Britannica Atlas

Encyclopædia Britannica, Inc.

CHICAGO • LONDON • TORONTO

GENEVA • SYDNEY • TOKYO • MANILA • SEOUL

INTERNATIONAL PLANNING CONFERENCE
INTERNATIONALE BERATER-KONFERENZ
CONFERENCIA INTERNACIONAL DE CONSULTORES
CONFÉRENCE INTERNATIONALE DE CONSEILLERS
CONFERÊNCIA INTERNACIONAL DE CONSULTORES

Dr. Manlio Castiglioni (deceased)
Chief Editor, Touring Club Italiano, Milano

Dr. S. P. Chatterjee
Chairman, National Committee for Geography, India

Dr. Arch C. Gerlach (deceased)
Chief Geographer, United States Geological Survey

Dr. Ir. Cornelis Koeman
Professor of Cartography, State University of Utrecht

Dr. André Libault
Department of Geography, Universidade de São Paulo

Brig. D. E. O. Thackwell
President (1964-1968), International Cartographic Association

Robert J. Voskuil
Adviser on Cartography,
United States Department of State

Dr. Akira Watanabe
Chairman, National Committee of Geography,
Science Council of Japan

CARTOGRAPHIC FIRMS
KARTOGRAPHISCHE FIRMEN
FIRMAS CARTOGRÁFICAS
MAISONS D'ÉDITIONS CARTOGRAPHIQUES
CASA DE EDIÇÕES CARTOGRÁPHICAS

RAND McNALLY & COMPANY, Chicago
Russell L. Voisin, Vice-President, Cartography
Jon M. Leverenz, Cartographic Editor

MONDADORI-McNALLY GmbH, Stuttgart
Helmut Schaub, Cartographic Editor

CARTOGRAPHIA, Budapest
Ervin Földi, Coordinator

ESSELTE MAP SERVICE, Stockholm
Gösta Lundqvist (deceased), General Supervisor
Paul R. Kraske, Head of Editorial Staff

GEORGE PHILIP & SON LIMITED, London
Harold Fullard, Director and Cartographic Editor

TEIKOKU-SHOIN CO., LTD., Tokyo
Kimio Moriya, General Supervisor

MAP ADVISERS
KARTOGRAPHISCHE BERATER
CONSEJEROS CARTOGRÁFICOS
CONSEILLERS CARTOGRAPHES
CONSELHEIROS CARTOGRÁFICOS

Europe
Prof. Dr. Emil Meynen
Direktor des Instituts für Landeskunde,
Bad Godesberg

Prof Sándor Radó
Director, Department of Cartography,
National Office of Lands and Mapping,
Budapest

Asia
Abba H. Salzman
Consultant on place names of Israel,
Chicago

Dr. Hisashi Sato
Science Faculty, Geographical Institute,
Tokyo University

Australia
Prof. R. O. Buchanan
Professor Emeritus, London School
of Economics and Political Science,
University of London

Anglo-America
Dr. Arch C. Gerlach (deceased)
Chief Geographer,
United States Geological Survey

Latin America
Dr. André Libault
Department of Geography,
Universidade de São Paulo

Dra. Consuelo Soto Mora
Directora del Instituto de Geografía,
Universidad Nacional
Autónoma de México

Dr. Jorge A. Vivó Escoto
Colegio de Geografía,
Facultad de Filosofía y Letras,
Universidad Nacional de México

Metropolitan Area Maps
Prof. Harold M. Mayer
Department of Geography,
Kent State University, Ohio

World Scene
Prof. Norton S. Ginsburg,
Prof. Chauncy D. Harris,
Prof. Marvin W. Mikesell
Department of Geography,
University of Chicago

CONTRIBUTORS—WORLD SCENE
MITARBEITER—WELT-PANORAMA
COLABORADORES—PERSPECTIVA DEL MUNDO
COLLABORATEURS—LE MONDE AUJOURD'HUI
COLABORADORES—PERSPECTIVA DO MUNDO

Robert C. Bergstrom
Director of Admissions and Registration,
Morton College, Cicero, Illinois

Prof. Wesley Calef
Department of Geography, Illinois State University, Normal

Nathaniel B. Guyol
Consulting Economist on Energy, Interenergie,
San Rafael, California

Prof. Edwin H. Hammond
Department of Geography, Syracuse University

Robert D. Hodgson
The Geographer,
United States Department of State

Prof. A. W. Küchler
Department of Geography-Meteorology,
The University of Kansas

Prof. G. Etzel Pearcy
Department of Geography,
California State College, Los Angeles

Prof. David E. Sopher
Department of Geography, Syracuse University

Prof. Richard S. Thoman
Department of Geography,
California State University, Hayward

Mrs. Evelyn Z. Thoman

Dr. William Van Royen
Director, Division of Environmental Sciences,
United States Army Research Office,
Durham, North Carolina

Prof. Philip L. Wagner
Department of Geography,
Simon Fraser University, British Columbia

Maps for the World Scene were designed
especially for *Encyclopædia Britannica*
by David L. Burke

EDITORS
HERAUSGEBER
REDACTORES
ÉDITEURS
EDITORES

Frank J. Sutley
Geography Editor

Staff: Research Geographers
William A. Cleveland
Mara Grubisic
Stephen P. Neher
Neil D. Shere
Joseph R. Sturgis

Will Gallagher
Art Director

Cynthia Peterson
Associate Art Director

Chris Leszczynski
Cartographic Supervisor

Staff: Cartographers
Ramón Goas
William W. Karpa
Mimi McCullough
Eugene Melchert

J. Thomas Beatty
Editorial Production Manager

Necia B. Kowalski
Chief Production Editor

Encyclopædia Britannica, Inc.
Robert P. Gwinn, Chairman of the Board
Charles E. Swanson, President
Charles Van Doren, Vice-President/Editorial

© 1969, 1970, 1972, 1974, 1977, 1979
Reprinted
ENCYCLOPÆDIA BRITANNICA, INC.
All rights reserved
No part of this work may be reproduced or utilized in any form or by any means, electronic or mechanical, including photocopying, recording, or by any information storage and retrieval system, without permission in writing from the publisher.
Map plates 1-280, pages vi-xvi, and tables and index beginning on I-1 from *The International Atlas*
© 1969, 1974, 1977, 1979 RAND McNALLY & COMPANY
Library of Congress Catalog Card Number: Map 69-1
International Standard Book Number: 0-85229-357-7
ISSN: 0068-1148
Printed in the U.S.A.

Foreword

Throughout history, educators have pointed out that a deep gulf may separate knowledge of something from the understanding of it. The *Britannica Atlas* presents the latest facts about the present-day world at the same time that it attempts to add substantially to man's understanding of it. To produce a work that may give a reader this deeper insight, the editors have departed from traditional atlas-making in two important particulars: (1) greater internationalism of content and (2) complete comparability among the maps.

Internationalism: Too often an atlas will cater to local prejudices and tastes. To avoid this pitfall, the publishers of this atlas—Encyclopædia Britannica, Inc., and Rand McNally & Company—assured the truly international character of the content at the earliest planning stage by inviting a group of eminent scholars and cartographic houses from various parts of the world to participate in the work. The original planning group included members from France, Germany, India, Italy, Japan, the Netherlands, Sweden, the United Kingdom, and the United States. Actual compilation of the maps was carried out in six countries—Germany, Hungary, Japan, Sweden, the United Kingdom, and the United States.

In keeping with the international outlook of the atlas, the metric system of measurement has been used throughout the reference maps, rather than the British-U.S. system. Map scales and elevation and depth scales on the map pages are given in both systems of measurement. In the Legend to Maps meter-foot and kilometer-mile equivalents are given.

Most of the atlas carries parallel texts in English, German, Spanish, French, and Portuguese. Names of inhabited places and of physical features situated within the boundaries of one country appear on the maps in the local language; where space permits, the English alternate also is given if the local name is likely to be unfamiliar. The names of countries are in English, because some country names are extremely unfamiliar in the local language—Druk-Yul (Bhutan), Magyarország (Hungary), Nihon (Japan). On the larger-scale maps, however, the local form of a country name is shown also. The names of large bodies of water, mountain ranges, and other major physical features that extend across international boundaries are given in English on smaller-scale maps, but on large-scale maps both the English and local forms will be found. In transliterating place names into English from languages not written in the roman alphabet, every effort has been made to use internationally accepted systems of transliteration.

Geographical terms such as lake, mountain, island, etc., appear on the maps in the local language. Five-language glossaries of selected terms used on a map are printed in the margins of most pages, and a glossary of all terms appears on pages **I •1–I •7**.

In the index, symbols are given with all entries except those naming cities or towns, to aid in identifying the features, e.g., **∧** for mountain, **≻** for cape, **≃** for river. The symbols represent graphically the broad categories of the features named. A five-language key at the bottom of the index pages associates each symbol with the class of terms it represents.

The World Scene is a separate section of topical maps. These maps summarize in cartographic form the patterns of man's physical environment and some of his more important economic activities, political alignments, and cultural distributions. Several maps are concerned with recent political history. In the maps that show climate, surface configurations, soils, natural vegetation, and drainage, the reader may identify the influence of the natural habitat on human settlement and activity.

Finally, the effort to ensure the international character of the atlas is manifest in the balanced coverage of the world's regions. The *Britannica Atlas* allots to each region of the world a map coverage that takes into account the region's economic and cultural significance, its population, and its surface area. Approximately two-thirds of the map pages are devoted to Anglo-America, Asia, and Europe, and about one-third to Africa, Australia/Oceania, Latin America, and the Soviet Union. A world map on pp. xiv-xv has blocked out on it the areas and page numbers of the various maps.

Comparability. All atlases have attempted, with varying degrees of success, to use uniform map scales wherever practical. This atlas has been prepared with a minimal number of map scales, selected to permit valid areal comparisons between all parts of the earth. At the beginning of the atlas there appear political and physical maps of the world at 1:75,000,000, maps of the oceans at 1:48,000,000, and relief maps of the continents at 1:24,000,000. Next, the major world regions are uniformly presented at 1:12,000,000 (190 miles to the inch).

Virtually the entire land area of the earth is portrayed again, in sections, at one of two larger scales. The less densely populated regions are at 1:6,000,000 (95 miles to the inch), and Europe, most of North America, and the most densely populated sections of South and East Asia are at 1:3,000,000 (47 miles to the inch). The 1:3,000,000 and 1:6,000,000 series are thoroughly comparable with one another. Both indicate the chief natural and man-made features of each region, showing elevations, rivers, major railroads and airports, two classes of highways, and even selected offshore water depths.

Finally, the scale of 1:1,000,000 (16 miles to the inch) has been used in presenting 43 key regions of the continents characterized by exceptional economic importance, high concentration of population, complexity of transportation development, or some combination of these. This scale is unusually large for a general atlas, and is ordinarily reserved for small inset maps dealing with special subjects. Its use in this atlas permits the inclusion of a multitude of place names and many other local details such as waterfalls, ruins, parks, bird and wildlife sanctuaries, shipyards, military installations, dams, and reservoirs.

At the back of the atlas is a 29-page section of 60 maps of the world's major urban centers, all at a scale of 1:300,000 (just under 5 miles to the inch). These maps display the land-use patterns and other local features of great metropolitan agglomerations. Nearly all of the most populous world metropolitan areas are shown, and a number of smaller but important areas are also included. Grouping these metropolitan maps in a separate section following the regional maps facilitates comparison between them and avoids interrupting continuity of the regional maps.

The arrangement of the maps is such that the reader gets a progressively more detailed, but always comparable, view of the earth's surface. There is first a global view of the world and of the oceans, then an overall survey of the continents, shown in hemispheres or quadrants of the earth. There follows a closer view of all regions within the continents, in maps that are primarily political. The regions are next shown in sections at a larger scale, with emphasis on the relationships between physical and cultural features. At a still larger scale, the cultural features of densely populated areas are shown in great detail. Finally, the close-up maps of cities and their environs include even more detail. A three-page Legend to Maps appears on pp. x-xii.

Collection and analysis of the map data have benefited from the recent accelerated progress in aerial and satellite surveying, radar and sonar technology, and electronic data processing. The shaded relief technique was used to give the maps the effect of a third dimension. All the resources of modern graphic arts were utilized to give form to the editorial plan.

Vorwort

Pädagogen haben schon immer darauf hingewiesen, dass blosses Wissen und wahres Verstehen zwei ganz verschiedene Dinge sein können. Der *Britannica Atlas* nun versucht, nicht nur die letzten Errungenschaften der Wissenschaft darzulegen, sondern auch das Verständnis der Welt bedeutend zu vertiefen. Um dem Leser diesen tieferen Einblick zu gewähren, sind die Herausgeber von der beim Zusammenstellen von Atlanten üblichen Methode in zwei wichtigen Punkten abgegangen: sie haben erstens einen grösseren Internationalismus des Inhalts, zweitens eine vollkommene Vergleichbarkeit der einzelnen Karten untereinander angestrebt.

Internationalismus. Es geschieht allzu oft, dass ein Atlas national und provinziell anmutet. Um dies zu vermeiden, haben die Verleger des vorliegenden Atlasses—Encyclopædia Britannica, Inc., und Rand McNally & Company—den internationalen Charakter des Inhalts dadurch gewährleistet, dass sie eminente Wissenschaftler und kartographische Firmen aus aller Welt von Anfang an mit dem Unternehmen assoziiert haben. Die ursprüngliche Planungsgruppe zählte Mitglieder aus Frankreich, Deutschland, Indien, Italien, Japan, den Niederlanden, Schweden, Grossbritannien und den Vereinigten Staaten. Zusammengestellt wurden die Karten in sechs Ländern: in Deutschland, Ungarn, Japan, Schweden, Grossbritannien und in den Vereinigten Staaten.

Das metrische und nicht das angelsächsische Masssystem wird in den Karten benutzt. Die Massstäbe der Karten sowie die Farbskalen für Höhen und Tiefen am Rand jeder Karte werden in beiden Masssystemen angeführt. In die Zeichenerklärung wird die Gleichwertigkeit zwischen Metern und "feet" sowie zwischen Kilometern und Meilen gegeben.

Fast alle Texte des Atlasses sind zugleich in Englisch, Deutsch, Spanisch, Französisch und Portugiesisch gedruckt. Die Namen bewohnter Orte und physischer Gepräge, die innerhalb der Grenzen eines Staates liegen, erscheinen auf den Karten in der Landessprache; wo es der Platz erlaubte, ist der englische Name dann hinzugefügt, wenn der landessprachliche wahrscheinlich unbekannt ist. Die Namen der Länder werden in Englisch wiedergegeben, da manche Ländernamen in ihrer landessprachlichen Form überhaupt nicht geläufig sind—Druk-Yul (Bhutan), Magyarország (Ungarn), Nihon (Japan). Auf den Karten in grösserem Massstab findet sich jedoch auch die lokale Form eines Ländernamens. Die Namen grosser Gewässer, die Namen von Gebirgen und anderen grösseren physischen Geprägen, die sich über das Gebiet mehrerer Staaten erstrecken, sind auf den Karten in kleinerem Massstab nur auf Englisch eingezeichnet, auf den Karten in grösserem Massstab ist jedoch die landessprachliche Form hinzugefügt. Viel Mühe wurde darauf verwendet, international anerkannte Transliterationssysteme zu benutzen, um Ortsnamen aus Sprachen mit nichtlateinischen Schriftzeichen in Englisch wiederzugeben.

Geographische Begriffe wie See, Berg, Insel usw, sind auf den Karten in der Landessprache gedruckt. Am Rand der meisten Karten befinden sich fünfsprachige Glossare der wichtigsten Begriffe, die in den Karten vorkommen. Ein Verzeichnis aller Begriffe ist auf den Seiten **I •1–I •7**.

Neben allen Namen, die im Register enthalten sind, ausgenommen Grossstädte und Städte, steht das entsprechende Symbol, das jeden Namen einer physischen Gegebenheit zuordnet: z.B. **∧** für Berg, **≻** für Kap, **≃** für Fluss. Die Symbole drücken in graphischer Form die Kategorien für die genannten physischen Gegebenheiten aus. Am Fuss der Registerseite befindet sich ein fünfsprachiges Verzeichnis, in dem jedes Symbol dem Begriff zugeordnet wird, den es darstellt.

Das World Scene (Welt-Panorama) ist eine besondere Reihe von thematischen Karten. Diese Karten stellen in kartographischer Weise die Gebilde der natürlichen Umgebung des Menschen dar. Sie zeigen ausserdem einige der bedeutenderen Wirtschaftsformen, politischen Verbände und Kulturgruppen. Die Reihe enthält einige Karten zur politischen Geschichte der jüngsten Vergangenheit. Mit Hilfe der Karten über Klima, Oberflächenformen, Bodenarten, natürliche Vegetation und Entwässerung kann der Leser den Einfluss der natürlichen Umbebung des Menschen auf menschliche Siedlungsformen und Tätigkeiten feststellen. Für diese Kartenreihe wurden die modernsten Informationen verwendet, die erhältlich waren.

Schliesslich zeigt die Auswahl der Karten das Bemühen um den internationalen Charakter des Atlasses. Der Kartenanteil, den der *Britannica Atlas* jeder Region einräumt, beachtet die ökonomische und kulturelle Bedeutung des Gebietes, seine Bevölkerungszahl und die Grösse des Territoriums. Ungefähr zwei Drittel der Kartenseiten stellen Anglo-Amerika, Asien und Europa dar, ungefähr ein Drittel Afrika, Australien/Ozeanien, Latein-Amerika und die Sowjetunion. Auf den Seiten xiv-xv sind die Gebiete und Seitenzahlen der verschiedenen Karten auf einer Erdkarte skizziert.

Vergleichsmöglichkeiten. Mit unterschiedlichem Erfolg haben alle Atlanten versucht, wo es praktisch erschien, einheitliche Massstäbe für Karten zu verwenden. Dieser Atlas gebraucht eine sehr geringe Zahl von Massstäben, um fundierte Vergleiche zwischen Gebieten aus allen Teilen der Erde zu ermöglichen. Am Anfang des Atlasses stehen politische und physische Erdkarten im Massstab 1:75 000 000, Ozeankarten im Massstab 1:48 000 000 und Reliefkarten der Erdteile im Massstab 1:24 000 000. Als nächstes werden die Hauptgebiete der Erde alle im Massstab 1:12 000 000 (1 cm = 120 km) dargestellt.

Fast das gesamte Landgebiet der Erde wird in Ausschnitten in einem der beiden grösseren Massstäbe dargestellt. Die weniger dicht besiedelten Gebiete der Erde werden in 1:6 000 000 (1 cm = 60 km) abgebildet; Europa, der grösste Teil Nordamerikas und die am dichtesten besiedelten Regionen von Süd- und Ostasien werden in 1:3 000 000 (1 cm = 30 km) dargestellt. Diese beiden Kartenreihen sind miteinander vollständig vergleichbar. Beide Reihen stellen die wichtigsten natürlichen Gebilde und die von Menschenhand ausgeführten Konstruktionen jeder Region dar sowie Erhebungen, Flüsse, grössere Eisenbahnlinien und Flughäfen, zwei Klassen von Autostrassen und sogar manche Meerestiefen.

Der Massstab 1:1 000 000 (1 cm = 10 km) wird schliesslich verwendet, um 43 Schlüsselgebiete darzustellen, die eine oder mehrere der folgenden Besonderheiten zeigen: ausserordentliche wirtschaftliche Bedeutung, dichte Besiedlung und Komplexität des Verkehrsnetzes. Dieser Massstab ist für einen allgemeinen Atlas ungewöhnlich gross und ist normalerweise nur für kleine Nebenkarten reserviert, die spezielle Themen darstellen. Er wird jedoch in diesem Atlas verwendet, um viele Ortsnamen verzeichnen zu können sowie andere lokale Einzelheiten, z.B. Wasserfälle, Ruinen, Naturschutzgebiete, Werften, Militäranlagen, Talsperren und Wasserreservoirs.

Am Schluss des Kartenteils dieses Atlasses befindet sich eine Reihe von 60 Karten, die auf 29 Seiten im Massstab 1:300 000 (1 cm = 3 km) die grössten städtischen Siedlungsgebiete der Erde abbilden. Diese Karten zeigen die Bodennutzung und andere örtliche Gebilde innerhalb der Stadtregionen. Die meist besiedelten Stadtregionen der

Erde sind fast alle abgebildet sowie auch eine Anzahl kleinerer und dennoch wichtiger Stadtregionen. Die Zusammenfassung dieser Stadtregionen in einem besonderen Kartenteil erleichtert den Vergleich zwischen ihnen, ausserdem wird die Folge der Regionalkarten nicht unterbrochen.

Die Karten sind so angeordnet, dass der Leser eine fortschreitend detailliertere, aber immer vergleichbare Ansicht der Erdoberfläche bekommt. Zuerst findet er eine globale Darstellung der Welt und der Ozeane, dann eine allgemeine Übersicht der Erdteile, die in Hemisphären oder Quadranten der Erde gezeigt werden. Darauf folgt eine detailliertere Darstellung aller Regionen jedes Erdteils auf Karten, die vorwiegend politisch sind. In grösserem Massstab werden danach die Regionen in Ausschnitten abgebildet, wobei die Beziehungen zwischen physischen und kulturellen Gebieten betont werden. In noch grösserem Massstab wird sehr detailliert das kulturelle Gepräge dicht besiedelter Gebiete vorgeführt. Schliesslich gibt die Kartenreihe der Städte und ihrer Umgebungen eine noch mehr in Einzelheiten gehende Darstellung. Die Zeichenerklärung ist auf den Seiten x-xii zu finden.

Sammlung und Analyse der Karteninformation hat von dem rapiden Fortschritt in der Technik der Luft- und Satellitenaufnahmen, in der Radar-und Sonartechnik und in der elektronischen Datenverarbeitung profitiert. Die sogenannte Schummerungstechnik, die den Karten einen dreidimensionalen Effekt gibt, wurde verwand. Alle Mittel der modernen Graphik wurden gebraucht, um dem Plan der Herausgeber Gestalt zu verleihen.

Prefacio

A través de la historia, los pedagogos han sabido muy bien, que el mero conocimiento y el legítimo entendimiento son conceptos que, pueden hallarse separados por un verdadero abismo. Una simple acumulación de datos muy bien puede resultar de escaso valor si el significado de los mismos y su interrelación no se comprenden plenamente.

Además de reflejar los últimos conocimientos que nos ofrece la ciencia, el *Britannica Atlas* tiene por meta el incrementar sustancialmente el grado de comprensión con que el hombre moderno mira a su mundo. Para lograr este fin, los editores se han apartado del curso tradicional en dos importantes sentidos: (1) más internacionalismo en cuanto al contenido y (2) una paridad metódica en el diseño de los mapas que permite su mejor comparación.

Internacionalismo. Frecuentemente, muchos atlas, tratan de satisfacer gustos y prejuicios locales. Para evitar esto, los responsables de la creación de esta obra—Encyclopædia Britannica, Inc., y Rand McNally & Company—desde un principio aseguraron el carácter verdaderamente internacional de su contenido al invitar a un grupo de eminentes geógrafos y firmas cartográficas de distintas partes del mundo a colaborar en su preparación. El grupo que participó en el proyecto original quedó constituido por representantes de Francia, Alemania, India, Italia, Japón, los Países Bajos, Suecia, el Reino Unido y los Estados Unidos de Norteamérica. La realización de los mapas en sí tuvo lugar en seis países—Alemania, Hungría, Japón, Suecia, el Reino Unido y los Estados Unidos de Norteamérica.

El sistema métrico ha sido usado en todos los mapas topográficos, en lugar del sistema anglo-norteamericano de medidas. Las escalas horizontales y las escalas verticales (alturas y profundidades) en las páginas de mapas se expresan en ambos sistemas, y en la Leyenda para los Mapas se ofrecen las equivalencias metro-pie y kilómetro-milla.

El inglés, el alemán, el español, el francés y el portugués se utilizan paralelamente en la mayor parte de la obra. Los nombres de los lugares habitados y de los accidentes geográficos situados dentro de los límites de un país dado se escriben en la lengua local; de permitirlo el espacio disponible, también se da el equivalente inglés si el nombre local no es fácilmente reconocible. Los nombres de los países se dan en inglés, puesto que algunos son muy difíciles de identificar si se expresan en el idioma local—Druk-Yul (Bhután), Magyarország (Hungría), Nihon (Japón). Ahora bien, en los mapas a mayor escala la forma local del nombre del país también se expresa. En cuanto a los nombres de grandes mares o lagos, cordilleras, u otros accidentes mayores que se extienden a través de las fronteras internacionales, éstos se dan en inglés en los mapas a escala reducida, y tanto en las formas locales como en inglés, en los mapas a mayor escala. A los efectos de "trasliterar" al inglés los nombres de lugares cuyas grafías originales no se escriben por medio del alfabeto latino, se ha puesto el mayor esfuerzo en seguir la guía de los sistemas de "trasliteración" más aceptados internacionalmente.

Términos geográficos tales como lago, monte, isla, etc., aparecen en los mapas en el idioma local. Sobre los márgenes de la mayor parte de las páginas se hallarán glosarios en cinco idiomas que incluyen la mayoría de las voces utilizadas en cada mapa, y en las páginas I•1–I•7 se incluye un glosario completo.

Todas las entradas del índice, a excepción de las ciudades o poblaciones, van acompañadas de un símbolo gráfico que las identifica a primera vista como nombre de, v. gr., montaña **Λ**, cabo **≻**, río **≃**, etc. Y al pie de cada página del índice se hallará una clave en cinco idiomas en la que se equiparan los símbolos con las amplias categorías de accidentes geográficos que representan.

La World Scene (Perspectiva del Mundo) constituye una sección aparte dedicada a mapas especializados. Estos mapas compendian cartográficamente el medio físico en que habita la humanidad, y algunas de sus actividades económicas, alineamientos políticos y aspectos culturales más importantes. Varios de los mapas se ocupan de la historia política más reciente. En los mapas que se ocupan de aspectos de geografía física tales como la distribución de climas, las estructuras geológicas, los suelos, la flora, el régimen de vertientes, podrá el lector observar la influencia que sobre el asiento de las comunidades humanas y sus actividades ha tenido el medio físico.

Por último, el esfuerzo por garantizarle a la obra su carácter internacional se hace palpable en el equilibrado tratamiento que se da a las regiones del mundo. El *Britannica Atlas* reparte entre las regiones del mundo su contenido cartográfico teniendo en cuenta la significación cultural, económica y demográfica de las mismas, aparte de sus dimensiones territoriales. La América Latina, junto con Africa, Australia/Oceanía y la Unión Soviética, comprenden aproximadamente una tercera parte de los mapas, estando el resto dedicado a la América anglosajona, Asia y Europa. Véase el mapamundi en las páginas xiv-xv, en el cual se han trazado las zonas, e indicado los folios, a que corresponden los distintos mapas.

Paridad de escalas. Todos los atlas intentan, con mayor o menor éxito, y siempre que sea práctico, utilizar escalas uniformes. En este atlas se ha utilizado el mínimo posible de escalas, y éstas se han escogido de manera que permitan la comparación entre todas las porciones de la tierra en cuanto a su extensión superficial. En la sección inicial aparecen varios grandes mapas: mapamundis con información política y fisiográfica, a una escala de 1:75 000 000; mapas oceánicos, a 1:48 000 000; y mapas topográficos de los continentes, a 1:24 000 000. Seguidamente se agrupan las principales regiones del mundo, a una escala uniforme de 1:12 000 000 (o sea, cada centímetro corresponde a 120 kilómetros).

El resto de la superficie terrestre, en su casi totalidad, queda representado, por secciones, a base de una u otra de dos escales mayores. La de 1:6 000 000 (60 kms. por cm.) se aplica a las regiones menos pobladas, y la de 1:3 000 000 (30 kms. por cm.), a Europa, casi toda la América del Norte y las regiones más densamente pobladas del Asia meridional y del extremo Oriente. Las dos series son perfectamente comparables entre sí, pues ambas indican los principales rasgos de cada región, tanto naturales como artificales, tales como las cumbres más elevadas, las corrientes fluviales, los principales aeropuertos y vías ferroviarias, dos tipos de carreteras, y aun profundidades marinas representativas.

Por último, la escala de 1:1 000 000 (10 kms. por cm.) se ha destinado a la representación de 43 regiones estratégicas, escogidas atendiendo a su excepcional importancia económica, su gran densidad de población, la complejidad de sus redes de communicaciones, o alguna combinación de estos factores. Esta escala es mucho mayor de la que se acostumbra utilizar en atlas generales, y a lo sumo se reserva para pequeños recuadros especializados que se insertan dentro del marco de mapas mayores. Su uso en esta obra permite abundar en una verdadera riqueza de detalles—saltos de agua, restos arqueológicos, parques forestales y santuarios de flora y fauna, astilleros, instalaciones militares, presas y embalses, además de muchas poblaciones.

Al final de la obra hay una sección de 29 páginas que contiene 60 planos de los principales complejos urbanos, trazados todos a una escala de 1:300 000 (tres kms. por cm.). En estos mapas se muestran, entre otras, las características demográfico-territoriales de las grandes aglomeraciones urbanas. Casi todas las metrópolis más populosas de la Tierra están representadas, así como algunas menores pero realmente importantes. Estos mapas se han agrupado al final del atlas a fin de facilitar la comparación entre sí y para no interrumpir la continuidad de los mapas regionales.

Los mapas están ordenados de modo que el lector vaya obteniendo progresivamente imágenes cada vez más detalladas, si bien siempre comparables de la superficie terrestre. Primero, la visión global del mundo y sus océanos; seguidamente, una visión panorámica de los continentes, mostrados en sus respectivos hemisferios o cuadrantes terrestres. A continuación, la vista más cercana de todas las regiones dentro de los continentes, con énfasis principalmente político. Después, las subregiones, a mayor escala, con énfasis principalmente en las relaciones entre los rasgos físicos y los culturales. A escala aun mayor, se muestran en gran detalle los rasgos culturales de las zonas densamente pobladas. Y por último, los planos de las ciudades y sus alrededores, que incluyen aun más detalles. La sección denominada Leyenda para los Mapas ocupa las tres páginas x a xii.

La compilación y el análisis de datos cartográficos se han beneficiado con el reciente y aceleradísimo progreso logrado en las técnicas del reconocimiento aéreo, y del efectuado por medio de satélites, del radar o del sonar, así como del procesamiento de datos por medios electrónicos. Se ha aprovechado plenamente el sombreado al relieve, que produce un efecto tridimensional en el mapa forzosamente plano de un atlas. Todos los más modernos recursos de las artes gráficas se han puesto en juego al estructurar el plan editorial.

Avant-propos

Tout au long de l'histoire, les éducateurs ont déploré le fossé profond qui sépare trop souvent le savoir accumulatif de la compréhension. Aussi *Britannica Atlas* ne se contente-t-il pas de rassembler les connaissances les plus récentes concernant la physionomie de la planète; il s'efforce d'élargir la compréhension qu'acquiert l'homme du monde au sein duquel il vit. Afin de dégager pour le lecteur le sens intime des faits, les éditeurs se sont écartés des méthodes traditionnelles: (1) par la présentation d'un contenu plus largement international; (2) en proposant une systématique complète de comparaison entre les cartes.

Caractère international. On constate souvent qu'en s'inspirant d'un certain esprit de clocher, tel atlas en arrive à ne plus guère refléter que les vues d'un nationalisme étriqué. Soucieux d'éviter cet écueil, c'est d'entrée de jeu que les éditeurs ont tenu à affirmer le caractère fondamentalement international du nouvel ouvrage. D'éminents spécialistes et plusieurs maisons d'éditions cartographiques du monde entier ont été invités à collaborer à cette œuvre. Des personnalités d'Allemagne, des États-Unis, de France, de Grande-Bretagne, de l'Inde, d'Italie, du Japon, des Pays-Bas et de Suède ont formé le groupe initial. Les documents cartographiques proviennent de six pays: l'Allemagne, les États-Unis, la Grande-Bretagne, la Hongrie, le Japon et la Suède.

On a utilisé dans l'ensemble des cartes les unités de mesure du système métrique de préférence à leurs équivalents anglo-américains. Toutefois, les échelles des cartes et les échelles altimétriques et bathymétriques sont indiquées dans les deux systèmes, métrique et anglo-américain. On trouvera, dans la légende des cartes, les rapports respectifs du mètre et du pied, du kilomètre et du mille.

La plupart des textes de l'Atlas sont présentés en cinq langues: anglais, allemand, espagnol, français et portugais. Les noms de lieux et de particularités géographiques sont, pour chaque pays, transcrits dans leur forme locale. Néanmoins, chaque fois que celle-ci risquait de paraître insolite, on l'a complétée par la variante anglaise pour autant que le permettait l'échelle de la carte. En ce qui concerne les noms de pays, on a eu recours à l'anglais, la version locale de certains d'entre eux risquant de demeurer hermétique au lecteur. Tel est le cas de Magyarország (Hongrie), Nihon (Japon) et Druk-Yul (Bhoutan). Cependant, les noms locaux apparaissent aussi sur les cartes à grande échelle. Dans le cas des océans, des

chaînes de montagnes et des autres unités géographiques qui ignorent les frontières politiques, les cartes à petite échelle ne font état que de la seule appellation anglaise, tandis que les projections à grande échelle comportent les deux versions, locale et anglaise. La transcription correspondant à la graphie et à la phonétique anglaises de caractères étrangers à l'alphabet romain a été établie avec le souci de respecter au plus près les systèmes de translittération internationalement reconnus.

On a conservé leur forme locale aux termes génériques s'appliquant à des unités géographiques telles que lac, montagne, île. C'est pourquoi des glossaires succincts en cinq langues figurent en marge de la grande majorité des cartes. En outre, ces renseignements sont complétés aux pages I•1–I•7 par un lexique exhaustif.

Exception faite pour les noms de villes, tous les mots figurant à l'index sont identifiés à l'aide de signes conventionnels représentant graphiquement les traits évocateurs des catégories considérées; c'est ainsi qu'on trouvera ⋀ pour montagne, ≻ pour cap, ≃ pour rivière. Une clé de cinq langues rappelle, en bas des pages d'index, la classe des termes associés à chaque signe conventionnel utilisé.

Une section séparée, intitulée World Scene (Le Monde Aujourd'hui), contient une série de cartes thématiques. Ces cartes présentent synthétiquement les différents types d'environnement physique auxquels l'homme se trouve associé et quelques-unes des activités économiques, dépendances politiques et aires culturelles les plus notables. Plusieurs cartes touchent à l'histoire politique récente. Dans les cartes consacrées aux climats, aux configurations de surface, aux sols, à la végétation naturelle et à l'hydrographie, le lecteur aura tout loisir de reconnaître les influences d'ordre écologique sur l'implantation et l'activité humaines.

Enfin, on retrouve ce caractère international de l'Atlas jusque dans l'équilibre respecté dans la représentation des différentes régions de la Terre. *Britannica Atlas* accorde à chaque région du monde une couverture cartographique tenant compte de son importance économique et culturelle, de sa densité démographique, de sa superficie. C'est ainsi qu'environ les deux tiers des pages de cartes portent sur le monde anglo-américain, l'Asie et l'Europe, tandis que le tiers restant se partage entre l'Afrique, l'Amérique latine, l'Australie et l'Océanie, et l'Union soviétique. La repérage et l'identification des surfaces cartographiées dans l'Atlas sont assurés par une mappemonde avec renvoi aux pages où elles figurent (voir pages xiv et xv).

Systématique de comparaison. Avec un succès plus ou moins affirmé, tous les atlas ont jusqu'ici tendu à utiliser une gamme d'échelles uniformisées, dans la mesure où l'opération était techniquement possible. *Britannica Atlas* comporte un nombre restreint d'échelles soigneusement déterminées, propres à rendre vraiment significatives les comparaisons entre les différentes parties du monde. Les premières planches de l'Atlas permettent une vue d'ensemble sur le monde physique et politique grâce à des cartes au 1:75 000 000. Des projections au 1:48 000 000 sont consacrées aux océans, tandis que la figuration du relief des continents est reproduite au 1:24 000 000 (1 cm = 240 km). Ensuite, les vastes régions du globe sont toutes uniformément représentées au 1:12 000 000 (1 cm = 120 km).

Dans un découpage à plus grande échelle, la quasi-totalité des régions du monde est présentée de nouveau à l'échelle de 1:6 000 000 (1 cm = 60 km), pour les régions de moindre population, et à celle de 1:3 000 000 (1 cm = 30 km), pour l'Europe, la plus grande partie de l'Amérique du Nord et pour les régions les plus peuplées du Sud et de l'Est de l'Asie. Les séries au 1:6 000 000 et au 1:3 000 000 sont parfaitement comparables. L'une et l'autre indiquent les accidents naturels et les aspects proprement humains de chaque région: l'altitude, le système fluvial, les grands réseaux ferroviaires, les principaux aéroports, deux catégories de réseaux routiers et même les indications bathymétriques marquantes au large des côtes.

Enfin, on a fait appel à l'échelle de 1:1 000 000 (1 cm = 10 km) pour représenter 43 régions essentielles, choisies soit pour leur importance économique exceptionnelle, leur forte densité démographique, la complexité de leur réseau de transports, soit pour telle ou telle combinaison de ces facteurs. C'est une échelle inhabituellement grande dans les atlas généraux; on la réserve, d'ordinaire, aux cartons illustrant des études particulières. Elle a permis d'introduire quantité de noms de lieux ainsi que de multiples particularités locales: chutes d'eau, ruines, parcs, réserves ornithologiques et zoologiques, chantiers navals, installations militaires, barrages et réservoirs.

À la fin de l'Atlas, une section de 29 pages comprend 60 cartes au 1:300 000 (1 cm = 3 km) des centres urbains les plus importants. On y trouve l'aménagement et les traits caractéristiques des grandes agglomérations urbaines. Les principales concentrations urbaines y sont presque toutes comprises. Il s'y ajoute quelques agglomérations moins compactes mais non sans importance. Ce regroupement des zones citadines à la suite des cartes par régions offre l'avantage d'éviter toute rupture dans la succession de ces dernières.

La succession des cartes a été ordonnée de telle sorte que la surface de la Terre se dévoile progressivement du général au particulier, sans que le lecteur cesse de disposer de termes de comparaison. C'est d'abord une vue d'ensemble de la planète et de ses océans; puis, un survol général des continents présentés par hémisphère ou par quadrant terrestre. Suit l'examen plus poussé, sur des cartes principalement politiques, de toutes les régions qu'ils englobent. Celles-ci sont à leur tour projetées à grande échelle; l'accent est alors mis sur les relations de l'évolution culturelle et de l'environnement. Sous un verre plus grossissant apparaissent dans le détail les particularités culturelles des zones de forte densité démographique. Enfin, les gros plans des métropoles et de leurs agglomérations apportent au lecteur un faisceau d'informations plus détaillées. Les pages x à xii présentent la légende des cartes.

La collecte et l'analyse des données d'ordre physique destinées à la réalisation des cartes ont bénéficié des progrès de plus en plus rapides qui interviennent dans le domaine de l'observation aérienne et par satellites, de la technologie du radar et du sonar, enfin du traitement électronique de l'information. Le "relief ombré" a permis de conférer à nos cartes un aspect tridimensionnel. En un mot, toutes les ressources de l'art graphique contemporain ont été mises en œuvre afin d'atteindre le but que s'étaient fixé les éditeurs.

Prefácio

Ao longo da história, sabem-no muito bem os pedagogos, o conhecimento das coisas e a sua compreensão são conceitos que podem estar separados por um verdadeiro abismo. Uma simples acumulação de dados pode valer muito pouco se o seu significado e sua inter-relação não forem plenamente compreendidos.

Além de refletir os mais recentes fatos em relação ao mundo de hoje, o *Britannica Atlas* tem por meta aumentar substancialmente o grau de compreensão que o homem moderno tem do mundo em que vive. Para atingir esse objetivo, os editores afastaram-se dos caminhos tradicionais em dois importantes aspectos: (1) maior internacionalismo de conteúdo, e (2) perfeita comparabilidade dos mapas.

Internacionalismo. Freqüentemente, muitos atlas procuram satisfazer gostos e preconceitos locais. Para evitar esse defeito, os responsáveis por esta obra—Encyclopaedia Britannica, Inc. e Rand McNally & Company—desde o princípio asseguraram o caráter verdadeiramente internacional de seu conteúdo convidando um grupo de eminentes geógrafos e firmas cartográficas de diversas partes do mundo para colaborar em seu preparo. O grupo que participou foi constituído por representantes do Brasil e Ibero-América, da França, Alemanha, Índia, Itália, Japão, Países Baixos, Suécia, Reino Unido, e os Estados Unidos.

O sistema métrico foi usado em todos os mapas topográficos em lugar do sistema anglo-americano de medidas. As escalas horizontais e verticais (altitudes e profundidades) são expressas, nas páginas dos mapas, em ambos os sistemas, e na *Legendas dos Mapas* figuram as equivalências metro-pé e quilômetro-milha.

O inglês, o alemão, o espanhol, o francês e o português são utilizados paralelamente na maior parte da obra. Os nomes dos lugares habitados e dos acidentes geográficos situados dentro dos limites de um dado país são escritos na língua local; se o espaço disponível o permitir, apresenta-se também o equivalente inglês, caso o nome local não seja facilmente reconhecível. Os nomes dos países são apresentados em inglês, uma vez que alguns são muito difíceis de identificar quando expressos na língua local: Druk-Yul (Butã), Magyarország (Hungria), Nihon (Japão). Contudo, nos mapas em escala maior figura também a forma local do nome do país. Os nomes dos grandes mares ou lagos, cordilheiras ou outros acidentes maiores, que se estendem através de fronteiras internacionais, são apresentados em inglês nos mapas em escala reduzida, e tanto nas formas locais como em inglês nos mapas em escala maior. Para fins de transliteração para o inglês dos topônimos em línguas que não utilizam o alfabeto latino, fez-se o maior esforço para seguir os sistemas de transliteração mais aceitos internacionalmente.

Termos geográficos tais como lago, monte, ilha etc., aparecem nos mapas na língua local. À margem da maior parte das páginas acham-se glossários, em cinco línguas, que incluem a maioria dos termos utilizados em cada mapa; um glossário completo figura às páginas I•1–I•7.

Todas as entradas no índice, exceto as de cidades ou outros centros urbanos, são acompanhadas de um símbolo gráfico que os identifica, como, por exemplo, montanha ⋀, cabo ≻, rio ≃ etc., e ao pé de cada página, encontra-se, em cinco línguas, a chave da equivalência dos símbolos às categorias maiores de acidentes geográficos que representam.

Esforço para assegurar à obra seu caráter internacional faz-se evidente no tratamento equilibrado dado às diversas regiões do mundo. O *Britannica Atlas* reparte entre as regiões do mundo o seu conteúdo cartográfico, levando em conta sua significação cultural, econômica, demográfica e territorial. A América Latina, juntamente com a África, Austrália/Oceania e a União Soviética, compreendem, aproximadamente, a terça parte dos mapas, sendo os restantes dois terços dedicados à Anglo-América, Ásia e Europa. No mapa-múndi nas páginas xii-xv foram traçadas as zonas e indicadas as páginas a que correspondem os diversos mapas.

Comparabilidade. Todos os atlas, com êxito maior ou menor, e sempre que possível procuram utilizar escalas uniformes. No *Britannica Atlas* utilizou-se o menor número possível de escalas, e estas foram escolhidas de modo a permitir a comparabilidade de todas as partes da Terra no tocante à área. Na seção inicial do Atlas, aparecem vários mapas grandes: mapasmúndi, com informações políticas e fisiográficas, em escala de 1:75 000 000; mapas oceânicos, em escala de 1:48 000 000; e mapas dos continentes, em escala 1:24 000 000. A seguir, agrupam-se as principais regiões do mundo a uma escala uniforme de 1:12 000 000 (seja, cada centímetro corresponde a 120 quilômetros).

O restante da superfície terrestre, em sua quase totalidade, foi representada por seções, utilizando-se uma ou outra das duas escalas maiores. A de 1:6 000 000 (60 km por cm) aplica-se às regiões menos povoadas, e a de 1:3 000 000 (30 km por cm), à Europa, quase toda a América do Norte e às regiões mais densamente povoadas da Ásia Meridional e do Extremo Oriente. As duas séries são perfeitamente comparáveis entre si, pois ambas indicam os principais acidentes de cada região, tanto naturais como artificiais, tais como os picos mais elevados, os rios, os principais aeroportos a ferrovias, duas categorias de rodovias, e, ainda, as profundidades submarinas mais representativas.

Por último, a escala de 1:1 000 000 (10 km por cm) foi destinada à representação de 43 regiões estratégicas, escolhidas de acordo com a excepcional importância econômica, grande densidade demográfica, complexidade da rede de comunicações, ou alguma combinação desses fatores. Essa escala, muito maior que a habitualmente utilizada em atlas gerais, costuma ser reservada aos mapas que focalizam temas especiais insertos em mapas maiores. Seu uso nesta obra proporciona uma grande riqueza de detalhes, tais como quedas d'água, sítios arqueológicos, parques florestais, reservas naturais e biológicas, estaleiros, instalações militares, represas e barragens, além de muitos centros urbanos menores.

No final do Atlas figura uma seção de 29 páginas que contêm 60/mapas dos principais centros urbanos, traçados à escala única de 1:300 000 (3 km por cm). Esses mapas mostram a forma de uso do solo e outras características demográfico-territoriais das grandes aglomerações urbanas. Quase todas as áreas metropolitanas mais populosas do Mundo estão aí representadas, assim como algumas menores, mas igualmente importantes. Esses mapas foram agrupados em uma seção especial no final do Atlas para fins de comparabilidade, bem como para evitar a interrupção da continuidade dos mapas regionais.

Os mapas estão ordenados de modo a permitir ao leitor uma visão progressivamente mais detalhada, mas sempre comparável, da superfície terrestre. Primeiro, vem uma visão global do Mundo e dos oceanos; em seguida, uma visão panorâmica dos continentes, apresentados em seus respectivos hemisférios ou quadrantes terrestres. Segue-se uma visão mais próxima de todas as regiões dentro dos continentes, em mapas primordialmente políticos. Depois, as subregiões, em escala maior, com ênfase principalmente nas relações entre os acidentes físicos e os culturais. A escala ainda maior, apresentam-se, em grande detalhe, os acidentes culturais das zonas densamente povoadas. E por último, os mapas das cidades e seus arredores, que incluem ainda mais detalhes. A seção denominada *Legendas dos Mapas* ocupa a três páginas, de x a xii.

A compilação e a análise dos dados cartográficos beneficiaram-se com o recente e aceleradíssimo progresso alcançado pelas técnicas dos levantamentos aerofotogramétricos e por meio de satélites, pela tecnologia do radar e do sonar, e pelo processamento electrônico de dados. Utilizou-se a técnica do sombreado para o relevo, com o objetivo de dar aos mapas um efeito tridimensional. Todos os recursos das artes gráficas atuais foram empregados na execução do projeto editorial.

SUMMARY OF CONTENTS

INHALTSVERZEICHNIS

SUMARIO DEL CONTENIDO

TABLE DES MATIÈRES

SUMÁRIO

List of Maps

WORLD, OCEAN, and CONTINENT MAPS

REGIONAL MAPS

Europe

Union of Soviet Socialist Republics

Asia

Africa

Australia/Oceania

Anglo-America

Latin America

METROPOLITAN AREA MAPS (1:300,000)

*Scale in millions

Kartenverzeichnis

WELTKARTEN, KARTEN DER OZEANE UND ERDTEILE

REGIONALKARTEN

EUROPA

Union der Sozialistischen Sowjetrepubliken

Asien

Afrika

Australien/Ozeanien

Anglo-Amerika

Latein-Amerika

KARTEN VON STADTREGIONEN (1:300 000)

*Im massstäb millionen

Lista de Mapas

MAPAS DEL MUNDO, OCÉANOS Y CONTINENTES

*Escala en millones

MAPAS REGIONALES

Europa

Unión de Repúblicas Socialistas Soviéticas

Asia

África

Australia/Oceanía

América Anglosajona

América Latina

MAPAS DE LAS ÁREAS METROPOLITANAS (1:300 000)

Liste des Cartes

CARTES DU MONDE, DES OCÉANS ET DES CONTINENTS

CARTES RÉGIONALES

Europe

Union des Républiques Socialistes Soviétiques

Asie

Afrique

Australie/Océanie

Amérique Anglo-Saxonne

*Echelle en millions

Amérique Latine

CARTES DES ZONES MÉTROPOLITAINES (1 :300 000)

Lista de Mapas

MAPAS DO MUNDO, DOS OCEANOS E DOS CONTINENTES

MAPAS REGIONAIS

Europa

União das Repúblicas Socialistas Soviéticas

Ásia

África

Austrália/Oceania

América Anglosaxônica

América Latina

MAPAS DAS ÁREAS METROPOLITANAS (1 :300 000)

*Escalas em milhões

Legend to Maps/Zeichenerklärung
Leyendas Para Mapas/Légende des Cartes/Legendas dos Mapas

The design and color of the map symbols are consistent throughout the Regional and Metropolitan Area maps, although the size of the symbol varies with scale. An asterisk marks those symbols which appear only on the 1:300,000 scale maps. Symbols for inhabited localities, boundaries, and capitals are given on page xi.

The symbol 80-81 in the margin of a map directs the reader to a map of the adjoining area.

A separate legend on page 1 identifies the land and submarine features which appear on the World, Ocean, and Continent maps.

Der Entwurf und die Farbe der Kartensymbole sind einheitlich für alle Regionalkarten und Karten von Stadtregionen, während die Grösse des Symbols sich mit dem Massstab ändert. Ein Stern kennzeichnet diejenigen Symbole, welche nur auf den Karten im Massstab 1:300 000 erscheinen. Symbole für bewohnte Orte, für Grenzen und Hauptstädte sind auf Seite xi angeführt.

Kennzeichen 80-81 am Rande einer Karte ist ein Hinweis für den Leser, die Karte eines angrenzenden Gebietes nachzuschlagen.

Eine andere Legende auf Seite 1 identifiziert die Land- und untermeerischen Phänomene, die auf den Weltkarten, Karten der Ozeane und Erdteile erscheinen.

El diseño y el color de los símbolos cartográficos son uniformes para todas los mapas regionales y de las áreas metropolitanas, aunque el tamaño del símbolo varía según la escala. Un asterisco distingue los símbolos que aparecen sólo en los mapas a 1:300 000. Los símbolos de lugares poblados, de límites y de capitales se hallan en la página xi.

El símbolo 80-81 al margen de un mapa dirige al lector a un mapa del área adyacente.

Otra leyenda, en la página 1, identifica la topografía terrestre y submarina que se encuentra en los mapas del Mundo, Océanos y Continentes.

La couleur et la forme des symboles cartographiques des cartes régionales et des cartes des zones métropolitaines sont identiques, bien que la grandeur des signes varie selon l'échelle. Un astérisque accompagne les symboles qui n'apparaissent que sur les cartes au 1:300 000°. La légende des signes conventionnels pour les lieux habités, les frontières et les capitales se trouve à la page xi.

Le symbole 80-81 en marge d'une carte renvoie le lecteur à une carte de la région voisine.

Pour les cartes du monde, des océans et des continents, une légende séparée, à la page 1, donne le sens des symboles représentant les paysages continentaux et les formes de relief sous-marin.

A cor e a forma dos símbolos cartográficos dos mapas regionais e das áreas metropolitanas são idênticos, ainda que a dimensão do símbolo varie segundo a escala. Um asterisco distingue os símbolos que só aparecem nos mapas da escala de 1:300 000. As legendas dos símbolos convencionais dos lugares povoados, fronteiras e capitais encontram-se à pág. xi.

O símbolo 80-81 à margem de um mapa, remete o leitor a um mapa da região vizinha.

Nos mapas do mundo, dos oceanos e dos continentes uma legenda separada, na pág. 1, indica o sentido dos símbolos representativos das paisagens continentais e das formas do relevo submarino.

Hydrographic Features / Hydrographische Objekte / Elementos Hidrográficos
Données Hydrographiques / Acidentes Hidrográficos

Shoreline/Uferlinie
Línea costanera/Trait de côte
Linha costeira

Undefined or Fluctuating Shoreline
Unbestimmte oder Veränderliche Uferlinie
Línea costanera indefinida o fluctuante
Trait de côte indéfini ou fluctuant
Linha costeira indefinida ou flutuante

Amur
River, Stream/Fluss, Strom
Río, Corriente/Rivière, Cours d'eau
Rio, curso d'água

Intermittent Stream/Periodischer Fluss
Corriente intermitente/Cours d'eau périodique
Rio, curso d'água intermitente

SALTO ANGEL
Rapids, Falls/Stromschnellen, Wasserfälle
Rápidos, Cascadas/Rapides, Chutes d'eau
Corredeiras, quedas d'água

764 ▽
Depth of Water/Wassertiefe
Profundidad del agua/Profondeur bathymétrique
Profundidade da água

8428 ▼
Greatest Depth (Atlantic, Indian, Pacific oceans)
Grösste Tiefe (Atlantischer, Indischer, Pazifischer Ozean)
Profundidad más grande (Océanos Atlántico, Índico, Pacífico)
Profondeur maximum (océans Atlantique, Indien, Pacifique))
Profundidade máxima (oceanos Atlântico, Índico, Pacífico)

Canal du Midi
Navigable Canal/Schiffbarer Kanal
Canal navegable/Canal navigable
Canal navegável

Irrigation or Drainage Canal
Be- oder Entwässerungskanal
Canal de irrigación o desagüe
Canal d'irrigation ou de drainage
Canal de irrigação ou drenagem

Los Angeles Aqueduct
Aqueduct/Aquädukt
Acueducto/Aqueduc
Aqueduto

Pier, Breakwater/Landungsbrücke, Wellenbrecher
Embarcadero, Rompeolas/Jetée, Brise-lames
Cais, Quebra-mar

GREAT BARRIER REEF
Reef/Riff
Arrecife/Récif
Recife

Kumdah
Uninhabited Oasis/Unbewohnte Oase
Oasis deshabitado/Oasis inhabitée
Oásis desabitado

L. Victoria
Lake, Reservoir/See, Stausee
Lago, Embalse/Lac, Réservoir
Lago, reservatório (represa)

Intermittent Lake, Reservoir
Periodischer See, Stausee
Lago o Embalse intermitente
Lac ou Réservoir périodique
Lago, reservatório (represa) **intermitente**

Tuz Gölü
Salt Lake/Salzsee
Lago salado/Lac salé
Lago salgado

Dry Lake Bed/Trockener Seeboden
Lecho de lago seco/Fond de lac asséché
Leito de lago seco

The Everglades
Swamp/Sumpf
Pantano/Marais
Pântano

RIMO GLACIER
Glacier/Gletscher
Glaciar/Glacier
Geleira

(395)
Lake Surface Elevation
Seehöhe
Elevación del lago
Cote du niveau du lac
Altitude do nível do lago

Topographic Features / Topographische Objekte / Elementos Topográficos
Données Topographiques / Acidentes Topográficos

Mt. Kenya 5199 △
Elevation Above Sea Level
Höhe über dem Meeresspiegel
Elevación sobre el nivel del mar
Cote au-dessus du niveau de la mer
Altitude acima do nível do mar

76 ▽
Elevation Below Sea Level
Höhe unter dem Meeresspiegel
Elevación bajo del nivel del mar
Cote au-dessous du niveau de la mer
Altitude abaixo do nível do mar

Mount Cook 3764 ▲
Highest Elevation in Country
Höchster Punkt des Landes
Elevación más alta en el país
Cote la plus élevée d'un pays
Altitude mais elevada de um país

133 ▼
Lowest Elevation in Country
Tiefster Punkt des Landes
Elevación más baja en el país
Cote la plus basse d'un pays
Altitude mais baixa de um país

(106)
Elevation of City
Höhenangabe einer Stadt
Elevación de ciudad
Altitude d'une ville
Altitude de uma cidade

Khyber Pass 1067
Mountain Pass/Pass
Paso/Col de montagne
Passo (de montanha)

*
Rock/Fels
Roca/Rocher
Rocha

Lava/Lava
Lava/Lave
Lava

Sand Area/Sandgebiet
Área de arena/Région sableuse, Erg
Região arenosa, Erg

Salt Flat/Salzebene
Salar/Dépression salée
Depressão salgada

Elevations and depths are given in meters
Höhen und Tiefen sind in Metern angegeben
Elevaciones y profundidades se dan en metros
Cotes et profondeurs sont indiquées en mètres
Altitudes e profundidades são apresentadas em metros

A N D E S
KUNLUNSHANMAI
Mountain Range, Plateau, Valley, etc.
Gebirge, Hochebene, Tal, usw.
Sierra, Meseta, Valle, etc.
Chaîne de montagnes, Plateau, Vallée, etc.
Cadeia de montanhas. Planalto, Vale etc.

BAFFIN ISLAND
NUNIVAK ISLAND
Island
Insel
Isla
Île
Ilha

POLUOSTROV KAMČATKA
CABO DE HORNOS
Peninsula, Cape, Point, etc.
Halbinsel, Kap, Landspitze, usw.
Península, Cabo, Punta, etc.
Péninsule, Cap, Pointe, etc.
Península, Cabo, Ponta etc.

Highest Elevation and Lowest Elevation of a continent are underlined
Höchster und tiefster Punkt innerhalb eines Erdteils sind unterstrichen
Elevación más alta y más baja de un continente se subrayan
La cote la plus haute et la cote la plus basse d'un continent sont soulignées
As altitudes mais e menos elevadas de um continente são sublinhadas

Legend to Maps/Zeichenerklärung
Leyendas Para Mapas/Légende des Cartes/Legendas dos Mapas

Inhabited Localities / Bewohnte Orte / Lugares Poblados / Lieux Habités / Lugares Habitados

The symbol represents the number of inhabitants within the locality/Die Signatur entspricht der Einwohnerzahl des Ortes
El símbolo representa el número de habitantes dentro del lugar/Le symbole représente le nombre d'habitants de la localité
O símbolo representa o número de habitantes do lugar

1:300,000 1:3,000,000	1:1,000,000 1:6,000,000		
		•	0—10,000
		○	10,000—25,000
		⊙	25,000—100,000
		⊡	100,000—250,000
		▣	250,000—1,000,000
		■	>1,000,000

1:12,000,000		
	•	0—50,000
	⊙	50,000—100,000
	⊡	100,000—250,000
	▣	250,000—1,000,000
	■	>1,000,000

1:24,000,000 1:48,000,000		
	•	0—100,000
	⊙	100,000—1,500,000
	■	>1,500,000

The size of type indicates the relative economic and political importance of the locality
Die Schriftgrösse entspricht der relativen wirtschaftlichen und politischen Bedeutung des Ortes
El tamaño del tipo de imprenta indica la relativa importancia económica y política del lugar
La dimension des caractères indique l'importance économique et politique relative d'une localité
A dimensão dos caracteres tipográficos indica a importância econômica e política relativa do lugar

Écommoy	Lisieux	**Rouen**
Trouville	**Orléans**	**PARIS**

Hollywood □ *Westminster* — **Section of a City, Neighborhood/Stadtteil, Nachbarschaft**
Sección de una ciudad, Barrio/Arrondissement, Quartier
Seção de uma cidade, Bairro

Northland Center ■ — * **Major Shopping Center/Haupteinkaufszentrum/Mercado principal**
Centre commercial important/Centro comercial importante

BYRD □ — **Scientific Station/Wissenschaftliche Station/Estación científica**
Station scientifique/Estação científica

Bi'r Safājah ° — **Inhabited Oasis/Bewohnte Oase/Oasis habitado**
Oasis habitée/Oásis habitado

Kumdah ° — **Uninhabited Oasis/Unbewohnte Oase/Oasis deshabitado**
Oasis inhabitée/Oásis desabitado

Urban Area (area of continuous industrial, commercial, and residential development)
Stadtgebiet (ausgedehntes industrie-, Geschäfts- und Wohngebiet)
Zona urbanizada (área de desarrollo industrial, comercial y residencial)
Zone urbanisée (zone d'occupation continue par des industries, des commerces, des habitations)
Zona urbanizada (área de ocupação contínua por indústrias, estabelecimentos comerciais e habitações)

* **Major Industrial Area/Hauptindustriegebiet/Zona principal industrial**
Région industrielle importante/Zona industrial importante

* **Wooded Area/Wald/Área de bosque**
Région boisée/Área verde

* **Local Park or Recreational Area/Park oder Erholungsgebiet**
Parque municipal o área de recreo/Parc municipal ou zone de loisirs
Parque municipal ou área de lazer

Political Boundaries / Politische Grenzen / Límites Políticos / Frontières Politiques / Fronteiras e Limites

International (First-order political unit) **/Staatsgrenze** (Politische Einheit erster Ordnung)
Internacionales (Unidad política de primer orden) **/Internationales** (Entités politiques de premier ordre)
Internacionais (Unidade política de primeiro nível)

1:300,000 1:1,000,000 1:3,000,000 1:6,000,000	1:24,000,000 1:48,000,000	1:12,000,000	
HUNGARY			**Demarcated, Undemarcated, and Administrative** **Markiert, unmarkiert, verwaltungstechnisch** **Demarcado, No demarcado, y Administrativo** **Délimitées, Non-délimitées, Administratives** **Delimitados, Não delimitados, Administrativos**
			Disputed de facto/Umstritten de facto **Disputado de hecho/Contestées de facto** **Contestados de fato**
			Disputed de jure/Umstritten de jure **Disputado de derecho/Contestées de jure** **Contestados de direito**
			Indefinite or Undefined/Unklar oder Unbestimmt **Indefinido o No determinado/Imprécises ou Non définies** **Imprecisos ou Não definidos**
			Demarcation Line/Demarkationslinie **Línea de demarcación/Ligne de démarcation** **Linha de demarcação** (utilizada na Coréia)

Internal/Verwaltungsgrenze/Internos/Intérieures/Limites Internos

PERNAMBUCO — **State, Province, etc.** (Second-order political unit)
Land, Provinz, usw. (Politische Einheit zweiter Ordnung)
Estado, Provincia, etc. (Unidad política de segundo orden)
État, Province, etc. (Subdivision administrative de deuxième ordre)
Estado, Província, etc. (Unidade política de segundo nível)

WESTCHESTER — **County, Oblast, etc.** (Third-order political unit)**/Grafschaft, Oblast, usw.** (Politische Einheit dritter Ordnung)
Condado, Oblast, etc. (Unidad política de tercer orden)
Comté, Oblast, etc. (Subdivision administrative de troisième ordre)
Condado, Oblast, etc. (Unidade política de terceiro nível)

ISERLOHN — **Okrug, Kreis, etc.** (Fourth-order political unit)**/Okrug, Kreis, usw.** (Politische Einheit vierter Ordnung)
Okrug, Kreis, etc. (Unidad política de cuarto orden)
Okrug, Kreis, etc. (Subdivision administrative de quatrième ordre)
Okrug, Kreis, etc. (Unidade política de quarto nível)

City or Municipality (may appear in combination with another boundary symbol)
Stadt oder Gemeinde (kann zusammen mit einem anderen Begrenzungssymbol erscheinen)
Ciudad o Municipio (puede aparecer en combinación con otro símbolo de límite)
Ville ou Municipalité (peut paraître en combinaison avec un autre symbole de limites politiques)
Cidade ou Municipalidade (Pode aparecer em combinação com outro símbolo de limite político)

A N D A L U C Í A — **Historical Region** (No boundaries indicated)
Historische Landschaft (Grenzen werden nicht gezeigt)
Región Histórica (Sin indicación de límites)
Région Historique (Sans indication de frontières)
Região Histórica (Sem indicação de fronteiras)

Capitals of Political Units
Hauptstädte politischer Einheiten
Capitales de Unidades Políticas
Capitales d'Entités Politiques
Capitais de Unidades Políticas

BUDAPEST — Independent Nation
Unabhängiger Staat
Nación independiente
État indépendant
Estado independente

Cayenne — Dependency
(Colony, protectorate, etc.)
Abhängiges Gebiet
(Kolonie, Protektorat, usw.)
Dependencia
(Colonia, protectorado, etc.)
Territoire dépendant
(Colonie, protectorat, etc.)
Dependência
(Colônia, protetorado, etc.)

GALAPAGOS (Ecuador) — Administering Country
Verwaltender Staat
País administrador
Pays administrateur
País administrador

Recife — State, Province, etc./Land, Provinz, usw.
Estado, Provincia, etc./État, Province, etc.
Estado, Província, etc.

White Plains — County, Oblast, etc./Grafschaft, Oblast, usw.
Condado, Oblast, etc./Comté, Oblast, etc.
Condado, Oblast, etc.

Iserlohn — Okrug, Kreis, etc./Okrug, Kreis, usw.
Okrug, Kreis, etc./Okrug, Kreis, etc.
Okrug, Kreis, etc.

Legend to Maps/Zeichenerklärung
Leyendas Para Mapas/Légende des Cartes/Legendas dos Mapas

Transportation / Verkehr / Transporte / Transports / Transporte

Road/Strasse/Camino/Route/Rodovia	1:300,000	1:1,000,000	1:3,000,000 1:6,000,000	1:12,000,000
Primary/Erster Ordnung/Principal/de premier ordre/Principal	PASSAIC EXPWY. (I-80)	PENNSYLVANIA TURNPIKE		
Secondary/Zweiter Ordnung/Secundario/de second ordre/Secundária	BERLINER RING			
Tertiary/Dritter Ordnung/Terciario/de troisième ordre/Terciária				
Minor Road, Trail/Weg, Pfad Rodera, Vereda/Route secondaire, Piste/Caminho, trilha				

Railway/Eisenbahn/Ferrocarril/Voie ferrée/Ferrovia				
Primary/Hauptbahn/Principal/Principale/Principal	CANADIAN NATIONAL	SANTA FE		
Secondary/Sonstige Bahn/Secundario/Secondaire/Secundária				
*Rapid Transit/Schnellverkehr/Tránsito rápido/Métro/Trânsito rápido (metrô)				
Airport/Flughafen/Aeropuerto/Aéroport/Aeroporto	LONDON (HEATHROW) AIRPORT	DULLES INTERNATIONAL AIRPORT		
*Rail or Air Terminal/Bahnhof oder Flughafengebäude Terminal ferroviaria o aéro/Gare ou aérogare Terminal ferroviário ou aéreo (estação)	SÜD-BAHNHOF			

REICHS-BRÜCKE — Bridge/Brücke/Puente/Pont/Ponte

GREAT ST. BERNARD TUNNEL — Tunnel/Tunnel/Túnel/Tunnel/Túnel

Houston Ship Channel — Shipping Channel/Schiffahrtsrinne
Canal maritimo/Chenal maritime
Canal marítimo

Canal du Midi — Navigable Canal/Schiffbarer Kanal
Canal navegable/Canal navigable
Canal navegável

Intracoastal Waterway/Küstenschiffahrtsweg
Via fluvial Intracostera/Canal côtier
Via costeira interna

TO MALMÖ — Ferry/Fähre
Balsadera/Bac
Balsa

Miscellaneous Cultural Features / Sonstige Objekte / Elementos Culturales Misceláneos
Éléments Culturels Divers / Acidentes Culturais Diversos

PARQUE NACIONAL LANÍN — National or State Park or Monument
National- oder Naturpark oder Denkmal
Parque o Monumento nacional o provincial
Parc ou Monument national ou régional
Parque ou Monumento nacional ou regional

EDISON NAT. HIST. SITE — National or State Historic(al) Site, Memorial
Historische Stätte, Gedenkstätte
Sitio histórico nacional o provincial, Monumento
Site historique national ou régional, Mémorial
Sítio histórico nacional ou regional, Monumento histórico

SEMINOLE IND. RES. — Indian Reservation/Indianerreservation
Reserva de indios/Réserve indienne
Reserva indígena

FORT DIX — Military Installation/Militäranlage
Instalación militar/Installation militaire
Instalação militar

GREENWOOD CEMETERY — * Cemetery/Friedhof
Cementerio/Cimetière/Cemitério

SORBONNE — **Point of Interest** (Battlefield, museum, temple, university, etc.)
Sehenswürdigkeit (Schlachtfeld, Museum, Tempel, Universität, usw.)
Punto de interés (Campo de batalla, museo, templo, universidad, etc.)
Curiosité (Champ de bataille, musée, temple, université, etc.)
Pontos de interesse (Campo de batalha, museu, templo, universidade, etc.)

STEPHANSDOM — Church, Monastery/Kirche, Kloster
Iglesia, Monasterio/Église, Monastère
Igreja, Mosteiro

UXMAL — Ruins/Ruinen/Ruinas/Ruines/Ruínas

WINDSOR CASTLE — Castle/Burg, Schloss/Castillo/Château/Castelo

* Lighthouse/Leuchtturm
Faro/Phare/Farol

ASWĀN DAM — Dam/Damm/Presa/Barrage
Represa (barragem)

* Lock/Schleuse/Esclusa
Écluse/Eclusa

Crib — * Water Intake Crib/Wasseraufnahmestation
Toma de agua/Prise d'eau/Captação de água

Quarry or Surface Mine
Steinbruch oder Tagebau
Cantera o Mina de hoyo abierto
Carrière ou Mine à ciel ouvert
Pedreira ou mina a céu aberto

Subsurface Mine/Bergwerk
Mina subterránea/Mine souterraine
Mina subterrânea

* Oil Well/Ölbohrturm
Pozo de petróleo/Puits de pétrole
Poço de petróleo

Metric-English Equivalents / Umrechnung metrischer Masse in englische Masse / Métrico-Equivalentes Ingleses
Equivalences métriques des mesures anglaises / Equivalentes métricos das medidas inglesas

Areas represented by one square centimeter at various map scales
Flächen die einem cm² in den verschiedenen Kartenmassstäben entsprechen
Áreas representados por un centímetro cuadrado a varias escalas de mapas
Surface représentée par un cm² aux échelles indiquées
Áreas representadas por cm² nas escalas indicadas nos mapas

Meter=3.28 feet — Meter² (m²)=10.76 square feet
Kilometer=0.62 mile — Kilometer² (km²)=0.39 square mile

1:300,000	9 km²	3.48 square miles
1:1,000,000	100 km²	39 square miles
1:3,000,000	900 km²	348 square miles
1:6,000,000	3,600 km²	1,390 square miles
1:12,000,000	14,400 km²	5,558 square miles
1:24,000,000	57,600 km²	22,234 square miles
1:48,000,000	230,400 km²	88,934 square miles

Elevation tints shown only on 1:3,000,000 and 1:6,000,000 scale maps
Höhenschichten erscheinen nur auf Karten im Massstab 1:3 000 000 und 1:6 000 000
Se indica las tintas de elevación sólo en los mapas de escala 1:3 000 000 y 1:6 000 000
Teintes hypsométriques exprimées seulement sur cartes à 1:3 000 000 et 1:6 000 000
Indicaram-se as graduações de cor hipsométricas somente nos mapas de escalas 1:3 000 000 e 1:6 000 000

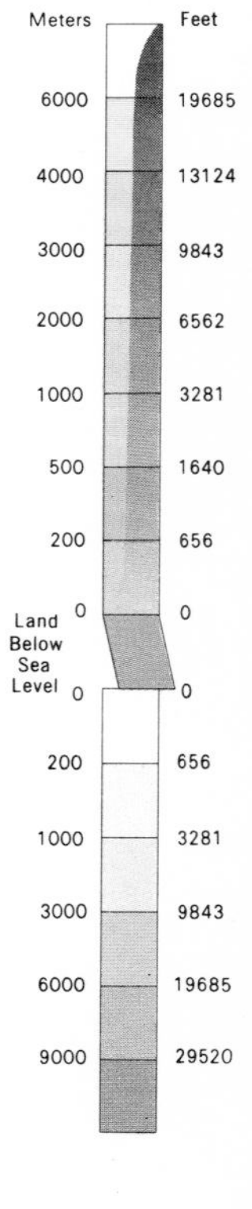

Meters
Feet
6000
19685
4000
13124
3000
9843
2000
6562
1000
3281
500
1640
200
656
0
0
Land Below Sea Level
0
0
200
656
1000
3281
3000
9843
6000
19685
9000
29520

Alternate Names / Alternative Namensformen / Nombres Alternativos
Variantes Toponymiques / Variantes Toponímicas

MOSKVA
MOSCOW

Basel
Bâle

English or second official language names are shown in reduced size lettering
Englische Namen oder Namen in einer zweiten offiziellen Sprache erscheinen in kleineren Schriftgrössen
Los nombres en inglés o un segundo idioma oficial se muestran en tipo de imprenta mas pequeño
Les toponymes en anglais ou dans la seconde langue officielle sont indiqués en caractères plus petits
Os topônimos em inglês ou num segundo idioma oficial aparecem em tipologia menor

VOLGOGRAD
(STALINGRAD)

Ventura
(San Buenaventura)

Historical or other alternates in the local language are shown in parentheses
Historische oder alternative Namensformen einheimischen Sprache erscheinen in Klammern
Los nombres históricos y alternativos locales se muestran en paréntesis
Les noms historiques de lieux ou les variantes toponymiques locales sont mis entre parenthèses
Os topônimos históricos ou as variantes toponímicas locais aparecem entre parênteses

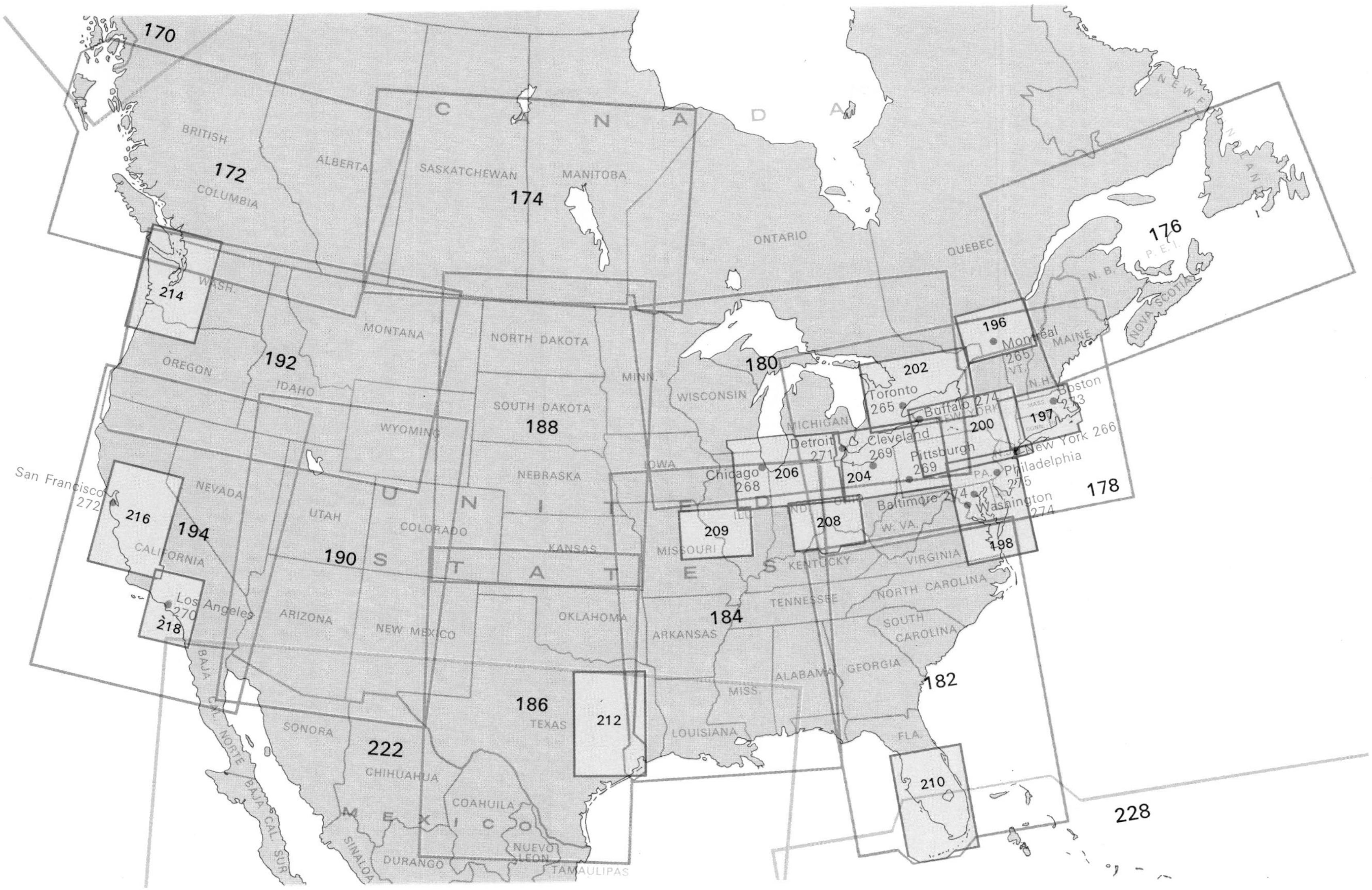
170
172
174
176
178
180
182
184
186
188
190
192
194
196
197
198
200
202
204
206
208
209
210
212
214
216
218
222
228
C A N A D A
U N I T E D S T A T E S
M E X I C O
BRITISH COLUMBIA
ALBERTA
SASKATCHEWAN
MANITOBA
ONTARIO
QUEBEC
N.B.
P.E.I.
NOVA SCOTIA
WASH.
OREGON
IDAHO
MONTANA
WYOMING
NORTH DAKOTA
SOUTH DAKOTA
NEBRASKA
MINN.
WISCONSIN
MICHIGAN
IOWA
NEVADA
UTAH
COLORADO
KANSAS
MISSOURI
CALIFORNIA
ARIZONA
NEW MEXICO
OKLAHOMA
ARKANSAS
TENNESSEE
KENTUCKY
VIRGINIA
W. VA.
NORTH CAROLINA
SOUTH CAROLINA
GEORGIA
ALABAMA
MISS.
LOUISIANA
TEXAS
FLA.
MAINE
VT.
N.H.
PA.
San Francisco 272
Los Angeles 270
Chicago 268
Detroit 271
Cleveland 269
Pittsburgh 269
Toronto 265
Buffalo 274
Montreal 265
Boston 273
New York 266
Philadelphia 275
Baltimore 274
Washington 274
SONORA
CHIHUAHUA
COAHUILA
NUEVO LEON
TAMAULIPAS
DURANGO
SINALOA
BAJA CAL. NORTE
BAJA CAL. SUR

24a
ICELAND
24
26
28
30
32
34
36
38
40
41
42
44
46
48
50
52
54
56
58
60
66
68
70
72
73
74
76
118
120
138
UNITED KINGDOM
IRE.
NORWAY
SWEDEN
FINLAND
DEN.
NETH.
BEL.
LUX.
FED. REP. OF GERMANY
GERMAN DEM. REP.
POLAND
CZECHOSLOVAKIA
FRANCE
SWITZ.
AUS.
HUNGARY
ROMANIA
YUGOSLAVIA
BUL.
ALB.
GREECE
ITALY
SPAIN
PORTUGAL
MOROCCO
ALGERIA
TUNISIA
MALTA
CYPRUS
LEBANON
SYRIA
IRAQ
IRAN
TURKEY
UNION OF SOVIET SOCIALIST REPUBLICS
Leningrad 255
Moskva 255
Manchester 252
London 250
Ruhr 253
Berlin 254
Paris 251
Wien 254
Budapest 254
Milano 256
Roma 257
Madrid 256
Lisboa 256
Barcelona 256
İstanbul 257
Athínai 257
Tehrān 257
Copyright © by Rand McNally & Co.
A-515300-964

MAP COVERAGE / KARTENAUSSCHNITTE
CONTENIDO DEL ATLAS / TABLEAU D'ASSEMBLAGE
ABRANGÊNCIA DO MAPA

Map Scale

Manila 259 • 1:300,000

1:1,000,000 | 1:6,000,000

1:3,000,000 | 1:12,000,000

138 **Page Reference / Seitenangabe**
Página de Referencia / Page de Référence / Página de Referência

Enlarged maps of Anglo-America and Europe on page xiii.
Vergrösserte Karten von Anglo-Amerika und Europa auf Seite xiii.
Mapas aumentados de América Anglosajona y Europa, página xiii.
Cartes à grande échelle de l'Amérique anglo-saxonne et de l'Europe à la page xiii.
Mapas ampliados da América Anglo-saxônica e da Europa, página xiii.

World, Ocean, and Continent maps on pages 2-19.
Weltkarten, Karten der Ozeane und Erdteile auf Seiten 2-19.
Mapas del Mundo, Océanos y Continentes, páginas 2-19.
Cartes du Monde, des Océans et des Continents aux pages 2-19.
Mapas do Mundo, dos Oceanos e dos Continentes, páginas 2-19.

Additional Pacific Ocean Island maps on pages 164-165.
Zusätzliche Karten der Inseln des Pazifischen Ozeans auf Seite 164-165.
Mapas adicionales de las Islas del Océano Pacifico, páginas 164-165.
Cartes supplémentaires des Îles de l'Océan Pacifique aux pages 164-165.
Mapas suplementares das ilhas do Oceano Pacifico, páginas 164-165.

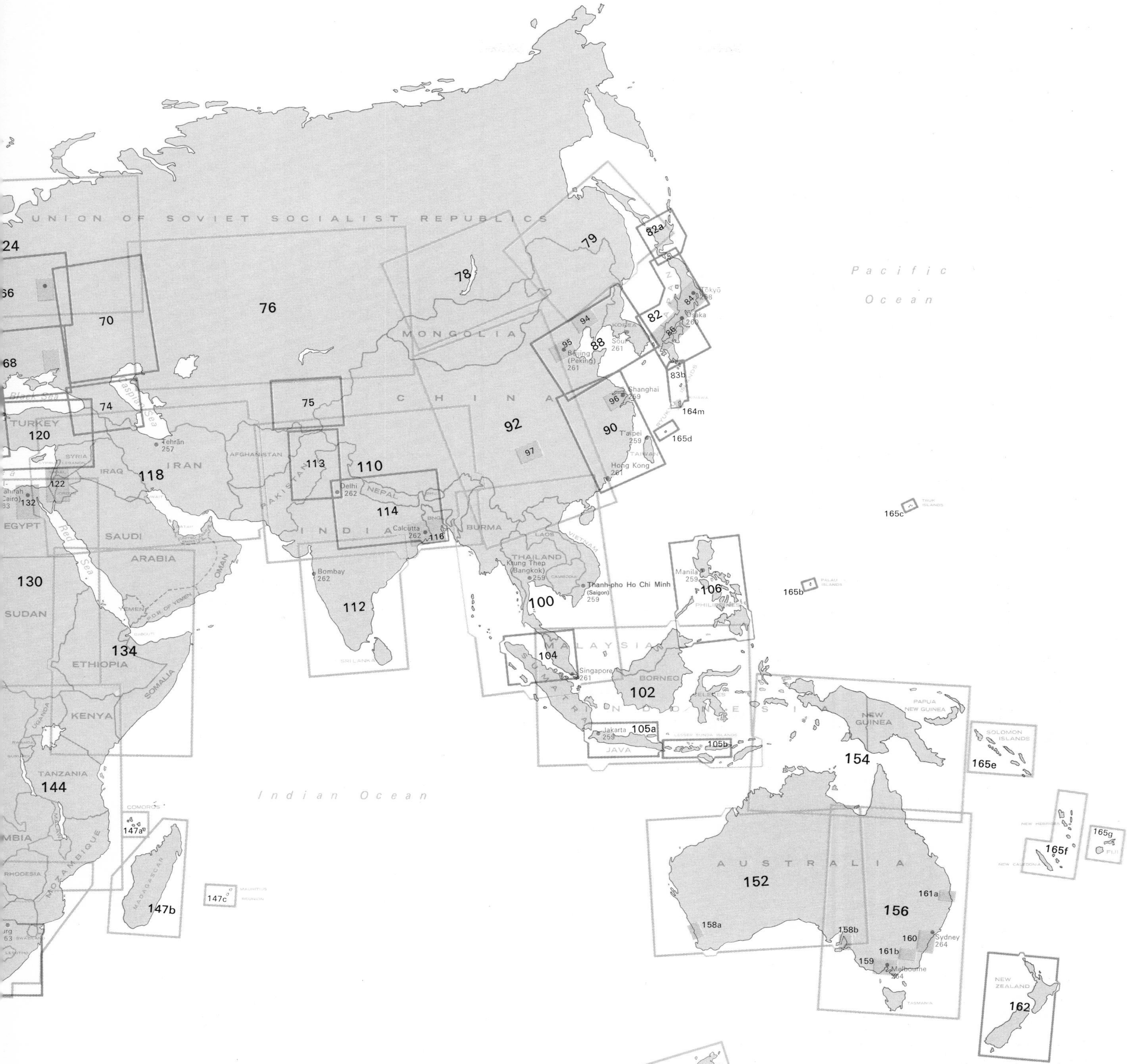
UNION OF SOVIET SOCIALIST REPUBLICS
Pacific Ocean
Indian Ocean
MONGOLIA
CHINA
KOREA
TURKEY
SYRIA
IRAQ
IRAN
AFGHANISTAN
PAKISTAN
NEPAL
INDIA
BURMA
EGYPT
SAUDI ARABIA
OMAN
SUDAN
ETHIOPIA
SOMALIA
KENYA
TANZANIA
MOZAMBIQUE
RHODESIA
MADAGASCAR
LAOS
VIETNAM
THAILAND
CAMBODIA
PHILIPPINES
MALAYSIA
BORNEO
SUMATRA
INDONESIA
JAVA
NEW GUINEA
PAPUA NEW GUINEA
SOLOMON ISLANDS
AUSTRALIA
NEW ZEALAND
Tehrān 257
Delhi 262
Calcutta 262
Bombay 262
Beijing (Peking) 261
Sŏul 261
Tōkyō 258
Ōsaka 260
Shanghai 259
T'aipei 259
Hong Kong 261
Krung Thep (Bangkok) 259
Thanh-pho Ho Chi Minh (Saigon) 259
Manila 259
Singapore 261
Jakarta 259
Sydney 264
Melbourne 264
24
66
68
70
74
75
76
78
79
82
82a
83b
84
86
88
90
92
94
95
96
97
100
102
104
105a
105b
106
110
112
113
114
116
118
120
122
130
132
134
144
147a
147b
147c
152
154
156
158a
158b
159
160
161a
161b
162
164m
165b
165c
165d
165e
165f
165g

166
168
220
232
234
22
62
64
80
108
124
126
128
98
150

THIS SECTION OPENS with World Political and World Physical maps at the scale of 1:75,000,000. There follow maps of the Pacific, Indian, and Atlantic oceans at the scale 1:48,000,000, the largest scale at which the total expanse of these bodies of water could be portrayed. Finally, a series of continent relief maps at the scale of 1:24,000,000 show a global view of the earth as it would appear from about 4,000 miles in space. The Azimuthal Equal-Area projection is used for the 1:24,000,000 maps, the scale being approximately that of a globe 20 inches in diameter.

The colors of the continent maps portray the land areas as if viewed from space during the growing season, without regard to the fact that the growing seasons are not concurrent in all areas. Underwater features and varying water depths are represented by shaded relief and different color tones. The result is a strong physical portrait of the earth's major land and submarine forms. The legend below shows how these different kinds of terrain and vegetation have been represented. The names of physical features—plateaus, basins, mountain ranges, seas, rivers, lakes, gulfs, trenches, bays, islands—predominate on these maps.

DIESER KARTENTEIL BEGINNT mit politischen und physischen Weltkarten im Massstab 1:75 Millionen. Dann folgen Karten des Pazifischen, Indischen und Atlantischen Ozeans in 1:48 Millionen, dem grössten Massstab, in dem diese Wasserflächen in ihrer ganzen Ausdehnung abgebildet werden konnten. Schliesslich folgt eine Reihe von Reliefkarten der Erdteile in 1:24 Millionen. Sie geben eine Übersicht der Erde, wie sie aus einer Entfernung von ungefähr 6 400 Kilometer aus dem Weltraum gewonnen würde. Den Karten im Massstab 1:24 Millionen liegt ein flächentreuer azimutaler Entwurf zugrunde, dieser Massstab entspricht ungefähr dem eines Globus von 50 cm Durchmesser.

Die Farben der Erdteilkarten bilden jedes Landgebiet so ab, wie es in der Vegetationsperiode aus der Vogelperspektive erschiene, ohne zu berücksichtigen, dass die Vegetationsperioden nicht in allen Gebieten gleichzeitig eintreten. Die Gliederung des Meeresbodens und die unterschiedlichen Meerestiefen werden durch Schummerung und verschiedene Farbstufen dargestellt. Das Ergebnis ist eine anschauliche physische Darstellung der wichtigsten terrestrischen und untermeerischen Formen der Erde. Die untenstehende Zeichenerklärung zeigt, wie diese verschiedenen Geländeformen und Vegetationsgebiete veranschaulicht werden. Namen physischer Objekte—Hochebenen, Becken, Gebirgszüge, Meere, Flüsse, Seen, Buchten, Gräben, Inseln—herrschen in diesen Karten vor.

ESTA SECCIÓN DA PRINCIPIO con los Mapas Políticos y Físicos del Mundo, a una escala de 1:75 000 000. A continuación están los mapas de los océanos Pacífico, Indico y Atlántico a una escala de 1:48 000 000, que es la mayor escala utilizable para la representación de esas masas de agua en toda su extensión. Por último, una serie de mapas del relieve de los continentes, a una escala de 1:24 000 000, proporcionan una vista global de la tierra tal como se apreciaría desde el espacio a una distancia aproximada de 6 400 kilómetros. La proyección azimutal equiárea se usa, para los mapas de 1:24 000 000, a una escala según la cual la tierra se reduciría a un globo de unos 50 cm de diámetro.

Los colores utilizados en los mapas de los continentes representan las diversas regiones de la tierra tal como se verían desde el espacio durante la estación en que la vegetación se desarrolla, sin tomar en cuenta que este fenómeno no se produce simultáneamente en todas las áreas. Las estructuras características del fondo marino y las variaciones de profundidad de los océanos se representan mediante relieve sombreado y distintos matices de color. El resultado es una imagen elocuente de las formas terrestres y submarinas más notables del planeta. La leyenda abajo explica cómo se representan estos diferentes tipos de terreno y vegetación. En estos mapas predomina la nomenclatura de elementos físicos: mesetas, cuencas, sierras, mares, ríos, lagos, golfos, bahías, trincheras, islas.

CETTE PARTIE comprend d'abord des cartes du monde politique et du monde physique à l'échelle de 1:75 000 000. Viennent ensuite les cartes des océans Pacifique, Indien et Atlantique à l'échelle de 1:48 000 000, la plus grande échelle qui a permis la reproduction complète de ces étendues d'eau. Pour terminer, une série de cartes en relief des continents à l'échelle de 1:24 000 000 donne une vue globale de la terre, telle qu'elle apparaîtrait vue de l'espace à une distance d'environ 6 400 kilomètres. La projection azimutale équivalente a été utilisée pour les cartes au 1:24 000 000e, dont l'échelle équivaut à celle d'un globe de 50 cm de diamètre environ.

Les couleurs des cartes font apparaître les continents tels qu'on les verrait de l'espace, pendant la saison de croissance végétale, mais sans tenir compte du fait que cette saison n'apparaît pas partout simultanément. Le relief sous-marin est représenté par un estompage et la profondeur des océans par une variation de la couleur. Il en résulte une reproduction vigoureuse des principaux paysages continentaux et des principales formes sous-marines. La légende ci-dessous indique de quelle façon ils sont cartographiés. Les noms d'éléments topographiques tels que plateaux, bassins, chaînes de montagnes, mers, cours d'eau, lacs, golfes, baies, crêtes, îles et fosses océaniques, prédominent dans ces cartes.

ESTA SEÇÃO PRINCIPIA com os mapas políticos e físicos do Mundo, em escala de 1:75 000 000. Seguem-se os mapas dos oceanos Pacífico, Índico e Atlântico na escala de 1:48 000 000, a maior escala que se pode utilizar para a representação dessas massas de água em toda a sua extensão. Finalmente, uma série de mapas de relevo dos continentes, na escala de 1:24 000 000, proporciona uma visão global da Terra tal como apareceria do espaço a uma distância aproximada de cerca de 6 400 km. A projeção azimutal equiárea foi usada para os mapas da escala de 1:24 000 000, segundo a qual a Terra se apresentaria como um globo de cerca de 50 cm de diâmetro.

As cores utilizadas nos mapas dos continentes representam as massas terrestres tal como apareceriam vistas do espaço durante a estação do crescimento vegetal, sem levar em conta que este fenômeno não se produz simultaneamente em todas as regiões. As características do fundo do mar e as variações de profundidade das águas são representadas por um relevo sombreado e por diferentes matizes de cor. O resultado proporciona uma imagem física eloqüente das principais formas terrestres e submarinas da Terra. As legendas abaixo explicam como foram representados os diversos tipos de terreno e de vegetação. Nestes mapas predomina a nomenclatura dos elementos físicos: planaltos, bacias, cadeias de montanhas, mares, rios, lagos, golfos, baías, fossas, ilhas.

Land Features / Land Phänomene / Elementos de la Tierra / Paysages Continentaux / Elementos da Terra

Ice and Snow
Eis und Schnee
Hielo y nieve
Glace et neige
Gelo e neve

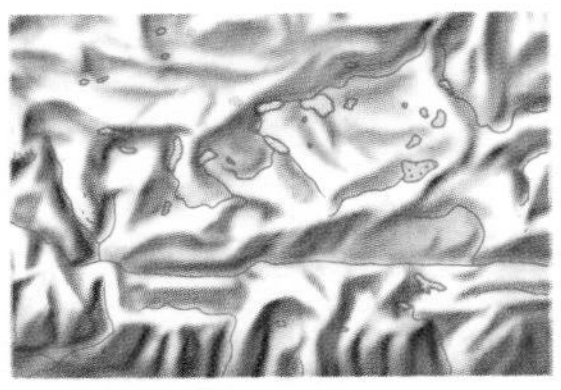

High Barren Area
Hochgebirgswüste
Alta zona árida
Région haute et aride
Alta zona árida

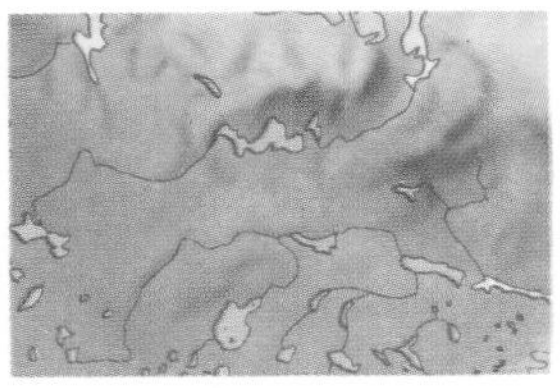

Tundra and Alpine
Tundra und Alpine Vegetation
Tundra y alpina
Toundra et végétation alpine
Tundra e vegetação alpina

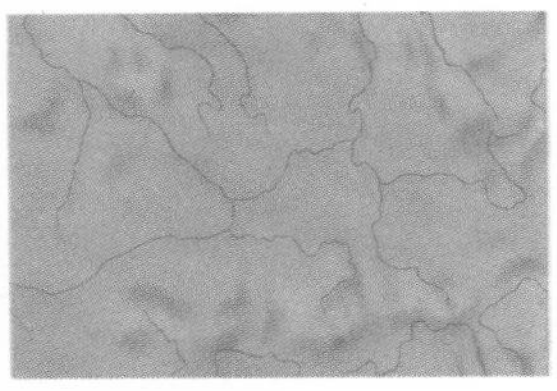

Needleleaf Trees
Nadelwälder
Coníferas
Forêt de conifères
Coníferas

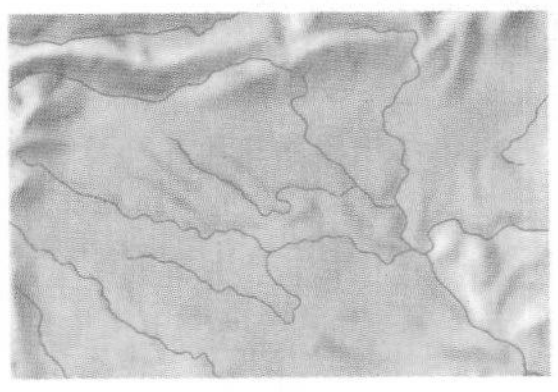

Broadleaf Trees
Laubwälder
Árboles de hojas anchas
Forêt à feuilles caduques
Árvores de folhas caducas

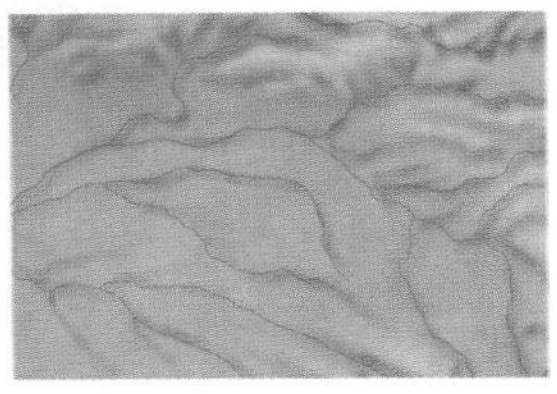

Tropical Rainforest
Tropischer Regenwald
Bosque tropical lluvioso
Forêt tropicale humide
Floresta tropical úmida

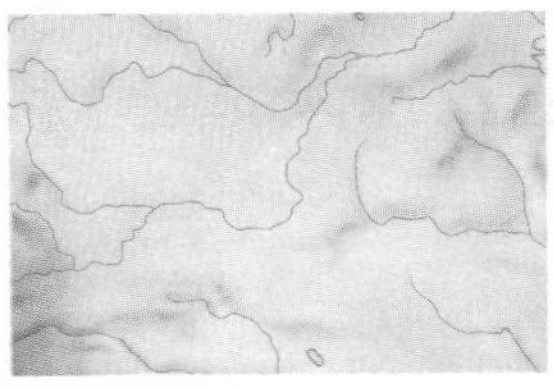

Grassland
Grasland
Pradera
Formations herbacées
Pradaria

Dry Scrub
Trockenes Buschland
Matorral
Brousse sèche
Caatinga

Desert
Wüste
Desierto
Désert
Deserto

Submarine Features / Untermeerische Phänomene / Elementos Submarinos / Formes de Relief Sous-marin / Elementos Submarinos

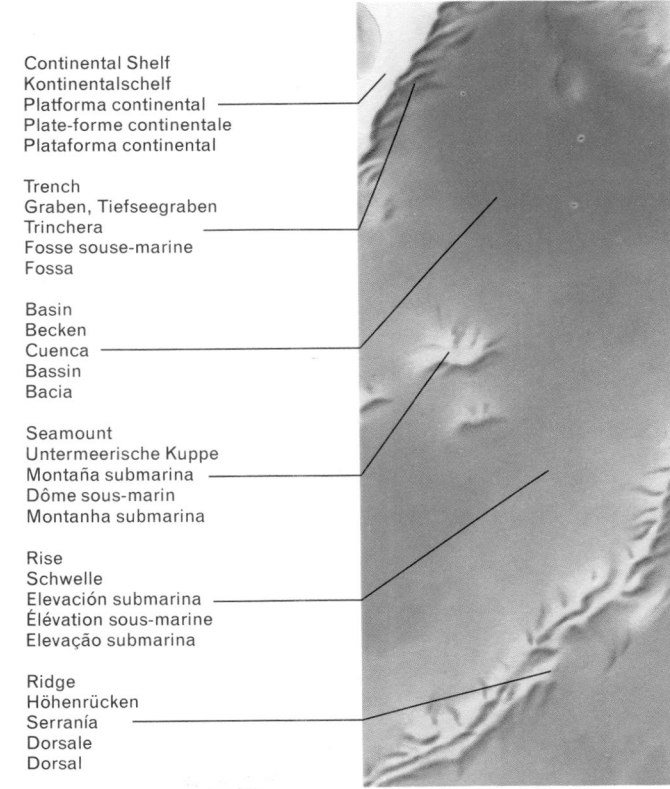

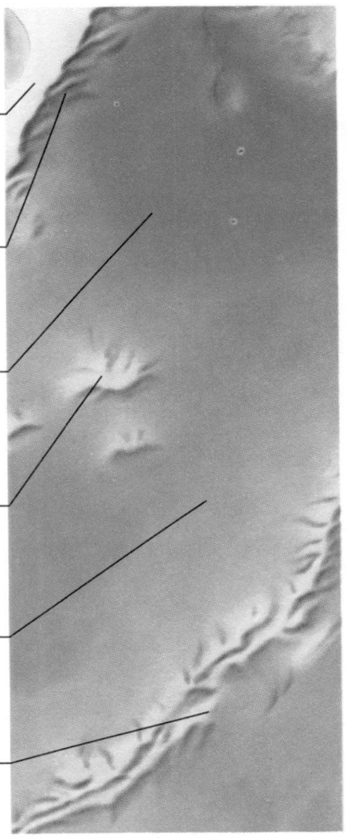
Continental Shelf
Kontinentalschelf
Platforma continental
Plate-forme continentale
Plataforma continental
Trench
Graben, Tiefseegraben
Trinchera
Fosse souse-marine
Fossa
Basin
Becken
Cuenca
Bassin
Bacia
Seamount
Untermeerische Kuppe
Montaña submarina
Dôme sous-marin
Montanha submarina
Rise
Schwelle
Elevación submarina
Élévation sous-marine
Elevação submarina
Ridge
Höhenrücken
Serranía
Dorsale
Dorsal

ARCTIC OCEAN
GREENLAND
(Den.)
Beaufort Sea
Baffin Bay
BAFFIN ISLAND
VICTORIA ISLAND
UNITED STATES
U.S.S.R.
ICELAND
Reykjavik
Godthåb
Thule
Godhavn
Angmagssalik
Nome
Fairbanks
Anchorage
Mount McKinley
Inuvik
Yellowknife
Hudson Bay
Churchill
Bering Sea
Gulf of Alaska
ALEUTIAN ISLANDS
C A N A D A
ROCKY MOUNTAINS
Edmonton
Calgary
Winnipeg
Vancouver
Seattle
Portland
Goose Bay
NEWFOUNDLAND
St. John's
Halifax
Québec
Montreal
Ottawa
Toronto
Minneapolis
DETROIT
CHICAGO
Boston
NEW YORK
PHILADELPHIA
Washington
NORTH AMERICA
UNITED STATES
Salt Lake City
Denver
St. Louis
SAN FRANCISCO
LOS ANGELES
San Diego
Phoenix
El Paso
Dallas
Atlanta
APPALACHIAN MOUNTAINS
Houston
New Orleans
Miami
BAHAMAS
BERMUDA
(U.K.)
ATLANTIC OCEAN
IRELAND
Dublin
Glasgow
PORTUGAL
Porto
Lisboa
GIBRALTAR
(U.K.)
Rabat
Casablanca
MOROCCO
AÇORES AZORES
(Port.)
ARQUIPÉLAGO DA MADEIRA
(Port.)
ISLAS CANARIAS
CANARY ISLANDS
(Sp.)
WESTERN SAHARA
MAURI-TANIA
Nouakchott
CAPE VERDE
SENEGAL
Dakar
GAMBIA
Banjul
GUINEA-BISSAU
GUINEA
Conakry
SIERRA LEONE
Freetown
Monrovia
LIBERIA
PACIFIC OCEAN
MIDWAY ISLANDS
(U.S.)
HAWAIIAN ISLANDS
(U.S.)
Honolulu
JOHNSTON ISLAND
(U.S.)
Tropic of Cancer
Gulf of Mexico
MEXICO
Monterrey
CABO SAN LUCAS
Guadalajara
CIUDAD DE MÉXICO
CUBA
La Habana
JAMAICA
Kingston
HAITI
Port-au-Prince
DOMINICAN REPUBLIC
Santo Domingo
PUERTO RICO (U.S.)
San Juan
GUADELOUPE (Fr.)
MARTINIQUE (Fr.)
BARBADOS
TRINIDAD AND TOBAGO
Port of Spain
Caribbean Sea
GUATEMALA
Guatemala
BELIZE
HONDURAS
Tegucigalpa
San Salvador
EL SALVADOR
NICARAGUA
Managua
San José
COSTA RICA
Panamá
PANAMA
CLIPPERTON
(Fr. Poly.)
Caracas
VENEZUELA
GUYANA
Georgetown
Paramaribo
SURINAME
FRENCH GUIANA
Medellín
Bogotá
Cali
COLOMBIA
Quito
ECUADOR
Guayaquil
ARCHIPIÉLAGO DE COLÓN
GALÁPAGOS ISLANDS
(Ec.)
LINE ISLANDS
Equator
POLYNESIA
CANTON AND ENDERBURY (U.K.–U.S.)
PHOENIX ISLANDS
TOKELAU ISLANDS
(N.Z.)
ÎLES MARQUISES
WALLIS AND FUTUNA
(Fr.)
W. SAMOA
AM. SAMOA
Apia
FIJI
TONGA
NIUE
(N.Z.)
COOK ISLANDS
(N.Z.)
ÎLES DE LA SOCIÉTÉ
SOCIETY ISLANDS
ÎLES TUAMOTU
FRENCH POLYNESIA
Manaus
Amazonas
Belém
Fortaleza
CABO DE SÃO ROQUE
Natal
Recife
Iquitos
Trujillo
Lima
PERU
B R A Z I L
SOUTH AMERICA
Salvador
Arequipa
La Paz
BOLIVIA
Sucre
Goiânia
Brasília
Belo Horizonte
PARAGUAY
SÃO PAULO
RIO DE JANEIRO
Santos
Curitiba
Asunción
Antofagasta
ISLA SAN AMBROSIO
(Chile)
CHILE
Tropic of Capricorn
PITCAIRN
(U.K.)
ISLA DE PASCUA
EASTER ISLAND
(Chile)
Córdoba
Porto Alegre
URUGUAY
Rosario
Valparaíso
Santiago
Co. Aconcagua
6959
BUENOS AIRES
Montevideo
ISLAS JUAN FERNÁNDEZ
(Chile)
ARGENTINA
Concepción
Mar del Plata
Bahía Blanca
ANDES
International Date Line
CHATHAM ISLAND
(N.Z.)
FALKLAND ISLANDS
ISLAS MALVINAS
(U.K.)
Punta Arenas
CABO DE HORNOS
CAPE HORN
SOUTH GEORGIA
(Falk. Is.)
SOUTH ORKNEY ISLANDS
(B.A.T.)
Antarctic Circle
LARSEN ICE SHELF
Bellingshausen Sea
Weddell Sea
Ross Sea
Vinson Massif
5140
A N T A R

Kilometers 0 1000 2000 3000 Km.

Statute Miles 0 1000 2000 3000 Mi.

One centimeter represents 750 kilometers.
One inch represents approximately 1200 miles.

Robinson Projection

Scale 1:75,000,000

ARCTIC OCEAN
GREENLAND
ELLESMERE ISLAND
QUEEN ELIZABETH ISLANDS
Beaufort Sea
Baffin Bay
BAFFIN ISLAND
Hudson Bay
Labrador Sea
LABRADOR BASIN
ICELAND
Bering Sea
Gulf of Alaska
ALEUTIAN BASIN
ALEUTIAN TRENCH
C A N A D A
N O R T H
A M E R I C A
U N I T E D S T A T E S
ROCKY MOUNTAINS
APPALACHIAN MOUNTAINS
GREAT BASIN
GREAT PLAINS
Gulf of Mexico
M E X I C O
Caribbean Sea
GREATER ANTILLES
P A C I F I C
O C E A N
MENDOCINO SEASCARP
MURRAY FRACTURE ZONE
Tropic of Cancer
HAWAIIAN ISLANDS
MARCUS-NECKER RIDGE
CENTRAL PACIFIC BASIN
CLARION FRACTURE ZONE
CLIPPERTON FRACTURE ZONE
EAST PACIFIC BASIN
Equator
P O L Y N E S I A
ATLANTIC
OCEAN
NORTH AMERICAN BASIN
NEWFOUNDLAND BASIN
MID-ATLANTIC RIDGE
CAPE VERDE BASIN
GUIANA BASIN
REYKJANES RIDGE
WEST EUROPEAN BASIN
S O U T H
A M E R I C A
B R A Z I L
Amazon
SELVAS
ANDES
BRAZIL BASIN
ARGENTINE BASIN
PAMPAS
PATAGONIA
Tropic of Capricorn
P A C I F I C
O C E A N
SOUTHWESTERN PACIFIC BASIN
SOUTHEAST PACIFIC BASIN
ALBATROSS CORDILLERA
CHILE RISE
FALKLAND ISLANDS
Scotia Sea
Drake Passage
Antarctic Circle
Weddell Sea
Bellingshausen Sea
Amundsen Sea
Ross Sea
ROSS ICE SHELF
BYRD LAND
QUEEN MAUD MOUNTAINS
WHITMORE MOUNTAINS
International Date Line

Kilometers 0 1000 2000 3000 Km.
Statute Miles 0 1000 2000 3000 Mi.

One centimeter represents 750 kilometers.
One inch represents approximately 1200 miles.
Robinson Projection
Scale 1:75,000,000

GREENLAND
Greenland Sea
Barents Sea
Arctic Circle
Norwegian Sea
ICELAND
Reykjavík
NORWAY
SWEDEN
FINLAND
Helsinki
LENINGRAD
Oslo
Stockholm
Baltic Sea
North Sea
UNITED KINGDOM
IRELAND
Dublin
LONDON
København
DENMARK
Amsterdam
NETH.
BERLIN
Warszawa
POLAND
PARIS
FRANCE
Wien
Budapest
HUNGARY
ROMANIA
Bucureşti
Beograd
YUGO.
BULGARIA
Sofija
MOSKVA
Volga
URAL'SKIJE GORY
URAL MOUNTAINS
UNION OF SOVIET SOCIALIST REPUBLICS
ZAPADNO-SIBIRSKAJA NIZMENNOST'
SREDNESIBIRSKOJE PLOSKOGORJE
Sea of Okhotsk
More Laptevych
Black Sea
Caspian Sea
Aral'skoje More
İstanbul
Ankara
TURKEY
MEDITERRANEAN SEA
Roma
Napoli
Barcelona
TUNISIA
Tunis
LIBYA
SAHARA
EGYPT
AL-QAHIRAH
CYPRUS
SYRIA
LEBANON
ISRAEL
JORDAN
IRAQ
Baghdad
IRAN
Tehrān
KUWAIT
SAUDI ARABIA
Ar-Riyad
QATAR
UNITED ARAB EMIRATES
OMAN
YEMEN
P.D.R. of YEMEN
Aden
Gulf of Aden
Red Sea
Tropic of Cancer
SUDAN
Al-Khurtūm
ETHIOPIA
Addis Abeba
DJIBOUTI
SOMALIA
Mogadisho
KENYA
Nairobi
UGANDA
RWANDA
BURUNDI
TANZANIA
Dar-es-Salaam
ZAIRE
ZAMBIA
Lusaka
MALAWI
MOZAMBIQUE
Maputo
RHODESIA
Salisbury
BOTSWANA
NAMIBIA
SOUTH AFRICA
Pretoria
Johannesburg
Durban
Cape Town
LESOTHO
SWAZILAND
MADAGASCAR
Mozambique Channel
AFRICA
AFGHANISTAN
Kābul
PAKISTAN
Karāchi
INDIA
Delhi
Bombay
CALCUTTA
Madras
Bangalore
Hyderābād
NEPAL
Mount Everest
BHUTAN
BNGL.
Dacca
SRI LANKA
Colombo
MALDIVES
ARABIAN SEA
Bay of Bengal
HIMALAYAS
TIEN SHAN
PAMIR
HINDU KUSH
ALTAY
MONGOLIA
GOBI
CHINA
BEIJING
Shanghai
Chongqing
Guangzhou
HONG KONG
Taipei
TAIWAN
KOREA
SOUL
Pyongyang
JAPAN
TŌKYŌ
Ōsaka
Sea of Japan
Yellow Sea
East China Sea
South China Sea
BURMA
Rangoon
THAILAND
Bangkok
KAM.
VIET-NAM
Ha-noi
Thanh-pho Ho Chi Minh
PHILIPPINES
Manila
Philippine Sea
MALAYSIA
Kuala Lumpur
Singapore
BRUNEI
BORNEO
SUMATERA
JAKARTA
GREATER SUNDA ISLANDS
INDONESIA
JAWA
SULAWESI
PAPUA NEW GUINEA
Arafura Sea
Timor Sea
AUSTRALIA
GREAT SANDY DESERT
GIBSON DESERT
GREAT VICTORIA DESERT
GREAT DIVIDING RANGE
GREAT BARRIER REEF
Perth
Adelaide
Melbourne
Sydney
Canberra
Brisbane
Great Australian Bight
TASMANIA
Hobart
Coral Sea
Gulf of Carpentaria
INDIAN OCEAN
Equator
Tropic of Capricorn
SEYCHELLES
MAURITIUS
RÉUNION
CHAGOS ARCHIPELAGO
COCOS ISLANDS
CHRISTMAS ISLAND
CENTRAL BASIN
ARABIAN BASIN
SOMALI BASIN
MASCARENE BASIN
WEST AUSTRALIAN BASIN
SOUTH AUSTRALIAN BASIN
CROZET BASIN
AGULHAS BASIN
MID-INDIAN RIDGE
CARLSBERG RIDGE
NINETY EAST RIDGE
WEST-INDIAN RIDGE
ATLANTIC-INDIAN RIDGE
ATLANTIC-INDIAN BASIN
SOUTH INDIAN BASIN
AUSTRALIAN-ANTARCTIC RISE
KERGUELEN-GAUSSBERG RIDGE
AMSTERDAM-NATURALISTE RIDGE
MADAGASCAR BASIN
MADAGASCAR PLATEAU
MOZAMBIQUE PLATEAU
JAVA TRENCH
ÎLES KERGUELEN
ÎLES CROZET
PRINCE EDWARD ISLANDS
BOUVETØYA
Antarctic Circle
ANTARCTICA
ENDERBY LAND
QUEEN MAUD LAND
PRINCESS MARTHA COAST
NEW SCHWABENLAND
AMERICAN HIGHLAND
WILKES LAND
AMERY ICE SHELF
WEST ICE SHELF
SHACKLETON ICE SHELF

ARCTIC OCEAN
Beaufort Sea
Chukchi Sea
BERING SEA
ALEUTIAN BASIN
ALEUTIAN TRENCH
Gulf of Alaska
GULF OF ALASKA SEAMOUNT PROVINCE
International Date Line
EMPEROR SEAMOUNT CHAIN
PACIFIC OCEAN
MENDOCINO SEASCARP
MURRAY FRACTURE ZONE
NORTH HAWAIIAN SEAMOUNT RANGE
MIDWAY ISLANDS
HAWAIIAN ISLANDS
HAWAIIAN RIDGE
Honolulu
Tropic of Cancer
WAKE ISLAND
MARCUS-NECKER RIDGE
JOHNSTON ISLAND
EAST PACIFIC BASIN
CENTRAL PACIFIC BASIN
MARSHALL ISLANDS
KINGMAN REEF
PALMYRA ATOLL
NORTHWEST CHRISTMAS ISLAND RIDGE
LINE ISLANDS
CHRISTMAS ISLAND
Equator
CANTON AND ENDERBURY
KIRIBATI
TUVALU
TOKELAU ISLANDS
W. SAMOA
AMERICAN SAMOA
WALLIS AND FUTUNA
FIJI
NORTH FIJI BASIN
TONGA
TONGA TRENCH
KERMADEC TRENCH
COOK ISLANDS
FRENCH POLYNESIA
ÎLES MARQUISES
TAHITI
ÎLES TUAMOTU
PITCAIRN
AUSTRAL SEAMOUNT CHAIN
Tropic of Capricorn
SOUTH FIJI BASIN
NORFOLK ISLAND
NORFOLK ISLAND RIDGE
LOUISVILLE RIDGE
NEW ZEALAND
NORTH ISLAND
SOUTH ISLAND
Auckland
Wellington
Christchurch
CHATHAM RISE
BOUNTY BASIN
CAMPBELL RISE
SOUTHWESTERN PACIFIC BASIN
EMERALD BASIN
ALBATROSS CORDILLERA
SOUTHEAST PACIFIC BASIN
CHILE RISE
ISLA DE PASCUA
EASTER ISLAND
ISLA SALA Y GÓMEZ
CLARION FRACTURE ZONE
CLIPPERTON FRACTURE ZONE
MIDDLE AMERICA TRENCH
GALÁPAGOS ISLANDS
CARNEGIE RIDGE
COCOS RIDGE
NORTH AMERICA
CANADA
UNITED STATES
ROCKY MOUNTAINS
ALASKA
Anchorage
Vancouver
Seattle
Portland
SAN FRANCISCO
LOS ANGELES
San Diego
Salt Lake City
Denver
Phoenix
El Paso
Dallas
Houston
New Orleans
Memphis
Saint Louis
CHICAGO
DETROIT
Minneapolis
Winnipeg
Edmonton
Calgary
Ottawa
Toronto
Montréal
Quebec
Buffalo
Cleveland
Washington
BOSTON
NEW YORK
PHILADELPHIA
Baltimore
Norfolk
Atlanta
Charleston
Jacksonville
Tampa
Miami
Hudson Bay
Labrador Sea
LABRADOR BASIN
GREENLAND
ICELAND
NEWFOUNDLAND
ATLANTIC
NORTH AMERICAN BASIN
OCEAN
BERMUDA
Gulf of Mexico
MEXICO
CIUDAD DE MÉXICO
Guadalajara
Monterrey
CUBA
La Habana
BAHAMAS
WEST INDIES
PUERTO RICO
HAITI
DOM. REP.
JAMAICA
BELIZE
GUATEMALA
HONDURAS
NICARAGUA
COSTA RICA
PANAMA
Caribbean Sea
VENEZUELA
COLOMBIA
Bogotá
ECUADOR
Quito
Guayaquil
PERU
Lima
SOUTH AMERICA
BRAZIL
Amazon
BOLIVIA
La Paz
PARAGUAY
Asunción
ATACAMA TRENCH
Antofagasta
Santiago
Valparaíso
ISLAS JUAN FERNÁNDEZ
Córdoba
Rosario
BUENOS AIRES
Montevideo
URUGUAY
Río de la Plata
PAMPAS
ARGENTINA
ARGENTINE BASIN
CHILE
ANDES
PATAGONIA
Punta Arenas
Estrecho de Magallanes
ISLA GRANDE DE TIERRA DEL FUEGO
FALKLAND ISLANDS
FALKLAND RISE
SOUTH GEORGIA RISE
Scotia Sea
Drake Passage
SOUTH SHETLAND ISLANDS
SOUTH ORKNEY ISLANDS
SOUTH SANDWICH ISLANDS
GRAHAM LAND
ANTARCTIC PENINSULA
ATLANTIC-INDIAN BASIN
Antarctic Circle
Bellingshausen Sea
Amundsen Sea
Weddell Sea
Ross Sea
Kilometers 0 400 800 1200 1600 Km.
Statute Miles 0 400 800 1200 1600 Mi.
Scale 1:48,000,000
at 35° latitude
One centimeter represents 480 kilometers.
One inch represents approximately 760 miles.
Modified Cylindrical Projection
Copyright © by Rand McNally & Co.
Map prepared by Rand McNally & Co.
A-514700-764 -13

Atlantic Ocean / Atlantischer Ozean
Océano Atlántico / Océan Atlantique
Oceano Atlântico

Antarctica / Antarktis
Antártida / Antarctique
Antártida

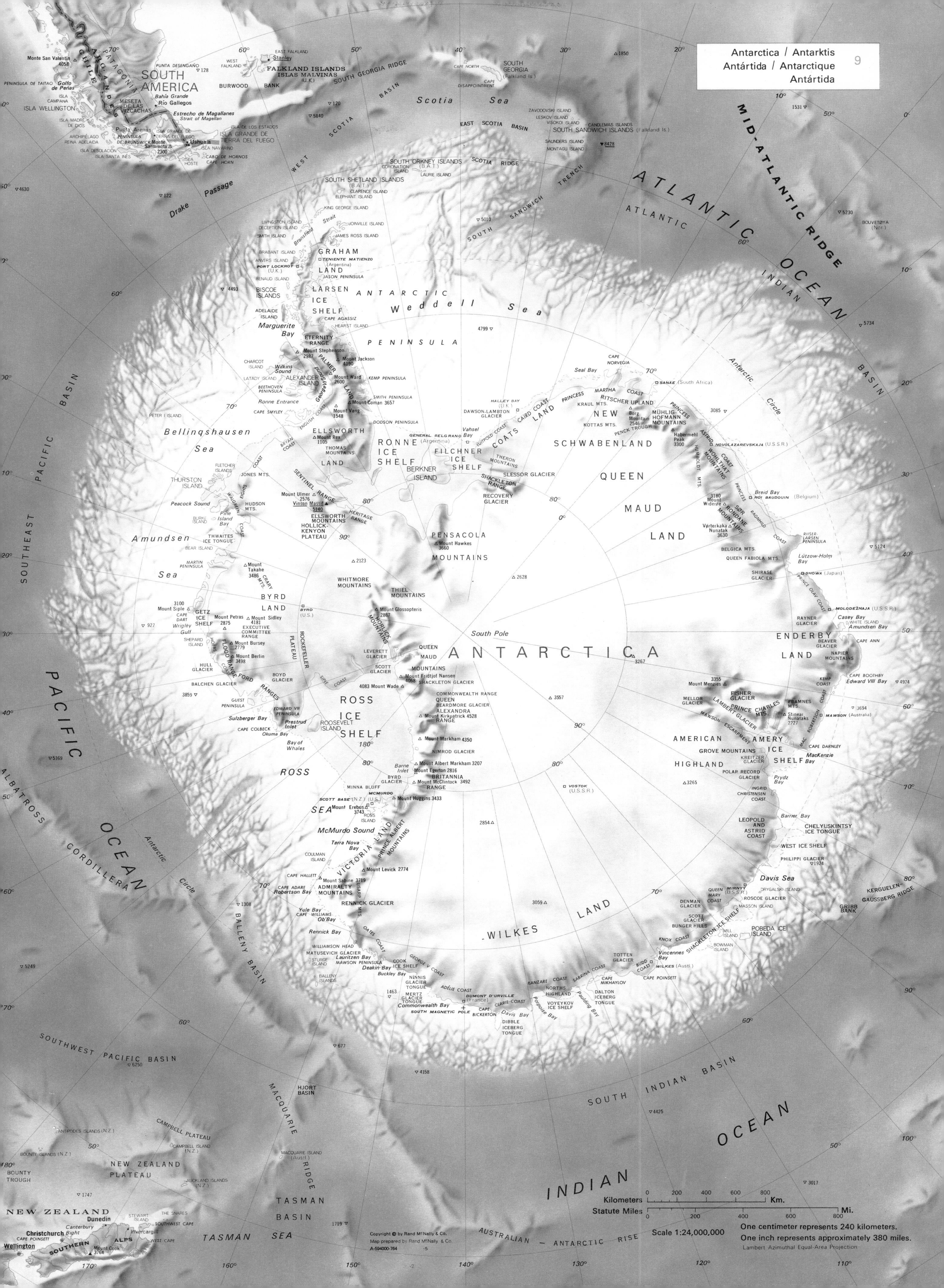

ATLANTIC OCEAN
EUROPE
ASIA
UNION OF SOVIET SOCIALIST REPUBLICS
CANADA
GREENLAND
ICELAND
NORWAY
SWEDEN
FINLAND
DENMARK
UNITED KINGDOM
IRELAND
NETH.
BEL.
LUX.
FED. REP. OF GER.
GER. DEM. REP.
POLAND
CZECHOSLOVAKIA
AUSTRIA
SWITZ.
HUNGARY
ROMANIA
YUGOSLAVIA
BULGARIA
ALBANIA
GREECE
ITALY
FRANCE
SPAIN
PORTUGAL
ANDORRA
TURKEY
ASIA MINOR
CYPRUS
SYRIA
LEBANON
ISRAEL
JORDAN
IRAQ
IRAN
KUWAIT
NEUTRAL ZONE
SAUDI ARABIA
ARABIAN PENINSULA
QATAR
BAHRAIN
UNITED ARAB EMIRATES
OMAN
EGYPT
LIBYA
TUNISIA
ALGERIA
MOROCCO
WESTERN SAHARA
MAURITANIA
SAHARA
MALTA
Labrador Sea
LABRADOR BASIN
Davis Strait
Denmark Strait
Greenland Sea
GREENLAND BASIN
Norwegian Sea
NORWEGIAN BASIN
MOHNS RIDGE
WEST JAN MAYEN RIDGE
SOUTH JAN MAYEN RIDGE
GREENLAND-ICELAND RISE
REYKJANES RIDGE
ROCKALL RISE
MID-ATLANTIC RIDGE
WEST EUROPEAN BASIN
IBERIAN BASIN
AZORES-GIBRALTAR RIDGE
AZORES PLATEAU
CANARY BASIN
CAPE VERDE TERRACE
Barents Sea
BARENTS TROUGH
MURMANSK RISE
WEST NOVAYA ZEMLYA TROUGH
NOVAYA ZEMLYA RIDGE
EAST NOVAYA ZEMLYA TROUGH
Karskoje More
Kara Sea
Beloje More
White Sea
North Sea
Baltic Sea
Gulf of Bothnia
Gulf of Finland
English Channel
Bay of Biscay
Mediterranean Sea
Tyrrhenian Sea
Adriatic Sea
Ionian Sea
Aegean Sea
Black Sea
Caspian Sea
Aral'skoje More
Persian Gulf
Gulf of Oman
Red Sea
Tropic of Cancer
Arctic Circle
URAL'SKIJE GORY
URAL MOUNTAINS
CARPATHIAN MOUNTAINS
ATLAS MOUNTAINS
ZAPADNO-SIBIRSKAJA NIZMENNOST'
SREDNERUSSKAJA VOZVYŠENNOST
PRIVOLŽSKAJA VOZVYŠENNOST
PRIKASPIJSKAJA NIZMENNOST
KYZYLKUM
KARAKUMY
MESOPOTAMIA
AS-SAHRA AL-LIBIYAH
Reykjavík
Oslo
Stockholm
Helsinki
København
LENINGRAD
MOSKVA
MOSCOW
Warszawa
BERLIN
Amsterdam
Bruxelles
LONDON
Dublin
PARIS
MADRID
Lisboa
BARCELONA
ROMA
WIEN
BUDAPEST
Praha
Beograd
Bucuresti
Sofija
Tirane
Athinai
İSTANBUL
Ankara
Tbilisi
Jerevan
BAKU
TEHRĀN
Baghdād
Dimashq
Bayrūt
Yerushalayim
'Ammān
AL-QĀHIRAH
CAIRO
Tunis
Alger
Rabat
Tarābulus
Ar-Riyāḍ
Al-Kuwayt
Al-Manāmah
Nouakchott
El-Aaiún

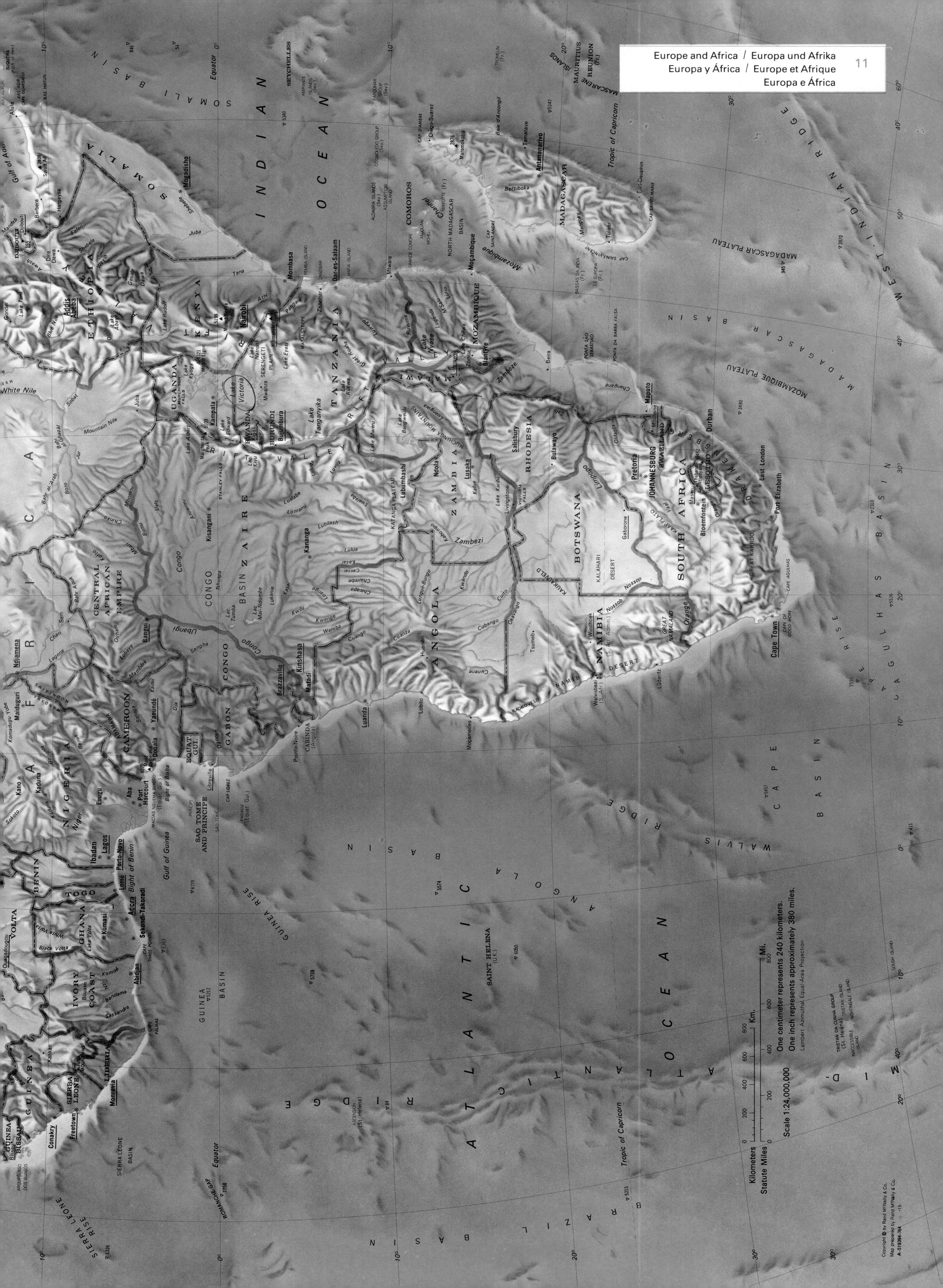
INDIAN OCEAN
ATLANTIC OCEAN
SOMALI BASIN
MADAGASCAR BASIN
MOZAMBIQUE PLATEAU
MADAGASCAR PLATEAU
WEST INDIAN RIDGE
AGULHAS BASIN
AGULHAS RISE
CAPE BASIN
WALVIS RIDGE
ANGOLA BASIN
GUINEA BASIN
GUINEA RISE
SIERRA LEONE BASIN
SIERRA LEONE RISE
BRAZIL BASIN
MID-ATLANTIC RIDGE
Gulf of Aden
Gulf of Guinea
Bight of Benin
Bight of Biafra
Mozambique Channel
Equator
Tropic of Capricorn
ETHIOPIA
SOMALIA
KENYA
UGANDA
RWANDA
BURUNDI
TANZANIA
ZAIRE
CONGO
GABON
CAMEROON
NIGERIA
BENIN
TOGO
GHANA
IVORY COAST
LIBERIA
SIERRA LEONE
GUINEA
GUINEA-BISSAU
UPPER VOLTA
CENTRAL AFRICAN EMPIRE
EQUAT. GUI.
SAO TOME AND PRINCIPE
CABINDA (Angola)
ANGOLA
ZAMBIA
MALAWI
MOZAMBIQUE
RHODESIA
BOTSWANA
NAMIBIA
SOUTH AFRICA
LESOTHO
SWAZILAND
MADAGASCAR
COMOROS
SEYCHELLES
MAURITIUS
REUNION (Fr.)
SAINT HELENA (U.K.)
Mogadisho
Nairobi
Addis Ababa
Kampala
Dar-es-Salaam
Mombasa
Kinshasa
Brazzaville
Luanda
Lusaka
Salisbury
Bulawayo
Pretoria
Johannesburg
Maputo
Durban
East London
Port Elizabeth
Cape Town
Antananarivo
Lagos
Ibadan
Accra
Abidjan
Monrovia
Freetown
Conakry
Ndjamena
Bangui
Yaoundé
Douala
Libreville
Lake Victoria
Lake Tanganyika
Lake Nyasa
Zambezi
Congo
Orange
Limpopo
KALAHARI DESERT
NAMIB DESERT
Kilometers
Statute Miles
Scale 1:24,000,000
One centimeter represents 240 kilometers.
One inch represents approximately 380 miles.
Lambert Azimuthal Equal-Area Projection
Copyright © by Rand McNally & Co.
Map prepared by Rand McNally & Co.

ATLANTIC OCEAN
ARCTIC OCEAN
North Pole
GREENLAND (Den.)
ICELAND
Reykjavík
Greenland Sea
Norwegian Sea
Barents Sea
Denmark Strait
Arctic Circle
SVALBARD
ZEML'A FRANCA-IOSIFA
FRANZ JOSEPH LAND
SEVERNAJA ZEML'A
NOVAJA ZEML'A
Karskoje More
Kara Sea
More Laptevych
Laptev Sea
NOVOSIBIRSKIJE OSTROVA
Vostočno-Sibirskoje More
East Siberian Sea
OSTROV VRANGEL'A
Chukchi Sea
Bering Strait
UNITED STATES
ALEUTIAN BASIN
Bering Sea
Sea of Okhotsk
KURIL'SKIJE OSTROVA
KURIL ISLANDS
OSTROV SACHALIN
Sea of Japan
UNITED KINGDOM
IRELAND
NORWAY
SWEDEN
FINLAND
North Sea
Baltic Sea
POLAND
CZECHOSLOVAKIA
HUNGARY
ROMANIA
BULGARIA
UNION OF SOVIET SOCIALIST REPUBLICS
EUROPE
ASIA
ZAPADNO-SIBIRSKAJA NIZMENNOST'
SREDNESIBIRSKOJE PLOSKOGORJE
CHREBET ČERSKOGO
URAL'SKIJE GORY
URAL MOUNTAINS
MOSKVA
LENINGRAD
Black Sea
Caspian Sea
Aral'skoje More
TURKEY
ASIA MINOR
SYRIA
IRAQ
IRAN
MONGOLIA
GOBI
TIEN SHAN
TALIMUPENDI
TAKLA MAKAN
KUNLUNSHANMAI
CHINA
NORTH KOREA
SOUTH KOREA
JAPAN
BEIJING
SHANGHAI
Yellow Sea
EAST CHINA

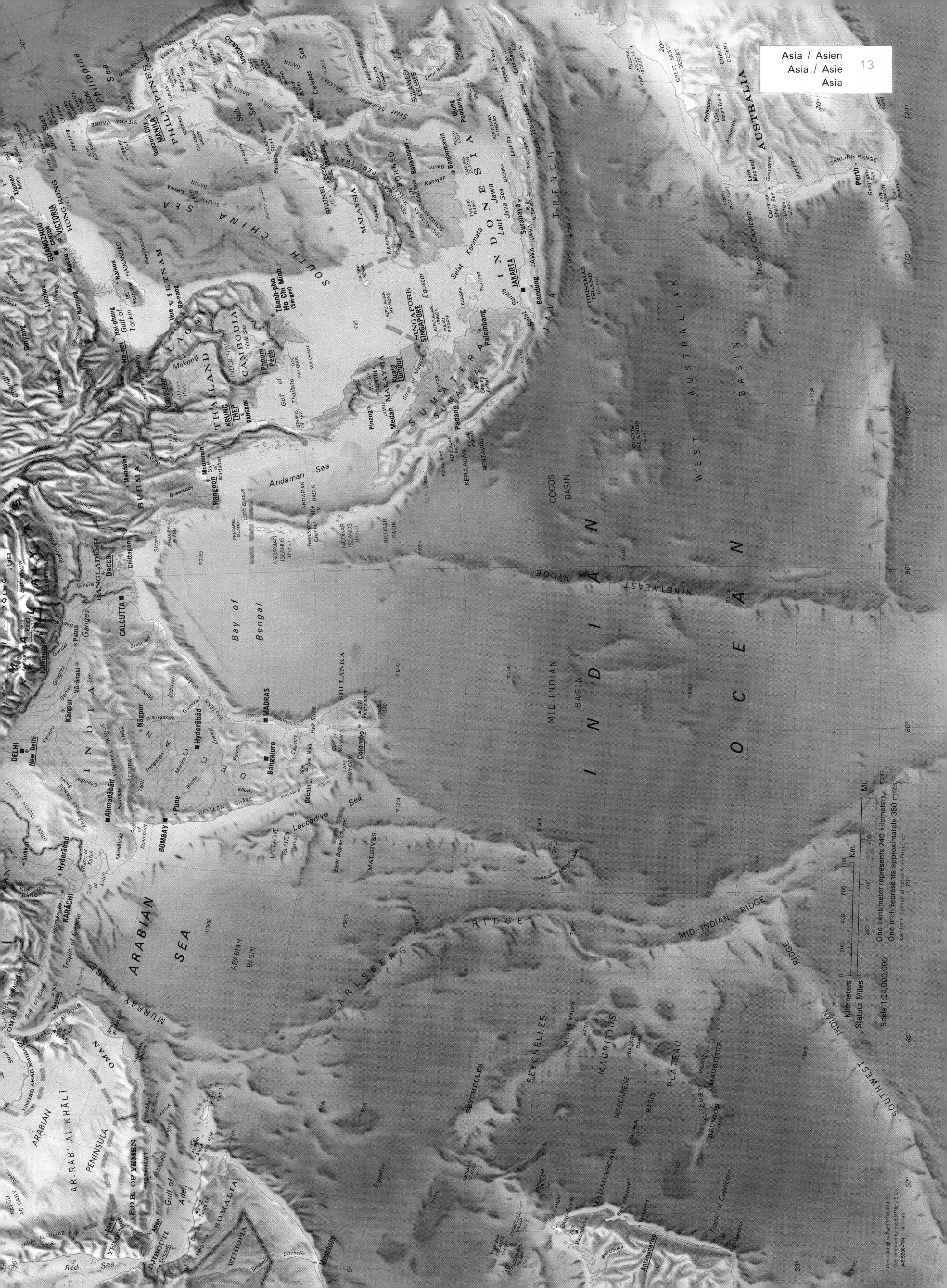
INDIAN OCEAN
ARABIAN SEA
Bay of Bengal
Andaman Sea
SOUTH CHINA SEA
Sulu Sea
Celebes Sea
Philippine Sea
Java Sea
Laccadive Sea
Gulf of Aden
Red Sea
Gulf of Oman
Gulf of Thailand
Gulf of Tonkin
Strait of Malacca
JAVA TRENCH
NINETYEAST RIDGE
CARLSBERG RIDGE
MURRAY RIDGE
MID-INDIAN RIDGE
SOUTHWEST INDIAN RIDGE
MID-INDIAN BASIN
ARABIAN BASIN
COCOS BASIN
WEST AUSTRALIAN BASIN
MASCARENE BASIN
MASCARENE PLATEAU
INDIA
SRI LANKA
BANGLADESH
BURMA
THAILAND
LAOS
CAMBODIA
VIETNAM
MALAYSIA
SINGAPORE
INDONESIA
PHILIPPINES
BRUNEI
AUSTRALIA
SOMALIA
ETHIOPIA
DJIBOUTI
YEMEN
P.D.R. OF YEMEN
OMAN
MADAGASCAR
SEYCHELLES
MAURITIUS
MALDIVES
ARABIAN PENINSULA
AR-RAB' AL-KHĀLĪ
BORNEO
SUMATERA
SULAWESI CELEBES
MINDANAO
LUZON
Equator
Tropic of Cancer
Tropic of Capricorn
DELHI
New Delhi
BOMBAY
CALCUTTA
MADRAS
Bangalore
Hyderābād
Nāgpur
Kānpur
Ahmadābād
Pune
Karāchi
Colombo
Dacca
Chittagong
Rangoon
Mandalay
KRUNG THEP
BANGKOK
Phnum Pénh
Ha-noi
Thanh-pho Ho Chi Minh (Sai-gon)
Kuala Lumpur
JAKARTA
Surabaya
Bandung
Palembang
Medan
MANILA
Quezon City
HONG KONG
VICTORIA
GUANGZHOU CANTON
Kunming
Perth
Aden
Mogadisho
Antananarivo
Scale 1:24,000,000
One centimeter represents 240 kilometers.
One inch represents approximately 380 miles.
Lambert Azimuthal Equal-Area Projection
Kilometers
Statute Miles
Copyright © by Rand McNally & Co.

CHONGQING
Changsha
Nanchang
Wenzhou
East China Sea
CHINA
ASIA
HIMALAYAS
Guiyang
Fuzhou
Kunming
Liuzhou
Xiamen
Amoy
T'aipei
Formosa Strait
TAIWAN
FORMOSA
RYUKYU TRENCH
NANSEI-SHOTŌ
RYUKYU ISLANDS
(Japan)
Naha
OKINAWA-JIMA
OGASAWARA-GUNTŌ
BONIN ISLANDS
(Jap.)
Tropic of Cancer
Nanning
GUANGZHOU
CANTON
VICTORIA
HONG KONG
(U.K.)
Macau
(Port.)
Luzon Strait
BATAN ISLANDS
Balintang Channel
Mandalay
BURMA
Zhanjiang
Ha-noi
Hai-phong
Gulf of Tonkin
Haikou
HAINANDAO
LAOS
Viangchan
Hue
Da-nang
VIETNAM
Moulmein
THAILAND
KRUNG THEP
BANGKOK
KAMPUCHEA
Phnum Penh
THANH-PHO HO CHI MINH
(SAI-GON)
Gulf of Thailand
ISTHMUS OF KRA
SOUTH CHINA SEA
SOUTH CHINA BASIN
LUZON
Lingayen Gulf
SIERRA MADRE
Quezon City
MANILA
PHILIPPINES
PHILIPPINE TRENCH
Sibuyan Sea
SAMAR
Cebu
Sulu Sea
SULU BASIN
MINDANAO
Davao
Zamboanga
Moro Gulf
Mount Apo
Davao Gulf
Balabac Strait
PHILIPPINE SEA
PHILIPPINE BASIN
KYUSHU-PALAU RIDGE
PALAU ISLANDS
WEST CAROLINE BASIN
CAROLINE
EAST CAROLINE BASIN
EAURIPIK RIDGE
HONSHU RIDGE
MARIANA RIDGE
MARIANA ISLANDS
MARIANA TRENCH
GUAM
(U.S.)
MARIANA BASIN
HALL ISLANDS
TRUK ISLANDS
MALAYSIA
Kota Kinabalu
Gunong Kinabalu
Bandar Seri Begawan
BRUNEI
(U.K.)
Celebes Sea
CELEBES BASIN
Manado
Pinang
MALAY PENINSULA
Medan
Kuala Lumpur
SINGAPORE
Strait of Malacca
SUMATERA
SUMATRA
Kuching
BORNEO
KALIMANTAN
Balikpapan
Equator
SULAWESI
CELEBES
Banjarmasin
Ujung Pandang
GREATER SUNDA ISLANDS
INDONESIA
MOLUCCAS
MALUKU
Padang
Palembang
Selat Karimata
Laut Jawa
Java Sea
JAKARTA
Bandung
Surabaya
JAWA
JAVA
Laut Flores
NUSA TENGGARA
Dili
Laut Sawu
SAVU BASIN
TIMOR TROUGH
Timor Sea
SAHUL SHELF
BANDA BASIN
Laut Banda
SERAM
Laut Seram
Jayapura
PEGUNUNGAN VAN REES
PEGUNUNGAN MAOKE
NEW GUINEA
Bismarck Sea
PAPUA NEW GUINEA
Rabaul
NEW BRITAIN
NEW BRITAIN TRENCH
BOUGAINVILLE
SOLOMON BASIN
Gulf of Papua
Port Moresby
OWEN STANLEY RANGE
Torres Strait
Arafura Sea
ARU BASIN
CAPE YORK
CAPE YORK PENINSULA
CORAL SEA BASIN
CORAL SEA PLATEAU
GREAT BARRIER REEF
Gulf of Carpentaria
GROOTE EYLANDT
WELLESLEY ISLANDS
Darwin
ARNHEM LAND
CAPE ARNHEM
Joseph Bonaparte Gulf
KIMBERLEY PLATEAU
Collier Bay
Broome
Birdum
BARKLY TABLELAND
Cairns
Townsville
GREAT DIVIDING RANGE
Mount Isa
SELWYN RANGE
TANAMI DESERT
GREAT SANDY DESERT
MACDONNELL RANGES
Alice Springs
SIMPSON DESERT
AUSTRALIA
Rockhampton
GIBSON DESERT
Mount Bruce
Mount Woodroffe
Lake Eyre
STURT DESERT
Lake Macleod
Carnarvon
Shark Bay
GREAT VICTORIA DESERT
Lake Torrens
Lake Frome
Broken Hill
Brisbane
Newcastle
SYDNEY
Canberra
Mount Kosciusko
MELBOURNE
Lake Everard
Lake Gairdner
EYRE PENINSULA
NULLARBOR PLAIN
Kalgoorlie
Spencer Gulf
Gulf Saint Vincent
Adelaide
Perth
DARLING RANGE
Great Australian Bight
SOUTH AUSTRALIAN BASIN
Bass Strait
Hobart
TASMAN
JAVA TRENCH
CHRISTMAS ISLAND
(Austl.)
COCOS ISLANDS
(Austl.)
WHARTON BASIN
WEST AUSTRALIAN BASIN
INDIAN OCEAN
Tropic of Capricorn
NINETY EAST RIDGE
BROKEN RIDGE
DIAMANTINA TROUGH
Kilometers 0 200 400 600 800 Km.
Statute Miles 0 100 200 300 400 500 600 Mi.
Scale 1:24,000,000
One centimeter represents 240 kilometers.
One inch represents approximately 380 miles.
Lambert Azimuthal Equal-Area Projection
Copyright © by Rand McNally & Co.
Map prepared by Rand McNally & Co.

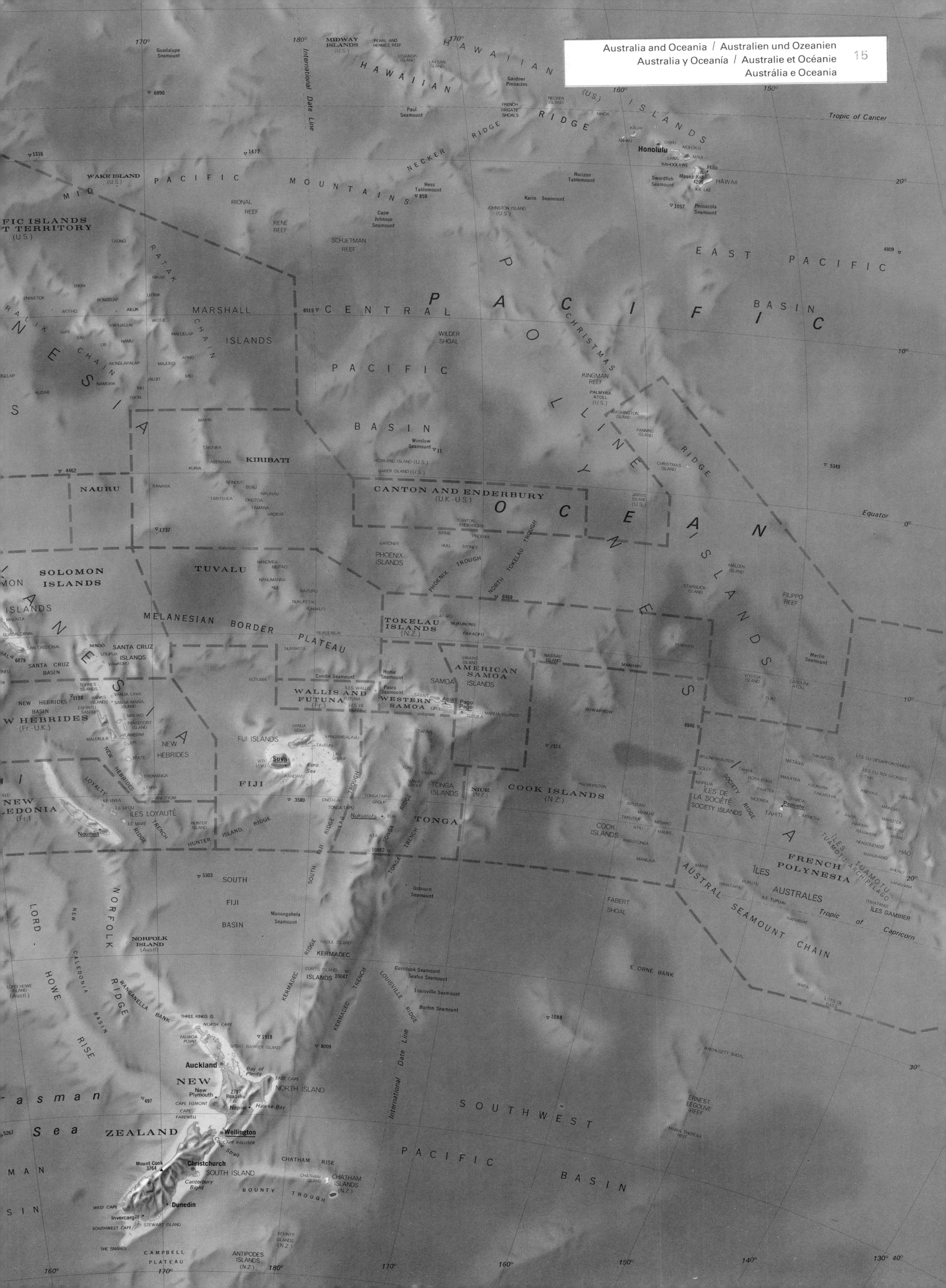
PACIFIC OCEAN
HAWAIIAN ISLANDS
HAWAIIAN RIDGE
Honolulu
Hilo
HAWAII
MIDWAY ISLANDS (U.S.)
WAKE ISLAND (U.S.)
JOHNSTON ISLAND (U.S.)
MID PACIFIC MOUNTAINS
NECKER RIDGE
International Date Line
Tropic of Cancer
Equator
Tropic of Capricorn
EAST PACIFIC BASIN
CENTRAL PACIFIC BASIN
MARSHALL ISLANDS
RATAK CHAIN
RALIK CHAIN
KIRIBATI
NAURU
TUVALU
CANTON AND ENDERBURY (U.K.-U.S.)
PHOENIX ISLANDS
PHOENIX TROUGH
NORTH TOKELAU TROUGH
TOKELAU ISLANDS (N.Z.)
SOLOMON ISLANDS
SANTA CRUZ ISLANDS
SANTA CRUZ BASIN
MELANESIAN BORDER PLATEAU
NEW HEBRIDES (Fr.-U.K.)
NEW HEBRIDES TRENCH
WALLIS AND FUTUNA (Fr.)
AMERICAN SAMOA
WESTERN SAMOA
Apia
Pago Pago
FIJI ISLANDS
FIJI
Suva
Koro Sea
LAU RIDGE
TONGA
TONGA ISLANDS
Nukualofa
TONGA TRENCH
NIUE (N.Z.)
COOK ISLANDS (N.Z.)
CHRISTMAS RIDGE
LINE ISLANDS
KINGMAN REEF
PALMYRA ATOLL (U.S.)
ÎLES DE LA SOCIÉTÉ
SOCIETY ISLANDS
Papeete
TAHITI
FRENCH POLYNESIA
ÎLES TUAMOTU
TUAMOTU ARCHIPELAGO
ÎLES GAMBIER
ÎLES AUSTRALES
AUSTRAL SEAMOUNT CHAIN
ÎLES LOYAUTÉ
NEW CALEDONIA (Fr.)
Nouméa
LOYALTY RIDGE
NORFOLK ISLAND (Austl.)
NORFOLK RIDGE
LORD HOWE ISLAND (Austl.)
LORD HOWE RISE
NEW CALEDONIA BASIN
SOUTH FIJI BASIN
KERMADEC ISLANDS
KERMADEC RIDGE
KERMADEC TRENCH
LOUISVILLE RIDGE
NEW ZEALAND
NORTH ISLAND
SOUTH ISLAND
Auckland
Wellington
Christchurch
Dunedin
Invercargill
Napier
New Plymouth
Mount Cook 3764
Cook Strait
Tasman Sea
CHATHAM RISE
CHATHAM ISLANDS (N.Z.)
BOUNTY TROUGH
CAMPBELL PLATEAU
ANTIPODES ISLANDS (N.Z.)
SOUTHWEST PACIFIC BASIN
10882

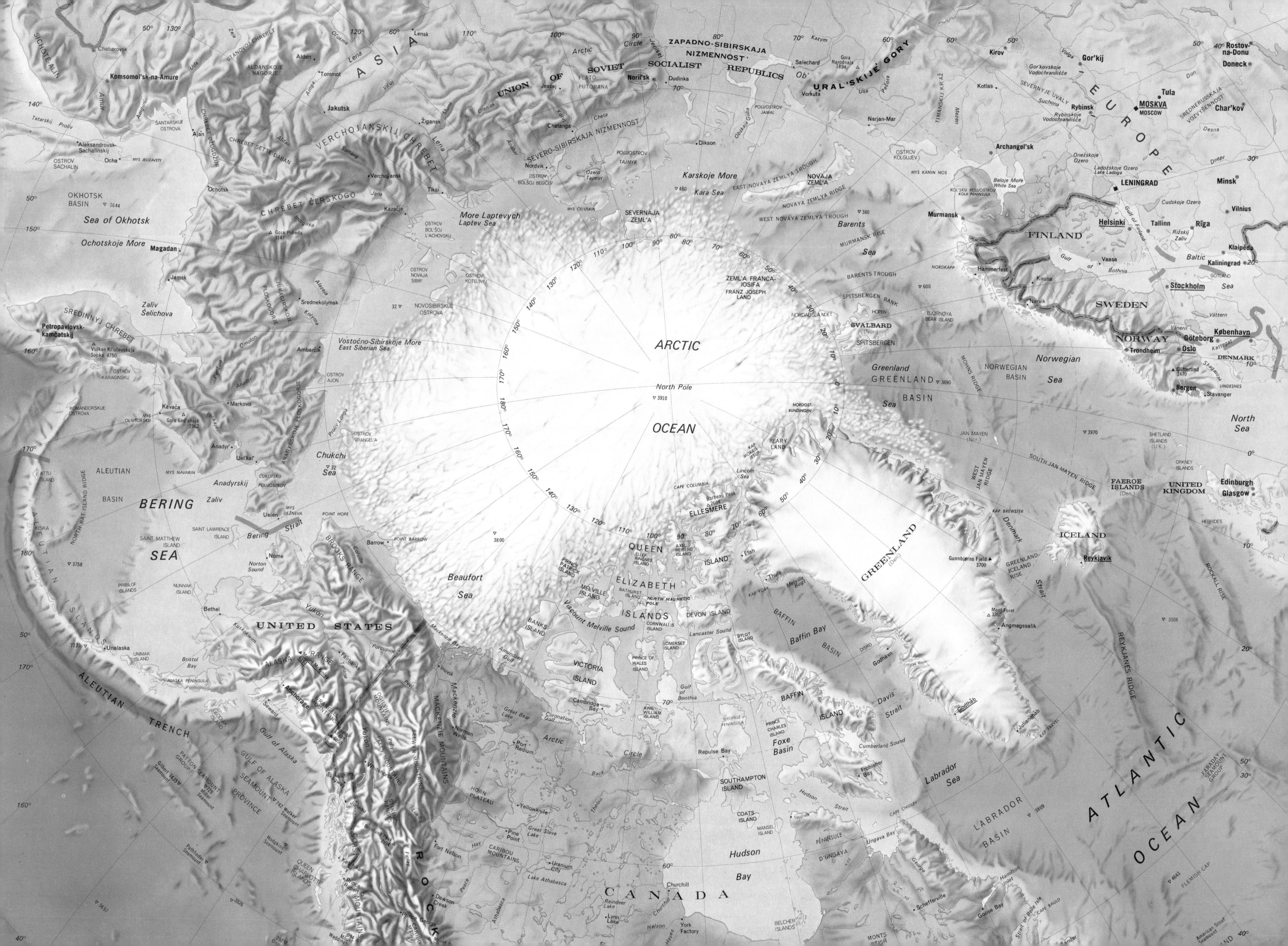
ARCTIC
OCEAN
North Pole
ASIA
UNION OF SOVIET SOCIALIST REPUBLICS
EUROPE
ATLANTIC
OCEAN
CANADA
UNITED STATES
GREENLAND
ICELAND
FINLAND
SWEDEN
NORWAY
UNITED KINGDOM
BERING
SEA
Sea of Okhotsk
Ochotskoje More
More Laptevych
Laptev Sea
Karskoje More
Kara Sea
Barents
Sea
Norwegian
Sea
Greenland
Sea
North
Sea
Beaufort
Sea
Chukchi
Sea
Vostočno-Sibirskoje More
East Siberian Sea
Baffin Bay
Hudson
Bay
Labrador
Sea
Davis
Strait
Denmark
Strait
Bering
Strait
ALEUTIAN
TRENCH
ALEUTIAN
BASIN
Gulf of Alaska
Foxe
Basin
QUEEN
ELIZABETH
ISLANDS
ELLESMERE
VICTORIA
ISLAND
BAFFIN
ISLAND
SVALBARD
ZEML'A FRANCA-IOSIFA
FRANZ JOSEPH LAND
NOVAJA ZEML'A
SEVERNAJA ZEML'A
URAL'SKIJE GORY
ZAPADNO-SIBIRSKAJA NIZMENNOST'
VERCHOJANSKIJ CHREBET
CHREBET ČERSKOGO
BROOKS RANGE
MACKENZIE MOUNTAINS
REYKJANES RIDGE
MOSKVA
MOSCOW
LENINGRAD
Helsinki
Stockholm
Oslo
København
Reykjavik
Murmansk
Anchorage

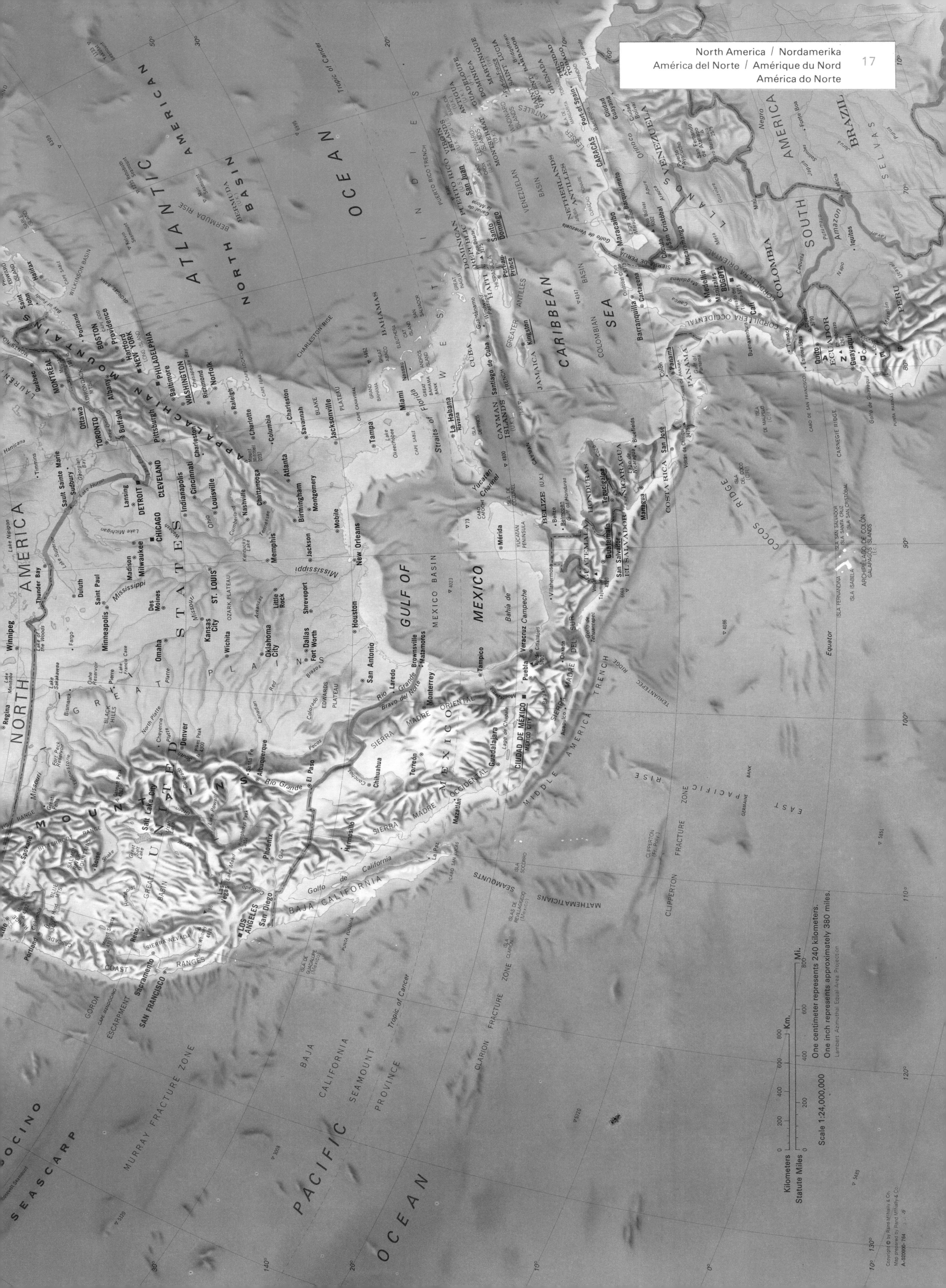
NORTH AMERICA
UNITED STATES
GREAT PLAINS
ROCKY MOUNTAINS
APPALACHIAN MOUNTAINS
ATLANTIC OCEAN
NORTH AMERICAN BASIN
BERMUDA RISE
PACIFIC OCEAN
GULF OF MEXICO
MEXICO BASIN
CARIBBEAN SEA
COLOMBIAN BASIN
VENEZUELAN BASIN
WEST INDIES
BAHAMAS
GREATER ANTILLES
LESSER ANTILLES
CUBA
JAMAICA
HAITI
DOMINICAN REPUBLIC
PUERTO RICO
SOUTH AMERICA
VENEZUELA
COLOMBIA
ECUADOR
PERU
BRAZIL
PANAMA
COSTA RICA
NICARAGUA
HONDURAS
EL SALVADOR
GUATEMALA
BELIZE
SIERRA MADRE OCCIDENTAL
SIERRA MADRE ORIENTAL
SIERRA MADRE DEL SUR
MIDDLE AMERICA TRENCH
EAST PACIFIC RISE
COCOS RIDGE
CARNEGIE RIDGE
CLIPPERTON FRACTURE ZONE
CLARION FRACTURE ZONE
MURRAY FRACTURE ZONE
BAJA CALIFORNIA SEAMOUNT PROVINCE
MATHEMATICIANS SEAMOUNTS
Tropic of Cancer
Equator
Kilometers
Statute Miles
Scale 1:24,000,000
One centimeter represents 240 kilometers.
One inch represents approximately 380 miles.
Lambert Azimuthal Equal-Area Projection

NORTH AMERICA
UNITED STATES
ROCKY MOUNTAINS
APPALACHIAN MOUNTAINS
GREAT PLAINS
MEXICO
SIERRA MADRE ORIENTAL
SIERRA MADRE DEL SUR
GULF OF MEXICO
MEXICO BASIN
CHICAGO
CLEVELAND
NEW YORK
PHILADELPHIA
Baltimore
WASHINGTON
Pittsburgh
Cincinnati
Charleston
Louisville
Nashville
Richmond
Norfolk
Raleigh
Atlanta
Savannah
Jacksonville
Tampa
Miami
Omaha
Des Moines
Kansas City
ST. LOUIS
Denver
Cheyenne
Wichita
Oklahoma City
Little Rock
Memphis
Birmingham
Montgomery
Jackson
Mobile
New Orleans
Albuquerque
El Paso
Fort Worth
Dallas
Houston
San Antonio
Laredo
Brownsville
Monterrey
Matamoros
Torreón
Tampico
Guadalajara
CIUDAD DE MEXICO
Puebla
Veracruz
Mérida
YUCATAN PENINSULA
Bahía de Campeche
NORTH AMERICAN BASIN
ATLANTIC OCEAN
BERMUDA (U.K.)
MID-ATLANTIC RIDGE
AZORES RIDGE
AÇORES (Port.)
CANARY BASIN
CAPE VERDE BASIN
GUIANA BASIN
Tropic of Cancer
SOUTHEAST NEWFOUNDLAND RIDGE
BAHAMAS
Nassau
Straits of Florida
WEST INDIES
CUBA
La Habana
Havana
Santiago de Cuba
CAYMAN ISLANDS (U.K.)
JAMAICA
Kingston
HISPANIOLA
HAITI
Port-au-Prince
DOMINICAN REPUBLIC
Santo Domingo
PUERTO RICO (U.S.)
San Juan
PUERTO RICO TRENCH
VIRGIN ISLANDS (U.K. and U.S.)
ANTIGUA (U.K.)
GUADELOUPE (Fr.)
DOMINICA
MARTINIQUE (Fr.)
Fort-de-France
SAINT LUCIA
BARBADOS
Bridgetown
SAINT VINCENT (U.K.)
GRENADA
TRINIDAD AND TOBAGO
Port of Spain
GREATER ANTILLES
LESSER ANTILLES
NETHERLANDS ANTILLES
CARIBBEAN SEA
VENEZUELAN BASIN
COLOMBIAN BASIN
Yucatan Channel
BELIZE
GUATEMALA
Guatemala
HONDURAS
Tegucigalpa
EL SALVADOR
San Salvador
NICARAGUA
Managua
COSTA RICA
San José
PANAMA
Panamá
MIDDLE AMERICA TRENCH
TEHUANTEPEC RIDGE
COCOS RIDGE
CARNEGIE RIDGE
ARCHIPIÉLAGO DE COLÓN
GALAPAGOS ISLANDS (Ec.)
Equator
SOUTH AMERICA
VENEZUELA
CARACAS
Maracaibo
Barquisimeto
Ciudad Bolívar
Ciudad Guayana
COLOMBIA
BOGOTÁ
Medellín
Cali
Barranquilla
Cartagena
Cúcuta
Bucaramanga
LLANOS
ECUADOR
Quito
Guayaquil
PERU
LIMA
Iquitos
GUYANA
Georgetown
SURINAME
Paramaribo
FRENCH GUIANA
Cayenne
BRAZIL
Manaus
Belém
São Luís
Fortaleza
Natal
João Pessoa
Recife
Maceió
Aracaju
Salvador
Teresina
Campina Grande
SELVAS
Amazon
Negro
Orinoco
Madeira
Purus
Tapajós
Xingu
Tocantins
CORDILLERA OCCIDENTAL
CORDILLERA ORIENTAL
SERRA DOS PARECIS
SERRA DO RONCADOR
SERRA DOS CARAJÁS
ILHA DE MARAJÓ

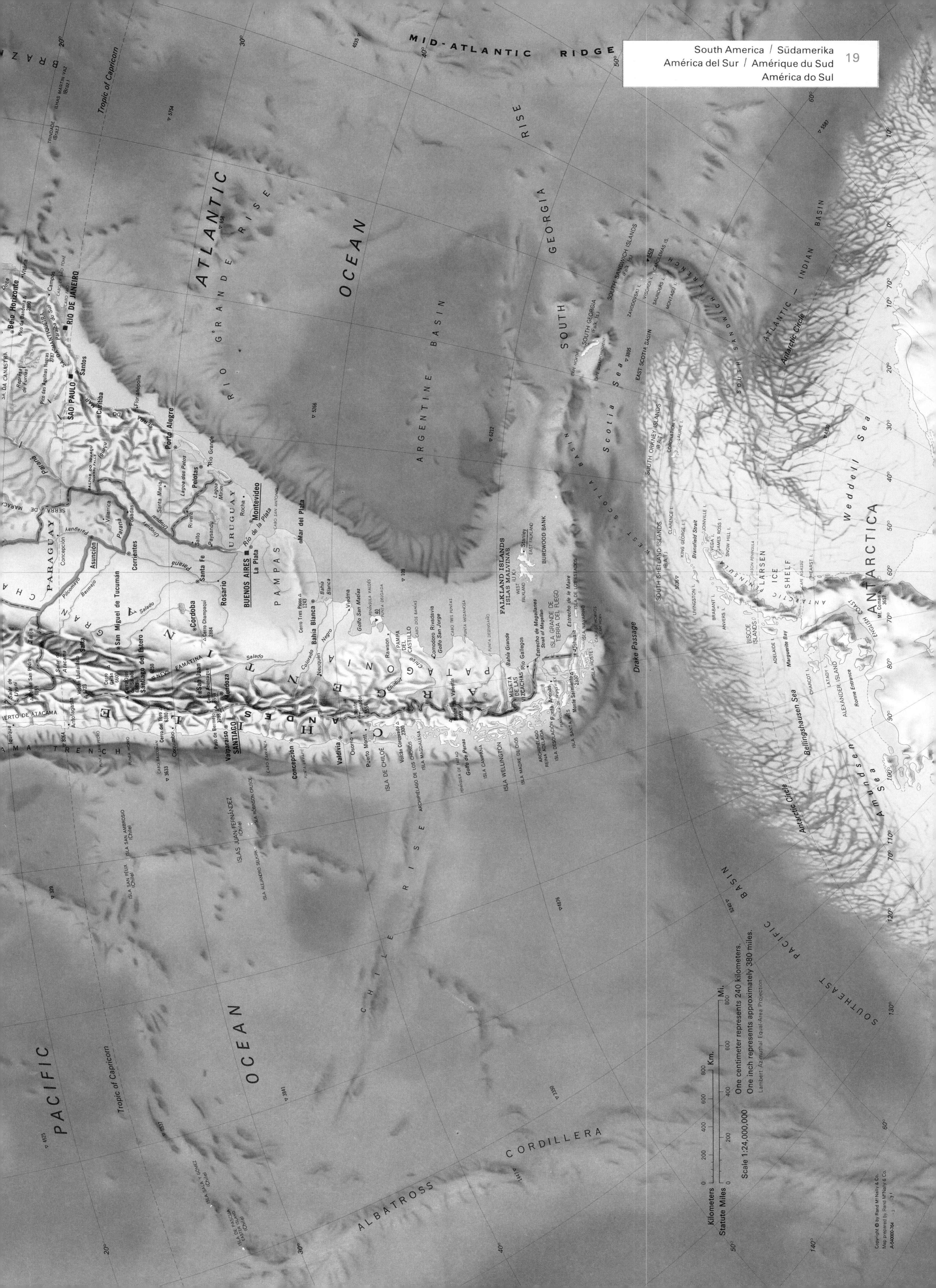
MID-ATLANTIC RIDGE
ATLANTIC
OCEAN
RIO GRANDE RISE
ARGENTINE BASIN
SOUTH GEORGIA RISE
Scotia Sea
Weddell Sea
ANTARCTICA
LARSEN ICE SHELF
SOUTH SANDWICH TRENCH
ATLANTIC — INDIAN BASIN
Antarctic Circle
Drake Passage
Bellingshausen Sea
Amundsen Sea
SOUTHEAST PACIFIC BASIN
CHILE RISE
ALBATROSS CORDILLERA
PACIFIC
OCEAN
Tropic of Capricorn
PARAGUAY
URUGUAY
PAMPAS
PATAGONIA
BUENOS AIRES
Montevideo
SANTIAGO
Asunción
RIO DE JANEIRO
SÃO PAULO
Belo Horizonte
Pôrto Alegre
Córdoba
Rosario
Mendoza
Valparaíso
Concepción
Mar del Plata
Bahía Blanca
FALKLAND ISLANDS
ISLAS MALVINAS
SOUTH GEORGIA
SOUTH SANDWICH ISLANDS
SOUTH ORKNEY ISLANDS
SOUTH SHETLAND ISLANDS
ALEXANDER ISLAND
ISLA GRANDE DE TIERRA DEL FUEGO
Estrecho de Magallanes
Kilometers
Statute Miles
Scale 1:24,000,000
One centimeter represents 240 kilometers.
One inch represents approximately 380 miles.
Lambert Azimuthal Equal-Area Projection
Copyright © by Rand McNally & Co.

THE REGIONAL MAPS consist of three basic series, each distinctive in style, but using common symbols to ensure ease of understanding (see Legend to Maps, pages x-xii). Every major land region, continent or subcontinent, is introduced by one or more maps at the scale of 1:12,000,000. There follow maps at 1:6,000,000 and 1:3,000,000 which cover the region in sections, in greater detail. Except for scale, the 1:6,000,000 and 1:3,000,000 maps are alike. Finally, selected areas of special importance in the region are shown at 1:1,000,000. Each scale is identified by a color bar, and a locater map with the same color may be found in the margin of the map page. A sample area at each of the scales, including centimeter-kilometer and inch-mile equivalents, appears on page 21.

The three basic series differ in content and emphasis. The 1:12,000,000 maps, which are primarily political, present an overview of each region. They show national boundaries and, in some cases, subordinate administrative subdivisions as well. These introductory maps make it possible to compare location, areal extent, and shape among the nations of the world. The distribution of cities, towns and metropolitan areas is shown in the context of broad physical configurations. A selection of the most important railways and highways also appears.

The 1:6,000,000 and 1:3,000,000 maps together constitute about half of the map pages and provide the basic reference coverage of the Atlas. They show sections of regions in great detail—in some cases individual countries (Japan and New Zealand), in others, parts of countries (central Mexico), in still others, larger regions (the Middle East). The more densely settled areas appear at the larger 1:3,000,000 scale, the remaining areas at 1:6,000,000. Maps at these two scales present political and cultural information against the background of a detailed physical portrait of the terrain, which is depicted by both shaded relief and a spectrum of altitude tints. Bathymetric tints are used to show offshore water depths. The transportation pattern shown includes major railways, two classes of roads, and airports that offer either international or jet service. The names and boundaries of political subdivisions are given for selected countries.

In the 1:1,000,000 series, strategic areas that are of special interest because of economic importance, dense settlement, or both, appear in even greater detail. This series is designed to show the pattern of cities, towns, roads, railways, bridges, airports, dams, reservoirs, and other interrelated features reflecting man's dense occupancy in these areas. The most important parks, places of historical interest, and recreational facilities are indicated. Three classes of highways and two classes of railways are shown, and major roads are named. All features are portrayed against a topographic background of shaded relief.

Inhabited places on the regional maps are classified in two distinct ways. Cities and towns of different *population size* are distinguished by the *size and shape of the symbol* that locates the place. The symbol reflects the population within the municipal or corporate limits, exclusive of any suburbs. In countries where the limits of a municipality include rural areas, the symbol represents only the urban or agglomerated population. The *relative political and economic importance* of a place which may be independent of the number of its inhabitants, is indicated by the *size of type* in which its name appears.

A key to all symbols and type sizes is shown on page xi of the Legend to Maps.

DIE REGIONALKARTEN bestehen aus drei Serien, die im Stil verschieden sind, der besseren Lesbarkeit halber aber gemeinsame Kartensignaturen verwenden (siehe "Zeichenerklärung" S. x-xii). Jede Grossregion, jeder Kontinent oder Subkontinent wird durch eine oder mehrere Karten im Massstab 1:12 Millionen eingeleitet. Es folgen sodann Karten in den Massstäben 1:6 und 1:3 Millionen, welche die Region in Teilen und grösseren Einzelheiten darstellen. Die Karten in 1:6 Millionen und 1:3 Millionen unterscheiden sich nur im Massstab. Schliesslich werden ausgewählte Gebiete von besonderer Bedeutung innerhalb der Region in 1:1 Million dargestellt. Jede Massstabsangabe ist durch ein Farbfeld gekennzeichnet, und ein Lagekärtchen in derselben Farbe erscheint am Rand der Kartenseite. Kartenausschnitte als Beispiele für jeden dieser Massstäbe mit Angabe des Verhältnisses Zentimeter zu Kilometer und Zoll zu Meilen sind auf Seite 21 aufgeführt.

Die drei Kartenreihen unterscheiden sich in Inhalt und Betonung. Die Karten in 1:12 Millionen, die vor allem politische Karten sind, geben einen Überblick über jede Region. Sie zeigen die Staatsgrenzen und in manchen Fällen auch die Grenzen von nachgeordneten Verwaltungseinheiten. Diese einführenden Karten ermöglichen einen Vergleich der Lage, Ausdehnung und Gestalt der Staaten der Erde. Die Verteilung der städtischen Ballungsgebiete, Grossstädte und Städte wird in ihrem Zusammenhang mit dem grossräumigen Formenschatz des Reliefs gezeigt. Gezeigt wird auch eine Auswahl der wichtigsten Eisenbahnlinien und Fernverkehrsstrassen.

Die Karten 1:6 Millionen und 1:3 Millionen machen zusammen mehr als die Hälfte der Kartenseiten aus und bilden den grundlegenden Teil des Atlasses. Sie zeigen sehr inhaltsreiche Ausschnitte von Regionen—in einigen Fällen einzelne Länder (Japan und Neuseeland), in anderen Landesteile (Zentralmexiko) und weider anderen Grossräume (Mittlerer Osten).

Die dichter besiedelten Gebiete sind in 1:3 Millionen dargestellt, die übrigen Gebiete in 1:6 Millionen. Die Karten in diesen beiden Massstäben liefern politische und kulturgeographische Informationen vor dem Hintergrund einer detaillierten Geländedarstellung, gekennzeichnet durch Reliefschummerung und eine Skala von Höhenschichten. Tiefenstufen werden verwendet, um die Wassertiefen jenseits der Küsten zu gliedern. Das abgebildete Verkehrsnetz umfasst wichtige Eisenbahnlinien, zwei Klassen von Strassen und Flughäfen, die entweder im internationalen Verkehr oder von Düsenflugzeugen angeflogen werden. Die Verwaltungsgliederung wird für eine grosse Zahl von Staaten gezeigt.

In der Kartenserie 1:1 Million sind mit noch zahlreicheren Einzelheiten zentrale Räume dargestellt, denen infolge ihrer wirtschaftlichen Bedeutung, dichten Besiedlung oder durch beide Faktoren bedingt, besonderes Interesse zukommt. Diese Kartenserie wurde entwickelt, um die Verteilung der Grossstädte, Städte, Strassen, Eisenbahnen, Brücken, Flughäfen, Dämme, Stauseen und anderer Objekte zu zeigen, die Ausdruck sind für die dichte Besiedlung. Verzeichnet sind auch die wichtigsten Parks, Örtlichkeiten von historischem Interesse und Erholungsstätten. Drei Strassenklassen und zwei Klassen von Eisenbahnlinien werden unterschieden. Die Darstellung ist unterlegt durch eine Reliefschummerung.

Die Siedlungen auf den Regionalkarten sind auf zwei bestimmte Arten klassifiziert. Grossstädte und Städte unterschiedlicher *Einwohnerzahl* sind durch *Grösse und Form der Signatur* unterschieden, die den Ort lokalisiert. Die Signatur entspricht der Zahl der Einwohner innerhalb der Stadtgrenzen, schliesst also nicht eingemeindete Vororte aus. In Staaten, in denen ländliche Gebiete in die Stadtgemeinden einbezogen sind, entsprechen die Signaturen nur der in den zentralen Siedlungen ansässigen Bevölkerung. Die *relative politische und wirtschaftliche Bedeutung* eines Ortes, die von der Zahl seiner Einwohner unabhängig sein kann, ist ausgedrückt durch die *Schriftgrösse,* in welcher der Ortsname erscheint.

Ein Schlüssel zu allen Signaturen und Schriftgrössen findet sich auf Seite xi der "Zeichenerklärung".

LOS MAPAS REGIONALES integran tres series básicas, cada una con su estilo propio; pero los símbolos usados son en todas los mismos para facilitar su comprensión (véanse las Leyendas para Mapas, páginas x-xii). Cada una de las grandes regiones, continentes o subcontinentes, se presenta a través de uno o varios mapas a la escala de 1:12 000 000. A continuación hay mapas a escalas de 1:6 000 000 y 1:3 000 000 que presentan la región correspondiente en secciones, con mayores detalles. Con excepción de su escala, los mapas de 1:6 000 000 y 1:3 000 000 tienen las mismas características. Por ultimo, aparecen a la escala de 1:1 000 000 áreas de cada región seleccionadas por su importancia. Cada escala se identifica por una barra de color, y un mapa-guía con el mismo color se presenta en el margen de la página de cada mapa. La página 21 ofrece como ejemplo un área-muestra a cada una de las escalas, incluyendo equivalentes en centímetros-kilómetros y pulgadas-millas.

Las tres series básicas son diferentes en contenido y en énfasis. Los mapas a escala de 1:12 000 000, fundamentalmente políticos, ofrecen una vista general de cada región. Indican las fronteras nacionales y, en algunos casos, las subdivisiones administrativas secundarias. Son mapas introductivos que permiten comparar la ubicación, extensión territorial y forma de las distintas naciones. La distribución de ciudades, poblados y áreas metropolitanas se aprecia en un contexto físico esbozado a grandes rasgos. Los detalles incluyen una selección de las vías férras y las carreteras más importantes.

Las series de mapas a 1:6 000 000 y a 1:3 000 000 ocupan entre ambas cerca de la mitad de los mapas del atlas y en ellas se concentra el material de consulta básico de la obra. Los mapas muestran secciones de regiones en gran detalle: en algunos casos países enteros, como Japón y Nueva Zelandia; en otros, partes de países, como el centro de México; y en otros, regiones mas extensas, como el Medio Oriente. Las áreas con mayor densidad de establecimientos humanos se presentan a una escala mayor, la de 1:3 000 000, y las demás a la escala de 1:6 000 000. En estas dos escalas los mapas contienen información política y cultural, sobre un fondo que ilustra en detalle la configuración física del terreno, utilizando sombreado para el relieve y toda una gama de tintes para indicar las altitudes. Un colorido batimétrico señala las variaciones de profundidad en el suelo marino. El esquema de las vías de comunicación incluye las principales vías férreas, dos clases de caminos, y los aeropuertos que ofrecen servicio nacional o internacional de jets. Las subdivisiones políticas secundarias se dan para una selección de varios países.

En la serie de mapas de 1:1 000 000, las áreas estratégicas de especial interés por su importancia económica, su densidad de población, o ambos factores combinados, aparecen aún con mayor detalle. Esta serie se diseñó para mostrar la distribución de ciudades, poblados, caminos, vías férreas, puentes, aeropuertos, presas, embalses y otros elementos similares, que reflejan la densidad de la ocupación humana. También se consignan los parques más importantes, los sitios de interés histórico, los campos de recreo, tres clases de carreteras, y dos de ferrocarriles, se da los nombres de los caminos más importantes. Todos estos elementos aparecen sobre un fondo topográfico de relieve sombreado.

En los mapas regionales se hacen dos clasificaciones distintas de los lugares habitados. Las ciudades y las poblaciones *de diferente densidad de habitantes* se distinguen por la *forma y tamaño del símbolo* que las localiza en el mapa. Este símbolo refleja el tamaño de la poblacióin dentro de sus límites municipales, sin tomar en cuenta los suburbios. En los países donde los límites de una municipalidad incluyen áreas rurales, el símbolo se limita a representar el conglomerado urbano de habitantes. La *importancia económica y política de un lugar,* la cual puede ser independiente del número de sus habitantes, se indica mediante el *tamaño del tipo de imprenta* en que aparece su nombre.

La clave de los símbolos y el valor de los tamaños de las letras se dan en la página xi de las Leyendas para Mapas.

LES CARTES RÉGIONALES sont de trois types principaux, chacun d'un style différent mais avec des symboles communs pour faciliter la compréhension (voir la légende des cartes pages x-xii). Chaque grande région, continent ou subcontinent, est représentée par une ou plusieurs cartes à l'échelle de 1:12 000 000e. Viennent ensuite des cartes au 1:6 000 000e et au 1:3 000 000e qui couvrent la région par sections plus détaillées; hormis la différence d'échelle, ces cartes sont semblables. Enfin, des secteurs particulièrement importants sont représentés au 1:1 000 000e. À chaque échelle correspond une bande colorée et une carte repère de même couleur, dans la marge de chaque page. Un échantillon de cartes aux diverses échelles est représenté à droite. Chaque carte est accompagnée d'une double échelle graphique donnant les rapports centimètre/kilomètre et inch/mille correspondants.

Les trois catégories de cartes diffèrent par le contenu et par ce qu'elles mettent en relief. Les cartes au 1:12 000 000e, qui sont essentiellement politiques, donnent un apercu général de chaque région. Elles indiquent les frontières nationales et, dans certains cas, les subdivisions administratives intérieures. Ces cartes d'introduction permettent de comparer la localisation, la superficie et la forme des pays du monde. La répartition des villes et des zones métropolitaines y apparaît dans le cadre des grandes régions naturelles. Les routes et les voies ferrées les plus importantes y figurent également.

Les cartes au 1:6 000 000e et au 1:3 000 000e forment la moitié de l'Atlas et en constituent la série cartographique essentielle. Elles représentent de façon plus détaillée une partie de pays (centre du Mexique), ou encore des régions plus vestes (Moyen-Orient) ou, parfois, des pays entiers (Japon, Nouvelle-Zélande). Les régions les plus peuplées sont représentées à plus grande échelle (1;3 000 000e) que les autres (1:6 000 000e). Ces cartes offrent des informations d'ordre politique et culturel sur un fond topographique précis où le relief est indiqué à la fois par un estompage et par des variations de couleur. Différentes teintes de bleu sont utilisées pour symboliser les profondeurs marines. Les réseaux de transport représentés comprennent les principales voies ferrées, deux catégories de routes et les aéroports internationaux ou desservis par des avions à réaction. Les subdivisions politiques d'un certain nombre de pays sont aussi tracées.

Dans la série de cartes au 1:1 000 000e, des régions très importantes, soit du fait de leur densité de population, soit du fait de leur rôle économique, sont représentées d'une manière encore plus détaillée. L'objectif de cette série de cartes est de montrer la répartition des villes, routes, voies ferrées, ponts, aéroports, barrages, lacs de barrages et autres données associées qui traduisent la densité de l'occupation humaine dans ces régions. Les parcs les plus importants, les sites historiques essentiels et les centres de loisirs sont indiqués. Toutes les informations se détachent sur un fond topographique où le relief apparaît en estompage.

Les centres urbains des cartes régionales sont classés de deux manières différentes. *L'importance de la population* des villes est indiquée par *la dimension et la forme du symbole* qui les situe sur la carte. Seule la population comprise dans les limites municipales est prise en considération; dans les pays où des espaces ruraux sont inclus dans les limites d'une municipalité, seule la population urbaine entre en ligne de compte. *L'importance politique et économique relative* d'une ville, qui n'est pas nécessairement liée au nombre d'habitants, est indiquée par la dimension des caractères qui composent son nom.

La signification de tous les symboles utilisés dans les cartes régionales est donnée par la légende des cartes aux pages x-xii.

OS MAPAS REGIONAIS compreendem três séries básicas, cada uma em estilo diferente, mas que empregam os mesmos símbolos para facilitar sua compreensão (Ver as *Legendas dos mapas*, pág. x-xii). Os mapas de cada uma das principais regiões terrestres, continentes ou subcontinentes, são introduzidos por um ou mais mapas na escala 1:12 000 000. Em seguida, vêm mapas, nas escalas de 1:6 000 000 e 1:3 000 000, que apresentam, com maiores detalhes, seções da região considerada. Exceto quanto à escala, os mapas de 1:6 000 000 e 1:3 000 000 têm as mesmas características. Finalmente, aparecem, na escala de 1:1 000 000, os mapas das áreas mais importantes da região considerada. A cada escala corresponde uma barra colorida e um indicador da mesma cor, que se encontra à margem da página de cada mapa. À página 21, acha-se um exemplo de cada escala, bem como a equivalência das relações centímetro/quilômetro e polegada/milha.

As três séries básicas de mapas são diferentes quanto ao conteúdo e à apresentação. Os mapas em escala de 1:12 000 000, que são essencialmente políticos, oferecem uma visão geral de cada região. Indicam as fronteiras nacionais e, em alguns casos, as subdivisões administrativas internas. Esses mapas servem de introdução e permitem avaliar e comparar a posição, superfície e forma dos países do Mundo. Neles está claramente indicada a distribuição das cidades e outros centros urbanos, bem como as principais características da configuração do solo. Encontra-se neles também uma seleção das ferrovias e rodovias mais importantes.

A série de mapas das escalas de 1:6 000 000 e de 1:3 000 000 constituem o principal material de referência do Atlas e representa cerca de metade do conjunto de mapas. Entre eles há mapas detalhados de parte de um país (centro do México), de um país inteiro (Japão e a Nova Zelândia) ou de uma região mais extensa (Oriente Médio). As áreas de maior densidade demográfica são apresentados em escala maior, a de 1:3 000 000, e as demais, na de 1:6 000 000. Nessas duas escalas, os mapas fornecem informações de ordem política e cultural sobre um fundo que indica a configuração detalhada das particularidades físicas do solo, cujo relevo se destaca por contrastes de sombras e cores. Diversos matizes do azul traduzem o mapa batimétrico da profundidade ao largo das costas. Indicam também os aeroportos internacionais, as principais ferrovias, duas categorias de rodovias. As subdivisões políticas internas de numerosos países estão igualmente assinalados.

Na série de mapas da escala de 1:1 000 000, certas áreas, de interesse estratégico conjugado à importância econômica, densidade demográfica, ou ambos os elementos combinados, aparecem em forma ainda mais detalhada. O objetivo dessa série é representar a distribuição dos grandes centros urbanos, cidades, rodovias, ferrovias, pontes, aeroportos, represas, reservatórios e outras características associadas às grandes densidades demográficas. Indicam-se, também, os parques mais importantes, os lugares de interesse histórico, as áreas de lazer, três categorias de rodovias, e duas de ferrovias; e a nomenclatura dos grandes itinerários rodoviários. Todos esses elementos destacam-se sobre um fundo topográfico do relevo, executado em matizes das diversas cores.

Nos mapas regionais, assinalam-se os centros urbanos de dois modos. A *grandeza da população* das grandes cidades e dos centros urbanos secundários é representada pela *dimensão e forma do símbolo* que as localiza no mapa. O símbolo só reflete a população situada dentro de limites administrativos, sem levar em conta os subúrbios. Nos países onde os limites de uma municipalidade incluem zonas rurais, o símbolo representa apenas a população. A *importância política e econômica* de uma cidade, que não se relaciona necessariamente com o número de seus habitantes, é indicada pela *dimensão* dos caracteres tipográficos com que se compõe o seu nome.

A chave dos símbolos e caracteres tipográficos empregados figura na pág. xi, nas *Legendas dos mapas*.

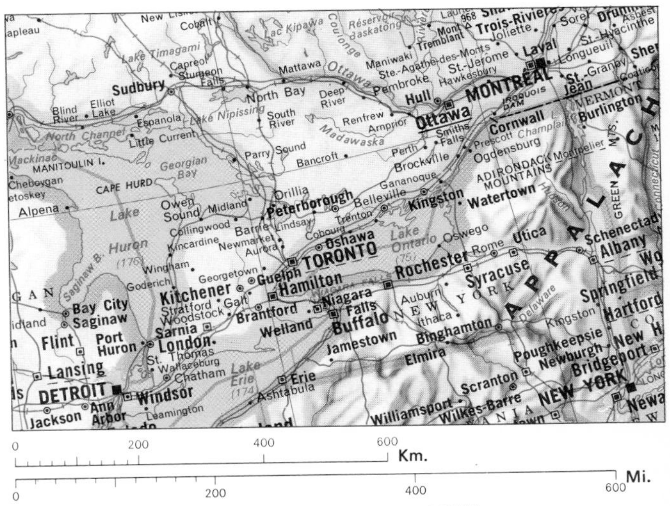

Scale 1:12,000,000
One centimeter represents 120 kilometers.
One inch represents approximately 190 miles.

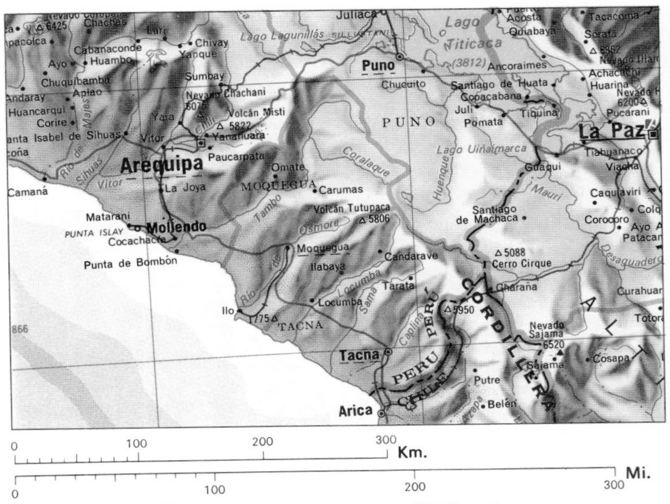

Scale 1:6,000,000
One centimeter represents 60 kilometers.
One inch represents approximately 95 miles.

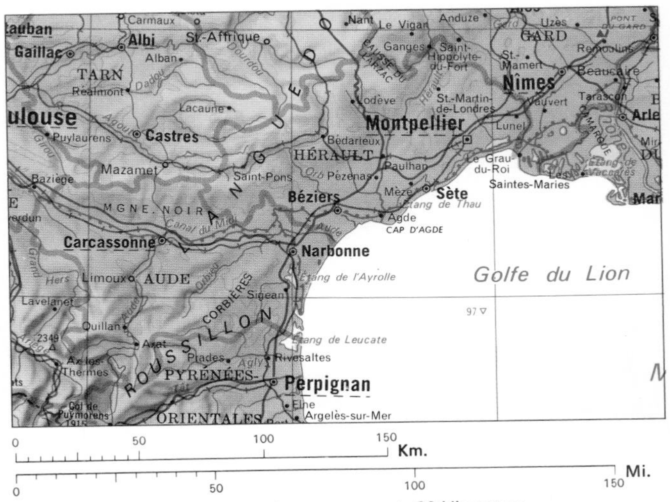

Scale 1:3,000,000
One centimeter represents 30 kilometers.
One inch represents approximately 47 miles.

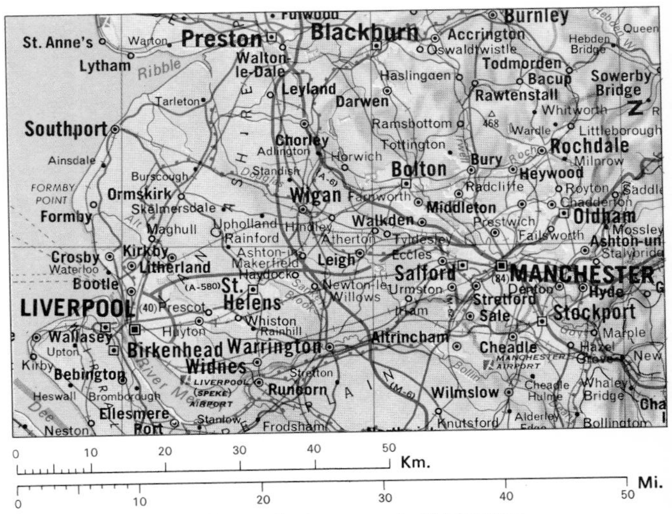

Scale 1:1,000,000
One centimeter represents 10 kilometers.
One inch represents approximately 16 miles.

MAP FORM	-älven	gora	île	islands	-øya	ozero	sea	vodochranilišče
ENGLISH	river	mountain	island	islands	island	lake	sea	reservoir
DEUTSCH	Fluss	Berg	Insel	Inseln	Insel	See	Meer	Stausee
ESPAÑOL	río	montaña	isla	islas	isla	lago	mar	embalse
FRANÇAIS	rivière	montagne	île	îles	île	lac	mer	réservoir
PORTUGUÊS	rio	montanha	ilha	ilhas	ilha	lago	mar	reservatório

For complete glossary see page I • 1.

UNION OF SOVIET SOCIALIST REPUBLICS
RUSSIAN SOVIET FEDERATED SOCIALIST REPUBLIC
URAL MOUNTAINS
URAL'SKIJE GORY
CAUCASUS
BLACK SEA
CASPIAN SEA
Barents Sea
White Sea
TURKEY
IRAN
IRAQ
SYRIA
CYPRUS
FINLAND
BULGARIA
ROMANIA
MOSCOW MOSKVA
LENINGRAD
Kijev
Char'kov
Volgograd (Stalingrad)
Kazan'
Gor'kij
Kujbyšev
Sverdlovsk
Čel'abinsk
Perm'
Saratov
Rostov-na-Donu
Odessa
Minsk
Riga
Tallinn
Helsinki
Vilnius
Tbilisi
Baku
Jerevan
Ankara
İstanbul
Bucureşti
Sofija
Athinai
TEHRĀN
Baghdād
Archangel'sk
Murmansk
Astrachan'
Orenburg
Ufa
Magnitogorsk
Kurgan
Omsk
Dnepropetrovsk
Doneck
Kišin'ov
L'vov
Kirov
Izevsk
Syktyvkar
Petrozavodsk

Kilometers 0 200 400 600 Km.
Statute Miles 0 200 400 600 Mi.

Scale 1:12,000,000

One centimeter represents 120 kilometers.
One inch represents approximately 190 miles.
Miller Oblated Stereographic Projection

62 · 65
108 · 109

a

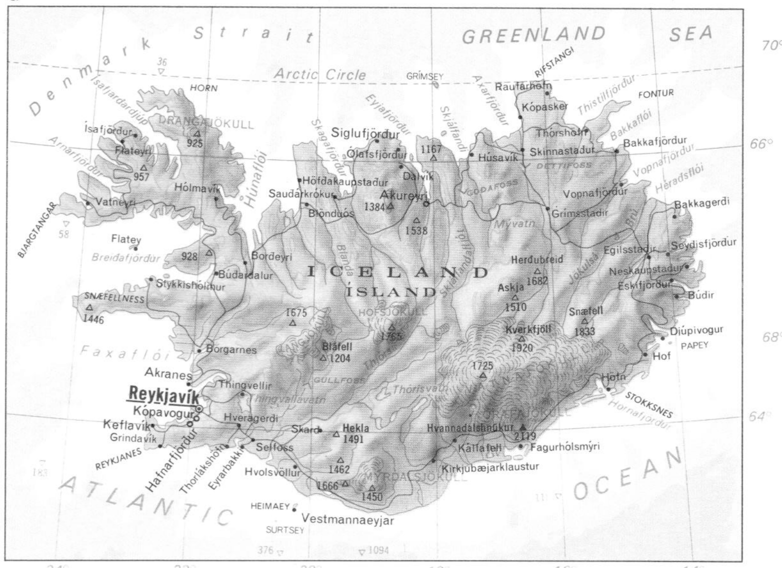

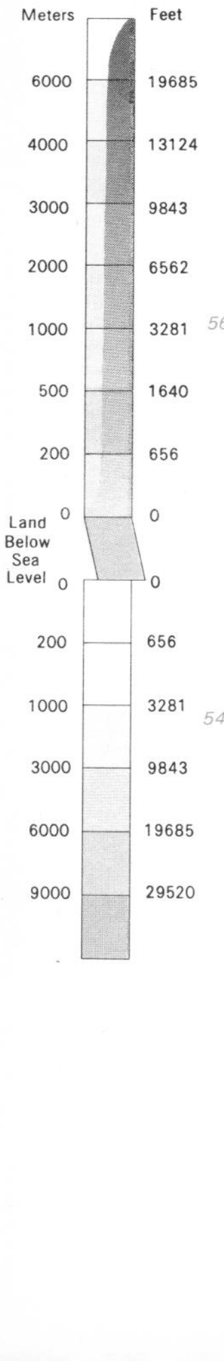

MAP FORM	-älven	-fjorden	guba	-joki	-jökull	lääni	-øya	ozero
ENGLISH	river	fjord, lake	bay	river	glacier	province	island	lake
DEUTSCH	Fluss	Fjord, See	Bucht	Fluss	Gletscher	Provinz	Insel	See
ESPAÑOL	río	fiordo, lago	bahía	río	glaciar	provincia	isla	lago
FRANÇAIS	rivière	fjord, lac	baie	rivière	glacier	province	île	lac
PORTUGUÊS	rio	fiorde, lago	baía	rio	geleira	província	ilha	lago

For complete glossary see page *I • 1*.

Kilometers 0 100 200 300 Km.

Statute Miles 0 100 200 300 Mi.

Scale 1:6,000,000

One centimeter represents 60 kilometers.
One inch represents approximately 95 miles.
Lambert Conformal Conic Projection

Meters	Feet
6000	19685
4000	13124
3000	9843
2000	6562
1000	3281
500	1640
200	656
0	0
Land Below Sea Level	
0	0
200	656
1000	3281
3000	9843
6000	19685
9000	29520

30-31

MAP FORM	-älven	bugt	-fjället	-fjell	-fjorden	-järvi	-joki	-ö, -ön	-sjön	-vesi
ENGLISH	river	bay	mountain	mountain	fjord, lake	lake	river	island	lake	lake
DEUTSCH	Fluss	Bucht	Berg	Berg	Fjord, See	See	Fluss	Insel	See	See
ESPAÑOL	río	bahía	montaña	montaña	fiordo, lago	lago	río	isla	lago	lago
FRANÇAIS	rivière	baie	montagne	montagne	fjord, lac	lac	rivière	île	lac	lac
PORTUGUÊS	rio	baía	montanha	montanha	fiorde, lago	lago	rio	ilha	lago	lago

For complete glossary see page *I•1*.

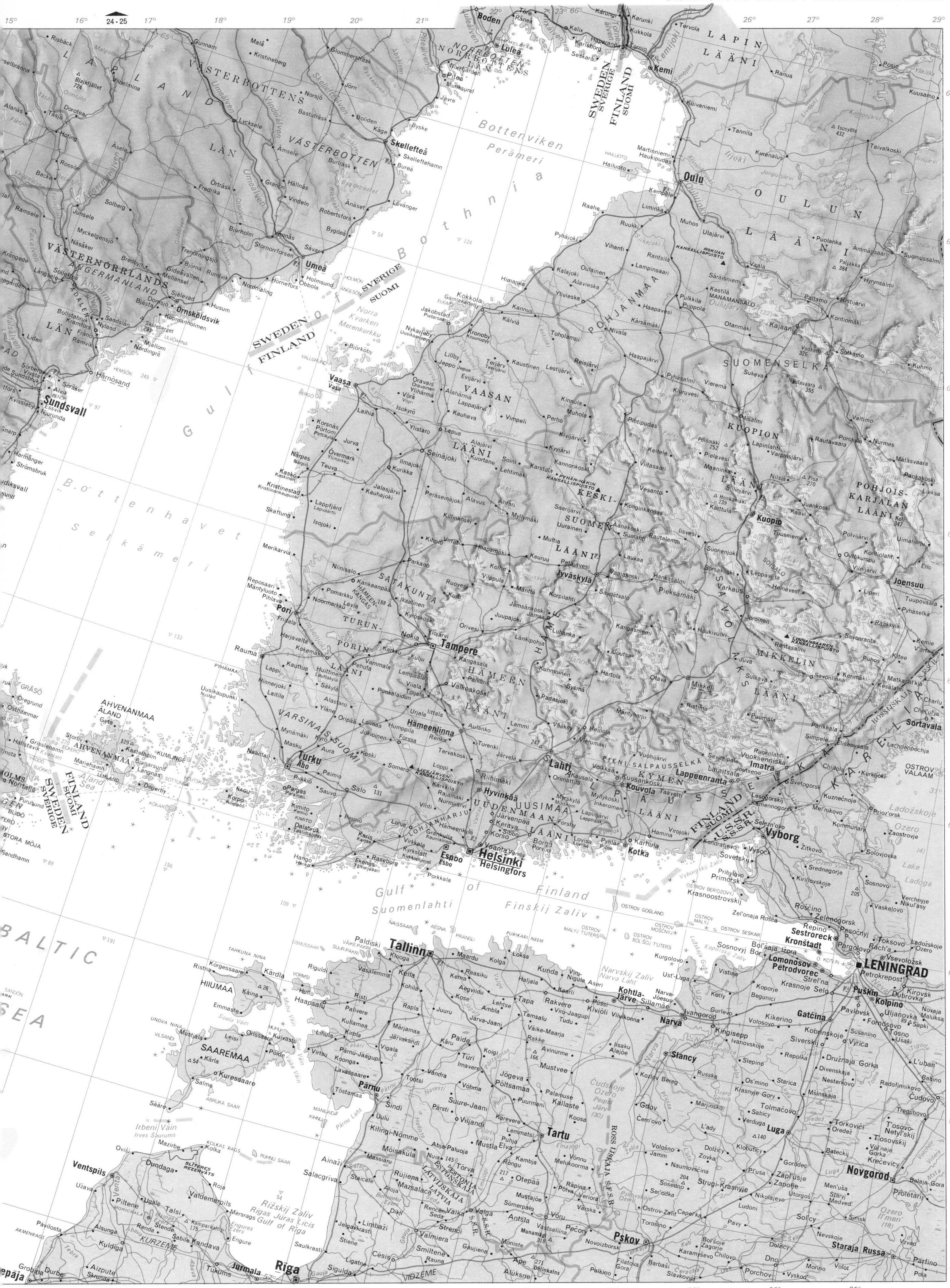

Kilometers 0 50 100 150 Km.
Statute Miles 0 50 100 150 Mi.

Scale 1:3,000,000

One centimeter represents 30 kilometers.
One inch represents approximately 47 miles.
Conic Projection, Two Standard Parallels

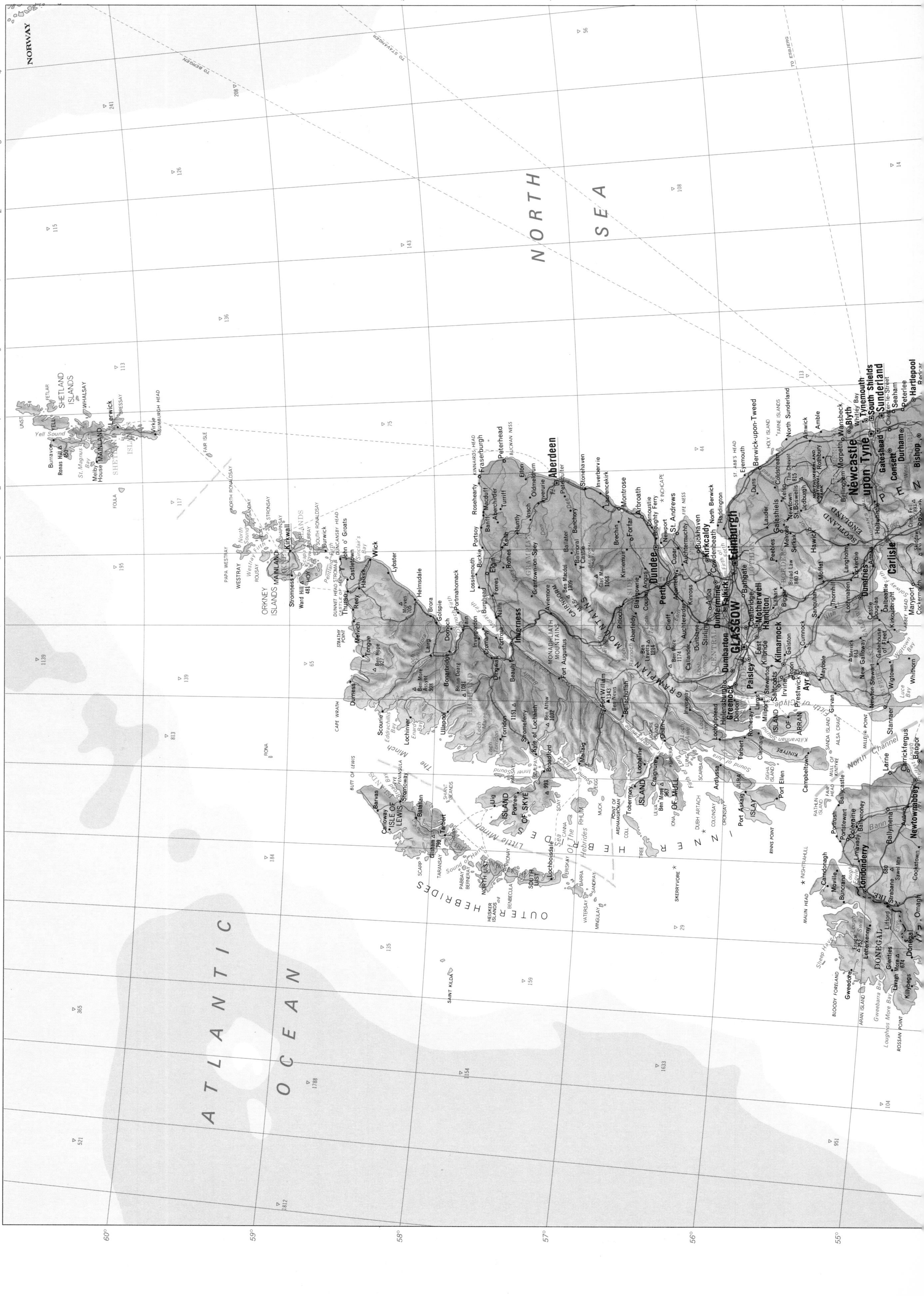
NORTH SEA
ATLANTIC OCEAN
NORWAY
SHETLAND ISLANDS
ORKNEY ISLANDS
OUTER HEBRIDES
Lerwick
Kirkwall
Wick
Thurso
Inverness
Aberdeen
Dundee
Perth
Edinburgh
GLASGOW
Stirling
Oban
Fort William
Stornoway
ISLE OF LEWIS
ISLAND OF SKYE
ISLAND OF MULL
ISLAY
ARRAN
Newcastle upon Tyne
Sunderland
South Shields
Carlisle
Durham
Dumfries
Ayr
Kilmarnock
Stranraer
Londonderry
Belfast
Bangor
Larne
Newtownabbey
ST. KILDA
GRAMPIAN MOUNTAINS
MONADHLIATH MOUNTAINS
60°
59°
58°
57°
56°
55°

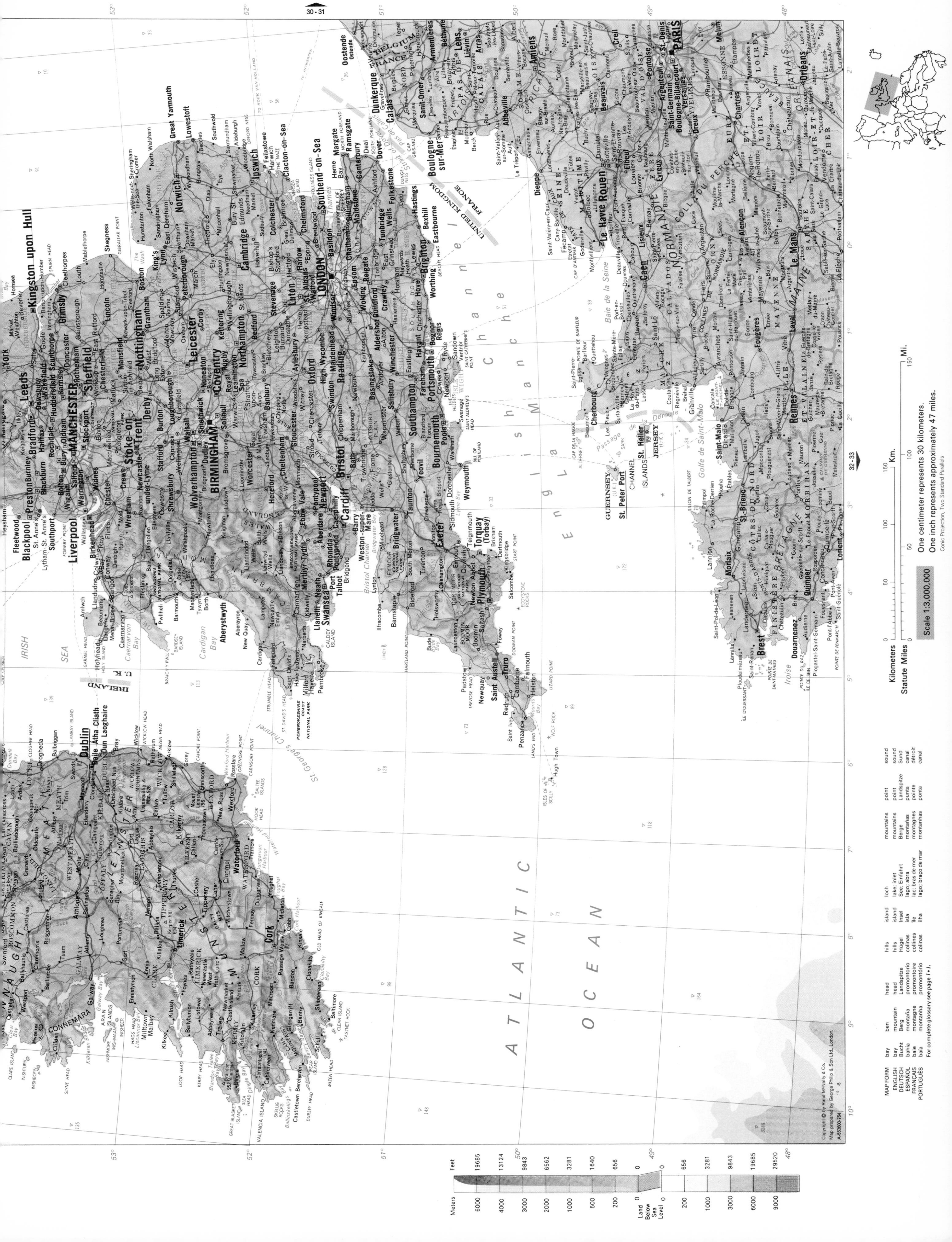
Scale 1:3,000,000
One centimeter represents 30 kilometers.
One inch represents approximately 47 miles.
Conic Projection, Two Standard Parallels
Kilometers
Statute Miles
ATLANTIC OCEAN
English Channel
IRISH SEA
LONDON
PARIS
DUBLIN
Copyright © by Rand McNally & Co.
Map prepared by George Philip & Son Ltd., London

Meters	Feet
6000	19685
4000	13124
3000	9843
2000	6562
1000	3281
500	1640
200	656
Land Below Sea Level 0	0
0	0
200	656
1000	3281
3000	9843
6000	19685
9000	29520

MAP FORM	Bucht	Gebirge	jezioro	Kanal	park narodowy	See	Wald
ENGLISH	bay	range	lake, lagoon	canal	national park	lake	forest, mountains
DEUTSCH	Bucht	Gebirge	See, Haff	Kanal	Nationalpark	See	Wald
ESPAÑOL	bahía	sierra	lago, laguna	canal	parque national	lago	bosque, montañas
FRANÇAIS	baie	chaîne	lac, lagune	canal	parc national	lac	forêt, montagnes
PORTUGUÊS	baía	serra	lago, laguna	canal	parque nacional	lago	bosque, montanhas

For complete glossary see page I•1.
For Budapest and Wien metropolitan maps see page 254.

Kilometers 0 50 100 150 Km.
Statute Miles 0 50 100 150 Mi.

Scale 1:3,000,000

One centimeter represents 30 kilometers.
One inch represents approximately 47 miles.
Conic Projection, Two Standard Parallels.

BALTIC SEA
Gulf of Danzig
Pomeranian Bay
Kaliningrad (Königsberg)
Gdańsk (Danzig)
Gdynia
Szczecin (Stettin)
Bydgoszcz
Toruń
Poznań
WARSZAWA WARSAW
Łódź
Wrocław (Breslau)
Kraków
Katowice
Lublin
Białystok
Dresden
PRAHA PRAGUE
Brno
Ostrava
Bratislava
WIEN VIENNA
Graz
Linz
BUDAPEST
Debrecen
Miskolc
Szeged
Košice
Kielce
Radom
Częstochowa
Olsztyn (Allenstein)
Brest
Grodno
POLAND
U.S.S.R.
CARPATHIAN MOUNTAINS

28 - 29

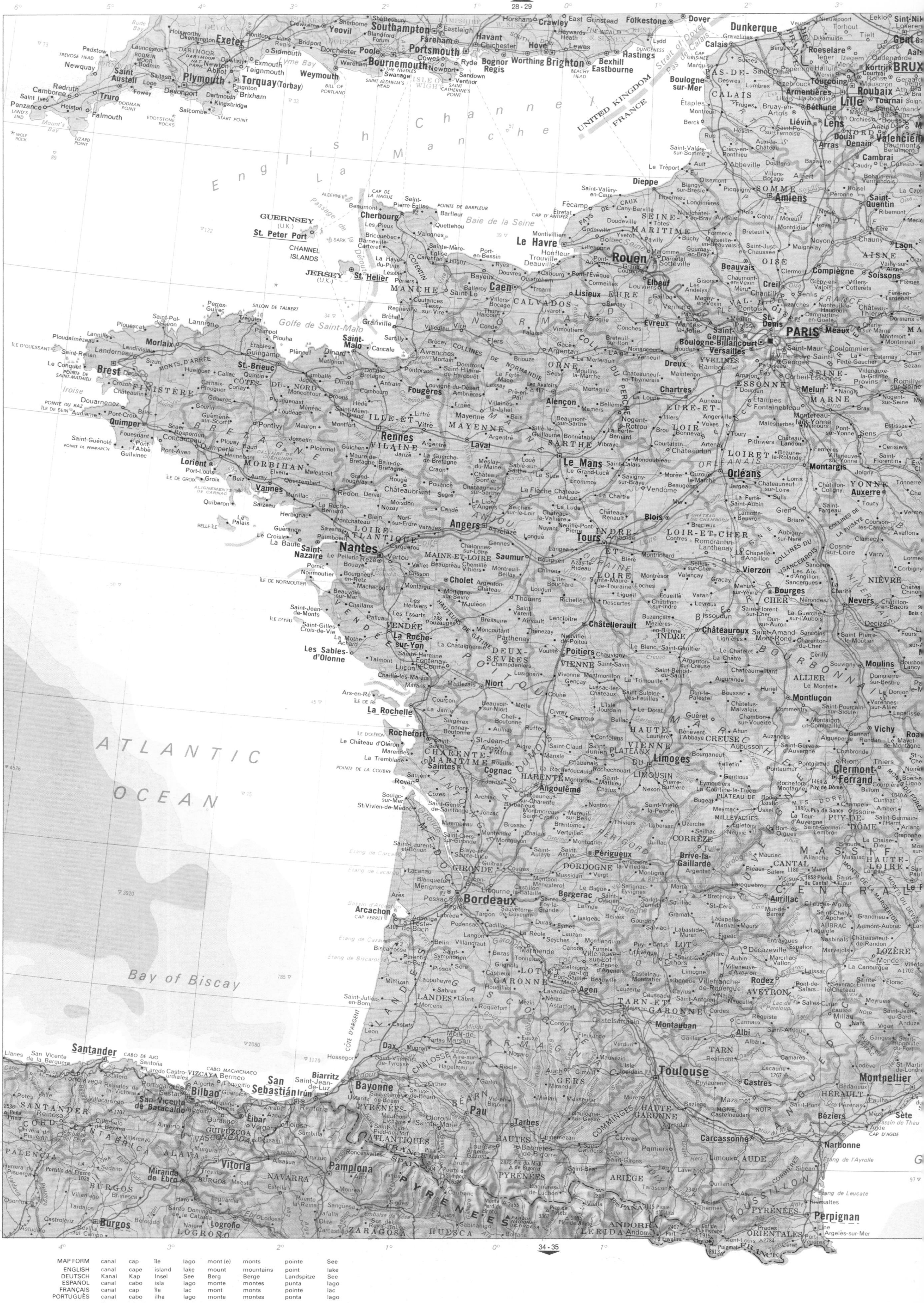

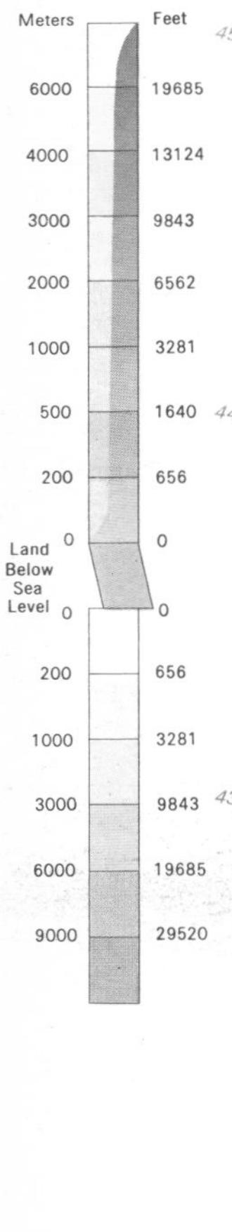

34 - 35

MAP FORM	canal	cap	île	lago	mont (e)	monts	pointe	See
ENGLISH	canal	cape	island	lake	mount	mountains	point	lake
DEUTSCH	Kanal	Kap	Insel	See	Berg	Berge	Landspitze	See
ESPAÑOL	canal	cabo	isla	lago	monte	montes	punta	lago
FRANÇAIS	canal	cap	île	lac	mont	mont	pointe	lac
PORTUGUÊS	canal	cabo	ilha	lago	monte	montes	ponta	lago

For complete glossary see page *I • 1*.

Kilometers 0 50 100 150 Km.

Statute Miles 0 50 100 150 Mi.

Scale 1:3,000,000

One centimeter represents 30 kilometers.

One inch represents approximately 47 miles.

Lambert Conformal Conic Projection

Spain and Portugal / Spanien und Portugal / España y Portugal / Espagne et Portugal / Espanha e Portugal

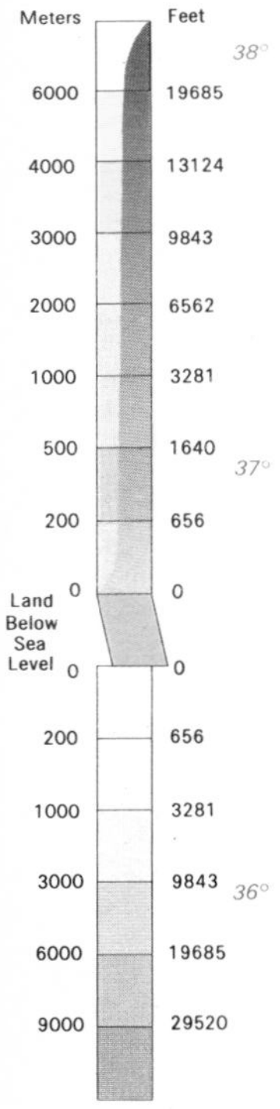

ESPAÑOL	bahía	cabo	isla	embalse	puerto	punta	ría	sierra
ENGLISH	bay	cape	island	reservoir	pass	point	estuary	mountains
DEUTSCH	Bucht	Kap	Insel	Stausee	Pass	Landspitze	Trichtermündung	Berge
FRANÇAIS	baie	cap	île	réservoir	col	pointe	estuaire	montagnes
PORTUGUÊS	baía	cabo	ilha	reservatório	porto	ponta	estuário	serra

For complete glossary see page I·1.
For Madrid, Barcelona and Lisboa metropolitan maps see page 256.

32 - 33

138 - 139

Kilometers 0 50 100 150 Km.
Statute Miles 0 50 100 150 Mi.

Scale 1:3,000,000

One centimeter represents 30 kilometers.
One inch represents approximately 47 miles.
Conic Projection, Two Standard Parallels

38-39

30-31

32-33

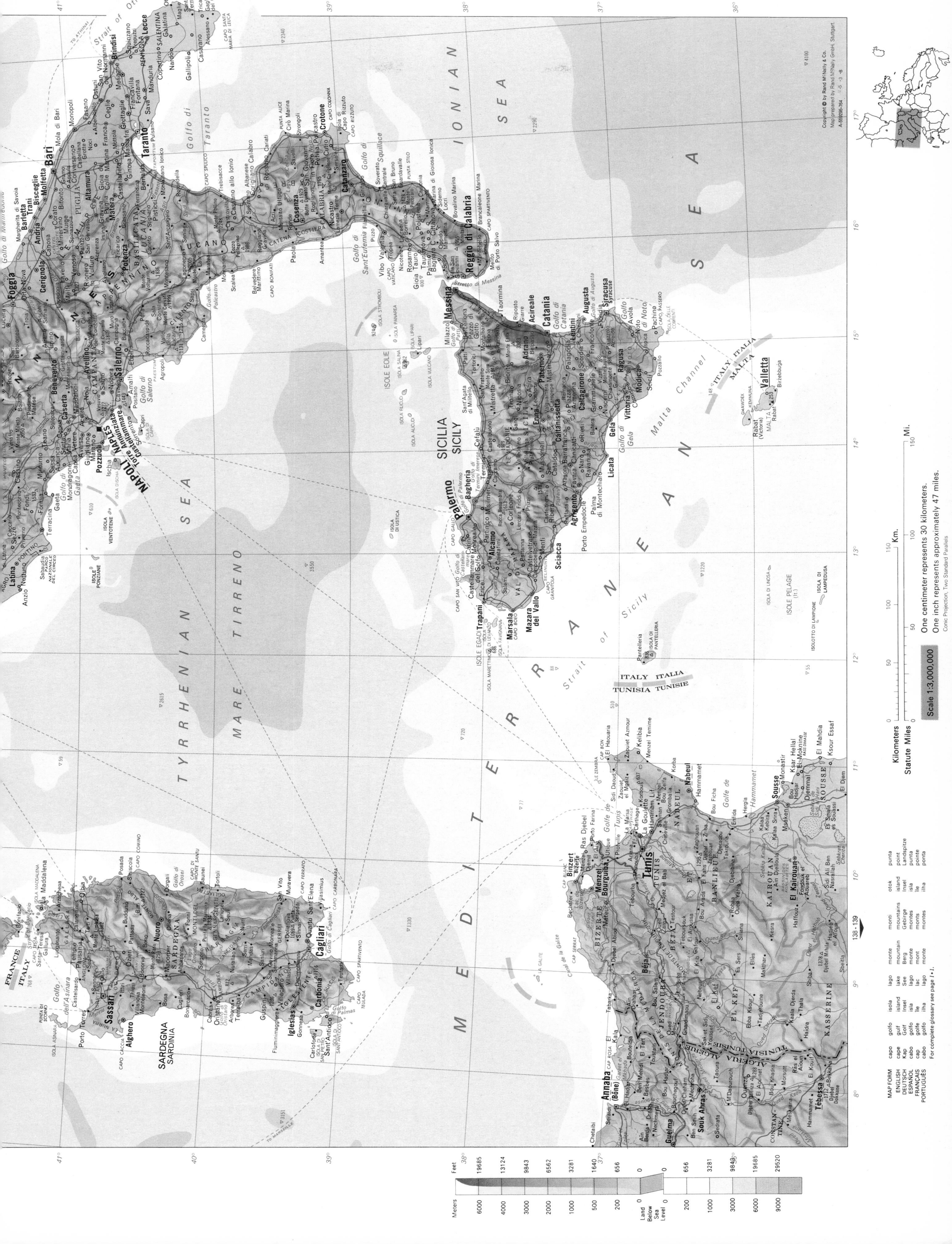
TYRRHENIAN SEA
MARE TIRRENO
IONIAN SEA
MEDITERRANEAN SEA
Strait of Sicily
Malta Channel
Strait of Otranto
Golfo di Taranto
SICILIA
SICILY
SARDEGNA
SARDINIA
Palermo
Messina
Catania
Cagliari
Sassari
Tunis
Bari
Taranto
Reggio di Calabria
Valletta
NAPOLI
NAPLES
ITALY ITALIA
TUNISIA TUNISIE
FRANCE
ITALY
Scale 1:3,000,000
One centimeter represents 30 kilometers.
One inch represents approximately 47 miles.
Conic Projection, Two Standard Parallels
Kilometers
Statute Miles
Copyright © by Rand McNally & Co.
Meters
Feet
138-139

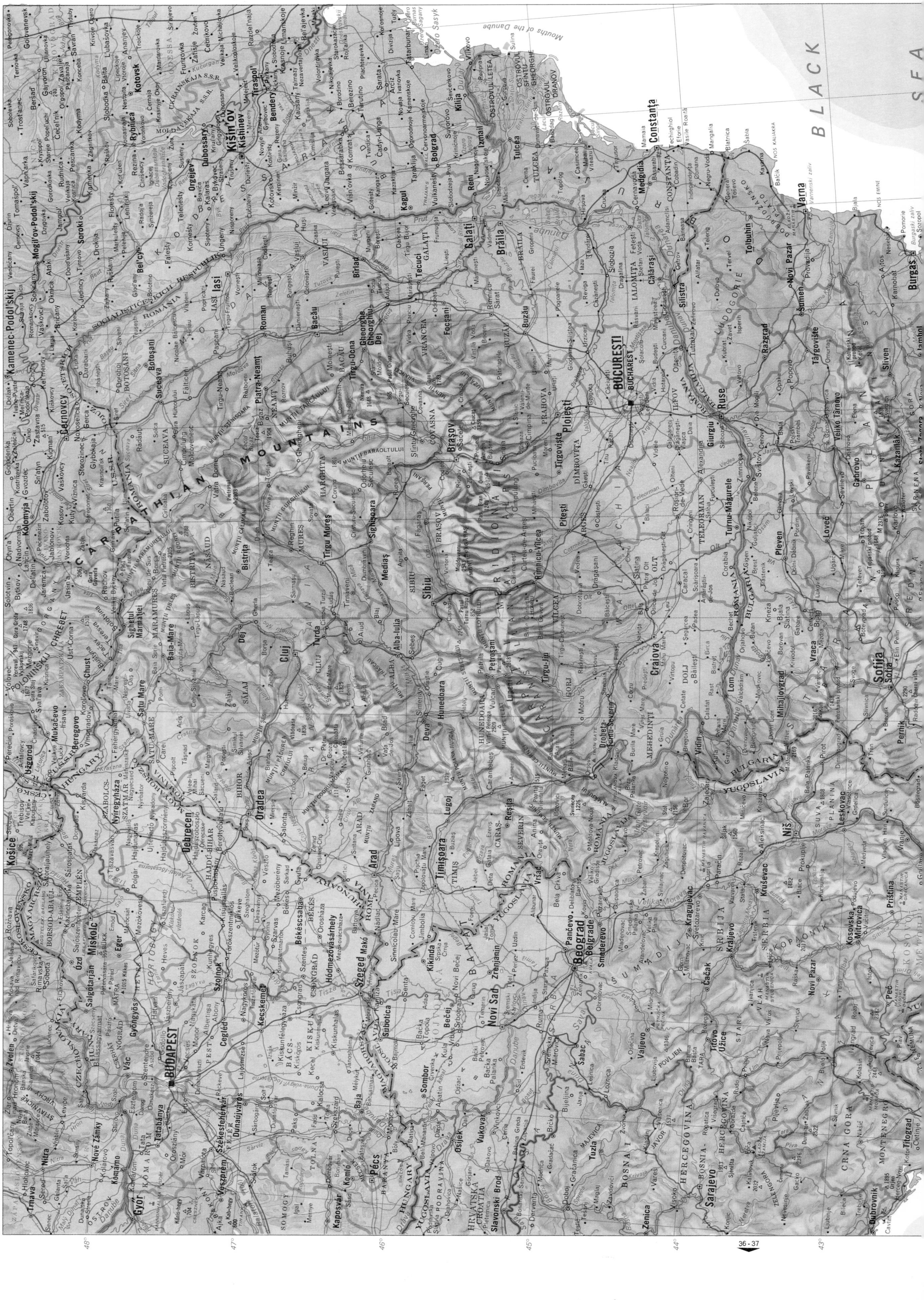

68-69
30-31
36-37

Kilometers 0 50 100 150 Km.
Statute Miles 0 50 100 150 Mi.

Scale 1:3,000,000

One centimeter represents 30 kilometers.
One inch represents approximately 47 miles.
Conic Projection, Two Standard Parallels

MAP FORM	ákra	kólpos	lacul	límni	manastir	munţii	prohod	sea
ENGLISH	cape	bay	lake	lake	monastery	mountains	pass	sea
DEUTSCH	Kap	Bucht	See	See	Kloster	Berge	Pass	Meer
ESPAÑOL	cabo	bahía	lago	lago	monasterio	montañas	paso	mar
FRANÇAIS	cap	baie	lac	lac	monastère	montagnes	col	mer
PORTUGUÊS	cabo	baía	lago	lago	mosteiro	montanhas	passo	mar

For complete glossary see page I•I.
For Athinai and Istanbul metropolitan maps, see page 257. Budapest, page 254.

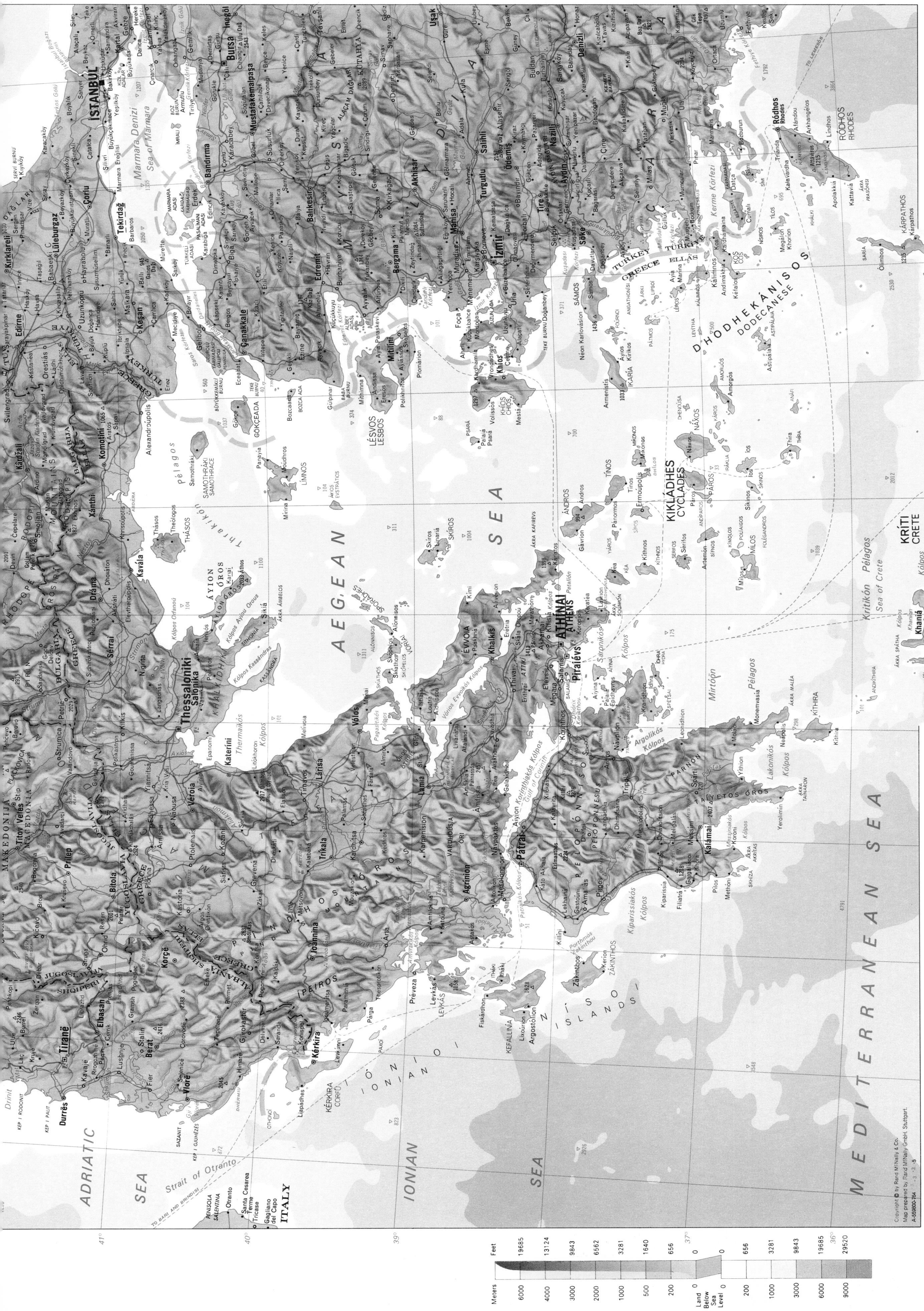
120 - 121
AEGEAN SEA
MEDITERRANEAN SEA
IONIAN SEA
ADRIATIC SEA
Strait of Otranto
ITALY
Sea of Marmara
Marmara Denizi
İSTANBUL
Bursa
İzmir
Thessaloníki
Salonika
ATHÍNAI
ATHENS
Piraiévs
Pátrai
Tiranë
Durrës
KÉRKIRA
CORFU
KRÍTI
CRETE
Iráklion
Khaniá
KIKLÁDHES
CYCLADES
DHODHEKÁNISOS
DODECANESE
RÓDHOS
RHODES
LÉSVOS
LESBOS
TURKEY
TÜRKIYE
GREECE
ELLÁS
IONIAN ISLANDS
PELOPÓNNISOS
Kritikón Pélagos
Sea of Crete
Mirtóön Pélagos
Copyright © by Rand McNally & Co.
Map prepared by Rand McNally GmbH, Stuttgart.

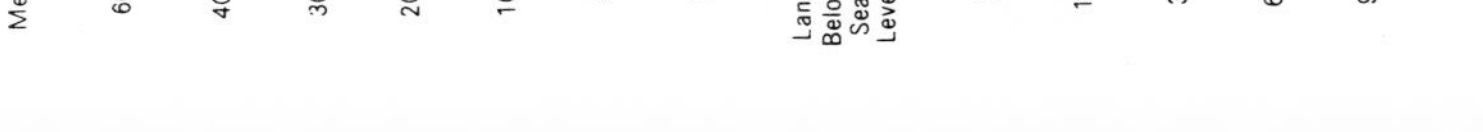
Feet
19685
13124
9843
6562
3281
1640
656
0
0
656
3281
9843
19685
29520
Meters
6000
4000
3000
2000
1000
500
200
0
Land Below Sea Level
0
200
1000
3000
6000
9000

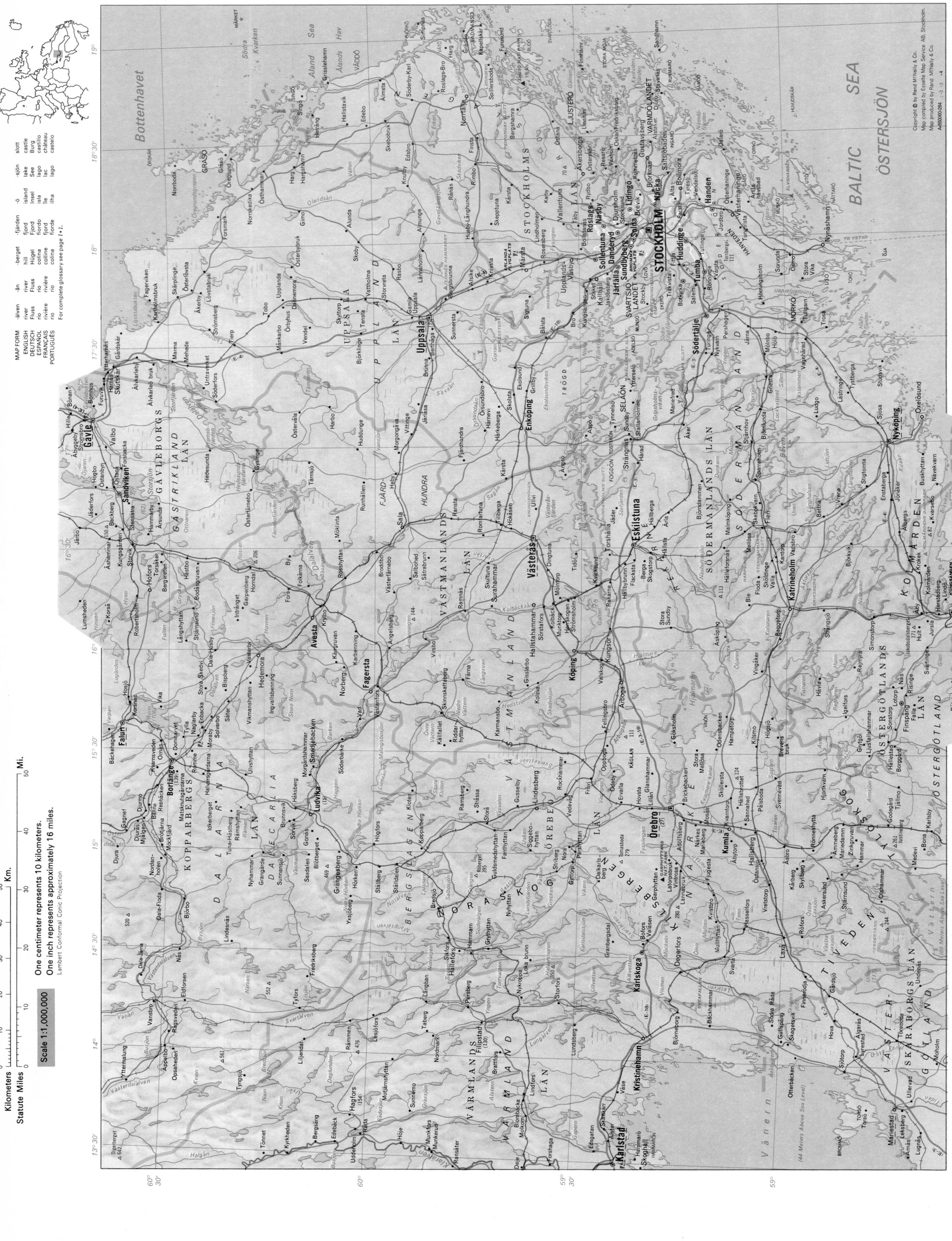
Kilometers 0 10 20 30 40 50 Km.
Statute Miles 0 10 20 30 40 50 Mi.
Scale 1:1,000,000
One centimeter represents 10 kilometers.
One inch represents approximately 16 miles.
Lambert Conformal Conic Projection
MAP FORM -älven -ån -berget -fjärden -ö -sjön slott
ENGLISH river river hill fjord island lake castle
DEUTSCH Fluss Fluss Hügel Fjord Insel See Burg
ESPAÑOL rio rio colina fiordo isla lago castillo
FRANÇAIS rivière rivière colline fjord île lac château
PORTUGUÊS rio rio colina fiorde ilha lago castelo
For complete glossary see page I • 1.
Copyright © by Rand McNally & Co.
Map compiled by Esselte Map Service AB, Stockholm.
Map produced by Rand McNally & Co.
BALTIC SEA
ÖSTERSJÖN
Bottenhavet
STOCKHOLM
Uppsala
Gävle
Västerås
Örebro
Karlstad
Norrköping
Nyköping
Eskilstuna
Falun
Borlänge
Vänern

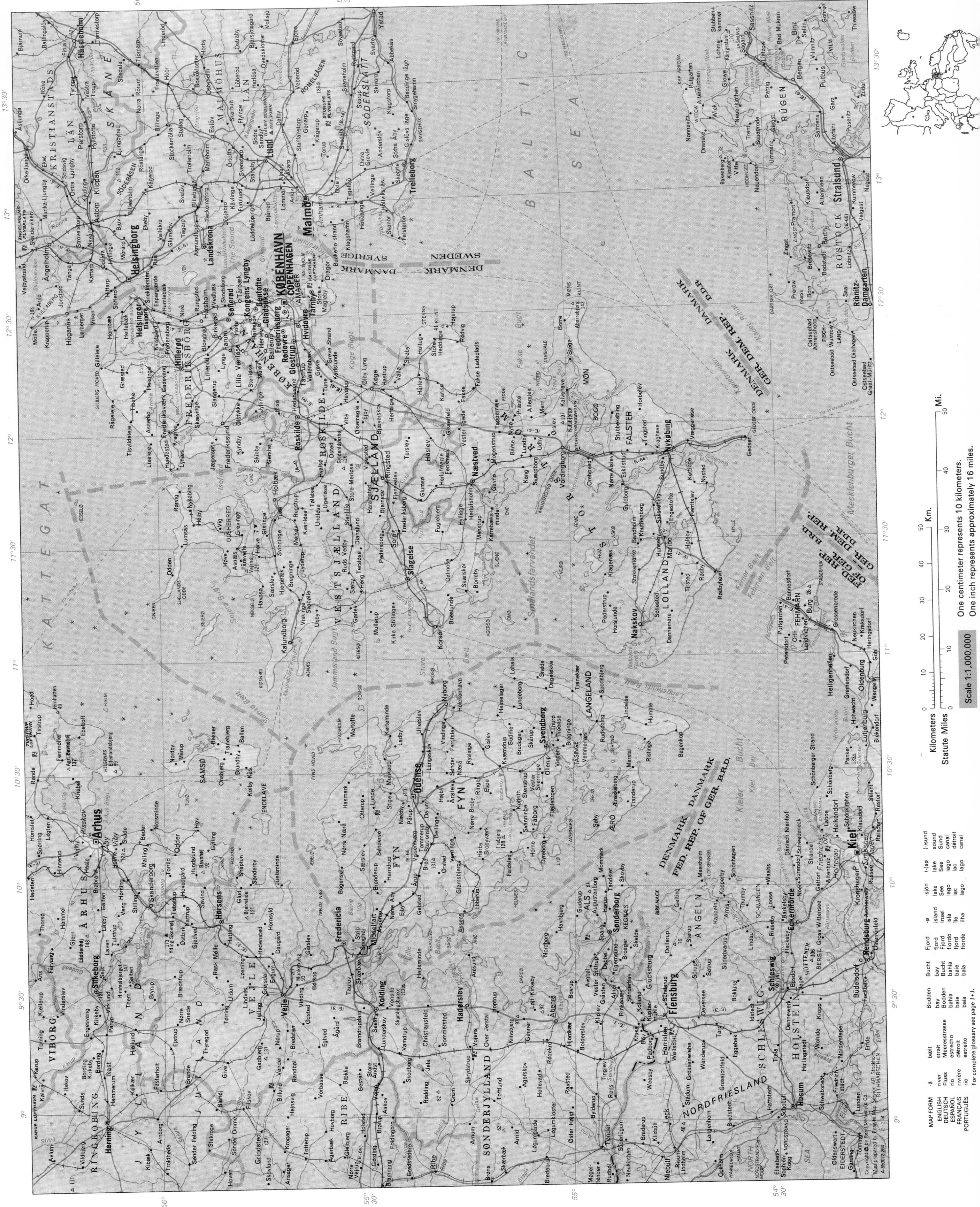
Scale 1:1,000,000
One centimeter represents 10 kilometers.
One inch represents approximately 16 miles.
Kilometers
Statute Miles
KØBENHAVN
COPENHAGEN
Malmö
Kiel
KATTEGAT
BALTIC SEA
SVERIGE
SWEDEN
DANMARK
DENMARK
SJÆLLAND
FYN
LOLLAND
FALSTER
RÜGEN
SKÅNE
JYLLAND
SCHLESWIG
HOLSTEIN
NORDFRIESLAND

GLASGOW
Paisley
Greenock
Kilmarnock
Ayr
Stirling
Falkirk
Motherwell
Hamilton
Dumfries
ISLAY
JURA
KINTYRE
ISLAND OF ARRAN
Campbeltown
North Channel
SCOTLAND
NORTHERN IRELAND
Londonderry
Belfast
Lisburn
Larne
Bangor
Newtownards
Lurgan
Portadown
Armagh
Newry
Dundalk
Dún Dealgan
Drogheda
Droichead Átha
DUBLIN BAILE ÁTHA CLIATH
Dun Laoghaire
Bray
IRISH SEA
ISLE OF MAN (U.K.)
Douglas
ANGLESEY
Holyhead
Bangor
Llandudno
Rhyl
Colwyn Bay
Workington
Whitehaven
Solway Firth
GALLOWAY
CARRICK
DONEGAL
MONAGHAN
CAVAN
LOUTH
MEATH
KILDARE
WICKLOW
IRELAND EIRE
UNITED KINGDOM
Copyright © by Rand McNally & Co.
Map prepared by George Philip & Son Ltd., London.
A-553695-264

MAP FORM	bay	dale	firth	forest	head	loch	moor	water
ENGLISH	bay	dale	estuary	forest	head	lake; inlet	moor	water (lake, river)
DEUTSCH	Bucht	Weites Tal	Trichtermündung	Wald	Landspitze	See; Einfahrt	Moor	See, Fluss
ESPAÑOL	bahia	valle	estuario	bosque	promontorio	lago; abra	páramo	lago, río
FRANÇAIS	baie	vallée	estuaire	forêt	promontoire	lac; bras de mer	lande	lac, rivière
PORTUGUÊS	baia	vale	estuário	bosque	promontório	lago; braço de mar	charco	lago, rio

For complete glossary see page I • 1.
For Manchester-Liverpool metropolitan map see page 252.

NORTH SEA
Berwick-upon-Tweed
Holy Island
Farne Islands
Bamburgh
Alnwick
Amble
Morpeth
Blyth
Whitley Bay
Tynemouth
South Shields
NEWCASTLE UPON TYNE
Gateshead
Sunderland
Seaham
Durham
Hartlepool
Middlesbrough
Redcar
Stockton-on-Tees
Darlington
Whitby
Robin Hood's Bay
Scarborough
Filey
Flamborough Head
Bridlington
NORTH YORK MOORS
VALE OF PICKERING
Harrogate
York
Beverley
Kingston upon Hull (Hull)
Grimsby
Cleethorpes
Spurn Head
Lincoln
Skegness
Gibraltar Point
LEEDS
Bradford
Wakefield
Huddersfield
Barnsley
Doncaster
Sheffield
Rotherham
Chesterfield
Mansfield
MANCHESTER
Stockport
Oldham
Rochdale
Bolton
Wigan
Blackburn
Burnley
Preston
Lancaster
Morecambe
Heysham
Kendal
Penrith
Carlisle
Hawick
Jedburgh
Kelso
Selkirk
Galashiels
Haddington
Dunbar
North Berwick
LAMMERMUIR HILLS
CHEVIOT HILLS
The Cheviot 815
NORTHUMBERLAND NATIONAL PARK
SCOTLAND
ENGLAND
YORKSHIRE DALES NATIONAL PARK
NORTH YORK MOORS NATIONAL PARK
PEAK DISTRICT NATIONAL PARK
Warrington
Widnes
St. Helens
Birkenhead
Chester
Macclesfield
Buxton
Matlock
Worksop
Gainsborough
Scunthorpe
Goole
Selby
Ripon
Richmond
Northallerton
Thirsk
Malton
Driffield
Hornsea
Withernsea
Louth
Mablethorpe
TO BERGEN, STAVANGER
TO GÖTEBORG
TO ROTTERDAM
Mouth of the Humber
3° 2° 30′ 2° 1° 30′ 1° 0° 30′ 0° 0° 30′
56° 55° 30′ 55° 54° 30′ 54° 53° 30′
44 - 45

Kilometers 0 10 20 30 40 50 Km.

Statute Miles 0 10 20 30 40 50 Mi.

Scale 1:1,000,000

One centimeter represents 10 kilometers.
One inch represents approximately 16 miles.

Lambert Conformal Conic Projection

ENGLISH	bay	drain	forest	head	hill	isle	marsh	point	vale
DEUTSCH	Bucht	Abzugsgraben	Wald	Landspitze	Hügel	Insel	Marsch	Landspitze	Tal
ESPAÑOL	bahía	acequia	bosque	promontorio	colina	isla	pantano	punta	valle
FRANÇAIS	baie	drainage	forêt	promontoire	colline	île	marais	pointe	dépression
PORTUGUÊS	baía	drenagem	bosque	promontório	colina	ilha	pântano	ponta	vale

For complete glossary see page *I* • *1*.
For London metropolitan map, see page 250.

Kilometers 0 10 20 30 40 50 Km.

Statute Miles 0 10 20 30 40 50 Mi.

Scale 1:1,000,000

One centimeter represents 10 kilometers.
One inch represents approximately 16 miles.
Lambert Conformal Conic Projection

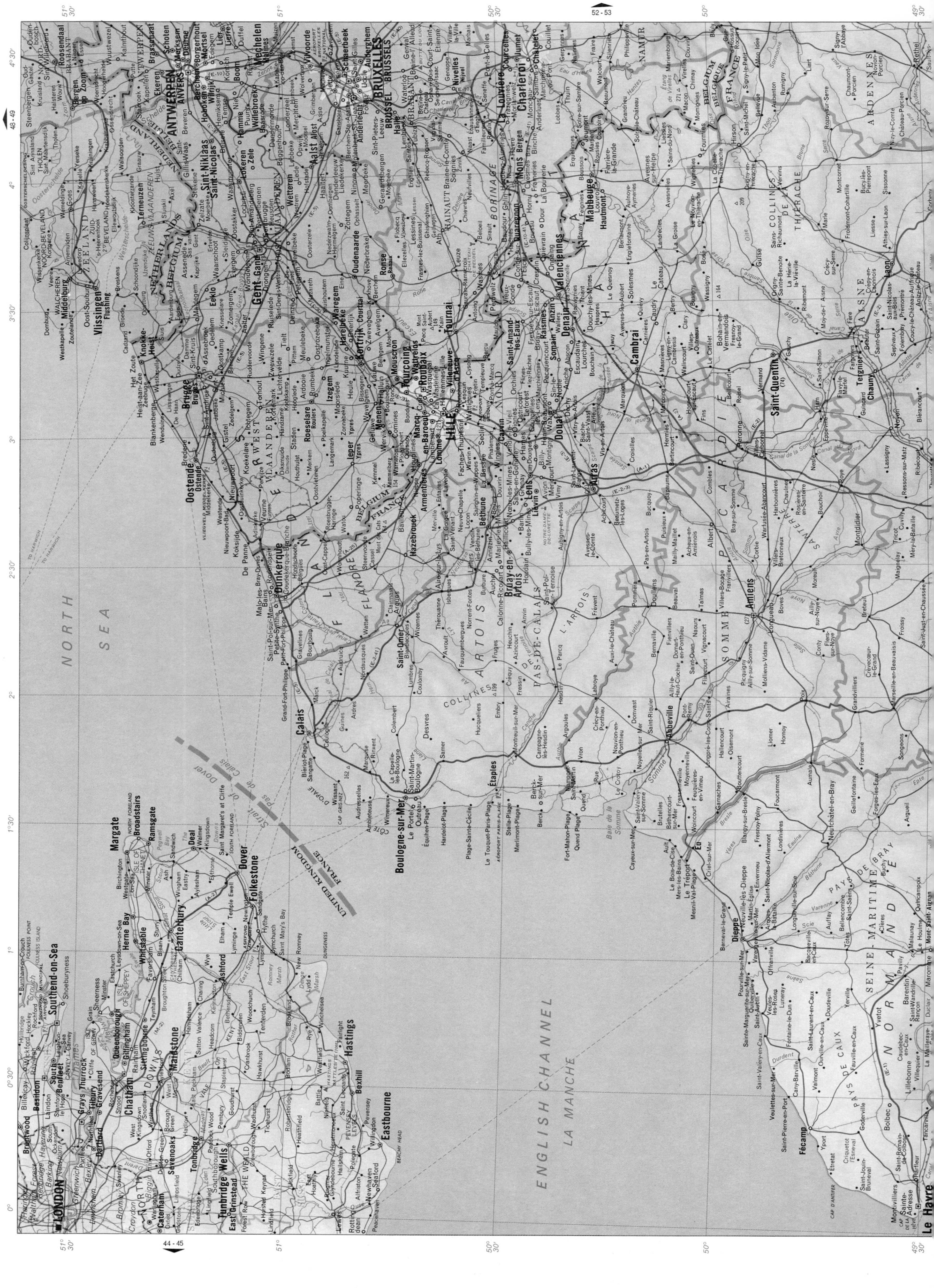
52 - 53
48 - 49
44 - 45
NORTH SEA
ENGLISH CHANNEL
LA MANCHE
Strait of Dover
Pas de Calais
UNITED KINGDOM
FRANCE
BELGIUM
NEDERLAND
LONDON
BRUXELLES
BRUSSEL
Paris — London — Bruxelles

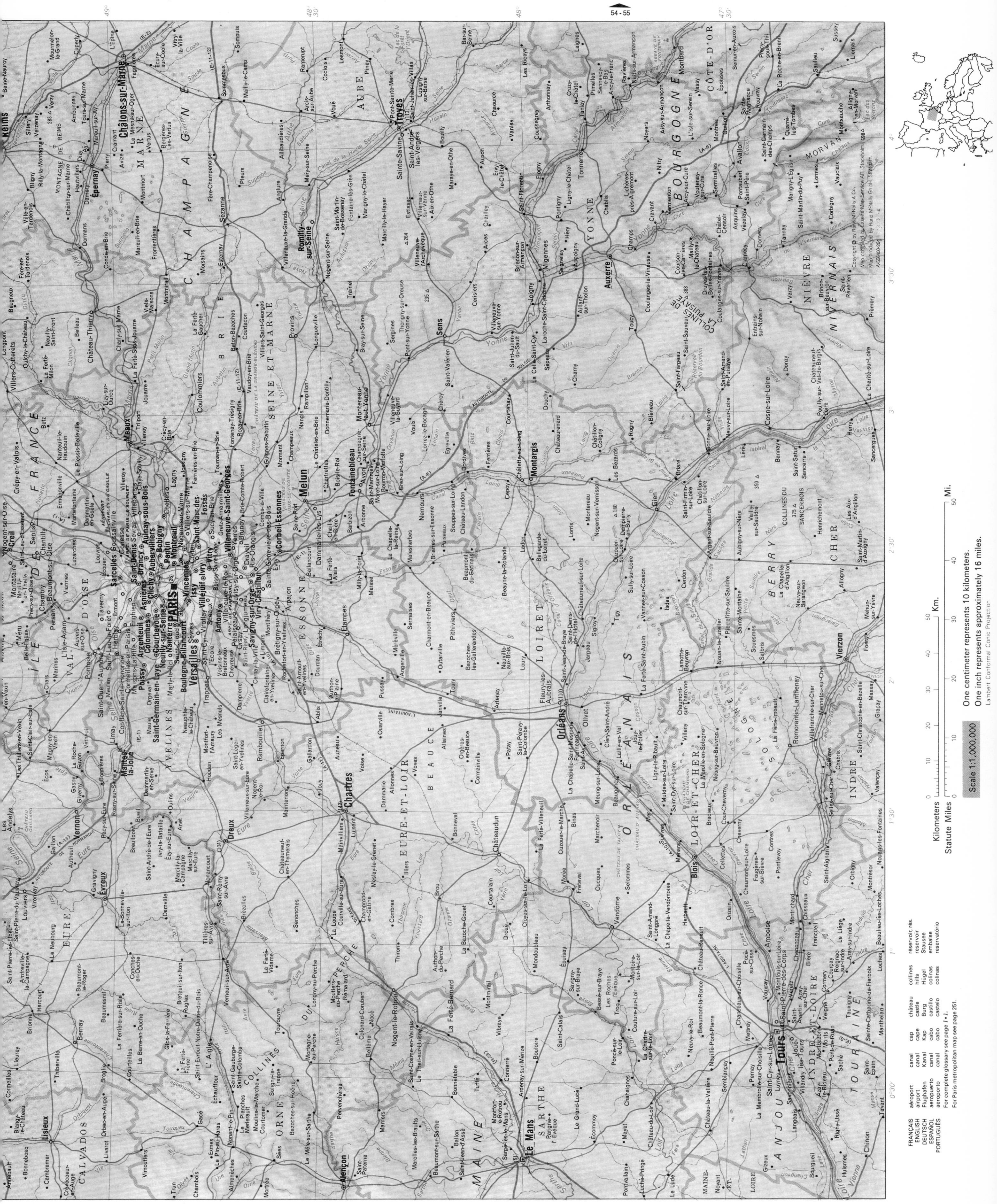
54 - 55
Reims
Châlons-sur-Marne
Épernay
Troyes
Paris
Versailles
Meaux
Melun
Fontainebleau
Sens
Auxerre
Montargis
Orléans
Chartres
Dreux
Évreux
Lisieux
Alençon
Le Mans
Tours
Blois
Vierzon
CHAMPAGNE
BRIE
ÎLE DE FRANCE
BEAUCE
ORLÉANAIS
SOLOGNE
BERRY
TOURAINE
ANJOU
MAINE
PERCHE
BOURGOGNE
NIVERNAIS
Kilometers
Statute Miles
Km.
Mi.
Scale 1:1,000,000
One centimeter represents 10 kilometers.
One inch represents approximately 16 miles.
Lambert Conformal Conic Projection
FRANÇAIS aéroport canal cap château collines réservoir, rés.
ENGLISH airport canal cape castle hills reservoir
DEUTSCH Flughafen Kanal Kap Burg Hügel Stausee
ESPAÑOL aeropuerto canal cabo castillo colinas embalse
PORTUGUÊS aeroporto canal cabo castelo colinas reservatório
For complete glossary see page I • I.
For Paris metropolitan map see page 251.

DEUTSCH	Gebirge	Kanal	Moor	Naturpark	Stausee	Talsperre	Wald
ENGLISH	range	canal	moor	reserve	reservoir	dam	forest, mountains
ESPAÑOL	sierra	canal	páramo	reserva	embalse	presa	bosque, montañas
FRANÇAIS	chaîne	canal	lande	réserve	réservoir	barrage	forêt, montagnes
PORTUGUÊS	serra	canal	charco	reserva	reservatório	represa	bosque, montanhas

For complete glossary see page *I • 1*.
For Ruhr metropolitan map see page 253.

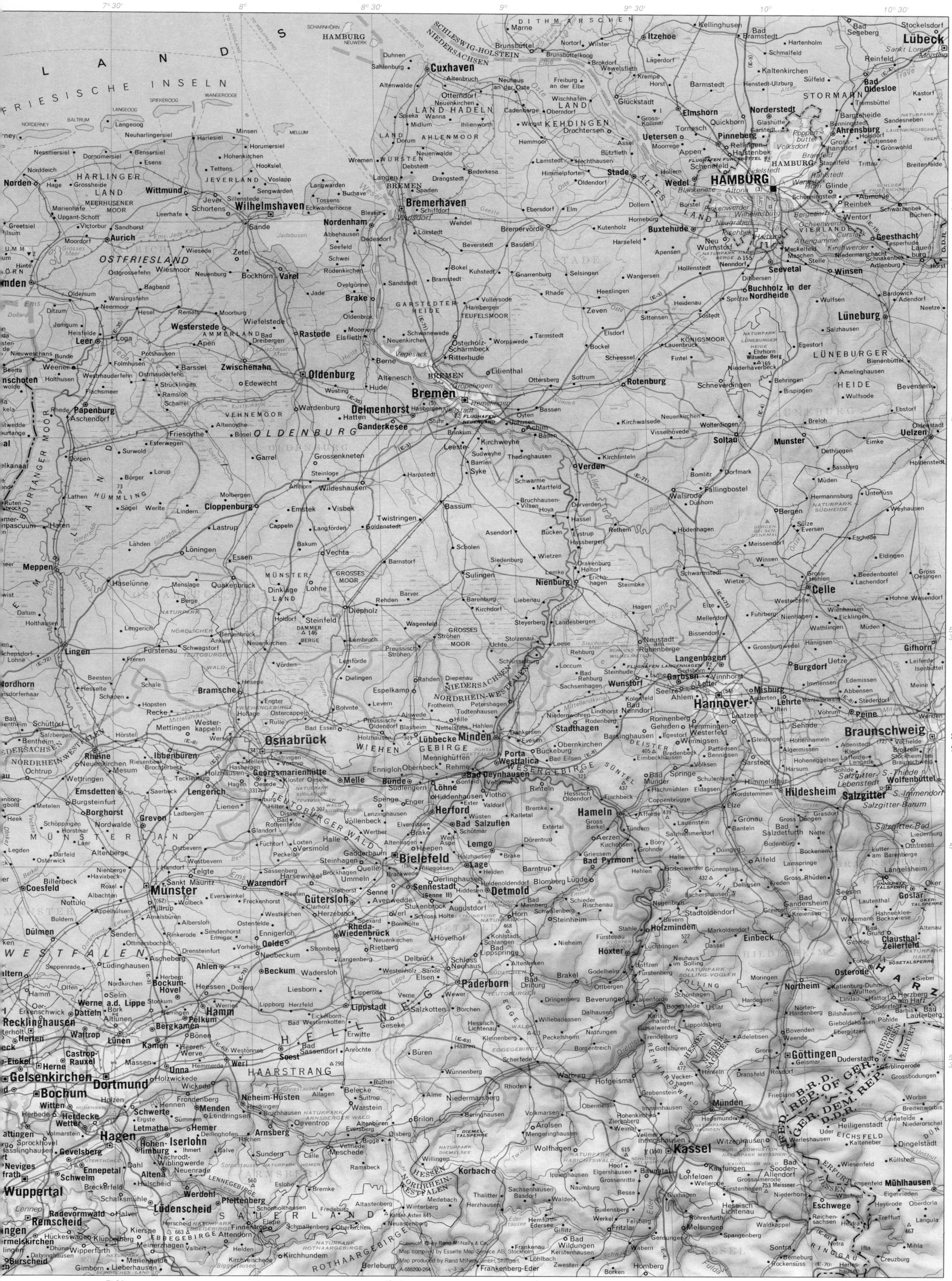

Kilometers 0 10 20 30 40 50 Km.

Statute Miles 0 10 20 30 40 50 Mi.

Scale 1:1,000,000

One centimeter represents 10 kilometers.

One inch represents approximately 16 miles.

Lambert Conformal Conic Projection

BALTIC SEA
Pomeranian Bay
Mecklenburger Bucht
Kieler Bucht
Lübecker Bucht
RÜGEN
FEHMARN
USEDOM
WOLIN
Szczecin (Stettin)
BERLIN (WEST)
(OST)
HAMBURG
Lübeck
Rostock
Stralsund
Kiel
Schwerin
Wismar
Greifswald
Neubrandenburg
Neustrelitz
Prenzlau
Anklam
Demmin
Güstrow
Parchim
Waren
Wolgast
Ribnitz-Damgarten
Bergen
Sassnitz
Eutin
Neustadt in Holstein
Bad Oldesloe
Ratzeburg
Mölln
Geesthacht
Lüneburg
Uelzen
Salzwedel
Stendal
Wittenberge
Perleberg
Ludwigslust
Neuruppin
Rathenow
Nauen
Oranienburg
Eberswalde
Schwedt
Angermünde
Templin
Pasewalk
Swinoujscie
Goleniów
Stargard Szczecinski
Kostrzyn
Chojna
POLSKA
D.D.R.
B.R.D.
POLAND
GER. DEM. REP.
FED. REP. OF GER.
MECKLENBURGISCHE SEENPLATTE
VORPOMMERN
MECKLENBURG
UCKERMARK
PRIGNITZ
HAVELLAND
ALTMARK
BARNIM
Elbe
Oder

48 - 49

Scale 1:1,000,000
One centimeter represents 10 kilometers.
One inch represents approximately 16 miles.
Lambert Conformal Conic Projection
Kilometers
Statute Miles
Km.
Mi.
For complete glossary see page I • I.
For Berlin metropolitan map see page 254.

52-53

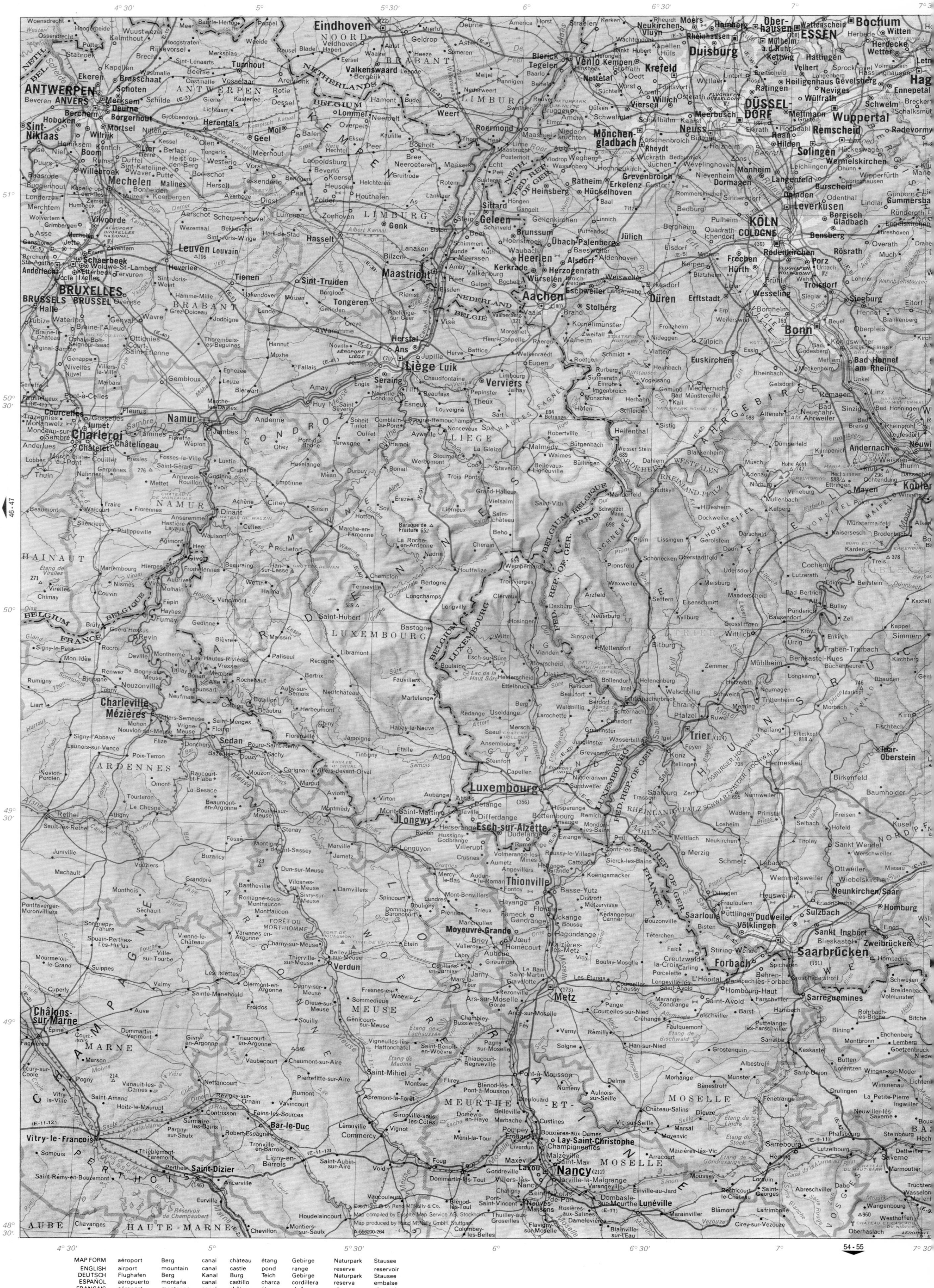

46-47

54-55

MAP FORM	aéroport	Berg	canal	chateau	étang	Gebirge	Naturpark	Stausee
ENGLISH	airport	mountain	canal	castle	pond	range	reserve	reservoir
DEUTSCH	Flughafen	Berg	Kanal	Burg	Teich	Gebirge	Naturpark	Stausee
ESPAÑOL	aeropuerto	montaña	canal	castillo	charca	cordillera	reserva	embalse
FRANÇAIS	aéroport	montagne	canal	château	étang	chaîne	réserve	réservoir
PORTUGUÊS	aeroporto	montanha	canal	castelo	lagoa	cordilheira	reserva	reservatório

For complete glossary see page I•1.
For Ruhr metropolitan map see page 253.

Kilometers 0 10 20 30 40 50 Km.

Statute Miles 0 10 20 30 40 50 Mi.

Scale 1:1,000,000

One centimeter represents 10 kilometers.
One inch represents approximately 16 miles.

Lambert Conformal Conic Projection

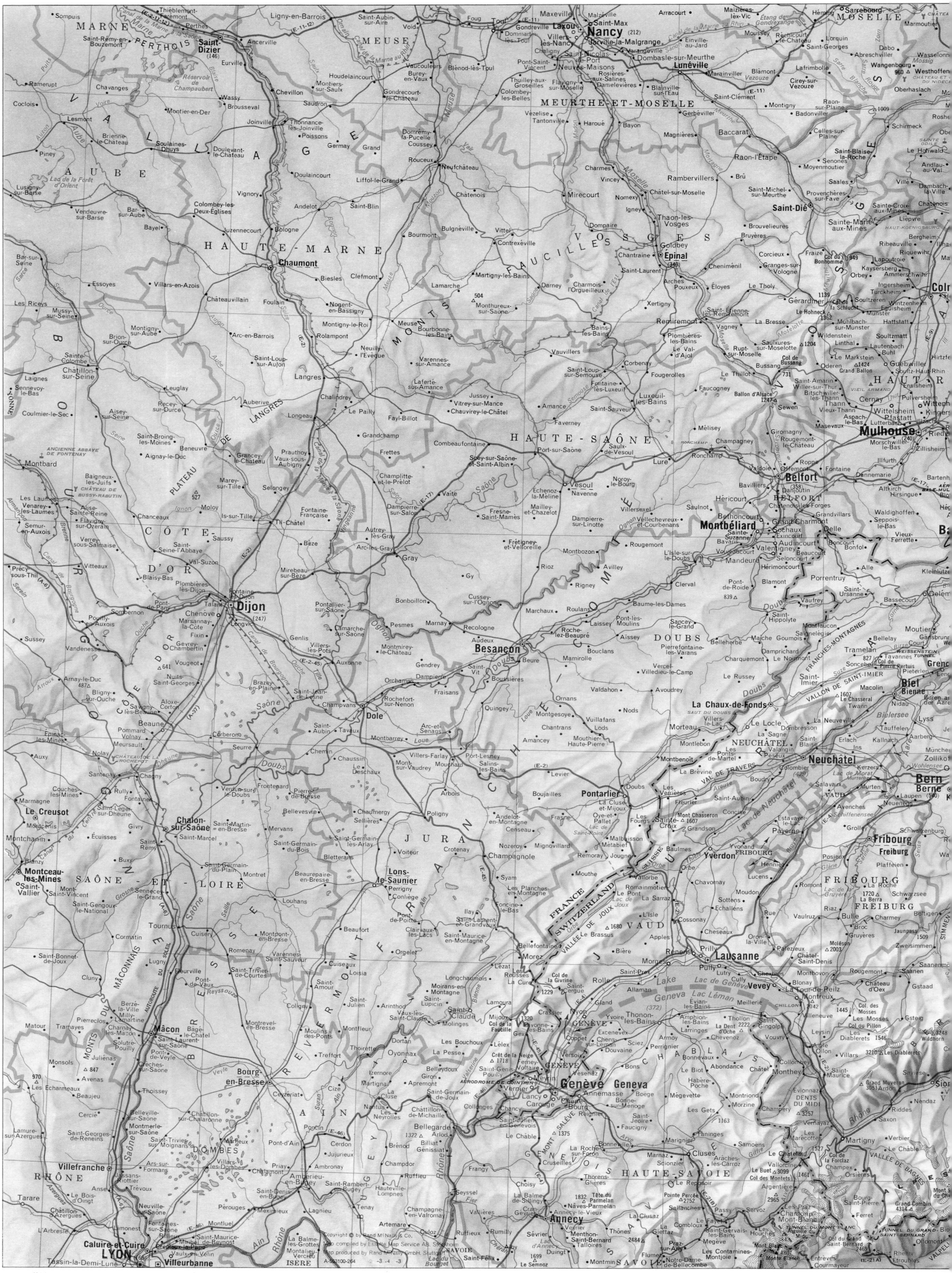

MAP FORM	col	Horn	lago	mont	passo	piz, -zo	See	Spitze	val
ENGLISH	pass	peak	lake	mount	pass	peak	lake	peak	valley
DEUTSCH	Pass	Horn	See	Berg	Pass	Gipfel	See	Spitze	Tal
ESPAÑOL	paso	pico	lago	monte	paso	pico	lago	pico	valle
FRANÇAIS	col	cime	lac	mont	col	cime	lac	cime	val
PORTUGUÊS	passo	pico	lago	monte	passo	pico	lago	pico	vale

For complete glossary see page I • 1.

Kilometers 0 10 20 30 40 50 Km.

Statute Miles 0 10 20 30 40 50 Mi.

Scale 1:1,000,000

One centimeter represents 10 kilometers.

One inch represents approximately 16 miles.

Lambert Conformal Conic Projection

MAP FORM	abbaye	capo	col	île, î.	lac, l.	monte	passo	pic	val (-le)
ENGLISH	abbey	cape	pass	island	lake	mountain	pass	peak	valley
DEUTSCH	Abtei	Kap	Pass	Insel	See	Berg	Pass	Gipfel	Tal
ESPAÑOL	abadía	cabo	paso	isla	lago	montaña	paso	pico	valle
FRANÇAIS	abbaye	cap	col	île	lac	montagne	col	cime	val
PORTUGUÊS	abadia	cabo	passo	ilha	lago	montanha	passo	pico	vale

For complete glossary see page I • 1.
For Milano metropolitan map see page 256.

Kilometers 0 10 20 30 40 50 Km.

Statute Miles 0 10 20 30 40 50 Mi.

Scale 1:1,000,000

One centimeter represents 10 kilometers.

One inch represents approximately 16 miles.

Lambert Conformal Conic Projection

54-55

ADRIATIC SEA
MARE ADRIATICO
Gulf of Venice
Golf of Trieste
Foci del Po
Mouths of the Po
LIGURIAN SEA
MAR LIGURE
Trieste
Venezia Venice
Padova
Vicenza
Verona
Brescia
Mantova
Cremona
Parma
Reggio nell'Emilia
Modena
Bologna
Ferrara
Rovigo
Ravenna
Rimini
Pesaro
Firenze Florence
Prato
Pistoia
Lucca
Massa
Carrara
La Spezia
Viareggio
Treviso
Chioggia
San Marino
Kilometers
Statute Miles
Km.
Mi.
Scale 1:1,000,000
One centimeter represents 10 kilometers.
One inch represents approximately 16 miles.
Lambert Conformal Conic Projection
60-61
56-57
MAP FORM Alpen Berg cima Gebirge monte piz Schloss See Spitze
ENGLISH mountains mountain peak range mountain peak castle lake peak
DEUTSCH Alpen Berg Gipfel Gebirge Berg Gipfel Schloss See Spitze
ESPAÑOL montañas montaña pico sierra montaña pico castillo lago pico
FRANÇAIS montagnes montagne cime chaîne montagne pico château lac cime
PORTUGUÊS montanhas montanha pico serra montanha pico castelo lago pico
For complete glossary see page I • I.
Copyright © by Rand McNally & Co.
Map compiled by Esselte Map Service AB, Stockholm.
Map produced by Rand McNally GmbH, Stuttgart.

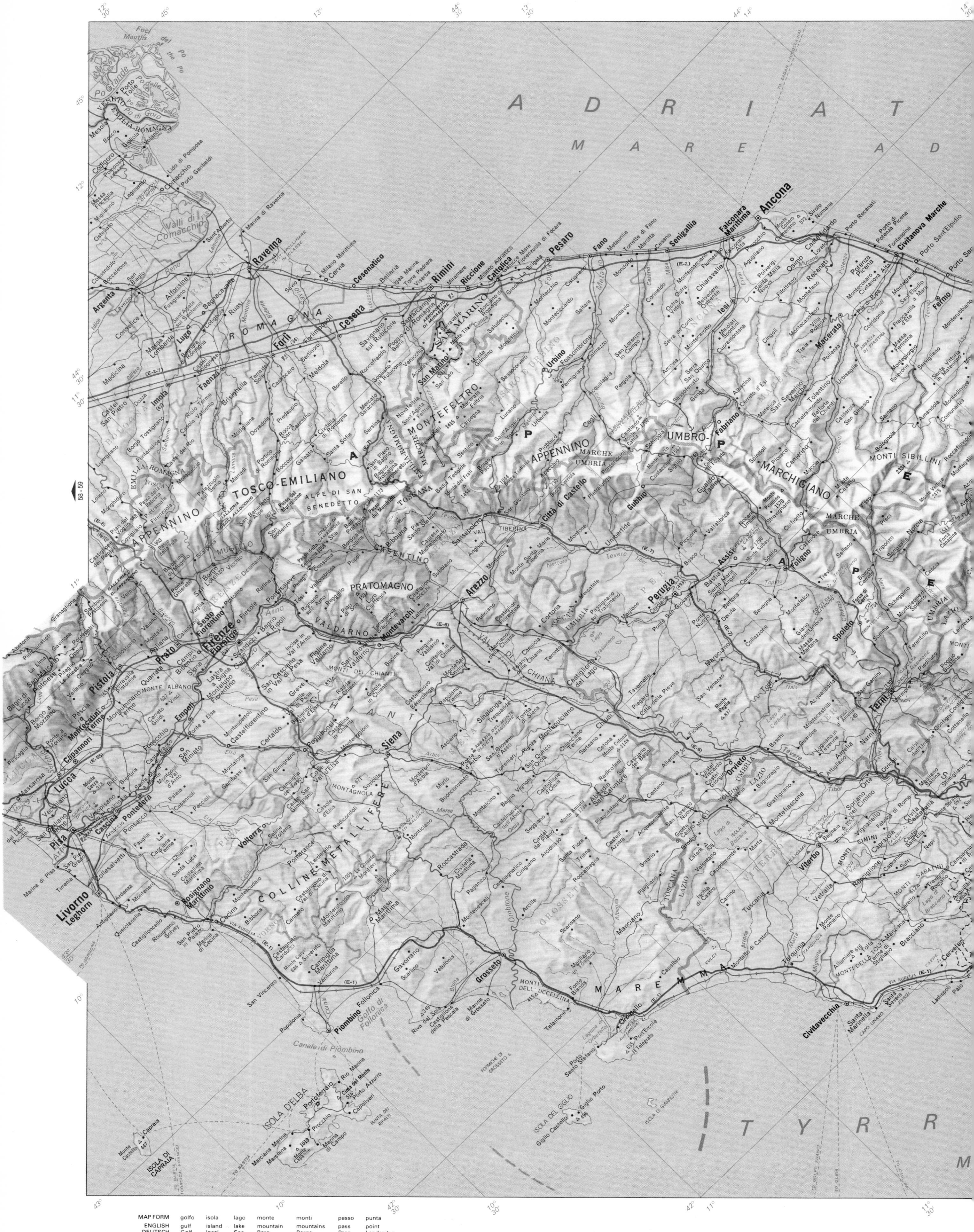

MAP FORM	golfo	isola	lago	monte	monti	passo	punta
ENGLISH	gulf	island	lake	mountain	mountains	pass	point
DEUTSCH	Golf	Insel	See	Berg	Berge	Pass	Landspitze
ESPAÑOL	golfo	isla	lago	montaña	montañas	paso	punta
FRANÇAIS	golfe	île	lac	montagne	montagnes	col	pointe
PORTUGUÊS	golfo	ilha	lago	montanha	montanhas	passo	ponta

For complete glossary see page *I* • *1*.
For Roma metropolitan map see page 257.

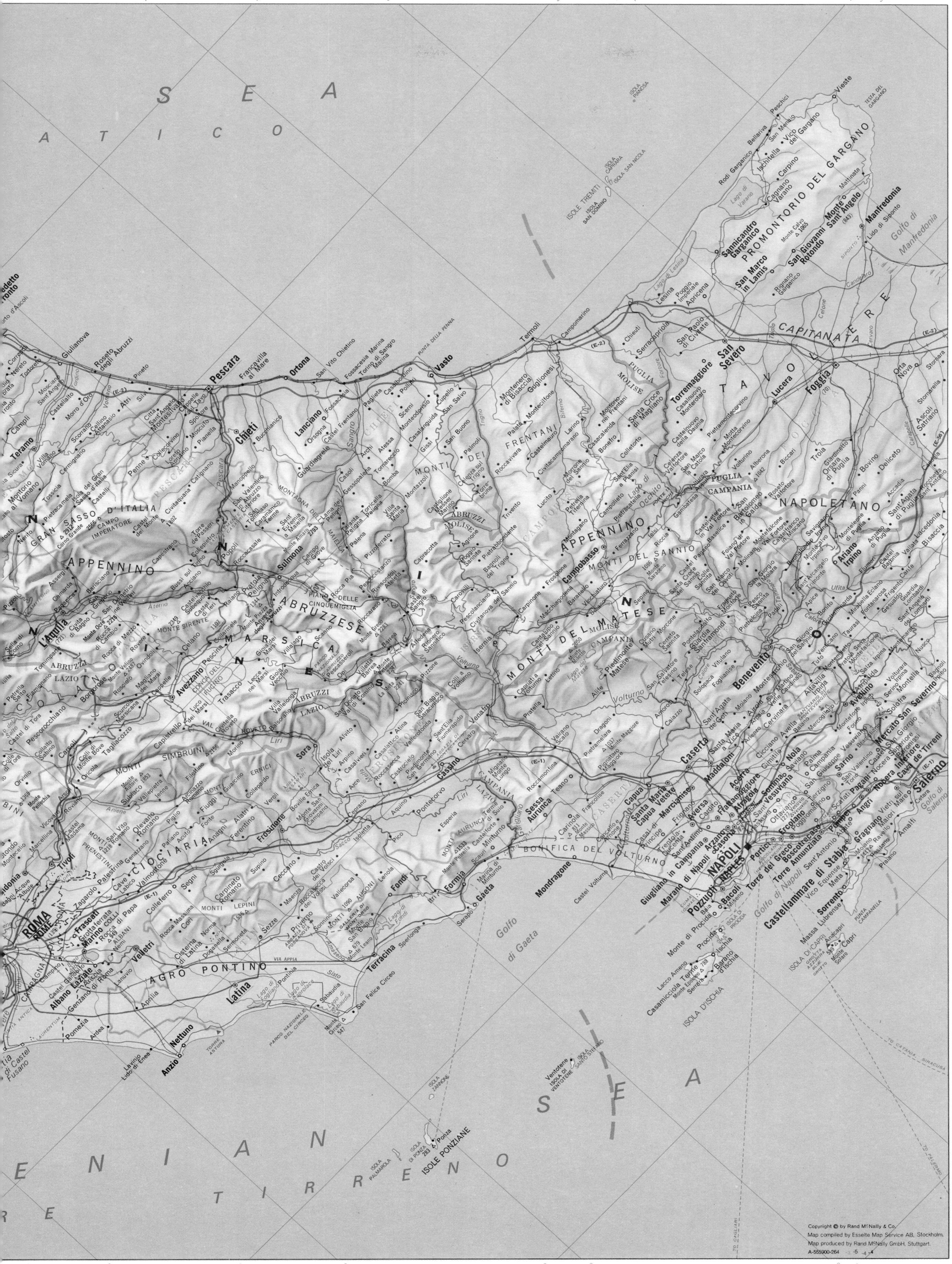

Kilometers 0 10 20 30 40 50 Km.

Statute Miles 0 10 20 30 40 50 Mi.

Scale 1:1,000,000

One centimeter represents 10 kilometers.

One inch represents approximately 16 miles.

Lambert Conformal Conic Projection

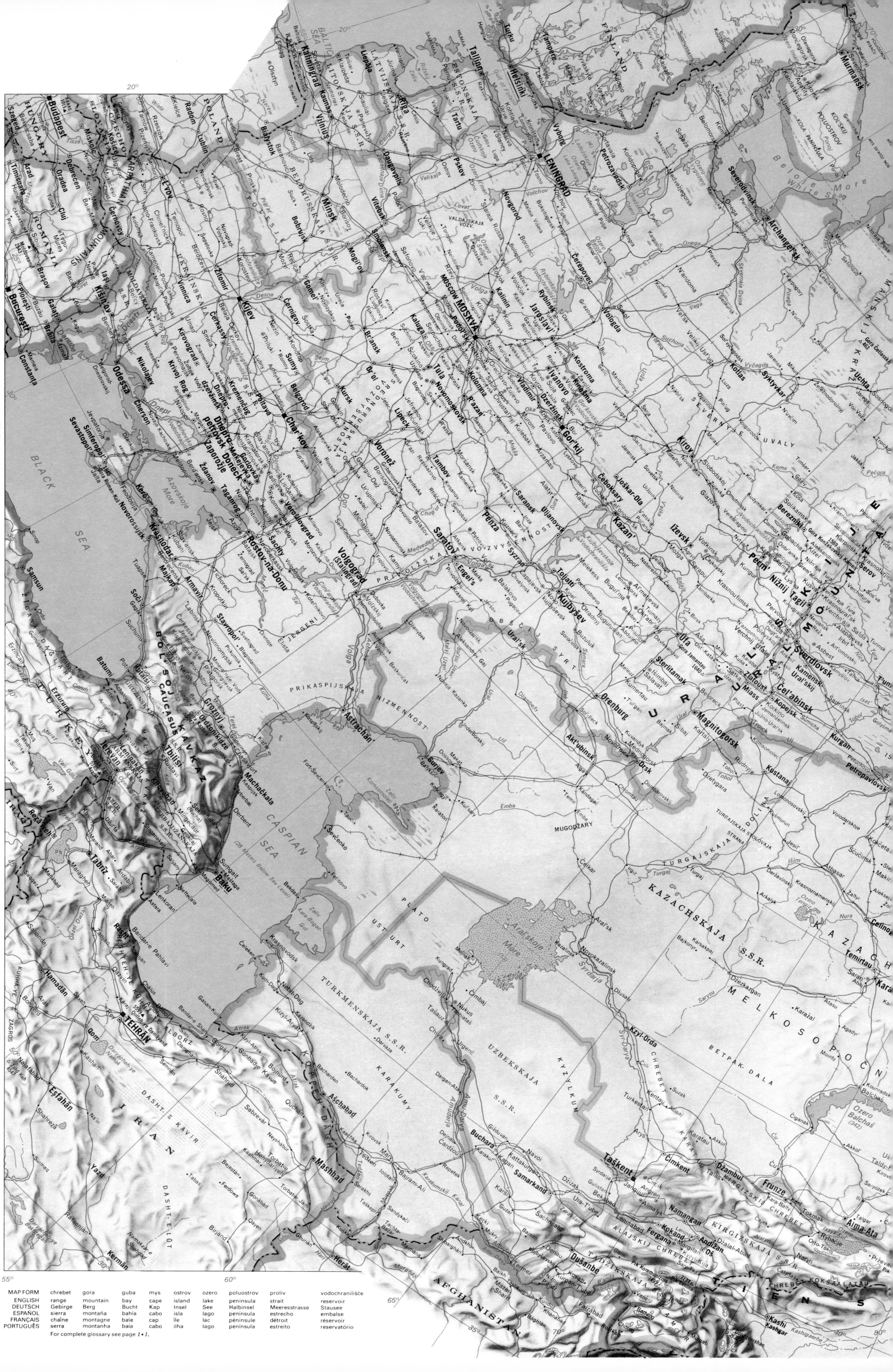

22 · 23

108 · 109

MAP FORM	chrebet	gora	guba	mys	ostrov	ozero	poluostrov	proliv	vodochranilišče
ENGLISH	range	mountain	bay	cape	island	lake	peninsula	strait	reservoir
DEUTSCH	Gebirge	Berg	Bucht	Kap	Insel	See	Halbinsel	Meeresstrasse	Stausee
ESPAÑOL	sierra	montaña	bahía	cabo	isla	lago	península	estrecho	embalse
FRANÇAIS	chaîne	montagne	baie	cap	île	lac	péninsule	détroit	réservoir
PORTUGUÊS	serra	montanha	baía	cabo	ilha	lago	península	estreito	reservatório

For complete glossary see page *I • 1*.

Copyright © by Rand McNally & Co.
Map prepared by Esselte Map Service AB, Stockholm.
A-579594-264

Kilometers 0 200 400 600 Km.
Statute Miles 0 200 400 600 Mi.

Scale 1:12,000,000

One centimeter represents 120 kilometers.
One inch represents approximately 190 miles.
Lambert Conformal Conic Projection

Eastern and Central Soviet Union / Östliche und zentrale Sowjetunion / Unión Soviética Oriental y Central
Union Soviétique Orientale et Centrale / União Soviética Oriental e Central

MAP FORM	chrebet	gora	guba	mys	ostrov	ozero	poluostrov	proliv	vodochranilišče
ENGLISH	range	mountain	bay	cape	island	lake	peninsula	strait	reservoir
DEUTSCH	Gebirge	Berg	Bucht	Kap	Insel	See	Halbinsel	Meeresstrasse	Stausee
ESPAÑOL	sierra	montaña	bahía	cabo	isla	lago	península	estrecho	embalse
FRANÇAIS	chaîne	montagne	baie	cap	île	lac	péninsule	détroit	réservoir
PORTUGUÊS	serra	montanha	baía	cabo	ilha	lago	peninsula	estreito	reservatório

For complete glossary see page *I • 1*.

Kilometers 0 200 400 600 Km.

Statute Miles 0 200 400 600 Mi.

Scale 1:12,000,000

One centimeter represents 120 kilometers.
One inch represents approximately 190 miles.
Lambert Conformal Conic Projection

ALASKA
UNITED STATES
Chukchi Sea
Bering Strait
OSTROV VRANGEL'A
VOSTOČNO-SIBIRSKOJE MORE
EAST SIBERIAN SEA
OSTROVA DE-LONGA
OSTROVA ANŽU
OSTROV NOVAJA SIBIR'
OSTROV KOTEL'NYJ
OSTROV BOL'ŠOJ L'ACHOVSKIJ
Proliv Dmitrija Lapteva
Proliv Sannikova
Proliv Longa
ČUKOTSKIJ POLUOSTROV
EKIATAPSKIJ CHREBET
Zaliv Kresta
Anadyrskij Zaliv
SAINT LAWRENCE ISLAND
SAINT MATTHEW ISLAND
NUNIVAK ISLAND
Anadyr'
ANADYRSKOJE PLOSKOGORJE
AN'UJSKIJ CHREBET
KOLYMSKAJA NIZMENNOST'
JUKAGIRSKOJE PLOSKOGORJE
KORJAKSKOJE NAGORJE
PENŽINSKIJ CHREBET
Bering Sea
Olutorskij Zaliv
Penžinskaja Guba
Gižiginskaja Guba
Zaliv Šelichova
MOMSKIJ CHREBET
CHREBET ČERSKOGO
Gora Pobeda
Pik Aborigen
CHREBET SUNTAR-CHAJATA
CHREBET SETTE-DABAN
Magadan
Ochotsk
Jakutsk
REPUBLICS
ALDANSKOJE NAGORJE
STANOVOJ CHREBET
CHREBET DŽUGDŽUR
SREDINNYJ CHREBET
POLUOSTROV KAMČATKA
Petropavlovsk-Kamčatskij
Kl'učevskaja Sopka
KOMANDORSKIJE OSTROVA
SEA OF OKHOTSK
OCHOTSKOJE MORE
ŠANTARSKIJE OSTROVA
OSTROV SACHALIN
SAKHALIN
Južno-Sachalinsk
Tatarskij Proliv
La Perouse Strait
KURIL'SKIJE OSTROVA
KURIL ISLANDS
Habomai, Shikotan, Kunashiri, and Etorofu, occupied by the U.S.S.R. since 1945, are claimed by Japan pending a final peace treaty.
BUREINSKIJ CHREBET
SICHOTE-ALIN'
Komsomol'sk-na-Amure
Chabarovsk
Blagoveščensk
Vladivostok
Ussurijsk
Haerbin
Qiqihaer Tsitsihar
Jiamusi
HEILONGJIANG
MANCHURIA
CHINA
NEIMENGGU ZIZHIQU
DAXINGANLINGSHANMAI
XIAOXINGANLINGSHANMAI
JILIN
HOKKAIDO
Sapporo
Hakodate
Asahikawa
Kushiro
Muroran
Otaru
HONSHU
Aomori
Akita
Morioka
Hachinohe
JAPAN
SEA OF JAPAN
PACIFIC OCEAN

Baltic and Moscow Regions / Baltenland und Mittelrussland / Regiones de Báltico y de Moscú
Républiques Baltes et la Région de Moscou / Regiões do Báltico e de Moscou

26 - 27
30 - 31
Meters
Feet
6000 19685
4000 13124
3000 9843
2000 6562
1000 3281
500 1640
200 656
0 0
Land Below Sea Level
200 656
1000 3281
3000 9843
6000 19685
9000 29520
The annexation of Lithuania, Latvia, and Estonia in 1940 by the Soviet Union has never been officially recognized by the United States Government.
Gulf of Finland
Suomenlahti
Finskij Zaliv
BALTIC SEA
Helsinki
Helsingfors
Tallinn
Riga
Vilnius
Kaunas
Minsk
LENINGRAD
Copyright © by Rand McNally & Co.
Map compiled by Cartographia, Budapest
Map produced by Rand McNally & Co.

MAP FORM	gr'ada	ostrov, o.	ozero, o.	vodochranilišče, vdchr.	vozvyšennost', vozv.	zaliv	zapovednik, zapov.
ENGLISH	ridge	island	lake	reservoir	upland	gulf; bay	reserve
DEUTSCH	Höhenrücken	Insel	See	Stausee	Bergland	Golf; Bucht	Reservat
ESPAÑOL	lomerío	isla	lago	embalse	tierras altas	golfo; bahía	reserva
FRANÇAIS	crête	île	lac	réservoir	hautes terres	golfe; baie	réserve
PORTUGUÊS	cordilheira	ilha	lago	reservatório	terras altas	golfo; baía	reserva

For complete glossary see page I • 1.
For Leningrad metropolitan map see page 255.

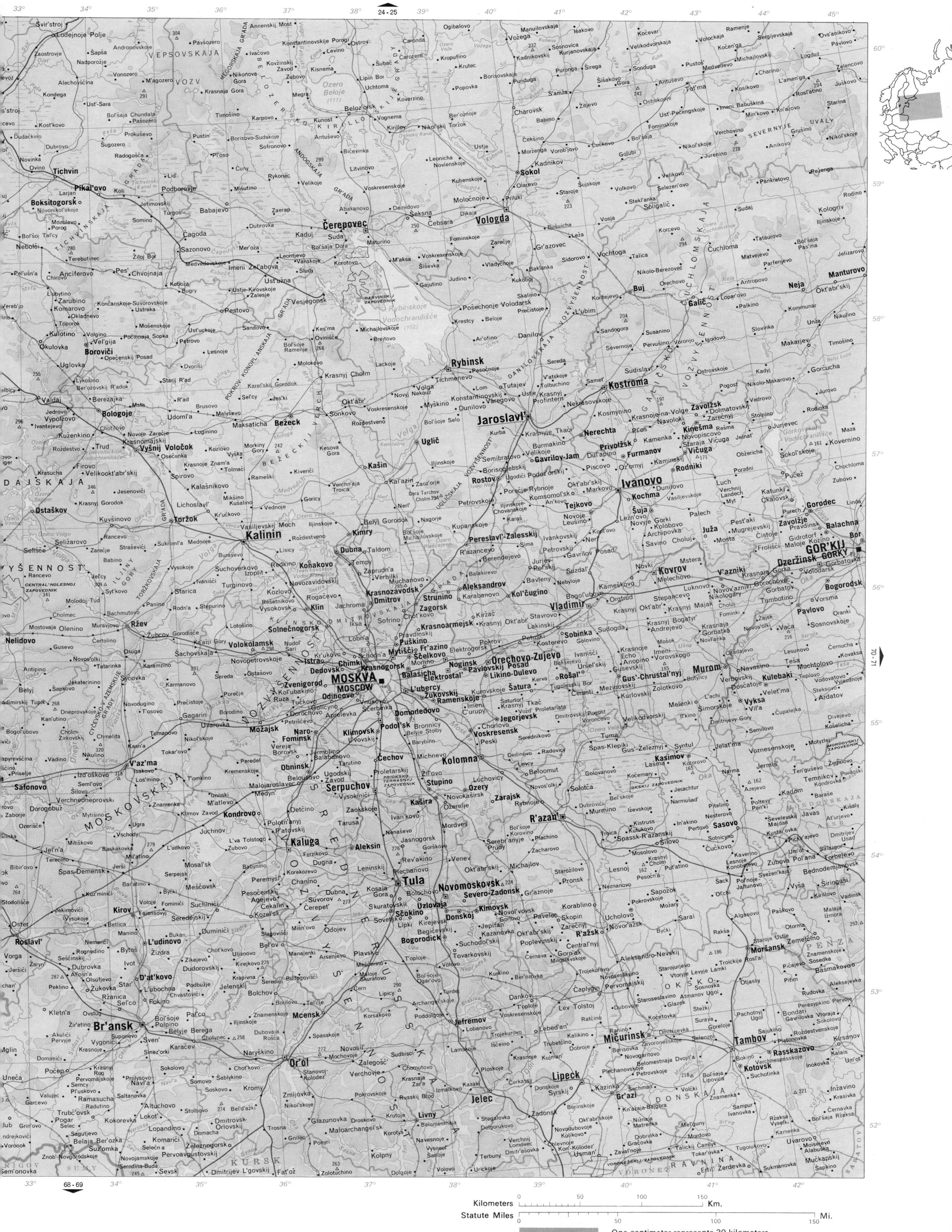

Kilometers 0 50 100 150 Km.
Statute Miles 0 50 100 150 Mi.

Scale 1:3,000,000

One centimeter represents 30 kilometers.
One inch represents approximately 47 miles.
Lambert Conformal Conic Projection

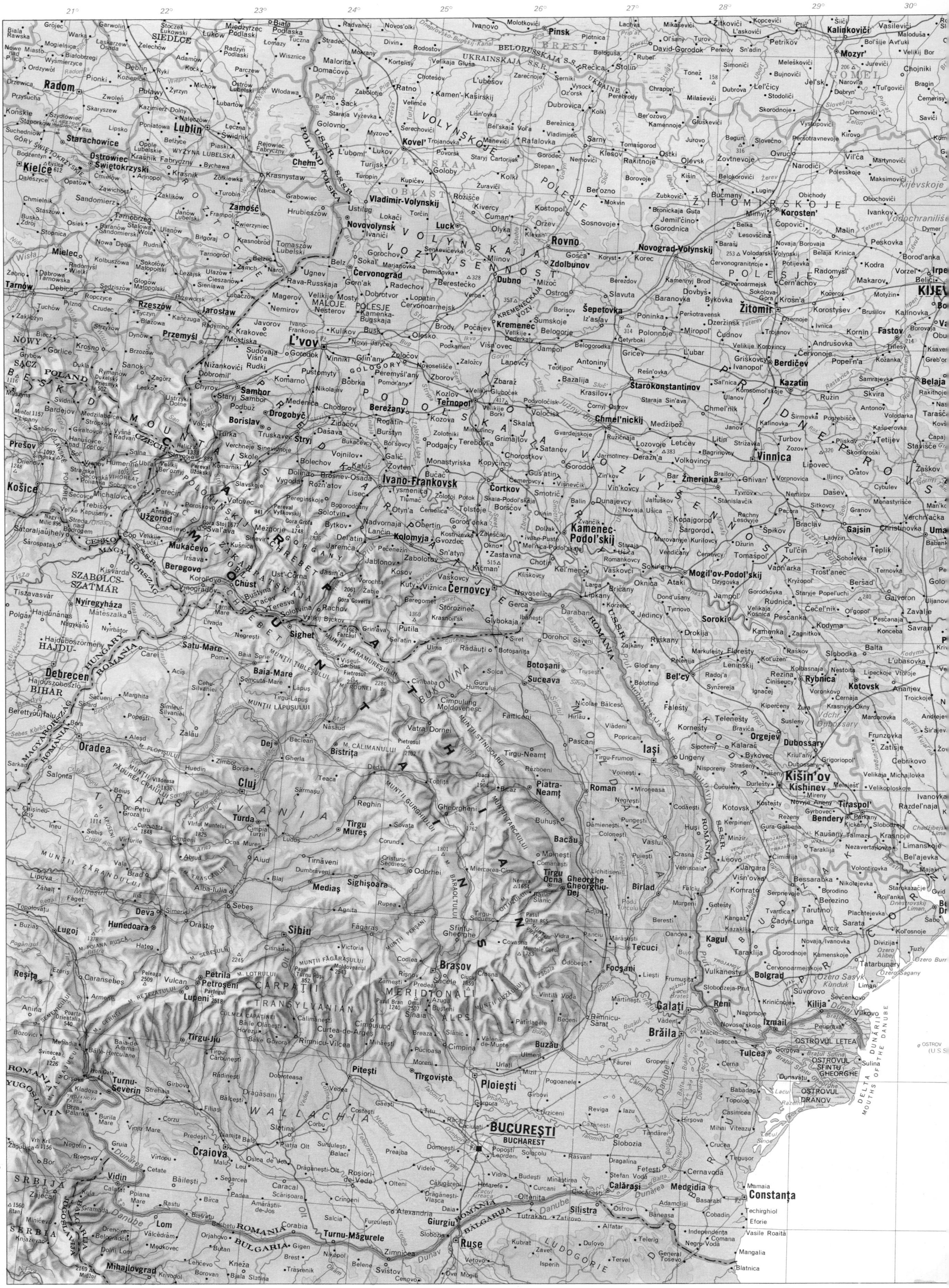

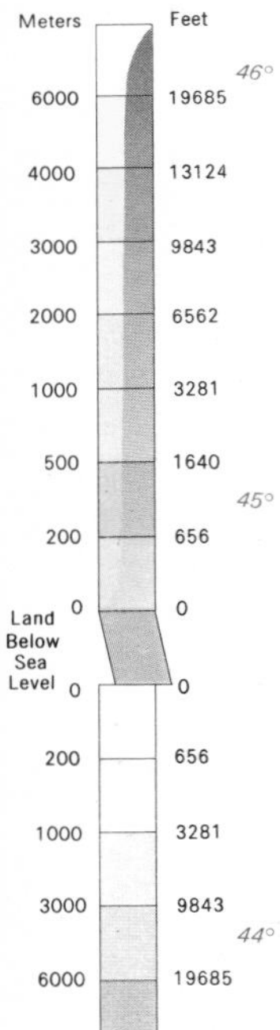

30·31

38·39

MAP FORM	gora	liman	mys	nizmennost', nizm.	ozero	vozvyšennost', vozv.	zaliv
ENGLISH	mountain	bay	cape	plain	lake	upland	bay
DEUTSCH	Berg	Bucht	Kap	Ebene	See	Bergland	Bucht
ESPAÑOL	montaña	bahía	cabo	llanno	lago	tierras altas	bahía
FRANÇAIS	montagne	baie	cap	plaine	lac	hautes terres	baie
PORTUGUÊS	montanha	baía	cabo	planície	lago	terras altas	baía

For complete glossary see page *I·1*.

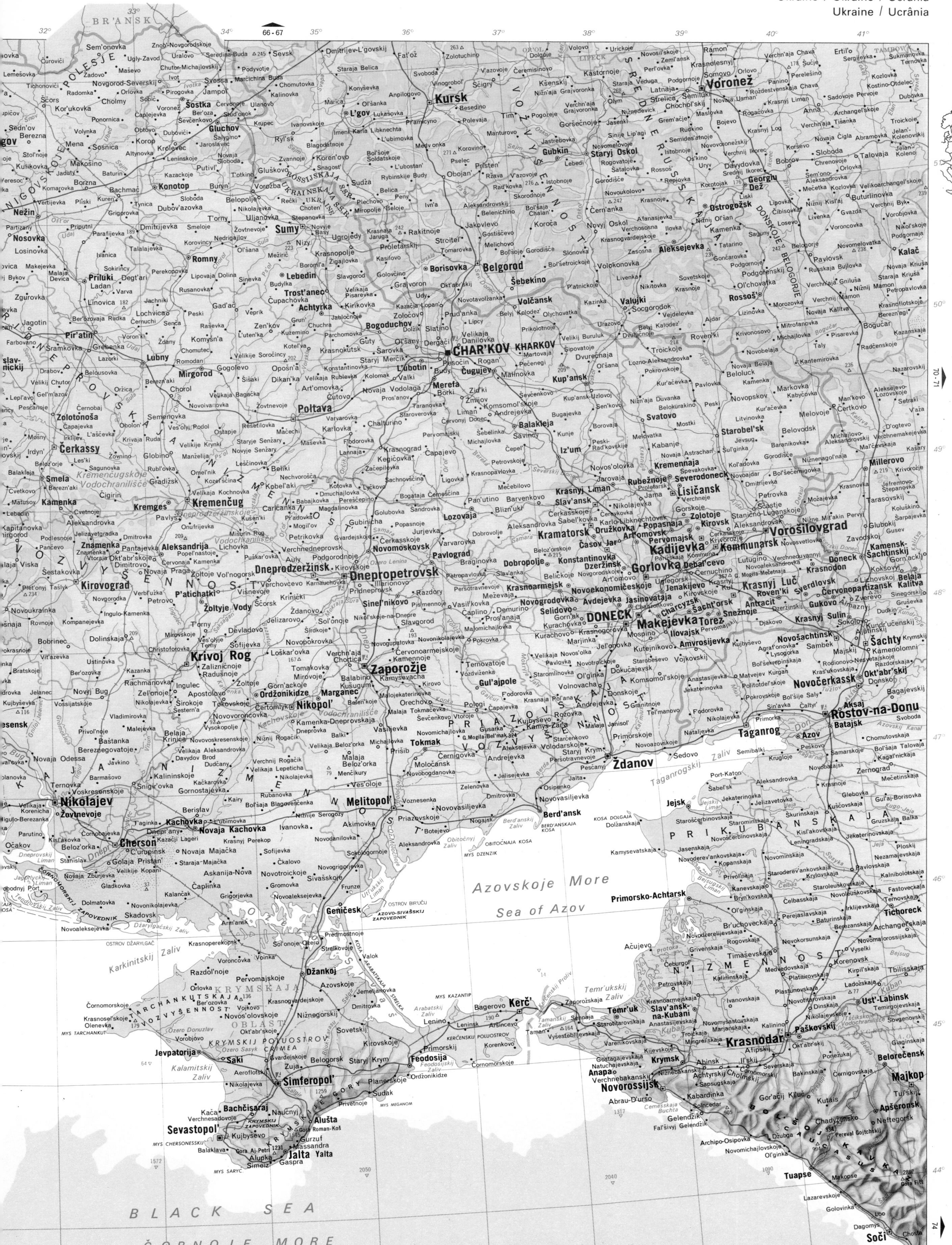

Kilometers 0 50 100 150 Km.

Statute Miles 0 50 100 150 Mi.

Scale 1:3,000,000

One centimeter represents 30 kilometers.

One inch represents approximately 47 miles.

Lambert Conformal Conic Projection

Volga Region / Wolgagebiet / Región del Volga
Région de la Volga / Região do Volga

24·25

66·67

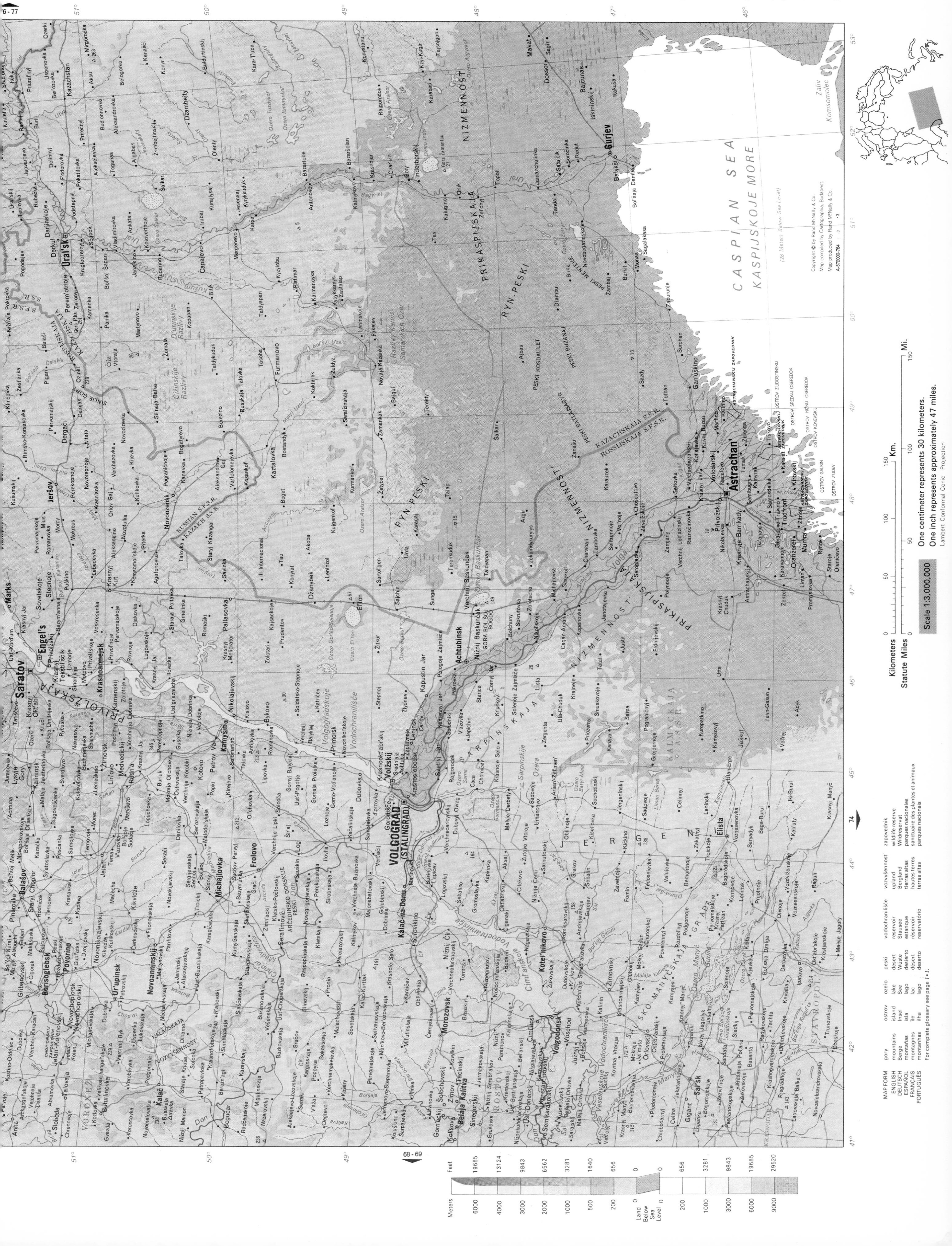
CASPIAN SEA
KASPIJSKOJE MORE
(28 Meters Below Sea Level)
Saratov
Engel's
Volgograd (Stalingrad)
Astrachan'
Ural'sk
Gurjev
Elista
PRIKASPIJSKAJA NIZMENNOST'
RYN-PESKI
Scale 1:3,000,000
One centimeter represents 30 kilometers.
One inch represents approximately 47 miles.
Lambert Conformal Conic Projection
Kilometers
Statute Miles
Copyright © by Rand McNally & Co.
Map compiled by Cartographia, Budapest.
Map produced by Rand McNally & Co.
A-572000-764
MAP FORM gory ostrov ozero peski vodochranilišče vozvyšennost' zapovednik
ENGLISH mountains island lake desert reservoir upland wildlife reserve
DEUTSCH Berge Insel See Wüste Stausee Bergland Wildreservat
ESPAÑOL montañas isla lago desierto embalse tierras altas parques nacionales
FRANÇAIS montagnes île lac désert réservoir hautes terres sanctuaire des plantes et animaux
PORTUGUÊS montanhas ilha lago deserto reservatório terras altas parques nacionais
For complete glossary see page I • I.
Meters
Feet
Land Below Sea Level
68-69
74
76-77

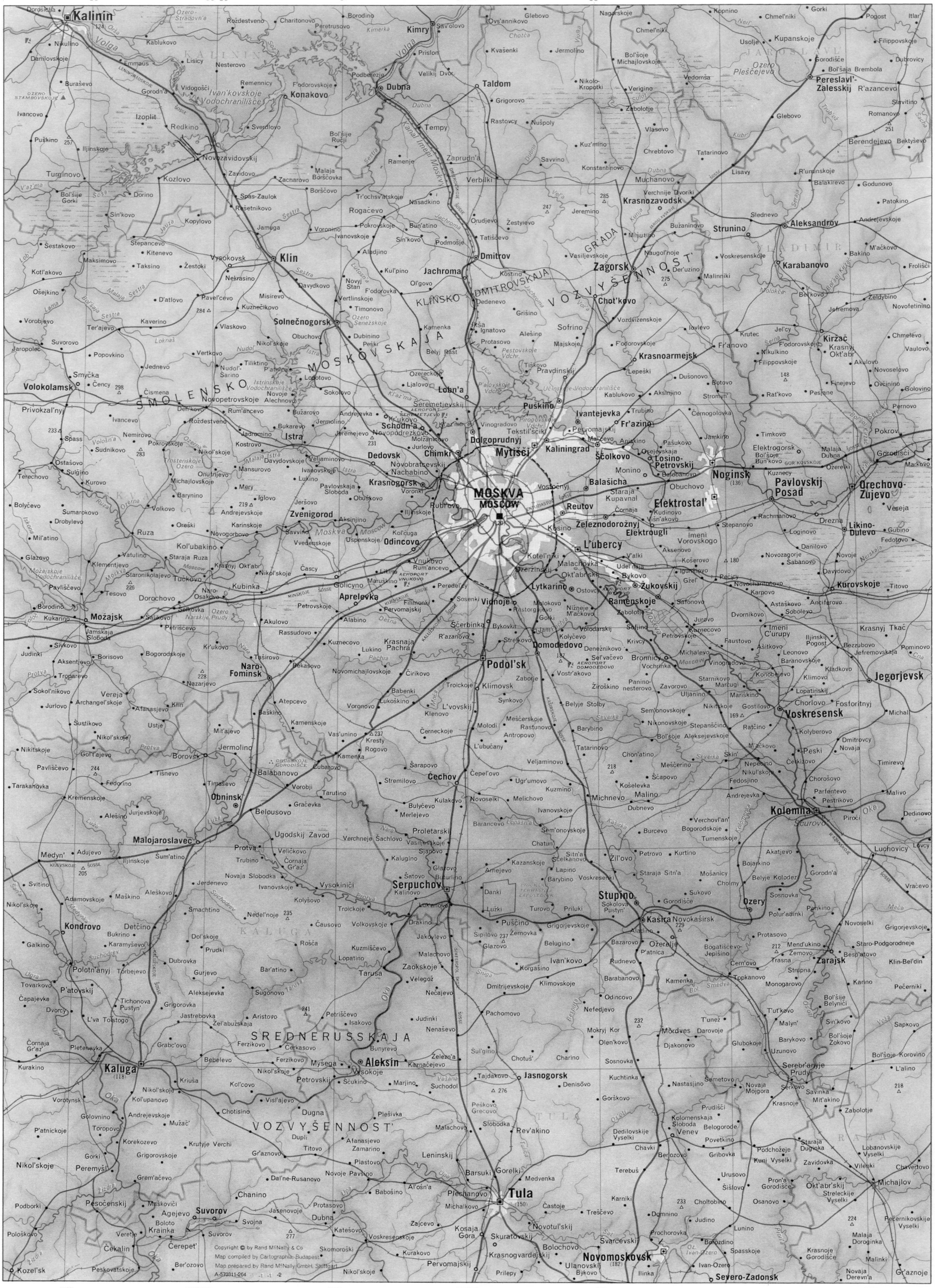

MAP FORM	gr'ada	ozero	vodochranilišče, vdchr.	vozvyšennost'	zapovednik
ENGLISH	ridge	lake	reservoir	upland	reserve
DEUTSCH	Höhenrücken	See	Stausee	Bergland	Reservat
ESPAÑOL	lomerío	lago	embalse	tierras altas	reserva
FRANÇAIS	crête	lac	réservoir	hautes terres	réserve
PORTUGUÊS	cordilheira	lago	reservatório	terras altas	reserva

For complete glossary see page *I* • *1*.
For Moskva metropolitan map see page 255.

Kilometers 0 10 20 30 40 50 Km.
Statute Miles 0 10 20 30 40 50 Mi.

Scale 1:1,000,000

One centimeter represents 10 kilometers.
One inch represents approximately 16 miles.
Lambert Conformal Conic Projection

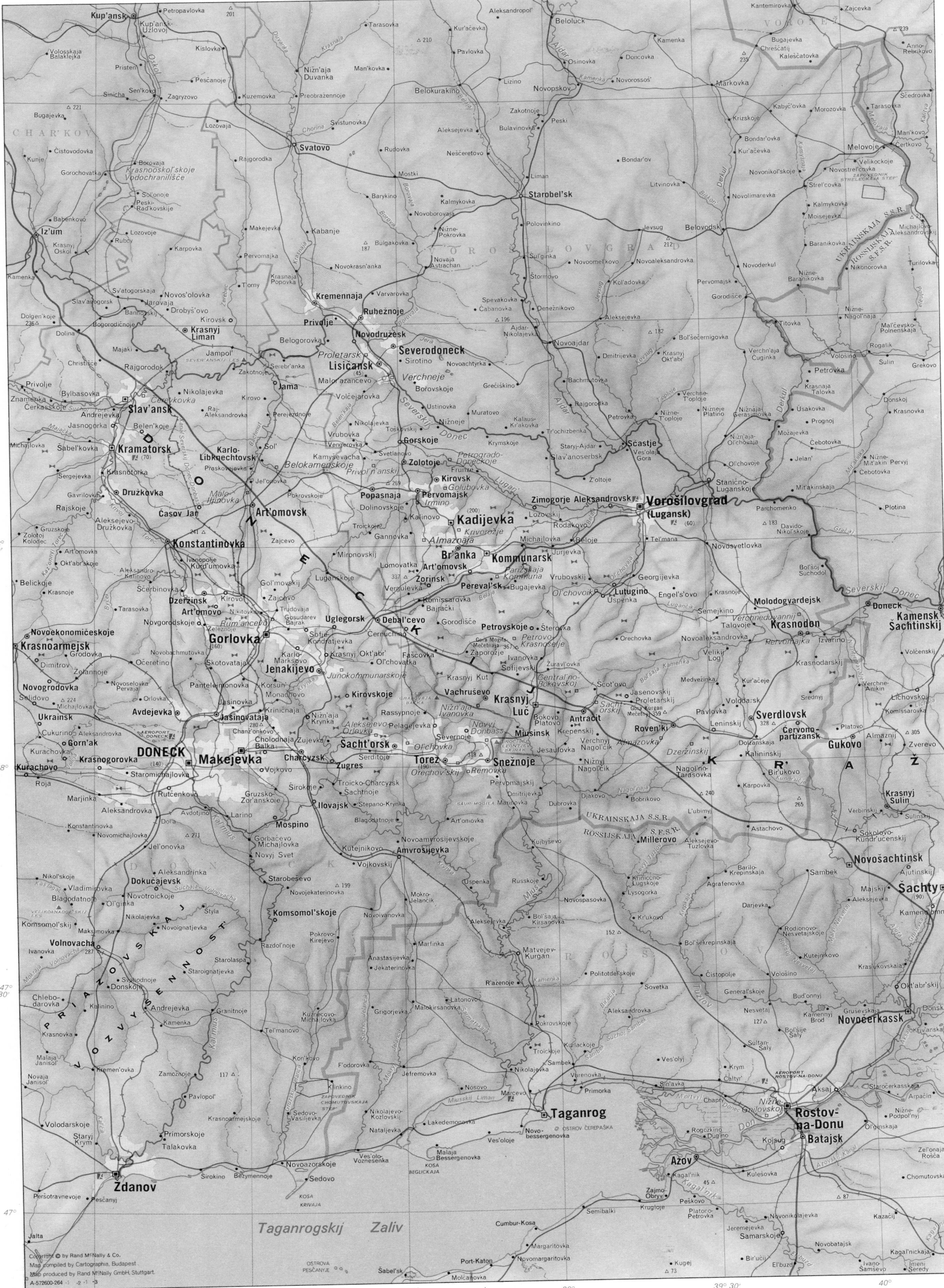

MAP FORM	kosa	ostrov, o.	vodochranilišče, vdchr.	vozvyšennost', vozv.	zaliv	zapovednik, zapov
ENGLISH	spit	island	reservoir	upland	bay	reserve
DEUTSCH	Landzunge	Insel	Stausee	Bergland	Bucht	Reservat
ESPAÑOL	lengua de tierra	isla	embalse	tierras altas	bahía	reserva
FRANÇAIS	flèche	île	réservoir	hautes terres	baie	réserve
PORTUGUÊS	ponta de terra	ilha	reservatório	terras altas	baía	reserva

For complete glossary see page I • 1.

Kilometers 0 10 20 30 40 50 Km.

Statute Miles 0 10 20 30 40 50 Mi.

Scale 1:1,000,000

One centimeter represents 10 kilometers.

One inch represents approximately 16 miles.

Lambert Conformal Conic Projection

Caucasus and Transcaucasia / Kaukasus und Transkaukasien / Cáucaso y Transcaucasia
Caucasie et Transcaucasie / Cáucaso e Transcaucásia

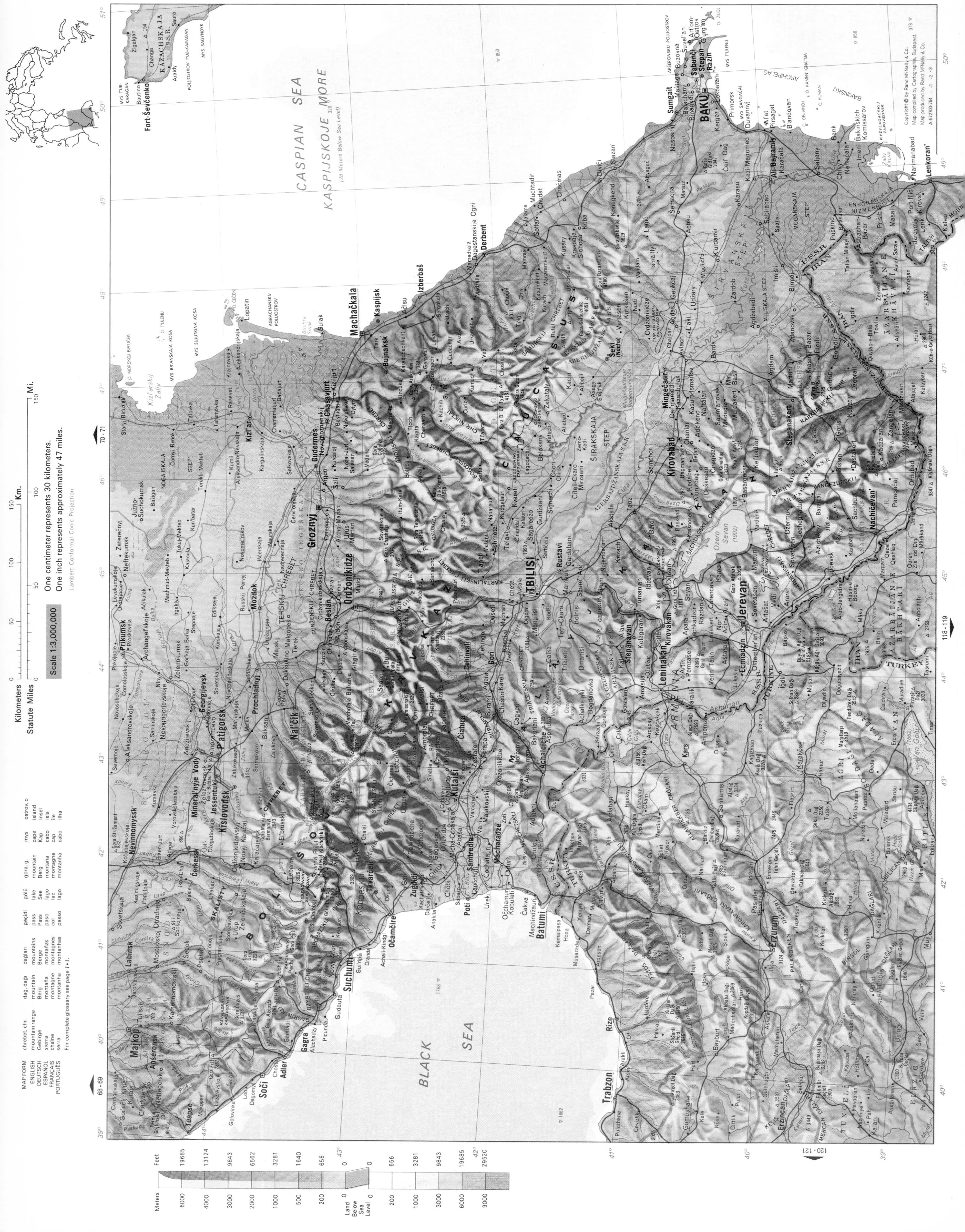

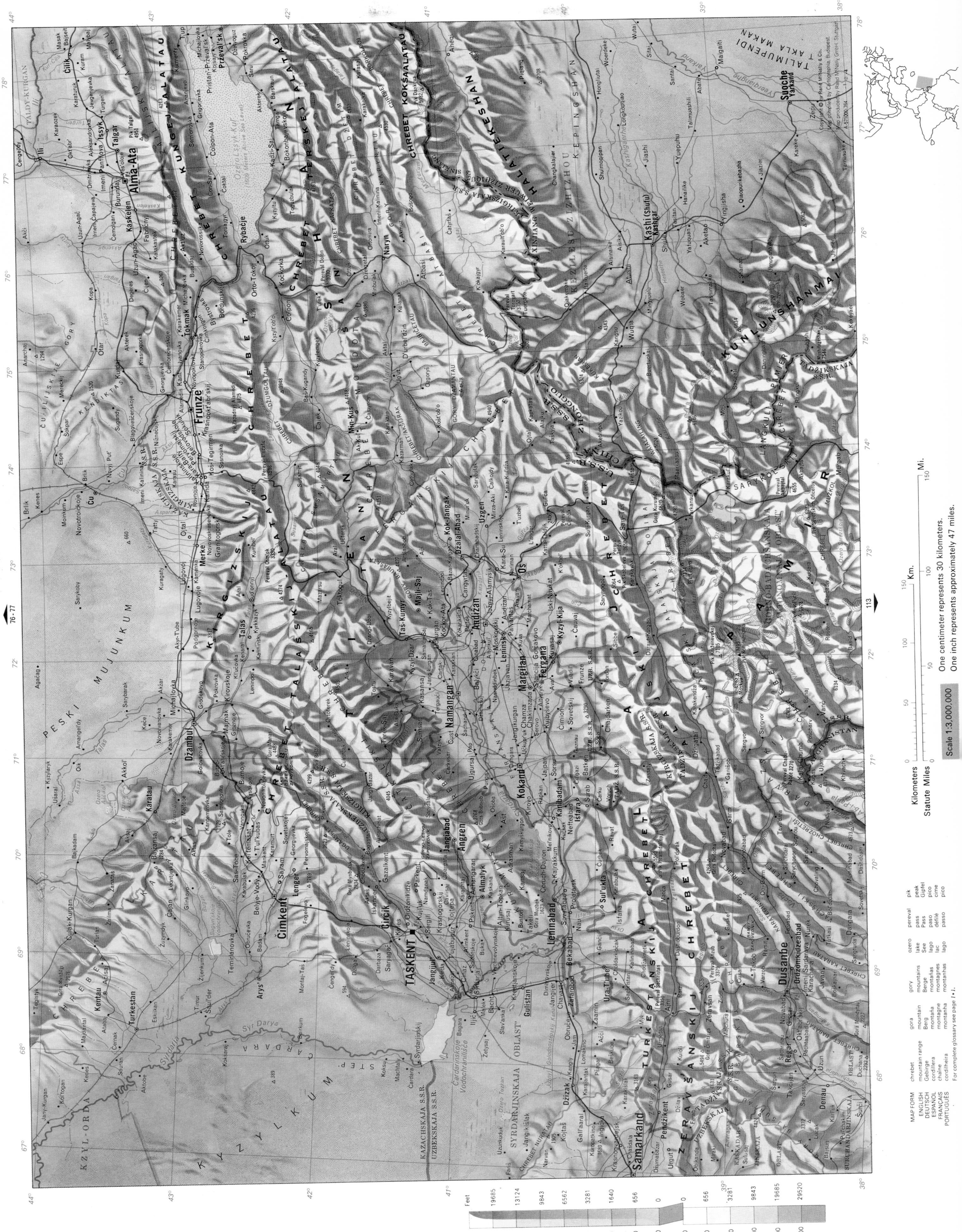
Alma-Ata
Frunze
Taškent
Dušanbe
Samarkand
Leninabad
Kokand
Fergana
Andižan
Namangan
Osh
Kašgar
Džambul
Čimkent
Kentau
Turkestan
Przeval'sk
Rybačje
Naryn
Talas
Tokmak
Issyk
Talgar
Kaskelen
Čirčik
Angren
Almalyk
Gulistan
Margilan
Suoche (Yarkand)
Ozero Issyk-Kul'
Syrdar'ja
KIRGIZSKAJA S.S.R.
KAZACHSKAJA S.S.R.
UZBEKSKAJA S.S.R.
TADŽIKSKAJA S.S.R.
XINJIANG WEIWUER ZIZHIQU
KYZYLKUM
PESKI MUJUNKUM
TALIMUPENDI TAKLA MAKAN
CHREBET KUNGEJ ALATAU
CHREBET TERSKEJ ALATAU
KIRGIZSKIJ CHREBET
TALASSKIJ ALATAU
CHREBET KOKŠAALATAU
ALAJSKIJ CHREBET
TURKESTANSKIJ CHREBET
ZERAVŠANSKIJ CHREBET
P A M I R
KUNLUNSHANMAI
TIEN SHAN
Scale 1:3,000,000
One centimeter represents 30 kilometers.
One inch represents approximately 47 miles.
Kilometers
Statute Miles
MAP FORM: chrebet, gora, gory, ozero, pereval, pik
ENGLISH: mountain range, mountain, mountains, lake, pass, peak
DEUTSCH: Gebirge, Berg, Berge, See, Pass, Gipfel
ESPAÑOL: cordillera, montaña, montañas, lago, paso, pico
FRANÇAIS: chaîne, montagne, montagnes, lac, défilé, cime
PORTUGUÊS: cordilheira, montanha, montanhas, lago, passo, pico
For complete glossary see page I•1.
Meters
Feet
Land Below Sea Level

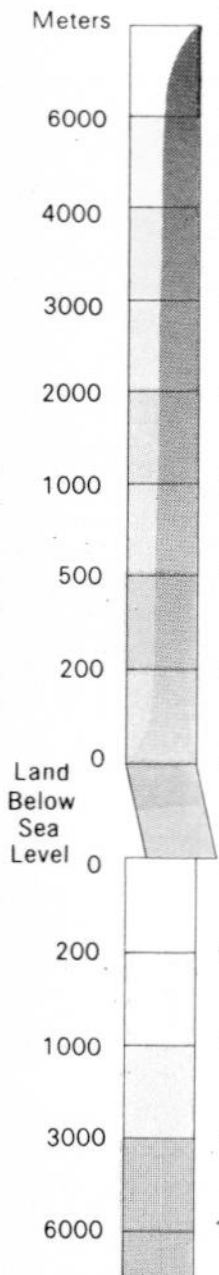

24-25
70-71
75

MAP FORM	chrebet	gora	-he	-hu	ozero	plato	porog
ENGLISH	mountain range	mountain	river	lake	lake	plateau	waterfall
DEUTSCH	Gebirge	Berg	Fluss	See	See	Hochebene	Wasserfall
ESPAÑOL	cordillera	montaña	río	lago	lago	meseta	cascada
FRANÇAIS	chaîne	montagne	rivière	lac	lac	plateau	chute d'eau
PORTUGUÊS	cordilheira	montanha	rio	lago	lago	meseta	cascata

For complete glossary see page *I • 1*.

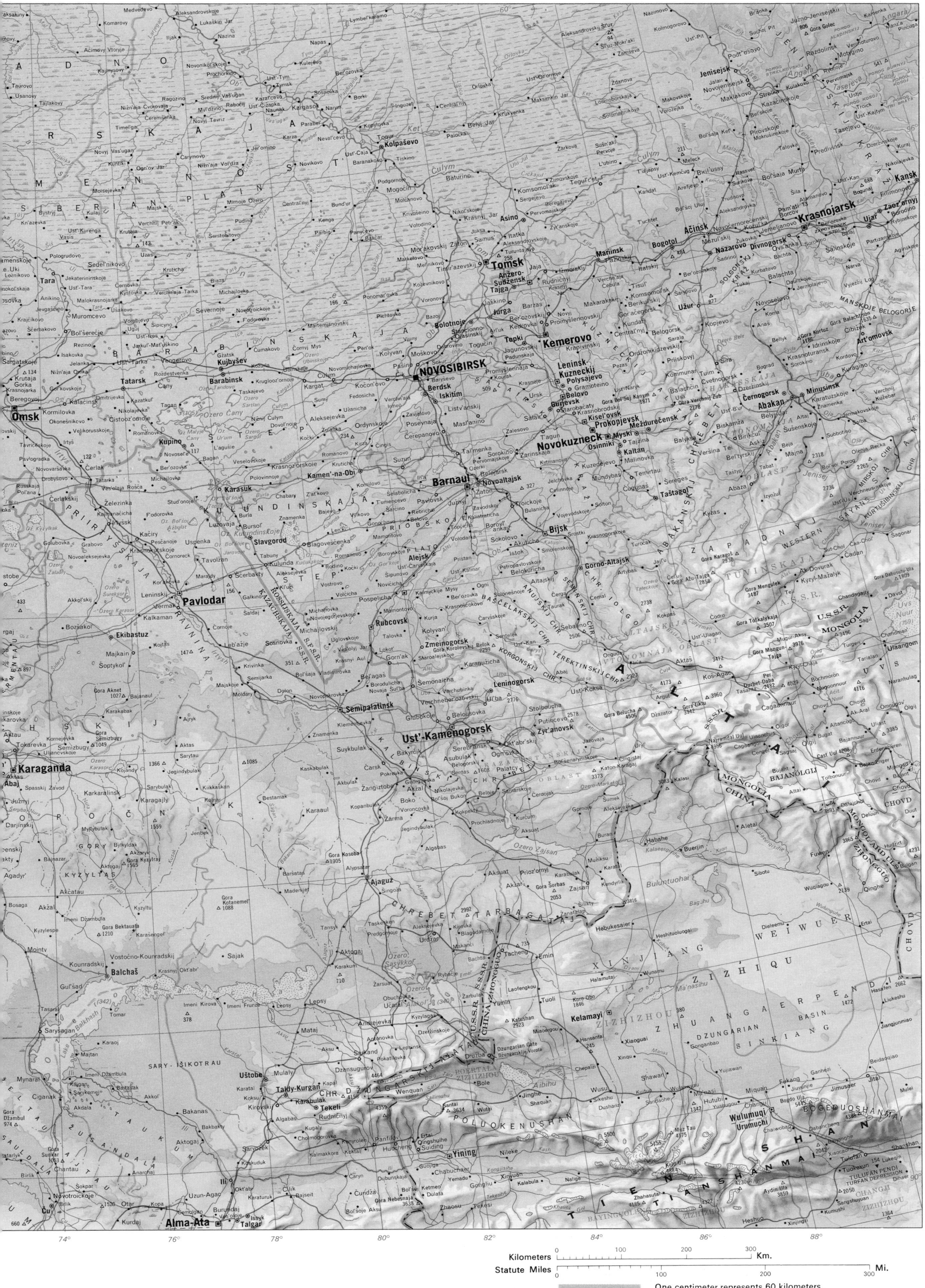

Kilometers 0 100 200 300 Km.

Statute Miles 0 100 200 300 Mi.

Scale 1:6,000,000

One centimeter represents 60 kilometers.
One inch represents approximately 95 miles.
Lambert Conformal Conic Projection

79

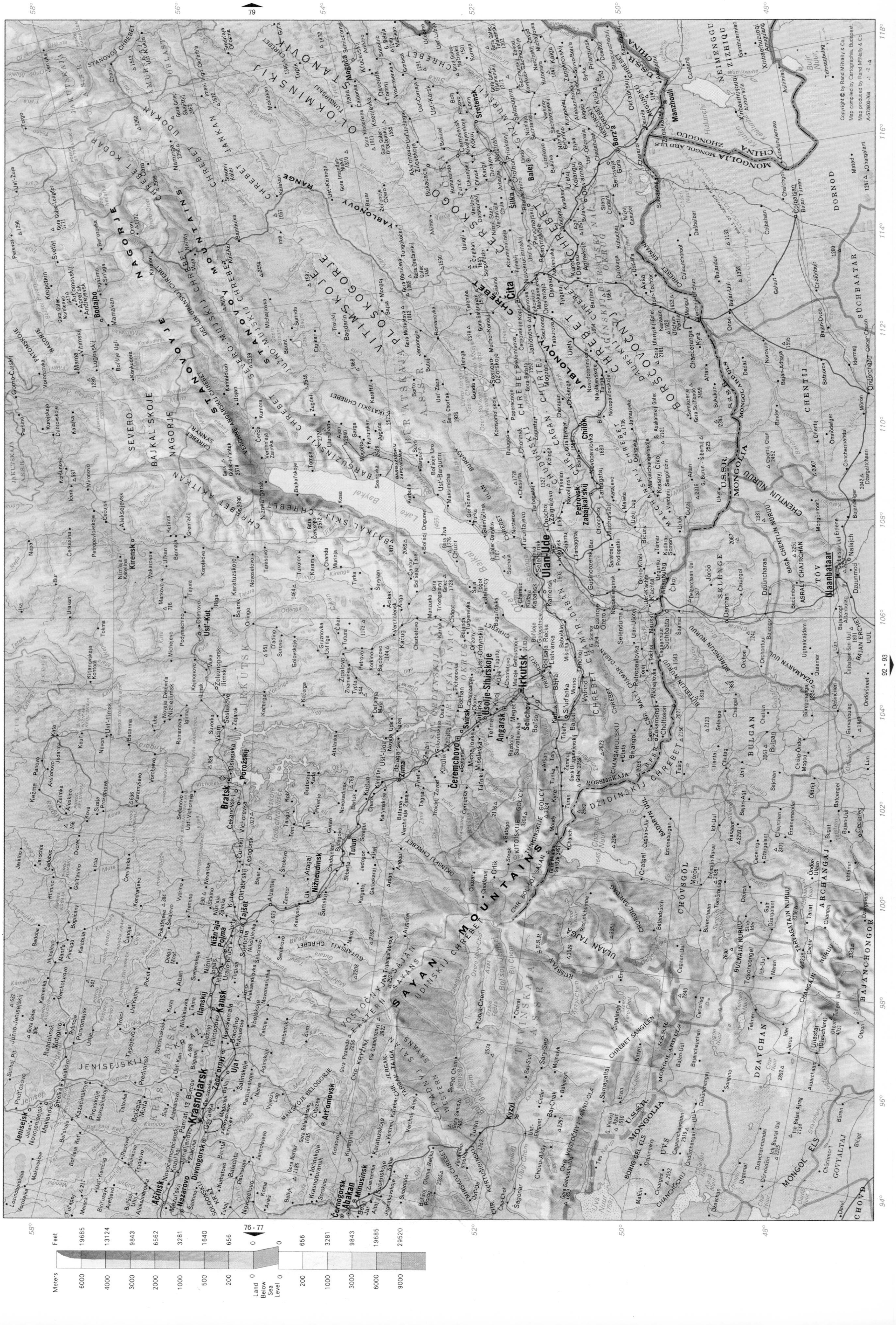

76 - 77
92 - 93

MAP FORM	chrebet	gora	nuruu	nuur	ozero, o.	porog	uul
ENGLISH	mountain range	mountain	mountain range	lake	lake	waterfall	mountains
DEUTSCH	Gebirge	Berg	Gebirge	See	See	Wasserfall	Berge
ESPAÑOL	cordillera	montaña	cordillera	lago	lago	cascada	montañas
FRANÇAIS	chaîne	montagne	chaîne	lac	lac	chute d'eau	montagnes
PORTUGUÊS	cordilheira	montanha	cordilheira	lago	lago	cascata	montanhas

For complete glossary see page J•1.

Scale 1:6,000,000

Kilometers 0 100 200 300 Km.
Statute Miles 0 100 200 300 Mi.

One centimeter represents 60 kilometers.
One inch represents approximately 95 miles.
Lambert Conformal Conic Projection

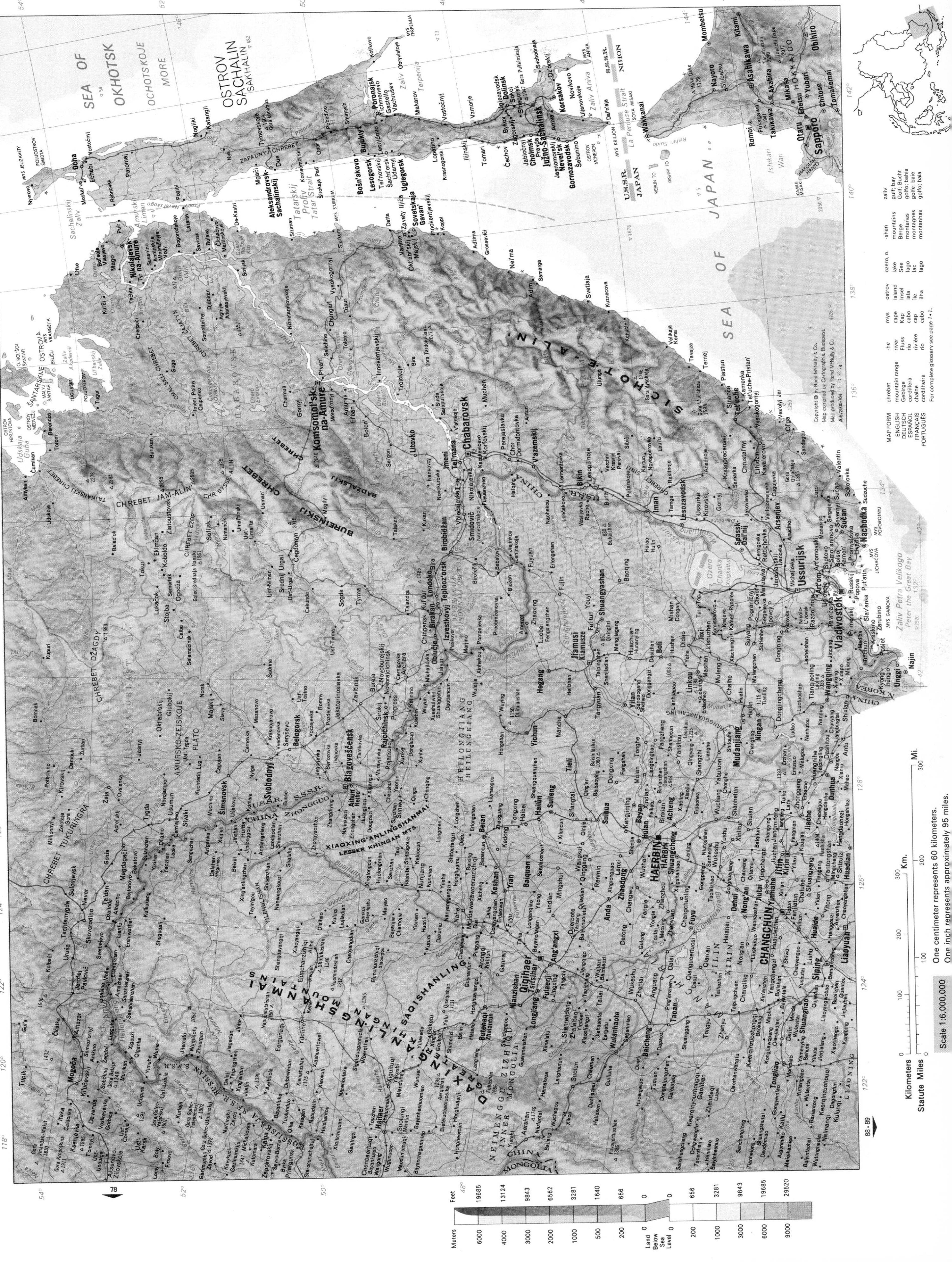
SEA OF OKHOTSK
OCHOTSKOJE MORE
OSTROV SACHALIN
SAKHALIN
SEA OF JAPAN
La Perouse Strait
Tatarskij Proliv
Tatar Strait
U.S.S.R.
JAPAN
NIHON
CHINA
ZHONGGUO
MONGOLIA
SICHOTE-ALIN'
CHREBET DŽAGDY
BUREINSKIJ CHREBET
XIAOXING'ANLINGSHANMAI
LESSER KHINGAN MTS.
DA HINGGAN LING
HEILONGJIANG
JILIN
Komsomol'sk-na-Amure
Chabarovsk
Vladivostok
Nachodka
Ussurijsk
Blagoveščensk
Južno-Sachalinsk
Nikolajevsk-na-Amure
Sovetskaja Gavan'
Birobidžan
HAERBIN
HARBIN
CHANGCHUN
Qiqihaer
Jiamusi
Mudanjiang
Sapporo
Asahikawa
Wakkanai
Amur
Heilongjiang
Songhuajiang
Zaliv Petra Velikogo
Peter the Great Bay
MAP FORM: chrebet, -he, mys, ostrov, ozero, o., -shan, zaliv
ENGLISH: mountain range, river, cape, island, lake, mountains, gulf, bay
DEUTSCH: Gebirge, Fluss, Kap, Insel, See, Berge, Golf, Bucht
ESPAÑOL: cordillera, río, cabo, isla, lago, montañas, golfo, bahía
FRANÇAIS: chaîne, rivière, cap, île, lac, montagnes, golfe, baie
PORTUGUÊS: cordilheira, rio, cabo, ilha, lago, montanhas, golfo, baía
For complete glossary see page I • 1.
Copyright © by Rand McNally & Co.
Map compiled by Cartographia, Budapest.
Map produced by Rand McNally & Co.
A-572900-764 -1 -2 -4
Scale 1:6,000,000
One centimeter represents 60 kilometers.
One inch represents approximately 95 miles.
Kilometers 0 100 200 300 Km.
Statute Miles 0 100 200 300 Mi.
Meters 6000 4000 3000 2000 1000 500 200 0
Feet 19685 13124 9843 6562 3281 1640 656 0
Land Below Sea Level
0 200 1000 2000 3000 6000 9000
0 656 3281 9843 19685 29520
82-83
78
88-89

62 - 65

108 - 109

MAP FORM	-dao	-he	-hu	-jiang	-jima	-shan	-shanmai	-shima
ENGLISH	island	river	lake	river	island	mountain(s)	mountains	island
DEUTSCH	Insel	Fluss	See	Fluss	Insel	Berg(e)	Berge	Insel
ESPAÑOL	isla	rio	lago	rio	isla	montaña(s)	montañas	isla
FRANÇAIS	île	rivière	lac	rivière	île	montagne(s)	montagnes	île
PORTUGUÊS	ilha	rio	lago	rio	ilha	montanha(s)	montanhas	ilha

For complete glossary see page *I • 1*.

98 - 99

Kilometers 0 200 400 600 Km.

Statute Miles 0 200 400 600 Mi.

Scale 1:12,000,000

One centimeter represents 120 kilometers.
One inch represents approximately 190 miles.
Lambert Conformal Conic Projection

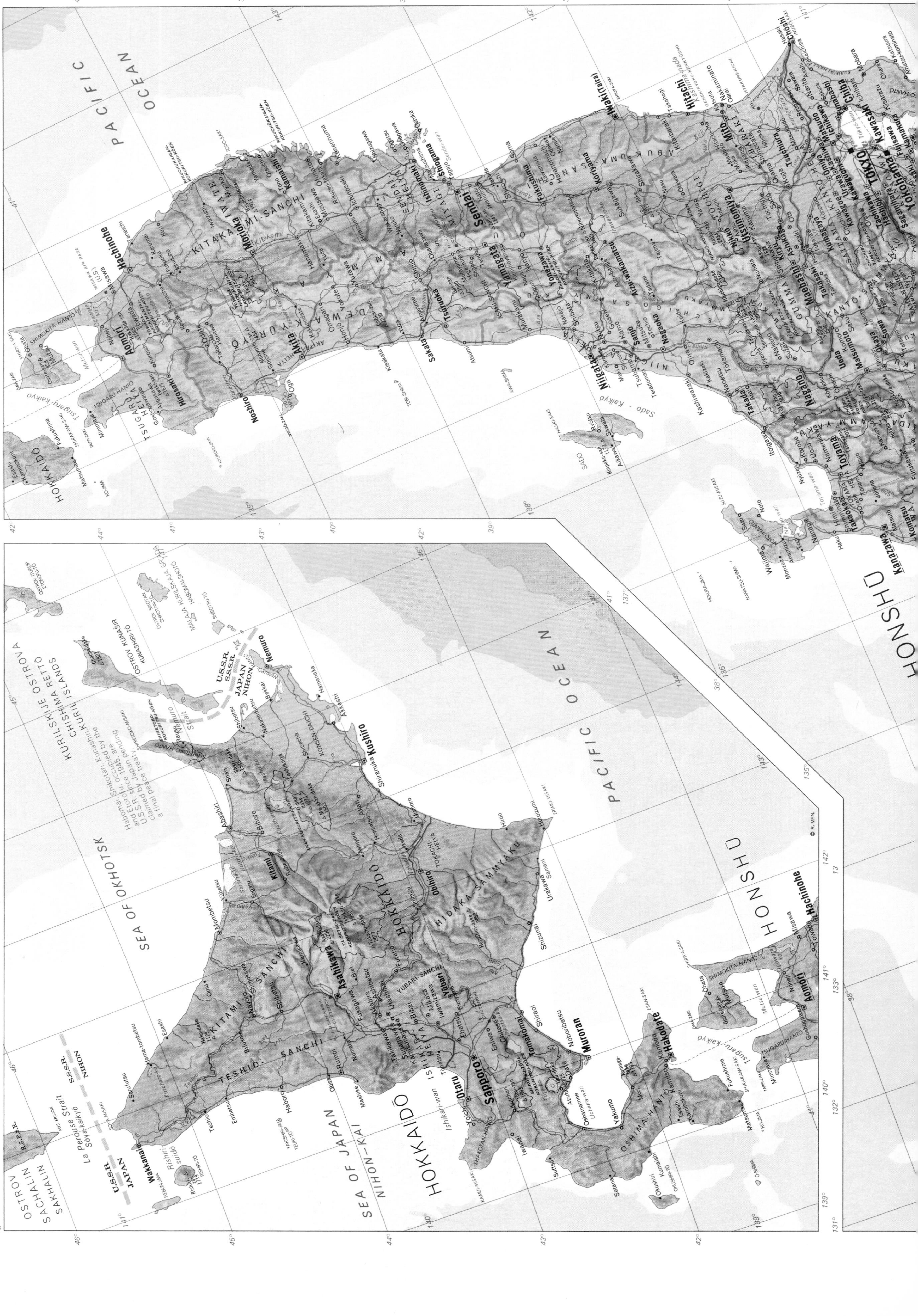
PACIFIC OCEAN
SEA OF OKHOTSK
SEA OF JAPAN
NIHON-KAI
HOKKAIDŌ
HONSHŪ
OSTROV SACHALIN SAKHALIN
KURIL'SKIJE OSTROVA CHISHIMA-RETTO KURIL ISLANDS
La Perouse Strait Sōya-kaikyō
Tsugaru-kaikyō
Sado-kaikyō
U.S.S.R.
JAPAN
NIHON
Sapporo
Asahikawa
Kushiro
Hakodate
Muroran
Otaru
Wakkanai
Nemuro
Aomori
Hachinohe
Akita
Sendai
Niigata
Yamagata
TŌKYŌ
Chiba
Kanazawa
Toyama
Mito
Hitachi
a

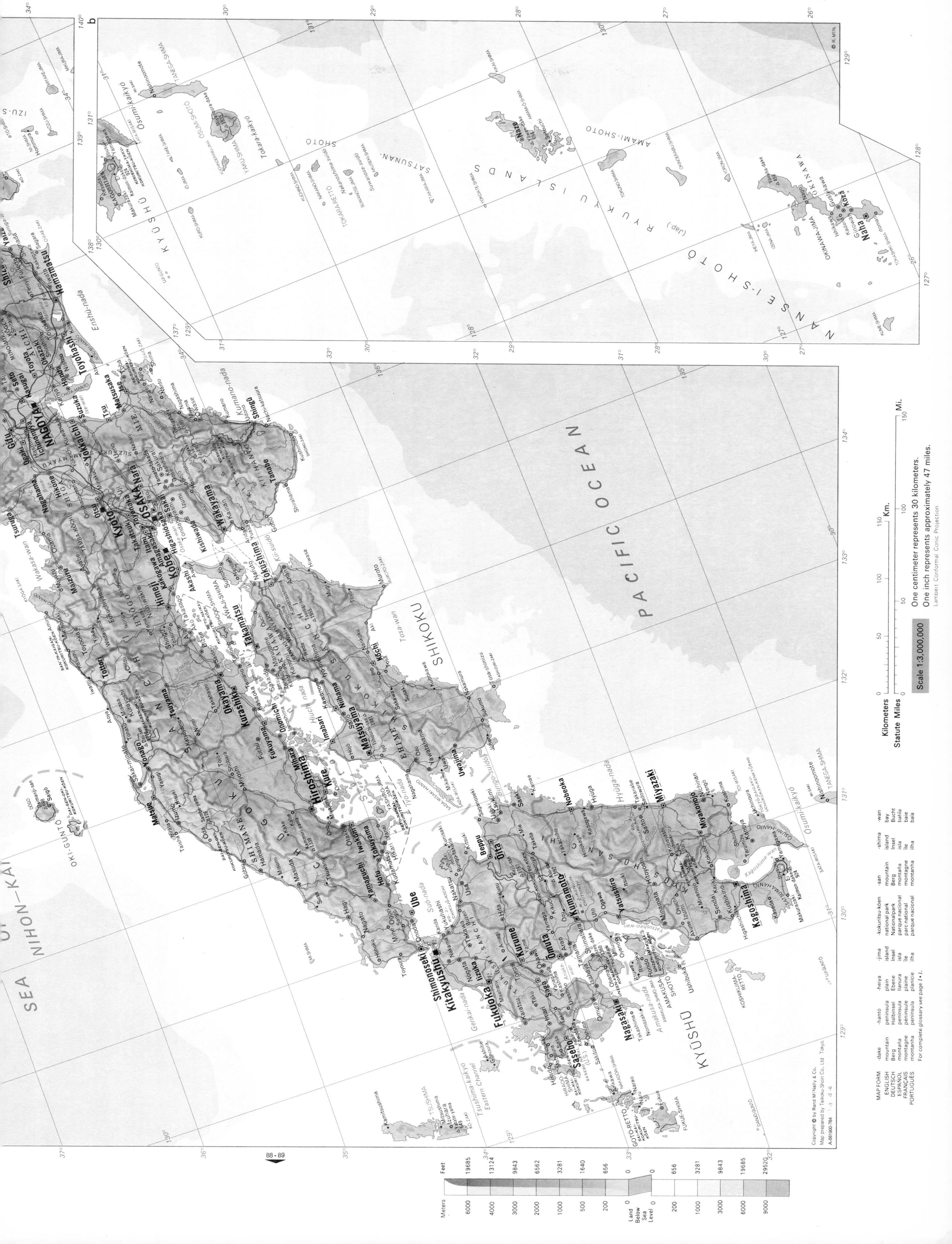
PACIFIC OCEAN
SHIKOKU
KYŪSHŪ
NANSEI-SHOTŌ
RYUKYU ISLANDS
Scale 1:3,000,000
One centimeter represents 30 kilometers.
One inch represents approximately 47 miles.
Lambert Conformal Conic Projection
Kilometers
Statute Miles
MAP FORM -dake -hanto -heiya -jima -kokuritsu-kōen -san -shima -wan
ENGLISH mountain peninsula plain island national park mountain island bay
DEUTSCH Berg Halbinsel Ebene Insel Nationalpark Berg Insel Bucht
ESPAÑOL montaña península llanura isla parque nacional montaña isla bahía
FRANÇAIS montagne péninsule plaine île parc national montagne île baie
PORTUGUÊS montanha península planície ilha parque nacional montanha ilha baía
For complete glossary see page I·1.
Copyright © by Rand McNally & Co.
Map prepared by Teikoku-Shoin Co., Ltd. Tokyo.
88-89
Meters
Feet
Land Below Sea Level

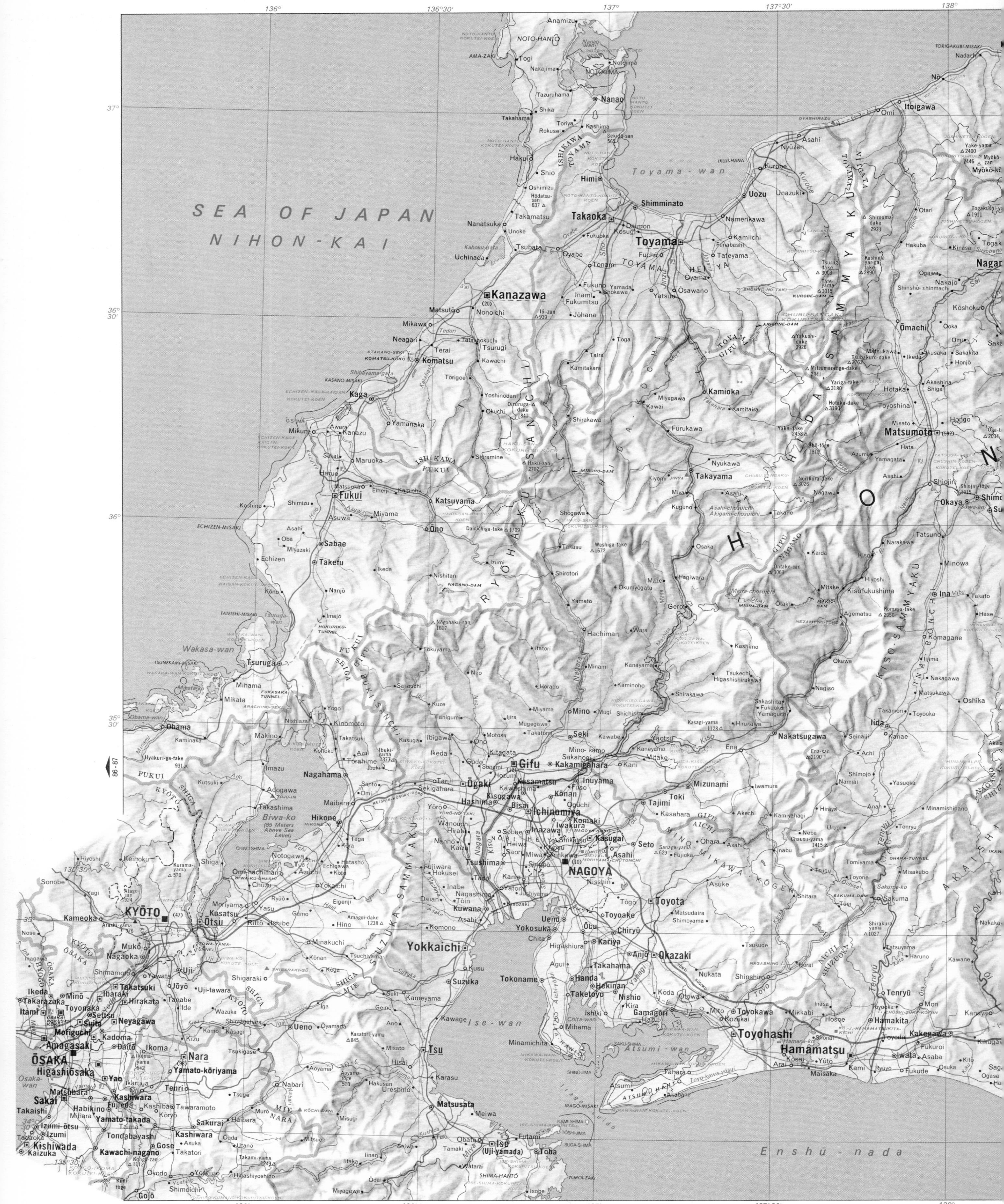

MAP FORM	-dake	-hantō	-kokuteikōen	-misaki	-san	-tōge	-wan	-yama	-zaki
ENGLISH	mountain	peninsula	national park	cape	mountain	pass	bay	mountain	point
DEUTSCH	Berg	Halbinsel	Nationalpark	Kap	Berg	Pass	Bucht	Berg	Landspitze
ESPAÑOL	montaña	península	parque nacional	cabo	montaña	paso	bahía	montaña	punta
FRANÇAIS	montagne	péninsule	parc national	cap	montagne	défilé	baie	montagne	pointe
PORTUGUÊS	montanha	península	parque nacional	cabo	montanha	passo	baía	montanha	ponta

For complete glossary see page *I • 1*.
For Tōkyō-Yokohama metropolitan map see page 258.

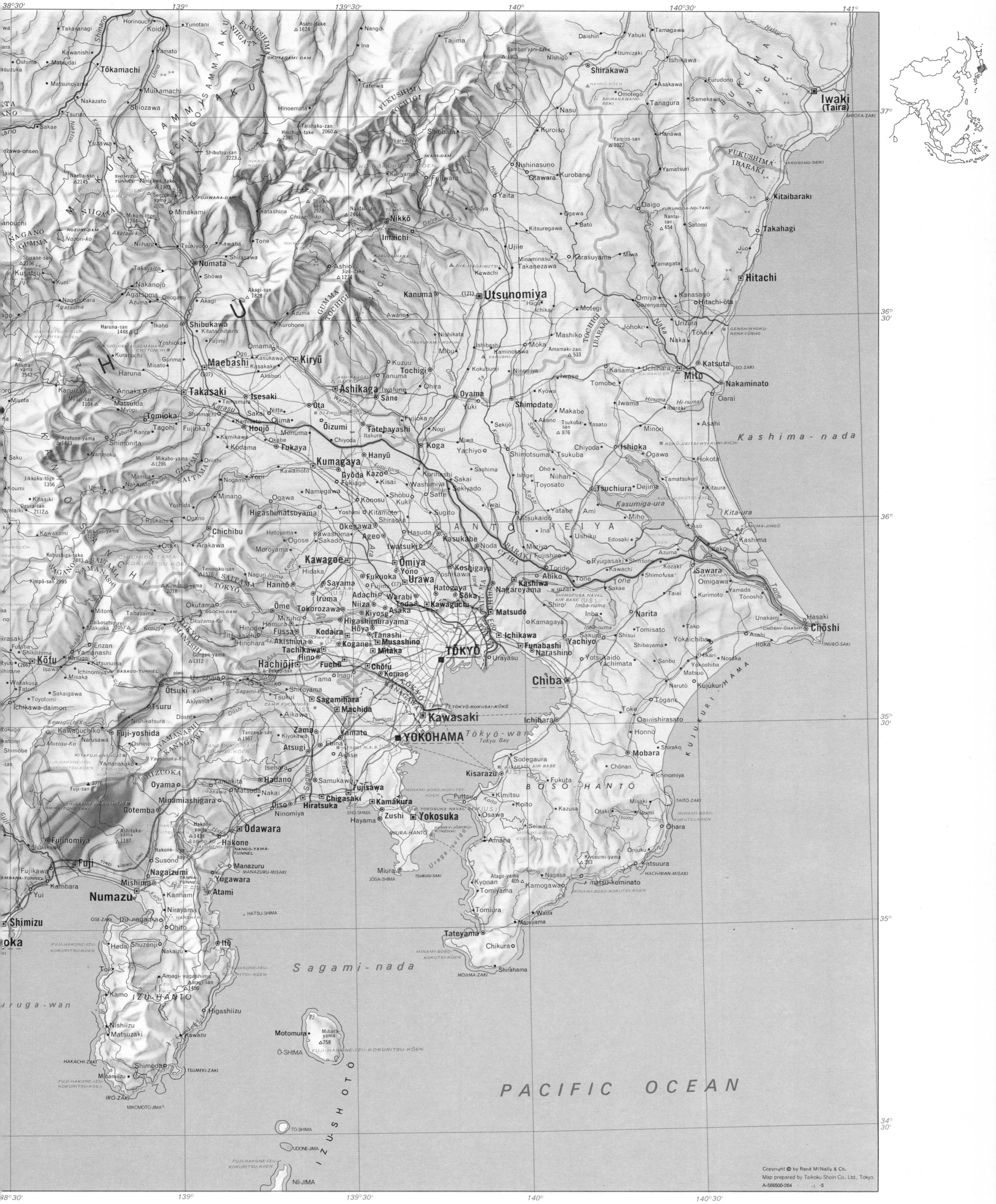

Kilometers 0 10 20 30 40 50 Km.

Statute Miles 0 10 20 30 40 50 Mi.

Scale 1:1,000,000

One centimeter represents 10 kilometers.
One inch represents approximately 16 miles.
Lambert Conformal Conic Projection

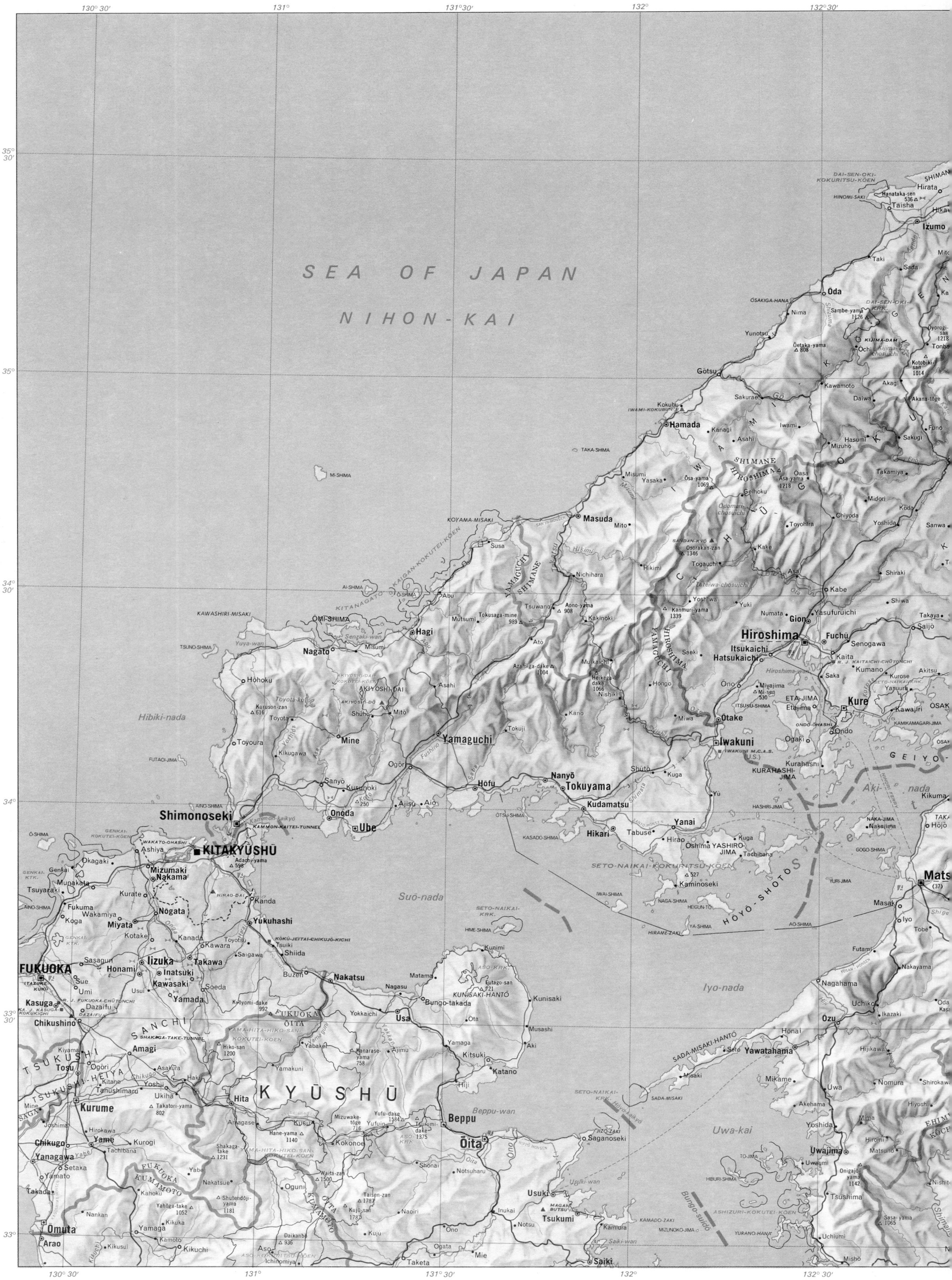

MAP FORM	-jima	-misaki	-san	-sen	-shima	-tōge	-yama	-zen
ENGLISH	island	cape	mountain	mountain	island	pass	mountain	mountain
DEUTSCH	Insel	Kap	Berg	Berg	Insel	Pass	Berg	Berg
ESPAÑOL	isla	cabo	montaña	montaña	isla	paso	montaña	montaña
FRANÇAIS	île	cap	montagne	montagne	île	défilé	montagne	montagne
PORTUGUÊS	ilha	cabo	montanha	montanha	ilha	passo	montanha	montanha

For complete glossary see page *I • 1*.
For Ōsaka-Kōbe-Kyōto metropolitan map, see page 260.

Kilometers 0 10 20 30 40 50 Km.

Statute Miles 0 10 20 30 40 50 Mi.

Scale 1:1,000,000

One centimeter represents 10 kilometers.
One inch represents approximately 16 miles.
Lambert Conformal Conic Projection

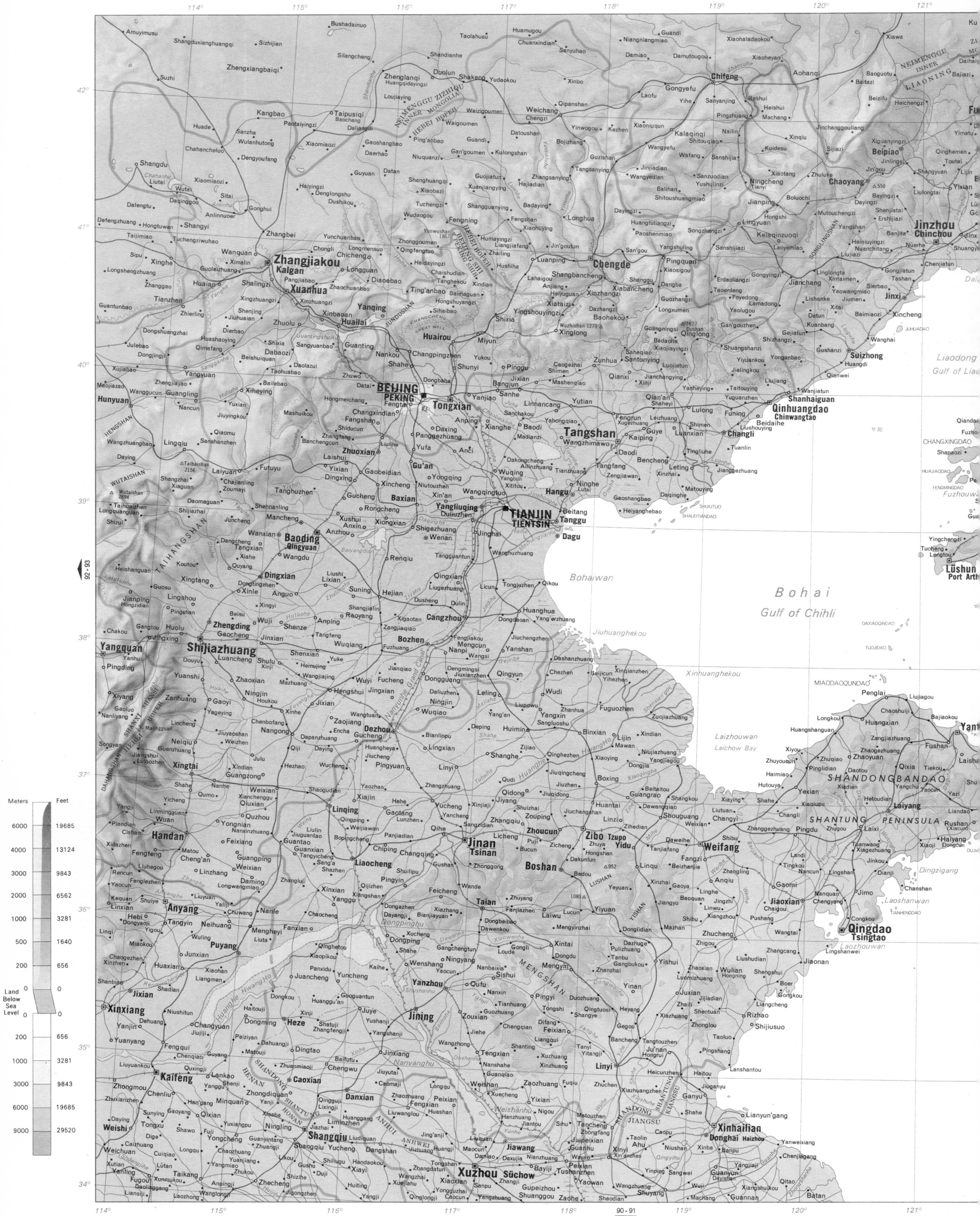

MAP FORM	-dao	-do	-gang	-he	-hu	-san	-shan	-wan
ENGLISH	island	island	river	river	lake	mountain	mountain	bay
DEUTSCH	Insel	Insel	Fluss	Fluss	See	Berg	Berg	Bucht
ESPAÑOL	isla	isla	río	río	lago	montaña	montaña	bahía
FRANÇAIS	île	île	rivière	rio	lac	montagne	montagne	baie
PORTUGUÊS	ilha	ilha	rio	rio	lago	montanha	montanha	baia

For complete glossary see page I•1.
For Sŏul metropolitan map, see page 261.

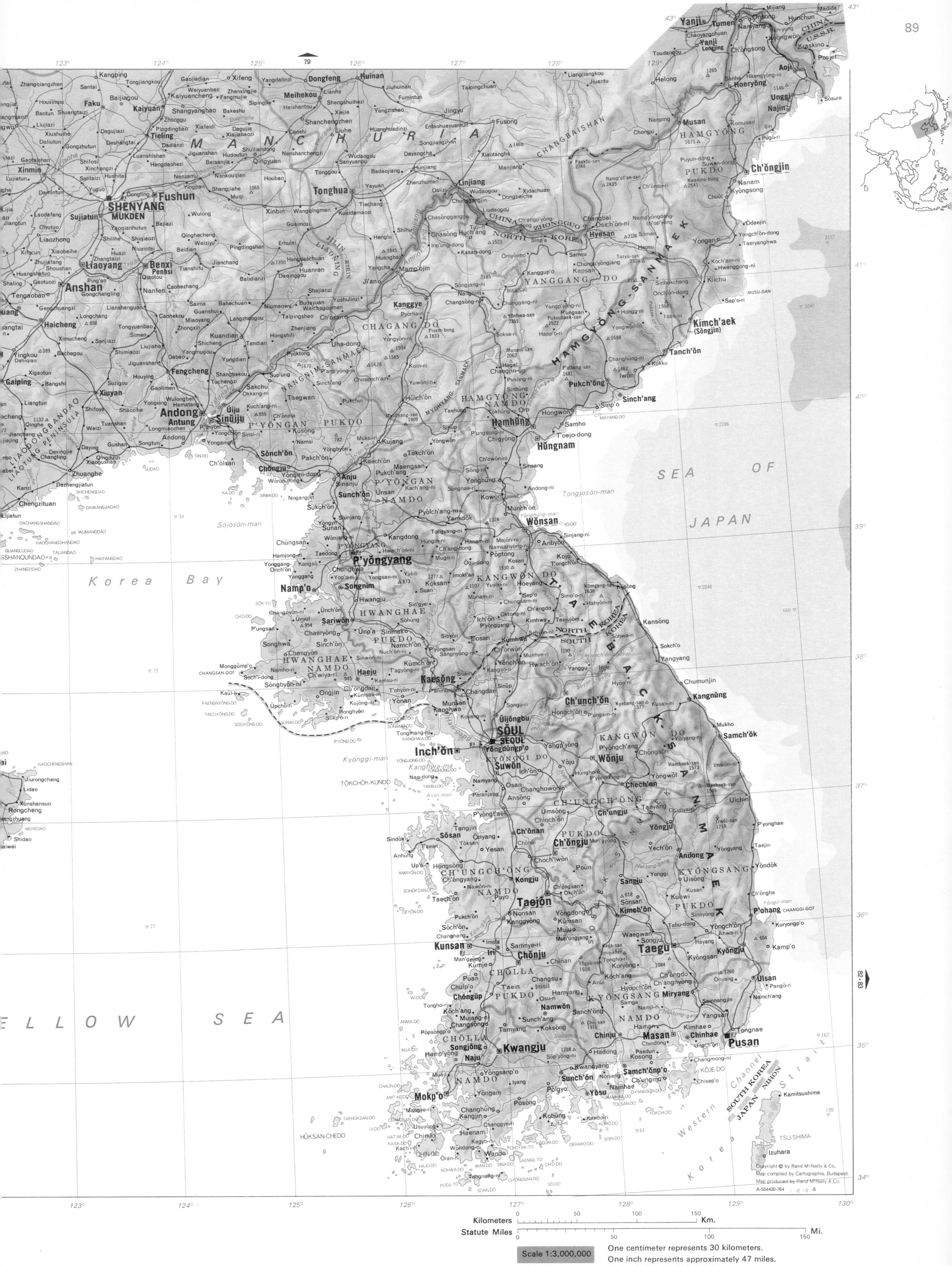

Kilometers 0 50 100 150 Km.

Statute Miles 0 50 100 150 Mi.

Scale 1:3,000,000

One centimeter represents 30 kilometers.
One inch represents approximately 47 miles.
Lambert Conformal Conic Projection

YELLOW SEA
HUANGHAI
SHANGHAI
NANJING
NANKING
WUHAN
Hangzhou
Hefei
Nanchang
DABIESHAN
JIULINGSHAN
MUFUSHAN
HUANGSHAN

88-89
92-93

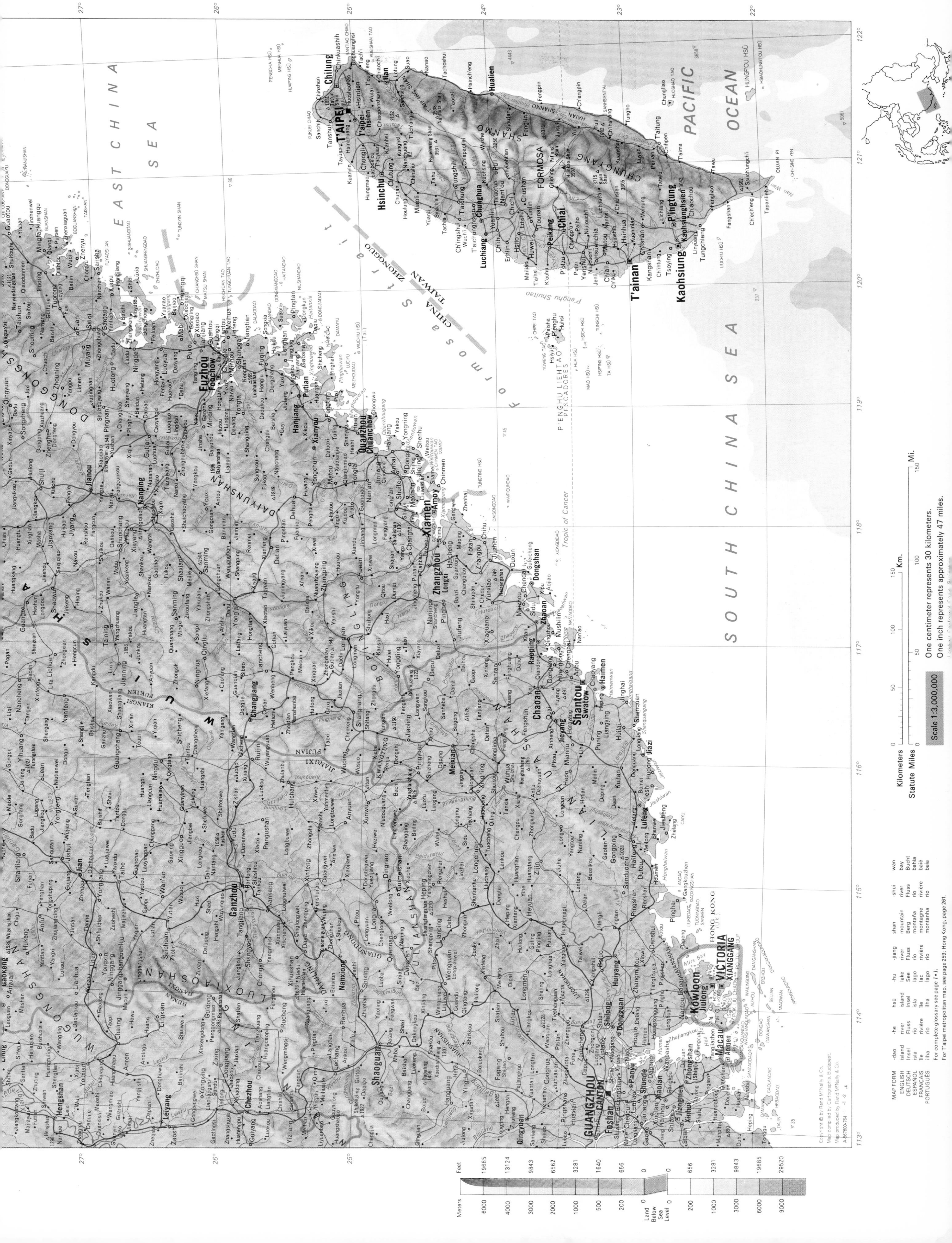
EAST CHINA SEA
PACIFIC OCEAN
SOUTH CHINA SEA
Formosa Strait
FORMOSA
Scale 1:3,000,000
One centimeter represents 30 kilometers.
One inch represents approximately 47 miles.

88-89
78
INNER MONGOLIA
NEIMENGGU ZIZHIQU
NINGXIA HUIZU ZIZHIQU
GANSU
QINGHAI
SHANXI
HEBEI
GOBI
ÖMNÖGÖV'
DORNOGOV'
DUNDGOV'
ÖVÖRCHANGAJ
BAJANCHONGOR
GOV'ALTAJ
XINJIANG WEIWUER ZIZHIQU
MONGOLIA
CHINA
Lanzhou
Xining
Yinchuan
Baotou
Hohhot
Taiyuan
Zhengzhou
Datong
Jiuquan
Dunhuang
Hami
Yumen

90 - 91
100 - 101
110 - 111
Scale 1:6,000,000
One centimeter represents 60 kilometers.
One inch represents approximately 95 miles.
Lambert Conformal Conic Projection
Kilometers
Statute Miles
Km.
Mi.
MAP FORM -he -hu -jiang -ling -shan -shanmai -shui uul
ENGLISH river lake river mountains mountain mountains river mountain
DEUTSCH Fluss See Fluss Berge Berg Berge Fluss Berg
ESPAÑOL río lago río montañas montaña montañas río montaña
FRANÇAIS rivière lac rivière montagnes montagne montagnes rivière montagne
PORTUGUÊS rio lago rio montanhas montanha montanhas rio montanha
For complete glossary see page I • I.
Feet
Meters
Land Below Sea Level
Copyright © by Rand McNally & Co.
Map compiled by Cartographia, Budapest.
Map produced by Rand McNally GmbH, Stuttgart.
SOUTH CHINA SEA
Gulf of Tonkin
GUANGZHOU (CANTON)
WUHAN
CHONGQING (CHUNGKING)
Chengdu
Kunming
Ha-noi
Mandalay
HUNAN
HUBEI
SICHUAN
YUNNAN
GUANGDONG
GUANGXI ZHUANG ZIZHIQU
GUIZHOU
XIZANG ZIZHIQU
KACHIN
SHAN
VIETNAM
LAOS
BURMA
THAILAND

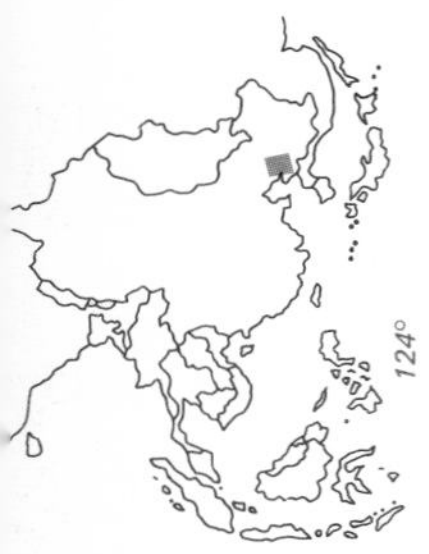

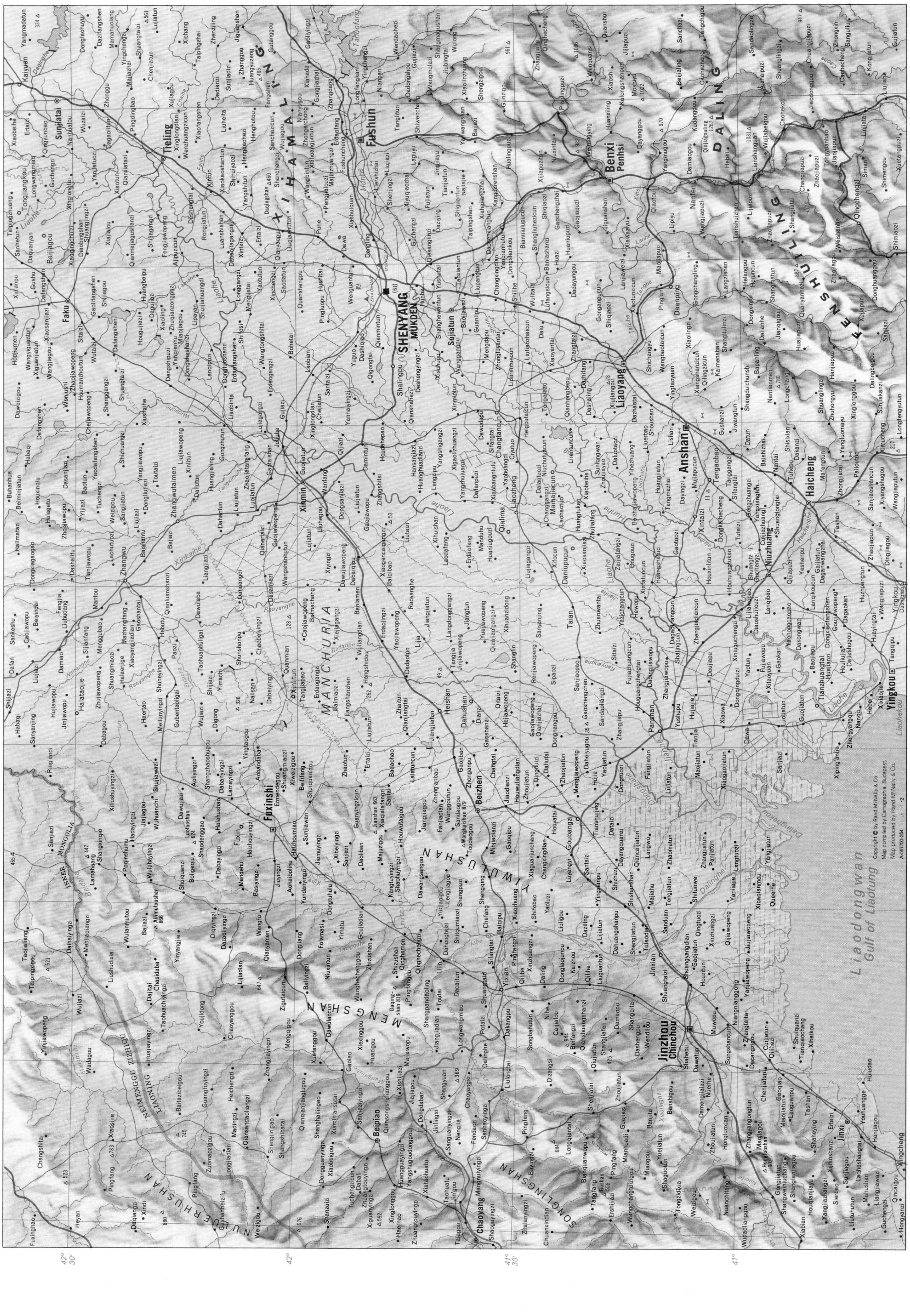

Kilometers 0 10 20 30 40 50 Km.
Statute Miles 0 10 20 30 40 50 Mi.

Scale 1:1,000,000

One centimeter represents 10 kilometers.
One inch represents approximately 16 miles.
Modified Polyconic Projection

MAP FORM	-he	-kou	-shan	-wan
ENGLISH	river	estuary	mountains	bay
DEUTSCH	Fluss	Trichtermündung	Berge	Bucht
ESPAÑOL	río	estuario	montañas	bahía
FRANÇAIS	rivière	estuaire	montagnes	baie
PORTUGUÊS	rio	estuário	montanhas	baía

For complete glossary see page I • 1.

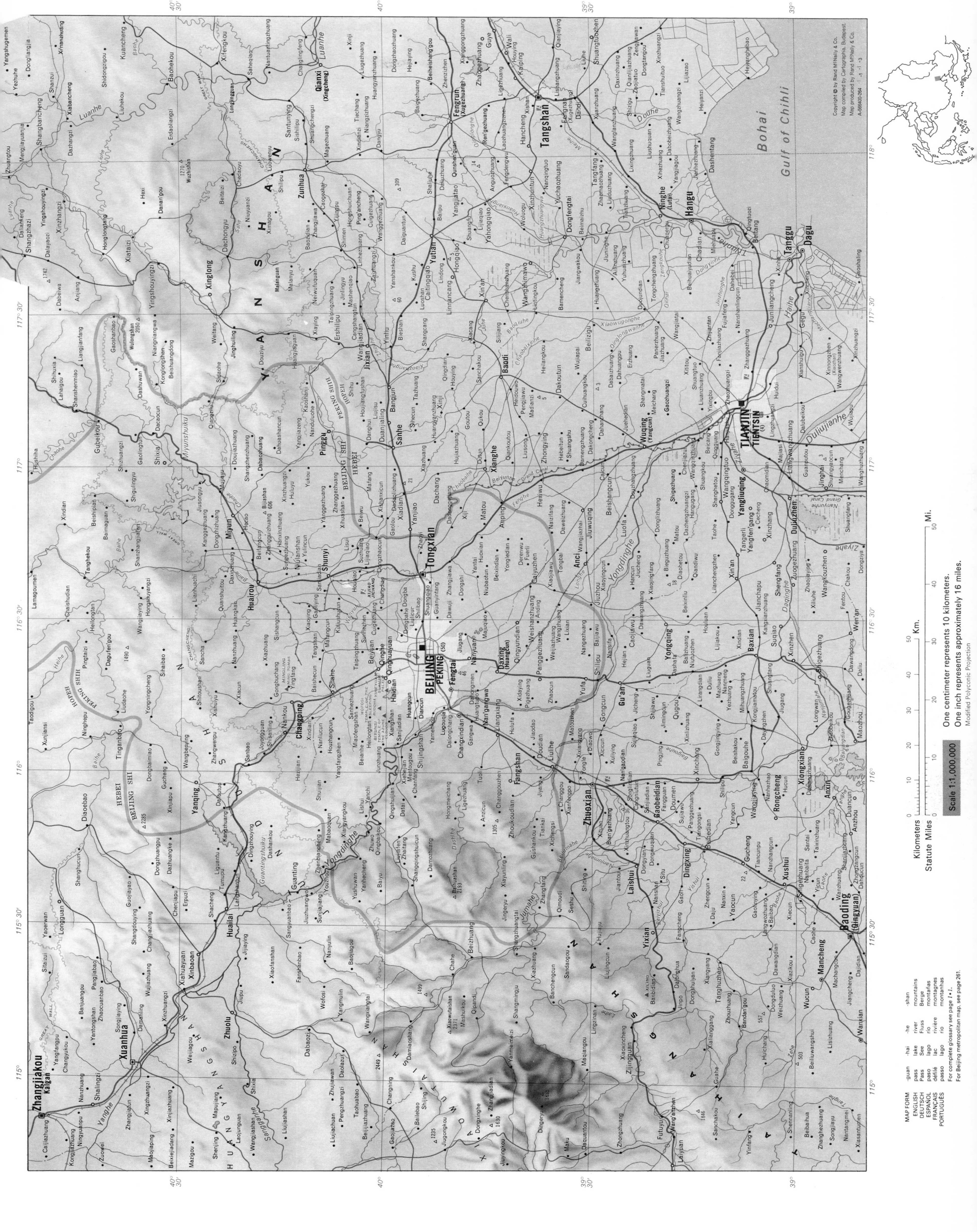
BEIJING
PEKING
TIANJIN
TIENTSIN
Bohai
Gulf of Chihli
Kilometers
Statute Miles
Scale 1:1,000,000
One centimeter represents 10 kilometers.
One inch represents approximately 16 miles.
Modified Polyconic Projection
For complete glossary see page I • 1.
For Beijing metropolitan map, see page 261.
Copyright © by Rand McNally & Co.
Map compiled by Cartographia, Budapest.
Map produced by Rand McNally & Co.

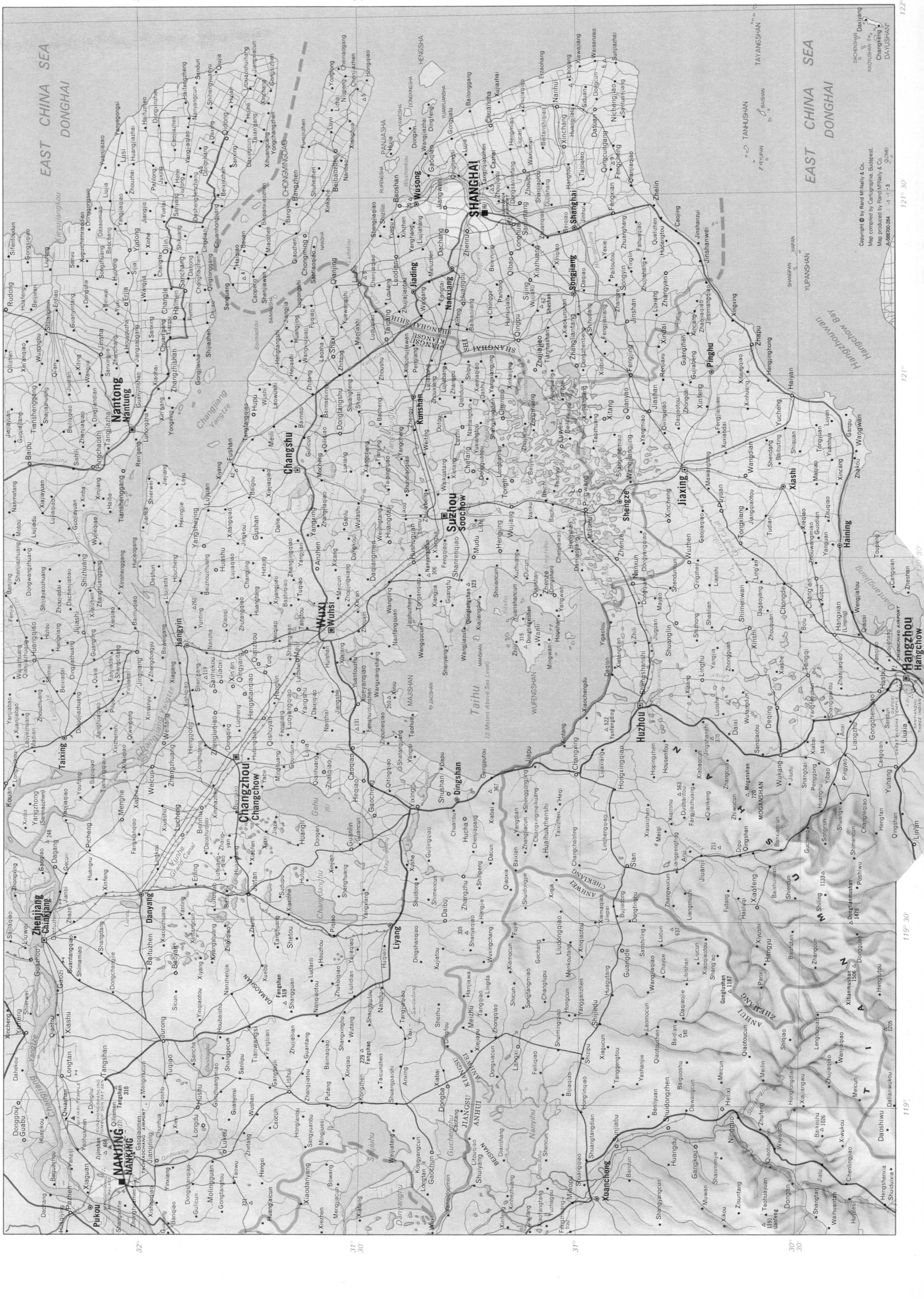

Kilometers 0 10 20 30 40 50 Km.
Statute Miles 0 10 20 30 40 50 Mi.

Scale 1:1,000,000

One centimeter represents 10 kilometers.
One inch represents approximately 16 miles.
Lambert Conformal Conic Projection

MAP FORM	-he	-hu	-jiang	-kou	-shan	-wan
ENGLISH	river	lake	river	river mouth	mountains	bay
DEUTSCH	Fluss	See	Fluss	Flussmündung	Berge	Bucht
ESPAÑOL	rio	lago	rio	desembocadura	montañas	bahía
FRANÇAIS	rivière	lac	rivière	embouchure	montagnes	baie
PORTUGUÊS	rio	lago	rio	desembocadura	montanhas	baía

For complete glossary see page I•1.
For Shanghai metropolitan map see page 259.

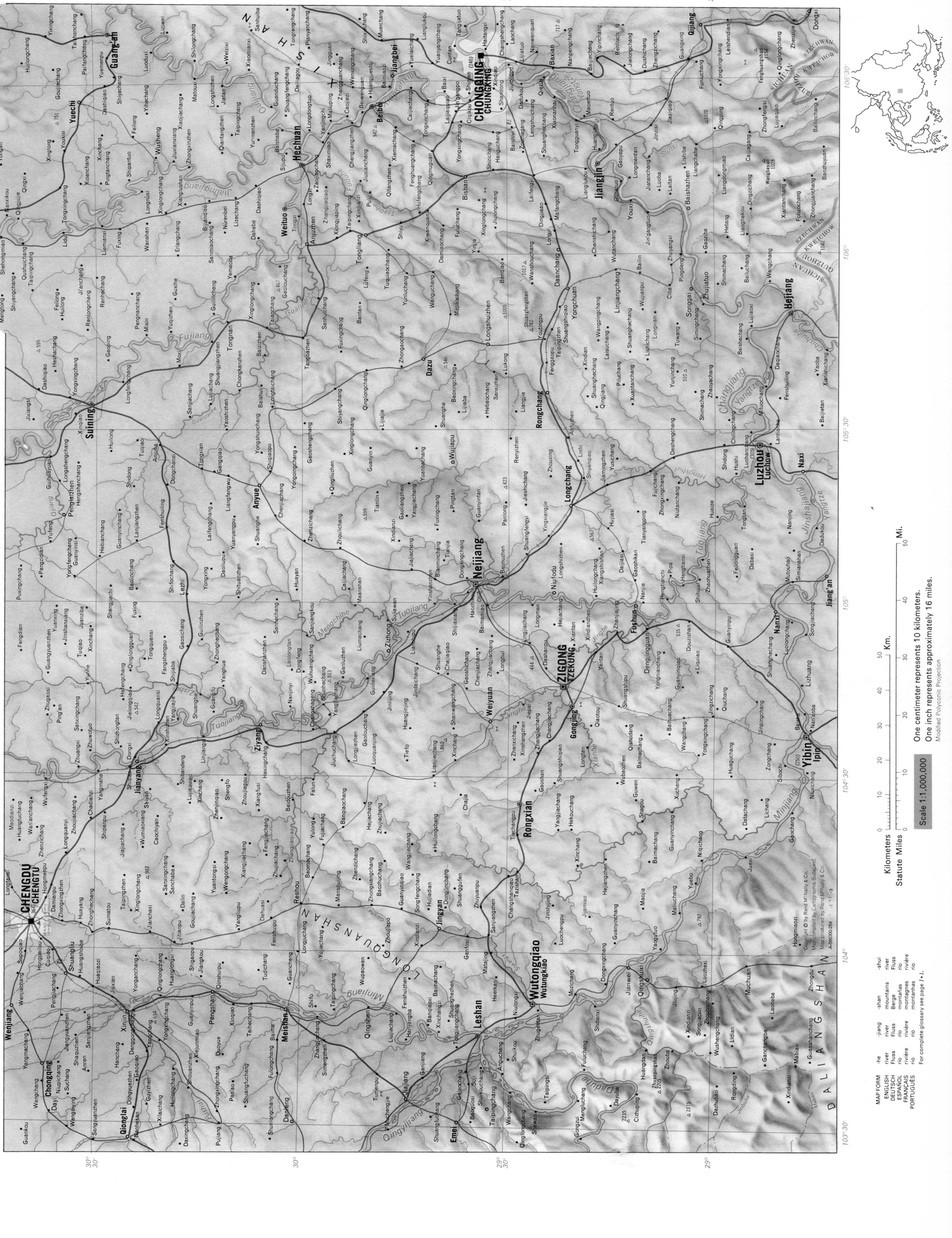
CHONGQING
CHUNGKING
CHENGDU
CHENGTU
ZIGONG
TZEKUNG
Neijiang
Luzhou
Luchow
Yibin
Ipin
Leshan
Suining
Hechuan
Guang'an
Wutongqiao
Wutungkiao
DALIANGSHAN
LONGQUANSHAN
Scale 1:1,000,000
One centimeter represents 10 kilometers.
One inch represents approximately 16 miles.
Modified Polyconic Projection
Kilometers
Statute Miles
MAP FORM -he -jiang -shan -shui
ENGLISH river river mountains river
DEUTSCH Fluss Fluss Berge Fluss
ESPAÑOL rio rio montañas rio
FRANÇAIS rivière rivière montagnes rivière
PORTUGUÊS rio rio montanhas rio
For complete glossary see page [•].
Copyright © by Rand McNally & Co.
Map compiled by Cartographia, Budapest.
Map produced by Rand McNally & Co.

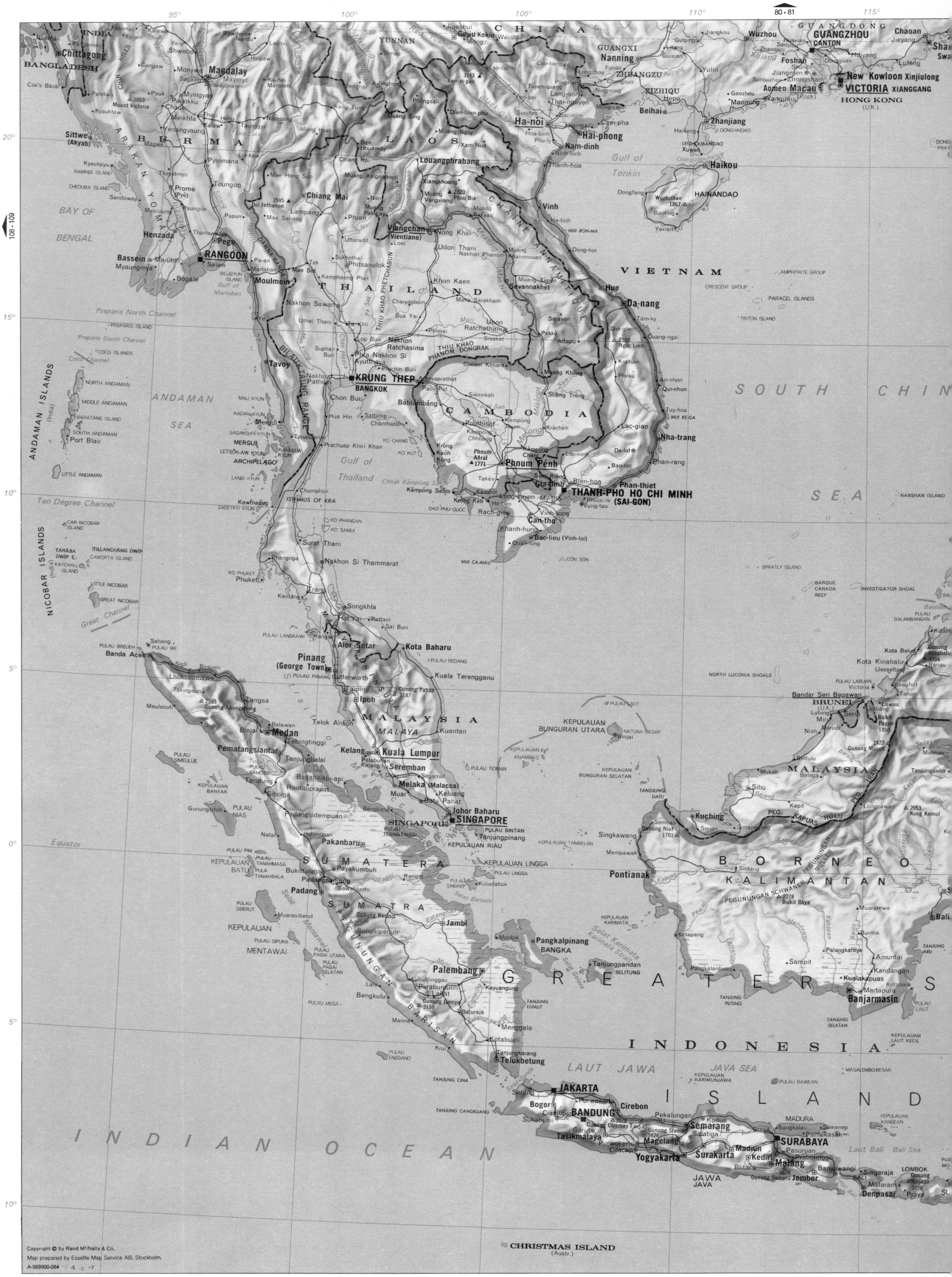

MAP FORM	gulf	gunung	island	kepulauan	pulau	sea	selat	strait
ENGLISH	gulf	mountain	island	islands	island	sea	strait	strait
DEUTSCH	Golf	Berg	Insel	Inseln	Insel	Meer	Meeresstrasse	Meeresstrasse
ESPAÑOL	golfo	montaña	isla	islas	isla	mar	estrecho	estrecho
FRANÇAIS	golfe	montagne	île	îles	île	mer	détroit	détroit
PORTUGUÊS	golfo	montanha	ilha	ilhas	ilha	mar	estreito	estreito

For complete glossary see page *I* • *1*.

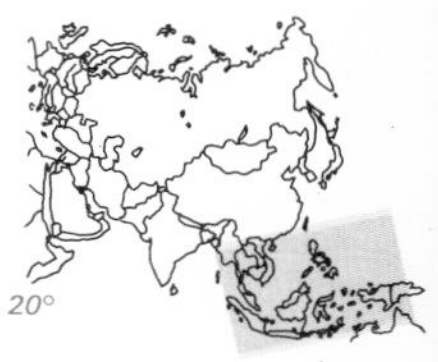

125°
130°
135°
140°
145°
Tropic of Cancer
Hualien
TAIWAN
FORMOSA
T'aitung
P'ingtung
Luzon Strait
BATAN ISLANDS
Balintang Channel
BABUYAN ISLANDS
Aparri
Tuguegarao
LUZON
Baguio
Cabanatuan
San Fernando
Quezon City
PHILIPPINES
Batangas
Naga
Mayon Volcano
Legazpi
Sorsogon
San Bernardino Strait
Sibuyan Sea
SAMAR
Catbalogan
Tacloban
PANAY
Iloilo
Bacolod
Cebu
LEYTE
Leyte Gulf
NEGROS
BOHOL
Dumaguete
Surigao
Mindanao Sea
Butuan
Cagayan de Oro
MINDANAO
Zamboanga
Moro Gulf
Cotabato
Davao
Davao Gulf
Jolo
SULU ARCHIPELAGO
CAPE SAN AGUSTIN
SARANGANI ISLANDS
PHILIPPINE SEA
PACIFIC OCEAN
OKINO-TORI-SHIMA (Japan)
MARIANA ISLANDS
PACIFIC ISLANDS TRUST TERRITORY (U.S.)
SAIPAN
TINIAN
ROTA
Agana
GUAM (U.S.)
YAP
ULITHI
PALAU ISLANDS
BABELTHUAP
Koror
ANGAUR
CAROLINE ISLANDS
SONSOROL ISLANDS
PULO ANNA
MERIR
TOBI
HELEN ISLAND
KEPULAUAN TALAUD
CELEBES SEA
KEPULAUAN SANGIHE
Manado
Gorontalo
HALMAHERA
Ternate
Tidore
MOROTAI
LAUT MALUKU
MOLUCCA SEA
MALUKU
PULAU OBI
KEPULAUAN SULA
KEPULAUAN BANGGAI
LAUT SERAM
CERAM SEA
SERAM
CERAM
BURU
Ambon
LAUT BANDA
BANDA SEA
KEPULAUAN KAI
Tual
KEPULAUAN ARU
KEPULAUAN TANIMBAR
YAMDENA
Saumlaki
KEPULAUAN BABAR
WETAR
TIMOR
Dili
Kupang
TIMOR SEA
FLORES
ARAFURA SEA
AUSTRALIA
CAPE WESSEL
CAPE YORK PENINSULA
Torres Strait
Gulf of Papua
WAIGEO
Sorong
Manokwari
BIAK
Teluk Cenderawasih
JAZIRAH DOBERAI
Jayapura (Sukarnapura)
PAPUA NEW GUINEA
Vanimo
Aitape
Wewak
Madang
PEGUNUNGAN VAN REES
PEGUNUNGAN MAOKE
Puncak Jaya
Puncak Trikora
Mandala
NEW GUINEA
Mount Wilhelm 4509
Mount Hagen
Mount Bosavi
Lake Murray
Fly
Kikori
Balimo
Daru
Merauke
PULAU YOS SUDARSA
TANJUNG VALS
Equator
0°
5°
10°
15°
20°

150 - 151

Kilometers 0 200 400 600 Km.
Statute Miles 0 200 400 600 Mi.

Scale 1:12,000,000
One centimeter represents 120 kilometers.
One inch represents approximately 190 miles.
Lambert Conformal Conic Projection

Kilometers 0 100 200 300 Km.
Statute Miles 0 100 200 300 Mi.

Scale 1:6,000,000
One centimeter represents 60 kilometers.
One inch represents approximately 95 miles.
Lambert Conformal Conic Projection

MAP FORM	gunung	island	-jiang	kepulauan	khao	kyun	pulau	-shan
ENGLISH	mountain	island	river	islands	mountain	island	island	mountain
DEUTSCH	Berg	Insel	Fluss	Inseln	Berg	Insel	Insel	Berg
ESPAÑOL	montaña	isla	río	islas	montaña	isla	isla	montaña
FRANÇAIS	montagne	île	rivière	îles	montagne	île	île	montagne
PORTUGUÊS	montanha	ilha	rio	ilhas	montanha	ilha	ilha	montanha

For complete glossary see page J•1.
For Krung Thep (Bangkok) and Thanh-pho Ho Chi Minh (Sai-gon) metropolitan maps see page 259.

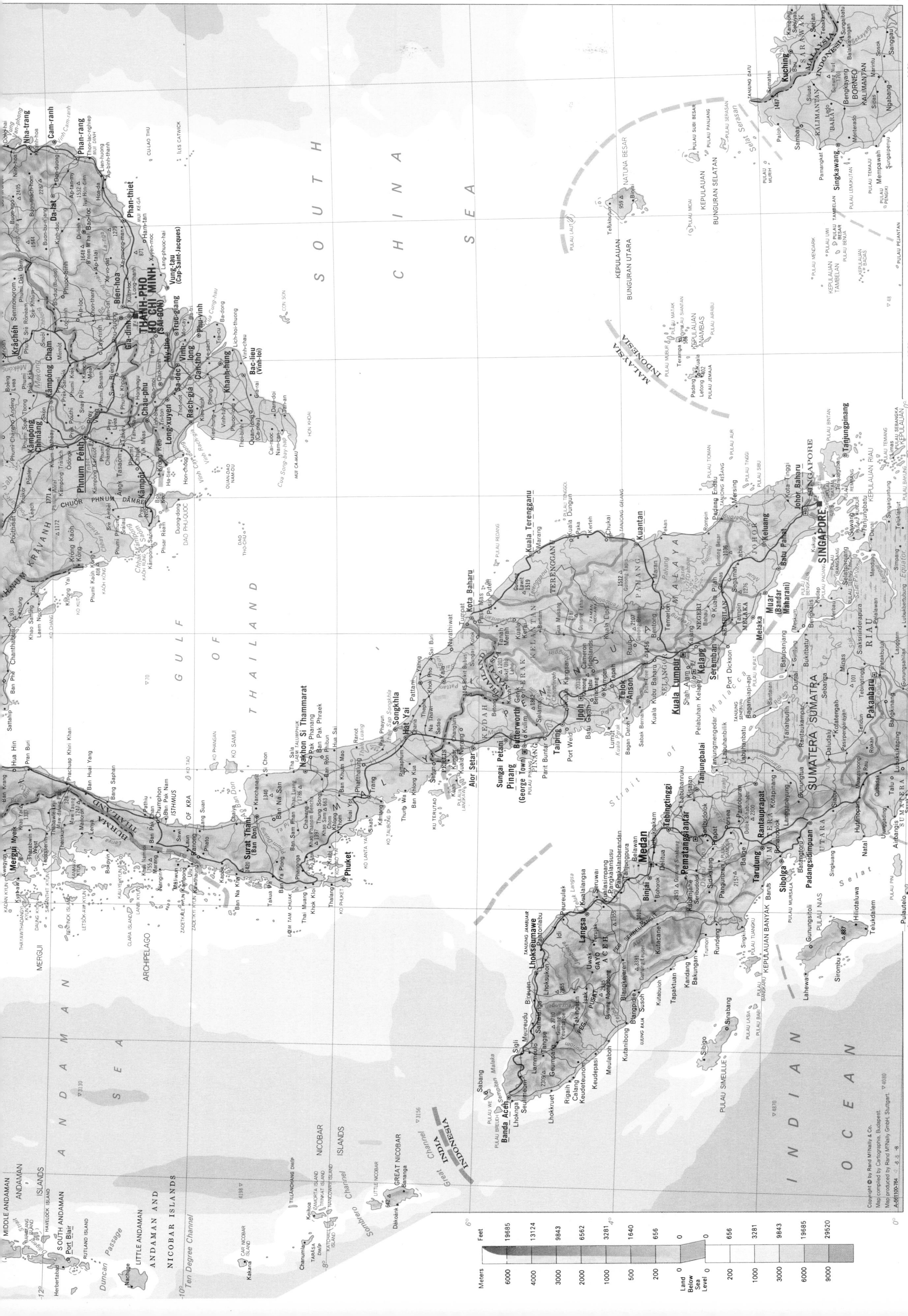
SOUTH CHINA SEA
GULF OF THAILAND
ANDAMAN SEA
INDIAN OCEAN
MALAYA
SUMATERA
SINGAPORE
Kuala Lumpur
THANH-PHO HO CHI MINH (SAI-GON)
Phnum Pénh
ANDAMAN AND NICOBAR ISLANDS
MERGUI ARCHIPELAGO
Ten Degree Channel
Duncan Passage
Sombrero Channel
Great Channel
102-103
Feet
Meters
Land Below Sea Level

SOUTH CHINA SEA
INDIAN OCEAN
LAUT JAVA
SUMATERA
SUMATRA
KALIMANTAN
JAWA
JAVA
MALAYA
SINGAPORE
JAKARTA
Kuala Lumpur
Pinang (George Town)
Ipoh
Melaka
Johor Baharu
Kuantan
Kuala Terengganu
Kota Baharu
Songkhla
Hat Yai
Pekanbaru
Padang
Bukittinggi
Jambi
Palembang
Bengkulu
Telukbetung
Tanjungkarang
Pangkalpinang
BANGKA
BELITUNG
Tanjungpandan
Pontianak
Kuching
Singkawang
Bandung
Bogor
Cirebon
Semarang
Surakarta
Yogyakarta
Tegal
Pekalongan
KEPULAUAN RIAU
KEPULAUAN LINGGA
KEPULAUAN ANAMBAS
KEPULAUAN BUNGURAN UTARA
KEPULAUAN BUNGURAN SELATAN
KEPULAUAN TAMBELAN
KEPULAUAN KARIMATA
KEPULAUAN KARIMUNJAWA
KEPULAUAN MENTAWAI
Equator
Selat Karimata
Selat Sunda
Selat Bangka
Selat Berhala
Selat Mentawai
Selat Serasan
CHRISTMAS ISLAND (Austl.)
Flying Fish Cove
Copyright © by Rand McNally & Co.
Map compiled by Cartographia, Budapest.
Map produced by Rand McNally GmbH, Stuttgart.
A-565500-764

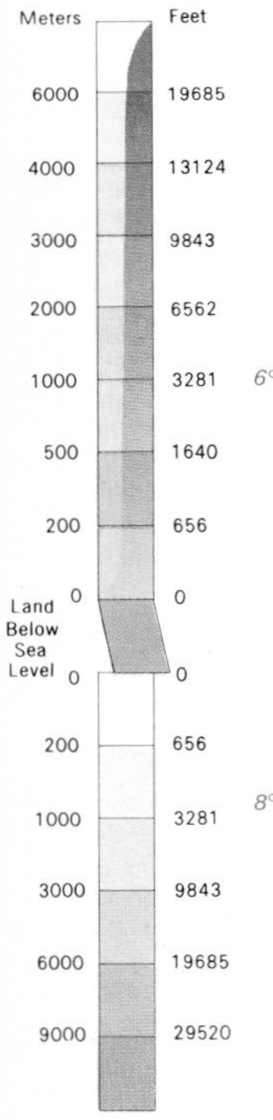
Meters
Feet
6000 19685
4000 13124
3000 9843
2000 6562
1000 3281
500 1640
200 656
0 0
Land Below Sea Level
0 0
200 656
1000 3281
3000 9843
6000 19685
9000 29520

MAP FORM	danau	gunung	kepulauan	pegunungan	pulau	selat	tanjung	teluk
ENGLISH	lake	mountain	islands	mountains	island	strait	cape	bay
DEUTSCH	See	Berg	Inseln	Berge	Insel	Meeresstrasse	Kap	Bucht
ESPAÑOL	lago	montaña	islas	montañas	isla	estrecho	cabo	bahía
FRANÇAIS	lac	montagne	îles	montagnes	île	détroit	cap	baie
PORTUGUÊS	lago	montanha	ilhas	montanhas	ilha	estreito	cabo	baía

For complete glossary see page I • 1.

PHILIPPINES
MALAYSIA
SULU SEA
CELEBES SEA
SULU ARCHIPELAGO
Zamboanga
Moro Gulf
MINDANAO
Davao
General Santos
Jolo
SABAH
Kota Kinabalu (Jesselton)
Sandakan
BRUNEI
Bandar Seri Begawan
Miri
Tawau
Tarakan
KALIMANTAN TIMUR
BORNEO
KALIMANTAN
Samarinda
Balikpapan
KALIMANTAN SELATAN
Banjarmasin
Makasar Strait
Selat Makasar
SULAWESI UTARA
Manado
Gorontalo
Teluk Tomini
SULAWESI TENGAH
Palu
Poso
LAUT MALUKU
MOLUCCA SEA
KEPULAUAN SULA
MALUKU
SULAWESI SELATAN
SULAWESI CELEBES
Ujung Pandang (Makasar)
Parepare
SULAWESI TENGGARA
Kendari
Teluk Bone
Baubau
LAUT BANDA
BANDA SEA
Laut Flores
Flores Sea
JAWA TIMUR
Laut Bali
Bali Sea
BALI
Denpasar
LOMBOK
Mataram
SUMBAWA
NUSA TENGGARA BARAT
FLORES
Ende
NUSA TENGGARA TIMUR
Laut Sawu
Savu Sea
SUMBA
TIMOR TIMUR
Dili
TIMOR
Kupang
TIMOR SEA
Equator
154-155

Kilometers 0 100 200 300 Km.
Statute Miles 0 100 200 300 Mi.

Scale 1:6,000,000
One centimeter represents 60 kilometers.
One inch represents approximately 95 miles.
Mercator Projection

Malaya, Singapore and Northern Sumatra / Malaya, Singapur und Nordsumatra / Malaya, Singapur y Sumatra Septentrional
Malaya, Singapour et Sumatra Septentrional / Malaia, Cingapura e Sumatra Setentrional

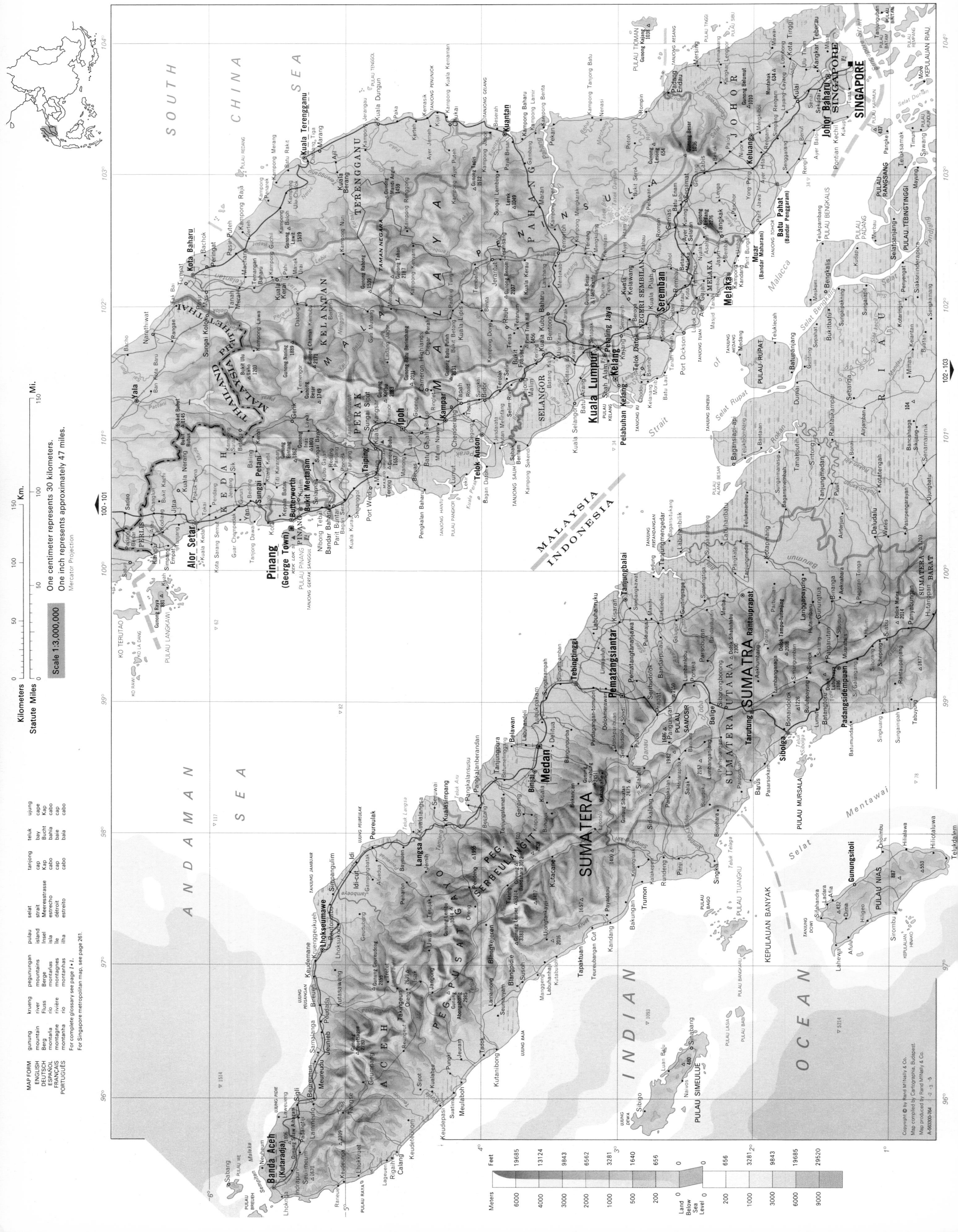

LAUT JAWA
JAVA SEA
JAWA
JAVA
INDIAN OCEAN
JAKARTA
BANDUNG
SEMARANG
SURABAYA
YOGYAKARTA
SURAKARTA
MADURA
BALI
LOMBOK
SUMBAWA
FLORES
SUMBA
NUSA TENGGARA
LESSER SUNDA ISLANDS
NUSA TENGGARA BARAT
NUSA TENGGARA TIMUR
Laut Flores
Flores Sea
Laut Sawu
Savu Sea
Selat Sunda
Selat Madura
Selat Lombok
Scale 1:3,000,000
One centimeter represents 30 kilometers.
One inch represents approximately 47 miles.
Kilometers
Statute Miles
Meters
Feet
Land Below Sea Level
MAP FORM | gunung | pulau | tanjung | teluk
ENGLISH | mountain | island | cape | bay
DEUTSCH | Berg | Insel | Kap | Bucht
ESPAÑOL | montaña | isla | cabo | bahía
FRANÇAIS | montagne | île | cap | baie
PORTUGUÊS | montanha | ilha | cabo | baía
For complete glossary see page I • I.
Copyright © by Rand McNally & Co.
Map compiled by Cartographia, Budapest.
Map produced by Rand McNally GmbH, Stuttgart.

Scale 1:3,000,000

One centimeter represents 30 kilometers.
One inch represents approximately 47 miles.
Lambert Conformal Conic Projection

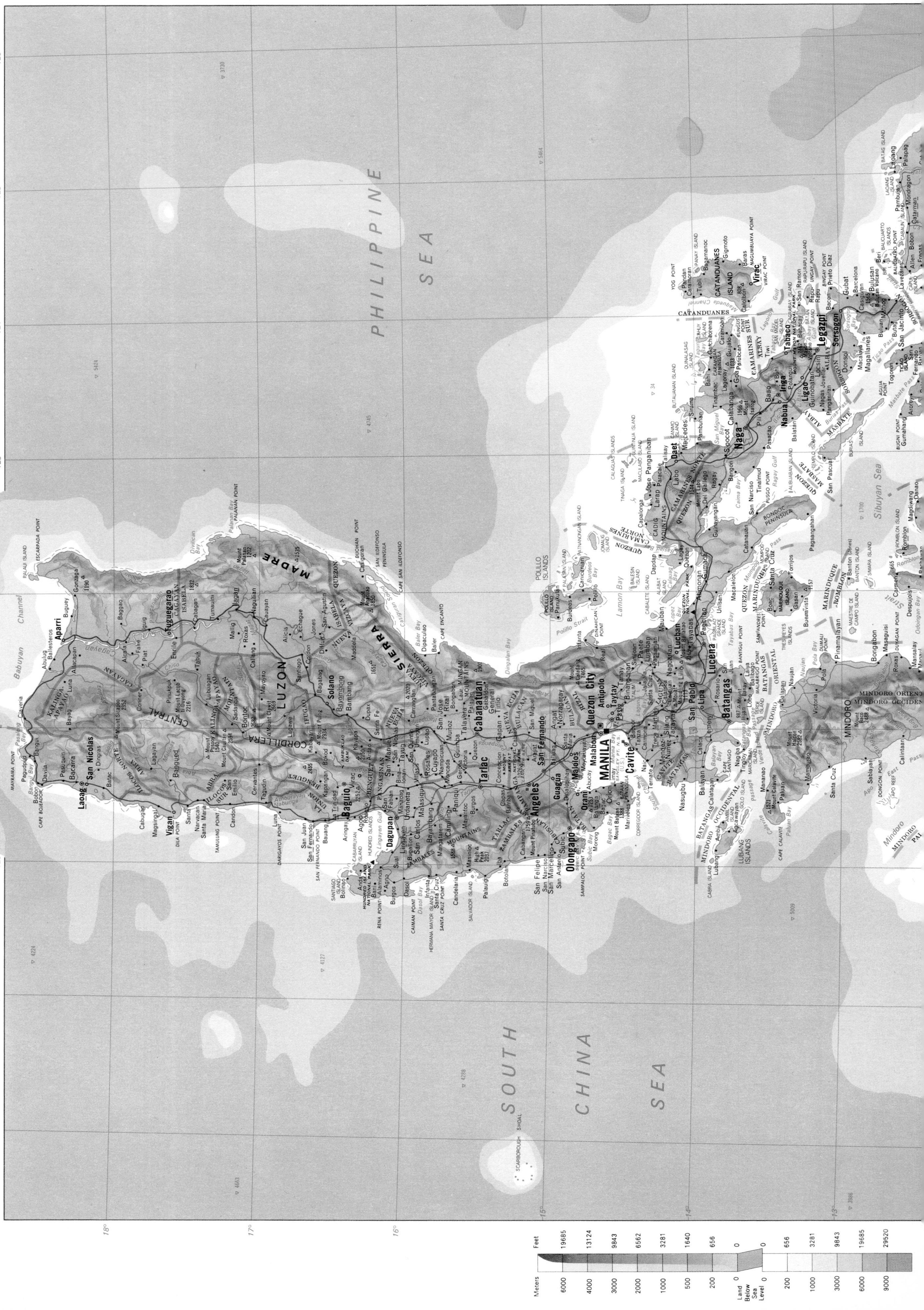
PHILIPPINE SEA
SOUTH CHINA SEA
LUZON
MANILA
Quezon City
Cavite
Batangas
Lucena
Baguio
Dagupan
Tarlac
Angeles
Olongapo
Aparri
Laoag
Vigan
San Fernando
Cabanatuan
Naga
Legazpi
Sorsogon
Daet
MINDORO
MARINDUQUE
CATANDUANES ISLAND
Virac
BABUYAN ISLANDS
Babuyan Channel
SIERRA MADRE
CORDILLERA CENTRAL
Lingayen Gulf
Manila Bay
Lamon Bay
Sibuyan Sea
SCARBOROUGH SHOAL
Meters
Feet
Land
Below Sea Level

MAP FORM	bay	channel	island, i.	mount, mt.	passage	peak, pk.	point	strait
ENGLISH	bay	channel	island	mount	passage	peak	point	strait
DEUTSCH	Bucht	Kanal	Insel	Berg	Durchfahrt	Gipfel	Landspitze	Meeresstrasse
ESPAÑOL	bahía	canal	isla	montaña	pasaje	pico	punta	estrecho
FRANÇAIS	baie	détroit	île	mont	passage	cime	pointe	détroit
PORTUGUÊS	baía	canal	ilha	montanha	passagem	pico	ponta	estreito

For complete glossary see page I•1.
For Manila metropolitan map see page 259.

SULU SEA
CELEBES SEA
Moro Gulf
MINDANAO
NEGROS
PANAY
CEBU
BOHOL
LEYTE
PALAWAN
BORNEO
KALIMANTAN
MALAYSIA
PHILIPPINES PILIPINAS
SULU ARCHIPELAGO
Mindanao Sea
Davao Gulf
Zamboanga
Davao
Cebu
Iloilo
Bacolod
Puerto Princesa
Sandakan
Cagayan de Oro
Tacloban
Copyright © by Rand McNally & Co.
Map prepared by Rand McNally & Co.

MAP FORM	gulf	-he	jabal	jazirat	range	ra's	-shan	-shanmai
ENGLISH	gulf	river	mountain	island	range	cape	mountain(s)	mountains
DEUTSCH	Golf	Fluss	Berg	Insel	Gebirge	Kap	Berg(e)	Berge
ESPAÑOL	golfo	río	montaña	isla	sierra	cabo	montaña(s)	montañas
FRANÇAIS	golfe	rivière	montagne	île	chaîne	cap	montagne(s)	montagnes
PORTUGUÊS	golfo	rio	montanha	ilha	serra	cabo	montanha(s)	montanhas

For complete glossary see page I • 1.

Kilometers 0 200 400 600 Km.
Statute Miles 0 200 400 600 Mi.

Scale 1:12,000,000

One centimeter represents 120 kilometers.
One inch represents approximately 190 miles.
Lambert Conformal Conic Projection

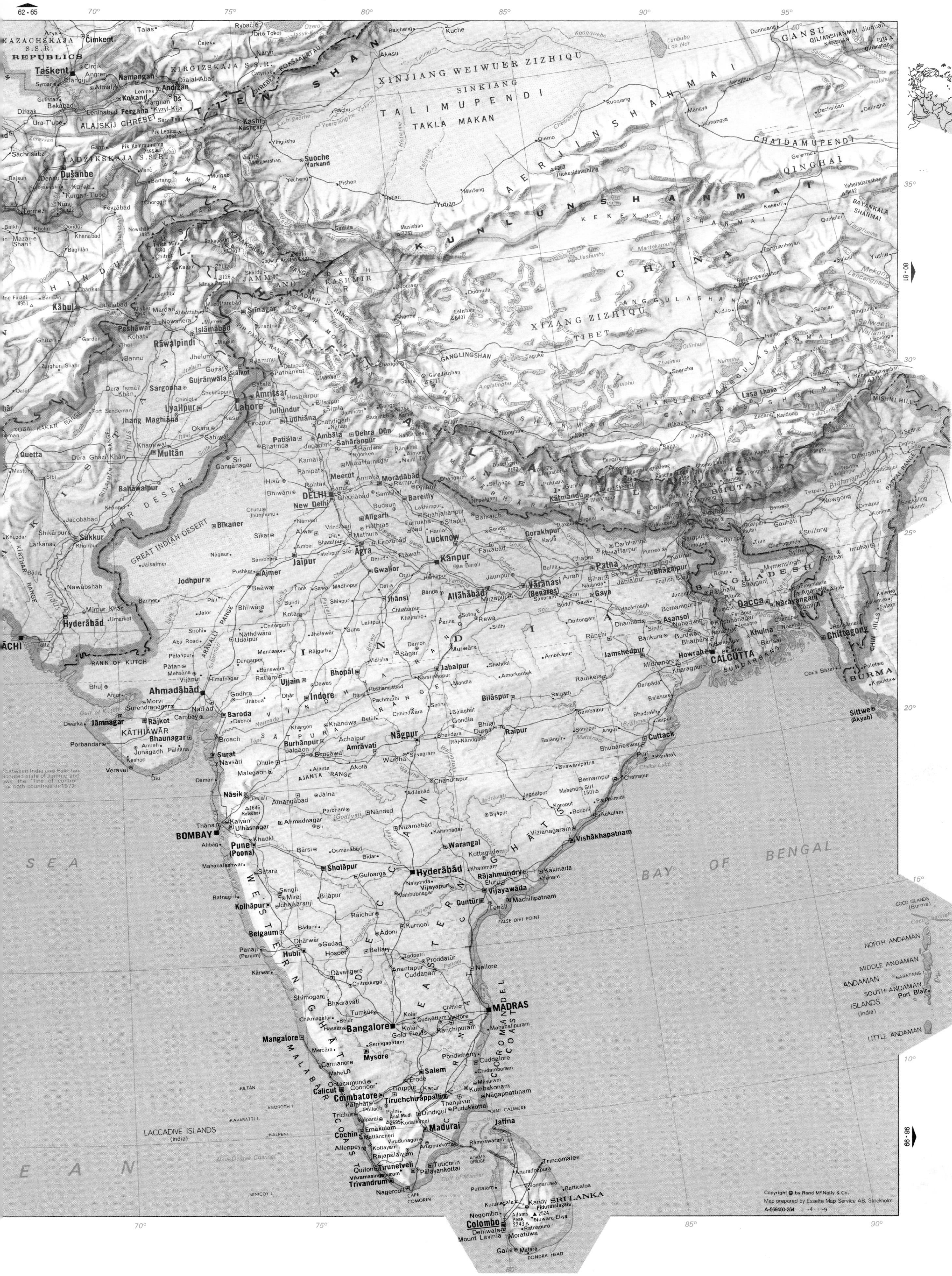
62 - 65
80 - 81
96 - 99
XINJIANG WEIWUER ZIZHIQU
SINKIANG
TALIMUPENDI
TAKLA MAKAN
TIEN SHAN
KUNLUN SHAN
ARJIN SHAN
CHAIDAMUPENDI
QINGHAI
GANSU
XIZANG ZIZHIQU
TIBET
CHINA
TANGGULA SHAN
NIANQINGTANGGULA SHAN
GANGDISE SHAN
HIMALAYA
NEPAL
BHUTAN
BANGLADESH
BURMA
INDIA
PAKISTAN
HINDU KUSH
KARAKORAM RANGE
JAMMU AND KASHMIR
THAR DESERT
GREAT INDIAN DESERT
RANN OF KUTCH
KĀTHIĀWĀR
SĀTPURA RANGE
VINDHYA RANGE
AJANTA RANGE
DECCAN
WESTERN GHĀTS
EASTERN GHĀTS
MALABAR COAST
COROMANDEL COAST
BAY OF BENGAL
LACCADIVE ISLANDS (India)
ANDAMAN ISLANDS (India)
NORTH ANDAMAN
MIDDLE ANDAMAN
SOUTH ANDAMAN
LITTLE ANDAMAN
SRI LANKA
Taškent
Dušanbe
Kābul
Peshāwar
Islāmābād
Rāwalpindi
Lahore
Multān
Quetta
Hyderābād
Srinagar
Amritsar
DELHI
New Delhi
Āgra
Jaipur
Kānpur
Lucknow
Allāhābād
Vārānasi (Benares)
Patna
Kātmāndu
Lhasa
Dacca
CALCUTTA
Chittagong
Ahmadābād
Baroda
Sūrat
BOMBAY
Pune (Poona)
Nāgpur
Hyderābād
MADRAS
Bangalore
Mysore
Madurai
Cochin
Trivandrum
Colombo
Kandy
Jaffna
Trincomalee
Copyright © by Rand McNally & Co.
Map prepared by Esselte Map Service AB, Stockholm.

Northern India and Pakistan / Nordindien und Pakistan / India Septentrional y Pakistán
Inde Septentrionale et Pakistan / Índia Setentrional e Paquistão

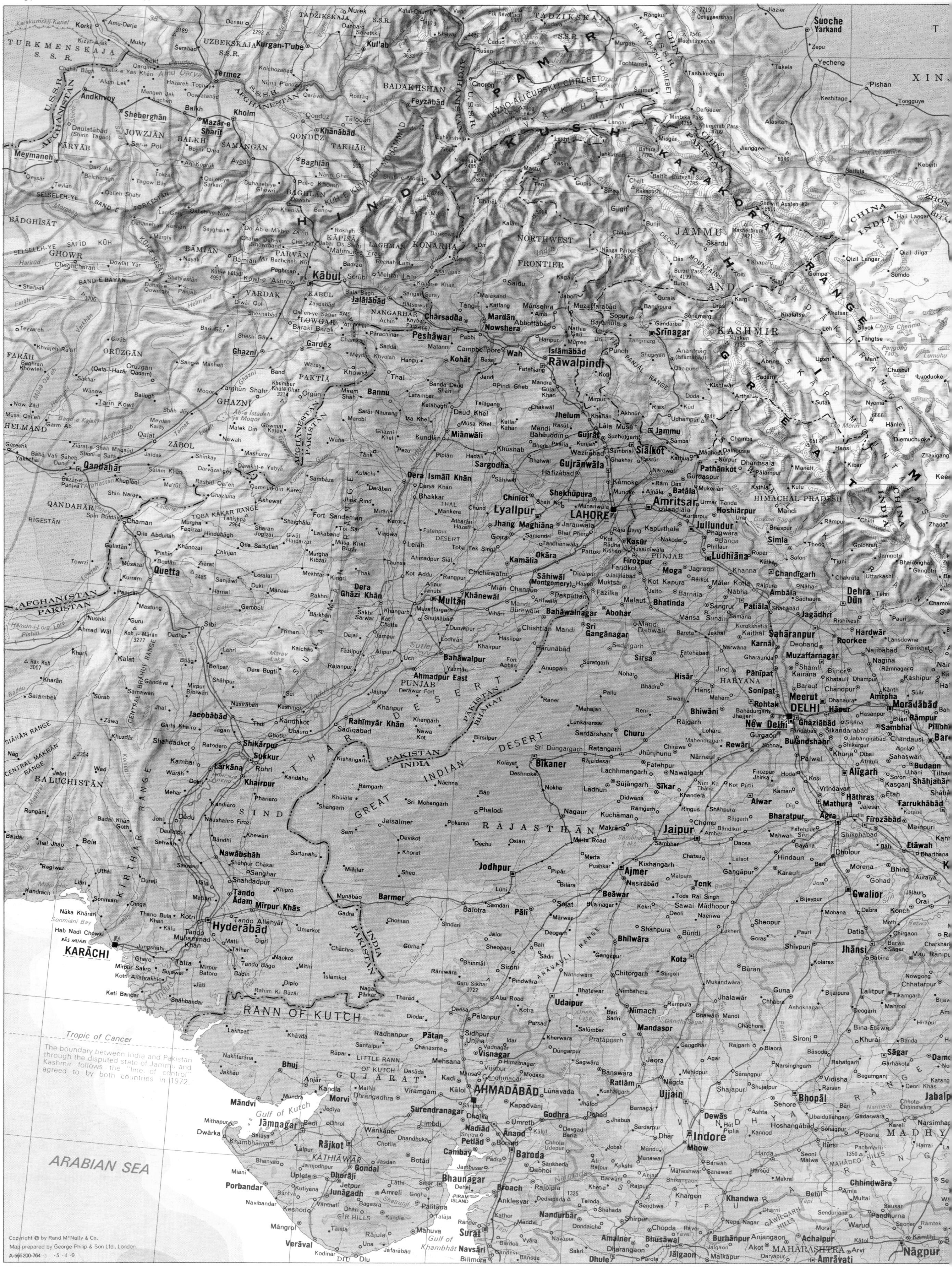

Meters	Feet
6000	19685
4000	13124
3000	9843
2000	6562
1000	3281
500	1640
200	656
0	0
Land Below Sea Level 0	0
200	656
1000	3281
3000	9843
6000	19685
9000	29520

MAP FORM	-chi	-he	-hu	-kou	range	-shan	-shanmai
ENGLISH	lake	river	lake	pass	range	mountain	mountains
DEUTSCH	See	Fluss	See	Pass	Gebirge	Berg	Berge
ESPAÑOL	lago	río	lago	paso	sierra	montaña	montañas
FRANÇAIS	lac	rivière	lac	col	chaîne	montagne	montagnes
PORTUGUÊS	lago	rio	lago	passo	serra	montanha	montanhas

For complete glossary see page *I·1*.

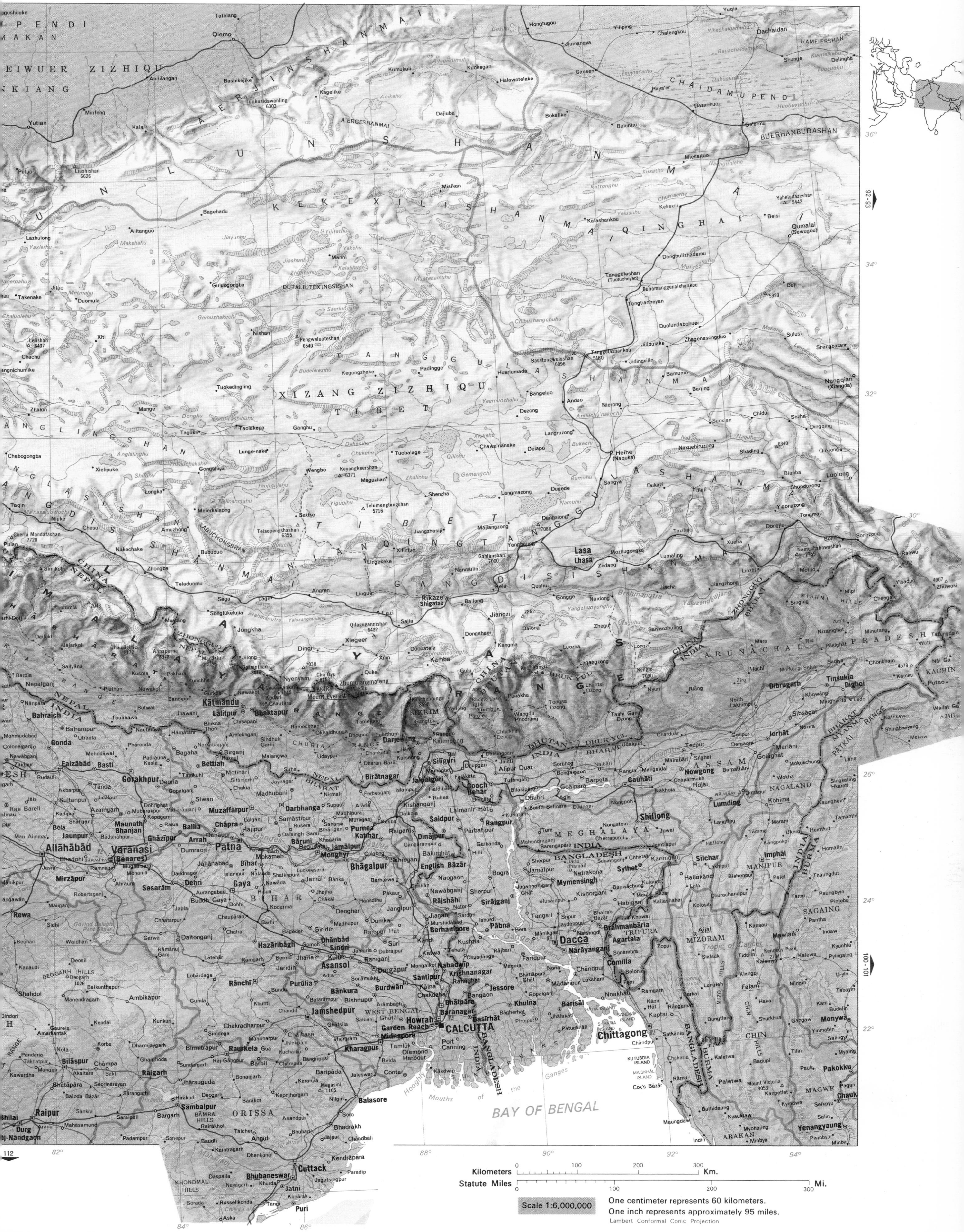

Kilometers 0 100 200 300 Km.
Statute Miles 0 100 200 300 Mi.

Scale 1:6,000,000
One centimeter represents 60 kilometers.
One inch represents approximately 95 miles.
Lambert Conformal Conic Projection

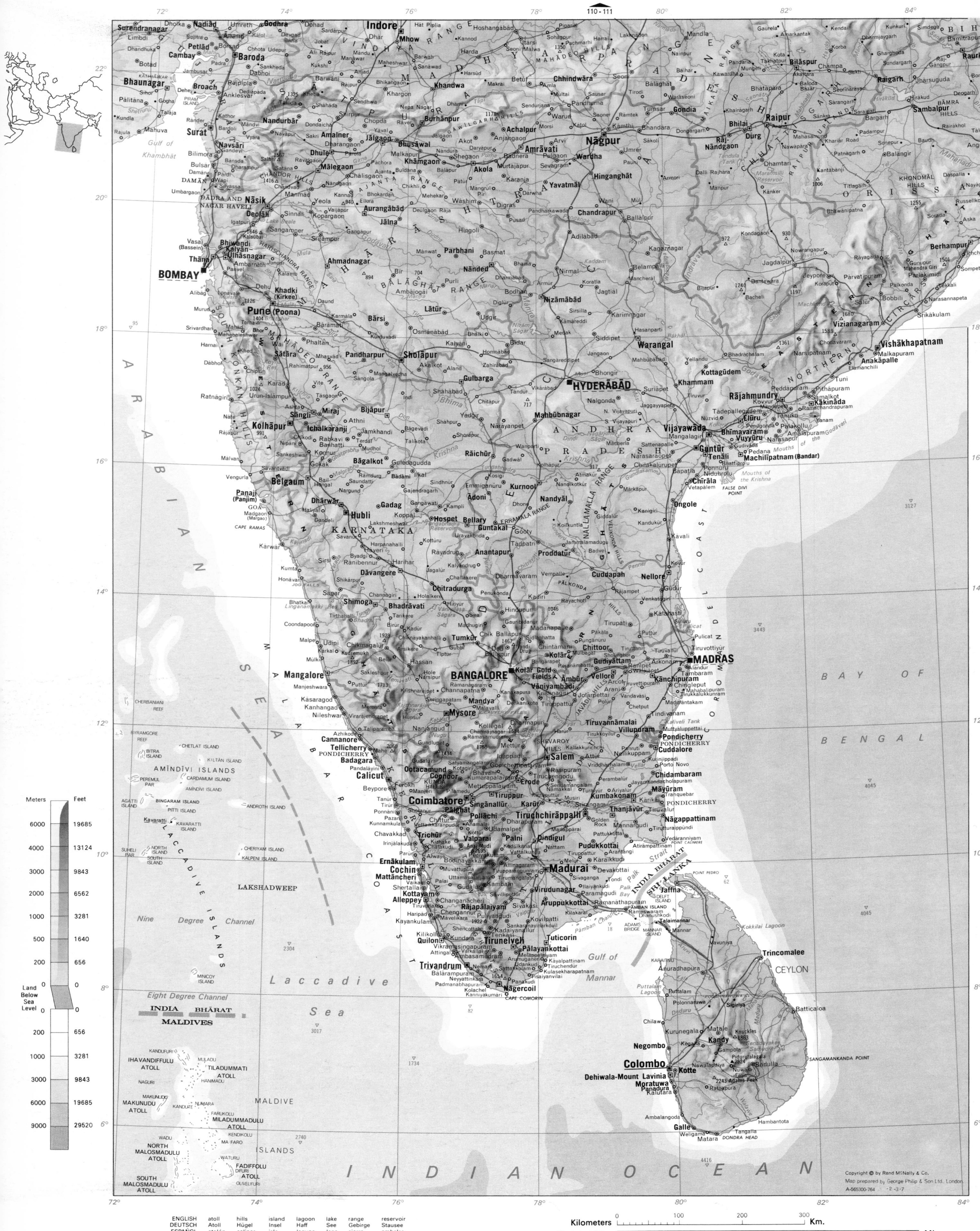

ENGLISH	atoll	hills	island	lagoon	lake	range	reservoir
DEUTSCH	Atoll	Hügel	Insel	Haff	See	Gebirge	Stausee
ESPAÑOL	atolón	colinas	isla	laguna	lago	sierra	embalse
FRANÇAIS	atoll	collines	île	lagune	lac	chaîne	réservoir
PORTUGUÊS	atol	colinas	ilha	laguna	lago	serra	reservatório

For complete glossary see page *I • 1*.
For Bombay metropolitan map, see page 262.

Kilometers 0 100 200 300 Km.
Statute Miles 0 100 200 300 Mi.

Scale 1:6,000,000

One centimeter represents 60 kilometers.
One inch represents approximately 95 miles.
Lambert Conformal Conic Projection

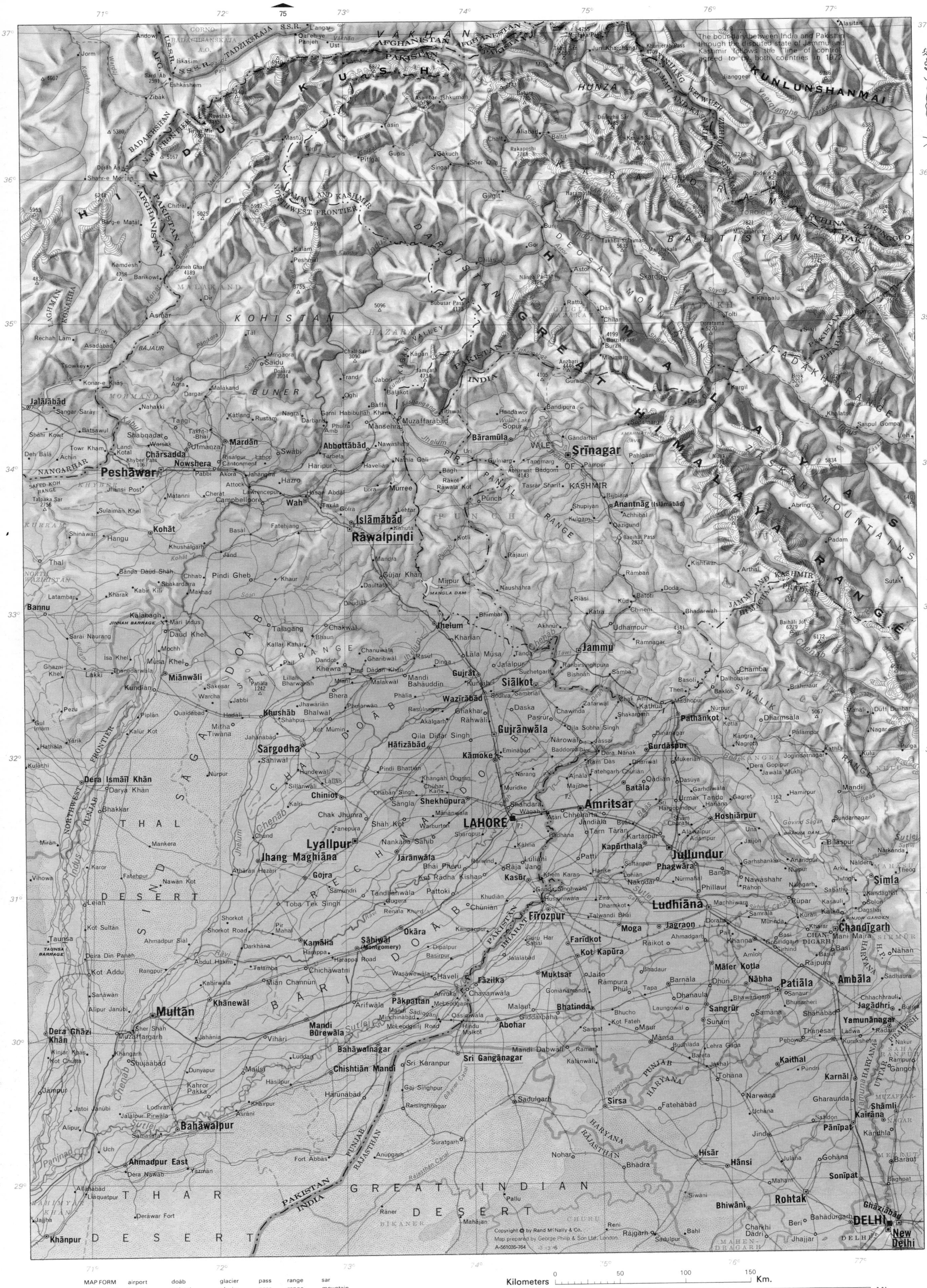

Meters	Feet
6000	19685
4000	13124
3000	9843
2000	6562
1000	3281
500	1640
200	656
0	0
Land Below Sea Level	
0	
200	656
1000	3281
3000	9843
6000	19685
9000	29520

Kilometers 0 50 100 150 Km.
Statute Miles 0 50 100 150 Mi.

Scale 1:3,000,000
One centimeter represents 30 kilometers.
One inch represents approximately 47 miles.
Lambert Conformal Conic Projection

MAP FORM	airport	doāb	glacier	pass	range	sar
ENGLISH	airport	upland	glacier	pass	range	mountain
DEUTSCH	Flughafen	Bergland	Gletscher	Pass	Gebirge	Berg
ESPAÑOL	aeropuerto	tierras altas	glaciar	paso	sierra	montaña
FRANÇAIS	aéroport	hautes terres	glacier	col	chaîne	montagne
PORTUGUÊS	aeroporto	terras altas	geleira	passo	serra	montanha

For complete glossary see page I • 1.
For Delhi metropolitan map, see page 262.

Ganges Lowland and Nepal / Gangestiefland und Nepal / Llanuras del Ganges y Nepal
Plaine du Gange et Népal / Planície do Ganges e Nepal

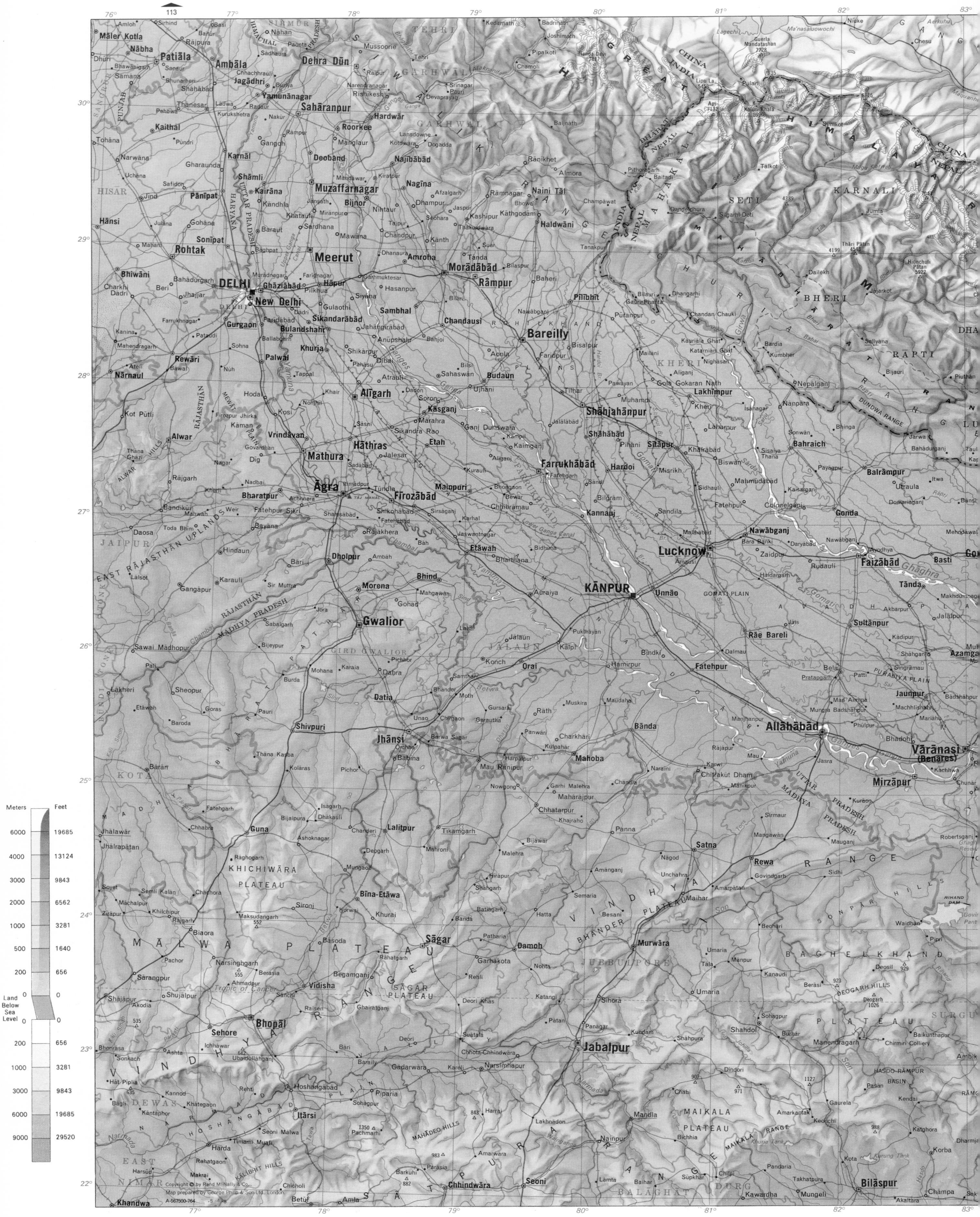

MAP FORM	hills	-hu	plains	plateau	range	-shan
ENGLISH	hills	lake	plains	plateau	range	mountains
DEUTSCH	Hügel	See	Ebenen	Hochebene	Gebirge	Berge
ESPAÑOL	colinas	lago	llanos	meseta	sierra	montañas
FRANÇAIS	collines	lac	plaines	plateau	chaîne	montagnes
PORTUGUÊS	colinas	lago	planícies	planalto	serra	montanhas

For complete glossary see page I·1.
For Delhi metropolitan map, see page 262.

Kilometers 0 50 100 150 Km.
Statute Miles 0 50 100 150 Mi.

Scale 1:3,000,000

One centimeter represents 30 kilometers.
One inch represents approximately 47 miles.
Lambert Conformal Conic Projection

84°
85°
86°
87°
88°
89°
90°
91°
29°
28°
27°
26°
25°
24°
X I Z A N G
T I B E T
Z I Z H I Q U
Brahmaputra Yaluzangbujiang
G A N G D I S I S H A N M A I
Lasa
Lhasa
Saga
Lage
Angren
Lingu
Lazi
Rikaze
Shigatse
Gyangzê
Jongkha
Dingri
Xigeer
Xêgar
Yangzhuoyonghu
Mount Everest
8848
Chö Oyu
8153
Makalu
8481
Kanchenjunga
8598
Dhaulagiri
Annapurna
Himalchuli
7864
Gosainthan
8013
G R E A T   H I M A L A Y A   R A N G E
BĀGMATI
Kātmāndu
Bhaktapur
Lalitpur
NĀRĀYANI
NEPAL
INDIA
JANAKPUR
SAGARMATHA
KOSI
MECHI
SIKKIM
Gangtok
Darjeeling
Kālimpong
BHUTAN
DRUK-YUL
Thimbu
Paro
Punakha
CHINA
Siliguri
Jalpaiguri
Cooch Behār
Dhubri
ASSAM
MEGHALAYA
Bettiah
Motihāri
Birganj
Biratnagar
Madhubani
Muzaffarpur
Darbhanga
Siwān
Chāpra
Hājīpur
Patna
Dānāpur
Arrah
Buxar
Ballia
Begusarai
Monghyr
Jamālpur
Bhāgalpur
Katihār
Purnea
Kishanganj
Raiganj
Bālurghāt
Dinājpur
Rangpur
Saidpur
BANGLADESH
BIHAR
Gaya
Bihar
Dehri
Jamūi
Deoghar
Giridih
Hazārībāgh
HAZĀRĪBĀGH PLATEAU
Dhanbād
Jharia
Sindri
Asansol
Rānīganj
Durgāpur
Rānchī
RĀNCHĪ PLATEAU
Purūlia
Bānkura
Bishnupur
Burdwān
Jamshedpur
Raurkela
Kharagpur
Midnapore
Howrah
CALCUTTA
Garden Reach
South Dum-Dum
Baranagar
Bhatpāra
Hooghly
Chinsura
Krishnanagar
Nabadwīp
Berhampore
Rājshāhi
Nawābganj
English Bāzār
Bogra
Sirājganj
Pābna
Kushtia
Jessore
Khulna
Faridpur
Dacca
Nārāyanganj
Mymensingh
Comilla
Chāndpur
Barisāl
Noākhāli
Jamālpur
Sherpur
Netrakona
G A N G E S   D E L T A
Ganges
Padma
Meghna
Tropic of Cancer
Mouths of the Ganges
BAY OF BENGAL
Hooghly
Haringhāta

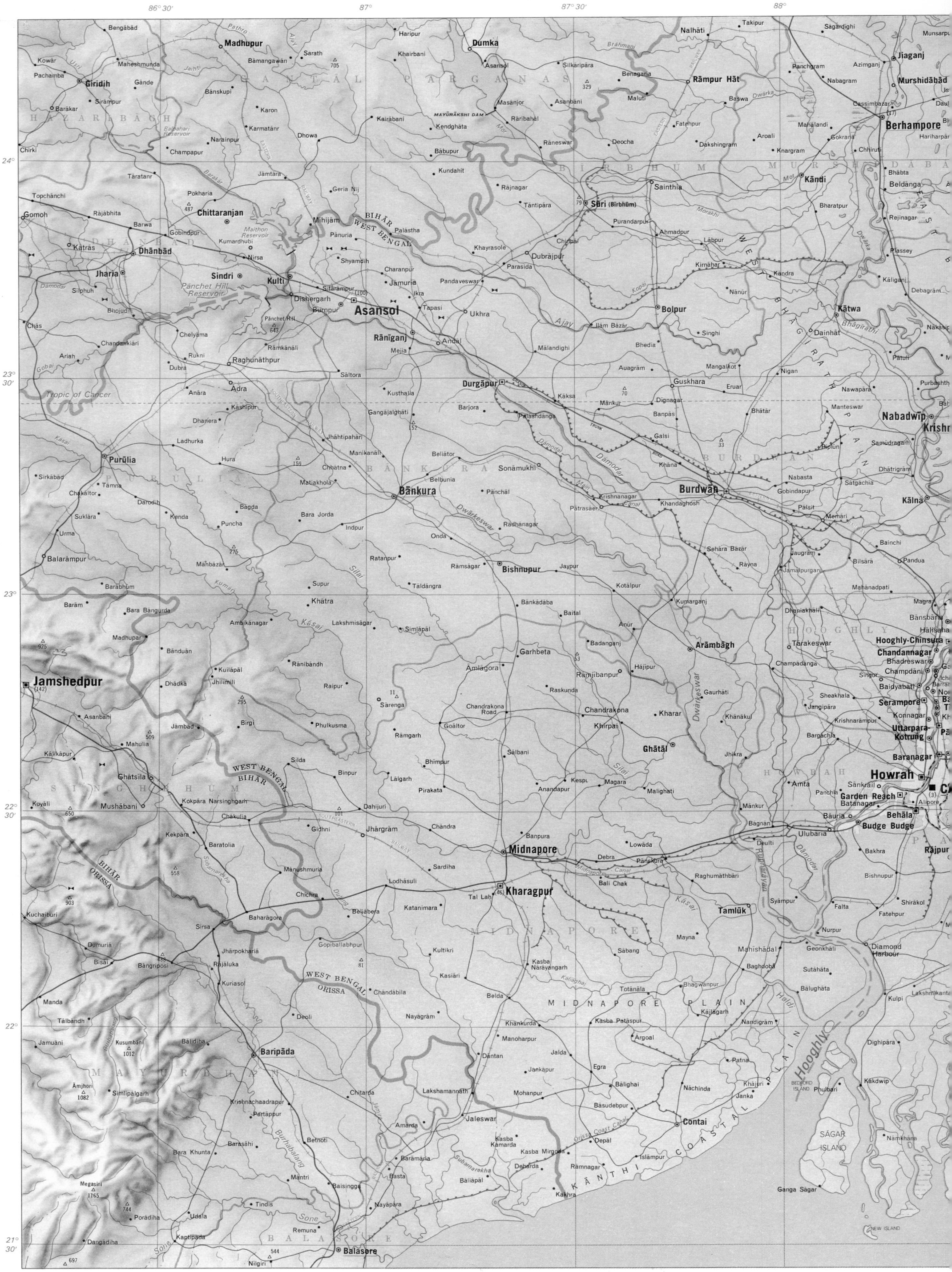

MAP FORM	bay	canal	char	delta	island	plain
ENGLISH	bay	canal	island	delta	island	plain
DEUTSCH	Bucht	Kanal	Insel	Delta	Insel	Ebene
ESPAÑOL	bahía	canal	isla	delta	isla	llanura
FRANÇAIS	baie	canal	île	delta	île	plaine
PORTUGUÊS	baía	canal	ilha	delta	ilha	planície

For complete glossary see page I • 1.
For Calcutta metropolitan map, see page 262.

89° 89° 30′ 90° 90° 30′

Kilometers 0 10 20 30 40 50 Km.

Statute Miles 0 10 20 30 40 50 Mi.

Scale 1:1,000,000

One centimeter represents 10 kilometers.
One inch represents approximately 16 miles.

Lambert Conformal Conic Projection

MAP FORM	harrat	jabal	jazireh	kūh	ra's	sabkhat	wādi
ENGLISH	lava flow	mountain	island	mountain	cape	salt marsh	wadi
DEUTSCH	Lavastrom	Berg	Insel	Berg	Kap	Salzmarsch	Wadi
ESPAÑOL	corriente de lava	montaña	isla	montaña	cabo	pantano salado	uadi
FRANÇAIS	coulée de lave	montagne	île	montagne	cap	marais salé	wadi
PORTUGUÊS	corrente de lava	montanha	ilha	montanha	cabo	pântano salgado	uádi

For complete glossary see page I•1.
For Tehrān metropolitan map see page 257.

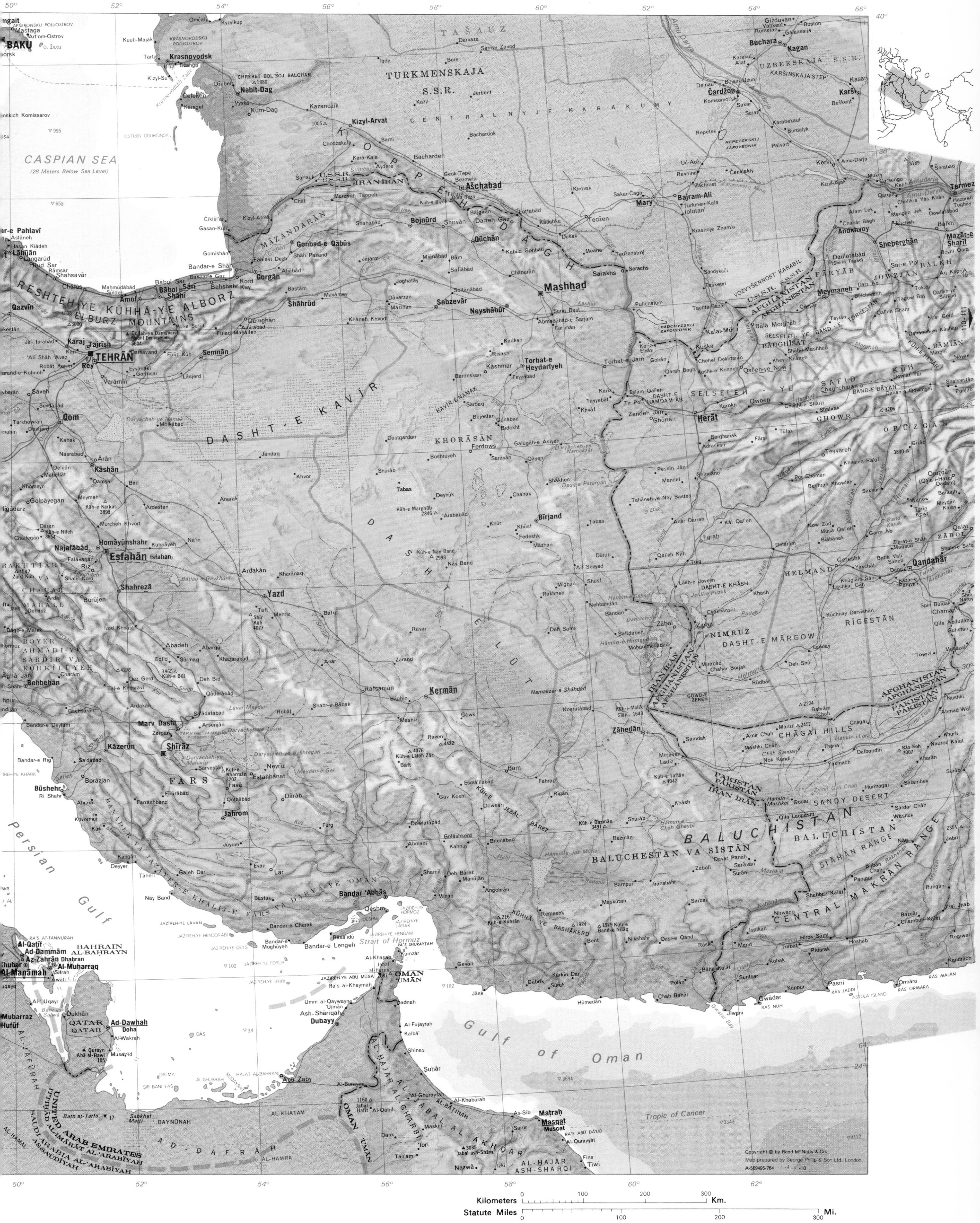

Kilometers 0 100 200 300 Km.
Statute Miles 0 100 200 300 Mi.

Scale 1:6,000,000
One centimeter represents 60 kilometers.
One inch represents approximately 95 miles.
Lambert Conformal Conic Projection

MAP FORM	burnu	dağ, dağı	dağları	gölü	jabal	körfezi	sabkhat
ENGLISH	cape	mountain	mountains	lake	mountains	bay, gulf	salt marsh
DEUTSCH	Kap	Berg	Berge	See	Berge	Bucht, Golf	Salzmarsch
ESPAÑOL	cabo	montaña	montañas	lago	montañas	bahía, golfo	pantano salado
FRANÇAIS	cap	montagne	montagnes	lac	montagnes	baie, golfe	marais salé
PORTUGUÊS	cabo	montanha	montanhas	lago	montanhas	baía, golfo	pântano salgado

For complete glossary see page *I • 1*.
For İstanbul metropolitan map see page 257.

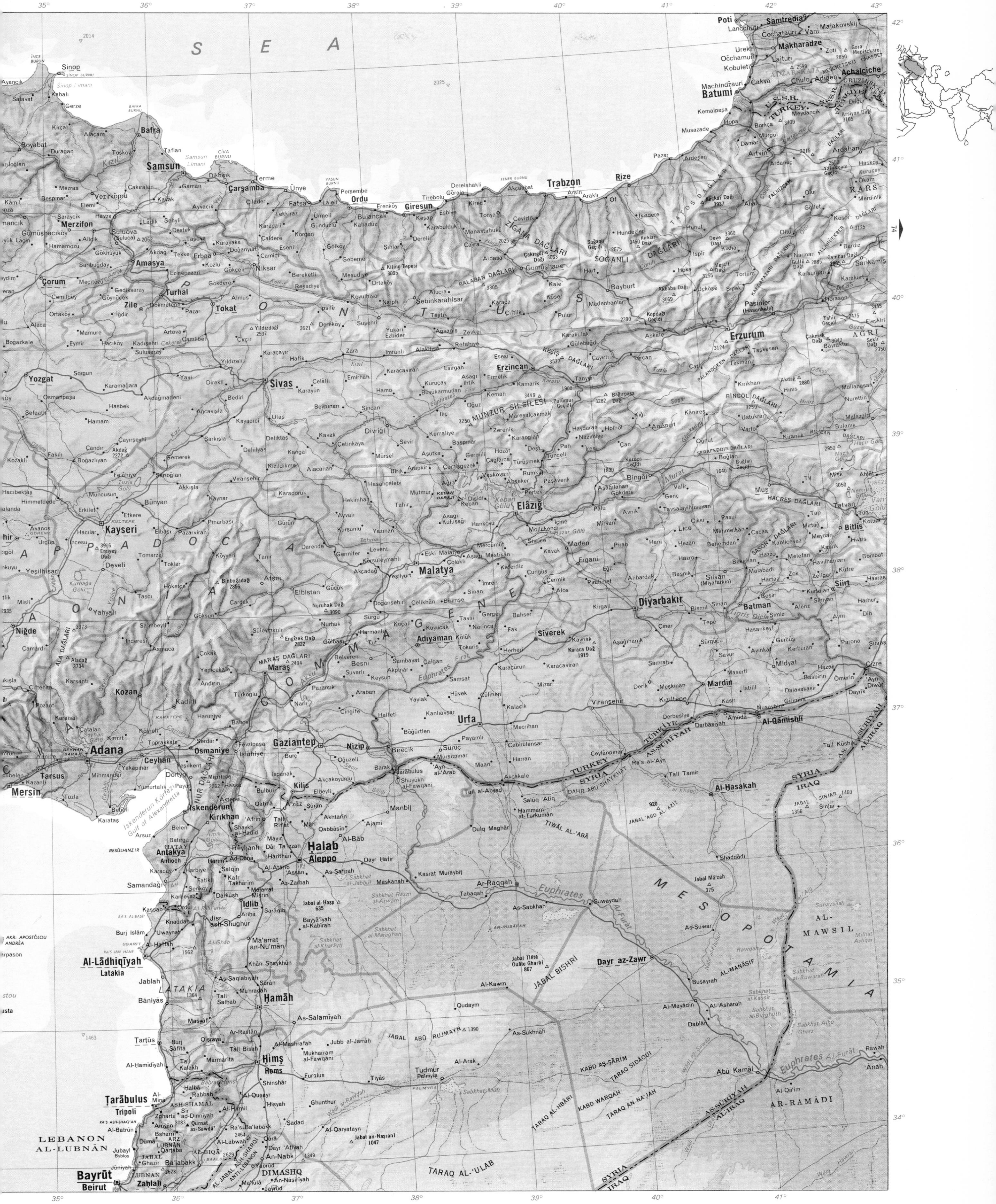

Kilometers 0 50 100 150 Km.
Statute Miles 0 50 100 150 Mi.

Scale 1:3,000,000
One centimeter represents 30 kilometers.
One inch represents approximately 47 miles.
Conic Projection, Two Standard Parallels

MEDITERRANEAN
SEA
Bayrūt
Beirut
Dimashq Damascus
'Ammān
TEL AVIV-YAFO
Hefa
Haifa
Şaydā
Sidon
Şūr
Tyre
Netanya
Ashdod
Irbid
Dar'ā
Az-Zarqā'
As-Suwaydā'
Nābulus
Jenin
Teverya
Tiberias
JABAL LUBNAN
DIMASHQ
AS-SUWAYDĀ'
DAR'Ā
AL-QUNAYŢIRAH
IRBID
AL-BALQĀ'
AL-QUDS
GOLAN HEIGHTS
SYRIA AS-SŪRIYAH
JORDAN AL-URDUN
LEBANON AL-LUBNAN
ISRAEL YISRA'EL

SAUDI ARABIA
JORDAN AL-URDUNN
ARD AS-SAWWAN
JIBAL WAQF AS-SIWWAN
AL-KARAK
QA' AL-JAFR
MA'AN
ASH-SHARAH
JORDAN AL-URDUNN
ISRAEL YISRA'EL
EGYPT MIŞR
HANEGEV
HADAROM
AL-KHALIL
WILDERNESS OF JUDEA
Yam HaMelah Dead Sea Al-Bahr al-Mayyit
Ghazzah Gaza
Khān Yūnus
Rafah
Al-'Arīsh
Be'er Sheva' Beersheba
Dimona
Al-Karak
Aṭ-Ṭafīlah
Ma'ān
Al-'Aqabah
Elat
SĪNĀ'
SHIBH JAZĪRAT SĪNĀ'
SINAI PENINSULA
JABAL AT TUBAYQ
Area occupied by Israel since June, 1967
Scale 1:1,000,000
One centimeter represents 10 kilometers.
One inch represents approximately 16 miles.
Kilometers
Statute Miles
MAP FORM har jabal nahr ra's sede-te'ufa tall
ENGLISH mountain mountain(s) river cape airport mountain wadi
DEUTSCH Berg Berg(e) Fluss Kap Flughafen Berg Wadi
ESPAÑOL montaña montaña(s) rio cabo aeropuerto montaña uadi
FRANÇAIS montagne montagne(s) rivière cap aéroport montagne wadi
PORTUGUÊS montanha montanha(s) rio cabo aeroporto montanha uadi
For complete glossary see page [•].

Western North Africa / West Nordafrika / Región Occidental de Africa Septentrional
Afrique du Nord Occidentale / África do Norte Ocidental

MAP FORM	bahr, baḥr	chott	jabal	lake	mountains	oued	wahát
ENGLISH	river, sea	salt marsh	mountain(s)	lake	mountains	wadi	oasis
DEUTSCH	Fluss, Meer	Salzmarsch	Berg(e)	See	Berge	Wadi	Oase
ESPAÑOL	río, mar	pantano salado	montaña(s)	lago	montañas	uadi	oasis
FRANÇAIS	rivière, mer	marais salé	montagne(s)	lac	montagnes	wadi	oasis
PORTUGUÊS	rio, mar	pântano salgado	montanha(s)	lago	montanhas	uádi	oásis

For complete glossary see page I • 1.

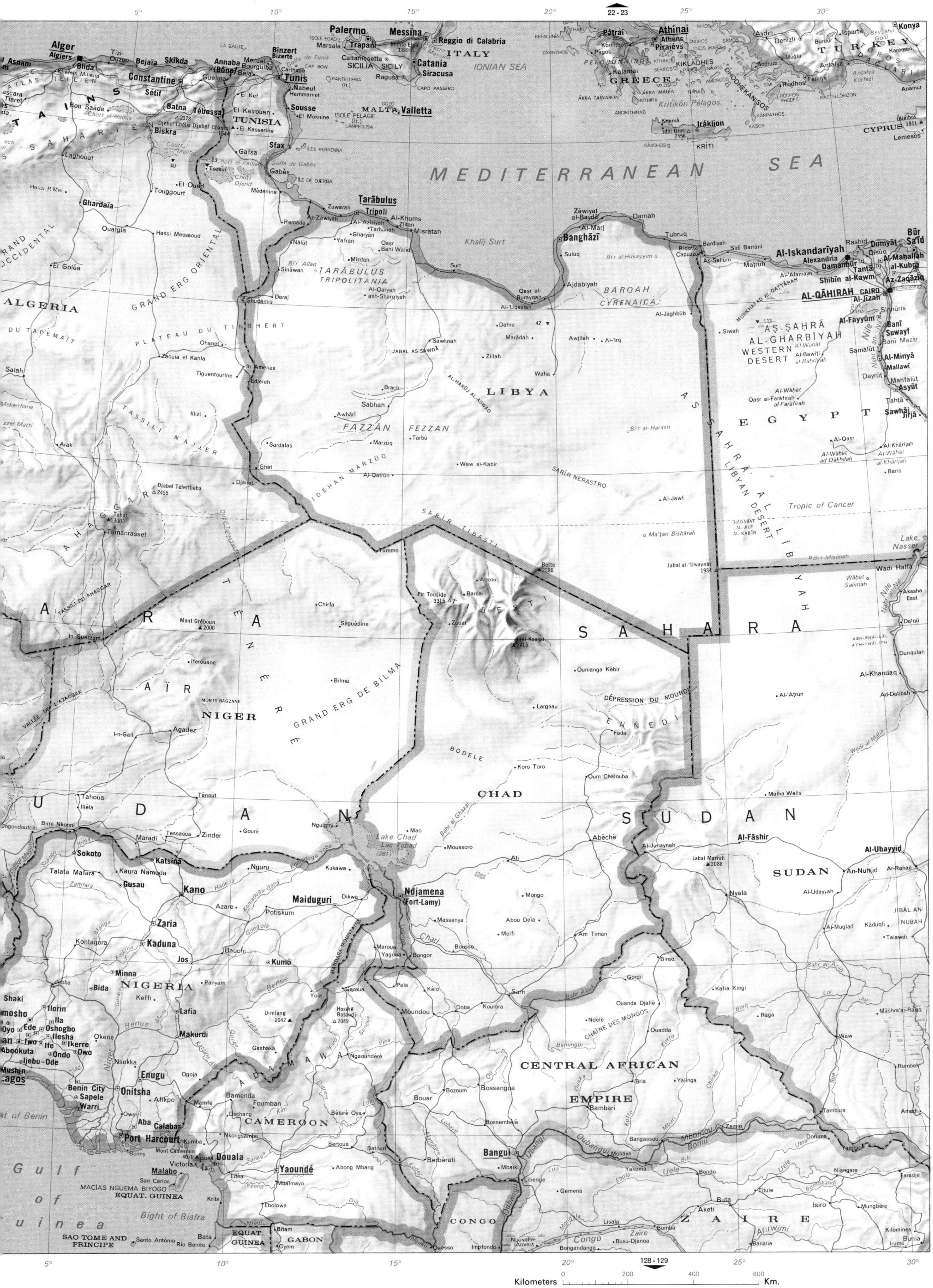

Kilometers 0 200 400 600 Km.
Statute Miles 0 200 400 600 Mi.

Scale 1:12,000,000

One centimeter represents 120 kilometers.
One inch represents approximately 190 miles.
Miller Oblated Stereographic Projection

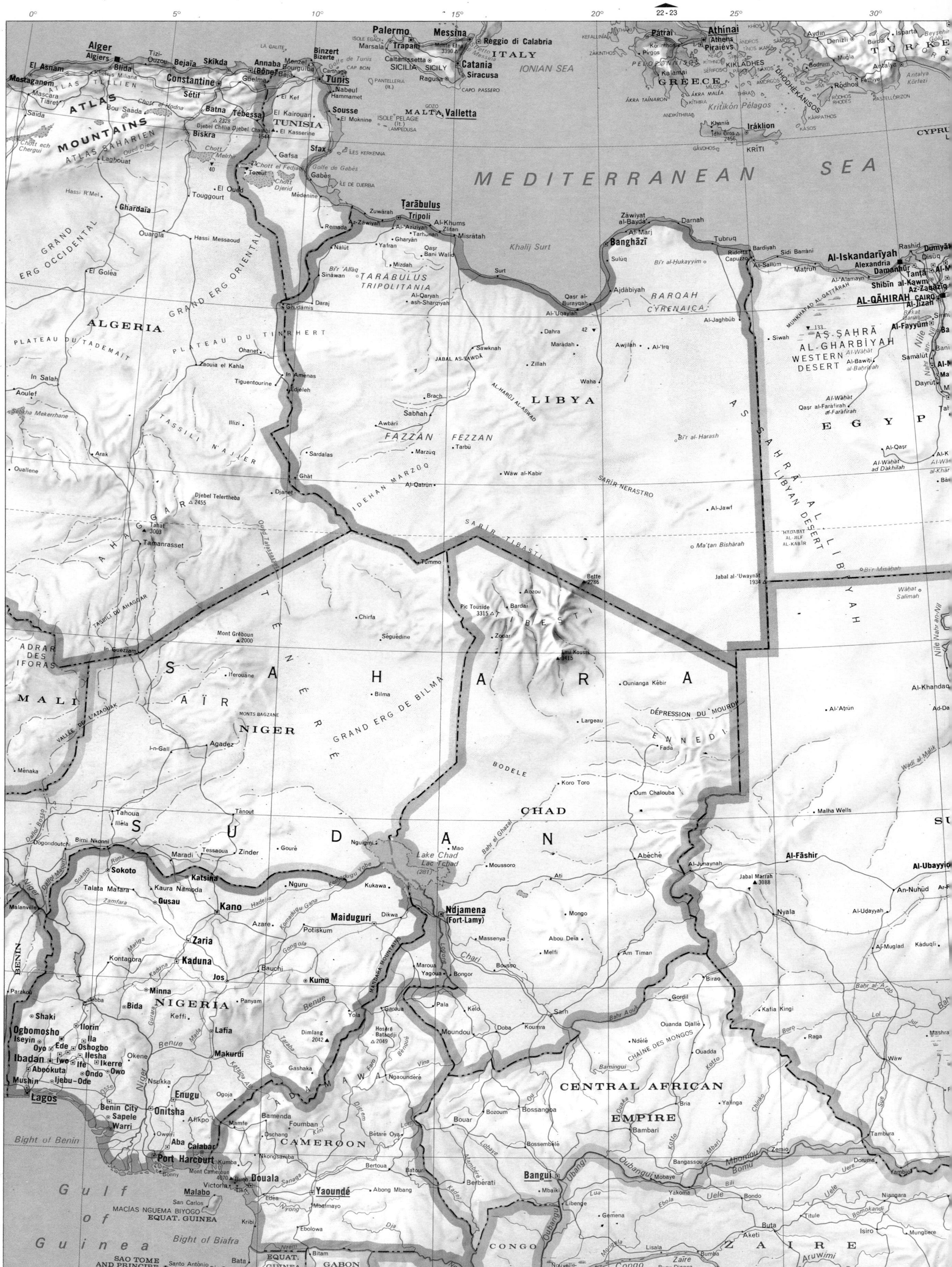

MAP FORM	bahr, bahr	chott	jabal	lake	mountains	oued	ra's; ras	wāhāt
ENGLISH	river, sea	salt marsh	mountain(s)	lake	mountains	wadi	cape	oasis
DEUTSCH	Fluss, Meer	Salzmarsch	Berg(e)	See	Berge	Wadi	Kap	Oase
ESPAÑOL	rio, mar	pantano salado	montaña(s)	lago	montañas	uadi	cabo	oasis
FRANÇAIS	rivière, mer	marais salé	montagne(s)	lac	montagnes	wadi	cap	oasis
PORTUGUÊS	rio, mar	pântano salgado	montanha(s)	lago	montanhas	uádi	cabo	oásis

For complete glossary see page I • 1.

Kilometers 0 200 400 600 Km.

Statute Miles 0 200 400 600 Mi.

Scale 1:12,000,000

One centimeter represents 120 kilometers.
One inch represents approximately 190 miles.
Miller Oblated Stereographic Projection

MAP FORM	cape	île	island	lake	mountains	plateau
ENGLISH	cape	island	island	lake	mountains	plateau
DEUTSCH	Kap	Insel	Insel	See	Berge	Hochebene
ESPAÑOL	cabo	isla	isla	lago	montañas	meseta
FRANÇAIS	cap	île	île	lac	montagnes	plateau
PORTUGUÊS	cabo	ilha	ilha	lago	montanhas	planalto

For complete glossary see page I • 1.

INDIAN OCEAN
SOMALIA
KENYA
Nairobi
Mombasa
Tanga
Zanzibar
Dar-es-Salaam
Arusha
Equator
SEYCHELLES
Victoria
MAHÉ ISLAND
LA DIGUE
PRASLIN ISLAND
SILHOUETTE
AMIRANTE ISLANDS (Sey.)
ÎLE DESROCHES (Sey.)
PLATTE ISLAND (Sey.)
ALPHONSE ISLAND (Sey.)
COETIVY ISLAND (Sey.)
ALDABRA ISLANDS (Sey.)
COSMOLEDO GROUP (Sey.)
ASSUMPTION ISLAND (Sey.)
ASTOVE ISLAND (Sey.)
SAINT PIERRE ISLAND (Sey.)
PROVIDENCE ISLAND (Sey.)
CERF ISLAND (Sey.)
FARQUHAR GROUP (Sey.)
AGALEGA ISLANDS (Mauritius)
COMOROS
Moroni
GRANDE COMORE
MOHELI
Mutsamudu
ANJOUAN
MAYOTTE (Fr.)
Dzaoudzi
ÎLES GLORIEUSES (Fr.)
BANC DU GEYSER
CAP D'AMBRE
Diégo-Suarez
Hell-Ville
MASSIF DU TSARATANANA
Maromokotro 2876
Majunga
Antalaha
Sambava
Vohémar
Ambilobe
Mananara
ÎLE SAINTE-MARIE
Fénérive
Tamatave
MADAGASCAR
Antananarivo
Antsirabe
Fianarantsoa
Ambositra
Manakara
Farafangana
Vangaindrano
Mananjary
Nosy Varika
Mahanoro
Vatomandry
Brickaville
Morondava
Belo
Maintirano
Tuléar
Betioky
Ampanihy
Androka
Tsihombe
Ambovombe
Fort-Dauphin
CAP SAINTE-MARIE
Tropic of Capricorn
TROMELIN (Fr.)
MAURITIUS
Port Louis
Curepipe
Mahébourg
REUNION (Fr.)
Saint-Denis
Le Port
Saint-Paul
Saint-Pierre
MASCARENE ISLANDS
BASSAS DA INDIA (Fr.)
ÎLE EUROPA (Fr.)
Mozambique Channel
MOZAMBIQUE
Beira
Nova Sofala
Quelimane
Chinde
Moçambique
Nampula
António Enes
Porto Amélia
Mocímboa da Praia
Inhambane
Inharrime
Vilanculos
Lake Nyasa
Zomba
Blantyre
Lilongwe
Mwanza
Mtwara
Lindi
Kilwa Kivinje
Kilwa Kisiwani
MAFIA ISLAND
Rhodesia unilaterally declared its independence from the United Kingdom on November 11, 1965
Copyright © by Rand McNally & Co.
Map prepared by Esselte Map Service AB, Stockholm.
A-589200-264

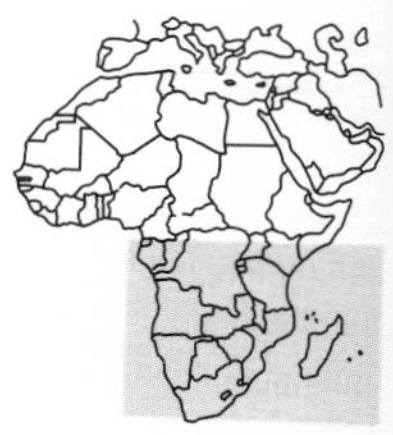

Kilometers 0 200 400 600 Km.

Statute Miles 0 200 400 600 Mi.

Scale 1:12,000,000

One centimeter represents 120 kilometers.
One inch represents approximately 190 miles.
Miller Oblated Stereographic Projection

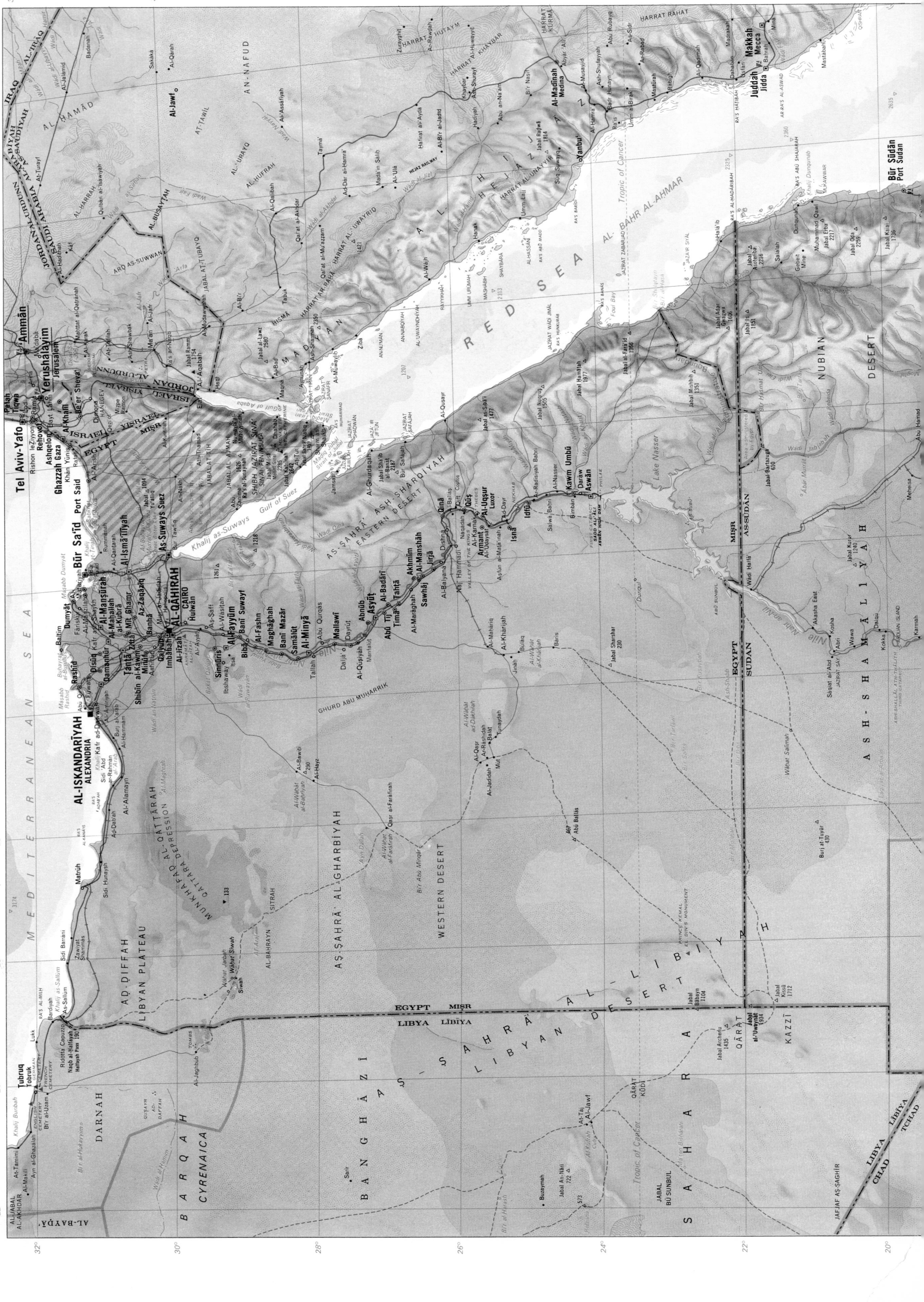
MEDITERRANEAN SEA
RED SEA
AL-BAHR AL-AHMAR
AL-ISKANDARĪYAH
ALEXANDRIA
AL-QĀHIRAH
CAIRO
Būr Sa'īd
Port Said
As-Suways Suez
Tel Aviv-Yafo
Yerushalayim
Jerusalem
'Ammān
Makkah
Mecca
Juddah
Jidda
Al-Madīnah
Medina
Būr Sūdān
Port Sudan
Aswān
Al-Uqṣur
Luxor
Asyūṭ
Lake Nasser
WESTERN DESERT
EASTERN DESERT
LIBYAN PLATEAU
LIBYAN DESERT
NUBIAN DESERT
EGYPT
MIṢR
SUDAN
AS-SŪDĀN
LIBYA
LĪBIYA
CHAD
TCHAD
ISRAEL
CYRENAICA
DARNAH
Tropic of Cancer
Gulf of Suez
Gulf of Aqaba

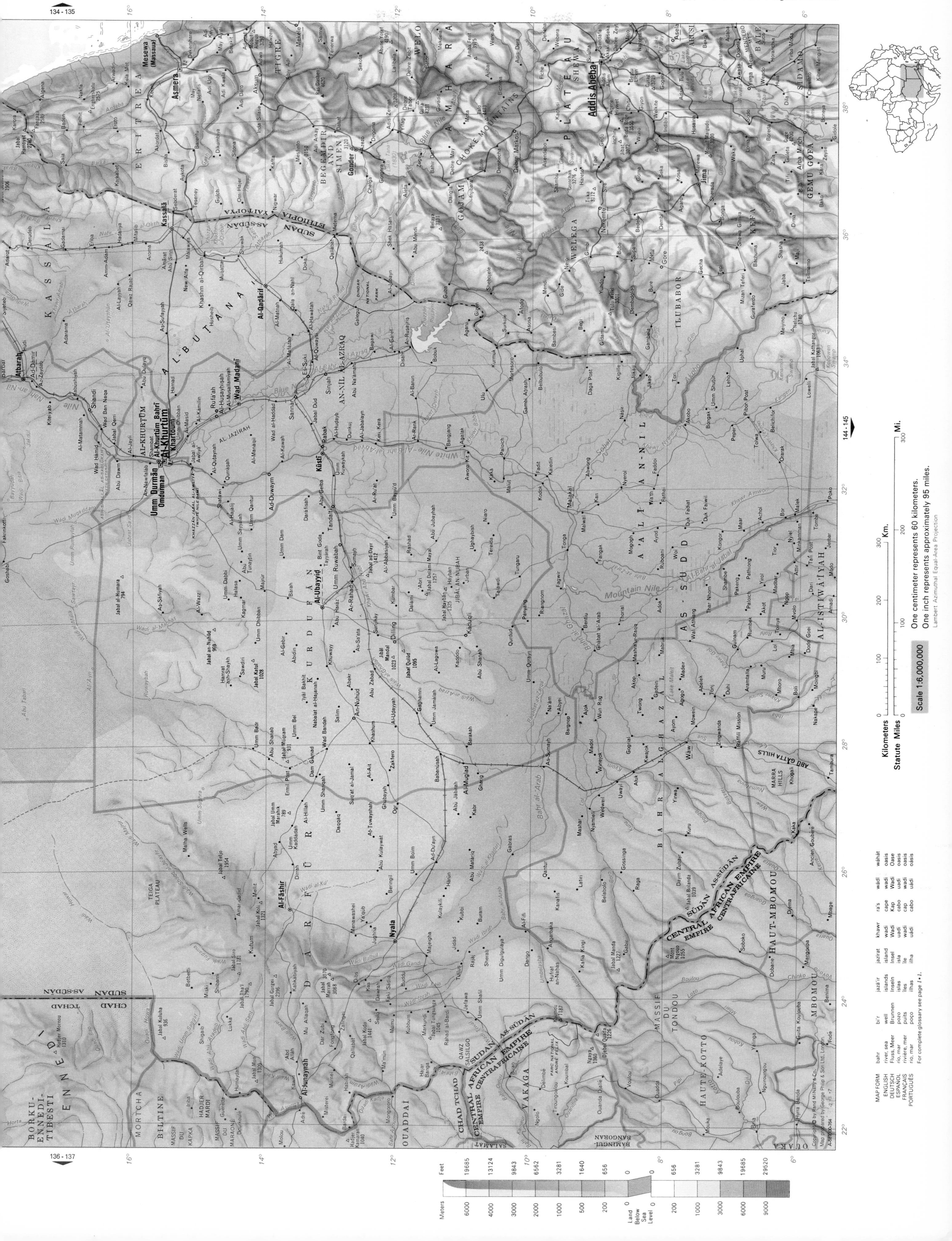
134 - 135
136 - 137
144 - 145
Scale 1:6,000,000
One centimeter represents 60 kilometers.
One inch represents approximately 95 miles.
Lambert Azimuthal Equal-Area Projection
Kilometers
Statute Miles
Km.
Mi.
Addis Abeba
Al-Kharṭūm
Umm Durmān
Asmera
Kassalā
Wad Madanī
Al-Ubayyiḍ
Nyala
Al-Fāshir
Al-Junaynah
Meters
Feet
Land Below Sea Level

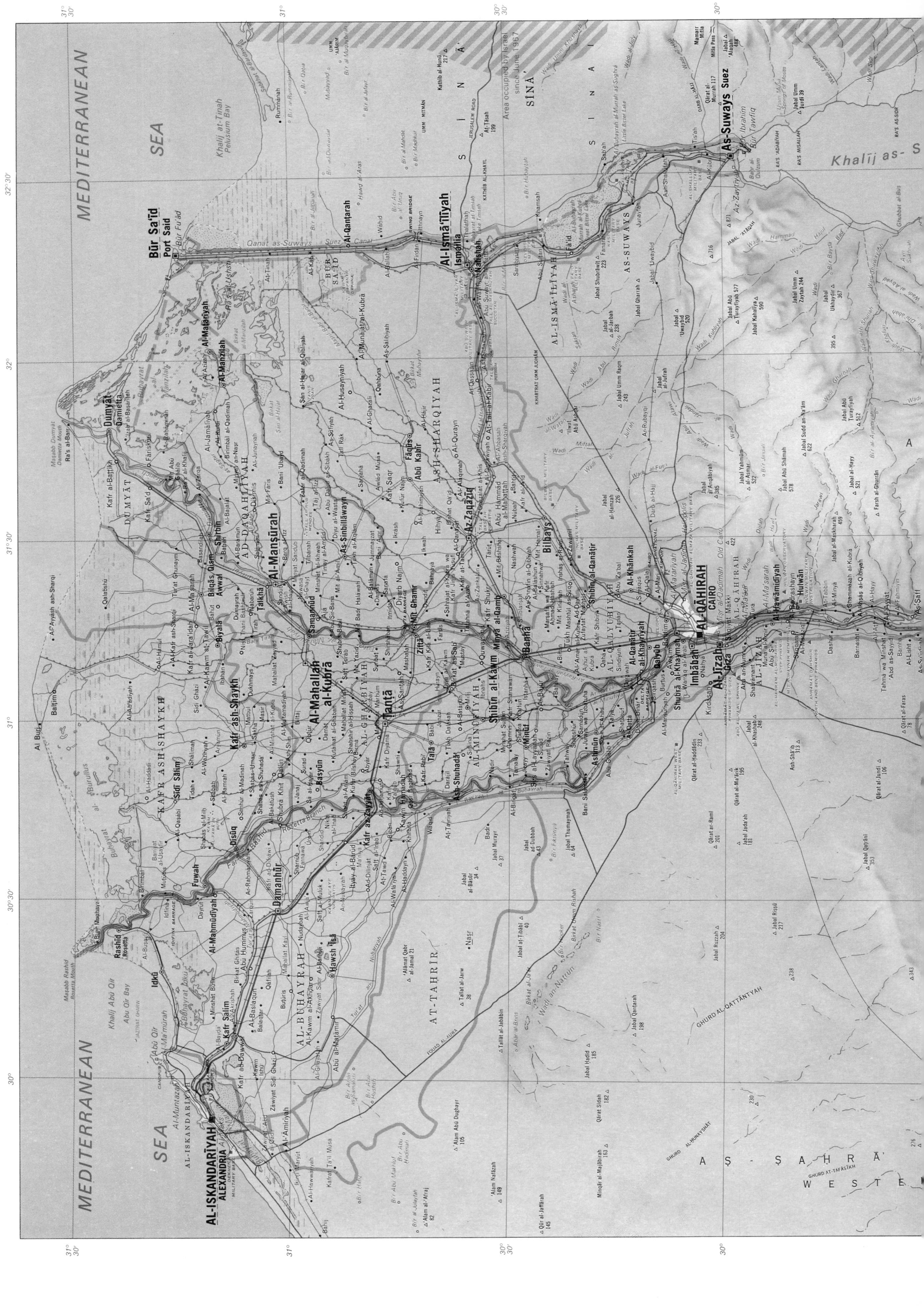
MEDITERRANEAN SEA
MEDITERRANEAN SEA
Būr Sa'īd
Port Said
Al-Ismā'īlīyah
Ismā'īlia
As-Suways Suez
AL-QĀHIRAH
CAIRO
AL-ISKANDARĪYAH
ALEXANDRIA
Al-Manṣūrah
Ṭanṭā
Al-Maḥallah al-Kubrā
Dumyāṭ
Damietta
Rashīd
Rosetta
Damanhūr
Az-Zaqāzīq
Banhā
Shibīn al-Kawm
Kafr ash-Shaykh
Al-Jīzah
Gīza
Ḥulwān
Imbābah
Bilbays
Fāqūs
Al-Qanṭarah
Khalīj as-Suways
Area occupied by Israel since June 1967
SĪNĀ'
S I N A I
AŞ-ŞAḤRĀ'
AT-TAHRIR
AL-BUḤAYRAH
AL-GHARBĪYAH
AL-MINŪFĪYAH
AL-QALYŪBĪYAH
ASH-SHARQIYAH
AD-DAQAHLĪYAH
KAFR ASH-SHAYKH
DUMYĀṬ
AS-SUWAYS
AL-ISMĀ'ĪLĪYAH
Qanāt as-Suways
Suez Canal
Khalīj at-Tīnah
Pelusium Bay
Khalīj Abū Qīr
Abū Qīr Bay
31° 30'
31°
30° 30'
30°
32° 30'
32°
31° 30'
31°
30° 30'
30°

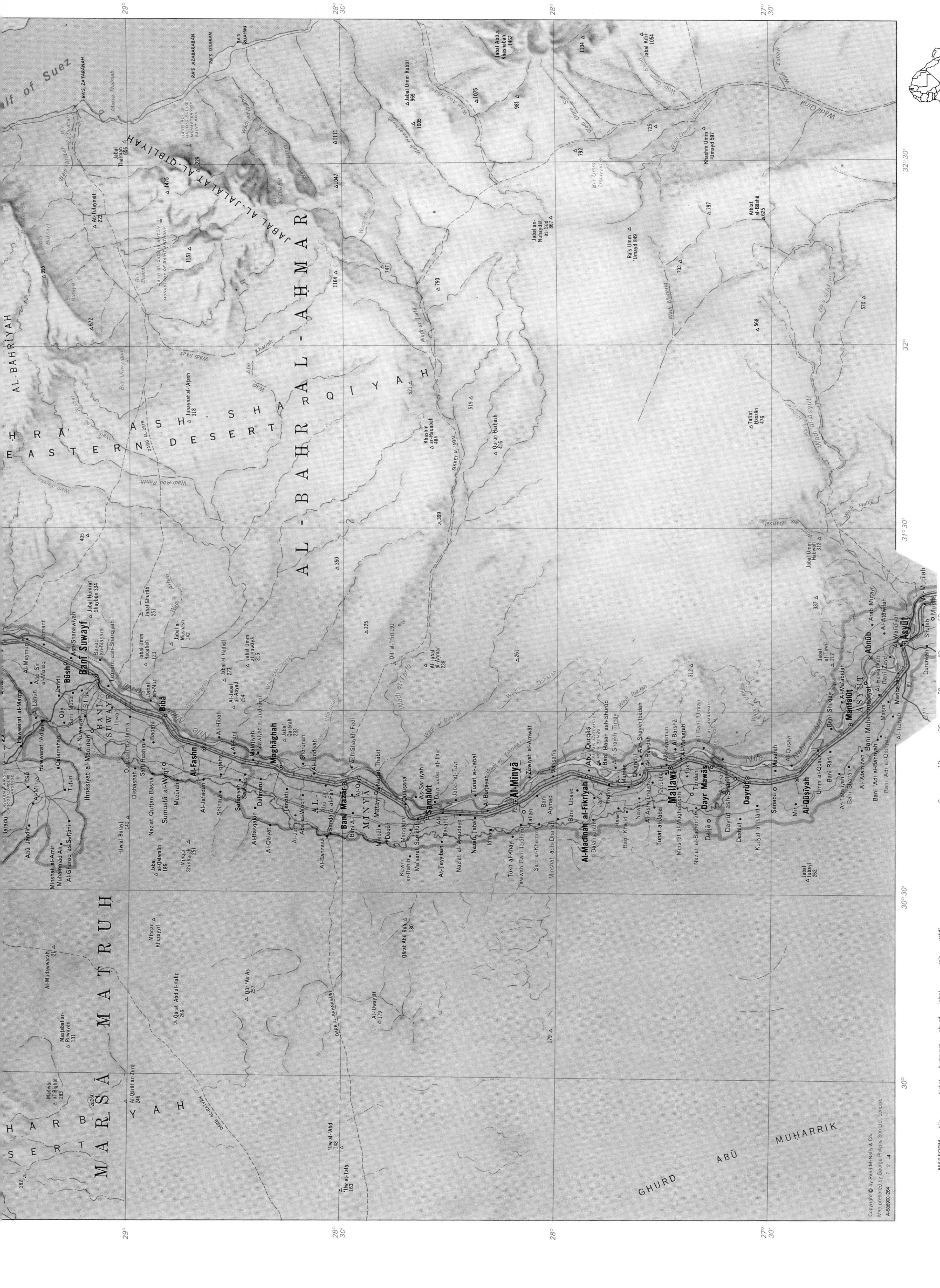
Gulf of Suez
JABAL AL-JALALAT AL-QIBLIYAH
EASTERN DESERT
ASH-SHARQIYAH
AL-BAHR AL-AHMAR
MARSĀ MATRŪH
AL-BAHRĪYAH
GHURD ABŪ MUHARRIK
Banī Suwayf
Al-Fashn
Maghāghah
Banī Mazār
Samālūt
Al-Minyā
Mallawī
Dayr Mawās
Dayrūt
Al-Qūsīyah
Manfalūt
Asyūt
Nile
Kilometers
Statute Miles
Km.
Mi.

Scale 1:1,000,000

One centimeter represents 10 kilometers.
One inch represents approximately 16 miles.
Lambert Conformal Conic Projection

MAP FORM	bi'r	birkat	buhayrat	ghurd	jabal	ra's	wādī
ENGLISH	well	lake	lake	dunes	mountain	cape	wadi
DEUTSCH	Brunnen	See	See	Dünen	Berg	Kap	Wadi
ESPAÑOL	pozo	lago	lago	dunas	montaña	cabo	uadi
FRANÇAIS	puits	lac	lac	dunes	montagne	cap	wadi
PORTUGUÊS	poço	lago	lago	dunas	montanha	cabo	uadi

For complete glossary see page I·1.
For Al-Qāhirah (Cairo) metropolitan map, see page 263.

118 - 119

130 - 131

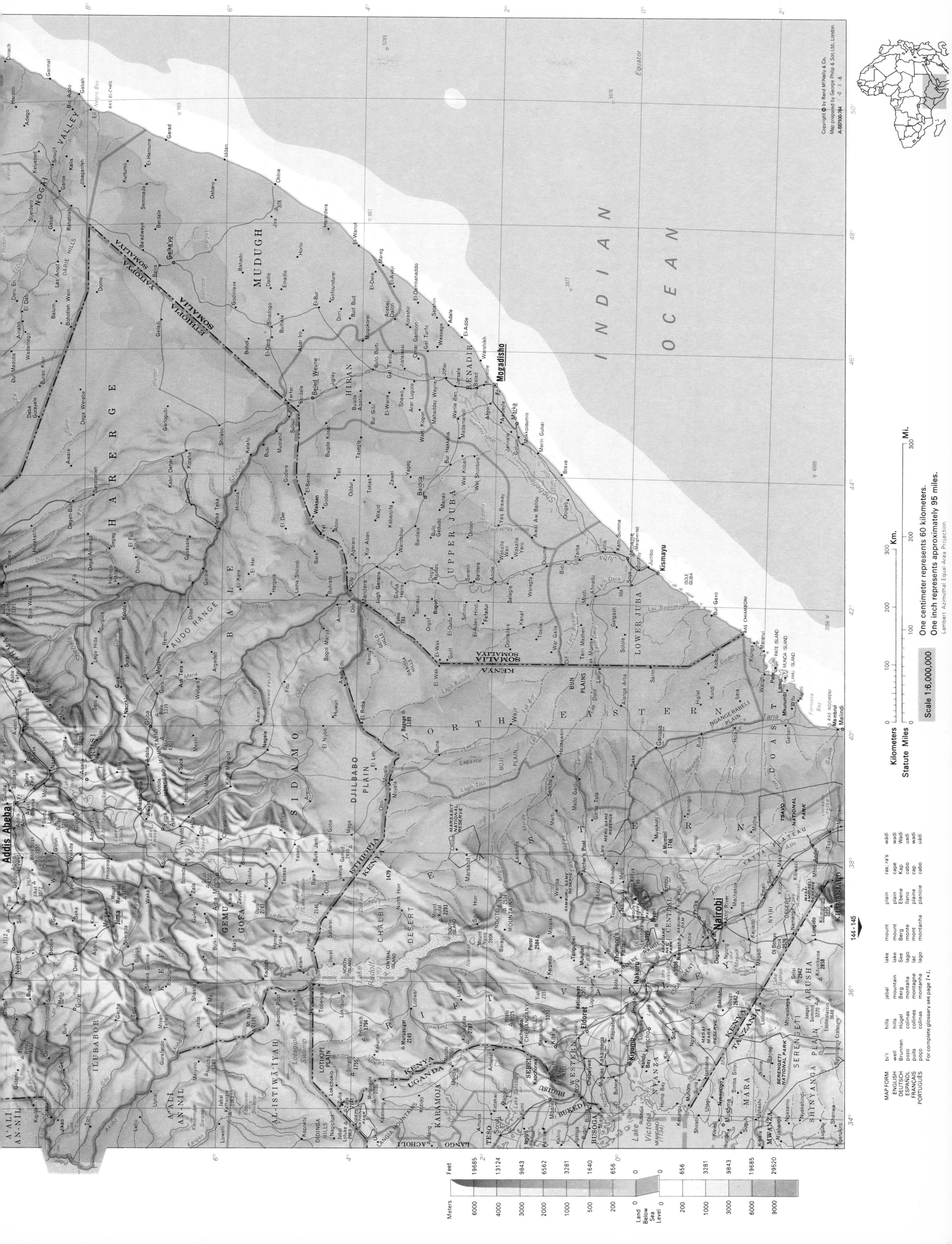
INDIAN OCEAN
Addis Abeba
Mogadisho
Nairobi
Kismayu
Equator
ETHIOPIA
SOMALIA
KENYA
UGANDA
TANZANIA
HARERGE
MUDUGH
BALE
SIDAMO
GEMU GOFA
KEFA
ILUBABOR
HIRAN
BENADIR
UPPER JUBA
LOWER JUBA
NORTH EASTERN
COAST
RIFT VALLEY
CHALBI DESERT
DJILBABO PLAIN
Lake Rudolf
Lake Victoria
144-145
Scale 1:6,000,000
One centimeter represents 60 kilometers.
One inch represents approximately 95 miles.
Lambert Azimuthal Equal-Area Projection
Kilometers
Statute Miles
Copyright © by Rand McNally & Co.
Map prepared by George Philip & Son Ltd. London
MAP FORM / ENGLISH / DEUTSCH / ESPAÑOL / FRANÇAIS / PORTUGUÊS
bi'r / well / Brunnen / pozo / puits / poço
hills / hills / Hügel / colinas / collines / colinas
jabal / mountain / Berg / montaña / montagne / montanha
lake / lake / See / lago / lac / lago
mount / mount / Berg / monte / mont / montanha
plain / plain / Ebene / llano / plaine / planicie
ras; ra's / cape / Kap / cabo / cap / cabo
wādī / wadi / Wadi / uadi / oued / uádi
For complete glossary see page I·1.
Feet
Meters
Land Below Sea Level

MEDITERRANEAN SEA
Khalīj Surt
Gulf of Sidra
Ṭarābulus
Tripoli
Banghāzī
Ajdābiyah
Darnah
Ṭubruq
Tobruk
Miṣrātah
Surt
Sabhah
Ghudāmis
Ghāt
Al-Jawf
Al-Jaghbūb
As-Sallūm
Siwah
Marsa Maṭrūḥ
EGYPT MIṢR
LIBYA LĪBIYĀ
SUDAN
TUNISIE
ALGERIA ALGÉRIE
NIGER
CHAD TCHAD
AṢ-ṢAḤRĀ' AL-LĪBĪYAH
LIBYAN DESERT
AṢ-ṢAḤRĀ' AL-GHARBĪYAH
AṢ-ṢAḤRĀ' AL-JANŪBĪYAH
BARQAH
CYRENAICA
ṬARĀBULUS
TRIPOLITANIA
FEZZAN
FAZZĀN
AL-JABAL AL-AKHḌAR
AL-HARŪJ AL-ASWAD
AL-ḤAMMĀDAH AL-ḤAMRĀ'
JABAL NAFŪSAH
SARĪR CALANSCIO
SARĪR TIBASTI
JABAL BŪ SUNBUL
SARĪR NERASTRO
REBIANA SAND SEA
AWBĀRĪ
MARZŪQ
IDEHAN MARZŪQ
TASSILI N'AJJER
TÉNÉRÉ DU TAFASSASSET
PLATEAU DU DJADO
PLATEAU DE MANGUENI
GRAND ERG ORIENTAL
TAMANRASSET
OUARGLA
GABÈS
MÉDENINE
Tropic of Cancer
Passe de Korizo

138 - 139

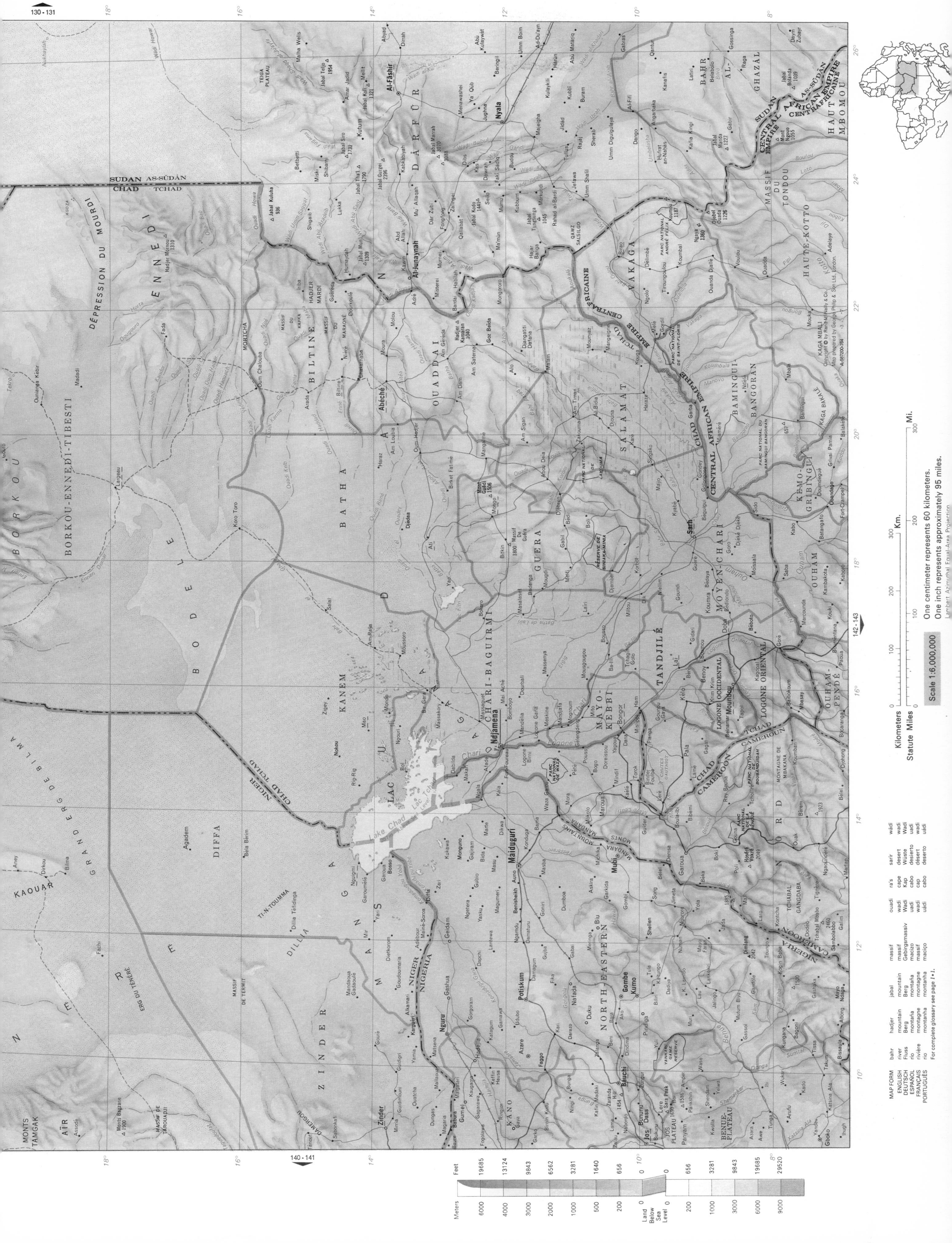
130-131
140-141
142-143
SUDAN
AS-SŪDĀN
CHAD
TCHAD
NIGER
NIGERIA
CAMEROUN
CENTRAL AFRICAN EMPIRE
EMPIRE CENTRAFRICAIN
BORKOU-ENNEDI-TIBESTI
ENNEDI
BORKOU
BODELE
BATHA
OUADDAI
BILTINE
KANEM
LAC
CHARI-BAGUIRMI
GUERA
SALAMAT
MAYO-KEBBI
TANDJILÉ
MOYEN-CHARI
LOGONE OCCIDENTAL
LOGONE ORIENTAL
DĀRFŪR
NORTH EASTERN
DIFFA
ZINDER
KANO
NORD
Lake Chad
Ndjamena
Abéché
Sarh
Moundou
Maiduguri
Nyala
Al-Fāshir
Al-Junaynah
Zinder
Kilometers
Statute Miles
Km.
Mi.
Scale 1:6,000,000
One centimeter represents 60 kilometers.
One inch represents approximately 95 miles.
Lambert Azimuthal Equal-Area Projection
Feet
Meters
Land Below Sea Level
MAP FORM | bahr | hadjer | jabal | massif | ouadi | ra's | sarir | wādi
ENGLISH | river | mountain | mountain | massif | wadi | cape | desert | wadi
DEUTSCH | Fluss | Berg | Berg | Gebirgsmassiv | Wadi | Kap | Wüste | Wadi
ESPAÑOL | río | montaña | montaña | macizo | uadi | cabo | desierto | uadi
FRANÇAIS | rivière | montagne | montagne | massif | wadi | cap | désert | wadi
PORTUGUÊS | rio | montanha | montanha | maciço | uádi | cabo | deserto | uádi
For complete glossary see page I • 1.
Copyright © by Rand McNally & Co.
Map prepared by George Philip & Son Ltd, London.

Northwestern Africa / Nordwestafrika / África Nor-occidental
Afrique du Nord-Ouest / África Norte-occidental

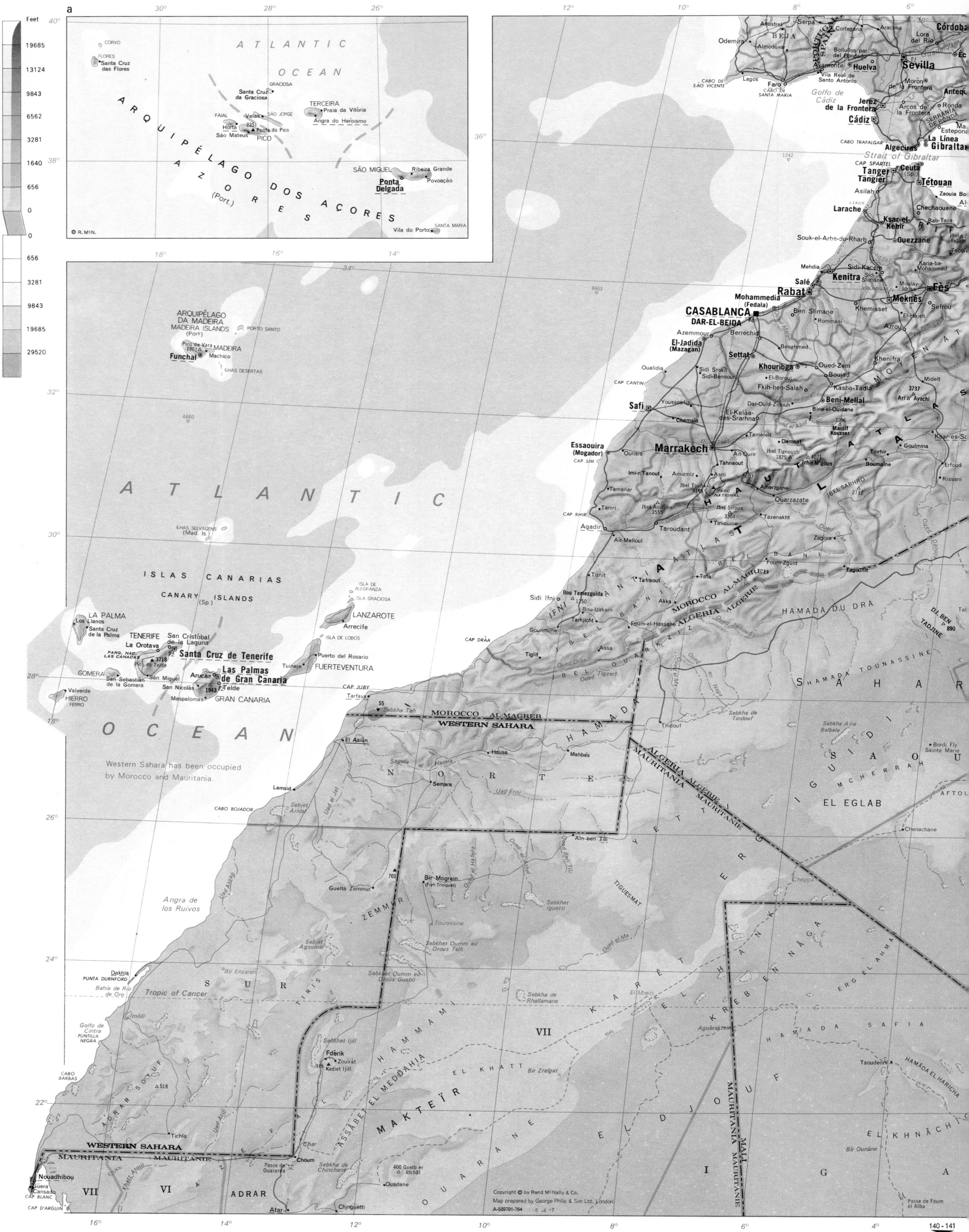

MAP FORM	cap	chott	djebel	erg	hamada	jbel	oued	sebkha
ENGLISH	cape	intermittent lake	mountain	sand desert	desert	mountain	wadi	salt flat
DEUTSCH	Kap	periodischer See	Berg	Sandwüste	Wüste	Berg	Wadi	Salzebene
ESPAÑOL	cabo	lago intermitente	montaña	desierto arenoso	desierto	montaña	uadi	salar
FRANÇAIS	cap	lac périodique	montagne	désert de sable	désert	montagne	wadi	saline
PORTUGUÊS	cabo	lago intermitente	montanha	deserto arenoso	deserto	montanha	uádi	salina

For complete glossary see page *I•1*.

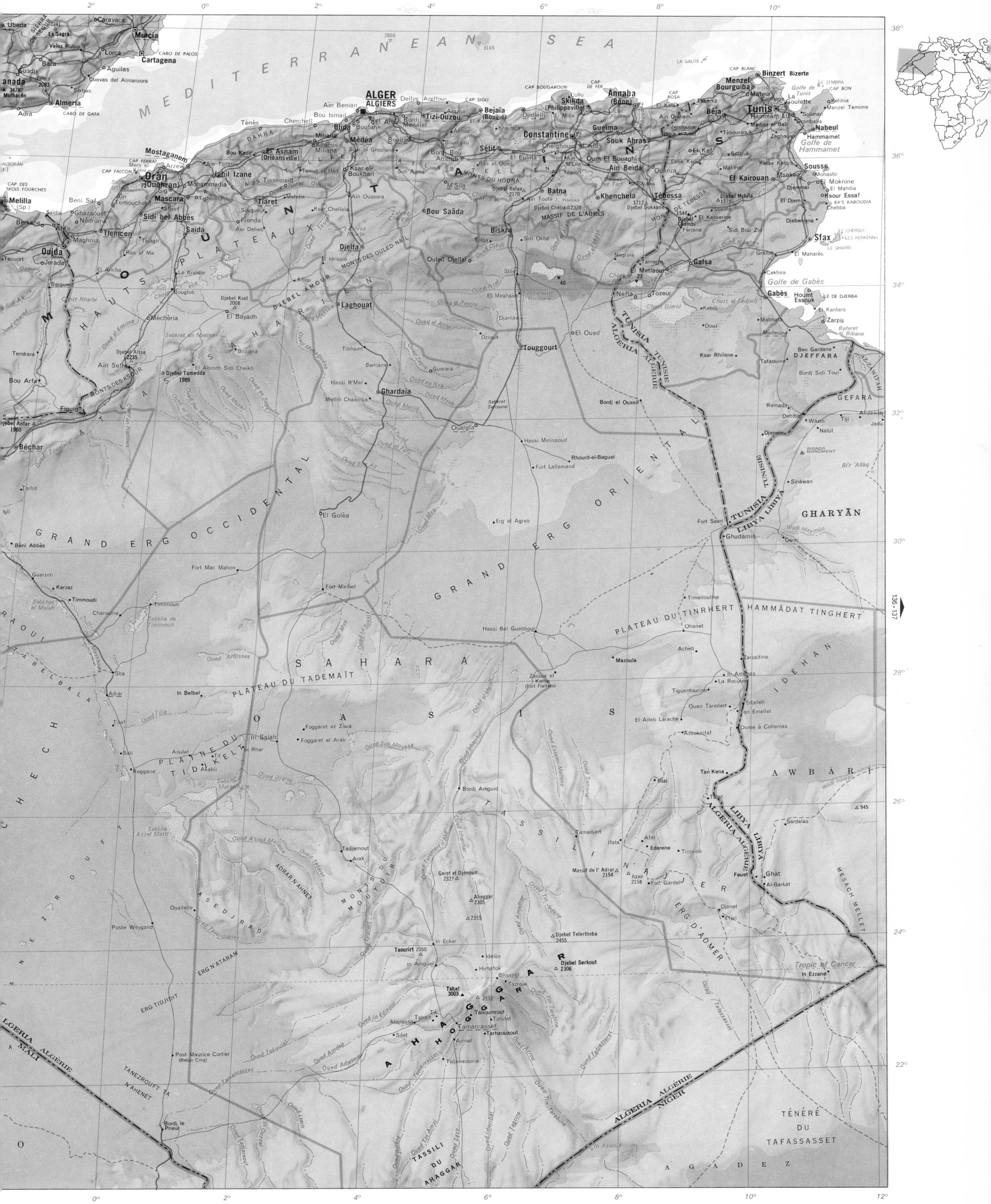
MEDITERRANEAN SEA
ALGER
ALGIERS
Oran
(Ouahran)
Constantine
Annaba
(Bône)
Tunis
Bizerte
Sousse
Sfax
Gabès
Melilla
Oujda
Tlemcen
Sidi bel Abbès
Mostaganem
Blida
Médéa
Sétif
Batna
Biskra
Djelfa
Laghouat
Ghardaïa
Ouargla
Touggourt
El Goléa
Tamanrasset
Murcia
Cartagena
Almería
HAUTS PLATEAUX
ATLAS SAHARIEN
GRAND ERG OCCIDENTAL
GRAND ERG ORIENTAL
PLATEAU DU TADEMAÏT
PLATEAU DU TINRHERT
SAHARA
OASIS
AHAGGAR
TASSILI N'AJJER
TÉNÉRÉ DU TAFASSASSET
GHARYĀN
AWBĀRĪ
TUNISIA
ALGERIA
LIBYA
ALGERIA ALGÉRIE
MALI
NIGER
Tropic of Cancer
136-137

Kilometers 0 100 200 300 Km.

Statute Miles 0 100 200 300 Mi.

Scale 1:6,000,000

One centimeter represents 60 kilometers.

One inch represents approximately 95 miles.

Lambert Azimuthal Equal-Area Projection

MAP FORM	coast	dhar	game reserve	ilha	lac	monts	mountains	vallée
ENGLISH	coast	escarpment	game reserve	island	lake	mountains	mountains	valley
DEUTSCH	Küste	Landstufe	Wildpark	Insel	See	Berge	Berge	Tal
ESPAÑOL	costa	escarpa	vedado de caza	isla	lago	montes	montañas	valle
FRANÇAIS	côte	escarpement	réserve à gibier	île	lac	monts	montagnes	vallée
PORTUGUÊS	costa	escarpa	reserva de caça	ilha	lago	montes	montanhas	vale

For complete glossary see page *1·1*.
For Lagos metropolitan map, see page 263.

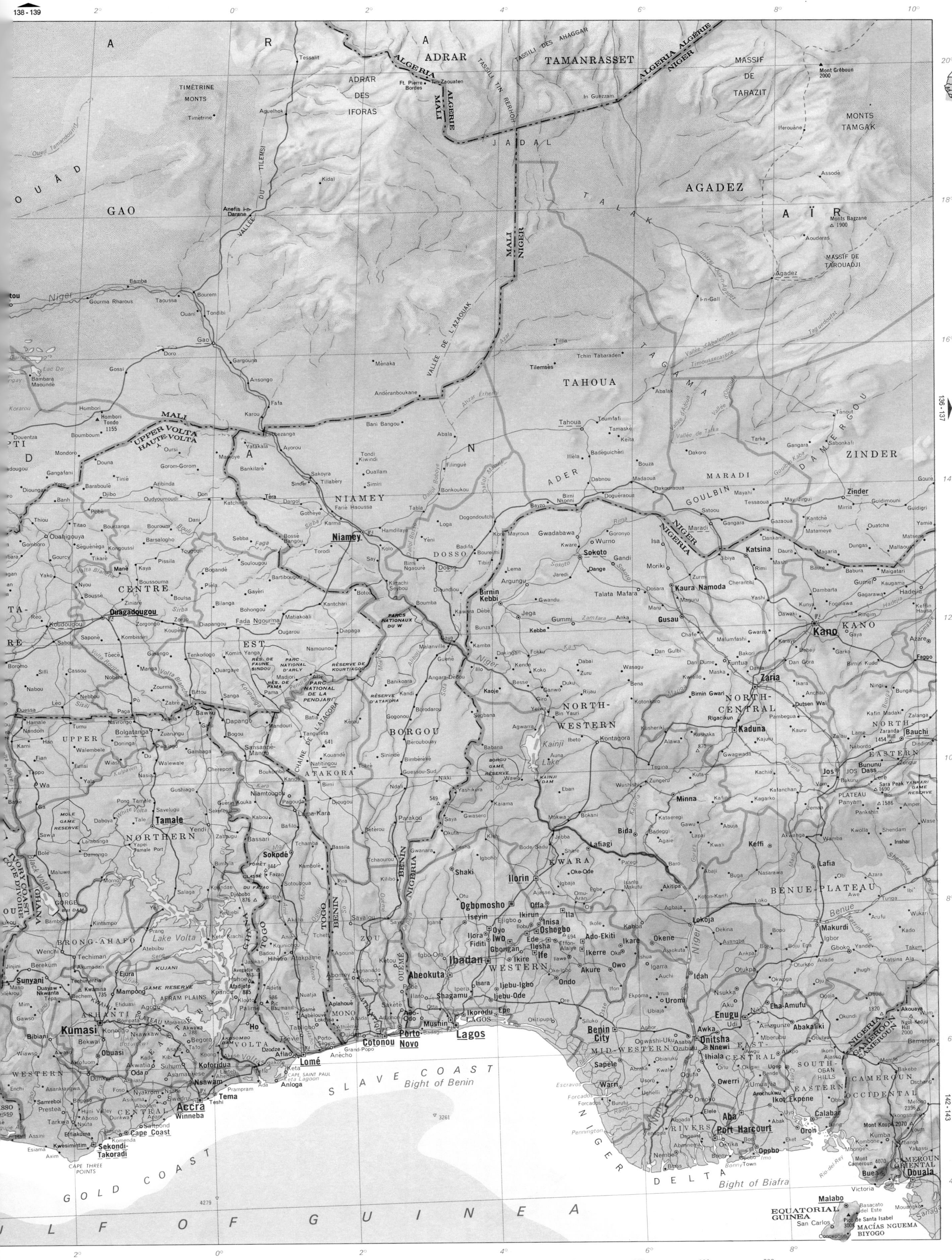

Kilometers 0 100 200 300 Km.

Statute Miles 0 100 200 300 Mi.

Scale 1:6,000,000

One centimeter represents 60 kilometers.

One inch represents approximately 95 miles.

Lambert Azimuthal Equal-Area Projection

Western Congo Basin / Westliches Kongobecken / Cuenca Occidental del Congo
Bassin du Congo, partie Occidentale / Bacia Ocidental do Congo

136 - 137

140 - 141

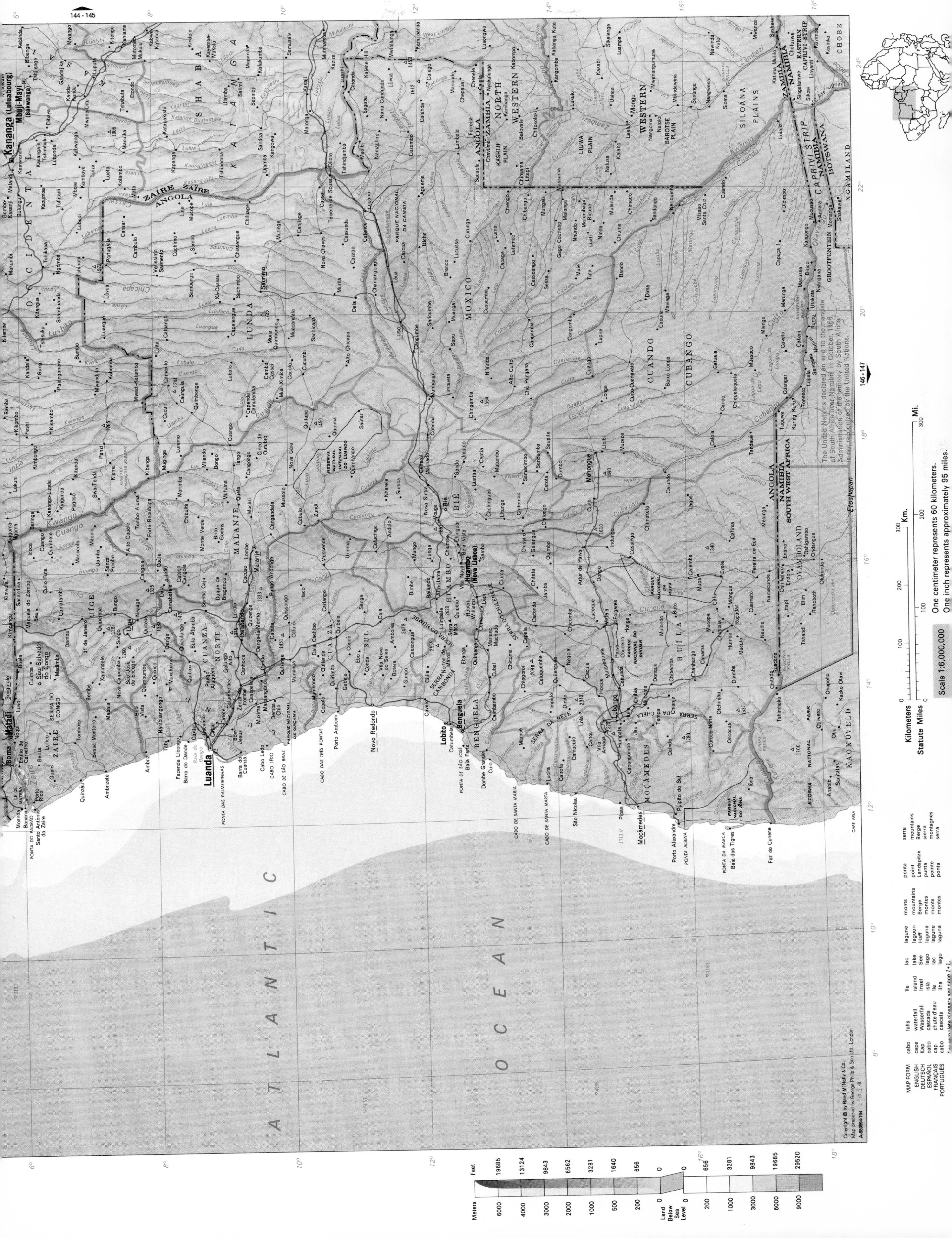
144 - 145
146 - 147
ATLANTIC
OCEAN
ANGOLA
ZAIRE
ZAMBIA
NAMIBIA
SOUTH WEST AFRICA
BOTSWANA
Luanda
Lobito
Benguela
Moçâmedes
Huambo (Nova Lisboa)
Malanje
Kananga (Luluabourg)
Mbuji-Mayi (Bakwanga)
Matadi
The United Nations declared an end to the mandate of South Africa over Namibia in October, 1966. Administration of the territory by South Africa is not recognized by the United Nations.
Scale 1:6,000,000
One centimeter represents 60 kilometers.
One inch represents approximately 95 miles.
Kilometers
Statute Miles
MAP FORM / ENGLISH / DEUTSCH / ESPAÑOL / FRANÇAIS / PORTUGUÊS
cabo / cape / Kap / cabo / cap / cabo
falls / waterfall / Wasserfall / cascada / chute d'eau / cascata
ile / island / Insel / isla / île / ilha
lac / lake / See / lago / lac / lago
lagune / lagoon / Haff / laguna / lagune / laguna
monts / mountains / Berge / montes / montes / montes
ponta / point / Landspitze / punta / pointe / ponta
serra / mountains / Berge / sierra / montagnes / serra
Copyright © by Rand McNally & Co.
Map prepared by George Philip & Son Ltd. London.
Meters
Feet
Land Below Sea Level

East Africa and Eastern Congo Basin / Ostafrika und Östliches Kongobecken / África Oriental y Cuenca Oriental del Congo
Afrique Orientale et Bassin du Congo, partie Orientale / África Oriental e Bacia Oriental do Congo

134 - 135

130-131

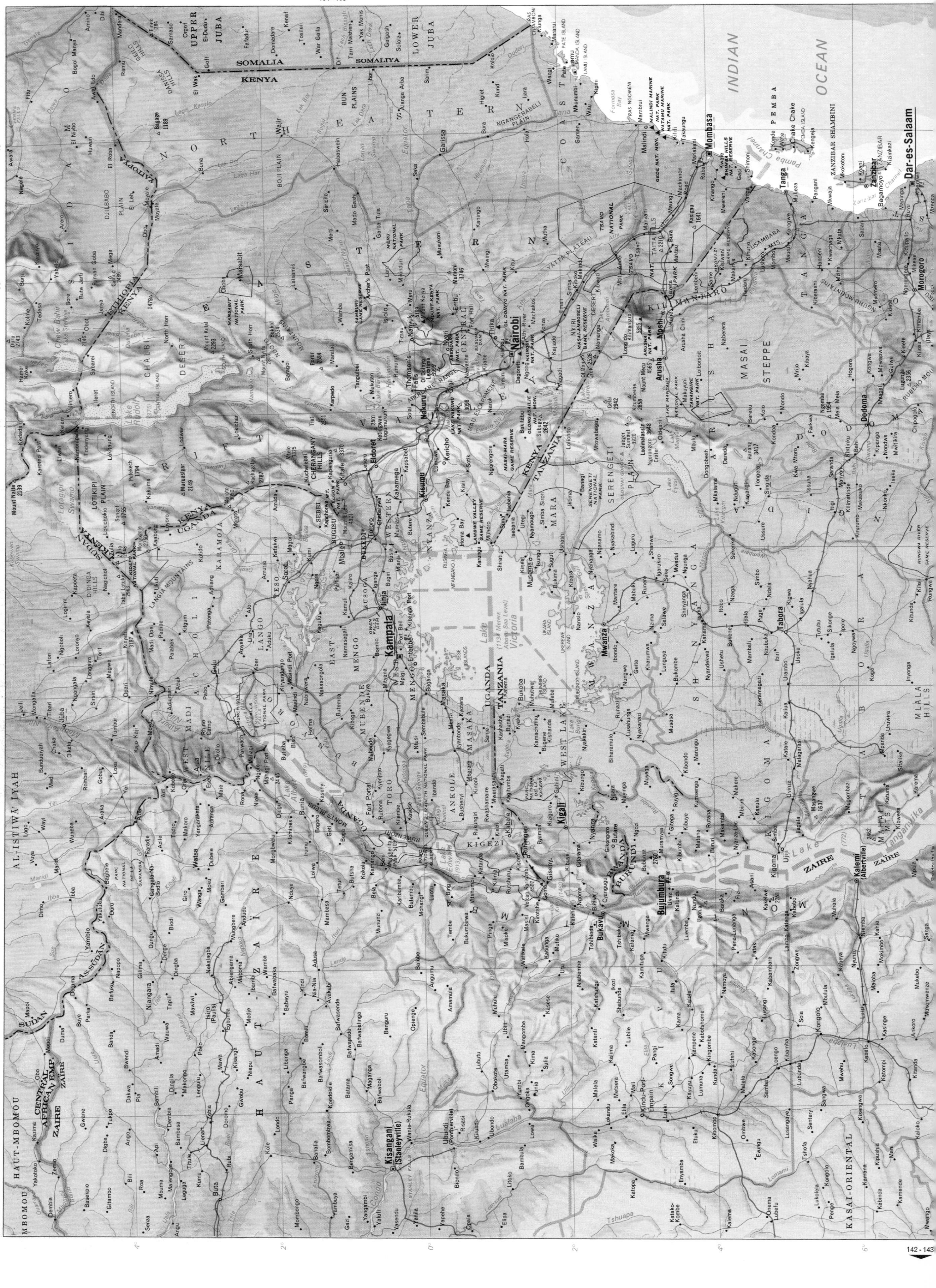

142 - 143

Kilometers 0 100 200 300 Km.

Statute Miles 0 100 200 300 Mi.

Scale 1:6,000,000

One centimeter represents 60 kilometers.
One inch represents approximately 95 miles.

Lambert Azimuthal Equal-Area Projection

ENGLISH	DEUTSCH	ESPAÑOL	FRANÇAIS	PORTUGUÊS
falls	Wasserfall	cascada	chute d'eau	cascata
game reserve	Wildreservat	vedado de caza	réserve à gibier	reserva de caça
island	Insel	isla	île	ilha
lake	See	lago	lac	lago
mountains	Berge	montañas	montagnes	montanhas
national park	Nationalpark	parque nacional	parc national	parque nacional
plain	Ebene	llano	plaine	planície
swamp	Sumpf	pantano	marais	pântano

For complete glossary see page I•I.

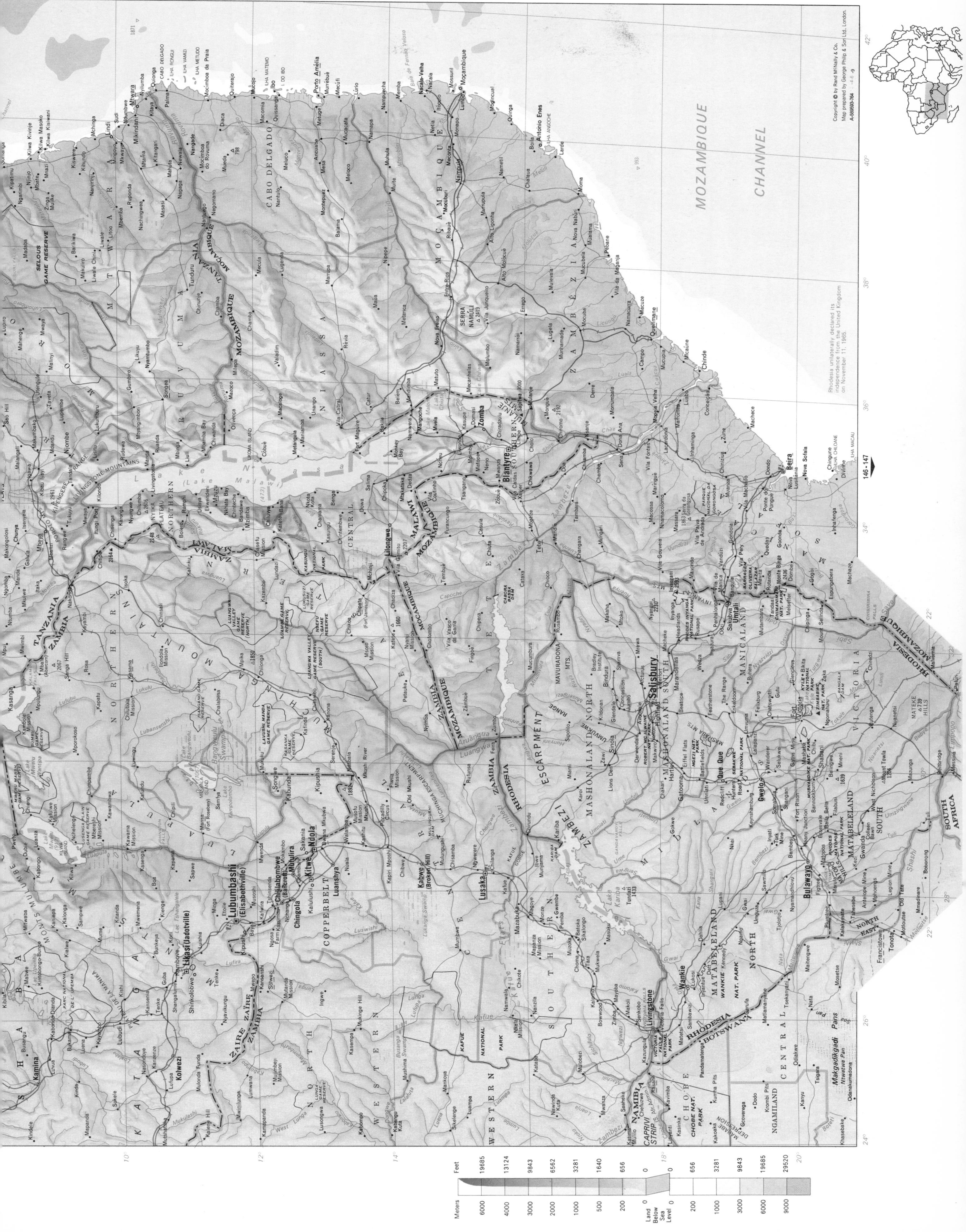
MOZAMBIQUE CHANNEL
TANZANIA
ZAMBIA
MALAWI
MOÇAMBIQUE
RHODESIA
BOTSWANA
NAMIBIA
SOUTH AFRICA
ZAIRE
Lake Nyasa (Lake Malawi)
Salisbury
Lusaka
Blantyre
Zomba
Lilongwe
Bulawayo
Lubumbashi (Elisabethville)
Likasi (Jadotville)
Kolwezi
Ndola
Kitwe
Kabwe (Broken Hill)
Livingstone
Beira
Moçambique
Porto Amélia
Quelimane
Tete
Umtali
Gwelo
Que Que
Wankie
Kamina
Rhodesia unilaterally declared its independence from the United Kingdom on November 11, 1965.
Copyright © by Rand McNally & Co.
Map prepared by George Philip & Son Ltd., London.
146 - 147
Feet
19685
13124
9843
6562
3281
1640
656
0
Meters
6000
4000
3000
2000
1000
500
200
0
Land Below Sea Level
0
656
3281
9843
19685
29520
0
200
1000
3000
6000
9000

Southern Africa and Madagascar / Südafrika und Madagaskar / África Meridional y Madagascar
Afrique Méridionale et Madagascar / África Meridional e Madagascar

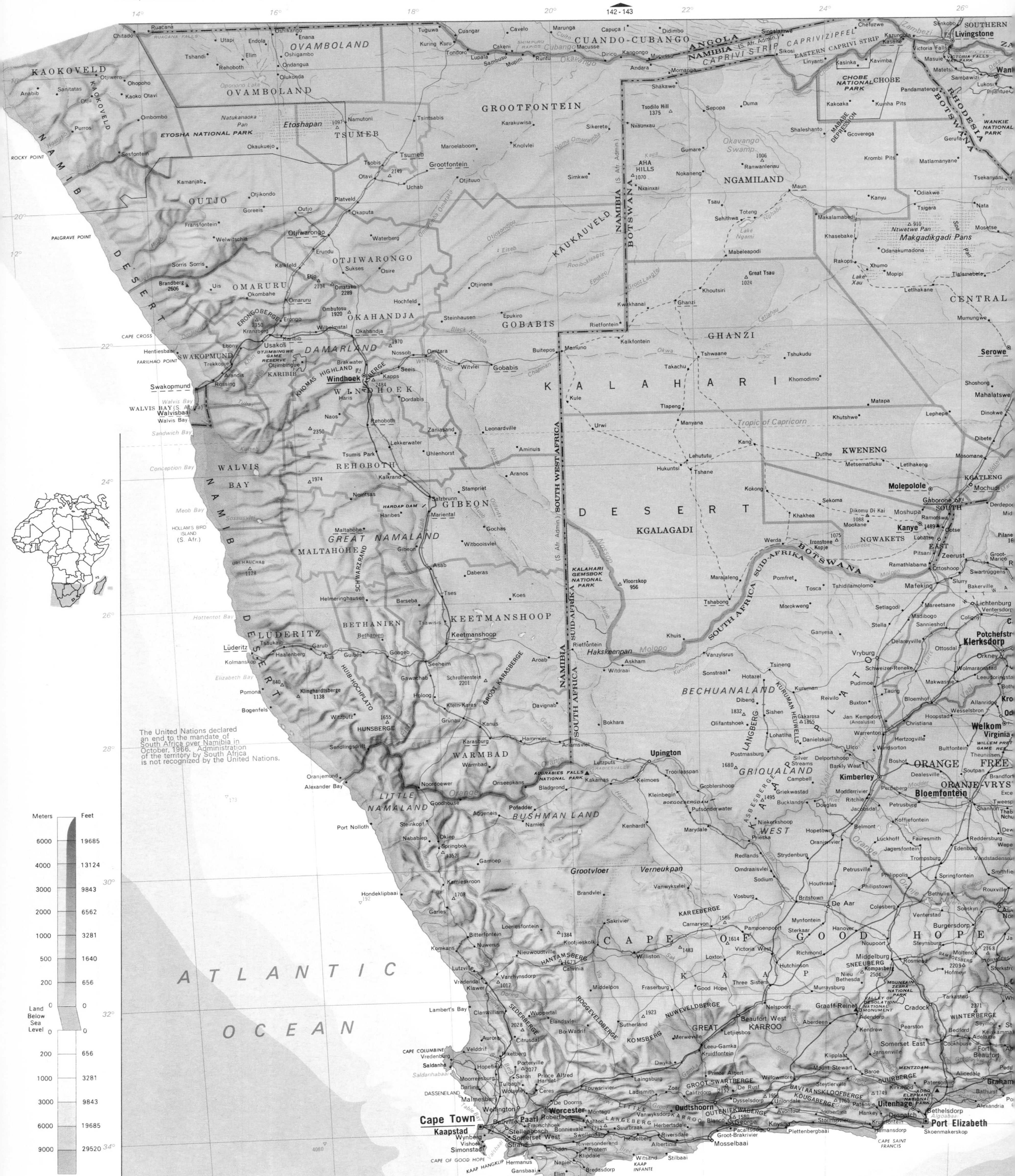

MAP FORM	bay	berg, berge	cape	game reserve	ilha	lake	national park
ENGLISH	bay	mountain, mountains	cape	game reserve	island	lake	national park
DEUTSCH	Bucht	Berg, Berge	Kap	Wildpark	Insel	See	Nationalpark
ESPAÑOL	bahia	montaña, montañas	cabo	vedado de caza	isla	lago	parque nacional
FRANÇAIS	baie	montagne, montagnes	cap	réserve à gibier	île	lac	parc national
PORTUGUÊS	baía	montanha, montanhas	cabo	reserva de caça	ilha	lago	parque nacional

For complete glossary see page *I•1*.

Kilometers 0 100 200 300 Km.
Statute Miles 0 100 200 300 Mi.

Scale 1:6,000,000

One centimeter represents 60 kilometers.
One inch represents approximately 95 miles.

Lambert Azimuthal Equal-Area Projection

144 - 145
a
INDIAN OCEAN
GRANDE COMORE
Moroni
COMOROS
COMORES
MOHELI
ANJOUAN
MAYOTTE (Fr.)
Dzaoudzi
MOZAMBIQUE CHANNEL
b
MOZAMBIQUE CHANNEL
MADAGASCAR
MADAGASIKARA
Antananarivo
Diégo-Suarez
Majunga
Tamatave
Fianarantsoa
Tuléar
Fort-Dauphin
INDIAN OCEAN
Tropic of Capricorn
c
INDIAN OCEAN
MAURITIUS
Port Louis
REUNION
Saint-Denis
MASCARENE ISLANDS
Salisbury
MASHONALAND SOUTH
MIDLANDS
MANICALAND
VICTORIA
MATABELELAND SOUTH
ZAMBEZIA
MANICA E SOFALA
Beira
INHAMBANE
GAZA
RHODESIA
MOZAMBIQUE
SOUTH AFRICA
Maputo (Lourenço Marques)
SWAZILAND
Mbabane
ZULULAND
NATAL
Pietermaritzburg
Durban
Ladysmith
Pietersburg
INDIAN OCEAN
WILD COAST
© R. McN.

South Africa / Republik Südafrika / Sudáfrica
Afrique du Sud / África do Sul

146 - 147

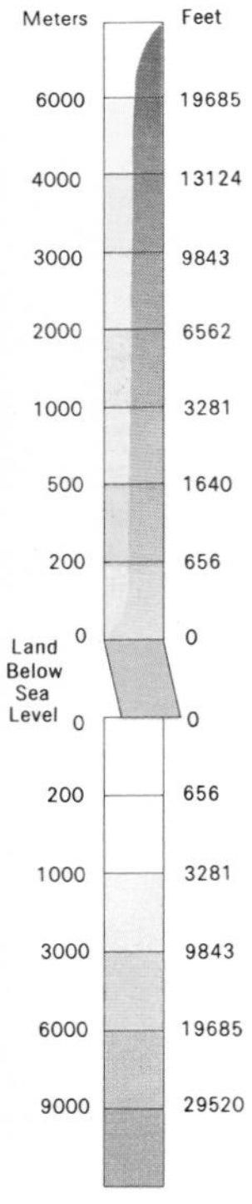

MAP FORM	bay	berge	cape	dam	game reserve	national park	pass	point
ENGLISH	bay	mountains	cape	dam	game reserve	national park	pass	point
DEUTSCH	Bucht	Berge	Kap	Damm	Wildpark	Nationalpark	Pass	Landspitze
ESPAÑOL	bahía	montañas	cabo	presa	vedado de caza	parque nacional	paso	punta
FRANÇAIS	baie	montagnes	cap	barrage	réserve à gibier	parc national	col	pointe
PORTUGUÊS	baía	montanhas	cabo	represa	reserva de caça	parque nacional	passo	ponta

For complete glossary see page *I* • *1*.
For Johannesburg metropolitan map, see page 263.

Pretoria
JOHANNESBURG
Krugersdorp
Benoni
Springs
Germiston
Vereeniging
Potchefstroom
Klerksdorp
Kroonstad
Welkom
Virginia
Bethlehem
Harrismith
Ladysmith
Newcastle
Dundee
Vryheid
Pietermaritzburg
DURBAN
Maputo
Mbabane
SWAZILAND
MOZAMBIQUE
MOÇAMBIQUE
LESOTHO
Maseru
SOUTH AFRICA
SUID AFRIKA
TRANSKEI
TEMBULAND
GRIQUALAND EAST
PONDOLAND
KAFFRARIA
ZULULAND
DRAKENSBERG
Queenstown
King William's Town
East London
Oos-Londen
Grahamstown
Port Alfred
Umtata
Port Shepstone
Aliwal North
Witbank
Standerton
Piet Retief
Stanger
Empangeni
Eshowe
WILD COAST
INDIAN
OCEAN
Copyright © by Rand McNally & Co.
Map prepared by George Philip & Son Ltd., London.

Kilometers 0 50 100 150 Km.
Statute Miles 0 50 100 150 Mi.

Scale 1:3,000,000

One centimeter represents 30 kilometers.
One inch represents approximately 47 miles.
Lambert Conformal Conic Projection

98 - 99
INDONESIA
JAWA
Yogyakarta
Surakarta
Malang
Jember
Madiun
Kediri
Magelang
Tasikmalaya
Cilacap
Blitar
Banyuwangi
BALI
Denpasar
Singaraja
LOMBOK
Mataram
Praya
Sumbawa Besar
SUMBAWA
NUSA TENGGARA
LESSER SUNDA ISLANDS
FLORES
Waingapu
Waikabubak
SUMBA
Baing
Laut Sawu
Savu Sea
PULAU SAWU
PULAU SEMAU
PULAU ROTI
Kupang
TIMOR
Soe
Timor Sea
HIBERNIA REEF
ASHMORE ISLANDS
CARTIER ISLAND (Austl.)
BROWSE ISLAND
SCOTT REEF
CAPE LONDONDERRY
Joseph Bonaparte Gulf
BONAPARTE ARCHIPELAGO
York Sound
Admiralty Gulf
BEAGLE REEF
ADÈLE ISLAND
BUCCANEER ARCHIPELAGO
Collier Bay
CAPE LEVEQUE
Yampi Sound
King Sound
KIMBERLEY PLATEAU
KING LEOPOLD RANGES
936
Mount Ord
DURACK RANGE
Derby
Broome
Fitzroy Crossing
Halls Creek
Gordon Downs
Wyndham
Kununurra
Lake Argyle
Victoria River Downs
Wave Hill
MELVILLE ISLAND
BATHURST ISLAND
CAPE CROKER
COBOURG PENINSULA
Van Diemen Gulf
Beagle Gulf
Clarence Strait
Darwin
POINT BLAZE
Rum Jungle
Pine Creek
ROWLEY SHOALS
INDIAN OCEAN
CAPE LATOUCHE TREVILLE
La Grange
EIGHTY MILE BEACH
TANAMI DESERT
Gregory Lake
NORTHERN TERRITORY
Port Hedland
Shay Gap
GREAT SANDY DESERT
MONTEBELLO ISLANDS
DAMPIER ARCHIPELAGO
Dampier
Roebourne
Marble Bar
BARROW ISLAND
Nullagine
MUIRON ISLANDS
NORTH WEST CAPE
Onslow
Pannawonica
HAMERSLEY RANGE
Wittenoom
Mount Brockman 1129
1235 Mount Bruce
Tom Price
Paraburdoo
Newman
Exmouth Gulf
POINT CLOATES
Lake Dora
Lake Auld (Dry)
Lake Disappointment (Dry Salt Lake)
Lake Wills
Lake Mackay (Dry Salt Lake)
Lake White (Dry)
Lake Macdonald (Dry)
Mount Leisler 901
Lake Neale
Lake Amadeus (Dry)
WESTERN AUSTRALIA
GIBSON DESERT
Mount Olga 1069
Ayers Rock 867
Mount Aloysius 1085
1439
Tropic of Capricorn
CAPE CUVIER
Lake Macleod
1105 Mount Augustus
906 Mount Essendon
Geographe Channel
Carnarvon
BERNIER ISLAND
DORRE ISLAND
Naturaliste Channel
Shark Bay
DIRK HARTOG ISLAND
STEEP POINT
Wooramel
ROBINSON RANGES
Peak Hill
Lake Carnegie (Dry)
Lake Gillen (Dry)
Lake Wells (Dry)
Wiluna
Meekatharra
Nannine
Cue
Lake Austin (Dry)
Sandstone
Boogardie
Mount Magnet
Agnew
Mount Redcliffe 576
Laverton
Yeo Lake (Dry)
GREAT VICTORIA DESERT
Lake Maurice (Dry)
Maralinga
Malcolm
Leonora
Lake Raeside (Dry)
Lake Carey (Dry Salt Lake)
Lake Ballard
Lake Minigwal (Dry)
Northampton
Mullewa
Yalgoo
HOUTMAN ABROLHOS
Geraldton
Dongara
Mongers Lake (Dry)
Lake Barlee (Dry Salt Lake)
Three Springs
Lake Moore (Dry)
Menzies
Kalgoorlie
Coolgardie
Boulder
Kanowna
Zanthus
Rawlinna
Haig
Forrest
Deakin
NULLARBOR PLAIN
Eucla
GREEN HEAD
Dalwallinu
Bonnie Rock
Bencubbin
Bullfinch
Southern Cross
Lake Lefroy (Dry)
Lake Cowan (Dry Salt Lake)
Norseman
Lake Dundas (Dry)
Eyre
CAPE ADIEU
Moora
Mochea
Stirling
Perth
Fremantle
Pinjarra
DARLING RANGE
Northam
Kellerberrin
Merredin
York
Beverley
Brookton
Hyden
Lake Johnston (Dry)
POINT CULVER
Great Australian Bight
Narrogin
Newdegate
Wagin
Ravensthorpe
Hopetoun
Esperance
CAPE ARID
Bunbury
Collie
Nyabing
Katanning
Gnowangerup
Geographe Bay
CAPE NATURALISTE
Busselton
Bridgetown
Manjimup
Bluff Knoll 1096
Mount Barker
Albany
HOOD POINT
CAPE KNOB
ARCHIPELAGO OF THE RECHERCHE
Esperance Bay
Augusta
CAPE LEEUWIN
Pemberton
Denmark
CAPE VANCOUVER
King George Sound
POINT D'ENTRECASTEAUX
WEST CAPE HOWE
INDIAN OCEAN
110° 115° 120° 125° 130°
10° 15° 20° 25° 30° 35° 40°
105° 110° 115° 120° 125° 130°
Copyright © by Rand McNally & Co.
Map prepared by Esselte Map Service AB, Stockholm.
A-590200-264

ENGLISH	bay	cape	island	lake	mount	point	range	reef
DEUTSCH	Bucht	Kap	Insel	See	Berg	Landspitze	Gebirge	Riff
ESPAÑOL	bahía	cabo	isla	lago	montaña	punta	cordillera	arrecife
FRANÇAIS	baie	cap	île	lac	mont	pointe	chaîne	récif
PORTUGUÊS	baía	cabo	ilha	lago	montanha	ponta	cordilheira	recife

For complete glossary see page *I* • *1*.

Kilometers 0 200 400 600 Km.

Statute Miles 0 200 400 600 Mi.

Scale 1:12,000,000

One centimeter represents 120 kilometers.
One inch represents approximately 190 miles.
Lambert Conformal Conic Projection

Western and Central Australia / West- und Mittelaustralien / Australia Centro-occidental
Australie Occidentale et Centrale / Austrália Centro-ocidental

ENGLISH	bay	cape	creek, cr.	island, i.	lake, l.	mount	point	range
DEUTSCH	Bucht	Kap	Bach	Insel	See	Berg	Landspitze	Gebirge
ESPAÑOL	bahía	cabo	riachuelo	isla	lago	montaña	punta	cordillera
FRANÇAIS	baie	cap	crique	île	lac	mont	pointe	chaîne
PORTUGUÊS	baía	cabo	riacho	ilha	lago	montanha	ponta	cordilheira

For complete glossary see page *I* • *1*.

Kilometers 0 100 200 300 Km.
Statute Miles 0 100 200 300 Mi.

Scale 1:6,000,000

One centimeter represents 60 kilometers.
One inch represents approximately 95 miles.
Lambert Conformal Conic Projection

MAP FORM	bay	cape	island	kepulauan	mount	pulau	range	tanjung
ENGLISH	bay	cape	island	islands	mount	island	range	cape
DEUTSCH	Bucht	Kap	Insel	Inseln	Berg	Insel	Gebirge	Kap
ESPAÑOL	bahía	cabo	isla	islas	montaña	isla	cordillera	cabo
FRANÇAIS	baie	cap	île	îles	mont	île	chaîne	cap
PORTUGUÊS	baía	cabo	ilha	ilhas	montanha	ilha	cordilheira	cabo

For complete glossary see page *I•1*.

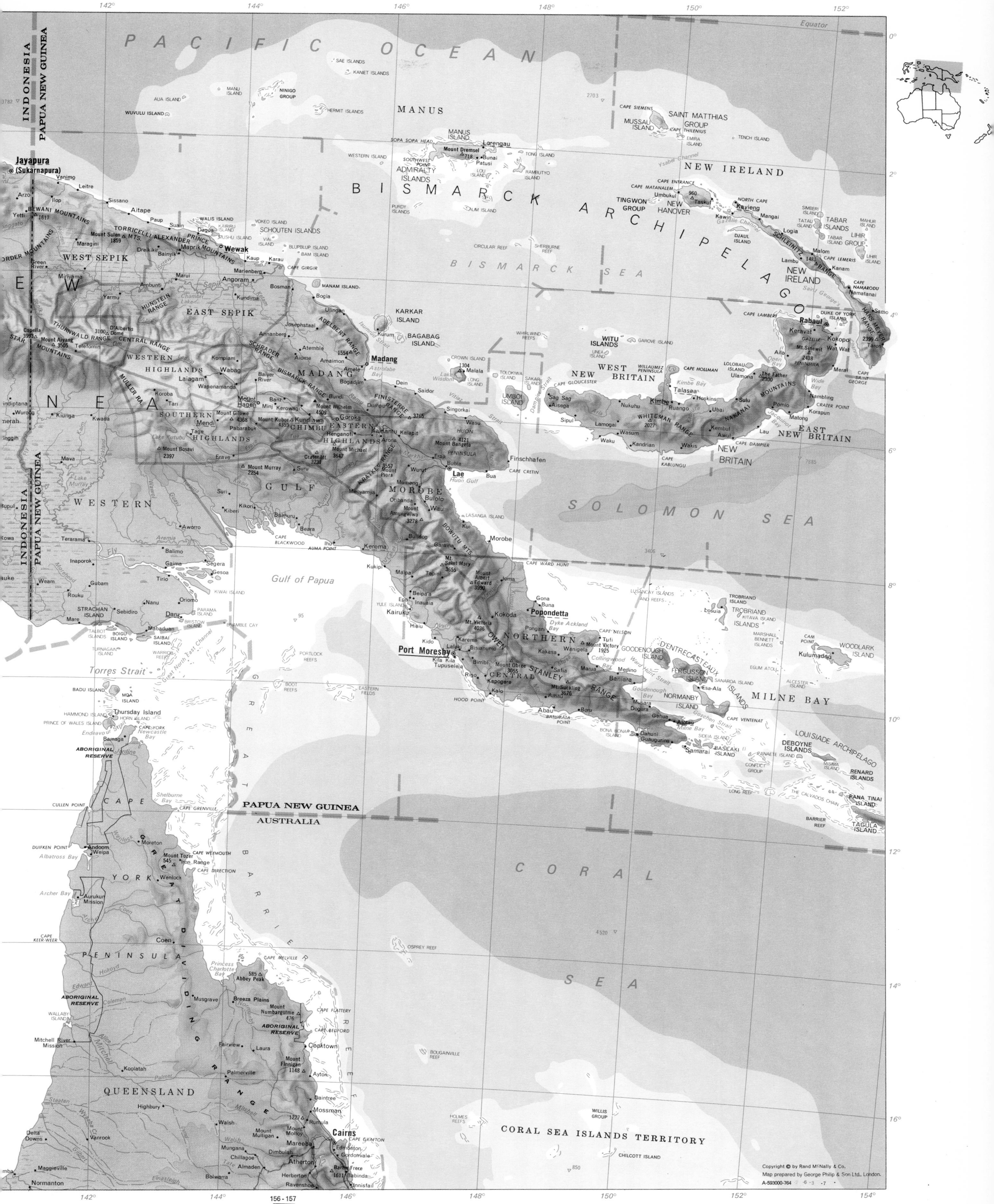

Kilometers 0 100 200 300 Km.
Statute Miles 0 100 200 300 Mi.

Scale 1:6,000,000
One centimeter represents 60 kilometers.
One inch represents approximately 95 miles.
Lambert Conformal Conic Projection

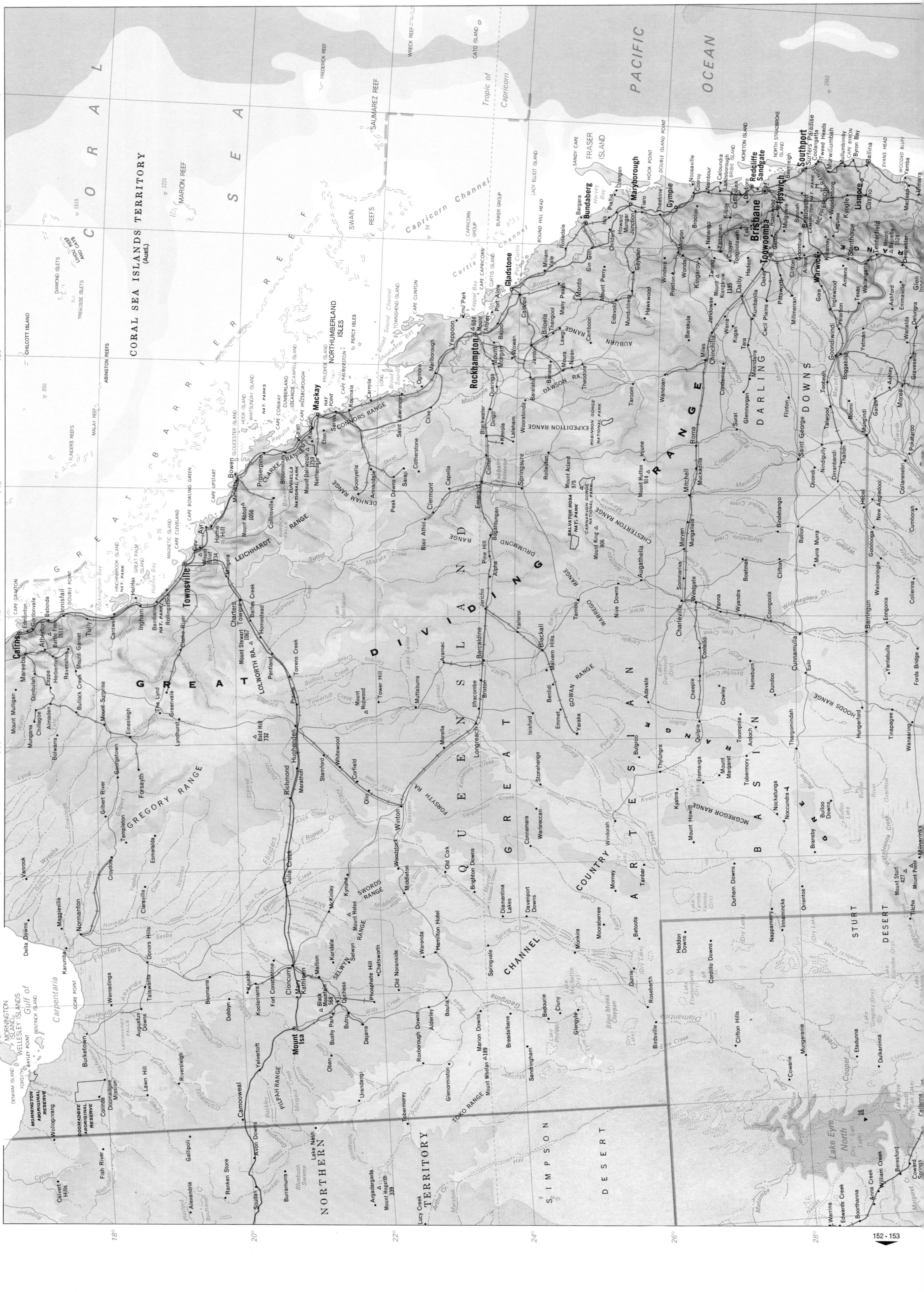

154 · 155
152 · 153

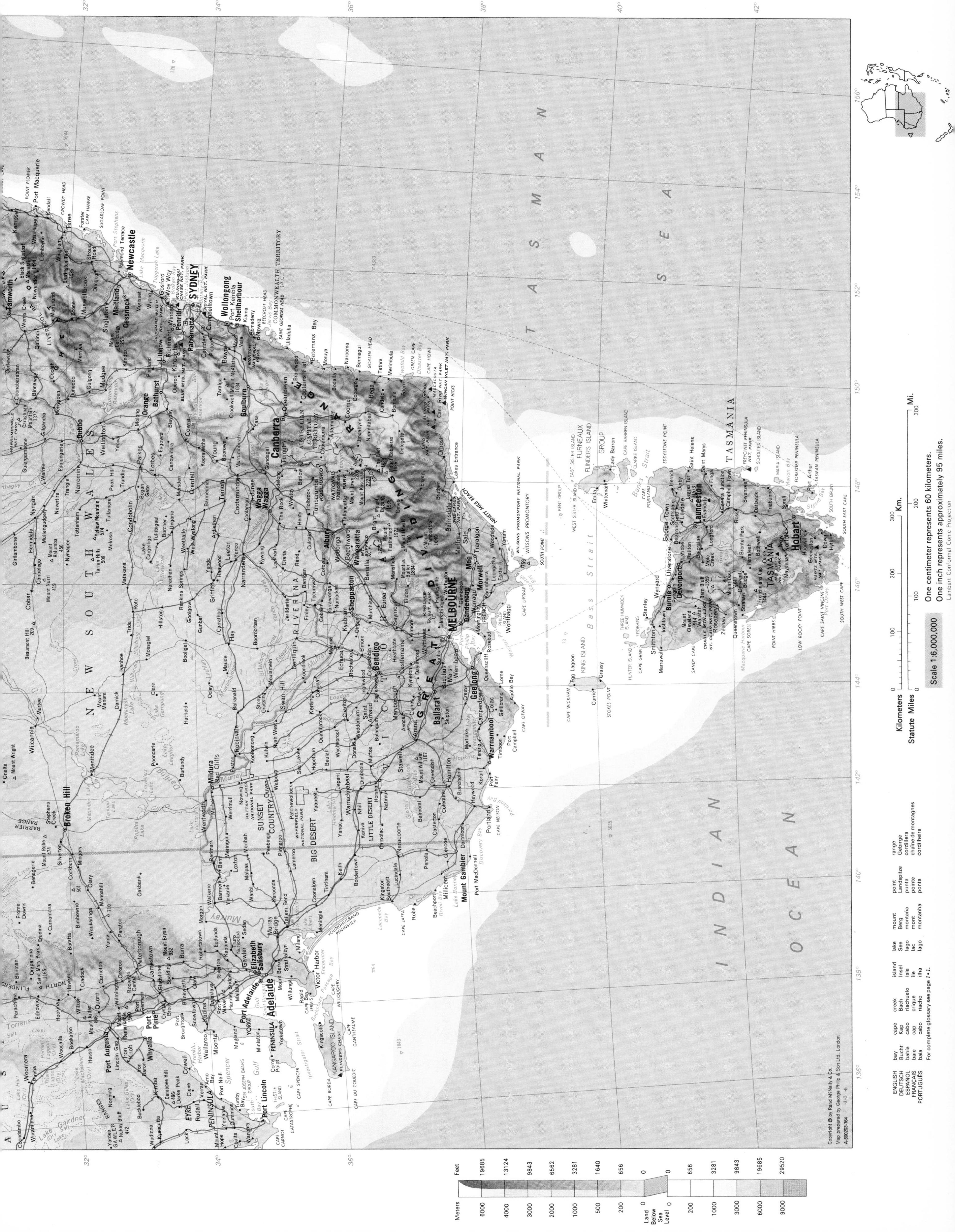
TASMAN SEA
INDIAN OCEAN
NEW SOUTH WALES
VICTORIA
TASMANIA
AUSTRALIAN CAPITAL TERRITORY
GREAT DIVIDING RANGE
Bass Strait
KING ISLAND
FLINDERS ISLAND
FURNEAUX GROUP
KANGAROO ISLAND
SYDNEY
MELBOURNE
Canberra
Adelaide
Hobart
Newcastle
Wollongong
Geelong
Ballarat
Bendigo
Launceston
Broken Hill
Mildura
Wagga Wagga
Albury
Port Augusta
Port Lincoln
Whyalla
Port Pirie
Scale 1:6,000,000
One centimeter represents 60 kilometers.
One inch represents approximately 95 miles.
Lambert Conformal Conic Projection
Kilometers
Statute Miles
ENGLISH bay cape creek island lake mount point range
DEUTSCH Bucht Kap Bach Insel See Berg Landspitze Gebirge
ESPAÑOL bahía cabo riachuelo isla lago montaña punta cordillera
FRANÇAIS baie cap crique île lac mont pointe chaîne de montagnes
PORTUGUÊS baía cabo riacho ilha lago montanha ponta cordilheira
For complete glossary see page I • 1.
Copyright © by Rand McNally & Co.
Map prepared by George Philip & Son Ltd., London.
Meters
Feet
Land Below Sea Level

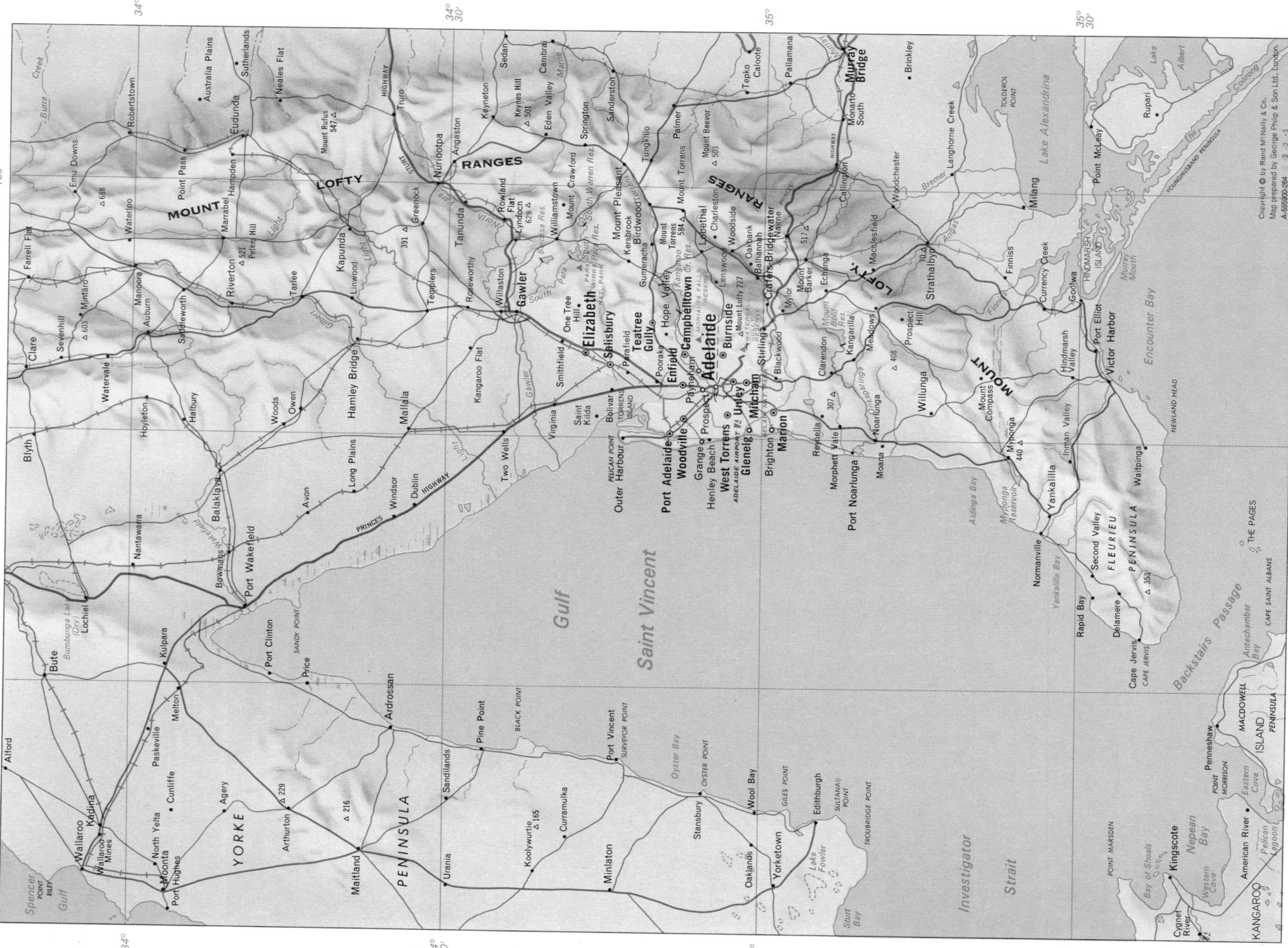

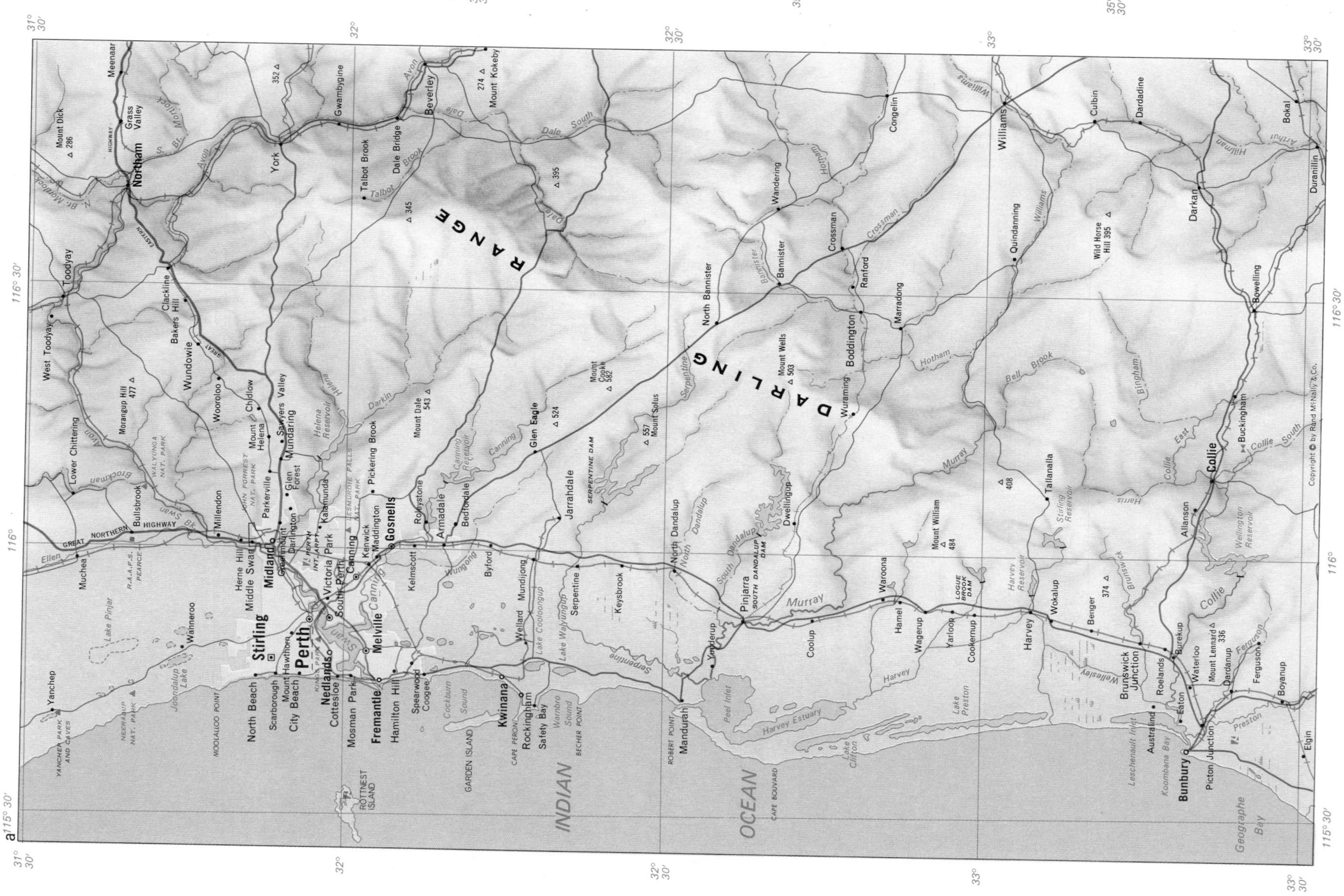

Scale 1:1,000,000

Kilometers / Statute Miles: 0 10 20 30 40 50

One centimeter represents 10 kilometers.
One inch represents approximately 16 miles.
Lambert Conformal Conic Projection

ENGLISH	DEUTSCH	ESPAÑOL	FRANÇAIS	PORTUGUÊS
bay, b.	Bucht	bahía	baie	baía
cape	Kap	cabo	cap	cabo
dam	Damm	diques	barrage	barragem
gulf	Golf	golfo	golfe	golfo
island	Insel	isla	île	ilha
lake, l.	See	lago	lac	lago
peninsula	Halbinsel	península	péninsule	península
point	Landspitze	punta	pointe	ponta

For complete glossary see page I•1.

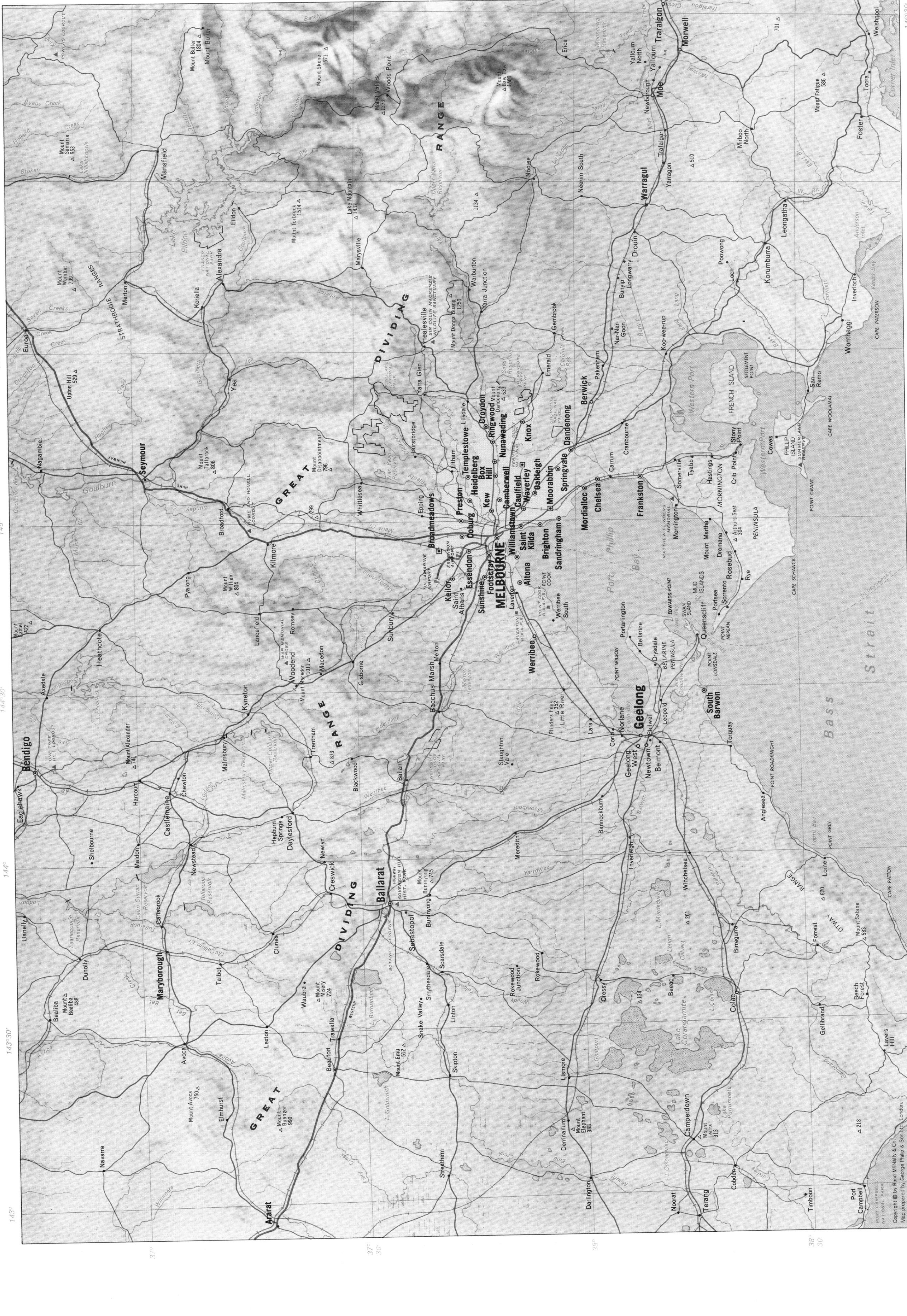

ENGLISH | bay, b. | cape | creek, cr. | lake, l. | mount, mt. | point | range, ra. | reservoir, res.
DEUTSCH | Bucht | Kap | Bach | See | Berg | Landspitze | Gebirge | Stausee
ESPAÑOL | bahía | cabo | riachuelo | lago | montaña | punta | cordillera | embalse
FRANÇAIS | baie | cap | crique | lac | mont | pointe | chaîne | réservoir
PORTUGUÊS | baía | cabo | riacho | lago | montanha | ponta | cordilheira | reservatório

For complete glossary see page I•J.
For Melbourne metropolitan map, see page 264.

Kilometers 0 10 20 30 40 50 Km.
Statute Miles 0 10 20 30 40 50 Mi.

Scale 1:1,000,000
One centimeter represents 10 kilometers.
One inch represents approximately 16 miles.

Copyright © by Rand McNally & Co.
Map prepared by George Philip & Son Ltd., London.

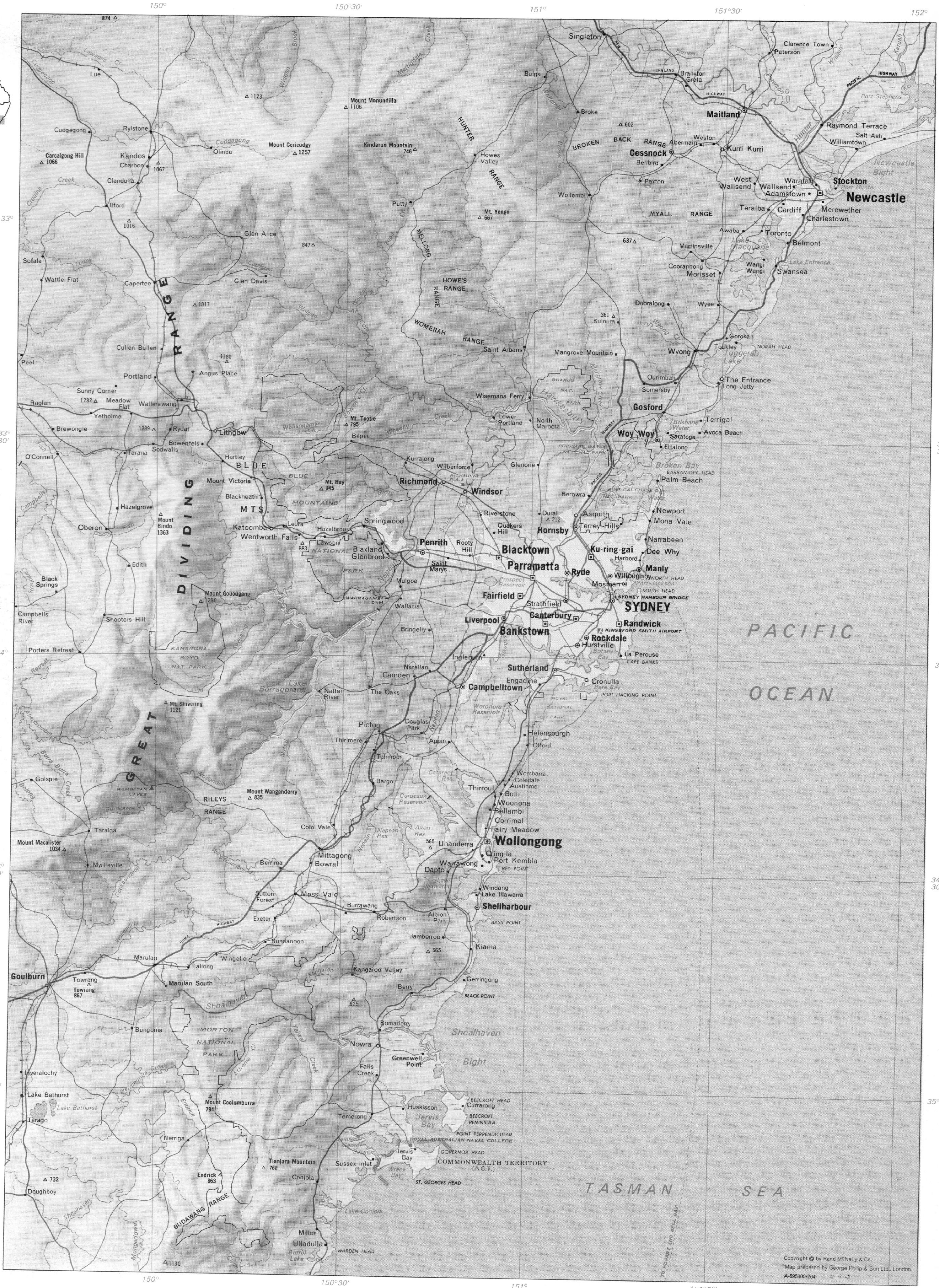

ENGLISH	bight	creek, cr.	head	mount	range	reservoir, res.
DEUTSCH	Bucht	Bach	Vorgebirge	Berg	Gebirge	Stausee
ESPAÑOL	ensenada pequeña	riachuelo	promontorio	montaña	cordillera	estanque
FRANÇAIS	anse	crique	promontoire	mont	chaîne	réservoir
PORTUGUÊS	enseada	riacho	promontório	montanha	cordilheira	reservatório

For complete glossary see page 1•1.
For Sydney metropolitan map, see page 264.

Kilometers 0 10 20 30 40 50 Km.
Statute Miles 0 10 20 30 40 50 Mi.

Scale 1:1,000,000

One centimeter represents 10 kilometers.
One inch represents approximately 16 miles.
Lambert Conformal Conic Projection

a

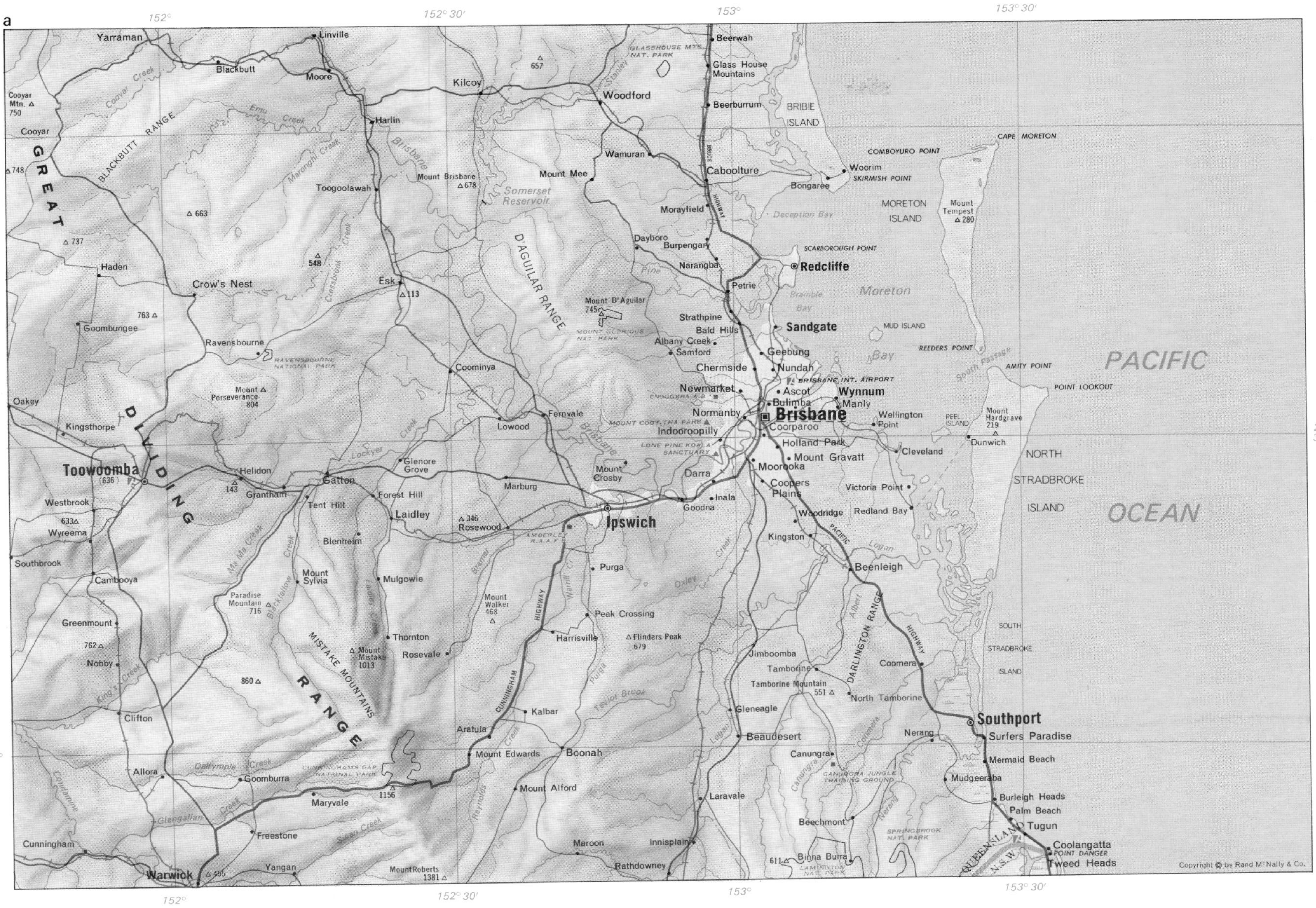

PACIFIC OCEAN
Brisbane
Ipswich
Toowoomba
Redcliffe
Sandgate
Wynnum
Manly
Southport
Surfers Paradise
Coolangatta
Tweed Heads
Warwick
Gatton
Laidley
Esk
Kilcoy
Woodford
Caboolture
Beerwah
Glass House Mountains
BRIBIE ISLAND
MORETON ISLAND
NORTH STRADBROKE ISLAND
SOUTH STRADBROKE ISLAND
Moreton Bay
GREAT DIVIDING RANGE
D'AGUILAR RANGE
MISTAKE MOUNTAINS
DARLINGTON RANGE
BLACKBUTT RANGE
Somerset Reservoir
Beenleigh
Cleveland
Dunwich
Boonah
Beaudesert
Yarraman
Linville
Crow's Nest
Oakey
Clifton
Allora
Cunningham
Copyright © by Rand McNally & Co.

b

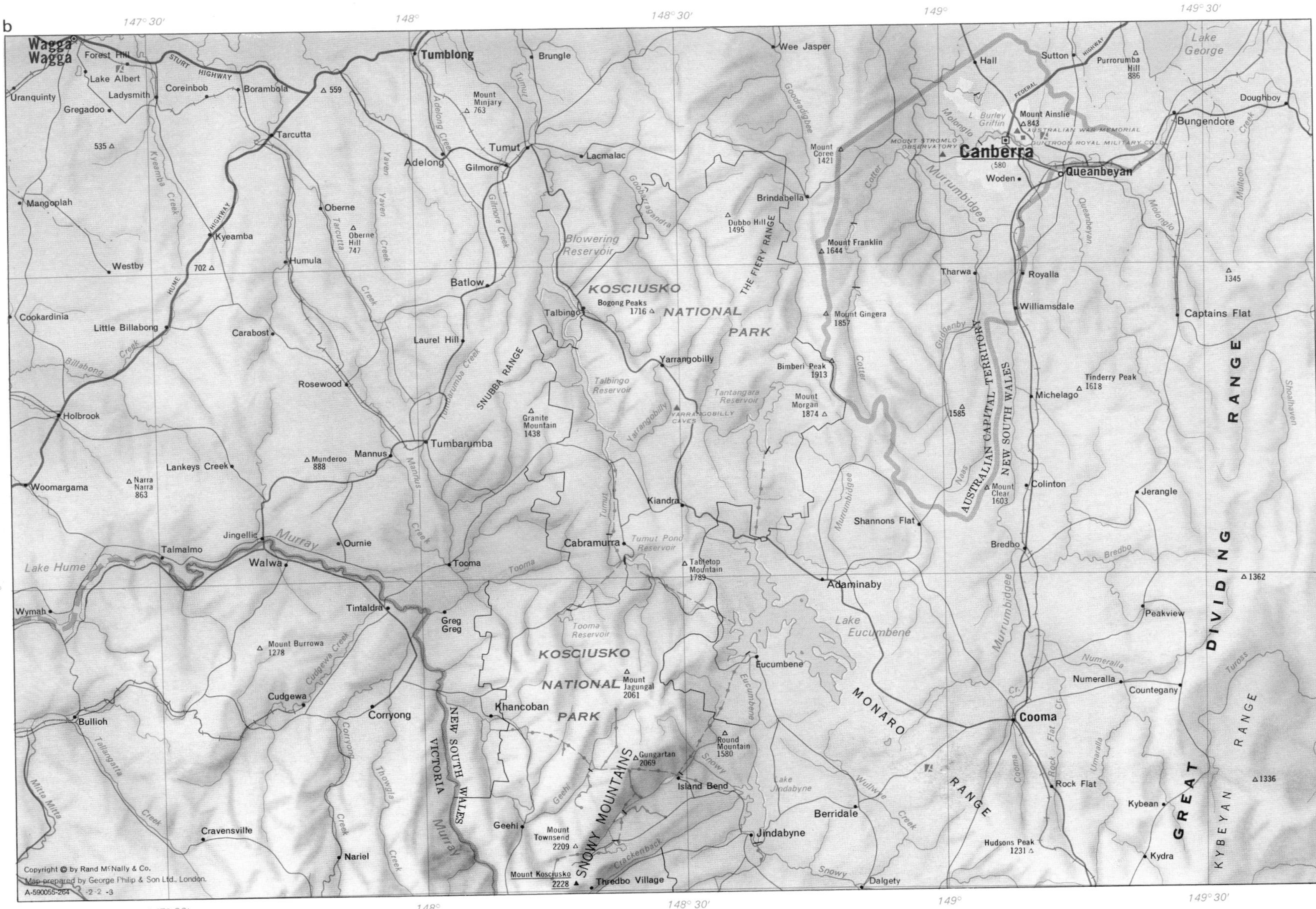

Wagga Wagga
Canberra
Queanbeyan
Tumut
Tumbarumba
Cooma
Jindabyne
Adaminaby
Kiandra
Cabramurra
Khancoban
Corryong
Holbrook
Bungendore
KOSCIUSKO NATIONAL PARK
SNOWY MOUNTAINS
Mount Kosciusko 2228
Thredbo Village
AUSTRALIAN CAPITAL TERRITORY
NEW SOUTH WALES
VICTORIA
GREAT DIVIDING RANGE
MONARO RANGE
KYBEYAN RANGE
Lake Hume
Lake Eucumbene
Lake Jindabyne
Lake George
Blowering Reservoir
Murray
Murrumbidgee
Copyright © by Rand McNally & Co.
Map prepared by George Philip & Son Ltd., London.

ENGLISH	creek	island	mount	peak	point	range	reservoir
DEUTSCH	Bach	Insel	Berg	Gipfel	Landspitze	Gebirge	Stausee
ESPAÑOL	riachuelo	isla	montaña	pico	punta	cordillera	embalse
FRANÇAIS	crique	île	mont	cime	pointe	chaîne	réservoir
PORTUGUÊS	riacho	ilha	montanha	pico	ponta	cordilheira	reservatório

For complete glossary see page *1•1*.

Kilometers 0 10 20 30 40 50 Km.
Statute Miles 0 10 20 30 40 50 Mi.

Scale 1:1,000,000

One centimeter represents 10 kilometers.
One inch represents approximately 16 miles.

Lambert Conformal Conic Projection

New Zealand / Neuseeland / Nueva Zelanda
Nouvelle Zélande / Nova Zelândia

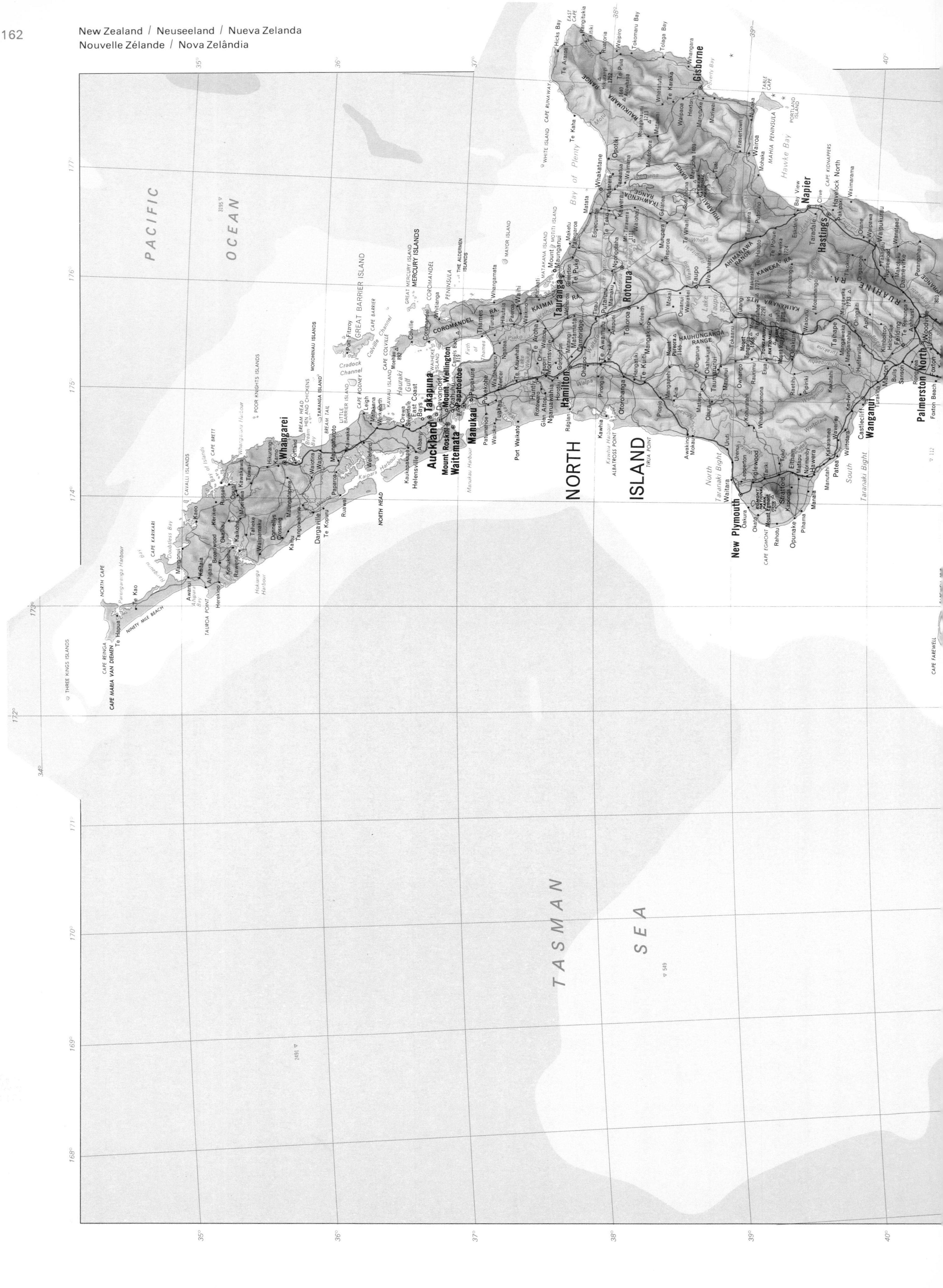
PACIFIC OCEAN
TASMAN SEA
NORTH ISLAND
Bay of Plenty
Hawke Bay
North Taranaki Bight
South Taranaki Bight
Hauraki Gulf
Firth of Thames
Lake Taupo
Auckland
Manukau
Hamilton
Tauranga
Rotorua
Gisborne
Napier
Hastings
New Plymouth
Wanganui
Palmerston North
Whangarei
Dargaville
Takapuna
Waitemata
Mount Wellington
Mount Roskill
Papatoetoe
Taupo
Whakatane
Opotiki
Wairoa
Thames
Coromandel
COROMANDEL PENINSULA
GREAT BARRIER ISLAND
MERCURY ISLANDS
POOR KNIGHTS ISLANDS
THREE KINGS ISLANDS
CAPE REINGA
CAPE MARIA VAN DIEMEN
NORTH CAPE
NINETY MILE BEACH
CAPE EGMONT
CAPE KIDNAPPERS
MAHIA PENINSULA
KAWEKA RA.
RUAHINE RA.
KAIMANAWA MTS.
RAUKUMARA RANGE
Kaipara Harbour
Manukau Harbour
Stratford
Hawera
Eltham
Patea
Feilding
Dannevirke
Te Kuiti
Te Awamutu
Cambridge
Matamata
Morrinsville
Waihi
Huntly
Pukekohe
Raglan
Kawhia
35°
36°
37°
38°
39°
40°
168°
169°
170°
171°
172°
173°
174°
175°
176°
177°

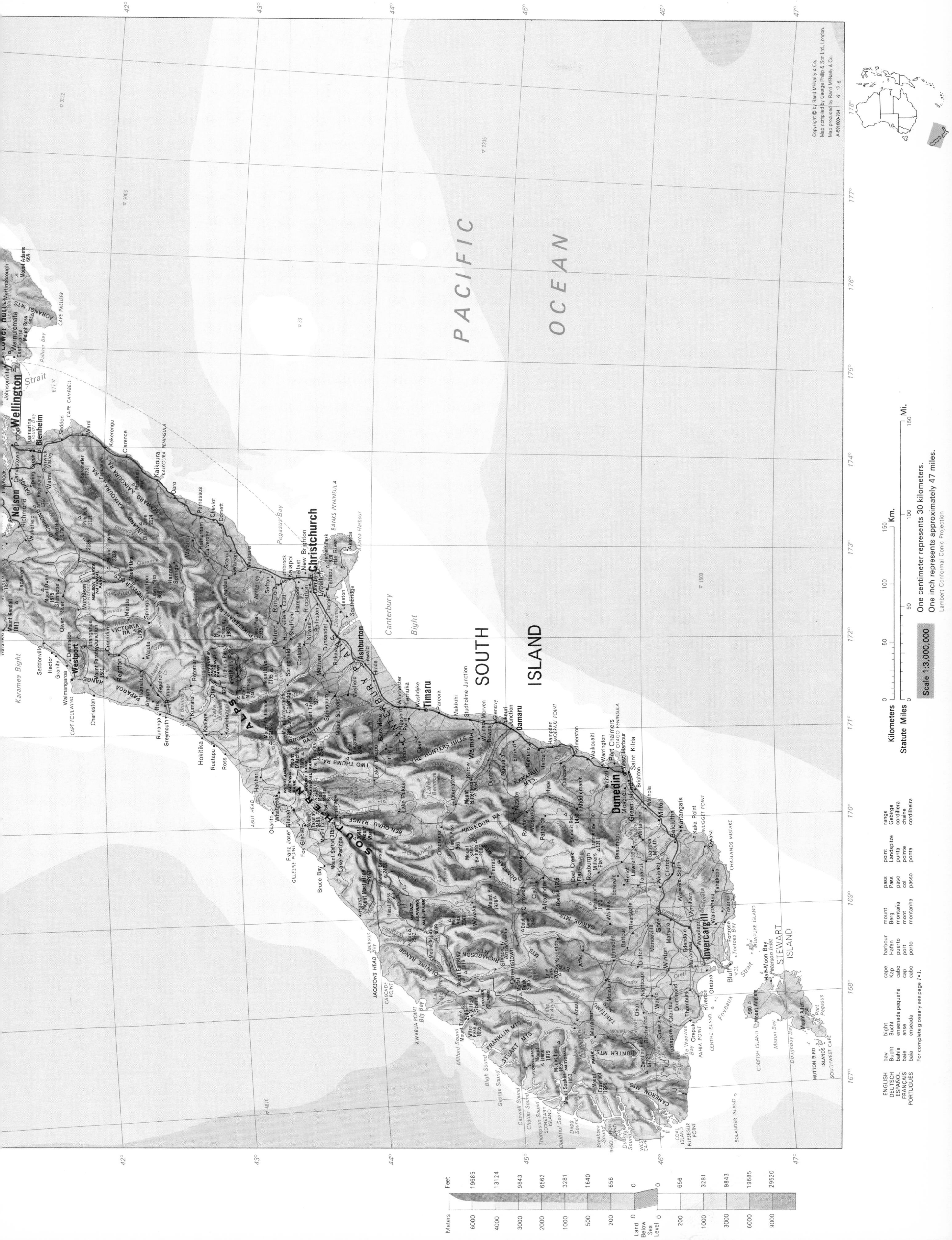
PACIFIC
OCEAN
SOUTH
ISLAND
STEWART ISLAND
SOUTHERN ALPS
Canterbury Bight
Pegasus Bay
Karamea Bight
Foveaux Strait
Wellington
Nelson
Blenheim
Christchurch
Ashburton
Timaru
Oamaru
Dunedin
Invercargill
Westport
Greymouth
Hokitika
Kaikoura
Queenstown
Scale 1:3,000,000
One centimeter represents 30 kilometers.
One inch represents approximately 47 miles.
Lambert Conformal Conic Projection
Kilometers
Statute Miles
Km.
Mi.
ENGLISH bay bight cape harbour mount pass point range
DEUTSCH Bucht Bucht Kap Hafen Berg Pass Landspitze Gebirge
ESPAÑOL bahía ensenada pequeña cabo puerto montaña paso punta cordillera
FRANÇAIS baie anse cap port mont col pointe chaîne
PORTUGUÊS baía enseada cabo porto montanha passo ponta cordilheira
For complete glossary see page I•1.
Copyright © by Rand McNally & Co.
Map compiled by George Philip & Son Ltd., London.
Map produced by Rand McNally & Co.
A-591600-764
Feet
Meters
Land Below Sea Level

a

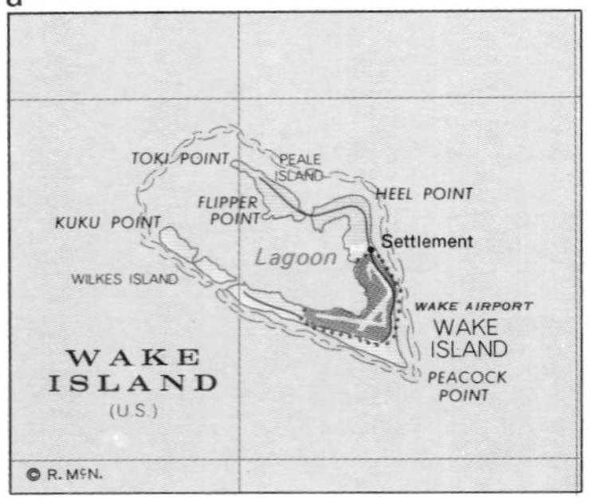

b

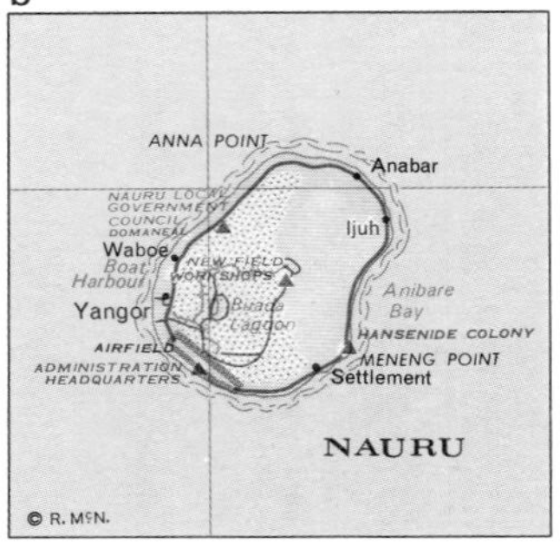

c

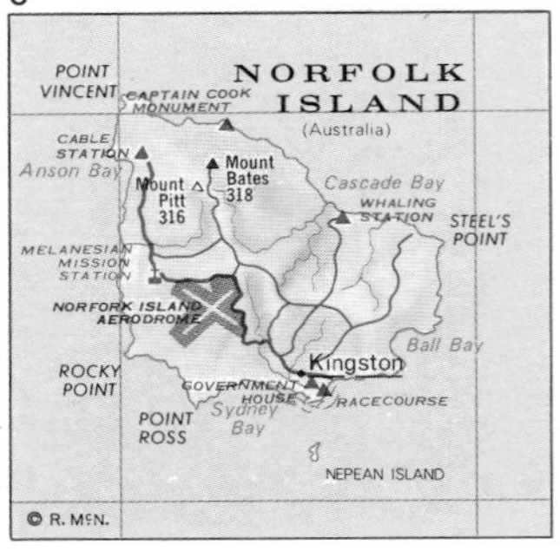

d

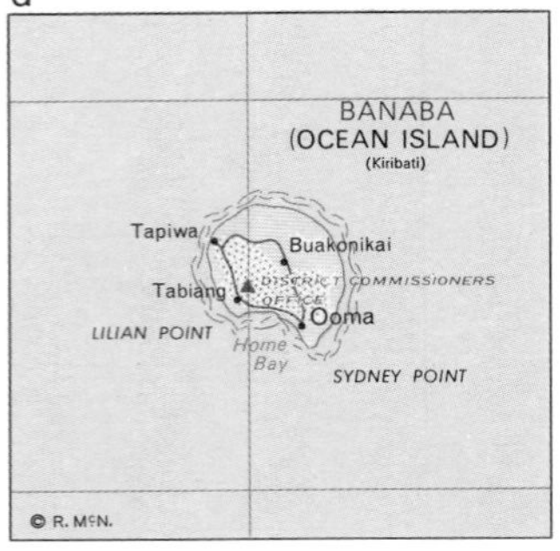

e

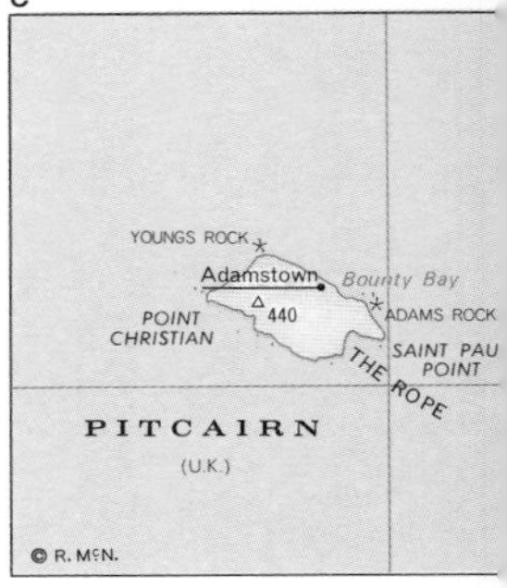

f

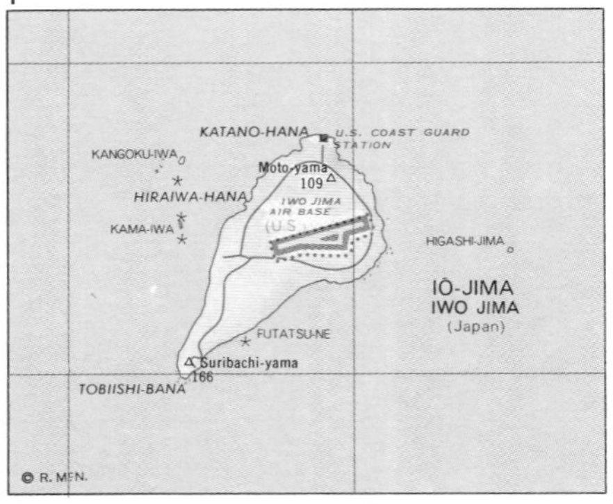

g

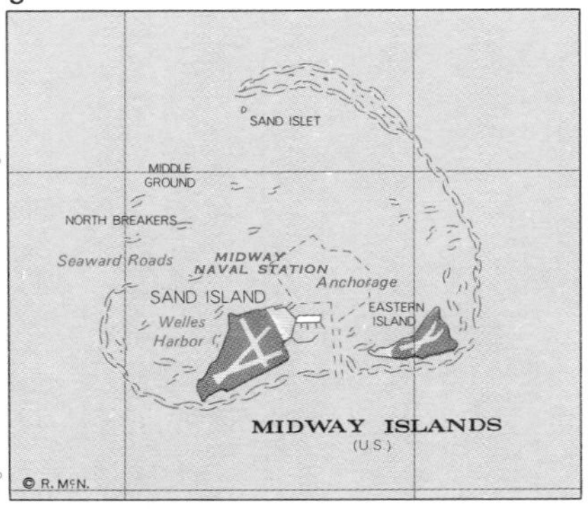

h

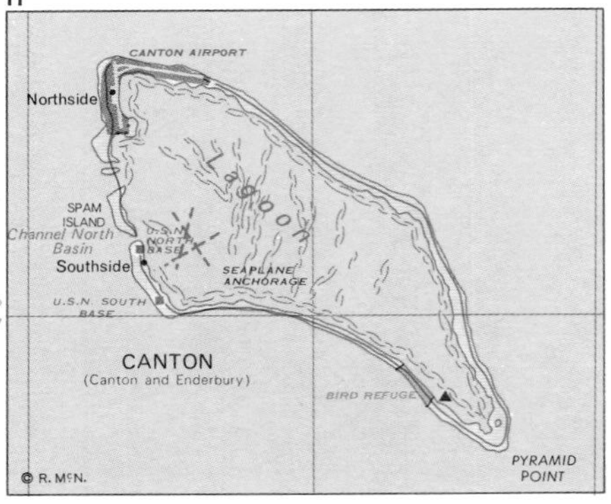

k

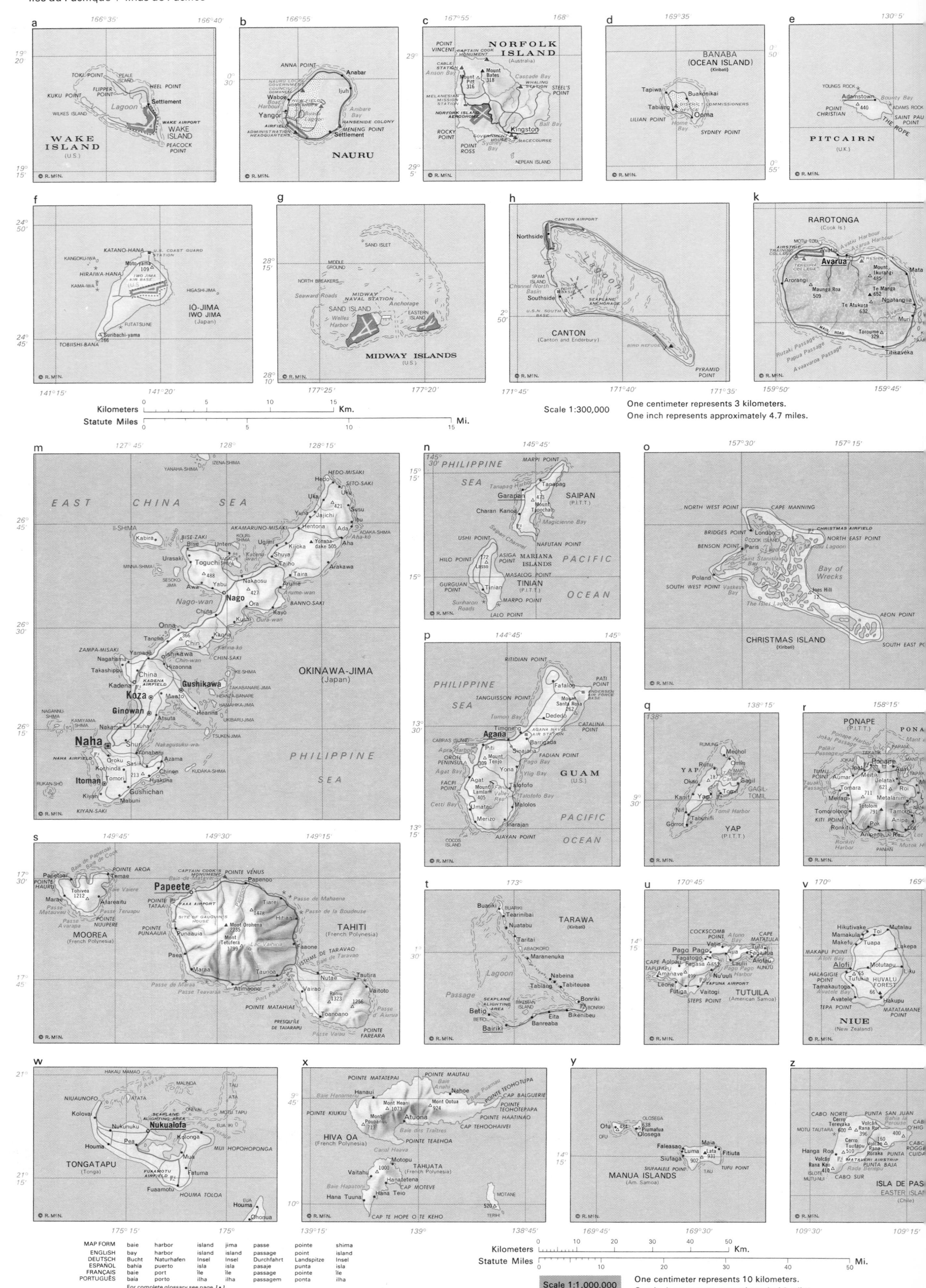

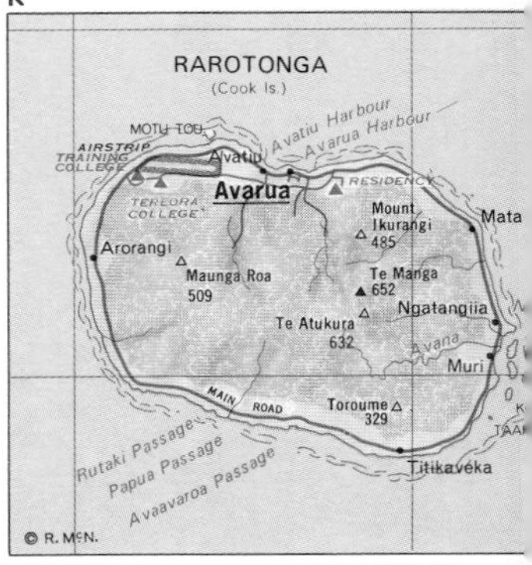

Kilometers 0 5 10 15 Km.
Statute Miles 0 5 10 15 Mi.

Scale 1:300,000
One centimeter represents 3 kilometers.
One inch represents approximately 4.7 miles.

m

n

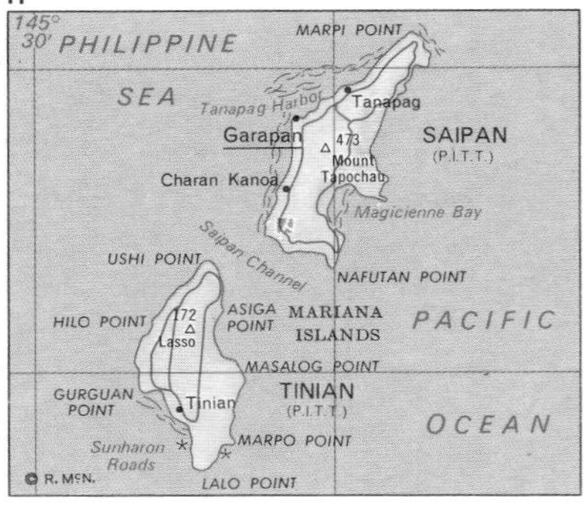

o

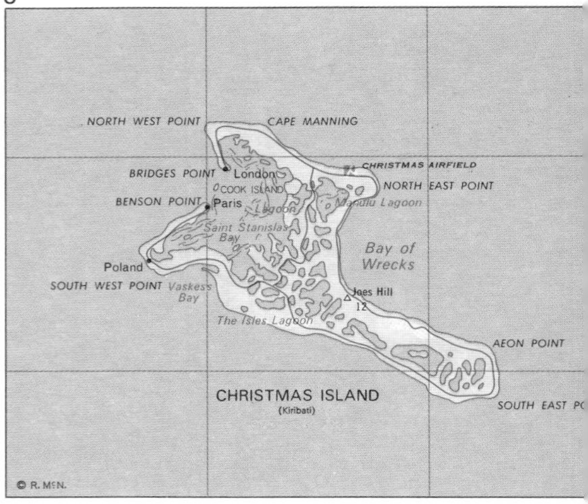

p

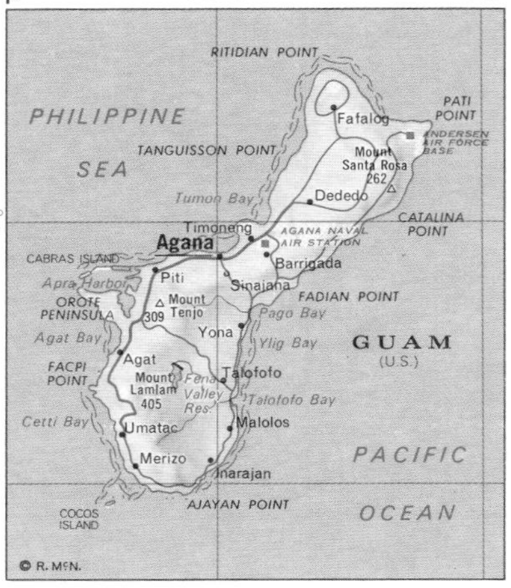

q

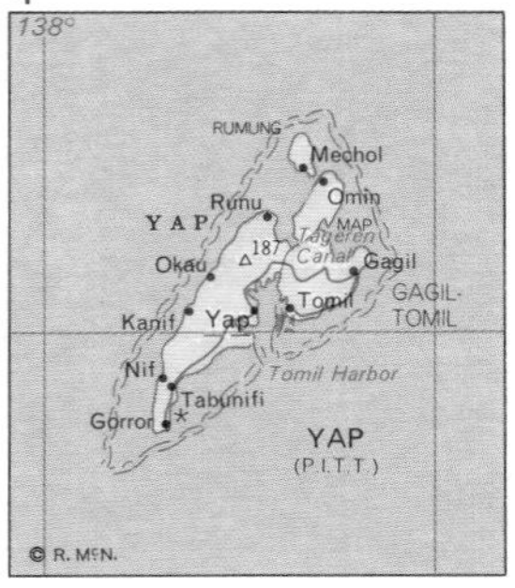

r

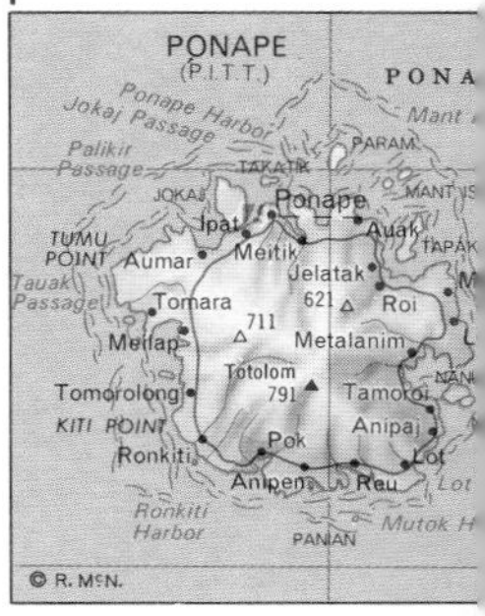

s

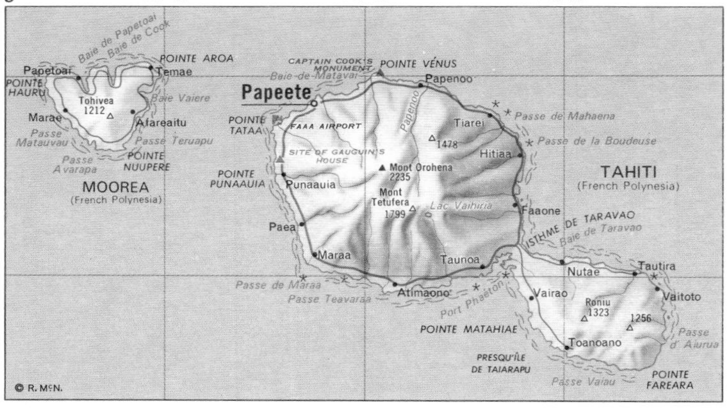

t

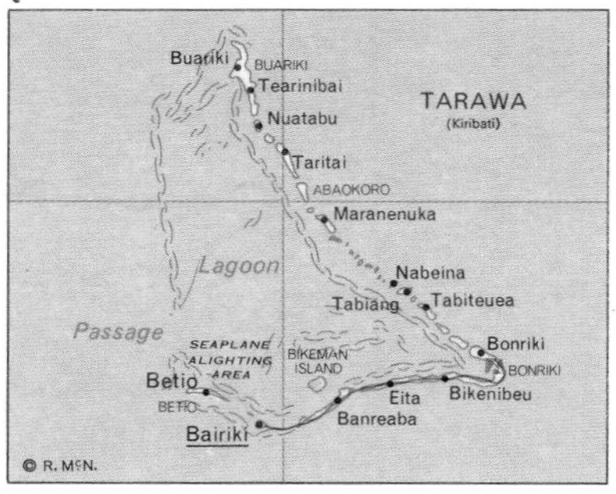

u

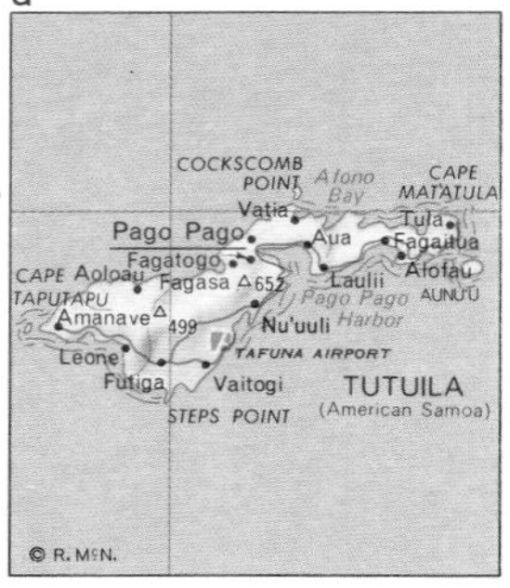

v

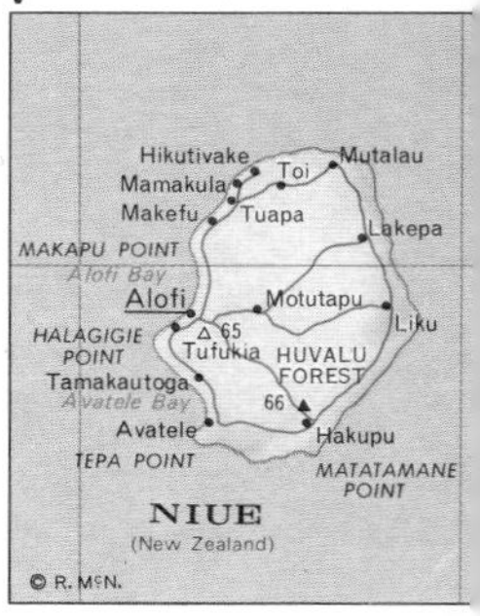

w

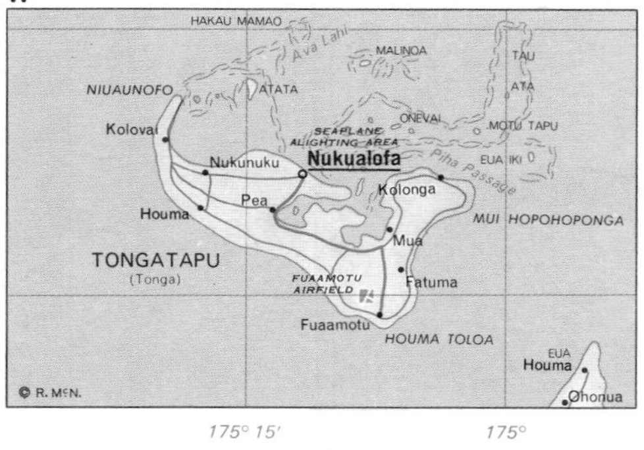

x

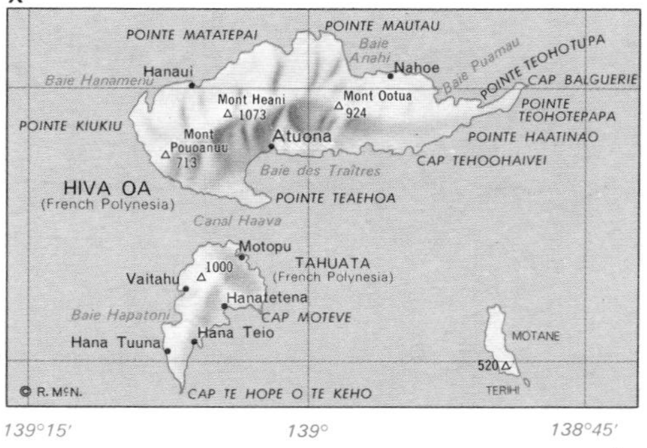

y

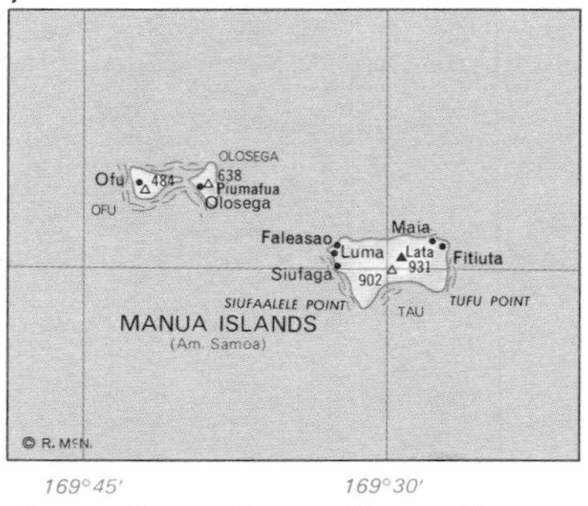

z

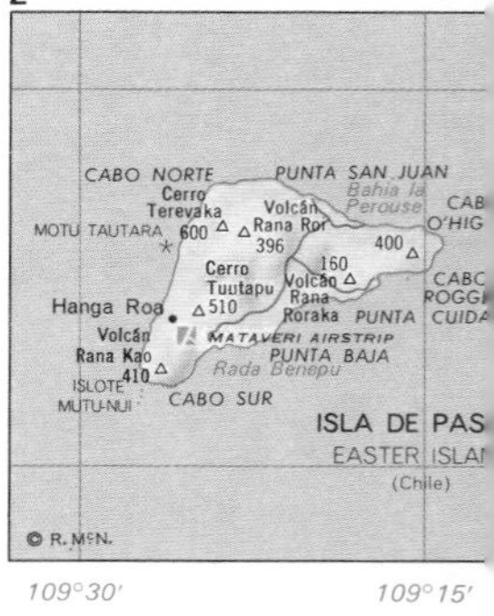

MAP FORM	baie	harbor	island	jima	passe	pointe	shima
ENGLISH	bay	harbor	island	island	passage	point	island
DEUTSCH	Bucht	Naturhafen	Insel	Insel	Durchfahrt	Landspitze	Insel
ESPAÑOL	bahía	puerto	isla	isla	pasaje	punta	isla
FRANÇAIS	baie	port	île	île	passage	pointe	île
PORTUGUÊS	baía	porto	ilha	ilha	passagem	ponta	ilha

For complete glossary see page I • 1.

Kilometers 0 10 20 30 40 50 Km.
Statute Miles 0 10 20 30 40 50 Mi.

Scale 1:1,000,000
One centimeter represents 10 kilometers.
One inch represents approximately 16 miles.
Transverse Mercator Projection

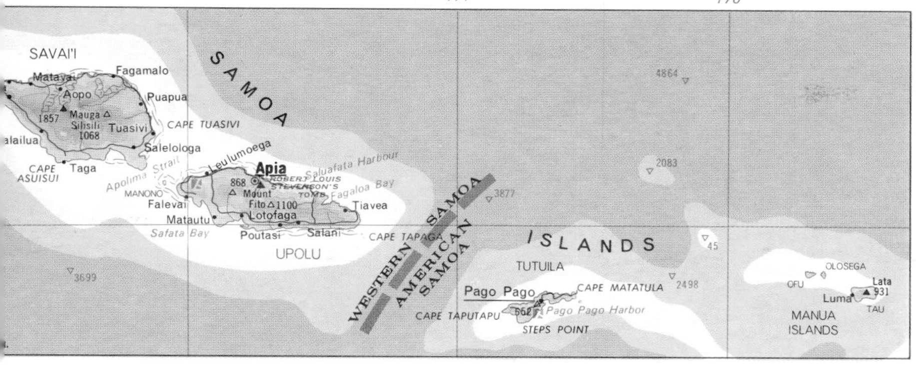

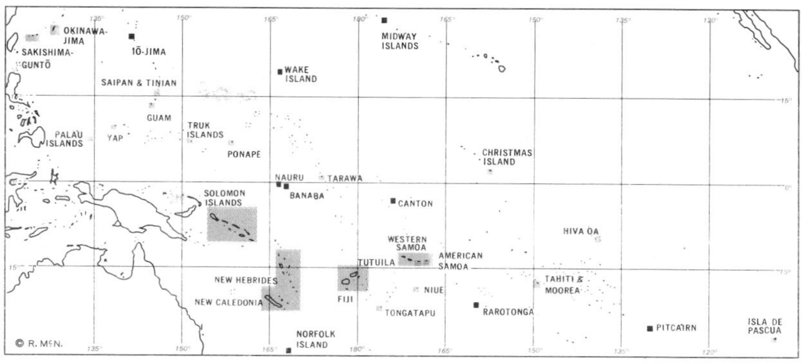

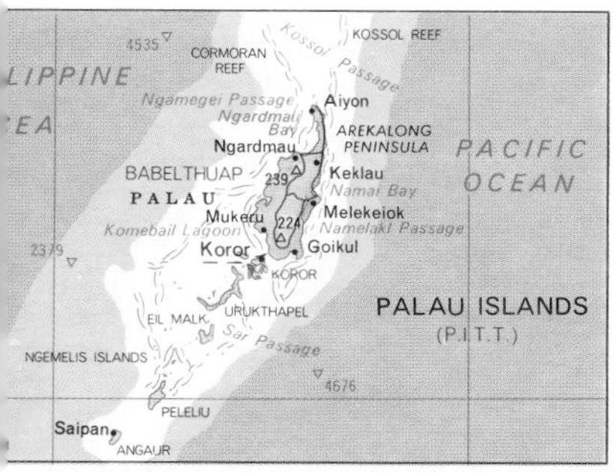

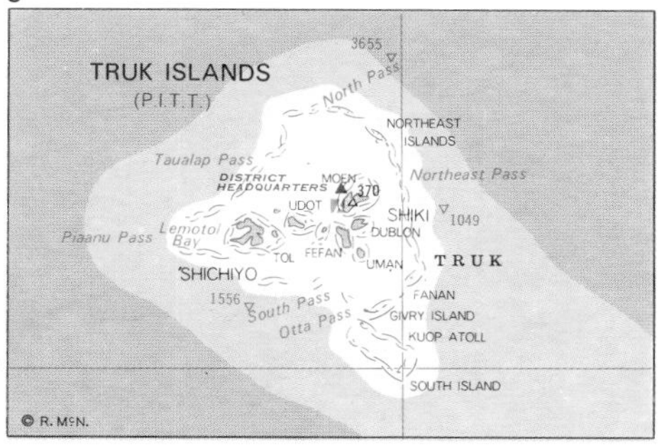

Kilometers 0 50 100 150 Km.
Statute Miles 0 50 100 150 Mi.

Scale 1:3,000,000
One centimeter represents 30 kilometers.
One inch represents approximately 47 miles.
Lambert Conformal Conic Projection

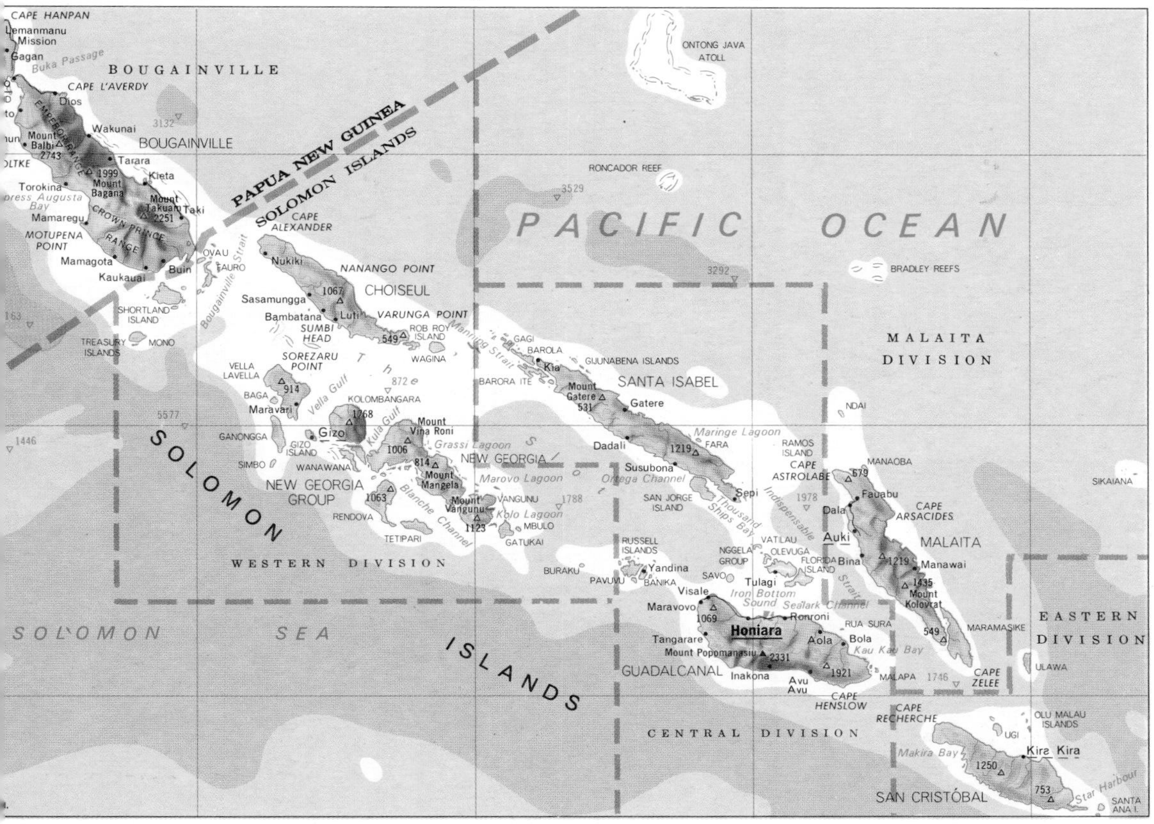

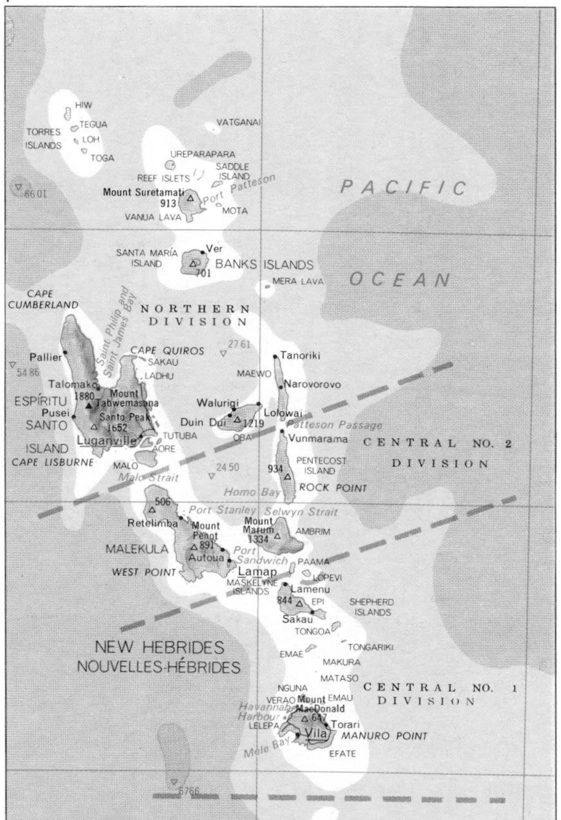

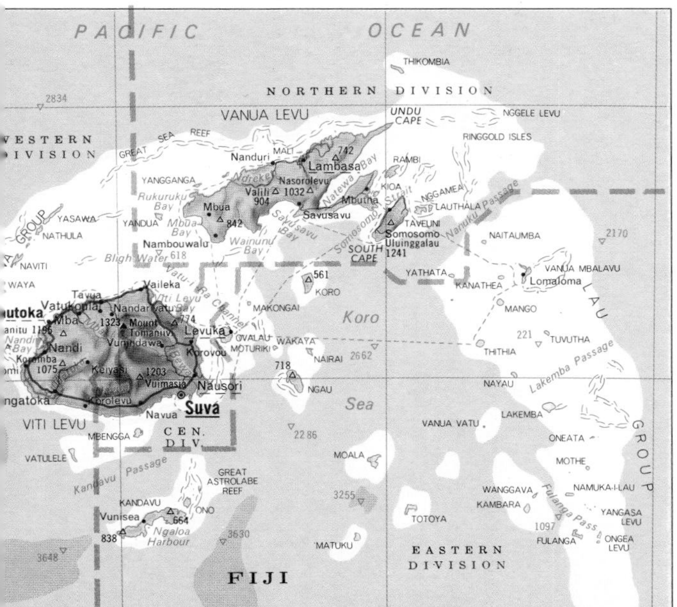

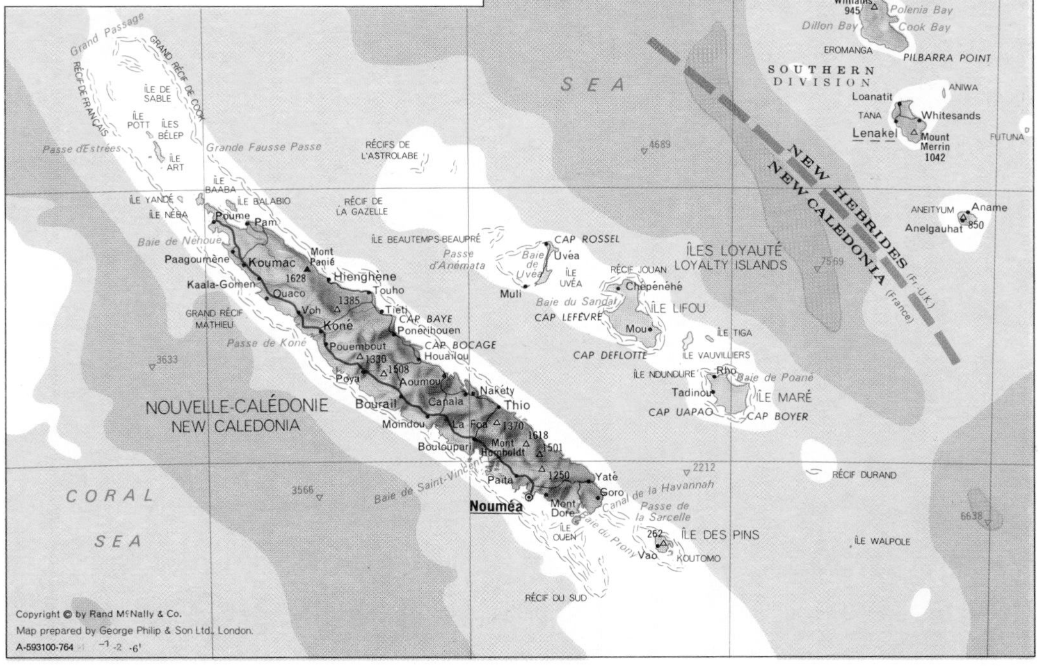

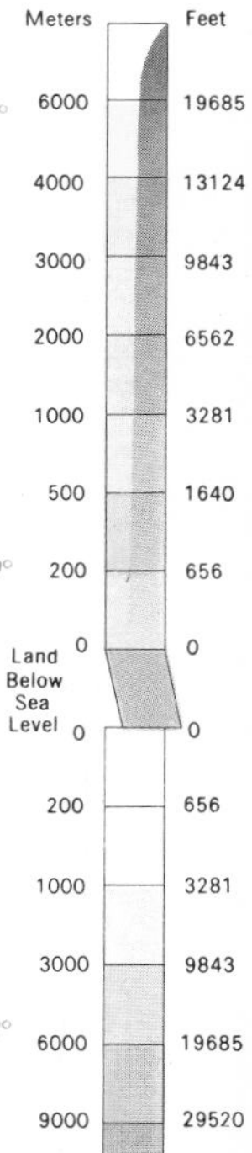

MAP FORM	bay	cape	île	lagoon	mount	point	passage	strait
ENGLISH	bay	cape	island	lagoon	mount	point	passage	strait
DEUTSCH	Bucht	Kap	Insel	Haff	Berg	Landspitze	Durchfahrt	Meeresstrasse
ESPAÑOL	bahía	cabo	isla	laguna	montaña	punta	pasaje	estrecho
FRANÇAIS	baie	cap	île	lagune	mont	pointe	passage	détroit
PORTUGUÊS	baía	cabo	ilha	laguna	montanha	ponta	passagem	estreito

For complete glossary see page 1 • 1.

Kilometers 0 100 200 300 Km.
Statute Miles 0 100 200 300 Mi.

Scale 1:6,000,000
One centimeter represents 60 kilometers.
One inch represents approximately 95 miles.
Lambert Conformal Conic Projection

168 - 169

ENGLISH	bay	cape	island	lake, l.	mountains, mts.	point	range	strait
DEUTSCH	Bucht	Kap	Insel	See	Berge	Landspitze	Gebirge	Meeresstrasse
ESPAÑOL	bahía	cabo	isla	lago	montañas	punta	sierra	estrecho
FRANÇAIS	baie	cap	île	lac	montagnes	pointe	chaîne	détroit
PORTUGUÊS	baía	cabo	ilha	lago	montanhas	ponta	serra	estreito

For complete glossary see page *I • 1*.

Kilometers 0 200 400 600 Km.

Statute Miles 0 200 400 600 Mi.

Scale 1:12,000,000

One centimeter represents 120 kilometers.
One inch represents approximately 190 miles.
Lambert Conformal Conic Projection

ENGLISH	bay	cape	desert	island	lake	mountains	peak	range
DEUTSCH	Bucht	Kap	Wüste	Insel	See	Berge	Gipfel	Gebirge
ESPAÑOL	bahía	cabo	desierto	isla	lago	montañas	pico	sierra
FRANÇAIS	baie	cap	désert	île	lac	montagnes	cime	chaîne
PORTUGUÊS	baía	cabo	deserto	ilha	lago	montanhas	pico	serra

For complete glossary see page *I • 1*.

166 - 167

Kilometers 0 200 400 600 Km.

Statute Miles 0 200 400 600 Mi.

Scale 1:12,000,000

One centimeter represents 120 kilometers.
One inch represents approximately 190 miles.
Albers Conical Equal-Area Projection

ARCTIC
Chukchi Sea
BERING SEA
UNION OF SOVIET SOCIALIST REPUBLICS
UNITED STATES
International Date Line
Arctic Circle
Anadyrskij Zaliv
ANADYRSKOJE PLOSKOGORJE
ČUKOTSKIJ POLUOSTROV
SEWARD PENINSULA
BROOKS
DE LONG MOUNTAINS
BAIRD MOUNTAINS
SCHWATKA MOUNTAINS
WARING MOUNTAINS
KUSKOKWIM
KILBUCK MOUNTAINS
AHKLUN MOUNTAINS
TAYLOR MOUNTAINS
KAIYUH MOUNTAINS
BEAVER MOUNTAINS
ZANE HILLS
LOOKOUT RIDGE
Norton Sound
Kotzebue Sound
Bering Strait
Kuskokwim Bay
Bristol Bay
SAINT LAWRENCE ISLAND
SAINT MATTHEW ISLAND
NUNIVAK ISLAND
NELSON ISLAND
PRIBILOF ISLANDS
Saint Paul Island
Saint George
ALEUTIAN ISLANDS
ANDREANOF ISLANDS
ISLANDS OF THE FOUR MOUNTAINS
FOX ISLANDS
UNIMAK ISLAND
UMNAK ISLAND
UNALASKA ISLAND
ATKA ISLAND
ADAK ISLAND
SHUMAGIN ISLANDS
KRENITZIN ISLANDS
ALASKA PENINSULA
PACIF
Barrow
Wainwright
Point Hope
Kotzebue
Kivalina
Noatak
Nome
Teller
Wales
Unalakleet
Saint Michael
Stebbins
Bethel
Dillingham
King Salmon
Naknek
Port Heiden
Port Moller
Cold Bay
Dutch Harbor
Unalaska
Anadyr'
Providenija
Uelen
Lavrentija
Gambell
Savoonga
Meters
6000
4000
3000
2000
1000
500
200
0
Land Below Sea Level
0
200
1000
3000
6000
9000
Feet
19685
13124
9843
6562
3281
1640
656
0
0
656
3281
9843
19685
29520
ENGLISH bay cape island, i. lake, l. mount, mt. peak, pk. point
DEUTSCH Bucht Kap Insel See Berg Gipfel Landspitze
ESPAÑOL bahia cabo isla lago monte pico punta
FRANÇAIS baie cap île lac mont cime pointe
PORTUGUÊS baía cabo ilha lago monte pico ponta
For complete glossary see page I • I.

Kilometers 0 100 200 300 Km.
Statute Miles 0 100 200 300 Mi.

Scale 1:6,000,000

One centimeter represents 60 kilometers.
One inch represents approximately 95 miles.
Lambert Conformal Conic Projection

ENGLISH	creek	Indian reserve	inlet	island	lake, l.	mountain	peak	provincial park	sound
DEUTSCH	Bach	Indianerreservation	Einfahrt	Insel	See	Berg	Gipfel	Provinz-Park	Sund
ESPAÑOL	riachuelo	reserva de Indios	abra	isla	lago	montaña	pico	parque de provincia	sonda
FRANÇAIS	crique	réserve indienne	bras de mer	île	lac	montagne	cime	parc provincial	détroit
PORTUGUÊS	riacho	reserva indígena	braço de mar	ilha	lago	montanha	pico	parque provincial	estreito

For complete glossary see page *I • 1*.

Kilometers 0 50 100 150 Km.
Statute Miles 0 50 100 150 Mi.

Scale 1:3,000,000

One centimeter represents 30 kilometers.
One inch represents approximately 47 miles.

Lambert Conformal Conic Projection

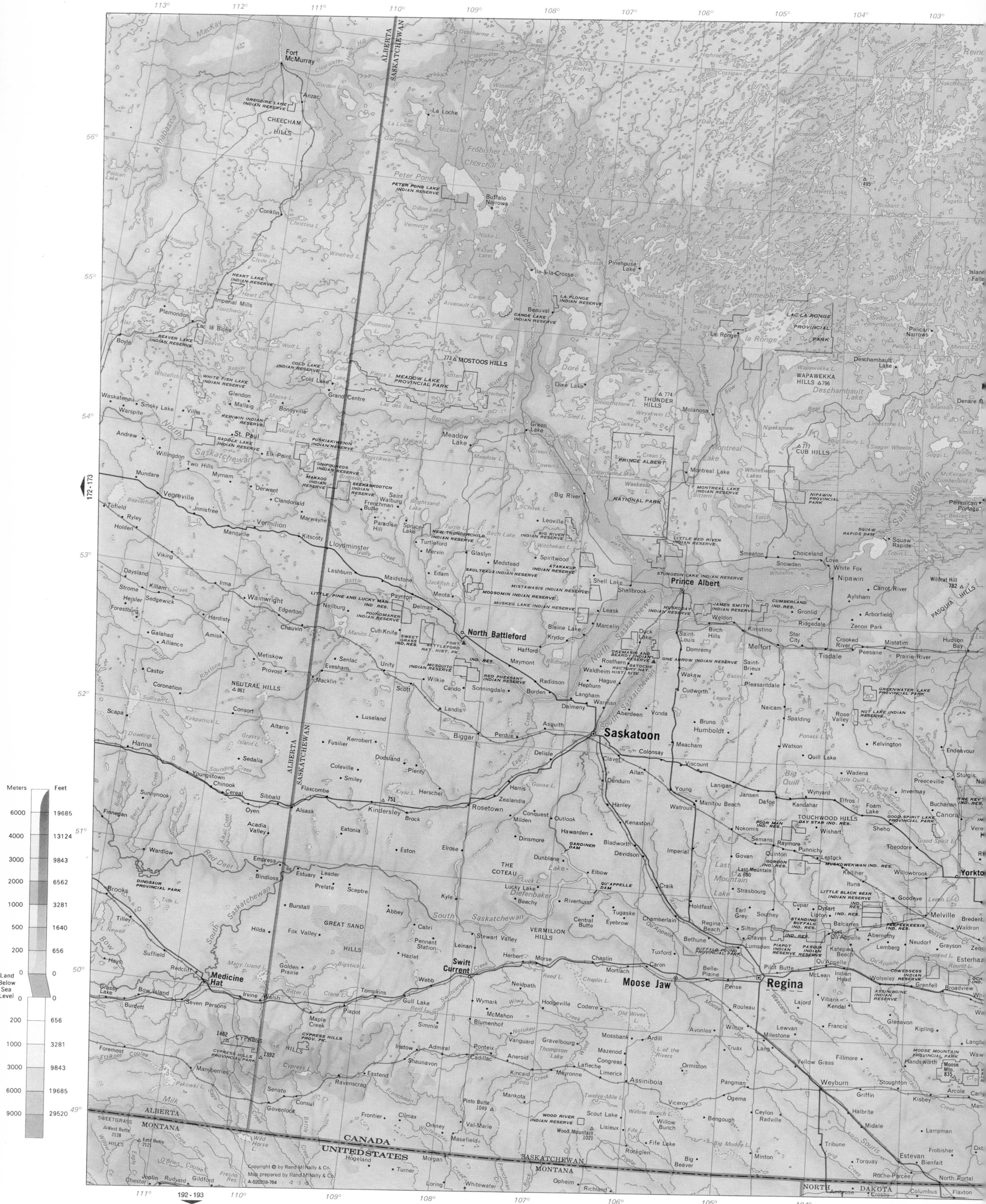

ENGLISH	creek, cr.	hills	Indian reserve	island, i.	lake, l.	provincial park
DEUTSCH	Bach	Hügel	Indianerreservation	Insel	See	Provinz-Park
ESPAÑOL	riachuelo	colinas	reserva de Indios	isla	lago	parque de provincia
FRANÇAIS	crique	collines	réserve indienne	île	lac	parc provincial
PORTUGUÊS	riacho	colinas	reserva indígena	ilha	lago	parque provincial

For complete glossary see page I • 1.

180 - 181

Kilometers 0 50 100 150 Km.

Statute Miles 0 50 100 150 Mi.

Scale 1:3,000,000

One centimeter represents 30 kilometers.
One inch represents approximately 47 miles.
Lambert Conformal Conic Projection

Meters
Feet
6000
19685
4000
13124
3000
9843
2000
6562
1000
3281
500
1640
200
656
0
0
Land Below Sea Level
0
0
200
656
1000
3281
3000
9843
6000
19685
9000
29520
178-179
Sept-Îles
Baie-Comeau
Hauterive
Matane
Gaspé
Chicoutimi
Jonquière
Québec
Lévis
Rivière-du-Loup
Rimouski
Edmundston
Campbellton
Bathurst
Newcastle
Chatham
Fredericton
Moncton
Saint John
Bangor
Lewiston
Portland
Augusta
Waterville
Halifax
Dartmouth
Charlottetown
Summerside
Truro
PRINCE EDWARD ISLAND
ÎLE D'ANTICOSTI
NOVA SCOTIA
Chaleur Bay
Northumberland
Fundy
Détroit de Jacques-Cartier
Détroit d'Honguedo
Saint Laurent
APPALACHIAN MOUNTAINS
NOTRE-DAME
QUÉBEC
NEW BRUNSWICK
CANADA
UNITED STATES
MAINE
NEWF.
QUÉ.

ENGLISH	bay	cape	dam	island	lake, l.	mountain	point	strait
DEUTSCH	Bucht	Kap	Damm	Insel	See	Berg	Landspitze	Meeresstrasse
ESPAÑOL	bahía	cabo	presa	isla	lago	montaña	punta	estrecho
FRANÇAIS	baie	cap	barrage	île	lac	montagne	pointe	détroit
PORTUGUÊS	baía	cabo	barragem	ilha	lago	montanha	ponta	estreito

For complete glossary see page *1•1*.

LABRADOR SEA
ATLANTIC OCEAN
NEWFOUNDLAND
LONG RANGE MOUNTAINS
Corner Brook
St. John's
Gander
Grand Falls
Windsor
Bishop's Falls
Botwood
Lewisporte
Deer Lake
Stephenville
Channel-Port-aux-Basques
Burgeo
Marystown
Grand Bank
Fortune
Burin
St. Lawrence
Placentia
Carbonear
Harbour Grace
Bay Roberts
Clarenville
Bonavista
St. Anthony
Blanc Sablon
Red Bay
White Bay
Notre Dame Bay
Bonavista Bay
Trinity Bay
Placentia Bay
Fortune Bay
St. Mary's Bay
Conception Bay
Saint George's Bay
Bay of Islands
AVALON PENINSULA
BURIN PENINSULA
GROS MORNE NATIONAL PARK
TERRA NOVA NATIONAL PARK
Cabot Strait
Strait of Belle Isle
SAINT PIERRE AND MIQUELON (France)
SAINT-PIERRE-ET-MIQUELON
MIQUELON
Saint-Pierre
LANGLADE
NEWFOUNDLAND
CANADA
CAPE BRETON ISLAND
CAPE BRETON HIGHLANDS NATIONAL PARK
Sydney
Glace Bay
North Sydney
Sydney Mines
New Waterford
Louisbourg
FORTRESS OF LOUISBOURG NATIONAL HISTORIC PARK
Ingonish
Chéticamp
Canso
SABLE ISLAND (N.S.)
ST. PAUL ISLAND (N.S.)
CAPE RACE
CAPE SPEAR
CAPE RAY
FUNK ISLAND
FOGO ISLAND
Fogo
Twillingate
Springdale
Baie Verte
Port Saunders
Daniel's Harbour
Rocky Harbour
Trout River
St. George's
Robinson
Cox's Cove
Millertown
Buchans
Badger
Harbour Breton
Hermitage
Ramea
François
Whitbourne
Trepassey
Ferryland
Renews
Cape Broyle
Witless Bay
Petty Harbour
Pouch Cove
Torbay
Wabana
61° 60° 59° 58° 57° 56° 55° 54° 53° 52°
51° 50° 49° 48° 47° 46° 45° 44°
Copyright © by Rand McNally & Co.
Map prepared by Rand McNally & Co.
A-520219-764 -2 -3 -4

Kilometers 0 50 100 150 Km.
Statute Miles 0 50 100 150 Mi.

Scale 1:3,000,000
One centimeter represents 30 kilometers.
One inch represents approximately 47 miles.
Lambert Conformal Conic Projection

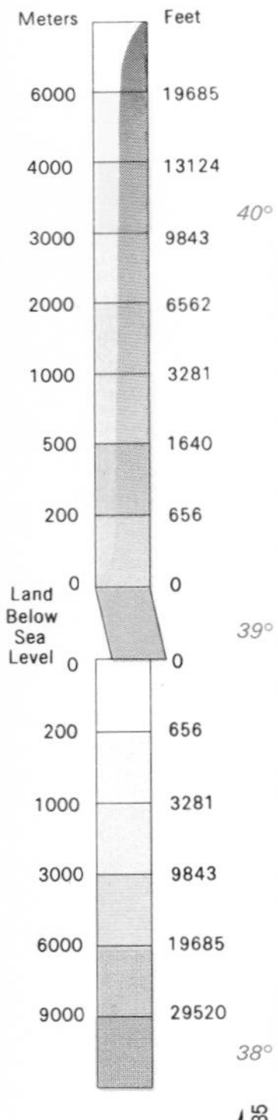

180 - 181
184 - 185
182 - 183

ENGLISH	bay	creek, cr.	island, i.	lake, l.	mountain, mtn.	point, pt.	reservoir, res.	state park, s.p.
DEUTSCH	Bucht	Bach	Insel	See	Berg	Landspitze	Stausee	Staatspark
ESPAÑOL	bahía	riachuelo	isla	lago	montaña	punta	embalse	parque del estado
FRANÇAIS	baie	crique	île	lac	montagne	pointe	réservoir	parc régional
PORTUGUÊS	baía	riacho	ilha	lago	montanha	ponta	reservatório	parque estadual

For complete glossary see page *I* • *1*.

Kilometers 0 50 100 150 Km.
Statute Miles 0 50 100 150 Mi.

Scale 1:3,000,000
One centimeter represents 30 kilometers.
One inch represents approximately 47 miles.
Albers Conical Equal-Area Projection

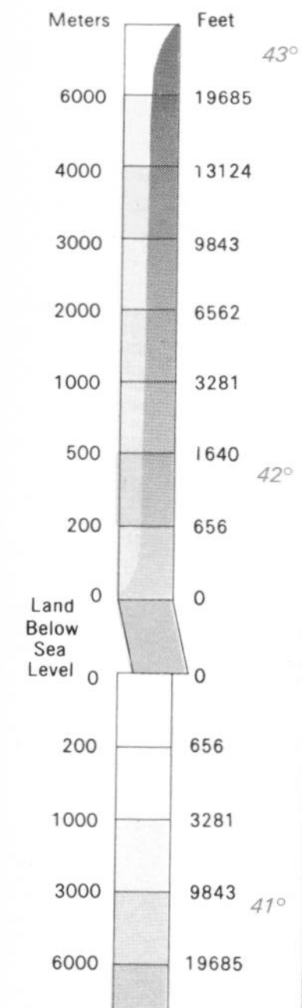

ENGLISH	bay	creek, cr.	Indian reservation	island, i.	lake, l.	point	reservoir, res.	state park, s.p.
DEUTSCH	Bucht	Bach	Indianerreservation	Insel	See	Landspitze	Stausee	Staatspark
ESPAÑOL	bahía	riachuelo	reserva de Indios	isla	lago	punta	embalse	parque del estado
FRANÇAIS	baie	crique	réserve indienne	île	lac	pointe	réservoir	parc régional
PORTUGUÊS	baía	riacho	reserva indígena	ilha	lago	ponta	reservatório	parque estadual

For complete glossary see page I • 1.

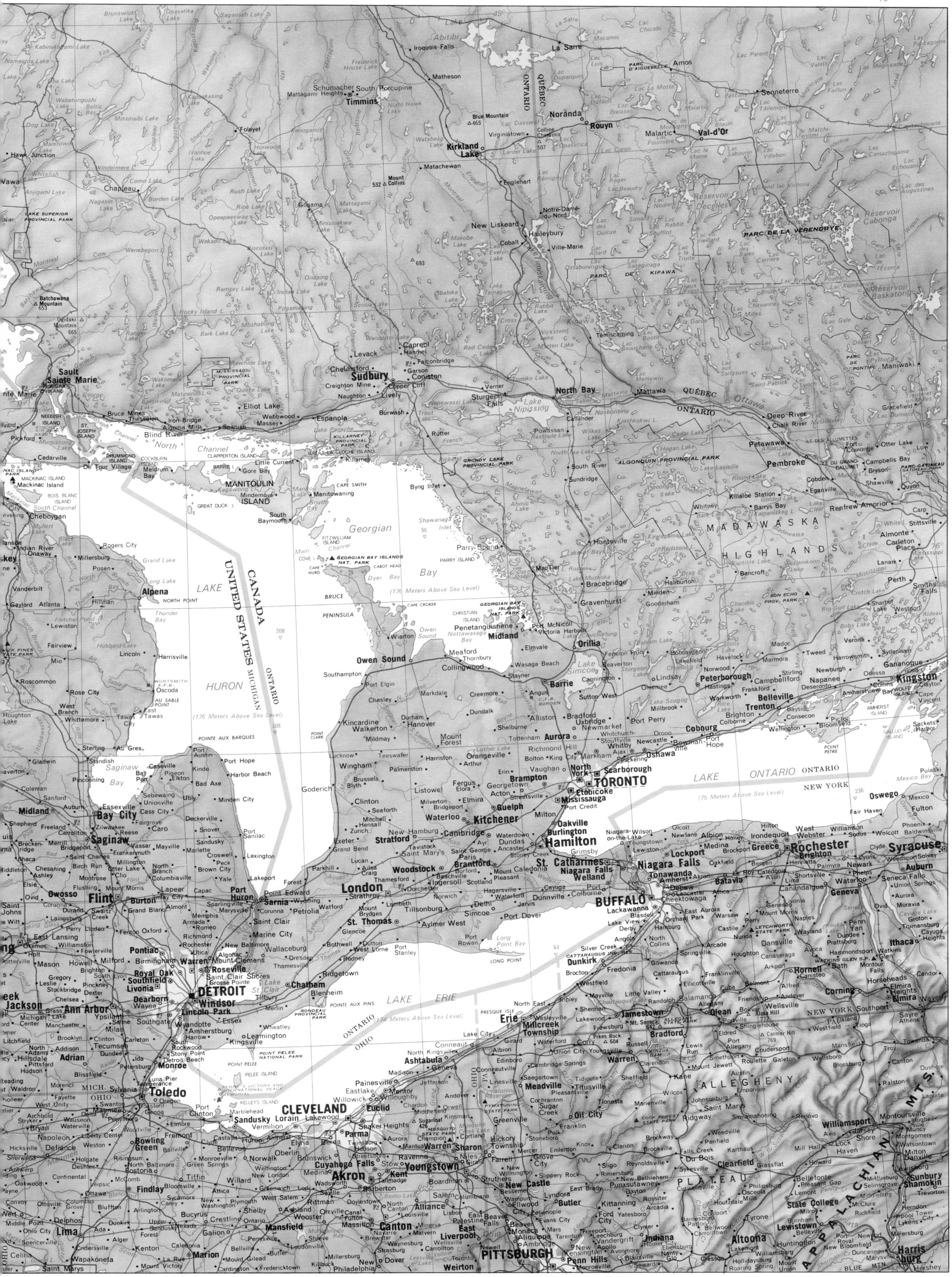

Scale 1:3,000,000

One centimeter represents 30 kilometers.
One inch represents approximately 47 miles.
Albers Conical Equal-Area Projection

Kilometers 0 50 100 150 Km.

Statute Miles 0 50 100 150 Mi.

Scale 1:3,000,000

One centimeter represents 30 kilometers.
One inch represents approximately 47 miles.

Albers Conical Equal-Area Projection

ENGLISH	bay	cape	creek, cr.	dam	island, i.	lake, l.	mountain, mtn.	state park, s.p.
DEUTSCH	Bucht	Kap	Bach	Damm	Insel	See	Berg	Staatspark
ESPAÑOL	bahía	cabo	riachuelo	presa	isla	lago	montaña	parque del estado
FRANÇAIS	baie	cap	crique	barrage	île	lac	montagne	parc régional
PORTUGUÊS	baía	cabo	riacho	barragem	ilha	lago	montanha	parque estadual

For complete glossary see page I•I.

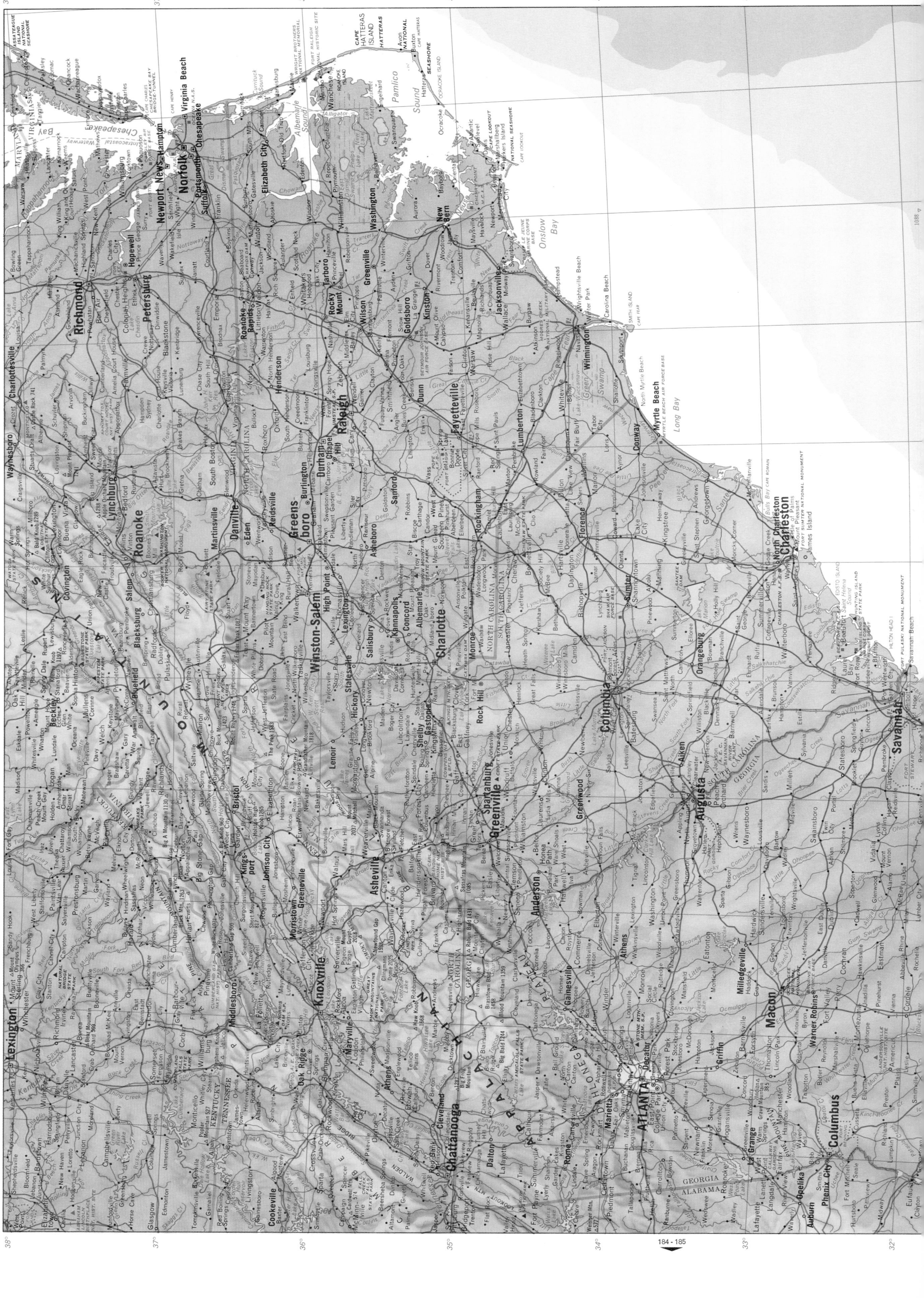

178-179

184-185

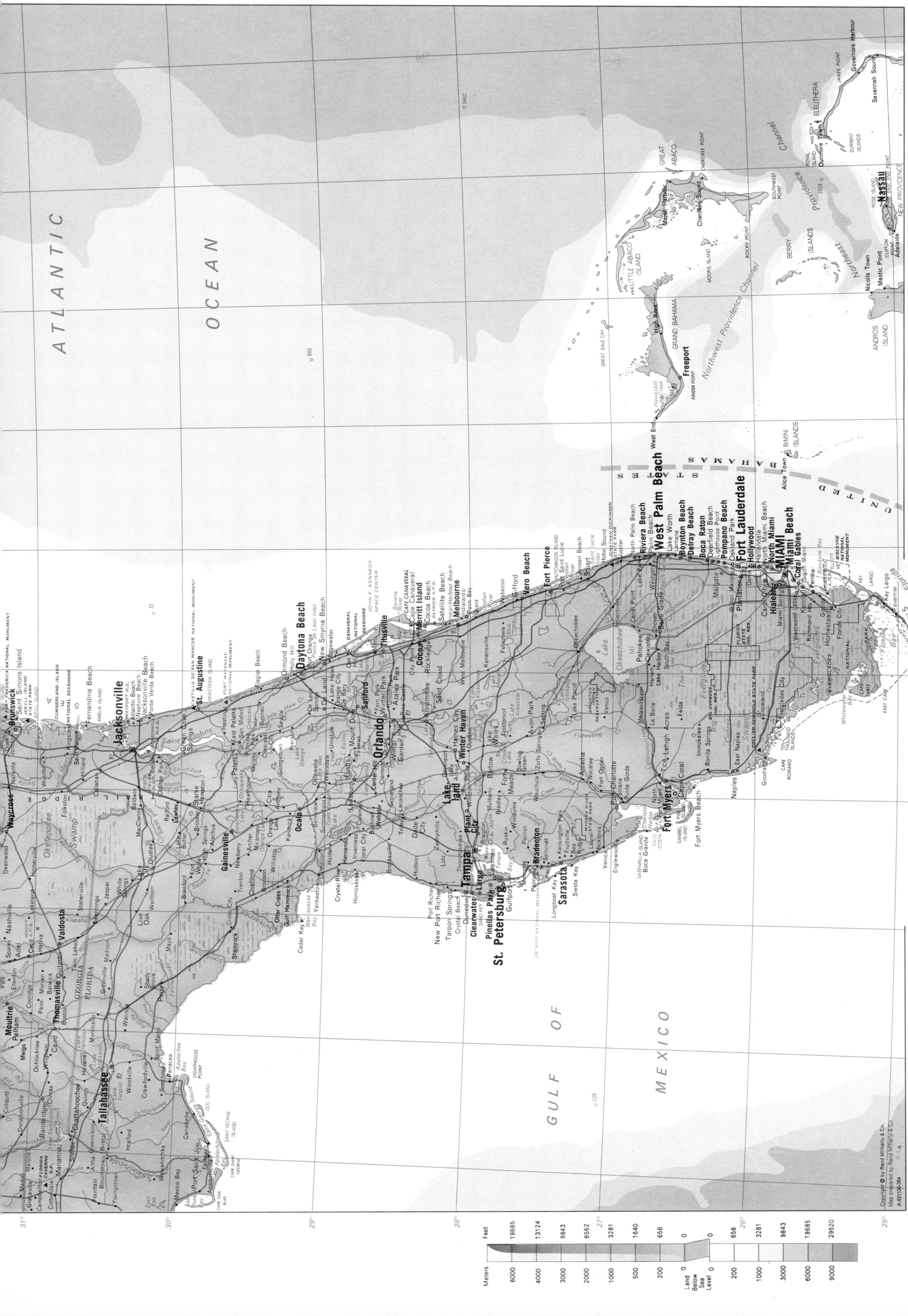
ATLANTIC
OCEAN
GULF OF MEXICO
BAHAMAS
UNITED STATES
Jacksonville
Tallahassee
Daytona Beach
Orlando
Tampa
St. Petersburg
Sarasota
Fort Myers
West Palm Beach
Fort Lauderdale
MIAMI
Key West
Freeport
Nassau
GRAND BAHAMA
Northwest Providence Channel
Straits of Florida
FLORIDA KEYS
Copyright © by Rand McNally & Co.
Map prepared by Rand McNally & Co.
Feet
Meters
Land Below Sea Level

178 - 179

180 - 181

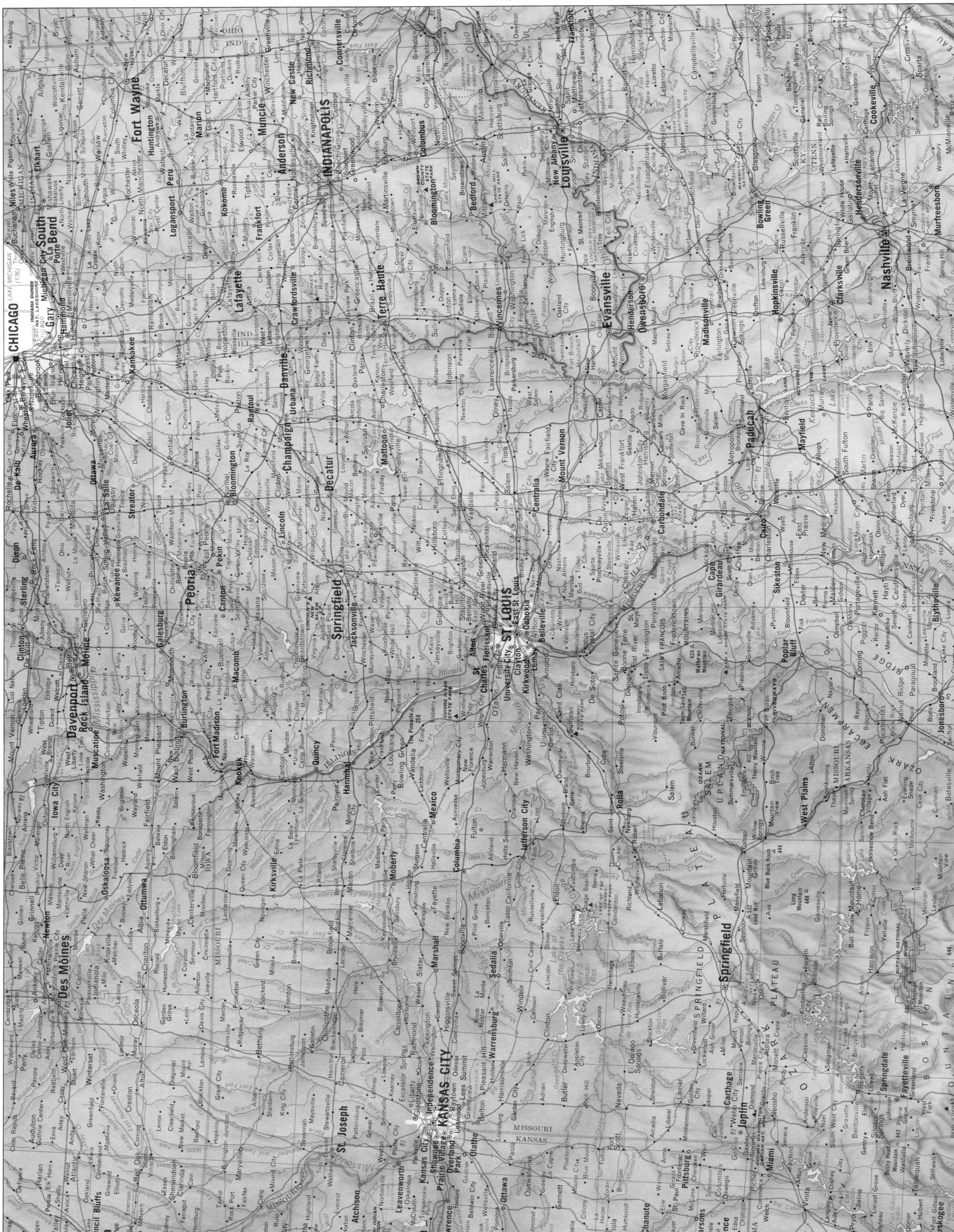

188 - 189

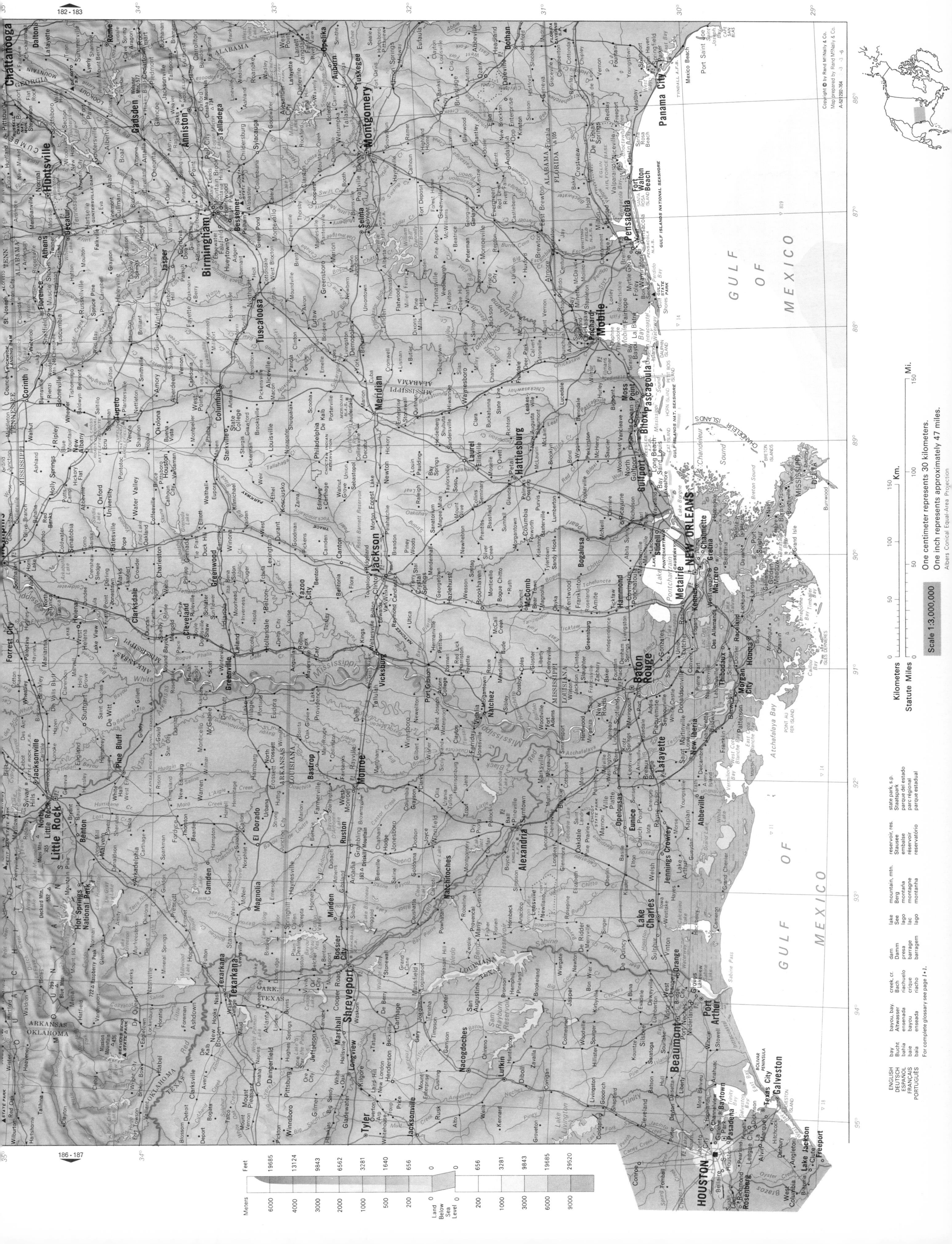
Scale 1:3,000,000
One centimeter represents 30 kilometers.
One inch represents approximately 47 miles.
Albers Conical Equal-Area Projection
GULF OF MEXICO

184 - 185

188 - 189

190 - 191

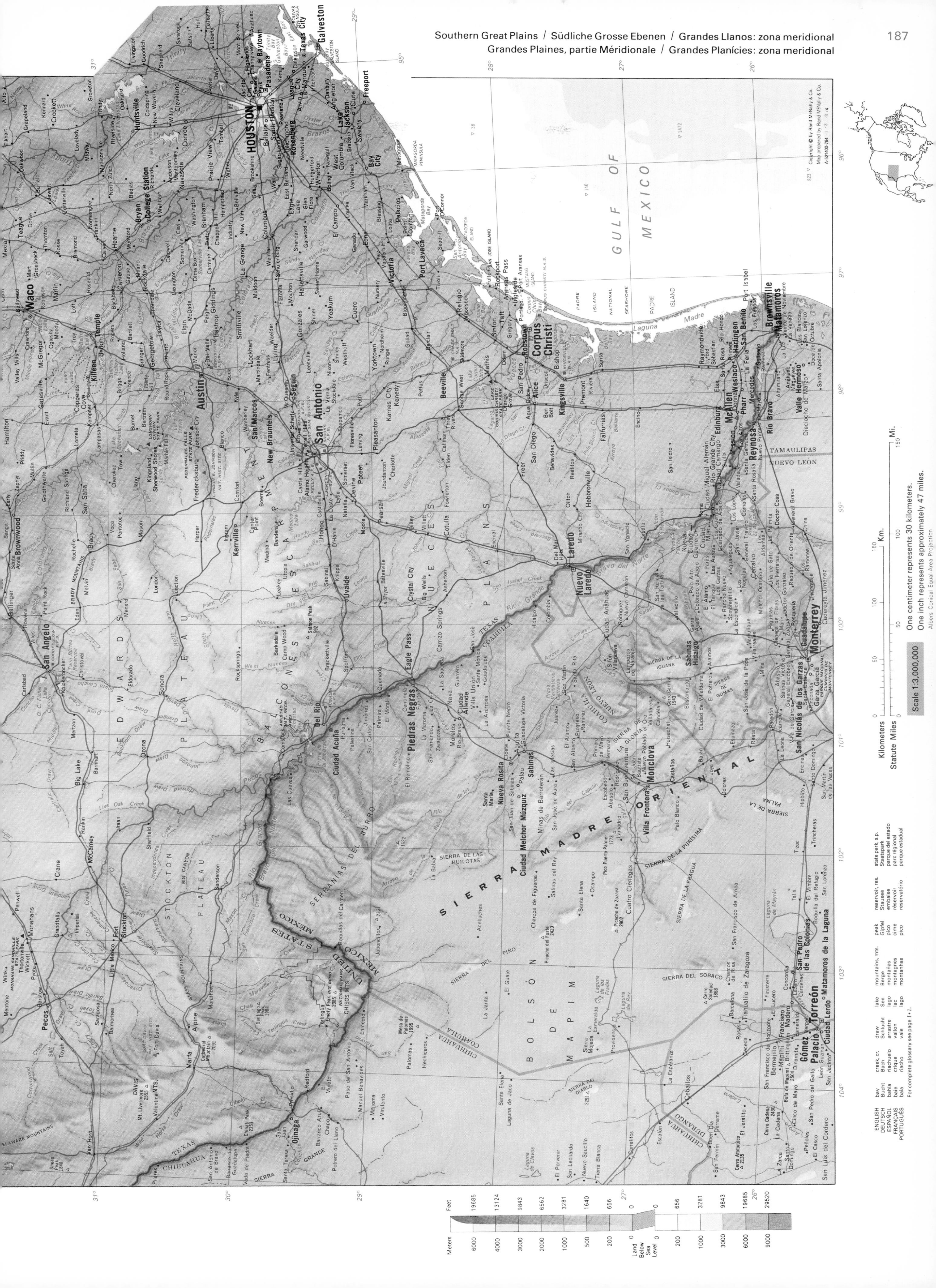
GULF OF MEXICO
HOUSTON
San Antonio
Austin
Corpus Christi
Monterrey
EDWARDS PLATEAU
STOCKTON PLATEAU
BALCONES ESCARPMENT
NUECES PLAINS
SIERRA MADRE ORIENTAL
BOLSÓN DE MAPIMÍ
TEXAS
COAHUILA
NUEVO LEON
TAMAULIPAS
CHIHUAHUA
DURANGO
UNITED STATES
MEXICO
Scale 1:3,000,000
One centimeter represents 30 kilometers.
One inch represents approximately 47 miles.
Albers Conical Equal-Area Projection
Kilometers
Statute Miles
Copyright © by Rand McNally & Co.
Map prepared by Rand McNally & Co.
Feet
Meters
Land Below Sea Level
For complete glossary see page I • I.

180-181
174-175
192-193
Winnipeg
Brandon
Grand Forks
Fargo
Moorhead
Bismarck
Minot
Williston
Jamestown
Aberdeen
Pierre
Rapid City
Dickinson
Miles City
St. Cloud
Brainerd
Bemidji
MANITOBA
SASKATCHEWAN
MINNESOTA
NORTH DAKOTA
SOUTH DAKOTA
MONTANA
WYOMING
ONTARIO
CANADA
UNITED STATES
COTEAU DU MISSOURI
SOURIS PLAIN
WILLISTON BASIN
BADLANDS
BLACK HILLS

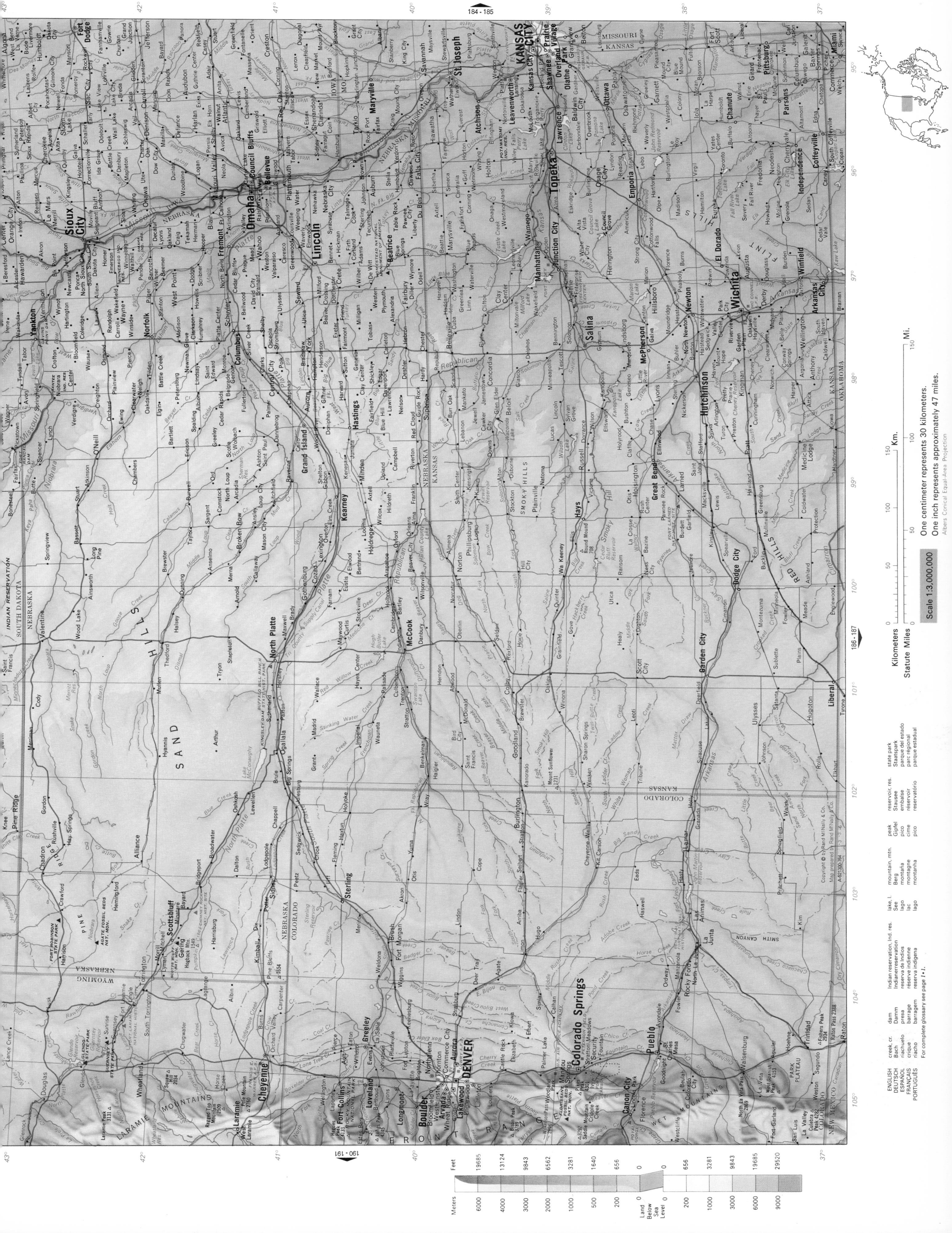
Scale 1:3,000,000
One centimeter represents 30 kilometers.
One inch represents approximately 47 miles.
Albers Conical Equal-Area Projection

188 - 189

192 - 193

194 - 195

186 - 187
Scale 1:3,000,000
One centimeter represents 30 kilometers.
One inch represents approximately 47 miles.
Albers Conical Equal-Area Projection
Kilometers
Statute Miles
ENGLISH creek, cr. Indian reservation lake mountains national monument, nat. mon. peak reservoir, res. wash
DEUTSCH Bach Indianerreservation See Berge Nationaldenkmal Gipfel Stausee Trockenfluss
ESPAÑOL riachuelo reserva de indios lago montañas monumental nacional pico reserva de agua uadi
FRANÇAIS crique réserve indienne lac montagnes monument national cime réservoir wadi
PORTUGUÊS riacho reserva indígena lago montanhas monumento nacional pico reservatório rio seco
For complete glossary see page I • 1.
Feet
Meters
Land Below Sea Level
Copyright © by Rand McNally & Co.

172 - 173

Meters	Feet
6000	19685
4000	13124
3000	9843
2000	6562
1000	3281
500	1640
200	656
0	0
Land Below Sea Level	
0	0
200	656
1000	3281
3000	9843
6000	19685
9000	29520

ENGLISH	creek, cr.	Indian reservation	lake, l.	mountain, mtn.	pass	peak	range	reservoir, res.
DEUTSCH	Bach	Indianerreservation	See	Berg	Pass	Gipfel	Gebirge	Stausee
ESPAÑOL	riachuelo	reserva de Indios	lago	montaña	paso	pico	sierra	embalse
FRANÇAIS	crique	réserve indienne	lac	montagne	col	cime	chaîne	réservoir
PORTUGUÊS	riacho	reserva indígena	lago	montanha	passo	pico	serra	reservatório

For complete glossary see page *I • 1*.

194 - 195

174 - 175

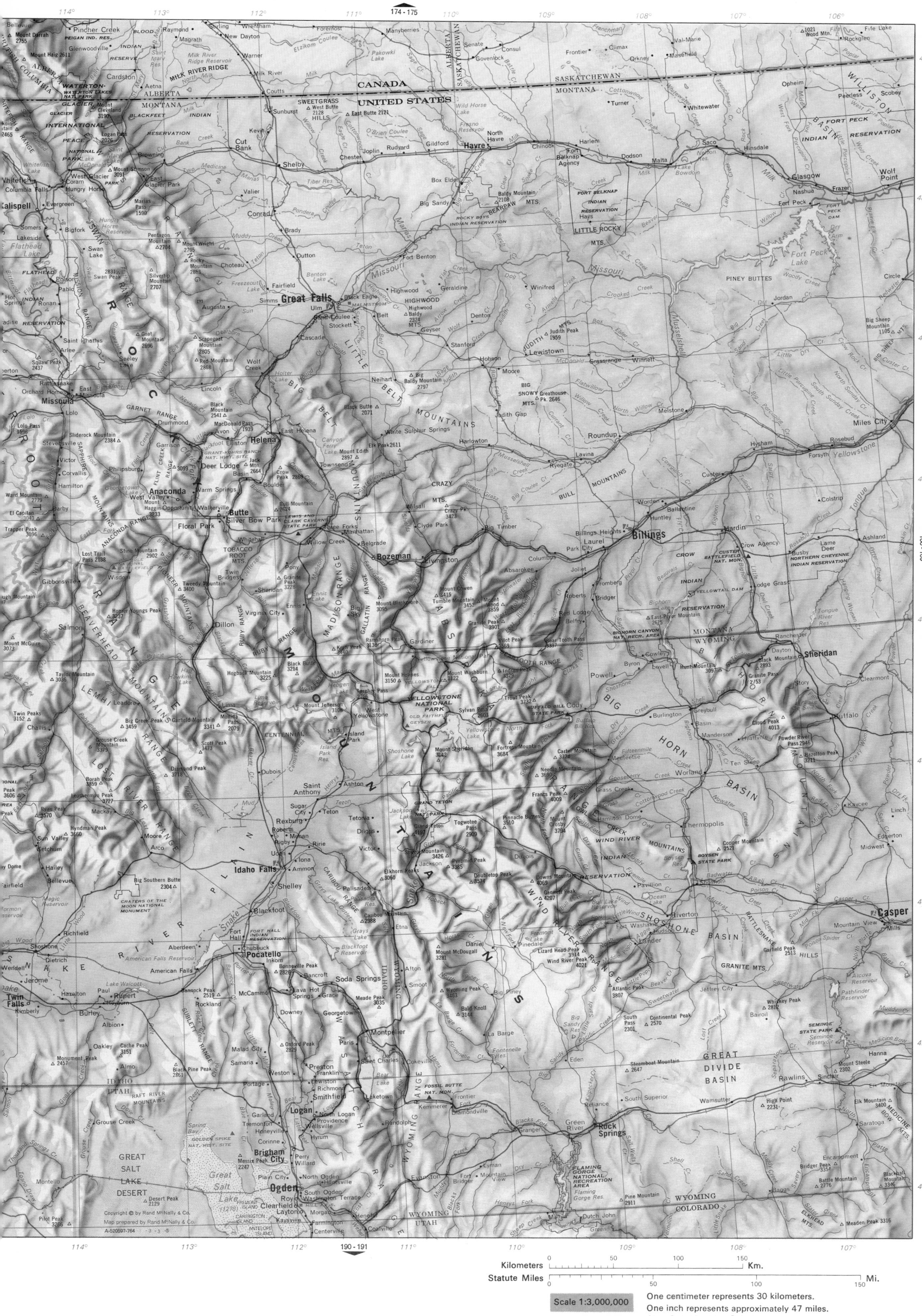

190 - 191
188 - 189

Kilometers 0 50 100 150 Km.
Statute Miles 0 50 100 150 Mi.

Scale 1:3,000,000
One centimeter represents 30 kilometers.
One inch represents approximately 47 miles.
Albers Conical Equal-Area Projection

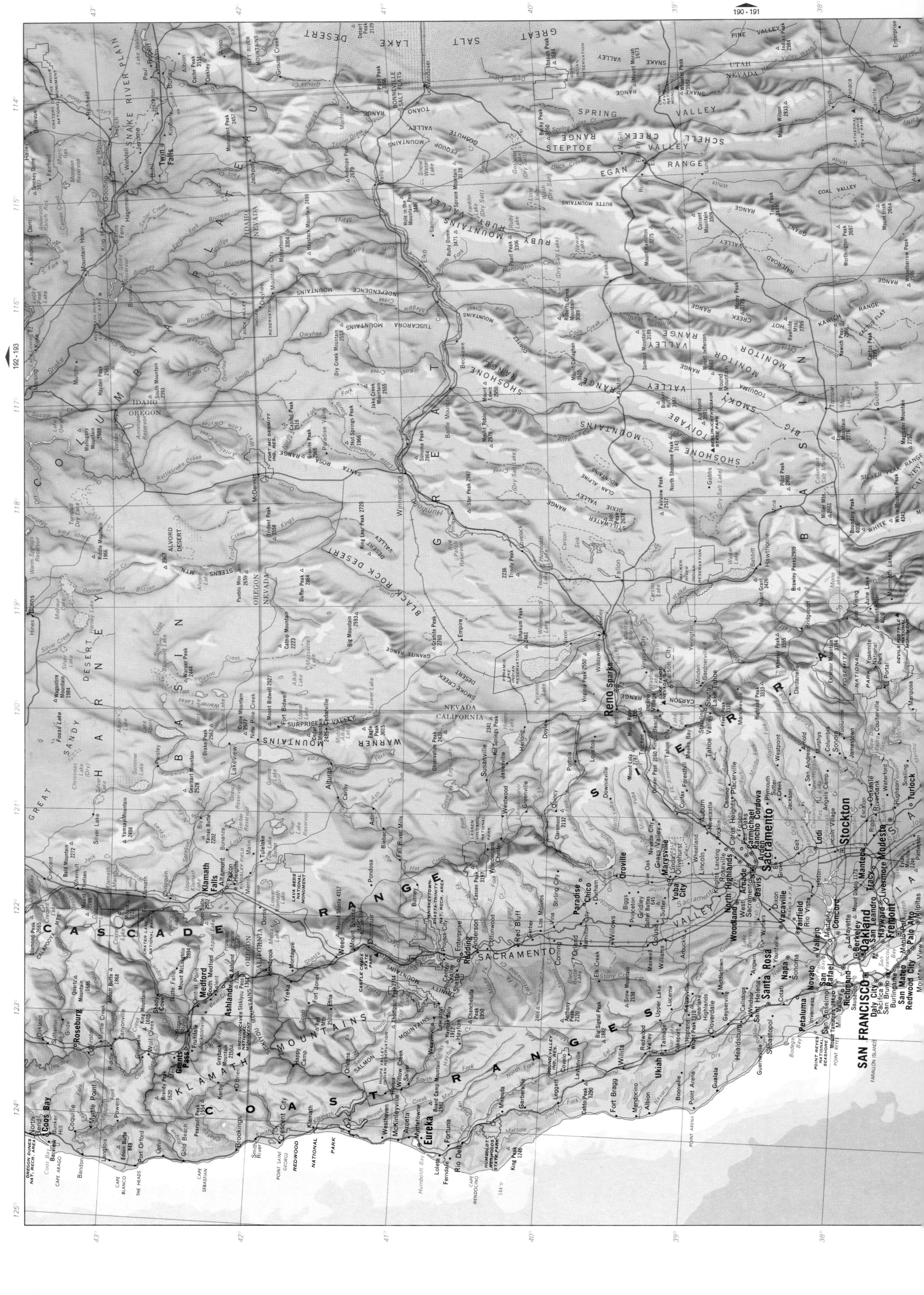
190 - 191
192 - 193
GREAT SALT LAKE DESERT
SNAKE RIVER PLAIN
COLUMBIA PLATEAU
GREAT BASIN
CASCADE RANGE
COAST RANGES
KLAMATH MOUNTAINS
SIERRA NEVADA
SACRAMENTO VALLEY
BLACK ROCK DESERT
RUBY MOUNTAINS
TOIYABE RANGE
SHOSHONE RANGE
IDAHO
NEVADA
OREGON
CALIFORNIA
UTAH
Twin Falls
Reno
Sparks
Carson City
Sacramento
Stockton
Oakland
SAN FRANCISCO
Berkeley
Fremont
Eureka
Redding
Chico
Medford
Klamath Falls
Grants Pass
Roseburg
Coos Bay
Santa Rosa
Winnemucca
Elko
Ely
Lakeview
Susanville
Alturas
Burns
Lake Tahoe
Pyramid Lake
Mount Shasta 4317
FARALLON ISLANDS
125°
124°
123°
122°
121°
120°
119°
118°
117°
116°
115°
114°
43°
42°
41°
40°
39°
38°

PACIFIC
OCEAN
LOS ANGELES
SAN DIEGO
Las Vegas
Tijuana
Mexicali
Kilometers
Statute Miles
Scale 1:3,000,000
One centimeter represents 30 kilometers.
One inch represents approximately 47 miles.
Albers Conical Equal-Area Projection
ENGLISH creek, cr. lake mountain, mtn. peak, pk. range reservoir, res. state park valley
DEUTSCH Bach See Berg Gipfel Gebirge Stausee Staatspark Tal
ESPAÑOL riachuelo lago montaña pico sierra embalse parque del estado valle
FRANÇAIS crique lac montagne cime chaîne réservoir parc régional vallée
PORTUGUÊS riacho lago montanha pico serra reservatório parque estadual vale
For complete glossary see page I • I.
Copyright © by Rand McNally & Co.
Map prepared by Rand McNally & Co.
Feet 19685 13124 9843 6562 3281 1640 656 0
Meters 6000 4000 3000 2000 1000 500 200 0
Land Below Sea Level
0 656 3281 9843 19685 29520
0 200 1000 3000 6000 9000

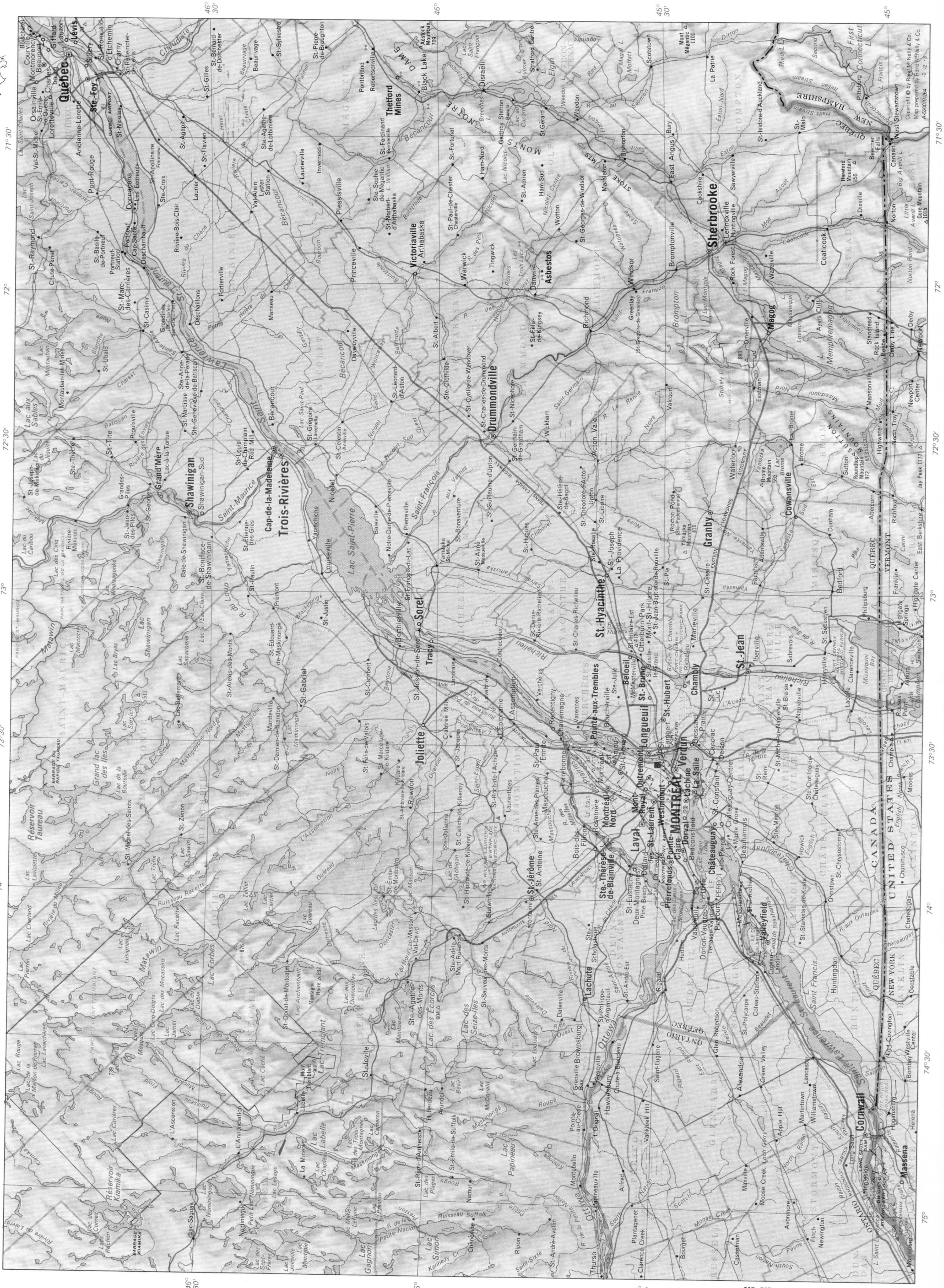

Kilometers 0 10 20 30 40 50 Km.
Statute Miles 0 10 20 30 40 50 Mi.

Scale 1:1,000,000
One centimeter represents 10 kilometers.
One inch represents approximately 16 miles.
Lambert Conformal Conic Projection

FRANÇAIS	aéroport	barrage	île	lac	montagne	parc	réservoir, rés.	rivière, r.
ENGLISH	airport	dam	island	lake	mountain	park	reservoir	river
DEUTSCH	Flughafen	Damm	Insel	See	Berg	Park	Stausee	Fluss
ESPAÑOL	aeropuerto	presa	isla	lago	montaña	parque	embalse	rio
PORTUGUÊS	aeroporto	barragem	ilha	lago	montanha	parque	reservatório	rio

For complete glossary see page I•1.
For Montréal metropolitan map, see page 265.

202 · 203

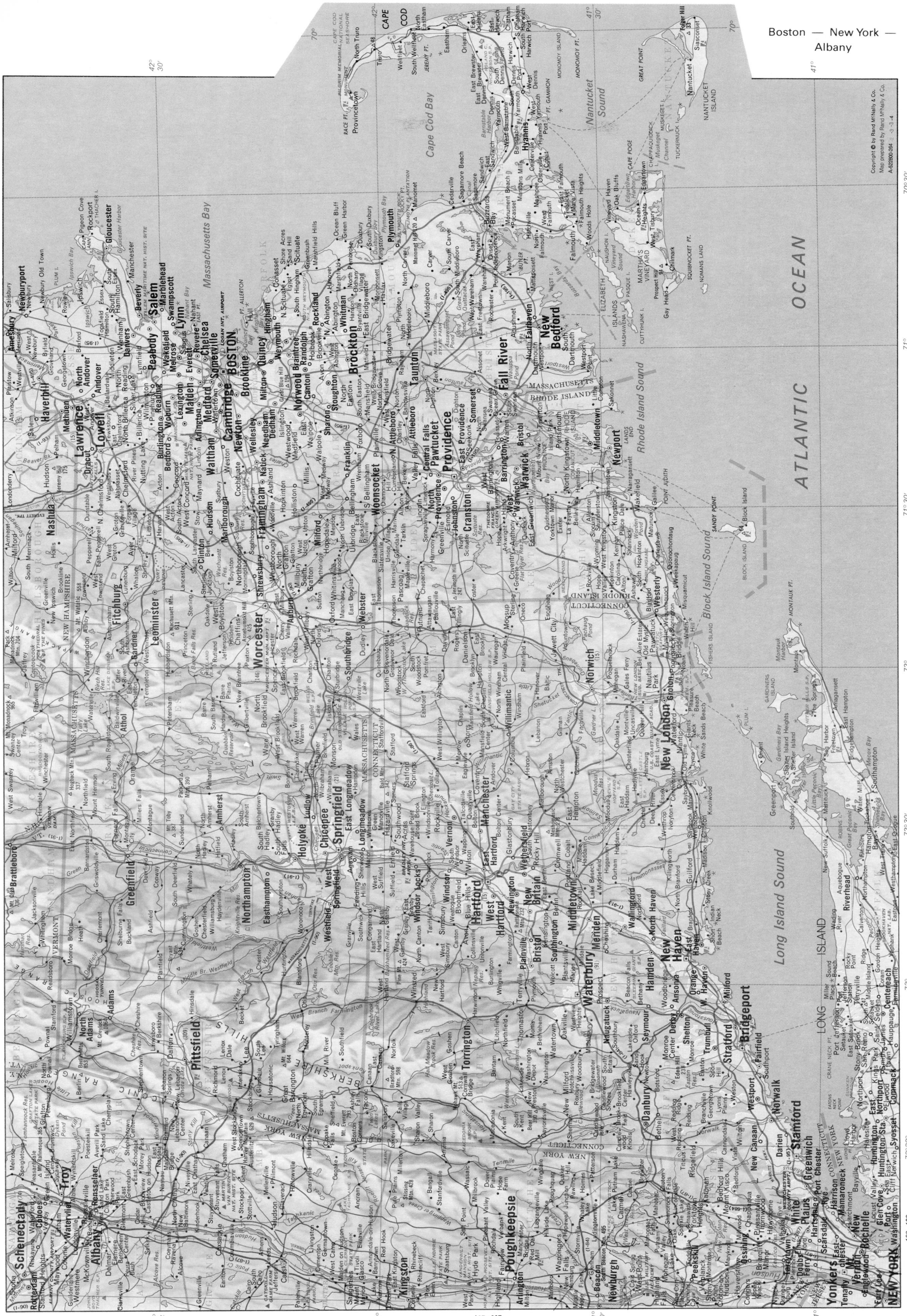
ATLANTIC OCEAN
Long Island Sound
Block Island Sound
Rhode Island Sound
Nantucket Sound
Cape Cod Bay
Massachusetts Bay
BOSTON
Providence
Hartford
New Haven
Albany
NEW YORK
Copyright © by Rand McNally & Co.

Scale 1:1,000,000

One centimeter represents 10 kilometers.
One inch represents approximately 16 miles.
Lambert Conformal Conic Projection

ENGLISH	bay	island, i.	lake, l.	mountain, mtn.	point, pt.	pond	reservoir, res.	sound
DEUTSCH	Bucht	Insel	See	Berg	Landspitze	Teich	Stausee	Sund
ESPAÑOL	bahia	isla	lago	montaña	punta	estanque	embalse	sonda
FRANÇAIS	baie	île	lac	montagne	pointe	étang	réservoir	détroit
PORTUGUÊS	baía	ilha	lago	montanha	ponta	lagoa	reservatório	estreito

For complete glossary see page I • I.
For Boston metropolitan map, see page 273. New York, pages 266-267.
198 - 199
200 - 201

NEW YORK
NEWARK
Jersey City
Elizabeth
Trenton
PHILADELPHIA
Camden
Wilmington
Chester
Atlantic City
Vineland
Allentown
Bethlehem
Reading
Lancaster
Harrisburg
York
BALTIMORE
Annapolis
WASHINGTON
Arlington
Alexandria
Frederick
Dover
Delaware Bay
200-201

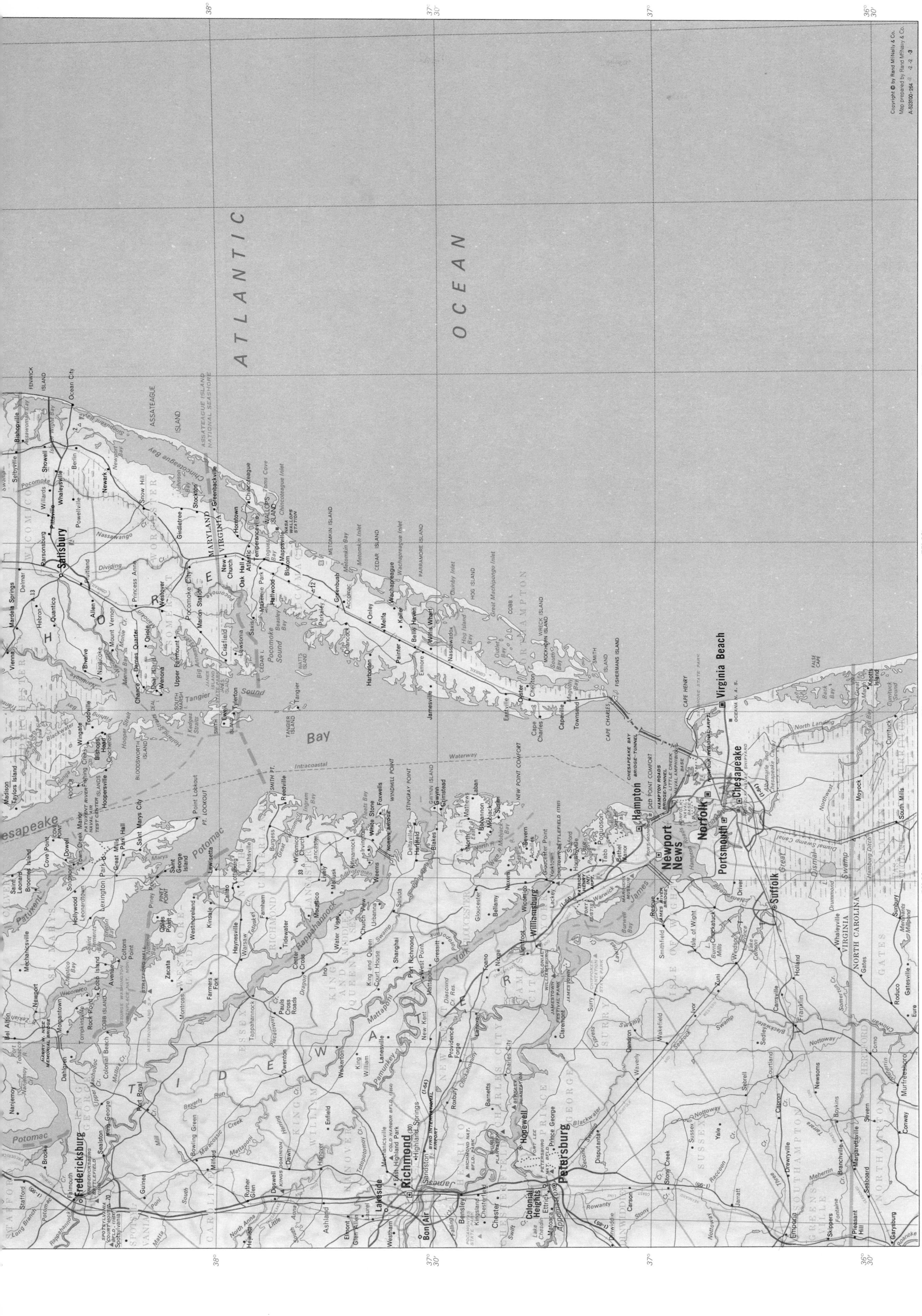

Scale 1:1,000,000

Kilometers 0 10 20 30 40 50 Km.

Statute Miles 0 10 20 30 40 50 Mi.

One centimeter represents 10 kilometers.
One inch represents approximately 16 miles.
Lambert Conformal Conic Projection

ENGLISH	airport, arpt.	bay	creek, cr.	inlet	island, i.	mountain	point, pt.	reservoir, res.	state park
DEUTSCH	Flughafen	Bucht	Bach	Einfahrt	Insel	Berg	Landspitze	Stausee	Naturpark
ESPAÑOL	aeropuerto	bahía	riachuelo	abra	isla	montaña	punta	embalse	parque provincial
FRANÇAIS	aéroport	baie	crique	bras de mer	île	montagne	pointe	réservoir	parc régional
PORTUGUÊS	aeroporto	baía	riacho	braço de mar	ilha	montanha	ponta	reservatório	parque estadual

For complete glossary see page *I • 1*.

For New York metropolitan map, see pages 266-267; Philadelphia, page 275; Baltimore and Washington, D.C., page 274.

ENGLISH	airport, arpt.	bay	creek, cr.	hill	island	lake	mountain	reservoir	state park, s.p.
DEUTSCH	Flughafen	Bucht	Bach	Hügel	Insel	See	Berg	Stausee	Naturpark
ESPAÑOL	aeropuerto	bahía	riachuelo	colina	isla	lago	montaña	embalse	parque provincial
FRANÇAIS	aéroport	baie	crique	colline	île	lac	montagne	réservoir	parc régional
PORTUGUÊS	aeroporto	baía	riacho	colina	ilha	lago	montanha	reservatório	parque estadual

For complete glossary see page I • 1.
For Buffalo metropolitan map, see page 274; New York, pages 266-267.

Kilometers 0 10 20 30 40 50 Km.

Statute Miles 0 10 20 30 40 50 Mi.

Scale 1:1,000,000

One centimeter represents 10 kilometers.
One inch represents approximately 16 miles.

Lambert Conformal Conic Projection

ENGLISH	airport	bay	canal	channel	creek, cr.	Indian reservation	island	lake, l.	point
DEUTSCH	Flughafen	Bucht	Kanal	Kanal	Bach	Indianerreservation	Insel	See	Landspitze
ESPAÑOL	aeropuerto	bahía	canal	canal	riachuelo	reserva de Indios	isla	lago	punta
FRANÇAIS	aéroport	baie	canal	canal	crique	réserve indienne	île	lac	pointe
PORTUGUÊS	aeroporto	baía	canal	canal	riacho	reserva indígena	ilha	lago	ponta

For complete glossary see page I•1.
For Toronto metropolitan map, see page 265; Buffalo, page 274.
204 - 205

Kilometers 0 10 20 30 40 50 Km.

Statute Miles 0 10 20 30 40 50 Mi.

Scale 1:1,000,000

One centimeter represents 10 kilometers.

One inch represents approximately 16 miles.

Lambert Conformal Conic Projection

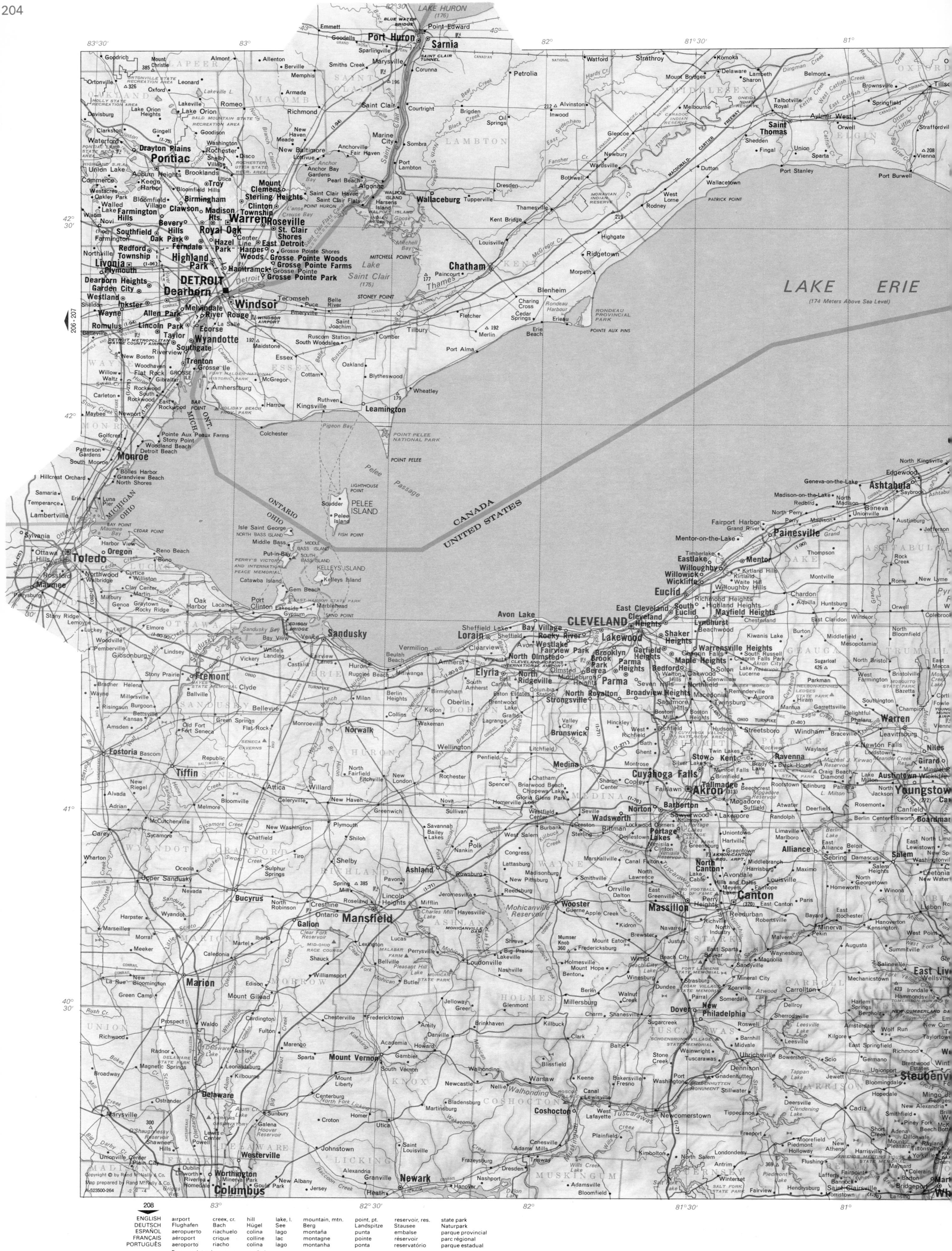

ENGLISH	airport	creek, cr.	hill	lake, l.	mountain, mtn.	point, pt.	reservoir, res.	state park
DEUTSCH	Flughafen	Bach	Hügel	See	Berg	Landspitze	Stausee	Naturpark
ESPAÑOL	aeropuerto	riachuelo	colina	lago	montaña	punta	embalse	parque provincial
FRANÇAIS	aéroport	crique	colline	lac	montagne	pointe	réservoir	parc régional
PORTUGUÊS	aeroporto	riacho	colina	lago	montanha	ponta	reservatório	parque estadual

For complete glossary see page *I* • *1*.
For Pittsburgh and Cleveland metropolitan maps, see page 269; Detroit, page 271; Buffalo, page 274.

Kilometers 0 10 20 30 40 50 Km.

Statute Miles 0 10 20 30 40 50 Mi.

Scale 1:1,000,000

One centimeter represents 10 kilometers.

One inch represents approximately 16 miles.

Lambert Conformal Conic Projection

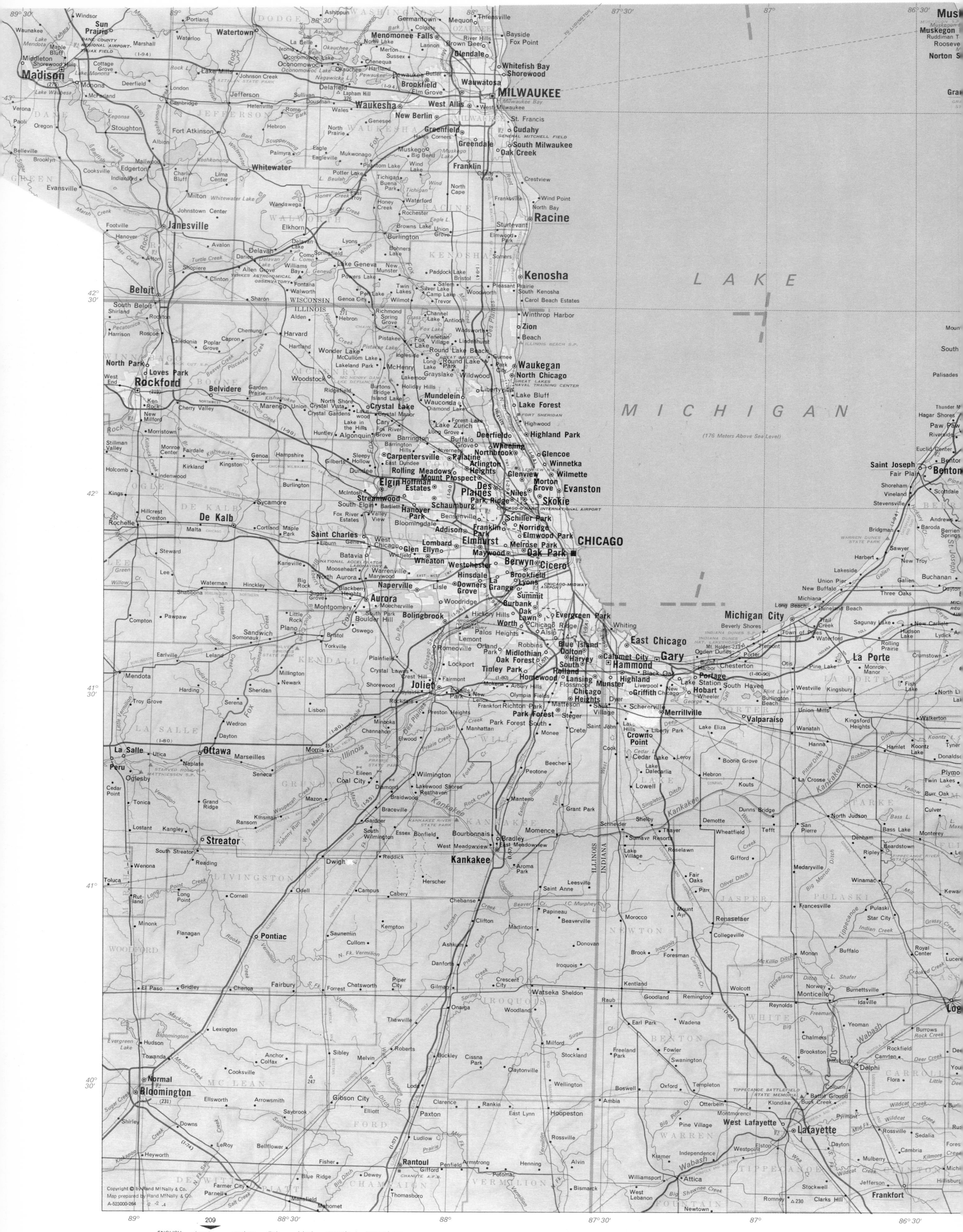

ENGLISH	airport	creek, cr.	ditch	lake, l.	reservoir	state park, s.p.
DEUTSCH	Flughafen	Bach	Graben	See	Stausee	Naturpark
ESPAÑOL	aeropuerto	riachuelo	acequia	lago	embalse	parque provincial
FRANÇAIS	aéroport	crique	fossé	lac	réservoir	parc régional
PORTUGUÊS	aeroporto	riacho	fosso	lago	reservatório	parque estadual

For complete glossary see page *I* • *1*.
For Chicago metropolitan map, see page 268; Detroit, page 271.

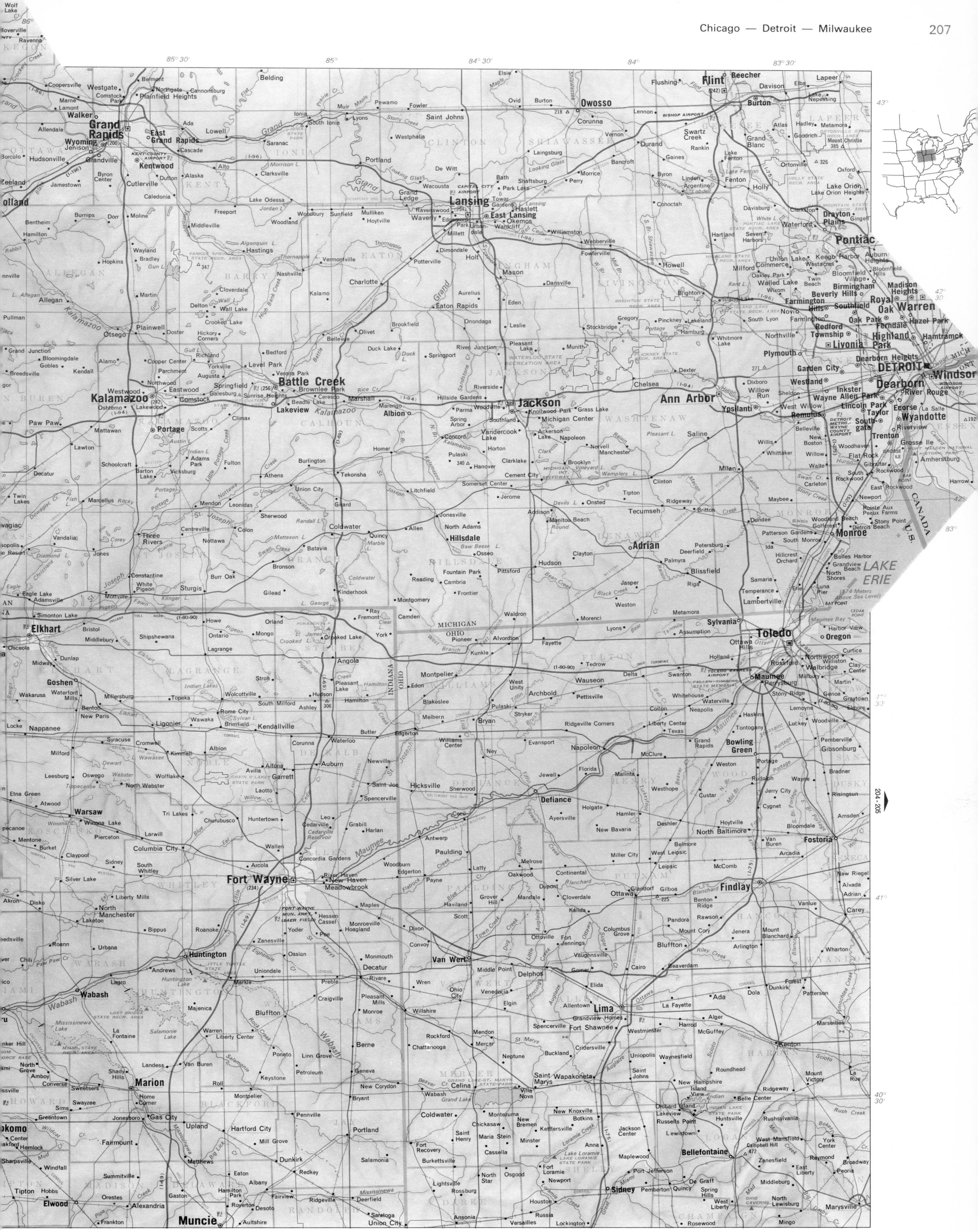

Kilometers 0 10 20 30 40 50 Km.
Statute Miles 0 10 20 30 40 50 Mi.

Scale 1:1,000,000

One centimeter represents 10 kilometers.
One inch represents approximately 16 miles.
Lambert Conformal Conic Projection

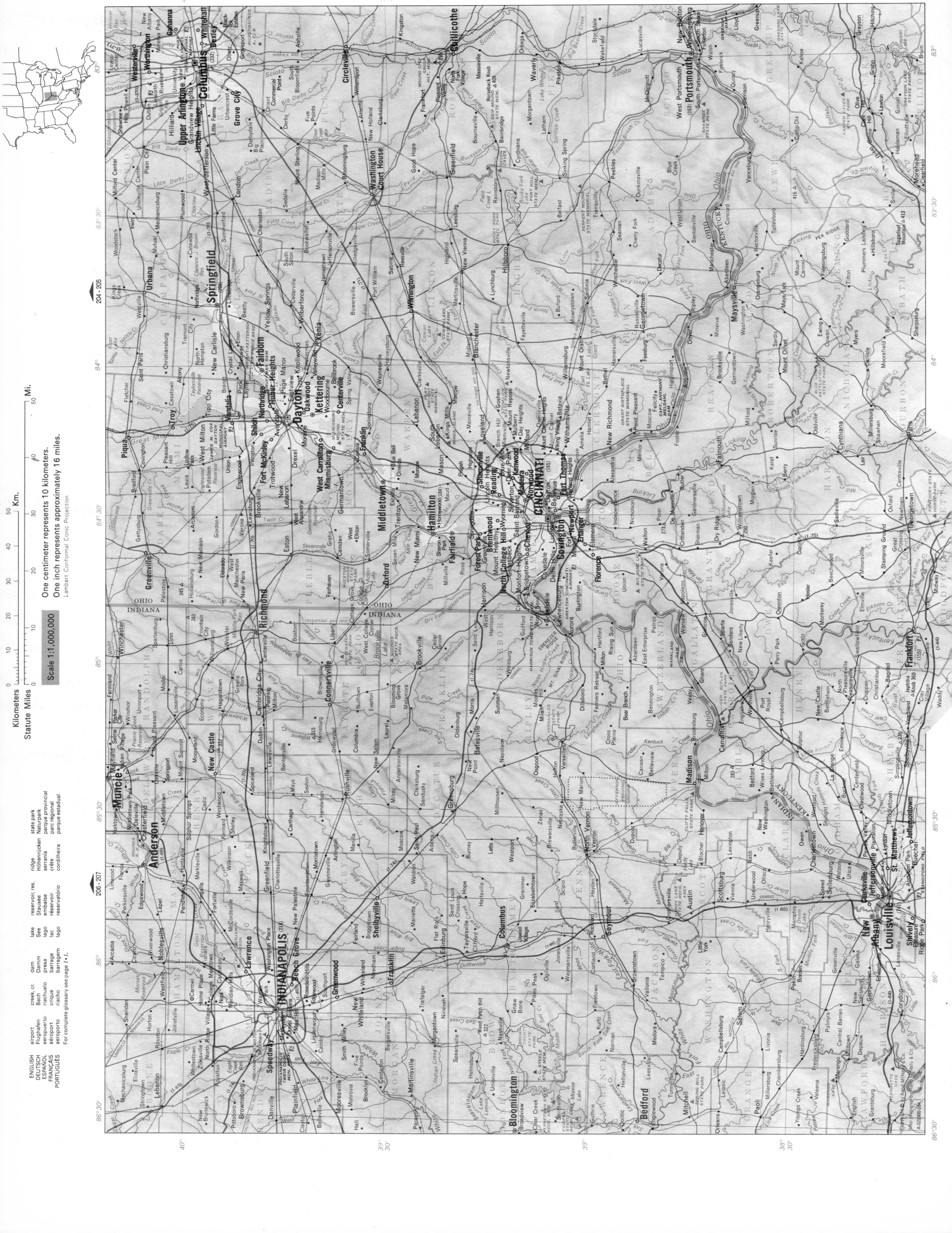
Scale 1:1,000,000
One centimeter represents 10 kilometers.
One inch represents approximately 16 miles.
Lambert Conformal Conic Projection

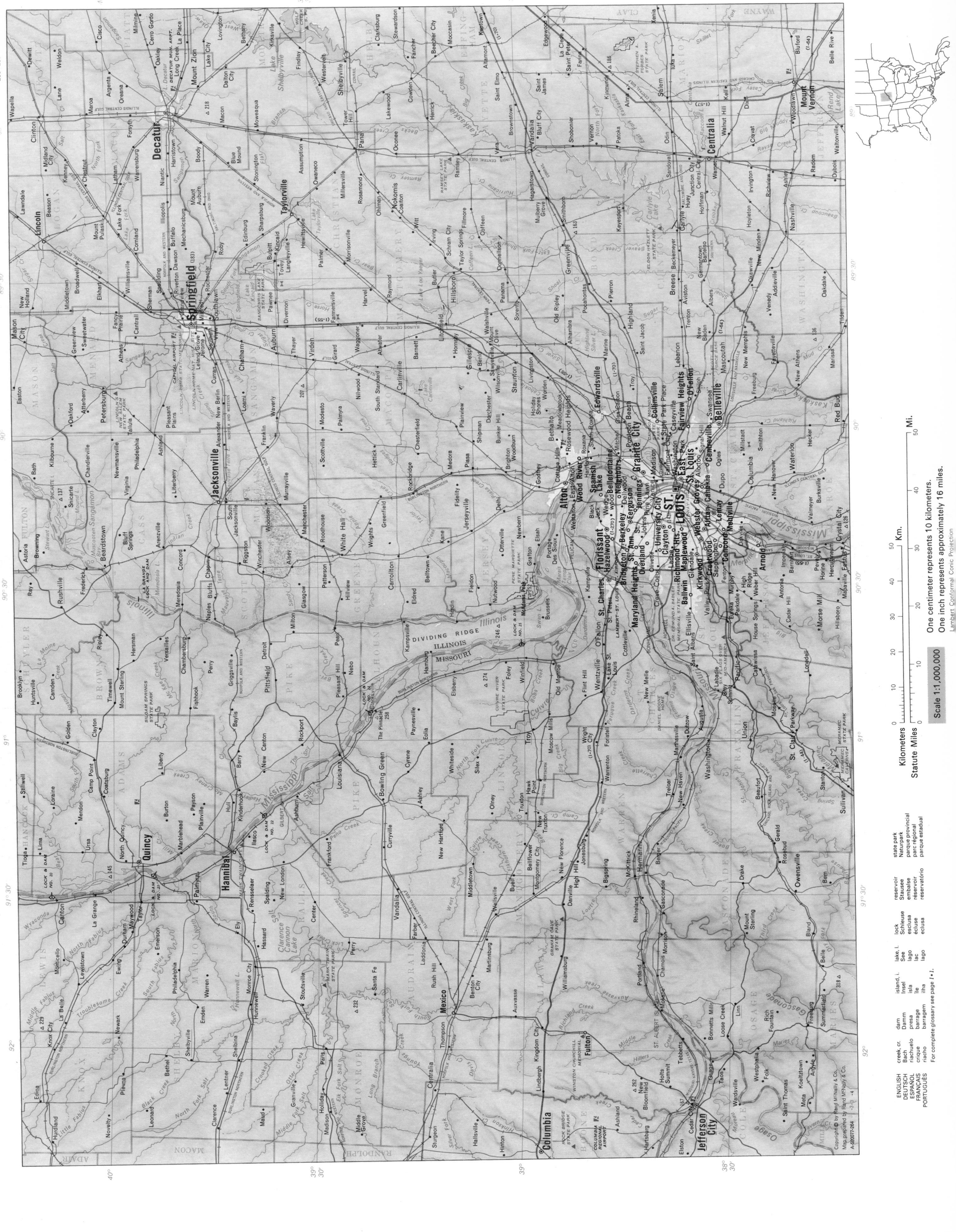

206-207
Scale 1:1,000,000
One centimeter represents 10 kilometers.
One inch represents approximately 16 miles.
Kilometers
Statute Miles
Km.
Mi.
Lambert Conformal Conic Projection
ENGLISH creek, cr. dam island, i. lake, l. lock reservoir state park
DEUTSCH Bach Damm Insel See Schleuse Stausee Naturpark
ESPAÑOL riachuelo presa isla lago esclusa embalse parque provincial
FRANÇAIS crique barrage île lac écluse réservoir parc régional
PORTUGUÊS riacho barragem ilha lago eclusa reservatório parque estadual
For complete glossary see page I•2.
Copyright © by Rand McNally & Co.
Map prepared by Rand McNally & Co.
Springfield
St. Louis
Decatur
Jacksonville
Quincy
Hannibal
Jefferson City
Columbia
Mexico
Centralia
Belleville
Alton
Mississippi
Illinois
Missouri

Kilometers 0 10 20 30 40 50 Km.

Statute Miles 0 10 20 30 40 50 Mi.

Scale 1:1,000,000

One centimeter represents 10 kilometers.
One inch represents approximately 16 miles.

Lambert Conformal Conic Projection

ENGLISH	bay	canal	cape	creek, cr.	inlet	island	key	lake, l.	swamp
DEUTSCH	Bucht	Kanal	Kap	Bach	Einfahrt	Insel	Klippe	See	Sumpf
ESPAÑOL	bahía	canal	cabo	riachuelo	abra	isla	cayo	lago	pantano
FRANÇAIS	baie	canal	cap	crique	bras de mer	île	caye	lac	marais
PORTUGUÊS	baía	canal	cabo	riacho	braço de mar	ilha	recife	lago	pântano

For complete glossary see page I•1.

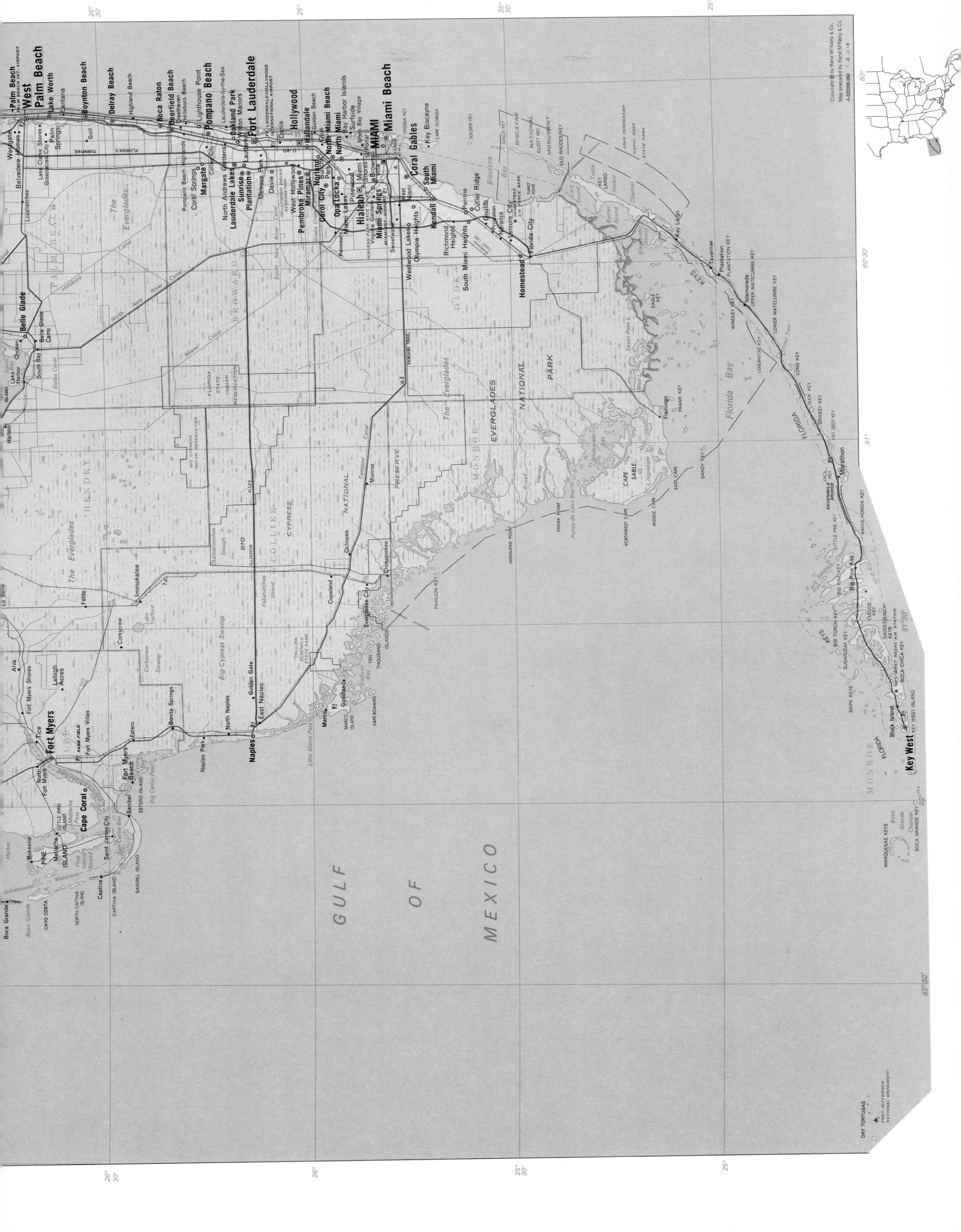
West Palm Beach
Palm Beach
Lake Worth
Lantana
Boynton Beach
Delray Beach
Highland Beach
Boca Raton
Deerfield Beach
Hillsboro Beach
Pompano Beach
Lighthouse Point
Margate
Coral Springs
Lauderdale-by-the-Sea
Oakland Park
Fort Lauderdale
Lauderdale Lakes
Sunrise
Plantation
Davie
Dania
Hollywood
Hallandale
Golden Beach
North Miami Beach
North Miami
Bay Harbor Islands
Surfside
Miami Beach
Miramar
Pembroke Pines
West Hollywood
Norland
Opa Locka
Carol City
Hialeah
Miami Springs
Miami Lakes
Pennsuco
MIAMI
Coral Gables
South Miami
West Miami
Key Biscayne
Westwood Lakes
Olympia Heights
Kendall
Perrine
Cutler Ridge
Goulds
Richmond Heights
South Miami Heights
Leisure City
Naranja
Princeton
Florida City
Homestead
Key Largo
Tavernier
Plantation
Islamorada
Marathon
Big Pine Key
Stock Island
Key West
Belle Glade
South Bay
Lake Harbor
Clewiston
Harlem
Immokalee
Felda
Corkscrew
Alva
Lehigh Acres
Fort Myers Shores
Tice
Fort Myers
North Fort Myers
Fort Myers Villas
Cape Coral
Estero
Bonita Springs
Fort Myers Beach
Sanibel
Saint James City
Bokeelia
Matlacha
Captiva
Boca Grande
Naples Park
North Naples
Naples
East Naples
Golden Gate
Marco
Goodland
Copeland
Ochopee
Everglades City
Chokoloskee
Monroe
Flamingo
GULF OF MEXICO
Florida Bay
EVERGLADES NATIONAL PARK
BIG CYPRESS
The Everglades
Big Cypress Swamp
BISCAYNE NATIONAL MONUMENT
TEN THOUSAND ISLANDS
CAPE SABLE
DRY TORTUGAS
FORT JEFFERSON NATIONAL MONUMENT
MARQUESAS KEYS
Copyright © by Rand McNally & Co.
Map prepared by Rand McNally & Co.

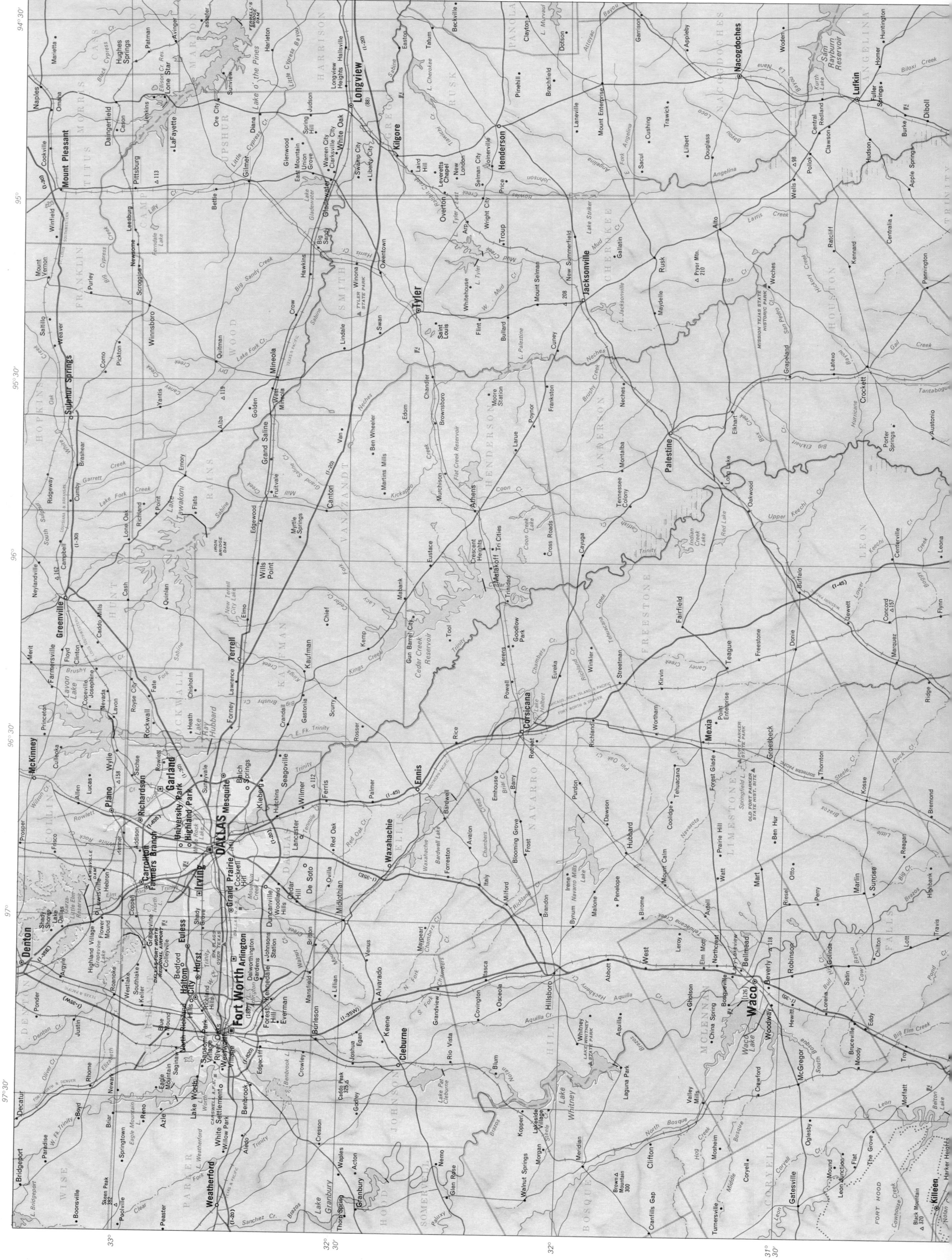
Dallas
Fort Worth
Arlington
Irving
Grand Prairie
Garland
Mesquite
Richardson
Plano
McKinney
Denton
Waco
Tyler
Longview
Kilgore
Henderson
Nacogdoches
Lufkin
Palestine
Jacksonville
Corsicana
Athens
Ennis
Waxahachie
Cleburne
Hillsboro
Mexia
Terrell
Greenville
Sulphur Springs
Mount Pleasant
Weatherford
Granbury
Killeen

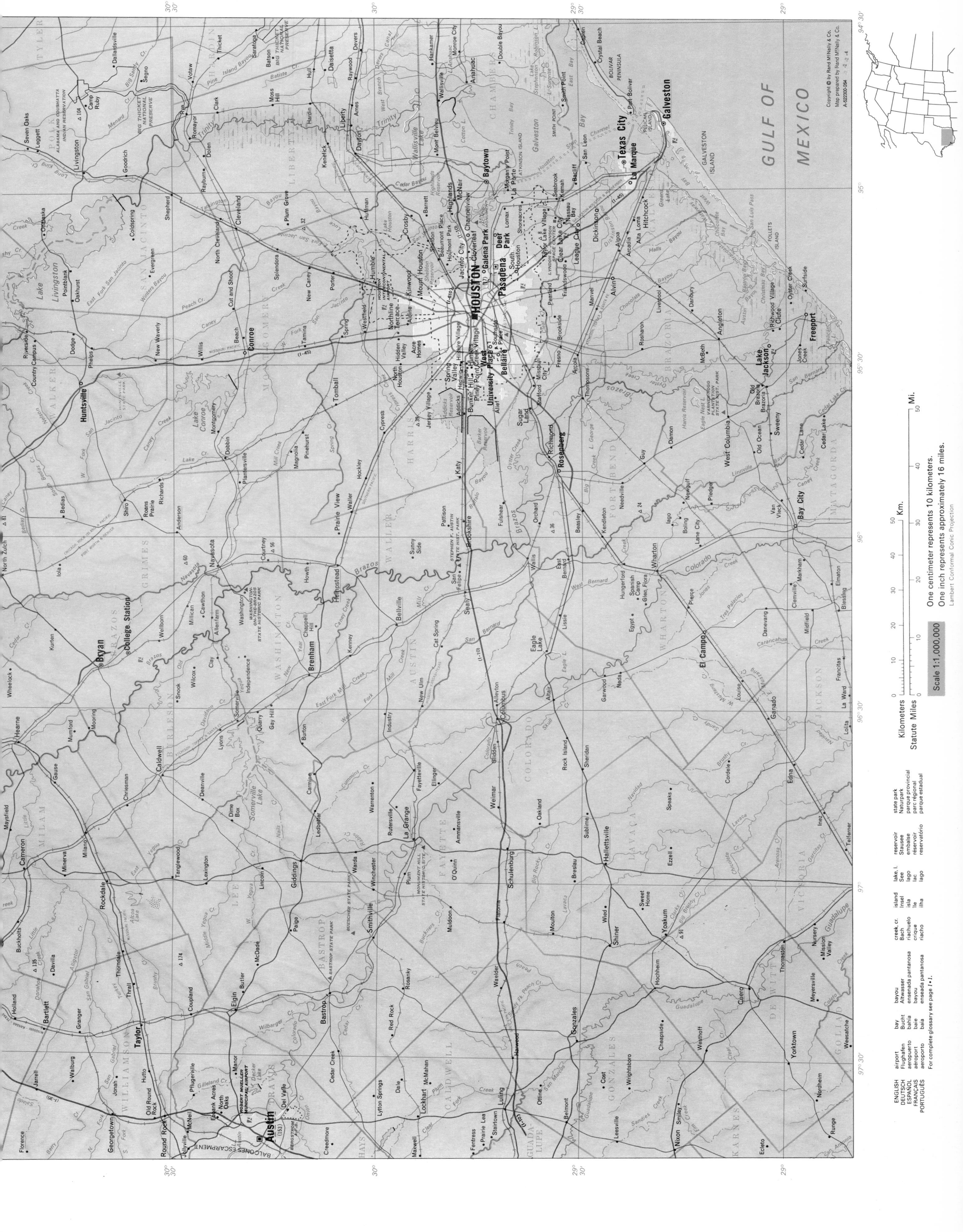
GULF OF MEXICO
HOUSTON
Galveston
Texas City
Baytown
Pasadena
Austin
Bryan
College Station
Huntsville
Conroe
Brenham
Taylor
Kilometers
Statute Miles
Km.
Mi.
Scale 1:1,000,000
One centimeter represents 10 kilometers.
One inch represents approximately 16 miles.
Lambert Conformal Conic Projection
Copyright © by Rand McNally & Co.
Map prepared by Rand McNally & Co.
ENGLISH DEUTSCH ESPAÑOL FRANÇAIS PORTUGUÊS
airport Flughafen aeropuerto aéroport aeroporto
bay Bucht bahía baie baía
bayou Altwasser ensenada pantanosa bayou enseada pantanosa
creek, cr. Bach riachuelo crique riacho
island Insel isla île ilha
lake, l. See lago lac lago
reservoir Stausee embalse réservoir reservatório
state park Naturpark parque provincial parc régional parque estadual
For complete glossary see page I • I.

VANCOUVER
New Westminster
Burnaby
Richmond
Victoria
Nanaimo
SEATTLE
Tacoma
Everett
Bellingham
Bremerton
Port Angeles
Mount Vernon
Anacortes
Strait of Georgia
Strait of Juan de Fuca
CANADA
UNITED STATES
BRITISH COLUMBIA
WASHINGTON
VANCOUVER ISLAND
OLYMPIC MOUNTAINS
CASCADE MOUNTAINS
WENATCHEE MOUNTAINS
SAN JUAN ISLANDS
WHIDBEY ISLAND

Scale 1:1,000,000

Kilometers 0 10 20 30 40 50 Km.

Statute Miles 0 10 20 30 40 50 Mi.

One centimeter represents 10 kilometers.
One inch represents approximately 16 miles.
Lambert Conformal Conic Projection

ENGLISH	bay	cape	channel	creek, cr.	island, i.	lake, l.	mount	peak	strait
DEUTSCH	Bucht	Kap	Kanal	Bach	Insel	See	Berg	Gipfel	Meeresstrasse
ESPAÑOL	bahía	cabo	canal	riachuelo	isla	lago	monte	pico	estrecho
FRANÇAIS	baie	cap	canal	crique	île	lac	mont	cime	détroit
PORTUGUÊS	baía	cabo	canal	riacho	ilha	lago	monte	pico	estreito

For complete glossary see page I•1.

Reno
Sparks
Carson City
South Lake Tahoe
Lake Tahoe
CARSON RANGE
CARSON VALLEY
PINE NUT MOUNTAINS
SIERRA NEVADA
Yosemite National Park
CATHEDRAL RANGE
Sacramento
West Sacramento
Roseville
Auburn
Placerville
Marysville
Yuba City
Oroville
Davis
Woodland
Stockton
Lodi
Modesto
Manteca
Tracy
Livermore
Pleasanton
Fremont
Hayward
Oakland
Berkeley
Alameda
San Leandro
SAN FRANCISCO
Daly City
San Mateo
Pacifica
Concord
Walnut Creek
Pittsburg
Antioch
Fairfield
Vacaville
Vallejo
Napa
Santa Rosa
Petaluma
Novato
SACRAMENTO VALLEY
NAPA VALLEY
SONOMA MOUNTAINS

PACIFIC OCEAN
Monterey Bay
SANTA CRUZ MOUNTAINS
SANTA CLARA VALLEY
GABILAN RANGE
COAST RANGES
SALINAS VALLEY
SIERRA DE SALINAS
SANTA LUCIA RANGE
DIABLO RANGE
CHOLAME HILLS
TEMBLOR RANGE
KETTLEMAN HILLS
CARRIZO PLAIN
LA PANZA RANGE
SAN JOAQUIN VALLEY
Santa Cruz
Watsonville
Gilroy
Hollister
Salinas
Monterey
Pacific Grove
Seaside
Carmel
Soledad
King City
San Lucas
San Ardo
Bradley
San Miguel
Paso Robles
Templeton
Atascadero
Morro Bay
San Luis Obispo
Cambria
San Simeon
Los Gatos
Saratoga
Campbell
Los Banos
Chowchilla
Madera
Fresno
Clovis
Sanger
Reedley
Selma
Kingsburg
Hanford
Visalia
Tulare
Lemoore
Coalinga
Avenal
Corcoran
Delano
Wasco
McFarland
Bakersfield
Oildale
Kerman
Mendota
Firebaugh
Huron
Five Points
Shandon
Cholame
McKittrick
Taft
Ford City
Fellows
Lost Hills
218
Copyright © by Rand McNally & Co.
Map prepared by Rand McNally & Co.
A-522500-264

ENGLISH	bay	canal	creek, cr.	lake, l.	mountain, mtn.	pass	range	reservoir	slough
DEUTSCH	Bucht	Kanal	Bach	See	Berg	Pass	Gebirge	Stausee	verlandene Wasserfläche
ESPAÑOL	bahía	canal	riachuelo	lago	montaña	paso	sierra	embalse	pantano
FRANÇAIS	baie	canal	crique	lac	montagne	col	chaîne	réservoir	fondrière
PORTUGUÊS	baía	canal	riacho	lago	montanha	passo	serra	reservatório	pântano

For complete glossary see page I • 1.
For San Francisco metropolitan map, see page 272.

Kilometers 0 10 20 30 40 50 Km.
Statute Miles 0 10 20 30 40 50 Mi.

Scale 1:1,000,000

One centimeter represents 10 kilometers.
One inch represents approximately 16 miles.

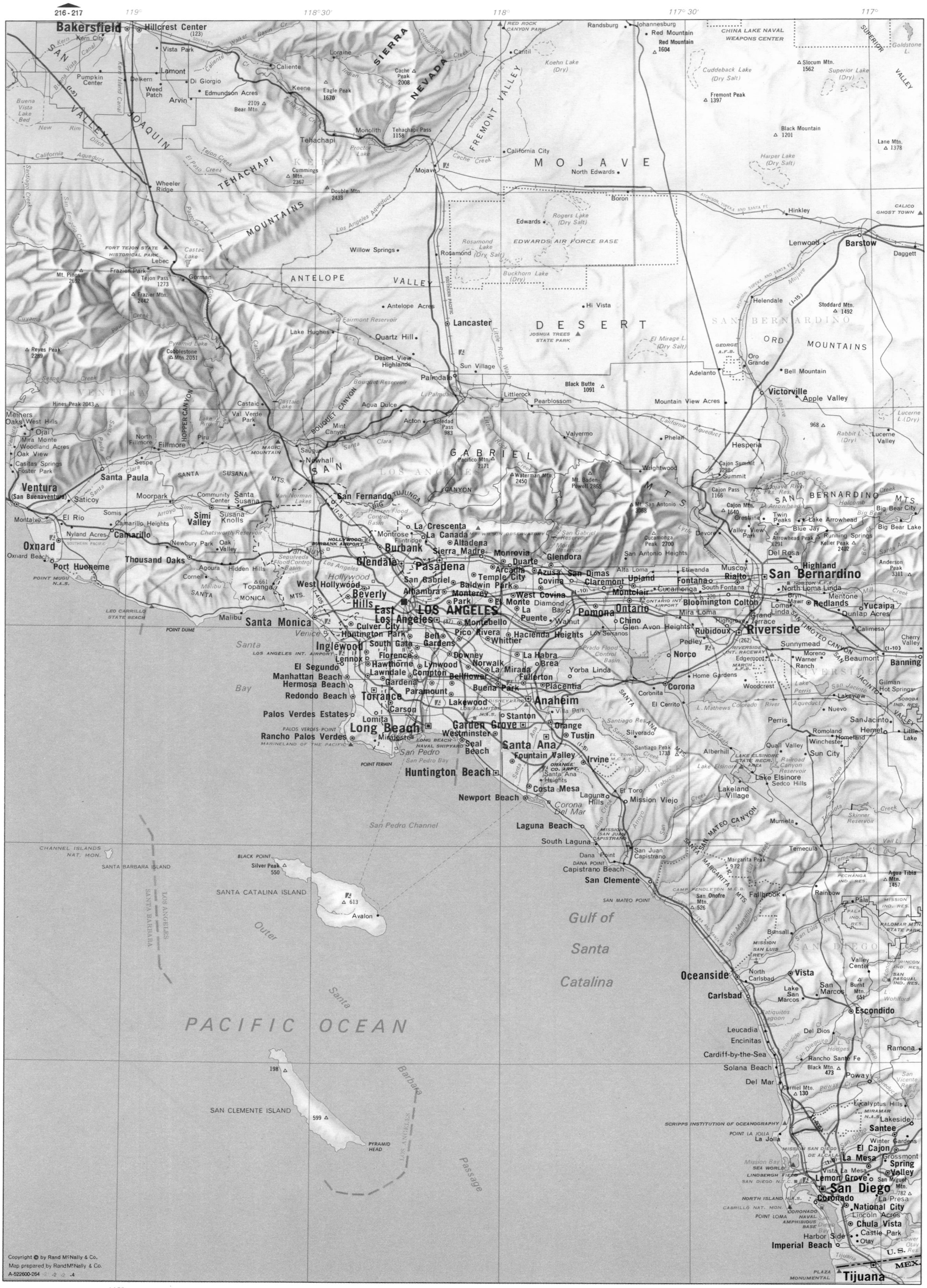
216-217
119°
118°30′
118°
117°30′
117°
35°
34°30′
34°
33°30′
33°
32°30′
Bakersfield
Hillcrest Center
SAN JOAQUIN VALLEY
SIERRA NEVADA
TEHACHAPI MOUNTAINS
Tehachapi
Tehachapi Pass 1158
Mojave
MOJAVE DESERT
California City
North Edwards
Boron
EDWARDS AIR FORCE BASE
Rogers Lake (Dry Salt)
Rosamond Lake (Dry Salt)
Rosamond
Willow Springs
ANTELOPE VALLEY
Lancaster
Palmdale
Quartz Hill
Lake Hughes
Gorman
Lebec
Mt. Pinos 2692
Frazier Mtn. 2442
Tejon Pass 1273
CHINA LAKE NAVAL WEAPONS CENTER
Randsburg
Johannesburg
Red Mountain
Hinkley
Barstow
Daggett
Lenwood
CALICO GHOST TOWN
SAN BERNARDINO
ORD MOUNTAINS
Victorville
Apple Valley
Adelanto
Hesperia
GEORGE A.F.B.
JOSHUA TREES STATE PARK
El Mirage L. (Dry Salt)
Black Butte 1091
Littlerock
Pearblossom
SAN GABRIEL MTS.
Mt. San Antonio 3068
Mt. Baden-Powell 2865
Waterman Mtn. 2450
Cajon Pass
SAN BERNARDINO MTS.
Big Bear Lake
Big Bear City
Lake Arrowhead
Running Springs
Ventura (San Buenaventura)
Oxnard
Port Hueneme
POINT MUGU N.A.S.
Camarillo
Santa Paula
Fillmore
Moorpark
Simi Valley
Thousand Oaks
Newhall
San Fernando
Burbank
Glendale
Pasadena
Malibu
Santa Monica
West Hollywood
Beverly Hills
LOS ANGELES
East Los Angeles
Culver City
Inglewood
El Segundo
Manhattan Beach
Hermosa Beach
Redondo Beach
Torrance
Palos Verdes Estates
Rancho Palos Verdes
Long Beach
San Pedro
Huntington Beach
Newport Beach
Costa Mesa
Santa Ana
Anaheim
Garden Grove
Fullerton
Pomona
Ontario
Upland
Riverside
San Bernardino
Redlands
Yucaipa
Banning
Beaumont
Corona
Norco
Irvine
Laguna Beach
Mission Viejo
San Juan Capistrano
Dana Point
San Clemente
CAMP PENDLETON M.C.B.
Temecula
Hemet
Perris
Lake Elsinore
Oceanside
Carlsbad
Vista
San Marcos
Escondido
Encinitas
Leucadia
Cardiff-by-the-Sea
Solana Beach
Del Mar
Poway
Ramona
La Jolla
San Diego
El Cajon
La Mesa
Santee
Lemon Grove
Spring Valley
Coronado
National City
Chula Vista
Imperial Beach
Tijuana
U.S.
MEX.
Santa Monica Bay
San Pedro Channel
Gulf of Santa Catalina
PACIFIC OCEAN
Outer Santa Barbara Passage
SANTA BARBARA ISLAND
CHANNEL ISLANDS NAT. MON.
SANTA CATALINA ISLAND
Avalon
SAN CLEMENTE ISLAND
PYRAMID HEAD
Copyright © by Rand McNally & Co.
Map prepared by Rand McNally & Co.
A-522600-264

ENGLISH	canyon	creek, cr.	lake, l.	mountain, mtn.	pass	peak	point	reservoir, res.
DEUTSCH	Cañon	Bach	See	Berg	Pass	Gipfel	Landspitze	Stausee
ESPAÑOL	cañon	riachuelo	lago	montaña	paso	pico	punta	embalse
FRANÇAIS	canyon	crique	lac	montagne	col	cime	pointe	réservoir
PORTUGUÊS	canhão	riacho	lago	montanha	passo	pico	ponta	reservatório

For complete glossary see page *I* • *1*.
For Los Angeles metropolitan map, see page 270.

Kilometers 0 10 20 30 40 50 Km.
Statute Miles 0 10 20 30 40 50 Mi.

Scale 1:1,000,000

One centimeter represents 10 kilometers.
One inch represents approximately 16 miles.

Lambert Conformal Conic Projection

a

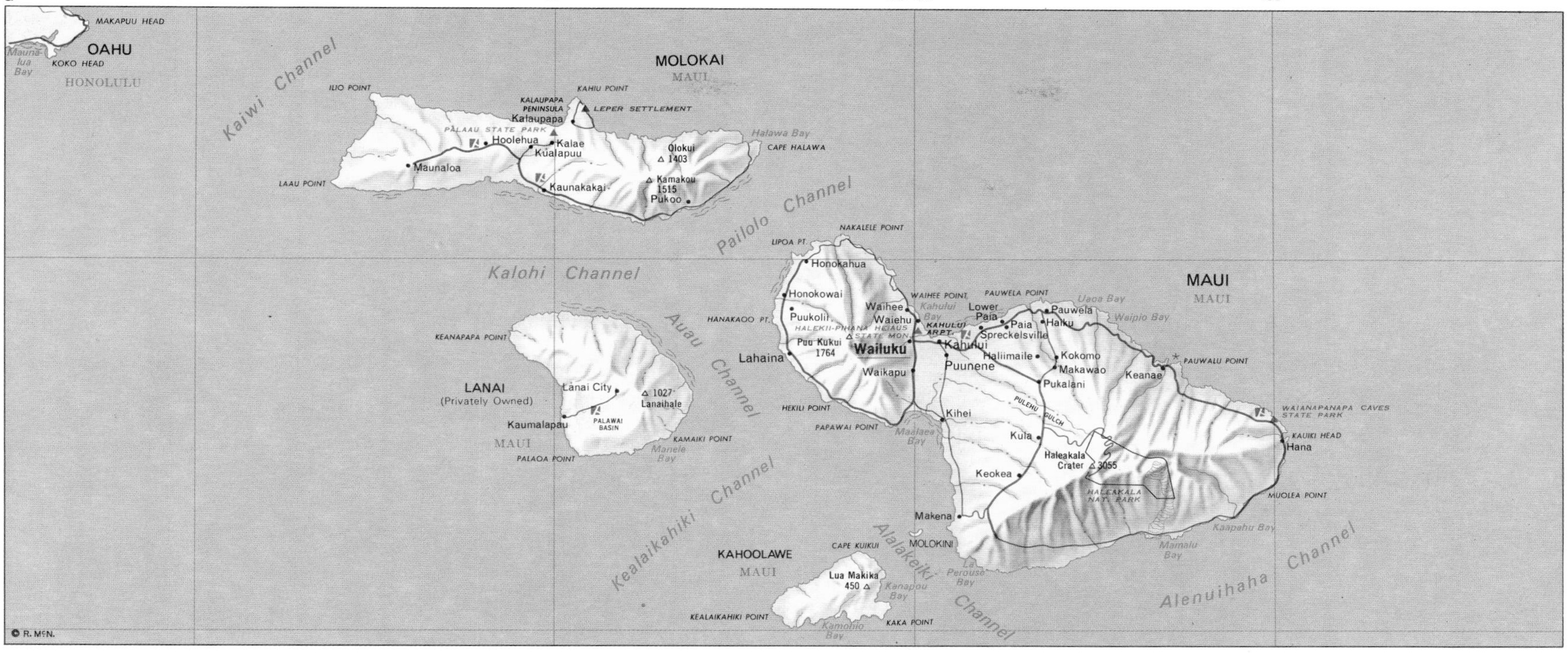

b

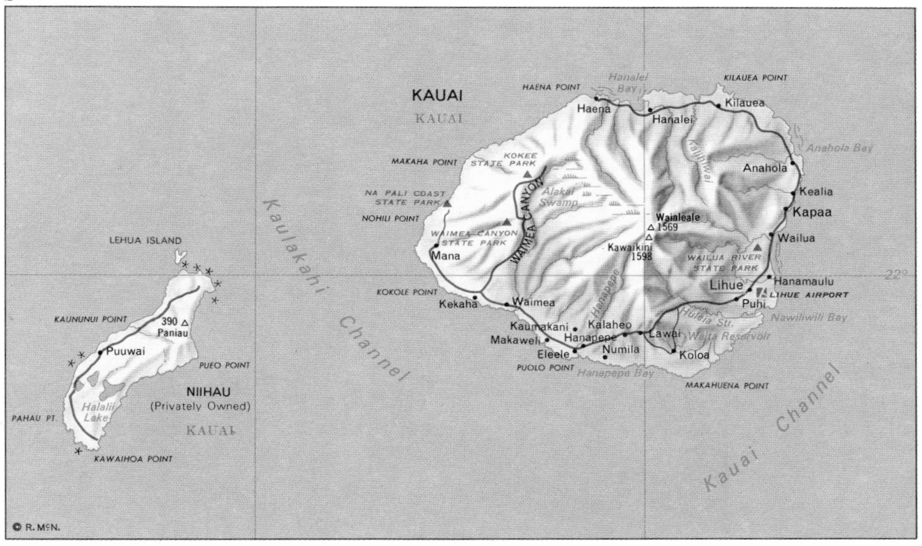

c

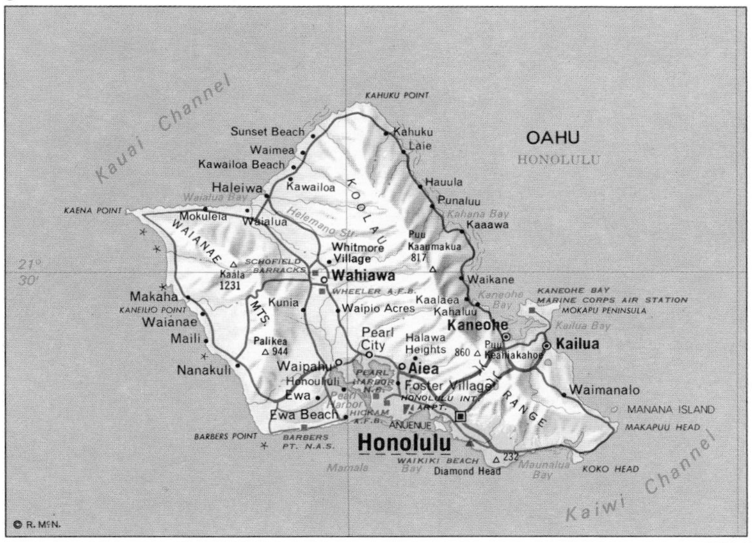

Kilometers 0 10 20 30 40 50 Km.
Statute Miles 0 10 20 30 40 50 Mi.

Scale 1:1,000,000

One centimeter represents 10 kilometers.
One inch represents approximately 16 miles.
Lambert Conformal Conic Projection

d

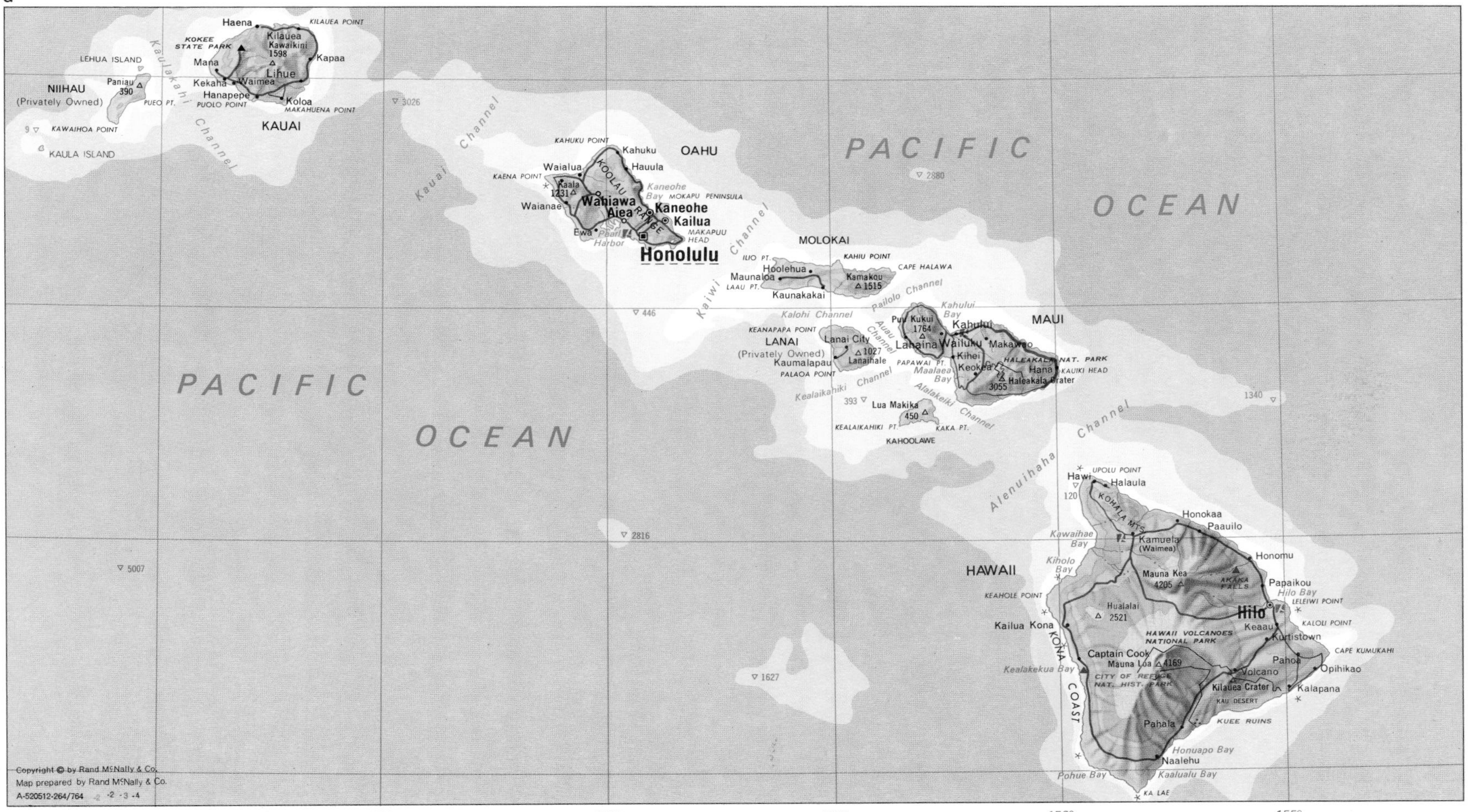

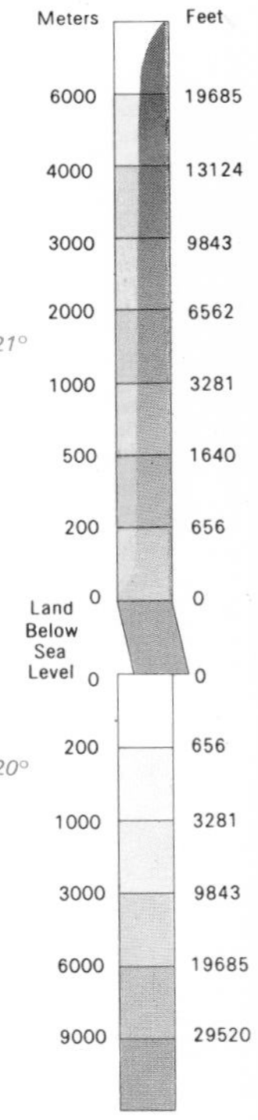

ENGLISH	bay	channel	head	mount	point	state park, s.p.
DEUTSCH	Bucht	Kanal	Landspitze	Berg	Landspitze	Staatspark
ESPAÑOL	bahía	canal	promontorio	monte	punta	parque del estado
FRANÇAIS	baie	détroit	promontoire	mont	pointe	parc régional
PORTUGUÊS	baía	canal	promontório	monte	ponta	parque estadual

For complete glossary see page *I • 1*.

Kilometers 0 50 100 150 Km.
Statute Miles 0 50 100 150 Mi.

Scale 1:3,000,000

One centimeter represents 30 kilometers.
One inch represents approximately 47 miles.
Lambert Conformal Conic Projection

168 - 169

ESPAÑOL	cabo	cordillera	golfo	isla, i.	lago, l.	punta	sierra	volcán, vol.
ENGLISH	cape	mountains	gulf	island	lake	point	mountains	volcano
DEUTSCH	Kap	Berge	Golf	Insel	See	Landspitze	Berge	Vulkan
FRANÇAIS	cap	montagnes	golfe	île	lac	pointe	montagnes	volcan
PORTUGUÊS	cabo	cordilheira	golfo	ilha	lago	ponta	serra	vulcão

For complete glossary see page I • 1.

ATLANTIC OCEAN
CARIBBEAN SEA
WEST INDIES
GREATER ANTILLES
LESSER ANTILLES
BAHAMAS
BERMUDA (U.K.)
Hamilton
Tropic of Cancer
TURKS AND CAICOS ISLANDS (U.K.)
CUBA
La Habana Havana
Santiago de Cuba
Camagüey
CAYMAN IS. (U.K.)
JAMAICA
Kingston
HAITI
Port-au-Prince
DOMINICAN REPUBLIC
Santo Domingo
HISPANIOLA
PUERTO RICO (U.S.)
San Juan
Nassau
ANDROS ISLAND
ANTIGUA (U.K.)
St. Johns
MONTSERRAT (U.K.)
GUADELOUPE (Fr.)
DOMINICA
Roseau
MARTINIQUE (Fr.)
Fort-de-France
SAINT LUCIA
Castries
SAINT VINCENT (U.K.)
Kingstown
BARBADOS
Bridgetown
GRENADA
St. George's
TRINIDAD AND TOBAGO
Port of Spain
NETHERLANDS ANTILLES
Willemstad
Oranjestad
VENEZUELA
Caracas
Maracaibo
Valencia
Barquisimeto
Ciudad Bolívar
Ciudad Guayana
COLOMBIA
Bogotá
Medellín
Cali
Barranquilla
Cartagena
Bucaramanga
Cúcuta
COSTA RICA
San José
Panamá
Colón
Gulf of Panama
BRAZIL
GUYANA
LLANOS
ANDES
Miami
Jacksonville
Tampa
St. Petersburg
Orlando
Savannah
Charleston
Atlanta
Columbia
Charlotte
Raleigh
Norfolk
Wilmington
GEORGIA
SOUTH CAROLINA
NORTH CAROLINA
VIRGINIA
FLORIDA
APPALACHIAN MTS
Straits of Florida
Windward Passage
Canal de la Mona
35°
30°
25°
20°
15°
10°
5°
85°
80°
75°
70°
65°
60°
55°

232 - 233

Kilometers 0 200 400 600 Km.

Statute Miles 0 200 400 600 Mi.

Scale 1:12,000,000

One centimeter represents 120 kilometers.
One inch represents approximately 190 miles.
Oblique Conic Conformal Projection

ESPAÑOL	bahía	cerro	isla	laguna	presa	punta	río	sierra
ENGLISH	bay	mountain	island	lagoon	reservoir	point	river	mountains
DEUTSCH	Bucht	Berg	Insel	Haff	Stausee	Landspitze	Fluss	Berge
FRANÇAIS	baie	montagne	île	lagune	réservoir	pointe	rivière	montagnes
PORTUGUÊS	baía	montanha	ilha	laguna	reservatório	ponta	rio	serra

For complete glossary see page *I* • *1*.

Kilometers 0 100 200 300 Km.
Statute Miles 0 100 200 300

Scale 1:6,000,000

One centimeter represents 60 kilometers.
One inch represents approximately 95 miles.

Lambert Conformal Conic Projection

GULF
OF
MEXICO
Bahía de Campeche
Golfo de Tehuantepec
Tropic of Cancer
T E X A S
LOUISIANA
MISSISSIPPI
ALABAMA
NUEVO LEON
TAMAULIPAS
YUCATAN
PENINSULA
QUINTANA ROO
CHIAPAS
TABASCO
VERACRUZ
GUATEMALA
BELIZE (U.K.)
HONDURAS
SIERRA MADRE ORIENTAL
SIERRA MADRE DEL SUR
SIERRA MADRE
Dallas
Fort Worth
Shreveport
Jackson
Houston
Galveston
San Antonio
Austin
Beaumont
Baton Rouge
New Orleans
Mobile
Corpus Christi
Brownsville
Matamoros
Nuevo Laredo
Laredo
Monterrey
Saltillo
Ciudad Victoria
Tampico
Ciudad Madero
San Luis Potosí
CIUDAD DE MÉXICO
MEXICO CITY
Puebla
Veracruz
Jalapa Enríquez
Oaxaca
Acapulco
Coatzacoalcos
Minatitlán
Villahermosa
Tuxtla Gutiérrez
Campeche
Mérida
Ciudad del Carmen
Ciudad Chetumal
Belize
Belmopan
Guatemala
Quezaltenango
Tapachula
Gulf of Honduras
226-227
228-229

222 - 223

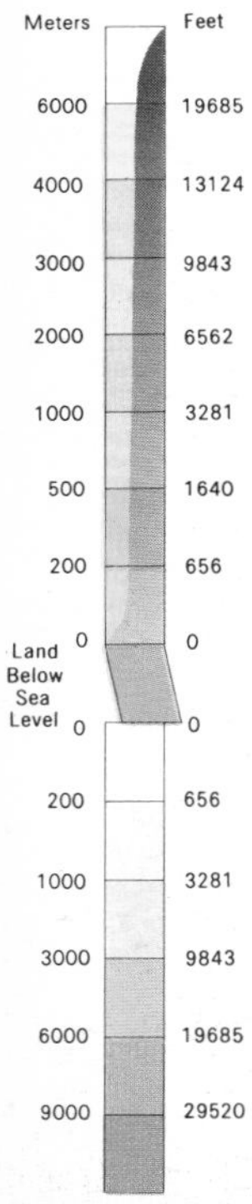

ESPAÑOL	arroyo	boca	cerro	lago	laguna	punta	río	sierra	volcán
ENGLISH	brook	entrance	butte	lake	lagoon	point	river	ranges	volcano
DEUTSCH	Bach	Einfahrt	Restberg	See	Haff	Landspitze	Fluss	Bergketten	Vulkan
FRANÇAIS	ruisseau	entrée	butte	lac	lagune	pointe	rivière	chaîne	volcan
PORTUGUÊS	arroio	entrada	cerro	lago	laguna	ponta	rio	serra	vulcão

For complete glossary see page *I • 1*.
For Ciudad de México metropolitan map, see page 276.

GULF OF MEXICO
Bahía de Campeche
Tropic of Cancer
Golfo de Tehuantepec
Bahía Coatzacoalcos
ISTMO DE TEHUANTEPEC
SIERRA MADRE ORIENTAL
SIERRA MADRE DEL SUR
SIERRA AZUL
TAMAULIPAS
VERACRUZ
SAN LUIS POTOSÍ
HIDALGO
PUEBLA
TLAXCALA
OAXACA
GUERRERO
TABASCO
CHIAPAS
Ciudad Victoria
Ciudad Mante
Ciudad Madero
Tampico
Pánuco
Tuxpan de Rodríguez Cano
Poza Rica de Hidalgo
Papantla
Pachuca
Tulancingo
Teziutlán
Jalapa Enríquez
Veracruz
CIUDAD DE MÉXICO
MEXICO CITY
Puebla
Atlixco
Tlaxcala
Apizaco
Córdoba
Orizaba
Ciudad Mendoza
Tehuacán
Izúcar de Matamoros
Alvarado
Tierra Blanca
San Andrés Tuxtla
Cosamaloapan
Coatzacoalcos
Minatitlán
Villahermosa
Oaxaca
Huajuapan de León
Juchitán
Salina Cruz
Tehuantepec
Ciudad Ixtepec
Tuxtla Gutiérrez
San Cristóbal las Casas
Puerto Escondido
Puerto Ángel
Pinotepa Nacional
Tonalá
Arriaga
Frontera
Cárdenas
Acayucan
Matías Romero
Miahuatlán de Porfirio Díaz
Tlacotalpan
Lerdo de Tejada
Catemaco
Tamazunchale
Huejutla de Reyes
Xicotepec de Juárez
Zacatlán
Perote
San Martín Texmelucan
Tecamachalco
Nautla
Misantla
Soto la Marina
La Pesca
Aldama
Altamira
Ebano
Tamuín
Tempoal
Tantoyuca
Naranjos
Cerro Azul
Álamo
Gutiérrez Zamora
Pijijiapan
Mapastepec
Arista
Ejutla de Crespo
Tlacolula
Zimatlán de Álvarez
Nochixtlán
Tlaxiaco
Putla de Guerrero
Ometepec
Tlapa
Chilapa de Díaz
Cuicatlán
Teotitlán del Camino
Juxtlahuaca
Sola de Vega
ISLA DE LOBOS
ISLA JUANA RAMÍREZ
CABO ROJO
PUNTA JEREZ
PUNTA DE PIEDRAS
PUNTA DEL MORRO
PUNTA ZEMPOALA
PUNTA GORDA
PUNTA ROCA PARTIDA
PUNTA ZAPOTITLÁN
PUNTA FRONTERA
PUNTA MALDONADO
Laguna Madre
Laguna de Tamiahua
Laguna Superior
Laguna Inferior
Laguna de Términos
Volcán San Martín 1400
Cerro Tres Picos 2058
Ixtaccíhuatl 5286
Popocatépetl 5452
Pico de Orizaba 5700
Cofre de Perote 4282
La Malinche 4461
Cerro Zempoaltépetl 3396
222–223
226–227

Kilometers 0 50 100 150 Km.
Statute Miles 0 50 100 150 Mi.

Scale 1:3,000,000
One centimeter represents 30 kilometers.
One inch represents approximately 47 miles.
Lambert Conformal Conic Projection

Central America / Zentralamerika / América Central
Amérique Centrale / América Central

222-223
224-225
92°
91°
90°
89°
88°
87°
16°
15°
14°
13°
12°
11°
10°
9°
8°
MEXICO
MÉXICO
GUATEMALA
BELIZE (U.K.)
HONDURAS
EL SALVADOR
CHIAPAS
EL PETÉN
ALTA VERAPAZ
BAJA VERAPAZ
IZABAL
EL QUICHÉ
HUEHUETENANGO
SAN MARCOS
QUEZALTENANGO
TOTONICAPÁN
SOLOLÁ
CHIMALTENANGO
SACATEPÉQUEZ
GUATEMALA
EL PROGRESO
ZACAPA
CHIQUIMULA
JALAPA
JUTIAPA
SANTA ROSA
ESCUINTLA
SUCHITEPÉQUEZ
RETALHULEU
COPÁN
OCOTEPEQUE
SANTA BÁRBARA
CORTÉS
YORO
ATLÁNTIDA
COMAYAGUA
INTIBUCÁ
LEMPIRA
LA PAZ
FRANCISCO MORAZÁN
EL PARAÍSO
VALLE
CHOLUTECA
CHINANDEGA
LEÓN
ESTELÍ
MADRIZ
NUEVA SEGOVIA
SIERRA MADRE
ALTOS CUCHUMATANES
SIERRA DE CHAMÁ
SIERRA DE SANTA CRUZ
SIERRA DE LAS MINAS
MONTAÑAS DEL MICO
Gulf of Honduras
Golfo de Fonseca
Bahía de Jiquilisco
Guatemala
San Salvador
Tegucigalpa
Managua
San Pedro Sula
Quezaltenango
Tapachula
Comitán
Escuintla
Santa Ana
San Miguel
San Vicente
Sonsonate
Puerto Barrios
Puerto Cortés
La Ceiba
Chinandega
León
Choluteca
Roatán
Utila
ISLA DE ROATÁN
PACIFIC
OCEAN
Copyright © by Rand McNally & Co.
Map prepared by Rand McNally & Co.
A-533600-764

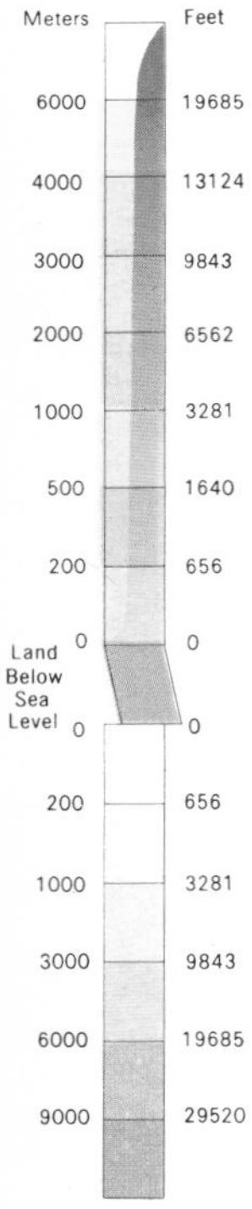
Meters
Feet
6000 19685
4000 13124
3000 9843
2000 6562
1000 3281
500 1640
200 656
0 0
Land Below Sea Level
0 0
200 656
1000 3281
3000 9843
6000 19685
9000 29520

ESPAÑOL	bahía	cerro	cordillera	isla	lago	laguna	punta	sierra	volcán
ENGLISH	bay	mountain	mountains	island	lake	lagoon	point	mountains	volcano
DEUTSCH	Bucht	Berg	Berge	Insel	See	Haff	Landspitze	Berge	Vulkan
FRANÇAIS	baie	montagne	montagnes	île	lac	lagune	pointe	montagnes	volcan
PORTUGUÊS	baía	cerro	cordilheira	ilha	lago	laguna	ponta	serra	vulcão

For complete glossary see page *I • 1*.

CARIBBEAN SEA
SAN ANDRÉS Y PROVIDENCIA (Colombia)
San Andrés
ISLA DE PROVIDENCIA
CAYOS DEL ESTE SUDESTE
CAYOS DE ALBUQUERQUE
CORN ISLANDS (Nic.)
SERRANILLA BANK (Col.)
SERRANA BANK (Col.)
RONCADOR BANK (Col.)
QUITA SUEÑO BANK (Col.)
CAYOS MISKITOS
Edinburgh Channel
Miskito Channel
GRACIAS A DIOS
Cabo Gracias a Dios
CABO FALSO
CABO CAMARÓN
Puerto Cabezas
COSTA DE MOSQUITOS
ZELAYA
Bluefields
San Juan del Norte
NICARAGUA
COSTA RICA
HONDURAS
JINOTEGA
MATAGALPA
BOACO
CHONTALES
Lake Nicaragua
ALAJUELA
HEREDIA
GUANACASTE
PUNTARENAS
SAN JOSÉ
CARTAGO
LIMÓN
San José
Alajuela
Heredia
Cartago
Puntarenas
Limón
Golfo de Nicoya
PENÍNSULA DE NICOYA
ARCHIPIÉLAGO DE BOCAS DEL TORO
BOCAS DEL TORO
CHIRIQUÍ
David
Golfo de Chiriquí
Golfo de los Mosquitos
VERAGUAS
COCLÉ
HERRERA
LOS SANTOS
COLÓN
PANAMÁ
Colón
Panamá
ISTHMUS OF PANAMA
Gulf of Panama
SERRANÍA DE TABASARÁ
CORDILLERA DE TALAMANCA
CORDILLERA DE GUANACASTE
CORDILLERA CENTRAL
CORDILLERA DE YOLAINA
CORDILLERA ISABELLA
MONTAÑAS DE COLÓN
MONTAÑAS DE HUAPÍ
RÍO SAN JUAN
Bahía de Coronado
Golfo Dulce
Península de Osa
Punta Burica
Santiago
Chitré
La Chorrera
Taboga
85° 84° 83° 82° 81° 80°
15° 14° 13° 12° 11° 10° 9° 8°

228 · 229

Kilometers 0 50 100 150 Km.
Statute Miles 0 50 100 150 Mi.

Scale 1:3,000,000
One centimeter represents 30 kilometers.
One inch represents approximately 47 miles.
Lambert Conformal Conic Projection

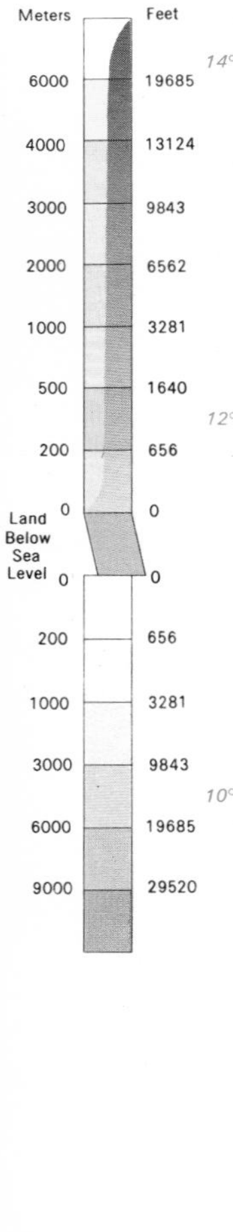

MAP FORM	bahía	cabo	cerro	channel	golfo	isla	passage	pico	punta
ENGLISH	bay	cape	mountain	channel	gulf	isle	passage	peak	point
DEUTSCH	Bucht	Kap	Berg	Kanal	Golf	Insel	Durchfahrt	Gipfel	Landspitze
ESPAÑOL	bahía	cabo	cerro	canal	golfo	isla	pasaje	pico	punta
FRANÇAIS	baie	cap	montagne	détroit	golfe	île	passage	cime	pointe
PORTUGUÊS	baía	cabo	cerro	canal	golfo	ilha	passagem	pico	ponta

For complete glossary see page *I • 1*.
For Caracas metropolitan map, see page 276.

ATLANTIC OCEAN
Tropic of Cancer
WEST INDIES
SEA
TURKS AND CAICOS ISLANDS (U.K.)
CAICOS ISLANDS
TURKS ISLANDS
Grand Turk
GREAT INAGUA
SILVER BANK
HAITI
HAÏTI
Cap-Haïtien
Port-au-Prince
HISPANIOLA
DOMINICAN REPUBLIC
REPÚBLICA DOMINICANA
Santo Domingo
Santiago
PUERTO RICO (U.S.)
San Juan
Ponce
Mayagüez
VIRGIN ISLANDS (U.S.)
VIRGIN ISLANDS (U.K.)
Charlotte Amalie
Road Town
SAINT CROIX
ANGUILLA (U.K.)
The Valley
SAINT KITTS-NEVIS (U.K.)
Basseterre
ANTIGUA (U.K.)
Saint Johns
MONTSERRAT (U.K.)
Plymouth
LEEWARD ISLANDS
LESSER ANTILLES
GUADELOUPE (Fr.)
Pointe-à-Pitre
Basse-Terre
DOMINICA
Roseau
MARTINIQUE (Fr.)
Fort-de-France
SAINT LUCIA
Castries
SAINT VINCENT (U.K.)
Kingstown
BARBADOS
Bridgetown
WINDWARD ISLANDS
GRENADINE IS.
GRENADA
Saint George's
TOBAGO
TRINIDAD AND TOBAGO
Port of Spain
San Fernando
NETHERLANDS ANTILLES
NEDERLANDSE ANTILLEN
ARUBA
Oranjestad
CURAÇAO
Willemstad
BONAIRE
Kralendijk
LA GUAJIRA
COLOMBIA
VENEZUELA
Maracaibo
Lago de Maracaibo
ZULIA
FALCÓN
Coro
LARA
Barquisimeto
Valencia
Maracay
CARACAS
La Guaira
Barcelona
Cumaná
SUCRE
Carúpano
Maturín
MONAGAS
ANZOÁTEGUI
ISLA DE MARGARITA
NUEVA ESPARTA
DELTA AMACURO
Orinoco
GUÁRICO
COJEDES
PORTUGUESA
TRUJILLO
Valera
APURE
72°
70°
68°
66°
64°
62°
60°
24°
22°
20°
18°
16°
14°
12°
10°

236-237

Kilometers 0 100 200 300 Km.
Statute Miles 0 100 200 300 Mi.

Scale 1:6,000,000
One centimeter represents 60 kilometers.
One inch represents approximately 95 miles.
Lambert Conformal Conic Projection

a

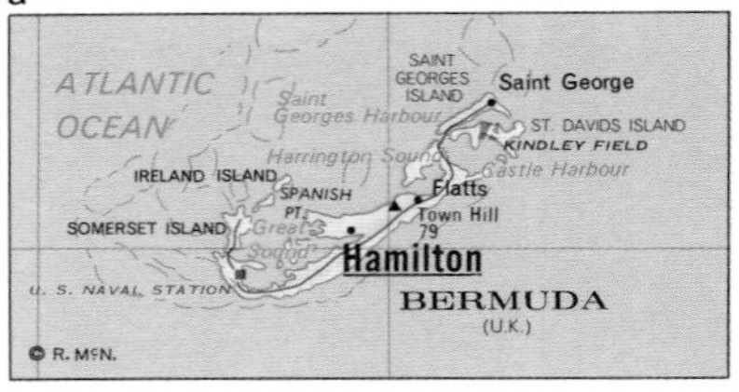
ATLANTIC OCEAN
Saint George
ST. DAVIDS ISLAND
KINDLEY FIELD
Castle Harbour
IRELAND ISLAND
SOMERSET ISLAND
Flatts
Town Hill
Hamilton
BERMUDA
(U.K.)
U. S. NAVAL STATION
32° 15′
64° 45′
65°

b

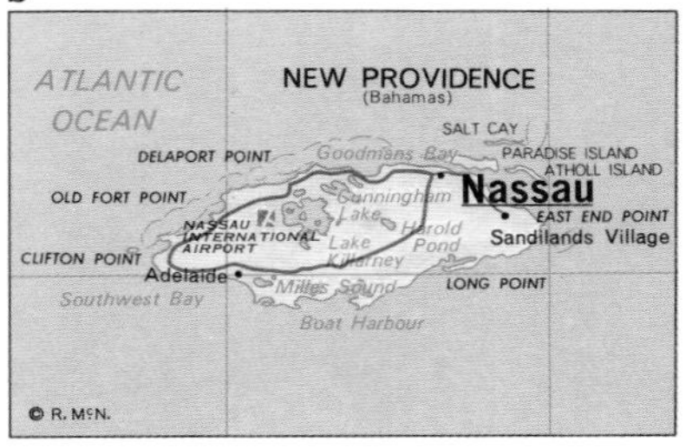
ATLANTIC OCEAN
NEW PROVIDENCE
(Bahamas)
SALT CAY
DELAPORT POINT
PARADISE ISLAND
ATHOLL ISLAND
OLD FORT POINT
Nassau
EAST END POINT
Sandilands Village
CLIFTON POINT
Adelaide
LONG POINT
Southwest Bay
Boat Harbour
25°
77° 30′
77° 15′

c

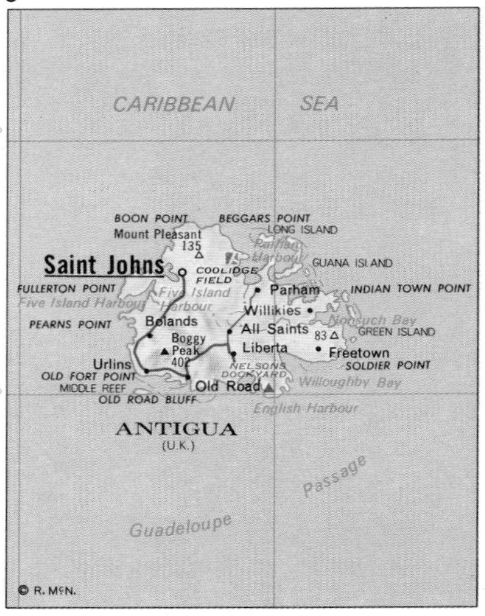
CARIBBEAN SEA
Saint Johns
BOON POINT
BEGGARS POINT
LONG ISLAND
Mount Pleasant
GUANA ISLAND
FULLERTON POINT
Parham
INDIAN TOWN POINT
Five Island Harbour
PEARNS POINT
Bolands
Willikies
All Saints
GREEN ISLAND
Liberta
Freetown
Urlins
Boggy Peak
Old Road
SOLDIER POINT
English Harbour
ANTIGUA
(U.K.)
Guadeloupe Passage
17° 15′
17°
61° 45′
62°

d

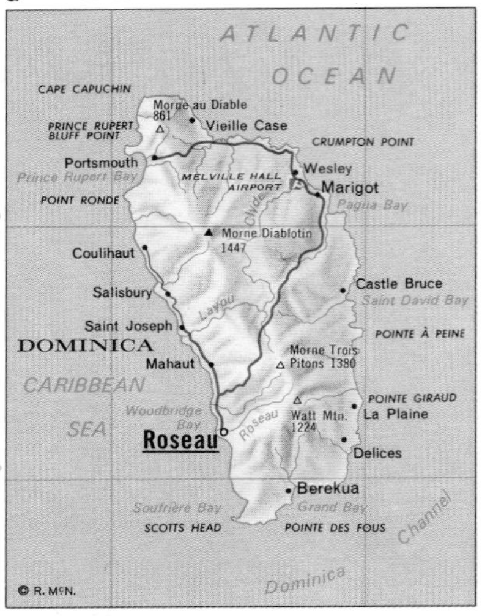
ATLANTIC OCEAN
CAPE CAPUCHIN
Morne au Diable
Vieille Case
PRINCE RUPERT BLUFF POINT
CRUMPTON POINT
Portsmouth
Wesley
Marigot
MELVILLE HALL AIRPORT
POINT RONDE
Morne Diablotin 1447
Coulihaut
Salisbury
Castle Bruce
Saint David Bay
Saint Joseph
POINTE À PEINE
DOMINICA
Mahaut
Morne Trois Pitons 1390
CARIBBEAN SEA
POINTE GIRAUD
La Plaine
Roseau
Watt Mtn. 1224
Delices
Berekua
Grand Bay
Soufrière Bay
SCOTTS HEAD
POINTE DES FOUS
Dominica Channel
15° 30′
15° 15′
61° 30′
61° 15′

e

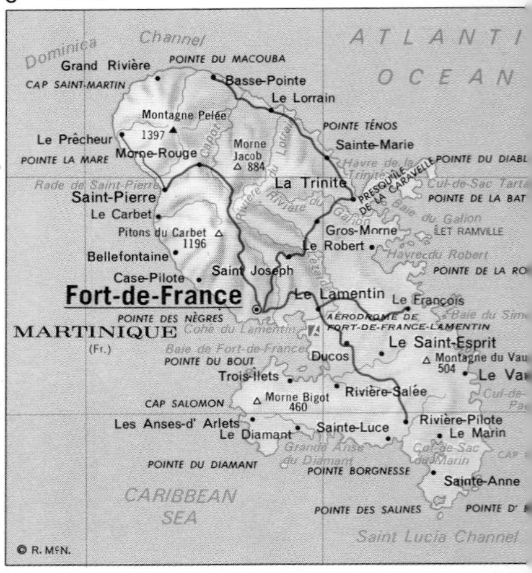
ATLANTIC OCEAN
Dominica Channel
Grand Rivière
POINTE DU MACOUBA
Basse-Pointe
Le Lorrain
CAP SAINT-MARTIN
Montagne Pelée 1397
POINTE TÉNOS
Le Prêcheur
Morne-Rouge
Sainte-Marie
POINTE LA MARE
Morne Jacob 884
La Trinité
Saint-Pierre
Le Carbet
Pitons du Carbet 1196
Bellefontaine
Le Robert
Case-Pilote
Saint Joseph
Fort-de-France
Le Lamentin
Le François
MARTINIQUE
(Fr.)
Ducos
Le Saint-Esprit
Trois-Ilets
Montagne du Vauclin 504
Le Vauclin
CAP SALOMON
Morne Bigot 460
Rivière-Salée
Rivière-Pilote
Les Anses-d'Arlets
Le Diamant
Sainte-Luce
Le Marin
POINTE DU DIAMANT
POINTE BORGNESSE
Sainte-Anne
CARIBBEAN SEA
POINTE DES SALINES
Saint Lucia Channel
14° 45′
14° 30′
61° 15′
61°

m

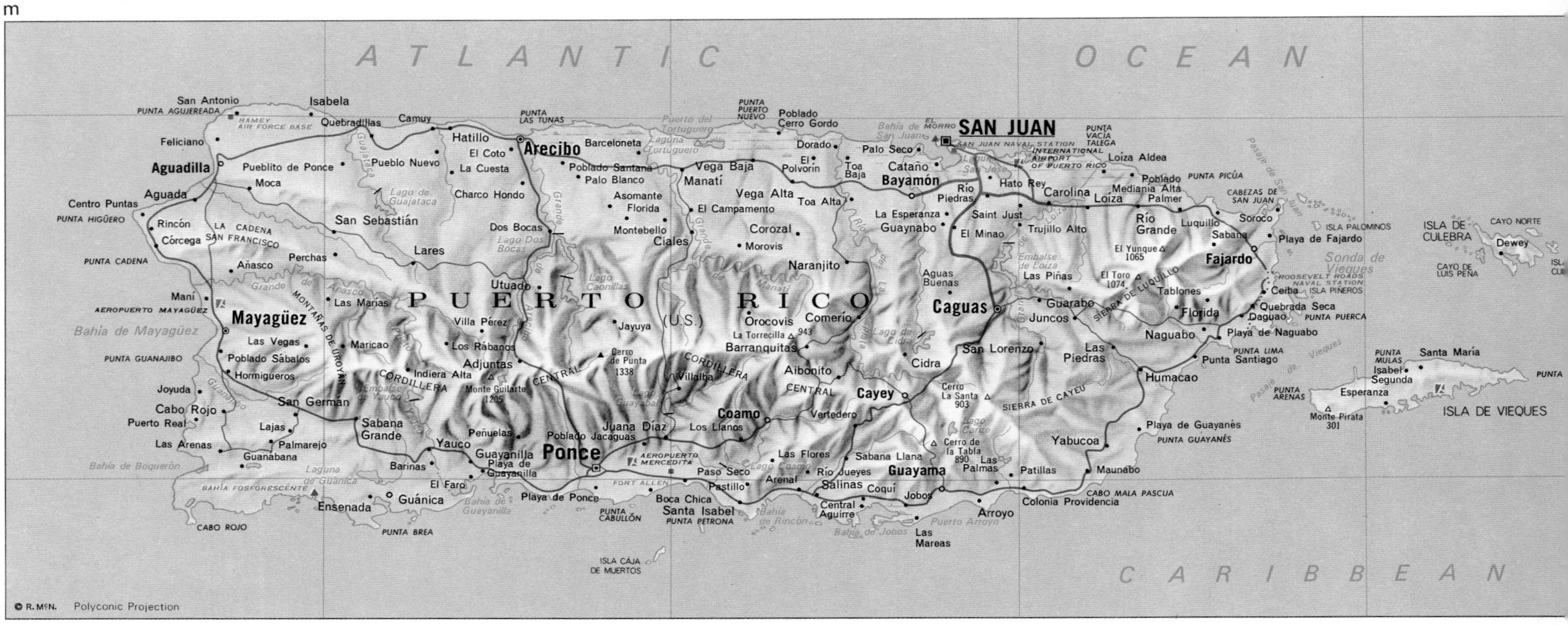
ATLANTIC OCEAN
CARIBBEAN
PUERTO RICO
(U.S.)
SAN JUAN
Aguadilla
Isabela
Arecibo
Quebradillas
Camuy
Hatillo
Barceloneta
Manatí
Vega Baja
Dorado
Bayamón
Cataño
Carolina
Loíza
Río Grande
Luquillo
Fajardo
Mayagüez
San Germán
Ponce
Caguas
Guayama
Cayey
Coamo
Humacao
Yabucoa
Arroyo
Maunabo
Utuado
Adjuntas
Jayuya
Orocovis
Barranquitas
Aibonito
Cidra
San Lorenzo
Juncos
Naguabo
Ceiba
Yauco
Guánica
Sabana Grande
Lajas
Cabo Rojo
Hormigueros
Añasco
Rincón
Moca
Lares
San Sebastián
Juana Díaz
Santa Isabel
Salinas
Patillas
ISLA DE CULEBRA
ISLA DE VIEQUES
Isabel Segunda
CABO ROJO
ISLA CAJA DE MUERTOS
Polyconic Projection
18° 30′
18°
67°
66° 30′
66°
65° 30′

p

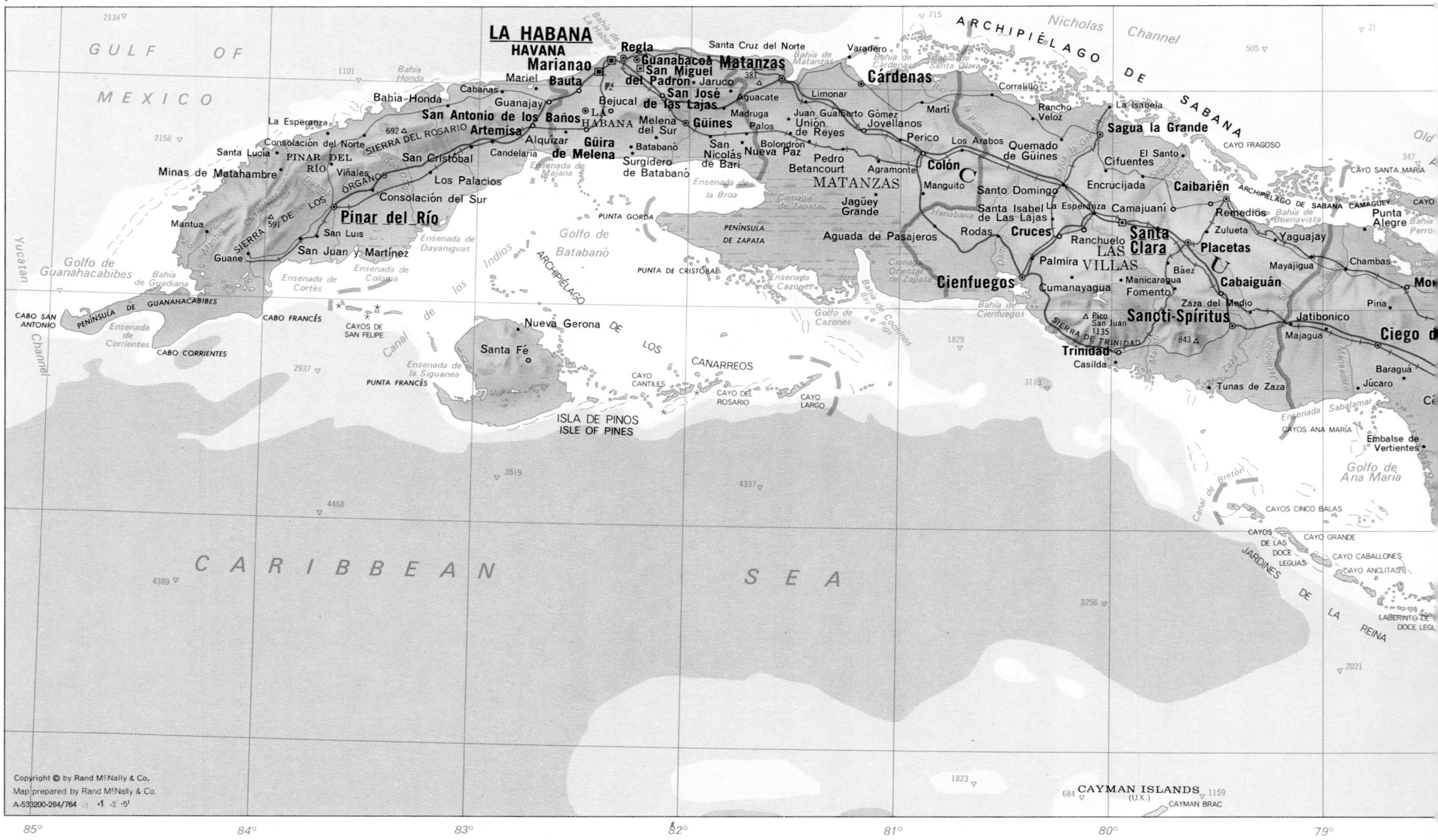
GULF OF MEXICO
CARIBBEAN SEA
LA HABANA
HAVANA
Marianao
Regla
Guanabacoa
Matanzas
Cárdenas
Bauta
Mariel
San Miguel del Padrón
San José de las Lajas
Güines
Bejucal
Artemisa
San Antonio de los Baños
Güira de Melena
Batabanó
Pinar del Río
San Cristóbal
Consolación del Sur
Minas de Matahambre
Guane
Mantua
San Juan y Martínez
San Luis
Colón
Jovellanos
Perico
MATANZAS
Cienfuegos
Santa Clara
LAS VILLAS
Sagua la Grande
Caibarién
Remedios
Placetas
Cabaiguán
Sancti-Spíritus
Trinidad
Ciego de Ávila
Nueva Gerona
Santa Fé
ISLA DE PINOS
ISLE OF PINES
ARCHIPIÉLAGO DE LOS CANARREOS
ARCHIPIÉLAGO DE SABANA
JARDINES DE LA REINA
Nicholas Channel
Yucatan Channel
Golfo de Guanahacabibes
Golfo de Batabanó
PENÍNSULA DE GUANAHACABIBES
CABO SAN ANTONIO
CABO CORRIENTES
PENÍNSULA DE ZAPATA
CAYMAN ISLANDS
(U.K.)
CAYMAN BRAC
Copyright © by Rand McNally & Co.
Map prepared by Rand McNally & Co.
23°
22°
21°
20°
85°
84°
83°
82°
81°
80°
79°

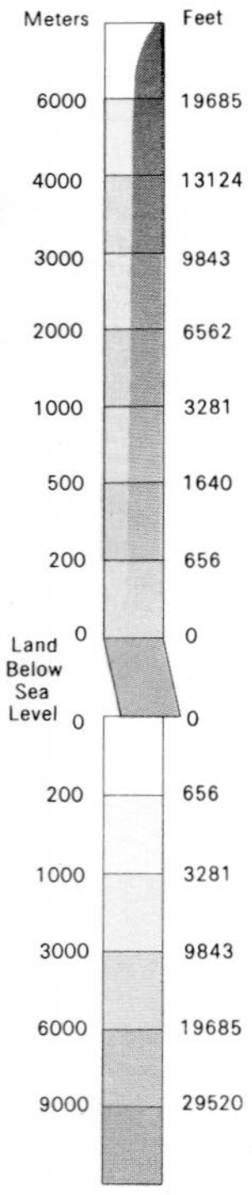
Meters
Feet
6000 19685
4000 13124
3000 9843
2000 6562
1000 3281
500 1640
200 656
0 0
Land Below Sea Level
0 0
200 656
1000 3281
3000 9843
6000 19685
9000 29520

MAP FORM	bahia	cayo	channel	ensenada	golfo	isla	mount	passage	point
ENGLISH	bay	cay	channel	bayou	gulf	island	mount	passage	point
DEUTSCH	Bucht	Klippe	Kanal	Altwasser	Golf	Insel	Berg	Durchfahrt	Landspitze
ESPAÑOL	bahía	cayo	canal	ensenada	golfo	isla	montaña	pasaje	punta
FRANÇAIS	baie	caye	détroit	bayou	golfe	île	mont	passage	pointe
PORTUGUÊS	baía	recife	canal	enseada	golfo	ilha	montanha	passagem	ponta

For complete glossary see page I • 1.
For La Habana metropolitan map, see page 276.

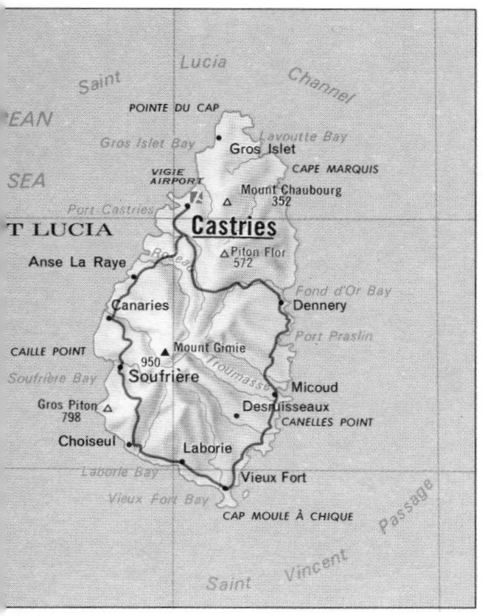

g

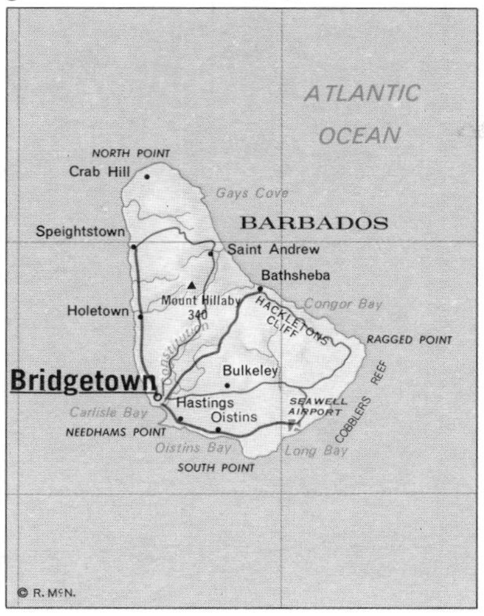

h

k

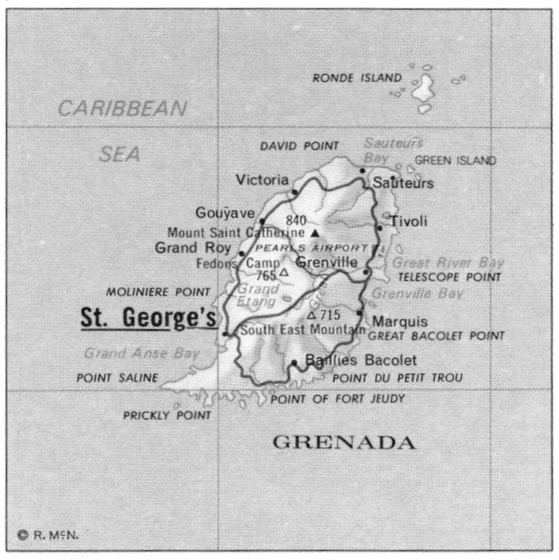

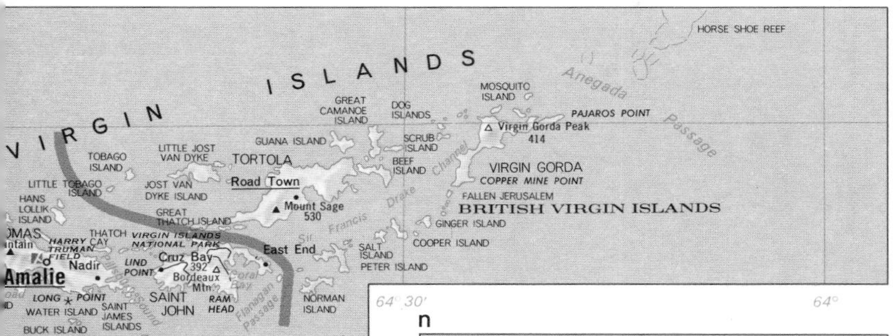

n

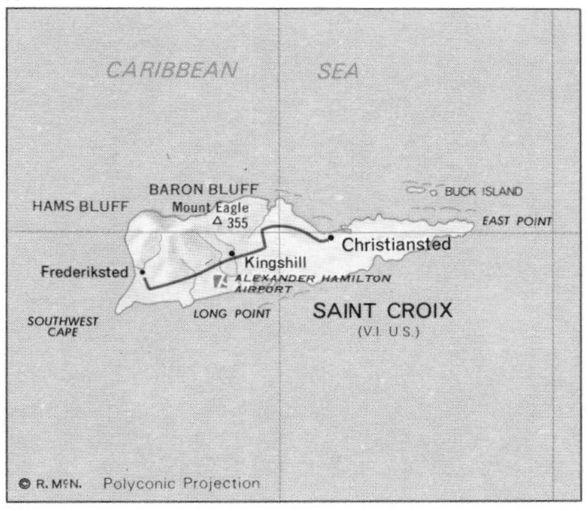

o

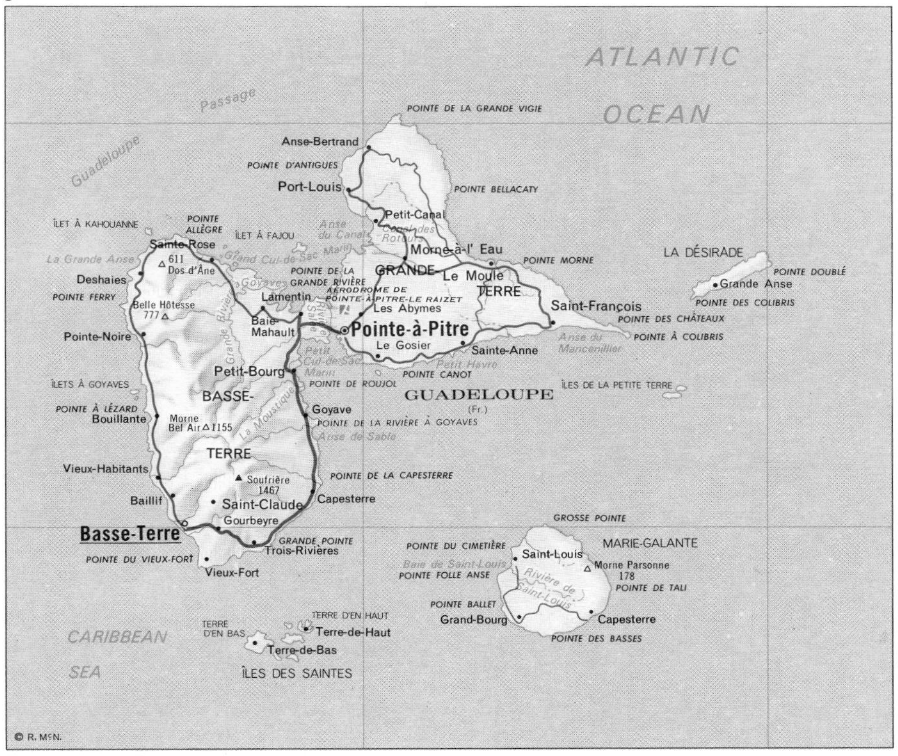

Kilometers 0 10 20 30 40 50 Km.
Statute Miles 0 10 20 30 40 50 Mi.

Scale 1:1,000,000

One centimeter represents 10 kilometers.
One inch represents approximately 16 miles.
Transverse Mercator Projection (except as noted)

q

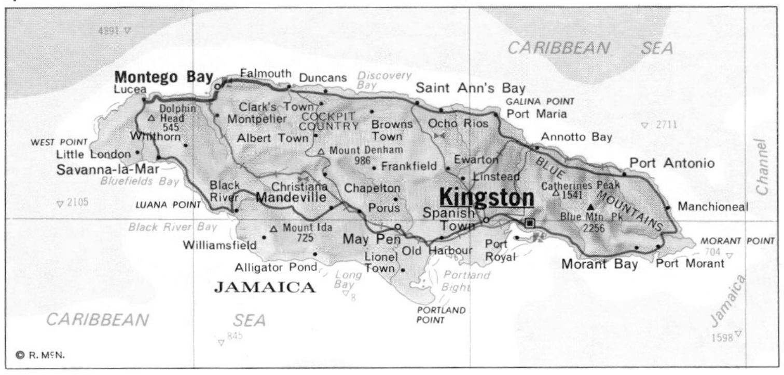

r

s

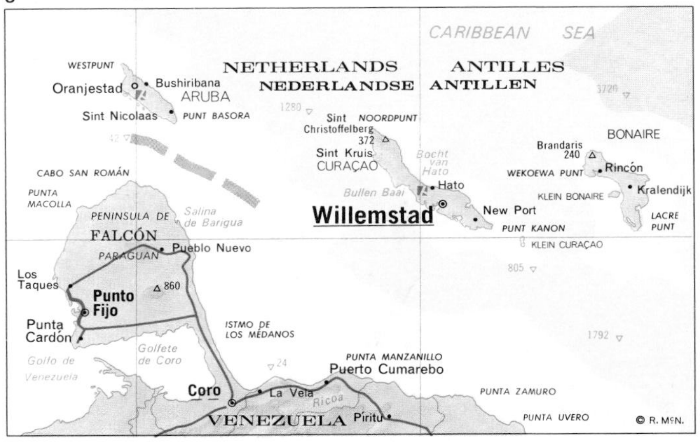

Kilometers 0 50 100 150 Km.
Statute Miles 0 50 100 150 Mi.

Scale 1:3,000,000

One centimeter represents 30 kilometers.
One inch represents approximately 47 miles.
Lambert Conformal Conic Projection

Kilometers 0 200 400 600 Km.

Statute Miles 0 200 400 600 Mi.

Scale 1:12,000,000

One centimeter represents 120 kilometers.
One inch represents approximately 190 miles.
Oblique Conic Conformal Projection

ATLANTIC OCEAN
BRAZIL
SURINAME
FRENCH GUIANA
Georgetown
Paramaribo
Cayenne
TUMUCHUMAC MOUNTAINS
ILHA DE MARAJÓ
Equator
Belém
São Luís
Fortaleza
Natal
João Pessoa
Recife
Maceió
Aracaju
Salvador
Teresina
Brasília
Goiânia
Belo Horizonte
Vitória
RIO DE JANEIRO
SÃO PAULO
Santos
Campinas
Cuiabá
Corumbá
Campo Grande
Santarém
Macapá
Amazonas
Xingu
Tocantins
PLANALTO DO MATO GROSSO
PLANALTO CENTRAL
SERRA DO CACHIMBO
SERRA DO RONCADOR
SERRA DOS CARAJÁS
CHAPADA DAS MANGABEIRAS
SERRA DO ESPINHAÇO
Tropic of Capricorn
CABO DE SÃO ROQUE
ATOL DAS ROCAS
ILHA FERNANDO DE NORONHA (Brazil)
234 - 235

MAP FORM	cerro	cordillera	ilha	lago	nevado	península	serra
ENGLISH	mountain	range	island	lake	mountain	peninsula	mountains
DEUTSCH	Berg	Gebirge	Insel	See	Berg	Halbinsel	Berge
ESPAÑOL	montaña	cordillera	isla	lago	montaña	península	montañas
FRANÇAIS	montagne	chaîne	île	lac	montagne	péninsule	montagnes
PORTUGUÊS	montanha	cordilheira	ilha	lago	montanha	península	montanhas

For complete glossary see page *I • 1*.

MAP FORM	cerro, co.	golfo	ilha	isla	lago	lagoa	monte	salar
ENGLISH	butte	gulf	island	isle	lake	lake	mountain	saltflat
DEUTSCH	Restberg	Golf	Insel	Insel	See	See	Berg	Salzebene
ESPAÑOL	cerro	golfo	isla	isla	lago	lago	montaña	salobral
FRANÇAIS	butte	golfe	île	île	lac	lac	montagne	salina
PORTUGUÊS	cerro	golfo	ilha	ilha	lago	lago	montanha	salina

For complete glossary see page *I • 1*.

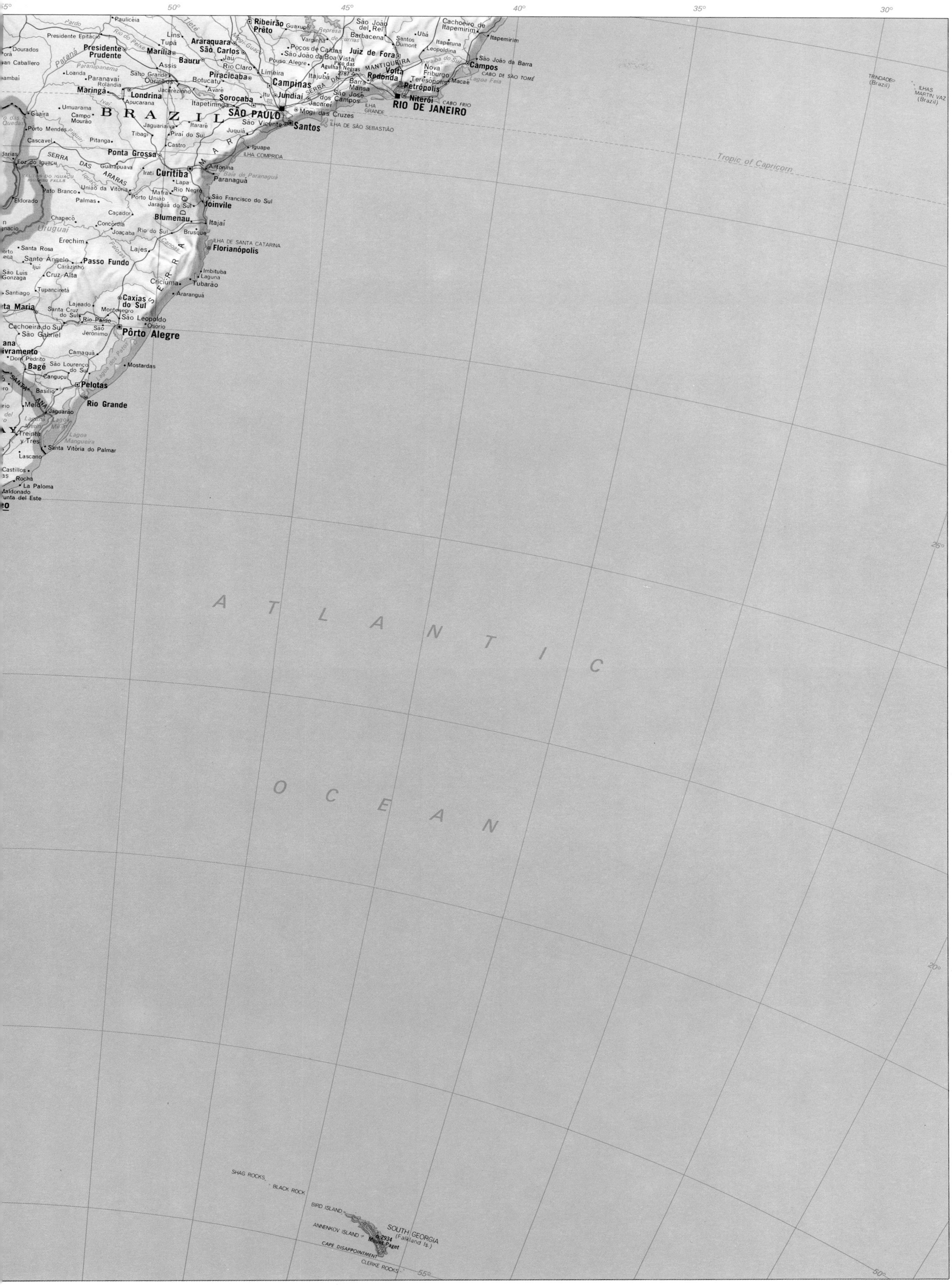

Kilometers 0 200 400 600 Km.

Statute Miles 0 200 400 600 Mi.

Scale 1:12,000,000

One centimeter represents 120 kilometers.
One inch represents approximately 190 miles.
Oblique Conic Conformal Projection

MAP FORM	bahía	cabo	cerro, co.	golfo	igarapé	isla, i.	lago, l.	punta	volcán, vol.
ENGLISH	bay	cape	butte	gulf	river	island	lake	point	volcano
DEUTSCH	Bucht	Kap	Restberg	Golf	Fluss	Insel	See	Landspitze	Vulkan
ESPAÑOL	bahía	cabo	cerro	golfo	río	isla	lago	punta	volcán
FRANÇAIS	baie	cap	butte	golfe	rivière	île	lac	pointe	volcan
PORTUGUÊS	baía	cabo	cerro	golfo	rio	ilha	lago	ponta	vulcão

For complete glossary see page I·1.
For Caracas metropolitan map, see page 276.

Kilometers 0 100 200 300 Km.
Statute Miles 0 100 200 300 Mi.

Scale 1:6,000,000

One centimeter represents 60 kilometers.
One inch represents approximately 95 miles.
Oblique Conic Conformal Projection

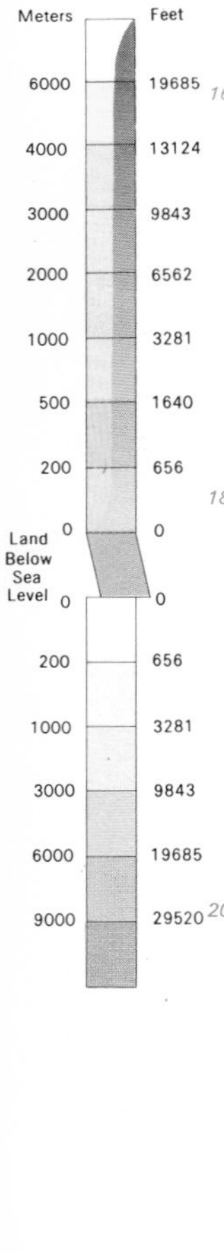

Copyright © by Rand McNally & Co.
Map prepared by Rand McNally & Co.
A-549792-764 -2 -3

MAP FORM	cerro	cordillera	isla, i.	lago, l.	nevado	punta	río	serra
ENGLISH	mountain	mountains	island	lake	mountain	point	river	mountains
DEUTSCH	Berg	Berge	Insel	See	Berg	Landspitze	Fluss	Berge
ESPAÑOL	montaña	montañas	isla	lago	nevado	punta	río	sierra
FRANÇAIS	montagne	montagnes	île	lac	montagne	pointe	rivière	montagnes
PORTUGUÊS	montanha	montanhas	ilha	lago	pico nevado	ponta	rio	serra

For complete glossary see page I • 1.
For Lima metropolitan map, see page 276.

Kilometers 0 100 200 300 Km.
Statute Miles 0 100 200 300 Mi.

Scale 1:6,000,000
One centimeter represents 60 kilometers.
One inch represents approximately 95 miles.
Oblique Conic Conformal Projection

236-237
236-239
245

MAP FORM	cabo	cachoeira, cach.	ilha, i.	lago, l.	riacho	ribeirão, rão.	rio, r.	serra, sa.
ENGLISH	cape	waterfall	island	lake	creek	creek	river	mountains
DEUTSCH	Kap	Wasserfall	Insel	See	Bach	Bach	Fluss	Berge
ESPAÑOL	cabo	cascada	isla	lago	riachuelo	riachuelo	río	montañas
FRANÇAIS	cap	chute d'eau	île	lac	crique	crique	rivière	montagnes
PORTUGUÊS	cabo	cascata	ilha	lago	riacho	riacho	rio	montanhas

For complete glossary see page *I* • *1*.

ATLANTIC OCEAN
Equator
FERNANDO DE NORONHA
ATOL DAS ROCAS
ILHA FERNANDO DE NORONHA
CEARÁ
RIO GRANDE DO NORTE
PARAÍBA
PERNAMBUCO
ALAGOAS
SERGIPE
PIAUÍ
BAHIA
Fortaleza
Teresina
Natal
João Pessoa
Recife
Olinda
Maceió
Aracaju
Parnaíba
Sobral
Mossoró
Campina Grande
Caruaru
Garanhuns
Juazeiro do Norte
Crato
Patos
Floriano
Caxias
Petrolina
Juàzeiro
Paulo Afonso
Alagoinhas
Jaboatão
Parangaba
Aracati
Quixadá
Crateús
Iguatu
Picos
Campo Maior
Sousa
Cajazeiras
Serra Talhada
Arcoverde
Jacobina
SERRA GRANDE
SERRA DA IBIAPABA
CHAPADA DO ARARIPE
CHAPADA DO APODI
PLANALTO DA BORBOREMA
CHAPADA DIAMANTINA
SERRA DAS MARRECAS
SERRA DO ESTREITO
SERRA DA TABATINGA
SERRA DE SANTA RITA
SERRA DE BATURITÉ
CABO DE SÃO ROQUE
44°
42°
40°
38°
36°
34°
32°
2°
0°
4°
6°
8°
10°
Copyright © by Rand McNally & Co.
Map prepared by Rand McNally & Co.
A-540396-764

Kilometers 0 100 200 300 Km.

Statute Miles 0 100 200 300 Mi.

Scale 1:6,000,000

One centimeter represents 60 kilometers.

One inch represents approximately 95 miles.

Oblique Conic Conformal Projection

238 - 239

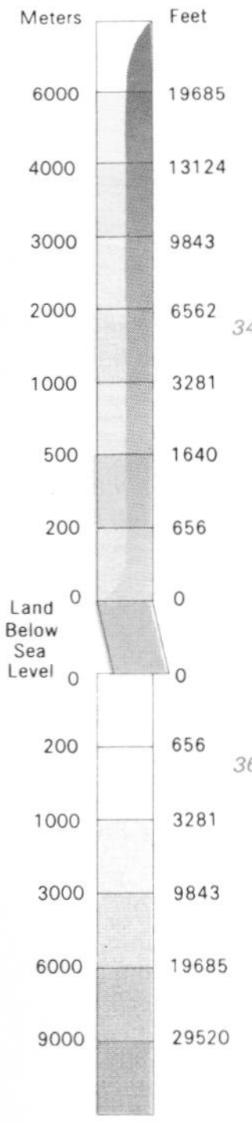

244

MAP FORM	cabo	cerro	cuchilla	ilha	laguna	punta	salar	sierra	volcán
ENGLISH	cape	mountain	hills	island	lagoon; lake	point	saltflat	mountains	volcano
DEUTSCH	Kap	Berg	Hügel	Insel	Haff; See	Landspitze	Salzebene	Berge	Vulkan
ESPAÑOL	cabo	cerro	cerro	isla	laguna	punta	salobral	sierra	volcán
FRANÇAIS	cap	montagne	collines	île	lagune; lac	pointe	salina	montagnes	volcan
PORTUGUÊS	cabo	cerro	colina	ilha	laguna	ponta	salina	serra	vulcão

For complete glossary see page *I • I*.
For Santiago metropolitan map, see page 276.

Kilometers 0 100 200 300 Km.
Statute Miles 0 100 200 300 Mi.

Scale 1:6,000,000
One centimeter represents 60 kilometers.
One inch represents approximately 95 miles.
Oblique Conic Conformal Projection

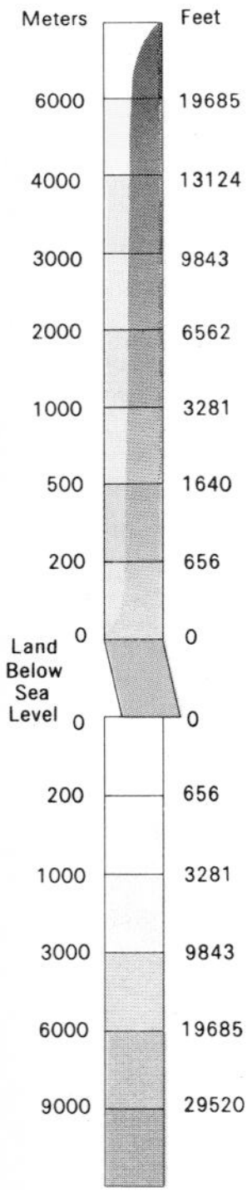

MAP FORM	bahía	cabo	cerro	isla	lago	monte	punta
ENGLISH	bay	cape	mountain, hill	isle	lake	mountain	point
DEUTSCH	Bucht	Kap	Berg, Hügel	Insel	See	Berg	Landspitze
ESPAÑOL	bahía	cabo	cerro	isla	lago	monte	punta
FRANÇAIS	baie	cap	montagne, colline	île	lac	montagne	pointe
PORTUGUÊS	baía	cabo	cerro	ilha	lago	monte	ponta

For complete glossary see page *I*•*1*.

Kilometers 0 100 200 300 Km.
Statute Miles 0 100 200 300 Mi.

Scale 1:6,000,000

One centimeter represents 60 kilometers.
One inch represents approximately 95 miles.
Oblique Conic Conformal Projection

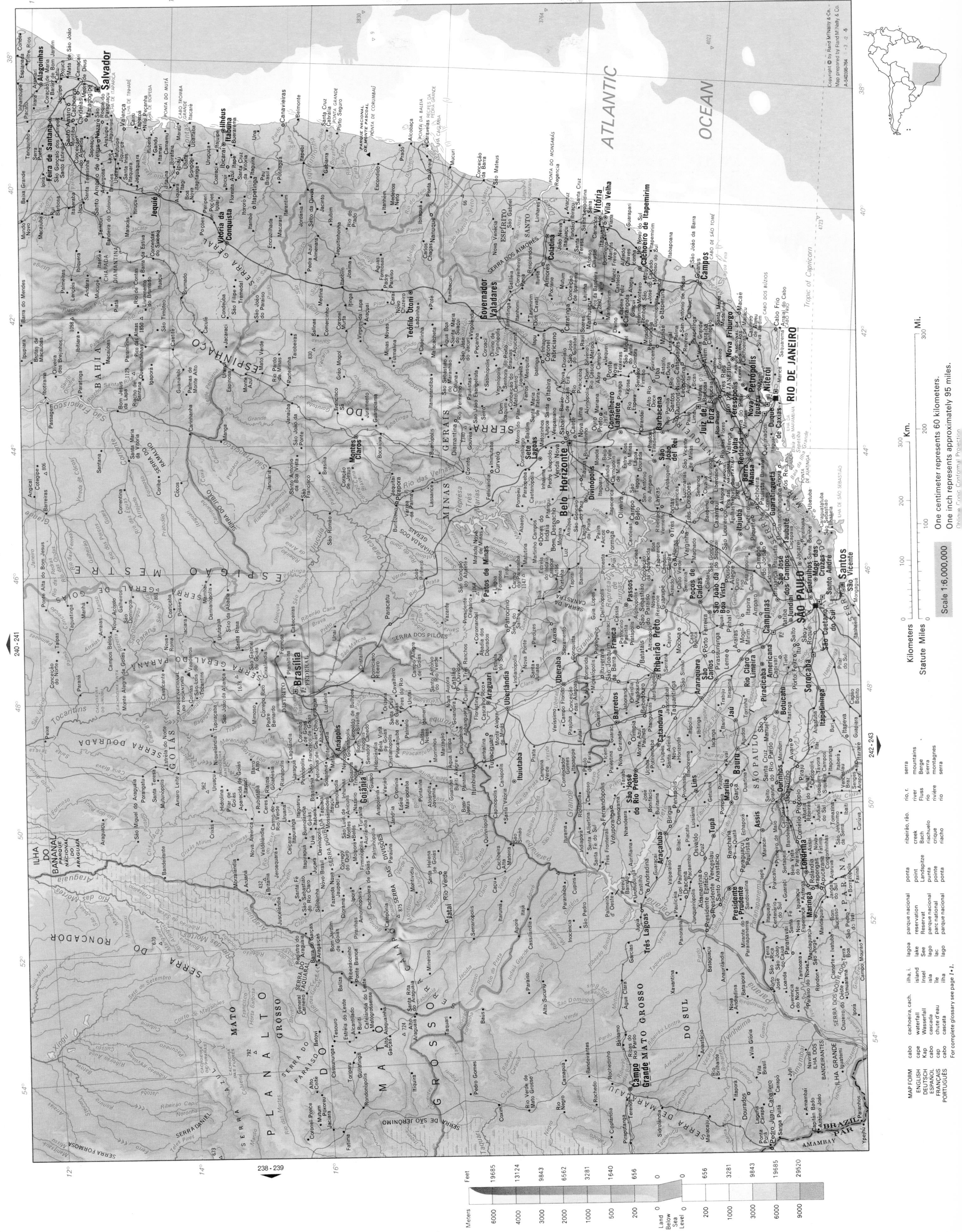
ATLANTIC
OCEAN
Salvador
Feira de Santana
Vitória da Conquista
Ilhéus
Itabuna
Jequié
Governador Valadares
Teófilo Otoni
Montes Claros
Vitória
Vila Velha
Cachoeiro de Itapemirim
Campos
RIO DE JANEIRO
Niterói
Petrópolis
Nova Friburgo
Juiz de Fora
Belo Horizonte
São Paulo
Santos
Campinas
Ribeirão Preto
Uberlândia
Uberaba
Brasília
Goiânia
Anápolis
Campo Grande
BAHIA
MINAS GERAIS
GOIÁS
MATO GROSSO
MATO GROSSO DO SUL
SÃO PAULO
PARANÁ
ESPÍRITO SANTO
SERRA DO ESPINHAÇO
ESPIGÃO MESTRE
SERRA DA MANTIQUEIRA
PLANALTO DO MATO GROSSO
SERRA DO RONCADOR
Tropic of Capricorn
Scale 1:6,000,000
One centimeter represents 60 kilometers.
One inch represents approximately 95 miles.
Oblique Conic Conformal Projection
Kilometers
Statute Miles
Copyright © by Rand McNally & Co.
Map prepared by Rand McNally & Co.
For complete glossary see page I • 1.
240-241
242-243
238-239
Feet
Meters
Land Below Sea Level

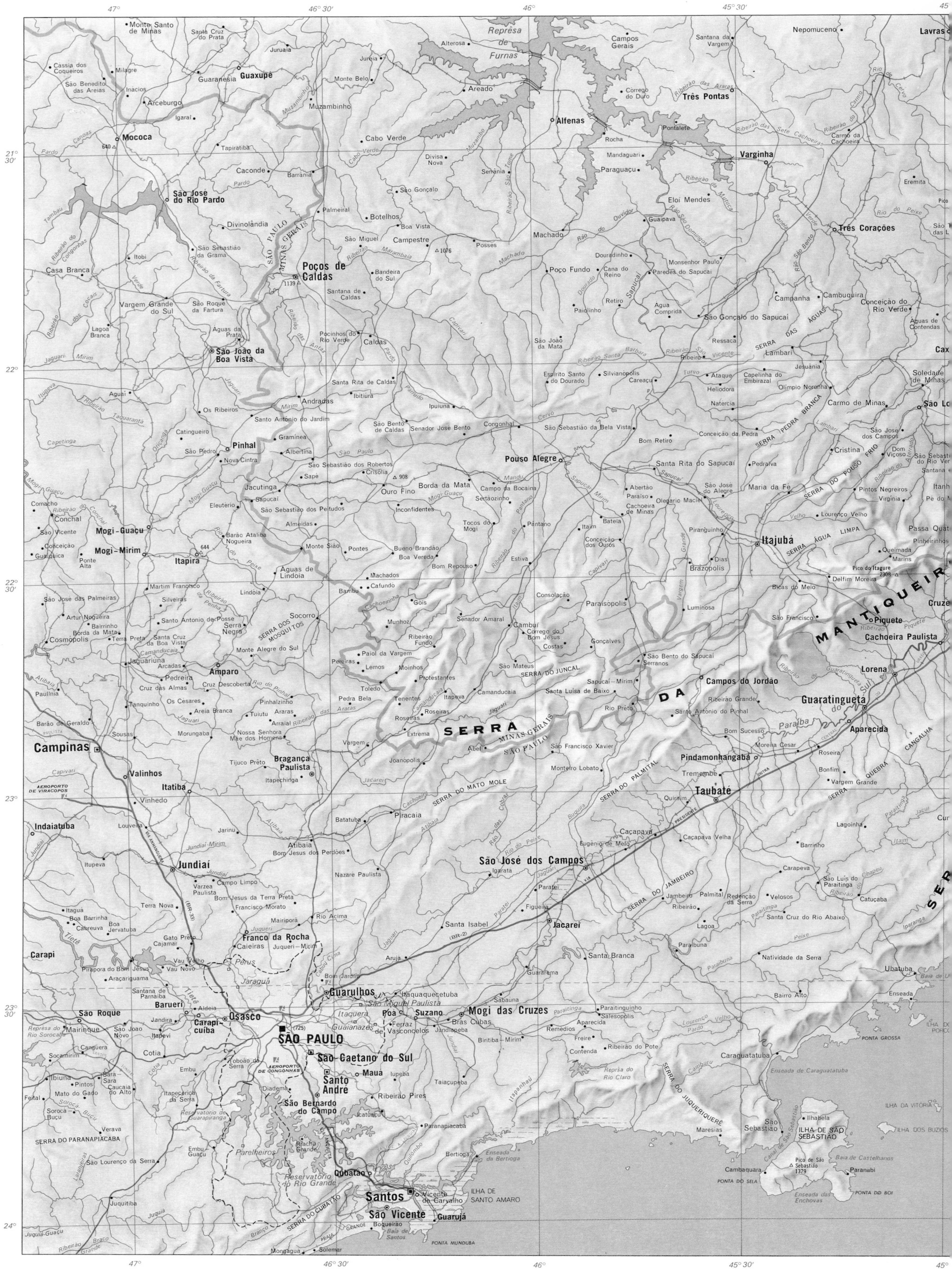

MAP FORM	baía	enseada	ilha	pico	ponta	represa	ribeirão	rio	serra
ENGLISH	bay	bay	island	peak	point	reservoir	stream	river	mountains
DEUTSCH	Bucht	Bucht	Insel	Gipfel	Landspitze	Stausee	Bach	Fluss	Berge
ESPAÑOL	bahía	bahía	isla	pico	punta	estanque	corriente de agua	río	sierra
FRANÇAIS	baie	baie	île	cime	pointe	réservoir	cours d'eau	rivière	montagnes
PORTUGUÊS	baía	enseada	ilha	pico	ponta	represa	ribeirão	rio	serra

For complete glossary see page *I*•*1*.
For Rio de Janeiro and São Paulo metropolitan maps, see page 277.

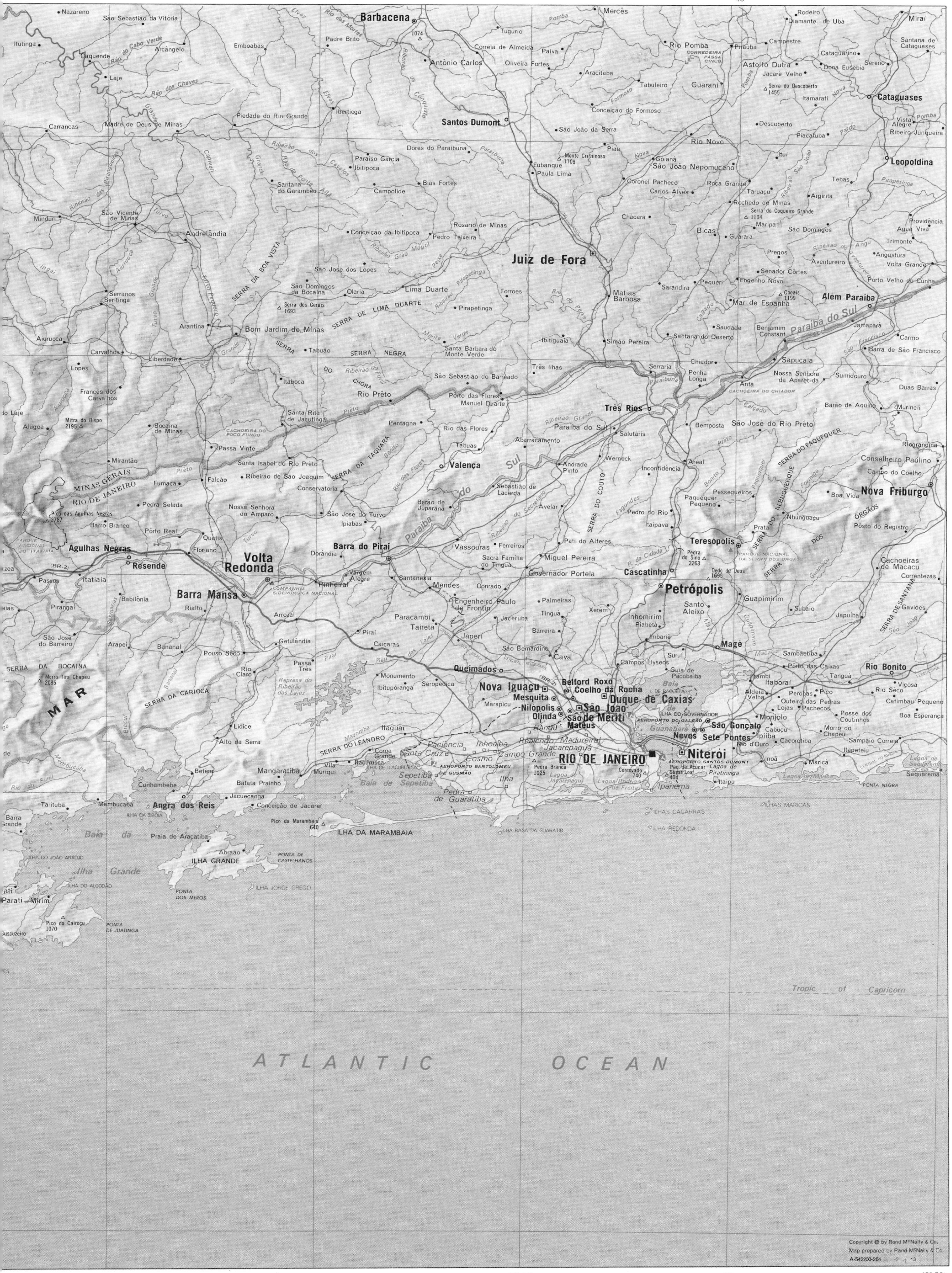

Kilometers 0 10 20 30 40 50 Km.

Statute Miles 0 10 20 30 40 50 Mi.

Scale 1:1,000,000

One centimeter represents 10 kilometers.
One inch represents approximately 16 miles.

Polyconic Projection

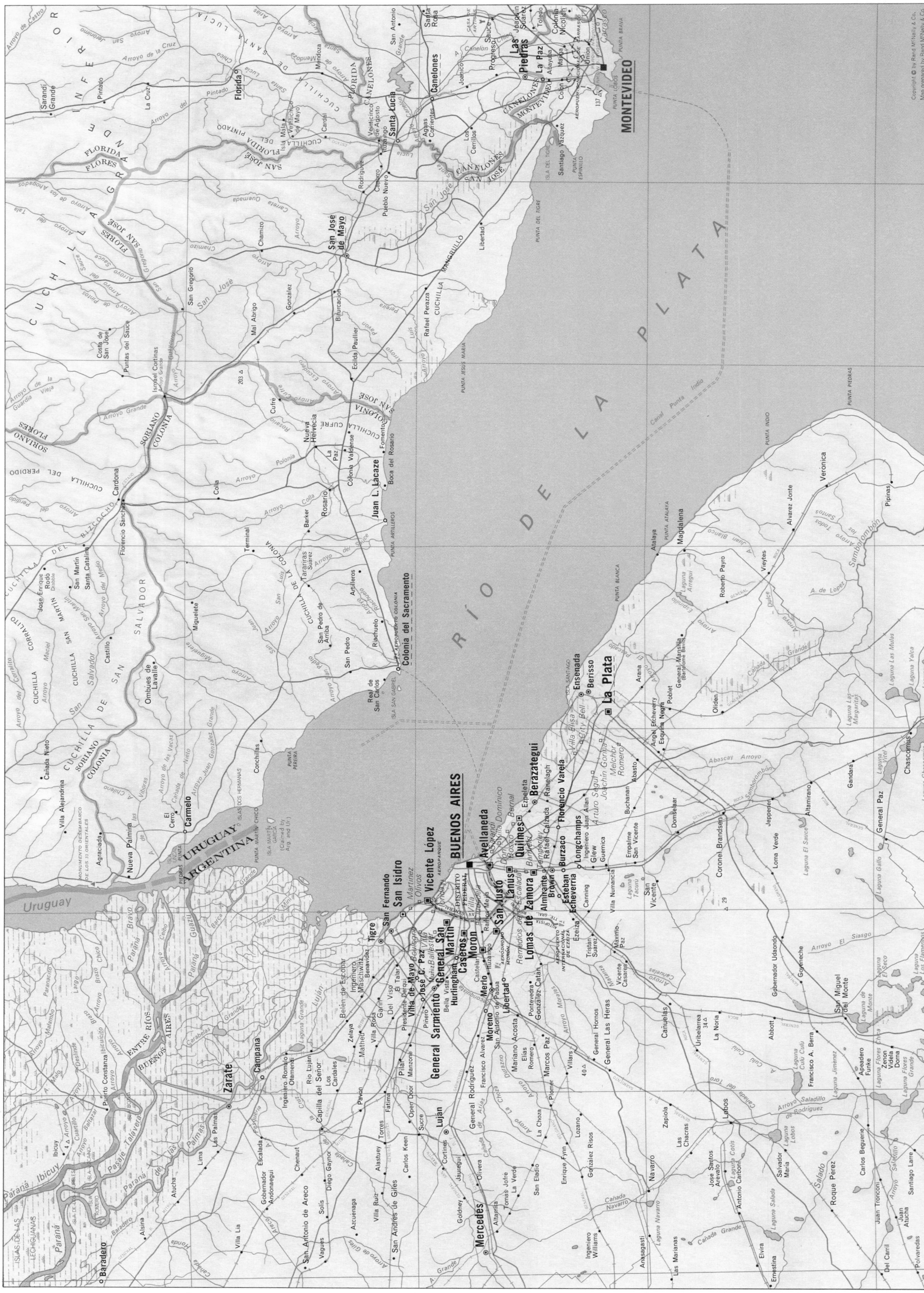

Kilometers 0 10 20 30 40 50 Km.
Statute Miles 0 10 20 30 40 50 Mi.

Scale 1:1,000,000

One centimeter represents 10 kilometers.
One inch represents approximately 16 miles.
Gauss-Krüger Projection

ESPAÑOL	aerodromo	arroyo, a.	cañada	cuchilla	isla	laguna	punta
ENGLISH	airport	brook	brook	hills	island	lake	point
DEUTSCH	Flughafen	Bach	Bach	Hügel	Insel	See	Landspitze
FRANÇAIS	aéroport	ruisseau	ruisseau	collines	île	lac	point
PORTUGUÊS	aeroporto	arroio	riacho	colina	ilha	laguna	ponta

For complete glossary see page I•1.
For Buenos Aires metropolitan map, see page 278.

THIS SECTION CONSISTS of 60 maps of the world's major metropolitan areas, at the scale of 1:300,000. The maps show the generalized land-use patterns in and around each city—the total urban extent, major industrial areas, parks and preserves, and wooded areas. Airports are shown, as are many details of the highway and rail transportation networks. Selected points of interest appear, such as Fisherman's Wharf and Chinatown in San Francisco, the Welcome monument in Jakarta, the Temple of the Jade Buddha in Shanghai, and the Cristo Redentor statue in Rio de Janeiro.

The maps name and locate a great number of towns, villages, and suburbs, and also sections or neighborhoods within limits of the larger cities. Prominent physical features, including elevations, named and unnamed, have been indicated to give a general impression of the local topography. Shaded relief has been omitted, however, to permit display of such details as streams, parks, airport runways, important public buildings and monuments, and the names of major streets. The corporate limits of major cities are also outlined. For the symbols used on these maps see the Legend to Maps, pages x-xii.

Maps of major world cities usually vary widely in scale, and heretofore have not been consistent in design and coverage. For this section, a special effort has been made to portray these varied metropolitan areas in as standard and comparable a fashion as possible. However, for a few cities (notably several in Asia) there has not been adequate source material to include certain information, such as major industrial areas and corporate limits.

The order of presentation is generally regional, with some exceptions where for ease of comparison major capitals or industrial centers or cities located in similar physical surroundings have been juxtaposed. Many American cities and some European cities, with their lower densities and more extensive areas, require larger maps than do Asiatic cities of comparable population. The total land area and population within the confines of each map are stated in the margin as a further aid to comparison. Additional data for these and other metropolitan areas with 1,000,000 or more inhabitants are listed in a table on page 279.

DIESER KARTENTEIL UMFASST 60 Karten der bedeutendsten Stadtregionen der Erde im Massstab 1:300 000. Die Karten zeigen in generalisierter Form die Landnutzung in und um jede Stadt: die gesamte Ausdehnung des verstädterten Gebietes, wichtige Industriegebiete, Parks, Landflächen in Gemeinbesitz und Wald. Flughäfen werden ebenso dargestellt wie viele Einzelheiten des Strassen- und Eisenbahnnetzes. Bekannte Sehenswürdigkeiten sind eingetragen wie die "Fisherman's Wharf" und "Chinatown" in San Francisco, das Willkomm-Denkmal in Jakarta, der Tempel des Jade-Buddhas in Shanghai und die "Cristo Redentor"-Statue in Rio de Janeiro.

Die Karten verzeichnen Name and Lage einer grossen Zahl von Städten, Dörfern, Vororten ebenso wie eingemeindete Ortsteile bei grösseren Städten. Hervortretende physische Formen wie benannte und unbenannte Erhebungen sind aufgenommen, um eine allgemeine Vorstellung des lokalen Reliefs zu geben. Auf die Schummerung wurde jedoch verzichtet, um klar solche Einzelheiten wie Flüsse, Parks, Start- und Landebahnen der Flughäfen, bedeutende öffentliche Gebäude und Denkmäler sowie die Namen der wichtigsten Strassen herausstellen zu können. Eingetragen sind ferner die Gemeindegrenzen der wichtigsten Städte. Zu den auf diesen Karten verwendeten Signaturen siehe "Zeichenerklärung" Seite x-xii.

Karten der bedeutendsten Weltstädte differieren normalerweise sehr stark in ihren Massstäben und sind daher uneinheitlich in ihrer Gestaltung und Begrenzung. Deshalb wurde in diesem Kartenteil besonderer Wert darauf gelegt, die verschiedenen städtischen Ballungsgebiete in möglichst einheitlicher und vergleichbarer Form darzustellen. Für einige Städte, vor allem mehrere asiatische, war das Quellenmaterial jedoch nicht ausreichend genug, um gewisse Informationen wie Hauptindustriegebiete oder Stadtgrenzen einzutragen.

Im allgemeinen sind diese Karten nach regionalen Gesichtspunkten geordnet. Um Vergleiche zu erleichtern wurden einige Ausnahmen gemacht, indem wichtige Hauptstädte, Industriezentren oder Städte in vergleichbarer landschaftlicher Lage einander gegenübergestellt wurden. Viele americkanische und einige europäische Städte mit ihrer geringen Bevölkerungsdichte, aber ausgedehnteren Fläche erfordern eine grössere Kartenfläche als asiatische Städte von vergleichbarer Bevölkerungszahl. Die gesamte Landfläche und die Bevölkerung innerhalb des dargestellten Gebietes ist am Kartenrand verzeichnet als ein weiteres Hilfsmittel für Vergleiche. Weitere Angaben über die dargestellten und andere Stadtregionen mit 1 000 000 oder mehr Bewohnern sind in einer Tabelle auf Seite 279.

INTEGRAN ESTA SECCION 60 mapas de las áreas metropolitanas más importantes del mundo, a la escala de 1:300 000. Los mapas muestran los patrones de uso del suelo dentro de cada ciudad y en sus alrededores—la extensión total del conglomerado urbano, las principales áreas industriales, parques y reservas, y zonas boscosas. Aparecen los aeropuertos, así como muchos otros detalles de las redes de carreteras y ferrocarriles. Se seleccionaron también puntos de interés, como el Muelle de los Pescadores y el Barrio Chino de San Francisco, el monumento de Bienvenida de Jakarta, el Templo del Buda de Jade de Shanghai y la estatua del Cristo Redentor de Rio de Janeiro.

Los mapas incluyen los nombres y la ubicación de gran número de ciudades, poblaciones menores, suburbios, e inclusive barrios y distritos de algunas de las ciudades más importantes. Las características físicas sobresalientes, e incluso algunas elevaciones con o sin nombre, están indicados para dar una impresión general de la topografía local. Se omitió sin embargo el relieve sombreado, lo cual permite mostrar detalles como ríos y arroyos, parques, pistas de aterrizaje, edificios y monumentos públicos notables y los nombres de las calles principales. También están marcados los límites territoriales de las ciudades más grandes. Para la interpretación de los símbolos usados en estos mapas, véanse Leyendas para Mapas en las páginas x-xii.

Los mapas de las ciudades más importantes del mundo varían generalmente en escala, y hasta ahora no han sido consistentes ni en diseño ni en contenido. En esta sección hemos hecho un esfuerzo de presentar las distintas áreas metropolitanas en la forma más uniforme posible, para facilitar sus comparaciones. Para algunas ciudades (la mayoría de ellas en Asia), no fué posible obtener de las propias fuentes material adecuado para la inclusión de ciertos datos, tales como las mayores áreas industriales y los límites municipales.

Los mapas de áreas metropolitanas se presentan por regiones, a excepción de unos cuantos que aparecen yuxtapuestos para facilitar la comparación entre grandes capitales, o centros comerciales, o ciudades ubicadas en contextos físicos similares. Muchas ciudades de América y algunas ciudades de Europa, por su baja densidad de población y su área extensa, requieren mapas más grandes que los ocupados por ciudades asiáticas con poblaciones comparables. Al margen de cada mapa se anotaron el área total y la población de territorio representado, lo cual facilita también las comparaciones. Datos adicionales acerca de éstas y otras áreas metropolitanas con un millón o más de habitantes, figuran en la tabla de la página 279.

CETTE PARTIE COMPREND 60 cartes des principales zones métropolitaines à l'échelle du 1:300 000ᵉ. Les cartes représentent les principaux types d'occupation du sol des villes et de leurs environs, c'est-à-dire de toute la zone urbanisée, les principales zones industrielles, les parcs et réserves naturelles, et les régions boisées. Les aéroports sont aussi représentés ainsi que de nombreux éléments des réseaux routier et ferroviaire. Certains lieux particulièrement intéressants sont indiqués, tels que le quai des pêcheurs et la ville chinoise à San Francisco, le monument de la Bienvenue à Jakarta, le temple du Bouddha de Jade à Shanghai et la statue du Christ Rédempteur à Rio de Janeiro.

Les cartes permettent de localiser un grand nombre de villes, villages et banlieues, ainsi que des quartiers de grandes villes. Les caractéristiques topographiques notables, comme les hauteurs sont indiquées même si elles ne portent pas de nom, pour donner une idée du site de l'aire métropolitaine. L'estompage du relief est omis cependant pour permettre de représenter cours d'eau, parcs, pistes d'envol des aéroports, monuments et bâtiments publics importants, noms des principales rues, ainsi que les limites municipales des grandes villes. (Pour la signification des symboles voir légende, pages x-xii.)

En général, les échelles des cartes des grandes villes du monde varient considérablement, et jusqu'ici la présentation et le contenu de ces cartes n'étaient pas comparables. Dans cette partie de l'Atlas, un effort spécial a été fait pour représenter les diverses zones métropolitaines de manière aussi homogène que possible. Cependant, dans certains cas (en Asie notamment), les documents de base n'étaient pas assez complets pour qu'il fût possible d'inclure avec précision des données comme les zones industrielles et les limites municipales.

L'ordre de présentation est régional, avec des exceptions quand, pour faciliter les comparaisons, de grandes capitales de grands centres industriels ou encore des villes possédant un même environnement naturel, sont juxtaposés. Beaucoup de villes américaines et quelques villes européennes ont une faible densité de population et une étendue considérable; elles requièrent, par conséquent, des cartes plus grandes que des villes asiatiques de population similaire. La superficie et la population de chaque carte sont indiquées dans la marge. Des informations supplémentaires concernant ces zones métropolitaines ou celles dont la population est au moins égale à un million d'habitants sont rassemblées dans la table, page 279.

INTEGRAM ESTA SEÇÃO 60 mapas das áreas metropolitanas mais importantes do mundo, em escala de 1:300 000. Os mapas mostram os principais tipos de uso do solo em cada cidade e seus arredores, seja, a extensão total da zona urbanizada, as principais áreas industriais, os parques e reservas, e as áreas florestais. Mostram os aeroportos, e muitos detalhes das redes rodo e ferroviária. Indicam também pontos de interesse, selecionados, tais como o Cais dos Pescadores e o Bairro Chinês de San Francisco, o monumento de Boasvindas, em Jakarta, o templo do Buda de Jade, em Shanghai, e a Estátua do Cristo Redentor, no Rio de Janeiro.

Os mapas apresentam o nome e a localização de grande número de cidades, vilas e subúrbios, e incluem bairros das cidades mais importantes. Foram indicadas as características físicas principais, inclusive elevações, com ou sem nome, com o objetivo de proporcionar uma idéia geral da topografia local. No entanto, omitiu-se o sombreado do relevo, para permitir a indicação de detalhes tais como cursos d'água, parques, pistas de aeroportos, edifícios públicos e monumentos notáveis, e os nomes das principais ruas, bem como os limites municipais das grandes cidades. Para a interpretação dos símbolos usados nesses mapas, ver as *Legendas dos mapas*, nas pág. x-xii.

Os mapas das cidades mais importantes do mundo variam consideravelmente, de modo geral, quanto à escala, e até o presente não são comparáveis nem na forma de apresentação nem no conteúdo. Nesta seção, fez-se um esforço especial para representar as diversas áreas metropolitanas do modo mais uniforme e comparável possível. No entanto, para algumas cidades, a maioria das quais da Ásia, não foi possível obter fontes fidedignas de informações, tais como áreas industriais principais e limites municipais.

A ordem de apresentação dos mapas das áreas metropolitanas é geralmente regional, exceto em certos casos em que, para facilidade de comparação, capitais ou centros industriais e cidades importantes localizadas em meio físico semelhante foram justapostos. Muitas cidades da América e algumas da Europa, por sua baixa densidade demográfica e áreas mais extensas, exigem mapas maiores que as cidades asiáticas de população comparável. À margem de cada mapa indicam-se a área terrestre e a população total do território representado, também para maior facilidade de comparação. Dados suplementares relativos a essas e outras áreas metropolitanas de um milhão de habitantes ou mais figuram na tabela de pág. 279.

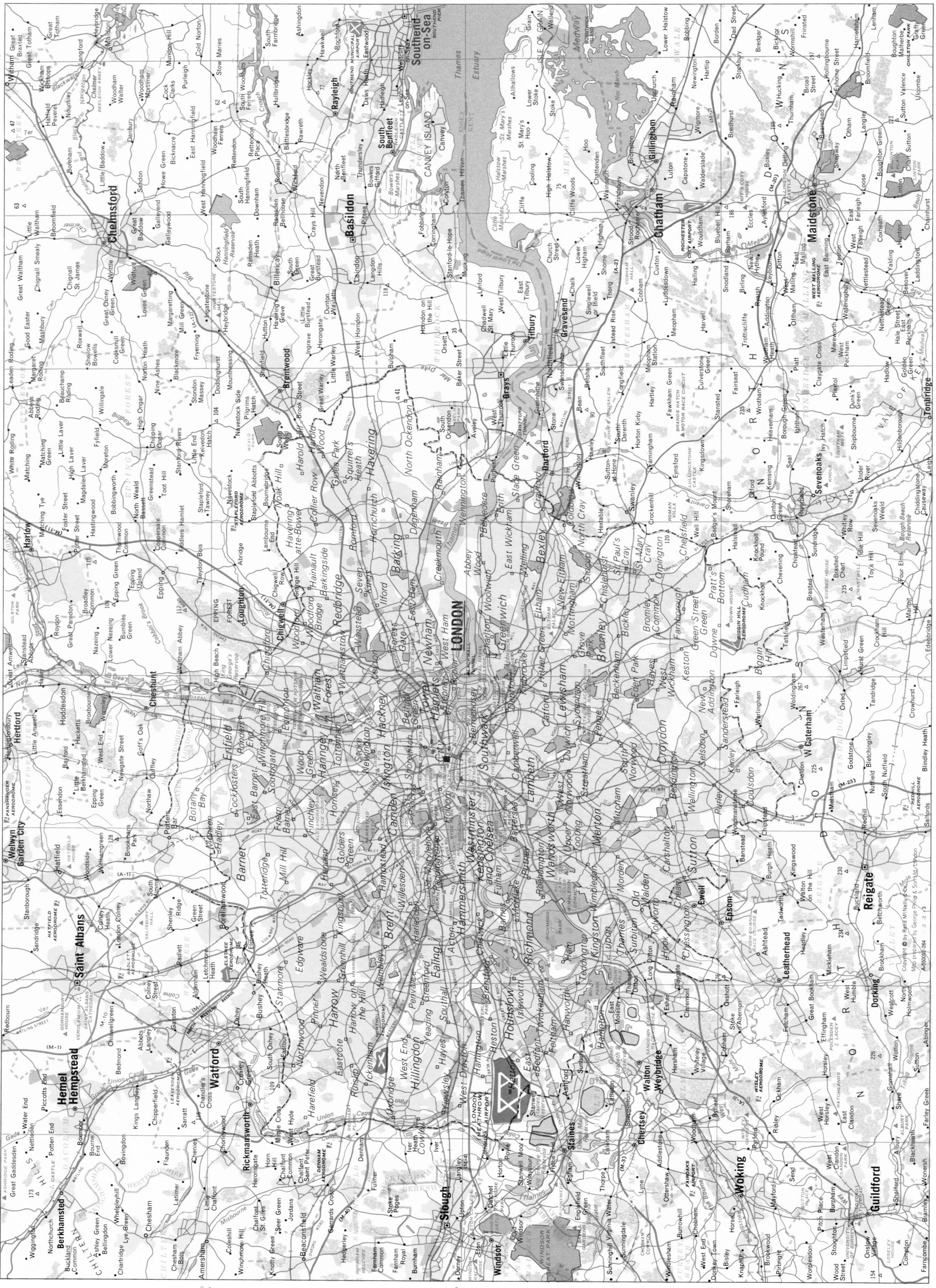
Kilometers 0 5 10 15 Km.
Statute Miles 0 5 10 15 Mi.
Scale 1:300,000
One centimeter represents 3 kilometers.
One inch represents approximately 4.7 miles.
ENGLISH aerodrome canal castle palace park race course road station
DEUTSCH Flughafen Kanal Burg Palast Park Rennbahn Landstrasse Bahnhof
ESPAÑOL aeropuerto canal castillo palacio parque hipódromo camino estación
FRANÇAIS aéroport canal château palais parc champ de course route gare
PORTUGUÊS aeroporto canal castelo palácio parque hipódromo estrada estação
For complete glossary see page I·1.
AREA: 6,400 km²
POPULATION: 10,325,000
LONDON
Chelmsford
Southend-on-Sea
Basildon
Brentwood
Chatham
Gillingham
Maidstone
Gravesend
Dartford
Tilbury
Grays
Sevenoaks
Tonbridge
Harlow
Hertford
Welwyn Garden City
Saint Albans
Hemel Hempstead
Berkhamsted
Watford
Rickmansworth
Slough
Windsor
Staines
Chertsey
Woking
Guildford
Dorking
Leatherhead
Epsom
Reigate
Croydon
Kingston upon Thames
Richmond
Hounslow
Heathrow London Airport

Kilometers 0 5 10 15 Km.
Statute Miles 0 5 10 15 Mi.

Scale 1:300,000

One centimeter represents 3 kilometers.
One inch represents approximately 4.7 miles.

AREA 6,500 km²
POPULATION 9,800,000

FRANÇAIS	aérodrome	bois	château	étang	forêt	ruisseau
ENGLISH	airport	woods	castle	pond	forest	brook
DEUTSCH	Flughafen	Gehölz	Burg	Teich	Wald	Bach
ESPAÑOL	aeropuerto	bosques	castillo	charca	bosque	arroyo
PORTUGUÊS	aeroporto	bosques	castelo	lagoa	bosque	arroio

For complete glossary see page I • I.

AREA 5,650 km²
POPULATION 6,275,000

ENGLISH	DEUTSCH	ESPAÑOL	FRANÇAIS	PORTUGUÊS
bank	Bank	banco	banc	banco
canal	Kanal	canal	canal	canal
hill	Hügel	colina	colline	colina
moor	Ried	páramo	lande	charneca
park	Park	parque	parc	parque
railway station	Bahnhof	terminal ferroviaria	gare	estação ferroviária
reservoir	Stausee	estanque	réservoir	reservatório
tower	Turm	torre	tour	torre

For complete glossary see page I•1.

Kilometers 0 5 10 15 Km.
Statute Miles 0 5 10 15 Mi.

Scale 1:300,000
One centimeter represents 3 kilometers.
One inch represents approximately 4.7 miles.

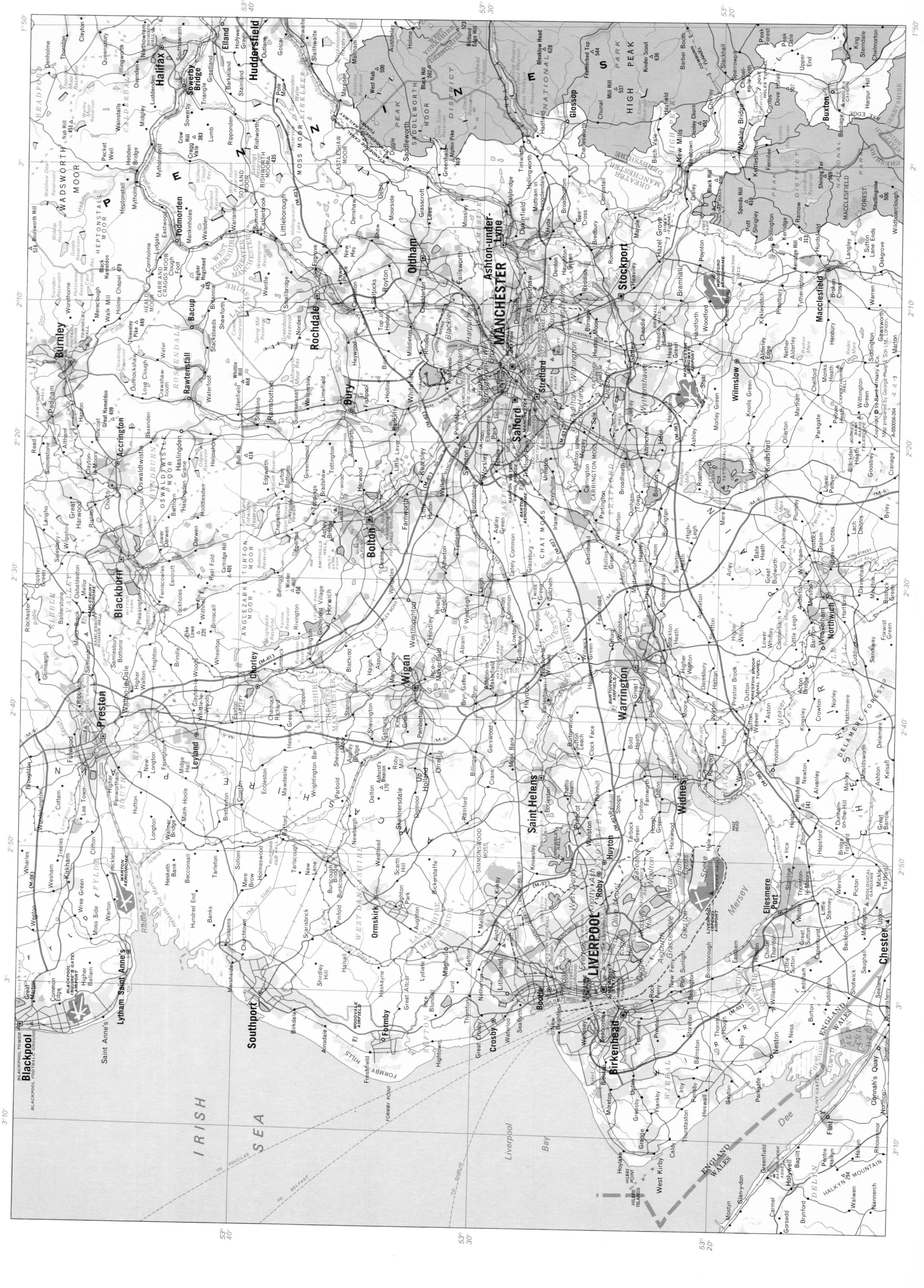

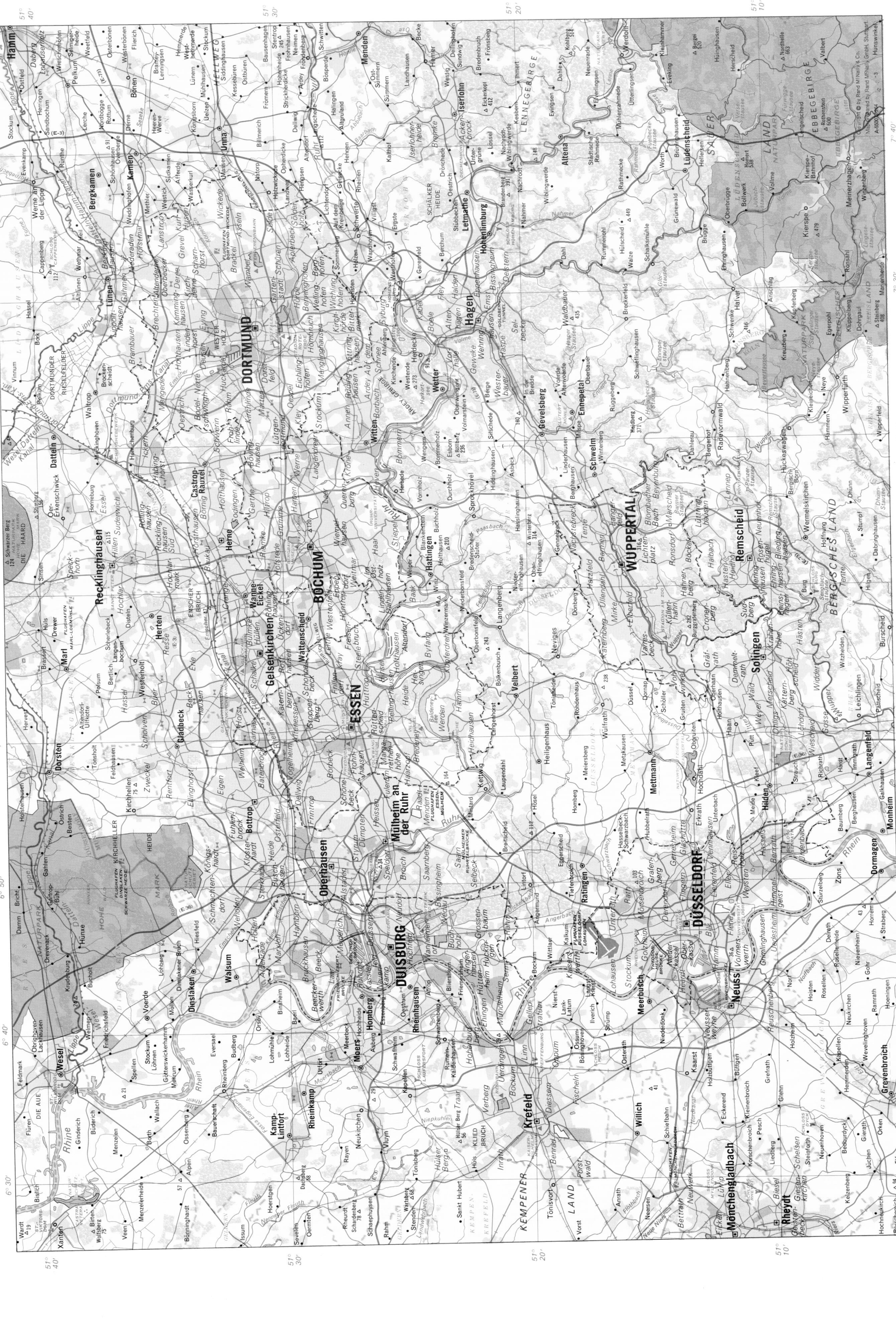

AREA: 6,500 km²
POPULATION: 8,450,000

DEUTSCH	Bach	Berg	Flughafen	Heide	Kanal	Schloss	Stausee
ENGLISH	creek	mountain	airport	heath	canal	castle	reservoir
ESPAÑOL	riachuelo	montaña	aeropuerto	matorral	canal	castillo	estanque
FRANÇAIS	crique	montagne	aéroport	lande	canal	château	réservoir
PORTUGUÊS	riacho	montanha	aeroporto	charneca	canal	castelo	reservatório

For complete glossary see page *I • 1*.

Kilometers 0 5 10 15 Km.
Statute Miles 0 5 10 15 Mi.

Scale 1:300,000
One centimeter represents 3 kilometers.
One inch represents approximately 4.7 miles.

a

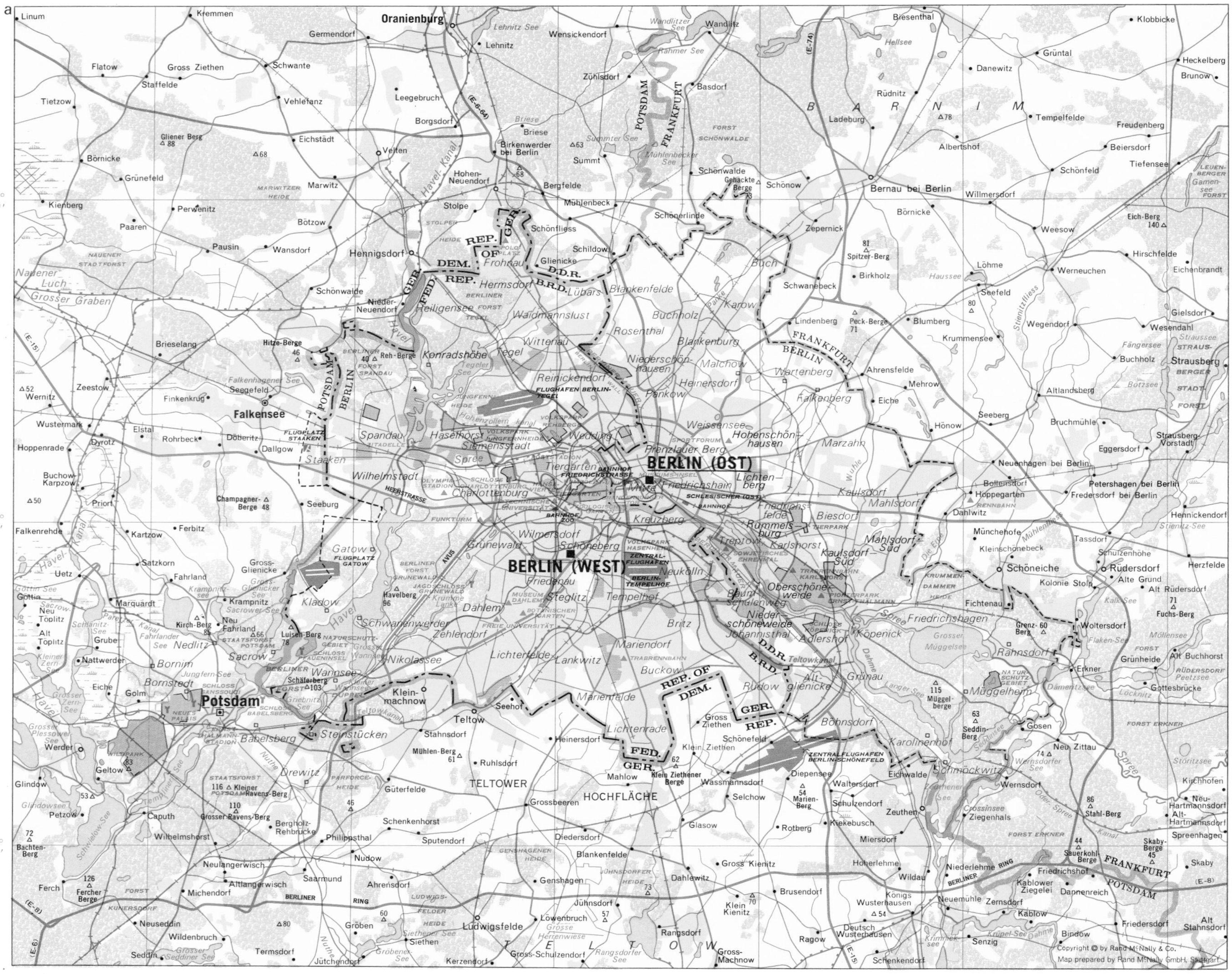

b

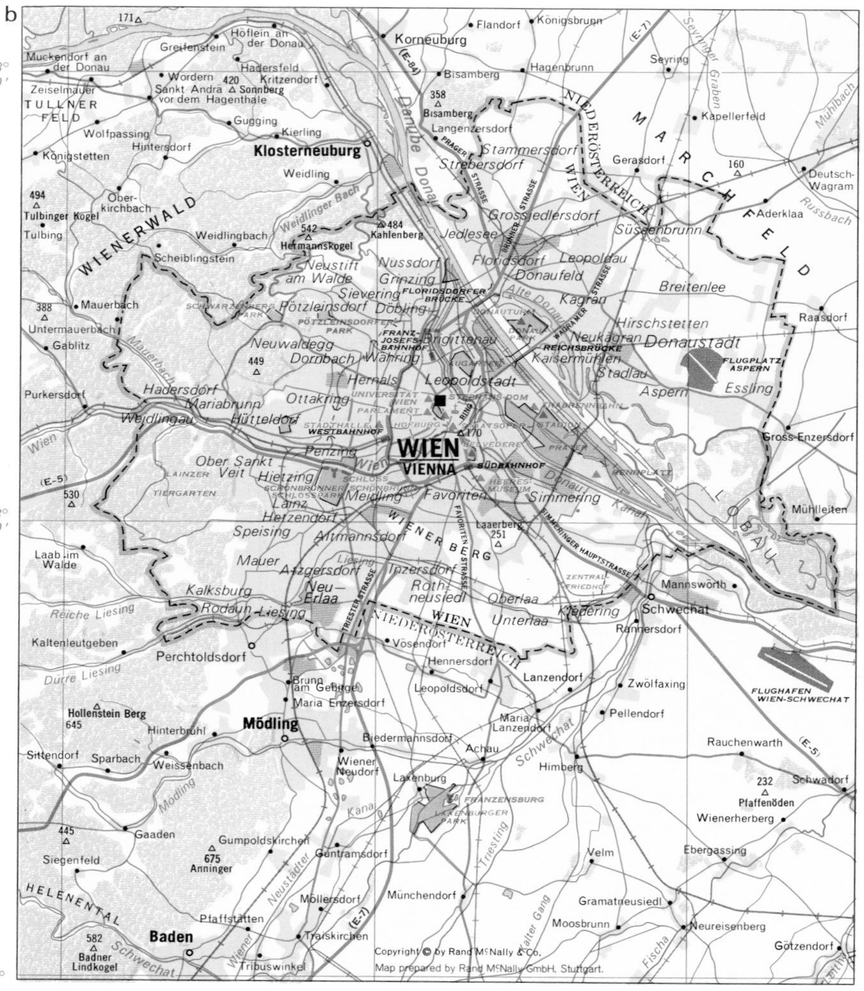

c

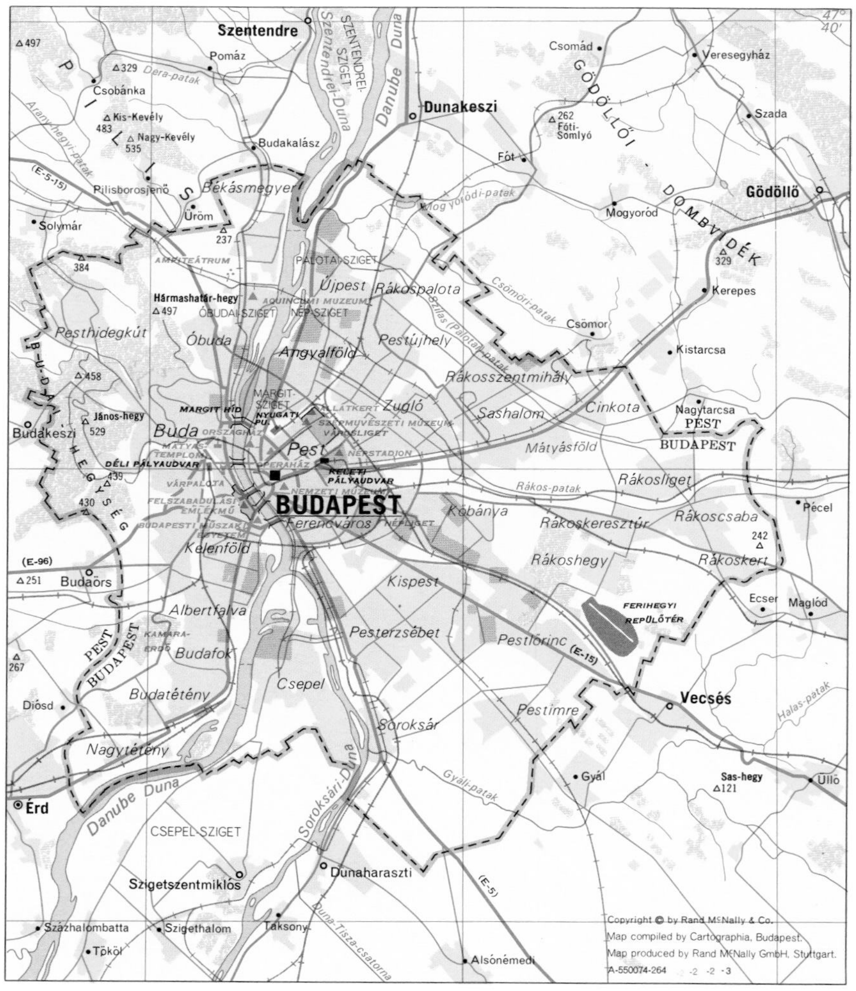

	AREA (km²)	POPULATION
BERLIN	3,700	3,550,000
WIEN	1,300	1,825,000
BUDAPEST	1,300	2,450,000

MAP FORM	Berg	Berge	hegy	Heide	Schloss	See	sziget
ENGLISH	hill	hills	mountain	heath	castle	lake	island
DEUTSCH	Berg	Berge	Berg	Heide	Schloss	See	Insel
ESPAÑOL	colina	colinas	montaña	matorral	castillo	lago	isla
FRANÇAIS	colline	collines	montagne	lande	château	lac	île
PORTUGUÊS	colina	colinas	montanha	charneca	castelo	lago	ilha

For complete glossary see page *I* • *1*.

Kilometers 0 5 10 15 Km.
Statute Miles 0 5 10 15 Mi.

Scale 1:300,000

One centimeter represents 3 kilometers.
One inch represents approximately 4.7 miles.

a

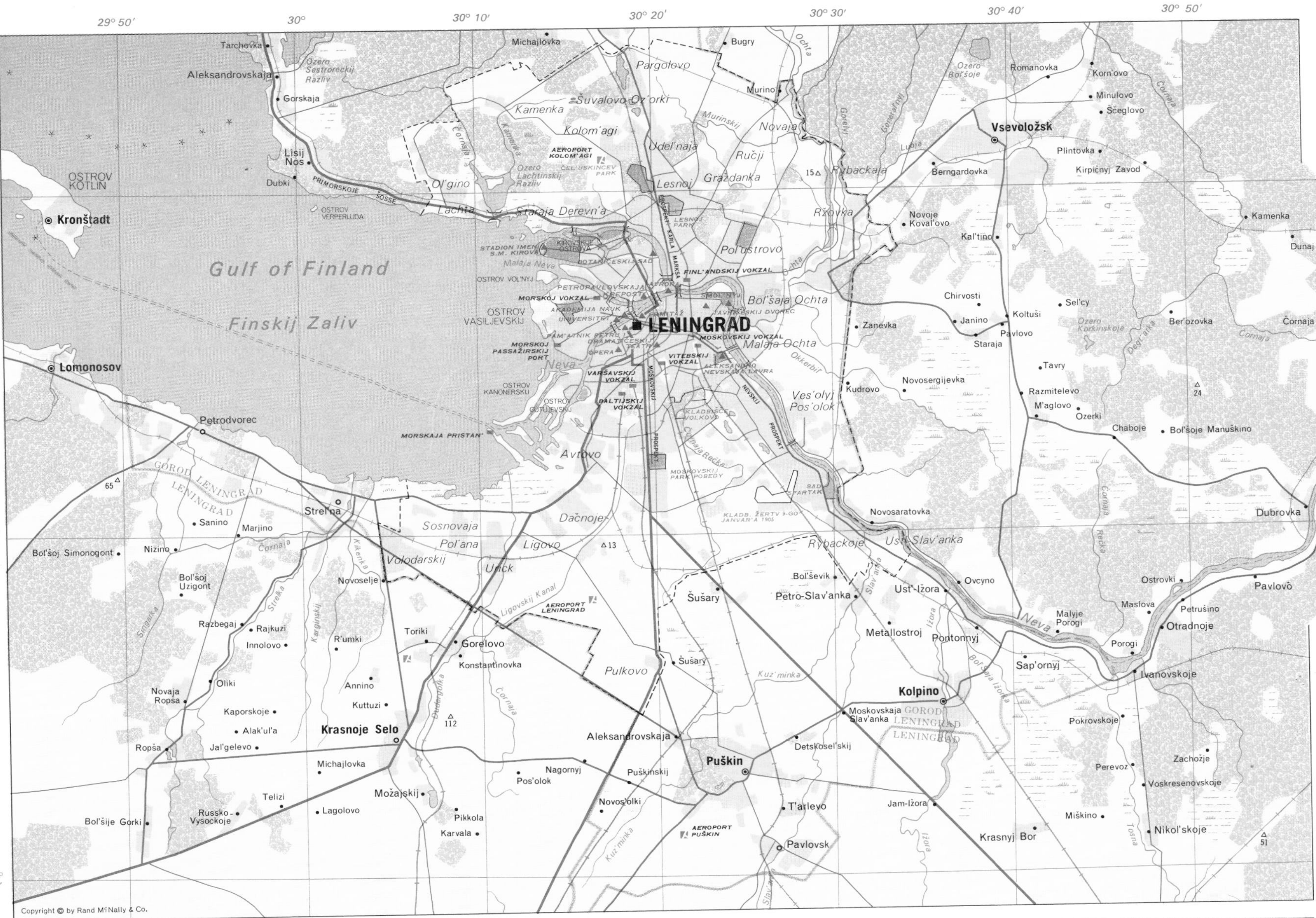

b

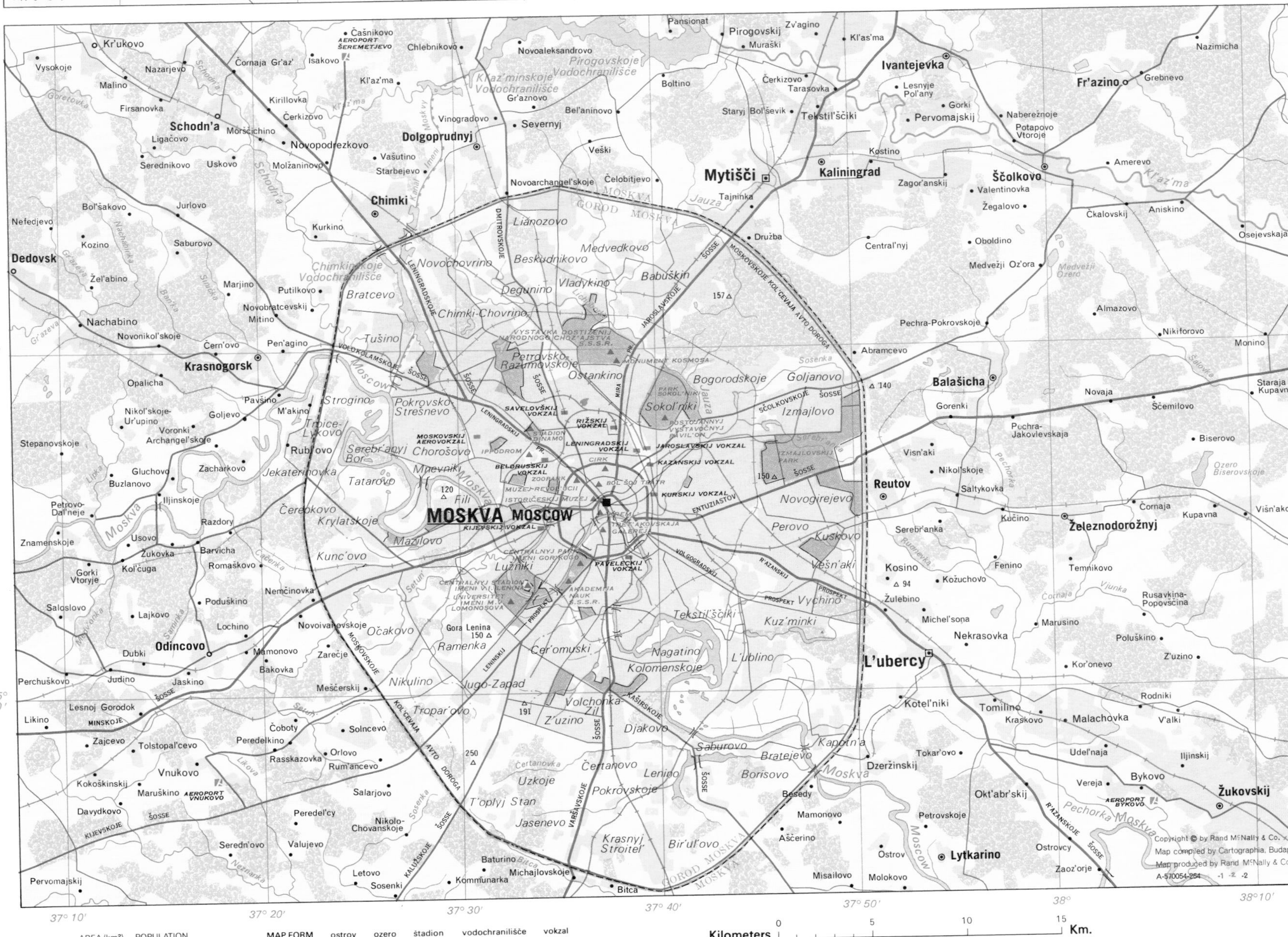

	AREA (km²)	POPULATION
LENINGRAD	2,800	4,850,000
MOSKVA	3,200	9,950,000

MAP FORM	ostrov	ozero	štadion	vodochranilišče	vokzal
ENGLISH	island	lake	stadium	reservoir	rail terminal
DEUTSCH	Insel	See	Stadion	Stausee	Bahnhof
ESPAÑOL	isla	lago	estadio	estanque	terminal ferroviaria
FRANÇAIS	île	lac	stade	réservoir	gare
PORTUGUÊS	ilha	lago	estádio	reservatório	estação ferroviária

For complete glossary see page I•1.

Kilometers 0 5 10 15 Km.

Statute Miles 0 5 10 15 Mi.

Scale 1:300,000

One centimeter represents 3 kilometers.
One inch represents approximately 4.7 miles.

MAP FORM	aeroporto	arroyo	estación	ponta	ribeira	riera
ENGLISH	airport	brook	station	point	creek	creek
DEUTSCH	Flughafen	Bach	Bahnhof	Landspitze	Bach	Bach
ESPAÑOL	aeropuerto	arroyo	estación	punta	riachuelo	riera
FRANÇAIS	aéroport	ruisseau	gare	pointe	crique	crique
PORTUGUÊS	aeroporto	arroio	estação	ponta	riacho	arroio

For complete glossary see page I • I.

	AREA (km²)	POPULATION
MADRID	1,250	3,675,000
MILANO	1,900	3,975,000
LISBOA	1,150	2,150,000
BARCELONA	950	3,825,000

Kilometers 0 5 10 15 Km.

Statute Miles 0 5 10 15 Mi.

Scale 1:300,000

One centimeter represents 3 kilometers.

One inch represents approximately 4.7 miles.

a

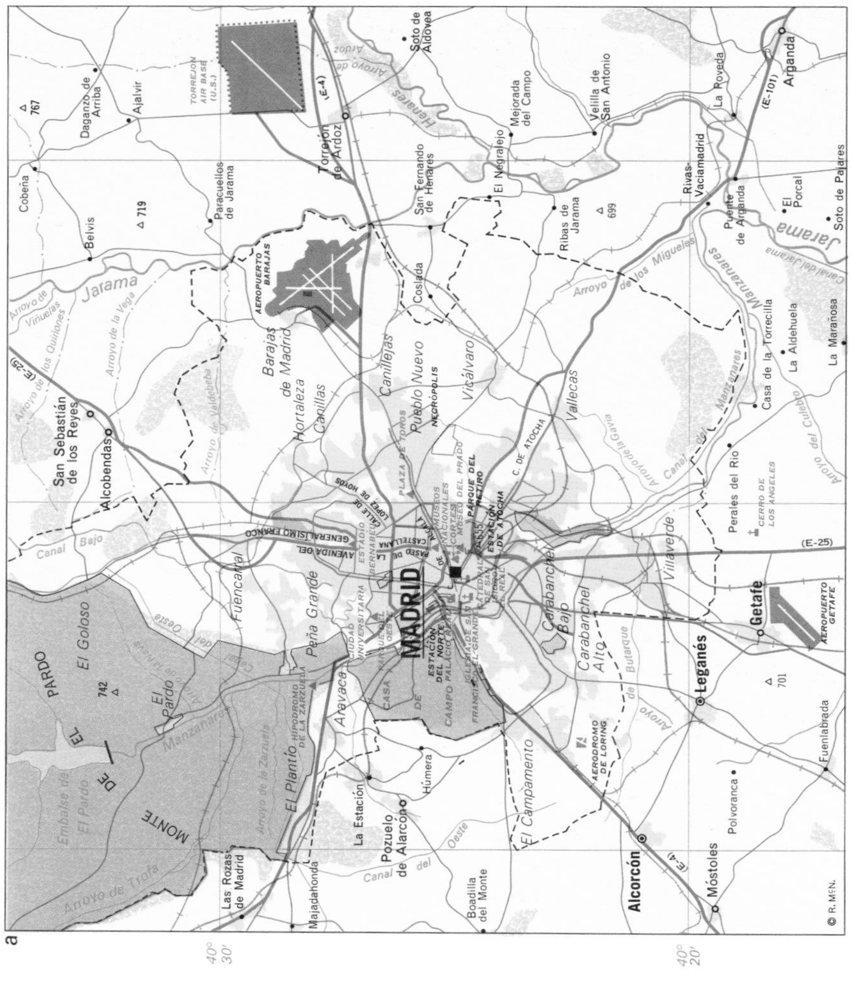

b

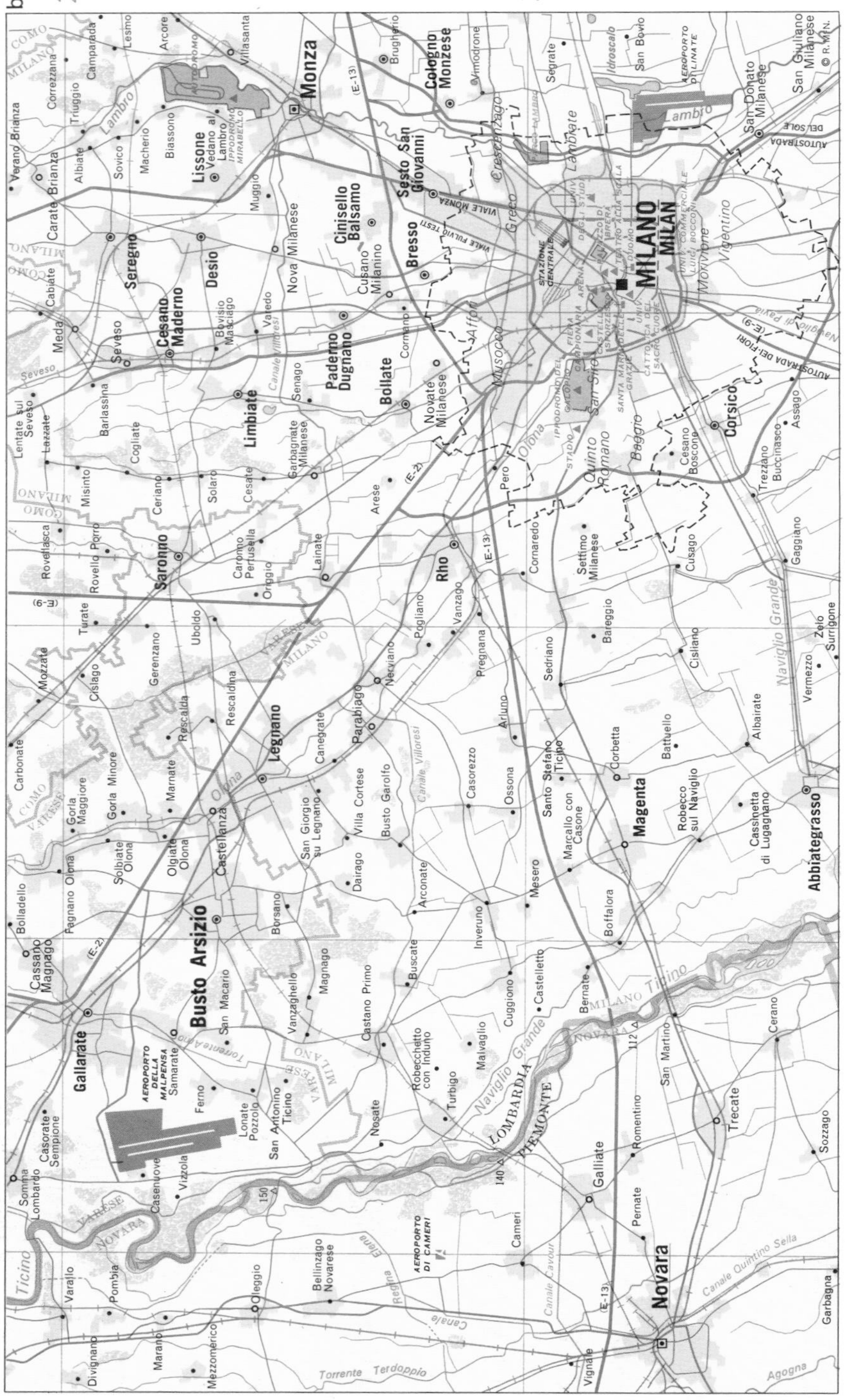

c

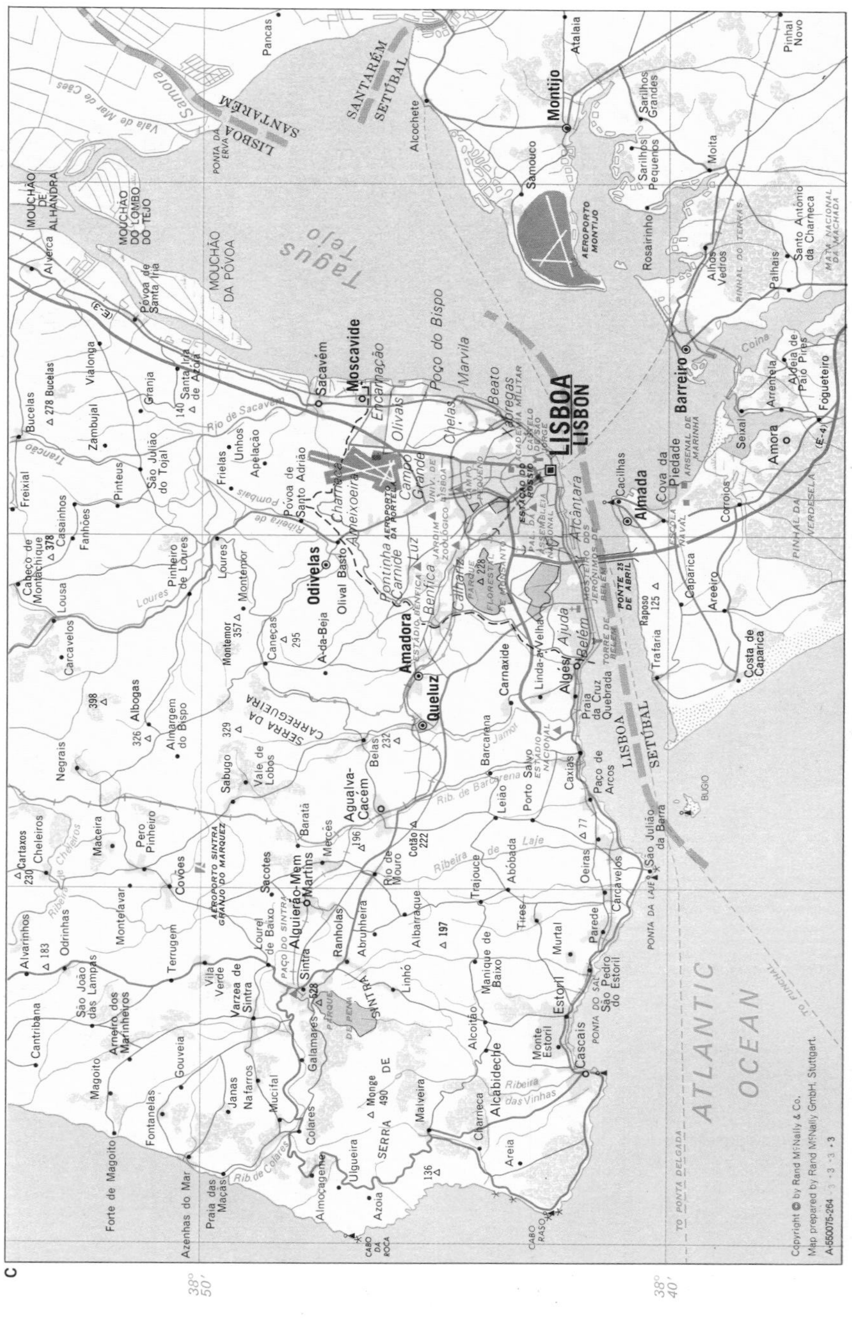

d

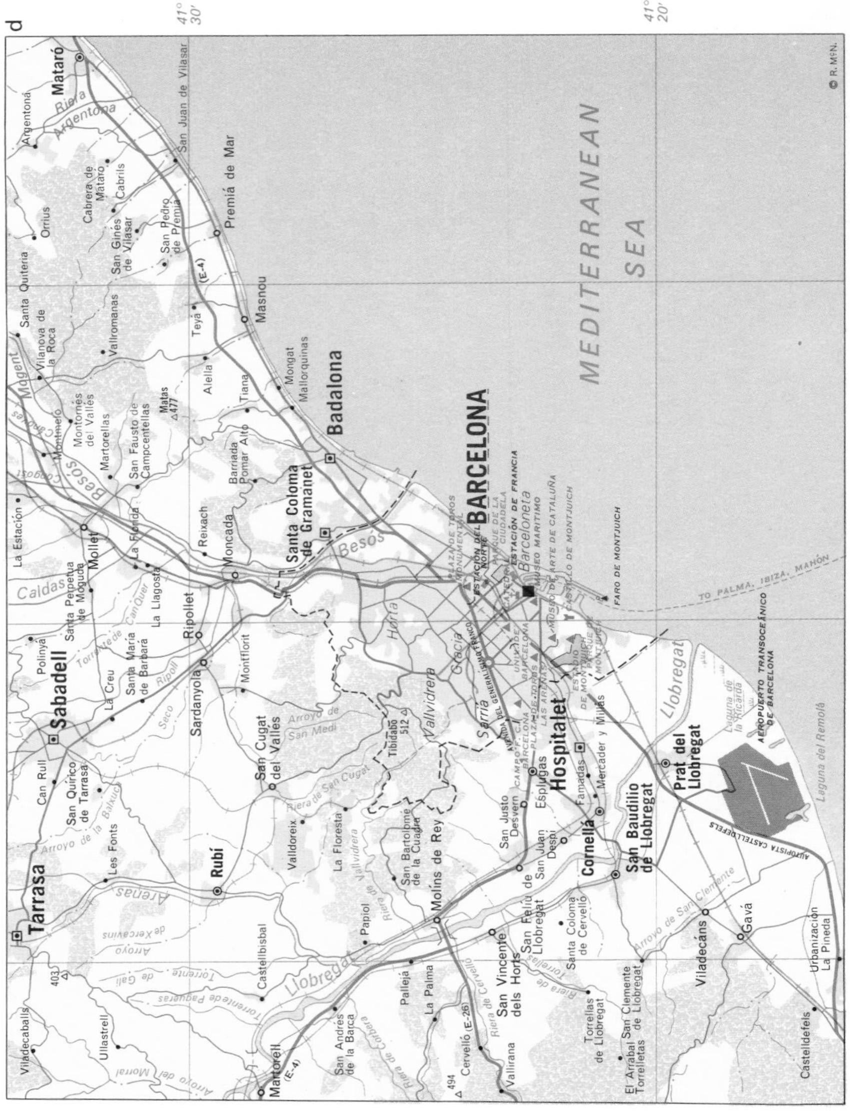

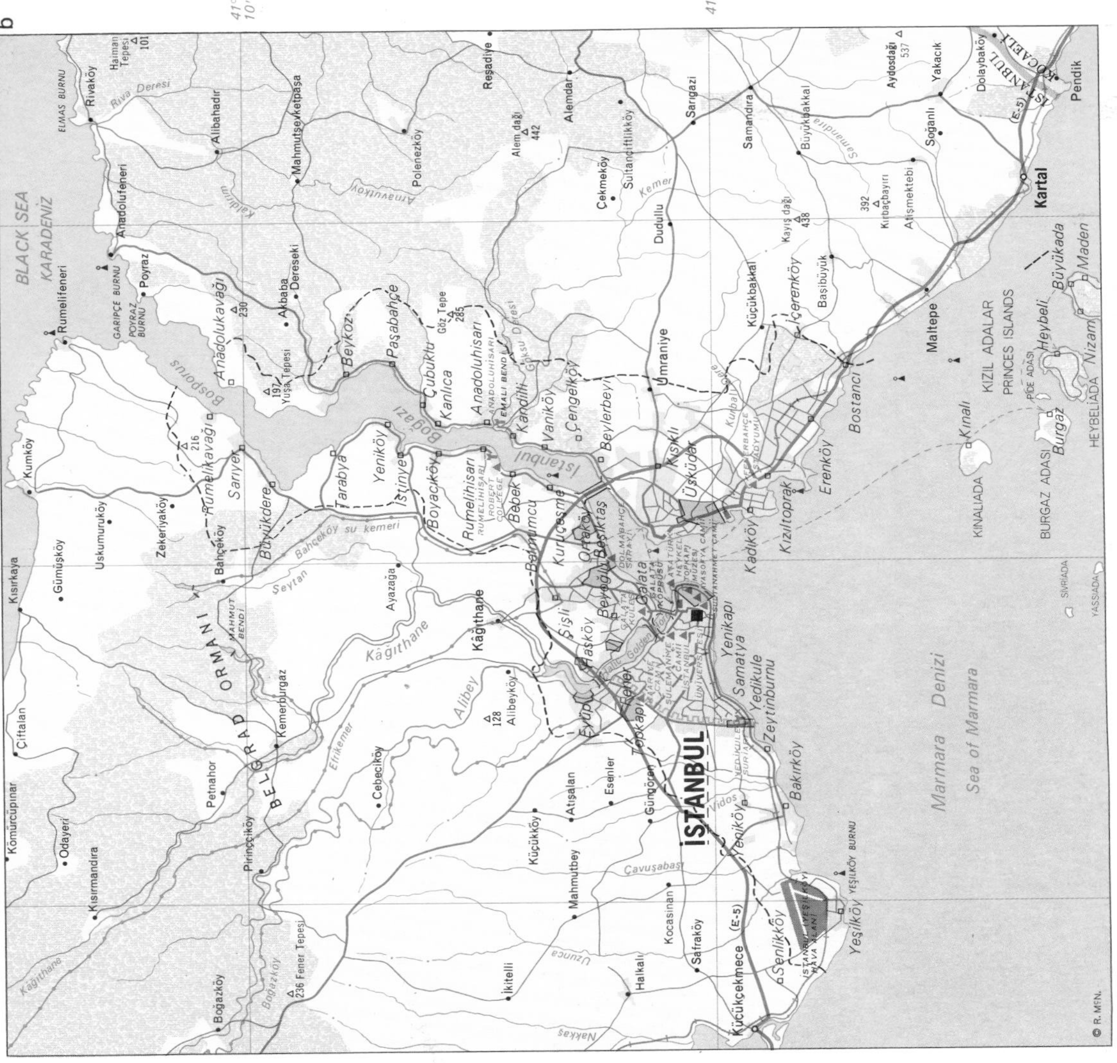
b
BLACK SEA
KARADENİZ
İSTANBUL
Boğaziçi
Bosporus
Üsküdar
Kadıköy
Beyoğlu
Beşiktaş
Sarıyer
BELGRAD ORMANI
Marmara Denizi
Sea of Marmara
KIZIL ADALAR
PRINCES ISLANDS
Kartal
Pendik
Maltepe
Bakırköy
Küçükçekmece
Yeşilköy
Büyükada
Heybeliada
Kınalıada
Burgazada
© R. McN.

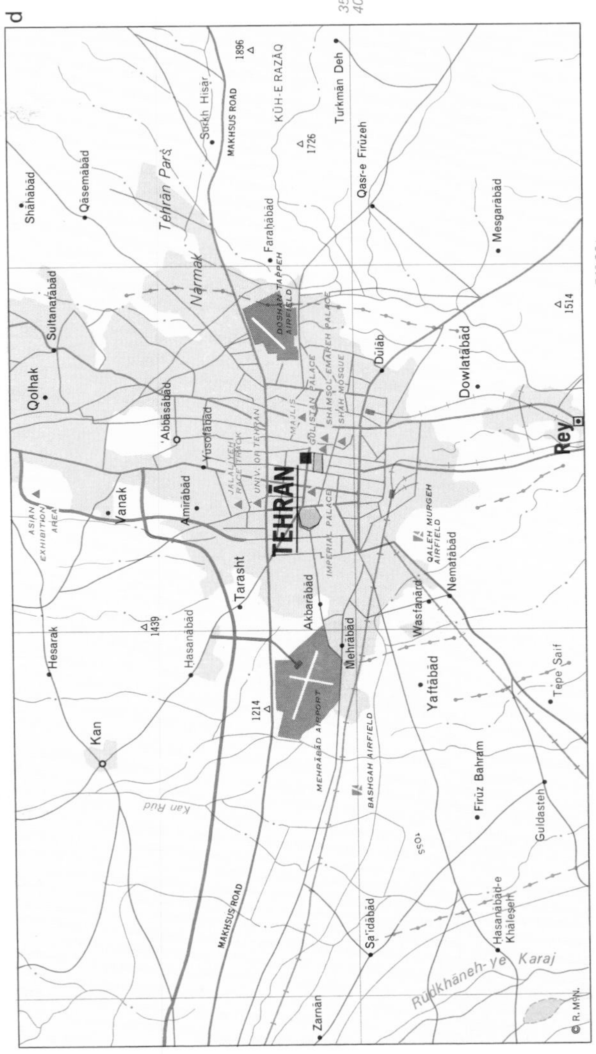
d
TEHRĀN
Rey
Tehrān Pārs
Mehrābād
Mehrābād Airport
Doshan Tappeh Airfield
Qaleh Morghī Airfield
KŪH-E RAZĀQ
Ṣāleḥābād
Shahābād
Qolhak
Tajrīsh
Vanak
Tarasht
Narmak
Dowlatābād
© R. McN.

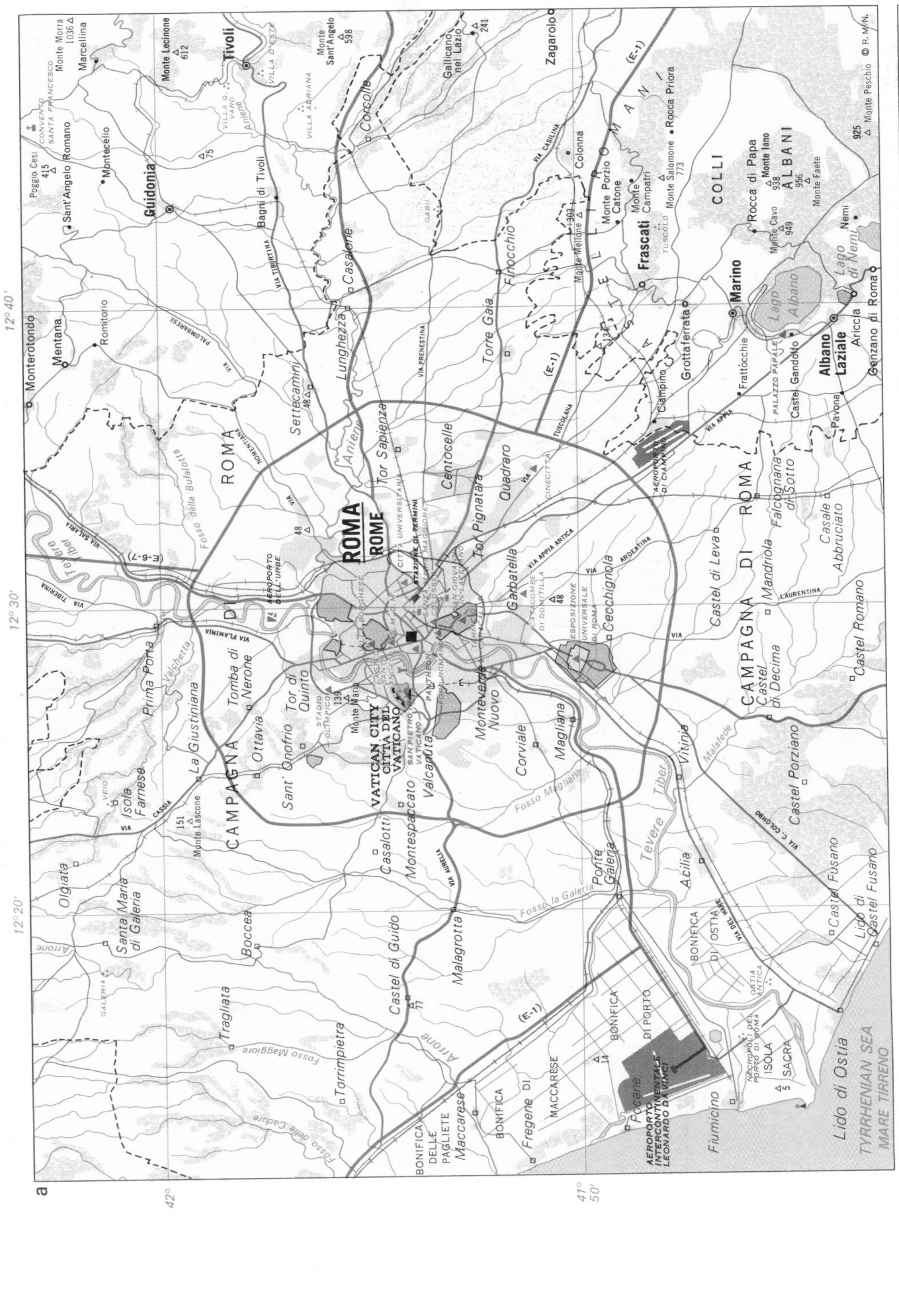
a
ROMA
ROME
VATICAN CITY
CITTÀ DEL VATICANO
CAMPAGNA DI ROMA
COLLI ALBANI
Tivoli
Guidonia
Frascati
Marino
Albano Laziale
Ariccia
Genzano di Roma
Lago Albano
Lago di Nemi
Fiumicino
Lido di Ostia
TYRRHENIAN SEA
MARE TIRRENO
AEROPORTO INTERCONTINENTALE LEONARDO DA VINCI
Tevere
Aniene
© R. McN.

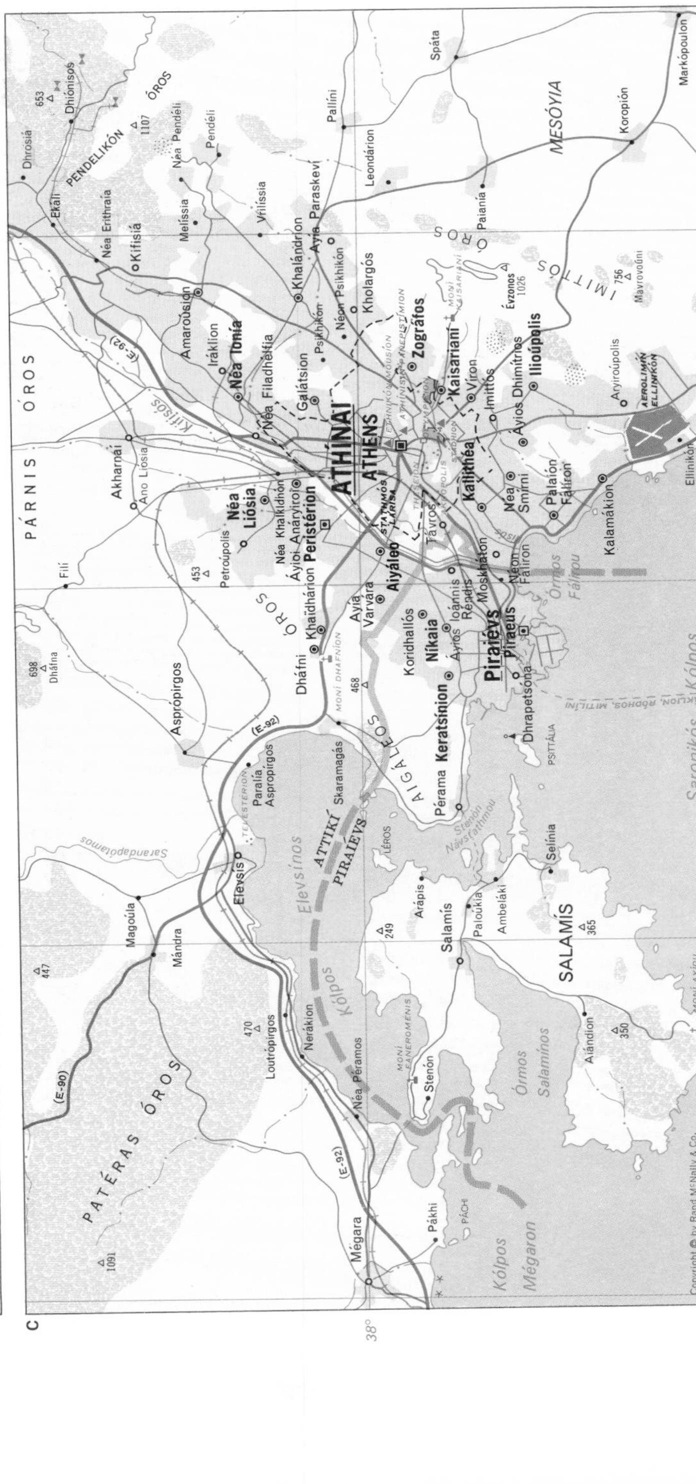
c
ATHÍNAI
ATHENS
PIRAIÉVS
PIRAEUS
PÁRNIS ÓROS
PENDELIKÓN ÓROS
IMITTÓS
AIGÁLEOS ÓROS
PATÉRAS ÓROS
SALAMÍS
Saronikós Kólpos
Kólpos Elevsínos
Kólpos Megáron
Mégara
Elevsís
Glifádha
Kifisiá
Marousi
Nikaia
Peristérion
Kallithéa
Néa Smírni
Palaión Fáliron
Ellinikón
MESOYIA
Spáta

Copyright © by Rand McNally & Co.
Map prepared by Rand McNally GmbH, Stuttgart
A-550076-264

Kilometers 0 5 10 15 Km.
Statute Miles 0 5 10 15 Mi.

Scale 1:300,000

One centimeter represents 3 kilometers.
One inch represents approximately 4.7 miles.

	AREA (km²)	POPULATION
ROMA	2,000	3,250,000
ATHÍNAI	1,100	3,350,000
İSTANBUL	1,300	4,300,000
TEHRĀN	950	5,200,000

MAP FORM	ada	burnu	camii	deresi	fosso	moní	monte
ENGLISH	island	cape	mosque	river	brook	monastery	mount
DEUTSCH	Insel	Kap	Moschee	Fluss	Bach	Kloster	Berg
ESPAÑOL	isla	cabo	mezquita	río	arroyo	monasterio	monte
FRANÇAIS	île	cap	mosquée	rivière	ruisseau	monastère	mont
PORTUGUÊS	ilha	cabo	mesquita	rio	arroio	mosteiro	monte

For complete glossary see page I • 1.

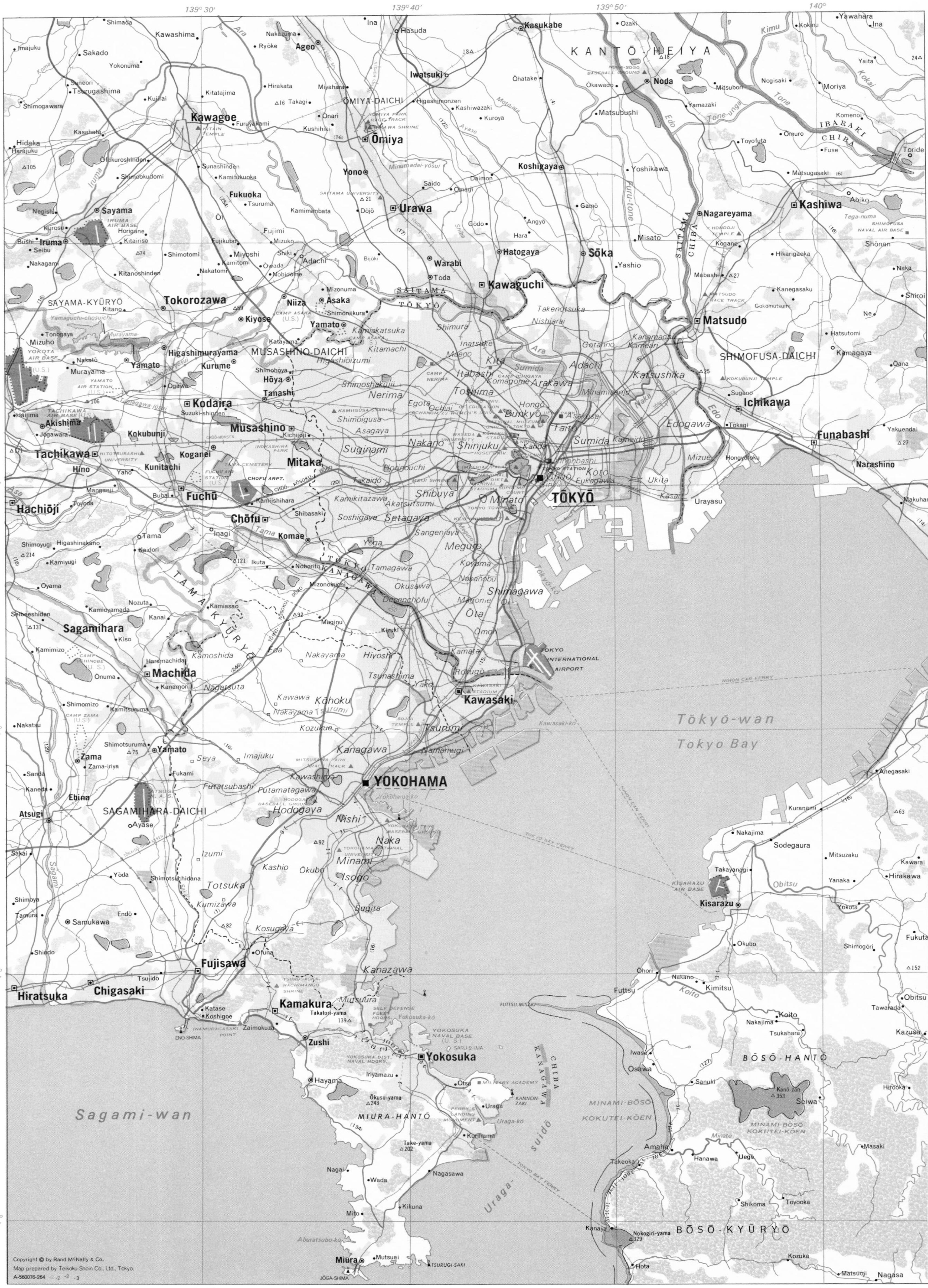

AREA (km²): 5,350
POPULATION: 24,350,000

MAP FORM	air base	camp	-daichi	-kō	-shima	temple	-yama
ENGLISH	air base	camp	plateau	harbor	island	temple	mountain
DEUTSCH	Luftstützpunkt	Lager	Hochebene	Hafen	Insel	Tempel	Berg
ESPAÑOL	base aérea	campo	meseta	puerto	isla	templo	montaña
FRANÇAIS	base aérienne	camp	plateau	port	île	temple	montagne
PORTUGUÊS	base aérea	campo	planalto	porto	ilha	templo	montanha

For complete glossary see page I • 1.

Kilometers 0 5 10 15 Km.
Statute Miles 0 5 10 15 Mi.

Scale 1:300,000
One centimeter represents 3 kilometers.
One inch represents approximately 4.7 miles.

a

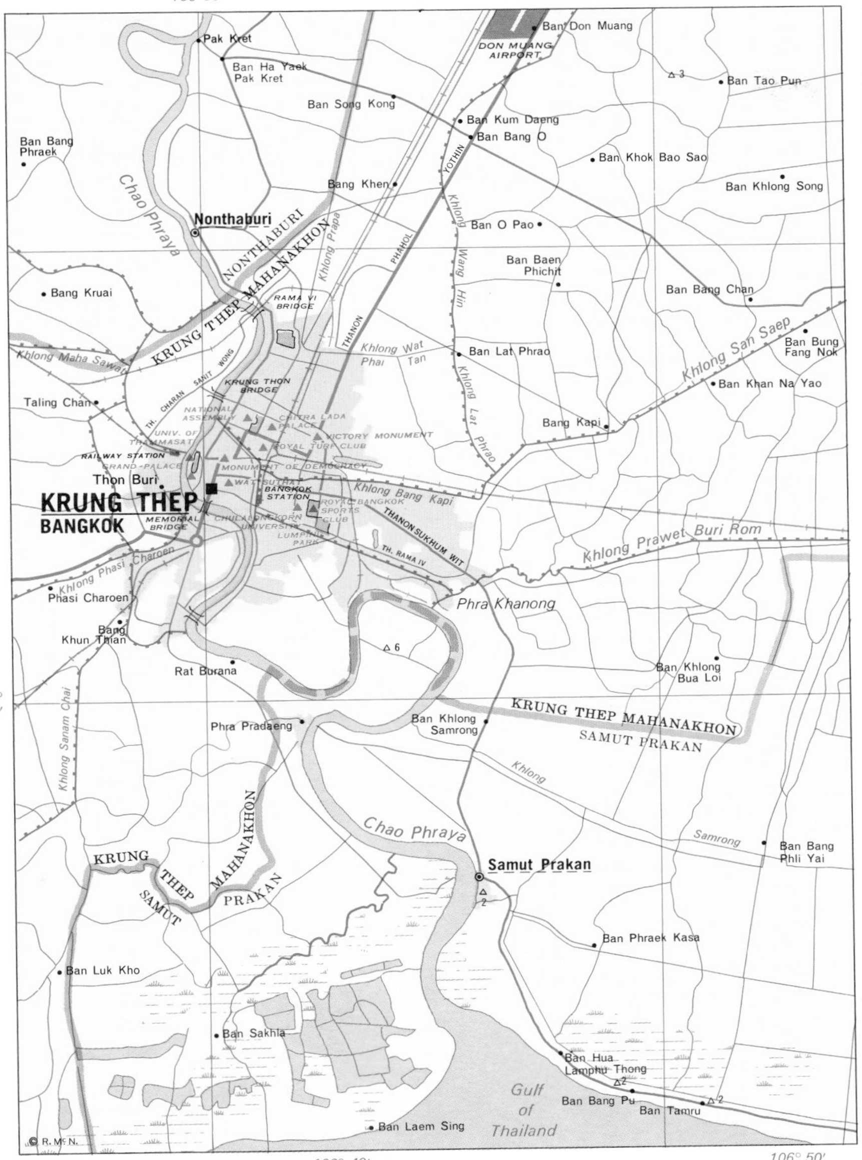

b

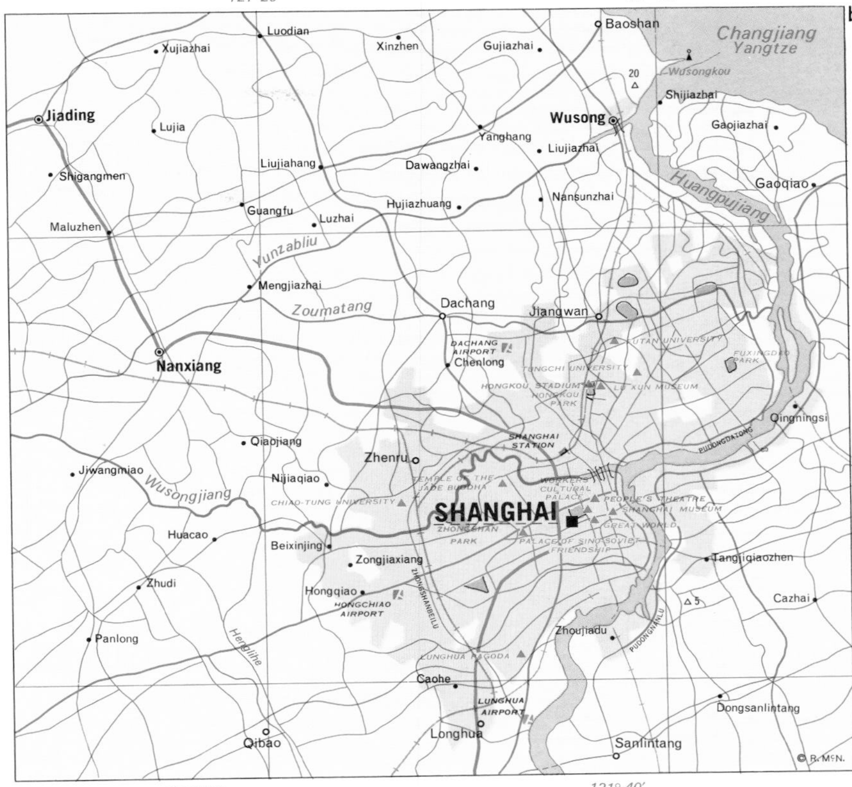

c

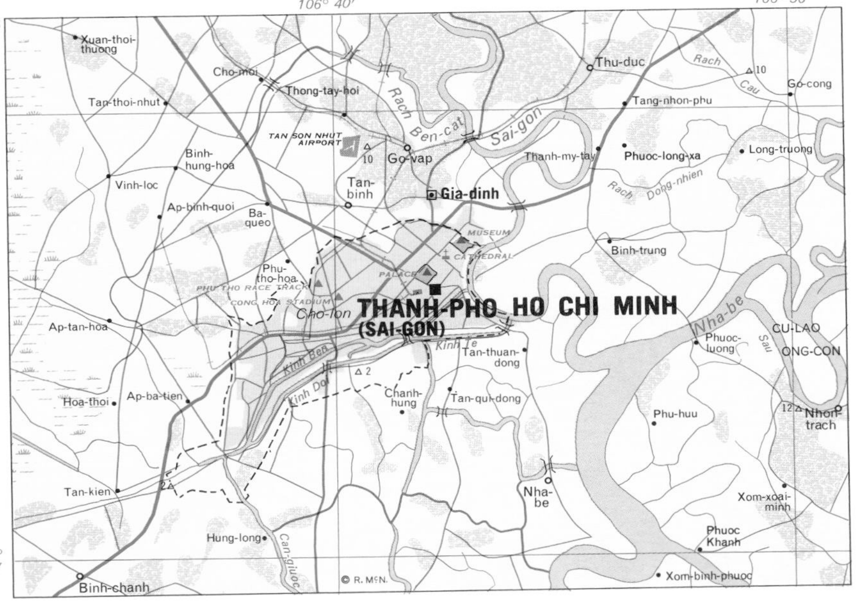

d

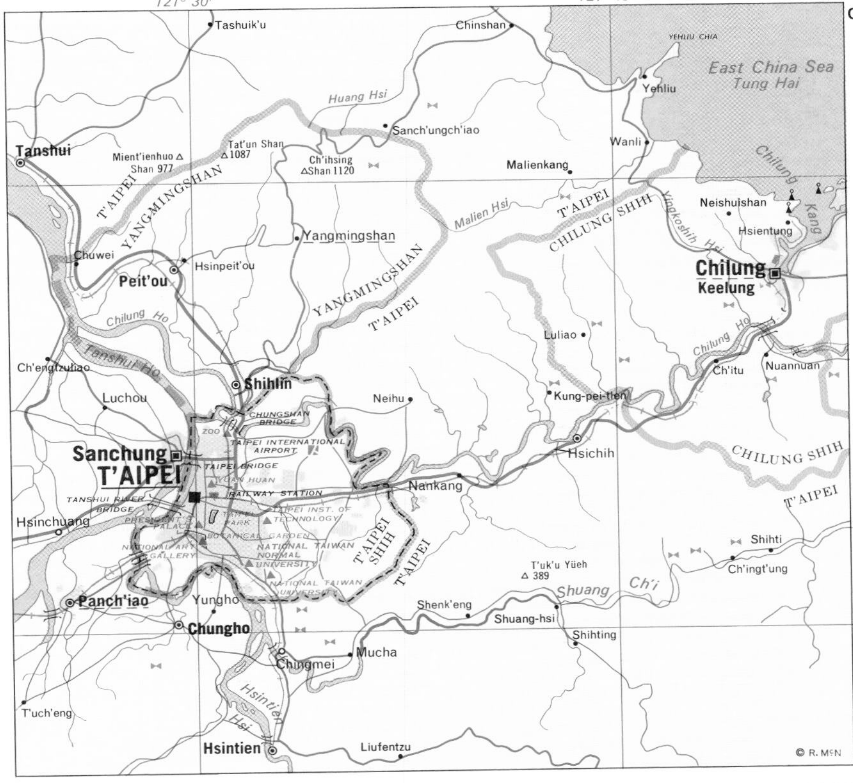

e

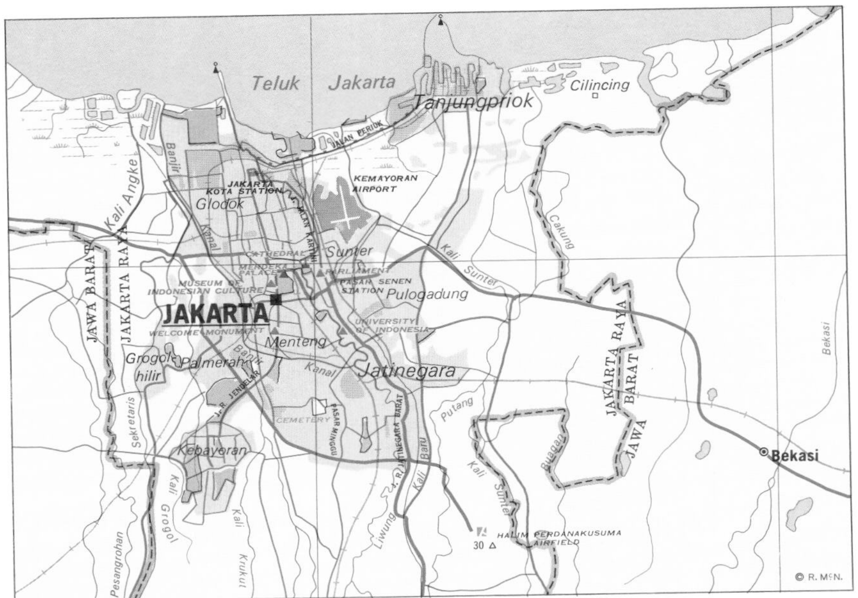

f

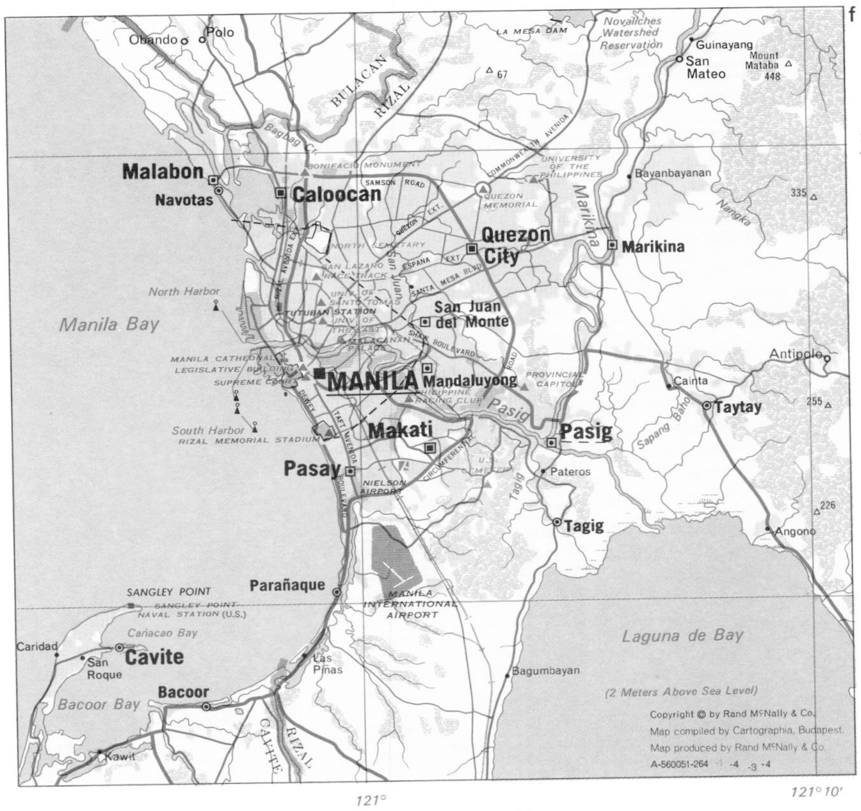

	AREA (km²)	POPULATION
KRUNG THEP (BANGKOK)	1,450	5,300,000
SAI-GON	750	2,400,000
JAKARTA	700	6,450,000
SHANGHAI	1,000	8,400,000
T'AIPEI	950	4,125,000
MANILA	650	5,900,000

MAP FORM	-jiang	kali	khlong	monument
ENGLISH	river	stream	stream	monument
DEUTSCH	Fluss	Bach	Bach	Denkmal
ESPAÑOL	río	corriente de agua	corriente de agua	monumento
FRANÇAIS	rivière	cours d'eau	cours d'eau	monument
PORTUGUÊS	rio	corrente de água	corrente de água	monumento

For complete glossary see page I•1.

Kilometers 0 5 10 15 Km.

Statute Miles 0 5 10 15 Mi.

Scale 1:300,000

One centimeter represents 3 kilometers.

One inch represents approximately 4.7 miles.

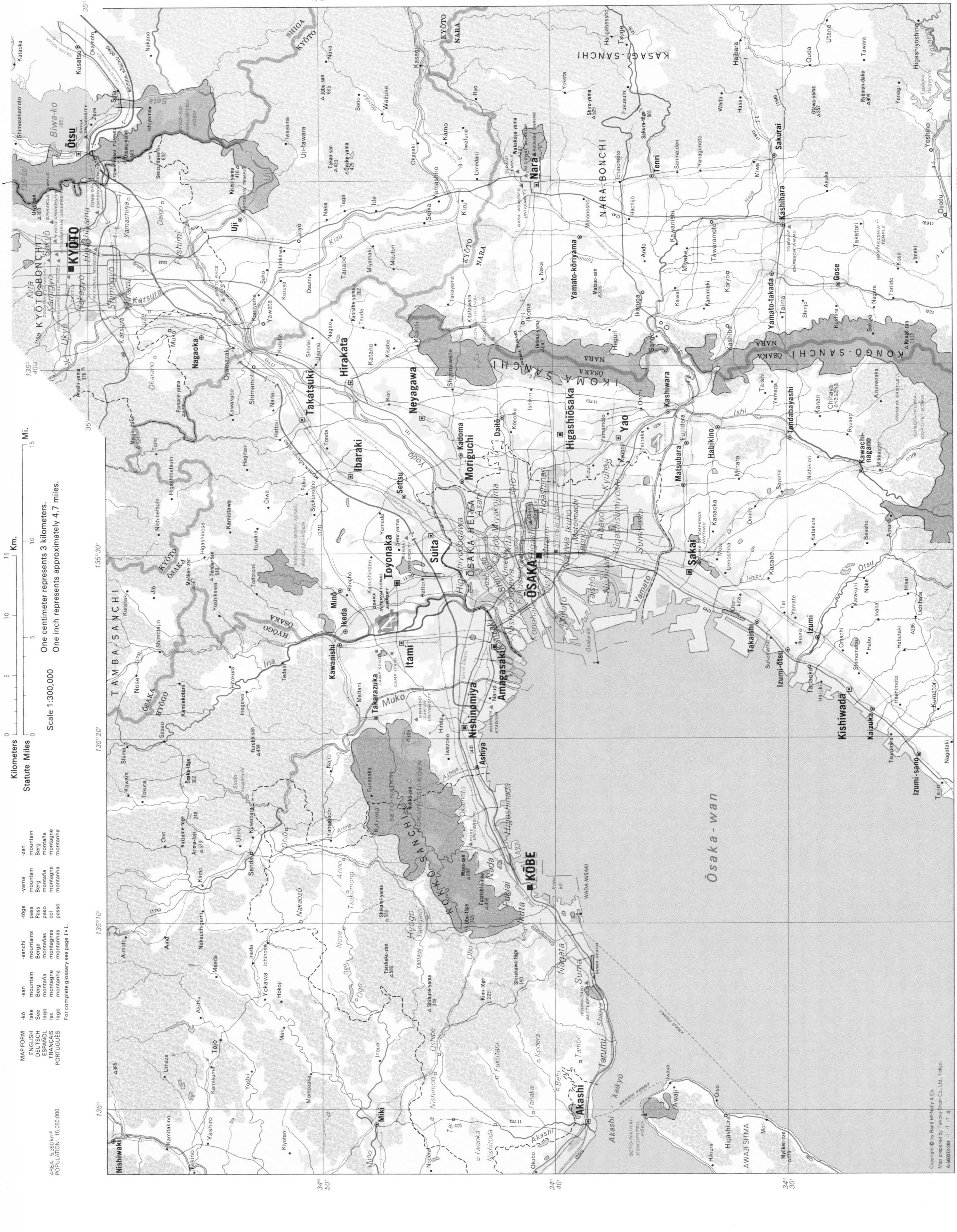
Kilometers 0 5 10 15 Km.
Statute Miles 0 5 10 15 Mi.
Scale 1:300,000
One centimeter represents 3 kilometers.
One inch represents approximately 4.7 miles.
MAP FORM -kō -san -sanchi -tōge -yama -zan
ENGLISH lake mountain mountains pass mountain mountain
DEUTSCH See Berg Berge Pass Berg Berg
ESPAÑOL lago montaña montañas paso montaña montaña
FRANÇAIS lac montagne montagnes col montagne montagne
PORTUGUÊS lago montanha montanhas passo montanha montanha
For complete glossary see page I•1.
AREA 5,350 km²
POPULATION 15,050,000
ŌSAKA
KŌBE
KYŌTO
Ōsaka-wan
Biwa-ko
Copyright © by Rand McNally & Co.
Map prepared by Teikoku-Shoin Co., Ltd. Tokyo.

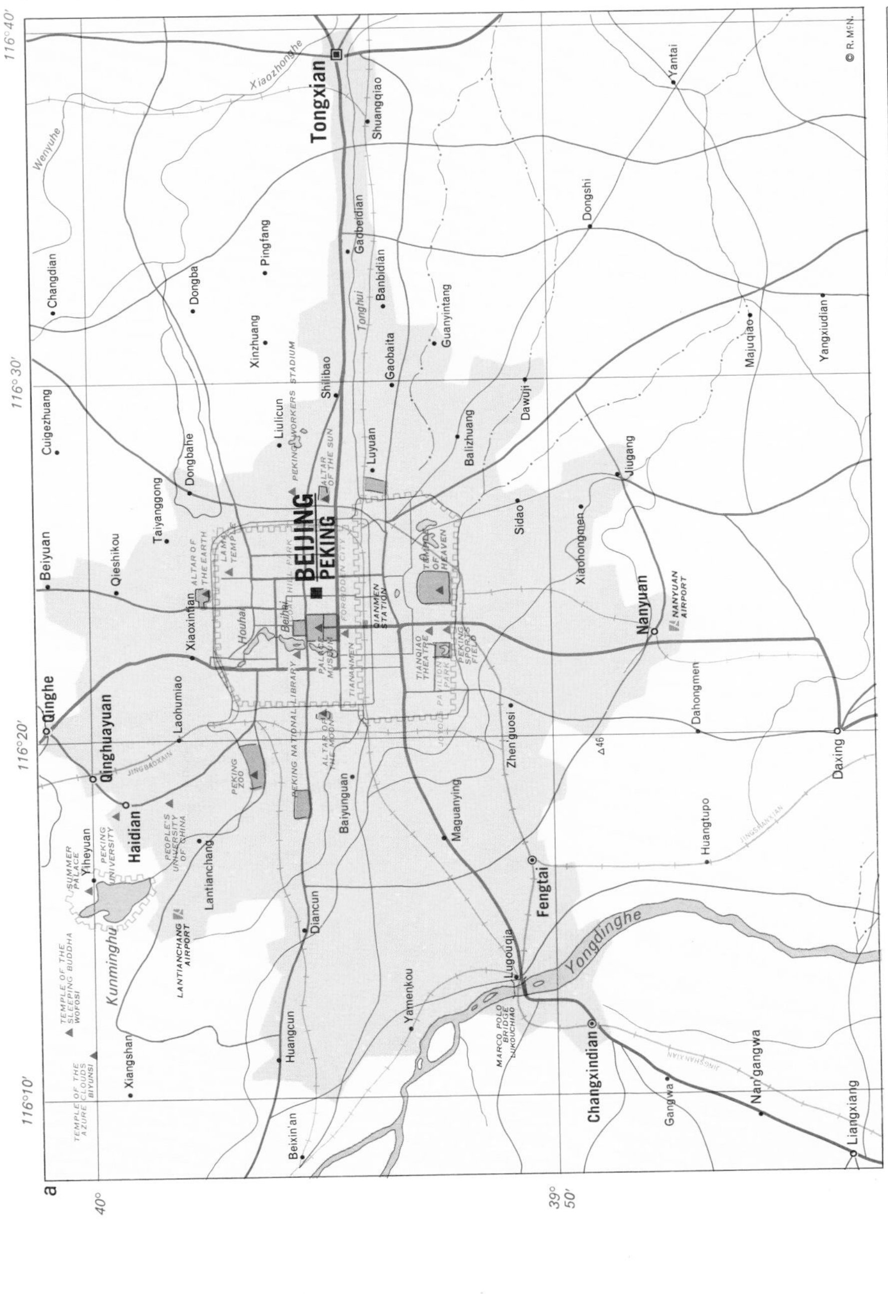

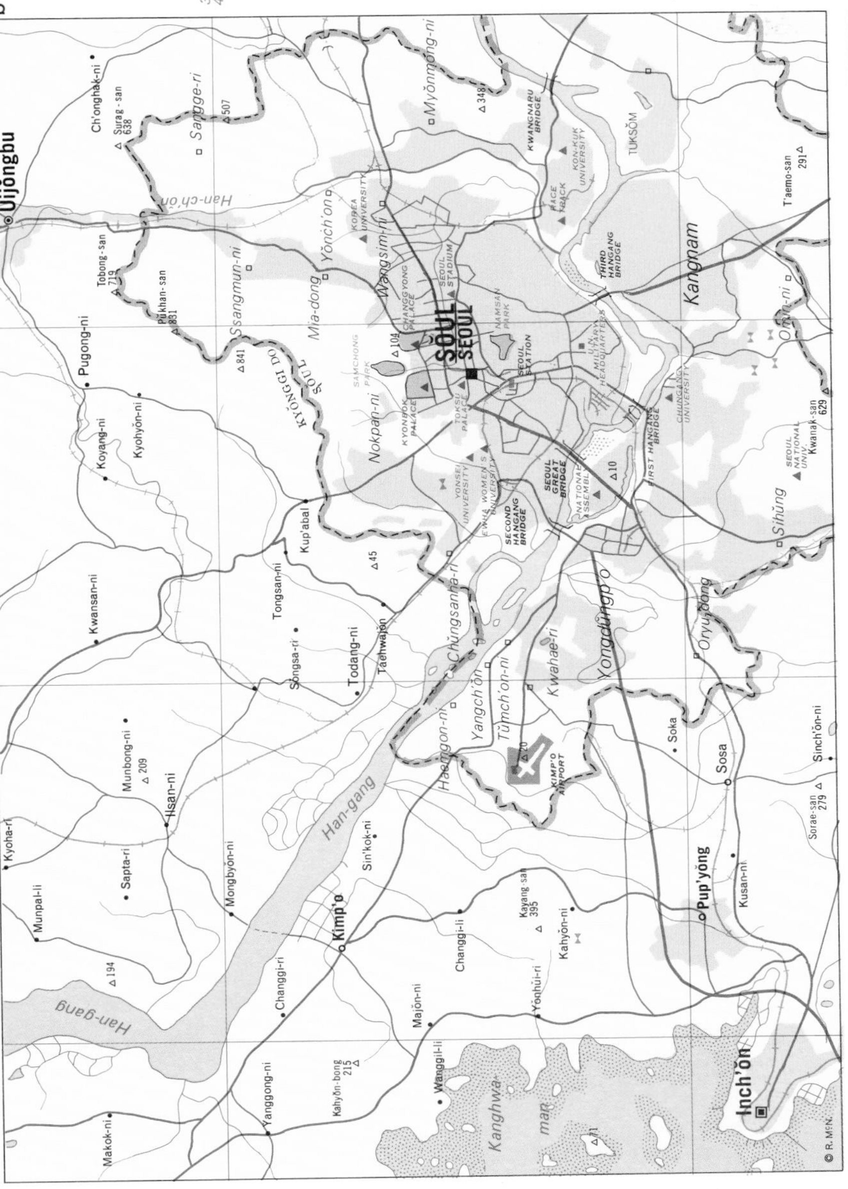

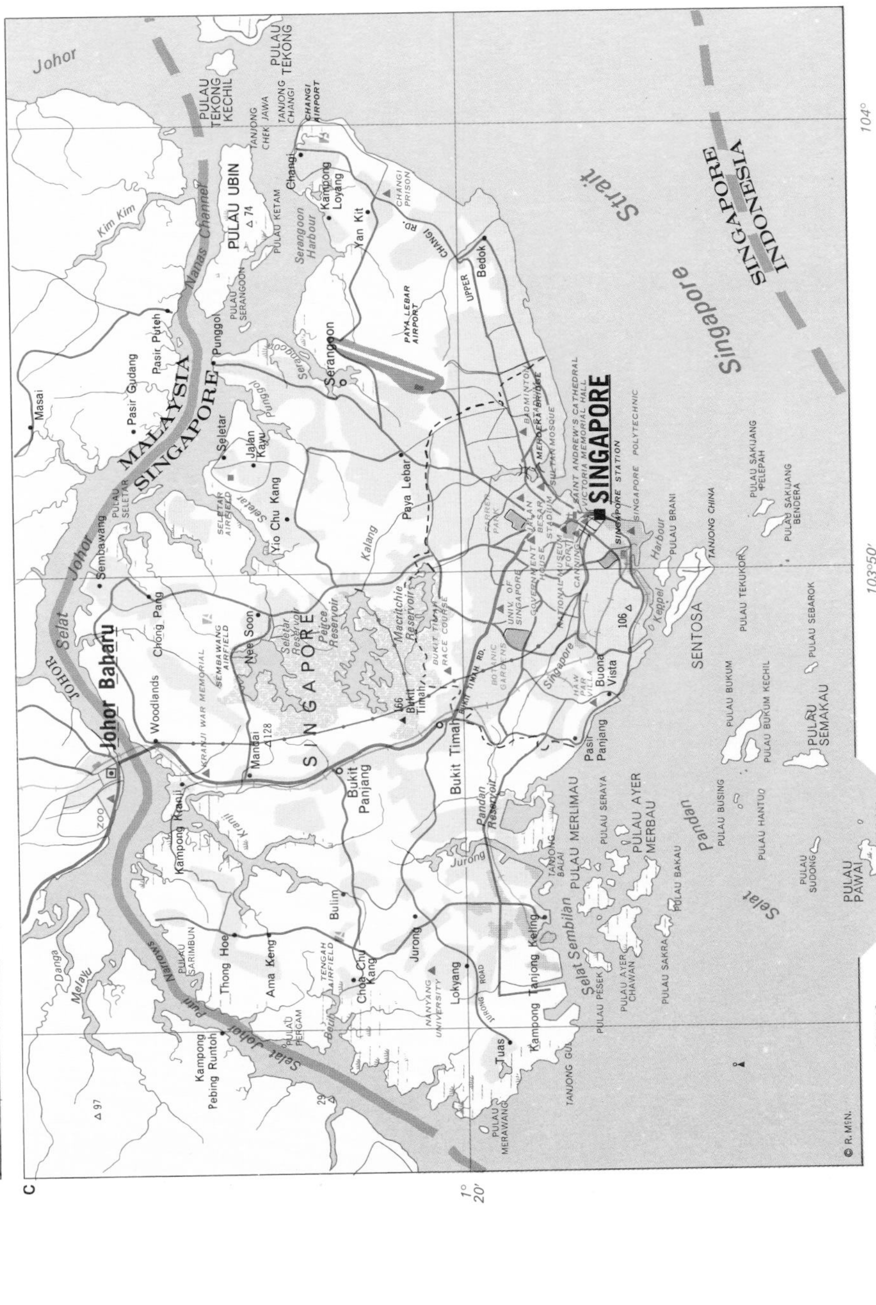

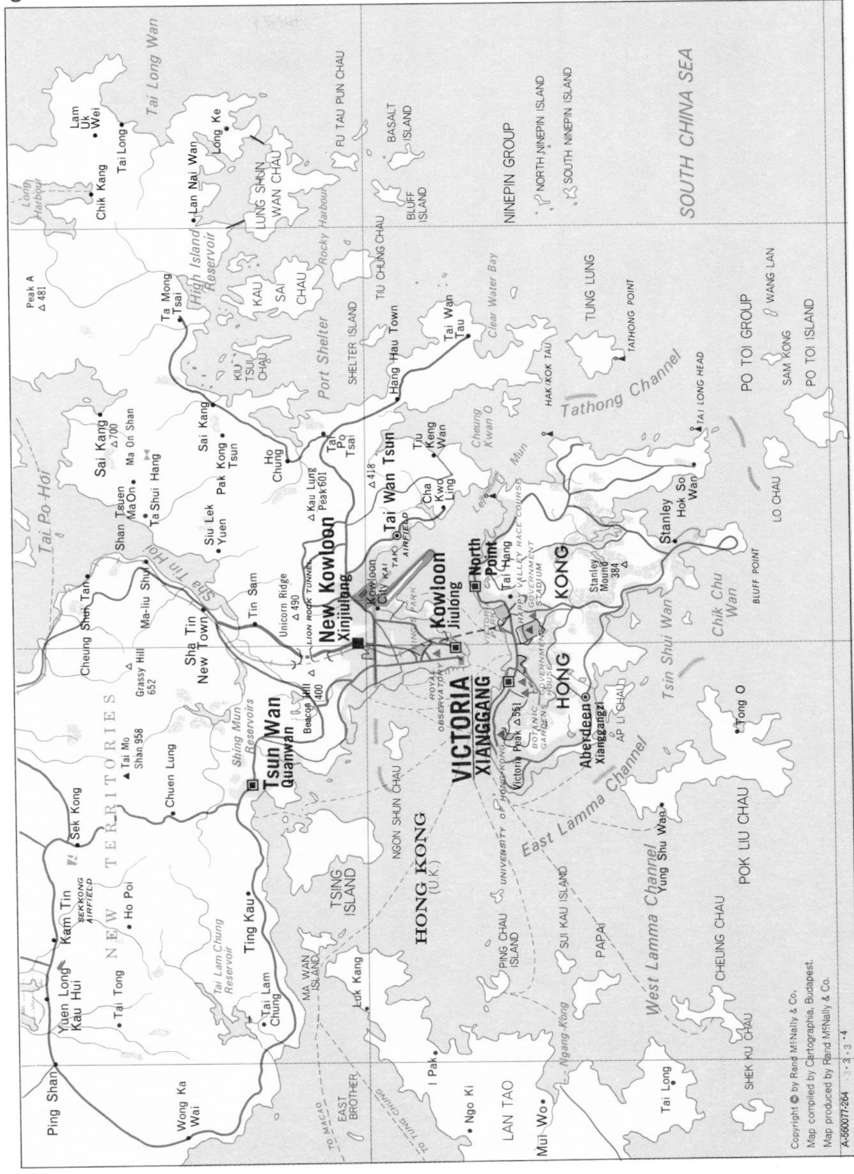

Kilometers 0 5 10 15 Km.

Statute Miles 0 5 10 15 Mi.

Scale 1:300,000

One centimeter represents 3 kilometers.

One inch represents approximately 4.7 miles.

	AREA (km²)	POPULATION
BEIJING (PEKING)	1,550	5,300,000
SŎUL	1,450	9,300,000
SINGAPORE	900	2,600,000
HONG KONG	650	4,450,000

MAP FORM	airport	chau	-he	island	park	peak	reservoir	wan
ENGLISH	airport	island	river	island	park	peak	reservoir	bay
DEUTSCH	Flughafen	Insel	Fluss	Insel	Park	Gipfel	Stausee	Bucht
ESPAÑOL	aeropuerto	isla	río	isla	parque	pico	estanque	bahía
FRANÇAIS	aéroport	île	rivière	île	parc	cime	réservoir	baie
PORTUGUÊS	aeroporto	ilha	rio	ilha	parque	pico	reservatório	baía

For complete glossary see page I•1.

Kilometers 0 5 10 15 Km.
Statute Miles 0 5 10 15 Mi.
Scale 1:300,000
One centimeter represents 3 kilometers.
One inch represents approximately 4.7 miles.

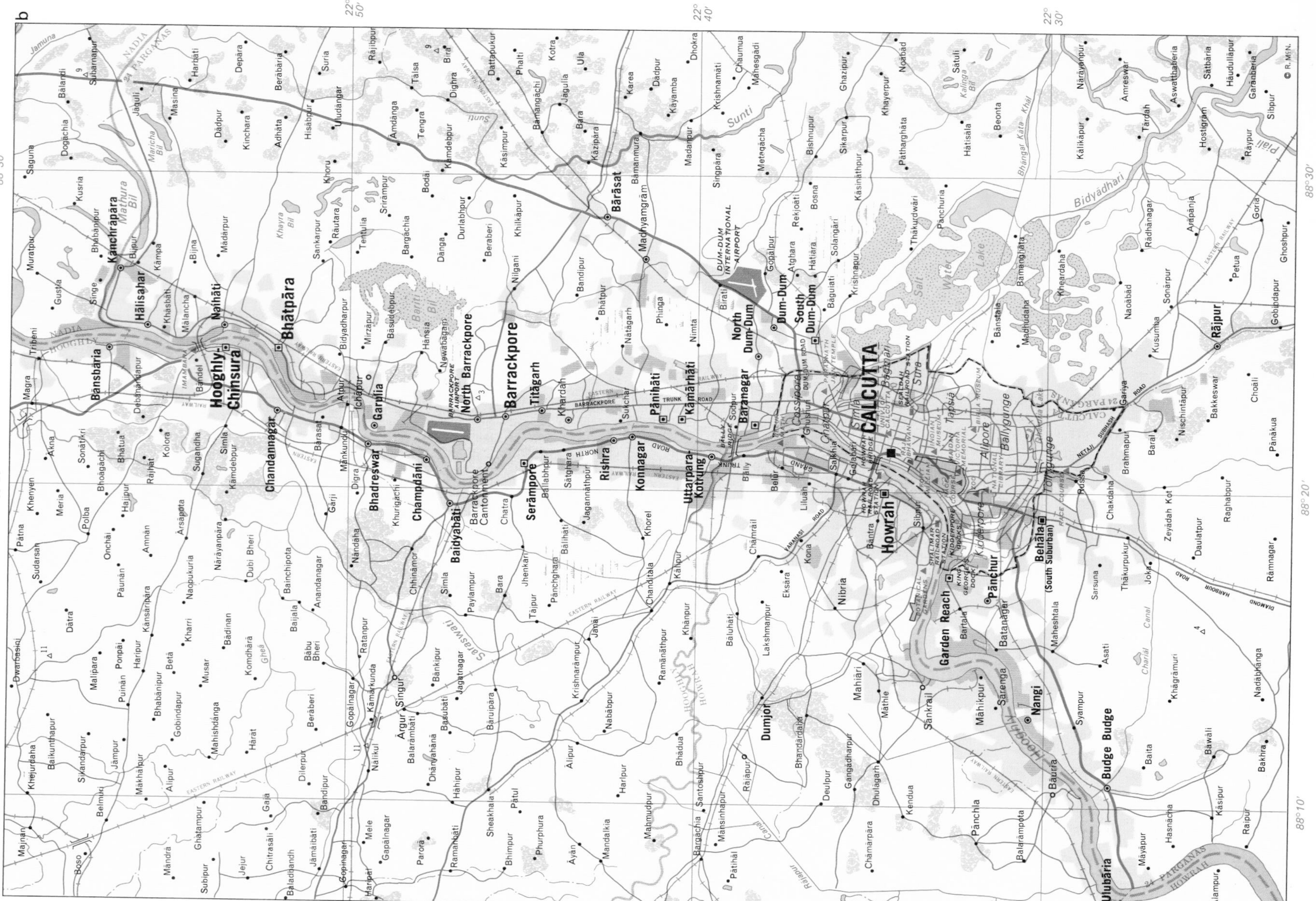

	AREA (km²)	POPULATION
DELHI	1,400	5,500,000
BOMBAY	1,050	8,250,000
CALCUTTA	3,100	11,200,000

ENGLISH	airport	dock	island	lake	point	railroad station	road	temple
DEUTSCH	Flughafen	Dock	Insel	See	Punkt	Bahnhof	Landstrasse	Tempel
ESPAÑOL	aeropuerto	muelle	isla	lago	punta	terminal ferroviaria	camino	templo
FRANÇAIS	aéroport	quai	île	lac	pointe	gare	route	temple
PORTUGUÊS	aeroporto	cais	ilha	lago	ponta	estação ferroviária	estrada	templo

For complete glossary see page [I•I].

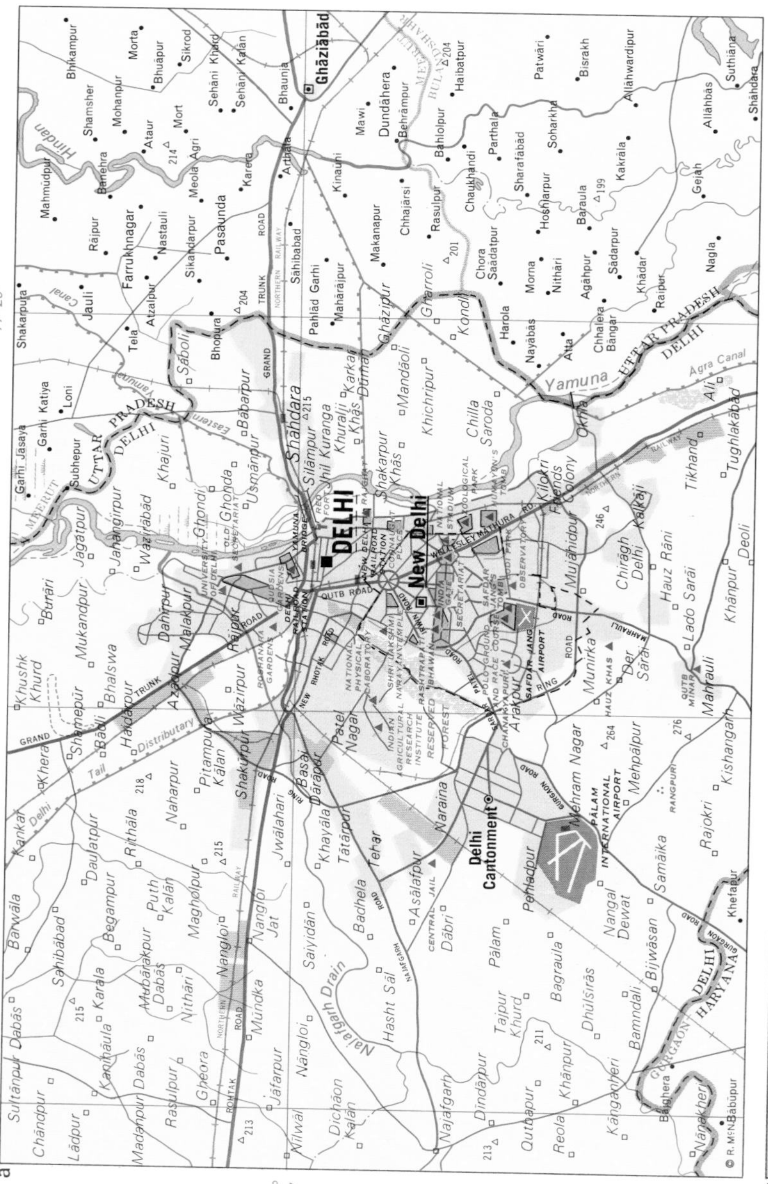

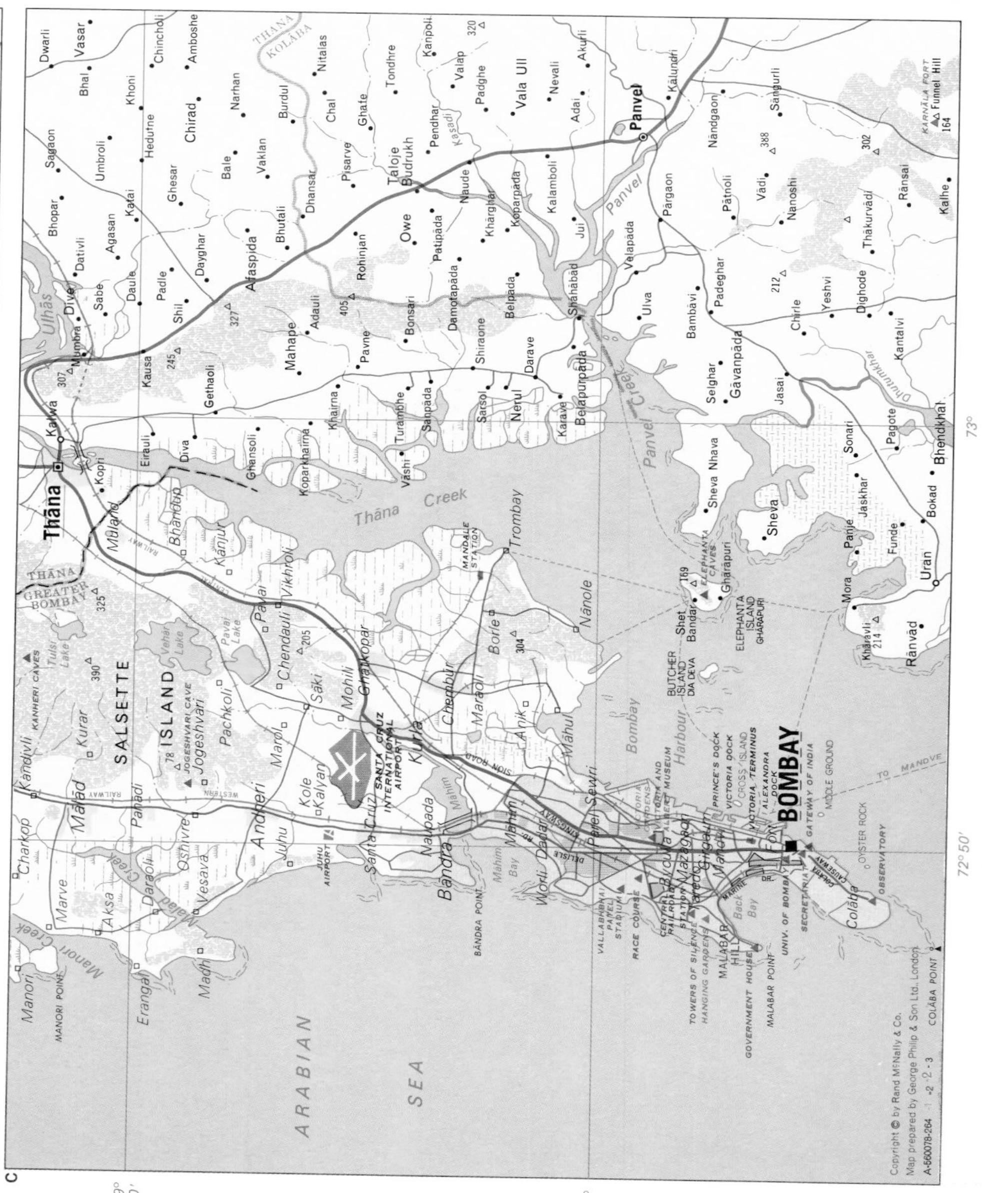

a

b
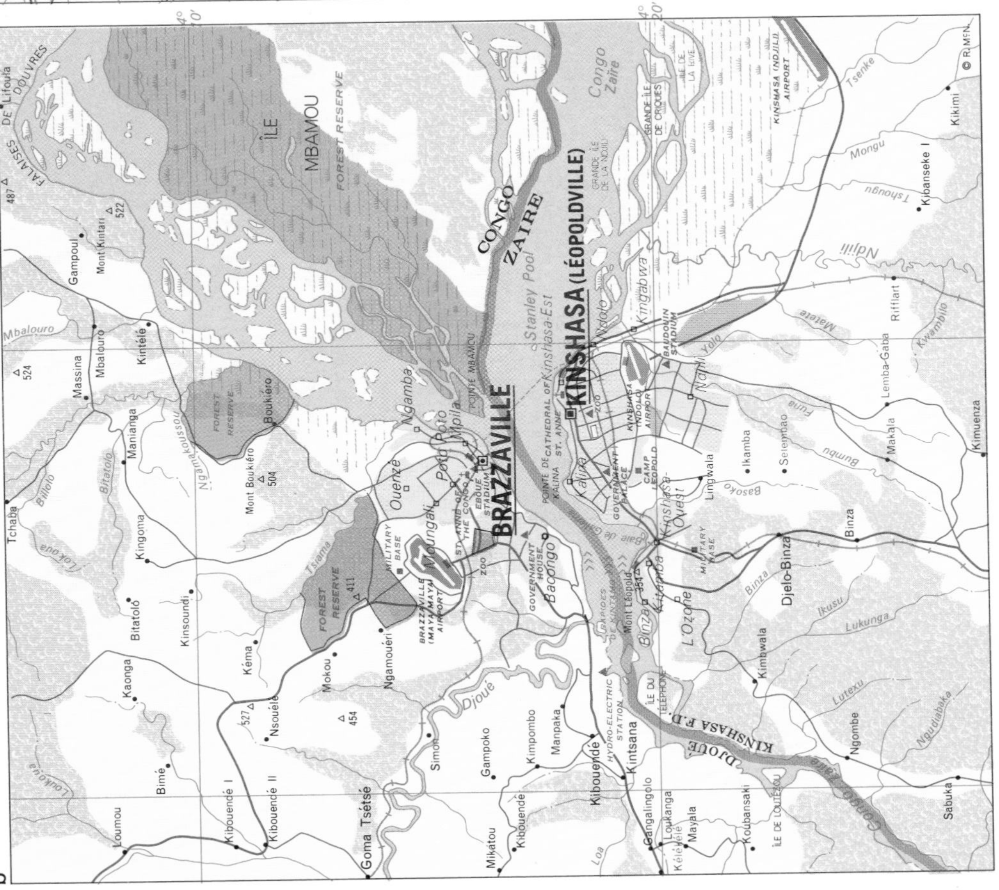

c
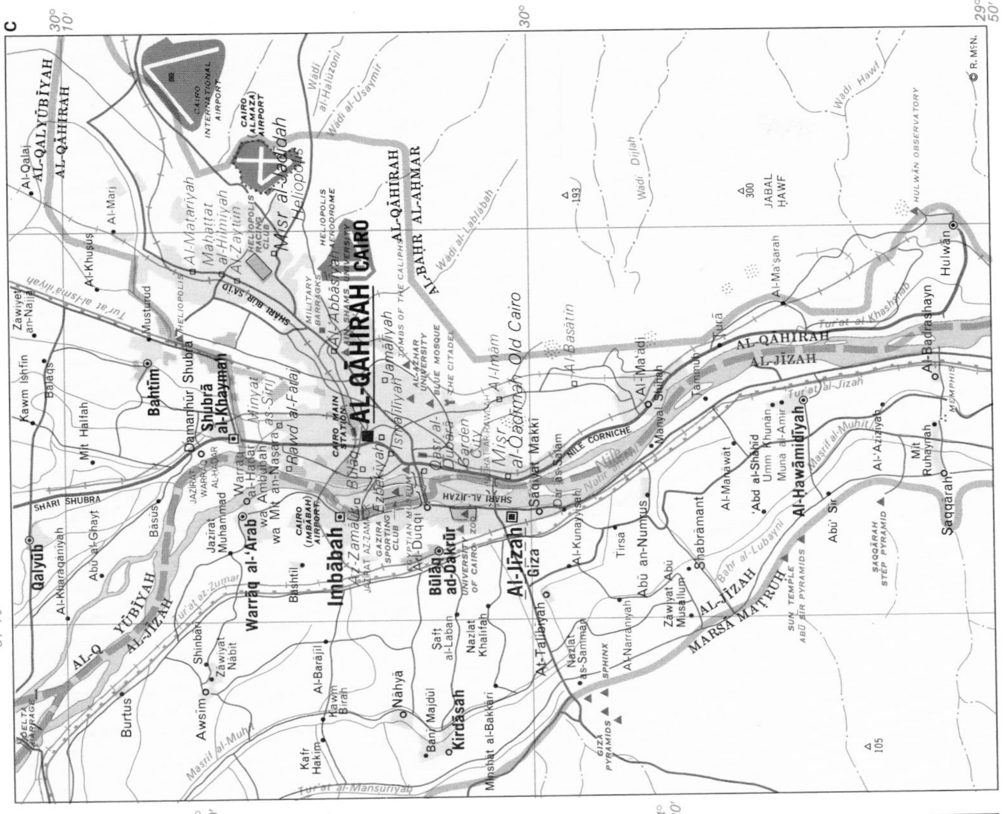

d
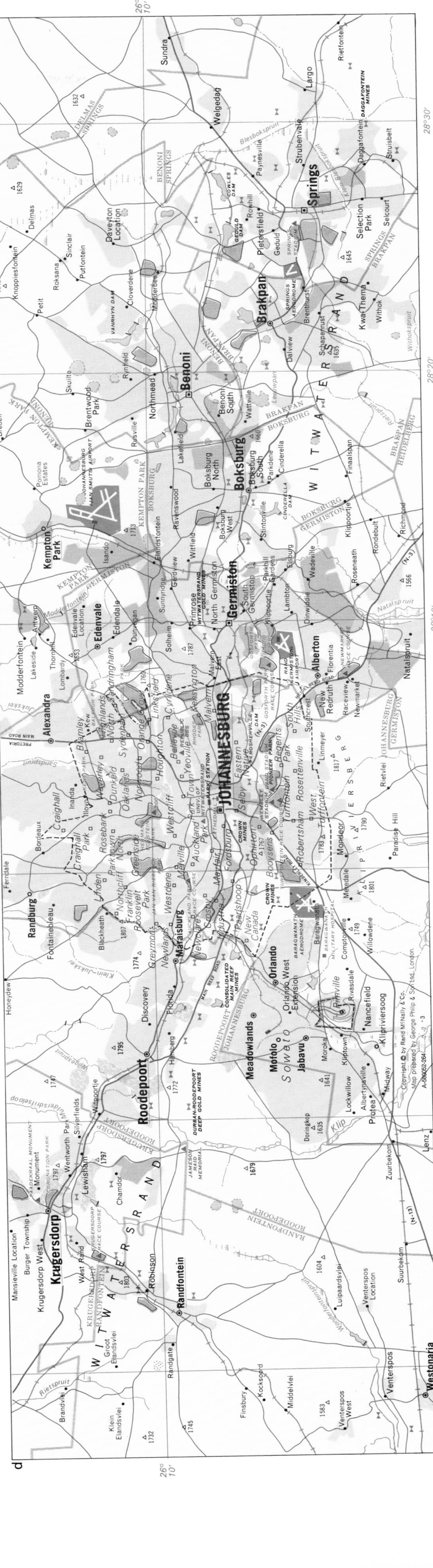

	AREA (km²)	POPULATON
LAGOS	750	2,400,000
KINSHASA–BRAZZAVILLE	1,150	2,750,000
AL QĀHIRAH (CAIRO)	1,200	8,900,000
JOHANNESBURG	2,650	3,300,000

MAP FORM	ENGLISH	DEUTSCH	ESPAÑOL	FRANÇAIS	PORTUGUÊS
airport	airport	Flughafen	aeropuerto	aéroport	aeroporto
creek	creek	Bach	riachuelo	crique	riacho
dam	dam	Damm	presa	barrage	barragem
île	island	Insel	isla	île	ilha
park	park	Park	parque	parc	parque
race course	race course	Rennbahn	hipódromo	champ de course	hipódromo
tur'at	canal	Kanal	canal	canal	canal
wadi	wadi	Wadi	uadi	wadi	uádi

For complete glossary see page I • 1.

Scale 1:300,000

One centimeter represents 3 kilometers.
One inch represents approximately 4.7 miles.

Kilometers 0 5 10 15 Km.
Statute Miles 0 5 10 15 Mi.

a

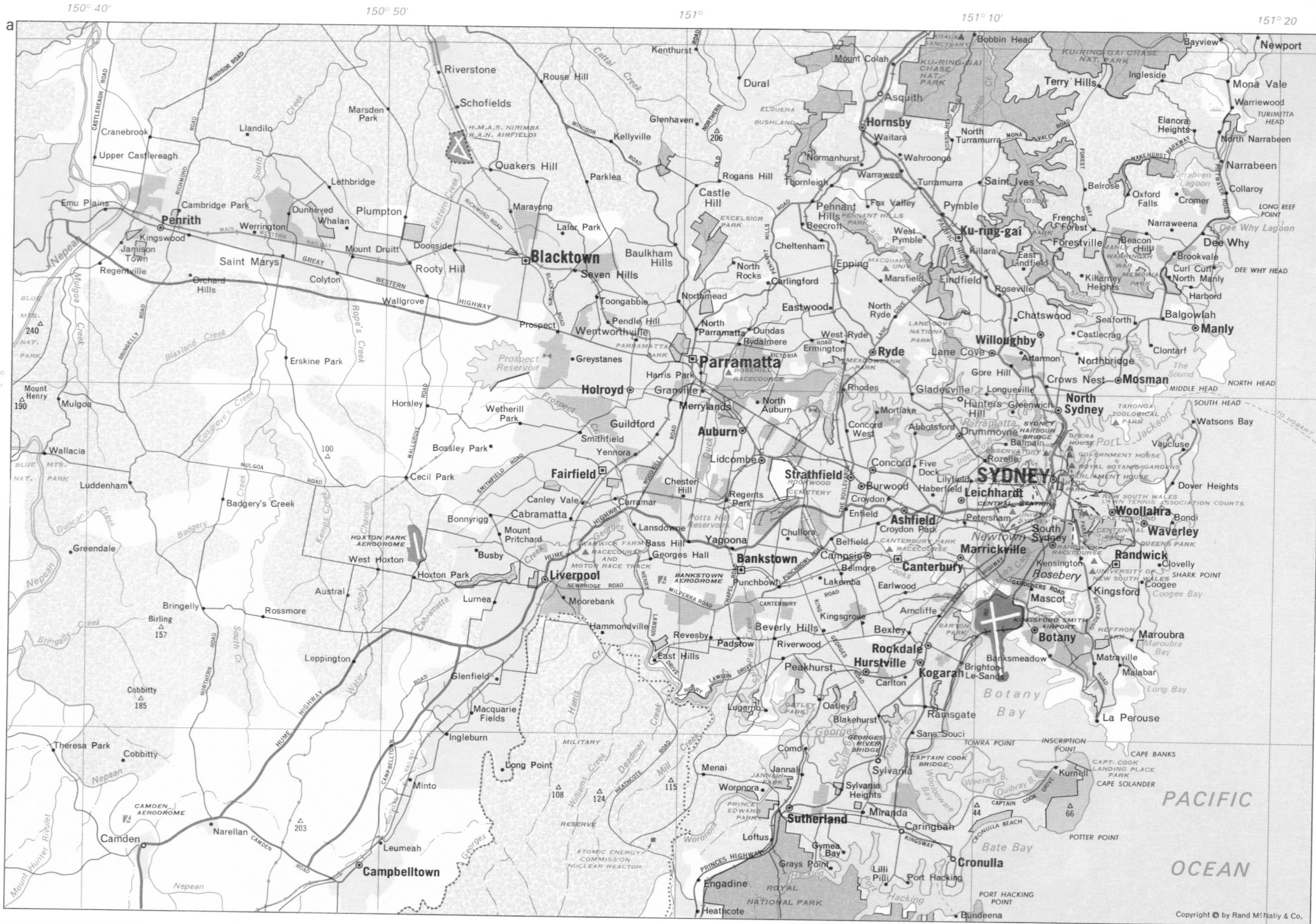

b

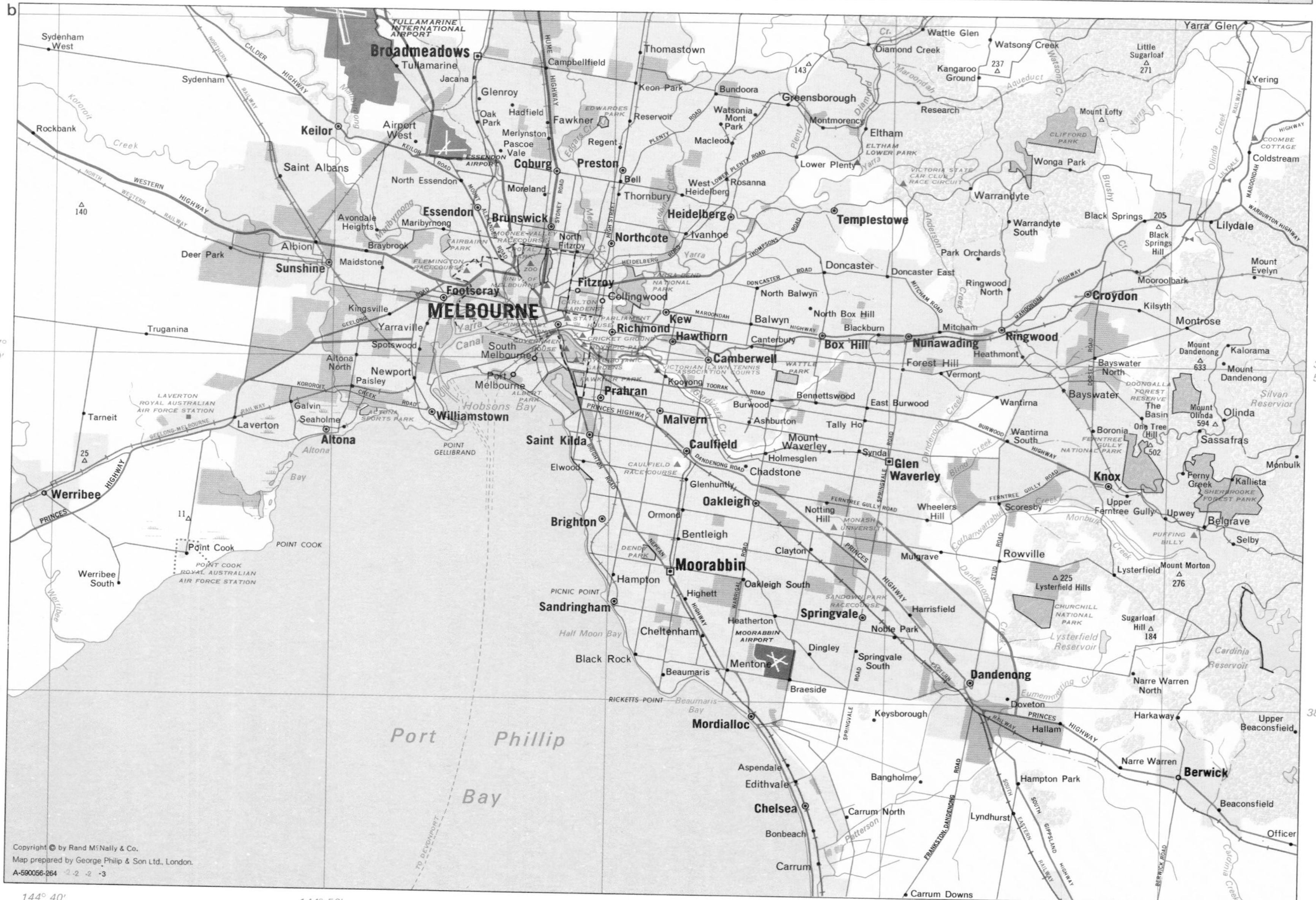

	AREA (km²)	POPULATION
MELBOURNE	2,600	2,425,000
SYDNEY	2,800	2,850,000

ENGLISH	bay, b.	bridge	creek, cr.	highway	point	road
DEUTSCH	Bucht	Brücke	Bach	Landstrasse	Landspitze	Landstrasse
ESPAÑOL	bahía	puente	riachuelo	camino	punta	camino
FRANÇAIS	baie	pont	crique	route	pointe	route
PORTUGUÊS	baía	ponte	riacho	estrada	ponta	estrada

For complete glossary see page *I • I*.

Kilometers 0 5 10 15 Km.

Statute Miles 0 5 10 15 Mi.

Scale 1:300,000

One centimeter represents 3 kilometers.

One inch represents approximately 4.7 miles.

a

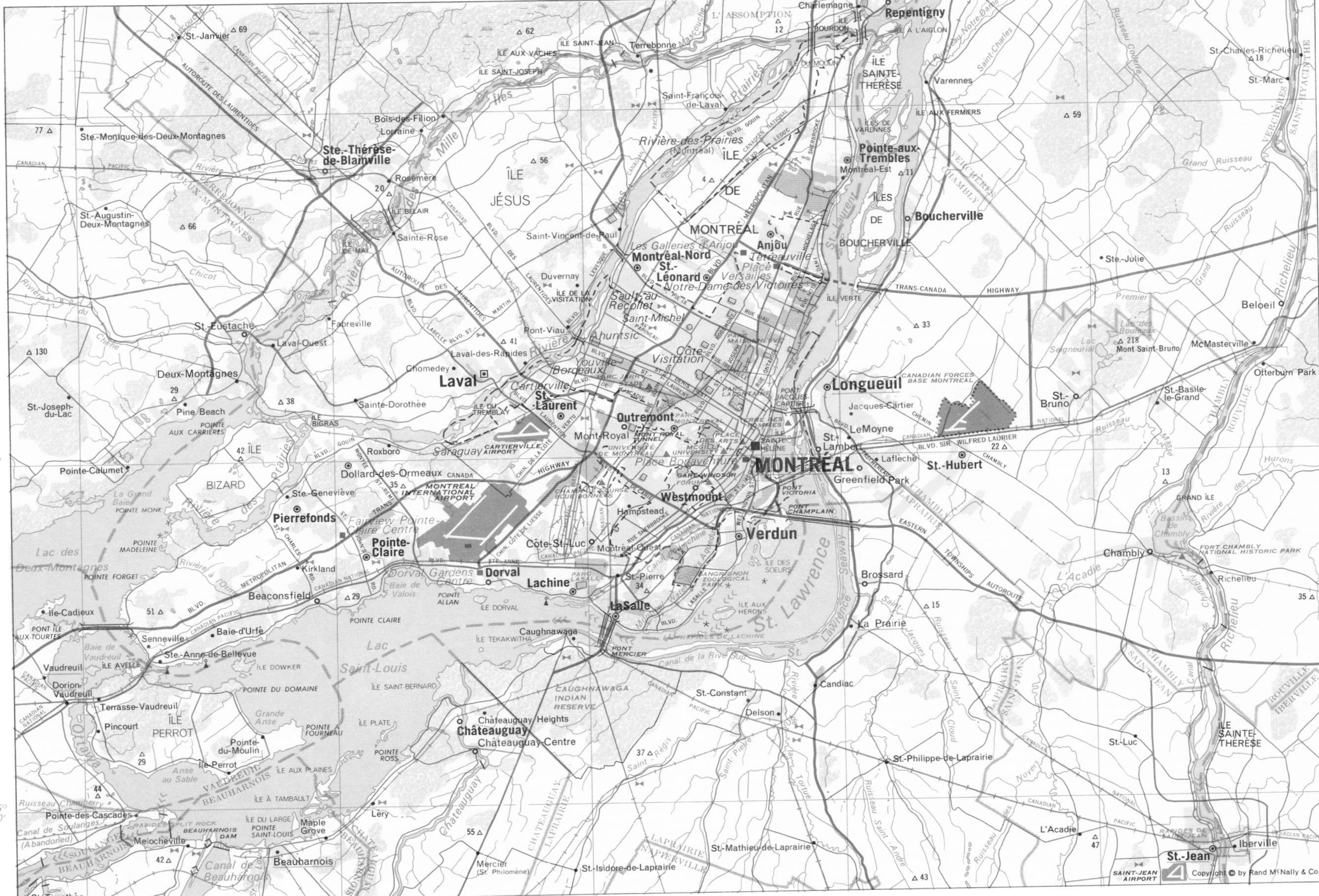
74° 00'
73° 50'
73° 40'
73° 30'
73° 20'
45° 40'
45° 30'
45° 20'
Repentigny
Charlemagne
Terrebonne
St.-Janvier
Ste.-Thérèse-de-Blainville
Bois-des-Filion
Lorraine
Rosemère
Ste.-Monique-des-Deux-Montagnes
St.-Augustin-Deux-Montagnes
Sainte-Rose
ÎLE JÉSUS
Laval
Ste.-Dorothée
Deux-Montagnes
St.-Eustache
Laval-Ouest
Fabreville
Chomedey
Laval-des-Rapides
Pont-Viau
Duvernay
St.-Joseph-du-Lac
Pine Beach
Pointe-Calumet
ÎLE BIZARD
Roxboro
Dollard-des-Ormeaux
Ste.-Geneviève
Pierrefonds
Pointe-Claire
Kirkland
Beaconsfield
Dorval
Lachine
LaSalle
Baie-d'Urfé
Senneville
Ste.-Anne-de-Bellevue
Île-Cadieux
Vaudreuil
Dorion-Vaudreuil
Terrasse-Vaudreuil
Pincourt
ÎLE PERROT
Pointe-du-Moulin
Île-Perrot
Lac des Deux Montagnes
Lac Saint-Louis
Caughnawaga
Châteauguay
Châteauguay Heights
Châteauguay-Centre
Léry
Maple Grove
Beauharnois
Melocheville
Pointe-des-Cascades
St.-Timothée
Canal de Beauharnois
Mercier
St.-Isidore-de-Laprairie
St.-Mathieu-de-Laprairie
St.-Philippe-de-Laprairie
St.-Constant
Delson
Candiac
La Prairie
Brossard
Greenfield Park
St.-Lambert
LeMoyne
Longueuil
Jacques-Cartier
St.-Hubert
Laflèche
Boucherville
ÎLES DE BOUCHERVILLE
Pointe-aux-Trembles
Montréal-Est
Varennes
ÎLE DE MONTRÉAL
Rivière-des-Prairies
Montréal-Nord
Anjou
St.-Léonard
Saint-Michel
Ahuntsic
Cartierville
St.-Laurent
Outremont
Mont-Royal
MONTRÉAL
Westmount
Verdun
Hampstead
Côte-St-Luc
Montréal-Ouest
St.-Pierre
St. Lawrence
MONTREAL INTERNATIONAL AIRPORT
CARTIERVILLE AIRPORT
CANADIAN FORCES BASE MONTREAL
St.-Bruno
Mont Saint-Bruno
Ste.-Julie
Beloeil
McMasterville
Otterburn Park
St.-Basile-le-Grand
Chambly
FORT CHAMBLY NATIONAL HISTORIC PARK
Richelieu
St.-Luc
L'Acadie
St.-Jean
Iberville
SAINT-JEAN AIRPORT
St.-Charles-Richelieu
St.-Marc
Rivière Richelieu
Copyright © by Rand McNally & Co.

b

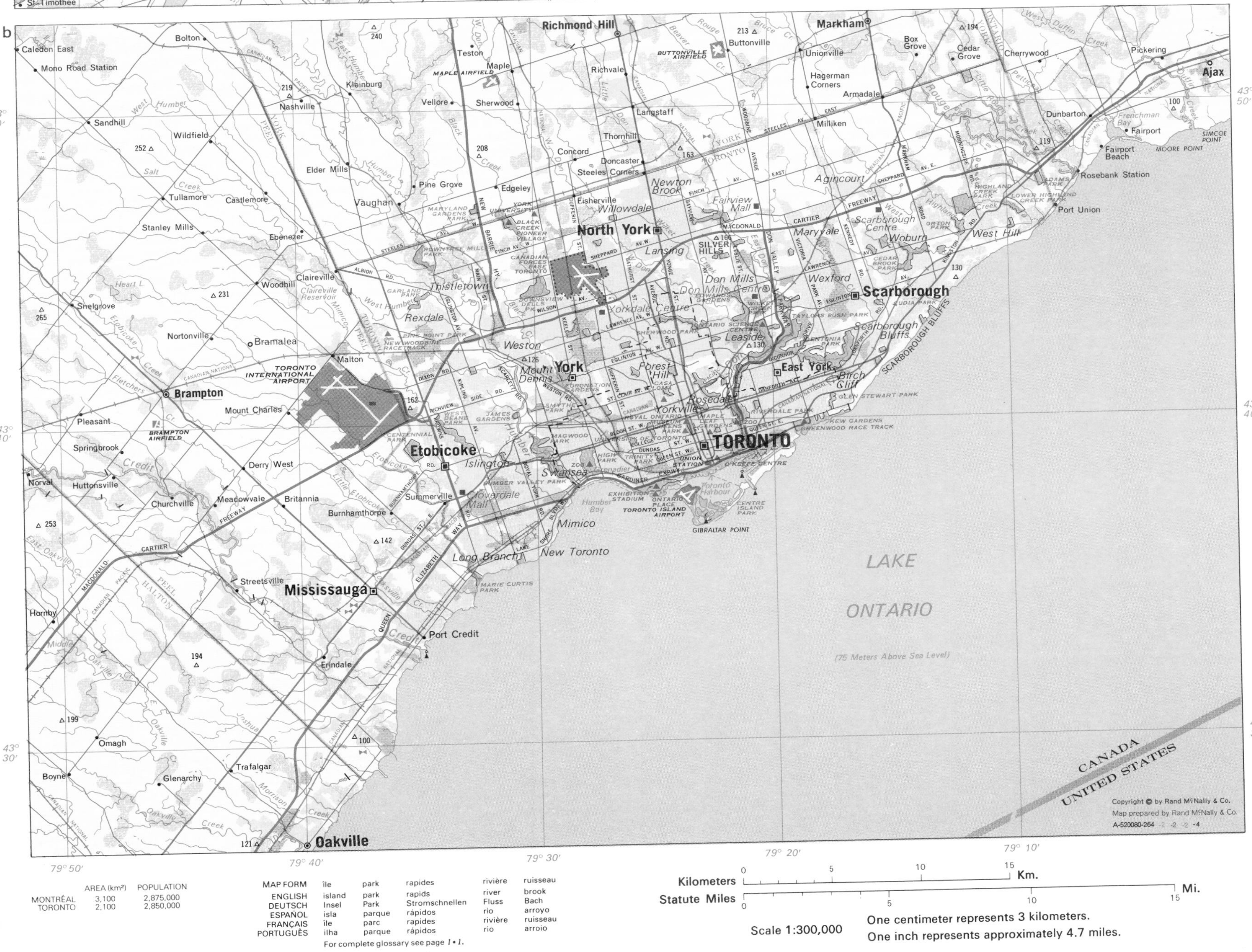
79° 50'
79° 40'
79° 30'
79° 20'
79° 10'
43° 50'
43° 40'
43° 30'
Caledon East
Mono Road Station
Bolton
Kleinburg
Nashville
Richmond Hill
Markham
Buttonville
BUTTONVILLE AIRFIELD
Unionville
Box Grove
Cedar Grove
Cherrywood
Pickering
Ajax
Teston
Maple
MAPLE AIRFIELD
Vellore
Sherwood
Richvale
Langstaff
Thornhill
Concord
Doncaster
Steeles Corners
Hagerman Corners
Armadale
Milliken
Dunbarton
Fairport
Fairport Beach
Rosebank Station
Port Union
Sandhill
Wildfield
Tullamore
Castlemore
Stanley Mills
Elder Mills
Pine Grove
Edgeley
Vaughan
Ebenezer
Woodbill
Claireville
Snelgrove
Nortonville
Bramalea
Malton
TORONTO INTERNATIONAL AIRPORT
Brampton
BRAMPTON AIRFIELD
Mount Charles
Pleasant
Springbrook
Norval
Huttonsville
Churchville
Meadowvale
Britannia
Derry West
Burnhamthorpe
Streetsville
Mississauga
Hornby
Port Credit
Erindale
Omagh
Trafalgar
Boyne
Glenarchy
Oakville
Etobicoke
Islington
Summerville
Rexdale
Thistletown
Weston
Mount Dennis
York
North York
Willowdale
Newton Brook
Fisherville
Lansing
Don Mills
Agincourt
Maryvale
Woburn
West Hill
Wexford
Scarborough
Scarborough Bluffs
Leaside
East York
Birch Cliff
Forest Hill
Yorkville
Rosedale
TORONTO
Swansea
Mimico
New Toronto
Long Branch
Toronto Harbour
TORONTO ISLAND AIRPORT
GIBRALTAR POINT
LAKE ONTARIO
(75 Meters Above Sea Level)
CANADA
UNITED STATES
Copyright © by Rand McNally & Co.
Map prepared by Rand McNally & Co.
A-520080-264

	AREA (km²)	POPULATION
MONTRÉAL	3,100	2,875,000
TORONTO	2,100	2,850,000

MAP FORM	île	park	rapides	rivière	ruisseau
ENGLISH	island	park	rapids	river	brook
DEUTSCH	Insel	Park	Stromschnellen	Fluss	Bach
ESPAÑOL	isla	parque	rápidos	río	arroyo
FRANÇAIS	île	parc	rapides	rivière	ruisseau
PORTUGUÊS	ilha	parque	rápidos	rio	arroio

For complete glossary see page I • 1.

Kilometers 0 5 10 15 Km.

Statute Miles 0 5 10 15 Mi.

Scale 1:300,000

One centimeter represents 3 kilometers.
One inch represents approximately 4.7 miles.

AREA: 8,900 km²
POPULATION: 15,800,000

ENGLISH	bay	brook, br.	creek	harbor	island	lake, l.	point	pond
DEUTSCH	Bucht	Bach	Bach	Hafen	Insel	See	Landspitze	Teich
ESPAÑOL	bahía	arroyo	riachuelo	puerto	isla	lago	punta	charca
FRANÇAIS	baie	ruisseau	crique	port	île	lac	pointe	étang
PORTUGUÊS	baía	arroio	riacho	porto	ilha	lago	ponta	lagoa

For complete glossary see page *I • 1*.

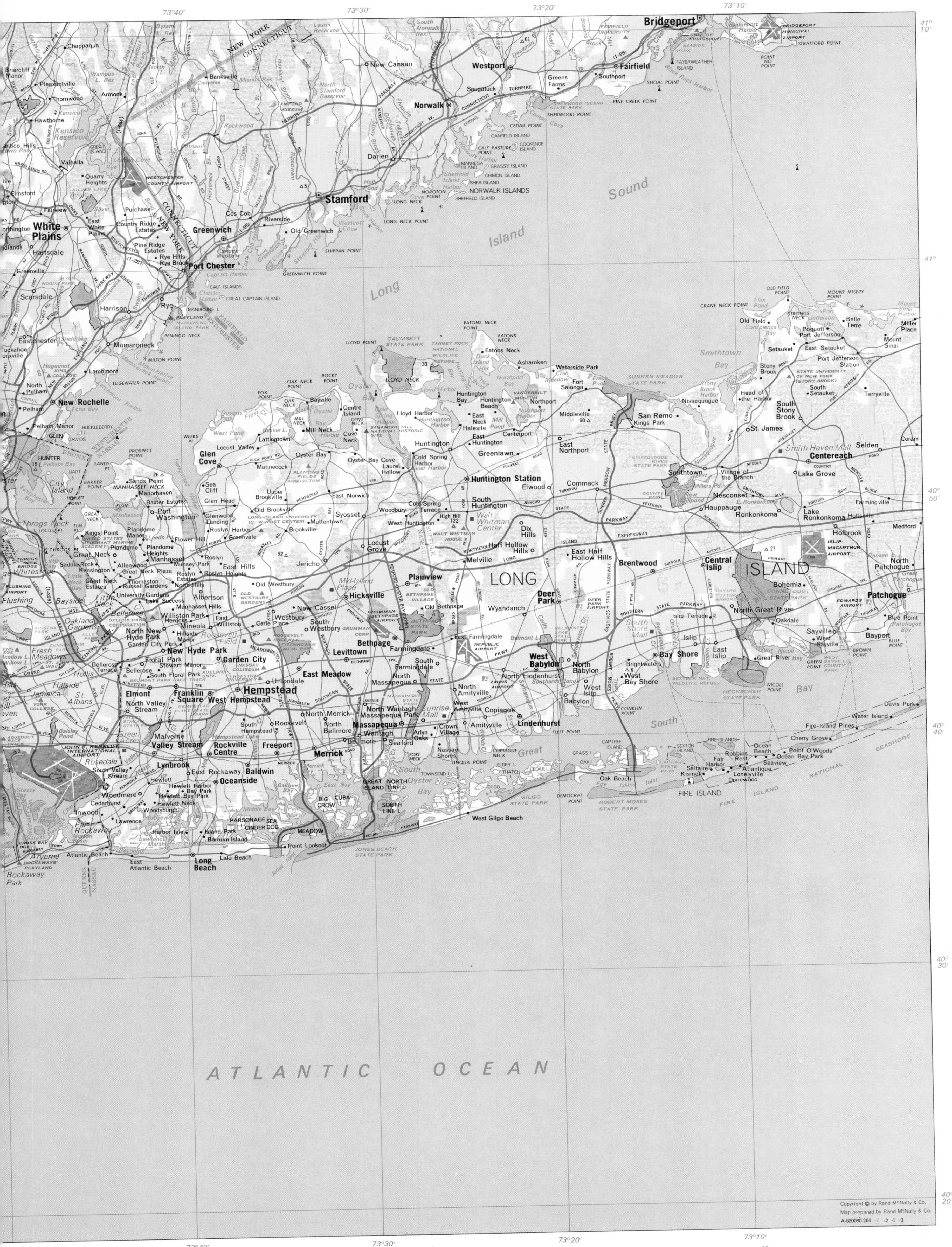

Kilometers 0 5 10 15 Km.

Statute Miles 0 5 10 15 Mi.

Scale 1:300,000

One centimeter represents 3 kilometers.
One inch represents approximately 4.7 miles.

AREA: 4,500 km²
POPULATION: 6,700,000

ENGLISH	airport	creek, cr.	harbor	lake, l.	park	woods
DEUTSCH	Flughafen	Bach	Hafen	See	Park	Gehölz
ESPAÑOL	aeropuerto	riachuelo	puerto	lago	parque	bosques
FRANÇAIS	aéroport	crique	port	lac	parc	bois
PORTUGUÊS	aeroporto	riacho	porto	lago	parque	bosques

For complete glossary see page 1 • 1.

Kilometers 0 5 10 15 Km.
Statute Miles 0 5 10 15 Mi.

Scale 1:300,000
One centimeter represents 3 kilometers.
One inch represents approximately 4.7 miles.

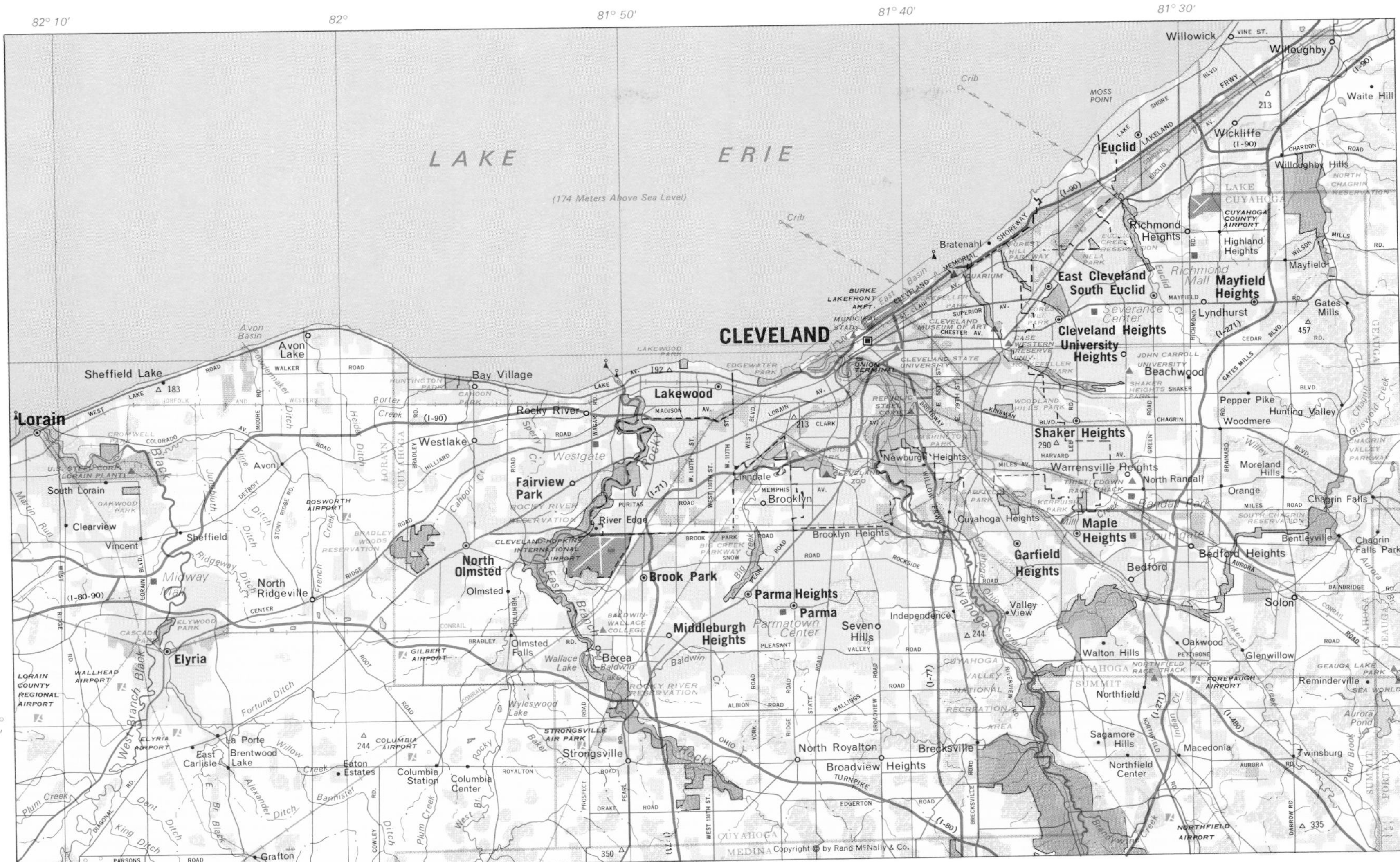

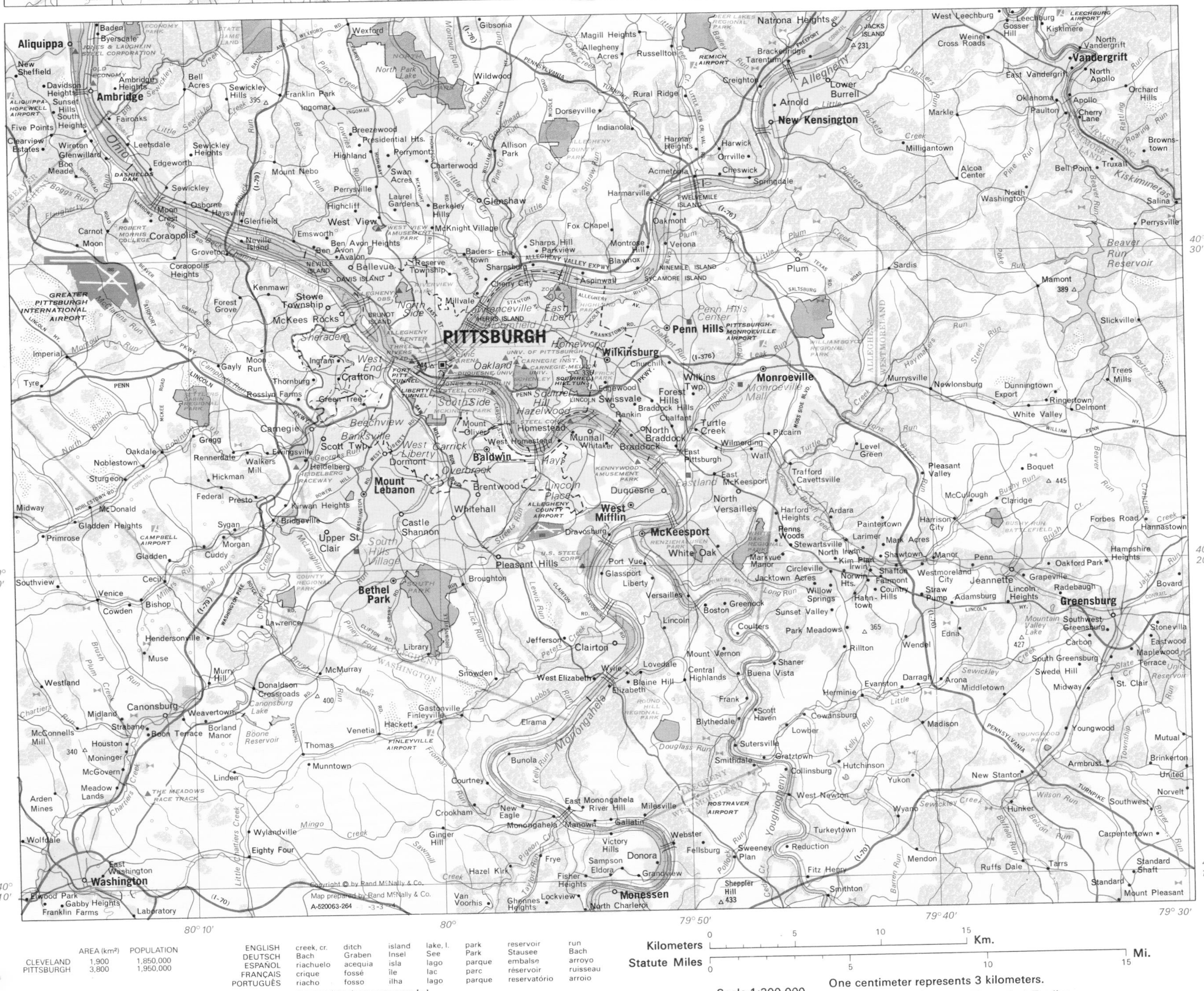

	AREA (km²)	POPULATION
CLEVELAND	1,900	1,850,000
PITTSBURGH	3,800	1,950,000

ENGLISH	creek, cr.	ditch	island	lake, l.	park	reservoir	run
DEUTSCH	Bach	Graben	Insel	See	Park	Stausee	Bach
ESPAÑOL	riachuelo	acequia	isla	lago	parque	embalse	arroyo
FRANÇAIS	crique	fossé	île	lac	parc	reservoir	ruisseau
PORTUGUÊS	riacho	fosso	ilha	lago	parque	reservatório	arroio

For complete glossary see page *I • 1*.

Kilometers 0 5 10 15 Km.
Statute Miles 0 5 10 15 Mi.

Scale 1:300,000
One centimeter represents 3 kilometers.
One inch represents approximately 4.7 miles.

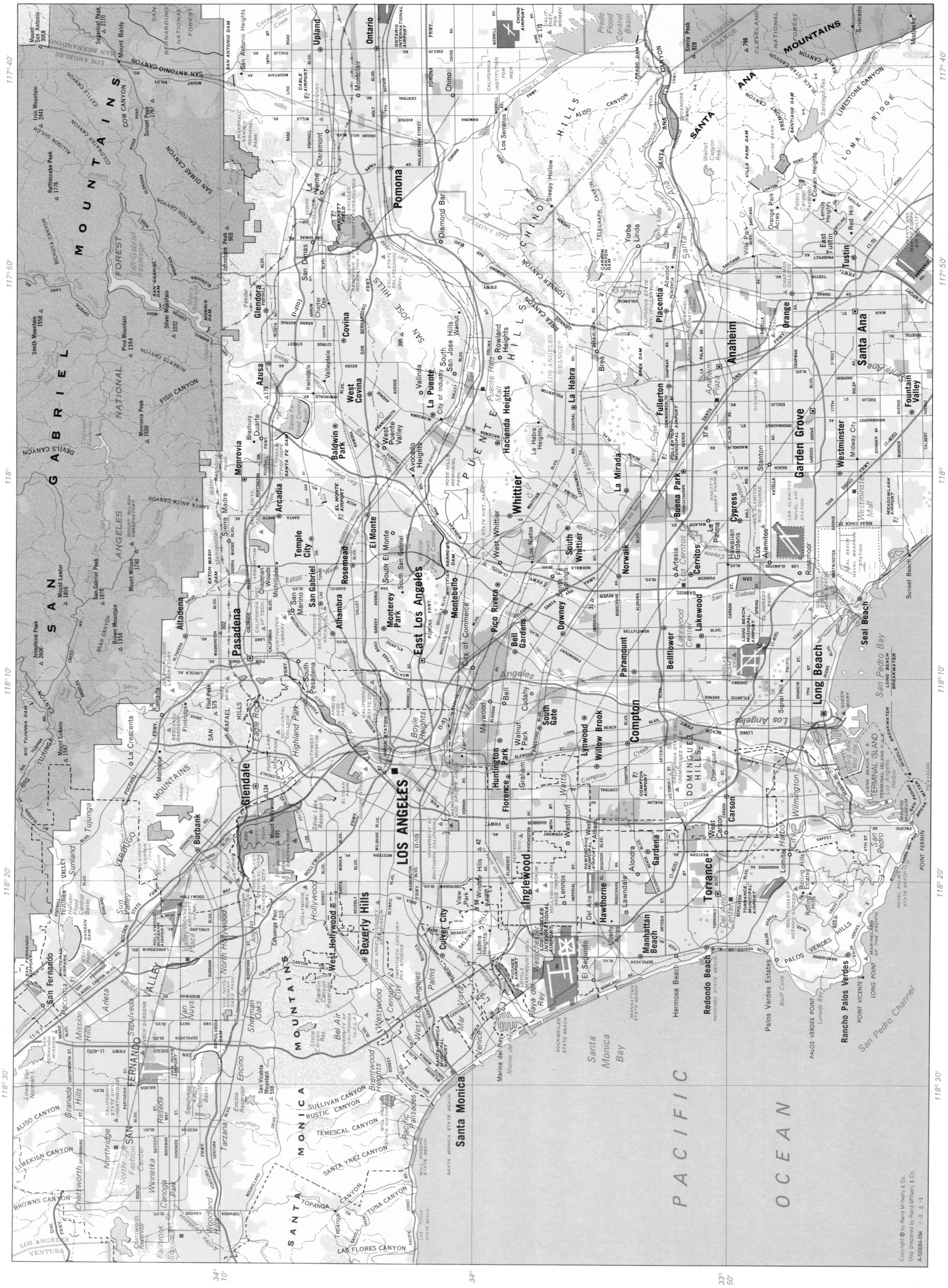

Kilometers 0 5 10 15 Km.
Statute Miles 0 5 10 15 Mi.

Scale 1:300,000
One centimeter represents 3 kilometers.
One inch represents approximately 4.7 miles.

ENGLISH	DEUTSCH	ESPAÑOL	FRANÇAIS	PORTUGUÊS
canyon	Cañon	cañon	canyon	canhão
college	College	escuela	collège	colégio
creek	Bach	riachuelo	crique	riacho
dam	Damm	diques	barrage	dique
hills	Hügel	colinas	collines	colinas
mount	Berg	montaña	mont	montanha
park	Park	parque	parc	parque
peak	Gipfel	pico	cime	pico
reservoir	Stausee	estanque	réservoir	reservatório

For complete glossary see page I • 1.

AREA 5,900 km²
POPULATION 8,375,000

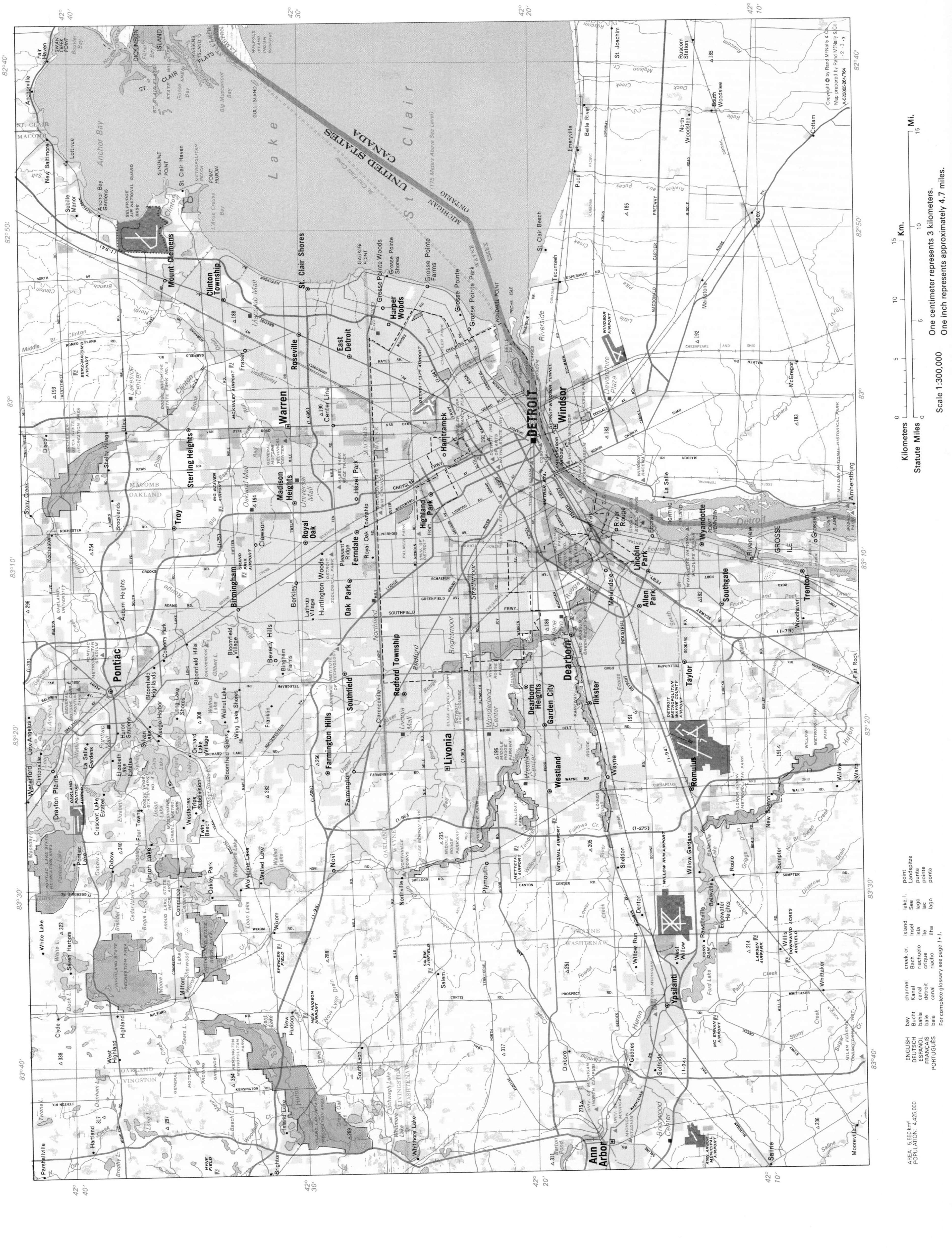
Scale 1:300,000
One centimeter represents 3 kilometers.
One inch represents approximately 4.7 miles.
Kilometers 0 5 10 15 Km.
Statute Miles 0 5 10 15 Mi.
Copyright © by Rand McNally & Co.
Map prepared by Rand McNally & Co.
AREA: 5,550 km²
POPULATION: 4,425,000
ENGLISH bay channel creek, cr. island lake, l. point
DEUTSCH Bucht Kanal Bach Insel See Landspitze
ESPAÑOL bahía canal riachuelo isla lago punta
FRANÇAIS baie canal crique île lac pointe
PORTUGUÊS baía canal riacho ilha lago ponta
For complete glossary see page I•1.
DETROIT
Windsor
UNITED STATES
CANADA
MICHIGAN
ONTARIO
Lake St. Clair
(175 Meters Above Sea Level)
Detroit
Ann Arbor
Ypsilanti
Pontiac
Warren
Dearborn
Livonia
Southfield
Troy
Royal Oak
Mount Clemens
Sterling Heights
Farmington Hills
Taylor
Wyandotte
Romulus
Westland
Highland Park
Hamtramck
Windsor
Amherstburg
Essex
Tecumseh
Belle River
Trenton
Grosse Ile
Redford Township
Clinton Township
St. Clair Shores
Roseville
East Detroit
Madison Heights
Ferndale
Oak Park
Birmingham
Inkster
Garden City
Dearborn Heights
Allen Park
Lincoln Park
Southgate
Wayne
Plymouth
Northville
Novi
Milford
Brighton
South Lyon
Saline
Belleville
Flat Rock
DETROIT METROPOLITAN WAYNE COUNTY AIRPORT
WILLOW RUN AIRPORT
WINDSOR AIRPORT

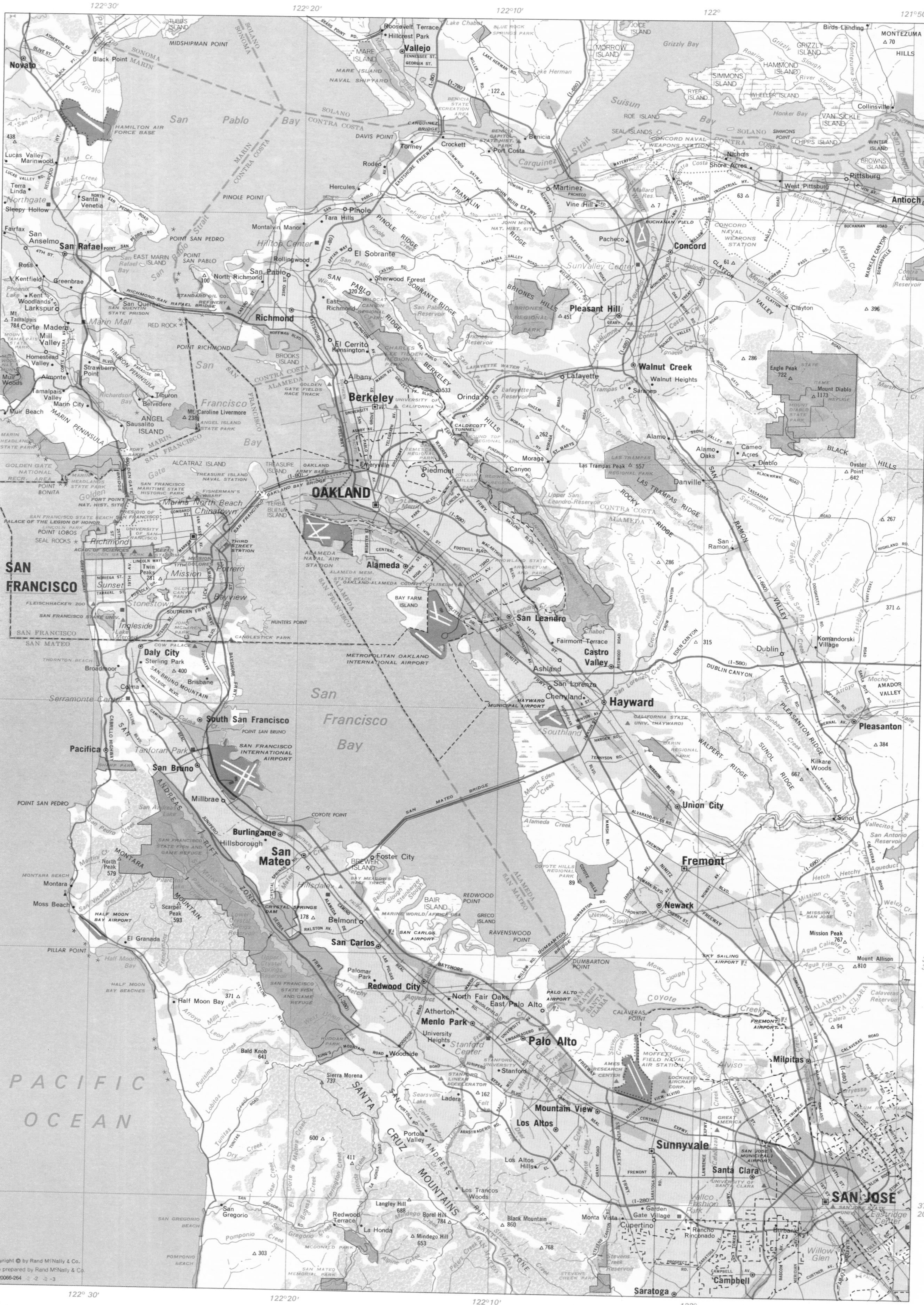

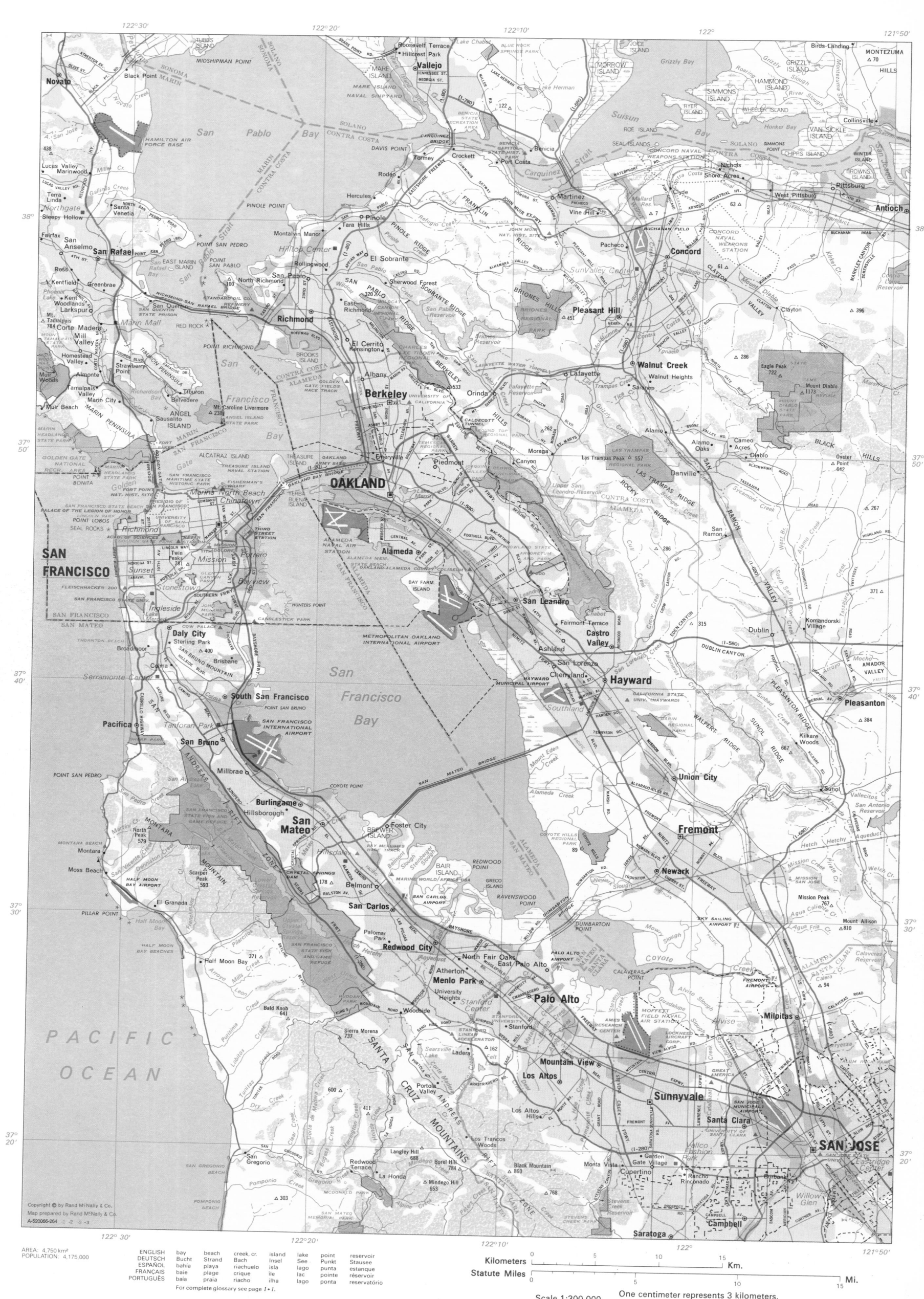

AREA: 4,750 km²
POPULATION: 4,175,000

ENGLISH	bay	beach	creek, cr.	island	lake	point	reservoir
DEUTSCH	Bucht	Strand	Bach	Insel	See	Punkt	Stausee
ESPAÑOL	bahia	playa	riachuelo	isla	lago	punta	estanque
FRANÇAIS	baie	plage	crique	île	lac	pointe	réservoir
PORTUGUÊS	baia	praia	riacho	ilha	lago	ponta	reservatório

For complete glossary see page I • 1.

Kilometers 0 5 10 15 Km.
Statute Miles 0 5 10 15 Mi.

Scale 1:300,000
One centimeter represents 3 kilometers.
One inch represents approximately 4.7 miles.

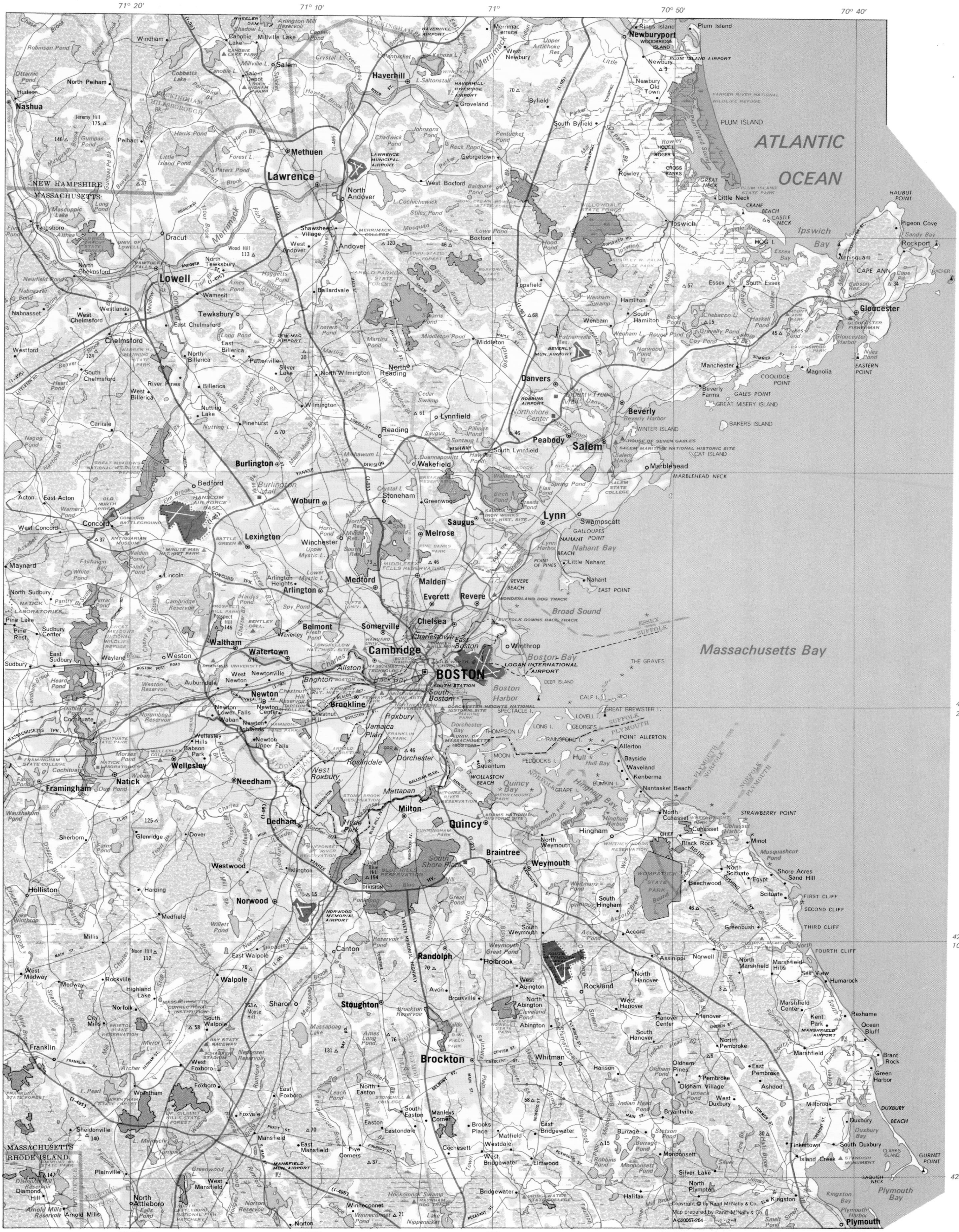

AREA: 5,150 km²
POPULATION: 3,625,000

ENGLISH	bay	brook	island, i.	lake, l.	point	pond	reservation
DEUTSCH	Bucht	Bach	Insel	See	Landspitze	Teich	Reservat
ESPAÑOL	bahía	arroyo	isla	lago	punta	charca	parque nacional
FRANÇAIS	baie	ruisseau	île	lac	pointe	étang	réservation
PORTUGUÊS	baía	arroio	ilha	lago	ponta	lagoa	parque nacional

For complete glossary see page I • 1.

Kilometers 0 5 10 15 Km.
Statute Miles 0 5 10 15 Mi.

Scale 1:300,000

One centimeter represents 3 kilometers.
One inch represents approximately 4.7 miles.

	AREA (km²)	POPULATION
BUFFALO	2,550	1,450,000
BALTIMORE	1,150	1,500,000
WASHINGTON	1,550	2,225,000

ENGLISH	airport	bridge	creek, cr.	island, i.	park	point	run	university
DEUTSCH	Flughafen	Brücke	Bach	Insel	Park	Landspitze	Bach	Universität
ESPAÑOL	aeropuerto	puente	riachuelo	isla	parque	punta	arroyo	universidad
FRANÇAIS	aéroport	pont	crique	île	parc	pointe	ruisseau	université
PORTUGUÊS	aeroporto	ponte	riacho	ilha	parque	ponta	arroio	universidade

For complete glossary see page [•].

Kilometers 0 5 10 15 Km.
Statute Miles 0 5 10 15 Mi.

Scale 1:300,000
One centimeter represents 3 kilometers.
One inch represents approximately 4.7 miles.

b

c

a

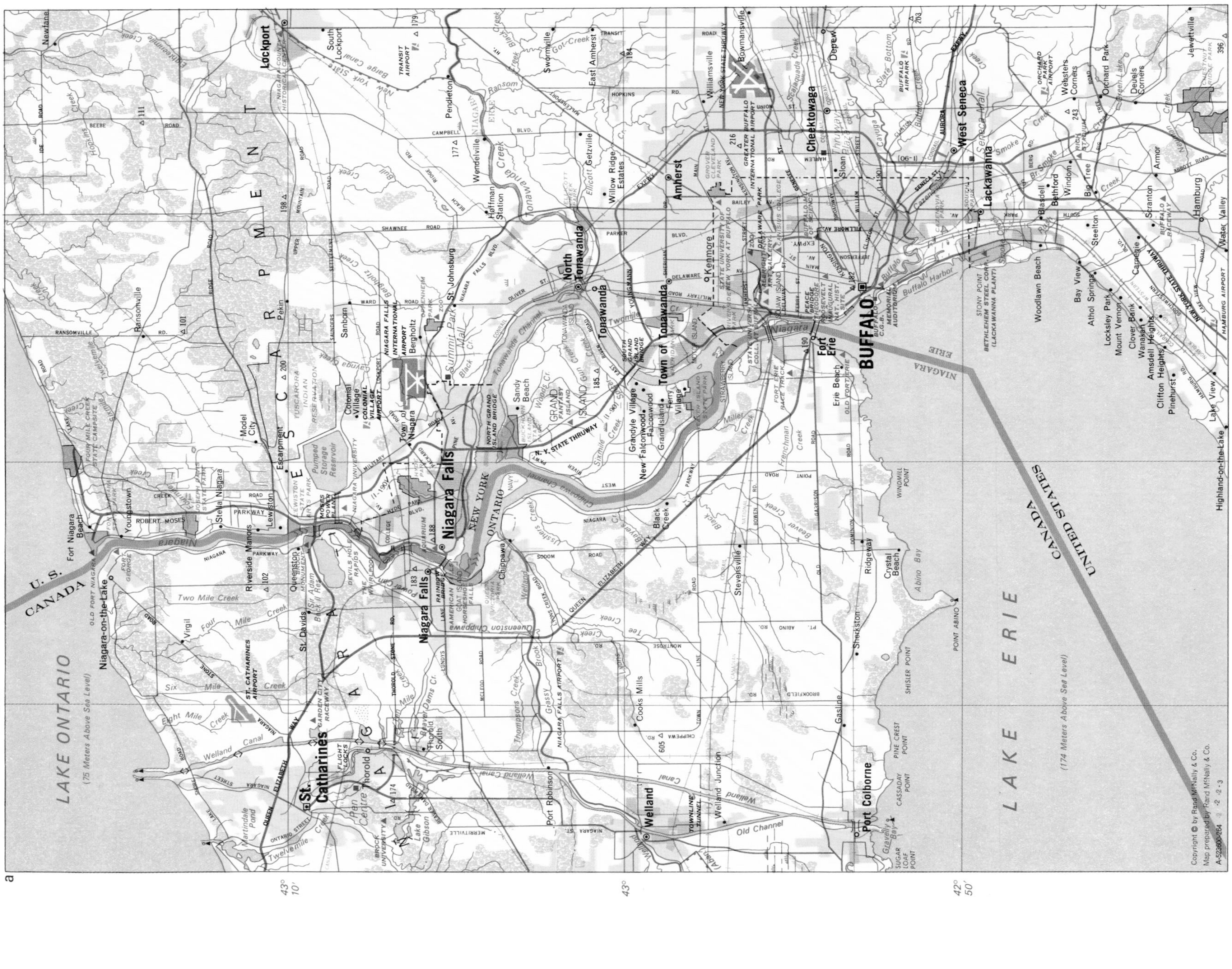

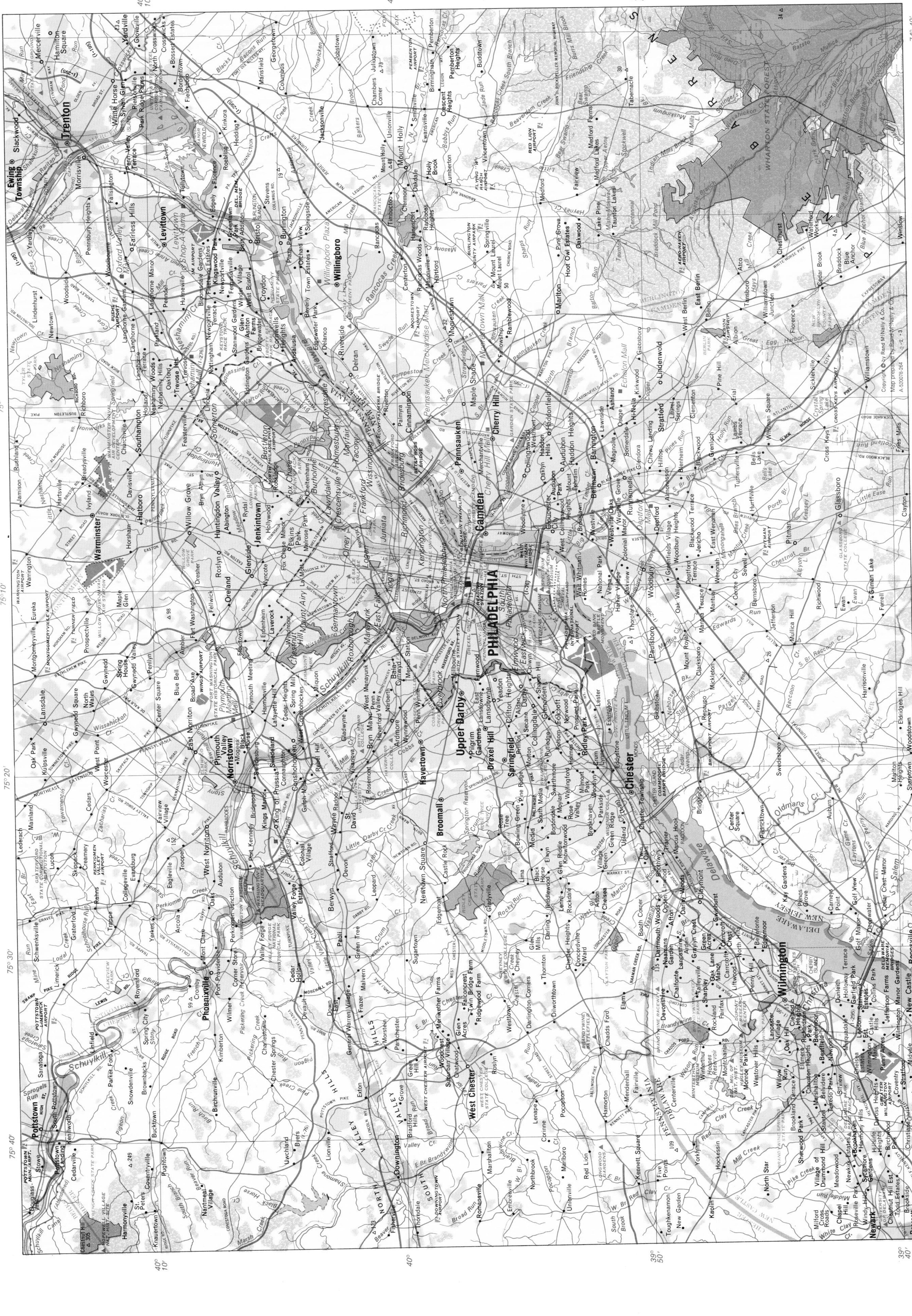
PHILADELPHIA
Camden
Trenton
Wilmington
Chester
Norristown
Scale 1:300,000
One centimeter represents 3 kilometers.
One inch represents approximately 4.7 miles.
Kilometers
Statute Miles
AREA: 6,500 km²
POPULATION: 5,150,000
ENGLISH airport bridge college creek, cr. island, I. lake, l. run state park
DEUTSCH Flughafen Brücke College Bach Insel See Bach Staatspark
ESPAÑOL aeropuerto puente escuela riachuelo isla lago arroyo parque del estado
FRANÇAIS aéroport pont collège crique île lac ruisseau parc régional
PORTUGUÊS aeroporto ponte escola riacho ilha lago arroio parque estadual
For complete glossary see page I • 1.

a

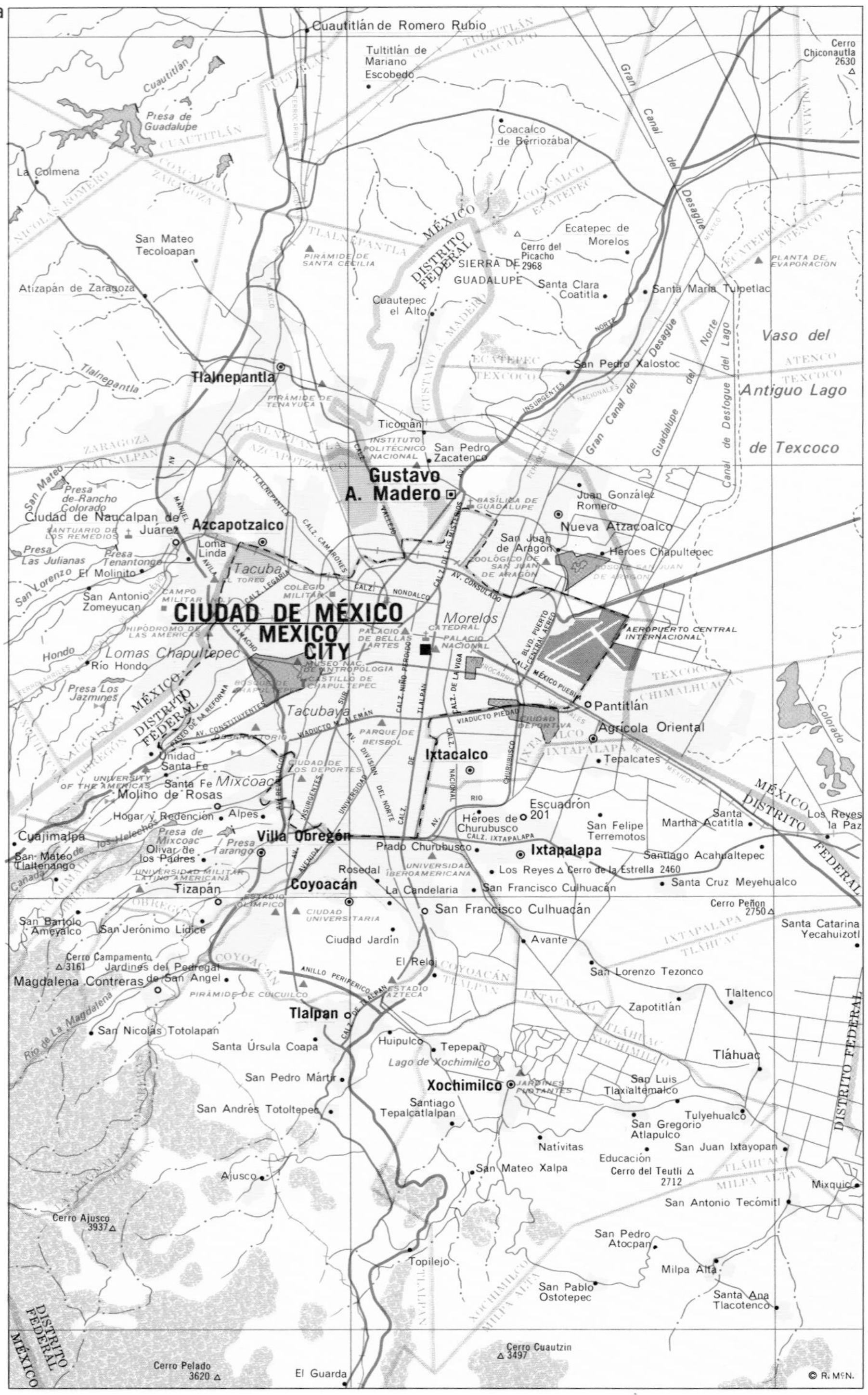

b

c

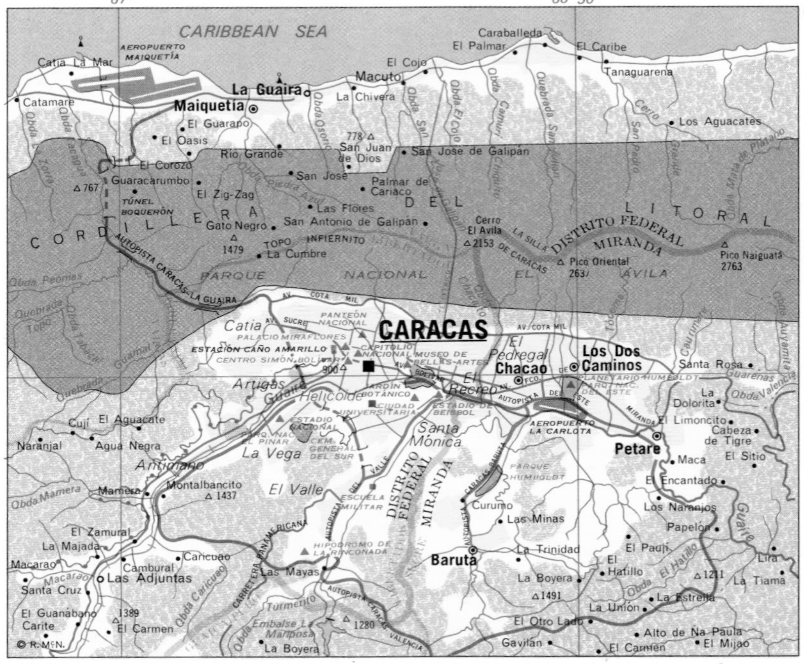

d

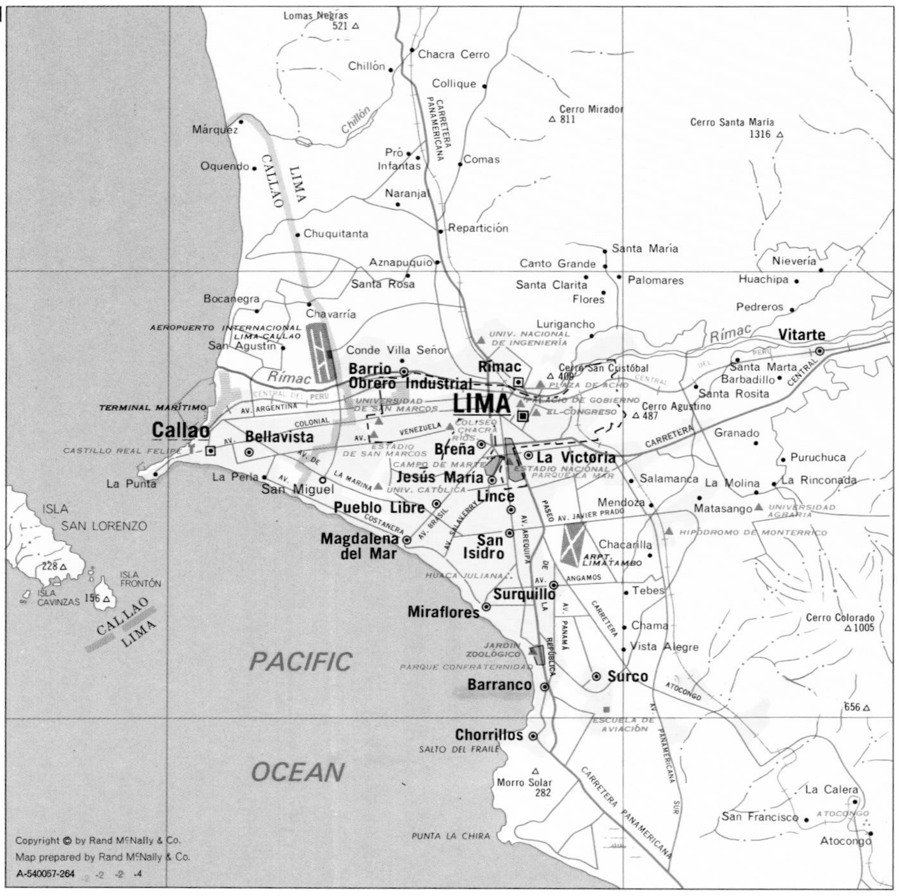

e

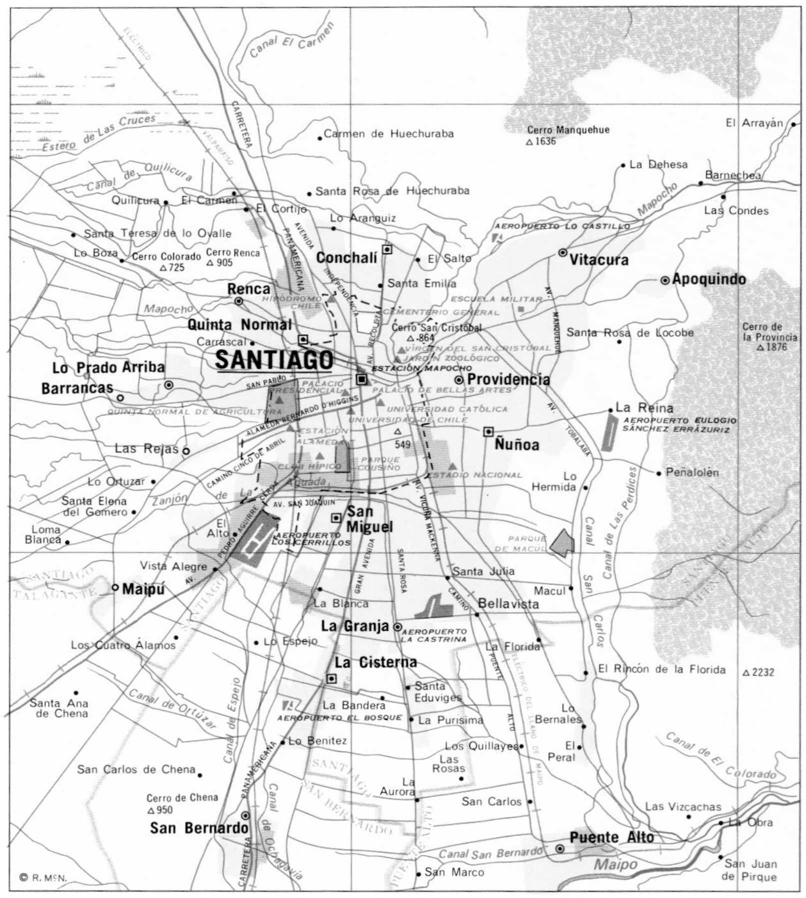

	AREA (km²)	POPULATION
CIUDAD DE MÉXICO	2,050	13,250,000
LA HABANA	750	2,050,000
CARACAS	750	2,950,000
LIMA	750	4,300,000
SANTIAGO	1,100	3,700,000

ESPAÑOL	arroyo	castillo	isla	laguna	presa	quebrada
ENGLISH	brook	castle	island	lagoon	reservoir	creek
DEUTSCH	Bach	Burg	Insel	Haff	Stausee	Bach
FRANÇAIS	ruisseau	château	île	lagune	réservoir	crique
PORTUGUÊS	arroio	castelo	ilha	laguna	reservatório	arroio

For complete glossary see page *I • 1*.

Kilometers 0 5 10 15 Km.

Statute Miles 0 5 10 15 Mi.

Scale 1:300,000

One centimeter represents 3 kilometers.
One inch represents approximately 4.7 miles.

a

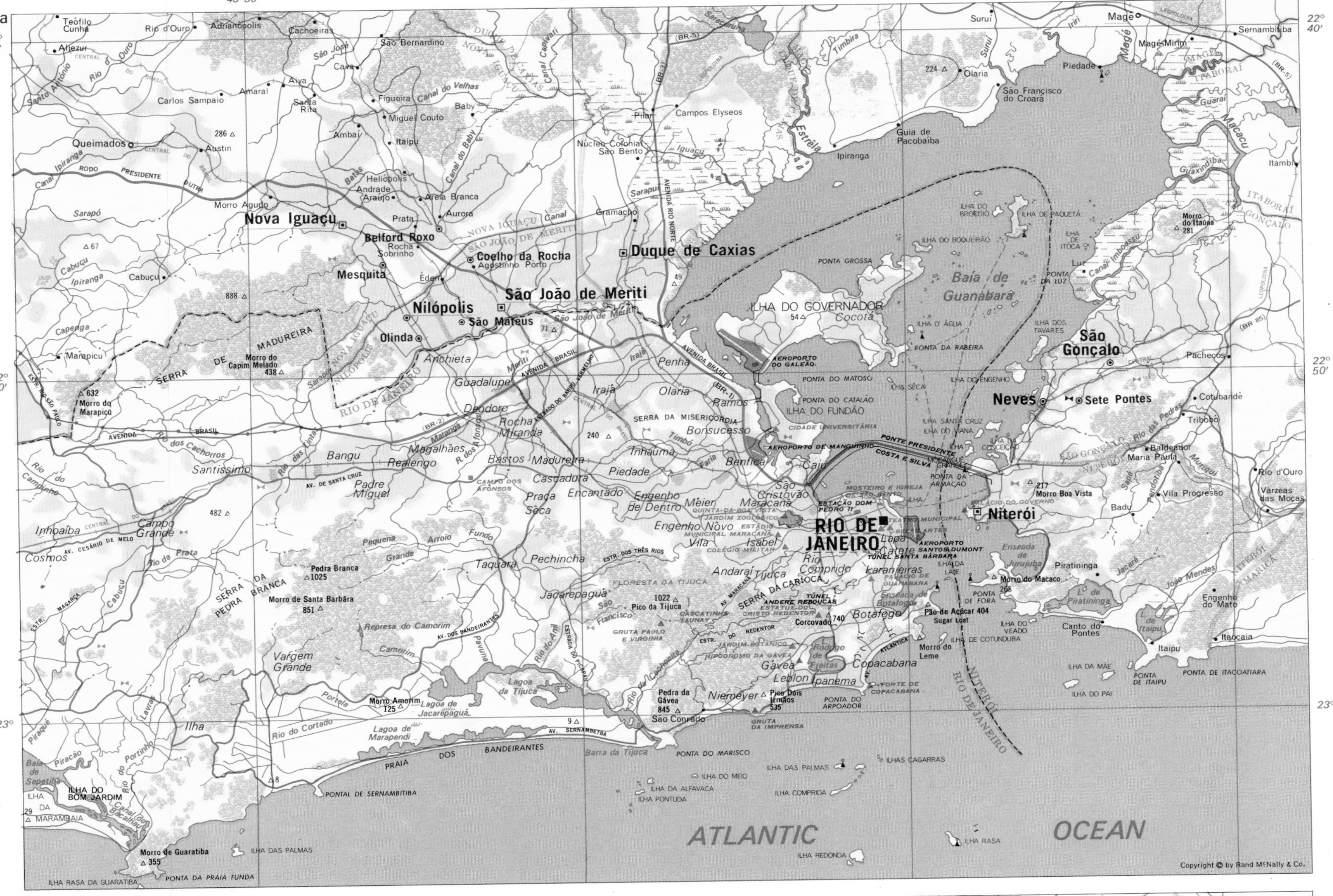
ATLANTIC
OCEAN
RIO DE JANEIRO
Niterói
Nova Iguaçu
Duque de Caxias
São João de Meriti
Nilópolis
Belford Roxo
Mesquita
São Gonçalo
Neves
Baía de Guanabara
ILHA DO GOVERNADOR
ILHA DO FUNDÃO
Copacabana
Ipanema
Leblon
Gávea
Botafogo
Tijuca
Pão de Açúcar 404
Corcovado 740
Pico da Tijuca 1022
Pedra Branca 1025
SERRA DA PEDRA BRANCA
SERRA DE MADUREIRA
Lagoa de Jacarepaguá
PRAIA DOS BANDEIRANTES
Barra da Tijuca
PONTE PRESIDENTE COSTA E SILVA
AEROPORTO DO GALEÃO
Magé
Copyright © by Rand McNally & Co.

b

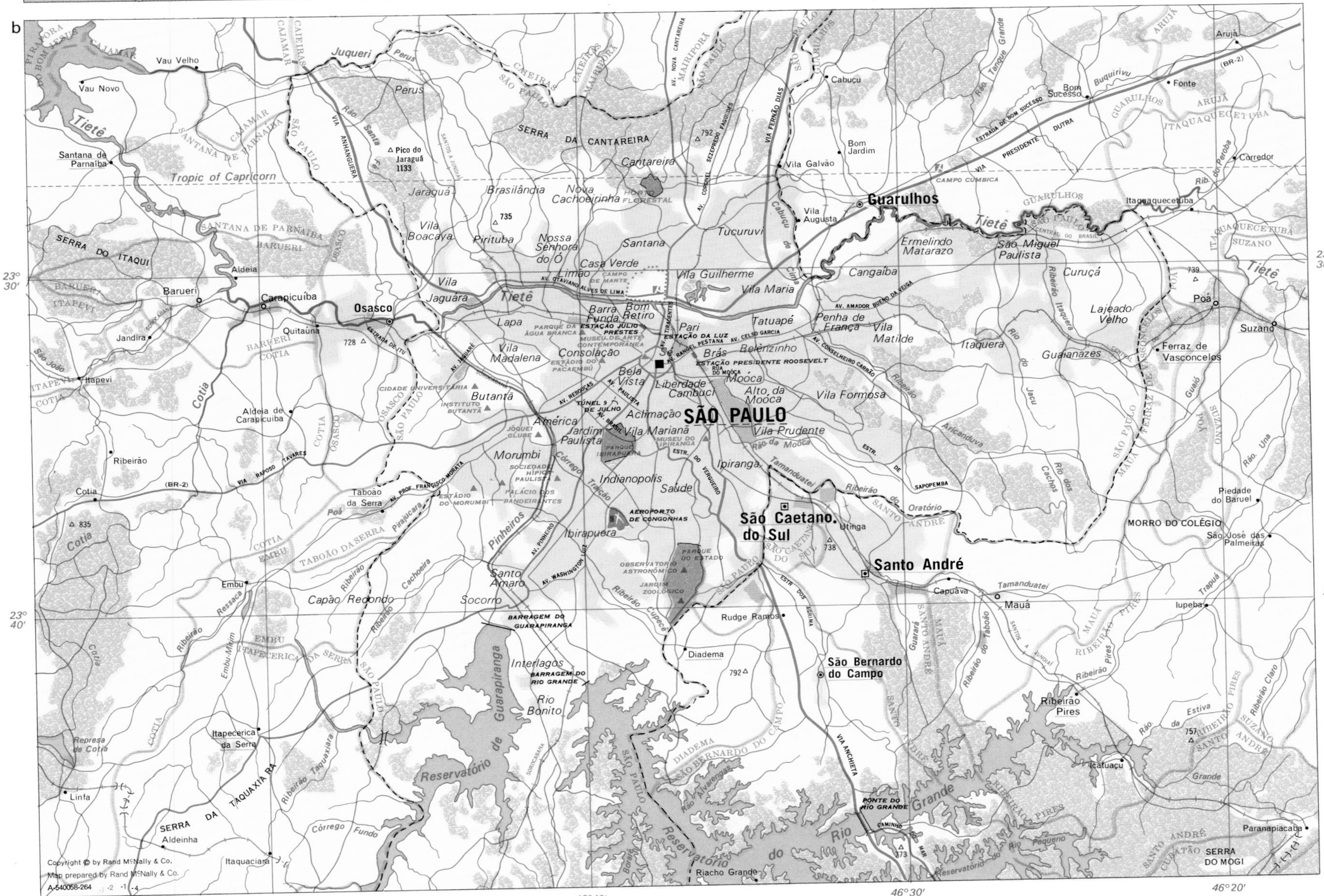
SÃO PAULO
Guarulhos
Osasco
Santo André
São Caetano do Sul
São Bernardo do Campo
Diadema
Mauá
Tietê
Tropic of Capricorn
SERRA DA CANTAREIRA
SERRA DO ITAQUI
Pico do Jaraguá 1133
Reservatório de Guarapiranga
Rio Grande
Santo Amaro
Interlagos
AEROPORTO DE CONGONHAS
Ibirapuera
Copyright © by Rand McNally & Co.
Map prepared by Rand McNally & Co.
A-540058-264

	AREA (km²)	POPULATION
RIO DE JANEIRO	2,200	8,200,000
SÃO PAULO	3,200	11,000,000

MAP FORM	ilha	lagoa, l.	morro	ponta	reservatório	ribeirão, rão.
ENGLISH	island	lagoon	hill	point	reservoir	creek
DEUTSCH	Insel	Haff	Hügel	Landspitze	Stausee	Bach
ESPAÑOL	isla	laguna	colina	punta	embalse	riachuelo
FRANÇAIS	île	lagune	colline	pointe	réservoir	crique
PORTUGUÊS	ilha	laguna	colina	ponta	reservatório	riacho

For complete glossary see page *I • 1*.

Kilometers 0 5 10 15 Km.
Statute Miles 0 5 10 15 Mi.

Scale 1:300,000

One centimeter represents 3 kilometers.
One inch represents approximately 4.7 miles.

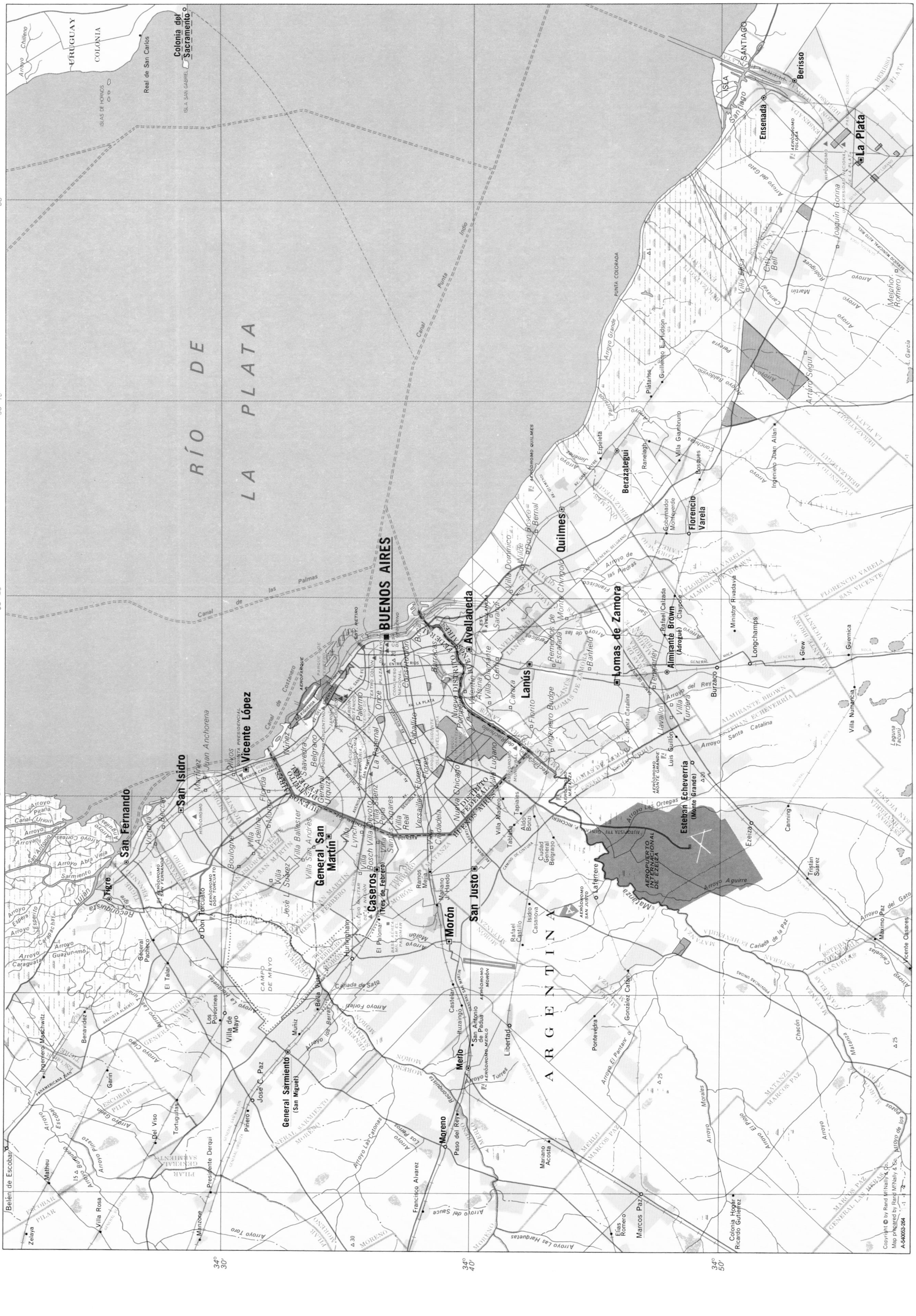
RÍO DE LA PLATA
BUENOS AIRES
URUGUAY
COLONIA
Colonia del Sacramento
Real de San Carlos
ARGENTINA
San Fernando
Tigre
San Isidro
Vicente López
General San Martín
Caseros
Morón
San Justo
Avellaneda
Lanús
Lomas de Zamora
Quilmes
Berazategui
Florencio Varela
Almirante Brown
Esteban Echeverría
Ensenada
Berisso
La Plata
Merlo
Moreno
General Sarmiento
AEROPUERTO INTERNACIONAL DE EZEIZA
Ezeiza
Marcos Paz
Canal Punta Indio
Canal de las Palmas
Copyright © by Rand McNally & Co.
Map prepared by Rand McNally & Co.
A-540053-264

Kilometers 0 5 10 15 Km.

Statute Miles 0 5 10 15 Mi.

Scale 1:300,000

One centimeter represents 3 kilometers.
One inch represents approximately 4.7 miles.

MAP FORM	ENGLISH	DEUTSCH	ESPAÑOL	FRANÇAIS	PORTUGUÊS
aeródromo	airport	Flughafen	aeropuerto	aéroport	aeroporto
arroyo	creek	Bach	riachuelo	crique	riacho
canal	navigation canal	Schiffahrtskanal	canal de navegación	canal navigable	canal navegável
estación	station	Bahnhof	estación	gare	estação
ilha	island	Insel	isla	île	ilha
parque	park	Park	parque	parc	parque
punta	point	Landspitze	punta	pointe	ponta

For complete glossary see page I • 1.

AREA: 4,700 km²
POPULATION: 10,450,000

THIS TABLE lists the major metropolitan areas of the world according to their estimated population on January 1, 1978. For convenience in reference, the areas are grouped by major region with the total for each region given. The number of areas by population classification is given in parentheses with each size group.

For ease of comparison, each metropolitan area has been defined by Rand McNally & Company according to consistent rules. A metropolitan area includes a central city, neighboring communities linked to it by continuous built-up areas, and more distant communities if the bulk of their population is supported by commuters to the central city. Some metropolitan areas have more than one central city; in such cases each central city is listed.

IN DIESER TABELLE sind die Hauptmetropolen der Welt verzeichnet, gemessen nach ihrer Bevölkerung, die nach dem Stand vom 1. Januar 1978 geschätzt wurde. Zur besseren Übersicht sind die Zonen nach grösseren Regionen gruppiert, wobei die Gesamtzahl für jede Region angegeben ist. Die Anzahl der Zonen ist nach Bevölkerung klassifiziert und in Klammern hinter denen nach Grössen sortierten Gruppen angegeben.

Zum einfacheren Vergleich ist jede Metropole von Rand McNally & Company nach übereinstimmenden Massstäben definiert worden. Eine Metropole schliesst eine zentrale Stadt mit benachbarten Gemeinden, die mit ihr durch ununterbrochen bebaute Gebiete verbunden sind ein, sowie weiter entfernte Gemeinden, wenn der grösste Teil ihrer Bevölkerung von den Pendlern unterhalten wird. Einige Metropolen haben mehr als eine zentrale Stadt; in solchen Fällen ist jede dieser zentralen Städte angeführt.

ESTA TABLA indica las principales áreas metropolitanas del mundo, de acuerdo con su población calculada al 1 de enero de 1978. Para facilitar las referencias, las áreas se han agrupado por regiones principales, indicándose el total para cada región. El número de áreas, clasificadas por población, se indica entre paréntesis en los grupos de cada tamaño.

Para facilitar las comparaciones, Rand McNally y Compañía ha definido cada área metropolitana de acuerdo con reglas consistentes. Un área metropolitana incluye una ciudad central, localidades vecinas vinculadas con ella mediante sectores construídos y contínuos, y localidades más distantes, si el grueso de su población lo constituye un núcleo que diariamente viaja a la ciudad central. Algunas áreas metropolitanas incluyen más de una ciudad central; en tales casos se indica cada una dichas ciudades.

CETTE TABLE contient la liste des aires métropolitaines les plus considérables dans le monde pour ce qui est du peuplement a la date du Ier janvier 1978. Afin de faciliter la consultation, on a groupé les aires par grandes régions en indiquant la population totale pour chaque région, et, entre parenthèses, le nombre d'aires comprises dans celle-ci.

Afin de rendre plus faciles les comparaisons, Rand McNally & Co. a défini chaque aire métropolitaine selon des règles cohérentes: une aire métropolitaine englobe une cité centrale ou métropole et l'environnement urbain continu qui s'y rattache; elle inclut également des agglomérations éloignées de la métropole lorsque la population de ces dernières est pour sa májorité constituée d'habitants se rendant quotidiennement dans la cité où est situé le lieu de travail de ceux-ci. On trouvera quelques aires métropolitaines pourvues de plus d'une métropole. Dans ce cas, chaque métropole est mentionnée.

A TABELA que se segue relaciona as principais áreas metropolitanas do mundo, de acordo com as respectivas populações, estimadas para 1 de janeiro de 1978. Para facilidade de referência, as áreas metropolitanas foram agrupadas dentro das regiões maiores, indicando-se, entre parênteses, os totais de cada região maior e o número de áreas metropolitanas, classificadas segundo a população, compreendidas em cada uma.

Para fins de comparabilidade, Rand McNally & Company definiu cada área metropolitana de acordo com regras uniformes. Uma área metropolitana inclui uma cidade central, as localidades vizinhas ligadas a ela por áreas construídas contínuas, e as localidades mais distantes, desde que a maior parte de suas respectivas populações dependa economicamente da cidade central e que para ela viaje diariamente. Algumas áreas metropolitanas incluem mais de uma cidade central; em tais casos, indicam-se ambas as cidades.

CLASSIFICATION KLASSIFIZIERT CLASIFICADAS CLASSIFICATION CLASSIFICAÇÃO	ANGLO-AMERICA ANGLO-AMERIKA AMÉRICA ANGLOSAJONA AMÉRIQUE ANGLO-SAXONNE AMÉRICA ANGLO-SAXÔNICA	LATIN AMERICA LATEIN-AMERIKA AMÉRICA LATINA AMÉRIQUE LATINE AMÉRICA LATINA	EUROPE EUROPA EUROPA EUROPE EUROPA	U.S.S.R U.S.S.R. U.R.S.S. U.R.S.S. U.R.S.S.	ASIA ASIEN ASIA ASIE ÁSIA	AFRICA-OCEANIA AFRIKA-OZEANIEN AFRICA-OCEANÍA AFRIQUE-OCÉANIE ÁFRICA-OCEANIA
OVER–15,000,000 (3)	New York				Ōsaka-Kōbe-Kyōto Tōkyō-Yokohama	
10,000,000–15,000,000 (5)		Ciudad de México (Mexico City) São Paulo	London	Moskva (Moscow)	Calcutta	
5,000,000–10,000,000 (17)	Chicago Los Angeles Philadelphia	Buenos Aires Rio de Janeiro	Essen-Dortmund-Duisburg (The Ruhr) Paris	Leningrad	Beijing (Peking) Bombay Delhi Jakarta Manila Shanghai Sŏul (Seoul) Tehrān	Al-Qāhirah (Cairo)
3,000,000–5,000,000 (27)	Boston Detroit-Windsor San Francisco-Oakland-San Jose Washington	Bogotá Caracas Lima Santiago	Athínai (Athens) Barcelona Berlin İstanbul Madrid Milano (Milan) Roma (Rome)		Baghdād Chongqing (Chungking) Karāchi Krung Thep (Bangkok) Madras Nagoya Shenyang (Mukden) T'aipei Tianjin (Tientsin) Victoria Wuhan	Sydney
2,000,000–3,000,000 (45)	Cleveland Dallas-Fort Worth Houston Miami-Fort Lauderdale Montréal Pittsburgh St. Louis San Diego-Tijuana Toronto	Belo Horizonte Guadalajara La Habana (Havana) Recife	Birmingham Bruxelles (Brussels) București (Bucharest) Budapest Hamburg Katowice-Bytom-Gliwice Lisboa (Lisbon) Manchester Napoli (Naples) Warszawa (Warsaw)	Doneck-Makejevka Kijev (Kiev)	Ahmadābād Bangalore Dacca Guangzhou (Canton) Haerbin (Harbin) Hyderābād Lahore Pusan Rangoon Singapore Surabaya Thanh-pho Ho Chi Minh (Sai-gon) Xi'an (Sian)	Alger (Algiers) Al-Iskandarīyah (Alexandria) Casablanca Johannesburg Kinshasa Lagos Melbourne
1,500,000–2,000,000 (32)	Atlanta Baltimore Buffalo Minneapolis-St. Paul Seattle-Tacoma	Medellín Monterrey Pôrto Alegre San Juan	Amsterdam Frankfurt am Main Glasgow København (Copenhagen) Köln (Cologne) Leeds-Bradford Liverpool München (Munich) Stuttgart Torino (Turin) Wien (Vienna)	Baku Char'kov (Kharkov) Gor'kij (Gorky) Taškent	Ankara Chengdu (Chengtu) Colombo Fukuoka Kānpur Kitakyūshū-Shimonoseki Nanjing (Nanking) Taiyuan	
1,000,000–1,500,000 (81)	Cincinnati Denver El Paso-Ciudad Juárez Hartford Indianapolis Kansas City Milwaukee New Orleans Phoenix Portland Vancouver	Cali Córdoba Fortaleza Guatemala Guayaquil Montevideo Rosario Salvador	Antwerpen (Anvers) Beograd (Belgrade) Düsseldorf Hannover Lille Łódź Lyon Mannheim Marseille Newcastle-Sunderland Nürnberg Porto Praha (Prague) Rotterdam Sofija (Sofia) Stockholm Valencia	Čel'abinsk (Chelyabinsk) Dnepropetrovsk Jerevan Kazan' Kujbyšev (Kuybyshev) Minsk Novosibirsk Odessa Omsk Perm Rostov-na-Donu Saratov Sverdlovsk Tbilisi Volgograd	Anshan Bandung Bayrūt (Beirut) Changchun (Hsinking) Chittagong Dimashq (Damascus) Fushun Ha-noi Hiroshima-Kure İzmir Jinan (Tsinan) Kaohsiung Kunming Lanzhou (Lanchow) Lucknow Lüda (Dairen) Nāgpur Pune (Poona) P'yongyang Qingdao (Tsingtao) Sapporo Shijiazhuang (Shihchiachuang) Taegu Tel Aviv-Yafo Zhengzhou (Chengchow)	Addis Abeba Brisbane Cape Town Durban Tunis
TOTAL / GESAMTZAHL TOTAL / TOTAL / TOTAL (210)	33	24	48	23	68	14

World Scene

World Scene

Table of Contents

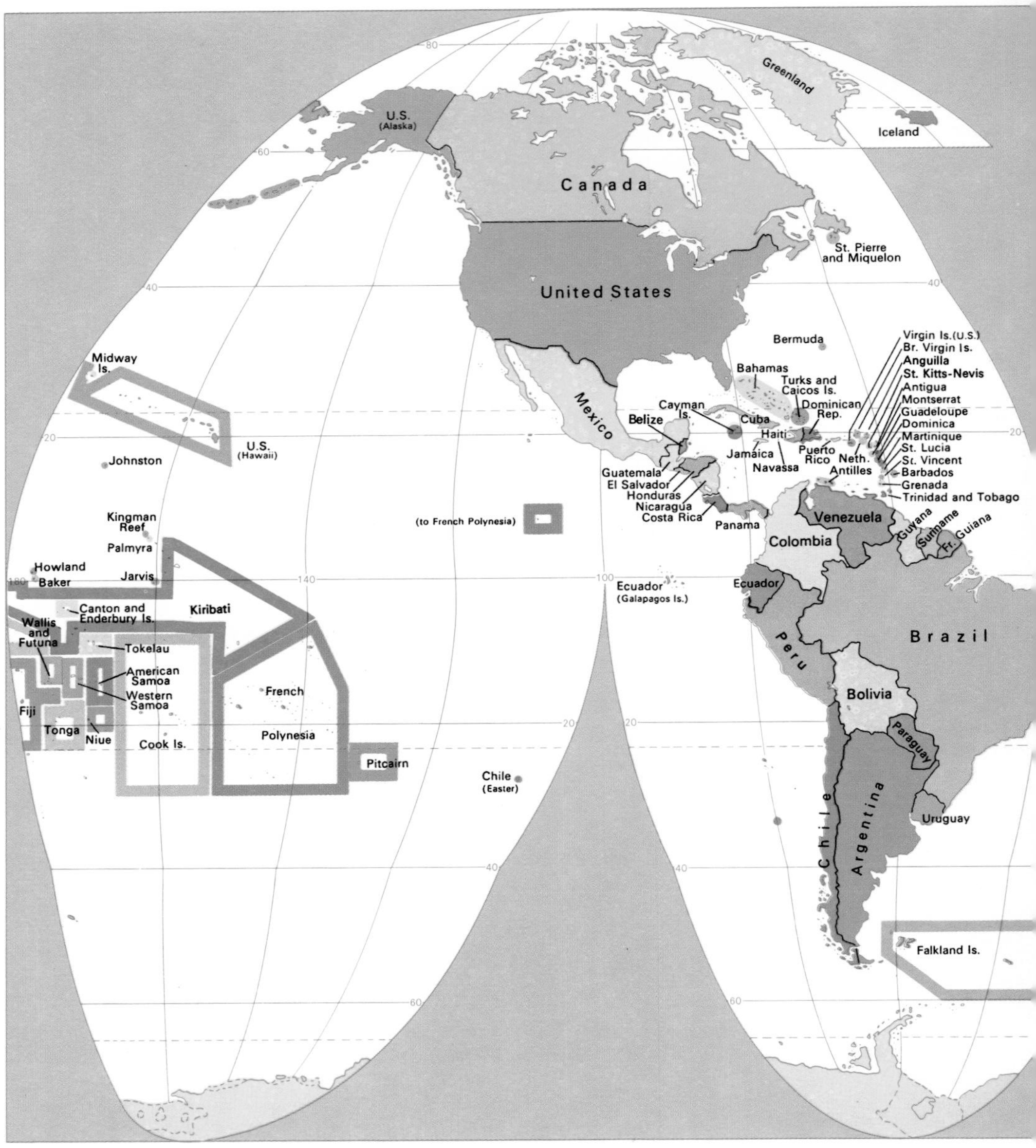

The World July 1, 1979

Every political entity that has a separate administration, whether it is independent or dependent, is named here and is distinguished from adjacent units by color. In all, over 200 political units are named. A noncontiguous part of a country has the same color as the country. If it lies at any distance, it is identified (for example, Alaska, a state of the United States), but if it lies close by, it is not (for example, the island of Corsica, which comprises two departments of France).

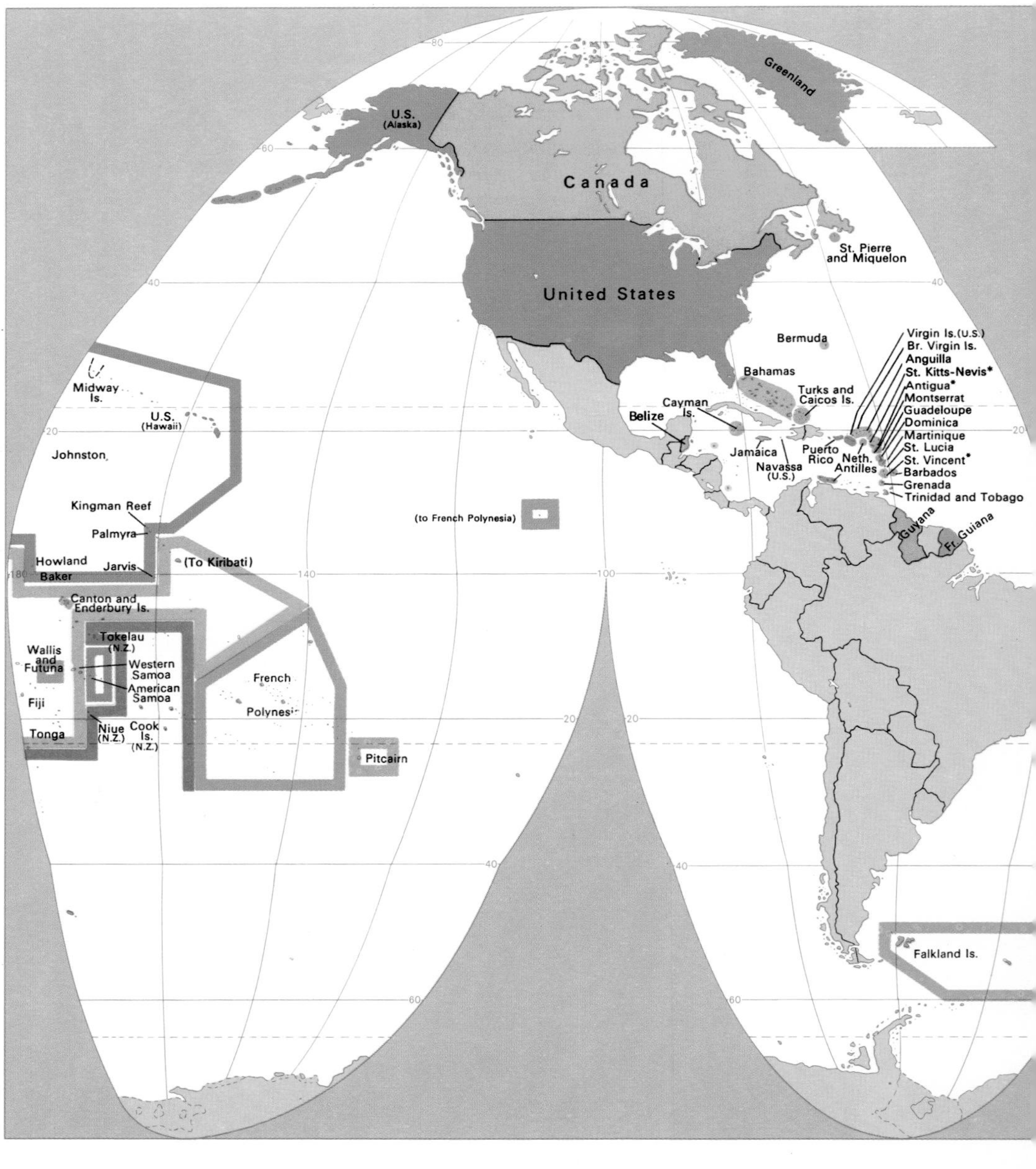

Politically Related Areas

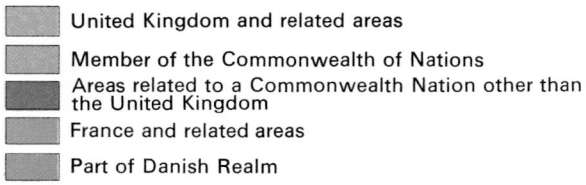

- United Kingdom and related areas
- Member of the Commonwealth of Nations
- Areas related to a Commonwealth Nation other than the United Kingdom
- France and related areas
- Part of Danish Realm
- Part of Netherlands Realm
- United States and related areas

*Virtually independent: major country primarily responsible for foreign relations and defense.

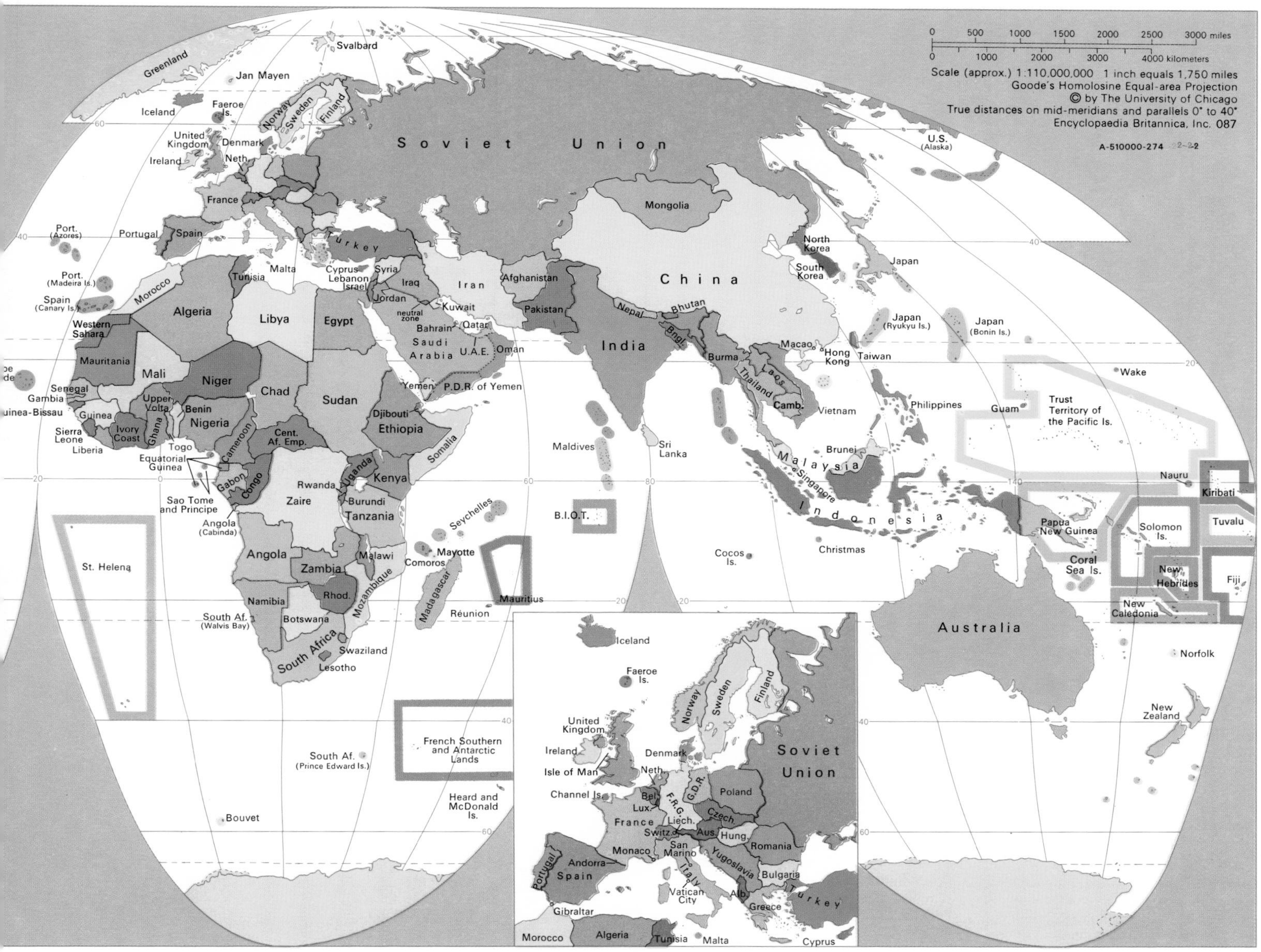
0 500 1000 1500 2000 2500 3000 miles
0 1000 2000 3000 4000 kilometers
Scale (approx.) 1:110,000,000 1 inch equals 1,750 miles
Goode's Homolosine Equal-area Projection
© by The University of Chicago
True distances on mid-meridians and parallels 0° to 40°
Encyclopaedia Britannica, Inc. 087
A-510000-274
Greenland
Svalbard
Jan Mayen
Iceland
Faeroe Is.
United Kingdom
Ireland
Denmark
Neth.
Norway
Sweden
Finland
Soviet Union
U.S. (Alaska)
Mongolia
France
Port. (Azores)
Portugal
Spain
Port. (Madeira Is.)
Spain (Canary Is.)
Morocco
Algeria
Tunisia
Malta
Libya
Egypt
Turkey
Cyprus
Lebanon
Israel
Syria
Iraq
Jordan
Iran
Afghanistan
Pakistan
Kuwait
neutral zone
Bahrain
Qatar
Saudi Arabia
U.A.E.
Oman
North Korea
South Korea
Japan
China
Nepal
Bhutan
Bngl.
India
Burma
Japan (Ryukyu Is.)
Japan (Bonin Is.)
Macao
Hong Kong
Taiwan
Thailand
Laos
Camb.
Vietnam
Philippines
Guam
Wake
Trust Territory of the Pacific Is.
Western Sahara
Mauritania
Mali
Niger
Chad
Sudan
Yemen
P.D.R. of Yemen
Senegal
Gambia
Guinea-Bissau
Guinea
Sierra Leone
Liberia
Ivory Coast
Ghana
Upper Volta
Benin
Nigeria
Togo
Cameroon
Cent. Af. Emp.
Djibouti
Ethiopia
Somalia
Equatorial Guinea
Sao Tome and Principe
Gabon
Congo
Rwanda
Uganda
Kenya
Zaire
Burundi
Tanzania
Seychelles
Maldives
Sri Lanka
B.I.O.T.
Brunei
Malaysia
Singapore
Indonesia
Nauru
Kiribati
Tuvalu
Papua New Guinea
Solomon Is.
Coral Sea Is.
New Hebrides
Fiji
New Caledonia
Christmas
Cocos Is.
Angola (Cabinda)
Angola
Zambia
Malawi
Comoros
Mayotte
Mauritius
Rhod.
Mozambique
Madagascar
Réunion
Namibia
Botswana
South Af. (Walvis Bay)
South Africa
Swaziland
Lesotho
St. Helena
Australia
Norfolk
New Zealand
French Southern and Antarctic Lands
South Af. (Prince Edward Is.)
Heard and McDonald Is.
Bouvet
Iceland
Faeroe Is.
United Kingdom
Ireland
Isle of Man
Channel Is.
Denmark
Neth.
Bel.
Lux.
F.R.G.
G.D.R.
Poland
Czech.
Soviet Union
France
Switz.
Liech.
Aus.
Hung.
Romania
Monaco
San Marino
Italy
Yugoslavia
Bulgaria
Portugal
Andorra
Spain
Vatican City
Alb.
Greece
Turkey
Gibraltar
Morocco
Algeria
Tunisia
Malta
Cyprus

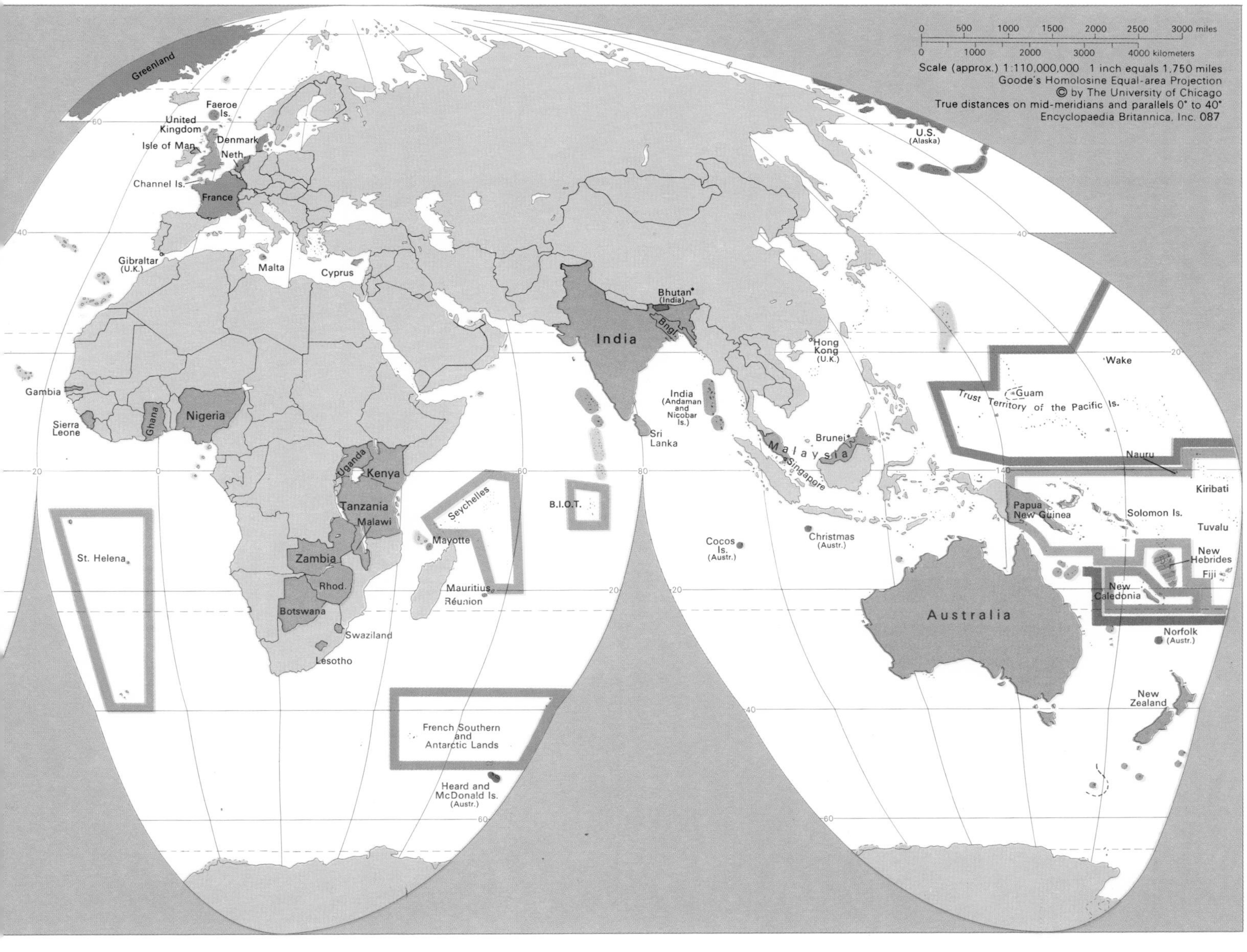
0 500 1000 1500 2000 2500 3000 miles
0 1000 2000 3000 4000 kilometers
Scale (approx.) 1:110,000,000 1 inch equals 1,750 miles
Goode's Homolosine Equal-area Projection
© by The University of Chicago
True distances on mid-meridians and parallels 0° to 40°
Encyclopaedia Britannica, Inc. 087
Greenland
Faeroe Is.
United Kingdom
Isle of Man
Denmark
Neth.
Channel Is.
France
U.S. (Alaska)
Gibraltar (U.K.)
Malta
Cyprus
Bhutan (India)
Bngl.
India
Hong Kong (U.K.)
Wake
Guam
Trust Territory of the Pacific Is.
Gambia
Sierra Leone
Ghana
Nigeria
India (Andaman and Nicobar Is.)
Sri Lanka
Brunei
Malaysia
Singapore
Nauru
Kiribati
Uganda
Kenya
Tanzania
Malawi
Seychelles
B.I.O.T.
Papua New Guinea
Solomon Is.
Tuvalu
St. Helena
Mayotte
Cocos Is. (Austr.)
Christmas (Austr.)
New Hebrides
Fiji
Zambia
Rhod.
Mauritius
Réunion
New Caledonia
Botswana
Swaziland
Lesotho
Australia
Norfolk (Austr.)
New Zealand
French Southern and Antarctic Lands
Heard and McDonald Is. (Austr.)

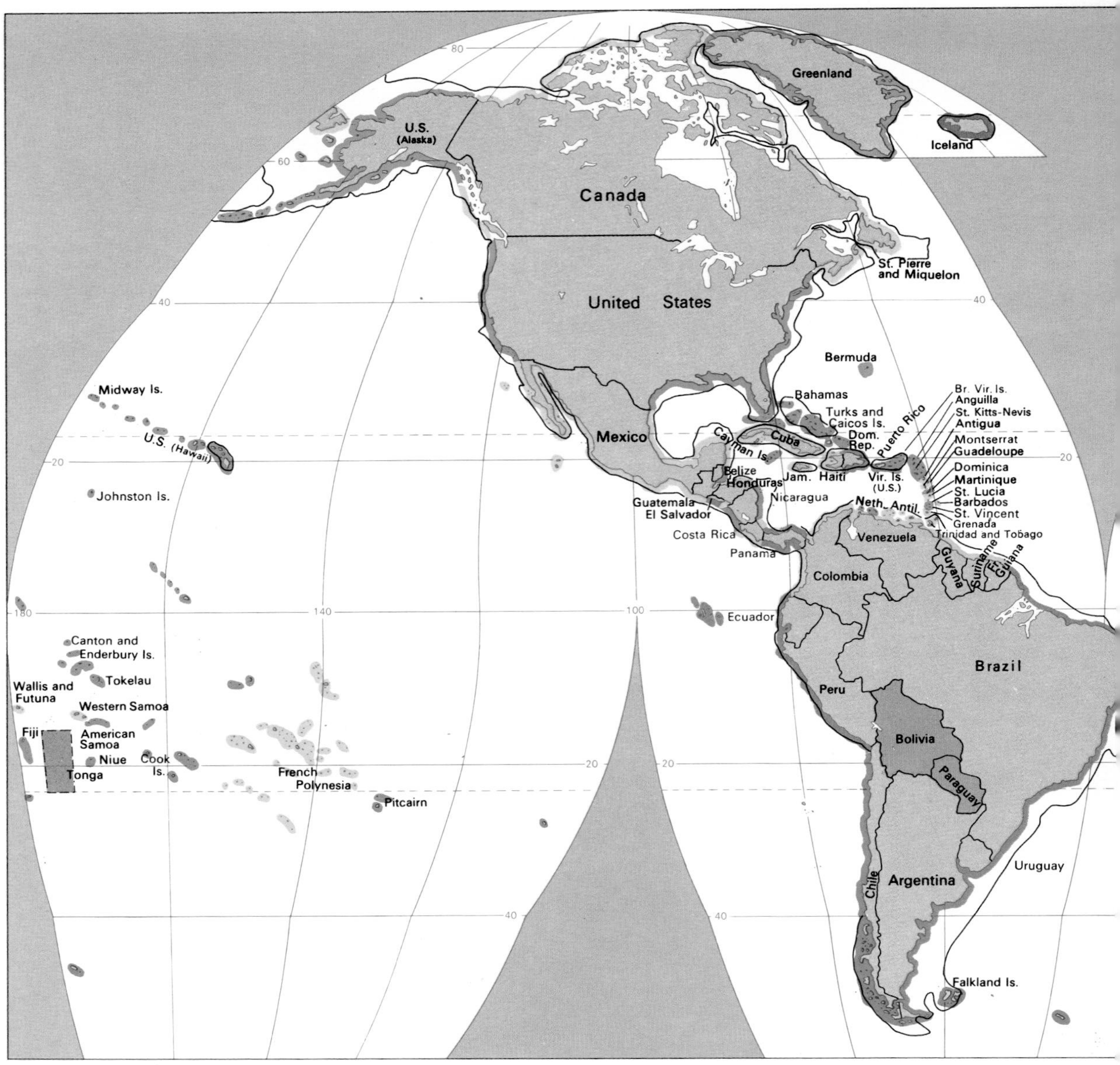

Seaward Claims

Common territorial sea claims

- 3 nautical miles
- 6 nautical miles
- 12 nautical miles

Less common claims

- 4 nautical miles
- 10 nautical miles
- Over 12 nautical miles
- Unusual claim

Other features

- Landlocked countries
- Continental shelf

Note: Territorial claims of outlying islands to their offshore waters are the same as those of the administering country.

Coastal states have long claimed jurisdiction over adjacent waters as a measure of defense from attack, in order to exploit offshore resources, and to control such matters as customs, sanitation, immigration, and criminal acts. Recently most states have become more aware of offshore fishing rights and of the resources on and under the floor of the sea.

Traditionally, the breadth of the territorial sea was generally three nautical miles, but in recent years greater claims have become more and more common. Today, the breadth varies sharply from place to place, for each state unilaterally establishes a limit according to its own political and economic objectives. The world map and table show the variety of claims.

Within the last few years a number of states have laid claim to offshore fishing zones for exclusive rights in waters previously accessible to fishermen from all states.

Numerous disputes involving conflicting claims prompted the United Nations to convene the several Law of the Sea conferences, the First in 1958, the Second in 1960, and the Third, sessions 1974-78. The diagrams *Offshore zones* illustrate the division of the waters adjacent to a coastal state into four zones as defined by the Law of the Sea Conventions: territorial sea, contiguous zone, high seas, and continental shelf. The low-water line along the coast has been defined as the baseline from which the limits of these various zones are measured. Each state has determined the breadth of its territorial sea where it may exercise sovereign control over the water, the seabed, and the airspace. Seaward of this zone a state may also establish a contiguous zone where it has limited jurisdictional rights. The high seas encompass all waters beyond the territorial sea; these are open to all states for navigation and other activities not precluded by convention or agreement.

The physical continental shelf may be very narrow or may extend seaward for hundreds of miles. The Law of the Sea Convention has therefore defined the limits of the continental shelf where a coastal state has the exclusive right to exploit seabed resources. This legal version of the shelf, as illustrated in the diagram, extends from the outer limit of the territorial sea to where the depth is 200 meters, or to greater depths if they will admit exploitation of the resources of the seabed and subsoil.

The thirty landlocked states must negotiate with coastal states for rights of transit to the sea, as well as for any rights within offshore jurisdictional zones.

Extended claims tend to decrease the area of the high seas and restrict or completely close narrow straits and channels that provide access to seas and gulfs. These broader claims could interfere seriously with established shipping lanes through which food and fuel resources pass. In addition, they could disrupt international air routes and impede military operations.

At the Law of the Sea conferences, many complex problems were faced in an effort to arrive at a territorial sea of uniform breadth and to promote international cooperation. Although the conferences were successful in resolving many legal maritime matters they failed to standardize the breadth of the territorial sea in a manner agreeable to all states. The small maps on this page illustrate the solutions for two types of claims. Conferences in the future may achieve international accord on jurisdictional issues.

Offshore zones

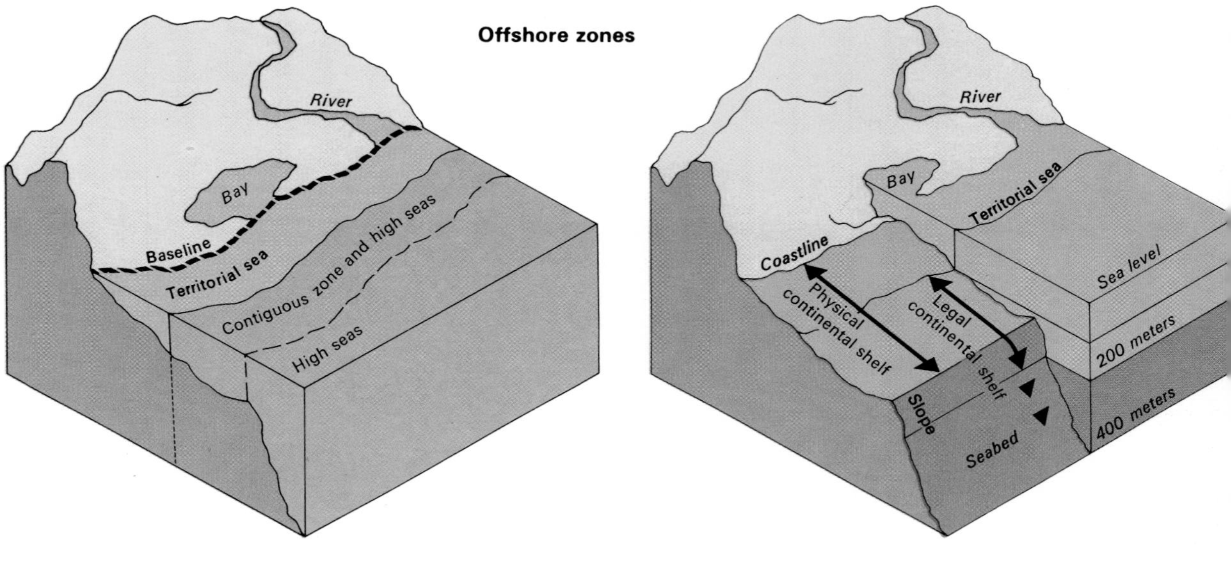

Irregular coastline of Norway

Norway measures its territorial sea from a straight baseline, which in general runs along the outer fringe of offshore islands and coastal promontories. The Law of the Sea Convention permits this type of claim in the case of highly irregular coastlines fringed with islands. In other cases the coastal features do not justify such claims to additional waters, and the claims may not be recognized.

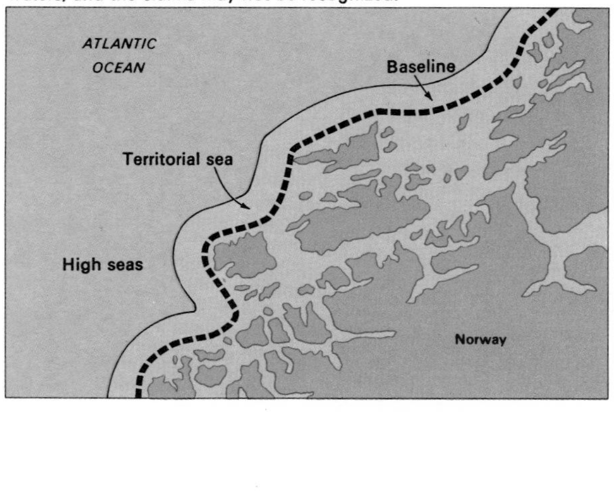

Overlapping claims in the Persian Gulf

The waters of the Persian Gulf are less than 200 meters in depth and the entire seabed is continental shelf. To determine the extent of jurisdiction that each state has over the resources of the seabed beyond its territorial sea, the Law of the Sea Convention provides for median lines, measured from the same baseline as the territorial sea. The median lines divide the continental shelf between opposite and adjacent states.

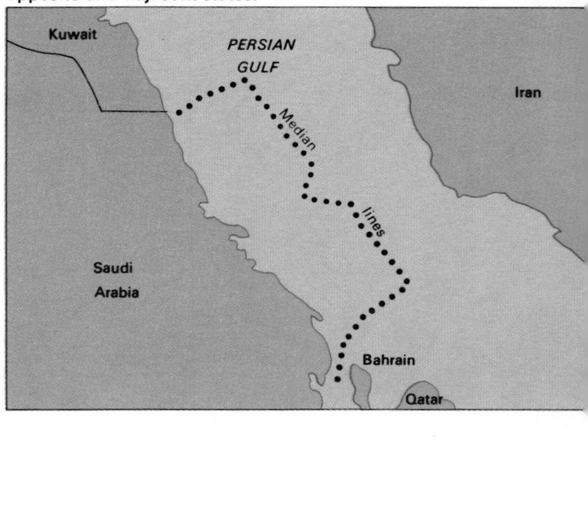

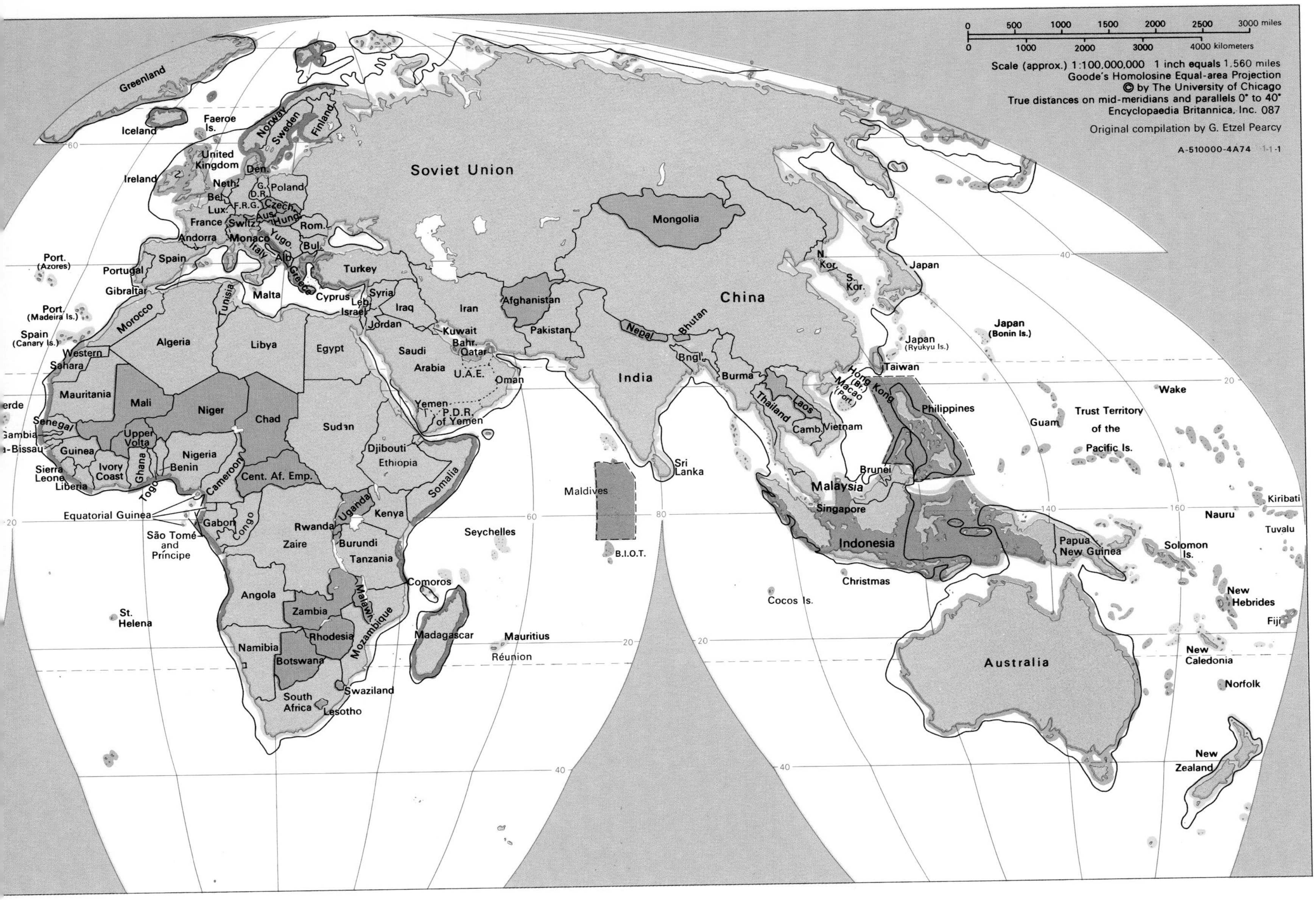

Political unit	Territorial sea claim*	Fishing claim*†
Albania	15 A	
Algeria	12	
Angola	20	200
Argentina	200 A	
Australia	3 A	12
Bahamas	3	200
Bahrain	3	
Bangladesh	12 A	200
Barbados	12	200
Belgium	3	6
Belize	3 B	
Benin	200	
Brazil	200 A	
Brunei	3 B	
Bulgaria	12	
Burma	12 A	200
Cambodia	12 A	200
Cameroon	50 A	
Canada	12 A	200
Cape Verde	12	200
Chile	3	200
China	12 A	
Colombia	12	200
Comoros	12	200
Congo	200	
Costa Rica	12	200
Cuba	12 A	200
Cyprus	12	
Denmark	3 A	200
Djibouti	12	
Dominican Republic	6 A	200
Ecuador	200 A	
Egypt	12 A	
El Salvador	200	
Equatorial Guinea	12	
Ethiopia	12 A	
Fiji	12 C	
Finland	4 A	12
France	12 A	200
French Guiana	12 B	80
Gabon	100 A	150
Gambia, The	50	
German Dem. Rep.	3 A	200
Germany, Fed. Rep. of	3 A	200
Ghana	200	
Gibraltar	3 B	
Greece	6	
Greenland	3 B	12
Grenada	12	200
Guatemala	12 A	200
Guinea	200 A	
Guinea-Bissau	12	200
Guyana	12	200
Haiti	12 A	200
Honduras	12	
Hong Kong	3 B	
Iceland	4 A	200
India	12	200
Indonesia	12 C	
Iran	12 A	50
Iraq	12	
Ireland	3 A	200
Israel	6	
Italy	12	
Ivory Coast	12	200
Jamaica	12	
Japan	12	200
Jordan	3	
Kenya	12 A	
Korea, North	12	200
Korea, South	12 A	200
Kuwait	12	
Lebanon	‡	6
Liberia	200	
Libya	12 A	
Madagascar	50 A	150
Malaysia	12 A	
Maldives		35–300
Malta	12 A	25
Mauritania	70 A	200
Mauritius	12 A	200
Mexico	12 A	200
Monaco	12	
Morocco	12	70
Mozambique	12 A	200
Namibia	6 B	12
Nauru	12	
Netherlands	3	200
New Caledonia	12 B	
New Zealand	12	200
Nicaragua	3	200
Nigeria	30	
Norway	4 A	200
Oman	12 A	200
Pakistan	12	200
Panama	200 A	
Papua New Guinea	12	200
Peru	200	
Philippines	C	
Poland	12 A	200
Portugal	12 A	200
Qatar	3	
Romania	12	
São Tomé and Príncipe	12	200
Saudi Arabia	12 A	
Senegal	150 A	200
Seychelles	12 D	200
Sierra Leone	200	
Singapore	3	
Solomon Islands	3 D	200
Somalia	200 A	
South Africa	12	200
Soviet Union	12 A	200
Spain	12	200
Sri Lanka	12 A	200
Sudan	12 A	
Suriname	12	200
Sweden	4 A	200
Syria	12 A	
Taiwan	3	12
Tanzania	50 A	
Thailand	12 A	
Togo	30	200
Tonga	C	
Trinidad and Tobago	12	
Tunisia	12 E	
Turkey	6–12 A	
United Arab Emirates	3 or 12	
United Kingdom	3 A	200
United States	3	200
Uruguay	200	
Venezuela	12 A	200
Vietnam	12	200
Western Sahara	6 D	
Western Samoa	12	
Yemen	12	
Yemen, P.D.R.	12	200
Yugoslavia	10 A	12
Zaire	12	

* Nautical miles.
† When claim is beyond the territorial sea.
‡ No specific claim.

A. Measured from a straight (or extended) baseline.
B. Same as that of administering country.
C. Extends beyond a perimeter drawn around archipelago.
D. Newly independent; assumed to be same as former metropole.
E. For part of the coast, the territorial sea follows the 50-meter isobath (max. breadth 65 mi.).

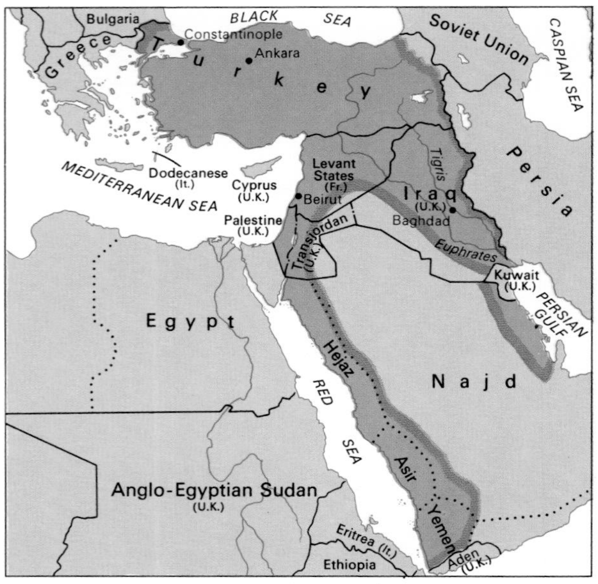

Dissolution of the Ottoman Empire

Ottoman Empire 1913

Administrative boundaries (1923) as a result of WW I settlements; dotted are indefinite

Dissolution of Austria-Hungary

Austria-Hungary 1913

Administrative boundaries (1923) as a result of WW I settlements

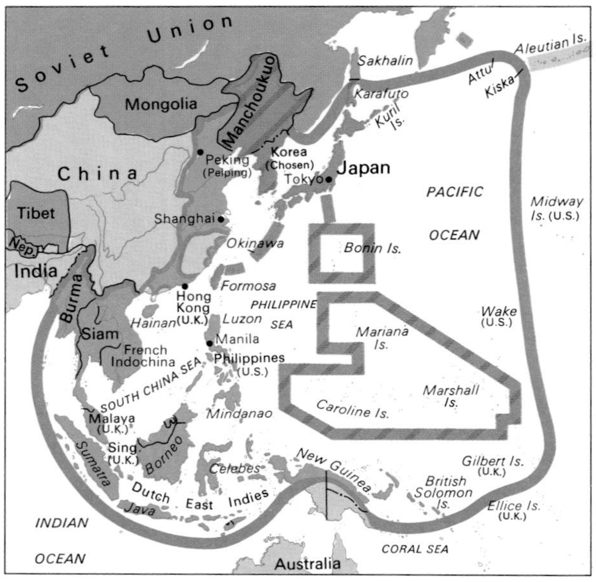

Japanese Expansion World War II

Japan 1939

Japanese dependencies 1939

Maximum occupation

Neutral states

States joining Allies 1945

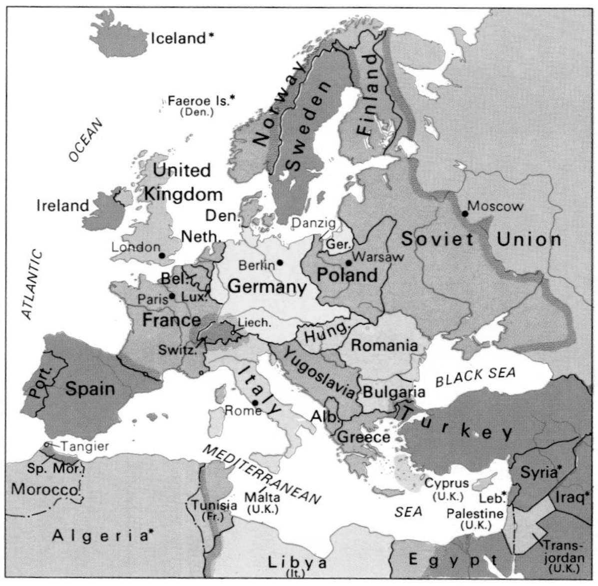

Axis Expansion World War II

Germany 1939

Other Axis Powers 1940-45

Maximum occupation

Neutral states

States joining Allies 1943-45

*Occupied by Allies

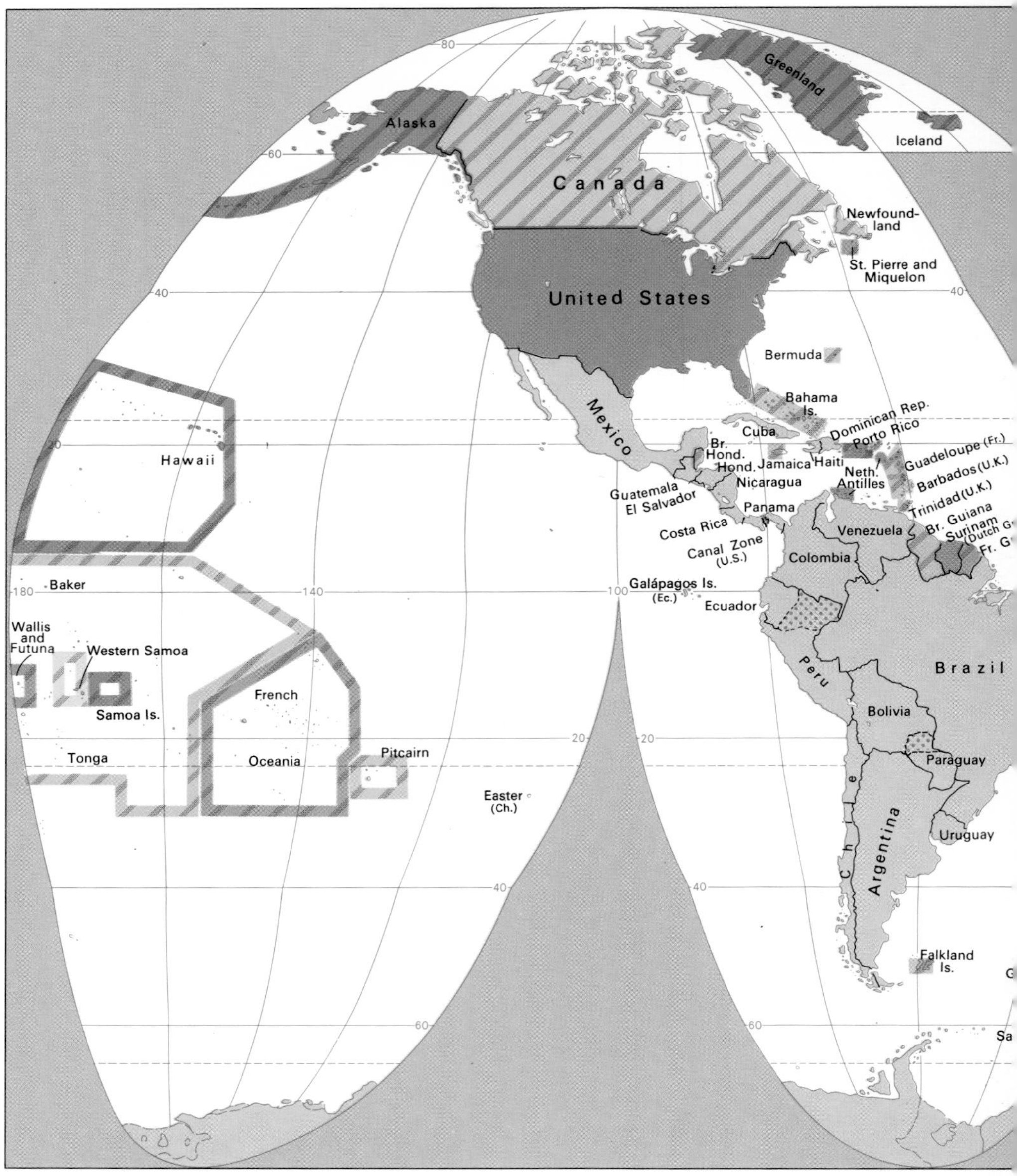

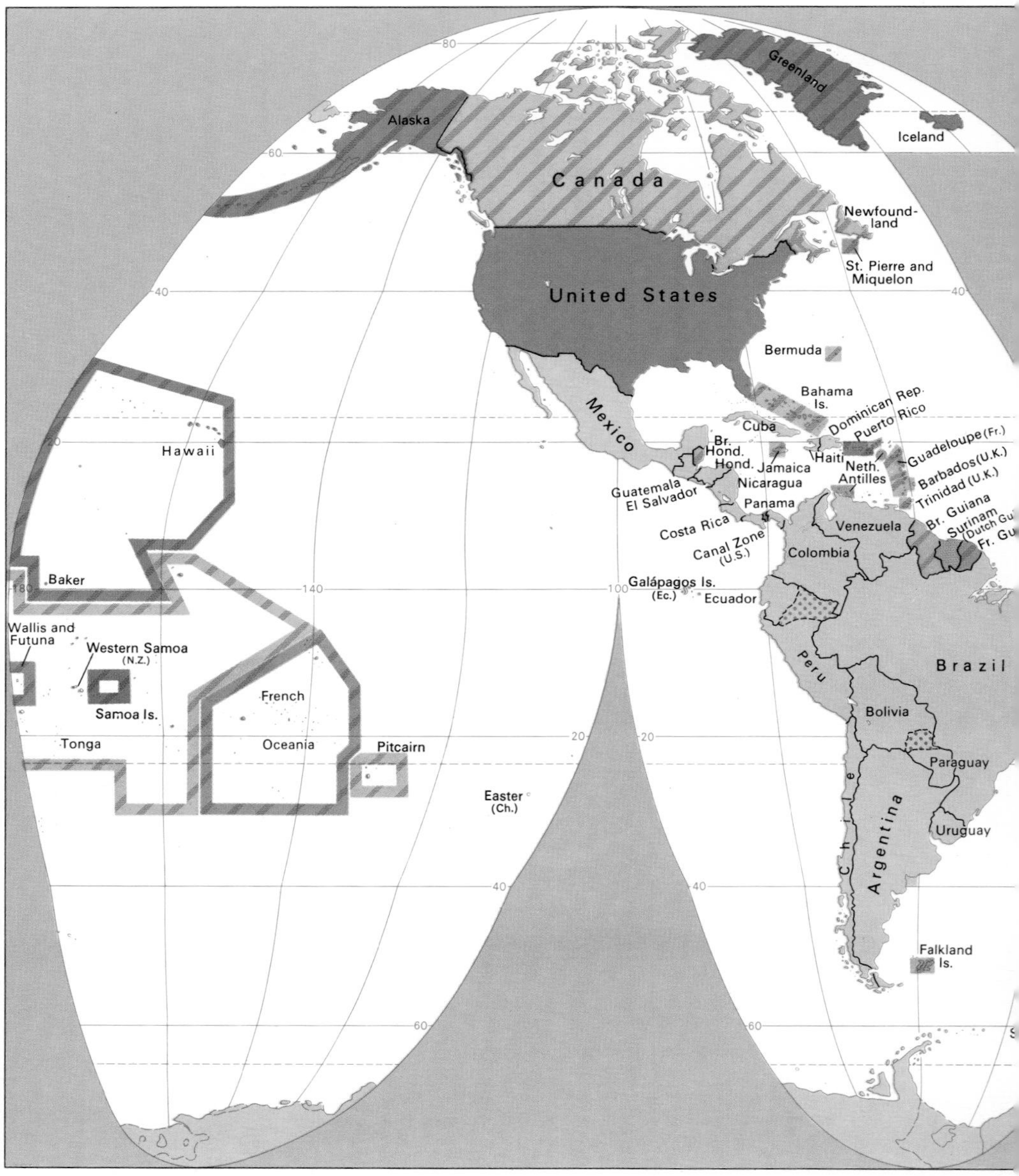

The World January 1, 1914

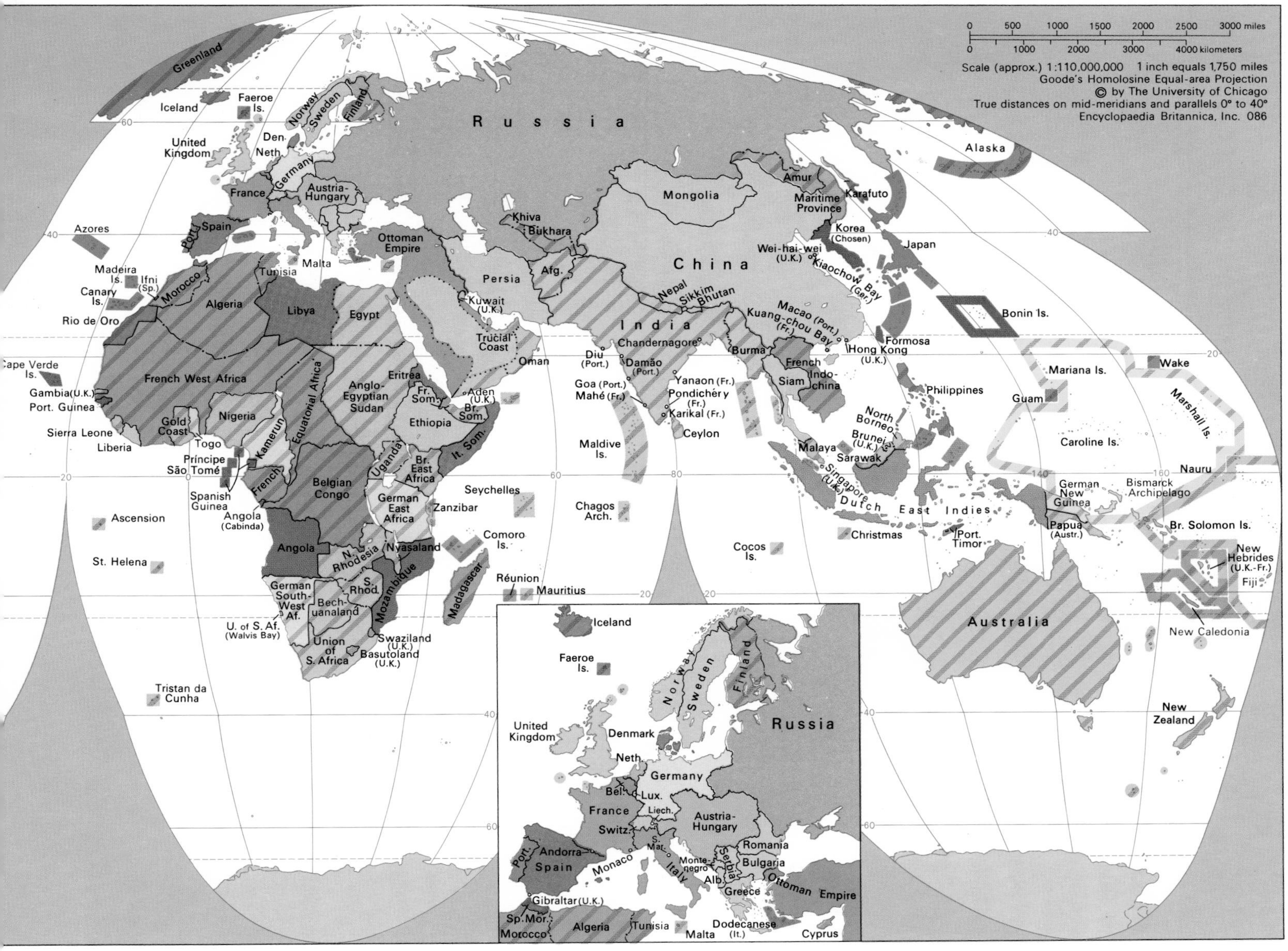

- United Kingdom
  - Related areas
- France
  - Related areas
- Portugal
  - Related areas
- Spain
  - Related areas
- Netherlands
  - Related areas
- Belgium
  - Related areas
- Germany
  - Related areas
- Denmark
  - Related areas
- Japan
  - Related areas
- Italy
  - Related areas
- United States
  - Related areas
- Ottoman Empire
- Russia
  - Related areas
- Austria-Hungary
- Countries without related areas
- Disputed areas
- Intercolonial boundary

The World January 1, 1937

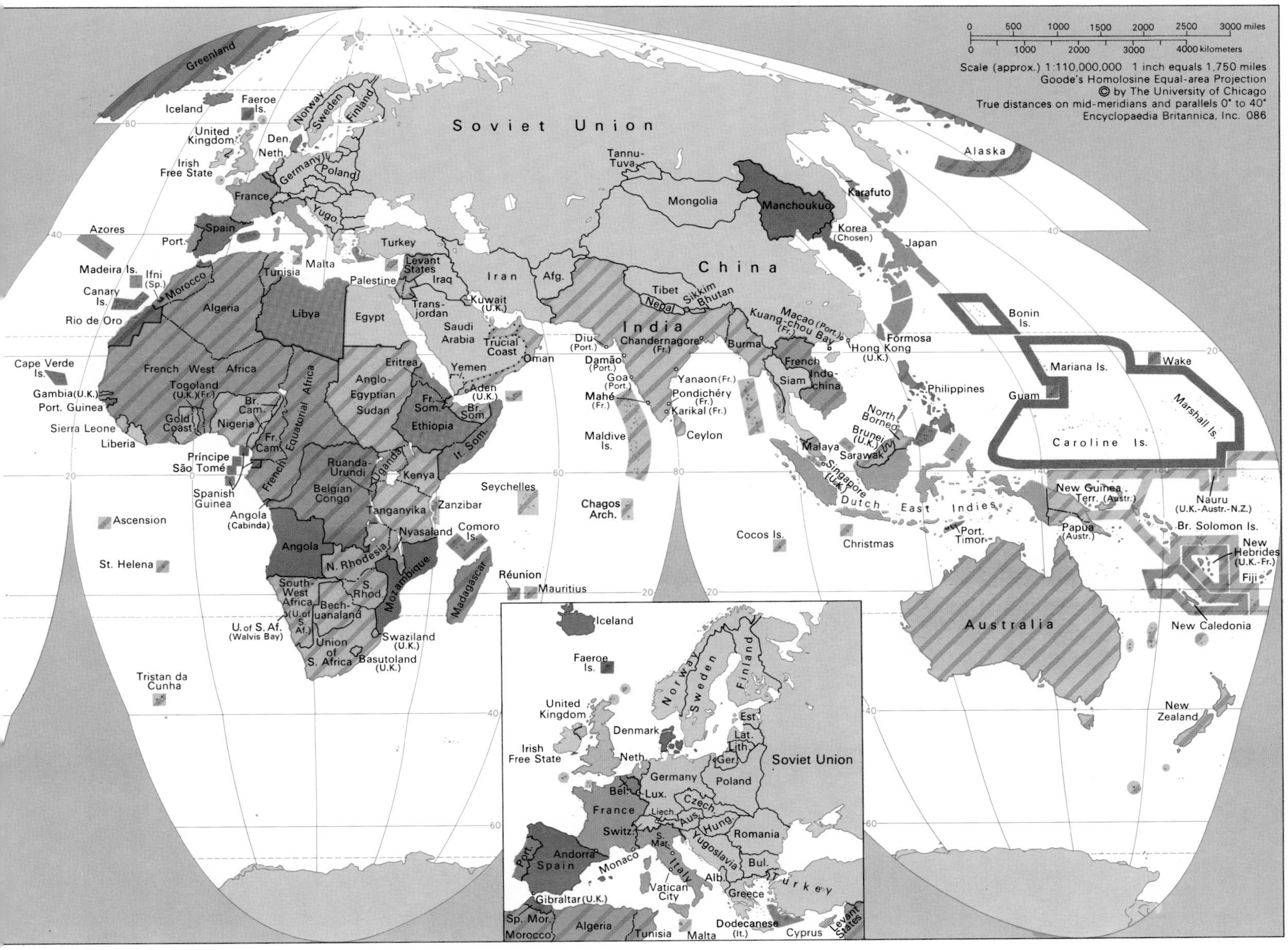

- United Kingdom
  - Related areas
- France
  - Related areas
- Portugal
  - Related areas
- Spain
  - Related areas
- Netherlands
  - Related areas
- Belgium
  - Related areas
- Denmark
  - Related areas
- Japan
  - Related areas
- Italy
  - Related areas
- United States
  - Related areas
- Countries without related areas
- Disputed areas
- Intercolonial boundary

Population

Extent of urbanization
Percent of total population urban

- 80% and more
- 60 to 79%
- 40 to 59%
- 20 to 39%
- Less than 20%

Major metropolitan areas

- 5,000,000 and more persons
- 3,000,000 to 4,999,999
- 2,000,000 to 2,999,999

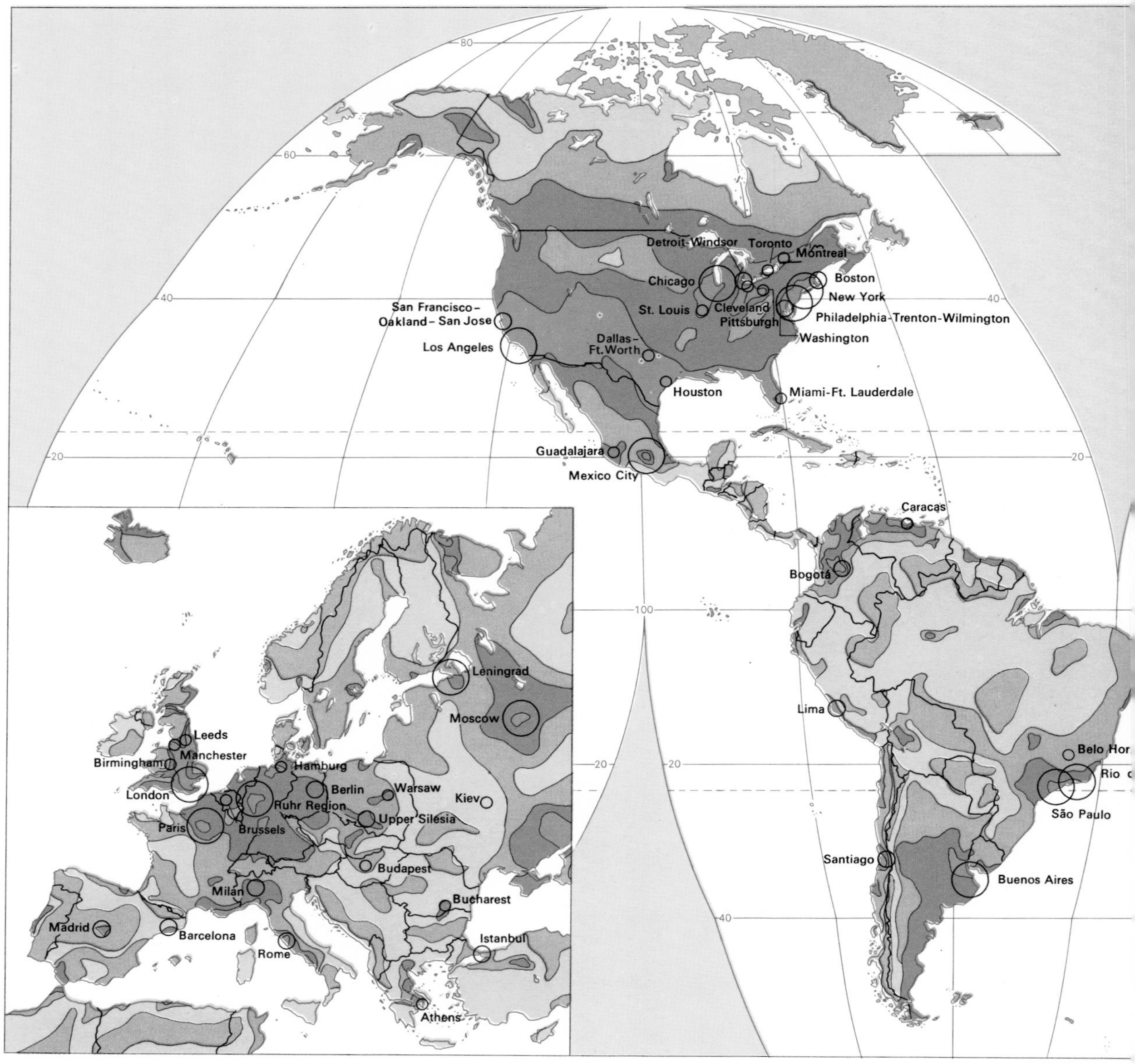

Detroit-Windsor
Toronto
Montreal
Boston
New York
Philadelphia-Trenton-Wilmington
Washington
Chicago
St. Louis
Cleveland
Pittsburgh
San Francisco-Oakland-San Jose
Los Angeles
Dallas-Ft. Worth
Houston
Miami-Ft. Lauderdale
Guadalajara
Mexico City
Caracas
Bogotá
Lima
Belo Hor
Rio
São Paulo
Santiago
Buenos Aires
Leningrad
Moscow
Kiev
Leeds
Manchester
Birmingham
London
Hamburg
Berlin
Warsaw
Ruhr Region
Upper Silesia
Paris
Brussels
Budapest
Milan
Bucharest
Madrid
Barcelona
Rome
Istanbul
Athens
80
60
40
20
100

The increase in the proportion of urban to total population reflects the change from a dispersed pattern of human settlement to a concentrated one. In industrialized countries the proportion of people living in cities increases mainly through movement from country to city, due to the attraction of higher wages and greater opportunities, a process which in most cases started about 100 years ago. In the underdeveloped countries, where in recent years the number of people living in cities has risen sharply, the proportion of urban population has not increased appreciably; here the urban growth is generally due not so much to rural-urban migration as it is to the natural population increase in both urban and rural areas, and to the decline in the urban mortality rate.

In population studies the definitions of "urban" differ from country to country, but generally take into account the total number of people in a settlement and the percent of the population engaged in nonagricultural activities. The map shows the degree of urbanization (the proportion of urban to total population), considering as urban those communities having no fewer than 2,000 inhabitants, more than half of them dependent on nonfarm occupations. Also indicated are selected metropolitan areas where cities have expanded beyond their boundaries into the surrounding regions in patterns of continuous settlement oriented toward the central cities.

Age and sex composition

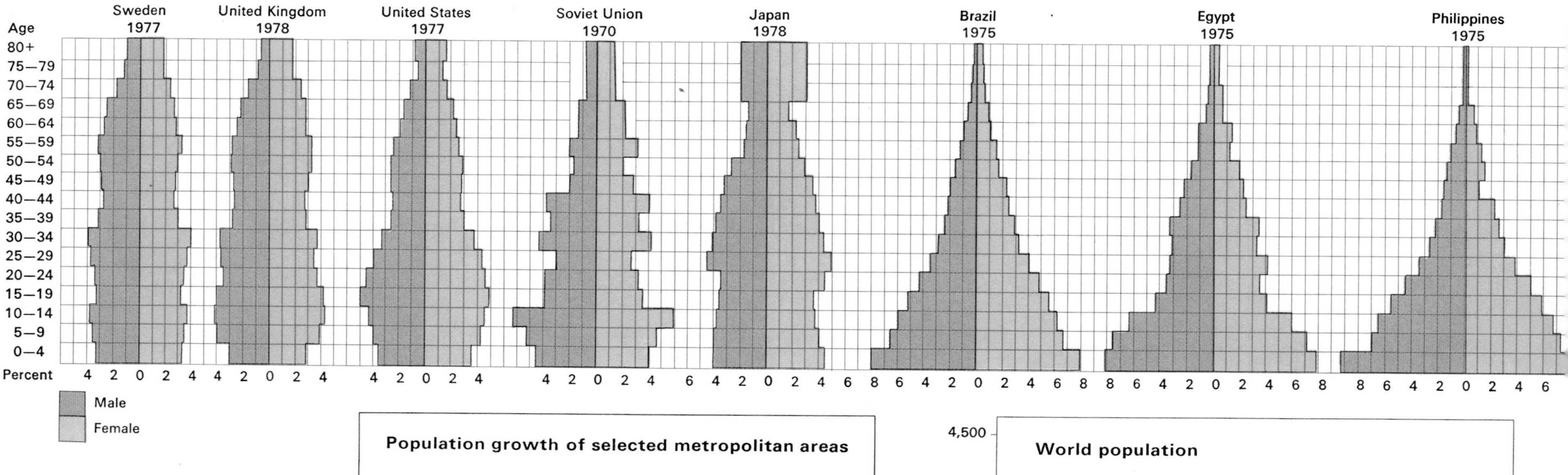

Sweden 1977
United Kingdom 1978
United States 1977
Soviet Union 1970
Japan 1978
Brazil 1975
Egypt 1975
Philippines 1975
Age
80+
75—79
70—74
65—69
60—64
55—59
50—54
45—49
40—44
35—39
30—34
25—29
20—24
15—19
10—14
5—9
0—4
Percent
4 2 0 2 4 4 2 0 2 4 4 2 0 2 4 4 2 0 2 4 6 4 2 0 2 4 6 8 6 4 2 0 2 4 6 8 8 6 4 2 0 2 4 6 8 8 6 4 2 0 2 4 6
Male
Female

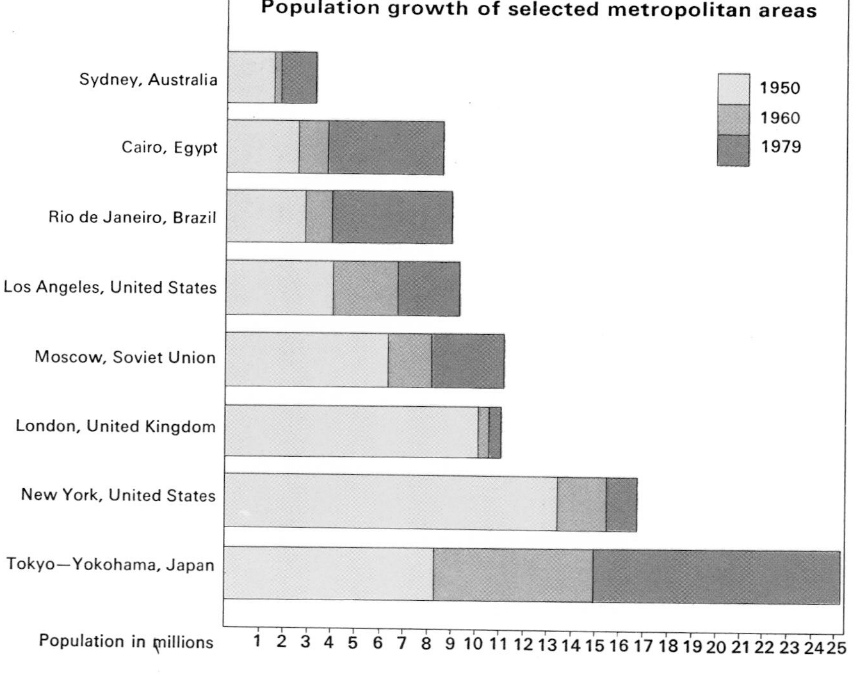

Population growth of selected metropolitan areas
1950
1960
1979
Sydney, Australia
Cairo, Egypt
Rio de Janeiro, Brazil
Los Angeles, United States
Moscow, Soviet Union
London, United Kingdom
New York, United States
Tokyo—Yokohama, Japan
Population in millions
1 2 3 4 5 6 7 8 9 10 11 12 13 14 15 16 17 18 19 20 21 22 23 24 25

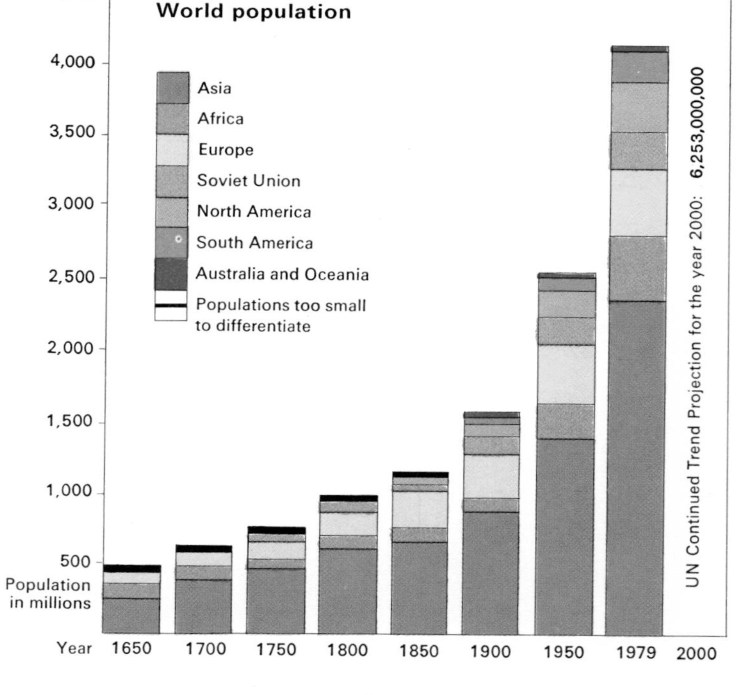

World population
Asia
Africa
Europe
Soviet Union
North America
South America
Australia and Oceania
Populations too small to differentiate
4,500
4,000
3,500
3,000
2,500
2,000
1,500
1,000
500
Population in millions
Year 1650 1700 1750 1800 1850 1900 1950 1979 2000
UN Continued Trend Projection for the year 2000: 6,253,000,000

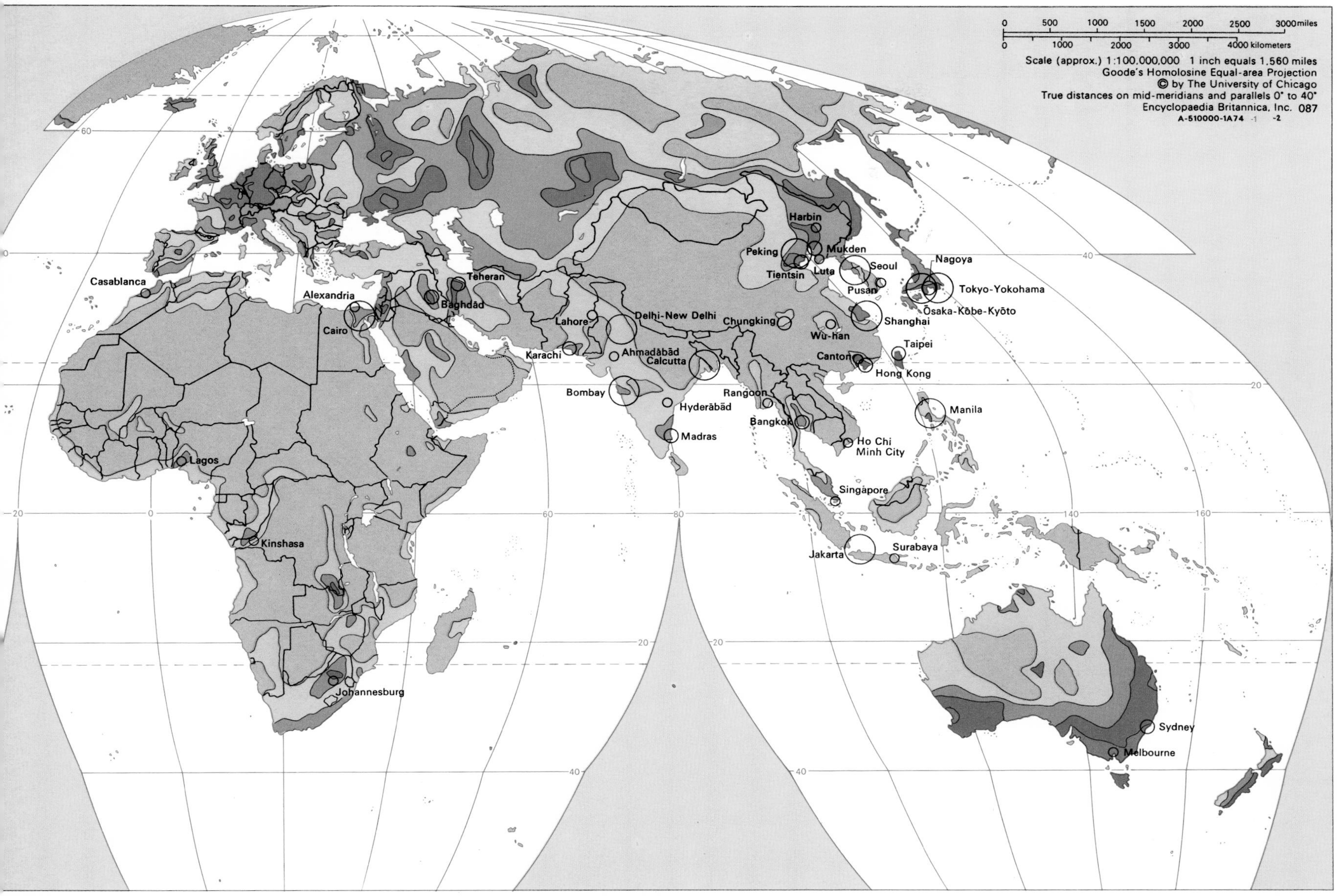
0 500 1000 1500 2000 2500 3000 miles
0 1000 2000 3000 4000 kilometers
Scale (approx.) 1:100,000,000 1 inch equals 1,560 miles
Goode's Homolosine Equal-area Projection
© by The University of Chicago
True distances on mid-meridians and parallels 0° to 40°
Encyclopaedia Britannica, Inc. 087
A-510000-1A74
Casablanca
Alexandria
Cairo
Teheran
Baghdād
Karachi
Lahore
Delhi-New Delhi
Ahmadābād
Calcutta
Bombay
Hyderābād
Madras
Rangoon
Bangkok
Ho Chi Minh City
Singapore
Jakarta
Surabaya
Manila
Chungking
Wu-han
Shanghai
Canton
Hong Kong
Taipei
Peking
Tientsin
Harbin
Mukden
Luta
Seoul
Pusan
Nagoya
Tokyo-Yokohama
Ōsaka-Kōbe-Kyōto
Lagos
Kinshasa
Johannesburg
Sydney
Melbourne

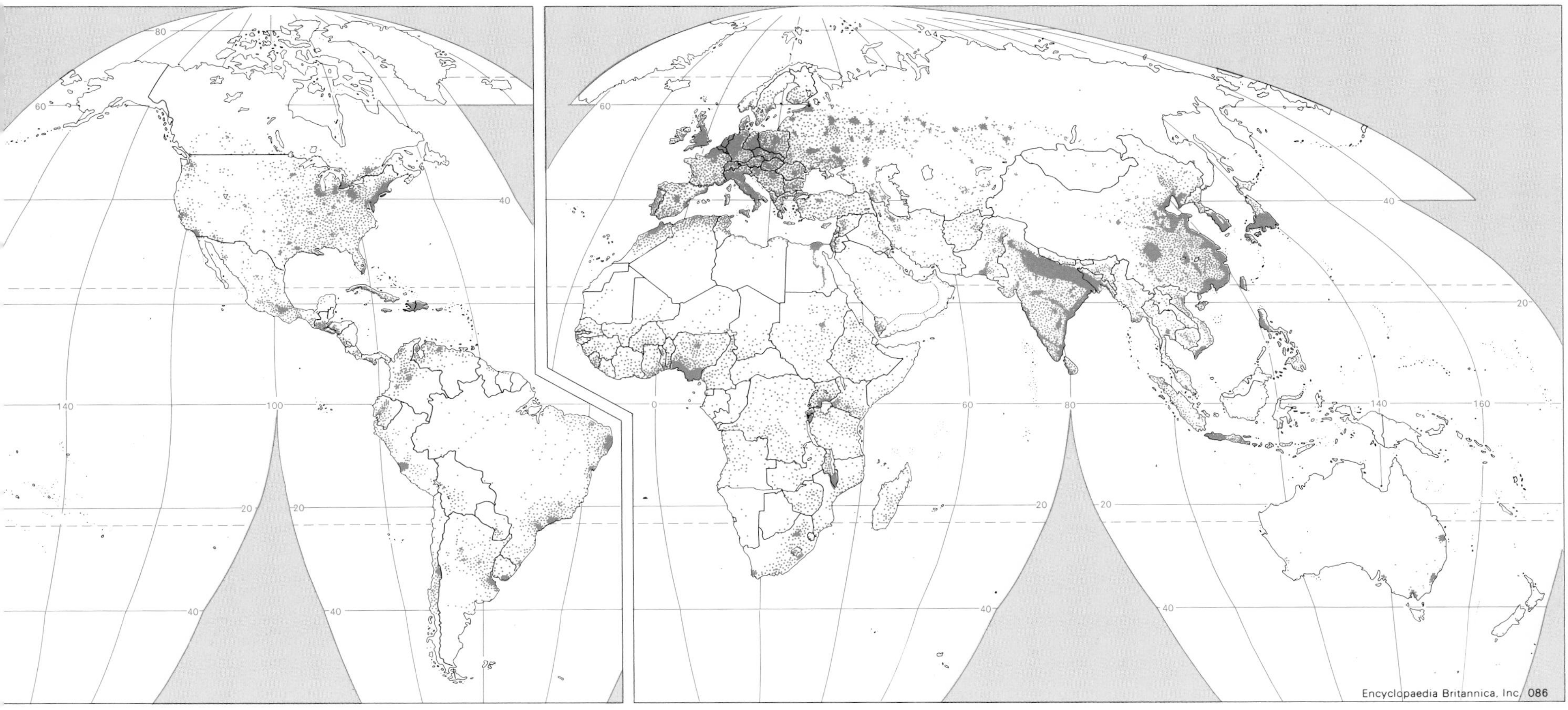
Encyclopaedia Britannica, Inc. 086

Distribution

Each dot represents 100,000 persons. The dots show the location of concentrated areas of population rather than the location of cities.

Religions

The majority of the inhabitants in each of the areas colored on the map share the religious tradition indicated. Letter symbols show religious traditions shared by at least 25% of the inhabitants within areal units no smaller than one thousand square miles. Therefore minority religions of city-dwellers have generally not been represented.

R	Roman Catholicism
P	Protestantism
E	Eastern Orthodox religions (including Armenian, Coptic, Ethiopian, Greek, and Russian Orthodox)
M	Mormonism
C	Christianity, undifferentiated by branch (chiefly mingled Protestantism and Roman Catholicism, neither predominant)
I	Islam, predominantly Sunni
Sh	Islam, predominantly Shia
	Theravada Buddhism
L	Lamaism
H	Hinduism
J	Judaism
Ch	Chinese religions*
Ja	Japanese religions*
	Korean religions*
	Vietnamese religions*
T	Simple ethnic (tribal) religions
Sk	Sikhism
	Countries under Communist regimes; traditional religions often subject to restraint
	Uninhabited

*In certain Eastern Asian areas, most of the people have plural religious affiliations. Chinese, Korean, and Vietnamese religions include Mahayana Buddhism, Taoism, Confucianism, and folk cults. The Japanese religions include Shinto and Mahayana Buddhism.

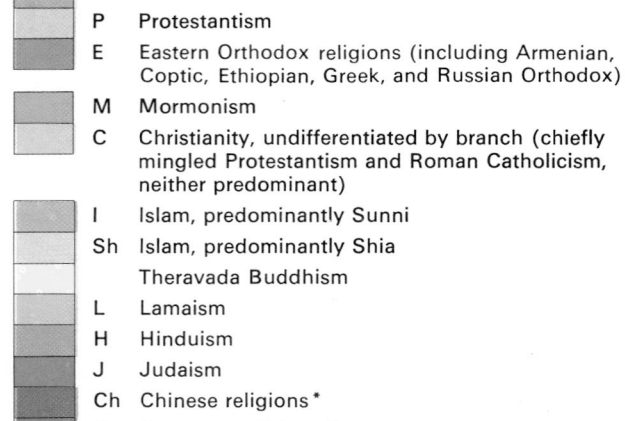

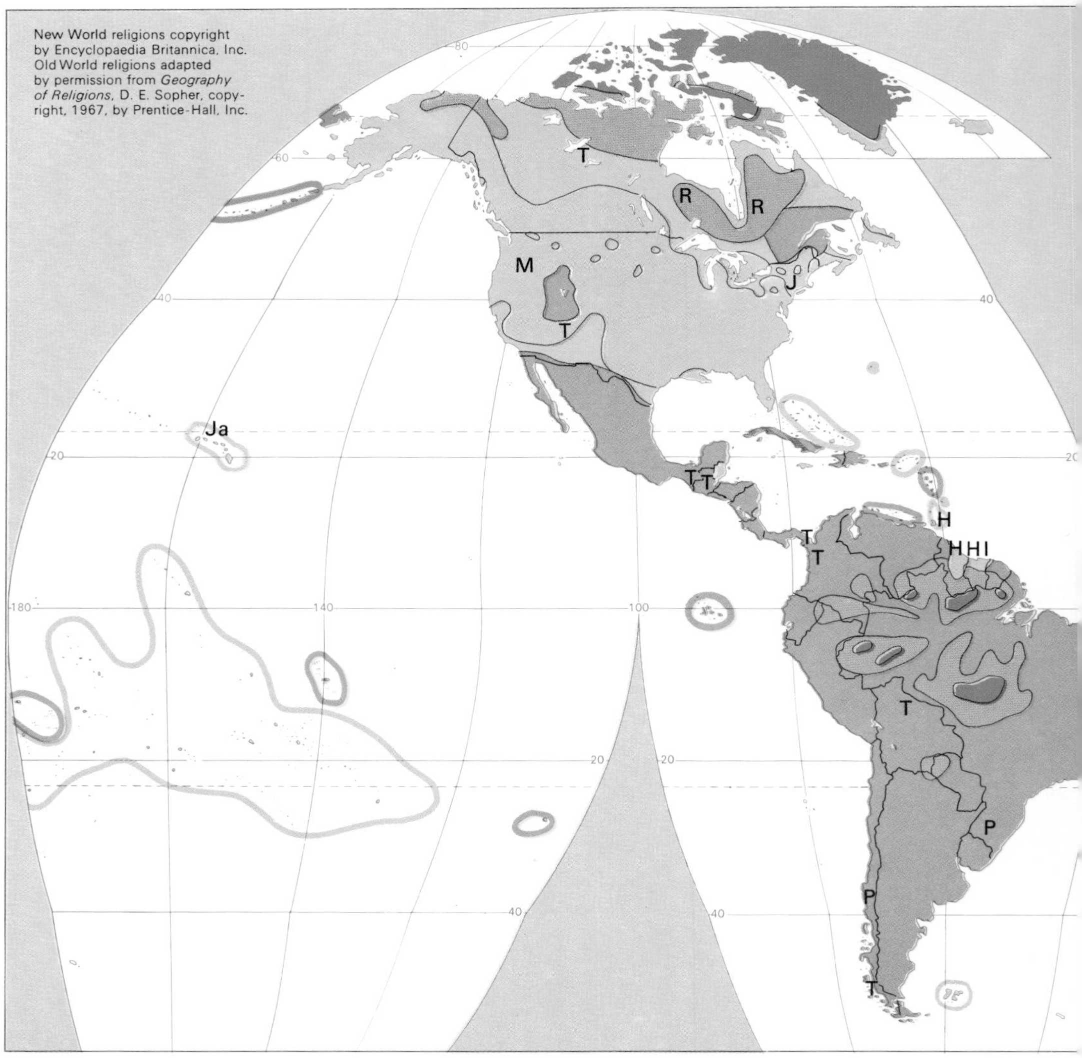
New World religions copyright by Encyclopaedia Britannica, Inc. Old World religions adapted by permission from *Geography of Religions*, D. E. Sopher, copyright, 1967, by Prentice-Hall, Inc.
T
R
R
M
J
T
Ja
T T
T
T
H
HHI
T
P
P
T

Languages

Languages of Europe

The following languages are ranked in descending order by number of speakers. Languages spoken by more than 4 million persons are indicated by color. Others listed, spoken by fewer than 4 million persons, are named on the map.

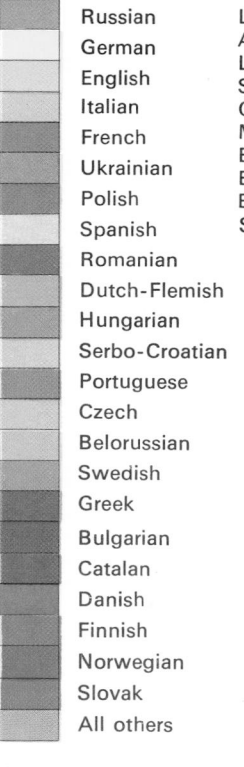

Russian
German
English
Italian
French
Ukrainian
Polish
Spanish
Romanian
Dutch-Flemish
Hungarian
Serbo-Croatian
Portuguese
Czech
Belorussian
Swedish
Greek
Bulgarian
Catalan
Danish
Finnish
Norwegian
Slovak
All others

Lithuanian	Macedonian	Icelandic	
Albanian	Turkish	Karelian	
Latvian	Welsh	Lusatian	
Slovenian	Mari	Lappish	
Chuvash	Romansh	Liv	
Mordvinian	Irish-Gaelic	Frisian	
Basque	Scots-Gaelic	Ladin	
Breton	Komi	Friulian	
Estonian	Maltese	Adyge	
Sardinian			

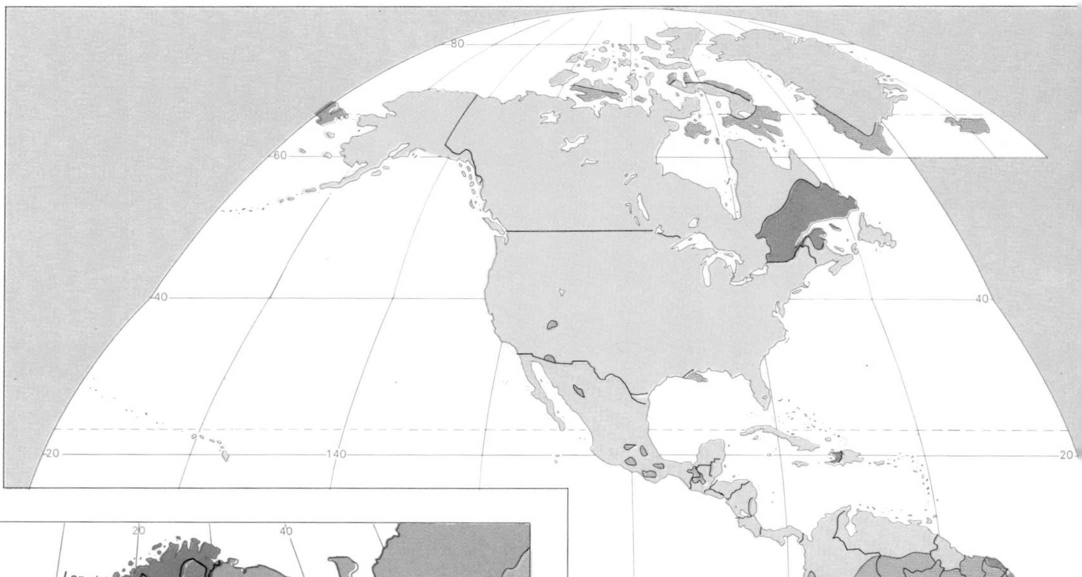
Quechua

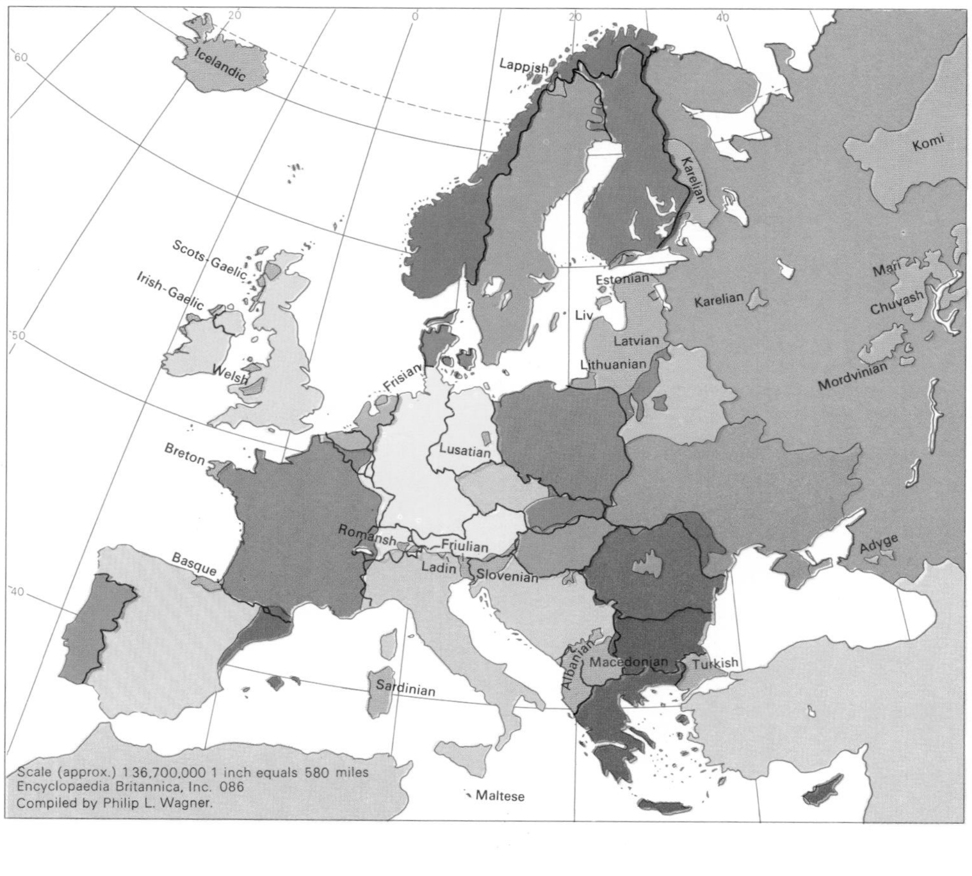
Icelandic
Lappish
Komi
Karelian
Scots-Gaelic
Irish-Gaelic
Estonian
Liv
Karelian
Mari
Chuvash
Latvian
Lithuanian
Welsh
Frisian
Mordvinian
Lusatian
Breton
Romansh
Friulian
Adyge
Basque
Ladin
Slovenian
Albanian
Macedonian
Turkish
Sardinian
Maltese
Scale (approx.) 1:36,700,000 1 inch equals 580 miles
Encyclopaedia Britannica, Inc. 086
Compiled by Philip L. Wagner.

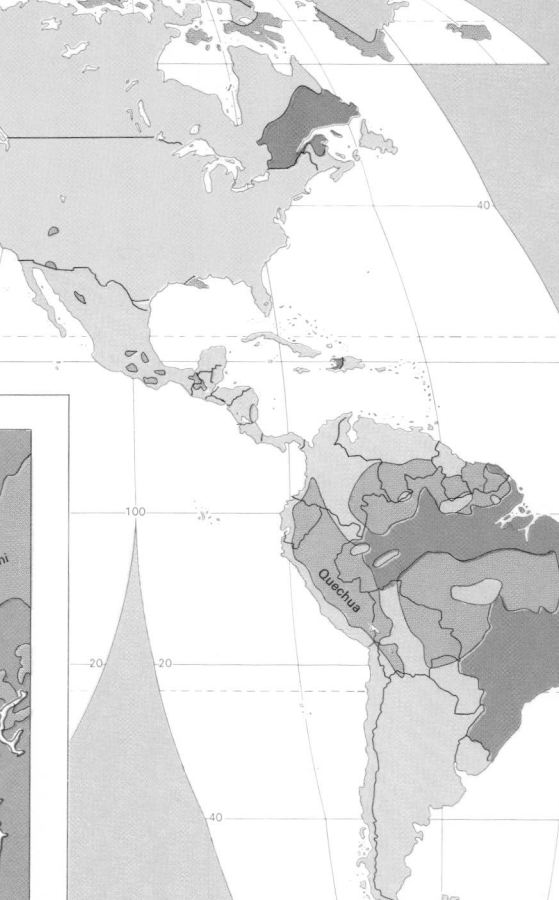

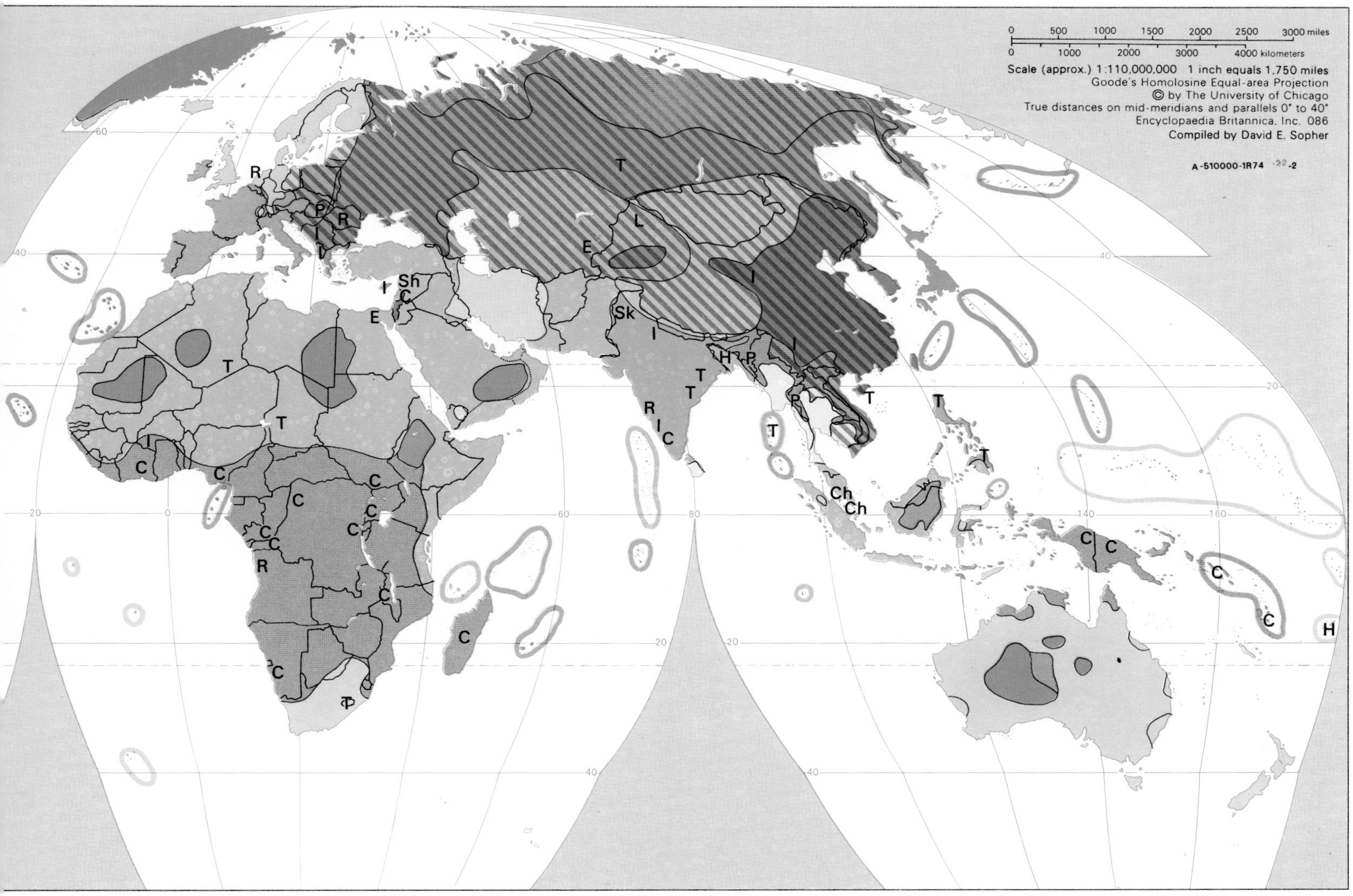

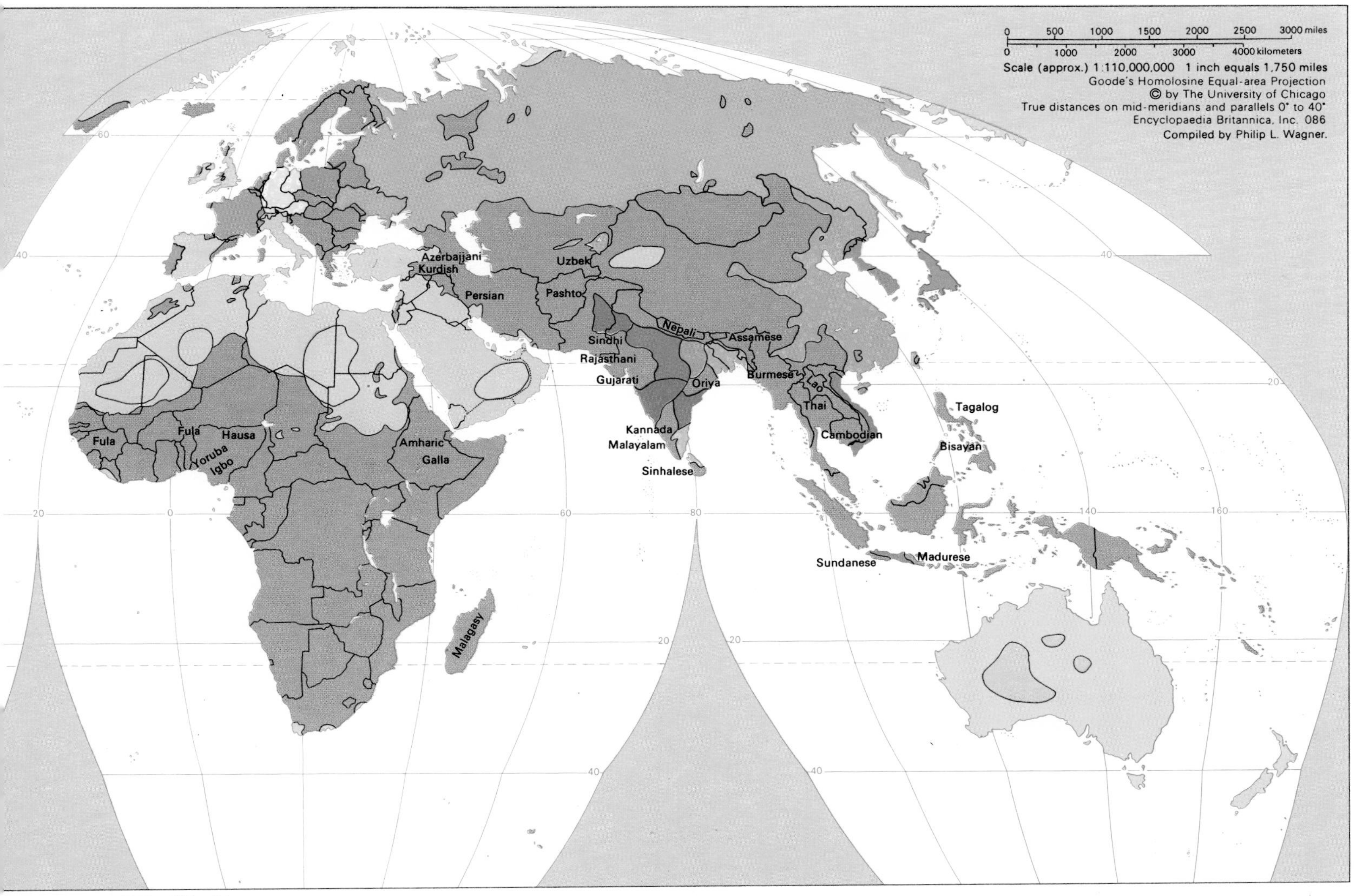

Languages of the World

The following languages are ranked in descending order by number of speakers. Languages spoken by more than 25 million persons are indicated by color. Others listed, spoken by 5–25 million persons, are named on the map.

Chinese
English
Spanish
Russian
Hindi
German
Japanese
Bengali
Portuguese
Arabic
French
Italian
Bihari
Javanese
Telugu
Ukrainian
Korean
Marathi
Tamil
Polish
Punjabi
Vietnamese
Turkish
All others
Uninhabited

Gujarati
Rajasthani
Kannada
Malayalam
Oriya
Burmese
Pashto
Thai
Sundanese
Bisayan
Amharic
Persian
Hausa
Quechua
Uzbek
Fula
Lao
Sinhalese
Yoruba
Azerbaijani
Sindhi
Igbo
Kurdish
Madurese
Assamese
Tagalog
Malagasy
Nepali
Cambodian
Galla

Agricultural Regions

- Cash crop and livestock farming
- Cash crop farming, grain or cotton dominant
- Crop and livestock farming with cash products minor
- Livestock ranching
- Dairying
- Mediterranean agriculture
- Specialized horticulture
- Plantation agriculture
- Intensive subsistence tillage, rice dominant
- Intensive subsistence tillage, with no dominant crop
- Rudimental sedentary farming
- Shifting cultivation
- Nomadic herding
- No agriculture

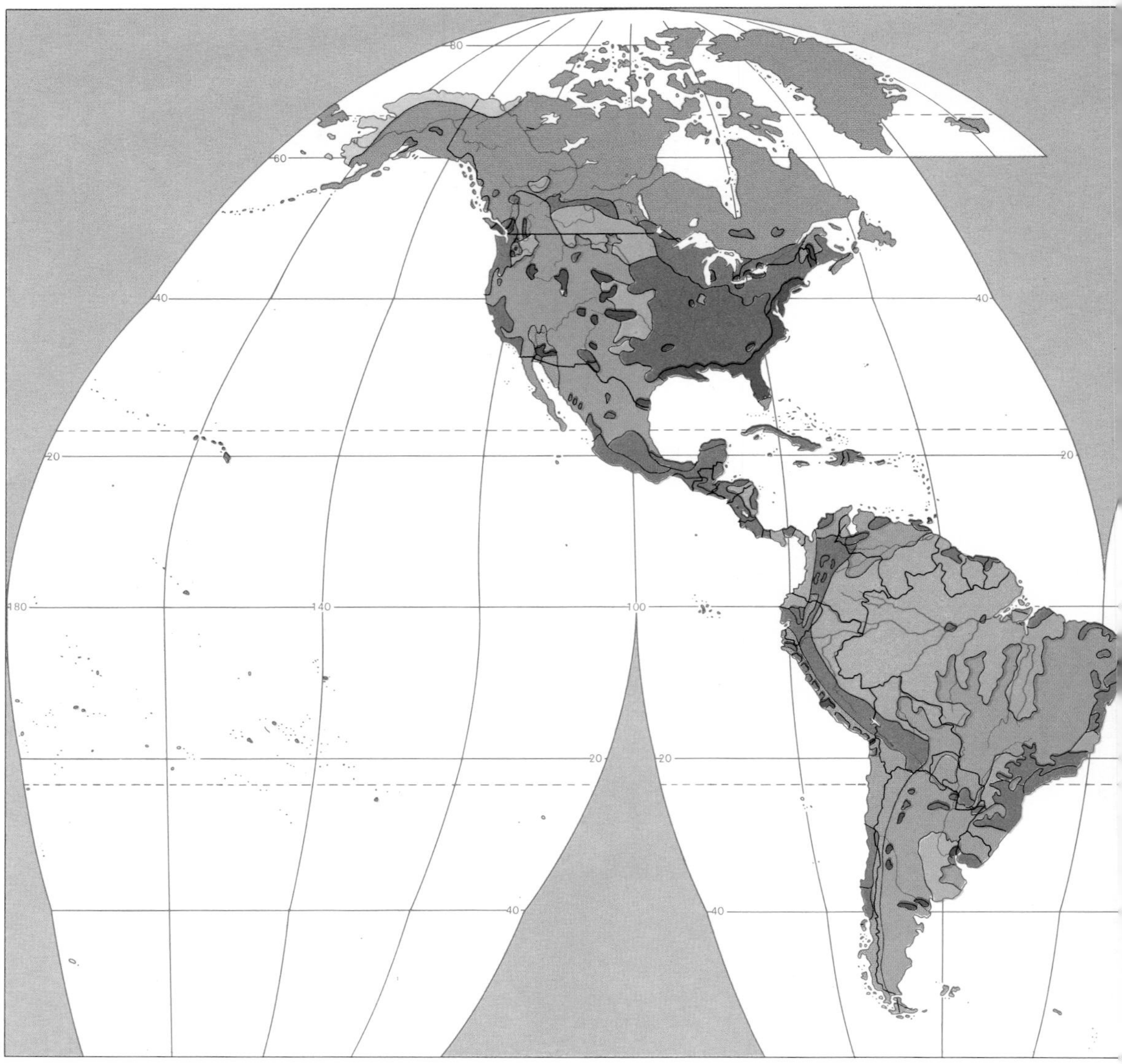

Forests and Fisheries

Forests

- Conifers: cedar, fir, hemlock, pine, redwood, spruce
- Regions of exploitation
- Tropical hardwoods: ebony, mahogany, rosewood, teak
- Regions of exploitation
- Temperate hardwoods: hickory, maple, oak, poplar, walnut, and some mixed hardwoods and conifers
- Regions of exploitation

Fisheries

- Pelagic fishing regions: anchoveta, anchovy, herring, menhaden, pilchard, sardine, sprat, tuna
- Ground fishing regions: cod, haddock, hake, horse mackerel, mackerel, pollack, redfish
- Mixed ground and pelagic fishing regions
- Shellfish: clam, crab, lobster, mussel, oyster, scallop, shrimp, squid
- Whales: blue, fin, minke, pilot, sei, sperm
  Each represents an average annual catch of about 300 whales; Each represents an average annual catch of less than 200 whales
- Fishing regions showing percentage of world catch (excluding whales)

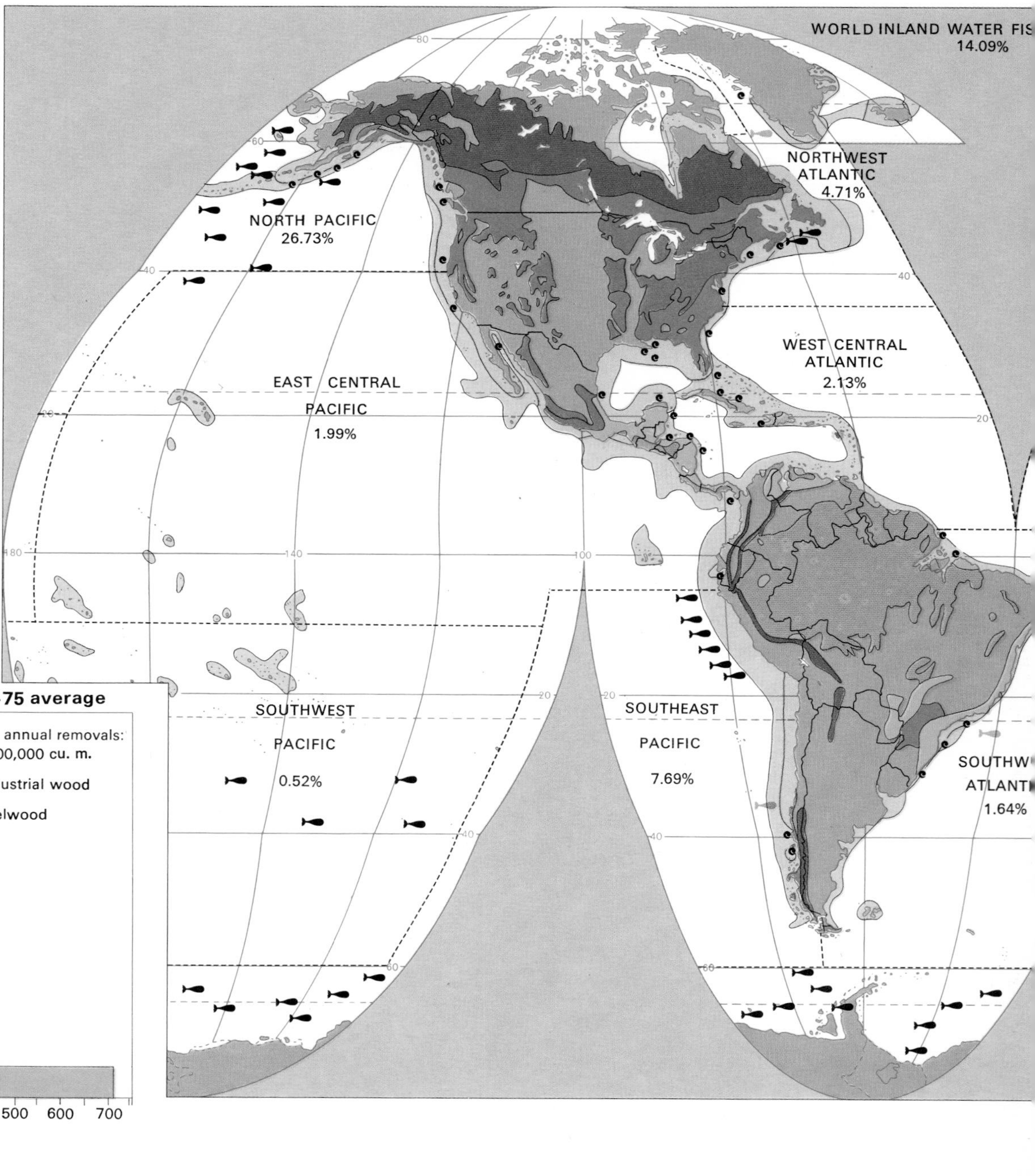
WORLD INLAND WATER FIS
14.09%
NORTHWEST
ATLANTIC
4.71%
NORTH PACIFIC
26.73%
WEST CENTRAL
ATLANTIC
2.13%
EAST CENTRAL
PACIFIC
1.99%
SOUTHWEST
PACIFIC
0.52%
SOUTHEAST
PACIFIC
7.69%
SOUTHW
ATLANT
1.64%

Fishing catch (live weight) 1971-75 average

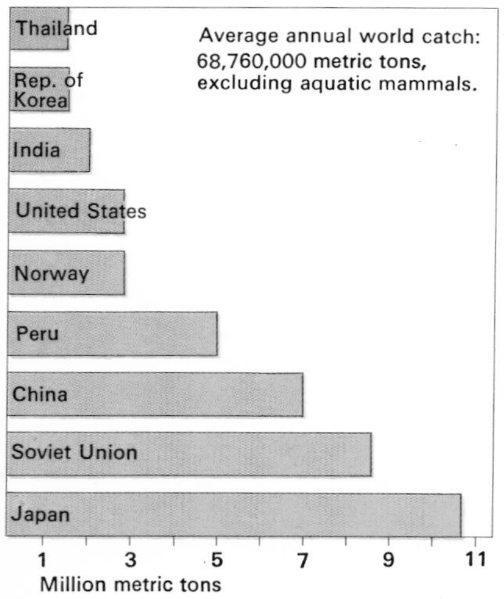
Average annual world catch:
68,760,000 metric tons,
excluding aquatic mammals.
Thailand
Rep. of Korea
India
United States
Norway
Peru
China
Soviet Union
Japan
1
3
5
7
9
11
Million metric tons

Forest removals 1971-75 average

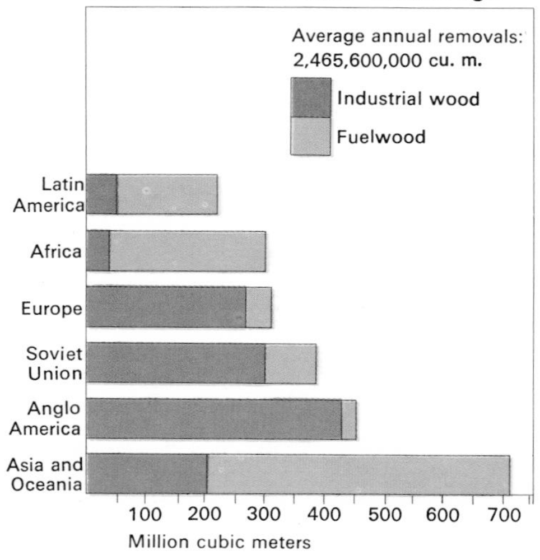
Average annual removals:
2,465,600,000 cu. m.
Industrial wood
Fuelwood
Latin America
Africa
Europe
Soviet Union
Anglo America
Asia and Oceania
100
200
300
400
500
600
700
Million cubic meters

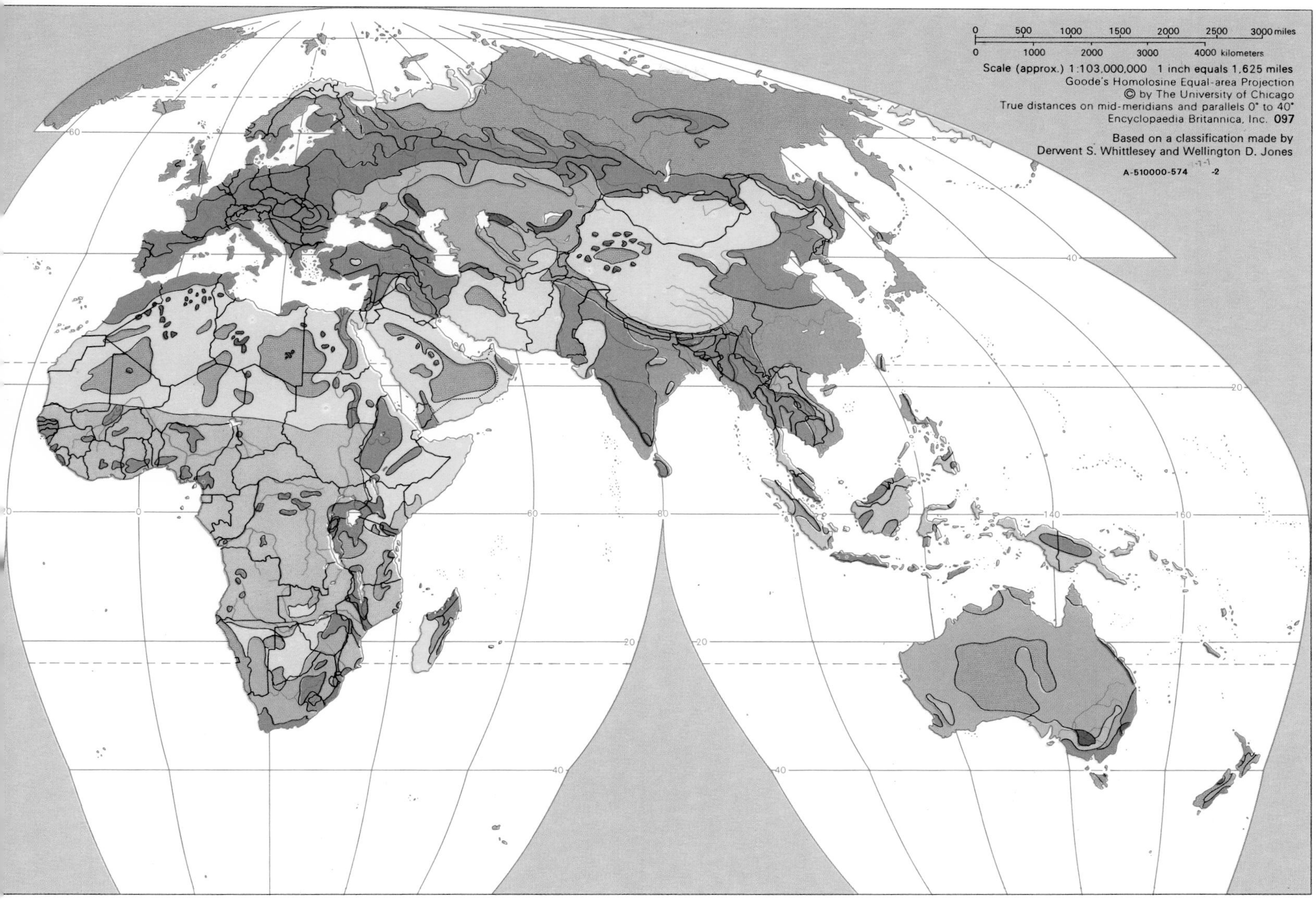
0 500 1000 1500 2000 2500 3000 miles
0 1000 2000 3000 4000 kilometers
Scale (approx.) 1:103,000,000 1 inch equals 1,625 miles
Goode's Homolosine Equal-area Projection
© by The University of Chicago
True distances on mid-meridians and parallels 0° to 40°
Encyclopaedia Britannica, Inc. 097
Based on a classification made by
Derwent S. Whittlesey and Wellington D. Jones
A-510000-574 -2

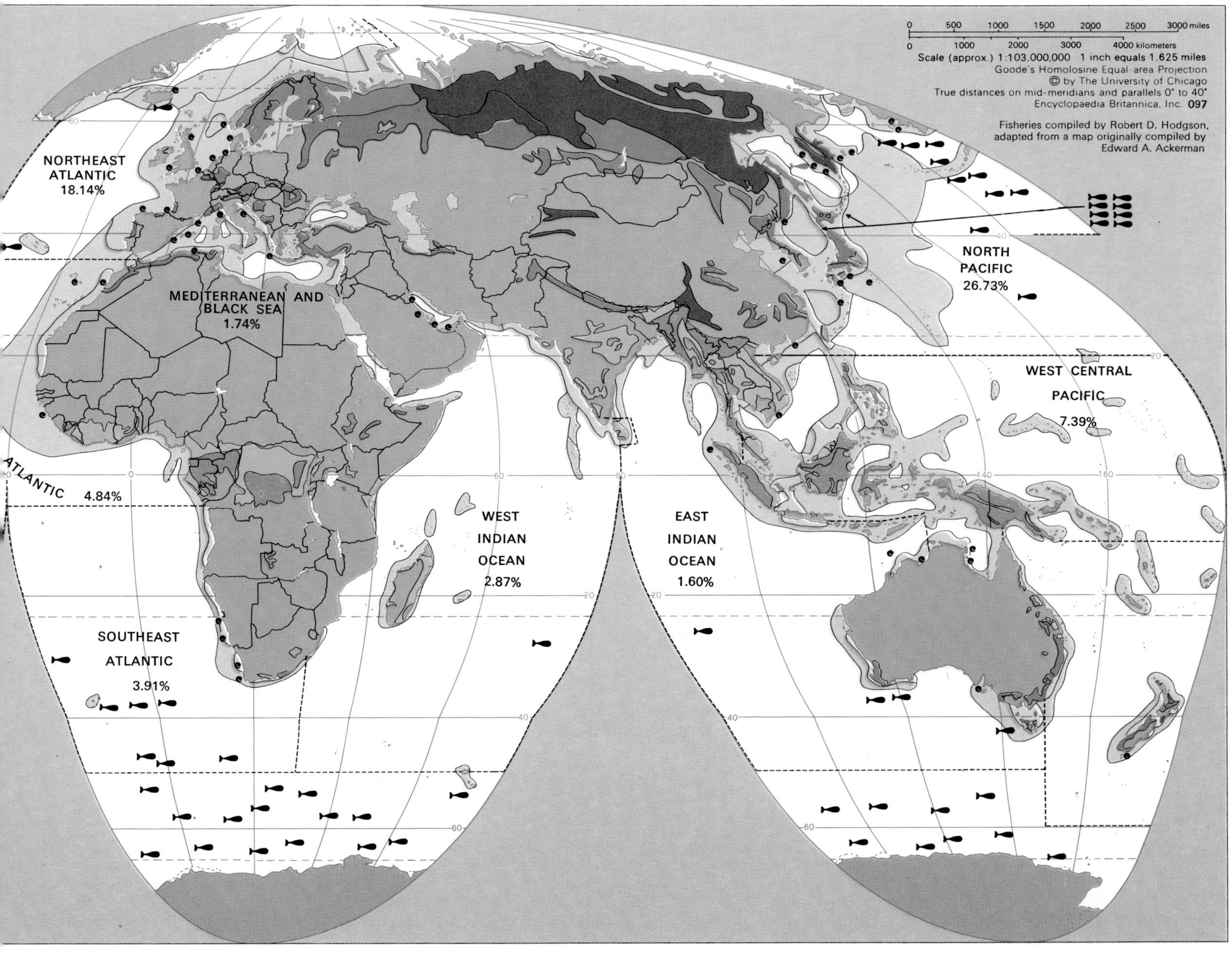
0 500 1000 1500 2000 2500 3000 miles
0 1000 2000 3000 4000 kilometers
Scale (approx.) 1:103,000,000 1 inch equals 1,625 miles
Goode's Homolosine Equal-area Projection
© by The University of Chicago
True distances on mid-meridians and parallels 0° to 40°
Encyclopaedia Britannica, Inc. 097
Fisheries compiled by Robert D. Hodgson,
adapted from a map originally compiled by
Edward A. Ackerman
NORTHEAST ATLANTIC 18.14%
MEDITERRANEAN AND BLACK SEA 1.74%
NORTH PACIFIC 26.73%
WEST CENTRAL PACIFIC 7.39%
ATLANTIC 4.84%
WEST INDIAN OCEAN 2.87%
EAST INDIAN OCEAN 1.60%
SOUTHEAST ATLANTIC 3.91%

Minerals

4-year world average production shown in graphs. Producing areas shown on maps

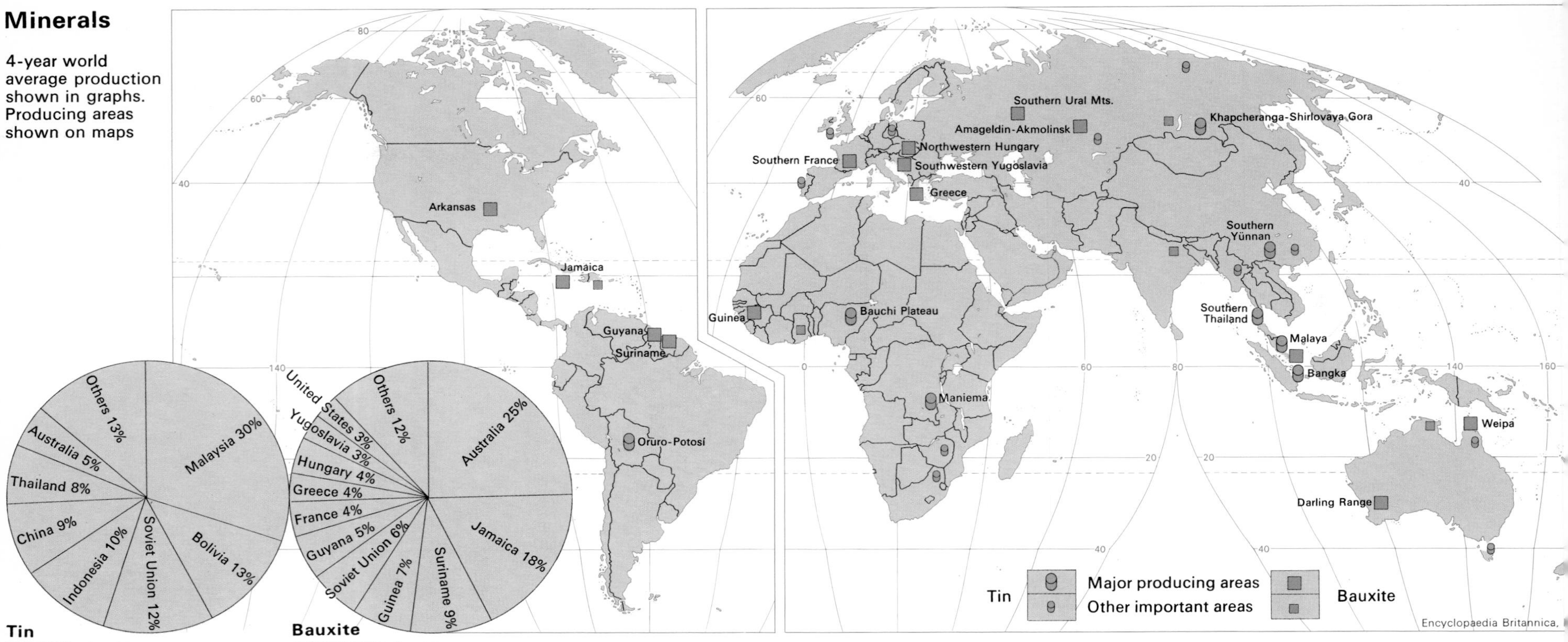
Others 13%
Australia 5%
Thailand 8%
China 9%
Indonesia 10%
Soviet Union 12%
Bolivia 13%
Malaysia 30%
United States 3%
Yugoslavia 3%
Hungary 4%
Greece 4%
France 4%
Guyana 5%
Soviet Union 6%
Guinea 7%
Suriname 9%
Jamaica 18%
Australia 25%
Others 12%
Arkansas
Jamaica
Guyana
Suriname
Oruro-Potosí
Southern Ural Mts.
Amageldin-Akmolinsk
Khapcheranga-Shirlovaya Gora
Northwestern Hungary
Southern France
Southwestern Yugoslavia
Greece
Southern Yünnan
Guinea
Bauchi Plateau
Southern Thailand
Malaya
Bangka
Maniema
Weipa
Darling Range
Tin
Major producing areas
Other important areas
Bauxite
Encyclopaedia Britannica,

Tin
259,300 short tons

Bauxite
72,117,500 short tons

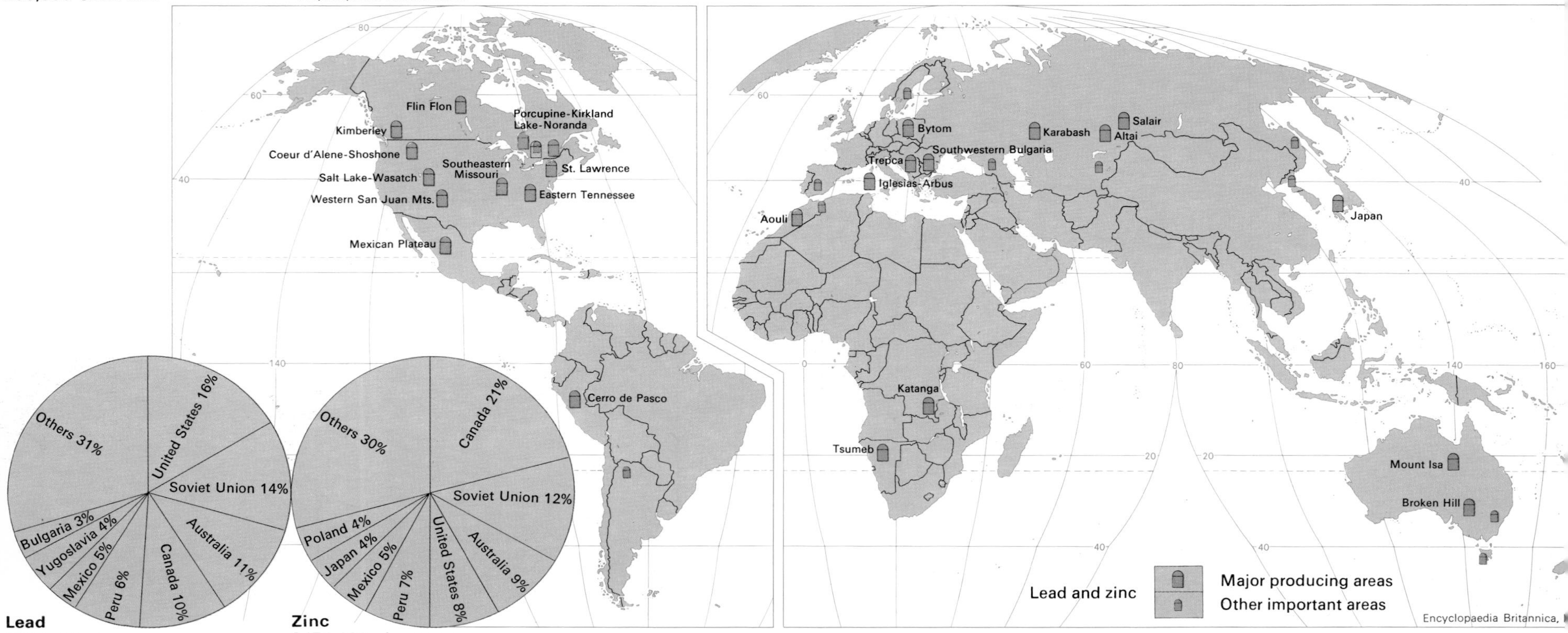
Others 31%
United States 16%
Soviet Union 14%
Australia 11%
Canada 10%
Peru 6%
Mexico 5%
Yugoslavia 4%
Bulgaria 3%
Others 30%
Canada 21%
Soviet Union 12%
Australia 9%
United States 8%
Peru 7%
Mexico 5%
Japan 4%
Poland 4%
Flin Flon
Kimberley
Porcupine-Kirkland Lake-Noranda
Coeur d'Alene-Shoshone
Southeastern Missouri
Salt Lake-Wasatch
St. Lawrence
Western San Juan Mts.
Eastern Tennessee
Mexican Plateau
Cerro de Pasco
Bytom
Karabash
Salair
Altai
Trepca
Southwestern Bulgaria
Iglesias-Arbus
Aouli
Japan
Katanga
Tsumeb
Mount Isa
Broken Hill
Lead and zinc
Major producing areas
Other important areas
Encyclopaedia Britannica,

Lead
3,816,300 short tons

Zinc
6,174,400 short tons

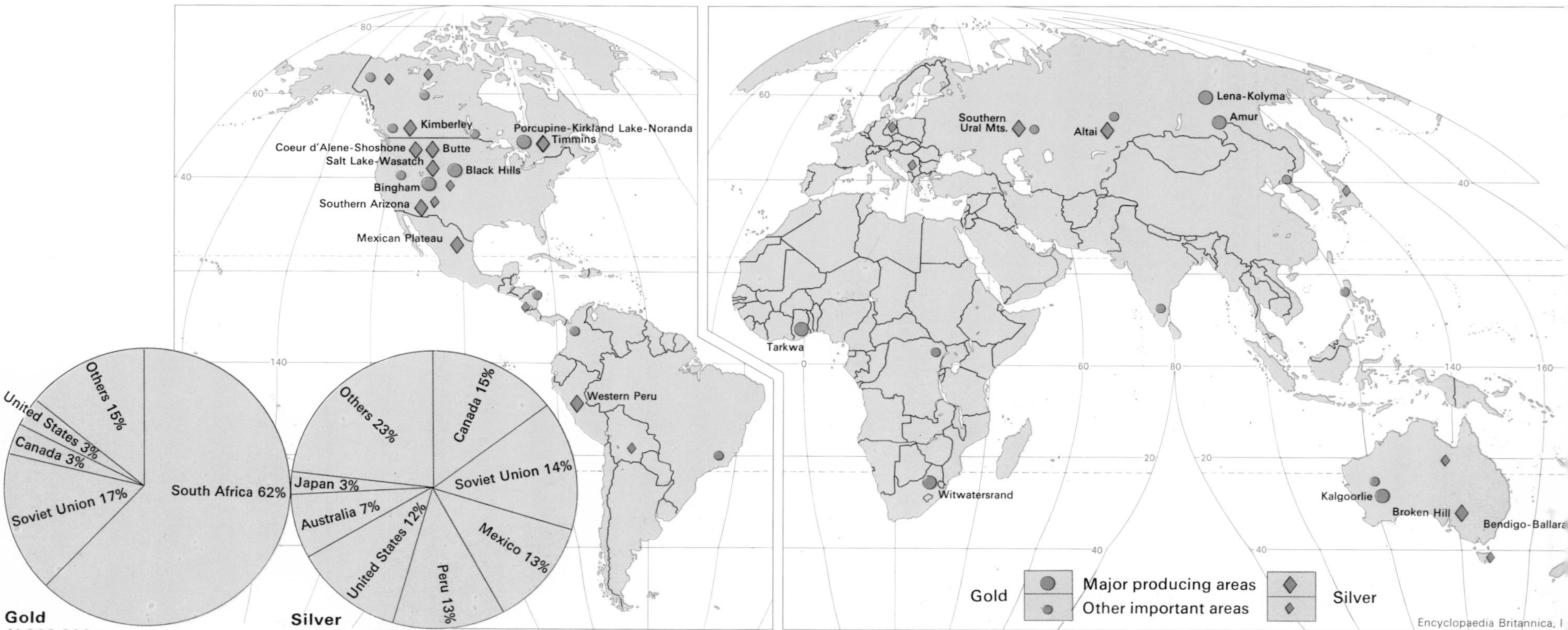
Others 15%
United States 3%
Canada 3%
Soviet Union 17%
South Africa 62%
Others 23%
Canada 15%
Soviet Union 14%
Mexico 13%
Peru 13%
United States 12%
Australia 7%
Japan 3%
Kimberley
Porcupine-Kirkland Lake-Noranda
Timmins
Coeur d'Alene-Shoshone
Butte
Salt Lake-Wasatch
Black Hills
Bingham
Southern Arizona
Mexican Plateau
Western Peru
Southern Ural Mts.
Altai
Lena-Kolyma
Amur
Tarkwa
Witwatersrand
Kalgoorlie
Broken Hill
Bendigo-Ballara
Gold
Major producing areas
Other important areas
Silver
Encyclopaedia Britannica, I

Gold
41,663,800 troy ounces

Silver
299,671,800 troy ounces

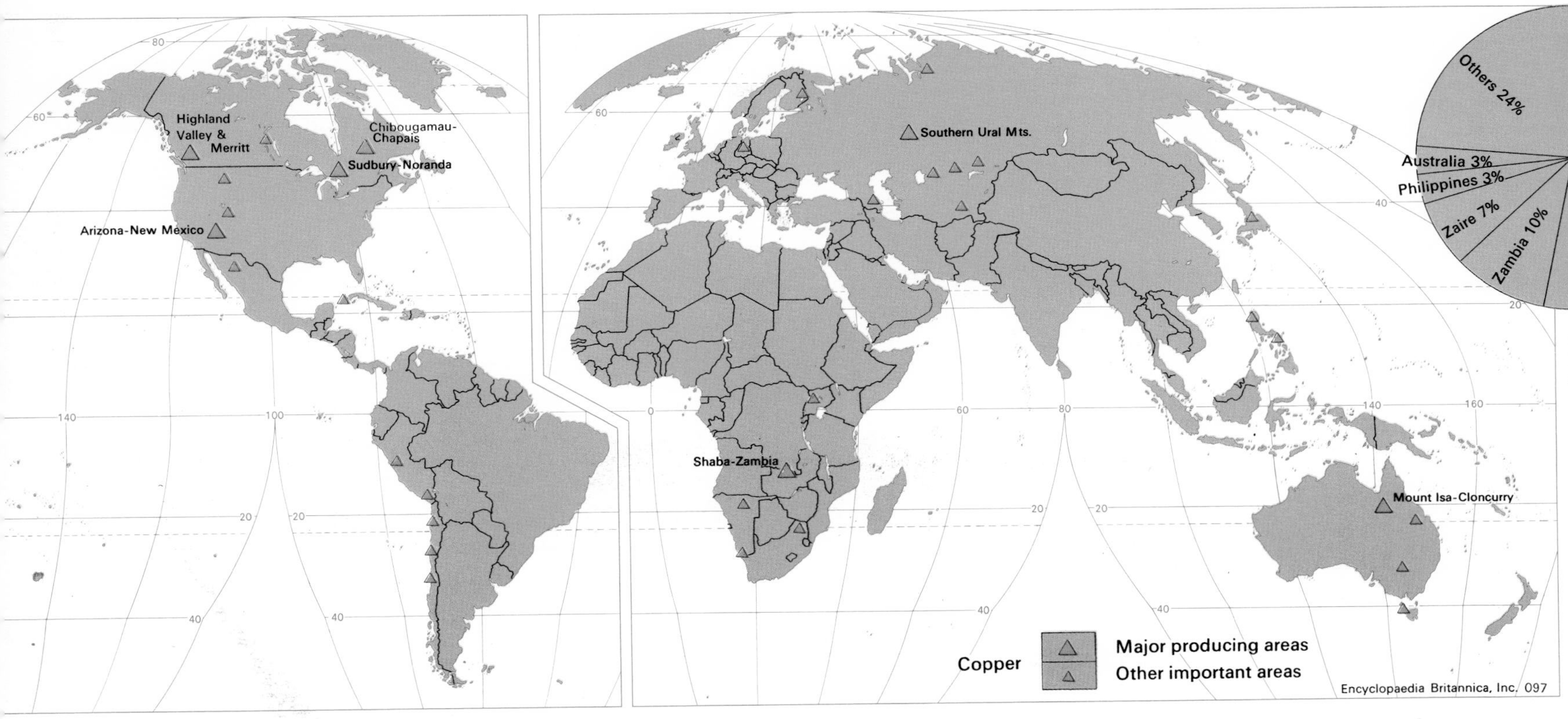
Highland Valley & Merritt
Chibougamau-Chapais
Sudbury-Noranda
Arizona-New Mexico
Southern Ural Mts.
Shaba-Zambia
Mount Isa-Cloncurry
Others 24%
United States 21%
Australia 3%
Philippines 3%
Chile 11%
Zaire 7%
Zambia 10%
Soviet Union 10%
Canada 11%
Copper
Major producing areas
Other important areas
Encyclopaedia Britannica, Inc. 097

Copper
7,727,300
short tons

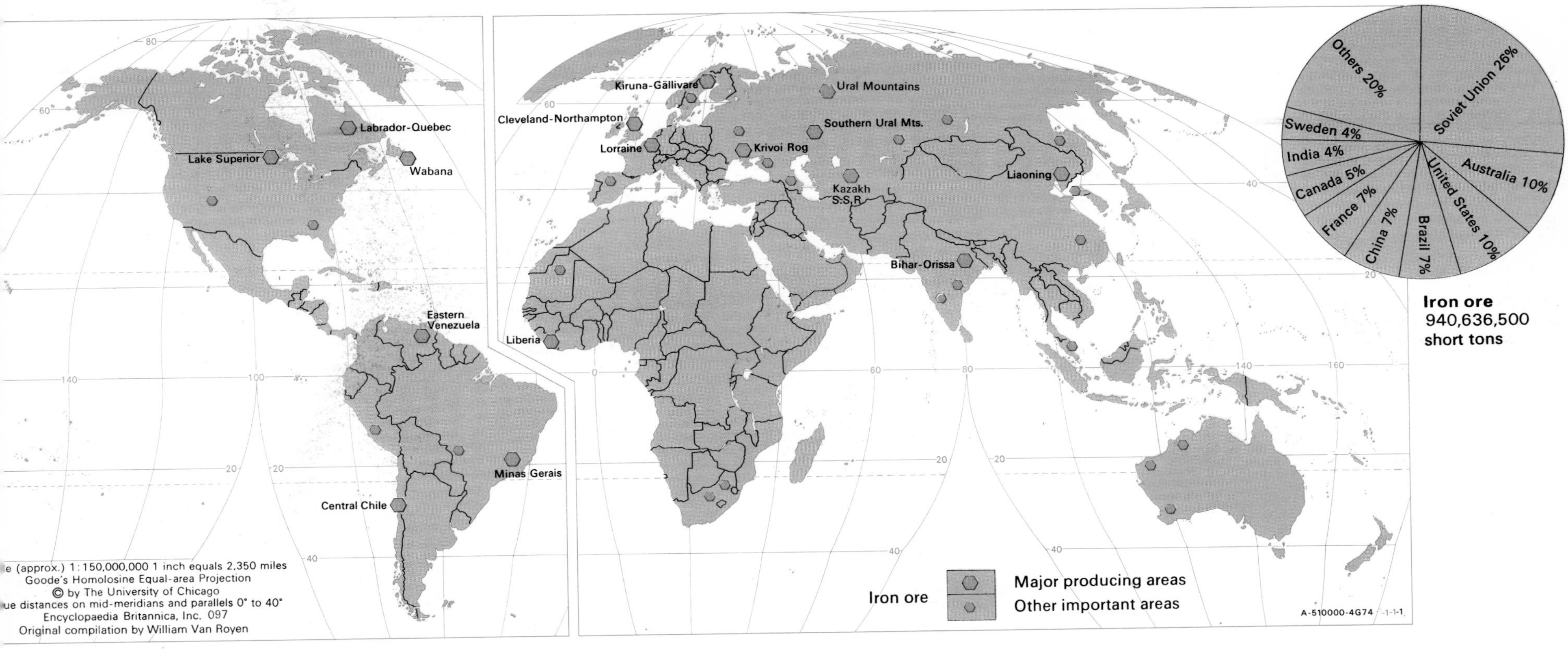
Labrador-Quebec
Lake Superior
Wabana
Eastern Venezuela
Minas Gerais
Central Chile
Kiruna-Gällivare
Cleveland-Northampton
Lorraine
Krivoi Rog
Ural Mountains
Southern Ural Mts.
Kazakh S.S.R.
Liaoning
Bihar-Orissa
Liberia
Others 20%
Soviet Union 26%
Sweden 4%
India 4%
Canada 5%
France 7%
China 7%
Brazil 7%
United States 10%
Australia 10%
Iron ore
Major producing areas
Other important areas
A-510000-4G74 -1-1-1

Scale (approx.) 1:150,000,000 1 inch equals 2,350 miles
Goode's Homolosine Equal-area Projection
© by The University of Chicago
True distances on mid-meridians and parallels 0° to 40°
Encyclopaedia Britannica, Inc. 097
Original compilation by William Van Royen

Iron ore
940,636,500
short tons

Ferroalloying Minerals

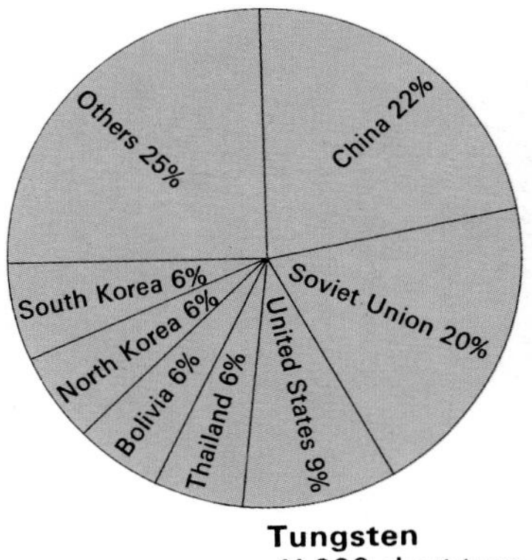
Others 25%
China 22%
South Korea 6%
North Korea 6%
Bolivia 6%
Thailand 6%
United States 9%
Soviet Union 20%

Tungsten
41,600 short tons

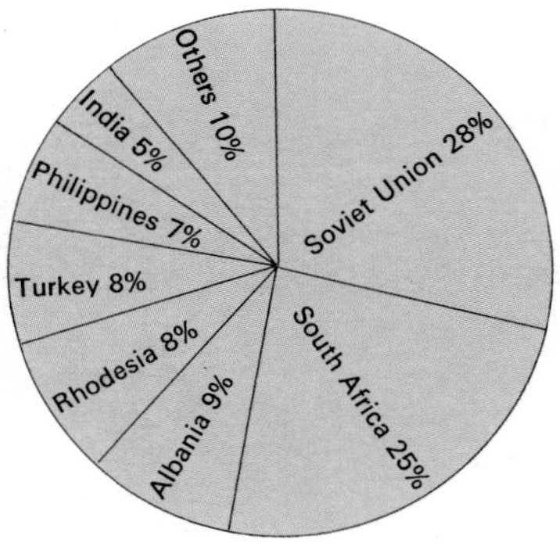
Others 10%
India 5%
Philippines 7%
Turkey 8%
Rhodesia 8%
Albania 9%
South Africa 25%
Soviet Union 28%

Chromite
7,758,500 short tons

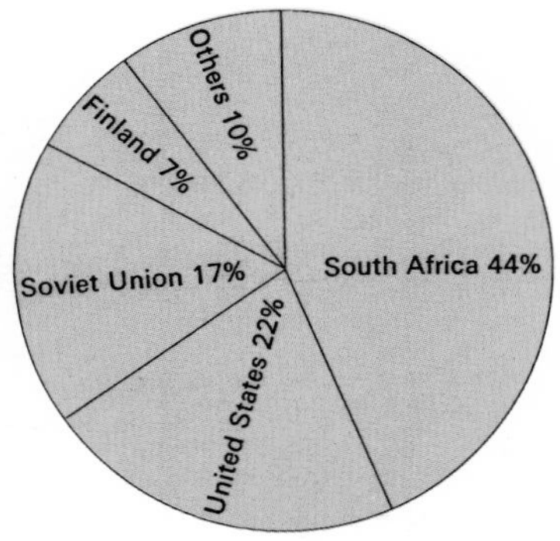
Others 10%
Finland 7%
Soviet Union 17%
United States 22%
South Africa 44%

Vanadium
21,700 short tons

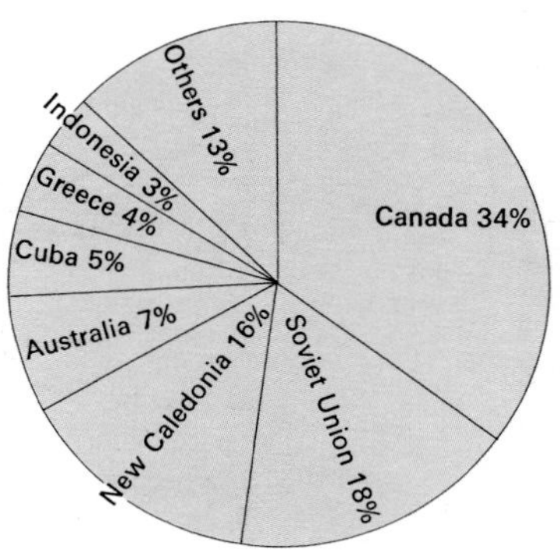
Others 13%
Indonesia 3%
Greece 4%
Cuba 5%
Australia 7%
New Caledonia 16%
Soviet Union 18%
Canada 34%

Nickel
806,900 short tons

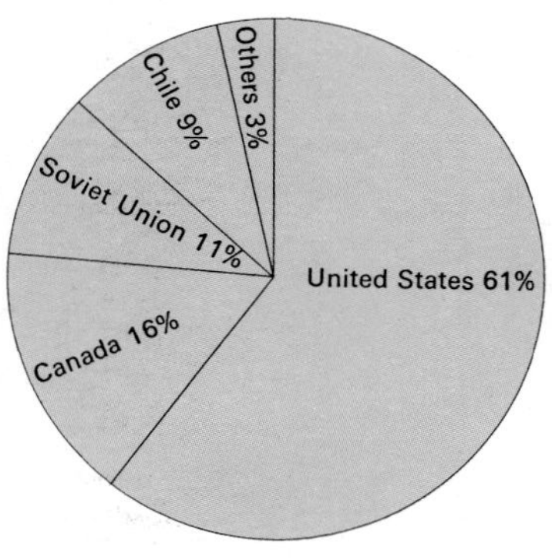
Others 3%
Chile 9%
Soviet Union 11%
Canada 16%
United States 61%

Molybdenum
91,300 short tons

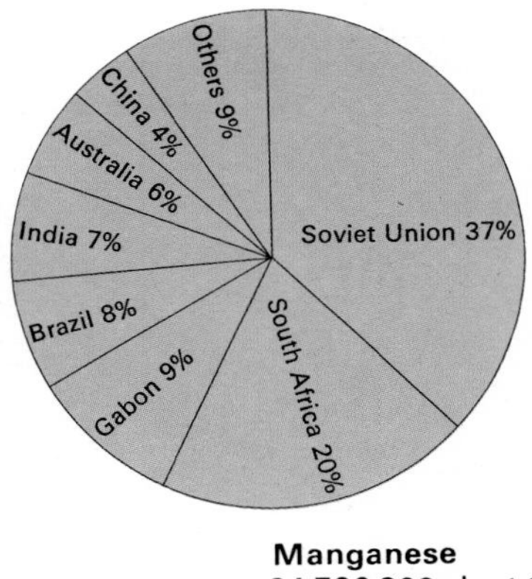
Others 9%
China 4%
Australia 6%
India 7%
Brazil 8%
Gabon 9%
South Africa 20%
Soviet Union 37%

Manganese
24,720,300 short tons

Energy Production and Consumption

Unit of measure is metric tons coal equivalent (m.t.c.e.)

Production

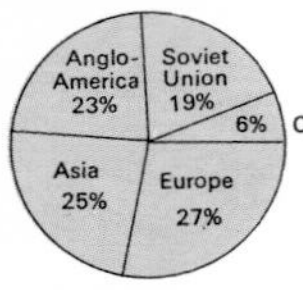
Anglo-America 23%
Soviet Union 19%
6% Others
Asia 25%
Europe 27%

Coal and lignite
World total: 2,640,000,000

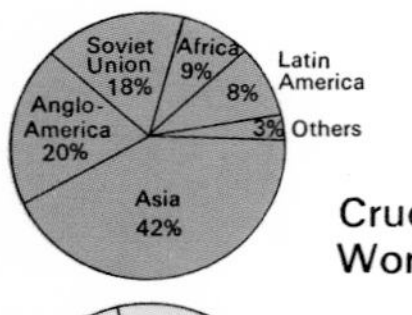
Soviet Union 18%
Africa 9%
Latin America 8%
3% Others
Anglo-America 20%
Asia 42%

Crude petroleum
World total: 4,035,000,000

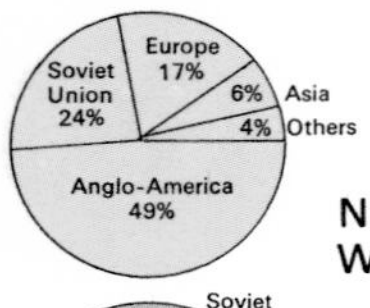
Soviet Union 24%
Europe 17%
6% Asia
4% Others
Anglo-America 49%

Natural gas
World total: 1,658,000,000

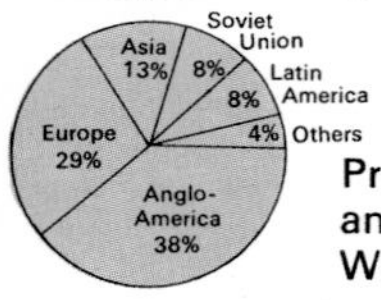
Asia 13%
Soviet Union 8%
Latin America 8%
4% Others
Europe 29%
Anglo-America 38%

Primary electricity (hydro-, geothermal, and nuclear)
World total: 221,000,000

Table of equivalents

Coal, anthracite and bituminous	1 metric ton = 1.0 m.t.c.e.
Lignite	1 metric ton = 0.3 – 0.6 m.t.c.e.
Petroleum	1 metric ton = 1.5 m.t.c.e.
Natural gas	1,000 cubic meters = 1.33 m.t.c.e.
Hydro-, geothermal, and nuclear electricity	1.0 megawatt-hour= 0.125 m.t.c.e.

Potential energy of 1 metric ton of coal equals 28,000,000 B.T.U.

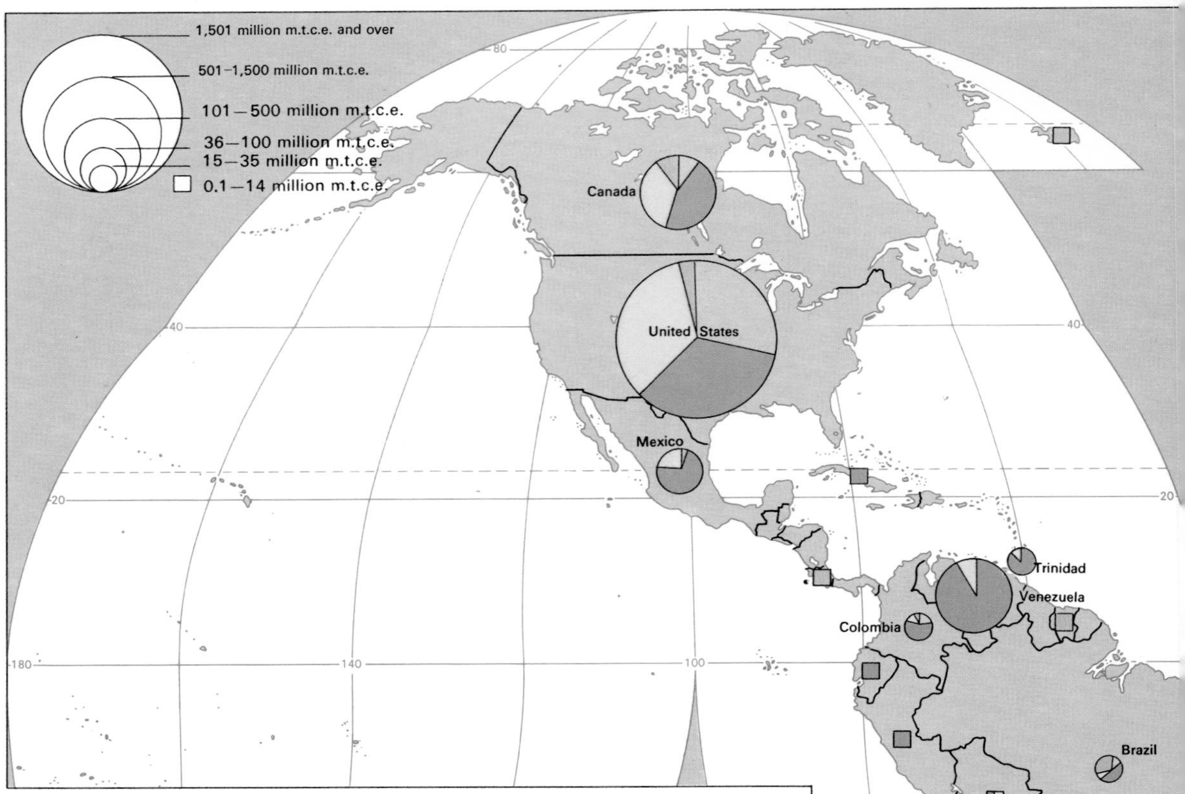
1,501 million m.t.c.e. and over
501–1,500 million m.t.c.e.
101—500 million m.t.c.e.
36—100 million m.t.c.e.
15—35 million m.t.c.e.
0.1—14 million m.t.c.e.
Canada
United States
Mexico
Trinidad
Venezuela
Colombia
Brazil
Argentina

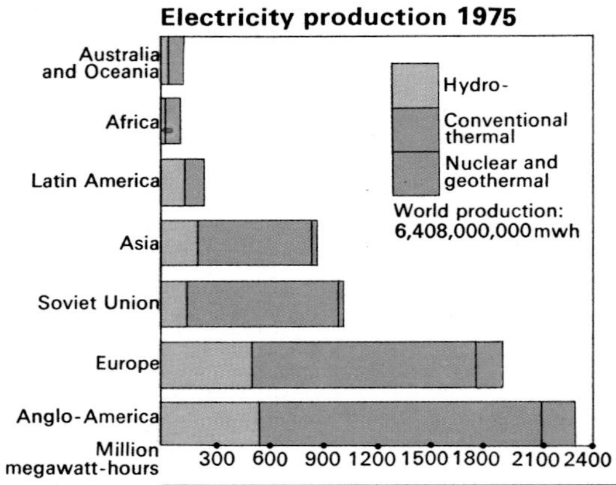
Electricity production 1975
Australia and Oceania
Africa
Latin America
Asia
Soviet Union
Europe
Anglo-America
Hydro-
Conventional thermal
Nuclear and geothermal
World production: 6,408,000,000 mwh
Million megawatt-hours
300 600 900 1200 1500 1800 2100 2400

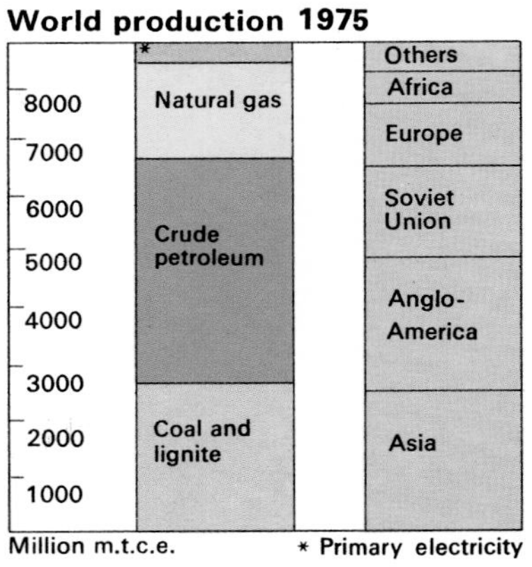
World production 1975
8000
7000
6000
5000
4000
3000
2000
1000
Million m.t.c.e.
*
Natural gas
Crude petroleum
Coal and lignite
Others
Africa
Europe
Soviet Union
Anglo-America
Asia
* Primary electricity

Consumption

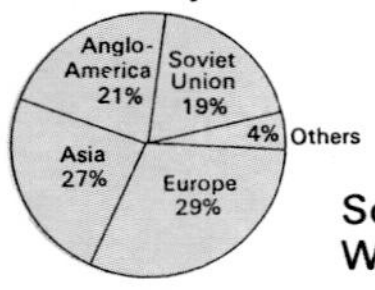
Anglo-America 21%
Soviet Union 19%
4% Others
Asia 27%
Europe 29%

Solid fuels
World total: 2,626,000,000

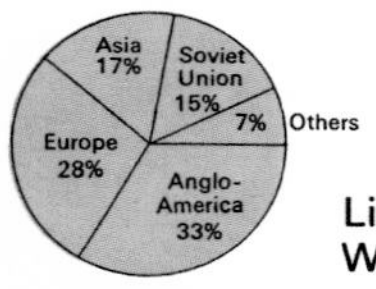
Asia 17%
Soviet Union 15%
7% Others
Europe 28%
Anglo-America 33%

Liquid fuels
World total: 3,525,000,000

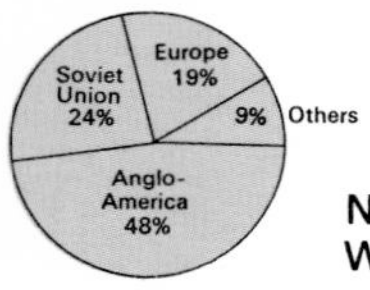
Soviet Union 24%
Europe 19%
9% Others
Anglo-America 48%

Natural and manufactured gas
World total: 1,633,000,000

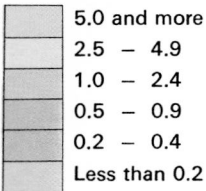

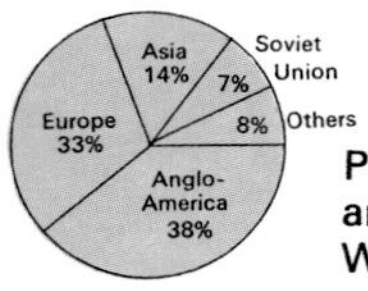
Asia 14%
Soviet Union 7%
8% Others
Europe 33%
Anglo-America 38%

Primary electricity (hydro-, geothermal, and nuclear)
World total: 221,000,000

Consumption totals exclude noncommercial fuels, fuels consumed by vessels engaged in international trade, and nonfuel petroleum products.

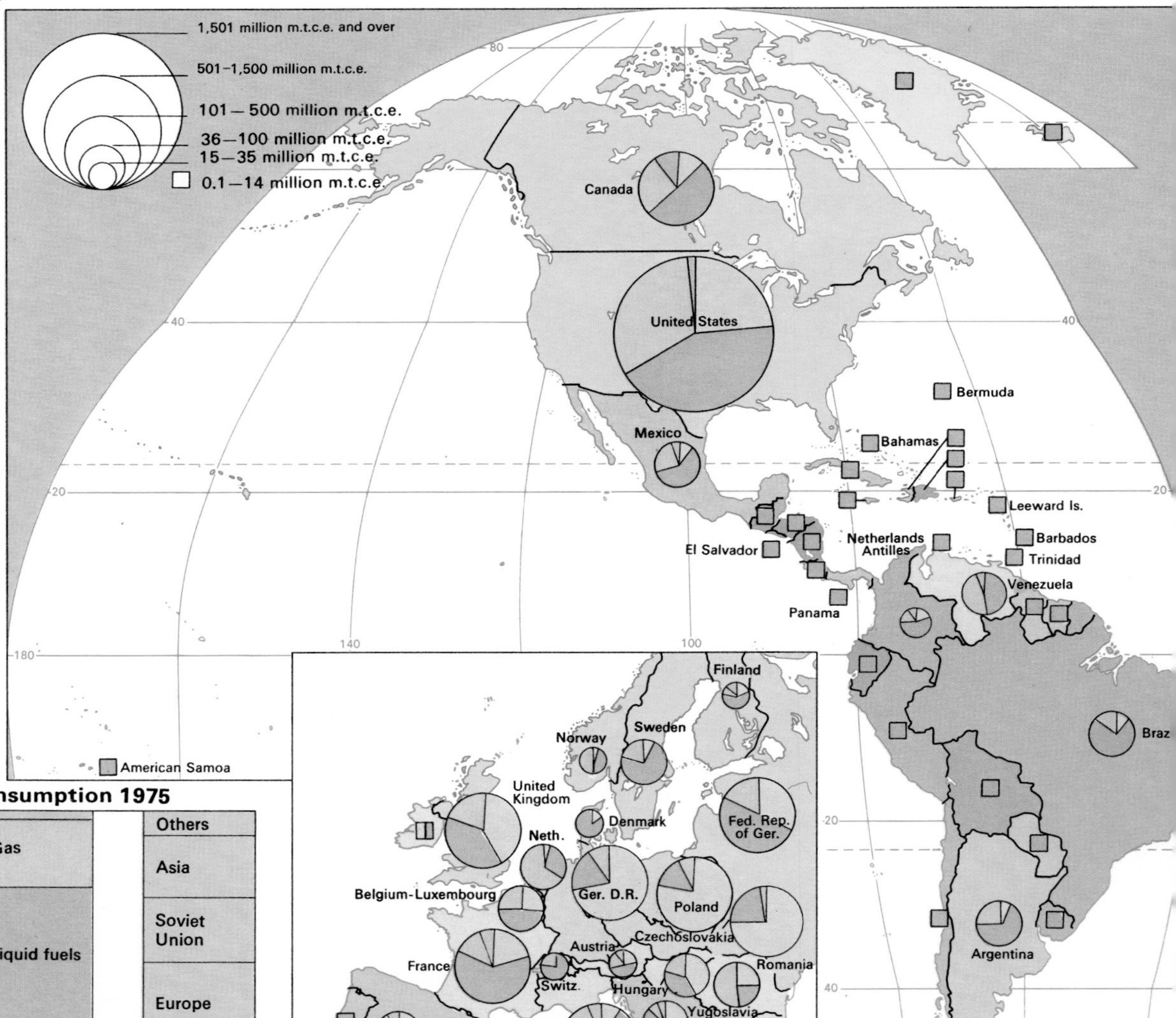
1,501 million m.t.c.e. and over
501–1,500 million m.t.c.e.
101—500 million m.t.c.e.
36—100 million m.t.c.e.
15—35 million m.t.c.e.
0.1—14 million m.t.c.e.
Canada
United States
Mexico
Bermuda
Bahamas
Leeward Is.
Barbados
Trinidad
Netherlands Antilles
El Salvador
Venezuela
Panama
American Samoa
Braz
Argentina
Finland
Norway
Sweden
United Kingdom
Denmark
Neth.
Fed. Rep. of Ger.
Belgium-Luxembourg
Ger. D.R.
Poland
Czechoslovakia
France
Austria
Switz.
Hungary
Romania
Yugoslavia
Spain
Italy
Bulgaria
Malta

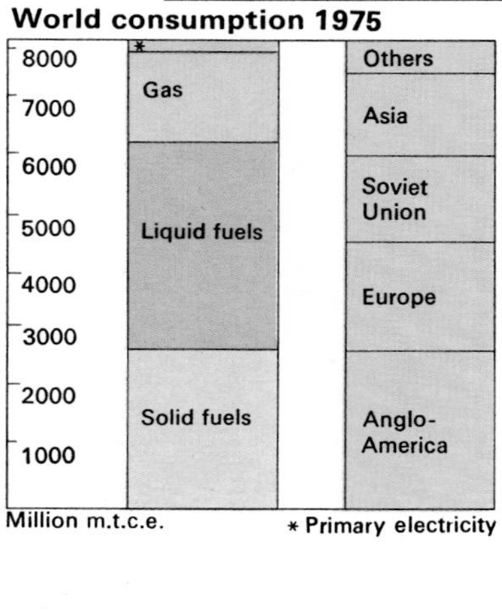
World consumption 1975
8000
7000
6000
5000
4000
3000
2000
1000
Million m.t.c.e.
*
Gas
Liquid fuels
Solid fuels
Others
Asia
Soviet Union
Europe
Anglo-America
* Primary electricity

Per capita consumption

- 5.0 and more
- 2.5 – 4.9
- 1.0 – 2.4
- 0.5 – 0.9
- 0.2 – 0.4
- Less than 0.2

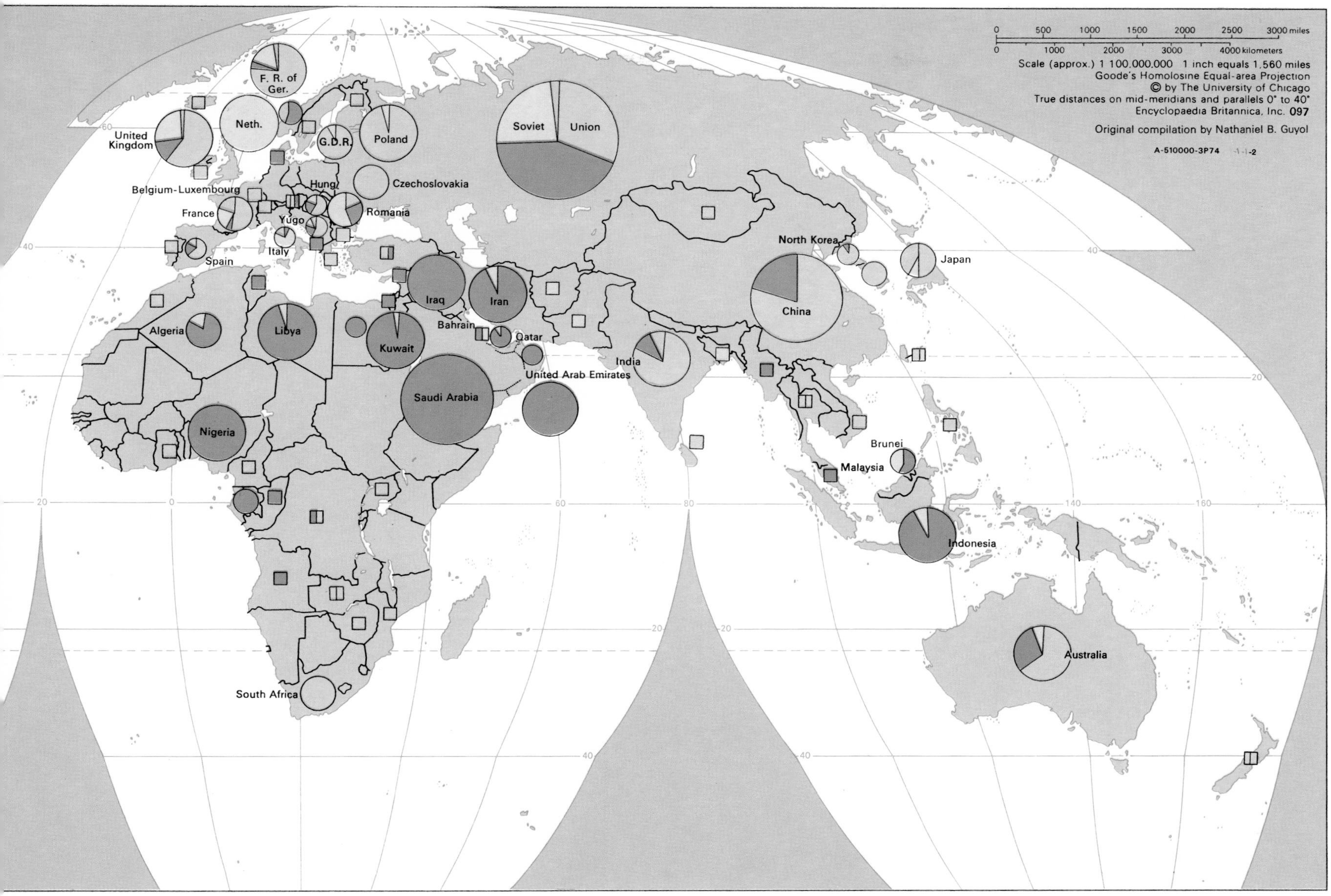
0 500 1000 1500 2000 2500 3000 miles
0 1000 2000 3000 4000 kilometers
Scale (approx.) 1:100,000,000 1 inch equals 1,560 miles
Goode's Homolosine Equal-area Projection
© by The University of Chicago
True distances on mid-meridians and parallels 0° to 40°
Encyclopaedia Britannica, Inc. 097
Original compilation by Nathaniel B. Guyol
A-510000-3P74
F. R. of Ger.
United Kingdom
Neth.
G.D.R.
Poland
Soviet
Union
Belgium-Luxembourg
Hung.
Czechoslovakia
France
Yugo.
Romania
Italy
Spain
North Korea
Japan
Iraq
Iran
Algeria
Libya
Kuwait
Bahrain
Qatar
China
India
United Arab Emirates
Saudi Arabia
Nigeria
Brunei
Malaysia
Indonesia
Australia
South Africa

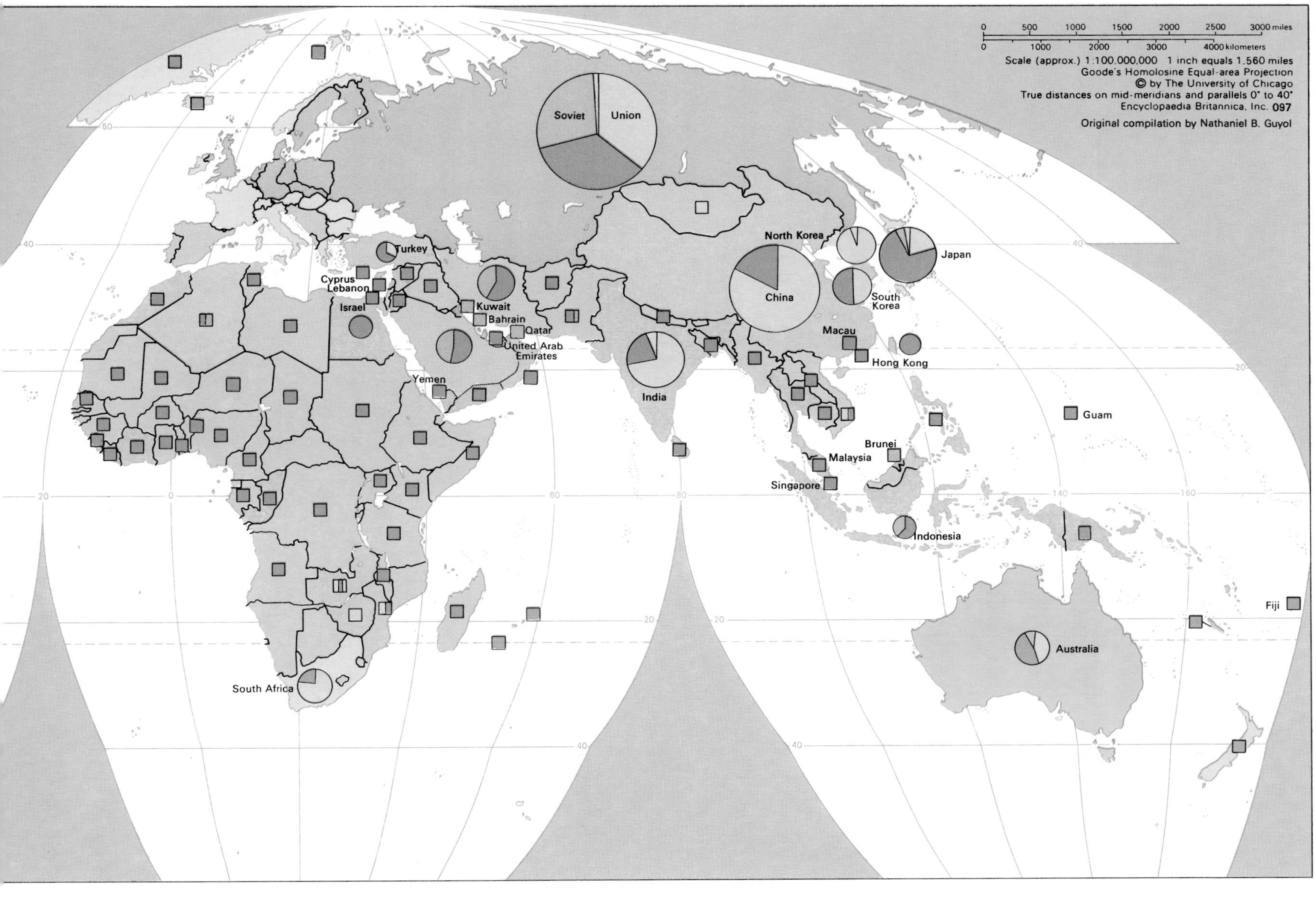
0 500 1000 1500 2000 2500 3000 miles
0 1000 2000 3000 4000 kilometers
Scale (approx.) 1:100,000,000 1 inch equals 1,560 miles
Goode's Homolosine Equal-area Projection
© by The University of Chicago
True distances on mid-meridians and parallels 0° to 40°
Encyclopaedia Britannica, Inc. 097
Original compilation by Nathaniel B. Guyol
Soviet
Union
North Korea
Japan
Turkey
Cyprus
Lebanon
Israel
Kuwait
Bahrain
Qatar
United Arab Emirates
China
South Korea
Macau
Hong Kong
Yemen
India
Guam
Brunei
Malaysia
Singapore
Indonesia
Fiji
Australia
South Africa

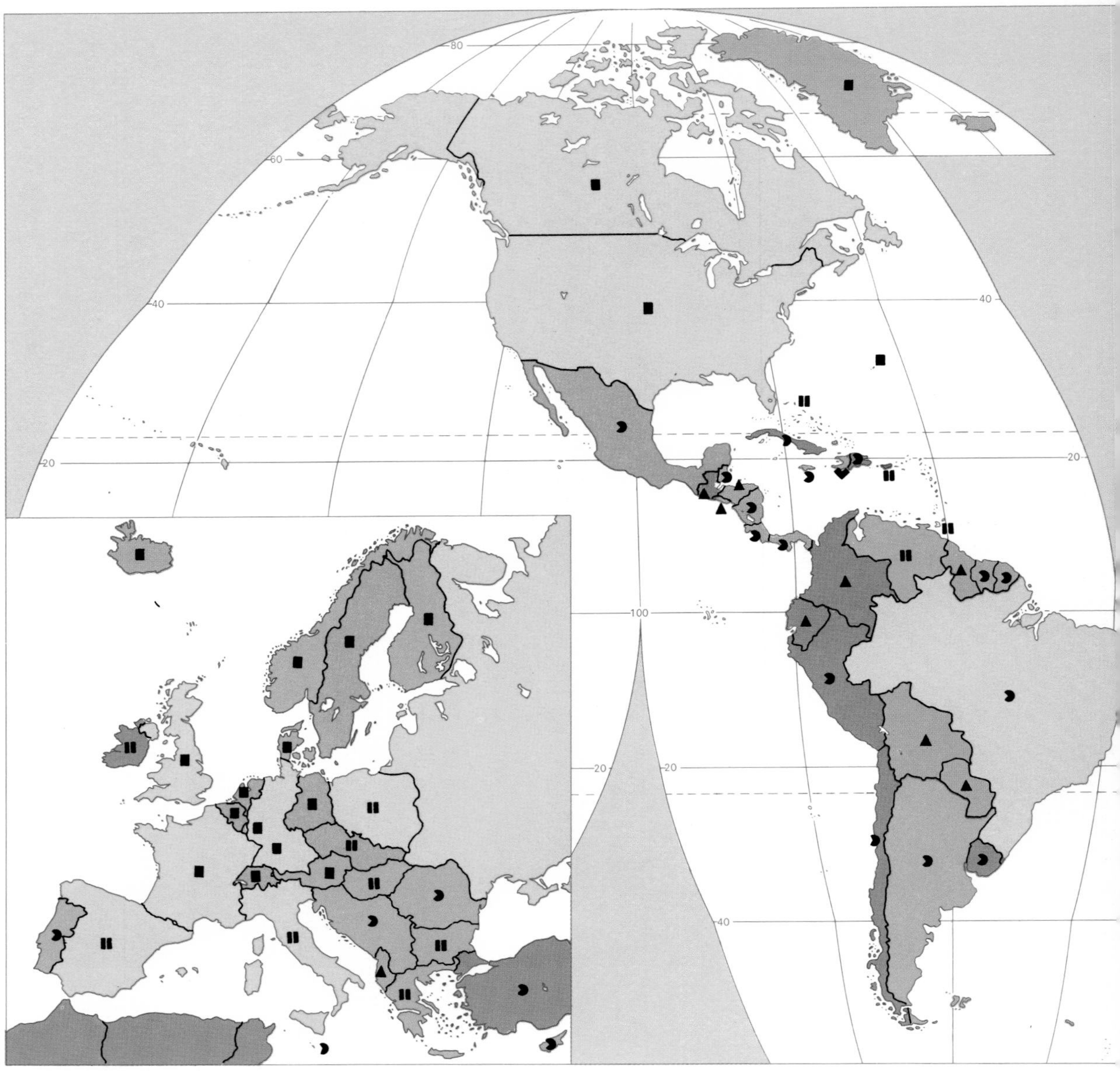

Gross National Product

Total per country at market price In U.S. $000,000	Number of countries
84,000 and more	13
42,000–83,999	9
14,000–41,999	21
4,667–13,999	23
2,334–4,666	16
Less than 2,334	101
No data available	

Per capita In U.S. dollars	Number of countries
■ 3,720 and more	34
▮▮ 1,860–3,719	24
◗ 620–1,859	42
▲ 207–619	51
❤ 104–206	26
● Less than 104	6

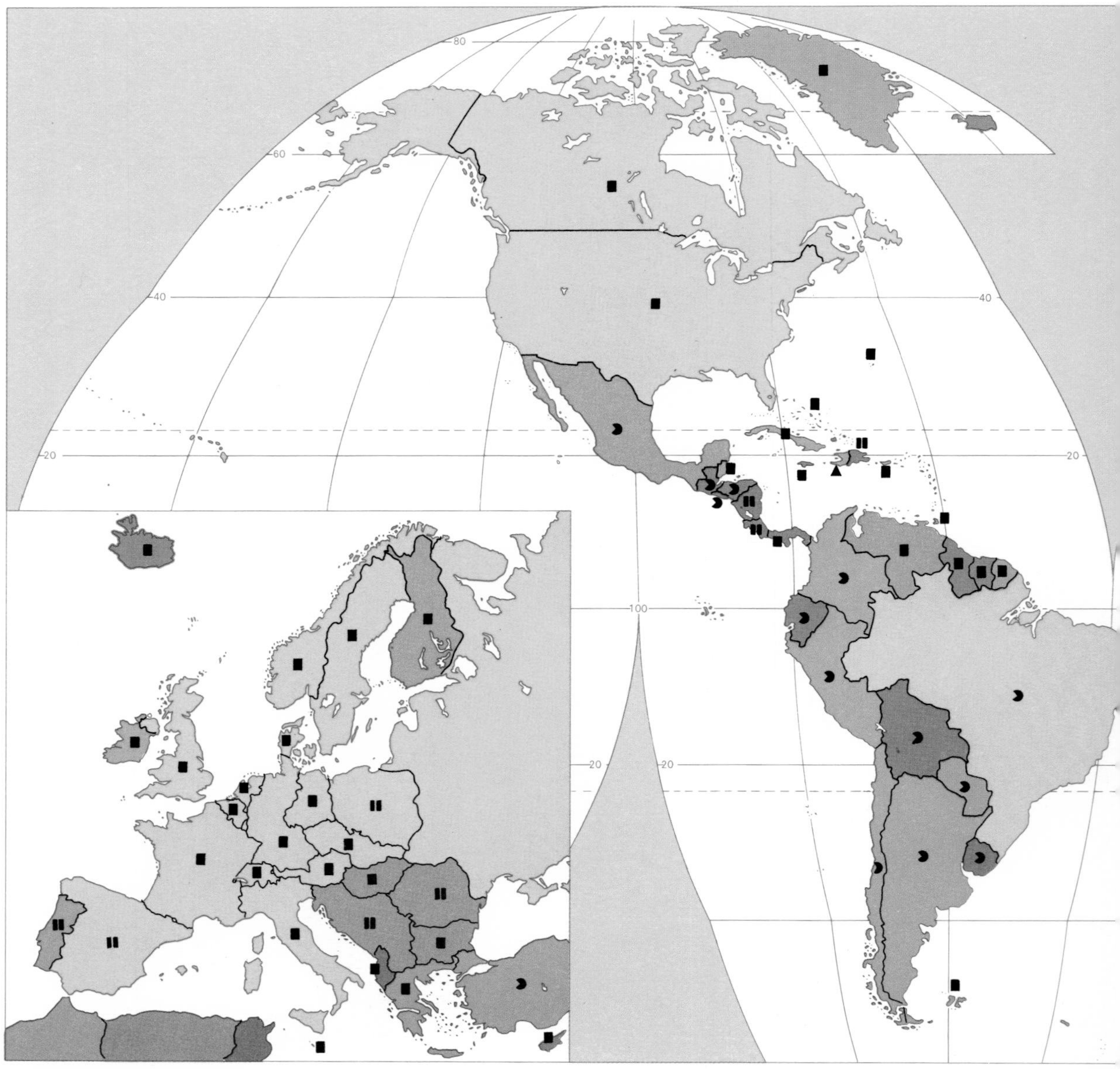

International Trade

Total per country In U.S. $000,000	Number of countries
15,174 and more	25
7,587–15,173	19
2,529–7,586	22
844–2,528	31
423–843	19
Less than 423	41
No data available	

Per capita In U.S. dollars	Number of countries
■ 702 and more	60
▮▮ 351–701	18
◗ 117–350	39
▲ 40–116	24
❤ 22–39	8
● Less than 22	9

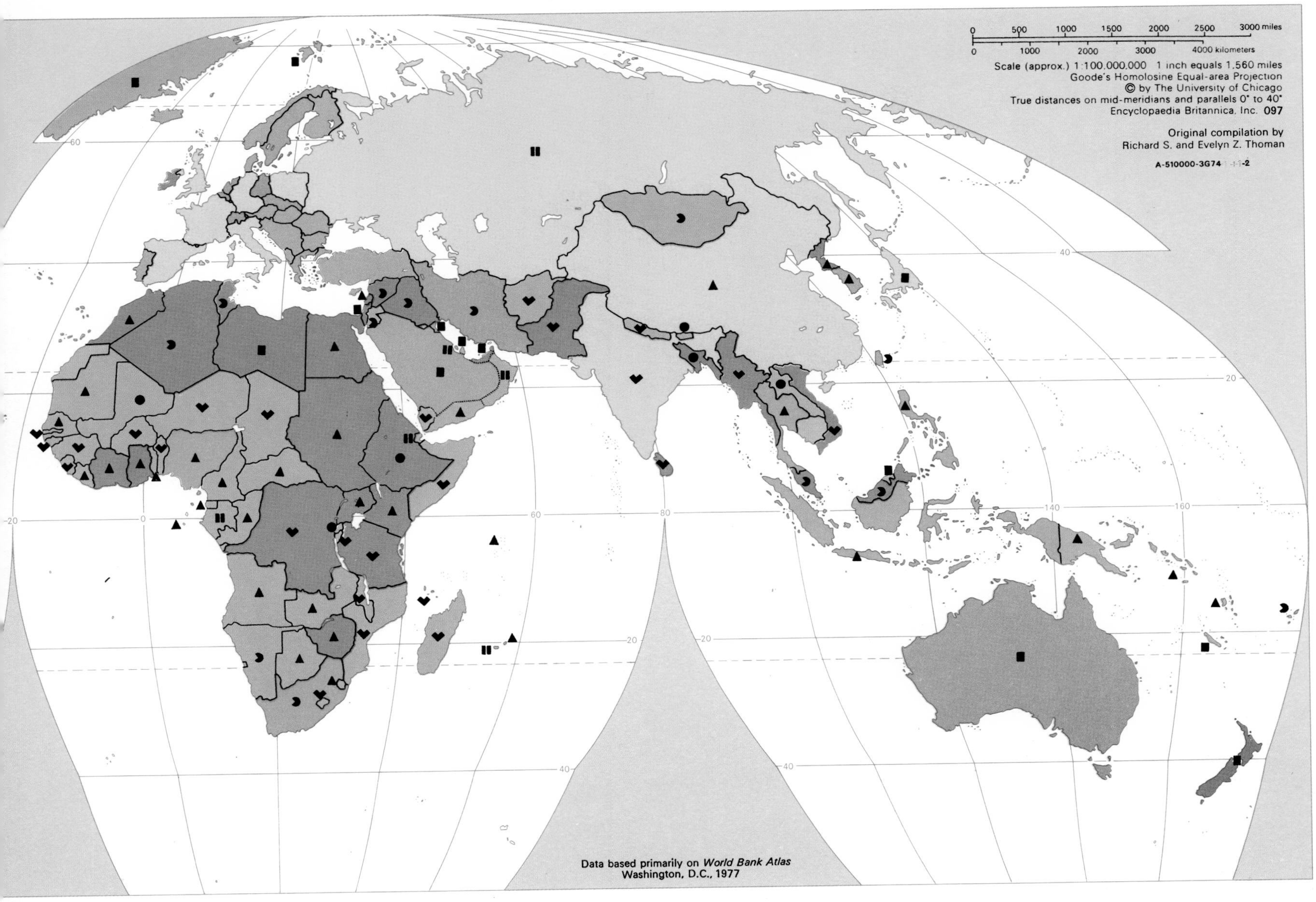
0 500 1000 1500 2000 2500 3000 miles
0 1000 2000 3000 4000 kilometers
Scale (approx.) 1:100,000,000 1 inch equals 1,560 miles
Goode's Homolosine Equal-area Projection
© by The University of Chicago
True distances on mid-meridians and parallels 0° to 40°
Encyclopaedia Britannica, Inc. 097
Original compilation by
Richard S. and Evelyn Z. Thoman
A-510000-3G74 -2
Data based primarily on *World Bank Atlas*
Washington, D.C., 1977

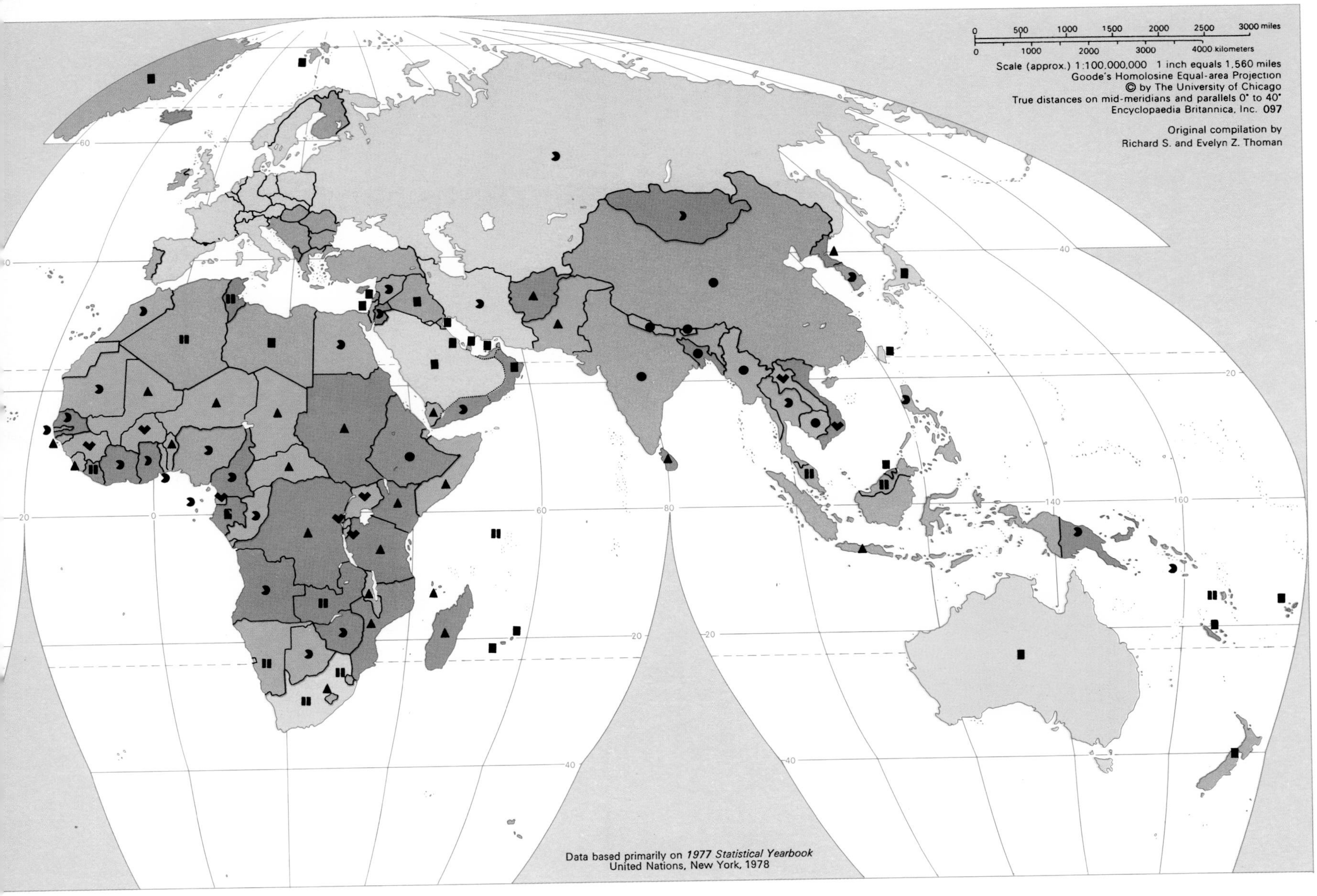
0 500 1000 1500 2000 2500 3000 miles
0 1000 2000 3000 4000 kilometers
Scale (approx.) 1:100,000,000 1 inch equals 1,560 miles
Goode's Homolosine Equal-area Projection
© by The University of Chicago
True distances on mid-meridians and parallels 0° to 40°
Encyclopaedia Britannica, Inc. 097
Original compilation by
Richard S. and Evelyn Z. Thoman
Data based primarily on *1977 Statistical Yearbook*
United Nations, New York, 1978

Intercontinental Air Connections

Scale (approx.) 1:70,000,000 1 inch equals 1100 miles
Center: 45° North Latitude, 10° East Longitude
Briesemeister Elliptical Equal-area Projection
Adapted by permission from the American Geographical Society
Encyclopaedia Britannica, Inc. 087
A-510000-4D74 -1-1-1

The routes shown represent the generalized pattern of principal world air flights between continents showing points of departure and arrival. Connecting flights between points on the same continent are not shown. The data are taken primarily from the *Official Airline Guide*, Worldwide edition (R. H. Donnelley Corp.), and *Air Distances Manual* (International Air Transport Association).

Great Circle Distances

	Statute miles	Kilo-meters
Beirut to Belgrade	1,107	1,782
Lagos	2,784	4,481
Paris	1,980	3,186
Rome	1,377	2,216
Cairo to Colombo	3,524	5,671
London	2,192	3,528
Moscow	1,808	2,910
Teheran	1,214	1,954
Caracas to Guatemala City	1,609	2,590
Las Palmas	3,540	5,696
Madrid	4,349	6,999
Miami	1,361	2,190
Copenhagen to Anchorage	4,310	6,935
Montreal	3,604	5,799
Sondre Stromfjord	2,129	3,427
Tel Aviv-Yafo	1,953	3,143
Dakar to Geneva	2,567	4,132
Madrid	1,964	3,161
New York	3,800	6,115
Recife	1,980	3,186
Honolulu to Brisbane	4,694	7,554
Los Angeles	2,551	4,106
Manila	5,292	8,515
Tokyo	3,846	6,189
Karachi to Addis Ababa	2,167	3,486
Athens	2,684	4,320
Cairo	2,210	3,556
Nairobi	2,713	4,367
Lima to Kingston	2,069	3,330
Miami	2,619	4,215
New York	3,642	5,861
Panama City	1,465	2,357
Lisbon to Luanda	3,588	5,774
Montreal	3,261	5,248
Paramaribo	3,679	5,920
Rio de Janeiro	4,791	7,710
London to Bermuda	3,428	5,514
Chicago	3,941	6,343
Los Angeles	5,439	8,753
Tunis	1,137	1,830
Los Angeles to Panama City	3,007	4,840
Papeete	4,105	6,607
Paris	5,659	9,108
Tokyo	5,473	8,808
Mexico City to Chicago	1,689	2,718
Lima	2,635	4,241
Vancouver	2,448	3,940
Washington, D.C.	1,879	3,024
Moscow to Amsterdam	1,330	2,142
Delhi	2,709	4,360
Peking	3,606	5,802
Teheran	1,545	2,486
New York to Bogotá	2,481	3,993
Brasília	4,238	6,821
London	3,440	5,536
Rome	4,263	6,861
Panama City to Brasília	2,754	4,433
Houston	1,772	2,852
Los Angeles	3,007	4,840
Quito	640	1,029
Paris to Colombo	5,292	8,516
Fort-de-France	4,255	6,848
Kano	2,559	4,115
Moscow	1,541	2,479
Rio de Janeiro to London	5,746	9,248
Monrovia	2,994	4,818
New York	4,800	7,725
Panama City	3,289	5,293
Rome to Delhi	3,685	5,929
Lagos	2,490	4,007
Nairobi	3,353	5,396
Tel Aviv-Yafo	1,416	2,280
Sydney to Auckland	1,341	2,159
Manila	3,888	6,258
Pago Pago	2,733	4,399
Singapore	3,912	6,296
Tokyo to Anchorage	3,457	5,563
San Francisco	5,145	8,280
Seattle	4,790	7,708
Wake	1,983	3,192

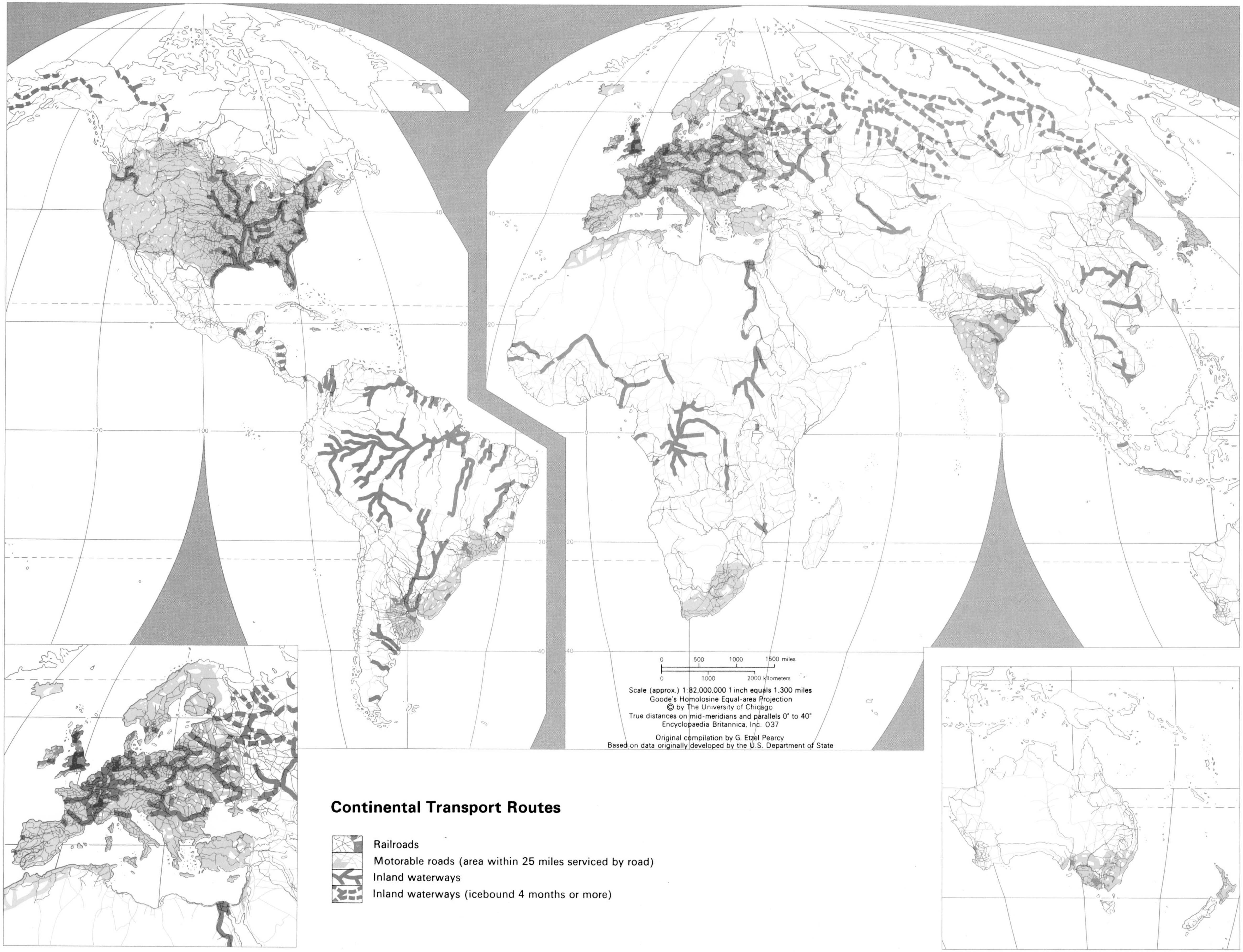
0 500 1000 1500 miles
0 1000 2000 kilometers
Scale (approx.) 1:82,000,000 1 inch equals 1,300 miles
Goode's Homolosine Equal-area Projection
© by The University of Chicago
True distances on mid-meridians and parallels 0° to 40°
Encyclopaedia Britannica, Inc. 037
Original compilation by G. Etzel Pearcy
Based on data originally developed by the U.S. Department of State
Railroads
Motorable roads (area within 25 miles serviced by road)
Inland waterways
Inland waterways (icebound 4 months or more)

Continental Transport Routes

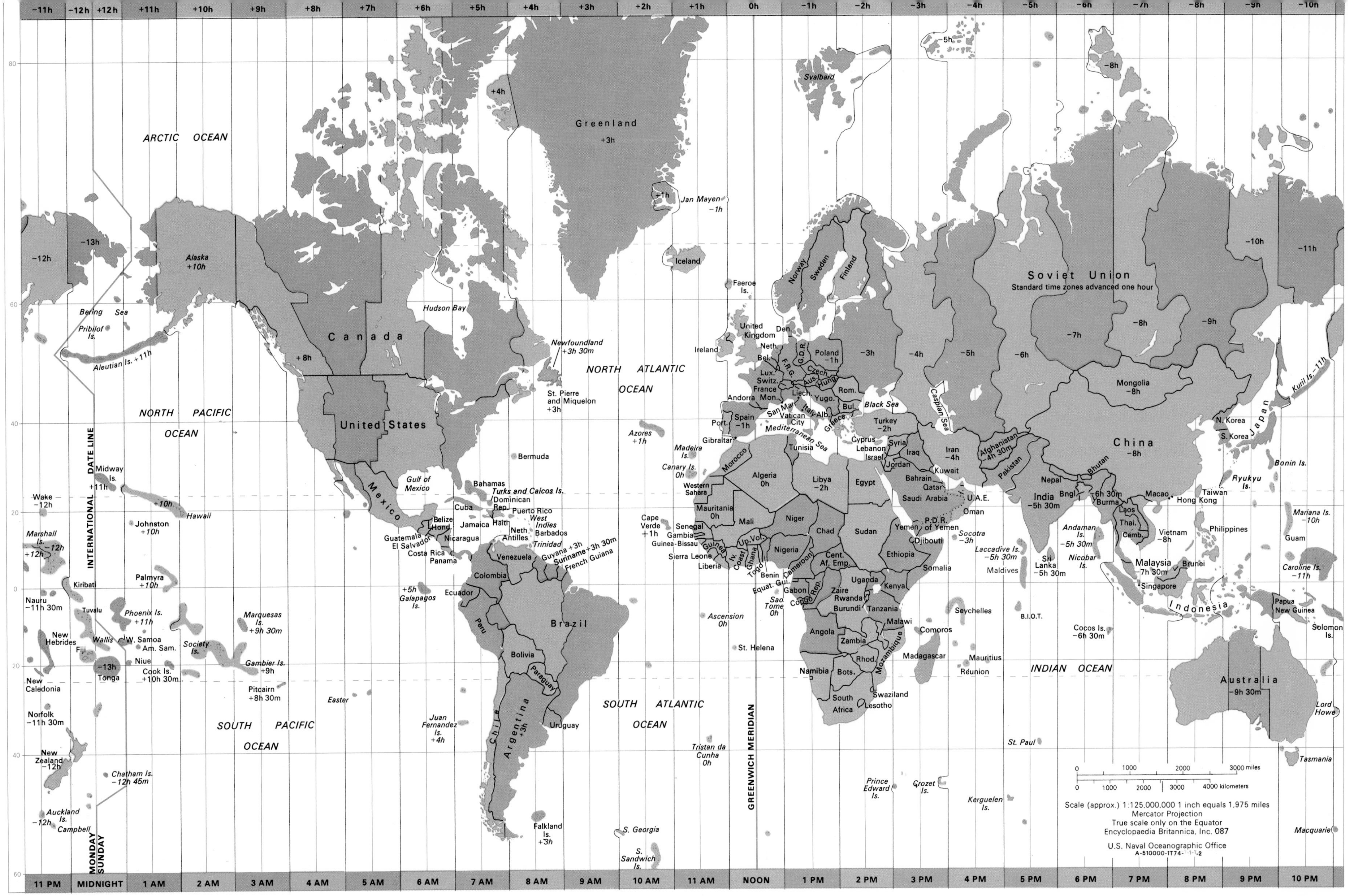

Time Zones

- Standard time zone of even-numbered hours from Greenwich time
- Standard time zone of odd-numbered hours from Greenwich time
- Time varies from the standard time zone by half an hour
- Time varies from the standard time zone by other than half an hour

h m hours, minutes

The standard time zone system, fixed by international agreement and by law in each country, is based on a theoretical division of the globe into 24 zones of 15° longitude each. The mid-meridian of each zone fixes the hour for the entire zone. The zero time zone extends 7½° east and 7½° west of the Greenwich meridian, 0° longitude. Since the earth rotates toward the east, time zones to the west of Greenwich are earlier, to the east, later.

Plus and minus hours at the top of the map are added to or subtracted from local time to find Greenwich time. Local standard time can be determined for any area in the world by adding one hour for each time zone counted in an easterly direction from one's own, or by subtracting one hour for each zone counted in a westerly direction. To separate one day from the next, the 180th meridian has been designated as the international date line. On both sides of the line the time of day is the same, but west of the line it is one day later than it is to the east.

Countries that adhere to the international zone system adopt the zone applicable to their location. Some countries, however, establish time zones based on political boundaries, or adopt the time zone of a neighboring unit. For all or part of the year some countries also advance their time by one hour, thereby utilizing more daylight hours each day.

Climate Graphs

Each graph below shows temperature and rainfall at a weather station that was selected to illustrate one of the climate regions described in the legend at the right. The weather stations are keyed by number to the maps. The elements of the graphs are identified in the sample graph at the top, with a temperature scale in degrees Fahrenheit and Celsius (Centigrade), and a precipitation scale in inches and millimeters.

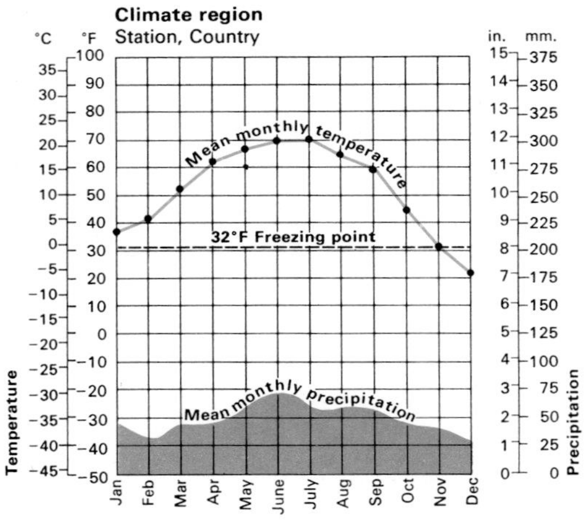

1 Rainy tropical
Manaus, Brazil

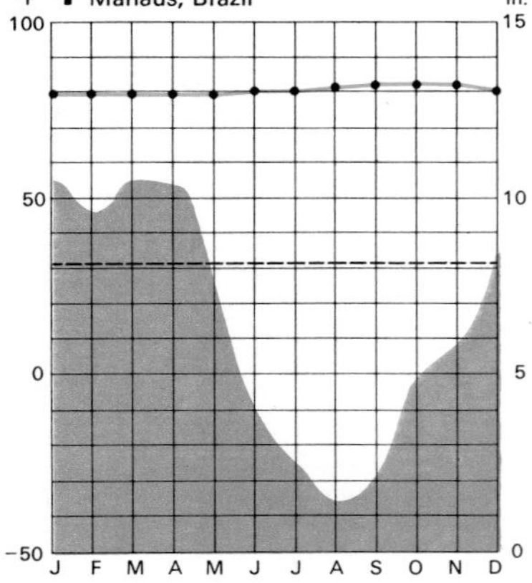

2 Wet and dry tropical
Madras, India

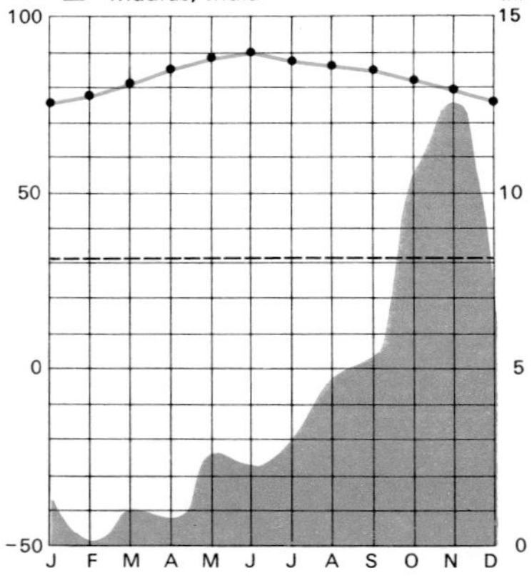

3 Semiarid tropical
Cloncurry, Australia

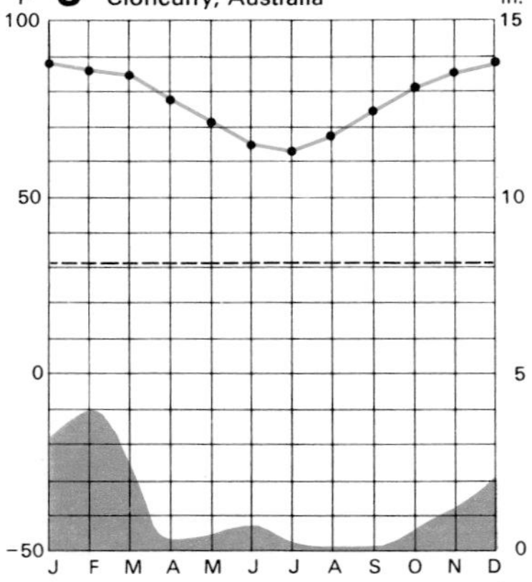

4 Hot arid
Aswan, Egypt

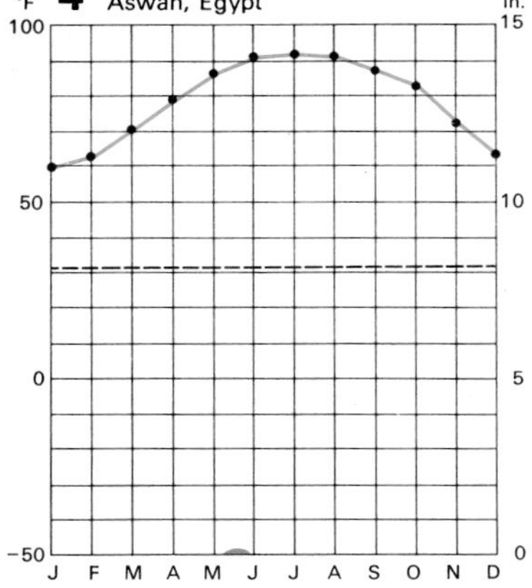

5 Humid subtropical
Tokyo, Japan

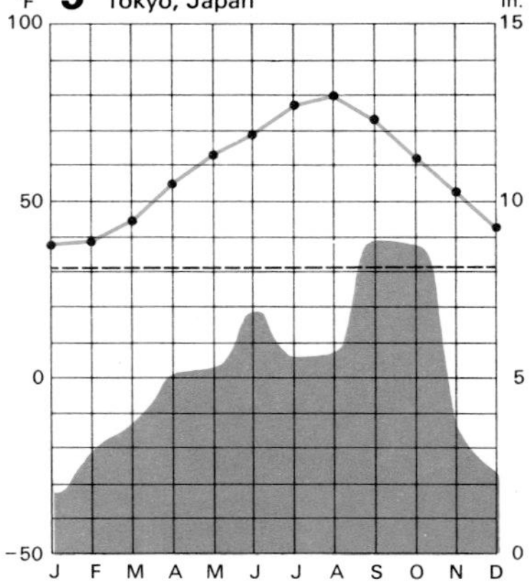

6 Dry subtropical
Oran, Algeria

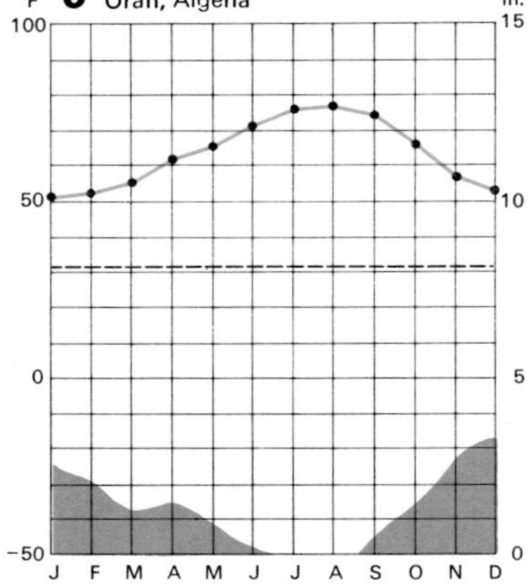

7 Humid mid-latitude
Chicago, United States

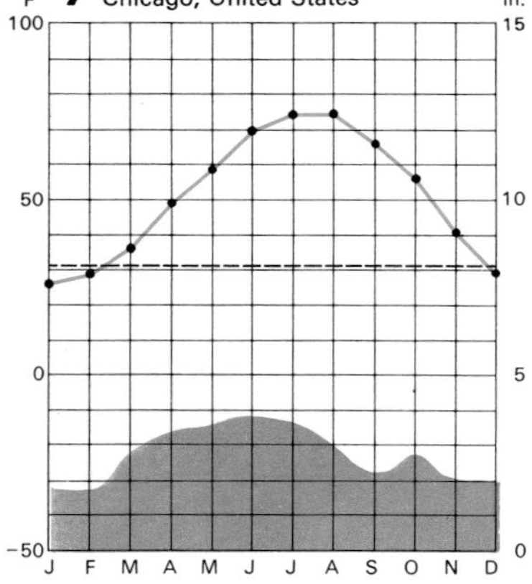

8 Temperate marine
Amsterdam, Netherlands

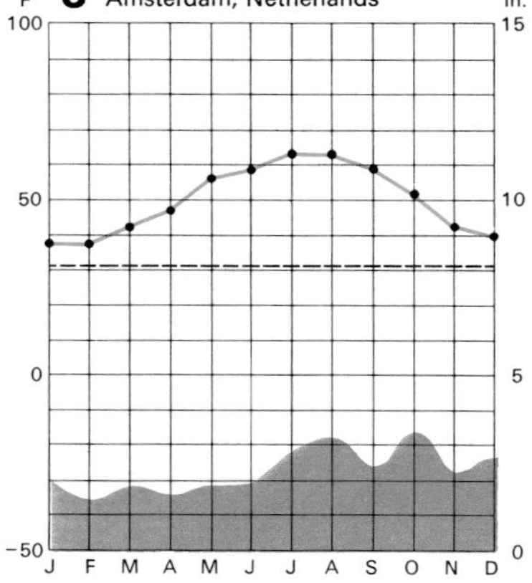

9 Semiarid mid-latitude
Ankara, Turkey

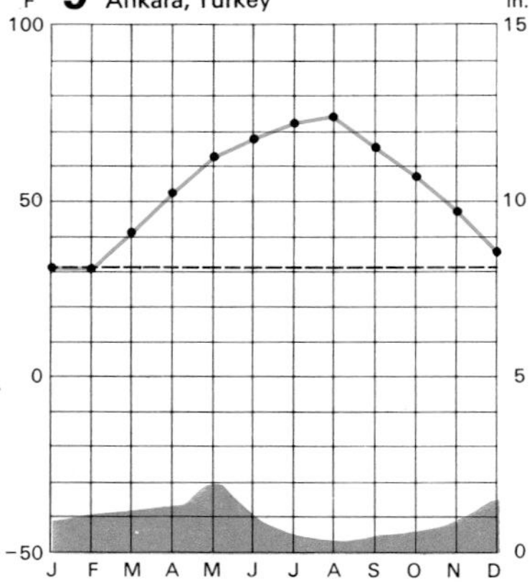

10 Arid mid-latitude
Las Vegas, United States

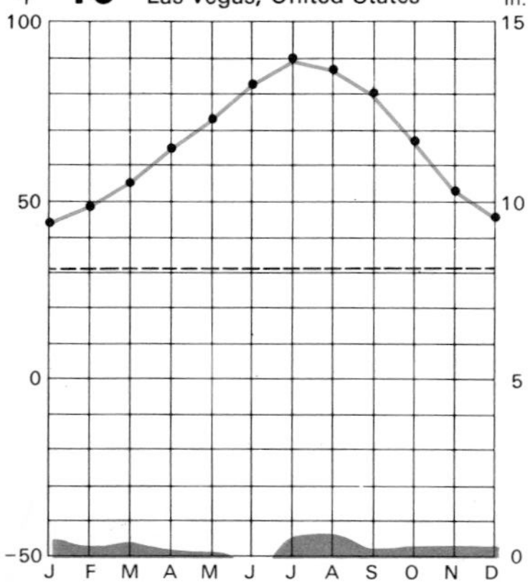

11 Subarctic
Yakutsk, Soviet Union

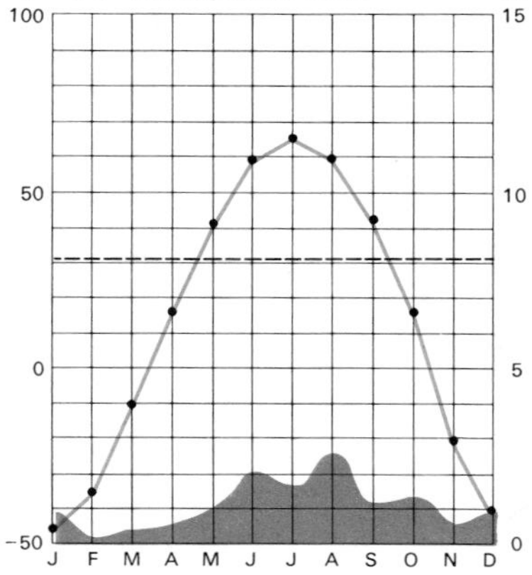

12 Arctic margin
Dikson, Soviet Union

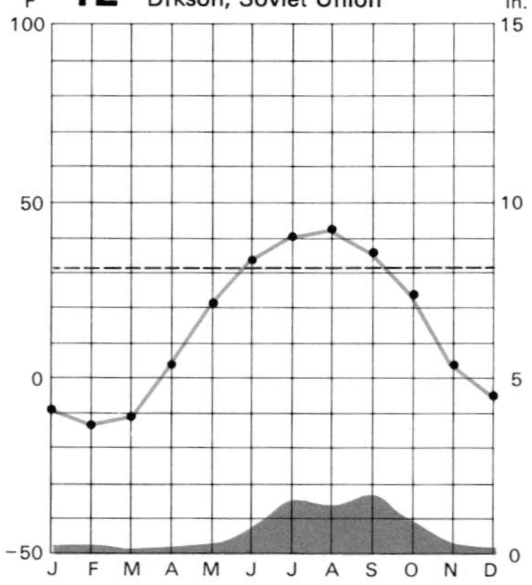

Climate Regions

- **Rainy tropical** At most, one or two dry months; all mor warm or hot
- **Wet and dry tropical** A well-developed dry season with one or two rainy seasons; all months warm or hot
- **Semiarid tropical** Light precipitation, rapid evaporation; all months warm or hot
- **Hot arid** Negligible precipitation, rapid evaporation; all months warm or hot
- **Humid subtropical** Precipitation in all seasons with maximum in summer; long warm summers, cool winters
- **Dry subtropical** Hot dry summers; cool, moderately rainy winters
- **Humid mid-latitude** Precipitation in all seasons with maximum in summer; warm or hot summers, cold winters
- **Temperate marine** Numerous rainy days in all seasons with moderate total precipitation, higher precipitation in highland areas; warm summers, cool winters
- **Semiarid mid-latitude** Light precipitation; warm or hot summers, cool or cold winters
- **Arid mid-latitude** Extremely light precipitation; warm or hot summers, cool or cold winters
- **Subarctic** Light precipitation; short cool summers, long very cold winters
- **Arctic margin** Extremely light precipitation; very short cold summers, extremely long cold winters
- **High altitude** Climate varies with elevation, latitude, and exposure

Mean Annual Temperature

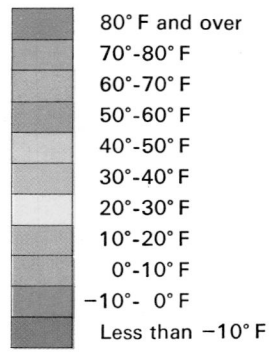

- 80° F and over
- 70°-80° F
- 60°-70° F
- 50°-60° F
- 40°-50° F
- 30°-40° F
- 20°-30° F
- 10°-20° F
- 0°-10° F
- −10°- 0° F
- Less than −10° F

Mean Annual Precipitation

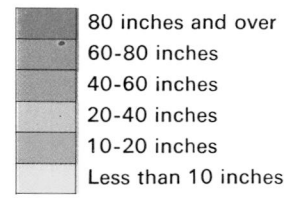

- 80 inches and over
- 60-80 inches
- 40-60 inches
- 20-40 inches
- 10-20 inches
- Less than 10 inches

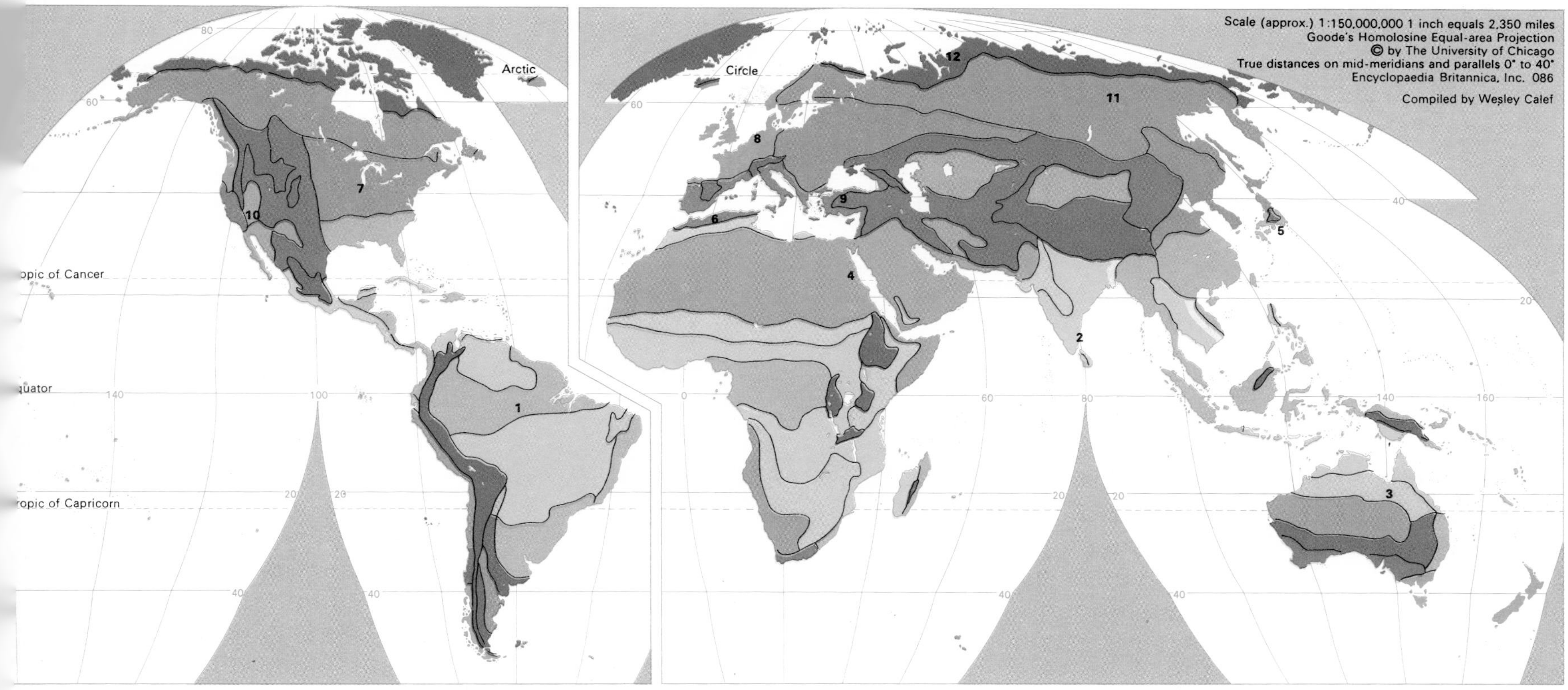
Scale (approx.) 1:150,000,000 1 inch equals 2,350 miles
Goode's Homolosine Equal-area Projection
© by The University of Chicago
True distances on mid-meridians and parallels 0° to 40°
Encyclopaedia Britannica, Inc. 086
Compiled by Wesley Calef
Arctic
Circle
Tropic of Cancer
Equator
Tropic of Capricorn
1
2
3
4
5
6
7
8
9
10
11
12

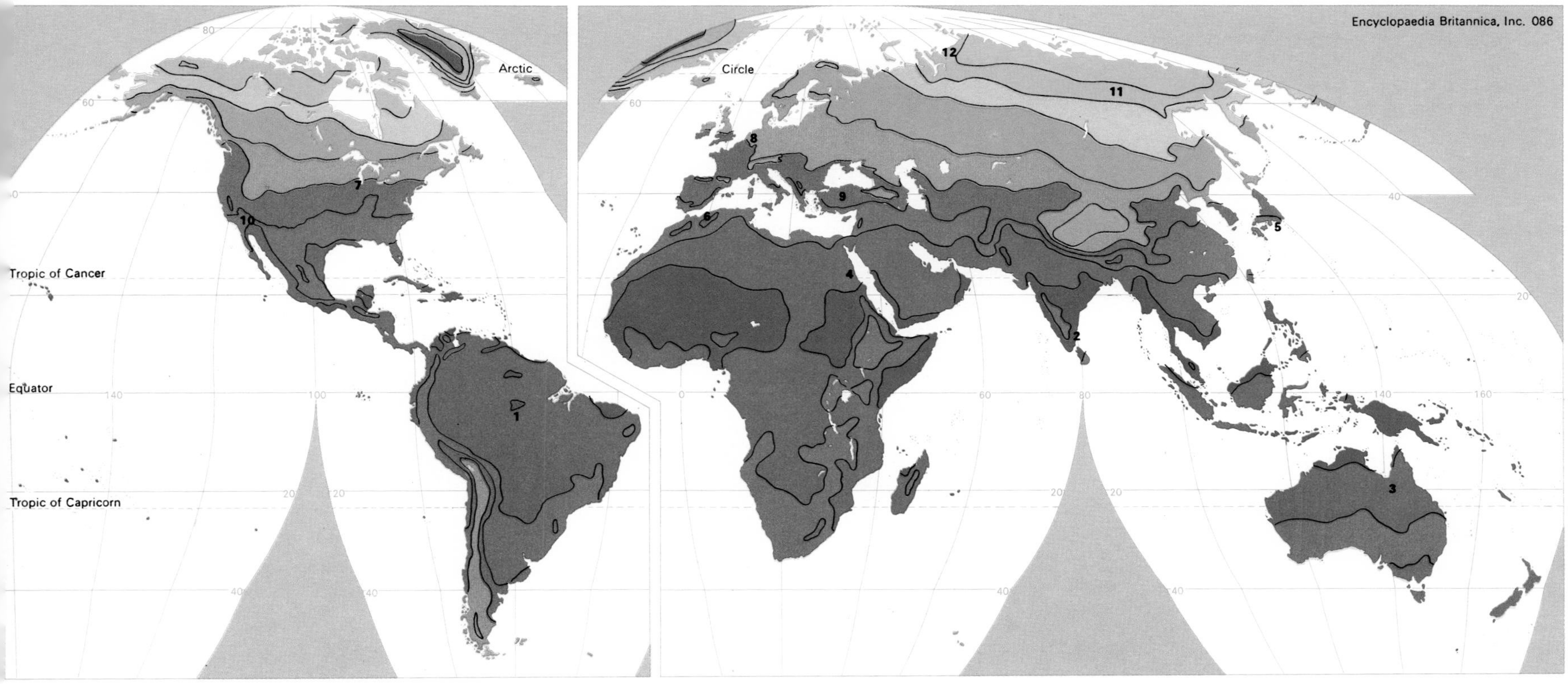
Encyclopaedia Britannica, Inc. 086
Arctic
Circle
Tropic of Cancer
Equator
Tropic of Capricorn
1
2
3
4
5
6
7
8
9
10
11
12

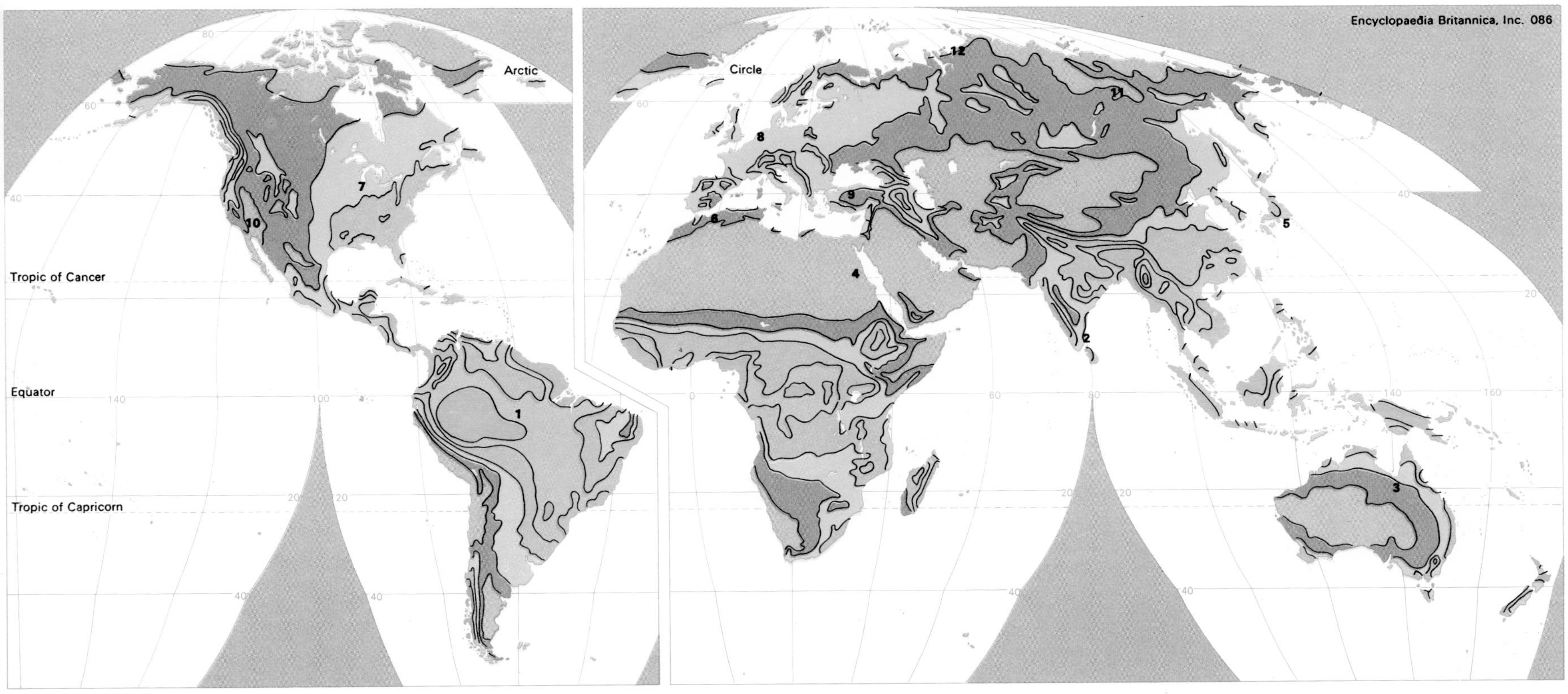
Encyclopaedia Britannica, Inc. 086
Arctic
Circle
Tropic of Cancer
Equator
Tropic of Capricorn
1
2
3
4
5
6
7
8
9
10
11
12

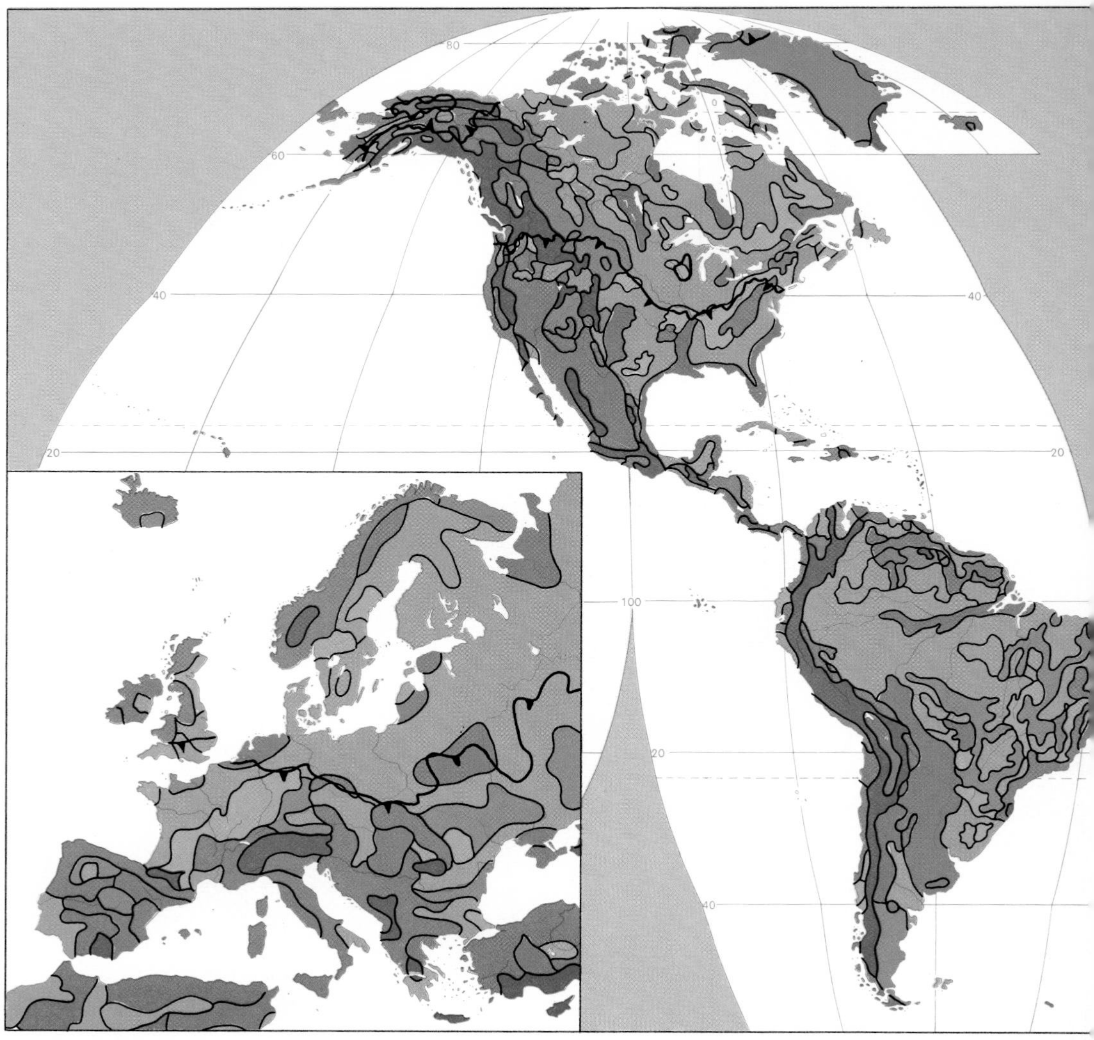

Surface Configuration

Smooth lands

- Level plains: nearly all slopes gentle; local relief less than 100 ft. (30 m.)
- Irregular plains: majority of slopes gentle; local relief 100-300 ft. (30-90 m.)

Broken lands

- Tablelands and plateaus: majority of slopes gentle, with the gentler slopes on the uplands; local relief more than 300 ft. (90 m.)
- Hill-studded plains: majority of slopes gentle, with the gentler slopes in the lowlands; local relief 300-1,000 ft. (90-300 m.)
- Mountain-studded plains: majority of slopes gentle, with the gentler slopes in the lowlands; local relief more than 1,000 ft. (300 m.)

Rough lands

- Hill lands: steeper slopes predominate; local relief less than 1,000 ft. (300 m.)
- Mountains: steeper slopes predominate; local relief 1,000-5,000 ft. (300-1,500 m.)
- Mountains of great relief: steeper slopes predominate; local relief more than 5,000 ft. (1,500 m.)

Other surfaces

- Ice caps: permanent ice
- Maximum extent of glaciation

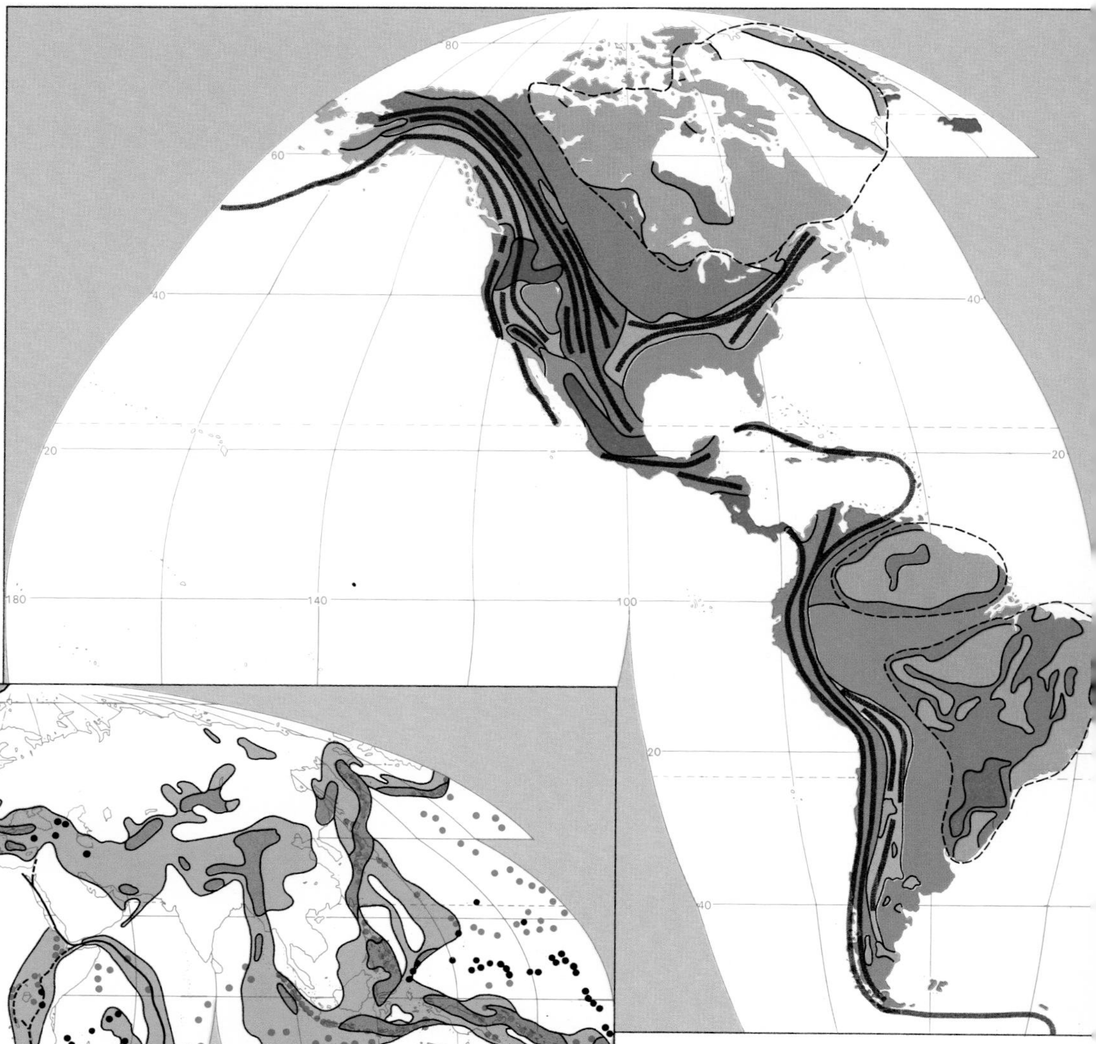

Earth Structure and Tectonics

- Precambrian stable shield areas
- Exposed Precambrian rock
- Paleozoic and Mesozoic flat-lying sedimentary rocks
- Principal Paleozoic and Mesozoic folded areas
- Cenozoic sedimentary rocks
- Principal Cenozoic folded areas
- Lava plateaus
- Major trends of folding

Geologic time chart

Precambrian—from formation of the earth (at least 4 billion years ago) to 600 million years ago

Paleozoic—from 600 million to 200 million years ago

Mesozoic—from 200 million to 70 million years ago

Cenozoic—from 70 million years ago to present time

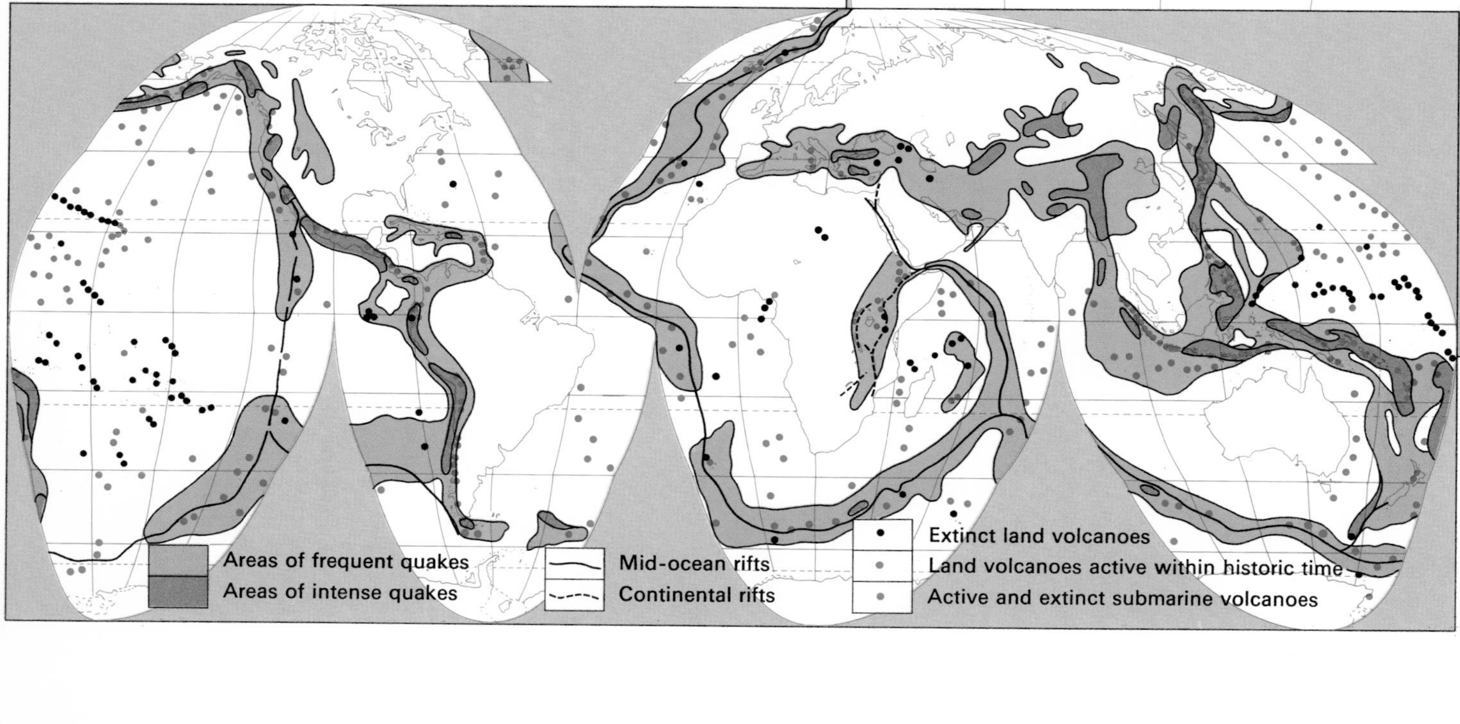
Areas of frequent quakes
Areas of intense quakes
Mid-ocean rifts
Continental rifts
Extinct land volcanoes
Land volcanoes active within historic time
Active and extinct submarine volcanoes

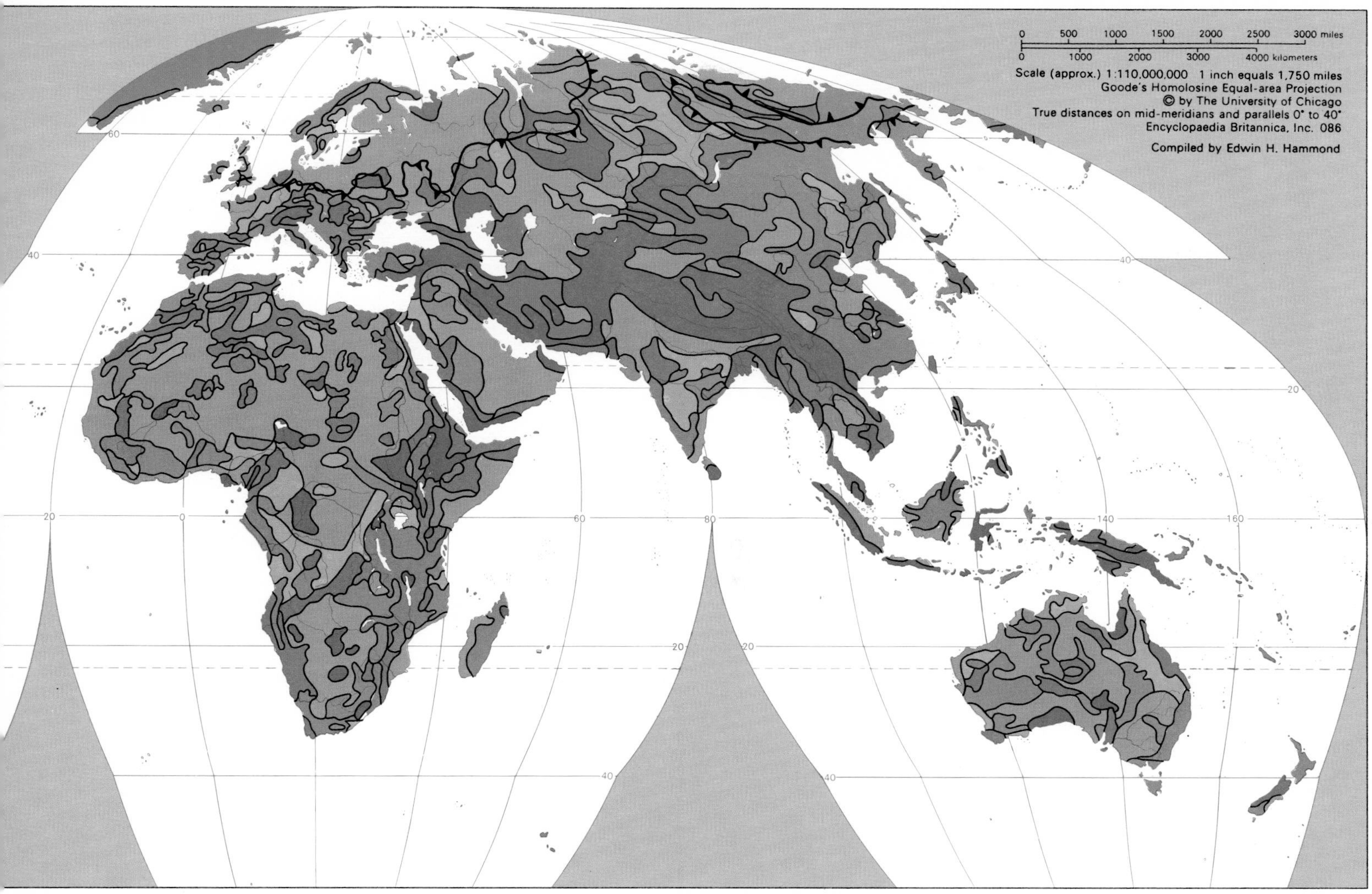
0 500 1000 1500 2000 2500 3000 miles
0 1000 2000 3000 4000 kilometers
Scale (approx.) 1:110,000,000 1 inch equals 1,750 miles
Goode's Homolosine Equal-area Projection
© by The University of Chicago
True distances on mid-meridians and parallels 0° to 40°
Encyclopaedia Britannica, Inc. 086
Compiled by Edwin H. Hammond

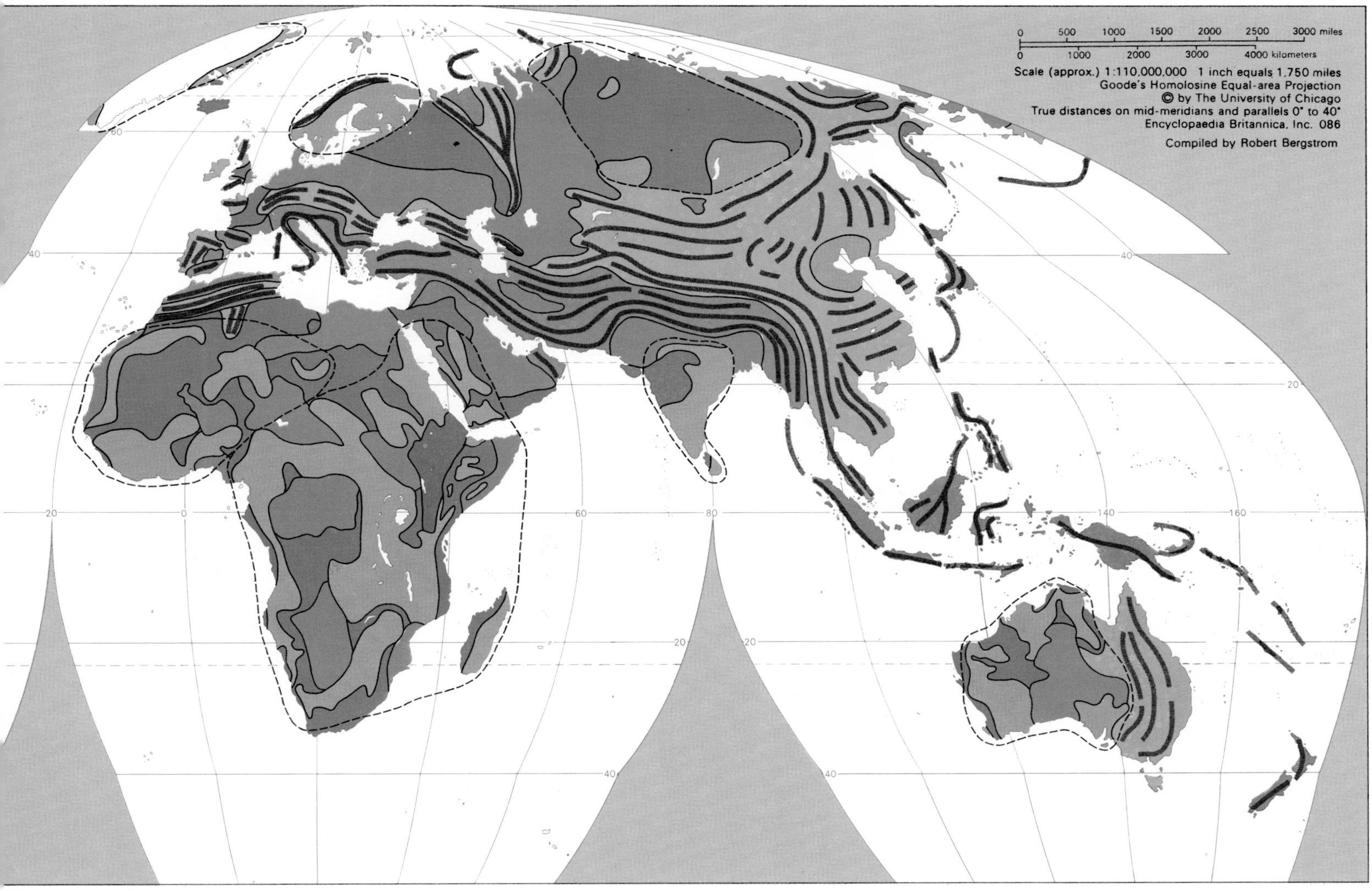
0 500 1000 1500 2000 2500 3000 miles
0 1000 2000 3000 4000 kilometers
Scale (approx.) 1:110,000,000 1 inch equals 1,750 miles
Goode's Homolosine Equal-area Projection
© by The University of Chicago
True distances on mid-meridians and parallels 0° to 40°
Encyclopaedia Britannica, Inc. 086
Compiled by Robert Bergstrom

Development of the earth's structure

The earth is in process of constant transformation. Movements in the hot, dense interior of the earth result in folding and fracture of the crust and transfer of molten material to the surface. As a result, large structures such as mountain ranges, volcanoes, lava plateaus, and rift valleys are created. The forces that bring about these structural changes are called *tectonic forces*.

The present continents have developed from stable nuclei, or *shields*, of ancient (Precambrian) rock. Erosive forces such as water, wind, and ice have worn away particles of the rock, depositing them at the edges of the shields, where they have accumulated and ultimately become sedimentary rock. Subsequently, in plaees, these extensive areas of flat-lying rock have been elevated, folded, or warped, by the action of tectonic forces, to form mountains. The shape of these mountains has been altered by later erosion. Where the forces of erosion have been at work for a long time, the mountains tend to have a low relief and rounded contours, like the Appalachians. Mountains more recently formed are high and rugged, like the Himalayas.

The map above depicts some of the major geologic structures of the earth and identifies them according to the period of their formation. A geologic time chart is included in the legend. The inset map shows the most important areas of earthquakes, rifts, and volcanic activity. Comparison of all the maps will show the close correlation between present-day mountain systems, recent (Cenozoic) mountain-building, and the areas of frequent earthquakes and active volcanoes.

Natural Vegetation

Broad-leaved evergreen vegetation
- Broad-leaved evergreen forest
- Broad-leaved evergreen shrub formation
- Scattered broad-leaved evergreen shrubs
- Scattered broad-leaved evergreen dwarf shrubs

Broad-leaved deciduous vegetation
- Broad-leaved deciduous forest
- Broad-leaved deciduous shrub formation
- Scattered broad-leaved deciduous shrubs
- Scattered broad-leaved deciduous dwarf shrubs

Coniferous vegetation
- Needle-leaved evergreen forest
- Scattered needle-leaved evergreen trees
- Needle-leaved deciduous forest

Mixed vegetation without grass
- Forest of broad-leaved evergreen and deciduous trees
- Forest of broad-leaved and needle-leaved evergreen trees
- Broad-leaved deciduous forests with broad-leaved evergreen shrubs
- Forest of broad-leaved deciduous and needle-leaved evergreen trees

Mixed vegetation with grass
- Grassland with scattered broad-leaved evergreen trees
- Grassland with broad-leaved evergreen shrubs
- Grassland with scattered broad-leaved deciduous trees
- Grassland with broad-leaved deciduous shrubs

Grassland, tundra, barren
- Grassland
- Patches of grass
- Lichens and grasses
- Lichens and mosses
- Barren

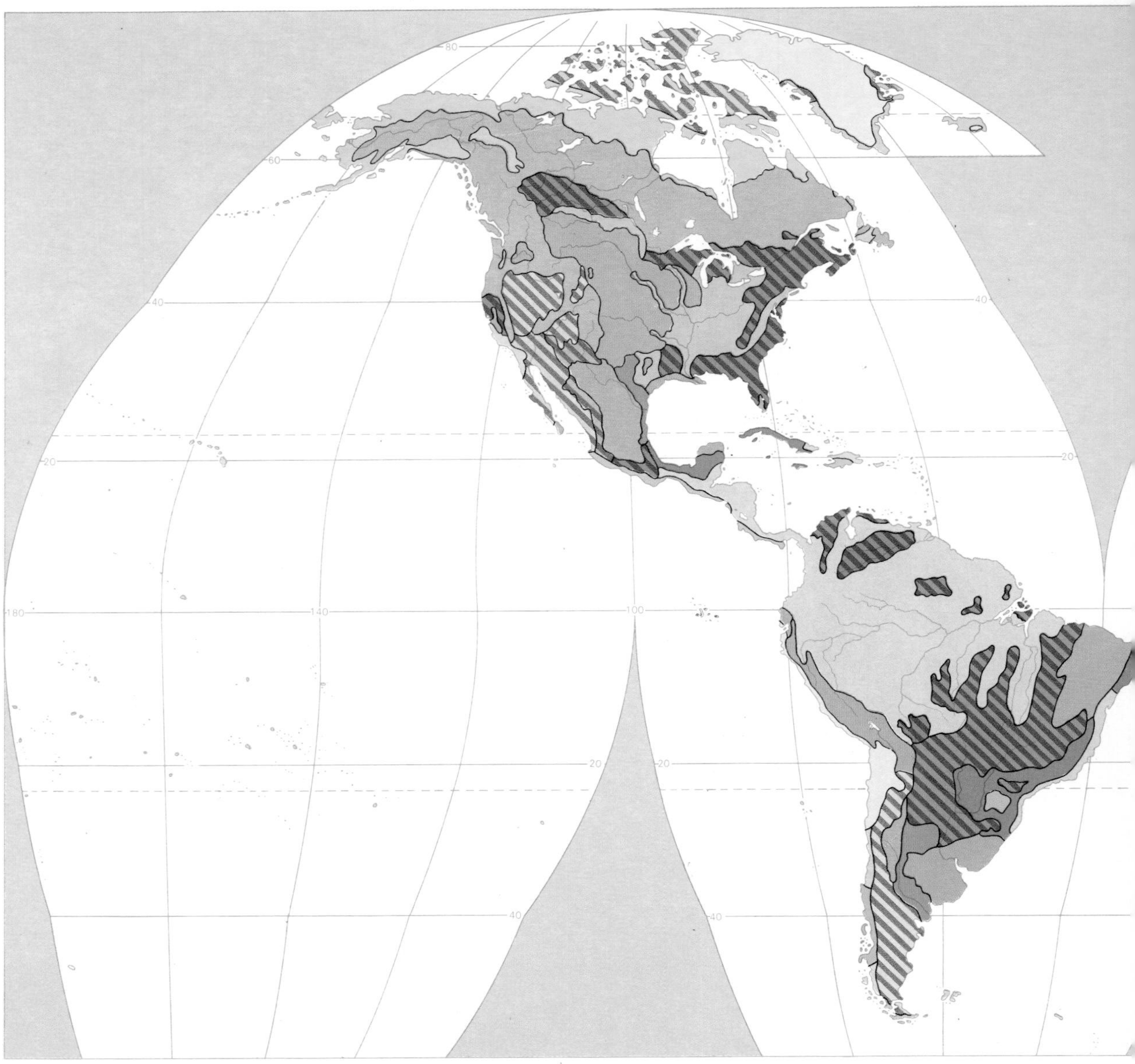

Soils

- Tundra soils of frigid climates; commonly with permanently frozen subsoil; supports dwarf shrubs, mosses, and lichens; some used for reindeer pasture
- Podzolic soils of humid, cool climates; covered with predominantly coniferous forest; some farming, mainly subsistence
- Podzolic soils of humid, temperate climates; originally covered with predominantly deciduous forest, much of it removed to accommodate extensive general farming, industry, and cities
- Podzolic soils of humid, warm climates; covered with coniferous or mixed forest; general farming
- Chernozemic soils of subhumid and semiarid, cool to tropical climates; supports mainly grasslands; extensive grain and livestock farming
- Latosolic soils of humid or wet-dry tropical and subtropical climates; supports forest or savanna; shifting cultivation with some plantation agriculture
- Grumusolic soils of humid to semiarid and temperate to tropical climates, with distinct wet and dry seasons; mainly grass-covered; livestock and grain farming
- Desertic soils of arid climates; includes many areas of shallow, stony soils; sparse cover of shrubs and grass, some suitable for grazing; fertile if irrigated; dry farming possible in some areas
- Mountain soils of all climates; shallow, stony; barren, grass-covered, or forested, depending on climate; includes many areas of other soils
- Alluvial soils of all climates; deposited by water in flood plains and deltas of rivers; intensive farming in most temperate and some tropical regions (many smaller areas not shown)
- Ice cap of polar regions

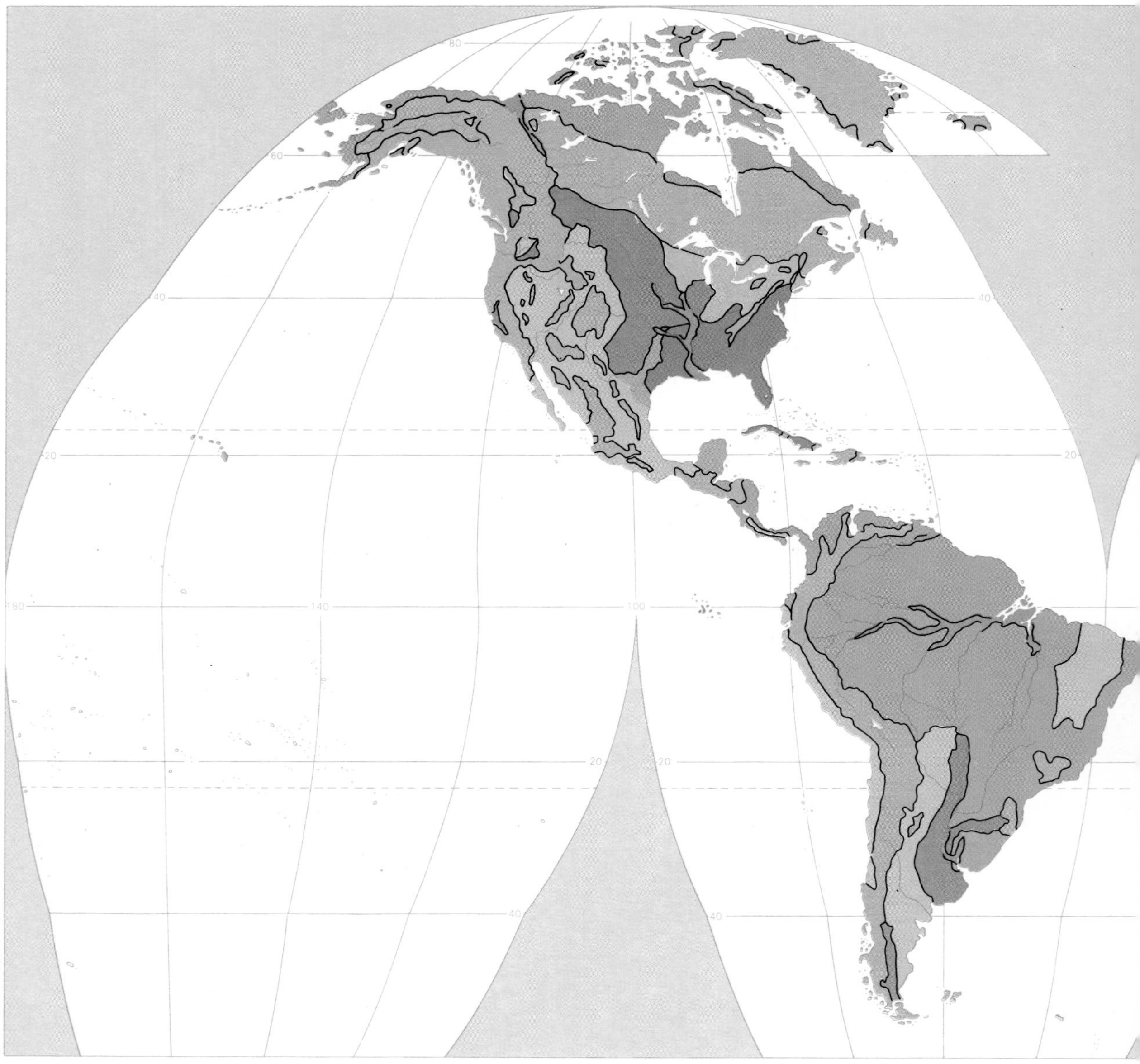

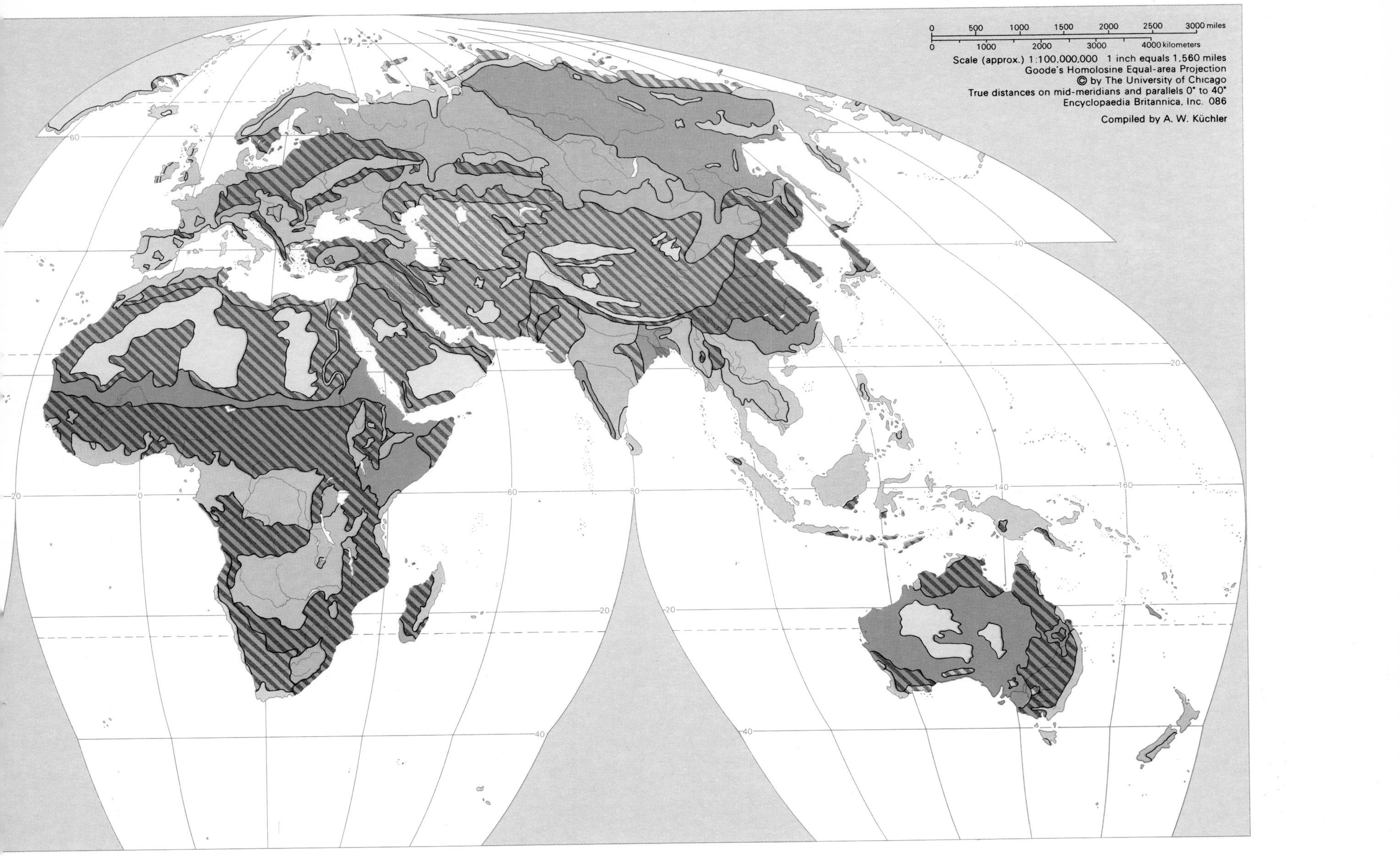

0 500 1000 1500 2000 2500 3000 miles
0 1000 2000 3000 4000 kilometers
Scale (approx.) 1:100,000,000 1 inch equals 1,560 miles
Goode's Homolosine Equal-area Projection
© by The University of Chicago
True distances on mid-meridians and parallels 0° to 40°
Encyclopaedia Britannica, Inc. 086
Compiled by A. W. Küchler

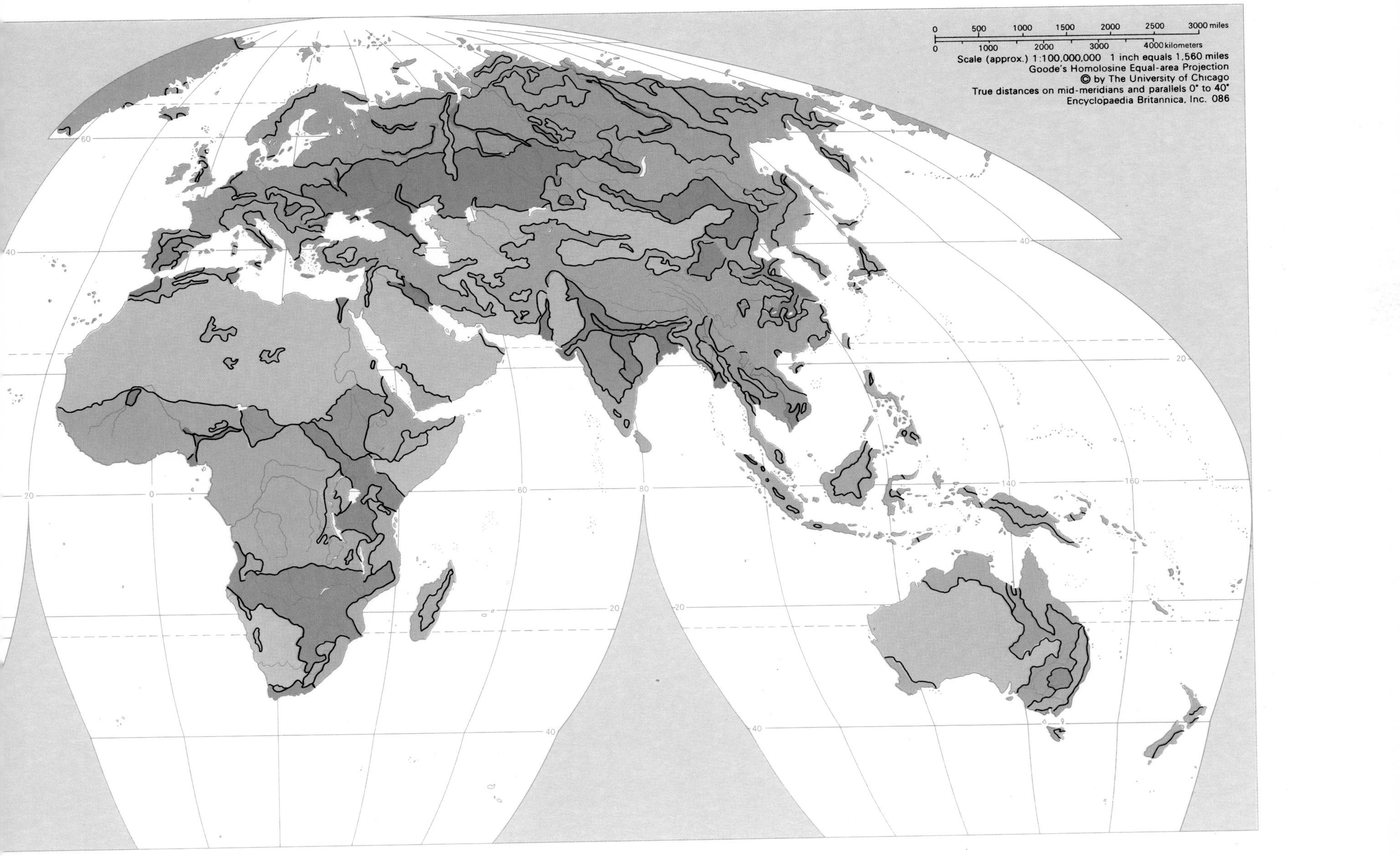

0 500 1000 1500 2000 2500 3000 miles
0 1000 2000 3000 4000 kilometers
Scale (approx.) 1:100,000,000 1 inch equals 1,560 miles
Goode's Homolosine Equal-area Projection
© by The University of Chicago
True distances on mid-meridians and parallels 0° to 40°
Encyclopaedia Britannica, Inc. 086

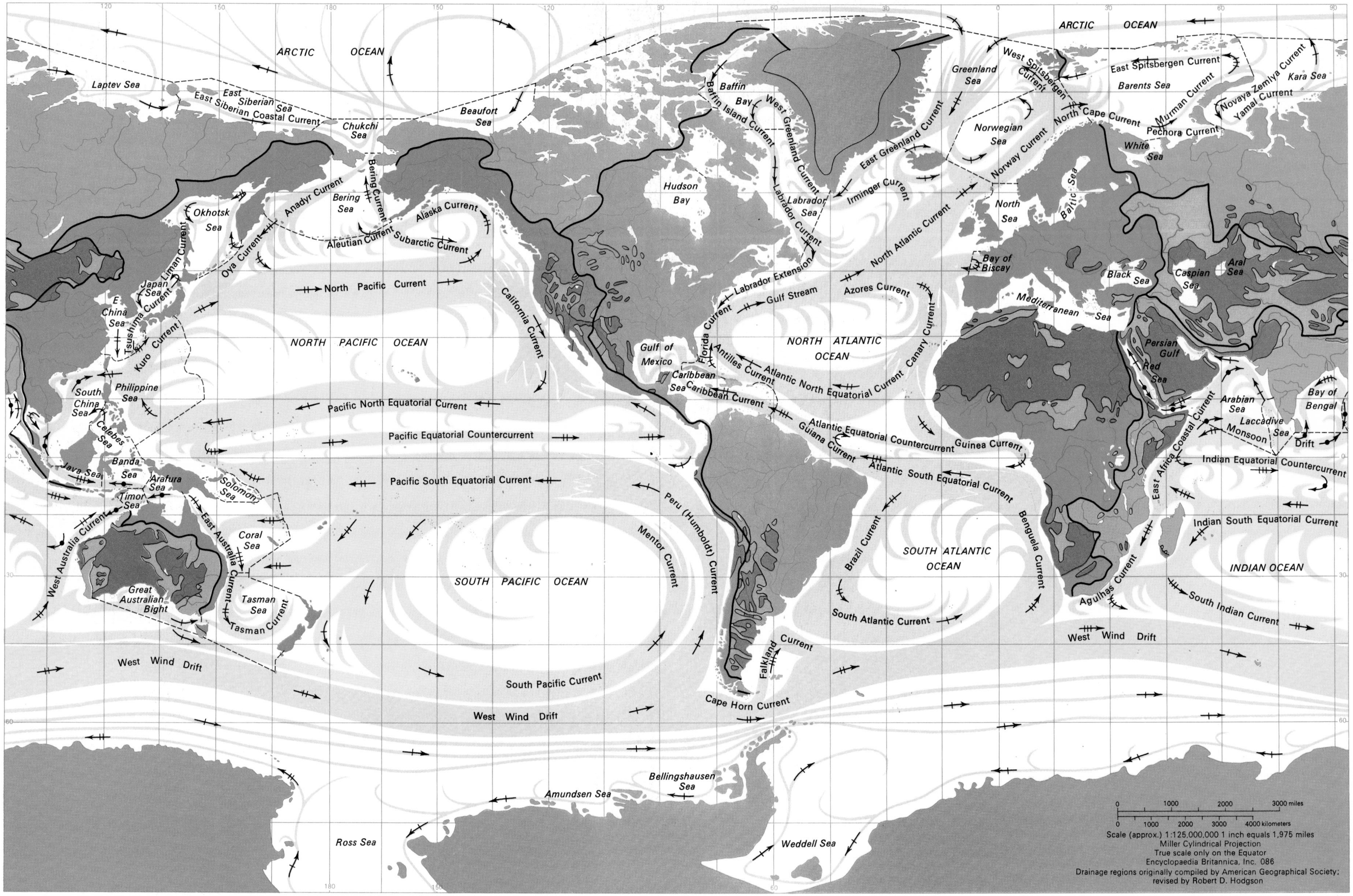

Drainage Regions and Ocean Currents

Currents during Northern Hemisphere winter

- Cold current
- Warm current
- Indicates a current that reverses direction during Northern Hemisphere summer

Speed of current

(1 knot=1 nautical mile[6,076 ft.] per hour)

- Less than 0.5 knots
- 0.5—0.8 knots
- Greater than 0.8 knots
- Limits of seas

Drainage regions

Surface drainage reaching an Ocean

- Outline of oceanic drainage regions
- Atlantic Ocean
- Pacific Ocean
- Indian Ocean
- Arctic Ocean

- Surface drainage not reaching an ocean
- Arid regions
- Ice cap

THE MAP FORM column of the Glossary lists in alphabetical order the geographical terms, including any abbreviations, that appear on the maps. Terms preceded by a hyphen are those which commonly appear as endings in map names (for example, -san in Fuji-san, -älven in Dalälven). The languages of the terms are identified by abbreviations in *italics* (see Abbreviations of Language Names below). The Glossary provides the English, German, Spanish, French, and Portuguese equivalent for each term.

As a rule, the translations were made from the map form to English, then from English into the other four languages. Since the glossary terms and translations refer to specific map features, some may vary from the customary dictionary definitions of the terms.

IN DER SPALTE "Geographische Begriffe" werden alle Begriffe und Abkürzungen in alphabetischer Ordnung aufgeführt, die in den Karten erscheinen. Begriffe mit vorgesetztem Bindestrich erscheinen normalerweise als Wortendungen in Kartennamen (z.B. -san in Fuji-san, -älven in Dalälven). In *Kursivschrift* sind die jeweiligen Abkürzungen angegeben für die Sprachen, in denen der Begriff wiedergegeben ist (siehe unten: Abkürzungen der Sprachen). Das Verzeichnis gibt für jeden Begriff den entsprechenden Ausdruck in englisch, deutsch, spanisch, französisch, und portugiesisch.

In der Regel wurde der Begriff in der Karte ins Englische übersetzt und dann vom Englischen in die vier anderen Sprachen. Da die Begriffe und Übersetzungen sich auf bestimmte Objekte in der Karte beziehen, können einige von ihnen von den in den üblichen Wörterbüchern aufgeführten Begriffsbestimmungen abweichen.

LOS TÉRMINOS GEOGRÁFICOS que aparecen en los mapas, incluyendo abreviaciones, son presentados en la columna de Términos Geográficas del Glosario, en orden alfabético. Los términos que están precedidos por un guión aparecen frecuentemente como terminaciones de los nombres en los mapas (por ejemplo, -san en Fuji-san, -älven en Dalälven). Los idiomas que representan los términos están identificados por medio de abreviaciones en *cursiva* (véase abajo, Abreviaciones de los Idiomas Extranjeros). El Glosario provee el equivalente para cada término en inglés, alemán, español, francés y portugués.

Generalmente las traducciones están hechas de las formas originales de la terminología de los mapas que aparecen primero en inglés, y luego se traducen a las otras cuatro lenguas. Algunos términos y traducciones pueden aparecer distintas a las usadas en los diccionarios generales porque se refieren a los rasgos particulares de los mapas.

LE GLOSSAIRE cite par ordre alphabétique les termes géographiques et les abréviations utilisées. Les mots précédés d'un tiret sont des suffixes (par exemple -san dans Fuji-san, -älven dans Dalälven). La langue d'origine du nom cité est indiquée par une abréviation en *italique* (voir Abréviations des noms de langues, ci-dessous). Le Glossaire donne chaque nom en anglais, allemand, espagnol, français, et portugais.

En général, les termes géographiques des cartes ont d'abord été traduits en anglais, puis de l'anglais dans les quatre autres langues. Les définitions de certains termes sont adaptées aux particularités de l'Atlas. Il peut arriver qu'elles diffèrent des définitions habituelles données par les dictionnaires.

A COLUNA 'TERMINOLOGIA', do *Glossário*, contém todos os termos geográficos que figuram nos mapas, em ordem alfabética e com as respectivas abreviações. Os termos precedidos por um hífen são os que freqüentemente aparecem nos mapas como sufixos de nomes tais como *-san* (em Fuji-san), *-älven* (em Dalälven). As línguas em que os termos são expressos estão identificadas por abreviações em *grifo* (ver abaixo, 'Abreviações das línguas estrangeiras'). O Glossário fornece o equivalente de cada termo em inglês, alemão, espanhol, português e francês.

De modo geral, as traduções foram feitas das formas originais da terminologia usada nos mapas para o inglês, e, em seguida, do inglês para as outras quatro línguas. Uma vez que os termos geográficos e traduções do *Glossário* referem-se a acidentes específicos de cada mapa, é possível que algumas definições sejam diferentes das consignadas nos dicionários gerais das línguas.

Abbreviations of Language Names / Abkürzungen der Nationalsprachen / Abreviaciones de los Idiomas Extranjeros / Abréviations des Noms de Langues / Abreviações dos Idiomas Estrangeiros

	ENGLISH	DEUTSCH	ESPAÑOL	FRANÇAIS	PORTUGUÊS
Afk.	Afrikaans	Afrikaans	Africano	Afrikaans	Afrikaans
Alb.	Albanian	Albanisch	Albanesa	Albanais	Albanês
Ara.	Arabic	Arabisch	Árabe	Arabe	Árabe
Ber.	Berber	Berberisch	Bereber	Berbère	Berbere
Ben.	Bengali	Bengali	Bengali	Bengali	Bengali
Blg.	Bulgarian	Bulgarisch	Búlgaro	Bulgare	Búlgaro
Bur.	Burmese	Burmanisch	Birmano	Birman	Birmanês
Cat.	Catalan	Katalanisch	Catalán	Catalan	Catalão
Cbd.	Cambodian	Kambod-schanisch	Camboyano	Cambodgien	Cambojano
Ch.	Chinese	Chinesisch	Chino	Chinois	Chinês
Czech	Czech	Tschechisch	Checo	Tchèque	Tcheco
Dan.	Danish	Dänisch	Danés	Danois	Dinamarquês
Du.	Dutch	Niederländisch	Holandés	Néerlandais	Holandês
Eng.	English	Englisch	Inglés	Anglais	Inglês
Est.	Estonian	Estnisch	Estonio	Esthonien	Estoniano
Finn.	Finnish	Finnisch	Finés	Finnois	Finlandês
Flm.	Flemish	Flämisch	Flamenco	Flamand	Flamengo
Fr.	French	Französisch	Francés	Français	Francês
Gae.	Gaelic	Gälisch	Gaélico	Gaélique	Gaélico
Ger.	German	Deutsch	Alemán	Allemand	Alemão
Gr.	Greek	Griechisch	Griego	Grec	Grego
Hau.	Hausa	Haussa	Hausa	Haoussa	Haussa
Heb.	Hebrew	Hebräisch	Hebreo	Hébreu	Hebreu
Hung.	Hungarian	Ungarisch	Húngaro	Hongrois	Húngaro
Ice.	Icelandic	Isländisch	Islandés	Islandais	Islandês
Indon.	Indonesian	Indonesisch	Indonesio	Indonésien	Indonésio
It.	Italian	Italienisch	Italiano	Italien	Italiano
Jap.	Japanese	Japanisch	Japonés	Japonais	Japonês
Kor.	Korean	Koreanisch	Coreano	Coréen	Coreano
Lao.	Laotian	Laotisch	Laosiano	Laotien	Laosiano
Lapp.	Lappish	Lappisch	Lapón	Lapon	Lapão
Latv.	Latvian	Lettisch	Letón	Letton	Letão
Lith.	Lithuanian	Litauisch	Lituano	Lithuanien	Lituano
Mal.	Malay	Malaiisch	Malayo	Malais	Malaio
Mong.	Mongolian	Mongolisch	Mogol	Mongol	Mongol
Nor.	Norwegian	Norwegisch	Norvego	Norvégien	Norueguês
Pas.	Pashto	Paschtu	Pushtu	Pachtou	Pachtu
Per.	Persian	Persisch	Persa	Persan	Persa
Pol.	Polish	Polnisch	Polaco	Polonais	Polonês
Poly.	Polynesian	Polynesisch	Polinesio	Polynésien	Polinésio
Port.	Portuguese	Portugiesisch	Portugués	Portugais	Português
Rom.	Romanian	Rumänisch	Rumano	Roumain	Romeno
Rus.	Russian	Russisch	Ruso	Russe	Russo
S./C.	Serbo-Croatian	Serbokroatisch	Servio-croata	Serbo-croate	Servo-croata
Sin.	Sinhalese	Singhalesisch	Cingalés	Cinghalais	Cingalês
Slo.	Slovak	Slowakisch	Eslovaco	Slovaque	Eslovaco
Sp.	Spanish	Spanisch	Español	Espagnol	Espanhol
Swe.	Swedish	Schwedisch	Sueco	Suédois	Sueco
Thai	Thai	Thai	Tai	Thaï	Tailandês
Tib.	Tibetan	Tibetisch	Tibetano	Tibétain	Tibetano
Tur.	Turkish	Türkisch	Turco	Turc	Turco
Viet.	Vietnamese	Vietnamesisch	Vietnamita	Vietnamien	Vietnamita
Welsh	Welsh	Walisisch	Galés	Gallois	Galês

ENGLISH	DEUTSCH	Map Form / Geographische Begriffe / Términos Geográficos / Termes Géographiques / Termos Geográficos	ESPAÑOL	FRANÇAIS	PORTUGUÊS
		A			
river	Fluss	**-å** *Dan., Nor., Swe.*	río	rivière	rio
brook	Bach	**a., arroyo** *Sp.*	arroyo	ruisseau	córrego
river	Fluss	**āb** *Per.*	río	rivière	rio
army base	Heeresstützpunkt	**a.b., army base** *Eng.*	base del ejército	base d'armée	base militar
well	Brunnen	**ābār** *Ara.*	pozo	puits	poço
abbey	Abtei	**abb., abbazia** *It.*	abadía	abbaye	abadia
abbey	Abtei	**abbaye** *Fr.*	abadía	abbaye	abadia
abbey	Abtei	**abbazia** *It.*	abadía	abbaye	abadia
abbey	Abtei	**abbey** *Eng.*	abadía	abbaye	abadia
aboriginal reserve	Eingeborenenschutzgebiet	**aboriginal reserve** *Eng.*	zona de aborígenes	réserve des indigènes	reserva indígena
abbey	Abtei	**Abtei** *Ger.*	abadía	abbaye	abadia
ditch	Graben	**acequia** *Sp.*	acequia	fossé	fosso
reservoir	Stausee	**açude** *Port.*	embalse	réservoir	açude
island(s)	Insel(n)	**ada(lar)** *Tur.*	isla(s)	île(s)	ilha(s)
island	Insel	**adası** *Tur.*	isla	île	ilha
mountains	Berge	**adrar** *Ber.*	montañas	montagnes	montanhas
Atomic Energy Commission	Atomenergiekommission	**A.E.C., Atomic Energy Commission** *Eng.*	Comisión de Energía Atomica	Commission de l'Énergie Atomique	Comissão de Energia Atômica
airport	Flughafen	**aérd., aérodrome** *Fr.*	aeródromo	aérodrome	aeródromo
airport	Flughafen	**aeródromo** *Port., Sp.*	aeródromo	aérodrome	aeródromo
airport	Flughafen	**aeroparque** *Sp.*	aeroparque	aéroport	aeroporto
airport	Flughafen	**aéroport** *Fr.*	aeropuerto	aéroport	aeroporto
airport	Flughafen	**aeroporto** *It., Port.*	aeropuerto	aéroport	aeroporto
airport	Flughafen	**aeropuerto** *Sp.*	aeropuerto	aéroport	aeroporto
air force base	Luftwaffenstützpunkt	**a.f.b., air force base** *Eng.*	base aeronáutica	base aérienne	base aérea
wadi	Wadi	**ahzar** *Ara.*	uadi	wadi	uádi
peak	Gipfel	**aiguille** *Fr.*	pico	aiguille	pico
air base	Luftstützpunkt	**air base** *Eng.*	base aérea	base aérienne	base aérea
airfield	Flugplatz	**airfield** *Eng.*	camp de aviación	aérodrome	campo de pouso
air force base	Luftwaffenstützpunkt	**air force base** *Eng.*	base aeronáutica	base aérienne	base aérea
airport	Flughafen	**airport** *Eng.*	aeropuerto	aéroport	aeroporto
cape	Kap	**ákra, akrotírion** *Gr.*	cabo	cap	cabo
hill	Hügel	**'alam, 'alāmat** *Ara.*	colina	colline	colina
avenue	Allee	**alameda** *Sp.*	alameda	avenue	avenida
alps	Alpen	**alpes** *Fr.*	alpes	alpes	alpes
alps	Alpen	**alpi** *It.*	alpes	alpes	alpes
mountains, hills	Berge, Hügel	**altos** *Sp.*	altos	montagnes, collines	montanhas, colinas
river	Fluss	**-älv, -älven** *Swe.*	río	rivière	rio
amusement park	Vergnügungspark	**amusement park** *Eng.*	parque de diversiones	parc récréatif	parque de diversões
river	Fluss	**-ån** *Swe.*	río	rivière	rio
anchorage	Ankerplatz	**anchorage** *Eng.*	ancladero	ancrage	ancoradouro
bay	Bucht	**angra** *Sp.*	angra	baie	baía
cove	kleine Bucht	**anse** *Fr.*	ensenada	anse	enseada
bay	Bucht	**ao** *Thai*	bahía	baie	baía
aqueduct	Aquädukt	**aqueduc** *Fr.*	acueducto	aqueduc	aqueduto
aqueduct	Aquädukt	**aqueduct** *Eng.*	acueducto	aqueduc	aqueduto
archipelago	Archipel	**archipel** *Fr.*	archipiélago	archipel	arquipélago
archipelago	Archipel	**archipelag** *Rus.*	archipiélago	archipel	arquipélago
archipelago	Archipel	**archipelago** *Eng.*	archipiélago	archipel	arquipélago
archipelago	Archipel	**archipiélago** *Sp.*	archipiélago	archipel	arquipélago
arm	Arm	**arm** *Eng.*	brazo	bras	braço de rio
army base	Heeresstützpunkt	**army base** *Eng.*	base del ejército	base d'armée	base militar
airport	Flughafen	**arpt., aéroport** *Fr.* **aeroporto** *It., Port.* **aeropuerto** *Sp.* **airport** *Eng.*	aeropuerto	aéroport	aeroporto
archipelago	Archipel	**arquipélago** *Port.*	archipiélago	archipel	arquipélago
reef	Riff	**arrecife** *Sp.*	arrecife	récif	recife
brook	Bach	**arroyo** *Sp.*	arroyo	ruisseau	córrego
hills	Hügel	**-ås, -åsen** *Swe.*	colinas	collines	colinas
ridge	Höhenrücken	**'assâbet** *Ara.*	sierra	crête	serra
atoll	Atoll	**atol** *Port.*	atolón	atoll	atol
atoll	Atoll	**atoll** *Eng., Fr.*	atolón	atoll	atol
auditorium	Auditorium	**aud., auditorium** *Eng.*	auditorio	auditorium	auditório
race course	Rennbahn	**autodrome** *Fr.*	autódromo	autodrome	autódromo
race course	Rennbahn	**autodromo** *It.*	autódromo	autodrome	autódromo
expressway	Autobahn	**autopista** *Sp.*	autopista	autoroute	via expressa
avenue	Allee	**av., avenida** *Port., Sp.* **avenue** *Eng., Fr.*	avenida	avenue	avenida
channel	Kanal	**ava** *Poly.*	canal, estrecho	canal, détroit	canal, estreito
avenue	Allee	**avenida** *Port., Sp.*	avenida	avenue	avenida
avenue	Allee	**avenue** *Eng., Fr.*	avenida	avenue	avenida
spring	Quelle	**'ayn** *Ara.*	manantial	source	manancial, fonte

Glossary and Abbreviations of Geographical Terms / Verzeichnis und Abkürzungen Geographischer Begriffe
Glosario y Abreviaciones de Términos Geográficos / Glossaire et Abréviations de Termes Géographiques
Glossário e Abreviações de Termos Geográficos

B

ENGLISH	DEUTSCH	Map Form Geographische Begriffe Términos Geográficos Termes Géographiques Termos Geográficos	ESPAÑOL	FRANÇAIS	PORTUGUÊS
bay	Bucht	**baai** *Du.*	bahía	baie	baía
strait	Meeresstrasse	**bab** *Ara.*	estrecho	détroit	estreito
brook, creek	Bach	**Bach** *Ger.*	arroyo, riachuelo	ruisseau, crique	córrego, arroio
hill	Hügel	**-backen** *Swe.*	colina	colline	colina
desert	Wüste	**bādiyat** *Ara.*	desierto	désert	deserto
strait	Meeresstrasse	**bælt** *Dan.*	estrecho	détroit	estreito
bay	Bucht	**bahía** *Sp.*	bahía	baie	baía
inlet	Einfahrt	**bahiret** *Ara.*	abra	bras de mer	enseada, estuário
railroad station	Bahnhof	**Bahnhof** *Ger.*	estación de ferrocarril	gare	estação ferroviária
river; sea	Fluss; Meer	**bahr, baḥr** *Ara.*	río; mar	rivière; mer	rio; mar
reservoir	Stausee	**baḥrat** *Ara.*	embalse	réservoir	reservatório
bay	Bucht	**baía** *Port.*	bahía	baie	baía
bay	Bucht	**baie** *Fr.*	bahía	baie	baía
reef, sand bar	Riff, Sandbarre	**bajo** *Sp.*	bajo	récif, banc de sable	recife, banco de areia
gorge	Schlucht	**balka** *Rus.*	garganta	gorge	garganta
dome	Kuppe	**ballon** *Fr.*	domo	ballon	domo
marsh	Marsch	**balta** *Rom.*	pantano	marais	pântano
cape	Kap	**-bana** *Jap.*	cabo	cap	cabo
marsh	Marsch	**bañados** *Sp.*	bañados	marais	pântano
island	Insel	**-banare** *Jap.*	isla	île	ilha
bank	Bank	**banco** *Sp.*	banco	banc	banco
peninsula	Halbinsel	**-bandao** *Ch.*	península	péninsule	península
bank	Bank	**bank** *Eng.*	banco	banc	banco
shoal	Untiefe	**-banken** *Swe.*	bajo	haut-fond	escolho
sand bar	Sandbarre	**barra** *Sp.*	barra	banc de sable	banco de areia
dam	Damm	**barrage** *Fr.*	presa	barrage	represa
ravine	Tobel	**barranca** *Sp.*	barranca	ravin	ravina
air base	Luftstützpunkt	**base aérea** *Sp.*	base aérea	base aérienne	base aérea
basilica	Basilika	**basílica** *Sp.*	basílica	basilique	basílica
basilica	Basilika	**basilique** *Fr.*	basílica	basilique	basílica
basin	Becken	**basin** *Eng.*	cuenca	bassin	bacia
basin	Becken	**bassin** *Fr.*	cuenca	bassin	bacia
marsh	Marsch	**batakliği** *Tur.*	pantano	marais	pântano
river	Fluss	**batang** *Indon.*	río	rivière	rio
river	Fluss	**batha** *Ara.*	río	rivière	rio
marsh	Marsch	**bāṭlāq** *Per.*	pantano	marais	pântano
battlefield	Schlachtfeld	**battlefield** *Eng.*	campo de batalla	champ de bataille	campo de batalha
mountain	Berg	**batu** *Mal.*	montaña	montagne	montanha
bay	Bucht	**bay** *Eng.*	bahía	baie	baía
bayou	Altwasser	**bayou** *Fr., Eng.*	ensenada pantanosa	bayou	enseada pantanosa
beach	Strand	**beach** *Eng.*	playa	plage	praia
mountain	Berg	**bein, beinn** *Gae.*	montaña	montagne	montanha
snowcapped mountains	Schneegipfel	**belogorje** *Rus.*	nevados	montagnes neigeuses	picos nevados
mountain	Berg	**ben** *Gae.*	montaña	montagne	montanha
mountain, hill	Berg	**Berg** *Ger.*	montaña, colina	montagne, colline	montanha, colina
mountains	Berge	**berg** *Afk.*	montañas	montagnes	montanhas
hill(s), mountain(s)	Hügel, Berg(e)	**-berg** *Swe.*	colina(s), montaña(s)	colline(s), montagne(s)	colina(s), montanha(s)
mountains	Berge	**Berge** *Ger.*	montañas	montagnes	montanhas
mountains	Berge	**berge** *Afk.*	montañas	montagnes	montanhas
hills, mountains	Hügel, Berge	**-bergen** *Swe.*	colinas, montañas	collines, montagnes	colinas, montanhas
hill, mountain	Hügel, Berg	**-berget** *Swe.*	colina, montaña	colline, montagne	colina, montanha
upland	Bergland	**Bergland** *Ger.*	tierras altas	hautes terres	terras altas
battlefield	Schlachtfeld	**bfld., battlefield** *Eng.*	campo de batalla	champ de bataille	campo de batalha
mountain, hill	Berg	**Bg., Berg** *Ger.*	montaña, colina	montagne, colline	montanha, colina
bridge	Brücke	**bge., bridge** *Eng.*	puente	pont	ponte
bight	Bucht	**bight** *Eng.*	bahía	baie	baía, enseada
bill (point)	Landspitze	**bill** *Eng.*	punta	pointe	ponta
valley	Tal	**biq'at** *Heb.*	valle	vallée	vale
well	Brunnen	**bi'r** *Ara.*	pozo	puits	poço
lake	See	**birkat** *Ara.*	lago	lac	lago
mountains	Berge	**bjeshkët** *Alb.*	montañas	montagnes	montanhas
brook	Bach	**bk., brook** *Eng.*	arroyo	ruisseau	córrego
upland	Bergland	**blaenau** *Welsh*	tierras altas	hautes terres	terras altas
bluff(s)	Steilufer	**bluff(s)** *Eng.*	acantilado(s)	falaise(s)	falésia(s)
boulevard	Boulevard	**blvd., boulevard** *Fr., Eng.*	bulevar	boulevard	bulevar
mountain	Berg	**b'nom** *Viet.*	montaña	montagne	montanha
lake	See	**-bo** *Ch.*	lago	lac	lago
river mouth	Flussmündung	**boca** *Sp.*	boca	embouchure	foz
river mouth; pass	Flussmündung; Pass	**bocca** *It.*	boca; paso	embouchure; col	foz; passo
bay	Bucht	**bocht** *Du.*	bahía	baie	baía
bay	Bodden	**Bodden** *Ger.*	bahía	baie	baía
bog	Moor	**bog** *Eng.*	pantano	fondrière	pântano
strait	Meeresstrasse	**boğazı** *Tur.*	estrecho	détroit	estreito
range	Gebirge	**bogd** *Mong.*	sierra	chaîne	cordilheira
woods	Gehölz	**bois** *Fr.*	bosque	bois	bosque
enclosed basin	Becken	**bolsón** *Sp.*	bolsón	bassin fermée	bacia fechada
forest	Wald	**bory** *Pol.*	bosque	forêt	floresta
forest	Wald	**bosque** *Sp.*	bosque	forêt	floresta
boulevard	Boulevard	**boulevard** *Fr., Eng.*	boulevar	boulevard	bulevar
branch	Arm	**br., branch** *Eng.*	brazo	bras	braço
stream distributary	Flussarm	**braţul** *Rom.*	brazo de río	bras	braço de rio
breakwater	Wellenbrecher	**breakwater** *Eng.*	rompeolas	brise-lames	quebra-mar
glacier	Gletscher	**-breen** *Nor.*	glaciar	glacier	galeira
bridge	Brücke	**bridge** *Eng.*	puente	pont	ponte
brook	Bach	**brook** *Eng.*	arroyo	ruisseau	córrego
marsh	Bruch	**Bruch** *Ger.*	pantano	marais	pântano
bridge	Brücke	**Brücke** *Ger.*	puente	pont	ponte
bridge	Brücke	**brug** *Du.*	puente	pont	ponte
bay	Bucht	**Bucht** *Ger.*	bahía	baie	baía
bay	Bucht	**buchta** *Rus.*	bahía	baie	baía
mountain	Berg	**bufa** *Sp.*	bufa	montagne	montanha
bay	Bucht	**bugt** *Dan.*	bahía	baie	baía
lake	See	**buḥayrah** *Ara.*	lago	lac	lago
lake, lagoon	See, Lagune, Haff	**buḥayrat** *Ara.*	lago, laguna	lac, lagune	lago, laguna
mountain, hill	Berg, Hügel	**bukit** *Indon., Mal.*	montaña, colina	montagne, colline	montanha, colina
bay	Bucht	**-bukten** *Swe.*	bahía	baie	baía
mountain	Berg	**bulu** *Indon.*	montaña	montagne	montanha
castle	Burg	**Burg** *Ger.*	castillo	château	castelo
hill	Hügel	**burj** *Ara.*	colina	colline	colina
creek	Bach	**burn** *Ger.*	riachuelo	crique	riacho
cape	Kap	**burnu, burun** *Tur.*	cabo	cap	cabo
bay	Busen	**Busen** *Ger.*	bahía	baie	baía
butte(s)	Restberg(e)	**butte(s)** *Eng., Fr.*	butte(s)	butte(s)	colina, outeiro

C

ENGLISH	DEUTSCH	Map Form	ESPAÑOL	FRANÇAIS	PORTUGUÊS
cape	Kap	**c., cabo** *Sp.* **cap** *Fr.* **cape** *Eng.*	cabo	cap	cabo
street	Strasse	**c., calle** *Sp.*	calle	rue	rua
peaks	Gipfel	**cabezas** *Sp.*	cabezas	cimes	picos

ENGLISH	DEUTSCH	Map Form Geographische Begriffe Términos Geográficos Termes Géographiques Termos Geográficos	ESPAÑOL	FRANÇAIS	PORTUGUÊS
cape	Kap	**cabo** *Port., Sp.*	cabo	cap	cabo
waterfall	Wasserfall	**cachoeira** *Port.*	cascada	chute d'eau	cachoeira
street	Strasse	**calle** *Sp.*	calle	rue	rua
parkway	Ferienstrasse	**calzada** *Sp.*	calzada	allée de parc	alameda de parque
mosque	Moschee	**camii** *Tur.*	mezquita	mosquée	mesquita
road	Weg	**camino** *Sp.*	camino	route	rodovia
camp	Lager	**camp** *Eng., Fr.*	campo	camp	campo
plain	Ebene	**campo** *It.*	llanura	plaine	planície
brook; ravine	Bach; Tobel	**cañada** *Sp.*	cañada	ruisseau; ravin	ravina
canal	Kanal	**canal** *Eng.*	canal	canal	canal
canal, channel	Kanal	**canal** *Fr., Port., Sp.*	canal	canal	canal
canal, channel	Kanal	**canale** *It.*	canal	canal	canal
stream distributary	Flussarm	**caño** *Sp.*	caño	bras	braço de rio, igarapé
canyon	Cañon	**cañón** *Sp.*	cañón	canyon	canhão
canyon	Cañon	**canyon** *Eng.*	cañón	canyon	canhão
plateau	Hochebene	**cao nguyen** *Viet.*	meseta	plateau	planalto
cape	Kap	**cap** *Fr.*	cabo	cap	cabo
cape	Kap	**cape** *Eng.*	cabo	cap	cabo
capitol	Kapitol	**capitolio** *Sp.*	capitolio	capitole	capitólio
cape	Kap	**capo** *It.*	cabo	cap	cabo
captain	Kapitän	**capt., captain** *Eng.*	capitán	capitaine	capitão
highway	Strasse	**carretera** *Sp.*	carretera	route	rodovia
valley	Tal	**carse** *Gae.*	valle	vallée	vale
waterfall	Wasserfall	**cascada** *Sp.*	cascada	chute d'eau	queda d'água
waterfall	Wasserfall	**cascata** *It.*	cascada	chute d'eau	queda d'água
castle	Burg, Schloss	**castel, castello** *It.*	castillo	château	castelo
castle	Burg, Schloss	**castelo** *Port.*	castillo	château	castelo
castle	Burg, Schloss	**castillo** *Sp.*	castillo	château	castelo
castle	Burg, Schloss	**castle** *Eng.*	castillo	château	castelo
cataracts	Katarakten	**cataratas** *Port., Sp.*	cataratas	cataractes	cataratas
cathedral	Kathedrale	**catedral** *Sp.*	catedral	cathédrale	catedral
range	Gebirge	**catena** *Sp.*	catena	chaîne	cordilheira
cathedral	Kathedrale	**cathedral** *Eng.*	catedral	cathédrale	catedral
causeway	Dammweg	**causeway** *Eng.*	calzada	chaussée	estrada elevada
upland	Bergland	**causse** *Fr.*	tierras altas	causse	terras altas
cave(s)	Höhle(n)	**cave(s)** *Eng.*	cueva(s)	caverne(s)	caverna(s)
cay	Klippe	**cay** *Eng.*	cayo	caye	baixio
cay(s)	Klippe(n)	**cayo(s)** *Sp.*	cayo(s)	cave(s)	baixio(s)
cemetery	Friedhof	**cementerio** *Sp.*	cementerio	cimetière	cemitério
cemetery	Friedhof	**cemetery** *Eng.*	cementerio	cimetière	cemitério
mountain(s), hill(s)	Berg(e), Hügel	**cerro(s)** *Sp.*	cerro(s)	montagne(s), colline(s)	montanha(s), colina(s)
range	Gebirge	**chaîne** *Fr.*	sierra	chaîne	cordilheira
channel	Kanal	**channel** *Eng.*	canal, estrecho	canal, détroit	canal, estreito
hills	Hügel	**chapada** *Port.*	colinas	collines	chapada
island	Insel	**char** *Ben.*	isla	île	ilha
castle	Burg, Schloss	**château** *Fr.*	castillo	château	castelo
island	Insel	**chau** *Ch.*	isla	île	ilha
road	Landstrasse	**chemin** *Fr.*	camino	chemin	rodovia
bay	Bucht	**chhāk** *Cbd.*	bahía	baie	baía
river	Fluss	**ch'i** *Ch.*	río	rivière	rio
lake	See	**-chi** *Ch.*	lago	lac	lago
cape	Kap	**chia** *Ch.*	cabo	cap	cabo
harbor	Hafen	**chiang** *Ch.*	puerto	port	porto
cape	Kap	**chiao** *Ch.*	cabo	cap	cabo
road	Landstrasse	**chin., chemin** *Fr.*	camino	chemin	rodovia
river	Fluss	**-ch'ŏn** *Kor.*	río	rivière	rio
reservoir	Stausse	**-chŏsuji** *Kor.*	embalse	réservoir	reservatório
intermittent lake, salt marsh	periodischer See, Salzmarsch	**chott** *Ara.*	lago intermitente, pantano salado	lac périodique, marais salé	lago intermitente, pântano salgado
range	Gebirge	**chr., chrebet** *Rus.*	sierra	chaîne	cordilheira
river	Fluss	**ch'uan** *Ch.*	río	rivière	rio
mountains	Berge	**chuŏr phnum** *Cbd.*	montañas	montagnes	montanhas
church	Kirche	**church** *Eng.*	iglesia	église	igreja
waterfalls	Wasserfälle	**chutes** *Fr.*	cascadas	chutes d'eau	quedas d'água
marsh	Marsch	**ciénaga** *Sp.*	ciénaga	marais	pântano
peak	Gipfel	**cima** *It., Sp.*	cima	cime	pico
peak	Gipfel	**cime** *Fr.*	cima	cime	pico
cemetery	Friedhof	**cimetière** *Fr.*	cementerio	cimetière	cemitério
city	Stadt	**città** *It.*	ciudad	ville	cidade
city	Stadt	**city** *Eng.*	ciudad	ville	cidade
city	Stadt	**ciudad** *Sp.*	ciudad	ville	cidade
claypan	Tonpfanne	**claypan** *Eng.*	capa de arcilla	couche argilleuse	camada de argila
cliff(s)	Kliff(e)	**cliff(s)** *Eng.*	risco(s)	falaise(s)	falésia(s)
mountain	Berg	**co** *Viet.*	montaña	montagne	montanha
mountain, hill	Berg, Hügel	**co., cerro** *Sp.*	cerro	montagne, colline	montanha, colina
coast	Küste	**coast** *Eng.*	costa	côte	costa
coast guard station	Küstenwachtstation	**coast guard station** *Eng.*	estación de los guardacostas	station des gardes de la côte	estação de guarda costeira
pass	Pass	**col** *Fr.*	paso	col	passo
college	Hochschule	**colegio** *Sp.*	colegio	collège	colégio
hill(s)	Hügel	**colina(s)** *Sp.*	colina(s)	colline(s)	colina(s)
college	Hochschule	**coll., college** *Eng.*	colegio	collège	colégio
hills	Hügel	**colli** *It.*	colinas	collines	colinas
hills	Hügel	**colline** *It.*	colinas	collines	colinas
hills	Hügel	**collines** *Fr.*	colinas	collines	colinas
common	Gemeindeland	**common** *Eng.*	campo común	commune	terra comum
islands	Inseln	**con** *Viet.*	islas	îles	ilhas
plain	Ebene	**conca** *It.*	llanura	plaine	planície
convent	Nonnenkloster	**convent** *Eng.*	convento	couvent	convento
convent	Nonnenkloster	**convento** *It., Port., Sp.*	convento	couvent	convento
range	Gebirge	**cord., cordillera** *Sp.*	cordillera	chaîne	cordilheira
mountain	Berg	**corno** *It.*	montaña	montagne	montanha
brook	Bach	**córrego** *Port.*	arroyo	ruisseau	córrego
coast	Küste	**costa** *Sp.*	costa	côte	costa
coast, hills	Küste, Hügel	**côte** *Fr.*	costa, colinas	côte	costa, colinas
hills	Hügel	**coteau** *Fr.*	colinas	coteau	colinas
coulee	breite Schlucht	**coulee** *Eng.*	rambla	coulée	barranco
coulee	breite Schlucht	**coulée** *Fr.*	rambla	coulée	barranco
county park	Park	**county park** *Eng.*	parque del condado	parc de comté	parque de condado
convent	Nonnenkloster	**couvent** *Fr.*	convento	couvent	convento
cove	kleine Bucht	**cove** *Eng.*	ensenada	anse	enseada
creek	Bach	**cr., creek** *Eng.*	riachuelo	crique	riacho
crag	Felsspitze	**crag** *Eng.*	despeñadero	pointe de rocher	despenhadeiro
crater	Krater	**crater** *Eng.*	cráter	cratère	cratera
crater	Krater	**cratère** *Fr.*	cráter	cratère	cratera
creek	Bach	**creek** *Eng.*	riachuelo	crique	riacho
peak	Gipfel	**croda** *It.*	pico	cime	pico
canal	Kanal	**csatorna** *Hung.*	canal	canal	canal
bay	Bucht	**cua** *Viet.*	bahía	baie	baía
hills, ridge	Hügel, Höhenrücken	**cuchilla** *Sp.*	cuchilla	collines, crête	coxilha
caves	Höhen	**cuevas** *Sp.*	cuevas	cavernes	cavernas
cove	kleine Bucht	**cul-de-sac** *Fr.*	ensenada	cul-de-sac	enseada
mountains	Berge	**culmea** *Rom.*	montañas	montagnes	montanhas
summit	Gipfel	**cumbre** *Sp.*	cumbre	sommet	cume

D

ENGLISH	DEUTSCH	Map Form	ESPAÑOL	FRANÇAIS	PORTUGUÊS
mountain	Berg	**dağ, dağı** *Tur.*	montaña	montagne	montanha
mountains	Berge	**dāgh** *Per.*	montañas	montagnes	montanhas
mountains	Berge	**dağlar, dağları** *Tur.*	montañas	montagnes	montanhas
hill	Hügel	**ḑahr** *Ara.*	colina	colline	colina
plateau	Hochebene	**-dai, -daichi** *Jap.*	meseta	plateau	planalto

ENGLISH	DEUTSCH	Map Form / Geographische Begriffe / Términos Geográficos / Termes Géographiques / Termos Geográficos	ESPAÑOL	FRANÇAIS	PORTUGUÊS
mountain	Berg	**-dake** *Jap.*	montaña	montagne	montanha
valley	Tal	**-dal, -dalen** *Nor., Swe.*	valle	vallée	vale
dale	weites Tal	**dale** *Eng.*	valle ancho	vallée large	vale aberto
dam	Damm	**dam** *Eng.*	presa	barrage	represa
lake	See	**danau** *Indon.*	lago	lac	lago
island	Insel	**-dao** *Ch., Viet.*	isla	île	ilha
marsh	Marsch	**daqq** *Per.*	pantano	marais	pântano
lake	See	**daryācheh** *Per.*	lago	lac	lago
desert	Wüste	**dasht** *Per.*	desierto	désert	deserto
monastery	Kloster	**dayr** *Ara.*	monasterio	monastère	mosteiro
deep	Tiefe	**deep** *Eng.*	fosa marina	fossé marin	fossa submarina
delta	Delta	**delta** *Eng., Fr., Sp.*	delta	delta	delta
sea	Meer	**deniz, denizi,** *Tur.*	mar	mer	mar
monument	Denkmal	**Denkmal** *Ger.*	monumento	monument	monumento
pass	Pass	**deo** *Viet.*	paso	col	passo
depression	Senke	**depression** *Eng.*	depresión	dépression	depressão
river	Fluss	**deresi** *Tur.*	río	rivière	rio
desert	Wüste	**desert** *Eng.*	desierto	désert	deserto
desert	Wüste	**desierto** *Sp.*	desierto	désert	deserto
strait	Meeresstrasse	**détroit** *Fr.*	estrecho	détroit	estreito
escarpment	Landstufe	**dhar** *Ara.*	escarpa	escarpement	escarpa
canal	Kanal	**dhiórix** *Gr.*	canal	canal	canal
lake	See	**-dian** *Ch.*	lago	lac	lago
channel	Kanal	**diep** *Du.*	canal, estrecho	canal, détroit	canal, estreito
dike	Deich	**dijk** *Du.*	dique	digue	dique
district	Distrikt	**district** *Eng.*	distrito	district	distrito
district	Distrikt	**distrito** *Sp.*	distrito	district	distrito
ditch	Graben	**ditch** *Eng.*	acequia	fossé	fosso
peninsula	Halbinsel	**djazirah** *Indon.*	península	péninsule	península
mountain(s)	Berg(e)	**djebel** *Ara.*	montaña(s)	montagne(s)	montanha(s)
fjord	Fjord	**-djúp** *Ice.*	fiordo	fjord	fiorde
channel, sound	Kanal, Sund	**-djupet** *Swe.*	canal, sonda	canal, détroit	canal, estreito
zoo	Zoo	**djurpark** *Swe.*	parque zoológico	zoo	jardim zoológico
island	Insel	**-do** *Kor.*	isla	île	ilha
interfluve	Erhebung	**doāb** *Per.*	interfluvio	interfluve	interflúvio
dock	Dock	**dock** *Eng.*	muelle	quai	doca
mountain	Berg	**doi** *Thai*	montaña	montagne	montanha
valley	Tal	**dolina** *Rus.*	valle	vallée	vale
mountain	Berg	**dolok** *Indo.*	montaña	montagne	montanha
hills	Hügel	**dombrovidék** *Hung.*	colinas	collines	colinas
hills	Hügel	**dombvidék** *Hung.*	colinas	collines	colinas
peak	Gipfel	**dos** *Fr.*	pico	dos	pico
downs (hills)	Hügelland	**downs** *Eng.*	colinas	collines	terras baixas (colinas)
drive	Fahrweg	**dr., drive** *Eng.*	calzada	avenue	avenida
drain	Abzugsgraben	**drain** *Eng.*	desaguadero	drainage	escoadouro
draw	kleines Tal	**draw** *Eng.*	valle pequeño	ravine	bacia, vale
drive	Fahrweg	**drive** *Eng.*	calzada	avenue	avenida
dry lake	Trockensee	**dry lake** *Eng.*	lago seco	lac asséché	lago seco
dunes	Dünen	**dunes** *Eng., Fr.*	dunas	dunes	dunas

E

ENGLISH	DEUTSCH	Map Form	ESPAÑOL	FRANÇAIS	PORTUGUÊS
east	Ost	**e., east** *Eng.*	este	est	leste
school	Schule	**école** *Fr.*	escuela	école	escola
mountain	Berg	**-egga** *Nor.*	montaña	montagne	montanha
memorial	Ehrenmal	**Ehrenmal** *Ger.*	monumento	memorial	monumento
river	Fluss	**-elv, -elva** *Nor.*	río	rivière	rio
reservoir	Stausee	**embalse** *Sp.*	embalse	réservoir	reservatório
pier	Landungsbrücke	**embarcadero** *Sp.*	embarcadero	jetée	cais
valley	Tal	**'emeq** *Heb.*	valle	vallée	vale
monument	Denkmal	**emlékmű** *Hung.*	monumento	monument	monumento
spring	Quelle	**'en** *Heb.*	manantial	source	fonte, manancial
cove	kleine Bucht	**enseada** *Port.*	ensenada	anse	enseada
cove	kleine Bucht	**ensenada** *Sp.*	ensenada	anse	enseada
entrance	Einfahrt	**entrance** *Eng.*	entrada	entrée	entrada
forest	Wald	**erdő** *Hung.*	bosque	forêt	floresta
sand desert	Sandwüste	**erg** *Ara.*	desierto arenoso	désert de sable	deserto arenoso
escarpment	Landstufe	**escarpment** *Eng.*	escarpa	escarpement	escarpa
school	Schule	**escuela** *Sp.*	escuela	école	escola
highland	Hochland	**espigão** *Port.*	región montañosa	pays montagneux	espigão
station	Bahnhof, Stützpunkt	**est., estação** *Port.* **estación** *Sp.*	estación	station	estação
stadium	Stadion	**estadio** *Sp.*	estadio	stade	estádio
reservoir	Stausee	**estanque** *Sp.*	estanque	réservoir	reservatório
estuary	Trichtermündung	**estero** *Sp.*	estero	estuaire	estuário
road	Landstrasse	**estr., estrada** *Port.*	camino	route	estrada
strait	Meeresstrasse	**estrecho** *Sp.*	estrecho	détroit	estreito
estuary	Trichtermündung	**estuary** *Eng.*	estuario	estuaire	estuário
pond	Teich	**étang** *Fr.*	charca	étang	lagoa, açude
expressway	Autobahn	**expy., expressway** *Eng.*	autopista	autoroute	via expressa
island	Insel	**-ey** *Ice.*	isla	île	ilha
lake	See	**ežeras** *Lith.*	lago	lac	lago
lake	See	**ezers** *Latv.*	lago	lac	lago

F

ENGLISH	DEUTSCH	Map Form	ESPAÑOL	FRANÇAIS	PORTUGUÊS
faculty (school)	Fakultät	**faculté** *Fr.*	facultad	faculté	faculdade
fairground	Ausstellungsgelände	**fairground** *Eng.*	campo para ferias	champ de foire	terreno para feiras
cliff	Kliff	**falaise** *Fr.*	risco	falaise	falésia
waterfall	Wasserfall	**fall(s)** *Eng.*	cascada	chute d'eau	queda d'água
waterfall	Wasserfall	**Fall** *Ger.*	cascada	chute d'eau	queda d'água
waterfall	Wasserfall	**-fallet** *Swe.*	cascada	chute d'eau	queda d'água
river	Fluss	**far'** *Ara.*	río	rivière	rio
lighthouse	Leuchtturm	**faro** *Sp.*	faro	phare	farol
upland	Bergland	**farsh** *Ara.*	tierras altas	hautes terres	terras altas
fell (mountain, hill)	ödes Hügelland	**fell** *Eng.*	colina rocosa	colline rocheuse	colina rochosa
mountain	Berg	**-fell** *Ice.*	montaña	montagne	montanha
mountain	Berg	**-feng** *Ch.*	montaña	montagne	montanha
upland	Bergland	**fennsík** *Hung.*	tierras altas	hautes terres	terras altas
ferry	Fähre	**ferry** *Eng.*	balsadera	bac	balsa
lake	See	**fertő** *Hung.*	lago	lac	lago
fortress	Feste	**Feste** *Ger.*	fortaleza	fort	fortaleza
estuary, strait	Trichtermündung, Meeresstrasse	**firth** *Gae.*	estuario, estrecho	estuaire, détroit	estuário, estreito
mountain(s)	Berg(e)	**fjäll(en)** *Swe.*	montaña(s)	montagne(s)	montanha(s)
mountain	Berg	**fjället** *Swe.*	montaña	montagne	montanha
fjord	Fjord	**fjärden** *Swe.*	fiordo	fjord	fiorde
mountain	Berg	**-fjell, -fjellet** *Nor.*	montaña	montagne	montanha
mountain	Berg	**fjöll** *Ice.*	montaña	montagne	montanha
fjord	Fjord	**-fjord** *Nor.*	fiordo	fjord	fiorde
fjord, lake	Fjord, See	**-fjorden** *Nor., Swe.*	fiordo, lago	fjord, lac	fiorde, lago
fjord, bay	Fjord, Bucht	**fjördur** *Ice.*	fiordo, bahía	fjord, baie	fiorde, baía
fork	Arm	**fk., fork** *Eng.*	brazo	bras	braço de rio
flat	Flachland	**flat** *Eng.*	llano	plat	planície
river	Fluss	**-fljót** *Ice.*	río	rivière	rio
bay	Bucht	**-flói** *Ice.*	bahía	baie	baía
flood control basin	Hochwasserrückhaltebecken	**flood control basin** *Eng.*	cuenca para controlar la inundación	bassin de contrôle d'inondation	bacia de controle de inundações
airport	Flughafen	**Flughafen** *Ger.*	aeropuerto	aéroport	aeroporto
airport	Flugplatz	**Flugplatz** *Ger.*	aeropuerto	aéroport	aeroporto
airport	Flugplatz	**flygplats** *Swe.*	aeropuerto	aéroport	aeroporto
river mouth; pass	Flussmündung; Pass	**foce** *It.*	desembocadura; paso	embouchure; col	desembocadura; foz; passo
canal	Kanal	**föcsatorna** *Hung.*	canal	canal	canal
glacier	Gletscher	**-fonn** *Nor.*	glaciar	glacier	geleira
spring	Quelle	**fontaine** *Fr.*	manantial	fontaine	manancial
pass	Pass	**forca** *It.*	paso	col	passo
inlet	Förde	**Förde** *Ger.*	abra	bras de mer	enseada
foreland	Vorland	**foreland** *Eng.*	promontorio	promontoire	promontório
forest	Wald	**forest** *Eng.*	bosque	forêt	floresta
forest reserve	Waldreservat	**forest reserve** *Eng.*	reserva de bosque	réserve forestière	reserva florestal
forest	Wald	**forêt** *Fr.*	bosque	forêt	floresta
waterfall	Wasserfall	**-forsen** *Swe.*	cascada	chute d'eau	queda d'água
forest	Forst	**Forst** *Ger.*	bosque	forêt	floresta
fort	Fort	**fort** *Eng., Fr.*	fuerte	fort	forte
waterfall	Wasserfall	**-foss** *Ice.*	cascada	chute d'eau	queda d'água
waterfall	Wasserfall	**-fossen** *Nor.*	cascada	chute d'eau	queda d'água
brook	Bach	**fosso** *It.*	arroyo	ruisseau	córrego
pass	Pass	**foum** *Ara.*	paso	col	passo
fracture zone	Bruchzone	**fracture zone** *Eng.*	zona de fractura	zone de faille	zona de fratura
freeway	Autobahn	**frwy., freeway** *Eng.*	autopista	autoroute	via expressa
fort	Fort	**ft., fort** *Eng., Fr.*	fuerte	fort	forte
stream distributary	Flussarm	**furo** *Port.*	brazo de río	bras	furo

G

ENGLISH	DEUTSCH	Map Form	ESPAÑOL	FRANÇAIS	PORTUGUÊS
mountain, hill	Berg, Hügel	**g., gora** *Rus.*	montaña, colina	montagne, colline	montanha, colina
mountain	Berg	**g., gunong** *Mal.* **gunung** *Indon.*	montaña	montagne	montanha
mountain	Berg	**-gai'sa** *Lapp.*	montaña	montagne	montanha
tunnel	Tunnel	**galleria** *It.*	túnel	tunnel	túnel
gallery	Galerie	**gallery** *Eng.*	galería	galerie	galeria
game farm	Wildfarm	**game farm** *Eng.*	criadero de caza	ferme de gibier	fazenda de caça
game park	Wildpark	**game park** *Eng.*	vedado de caza	parc à gibier	parque de caça
game refuge	Wildgehege	**game refuge** *Eng.*	refugio de caza	refuge de gibier	refúgio de caça
game reserve	Wildreservat	**game reserve** *Eng.*	vedado de caza	réserve à gibier	reserva de caça
game sanctuary	Wildschutzgebiet	**game sanctuary** *Eng.*	vedado de caza	réserve à gibier	santuário de caça
bay	Bucht	**-gang** *Ch.*	bahía	baie	baía
river	Fluss	**-gang** *Kor.*	río	rivière	rio
gap	Pass	**gap** *Eng.*	paso	col	passo
intermittent lake	periodischer See	**garaet** *Ara.*	lago intermitente	lac périodique	lago intermitente
garden	Garten	**gard., garden** *Eng.*	jardín	jardin	jardim
gardens	Gärten	**gardens** *Eng.*	jardines	jardins	jardins
mountain	Berg	**garet** *Ara.*	montaña	montagne	montanha
station	Bahnhof, Stützpunkt	**garı** *Tur.*	estación	station	estação
lake	See	**-gata** *Jap.*	lago	lac	lago
gate	Tor	**gate** *Eng.*	puerta	porte	portão
mountain torrent	Wildbach	**gave** *Fr.*	torrente	gave	torrente
range	Gebirge	**gebergte** *Du.*	sierra	chaîne	cordilheira
range	Gebirge	**Gebirge** *Ger.*	sierra	chaîne	cordilheira
pass	Pass	**geçidi** *Tur.*	paso	col	passo
oasis, well	Oase, Brunnen	**ghadīr** *Ara.*	oasis, pozo	oasis, puits	oásis, poço
mountains	Berge	**ghar** *Pas.*	montañas	montagnes	montanhas
spring	Quelle	**ghayl** *Ara.*	manantial	source	manancial
bay	Bucht	**ghubbat** *Ara.*	bahía	baie	baía
dunes	Dünen	**ghurd** *Ara.*	dunas	dunes	dunas
island	Insel	**gili** *Indon.*	isla	île	ilha
peak	Gipfel	**Gipfel** *Ger.*	pico	cime	pico
hill	Hügel	**giva't** *Heb.*	colina	colline	colina
bay	Bucht	**gji** *Alb.*	bahía	baie	baía
glacier	Gletscher	**glacier** *Eng., Fr.*	glaciar	glacier	geleira
river	Fluss	**gol** *Mong.*	río	rivière	rio
lake	See	**göl** *Tur.*	lago	lac	lago
bald mountains	kahle Berge	**gol'cy** *Rus.*	montañas calvas	monts chauves	montanhas calvas
golf course	Golfplatz	**golf course** *Eng.*	campo de golf	champ de golf	campo de golfe
gulf	Golf	**golfe** *Fr.*	golfo	golfe	golfo
bay	Bucht	**golfete** *Sp.*	golfete	baie	baía
gulf	Golf	**golfo** *It., Sp.*	golfo	golfe	golfo
lake	See	**gölü** *Tur.*	lago	lac	lago
mountain, hill	Berg, Hügel	**gora** *Rus.*	montaña, colina	montagne, colline	montanha, colina
mountains	Berge	**gora** *S./C.*	montañas	montagnes	montanhas
mountain	Berg	**góra** *Pol.*	montaña	montagne	montanha
gorge	Schlucht	**gorge** *Eng., Fr.*	garganta	gorge	garganta
mountains, hills	Berge, Hügel	**gorje** *S./C.*	montañas, colinas	montagnes, collines	montanhas, colinas
ruins	Ruinen	**gorodišče** *Rus.*	ruinas	ruines	ruínas
mountains, hills	Berge, Hügel	**gory** *Rus.*	montañas, colinas	montagnes, collines	montanhas, colinas
mountains	Berge	**góry** *Pol.*	montañas	montagnes	montanhas
river	Fluss	**-gou** *Ch.*	río	rivière	rio
sinkhole	Schluckloch	**gouffre** *Fr.*	sumidero	gouffre	sumidouro
wadi	Wadi	**goulbin** *Hau.*	uadi	wadi	uádi
ditch	Graben	**Graben** *Ger.*	acequia	fossé	fosso
ridge	Höhenrücken	**gr'ada** *Rus.*	sierra	crête	cordilheira
mountain	Berg	**gradište** *Blg.*	montaña	montagne	montanha
ridges	Höhenrücken	**gr'ady** *Rus.*	sierras	crêtes	cordilheira
general	General	**gral., general** *Eng., Sp.*	general	général	geral
ridge	Grat	**Grat** *Ger.*	sierra	crête	cordilheira
grotto	Grotte	**grotta** *It.*	gruta	grotte	gruta
grotto	Grotte	**grotte** *Fr.*	gruta	grotte	gruta
group	Gruppe	**group** *Eng.*	grupo	groupe	grupo
island	Insel	**-grund** *Swe.*	isla	île	ilha
group	Gruppe	**grupo** *Sp.*	grupo	groupe	grupo
group	Gruppe	**gruppo** *It.*	grupo	groupe	grupo
pass	Pass	**-guan** *Ch.*	paso	col	passo
bay	Bucht	**guba** *Rus.*	bahía	baie	baía
mountain	Berg	**guelb** *Ara.*	montaña	montagne	montanha
gulch	Wildbachschlucht	**gulch** *Eng.*	quebrada	ravin	quebrada
gulf	Golf	**gulf** *Eng.*	golfo	golfe	golfo
mountain	Berg	**gunong** *Mal.*	montaña	montagne	montanha
mountain	Berg	**gunung** *Indon.*	montaña	montagne	montanha
islands	Inseln	**-guntō** *Jap.*	islas	îles	ilhas

H

ENGLISH	DEUTSCH	Map Form	ESPAÑOL	FRANÇAIS	PORTUGUÊS
upland	Bergland	**haḍabat** *Ara.*	tierras altas	hautes terres	terras altas
mountain	Berg	**hadjer** *Ara.*	montaña	montagne	montanha
lagoon	Haff	**Haff** *Ger.*	laguna	lagune	laguna
sea, lake	Meer, See	**-hai** *Ch.*	mar, lago	mer, lac	mar, lago
strait	Meeresstrasse	**-haixia** *Ch.*	estrecho	détroit	estreito
reef	Riff	**hakau** *Poly.*	arrecife	récif	recife
peninsula	Halbinsel	**Halbinsel** *Ger.*	península	péninsule	península
hall	Halle	**hall** *Eng., Fr.*	salón	hall	hall
peninsula	Halbinsel	**-halvøya** *Nor.*	península	péninsule	península
beach	Strand	**-hama** *Jap.*	playa	plage	praia
desert	Wüste	**hamada** *Ara.*	desierto	désert	deserto
plateau	Hochebene	**ḥammādat** *Ara.*	meseta	plateau	planalto
lake, marsh	See, Marsch	**hāmūn** *Per.*	lago, pantano	lac, marais	lago, pântano
point	Landspitze	**-hana** *Jap.*	punta	pointe	ponta
peninsula	Halbinsel	**-hantō** *Jap.*	península	péninsule	península
mountain, hill	Berg, Hügel	**har** *Heb.*	montaña, colina	montagne, colline	montanha, colina
harbor, harbour	Hafen	**harbor, harbour** *Eng.*	puerto	port	porto
mountains, hills	Berge, Hügel	**hare** *Heb.*	montañas, colinas	montagnes, collines	montanhas, colinas
ridge	Höhenrücken	**-harju** *Finn.*	sierra	crête	cordilheira
lava flow	Lavastrom	**ḥarrat** *Ara.*	corriente de lava	coulée de lave	corrente de lava
hills	Hügel	**hauteurs** *Fr.*	colinas	hauteurs	colinas

Glossary and Abbreviations of Geographical Terms / Verzeichnis und Abkürzungen Geographischer Begriffe
Glosario y Abreviaciones de Términos Geográficos / Glossaire et Abréviations de Termes Géographiques
Glossário e Abreviações de Termos Geográficos

ENGLISH	DEUTSCH	Map Form / Geographische Begriffe / Términos Geográficos / Termes Géographiques / Termos Geográficos	ESPAÑOL	FRANÇAIS	PORTUGUÊS
sea, bay	Meer, Bucht	**-hav** *Swe.*	mar, bahía	mer, baie	mar, baía
harbor	Hafen	**havre** *Fr.*	puerto	havre	porto
oasis	Oase	**ḥawḍ** *Ara.*	oasis	oasis	oásis
lake	See	**hawr** *Ara.*	lago	lac	lago
harbor, harbour	Hafen	**hbr., harbor, harbour** *Eng.*	puerto	port	porto
headquarters	Hauptquartier	**hdqrs., headquarters** *Eng.*	cuartel general	guartier général	quartel-general
river	Fluss	**-he** *Ch.*	río	rivière	rio
head (headland)	Landspitze	**head** *Eng.*	promontorio	promontoire	promontório
heath	Heide	**heath** *Eng.*	matorral	lande	charneca
mountain(s)	Berg(e)	**hegy(ség)** *Hung.*	montaña(s)	montagne(s)	montanha(s)
heath	Heide	**Heide** *Ger.*	matorral	lande	charneca
plain	Ebene	**-heiya** *Jap.*	llanura	plaine	planície
river mouth	Flussmündung	**-hekou** *Ch.*	desembocadura	embouchure	desembocadura
hills	Hügel	**heuwells** *Afk.*	colinas	collines	colinas
highland	Hochland	**highland** *Eng.*	región montañosa	pays montagneux	terras altas
highway	Strasse	**highway** *Eng.*	carretera	route	rodovia
hill(s)	Hügel	**hill(s)** *Eng.*	colina(s)	colline(s)	colina(s)
race course	Rennbahn	**hipódromo** *Sp.*	hipódromo	hippodrome	hipódromo
race course	Rennbahn	**hippodrome** *Fr.*	hipódromo	hippodrome	hipódromo
historical	historisch	**hist., historical** *Eng.*	histórico	historique	histórico
historical park	historischer Park	**historical park** *Eng.*	parque histórico	parc historique	parque histórico
historic(al) site	historische Stätte	**historic(al) site** *Eng.*	sitio histórico	site historique	sítio histórico
river	Fluss	**hka** *Bur.*	río	rivière	rio
Her Majesty's Air Station (U.K.)	Luftwaffenstützpunkt (U.K.)	**H.M.A.S., Her Majesty's Air Station** *Eng.*	Real Estación Aeronáutica (U.K.)	Station Aérienne Royale (U.K.)	Real Estação Aeronáutica (U.K.)
river	Fluss	**ho** *Ch.*	río	rivière	rio
reservoir	Stausse	**-ho** *Kor.*	embalse	réservoir	reservatório
mountain	Berg	**-hø** *Nor.*	montaña	montagne	montanha
plateau	Hochebene	**Hochebene** *Ger.*	meseta	plateau	planalto
forest	Hochwald	**Hochwald** *Ger.*	bosque	forêt	floresta
mountain	Berg	**-högarna** *Swe.*	montaña	montagne	montanha
height	Höhe	**Höhe** *Ger.*	altura	hauteur	elevação
cave(s)	Höhle(n)	**Höhle(n)** *Ger.*	cueva(s)	caverne(s)	caverna(s)
bay	Bucht	**hoi** *Ch.*	bahía	baie	baía
island	Insel	**-holm** *Dan.*	isla	île	ilha
hook	Haken	**hook** *Eng.*	gancho	crochet	cabo, promontório
mountain	Berg	**hora** *Czech., Slo.*	montaña	montagne	montanha
point; peak	Horn	**Horn** *Ger.*	punta; pico	pointe; cime	ponta; pico
ruin	Ruine	**horva** *Heb.*	ruina	ruine	ruína
mountains	Berge	**hory** *Czech., Slo.*	montañas	montagnes	montanhas
hospital	Krankenhaus	**hospital** *Eng., Sp.*	hospital	hôpital	hospital
point	Landspitze	**houma** *Poly.*	punta	pointe	ponta
house	Haus	**house** *Eng.*	casa	maison	casa
island	Insel	**hsü** *Ch.*	isla	île	ilha
lake	See	**-hu** *Ch.*	lago	lac	lago
hill	Hügel	**Hügel** *Ger.*	colina	colline	colina
cape	Huk	**Huk** *Ger.*	cabo	cap	cabo
cape	Huk	**-huk** *Swe.*	cabo	cap	cabo
highway	Strasse	**hy., highway** *Eng.*	carretera	route	rodovia

I

ENGLISH	DEUTSCH	Map Form	ESPAÑOL	FRANÇAIS	PORTUGUÊS
island	Insel	**i., isla** *Sp.* **island** *Eng.*	isla	île	ilha
icefield	Eisdecke	**icefield** *Eng.*	helero	champ de glace	geleira
ice shelf	Schelfeis	**ice shelf** *Eng.*	corniza glacial	barrière de glace	banco de gelo
ice tongue	Eiszunge	**ice tongue** *Eng.*	lengua de glaciar	langue glaciaire	língua de geleira
dunes	Dünen	**idehan** *Ber.*	dunas	dunes	dunas
river	Fluss	**ig., igarapé** *Port.*	río	rivière	igarapé
church	Kirche	**iglesia** *Sp.*	iglesia	église	igreja
lake	See	**-ike** *Jap.*	lago	lac	lago
island(s)	Insel(n)	**île(s)** *Fr.*	isla(s)	île(s)	ilha(s)
islet(s)	kleine Insel(n)	**îlet(s)** *Fr.*	isleta(s)	îlet(s)	ilhota(s)
island(s)	Insel(n)	**ilha(s)** *Port.*	isla(s)	île(s)	ilha(s)
islet(s)	kleine Insel(n)	**ilhéu(s)** *Port.*	isleta(s)	îlot(s)	ilhéu(s)
hill, upland	Hügel, Bergland	**'ilw** *Ara.*	colina, tierras altas	colline, hautes terres	colina, terras altas
hill	Hügel	**'ilwat** *Ara.*	colina	colline	colina
lake	See	**in** *Bur.*	lago	lac	lago
Indian reservation	Indianerreservation	**Ind. res., Indian reservation, Indian reserve** *Eng.*	reserva de Indios	réserve Indienne	reserva indígena
inlet	Einfahrt	**inlet** *Eng.*	abra	bras de mer	enseada
island(s)	Insel(n)	**Insel(n)** *Ger.*	isla(s)	île(s)	ilha(s)
institute	Institut	**inst., institute** *Eng.*	instituto	institut	instituto
international	international	**int., international** *Eng.*	internacional	international	internacional
race course	Rennbahn	**ippodromo** *It.*	hipódromo	hippodrome	hipódromo
wadi	Wadi	**irhazer** *Ber.*	uadi	wadi	uádi
dunes	Dünen	**'irq** *Ara.*	dunas	dunes	dunas
islands	Inseln	**is., islands** *Eng.* **islas** *Sp.*	islas	îles	ilhas
island	Insel	**isla** *Sp.*	isla	île	ilha
island(s)	Insel(n)	**island(s)** *Eng.*	isla(s)	île(s)	ilha(s)
islands	Inseln	**islas** *Sp.*	islas	îles	ilhas
isle(s)	Insel(n)	**isle(s)** *Eng.*	isla(s)	île(s)	ilha(s)
islet(s)	kleine Insel(n)	**islet(s)** *Eng.*	isleta(s)	îlot(s)	ilhota(s)
islet	kleine Insel	**islote** *Sp.*	islote	îlot	ilhota
island	Insel	**isola** *It.*	isla	île	ilha
islands	Inseln	**isole** *It.*	islas	îles	ilhas
islet	kleine Insel	**isolotto** *It.*	isleta	îlot	ilhota
isthmus	Landenge	**isthme** *Fr.*	istmo	isthme	istmo
isthmus	Landenge	**isthmus** *Eng.*	istmo	isthme	istmo
isthmus	Landenge	**istmo** *Sp.*	istmo	isthme	istmo
island	Insel	**-iwa** *Jap.*	isla	île	ilha

J

ENGLISH	DEUTSCH	Map Form	ESPAÑOL	FRANÇAIS	PORTUGUÊS
mountain(s)	Berg(e)	**jabal** *Ara.*	montaña(s)	montagne(s)	montanha(s)
garden	Garten	**jardin** *Fr.*	jardín	jardin	jardim
garden	Garten	**jardín** *Sp.*	jardín	jardin	jardim
gardens	Gärten	**jardines** *Sp.*	jardines	jardins	jardins
lake	See	**järv** *Est.*	lago	lac	lago
lake	See	**-järvi** *Finn.*	lago	lac	lago
mountains	Berge	**jary** *Rus.*	montañas	montagnes	montanhas
cave	Höhle	**jaskyně** *Slo.*	cueva	caverne	caverna
lake	See	**-jaur** *Lapp.*	lago	lac	lago
islands	Inseln	**jazā'ir** *Ara.*	islas	îles	ilhas
island	Insel	**jazīrat** *Ara.*	isla	île	ilha
island	Insel	**jazīreh** *Per.*	isla	île	ilha
reservoir	Stausee	**jazovir** *Blg.*	embalse	réservoir	reservatório
mountain(s)	Berg(e)	**jbel** *Ara.*	montaña(s)	montagne(s)	montanha(s)
lake	See	**jezero** *S./C.*	lago	lac	lago
lake, lagoon	See, Lagune, Haff	**jezioro** *Pol.*	lago, laguna	lac, lagune	lago, laguna
river	Fluss	**-jiang** *Ch.*	río	rivière	rio
cape	Kap	**-jiao** *Ch.*	cabo	cap	cabo
mountains	Berge	**jibāl** *Ara.*	montañas	montagnes	montanhas
island	Insel	**-jima** *Jap.*	isla	île	ilha
saddle	Joch	**Joch** *Ger.*	paso	col	passo
river	Fluss	**-joki** *Finn.*	río	rivière	rio
glacier	Gletscher	**-jøkulen** *Nor.*	glaciar	glacier	geleira
glacier	Gletscher	**-jökull** *Ice.*	glaciar	glacier	geleira
gulf	Golf	**jūras līcis** *Latv.*	golfo	golfe	golfo
islands	Inseln	**juzur** *Ara.*	islas	îles	ilhas

K

ENGLISH	DEUTSCH	Map Form	ESPAÑOL	FRANÇAIS	PORTUGUÊS
mountains	Berge	**kabīr** *Per.*	montañas	montagnes	montanhas
dunes	Dünen	**kahal** *Ara.*	dunas	dunes	dunas
sea	Meer	**-kai** *Jap.*	mar	mer	mar
strait	Meeresstrasse	**-kaikyō** *Jap.*	estrecho	détroit	estreito
mountain	Berg	**-kaise** *Lapp.*	montaña	montagne	montanha
navy installation	Anlage der Marine	**ka.j., kaijō-jieitai** *Jap.*	estación de la marina	installation navale	instalação naval
creek	Bach	**kali** *Indon.*	riachuelo	crique	riacho
mountain	Berg	**kalns** *Latv.*	montaña	montagne	montanha
ridge	Kamm	**Kamm** *Ger.*	sierra	crête	serra
canal	Kanal	**kanaal** *Du.*	canal	canal	canal
canal, channel	Kanal	**Kanal** *Ger.*	canal	canal	canal
canal, channel	Kanal	**kanal** *Rus., S./C., Swe.*	canal	canal	canal
canal, channel	Kanal	**kanał** *Pol.*	canal	canal	canal
canal, channel	Kanal	**Kanalen** *Swe.*	canal	canal	canal
canal, channel	Kanal	**kanava** *Finn.*	canal	canal	canal
pass	Pass	**kandao** *Pas.*	paso	col	passo
river	Fluss	**-kang** *Kor.*	río	rivière	rio
moor	Moor	**-kangas** *Finn.*	páramo	lande	charneca
national park	Nationalpark	**kansallis-puisto** *Finn.*	parque nacional	parc national	parque nacional
island	Insel	**kaôh** *Cbd.*	isla	île	ilha
cape	Kap	**Kap** *Ger.*	cabo	cap	cabo
gorge	Schlucht	**kapija** *S./C.*	garganta	gorge	garganta
cape	Kap	**-kapp** *Nor.*	cabo	cap	cabo
dunes	Dünen	**kathīb** *Ara.*	dunas	dunes	dunas
desert	Wüste	**kavīr** *Per.*	desierto	désert	deserto
mountain	Berg	**kawlat** *Ara.*	montaña	montagne	montanha
hill	Hügel	**kawm** *Ara.*	colina	colline	colina
mountain	Berg	**kediet** *Ara.*	montaña	montagne	montanha
lake	See	**kenohan** *Indon.*	lago	lac	lago
cape	Kap	**kep** *Alb.*	cabo	cap	cabo
islands	Inseln	**kepulauan** *Indon.*	islas	îles	ilhas
key(s), cay(s)	Klippe(n)	**key(s)** *Eng.*	cayo(s)	caye(s)	baixio(s)
intermittent lake	periodischer See	**khabrat** *Ara.*	lago intermitente	lac périodique	lago intermitente
gulf	Golf	**khalīj** *Ara.*	golfo	golfe	golfo
mountain	Berg	**khao** *Bur., Thai*	montaña	montagne	montanha
mountain	Berg	**khashm** *Ara.*	montaña	montagne	montanha
wadi	Wadi	**khatt** *Ara.*	uadi	wadi	uádi
wadi, river	Wadi, Fluss	**khawr** *Ara.*	uadi, río	wadi, rivière	uádi, rio
dam	Damm	**khazzān** *Ara.*	presa	barrage	represa
river, canal	Fluss, Kanal	**khlong** *Thai*	río, canal	rivière, canal	rio, canal
dunes	Dünen	**khubb** *Ara.*	dunas	dunes	dunas
kill (river, channel)	Fluss, Kanal	**kill** *Eng.*	río, canal	rivière, canal	rio, canal
cemetery	Friedhof	**kladb., kladbišče** *Rus.*	cementerio	cimetière	cemitério
cloister	Kloster	**klasztory** *Pol.*	claustro	cloître	claustro, convento
cloister, monastery	Kloster	**Kloster** *Ger.*	claustro, monasterio	cloître, monastère	claustro, mosteiro
knob	Kuppe	**knob** *Eng.*	protuberancia	bosse	cerro, colina
island	Insel	**ko** *Thai*	isla	île	ilha
lake, lagoon	See, Lagune, Haff	**-ko** *Jap.*	lago, laguna	lac, lagune	lago, laguna
harbor	Hafen	**-kō** *Jap.*	puerto	port	porto
highland	Hochland	**-kōchi** *Jap.*	región montañosa	pays montagneux	terras altas
mountain	Kogel	**Kogel** *Ger.*	montaña	montagne	montanha
plateau	Hochebene	**-kogen** *Jap.*	meseta	plateau	planalto
mountains	Berge	**koh** *Per.*	montañas	montagnes	montanhas
air force installation	Anlage der Luftwaffe	**ko.j., kōkū-jieitai** *Jap.*	estación aeronáutica	installation aérienne	instalação da força aérea
national park	Nationalpark	**-kokuritsu-kōen** *Jap.*	parque nacional	parc national	parque nacional
national park	Nationalpark	**-kokutei-kōen** *Jap.*	parque nacional	parc national	parque nacional
bay	Bucht	**kólpos** *Gr.*	bahía	baie	baía
bay	Bucht	**kong** *Ch.*	bahía	baie	baía
mountain	Berg	**kong** *Indon.*	montaña	montagne	montanha
peak	Kopf	**Kopf** *Ger.*	pico	cime	pico
bridge	Brücke	**köprüsü** *Tur.*	puente	pont	ponte
gulf, bay	Golf, Bucht	**körfezi** *Tur.*	golfo, bahía	golfe, baie	golfo, baía
spit	Landzunge	**kosa** *Rus.*	lengua de tierra	flèche	ponta de terra
rapids	Stromschnellen	**-koski** *Finn.*	rápidos	rapides	rápidos
pass	Pass	**kotal** *Per.*	paso	col	passo
basin	Becken	**kotlina** *Pol.*	cuenca	bassin	bacia
bay; pass	Bucht; Pass	**-kou** *Ch.*	bahía; paso	baie; col	baía; passo
mountains	Berge	**kras** *Slo.*	montañas	montagnes	montanhas
ridge	Höhenrücken	**kr'až** *Rus.*	sierra	crête	serra
escarpment	Landstufe	**kreb** *Ara.*	escarpa	escarpement	escarpa
fort	Fort	**krepost'** *Rus.*	fuerte	fort	forte
national park	Nationalpark	**krk., kokuritsu-kōen** *Jap.*	parque nacional	parc national	parque nacional
river	Fluss	**krueng** *Indon.*	río	rivière	rio
national park	Nationalpark	**ktk., kokutei-kōen** *Jap.*	parque nacional	parc national	parque nacional
river mouth	Flussmündung	**-ku** *Ch.*	desembocadura	embouchure	desembocadura
bay	Bucht	**kuala** *Mal.*	bahía	baie	baía
mountain(s)	Berg(e)	**kūh(ha)** *Per.*	montaña(s)	montagne(s)	montanha(s)
hill	Hügel	**-kulle** *Swe.*	colina	colline	colina
dome	Kuppe	**Kuppe** *Ger.*	domo	dôme	domo
strait	Meeresstrasse	**-kurkku** *Finn.*	estrecho	détroit	estreito
channel	Kanal	**kyle** *Gae.*	canal, estrecho	canal, détroit	canal, estreito
island	Insel	**kyun** *Bur.*	isla	île	ilha
hills	Hügel	**-kyūryū** *Jap.*	colinas	collines	colinas

L

ENGLISH	DEUTSCH	Map Form	ESPAÑOL	FRANÇAIS	PORTUGUÊS
lake	See	**l., lac** *Fr.* **lago** *It., Sp.* **lagoa** *Port.* **lake** *Eng.*	lago	lac	lago, lagoa
pass	Pass	**la** *Tib.*	paso	col	passo
province	Provinz	**lääni** *Finn.*	provincia	province	província
lake(s)	See(n)	**lac(s)** *Fr.*	lago(s)	lac(s)	lago(s)
lake	See	**lacul** *Rom.*	lago	lac	lago
river	Fluss	**lae** *Indon.*	río	rivière	rio
cape	Kap	**laem** *Thai*	cabo	cap	cabo
lagoon, lake	Lagune, Haff, See	**lag., laguna** *Sp.*	laguna	lagune, lac	laguna
lake	See	**lago** *It., Port., Sp.*	lago	lac	lago
lake, lagoon	See, Lagune, Haff	**lagoa** *Port.*	lago, laguna,	lac, lagune	lagoa
lagoon	Lagune, Haff	**lagoon** *Eng.*	laguna	lagune	laguna
lakes	Seen	**lagos** *Port., Sp.*	lagos	lacs	lagos
lagoon, lake	Lagune, Haff, See	**laguna** *Sp.*	laguna	lagune, lac	laguna, lago
lagoon	Lagune, Haff	**lagune** *Fr.*	laguna	lagune	laguna
bay	Bucht	**laht** *Est.*	bahía	baie	baía
gulf	Golf	**-lahti** *Finn.*	golfo	golfe	golfo
lake(s)	See(n)	**lake(s)** *Eng.*	lago(s)	lac(s)	lago(s)
county	Grafschaft	**län** *Swe.*	condado	comté	condado
lake	Lanke (See)	**Lanke** *Ger.*	lago	lac	lago
sea	Meer	**laut** *Indon.*	mar	mer	mar
lava flow	Lavastrom	**lava flow** *Eng.*	corriente de lava	coulée de lave	corrente de lava
hill, mountain	Hügel, Berg	**law** *Gae.*	colina, montaña	colline, montagne	colina montanha
mountains; forest	Berge; Wald	**les** *Czech*	montañas; bosque	montagnes; forêt	montanhas; floresta
forest	Wald	**les** *Rus.*	bosque	forêt	floresta
level (plain)	Niveau (Ebene)	**level** *Eng.*	nivel (llano)	niveau (plaine)	planície
islands	Inseln	**liehtao** *Ch.*	islas	îles	ilhas
lighthouse	Leuchtturm	**lighthouse** *Eng.*	faro	phare	farol
estuary	Trichtermündung	**liman** *Rus.*	estuario	estuaire	estuário

ENGLISH	DEUTSCH	Map Form Geographische Begriffe Términos Geográficos Termes Géographiques Termos Geográficos	ESPAÑOL	FRANÇAIS	PORTUGUÊS
bay	Bucht	**limanı** *Tur.*	bahía	baie	baía
lake	See	**límni** *Gr.*	lago	lac	lago
peak	Gipfel	**-ling** *Ch.*	pico	cime	pico
plain	Ebene	**llano** *Sp.*	llano	plaine	planície
plains	Ebenen	**llanos** *Sp.*	llanos	plaines	planícies
lake, inlet	See, Einfahrt	**loch** *Gae.*	lago, abra	lac, bras de mer	lago, angra
lock	Schleuse	**lock** *Eng.*	esclusa	écluse	eclusa
lock and dam	Damm mit Schleuse	**lock and dam** *Eng.*	presa y esclusa	écluse et barrage	represa e eclusa
gorge	Schlucht	**log** *Rus.*	garganta	gorge	garganta
mountain	Berg	**loi** *Bur.*	montaña	montagne	montanha
hills	Hügel	**lomas** *Sp.*	lomas	collines	colinas
lake	See	**lough** *Gae.*	lago	lac	lago
lowland	Tiefland	**lowland** *Eng.*	tierra baja	terrain bas	terras baixas
marsh	Luch (Bruch)	**Luch** *Ger.*	pantano	marais	pântano
airport	Flughafen	**luchthaven** *Du.*	aeropuerto	aéroport	aeroporto
island	Insel	**-luoto** *Finn.*	isla	île	ilha

M

ENGLISH	DEUTSCH	Map Form	ESPAÑOL	FRANÇAIS	PORTUGUÊS
mountains	Berge	**m., munţii** *Rom.*	montañas	montagnes	montanhas
island	Insel	**-maa** *Est.*	isla	île	ilha
river	Fluss	**mae** *Thai*	río	rivière	rio
strait	Meeresstrasse	**maḍiq** *Ara.*	estrecho	détroit	estreito
depression	Senke	**makhtesh** *Heb.*	depresión	dépression	depressão
bay	Bucht	**-man** *Kor.*	bahía	baie	baía
monastery	Kloster	**manastir** *S./C.*	monasterio	monastère	mosteiro
sea	Meer	**mar** *Sp.*	mar	mer	mar
marsh	Marsch	**marais** *Fr.*	pantano	marais	pântano
sea	Meer	**mare** *It.*	mar	mer	mar
Marine Corps Air Station	Flugstützpunkt des Marine-Corps	**Marine Corps Air Station** *Eng.*	estación aeronáutica de la infantería de marina	station aérienne des fusiliers marins	estação aérea de fuzileiros navais
Marine Corps Base	Marine-Corps-Stützpunkt	**Marine Corps Base** *Eng.*	base de la infantería de marina	base des fusiliers marins	base de fuzileiros navais
bay	Bucht	**marsā** *Ara.*	bahía	baie	baía
marsh	Marsch	**Marsch** *Ger.*	pantano	marais	pântano
marsh(es)	Marsch(en)	**marsh(es)** *Eng.*	pantano(s)	marais	pântano(s)
river mouth	Flussmündung	**maṣabb** *Ara.*	desembocadura	embouchure	desembocadura
canal	Kanal	**maṣrif** *Ara.*	canal	canal	canal
massif	Gebirgsmassiv	**massif** *Eng., Fr.*	macizo	massif	maciço
Marine Corps Air Station	Flugstützpunkt des Marine-Corps	**M.C.A.S., Marine Corps Air Station** *Eng.*	estación aeronáutica de la infantería de marina	station aérienne des fusiliers marins	estação aérea de fuzileiros navais
Marine Corps Base	Marine-Corps-Stützpunkt	**M.C.B., Marine Corps Base** *Eng.*	base de la infantería de marina	base des fusiliers marins	base de fuzileiros navais
meadow	Wiese	**meadow** *Eng.*	prado	prairie	pradaria
dunes	Dünen	**médanos** *Sp.*	médanos	dunes	dunas
sea, lake	Meer	**Meer** *Ger.*	mar, lago	mer, lac	mar, lago
sea, lake	Meer	**meer** *Afk., Du.*	mar, lago	mer, lac	mar, lago
hills	Hügel	**melkosopočnik** *Rus.*	colinas	collines	colinas
memorial	Gedenkstätte	**mem., memorial** *Eng., Fr.*	monumento	memorial	monumento
peninsula	Halbinsel	**menandjung** *Indon.*	península	péninsule	península
sea	Meer	**mer** *Fr.*	mar	mer	mar
mesa	Tafelberg	**mesa** *Sp.*	mesa	mesa	mesa
plateau	Hochebene	**meseta** *Sp.*	meseta	plateau	planalto
middle	Mittel-	**mid., middle** *Eng.*	medio	moyen	médio, central
spit	Landzunge	**mierzeja** *Pol.*	lengua de tierra	flèche	ponta de terra
bay	Bucht	**mifraz** *Heb.*	bahía	baie	baía
mines	Bergwerke	**mikhrot** *Heb.*	minas	mines	minas
military	militärisch	**mil., military** *Eng.*	militar	militaire	militar
harbor	Hafen	**-minato** *Jap.*	puerto	port	porto
mine	Bergwerk	**mine** *Eng., Fr.*	mina	mine	mina
mountain	Berg	**-mine** *Jap.*	montaña	montagne	montanha
cliff	Kliff	**minqār** *Ara.*	risco	falaise	falésia
cape	Kap	**-misaki** *Jap.*	cabo	cap	cabo
mission	Mission	**mission** *Eng., Fr.*	misión	mission	missão
monument	Denkmal	**mon., monument** *Eng. Fr.*	monumento	monument	monumento
monastery	Kloster	**monasterio** *Sp.*	monasterio	monastère	mosteiro
monastery	Kloster	**monastero** *It.*	monasterio	monastère	mosteiro
monastery	Kloster	**monastery** *Eng.*	monasterio	monastère	mosteiro
monastery	Kloster	**moni** *Gr.*	monasterio	monastère	mosteiro
mount	Berg	**mont** *Fr.*	monte	mont	monte
mountain	Berg	**montagna** *It.*	montaña	montagne	montanha
mountain(s)	Berg(e)	**montagne(s)** *Fr.*	montaña(s)	montagne(s)	montanha(s)
mountain(s)	Berg(e)	**montaña(s)** *Sp.*	montaña(s)	montagne(s)	montanha(s)
mount	Berg	**monte** *It., Port., Sp.*	monte	mont	monte
mountains	Berge	**montes** *Port., Sp.*	montes	monts	montes
mountains	Berge	**monti** *It.*	montes	monts	montes
mountains	Berge	**monts** *Fr.*	montes	monts	montes
monument	Denkmal	**monument** *Eng., Fr.*	monumento	monument	monumento
moor	Moor	**moor** *Eng.*	páramo	lande	charneca
moor	Moos	**Moos** *Ger.*	páramo	lande	charneca
sea	Meer	**more** *Rus.*	mar	mer	mar
mountain	Berg	**-mori** *Jap.*	montaña	montagne	montanha
mountain	Berg	**morne** *Fr.*	montaña	morne	montanha
hill, mountain	Hügel, Berg	**morro** *Port., Sp.*	morro	colline, montagne	morro
mosque	Moschee	**mosque** *Eng.*	mezquita	mosquée	mesquita
island, rock	Insel, Fels	**motu** *Poly.*	isla, roca	île, rocher	ilha, rochedo
island	Insel	**mouchão** *Port.*	isla	île	mouchão
mound	Erdhügel	**mound** *Eng.*	montículo	tertre	montículo
mount	Berg	**mount** *Eng.*	monte	mont	monte
mountain(s)	Berg(e)	**mountain(s)** *Eng.*	montaña(s)	montagne(s)	montanha(s)
mouth	Mündung	**mouth** *Eng.*	desembocadura	embouchure	desembocadura
mount	Berg	**mt., mount** *Eng.*	monte	mont	monte
mountain	Berg	**mtn., mountain** *Eng.*	montaña	montagne	montanha
mountains	Berge	**mts., mountains** *Eng.*	montañas	montagnes	montanhas
point	Landspitze	**mui** *Viet.*	punta	pointe	ponta
headland	Landspitze	**mull** *Gae.*	promontorio	promontoire	promontório
channel	Kanal	**mun** *Ch.*	canal, estrecho	canal, détroit	canal, estreito
depression	Senke	**munkhafaḍ** *Ara.*	depresión	dépression	depressão
mountain	Berg	**muntele** *Rom.*	montaña	montagne	montanha
mountains	Berge	**munţii** *Rom.*	montañas	montagnes	montanhas
museum	Museum	**museo** *It., Sp.*	museo	musée	museu
museum	Museum	**Museum** *Ger.*	museo	musée	museu
museum	Museum	**museum** *Eng.*	museo	musée	museu
museum	Museum	**múzeum** *Hung.*	museo	musée	museu
museum	Museum	**muzej** *Rus.*	museo	musée	museu
cape	Kap	**mys** *Rus.*	cabo	cap	cabo

N

ENGLISH	DEUTSCH	Map Form	ESPAÑOL	FRANÇAIS	PORTUGUÊS
north	Nord	**n., north** *Eng.*	norte	nord	norte
sea, gulf	Meer, Golf	**-nada** *Jap.*	mar, golfo	mer, golfe	mar, golfo
desert	Wüste	**nafūd** *Ara.*	desierto	désert	deserto
plateau, mountains	Hochebene, Berge	**nagorje** *Rus.*	meseta, montañas	plateau, montagnes	planalto, montanhas
river	Fluss	**nahr** *Ara.*	río	rivière	rio
sea	Meer	**-naikai** *Jap.*	mar	mer	mar
salt flat	Salzebene	**namakzār** *Per.*	salar	saline	salina
narrows	Meeresenge	**narrows** *Eng.*	angostura	goulet	estreito
peninsula	Halbinsel	**-näs** *Swe.*	península	péninsule	península
naval air station	Flugstützpunkt der Marine	**n.a.s., naval air station** *Eng.*	estación aeronáutica de la marina	station des forces aériennes navales	estação aérea da marinha
National Aeronautics and Space Administration	Nationale Aeronautik- und Weltraum-Behörde	**N.A.S.A., National Aeronautics and Space Administration** *Eng.*	Administración Nacional Aeronáutica y Espacial	Administration Nationale de l'Espace et Aéronautique	Administração Nacional do Espaço e Aeronâutica
national park	Nationalpark	**nasjonal park** *Nor.*	parque nacional	parc national	parque nacional
national	national	**nat., national** *Eng., Fr.*	nacional	national	nacional
national battlefield site	Schlachtfeld	**national battlefield site** *Eng.*	campo de batalla nacional	champ de bataille national	campo de batalha nacional
national cemetery	National-friedhof	**national cemetery** *Eng.*	cementerio nacional	cimetière national	cemitério nacional
national forest	Wald in Gemeinbesitz	**national forest** *Eng.*	bosque nacional	forêt nationale	floresta nacional
national historical park	Park an historischer Stätte	**national historical park** *Eng.*	parque histórico nacional	parc historique national	parque histórico nacional
national historical site	historische Stätte	**national historical site** *Eng.*	lugar histórico nacional	site historique national	sítio histórico nacional
national laboratory	staatliche Forschungsanstalt	**national laboratory** *Eng.*	laboratorio nacional	laboratoire national	laboratório nacional
national memorial	nationale Gedenkstätte	**national memorial** *Eng.*	monumento nacional	memorial national	monumento nacional
national military park	Park bei einem Schlachtfeld	**national military park** *Eng.*	parque militar nacional	parc militaire national	parque militar nacional
national monument	Nationaldenkmal	**national monument** *Eng.*	monumento nacional	monument national	monumento nacional
national park	Nationalpark	**national park** *Eng.*	parque nacional	parc national	parque nacional
natioanal recreation area	Ausflugsgebiet	**national recreation area** *Eng.*	campo nacional de recreo	région de récréation nationale	área de lazer nacional
national seashore	öffentlicher Badestrand	**national seashore** *Eng.*	playa nacional	plage nationale	praia nacional
reserve	Naturpark	**Naturpark** *Ger.*	reserva natural	réserve naturelle	reserva natural
nature reserve	Naturschutzgebiet	**Naturschutzgebiet** *Ger.*	reserva natural	réserve naturelle	reserva natural
naval air station	Flugstützpunkt der Marine	**naval air station** *Eng.*	estación aeronáutica de la marina	station des forces aériennes navales	estação aérea da marinha
naval base	Flottenstützpunkt	**naval base** *Eng.*	base naval	base navale	base naval
naval station	Marinestation	**naval station** *Eng.*	estación naval	station navale	estação naval
naval base	Flottenstützpunkt	**n.b., naval base** *Eng.*	base naval	base navale	base naval
rock	Fels	**-ne** *Jap.*	roca	rocher	rochedo
neck	Landenge	**neck** *Eng.*	istmo	isthme	istmo
necropolis	Friedhof	**necrópolis** *Sp.*	necrópolis	nécropole	necrópole
cape	Kap	**neem** *Est.*	cabo	cap	cabo
peninsula, point	Halbinsel, Landspitze	**-nes** *Ice., Nor.*	península, punta	péninsule, pointe	península, ponta
promontory	Vorgebirge	**ness** *Gae.*	promontorio	promontoire	promontório
snowcapped mountain(s)	Schneegipfel	**nev(s)., nevado(s)** *Sp.*	nevado(s)	montagne(s) neigeuse(s)	pico(s) nevado(s)
mountain	Berg	**ngoc** *Viet.*	montaña	montagne	montanha
cape	Kap	**nina** *Est.*	cabo	cap	cabo
islands	Inseln	**nísoi** *Gr.*	islas	îles	ilhas
island	Insel	**nísos** *Gr.*	isla	île	ilha
lowland	Tiefland	**nizina** *Rus.*	tierra baja	terrain bas	terras baixas
lowland	Tiefland	**nižina** *Slo.*	tierra baja	terrain bas	terras baixas
lowland	Tiefland	**nizmennost'** *Rus.*	tierra baja	terrain bas	terras baixas
cape	Kap	**nos** *Blg.*	cabo	cap	cabo
naval station	Marinestation	**n.s., naval station** *Eng.*	estación naval	station navale	estação naval
nature reserve	Naturschutzgebiet	**Nsg., Naturschutzgebiet** *Ger.*	reserva natural	réserve naturelle	reserva natural
mountain	Berg	**nui** *Viet.*	montaña	montagne	montanha
lake	See	**-numa** *Jap.*	lago	lac	lago
mountains	Berge	**nuruu** *Mong.*	montañas	montagnes	montanhas
island	Insel	**nusa** *Indon.*	isla	île	ilha
lake	See	**nuur** *Mong.*	lago	lac	lago

O

ENGLISH	DEUTSCH	Map Form	ESPAÑOL	FRANÇAIS	PORTUGUÊS
bay	Bucht	**o** *Ch.*	bahía	baie	baía
island	Insel	**-ø** *Dan., Nor.*	isla	île	ilha
island	Insel	**-ö** *Swe.*	isla	île	ilha
island	Insel	**o., ostrov** *Rus.*	isla	île	ilha
islands	Inseln	**-öarna** *Swe.*	islas	îles	ilhas
oasis	Oase	**oasis** *Eng., Fr., Sp.*	oasis	oasis	oásis
observatory	Observatorium	**observatorio** *Sp.*	observatorio	observatoire	observatório
observatory	Observatorium	**observatory** *Eng.*	observatorio	observatoire	observatório
ocean	Ozean	**ocean** *Eng.*	océano	océan	oceano
island	Insel	**-ön** *Swe.*	isla	île	ilha
mountains	Berge	**óri** *Gr.*	montañas	montagnes	montanhas
bay	Bucht	**órmos** *Gr.*	bahía	baie	baía
mountain(s)	Berg(e)	**óros** *Gr.*	montaña(s)	montagne(s)	montanha(s)
island(s)	Insel(n)	**ostrov(a)** *Rus.*	isla(s)	île(s)	ilha(s)
island	Insel	**ostrovul** *Rom.*	isla	île	ilha
islands	Inseln	**otoci** *S./C.*	islas	îles	ilhas
island	Insel	**otok** *S./C.*	isla	île	ilha
wadi	Wadi	**ouadi** *Ara.*	uadi	wadi	uádi
wadi	Wadi	**oued** *Ara.*	uadi	wadi	uádi
outlet	Abfluss	**outlet** *Eng.*	desagüe	débouché	escoadouro
island	Insel	**-øy, -øya** *Nor.*	isla	île	ilha
lake	See	**oz., ozero** *Rus.*	lago	lac	lago
lakes	Seen	**ozera** *Rus.*	lagos	lacs	lagos

P

ENGLISH	DEUTSCH	Map Form	ESPAÑOL	FRANÇAIS	PORTUGUÊS
hills	Hügel	**pahorkatina** *Czech.*	colinas	collines	colinas
palace	Palast	**pal., palace** *Eng.*	palacio	palais	palácio
palace	Palast	**palacio** *Sp.*	palacio	palais	palácio
palace	Palast	**palais** *Fr.*	palacio	palais	palácio
palace	Palast	**palazzo** *It.*	palacio	palais	palácio
palace	Palast	**paleis** *Du.*	palacio	palais	palácio
railroad station	Bahnhof	**pályaudvar** *Hung.*	estación ferrocarril	gare	estação ferroviária
monument	Denkmal	**pam'atnik** *Rus.*	monumento	monument	monumento
plain	Ebene	**pampa** *Sp.*	pampa	plaine	pampa
basin	Becken	**pánev** *Czech*	cuenca	bassin	bacia
swamp	Sumpf	**pantanal** *Port., Sp.*	pantanal	marais	pantanal
marsh, swamp; reservoir	Marsch, Sumpf; Stausee	**pantano** *Sp.*	pantano	marais; réservoir	pântano
moor	Moor	**páramo** *Sp.*	páramo	lande	charneca
park	Park	**parc** *Fr.*	parque	parc	parque
national park	National park	**parc national** *Fr.*	parque nacional	parc national	parque nacional
park	Park	**parco** *It.*	parque	parc	parque
national park	Nationalpark	**parco nazionale** *It.*	parque nacional	parc national	parque nacional
provincial park	Naturpark	**parc provincial** *Fr.*	parque de la provincia	parc provincial	parque provincial
park	Park	**Park** *Ger.*	parque	parc	parque
park	Park	**park** *Eng.*	parque	parc	parque
national park	Nationalpark	**park narodowy** *Pol.*	parque nacional	parc national	parque nacional
parkway	Ferienstrasse	**parkway** *Eng.*	calzada	allée de parc	alameda de parque
park	Park	**parque** *Port., Sp.*	parque	parc	parque
national park	Nationalpark	**parq. nac., parque nacional** *Port., Sp.*	parque nacional	parc national	parque nacional
beach	Strand	**part** *Hung.*	playa	plage	praia
strait	Meeresstrasse	**pas** *Fr.*	estrecho	détroit	estreito
passage	Durchfahrt	**pasaje** *Sp.*	pasaje	passage	passagem
pass	Pass	**paso** *Sp.*	paso	col	passo
pass	Pass	**Pass** *Ger.*	paso	col	passo
pass	Pass	**pass** *Eng.*	paso	col	passo
passage	Durchfahrt	**passage** *Eng., Fr.*	pasaje	passage	passagem
passage	Durchfahrt	**passe** *Fr.*	pasaje	passe	passagem

Glossary and Abbreviations of Geographical Terms / Verzeichnis und Abkürzungen Geographischer Begriffe
Glosario y Abreviaciones de Términos Geográficos / Glossaire et Abréviations de Termes Géographiques
Glossário e Abreviações de Termos Geográficos

ENGLISH	DEUTSCH	Map Form / Geographische Begriffe / Términos Geográficos / Termes Géographiques / Termos Geográficos	ESPAÑOL	FRANÇAIS	PORTUGUÊS
pass	Pass	**passo** *It.*	paso	col	passo
pass	Pass	**pasul** *Rom.*	paso	col	passo
creek	Bach	**patak** *Hung.*	riachuelo	crique	riacho
peak(s)	Gipfel	**peak(s)** *Eng.*	pico(s)	pic(s)	pico(s)
cave	Höhle	**pećina** *S./C.*	cueva	caverne	caverna
mountains	Berge	**peg., pegunungan** *Indon.*	montañas	montagnes	montanhas
sea	Meer	**pélagos** *Gr.*	mar	mer	mar
bay	Bucht	**pellg** *Alb.*	bahía	baie	baía
peninsula	Halbinsel	**pen., peninsula** *Eng.*	península	péninsule	península
peak; rock	Gipfel; Fels	**peña** *Sp.*	peña	pic; rocher	penha
peak; large rock	Gipfel; grosser Fels	**peñasco** *Sp.*	peñasco	pic; rocher	penhasco
basin	Becken	**-pendi** *Ch.*	cuenca	bassin	bacia
peninsula	Halbinsel	**peninsula** *Eng.*	península	péninsule	península
peninsula	Halbinsel	**península** *Sp.*	península	péninsule	península
peninsula	Halbinsel	**péninsule** *Fr.*	península	péninsule	península
rock	Fels	**peñón** *Sp.*	peñón	rocher	rochedo
pass	Pass	**pereval** *Rus.*	paso	col	passo
strait	Meeresstrasse	**pertuis** *Fr.*	estrecho	pertuis	estreito
sand desert	Sandwüste	**peski** *Rus.*	desierto arenoso	désert de sable	deserto arenoso
mountain	Berg	**phnum** *Cbd.*	montaña	montagne	montanha
mountain	Berg	**phou** *Lao.*	montaña	montagne	montanha
mountain	Berg	**phu** *Thai*	montaña	montagne	montanha
cape	Kap	**pi** *Ch.*	cabo	cap	cabo
plain	Ebene	**piano** *It.*	llanura	plaine	planície
peak	Gipfel	**pic** *Fr.*	pico	pic	pico
peak	Gipfel	**picacho** *Sp.*	picacho	pic	pico
peak	Gipfel	**picco** *It.*	pico	pic	pico
peak(s)	Gipfel	**pico(s)** *Port., Sp.*	pico(s)	pic(s)	pico(s)
pier	Landungsbrücke	**pier** *Eng.*	embarcadero	jetée	cais
mountain	Berg	**-piggen** *Nor.*	montaña	montagne	montanha
peak	Gipfel	**pik** *Rus.*	pico	pic	pico
forest	Wald	**pinhal** *Port.*	bosque	forêt	pinhal
peak	Gipfel	**pique** *Fr.*	pico	pique	pico
pyramid	Pyramide	**pirámide** *Sp.*	pirámide	pyramide	pirâmide
peak(s)	Gipfel	**piton(s)** *Fr.*	pico(s)	piton(s)	pico(s)
peak	Gipfel	**piz, pizzo** *It.*	pico	pic	pico
peak	Gipfel	**pk., peak** *Eng.*	pico	pic	pico
parkway	Ferienstrasse	**pkwy., parkway** *Eng.*	calzada	allée de parc	alameda de parque
plain	Ebene	**plain** *Eng.*	llanura	plaine	planície
plain	Ebene	**plaine** *Fr.*	llanura	plaine	planície
plains	Ebenen	**plains** *Eng.*	llanura	plaines	planícies
plateau	Hochebene	**planalto** *Port.*	meseta	plateau	planalto
planetarium	Planetarium	**planetario** *Sp.*	planetario	planétarium	planetário
planetarium	Planetarium	**planetarium** *Eng.*	planetario	planétarium	planetário
mountain, range	Berg, Gebirge	**planina** *S./C.*	montaña, sierra	montagne, chaîne	montanha, cordilheira
plateau	Hochebene	**plateau** *Eng., Fr.*	meseta	plateau	planalto
plateau	Hochebene	**plato** *Afk., Blg., Rus.*	meseta	plateau	planalto
beach	Strand	**playa** *Sp.*	playa	plage	praia
square	Platz	**plaza** *Sp.*	plaza	place	praça
plateau	Hochebene	**plošina** *Czech*	meseta	plateau	planalto
plateau	Hochebene	**ploskogorje** *Rus.*	meseta	plateau	planalto
pass	Pass	**poarta** *Rom.*	paso	col	passo
hill	Hügel	**poggio** *It.*	colina	colline	colina
mountains	Berge	**pohorie** *Slo.*	montañas	montagnes	montanhas
point	Landspitze	**point** *Eng.*	punta	pointe	ponta
point	Landspitze	**pointe** *Fr.*	punta	pointe	ponta
island	Insel	**pol** *Du.*	isla	île	ilha
plain, basin	Ebene, Becken	**polje** *S./C.*	llanura, cuenca	plaine, bassin	planície, bacia
peninsula	Halbinsel	**poluostrov** *Rus.*	península	péninsule	península
peninsula	Halbinsel	**poluotok** *S./C.*	península	péninsule	península
pond	Teich	**pond** *Eng.*	charca	étang	lago
peak	Gipfel	**-pong** *Kor.*	pico	cime	pico
bridge	Brücke	**pont** *Fr.*	puente	pont	ponte
point	Landspitze	**ponta, pontal** *Port.*	punta	pointe	ponta, pontal
bridge	Brücke	**ponte** *Port.*	puente	pont	ponte
pool	Tümpel	**pool** *Eng.*	charco	étang	charco
rapids	Stromschnellen	**porog** *Rus.*	rápidos	rapides	rápidos
port	Hafen	**port** *Eng., Fr.*	puerto	port	porto
port	Hafen	**porto** *It.*	puerto	port	porto
strait	Meeresstrasse	**porthmós** *Gr.*	estrecho	détroit	estreito
provincial park	Naturpark	**p.p., provincial park** *Eng.*	parque de la provincia	parc provincial	parque provincial
beach	Strand	**praia** *Port.*	playa	plage	praia
reservoir	Stausee	**přehr., přehradová nádrž** *Czech*	embalse	réservoir	reservatório
reservoir, dam	Stausee, Damm	**presa** *Sp.*	presa	réservoir, barrage	represa
peninsula	Halbinsel	**presqu'île** *Fr.*	península	presqu'île	península
pass	Pass	**priesmyk** *Slo.*	paso	col	passo
reservoir	Stausee	**priehradová nádrž** *Slo.*	embalse	réservoir	reservatório
prison	Gefängnis	**prison** *Eng.*	prisión	prison	prisão
pass	Pass	**prohod** *Blg.*	paso	col	passo
strait	Meeresstrasse	**proliv** *Rus.*	estrecho	détroit	estreito
promontory	Vorgebirge	**promontorio** *It., Sp.*	promontorio	promontoire	promontório
promontory	Vorgebirge	**promontory** *Eng.*	promontorio	promontoire	promontório
provincial park	Naturpark	**prov. park, provincial park** *Eng.*	parque de la provincia	parc provincial	parque provincial
reservoir	Stausee	**prudy** *Rus.*	embalse	réservoir	reservatório
pass	Pass	**průsmyk** *Czech*	paso	col	passo
pass	Pass	**przełęcz** *Pol.*	paso	col	passo
cape	Kap	**przylądek** *Pol.*	cabo	cap	cabo
point	Landspitze	**pt., point** *Eng.*	punta	pointe	ponta
railroad station	Bahnhof	**pu., pályaudvar** *Hung.*	estación de ferrocarril	gare	estação ferroviária
port	Hafen	**puerto** *Sp.*	puerto	port	porto
peak	Gipfel	**puig** *Cat.*	pico	cime	pico
island	Insel	**pulau** *Indon., Mal.*	isla	île	ilha
islands	Inseln	**pulau-pulau** *Indon.*	islas	îles	ilhas
upland	Bergland	**puna** *Sp.*	puna	hautes terres	terras altas
point	Landspitze	**punt** *Du.*	punta	pointe	ponta
point, peak	Landspitze, Gipfel	**punta** *It., Sp.*	punta	pointe, cime	ponta
point	Landspitze	**puntilla** *Sp.*	puntilla	pointe	ponta pequena
peak	Gipfel	**puntjak** *Indon.*	pico	cime	pico
forest	Wald	**puszcza** *Pol.*	bosque	forêt	floresta
pyramid	Pyramide	**pyramid** *Eng.*	pirámide	pyramide	pirâmide

Q

ENGLISH	DEUTSCH	Map Form	ESPAÑOL	FRANÇAIS	PORTUGUÊS
salt flat	Salzebene	**qā'** *Ara.*	salar	saline	salina
pass	Pass	**qaf'** *Alb.*	paso	col	passo
canal	Kanal	**qanāt** *Ara.*	canal	canal	canal
hill	Hügel	**qārat** *Ara.*	colina	colline	colina
hills	Hügel	**qārāt** *Ara.*	colinas	collines	colinas
dunes	Dünen	**qawz** *Ara.*	dunas	dunes	dunas
creek	Bach	**qbda, quebrada** *Sp.*	quebrada	crique	arroio
mountain	Berg	**qolleh** *Per.*	montaña	montagne	montanha
canal	Kanal	**-qu** *Ch.*	canal	canal	canal
quarry	Steinbruch	**quarry** *Eng.*	cantera	carrière	pedreira
creek	Bach	**quebrada** *Sp.*	quebrada	crique	arroio
rapids	Stromschnellen	**quedas** *Port.*	rápidos	rapides	quedas
islands	Inseln	**-qundao** *Ch.*	islas	îles	ilhas
hill	Hügel	**qūr** *Ara.*	colina	colline	colina
mountain	Berg	**qurnat** *Ara.*	montaña	montagne	montanha

R

ENGLISH	DEUTSCH	Map Form	ESPAÑOL	FRANÇAIS	PORTUGUÊS
river	Fluss	**r., rio** *Port.* **río** *Sp.*	río	rivière	rio
		river *Eng.* **rivière** *Fr.*			
range	Gebirge	**ra., range** *Eng.*	sierra	chaîne	cordilheira
Royal Australian Air Force Station	Luftwaffenstützpunkt (Austl.)	**R.A.A.F.S., Royal Australian Air Station** *Eng.*	Real Estación Aeronáutica (Austl.)	Station Aérienne Royale (Austl.)	Real Estação da Força Aérea Australiana
race course	Rennbahn	**race course** *Eng.*	hipódromo	champ de course	hipódromo
race track	Rennbahn	**race track** *Eng.*	hipódromo	champ de course	hipódromo
raceway	Rennbahn	**raceway** *Eng.*	hipódromo	champ de course	hipódromo
river	Fluss	**rach** *Viet.*	río	rivière	rio
anchorage	Ankerplatz	**rada** *Sp.*	rada	ancrage	ancoradouro
cape	Kap	**rags** *Latv.*	cabo	cap	cabo
railroad	Eisenbahn	**railroad** *Eng.*	ferrocarril	chemin de fer	ferrovia
railway	Eisenbahn	**railway** *Eng.*	ferrocarril	chemin de fer	ferrovia
railway station	Bahnhof	**railway station** *Eng.*	estación de ferrocarril	gare	estação ferroviária
dunes	Dünen	**ramlat** *Ara.*	dunas	dunes	dunas
range(s)	Gebirge	**range(s)** *Eng.*	sierra(s)	chaîne(s)	cordilheira(s)
river	Fluss	**rāo., ribeirão** *Port.*	río	rivière	rio, ribeirão
rapids	Stromschnellen	**rapides** *Fr.*	rápidos	rapides	rápidos
rapids	Stromschnellen	**rapids** *Eng.*	rápidos	rapides	rápidos
wadi	Wadi	**raqabat** *Ara.*	uadi	wadi	uádi
cape	Kap	**ras, ra's** *Ara.*	cabo	cap	cabo
cape	Kap	**rās** *Per.*	cabo	cap	cabo
ravine	Tobel	**ravine** *Eng.*	barranca	ravin	ravina
plain	Ebene	**ravnina** *Rus.*	llanura	plaine	planície
canal	Kanal	**rayyāḥ** *Ara.*	canal	canal	canal
flood plain	Überschwemmungsebene	**razlivy** *Rus.*	llanura de inundación	lit d'inondation	planície de inundação
road	Landstrasse	**rd., road** *Eng.*	camino	route	rodovia
reef	Riff	**récif** *Fr.*	arrecife	récif	recife
reefs	Riffe	**recifes** *Port.*	arrecifes	récifs	recifes
reefs	Riffe	**récifs** *Fr.*	arrecifes	récifs	recifes
reef(s)	Riff(e)	**reef(s)** *Eng.*	arrecife(s)	récif(s)	recife(s)
regional park	Regionalpark	**regional park** *Eng.*	parque regional	parc régional	parque regional
mountain	Berg	**-rei** *Jap.*	montaña	montagne	montanha
race course	Rennbahn	**Rennbahn** *Ger.*	hipódromo	champ de course	hipódromo
dam; reservoir	Damm; Stausee	**represa** *Port.*	presa; embalse	barrage; réservoir	represa
airport	Flughafen	**repülőtér** *Hung.*	aeropuerto	aéroport	aeroporto
reservoir	Stausee	**res., reservoir** *Eng.*	embalse	réservoir	reservatório
reservation	Reservat	**reservation** *Eng.*	reservación	réservation	reserva
reservoir	Stausee	**reservatório** *Port.*	embalse	réservoir	reservatório
reserve	Reservat	**reserve** *Eng.*	reserva	réserve	reserva
reserve	Reservat	**réserve** *Fr.*	reserva	réserve	reserva
game reserve	Wildreservat	**réserve de chasse** *Fr.*	vedado de caza	réserve de chasse	reserva de caça
reservoir	Stausee	**reservoir** *Eng.*	embalse	réservoir	reservatório
reservoir	Stausee	**réservoir** *Fr.*	embalse	réservoir	reservatório
islands	Inseln	**-retto** *Jap.*	islas	îles	ilhas
ria	Ria	**ría** *Sp.*	ría	ria	ria
creek	Bach	**riacho** *Port., Sp.*	riacho	crique	riacho
creek	Bach	**riachuelo** *Sp.*	riachuelo	crique	riacho
creek	Bach	**rib., ribeira** *Port.*	riachuelo	crique	ribeira
river	Fluss	**ribeirão** *Port.*	río	rivière	ribeirão
ridge	Höhenrücken	**ridge** *Eng.*	sierra	crête	serra
moor	Ried	**Ried** *Ger.*	páramo	lande	charneca
creek	Bach	**riera** *Sp.*	riera	crique	riacho
national museum	Reichsmuseum	**rijksmuseum** *Du.*	museo nacional	musée national	museu nacional
army installation	Anlage des Heeres	**rikujō-jieitai** *Jap.*	estación del ejército	installation militaire	instalação militar
river	Fluss	**rio** *Port.*	río	rivière	rio
river	Fluss	**río** *Sp.*	río	rivière	rio
river	Fluss	**riozinho** *Port.*	río	rivière	riozinho
rise (submarine)	Schwelle (untermeerische)	**rise** *Eng.*	elevación (submarina)	élévation (sous-marine)	elevação (submarina)
river	Fluss	**river** *Eng.*	río	rivière	rio
brook	Bach	**rivera** *Sp.*	rivera	ruisseau	córrego
coast	Küste	**riviera** *It.*	costa	côte	costa
river	Fluss	**rivière** *Fr.*	río	rivière	rio
army installation	Anlage des Heeres	**r.j., rikujō-jieitai** *Jap.*	estación del ejército	installation militaire	instalação do exército
road	Landstrasse	**road** *Eng.*	camino	route	rodovia
roads (anchorage)	Ankerplatz	**roads** *Eng.*	ancladero	ancrage	ancoradouro
rock	Fels	**roca** *Sp.*	roca	rocher	rochedo
rock, mountain	Fels, Berg	**rocca** *It.*	roca, montaña	rocher, montagne	rochedo, montanha
rock(s)	Fels(en)	**rock(s)** *Eng.*	roca(s)	rocher(s)	rochedo(s)
cape	Kap	**rt** *S./C.*	cabo	cap	cabo
brook	Bach	**rů** *Fr.*	arroyo	rû	córrego
mountains	Berge	**rudohorie** *Slo.*	montañas	montagnes	montanhas
brook	Bach	**ruisseau** *Fr.*	arroyo	ruisseau	córrego
mountain	Berg	**rujm** *Ara.*	montaña	montagne	montanha
run	Bach	**run** *Eng.*	arroyo	ruisseau	córrego

S

ENGLISH	DEUTSCH	Map Form	ESPAÑOL	FRANÇAIS	PORTUGUÊS
south	süd	**s., south** *Eng.*	sur	sud	sul
range	Gebirge	**sa., serra** *Port.*	sierra	chaîne	cordilheira
island	Insel	**saar** *Est.*	isla	île	ilha
savanna	Savanne	**sabana** *Sp.*	sabana	savane	savana
salt marsh; lagoon	Salzmarsch; Lagune, Haff	**sabkhat** *Ara.*	pantano salado; laguna	marais salé; lagune	pântano salgado; laguna
dam	Damm	**sadd** *Ara.*	presa	barrage	represa
wadi	Wadi	**saguia** *Ara.*	uadi	wadi	uádi
desert	Wüste	**ṣaḥrā'** *Ara.*	desierto	désert	deserto
cape	Kap	**-saki** *Jap.*	cabo	cap	cabo
salt flat	Salzebene	**salar** *Sp.*	salar	saline	salina
salt marsh, salt flat	Salzmarsch, Salzebene	**salina(s)** *Sp.*	salina(s)	marais salé, saline	salina(s)
salt marsh, salt flat	Salzmarsch, Salzebene	**salines** *Fr.*	pantano salado, salinas, salar	salines	pântano salgado, salinas
salt flat	Salzebene	**salt flat** *Eng.*	salar	saline	salina
salt lake	Salzsee	**salt lake** *Eng.*	lago salado	lac salé	lago salgado
salt marsh	Salzmarsch	**salt marsh** *Eng.*	pantano salado	marais salé	pântano salgado
waterfall	Wasserfall	**salto(s)** *Port., Sp.*	salto(s)	chute d'eau	salto(s)
reservoir	Stausee	**samudra** *Sin.*	embalse	réservoir	reservatório
range	Gebirge	**-sammyaku** *Jap.*	sierra	chaîne	cordilheira
mountain	Berg	**-san** *Jap., Kor.*	montaña	montagne	montanha
mountains	Berge	**-sanchi** *Jap.*	montañas	montagnes	montanhas
mountains	Berge	**-sanmaek** *Kor.*	montañas	montagnes	montanhas
shrine	Schrein	**santuario** *It., Sp.*	santuario	châsse	santuário
mountain	berg	**sar** *Pas.*	montaña	montagne	montanha
island	Insel	**sari** *Est.*	isla	île	ilha
desert	Wüste	**sarīr** *Ara.*	desierto	désert	deserto
saddle	Sattel	**Sattel** *Ger.*	paso	col	passo
strait	Meeresstrasse	**šaurums** *Latv.*	estrecho	détroit	estreito
waterfall	Wasserfall	**saut** *Fr.*	cascada	saut	queda d'água
castle	Schloss	**Schloss** *Ger.*	castillo	château	castelo
gorge	Schlucht	**Schlucht** *Ger.*	garganta	gorge	garganta
school	Schule	**school** *Eng.*	escuela	école	escola
sea	Meer	**sea** *Eng.*	mar	mer	mar
seamount	untermeerische Kuppe	**seamount** *Eng.*	montaña submarina	montagne sous-marine	montanha submarina
sea scarp	Abbruch	**sea scarp** *Eng.*	cantil	escarpement sous-marine	escarpa submarina
dry lake	Trockensee	**sebjet** *Ara.*	lago seco	lac asséché	lago seco
salt flat	Salzebene	**sebkha** *Ara.*	salar	saline	salina
intermittent lake	periodischer See	**sebkra** *Ara.*	lago intermitente	lac périodique	lago intermitente
salt marsh	Salzmarsch	**sebkret** *Ara.*	pantano salado	marais salé	pântano salgado
airport	Flughafen	**sede-te'ufa** *Heb.*	aeropuerto	aéroport	aeroporto
saddle	Sattel	**sedlo** *Czech*	paso	col	passo
lake(s)	See(n)	**See(n)** *Ger.*	lago(s)	lac(s)	lago(s)

ENGLISH	DEUTSCH	Map Form Geographische Begriffe Términos Geográficos Termes Géographiques Termos Geográficos	ESPAÑOL	FRANÇAIS	PORTUGUÊS
strait	Meeresstrasse	**selat** *Indon.*	estrecho	détroit	estreito
peninsula	Halbsinel	**semenandjung** *Indon.*	península	péninsule	península
seminary	Seminar	**seminary** *Eng.*	seminario	séminaire	seminário
mountain	Berg	**-sen** *Jap.*	montaña	montagne	montanha
sound	Sund	**seno** *Sp.*	seno	détroit	estreito
range, mountain	Gebirge, Berg	**serra** *Port.*	sierra	chaîne, montagne	serra
ridge(s)	Höhenrücken	**serranía(s)** *Sp.*	serranía(s)	crête(s)	serrania(s)
rapids	Stromschnellen	**shallāl** *Ara.*	rápidos	rapides	rápidos
mountain(s); island	Berg(e); Insel	**-shan** *Ch.*	montaña(s); isla	montagne(s); île	montanha(s) ilha
pass	Pass	**-shankou** *Ch.*	paso	col	passo
mountains	Berge	**-shanling, -shanmai, -shanmo** *Ch.*	montañas	montagnes	montanhas
bay	Bucht	**sharm** *Ara.*	bahía	baie	baía
peninsula	Halbinsel	**shibh jazīrat** *Ara.*	península	péninsule	península
island	Insel	**-shima** *Jap.*	isla	île	ilha
reef	Riff	**-shō** *Jap.*	arrecife	récif	recife
shoal(s)	Untiefe(n)	**shoal(s)** *Eng.*	bajo(s)	haut-fond(s)	baixio(s)
islands	Inseln	**-shotō** *Jap.*	islas	îles	ilhas
shrine	Schrein	**shrine** *Eng.*	santuario	châsse	santuário
river	Fluss	**-shui** *Ch.*	río	rivière	rio
reservoir	Stausee	**-shuiku** *Ch.*	embalse	réservoir	reservatório
strait	Meeresstrasse	**shuitao** *Ch.*	estrecho	détroit	estreito
temple	Tempel	**-si** *Ch.*	templo	temple	templo
range, ridge	Gebirge, Höhenrücken	**sierra** *Sp.*	sierra	chaîne, crête	serra
range	Gebirge	**silsilesi** *Tur.*	sierra	chaîne	cordilheira
rapids	Stromschnellen	**šivera** *Rus.*	rápidos	rapides	rápidos
lake	See	**-sjø** *Nor.*	lago	lac	lago
lakes	Seen	**-sjöarna** *Swe.*	lagos	lacs	lagos
lake	See	**-sjøen** *Nor.*	lago	lac	lago
lake, bay	See, Bucht	**-sjön** *Swe.*	lago, bahía	lac, baie	lago, baía
island	Insel	**-skär** *Swe.*	isla	île	ilha
forest	Wald	**-skog, -skogen** *Swe.*	basque	forêt	floresta
mountain	Berg	**slieve** *Gae.*	montaña	montagne	montanha
castle	Schloss	**slot** *Du.*	castillo	château	castelo
castle	Schloss	**slott** *Swe.*	castillo	château	castelo
slough	verlandende Wasserfläche	**slough** *Eng.*	pantano	fondrière	pântano, brejo
ridge	Höhenrücken	**snía., serranía** *Sp.*	serranía	crête	serrania
snowfield	Schneefeld	**snowfield** *Eng.*	ventisquero	champ de neige	campo de neve
lake	See	**-sø** *Dan.*	lago	lac	lago
sound	Sund	**sonda** *Sp.*	sonda	détroit	estreito
sound	Sund	**sound** *Eng.*	sonda	détroit	estreito
cave, tunnel	Höhle, Tunnel	**souterrain** *Fr.*	cueva, túnel	souterrain	caverna, túnel
state park	Naturpark	**s.p., state park** *Eng.*	parque provincial	parc régional	parque estadual
cave	Höhle	**špilja** *S./C.*	cueva	caverne	caverna
spit	Landzunge	**spit** *Eng.*	lengua de tierra	flèche	ponta de terra
peak	Spitze	**Spitze** *Ger.*	pico	cime	pico
spring	Quelle	**spr., spring** *Eng.*	manantial	source	manancial
square	Platz	**sq., square** *Eng.*	plaza	place	praça
range, ridge	Gebirge Höhenrücken	**srra., sierra** *Sp.*	sierra	chaîne, crête	serra
saint	Sankt	**st., saint** *Eng., Fr.*	san, santa, santo	saint	são, santa, santo
street	Strasse	**st., street** *Eng.*	calle	rue	rua
saint	Sankt	**sta., santa** *Port., Sp.*	santa	sainte	santa
station	Bahnhof, Stützpunkt	**sta., station** *Eng., Fr.*	estación	station	estação
stadium	Stadion	**stad., stadium** *Eng.*	estadio	stade	estádio
stadium	Stadion	**stadio** *It.*	estadio	stade	estádio
stadium	Stadion	**Stadion** *Ger.*	estadio	stade	estádio
stadium	Stadion	**stadion** *Rus.*	estadio	stade	estádio
stadium	Stadion	**stadium** *Eng.*	estadio	stade	estádio
state beach	öffentlicher Badestrand	**state beach** *Eng.*	playa provincial	plage régionale	praia estadual
state forest	Wald in Gemeinbesitz	**state forest** *Eng.*	bosque provincial	forêt régionale	floresta estadual
state historical park	Park an historischer Stätte	**state historical park** *Eng.*	parque histórico provincial	parc historique régional	parque histórico estadual
state park	Naturpark	**state park** *Eng.*	parque provincial	parc régional	parque estadual
state recreation area	Ausflugsgebiet	**state recreation area** *Eng.*	zona de recreo provincial	zone récréative regional	área de lazer estadual
station	Bahnhof, Stützpunkt	**station** *Eng., Fr.*	estación	station	estação
reservoir	Stausee	**Stausee** *Ger.*	embalse	réservoir	reservatório
station	Bahnhof, Stützpunkt	**stazione** *It.*	estación	station	estação
saint	Sankt	**ste., sainte** *Fr.*	santa	sainte	santa
mountains	Berge	**stěny** *Czech*	montañas	montagnes	montanhas
steppe	Steppe	**step'** *Rus.*	estepa	steppe	estepe
peak	Gipfel	**štít** *Slo.*	pico	cime	pico
saint	Sankt	**sto., santo** *Port., Sp.*	santo	saint	santo
strait(s)	Meeresstrasse	**strait(s)** *Eng.*	estrecho	détroit	estreito
stream	Strom	**stream eng.**	corriente de agua	cours d'eau	curso d'água
street	Strasse	**street** *Eng.*	calle	rue	rua
strait	Meeresstrasse	**stretto** *It.*	estrecho	détroit	estreito
stream	Strom	**Strom** *Ger.*	corriente de agua	cours d'eau	curso d'água
stream	Strom	**-ström, -strömmen** *Swe.*	corriente de agua	cours d'eau	curso d'água
river	Fluss	**-su** *Kor.*	río	rivière	rio
channel	Kanal	**-suidō** *Jap.*	canal, estrecho	canal, détroit	canal, estreito
sound	Sund	**Sund** *Ger.*	sonda	détroit	estreito
sound	Sund	**-sund** *Swe.*	sonda	détroit	estreito
river	Fluss	**suyu** *Tur.*	río	rivière	rio
swamp	Sumpf	**swamp** *Eng.*	pantano	marais	pântano
ridge	Höhenrücken	**syrt** *Tur.*	sierra	crête	serra
island	Insel	**sziget** *Hung.*	isla	île	ilha

T

ENGLISH	DEUTSCH	Map Form	ESPAÑOL	FRANÇAIS	PORTUGUÊS
tableland	Tafelland	**tableland** *Eng.*	mesa, altiplano	plateau	planalto
woods	Gehölz	**tailis** *Fr.*	bosque	taillis	bosque
reef	Riff	**taka** *Indon.*	arrecife	récif	recife
mountain	Berg	**-take** *Jap.*	montaña	montagne	montanha
waterfall	Wasserfall	**-taki** *Jap.*	cascada	chute d'eau	queda d'água
valley	Tal	**Tal** *Ger.*	valle	vallée	vale
mountain	Berg	**tall** *Ara.*	montaña	montagne	montanha
mountain, hill	Berg, Hügel	**tallat** *Ara.*	montaña, colina	montagne, colline	montanha, colina
hills	Hügel	**tallāt** *Ara.*	colinas	collines	colinas
dam	Talsperre	**Talsperre** *Ger.*	presa	barrage	represa
cape	Kap	**tandjung** *Indon.*	cabo	cap	cabo
point	Landspitze	**-tangar, -tangi** *Ice.*	punta	pointe	ponta
cape	Kap	**tanjong** *Mal.*	cabo	cap	cabo
island	Insel	**tao** *Ch.*	isla	île	ilha
hills	Hügel	**ṭaraq** *Ara.*	colinas	collines	colinas
lake	See	**tasek** *Mal.*	lago	lac	lago
lake	See	**tasik** *Indon.*	lago	lac	lago
plateau	Hochebene	**tassili** *Ber.*	meseta	plateau	planalto
mountain	Berg	**taung** *Bur.*	montaña	montagne	montanha
range	Gebirge	**taungdan** *Bur.*	sierra	chaîne	cordilheira
theatre	Theater	**teatro** *It., Sp.*	teatro	théâtre	teatro
bay	Bucht	**teluk** *Indon.*	bahía	baie	baía
temple	Tempel	**temple** *Eng., Fr.*	templo	temple	templo
church	Kirche	**templom** *Hung.*	iglesia	église	igreja
desert	Wüste	**ténéré** *Ber.*	desierto	désert	deserto
peak, hill	Gipfel, Hügel	**tepe, tepesi** *Tur.*	pico, colina	cime, colline	pico, colina
territory	Territorium	**territory** *Eng.*	territorio	territoire	território
lagoon	Lagune, Haff	**thale** *Thai*	laguna	lagune	laguna
mountains	Berge	**thiu khao** *Thai*	montañas	montagnes	montanhas
mountain	Berg	**-tind, -tinderne** *Nor.*	montaña	montagne	montanha
ridge	Höhenrücken	**ṭiwāl** *Ara.*	sierra	crête	serra
mountain	Berg	**-tjåkko, -tjöure** *Lapp.*	montaña	montagne	montanha
island	Insel	**-to** *Kor.*	isla	île	ilha
island	Insel	**-tō** *Jap.*	isla	île	ilha
lake	See	**tó** *Hung.*	lago	lac	lago
pass	Pass	**-tōge** *Jap.*	paso	col	passo
island	Insel	**tokong** *Mal.*	isla	île	ilha
lake	See	**tônlé** *Cbd.*	lago	lac	lago
mountain torrent	Wildbach	**torrente** *It., Sp.*	torrente	torrent	torrente
tower	Turm	**tower** *Eng.*	torre	tour	torre
turnpike	gebührenpflichtige Autobahn	**tpk., turnpike** *Eng.*	camino con peaje	grande route à péage	rodovia com pedágio
lake	See	**-träsk** *Swe.*	lago	lac	lago
trench	Tiefseegraben	**trench** *Eng.*	trinchera	tranchée	fossa submarina
trough	Tiefseegraben	**trough** *Eng.*	trinchera	tranchée	fossa submarina
volcano	Vulkan	**tulūl** *Ara.*	volcán	volcan	vulcão
tunnel	Tunnel	**túnel** *Sp.*	túnel	tunnel	túnel
tunnel	Tunnel	**tunnel** *Eng., Fr.*	túnel	tunnel	túnel
hill, mountain	Hügel, Berg	**-tunturi** *Finn.*	colina, montaña	colline, montagne	colina, montanha
island	Insel	**-tuo** *Ch.*	isla	île	ilha
canal	Kanal	**tur'at** *Ara.*	canal	canal	canal
turnpike	gebührenpflichtige Autobahn	**turnpike** *Eng.*	camino con peaje	grande route à péage	rodovia com pedágio

U-V

ENGLISH	DEUTSCH	Map Form	ESPAÑOL	FRANÇAIS	PORTUGUÊS
cape	Kap	**udjung** *Indon.*	cabo	cap	cabo
lagoon	Lagune, Haff	**-umi** *Jap.*	laguna	lagune	laguna
United Nations	Vereinte Nationen	**U.N., United Nations** *Eng.*	Naciones Unidas	Nations Unies	Nações Unidas
canal	Kanal	**-unga** *Jap.*	canal	canal	canal
university	Universität	**univ., universidad** *Sp.* **universidade** *Port.* **università** *It.* **university** *Eng.*	universidad	université	universidade
university	Universität	**Universität** *Ger.*	universidad	université	universidade
university	Universität	**université** *Fr.*	universidad	université	universidade
university	Universität	**universitet** *Rus.*	universidad	université	universidade
upland	Bergland	**upland** *Eng.*	tierras altas	hautes terres	terras altas
lake	See	**-ura** *Jap.*	lago	lac	lago
mountain(s)	Berg(e)	**uul** *Mong.*	montaña(s)	montagne(s)	montanha(s)
elevation(s)	Höhe(n)	**uval(y)** *Rus.*	altura(s)	élévation(s)	elevação(ões)
spring	Quelle	**'uyūn** *Ara.*	manantial	source	manancial
hill	Hügel	**-vaara** *Finn.*	colina	colline	colina
strait	Meeresstrasse	**väin** *Est.*	estrecho	détroit	estreito
valley	Tal	**val** *Fr., It.*	valle	val	vale
valley	Tal	**valle** *It., Sp.*	valle	vallée	vale
valley	Tal	**vallée** *Fr.*	valle	vallée	vale
waterfall	Wasserfall	**vallen** *Du.*	cascada	chute d'eau	queda d'água
valley	Tal	**valley** *Eng.*	valle	vallée	vale
valley	Tal	**vallon** *Fr.*	valle	vallon	vale
lake	See	**-vatn** *Ice., Nor.*	lago	lac	lago
lake	See	**-vatnet** *Nor.*	lago	lac	lago
lake	See	**-vattnett** *Swe.*	lago	lac	lago
reservoir	Stausee	**vdchr., vodochranilišče** *Rus.*	embalse	réservoir	reservatório
hills	Hügel	**-veden** *Swe.*	colinas	collines	colinas
upland	Bergland	**verch** *Rus.*	tierras altas	hautes terres	terras altas
lake	See	**-vesi** *Finn.*	lago	lac	lago
viaduct	Viadukt	**viaducto** *Sp.*	viaducto	viaduc	viaduto
plateau	Hochebene	**-vidda** *Nor.*	meseta	plateau	planalto
gulf	Golf	**-viken** *Swe.*	golfo	golfe	golfo
bay	Bucht	**vinh** *Viet.*	bahía	baie	baía
mountain	Berg	**virful** *Rom.*	montaña	montagne	montanha
airport	Flughafen	**vliegveld** *Du.*	aeropuerto	aéroport	aeroporto
channel	Kanal	**vliet** *Du.*	canal, estrecho	canal, détroit	canal, estreito
canal	Kanal	**vodnyj put'** *Rus.*	canal	canal	canal
reservoir	Stausee	**vodochranilišče** *Rus.*	embalse	réservoir	reservatório
railroad station	Bahnhof	**vokzal** *Rus.*	estación de ferrocarril	gare	estação ferroviária
volcano	Vulkan	**vol., volcán** *Sp.* **volcano** *Eng.*	volcán	volcan	vulcão
pass	Pass	**vorota** *Rus.*	paso	col	passo
upland	Bergland	**vozvyšennost'** *Rus.*	tierras altas	hautes terres	terras altas
mountain	Berg	**vrâh** *Blg.*	montaña	montagne	montanha
mountains	Berge	**vrchovina** *Czech, Slo.*	montañas	montagnes	montanhas
peak	Gipfel	**vrh** *S./C.*	pico	cime	pico
volcano	Vulkan	**vulkan** *Rus.*	volcán	volcan	vulcão
bay	Bucht	**vung** *Viet.*	bahía	baie	baía
mountain, hill	Berg, Hügel	**-vuori** *Finn.*	montaña, colina	montagne, colline	montanha, colina

W-Z

ENGLISH	DEUTSCH	Map Form	ESPAÑOL	FRANÇAIS	PORTUGUÊS
west	West	**w., west** *Eng.*	oeste	ouest	oeste
wadi	Wadi	**wādī** *Ara.*	uadi	wadi	uádi
oasis	Oase	**wāḥat, wāḥāt** *Ara.*	oasis	oasis	oásis
forest; mountains	Wald	**Wald** *Ger.*	bosque; montañas	forêt; montagnes	floresta; montanhas
bay	Bucht	**-wan** *Ch., Jap.*	bahía	baie	baía
wash	Wadi	**wash** *Eng.*	uadi	wadi	uádi
waterfalls	Wasserfälle	**Wasserfälle** *Ger.*	cascadas	chutes d'eau	quedas d'água
water (lake; river)	Wasser (See; Fluss)	**water** *Eng.*	agua (lago;rio)	eau (lac; rivière)	água (lago, rio)
waterway	Wasserstrasse	**waterway** *Eng.*	canal	canal	canal
pond	Weiher	**Weiher** *Ger.*	charca	étang	charco
well	Brunnen	**well** *Eng.*	pozo	puits	poço
bay	Wiek	**Wiek** *Ger.*	bahía	baie	baía
woods	Gehölz	**woods** *Eng.*	bosque	bois	bosque
water (lake; river)	Wasser (See; Fluss)	**wr., water** *Eng.*	agua (lago; rio)	eau (lac; rivière)	água (lago, rio)
river	Fluss	**-xi** *Ch.*	río	rivière	rio
strait	Meeresstrasse	**-xia** *Ch.*	estrecho	détroit	estreito
lake, sea	See, Meer	**yam** *Heb.*	lago, mar	lac, mer	lago, mar
mountain	Berg	**-yama** *Jap.*	montaña	montagne	montanha
sea, bay, lake	Meer, Bucht, See	**-yang** *Ch.*	mar, bahía, lago	mer, baie, lac	mar, baía, lago
peninsula	Halbinsel	**yarımadası** *Tur.*	península	péninsule	península
mountain	Berg	**yebel** *Ara.*	montaña	montagne	montanha
rock, island	Fels, Insel	**yen** *Ch.*	roca, isla	rocher,île	rochedo, ilha
mountains	Berge	**yoma** *Bur.*	montañas	montagnes	montanhas
island	Insel	**-yu** *Ch.*	isla	île	ilha
intermittent lake	periodischer See	**zahrez** *Ara.*	lago intermitente	lac périodique	lago intermitente
point	Landspitze	**-zaki** *Jap.*	punta	pointe	ponta
lagoon	Lagune, Haff	**zalew** *Pol.*	laguna	lagune	laguna
gulf, bay	Golf, Bucht	**zaliv** *Rus.*	golfo, bahía	golfe, baie	golfo, baía
reserve	Reservat	**zapov., zapovednik** *Rus.*	reserva	réserve	reserva
sea, lake	Meer, See	**zee** *Du.*	mar, lago	mer, lac	mar, lago
autonomous province	autonome Provinz	**zizhiqu** *Ch.*	provincia autónoma	province autonome	província autônoma
autonomous district	autonomer Distrikt	**zizhizhou** *Ch.*	distrito autónomo	district autonome	distrito autônomo
zoo	Zoo	**zoo** *Eng.*	parque zoológico	zoo	jardim zoológico

THIS TABLE gives the area, population, population density, capital, and political status for every country in the world. The political units listed are categorized by political status in the last column of the table, as follows: A—independent countries; B—internally independent political entities which are under the protection of another country in matters of defense and foreign affairs; C—colonies and other dependent political units; and D—the major administrative subdivisions of Australia, Canada, China, the Soviet Union, the United Kingdom, and the United States. For comparison, the table also includes the continents and the world. For units categorized B, the names of protecting countries are specified in the political-status column. For units categorized C, the names of administering countries are given in parentheses in the first column. A key to abbreviations of country names appears on page I•26. All footnotes to this table appear on page I•11.

The populations are estimates for January 1, 1978, made by Rand McNally & Company on the basis of official data, United Nations estimates, and other available information.

IN DIESER ÜBERSICHT sind Fläche, Bevölkerung, Bevölkerungsdichte, Hauptstadt und politischer Status für jedes Land der Erde aufgeführt. Die politischen Einheiten sind in der letzten Spalte der Tabelle nach ihrem politischen Status wie folgt gegliedert: A—souveräne Staaten; B—innenpolitisch unabhängige Länder unter der Protektion eines anderen Landes in Angelegenheiten der Aussenpolitik und Verteidigung; C—Kolonien oder anderweitig abhängige Gebiete; D—die wichtigsten Verwaltungseinheiten von Australien, Kanada, China, der Sowjetunion, dem Vereinigten Königreich und den Vereinigten Staaten. Für Vergleiche enthält die Übersicht auch Angaben über die Kontinente und die Welt. Für die unter B eingestuften Einheiten ist der Name des Schutzstaates in der Spalte Politischer Status aufgeführt. Für die unter C eingestuften Gebiete steht der Name des die Verwaltung ausübenden Landes in Klammern in der ersten Spalte. Ein Verzeichnis der Abkürzungen der Ländernamen findet sich auf Seite I•26. Alle Fussnoten zu dieser Übersicht erscheinen auf Seite I•11.

Die Bevölkerungsangaben sind Schätzungen zum 1. Januar 1978, die Rand McNally & Company auf der Grundlage amtlicher Zahlen, Schätzungen der Vereinten Nationen und anderer zugänglicher Informationen berechnet hat.

EL CUADRO ABAJO incluye la extensión, población y densidad de población, la capital y el estado político de todos los países del mundo. Las entidades políticas nombradas están clasificadas de acuerdo a su estado político en la última columna de la tabla, de esta manera: A—países independientes; B—entidades políticas internamente independientes las cuales se encuentran bajo la protección de otro país en cuanto a asuntos de defensa nacional y relaciones con el extranjero; C—colonias y otras entidades políticas dependientes; y D—las mayores subdivisiones administrativas de Australia, Canadá, China, la Unión Soviética, el Reino Unido, y los Estados Unidos. Para servir de medida comparativa, el cuadro también incluye los continentes y el mundo. Para las entidades de la clasificación B, los nombres de los países protectores están especificados en la columna de estado político. Para las unidades bajo la categoría C, los nombres de los países administradores se encuentran entre paréntesis en la primera columna. El código de las abreviaciones de los nombres de los países aparece en la págîna I•26. Todas las notas para este cuadro se encuentran en la página I•11.

Las poblaciones son los estimados de Rand McNally & Company, tomados el 1o. de Enero de 1978, en base a datos oficiales, estimados de las Naciones Unidas y varias otras informaciones disponibles.

CETTE TABLE donne, pour chaque pays du monde, les renseignements suivants: superficie, population, densité de population, capitale, statut politique. Les entités politiques sont classées, selon leur statut, dans la dernière colonne du tableau: A—pays indépendants; B—entités politiques indépendants intérieurement, mais qui se trouvent sous la protection d'un autre pays pour leur défense et leurs relations extérieures; C—colonies et autres entités politiques dépendantes; D—principales subdivisions administratives de l'Australie, du Canada, de la Chine, de l'U.R.S.S., du Royaume-Uni, des États-Unis. Pour permettre les comparaisons, la table comprend aussi les continents et le monde. Pour les entités politiques de la catégorie B, les noms des pays protecteurs sont spécifiés dans la colonne "statut politique". Pour celles de la catégorie C, les noms des pays administrateurs sont mis entre parenthèses dans la première colonne. Un index des abréviations des noms de pays se trouve à la page I•26. Toutes les notes et renvois relatifs à cette table se trouvent à la page I•11.

Les chiffres concernant la population sont des estimations au 1er janvier 1978, établies par Rand McNally & Company, d'après les sources officielles, les estimations des Nations Unies et autres informations disponibles.

A TABELA que se segue apresenta a área, a população, a densidade demográfica, a capital e o estatuto político de todos os países do mundo. As unidades políticas relacionadas na tabela estão classificadas de acordo com o respectivo estatuto político na última coluna, do seguinte modo: A—países independentes; B—unidades políticas internamente independentes mas que se encontram sob a proteção de outro país no tocante a assuntos de defesa nacional e negócios externos; C—colônias e outras unidades políticas dependentes; e D—subdivisões administrativas principais da Austrália, Canadá, China, União Soviética, Reino Unido e Estados Unidos. Para fins de comparabilidade, a tabela também inclui os continentes e o mundo. No tocante às unidades classificadas em B, os nomes dos países protetores estão especificados na coluna relativa ao estatuto político. Para as unidades da categoria C, os nomes dos países administradores figuram entre parênteses na primeira coluna. Uma lista das abreviaturas dos nomes dos países aparece à pág. I•26. Todas as chamadas de pé-de-página da tabela encontram-se à pág. I•11.

Os dados relativos à população são estimativas de Rand McNally & Company para 1 de janeiro de 1978, com base em dados oficiais, estimativas das Nações Unidas e outras informações disponíveis.

NAME / NAME / NOMBRE / NOM / NOME English / Englisch Inglés / Anglais / Inglês	 Local / Einheimisch Local / Local / Local	AREA / FLÄCHE AREA / SUPERFICIE / ÁREA km²	 sq. mi.	POPULATION BEVÖLKERUNG POBLACIÓN POPULATION POPULAÇÃO	DENSITY PER BEVÖLKERUNGSDICHTE PRO / DENSIDAD POR DENSITÉ / DENSIDÁDE POR km²	 sq. mi.	CAPITAL HAUPTSTADT CAPITAL CAPITALE CAPITAL	POLITICAL STATUS POLITISCHER STATUS ESTADO POLÍTICO STATUT POLITIQUE ESTATUTO POLÍTICO
†Afghanistan	Afghānestān	647,500	250,000	20,565,000	32	82	Kābul	A
Africa	...	30,264,000	11,685,000	429,400,000	14	37	...	...
Alabama, U.S.	Alabama	133,667	51,609	3,725,300	28	72	Montgomery	D
Alaska, U.S.	Alaska	1,518,800	586,412	407,500	0.3	0.7	Juneau	D
†Albania	Shqipëri	28,748	11,100	2,655,000	92	239	Tiranë	A
Alberta, Can.	Alberta	661,185	255,285	1,889,000	2.9	7.4	Edmonton	D
†Algeria	Algérie	2,381,741	919,595	18,073,000	7.6	20	Alger (Algiers)	A
American Samoa (U.S.)	American Samoa	197	76	33,000	168	434	Pago Pago	C
Andorra	Andorra	453	175	28,000	62	160	Andorra	A
†Angola	Angola	1,246,700	481,353	7,214,000	5.8	15	Luanda	A
Anguilla (U.K.)	Anguilla	91	35	6,000	66	171	The Valley	C
Anhwei, China	Anhui	139,900	54,000	44,490	318	824	Hefei (Hofei)	D
Antarctica	...	13,209,000	5,100,000	(1)	...	...	...	...
Antigua (incl. Barbuda)	Antigua	442	171	75,000	170	439	Saint Johns	B (U.K.)
†Argentina	Argentina	2,776,889	1,072,162	26,075,000	9.4	24	Buenos Aires	A
Arizona, U.S.	Arizona	295,023	113,909	2,359,600	8.0	21	Phoenix	D
Arkansas, U.S.	Arkansas	137,539	53,104	2,143,700	16	40	Little Rock	D
Armenia, U.S.S.R.	Arm'anskaja S.S.R.	29,800	11,500	2,887,000	97	251	Jerevan	D
Asia	...	44,250,000	17,085,000	2,432,000,000	55	142	...	...
†Australia	Australia	7,686,849	2,967,909	13,858,000	1.8	4.7	Canberra	A
Australian Capital Territory, Austl.	Australian Capital Territory	2,432	939	202,000	83	215	Canberra	D
†Austria	Österreich	83,849	32,374	7,500,000	89	232	Wien (Vienna)	A
Azerbaidzhan, U.S.S.R.	Azerbajdžanskaja S.S.R.	86,600	33,450	5,801,000	67	173	Baku	D
†Bahamas	Bahamas	13,935	5,380	222,000	16	41	Nassau	A
†Bahrain	Al-Baḥrayn	598	231	268,000	448	1,160	Al-Manāmah	A
†Bangladesh	Bangladesh	142,775	55,126	84,605,000	593	1,535	Dacca	A
†Barbados	Barbados	430	166	250,000	581	1,506	Bridgetown	A
†Belgium	Belgique (French) België (Dutch)	30,513	11,781	10,005,000	328	849	Bruxelles (Brussels)	A
Belize (U.K.)	Belize	22,965	8,867	150,000	7.0	17	Belmopan	C
†Benin	Benin	112,622	43,484	3,405,000	30	78	Porto Novo	A
Bermuda (U.K.)	Bermuda	54	21	59,000	1,093	2,810	Hamilton	C
†Bhutan	Druk-Yul	47,000	18,200	1,245,000	26	68	Paro and Thimbu	B (India)
†Bolivia	Bolivia	1,098,581	424,164	4,887,000	4.4	12	Sucre and La Paz	A
†Botswana	Botswana	600,372	231,805	718,000	1.2	3.1	Gaborone	A
†Brazil	Brasil	8,511,965	3,286,487	113,815,000	13	35	Brasília	A
British Antarctic Territory (excl. Antarctic mainland) (U.K.)	British Antarctic Territory	5,284	2,040	(1)	...	...	Stanley, Falkland Islands	C
British Columbia, Can.	British Columbia	948,596	366,255	2,534,000	2.7	6.9	Victoria	D
British Indian Ocean Territory (U.K.)	British Indian Ocean Territory	47	18	(1)	...	...	Victoria, Seychelles	C
British Virgin Islands (U.K.)	British Virgin Islands	153	59	10,000	65	170	Road Town	C
Brunei	Brunei	5,765	2,226	190,000	33	85	Bandar Seri Begawan	B (U.K.)
†Bulgaria	Bâlgarija	110,912	42,823	8,820,000	80	206	Sofija (Sofia)	A
†Burma	Myanma	678,033	261,790	31,815,000	47	122	Rangoon	A
†Burundi	Burundi	27,834	10,747	4,003,000	144	372	Bujumbura	A
†Byelorussia, U.S.S.R.	Belorusskaja S.S.R.	207,600	80,150	9,520,000	46	119	Minsk	D
California, U.S.	California	411,013	158,693	22,017,500	54	139	Sacramento	D
†Cambodia	Kampuchea	181,035	69,898	8,712,000	48	125	Phnum Pénh	A
†Cameroon	Cameroun	475,442	183,569	6,725,000	14	37	Yaoundé	A
†Canada	Canada	9,976,139	3,851,809	23,625,000	2.4	6.0	Ottawa	A
Canton and Enderbury (U.K.-U.S.)	Canton and Enderbury	70	27	...	...	...	...	C
†Cape Verde	Cabo Verde	4,033	1,557	314,000	78	202	Praia	A
Cayman Islands (U.K.)	Cayman Islands	260	100	12,000	46	120	Georgetown	C
†Central African Empire	Empire centrafricaine	622,984	240,535	1,923,000	3.1	8.0	Bangui	A
†Chad	Tchad	1,284,000	495,800	4,255,000	3.3	9.0	Ndjamena	A
Chekiang, China	Zhejiang	101,800	39,300	34,220,000	336	871	Hangzhou (Hangchow)	D
†Chile	Chile	756,945	292,258	10,740,000	14	37	Santiago	A
†China (excl. Taiwan)	Zhongguo	9,561,000	3,691,500	855,546,000	89	232	Beijing (Peking)	A
Christmas Island (Austl.)	Christmas Island	135	52	3,600	27	52	The Settlement	C
Cocos (Keeling) Islands (Austl.)	Cocos (Keeling) Islands	14	5	700	50	140	...	C
†Colombia	Colombia	1,138,914	439,737	25,460,000	22	58	Bogotá	A
Colorado, U.S.	Colorado	269,998	104,247	2,644,400	9.8	25	Denver	D
†Comoros	Comores	2,079	803	314,000	151	391	Moroni	A
†Congo	Congo	342,000	132,000	1,455,000	4.3	11	Brazzaville	A

NAME / NAME / NOMBRE / NOM / NOME — English / Englisch / Inglés / Anglais / Inglês	Local / Einheimisch / Local / Local / Local	AREA / FLÄCHE / AREA / SUPERFICIE / ÁREA km²	sq. mi.	POPULATION / BEVÖLKERUNG / POBLACIÓN / POPULATION / POPULAÇÃO	DENSITY PER / BEVÖLKERUNGSDICHTE / PRO / DENSIDAD POR / DENSITÉ / DENSIDADE POR km²	sq. mi.	CAPITAL / HAUPTSTADT / CAPITAL / CAPITALE / CAPITAL	POLITICAL STATUS / POLITISCHER STATUS / ESTADO POLÍTICO / STATUT POLITIQUE / ESTATUTO POLÍTICO
Connecticut, U.S.	Connecticut	12,973	5,009	3,142,500	242	627	Hartford	D
Cook Islands (N.Z.)	Cook Islands	241	93	18,000	75	194	Avarua	C
Coral Sea Islands (Austl.)	Coral Sea Islands	2.6	1	(1)	...	...	Canberra, Australia	C
†Costa Rica	Costa Rica	50,900	19,650	2,079,000	41	106	San José	A
†Cuba	Cuba	114,524	44,218	9,678,000	85	219	La Habana (Havana)	A
†Cyprus	Kípros (Greek) Kıbrıs (Turkish)	9,251	3,572	645,000	70	181	Levkósia (Nicosia)	A
†Czechoslovakia	Československo	127,876	49,373	15,095,000	118	306	Praha (Prague)	A
Delaware, U.S.	Delaware	5,328	2,057	587,600	110	286	Dover	D
†Denmark	Danmark	43,069	16,629	5,090,000	118	306	København (Copenhagen)	A
District of Columbia, U.S.	District of Columbia	174	67	689,000	3,960	10,284	Washington	D
†Djibouti	Djibouti	23,000	8,900	152,000	6.6	17	Djibouti	A
Dominica	Dominica	751	290	77,000	103	266	Roseau	A
†Dominican Republic	República Dominicana	48,734	18,816	5,041,000	103	268	Santo Domingo	A
†Ecuador	Ecuador	283,561	109,483	8,180,000	29	75	Quito	A
†Egypt(2)	Mişr	1,002,000	386,900	39,320,000	39	102	Al-Qāhirah (Cairo)	A
†El Salvador	El Salvador	21,393	8,260	4,290,000	201	519	San Salvador	A
England, U.K.	England	130,359	50,332	46,386,000	356	922	London	D
†Equatorial Guinea	Guinea Ecuatorial	28,051	10,830	325,000	12	30	Malabo	A
Estonia, U.S.S.R.	Estonskaja S.S.R.	45,100	17,400	1,456,000	32	84	Tallinn	D
†Ethiopia	Yaitopya	1,221,900	471,778	29,775,000	24	63	Addis Abeba	A
Europe	...	9,907,000	3,825,000	654,000,000	66	171	...	...
Faeroe Islands (Den.)	Føroyar	1,399	540	40,000	29	74	Tórshavn	C
Falkland Islands (Islas Malvinas) (excl. Dependencies) (U.K.)(3)	Falkland Islands	11,961	4,618	1,900	0.2	0.4	Stanley (Port Stanley)	C
†Fiji	Fiji	18,272	7,055	595,000	33	84	Suva	A
†Finland	Suomi	337,032	130,129	4,770,000	14	37	Helsinki (Helsingfors)	A
Florida, U.S.	Florida	151,670	58,560	8,651,600	57	148	Tallahassee	D
†France	France	543,998	210,039	53,208,000	98	253	Paris	A
French Guiana (Fr.)	Guyane française	91,000	35,100	66,000	0.7	1.9	Cayenne	C
French Polynesia (Fr.)	Polynésie française	4,000	1,550	138,000	35	89	Papeete	C
French Southern and Antarctic Territories (excl. Adelie Coast) (Fr.)	Terres australes et antarctiques françaises	7,557	2,918	200	0.03	0.07	...	C
Fukien, China	Fujian	123,000	47,500	19,680,000	160	414	Fuzhou (Foochow)	D
†Gabon	Gabon	267,667	103,347	537,000	2.0	5.2	Libreville	A
†Gambia	Gambia	11,295	4,361	559,000	49	128	Banjul	A
Georgia, U.S.S.R.	Gruzinskaja S.S.R.	69,700	26,900	5,046,000	72	188	Tbilisi	D
Georgia, U.S.	Georgia	152,488	58,876	5,032,400	33	85	Atlanta	D
†German Democratic Republic	Deutsche Demokratische Republik	108,178	41,768	16,695,000	154	400	Berlin (Ost) (East Berlin)	A
†Germany, Federal Republic of (incl. West Berlin)	Bundesrepublik Deutschland	248,533	95,959	61,070,000	246	636	Bonn	A
†Ghana	Ghana	238,537	92,100	10,905,000	46	118	Accra	A
Gibraltar (U.K.)	Gibraltar	6	2	30,000	5,000	15,000	Gibraltar	C
†Greece	Ellás	131,944	50,944	9,340,000	71	183	Athínai (Athens)	A
Greenland (Den.)	Grønland	2,175,600	840,000	50,000	0.02	0.06	Godthåb	C
†Grenada	Grenada	344	133	114,000	331	857	Saint George's	A
Guadeloupe (incl. Dependencies) (Fr.)	Guadeloupe	1,780	687	371,000	208	540	Basse-Terre	C
Guam (U.S.)	Guam	549	212	96,000	175	453	Agana	C
†Guatemala	Guatemala	108,889	42,042	6,525,000	60	155	Guatemala	A
Guernsey (incl. Dependencies) (U.K.)	Guernsey	78	30	54,000	692	1,800	St. Peter Port	C
†Guinea	Guinée	245,857	94,926	4,695,000	19	49	Conakry	A
†Guinea-Bissau	Guinea-Bissau	36,125	13,948	539,000	15	39	Bissau	A
†Guyana	Guyana	214,969	83,000	781,000	3.6	9.4	Georgetown	A
†Haiti	Haïti	27,750	10,714	4,800,000	173	448	Port-au-Prince	A
Hawaii, U.S.	Hawaii	16,705	6,450	914,200	55	142	Honolulu	D
Heilungkiang, China	Heilongjiang	705,300	272,300	20,000,000	28	73	Haerbin (Harbin)	D
Honan, China	Henan	166,800	64,400	64,425,000	386	1,000	Zhengzhou (Chengchow)	D
†Honduras	Honduras	112,088	43,277	2,946,000	26	68	Tegucigalpa	A
Hong Kong (U.K.)	Hong Kong	1,034	399	4,445,000	4,299	11,140	Victoria (Hong Kong)	C
Hopeh (incl. Peking and Tientsin), China	Hebei	214,200	82,700	56,465,000	327	848	Tianjin (Tientsin)	D
Hunan, China	Hunan	210,600	81,300	51,335,000	244	631	Changsha	D
†Hungary	Magyarország	93,032	35,920	10,690,000	115	298	Budapest	A
Hupeh, China	Hubei	187,500	72,400	42,225,000	225	583	Wuhan	D
†Iceland	Ísland	103,000	39,800	225,000	2.2	5.7	Reykjavík	A
Idaho, U.S.	Idaho	216,412	83,557	854,900	4.0	10	Boise	D
Illinois, U.S.	Illinois	146,075	56,400	11,277,200	77	200	Springfield	D
†India (incl. part of Kashmir)	Bhārat	3,183,643	1,229,210	627,990,000	197	511	New Delhi	A
Indiana, U.S.	Indiana	93,993	36,291	5,306,100	56	146	Indianapolis	D
†Indonesia	Indonesia	1,919,270	741,034	138,180,000	72	186	Jakarta	A
Inner Mongolia, China	Neimenggu Zizhiqu	424,500	163,900	12,175,000	29	74	Huhehaote	D
Iowa, U.S.	Iowa	145,790	56,290	2,880,900	20	51	Des Moines	D
†Iran	Īrān	1,648,000	636,300	34,160,000	21	54	Tehrān	A
†Iraq	Al-'Irāq	434,924	167,925	12,069,000	28	72	Baghdād	A
†Ireland	Eire	70,285	27,137	3,210,000	46	118	Dublin (Baile Átha Cliath)	A
Isle of Man (U.K.)	Isle of Man	588	227	64,000	109	282	Douglas	C
†Israel(2)	Yisra'el	20,770	8,019	3,610,000	174	450	Yerushalayim (Jerusalem)	A
†Italy	Italia	301,250	116,313	56,710,000	188	488	Roma (Rome)	A
†Ivory Coast	Côte d'Ivoire	322,463	124,504	7,095,000	22	57	Abidjan	A
†Jamaica	Jamaica	10,962	4,232	2,080,000	190	491	Kingston	A
†Japan	Nihon	372,197	143,706	114,650,000	308	798	Tōkyō	A
Jersey (U.K.)	Jersey	116	45	75,000	647	1,667	St. Helier	C
†Jordan(2)	Al-Urdunn	97,740	37,738	2,900,000	30	77	'Ammān	A
Kansas, U.S.	Kansas	213,063	82,264	2,337,200	11	28	Topeka	D
Kansu, China	Gansu	720,300	278,100	17,110,000	24	62	Lanzhou (Lanchow)	D
Kazakh S.S.R., U.S.S.R.	Kazachskaja S.S.R.	2,715,000	1,048,300	14 592,000	5.4	14	Alma-Ata	D
Kentucky, U.S.	Kentucky	104,623	40,395	3,482,400	33	86	Frankfort	D
†Kenya	Kenya	582,644	224,960	14,545,000	25	65	Nairobi	A
Kiangsi, China	Jiangxi	164,700	63,600	23,955,000	145	377	Nanchang	D
Kiangsu (incl. Shanghai), China	Jiangsu	108,000	41,700	56,465,000	721	1,867	Nanjing (Nanking)	D
Kirghiz S.S.R., U.S.S.R.	Kirgizskaja S.S.R.	198,500	76,650	3,433,000	17	45	Frunze	D
Kiribati	Kiribati	857	331	58,000	68	175	Bairiki	A
Kirin, China	Jilin	271,700	104,900	17,110,000	63	163	Changchun	D
Korea, North	Chosŏn Minjujuŭi In'min Konghwaguk	120,538(4)	46,540(4)	16,855,000	140	362	P'yŏngyang	A
Korea, South	Taehan-Min'guk	98,477(4)	38,022(4)	36,735,000	373	966	Sŏul (Seoul)	A
†Kuwait	Al-Kuwayt	16,000	6,200	1,091,000	68	176	Al-Kuwayt	A
Kwangsi Chuang, China	Guangxi Zhuang Zizhiqu	240,100	92,700	25,665,000	107	277	Nanning	D
Kwangtung, China	Guangdong	211,600	81,700	51,335,000	243	628	Guangzhou (Canton)	D
Kweichow, China	Guizhou	174,000	67,200	22,330,000	128	332	Guiyang (Kweiyang)	D
†Laos	Lao	236,800	91,400	3,485,000	15	38	Viangchan (Vientiane)	A
Latvia, U.S.S.R.	Latvijskaja S.S.R.	63,700	24,600	2,601,000	40	106	Rīga	D
†Lebanon	Al-Lubnān	10,230	3,950	3,096,000	303	784	Bayrūt (Beirut)	A
†Lesotho	Lesotho	30,355	11,720	1,622,000	53	138	Maseru	A
Liaoning, China	Liaoning	229,500	88,600	34,220,000	149	386	Shenyang (Mukden)	D
†Liberia	Liberia	111,369	43,000	1,810,000	16	42	Monrovia	A
†Libya	Lībiyā	1,759,540	679,362	2,678,000	1.5	4.0	Ṭarābulus (Tripoli)	A
Liechtenstein	Liechtenstein	160	62	25,000	156	403	Vaduz	A
Lithuania, U.S.S.R.	Litovskaja S.S.R.	65,200	25,150	3,381,000	52	134	Vilnius	D
Louisiana, U.S.	Louisiana	125,674	48,523	3,905,500	31	80	Baton Rouge	D
†Luxembourg	Luxembourg	2,586	998	365,000	141	366	Luxembourg	A
Macau (Port.)	Macau	16	6	284,000	17,750	47,333	Macau	C
†Madagascar	Madagasikara	587,041	226,658	8,399,000	14	37	Antananarivo	A
Maine, U.S.	Maine	86,026	33,215	1,086,800	13	33	Augusta	D
†Malawi	Malawi	118,484	45,747	5,385,000	45	118	Lilongwe	A
†Malaysia	Malaysia	332,633	128,430	12,845,000	39	100	Kuala Lumpur	A
†Maldives	Maldives	298	115	141,000	473	1,226	Male	A
†Mali	Mali	1,239,710	478,655	6,050,000	4.9	13	Bamako	A
†Malta	Malta	316	122	275,000	870	2,254	Valletta	A

NAME / NAME / NOMBRE / NOM / NOME English / Englisch Inglés / Anglais / Inglês	Local / Einheimisch Local / Local / Local	AREA / FLÄCHE AREA / SUPERFICIE / ÁREA km²	sq. mi.	POPULATION BEVÖLKERUNG POBLACIÓN POPULATION POPULAÇÃO	DENSITY PER BEVÖLKERUNGSDICHTE PRO / DENSIDAD POR DENSITÉ / DENSIDADE POR km²	sq. mi.	CAPITAL HAUPTSTADT CAPITAL CAPITALE CAPITAL	POLITICAL STATUS POLITISCHER STATUS ESTADO POLÍTICO STATUT POLITIQUE ESTATUTO POLÍTICO
Manitoba, Can.	Manitoba	650,087	251,000	1,050,000	1.6	4.2	Winnipeg	D
Martinique (Fr.)	Martinique	1,100	425	378,000	344	889	Fort-de-France	C
Maryland, U.S.	Maryland	27,394	10,577	4,190,000	153	396	Annapolis	D
Massachusetts, U.S.	Massachusetts	21,386	8,257	5,832,600	273	706	Boston	D
†Mauritania	Mauritanie	1,030,700	397,950	1,484,000	1.4	3.7	Nouakchott	A
†Mauritius (incl. Dependencies)	Mauritius	2,045	789	901,000	441	1,142	Port Louis	A
Mayotte (Fr.)	Mayotte	373	144	43,000	115	299	Dzaoudzi	C
†Mexico	México	1,972,546	761,604	65,555,000	33	86	Ciudad de México (Mexico City)	A
Michigan, U.S.	Michigan	150,779	58,216	9,121,800	60	157	Lansing	D
Midway Islands (U.S.)	Midway Islands	5	2	2,000	400	1,000	. . .	C
Minnesota, U.S.	Minnesota	217,735	84,068	4,026,900	18	48	St. Paul	D
Mississippi, U.S.	Mississippi	123,584	47,716	2,379,200	19	50	Jackson	D
Missouri, U.S.	Missouri	180,486	69,686	4,800,800	27	69	Jefferson City	D
Moldavia, U.S.S.R.	Moldavskaja S.S.R.	33,700	13,000	3,902,000	116	300	Kišin'ov (Kishinev)	D
Monaco	Monaco	1.5	0.6	26,000	17,333	43,333	Monaco	A
†Mongolia	Mongol Ard Uls	1,565,000	604,200	1,552,000	1.0	2.6	Ulaanbaatar (Ulan Bator)	A
Montana, U.S.	Montana	381,086	147,138	763,800	2.0	5.2	Helena	D
Montserrat (U.K.)	Montserrat	101	39	14,000	139	359	Plymouth	C
†Morocco	Al-Magreb	446,550	172,415	18,575,000	42	108	Rabat	A
†Mozambique	Moçambique	783,763	303,771	9,745,000	12	32	Maputo	A
Namibia (excl. Walvis Bay) (S. Afr.)[6]	Namibia	823,168	317,827	910,000	1.1	3.0	Windhoek	C
Nauru	Nauru	21	8	7,300	348	913	. . .	A
Nebraska, U.S.	Nebraska	200,017	77,227	1,564,900	7.8	20	Lincoln	D
†Nepal	Nepāl	140,797	54,362	13,280,000	94	244	Kāthmāndu	A
†Netherlands	Nederland	40,844	15,770	13,945,000	341	884	Amsterdam and 's-Gravenhage (The Hague)	A
Netherlands Antilles (Neth.)	Nederlandse Antillen	961	371	242,000	252	652	Willemstad	C
Nevada, U.S.	Nevada	286,297	110,540	637,000	2.2	5.8	Carson City	D
New Brunswick, Can.	New Brunswick	73,437	28,354	696,000	9.5	25	Fredericton	D
New Caledonia (incl. Dependencies) (Fr.)	Nouvelle-Calédonie	19,058	7,358	141,000	7.4	19	Nouméa	C
Newfoundland, Can.	Newfoundland	404,517	156,185	573,000	1.4	3.7	St. John's	D
New Hampshire, U.S.	New Hampshire	24,097	9,304	838,000	35	90	Concord	D
New Hebrides (Fr.-U.K.)	New Hebrides (English) Nouvelles-Hébrides (French)	14,760	5,700	100,000	6.8	18	Vila	C
New Jersey, U.S.	New Jersey	20,295	7,836	7,358,700	363	939	Trenton	D
New Mexico, U.S.	New Mexico	315,113	121,666	1,201,600	3.8	9.9	Santa Fe	D
New South Wales, Austl.	New South Wales	801,428	309,433	4,886,000	6.1	16	Sydney	D
New York, U.S.	New York	128,401	49,576	18,102,300	141	365	Albany	D
†New Zealand	New Zealand	268,675	103,736	3,245,000	12	31	Wellington	A
†Nicaragua	Nicaragua	130,000	50,200	2,347,000	18	47	Managua	A
†Niger	Niger	1,267,000	489,200	4,925 000	3.9	10	Niamey	A
†Nigeria	Nigeria	923,768	356,669	66,190,000	72	186	Lagos	A
Ningsia Hui, China	Ningxia Huizu Zizhiqu	66,300	25,600	2,565,000	39	100	Yinchuan (Yinchwan)	D
Niue (N.Z.)	Niue	259	100	3,000	12	30	Alofi	C
Norfolk Island (Austl.)	Norfolk Island	36	14	2,000	56	143	Kingston	C
North America	. . .	24,398,000	9,420,000	355,200,000	15	38	. . .	. . .
North Carolina, U.S.	North Carolina	136,197	52,586	5,538,600	41	105	Raleigh	D
North Dakota, U.S.	North Dakota	183,022	70,665	650,500	3.6	9.2	Bismarck	D
Northern Ireland, U.K.	Northern Ireland	14,120	5,452	1,537,000	109	282	Belfast	D
Northern Territory, Austl.	Northern Territory	1,347,519	520,280	100,000	0.07	0.2	Darwin	D
Northwest Territories, Can.	Northwest Territories	3,379,683	1,304,903	44,000	0.01	0.03	Yellowknife	D
†Norway	Norge	323,878	125,050	4,060,000	13	32	Oslo	A
Nova Scotia, Can.	Nova Scotia	55,491	21,425	851,000	15	40	Halifax	D
Oceania (incl. Australia)	. . .	8,534,000	3,295,000	21,900,000	2.6	6.6	. . .	. . .
Ohio, U.S.	Ohio	106,764	41,222	10,669,100	100	259	Columbus	D
Oklahoma, U.S.	Oklahoma	181,089	69,919	2,823,100	16	40	Oklahoma City	D
†Oman	'Umān	212,457	82,030	824,000	3.9	10	Masqaṭ (Muscat)	A
Ontario, Can.	Ontario	1,068,582	412,582	8,492,000	7.9	21	Toronto	D
Oregon, U.S.	Oregon	251,180	96,981	2,372,700	9.4	24	Salem	D
Pacific Islands Trust Territory (U.S.)	Pacific Islands Trust Territory	1,857	717	129,000	69	180	Saipan	C
†Pakistan (incl. part of Kashmir)	Pākistān	895,496	345,753	77,040,000	86	223	Islāmābād	A
†Panama	Panamá	77,096	29,767	1,835,000	24	62	Panamá	A
†Papua New Guinea	Papua New Guinea	461,691	178,260	2,950,000	6.4	17	Port Moresby	A
†Paraguay	Paraguay	406,752	157,048	2,839,000	7.0	18	Asunción	A
Pennsylvania, U.S.	Pennsylvania	117,412	45,333	11,896,700	101	262	Harrisburg	D
†Peru	Perú	1,285,216	496,224	16,795,000	13	34	Lima	A
†Philippines	Pilipinas	300,000	115,831	44,505,000	148	384	Manila	A
Pitcairn (excl. Dependencies) (U.K.)	Pitcairn	5	2	70	14	35	Adamstown	C
†Poland	Polska	312,677	120,725	34,865,000	112	289	Warszawa (Warsaw)	A
†Portugal	Portugal	92,082	35,553	9,660,000	105	272	Lisboa (Lisbon)	A
Prince Edward Island, Can.	Prince Edward Island	5,657	2,184	121,000	21	55	Charlottetown	D
Puerto Rico (U.S.)	Puerto Rico	8,897	3,435	3,345,000	376	974	San Juan	C
†Qatar	Qaṭar	11,000	4,247	100,000	9.1	24	Ad-Dawḥah (Doha)	A
Quebec, Can.	Québec	1,540,680	594,860	6,406,000	4.2	11	Québec	D
Queensland, Austl.	Queensland	1,727,522	667,000	2,084,000	1.2	3.1	Brisbane	D
Reunion (Fr.)	Réunion	2,510	969	525,000	209	542	Saint-Denis	C
Rhode Island, U.S.	Rhode Island	3,144	1,214	922,400	293	760	Providence	D
Rhodesia (U.K.)[5]	Rhodesia	390,580	150,804	6,860,000	18	45	Salisbury	C
†Romania	România	237,500	91,699	21,760,000	92	237	Bucureşti (Bucharest)	A
Russian Soviet Federated Socialist Republic, U.S.S.R.	Rossijskaja S.F.S.R.	17,075,400	6,592,850	137,053,000	8.0	21	Moskva (Moscow)	D
†Rwanda	Rwanda	26,338	10,169	4,421,000	168	435	Kigali	A
St. Helena (incl. Dependencies) (U.K.)	St. Helena	419	162	8,000	19	49	Jamestown	C
St. Kitts-Nevis	St. Kitts-Nevis	267	103	48,000	178	466	Basseterre	B (U.K.)
St. Lucia	St. Lucia	616	238	117,000	190	492	Castries	A
St. Pierre and Miquelon (Fr.)	St.-Pierre-et-Miquelon	242	93	6,000	25	65	Saint-Pierre	C
St. Vincent	St. Vincent	388	150	117,000	302	780	Kingstown	B (U.K.)
San Marino	San Marino	61	24	21,000	344	875	San Marino	A
†Sao Tome and Principe	São Tomé e Príncipe	964	372	83,000	86	223	São Tomé	A
Saskatchewan, Can.	Saskatchewan	651,900	251,700	947,000	1.5	3.8	Regina	D
†Saudi Arabia	Al-'Arabīyah as-Sa'ūdīyah	2,149,690	830,000	9,645,000	4.5	12	Ar-Riyāḍ (Riyadh)	A
Scotland, U.K.	Scotland	78,772	30,414	5,202,000	66	171	Edinburgh	D
†Senegal	Sénégal	196,722	75,955	5,295,000	27	70	Dakar	A
†Seychelles (U.K.)	Seychelles	404	156	61,000	136	352	Victoria	A
Shansi, China	Shānxī	157,200	60,700	21,385,000	159	411	Taiyuan (Taiyüan)	D
Shantung, China	Shandong	153,600	59,300	72,715,000	463	1,198	Jinan (Tsinan)	D
Shensi, China	Shǎnxī	195,800	75,600	25,665,000	131	339	Xi'an (Sian)	D
†Sierra Leone	Sierra Leone	71,740	27,699	3,252,000	45	117	Freetown	A
†Singapore	Singapore	581	224	2,320,000	3,993	10,357	Singapore	A
Sinkiang Uighur, China	Xinjiang Weiwuer Zizhiqu	1,646,700	635,800	7,700,000	4.7	12	Wulumuqi (Urumchi)	D
†Solomon Islands	Solomon Islands	29,785	11,500	215,000	7.2	19	Honiara	A
†Somalia	Somaliya	637,657	246,201	3,391,000	5.3	14	Mogadisho	A
†South Africa (incl. Walvis Bay)	South Africa (English) Suid-Afrika (Afrikaans)	1,222,161	471,879	27,061,000	22	57	Pretoria and Cape Town	A
South America	. . .	17,793,000	6,870,000	226,000,000	13	33	. . .	. . .
South Australia, Austl.	South Australia	984,377	380,070	1,273,000	1.3	3.3	Adelaide	D
South Carolina, U.S.	South Carolina	80,432	31,055	2,900,500	36	93	Columbia	D
South Dakota, U.S.	South Dakota	199,551	77,047	688,400	3.4	8.9	Pierre	D
†Spain	España	504,750	194,885	36,530,000	72	187	Madrid	A
Spanish North Africa (Sp.)[7]	Plazas de Soberanía en el Norte de África	32	12	116,000	3,625	9,667	. . .	C
†Sri Lanka	Sri Lanka	65,610	25,332	14,085,000	215	556	Colombo	A
†Sudan	As-Sūdān	2,505,813	967,500	16,726,000	6.7	17	Al-Kharṭūm (Khartoum)	A
†Suriname	Suriname	163,265	63,037	454,000	2.8	7.2	Paramaribo	A
Svalbard and Jan Mayen (Nor.)	Svalbard og Jan Mayen	62,423	24,102	[1]	. . .	. . .	Longyearbyen	C
†Swaziland	Swaziland	17,366	6,705	515,000	30	77	Mbabane	A

NAME / NAME / NOMBRE / NOM / NOME — English / Englisch / Inglés / Anglais / Inglês	Local / Einheimisch / Local / Local / Local	AREA / FLÄCHE / AREA / SUPERFICIE / ÁREA km²	sq. mi.	POPULATION / BEVÖLKERUNG / POBLACIÓN / POPULATION / POPULAÇÃO	DENSITY PER / BEVÖLKERUNGSDICHTE PRO / DENSIDAD POR / DENSITÉ / DENSIDÁDE POR km²	sq. mi.	CAPITAL / HAUPTSTADT / CAPITAL / CAPITALE / CAPITAL	POLITICAL STATUS / POLITISCHER STATUS / ESTADO POLÍTICO / STATUT POLITIQUE / ESTATUTO POLÍTICO
†Sweden	Sverige	449,750	173,649	8,265,000	18	48	Stockholm	A
Switzerland	Schweiz (German); Suisse (French); Svizzera (Italian)	41,288	15,941	6,270,000	152	393	Bern	A
†Syria(2)	As-Sūriyah	185,180	71,498	7,968,000	43	111	Dimashq (Damascus)	A
Szechwan, China	Sichuan	569,000	219,700	95,820,000	168	436	Chengdu (Chengtu)	D
Tadzhik S.S.R., U.S.S.R.	Tadžikskaja S.S.R.	143,100	55,250	3,538,000	25	64	Dušanbe	D
Taiwan	T'aiwan	35,961	13,885	16,770,000	466	1,208	T'aipei	A
†Tanzania	Tanzania	945,087	364,900	16,154,000	17	44	Dar-es-Salaam	A
Tasmania, Austl.	Tasmania	68,332	26,383	412,000	6.0	16	Hobart	D
Tennessee, U.S.	Tennessee	109,411	42,244	4,276,400	39	101	Nashville	D
Texas, U.S.	Texas	692,405	267,339	12,834,700	19	48	Austin	D
†Thailand	Prathet Thai	514,000	198,500	44,600,000	87	225	Krung Thep (Bangkok)	A
Tibet, China	Xizang Zizhiqu	1,221,700	471,700	1,710,000	3.9	10	Lasa (Lhasa)	D
†Togo	Togo	56,000	21,600	2,366,000	42	110	Lomé	A
Tokelau Islands (N.Z.)	Tokelau Islands	10	4	1,600	160	400	...	C
Tonga	Tonga	699	270	92,000	132	341	Nukualofa	A
†Trinidad and Tobago	Trinidad and Tobago	5,128	1,980	1,118,000	218	565	Port of Spain	A
Tsinghai, China	Qinghai	721,000	278,400	2,565,000	3.6	9.2	Xining (Sining)	D
†Tunisia	Tunisie	164,150	63,379	5,875,000	36	93	Tunis	A
†Turkey	Türkiye	780,576	301,382	41,605,000	53	138	Ankara	A
Turkmen S.S.R., U.S.S.R.	Turkmenskaja S.S.R.	488,100	188,450	2,627,000	5.4	14	Aščhabad	D
Turks and Caicos Islands (U.K.)	Turks and Caicos Islands	430	166	5,000	12	30	Grand Turk	C
Tuvalu (U.K.)	Tuvalu	23	9.1	7,000	304	769	Funafuti	C
†Uganda	Uganda	235,886	91,076	12,521,000	53	137	Kampala	A
†Ukraine, U.S.S.R.	Ukrainskaja S.S.R.	603,700	233,100	49,941,000	83	214	Kijev (Kiev)	D
†Union of Soviet Socialist Republics	Sojuz Sovetskich Socialističeskich Respublik	22,274,900	8,600,350	260,110,000	12	30	Moskva (Moscow)	A
†United Arab Emirates	Ittiḥād al-Imārāt al-'Arabīyah	83,600	32,300	239,000	2.9	7.4	Abū Ẓaby	A
†United Kingdom	United Kingdom	244,013	94,214	55,890,000	229	593	London	A
†United States	United States	9,519,617(8)	3,675,545(8)	217,513,000	23	59	Washington, D.C.	A
†Upper Volta	Haute-Volta	274,200	105,800	6,376,000	23	60	Ouagadougou	A
†Uruguay	Uruguay	177,508	68,536	2,826,000	16	41	Montevideo	A
Utah, U.S.	Utah	219,931	84,916	1,263,800	5.7	15	Salt Lake City	D
Uzbek S.S.R., U.S.S.R.	Uzbekskaja S.S.R.	449,600	173,600	14,332,000	32	83	Taškent	D
Vatican City	Città del Vaticano	0.4	0.2	1,000	2,500	5,000	Città del Vaticano (Vatican City)	A
†Venezuela	Venezuela	912,050	352,144	13,047,000	14	37	Caracas	A
Vermont, U.S.	Vermont	24,887	9,609	483,300	19	50	Montpelier	D
Victoria, Austl.	Victoria	227,618	87,884	3,730,000	16	42	Melbourne	D
†Vietnam	Viet-nam	332,559	128,402	48,475,000	146	378	Ha-noi	A
Virginia, U.S.	Virginia	105,716	40,817	5,114,200	48	125	Richmond	D
Virgin Islands (U.S.)	Virgin Islands	344	133	102,000	297	766	Charlotte Amalie	C
Wake Island (U.S.)	Wake Island	8	3	1,000	125	333	...	C
Wales, U.K.	Wales	20,761	8,016	2,765,000	133	345	Cardiff	D
Wallis and Futuna (Fr.)	Wallis et Futuna	255	98	9,500	37	97	Mata-Utu	C
Washington, U.S.	Washington	176,616	68,192	3,697,200	21	54	Olympia	D
Western Australia, Austl.	Western Australia	2,527,621	975,920	1,171,000	0.5	1.2	Perth	D
Western Sahara	...	266,000	102,700	139,000	0.5	1.4	El Aaiún	C
†Western Samoa	Western Samoa	2,842	1,097	170,000	60	155	Apia	A
West Virginia, U.S.	West Virginia	62,628	24,181	1,846,100	29	76	Charleston	D
Wisconsin, U.S.	Wisconsin	145,438	56,154	4,616,500	32	82	Madison	D
Wyoming, U.S.	Wyoming	253,596	97,914	406,900	1.6	4.2	Cheyenne	D
†Yemen	Al-Yaman	195,000	75,300	5,690,000	29	76	Ṣan'ā'	A
†Yemen, People's Democratic Republic of	Al-Yamin ash-Sha'bīyah	287,683	111,075	1,825,000	6.3	16	Aden	A
†Yugoslavia	Jugoslavija	255,804	98,766	21,875,000	86	221	Beograd (Belgrade)	A
Yukon, Can.	Yukon	536,324	207,076	22,000	0.04	0.1	Whitehorse	D
Yunnan, China	Yunnan	436,100	168,400	25,665,000	59	152	Kunming	D
†Zaire	Zaïre	2,345,409	905,567	26,705,000	11	29	Kinshasa (Léopoldville)	A
†Zambia	Zambia	752,614	290,586	5,406,000	7.2	19	Lusaka	A
WORLD	...	**148,354,000**	**57,280,000**	**4,119,000,000**	**28**	**72**	...	...

† Member of the United Nations (1978).
... None, or not applicable.
(1) No permanent population.
(2) Data do not reflect de facto changes during 1967.
(3) Claimed by Argentina.
(4) The 1,262 km² or 487 sq. mi. of the demilitarized zone are not included in either North or South Korea.
(5) On November 11, 1965, Rhodesia unilaterally declared its independence from the United Kingdom.
(6) In October 1966 the United Nations terminated the South African mandate over Namibia, a decision which South Africa did not accept.
(7) Comprises Ceuta, Melilla, and several small islands.
(8) Total area of the United States includes 156,492 km² or 60,422 sq. mi. of Great Lakes area, not included in any State.

† Membre des Nations Unies (1978).
... Pas d'information, ou pas applicable.
(1) Pas de population permanente.
(2) Ces données ne reflètent pas les changements de facto depuis 1967.
(3) Revendiqué par l'Argentine.
(4) Les 1 262 km² ou 487 sq. mi. de la zone démilitarisée ne sont inclus ni dans la Corée du Nord ni dans celle du Sud.
(5) Le 11 novembre 1965, la Rhodésie s'est proclamée unilatéralement indépendante du Royaume-Uni.
(6) En octobre 1966, les Nations Unies ont mis fin au mandat de l'Afrique du Sud sur le Namibie; l'Afrique du Sud n'a pas accepté cetta décision.
(7) Inclus Ceuta, Melilla et plusieurs petites îles.
(8) La superficie totale des États-Unis comprend les 156 492 km² ou 60 422 sq. mi. des Grands Lacs qui ne sont inclus dans aucun des États.

† Mitglied der Vereinten Nationen (1978).
... Kein(e), oder nicht anwendbar.
(1) Bevölkerungszahl schwankend.
(2) Die Angaben zeigen nicht die de facto Veränderungen des Jahres 1967.
(3) Von Argentinien beansprucht.
(4) Die 1 262 km² oder 487 sq. mi. entmilitarisierter Zone sind weder in Nord-noch in Südkorea eingetragen.
(5) Am 11.November 1965 erklärte Rhodesien einseitig seine Unabhängigkeit von dem Vereinigten Königreich.
(6) Im Oktober 1966 setzten die Vereinten Nationen dem Mandat Südafrikas über Namibia ein Ende; Südafrika erkannte diese Entscheidung nicht an.
(7) Umfasst Ceuta, Melilla und mehrere kleine Inseln.
(8) Die Gesamtfläche der Vereinigten Staaten schliesst die 156 492 km² oder 60 422 sq. mi. der grossen Seen ein, die jedoch in der Flächenangabe keines Einzelstaates enthalten sind.

Membro das Nações Unidas (1978).
... Inexistente ou não aplicável.
(1) Sem população permanente.
(2) Os dados não refletem as mudanças de fato durante 1967.
(3) Reivindicado pela Argentina.
(4) Exclusive 1 262 km² (487 milhas quadradas) da zona desmilitarizada.
(5) A 11 de novembro de 1965, a Rodésia declarou unilateralmente sua independência do Reino Unido.
(6) Em outubro de 1966, as Nações Unidas terminaram o mandato da África do Sul sobre o Sudoeste Africano [Namíbia], decisão não acatada pela África do Sul.
(7) Compreende Ceuta, Melilla e várias ilhas pequenas.
(8) A área total dos Estados Unidos inclui 156 492 km² (60 422 milhas quadradas) referentes à área dos Grandes Lagos, não incluída em nenhum Estado.

† Miembro de las Naciones Unidas (1978).
... Ninguno, o no se aplica.
(1) Sin población permanente.
(2) Los datos no indican ningunos cambios de facto durante 1967.
(3) Reclamado por la Argentina.
(4) Los 1 262 km² o 487 sq. mi. de la zona desmilitarizada, no están incluídos para Corea del Norte o del Sur.
(5) El 11 de noviembre de 1965, Rhodesia declaró unilateralmente su independencia del Reino Unido.
(6) En octubre de 1966, las Naciones Unidas terminaron el mandato asignado sobre Namibia, dicha decisión no fue aceptada por Sudáfrica.
(7) Comprende Ceuta, Melilla y varias islas pequeñas.
(8) Área total de los Estados Unidos que encluye 156 492 km² o 60 422 sq. mi. del área de los Grandes Lagos que no se encluye en el total de ninguno de los estados.

ALL URBAN CENTERS of 50,000 or more population and many other important or well-known cities and towns are listed in the following table. The populations are from recent censuses (designated C) or official estimates (designated E) for the dates specified. For a few cities, only unofficial estimates are available (designated UE). For comparison, the total population of each country is also given. For each country, the date stated for the total population also applies to the cities, except those for which another date is specified.

Population estimates for 1978 for countries may be found in the World Information Table (pages *I•8–I•11*).

A population figure in parentheses and preceded by a star (★) is the population of a city's entire metropolitan area. To permit meaningful comparisons of metropolitan areas, these have been defined by Rand McNally according to consistent rules (see introduction to Metropolitan Areas Table, page 279), and in some cases may differ somewhat from the officially recognized metropolitan areas. Where a town is located within the metropolitan area of another city, that city's name is given in parentheses preceded by a star (★). The capital of a country is denoted by CAPITAL letters.

ALLE STÄDTISCHEN ZENTREN mit 50 000 oder mehr Einwohnern und zahlreiche andere bedeutende oder bekannte Städte sind in der folgenden Tabelle zusammengestellt. Die Bevölkerungszahlen stammen von neuesten Zählungen (mit C gekennzeichnet) oder amtlichen Schätzungen (E) zu den angegebenen Zeitpunkten. Für einige wenige Städte waren lediglich inoffizielle Schätzungen erhältlich (UE). Zu Vergleichszwecken ist ferner die Gesamtbevölkerung jedes Landes angegeben. Das Bezugsjahr für die Einwohnerzahl eines Landes betrifft auch die Städte mit Ausnahme jener, bei denen ein anderes Datum angegeben ist.

Schätzungen der Bevölkerungszahlen der Länder für 1978 finden sich in der Welt-Informationstabelle (Seite *I•8–I•11*).

Bevölkerungszahlen in Klammern mit vorangestelltem Stern (★) beziehen sich auf die gesamte Stadtregion einer Stadt. Um sinnvolle Vergleiche von Stadtregionen zu ermöglichen, wurden diese von Rand McNally nach einheitlichen Regeln festgelegt (siehe Einleitung: Tabelle der Stadtregionen, Seite 279), weshalb sie in einigen Fällen etwas von der offiziellen Abgrenzung von Stadtregionen abweichen können. Ist eine Stadt in die Stadtregion einer anderen Grossstadt einbezogen, so wird der Name der Stadtregion mit vorangestelltem Stern (★) in Klammern aufgeführt. Die Hauptstadt eines Landes wird durch GROSSBUCHSTABEN hervorgehoben.

TODAS LOS CENTROS URBANOS de 50 000 habitantes o más y muchos otros de importancia así como bien conocidas ciudades y pueblos están incluídos en la tabla que se presenta a continuación. El número de habitantes indicados está tomado del censo más reciente (cifras identificadas con la letra C) o estimados oficiales (E) para las fechas especificadas. Para algunas ciudades, sólo existen informes no oficiales (UE). Para medida de comparación, la población total de cada país se encuentra incluída también.

Para permitir una comparación, se da la población total de cada país, referente al mismo año que se usa para las ciudades principles, excepto para aquellas en las que se especifica otra fecha. El número de habitantes para 1978 para los países, se encuentra en la Tabla de Información Mundial (páginas *I•8–I•11*).

La segunda cifra para la población que aparece en paréntesis y está precedida por una estrella (★) constituye la población de un área metropolitana entera. Para permitir comparaciones validas de áreas metropolitanas, éstas fueron definidas por Rand McNally siguiendo las reglas establecidas para estos propósitos (véase la Introducción a la Tabla de las Áreas Metropolitanas, página 279), y en algunas ocasiones pueden ser un poco distintas de las áreas metropolitanas oficialmente reconocidas. Cuando una población se encuentra dentro de los límites de un área metropolitana de otra ciudad, el nombre de ésta se da entre paréntesis precedido por una (★). La capital de un país se indica con letras MAYÚSCULAS.

TOUTES LES VILLES de plus de 50 000 habitants et des villes moins peuplées, mais célèbres ou importantes, sont mentionnées dans la table ci-dessous. Les chiffres donnant la population proviennent de recensements récents (référence C), ou d'estimations officielles (référence E), aux dates indiquées. Pour quelques villes, on dispose seulement d'estimations non officielles (référence UE). La population totale de chaque pays est également donnée, ce qui permet des comparaisons. Dans chaque pays, la date des renseignements est identique pour les villes et le pays, sauf indication contraire.

On trouvera dans la table d'informations mondiales (pages *I•8* à *I•11*) les estimations de la population en 1978 pour chaque pays.

Les chiffres entre parenthèses, précédés d'une étoile (★), indiquent la population de l'ensemble de la zone métropolitaine. Pour permettre d'établir des comparaisons significatives entre les zones métropolitaines, ces dernières ont été définies selon des critères uniformes par Rand McNally & Company (voir l'introduction à la table des zones métropolitaines, page 279). Parfois, les limites des zones métropolitaines ainsi définies diffèrent des limites officielles. Quand une ville fait partie de la zone métropolitaine d'une autre ville, le nom de celle-ci, précédé d'une étoile (★), est mis entre parenthèses. Le nom des capitales de pays est écrit en lettres MAJUSCULES.

TODOS OS CENTROS URBANOS de 50 000 habitantes e mais, bem como muitas outras cidades e vilas importantes ou muito conhecidas figuram na tabela que se apresenta em seguida. Os dados relativos à população referem-se a censos recentes (identificadas com a letra C), ou a estimativas oficiais (E) nas datas indicadas. Para algumas cidades só existem estimativas não oficiais (UE). Para fins de comparabilidade, apresenta-se também a população total de cada país.

Para cada país, a data de referência da população total aplica-se também às cidades exceto quando especificado em contrário. As estimativas da população dos países para 1978 encontra-se na *Tabela de informações mundiais* (páginas *I•8–I•11*).

Um dado de população apresentado entre parênteses e precedido por uma estrela (★), refere-se à população de toda a área metropolitana. Para fins de comparabilidade, as áreas metropolitanas foram definidas por Rand McNally segundo regras coerentes (ver a 'Introdução' à *Tabela das áreas metropolitanas*, página 279), e em certos casos podem ser um pouco diferentes das áreas metropolitanas oficialmente reconhecidas. Quando um centro urbano esta localizado dentro dos limites da área metropolitana de outro, seu nome figura entre parênteses precedido por uma estrela (★). A capital de um país é indicada por letras MAIÚSCULAS.

AFGHANISTAN / Afghānestān	
1975 E	19,280,000
Bāghlān (1973 E)	110,900
Chārikār (1973 E)	110,400
Herāt	157,000
•KĀBUL (1971 E) (★498,800)	318,094
Qandahār	209,000
ALBANIA / Shqipëri	
1971 E	2,188,000
Durrës	55,000
Shkodër	56,500
•TIRANË	174,800
Vlorë (Valona)	51,400
ALGERIA / Algérie	
1974 E	16,275,000
•ALGER (ALGIERS) (★1,800,000)	1,503,720
Annaba (Bône)	313,174
Batna (115,138▲)	91,500
Béchar (Colomb-Béchar)	71,081
Bejaïa (Bougie) (103,996▲)	80,000
Biskra	84,971
Blida	158,947
Bordj Bou Arreridj (85,545▲)	66,400
Bordj Ménaïe (87,736▲)	38,700
Boufarik (109,234▲)	77,700
Constantine	350,183
Djidjelli (61,545▲)	43,500
Douéra	55,993
El Affroun (67,566▲)	47,500
El Asnam (Orléansville) (114,327▲)	80,500
Ghardaïa (85,230▲)	55,200
Ighil Izane (Relizane)	65,918
Khemis Miliana (63,370▲)	41,400
Laghouat (60,249▲)	41,900
Mascara (82,468▲)	70,600
Médéa (102,336▲)	70,700
Mostaganem	101,780
Oran (Ouahran)	485,139
Saïda (59,344▲)	51,800
Sétif	157,065
Sidi bel Abbès	151,148
Skikda (Philippeville)	127,968
Souk Ahras (60,551▲)	48,800
Tébessa	58,008
Tiaret	63,039
Tizi-Ouzou (223,702▲)	108,000
Tlemcen	115,054
Touggourt (65,935▲)	34,800
AMERICAN SAMOA	
1970 C	27,159
•PAGO PAGO	2,451
ANDORRA	
1971 C	20,550
•ANDORRA	2,000
ANGOLA	
1970 C	5,673,046
Huambo (Nova Lisboa)	61,885
Lobito	59,528
•LUANDA	475,328
ANGUILLA	
1974 C	6,519
•South Hill	774
THE VALLEY	760
ANTIGUA	
1970 C	65,525
•SAINT JOHNS	21,814
ARGENTINA	
1970 C	23,362,204
Almirante Brown (★Buenos Aires)	245,017
Avellaneda (★Buenos Aires)	337,538
Bahía Blanca	182,158
Berazategui (★Buenos Aires)	127,740
Berisso (★La Plata)	58,833
•BUENOS AIRES (★8,625,000)	2,972,453
Caseros (Tres de Febrero) (★Buenos Aires)	313,460
Catamarca (★64,410)	57,228
Comodoro Rivadavia	72,906
Concordia	72,136
Córdoba (★825,000)	798,663
Corrientes	136,924
Esteban Echeverría (★Buenos Aires)	111,150
Florencio Varela (★Buenos Aires)	98,446
Formosa	61,071
General San Martín (★Buenos Aires)	360,573
General Sarmiento (San Miguel) (★Buenos Aires)	315,457
Godoy Cruz (★Mendoza)	112,481
Guaymallén (★Mendoza)	112,081
Junín	59,020
Lanús (★Buenos Aires)	449,824
La Plata (★510,000)	408,300
Las Heras (★Mendoza)	67,789
Lomas de Zamora (★Buenos Aires)	410,806
Mar del Plata	302,282
Mendoza (★500,000)	118,568
Merlo (★Buenos Aires)	188,868
Moreno (★Buenos Aires)	114,041
Morón (★Buenos Aires)	485,983
Olavarría	52,453
Paraná	127,635
Pergamino	56,078
Posadas	97,514
Quilmes (★Buenos Aires)	355,265
Resistencia	142,848
Río Cuarto	88,852
Rosario (★875,000)	750,455
Salta	176,216
San Fernando (★Buenos Aires)	119,565
San Isidro (★Buenos Aires)	250,008
San Juan (★225,000)	112,500
San Justo (★Buenos Aires)	659,193
San Lorenzo (★Rosario)	56,487
San Luis	50,771
San Miguel de Tucumán (★380,000)	321,567
San Nicolás de los Arroyos	64,730
San Rafael	58,237
San Salvador de Jujuy	82,637
Santa Fe	244,655
Santiago del Estero (★140,000)	105,127
Tandil	65,876
Tigre (★Buenos Aires)	152,335
Vicente López (★Buenos Aires)	285,178
Villa María	56,087
Zárate	54,772
AUSTRALIA	
1976 C	13,546,154
Adelaide (★900,379)	13,773
Ballarat (★58,500)	37,863
Bankstown (★Sydney)	155,830
Blacktown (★Sydney)	159,724
Box Hill (★Melbourne)	50,280
Brisbane (★957,710)	725,000
Broadmeadows (★Melbourne)	108,736
Camberwell (★Melbourne)	89,865
Campbelltown (★Sydney)	52,285
CANBERRA (★215,414)	193,000
Canterbury (★Sydney)	128,669
Caulfield (★Melbourne)	73,604
Coburg (★Melbourne)	58,379
Darwin (1973 C) (★42,858)	36,900
Doncaster and Templestowe (★Melbourne)	82,090
Enfield (★Adelaide)	73,504
Essendon (★Melbourne)	51,112
Fairfield (★Sydney)	114,581
Footscray (★Melbourne)	51,681
Frankston (★Melbourne)	71,894
Geelong (★131,000)	15,727
Heidelberg (★Melbourne)	66,107
Hobart (★162,059	50,381
Holroyd (★Sydney)	79,861
Hurstville (★Sydney)	66,348
Ipswich (★Brisbane) (1975 E)	67,500
Keilor (★Melbourne)	70,591
Knox (★Melbourne)	74,386
Ku-ring-gai (★Sydney)	100,100
Launceston (★64,000)	32,947
Leichhardt (★Sydney)	62,540
Liverpool (★Sydney)	89,656
Marion (★Adelaide)	67,280
Marrickville (★Sydney)	87,796
Melbourne (★2,603,578)	65,065
Melville (★Perth)	54,377
Mitcham (★Adelaide)	59,885
Moorabbin (★Melbourne)	103,056
Newcastle (★362,980)	138,696
Northcote (★Melbourne)	54,883
Nunawading (★Melbourne)	94,324
Oakleigh (★Melbourne)	54,531
Parramatta (★Sydney)	131,655
Penrith (★Sydney)	79,038

▲ Population of an entire municipality, commune, or district, including rural area.
• Largest city in country.
★ Population or designation of the metropolitan area, including suburbs.
C Census. **E** Official estimate. **UE** Unofficial estimate.
L Population within municipal limits of year specified.

▲ Bevölkerung eines ganzen städtischen Verwaltungsgebietes, eines Kommunalbezirkes oder eines Distrikts, einschliesslich ländlicher Gebiete.
• Grösste Stadt des Landes.
★ Bevölkerung oder Bezeichnung der Stadtregion einschliess lich Vororte.
C Volkszählung. **E** Offizielle Schätzung.
UE Inoffizielle Schätzung.
L Bevölkerung innerhalb der städtischen Verwaltungseinheit des angegebenen Jahres.

Perth (★805,489) 87,576
Preston (★Melbourne) 88,380
Randwick (★Sydney) 119,460
Rockdale (★Sydney) 83,789
Rockhampton (1975 E) 51,500
Ryde (★Sydney) 89,130
St. Kilda (★Melbourne) 52,158
Salisbury (★Adelaide) 77,476
Southport (Gold Coast) (1975 E) 80,250
Springvale (★Melbourne) 72,473
Stirling (★Perth) 162,163
Sunshine (★Melbourne) 88,165
•Sydney (★3,021,299) 52,152
Tea Tree Gully (★Adelaide) 56,039
Toowoomba (1975 E) 62,900
Townsville (1975 E) 82,500
Waverley (★Melbourne) 117,143
Waverley (★Sydney) 61,724
Willoughby (★Sydney) 51,523
Wollongong (★211,122) 165,143
Woodville (★Adelaide) 75,269
Woollahra (★Sydney) 53,207

AUSTRIA / Österreich
1971 C 7,456,745
Graz (★270,000) 248,500
Innsbruck (★140,000) 115,197
Klagenfurt (1973 L) 82,512
Leoben (★48,000) 35,153
Linz (★275,000) 202,874
Salzburg (★150,000) 128,845
Sankt Pölten (1973 L) 50,144
Steyr (★54,000) 40,578
Villach (1973 L) 50,993
Wels (★59,000) 47,279
•WIEN (VIENNA) (★1,940,000) 1,614,841

BAHAMAS
1970 C 168,812
•NASSAU (★101,503) 3,233

BAHRAIN / Al-Baḥrayn
1971 C 216,078
•AL-MANĀMAH (★145,000) 89,112
Al-Muḥarraq (★Al-Manāmah) 37,577

BANGLADESH
1974 C 71,479,071
Barisāl 98,127
Brāhmanbāria 62,407
Chāndpur 51,668
Chittagong (★1,050,000) 416,733
Comilla 86,446
•DACCA (★2,400,000) 1,310,976
Dinājpur 61,866
Doublemooring (★Chittagong) 125,453
Harirāmpur (★Dacca) 71,429
Jamālpur 60,261
Jessore (★82,817) 76,168
Khulna 437,304
Mīrpur (★Dacca) 91,525
Mymensingh (Nasirābād) (★182,153) 76,036
Nārāyanganj (★Dacca) 176,459
Pābna 62,254
Pānchlāish (★Chittagong) 127,839
Rājshāhi (Rampur Boalia) (★132,909) 96,645
Rangpur 72,829
Saidpur 90,132
Sirājganj 74,457
Sītākunda (★Chittagong) 99,929
Sylhet 59,546
Tangail 51,863
Tongi (★Dacca) 67,420

BARBADOS
1970 C 238,141
•BRIDGETOWN (★115,000) 8,789

BELGIUM / Belgique / België
1976 E 9,823,302
Aalst (Alost) (★Bruxelles) (1977 L) 82,195
Anderlecht (★Bruxelles) 99,942
Antwerpen (Anvers) (★1,065,000) 206,786
Brugge (Bruges) 119,351
•BRUXELLES (BRUSSEL) (BRUSSELS) (★2,040,000) 152,850
Charleroi (1977 L) (★365,000) 229,474
Deurne (★Antwerpen) 80,427
Forest (Vorst) (★Bruxelles) 52,631
Genk 61,156
Gent (Grand) (1977 L) (★335,000) 248,671
Hasselt (1977 L) 62,755
Ixelles (Elsene) (★Bruxelles) 80,151
Kortrijk (Courtrai) (1977 L) (★174,000) 75,535
La Louvière (1977 L) (★130,000) 76,167
Leuven (Louvain) (1977 L) (★108,000) 81,932
Liège (Luik) (1977 L) (★545,000) 221,404
Mechelen (Malines) (1977 L) 77,868
Molenbeek-St.-Jean (Sint-Jans-Molenbeek) (★Bruxelles) 71,991
Mons (Bergen) (1977 L) (★203,000) 93,332
Mouscron (Moeskroen) (★Lille, France) (1977 L) 54,690
Namur (1977 L) 100,039
Oostende (Ostende) (★82,000) 71,446
Roeselare (Roulers) (1977 L) 51,247
Saint-Gilles (Sint-Gillis) (★Bruxelles) 51,135
Schaerbeek (Schaarbeek) (★Bruxelles) 112,649
Seraing (★Liège) (1977 L) 75,050
Sint-Niklaas (Saint-Nicolas) 48,680
Tournai (Doornik) (1977 L) 70,743
Uccle (Ukkel) (★Bruxelles) 77,369
Verviers (1977 L) (★80,000) 56,109

BELIZE
1972 E 127,200
•Belize 41,500
BELMOPAN (1971 E) 5,000

BENIN
1975 E 3,112,000
•Cotonou 178,000
PORTO-NOVO 104,000

BERMUDA
1970 C 52,330
•HAMILTON (★13,757) 2,060

BOLIVIA
1976 C 4,687,718
Cochabamba 204,414
•LA PAZ 654,713
Oruro 124,121
Potosí 77,233
Santa Cruz 255,568
SUCRE 63,259

BOTSWANA
1971 C 574,094
•Francistown 18,613
GABORONE (GABERONES) 17,718

BRAZIL / Brasil
1970 C 93,215,301
Alagoinhas 53,891
Americana 62,387
Anápolis 89,405
Aracaju 179,512
Araçatuba 85,660
Araraquara 82,607
Bagé 57,036
Barbacena 57,766
Barra Mansa (★Volta Redonda) 75,006
Barretos 53,050
Bauru 120,178
Belém (★660,000) 565,097
Belford Roxo (★Rio de Janeiro) 173,427
Belo Horizonte (1975 E) (★1,945,000) 1,557,464
Blumenau 85,942
BRASÍLIA (1975 UE) (★750,000) 350,000
Cachoeira do Sul 50,001
Cachoeiro de Itapemirim 58,968
Campina Grande 163,206
Campinas 328,629
Campo Grande 130,792
Campos 153,310
Campos Elyseos (★Rio de Janeiro) 104,636
Canoas (★Pôrto Alegre) 148,798
Carapicuíba (★São Paulo) 54,907
Caruaru 101,006
Cavaleiro (★Recife) 58,811
Caxias do Sul 107,487
Coelho da Rocha (★Rio de Janeiro) 100,781
Criciúma 50,430
Cuiabá 83,621
Curitiba (★680,000) 483,038
Diadema (★São Paulo) 68,552
Divinópolis 69,872
Duque de Caxias (★Rio de Janeiro) 256,582
Feira de Santana 127,105
Florianópolis 115,665
Fortaleza (1975 E) (★1,175,000) 1,109,837
Franca 86,852
Goiânia 362,152
Governador Valadares 125,174
Guaratinguetá 55,069
Guarulhos (★São Paulo) 221,639
Ilhéus 58,529
Ipiíba (★Rio de Janeiro) 55,486
Itabuna 89,928
Itajaí 54,135
Itaquari (★Vitória) 64,559
Jaboatão (★Recife) 52,537
Jequié 62,341
João Pessoa (★310,000) 197,398
Joinvile 77,760
Juàzeiro do Norte 79,796
Juiz de Fora 218,832
Jundiaí 145,785
Lajes 82,325
Limeira 77,243
Londrina 156,670
Macapá 51,563
Maceió 242,867
Manaus 284,118
Marília 73,165
Maringá 51,620
Mauá (★São Paulo) 101,569
Mesquita (★Rio de Janeiro) 93,926
Mogi das Cruzes (★São Paulo) 90,330
Montes Claros 81,572
Mossoró 77,251
Muribeca dos Guararapes (★Recife) 74,963
Natal 250,787
Neves (★Rio de Janeiro) 112,912
Nilópolis (★Rio de Janeiro) 86,720
Niterói (★Rio de Janeiro) (1975 E) 376,033
Nova Friburgo 65,732
Nova Iguaçu (★Rio de Janeiro) 331,457
Nôvo Hamburgo (★Pôrto Alegre) 81,248
Olinda (★Recife) 187,553
Osasco (★São Paulo) 283,303
Paranaguá 51,510
Parnaíba 57,031
Parque Industrial (★Belo Horizonte) 80,572
Passo Fundo 69,135
Pelotas 150,278
Petrópolis (★Rio de Janeiro) 116,080
Pinheirinho (★Curitiba) 50,302
Piracicaba 125,490
Poços de Caldas 51,844
Ponta Grossa 92,344
Pôrto Alegre (1975 E) (★1,760,000) 1,043,964
Presidente Prudente 91,188
Queimados (★Rio de Janeiro) 62,560
Recife (1975 E) (★2,100,000) 1,249,821
Ribeirão Prêto 190,897
Rio Claro 69,240
Rio de Janeiro (1975 E) (★8,235,000) 4,857,716
Rio Grande 98,863
Salvador (1975 E) (★1,270,000) 1,237,373
Santa Maria 120,667
Santarém 51,123
Santo André (★São Paulo) 415,025
Santos (★610,000) 341,317
São Bernardo do Campo (★São Paulo) 187,368
São Caetano do Sul (★São Paulo) 150,171
São Carlos 74,835
São Gonçalo (★Rio de Janeiro) 161,392
São João de Meriti (★Rio de Janeiro) 163,934
São José do Rio Prêto 108,319
São José dos Campos 130,118
São Leopoldo (★Pôrto Alegre) 62,861
São Luís 167,529
•São Paulo (1975 E) (★9,900,000) 7,198,608
São Vicente (★Santos) 116,075
Sete Lagoas 61,063
Sete Pontes (★Rio de Janeiro) 53,766
Sobral 51,864
Sorocaba 165,990
Taubaté 98,933
Teófilo Otoni 64,568
Teresina 181,071
Teresópolis 53,462
Tubarão 51,121
Uberaba 108,576
Uberlândia 110,463
Uruguaiana 60,667
Vicente de Carvalho (★Santos) 59,767
Vitória (★345,000) 121,978
Vitória da Conquista 82,477
Volta Redonda (★205,000) 120,645

BRUNEI
1971 C 136,256
•BANDAR SERI BEGAWAN (BRUNEI) (★37,000) 17,410

BULGARIA / Bâlgarija
1973 E 8,619,000
Burgas 143,100
Gabrovo (1969 E) 71,800
Haskovo (Khaskovo) (1969 E) 66,900
Jambol (Yambol) (1969 E) 70,300
Kazanlâk (1969 E) 50,300
Pazardžik (1969 E) 61,400
Pernik (Dimitrovo) (1969 E) 79,900
Pleven 110,500
Plovdiv 274,700
Ruse 165,000
Sliven (1969 E) 81,100
•SOFIJA (SOFIA) (★1,060,000) 937,100
Stara Zagora 118,400
Šumen (Shumen) (Kolarovgrad) (1969 E) 69,600
Tolbuhin (Dobrich) (1969 E) 64,100
Varna 255,900

BURMA / Myanma
1970 E 27,584,000
Bassein 136,000
Henzada 85,000
Mandalay 402,000
Moulmein 173,000
Myingyan 65,000
Pegu 125,000
•RANGOON (1973 E) 2,055,365
Pyè (Prome) 65,000
Sittwe (Akyab) 82,000
Tavoy 53,000

BURUNDI
1970 E 3,540,000
•BUJUMBURA 78,810

CAMBODIA / Kampuchea
1962 C 5,728,771
•PHNUM PÉNH 393,995

CAMEROON / Cameroun
1970 E 5,836,000
•Douala 230,000
YAOUNDÉ (1969 E) 165,800

CANADA
1976 C 22,992,604
Beauport, Québec (★Québec) 55,339
Brampton, Ontario (★Toronto) 103,459
Brantford, Ontario (★82,800) 66,950
Burlington, Ontario (★Hamilton) 104,314
Burnaby, British Columbia (★Vancouver) 131,599
Calgary, Alberta 469,917
Cambridge (Galt), Ontario (★Kitchener) 72,383
Charlesbourg, Québec (★Québec) 63,147
Charlottetown, Prince Edward Island (★24,837) 17,063
Chicoutimi, Québec (★128,643) 57,737
Dartmouth, Nova Scotia (★Halifax) 65,341
East York, Ontario (★Toronto) 106,950
Edmonton, Alberta (★554,228) 461,361
Etobicoke, Ontario (★Toronto) 297,109
Gatineau, Québec (★Ottawa) 73,479
Guelph, Ontario (★70,388) 67,538
Halifax, Nova Scotia (★267,991) 117,882
Hamilton, Ontario (★529,371) 312,003
Hull, Québec (★Ottawa) 61,039
Jonquière, Québec (★Chicoutimi) 60,691
Kingston, Ontario (★90,741) 56,032
Kitchener, Ontario (★272,158) 131,870
Lachine (★Montréal) 41,503
LaSalle, Québec (★Montréal) 76,713
Laval, Québec (★Montréal) 246,243
London, Ontario (★270,383) 240,392
Longueuil, Québec (★Montréal) 122,429
Markham, Ontario (★Toronto) 56,206
Mississauga, Ontario (★Toronto) 250,017
Moncton, New Brunswick (★77,571) 55,934
•Montréal, Québec (★2,802,485) 1,080,546
Montréal-Nord, Québec (★Montréal) 97,250
Niagara Falls, Ontario (★Buffalo) 69,423
North Bay, Ontario (★53,961) 51,639
North York, Ontario (★Toronto) 558,398
Oakville, Ontario (★Toronto) 68,950
Oshawa, Ontario (★135,196) 107,023
OTTAWA, Ontario (★693,288) 304,462
Peterborough, Ontario (★65,293) 59,683
Prince George, British Columbia 59,929
Québec, Québec (★542,158) 177,082
Regina, Saskatchewan (★151,191) 149,593
Richmond, British Columbia (★Vancouver) 80,034
Saint Catharines, Ontario (★Buffalo) 123,351
Sainte-Foy, Québec (★Québec) 71,237
Saint John, New Brunswick (★112,974) 85,956
Saint John's, Newfoundland (★143,390) 86,576
Saint-Laurent, Québec (★Montréal) 64,404
Saint-Léonard, Québec (★Montréal) 78,452
Sarnia, Ontario (★81,342) 55,576
Saskatoon, Saskatchewan 133,750
Sault Sainte Marie, Ontario (★81,992) 81,048
Scarborough, Ontario (★Toronto) 387,149
Shawinigan, Québec (★55,414) 24,921
Sherbrooke, Québec (★104,505) 76,804
Sudbury, Ontario (★157,030) 97,604
Sydney, Nova Scotia (★88,614) 30,645
Thunder Bay, Ontario (★119,253) 111,476
Toronto, Ontario (★2,803,101) 633,318
Trois-Rivières, Québec (★98,583) 52,518
Vancouver, British Columbia (★1,166,348) 410,188
Verdun, Québec (★Montréal) 68,013
Victoria, British Columbia (★218,250) 62,551
Windsor, Ontario (★Detroit) 196,526
Winnipeg, Manitoba (★578,217) 560,874
Yellowknife 8,256
York, Ontario (★Toronto) 141,367

CAPE VERDE / Cabo Verde
1970 C 272,071
•Mindelo 28,797
PRAIA 21,494

CENTRAL AFRICAN EMPIRE / Empire centrafricaine
1971 E 1,637,000
Bambari (1968 E) 35,300
•BANGUI 187,000

CHAD / Tchad
1972 E 3,791,000
Moundou (1970 E) 35,000
•NDJAMENA 179,000
Sarh (1970 E) 38,000

CHILE
1970 C 8,880,889
Antofagasta 138,821
Apoquindo (★Santiago) 90,722
Arica 87,726
Chillán 87,555
Concepción (★395,000) 175,853
Conchalí (★Santiago) 246,046
Coquimbo 50,405
Iquique 65,040
La Cisterna (★Santiago) 246,537
La Granja (★Santiago) 163,882
La Serena 61,897
Lo Prado Arriba (★Santiago) 112,548
Los Angeles 49,175
Lota 48,166
Ñuñoa (★Santiago) 280,733
Osorno 68,815
Providencia (★Santiago) 85,678
Puente Alto (★Santiago) 61,077
Puerto Montt 62,726
Punta Arenas 61,813
Quinta Normal (★Santiago) 138,007
Rancagua 86,404
Renca (★Santiago) 68,440
San Bernardo (★Santiago) 100,225
San Miguel (★Santiago) 320,883
•SANTIAGO (★2,925,000) 517,473
Talca 94,449
Talcahuano (★Concepción) 152,755
Temuco 110,335
Valdivia 82,362
Valparaíso (★530,000) 250,358
Viña del Mar (★Valparaíso) 188,811

▲ Población de un municipio, comuna o distrito entero, incluyendo sus áreas rurales.
• Ciudad más grande de un país.
★ Población o designación de un área metropolitana, incluyendo los suburbios.
C Censo. E Estimado oficial.
UE Estimado no oficial.
L Población dentro de los límites municipales de un año específico.

▲ Population d'une municipalité, d'une commune ou d'un district, zone rurale incluse.
• Ville la plus peuplée du pays.
★ Population de l'agglomération (ou nom de la zone métropolitaine englobante).
C Recensement. E Estimation officielle.
UE Estimation non officielle.
L Population comprise dans les limites municipales de l'année indiquée.

▲ População de um município, comuna ou distrito, inclusive as respectivas áreas rurais.
• Maior cidade de um país.
★ População ou indicação de uma área metropolitana, inclusive subúrbios.
C Censo. E Estimativa oficial.
UE Estimativa não oficial.
L População dentro dos limites municipais no ano indicado.

CHINA / Zhongguo
1958 UE 650,000,000
Andong (Antung) 370,000
Anqing (Anking) (1953 C) 105,300
Anshan 833,000
Anyang (1953 C) 124,900
Baiyinchang (Paiyin) 50,000
Bangbu (Pengpu) 330,000
Baoding (Paoting) (1957 E) 265,000
Baoji (Paoki) 180,000
Baotou (Paotow) 490,000
Beian (Peian) (1953 UE) 70,000
Beihai (Pakhoi) (1953 C) 80,000
BEIJING (PEKING) (1970 E) (7,570,000▲) 4,800,000
Benxi (Penki) (1953 C) 449,000
Boshan (Tzupo) (875,000▲) 250,000
Boxian (Pohsien) (1953 UE) 90,000
Cangzhou (1953 UE) 60,000
Changchun (Hsinking) 988,000
Changde (Changte) (1953 C) 94,800
Changsha 709,000
Changshu (1953 C) 101,400
Changzhi (Changchih) 180,000
Changzhou (Changchow) 300,000
Chaoan 101,300
Chengde (Chengteh) 120,000
Chengdu (Chengtu) 1,135,000
Chifeng (Chihfeng) (1953 C) 49,000
Chongqing (Chungking) 2,165,000
Datong (Tatung) (1953 C) 228,500
Duyun (Tuyün) 60,000
Foshan (Fatshan) 120,000
Fuling (Fowling) (1953 UE) 60,000
Fushun 1,019,000
Fuxian (Fuhsien) (1953 UE) 70,000
Fuxinshi (Fusin) 290,000
Fuyang (Fowyang) (1953 UE) 65,000
Fuzhou (Foochow) 623,000
Ganzhou (Kanchow) (1953 C) 98,600
Gejiu (Kokiu) 180,000
Guangzhou (Canton) 1,867,000
Guilin (Kweilin) 170,000
Guiyang (Kweiyang) 530,000
Haerbin (Harbin) (1959 E) 1,814,000
Haicheng (1953 UE) 80,000
Haikou (Hoihow) 402,000
Hailaer (Hailar) 60,000
Handan (Hantan) 380,000
Hangu (Hanku) (1953 UE) 50,000
Hangzhou (Hangchow) 794,000
Hanzhong (Hanchung) (1953 C) 70,000
Hechuan (Hochwan) (1953 UE) 50,000
Hefei (Hofei) 360,000
Hegang (Hokang) 200,000
Hengyang 240,000
Huaian (Hwaian) (1953 UE) 55,000
Huaide (Hwaite) 60,000
Huainan (Hwainan) 280,000
Huaiyin (Hwaiyin) (1953 C) 77,000
Huangshi (Hwangshih) (1953 C) 110,500
Huhehaote (Kweisui) 320,000
Huiyang (Waiyeung) 73,000
Hulan (1953 UE) 60,000
Huzhou (Huchow) 120,000
Jiamusi (Kiamusze) 232,000
Ji'an (Kian) (1953 C) 52,800
Jiangmen (Kongmoon) 110,000
Jiaozuo (Tsiaotso) 250,000
Jiaxing (Kashing) 132,000
Jieyang (Kityang) (1953 UE) 55,000
Jilin (Kirin) 583,000
Jinan (Tsinan) 882,000
Jingdezhen (Kingtechen) 266,000
Jinhua (Kinhwa) (1953 C) 46,200
Jining 100,000
Jining (Tsining) (1953 C) 86,200
Jinshi (Tsingshih) (1953 UE) 50,000
Jinxian (Chinhsien) (1953 UE) 60,000
Jinzhou (Chinchow) 400,000
Jiujiang (Kiukiang) (1953 C) 64,600
Jixi (Chihsi) 253,000
Kaifeng (1953 C) 299,100
Kashi (Kashgar) 100,000
Kelamayi (Karamai) 43,000
Kunming 900,000
Lanzhou (Lanchow) 732,000
Lasa (Lhasa) (1953 C) 70,000
Leshan (Loshan) (1953 UE) 60,000
Liaoyang 169,000
Liaoyuan (Shwangliao) 177,000
Linxia (Linsia) (1953 UE) 50,000
Liuzhou (Liuchow) 190,000
Luda (Dairen) (1,590,000▲) 1,000,000
Luohe (Loho) (1953 UE) 50,000
Luoyang (Loyang) 500,000
Lüshun (Port Arthur) (1953 C) 126,000
Luzhou (Luchow) 130,000
Meixian (Meihsien) (1953 UE) 45,000
Mudanjiang (Mutankiang) 251,000
Nanchang 520,000
Nanchong (Nanchung) (1953 C) 164,700
Nanjing (Nanking) 1,455,000
Nanning (1957 E) 264,000
Nantong (Nantung) 240,000
Nanyang (1953 UE) 50,000
Neijiang (Neikiang) 180,000
Ningbo (Ningpo) 280,000
Pingdingshan 70,000
Pingliang (1953 C) 60,000
Qingdao (Tsingtao) 1,144,000
Qinhuangdao (Chinwangtao) 210,000
Qiqihaer (Tsitsihar) 704,000
Quanzhou (Chüanchow) 110,000
Rugao (Jukao) (1953 UE) 40,000
•Shanghai (1970 E) (10,820,000▲) 7,900,000
Shangqiu (Shangkiu) (1953 C) 134,400
Shangrao (Shangjao) (1953 UE) 50,000
Shangshui (Chowkiakow) (1953 C) 85,500
Shantou (Swatow) 250,000
Shaoguan (Kükong) (1953 C) 81,700
Shaoxing (Shaohing) (1953 C) 130,600
Shaoyang 170,000
Shashi (Shasi) (1953 C) 85,800
Shenyang (Mukden) 2,423,000
Shijiazhuang (Shihkiachwang) 623,000
Shuangcheng (1953 UE) 80,000
Shuangyashan 110,000
Siping (Szeping) 130,000
Suihua (Suihwa) (1953 UE) 55,000
Suining (1953 UE) 50,000
Suouche (Yarkand) (1953 C) 80,000
Suzhou (Soochow) 651,000
Taiyuan (Taiyüan) 1,053,000
Taizhou (Taichow) (1953 C) 159,800
Tangshan 812,000
Taoan (1953 UE) 65,000
Tianjin (Tientsin) (1970 E) (4,280,000▲) 3,800,000
Tianshui (Tienshui) (1953 C) 63,000
Tieling (Tiehling) (1953 UE) 65,000
Tonghua (Tunghwa) (1953 C) 129,100
Tongxian (1953 UE) 55,000
Tunxi (Tunki) (1953 UE) 50,000
Wanxian (Wanhsien) (1953 UE) 90,000
Weifang 190,000
Wenzhou (Wenchow) 210,000
Wuhan (Hankow) 2,226,000
Wuhu 240,000
Wulanhaote (Ulanhot) (1953 C) 51,400
Wulumuqi (Urumchi) 320,000
Wutongqiao (Wutungkiao) 140,000
Wuxi (Wusih) 616,000
Wuzhou (Wuchow) 120,000
Xiamen (Amoy) 308,000
Xi'an (Sian) 1,368,000
Xiangfan (Siangfan) (1953 C) 73,300
Xiangtan (Siangtan) 247,000
Xianyang (Sienyang) (1953 C) 70,000
Xinghua (Hinghwa) (1953 UE) 85,000
Xingtai (Singtai) (1953 UE) 70,000
Xinhailian (Sinhailien) 210,000
Xining (Sining) (1957 E) 300,000
Xinxiang (Sinsiang) 203,000
Xinyang (Sinyang) (1953 UE) 50,000
Xuanhua (Süanhwa) (1953 C) 114,100
Xuchang (Hsüchang) (1953 C) 58,000
Xuzhou (Süchow) 710,000
Yaan (1953 C) 55,200
Yancheng (1953 UE) 50,000
Yangjiang (Yeungkong) (1953 UE) 50,000
Yangquan (Yangchüan) 200,000
Yangzhou (Yangchow) 160,000
Yanji (Yenki) 80,000
Yantai (Chefoo) 140,000
Yibin (Ipin) 190,000
Yichang (Ichang) (1953 UE) 85,000
Yichun (Ichun) 200,000
Yinchuan (Yinchwan) 91,000
Yingkou (Yingkow) (1953 C) 131,400
Yining (Kuldja) 85,000
Yiyang (Iyang) (1953 UE) 80,000
Yuci (Yütze) 100,000
Yumen (Yümen) 200,000
Zhangjiakou (Kalgan) (480,000▲) 350,000
Zhangzhou (1953 C) 81,200
Zhanjiang (Tsamkong) 170,000
Zhaoqing (Kaoyao) 70,000
Zhengzhou (Chengchow) 785,000
Zhenjiang (Chinkiang) 190,000
Zhongshan (Shekki) (1953 C) 93,000
Zhuzhou (Chuchow) 190,000
Zigong (Tzekung) 280,000
Zunyi (Tsunyi) 200,000

COLOMBIA
1973 C 21,070,115
Armenia 135,615
Barrancabermeja (99,155▲) 87,191
Barranquilla (★730,000) 661,920
Bello (★Medellín) 121,204
•BOGOTÁ (★2,925,000) 2,855,065
Bucaramanga 298,051
Buenaventura (139,839▲) 115,770
Buga (84,057▲) 71,016
Cali 923,446
Cartagena 313,305
Cartago (77,890▲) 69,154
Ciénaga (89,723▲) 42,546
Cúcuta 269,565
Envigado (★Medellín) (69,921▲) 63,584
Girardot (61,829▲) 59,165
Ibagué (204,810▲) 176,223
Itagüí (★Medellín) 96,972
Manizales 231,066
Medellín (★1,500,000) 1,100,082
Montería (149,442▲) 89,583
Neiva (121,432▲) 105,476
Palmira (180,801▲) 140,481
Pasto (149,620▲) 119,339
Pereira (210,543▲) 174,128
Popayán (94,120▲) 77,669
Santa Marta 128,577
Sincelejo (76,701▲) 68,797
Sogamoso (67,738▲) 48,891
Soledad (★Barranquilla) 64,469
Tuluá (109,437▲) 86,736
Tunja (77,473▲) 51,620
Valledupar (110,038▲) 87,425
Villavicencio (92,814▲) 82,869

COMOROS / Comores
1974 E 292,000
•MORONI 12,000

CONGO
1970 C 1,089,300
•BRAZZAVILLE 175,000
Pointe-Noire 135,000

COSTA RICA
1976 E 1,993,800
Alajuela 35,000
Desamparados (★San José) 32,700
Limón (43,800▲) 31,900
Puntarenas 29,000
•SAN JOSÉ (★493,300) 228,300

CUBA
1970 C 8,553,400
Bayamo (92,700▲) 71,700
Camagüey 196,900
Cárdenas (55,700▲) 55,200
Chaparra (51,000▲) 8,400
Ciego de Avila (70,200▲) 60,900
Cienfuegos (90,700▲) 85,200
Guanabacoa (★La Habana) 69,700
Guantánamo (131,500▲) 130,100
Holguín (163,100▲) 131,500
•LA HABANA (HAVANA) (★1,800,000) 1,755,400
Manzanillo (88,900▲) 77,900
Matanzas 85,400
Palma Soriano (59,600▲) 41,200
Pinar del Río 73,200
Sancti-Spiritus (66,500▲) 57,700
Santa Clara (154,500▲) 131,500
Santiago de Cuba 276,000
Victoria de las Tunas (65,000▲) 53,700

CYPRUS / Kípros / Kıbrıs
1974 E 639,000
Lemesós (Limassol) (★80,600) 55,000
•LEVKOSÍA (NICOSIA) (★117,100) 51,000

CZECHOSLOVAKIA / Československo
1975 E 14,857,145
Banská Bystrica 55,832
Bratislava 340,902
Brno 359,540
České Budějovice (Budweis) 82,528
Gottwaldov (Zlín) 69,788
Havířov (★Ostrava) 91,653
Hradec Králové 87,217
Karlovy Vary (Karlsbad) (★57,000) 50,386
Karviná (★Ostrava) 81,394
Kladno (★80,000) 62,019
Košice 174,388
Liberec (★92,000) 76,441
Most 59,909
Nitra 57,105
Olomouc 96,207
Opava 54,873
Ostrava (★710,000) 300,945
Pardubice 79,869
Plzeň (Pilsen) 156,461
•PRAHA (PRAGUE) (★1,250,000) 1,169,567
Prešov 62,429
Teplice 52,810
Trnava 50,948
Ústí nad Labem (★96,000) 75,724
Žilina 58,142

DENMARK / Danmark
1976 E 5,065,313
Ålborg 154,646
Århus 246,355
Ballerup-Måløv (★København) 50,988
Esbjerg 79,160
Frederiksberg (★København) 93,692
Gentofte (★København) 70,253
Gladsakse (★København) 68,684
Helsingør (Elsinore) 55,964
Herning (54,871▲) 46,900
Horsens 53,966
Hvidovre (★København) 51,213
•KØBENHAVN (COPENHAGEN) (★1,505,000) 545,350
Kolding 54,434
Lyngby (Kongens Lyngby)-Tårbæk (★København) 55,401
Odense 168,206
Randers 64,193
Rønne 15,399
Roskilde 49,388
Vejle 48,848

DJIBOUTI
1970 E 95,000
•DJIBOUTI 62,000

DOMINICA
1970 C 70,302
•ROSEAU 10,157

DOMINICAN REPUBLIC / República Dominicana
1970 C 4,006,405
San Francisco de Macorís 44,620
Santiago [de los Caballeros] 155,000
•SANTO DOMINGO 673,470

ECUADOR
1974 C 6,500,845
Ambato 77,052
Cuenca 104,667
Esmeraldas 60,132
•Guayaquil 814,064
Machala 68,379
Manta 63,514
Milagro 53,058
Portoviejo 59,404
QUITO 597,133
Riobamba 58,029

EGYPT / Misr
1966 C 30,083,419
Al-Fayyūm (1970 E) 151,000
Al-Iskandarīyah (Alexandria) (1976 C) (★2,425,000) 2,161,916
Al-Ismā'īlīyah (★180,000) 144,163
Al-Jīzah (Giza) (★Al-Qāhirah) (1976 C) 1,246,054
Al-Mahallah al-Kubrā (1970 E) 256,000
Al-Manṣūrah (1970 E) (★238,000) 212,000
Al-Minyā (1970 E) 122,000
•AL-QĀHIRAH (CAIRO) (1976 C) (★8,000,133) 5,084,463
Al-Uqṣur (Luxor) 77,578
As-Suways (Suez) (1976 C) 194,001
Aswān (1970 E) 202,000
Asyūṭ (1970 E) 176,000
Az-Zaqāzīq (1970 E) 173,000
Banhā 63,849
Banī Suwayf 90,425
Bilbays 58,070
Būlāq ad-Dakrūr (★Al-Qāhirah) 75,130
Būr Sa'īd (Port Said) (1976 C) 262,620
Damanhūr (1970 E) 161,000
Dumyāṭ (Damietta) 86,327
Kafr ash-Shaykh 51,544
Mallawī 59,938
Minūf 48,256
Mīt Ghamr (★82,000) 43,665
Qalyūb 49,303
Qinā 68,536
Sawhāj 74,753
Shibīn al-Kawm 66,290
Shubrā al-Khaymah (★Al-Qāhirah) (1976 C) 393,700
Ṭanṭā (1970 E) 254,000

EL SALVADOR
1974 E 3,980,000
Mejicanos (★San Salvador) 62,900
San Miguel 66,900
•SAN SALVADOR (★655,000) 366,000
Santa Ana 105,300

EQUATORIAL GUINEA / Guinea Ecuatorial
1965 C 254,684
•MALABO (37,152▲) 17,500

ETHIOPIA / Yaitopya
1974 E 27,800,800
•ADDIS ABEBA (1975 E) 1,161,300
Asmera (1975 E) 318,000
Dese 54,910
Dire Dawa 72,860
Gonder 43,040
Harer 53,560
Jima 52,420
Mitsiwa (Massaua) 23,880
Nazeret 50,550

FAEROE ISLANDS / Føroyar
1975 E 40,441
•TÓRSHAVN 11,329

FIJI
1966 C 476,727
•SUVA (★80,269) 54,157

FINLAND / Suomi
1975 E 4,727,666
Espoo (Esbo) (★Helsinki) 117,090
Hämeenlinna 40,761
•HELSINKI (HELSINGFORS) (★863,000) 502,961
Jyväskylä (★84,000) 61,209
Kotka (★63,000) 34,026
Kouvola (★52,000) 29,383
Kuopio 71,684
Lahti (★108,000) 94,864
Lappeenranta 52,682
Oulu (★110,000) 93,707
Pori 80,343
Tampere (★239,000) 168,118
Turku (Åbo) (★217,000) 164,857
Vaasa (Vasa) 54,402
Vantaa (Vanda) (★Helsinki) 113,176

FRANCE
1975 C 52,655,802
Aix-en-Provence 110,659
Ajaccio 50,726
Albi 46,162
Alès (★67,513) 44,245
Amiens (★512,997) 131,476
Angers (★188,695) 137,587
Angoulême (★100,528) 47,221
Annecy (★103,543) 53,262
Antibes (★Cannes) 55,960
Antony (★Paris) 57,540
Argenteuil (★Paris) 102,530
Arles (50,059▲) 37,340
Armentières (★58,000) 26,346
Arras (★79,783) 46,446
Asnières [-sur-Seine] (★Paris) 75,431
Aubervilliers (★Paris) 72,976
Aulnay-sous-Bois (★Paris) 78,137
Avignon (★162,562) 90,786
Bastia (★56,984) 50,718
Bayonne (★121,474) 42,938
Beauvais 54,089
Belfort (★75,795) 54,615
Besancon (★126,349) 120,315
Béthune (★145,155) 26,982
Béziers (★88,619) 84,029
Blois 49,778
Bondy (★Paris) 48,333
Bordeaux (★612,456) 223,131
Boulogne-Billancourt (★Paris) 103,578
Boulogne-sur-Mer (★100,581) 48,440
Bourge-en-Bresse 42,181
Bourges (★86,041) 77,300
Brest (★190,812) 166,826
Brive-la-Gaillarde 51,864
Bruay-en-Artois (★116,340) 25,714
Caen (★181,390) 119,474
Calais (★100,327) 78,820
Cambrai (★51,357) 39,049
Cannes (★210,000) 70,527
Carcassonne 42,154
Castres 45,978
Châlons-sur-Marne (★63,407) 52,275
Chalon-sur-Saône (★72,407) 58,187
Chambéry (★88,081) 54,415
Champigny-sur-Marne (★Paris) 80,291
Charleville-Mézières (★69,124) 60,176
Chartres (★72,246) 38,928
Châteauroux (★66,836) 53,429

▲ Population of an entire municipality, commune, or district, including rural area.
• Largest city in country.
★ Population or designation of the metropolitan area, including suburbs.
C Census. E Official estimate. UE Unofficial estimate.
L Population within municipal limits of year specified.

▲ Bevölkerung eines ganzen städtischen Verwaltungsgebietes, eines Kommunalbezirkes oder eines Distrikts, einschliesslich ländlicher Gebiete.
• Grösste Stadt des Landes.
★ Bevölkerung oder Bezeichnung der Stadtregion einschliess lich Vororte.
C Volkszählung. E Offizielle Schätzung.
UE Inoffizielle Schätzung.
L Bevölkerung innerhalb der städtischen Verwaltungseinheit des angegebenen Jahres.

Châttellerault (★66,836) 37,080
Cherbourg (★82,539) 32,536
Cholet 52,976
Clamart (★Paris) 52,952
Clermont-Ferrand (★253,244) 156,900
Clichy (★Paris) 47,764
Cognac 22,237
Colmar (★83,435) 64,771
Colombes (★Paris) 83,390
Compiègne (★57,210) 37,699
Courbevoie (★Paris) 54,488
Creil (★77,225) 32,509
Créteil (★Paris) 59,023
Denain (★Valenciennes) 26,204
Dieppe (★40,000) 25,822
Dijon (★208,432) 151,705
Douai (★210,508) 45,239
Drancy (★Paris) 64,430
Dunkerque (★186,314) 83,163
Elbeuf (★48,000) 19,116
Épinal (★53,522) 39,525
Fontainebleau (★36,000) 16,778
Forbach (★62,000) 25,244
Fréjus (★50,000) 28,851
Gennevilliers (★Paris) 50,290
Grenoble (★389,088) 166,037
Hayange (★75,000) 20,426
Issy-les-Moulineaux (★Paris) 47,561
Ivry-sur-Seine (★Paris) 62,856
La Rochelle (★100,649) 75,367
La Seyne-sur-Mer (★Toulon) 51,155
Laval 51,544
Le Blanc-Mesnil (★Paris) 49,107
Le Havre (★264,422) 217,881
Le Mans (★192,057) 152,285
Lens (★328,741) 40,199
Le Puy [-en-Velay] (★41,000) 26,594
Levallois-Perret (★Paris) 52,523
Lille (★1,015,000) 172,280
Limoges (★167,664) 143,689
Longwy (★83,000) 20,131
Lorient (★105,797) 69,769
Lourdes 17,870
Lyon (★1,170,660) 456,716
Mâcon 39,344
Maisons-Alfort (★Paris) 54,146
Mantes [-la-Jolie] 42,465
Marseille (★1,070,912) 908,600
Maubeuge (★105,000) 35,399
Melun (★77,272) 37,705
Menton (★34,000) 25,129
Mérignac (★Bordeaux) 50,652
Metz (★181,191) 111,869
Meudon (★Paris) 52,806
Montargis (★50,200) 18,380
Montbéliard (★132,343) 30,425
Montceau-les-Mines (★51,385) 28,177
Montluçon (★71,988) 56,468
Montpellier (★211,430) 191,354
Montreuil-sous-Bois (★Paris) 96,587
Moyeuvre [-Grande] (★77,000) 12,523
Mulhouse (★218,743) 117,013
Nancy (★280,569) 107,902
Nanterre (★Paris) 95,032
Nantes (★453,500) 256,693
Neuilly-sur-Seine (★Paris) 65,983
Nevers (★59,424) 45,480
Nice (★437,566) 344,481
Nîmes (★131,638) 127,933
Niort (★64,128) 62,267
Noisy-le-Sec (★Paris) 37,734
Orléans (★209,234) 106,246
Pantin (★Paris) 42,739
•PARIS (★9,150,000) 2,299,830
Pau (★126,859) 83,498
Périgueux (★57,830) 35,120
Perpignan (★117,689) 106,426
Pessac (★Bordeaux) 51,360
Poissy (★Paris) 37,431
Poitiers (★98,554) 81,313
Quimper 55,977
Reims (★197,021) 178,381
Rennes (★229,310) 198,305
Roanne (★83,561) 55,195
Roubaix (★Lille) 109,553
Rouen (★388,711) 114,927
Rueil-Malmaison (★Paris) 62,727
Saint-Brieuc (★82,148) 52,559
Saint-Chamond 40,250
Saint-Denis (★Paris) 96,132
Saint-Dizier 37,266
Saint-Étienne (★334,846) 220,070
Saint-Malo 45,030
Saint-Maur-des-Fossés (★Paris) 80,920
Saint-Nazaire (★119,418) 69,251
Saint-Ouen (★Paris) 43,588
Saint-Quentin (★75,056) 67,243
Sarcelles (★Paris) 55,007
Soissons (★49,000) 30,009
Strasbourg (★390,000) 253,384
Suresnes (★Paris) 37,537
Tarbes (★78,645) 54,897
Thionville (★141,881) 43,020
Toulon (★378,430) 181,801
Toulouse (★509,939) 373,796
Tourcoing (★Lille) 102,239
Tours (★245,631) 140,686
Troyes (★126,611) 72,167
Valence (★104,330) 68,604
Valenciennes (★350,599) 42,473
Vénissieux (★Lyon) 74,347
Verdun 23,621
Versailles (★Paris) 94,145
Vichy (★59,062) 32,117
Villejuif (★Paris) 55,606
Villeurbanne (★Lyon) 116,535
Vitry-sur-Seine (★Paris) 87,316

FRENCH GUIANA / Guyane française
1967 C 44,392
•CAYENNE 24,518

FRENCH POLYNESIA / Polynésie française
1971 C 119,168
•PAPEETE (★36,784) 25,342

GABON
1970 E 500,000
•LIBREVILLE (1969 C) 73,000
Port-Gentil (1970 C) 31,000

GAMBIA
1974 E 510,000
•BANJUL (BATHURST) (★80,000) 41,047

GAZA STRIP
1967 C 356,261
•GHAZZAH (GAZA) 118,272
Khān Yūnus 52,997
Rafaḥ 49,812

GERMAN DEMOCRATIC REPUBLIC (EAST GERMANY) / Deutsche Demokratische Republik
1974 E 16,890,760
Altenburg 51,193
•BERLIN, OST-(EAST BERLIN) (★Berlin) 1,094,147
Bitterfeld (★110,000) 27,062
Brandenburg 94,071
Cottbus 94,293
Dessau (★135,000) 100,820
Dresden (★640,000) 507,692
Erfurt 202,979
Frankfurt an der Oder 70,817
Freiberg 50,815
Gera 113,108
Görlitz 84,658
Gotha 59,243
Greifswald 53,940
Halle (★475,000) 241,425
Halle-Neustadt (★Halle) 67,956
Hoyerswerda 64,904
Jena 99,431
Karl-Marx-Stadt (Chemnitz) (★460,000) 303,811
Leipzig (★725,000) 570,972
Magdeburg (★390,000) 276,089
Merseburg (★Halle) 54,269
Neubrandenburg 59,971
Plauen 80,353
Potsdam (★Berlin) 117,236
Rostock 210,167
Schwerin 104,984
Stralsund 72,167
Weimar 63,144
Wismar 56,765
Wittenberg 51,364
Zwickau (★175,000) 123,069

GERMANY, FEDERAL REPUBLIC OF (WEST GERMANY) / Bundesrepublik Deutschland
1974 E 61,991,300
Aachen (★540,000) 242,416
Aalen (★78,000) 50,762
Ahlen (1975 L) 54,714
Albstadt (1975 L) 51,488
Alsdorf (★Aachen) 48,085
Amberg 47,432
Ansbach 39,673
Arnsberg (1975 L) 81,049
Aschaffenburg (★140,000) 54,535
Augsburg (★385,000) 254,053
Baden-Baden (1975 L) 50,201
Bad Homburg (★Frankfurt am Main) 51,465
Bad Kreuznach 43,047
Bad Oeynhausen 44,839
Bad Salzuflen (★Herford) 51,635
Bamberg (★120,000) 75,378
Bayreuth (★85,000) 66,936
Bergisch Gladbach (★Köln) (1975 L) 98,679
Berlin, West-(★3,850,000) 2,023,987
Bielefeld 319,611
Bocholt (1975 L) 65,675
Bochum (★Essen) (1975 L) 417,336
BONN (★535,000) 283,891
Bottrop (★Essen) (1975 E) 101,495
Braunschweig (Brunswick) (★340,000) 271,213
Bremen (★805,000) 579,430
Bremerhaven (★190,000) 144,529
Brühl (★Köln) (1975 L) 44,084
Castrop-Rauxel (★Essen) (1975 L) 83,421
Celle 74,845
Coburg 46,646
Cuxhaven 60,669
Darmstadt (★295,000) 138,871
Delmenhorst (★Bremen) 70,992
Detmold 65,677
Dinslaken (★Essen) (1975 L) 56,741
Dormagen (★Köln) (1975 L) 54,894
Dorsten (★Essen) (1975 L) 64,761
Dortmund (★Essen) (1975 L) 636,954
Duisburg (★Essen) (1975 L) 599,799
Düren (★107,000) 88,579
Düsseldorf (1975 L) (★1,150,000) 675,437
Emden 53,911
Erlangen (★Nürnberg) 100,550
Eschweiler (★Aachen) 53,999
•Essen (1975 L) (★5,350,000) 684,147
Esslingen (★Stuttgart) 97,029
Euskirchen 43,695
Flensburg (★107,000) 94,528
Frankfurt am Main (★1,825,000) 652,037
Freiburg (★210,000) 179,196
Friedrichshafen (1975 L) 51,930
Fulda (★78,000) 59,696
Fürth (★Nürnberg) 103,238
Garbsen (★Hannover) 56,356
Gelsenkirchen (★Essen) 327,591
Giessen (★155,000) 76,217
Gladbeck (1975 E) 81,220
Göppingen (1975 L) (★150,000) 55,415
Goslar (★82,000) 54,041
Göttingen 122,428
Grevenbroich (1975 L) 56,935
Gütersloh 78,195
Hagen (★Essen) (1975 L) 231,840
Hamburg (★2,250,000) 1,733,802
Hameln (★70,000) 61,722
Hamm (1975 L) 172,686
Hanau (★Frankfurt am Main) 88,017
Hannover (★980,000) 562,951
Hattingen (★Essen) 58,929
Heidelberg (★Mannheim) (1975 E) 129,368
Heidenheim (★85,000) 50,765
Heilbronn (★225,000) 115,924
Herford (★120,000) 64,675
Herne (★Essen) (1975 L) 193,831
Herten (★Essen) (1975 L) 70,795
Hilden (★Düsseldorf) (1975 L) 52,852
Hildesheim (★137,000) 106,734
Hof 55,041
Hürth (★Köln) (1975 L) 52,526
Ingolstadt (★130,000) 90,357
Iserlohn (1975 L) 97,194
Kaiserslautern (★136,000) 102,119
Karlsruhe (1975 E) (★500,000) 280,448
Kassel (★365,000) 210,042
Kempten 57,022
Kiel (★345,000) 264,290
Koblenz (★175,000) 119,295
Köln (Cologne) (1975 L) (★1,700,000) 1,022,075
Konstanz (1975 L) 65,963
Krefeld (★Essen) (1975 L) 231,642
Landshut 56,405
Leverkusen (★Köln) (1975 L) 167,671
Lippstadt (1975 L) 63,983
Lübeck (★275,000) 234,510
Lüdenscheid 78,002
Ludwigsburg (★Stuttgart) (1975 L) 85,236
Ludwigshafen (★Mannheim) 173,976
Lüneburg 65,301
Lünen (★Essen) (1975 L) 85,876
Mainz (★Wiesbaden) 184,030
Mannheim (★1,390,000) 320,508
Marburg an der Lahn 71,604
Marl (★Essen) (1975 L) 91,779
Meerbusch (★Düsseldorf) 50,631
Menden [Sauerland] (1975 L) 53,530
Minden (★120,000) 79,739
Moers (★Essen) (1975 L) 101,738
Mönchengladbach (1975 L) (★390,000) 263,356
Mülheim an der Ruhr (★Essen) (1975 L) 190,689
München (Munich) (★1,850,000) 1,323,434
Münster (1975 L) 262,567
Neumünster 85,645
Neunkirchen (★135,000) 55,884
Neuss (★Düsseldorf) (1975 L) 147,833
Neustadt [an der Weinstrasse] 51,124
Neuwied (★145,000) 62,598
Norderstedt (★Hamburg) 61,452
Nordhorn 49,844
Nürnberg (★1,035,000) 509,813
Oberhausen (★Essen) 239,309
Offenbach (★Frankfurt am Main) 117,947
Offenburg (1975 L) 51,888
Oldenburg 134,280
Osnabrück (★265,000) 163,674
Paderborn (1975 L) 103,230
Passau 50,669
Pforzheim (1975 E) (★220,000) 108,635
Pirmasens 54,631
Ratingen (★Düsseldorf) (1975 L) 84,634
Recklinghausen (★Essen) 123,229
Regensburg (★190,000) 133,183
Remscheid (★Wuppertal) (1975 L) 135,810
Reutlingen (1975 L) (★148,000) 96,157
Rheine (1975 L) 71,900
Rüsselsheim (★Wiesbaden) 60,221
Saarbrücken (★405,000) 205,987
Saarlouis (★115,000) 40,057
Salzgitter 120,090
Schwäbisch Gmünd (1975 L) 57,212
Schweinfurt (★110,000) 56,976
Siegen (1975 L) (★205,000) 117,224
Sindelfingen (★Stuttgart) 54,638
Singen (1975 L) 46,609
Solingen (★Wuppertal) (1975 L) 175,298
Stolberg (★Aachen) 57,583
Stuttgart (★1,875,000) 613,263
Trier (★125,000) 101,145
Troisdorf (★Bonn) 56,725
Tübingen 71,175
Ulm (1975 L) (★200,000) 98,499
Unna (★Essen) 53,897
Velbert (★Essen) (1975 L) 97,021
Viersen (★Mönchengladbach) 85,175
Villingen-Schwenningen (1975 L) 81,772
Wesel (1975 L) 56,493
Wetzlar (★100,000) 36,640
Wiesbaden (★750,000) 252,017
Wilhelmshaven (★135,000) 104,218
Witten (★Essen) (1975 L) 109,554
Wolfenbüttel (★Braunschweig) 53,064
Wolfsburg 130,232
Worms 76,316
Wuppertal (1975 L) (★920,000) 412,403
Würzburg (★195,000) 113,121

GHANA
1970 C 8,559,313
•ACCRA (★738,498) 633,880
Cape Coast 71,594
Koforidua 46,235
Kumasi 345,117
Sekondi-Takoradi 160,868
Tamale 83,653
Tema 60,767

GIBRALTAR
1976 E 30,000
•GIBRALTAR 30,000

GREECE / Ellás
1971 C 8,768,641
Agrínion (★41,794) 30,973
Aiyáleo (★Athínai) 79,961
Árgos 18,890
•ATHÍNAI (ATHENS) (★2,540,241) 867,023
Ilioúpolis (★Athínai) 49,215
Ioánnina (Yanina) 40,130
Iráklion (Candia) (★84,710) 77,506
Kalámai (★40,402) 39,133
Kallithéa (★Athínai) 82,438
Kavála 46,234
Keratsínion (★Athínai) 67,672
Khalkís (Chalcis) 36,300
Khaniá (Canea) (★53,026) 40,564
Khíos (Chios) (★30,021) 24,084
Koridhallós (★Athínai) 47,335
Kórinthos (Corinth) 20,773
Lárisa 72,336
Mégara 17,294
Néa Ionía (★Athínai) 54,906
Néa Liósia (★Athínai) 56,217
Níkaia (★Athínai) 86,269
Pátrai (Patras) (★120,847) 111,607
Peristérion (★Athínai) 118,413
Piraiévs (Piraeus) (★Athínai) 187,362
Ródhos (Rhodes) 32,092
Spárti (Sparta) (★13,432) 10,549
Thessaloníki (Salonika) (★557,360) 345,799
Thívai (Thebes) 15,971
Tríkkala 34,794
Vólos (★88,096) 51,290
Zografós (★Athínai) 56,722

GREENLAND / Grønland
1975 E 49,502
•GODTHÅB 8,328

GRENADA
1970 C 93,858
•SAINT GEORGE'S (★23,000) 7,303

GUADELOUPE
1967 C 312,724
BASSE-TERRE (★25,985) 15,690
•Pointe-à-Pitre (★54,519) 33,107

GUAM
1970 C 84,996
•AGANA (★29,000) 2,119

GUATEMALA
1973 C 5,211,929
•GUATEMALA (★945,000) 717,322
Quezaltenango 45,977

GUERNSEY
1971 C 53,734
•ST. PETER PORT (★36,000) 16,303

GUINEA / Guinée
1967 E 3,702,000
•CONAKRY (1967 C) 197,267

GUINEA-BISSAU
1970 C 487,448
•BISSAU 71,169

GUYANA
1970 C 699,848
•GEORGETOWN (★164,039) 63,184

HAITI / Haïti
1971 C 4,314,628
Cap-Haïtien 46,217
•PORT-AU-PRINCE (★493,932) 458,675

HONDURAS
1974 C 2,656,948
San Pedro Sula 150,991
•TEGUCIGALPA 273,894

HONG KONG
1971 C 3,950,802
Kowloon (★Victoria) 715,440
New Kowloon (★Victoria) 1,479,417
North Point (★Victoria) (1966 E) 350,000
Tai Wan Tsun (Ngau Tau Kok) (★Victoria) (1961 C) 53,836
Tsun Wan (★Victoria) 267,670
•VICTORIA (HONG KONG) (★3,575,000) 521,612

HUNGARY / Magyarország
1977 E 10,625,300
Békéscsaba (64,000▲) 55,700
•BUDAPEST (★2,535,000) 2,081,700
Debrecen 190,000
Dunaújváros 57,000
Eger 59,000
Győr 120,000
Hódmezővásárhely (54,000▲) 45,200
Kaposvár 70,000
Kecskemét (92,000▲) 73,400
Miskolc 203,000
Nyíregyháza (95,000▲) 75,000
Pécs 164,000
Sopron 54,000
Szeged 171,000
Székesfehérvár 98,000
Szolnok 73,000
Szombathely 79,000
Tatabánya 73,000
Veszprém 51,000
Zalaegerszeg 51,000

ICELAND / Ísland
1976 E 220,918
•REYKJAVÍK (★117,761) 84,493

▲ Población de un municipio, comuna o distrito entero, incluyendo sus áreas rurales.
• Ciudad más grande de un país.
★ Población o designación de un área metropolitana, incluyendo los suburbios.
C Censo. E Estimado oficial.
UE Estimado no oficial.
L Población dentro de los límites municipales de un año especifico.

▲ Population d'une municipalité, d'une commune ou d'un district, zone rurale incluse.
• Ville la plus peuplée du pays.
★ Population de l'agglomération (ou nom de la zone métropolitaine englobante).
C Recensement. E Estimation officielle.
UE Estimation non officielle.
L Population comprise dans les limites municipales de l'année indiquée.

▲ População de um município, comuna ou distrito, inclusive as respectivas áreas rurais.
• Maior cidade de um país.
★ População ou indicação de uma área metropolitana, inclusive subúrbios.
C Censo. E Estimativa oficial.
UE Estimativa não oficial.
L População dentro dos limites municipais no ano indicado.

INDIA / Bhārat

1971 C....................547,949,809
Abohar.................... 58,925
Achalpur (Ellichpur) (★66,451).. 42,326
Ādoni.................... 85,311
Agartala (★100,264)............ 59,625
Āgra (★634,622)................591,917
Ahmadābād (★1,950,000)......1,585,544
Ahmadnagar (★148,405).........118,236
Ajmer (★264,291)...............262,851
Akola.........................168,438
Alandur (★Madras)............ 65,039
Alīgarh.......................252,314
Alīpur Duār (★54,454).......... 36,667
Allahābād (★513,036)...........490,622
Alleppey......................160,166
Alwar.........................100,378
Amalner...................... 55,544
Ambāla (★186,126)............ 83,633
Ambāla Cantonment
(★Ambāla)...................102,493
Ambarnāth (★Bombay)......... 56,276
Āmbūr........................ 54,011
Amrāvati (Amraoti) (★221,277)..193,800
Amritsar (★458,029)............407,628
Amroha........................ 82,702
Anakapalle.................... 57,273
Ānand......................... 59,155
Anantapur..................... 80,069
Arcot (★75,911)............... 30,230
Arrah......................... 92,919
Aruppukkottai................. 62,223
Asansol (★925,000)............155,968
Aurangābād (★165,253).........150,483
Avadi (★Madras).............. 77,413
Badagara...................... 53,938
Bāgalkot...................... 51,746
Bahraich...................... 73,931
Baidyabāti (★Calcutta)......... 54,130
Ballia........................ 47,101
Bālurghāt..................... 67,088
Bānda......................... 50,575
Bangalore (★1,750,000)........1,540,741
Bangaon....................... 50,538
Bānkura....................... 79,129
Bansbāria (★Calcutta)......... 61,748
Baranagar (★Calcutta).........136,842
Bareilly (★326,106)...........296,248
Baroda (Vadodara) (★467,487)...466,696
Barrackpore (★Calcutta)....... 96,889
Bārsi......................... 62,374
Basīrhāt...................... 63,816
Batāla (★76,488).............. 58,200
Beāwar........................ 66,114
Behāla (South Suburban)
(★Calcutta)..................272,600
Belgaum (★213,872)............192,427
Bellary.......................125,183
Berhampore *(West Bengal St.)*
(★78,909).................... 72,605
Berhampur *(Orissa St.)*..........117,662
Bettiah....................... 51,018
Bhadrāvati (★101,358)......... 40,203
Bhāgalpur.....................172,202
Bharatpur (★69,902)........... 68,036
Bhatinda (★65,318)............ 53,684
Bhātpāra (★Calcutta)..........204,750
Bhaunagar (★225,974)..........225,358
Bhavāni (★56,696)............. 23,114
Bhilai (Bhilainagar)
(★245,124)...................157,173
Bhīlwāra...................... 82,155
Bhīmavaram.................... 63,762
Bhiwandi (★Bombay)........... 79,576
Bhiwāni....................... 73,086
Bhopāl (★384,859).............298,022
Bhubaneswar...................105,491
Bhuj (★52,861)................ 52,177
Bhusāwal (★104,708)........... 96,800
Bīdar......................... 50,670
Bihar.........................100,046
Bijāpur.......................103,931
Bīkaner (★208,894)............188,518
Bilāspur (★130,740)........... 98,410
Bīr (Bhir).................... 49,965
Bodināyakkanūr................ 54,176
Bokāro Steel City (★107,159).... 94,007
Bombay (★6,750,000)..........5,970,575
Broach (Bharuch) (★92,251)..... 91,589
Budaun........................ 72,204
Budge Budge (★Calcutta)...... 51,039
Bulandshahr................... 59,505
Bulsār (Valsad) (★54,966)....... 43,254
Burdwān.......................143,318
Burhānpur (★105,335)..........105,246
•Calcutta (★9,100,000).........3,148,746
Calicut (Kozhikode)...........333,979
Cambay........................ 62,097
Cannanore (★59,912)........... 55,162
Champdāni (★Calcutta)......... 58,596
Chandannagar (Chandernagore)
(★Calcutta).................. 75,238
Chandausi..................... 53,393
Chandīgarh (★232,940).........218,743
Chandrapur.................... 75,134
Chāpra (★98,401).............. 83,101
Chhindwāra (★53,508).......... 53,492
Chidambaram (★57,658)........ 48,811
Chīrāla....................... 54,487
Chitradurga................... 50,254
Chittoor...................... 63,035
Churu (★53,185)............... 52,502
Cochin........................439,066
Coimbatore (★750,000).........356,368
Cooch Behār (★62,664)......... 53,684
Coonoor (★70,813)............. 38,007
Cuddalore.....................101,335
Cuddapah...................... 66,195
Cuttack (★205,759)............194,068
Damoh (★59,983).............. 59,489
Darbhanga.....................132,059
Darjeeling.................... 42,873
Dāvangere.....................121,110
Dehra Dūn (★203,464)..........166,073
Delhi (★4,500,000)............3,706,558
Delhi Cantonment (★Delhi)..... 57,339
Deolāli (★Nāsik).............. 55,436
Dewās (★51,866)............... 51,545
Dhānbād (★600,000)............ 79,838
Dhorāji (★60,080)............. 59,773
Dhule (Dhulia)................137,129
Dibrugarh..................... 80,348
Dindigul......................128,429
Dohad (★51,406)............... 44,506
Dombivli (★Bombay)........... 51,108
Durg (★Bhilai)................ 67,892
Durgapur......................206,638
Elūru (Ellore).................127,023
English Bāzār (★68,026)......... 61,335
Erode (★169,613)..............105,111
Etāwah........................ 85,894
Faizābād (★109,806)...........102,835
Farīdābād New Township
(★Delhi)..................... 85,762
Farrukhābād (★110,835)........102,768
Fatehpur...................... 54,665
Fīrozābād.....................133,863
Fīrozpur (Ferozepore) (★97,709). 49,545
Gadag......................... 95,426
Garden Reach (★Calcutta)......154,913
Gauhāti (★200,377)............123,783
Gaya..........................179,884
Ghāziābād (★Delhi)...........118,836
Godhra (★66,853).............. 66,403
Gonda......................... 52,662
Gondal (★55,329).............. 54,928
Gondia........................ 77,992
Gorakhpur.....................230,911
Govindpura (★Bhopāl)......... 53,922
Gudivāda...................... 61,068
Gudiyāttam (★67,966).......... 63,007
Gulbarga......................145,588
Guntakal...................... 66,320
Guntūr........................269,991
Gurgaon....................... 57,151
Gwalior (★406,140)............384,772
Hābra (★93,351)............... 51,435
Haldwāni...................... 52,205
Hālisahar (★Calcutta)......... 68,906
Hāpur......................... 71,266
Hardwār (★79,277)............. 77,864
Hassan........................ 51,325
Hāthras....................... 74,349
Hazāribāgh.................... 54,818
Hisār......................... 89,437
Hooghly-Chinsura (★Calcutta)..105,241
Hoshiārpur.................... 57,691
Hospet........................ 65,196
Howrah (★Calcutta)............737,877
Hubli-Dhārwār.................379,166
Hyderābād (★2,000,000).......1,607,396
Ichalkaranji.................. 87,731
Imphāl........................100,366
Indore (★560,936).............543,381
Jabalpur (★534,845)...........426,224
Jabalpur Cantonment
(★Jabalpur).................. 50,195
Jagādhri (★115,020)........... 35,094
Jagannāthnagar (★Rānchi)...... 55,663
Jaipur........................615,258
Jālgaon.......................106,711
Jālna......................... 91,099
Jalpaiguri.................... 55,159
Jamālpur (★Monghyr).......... 61,731
Jammu (★164,207)..............155,338
Jāmnagar (★227,640)...........199,709
Jamshedpur (★456,146).........341,576
Jaunpur....................... 80,737
Jhānsi (★198,135).............173,292
Jodhpur.......................317,612
Jorhāt (★70,674).............. 30,247
Jullundur (★329,830)..........296,106
Junāgadh (★95,900)............ 95,485
Kadaiyanallūr................. 50,295
Kākināda......................164,200
Kālol (★Ahmadābād)........... 50,321
Kalyān (★Bombay)............. 99,547
Kamarhati (★Calcutta).........169,404
Kāmthi (★Nāgpur)............. 53,412
Kānchipuram (Conjeeveram)
(★119,693)...................110,657
Kānchrāpāra (★Calcutta)....... 78,768
Kānpur (★1,320,000)..........1,154,388
Kānpur Cantonment (★Kānpur). 69,452
Kāraikkudi (★88,371).......... 55,449
Karnāl........................ 92,784
Karūr......................... 65,706
Katihār (★80,121)............. 67,014
Kayankulam (Kayamkulam).... 54,102
Kerkend (★Dhānbād)........... 51,314
Khadki (Kirkee) (★Pune)....... 65,497
Khāmgaon...................... 53,692
Khammam....................... 56,919
Khandwa (★85,403)............. 84,517
Kharagpur (★161,257).......... 61,783
Khurja........................ 50,245
Kolar Gold Fields (★118,861).... 76,112
Kolhāpur (★267,513)...........259,050
Kota..........................212,991
Kottagūdem.................... 75,542
Kottayam...................... 59,714
Krishnanagar.................. 85,923
Kumbakonam (★119,655).........113,130
Kurnool.......................136,710
Lātūr......................... 70,156
Lucknow (★840,000)............749,239
Ludhiāna (★401,176)...........397,850
Machilīpatnam (Bandar)........112,612
Madras (★3,200,000)..........2,469,449
Madurai (★725,000)............549,114
Mahbūbnagar................... 51,756
Mālegaon......................191,847
Mandasor (★56,988)............ 52,347
Mandya........................ 72,132
Mangalore (★215,122)..........165,174
Mathura (★140,150)............132,028
Maunath Bhanjan............... 64,058
Māyūram....................... 60,195
Meerut (★367,754).............270,993
Meerut Cantonment (★Meerut). 85,415
Mehsāna (Mahesāna) (★51,713). 51,598
Mhow (★63,739)................ 59,037
Midnapore..................... 71,326
Miraj (★Sāngli)............... 77,606
Mirzāpur......................105,939
Moga (★61,625)................ 55,270
Monghyr (★164,205)............102,474
Morādābād (★272,652)..........258,590
Morvi......................... 60,976
Murwāra (Katni) (★86,535)...... 54,864
Muzaffarnagar.................114,783
Muzaffarpur...................126,379
Mysore........................355,685
Nabadwīp...................... 94,204
Nadiād........................108,269
Nāgappattinam (★74,019)....... 68,026
Nāgercoil.....................141,288
Nāgpur (★950,000).............866,076
Naihāti (★Calcutta)........... 82,080
Nānded........................126,538
Nandurbār..................... 54,070
Nandyāl....................... 63,193
Nāsik (★271,681)..............176,091
Navsāri (★80,101)............. 72,979
Nellore.......................133,590
NEW DELHI (★Delhi)...........301,801
Neyveli....................... 58,285
Nizāmābād.....................115,640
North Barrackpore (★Calcutta). 76,335
North Dum-Dum (★Calcutta)... 63,873
Nowgong....................... 56,537
Ongole........................ 53,330
Ootacamund.................... 63,310
Outer Burnpur (★Asansol)...... 56,900
Pālayankottai (★Tirunelveli).... 70,070
Pālghāt....................... 95,788
Pallavaram (★Madras)......... 51,374
Palni (★51,664)............... 49,575
Panaji (Panjim) (Nova Goa)
(★59,258).................... 34,953
Pānchur (★Calcutta)........... 59,021
Pandharpur.................... 53,638
Pānihāti (★Calcutta)..........148,046
Pānīpat....................... 87,981
Parbhani...................... 61,570
Pātan......................... 64,519
Pathānkot (★78,192)........... 76,355
Patiāla (★151,041)............148,686
Patna (★625,000)..............473,001
Phagwāra (★55,012)............ 50,863
Pīlībhīt...................... 68,273
Pimpri-Chinchwad (★Pune).... 83,542
Pollāchi (★93,838)............ 68,655
Pondicherry (★153,325)........ 90,637
Porbandar (★106,727).......... 96,881
Proddatūr..................... 70,822
Pudukkottai................... 66,384
Pune (Poona) (★1,175,000)......856,105
Pune Cantonment (★Pune)..... 77,774
Puri.......................... 72,674
Purnea (★71,311).............. 56,484
Purūlia....................... 57,708
Quilon........................124,208
Rāichūr....................... 79,831
Raipur (★205,986).............174,518
Rājahmundry (★188,805)........165,912
Rājapālaiyam.................. 86,952
Rājkot........................300,612
Rāj-Nāndgaon (★55,827)........ 41,183
Rāmpur........................161,417
Rānchī (★255,551).............175,934
Ratlām (★119,247).............106,666
Raurkela (★172,502)...........125,426
Rewa.......................... 69,182
Rishra (★Calcutta)............ 63,486
Rohtak........................124,755
Roorkee (★62,456)............. 47,561
Sāgar (★154,785)..............118,574
Sahāranpur....................225,396
Salem (★416,440)..............308,716
Sambalpur (★105,085).......... 64,675
Sambhal....................... 86,323
Sāngli (★201,597).............115,138
Sāntipur...................... 61,166
Sātāra........................ 66,433
Satna (★62,162)............... 57,531
Secunderābād Cantonment
(★Hyderābād)................ 94,416
Serampore (★Calcutta).........102,023
Shāhjahānpur (★144,065).......135,604
Shillong (★122,752)........... 87,659
Shimoga.......................102,709
Shivpuri (★50,858)............ 42,120
Sholāpur......................398,361
Sīkar......................... 70,987
Silchar....................... 52,596
Silīguri...................... 97,484
Simla......................... 55,368
Singānallūr (★Coimbatore).....112,206
Sītāpur....................... 66,715
Sivakāsi (★60,753)............ 44,883
Sonīpat....................... 62,393
South Dum-Dum (★Calcutta)..174,342
Sri Gangānagar (Gangānagar).. 90,042
Srīnagar (★415,271)...........403,413
Srīrangam (★Tiruchchirāppalli) .51,069
Srīvilliputtūr................ 53,855
Surat (★493,001)..............471,656
Surendranagar (★97,251)....... 66,667
Tāmbaram (★Madras)........... 58,805
Tellicherry................... 68,759
Tenāli........................102,937
Thāna (★Bombay)..............170,675
Thanjāvūr (Tanjore)...........140,547
Tinsukia...................... 54,911
Tiruchchirāppalli (Trichinopoly)
(★475,000)...................307,400
Tiruchendūr (★55,636)......... 18,126
Tirunelveli (★266,688)........108,498
Tirupati (★71,984)............ 65,843
Tiruppur (★151,127)...........113,302
Tiruvannāmalai................ 61,370
Tiruvottiyūr (★Madras)........ 82,853
Titāgarh (★Calcutta).......... 88,218
Tonk.......................... 55,866
Trichūr....................... 76,241
Trivandrum....................409,627
Tumkūr........................ 70,476
Tuticorin (★181,913)..........155,310
Udaipur.......................161,278
Ujjain (★208,561).............203,278
Ulhāsnagar (★Bombay).........168,462
Uttarpara-Kotrung (★Calcutta). 67,568
Valparai...................... 95,175
Vāniyambādi (★57,686)......... 51,810
Vārānasi (Benares) (★606,271)..583,856
Vellore (★178,554)............139,082
Verāval (★75,520)............. 58,771
Vijayawāda (★344,607).........317,258
Villupuram.................... 60,242
Virudunagar................... 61,902
Vishākhapatnam (★363,467).....352,504
Vizianagaram.................. 86,608
Warangal......................207,520
Wardha........................ 69,037
Yamunānagar (★Jagādhri)..... 72,594
Yavatmāl...................... 64,836

INDONESIA

1971 C....................119,232,499
Ambon (Amboina).............. 79,636
Balikpapan....................137,340
Banda Aceh (Kutaradja)....... 53,668
Bandung (★1,250,000).........1,201,730
Banjarmasin...................281,673
Banyuwangi.................... 89,303
Binjai........................ 59,882
Blitar........................ 67,856
Blora......................... 53,504
Bogor.........................195,882
Bojonegoro.................... 52,597
Bukittinggi................... 63,132
Cianjur (Tjiandjur)...........144,803
Cilacap (Tjilatjap)............ 82,043
Cimahi (Tjimahi).............. 72,367
Cirebon (Tjirebon)............178,529
Denpasar...................... 88,142
Garut......................... 81,234
Gorontalo..................... 82,328
•JAKARTA (DJAKARTA)
(★4,650,000).................4,576,009
Jambi (Telanaipura)...........158,559
Jember........................122,712
Jombang....................... 45,450
Kediri........................178,865
Krawang....................... 61,361
Kudus......................... 87,767
Kupang........................ 52,698
Langsa........................ 55,016
Madiun........................136,147
Magelang......................110,308
Malang........................422,428
Manado........................169,684
Martapura..................... 69,729
Medan.........................635,562
Mojokerto..................... 60,013
Padang........................196,339
Pakanbaru.....................145,030
Palembang.....................582,961
Pangkalpinang................. 74,733
Parepare...................... 72,538
Pasuruan...................... 75,266
Payakumbuh.................... 63,388
Pekalongan....................111,537
Pemalang...................... 77,672
Pematangsiantar...............129,232
Ponorogo...................... 67,711
Pontianak.....................217,555
Probolinggo................... 82,008
Purwakarta.................... 49,703
Purwokerto.................... 94,023
Purworejo..................... 52,956
Salatiga...................... 69,831
Samarinda.....................137,521
Semarang......................646,590
Serang........................ 56,263
Situbondo..................... 55,348
Solok......................... 24,771
Sukabumi...................... 96,242
Surabaya (★1,650,000).........1,556,255
Surakarta.....................414,285
Tangerang..................... 50,893
Tanjungkarang-Telukbetung...198,986
Tasikmalaya...................136,004
Tegal.........................105,752
Tulungagung................... 68,899
Ujung Pandang (Makasar).....434,766
Watampone (Bone)............. 54,720
Yogyakarta (Jogjakarta).......342,267

IRAN / Īrān

1966 C.....................25,323,064
Ābādān (1972 E)...............306,000
Ahvāz (1972 E)................286,000
Arāk.......................... 71,925
Ardabīl....................... 83,596
Bābol......................... 49,973
Borūjerd...................... 71,486
Dezfūl........................ 84,499
Eşfahān (Isfahan) (1972 E)......575,000
Gorgān........................ 51,181
Hamadān (1971 E)..............141,000
Kāshān........................ 58,468
Kermān (1972 E)...............100,000
Kermānshāh (1972 E)...........239,000
Khorramābād................... 59,578
Khorramshahr.................. 88,536
Marāgheh...................... 54,106
Mashhad (Meshed) (1972 E)....562,000
Masjed Soleymān............... 64,488
Qazvīn (1972 E)...............104,000
Qom (1972 E)..................164,000
Rasht (1972 E)................170,000
Rey (★Tehrān).................102,825
Reżā'īyeh (1972 E)............148,000
Sanandaj...................... 54,578
Shīrāz (1972 E)...............356,000
Tabrīz (1972 E)...............493,000
Tajrīsh (★Tehrān).............157,486
•TEHRĀN (1973 E) (★4,350,000)..3,774,000
Yazd (1972 E).................117,000
Zanjān........................ 58,714

▲ Population of an entire municipality, commune, or district, including rural area.
• Largest city in country.
★ Population or designation of the metropolitan area, including suburbs.
C Census. E Official estimate. UE Unofficial estimate.
L Population within municipal limits of year specified.

▲ Bevölkerung eines ganzen städtischen Verwaltungsgebietes, eines Kommunalbezirkes oder eines Distrikts, einschliesslich ländlicher Gebiete.
• Grösste Stadt des Landes.
★ Bevölkerung oder Bezeichnung der Stadtregion einschliess lich Vororte.
C Volkszählung. E Offizielle Schätzung.
UE Inoffizielle Schätzung.
L Bevölkerung innerhalb der städtischen Verwaltungseinheit des angegebenen Jahres.

IRAQ / Al-ʿIrāq
1970 E. 9,465,800
Ad-Dīwānīyah 62,300
Al-ʿAmārah 80,100
Al-Baṣrah (Basra) 370,900
Al-Ḥillah (Hilla) 128,800
Al-Mawṣil (Mosul) 293,100
An-Najaf 179,200
An-Nāṣirīyah 62,400
As-Sulaymānīyah 98,100
•BAGHDĀD (★2,183,800) 1,300,000
Irbīl 107,400
Karbalā' 107,500
Kirkūk 207,900

IRELAND / Eire
1971 C 2,978,248
Cork (Corcaigh) (★134,430) 128,645
•DUBLIN (BAILE ÁTHA CLIATH) (★835,000) 567,866
Dún Laoghaire (★Dublin) 53,171
Limerick (Luimneach) (★63,002) 57,161
Waterford (Port Láirge) (★33,676) 31,968

ISLE OF MAN
1971 C 56,289
•DOUGLAS (★28,000) 20,389

ISRAEL / Yisra'el
1975 E 3,493,200
Ashdod 52,500
Bat Yam (★Tel Aviv-Yafo) 118,100
Be'er Sheva' (Beersheba) 96,500
Bene Beraq (★Tel Aviv-Yafo) 83,000
Giv'atayim (★Tel Aviv-Yafo) 50,000
Ḥefa (Haifa) (★395,000) 227,200
Ḥolon (★Tel Aviv-Yafo) 114,000
Naẕerat (Nazareth) (★58,000) 36,700
Netanya 82,400
Petaḥ Tiqwa (★Tel Aviv-Yafo) 106,800
Ramat Gan (★Tel Aviv-Yafo) 121,100
Rehovot 50,100
Rishon leẔiyyon (★Tel Aviv-Yafo) 68,300
•Tel Aviv-Yafo (Tel Aviv-Jaffa) (★1,260,000) 353,800
YERUSHALAYIM (AL-QUDS) (JERUSALEM) (incl. Old City) (★375,000) 355,500

ITALY / Italia
1976 E 56,322,605
Afragola (★Napoli) 57,488
Agrigento 49,979
Alessandria 102,910
Ancona 107,829
Andria 81,646
Arezzo 91,299
Ascoli Piceno 56,448
Asti 80,021
Avellino 58,574
Aversa 50,374
Bari 384,374
Barletta 78,991
Benevento (61,856▲) 52,300
Bergamo (★335,000) 127,816
Biella 56,148
Bologna (★560,000) 485,643
Bolzano (Bozen) 106,913
Brescia 215,156
Brindisi 87,160
Busto Arsizio (★Milano) 82,037
Cagliari (★295,000) 240,256
Caltanissetta (60,713▲) 54,100
Carpi (58,763▲) 50,900
Carrara (★Massa) 70,181
Caserta 65,074
Casoria (★Napoli) 64,515
Castellammare di Stabia 73,049
Catania 399,773
Catanzaro 91,989
Cerignola (50,188▲) 44,200
Cesena (89,527▲) 67,500
Chieti 55,530
Chioggia (53,038▲) 37,800
Cinisello Balsamo (★Milano) 79,720
Cologno Monzese (★Milano) 50,461
Como (★160,000) 97,319
Cosenza 102,375
Cremona 82,489
Crotone 55,364
Cuneo 56,088
Ercolano (Resina) (★Napoli) 55,013
Faenza (55,635▲) 40,300
Fano (52,046▲) 42,900
Ferrara (155,172▲) 127,200
Firenze (Florence) (★660,000) 464,792
Foggia 153,334
Foligno (52,086▲) 45,700
Forlì (109,618▲) 91,800
Gela 73,268
Genova (Genoa) (★870,000) 800,532
Grosseto (68,345▲) 60,300
Imola (59,649▲) 47,500
L'Aquila 65,451
La Spezia (★193,000) 121,075
Latina (90,515▲) 79,400
Lecce 88,499
Lecco 54,335
Livorno (Leghorn) 177,687
Lucca 91,658
Manfredonia (51,158▲) 44,100
Mantova 65,574
Marsala (84,014▲) 49,200
Massa (★144,000) 65,332
Messina 265,318
•Milano (Milan) (★3,780,000) 1,705,086
Modena 178,530
Molfetta 65,643
Moncalieri (★Torino) 63,104
Monza (★Milano) 120,574
Napoli (Naples) (★2,030,000) 1,223,927
Nicastro (Lamezia Terme) (60,257▲) 29,000
Nocera Inferiore (51,459▲) 43,200
Novara 102,132
Padova (★280,000) 242,186
Palermo 673,163
Parma 177,894
Pavia 87,909
Perugia 136,799
Pesaro 89,890
Pescara 135,167
Piacenza 109,250
Pisa 103,479
Pistoia (94,684▲) 84,700
Pordenone 52,319
Portici (★Napoli) 83,135
Potenza 62,440
Pozzuoli (★Napoli) (67,510▲) 58,800
Prato (★196,000) 154,362
Ragusa (64,789▲) 53,700
Ravenna (138,172▲) 101,400
Reggio di Calabria 177,883
Reggio nell'Emilia 129,674
Rimini 125,815
Rivoli (★Torino) 50,003
ROMA (ROME) (★3,150,000) 2,883,996
Rovigo 51,784
Salerno (★235,000) 161,645
San Giorgio a Cremano (★Napoli) 61,516
San Remo (64,376▲) 53,200
San Severo 53,810
Sassari 115,990
Savona (★122,000) 79,662
Scandicci (★Firenze) 53,555
Sesto San Giovanni (★Milano) 98,702
Siena 64,941
Siracusa 120,569
Taranto 243,750
Teramo (50,353▲) 39,900
Terni 112,523
Torino (Turin) (★1,675,000) 1,910,621
Torre Annunziata 57,427
Torre del Greco (★Napoli) 98,532
Trapani (70,055▲) 60,600
Trento 97,722
Treviso 90,727
Trieste 267,857
Udine (★127,000) 103,627
Varese 89,762
Venezia (Venice) (★445,000) 362,494
Vercelli 55,321
Verona 271,381
Viareggio 58,799
Vicenza 119,132
Vigevano 67,725
Viterbo (57,330▲) 49,000

IVORY COAST / Côte d'Ivoire
1969 E 4,618,600
•ABIDJAN 510,000
Bouaké 161,300

JAMAICA
1973 E 1,997,908
•KINGSTON 603,717
Montego Bay (1970 C) 43,754

JAPAN / Nihon
1976 E 113,085,811
Abiko (★Tōkyō) (1975 C) 76,218
Ageo (★Tōkyō) 150,805
Aizu-wakamatsu 109,859
Akashi (★Ōsaka) 239,401
Akishima (★Tōkyō) (1975 C) 83,864
Akita 266,779
Amagaski (★Ōsaka) 544,291
Anan (1975 C) (60,439▲) 37,200
Anjō 113,113
Aomori 270,012
Arao (★Ōmuta) (1975 C) (58,296▲) 47,300
Asahikawa (1975 C) 320,526
Asaka (★Tōkyō) (1975 C) 81,755
Ashikaga 163,109
Ashiya (★Ōsaka) (1975 C) 76,211
Atami (1975 C) 51,437
Atsugi (★Tōkyō) 113,379
Ayase (★Tōkyō) (1975 C) 50,365
Beppu 135,402
Bisai (1975 C) 54,247
Chiba (★Tōkyō) 683,514
Chichibu (1975 C) 61,798
Chigasaki (★Tōkyō) 156,630
Chita (★Nagoya) (1975 C) 56,560
Chitose (1975 C) 61,031
Chōfu (★Tōkyō) 177,177
Chōshi (1975 C) 90,374
Daitō (★Ōsaka) 111,850
Ebetsu (1975 C) 77,624
Ebina (Tōkyō) (1975 C) 59,783
Fuchū (★Tōkyō) 184,818
Fuchū (1975 C) 50,217
Fuji (★320,000) 200,958
Fujieda (1975 C) (90,358▲) 64,300
Fujiidera (★Ōsaka) (1975 C) 59,515
Fujimi (★Tōkyō) (1975 C) 70,391
Fujinomiya (★Fuji) (102,301▲) 79,400
Fujisawa (★Tōkyō) 271,291
Fuji-yoshida (1975 C) 51,976
Fukaya (1975 C) (75,748▲) 53,100
Fukuchiyama (1975 C) (60,003▲) 43,000
Fukui 234,001
Fukuoka (★1,445,000) 1,021,623
Fukushima 250,441
Fukuyama 334,848
Funabashi (★Tōkyō) 431,940
Futtsu (1975 C) 56,653
Gamagōri (1975 C) 85,282
Gifu 409,404
Ginowan (1975 C) 53,835
Gyōda (1975 C) 66,069
Habikino (★Ōsaka) (1975 C) 94,160
Hachinohe 227,731
Hachiōji (★Tōkyō) 337,405
Hadano (★Tōkyō) 106,968
Hakodate 307,453
Hamada (1975 C) 50,316
Hamamatsu 472,052
Handa (1975 C) 85,824
Hannō (★Tōkyō) (1975 C) 55,926
Hatogaya (★Tōkyō) (1975 C) 56,693
Hekinan (1975 C) 60,680
Higashihiroshima (★Hiroshima) (1975 C) 66,231
Higashikurume (★Tōkyō) 103,075
Higashimatsuyama (1975 C) 57,684
Higashimurayama (★Tōkyō) 115,045
Higashiōsaka (★Ōsaka) 524,723
Higashiyamato (★Tōkyō) (1975 C) 58,464
Hikone (1975 C) 85,066
Himeji 439,717
Hino (★Tōkyō) 131,231
Hirakata (★Ōsaka) 309,786
Hiratsuka (★Tōkyō) 199,021
Hirosaki (167,815▲) 108,600
Hiroshima (★1,425,000) 863,273
Hita (1975 C) (63,969▲) 47,300
Hitachi 202,009
Hōfu (107,175▲) 84,000
Honjō (1975 C) 51,090
Hōya (★Tōkyō) (1975 C) 91,546
Ibaraki (★Ōsaka) 214,580
Ichihara (★Tōkyō) 198,896
Ichikawa (★Tōkyō) 331,019
Ichinomiya 241,150
Iida (1975 C) (77,112▲) 51,900
Iizuka (1975 C) (★103,000) 75,417
Ikeda (★Ōsaka) 101,689
Imabari 121,500
Inazawa (★Nagoya) (1975 C) 88,606
Inuyama (★Nagoya) (1975 C) 58,731
Iruma (★Tōkyō) (1975 C) 83,997
Isahaya (1975 C) (73,341▲) 49,400
Ise (Uji-yamada) 105,252
Isehara (★Tōkyō) (1975 C) 61,616
Isesaki (1975 C) 97,841
Ishinomaki (1975 C) 115,085
Itami (★Ōsaka) 175,051
Itō (1975 C) 68,072
Itsukaichi (★Hiroshima) (1975 C) 64,885
Iwaki (Taira) (332,838▲) 262,100
Iwakuni 111,136
Iwamizawa (1975 C) (72,305▲) 56,800
Iwata (1975 C) 67,665
Iwatsuki (★Tōkyō) (1975 C) (83,825▲) 60,900
Izumi (★Ōsaka) 120,153
Izumi (★Sendai) (1975 C) 70,087
Izumi-ōtsu (★Ōsaka) (1975 C) 66,250
Izumi-sano (★Ōsaka) (1975 C) 86,139
Joetsu (Takada) 124,158
Jōyō (★Ōsaka) (1975 C) 58,923
Kadoma (★Ōsaka) 142,993
Kaga (1975 C) (61,599▲) 47,400
Kagamigahara (1975 C) 94,192
Kagoshima 468,649
Kainan (1975 C) 53,250
Kaizuka (★Ōsaka) (1975 C) 79,506
Kakogawa (★Ōsaka) 176,558
Kamagaya (★Tōkyō) (1975 C) 63,288
Kamaishi (1975 C) 68,981
Kamakura (★Tōkyō) 168,183
Kamifukuoka (★Tōkyō) (1975 C) 58,332
Kanazawa 400,411
Kanoya (1975 C) (67,951▲) 38,500
Kanuma (1975 C) (81,799▲) 55,800
Karatsu (1975 C) 75,224
Kariya (★Nagoya) (1975 C) 96,152
Kasaoka (1975 C) (63,413▲) 42,700
Kashihara (★Ōsaka) (1975 C) 95,701
Kashiwa (★Tōkyō) 211,611
Kashiwara (★Ōsaka) (1975 C) 63,586
Kashiwazaki (1975 C) (80,351▲) 53,500
Kasuga (★Fukuoka) (1975 C) 55,160
Kasugai (★Nagoya) 222,335
Kasukabe (★Tōkyō) 129,958
Katano (★Ōsaka) (1975 C) 52,732
Katsuta (1975 C) 79,996
Kawachi-nagano (★Ōsaka) (1975 C) 66,936
Kawagoe (★Tōkyō) 233,974
Kawaguchi (★Tōkyō) 351,802
Kawanishi (★Ōsaka) 119,562
Kawasaki (★Tōkyō) 1,025,455
Kesennuma (1975 C) 66,616
Kimitsu (1975 C) 76,016
Kiryū 134,127
Kisarazu 100,131
Kishiwada (★Ōsaka) 175,899
Kitakyūshū (★1,510,000) 1,063,990
Kitami (1975 C) (91,519▲) 73,000
Kiyose (★Tōkyō) (1975 C) 60,574
Kōbe (★Ōsaka) 1,363,992
Kōchi 286,629
Kodaira (★Tōkyō) 157,540
Kōfu 195,009
Koga (★Tōkyō) (1975 C) 55,973
Koganei (★Tōkyō) 102,489
Kokubunji (★Tōkyō) (1975 C) 88,159
Komae (★Tōkyō) (1975 C) 70,043
Komaki (★Nagoya) (1975 C) 97,445
Komatsu 101,232
Kōnan (1975 C) 90,426
Kōnosu (★Tōkyō) (1975 C) 51,632
Kōriyama (269,082▲) 183,700
Koshigaya (★Tōkyō) 202,000
Kudamatsu (★Tokuyama) (1975 C) 55,825
Kumagaya 132,259
Kumamoto 495,811
Kunitachi (★Tōkyō) (1975 C) 64,495
Kurashiki 396,020
Kure (★Hiroshima) 241,961
Kurume 207,586
Kusatsu (★Ōsaka) (1975 C) 64,873
Kushiro (1975 C) 206,840
Kuwana (1975 C) 83,440
Kyōto (★Ōsaka) 1,461,567
Machida (★Tōkyō) 263,758
Maebashi 253,552
Maizuru (1975 C) (97,780▲) 82,600
Marugame (1975 C) 65,662
Matsubara (★Ōsaka) 135,349
Matsudo (★Tōkyō) 358,139
Matsue 129,277
Matsumoto 187,225
Matsuyama 374,492
Matsuzaka (109,889▲) 79,600
Mihara (1975 C) 83,679
Minō (★Ōsaka) (1975 C) 79,621
Misato (★Tōkyō) (1975 C) 79,355
Mishima (★Numazu) (1975 C) 89,248
Mitaka (★Tōkyō) 166,249
Mito 201,787
Miyako (1975 C) 61,912
Miyakonojō (120,730▲) 77,800
Miyazaki 240,001
Mobara (1975 C) 64,942
Moriguchi (★Ōsaka) 172,785
Morioka 220,051
Muroran (1975 C) (★210,000) 158,715
Musashi-murayama (★Tōkyō) (1975 C) 50,842
Musashino (★Tōkyō) 139,204
Nagahama (1975 C) 54,064
Nagano (310,593▲) 234,000
Nagaoka 173,375
Nagaokakyo (★Ōsaka) (1975 C) 65,557
Nagareyama (★Tōkyō) (1975 C) 82,936
Nagasaki 449,371
Nagoya (★3,565,000) 2,080,050
Naha 295,547
Nara (★Ōsaka) 264,739
Narashino (★Tōkyō) 119,476
Naruto (1975 C) (61,959▲) 50,600
Neyagawa (★Ōsaka) 259,456
Niigata 429,146
Niihama 132,693
Niiza (★Tōkyō) 111,922
Nishinomiya (★Ōsaka) 403,756
Nishio (1975 C) (82,524▲) 62,600
Nobeoka 135,882
Noboribetsu (★Muroran) (1975 C) 50,885
Noda (★Tōkyō) (1975 C) 78,193
Nōgata (1975 C) 58,551
Numazu (★420,000) 200,390
Obihiro (1975 C) 141,774
Ōbu (★Nagoya) (1975 C) 56,211
Ōdate (1975 C) (71,828▲) 50,200
Odawara 175,136
Ōgaki 140,368
Ōita 329,456
Ōkawa (1975 C) 50,395
Okaya (1975 C) 61,776
Okayama 520,469
Okazaki 239,612
Okinawa (1975 C) 91,347
Ōme (★Tōkyō) (1975 C) 86,152
Ōmiya (★Tōkyō) 334,608
Ōmuta (★225,000) 165,435
Onojo (★Fukuoka) (1975 C) 52,169
Onomichi 103,105
Ōsaka (★14,800,000) 2,750,418
Ōta 113,624
Otaru (1975 C) 184,406
Ōtsu (★Ōsaka) 195,414
Oyama (121,648▲) 78,500
Saga 154,631
Sagamihara (★Tōkyō) 390,851
Sakado (★Tōkyō) (1975 C) 51,230
Sakai (★Ōsaka) 768,702
Sakaide (1975 C) 67,624
Sakata (1975 C) (97,723▲) 71,200
Sakura (★Tōkyō) (1975 C) (80,804▲) 61,500
Sanjō (1975 C) 81,806
Sano (1975 C) 75,844
Sapporo (★1,315,000) 1,276,547
Sasebo 251,607
Sayama (★Tōkyō) 109,069
Seki (1975 C) 53,881
Sendai (*Kagoshlma-ken*) (1975 C) (61,788▲) 34,700
Sendai (*Miyagi-ken*) (1975 C) (★815,000) 615,473
Seto 115,817
Settsu (★Ōsaka) (1975 C) 76,704
Shibata (1975 C) (74,025▲) 48,700
Shijōnawate (★Ōsaka) (1975 C) 52,368
Shimada (1975 C) 68,820
Shimizu (★Shizuoka) 242,951
Shimonoseki (★Kitakyūshū) 268,385
Shiogama (★Sendai) (1975 C) 59,235
Shizuoka (★730,000) 450,322
Sōka (★Tōkyō) 172,401
Suita (★Ōsaka) 306,568
Suzuka (143,611▲) 100,800
Tachikawa (★Tōkyō) 138,556
Tajimi (1975 C) 68,901
Takaishi (★Ōsaka) (1975 C) 66,824
Takamatsu 302,397
Takaoka (★215,000) 171,041
Takarazuka (★Ōsaka) 166,007
Takasago (★Ōsaka) (1975 C) 77,080
Takasaki 214,384
Takatsuki (★Ōsaka) 337,264
Takawa (1975 C) 61,464
Takayama (1975 C) 60,504
Takikawa (1975 C) 50,090
Tama (★Tōkyō) (1975 C) 55,465
Tamano (1975 C) 78,516
Tanabe (1975 C) (66,999▲) 51,800
Tanashi (★Tōkyō) (1975 C) 67,433
Tatebayashi (1975 C) 66,410
Tochigi (1975 C) 83,189
Toda (★Tōkyō) (1975 C) 77,137
Tokai (★Nagoya) (1975 C) 95,457
Toki (1975 C) 63,324
Tokoname (1975 C) 54,865
Tokorozawa (★Tōkyō) 204,636

▲ Población de un municipio, comuna o distrito entero, incluyendo sus áreas rurales.
• Ciudad más grande de un país.
★ Población o designación de un área metropolitana, incluyendo los suburbios.
C Censo. E Estimado oficial.
UE Estimado no oficial.
L Población dentro de los límites municipales de un año específico.

▲ Population d'une municipalité, d'une commune ou d'un district, zone rurale incluse.
• Ville la plus peuplée du pays.
★ Population de l'agglomération (ou nom de la zone métropolitaine englobante).
C Recensement. E Estimation officielle.
UE Estimation non officielle.
L Population comprise dans les limites municipales de l'année indiquée.

▲ População de um município, comuna ou distrito, inclusive as respectivas áreas rurais.
• Maior cidade de um país.
★ População ou indicação de uma área metropolitana, inclusive subúrbios.
C Censo. E Estimativa oficial.
UE Estimativa não oficial.
L População dentro dos limites municipais no ano indicado.

JAPAN *continued*
Tokushima 241,033
Tokuyama (★250,000) 108,294
•TŌKYŌ (★24,700,000) 8,590,142
Tomakomai (1975 C) 132,477
Tondabayashi (★Ōsaka) (1975 C) 91,393
Toride (★Tōkyō) (1975 C) 52,816
Tosu (1975 C) 50,733
Tottori 124,135
Toyama 293,318
Toyohashi 287,725
Toyokawa (1975 C) 98,223
Toyonaka (★Ōsaka) 399,160
Toyota 255,827
Tsu 140,692
Tsuchiura 105,773
Tsuruga (1975 C) 60,205
Tsuruoka (1975 C) (95,932▲) 74,600
Tsushima (1975 C) 58,241
Tsuyama (1975 C) (79,907▲) 56,500
Ube (★218,000) 163,696
Ueda 106,562
Uji (★Ōsaka) 139,974
Urawa (★Tōkyō) 338,275
Utsunomiya 351,591
Uwajima (1975 C) 70,428
Wakayama (1975 C) 389,717
Wakkanai (1975 C) 55,464
Warabi (★Tōkyō) (1975 C) 76,311
Yachiyo (★Tōkyō) 117,707
Yaizu (1975 C) 94,102
Yamagata 223,852
Yamaguchi (107,363▲) 77,600
Yamato (★Tōkyō) 152,074
Yamato-kōriyama (★Ōsaka) (1975 C) 71,001
Yamato-takada (★Ōsaka) (1975 C) 58,637
Yao (★Ōsaka) 266,117
Yashio (★Tōkyō) (1975 C) 56,127
Yatsushiro (104,469▲) 78,000
Yawata (★Ōsaka) (1975 C) 50,131
Yokkaichi 249,470
Yokohama (★Tōkyō) 2,658,545
Yokosuka (★Tōkyō) 395,802
Yonago 120,122
Yonezawa (1975 C) (91,974▲) 71,400
Yono (★Tōkyō) (1975 C) 71,044
Yūbari (1975 C) 50,131
Zama (★Tōkyō) (1975 C) 80,562
Zushi (★Tōkyō) (1975 C) 56,298

JERSEY
1971 C 72,629
•ST. HELIER (★45,000) 28,135

JORDAN / Al-Urdunn
1973 E 2,555,000
Al-Quds (Jerusalem, Old City) (1961 C: 60,488; → Yerushalayim, Israel)
•'AMMĀN (1971 C) 520,720
Az-Zarqā' 214,000
Bayt Lahm (Bethlehem) (1967 C/Israel) 16,313
Irbid 113,000

KENYA
1973 E 12,482,000
Mombasa 301,000
•NAIROBI 630,000

KOREA, NORTH / Chosŏn Minjujuŭi In'min Konghwaguk
1967 E 12,780,000
Ch'ŏngjin 265,000
Haeju 115,000
Hamhŭng (1944 C) 112,184
Hŭngnam (1944 C) 143,600
Kaesŏng 140,000
Kimch'aek (Sŏngjin) 265,000
Namp'o (Chinnamp'o) 130,000
•P'YŎNGYANG 840,000
Sinŭiju 165,000
Songnim (1944 C) 53,035
Wŏnsan 215,000

KOREA, SOUTH / Taehan-Min'guk
1975 C 34,708,542
Andong (95,449▲) 79,900
Anyang (★Sŏul) 134,862
Bucheon (★Sŏul) 109,236
Chech'ŏn (74,239▲) 51,300
Cheju (135,189▲) 73,700
Chinhae 103,657
Chinju (154,676▲) 121,400
Ch'ŏnan (96,789▲) 68,000
Ch'ŏngju 192,734
Chŏnju 311,432
Ch'unch'ŏn 140,521
Ch'ungju (105,143▲) 73,100
Chungmu (66,817▲) 55,900
Inch'ŏn (★Sŏul) 799,982
Iri (117,111▲) 97,200
Kangnŭng (85,040▲) 55,900
Kimch'ŏn (67,066▲) 50,700
Kunsan 154,485
Kwangju 607,058
Kyŏngju (108,447▲) 64,800
Masan 371,937
Mokp'o 192,927
P'ohang (134,404▲) 110,000
Pusan 2,454,051
Seongnam (★Sŏul) 272,329
Sŏkch'o 71,475
•SŎUL (SEOUL) (★8,625,000) 6,889,470
Sunch'ŏn (108,034▲) 72,500
Suwŏn 224,177
Taegu 1,311,078
Taejŏn 506,703
Ŭijŏngbu (★Sŏul) 108,365
Ulsan (252,639▲) 171,200
Wŏnju 120,335
Yŏngju (70,793▲) 50,800
Yŏsu 130,641

KUWAIT / Al-Kuwayt
1975 C 994,837
Abraq Khīţān (★Al-Kuwayt) 59,443
Al-Jahrah (★Al-Kuwayt) 52,302
•AL-KUWAYT (★780,000) 78,116
Hawalli (★Al-Kuwayt) 130,565
Salmiya (★Al-Kuwayt) 113,943

LAOS / Lao
1973 E 3,181,000
Louangphrabang 43,000
Savannakhet 50,691
•VIANGCHAN (VIENTIANE) 174,229

LEBANON / Al-Lubnān
1970 E 2,126,355
•BAYRŪT (BEIRUT) (★1,010,000) 474,870
Ţarābulus (Tripoli) 157,320

LESOTHO
1972 E 972,000
•MASERU 17,000

LIBERIA
1970 E 1,200,000
•MONROVIA 100,000

LIBYA / Lībiyā
1970 E 1,938,000
Banghāzi (Bengasi) 170,000
•ŢARĀBULUS (TRIPOLI) 264,000

LIECHTENSTEIN
1974 E 23,745
•VADUZ 4,382

LUXEMBOURG
1973 E 353,000
Esch-sur-Alzette (1970 C) (★96,000) 27,574
•LUXEMBOURG (★104,000) 78,300

MACAU
1970 C 248,316
•MACAU (★248,636) 241,413

MADAGASCAR / Madagasikara
1972 E 7,928,868
•ANTANANARIVO 366,530
Antsirabe (70,003▲) 33,287
Fianarantsoa 58,818
Majunga 67,456
Tamatave 59,503

MALAWI
1975 E 5,044,000
•Blantyre (1972 E) 163,921
LILONGWE 102,000

MALAYSIA
1970 C 10,452,309
Alor Setar (★85,748) 66,179
Batu Pahat (Bandar Penggaram) 53,291
Butterworth (★Pinang) 61,187
Ipoh (★257,309) 247,689
Johor Baharu (★Singapore) 136,229
Kelang 113,607
Kota Baharu (★69,756) 55,052
•KUALA LUMPUR (★750,000) 451,728
Kuala Terengganu (★59,494) 53,353
Kuching 63,535
Melaka (Malacca) (★99,782) 86,357
Muar (Bandar Maharani) 61,218
Petaling Jaya (★Kuala Lumpur) 93,447
Pinang (George Town) (★450,000) 270,019
Seremban (★90,062) 79,915
Sibu 50,635
Taiping 54,645

MALDIVES
1970 C 114,469
•MALE 13,610

MALI
1972 E 5,257,000
•BAMAKO 237,000
Mopti 43,000
Tombouctou (Timbuktu) (1971 E) 11,900

MALTA
1972 E 318,500
•VALLETTA (★202,000) 15,200

MARTINIQUE
1967 C 320,030
•FORT-DE-FRANCE (★110,184) 96,943

MAURITANIA / Mauritanie
1971 E 1,190,000
•NOUAKCHOTT 35,000

MAURITIUS
1975 E 867,191
Beau Bassin (★Port Louis) 82,951
Curepipe (★Port Louis) 53,793
•PORT LOUIS (★395,000) 139,592
Quatre Bornes (★Port Louis) 52,884
Vacoas (★Port Louis) 49,825

MEXICO / México
1974 E 58,118,000
Acapulco [de Juárez] 309,300
Aguascalientes 213,400
Campeche (1970 C) 69,506
Celaya (1970 C) 79,977
Chihuahua 327,300
•CIUDAD DE MÉXICO (MEXICO CITY) (★11,250,000) 8,299,200
Ciudad Juárez (★El Paso, Tex.) 497,300
Ciudad Madero (★Tampico) 115,300
Ciudad Mante (1970 C) 51,247
Ciudad Obregón 144,800
Ciudad Victoria (1970 C) 83,897
Coatzacoalcos (1970 C) 69,753
Colima (1970 C) 58,450
Córdoba (1970 C) 78,495
Cuernavaca 239,800
Culiacán 228,000
Delicias (1970 C) 52,446
Durango 182,600
Ensenada (1970 C) 77,687
Gómez Palacio (★Torreón) (1970 C) 79,650
Guadalajara (★1,900,000) 1,478,400
Guadalupe (★Monterrey) (1970 C) 51,899
Guaymas (1970 C) 57,492
Hermosillo 232,700
Hidalgo del Parral (1970 C) 57,619
Irapuato 135,600
Jalapa Enríquez 161,400
León [de los Aldamas] 468,900
Los Mochis (1970 C) 67,953
Matamoros (★Brownsville, Tex.) 165,100
Mazatlán 147,000
Mérida 233,900
Mesa de Tijuana (★San Diego, Calif.) (1970 C) 50,094
Mexicali (★330,000) 317,200
Minatitlán (1970 C) 68,397
Monclova (1970 C) 78,134
Monterrey (★1,550,000) 1,006,200
Morelia 199,100
Netzahualcóyotl (★Ciudad de México) (1970 C) 580,438
Nogales (1970 C) 52,108
Nuevo Laredo (★Laredo, Tex.) 184,600
Oaxaca [de Juárez] 114,900
Orizaba (★235,000) 105,200
Pachuca [de Soto] (1970 C) 83,892
Poza Rica de Hidalgo 152,300
Puebla [de Zaragoza] 466,000
Querétaro 142,400
Reynosa 181,600
Salamanca (1970 C) 61,039
Saltillo 200,700
San Luis Potosí 271,100
Tampico (★365,000) 212,200
Tapachula (1970 C) 60,620
Tepic 108,900
Tijuana (★San Diego, Calif.) 363,200
Tlaquepaque (★Guadalajara) (1970 C) 59,760
Toluca [de Lerdo] 136,100
Torreón (★400,000) 244,300
Tuxtla Gutiérrez (1970 C) 66,851
Uruapan [del Progreso] 108,100
Veracruz [Llave] (★320,000) 255,600
Villahermosa 133,200
Zacatecas (1970 C) 50,251
Zamora de Hidalgo (1970 C) 57,775

MONACO
1975 E 25,000
•MONACO (★50,000) 25,000

MONGOLIA / Mongol Ard Uls
1969 C 1,197,600
•ULAANBAATAR (ULAN BATOR) 267,400

MOROCCO / Al-Magreb
1971 C 15,379,259
Agadir 61,192
Beni-Mellal 53,826
•Casablanca (Dar-el-Beida) (★1,575,000) 1,506,373
El-Jadida (Mazagan) 55,501
Fès (Fez) 325,327
Kenitra 139,206
Khouribga 73,667
Marrakech 332,741
Meknès 248,369
Mohammedia (Fedala) 70,392
Oujda 175,532
RABAT (★540,000) 367,620
Safi 129,113
Salé (★Rabat) 155,557
Tanger (Tangier) 187,894
Taza 55,157
Tétouan 139,105

MOZAMBIQUE / Moçambique
1970 C 8,168,933
Beira 110,752
João Belo 63,494
•MAPUTO (LOURENÇO MARQUES) 341,922
Nampula 120,188
Quelimane 71,289
Tete 51,453

NAMIBIA
1970 C 722,867
•WINDHOEK 61,260

NEPAL / Nepāl
1971 C 11,555,983
•KĀTHMĀNDU (★215,000) 150,402
Lalitpur (★Kāthmāndu) 59,049

NETHERLANDS / Nederland
1977 E 13,815,680
Alkmaar (★103,000) 67,554
Almelo 62,501
Amersfoort (★127,931) 87,203
Amstelveen (★Amsterdam) 70,924
•AMSTERDAM (★1,760,000) 740,650
Apeldoorn 135,251
Arnhem (★282,000) 125,570
Breda (★152,000) 118,845
Delft (★'s-Gravenhage) 85,118
Den Helder 60,828
Deventer 65,140
Dordrecht (★190,000) 102,688
Ede (80,142▲) 42,000
Eindhoven (★362,000) 192,566
Emmen (87,355▲) 34,600
Enschede (★280,000) 141,423
Geleen (★180,000) 36,110
Gouda 57,773
Groningen (★201,000) 161,825
Haarlem (★Amsterdam) 162,774
Haarlemmermeer (74,271▲) 10,100
Heerlen (★266,000) 70,928
Helmond 58,930
Hengelo (★Enschede) 73,084
Hilversum (★Amsterdam) 93,951
IJmuiden (Velsen) (★Amsterdam) 63,023
Leeuwarden 85,435
Leiden (★170,000) 101,524
Maastricht (★145,000) 110,191
Nijmegen (★215,000) 148,073
Rijswijk (★'s-Gravenhage) 53,532
Roosendaal 52,652
Rotterdam (★1,090,000) 600,978
Schiedam (★Rotterdam) 76,865
's-GRAVENHAGE (THE HAGUE) (★800,000) 471,137
's-Hertogenbosch (★181,000) 86,809
Tilburg (★213,000) 150,738
Utrecht (★465,000) 245,269
Venlo (★86,000) 61,636
Vlaardingen (★Rotterdam) 79,068
Vlissingen (Flushing) (43,415▲) 24,800
Zaanstad (Zaandam) (★Amsterdam) 125,409
Zeist (★Utrecht) 58,910
Zwolle 78,585

NETHERLANDS ANTILLES / Nederlandse Antillen
1965 E 209,000
•WILLEMSTAD (1960 C) (★94,133) 43,547

NEW CALEDONIA / Nouvelle-Calédonie
1975 E 136,000
•NOUMÉA 60,200

NEW HEBRIDES / Nouvelles-Hébrides
1974 E 93,000
•VILA (1972 C) (★9,242) 4,292

NEW ZEALAND
1976 C 3,129,383
•Auckland (★765,000) 150,708
Christchurch (★306,000) 171,987
Dunedin (★114,000) 82,546
Hamilton (★94,777) 87,968
Invercargill (★53,762) 49,738
Lower Hutt (★Wellington) 64,553
Manukau (★Auckland) 139,059
Napier (★100,978) 46,994
Palmerston North (★63,873) 57,931
Rotorua (★46,650) 37,229
Takapuna (★Auckland) 62,220
Waitemala (★Auckland) 79,883
WELLINGTON (★349,628) 139,566

NICARAGUA
1971 C 1,877,952
León 54,841
•MANAGUA 375,278

NIGER
1975 E 4,600,000
•NIAMEY 130,000

NIGERIA
1971 E 56,510,000
Aba 158,000
Abeokuta 226,000
Ado-Ekiti 190,000
Akure (1963 C) 71,106
Benin City 122,000
Bida (1963 C) 55,007
Calabar (1963 C) 76,418
Deba (1963 C) 60,679
Ede 163,000
Effon Alaiye (1963 C) 67,090
Enugu 167,000
Gusau (1963 C) 69,231
Ibadan 758,000
Ife 157,000
Ijebu-Ode (1963 C) 68,543
Ikare (1963 C) 61,696
Ikerre 130,000
Ikire (1963 C) 54,022
Ikirun (1963 C) 79,516
Ikorodu (1963 C) 81,024
Ila 139,000
Ilawe (1963 C) 80,833
Ilesha 200,000
Ilobu (1963 C) 87,223
Ilorin 252,000
Inisa (1963 C) 52,482
Iseyin 115,000
Iwo 192,000
Jos (1963 C) 90,402
Kaduna 181,000
Kano 357,000
Katsina 109,000
Kumo (1963 C) 64,878
Lafia (1963 C) 53,667
•LAGOS (★1,250,000) 901,000
Maiduguri 169,000
Makurdi (1963 C) 53,967
Minna (1963 C) 59,988
Mushin (★Lagos) 176,000
Offa (1963 C) 86,425
Ogbomosho 387,000
Oka (1963 C) 62,761
Ondo (1963 C) 74,343
Onitsha 197,000
Oshogbo 253,000
Owo (1963 C) 89,693
Oyo 136,000
Port Harcourt 217,000
Sapele (1963 C) 61,007

▲ Population of an entire municipality, commune, or district, including rural area.
• Largest city in country.
★ Population or designation of the metropolitan area, including suburbs.
C Census. E Official estimate. UE Unofficial estimate.
L Population within municipal limits of year specified.

▲ Bevölkerung eines ganzen städtischen Verwaltungsgebietes, eines Kommunalbezirkes oder eines Distrikts, einschliesslich ländlicher Gebiete.
• Grösste Stadt des Landes.
★ Bevölkerung oder Bezeichnung der Stadtregion einschliess lich Vororte.
C Volkszählung. E Offizielle Schätzung.
UE Inoffizielle Schätzung.
L Bevölkerung innerhalb der städtischen Verwaltungseinheit des angegebenen Jahres.

- Shagamu (1963 C) 51,371
- Shaki (1963 C) 76,290
- Shomolu (★Lagos) (1963 C) 64,731
- Sokoto (1963 C) 89,817
- Warri (1963 C) 55,254
- Zaria 201,000

NORWAY / Norge

- 1977 E 4,035,365
- Bergen (★240,000) 212,692
- Drammen (★70,500) 50,834
- Fredrikstad (★49,000) 28,925
- Kristiansand 60,048
- •OSLO (★725,000) 461,881
- Skien (★79,049) 47,337
- Stavanger (★124,000) 87,402
- Trondheim 135,592

OMAN / 'Umān

- 1962 E 565,000
- MASQAṬ (MUSCAT) 6,000
- •Maṭraḥ 14,000

PAKISTAN / Pākistān

- 1972 C 64,979,732
- Bahāwalpur 133,956
- Burewala 56,894
- Chiniot 69,124
- Dera Ghāzi Khān 71,429
- Dera Ismāīl Khān (★59,892) 57,500
- Gujrānwāla 360,419
- Gujrāt 100,581
- Hāfizābād 61,413
- Hyderābād (★660,000) 600,000
- ISLĀMĀBĀD (★Rāwalpindi) 77,318
- Jacobābād 57,292
- Jhang Maghiāna 135,722
- Jhelum (★63,653) 51,000
- Kamālia 52,000
- Kāmoke 50,139
- •Karāchi (★3,498,634) 2,850,000
- Kasūr 102,531
- Khānewāl 67,617
- Kohāt (★64,634) 48,091
- Lahore (★2,200,000) 2,050,000
- Lahore Cantonment (★Lahore) 147,165
- Lārkāna 71,943
- Lyallpur 822,263
- Mardān 115,218
- Mīrpur Khās 81,617
- Multān (★542,195) 520,000
- Nawābshāh 80,779
- Nowshera (★56,117) 31,103
- Okāra 101,791
- Peshāwar (★268,366) 210,000
- Quetta (★155,627) 120,000
- Rahīmyār Khān 74,407
- Rāwalpindi (★725,000) 375,000
- Rāwalpindi Cantonment (★Rāwalpindi) (1961 C) 142,805
- Sāhiwāl (Montgomery) 106,213
- Sargodha (★201,407) 140,000
- Shekhūpura 82,083
- Shikārpur 70,301
- Siālkot (★203,779) 185,000
- Sukkur 158,876
- Wah Cantonment 107,671

PANAMA / Panamá

- 1970 C 1,472,280
- Balboa (★Panamá) 2,569
- Colón (1972 E) (★78,000) 69,650
- •PANAMÁ (1972 E) (★500,000) 371,070
- San Miguelito (★Panamá) 68,400

PAPUA NEW GUINEA

- 1971 C 2,490,037
- Lae 38,707
- •PORT MORESBY 76,507
- Rabaul 26,619

PARAGUAY

- 1972 C 2,354,071
- •ASUNCIÓN (★540,000) 392,753

PERU / Perú

- 1972 C 13,572,052
- Arequipa (★304,653) 98,605
- Ayacucho (★43,304) 34,593
- Barrio Obrero Industrial (★Lima) 238,402
- Breña (★Lima) 123,345
- Callao (★Lima) 196,919
- Cerro de Pasco (★47,178) 35,975
- Chiclayo (★189,685) 148,932
- Chimbote 159,045
- Chorrillos (★Lima) 87,021
- Cuzco (★120,881) 67,658
- Huancayo (★115,693) 64,777
- Ica 73,883
- Iquitos 111,327
- Jesús María (★Lima) 82,988
- La Victoria (★Lima) 265,157
- •LIMA (★3,350,000) 340,339
- Lince (★Lima) 82,749
- Magdalena del Mar (★Lima) 54,855
- Miraflores (★Lima) 93,926
- Piura (★126,702) 81,683
- Pueblo Libre (★Lima) 76,279
- Rímac (★Lima) 165,340
- San Isidro (★Lima) 61,682
- Sullana (1961 C) (★53,000) 34,501
- Surco (★Lima) 70,949
- Surquillo (★Lima) 89,201
- Tacna 55,752
- Trujillo (★241,882) 127,535
- Vitarte (★Lima) 54,417

PHILIPPINES / Pilipinas

- 1970 C 36,684,486
- Angeles (1975 E) 175,700
- Bacolod (1975 E) 196,500
- Baguio (1975 E) 100,200
- Baliuag 52,133
- Batangas (1975 E) (125,300▲) 20,000
- Biñan (★Manila) 58,290
- Butuan (1975 E) (173,400▲) 71,400
- Cabanatuan (1975 E) (118,000▲) 34,200
- Cadiz (1975 E) (130,200▲) 26,000
- Cagayan de Oro (1975 E) (163,200▲) 34,300
- Calbayog (1975 E) (101,700▲) 11,800
- Caloocan (★Manila) (1975 E) 364,100
- Cavite (★140,000) 75,739
- Cebu (1975 E) (★485,000) 418,500
- Cotabato (61,184▲) 51,328
- Dadiangas (1975 E) (108,300▲) 57,400
- Dagupan 83,582
- Davao (1975 E) (515,500▲) 190,700
- Iligan (1975 E) (129,500▲) 11,700
- Iloilo (1975 E) 248,000
- Isabela (Basilan) (1975 E) (171,300▲) 17,100
- Laoag (61,727▲) 30,203
- Lapu-Lapu 69,268
- Legazpi (84,090▲) 35,911
- Lipa (1975 E) (112,000▲) 21,300
- Lucena 77,006
- Makati (★Manila) 264,918
- Malabon (★Manila) 141,514
- Malolos 73,996
- Mandaluyong (★Manila) 149,407
- Mandaue (★Cebu) 58,579
- •MANILA (1975 E) (★5,375,000) 1,438,300
- Marawi 55,708
- Marikina (★Manila) 113,400
- Mecauayan (★Manila) 50,977
- Muntinglupa (★Manila) 65,057
- Naga 79,846
- Navotas (★Manila) 83,245
- Olongapo (1975 E) 134,500
- Ormoc (84,563▲) 14,126
- Parañaque (★Manila) 97,214
- Pasay (★Manila) (1975 E) 240,900
- Pasig (★Manila) 156,492
- Quezon City (★Manila) (1975 E) 994,700
- San Carlos (90,058▲) 22,692
- San Fernando 84,362
- San Juan del Monte (★Manila) 104,559
- San Pablo (1975 E) (125,700▲) 49,000
- Tacloban (76,531▲) 52,432
- Taguig (★Manila) 55,257
- Tarlac (135,128▲) 26,519
- Valenzuela (★Manila) 98,456
- Zamboanga (1975 E) (240,100▲) 50,400

POLAND / Polska

- 1975 E 34,186,000
- Bedzin (★Katowice) 59,400
- Białystok 195,900
- Bielsko-Biała 120,900
- Bydgoszcz 322,700
- Bytom (Beuthen) (★Katowice) 234,400
- Chorzów (★Katowice) 156,300
- Częstochowa 200,300
- Dąbrowa Górnicza (★Katowice) 79,600
- Dzierżoniów (Reichenbach) (★85,000) 35,400
- Elbląg (Elbing) 97,300
- Gdańsk (Danzig) (★775,000) 421,000
- Gdynia (★Gdańsk) 221,100
- Gliwice (Gleiwitz) (★Katowice) 197,200
- Gniezno 55,100
- Gorzów Wielkopolski 87,200
- Grudziądz 82,200
- Inowrocław 59,700
- Jastrzębie Zdrój 90,900
- Jaworzno (★Katowice) 74,500
- Jelenia Góra (★87,000) 58,800
- Kalisz 87,300
- •Katowice (★2,450,000) 343,700
- Kędzierzyn-Koźle (Heydebreck) 69,300
- Kielce 151,200
- Konin 49,800
- Koszalin (Köslin) 77,600
- Kraków 684,600
- Legnica (Liegnitz) 82,100
- Lodź (★980,000) 798,300
- Lublin 272,000
- Mysłowice (★Katowice) 61,700
- Olsztyn (Allenstein) 112,700
- Opole (Oppeln) 106,000
- Ostrowiec Świętokrzyski 57,300
- Ostrów Wielkopolski 54,100
- Pabianice (★Łódź) 66,800
- Piekary Śląskie (★Katowice) 62,100
- Piotrków Trybunalski 64,200
- Płock 87,800
- Poznań (★585,000) 516,000
- Przemyśl 57,400
- Radom 175,300
- Ruda Śląska (★Katowice) 149,600
- Rybnik 103,000
- Rzeszów 95,800
- Siemianowice Śląskie (★Katowice) 72,100
- Słupsk (Stolp) 77,600
- Sopot (Zoppot) (★Gdańsk) 51,700
- Sosnowiec (★Katowice) 195,700
- Starachowice 45,900
- Stargard Szczeciński 51,400
- Świdnica (Schweidnitz) 51,600
- Świętochłowice (★Katowice) 58,400
- Szczecin (Stettin) 369,700
- Tarnów 97,800
- Tarnowskie Góry (★Katowice) 62,300
- Tomaszów Mazowiecki 58,300
- Toruń 149,200
- Tychy (★Katowice) 135,600
- Wałbrzych (★185,000) 128,000
- WARSZAWA (WARSAW) (★1,950,000) 1,436,100
- Włocławek 90,500
- Wodzisław Śląski 101,900
- Wrocław (Breslau) 575,900
- Zabrze (Hindenburg) (★Katowice) 203,700
- Zawiercie 51,200
- Zielona Góra (Grünberg) 84,200

PORTUGAL

- 1970 C 8,663,252
- Amadora (★Lisboa) 65,870
- Barreiro (★Lisboa) 53,690
- Çoimbra 55,985
- •LISBOA (LISBON) (1975 E) (★1,950,000) 829,900
- Ponta Delgada (*Açores*) 20,190
- Porto (1975 E) (★1,150,000) 335,700
- Vila Nova de Gaia (★Porto) 50,805

PUERTO RICO

- 1970 C 2,712,033
- Bayamón (★San Juan) 147,552
- Caguas (★San Juan) (95,661▲) 63,215
- Carolina (★San Juan) 94,271
- Guaynabo (★San Juan) 55,310
- Mayagüez (★116,100) 68,872
- Ponce (★213,984) 128,233
- •SAN JUAN (★1,185,000) 452,749

QATAR / Qaṭar

- 1971 E 160,000
- •AD-DAWḤAH (DOHA) 95,000

REUNION / Réunion

- 1971 E 455,200
- •SAINT-DENIS (94,100▲) 85,400

RHODESIA

- 1975 E 6,420,000
- Bulawayo (★340,000) 80,200
- Gwelo (★64,000) 20,600
- Harari (★Salisbury) (1969 C) 58,007
- Highfield (★Salisbury) (1969 C) 52,560
- •SALISBURY (★569,000) 107,600
- Umtali (★62,000) 20,500

ROMANIA / România

- 1977 E 21,559,416
- Arad 171,110
- Bacău 126,654
- Baia-Mare 100,992
- Bîrlad 55,937
- Brăila 194,633
- Brașov 257,150
- •BUCUREȘTI (BUCHAREST) (★2,000,000) 1,807,044
- Buzău 97,787
- Cluj 262,421
- Constanța (★290,226) 256,875
- Craiova 222,399
- Deva 60,538
- Drobeta-Turnu-Severin 76,955
- Galați 239,306
- Hunedoara 79,630
- Iași 264,947
- Mediaș 64,861
- Oradea 171,258
- Petroșani (★73,000) 40,684
- Piatra-Neamț 78,100
- Pitești 123,943
- Ploiești (★254,592) 199,269
- Reșița 84,998
- Satu-Mare 103,612
- Sibiu 151,120
- Suceava 62,869
- Timișoara 268,785
- Tîrgu-Mureș 130,051
- Turda 55,256

RWANDA

- 1970 E 3,736,000
- •KIGALI 59,100

ST. KITTS-NEVIS

- 1970 C 47,457
- •BASSETERRE (*St. Kitts*) 13,055
- Charlestown (*Nevis*) 1,880

ST. LUCIA

- 1970 C 101,064
- •CASTRIES 39,132

ST. PIERRE AND MIQUELON / Saint-Pierre-et-Miquelon

- 1974 C 5,840
- •SAINT-PIERRE 5,232

ST. VINCENT

- 1970 C 89,129
- •KINGSTOWN (★23,782) 17,258

SAN MARINO

- 1973 E 19,000
- •SAN MARINO 4,400

SAO TOME AND PRINCIPE / São Tomé e Príncipe

- 1970 C 73,631
- •SÃO TOMÉ 17,380

SAUDI ARABIA / Al-'Arabiyah as-Sa'ūdiyah

- 1974 C 7,012,642
- Abhā 30,150
- Ad-Dammām 127,844
- Al-Hufūf (Hofuf) 101,271
- Al-Madīnah (Medina) 198,186
- Al-Mubarraz 54,325
- •AR-RIYĀD (RIYADH) 666,840
- Aṭ-Ṭā'if 204,857
- Buraydah 69,940
- Juddah (Jidda) 561,104
- Makkah (Mecca) 366,801
- Tabūk 74,825
- 'Unayzah (1961 UE) 50,000

SENEGAL / Sénégal

- 1973 E 4,227,000
- •DAKAR (1974 E) (★735,000) 667,000
- Kaolack 114,000
- Rufisque (★Dakar) 54,000
- Saint-Louis 99,000
- Thiès 105,000
- Ziguinchor 58,000

SEYCHELLES

- 1971 C 52,437
- •VICTORIA 13,622

SIERRA LEONE

- 1974 C 2,730,000
- •FREETOWN (★335,000) 274,000

SINGAPORE

- 1970 C 2,074,507
- •SINGAPORE (★2,225,000) 2,074,507

SOLOMON IS.

- 1970 C 160,998
- •HONIARA 11,911

SOMALIA / Somaliya

- 1972 E 2,941,000
- Hargeysa (1966 E) 42,000
- •MOGADISHO 230,000

SOUTH AFRICA / Suid-Afrika

- 1970 C 21,794,328
- Alexandra (★Johannesburg) 57,040
- Benoni (★Johannesburg) 151,294
- Bloemfontein (★182,329) 149,836
- Boksburg (★Johannesburg) 106,126
- Brakpan (★Johannesburg) 73,210
- CAPE TOWN (KAAPSTAD) (★1,125,000) 697,514
- Carletonville 93,096
- Durban (★1,040,000) 736,852
- East London (Oos-Londen) (★190,000) 119,727
- Elsies River (★Cape Town) 64,539
- Germiston (★Johannesburg) 221,972
- •Johannesburg (★2,550,000) 654,232
- Kimberley 105,258
- Klerksdorp (★175,000) 63,558
- Kroonstad 51,988
- Krugersdorp (★Johannesburg) 92,725
- Mdantsane (★East London) 67,501
- Parow (★Cape Town) 60,768
- Pietermaritzburg (★160,855) 114,822
- Port Elizabeth (★475,869) 392,231
- Potchefstroom 57,443
- PRETORIA (★575,000) 545,450
- Randfontein (★Johannesburg) 50,481
- Roodepoort-Maraisburg (★Johannesburg) 115,366
- Soweto (★Johannesburg) 602,043
- Springs (★Johannesburg) 142,812
- Tembisa (★Johannesburg) 83,637
- Uitenhage (★Port Elizabeth) 70,517
- Umlazi (★Durban) 123,495
- Vanderbijlpark (★Vereeniging) 80,375
- Vereeniging (★310,188) 172,549
- Welkom (★132,880) 67,472

SPAIN / España

- 1975 E 35,472,000
- Albacete (101,249▲) 89,700
- Alcalá de Henares (★Madrid) (1970 C) 59,783
- Alcoy (1970 C) 61,371
- Algeciras (1970 C) 81,662
- Alicante 214,760
- Almería 120,072
- Avilés (1970 C) (★108,000) 81,710
- Badajoz (102,827▲) 81,700
- Badalona (★Barcelona) (1970 C) 162,888
- Baracaldo (★Bilbao) (1970 C) 108,757
- Barcelona (1974 E) (★3,455,000) 1,816,623
- Bilboa (★910,000) 431,347
- Burgos 132,913
- Cáceres 58,870
- Cádiz 140,862
- Cartagena (1970 C) (146,904▲) 120,000
- Castellón de la Plana 108,650
- Córdoba 250,903
- Cornellá (★Barcelona) (1970 C) 77,314
- Elche (1970 C) (122,663▲) 101,271
- El Ferrol del Caudillo (1970 C) (★116,000) 87,736
- Gerona 75,109
- Getafe (★Madrid) (1970 C) 69,424
- Gijón (1970 C) 187,612
- Granada 214,230
- Guadalajara 45,060
- Hospitalet (★Barcelona) (1970 C) 241,978
- Huelva 112,091
- Huesca 36,479
- Jaén 82,050
- Jerez de la Frontera (1970 C) (149,867▲) 112,411
- La Coruña 206,776
- La Línea (★Gibraltar) (1970 C) 52,127
- Las Palmas de Gran Canaria (*Is. Canarias*) 327,489
- Leganés (★Madrid) (1970 C) 57,537
- León (★130,000) 113,339
- Lérida (100,872▲) 81,200
- Linares (1970 C) (50,516▲) 45,330
- Logrono 96,546
- Lorca (1970 C) (60,609▲) 25,208
- Lugo (67,905▲) 56,900
- •MADRID (1974 E) (★3,860,000) 3,274,043
- Málaga 408,458
- Manresa (1970 C) 57,846
- Mataró (1970 C) 73,129
- Mieres (1970 C) (64,552▲) 22,790
- Murcia (262,071▲) 172,000
- Orense (80,210▲) 69,500
- Oviedo 159,652
- Palencia 62,186
- Palma [de Mallorca] 262,948
- Pamplona 163,197
- Pontevedra (60,301▲) 31,200
- Puertollano (1970 C) 53,001
- Reus (1970 C) 59,095
- Sabadell (★Barcelona) (1970 C) 159,408

▲ Población de un municipio, comuna o distrito entero, incluyendo sus áreas rurales.
• Ciudad más grande de un país.
★ Población o designación de un área metropolitana, incluyendo los suburbios.
C Censo. E Estimado oficial.
UE Estimado no oficial.
L Población dentro de los límites municipales de un año especifico.

▲ Population d'une municipalité, d'une commune ou d'un district, zone rurale incluse.
• Ville la plus peuplée du pays.
★ Population de l'agglomération (ou nom de la zone métropolitaine englobante).
C Recensement. E Estimation officielle.
UE Estimation non officielle.
L Population comprise dans les limites municipales de l'année indiquée.

▲ População de um município, comuna ou distrito, inclusive as respectivas áreas rurais.
• Maior cidade de um país.
★ População ou indicação de uma área metropolitana, inclusive subúrbios.
C Censo. E Estimativa oficial.
UE Estimativa não oficial.
L População dentro dos limites municipais no ano indicado.

SPAIN, *continued*

Sagunto (1970 C)	47,026
Salamanca	131,374
San Baudilio de Llobregat (★Barcelona) (1970 C)	50,051
San Cristóbal de la Laguna *(Is. Canarias)* (1970 C) (79,963▲)	17,483
San Fernando (1970 C)	60,187
San Sebastián (★265,000)	166,250
Santa Coloma de Gramanet (1970 C) (★Barcelona)	106,711
Santa Cruz de Tenerife (Is. Canarias)	175,950
Santander	164,994
Santiago de Compostela (1970 C) (70,893▲)	51,620
Segovia	46,954
Sevilla (Seville) (★680,000)	589,721
Tarragona	100,786
Tarrasa (★Barcelona) (1970 C)	138,697
Toledo	51,429
Valencia (★1,040,000)	707,915
Valladolid	285,960
Vigo (1970 C)	197,144
Vitoria	169,780
Zamora	51,978
Zaragoza (Saragossa)	528,704

SPANISH NORTH AFRICA / Plazas de Soberanía en el Norte de África

1974 E	123,548
•Ceuta	65,235
Melilla	58,313

SRI LANKA

1972 E	13,022,000
•COLOMBO (1973 E) (★1,475,000)	618,000
Dehiwala-Mount Lavinia (★Colombo) (1973 E)	136,000
Galle	80,000
Jaffna (1973 E)	112,000
Kandy	85,000
Kotte (★Colombo)	89,000
Moratuwa	93,000
Negombo	56,000
Trincomalee	44.000

SUDAN / As-Sūdān

1973 C	12,427,795
Al-Fāshir	51,932
•AL-KHURṬŪM (KHARTOUM) (★790,000)	333,921
Al-Khurṭūm Bahrī (Khartoum North) (★Al-Khurṭūm)	150,991
Al-Qaḍārif	66,465
Al-Ubayyid (El Obeid)	90,060
'Atbarah	66,116
Būr Sūdān (Port Sudan)	132,631
Jūbā	56,737
Kassalā	98,751
Kūstī	65,257
Nyala	59,852
Umm Durmān (Omdurman) (★Al-Khurṭūm)	299,401
Wad Madanī	106,776
Wāw	52,752

SURINAME

1971 C	384,900
•PARAMARIBO (★175,000)	102,300

SWAZILAND

1976 C	496,800
•MBABANE	22,000

SWEDEN / Sverige

1975 E	8,208,442
Borås	105,177
Borlänge	46,208
Eskilstuna	92,663
Gävle	86,911
Göteborg (Gothenburg) (★665,000)	444,651
Halmstad (74,292▲)	64,400
Helsingborg	101,685
Huddinge (★Stockholm)	62,576
Järfälla (★Stockholm)	51,549
Jönköping (108,500▲)	89,300
Kalmar (52,385▲)	44,500
Karlskrona (60,013▲)	50,100
Karlstad	72,369
Kristianstad (67,499▲)	44,300
Linköping	109,236
Luleå	66,290
Lund	76,284
Malmö (★315,000)	243,591
Mölndal (★Göteborg)	47,295
Nacka (★Stockholm)	55,321
Norrköping	119,169
Nykoping (62,561▲)	38,900
Örebro	117,837
Örnsköldsvik (60,378▲)	36,600
Ostersund (54,135▲)	47,100
Skellefteå (72,492▲)	42,000
Södertälje (★Stockholm)	77,695
Solna (★Stockholm)	53,878
•STOCKHOLM (★1,357,558)	665,202
Sundsvall	93,992
Trollhättan	50,225
Umeå (75,290▲)	64,100
Uppsala	138,116
Västerås	117,911
Växjö (62,048▲)	44,200

SWITZERLAND / Schweiz / Suisse

1977 E	6,297,600
Aarau (★51,200)	15,900
Baden (★66,800)	13,700
Basel (Bâle) (★555,000)	188,800
Bellinzona (★33,400)	17,400
BERN (BERNE) (★283,500)	146,800
Biel (Bienne) (★88,600)	59,200
Fribourg (Freiburg) (★53,600)	39,800
Genève (Geneva) (★400,000)	152,600
Lausanne (★227,300)	132,800
Locarno (★41,100)	15,300
Lugano (★68,100)	28,400
Luzern (Lucerne) (★156,200)	64,200
Neuchâtel (Neuenburg) (★59,900)	35,800
Olten (★48,000)	19,900
Sankt Gallen (St. Gall) (★113,000)	76,300
Schaffhausen (Schaffhouse) (★52,400)	32,900
Solothurn (Soleure) (★34,900)	15,900
Thun (Thoune) (★64,700)	36,900
Vevey (★60,400)	16,300
Winterthur (★107,300)	87,900
Zug (Zoug) (★52,200)	22,300
•Zürich (★775,000)	383,000

SYRIA / As-Sūrīyah

1970 C	6,304,685
Al-Lādhiqīyah (Latakia)	125,716
Al-Qāmishlī	47,714
Dayr as-Zawr	66,164
•DIMASHQ (DAMASCUS) (★1,100,000)	836,668
Ḥalab (Aleppo)	639,428
Ḥamāh	137,421
Ḥimṣ (Homs)	215,423
Mukhayyam al-Yarmūk (★Dimashq)	64,273

TAIWAN / T'aiwan

1973 E	15,426,939
Changhua (146,868▲)	111,000
Chiai	246,513
Chilung (Keelung) (1975 E)	341,400
Chungho (★T'aipei)	99,755
Chungli (Chunli) (146,140▲)	121,000
Hsinchu	220,302
Hualien	96,175
Ilan (73,860▲)	59,500
Kaohsiung (1975 E) (★1,145,000)	998,900
Kaohsiunghsien (Fengshan) (★Kaohsiung)	128,565
P'ingtung	169,657
Sanch'ung (★T'aipei)	259,837
T'aichung (1975 E) (546,800▲)	420,000
T'aichunghsien (Fengyüan)	84,000
T'ainan (1975 E)	523,600
•T'AIPEI (1975 E) (★3,175,000)	2,043,300
T'aipeihsien (Panch'iao) (★T'aipei)	159,566
T'aitung	60,000
T'aoyüan	124,821
Yungho (★T'aipei)	108,912

TANZANIA

1967 C	12,313,469
•DAR-ES-SALAAM (1970 E)	343,900
Tanga	61,058
Zanzibar	68,490

THAILAND / Prathet Thai

1972 E	36,286,000
Chiang Mai	93,353
Hat Yai	57,255
•KRUNG THEP (BANGKOK) (★3,375,000)	3,133,834
Nakhon Ratchasima	77,397
Nakhon Sawan	51,378
Nakhon Si Thammarat	50,761
Phitsanulok	70,649
Songkhla	50,687
Ubon Ratchathani	52,171
Udon Thani	70,110

TOGO

1971 E	1,914,000
•LOMÉ	144,300

TONGA

1966 C	77,429
•NUKUALOFA	15,545

TRINIDAD AND TOBAGO

1973 E	1,061,850
•PORT OF SPAIN (★350,000)	60,450
San Fernando (★73,000)	36,650

TUNISIA / Tunisie

1975 C	5,588,209
Binzert (Bizerte)	62,856
Kairouan	54,546
Sfax	171,297
Sousse	69,530
•TUNIS (★950,000)	550,404

TURKEY / Türkiye

1975 C	40,197,669
Adana	467,122
Adapazarı	113,411
Afyon	60,117
Akhisar	53,027
ANKARA (★1,750,000)	1,698,542
Antakya (Antioch)	77,437
Antalya	130,759
Aydın	59,228
Balıkesir	99,334
Batman	64,305
Buca (★Izmir) (1970 C)	52,526
Bursa	346,084
Ceyhan	62,861
Çorum	64,839
Denizli	106,704
Diyarbakır	169,746
Edirne	63,290
Elâzığ	131,116
Ereğli	50,402
Erzincan	60,459
Erzurum	162,925
Eskişehir	258,266
Gaziantep	300,801
Gelibolu (Gallipoli)	13,426
İskenderun (Alexandretta)	103,164
İsparta	62,873
•İstanbul (★3,675,000)	2,534,839
İzmir (Smyrna) (★945,000)	636,078
İzmit (Kocaeli)	164,675
Kâğithane (★İstanbul) (1970 C)	111,427
Karabük	69,070
Kars	54,787
Kartal (★İstanbul)	52,964
Kayseri	207,039
Kilis	54,012
Kırıkkale	138,015
Konya	246,381
Kütahya	82,400
Malatya	154,056
Manisa	78,133
Maraş	128,891
Mersin	152,186
Nazilli	52,019
Osmaniye	61,561
Sağmalcılar (★İstanbul) (1970 C)	124,085
Samsun	169,060
Sivas	149,155
Tarsus	101,690
Trabzon	97,208
Urfa	132,982
Uşak	58,561
Van	63,727
Zile	32,108
Zonguldak (★160,000)	90,110

UGANDA

1969 C	9,548,847
Jinja	52,509
•KAMPALA	330,700

UNION OF SOVIET SOCIALIST REPUBLICS / Sojuz Sovetskich Socialističeskich Respublik

1977 E	257,824,000
Abakan	123,000
Ačinsk (Achinsk)	117,000
Akt'ubinsk (Aktyubinsk)	184,000
Alapajevsk	52,000
Aleksandrija	79,000
Aleksandrov	58,000
Aleksin	66,000
Alma-Ata (★905,000)	871,000
Almalyk	97,000
Al'metjevsk	104,000
Alytus	51,000
Andižan (Andizhan)	224,000
Angarsk	233,000
Angren	102,000
Antracit (★Krasnjy Luč)	60,000
Anžero-Sudžensk	105,000
Apatity	58,000
Archangel'sk (Archangel)	391,000
Armavir	158,000
Arsenjev	60,000
Art'om (Artem)	70,000
Art'omovsk (Artemovsk)	91,000
Arzamas	89,000
Asbest	80,000
Aščhabad (Ashkhabad)	302,000
Astrachan' (Astrakhan')	466,000
Azov	75,000
Baku (★1,625,000)	961,000
Balakovo	140,000
Balašicha (★Moskva)	108,000
Balašov (Balashov)	91,000
Balchaš (Balkhash)	79,000
Baranoviči (Baranovichi)	126,000
Barnaul (★585,000)	522,000
Batajsk (★Rostov-na-Donu)	102,000
Batumi	118,000
Bekabad	63,000
Belaja Cerkov'	141,000
Bel'cy (Bel'tsy)	123,000
Belgorod	227,000
Belogorsk	65,000
Beloreck (Beloretsk)	72,000
Belovo	112,000
Bendery	100,000
Berd'ansk (Berdyansk)	119,000
Berdičev (Berdichev)	80,000
Berdsk (★Novosibirsk)	64,000
Berezniki	176,000
Bijsk (Biysk)	212,000
Birobidžan (Birobidzhan)	67,000
Blagoveščensk	177,000
Bobrujsk (Bobruysk)	192,000
Bor (★Gor'kij)	62,000
Borisoglebsk	69,000
Borisov	106,000
Boroviči (Borovichi)	59,000
Br'anka (★Kadijevka)	67,000
Br'ansk (Bryansk)	385,000
Bratsk	203,000
Brest	167,000
Brovary (★Kijev)	50,000
Buchara (Bukhara)	147,000
Bugul'ma	82,000
Buguruslan	53,000
Buzuluk	76,000
Čajkovskij (Chaykovskij)	64,000
Čapajevsk (Chapayevsk)	87,000
Čardžou (Chardzhou)	113,000
Čeboksary (Cheboksary)	292,000
Čel'abinsk (★1,195,000)	1,007,000
Celinograd (Tselinograd)	222,000
Čeremchovo (Cheremkhovo)	87,000
Čerepovec (Cherepovets)	246,000
Čerkassy (Cherkassy)	229,000
Čerkessk (Cherkessk)	85,000
Černigov (Chernigov)	233,000
Černogorsk (Chernogorsk)	70,000
Černovcy (Chernovtsy)	214,000
Červonograd (Chervonograd)	53,000
Chabarovsk (Khabarovsk)	524,000
Charcyzsk (★Doneck)	60,000
Char'kov (Kharkov) (★1,680,000)	1,405,000
Chasavjurt (Khasavyurt)	66,000
Cherson (Kherson)	324,000
Chimki (Khimki) (★Moskva)	106,000
Chmel'nickij (Khmel'nitskiy)	167,000
Čimkent (Chimkent)	303,000
Čirčik (Chirchik) (★Taškent)	131,000
Čistopol' (Chistopol')	67,000
Čita (Chita)	294,000
Čusovoj (Chusovoy)	59,000
Daugavpils	114,000
Derbent	69,000
Dimitrov (★Krasnoarmejsk)	58,000
Dimitrovgrad (Melekess)	99,000
Dmitrov	50,000
Dneprodzeržinsk (★Dnepropetrovsk)	251,000
Dnepropetrovsk (★1,410,000)	995,000
Dolgoprudnyj (★Moskva)	64,000
Doneck (Donetsk) (★2,025,000)	984,000
Drogobyč (Drogobych)	68,000
Družkovka (★Kramatorsk)	61,000
Dubna	51,000
Dušanbe (Dushanbe)	460,000
Džalal-Abad	54,000
Džambul (Dzhambul)	252,000
Dzeržinsk (★Gor'kij)	248,000
Džezkazgan (Dzhezkazgan)	85,000
Džizak	59,000
Ekibastuz	55,000
Elektrostal'	135,000
Elista	63,000
Engel's (★Saratov)	163,000
Feodosija	77,000
Fergana	135,000
Frunze	511,000
Gatčina (★Leningrad)	74,000
Georgijevsk	51,000
Georgiu-Dež (Liski)	52,000
Glazov	82,000
Gomel'	360,000
Gori	54,000
Gor'kij (Gorky) (★1,835,000)	1,319,000
Gorlovka (★705,000)	342,000
Gorno-Altajsk (1975 E)	39,000
Grodno	182,000
Groznyj (Groznyy)	387,000
Gubkin	68,000
Gukovo	71,000
Gurjev (Gur'yev)	134,000
Gus'-Chrustal'nyj	70,000
Igarka (1974 E)	16,000
Inta	52,000
Irbit	52,000
Irkutsk	532,000
Išim (Ishim)	63,000
Išimbaj (Ishimbay)	58,000
Iskitim	59,000
Ivano-Frankovsk	142,000
Ivanovo	461,000
Iževsk (Izhevsk)	534,000
Izmail	79,000
Iz'um	58,000
Jakutsk (Yakutsk)	149,000
Jalta (Yalta)	77,000
Jangijul' (Yangiyul')	62,000
Jaroslavl' (Yaroslavl')	584,000
Jefremov (Yefremov)	53,000
Jegorjevsk (Yegor'yevsk)	71,000
Jejsk (Yeysk)	71,000
Jelec (Yelets)	113,000
Jelgava	65,000
Jenakijevo (★Gorlovka)	114,000
Jerevan (Yerevan) (★1,065,000)	956,000
Jessentuki (Yessentuki)	74,000
Jevpatorija (Yevpatoriya)	94,000
Joškar-Ola (Yoshkar-Ola)	216,000
Jurga (Yurga)	75,000
Jūrmala (★Rīga)	59,000
Južno-Sachalinsk	134,000
Kadijevka (★600,000)	141,000
Kalinin	401,000
Kaliningrad (★Moskva)	121,000
Kaliningrad (Königsberg)	353,000
Kaluga	262,000
Kaluš	57,000
Kamenec-Podol'skij	79,000
Kamensk-Šachtinskij	76,000
Kamensk-Ural'skij	187,000
Kamyšin (Kamyshin)	109,000
Kansk	98,000
Karaganda	576,000
Karši (Karshi)	95,000
Kattakurgan	51,000
Kaunas	359,000
Kazan' (★1,015,000)	970,000
Kemerovo	454,000
Kentau	61,000
Kerč (Kerch')	154,000
Kijev (Kiev) (★2,290,000)	2,079,000
Kimry	59,000
Kinešma (Kineshma)	101,000
Kirov	381,000
Kirovabad	216,000
Kirovakan	133,000
Kirovo-Čepeck	64,000
Kirovograd	228,000
Kisel'ovsk (★Prokopjevsk)	124,000
Kišin'ov (Kishinev)	489,000
Kislovodsk	98,000
Kizel (1974 E)	42,000
Klaipėda (Memel)	173,000
Klimovsk (★Moskva)	52,000
Klin	89,000
Klincy (Klintsy)	66,000
Kohtla-Järve	72,000
Kokand	155,000
Kokčetav (Kokchetav)	98,000
Kolomna	145,000
Kolomyja	51,000
Kolpino (★Leningrad)	104,000
Kommunarsk (★Kadijevka)	129,000
Komsomol'sk-na-Amure	252,000
Konotop	77,000
Konstantinovka	111,000

▲ Population of an entire municipality, commune, or district, including rural area.
• Largest city in country.
★ Population or designation of the metropolitan area, including suburbs.
C Census. **E** Official estimate. **UE** Unofficial estimate.
L Population within municipal limits of year specified.

▲ Bevölkerung eines ganzen städtischen Verwaltungsgebietes, eines Kommunalbezirkes oder eines Distrikts, einschliesslich ländlicher Gebiete.
• Grösste Stadt des Landes.
★ Bevölkerung oder Bezeichnung der Stadtregion einschliess lich Vororte.
C Volkszählung. **E** Offizielle Schätzung.
UE Inoffizielle Schätzung.
L Bevölkerung innerhalb der städtischen Verwaltungseinheit des angegebenen Jahres.

Kopejsk (★Čel'abinsk) 157,000
Korkino 66,000
Korosten' 62,000
Kostroma 250,000
Kotlas 63,000
Kovrov 140,000
Kramatorsk (1976 E) (★420,000) 167,000
Krasnoarmejsk (★150,000) 59,000
Krasnodar 552,000
Krasnodon (1974 E) 46,000
Krasnogorsk (★Moskva) 72,000
Krasnojarsk (Krasnoyarsk) 769,000
Krasnokamsk 58,000
Krasnoturjinsk 60,000
Krasnovodsk 55,000
Krasnyj Luč (★220,000) 105,000
Kremenčug (Kremenchug) 206,000
Krivoj Rog (Krivoy Rog) 641,000
Kronštadt (Kronshtadt)
(★Leningrad) (1970 C) 39,477
Kropotkin 74,000
Kstovo (★Gor'kij) 56,000
Kujbyšev (Kuybyshev)
(★1,420,000) 1,204,000
Kul'ab 51,000
Kumertau 54,000
Kungur 83,000
Kurgan 304,000
Kursk 373,000
Kustanaj (Kustanay) 154,000
Kutaisi 182,000
Kuzneck (Kuznetsk) 96,000
Kyzyl 59,000
Kzyl-Orda 148,000
Labinsk 57,000
Leninabad 123,000
Leninakan 192,000
Leningrad (★5,150,000) 3,963,000
Leninogorsk (*Tatarsk obl.*) 52,000
Leninogorsk (*Vostochno-Kazakh obl.*) 69,000
Leninsk-Kuzneckij 131,000
Lida 56,000
Liepāja 104,000
Lipeck (Lipetsk) 375,000
Lisičansk (★365,000) 123,000
L'ubercy (★Moskva) 156,000
Lubny 51,000
Luck (Lutsk) 133,000
L'vov 642,000
Lys'va 76,000
Machačkala (Makhachkala) 239,000
Magadan 116,000
Magnitogorsk 398,000
Majkop (Maykop) 128,000
Makejevka (★Doneck) 437,000
Margilan 115,000
Mary 72,000
Melitopol' 157,000
Meždurečensk 91,000
Miass 146,000
Michajlovka (Mikhaylovka) 58,000
Mičurinsk (Michurinsk) 102,000
Mineral'nyje Vody 64,000
Mingečaur 54,000
Minsk (★1,250,000) 1,216,000
Minusinsk 51,000
Mogil'ov (Mogilev) 275,000
Molodečno (Molodechno) 66,000
Moršansk 50,000
•MOSKVA (MOSCOW)
(★10,925,000) 7,644,000
Mozyr' 72,000
Mukačevo (Mukachevo) 71,000
Murmansk 374,000
Murom 112,000
Mytišči (Mytishchi) (★Moskva) 136,000
Nabereżnyje Čelny
(Naberezhnyye Chelny) 253,000
Nachodka (Nakhodka) 129,000
Nal'čik (Nal'chik) 199,000
Namangan 224,000
Naro-Fominsk 54,000
Narva 72,000
Navoi 87,000
Nebit-Dag 67,000
Neftekamsk 63,000
Nevinnomyssk 101,000
Nežin (Nezhin) 70,000
Nikolajev (Nikolayev) 447,000
Nikopol' 146,000
Nižnekamskij (Nizhnekamsk) 120,000
Nižnevartovsk 76,000
Nižnij Tagil (Nizhniy Tagil) 399,000
Noginsk 112,000
Noril'sk 173,000
Novgorod 179,000
Novoaltajsk (★Barnaul) 53,000
Novočeboksarsk 74,000
Novočerkassk 184,000
Novokujbyševsk (★Kujbyšev) 114,000
Novokuzneck (Novokuznetsk) 537,000
Novomoskovsk
(*Dnepropetrovsk obl.*) 70,000
Novomoskovsk (*Tula obl.*)
(1976 E) (★365,000) 146,000
Novopolock 65,000
Novorossijsk (Novorossiysk) 153,000
Novošachtinsk 101,000
Novosibirsk (★1,435,000) 1,304,000
Novotroick (Novotroitsk) 96,000
Nukus 100,000
Obninsk 69,000
Odessa (★1,100,000) 1,039,000
Odincovo (★Moskva) 80,000
Okt'abr'skij (Oktyabr'skiy) 88,000
Omsk 1,026,000
Ordžonikidze (Ordzhonikidze) 281,000
Orechovo-Zujevo (1976 E)
(★195,000) 128,000
Orenburg 446,000
Or'ol (Orel) 289,000
Orša (Orsha) 116,000
Orsk 244,000
Oš (Osh) 161,000

Osinniki 60,000
Panevėžys 97,000
Pärnu 50,000
P'atigorsk (Pyatigorsk) 105,000
Pavlodar 258,000
Pavlograd 100,000
Pavlovo 68,000
Pavlovskij Posad 69,000
Penza 443,000
Perm' (★1,045,000) 972,000
Pervomajsk 75,000
Pervomajsk (★Kadijevka)
(1974 E) 46,000
Pervoural'sk 126,000
Petrodvorec (Petrodvorets)
(★Leningrad) 65,000
Petropavlovsk 199,000
Petropavlovsk-Kamčatskij 207,000
Petrozavodsk 220,000
Pinsk 87,000
Podol'sk (★Moskva) 193,000
Polevskoj (Polevskoy) 64,000
Polock (Polotsk) 76,000
Poltava 274,000
Poti 54,000
Priluki 66,000
Prokopjevsk (Prokop'yevsk)
(1976 E) (★395,000) 267,000
Prževal'sk 51,000
Pskov 167,000
Puškin (★Leningrad) 86,000
Puškino (Pushkino) 65,000
Ramenskoje (★Moskva) 73,000
R'azan' (Ryazan') 442,000
Rečica (Rechitsa) 60,000
Reutov (★Moskva) 59,000
Revda 61,000
Rīga (★895,000) 816,000
Romny 51,000
Roslavl' 55,000
Rostov-na-Donu (★1,065,000) 921,000
Roven'ki 62,000
Rovno 167,000
Rubcovsk (Rubtsovsk) 173,000
Rubežnoje (★Lisičansk) 68,000
Rudnyj (Rudnyy) 108,000
Rustavi (★Tbilisi) 131,000
Rybinsk 237,000
Ržev (Rzhev) 69,000
Sachtinsk 52,000
Šach'torsk (★Torez) 73,000
Šachty (Shakhty) 223,000
Šadrinsk (Shadrinsk) 82,000
Safonovo 53,000
Salavat 131,000
Salsk 57,000
Samarkand 312,000
Saran' 55,000
Saransk 248,000
Sarapul 108,000
Saratov (★1,075,000) 856,000
Ščelkovo (★Moskva) 91,000
Ščokino (Shchekino) 72,000
Semipalatinsk 282,000
Serov 101,000
Serpuchov (Serpukhov) 132,000
Sevastopol' 283,000
Ševčenko (Shevchenko) 111,000
Severodoneck (★Lisičansk) 111,000
Severodvinsk 188,000
Šiauliai 115,000
Simferopol' 291,000
Slav'ansk (★Kramatorsk) 138,000
Slav'ansk-na-Kubani 57,000
Smela 60,000
Smolensk 264,000
Snežnoje (★Torez) 63,000
Soči (Sochi) 255,000
Sokol (1974 E) 48,000
Soligorsk 57,000
Solikamsk 97,000
Solncevo (★Moskva) 51,000
Šostka (Shostka) 64,000
Spassk-Dal'nij 52,000
Staryj Oskol 92,000
Stavropol' 245,000
Sterlitamak 211,000
Stryj 57,000
Stupino 64,000
Suchumi (Sukhumi) 120,000
Šuja (Shuya) 72,000
Sumgait (★Baku) 174,000
Sumy 203,000
Surgut 74,000
Sverdlovsk (*Sverdlovsk obl.*)
(★1,400,000) 1,187,000
Sverdlovsk (*Vorosilovgrad obl.*) 72,000
Svetlogorsk 57,000
Svobodnyj 72,000
Syktyvkar 161,000
Syzran' 187,000
Taganrog 285,000
Taldy-Kurgan 84,000
Tallinn 415,000
Tambov 265,000
Tartu 100,000
Tašauz (Tashauz) 84,000
Taškent (Tashkent)
(★1,880,000) 1,689,000
Tbilisi (★1,205,000) 1,042,000
Temirtau 202,000
Termez 57,000
Ternopol' 133,000
Tichoreck (Tikhoretsk) 63,000
Tichvin 54,000
Tiraspol' 142,000
Tobol'sk 53,000
Tokmak 56,000
Toljatti (Togliatti) 479,000
Tomsk 423,000
Torez (Thorez) (★290,000) 96,000
Toržok 50,000
Troick (Troitsk) 92,000
Tuapse 63,000
Tula (★605,000) 510,000

Tulun 51,000
T'umen' (Tyumen') 347,000
Turkestan 61,000
Uchta (Ukhta) 77,000
Ufa 942,000
Uglič (Uglich) (1974 E) 37,000
Ulan-Ude 308,000
Uljanovsk (Ul'yanovsk) 447,000
Uman' 81,000
Ural'sk 162,000
Urgenč (Urgench) 94,000
Usolje-Sibirskoje 101,000
Ussurijsk 147,000
Ust-Ilimsk 53,000
Ust'-Kamenogorsk 267,000
Užgorod (Uzhgorod) 85,000
Uzlovaja (★Novomoskovsk) 64,000
V'az'ma (Vyaz'ma) 51,000
Velikije Luki 103,000
Ventspils (1974 E) 44,000
Verchn'aja Salda 52,000
Vičuga (Vichuga) 52,000
Vilnius 458,000
Vinnica (Vinnitsa) 297,000
Vitebsk 286,000
Vladimir 284,000
Vladivostok 536,000
Volgodonsk 54,000
Volgograd (Stalingrad)
(★1,205,000) 931,000
Vologda 224,000
Vol'sk 72,000
Volžsk 54,000
Volžskij (★Volgograd) 203,000
Vorkuta 96,000
Voronež (Voronezh) 779,000
Vorošilovgrad (Lugansk) 445,000
Voskresensk 74,000
Votkinsk 88,000
Vyborg 72,000
Vyšnij Voločok 75,000
Zagorsk 101,000
Zaporožje (Zaporozh'ye) 772,000
Ždanov (Zhdanov) 474,000
Zelenograd (★Moskva) 125,000
Železnodorožnyj (★Moskva) 72,000
Železnogorsk 60,000
Zel'onodol'sk (Zelenodol'sk) 86,000
Žigulevsk (Zhigulevsk) 50,000
Zima 51,000
Žitomir (Zhitomir) 236,000
Zlatoust 197,000
Žoltyje Vody 52,000
Žukovskij (Zhukovskiy) 87,000
Zyr'anovsk (Zyryanovsk) 55,000

UNITED ARAB EMIRATES / Ittiḥād al-Imārāt al-'Arabiyah

1973 E 208,000
ABŪ ZABY 50,000
•Dubayy (1970 E) 60,000

UNITED KINGDOM†

1976 E 55,927,500
Aberdeen, Scot. 209,831
Accrington (Hyndburn)
(★Blackburn) 80,400
Adur (★Brighton) 57,500
Aldershot (Rushmoor)
(★London) 82,400
Ashton-under-Lyne (Tameside)
(★Manchester) 222,100
Aylesbury (1973 E) 41,420
Ayr, Scot. (1974 E) (★97,000) 47,991
Barnsley 224,400
Barrow-in-Furness 73,400
Basildon (★London) 141,700
Basingstoke (1973 E) 60,910
Bath 83,100
Bedford (1973 E) 74,390
Beeston and Stapleford
(★Nottingham) (1973 E) 65,360
Belfast, N. Ire. (★710,000) 363,000
Benfleet (Castle Point)
(★London) 82,900
Birkenhead (Wirral)
(★Liverpool) 348,200
Birmingham (★2,680,000) 1,058,800
Blackburn (★222,900) 142,500
Blackpool (★285,000) 149,000
Blyth (Blyth Valley) 69,300
Bolton (★Manchester) 261,000
Bootle (★Liverpool) (1973 E) 71,160
Bournemouth (★305,000) 144,100
Bradford (★Leeds) 458,900
Brentwood (★London) (1973 E) 58,690
Brighton (★425,000) 156,500
Bristol (★640,000) 416,300
Burnley (★160,000) 92,100
Burton upon Trent (1973 E) 49,480
Bury (★Manchester) 181,200
Bury St. Edmunds (1973 E) 26,800
Camborne-Redruth (1973 E) 43,970
Cambridge 106,400
Cannock (Cannock Chase)
(★Birmingham) 84,800
Cardiff, Wales (★625,000) 281,500
Carlisle (1973 E) 70,930
Carlton (Gedling)
(★Nottingham) 101,600
Castlereagh, N. Ire. (★Belfast)
(1975 E) 63,600
Chatham (Medway) (★London) 144,500
Chelmsford (★London)
(1973 E) 58,320
Cheltenham 86,500
Chertsey (Runnymede)
(★London) 74,800
Cheshunt (Broxbourne)
(★London) 76,800
Chester (1973 E) 61,370
Chesterfield (★125,000) 93,900
Chigwell (★London) (1973 E) 54,220
Clacton-on-Sea (1973 E) 39,380

Clydebank, Scot. (★Glasgow) 55,902
Colchester (1973 E) 79,600
Corby 55,600
Coventry (★650,000) 336,800
Crawley (★London) 72,600
Crewe (1973 E) 50,450
Crosby (★Liverpool) (1973 E) 56,750
Darlington (1973 E) 85,120
Dartford (★London) (1973 E) 44,130
Derby (★270,000) 213,700
Dewsbury (★Leeds) (1973 E) 50,560
Doncaster (1973 E) (★160,000) 81,530
Dover (1973 E) 34,160
Dudley (★Birmingham) 300,200
Dundee, Scot. 194,420
Dunfermline, Scot. (1974 E)
(★124,893) 53,418
Durham (1973 E) 29,490
Eastbourne 73,200
East Kilbride, Scot. (★Glasgow)
(1974 E) 67,834
Edinburg, Scot. (★650,000) 467,097
Ellesmere Port (★Liverpool)
(1973 E) 63,870
Epsom and Ewell (★London) 70,700
Exeter 93,300
Falkirk, Scot. (1974 E)
(★142,058) 36,589
Fareham (★Portsmouth) 86,300
Folkestone (1973 E) 45,610
Gateshead (★Newcastle) 222,000
Gillingham (★London) 93,900
Glasgow, Scot. (★1,890,000) 856,012
Gloucester (★113,000) 91,600
Gosport (★Portsmouth) 82,300
Gravesend (Gravesham)
(★London) 96,000
Great Yarmouth (1973 E) 49,410
Grimsby (★150,000) 93,800
Guildford (★London) (1973 E) 58,470
Halifax (1973 E) (★164,000) 88,580
Haltemprice (★Hull) (1973 E) 54,850
Hamilton, Scot. (★Glasgow) 107,178
Harlow (★London) 80,000
Harrogate (1973 E) 64,620
Hartlepool (★Middlesbrough) 97,100
Hastings 74,600
Havant (★Portsmouth) 116,400
Hemel Hempstead (★London)
(1973 E) 71,150
Hereford 47,800
Hertford (★London) (1973 E) 20,760
Hertsmere (★London) 87,400
High Wycombe (1973 E) 61,190
Hove (★Brighton) 88,100
Huddersfield (1973 E)
(★209,000) 130,060
Huyton-with-Roby (Knowsley)
(★Liverpool) 189,700
Iverclyde (Greenock), Scot. 104,116
Ipswich 121,500
Irvine, Scot. (★89,000) 50,900
Islwyn, Wales (★Newport) 66,200
Kidderminster (1973 E) 49,960
Kilmarnock, Scot. (1974 E)
(★82,000) 50,318
Kingston upon Hull (Hull)
(★355,000) 276,600
Kingswood (★Bristol) 78,800
Kirkcaldy, Scot. (1974 E)
(★148,028) 50,063
Lancaster (1973 E) (★100,000) 50,570
Leeds (★1,555,000) 744,500
Leicester (★495,000) 289,400
Leyland (South Ribble)
(★Preston) 92,000
Lincoln 73,700
Liverpool (★1,575,000) 539,700
•LONDON (★11,175,000) 7,028,200
Londonderry, N. Ire.
(1973 E) (★87,000) 51,200
Loughborough (1973 E) 49,010
Lowestoft (1973 E) 53,260
Lurgan, N. Ire. (1971 C)
(★59,000) 25,431
Luton (★210,000) 164,500
Macclesfield (1973 E) 45,420
Maidenhead (★London) (1973 E) 48,210
Maidstone (1973 E) 72,110
Manchester (★2,835,000) 490,000
Mansfield (1973 E) (★198,000) 58,450
Margate (1973 E) 50,290
Merthyr Tydfil, Wales (1973 E) 53,680
Middlesbrough (Teesside)
(★580,000) 153,900
Monklands (Coatbridge),
Scot. 107,561
Motherwell, Scot. (★Glasgow) 161,104
Newcastle-under-Lyme
(★Stoke-on-Trent) (1973 E) 75,940
Newcastle-upon-Tyne
(★1,325,000) 295,800
Newport (Wales) (★310,000) 134,100
Newtownabbey, N. Ire.
(★Belfast) (1975 E) 71,500
Northampton 142,000
North Down (Bangor), N. Ire.
(★Belfast) (1975 E) 59,600
Norwich (★201,000) 119,200
Nottingham (★655,000) 280,300
Nuneaton (★Coventry) 111,100
Oadby and Wigston
(★Leicester) 52,400
Oldham (★Manchester) 227,500
Oxford (★215,000) 117,400
Penzance (1973 E) 19,360
Perth, Scot. (1974 E) 44,066
Peterborough (1973 E) 72,270
Plymouth (★295,000) 259,100
Pontypcol (Torfaen), Wales
(★Newport) 88,700
Poole (★Bournemouth) 110,600
Portsmouth (★500,000) 198,500
Port Talbot, Wales (1973 E)
(★132,000) 50,200

▲ Población de un municipio, comuna o distrito entero, incluyendo sus áreas rurales.
• Ciudad más grande de un país.
★ Población o designación de un área metropolitana, incluyendo los suburbios.
C Censo. E Estimado oficial.
UE Estimado no oficial.
L Población dentro de los límites municipales de un año específico.

▲ Population d'une municipalité, d'une commune ou d'un district, zone rurale incluse.
• Ville la plus peuplée du pays.
★ Population de l'agglomération (ou nom de la zone métropolitaine englobante).
C Recensement. E Estimation officielle.
UE Estimation non officielle.
L Population comprise dans les limites municipales de l'année indiquée.

▲ População de um município, comuna ou distrito, inclusive as respectivas áreas rurais.
• Maior cidade de um país.
★ População ou indicação de uma área metropolitana, inclusive subúrbios.
C Censo. E Estimativa oficial.
UE Estimativa não oficial.
L População dentro dos limites municipais no ano indicado.

UNITED KINGDOM, *continued*

Preston (★245,000)	131,200
Ramsgate (1973 E)	40,090
Reading (★201,000)	131,200
Redditch (★Birmingham)	51,600
Reigate and Banstead (★London)	112,400
Renfrew, Scot. (★Glasgow)	209,476
Rhondda, Wales (★Cardiff)	85,400
Rochdale (★Manchester)	210,200
Rotherham (★Sheffield)	249,400
Rugby (1973 E)	60,380
Saint Albans (★London)	123,800
Saint Helens	194,400
Salford (★Manchester)	261,100
Salisbury (1973 E)	35,460
Scarborough (1973 E)	43,300
Scunthorpe	68,100
Sheffield (★725,000)	558,000
Shrewsbury (1973 E)	56,120
Slough (★London)	99,700
Smethwick (Sandwell) (★Birmingham)	312,900
Solihull (★Birmingham)	199,600
Southampton (★400,000)	213,700
Southend-on-Sea (★London)	159,300
Southport (★Liverpool) (1973 E)	86,030
South Shields (South Tyneside) (★Newcastle)	166,800
Stafford (1973 E)	54,860
Staines (Spelthorne) (★London)	95,900
Stevenage	72,600
Stirling, Scot. (1974 E) (★58,000)	29,818
Stockport (★Manchester)	292,900
Stockton-on-Tees (★Middlesbrough)	165,400
Stoke-on-Trent (★445,000)	256,200
Stratford-upon-Avon (1973 E)	20,080
Stretford (Trafford) (★Manchester)	227,400
Sunderland (★Newcastle)	295,700
Swansea, Wales (★270,000)	190,800
Swindon (Thamesdown)	142,700
Tamworth	52,800
Taunton (1973 E)	37,570
Thurrock (★London)	127,700
Torquay (Torbay)	109,900
Tunbridge Wells (1973 E)	44,800
Tynemouth (North Tyneside) (★Newcastle)	202,600
Wakefield (★Leeds) (1973 E)	58,490
Walsall (★Birmingham)	268,600
Walton and Weybridge (Elmbridge) (★London)	112,300
Wansbeck	62,300
Warrington	166,200
Watford (★London)	77,000
Weston-super-Mare (1973 E)	51,960
Weymouth and Portland	57,000
Widnes (Halton)	113,100
Wigan (★Manchester)	310,700
Woking (★London)	79,300
Wolverhampton (★Birmingham)	266,400
Worcester	73,900
Worthing (★Brighton)	89,100
Wrexham, Wales (1973 E)	39,530
York (★140,000)	101,900

UNITED STATES[1]

1978 UE[2]	217,265,200
Abilene, Tex. (★103,200)	99,400
Akron, Ohio (★614,000)	242,600
Alameda, Calif. (★San Francisco)	69,300
Albany, Ga. (★92,300)	72,500
Albany, N.Y. (★736,400)	106,600
Albuquerque, N. Mex. (★395,000)	288,600
Alexandria, La. (★99,600)	50,200
Alexandria, Va. (★Washington)	108,700
Alhambra, Calif. (★Los Angeles)	60,600
Allentown, Pa. (★527,000)	104,900
Alliance, Ohio (★51,600)	25,600
Altoona, Pa. (★119,900)	57,400
Amarillo, Tex. (★146,000)	140,500
Ames, Iowa (★58,400)	45,200
Amherst, N.Y. (★Buffalo)	64,900
Anaheim, Calif. (★Los Angeles)	203,000
Anchorage, Alaska (★178,600)	178,600
Anderson, Ind. (★148,000)	68,600
Anderson, S.C. (★65,500)	29,000
Annapolis, Md. (★70,200)	33,300
Ann Arbor, Mich. (★Detroit)	104,500
Anniston, Ala. (★102,900)	31,100
Antioch, Calif. (★93,700)	35,900
Appleton, Wis. (★164,000)	60,500
Arcadia, Calif. (★Los Angeles)	48,700
Arden, Calif. (★Sacramento)	52,900
Arlington, Mass. (★Boston)	48,000
Arlington, Tex. (★Dallas)	121,500
Arlington, Va. (★Washington)	152,300
Arlington Heights, Ill. (★Chicago)	72,200
Arvada, Colo. (★Denver)	83,200
Asheville, N.C. (★133,200)	58,000
Ashtabula, Ohio (★44,700)	24,000
Athens, Ga. (★86,600)	50,500
Atlanta, Ga. (★1,760,000)	406,000
Atlantic City, N.J. (★166,300)	43,100
Auburn, N.Y. (★48,000)	32,000
Augusta, Ga. (★217,000)	51,200
Augusta, Maine (★51,400)	20,600
Aurora, Colo. (★Denver)	128,000
Aurora, Ill. (★Chicago)	79,600
Austin, Tex. (★394,000)	326,000
Bakersfield, Calif. (★215,000)	85,500
Baltimore, Md. (★1,895,000)	814,000
Bangor, Maine (★86,500)	31,900
Baton Rouge, La. (★388,000)	198,000
Battle Creek, Mich. (★106,000)	37,900
Bay City, Mich. (★183,700)	46,100
Bayonne, N.J. (★New York)	74,100
Baytown, Tex. (★Houston)	48,900
Beaumont, Tex. (★324,000)	112,700
Beckley, W.Va. (★62,300)	21,200
Belleville, Ill. (★St. Louis)	45,000
Bellevue, Wash. (★Seattle)	68,600
Bellflower, Calif. (★Los Angeles)	51,300
Bellingham, Wash. (★64,300)	43,800
Beloit, Wis. (★57,800)	34,600
Benton Harbor, Mich. (★101,500)	15,300
Berkeley, Calif. (★San Francisco)	108,500
Berwyn, Ill. (★Chicago)	47,800
Bethesda, Md. (★Washington)	77,700
Bethlehem, Pa. (★Allentown)	72,900
Billings, Mont. (★94,700)	72,100
Biloxi, Miss. (★Gulfport)	45,200
Binghamton, N.Y. (★249,900)	59,500
Birmingham, Ala. (★695,000)	267,500
Bismarck, N.Dak. (★56,300)	40,600
Bloomfield, N.J. (★New York)	52,100
Bloomington, Ill. (★88,200)	43,300
Bloomington, Ind. (★90,400)	49,500
Bloomington, Minn. (★Minneapolis)	79,000
Boise, Idaho (★138,500)	107,600
Boston, Mass. (★3,825,000)	624,000
Boulder, Colo. (★96,700)	79,900
Bowling Green, Ky. (★50,200)	38,300
Bremerton, Wash. (★110,500)	39,600
Bridgeport, Conn. (★444,400)	136,800
Bristol, Conn. (★Hartford)	58,400
Bristol, Tenn. (★72,300)	27,400
Brockton, Mass. (★Boston)	96,000
Brookline, Mass. (★Boston)	49,300
Brownsville, Tex. (★282,000)	78,000
Brunswick, Ga. (★45,900)	18,100
Bryan, Tex. (★71,100)	37,400
Buena Park, Calif. (★Los Angeles)	62,500
Buffalo, N.Y. (★1,225,000)	387,000
Burbank, Calif. (★Los Angeles)	85,200
Burlington, N.C. (★91,800)	37,200
Burlington, Vt. (★107,100)	36,800
Butler, Pa. (★78,300)	17,400
Butte, Mont. (★39,500)	39,500
Cambridge, Mass. (★Boston)	103,400
Camden, N.J. (★Philadelphia)	87,600
Canton, Ohio (★309,000)	97,600
Cape Girardeau, Mo. (★49,300)	32,400
Carson, Calif. (★Los Angeles)	78,500
Carson City, Nev.	28,700
Casper, Wyo. (★55,200)	43,700
Catonsville, Md. (★Baltimore)	47,000
Cedar Rapids, Iowa (★154,400)	110,400
Champaign, Ill. (★126,000)	60,100
Charleston, S.C. (★326,000)	56,300
Charleston, W.Va. (★235,000)	64,800
Charlotte, N.C. (★454,000)	283,400
Charlottesville, Va. (★68,800)	41,300
Chattanooga, Tenn. (★334,700)	154,600
Cheektowaga, N.Y. (★Buffalo)	99,800
Cherry Hill, N.J. (★Philadelphia)	69,500
Chesapeake (South Norfolk), Va. (★Norfolk)	112,000
Chester, Pa. (★Philadelphia)	45,500
Cheyenne, Wyo. (★59,500)	47,000
Chicago, Ill. (★7,635,000)	2,980,000
Chico, Calif. (★59,400)	25,200
Chicopee, Mass. (★Springfield)	55,000
Chula Vista, Calif. (★San Diego)	79,900
Cicero, Ill. (★Chicago)	61,600
Cincinnati, Ohio (★1,425,000)	390,000
Clarksburg, W.Va. (★55,400)	22,800
Clarksville, Tenn. (★82,600)	57,400
Clearwater, Fla. (★St. Petersburg)	72,300
Cleveland, Ohio (★2,255,000)	595,000
Cleveland Heights, Ohio (★Cleveland)	47,400
Clifton, N.J. (★New York)	77,500
Clinton, Iowa (★45,300)	33,200
Clinton Township, Mich. (★Detroit)	65,500
Coatesville, Pa. (★76,000)	12,400
Cocoa, Fla. (★90,000)	14,900
Colorado Springs, Colo. (★274,000)	183,500
Columbia, Mo. (★69,800)	62,400
Columbia, S.C. (★342,000)	111,000
Columbus, Ga. (★219,700)	160,000
Columbus, Ind. (★66,700)	27,700
Columbus, Ohio (★922,000)	527,000
Compton, Calif. (★Los Angeles)	76,400
Concord, Calif. (★San Francisco)	99,700
Concord, N.H. (★54,600)	29,100
Corpus Christi, Tex. (★262,000)	216,000
Corvallis, Oreg. (★50,400)	38,600
Costa Mesa, Calif. (★Los Angeles)	78,300
Council Bluffs, Iowa (★Omaha)	58,400
Covington, Ky. (★Cincinnati)	43,300
Cranston, R.I. (★Providence)	72,800
Cumberland, Md. (★81,100)	26,200
Dallas, Tex. (★2,495,000)	800,000
Daly City, Calif. (★San Francisco)	74,200
Danbury, Conn. (★129,000)	56,500
Danville, Ill. (★82,800)	43,800
Danville, Va. (★71,900)	45,300
Davenport, Iowa (★320,700)	101,500
Dayton, Ohio (★905,000)	187,400
Daytona Beach, Fla. (★130,500)	49,000
Dearborn, Mich. (★Detroit)	95,500
Dearborn Heights, Mich. (★Detroit)	78,000
Decatur, Ala. (★59,000)	39,500
Decatur, Ill. (★117,200)	88,900
De Kalb, Ill. (★44,500)	29,800
Denver, Colo. (★1,305,000)	473,900
Des Moines, Iowa (★323,000)	191,000
Des Plaines, Ill. (★Chicago)	54,700
Detroit, Mich. (★4,660,000)	1,245,000
Dothan, Ala. (★61,100)	45,600
Dover, Del. (★73,300)	23,100
Dover, N.H. (★69,700)	20,600
Downey, Calif. (★Los Angeles)	86,400
Dubuque, Iowa (★82,100)	63,200
Duluth, Minn. (★146,200)	93,000
Dundalk, Md. (★Baltimore)	88,800
Durham, N.C. (★193,800)	105,400
East Chicago, Ind. (★Chicago)	42,700
East Detroit, Mich. (★Detroit)	40,100
East Hartford, Conn. (★Hartford)	52,200
East Lansing, Mich. (★Lansing)	51,600
East Liverpool, Ohio (★64,700)	21,200
East Los Angeles, Calif. (★Los Angeles)	100,700
East Orange, N.J. (★New York)	72,300
East Providence, R.I. (★Providence)	49,900
East St. Louis, Ill. (★St. Louis)	53,600
Eau Claire, Wis. (★84,300)	49,500
Edina, Minn. (★Minneapolis)	49,300
Edison, N.J. (★New York)	65,400
El Cajon, Calif. (★San Diego)	68,100
Elgin, Ill. (★Chicago)	62,800
Elizabeth, N.J. (★New York)	100,600
Elmira, N.Y. (★130,300)	35,600
El Monte, Calif. (★Los Angeles)	67,500
El Paso, Tex. (★1,020,000)	402,000
Elyria, Ohio (★Cleveland)	50,600
Enid, Okla. (★54,400)	51,400
Erie, Pa. (★239,500)	126,400
Escondido, Calif. (★San Diego)	56,200
Euclid, Ohio (★Cleveland)	60,300
Eugene, Oreg. (★205,000)	97,900
Eureka, Calif. (★69,800)	24,100
Evanston, Ill. (★Chicago)	75,300
Evansville, Ind. (★214,000)	131,100
Everett, Wash. (★Seattle)	48,600
Fairbanks, Alaska (★49,000)	35,100
Fairfield, Calif. (★99,300)	54,200
Fairfield, Conn. (★Bridgeport)	59,100
Fairmont, W.Va. (★53,700)	26,200
Fall River, Mass. (★169,900)	101,100
Fargo, N.Dak. (★101,400)	58,100
Farmington Hills, Mich. (★Detroit)	55,600
Fayetteville, Ark. (★77,600)	34,500
Fayetteville, N.C. (★225,000)	67,200
Fitchburg, Mass. (★100,400)	36,600
Flint, Mich. (★543,000)	164,100
Florence, Ala. (★93,300)	34,600
Florence, S.C. (★57,000)	33,800
Florissant, Mo. (★St. Louis)	74,100
Fond du Lac, Wis. (★49,200)	36,400
Fort Collins, Colo. (★70,800)	58,500
Fort Lauderdale, Fla. (★Miami)	153,600
Fort Myers, Fla. (★99,500)	36,600
Fort Pierce, Fla. (★67,900)	33,200
Fort Smith, Ark. (★99,900)	68,600
Fort Walton Beach, Fla. (★88,400)	21,900
Fort Wayne, Ind. (★301,000)	184,800
Fort Worth, Tex. (★Dallas)	340,000
Fountain Valley, Calif. (★Los Angeles)	54,800
Framingham, Mass. (★Boston)	66,200
Frankfort, Ky	23,200
Freeport, Tex. (★68,100)	11,500
Fremont, Calif. (★San Francisco)	117,700
Fresno, Calif. (★356,000)	191,000
Fullerton, Calif. (★Los Angeles)	95,700
Gadsden, Ala. (★83,600)	49,100
Gainesville, Fla. (★106,200)	72,300
Galesburg, Ill. (★42,700)	34,100
Galveston, Tex. (★152,500)	60,200
Garden Grove, Calif. (★Los Angeles)	117,300
Garland, Tex. (★Dallas)	127,900
Gary, Ind. (★Chicago)	157,000
Gastonia, N.C. (★116,500)	48,500
Glendale, Ariz. (★Phoenix)	76,700
Glendale, Calif. (★Los Angeles)	135,700
Glens Falls, N.Y. (★63,200)	17,100
Goldsboro, N.C. (★64,000)	27,300
Grand Forks, N.Dak. (★53,700)	42,900
Grand Island, Nebr. (★38,500)	33,400
Grand Junction, Colo. (★54,900)	25,600
Grand Prairie, Tex. (★Dallas)	59,000
Grand Rapids, Mich. (★471,000)	182,600
Great Falls, Mont. (★74,900)	60,300
Greece, N.Y. (★Rochester)	62,500
Greeley, Colo. (★63,100)	49,200
Green Bay, Wis. (★155,200)	89,700
Greensboro, N.C. (★358,500)	161,200
Greenville, Miss. (★51,500)	42,900
Greenville, S.C. (★307,000)	56,400
Greenwich, Conn. (★New York)	59,700
Gulfport, Miss. (★174,500)	44,200
Hackensack, N.J. (★New York)	34,200
Hagerstown, Md. (★141,500)	37,000
Hamden, Conn. (★New Haven)	50,500
Hamilton, Ohio (★Cincinnati)	64,400
Hammond, Ind. (★Chicago)	103,000
Hampton, Va. (★Newport News)	130,100
Hanover, Pa. (★51,900)	14,400
Harlingen, Tex. (★79,000)	42,900
Harrisburg, Pa. (★398,000)	55,200
Hartford, Conn. (★1,071,000)	130,100
Hattiesburg, Miss. (★61,100)	39,600
Hawthorne, Calif. (★Los Angeles)	56,300
Hayward, Calif. (★San Francisco)	98,100
Hazleton, Pa. (★71,900)	28,900
Helena, Mont	27,700
Hialeah, Fla. (★Miami)	123,700
Hickory, N.C. (★76,500)	19,100
Hicksville, N.Y. (★New York)	50,200
High Point, N.C. (★Greensboro)	60,900
Hilo, Haw	29,300
Hoboken, N.J. (★New York)	38,300
Holland, Mich. (★62,000)	28,600
Hollywood, Fla. (★Miami)	119,000
Honolulu, Haw. (★728,000)	328,000
Hot Springs National Park, Ark. (★57,400)	37,800
Houma, La. (★57,600)	30,700
Houston, Tex. (★2,345,000)	1,460,000
Huntington, W.Va. (★254,600)	68,200
Huntington Beach, Calif. (★Los Angeles)	163,500
Huntsville, Ala. (★193,600)	137,800
Hutchinson, Kans. (★49,200)	41,900
Idaho Falls, Idaho (★51,100)	37,200
Independence, Mo. (★Kansas City)	110,700
Indianapolis, Ind. (★1,078,000)	711,000
Inglewood, Calif. (★Los Angeles)	89,000
Iowa City, Iowa (★66,800)	49,100
Irondequoit, N.Y. (★Rochester)	57,900
Irving, Tex. (★Dallas)	104,800
Irvington, N.J. (★New York)	57,300
Ithaca, N.Y. (★76,700)	30,700
Jackson, Mich. (★134,100)	42,100
Jackson, Miss. (★277,500)	193,000
Jackson, Tenn. (★56,200)	41,300
Jacksonville, Fla. (★619,000)	547,000
Jacksonville, N.C. (★85,100)	19,100
Jamestown, N.Y. (★68,500)	36,600
Janesville, Wis. (★62,800)	49,200
Jefferson City, Mo. (★44,000)	35,900
Jersey City, N.J. (★New York)	236,900
Johnson City, Tenn. (★104,300)	51,700
Johnstown, Pa. (★174,000)	38,300
Joliet, Ill. (★Chicago)	70,900
Joplin, Mo. (★70,400)	40,200
Juneau, Alaska	18,400
Kalamazoo, Mich. (★213,000)	77,200
Kankakee, Ill. (★76,500)	27,700
Kannapolis, N.C. (★89,600)	37,000
Kansas City, Kans. (★Kansas City)	166,800
Kansas City, Mo. (★1,235,000)	454,000
Kenosha, Wis. (★109,000)	81,900
Kettering, Ohio (★Dayton)	68,700
Key West, Fla	24,500
Killeen, Tex. (★136,000)	54,700
Kingsport, Tenn. (★115,700)	33,000
Kingston, N.Y. (★89,900)	23,900
Knoxville, Tenn. (★466,000)	186,200
Kokomo, Ind. (★92,400)	52,300
La Crosse, Wis. (★82,600)	48,900
Lafayette, Ind. (★107,900)	48,800
Lafayette, La. (★144,800)	77,700
Lake Charles, La. (★133,400)	75,700
Lakeland, Fla. (★120,000)	48,800
Lakewood, Calif. (★Los Angeles)	80,900
Lakewood, Colo. (★Denver)	125,800
Lakewood, Ohio (★Cleveland)	63,800
Lakewood Center, Wash. (★Seattle)	51,400
Lancaster, Calif. (★76,300)	37,300
Lancaster, Ohio (★54,500)	39,700
Lancaster, Pa. (★201,500)	53,300
Lansing, Mich. (★320,500)	124,100
Laredo, Tex. (★300,000)	80,000
Las Cruces, N.Mex. (★63,800)	41,500
Las Vegas, Nev. (★346,000)	155,800
Lawrence, Kans. (★52,900)	51,900
Lawrence, Mass. (★Boston)	67,000
Lawton, Okla. (★99,400)	83,200
Lebanon, Pa. (★79,200)	27,900
Levittown, N.Y. (★New York)	65,500
Levittown, Pa. (★Philadelphia)	78,500
Lewiston, Maine (★86,600)	40,300
Lexington, Ky. (★243,800)	190,900
Lima, Ohio (★98,600)	50,000
Lincoln, Nebr. (★174,200)	165,100
Little Rock, Ark. (★357,000)	142,700
Livermore, Calif. (★San Francisco)	48,600
Livonia, Mich. (★Detroit)	115,600
Lockport, N.Y. (★64,900)	26,300
Lompoc, Calif. (★47,300)	25,300
Long Beach, Calif. (★Los Angeles)	341,200
Longview, Tex. (★76,600)	53,000
Longview, Wash. (★60,000)	29,500
Lorain, Ohio (★Cleveland)	81,000
Los Angeles, Calif. (★9,200,000)	2,765,000
Louisville, Ky. (★867,000)	319,800
Lowell, Mass. (★Boston)	90,100
Lubbock, Tex. (★194,500)	169,000
Lufkin, Tex. (★45,700)	28,100
Lynchburg, Va. (★115,500)	65,400
Lynn, Mass. (★Boston)	77,400
McAllen, Tex. (★116,600)	52,000
Macon, Ga. (★223,600)	120,700
Madison, Wis. (★266,000)	168,700
Malden, Mass. (★Boston)	55,700
Manchester, Conn. (★Hartford)	51,300
Manchester, N.H. (★126,500)	80,600
Manitowoc, Wis. (★55,600)	32,000
Mankato, Minn. (★46,100)	28,400
Mansfield, Ohio (★111,300)	55,700
Marion, Ind. (★75,600)	40,200
Marion, Ohio (★55,500)	39,200
Martinsville, Va. (★67,200)	18,600

[1] For abbreviations of state names, see Index, page *I* • *26*.
[2] Rand McNally & Company estimates.
• Largest city in country.
★ Population or designation of the metropolitan area, including suburbs.
C Census. **E** Official estimate. **UE** Unofficial estimate.

[1] Für die Abkürzungen der Namen der Staaten siehe Register, S. *I* • *26*.
[2] Schätzungen der Rand McNally & Company.
• Grösste Stadt des Landes.
★ Bevölkerung oder Bezeichnung der Stadtregion einschliesslich Vororte.
C Volkszählung. **E** Offizielle Schätzung.
UE Inoffizielle Schätzung.

Marysville, Calif. (★75,700)...... 9,600
Mason City, Iowa (★40,300)..... 30,200
Medford, Mass. (★Boston)..... 58,900
Medford, Oreg. (★78,500)....... 33,100
Melbourne, Fla. (★94,500)...... 38,600
Memphis, Tenn. (★825,000).....655,000
Merced, Calif. (★74,100)........ 33,100
Meriden, Conn. (★New Haven). 58,100
Meridian, Miss. (★59,400)....... 44,500
Mesa, Ariz. (★Phoenix)........112,400
Mesquite, Tex. (★Dallas)........ 64,600
Metairie, La. (★New Orleans)...168,100
Miami, Fla. (★2,420,000).........348,000
Miami Beach, Fla. (★Miami)... 90,800
Michigan City, Ind. (★64,000)... 40,800
Middletown, N.Y. (★78,200)...... 25,700
Middletown, Ohio (★106,600).... 46,600
Midland, Tex. (★71,700)......... 66,500
Midwest City, Okla. (★Oklahoma City)............ 51,500
Milford, Conn. (★Bridgeport)... 52,200
Milwaukee, Wis. (★1,382,000)....641,000
Minneapolis, Minn. (★1,950,000)..................359,000
Minot, N.Dak. (★37,500)........ 33,300
Missoula, Mont. (★58,900)...... 29,800
Mobile, Ala. (★348,000).........208,100
Modesto, Calif. (★177,600)....... 94,800
Monroe, La. (★118,600).......... 63,200
Monroe, Mich. (★59,400)........ 24,600
Monterey, Calif. (★130,500)...... 28,000
Monterey Park, Calif. (★Los Angeles).................... 52,400
Montgomery, Ala. (★214,200)....161,000
Montpelier, Vt. (★36,600)....... 8,200
Morgantown, W.Va. (★62,400)... 30,100
Mountain View, Calif. (★San Francisco).................. 55,400
Mount Prospect, Ill. (★Chicago)................... 52,400
Mount Vernon, N.Y. (★New York)......................... 66,600
Muncie, Ind. (★126,800)......... 76,700
Muskegon, Mich. (★178,700)..... 44,200
Muskogee, Okla. (★50,400)...... 38,900
Nashua, N.H. (★117,000)........ 63,300
Nashville, Tenn. (★560,000).....459,000
Natchez, Miss. (★42,900)........ 23,400
National City, Calif. (★San Diego)........................ 52,100
Newark, N.J. (★New York)......324,000
Newark, Ohio (★77,700)......... 37,600
New Bedford, Mass. (★162,400). 98,200
New Britain, Conn. (★Hartford). 75,900
Newburgh, N.Y. (★113,700)...... 25,200
New Castle, Pa. (★65,300)....... 34,400
New Haven, Conn. (★501,500)...121,200
New London, Conn. (★250,900).. 30,100
New Orleans, La. (★1,125,000)...560,000
Newport, R.I. (★63,500).......... 28,100
Newport Beach, Calif. (★Los Angeles)..................... 65,000
Newport News, Va. (★324,000)...141,400
New Rochelle, N.Y. (★New York)......................... 70,500
Newton, Mass. (★Boston)...... 87,200
•New York, N.Y. (★17,040,000)..7,420,000
Niagara Falls, N.Y. (★Buffalo).. 78,400
Nogales, Ariz. (★80,200)........ 11,700
Norfolk, Va. (★764,000)..........266,400
Norman, Okla. (★Oklahoma City)......................... 62,500
Northampton, Mass. (★35,800).. 30,300
North Charleston, S.C. (★Charleston)................ 60,400
North Little Rock, Ark. (★Little Rock)....................... 61,700
Norwalk, Calif. (★Los Angeles). 84,900
Norwalk, Conn. (★New York)... 76,100
Oakland, Calif. (★San Francisco)..................326,000
Oak Lawn, Ill. (★Chicago)...... 63,100
Oak Park, Ill. (★Chicago)........ 58,400
Oceanside, Calif. (★173,000)..... 65,000
Odessa, Tex. (★101,800)......... 90,400
Ogden, Utah (★196,400)......... 66,900
Oklahoma City, Okla. (★691,000).371,000
Olympia, Wash. (★87,500)....... 25,800
Omaha, Nebr. (★576,000)........382,900
Ontario, Calif. (★Los Angeles).. 69,200
Opelika, Ala. (★53,100).......... 22,600
Orange, Calif. (★Los Angeles).. 84,800
Orlando, Fla. (★492,000).........114,000
Oshkosh, Wis. (★68,400)......... 49,600
Overland Park, Kans. (★Kansas City).............. 83,100
Owensboro, Ky. (★63,100)........ 51,100
Oxnard, Calif. (★Ventura)...... 95,900
Paducah, Ky. (★67,900).......... 30,100
Palo Alto, Calif. (★San Francisco)................... 54,600
Panama City, Fla. (★88,200)..... 39,700
Parkersburg, W.Va. (★89,900).... 36,300
Parma, Ohio (★Cleveland)...... 99,100
Pasadena, Calif. (★Los Angeles).....................106,200
Pasadena, Tex. (★Houston).... 98,100
Pascagoula, Miss. (★72,200)..... 31,300
Pasco, Wash. (★98,500).......... 15,600
Passaic, N.J. (★New York)...... 47,100
Paterson, N.J. (★New York).....131,100
Pawtucket, R.I. (★Providence).. 68,100
Penn Hills, Pa. (★Pittsburgh).. 62,200
Pensacola, Fla. (★222,600)....... 65,900
Peoria, Ill. (★319,000)...........126,000
Petersburg, Va. (★125,800)....... 47,800
Philadelphia, Pa. (★5,320,000).1,805,000
Phoenix, Ariz. (★1,270,000)......669,000
Pico Rivera, Calif. (★Los Angeles)..................... 50,500
Pierre, S.Dak................... 11,700
Pine Bluff, Ark. (★69,900)....... 53,900
Pittsburgh, Pa. (★2,190,000).....430,000
Pittsfield, Mass. (★97,600)...... 53,600
Pocatello, Idaho (★50,300)...... 42,500
Pomona, Calif. (★Los Angeles). 83,400

Pompano Beach, Fla. (★Miami)...................... 53,000
Pontiac, Mich. (★Detroit)....... 76,000
Port Arthur, Tex. (★Beaumont). 52,200
Port Huron, Mich. (★152,000)... 34,200
Portland, Maine (★213,500)...... 56,700
Portland, Oreg. (★1,109,000).....348,000
Portsmouth, N.H. (★56,000)..... 24,100
Portsmouth, Ohio (★68,100)...... 24,600
Portsmouth, Va. (★Norfolk)....105,300
Pottstown, Pa. (★80,200)......... 26,000
Pottsville, Pa. (★58,900)......... 18,400
Poughkeepsie, N.Y. (★224,200).. 31,000
Providence, R.I. (★871,000)......158,600
Provo, Utah (★172,300).......... 55,200
Pueblo, Colo. (★117,500).........103,800
Quincy, Ill. (★53,800)............ 43,000
Quincy, Mass. (★Boston)....... 92,700
Racine, Wis. (★133,900)......... 91,800
Raleigh, N.C. (★265,000).........139,600
Rapid City, S.Dak. (★72,200).... 49,500
Reading, Pa. (★211,000)......... 78,200
Redding, Calif. (★82,800)........ 40,400
Redford Township, Mich. (★Detroit)................... 64,500
Redondo Beach, Calif. (★Los Angeles)..................... 64,400
Redwood City, Calif. (★San Francisco).................. 54,900
Reno, Nev. (★147,800)........... 80,900
Richardson, Tex. (★Dallas)..... 63,700
Richmond, Calif. (★San Francisco).................. 69,700
Richmond, Ind. (★63,200)........ 43,100
Richmond, Va. (★540,000).......222,600
Riverside, Calif. (★San Bernardino)..................152,600
Roanoke, Va. (★199,500).........100,300
Rochester, Minn. (★80,400)...... 58,800
Rochester, N.Y. (★808,500)......258,100
Rockford, Ill. (★243,000).........143,900
Rock Hill, S.C. (★60,300)........ 36,400
Rock Island, Ill. (★Davenport).. 46,600
Rocky Mount, N.C. (★65,400).... 38,800
Rome, Ga. (★71,100)............. 29,100
Rome, N.Y. (★Utica)........... 48,300
Roseville, Mich. (★Detroit)...... 55,600
Royal Oak, Mich. (★Detroit).... 74,800
Sacramento, Calif. (★783,000)...261,500
Saginaw, Mich. (★183,000)...... 82,100
St. Clair Shores, Mich. (★Detroit)................... 83,000
St. Cloud, Minn. (★71,300)....... 40,200
St. Joseph, Mo. (★88,700)....... 77,500
St. Louis, Mo. (★2,250,000).......495,000
St. Paul, Minn. (★Minneapolis).271,000
St. Petersburg, Fla. (★649,000)..238,200
Salem, Oreg. (★148,000)......... 83,100
Salina, Kans. (★46,800).......... 42,100
Salinas, Calif. (★100,200)....... 76,000
Salisbury, Md. (★52,100)......... 16,000
Salisbury, N.C. (★55,400)........ 25,100
Salt Lake City, Utah (★594,500)..164,500
San Angelo, Tex. (★73,100)...... 69,600
San Antonio, Tex. (★960,000)....804,000
San Bernardino, Calif. (★665,000)......................104,400
San Diego, Calif. (★2,100,000)....820,000
Sandusky, Ohio (★61,900)........ 31,700
San Francisco, Calif. (★4,500,000).....................658,000
San Jose, Calif. (★San Francisco)..................590,100
San Leandro, Calif. (★San Francisco).................. 67,200
San Mateo, Calif. (★San Francisco).................. 78,800
Santa Ana, Calif. (★Los Angeles)......................183,800
Santa Barbara, Calif. (★163,600). 74,200
Santa Clara, Calif. (★San Francisco).................. 84,100
Santa Cruz, Calif. (★127,300)..... 38,600
Santa Fe, N.Mex. (★52,000)...... 46,500
Santa Maria, Calif. (★59,800).... 35,600
Santa Monica, Calif. (★Los Angeles)..................... 91,100
Santa Rosa, Calif. (★156,500).... 72,200
Sarasota, Fla. (★249,000)......... 47,100
Savannah, Ga. (★196,300).........112,500
Schenectady, N.Y. (★Albany)...... 72,100
Scottsdale, Ariz. (★Phoenix).... 79,300
Scranton, Pa. (★477,000)......... 92,600
Seattle, Wash. (★1,855,000)......481,000
Sharon, Pa. (★90,000)............ 22,600
Sheboygan, Wis. (★72,500)....... 48,500
Sherman, Tex. (★59,300)......... 25,500
Shreveport, La. (★277,000).......187,600
Silver Spring, Md. (★Washington)............... 83,700
Simi (Simi Valley), Calif. (★Los Angeles)................ 72,500
Sioux City, Iowa (★102,300)...... 85,100
Sioux Falls, S. Dak. (★85,600).... 74,700
Skokie, Ill. (★Chicago).......... 67,400
Somerville, Mass. (★Boston).... 77,100
South Bend, Ind. (★422,000).....111,500
Southfield, Mich. (★Detroit).... 77,700
South Gate, Calif. (★Los Angeles)..................... 55,700
South San Francisco, Calif. (★San Francisco)........... 49,300
Spartanburg, S.C. (★143,000).... 46,900
Spokane, Wash. (★294,000).......174,000
Springfield, Ill. (★150,500)....... 86,300
Springfield, Mass. (★504,000)....168,000
Springfield, Mo. (★170,700)......132,600
Springfield, Ohio (★Dayton)..... 73,700
Stamford, Conn. (★New York)..105,000
State College, Pa. (★78,600)...... 37,100
Sterling Heights, Mich. (★Detroit)................... 98,200
Steubenville, Ohio (★141,500)... 26,900
Stockton, Calif. (★256,000).......124,500
Stratford, Conn. (★Bridgeport). 51,300
Sumter, S.C. (★70,000)........... 24,300

Sunnyvale, Calif. (★San Francisco)..................105,600
Syracuse, N.Y. (★559,000).......177,000
Tacoma, Wash. (★Seattle).......150,000
Tallahassee, Fla. (★121,800)..... 86,400
Tampa, Fla. (★541,000)...........278,000
Taunton, Mass. (★56,700)....... 40,500
Taylor, Mich. (★Detroit)......... 78,500
Tempe, Ariz. (★Phoenix)....... 92,400
Temple, Tex. (★58,100)......... 41,000
Terre Haute, Ind. (★126,700).... 61,800
Texarkana, Tex. (★76,500)....... 34,200
Texas City, Tex. (★Galveston).. 41,200
Thousand Oaks, Calif. (★Los Angeles)............... 65,500
Toledo, Ohio (★573,000).........366,000
Topeka, Kans. (★151,000).........121,300
Torrance, Calif. (★Los Angeles).134,900
Town of Tonawanda, N.Y. (★Buffalo).................. 79,200
Towson, Md. (★Baltimore)...... 83,600
Trenton, N.J. (★Philadelphia).. 98,100
Troy, Mich. (★Detroit).......... 62,000
Troy, N.Y. (★Albany)........... 57,400
Tucson, Ariz. (★435,000).........301,600
Tulsa, Okla. (★505,000)..........334,700
Tuscaloosa, Ala. (★108,600)..... 71,000
Tyler, Tex. (★87,800)............ 62,400
Union, N.J. (★New York)....... 50,100
Union City, N.J. (★New York)... 50,700
Uniontown, Pa (★53,800) 15,400
University City, Mo. (★St. Louis)......................... 45,000
Upper Darby, Pa. (★Philadelphia)............... 50,600
Utica, N.Y. (★266,600)........... 79,100
Valdosta, Ga. (★53,900).......... 35,800
Vallejo, Calif. (★San Francisco). 70,500
Vancouver, Wash. (★Portland). 46,000
Ventura (San Buenaventura), Calif. (★283,000)............... 67,800
Vicksburg, Miss. (★45,100)...... 31,000
Victoria, Tex. (★50,500).......... 46,700
Vineland, N.J. (★103,000)........ 55,800
Virginia Beach, Va. (★Norfolk).233,600
Visalia, Calif. (★76,300)......... 40,800
Waco, Tex. (★132,500)........... 97,300
Walnut Creek, Calif. (★San Francisco).................. 49,300
Waltham, Mass. (★Boston)..... 53,700
Warren, Mich. (★Detroit).......165,600
Warren, Ohio (★Youngstown)... 59,500
Warwick, R.I. (★Providence).... 85,900
WASHINGTON, D.C. (★3,200,000)....................689,000
Washington, Pa. (★54,100)....... 20,300
Waterbury, Conn. (★213,700)....106,400
Waterloo, Iowa (★133,500)....... 75,300
Waukegan, Ill. (★Chicago)...... 64,400
Wausau, Wis. (★61,400).......... 33,100
Wauwatosa, Wis. (★Milwaukee)................ 55,300
Wayne, N.J. (★New York)....... 48,800
West Allis, Wis. (★Milwaukee).. 67,700
West Covina, Calif. (★Los Angeles)..................... 78,300
West Hartford, Conn. (★Hartford).................. 65,900
West Haven, Conn. (★New Haven)....................... 53,000
Westland, Mich. (★Detroit)..... 94,000
Westminster, Calif. (★Los Angeles)..................... 69,100
West Palm Beach, Fla. (★325,000).................... 62,000
West Seneca, N.Y. (★Buffalo).. 56,500
Weymouth, Mass. (★Boston).... 57,500
Wheaton, Md. (★Washington).. 73,000
Wheeling, W.Va. (★154,700)...... 43,200
Whittier, Calif. (★Los Angeles). 69,800
Wichita, Kans. (★359,000) 269,000
Wichita Falls, Tex. (★116,000)... 95,100
Wilkes-Barre, Pa. (★Scranton).. 55,500
Williamsport, Pa. (★89,900)...... 34,900
Wilmington, Del. (★Philadelphia).............. 73,500
Wilmington, N.C. (★97,900)...... 55,700
Winston-Salem, N.C. (★255,000).143,100
Winter Haven, Fla. (★75,800).... 19,100
Worcester, Mass. (★367,000).....168,300
Wyoming, Mich. (★Grand Rapids)...................... 58,400
Yakima, Wash. (★98,000)........ 48,800
Yonkers, N.Y. (★New York).....188,600
York, Pa. (★207,000)............. 44,800
Youngstown, Ohio (★496,000)....118,600
Yuma, Ariz. (★46,800)........... 32,600
Zanesville, Ohio (★58,800)....... 37,400

UPPER VOLTA / Haute-Volta

1975 C.........................6,144,013
Bobo Dioulasso..................115,063
•OUAGADOUGOU 172,661

URUGUAY

1975 C.........................2,763,964
Las Piedras (★Montevideo)..... 53,983
Melo............................ 38,260
Mercedes....................... 34,667
Minas.......................... 35,433
•MONTEVIDEO (★1,350,000)....1,229,748
Paysandú...................... 62,412
Rivera......................... 49,013
Salto........................... 71,881

VATICAN CITY

1976 E............................ 1,000

VENEZUELA

1971 C........................10,721,522
Acarigua....................... 56,743
Barcelona...................... 78,201
Barinas........................ 56,329
Barquisimeto..................330,815
Baruta (★Caracas)..............121,066
Cabimas.........................118,037
•CARACAS (★2,475,000).........1,658,500
Carúpano....................... 50,935
Catia La Mar (★Caracas)....... 62,200
Chacao (★Caracas)............. 78,528
Ciudad Bolívar.................103,728
Ciudad Guayana (Santo Tomé de Guayana)..................143,540
Ciudad Ojeda (Lagunillas)...... 83,083
Coro............................ 68,701
Cumaná.........................119,751
El Tigre......................... 49,801
Los Dos Caminos (★Caracas).. 59,211
Los Teques...................... 63,106
Maiquetía (★Caracas).......... 59,238
Maracaibo......................651,574
Maracay........................255,134
Maturín......................... 98,188
Mérida.......................... 74,214
Petare (★Caracas)..............227,727
Puerto Cabello.................. 72,103
Puerto la Cruz.................. 63,276
Punto Fijo...................... 55,483
San Cristóbal....................151,717
Valencia........................367,171
Valera........................... 76,740

VIETNAM / Viet-nam Dan-chu Cong-hoa

1967 E........................37,073,000
Bien-hoa....................... 52,200
Can-tho........................ 61,100
Da-lat (1971 E)................. 86,600
Da-nang (1971 E)................437,700
Gia-dinh (★Sai-gon) (1968 E)....151,100
Hai-phong (1960 C) (369,248▲)...182,496
HA-NOI (1960 C) (★643,576)......414,620
Hue (1971 E)....................199,900
My-tho.......................... 62,700
Nam-dinh (1960 C).............. 86,132
Nha-trang...................... 59,600
Phan-thiet..................... 58,300
Phu-vinh (1971 E)............... 51,500
Qui-nhon....................... 50,000
Rach-gia........................ 56,000
•Thanh-pho Ho Chi Minh (Sai-gon) (1971 E) (★2,750,000)..............1,804,880
Vung-tau (Cap-St.-Jacques)..... 54,200

VIRGIN ISLANDS

1970 C.......................... 62,468
•CHARLOTTE AMALIE........... 12,220

WESTERN SAMOA

1971 E..........................148,565
•APIA........................... 30,593

YEMEN / Al-Yaman

1975 C.........................5,237,893
Al-Ḥudaydah (Hodeida)........ 80,000
•ṢAN'Ā'.........................135,000
Ta'izz.......................... 79,000

YEMEN, PEOPLE'S DEMOCRATIC REPUBLIC OF / Al-Yaman ash-Sha'biyah

1973 E..........................1,555,000
•ADEN...........................264,300
Al-Mukallā (1970 E)............ 65,000

YUGOSLAVIA / Jugoslavija

1971 C........................20,504,516
Banja Luka..................... 89,866
•BEOGRAD (BELGRADE) (★1,150,000).................770,140
Bitola.......................... 65,851
Kragujevac..................... 71,180
Ljubljana.......................173,662
Maribor......................... 97,167
Niš.............................127,178
Novi Sad........................141,712
Osijek.......................... 93,912
Pančevo (★Beograd)........... 54,269
Priština......................... 69,524
Rijeka..........................132,933
Šabac........................... 42,307
Sarajevo........................244,045
Skopje..........................312,092
Sombor.......................... 43,971
Split............................151,875
Subotica........................ 88,787
Titograd........................ 54,509
Tuzla........................... 53,825
Vršac........................... 34,231
Vukovar......................... 30,149
Zadar........................... 43,187
Zagreb..........................566,084
Zaječar......................... 27,677
Zenica.......................... 51,279
Zrenjanin....................... 59,580

ZAIRE / Zaïre

1974 E........................24,222,000
Bandundu (1970 C)............. 74,467
Bukavu..........................182,000
Kananga (Luluabourg).........601,000
Kikwit..........................150,000
•KINSHASA (LÉOPOLDVILLE)..2,008,000
Kisangani (Stanleyville).......311,000
Likasi (Jadotsville) (1970 C)....146,394
Lubumbashi (Élisabethville)....404,000
Matadi..........................144,000
Mbandaka (Coquilhatville)......134,000
Mbuji-Mayi (Bakwanga).......337,000

ZAMBIA

1976 E.........................5,138,000
Chililabombwe (Bancroft)...... 64,000
Chingola........................156,000
Kabwe (Broken Hill)............115,000
Kitwe...........................281,000
Livingstone..................... 65,000
Luanshya.......................135,000
•LUSAKA........................483,000
Mufulira........................154,000
Ndola...........................260,000

[1] Para las abreviaciones de los nombres de estado véase el Índice, página *I • 26*.
[2] Cifras de Rand McNally y Compañia.
• Ciudad más grande de un país.
★ Población o designación de un área metropolitana, incluyendo los suburbios.
C Censo. **E** Estimado oficial. **UE** Estimado no oficial.

[1] Pour les abréviations des noms des États, voir Index page *I • 26*.
[2] Estimations de Rand McNally & Company.
• Ville la plus peuplée du pays.
★ Population de l'agglomération (ou nom de la zone métropolitaine englobante).
C Recensement. **E** Estimation officielle.
UE Estimation non officielle.

[1] Para as abreviaturas dos nomes dos Estados, ver o Índice, pág. *I • 26*.
[2] Estimativas de Rand McNally & Company.
• Maior cidade do país.
★ População ou indicação de uma área metropolitana, inclusive subúrbios.
C Censo. **E** Estimativa oficial.
UE Estimativa não oficial.

The Index includes in a single alphabetical list some 160,000 names appearing on the maps. Each name is followed by a page reference to one or more maps and by the location of the feature on the map, in coordinates of latitude and longitude. If a page contains several maps, a lowercase letter identifies the particular map. The page reference for two-page maps is always to the left-hand page.

Most map features are indexed to the largest-scale map on which they appear. However, a feature usually is not indexed to a Metropolitan Area map if it is also shown on another map where it can be seen in a broader setting. Countries, mountain ranges, and other extensive features are generally indexed to the largest-scale map that shows them in their entirety.

The order in which index information is presented is shown in the English, German, Spanish, French, and Portuguese headings at the center of each two-page spread.

For example:

ENGLISH

Name	Page	Lat.°′	Long.°′

The features indexed are of three types: *point*, *areal*, and *linear*. For *point* features (for example, cities, mountain peaks, dams), latitude and longitude coordinates give the location of the point on the map. For *areal* features (countries, mountain ranges, etc.), the coordinates generally indicate the approximate center of the feature. For *linear* features (rivers, canals, aqueducts), the coordinates locate a terminating point—for example, the mouth of a river, or the point at which a feature reaches the map margin.

Name Forms Names in the Index, as on the maps, are generally in the local language and insofar as possible are spelled according to official practice. Diacritical marks are included, except that those used to indicate tone, as in Vietnamese, are usually not shown. Most features that extend beyond the boundaries of one country have no single official name, and these are usually named in English. Many English, German, Spanish, French, and Portuguese names, which may not be shown on the maps, appear in the Index as cross references. All cross references are indicated by the symbol →. A name that appears in a shortended version on the map due to space limitations is given in full in the Index, with the portion that is omitted on the map enclosed in brackets, for example, Acapulco [de Juárez].

Transliteration For names in languages not written in the Roman alphabet, the locally official transliteration system has been used where one exists. Thus, names in the Soviet Union and Bulgaria have been transliterated according to the systems adopted by the academies of science of these countries. Similarly, the transliteration for mainland Chinese names follows the Pinyin system, which has been officially adopted in mainland China. For languages with no one locally accepted transliteration system, notably Arabic, transliteration in general follows closely a system adopted by the United States Board on Geographic Names.

Alphabetization Names are alphabetized in the order of the letters of the English alphabet. Spanish *ll* and *ch*, for example, are not treated as distinct letters. Furthermore, diacritical marks are disregarded in alphabetization—German or Scandinavian *ä* or *ö* are treated as *a* or *o*.

The names of physical features may appear inverted, since they are always alphabetized under the proper, not the generic, part of the name, thus: "Gibralter, Strait of ʉ." Otherwise every entry, whether consisting of one word or more, is alphabetized as a single continuous entity. "Lakeland," for example, appears after "La Crosse" and before "La Salle." Names beginning with articles (Le Havre, Den Helder, A-Qāhirah, As-Suways) are not inverted. Names beginning "Mc" are alphabetized as though spelled "Mac," and names beginning "St." and "Sainte" as though spelled "Saint."

In the case of identical names, towns are listed first, then political divisions, then physical features. Entries that are completely identical (including symbols, discussed below) are distinguished by abbreviations of their official country names and are sequenced alphabetically by country name. The many duplicate names in Canada, the United Kingdom, and the United States are further distinguished by abbreviations of the names of their primary subdivisions. (See list of abbreviations on pages I• 26 through I• 28.)

Abbreviation and Capitalization Abbreviation and styling have been standardized for all languages. A period is used after every abbreviation even when this may not be the local practice. The abbreviation "St." is used only for "Saint." "Sankt" and other forms of the term are spelled out.

All names are written with an initial capital letter except for a few Dutch names, such as 's-Gravenhage. Capitalization of noninitial words in a name generally follows local practice.

Symbol The symbols that appear in the Index represent graphically the broad categories of the features named, for example, ʌ for mountain (Everest, Mount ʌ). An abbreviated key to the symbols, in the five Atlas languages, appears at the foot of each pair of Index pages. Superior numbers following some symbols in the Index indicate finer distinctions, for example, ʌ^1 for volcano (Fuji-san ʌ^1). A complete list of the symbols and superior numbers is given on page I• 26.

Das Register umfasst in alphabetischer Anordnung etwa 160 000 in den Karten erscheinende Namen. Nach jedem Namen folgt die Seitenangabe zu einer oder mehreren Karten und die Lageangabe des Objektes in der Karte mit geographischer Länge und Breite. Enthält eine Seite mehrere Karten, so wird die betreffende Karte durch einen Kleinbuchstaben gekennzeichnet. Die Seitenangabe für Doppelseiten bezieht sich immer auf die linke Seite.

Die Verweise für die meisten Objekte in den Karten beziehen sich auf die Karte mit dem grössten Massstab. Normalerweise werden jedoch Verweise auf Objekte in den Karten der Stadtregionen nicht gegeben, wenn sie auf einer anderen Karte in grösserem Zusammenhang dargestellt sind. Die Lageangaben für Länder, Gebirgszüge und andere ausgedehnte Objekte beziehen sich allgemein auf die Karte grössten Massstabes, die sie in ihrer ganzen Ausdehnung zeigt.

Die Anordnung, in welcher die Lageangabe erfolgt, geht aus den englischen, deutschen, spanischen, französischen und portugiesischen Überschriften in der Mitte jeder Doppelseite hervor.

Zum Beispiel:

DEUTSCH

Name	Seite	Breite°′	Länge°′ E=Ost

Die aufgeführten Objekte gliedern sich in drei Gruppen: *punkt-*, *flächen-* und *linienförmige* Objekte. Bei *punktförmigen* Objekten (z.B. Städte, Berge, Dämme) beziehen sich die Angaben nach Länge und Breite auf die Signatur in der Karte. Bei *flächenhaften* Objekten (Länder, Gebirgszüge usw.) verweisen die Koordinaten im allgemeinen auf das ungefähre Zentrum des Objektes. Bei *linienhaften* Objekten (Flüsse, Kanäle, Wasserleitungen) beziehen sich die Koordinaten auf einen bestimmten Punkt, z.B. die Mündung eines Flusses oder den Punkt, an dem das Objekt den Kartenrand schneidet.

Namengebung Wie in den karten so sind auch im Register die Namen im allgemeinen in der örtlichen Namensform wiedergegeben und soweit als möglich in der amtlichen Schreibweise. Diakritische Zeichen wurden gesetzt; sie wurden nur dort weggelassen, wo sie, wie im Vietnamesischen, Tonhöhen kennzeichnen. Meist haben Objekte, die sich über die Grenzen eines Landes hinaus erstrecken, keinen einzelnen offiziellen Namen; normalerweise sind sie daher englisch beschriftet. Viele englische, deutsche, spanische, französische und portugiesische Namensformen, die nicht in den Karten enthalten sind, erscheinen im Register als Kreuzverweis. Alle Kreuzverweise werden durch das Symbol → gekennzeichnet. Namen, die aus Platzgründen in abgekürzter Form in der Karte erscheinen, werden im Register voll ausgeschrieben, wobei der auf der Karte weggelassene Teil in Klammern gesetzt ist, z.B. Acapulco [de Juárez].

Transkription Für die Transkription von Namen aus Sprachen, die nicht im lateinischen Alphabet geschrieben werden, wurde das offizielle Transkriptionssystem benutzt, sofern ein solches vorhanden ist. So wurden die Namen in der Sowjetunion und in Bulgarien nach dem von den wissenschaftlichen Akademien dieser Länder angewandten System transkribiert. Entsprechend wurden die Namen auf dem chinesischen Festland nach dem Pinyin-System übertragen, das offiziell in der Volksrepublik China eingeführt wurde. Bei Sprachen, für die ein allgemein anerkanntes Transkriptionssystem nicht vorliegt, vor allem für Arabisch, erfolgte die Transkription in enger Anlehnung an das vom United States Board on Geographic Names angewandte System.

Alphabetische Ordnung Die alphabetische Ordnung der Namen entspricht der Reihenfolge der Buchstaben im englischen Alphabet. So werden z.B. das spanische *ll* und *ch* nicht als besondere Buchstaben behandelt. Ferner wurden diakritische Zeichen beim Alphabetisieren nicht berücksichtigt, das deutsche oder skandinavische *ä* oder *ö* als *a* oder *o* behandelt.

Physische Objekte können umgestellt erscheinen, da sie immer nach dem Eigennamen und nicht nach dem Gattungsbegriff eingeordnet wurden, z.B. "Gibraltar, Strait of ʉ". Ansonsten wurde jeder Eintrag, ob er aus einem Wort oder aus mehreren besteht, als eine einzige Einheit behandelt. So ist z.B. "Lakeland" nach "La Crosse," aber vor "La Salle" aufgeführt. Namen, die mit einem Artikel beginnen, wirden nicht umgestellt (Le Havre, Den Helder, Al-Qāhirah, As-Suways). Namen, die mit "Mc" beginnen, sind der Schreibweise "Mac" nach eingeordnet und Namen, die mit "St." und "Sainte" beginnen, entsprechend der Schreibweise "Saint".

Wo Namensgleichheit besteht, werden zunächst die Städte aufgeführt, dann politische Einheiten und schliesslich physische Objekte. Eintragungen, die vollkommen identisch sind (einschliesslich der weiter unten erläuterten Symbole), werden durch Hinzufügung der Abkürzung des offiziellen Ländernamens unterschieden und sind den Ländernamen nach alphabetisch geordnet. Die zahlreichen identischen Namen in Kanada, dem Vereinigten Königreich und den Vereinigten Staaten sind darüber hinaus noch durch Abkürzungen der obersten Verwaltungseinheit unterschieden. (Siehe Verzeichnis der Abkürzungen, Seite I• 26—I• 28.)

Abkürzungen und Grossschreibung Abkürzung und Schreibweise wurden für alle Sprachen vereinheitlicht. Nach jeder Abkürzung steht ein Punkt, auch wenn dies nicht der jeweiligen Gepflogenheit entspricht. Die Abkürzung "St." wird ausschliesslich für "Saint" gebraucht. "Sankt" und andere Formen dieses Begriffes werden ausgeschrieben.

Der erste Buchstabe eines Namens wird gross geschrieben, ausgenommen einige holländische Namen wie 's-Gravenhage. Die Grossschriebung der weiteren Worte eines zusammengesetzten Namens folgt im allgemeinen der landesüblichen Schreibweise.

Symbole Die im Register verwendeten Symbole veranschaulichen graphisch die zahlreichen Kategorien der benannten Objekte, z.B. ʌ = Berg (Everest, Mount ʌ). Eine Kurzgefasste Erläuterung der Symbole erscheint in jeder die fünf Sprachen des Atlas am Fusse jeder Doppelseite des Registers. Hochgestellte Ziffern hinter Symbolen im Register bezeichnen feinere Unterscheidungen, z.B. ʌ^1= Vulkan (Fuji-san ʌ^1). Eine vollständige Übersicht der Symbole und hochgestellten Ziffern findet sich auf Seite I• 26.

El Índice contiene en una sola lista alfabética, alrededor de 160 000 nombres que aparecen en los mapas. Después de cada nombre está indicada la página o las páginas de referencia, en los cuales se encuentran los mismos, y las coordinadas de la latitud y la longitud del lugar del rasgo. Si una página contiene various mapas, letras minúsculas identifican el mapa correspondiente. Para mapas que ocupan dos páginas, la página de referencia siempre es la de la izquierda.

La mayoría de los nombres que figuran en el Índice, se refiere a los mapas en la escala más grande. Sin embargo, un nombre no se refiere en un mapa metropolitano si ya aparece en otro mapa, donde se muestra en un marco de mayor proporción. Los países, sierras y otros rasgos extensivos se refieren generalmente en el Índice en los mapas de escalas mayores en que se muestran completos.

El orden en que la información del Índice se presenta, aparece en un encabezamiento al centro de cada par de páginas, en inglés, alemán, español, francés y portugués.

Por ejemplo:

ESPAÑOL

Nombre	Página	Lat.°′	Long.°′ W=Oeste

Los rasgos anotados en el Índice son de tres tipos: *el punto*, *el área y la extensión linear*. Para rasgos que indican *el punto* (como por ejemplo, las ciudades, picos de montañas, presas), las coordinadas de latitud y longitud indican la posición exacta del punto sobre el mapa. Respecto a *las áreas* (como países, sierras, etc.), las coordinadas indican usualmente el centro aproximado del rasgo particular. En cuanto a *los rasgos lineares* (ríos, canales, acueductos) las coordinadas indican los puntos terminales, por ejemplo, la boca de un río, o el punto en que un rasgo físico alcanza el margen del mapa.

Las Formas de los Nombres Los nombres que aparecen en el Índice, así como también en los mapas, se dan en general en el idioma local, y en tanto que es posible siguen la ortografía oficialmente aceptada. Incluímos también marcas diacríticas, excepto las que se usan para indicar tono, como en la lengua vietnamita. A causa de que la mayoría de los rasgos que se extienden más allá de las fronteras de un país no tienen un solo nombre oficial, éstos se denominan usualmente en inglés. Muchos nombres, en inglés, alemán, español, francés y portugués, que pueden no figurar en el mapa, se dan como referencia de una página a otra en el Índice. Todas las referencias que pasan a otras páginas se indican con el símbolo →. Un nombre que aparece en el mapa en forma abreviada, debido a la limitación de espacio, en el Índice figura en su forma completa, poniendo entre paréntesis angulares la parte omitida en el mapa, por ejemplo Acapulco [de Juárez].

"Trasliteración" Para los nombres escritos en los idiomas que no usan el alfabeto latino, el sistema oficial de trasliteración ha sido utilizado donde localmente existe. Así,

los nombres de la Unión Soviética y de Bulgaria se trasliteran conforme a los sistemas aceptados por las academias de las ciencias de sus respectivos países. De la misma manera, la trasliteración de los nombres en chino continental siguen el sistema Pinyin que ha sido oficialmente adoptado en este país. Para idiomas sin ningún sistema localmente aceptado de trasliteración, particularmente para el árabe, éstos se trasliteran usando por lo general un sistema adoptado por el United States Board on Geographic Names.

Alfabetización Los nombres se han ordenado de acuerdo con el alfabeto inglés. Las letras del alfabeto en español *ll* y *ch* por ejemplo, no se han considerado letras separadas. Además, los signos diacríticos no se toman en cuenta en la alfabetización—en alemán o escadinavo letras *ä* u *ö* se tratan como *a* u *o*.

Los nombres de los rasgos físicos algunas veces se invierten, ya que se ordenan alfabéticamente según la parte propia y no genérica del nombre. Así por ejemplo, en el caso del Estrecho de Gibraltar aparece: Gibraltar, Strait of u . Por lo demás, cada renglón, sea una palabra o una frase, se alfabetiza como una unidad. Por ejemplo, "Lakeland" aparece después de "La Crosse" y antes de "La Salle". Los nombres que comienzan con artículos (Le Havre, Den Helder, Al-Qāhirah, As-Suways) no están invertidos. Nombres que empiezan con "Mc" se tratan como si fueran del grupo de "Mac", y los que comienzan con "St." y "Sainte" se incluyen con "Saint".

En los casos de nombres idénticos, las poblaciones aparecen primero, las divisiones políticas después y finalmente los rasgos físicos. En caso de ser completamente idénticos (incluyendo los símbolos, discutidos más abajo) se distinguen por medio de abreviaciones de los nombres oficiales de los países a que pertenecen y son puestos en orden alfabético, de acuerdo al nombre de cada país. Hay muchos nombres duplicados en Canadá, el Reino Unido y los Estados Unidos de América, y éstos se distinguen además, por sus subdivisiones primarias. (Vease abajo, la lista de abreviaciones en las páginas I•26-I•28.)

Abreviaciones y Mayúsculas Las abreviaciones y el uso de las mayúsculas se han hecho uniformes para todos los idiomas. Se usa un punto al final de la abreviación, aun cuando en algunos casos no sea ésta la práctica local. La abreviación "St." se usa sólo para "Saint". Las otras formas del mismo término, como "Sankt", se escriben completas.

La mayúscula se usa al comienzo de todos los nombres a excepción de algunos holandeses, como 's-Gravenhage. Las palabras que no son iniciales, se dan con mayúscula o minúscula, según la práctica local.

Símbolos Los símbolos que aparecen en el Índice representan gráficamente las grandes categorías de los rasgos que se han ido nombrando, por ejemplo, ∧ para montaña (Everest, Mount ∧). Una clave abreviada para los símbolos aparece en los cinco idiomas del Atlas al pie de cada par de páginas del Índice. Los números que siguen más arriba del símbolo indican alguna diferencia más precisa, por ejemplo, ∧¹ para un volcán (Fuji-san ∧¹). Una lista completa de símbolos y números superiores aparece en la página I•26.

L'index rassemble en une seule liste alphabétique, quelque 160 000 noms qui figurent sur les cartes. Chaque nom est suivi d'un renvoi à une ou plusieurs pages de cartes et de coordonnées géographiques qui permettent de localiser ce qu'il désigne. Si une page contient plusieurs cartes, une lettre minuscule permet d'identifier chaque carte. Pour les cartes en double page, la référence indiquée est toujours celle de la page de gauche.

En général, l'index renvoie aux cartes où l'information recherchée est reproduite à la plus grande échelle; cependant, les cartes de zones métropolitaines ne sont pas utilisées si le terme géographique figure sur une autre carte dans un contexte plus large. Pour les éléments de grande dimension comme les pays et les chaînes de montagnes, l'index renvoie généralement à la carte à grande échelle qui les représente en entier.

L'ordre des informations de l'index est rappelé en tête de chaque double page dans les cinq langues: anglais, allemand, espagnol, français et portugais.

Par exemple:

FRANÇAIS

Nom	Page	Lat.°'	Long.°' W=Ouest

Les termes de l'index désignent des réalités géographiques de type *ponctuel*, *spatial* ou *linéaire*. Leur position est déterminée par les coordonnées géographiques du lieu quand les données sont de type *ponctuel* (villes, sommets, barrages, etc.), quand elles sont de type *spatial* (pays, chaînes de montagnes, etc.) par les coordonnées du centre approximatif de la zone considérée, et, quand elles sont du type *linéaire* (aqueducs, canaux, etc.) par les coordonnées soit d'un point terminal comme l'embouchure d'un cours d'eau, soit du point où les limites de la carte les interrompent.

Forme des Toponymes Les noms de l'index comme ceux des cartes sont généralement reproduits dans la langue locale et, dans la mesure du possible, selon leur orthographe officielle. Les signes diacritiques sont conservés, à l'exclusion de ceux qui servent à indiquer le ton, comme en vietnamien. La plupart des données géographiques qui s'étendent au-delà des frontières d'un pays sont nommées souvent en anglais, car elles n'ont pas de nom officiel unique. Beaucoup de noms anglais, allemands, espagnols, français et portugais, qui ne se trouvent pas sur les cartes, sont cités dans l'index sous forme de renvois. Tous les renvois sont signalés par le symbole (→). Un nom écrit sur la carte sous forme abrégée, par manque de place, figure en entier dans l'index; la partie omise est entre crochets, par exemple: Acapulco [de Juárez].

Transcription des Noms Pour les noms qui viennent de langues n'utilisant pas l'alphabet romain, le système local et officiel de transcription a été utilisé là où il existait. Ainsi, les noms russes et bulgares ont été transcrits selon les systèmes adoptés par les académies des sciences de ces pays. De même, pour la transcription des noms de la Chine continentale, on a employé le système Pinyin, officiellement adopté en Chine continentale. Pour les langues qui n'ont pas de système officiel de transcription en alphabet romain, notamment l'arabe, la transcription suit généralement de près le système adopté par le United States Board on Geographic Names (Comité américain pour les noms géographiques).

Orde Alphabétique Les noms sont classés dans l'ordre de l'alphabet anglais. Les *ll* et *ch* espagnols, par exemple, ne sont pas traités comme des lettres séparées. De plus, on ne tient pas compte des signes diacritiques: le *ä* et le *ö* allemand ou scandinave correspondent au *a* et *o* sans tréma.

Les noms des données physiques peuvent se trouver inversés car ils sont toujours classés suivant le nom propre. Exemple: "Gibraltar, Strait of u ". Par ailleurs, les noms composés d'un ou plusieurs mots sont considérés comme une seule entité. Exemple: "Lakeland" est inscrit après "La Crosse" et avant "La Salle". Les noms qui commencent par un article (Le Havre, Den Helder, Al-Qāhirah, As-Suways) ne sont pas inversés. Les noms qui commencent par "Mc" sont classés comme s'ils s'écrivaient "Mac" et les noms qui commencent par "St." ou "Sainte" sont classés comme s'ils s'écrivaient "Saint".

Dans le cas de noms identiques, les villes sont inscrites d'abord, puis les divisions politiques, et ensuite les données physiques. Les noms qui sont tout à fait identiques (y compris les symboles qui s'y rapportent) se distinguent par leur pays d'origine, noté en abrégé dans l'ordre alphabétique. Les noms que l'on rencontre plusieurs fois, au Canada, au Royaume-Uni et aux Etats-Unis se distinguent grâce à l'abréviation de la première subdivision administrative de ce pays (voir la liste des abréviations de la page I•26 à la page I•28).

Abréviations et Majuscules L'usage des abréviations a été standardisé pour toutes les langues. Un point suit chaque abréviation, même quand ce n'est pas l'usage dans certaines langues. L'abréviation "St." sert uniquement pour le mot "Saint". "Sankt" et les autres formes du mot "Saint" sont écrites en entier.

Tous les noms commencent par une majuscule, sauf quelques noms des Pays-Bas comme 's-Gravenhage. Certains noms prennent une majuscule, même s'ils ne se trouvent pas au début du terme; on a adopté, en général, l'orthographe locale.

Symboles Les symboles utilisés dans l'index donnent une représentation graphique des réalités géographiques mentionnées. Par exemple, ∧ pour une montagne (Everest, Mount ∧). Une explication abrégée des symboles dans les cinq langues de l'Atlas se trouve au bas de chaque double page de l'index. Les indices qui accompagnent certains symboles permettent une distinction plus précise. Par exemple, ∧¹ pour volcan (Fujisan ∧¹). Une liste complète des symboles et indices est donnée à la page I•26.

O Índice contém, numa só lista alfabética, cerca de 160 000 nomes que figuram nos mapas. Segue-se a cada nome a referência a um ou mais mapas e a localização do acidente geográfico no mapa pelas respectivas coordenadas de latitude e longitude. A referência a mapas que ocupam duas páginas fica sempre na página da esquerda. A maior parte dos acidentes geográficos estão indexados no mapa em que aparecem em escala maior. No entanto, um acidente geográfico não é geralmente indexado num mapa de Área Metropolitana se também figura em outro mapa em que aparece em contexto mais amplo. Os países, cordilheiras e outros acidentes geográficos de maior extensão estão geralmente indexados no mapa em escala maior que os apresente em seu todo.

A ordem em que as informações são apresentadas no Índice figura no cabeçalho, a cada duas páginas, em inglês, alemão, espanhol, francês e PORTUGUÊS.

Por exemplo:

PORTUGUÊS

Nome	Página	Lat.°'	Long.°' W=Oeste

Os acidentes indexados são de três tipos: *ponto*, *espacial* (área) e *linear* (extensão). Para acidentes que indicam *pontos* (como, por exemplo, cidades, picos de montanhas, represas), as coordenadas de latitude e longitude indicam a posição exata do ponto no mapa. No que se refere aos acidentes espaciais (como países, cordilheiras etc.), as coordenadas geralmente indicam o centro aproximado do acidente específico. Quanto aos *acidentes lineares* (rios, canais, aquedutos), as coordenadas localizam os pontos terminais, como, por exemplo, a foz de um rio, ou o ponto em que um acidente físico atinge a margem do mapa.

Formas dos nomes Os nomes que aparecem no Índice, assim como também nos mapas, são geralmente apresentados na língua local, e tanto quanto possível, seguem a ortografia oficial. Usam-se, também, os sinais diacríticos, exceto os que indicam tom, como na língua vietnamita. A maioria dos acidentes geográficos que se estendem além das fronteiras de um só país não possuem um nome oficial único; nesses casos, estão geralmente indicados em inglês. Muitos nomes em inglês, alemão, espanhol, português e francês podem não figurar nos mapas, mas aparecem no Índice como referências remissivas. Todas essas referências são indicadas pelo símbolo (→). Um nome que aparece no mapa em forma abreviada devido a limitações de espaço, figura no Índice em sua forma completa, com a parte omitida no mapa entre chaves (por exemplo, Acapulco [de Juárex]).

Transliteração Para os nomes escritos em línguas que não usam o alfabeto latino, foi utilizado o sistema oficial de transliteração, sempre que este existia. Assim, os nomes da União Soviética e da Bulgária foram transliterados de acordo com os sistemas adotados pelas academias de ciências desses países. Do mesmo modo, a transliteração dos nomes da China continental seguem o sistema Pinyin, que foi oficialmente adotado nesse país. Para as línguas que não possuem um sistema de transliteração adotado oficialmente, em especial o árabe, a transliteração geralmente segue de perto o sistema adotado pelo Conselho de Nomes Geográficos dos Estados Unidos (United States Board on Geographic Names).

Alfabetação Os nomes foram ordenados de acordo com o alfabeto inglês. Por exemplo, o espanhol *ll* e *ch* não foram considerados como letras separadas. Ademais, os sinais diacríticos não foram considerados na alfabetação. Por exemplo, em alemão ou escandinavo as letras *ä* ou *ö* foram tratradas como *a* ou *o*.

Os nomes dos acidentes físicos podem aparecer, às vezes, invertidos, já que foram sempre alfabetados pela parte específica e não genérica do nome, como, por exemplo, *Gibraltar, estreito de* u . Por outro lado, cada entrada do Índice, quer constituída por uma só palavra ou mais de uma, foi alfabetada como uma unidade contínua. Por exemplo, "Lakeland" aparece depois de "La Grosse" e antes de "La Salle". Os nomes que começam por artigo (Le Havre, Den Helder, Al-Qāhirah, As-Suways) não são invertidos. Os nomes que começam por "Mc" são alfabetados como se fossem soletrados "Mac", e os que começam por "St." e "Sainte" como se fossem soletrados "Saint".

Nos casos de nomes idênticos, as cidades estão relacionadas em primeiro lugar; depois as divisões políticas e em seguida os acidentes físicos. As entradas completamente idênticas (inclusive símbolos, mencionados mais abaixo), distinguem-se pelas abreviaturas dos nomes oficiais dos países a que pertencem e são arrolados na ordem alfabética do nome do país. Os muitos nomes repetidos no Canadá, no Reino Unido e nos Estados Unidos, são ainda diferenciados pelas abreviaturas dos nomes das respectivas subdivisões primárias (Ver a lista de abreviaturas, das páginas I•26 a I•28.)

Abreviações e uso de maiúsculas As abreviaturas e o estilo foram normalizados em todas as línguas. Usa-se um ponto depois de cada abreviatura, mesmo que não seja essa a prática local. A abreviatura "St." só é usada para "Saint". As outras formas do termo, tal como "Sankt", são escritas por extenso.

Todos os nomes são escritos com a inicial maiúscula exceto em alguns nomes holandeses, como 's-Gravenhage. O uso de maiúsculas em palavras não iniciais de um nome segue geralmente a prática local.

Símbolos Os símbolos que aparecem no Índice representam graficamente as grandes categorias dos acidentes indicados, por exemplo, ∧ para montanha (Everest, Mount ∧). Uma chave abreviada dos símbolos nas cinco línguas do Atlas figura no pé de cada par de páginas do Índice. Os números altos que acompanham certos símbolos do Índice indicam diferenças mais precisas, como, por exemplo, ∧¹ para vulcão (Fuji-san ∧¹). Uma lista completa de símbolos e números altos aparece à pág. I•26.

Key to Index Symbols

The symbols below represent the categories into which the physical and cultural features are classified in the Index. Broad categories appear in **boldface** type. Symbols with superior numbers identify subcategories.

Schlüssel zu den Symbolen des Registers

Die folgenden Symbole veranschaulichen die Kategorien, nach denen physische und kulturgeographische Objekte im Register geordnet sind. Die Oberbegriffe sind in **Fettdruck** hervorgehoben. Symbole mit hochgestellten Nummern kennzeichnen Unterbegriffe.

Clave de los Símbolos del Índice

Los símbolos abajo representan las categorías dentro de las cuales están clasificados los rasgos físicos y culturales que están incluídos en el Índice. Las grandes categorías aparecen en **negrilla.** Los símbolos que tienen números en su parte superior identifican las subcategorías.

Signification des Symboles de l'Index

Les symboles ci-dessous représentent les catégories sous lesquelles les données physiques et culturelles sont classées dans l'index. Les symboles en caractères **gras** correspondent aux catégories principales. Ceux suivis d'un indice désignent les subdivisions d'une même catégorie.

Chave dos Símbolos do Índice

Os símbolos abaixo representam as categorias em que estão classificados os acidentes físicos e culturais no Índice. As grandes categorias aparecem em **negrito.** Os símbolos acompanhados de números altos identificam as subcategorias.

ENGLISH	DEUTSCH	ESPAÑOL	FRANÇAIS	PORTUGUÊS
Mountain	**Berg**	**Montaña**	**Montagne**	**Montanha**
^{1} Volcano	^{1} Vulkan	^{1} Volcán	^{1} Volcan	^{1} Vulcão
^{2} Hill	^{2} Hügel	^{2} Colina	^{2} Colline	^{2} Colina
Mountains	**Berge**	**Montañas**	**Montagnes**	**Montanhas**
^{1} Plateau	^{1} Hochebene	^{1} Meseta	^{1} Plateau	^{1} Planalto
^{2} Hills	^{2} Hügel	^{2} Colinas	^{2} Collines	^{2} Colinas
Pass	**Pass**	**Paso**	**Col**	**Passo**
Valley, Canyon	**Tal, Cañon**	**Valle, Cañón**	**Vallée, Canyon**	**Vale, Canhão**
Plain	**Ebene**	**Llano**	**Plaine**	**Planície**
^{1} Basin	^{1} Becken	^{1} Cuenca	^{1} Bassin	^{1} Bacia
^{2} Delta	^{2} Delta	^{2} Delta	^{2} Delta	^{2} Delta
Cape	**Kap**	**Cabo**	**Cap**	**Cabo**
^{1} Peninsula	^{1} Halbinsel	^{1} Península	^{1} Péninsule	^{1} Península
^{2} Spit, Sand Bar	^{2} Landzunge, Sandbarre	^{2} Lengua de Tierra, Bajo	^{2} Flèche, Banc de sable	^{2} Ponta de Terra, Banco de Areia
Island	**Insel**	**Isla**	**Île**	**Ilha**
^{1} Atoll	^{1} Atoll	^{1} Atolón	^{1} Atoll	^{1} Atol
^{2} Rock	^{2} Fels	^{2} Roca	^{2} Rocher	^{2} Rochedo
Islands	**Inseln**	**Islas**	**Îles**	**Ilhas**
^{1} Rocks	^{1} Felsen	^{1} Rocas	^{1} Rochers	^{1} Rochedos
Other Topographic Features	**Andere Topographische Objekte**	**Otros Elementos Topográficos**	**Autres données topographiques**	**Outros Acidentes Topográficos**
^{1} Continent	^{1} Erdteil	^{1} Continente	^{1} Continent	^{1} Continente
^{2} Coast, Beach	^{2} Küste, Strand	^{2} Costa, Playa	^{2} Côte, Plage	^{2} Costa, Praia
^{3} Isthmus	^{3} Landenge	^{3} Istmo	^{3} Isthme	^{3} Istmo
^{4} Cliff	^{4} Kliff	^{4} Risco	^{4} Falaise	^{4} Falésia
^{5} Cave, Caves	^{5} Höhle, Höhlen	^{5} Cueva, Cuevas	^{5} Caverne, Cavernes	^{5} Caverna, Cavernas
^{6} Crater	^{6} Krater	^{6} Cráter	^{6} Cratère	^{6} Cratera
^{7} Depression	^{7} Senke	^{7} Depresión	^{7} Dépression	^{7} Depressão
^{8} Dunes	^{8} Dünen	^{8} Dunas	^{8} Dunes	^{8} Dunas
^{9} Lava Flow	^{9} Lavastrom	^{9} Corriente de Lava	^{9} Coulée de lave	^{9} Corrente de Lava
River	**Fluss**	**Río**	**Rivière, Fleuve**	**Rio**
^{1} River Channel	^{1} Flussarm	^{1} Brazo de Río	^{1} Bras de rivière	^{1} Canal de Rio
Canal	**Kanal**	**Canal**	**Canal**	**Canal**
^{1} Aqueduct	^{1} Aquädukt	^{1} Acueducto	^{1} Aqueduc	^{1} Aqueduto
Waterfall, Rapids	**Wasserfall Stromschnellen**	**Cascada, Rápidos**	**Chute d'eau, Rapides**	**Quedas d'água, Rápidos**
Strait	**Meeresstrasse**	**Estrecho**	**Détroit**	**Estreito**
Bay, Gulf	**Bucht, Golf**	**Bahía, Golfo**	**Baie, Golfe**	**Baía, Golfo**
^{1} Estuary	^{1} Trichtermündung	^{1} Estuario	^{1} Estuaire	^{1} Estuário
^{2} Fjord	^{2} Fjord	^{2} Fiordo	^{2} Fjord	^{2} Fiorde
^{3} Bight	^{3} Bucht	^{3} Bahía	^{3} Baie	^{3} Enseada
Lake, Lakes	**See, Seen**	**Lago, Lagos**	**Lac, Lacs**	**Lago, Lagos**
^{1} Reservoir	^{1} Stausee	^{1} Embalse	^{1} Réservoir, Retenue	^{1} Reservatório
Swamp	**Sumpf**	**Pantano**	**Marais**	**Pântano**
Ice Features, Glacier	**Eis- und Gletscherformen**	**Accidentes Glaciales, Glaciar**	**Formes glaciaires, Glacier**	**Acidentes Glaciares, Geleira**
Other Hydrographic Features	**Andere Hydrographische Objekte**	**Otros Elementos Hidrográficos**	**Autres données hydrographiques**	**Outros Acidentes Hidrográficos**
^{1} Ocean	^{1} Ozean	^{1} Océano	^{1} Océan	^{1} Oceano
^{2} Sea	^{2} Meer	^{2} Mar	^{2} Mer	^{2} Mar

ENGLISH	DEUTSCH	ESPAÑOL	FRANÇAIS	PORTUGUÊS
Other Hydrographic Features	**Andere Hydrographische Objekte**	**Otros Elementos Hidrográficos**	**Autres données hydrographiques**	**Outros Acidentes Hidrográficos**
^{3} Anchorage	^{3} Ankerplatz	^{3} Ancladero	^{3} Ancrage	^{3} Ancoradouro
^{4} Oasis, Well, Spring	^{4} Oase, Brunnen, Quelle	^{4} Oasis, Pozo, Manantial	^{4} Oasis, Puits, Source	^{4} Oásis, Poço, Fonte, Manancial
Submarine Features	**Untermeerische Objekte**	**Accidentes Submarinos**	**Formes de relief sous-marin**	**Acidentes Submarinos**
^{1} Depression	^{1} Senke	^{1} Depresión	^{1} Dépression	^{1} Depressão
^{2} Reef, Shoal	^{2} Riff, Untiefe	^{2} Arrecife, Bajo	^{2} Récif, Haut-fond	^{2} Recife, Baixio
^{3} Mountain, Mountains	^{3} Berg, Berge	^{3} Montaña, Montañas	^{3} Montagne, Montagnes	^{3} Montanha, Montanhas
^{4} Slope, Shelf	^{4} Abhang, Schelf	^{4} Talud, Plataforma	^{4} Talus, Plateau continental	^{4} Talude, Plataforma
Political Unit	**Politische Einheit**	**Unidad Política**	**Entité politique**	**Unidade Política**
^{1} Independent Nation	^{1} Unabhängiger Staat	^{1} Nación Independiente	^{1} État indépendant	^{1} País Independente
^{2} Dependency	^{2} Abhängiges Gebiet	^{2} Dependencia	^{2} Dépendance	^{2} Dependência
^{3} State, Canton, Republic	^{3} Land, Kanton, Republik	^{3} Estado, Cantón, República	^{3} État, Canton, République	^{3} Estado, Cantão, República
^{4} Province, Region, Oblast	^{4} Provinz, Landschaft, Oblast	^{4} Provincia, Región, Oblast	^{4} Province, Région, Oblast	^{4} Província, Região, Oblast
^{5} Department, District, Prefecture	^{5} Département, Distrikt, Präfektur	^{5} Departamento, Distrito, Prefectura	^{5} Département, District, Préfecture	^{5} Departamento, Distrito, Prefeitura
^{6} County	^{6} Grafschaft	^{6} Condado	^{6} Comté	^{6} Condado
^{7} City, Municipality	^{7} Stadt, Stadtkreis	^{7} Ciudad, Municipalidad	^{7} Ville, Municipalité	^{7} Cidade, Municipalidade
^{8} Miscellaneous	^{8} Verschiedenes	^{8} Misceláneo	^{8} Divers	^{8} Diversos
^{9} Historicai	^{9} Historisch	^{9} Histórico	^{9} Historique	^{9} Sítio Histórico
Cultural Institution	**Kulturelle Institution**	**Institución Cultural**	**Institution culturelle**	**Instituição Cultural**
^{1} Religious Institution	^{1} Religiöse Institution	^{1} Institución Religiosa	^{1} Institution religieuse	^{1} Instituição Religiosa
^{2} Educational Institution	^{2} Erziehungs-institution	^{2} Institución Educacional	^{2} Établissement d'éducation	^{2} Estabelecimento de Ensino
^{3} Scientific, Industrial Facility	^{3} Wissenschaftliche, Industrielle Anlage	^{3} Institución Científica o Industrial	^{3} Établissement scientifique ou industriel	^{3} Estabelecimento Científico ou Industrial
Historical Site	**Historische Stätte**	**Sitio Histórico**	**Site historique**	**Sítio Histórico**
Recreational Site	**Erholungs- und Ferienort**	**Sitio de Recreo**	**Centre de loisirs**	**Área de Lazer**
Airport	**Flughafen**	**Aeropuerto**	**Aéroport**	**Aeroporto**
Military Installation	**Militäranlage**	**Instalación Militar**	**Installation militaire**	**Instalação Militar**
Miscellaneous	**Verschiedenes**	**Misceláneo**	**Divers**	**Diversos**
^{1} Region	^{1} Region	^{1} Región	^{1} Région	^{1} Região
^{2} Desert	^{2} Wüste	^{2} Desierto	^{2} Désert	^{2} Deserto
^{3} Forest, Moor	^{3} Wald, Moor	^{3} Bosque, Páramo	^{3} Forêt, Lande	^{3} Floresta, Pântano
^{4} Reserve, Reservation	^{4} Reservat	^{4} Reserva, Reservación	^{4} Réserve	^{4} Reserva
^{5} Transportation	^{5} Verkehr	^{5} Transporte	^{5} Transport	^{5} Transporte
^{6} Dam	^{6} Damm	^{6} Presa	^{6} Barrage	^{6} Represa
^{7} Mine, Quarry	^{7} Bergwerk, Steinbruch	^{7} Mina, Cantera	^{7} Mine, Carrière	^{7} Mina, Pedreira
^{8} Neighborhood	^{8} Nachbarschaft	^{8} Barrio	^{8} Quartier	^{8} Arredores, Vizinhança
^{9} Shopping Center	^{9} Einkaufszentrum	^{9} Mercado	^{9} Centre commercial	^{9} Shopping Center

List of Abbreviations / Verzeichnis der Abkürzungen
Lista de Abreviaciones / Liste des Abréviations / Lista de Abreviaturas

	LOCAL NAME	ENGLISH	DEUTSCH	ESPAÑOL	FRANÇAIS	PORTUGUÊS
Afg.	Afghānestān	Afghanistan	Afghanistan	Afganistán	Afghanistan	Afeganistão
Afr.	—	Africa	Afrika	Africa	Afrique	África
Ala., U.S.	Alabama	Alabama	Alabama	Alabama	Alabama	Alabama
Alaska, U.S.	Alaska	Alaska	Alaska	Alaska	Alaska	Alasca
Alg.	Algérie	Algeria	Algerien	Argelia	Algérie	Argélia
Alta., Can.	Alberta	Alberta	Alberta	Alberta	Alberta	Alberta
Am. Sam.	American Samoa	American Samoa	Amerikanisch-Samoa	Samoa Americana	Samoa américaines	Samoa Americana
And.	Andorra	Andorra	Andorra	Andorra	Andorre	Andorra
Ang.	Angola	Angola	Angola	Angola	Angola	Angola
Anguilla	Anguilla	Anguilla	Anguilla	Anguilla	Anguilla	Anguilla
Ant.	—	Antarctica	Antarktis	Antártida	Antarctique	Antártida
Antig.	Antigua	Antigua	Antigua	Antigua	Antigua	Antígua
Arc. O.	—	Arctic Ocean	Nördliches Eismeer	Océano Artico	Océan Glacial arctique	Ártico, Oceano
Arg.	Argentina	Argentina	Argentinien	Argentina	Argentine	Argentina
Ariz., U.S.	Arizona	Arizona	Arizona	Arizona	Arizona	Arizona
Ark., U.S.	Arkansas	Arkansas	Arkansas	Arkansas	Arkansas	Arkansas
Ar. Sa.	Al-'Arabīyah as-Sa'ūdīyah	Saudi Arabia	Saudi-Arabien	Arabia Saudita	Arabie Saoudite	Arábia Saudita
As.	—	Asia	Asien	Asia	Asie	Ásia
Atl. O.	—	Atlantic Ocean	Atlantischer Ozean	Océano Atlántico	Océan Atlantique	Atlântico, Oceano
Austl.	Australia	Australia	Australien	Australia	Australie	Austrália
Ba.	Bahamas	Bahamas	Bahama-Inseln	Bahamas	Bahama	Bahamas
Baḥr.	Al-Baḥrayn	Bahrain	Bahrain	Bahrein	Bahreïn	Bahrein
Barb.	Barbados	Barbados	Barbados	Barbados	Barbade	Barbados
B.A.T.	British Antarctic Territory	British Antarctic Territory	Britisches Antarktis-Territorium	Territorio Antártico Británico	Terre antarctique britannique	Território Antártico Britânico
B.C., Can.	British Columbia	British Columbia	Britisch Kolumbien	Columbia Británica	Colombie-Britannique	Colúmbia Britânica
Bdi.	Burundi	Burundi	Burundi	Burundi	Burundi	Burundi
Bel.	Belgique België	Belgium	Belgien	Bélgica	Belgique	Bélgica
Belize	Belize	Belize	Belize	Belize	Belize	Belize
Benin	Benin	Benin	Benin	Benin	Benin	Benin
Ber.	Bermuda	Bermuda	Bermuda	Bermudas	Bermudes	Bermudas
Ber. S.	—	Bering Sea	Beringmeer	Mar de Bering	Mer de Bering	Bering, Mar de
Bhārat	Bhārat	India	Indien	India	Inde	Índia
B.I.O.T.	British Indian Ocean Territory	British Indian Ocean Territory	Britisches Indischer Ozean-Territorium	Territorio Británico del Océano Indico	Territoire britannique de l'océan Indien	Território Britânico do Oceano Índico
Blg.	Bâlgarija	Bulgaria	Bulgarien	Bulgaria	Bulgarie	Bulgária
Bngl.	Bangladesh	Bangladesh	Bangladesch	Bangladesh	Bangla Desh	Bangladesh
Bol.	Bolivia	Bolivia	Bolivien	Bolivia	Bolivie	Bolívia
Bots.	Botswana	Botswana	Botswana	Botswana	Botswana	Botsuana
Bra.	Brasil	Brazil	Brasilien	Brasil	Brésil	Brasil
B.R.D.	Bundesrepublik Deutschland	Federal Republic of Germany	Bundesrepublik Deutschland	República Federal de Alemania	République fédérale d' Allemagne	Alemanha, República Federal da
Bru.	Brunei	Brunei	Brunei	Brunei	Brunéi	Brunei
Br. Vir. Is.	British Virgin Islands	British Virgin Islands	Britischen Jungferninseln	Islas Vírgenes Británicas	Îles Vierges britanniques	Virgens Britânicas, Ilhas
Calif., U.S.	California	California	Kalifornien	California	Californie	Califórnia
Cam.	Cameroun	Cameroon	Kamerun	Camerún	Cameroun	Camarão
Can.	Canada	Canada	Kanada	Canadá	Canada	Canadá
Can./End.	Canton and Enderbury	Canton and Enderbury	Canton und Enderbury	Islas Canton y Enderbury	Îles Canton et Enderbury	Cantão e Enderbury
Carib. S.	—	Caribbean Sea	Karibisches Meer	Mar Caribe	Mer des Caraïbes	Caribe, Mar do
Cay. Is.	Cayman Islands	Cayman Islands	Kaiman-Inseln	Islas Caimán	Îles Caïmanes	Cayman, Ilhas
Centraf.	Empire centrafricain	Central African Empire	Zentralafrikanisches Reich	Imperio Centroafrican	Empire centrafricain	Centro-Africano, Império
Česko.	Československo	Czechoslovakia	Tschechoslowakei	Checoslovaquia	Tchécoslovaquie	Tchecoslováquia
Chile	Chile	Chile	Chile	Chile	Chili	Chile
Christ. I.	Christmas Island	Christmas Island	Weihnachtsinsel	Isla Christmas	Île Christmas	Christmas, Ilha
C.Iv.	Côte d'Ivoire	Ivory Coast	Elfenbeinküste	Costa de Marfil	Côte d'Ivoire	Costa do Marfim
C.M.I.K.	Chosŏn Minjujuŭi In'min Konghwaguk	North Korea	Nordkorea	Corea del Norte	Corée du Nord	Coréia do Norte

	LOCAL NAME	ENGLISH	DEUTSCH	ESPAÑOL	FRANÇAIS	PORTUGUÊS
Cocos Is.	Cocos (Keeling) Islands	Cocos (Keeling) Islands	Kokos-Inseln	Islas Cocos (Keeling)	Îles des Cocos (Keeling)	Cocos (Keeling), Ilhas
Col.	Colombia	Colombia	Kolumbien	Colombia	Colombie	Colômbia
Colo., U.S.	Colorado	Colorado	Colorado	Colorado	Colorado	Colorado
Comores	Comores	Comoros	Komoren	Comoras	Comores	Comores
Congo	Congo	Congo	Kongo	Congo	Congo	Congo
Conn., U.S.	Connecticut	Connecticut	Connecticut	Connecticut	Connecticut	Connecticut
Cook Is.	Cook Islands	Cook Islands	Cook-Inseln	Islas Cook	Îles Cook	Cook, Ilhas
C.R.	Costa Rica	Costa Rica	Costa Rica	Costa Rica	Costa Rica	Costa Rica
Cuba	Cuba	Cuba	Kuba	Cuba	Cuba	Cuba
C.V.	Cabo Verde	Cape Verde	Kap Verde	Cabo Verde	Cap-Vert	Cabo Verde
C.Z.	Canal Zone	Canal Zone	Panama-kanal-Zone	Zona del Canal de Panamá	Zone du Canal de Panama	Zona do Canal
Dan.	Danmark	Denmark	Dänemark	Dinamarca	Danemark	Dinamarca
D.C., U.S.	District of Columbia	District of Columbia	District of Columbia	District of Columbia	District of Columbia	Distrito de Columbia
D.D.R.	Deutsche Demokratische Republik	German Democratic Republic	Deutsche Demokratische Republik	República Democrática Alemana	Republique démocratique allemande	Alemã, República Democrática
Del., U.S.	Delaware	Delaware	Delaware	Delaware	Delaware	Delaware
Den.	Danmark	Denmark	Dänemark	Dinamarca	Danemark	Dinamarca
Dji.	Djibouti	Djibouti	Djibouti	Djibouti	Djibouti	Djibouti
Dom.	Dominica	Dominica	Dominica	Dominica	Dominique	Dominica
D.Y.	Druk-Yul	Bhutan	Bhutan	Bhután	Bhoutan	Butã
Ec.	Ecuador	Ecuador	Ecuador	Ecuador	Équateur	Equador
Eire	Eire	Ireland	Irland	Irlanda	Irlande	Irlanda
Ellás	Ellás	Greece	Griechenland	Grecia	Grèce	Grécia
El Sal.	El Salvador	El Salvador	El Salvador	El Salvador	El Salvador	El Salvador
Eng., U.K.	England	England	England	Inglaterra	Angleterre	Inglaterra
Esp.	España	Spain	Spanien	España	Espagne	Espanha
Eur.	—	Europe	Europa	Europa	Europe	Europa
Falk. Is.	Falkland Islands	Falkland Islands (Islas Malvinas)	Falkland-Inseln	Islas Malvinas	Îles Falkland	Falkland (Malvinas), Ilhas
Fiji	Fiji	Fiji	Fidschi	Fiji	Fidji	Fiji (Fidji)
Fla., U.S.	Florida	Florida	Florida	Florida	Floride	Flórida
Før.	Føroyar	Faeroe Islands	Färöer	Islas Feroe	Îles Féroé	Faeroe, Ilhas
Fr.	France	France	Frankreich	Francia	France	França
Ga., U.S.	Georgia	Georgia	Georgia	Georgia	Géorgie	Geórgia
Gabon	Gabon	Gabon	Gabun	Gabón	Gabon	Gabão
Gam.	Gambia	Gambia	Gambia	Gambia	Gambie	Gâmbia
Gaza	—	Gaza Strip	Ghaza	Área de Gaza	Zone de Gaza	Gaza
Ghana	Ghana	Ghana	Ghana	Ghana	Ghana	Gana
Gib.	Gibraltar	Gibraltar	Gibraltar	Gibraltar	Gibraltar	Gibraltar
Gren.	Grenada	Grenada	Grenada	Granada	Grenade	Grenada
Grn.	Grønland	Greenland	Grönland	Groenlandia	Groenland	Groenlândia
Guad.	Guadeloupe	Guadeloupe	Guadeloupe	Guadalupe	Guadeloupe	Guadalupe
Guam	Guam	Guam	Guam	Guam	Guam	Guam
Guat.	Guatemala	Guatemala	Guatemala	Guatemala	Guatemala	Guatemala
Guer.	Guernsey	Guernsey	Guernsey	Guernesey	Guernesey	Guernsey
Gui. B.	Guinea-Bissau	Guinea-Bissau	Guina-Bissau	Guinea-Bissau	Guinée-Bissau	Guiné-Bissau
Gui. Ecu.	Guinea Ecuatorial	Equatorial Guinea	Äquatorial-Guinea	Guinea Ecuatorial	Guinée équatoriale	Guiné Equatorial
Guinée	Guinée	Guinea	Guinea	Guinea	Guinée	Guiné
Guy.	Guyana	Guyana	Guayana	Guyana	Guyane	Guiana
Guy. fr.	Guyane française	French Guiana	Französisch-Guayana	Guayana Francesa	Guyane française	Guiana Francesa
Haï.	Haïti	Haiti	Haiti	Haití	Haïti	Haiti
Haw., U.S.	Hawaii	Hawaii	Hawaii	Hawaii	Hawaii	Havaí
H.K.	Hong Kong	Hong Kong	Hongkong	Hong Kong	Hong-kong	Hong Kong
Hond.	Honduras	Honduras	Honduras	Honduras	Honduras	Honduras
H. Vol.	Haute-Volta	Upper Volta	Obervolta	Alto Volta	Haute-Volta	Alto Volta
Idaho, U.S.	Idaho	Idaho	Idaho	Idaho	Idaho	Idaho
I.I.A.	Ittihād al-Imārāt al-'Arabīyah	United Arab Emirates	Vereinigte Arabische Emirate	Emiratos Arabes Unidos	Union des Émirats Arabes	Emirados Árabes Unidos
Ill., U.S.	Illinois	Illinois	Illinois	Illinois	Illinois	Illinois
Ind., U.S.	Indiana	Indiana	Indiana	Indiana	Indiana	Indiana
Ind. O.	—	Indian Ocean	Indischer Ozean	Océano Índico	Océan Indien	Índico, Oceano
Indon.	Indonesia	Indonesia	Indonesien	Indonésia	Indonésie	Indonésia
I. of Man	Isle of Man	Isle of Man	Insel Man	Isla de Man	Île de Man	Man, Ilha de
Iowa, U.S.	Iowa	Iowa	Iowa	Iowa	Iowa	Iowa
Īrān	Īrān	Iran	Iran	Irán	Iran	Irã
'Irāq	Al-'Irāq	Iraq	Irak	Irak	Irak	Iraque
Ísland	Ísland	Iceland	Island	Islandia	Islande	Islândia
It.	Italia	Italy	Italien	Italia	Italie	Itália
Jam.	Jamaica	Jamaica	Jamaika	Jamaica	Jamaïque	Jamaica
Jersey	Jersey	Jersey	Jersey	Jersey	Jersey	Jersey
Jugo.	Jugoslavija	Yugoslavia	Jugoslawien	Yugoslavia	Yougoslavie	Iugoslávia
Kam.	Kâmpŭchea	Cambodia	Kambodscha	Camboya	Cambodge	Camboja
Kans., U.S.	Kansas	Kansas	Kansas	Kansas	Kansas	Kansas
Kenya	Kenya	Kenya	Kenia	Kenia	Kenya	Quênia
Kípros	Kípros Kıbrıs	Cyprus	Zypern	Chipre	Chypre	Chipre
Kiribati	Kiribati	Kiribati	Kiribati	Kiribati	Kiribati	Kiribati
Kuwayt	Al-Kuwayt	Kuwait	Kuwait	Kuwait	Koweït	Kuwait
Ky., U.S.	Kentucky	Kentucky	Kentucky	Kentucky	Kentucky	Kentucky
La., U.S.	Louisiana	Louisiana	Louisiana	Luisiana	Louisiane	Louisiana
Lao	Lao	Laos	Laos	Laos	Laos	Lao
Leso.	Lesotho	Lesotho	Lesotho	Lesotho	Lesotho	Lesoto
Liber.	Liberia	Liberia	Liberia	Liberia	Libéria	Libéria
Lībiyā	Lībiyā	Libya	Libyen	Libia	Libye	Líbia
Liech.	Liechtenstein	Liechtenstein	Liechtenstein	Liechtenstein	Liechtenstein	Liechtenstein
Lubnān	Al-Lubnān	Lebanon	Libanon	Líbano	Liban	Líbano
Lux.	Luxembourg	Luxembourg	Luxemburg	Luxemburgo	Luxembourg	Luxemburgo
Macau	Macau	Macau	Macau	Macao	Macao	Macau
Madag.	Madagasikara	Madagascar	Madagaskar	Madagascar	Madagascar	Madagascar
Magreb	Al-Magreb	Morocco	Marokko	Marruecos	Maroc	Marrocos
Magy.	Magyarország	Hungary	Ungarn	Hungría	Hongrie	Hungria
Maine, U.S.	Maine	Maine	Maine	Maine	Maine	Maine
Malawi	Malawi	Malawi	Malawi	Malawi	Malawi	Malaui
Malay.	Malaysia	Malaysia	Malaysia	Malasia	Malaisie	Malásia
Mald.	Maldives	Maldives	Malediven	Maldivas	Maldives	Maldivas
Mali	Mali	Mali	Mali	Malí	Mali	Mali
Malta	Malta	Malta	Malta	Malta	Malte	Malta
Man., Can.	Manitoba	Manitoba	Manitoba	Manitoba	Manitoba	Manitoba
Mart.	Martinique	Martinique	Martinique	Martinica	Martinique	Martinica
Mass., U.S.	Massachusetts	Massachusetts	Massachusetts	Massachusetts	Massachusetts	Massachusetts
Maur.	Mauritanie	Mauritania	Mauretanien	Mauritania	Mauritanie	Mauritânia
Maus.	Mauritius	Mauritius	Mauritius	Mauricio	Maurice	Maurício
Mayotte	Mayotte	Mayotte	Mayotte	Mayotte	Mayotte	Mayotte
Md., U.S.	Maryland	Maryland	Maryland	Maryland	Maryland	Maryland
Medit. S.	—	Mediterranean Sea	Mittelmeer	Mar Mediterráneo	Méditerranée, Mer	Mediterrâneo, Mar
Mex.	México	Mexico	Mexiko	México	Mexique	México
Mich., U.S.	Michigan	Michigan	Michigan	Michigan	Michigan	Michigan
Mid. Is.	Midway Islands	Midway Islands	Midway-Inseln	Islas Midway	Îles Midway	Midway, Ilhas
Minn., U.S.	Minnesota	Minnesota	Minnesota	Minnesota	Minnesota	Minnesota
Mişr	Mişr	Egypt	Ägypten	Egipto	Égypte	Egito
Miss., U.S.	Mississippi	Mississippi	Mississippi	Misisipí	Mississippi	Mississippi
Mo., U.S.	Missouri	Missouri	Missouri	Misuri	Missouri	Missouri
Moç.	Moçambique	Mozambique	Mosambik	Mozambique	Mozambique	Moçambique
Monaco	Monaco	Monaco	Monaco	Mónaco	Monaco	Mônaco
Mong.	Mongol Ard Uls	Mongolia	Mongolei	Mongolia	Mongolie	Mongólia
Mont., U.S.	Montana	Montana	Montana	Montana	Montana	Montana
Monts.	Montserrat	Montserrat	Montserrat	Montserrat	Montserrat	Montserrat
Mya.	Myanma	Burma	Birma	Birmania	Birmanie	Birmânia
N.A.	—	North America	Nordamerika	América del Norte	Amérique du Nord	América do Norte
Namibia	Namibia	Namibia	Namibia	Namibia	Namibie	Namíbia
Nauru	Nauru	Nauru	Nauru	Nauru	Nauru	Nauru

	LOCAL NAME	ENGLISH	DEUTSCH	ESPAÑOL	FRANÇAIS	PORTUGUÊS
N.B., Can.	New Brunswick	New Brunswick	Neubraun-schweig	Nueva Brunswick	Nouveau-Brunswick	Nova Brunswick
N.C., U.S.	North Carolina	North Carolina	Nord Karolina	Carolina del Norte	Caroline du Nord	Carolina do Norte
N. Cal.	Nouvelle-Calédonie	New Caledonia	Neukaledonien	Nueva Caledonia	Nouvelle-Calédonie	Nova Caledônia
N. Dak., U.S.	North Dakota	North Dakota	Nord Dakota	Dakota del Norte	Dakota du Nord	Dakota do Norte
Nebr., U.S.	Nebraska	Nebraska	Nebraska	Nebraska	Nebraska	Nebraska
Ned.	Nederland	Netherlands	Niederlande	Países Bajos	Pays-Bas	Países Baixos
Ned. Ant.	Nederlandse Antillen	Netherlands Antilles	Niederländische Antillen	Antillas Neerlandesas	Antilles néerlandaises	Antilhas Holandesas
Nepāl	Nepāl	Nepal	Nepal	Nepal	Népal	Nepal
Nev., U.S.	Nevada	Nevada	Nevada	Nevada	Nevada	Nevada
Newf., Can.	Newfoundland	Newfoundland	Neufundland	Terranova	Terre-Neuve	Terra Nova
N.H., U.S.	New Hampshire	New Hampshire	New Hampshire	Nuevo Hampshire	New Hampshire	Nova Hampshire
N. Heb.	New Hebrides Nouvelles-Hébrides	New Hebrides	Neuen Hebriden	Nuevas Hébridas	Nouvelles-Hébrides	Novas Hébridas
Nic.	Nicaragua	Nicaragua	Nicaragua	Nicaragua	Nicaragua	Nicarágua
Nig.	Nigeria	Nigeria	Nigeria	Nigeria	Nigéria	Nigéria
Niger	Niger	Niger	Niger	Niger	Niger	Níger
Nihon	Nihon	Japan	Japan	Japón	Japon	Japão
N. Ire., U.K.	Northern Ireland	Northern Ireland	Nord Irland	Irlanda del Norte	Irlande du Nord	Irlanda do Norte
Niue	Niue	Niue	Niue	Niue	Niue	Niue
N.J., U.S.	New Jersey	New Jersey	New Jersey	Nueva Jersey	New Jersey	Nova Jersey
N. Mex., U.S.	New Mexico	New Mexico	New Mexico	Nueva Mexico	Nouveau Mexique	Nova México
Nor.	Norge	Norway	Norwegen	Noruega	Norvège	Noruega
Norf. I.	Norfolk Island	Norfolk Island	Norfolk-Insel	Islas Norfolk	Îles Norfolk	Norfolk, Ilha
N.S., Can.	Nova Scotia	Nova Scotia	Neu Schottland	Nueva Escocia	Nouvelle-Écosse	Nova Scotia
N.W. Ter., Can.	Northwest Territories	Northwest Territories	Nord-West Territorien	Territorios del Noroeste	Territoires du Nord-Ouest	Territórios do Noroeste
N.Y., U.S.	New York	New York	New York	Nueva York	New York	Nova York
N.Z.	New Zealand	New Zealand	Neuseeland	Nueva Zelanda	Nouvelle-Zélande	Nova Zelândia
Oc.	—	Oceania	Ozeanien	Oceanía	Océanie	Oceania
Ohio, U.S.	Ohio	Ohio	Ohio	Ohio	Ohio	Ohio
Okla., U.S.	Oklahoma	Oklahoma	Oklahoma	Oklahoma	Oklahoma	Oklahoma
Ont., Can.	Ontario	Ontario	Ontario	Ontario	Ontario	Ontário
Oreg., U.S.	Oregon	Oregon	Oregon	Oregón	Oregon	Oregon
Öst.	Österreich	Austria	Österreich	Austria	Autriche	Áustria
Pa., U.S.	Pennsylvania	Pennsylvania	Pennsylvanien	Pensilvania	Pennsylvanie	Pennsylvania
Pac. O.	—	Pacific Ocean	Pazifischer Ozean	Océano Pacífico	Océan Pacifique	Pacífico, Oceano
Pāk.	Pākistān	Pakistan	Pakistan	Paquistán	Pakistan	Paquistão
Pan.	Panamá	Panama	Panama	Panamá	Panama	Panamá
Pap. N. Gui.	Papua New Guinea	Papua New Guinea	Papua Neuguinea	Papua Nueva Guinea	Papua Nouvelle-Guinée	Papua-Nova Guiné
Para.	Paraguay	Paraguay	Paraguay	Paraguay	Paraguay	Paraguai
P.E.I., Can.	Prince Edward Island	Prince Edward Island	Prinz Edward-Insel	Isla Príncipe Eduardo	Île-du-Prince-Édouard	Príncipe Eduardo, Ilha do
Perú	Perú	Peru	Peru	Perú	Pérou	Peru
Pil.	Pilipinas	Philippines	Philippinen	Filipinas	Philippines	Filipinas
Pit.	Pitcairn	Pitcairn	Pitcairn	Pitcairn	Pitcairn	Pitcairn
P.I.T.T.	Pacific Islands Trust Territory	Pacific Islands Trust Territory	Treuhandgebiet Pazifische Inseln	Territorio Fidei-cometido de las Islas Pacificas	Îles du Pacifique (Territoire sous tutelle)	Pacífico, Ilhas do (Território sob Tutela)
Pol.	Polska	Poland	Polen	Polonia	Pologne	Polônia
Poly. fr.	Polynésie française	French Polynesia	Französisch-Polynesien	Polinesia Francesa	Polynésie française	Polinésia Francesa
Port.	Portugal	Portugal	Portugal	Portugal	Portugal	Portugal
P.R.	Puerto Rico	Puerto Rico	Puerto Rico	Puerto Rico	Porto Rico	Porto Rico
P.S.N.À.	Plazas de Soberanía en el Norte de Africa	Spanish North Africa	Spanisch-Nordafrika	Plazas de Soberanía en el Norte de África	Afrique du Nord espagnole	África do Norte Espanhola
Qaṭar	Qaṭar	Qatar	Katar	Qatar	Qatar	Qatar
Que., Can.	Québec	Quebec	Quebec	Quebec	Québec	Québec
Rep. Dom.	República Dominicana	Dominican Republic	Dominikanische Republik	República Dominicana	République Dominicaine	Dominicana, República
Réu.	Réunion	Reunion	Réunion	Reunión	Réunion	Reunião
Rh.	Rhodesia	Rhodesia	Rhodesien	Rhodesia	Rhodésie	Rodésia
R.I., U.S.	Rhode Island	Rhode Island	Rhode Island	Rhode Island	Rhode Island	Rhode Island
Rom.	România	Romania	Rumänien	Rumania	Roumanie	Romênia
Rw.	Rwanda	Rwanda	Ruanda	Rwanda	Rwanda	Ruanda
S.A.	—	South America	Südamerika	América del Sur	Amérique du Sud	América do Sul
S. Afr.	South Africa Suid-Afrika	South Africa	Südafrika	Sudáfrica	Afrique du Sud	África do Sul
Sah. Occ.	Sahara Occidentale	Western Sahara	Westliche Sahara	Sahara Occidental	Sahara Occidentale	Saara Ocidental
Sask., Can.	Saskatchewan	Saskatchewan	Saskatchewan	Saskatchewan	Saskatchewan	Saskatchewan
S.C., U.S.	South Carolina	South Carolina	Süd Karolina	Carolina del Sur	Caroline du Sud	Carolina do Sul
S. Ch. S.	—	South China Sea	Südchinesisches Meer	Mar de China Meridional	Mer de Chine Méridionale	China do Sul, Mar da
Schw.	Schweiz Suisse Svizzera	Switzerland	Schweiz	Suiza	Suisse	Suíça
Scot., U.K.	Scotland	Scotland	Schottland	Escocia	Écosse	Escócia
S., Dak., U.S.	South Dakota	South Dakota	Süd Dakota	Dakota del Sur	Dakota du Sud	Dakota do Sul
Sén.	Sénégal	Senegal	Senegal	Senegal	Sénégal	Senegal
Sey.	Seychelles	Seychelles	Seychellen	Seychelles	Seychelles	Seychelles
Shq.	Shqipëri	Albania	Albanien	Albania	Albanie	Albânia
Sing.	Singapore	Singapore	Singapur	Singapur	Singapour	Cingapura
S.L.	Sierra Leone	Sierra Leone	Sierra Leone	Sierra Leone	Sierra Leone	Serra Leoa
S. Lan.	Sri Lanka	Sri Lanka	Sri Lanka	Sri Lanka	Sri Lanka	Sri Lanka
S. Mar.	San Marino	San Marino	San Marino	San Marino	Saint-Marin	San Marino
Sol. Is.	Solomon Islands	Solomon Islands	Salomon-Inseln	Islas Salomón	Îles Salomon	Salomão, Ilhas
Som.	Somaliya	Somalia	Somaliland	Somalia	Somalie	Somália
Sp.	España	Spain	Spanien	España	Espagne	Espanha
S.S.R.	Sovetskaja Socialist-ičeskaja Respublika	Soviet Socialist Republic	Sowjetische Sozialistische Republik	República Socialista Soviética	République socialiste soviétique	República Socialista Soviética
S.S.S.R.	Sojuz Sovetskich Socialist-ičeskich Respublik	Union of Soviet Socialist Republics	Union der Sozialistischen Sowjet-republiken	Unión de Repúblicas Socialistas Soviéticas	Union des Républiques socialistes soviétiques	União das Repúblicas Socialistas Soviéticas
St. Hel.	St. Helena	St. Helena	Sankt Helena	Santa Elena	Sainte-Hélène	Santa Helena
St. K.-N.	St. Kitts-Nevis	St. Kitts-Nevis	Sankt Christo-pher-Nevis	San Cristóbal-Nevis	Saint-Christo-phe-Nevis	São Cristóvão-Neves
St. Luc.	St. Lucia	St. Lucia	Santa Lucia	Santa Lucía	Sainte-Lucie	Santa Lúcia
S. Tom./P.	São Tomé e Príncipe	Sao Tome and Principe	São Tomé und Principe	São Tomé y Príncipe	Sao Tomé et Principe	São Tomé e Príncipe
St. P./M.	St.-Pierre-et-Miquelon	St. Pierre and Miquelon	Saint-Pierre und Miquelon	San Pedro y Miquelón	Saint-Pierre-et-Miquelon	São Pedro e Miquelon
St. Vin.	St. Vincent	St. Vincent	Sankt Vincent	San Vicente	Saint-Vincent	São Vicente
Sūd.	As-Sūdān	Sudan	Sudan	Sudán	Soudan	Sudão
Suomi	Suomi	Finland	Finnland	Finlandia	Finlande	Finlândia
Sur.	Suriname	Suriname	Suriname	Suriname	Suriname	Suriname
Sūrīy.	As-Sūrīyah	Syria	Syrien	Siria	Syrie	Síria
Sval.	Svalbard og Jan Mayen	Svalbard and Jan Mayen	Svalbard und Jan Mayen	Svalbard e Isla de Jan Mayen	Svalbard et Île Jan Mayen	Svalbard e Jan Mayen, Ilhas
Sve.	Sverige	Sweden	Schweden	Suecia	Suède	Suécia
Swaz.	Swaziland	Swaziland	Swasiland	Swazilandia	Swaziland	Suazilândia
T.a.a.f.	Terres australes et antarctiques françaises	French Southern and Antarctic Territories	Französische Süd- und Antarktis-Gebiete	Tierras Australes y Antárticas Francesas	Terres australes antarctiques françaises	Terras Austrais e Antárticas Francesas

	LOCAL NAME	ENGLISH	DEUTSCH	ESPAÑOL	FRANÇAIS	PORTUGUÊS
Taehan	Taehan-Min'guk	South Korea	Südkorea	Corea del Sur	Corée du Sud	Coréia do Sul
T'aiwan	T'aiwan	Taiwan	Taiwan	Taiwán	Taïwan	Taiwan (Formosa)
Tan.	Tanzania	Tanzania	Tansania	Tanzania	Tanzanie	Tanzania
Tchad	Tchad	Chad	Tschad	Chad	Tchad	Tchad
T./C. Is.	Turks and Caicos Islands	Turks and Caicos Islands	Turks- und Caicos-Inseln	Islas Turcas y Caicos	Îles Turques et Caïques	Turcas e Caicos, Ilhas
Tenn., U.S.	Tennessee	Tennessee	Tennessee	Tennessee	Tennessee	Tennessee
Tex., U.S.	Texas	Texas	Texas	Texas	Texas	Texas
Thai.	Prathet Thai	Thailand	Thailand	Tailandia	Thaïlande	Tailândia
Togo	Togo	Togo	Togo	Togo	Togo	Togo
Tok. Is.	Tokelau Islands	Tokelau Islands	Tokelau-Inseln	Islas Tokelau	Îles Tokelaou	Tokelau, Ilhas
Tonga	Tonga	Tonga	Tonga	Tonga	Tonga	Tonga
Trin.	Trinidad and Tobago	Trinidad and Tobago	Trinidad und Tobago	Trinidad y Tabago	Trinité-et-Tobago	Trinidad e Tobago
Tun.	Tunisie	Tunisia	Tunesien	Túnez	Tunisie	Tunísia
Tür.	Türkiye	Turkey	Türkei	Turquía	Turquie	Turquia
Tuvalu	Tuvalu	Tuvalu	Tuvalu	Tuvalu	Tuvalu	Tuvalu
Ug.	Uganda	Uganda	Uganda	Uganda	Ouganda	Uganda
U.K.	United Kingdom	United Kingdom	Vereinigtes Königreich	Reino Unido	Royaume-Uni	Reino Unido
'Uman	'Umān	Oman	Oman	Omán	Oman	Omã
Ur.	Uruguay	Uruguay	Uruguay	Uruguay	Uruguay	Uruguai
Urd.	Al-Urdunn	Jordan	Jordanien	Jordania	Jordania	Jordânia
U.S.	United States	United States	Vereinigte Staaten	Estados Unidos	États-Unis	Estados Unidos
U.S.S.R.	Sojuz Sovetskich Socialist-ičeskich Respublik	Union of Soviet Socialist Republics	Union der Sozialistischen Sowjet-republiken	Unión de Repúblicas Socialistas Soviéticas	Union des Républiques socialistes soviétiques	União das Repúblicas Socialistas Soviéticas
Utah, U.S.	Utah	Utah	Utah	Utah	Utah	Utah

	LOCAL NAME	ENGLISH	DEUTSCH	ESPAÑOL	FRANÇAIS	PORTUGUÊS
Va., U.S.	Virginia	Virginia	Virginia	Virginia	Virginie	Virgínia
Vat.	Città del Vaticano	Vatican City	Vatikanstadt	Ciudad del Vaticano	Cité du Vatican	Vaticano
Ven.	Venezuela	Venezuela	Venezuela	Venezuela	Venezuela	Venezuela
Viet.	Viet-nam	Vietnam	Vietnam	Viet-Nam	Viet-Nam	Vietnam
Vir. Is., U.S.	Virgin Islands	Virgin Islands (U.S.)	Amerikanische Jungferninseln	Islas Vírgenes (americanas)	Îles Vierges (américaines)	Virgens Americanas, Ilhas
Vt., U.S.	Vermont	Vermont	Vermont	Vermont	Vermont	Vermont
Wake I.	Wake Island	Wake Island	Wake	Isla Wake	Île de Wake	Wake
Wales, U.K.	Wales	Wales	Wales	Gales	Galles	Gales
Wal./F.	Wallis et Futuna	Wallis and Futuna	Wallis und Futuna	Wallis y Futuna	Wallis et Futuna	Wallis e Futuna
Wash., U.S.	Washington	Washington	Washington	Washington	Washington	Washington
Wis., U.S.	Wisconsin	Wisconsin	Wisconsin	Wisconsin	Wisconsin	Wisconsin
W. Sam.	Western Samoa	Western Samoa	Westsamoa	Samoa Occidental	Samoa-Occidentale	Samoa Ocidental
W. Va., U.S.	West Virginia	West Virginia	West Virginia	Virginia Occidental	Virginie Occidentale	Virgínia Ocidental
Wyo., U.S.	Wyoming	Wyoming	Wyoming	Wyoming	Wyoming	Wyoming
Yai.	Yaitopya	Ethiopia	Äthiopien	Etiopía	Ethiopie	Etiópia
Yaman	Al-Yaman	Yemen	Jemen	Yemen	Yémen	Iêmen
Yam. S.	Al-Yaman ash-Sha'bīyah	People's Democratic Republic of Yemen	Volksrepublik Jemen	República Popular Democrática del Yemen	République démocratique populaire du Yémen	Iêmen, República Popular Democrática do
Yis.	Yisra'el	Israel	Israel	Israel	Israël	Israel
Yukon, Can.	Yukon	Yukon	Yukon	Yukón	Yukon	Yukon
Zaïre	Zaïre	Zaire	Zaire	Zaire	Zaïre	Zaire
Zam.	Zambia	Zambia	Sambia	Zambia	Zambie	Zâmbia
Zhg.	Zhongguo	China	China	China	Chine	China

Index / Register / Indice / Index / Indice

ENGLISH Name / DEUTSCH Name	Page / Seite	Lat. / Breite °′	Long. / Länge °′ E=Ost
A			
A, Peak ∧	261d	22.27 N	114.18 E
Aa ≃	46	51.01 N	2.06 E
Aach, B.R.D.	54	47.50 N	8.51 E
Aach, B.R.D.	54	47.31 N	9.58 E
Aachen	52	50.47 N	6.05 E
Aach im Allgäu	54	47.31 N	9.58 E
Aach-Linz	54	47.54 N	9.11 E
Aadorf	54	47.30 N	8.54 E
Aaiun → El Aaiún	138	27.09 N	13.12 W
Aalen	52	48.50 N	10.05 E
A'alī an-Nīl □[4]	130	9.00 N	32.00 E
Aalsmeer	48	52.16 N	4.45 E
Aalst (Alost), Bel.	46	50.56 N	4.02 E
Aalst, Ned.	48	51.23 N	5.29 E
Aalten	48	51.56 N	6.35 E
Aalter	46	51.05 N	3.27 E
Aalwynsfontein	148	30.27 S	18.38 E
Äänekoski	26	62.36 N	25.44 E
Aansluit	148	26.44 S	22.28 E
Aarau	54	47.23 N	8.03 E
Aarberg	54	47.03 N	7.16 E
Aarburg	54	47.19 N	7.54 E
Aardenburg	48	51.16 N	3.27 E
Aare ≃	54	47.37 N	8.13 E
Aareschlucht ♠	54	46.44 N	8.12 E
Aargau □[3]	54	47.30 N	8.10 E
Aarle-Rixtel	48	51.31 N	5.38 E
Aaronsburg	200	40.54 N	77.27 W
Aarschot	52	50.59 N	4.50 E
Aarwangen	54	47.15 N	7.46 E
Aazanèn	34	35.13 N	3.10 W
Aba, Nig.	140	5.06 N	7.21 E
Aba, Zaïre	144	3.52 N	30.14 E
Aba, Zhg.	92	33.06 N	101.59 E
'Abā, Ţiwāl al- ∧	120	36.20 N	39.22 E
Abā al-Bawl, Qurayn ∧[2]	118	24.57 N	51.13 E
Abā al-Waqf	132	28.35 N	30.46 E
Abacaxis ≃	232	3.54 S	58.47 W
Abadab, Jabal ∧	130	18.53 N	35.59 E
Ābādān	118	30.20 N	48.16 E
Ābādeh	118	31.10 N	52.37 E
Abadia dos Dourados	245	18.28 S	47.24 W
Abadiânia	245	16.06 S	48.48 W
Abadla	138	31.01 N	2.44 W
Abaeté	245	19.09 S	45.27 W
Abaeté ≃	245	18.02 S	45.12 W
Abaetetuba	240	1.42 S	48.54 W
Abagajtuj	78	49.35 N	117.49 E
Abagaqi (Hanbumiao)	92	43.41 N	114.40 E
Abai, Malay.	106	5.41 N	118.23 E
Abaí, Para.	242	25.58 S	55.57 W
Abaj, S.S.S.R.	76	50.27 N	85.05 E
Abaj, S.S.S.R.	76	49.38 N	72.52 E
Abaji	140	8.28 N	6.57 E
Abajo Mountains ⛰	190	37.50 N	109.25 W
Abajo Peak ∧	190	37.51 N	109.28 W
Abak	140	4.57 N	7.47 E
Abakaliki	140	6.21 N	8.06 E
Abakan	76	53.43 N	91.26 E
Abakan ≃	76	53.43 N	91.30 E
Abakanovo	66	59.18 N	37.39 E
Abakanskij Chrebet ⛰	76	52.20 N	88.50 E
Abala, Congo	142	1.21 S	15.30 E
Abala, Niger	140	14.56 N	3.26 E
Abalak, Niger	140	15.27 N	6.17 E
Abalak, S.S.S.R.	76	58.08 N	68.36 E
Abalemma, Vallée d' ∨	140	15.34 N	6.23 E
Aban	78	56.41 N	96.04 E
Abancay	238	13.35 S	72.55 W
Abanga ≃	142	0.20 S	10.30 E
Abano Terme	58	45.21 N	11.47 E
Abaokoro I	164t	1.30 N	173.01 E
Abar Irir	134	4.54 N	46.18 E
Abarqū	118	31.08 N	53.17 E
Abarracamento	246	22.12 S	43.30 W
Abaša	74	42.12 N	42.13 E
Abashiri	82a	44.01 N	144.17 E
Abasolo, Méx.	186	25.57 N	100.24 W
Abasolo, Méx.	186	27.12 N	101.24 W
Abasolo, Méx.	194	32.39 N	115.21 W
Abasolo, Méx.	222	24.04 N	98.22 W
Abasolo, Méx.	222	25.18 N	104.40 W
Abasolo, Méx.	224	20.27 N	101.32 W
Abasolo del Valle	224	17.44 N	95.29 W
Abastumani	74	41.46 N	42.50 E
Abate	75	39.03 N	77.36 E
Abatiá	245	23.19 S	50.18 W
Abatskij	76	56.18 N	70.28 E
Abau	154	10.11 S	148.42 E
Abava ≃	66	57.06 N	21.54 E
Abay → Blue Nile ≃	130	15.38 N	32.31 E
Abaya, Lake ◎	134	6.20 N	37.55 E
Abayita, Lake ◎	134	7.37 N	38.35 E
Abayuba	248	34.51 S	56.14 W
Abaza	76	52.39 N	90.06 E
Abba	142	5.20 N	15.11 E
Abbabach ≃	253	51.28 N	7.41 E
'Abbādah	122	33.30 N	36.33 E
Abbadia San Salvatore	60	42.53 N	11.41 E
'abbāsābād	257d	35.44 N	51.25 E
Abbasanta	36	40.08 N	8.50 E
Abbaye, Étang de l' ◎	251	48.41 N	1.56 E
Abbaynagar	116	23.01 N	89.28 E
Abbé, Lac (Lake Abe) ◎	134	11.09 N	41.47 E
Abbehausen	48	53.29 N	8.26 E
Abbekås	41	55.24 N	13.36 E
Abbensen	48	52.23 N	10.11 E
Abbess Roding	250	51.47 N	0.17 E
Abbeville, Fr.	46	50.06 N	1.50 E
Abbeville, Ga., U.S.	182	31.59 N	83.18 W
Abbeville, La., U.S.	184	29.58 N	92.08 W
Abbeville, Miss., U.S.	184	34.25 N	89.37 W
Abbeville, S.C., U.S.	182	34.11 N	82.23 W
Abbey	174	50.43 N	108.45 W
Abbeyfeale	28	52.24 N	9.18 W
Abbey Head ≻	28	54.46 N	3.58 W
Abbeyleix	28	52.55 N	7.20 W
Abbey Peak ∧	154	14.18 S	144.29 E
Abbey Town	42	54.50 N	3.17 W
Abbey Wood ↣[8]	250	51.29 N	0.08 E
Abbiategrasso	56	45.24 N	8.54 E
Abbot, Mount ∧	156	20.03 S	147.45 E
Abbotsbury	44	50.40 N	2.36 W
Abbotsford, Austl.	264a	33.51 S	151.08 E
Abbotsford, B.C., Can.	172	49.03 N	122.17 W
Abbotsford, Wis., U.S.	180	44.57 N	90.19 W
Abbots Langley	44	51.43 N	0.25 W
Abbott	212	31.53 N	97.04 W
Abbottābād	113	34.09 N	73.13 E
Abbott Butte ∧	192	42.57 N	122.33 W
Abbottstown	198	39.53 N	76.59 W
Abchazskaja Avtonomnaja Sovetskaja Socialističeskaja Respublika □[3]	74	43.10 N	41.00 E
Abchazskij Chrebet ⛰	74	43.15 N	41.20 E
Abcoude	48	52.16 N	4.58 E
'Abd, 'Ilw al- ∧[2]	132	28.30 N	29.45 E
'Abd al-'Azīz, Jabal ⛰	120	36.25 N	40.20 E
'Abd al-Ḥafiẓ, Qārat ∧[2]	132	28.53 N	30.08 E
'Abd al-Kūrī I	108	12.12 N	52.15 E
'Abd Allāh	130	13.30 N	23.02 E
'Abd Allāh, Khawr ⊔	118	29.50 N	48.20 E
'abd al-Shāhīd	263c	29.55 N	31.13 E
Ābdānān	118	32.58 N	47.26 E
Ábdēra ⊥	38	40.59 N	24.58 E
Abdrachmanovo	70	54.46 N	52.30 E
Abdul Ghadir	134	10.32 N	42.52 E
Abdul Hakīm	113	30.33 N	72.07 E
Abdulino	70	53.42 N	53.40 E
Abdulovo	70	54.16 N	53.27 E
Abe ≃	84	34.56 N	138.24 E
Abe, Lake (Lac Abbé) ◎	134	11.06 N	41.50 E
Abéché	136	13.49 N	20.49 E
Abéjar	34	41.48 N	2.47 W
Abejonal, Cerro ∧	226	11.39 N	86.10 W
Abejorral	236	5.47 N	75.26 W
Abekr	130	12.43 N	28.55 E
Abel	246	22.54 S	46.08 W
Abelardo L. Rodríguez, Presa ◎[1]	222	29.03 N	110.52 W
Abelek	130	7.23 N	28.46 E
Abêlessa	138	22.54 N	4.50 E
Abel Tasman National Park ♠	162	40.55 S	173.00 E
Abelti	134	8.10 N	37.37 E
Abemama I[1]	14	0.21 N	173.51 E
Abenberg	52	49.14 N	10.57 E
Abengourou	140	6.44 N	3.29 W
Abengourou □[5]	140	6.30 N	3.30 W
Abeno ↣[8]	260	34.38 N	135.30 E
Abenójar	34	38.53 N	4.21 W
Åbenrå	41	55.02 N	9.26 E
Åbenrå Fjord C	41	55.03 N	9.34 E
Abensberg	30	48.49 N	11.51 E
Abeokuta	140	7.10 N	3.26 E
Aber	144	2.12 N	32.21 E
Aberaman	44	51.42 N	3.25 W
Aberavon → Port Talbot	44	51.36 N	3.47 W
Aberayron	44	52.15 N	4.15 W
Abercarn	44	51.39 N	3.08 W
Aberchirder	28	57.33 N	2.38 W
Abercorn, Qué., Can.	196	45.02 N	72.40 W
Abercorn → Mbala, Zam.	144	8.50 S	31.22 E
Abercrombie ≃	160	34.09 S	149.40 E
Aberdare	44	51.43 N	3.27 W
Aberdare National Park ♠	144	0.30 S	36.45 E
Aberdare Range ⛰	144	0.25 S	36.38 E
Aberdaron	44	52.49 N	4.43 W
Aberdeen, Sask., Can.	174	52.19 N	106.17 W
Aberdeen (Xianggangzi), H.K.	261d	22.15 N	114.09 E
Aberdeen, S. Afr.	148	32.29 S	24.03 E
Aberdeen, Scot., U.K.	28	57.10 N	2.04 W
Aberdeen, Idaho, U.S.	192	42.57 N	112.50 W
Aberdeen, Md., U.S.	198	39.30 N	76.10 W
Aberdeen, Miss., U.S.	184	33.49 N	88.33 W
Aberdeen, N.C., U.S.	182	35.08 N	79.26 W
Aberdeen, Ohio, U.S.	208	38.39 N	83.46 W
Aberdeen, S. Dak., U.S.	188	45.28 N	98.29 W
Aberdeen, Wash., U.S.	214	46.59 N	123.50 W
Aberdeen Lake ◎	166	64.27 N	99.00 W
Aberdeen Proving Ground ■	198	39.25 N	76.10 W
Aberdour	42	56.03 N	3.19 W
Aberdovey	44	52.33 N	4.02 W
Aberdulais	44	51.41 N	3.48 W
Aberfeldy	28	56.37 N	3.54 W
Abergavenny	44	51.50 N	3.00 W
Abergele	42	53.17 N	3.34 W
Abergwynfi	44	51.40 N	3.35 W
Abergynolwyn	44	52.40 N	3.58 W
Aberjona ≃	273	42.27 N	71.08 W
Abermain	160	32.49 S	151.25 E
Abernathy	186	33.50 N	101.51 W
Abernethy, Sask., Can.	174	50.45 N	103.25 W
Abernethy, Scot., U.K.	28	56.20 N	3.19 W
Aberporth	44	52.09 N	4.33 W
Abersee ◎	58	47.44 N	13.26 E
Abersoch	44	52.50 N	4.29 W
Abersychan	44	51.44 N	3.04 W
Abert, Lake ◎	192	42.38 N	120.13 W
Abertão	246	22.18 S	45.47 W
Abertillery	44	51.45 N	3.09 W
Aberystwyth	44	52.25 N	4.05 W
Abessinien, Hochland von → Amhara Plateau ⛰[1]	134	9.00 N	38.00 E
Abetone	60	44.08 N	10.40 E
Abez'	24	66.32 N	61.42 E
Abhā	134	18.13 N	42.30 E
Abhar	118	36.09 N	49.13 E
Abharwat ∧	113	34.02 N	74.25 E
Abhayāpuri	114	26.20 N	90.40 E
Abiaca Creek ≃	184	33.20 N	90.15 W
Abid, Oued el ≃	138	32.18 N	7.03 W
'Ābidīn	130	13.33 N	29.38 E
'Abīdīyah	130	18.14 N	33.57 E
Abidjan	140	5.19 N	4.02 W
Abidjan □[5]	140	5.30 N	4.30 W
'Ābid Mār, Tall ∧	122	32.26 N	36.42 E
Abiengama	144	2.35 N	27.46 E
Abiko	84	35.52 N	140.03 E
Abilene, Kans., U.S.	188	38.55 N	97.13 W
Abilene, Tex., U.S.	186	32.27 N	99.44 W
Abingdon, Eng., U.K.	44	51.41 N	1.17 W
Abingdon, Va., U.S.	182	36.43 N	81.59 W
Abinger	250	51.12 N	0.24 W
Abington, Conn., U.S.	197	41.52 N	72.01 W
Abington, Mass., U.S.	197	42.07 N	70.57 W
Abington, Pa., U.S.	198	40.07 N	75.08 W
Abington Reefs ⌇[2]	156	18.00 S	149.36 E
Abino, Point ≻	202	42.50 N	79.05 W
Abino Bay C	274a	42.51 N	79.05 W
Abinsk	68	44.52 N	38.09 E
Āb-i-Panja (P'andž) ≃	62	37.06 N	68.20 E
Abiquiu	190	36.12 N	106.19 W
Abiquiu Reservoir ◎[1]	190	36.18 N	106.32 W
Abiseo ≃	238	7.18 S	76.50 W
Abisko	24	68.20 N	18.51 E
Abisko Nationalpark ♠	24	68.20 N	18.30 E
Abita Springs	184	30.29 N	90.02 W
Abitau ≃	166	59.53 N	109.03 W
Abitibi ≃	166	51.03 N	80.55 W
Abitibi, Lake ◎	180	48.42 N	79.45 W
Abiy Adi	134	13.36 N	39.00 E
Abja-Paluoja	66	58.08 N	25.21 E
Ableiges	251	49.05 N	1.59 E
Ablis	46	48.31 N	1.50 E
Ablon-sur-Seine	251	48.43 N	2.25 E
Abminga	152	26.07 S	134.52 E
Abnūb	132	27.16 N	31.09 E
Åbo → Turku	26	60.27 N	22.17 E
Abóbada	256c	38.43 N	9.20 W
Abodom	140	5.32 N	0.49 W
Abohar	113	30.09 N	74.11 E
Aboisso	140	5.28 N	3.12 W
Aboisso □[5]	140	5.30 N	3.15 W
Abomey	140	7.11 N	1.59 E
Abondance	54	46.17 N	6.44 E
Abong	136	6.59 N	10.44 E
Abongabong, Gunung ∧	104	4.15 N	96.48 E
Abong Mbang	142	3.59 N	13.10 E
Abonnema	140	4.43 N	6.47 E
Abony	30	47.11 N	20.01 E
Aborigen, Pik ∧	64	61.59 N	149.19 E
Aborlan	106	9.26 N	118.33 E
Aborrebjerg ∧[2]	41	54.59 N	12.32 E
Aboso	140	5.22 N	1.56 W
Abō-tōge)(	84	36.11 N	137.35 E
Abou	134	4.27 N	43.05 E
Abou Arak, Ouadi ∨	136	13.15 N	19.40 E
Abou Deïa	136	11.27 N	19.17 E
Abounamy ≃	240	4.24 N	54.26 W
Abra □[4]	106	17.35 N	120.50 E
Abra ≃	106	17.31 N	120.23 E
Abraão	246	23.08 S	44.10 W
Abrahamsdam	148	29.08 S	22.39 E
Abraka	140	5.50 N	6.05 E
Abram	252	53.31 N	2.35 W
Abramcevo	255b	55.50 N	37.50 E
Abramovka	68	51.12 N	41.01 E
Abramovskaja	24	65.11 N	51.43 E
Abram S. Hewitt State Forest ♠	266	41.11 N	74.22 W
Abrantes	34	39.28 N	8.12 W
Abra Pampa	242	22.43 S	65.42 W
Abraq, Wādī al- ∨	136	26.27 N	18.48 E
Abrau-D'urso	68	44.43 N	37.37 E
Abra Vieja, Arroyo ≃	278	34.26 S	58.34 W
Abre Campo	245	20.18 S	42.29 W
Ábrego	236	8.05 N	73.13 W
Abreojos, Punta ≻	222	26.42 N	113.35 W
Abreschviller	54	48.38 N	7.06 E
Abreu e Lima	240	7.54 S	34.53 W
'Abrī, Sūd.	130	20.48 N	30.20 E
'Abrī, Sūd.	130	11.40 N	30.28 E
Abridge	250	51.39 N	0.07 E
Abriès	56	44.47 N	6.56 E
Abring	113	33.42 N	76.35 E
Abrud	38	46.17 N	23.04 E
Abruka Saar I	66	58.10 N	22.30 E
Abrunheira	256c	38.46 N	9.21 W
Abruzzi □[4]	60	42.20 N	13.45 E
Abruzzo, Parco Nazionale d' ♠	60	41.45 N	13.45 E
Absam	58	47.18 N	11.30 E
Absaroka Range ⛰	192	44.45 N	109.50 W
Absarokee	192	45.31 N	109.27 W
Abscon	46	50.20 N	3.18 E
Absecon	198	39.26 N	74.30 W
Absecon Bay C	198	39.24 N	74.28 W
Abşeker	120	38.55 N	39.11 E
Abtenau	58	47.33 N	13.21 E
Abtsgmünd	52	48.54 N	10.00 E
Abu	86	34.30 N	131.28 E
Abu ≃	86	34.25 N	131.24 E
Abū Āhl ⍑[4]	118	34.06 N	43.45 E
Abū 'Alāwī, Wādī ∨	132	30.07 N	31.51 E
Abū al-Ghayṭ	263c	30.09 N	31.11 E
Abū al-Ḥamām, Jabal ∧	122	30.27 N	35.38 E
Abū al-Hawl (Sphinx) ⊥	132	29.59 N	31.08 E
Abū 'Alī I	118	27.20 N	49.33 E
Abū al-Khaṣīb	118	30.27 N	47.59 E
Abū al-Maṭāmīr	132	30.55 N	30.11 E
Abū al-'Urūq, Bi'r ⍑[4]	132	30.45 N	32.23 E
Abū an-Na'am	118	25.15 N	38.51 E
Abū an-Numrus	132	29.57 N	31.12 E
Abū 'Aradeib, Wādī ∨	130	14.12 N	23.06 E
Abū 'Arīsh	134	16.57 N	42.50 E
Abū Ashqar, 'Ilwat ∧[2]	132	30.22 N	31.46 E
Abū Ballās ∧[2]	130	24.26 N	27.39 E
Abucay	106	14.45 N	120.30 E
Abū Daraj, Ra's ≻	132	29.23 N	32.34 E
Abū Dā'ūd, Ra's ≻	118	23.20 N	58.55 E
Abū Dā'ūd as-Sibākh	132	30.55 N	31.34 E
Abū Dawm	130	16.16 N	32.36 E
Abū Dawm, Wādī ∨	130	18.28 N	31.49 E
Abū Dhi'ābah, Wādī ∨	132	29.37 N	32.06 E
Abū Dīs	130	19.08 N	33.34 E
Abū Dughayr, 'Alam ∧[2]	132	30.36 N	29.46 E
Abū Dulayq	130	15.54 N	33.49 E
Abufari	238	5.25 S	62.59 W
Abū Gatta Hills ⛰[2]	130	6.06 N	27.44 E
Abū Gelba	130	13.11 N	31.52 E
Abū Ghālib	132	30.16 N	30.56 E
Abū Ghaush	122	31.48 N	35.06 E
Abū Ḥabl, Khawr ∨	130	12.49 N	31.15 E
Abū Ḥād, Wādī ∨	132	28.20 N	32.49 E
Abū Ḥadīmah, Bi'r ⍑[4]	132	30.44 N	29.51 E
Abū Ḥamad	130	19.32 N	33.19 E
Abū Ḥammād al-Maḥaṭṭah	132	30.32 N	31.40 E
Abū Ḥarāz, Sūd.	130	19.04 N	32.07 E
Abū Ḥarāz, Sūd.	130	12.58 N	29.52 E
Abū Ḥasan, Jabal ∧	134	17.42 N	42.54 E
Abū Ḥummuṣ	132	31.06 N	30.19 E
Abū Ḥushsh, Bi'r ⍑[4]	132	30.49 N	29.57 E
Abuja	140	9.12 N	7.11 E
Abū Jābirah	130	11.04 N	26.51 E
Abū Jandīr	132	29.14 N	30.41 E
Abū Jirj	132	28.32 N	30.47 E
Abū Jubayhah	130	11.27 N	31.14 E
Abū Kabīr	132	30.44 N	31.40 E
Abū Kamāl	120	34.27 N	40.55 E
Abū Kharjah, Wādī ∨	132	28.38 N	31.44 E
Abū Khashabah, Jabal ∧	132	28.08 N	32.52 E
Abūksāh	132	29.23 N	30.42 E
Abū Kulaywāt	130	12.20 N	26.00 E
Abukuma ≃	82	38.02 N	140.56 E
Abukuma-sanchi ⛰	84	37.30 N	140.45 E
Abū Latt I	134	19.58 N	40.08 E
Abulug	106	18.27 N	121.27 E
Abulug ≃	106	18.29 N	121.25 E
Abū Madd, Ra's ≻	118	24.50 N	37.07 E
Abū Makhlūf, Bi'r ⍑[4]	132	30.45 N	29.42 E
Abū Maṭāriq	130	10.58 N	26.17 E
Abu Mendi	134	11.47 N	35.43 E
Abū Minqār, Bi'r ⍑[4]	130	26.30 N	27.35 E
Abumombazi	142	3.42 N	22.10 E
Abū Muḥammad, Bi'r ⍑[4]	122	29.43 N	34.13 E
Abū Muḥarrik, Ghurd ⏏[8]	130	27.50 N	29.40 E
Abū Mūsā, Jazīreh-ye I	118	25.52 N	55.03 E
Abunã	238	9.42 S	65.23 W
Abuná ≃	238	9.41 S	65.23 W
Abū Na'āmah	130	12.44 N	34.08 E
Abune Yosef ∧	134	12.10 N	39.12 E
Abū Qarḍī, Qā' ⌣	122	32.08 N	37.11 E
Abū Qashash	122	31.57 N	35.11 E
Abū Qīr	132	31.19 N	30.04 E
Abū Qīr, Khalīj C	132	31.23 N	30.13 E
Abū Qurqāṣ	132	27.56 N	30.50 E
Aburatsubo-kō C	258	35.09 N	135.38 E
Abū Rimth, Wādī ∨	132	28.45 N	31.27 E
Abū Rīshat, Wādī ∨	132	28.54 N	31.37 E
Abu Road	110	24.29 N	72.47 E
Abū Rubayq	118	23.44 N	39.42 E
Abū Rūḥ, Qārat ∧[2]	132	28.21 N	30.25 E
Abū Rujmayn, Jabal ⛰	120	34.52 N	38.20 E
Abū Sanṭ, Wādī ∨	130	14.11 N	23.06 E
Abū Shajarah, Ra's ≻	130	21.04 N	37.14 E
Abū Shāmah, Jabal ∧	132	29.52 N	31.38 E
Abū Shanab, Sūd.	130	10.47 N	29.32 E
Abū Shanab, Sūd.	130	13.57 N	27.47 E
Abū Shaykhāt, Ḍahr ∧[2]	120	36.36 N	39.40 E
Abu Simbel → Abū Sunbul ⊥	130	22.22 N	31.38 E
Abū Ṣīr	263c	29.53 N	31.13 E
Abu Ṣīr al-Malaq	132	29.15 N	31.05 E
Abū Ṣīr-Banā	132	30.55 N	31.15 E
Abū Ṣīr Pyramids ⊥	263c	29.54 N	31.12 E
Abū Sulṭan	132	30.25 N	32.19 E
Abū Sunbul ⊥	130	22.22 N	31.38 E
Abū Ṣuwayr al-Maḥaṭṭah	132	30.34 N	32.07 E
Abū Ṣuwayr Military Base ■	132	30.34 N	32.06
Abuta	82a	42.33 N	140.46 E
Abū Ṭabarī ⍑[4]	130	17.35 N	28.31 E
Abut Head ≻	162	43.07 N	170.15 E
Abū Tīj	130	27.02 N	31.19 E
Abū Ṭunayṭin	130	14.24 N	31.01 E
Abū Ṭurayfīyah, Jabal ∧, Miṣr	132	29.58 N	32.06 E
Abū Ṭurayfīyah, Jabal ∧, Miṣr	132	29.42 N	31.49 E
Abū 'Uwayjilah ⍑[4]	122	30.50 N	34.07 E
Abuye Meda ∧	134	10.28 N	39.44 E
Abuyog	106	10.45 N	125.01 E
Abū Zabad	130	12.21 N	29.15 E
Abū Za'bal	132	30.15 N	31.21 E
Abū Ẓaby	118	24.28 N	54.22 E
Abū Zanīmah	130	29.03 N	33.06 E
Abwong	130	9.07 N	32.12 E
Åby	40	58.40 N	16.11 E
Åby ↣[8]	41	56.09 N	10.10 E
Aby, Lagune C	140	5.15 N	3.14 W
Abyaḍ	130	13.46 N	26.28 E
Abyaḍ, Wādī al- ∨	132	29.38 N	32.13 E
Åbyälven ≃	26	65.01 N	21.24 E
Abyār	132	30.50 N	30.52 E
Abyār 'Alī	118	24.25 N	39.32 E
Åbybro	26	57.09 N	9.45 E
Abydos	152	21.25 S	118.54 E
Abyei	130	9.36 N	28.26 E
Åbyggeby	40	60.44 N	17.07 E
Åbytorp	40	59.07 N	15.04 E
Abzanovo, S.S.S.R.	76	51.51 N	56.46 E
Abzanovo, S.S.S.R.	76	53.50 N	58.36 E
Acacías	236	3.59 N	73.46 W
Acacio	222	24.50 N	102.44 W
Academia	204	40.25 N	82.28 W
Academy Corners	198	41.57 N	77.23 W
Academy of Sciences ☉[3]	272	37.46 N	122.28 W
Acadia National Park ♠	178	44.18 N	68.15 W
Acadia Valley	174	51.08 N	110.13 W
Acahay	242	25.55 S	57.09 W
Acajete	224	19.06 N	97.57 W
Acajutiba	240	11.40 S	38.01 W
Acajutla	226	13.36 N	89.50 W
Acala	224	16.34 N	92.48 W
Acalayong	142	1.05 N	9.40 E
Acámbaro	224	20.02 N	100.44 W
Acampo	216	38.10 N	121.13 W
Acandí	236	8.32 N	77.14 W
Acaponeta	224	22.30 N	105.22 W
Acaponeta, Río de ≃	224	22.20 N	105.37 W
Acapulco [de Juárez]	224	16.51 N	99.55 W
Acará	240	1.57 S	48.11 W
Acará ≃	240	1.40 S	48.25 W
Acará, Cachoeira ⌊	238	5.47 S	59.12 W
Acará, Lago ◎	236	3.39 S	62.40 W
Acaraí ≃	240	2.02 S	52.15 W
Acarai Mountains ⛰	236	1.50 N	57.40 W
Acará-Miri ≃	240	1.58 S	48.12 W
Acaraú	240	2.53 S	40.07 W
Acaraú ≃	240	2.51 S	40.08 W
Acaray ≃	242	25.29 S	54.42 W
Acari, Bra.	240	6.31 S	36.38 W
Acarí, Perú	238	15.26 S	74.37 W
Acari ≃, Bra.	238	5.18 S	59.42 W
Acari ≃, Bra.	245	16.00 S	45.03 W
Acarí, Río de ≃	238	15.39 S	74.39 W
Acarigua	236	9.33 N	69.12 W
Acatic	224	20.47 N	102.53 W
Acatlán	224	20.09 N	98.27 W
Acatlán ≃	224	18.04 N	98.19 W
Acatlán de Juárez	224	20.26 N	103.38 W
Acatlán [de Osorio]	224	18.12 N	98.03 W

Symbols in the index entries represent the broad categories identified in the key at the right. Symbols with superior numbers (⛰[2]) identify subcategories (see complete key on page *I* · *26*).

Kartensymbole in dem Registerverzeichnis stellen die rechts in Schlüssel erklärten Kategorien dar. Symbole mit hochgestellten Ziffern (⛰[2]) bezeichnen Unterabteilungen einer Kategorie (vgl. vollständiger Schlüssel auf Seite *I* · *26*).

Los símbolos incluídos en el texto del índice representan las grandes categorias identificadas con la clave a la derecha. Los símbolos con numeros en su parte superior (⛰[2]) identifican las subcategorías (véase la clave completa en la página *I* · *26*).

Les symboles de l'index représentent les catégories indiquées dans la légende à droite. Les symboles suivis d'un indice (⛰[2]) représentent des sous-catégories (voir légende complète à la page *I* · *26*).

Os símbolos incluídos no texto do índice representam as grandes categorias identificadas com a chave à direita. Os símbolos com números em sua parte superior (⛰[2]) identificam as subcategorias (veja-se a chave completa à página *I* · *26*).

Symbol	English	Deutsch	Español	Français	Português
∧	Mountain	Berg	Montaña	Montagne	Montanha
⛰	Mountains	Berge	Montañas	Montagnes	Montanhas
)(	Pass	Pass	Paso	Col	Passo
∨	Valley, Canyon	Tal, Cañon	Valle, Cañón	Vallée, Canyon	Vale, Canhão
⌣	Plain	Ebene	Llano	Plaine	Planície
≻	Cape	Kap	Cabo	Cap	Cabo
I	Island	Insel	Isla	Île	Ilha
II	Islands	Inseln	Islas	Îles	Ilhas
⏏	Other Topographic Features	Andere Topographische Objekte	Otros Elementos Topográficos	Autres données topographiques	Outros Elementos Topográficos

ESPAÑOL

Nombre	Página	Lat.°′	Long.°′ W=Oeste
Acatlán [de Pérez Figueroa]	224	18.32 N	96.37 W
Acatzingo [de Hidalgo]	224	18.59 N	97.47 W
Acay, Nevado de ∧	242	24.21 S	66.12 W
Acayucan	224	17.57 N	94.55 W
Accadia	60	41.10 N	15.20 E
Acceglio	56	44.28 N	7.00 E
Aččen, Mys ≻	170	64.45 N	175.30 W
Aččhoj-Martan	74	43.11 N	45.18 E
Ačči	75	39.57 N	68.14 E
Acciano	60	42.10 N	13.43 E
Accokeek	198	38.40 N	77.02 W
Accomac	198	37.43 N	75.40 W
Accomack □6	198	37.45 N	75.40 W
Accord, Mass., U.S.	273	42.10 N	70.53 W
Accord, N.Y., U.S.	200	41.48 N	74.13 W
Accord Brook ≃	273	42.10 N	70.53 W
Accord Pond @	273	42.10 N	70.53 W
Accotink Creek ≃	274c	38.46 N	77.13 W
Accotink Creek, Bear Branch ≃	274c	38.52 N	77.15 W
Accotink Creek, Long Branch ≃	274c	38.48 N	77.13 W
Accoville	182	37.46 N	81.50 W
Accra	140	5.33 N	0.13 W
Accrington	42	53.46 N	2.21 W
Accumoli	60	42.42 N	13.15 E
Acebal	242	33.14 S	60.50 W
Acebuches	222	28.15 N	102.43 W
Aceguá	242	31.52 S	54.12 W
Aceh □4	104	4.00 N	97.00 E
Aceh ≃	104	5.36 N	95.20 E
Acerenza	36	40.48 N	15.57 E
Acerra	60	40.57 N	14.22 E
Acevedo	242	33.45 S	60.27 W
Achacachi	238	16.03 S	68.43 W
Achaguas	236	7.46 N	68.14 W
Achalciche	74	41.38 N	42.59 E
Achali-Kindgi	74	42.48 N	41.16 E
Achalkalaki	74	41.25 N	43.29 E
Achalpur	110	21.16 N	77.31 E
Achangaran	75	40.54 N	69.37 E
Achao	244	42.28 S	73.30 W
Achar	242	32.25 S	56.10 W
Achar Uul ∧	92	45.10 N	103.45 E
Achau	254b	48.05 N	16.23 E
Acheb	138	28.23 N	9.05 E
Achêne	52	50.16 N	5.03 E
Acheng	79	45.32 N	126.59 E
Achenkirch	58	47.31 N	11.42 E
Achen Pass)(	58	47.35 N	11.38 E
Achen See @	58	47.28 N	11.42 E
Achères	251	48.58 N	2.04 E
Achern	52	48.37 N	8.04 E
Acheron ≃	159	37.14 S	145.42 E
Acheux-en-Amiénois	46	50.04 N	2.32 E
Achhībal	113	33.41 N	75.14 E
Achhnera	114	27.11 N	77.46 E
Achí, Col.	236	8.34 N	74.33 W
Achi, Nihon	84	35.27 N	137.45 E
Achiasi	140	5.52 N	1.00 W
Achicourt	46	50.16 N	2.46 E
Achigan, Lac de l' @	196	45.56 N	73.58 W
Achiguate ≃	226	13.55 N	90.55 W
Achill	28	53.56 N	9.54 W
Achilles	198	37.17 N	76.27 W
Achill Head ≻	28	53.59 N	10.13 W
Achill Island I	28	54.00 N	10.00 W
Achim	48	53.00 N	9.02 E
Āchīn	110	34.08 N	70.42 E
Achiras	242	33.10 S	65.00 W
Achmeta	74	42.02 N	45.13 E
Acho, Plaza de ♠	276d	12.02 S	77.02 W
Achol	130	6.34 N	31.31 E
Acholi □5	144	3.00 N	32.30 E
Achsu	74	40.34 N	48.24 E
Achterwasser C	50	54.00 N	13.57 E
Achterwehr	41	54.19 N	9.57 E
Achthuizen	48	51.42 N	4.16 E
Achtuba	70	51.37 N	44.22 E
Achtuba ≃	70	46.42 N	48.00 E
Achtubinsk	70	48.17 N	46.10 E
Achty	74	41.28 N	47.43 E
Achtyrka	68	50.19 N	34.55 E
Achtyrskij	68	44.52 N	38.20 E
Achuapa	226	13.03 N	86.35 W
Achur'an (Arpa) ≃	74	40.06 N	43.39 E
Ači	75	41.17 N	73.02 E
Acıgöl	120	38.35 N	34.31 E
Acı Göl @	120	37.50 N	29.54 E
Acikak	78	54.11 N	106.18 E
Acikehu @	110	37.05 N	88.05 E
Ačikulak	74	44.34 N	44.50 E
Acilia ◆8	257a	41.47 N	12.22 E
Ačimovy Vtoryje	76	60.04 N	75.12 E
Ačinsk	76	56.17 N	90.30 E
Acıpayam	120	37.25 N	29.22 E
Acireale	36	37.37 N	15.10 E
Aciș	38	47.33 N	22.47 E
Ačisaj	75	43.35 N	68.53 E
Ačisu	74	42.38 N	47.40 E
Ačit	76	56.48 N	57.54 E
Ačit Nuur @	76	49.28 N	90.33 E
Ackenbrock ◆8	253	51.21 N	7.40 E
Ackerly	186	32.32 N	101.43 W
Ackerman	184	33.19 N	89.10 W
Ackermanville	200	40.49 N	75.17 W
Ackerson Lake	206	42.11 N	84.20 W
Ackley	180	42.33 N	93.03 W
Acklins, The Bight of C3	228	22.30 N	74.15 W
Acklins Island I	228	22.26 N	73.58 W
Acland, Mount ∧	156	24.55 S	148.05 E
Aclan Point ≻	106	11.44 N	122.22 E
Acle	44	52.38 N	1.33 E
Aclimação ◆8	277b	23.34 S	46.37 W
Acme, Alta., Can.	172	51.30 N	113.30 W
Acme, Pa., U.S.	204	40.08 N	79.26 W
Acme, Wash., U.S.	214	49.43 N	122.12 W
Acmetonia	269b	40.32 N	79.49 W
Acobamba	238	12.48 S	74.34 W
Acolla	238	11.44 S	75.34 W
Acolman □7	276a	19.37 N	98.58 W
Acoma Indian Reservation ◆4	190	34.52 N	107.40 W
Acomayo, Perú	238	13.55 S	71.41 W
Acomayo, Perú	238	9.46 S	76.05 W
Acomita	190	35.03 N	107.35 W
Aconcagua □4	242	32.15 S	70.50 W
Aconcagua, Cerro ∧	242	32.39 S	70.01 W
Aconchi	222	29.50 N	110.12 W
Aconibe	142	1.18 N	10.56 E
Aconquija, Sierra del ⋀	242	27.00 S	65.55 W
Acopiara	240	6.06 S	39.27 W
Açores, Arquipélago dos II	138a	38.30 N	28.00 W
Acoria	238	12.37 S	74.53 W
Acorizal	238	15.12 S	56.22 W
Acornhoek	146	24.37 S	31.02 E
Acosta	204	40.07 N	79.04 W
Acoyapa	226	11.58 N	85.10 W
Acqualagna	60	43.37 N	12.40 E
Acquanegra sul Chiese	58	45.10 N	10.26 E
Acquapendente	60	42.44 N	11.52 E
Acquarossa	54	46.28 N	8.57 E
Acquasanta Terme	60	42.46 N	13.24 E
Acquasparta	60	42.41 N	12.33 E
Acquaviva, It.	60	43.57 N	12.25 E
Acquaviva, S. Mar.	60	43.57 N	12.25 E
Acqui Terme	56	44.41 N	8.28 E
Acra	200	42.19 N	74.03 W
Acraman, Lake @	152	32.02 S	135.26 E
Acre → 'Akko	122	32.55 N	35.05 E
Acre □3	238	9.00 S	70.00 W
Acre ≃	238	8.45 S	67.22 W
Acre Homes	212	29.53 N	95.27 W
Acri	36	39.29 N	16.23 E

FRANÇAIS

Nom	Page	Lat.°′	Long.°′ W=Ouest
Acropolis → Akrópolis ⊥	257c	37.58 N	23.43 E
Acrotambo, Cumbre de ∧	238	8.50 S	76.50 W
Acton, Ont., Can.	202	43.37 N	80.02 W
Acton, Calif., U.S.	218	34.26 N	118.09 W
Acton, Mass., U.S.	197	42.29 N	71.26 W
Acton, Tex., U.S.	212	32.27 N	97.41 W
Acton ◆8	250	51.30 N	0.16 W
Acton Bridge	252	53.16 N	2.36 W
Acton Homes	148	28.36 S	29.26 E
Acton Lake @	208	39.34 N	84.45 W
Acton Turville	44	51.32 N	2.17 W
Acton Vale	196	45.39 N	72.34 W
Actopan	224	20.16 N	98.56 W
Actopan ≃	224	19.25 N	96.20 W
Açu	240	5.34 S	36.54 W
Açu, Igarapé ≃	240	3.44 S	55.31 W
Açuã ≃	238	7.12 S	64.11 W
Açucena	245	19.04 S	42.32 W
Acuitzio del Canje	224	19.29 N	101.20 W
Ačujevo	68	45.43 N	37.45 E
Acuña	242	29.55 S	57.58 W
Acuracay	238	5.35 S	74.10 W
Acurauá ≃	238	7.37 S	70.48 W
Acure ≃	236	8.28 N	61.02 W
Acushnet	197	41.41 N	70.55 W
Acuto	60	41.47 N	13.10 E
Acvež	70	58.21 N	47.46 E
Acworth	182	34.04 N	84.41 W
Ada, Ghana	140	5.47 N	0.24 E
Ada, Jugo.	38	45.48 N	20.08 E
Ada, Nihon	164m	26.44 N	128.19 E
Ada, Mich., U.S.	206	42.57 N	85.29 W
Ada, Minn., U.S.	188	47.18 N	96.31 W
Ada, Ohio, U.S.	206	40.46 N	83.49 W
Ada, Okla., U.S.	186	34.46 N	96.41 W
Ada, Mount ∧	170	56.41 N	134.41 W
Adab ⊥	118	31.59 N	45.45 E
Adaba	134	7.07 N	39.20 E
Adabai ≃	134	10.10 N	38.21 E
A-da-Beja	256c	38.47 N	9.14 W
'Adabīyah, Ra's ≻	132	29.52 N	32.30 E
Adachi	84	35.49 N	139.35 E
Adachi ◆8	258	35.45 N	139.48 E
Adachi-yama ∧	86	33.51 N	130.55 E
Adado, Ras ≻	134	11.20 N	48.45 E
Adâfer el Abiod ◆1	140	19.30 N	10.00 W
Adagide	120	38.06 N	28.02 E
Adai	262c	19.01 N	73.08 E
Adainville	251	48.43 N	1.39 E
Adair, Iowa, U.S.	188	41.30 N	94.39 W
Adair, Okla., U.S.	186	36.26 N	95.16 W
Adair □6	209	40.08 N	92.22 W
Adair, Bahía de C	222	31.30 N	113.48 W
Adair, Cape ≻	166	71.24 N	71.13 W
Adairsville	182	34.22 N	84.56 W
Adairville	184	36.40 N	86.51 W
Adaja ≃	34	41.32 N	4.52 W
Adak, S.S.S.R.	24	66.30 N	59.38 E
Adak, Alaska, U.S.	170	51.54 N	176.35 W
Adaka-shima I	164m	26.45 N	128.20 E
Adak Island I	170	51.45 N	176.40 W
Adala	120	38.34 N	28.17 E
Adale	134	2.47 N	46.27 E
Ådalen ∨	26	63.10 N	17.16 E
Ādam	108	22.24 N	57.32 E
Adam, Mount ∧	244	51.36 S	59.55 W
Adamantina	245	21.42 S	51.04 W
Adamaoua ⋀	142	7.00 N	12.00 E
Adamawa ⋀	124	7.00 N	12.00 E
Adamclisi	38	44.05 N	27.57 E
Adamello ⋀	58	46.10 N	10.35 E
Adamello, Monte ∧	58	46.09 N	10.30 E
Adaminaby	161b	36.03 S	148.43 E
Adami Tulu	134	7.52 N	38.40 E
Adamovka	76	51.32 N	59.56 E
Adamovskoje	72	54.52 N	35.57 E
Adamów	30	51.45 N	22.17 E
Ādampur	113	31.26 N	75.43 E
Adams, Ind., U.S.	208	39.23 N	85.34 W
Adams, Mass., U.S.	197	42.37 N	73.07 W
Adams, Minn., U.S.	180	43.34 N	92.43 W
Adams, Nebr., U.S.	188	40.28 N	96.31 W
Adams, N. Dak., U.S.	188	48.25 N	98.05 W
Adams, N.Y., U.S.	202	43.49 N	76.01 W
Adams, Tenn., U.S.	184	36.35 N	87.04 W
Adams, Wis., U.S.	180	43.58 N	89.49 W
Adams □6, Ill., U.S.	209	39.56 N	91.23 W
Adams □6, Ind., U.S.	206	40.50 N	84.56 W
Adams □6, Ohio, U.S.	208	38.48 N	83.32 W
Adams □6, Pa., U.S.	198	39.48 N	77.15 W
Adams ≃	172	50.52 N	119.35 W
Adams, Mount ∧, N.Z.	162	41.19 S	175.46 E
Adams, Mount ∧, Wash., U.S.	214	46.12 N	121.28 W
Adams Bridge ✣2	112	9.04 N	79.37 E
Adamsburg	269b	40.19 N	79.40 W
Adams Center	202	43.52 N	76.00 W
Adams Creek ≃	214	46.18 N	121.40 W
Adams Lake @	172	51.13 N	119.33 W
Adams Mills	204	40.09 N	81.57 W
Adams National Historic Site ⊥	273	42.15 N	71.01 W
Adams Park	206	42.08 N	85.29 W
Adams Park ♠	265b	43.48 N	79.09 W
Adams Peak ∧	112	6.48 N	80.30 E
Adams Rock I2	164e	25.04 S	130.05 W
Adamston	198	40.03 N	74.04 W
Adamstown, Austl.	160	32.56 S	151.44 E
Adamstown, Pit.	164e	25.04 S	130.05 W
Adamstown, Md., U.S.	198	39.19 N	77.29 W
Adamstown, Pa., U.S.	198	40.15 N	76.03 W
Adamsville, Qué., Can.	196	45.17 N	72.47 W
Adamsville, Mich., U.S.	206	41.47 N	86.00 W
Adamsville, Ohio, U.S.	204	40.04 N	81.53 W
Adamsville, Pa., U.S.	204	41.31 N	80.22 W
Adamsville, Tenn., U.S.	184	35.14 N	88.23 W
Adana	120	37.01 N	35.18 E
Adana □4	120	37.20 N	35.45 E
Adanero	34	40.56 N	4.36 W
Adapazarı	120	40.46 N	30.24 E
Adarama	130	17.05 N	34.54 E
Adare, Cape ≻	9	71.17 S	170.14 E
Adar Gwagwa, Jabal ∧	134	22.15 N	35.20 E
Adarot	130	17.50 N	36.07 E
Adaševo	70	53.56 N	44.19 E
Adauli	262c	19.06 N	73.02 E
Adaut	154	8.08 S	131.07 E
Adavale	156	25.55 S	144.36 E
Adayto	134	14.25 N	40.53 E
Adda ≃, It.	36	45.08 N	9.53 E
Adda ≃, Sūd.	130	9.51 N	24.50 E
Ad-Dab'ah	130	31.02 N	28.26 E
Ad-Dabbah	130	18.03 N	30.57 E
Ad-Dafīnah	118	23.18 N	41.58 E
Aḍ-Ḍafrah ◆1	118	23.25 N	53.25 E
Ad-Dahnā' ◆2	118	24.30 N	48.10 E
Ad-Daljamūn	132	30.48 N	30.50 E
Ad-Dāmir	134	17.35 N	33.58 E
Ad-Dammām	118	26.26 N	50.07 E
Ad-Dāmūr	122	33.44 N	35.27 E
Ad-Dānā	120	36.13 N	36.46 E
Ad-Daqahlīyah □4	132	30.55 N	31.30 E
Ad-Dār al-Ḥamrā'	118	27.19 N	37.44 E
Ad-Darb	134	17.43 N	42.15 E
Ad-Dawādimī	118	24.28 N	44.18 E
Ad-Dawḥah (Doha)	118	25.17 N	51.32 E
Ad-Dayr, Miṣr	130	25.20 N	32.35 E
Ad-Dayr, Miṣr	132	30.20 N	31.16 E
Ad-Dayr, Sūrīy.	122	32.28 N	36.27 E
Adderbury	44	52.00 N	1.17 W
Ad-Dibdibah ◆1	118	28.00 N	46.30 E
Addicks	212	29.47 N	95.39 W
Addicks Reservoir @1	212	29.49 N	95.40 W

PORTUGUÊS

Nome	Página	Lat.°′	Long.°′ W=Oeste
Addieville	209	38.23 N	89.29 W
Ad-Diffah (Libyan Plateau) ⋀1	130	30.30 N	25.30 E
Ad-Dilam	118	23.59 N	47.12 E
Ad-Dilinjāt	132	30.50 N	30.30 E
Ad-Dīmās	122	33.35 N	36.05 E
Addingham	42	53.57 N	1.53 W
Addington	250	51.18 N	0.23 E
Addis	184	30.21 N	91.16 W
Addis Ababa → Addis Abeba	134	9.00 N	38.50 E
Addis Abeba	134	9.00 N	38.50 E
Addis Alem	134	9.02 N	38.23 E
Addison, Ill., U.S.	206	41.55 N	88.00 W
Addison, Mich., U.S.	206	41.59 N	84.21 W
Addison, N.Y., U.S.	200	42.06 N	77.14 W
Addison, Tex., U.S.	212	32.58 N	96.50 W
Addison Creek ≃	268	41.51 N	87.51 W
Ad-Dīwānīyah	118	31.59 N	44.56 E
Addlestone	250	51.22 N	0.30 W
Addo	148	33.32 S	25.45 E
Addo Elephant National Park ♠	148	33.29 S	25.46 E
Ad-Du'ayn	130	11.26 N	26.09 E
Ad-Duhayr	122	31.10 N	32.00 E
Ad-Dūqah	134	19.36 N	40.54 E
Ad-Duqqī	263c	30.04 N	31.15 E
Ad-Duwayd	118	30.15 N	42.17 E
Ad-Duwaym	130	14.00 N	32.19 E
Ad-Duwayr	122	33.23 N	35.25 E
Adébour	136	13.20 N	11.54 E
Adegem	46	51.12 N	3.29 E
Adego	134	8.57 N	49.35 E
Adel, Ga., U.S.	182	31.08 N	83.25 W
Adel, Iowa, U.S.	180	41.37 N	94.01 W
Adelaida → Adelaide	158b	34.55 S	138.35 E
Adelaide, Austl.	158b	34.55 S	138.35 E
Adelaide, Ba.	230b	25.00 N	77.31 W
Adelaide, S. Afr.	148	32.42 S	26.20 E
Adelaide Airport ⊠	158b	34.58 S	138.32 E
Adelaide Island I	9	67.15 S	68.30 W
Adelaide Peninsula ≻1	166	68.09 N	97.45 W
Adelaide River	154	13.15 S	131.06 E
Adelanto	218	34.35 N	117.24 W
Adelaye	142	7.07 N	22.49 E
Adelbert Range ⋀	154	4.35 S	145.10 E
Adelboden	54	46.30 N	7.33 E
Adelebsen	48	51.34 N	9.45 E
Adèle Island I	150	15.32 S	123.09 E
Adélie Coast •2	9	67.00 S	139.00 E
Adelong Creek ≃	161b	35.06 S	148.02 E
Adelphi	274c	39.00 N	76.58 W
Adelphia	198	40.13 N	74.15 W
Adelphi University ⊎2	266	40.43 N	73.36 W
Adelsheim	52	49.24 N	9.23 E
Adelsö I	40	59.23 N	17.30 E
Aden	134	12.45 N	45.12 E
Aden, Gulf of C	134	12.30 N	48.00 E
Adena	204	40.13 N	80.53 W
Adenau	52	50.23 N	6.55 E
Adendorf	48	53.17 N	10.26 E
Adendorp	148	32.20 S	24.33 E
Adenstedt	48	52.15 N	10.10 E
Ader ⋀1	140	14.10 N	5.05 E
Aderklaa	254b	48.17 N	16.32 E
Adéta	140	7.08 N	0.44 E
Adhāta	262b	22.52 N	88.32 E
'Adhrā'	122	33.37 N	36.30 E
Adi	144	3.24 N	30.48 E
Adi, Pulau I	154	4.18 S	133.26 E
Adiaké	140	5.16 N	3.17 W
Adi Arkay	134	13.17 N	13.17 E
Adi Daro	134	14.27 N	38.16 E
Adieu, Cape ≻	152	31.59 S	132.09 E
Adigala	134	10.25 N	42.17 E
Adige (Etsch) ≃	58	45.10 N	12.20 E
Adigeni	74	41.42 N	42.42 E
Adigrat	134	14.18 N	39.31 E
Adi Keyih	134	14.49 N	39.23 E
Adi Kwala	134	14.39 N	38.53 E
Ādilābād	112	19.40 N	78.32 E
Adilang	144	2.44 N	33.29 E
Adilcevaz	74	38.44 N	42.44 E
Adimi	79	47.20 N	138.56 E
Adin	194	41.12 N	120.57 W
Adirondack Mountains ⋀	178	44.00 N	74.00 W
Adirondack Park ♠	178	44.00 N	74.20 W
Adis Dera	134	10.15 N	38.50 E
Adis Zemen	134	12.07 N	37.47 E
Adi Ugri	134	14.55 N	38.53 E
Adiwerna	105a	6.56 S	109.07 E
Adıyaman	120	37.46 N	38.17 E
Adıyaman □4	120	37.45 N	38.30 E
Adjan	102	2.11 N	113.12 E
Adjelman, Oued ∨	138	22.09 N	3.47 E
Adjohon	140	6.42 N	2.28 E
Adjud	38	46.04 N	27.11 E
Adjumani	144	3.22 N	31.47 E
Adjuntas	230m	18.10 N	66.43 W
Adler	68	43.27 N	39.55 E
Adler Planetarium ⊎	268	41.52 N	87.37 W
Adlershof ◆8	254a	52.26 N	13.33 E
Adlington	42	53.37 N	2.36 W
Adlington Hall ⊥	252	53.19 N	2.09 W
Adliswil	54	47.19 N	8.32 E
Admer, Erg d' ◆2	138	24.00 N	9.15 E
Admiral	174	49.43 N	108.01 W
Admiralitäts-Inseln → Admiralty Islands II	154	2.10 S	147.00 E
Admiralty Bay C, St. Vin.	231h	13.00 N	61.16 W
Admiralty Bay C, Alaska, U.S.	170	70.53 N	155.45 W
Admiralty Gulf C	150	14.20 S	125.50 E
Admiralty Inlet C, N.W. Ter., Can.	166	73.00 N	86.00 W
Admiralty Inlet C, Wash., U.S.	214	48.05 N	122.39 W
Admiralty Island I, N.W. Ter., Can.	166	69.30 N	101.00 W
Admiralty Island I, Alaska, U.S.	170	57.50 N	134.30 W
Admiralty Islands II	154	2.10 S	147.00 E
Admiralty Mountains ⋀	9	71.45 S	168.30 E
Adna	214	46.38 N	123.04 W
Ado ≃	84	35.19 N	136.05 E
Adobe Creek ≃, Calif., U.S.	272	37.26 N	122.06 W
Adobe Creek ≃, Colo., U.S.	188	38.05 N	103.18 W
Ado-Ekiti	140	7.38 N	5.12 E
Adogawa	84	35.20 N	136.02 E
Adok	130	8.11 N	30.19 E
Adolfo López Mateos, Presa @1	222	25.13 N	107.25 W
Adolfo Ruiz Cortines	222	25.40 N	108.40 W
Adolfsberg	40	59.15 N	15.10 E
Adolphus Reach ⩌	202	44.05 N	76.55 W
Adonara, Pulau I	102	8.20 S	123.10 E
Ādoni	112	15.38 N	77.17 E
Ado-Odo	140	6.36 N	2.56 E
Adorf	50	50.19 N	12.15 E
Adoua, Vallée d' ∨	140	14.37 N	6.40 E
Adour ≃	32	43.32 N	1.32 E
Adowa → Adwa	134	14.10 N	38.55 E
Ādra, Bhārat	116	23.30 N	86.40 E
Adra, Esp.	34	36.44 N	3.01 W
Adranga	144	2.55 N	29.58 E
Adrano	36	37.40 N	14.50 E
Adrar	138	27.54 N	0.17 W
Adrar ◆1	124	20.30 N	13.30 W
Adrar, Massif de l' ∧	138	25.03 N	7.55 W
Adraskan	118	33.39 N	62.16 E
Adrasman	75	40.38 N	69.58 E

Adré	136	13.28 N	22.12 E
Adrī	136	27.32 N	13.14 E
Adria	58	45.03 N	12.03 E
Adrian, Ga., U.S.	182	32.32 N	82.35 W
Adrian, Mich., U.S.	206	41.54 N	84.02 W
Adrian, Minn., U.S.	188	43.38 N	95.56 W
Adrian, Mo., U.S.	184	38.24 N	94.21 W
Adrian, Ohio, U.S.	204	41.03 N	83.20 W
Adrian, Oreg., U.S.	192	43.44 N	117.04 W
Adrian, Pa., U.S.	204	40.53 N	79.32 W
Adrian, Tex., U.S.	186	35.16 N	102.40 W
Adrian, W. Va., U.S.	178	38.54 N	80.17 W
Adrianople → Edirne	120	41.40 N	26.34 E
Adrianópolis	277a	22.39 S	43.30 W
Adrianovka	78	51.34 N	114.30 E
Adriatico Mar → Adriatic Sea ⫧2	22	42.30 N	16.00 E
Adriatic Sea ⫧2	22	42.30 N	16.00 E
Adriatique, Mer → Adriatic Sea ⫧2	22	42.30 N	16.00 E
Adriatisches Meer → Adriatic Sea ⫧2	22	42.30 N	16.00 E
Adro	58	45.37 N	9.57 E
Adrogué → Almirante Brown	248	34.48 S	58.23 W
Adstock Mountain ∧	196	46.02 N	71.12 W
Adua	154	1.55 S	129.50 E
Aduard	48	53.15 N	6.26 E
Adujevo	72	54.59 N	35.59 E
Aduku	144	2.01 N	32.43 E
Adur ≃	44	50.49 N	0.16 W
Adusa	144	1.23 N	28.01 E
Adutiškis	66	55.09 N	26.36 E
Advance	184	37.06 N	89.55 W
Adventure, Bahía ⩌	244	44.50 S	74.45 W
Advocate Harbour	176	45.20 N	64.47 W
Adwa	134	14.10 N	38.55 E
'Adwān, Wādī ∨	136	31.35 N	21.13 E
Adwick le Street	42	53.34 N	1.11 W
Adyča ≃	64	68.13 N	134.41 E
Adyge	74	44.19 N	41.57 E
Adygejskaja Avtonomnaja Oblast' □8	74	44.30 N	40.00 E
Adyk	70	45.48 N	45.38 E
Adžarskaja Avtonomnaja Sovetskaja Socialističeskaja Respublika □3	74	41.40 N	42.00 E
Adž Bogd Uul ⋀	92	44.52 N	95.10 E
Adžikend	74	40.31 N	46.21 E
Adžima	79	48.08 N	139.40 E
Adzopé	140	6.06 N	3.52 W
Adzopé □5	140	6.00 N	3.30 W
Adzragyn ≃	78	49.54 N	104.09 E
Adz'va ≃	24	66.36 N	59.28 E
Adz'vavom	24	66.36 N	59.12 E
Ae, Water of ≃	42	55.08 N	3.27 W
Æbelø I	41	55.38 N	10.12 E
Aegean Sea ⫧2	38	38.30 N	25.00 E
Aegerisee @	54	47.07 N	8.38 E
Aegina → Aíyina I	38	37.46 N	23.26 E
Aegna I	66	59.35 N	24.48 E
Aegviidu	66	59.17 N	25.37 E
Aekhumbang	104	1.59 N	99.11 E
Aeon Point ≻	164o	1.46 N	157.11 W
A'ergeshanmai ⋀	110	36.40 N	88.00 E
Aerhuola	79	51.01 N	120.10 E
A'erjinshanmai ⋀	80	37.30 N	86.30 E
Aerjisumu	92	42.58 N	111.08 E
Aerkuhu @	110	30.43 N	82.55 E
Ærø I	41	54.53 N	10.20 E
Aeroflotskij	68	45.03 N	34.01 E
Aero-Haven Airport ⊠	275	39.49 N	74.54 W
Aeron ≃	44	52.14 N	4.16 W
Aeroparque ⊠	278	34.35 S	58.24 W
Ærøskøbing	41	54.53 N	10.25 E
Aerqishan ∧	79	48.35 N	121.07 E
Aershan	79	47.11 N	119.57 E
Aershatu	92	44.11 N	113.36 E
Aerzen	48	52.03 N	9.16 E
Aesch	54	47.28 N	7.36 E
Aeschi	54	46.40 N	7.42 E
Aetna	172	49.08 N	113.15 W
Afade	136	12.14 N	14.38 E
Afadjoto ∧2	140	7.05 N	0.35 E
'Afak	118	32.04 N	45.15 E
Afanasjevka	68	50.47 N	38.36 E
Afanasjevo, S.S.S.R.	72	54.20 N	37.01 E
Afanasjevo, S.S.S.R.	72	55.18 N	36.12 E
Afanasjevskoje	76	56.49 N	58.17 E
Afándou	38	36.17 N	28.10 E
Afar	138	25.30 N	8.22 E
Afareaitu	164s	17.33 S	149.47 W
Afars and Issas → Djibouti □1	134	11.30 N	43.00 E
Afaspida	262c	19.08 N	73.04 E
Afdem	134	9.26 N	41.02 E
Afferde, B.R.D.	48	52.06 N	9.25 E
Afferde, B.R.D.	253	51.34 N	7.39 E
Affi	58	45.33 N	10.46 E
Affing	54	48.27 N	10.58 E
Afflisses, Oued ∨	138	28.29 N	1.09 E
Affollé ⋀2	140	16.55 N	10.25 W
Affoltern am Albis	54	47.17 N	8.27 E
Affori ◆8	256b	45.31 N	9.10 E
Affton	209	38.33 N	90.20 W
Afghānestān → Afghanistan □1	108	33.00 N	65.00 E
Afghanistan □1	108	33.00 N	65.00 E
Afgoi	134	2.10 N	45.09 E
'Afīf	118	23.55 N	42.56 E
Afikpo	140	5.53 N	7.56 E
Afipskij	68	44.55 N	38.50 E
Afiqim	122	32.40 N	35.35 E
Åfjord	26	63.58 N	10.12 E
Aflao	140	6.05 N	1.08 E
Aflou	138	34.07 N	2.06 E
Afmadu	134	0.32 N	42.10 E
Afodo	134	10.17 N	34.50 E
Afogados da Ingàzeira	240	7.45 S	37.39 W
Afognak Island I	170	58.15 N	152.30 W
Afonicha	24	68.13 N	53.17 E
Afono Bay C	164u	14.15 S	170.39 W
Afonso Bezerra	240	5.30 S	36.30 W
Afonso Cláudio	245	20.05 S	41.08 W
Afonsos, Campo dos ■	277a	22.53 S	43.23 W
Afonsos, Rio dos ≃	277a	22.51 S	43.23 W
'Afrā', Wādī ∨	118	30.59 N	35.38 E
Afragola	60	40.55 N	14.18 E
'Afraj, 'Alam al- ∧2	132	30.40 N	29.37 E
Afram ≃	140	7.00 N	0.52 E
Afram Plains ⊻	140	6.50 N	0.10 W
Africa •1	10	10.00 N	22.00 E
Africa del Sur → South Africa □1	146	30.00 S	26.00 E
Afrika → Africa •1	10	10.00 N	22.00 E
Afrikanda	24	67.25 N	32.43 E
'Afrīn	120	36.31 N	36.52 E
'afrīn ≃	120	36.22 N	36.28 E
Afrique → Africa •1	10	10.00 N	22.00 E
Afrique du Sud (République d') → South Africa □1	146	30.00 S	26.00 E
Afritz	58	46.43 N	13.48 E
Afşin	120	38.15 N	36.55 E
Afsluitdijk ◆5	48	53.00 N	5.15 E
Afton, Iowa, U.S.	184	41.02 N	94.12 W
Afton, N.Y., U.S.	200	42.14 N	75.32 W
Afton, Okla., U.S.	186	36.42 N	94.58 W
Afton, Wis., U.S.	206	42.36 N	89.04 W
Afton, Wyo., U.S.	190	42.44 N	110.56 W
Aftout ◆1	138	26.40 N	3.48 W
Afuá	240	0.10 S	50.23 W

'Afula	122	32.36 N	35.17 E
'Afula 'Illit	122	32.38 N	35.20 E
Afyon	120	38.45 N	30.33 E
Afyon □4	120	38.40 N	30.30 E
Afyonkarahisar → Afyon	120	38.45 N	30.33 E
Afzalgarh	114	29.24 N	78.41 E
Āg ≃	74	38.59 N	45.27 E
Aga, Nor.	26	60.18 N	6.36 E
Aga, S.S.S.R.	78	51.12 N	115.10 E
Aga ≃	78	51.30 N	115.50 E
Agačag	75	44.03 N	71.58 E
Agadem	136	16.50 N	13.17 E
Agadez	140	16.58 N	7.59 E
Agadez □5	136	19.45 N	12.00 E
Agadir	138	30.26 N	9.36 W
Agadyr'	76	48.17 N	72.53 E
Agafonovka	70	50.36 N	47.26 E
Agāhpur	262a	28.34 N	77.22 E
Agaie	140	9.03 N	6.18 E
Ägäisches Meer → Aegean Sea ⫧2	38	38.30 N	25.00 E
Agalak	130	11.01 N	32.42 E
Agalega Islands II	128	10.24 S	56.37 E
Agalta, Cordillera de ⋀	226	15.00 N	85.53 W
Agan ≃	62	61.23 N	74.35 E
Agana	164p	13.28 N	144.45 E
Agana Naval Air Station ■	164p	13.29 N	144.48 E
Agano ≃	82	37.57 N	139.08 E
Agapa	64	71.27 N	89.15 E
Agapovka	76	53.18 N	59.28 E
Agar	110	23.42 N	76.01 E
Agara	74	42.03 N	43.49 E
Ågård	41	55.35 N	9.26 E
Agaro	134	7.50 N	36.40 E
Agartala	110	23.49 N	91.16 E
Agaru	130	10.59 N	34.44 E
Agaruut	92	43.11 N	109.28 E
Agasan	262c	19.11 N	73.04 E
Agassiz	172	49.14 N	121.46 W
Agassiz, Cape ≻	9	68.29 S	62.56 W
Agat	164p	13.24 N	144.39 E
Agat Bay C	164p	13.24 N	144.39 E
Agate	188	39.28 N	103.56 W
Agate Beach	192	44.41 N	124.04 W
Agats	154	5.33 S	138.08 E
Agatsuma	84	36.34 N	138.50 E
Agatsuma ≃	84	36.30 N	139.01 E
Agatti Island I	112	10.50 N	72.12 E
Agattu Island I	171a	52.25 N	173.35 E
Agattu Strait ⩌	171a	52.35 N	173.25 E
Agawa	86	33.34 N	133.10 E
Agawa ≃	180	47.21 N	84.38 W
Agawa Bay C	180	47.20 N	84.42 W
Agawam, Mass., U.S.	197	42.05 N	72.37 W
Agawam, Mont., U.S.	172	48.00 N	112.10 W
Agay	56	43.26 N	6.51 E
Agazzano	56	44.57 N	9.31 E
Agbaja	140	7.58 N	6.38 E
Agbede	263a	6.40 N	3.29 E
Agbélouvé	140	6.40 N	1.10 E
Agboju	263a	6.28 N	3.17 E
Agbor	140	6.18 N	6.11 E
Agboville	140	5.56 N	4.13 W
Agboville □5	140	5.45 N	4.10 W
Agboyi Creek ≃	263a	6.34 N	3.25 E
Ağcakışla	120	39.33 N	36.22 E
Agcawayan	106	13.46 N	120.16 E
Agdam	74	39.59 N	46.57 E
Agdaš	74	40.38 N	47.28 E
Agde	32	43.19 N	3.28 E
Agde, Cap d' ≻	32	43.16 N	3.30 E
Agdžabedi	74	40.03 N	47.28 E
Agege	140	6.37 N	3.20 E
Agejevo	72	54.10 N	36.29 E
Agematsu	84	35.47 N	137.42 E
Agen	32	44.12 N	0.37 E
Agency	180	41.00 N	92.18 W
Agency Lake @	192	42.32 N	121.58 W
Ageo	84	35.58 N	139.36 E
Agepsta, Gora ∧	74	43.32 N	40.30 E
Ager ≃	58	48.05 N	13.51 E
Ageraro	134	4.08 N	42.40 E
Agerbæk	41	55.36 N	8.48 E
Agere Hiywet	134	8.56 N	37.56 E
Agerskov	41	55.07 N	9.08 E
Agersø I	41	55.12 N	11.12 E
Ager Tay •4	136	20.15 N	17.31 E
Agery	158b	34.10 S	137.44 E
Aggeneis	148	29.03 S	18.51 E
Agger ≃	52	50.48 N	7.11 E
Aggteleki Barlang •5	30	48.30 N	20.32 E
Āghā Jārī	118	30.42 N	49.50 E
Agia	114	26.05 N	90.32 E
Agidingbi	263a	6.38 N	3.21 E
Agimont	52	50.10 N	4.48 E
Ağın	120	38.57 N	38.43 E
Agincourt ◆8	265b	43.48 N	79.17 W
Aginskij Bur'atskij Nacional'nyj Okrug □8	78	51.00 N	114.00 E
Aginskoje, S.S.S.R.	76	55.15 N	94.55 E
Aginskoje, S.S.S.R.	78	51.06 N	114.32 E
Agira	36	37.39 N	14.32 E
Aglasterhausen	52	49.21 N	8.59 E
Ağlasun	120	37.40 N	30.32 E
Agliana	60	43.54 N	11.00 E
Agliano	56	44.47 N	8.15 E
Agly ≃	32	42.47 N	3.02 E
Agna	58	45.10 N	11.58 E
Agnadello	56	45.26 N	9.33 E
Agnes, Mount ∧	152	26.51 S	128.59 E
Agnes Lake @	180	48.13 N	91.21 W
Agnew	152	28.01 S	120.30 E
Agnews Hill ∧2	42	54.51 N	5.56 W
Agnibilékrou	140	7.08 N	3.12 W
Agnije-Afanasjevskij	79	51.57 N	138.45 E
Agnita	38	45.59 N	24.38 E
Agno, Pil.	106	16.07 N	119.48 E
Agno, Schw.	54	46.00 N	8.54 E
Agno ≃, It.	58	45.15 N	11.28 E
Agno ≃, Pil.	106	16.02 N	120.08 E
Agnone	60	41.48 N	14.22 E
Ago	82	34.20 N	136.51 E
Agogna ≃	56	45.04 N	8.54 E
Agogo, Ghana	140	6.47 N	1.04 W
Agogo, Sūd.	130	7.49 N	28.52 E
Agoo	106	16.20 N	120.22 E
Agordat → Akordat	134	15.35 N	37.54 E
Agordo	58	46.17 N	12.02 E
Agostinho Pôrto	277a	22.47 S	43.23 W
Agostitlán	224	19.33 N	100.41 W
Agouma	142	1.32 S	10.11 E
Agouna	140	7.34 N	1.42 E
Agoura	218	34.08 N	118.45 W
Agout ≃	32	43.47 N	1.41 E
Agoza ⊥	136	18.30 N	23.45 E
Āgra	114	27.11 N	78.01 E
Āgra □5	114	27.10 N	78.00 E
Āgra Canal ☰	262a	28.34 N	77.18 E
Agrachanskij Poluostrov ≻1	74	43.42 N	47.36 E
Agraciada	248	33.48 S	58.15 W
Agrado	236	2.15 N	75.46 W
Agrafenovka	73	47.45 N	39.29 E
Agram → Zagreb	36	45.48 N	15.58 E
Agramonte	230p	22.41 N	81.07 W
Agrate Brianza	56	45.34 N	9.21 E
Ágreda	34	41.51 N	1.56 W
Agrestina	240	8.27 S	35.57 W
Agri → Karaköse	74	39.44 N	43.03 E
Ağrı □4	74	39.30 N	43.15 E
Agri ≃	36	40.13 N	16.44 E
Agri Bavnehøj ∧2	41	56.14 N	10.33 E
Agrícola Oriental	276a	19.24 N	99.05 W
Agrigento	36	37.18 N	13.35 E
Agrihan I	98	18.46 N	145.40 E

Agrínion	38	38.37 N	21.24 E
Agrio ≃	242	38.21 S	69.43 W
Agropoli	36	40.21 N	15.00 E
Agro Pontino ◆1	60	41.25 N	12.55 E
Agryz	70	56.33 N	53.00 E
Agsumal, Sebjet @	138	24.21 N	12.52 W
Agtuuganon, Mount ∧	106	7.48 N	126.12 E
Agua, Ilha d' I	277a	22.49 S	43.10 W
Agua, Volcán de ∧1	226	14.28 N	90.45 W
Água Boa	245	17.59 S	42.24 W
Água Branca, Bra.	240	5.53 S	42.38 W
Água Branca, Bra.	240	9.17 S	37.55 W
Água Branca, Bra.	240	7.31 S	37.40 W
Água Branca, Parque da ♠	277b	23.32 S	46.40 W
Agua Brava, Laguna de C	224	22.10 N	105.32 W
Agua Caliente	224	23.20 N	105.20 W
Agua Caliente, Cerro ∧	222	26.27 N	106.12 W
Agua Caliente Creek ≃	272	37.29 N	121.56 W
Agua Caliente de Chínipas	222	27.27 N	108.32 W
Agua Caliente Grande	222	26.31 N	108.22 W
Aguacate	230p	22.59 N	81.49 W
Aguachica	236	8.19 N	73.38 W
Água Clara	245	20.27 S	52.52 W
Água Comprida, Bra.	245	20.04 S	48.08 W
Água Comprida, Bra.	246	21.54 S	45.40 W
Aguada	230m	18.23 N	67.11 W
Aguada Cecilio	244	40.51 S	65.51 W
Aguada de Guerra	244	41.04 S	68.25 W
Aguada de Pasajeros	230p	22.23 N	80.51 W
Aguadas	236	5.37 N	75.27 W
Agua de Afuera, Sierra del ⋀	224	23.53 N	99.45 W
Agua de Dios	236	4.23 N	74.40 W
Aguadilla	230m	18.26 N	67.09 W
Água Doce	242	27.00 S	51.33 W
Agua Dulce, Méx.	224	18.08 N	94.08 W
Aguadulce, Pan.	226	8.15 N	80.33 W
Agua Dulce, Calif., U.S.	218	34.30 N	118.23 W
Agua Escondida	224	19.08 N	103.27 W
Agua Fría ≃, C.R.	226	10.34 N	83.34 W
Agua Fria ≃, Ariz., U.S.	190	33.23 N	112.21 W
Agua Fria Creek ≃	272	37.28 N	121.56 W
Aguaí	246	22.04 S	46.58 W
Aguaje Copal, Cerro ∧	224	16.33 N	95.15 W
Agualeguas	222	26.18 N	99.34 W
Água Limpa	245	18.06 S	48.46 W
Água Limpa, Serra ⋀	246	22.30 S	45.25 W
Agualva-Cacém	256c	38.46 N	9.18 W
Aguán ≃	226	15.57 N	85.44 W
Aguanaval ≃	222	25.28 N	102.53 W
Agua Negra	276c	10.28 N	67.01 W
Aguanish	176	50.13 N	62.05 W
Aguanus ≃	176	50.13 N	62.05 W
Aguapeí ≃	238	15.53 S	58.25 W
Aguapeí, Serra do ⋀	238	16.00 S	59.35 W
Aguapepito	222	24.33 N	107.39 W
Aguapey ≃	242	29.07 S	56.36 W
Aguapira ≃	236	4.11 N	62.58 W
Água Preta, Igarapé ≃	236	1.41 S	63.48 W
Agua Prieta	222	31.18 N	109.34 W
Aguaragüe, Cordillera de ⋀	238	21.30 S	63.40 W
Aguaray	242	22.16 S	63.44 W
Aguaray Guazú ≃, Para.	242	24.47 S	57.19 W
Aguaray Guazú ≃, Para.	242	24.05 S	56.40 W
Aguarico ≃	236	0.59 S	75.11 W
Aguaruto	222	24.47 N	107.29 W
Aguas ≃	34	37.09 N	1.49 W
Águas, Serra das ∧	246	21.55 S	45.25 W
Aguasabon ≃	180	48.46 N	87.07 W
Águas Belas	240	9.07 S	37.07 W
Aguas Buenas	230m	18.15 N	66.06 W
Aguascalientes, Méx.	190	32.18 N	115.10 W
Aguascalientes, Méx.	224	21.53 N	102.18 W
Aguascalientes □3	224	22.00 N	102.30 W
Aguascalientes, Río de ≃	224	21.23 N	102.28 W
Aguas Corrientes	248	34.31 S	56.24 W
Águas da Prata	246	21.56 S	46.43 W
Águas de Contendas	246	21.54 S	45.01 W
Águas de Lindóia	246	22.29 S	46.39 W
Águas Formosas	245	17.05 S	40.57 W
Aguasvivas ≃	34	41.20 N	0.25 W
Agua Tibia ∧	218	33.24 N	116.59 W
Água Verde ≃	238	13.42 S	56.43 W
Água Viva	246	21.41 S	42.33 W
Aguayo	242	31.40 S	65.54 W
Aguaytia ≃	238	8.08 S	74.37 W
Agua Zarca, Méx.	190	31.10 N	110.59 W
Agua Zarca, Méx.	224	23.10 N	104.28 W
Agu Bay C	166	70.18 N	86.30 W
Agudo	242	29.38 S	53.15 W
Agudos	245	22.28 S	49.00 W
Águeda	34	40.34 N	8.27 W
Águeda ≃	34	41.02 N	6.56 W
Aguelhok	140	19.28 N	0.52 E
Aguema	142	12.03 S	21.49 E
Aguenier, Lac @	176	50.43 N	68.13 W
Agugliano	60	43.32 N	13.23 E
Agui	84	34.55 N	136.55 E
Aguijan I	98	14.51 N	145.34 E
Aguila	190	33.56 N	113.11 W
Águila, Cerro del ∧	222	26.58 N	112.28 W
Aguilar, Esp.	34	37.31 N	4.39 W
Aguilar, Colo., U.S.	188	37.24 N	104.46 W
Aguilar, Salar de ⊻	242	25.49 S	68.53 W
Aguilares, Arg.	242	27.26 S	65.37 W
Aguilares, El Sal.	226	13.58 N	89.12 W
Águilas	34	37.24 N	1.35 W
Aguililla	224	18.44 N	102.44 W
Aguirre, Arroyo ≃	278	34.46 S	58.35 W
Aguirre, Bahía C	244	54.57 S	65.50 W
Aguja, Cerro ∧	244	42.11 S	71.51 W
Aguja, Punta ≻	238	5.48 S	81.06 W
Aguja Point ≻	106	12.42 N	123.23 E
Agujas, Cabo de las → Agulhas, Cape ≻	148	34.52 S	20.00 E
Agujereada, Punta ≻	230m	18.31 N	67.08 W
Agujita	186	27.53 N	101.09 W
Agul ≃	78	55.44 N	95.41 E
Agulaa	134	13.42 N	39.35 E
Agulhas	148	34.50 S	20.00 E
Agulhas, Cape ≻	148	34.52 S	20.00 E
Agulhas Basin ✣1	8	45.00 S	25.00 E
Agulhas Negras	246	22.28 S	44.27 W
Agulhas Negras, Pico das ∧	246	22.23 S	44.38 W
Agung, Gunung ∧	105b	8.21 S	115.30 E
Agusan □4	106	8.35 N	125.35 E
Agusan ≃	106	9.00 N	125.31 E
Agustín Codazzi	236	10.02 N	73.14 W
Agustino, Cerro ∧	276d	12.04 S	77.00 W
Agutaya	106	11.09 N	120.56 E
Agutaya Island I	106	11.09 N	120.58 E
Ağva	120	41.09 N	29.50 E
Agvali	74	42.33 N	46.06 E
Ağvaniş	120	40.04 N	38.37 E
Agwarra	140	10.42 N	4.35 E
Ägypten → Egypt □1	130	27.00 N	30.00 E
Aha	164m	26.43 N	128.17 E
Ahaggar (Hoggar) ⋀	138	23.00 N	6.30 E
Ahaggar, Tassili des ⋀	140	20.20 N	4.40 E

≃	River	Fluss	Río	Rivière	Rio
☰	Canal	Kanal	Canal	Canal	Canal
↳	Waterfall, Rapids	Wasserfall, Stromschnellen	Cascada, Rápidos	Chute d'eau, Rapides	Cascata, Rápidos
⩌	Strait	Meeresstrasse	Estrecho	Détroit	Estreito
C	Bay, Gulf	Bucht, Golf	Bahía, Golfo	Baie, Golfe	Baía, Golfo
@	Lake, Lakes	See, Seen	Lago, Lagos	Lac, Lacs	Lago, Lagos
≋	Swamp	Sumpf	Pantano	Marais	Pântano
⍓	Ice Features, Glacier	Eis- und Gletscherformen	Accidentes Glaciales	Formes glaciaires	Acidentes Glaciares
⫧	Other Hydrographic Features	Andere Hydrographische Objekte	Otros Elementos Hidrográficos	Autres données hydrographiques	Outros Elementos Hidrográficos

✣	Submarine Features	Untermeerische Objekte	Accidentes Submarinos	Formes de relief sous-marin	Acidentes Submarinos
□	Political Unit	Politische Einheit	Unidad Politica	Entité politique	Unidade Política
⊎	Cultural Institution	Kulturelle Institution	Institución Cultural	Institution culturelle	Instituição Cultural
⊥	Historical Site	Historische Stätte	Sitio Histórico	Site historique	Sitio Histórico
♠	Recreational Site	Erholungs- und Ferienort	Sitio de Recreo	Centre de loisirs	Sítio de Lazer
⊠	Airport	Flughafen	Aeropuerto	Aéroport	Aeroporto
■	Military Installation	Militäranlage	Instalación Militar	Installation militaire	Instalação Militar
◆	Miscellaneous	Verschiedenes	Misceláneo	Divers	Miscelânea

Symbols in the index entries represent the broad categories identified in the key at the right. Symbols with superior numbers (▲²) identify subcategories (see complete key on page I · 26).

Kartensymbole in dem Registerverzeichnis stellen die rechts in Schlüssel erklärten Kategorien dar. Symbole mit hochgestellten Ziffern (▲²) bezeichnen Unterabteilungen einer Kategorie (vgl. vollständiger Schlüssel auf Seite I · 26).

Los símbolos incluídos en el texto del índice representan las grandes categorias identificadas con la clave a la derecha. Los símbolos con numeros en su parte superior (▲²) identifican las subcategorías (véase la clave completa en la página I · 26).

Les symboles de l'index représentent les catégories indiquées dans la légende à droite. Les symboles suivis d'un indice (▲²) représentent des sous-catégories (voir légende complète à la page I · 26).

Os símbolos incluídos no texto do índice representam as grandes categorias identificadas com a chave à direita. Os símbolos com números em sua parte superior (▲²) identificam as subcategorias (veja-se a chave completa à página I · 26).

Mountain	Berg	Montaña	Montagne	Montanha
Mountains	Berge	Montañas	Montagnes	Montanhas
Pass	Pass	Paso	Col	Passo
Valley, Canyon	Tal, Cañon	Valle, Cañón	Vallée, Canyon	Vale, Canhão
Plain	Ebene	Llano	Plaine	Planície
Cape	Kap	Cabo	Cap	Cabo
Island	Insel	Isla	Île	Ilha
Islands	Inseln	Islas	Îles	Ilhas
Other Topographic Features	Andere Topographische Objekte	Otros Elementos Topográficos	Autres données topographiques	Outros Elementos Topográficos

SPAÑOL — FRANÇAIS — PORTUGUÊS

Nombre / Nom / Nome	Página / Page	Lat.°′	Long.°′ W=Oeste / W=Ouest
Al-Bājūr	132	30.26 N	31.02 E
Al-Bakātūsh	132	31.03 N	30.48 E
Al-Balāmūn	132	30.49 N	31.26 E
Al-Balāshūn	132	30.26 N	31.26 E
Al-Ballaḥ	132	30.46 N	32.19 E
Al-Ballāṣ	130	26.01 N	32.46 E
Al-Balqā' □[8]	122	31.50 N	35.40 E
Al-Bālū'ah ◎	120	35.55 N	36.28 E
Al-Balyanā	130	26.14 N	32.00 E
Alban	32	43.54 N	2.28 E
Albanel, Lac ◎	166	50.55 N	73.12 W
Albani, Colli ⋀[2]	60	41.45 N	12.45 E
Albania □[1]	22		
	38	41.00 N	20.00 E
Albanie → Albania □[1]	38	41.00 N	20.00 E
Albanien → Albania □[1]	38	41.00 N	20.00 E
Albano, Lago ◎	60	41.45 N	12.40 E
Albano, Monte ∧	60	43.50 N	10.58 E
Albano Laziale	60	41.44 N	12.39 E
Albany, Austl.	152	35.02 S	117.53 E
Albany, N.Z.	162	36.43 S	174.42 E
Albany, Calif., U.S.	216	37.53 N	122.18 W
Albany, Ga., U.S.	182	31.35 N	84.10 W
Albany, Ill., U.S.	180	41.47 N	90.13 W
Albany, Ind., U.S.	206	40.18 N	85.14 W
Albany, Ky., U.S.	184	36.42 N	85.08 W
Albany, Minn., U.S.	180	45.38 N	94.34 W
Albany, Mo., U.S.	184	40.15 N	94.20 W
Albany, N.Y., U.S.	197	42.39 N	73.45 E
Albany, N.Y., U.S.	200	42.39 N	73.45 W
Albany, Ohio, U.S.	178	39.14 N	82.12 W
Albany, Oreg., U.S.	192	44.38 N	123.06 W
Albany, Tex., U.S.	186	32.44 N	99.18 W
Albany, Wis., U.S.	180	42.43 N	89.26 W
Albany □[6]	200	42.39 N	73.45 W
Albany ≃	166	52.17 N	81.31 W
Albany County Airport ⊠	200	42.45 N	73.48 W
Albany Park ◆[8]	268	41.58 N	87.43 W
Al-Barājīl	263c	30.04 N	31.09 E
Al-Barāmūn	132	31.07 N	31.26 E
Albardón	242	31.26 S	68.32 W
Albaredo d'Adige	58	45.19 N	11.16 E
Al-Bāriḥah	122	32.34 N	35.50 E
Al-Barkāt	136	24.54 N	10.11 E
Al-Barnūjī	132	30.56 N	30.23 E
Albaron	56	43.37 N	4.28 E
Albaron ∧	56	45.20 N	7.07 E
Albarracín	34	40.25 N	1.26 W
Albarradas	224	16.50 N	96.15 W
Al-Barrah	118	24.55 N	45.52 E
Albarraque	256c	38.46 N	9.21 W
Al-Barshā	132	27.43 N	30.54 E
Al-Barun	130	11.44 N	33.30 E
Al-Basātīn ◆[8]	263c	29.59 N	31.16 E
Al-Baslaqūn	132	31.06 N	30.08 E
Al-Basqalūn	132	28.42 N	30.44 E
Al-Baṣrah (Basra)	118	30.30 N	47.47 E
Al-Baṣrah □[4]	118	30.30 N	47.47 E
Al-Batānūn	132	30.37 N	30.59 E
Al-Baṭḥā'	118	31.06 N	45.53 E
Al-Bāṭinah ◆[1]	118	23.45 N	57.20 E
Albatross Bay ⊂	154	12.45 S	141.43 E
Albatross Cordillera ⟡[3]	9	62.00 S	155.00 W
Albatross Point ≻	162	38.06 S	174.41 E
Al-Batrūn	120	34.15 N	35.39 E
Al-Baṭrūnah	122	33.39 N	36.02 E
Al-Bauga	130	18.16 N	33.55 E
Al-Bawīṭī	130	28.21 N	28.52 E
Albay □[4]	106	13.00 N	123.40 E
Al-Bayahū	132	28.16 N	30.44 E
Al-Bayḍā (Beida), Lībīya	136	28.22 N	18.55 E
Al-Bayḍā', Miṣr	132	31.10 N	30.05 E
Al-Bayḍā' □[4]	136	32.30 N	21.30 E
Albay Gulf ⊂	106	13.10 N	124.00 E
Albazino	79	53.23 N	124.05 E
Albbruck	54	47.35 N	8.07 E
Albegna ≃	60	42.30 N	11.11 E
Albemarle	182	35.21 N	80.12 W
Albemarle and Chesapeake Canal ≊	198	36.43 N	76.15 W
Albemarle Sound ⊔	182	36.03 N	76.12 W
Albenga	56	44.03 N	8.13 E
Albens	56	45.47 N	5.57 E
Alberche ≃	34	39.58 N	4.46 W
Alberdi	242	26.10 S	58.09 W
Alberene	182	37.53 N	78.37 W
Alberga, Austl.	152	27.12 S	135.28 E
Ålberga, Sve.	40	58.44 N	16.34 E
Alberga Creek ≃	152	27.06 S	135.33 E
Albergaria-a-Velha	34	40.42 N	8.29 W
Alberhill	218	33.44 N	117.23 W
Alberique	34	39.07 N	0.31 W
Alberni Inlet ⊂	214	49.07 N	124.50 W
Alberobello	36	40.47 N	17.15 E
Alberona	60	41.26 N	15.07 E
Albers	209	38.33 N	89.37 W
Alberschwende	54	47.27 N	9.49 E
Albersloh	48	51.52 N	7.43 E
Albert	46	50.00 N	2.39 E
Albert ≃	161a	27.42 S	153.15 E
Albert, Lake ◎, Afr.	144	1.40 N	31.00 E
Albert, Lake ◎, Austl.	156	35.38 S	139.17 E
Albert, Parc National ♠	144	1.00 S	29.15 E
Alberta, Ala., U.S.	184	32.14 N	87.25 W
Alberta, Zaïre	142	2.12 N	22.21 E
Alberta □[4]	166	54.00 N	113.00 W
Alberta, Mount ∧	172	52.18 N	117.28 W
Albert Canyon	172	51.08 N	117.52 W
Albert City	188	42.47 N	94.57 W
Albert Edward, Mount ∧	154	8.23 S	147.24 E
Albert Edward Bay ⊂	166	69.32 N	103.00 W
Albert Falls	148	29.27 S	30.25 E
Albertfalva ◆[8]	254c	47.27 N	19.02 E
Alberti	242	35.02 S	60.16 W
Al'bertin	66	53.05 N	25.23 E
Albertina	246	22.12 S	46.37 W
Albertinia	148	34.13 S	21.36 E
Albertirsa	30	47.15 N	19.38 E
Albert Kanaal ≊	52	50.39 N	5.37 E
Albert Lea	180	43.39 N	93.22 W
Albert Markham, Mount ∧	9	81.23 S	158.12 E
Albert Nile ≃	144	3.36 N	32.02 E
Alberto, Lago → Albert, Lake ◎	144	1.40 N	31.00 E
Alberto Eduardo → Albert Edward, Mount ∧	154	8.23 S	147.24 E
Alberton, P.E.I., Can.	176	46.49 N	64.04 W
Alberton, S. Afr.	263d	26.16 S	28.08 E
Alberton, Mont., U.S.	192	47.00 N	114.29 W
Albert Park ♠	264b	37.51 S	144.57 E
Albertshof	254a	52.42 N	13.40 E
Albertson	266	40.46 N	73.39 W
Albertson Brook ≃	275	39.41 N	74.43 W
Albertson Brook, Blue Anchor Branch ≃	275	39.42 N	74.49 W
Albertson Brook, Pump Branch ≃	275	39.42 N	74.49 W
Albert Town	231q	18.17 N	77.33 W
Albertville, Fr.	56	45.41 N	6.23 E
Albertville, Ala., U.S.	184	34.16 N	86.12 W
Albertville → Kalemi, Zaïre	144	5.56 S	29.12 E
Albertville ◆[8]	263d	26.10 S	27.59 E
Albertynsville	263d	26.17 S	27.52 E
Albestroff	52	48.56 N	6.51 E
Albettone	58	45.21 N	11.35 E
Albi	32	43.56 N	2.09 E
Albia, Iowa, U.S.	180	41.02 N	92.48 W
Albia, N.Y., U.S.	200	42.43 N	73.39 W
Albiate	256b	45.39 N	9.15 E
Al-Bid'	118	28.25 N	35.04 E
Al Bidia	136	10.33 N	20.13 E
Albignasego	58	45.21 N	11.52 E
Albin	188	41.25 N	104.06 W
Albina	240	5.30 N	54.03 W
Albina, Ponta ≻	142	15.51 S	11.44 E
Albinea	58	44.37 N	10.36 E
Albino	56	45.46 N	9.47 E
Albion, Austl.	264b	37.47 S	144.49 E
Albion, B.C., Can.	214	49.11 N	122.33 W
Albion, Calif., U.S.	194	39.13 N	123.46 W
Albion, Idaho, U.S.	192	42.25 N	113.35 W
Albion, Ill., U.S.	184	38.23 N	88.04 W
Albion, Ind., U.S.	206	41.24 N	85.25 W
Albion, Iowa, U.S.	180	42.07 N	92.59 W
Albion, Mich., U.S.	206	42.15 N	84.45 W
Albion, Nebr., U.S.	188	41.42 N	98.00 W
Albion, N.J., U.S.	275	39.47 N	74.56 W
Albion, N.Y., U.S.	200	43.15 N	78.12 W
Albion, Pa., U.S.	204	41.53 N	80.22 W
Albion, R.I., U.S.	197	41.57 N	71.27 W
Albion, Wash., U.S.	192	46.48 N	117.15 W
Albion, Wis., U.S.	206	42.53 N	89.04 W
Albion Airstrip ⊠	275	39.46 N	74.58 W
Albion Park	160	34.34 S	150.47 E
Al-Biqā' □[4]	120	34.00 N	36.00 E
Al-Bi'r	118	28.50 N	36.19 E
Al-Bīrah	122	31.54 N	35.13 E
Al-Bi'r al-Jadīd	118	26.01 N	38.29 E
Al-Birīgāt	132	30.30 N	30.49 E
Al-Birk	134	18.13 N	41.33 E
Al-Birkah ╤[4]	134	22.12 N	40.43 E
Albisola Marina	56	44.19 N	8.30 E
Albisola Superiore	56	44.20 N	8.31 E
Albizzate	56	45.43 N	8.44 E
Alblasserdam	48	51.52 N	4.40 E
Albo, Monte ∧	36	40.29 N	9.33 E
Albocácer	34	40.21 N	0.02 E
Albogas	256c	38.51 N	9.15 W
Alborán, Isla de I	34	35.58 N	3.02 W
Ålborg	26	57.03 N	9.56 E
Ålborg Bugt ⊂	26	56.45 N	10.30 E
Alborz, Reshteh-ye Kūhhā-ye ⋀	118	36.00 N	53.00 E
Albreda	172	52.38 N	119.09 W
Albrighton	44	52.38 N	2.16 W
Al-Bu'ayrāt	136	31.24 N	15.44 E
Albuch ⋀	52	48.15 N	9.50 E
Albuera	106	10.55 N	124.42 E
Albufeira	34	37.05 N	8.15 W
Ālbū Gharz, Sabkhat ◎	120	34.45 N	41.15 E
Al-Buḥayrah □[4]	132	30.59 N	30.12 E
Albula ≃	54	46.42 N	9.27 E
Al-Bunbah	136	32.24 N	23.08 E
Albuñol	34	36.47 N	3.12 W
Albuquerque	190	35.05 N	106.40 W
Albuquerque, Cayos de II	226	12.10 N	81.50 W
Albuquerque, Serra do ⋀	246	22.20 S	42.55 W
Al-Buraymī	118	24.15 N	55.45 E
Alburg	178	44.59 N	73.18 W
Al-Burj	132	31.35 N	30.59 E
Al-Burjāyah	132	28.09 N	30.44 E
Alburquerque	34	39.13 N	7.00 W
Alburtis	198	40.31 N	75.36 W
Al-Burumbul	132	29.19 N	31.14 E
Albury, Austl.	156	36.05 S	146.55 E
Albury, N.Z.	162	44.14 S	170.52 E
Albury, Eng., U.K.	250	51.13 N	0.30 W
Albury Park ♠	250	51.13 N	0.29 W
Al-Buṣaylī	132	31.20 N	30.24 E
Al-Busayṭah ≚	118	29.30 N	38.45 E
Al-Buṭanah ◆[1]	130	15.00 N	34.40 E
Al-Buṭaynah	122	32.57 N	36.42 E
Al-Buwayḍah	122	32.28 N	36.04 E
Albuzzano	56	45.11 N	9.16 E
Alby, Fr.	56	45.49 N	6.01 E
Alby, Sve.	26	62.30 N	15.28 E
Alca	238	15.08 S	72.46 W
Alcabideche	256c	38.44 N	9.24 W
Alcácer do Sal	34	38.22 N	8.30 W
Alcains	34	39.55 N	7.27 W
Alcala	106	17.54 N	121.39 E
Alcalá de Guadaira	34	37.20 N	5.50 W
Alcalá de Henares	34	40.29 N	3.22 W
Alcalá la Real	34	37.28 N	3.56 W
Alcalde	190	36.05 N	106.03 W
Alcamo	36	37.59 N	12.58 E
Alčan ≃	79	46.38 N	134.22 E
Alcanadre ≃	34	41.37 N	0.12 W
Alcanar	34	40.33 N	0.29 E
Alcañices	34	41.42 N	6.21 W
Alcañiz	34	41.03 N	0.08 W
Alcântara, Bra.	240	2.24 S	44.24 W
Alcántara, Esp.	34	39.43 N	6.53 W
Alcantara, Pil.	106	12.16 N	122.03 E
Alcântara ◆[8]	256c	38.42 N	9.10 W
Alcántara, Embalse de ◎[1]	34	39.45 N	6.25 W
Alcantarilla	34	37.58 N	1.13 W
Alcantilado	245	16.23 S	53.31 W
Alcaraz	34	38.40 N	2.29 W
Alcarrache ≃	34	38.16 N	7.24 W
Alcatraz Island I	272	37.49 N	122.26 W
Alcaudete	34	37.36 N	4.05 W
Alcázar de San Juan	34	39.24 N	3.12 W
Alcazarquivir → Ksar-el-Kebir	138	35.01 N	5.54 W
Alcester, Eng., U.K.	44	52.13 N	1.52 W
Alcester, S. Dak., U.S.	188	43.01 N	96.38 W
Alcester Island I	154	9.35 S	152.25 E
Alcihuatl	224	19.55 N	104.34 W
Alcira (Gigena), Arg.	242	32.45 S	64.20 W
Alcira, Esp.	34	39.09 N	0.26 W
Alcoa	182	35.48 N	83.59 W
Alcoa Center	269b	40.33 N	79.39 W
Alcoa Lake ◎[1]	212	30.34 N	97.03 W
Alcobaça, Bra.	245	17.30 S	39.13 W
Alcobaça, Port.	34	39.33 N	8.59 W
Alcobendas	34	40.32 N	3.38 W
Alcochete	256c	38.45 N	8.58 W
Alcockspruit	148	27.55 S	30.01 E
Alcoitão	256c	38.44 N	9.24 W
Alcolea del Piuar	34	41.02 N	2.28 W
Alcomunga	224	18.25 N	97.02 W
Alconbury Brook ≃	44	52.19 N	0.12 W
Alconchel	34	38.31 N	7.04 W
Alcony	208	40.01 N	84.04 W
Alcorcón	256a	40.21 N	3.50 W
Alcorn College	184	31.52 N	91.09 W
Alcorta	242	33.32 S	61.07 W
Alcoutim	34	37.28 N	7.28 W
Alcova Reservoir ◎[1]	190	42.32 N	106.45 W
Alcove	200	42.28 N	73.55 W
Alcove Reservoir ◎[1]	200	42.29 N	73.57 W
Alcovy ≃	182	33.26 N	83.50 W
Alcoy	34	38.42 N	0.28 W
Alcoy, Nevado ∧	238	11.17 S	76.30 W
Alcubierre	34	41.48 N	0.27 W
Alcudia	34	39.52 N	3.07 E
Alcudia, Bahía de ⊂	34	39.48 N	3.13 E
Alcyon Lake ◎	275	39.44 N	75.08 W
Aldabra Islands I[1]	128	9.25 S	46.22 E
Aldama, Méx.	222	28.51 N	105.54 W
Aldama, Méx.	224	22.55 N	98.04 W
Aldama, Arroyo ≃	276b	23.05 N	82.15 W
Aldan, S.S.S.R.	64	58.37 N	125.24 E
Aldan, Pa., U.S.	275	39.55 N	75.17 W
Aldan ≃	64	63.28 N	129.35 E
Aldanskoje Nagorje ⋀[1]	64	57.00 N	127.00 E
Aldbourne	44	51.31 N	1.37 W
Aldbrough	42	53.50 N	0.07 W
Aldbury	44	51.48 N	0.36 W
Alde ≃	44	52.03 N	1.28 E
Aldea Apeleg	244	44.41 S	70.51 W
Aldeburgh	44	52.09 N	1.35 E
Aldecoa ◆[8]	276b	23.07 N	82.24 W
Aldeia	246	23.30 S	46.51 W
Aldeia de Carapicuiba	277b	23.35 S	46.48 W
Aldeia de Paio Pires	256c	38.38 N	9.05 W
Aldeia Nova de Santo Bento	34	37.55 N	7.25 W
Aldeia Velha	246	22.47 S	42.55 W
Aldeinha	277b	23.45 S	46.53 W
Alden, Ill., U.S.	206	42.27 N	88.31 W
Alden, Iowa, U.S.	180	42.31 N	93.23 W
Alden, Mich., U.S.	180	44.53 N	85.17 W
Alden, Minn., U.S.	180	43.40 N	93.34 W
Alden, N.Y., U.S.	200	42.54 N	78.30 W
Alden, Pa., U.S.	200	41.11 N	75.59 W
Alden Center	202	42.55 N	78.32 W
Aldenham	250	51.40 N	0.21 W
Aldenhoven	52	50.53 N	6.16 E
Aldenrade ◆[8]	253	51.31 N	6.44 E
Alder Creek ≃	192	45.50 N	119.56 W
Aldergrove	214	49.04 N	122.28 W
Alder Lake ◎[1]	214	46.45 N	122.15 W
Alderley	156	22.39 S	139.44 E
Alderley Edge	42	53.18 N	2.15 W
Aldermaston	44	51.23 N	1.09 W
Alderney I	28	49.43 N	2.12 W
Alder Peak ∧	216	35.53 N	121.22 W
Aldershot	44	51.15 N	0.47 W
Alderson	182	37.43 N	80.39 W
Alderton	214	47.10 N	122.14 W
Alderwood Manor	214	47.49 N	122.17 W
Aldine	212	29.54 N	95.24 W
Aldinga Bay ⊂	158b	35.20 S	138.25 E
Aldingen	54	48.05 N	8.41 E
Aldino	58	46.23 N	11.20 E
Aldo Bonzi	278	34.42 S	58.31 W
Aldridge	44	52.36 N	1.55 W
Aldwell, Lake ◎[1]	214	48.05 N	123.34 W
Alechovščina	66	60.25 N	33.52 E
Aled ≃	42	53.14 N	3.34 W
Aledo, Ill., U.S.	180	41.12 N	90.45 W
Aledo, Tex., U.S.	212	32.42 N	97.36 W
Aleg	140	17.03 N	13.55 W
Alegranza, Isla de I	138	29.23 N	13.30 W
Alegre	245	20.46 S	41.32 W
Alegre ≃, Bra.	238	15.01 S	59.57 W
Alegre ≃, Bra.	245	18.50 S	50.26 W
Alegre, Riacho ≃	242	22.06 S	58.00 W
Alegrete	242	29.46 S	55.46 W
Alegros Mountain ∧	190	34.09 N	108.11 W
Alegua, Mount ∧	134	14.12 N	39.40 E
Alej ≃	76	52.52 N	83.36 E
Alejandría → Al-Iskandarīyah	132	31.12 N	29.54 E
Alejandro, Isla → Alexander Island I	9	71.00 S	70.00 W
Alejandro Roca	242	33.21 S	63.43 W
Alejandro Selkirk, Isla (Isla Más Afuera) I	234	33.45 S	80.46 W
Alejo Ledesma	242	33.37 S	62.37 W
Alejsk	76	52.28 N	82.45 E
Aleknagik	170	59.17 N	158.38 W
Aleknagik, Lake ◎	170	59.20 N	158.45 W
Aleksandrija	68	48.40 N	33.07 E
Aleksandrijskaja	74	43.54 N	47.08 E
Aleksandrinka	73	47.47 N	37.41 E
Aleksandro-Kalinovo	73	48.25 N	37.40 E
Aleksandro-Nevskaja	74	43.55 N	46.35 E
Aleksandro Nevskaja Lavra ʋ[1]	255a	59.55 N	30.24 E
Aleksandro-Nevskij	70	53.28 N	40.13 E
Aleksandropol'	73	49.42 N	38.50 E
Aleksandrov	72	56.24 N	38.43 E
Aleksandrov Gaj	70	50.09 N	48.34 E
Aleksandrovka, S.S.S.R.	68	48.57 N	32.14 E
Aleksandrovka, S.S.S.R.	68	46.32 N	35.29 E
Aleksandrovka, S.S.S.R.	68	47.42 N	31.16 E
Aleksandrovka, S.S.S.R.	68	46.47 N	39.01 E
Aleksandrovka, S.S.S.R.	68	48.43 N	36.55 E
Aleksandrovka, S.S.S.R.	70	52.36 N	50.37 E
Aleksandrovka, S.S.S.R.	70	50.47 N	52.59 E
Aleksandrovka, S.S.S.R.	73	48.05 N	37.27 E
Aleksandrovka, S.S.S.R.	73	47.55 N	37.35 E
Aleksandrovka, S.S.S.R.	73	47.26 N	39.13 E
Aleksandrovka, S.S.S.R.	75	43.27 N	77.20 E
Aleksandrovka, S.S.S.R.	76	56.32 N	90.47 E
Aleksandrovka, S.S.S.R.	76	52.43 N	54.17 E
Aleksandrovka, S.S.S.R.	76	53.07 N	69.50 E
Aleksandrovsk	73	48.35 N	39.12 E
Aleksandrovskaja, S.S.S.R.	255a	59.44 N	30.21 E
Aleksandrovskaja, S.S.S.R.	255a	50.03 N	29.59 E
Aleksandrovskij	68	51.03 N	36.44 E
Aleksandrovskij Šl'uz	76	59.26 N	89.20 E
Aleksandrovskij Zavod	78	50.55 N	117.57 E
Aleksandrovskoje, S.S.S.R.	74	44.42 N	43.00 E
Aleksandrovskoje, S.S.S.R.	76	56.44 N	85.23 E
Aleksandrovskoje, S.S.S.R.	76	60.26 N	77.50 E
Aleksandrovsk-Sachalinskij	79	50.54 N	142.10 E
Aleksandrów Kujawski	30	52.52 N	18.42 E
Aleksandrów Łódzki	30	51.49 N	19.19 E
Aleksaškino	70	50.57 N	47.42 E
Aleksejevka, S.S.S.R.	68	50.37 N	38.42 E
Aleksejevka, S.S.S.R.	68	47.14 N	36.32 E
Aleksejevka, S.S.S.R.	70	53.15 N	50.30 E
Aleksejevka, S.S.S.R.	70	53.02 N	42.46 E
Aleksejevka, S.S.S.R.	70	52.18 N	48.01 E
Aleksejevka, S.S.S.R.	70	51.49 N	43.56 E
Aleksejevka, S.S.S.R.	70	52.35 N	51.17 E
Aleksejevka, S.S.S.R.	70	50.58 N	52.25 E
Aleksejevka, S.S.S.R.	72	54.41 N	36.34 E
Aleksejevka, S.S.S.R.	73	49.25 N	38.46 E
Aleksejevka, S.S.S.R.	73	49.01 N	39.11 E
Aleksejevka, S.S.S.R.	73	47.41 N	39.54 E
Aleksejevka, S.S.S.R.	73	47.38 N	38.49 E
Aleksejevka, S.S.S.R.	76	52.30 N	79.33 E
Aleksejevka, S.S.S.R.	76	53.31 N	69.30 E
Aleksejevka, S.S.S.R.	76	54.31 N	81.08 E
Aleksejevka, S.S.S.R.	76	48.25 N	85.40 E
Aleksejevka, S.S.S.R.	76	47.16 N	81.34 E
Aleksejevka, S.S.S.R.	76	55.22 N	72.03 E
Aleksejevka, S.S.S.R.	76	51.59 N	70.59 E
Aleksejevo-Družkovka	73	48.34 N	37.36 E
Aleksejevo-Lozovskoje	68	49.24 N	40.39 E
Aleksejevo-Orlovka ◆[8]	73	48.04 N	38.25 E
Aleksejevo-Tuzlovka	73	47.50 N	39.24 E
Aleksejevsk	78	57.50 N	108.23 E
Aleksejevskaja	70	50.17 N	42.11 E
Aleksejevskoje	70	55.18 N	50.06 E
Aleksin	72	54.31 N	37.05 E
Aleksinac	38	43.32 N	21.43 E
Alella	256d	41.30 N	2.18 E
Alemana, República Democrática → German Democratic Republic □[1]	30	52.00 N	12.30 E
Alemania, Arg.	242	25.36 S	65.38 W
Alemania, Chile	242	25.10 S	69.55 W
Alemania, República Federal de → Germany, Federal Republic Of □[1]	30	51.00 N	9.00 E
Alem Dağı ∧	257b	41.05 N	29.12 E
Alemdar	257b	41.03 N	29.14 E
Além Paraíba	246	21.52 S	42.41 W
Alençon	46	48.26 N	0.05 E
Alenquer	240	1.56 S	54.46 W
Alentejo □[9]	34	38.00 N	8.00 W
Alenuihaha Channel ⊔	219a	20.26 N	156.00 W
Alenz	120	37.51 N	41.36 E
Aléoutiennes, Îles → Aleutian Islands II	170	52.00 N	176.00 W
Alep → Ḥalab	120	36.12 N	37.10 E
Aleppo → Ḥalab	120	36.12 N	37.10 E
Alerces, Parque Nacional ♠	244	42.50 S	71.52 W
Aléria	36	42.05 N	9.30 E
Alert Bay	172	50.35 N	126.55 W
Alès	56	44.08 N	4.05 E
Aleșd	38	47.04 N	22.24 E
Alešino, S.S.S.R.	72	55.04 N	36.05 E
Alešino, S.S.S.R.	72	56.09 N	37.45 E
Aleški	70	51.38 N	41.46 E
Aleškino	78	58.35 N	100.32 E
Aleškovo	72	54.53 N	36.23 E
Alessandria	56	44.54 N	8.37 E
Alessandria □[4]	56	44.49 N	8.42 E
Alessano	36	39.53 N	18.20 E
Ålesund	26	62.28 N	6.09 E
Aleta	134	11.53 N	36.56 E
Aletai	76	47.52 N	88.07 E
Aletschhorn ∧	54	46.28 N	8.00 E
Alëuten → Aleutian Islands II	170	52.00 N	176.00 W
Aleutianas, Islas → Aleutian Islands II	170	52.00 N	176.00 W
Aleutian Basin ⟡[1]	16	57.00 N	179.00 E
Aleutian Islands II	170	52.00 N	176.00 W
Aleutian Range ⋀	170	59.00 N	155.00 W
Aleutian Trench ⟡[1]	16	52.00 N	170.00 W
Alevina, Mys ≻	64	58.50 N	151.20 E
Ale Water ≃	42	55.31 N	2.35 W
Alex	186	34.55 N	97.47 W
Alexander, Man., Can.	174	49.50 N	100.17 W
Alexander, Ill., U.S.	209	39.43 N	90.02 W
Alexander, N. Dak., U.S.	188	47.51 N	103.39 W
Alexander, N.Y., U.S.	200	42.54 N	78.16 W
Alexander ≃	122	32.24 N	34.52 E
Alexander, Cape ≻	165e	6.35 S	156.30 E
Alexander, Mount ∧	152	22.39 S	115.32 E
Alexander Archipelago II	170	56.30 N	134.00 W
Alexander Bay	146	28.40 S	16.30 E
Alexander City	184	32.56 N	85.57 W
Alexander Ditch ≊	269a	41.20 N	82.05 W
Alexander Hamilton Airport ⊠	231n	17.42 N	64.48 W
Alexander Indian Reserve ◆[4]	172	53.09 N	113.58 W
Alexander Island I	9	71.00 S	70.00 W
Alexandra, Austl.	159	37.12 S	145.43 E
Alexandra, N.Z.	162	45.15 S	169.24 E
Alexandra, S. Afr.	263d	26.06 S	28.05 E
Alexandra ≃	156	18.14 S	139.54 E
Alexandra Canal ≊	264a	33.56 S	151.10 E
Alexandra Falls ⌊	166	60.29 N	116.18 W
Alexandra Park ♠	252	53.27 N	2.15 W
Alexandra Park Race Course ♠	250	51.36 N	0.08 W
Alexandretta → İskenderun	120	36.37 N	36.07 E
Alexandretta, Gulf of → İskenderun Körfezi ⊂	120	36.30 N	35.40 E
Alexandria, Austl.	156	19.05 S	136.40 E
Alexandria, Bra.	240	6.25 S	38.01 W
Alexandria, B.C., Can.	172	52.38 N	122.27 W
Alexandria, Ont., Can.	196	45.19 N	74.38 W
Alexandria → Al-Iskandarīyah, Miṣr	132	31.12 N	29.54 E
Alexandria, Rom.	38	43.58 N	25.20 E
Alexandria, S. Afr.	148	33.39 S	26.24 E
Alexandria, Scot., U.K.	42	55.59 N	4.36 W
Alexandria, Ind., U.S.	206	40.16 N	85.41 W
Alexandria, Ky., U.S.	208	38.58 N	84.23 W
Alexandria, La., U.S.	184	31.18 N	92.27 W
Alexandria, Minn., U.S.	188	45.53 N	95.22 W
Alexandria, Mo., U.S.	184	40.27 N	91.28 W
Alexandria, Nebr., U.S.	188	40.15 N	97.23 W
Alexandria, Ohio, U.S.	204	40.05 N	82.37 W
Alexandria, Pa., U.S.	204	40.34 N	78.06 W
Alexandria, S. Dak., U.S.	188	43.39 N	97.47 W
Alexandria, Tenn., U.S.	184	36.05 N	86.02 W
Alexandria, Va., U.S.	198	38.48 N	77.03 W
Alexandria Airport ⊠	132	31.11 N	29.57 E
Alexandria Bay	202	44.20 N	75.55 W
Alexandrie → Al-Iskandarīyah	132	31.12 N	29.54 E
Alexandrina, Lake ◎	158b	35.26 S	139.10 E
Alexandroúpolis	38	40.50 N	25.52 E
Alexis	180	41.04 N	90.33 W
Alexis Creek	172	52.05 N	123.17 W
Alexis Indian Reserve ◆[4]	172	53.46 N	114.30 W
Alf	52	50.03 N	7.07 E
Ālfādānga	116	23.18 N	89.42 E
Al-Fahmīyīn	132	29.36 N	31.17 E
Al-Fallūjah	118	33.20 N	43.46 E
Alfambra	34	40.33 N	1.02 W
Alfambra ≃	34	40.21 N	1.07 W
Al-Fant	132	28.46 N	30.53 E
Alfarata	198	40.39 N	77.27 W
Al-Farḍah	134	14.51 N	48.27 E
Alfaro, Ec.	236	2.12 S	79.50 W
Alfaro, Esp.	34	42.11 N	1.45 W
Alfarrás	34	41.49 N	0.35 E
Al-Fāshir	130	13.38 N	25.21 E
Al-Fashn	132	28.49 N	30.54 E
Alfatar	38	43.57 N	27.17 E
Alfavaca, Ilha da I	277a	23.02 S	43.18 W
Al-Fāw	118	29.58 N	48.29 E
Al-Fayyūm	132	29.19 N	30.50 E
Al-Fayyūm □[4]	132	29.19 N	30.48 E
Alfbach ≃	52	50.03 N	7.08 E
Alfedena	60	41.44 N	14.02 E
Alfeld	48	51.59 N	9.50 E
Alfenas	246	21.25 S	45.57 W
Alfianello	58	45.16 N	10.10 E
Al-Fifi	130	10.03 N	25.01 E
Alfiós ≃	38	37.40 N	21.33 E
Al-Firdān	132	30.41 N	32.20 E
Alfonsine	60	44.30 N	12.03 E
Alford, Austl.	158b	33.49 S	137.49 E
Alford, Eng., U.K.	42	53.16 N	0.10 E
Alfortville	251	48.49 N	2.25 E
Ålfotbreen I	26	61.45 N	5.40 E
Alfred, Ont., Can.	196	45.34 N	74.53 W
Alfred, Maine, U.S.	178	43.29 N	70.43 W
Alfred, N.Y., U.S.	200	42.15 N	77.47 W
Alfred National Park ♠	156	37.35 S	149.20 E
Alfredo Chaves	245	20.38 S	40.45 W
Alfredo M. Terrazas	224	21.28 N	98.51 W
Alfreton	44	53.06 N	1.23 W
Alfriston	44	50.48 N	0.10 E
Alfta	26	61.21 N	16.05 E
Al-Fujayrah	118	25.06 N	56.21 E
Al-Fuqahā'	136	27.50 N	16.22 E
Al-Furāt → Euphrates ≃	118	31.00 N	47.25 E
Al-Furzul	122	33.52 N	35.56 E
Alga	76	49.46 N	57.20 E
Algabas, S.S.S.R.	70	50.39 N	52.07 E
Algabas, S.S.S.R.	76	48.21 N	81.39 E
Algabas, S.S.S.R.	76	44.41 N	78.06 E
Algači	78	50.43 N	117.47 E
Älgarås	40	58.48 N	14.14 E
Ålgård	26	58.46 N	5.51 E
Al-Garef	134	12.03 N	34.19 E
Algarrobal	242	28.08 S	70.39 W
Algarrobo, Arg.	242	38.53 S	63.08 W
Algarrobo, Chile	242	27.03 S	70.35 W
Algarrobo, Chile	242	33.22 S	71.40 W
Algarrobo del Águila	242	36.26 S	67.09 W
Algarrobo Verde	242	31.44 S	68.18 W
Algarve □[9]	34	37.10 N	8.15 W
Algasovo	66	53.41 N	41.40 E
Al-Gebir	130	13.43 N	29.49 E
Algeciras, Col.	236	2.35 N	75.18 W
Algeciras, Esp.	34	36.08 N	5.30 W
Algemesí	34	39.11 N	0.26 W
Algena	134	16.20 N	38.34 E
Alger (Algiers), Alg.	138	36.47 N	3.03 E
Alger, Ohio, U.S.	206	40.42 N	83.51 W
Alger, Baie d' ⊂	34	36.50 N	3.15 E
Algeria □[1]	124		
	138	28.00 N	3.00 E
Algérie → Algeria □[1]	138	28.00 N	3.00 E
Algerien → Algeria □[1]	138	28.00 N	3.00 E
Algermissen	48	52.15 N	9.58 E
Algés	256c	38.42 N	9.13 W
Al-Ghāb ◎	120	35.30 N	36.18 E
Al-Gharaq as-Sulṭānī	132	29.08 N	30.42 E
Al-Gharbīyah □[4]	132	31.08 N	31.00 E
Al-Ghārīyah	122	32.23 N	36.39 E
Al-Ghāṭ	118	26.00 N	45.03 E
Al-Ghawr ∨	122	31.50 N	35.30 E
Al-Ghayatah	132	30.57 N	30.06 E
Al-Ghayḍah	108	16.12 N	52.15 E
Al-Ghazālah	118	26.48 N	41.19 E
Al-Ghazālī	132	30.49 N	31.49 E
Al-Ghāzīyah	122	33.31 N	35.22 E
Alghero	36	40.34 N	8.19 E
Al-Ghizlānīyah	122	33.23 N	36.27 E
Al-Ghubbah I	118	24.18 N	53.18 E
Al-Ghulayfiqah	134	14.27 N	43.02 E
Al-Ghurayfah	118	24.00 N	56.29 E
Al-Ghurdaqah	130	27.14 N	33.50 E
Algier → Alger	138	36.47 N	3.03 E
Algiers → Alger	138	36.47 N	3.03 E
Alginet	34	39.16 N	0.28 W
Algoa	212	29.24 N	95.11 W
Algoabaai ⊂	148	33.50 S	25.65 E
Algodão, Ilha do I	246	23.13 S	44.36 W
Algodón ≃	236	2.23 S	71.56 W
Algodones	190	35.23 N	106.29 W
Algodor ≃	34	39.55 N	3.53 W
Algoma	180	44.36 N	87.27 W
Algoma Mills	180	46.10 N	82.50 W
Algona, Iowa, U.S.	180	43.04 N	94.14 W
Algona, Wash., U.S.	214	47.17 N	122.15 W
Algonac	204	42.37 N	82.32 W
Algonquin	206	42.10 N	88.18 W
Algonquin Lake ◎	206	42.40 N	85.20 W
Algonquin Provincial Park ♠	180	45.27 N	78.26 W
Algood	184	36.12 N	85.27 W
Algorta, Esp.	34	43.22 N	3.01 W
Algorta, Ur.	242	32.25 S	57.23 W
Algoy ≃	76	42.50 N	88.40 E
Alguierão-Mem Martins	256c	38.48 N	9.20 W
Al-Ḥaddādī	132	31.20 N	30.47 E
Al-Ḥaddayn	132	30.44 N	30.38 E
Al-Ḥadīthah, Ar. Sa.	118	31.30 N	37.09 E
Al-Ḥadīthah, 'Irāq	118	34.07 N	42.23 E
Al-Ḥaḍr	118	35.35 N	42.44 E
Al-Ḥaffah	120	35.35 N	36.02 E
Al-Ḥafīr al-Fawqānī	122	33.42 N	36.28 E
Al-Ḥajālīj	130	14.36 N	31.54 E
Al-Ḥajarah ◆[1]	118	30.00 N	44.00 E
Al-Ḥajar al-Gharbī ⋀	118	24.22 N	56.17 E
Al-Ḥajar ash-Sharqī ⋀	118	23.00 N	59.00 E
Al-Ḥājir	132	30.41 N	31.49 E
Al-Halfāyah	118	31.49 N	47.26 E
Al-Ḥamād ≚	118	32.00 N	39.30 E
Alhama de Granada	34	37.00 N	3.59 W
Alhama de Murcia	34	37.51 N	1.25 W
Al-Hamal ◆[1]	118	23.30 N	49.45 E
Alhambra, Calif., U.S.	218	34.06 N	118.08 W
Alhambra, Ill., U.S.	209	38.53 N	89.44 W
Al-Ḥamīdīyah	120	34.43 N	35.56 E
Al-Ḥammām	130	30.50 N	29.23 E
Al-Ḥamrā'	118	23.57 N	38.52 E
Al-Ḥamrā' ◆[1]	118	22.40 N	55.05 E
Al-Ḥamrah	132	31.10 N	30.52 E
Al-Ḥāmūl	132	31.19 N	31.10 E
Alhandra	240	7.26 S	34.54 W
Alhandra, Mouchão de I	256c	38.54 N	9.00 W
Al-Ḥanīsh al-Kabīr I	134	13.43 N	42.45 E
Al-Ḥarāk	122	32.44 N	36.18 E
Al-Ḥarīq	118	23.37 N	46.31 E
Al-Ḥārrah	122	33.03 N	36.00 E
Al-Ḥarrah ⊻[9]	118	31.00 N	38.30 E
Al-Ḥarūj al-Aswad ⋀[2]	136	27.00 N	17.10 E
Al-Ḥasakah	120	36.29 N	40.45 E
Al-Ḥasakah □[8]	120	36.30 N	41.00 E
Al-Ḥassānī I	118	24.58 N	37.05 E
Alhaurín el Grande	34	36.38 N	4.41 W
Al-Ḥawāmidīyah	263c	29.54 N	31.15 E
Al-Ḥawātah	134	13.25 N	34.38 E
Al-Ḥawātikah	132	27.16 N	31.01 E
Al-Ḥawrah	134	13.49 N	47.37 E
Al-Ḥawṭah, Ar. Sa.	118	23.27 N	46.46 E
Al-Ḥawṭah, Yam. S.	134	15.50 N	48.27 E
Al-Ḥawwārīyah	132	30.58 N	29.41 E
Al-Ḥayy, 'Irāq	118	32.10 N	46.03 E
Al-Ḥayy, Miṣr	132	29.39 N	31.18 E
Al-Ḥayyānīyah	118	28.38 N	42.45 E
Al-Ḥayz	130	28.02 N	28.39 E
Al-Ḥībah	132	28.45 N	30.55 E
Al-Ḥījānah	122	33.21 N	36.33 E
Al-Ḥijāz ◆[1]	108	24.30 N	38.30 E
Al-Ḥillah, 'Irāq	118	32.29 N	44.25 E
Al-Ḥillah, Sūd.	130	13.27 N	27.08 E
Al-Ḥillah □[4]	118	32.40 N	44.35 E
Al-Ḥilmīyah ◆[8]	263c	30.07 N	31.19 E
Al-Hindīyah	118	32.33 N	44.13 E
Al-Ḥiṣn	122	32.29 N	35.52 E
Al-Hoceima	138	35.15 N	3.55 W
Al Hoceima, Baie d' ⊂	34	35.20 N	3.50 W
Alhos Vedros	256c	38.39 N	9.02 W
Alhucemas, Islas de II	34	35.13 N	3.53 W
Al-Ḥudayb	130	13.00 N	32.50 E
Al-Ḥudaydah	134	14.48 N	42.57 E
Al-Ḥufrah	136	29.10 N	18.02 E
Al-Ḥufrah ◆[1]	118	28.40 N	38.30 E
Al-Hufūf	118	25.22 N	49.34 E
Al-Ḥulwah	118	23.27 N	46.47 E
Al-Ḥumayshī	134	13.41 N	45.52 E
Al-Ḥuṣayḥiṣah	130	14.44 N	33.18 E
Al-Ḥusaynīyah	132	30.52 N	31.55 E
Al-Ḥuṣaynīyah ╤[4]	134	17.48 N	44.27 E
Al-Ḥuwaymī	134	14.05 N	47.44 E
Al-Ḥuwayyiṭ	118	25.36 N	40.23 E
Ali ◆[8]	262a	28.31 N	77.18 E
'Ālī, Sadd al- (Aswān High Dam) ◆[6]	130	23.58 N	32.52 E
Alía	34	39.27 N	5.13 W
'Alīābād, Īrān	118	36.57 N	54.59 E
Aliabād, Pāk.	113	36.18 N	74.37 E
Aliabad, S.S.S.R.	74	41.29 N	46.37 E
Aliade	140	7.16 N	8.28 E
Aliaga	34	40.40 N	0.42 W
Aliağaçiftliği	120	38.48 N	26.59 E
Aliákmon ≃	38	40.30 N	22.36 E
Aliaksin, Cape ≻	170	55.30 N	160.43 W
'Alī al-Gharbī	118	32.27 N	46.41 E
Aliança	240	7.35 S	35.13 W
'Alī an-Nahrī	122	33.51 N	36.01 E
Alībāg	112	18.39 N	72.54 E
Alibahadır	257b	41.11 N	29.12 E
Ali-Bajramly	74	39.56 N	48.56 E
Alibardak	120	38.06 N	40.25 E
Alibej, Ozero ◎	68	45.48 N	30.02 E
Alibejli	74	41.23 N	46.49 E
Alibey ≃	257b	41.03 N	28.56 E
Alibey Adası I	120	39.20 N	26.38 E
Alibeyköy	257b	41.04 N	28.56 E
Alibijaban Island I	106	13.20 N	122.43 E
Alibori ≃	140	11.56 N	3.17 E
Al-Ibrāhīmīyah	132	30.57 N	30.35 E
Alibunar	38	45.05 N	20.58 E
Alicante	34	38.21 N	0.29 W
Alice, S. Afr.	148	32.47 S	26.50 E
Alice, Tex., U.S.	186	27.45 N	98.04 W
Alice ≃	156	24.02 S	144.50 E
Alice, Punta ≻	36	39.24 N	17.10 E
Alice Arm	172	55.29 N	129.29 W
Alicedale	148	33.18 S	26.05 E
Alice Downs	152	17.45 S	127.56 E
Alice Springs	152	23.42 S	133.53 E
Alice Superiore	56	45.28 N	7.47 E
Alice Town	228	25.44 N	79.17 W
Aliceville	184	33.08 N	88.09 W
Alicia, Pil.	106	16.45 N	121.42 E
Alicia, Pil.	106	7.30 N	122.55 E
Alıcık	120	40.49 N	35.21 E
Alick Creek ≃	156	20.25 S	142.00 E
Alicudi, Isola I	36	38.33 N	14.21 E
Al-'Idwah	132	29.21 N	30.55 E
Alief	212	29.43 N	95.35 W
Alife	60	41.20 N	14.20 E
Al-Ifranj	122	31.11 N	35.41 E
Alīganj, Bhārat	114	28.07 N	80.36 E
Alīganj, Bhārat	114	27.30 N	79.11 E
Alignements de Carnac ⊥	32	47.35 N	3.05 W
Alīgūdarz	118	33.24 N	49.41 E
Alijos, Escollos II[1]	222	24.57 N	115.44 W
'Alī Khēl	110	33.57 N	69.43 E
Al-Ikhṣāṣ al-Qiblīyah	132	29.42 N	31.17 E
Alikovo	70	55.45 N	46.45 E
Alima ≃	142	1.36 S	16.36 E
Al-'Imārīyah	132	27.37 N	30.53 E
Alim Island I	154	2.55 S	147.05 E
Alimkent	75	40.58 N	69.11 E
Alimodian	106	10.49 N	122.26 E
Alindao	142	5.02 N	21.13 E
Alingsås	26	57.56 N	12.31 E
Alip Mountains ⋀	106	6.44 N	125.05 E
Alipore	116	22.31 N	88.20 E
Alipur, Bhārat	262b	22.55 N	88.11 E
Ālipur, Bhārat	262b	22.43 N	88.12 E
Alīpur, Pāk.	113	29.23 N	70.55 E
Alīpur Duār	114	26.29 N	89.44 E
Alīpur Janūbi	113	30.13 N	71.18 E
Aliquippa	204	40.37 N	80.15 W
Aliquippa-Hopewell Airport ⊠	269b	40.35 N	80.17 W
Āli Rājpur	110	22.19 N	74.21 E
Al-'Irāq	122	31.05 N	35.39 E
Al-'Irāq → Iraq □[1]	118	33.00 N	44.00 E
Al-'Irq	136	29.02 N	21.33 E
Al-'Irqah	134	13.30 N	47.22 E
Ali-Sabieh	134	11.09 N	42.42 E
Aliseda	34	39.26 N	6.41 W
Alise-Sainte-Reine	54	47.32 N	4.29 E
Alī Seyyed	118	32.09 N	59.52 E
'Alī Shāh 'Avaẕ	118	35.39 N	51.04 E
Ali Shan ⋀	90	23.32 N	120.48 E
Alīshārī	74	39.02 N	47.15 E
Al-Iskandarīyah (Alexandria)	132	31.12 N	29.54 E
Al-Iskandarīyah □[4]	132	31.10 N	29.53 E
Al-Ismā'īlīyah (Ismailia)	132	30.35 N	32.16 E
Al-Ismā'īlīyah □[4]	132	30.30 N	32.15 E
Al-Ismā'īlīyah Military Base ■	132	30.35 N	32.14 E
Aliso Canyon ∨, Calif., U.S.	270	33.53 N	117.40 W
Aliso Canyon ∨, Calif., U.S.	270	34.18 N	118.33 W
Aliso Creek ≃	218	33.31 N	117.45 W
Alisos ≃	190	30.51 N	110.52 W
Al-Istiwā'īyah □[4]	130	5.00 N	31.00 E
Alistráti	38	41.04 N	23.57 E
Alitak, Cape ≻	170	56.51 N	154.21 W
Alitak Bay ⊂	170	57.00 N	154.05 W
Alitanguo	110	35.10 N	83.30 E
Al-Ittiḥād → Madīnat ash-Sha'b	134	12.50 N	44.56 E
Alivérion	38	38.24 N	24.02 E
Aliwal North	148	30.45 S	26.45 E
Alix	172	52.24 N	113.11 W
Al-'Izzīyah	132	27.13 N	30.59 E
Al-Jabal al-Abyaḍ ∧[2]	132	28.46 N	31.00 E
Al-Jabal al-Aḥmar ∧[2]	132	28.19 N	31.07 E
Al-Jabal al-Akhḍar ⋀, Lībīya	136	32.30 N	21.30 E
Al-Jabal al-Akhḍar ⋀, 'Umān	118	23.15 N	57.20 E
Al-Jabal ash-Sharqī (Anti-Lebanon) ⋀	122	33.35 N	36.00 E
Al-Jabalayn	130	12.36 N	32.48 E
Al-Jadīdah	130	25.34 N	28.51 E
Al-Jafādūn	132	28.50 N	30.48 E
Al-Jafr	122	30.18 N	36.13 E
Al-Jāfūrah ◆[2]	118	24.14 N	50.00 E
Al-Jaghbūb	136	29.45 N	24.31 E
Al-Jahrah	118	29.20 N	47.40 E
Al-Jalāmīd	118	31.20 N	39.56 E
Al-Jamālīyah	132	31.11 N	31.51 E
Al-Janūb □[4]	122	33.20 N	35.30 E
Al-Jarnūs	132	28.36 N	30.43 E
Al-Jawārah	108	18.55 N	57.17 E
Al-Jawf, Ar. Sa.	118	29.50 N	39.52 E
Al-Jawf, Lībīya	136	24.11 N	23.19 E
Al-Jawsh	136	32.00 N	11.40 E
Al-Jaylī	130	16.01 N	32.36 E
Al-Jazīrah ╤[4]	136	25.42 N	21.07 E
Al-Jazīrah ◆[1]	130	14.25 N	33.00 E
Aljezur, Bra.	277a	22.40 S	43.36 W
Aljezur, Port.	34	37.19 N	8.48 W
Al-Jibāb	122	33.06 N	36.15 E
Al-Jīzah (Giza)	132		
	263c	30.01 N	31.13 E
Al-Jīzah □[4]	132	29.46 N	31.18 E
Al-Jubayn	130	12.07 N	35.10 E
Aljucén ≃	34	38.56 N	6.25 W
Al-Judayyidah, Urd.	122	31.32 N	35.39 E
Al-Judayyidah, Urd.	122	31.15 N	35.49 E
Al-Julaydah ╤[4]	118	29.03 N	45.38 E
Al-Junaynah, Miṣr	132	31.06 N	31.41 E
Al-Junaynah, Sūd.	130	13.27 N	22.27 E
Al-Junaynah, Sūrīy.	122	32.54 N	36.44 E
Al-Jundīyah	132	28.34 N	30.50 E
Aljustrel	34	37.52 N	8.10 W
Al-Kāb, Miṣr	132	30.57 N	32.18 E
Al-Kāb, Sūd.	130	19.18 N	32.43 E

≃ River	Fluss	Río	Rivière	Rio
≊ Canal	Kanal	Canal	Canal	Canal
⌊ Waterfall, Rapids	Wasserfall, Stromschnellen	Cascada, Rápidos	Chute d'eau, Rapides	Cascata, Rápidos
⊔ Strait	Meeresstrasse	Estrecho	Détroit	Estreito
⊂ Bay, Gulf	Bucht, Golf	Bahía, Golfo	Baie, Golfe	Baía, Golfo
◎ Lake, Lakes	See, Seen	Lago, Lagos	Lac, Lacs	Lago, Lagos
☷ Swamp	Sumpf	Pantano	Marais	Pântano
⍓ Ice Features, Glacier	Eis- und Gletscherformen	Accidentes Glaciales	Formes glaciaires	Acidentes Glaciares
╤ Other Hydrographic Features	Andere Hydrographische Objekte	Otros Elementos Hidrográficos	Autres données hydrographiques	Outros Elementos Hidrográficos

⟡ Submarine Features	Untermeerische Objekte	Accidentes Submarinos	Formes de relief sous-marin	Acidentes Submarinos
□ Political Unit	Politische Einheit	Unidad Politica	Entité politique	Unidade Política
ʋ Cultural Institution	Kulturelle Institution	Institución Cultural	Institution culturelle	Instituição Cultural
⊥ Historical Site	Historische Stätte	Sitio Histórico	Site historique	Sitio Histórico
♠ Recreational Site	Erholungs- und Ferienort	Sitio de Recreo	Centre de loisirs	Sítio de Lazer
⊠ Airport	Flughafen	Aeropuerto	Aéroport	Aeroporto
■ Military Installation	Militäranlage	Instalación Militar	Installation militaire	Instalação Militar
◆ Miscellaneous	Verschiedenes	Misceláneo	Divers	Miscelânea

Al-Kabrit Military Base ■ 132 30.15 N 32.29 E
Al-Kafr 122 32.38 N 36.38 E
Al-Kafr ash-Sharqī 132 37.17 N 31.10 E
Al-Kahfah 118 27.04 N 43.02 E
Alkali Creek ≃, Alta., Can. 174 50.52 N 110.30 W
Alkali Creek ≃, Wyo., U.S. 192 43.16 N 107.40 W
Alkali Lake 172 51.47 N 122.14 W
Alkali Lake ⊜, Nev., U.S. 194 41.42 N 119.50 W
Alkali Lake ⊜, Oreg., U.S. 192 43.10 N 120.02 W
Alkamari 136 13.24 N 11.07 E
Al-Kāmilīn 130 15.05 N 33.11 E
Al-Karabah 130 18.33 N 33.42 E
Al-Karak 122 31.11 N 35.42 E
Al-Karak □[8] 122 31.03 N 35.44 E
Al-Karnak 130 25.43 N 32.39 E
Al-Kawah 130 13.44 N 32.30 E
Al-Kawd 134 13.05 N 45.22 E
Al-Kawm 120 35.11 N 38.52 E
Al-Kawm al-Akhḍar 132 30.58 N 30.17 E
Al-Kawm aṭ-Ṭawīl 132 31.12 N 31.05 E
Al-Kāẓimīyah 118 33.22 N 44.20 E
Alken 52 50.15 N 7.26 E
Al-Khabrā' 118 25.59 N 43.39 E
Al-Khābūrah 118 23.59 N 57.08 E
Al-Khalīl (Hebron) 122 31.32 N 35.06 E
Al-Khalīl □[8] 122 31.32 N 35.06 E
Al-Khālis 118 33.49 N 44.32 E
Al-Khandaq 130 18.36 N 30.34 E
Al-Khānkah 132 30.13 N 31.21 E
Al-Kharaqānīyah 263c 30.10 N 31.10 E
Al-Khārijah 130 25.26 N 30.33 E
Al-Khaṣab 118 26.12 N 56.15 E
Al-Khatam ⬥[1] 118 24.16 N 55.10 E
Al-Khirbah as-Samrā' 122 32.11 N 36.10 E
Al-Khiyām 122 33.19 N 35.36 E
Al-Khubar 118 26.17 N 50.12 E
Al-Khums (Homs) 136 32.39 N 14.16 E
Al-Khums □[4] 136 32.00 N 14.00 E
Al-Khuraybah, Urd. 122 32.40 N 35.52 E
Al-Khuraybah, Yam. S. 134 15.06 N 48.19 E
Al-Khurmah 134 21.54 N 42.03 E
Al-Khurṭūm (Khartoum) 130 15.36 N 32.32 E
Al-Khurṭūm □[4] 130 15.45 N 32.30 E
Al-Khurṭūm Baḥrī 130 15.38 N 32.33 E
Al-Khushnīyah 122 33.00 N 35.48 E
Al-Khuṣūṣ 263c 30.09 N 31.19 E
Al-Kifl 118 32.14 N 44.22 E
Al-Kiswah 122 33.21 N 36.14 E
Alkmaar 48 52.37 N 4.44 E
Al-kūbrī 132 30.02 N 32.33 E
Al-Kūfah 118 32.02 N 44.24 E
Al-Kufayr 122 33.26 N 35.44 E
Al-Kufrah (Cufra) ⬥[1] 136 24.20 N 23.15 E
Al-Kunayyisah 263c 29.59 N 31.11 E
Al-Kuntillah 130 30.00 N 34.41 E
Al-Kurdī 132 31.05 N 30.49 E
Al-Kūt 118 32.25 N 45.49 E
Al-Kūt □[4] 118 32.45 N 45.25 E
Al-Kuwayt 118 29.20 N 47.59 E
Al-Kuwayt → Kuwait □[1] 118 29.30 N 47.45 E
Alkvettern ⊜ 40 59.25 N 14.21 E
Allaben 200 42.07 N 74.22 W
Al-Labwah 120 34.12 N 36.21 E
Allacapan 106 18.15 N 121.35 E
Allach-Jun' 64 61.08 N 138.03 E
Allada 140 6.39 N 2.09 E
Al-Lādhiqīyah (Latakia) 120 35.31 N 35.47 E
Al-Lādhiqīyah □[8] 120 35.10 N 36.10 E
Allagash ≃ 176 47.05 N 69.02 W
Allagen 52 51.28 N 8.14 E
Al-Lagowa 130 11.24 N 29.08 E
Allāhābād, Bhārat 114 25.27 N 81.51 E
Allāhābād, Pāk. 113 34.51 N 72.26 E
Allahābād □[5] 114 25.20 N 82.00 E
Allāhbās 262a 28.31 N 77.25 E
Allahüekber Dağları ⋀⋀ 120 40.35 N 42.32 E
Al-Lāhūn 132 29.13 N 30.59 E
Allāhwardipur 262a 28.33 N 77.26 E
Allaines 46 48.12 N 1.50 E
Allaire State Park ♠ 198 40.08 N 74.08 W
Allakaket 170 66.34 N 152.41 W
Allaman 54 46.28 N 6.24 E
Allamuchy 200 40.55 N 74.49 W
Allan 174 51.53 N 106.04 W
Allan, Pointe ≻ 265a 45.26 N 73.45 W
Allanche 32 45.14 N 2.56 E
Allandale 210 29.07 N 80.58 W
Allan Island ❙ 214 48.28 N 122.42 W
Allanmyo 100 19.22 N 95.13 E
Allanridge 148 27.55 S 26.44 E
Allanson 158a 33.20 S 116.06 E
Allapattah Flats ≚ 210 27.29 N 82.34 W
'Allāq, Bi'r ⍑[4] 136 31.05 N 11.42 E
'Allāqī, Wādī al- ∨ 130 23.07 N 32.47 E
Allard, Lac ⊜, Qué., Can. 176 50.32 N 63.31 W
Allard, Lac ⊜, Qué., Can. 180 47.20 N 78.51 W
Allardt 184 36.23 N 84.53 W
Allariz 34 42.11 N 7.48 W
Állatkert ♠ 254c 47.31 N 19.05 E
Allatoona Lake ⊜[1] 182 34.08 N 84.38 W
Allauch 56 43.20 N 5.29 E
Al-Layyah 130 16.16 N 35.25 E
Alldays 146 22.44 S 29.04 E
Alle, Bel. 52 49.51 N 4.58 E
Alle, Schw. 54 47.26 N 7.08 E
Älleberg ⋀[2] 26 58.08 N 13.36 E
Allegan 206 42.32 N 85.51 W
Allegan □[6] 206 42.35 N 85.53 W
Allegan, Lake ⊜ 206 42.33 N 85.55 W
Allegany 200 42.06 N 78.30 W
Allegany □[6] 200 42.13 N 78.02 W
Allegany Indian Reservation ⬥[4] 200 42.10 N 78.47 W
Allegany State Park ♠ 200 42.04 N 78.44 W
Alleghany 216 39.28 N 120.51 W
Alleghe 58 46.24 N 12.01 E
Allegheny □[6] 204 40.26 N 79.59 W
Allegheny ≃ 204 40.27 N 80.00 W
Allegheny Acres 269b 40.37 N 79.53 W
Allegheny Center ʋ 269b 40.27 N 80.01 W
Allegheny County Airport ⊠ 269b 40.21 N 79.56 W
Allegheny County Park ♠ 269b 40.34 N 79.55 W
Allegheny Mountains ⋀⋀ 178 38.30 N 80.00 W
Allegheny Observatory ʋ[3] 269b 40.29 N 80.01 W
Allegheny Plateau ⋀⋀[1] 178 41.30 N 78.00 W
Allegheny Portage Railroad National Historic Site ⊥ 204 40.28 N 78.32 W
Allegheny Reservoir ⊜[1] 204 42.00 N 78.56 W
Allègre 56 45.12 N 3.42 E
Allègre, Pointe ≻ 231o 16.22 N 61.45 W
Allemagne, République fédérale d' → Germany, Federal Republic Of □[1] 30 51.00 N 9.00 E
Allemande,, République démocratique → German Democratic Republic □[1] 30 52.00 N 12.30 E
Allemanskraaldam ⬥[6] 148 28.16 S 27.07 E
Allemant 251 48.45 N 1.37 E
Allemont 56 45.08 N 6.02 E
Allen, Arg. 242 38.58 S 67.50 W
Allen, Pil. 106 12.30 N 124.17 E
Allen, Md., U.S. 198 38.17 N 75.42 W
Allen, Mich., U.S. 206 41.57 N 84.46 W
Allen, Nebr., U.S. 188 42.25 N 96.51 W
Allen, Okla., U.S. 186 34.53 N 96.25 W
Allen, Pa., U.S. 198 40.10 N 77.05 W
Allen, S. Dak., U.S. 188 43.17 N 101.55 W
Allen, Tex., U.S. 212 33.06 N 96.40 W
Allen, Wash., U.S. 214 48.31 N 122.23 W
Allen □[6], Ind., U.S. 206 41.04 N 85.09 W
Allen □[6], Ohio, U.S. 206 40.46 N 84.06 W
Allen ≃ 42 54.58 N 2.19 W
Allen, Lough ⊜ 28 54.08 N 8.08 W
Allen, Mount ⋀, N.Z. 162 47.05 S 167.48 E
Allen, Mount ⋀, Alaska, U.S. 170 62.14 N 142.13 W
Allenby Bridge ⬥[5] 122 31.52 N 35.52 E
Allendale, Ill., U.S. 184 38.32 N 87.43 W
Allendale, Mich., U.S. 206 42.58 N 85.57 W
Allendale, N.J., U.S. 266 41.02 N 74.08 W
Allendale, S.C., U.S. 182 33.06 N 81.18 W
Allendale Town 42 54.54 N 2.15 W
Allende, Méx. 222 25.17 N 100.01 W
Allende, Méx. 224 18.09 N 94.16 W
Allendorf, B.R.D. 52 51.16 N 9.58 E
Allendorf, B.R.D. 52 51.02 N 8.38 E
Allenfarm 212 30.24 N 96.14 W
All England Lawn Tennis Club ♠ 250 51.26 N 0.13 W
Allen Grove 206 42.35 N 88.41 W
Allen Park 206 42.15 N 83.13 W
Allenport, Pa., U.S. 204 40.06 N 79.51 W
Allenport, Pa., U.S. 204 40.20 N 77.53 W
Allensbach 54 47.43 N 9.03 E
Allenstein → Olsztyn 30 53.48 N 20.29 E
Allensville 204 40.32 N 77.49 W
Allenton, Mich., U.S. 204 42.55 N 82.57 W
Allenton, R.I., U.S. 197 41.32 N 71.29 W
Allentown, N.J., U.S. 198 40.11 N 74.35 W
Allentown, N.Y., U.S. 200 42.05 N 78.04 W
Allentown, Ohio, U.S. 206 40.46 N 84.12 W
Allentown, Pa., U.S. 198 40.36 N 75.29 W
Allentsteig 30 48.42 N 15.20 E
Allenwood, N.J., U.S. 198 40.09 N 74.06 W
Allenwood, N.Y., U.S. 266 40.48 N 73.44 W
Allenwood, Pa., U.S. 200 41.07 N 76.54 W
Alleppey 112 9.29 N 76.19 E
Aller ≃ 30 52.57 N 9.11 E
Allerona 60 42.49 N 11.58 E
Allerslev 41 55.05 N 12.03 E
Allerton, Iowa, U.S. 180 40.42 N 93.22 W
Allerton, Mass., U.S. 273 42.18 N 70.53 W
Allerton ⬥[8] 252 53.22 N 2.53 W
Allerton, Point ≻ 197 42.18 N 70.53 W
Allestree 44 52.57 N 1.29 W
Allevard 56 45.24 N 6.04 E
Alley Park ♠ 266 40.45 N 73.44 W
Alleyton 212 29.43 N 96.29 W
Allgäu ⬥[1] 54 47.35 N 10.10 E
Allgäuer Alpen ⋀⋀ 54 47.20 N 10.25 E
Allhallows 250 51.28 N 0.39 E
Alliance, Alta., Can. 172 52.26 N 111.47 W
Alliance, Nebr., U.S. 188 42.06 N 102.52 W
Alliance, Ohio, U.S. 204 40.55 N 81.06 W
Allibaudières 46 48.35 N 4.07 E
Al-Lidām 134 20.29 N 44.50 E
Allier □[5] 32 46.25 N 3.00 E
Allier ≃ 56 45.05 N 3.35 E
Alligator ≃ 182 35.58 N 75.58 W
Alligator Creek ≃, Ga., U.S. 182 31.58 N 82.22 W
Alligator Creek ≃, Tex., U.S. 212 30.42 N 97.07 W
Alligator Lake ⊜ 210 28.13 N 81.13 W
Alligator Pond 231q 17.52 N 77.34 W
Alligny-en-Morvan 46 47.12 N 4.10 E
Allinagaram 112 10.02 N 77.30 E
Allinge 26 55.16 N 14.49 E
Allipén ≃ 244 39.00 S 72.31 W
Al-Lisān ≻[1] 122 31.17 N 35.28 E
Al-Lisht 132 29.34 N 31.14 E
Allison 180 42.45 N 92.48 W
Allison, Mount ⋀ 272 37.30 N 121.52 W
Allison Gulch ∨ 270 34.16 N 117.44 W
Allison Harbour 172 51.03 N 127.30 W
Allison Park 204 40.34 N 79.57 W
Alliston 202 44.09 N 79.52 W
Al-Līth 134 20.09 N 40.16 E
Al-Imām ⬥[8] 263c 30.01 N 31.10 E
Allmendingen 54 48.20 N 9.43 E
Alloa 42 56.07 N 3.49 W
Allochio, Galleria degli ⬥[5] 60 44.03 N 11.30 E
Allogny 46 47.13 N 2.19 E
Allonby 42 54.46 N 3.25 W
Allone Abba 122 32.44 N 35.10 E
Allonnes 46 48.20 N 1.40 E
Allora 161a 28.02 S 151.59 E
Allos 56 44.14 N 6.38 E
Allott, Mount ⋀[2] 152 26.06 S 124.46 E
Allouez 180 44.29 N 88.01 W
Alloway 198 39.34 N 75.22 W
Alloway Creek ≃ 198 39.27 N 75.30 W
Allport 204 40.58 N 78.12 W
All Saints 230c 17.03 N 61.48 W
Allschwil 54 47.33 N 7.33 E
Allstedt 50 51.24 N 11.23 E
Allston ⬥[8] 273 42.22 N 71.08 W
Al-Lubnān → Lebanon □[1] 118 33.50 N 35.50 E
Alluets, Forêt des ♠ 251 48.55 N 1.55 E
Al-Luḥayyah 134 15.42 N 42.42 E
Allumette Lake ⊜ 180 45.53 N 77.13 W
Allumettes, Île des ❙ 180 45.50 N 77.05 W
Allumiere 60 42.09 N 11.54 E
Allview Estates 198 39.12 N 76.51 W
Allyn 214 47.23 N 122.50 W
Alm 58 47.24 N 12.54 E
Alm ≃ 58 48.05 N 13.55 E
Alma, Qué., Can. 176 48.33 N 71.39 W
Alma, Ark., U.S. 184 35.29 N 94.13 W
Alma, Ga., U.S. 182 31.33 N 82.28 W
Alma, Ill., U.S. 209 38.43 N 88.55 W
Alma, Kans., U.S. 188 39.01 N 96.17 W
Alma, Mich., U.S. 180 43.23 N 84.39 W
Alma, Nebr., U.S. 188 40.06 N 99.22 W
Alma, N.Y., U.S. 200 42.01 N 78.03 W
Alma, Wis., U.S. 180 44.20 N 91.55 W
Al-Ma'ābidah 132 27.20 N 31.01 E
Al-Ma'ādī ⬥[8] 132 29.58 N 31.15 E
Al-Ma'ānīyah 118 30.44 N 43.00 E
Alma-Ata 75 43.15 N 76.57 E
Alma-Ata □[4] 75 44.00 N 76.00 E
Alma Center 180 44.26 N 90.55 W
Almada 34 38.41 N 9.09 W
Almaden, Austl. 156 17.20 S 144.41 E
Almadén, Esp. 34 38.46 N 4.50 W
Almadén de la Plata 34 37.52 N 6.04 W
Al-Madīnah (Medina) 118 24.28 N 39.36 E
Al-Madīnah al-Fikrīyah 132 27.56 N 30.49 E
Al-Mado ⋀ 134 11.02 N 48.20 E
Al-Madwar 122 32.17 N 36.00 E
Al-Mafāzah 130 13.36 N 34.33 E
Al-Mafraq 122 32.21 N 36.12 E
Almafuerte 242 32.12 S 64.15 W
Al-Maghārīm 134 15.01 N 47.51 E
Al-Maghrah ⊜ 130 30.15 N 28.56 E
Almagor 122 32.55 N 35.36 E
Almagre, Laguna C 224 23.48 N 97.48 W
Al-Magreb → Morocco □[1] 138 32.00 N 5.00 W
Almagro 34 38.53 N 3.43 W
Almagro Island ❙ 106 11.56 N 124.18 E
Al-Maḥallah al-Kubrā 132 30.58 N 31.10 E
Al-Maḥārīq 130 25.37 N 30.39 E
Alma Hill ⋀[2] 200 42.03 N 78.01 W
Al-Maḥmūdīyah 132 31.11 N 30.32 E
Al-Maḥraṣ 132 27.49 N 30.48 E
Al-Maḥsamah 132 30.34 N 32.01 E
Al-Majdal 122 32.47 N 36.30 E
Almăjului, Munții ⋀⋀ 38 44.43 N 22.12 E
Al-Makīlī 136 32.09 N 22.17 E
Al-Maks 132 31.09 N 29.51 E
Almalyk 75 40.50 N 69.35 E
Al-Ma'mūrah 132 31.18 N 30.03 E
Al-Manāmah 118 26.13 N 50.35 E
Al-Manāqil 130 14.15 N 32.59 E
Al-Manāṣif ⬥[1] 120 35.13 N 40.54 E
Al-Manāwāt 263c 29.55 N 31.14 E
Almanor, Lake ⊜ 194 40.15 N 121.08 W
Almansa 34 38.52 N 1.05 W
Al-Manshāh 130 26.28 N 31.48 E
Almansor ≃ 34 38.56 N 8.54 W
Al-Manṣūrah 132 31.03 N 31.23 E
Al-Manṣūrīyah 132 30.08 N 31.05 E
Almanza 34 42.39 N 5.02 W
Al-Manzilah 132 31.09 N 31.56 E
Almanzor, Pico de ⋀ 34 40.15 N 5.18 W
Almanzora ≃ 34 37.14 N 1.46 W
Al-Maqnāh 118 28.24 N 34.45 E
Almar ≃ 34 40.54 N 5.29 W
Al-Marāghah 130 26.42 N 31.36 E
Al-Marāzīq 132 29.49 N 31.16 E
Almargem do Bispo 256c 38.51 N 9.16 W
Al-Marj 136 32.30 N 20.54 E
Al-Marj ⬥[8] 263c 30.09 N 31.20 E
Almas 240 11.33 S 47.09 W
Almaș ≃ 38 47.14 N 23.19 E
Almas, Pico das ⋀ 245 13.33 S 41.56 W
Al-Ma'ṣarah, Miṣr 132 27.42 N 30.52 E
Al-Ma'ṣarah, Miṣr 132 29.54 N 31.17 E
Al-Ma'ṣarah, Miṣr 132 31.13 N 31.19 E
Al-Mashqūq 122 32.24 N 36.43 E
Al-Mashrafah 120 34.50 N 36.52 E
Al-Masīd 130 15.15 N 32.57 E
Al-Maṣīrah ❙ 108 20.25 N 58.50 E
Al-Matammah 130 16.43 N 33.22 E
Al-Maṭarīyah 132 31.11 N 32.02 E
⬥[8]Maṭarīyah 132 30.07 N 31.19
Al-Matnah 130 13.47 N 35.03 E
Al-Mawṣil (Mosul) 118 36.20 N 43.08 E
Al-Mawṣil □[4] 118 36.10 N 42.35 E
Al-Mayādīn 120 35.01 N 40.27 E
Al-Maymūn 132 29.14 N 31.12 E
Almazán 34 41.29 N 2.32 W
Almazar, S.S.S.R. 75 40.59 N 68.54 E
Al-Mazār, Urd. 122 31.04 N 35.42 E
Almaznaja ⬥[8] 73 48.31 N 38.35 E
Almaznij 73 48.02 N 40.03 E
Almazora 34 39.57 N 0.03 W
Almazovka ⬥[8] 73 48.04 N 39.18 E
Almazovo 255b 55.51 N 38.02 E
Al-Mazra'ah 122 31.16 N 35.31 E
Al-Mazzah 122 33.30 N 36.15 E
Alme 52 51.28 N 8.37 E
Almeida 34 40.43 N 6.54 W
Almeidas 246 22.22 S 46.32 W
Almeirim, Bra. 240 1.32 S 52.34 W
Almeirim, Port. 34 39.12 N 8.38 W
Almejas, Bahía C 222 24.29 N 111.44 W
Almelo 48 52.21 N 6.39 E
Almelo-Nordhorn, Kanaal ≊ 48 52.20 N 6.40 E
Almena 188 39.54 N 99.43 W
Almenar 34 41.48 N 2.34 W
Almenara 245 16.11 S 40.42 W
Almenar de Soria 34 41.41 N 2.12 W
Almendares ≃ 276b 23.08 N 82.25 W
Almendra, Embalse de ⊜[1] 34 41.15 N 6.10 W
Almendralejo 34 38.41 N 6.24 W
Almenêches 46 48.42 N 0.07 E
Al'menevo 76 54.57 N 63.34 E
Almenno San Salvatore 56 45.45 N 9.35 E
Almería 34 36.50 N 2.27 W
Almería, Golfo de C 34 36.46 N 2.30 W
Al'metjevsk 70 54.53 N 52.20 E
Al'meż 24 60.03 N 48.03 E
Älmhult 26 56.33 N 14.08 E
Al-Midhnab 118 25.54 N 44.14 E
Al-Mīnā' 120 34.27 N 35.49 E
Almina, Punta ≻ 34 35.53 N 5.15 W
Almino Afonso 240 6.09 S 37.46 W
Al-Minshāt al-Kubrā 132 31.03 N 30.54 E
Al-Minūfīyah □[4] 132 30.30 N 31.00 E
Al-Minyā, Miṣr 132 28.06 N 30.45 E
Al-Minyā, Miṣr 132 29.45 N 31.18 E
Al-Minyā, Miṣr 132 29.14 N 30.45 E
Al-Minyā □[4] 132 28.26 N 30.42 E
Almira 192 47.43 N 118.56 W
Almirantazgo → Admiralty Mountains ⋀⋀ 9 71.45 S 168.30 E
Almirantazgo, Islas → Admiralty Islands ❙❙ 154 2.10 S 147.00 E
Almirante 226 9.18 N 82.24 W
Almirante, Bahía de C 226 9.20 N 82.18 W
Almirante Brown 248 34.48 S 58.23 W
Almirante Brown □[5] 278 34.50 S 58.20 W
Almirante Guillermo Brown, Parque ♠ 278 34.40 S 58.28 W
Almirante Latorre 242 29.38 S 70.58 W
Almirante Montt, Golfo Ⴎ 244 51.55 S 72.45 W
Almirós 38 39.11 N 22.46 E
Almiroú, Kólpos C 38 35.23 N 24.20 E
Al-Mismīyah 122 33.08 N 36.23 E
Almo 192 42.06 N 113.38 W
Almoçageme 256c 38.48 N 9.28 W
Almodôvar 34 37.31 N 8.04 W
Almodóvar del Campo 34 38.43 N 4.10 W
Almolonga 226 14.49 N 91.30 W
Almond, N.Y., U.S. 200 42.19 N 77.44 W
Almond, Wis., U.S. 180 44.16 N 89.24 W
Almond ≃ 42 55.58 N 3.18 W
Almondsbury 44 51.34 N 2.34 W
Almonesson 198 39.49 N 75.06 W
Almont 204 42.55 N 83.03 W
Almont ≃ 251 48.32 N 2.40 E
Almonte, Ont., Can. 202 45.14 N 76.12 W
Almonte, Esp. 34 37.15 N 6.31 W
Almonte, Calif., U.S. 272 37.53 N 122.32 W
Almonte ≃ 34 39.42 N 6.28 W
Almora 114 29.37 N 79.40 E
Almōra □[5] 114 29.45 N 79.35 E
Almsee ⊜ 58 47.45 N 13.57 E
Ålmsta 40 59.58 N 18.48 E
Al-Mu'allaqah 122 33.50 N 35.54 E
Al-Mu'aẓẓamīyah 122 33.45 N 36.39 E
Al-Mubarraz, Ar. Sa. 118 25.55 N 49.36 E
Al-Mubarraz, Ar. Sa. 134 22.17 N 46.44 E
Al-Mudawwarah 118 29.19 N 36.01 E
Al-Mudawwarah ⋀[2] 132 29.11 N 30.21 E
Almudébar 34 42.03 N 0.35 W
Al-Muglad 130 11.02 N 27.44 E
Al-Muḥarraq 118 26.16 N 50.37 E
Al-Mukallā 134 14.32 N 49.08 E
Al-Mukhā (Mocha) 134 13.19 N 43.15 E
Al-Munājāt al-Kubrā 132 30.50 N 32.01 E
Almuñécar 34 36.43 N 3.41 W
Almunge 40 59.53 N 18.03 E
Al-Muntazah 132 31.17 N 30.01 E
al-Murrah al-Rubrā, Al-Buḥayrah (Great Bitter Lake) ⊜ 132 30.20 N 32.23 E
al-Murrah aṣugarā, Al-Buạayrah (Little Bitter Lake) ⊜ 132 30.13 N 32.33 E
Almus 120 40.23 N 36.55 E
Al-Musallamīyah 130 14.34 N 33.21 E
Al-Musayfirah 122 32.37 N 36.20 E
Al-Musayjid 118 24.05 N 39.06 E
Al-Musayyib 118 32.47 N 44.18 E
Al-Mushannaf 122 32.44 N 36.46 E
Al-Musharrak Qiblī 132 29.23 N 30.34 E
Al-Mutā'iyah 122 32.29 N 36.17 E
Al-Mu'tamadīyah 132 31.02 N 31.05 E
Al-Mutayn 122 33.54 N 35.44 E
Al-Muṭī'ah 132 27.08 N 31.18 E
Al-Muwaqqar ⊥ 122 31.49 N 36.06 E
Al-Muwassam 134 16.25 N 42.20 E
Al-Muwayh 134 22.45 N 41.36 E
Al-Muwayliḥ 118 27.41 N 35.27 E
Aln ≃ 42 55.23 N 1.37 W
Alnarp 41 55.39 N 13.05 E
Al'n'aš 70 56.44 N 54.43 E
Alnaši 70 56.11 N 52.28 E
Al-Nasser 130 24.32 N 32.55 E
Alne ≃ 44 52.13 N 1.52 W
Alnmouth 42 55.23 N 1.36 W
Alnön ❙ 26 62.25 N 17.26 E
Alnor 41 54.55 N 9.36 E
Alnwick 42 55.25 N 1.42 W
Alnwick Indian Reserve ⬥[4] 202 44.10 N 78.06 W
Alo 136 11.47 N 20.53 E
Aloândia 245 17.43 S 49.29 W
Alofau 164u 14.16 S 170.36 W
Alofi 164v 19.01 S 169.55 W
Alofi Bay C 164v 19.01 S 169.56 W
Aloha 214 45.29 N 122.52 W
Aloha, Lake ⊜ 216 38.52 N 120.09 W
Aloi 144 2.17 N 33.10 E
Aloja 66 57.46 N 24.53 E
Alondra 270 33.54 N 118.19 W
Alónnisos 38 39.08 N 23.50 E
Alónnisos ❙ 38 39.13 N 23.55 E
Alor, Kepulauan ❙❙ 102 8.15 S 124.30 E
Alor, Pulau ❙ 102 8.15 S 124.45 E
Alor, Selat Ⴎ 102 8.20 S 123.48 E
Álora 34 36.48 N 4.42 W
Alor Gajah 104 2.23 N 102.13 E
Alor Setar 104 6.07 N 100.22 E
Alor Star → Alor Setar 104 6.07 N 100.22 E
Alorton 209 38.36 N 96.08 W
Alos 120 38.07 N 39.32 E
Al'ošn'a, S.S.S.R. 66 53.38 N 33.29 E
Al'ošn'a, S.S.S.R. 72 54.14 N 37.16 E
Alosno 34 37.33 N 7.07 W
Alost → Aalst 46 50.56 N 4.02 E
Alouette ≃ 214 49.16 N 122.42 W
Alouette Lake ⊜ 214 49.19 N 122.28 W
Alovo 70 54.38 N 46.27 E
Aloxe-Corton 54 47.04 N 4.52 E
Aloysius, Mount ⋀ 152 26.01 S 128.34 E
Alpachiri 242 37.22 S 63.46 W
Alpaugh 216 35.53 N 119.29 W
Alpen 48 51.35 N 6.30 E
Alpen → Alps ⋀⋀ 32 46.25 N 10.00 E
Alpena, Ark., U.S. 184 36.17 N 93.18 W
Alpena, Mich., U.S. 180 45.04 N 83.26 W
Alpena, S. Dak., U.S. 188 44.11 N 98.22 W
Alpercatas ≃ 240 6.02 S 44.19 W
Alpercatas, Serra das ⋀⋀[2] 240 6.00 S 45.00 W
Alpes 276a 19.22 N 99.12 W
Alpes → Alps ⋀⋀ 32 46.25 N 10.00 E
Alpes Dináricos → Dinara ⋀⋀ 36 43.50 N 16.35 E
Alpes Maritimes □[5] 56 44.00 N 7.10 E
Alpes Marítimos → Maritime Alps ⋀⋀ 56 44.15 N 7.10 E
Alpes Transilvanos → Carpații Meridionali ⋀⋀ 38 45.30 N 24.15 E
Alpha, Austl. 156 23.39 S 146.38 E
Alpha, Ill., U.S. 180 41.12 N 90.23 W
Alpha, Mich., U.S. 180 46.02 N 88.22 W
Alpha, N.J., U.S. 200 40.40 N 75.09 W
Alpharetta 182 34.04 N 84.18 W
Alphen aan den Rijn 48 52.07 N 4.40 E
Alphington 44 50.42 N 3.31 W
Alphin Pike ⋀[2] 252 53.31 N 2.00 W
Alphonse Island ❙ 128 7.00 S 52.45 E
Alpi → Alps ⋀⋀ 32 46.25 N 10.00 E
Alpiarça 34 39.15 N 8.35 W
Alpi Dinariche → Dinara ⋀⋀ 36 43.50 N 16.35 E
Alpignano 56 45.06 N 7.31 E
Alpilles, Chaîne des ⋀⋀[2] 56 43.45 N 4.50 E
Alpine, Ariz., U.S. 190 33.51 N 109.09 W
Alpine, Calif., U.S. 194 32.50 N 116.47 W
Alpine, N.J., U.S. 266 40.56 N 73.56 W
Alpine, N.Y., U.S. 200 42.19 N 76.44 W
Alpine, Tex., U.S. 186 30.22 N 103.40 W
Alpine □[6] 216 38.41 N 119.47 W
Alpine Creek ≃ 272 37.19 N 122.17 W
Alpinópolis 245 20.52 S 46.23 W
Alpi Retiche → Rhaetian Alps ⋀⋀ 54 46.30 N 10.00 E
Alpirsbach 54 48.21 N 8.23 E
Alplaus Kill ≃ 200 42.51 N 73.54 W
Alpnachstad 54 46.57 N 8.17 E
Alps ⋀⋀ 22 46.25 N 10.00 E
Alpsee ⊜ 54 47.34 N 10.10 E
Alpu 120 39.47 N 30.58 E
Al-Qābil 118 23.57 N 55.48 E
Al-Qābūn 122 33.33 N 36.20 E
Al-Qadam 122 33.28 N 36.17 E
Al-Qaḍārif 130 14.02 N 35.24 E
Al-Qaddāḥīyah 136 31.22 N 15.14 E
Al-Qaḍīmah 134 22.21 N 39.09 E
Al-Qāhirah (Cairo) 132 / 263c 30.03 N 31.15 E
Al-Qāhirah □[4] 132 30.02 N 31.13 E
Al-Qaḥmah 134 18.00 N 41.41 E
Al-Qā'im 118 34.21 N 41.07 E
Al-Qā'īyah ⍑[4] 118 26.27 N 45.35 E
Al-Qāiyāt 132 28.40 N 30.41 E
Al-Qalaj 263c 30.11 N 31.21 E
Al-Qalībah 118 28.32 N 37.42 E
Al-Qalyūbīyah □[4] 132 30.18 N 31.18 E
Al-Qāmishlī 120 37.02 N 41.14 E
Al-Qanāṭir al-Khayrīyah 132 30.12 N 31.08 E
Al-Qanāyāt 132 30.37 N 31.28 E
Al-Qanṭarah 132 30.52 N 32.19 E
Al-Qārah 118 29.52 N 40.15 E
Al-Qārāt az-Zurq ⋀[2] 132 29.00 N 29.55 E
Al-Qaryah ash-Sharqīyah 136 30.24 N 13.36 E
Al-Qaryatayn 120 34.14 N 37.14 E
Al-Qaṣabāt 136 32.35 N 14.03 E
Al-Qaṣābī 132 31.16 N 30.41 E
Al-Qaṣr, Miṣr 130 25.42 N 28.53 E
Al-Qaṣr, Urd. 122 31.19 N 35.45 E
Al-Qaṣṣāṣīn 132 30.34 N 31.56 E
Al-Qaṭīf 118 26.33 N 50.00 E
Al-Qaṭrūn 136 24.56 N 14.38 E
Al-Qaṭṭā 132 30.13 N 30.58 E
Al-Qaṭṭāwīyah 132 30.33 N 31.40 E
Al-Qays 132 28.29 N 30.47 E
Al-Qayṣūmah 118 28.16 N 46.03 E
Al-Qir'awn 122 33.34 N 35.43 E
Al-Qiṣfah 122 32.38 N 35.52 E
Al-Quds → Yerushalayim 122 31.46 N 35.14 E
Al-Quds □[8] 122 31.45 N 35.20 E
Alqueva, Barragem de ⬥[6] 34 38.14 N 7.29 W
Alquízar 230p 22.48 N 82.35 W
Al-Qunayṭirah 122 33.07 N 35.49 E
Al-Qunayṭirah □[8] 122 33.00 N 35.50 E
Al-Qunfudhah 134 19.08 N 41.05 E
Al-Qurayn 132 30.37 N 31.44 E
Al-Qurayyah 122 32.32 N 36.36 E
Al-Qurayyāt 118 23.17 N 58.55 E
Al-Qurnah 118 31.00 N 47.26 E
Al-Quṣaymah 122 30.40 N 34.22 E
Al-Quṣayr, Miṣr 118 26.06 N 34.17 E

ENGLISH

Name Page Lat.°′ Long.°′

Al-Quṣayr, Miṣr 132 27.27 N 30.52 E
Al-Quṣayr, Sūrīy. 120 34.31 N 36.35 E
Al-Qūṣīyah 132 27.26 N 30.49 E
Al-Quṭayfah 122 33.44 N 36.36 E
Al-Quṭaynah 130 14.52 N 32.21 E
Al-Quway'īyah 118 24.03 N 45.15 E
Al-Quwaysī 130 13.20 N 34.05 E
Alright, Île ❙ 176 47.25 N 61.47 W
Alrø ❙ 41 55.51 N 10.05 E
Alroy Downs 152 19.18 S 136.04 E
Als ❙ 41 54.59 N 9.55 E
Alsace □[9] 54 48.30 N 7.30 E
Alsace, Ballon d' ⋀ 54 47.50 N 6.51 E
Alsager 44 53.06 N 2.17 W
Alsask 174 51.23 N 109.59 W
Alsasua 34 42.54 N 2.10 W
Alsdorf 52 50.53 N 6.10 E
Alsea 192 44.23 N 123.36 W
Alsea ≃ 192 44.26 N 124.05 W
Alsek ≃ 170 59.10 N 138.10 W
Alsen 188 48.38 N 98.42 W
Alseno 58 44.54 N 9.59 E
Alsenz 52 49.43 N 7.49 E
Alsenz ≃ 52 49.49 N 7.51 E
Alsey 209 39.34 N 90.25 W
Alsfeld 52 50.45 N 9.16 E
Als Fjord C[2] 41 55.02 N 9.38 E
Al-Shallūfa Military Base ■ 132 30.03 N 32.32 E
Alsike 40 59.45 N 17.45 E
Alsina 242 33.54 S 59.23 W
Alsip 206 41.40 N 87.44 W
Alsleben 50 51.42 N 11.41 E
Alsónémedi 254c 47.19 N 19.10 E
Alstaden ⬥[8] 253 51.28 N 6.50 E
Ålstäket 40 59.20 N 18.28 E
Alstätte 48 52.08 N 6.55 E
Alstead ≃ 174 55.50 N 107.26 W
Alster 40 59.24 N 13.36 E
Alster ≃ 48 53.36 N 9.59 E
Alsterbro 26 56.57 N 15.55 E
Alstern ⊜ 40 59.40 N 13.55 E
Alston 42 54.49 N 2.26 W
Alsunga 66 56.59 N 21.34 E
Alswede 48 52.20 N 8.33 E
Alt ≃ 42 53.32 N 3.03 W
Alta, Nor. 24 69.55 N 23.12 E
Älta, Sve. 40 59.16 N 18.11 E
Alta, Calif., U.S. 216 39.12 N 120.49 W
Alta, Iowa, U.S. 188 42.40 N 95.18 W
Alta, Cachoeira ᒪ 240 5.46 S 54.28 W
Alta, Mount ⋀ 162 44.30 S 168.58 E
Altadena 218 34.12 N 118.08 W
Alta Gracia, Arg. 242 31.40 S 64.26 W
Alta Gracia, Nic. 226 11.34 N 85.35 W
Altagracia de Orituco 236 9.52 N 66.23 W
Alta Hill 216 39.14 N 121.04 W
Al Tahoe 216 38.57 N 119.59 W
Altai ⋀⋀ 80 48.00 N 90.00 E
Altair 212 29.34 N 96.28 W
Altaj, Mong. 76 48.18 N 89.35 E
Altaj (Jesönbulag), Mong. 80 46.25 N 96.20 E
Altaj, S.S.S.R. 76 53.27 N 91.48 E
Altajskij 76 51.58 N 85.22 E
Alta Loma, Calif., U.S. 218 34.07 N 117.36 W
Alta Loma, Tex., U.S. 212 29.22 N 95.04 W
Altamachi ≃ 238 16.08 S 66.50 W
Altamaha ≃ 182 31.19 N 81.17 W
Altamira, Bra. 240 3.12 S 52.12 W
Altamira, Chile 242 25.47 S 69.51 W
Altamira, C.R. 226 10.30 N 84.23 W
Altamira, Méx. 224 22.24 N 97.55 W
Altamira, Las Cuevas de •[5] 34 43.18 N 4.08 W
Altamirano 186 25.55 N 97.47 W
Altamont, Ill., U.S. 209 39.04 N 88.46 W
Altamont, Kans., U.S. 188 37.12 N 95.18 W
Altamont, N.Y., U.S. 200 42.42 N 74.02 W
Altamont, Oreg., U.S. 192 42.12 N 121.44 W
Altamont, Tenn., U.S. 184 35.26 N 85.43 W
Altamonte Springs 210 28.40 N 81.22 W
Altamura 36 40.50 N 16.33 E
Altamura, Isla ❙ 222 25.00 N 108.10 W
Altan, S.S.S.R. 78 49.31 N 111.32 E
Altan, S.S.S.R. 78 49.53 N 109.04 E
Altanbulag, Mong. 78 50.19 N 106.30 E
Altanbulag, Mong. 78 47.41 N 106.22 E
Altancögc 76 49.03 N 90.27 E
Altanširee 92 45.31 N 110.29 E
Altar 222 30.43 N 111.44 W
Altar ≃ 222 30.39 N 111.53 W
Altar, Desierto de ⬥[2] 222 31.50 N 114.15 W
Altare 56 44.20 N 8.20 E
Altario 174 51.55 N 110.09 W
Altarnun 44 50.37 N 4.30 W
Altar of the Earth ʋ[1] 261a 39.57 N 116.24 E
Altar of the Moon ʋ[1] 261a 39.55 N 116.20 E
Altar of the Sun ʋ[1] 261a 39.54 N 116.27 E
Altar Wash ∨ 190 32.05 N 111.19 W
Altaskij Kraj □[8] 76 52.30 N 83.00 E
Altastenberg 52 51.11 N 8.28 E
Altata, Méx. 222 24.38 N 107.55 W
Altata, S.S.S.R. 70 51.07 N 48.44 E
Alta Verapaz □[5] 226 15.40 N 90.00 W
Altavilla Irpina 60 41.00 N 14.47 E
Altaville 216 38.05 N 120.33 W
Alta Vista, Kans., U.S. 188 38.52 N 96.29 W
Altavista, Va., U.S. 182 37.06 N 79.17 W
Altay 76 60.20 N 68.58 E
Alt Buchhorst 254a 52.26 N 13.51 E
Altdamm → Dąbie ⬥[8] 50 53.24 N 14.40 E
Altdöbern 50 51.39 N 14.02 E
Altdorf 54 46.53 N 8.39 E
Alte Donau ⊜ 254b 48.14 N 16.26 E
Alteelva ≃ 24 69.58 N 23.23 E
Altefähr 50 54.20 N 13.07 E
Alte Grund 254a 52.28 N 13.47 E
Altena 52 51.17 N 7.40 E
Altenahr 52 50.31 N 6.59 E
Altenau 48 51.48 N 10.26 E
Altenbeken 48 51.46 N 8.56 E
Altenberg 50 50.46 N 13.45 E
Altenberge 48 52.03 N 7.27 E
Altenbruch 48 53.49 N 8.46 E
Altenbüren 52 51.23 N 8.30 E
Altenburg 50 50.59 N 12.26 E
Altenderne Oberbecker ⬥[8] 253 51.35 N 7.33 E
Altendorf 253 51.29 N 7.40 E
Altendorf ⬥[8] 253 51.25 N 7.06 E
Altendorf-Ulfkotte 253 51.38 N 7.00 E
Altenesch 48 53.08 N 8.37 E
Altenessen ⬥[8] 253 51.29 N 7.00 E
Altengamme ⬥[8] 48 53.25 N 10.16 E
Altenhagen, B.R.D. 48 52.03 N 8.38 E
Altenhagen, D.D.R. 50 53.45 N 13.06 E
Altenhagen ⬥[8] 253 51.22 N 7.28 E
Altenhof 50 52.55 N 13.43 E
Altenholz 41 54.24 N 10.07 E
Altenkirchen (Westerwald), B.R.D. 52 50.41 N 7.38 E
Altenkirchen, D.D.R. 50 54.38 N 13.20 E
Altenkrempe 50 54.08 N 10.49 E
Altenkunstadt 50 50.07 N 11.14 E
Altenmarkt an der Alz 58 48.00 N 12.32 E
Altenoythe 48 53.02 N 7.52 E
Altenpleen 50 54.21 N 12.57 E
Altensteig 52 48.35 N 8.37 E
Altentreptow 50 53.42 N 13.14 E
Altenvoerde 253 51.18 N 7.22 E
Altenwalde 48 53.49 N 8.40 E
Altenweddingen 50 52.00 N 11.31 E
Alte Oder ≃ 50 52.52 N 14.09 E
Alter do Chão 34 39.12 N 7.40 W
Alterosa 246 21.15 S 46.08 W
Alter Rhein ≃ 253 51.35 N 6.36 E
Altes Land ⬥[1] 48 53.33 N 9.38 E
Altfriedland 50 52.38 N 14.12 E
Altglashütten 54 47.51 N 8.06 E
Alt-glienicke ⬥[8] 254a 52.25 N 13.32 E

DEUTSCH

Name Seite Breite°′ Länge°′ E=Ost

Altgruland 253 51.27 N 7.41 E
Altha 182 30.34 N 85.08 W
Altham 252 53.47 N 2.21 W
Alt-Hartmannsdorf 254a 52.21 N 13.50 E
Althea Lake ⊜ 273 42.40 N 71.23 W
Altheimer 184 34.19 N 91.51 W
Althofen 30 46.54 N 14.27 E
Altinho 240 8.29 S 36.04 W
Altinópolis 245 21.02 S 47.23 W
Altıntaş 120 39.04 N 30.07 E
Altiplano ⋀⋀[1] 238 18.00 S 68.00 W
Alt Käbelich 50 53.29 N 13.29 E
Altkirch 54 47.37 N 7.15 E
Altlandsberg 50 52.33 N 13.43 E
Altlangerwisch 254a 52.19 N 13.04 E
Altlewin 50 52.42 N 14.16 E
Altlüdersdorf 50 53.02 N 13.11 E
Altlünen 48 51.38 N 7.31 E
Altmannsdorf ⬥[8] 254b 48.10 N 16.20 E
Altmar 202 43.31 N 76.00 W
Altmark □[9] 50 52.40 N 11.20 E
Altmittweida 50 50.58 N 12.57 E
Altmühl ≃ 30 48.55 N 11.52 E
Altmünster 58 47.54 N 13.45 E
Alto, Mich., U.S. 206 42.51 N 85.23 W
Alto, Tex., U.S. 212 31.39 N 95.04 W
Alto, Cerro ⋀, Perú 238 6.38 S 78.15 W
Alto, Cerro ⋀, Calif., U.S. 216 35.25 N 120.43 W
Alto Anapu ≃ 240 2.15 S 51.27 W
Alto Araguaia 245 17.19 S 53.12 W
Alto Cauale 142 7.34 S 16.16 E
Alto Cedro 230p 20.31 N 75.58 W
Alto Chicapa 142 10.53 S 19.14 E
Alto Coité 245 15.47 S 54.20 W
Alto Cuito 142 13.27 S 18.49 E
Alto da Moóca ⬥[8] 277b 23.34 S 46.35 W
Alto da Serra 246 22.53 S 44.14 W
Alto del Carmen 242 28.46 S 70.30 W
Alto de Ña Paula 276c 10.24 N 66.48 W
Alto Garças 245 16.56 S 53.32 W
Alto Ligonha 144 15.30 S 38.20 E
Alto Longá 240 5.15 S 42.12 W
Alto Lucero 224 19.37 N 96.43 W
Alto Madre de Dios ≃ 238 12.17 S 70.52 W
Alto Molócuè 144 15.38 S 37.42 E
Altomünster 30 48.28 N 11.58 E
Alton, Ont., Can. 202 43.52 N 80.04 W
Alton, Eng., U.K. 44 51.09 N 0.59 W
Alton, Ill., U.S. 209 38.54 N 90.10 W
Alton, Iowa, U.S. 188 42.59 N 96.01 W
Alton, Kans., U.S. 188 39.28 N 98.57 W
Alton, Ky., U.S. 208 38.04 N 84.55 W
Alton, Mo., U.S. 184 36.42 N 91.24 W
Alton, N.H., U.S. 178 43.27 N 71.13 W
Alton, N.Y., U.S. 200 43.13 N 76.59 W
Alton, R.I., U.S. 197 41.26 N 71.43 W
Altona, Austl. 152 27.34 S 120.00 E
Altona, Austl. 159 37.52 S 144.50 E
Altona, Man., Can. 174 49.06 N 97.33 W
Altona, Ind., U.S. 206 41.21 N 85.10 W
Altona ⬥[8] 48 53.32 N 9.56 E
Altona Bay C 264b 37.53 S 144.50 E
Altona North 264b 37.50 S 144.51 E
Altona Sports Park ♠ 264b 37.52 S 144.52 E
Altoona, Ala., U.S. 184 34.02 N 86.20 W
Altoona, Fla., U.S. 210 28.58 N 81.39 W
Altoona, Iowa, U.S. 180 41.39 N 93.28 W
Altoona, Kans., U.S. 188 37.32 N 95.40 W
Altoona, Pa., U.S. 204 40.30 N 78.24 W
Altoona, Wash., U.S. 214 46.16 N 123.39 W
Altoona, Wis., U.S. 180 44.48 N 91.26 W
Alto Pacajá ≃ 240 3.07 S 50.20 W
Alto Paraguai 238 14.30 S 56.31 W
Alto Paraná □[5] 242 25.00 S 54.50 W
Alto Parnaíba 240 9.06 S 45.57 W
Alto Purus ≃ 238 9.34 S 70.36 W
Alto Rio Doce 245 21.02 S 43.25 W
Alto Río Senguerr 244 45.02 S 70.50 W
Altos 240 5.03 S 42.28 W
Alto Santo 240 5.31 S 38.15 W
Alto Sucuriu 245 19.19 S 52.47 W
Altotonga 224 19.46 N 97.14 W
Altötting 30 48.13 N 12.40 E
Alto-Uama 142 12.14 S 15.33 E
Alto Volta → Upper Volta □[1] 140 13.00 N 2.00 W
Alto Yurua ≃ 238 9.24 S 72.43 W
Altrincham 42 53.24 N 2.21 W
Altruppin 50 52.56 N 12.50 E
Altshausen 54 47.56 N 9.32 E
Alt Stahnsdorf 254a 52.17 N 13.53 E
Altstätten, Öst. 36 47.28 N 9.30 E
Altstätten, Schw. 54 47.23 N 9.33 E
Alt Töplitz 254a 52.26 N 12.55 E
Altuchovo 66 52.40 N 34.20 E
Āltūn Kūprī 118 35.45 N 44.09 E
Altunoluk 120 39.34 N 26.44 E
Altunova 120 39.13 N 26.47 E
Alturas 194 41.29 N 120.32 W
Altus, Ark., U.S. 184 35.27 N 93.46 W
Altus, Okla., U.S. 186 34.38 N 99.20 W
Altus, Lake ⊜[1] 186 34.56 N 99.18 W
Altus Air Force Base ■ 186 34.40 N 99.16 W
Altusried 54 47.48 N 10.13 E
Altyagač 74 40.50 N 48.54 E
Altyaryk 75 40.23 N 71.30 E
Altykarasu 76 49.12 N 55.52 E
Altynaj 76 57.04 N 62.00 E
Altynasar ⊥ 76 45.10 N 63.07 E
Altynkul' 75 40.48 N 72.10 E
Altynovka 68 51.27 N 33.10 E
Altyntau 76 44.08 N 68.03 E
Altyn-Topkan 75 40.38 N 69.35 E
Al-'Ubaylah 134 21.59 N 50.57 E
Al-Ubayyiḍ 130 13.11 N 30.13 E
Alubijid 106 8.35 N 124.29 E
Alucra 120 40.20 N 38.46 E
Al-'Udaysāt 130 25.35 N 32.29 E
Al-Uḍayyah 130 12.03 N 28.17 E
Aluedua 104 4.47 N 97.47 E
Aluk 130 8.26 N 27.27 E
Alūksne 66 57.25 N 27.03 E
Al-'Ulā, Ar. Sa. 118 26.37 N 37.52 E
'Alula, Som. 134 11.58 N 50.48 E
Alum Bank 204 40.14 N 78.34 W
Alum Creek Lake ⊜[1] 204 40.15 N 82.58 W
Aluminé 244 39.13 S 70.57 W
Aluminé ≃ 244 39.50 S 70.53 W
Aluminé, Lago ⊜ 242 38.55 S 71.09 W
Alum Rock 216 37.23 N 121.50 W
Alum Rock Park ♠ 272 37.24 N 121.49 W
Alunda 40 60.04 N 18.05 E
Alunitdag 74 40.32 N 46.03 E
Alupka 68 44.26 N 34.03 E
Al-'Uqaylah 136 30.16 N 19.12 E
Al-'Uqayr 118 25.39 N 50.12 E
Al-Uqṣur (Luxor) 130 25.41 N 32.39 E
Al-'Urayq •[8] 118 29.10 N 39.15 E
Al-'Urayq ⬥[1] 118 24.47 N 42.55 E
Al-Urdunn → Jordan □[1] 118 31.00 N 36.00 E
Al-Urdunn → Jordan ≃ 122 31.46 N 35.33 E
Alušta 68 44.42 N 34.24 E
Al-'Uṭayshān ⍑[4] 130 16.25 N 34.30 E
Al-'Uwayjāt ⋀[2] 132 28.25 N 30.08 E
Al-'Uwaynidhīyah ❙ 118 26.37 N 36.05 E
Al-'Uyaynah 118 24.54 N 46.23 E
Alva, Fla., U.S. 210 26.43 N 81.37 W
Alva, Okla., U.S. 186 36.48 N 98.40 W
Alva ≃ 34 40.18 N 8.15 W
Alvada 204 41.03 N 83.24 W
Alvaiázere 34 39.49 N 8.23 W
Alvaneu-bad 54 46.40 N 9.39 E
Älvängen 26 57.58 N 12.07 E
Alvanley 252 53.16 N 2.45 W
Alvarado, Méx. 224 18.46 N 95.46 W
Alvarado, Tex., U.S. 212 32.24 N 97.13 W
Alvarães 236 3.12 S 64.50 W

Symbols in the index entries represent the broad categories identified in the key at the right. Symbols with superior numbers (⋀⋀[2]) identify subcategories (see complete key on page *I* · *26*).

Kartensymbole in dem Registerverzeichnis stellen die rechts in Schlüssel erklärten Kategorien dar. Symbole mit hochgestellten Ziffern (⋀⋀[2]) bezeichnen Unterabteilungen einer Kategorie (vgl. vollständiger Schlüssel auf Seite *I* · *26*).

Los símbolos incluídos en el texto del índice representan las grandes categorias identificadas con la clave a la derecha. Los símbolos con numeros en su parte superior (⋀⋀[2]) identifican las subcategorías (véase la clave completa en la página *I* · *26*).

Les symboles de l'index représentent les catégories indiquées dans la légende à droite. Les symboles suivis d'un indice (⋀⋀[2]) représentent des sous-catégories (voir légende complète à la page *I* · *26*).

Os símbolos incluídos no texto do índice representam as grandes categorias identificadas com a chave à direita. Os símbolos com números em sua parte superior (⋀⋀[2]) identificam as subcategorias (veja-se a chave completa à página *I* · *26*).

⋀	Mountain	Berg	Montaña	Montagne	Montanha
⋀⋀	Mountains	Berge	Montañas	Montagnes	Montanhas
)(	Pass	Pass	Paso	Col	Passo
∨	Valley, Canyon	Tal, Cañon	Valle, Cañón	Vallée, Canyon	Vale, Canhão
≚	Plain	Ebene	Llano	Plaine	Planície
≻	Cape	Kap	Cabo	Cap	Cabo
❙	Island	Insel	Isla	Île	Ilha
❙❙	Islands	Inseln	Islas	Îles	Ilhas
•	Other Topographic Features	Andere Topographische Objekte	Otros Elementos Topográficos	Autres données topographiques	Outros Elementos Topográficos

SPAÑOL · FRANÇAIS · PORTUGUÊS

Nombre / Nom / Nome	Página / Page / Página	Lat.°'	Long.°' W=Oeste / W=Ouest / W=Oeste
Alvarengas, Ribeirão ≃	277b	23.45 S	46.37 W
Alvarinhos	256c	38.54 N	9.22 W
Álvaro Obregón	224	19.50 N	101.05 W
Álvaro Obregón, Presa ⊜[1]	222	27.55 N	109.52 W
Alvastra ⊥	26	58.18 N	14.39 E
Alvdal	26	62.07 N	10.39 E
Älvdalen	26	61.14 N	14.02 E
Alvear	242	29.06 S	56.33 W
Alvechurch	44	52.21 N	1.57 W
Alverca	34	38.54 N	9.02 W
Alverda	204	40.38 N	78.52 W
Alverton	204	40.08 N	79.35 W
Alvesta	26	56.54 N	14.33 E
Alveston	44	51.36 N	2.32 W
Ålvik, Nor.	26	60.26 N	6.26 E
Alvik, Sve.	26	62.25 N	17.24 E
Alvin, Ill., U.S.	206	40.19 N	87.37 W
Alvin, Tex., U.S.	212	29.25 N	95.15 W
Alvinópolis	245	20.06 S	43.03 W
Alvinston	204	42.49 N	81.52 W
◆[8]So	272	37.26 N	121.58
Alviso Slough ≃	272	37.27 N	122.02 W
Alvito, It.	60	41.41 N	13.45 E
Alvito, Port.	34	38.15 N	7.59 W
Älvkarleby	40	60.34 N	17.27 E
Älvkarleö bruk	40	60.32 N	17.24 E
Alvord	186	33.22 N	97.42 W
Alvord Desert ◆[2]	192	42.30 N	118.25 W
Alvord Lake ⊜	192	42.23 N	118.36 W
Alvordton	206	41.40 N	84.26 W
Alvra, Pass d')(	54	46.35 N	9.50 E
Älvros	26	62.03 N	14.39 E
Älvsborgs Län □[6]	26	58.00 N	12.30 E
Älvsbyn	24	65.39 N	20.59 E
Älvsnabben ⊥	40	58.59 N	18.10 E
Al-Wafā'īyah	132	30.46 N	30.36 E
Al-Wāḥāt ad-Dākhilah ⍑[4]	130	25.30 N	29.05 E
Al-Wāḥāt al-Baḥrīyah ⍑[4]	130	28.15 N	28.57 E
Al-Wāḥat al-Farāfirah ⍑[4]	130	27.15 N	28.10 E
Al-Wāḥāt al-Khārijah ⍑[4]	130	25.20 N	30.35 E
Al-Wajh	118	26.15 N	36.26 E
Al-Wakrah	118	25.10 N	51.36 E
Al-Walīdīyah	132	27.12 N	31.10 E
Alwar	114	27.34 N	76.36 E
Alwar □[5]	114	27.40 N	76.35 E
Alwar Hills ⩕[2]	114	27.20 N	76.15 E
Al-Wāṣifīyah	132	30.35 N	32.10 E
Al-Wāsiṭah	132	29.20 N	31.12 E
Alwaye	112	10.07 N	76.21 E
Al-Wazīrīyah	132	31.11 N	30.57 E
Al-Wazz	130	15.01 N	30.10 E
Alwen ≃	44	52.58 N	3.24 W
Al-Widy	132	29.31 N	31.16 E
Al-Yamāmah → As-Sulaymānīyah	118	24.09 N	47.19 E
Al-Yaman → Yemen □[1]	134	15.00 N	44.00 E
Al-Yaman ash-Sha'bīyah → Yemen, People's Democratic Republic □[1]	134	15.00 N	48.00 E
Al Yāmūn	122	32.29 N	35.14 E
Alygdžer	78	53.38 N	98.16 E
Alyn and Deeside □[8]	252	53.16 N	3.02 W
Alypsatar	76	48.03 N	80.21 E
Alytus	66	54.24 N	24.03 E
Alz ≃	58	48.10 N	12.48 E
Alzamaj	78	55.33 N	98.39 E
Alzano Lombardo	56	45.44 N	9.43 E
Al-Zarqa	132	31.13 N	31.38 E
Alzenau	52	50.05 N	9.04 E
Alzette ≃	52	49.22 N	6.09 E
Alzey	52	49.45 N	8.07 E
Amab, Khawr ∨	130	17.08 N	34.51 E
Amacuro ≃	236	8.32 N	60.28 W
Amacuzac ≃	224	17.53 N	99.12 W
Amadeus, Lake ⊜	152	24.50 S	130.45 E
Āmādi, Bngl.	116	22.28 N	89.19 E
Amadi, Sūd.	130	5.31 N	30.20 E
Amadi, Zaïre	144	3.35 N	26.47 E
Amadjuak Lake ⊜	166	65.00 N	71.00 W
Amador □[6]	216	38.21 N	120.46 W
Amadora	256c	38.45 N	9.14 W
Amador City	216	38.25 N	120.56 W
Amadores	224	22.51 N	99.43 W
Amador Valley ∨	272	37.41 N	121.51 W
Amadror, Oued ∨	138	24.55 N	6.30 E
Amagansett	197	40.58 N	72.08 W
Amagasaki	86	34.43 N	135.25 E
Amagase	86	33.15 N	131.02 E
Amager I	41	55.37 N	12.37 E
Amagi	86	33.25 N	130.39 E
Amagi-san ∧	84	34.51 N	139.00 E
Amagi-yugashima	84	34.53 N	138.56 E
Amagoi-dake ∧	84	35.01 N	136.23 E
Amagunze	140	6.20 N	7.40 E
Amaha	84	35.13 N	139.52 E
Amahai	154	3.20 S	128.55 E
Amaichá del Valle	242	26.36 S	65.55 W
Amaimon	154	5.10 S	145.25 E
Amajac ≃	224	21.15 N	98.46 W
Ama Keng	261c	1.24 N	103.42 E
Amak Island I	170	55.25 N	163.07 W
Amakusa-nada ⍑[2]	82	32.35 N	130.05 E
Amakusa-shimo-jima I	82	32.20 N	130.05 E
Amakusa-shotō II	82	32.20 N	130.15 E
Amal, Lībīya	136	29.25 N	21.10 E
Åmål, Sve.	26	59.03 N	12.42 E
Amalāpuram	112	16.35 N	82.01 E
Amalat ≃	78	54.49 N	115.12 E
Amalfi, Col.	236	6.55 N	75.04 W
Amalfi, It.	60	40.38 N	14.36 E
Amalia	148	27.16 S	25.03 E
Amaliás	38	37.49 N	21.23 E
Amalner	110	21.03 N	75.04 E
Amamaki-zan ∧	84	36.25 N	140.09 E
Amambahag Point ≻	106	11.41 N	124.32 E
Amambaí	245	23.05 S	55.13 W
Amambaí ≃	245	23.22 S	53.56 W
Amambay □[5]	242	23.00 S	56.00 W
Amambay, Cordillera de ⩕	242	23.10 S	55.30 W
Amami-Ō-shima I	83b	28.15 N	129.20 E
Amami-shotō II	83b	28.16 N	129.21 E
Amamula	144	0.18 S	27.50 E
Amana	180	41.48 N	91.52 W
Amaná ≃, Bra.	240	4.25 S	57.34 W
Amana ≃, Ven.	228	9.45 N	62.39 W
Amaná, Lago ⊜	236	2.35 S	64.40 W
Amanave	164u	14.19 S	170.49 W
Amanavení, Brazo ≃[1]	236	3.43 N	68.58 W
Amance	54	47.48 N	6.04 E
Amancey	54	47.02 N	6.05 E
Amanda	178	39.39 N	82.45 W
Amanda Park	214	47.28 N	123.54 W
Amandola	60	42.59 N	13.21 E
Amānganj	114	24.26 N	80.02 E
Amāngarh	113	34.00 N	71.55 E
Amangel'dy, S.S.S.R.	75	43.43 N	71.07 E
Amangel'dy, S.S.S.R.	76	49.52 N	59.00 E
Amangel'dy, S.S.S.R.	76	50.10 N	65.13 E
Åmänningen ⊜	40	59.57 N	15.56 E
Amano	260	34.26 N	135.33 E
Amanotkel'	76	46.07 N	61.34 E
Amantea	36	39.08 N	16.05 E
Amantogaj	76	50.22 N	65.33 E
Amanu I[1]	14	17.48 S	140.46 W
Amapá	240	2.03 N	50.48 W
Amapá □[8]	240	1.00 N	52.00 W
Amapá Grande ≃	240	2.08 N	50.42 W
Amapala	226	13.17 N	87.40 W
Amapala, Punta ≻	226	13.10 N	87.54 W
Amapari ≃	240	0.43 N	51.32 W
Amaraji	240	8.24 S	35.27 W
Amaral	277a	22.42 S	43.29 W
Amarante	240	6.14 S	42.50 W
Amarante do Maranhão	240	5.36 S	46.45 W
Amaranth	174	50.36 N	98.43 W
Amarapura	100	21.54 N	96.03 E
Amărăştii-de-Jos	38	43.59 N	24.10 E
'Amārat Abū Sinn	130	15.21 N	35.45 E
Amarāvati ≃	112	10.51 N	78.11 E
Amarda	116	21.47 N	87.08 E
Amareleja	34	38.12 N	7.14 W
Amares	34	41.38 N	8.21 W
Amarete (Charazani)	238	15.14 S	68.58 W
Amargosa	245	13.02 S	39.36 W
Amargosa ≃	194	36.13 N	116.48 W
Amargosa Range ⩕	194	36.30 N	116.45 W
Amarillo	186	35.13 N	101.49 W
Amarillo, Mar → Yellow Sea ⍑[2]	80	36.00 N	123.00 E
'Amar Jadīd	130	14.28 N	25.14 E
Amarkantak	114	22.40 N	81.45 E
Amarnāth Cave ◆[5]	113	34.13 N	75.31 E
Amaro, Monte ∧	60	42.05 N	14.05 E
Amaro Leite	245	13.58 S	49.09 W
Amaroúsion	257c	38.03 N	23.49 E
Amarpātan	114	24.19 N	80.59 E
Amarti	134	14.16 N	41.10 E
Amarume	82	38.50 N	139.55 E
Amarwāra	114	22.18 N	79.10 E
Amasa	180	46.14 N	88.27 W
Amaseno ≃	60	41.34 N	13.13 E
Amasija	74	40.58 N	43.46 E
Amasra	120	41.45 N	32.24 E
Amasya	120	40.39 N	35.51 E
Amasya □[4]	120	40.45 N	35.30 E
Amataurá	236	3.29 S	68.06 W
Amatenango de la Frontera	226	15.26 N	92.07 W
Amatignak Island I	171a	51.15 N	179.08 W
Amatikulu	148	29.06 S	31.27 E
Amatique, Bahía de C	226	15.55 N	88.45 W
Amatitán	224	20.50 N	103.43 W
Amatitlán	226	14.29 N	90.37 W
Amatitlán, Lago de ⊜	226	14.27 N	90.34 W
Amatlán de Cañas	224	20.52 N	104.27 W
Amatlán de los Reyes	224	18.50 N	96.55 W
Amatrice	60	42.38 N	13.17 E
Amatsu-kominato	84	35.07 N	140.10 E
Amau	154	10.02 S	148.34 E
Amausi	114	26.46 N	80.51 E
Amawalk	200	41.17 N	73.46 W
Amay	52	50.33 N	5.19 E
Ama-zaki ≻	84	37.08 N	136.40 E
Amazar	79	53.54 N	120.53 E
Amazhaer	79	53.25 N	122.03 E
Amazon (Solimões) (Amazonas) ≃	232	0.05 S	50.00 W
Amazonas □[3]	236	2.00 S	64.00 W
Amazonas □[5], Col.	236	1.00 S	72.00 W
Amazonas □[5], Perú	238	5.30 S	78.00 W
Amazonas □[8]	236	3.30 N	66.00 W
Amazonas → Amazon ≃	232	0.05 S	50.00 W
Amb	113	34.19 N	72.51 E
Amba Ferit ∧	134	10.53 N	38.54 E
Ambāh	114	26.43 N	78.14 E
Ambahikily	147b	21.36 S	43.41 E
Ambahita	147b	24.01 S	45.16 E
Ambaí	277a	22.43 S	43.28 W
Ambājogāi	112	18.44 N	76.23 E
Ambakaka	147b	24.10 S	46.17 E
Ambāla	114	30.21 N	76.50 E
Ambāla □[5]	114	30.20 N	77.05 E
Ambāla Airport ⊠	113	30.22 N	76.50 E
Ambalabe	147b	18.24 S	49.10 E
Ambalangoda	112	6.14 N	80.03 E
Ambalanjanakomby	147b	16.42 S	47.05 E
Ambalavao	147b	21.50 S	46.56 E
Ambalema	236	4.47 N	74.46 W
Ambam	142	2.23 N	11.17 E
Ambanja	147b	13.41 S	48.27 E
Ambar	238	10.44 S	77.16 W
Ambararata	147b	15.03 S	48.33 E
Ambarawa	105a	7.15 S	110.24 E
Ambarčik, S.S.S.R.	64	69.39 N	162.20 E
Ambarčik, S.S.S.R.	78	55.09 N	95.46 E
Ambarijeby	147b	14.56 S	47.41 E
Ambarnāth	112	19.11 N	73.10 E
Ambarnyj	24	65.56 N	33.43 E
Ambaro, Baie d' C	147b	13.23 S	48.38 E
Ambāsamudram	112	8.42 N	77.28 E
Ambassador Bridge ◆[5]	271	42.20 N	83.05 W
Ambato, Ec.	236	1.15 S	78.37 W
Ambato, Madag.	147b	13.24 S	48.29 E
Ambato Boeni	147b	16.28 S	46.43 E
Ambatofinandrahana	147b	20.33 S	46.48 E
Ambatolampy	147b	19.23 S	47.25 E
Ambatomainty	147b	17.41 S	45.40 E
Ambatomanoina	147b	18.18 S	47.37 E
Ambatondrazaka	147b	17.50 S	48.25 E
Ambatosoratra	147b	17.34 S	48.32 E
Ambeláki	257c	37.57 N	23.32 E
Ambelau, Pulau I	154	3.51 S	127.12 E
Ámbelos, Ákra ≻	38	39.56 N	23.55 E
Ambenja	147b	15.17 S	46.58 E
Amber	110	26.59 N	75.52 E
Amber ≃	44	53.02 N	1.29 W
Amberes → Antwerpen	46	51.13 N	4.25 E
Amberg, B.R.D.	30	49.27 N	11.52 E
Amberg, Wis., U.S.	180	45.30 N	88.00 W
Ambérieu-en-Bugey	54	45.57 N	5.21 E
Amberley	162	43.10 S	172.44 E
Amberley Royal Australian Air Force Base ■	161a	27.37 S	152.41 E
Amberson	204	40.10 N	77.41 W
Ambert	56	45.33 N	3.45 E
Ambevongo	147b	15.27 S	47.27 E
Ambia	206	40.30 N	87.31 W
Ambidédi	140	14.35 N	11.47 W
Ambikānagar	116	22.57 N	86.46 E
Ambikāpur	114	23.07 N	83.12 E
Ambil	106	13.49 N	120.20 E
Ambil Island I	106	13.48 N	120.18 E
Ambilobe	147b	13.12 S	49.04 E
Ambinanyndrano	147b	20.20 S	48.19 E
Ambinanytelo	147b	15.21 S	49.35 E
Ambinda	147b	16.25 S	45.52 E
Ambivy	147b	21.31 S	44.02 E
Ambjörby	26	60.30 N	13.10 E
Ambla	66	59.11 N	25.51 E
Amble	42	55.20 N	1.34 W
Amblecote	44	52.28 N	2.09 W
Ambler, Alaska, U.S.	170	67.05 N	157.52 W
Ambler, Pa., U.S.	198	40.09 N	75.13 W
Ambleside	42	54.26 N	2.58 W
Ambleteuse	46	50.49 N	1.36 E
Amblève ≃	52	50.28 N	5.36 E
Ambo	238	10.07 S	76.10 W
Amboahangy	147b	24.15 S	46.22 E
Amboasary, Madag.	147b	18.26 S	48.16 E
Amboasary, Madag.	147b	25.02 S	46.23 E
Ambodifototra	147b	16.59 S	49.52 E
Ambodilazana	147b	18.06 S	49.10 E
Ambodiriana	147b	17.55 S	49.18 E
Ambohibary	147b	19.20 S	46.17 E
Ambohidratrimo	147b	18.50 S	47.26 E
Ambohidray	147b	18.36 S	48.18 E
Ambohimahamasina	147b	21.56 S	47.11 E
Ambohimahasoa	147b	21.07 S	47.13 E
Ambohimanga du Sud	147b	20.52 S	47.36 E
Ambohimitombo	147b	20.43 S	47.26 E
Amboina → Ambon	154	3.43 S	128.12 E
Amboise	46	47.25 N	0.59 E
Amboiva	142	11.32 S	14.44 E
Ambon	154	3.43 S	128.12 E
Ambon, Pulau I	154	3.40 S	128.10 E
Ambondro	147b	25.13 S	45.44 E
Ambonnay	46	49.04 N	4.10 E
Amboseli, Lake ⊜	144	2.37 S	37.08 E
Amboshe	262c	19.09 N	73.08 E
Ambositra	147b	20.31 S	47.15 E
Ambovombe	147b	25.11 S	46.05 E
Amboy, Ill., U.S.	180	41.44 N	89.20 W
Amboy, Ind., U.S.	206	40.36 N	85.56 W
Amboy, Minn., U.S.	180	43.59 N	94.10 W
Amboy, Wash., U.S.	214	45.55 N	122.27 W
Ambre, Cap d' ≻	147b	11.57 S	49.17 E
Ambre, Montagne d' ∧	147b	12.30 S	49.10 E
Ambridge	204	40.36 N	80.14 W
Ambridge Heights	204	40.36 N	80.13 W
Ambrières	32	48.24 N	0.38 W
Ambrim I	165f	16.15 S	168.10 E
Ambriz	142	7.50 S	13.06 E
Ambrizete	142	7.14 S	12.52 E
Ambrolauri	74	42.31 N	43.09 E
Ambronay	54	46.00 N	5.21 E
Ambrose	188	48.57 N	103.29 W
Ambrose Brook ≃	266	40.33 N	74.32 W
Ambrosia Lake	190	35.26 N	107.54 W
Ambuklao Dam ◆[6]	106	16.28 N	120.45 E
Ambulong Island I	106	12.12 N	121.01 E
Ambulu	105a	8.21 S	113.36 E
Ambuntentimur	105a	6.54 S	113.45 E
Ambunti	154	4.14 S	142.50 E
Āmbūr	112	12.47 N	78.42 E
Amburambur	105b	8.15 S	116.18 E
Amburayan Nabunge ≃	106	16.55 N	120.27 E
Amby	52	50.53 N	5.44 E
Amchitka Island I	171a	51.30 N	179.00 E
Amchitka Pass ⋓	171a	51.30 N	179.30 W
'Amd	134	15.18 N	48.00 E
Am Dam	136	12.46 N	20.29 E
Āmdānga	262b	22.49 N	88.31 E
Amded, Oued ∨	138	22.09 N	3.15 E
Amden	54	47.09 N	9.11 E
Amderma	62	69.45 N	61.39 E
Ameagle	178	37.57 N	81.25 W
Ameca	224	20.33 N	104.02 W
Ameca ≃	224	20.41 N	105.18 W
Amecameca [de Juárez]	224	19.07 N	98.46 W
Ameghino	242	34.50 S	62.27 W
Ameglia	58	44.04 N	9.57 E
Ameixoeira ◆[8]	256c	38.47 N	9.10 W
Ameland I	48	53.25 N	5.45 E
Amele	154	5.16 S	145.42 E
Amelia, It.	60	42.33 N	12.25 E
Amelia, Ohio, U.S.	208	39.02 N	84.13 W
Amelia, Passo d')(	60	42.36 N	12.32 E
Amelia Court House	182	37.21 N	77.59 W
Amelia Earhart Peak ∧	216	37.47 N	119.17 W
Amelia Island I	182	30.37 N	81.27 W
Amelinghausen	48	53.08 N	10.13 E
Amelsbüren	48	51.53 N	7.37 E
Ameng	92	23.50 N	104.32 E
Amenia	200	41.51 N	73.33 W
Amenucourt	251	49.06 N	1.39 E
Amerang	58	48.00 N	12.18 E
Amerevo	255b	55.55 N	38.03 E
America	48	51.26 N	5.59 E
América del Norte → North America ◆[1]	16	45.00 N	100.00 W
América del Sur → South America ◆[1]	18	15.00 S	60.00 W
American ≃, Calif., U.S.	216	38.36 N	121.30 W
American ≃, Wash., U.S.	214	46.58 N	121.08 W
American, Middle Fork ≃	216	38.55 N	121.02 W
American, North Fork ≃	216	38.43 N	121.09 W
American, South Fork ≃	216	38.43 N	121.09 W
Americana	245	22.45 S	47.20 W
American Canyon	216	38.10 N	122.15 W
American Falls	192	42.47 N	112.51 W
American Falls ↳	274a	43.05 N	79.04 W
American Falls Reservoir ⊜[1]	192	43.00 N	113.00 W
American Fork	190	40.23 N	111.48 W
American Highland ⩕[1]	9	72.30 S	78.00 E
American Lake ⊜	214	47.07 N	122.34 W
American Museum of Natural History ⚜	266	40.47 N	73.59 W
Americano	240	1.19 S	48.04 W
American River	158b	35.47 S	137.47 E
American Samoa □[2]	14		
	165a	14.20 S	170.00 W
American Scout Seamount ✣[3]	16	46.20 N	37.40 W
American University ⚜[2]	274c	38.56 N	77.05 W
Américas, Hipódromo de las ♠	276a	19.26 N	99.13 W
Americas, University of the ⚜[2]	276a	19.23 N	99.15 W
Americus, Ga., U.S.	182	32.04 N	84.14 W
Americus, Kans., U.S.	188	38.30 N	96.16 W
Amerikanisches Hochland → American Highland ⩕[1]	9	72.30 S	78.00 E
Amerique, Sierra de ⩕	226	12.12 N	85.19 W
Amérique du Nord → North America ◆[1]	16	45.00 N	100.00 W
Amern	52	51.14 N	6.15 E
Amerongen	48	52.00 N	5.27 E
Amersfoort, Ned.	48	52.09 N	5.24 E
Amersfoort, S. Afr.	148	26.59 S	29.53 E
Amersham	44	51.40 N	0.38 W
Amery, Austl.	152	31.09 S	117.05 E
Amery, Man., Can.	174	56.34 N	94.03 W
Amery, Wis., U.S.	180	45.19 N	92.22 W
Amery Ice Shelf ⍓	9	69.30 S	72.00 E
Amerzgane	138	31.00 N	7.10 W
Ames, Iowa, U.S.	180	42.02 N	93.37 W
Ames, N.Y., U.S.	200	42.50 N	74.36 W
Ames, Tex., U.S.	212	30.03 N	94.46 W
Amesbury, Eng., U.K.	44	51.10 N	1.45 W
Amesbury, Mass., U.S.	197	42.51 N	70.56 W
Ames Long Pond ⊜	273	42.05 N	71.07 W
Ames Nowell State Park ♠	273	42.07 N	70.59 W
Ames Pond ⊜	273	42.38 N	71.13 W
Ames Research Center ⚜[3]	272	37.25 N	122.04 W
Amet Sound ⋓	176	45.47 N	63.13 W
Amfíklia	38	38.38 N	22.35 E
Amfilokhía	38	38.51 N	21.10 E
Ámfissa	38	38.31 N	22.24 E
Amfiteátrum ⊥	254c	47.35 N	19.03 E
Amfreville-la-Campagne	46	49.13 N	0.57 E
Amfreville-les-Champs	46	49.42 N	0.49 E
Amga	64	60.53 N	132.00 E
Amga ≃	64	62.38 N	134.32 E
Am Géréda	136	12.52 N	21.10 E
Amguema	170	66.58 N	179.16 W
Amguema ≃	170	68.10 N	177.40 W
Amgun' ≃	79	52.56 N	139.40 E
Amhara Plateau ⩕[1]	134	9.00 N	38.00 E
Amherst, N.S., Can.	176	45.49 N	64.14 W
Amherst, Mass., U.S.	197	42.23 N	72.31 W
Amherst, N.H., U.S.	197	42.52 N	71.38 W
Amherst, N.Y., U.S.	200	42.58 N	78.48 W
Amherst, Ohio, U.S.	204	41.24 N	82.14 W
Amherst, Tex., U.S.	186	34.01 N	102.25 W
Amherst, Va., U.S.	182	37.35 N	79.03 W
Amherst, Wis., U.S.	180	44.27 N	89.17 W
Amherst, Île I	176	47.13 N	62.57 W
Amherst, Mount ∧	152	18.11 S	126.59 E
Amherstburg	204	42.06 N	83.06 W
Amherstdale	178	37.47 N	81.49 W
Amherst Island I	202	44.08 N	76.45 W
Amherstview	202	44.13 N	76.38 W
Ami	84	36.02 N	140.14 E
Amiata, Monte ∧	60	42.53 N	11.37 E
Amidon	188	46.29 N	103.19 W
Amiens, Austl.	156	28.35 S	151.49 E
Amiens, Fr.	46	49.54 N	2.18 E
Amik Gölü ⊜	120	36.22 N	36.17 E
Amili, Bhārat	110	28.26 N	95.52 E
Amili, Zhg.	110	28.25 N	95.52 E
Amīn as-Samālūsī, Bi'r ⍑[4]	132	29.52 N	30.02 E
Amīndīvi I	112	11.07 N	72.44 E
Amīndīvi Islands II	112	11.23 N	72.23 E
Aminga	242	28.50 S	66.54 W
Amino, Nihon	86	35.41 N	135.02 E
Amino, Yai.	134	4.22 N	41.56 E
Aminuis	146	23.43 S	19.21 E
Amīrābād	118	36.04 N	54.10 E
Amirante Islands II	128	6.00 S	53.10 E
Amirauté, Îles de l' → Admiralty Islands II	154	2.10 S	147.00 E
Amīr Chāh	118	29.13 N	62.28 E
Amisk	172	52.33 N	111.04 W
Amisk Lake ⊜	174	54.35 N	102.13 W
Amistad National Recreation Area ♠	186	29.32 N	101.12 W
Amistad Reservoir (Presa de la Amistad) ⊜[1]	186	29.34 N	101.15 W
Amite	184	30.44 N	90.30 W
Amite ≃	184	30.12 N	90.35 W
Amite, East Fork ≃	184	30.58 N	90.51 W
Amiterno ⊥	60	42.21 N	13.42 E
Amitori	165d	24.18 N	123.41 E
Amity, Ark., U.S.	184	34.16 N	93.28 W
Amity, Ohio, U.S.	204	40.03 N	83.17 W
Amity, Oreg., U.S.	214	45.07 N	123.12 W
Amity Point ≻	161a	27.24 S	153.27 E
Amityville	266	40.40 N	73.25 W
Amixtlán	224	20.03 N	97.48 W
Amizmiz	138	31.14 N	8.14 W
Āmjhori ∧	116	21.51 N	86.19 E
Āmjhupi	116	23.45 N	88.42 E
Āmla, Bhārat	114	21.56 N	78.07 E
Āmla, Bngl.	116	23.54 N	88.56 E
Āmlāgora	116	22.50 N	87.20 E
Amlekhganj	114	27.17 N	84.59 E
Åmli	26	58.47 N	8.30 E
Amlia Island I	170	52.06 N	173.30 W
Amloh	114	30.37 N	76.14 E
Am Loubia	136	13.39 N	20.08 E
Amlwch	42	53.25 N	4.20 W
'Amm-Adām	130	16.22 N	36.06 E
Ammagan	75	38.56 N	67.15 E
'Ammān	122	31.57 N	35.56 E
Amman Airport ⊠	122	35.57 N	35.58 E
Ammanford	44	51.45 N	0.35 W
Ämmänsaari	26	64.53 N	28.55 E
Ammansville	212	29.47 N	96.51 W
'Ammār, Tall ∧[2]	122	32.53 N	36.29 E
Ammarnäs	24	65.56 N	16.09 E
Ammaroo	152	21.45 S	135.15 E
Ämmeberg	40	58.52 N	15.00 E
Ammeloe	48	52.05 N	6.47 E
Ammendorf ◆[8]	50	51.25 N	11.59 E
Ammer ≃	58	47.57 N	11.08 E
Ammerån ≃	26	63.09 N	16.13 E
Ammerland ◆[1]	48	53.15 N	8.00 E
Ammerman Mountain ∧	170	68.21 N	141.03 W
Ammerschwihr	54	48.07 N	7.17 E
Ammersee ⊜	58	48.00 N	11.08 E
Ammókhostos (Famagusta)	120	35.07 N	33.57 E
Ammókhostou, Kólpos C	120	35.15 N	34.10 E
Ammon	192	43.30 N	111.57 W
Ammonoosuc ≃	178	44.10 N	72.02 W
Amnān	262b	22.56 N	88.18 E
Amnat Charoen	100	15.51 N	104.38 E
Amnay ≃	106	12.58 N	120.46 E
Amne Machin Shan → Animaqingshanmai ⩕	92	34.24 N	100.10 E
Amnicon ≃	180	46.41 N	91.52 W
Amnok-kang (Yalujiang) ≃	88	39.55 N	124.22 E
Amo ≃	114	26.16 N	89.36 E
Amohe ≃	92	22.58 N	101.44 E
Āmol	118	36.23 N	52.20 E
Amolar	238	18.01 S	57.30 W
Amöneburg	52	50.48 N	8.55 E
Amora	256c	38.37 N	9.07 W
Amorbach	52	49.39 N	9.13 E
Amorgós	38	36.50 N	25.54 E
Amorgós I	38	36.50 N	25.59 E
Amorim, Morro ∧[2]	277a	23.00 S	43.26 W
Amorinópolis	245	16.36 S	51.08 W
Amorosi	60	41.12 N	14.28 E
Amory	184	33.59 N	88.29 W
Amos	180	48.35 N	78.07 W
Åmose Å ≃	41	55.35 N	11.18 E
Åmot, Nor.	26	59.35 N	8.00 E
Åmot, Nor.	26	59.54 N	9.54 E
Åmotfors	26	59.46 N	12.22 E
Amour, Djebel ⩕	138	34.00 N	2.15 E
Amoy → Xiamen	90	24.28 N	118.07 E
Amozoc	224	19.02 N	98.03 W
Ampana	102	0.51 S	121.32 E
Ampanavoana	147b	15.41 S	50.22 E
Ampang	105b	8.47 S	118.00 E
Ampanihy	147b	24.42 S	44.45 E
Ampaoid, Mount ∧	106	7.57 N	125.41 E
Amparafaravola	147b	17.35 S	48.13 E
Amparihy, Madag.	147b	16.40 S	44.49 E
Amparihy, Madag.	147b	23.57 S	47.20 E
Amparo, Bra.	246	22.42 S	46.45 W
Amparo, Cuba	276b	23.01 N	82.31 W
Ampasibe	147b	22.56 S	46.58 E
Ampasilava, Baie d' C	147b	21.16 S	43.43 E
Ampasinambo	147b	20.31 S	48.00 E
Ampasindava, Baie d' C	147b	13.16 S	48.43 E
Ampel	105a	7.27 S	110.32 E
Amper	140	9.20 N	9.43 E
Amper ≃	58	48.10 N	11.50 E
Ampezzo	58	46.25 N	12.48 E
Ampezzo, Valle d' ∨	58	46.30 N	12.10 E
Ampflwang	58	48.05 N	13.34 E
Amphion-les-Bains	54	46.23 N	6.32 E
Amphitrite Group II	98	17.00 N	112.25 E
Ampitsikinana	147b	12.57 S	49.49 E
Ampiyacu ≃	236	3.19 S	71.51 W
Ampleforth	42	54.12 N	1.06 W
Ampombiantambo	147b	12.42 S	48.57 E
Amposta	34	40.43 N	0.35 E
Ampotaka	147b	25.03 S	44.41 E
Ampoza	147b	22.20 S	44.44 E
Ampthill	44	52.02 N	0.30 W
Ampuis	56	45.29 N	4.49 E
Ampus	56	43.36 N	6.23 E
Amqui	176	49.28 N	67.26 W
Āmr, Jabal al- ⩕	122	30.45 N	34.20 E
Amraoti → Amrāvati	110	20.56 N	77.45 E
Amrāvati	110	20.56 N	77.45 E
Am-Raya	136	14.00 N	16.35 E
Amreli	110	21.37 N	71.14 E
Āmreswar	262b	22.28 N	88.34 E
Amriswil	54	47.33 N	9.18 E
Amritsar	113	31.35 N	74.53 E
Amroha	114	28.55 N	78.28 E
Amrūka	113	30.19 N	73.53 E
Amrum I	30	54.39 N	8.21 E
Am Saterna	136	12.26 N	21.25 E
Amsden	204	41.13 N	83.20 W
Åmsel	138	22.37 N	5.26 E
Åmsele	26	64.32 N	19.20 E
Am Sigan	136	11.41 N	19.51 E
Amsoldingen	54	46.43 N	7.35 E
Amsteg	54	46.46 N	8.41 E
Amstel ≃	48	52.22 N	4.54 E
Amstelmeer ⊜	48	52.52 N	4.45 E
Amstelveen	48	52.18 N	4.51 E
Amsterdam, Ned.	48	52.22 N	4.54 E
Amsterdam, S. Afr.	148	26.35 S	30.45 E
Amsterdam, N.Y., U.S.	200	42.57 N	74.11 W
Amsterdam, Ohio, U.S.	204	40.28 N	80.55 W
Amsterdam-Naturaliste Ridge ✣[3]	14	30.00 S	90.00 E
Amsterdam-Rijn-Kanaal ≅	48	51.57 N	5.20 E
Amstetten	30	48.07 N	14.53 E
Amston	197	41.38 N	72.21 W
Amta	116	22.35 N	88.01 E
Āmtala	116	23.55 N	88.27 E
Amtāli	116	22.08 N	90.14 E
Am Timan	136	11.02 N	20.17 E
Amtrak Station ◆[5]	271	42.19 N	83.04 W
Amubri	226	9.31 N	82.56 W
'Āmūdā	120	37.05 N	40.54 E
Amu-Darja	118	37.56 N	65.15 E
Amu Darya (Amudarja) ≃	62	43.40 N	59.01 E
Amugulang → Xinbaerhuzuoqi	78	48.14 N	118.18 E
Amukta Island I	170	52.29 N	171.15 W
Amukta Pass ⋓	170	52.25 N	172.00 W
Amun	165e	5.57 S	154.45 E
Amundsen Bay C	9	66.55 S	50.00 E
Amundsen Gulf C	166	71.00 N	124.00 W
Amundsen Sea ⍑[2]	9	72.30 S	112.00 W
Amungen ⊜	26	61.09 N	15.39 E
Amuntai	102	2.26 S	115.15 E
'Amūr, Wādī ∨	130	18.56 N	33.34 E
Amurang	102	1.11 N	124.35 E
Amurd	75	38.12 N	71.21 E
Amuria	144	2.01 N	33.38 E
Amurrio	34	43.04 N	3.00 W
Amursk	79	50.13 N	136.52 E
Amurskaja Oblast' □[4]	79	53.00 N	129.00 E
Amurskij Liman C	79	52.45 N	141.40 E
Amurzet	79	47.43 N	131.06 E
Amusgos	224	16.39 N	98.06 W
Amutag	106	12.23 N	123.16 E
Amuwo	263a	6.28 N	3.18 E
Amuyimusu	88	42.25 N	113.21 E
Amuzhong	110	30.33 N	84.28 E
Amvamg	142	1.45 N	10.29 E
Amvrakikós Kólpos C	38	39.00 N	21.00 E
Amvrosijevka	73	47.47 N	38.29 E
Amwom, Khawr ∨	130	7.50 N	31.13 E
Amyl ≃	76	53.47 N	92.54 E
Amyūn	120	34.18 N	35.49 E
Amz'a	70	56.13 N	54.23 E
An	100	19.47 N	94.02 E
Anaa I[1]	14	17.25 S	145.30 W
Anabanua	102	3.57 S	120.04 E
Anabar	164b	0.30 S	166.57 E
Anabar ≃	64	73.08 N	113.36 E
Anabib	142	18.08 S	12.30 E
'Anabtā	122	32.19 N	35.07 E
Anabuki	86	34.02 N	134.11 E
Anacapri	60	40.33 N	14.13 E
Anaco	236	9.27 N	64.28 W
Anacoco	184	31.15 N	93.20 W
Anacoco, Bayou ≃	184	30.52 N	93.34 W
Anaconda	192	46.08 N	112.57 W
Anaconda Range ⩕	192	45.55 N	113.30 W
Anacortes	214	48.30 N	122.37 W
Anacostia ◆[8]	274c	38.52 N	76.59 W
Anacostia ≃	274c	38.52 N	77.01 W
Anacostia, Little Paint Branch ≃	274c	39.01 N	76.56 W
Anacostia, Northeast Branch ≃	274c	38.57 N	76.57 W
Anacostia, Paint Branch ≃	274c	38.58 N	76.55 W
Anacuao, Mount ∧	106	16.16 N	121.53 E
Anadarko	186	35.04 N	98.15 W
Anadia	240	9.42 S	36.18 W
Anadolufeneri	257b	41.12 N	29.09 E
Anadoluhisarı ⊥	257b	41.04 N	29.03 E
Anadolukavaği ◆[8]	257b	41.10 N	29.05 E
Anadyr'	170	64.45 N	177.29 E
Anadyr' ≃	64	64.55 N	176.05 E
Anadyrskaja Nizmennost' ≋	170	65.30 N	176.00 E
Anadyrskij Liman C	170	64.30 N	177.45 E
Anadyrskij Zaliv C	170	64.00 N	179.00 W
Anadyrskoje Ploskogorje ⩕[1]	170	67.00 N	174.00 E
Anáfi I	38	36.21 N	25.50 E
Anagekumuhu ⊜	110	37.33 N	89.15 E
Anagni	60	41.44 N	13.09 E
'Ānah	118	34.28 N	41.56 E
Anaheim	218		
	270	33.51 N	117.57 W
Anaheim Plaza ◆[9]	270	33.51 N	117.56 W
Anaheim Stadium ♠	270	33.51 N	117.57 W
Anaheim Union Canal ≅	270	33.54 N	117.52 W
Anahi, Baie C	164x	9.45 S	138.56 W
Anahim Lake	172	52.28 N	125.18 W
Anahola	219b	22.09 N	159.19 W
Anahola Bay C	219b	22.09 N	159.18 W
Anáhuac, Méx.	186	25.48 N	97.45 W
Anahuac, Tex., U.S.	212	29.46 N	94.41 W
Anahuac, Lake ⊜	212	29.48 N	94.41 W
Ānai Mudi ∧	112	10.10 N	77.04 E
Anajás	240	0.59 S	49.57 W
Anajás ≃	240	0.31 S	50.44 W
Anajás, Ilha I	240	0.20 S	50.30 W
Anajatuba	240	3.16 S	44.37 W
Anakāpalle	112	17.41 N	83.01 E
Anaklia	74	42.24 N	41.34 E
Anaktuvuk ≃	170	69.32 N	151.30 W
Anaktuvuk Pass	170	68.10 N	151.50 W
Analalava	147b	14.38 S	47.45 E
Analamaitso, Plateau d' ⩕[1]	147b	16.15 S	48.15 E
Analapetsa	147b	25.10 S	46.42 E
Analavoka	147b	22.33 S	46.30 E
Analomink	200	41.03 N	75.13 W
Anamã	236	3.35 S	61.22 W
Anamã, Lago ⊜	236	3.32 S	61.35 W
Anama Bay	174	51.56 N	98.05 W
Anamalai	112	10.35 N	76.56 E
Ana María, Cayos II	230p	21.29 N	78.46 W
Ana María, Golfo de C	230p	21.25 N	78.40 W
Anamas Dağı ∧	120	37.47 N	31.13 E
Anambas, Kepulauan II	102	3.00 N	106.00 E
Aname	165f	20.08 S	169.47 E
Anamizu	84	37.14 N	136.54 E
Anamoose	188	47.53 N	100.15 W
Anamosa	180	42.07 N	91.17 W
Anamu ≃	240	0.56 N	57.03 W
Anamur	120	36.06 N	32.50 E
Anamur Burnu ≻	120	36.03 N	32.48 E
Anan, Nihon	84	35.19 N	137.49 E
Anan, Nihon	86	33.55 N	134.39 E
Ānand	110	22.34 N	72.56 E
Ananda	140	7.17 N	4.16 W
Anandanagar	262b	22.51 N	88.16 E
Anandapur	116	22.34 N	87.25 E
Anandpur	113	31.15 N	76.30 E
Ananindeua	240	1.22 S	48.23 W
Ananjev	68	47.40 N	29.55 E
Ananjevo	75	42.45 N	77.40 E
Anantapur	112	14.41 N	77.36 E
Anantnāg (Islāmābād)	113	33.44 N	75.09 E
Anao-aon	106	9.47 N	125.25 E
Anapa	68	44.53 N	37.19 E
Anápolis	245	16.20 S	48.58 W
Anapu ≃	240	1.53 S	50.53 W
Anār, Īrān	118	30.53 N	55.18 E
Anar, S.S.S.R.	76	50.38 N	72.27 E
Anāra	116	23.28 N	86.33 E
Anārak	118	33.20 N	53.42 E
Anarchaj	75	44.02 N	75.15 E
Anār Darreh	118	32.46 N	61.39 E
Anaš	76	54.52 N	91.00 E
Anasagasti	248	35.01 S	59.24 W
Añasco	230m	18.17 N	67.08 W
Ånäset	26	64.16 N	21.03 E
Anasofya Camii ⚜[1]	257b	41.00 N	28.58 E
Anastácio	245	21.31 S	54.08 W
Anastasia Island I	182	29.48 N	81.16 W
Anastasijevka	73	47.34 N	38.31 E
Anastasijevskaja	68	45.13 N	37.53 E
'Anātā	122	31.49 N	35.16 E
Anatahan I	98	16.22 N	145.40 E
Anatoljevka	68	46.48 N	31.13 E
Añatuya	242	28.28 S	62.50 W
Anauá ≃	236	0.58 N	61.21 W
Anaurilândia	245	22.03 S	52.45 W
Anavelona ∧	147b	22.37 S	44.10 E
Anavilhanas, Arquipélago das II	236	2.42 S	60.45 W
Anawalt	182	37.15 N	81.26 W
'Anazah, Jabal ∧	118	32.12 N	39.18 E
Anbanjing	92	23.57 N	100.55 E
Anbei, Zhg.	92	40.45 N	96.06 E
Anbei, Zhg.	92	40.49 N	108.56 E
Anbianbao	92	37.39 N	108.11 E
Anbo	88	39.51 N	122.19 E
Anbu	90	23.28 N	116.44 E
Anbyŏn	88	39.03 N	127.32 E
Ancarano	60	42.50 N	13.44 E
Ancash □[5]	238	9.30 S	77.45 W
Ancaster, Ont., Can.	202	43.12 N	80.00 W
Ancaster, Eng., U.K.	44	52.59 N	0.32 W
Ancasti	242	28.49 S	65.30 W
Ancasti, Sierra de ⩕	242	28.50 S	65.39 W
Ance ≃, Fr.	56	44.58 N	3.40 E
Ance ≃, Fr.	56	45.17 N	4.08 E
Ancenis	32	47.22 N	1.11 W
Ancerville	54	48.38 N	5.02 E
Anchang	90	30.09 N	120.30 E
Anchau	140	10.59 N	8.23 E
Anchieta ◆[8]	277a	22.49 S	43.24 W
Anch'ing → Anqing	90	30.31 N	117.02 E
Ancholme ≃	42	53.41 N	0.32 W
Anchor	206	40.34 N	88.32 W
Anchorage	170	61.13 N	149.53 W
Anchor Bay C	204	42.38 N	82.45 W
Anchor Bay Gardens	204	42.39 N	82.46 W
Anchorena	242	35.41 S	65.27 W
Anchor Point	170	59.46 N	151.52 W
Anchor Point ≻	170	59.47 N	151.52 W
Anchorville	204	42.42 N	82.41 W
Anchuras	34	39.29 N	4.50 W
Anci (Langfang)	95	39.31 N	116.41 E
Ancien Goubéré	130	5.51 N	26.46 E
Ancienne-Lorette	196	46.48 N	71.21 W
Anciferovo, S.S.S.R.	66	58.58 N	34.01 E
Anciferovo, S.S.S.R.	72	55.33 N	38.49 E
Anclitas, Cayo I	230p	20.48 N	78.54 W
Anclote ≃	210	39.59 N	88.49 W
Anclote Keys II	210	28.12 N	82.51 W
Ancón, Méx.	224	22.35 N	101.11 W
Ancón, Perú	238	11.47 S	77.11 W
Ancona, It.	60	43.38 N	13.30 E
Ancona, S. Afr.	148	27.40 S	26.32 E
Ancona □[4]	60	43.33 N	13.10 E
Ancón de Sardinas, Bahía de C	236	1.30 N	79.00 W
Ancoraimes	238	15.54 S	68.58 W
Ancram	200	42.03 N	73.38 W
Ancre ≃	46	49.54 N	2.28 E
Ancrum	42	55.31 N	2.35 W
Ancuabe	144	12.58 S	39.54 E
Ancud	244	41.52 S	73.50 W
Ancud, Golfo de C	244	42.05 S	73.00 W
Ancy-le-Franc	46	47.46 N	4.10 E
Ancy-sur-Moselle	52	49.03 N	6.04 E
Anda, Pil.	106	16.17 N	119.57 E
Anda, Zhg.	79	46.24 N	125.19 E
Andacollo, Arg.	242	37.11 S	70.41 W
Andacollo, Chile	242	30.14 S	71.06 W
Andahuaylas	238	13.39 S	73.23 W
Andaingo	147b	18.12 S	48.17 E
Andāl	114	23.36 N	87.12 E
Andalgalá	242	27.36 S	66.19 W
Åndalo	58	46.10 N	11.00 E
Åndalsnes	26	62.34 N	7.42 E
Andalucía □[9]	34	37.36 N	4.30 W
Andalusia	184	31.19 N	86.29 W
Andaman Basin ✣[1]	12	10.00 N	95.00 E
Andamanen → Andaman Islands II	100	12.30 N	92.45 E
Andaman Islands II	100	12.00 N	92.45 E
Andaman Sea ⍑[2]	100	10.00 N	95.00 E
Andamarca, Bol.	238	18.49 S	67.31 W
Andamarca, Perú	238	11.46 S	74.44 W
Andamooka	156	30.27 S	137.12 E
Andance	56	45.14 N	4.47 E
Andao I	90	22.37 N	114.57 E
Andapa	147b	14.39 S	49.39 E
Andara	142	18.03 S	21.27 E
Andaraí	245	12.48 S	41.20 W
Andaraí ◆[8]	277a	22.56 S	43.15 W
Andarax ≃	34	36.48 N	2.26 W
Andaray	238	15.49 S	72.50 W
Andechs, Kloster ⚜[1]	58	47.58 N	11.10 E
Andeer	54	46.36 N	9.26 E
Andelfingen	54	47.36 N	8.41 E
Andelle ≃	46	49.19 N	1.44 E
Andelot	54	48.15 N	5.18 E
Andelot-en-Montagne	54	46.51 N	5.56 E
Andelu	251	48.53 N	1.50 E
Anden → Andes ⩕	18	20.00 S	68.00 W
Andenes	24	69.16 N	16.08 E
Andenne	52	50.29 N	5.06 E
Andéranboukane	140	15.26 N	3.02 E
Ånderdalen Nasjonalpark ♠	24	69.14 N	17.17 E
Andere Reboucas, Túnel ◆[5]	277a	22.56 S	43.14 W
Anderlecht	46	50.50 N	4.18 E
Anderlues	46	50.24 N	4.16 E
Andermatt	54	46.38 N	8.36 E
Andernach	52	50.26 N	7.24 E
Andersen Air Force Base ■	164p	13.35 N	144.56 E
Anderslöv	41	55.26 N	13.22 E
Anderson, Ala., U.S.	184	34.50 N	87.16 W
Anderson, Alaska, U.S.	170	64.21 N	149.10 W
Anderson, Calif., U.S.	194	40.27 N	122.18 W
Anderson, Ind., U.S.	208	40.10 N	85.41 W
Anderson, Mo., U.S.	184	36.39 N	94.27 W
Anderson, S.C., U.S.	182	34.31 N	82.39 W
Anderson, Tex., U.S.	212	30.29 N	95.59 W
Anderson □[6], Ky., U.S.	208	38.05 N	84.55 W
Anderson □[6], Tex., U.S.	212	31.47 N	95.40 W
Anderson ≃	170	69.43 N	128.58 W
Anderson, Mount ∧	214	47.43 N	123.20 W

≃ River	Fluss	Río	Rivière	Rio	
≅ Canal	Kanal	Canal	Canal	Canal	
↳ Waterfall, Rapids	Wasserfall, Stromschnellen	Cascada, Rápidos	Chute d'eau, Rapides	Cascata, Rápidos	
⋓ Strait	Meeresstrasse	Estrecho	Détroit	Estreito	
C Bay, Gulf	Bucht, Golf	Bahía, Golfo	Baie, Golfe	Baía, Golfo	
⊜ Lake, Lakes	See, Seen	Lago, Lagos	Lac, Lacs	Lago, Lagos	
≋ Swamp	Sumpf	Pantano	Marais	Pântano	
⍓ Ice Features, Glacier	Eis- und Gletscherformen	Accidentes Glaciales	Formes glaciaires	Acidentes Glaciares	
⍑ Other Hydrographic Features	Andere Hydrographische Objekte	Otros Elementos Hidrográficos	Autres données hydrographiques	Outros Elementos Hidrográficos	

✣ Submarine Features	Untermeerische Objekte	Accidentes Submarinos	Formes de relief sous-marin	Acidentes Submarinos
□ Political Unit	Politische Einheit	Unidad Política	Entité politique	Unidade Política
⚜ Cultural Institution	Kulturelle Institution	Institución Cultural	Institution culturelle	Instituição Cultural
⊥ Historical Site	Historische Stätte	Sitio Histórico	Site historique	Sitio Histórico
♠ Recreational Site	Erholungs- und Ferienort	Sitio de Recreo	Centre de loisirs	Sítio de Lazer
⊠ Airport	Flughafen	Aeropuerto	Aéroport	Aeroporto
■ Military Installation	Militäranlage	Instalación Militar	Installation militaire	Instalação Militar
◆ Miscellaneous	Verschiedenes	Misceláneo	Divers	Miscelânea

Anderson Creek ≃ 184 33.18 N 94.26 W
Anderson Dam 192 43.30 N 115.30 W
Anderson Inlet C 159 38.39 S 145.48 E
Anderson Island I 214 47.10 N 122.42 W
Anderson Lake ⊜ 172 50.41 N 122.07 W
Anderson Lake ⊜[1] 216 37.11 N 121.37 W
Anderson Peak ∧ 218 34.08 N 116.53 W
Anderson Ranch Reservoir ⊜[1] 192 43.25 N 115.20 W
Andersonville 208 39.30 N 85.17 W
Anderstorp 26 57.17 N 13.38 E
Anderten 48 52.21 N 9.51 E
Anderton 252 53.17 N 2.32 W
Andes, Col. 236 5.40 N 75.53 W
Andes, N.Y., U.S. 200 42.12 N 74.47 W
Andes ⩕ 18 20.00 S 68.00 W
Andes, Lake ⊜ 188 43.11 N 98.27 W
Andeville 46 49.15 N 2.10 E
Andevoranto 147b 18.57 S 49.06 E
Andfjorden ⋓ 24 69.10 N 16.20 E
Andheri ⇾[8] 262c 19.07 N 72.51 E
Andhra Lake ⊜ 112 18.54 N 73.32 E
Andhra Pradesh □[3] 112 16.00 N 79.00 E
Andijk 48 52.45 N 5.12 E
Andijskij Chrebet ⩕ 74 42.50 N 46.25 E
Andijskoje Kojsu ≃ 74 42.47 N 46.48 E
Andikíthira I 38 35.52 N 23.18 E
Andilamena 147b 17.01 S 48.35 E
Andilangan 110 37.36 N 83.50 E
Andimákhia 38 36.48 N 27.07 E
Andīmeshk 118 32.27 N 48.21 E
Anding 95 39.38 N 116.29 E
Andingbao 92 37.58 N 107.02 E
Andinkerke 46 51.04 N 2.36 E
Andirá ≃ 240 2.45 S 56.49 W
Andirá, Riozinho do ≃ 238 9.21 S 67.31 W
Andırın 120 37.34 N 36.20 E
Andisleben 50 51.04 N 10.56 E
Ándissa 38 39.14 N 25.59 E
Andižan 75 40.45 N 72.22 E
Andižan □[4] 75 40.45 N 72.00 E
Andjeguéré 142 6.41 N 21.03 E
Andkhvoy 110 36.56 N 65.08 E
Andlau-au-Val 54 48.23 N 7.25 E
Ando 260 34.37 N 135.46 E
Andoas 236 2.50 S 76.30 W
Andoga ≃ 66 59.10 N 37.27 E
Andogskaja Gr'ada ∧ 66 59.25 N 37.30 E
Andolsheim 54 48.04 N 7.25 E
Andomskij Pogost 24 61.14 N 36.36 E
Andong, Taehan 88 36.35 N 128.44 E
Andong (Antung), Zhg. 88 40.08 N 124.20 E
Andong, Zhg. 88 39.54 N 124.09 E
Andong, Zhg. 90 30.16 N 121.13 E
Andong-ni 88 39.28 N 127.27 E
Andora 56 43.59 N 8.08 E
Andorno Micca 56 45.37 N 8.03 E
Andorra 34 42.30 N 1.31 E
Andorra □[1] 22; 34 42.30 N 1.30 E
Andorre → Andorra □[1] 34 42.30 N 1.30 E
Andover, Eng., U.K. 44 51.13 N 1.28 W
Andover, Conn., U.S. 197 41.44 N 72.23 W
Andover, Maine, U.S. 178 44.38 N 70.45 W
Andover, Mass., U.S. 197 42.39 N 71.08 W
Andover, N.J., U.S. 200 40.59 N 74.45 W
Andover, N.Y., U.S. 200 42.09 N 77.48 W
Andover, Ohio, U.S. 204 41.36 N 80.34 W
Andover, S. Dak., U.S. 188 45.25 N 97.54 W
Andowj 113 37.02 N 71.27 E
Andøya I 24 69.08 N 15.54 E
Andradas 246 22.04 S 46.34 W
Andrade Araújo 277a 22.45 S 43.26 W
Andrade Pinto 246 22.14 S 43.22 W
Andradina 245 20.54 S 51.23 W
Andramaimba, Baie C 147b 12.15 S 48.50 E
Andramasina 147b 19.11 S 47.35 E
Andranopasy 147b 21.17 S 43.44 E
Andranovory 147b 23.08 S 44.10 E
Andrate 56 45.32 N 7.53 E
Andreafsky ≃ 170 52.02 N 163.16 W
Andreafsky, East Fork ≃ 170 62.03 N 163.07 W
Andreanof Islands II 170 52.00 N 176.00 W
Andreapol' 66 56.39 N 32.15 E
Andreas 198 40.45 N 75.48 W
Andreashütte → Zawadzkie 30 50.37 N 18.29 E
André Félix, Parc National ♠ 136 9.25 N 23.20 E
Andrejevka, S.S.S.R. 68 49.32 N 36.38 E
Andrejevka, S.S.S.R. 68 47.06 N 36.35 E
Andrejevka, S.S.S.R. 70 52.19 N 51.55 E
Andrejevka, S.S.S.R. 70 55.42 N 54.23 E
Andrejevka, S.S.S.R. 72 55.07 N 38.37 E
Andrejevka, S.S.S.R. 72 55.59 N 37.08 E
Andrejevka, S.S.S.R. 73 47.28 N 37.39 E
Andrejevka, S.S.S.R. 73 48.49 N 37.33 E
Andrejevka, S.S.S.R. 76 45.50 N 80.35 E
Andrejevka, S.S.S.R. 76 52.59 N 67.23 E
Andrejevo 70 55.56 N 41.08 E
Andrejevo-Ivanovka 68 47.28 N 30.28 E
Andrejevsk 78 58.06 N 114.08 E
Andrejevskaja 70 47.21 N 43.02 E
Andrejevskoje, S.S.S.R. 72 55.46 N 36.35 E
Andrejevskoje, S.S.S.R. 72 56.24 N 39.01 E
Andrejevskoje, S.S.S.R. 72 54.23 N 36.12 E
Andrejkoviči 66 52.25 N 33.00 E
Andrelândia 246 21.44 S 44.18 W
Andrésy 251 48.59 N 2.04 E
Andrew 172 53.53 N 112.21 W
Andrew, Mount ∧ 152 32.52 S 122.56 E
Andrew Gordon Bay C 166 64.23 N 75.30 W
Andrews, Ind., U.S. 206 40.52 N 85.36 W
Andrews, Mich., U.S. 206 41.57 N 86.22 W
Andrews, N.C., U.S. 182 35.12 N 83.49 W
Andrews, S.C., U.S. 182 33.27 N 79.34 W
Andrews, Tex., U.S. 186 32.19 N 102.33 W
Andrews Air Force Base ▪ 198 38.48 N 76.52 W
Andrezel 251 48.37 N 2.49 E
Andrézieux Bouthéon 56 45.32 N 4.16 E
Andria 36 41.13 N 16.18 E
Andriamena 147b 17.26 S 47.30 E
Andriandampy 147b 22.45 S 45.41 E
Andriba 147b 17.36 S 46.55 E
Andrija, Otok I 36 43.02 N 15.45 E
Andrijevica 38 42.44 N 19.46 E
Androka 147b 25.02 S 44.05 E
Andronovskoje 66 60.39 N 34.46 E
Ándros 38 37.50 N 24.57 E
Ándros I 38 37.45 N 24.42 E
Androscoggin ≃ 178 43.55 N 69.55 W
Andros Island I 228 24.26 N 77.57 W
Androsovka 70 52.41 N 49.35 E
Andros Town 228 24.43 N 77.47 W
Androth Island I 112 10.50 N 73.41 E
Andrupene 66 56.11 N 27.23 E
Andr'ušino 76 59.12 N 62.59 E
Andrušovka 68 50.01 N 29.01 E
Andrychów 30 49.52 N 19.21 E
Anducha'nakechi ⊜ 110 32.00 N 91.15 E
Andudu 144 2.29 N 28.41 E
Andújar 34 38.03 N 4.04 W
Andulo 142 11.30 S 16.45 E
Anduo 110 32.18 N 91.04 E
Anduze 56 44.03 N 3.59 E
Andžijevskij 74 44.14 N 43.05 E
Âne, Dos d' ∧ 231o 16.19 N 61.46 W
Aneby 26 57.50 N 14.48 E
Anécho 140 6.14 N 1.36 E
Anecón Grande, Cerro ∧ 244 41.25 S 70.16 W
Anefis I-n-Darane 140 18.03 N 0.36 E
Anegada I 228 18.45 N 64.20 W
Anegada, Bahía C 244 40.15 S 62.15 W
Anegada Passage ⋓ 228 18.30 N 63.40 W
Anegam 190 32.23 N 112.02 W
Anegasaki 258 35.28 N 140.02 E
Aneityum I 165f 20.12 S 169.45 E
Anelgauhat 165f 20.14 S 169.44 E
Añelo 242 38.21 S 68.47 W
Anémata, Passe d' ⋓ 165f 20.31 S 166.12 E
Anepahan Peak ∧ 106 9.40 N 118.25 E
Aneroid 174 49.43 N 107.20 W
Anet 46 48.51 N 1.26 E
Aneta 188 47.41 N 97.59 W
Aneto, Pico de ∧ 34 42.38 N 0.40 E
Aney 136 19.24 N 12.56 E
Añez 238 17.19 S 63.43 W
Anfeng 90 32.44 N 120.24 E
Anfengqiao 90 26.41 N 118.08 E
Anfengying 92 24.59 N 102.18 E
Anfo 58 45.46 N 10.29 E
Anfu 90 27.23 N 114.37 E
Anfuzhen 97 29.21 N 105.28 E
Anga 78 53.58 N 106.12 E
Angamacutiro [de la Unión] 224 20.10 N 101.41 W
Angamos, Punta ≻ 242 23.01 S 70.32 W
Angangueo 224 19.37 N 100.18 W
Ang'angxi 79 47.09 N 123.48 E
An'ganka 79 52.18 N 126.17 E
Angao 90 33.08 N 112.22 E
Angar 154 3.39 S 130.50 E
Angara ≃ 78 58.06 N 93.00 E
Angara-Débou 140 11.19 N 3.03 E
Angarbaka 130 9.44 N 24.44 E
Āngāria 116 22.29 N 90.22 E
Angarsk 78 52.34 N 103.54 E
Angas ≃ 158b 35.23 S 138.59 E
Angas Downs 152 24.49 S 132.14 E
Angas Hills ⩕[2] 152 22.55 S 128.00 E
Angastaco 242 25.38 S 66.11 W
Angaston 158b 34.30 S 139.02 E
Angat 106 14.56 N 121.02 E
Angat ≃ 106 14.53 N 120.46 E
Angathonísi I 38 37.28 N 27.00 E
Angatuba 245 23.29 S 48.25 W
Angaul 78 53.49 N 100.18 E
Angaur I 165b 6.54 N 134.09 E
Angden Pass)(114 29.43 N 86.17 E
Angduo 92 32.20 N 98.55 E
Ånge 26 62.31 N 15.37 E
Ángel, Cerro ∧ 224 22.49 N 102.34 W
Ángel, Salto (Angel Falls) ↳ 236 5.57 N 62.30 W
Angel Albino Corzo 224 15.55 N 92.43 W
Angel City 210 28.20 N 80.10 W
Ángel de la Guarda, Isla I 222 29.20 N 113.25 W
Angeles 106 15.09 N 120.35 E
Angeles, Sierra de los ⩕ 224 23.30 N 99.33 W
Angeles National Forest ♠ 270 34.15 N 117.56 W
Angel Etcheverry 248 35.02 S 58.04 W
Angel Falls → Ángel, Salto ↳ 236 5.57 N 62.30 W
Ängelholm 41 56.15 N 12.51 E
Angelica 200 42.18 N 78.01 W
Angelim 240 8.53 S 36.17 W
Angelina □[6] 212 31.17 N 94.42 W
Angelina ≃ 184 30.53 N 94.12 W
Angelina, East Fork ≃ 212 31.50 N 94.56 W
Angel Island I 272 37.52 N 122.26 W
Angellala Creek ≃ 156 26.40 S 146.08 E
Angeln ⇾[1] 41 54.39 N 9.44 E
Angelo ≃ 152 23.43 S 117.45 E
Ängelsberg 40 59.58 N 16.00 E
Angels Camp 216 38.04 N 120.32 W
Angels Creek ≃ 216 38.01 N 120.33 W
Angelus, Lake ⊜ 271 42.41 N 83.20 W
Angemuk ∧ 154 3.30 S 138.34 E
Anger ≃ 134 9.37 N 36.06 E
Angera 56 45.46 N 8.35 E
Angerbach ≃ 253 51.23 N 6.44 E
Angerburg → Węgorzewo 30 54.14 N 21.44 E
Angereb ≃ 134 13.45 N 36.40 E
Angeren 48 51.55 N 5.58 E
Angerhausen ⇾[8] 253 51.23 N 6.44 E
Ångermanälven ≃ 26 62.48 N 17.56 E
Ångermanland □[9] 26 63.30 N 18.05 E
Angermund 253 51.20 N 6.47 E
Angermünde 50 53.01 N 14.00 E
Angern 50 52.21 N 11.44 E
Angers 32 47.28 N 0.33 W
Angerville 46 48.19 N 2.00 E
Angervilliers 251 48.36 N 2.04 E
Ängesön I 26 63.43 N 20.55 E
Angevillers 52 49.23 N 6.02 E
Anggowala, Bukit ∧ 102 4.14 S 121.43 E
Anghiari 60 43.32 N 12.03 E
Angical 245 12.00 S 44.42 W
Angical do Piauí 240 6.05 S 42.44 W
Angicos 240 5.40 S 36.36 W
Angier 182 35.31 N 78.44 W
Angijak Island I 166 65.40 N 62.15 W
Angikuni Lake ⊜ 166 62.13 N 99.50 W
Angke, Kali ≃ 259e 6.06 S 106.46 E
Angkor, Ruines d' ⊥ 100 13.26 N 103.52 E
Ângk Tasaôm 100 11.01 N 104.41 E
Anglais, Baie des C 176 49.15 N 68.07 W
Anglais, Jardin ♠ 251 48.38 N 1.49 E
Anglalinghu ⊜ 110 31.40 N 83.00 E
Angle 44 51.41 N 5.06 W
Angle Inlet 188 49.21 N 95.04 W
Anglem, Mount ∧ 162 46.44 S 167.56 E
Anglesea 159 38.25 S 144.11 E
Angleterre → England □[8] 28 52.30 N 1.30 W
Angleton 212 29.10 N 95.26 W
Anglezarke Moor ⇾[3] 252 53.40 N 2.33 W
Anglezarke Reservoir ⊜[1] 252 53.39 N 2.35 W
Angling ≃ 174 56.45 N 93.36 W
Angling Lake ⊜ 174 53.55 N 93.52 W
Anglona ⇾[1] 36 40.50 N 8.45 E
Anglo-Normandes, Îles → Channel Islands II 28 49.20 N 2.20 W
Anglure 46 48.35 N 3.49 E
Angmagssalik 166 65.36 N 37.41 W
Angmering 44 50.48 N 0.28 W
Ango 144 4.02 N 25.52 E
Angoche, Ilha I 144 16.20 S 39.50 E
Angohrān 118 26.35 N 57.54 E
Angol 242 37.48 S 72.43 W
Angola, Ind., U.S. 206 41.38 N 85.00 W
Angola, N.Y., U.S. 200 42.38 N 79.02 W
Angola □[1] 128; 142 12.30 S 18.30 E
Angola Basin ⊹[1] 10 15.00 S 2.00 E
Angola Lake Shore 204 42.37 N 79.05 W
Angono 259f 14.31 N 121.09 E
Angoon 170 57.30 N 134.35 W
Angora → Ankara 120 39.56 N 32.52 E
Angoram 154 4.04 S 144.04 E
Angostura, Méx. 222 25.22 N 108.11 W
Angostura → Ciudad Bolívar, Ven. 236 8.08 N 63.33 W
Angostura Reservoir ⊜[1] 188 43.18 N 103.27 W
Angoulême 32 45.39 N 0.09 E
Angoumois □[9] 32 45.30 N 0.05 W
Angra, Pulau I 154 2.42 S 134.50 E
Angra do Heroísmo 138a 38.39 N 27.13 W
Angra dos Reis 246 23.00 S 44.18 W
Angren, S.S.S.R. 75 41.01 N 70.12 E
Angren, Zhg. 110 29.25 N 86.40 E
Angren ≃ 75 40.48 N 68.53 E
Angri 60 40.44 N 14.34 E
Angrignon Zoological Park ♠ 265a 45.26 N 73.36 W
Angrogna 56 44.50 N 7.13 E
Ängsö 40 59.32 N 16.51 E
Ängsö Nationalpark ♠ 40 59.39 N 18.44 E
Ang Thong 100 14.35 N 100.27 E
Angu 144 3.33 N 24.28 E
Angu ≃ 246 21.48 S 42.30 W
Angualasto 242 30.03 S 69.09 W
Anguang 79 45.31 N 123.45 E
Anguchang 97 29.30 N 103.39 E
Anguilas, Arroyo ≃ 278 34.26 S 58.31 W
Anguilla 184 32.58 N 90.50 W
Anguilla □[2] 220 18.15 N 63.05 W
Anguilla □[2] 228 18.13 N 63.03 W
Anguilla I 220 18.15 N 63.05 W
Anguilla Cays II 228 23.31 N 79.33 W
Anguillara Sabazia 60 42.05 N 12.16 E
Anguillara Veneta 58 45.08 N 11.53 E
Anguille, Cape ≻ 176 47.55 N 59.25 W
Angul 110 20.51 N 85.06 E
Angumu 144 0.07 S 27.42 E
Anguo 88 38.25 N 115.19 E
Anguozhuang 95 39.44 N 117.59 E
Angus 202 44.19 N 79.53 W
Angus Place 160 33.20 S 150.06 E
Angustura 246 21.45 S 42.41 W
Angusville 174 50.44 N 101.01 W
Angwa ≃ 144 15.51 S 30.35 E
Angwin 216 38.34 N 122.26 W
Angyalföld ⇾[8] 254c 47.33 N 19.05 E
Angyō 258 35.51 N 139.46 E
An-hai, Viet. 100 15.13 N 108.56 E
Anhai, Zhg. 90 24.45 N 118.27 E
Anhandui ≃ 245 21.37 S 52.59 W
Anhangá 240 1.11 S 47.49 W
Anhanguera 245 18.19 S 48.14 W
Anholt 48 51.52 N 6.27 E
Anholt I 26 56.42 N 11.34 E
Anhovo 58 46.03 N 13.37 E
Anhua 92 28.18 N 111.14 E
Anhuai 90 33.04 N 117.50 E
Anhui □[4] 90 32.00 N 117.00 E
Anhŭng 88 36.41 N 126.10 E
Anhwei → Anhui □[4] 90 32.00 N 117.00 E
Aniak 170 61.35 N 159.33 W
Aniak ≃ 170 61.34 N 159.30 W
Anibare Bay C 164b 0.32 S 166.57 E
Aniche 46 50.20 N 3.15 E
Anichovka 76 51.29 N 60.15 E
Anicuns 245 16.28 S 49.58 W
Anié 140 7.45 N 1.12 E
Anié ≃ 140 7.40 N 1.18 E
Anie, Pic d' ∧ 32 42.57 N 0.43 W
Aniene ≃ 60 41.56 N 12.30 E
Anif 58 47.45 N 13.04 E
Anik ⇾[8] 262c 19.02 N 72.53 E
Anikino, S.S.S.R. 76 56.32 N 73.56 E
Anikino, S.S.S.R. 78 53.26 N 120.20 E
Anikovo 66 59.23 N 43.45 E
Anil 240 2.32 S 44.14 W
Anil, Rio do ≃ 277a 22.59 S 43.21 W
Animaqingshanmai (Jishishan) ⩕ 92 34.24 N 100.10 E
Animas 190 31.57 N 108.48 W
Animas ≃ 190 36.43 N 108.13 W
Ánimas, Cerro de las ∧ 242 34.46 S 55.19 W
Animas Peak ∧ 190 31.35 N 108.47 W
Animas Valley ∨ 190 32.05 N 108.50 W
Anin 100 15.40 N 97.46 E
Anina 38 45.05 N 21.51 E
Anipaj 164r 6.50 N 158.19 E
Anipemza 74 40.27 N 43.37 E
Anipen 164r 6.49 N 158.14 E
Aniskino 72 55.54 N 38.06 E
Añisoc 142 1.51 N 10.46 E
Anita, Iowa, U.S. 188 41.27 N 94.46 W
Anita, Pa., U.S. 204 41.00 N 78.58 W
Aniva 79 46.43 N 142.32 E
Aniva, Mys ≻ 79 46.01 N 143.25 E
Aniva, Zaliv C 79 46.16 N 142.48 E
Anivorano 147b 18.44 S 48.58 E
Anivorano Nord 147b 12.44 S 49.13 E
Aniwa I 165f 19.17 S 169.35 E
Anizy-le-Château 46 49.30 N 3.27 E
Anjad 110 22.02 N 75.03 E
Anjan 26 63.41 N 12.49 E
Anjangaon 110 21.10 N 77.18 E
Anjār 110 23.08 N 70.01 E
'Anjarah 122 32.18 N 35.45 E
Anjavimihavana 147b 12.32 S 49.16 E
Anji 96 30.45 N 119.41 E
Anjiabe 147b 12.07 S 49.20 E
Anjiang, Zhg. 92 27.11 N 110.04 E
Anjiang, Zhg. 95 40.45 N 117.38 E
Anjigami Lake ⊜ 180 47.51 N 84.34 W
Anjō 84 34.57 N 137.05 E
Anjou 196 45.36 N 73.33 W
Anjou □[9] 32 47.20 N 0.30 W
Anjouan I 147a 12.15 S 44.25 E
Anjozorobe 147b 18.24 S 47.52 E
Anju 88 39.36 N 125.40 E
Anjuba 97 30.21 N 105.27 E
Anjudin 24 62.33 N 58.12 E
Anjuzhen 97 29.59 N 106.02 E
Anka 140 12.07 N 5.55 E
Ankang 92 32.31 N 109.19 E
Ankara 120 39.56 N 32.52 E
Ankara □[4] 120 39.50 N 32.50 E
Ankara ≃ 120 39.51 N 31.55 E
Ankaramena 147b 21.57 S 46.39 E
Ankaratra ⩕ 147b 19.25 S 47.12 E
Ankarimbelo 147b 22.08 S 47.20 E
Ankaroaka ∧ 147b 17.48 S 48.32 E
Ankarsrum 26 57.42 N 16.19 E
Ankasakasa 147b 16.21 S 44.52 E
Ankata 70 50.44 N 51.34 E
Ankavandra 147b 18.46 S 45.18 E
Ankazoabo 147b 22.18 S 44.31 E
Ankazobe 147b 18.21 S 47.07 E
Ankazomiriotra 147b 19.38 S 46.32 E
Ankeny 180 41.44 N 93.36 W
Ankhor 134 10.47 N 46.17 E
Ankiabe 147b 13.13 S 48.56 E
Ankilimalinika 147b 22.58 S 43.45 E
Ankilizato 147b 20.25 S 45.01 E
Anking → Anqing 90 30.31 N 117.02 E
Ankisabe 147b 19.17 S 46.29 E
Anklam 50 53.51 N 13.41 E
Anklesvar 110 21.36 N 73.00 E
Ankober 134 9.30 N 39.44 E
Ankole □[5] 144 0.30 S 30.30 E
Ankoro 144 6.45 S 26.57 E
Ankororoka 147b 25.30 S 45.11 E
Ankou 90 25.03 N 113.24 E
An'kovo 70 56.57 N 39.57 E
Ankpa 140 7.23 N 7.37 E
Ankum 48 52.32 N 7.52 E
Anlaby 42 53.45 N 0.27 W
Anlinhu ⊜ 88 41.13 N 114.32 E
Anlinnuoer 88 41.11 N 114.31 E
Anliu 90 23.42 N 115.42 E
An-loc 100 11.39 N 106.36 E
Anloga 140 5.47 N 0.50 E
Anlong 92 25.02 N 105.31 E
Ânlóng Vêng 100 14.14 N 104.05 E
Anlu 90 31.17 N 113.40 E
Ann ⊜ 26 63.16 N 12.34 E
Ann, Cape ≻, Ant. 9 66.10 S 51.22 E
Ann, Cape ≻, Mass., U.S. 273 42.39 N 70.38 W
Anna, S.S.S.R. 68 51.29 N 40.25 E
Anna, Ill., U.S. 184 37.28 N 89.15 W
Anna, Ohio, U.S. 206 40.24 N 84.10 W
Anna, Tex., U.S. 186 33.21 N 96.33 W
Anna, Lake ⊜[1] 178 38.04 N 77.45 W
Annaba (Bône) 138 36.54 N 7.46 E
Annaba □[5] 138 35.35 N 8.00 E
An-Nabaṭīyah at-Taḥtā 122 33.23 N 35.29 E
Annaberg 58 47.31 N 13.26 E
Annaberg-Buchholz 50 50.35 N 13.00 E
An-Nabī Shīt 122 33.52 N 36.07 E
An-Nabk 120 34.01 N 36.44 E
An-Nabqīyah I 118 26.44 N 36.01 E
Annaburg 50 51.44 N 13.03 E
Annaburger Heide ⇾[3] 50 51.40 N 13.05 E
Anna Creek 156 28.51 S 136.08 E
An-Nafī 118 24.57 N 43.42 E
An-Nafūd ⇾[2] 118 28.30 N 41.00 E
Annagassan 42 53.53 N 6.20 W
Annahütte 50 51.34 N 13.53 E
An-Najaf 118 31.59 N 44.20 E
Annaka 84 36.19 N 138.54 E
An-Nakhl, Miṣr 130 29.55 N 33.45 E
An-Nakhl, Sūrīy. 122 33.00 N 36.07 E
Annalee ≃ 28 54.03 N 7.24 W
Annalee Heights 198 38.52 N 77.11 W
Anna Maria 210 27.32 N 82.44 W
Anna Maria Island I 210 27.30 N 82.43 W
An-Nāmir 122 32.47 N 36.13 E
Annan 42 54.59 N 3.16 W
Annan ≃ 42 54.59 N 3.16 W
Annanberg 154 4.55 S 144.40 E
Annandale, Austl. 156 21.57 S 148.22 E
Annandale, Minn., U.S. 180 45.16 N 94.08 W
Annandale, N.J., U.S. 200 40.39 N 74.53 W
Annandale, Va., U.S. 198 38.50 N 77.12 W
Annandale ∨ 42 55.10 N 3.25 W
Annandale-on-Hudson 200 42.01 N 73.54 W
Anna Pink, Bahía C 244 45.50 S 74.50 W
Anna Plains 152 19.17 S 121.37 E
Anna Point ≻ 164b 0.30 S 166.56 E
Annapolis 198 38.59 N 76.30 W
Annapolis Basin C 176 44.39 N 65.42 W
Annapolis Royal 176 44.45 N 65.31 W
Annapurna ∧ 114 28.34 N 83.50 E
An-Naqīrah ⊤[4] 118 27.53 N 48.15 E
An-Nāqūrah 122 33.07 N 35.08 E
Ann Arbor 206 42.18 N 83.45 W
Ann Arbor Municipal Airport ⊠ 271 42.14 N 83.45 W
Annaricken Brook ≃ 275 40.03 N 74.42 W
An-Narrānīyah 263c 29.58 N 31.10 E
An-Nāṣirīyah, 'Irāq 118 31.02 N 46.16 E
An-Nāṣirīyah, Sūrīy. 120 33.52 N 36.49 E
An-Nāṣirīyah □[4] 118 31.00 N 46.15 E
An-Nawfalāb 130 15.52 N 32.32 E
An-Nawfalīyah 136 30.47 N 17.50 E
An-Nazlah 122 31.32 N 34.29 E
An-Nazlat 132 29.19 N 30.39 E
Annean, Lake ⊜ 152 26.54 S 118.14 E
Anne Arundel □[6] 198 38.59 N 76.30 W
Annebault 46 49.15 N 0.04 E
Annecy 54 45.54 N 6.07 E
Annecy, Lac d' ⊜ 54 45.51 N 6.11 E
Annecy-le-Vieux 54 45.55 N 6.09 E
Annemasse 54 46.12 N 6.15 E
Annen ⇾[8] 253 51.27 N 7.22 E
Annenkov Island I 234 54.29 S 37.05 W
Annenskij Most 66 60.45 N 37.10 E
Annenskoje 76 53.08 N 60.26 E
Annet-sur-Marne 251 48.56 N 2.43 E
Annette 170 55.03 N 131.34 W
Annette Island I 170 55.10 N 131.28 W
Annevoie-Rouillon 52 50.21 N 4.50 E
Annezin 46 50.32 N 2.37 E
Annfield Plain 42 54.51 N 1.45 W
An-nhon 100 13.53 N 109.06 E
Anniangniang 79 51.33 N 125.49 E
Annicco 56 45.14 N 9.52 E
Annieopsquotch Mountains ⩕ 176 48.20 N 57.30 W
An-Nīl al-Azraq □[4] 130 13.00 N 33.00 E
Anningdu 92 36.56 N 104.31 E
Anninger ∧ 254b 48.03 N 16.15 E
Annino 255a 59.46 N 30.03 E
Anninskije Mineral'nyje Vody 79 52.44 N 140.12 E
Annisquam 273 42.39 N 70.41 W
Annisquam ≃ 273 42.39 N 70.41 W
Anniston 184 33.40 N 85.50 W
Annobón → Pagalu I 128 1.25 S 5.36 E
Annonay 56 45.14 N 4.40 E
Annopol 30 50.54 N 21.52 E
Anno-Rebrikovo 73 49.36 N 40.12 E
Annot 56 43.58 N 6.40 E
Annotto Bay 231q 18.16 N 76.46 W
Annsjön ⊜ 40 58.48 N 15.26 E
An-Nubayrah 132 30.54 N 30.35 E
An-Nuhūd 130 12.42 N 28.26 E
An-Nu'mān I 118 27.08 N 35.46 E
An-Nuwayrah 132 29.06 N 30.59 E
Ann'val'kal', Mys ≻ 170 65.36 N 180.40 E
Annville, Ky., U.S. 182 37.19 N 83.58 W
Annville, Pa., U.S. 198 40.19 N 76.31 W
Annweiler am Trifels 52 49.12 N 7.58 E
Anō 84 34.46 N 136.27 E
Anoka 180 45.11 N 93.23 W
Anole 134 2.01 N 42.20 E
Áno Liósia 257c 38.05 N 23.42 E
Año Nuevo Bay C 216 37.07 N 122.19 W
Anopino 70 55.42 N 40.40 E
Anori, Bra. 236 3.47 S 61.38 W
Anorí, Col. 236 7.05 N 75.08 W
Anorotsangana 147b 13.56 S 47.55 E
Anosibe 147b 19.26 S 48.13 E
Anotaie ≃ 240 3.29 N 52.04 W
Anpilogovo 68 51.47 N 36.01 E
Anping, Zhg. 88 38.16 N 115.30 E
Anping, Zhg. 95 39.43 N 116.53 E
Anpingji 88 34.01 N 115.07 E
Anpingsi 90 26.33 N 113.22 E
Anpu 92 21.27 N 110.00 E
'Anqābīyah, Jabal al- ∧[2] 132 30.01 N 31.37 E
Anqing 90 30.31 N 117.02 E
Anqiu 88 36.25 N 119.10 E
Anrath 52 51.17 N 6.28 E
Anren, Zhg. 90 28.04 N 119.20 E
Anren, Zhg. 90 26.42 N 113.16 E
Anren, Zhg. 97 30.31 N 103.38 E
Anrenzhen 79 43.04 N 125.03 E
Anröchte 48 51.33 N 8.19 E
Ans, Bel. 52 50.39 N 5.32 E
Ans, Dan. 41 56.19 N 9.36 E
Anṣāb, Ar. Sa. 118 29.11 N 44.43 E
Anṣāb, Yam. S. 134 14.31 N 46.30 E
Ansager 41 55.42 N 8.45 E
Ansai 92 36.54 N 109.10 E
Anṣār 122 33.23 N 35.21 E
Ansbach 52 49.17 N 10.34 E
Anschan → Anshan 94 41.08 N 122.59 E
Anschlag 253 51.10 N 7.29 E
Anse 54 45.56 N 4.43 E
Anseba ≃ 134 16.00 N 38.30 E
Anse-Bertrand 231o 16.29 N 61.31 W
Anse-d'Hainault 228 18.30 N 74.27 W
Anse La Raye 231f 13.57 N 61.03 W
Anselmo 188 41.37 N 99.52 W
Anseremme 52 50.15 N 4.54 E
Anserma 236 5.13 N 75.48 W
Ansermanuevo 236 4.48 N 75.59 W
Ansha 90 26.04 N 117.04 E
Anshan 94 41.08 N 122.59 E
Anshanhu ⊜ 90 32.57 N 118.03 E
Anshun 92 26.19 N 105.50 E
Ansina 242 31.54 S 55.28 W
Ansley 188 41.18 N 99.23 W
Anson 186 32.45 N 99.54 W
Anson Bay C, Austl. 154 13.20 S 130.06 E

ENGLISH

Name	Page	Lat. °′	Long. °′

Anson Bay C, Norf. I. 164c 29.01 S 167.55 E
Anson Creek ≃ 202 44.53 N 79.03 W
Ansŏng 88 37.02 N 127.16 E
Ansongo 140 15.40 N 0.30 E
Ansonia, Conn., U.S. 197 41.20 N 73.05 W
Ansonia, Ohio, U.S. 206 40.13 N 84.38 W
Anson Lake ⊜ 174 56.45 N 100.47 W
Ansonville, N.C., U.S. 182 35.06 N 80.07 W
Ansonville, Pa., U.S. 204 40.51 N 78.34 W
Ansouis 56 43.44 N 5.28 E
Anspach 52 50.17 N 8.29 E
Ansted 178 38.08 N 81.06 W
Anstey 44 52.40 N 1.11 W
Anstruther Lake ⊜ 202 44.45 N 78.12 W
Ansudu 154 2.08 S 139.20 E
Ansus 154 1.44 S 135.49 E
Anta, Bra. 246 22.03 S 42.59 W
Anta, Perú 238 13.29 S 72.09 W
Anta, Cachoeira ↳ 245 13.06 S 48.09 W
Anta, Cachoeira da ↳ 238 7.29 S 61.51 W
Antabamba 238 14.19 S 72.55 W
Antakya (Antioch) 120 36.14 N 36.07 E
Antalaha 147b 14.53 S 50.16 E
Antalieptė 66 55.40 N 25.51 E
Antalovcy 68 48.38 N 22.31 E
Antalya 120 36.53 N 30.42 E
Antalya □[4] 120 37.00 N 31.00 E
Antalya, Gulf of → Antalya Körfezi C 120 36.30 N 31.00 E
Antalya Körfezi C 120 36.30 N 31.00 E
Antambohobe 147b 22.20 S 46.47 E
An-tan 100 15.26 N 108.39 E
Antanambao Manampotsy 147b 19.29 S 48.34 E
Antanambe 147b 16.26 S 49.52 E
Antananarivo 147b 18.55 S 47.31 E
Antanetibe 147b 18.27 S 46.42 E
Antanifotsy 147b 19.39 S 47.19 E
Antanimora 147b 24.49 S 45.40 E
Antar, Djebel ∧ 138 31.57 N 1.56 W
Antarctica ●[1] 9 90.00 S 0.00
Antarctic Peninsula ≻[1] 9 69.30 S 65.00 W
Antarctique, Péninsule → Antarctic Peninsula ≻[1] 9 69.30 S 65.00 W
Antarctiques territoires britanniques → British Antarctic Territory □[2] 9 60.00 S 45.00 W
Antarktis → Antarctica ●[1] 9 90.00 S 0.00
Antártica, Península → Antarctic Peninsula ≻[1] 9 69.30 S 65.00 W
Antas 240 10.23 S 38.20 W
Antas, Ribeirão das ≃ 246 21.47 S 46.36 W
Antas, Rio das ≃ 242 29.04 S 51.21 W
Antegnate 56 45.29 N 9.47 E
Antela, Laguna de ⊜ 34 42.07 N 7.41 W
Antelope Acres 218 34.44 N 118.19 W
Antelope Creek ≃, Nev., U.S. 194 40.00 N 117.24 W
Antelope Creek ≃, Oreg., U.S. 192 42.28 N 117.13 W
Antelope Creek ≃, S. Dak., U.S. 188 45.19 N 102.27 W
Antelope Creek ≃, Wyo., U.S. 188 43.29 N 105.23 W
Antelope Island I 192 40.57 N 112.12 W
Antelope Mine 144 21.02 S 28.27 E
Antelope Peak ∧ 194 41.19 N 114.58 W
Antelope Reservoir ⊜[1] 192 42.54 N 117.13 W
Antelope Valley ∨ 218 34.45 N 118.20 W
Antelope Wash ∨ 194 39.33 N 116.17 W
Antenor Navarro 240 6.44 S 38.27 W
Antequera, Bol. 238 18.29 S 66.53 W
Antequera, Esp. 34 37.01 N 4.33 W
Antequera, Para. 242 24.08 S 57.07 W
Antero Reservoir ⊜[1] 190 39.00 N 105.55 W
Anterselva, Lago d' ⊜ 58 46.53 N 12.10 E
Anterselva di Sopra 58 46.52 N 12.08 E
Antes Fort 200 41.12 N 77.14 W
Antetikireja 147b 14.42 S 47.29 E
Antevamena 147b 21.02 S 44.08 E
Antey-Saint-André 56 45.48 N 7.36 E
Anthéor 56 43.26 N 6.53 E
Anthon 188 42.23 N 95.52 W
Anthony, Fla., U.S. 182 29.18 N 82.07 W
Anthony, Kans., U.S. 188 37.09 N 98.02 W
Anthony, R.I., U.S. 197 41.42 N 71.32 W
Anthony Chabot Regional Park ♠ 272 37.45 N 122.06 W
Anthony Creek ≃ 178 37.54 N 80.20 W
Anthony Lagoon 152 17.59 S 135.32 E
Anthony Peak ∧ 194 39.51 N 122.58 W
Anti Atlas ⩕ 138 30.00 N 8.30 W
Antibes 56 43.35 N 7.07 E
Antibes, Cap d' ≻ 56 43.32 N 7.07 E
Anticosti, Île d' I 176 49.30 N 63.00 W
Antietam Creek, West Branch ≃ 198 39.41 N 77.37 W
Antietam National Battlefield Site ⊥ 178 39.24 N 77.47 W
Antifer, Cap d' ≻ 46 49.41 N 0.10 E
Antignano 60 43.30 N 10.19 E
Antigo 180 45.09 N 89.09 W
Antigonish 176 45.35 N 61.55 W
Antigorio, Valle ∨ 54 46.18 N 8.20 E
Antigua □[1] 220; 230c 17.03 N 61.48 W
Antigua Guatemala 226 14.34 N 90.44 W
Antigues, Pointe d' ≻ 231o 16.26 N 61.33 W
Antiguo Morelos 224 22.33 N 99.05 W
Anti-Lebanon → Al-Jabal ash-Sharqī ⩕ 122 33.35 N 36.00 E
Antilla, Arg. 242 26.07 S 64.36 W
Antilla, Cuba 230p 20.50 N 75.45 W
Antillas Holandesas → Netherlands Antilles □[2] 231s 12.15 N 69.00 W
Antilles hollandaise → Netherlands Antilles □[2] 231s 12.15 N 69.00 W
Antilyās 122 33.55 N 35.35 E
Antímano ⇾[8] 276c 10.28 N 66.59 W
Antimari ≃ 238 9.04 S 67.23 W
Antimony 190 38.07 N 111.55 W
Anting 96 31.18 N 121.09 E
Antioch → Antakya, Tür. 120 36.14 N 36.07 E
Antioch, Calif., U.S. 216 38.01 N 121.49 W
Antioch, Ill., U.S. 206 42.29 N 88.06 W
Antioquia 236 6.33 N 75.50 W
Antioquia □[5] 236 7.00 N 75.30 W
Antipino, S.S.S.R. 66 55.55 N 33.16 E
Antipino, S.S.S.R. 76 59.01 N 55.10 E
Antipino, S.S.S.R. 76 57.49 N 66.34 E
Antipodes Islands II 9 49.40 S 178.47 E
Antipolo 106 14.35 N 121.10 E
Antipovka 70 49.50 N 45.20 E
Antique □[4] 106 11.00 N 121.45 E
Antisana ≃ 236 0.59 S 78.01 W
Antler ≃ 174 49.08 N 101.00 W
Antlers 186 34.14 N 95.37 W
Antoetra 147b 20.46 S 47.20 E
Antofagasta 242 23.39 S 70.24 W
Antofagasta □[4] 242 23.30 S 69.00 W
Antofagasta de la Sierra 242 26.04 S 67.25 W
Antofalla, Salar de ≚ 242 25.44 S 67.45 W

DEUTSCH

Name	Seite	Breite °′	Länge ° E=Ost

Antofalla, Volcán ∧[1] 242 25.34 S 67.55 W
Antoing 46 50.34 N 3.27 E
Antolana ∧ 147b 17.04 S 48.09 E
Antón, Pan. 226 8.24 N 80.16 W
Anton, Tex., U.S. 186 33.49 N 102.10 W
Anton Chico 190 35.12 N 105.09 W
Antongil, Baie d' C 147b 15.45 S 49.50 E
Antonia 209 38.20 N 90.29 W
Antonibe 147b 15.07 S 47.24 E
Antonina 242 25.27 S 48.43 W
Antonina do Norte 240 6.43 S 39.58 W
Antoniny 68 49.49 N 26.52 E
Antonio Amaro 222 24.16 N 104.01 W
Antônio Bezerra 240 3.44 S 38.35 W
Antônio Carlos 246 21.19 S 43.45 W
Antonio de Biedma 244 47.29 S 66.30 W
Antônio Diogo 240 4.18 S 38.45 W
António Enes 144 16.14 S 39.58 E
Antonio Escobedo 224 20.46 N 103.57 W
Antônio João 245 23.15 S 55.31 W
Antônio Lemos 240 1.22 S 50.50 W
Antônio Prado 242 28.51 S 51.17 W
Antonio Varas, Península ≻[1] 244 51.40 S 72.55 W
Antonito 190 37.05 N 106.00 W
Antón Lizardo, Punta de ≻ 224 19.03 N 95.58 W
Antonov 68 49.37 N 29.47 E
Antonovka, S.S.S.R. 70 54.55 N 49.30 E
Antonovka, S.S.S.R. 76 45.38 N 80.15 E
Antonovka, S.S.S.R. 76 53.19 N 68.26 E
Antonovo 70 49.23 N 51.47 E
Antony 46 48.45 N 2.18 E
Antopol' 66 52.12 N 24.47 E
Antou 90 26.07 N 118.11 E
Antracit 73 48.06 N 39.06 E
Antraigues 56 44.43 N 4.21 E
Antrain 32 48.27 N 1.29 W
Antratsit → Antracit 73 48.06 N 39.06 E
Antrift ≃ 52 50.54 N 9.15 E
Antrim, N. Ire., U.K. 42 54.43 N 6.13 W
Antrim, Ohio, U.S. 204 40.06 N 81.23 W
Antrim, Pa., U.S. 200 41.37 N 77.18 W
Antrodoco 60 42.25 N 13.05 E
Antronapiana 54 46.03 N 8.07 E
Antropovo, S.S.S.R. 70 58.26 N 43.00 E
Antropovo, S.S.S.R. 72 55.15 N 37.39 E
Antsahe 147a 12.21 S 44.32 E
Antsakabary 147b 15.03 S 48.56 E
Antsalova 147b 18.40 S 44.37 E
Antsenavolo 147b 21.24 S 48.03 E
Antsiafabositra 147b 17.18 S 46.57 E
Antsirabe, Madag. 147b 19.51 S 47.02 E
Antsirabe, Madag. 147b 14.00 S 49.59 E
Antsirabe, Madag. 147b 15.57 S 48.58 E
Antsirane → Diégo-Suarez 147b 12.16 S 49.17 E
Antsla 66 57.50 N 26.32 E
Antsohihy 147b 14.52 S 47.59 E
Anttis 24 67.16 N 22.52 E
Antu 79 43.07 N 128.54 E
An-tuc (An-khe) 100 13.57 N 108.39 E
Antūfash, Jazīrat I 134 15.45 N 42.22 E
Antun' 79 47.36 N 135.46 E
Antung → Andong 88 40.08 N 124.20 E
Antuševo, S.S.S.R. 66 59.59 N 42.18 E
Antuševo, S.S.S.R. 66 59.54 N 37.40 E
Antwerp → Antwerpen, Bel. 46 51.13 N 4.25 E
Antwerp, S. Afr. 263d 26.06 S 28.10 E
Antwerp, N.Y., U.S. 202 44.12 N 75.37 W
Antwerp, Ohio, U.S. 206 41.11 N 84.45 W
Antwerpen (Anvers) 46 51.13 N 4.25 E
Antwerpen □[4] 52 51.10 N 4.50 E
Antykan 79 54.55 N 135.12 E
An Uaimh → Navan 28 53.39 N 6.41 W
Anučino, S.S.S.R. 70 52.58 N 43.52 E
Anučino, S.S.S.R. 79 43.58 N 133.02 E
Añueque, Sierra ⩕ 244 41.52 S 69.15 W
Anŭi 88 35.38 N 127.48 E
An'uj ≃ 79 49.18 N 136.27 E
An'ujsk 64 68.18 N 161.38 E
Anujskij Chrebet ⩕ 76 51.30 N 84.55 E
Anundshögen ⊥ 40 59.25 N 16.32 E
Anūpgarh 113 29.11 N 73.13 E
Anūpshahr 114 28.22 N 78.16 E
Ānūr 116 22.55 N 87.39 E
Anuradhapura 112 8.21 N 80.23 E
Anvers → Antwerpen 46 51.13 N 4.25 E
Anversa degli Abruzzi 60 41.59 N 13.48 E
Anvers Island I 9 64.33 S 63.35 W
Anvik 170 62.40 N 160.12 W
Anvik ≃ 170 62.39 N 160.14 W
Anvil Peak ∧ 171a 52.00 N 179.35 E
Anvil Range ⩕ 170 62.30 N 133.50 W
Anvin 46 50.27 N 2.15 E
Anxi, Zhg. 90 25.06 N 118.12 E
Anxi, Zhg. 92 40.32 N 95.51 E
Anxi, Zhg. 96 30.25 N 120.01 E
Anxian 92 31.40 N 104.32 E
Anxiang 92 29.23 N 112.09 E
Anxin 95 38.55 N 115.55 E
Anxing 96 31.24 N 119.06 E
Anxious Bay C 152 33.25 S 134.35 E
Anxiwei 90 25.15 N 115.06 E
Anyama 140 5.30 N 4.03 W
Anyang 88 36.06 N 114.21 E
Anyanghe ≃ 88 36.01 N 114.46 E
Anyeke 144 2.24 N 32.31 E
Anyer-kidul 105a 6.04 S 105.53 E
Anyi 90 28.50 N 115.31 E
Anykščiai 66 55.32 N 25.06 E
Anysberg 148 33.31 S 20.46 E
Anyuan, Zhg. 90 25.08 N 115.28 E
Anyuan, Zhg. 90 26.36 N 116.38 E
Anyuan, Zhg. 90 27.37 N 113.54 E
Anyuanyi → Tianzhu 92 37.14 N 102.59 E
Anyue 97 30.06 N 105.21 E
Anza ≃ 54 46.00 N 8.17 E
Anza-Borrego Desert State Park ♠ 194 33.00 N 116.26 W
Anzac 174 56.27 N 111.02 W
Anzaldo 238 17.50 S 65.55 W
Anzano di Puglia 60 41.07 N 15.17 E
Anzbari ∧ 113 34.40 N 74.50 E
Anze 92 36.10 N 112.10 E
Anžero-Sudženšk 76 56.07 N 86.00 E
Anzhen 96 31.36 N 120.28 E
Anzhou 95 38.52 N 115.49 E
Anzhuang 96 31.04 N 121.01 E
Anzi 142 0.52 S 23.24 E
Anzicun 95 39.46 N 115.50 E
Anzin 46 50.22 N 3.30 E
Anzio 60 41.27 N 12.37 E
Anzoátegui □[3] 236 9.00 N 64.30 W
Anzob 75 39.10 N 68.48 E
Anzob, Pereval)(75 39.07 N 68.52 E
Anzola dell'Emilia 58 44.33 N 11.11 E
Anzon ≃ 56 45.45 N 3.57 E
Anžu, Ostrova II 64 75.30 N 143.00 E
Aogaki 86 35.14 N 135.00 E
Aoga-shima I 80 32.28 N 139.46 E
Aohaibolihu 94 42.01 N 121.32 E
Aohandaba 94 42.05 N 121.59 E
Aohanqi 88 42.19 N 119.59 E
Aoíz 34 42.47 N 1.22 W
Aoji 88 42.31 N 130.23 E
Aojiao 90 23.37 N 117.26 E
Aola 165e 9.32 S 160.29 E
Aoliyingzi 94 42.14 N 121.58 E
Aoloau 164u 14.18 S 170.46 W
Ao Luk 100 8.23 N 98.43 E
Aomar 34 36.30 N 3.47 E
Aomen → Macau 90 22.14 N 113.35 E
Aomori 82 40.49 N 140.45 E
Aonla 114 28.17 N 79.09 E
Aono-yama ∧ 86 34.27 N 131.48 E

Symbols in the index entries represent the broad categories identified in the key at the right. Symbols with superior numbers (⩕[2]) identify subcategories (see complete key on page I · 26).

Kartensymbole in dem Registerverzeichnis stellen die rechts in Schlüssel erklärten Kategorien dar. Symbole mit hochgestellten Ziffern (⩕[2]) bezeichnen Unterabteilungen einer Kategorie (vgl. vollständiger Schlüssel auf Seite I · 26).

Los símbolos incluídos en el texto del índice representan las grandes categorias identificadas con la clave a la derecha. Los símbolos con numeros en su parte superior (⩕[2]) identifican las subcategorías (véase la clave completa en la página I · 26).

Les symboles de l'index représentent les catégories indiquées dans la légende à droite. Les symboles suivis d'un indice (⩕[2]) représentent des sous-catégories (voir légende complète à la page I · 26).

Os símbolos incluídos no texto do índice representam as grandes categorias identificadas com a chave à direita. Os símbolos com números em sua parte superior (⩕[2]) identificam as subcategorias (veja-se a chave completa à página I · 26).

∧ Mountain	Berg	Montaña	Montagne	Montanha
⩕ Mountains	Berge	Montañas	Montagnes	Montanhas
)(Pass	Pass	Paso	Col	Passo
∨ Valley, Canyon	Tal, Cañon	Valle, Cañón	Vallée, Canyon	Vale, Canhão
≚ Plain	Ebene	Llano	Plaine	Planície
≻ Cape	Kap	Cabo	Cap	Cabo
I Island	Insel	Isla	Île	Ilha
II Islands	Inseln	Islas	Îles	Ilhas
● Other Topographic Features	Andere Topographische Objekte	Otros Elementos Topográficos	Autres données topographiques	Outros Elementos Topográficos

Nombre / Nom / Nome	Página / Page	Lat.°′	Long.°′ W=Oeste / W=Ouest
Aôös (Vijosë) ≃	38	40.37 N	19.20 E
Aopo	165a	13.29 S	172.30 W
Aôral, Phnum ∧	100	12.02 N	104.10 E
Aorangi Mountains ∧∧	162	41.26 S	175.20 E
Aore I	165f	15.35 S	167.10 E
Aorere ≃	162	40.41 S	172.40 E
Aoshan I	90	29.56 N	122.14 E
Aoshang	90	25.42 N	113.00 E
Ao-shima I, Nihon	86	33.55 N	134.44 E
Ao-shima I, Nihon	86	33.44 N	132.29 E
Aosta	56	45.44 N	7.20 E
Aosta □[4]	54	45.45 N	7.20 E
Aosta, Valle d' ∨	56	45.46 N	7.25 E
Aoste	56	45.35 N	5.36 E
Aotou	90	22.44 N	114.33 E
Aoudaghost ⊥	140	17.25 N	10.40 W
Aouderas	140	17.37 N	8.26 E
Aoudour, Oued ≃	34	35.02 N	5.02 W
Aouis, Ouadi ∨	136	11.03 N	19.47 E
Aouk, Bahr ≃	136	8.51 N	18.53 E
Aoukalé ≃	136	9.17 N	22.42 E
Aoukâr ◆[1]	140	18.00 N	9.30 W
Aoulef	138	26.58 N	1.05 E
Aoulime, Jbel ∧	138	30.48 N	8.50 W
Aoumou	165f	21.24 S	165.50 E
Aourou	140	14.57 N	11.35 W
Aoya	86	35.31 N	133.59 E
Aoyama	84	34.40 N	136.11 E
Aoyama-tōge)(	84	34.40 N	136.16 E
Aozi	136	21.04 N	18.41 E
Aozou	136	21.49 N	17.25 E
Apa ≃	242	22.06 S	58.00 W
Apache	186	34.54 N	98.22 W
Apache Lake ◎[1]	190	33.18 N	111.16 W
Apache Peak ∧	190	31.49 N	110.25 W
Apalachee ≃	182	33.32 N	83.17 W
Apalachee Bay C	182	30.00 N	84.13 W
Apalaches → Appalachian Mountains ∧∧	168	41.00 N	77.00 W
Apalachicola	182	29.44 N	84.59 W
Apalachicola ≃	182	29.44 N	84.59 W
Apalachicola Bay C	182	29.40 N	85.00 W
Apalachin	200	42.04 N	76.09 W
Apam, Ghana	140	5.17 N	0.44 W
Apam, Méx.	224	19.43 N	98.25 W
Apanás, Lago de ◎[1]	226	13.11 N	85.59 W
Apango	224	17.44 N	99.20 W
Apapa ◆[8]	263a	6.27 N	3.22 E
Apapa Wharf ◆[5]	263a	6.23 N	3.23 E
Apaporis ≃	236	1.23 S	69.25 W
Aparados da Serra, Parque Nacional dos ♠	242	29.30 S	50.32 W
Aparan	74	40.36 N	44.23 E
Aparecida, Bra.	246	23.33 S	45.53 W
Aparecida, Bra.	246	22.50 S	45.14 W
Aparecida de Goiás	245	14.57 S	49.47 W
Aparima ≃	162	46.20 S	168.01 E
Aparri	106	18.22 N	121.39 E
Apaseo el Grande	224	20.33 N	100.41 W
Apastovo	70	55.11 N	48.30 E
Apatin	38	45.40 N	18.59 E
Apatity	24	67.34 N	33.18 E
Apatzingán [de la Constitución]	222	19.05 N	102.21 W
Apaxtla de Castrejón	224	18.09 N	99.52 W
Ap-ba-tien	259c	10.44 N	106.36 E
Ap-binh-quoi	259c	10.48 N	106.36 E
Ap-binh-thanh	100	11.11 N	108.42 E
Apcheron, Péninsule de l' → Apšeronskij Poluostrov ≻[1]	74	40.30 N	50.00 E
Ape	66	57.32 N	26.40 E
Apeadero Funke	248	35.28 S	58.59 W
Apecchio	60	43.33 N	12.25 E
Ape Dale ∨	44	52.30 N	2.45 W
Apeganau Lake ◎	174	55.35 N	99.35 W
Apelação	256c	38.49 N	9.08 W
Apeldoorn	52	52.13 N	5.58 E
Apeleg, Arroyo ≃	244	44.58 S	70.07 W
Apen	48	53.13 N	7.48 E
Apenes	214	49.16 N	124.41 W
Apeninos → Appennino ∧∧	36	43.00 N	13.00 E
Apenninen → Appennino ∧∧	36	43.00 N	13.00 E
Apennines → Appennino ∧∧	36	43.00 N	13.00 E
Apennins → Appennino ∧∧	36	43.00 N	13.00 E
Apensen	48	53.26 N	9.37 E
Apere ≃	238	13.44 S	65.18 W
Apese ◆[8]	263a	6.25 N	3.25 E
Apeú	240	1.18 S	47.59 W
Apex	182	35.44 N	78.51 W
Apex Mountain ∧	170	62.28 N	138.04 W
Api	144	3.40 N	25.26 E
Api ∧	114	30.00 N	80.57 E
Api, Tanjung ≻	102	0.48 S	121.39 E
Apia, Col.	236	5.05 N	75.58 W
Apia, W. Sam.	165a	13.50 S	171.44 W
Apiacá	238	21.08 S	41.34 W
Apiacá ≃	240	9.16 S	57.03 W
Apiacás, Serra dos ∧∧[1]	238	10.15 S	57.15 W
Apiaí	242	24.31 S	48.50 W
Apiaí Guaçu ≃	242	23.35 S	48.36 W
Apiaú ≃	238	2.39 N	61.12 W
Apice	60	41.07 N	14.56 E
Apidiá ≃	238	11.39 S	61.11 W
Apinajé	240	11.31 S	48.18 W
Apipilulco	224	18.11 N	99.41 W
Apishapa ≃	188	38.08 N	103.57 W
Apiti	162	39.58 S	175.53 E
Apizaco	224	19.25 N	98.09 W
Apizolaya	222	24.50 N	102.15 W
Aplao	238	16.05 S	72.31 W
Aplerbeck ◆[8]	253	51.29 N	7.33 E
Ap Li Chau I	261d	22.15 N	114.09 E
Aplinskij, Porog ∟	78	58.28 N	100.32 E
Apo	224	19.25 N	102.25 W
Apo, Mount ∧	106	6.59 N	125.16 E
Apodi	240	5.39 S	37.48 W
Apodi ≃	240	4.56 S	37.10 W
Apodi, Chapada do ∧∧[1]	240	5.10 S	37.45 W
Apo East Pass ⊔	106	12.40 N	120.40 E
Apolakkiá	38	36.06 N	27.50 E
Apolda	50	51.01 N	11.31 E
Apolima Strait ⊔	165a	14.50 S	172.10 W
Apolinario Saravia	248	24.25 S	64.02 W
Apollo	204	40.35 N	79.34 W
Apollo Bay	156	38.45 S	143.40 E
Apollo Beach	210	27.45 N	82.25 W
Apollonia ⊥	136	32.54 N	21.58 E
Apolo	238	14.43 S	68.31 W
Apón ≃	236	10.06 N	72.23 W
Aponguao ≃	236	4.48 N	61.36 W
Apopa	226	13.48 N	89.11 W
Apopka	210	28.40 N	81.30 W
Apopka, Lake ◎	210	28.37 N	81.38 W
Apoquindo	276e	33.24 S	70.32 W
Aporá	240	11.39 S	38.05 W
Aporé	246	18.58 S	52.01 W
Aporé ≃	245	19.27 S	50.57 W
Apo Reef ✣[2]	106	12.40 N	120.29 E
Aporema	240	1.14 N	50.49 W
Aporo	224	19.41 N	100.25 W
Apostle Islands II	180	46.50 N	90.30 W
Apostle Islands National Lakeshore ♠	180	46.55 N	91.00 W
Apóstoles	242	27.55 S	55.46 W
Apostolou Andréa, Akrotírion ≻	120	35.42 N	34.35 E
Apostolovo	68	47.39 N	33.44 E
Apozolco	224	21.22 N	104.00 W
Appalachen → Appalachian Mountains ∧∧	168	41.00 N	77.00 W
Appalaches, Monts → Appalachian Mountains ∧∧	168	41.00 N	77.00 W
Appalachia	182	36.54 N	82.47 W
Appalachian Mountains ∧∧	168	41.00 N	77.00 W
Äppelbo	40	60.30 N	14.00 E
Appelhülsen	48	51.54 N	7.25 E
Appen	48	53.40 N	9.44 E
Appennino (Appennines) ∧∧	36	43.00 N	13.00 E
Appennino, Galleria dell ◆[5]	60	44.10 N	11.10 E
Appennino Abruzzese ∧∧	60	42.00 N	14.00 E
Appennino Calabrese ∧∧	36	39.00 N	16.30 E
Appennino Ligure ∧∧	56	44.30 N	9.00 E
Appennino Lucano ∧∧	36	40.30 N	16.00 E
Appennino Napoletano ∧∧	60	41.30 N	15.00 E
Appennino Tosco-Emiliano ∧∧	36	44.00 N	11.30 E
Appennino Umbro-Marchigiano ∧∧	60	43.00 N	13.00 E
Appenweier	54	48.32 N	7.58 E
Appenzell	54	47.20 N	9.25 E
Appenzell-Ausser Rhoden □[3]	54	47.22 N	9.28 E
Appiano (Eppan)	58	46.28 N	11.15 E
Appiano Gentile	56	45.44 N	8.59 E
Appin	160	34.12 S	150.47 E
Appingedam	48	53.18 N	6.52 E
Apple ≃, U.S.	180	42.11 N	90.14 W
Apple ≃, Wis., U.S.	180	45.09 N	92.45 W
Appleby, S. Afr.	148	27.39 S	22.36 E
Appleby, Eng., U.K.	42	54.36 N	2.29 W
Appleby, Tex., U.S.	212	31.43 N	94.36 W
Apple Creek	204	40.45 N	81.50 W
Apple Creek ≃, Ill., U.S.	209	39.22 N	90.37 W
Apple Creek ≃, Mo., U.S.	184	37.35 N	89.32 W
Apple Creek ≃, N. Dak., U.S.	188	46.40 N	100.46 W
Appledore	44	51.03 N	4.10 W
Applegate	216	39.06 N	120.59 W
Applegate ≃	192	42.26 N	123.27 W
Apple Hill	196	45.13 N	74.46 W
Apple Orchard Mountain ∧	182	37.31 N	79.31 W
Apples	54	46.34 N	6.25 E
Apple Springs	212	31.13 N	94.58 W
Appleton, Eng., U.K.	252	53.21 N	2.33 W
Appleton, Minn., U.S.	180	45.12 N	96.01 W
Appleton, Wash., U.S.	214	45.49 N	121.16 W
Appleton, Wis., U.S.	180	44.16 N	88.25 W
Appleton City	184	38.11 N	94.02 W
Apple Valley	218	34.32 N	117.14 W
Applewold	204	40.47 N	79.36 W
Appley Bridge	252	53.35 N	2.43 W
Appling	182	33.33 N	82.19 W
Appomattox	182	37.21 N	78.50 W
Appomattox ≃	182	37.18 N	77.18 W
Appomattox Court House National Historical Park ♠	182	37.23 N	78.48 W
Approuague ≃	240	4.38 N	51.58 W
Apra Harbor C	164p	13.27 N	144.38 E
Aprelevka	72	55.33 N	37.04 E
Aprel'sk	78	58.10 N	114.34 E
Aprel'skij	79	53.30 N	126.16 E
Apremont	54	46.13 N	5.40 E
Apremont-la-Forêt	52	48.51 N	5.38 E
Aprica, Passo d')(	58	46.09 N	10.09 E
Apricena	60	41.47 N	15.27 E
April ≃	154	4.18 S	142.26 E
Aprilia	60	41.36 N	12.39 E
Apscheron → Apšeronskij Poluostrov ≻[1]	74	40.30 N	50.00 E
Apšeronsk	74	44.28 N	39.44 E
Apšeronskij Poluostrov ≻[1]	74	40.30 N	50.00 E
Apshawa	266	41.01 N	74.22 W
Apsley	202	44.45 N	78.06 W
Apt	56	43.53 N	5.24 E
Aptakisic	268	42.12 N	87.56 W
Ap-talai	100	11.24 N	107.23 E
Ap-tan-hoa	259c	10.45 N	106.35 E
Ap-tan-my	100	11.43 N	108.49 E
Aptos	216	36.59 N	121.54 W
Apuane, Alpi ∧∧	58	44.09 N	10.15 E
Apuaú	236	2.25 S	60.53 W
Apucarana	245	23.33 S	51.29 W
Apuiarés	240	3.56 S	39.24 W
Apulia Station	200	42.49 N	76.05 W
Apure □[3]	236	7.10 N	68.50 W
Apure ≃	236	7.37 N	66.25 W
Apurímac □[5]	238	14.00 S	73.00 W
Apurímac ≃	238	11.48 S	74.03 W
Apurito	236	7.56 N	68.27 W
Aqaba, Gulf of C	118	29.00 N	34.40 E
'Aqabah, Wādī al- ∨	122	30.14 N	33.53 E
Āqbolāgh	74	38.54 N	44.32 E
Āqcheh	110	36.56 N	66.11 E
'Aqīq	130	18.14 N	38.12 E
'Aqīq, Khalīj C	130	18.20 N	38.10 E
'Aqīq, Wādī al- ∨	118	24.17 N	40.10 E
Āq Köprük	116	36.05 N	66.51 E
'Aqrabā	122	33.06 N	36.00 E
'Aqrah	118	36.45 N	43.54 E
Aquarius Plateau ∧∧[1]	190	38.05 N	111.40 W
Aquasco	198	38.35 N	76.43 W
Aquashicola	200	40.49 N	75.35 W
Aquashicola Creek ≃	200	40.48 N	75.37 W
Äquatorial-Guinea → Equatorial Guinea □[1]	142	2.00 N	9.00 E
Aquebogue	197	40.57 N	72.37 W
Aqueduct Race Track ◆	266	40.40 N	73.50 W
Aquia Creek ≃	198	38.23 N	77.18 W
Aquiaulne ≃	46	47.37 N	2.30 E
Aquibi, Cachoeira ∟	240	11.08 S	55.22 W
Aquidabã	240	10.17 S	37.02 W
Aquidabã ≃	238	20.58 S	57.50 W
Aquidabán ≃	242	23.11 S	57.32 W
Aquidauana	238	20.28 S	55.48 W
Aquidauana ≃	238	19.44 S	56.50 W
Aquila, Méx.	224	18.36 N	103.30 W
Aquila, Schw.	54	46.31 N	8.57 E
Aquileia	58	45.46 N	13.22 E
Aquiles Serdán	222	28.36 N	105.53 W
Aquilla, Ohio, U.S.	204	41.34 N	81.09 W
Aquilla, Tex., U.S.	212	31.51 N	97.13 W
Aquilla Creek ≃	212	31.40 N	97.10 W
Aquin	228	18.17 N	73.24 W
Aquincumi Múzeum ◆	254c	47.34 N	19.03 E
Aquino	60	41.30 N	13.42 E
Aquio ≃	236	2.42 N	67.34 W
Ara ≃, Esp.	34	42.24 N	0.09 E
Ara ≃, Nihon	84	35.39 N	139.51 E
Arab	182	34.19 N	86.29 W
'Arab, Bahr al- ≃	130	9.02 N	29.28 E
'Arab, Khalīj al- C	130	30.55 N	29.05 E
Arab, Oued el ∨	138	34.41 N	6.31 E
'Arab, Shaṭṭ al- ≃	118	29.57 N	48.34 E
'Arab, Wādī al- ∨	122	32.35 N	35.35 E
'Arabābād	118	33.02 N	57.41 E
'Arabah, Wādī ∨	132	29.07 N	32.40 E
Araban	120	37.26 N	37.41 E
Arabatskaja Strelka, Kosa ≻[2]	68	45.40 N	35.00 E
Arabatskij Zaliv C	68	45.20 N	35.30 E
Arabba	58	46.30 N	11.52 E
Arabei Dalon	134	3.34 N	46.30 E
Arabelo	236	4.55 N	64.13 W
Arabi	184	29.57 N	90.02 W
Arabian Basin ✣[1]	12	10.00 N	65.00 E
Arabian Peninsula ≻[1]	12	25.00 N	45.00 E
Arabian Sea ✣[2]	108	15.00 N	65.00 E
Arabia Saudita → Saudi Arabia □[1]	108	25.00 N	45.00 E
Arabie, Mer d' → Arabian Sea ✣[2]	108	15.00 N	65.00 E
Arabie Saoudite → Saudi Arabia □[1]	108	25.00 N	45.00 E
Arabique, Péninsule → Arabian Peninsula ≻[1]	12	25.00 N	45.00 E
Arabisches Meer → Arabian Sea ✣[2]	108	15.00 N	65.00 E
Arab-Jengidža	74	39.29 N	44.58 E
'Arab Muṭayr	132	27.16 N	31.14 E
Ara-Bure, Porog ∟	78	53.00 N	100.12 E
Araç	120	41.15 N	33.21 E
Aracá ≃	236	0.25 S	62.55 W
Aracaju	240	10.55 S	37.04 W
Araçariguama	246	23.26 S	47.04 W
Aracataca	236	10.36 N	74.12 W
Aracati	240	4.34 S	37.46 W
Aracatiaçu, Açude ◎[1]	240	3.56 S	39.59 W
Araçatuba	245	21.12 S	50.25 W
Araceli	106	10.33 N	119.59 E
Aracena	34	37.53 N	6.33 W
Arâches-les-Carroz	54	46.02 N	6.39 E
Arachino-seki ⊥	84	35.33 N	136.05 E
Arachlej, Ozero ◎	78	52.12 N	112.52 E
Araci	240	11.20 S	38.57 W
Aracitaba	246	21.20 S	43.23 W
Aracoiaba	240	4.23 S	38.49 W
Aracruz	245	19.49 S	40.16 W
Aracu ≃	236	4.20 S	59.15 W
Araçuaí	245	16.52 S	42.04 W
Araçuaí ≃	245	16.46 S	42.02 W
Arad, Rom.	38	46.11 N	21.20 E
'Arad, Yis.	122	31.15 N	35.13 E
Arad □[5]	38	46.20 N	21.40 E
Arada, Hond.	226	14.48 N	88.18 W
Arada, Tchad	136	15.01 N	20.40 E
Aradhippou	120	34.57 N	33.35 E
Arafune-yama ∧	84	36.12 N	138.38 E
Arafura Sea ✣[2]	154	9.00 S	133.00 E
Aragarças	245	15.55 S	52.15 W
Arago, Cape ≻	192	43.18 N	124.25 W
Aragoiânia	245	16.57 S	49.30 W
Aragon	182	34.03 N	85.03 W
Aragón □[9]	34	41.00 N	1.00 W
Aragón ≃	34	42.13 N	1.44 W
Aragona	36	37.24 N	13.37 E
Aragona □[3]	236	10.00 N	67.10 W
Araguacema	240	8.50 S	49.34 W
Araguaçu	245	12.49 S	49.51 W
Aragua de Barcelona	236	9.28 N	64.49 W
Aragua de Maturín	236	9.58 N	63.29 W
Araguaia ≃	232	5.21 S	48.41 W
Araguaia, Parque Nacional do ♠	240	12.00 S	50.20 W
Araguaína	240	7.12 S	48.12 W
Araguainha	245	16.49 S	53.05 W
Araguao, Caño ≃[1]	236	9.15 N	60.50 W
Araguari	245	18.38 S	48.11 W
Araguari ≃, Bra.	240	1.15 N	49.55 W
Araguari ≃, Bra.	245	18.21 S	48.40 W
Araguatins	240	5.38 S	48.07 W
Aragvi ≃	74	41.50 N	44.43 E
Arai, Nihon	84	34.41 N	137.34 E
Arai, Nihon	84	37.01 N	138.15 E
Arāihāzār	116	23.47 N	90.40 E
Araioses	240	2.53 S	41.55 W
Arak, Alg.	138	25.18 N	3.45 E
Arāk, Īrān	118	34.05 N	49.41 E
Araka	144	4.20 N	30.23 E
Arakamčečen, Ostrov I	170	64.45 N	172.30 W
Arakan □[8]	100	19.00 N	94.15 E
Arakan, Porog ∟	78	57.35 N	96.36 E
Arakan Yoma ∧∧	100	19.00 N	94.40 E
Arakawa, Nihon	86	35.57 N	139.02 E
Arakawa, Nihon	164m	26.39 N	128.15 E
Arakawa ≃	258	35.47 N	139.44 E
Arakawa-dake ∧	84	35.30 N	138.10 E
Arákhova	38	38.29 N	22.35 E
Arákhthos ≃	38	39.01 N	21.03 E
Araklı	120	40.57 N	40.03 E
Arakmeer, Gora ∧	74	42.38 N	46.49 E
Arakpur ◆[8]	262a	28.35 N	77.10 E
Araks (Aras) ≃	74	40.01 N	48.28 E
Aral, S.S.S.R.	75	41.50 N	73.03 E
Aral, S.S.S.R.	75	42.32 N	72.40 E
Araldy	74	44.18 N	50.24 E
Aral Sea → Aral'skoje More ✣[2]	76	45.00 N	60.00 E
Aral'sk	76	46.48 N	61.40 E
Aral'skoje More ✣[2]	76	45.00 N	60.00 E
Aralsor, Ozero ◎, S.S.S.R.	70	49.05 N	48.12 E
Aralsor, Ozero ◎, S.S.S.R.	70	48.42 N	52.24 E
Aralsul'fat	76	46.50 N	61.58 E
Aramac	156	22.59 S	145.14 E
Aramac ≃	156	23.02 S	144.31 E
Aramari	245	12.04 S	38.30 W
Arāmbāgh	116	22.53 N	87.47 E
Arambaza	236	2.04 S	73.06 W
Aramberri	222	24.06 N	99.49 W
Aramia ≃	154	7.45 S	142.20 E
Aramil'	76	56.46 N	60.50 E
Aramon	56	43.53 N	4.41 E
Arampampa	238	17.55 S	66.04 W
Aramtalla	130	6.47 N	29.13 E
Ārān	118	34.04 N	51.29 E
Arana	248	35.00 S	57.54 W
Arana, Sierra ∧∧	34	37.20 N	3.30 W
Aranda de Duero	34	41.41 N	3.41 W
Arandai	154	2.10 S	133.01 E
Arandas	224	20.42 N	102.21 W
Aranđelovac	38	44.18 N	20.35 E
Arandis	146	22.24 S	15.00 E
Aran Fawddwy ∧	44	52.47 N	3.41 W
Arang	110	21.12 N	81.58 E
Ārani, Bhārat	112	12.40 N	79.17 E
Ārāni, Bngl.	116	24.17 N	88.52 E
Arani, Bol.	238	17.34 S	65.46 W
Aran Island I	28	54.58 N	8.33 W
Aran Islands II	28	53.07 N	9.43 W
Aranjuez	34	40.02 N	3.36 W
Aranos	146	24.09 S	19.09 E
Aransas ≃	186	28.04 N	97.14 W
Aransas Pass	186	27.54 N	97.09 W
Arantāngi	112	10.10 N	78.59 E
Arantes, Ribeirão das ≃	245	19.17 S	50.57 W
Arantina	246	21.56 S	44.15 W
Aranyaprathet	100	13.41 N	102.30 E
Arany-hegyi-patak ≃	254c	47.34 N	19.04 E
Aranzazu	236	5.16 N	75.30 W
Arao	86	33.00 N	130.28 E
Araouane	138	18.54 N	3.33 W
Arapa, Lago ◎	238	15.10 S	70.01 W
Arapaho	186	35.34 N	98.57 W
Arapahoe	188	40.18 N	99.54 W
Arapãnja	262b	22.26 N	88.28 E
Arapawa Island I	162	41.11 S	174.19 E
Arapeí	242	22.41 S	44.27 W
Arapey	242	30.58 S	57.32 W
Arapey Chico ≃	242	30.57 S	57.49 W
Arapey Grande ≃	242	30.55 S	57.49 W
Arapiraca	240	9.45 S	36.39 W
Arapiri, Ilha I	240	2.04 S	54.56 W
Arápis	257c	37.59 N	23.32 E
Arapkir	120	39.03 N	38.30 E
Arapongas	245	23.23 S	51.27 W
Arapoti	245	24.08 S	49.50 W
Arapuni	162	38.04 S	175.39 E
Araquari	242	26.23 S	48.43 W
Araquil ≃	34	42.48 N	1.45 W
'Ar'ar	118	13.53 N	44.50 E
'Ar'ar, Wādī ∨	118	31.23 N	42.26 E
Araranguá	242	28.56 S	49.29 W
Araraquara	245	21.47 S	48.10 W
Araras, Bra.	245	22.22 S	47.23 W
Araras, Bra.	246	22.49 S	46.36 W
Araras, Açude ◎[1]	240	4.20 S	40.28 W
Araras, Ribeirão das ≃, Bra.	246	21.18 S	45.45 W
Araras, Ribeirão das ≃, Bra.	246	22.52 S	46.37 W
Ararat, Austl.	159	37.17 S	142.56 E
Ararat, S.S.S.R.	74	39.50 N	44.42 E
Ararat, Mount → Büyük Ağrı Dağı ∧	74	39.42 N	44.18 E
Arari	240	3.28 S	44.47 W
Arāria	114	26.08 N	87.24 E
Araripe	240	7.12 S	40.08 W
Araripe, Chapada do ∧∧[1]	240	7.20 S	40.00 W
Araripina	240	7.33 S	40.34 W
Ararirá ≃	236	0.30 S	63.33 W
Arar Lugole	134	3.17 N	45.28 E
Araruna	240	6.32 S	35.44 W
Araruva	245	23.45 S	51.19 W
Aras (Araks) ≃	74	40.01 N	48.28 E
'Aras, Ḥawḍ al- ⊤[4]	132	30.51 N	32.32 E
Arashi-yama ∧[2]	260	35.01 N	135.40 E
Åråsviken C	40	59.02 N	14.01 E
Arataú ≃	240	2.35 S	50.41 W
Aratiba	242	27.24 S	52.19 W
Araticu	240	1.58 S	49.51 W
Araticu ≃	240	1.55 S	49.51 W
Áratos	38	41.05 N	25.33 E
Aratuípe	245	13.05 S	39.00 W
Aratula	161a	27.59 S	152.32 E
Arau	104	6.26 N	100.16 E
Arauá	240	11.16 S	37.37 W
Arauá ≃, Bra.	236	4.06 S	63.36 W
Arauã ≃, Bra.	238	7.59 S	65.14 W
Arauá ≃, Bra.	238	5.40 S	60.48 W
Arauca	236	7.05 N	70.45 W
Arauca □[5]	236	6.40 N	71.00 W
Arauca ≃	236	7.24 N	66.35 W
Araucária	242	25.35 S	49.25 W
Arauco	242	37.15 S	73.19 W
Arauco □[4]	242	37.50 S	73.15 W
Arauco, Bahía de C	242	37.11 S	73.25 W
Araújos	245	19.56 S	45.04 W
Arauquita	236	7.02 N	71.25 W
Araure	236	9.34 N	69.13 W
Aravaca ◆[8]	256a	40.28 N	3.46 W
Aravaipa Creek ≃	190	32.50 N	110.43 W
Arāvalli Range ∧∧	110	25.00 N	73.30 E
Aravan	75	40.32 N	72.30 E
Araviana ≃	34	41.41 N	2.07 W
Arawa	134	9.55 N	41.59 E
Arawata ≃	162	44.00 S	168.41 E
Araxá	245	19.35 S	46.55 W
Araya	236	10.34 N	64.15 W
Arayat	106	15.10 N	120.46 E
Arba	134	9.00 N	40.26 E
Arba ≃	34	41.52 N	1.18 W
Arbagar	78	51.56 N	116.15 E
Arbagia ◆[1]	36	40.00 N	9.10 E
Arba Gugu ∧	134	8.10 N	40.00 E
'Arbah, Wādī ∨	134	17.30 N	51.25 E
Ārbālia	116	22.41 N	88.47 E
Arba Minch	134	6.02 N	37.40 E
Arbaoua	34	34.54 N	5.56 W
Arbaž	70	57.41 N	48.18 E
Arbedo	54	46.12 N	9.03 E
Arbel	122	32.49 N	35.29 E
Arbia ≃	60	43.08 N	11.28 E
Arboga	40	59.24 N	15.50 E
Arbogaån ≃	40	59.26 N	16.04 E
Arbois	54	46.54 N	5.46 E
Arboledas	242	36.53 S	61.29 W
Arboletes	236	8.51 N	76.26 W
Arbon	54	47.31 N	9.26 E
Arbonne	46	48.25 N	2.34 E
Arborea	36	39.47 N	8.34 E
Arborea ◆[1]	36	39.55 N	8.50 E
Arborfield	174	53.06 N	103.39 W
Arborg	174	50.55 N	97.15 W
Arbrå	26	61.29 N	16.23 E
Arbroath	28	56.34 N	2.35 W
Arbuckle	216	39.01 N	122.03 W
Arbuckle, Lake ◎	210	27.41 N	81.24 W
Arbuckle Creek ≃	210	27.26 N	81.17 W
Arbuckle Mountains ∧∧	186	34.25 N	97.20 W
Arbury Hills	206	41.33 N	87.51 W
Arbutus Lake ◎	266	40.31 N	74.10 W
Arbuzinka	68	47.53 N	31.19 E
Arbuzovo	66	56.21 N	32.27 E
Arc ≃, Fr.	56	43.31 N	5.07 E
Arc ≃, Fr.	56	45.34 N	6.12 E
Arc, Bayou des ≃	184	35.00 N	91.30 W
Arcachon	32	44.37 N	1.12 W
Arcachon, Bassin d' C	32	44.40 N	1.10 W
Arcadas	246	22.42 S	46.52 W
Arcade, It.	58	45.47 N	12.13 E
Arcade, Calif., U.S.	216	34.02 N	118.15 W
Arcade, N.Y., U.S.	200	42.32 N	78.25 W
Arcadia, Calif., U.S.	218	34.08 N	118.01 W
Arcadia, Fla., U.S.	210	27.14 N	81.52 W
Arcadia, Ind., U.S.	208	40.11 N	86.01 W
Arcadia, Iowa, U.S.	188	42.05 N	95.03 W
Arcadia, Kans., U.S.	188	37.38 N	94.37 W
Arcadia, La., U.S.	184	32.33 N	92.55 W
Arcadia, Mich., U.S.	180	44.30 N	86.14 W
Arcadia, Nebr., U.S.	188	41.25 N	99.07 W
Arcadia, Ohio, U.S.	206	41.07 N	83.31 W
Arcadia, Pa., U.S.	204	40.47 N	78.51 W
Arcadia, S.C., U.S.	182	34.57 N	82.00 W
Arcadia, Tex., U.S.	212	29.23 N	95.07 W
Arcadia, Wis., U.S.	180	44.15 N	91.30 W
Arcângelo	246	21.18 S	44.19 W
Arcanum	208	39.59 N	84.33 W
Arcata	194	40.52 N	124.05 W
Arcatao	226	14.05 N	88.45 W
Arc de Triomphe ⊥	251	48.53 N	2.17 E
Arc Dome ∧	194	38.51 N	117.22 W
Arce	60	41.35 N	13.34 E
Arceburgo	246	21.22 S	46.56 W
Arčeda ≃	70	49.52 N	43.10 E
Arčedinsko-Donskije Peski ◆[2]	70	49.33 N	43.15 E
Arcelia	224	18.17 N	100.16 W
Arcen	48	51.29 N	6.11 E
Arc-en-Barrois	54	47.57 N	5.00 E
Arces	46	48.05 N	3.36 E
Arc-et-Senans	54	47.02 N	5.46 E
Arcevia	60	43.30 N	12.56 E
Archambault, Lac ◎	196	46.18 N	74.15 W
Archangaj □[8]	78	48.00 N	101.30 E
Archangel → Archangel'sk	24	64.34 N	40.32 E
Archangel'sk	24	64.34 N	40.32 E
Archangel'skaja	68	45.41 N	40.15 E
Archangel'skoje, S.S.S.R.	66	53.16 N	37.42 E
Archangel'skoje, S.S.S.R.	68	51.27 N	40.55 E
Archangel'skoje, S.S.S.R.	70	55.13 N	44.05 E
Archangel'skoje, S.S.S.R.	70	54.26 N	48.40 E
Archangel'skoje, S.S.S.R.	72	55.19 N	35.58 E
Archangel'skoje, S.S.S.R.	74	44.37 N	44.05 E
Archangel'skoje, S.S.S.R.	255b	55.47 N	37.18 E
Archara	79	49.27 N	130.07 E
Archara ≃	79	49.13 N	129.53 E
Archbald	200	41.30 N	75.32 W
Archbold	206	41.31 N	84.18 W
Archdale	182	35.56 N	79.57 W
Archenu, Jabal ∧	136	22.13 N	24.41 E
Archer	182	29.32 N	82.31 W
Archer ≃	154	13.28 S	141.41 E
Archer, Lake ◎	273	42.04 N	71.20 W
Archer Bay C	154	13.25 S	141.43 E
Archer City	186	33.36 N	98.38 W
Archer's Post	144	0.39 N	37.41 E
Arches	54	48.07 N	6.32 E
Arches National Park ♠	190	38.42 N	109.45 W
Archi	60	42.05 N	14.23 E
Archiac	32	45.31 N	0.18 W
Archibald Makin National Park ♠	156	35.50 S	140.25 E
Archidona	34	37.05 N	4.23 W
Archipo-Osipovka	68	44.22 N	38.33 E
Archipovka	70	56.38 N	41.14 E
Archipovo	24	66.26 N	45.52 E
Archonskaja	74	43.07 N	44.30 E
Archshofen	52	49.27 N	10.04 E
Archville	266	41.07 N	73.52 W
Arcidosso	60	42.52 N	11.33 E
Arcille	60	42.48 N	11.15 E
Arcinazzo Romano	60	41.48 N	13.12 E
Arcisate	56	45.54 N	8.52 E
Arcis-sur-Aube	46	48.32 N	4.08 E
Arciz	68	46.00 N	29.26 E
Arckaringa	152	27.56 S	134.45 E
Arckaringa Creek ≃	152	28.10 S	135.22 E
Arc-les-Gray	54	47.27 N	5.35 E
Arco, It.	58	45.55 N	10.53 E
Arco, Idaho, U.S.	192	43.38 N	113.18 W
Arco de Baúlhe	34	41.29 N	7.58 W
Arcola, Sask., Can.	174	49.37 N	102.30 W
Arcola, It.	58	44.07 N	9.47 E
Arcola, Ill., U.S.	184	39.41 N	88.19 W
Arcola, Ind., U.S.	206	41.06 N	85.18 W
Arcola, Miss., U.S.	184	33.16 N	90.53 W
Arcola, Pa., U.S.	275	40.09 N	75.27 W
Arcola, Tex., U.S.	212	29.31 N	95.27 W
Arconate	256b	45.32 N	8.51 E
Arcore	256b	45.38 N	9.19 E
Arcos	245	20.17 S	45.32 W
Arcos de la Frontera	34	36.45 N	5.48 W
Arcot	112	12.54 N	79.20 E
Arcoverde	240	8.25 S	37.04 W
Arctic Bay	166	73.02 N	85.11 W
Arctic Ocean ✣[1]	16	85.00 N	170.00 E
Arctic Red ≃	170	67.27 N	133.46 W
Arctic Red River	170	67.27 N	133.46 W
Arctic Village	170	68.08 N	145.19 W
Arctique, Océan Glacial → Arctic Ocean ✣[1]	16	85.00 N	170.00 E
Arcturus	144	17.47 S	31.20 E
Arcueil	251	48.48 N	2.20 E
Arcy-sur-Cure	46	47.36 N	3.45 E
Arḍ, Ra's al- ≻	118	29.21 N	48.05 E
Arda ≃, Eur.	38	41.39 N	26.29 E
Arda ≃, It.	58	45.02 N	10.02 E
Ardabīl	118	38.15 N	48.18 E
Ardahan	120	41.07 N	42.41 E
Ardakān, Īrān	118	30.16 N	52.01 E
Ardakān, Īrān	118	32.19 N	53.59 E
Ardal	118	31.59 N	50.39 E
Årdalsfjorden C[2]	26	61.12 N	7.30 E
Årdalstangen	26	61.14 N	7.43 E
Ardanuç	120	41.08 N	42.04 E
Ardara	269b	40.22 N	79.44 W
Ardasa	120	40.35 N	39.18 E
Ardatov, S.S.S.R.	70	55.15 N	43.06 E
Ardatov, S.S.S.R.	70	54.51 N	46.13 E
Ardbeg	42	55.39 N	6.05 W
Ardea	60	41.36 N	12.33 E
Ardèche □[5]	56	44.40 N	4.20 E
Ardèche ≃	56	44.16 N	4.39 E
Ardee	28	53.52 N	6.33 W
Arden, Man., Can.	174	50.17 N	99.14 W
Arden, Calif., U.S.	216	38.36 N	121.23 W
Arden, Del., U.S.	198	39.48 N	75.29 W
Arden, Forest of ◆[3]	44	52.23 N	1.42 W
Arden, Mount ∧	156	32.09 S	137.59 E
Ardenay-sur-Mérize	46	48.00 N	0.25 E
Arden Mines	269b	40.12 N	80.17 W
Ardennes □[5]	46	49.40 N	4.40 E
Ardennes ◆[1]	52	50.10 N	5.45 E
Ardennes, Canal des ≡	46	49.26 N	4.02 E
Ardenno	54	46.10 N	9.39 E
Ardentinny	42	56.03 N	4.55 W
Ardenza	60	43.31 N	10.19 E
Ardeşen	120	41.12 N	41.00 E
Ardestān	118	33.22 N	52.23 E
Ardey	253	51.28 N	7.43 E
Ardey ◆[8]	253	51.26 N	7.23 E
Ardeygebirge ∧∧[2]	253	51.25 N	7.20 E
Ardez	54	46.46 N	10.11 E
Ardglass	42	54.16 N	5.37 W
Ardila ≃	34	38.12 N	7.28 W
Ardill	174	49.53 N	105.49 W
Ardino	38	41.35 N	25.08 E
Ardlethan	156	34.21 S	146.54 E
Ardlussa	28	56.02 N	5.47 W
Ardmore, Ala., U.S.	184	34.59 N	86.52 W
Ardmore, Ind., U.S.	206	41.42 N	86.19 W
Ardmore, Md., U.S.	274c	38.56 N	76.52 W
Ardmore, Okla., U.S.	186	34.10 N	97.08 W
Ardmore, Pa., U.S.	198	40.01 N	75.18 W
Ardmore Point ≻	42	55.42 N	6.01 W
Ardnamurchan, Point of ≻	28	56.44 N	6.12 W
Ardnave Point ≻	42	55.54 N	6.20 W
Ardoch	156	27.26 S	144.08 E
Ardon, Schw.	54	46.13 N	7.15 E
Ardon, S.S.S.R.	74	43.12 N	44.18 E
Ardon ≃	74	43.17 N	44.18 E
Ardon, Har ∧	122	30.38 N	34.57 E
Ardooie	46	50.59 N	3.12 E
Ardoux ≃	46	47.42 N	1.35 E
Ardoz, Arroyo de ≃	256a	40.26 N	3.27 W
Ardres	46	50.51 N	1.59 E
Ardres ≃	46	49.18 N	3.40 E
Ardrossan, Austl.	158b	34.25 S	137.55 E
Ardrossan, Scot., U.K.	42	55.39 N	4.49 W
Ardsley, Eng., U.K.	42	53.32 N	1.28 W
Ardsley, N.Y., U.S.	266	41.01 N	73.51 W
Arduan Island I	130	19.55 N	30.22 E
Ardusson ≃	46	48.30 N	3.32 E
Åre	26	63.24 N	13.04 E
Areado	246	21.21 S	46.09 W
Areal	246	22.14 S	43.07 W
Arèches	56	45.41 N	6.34 E
Arecibo	230m	18.28 N	66.43 W
Areco ≃	248	33.56 S	59.16 W
Areeiro	256c	38.39 N	9.12 W
Arefjevo	76	57.01 N	90.40 E
Areguá	242	25.18 S	57.25 W
Areia, Bra.	240	6.58 S	35.42 W
Areia, Port.	256c	38.43 N	9.08 W
Areia, Ribeirão da ≃	245	16.07 S	45.52 W
Areia Branca, Bra.	240	4.56 S	37.07 W
Areia Branca, Bra.	246	22.48 S	46.51 W
Areia Branca, Bra.	277a	22.44 S	43.25 W
Areias	246	22.35 S	44.42 W
Arekalong Peninsula ≻[1]	165b	7.40 N	134.38 E
Arena, Point ≻	194	38.57 N	123.44 W
Arena, Punta ≻	222	23.33 N	109.28 W
Arena de la Ventana, Punta ≻	222	24.04 N	109.52 W
Arena Island I	106	9.14 N	120.46 E
Arenal, C.R.	226	10.29 N	84.53 W
Arenal, P.R.	230m	17.59 N	66.19 W
Arenal, Laguna de ◎	226	10.32 N	84.56 W
Arenal, Punta del ≻	231r	10.03 N	61.56 W
Arenal, Volcán ∧[1]	226	10.28 N	84.44 W
Arenales, Cerro ∧	244	47.07 S	73.35 W
Arenápolis	238	14.26 S	56.49 W
Arenas ≃	256d	41.26 N	2.00 E
Arenas, Punta ≻, Chile	238	21.39 S	70.10 W
Arenas, Punta ≻, P.R.	230m	18.07 N	65.35 W
Arenas, Punta de ≻, Arg.	244	53.09 S	68.13 W
Arenas, Punta de ≻, Ven.	236	10.29 N	64.14 W
Arenas de San Pedro	34	40.12 N	5.05 W
Arenberg	52	50.22 N	7.39 E
Arendal	26	58.27 N	8.48 E
Arendonk	52	51.19 N	5.05 E
Arendsee	50	52.53 N	11.30 E
Arendsee ◎	50	52.53 N	11.30 E
Arendtsville	198	39.55 N	77.18 W
Arenillas	236	3.33 S	80.04 W
Arennig Fawr ∧	44	52.55 N	3.45 W
Arenosa Creek ≃	186	28.52 N	96.44 W
Arenys de Mar	34	41.35 N	2.33 E
Arenzano	56	44.24 N	8.41 E
Arenzville	209	39.53 N	90.22 W
Areq, Sebkha Bou C	34	35.10 N	2.45 W
Arequipa	238	16.24 S	71.33 W
Arequipa □[5]	238	16.00 S	72.15 W
Arequito	242	33.09 S	61.28 W
Arero	134	4.42 N	38.47 E
Arês, Bra.	240	6.11 S	35.09 W
Arès, Fr.	32	44.46 N	1.08 W
Arese	256b	45.33 N	9.05 E
Åreskutan ∧	26	63.26 N	13.06 E
Areuse ≃	54	46.56 N	6.53 E
Arévalo	34	41.04 N	4.43 W
Arezzo	60	43.25 N	11.53 E
Arezzo □[4]	60	43.32 N	11.50 E
Arfa', Jabal ∧	122	29.51 N	35.27 E
'arfā', Wādī al- ∨	122	30.16 N	36.34 E
Arga ≃	34	42.18 N	1.47 W
Argada	78	54.14 N	110.41 E
Argadargada	156	21.40 S	136.40 E
Argajaš	76	55.29 N	60.52 E
Argamasilla de Alba	34	39.07 N	3.06 W
Arganda	34	40.18 N	3.26 W
Argao	106	9.52 N	123.36 E
Arga-Sala ≃	64	68.30 N	112.12 E
Argedeb	134	6.10 N	41.10 E
Argegno	54	45.56 N	9.08 E
Western Desert → Aṣ-Ṣaḥrā' al-Gharbīyah ◆[2]	138	36.47 N	3.03 E
Argelès-Gazost	32	43.01 N	0.06 E
Argelès-sur-Mer	32	42.33 N	3.01 E
Argelia → Algeria □[1]	138	28.00 N	3.00 E
Argen ≃	54	47.35 N	9.33 E
Argens ≃	56	43.24 N	6.44 E
Argent	148	26.04 S	28.50 E
Argenta, It.	60	44.37 N	11.50 E
Argenta, Ill., U.S.	209	39.59 N	88.49 W
Argentan	32	48.45 N	0.01 W
Argentario, Monte ∧	60	42.24 N	11.09 E
Argentat	32	45.06 N	1.56 E
Argentera	56	44.24 N	6.57 E
Argentera ∧	56	44.10 N	7.18 E
Argenteuil	46	48.57 N	2.15 E
Argenteuil □[6]	196	45.45 N	74.30 W
Argentia	176	47.18 N	53.59 W
Argentière	54	45.59 N	6.56 E
Argentières	251	48.39 N	2.52 E
Argentina □[1]	234	34.00 S	64.00 W
Argentina ≃	56	43.50 N	7.51 E
Argentine	206	42.47 N	83.51 W
Argentine → Argentina □[1]	234	34.00 S	64.00 W
Argentine Basin ✣[1]	18	45.00 S	45.00 W
Argentinien → Argentina □[1]	234	34.00 S	64.00 W
Argentino, Hipódromo ♠	278	34.34 S	58.26 W
Argentino, Lago ◎	244	50.13 S	72.25 W
Argentona	256d	41.33 N	2.24 E
Argentona, Riera ≃	256d	41.31 N	2.26 E
Argenton-Château	32	46.59 N	0.27 W
Argenton-sur-Creuse	32	46.35 N	1.31 E
Argentré	32	48.05 N	0.39 W
Argent-sur-Sauldre	46	47.33 N	2.27 E
Argeș □[4]	38	45.00 N	24.45 E
Argeș ≃	38	44.04 N	26.37 E
Arghandāb ≃	118	31.27 N	64.23 E
Arghastān ≃	110	31.23 N	65.45 E
Argirita	246	21.37 S	42.50 W
Argıthanı	120	38.17 N	31.43 E
Argo	130	19.31 N	30.25 E
Ārgoal	116	21.58 N	87.38 E
Argo Island I	130	19.25 N	30.27 E
Argolikós Kólpos C	38	37.33 N	22.45 E
Argolís □[5]	38	37.40 N	22.50 E
Argonia	188	37.16 N	97.46 W
Argonne	180	45.40 N	88.53 W
Argonne ◆[1]	52	49.30 N	5.00 E
Argonne National Laboratory υ[3]	206	41.43 N	87.58 W
Argopuro, Gunung ∧	105a	7.57 S	113.33 E
Árgos, Ellás	38	37.39 N	22.44 E
Argos, Ind., U.S.	206	41.14 N	86.15 W
Árgos Orestikón	38	40.28 N	21.16 E
Argostólion	38	38.10 N	20.30 E
Argoules	46	50.21 N	1.50 E
Argueil	46	49.32 N	1.31 E
Arguello, Point ≻	194	34.35 N	120.39 W
Arguin, Cap d' ≻	138	20.34 N	16.32 W
Argun	74	43.16 N	45.52 E
Argun ≃	74	43.22 N	45.55 E
Argungu	140	12.45 N	4.31 E
Arguni, Teluk C	154	3.06 S	133.42 E
Argunskij Chrebet ∧∧	78	50.05 N	118.20 E
Ārgur	262b	22.48 N	88.13 E
Argut	76	49.51 N	87.03 E
Argut ≃	76	50.16 N	86.43 E
Argyle, Minn., U.S.	188	48.20 N	96.49 W
Argyle, Mo., U.S.	209	38.18 N	92.02 W
Argyle, N.Y., U.S.	200	43.14 N	73.30 W
Argyle, Tex., U.S.	212	33.07 N	97.11 W
'Arhāb, Wādī ∨	132	28.55 N	31.09 E
Arhrîjît	140	18.24 N	9.15 W
Århus	41	56.09 N	10.13 E
Århus □[6]	41	56.15 N	10.05 E
Århus Bugt C	41	56.09 N	10.18 E
Aria	162	38.33 S	174.59 E
Aria ≃	154	5.45 S	149.15 E
Ariadnoje	79	45.08 N	134.25 E
Ariah	116	23.33 N	86.20 E
Ariake-wan C	82	31.28 N	131.08 E
Ariāl Khān ≃	116	23.56 N	90.46 E
Ariāl Khān ≃[1]	116	22.38 N	90.32 E
Ariamsvlei	146	28.08 S	19.50 E
Ariana	36	36.52 N	10.12 E
Ariano, Isola d' I	58	45.10 N	12.10 E
Ariano Irpino	60	41.09 N	15.05 E
Ariano nel Polesine	58	44.56 N	12.07 E
Ariari ≃	236	2.35 N	72.47 W
Arias	242	33.38 S	62.25 W
Arias, Arroyo de ≃	248	34.17 S	56.06 W
Arias, Cañada de ≃	248	34.39 S	58.59 W
Ariaú	240	3.11 S	57.14 W
Aribinda	140	14.14 N	0.52 W
Arica, Chile	238	18.29 S	70.20 W
Arica, Col.	236	2.08 S	71.47 W
Aricanduva, Ribeirão ≃	277b	23.32 S	46.33 W
Ariccia	60	41.43 N	12.40 E
Arichat	176	45.31 N	61.01 W
Arichuna	236	7.42 N	67.08 W
Arid, Cape ≻	152	34.00 S	123.09 E
Arida, Nig.	263a	6.34 N	3.16 E
Arida, Nihon	86	34.05 N	135.07 E
Arida ≃	86	34.05 N	135.06 E
Aridal, Sebjet ◎	138	26.12 N	14.05 W
Aridhaía	38	40.59 N	22.03 E
Ariège □[5]	32	43.00 N	1.30 E

	English	Deutsch	Español	Français	Português
≃	River	Fluss	Río	Rivière	Rio
≡	Canal	Kanal	Canal	Canal	Canal
∟	Waterfall, Rapids	Wasserfall, Stromschnellen	Cascada, Rápidos	Chute d'eau, Rapides	Cascata, Rápidos
⊔	Strait	Meeresstrasse	Estrecho	Détroit	Estreito
C	Bay, Gulf	Bucht, Golf	Bahía, Golfo	Baie, Golfe	Baía, Golfo
◎	Lake, Lakes	See, Seen	Lago, Lagos	Lac, Lacs	Lago, Lagos
	Swamp	Sumpf	Pantano	Marais	Pântano
	Ice Features, Glacier	Eis- und Gletscherformen	Accidentes Glaciales	Formes glaciaires	Acidentes Glaciares
⊤	Other Hydrographic Features	Andere Hydrographische Objekte	Otros Elementos Hidrográficos	Autres données hydrographiques	Outros Elementos Hidrográficos
✣	Submarine Features	Untermeerische Objekte	Accidentes Submarinos	Formes de relief sous-marin	Acidentes Submarinos
□	Political Unit	Politische Einheit	Unidad Politica	Entité politique	Unidade Política
υ	Cultural Institution	Kulturelle Institution	Institución Cultural	Institution culturelle	Instituição Cultural
⊥	Historical Site	Historische Stätte	Sitio Histórico	Site historique	Sitio Histórico
♠	Recreational Site	Erholungs- und Ferienort	Sitio de Recreo	Centre de loisirs	Sítio de Lazer
	Airport	Flughafen	Aeropuerto	Aéroport	Aeroporto
	Military Installation	Militäranlage	Instalación Militar	Installation militaire	Instalação Militar
◆	Miscellaneous	Verschiedenes	Misceláneo	Divers	Miscelânea

Name	Page	Lat. °′	Long. °′
Ariège ≃	32	43.31 N	1.25 E
Ariel	214	45.57 N	122.34 W
Arienzo	60	41.01 N	14.30 E
Arieș ≃	38	46.26 N	23.59 E
'Arif, Har ∧	122	30.26 N	34.44 E
Ārifwāla	113	30.17 N	73.04 E
Ariguanabo, Laguna de ⊜	276b	22.56 N	82.33 W
Ariguaní ≃	236	9.35 N	73.46 W
Arīḥā, Sūrīy.	120	35.48 N	35.36 E
Arīḥā, Urd.	122	31.25 N	35.47 E
Arīḥā (Jericho), Urd.	122	31.52 N	35.27 E
Arikaree ≃	188	40.01 N	101.56 W
Arikaree, North Fork ≃	188	39.39 N	102.57 W
Arikaree, South Fork ≃	188	39.39 N	102.57 W
Arikawa	82	32.59 N	129.07 E
Arild	41	56.16 N	12.34 E
Arima	231r	10.38 N	61.17 W
Arima ◆[8]	260	34.48 N	135.15 E
Arima ≃	260	34.52 N	135.15 E
Arima-fuji ∧[2]	260	34.55 N	135.14 E
Arimine-dam ◆[6]	84	36.29 N	137.27 E
Aringay	106	16.26 N	120.21 E
Arino ◆[8]	260	34.50 N	135.14 E
Arinos ≃	238	10.25 S	58.20 W
Arinthod	54	46.23 N	5.34 E
Ario de Rosales	224	19.12 N	101.43 W
Ariogala	66	55.16 N	23.30 E
Aripeka	210	28.26 N	82.40 W
Ariporo ≃	236	6.03 N	69.54 W
Aripuanã	238	9.10 S	60.38 W
Aripuanã ≃	238	5.07 S	60.24 W
Ariquemes	238	9.56 S	63.04 W
Ariranha, Igarapé ≃	240	1.08 S	55.57 W
'Arīsh, Wādī al- ∨	130	31.09 N	33.49 E
Arismendi	236	8.29 N	68.22 W
Arista, Méx.	224	15.56 N	93.48 W
Arista, Méx.	224	22.39 N	100.50 W
Aristazabal Island I	172	52.30 N	129.05 W
Aristes	200	40.49 N	76.20 W
Aristizábal, Cabo ≻	244	45.13 S	66.31 W
Aristovo	72	54.37 N	36.40 E
Aritao	106	16.18 N	121.02 E
Ariton	184	31.36 N	85.43 W
Arivonimamo	147b	19.01 S	47.15 E
Ariyalūr	112	11.08 N	79.05 E
Arizaro, Salar de ⊻	242	24.42 S	67.45 W
Arizgoiti	34	43.01 N	2.24 W
Arizona	242	35.43 S	65.18 W
Arizona □[3]	168		
	190	34.00 N	112.00 W
Arizpe	222	30.20 N	110.10 W
Arja	70	57.31 N	45.59 E
Årjäng	26	59.23 N	12.08 E
Arjasa	102	6.51 S	115.16 E
Arjawinangun	105a	6.39 S	108.24 E
Arjeplog	24	66.00 N	17.58 E
Arjona, Col.	236	10.15 N	75.21 W
Arjona, Esp.	34	37.56 N	4.03 W
Arka	64	60.03 N	142.12 E
Arkadak	70	51.58 N	43.28 E
Arkadelphia	184	34.07 N	93.04 W
Arkalyk	76	50.13 N	66.50 E
Arkansas □[3]	168	34.50 N	93.40 W
Arkansas ≃	168	33.48 N	91.04 W
Arkansas, Salt Fork ≃	186	36.36 N	97.03 W
Arkansas City, Ark., U.S.	184	33.36 N	91.12 W
Arkansas City, Kans., U.S.	188	37.04 N	97.02 W
Arkansas Post National Memorial ⊥	184	33.55 N	91.26 W
Arken-Ahon ∧	136	20.05 N	18.25 E
Arkhangélos	38	36.12 N	28.08 E
Arkhangel'sk → Archangel'sk	24	64.34 N	40.32 E
Arki	113	31.09 N	76.58 E
Árki I	38	37.22 N	26.45 E
Arkit	75	41.47 N	71.58 E
Arklow	28	52.48 N	6.09 W
Arkona, Kap ≻	50	54.41 N	13.26 E
Arkonam	112	13.06 N	79.40 E
Arkösund	26	58.30 N	16.56 E
Arkport	200	42.24 N	77.42 W
Arktičeskij, Mys ≻	64	81.15 N	95.45 E
Arktičeskogo Instituta, Ostrova II	64	75.20 N	81.55 E
Arkul'	70	57.17 N	50.03 E
Arkville	200	42.09 N	74.37 W
Arkwright	197	41.43 N	71.33 W
Ärla	40	59.17 N	16.40 E
Arlan	70	55.58 N	54.15 E
Arlanc	56	45.25 N	3.44 E
Arlanda flygplats ⊠	40	59.37 N	17.55 E
Arlanza ≃	34	42.06 N	4.09 W
Arlanzón ≃	34	42.03 N	4.17 W
Arlbergpass)(	58	47.08 N	10.12 E
Arlberg-Tunnel ◆[5]	54	47.08 N	10.12 E
Arlee	192	47.10 N	114.05 W
Arles	56	43.40 N	4.38 E
Arles à Port de Bouc, Canal d ≍	56	43.40 N	4.37 E
Arlesheim	54	47.30 N	7.37 E
Arleta ◆[8]	270	34.15 N	118.26 W
Arleux	46	50.17 N	3.06 E
Arley	252	53.19 N	2.30 W
Arlington, S. Afr.	148	28.06 S	27.54 E
Arlington, Ga., U.S.	182	31.27 N	84.44 W
Arlington, Ind., U.S.	208	39.39 N	85.35 W
Arlington, Iowa, U.S.	180	42.45 N	91.40 W
Arlington, Kans., U.S.	188	37.54 N	98.11 W
Arlington, Ky., U.S.	184	36.47 N	89.01 W
Arlington, Mass., U.S.	197	42.25 N	71.09 W
Arlington, Minn., U.S.	180	44.36 N	94.05 W
Arlington, Nebr., U.S.	188	41.27 N	96.21 W
Arlington, N.Y., U.S.	200	41.42 N	73.54 W
Arlington, Ohio, U.S.	206	40.54 N	83.39 W
Arlington, Oreg., U.S.	192	45.16 N	120.13 W
Arlington, S. Dak., U.S.	188	44.22 N	97.08 W
Arlington, Tenn., U.S.	184	35.18 N	89.40 W
Arlington, Tex., U.S.	212	32.44 N	97.07 W
Arlington, Vt., U.S.	178	43.05 N	73.09 W
Arlington, Va., U.S.	198	38.52 N	77.05 W
Arlington, Wash., U.S.	214	48.12 N	122.08 W
Arlington □[6]	274c	38.50 N	77.10 W
Arlington, Lake ⊜[1]	212	32.42 N	97.13 W
Arlington Heights, Ill., U.S.	206	42.05 N	87.59 W
Arlington Heights, Mass., U.S.	273	42.25 N	71.11 W
Arlington Memorial Bridge ◆[5]	274c	38.53 N	77.03 W
Arlington Mill Reservoir ⊜[1]	273	42.48 N	71.13 W
Arlington National Cemetery ◆	274c	38.53 N	77.04 W
Arlington Park Race Track ♠	268	42.05 N	88.01 W
Arlod	54	46.06 N	5.49 E
Arlon	52	49.41 N	5.49 E
Arlöv	41	55.39 N	13.05 E
Arltunga	152	23.26 S	134.41 E
Arl'uk	76	55.26 N	84.50 E
Arluno	56	45.30 N	8.56 E
Arly	140	11.35 N	1.28 E
Arly ≃	56	45.40 N	6.23 E
Arly, Parc National d' ♠	140	11.35 N	1.15 E
Arlyn Oaks	266	40.40 N	73.27 W
Arm ≃	174	50.46 N	105.00 W
Arma	188	37.33 N	94.42 W
Armação, Ponta da ≻	277a	22.53 S	43.08 W
Armada	204	42.51 N	82.53 W
Armadale, Austl.	158a	32.09 S	116.00 E
Armadale, Ont., Can.	265b	43.50 N	79.15 W
Armadale, Scot., U.K.	42	55.54 N	3.42 W
Arma di Taggia	56	43.50 N	7.51 E
Armagh, N. Ire., U.K.	42	54.21 N	6.39 W
Armagh, Pa., U.S.	204	40.27 N	79.02 W
Armagnac □[9]	32	43.45 N	0.10 E
Armāh, Wādī ∨	134	18.15 N	51.00 E
Armainvilliers, Étang d' ⊜	251	48.45 N	2.44 E
Armainvilliers, Forêt d' ♠	251	48.45 N	2.45 E
Armance ≃	46	47.26 N	3.33 E
Armançon ≃, Fr.	46	47.57 N	3.30 E
Armançon ≃, Fr.	54	47.33 N	4.17 E
Arm'ansk	68	46.07 N	33.41 E
Arm'anskaja Sovetskaja Socialističeskaja Respublika □[3]	74	40.00 N	45.00 E
Armant	130	25.37 N	32.32 E
Armavir	62	45.00 N	41.08 E
Armazém	242	28.16 S	49.01 W
Armbrust	204	40.13 N	79.33 W
Armells Creek ≃	192	47.37 N	108.40 W
Armenia	236	4.31 N	75.41 W
Armenia □[9]	74	40.00 N	45.00 E
Armenian Soviet Socialist Republic → Arm'anskaja Sovetskaja Socialističeskaja Respublika □[3]	74	40.00 N	43.00 E
Armeniș	38	45.12 N	22.19 E
Armenistís	38	37.36 N	26.08 E
Armeno	56	45.49 N	8.26 E
Armenonville-les-Gâtineaux	251	48.33 N	1.39 E
Armentières	46	50.41 N	2.53 E
Armería	224	18.56 N	103.58 W
Armería ≃	224	18.52 N	103.59 W
Armero	236	4.58 N	74.54 W
Armidale	156	30.31 S	151.39 E
Armijo	190	35.03 N	106.41 W
Armil Island I	134	16.25 N	40.12 E
Armit Lake ⊜	166	64.10 N	91.32 W
Armizonskoje	76	55.57 N	67.42 E
Armona	216	36.19 N	119.42 W
Armonk	266	41.08 N	73.43 W
Armor	200	42.44 N	78.48 W
Armori	112	20.28 N	79.59 E
Armour	188	43.19 N	98.21 W
Armoy	54	46.21 N	6.31 E
Armstrong, Arg.	242	32.47 S	61.36 W
Armstrong, B.C., Can.	172	50.27 N	119.12 W
Armstrong, Ill., U.S.	206	40.18 N	87.53 W
Armstrong, Iowa, U.S.	188	43.24 N	94.29 W
Armstrong, Mo., U.S.	184	39.16 N	92.42 W
Armstrong □[6]	204	40.49 N	79.32 W
Armstrong ≃	154	16.46 S	131.12 E
Armstrong, Mount ∧	170	63.12 N	133.16 W
Armstrong Station	166	50.18 N	89.02 W
Armthorpe	42	53.32 N	1.03 W
Ārmūr	112	18.48 N	78.17 E
Armutlu	120	40.31 N	28.50 E
Arnå ≃	41	54.57 N	8.53 E
Arnaccio	60	43.40 N	10.17 E
Arnaía	38	40.29 N	23.35 E
Arnarfjörđur C[2]	24a	65.45 N	23.40 W
Årnäs	40	58.41 N	13.35 E
Arnaud ≃	166	59.59 N	69.46 W
Arnaudville	184	30.24 N	91.56 W
Arnavutköy ≃	257b	41.13 N	29.12 E
Arnay-le-Duc	54	47.08 N	4.29 E
Arnaz	56	45.38 N	7.43 E
Arnborg	41	56.01 N	8.59 E
Arncliffe	264a	33.56 S	151.09 E
Arneburg	50	52.40 N	12.00 E
Arnedo	34	42.13 N	2.06 W
Arneiro dos Marinheiros	256c	38.51 N	9.25 W
Arneiroz	240	6.20 S	40.08 W
Arnejevo	72	54.58 N	37.35 E
Arnemuiden	48	51.30 N	3.41 E
Årnes	26	60.09 N	11.28 E
Arnett	186	36.08 N	99.46 W
Arnhem	48	51.59 N	5.55 E
Arnhem, Cape ≻	154	12.21 S	136.21 E
Arnhem Bay C	154	12.20 S	136.12 E
Arnhem Land ◆[1]	154	13.10 S	134.30 E
Arnhem Land Aboriginal Reserve ◆[4]	154	13.10 S	134.30 E
Arni	58	44.04 N	10.15 E
Arnis	41	54.38 N	9.56 E
Árnissa	38	40.48 N	21.50 E
Arno I[1]	14	7.05 N	171.41 E
Arno ≃	60	43.41 N	10.17 E
Arno Bay	156	33.54 S	136.34 E
Arnold, B.C., Can.	214	49.08 N	122.03 W
Arnold, Eng., U.K.	44	53.00 N	1.08 W
Arnold, Calif., U.S.	194	38.15 N	120.21 W
Arnold, Minn., U.S.	180	46.53 N	92.05 W
Arnold, Mo., U.S.	209	38.26 N	90.23 W
Arnold, Nebr., U.S.	188	41.26 N	100.12 W
Arnold, Pa., U.S.	204	40.35 N	79.45 W
Arnold Mills	273	41.59 N	71.24 W
Arnolds Park	188	43.22 N	95.08 W
Arnoldstein	58	46.33 N	13.43 E
Arnon ≃	46	48.16 N	0.38 E
Arnos Vale Airfield ⊠	231h	13.09 N	61.13 W
Arnot	200	41.40 N	77.07 W
Arnouville-lès-Gonesse	251	49.00 N	2.25 E
Arnouville-lès-Mantes	251	48.55 N	1.44 E
Arnoya ≃	34	42.15 N	8.09 W
Arnprior	202	45.26 N	76.21 W
Arnsberg	52	51.24 N	8.03 E
Arnsberg □[5]	48	51.20 N	7.15 E
Arnsberger Wald, Naturpark ♠	52	51.25 N	8.20 E
Arnsdorf	50	51.05 N	13.59 E
Arnstadt	50	50.50 N	10.57 E
Arnstein	52	49.58 N	9.58 E
Arnswalde → Choszczno	30	53.10 N	15.26 E
Arnum	41	55.15 N	8.59 E
Arø I	41	55.15 N	9.45 E
Aro ≃	236	8.01 N	64.11 W
Aroa	236	10.26 N	68.54 W
Aroa ≃	236	10.40 N	68.19 W
Aroa, Pointe ≻	164s	17.28 S	149.46 W
Aroab	146	26.47 S	19.40 E
Aroali	116	24.03 N	87.56 E
Arochukwu	140	5.23 N	7.55 E
Aroeiras	240	7.31 S	35.41 W
Ar'ofino	70	58.16 N	39.15 E
Arolla	54	46.02 N	7.29 E
Arolsen	52	51.23 N	9.01 E
Aroma	130	15.49 N	36.08 E
Aroma, Quebrada de ≃	238	19.55 S	69.45 W
Aroma Park	206	41.05 N	87.48 W
Aromas	216	36.53 N	121.39 W
Aromaševo	76	56.52 N	68.39 E
Aron ≃	46	47.15 N	2.02 E
Arona, It.	56	45.46 N	8.34 E
Arona, Pap. N. Gui.	154	6.20 S	146.00 E
Arona, Pa., U.S.	269b	40.16 N	79.39 W
Arongqi (Najitun)	79	48.07 N	123.28 E
Aroostook ≃	176	46.48 N	67.45 W
Aropuk Lake ⊜	170	61.12 N	163.50 W
Arorae I	14	2.38 S	176.49 E
Arorangi	164k	21.13 S	159.49 W
Aroroy	106	12.31 N	123.24 E
Arosa	54	46.47 N	9.41 E
Arosa, Ría de C[1]	34	42.28 N	8.57 W
Arosbaya	105a	6.56 S	112.51 E
Årøsund	41	55.16 N	9.45 E
Arotali	134	15.02 N	39.43 E
Aro Usu, Tanjung ≻	154	8.20 S	130.45 E
Arowhana ∧	162	38.07 S	177.52 E
Arp	212	32.13 N	95.04 W
Arpa (Achur'an) ≃, As.	74	40.06 N	43.39 E
Arpa ≃, S.S.S.R.	74	39.28 N	44.57 E
Arpaçay	74	40.52 N	43.20 E
Arpačin	73	47.14 N	40.11 E
Arpaia	60	41.02 N	14.33 E
Arpajon	46	48.35 N	2.15 E
Ārpāra	116	23.23 N	89.23 E
Arpino	60	41.39 N	13.36 E
Arpoador, Ponta do ≻, Bra.	242	24.25 S	47.00 W
Arpoador, Ponta do ≻, Bra.	277a	22.59 S	43.12 W
Arquà Petrarca	58	45.16 N	11.43 E
Arquà Polesine	58	45.01 N	11.45 E
Arquata del Tronto	60	42.46 N	13.18 E
Arquata Scrivia	56	44.41 N	8.53 E
Arque	238	17.48 S	66.23 W
Arques	46	50.44 N	2.17 E
Arques-la-Bataille	46	49.53 N	1.08 E
Arra	140	6.40 N	3.58 W
Ar-Rabaḍ	118	23.11 N	39.32 E
Ar-Rab' al-Khālī ◆[2]	126	20.00 N	51.00 E
Ar-Rabbah	122	31.16 N	35.44 E
Arracourt	54	48.44 N	6.32 E
Ar-Radīsīyah Baḥrī	130	24.57 N	32.53 E
Ar-Rafīd	122	32.57 N	35.53 E
Arraga	242	28.04 S	64.14 W
Arrah	114	25.34 N	84.40 E
Ar-Rahad	130	12.43 N	30.39 E
Ar-Raḥāminah	132	31.18 N	31.45 E
Ar-Raḥmānīyah	132	31.06 N	30.38 E
Arraial	246	22.50 S	46.39 W
Arraial do Cabo	245	22.58 S	42.01 W
Arraias	245	12.56 S	46.57 W
Arraias ≃, Bra.	240	11.10 S	53.35 W
Arraias ≃, Bra.	245	12.28 S	47.18 W
Ar-Ramādī	118	33.25 N	43.17 E
Ar-Ramādī □[4]	118	33.30 N	43.00 E
Ar-Ramthā	122	32.34 N	36.00 E
Arran, Island of I	42	55.35 N	5.15 W
Ar-Rank	130	11.45 N	32.48 E
Arran Lake ⊜	202	44.29 N	81.16 W
Ar-Raqqah	120	35.56 N	39.01 E
Ar-Raqqah □[8]	120	36.00 N	39.00 E
Arras	46	50.17 N	2.47 E
Ar-Ra's al-Aswad ≻	134	21.20 N	39.07 E
Ar-Rāshidah	130	25.35 N	28.56 E
Ar-Rass	118	25.52 N	43.28 E
Ar-Rastān	120	34.55 N	36.44 E
Arrats ≃	32	44.06 N	0.52 E
Ar-Rawḍah, Ar. Sa.	118	26.05 N	40.37 E
Ar-Rawḍah, Miṣr	132	27.48 N	30.52 E
Ar-Rawḍah, Miṣr	132	29.27 N	31.00 E
Ar-Rawḍah, Yam. S.	134	14.28 N	47.17 E
Ar-Rāwuk	134	15.45 N	48.54 E
Ar-Rayramūn	132	27.45 N	30.52 E
Ar-Rayyāḥ ar-Minūfīya ≍	132	30.20 N	31.00 E
Ar-Rayyāḥ at-Tawfīqī ≍	132	30.11 N	31.07 E
Arrecife	138	28.57 N	13.32 W
Arrecifes	242	34.03 S	60.07 W
Arrée, Montagnes d' ∧∧	32	48.26 N	3.55 W
Arregui, Laguna ⊜	248	35.05 S	57.33 W
Arrentela	256c	38.38 N	9.06 W
Arresø ⊜	41	55.58 N	12.08 E
Arrey	190	32.51 N	107.19 W
Arriaga	224	16.14 N	93.54 W
Arriba	188	39.17 N	103.17 W
Arrild	41	55.09 N	8.58 E
Ar-Rimāh	118	25.34 N	47.09 E
Ar-Riyāḍ (Riyadh)	118	24.38 N	46.43 E
Arroio Grande	242	32.14 S	53.05 W
Arrojado ≃	245	13.24 S	44.20 W
Arronches	34	39.07 N	7.17 W
Arrone ≃, It.	60	42.18 N	11.38 E
Arrone ≃, It.	60	41.52 N	12.11 E
Arros ≃	32	43.40 N	0.02 W
Arroscia ≃	56	44.03 N	8.11 E
Arroux ≃	32	46.29 N	3.58 E
Arrow ≃, Eng., U.K.	44	52.09 N	1.53 W
Arrow ≃, Eng., U.K.	44	52.12 N	2.43 W
Arrow Creek ≃	192	47.43 N	109.50 W
Arrow Dam ◆[6]	172	49.20 N	117.49 W
Arrowhead, Lake ⊜[1]	218	34.15 N	117.11 W
Arrowhead Peak ∧	218	34.13 N	117.16 W
Arrowhead Village	198	40.04 N	74.07 W
Arrow Lake ⊜	180	48.08 N	90.18 W
Arrowrock Reservoir ⊜[1]	192	43.36 N	115.51 W
Arrowsmith	206	40.27 N	88.38 W
Arrowsmith, Mount ∧, Austl.	156	30.09 S	141.50 E
Arrowsmith, Mount ∧, N.Z.	162	43.21 S	170.59 E
Arrowsmith Bay C	166	68.00 N	95.15 W
Arrowsmith Range ∧∧	162	43.18 S	171.00 E
Arrowtown	162	44.56 S	168.50 E
Arrowwood	172	50.44 N	113.09 W
Arroyan, Arroyo ≃[1]	278	34.24 S	58.32 W
Arroyito	242	31.25 S	63.03 W
Arroyo	230m	17.58 N	66.04 W
Arroyo, Puerto C	230m	17.58 N	66.05 W
Arroyo Arenas	276b	23.02 N	82.28 W
Arroyo de la Luz	34	39.29 N	6.35 W
Arroyo Frío	224	17.26 N	100.35 W
Arroyo Grande, Calif., U.S.	194	35.07 N	120.34 W
Arroyo Grande → Ismael Cortinas, Ur.	248	33.58 S	57.06 W
Arroyo Hondo	190	36.32 N	105.40 W
Arroyo Naranjo ◆[8]	276b	23.02 N	82.23 W
Arroyo Seco Park ♠	270	34.06 N	118.12 W
Arroyos y Esteros	242	25.04 S	57.06 W
Arrozal	246	22.37 S	44.03 W
Ar-Ru'at	130	12.21 N	32.17 E
Ar-Rubayqī	132	30.10 N	31.46 E
Ar-Ruḥaybah	122	33.45 N	36.42 E
Ar-Rukhaymīyah ⊤[4]	118	29.14 N	45.35 E
Ar-Rumaythah	118	31.32 N	45.12 E
Ar-Rummān	122	32.10 N	35.50 E
Ar-Ruqayyah ⊥	122	32.47 N	37.05 E
Ar-Ruṣāfah ⊥	120	35.37 N	38.45 E
Ar-Ruṣayriș	134	11.51 N	34.23 E
Ar-Rushaydah	122	32.40 N	36.50 E
Ar-Ruṭbah	118	33.02 N	40.17 E
Ar-Ru'ūs	132	29.21 N	31.04 E
Års	26	56.48 N	9.32 E
Arsacides, Cape ≻	165e	8.39 S	161.01 E
Aršan, S.S.S.R.	78	51.54 N	102.27 E
Aršan, S.S.S.R.	78	53.54 N	99.54 E
Aršan'-Zel'men'	70	47.36 N	44.36 E
Ārsāpota	262b	22.55 N	88.18 E
Arsbeck	52	51.08 N	6.12 E
Arsenal de Marinha ■	256c	38.39 N	9.09 W
Arsenal Football Club ♠	250	51.33 N	0.06 W
Arsenault Lake ⊜	174	55.06 N	108.30 W
Arsenjān	118	29.56 N	53.18 E
Arsenjev	79	44.10 N	133.15 E
Arsenjevo	66	53.44 N	36.40 E
Arsiè	58	45.59 N	11.45 E
Arsiero	58	45.48 N	11.21 E
Arsikere	112	13.20 N	76.15 E
Arsin	120	40.58 N	39.56 E
Aršincevo	68	45.17 N	36.25 E
Arsıyan Dağı ∧	120	41.24 N	42.30 E
Arsk	70	56.06 N	49.54 E
Arslanbob	75	41.21 N	72.56 E
Årslev	41	55.18 N	10.29 E
Arsoli	60	42.02 N	13.01 E
Ars-on-Ré	32	46.12 N	1.31 W
Ársos	120	34.50 N	32.46 E
Ars-sur-Formans	54	45.59 N	4.49 E
Ars-sur-Moselle	52	49.05 N	6.04 E
Årsta havsbad	40	59.05 N	18.10 E
Arsufhsa ≃	74	39.08 N	46.50 E
Årsunda	40	60.32 N	16.44 E
Arsuz	120	36.27 N	35.51 E
Art, Île I	165f	19.43 S	163.38 E
Árta, Ellás	38	39.09 N	20.59 E
Artá, Esp.	34	39.42 N	3.21 E
Artarmon	264a	33.49 S	151.11 E
Artašat	74	39.59 N	44.33 E
Arta Terme	58	46.28 N	13.01 E
Arteaga	224	18.28 N	102.25 W
Arteche	106	12.17 N	125.22 E
Artegna	58	46.14 N	13.09 E
Artemare	56	45.52 N	5.42 E
Artemisa	230p	22.49 N	82.46 W
Artemón	38	36.59 N	24.43 E
Artémou	140	15.31 N	12.16 W
Artemovsk → Art'omovsk	73	48.35 N	38.00 E
Artèn	58	46.00 N	11.50 E
Artenay	46	48.05 N	1.53 E
Artern	50	51.22 N	11.17 E
Artesia → Mosomane, Bots.	146	24.04 S	26.15 E
Artesia, Calif., U.S.	270	33.52 N	118.05 W
Artesia, Miss., U.S.	184	33.25 N	88.39 W
Artesia, N. Mex., U.S.	186	32.51 N	104.24 W
Artesia Lake ⊜	216	38.57 N	119.22 W
Artesian	188	44.00 N	97.55 W
Arth	54	47.04 N	8.31 E
Arthabaska	196	46.02 N	71.55 W
Arthabaska □[6]	196	46.05 N	72.00 W
Arthal	113	33.16 N	76.11 E
Arthala	262a	28.40 N	77.24 E
Arthies	251	49.06 N	1.48 E
Arthonnay	46	47.56 N	4.13 E
Arthur, Ont., Can.	202	43.50 N	80.32 W
Arthur, Ill., U.S.	184	39.43 N	88.28 W
Arthur, Nebr., U.S.	188	41.35 N	101.41 W
Arthur, N. Dak., U.S.	188	47.06 N	97.13 W
Arthur, Tenn., U.S.	182	36.33 N	83.40 W
Arthur ≃	158a	33.31 S	116.50 E
Arthur, Lake ⊜[1]	204	40.57 N	80.05 W
Arthur Fiord C[2]	166	76.33 N	93.11 W
Arthur Kill ⋓	266	40.30 N	74.15 W
Arthur's Pass	162	42.57 S	171.34 E
Arthur's Pass)(	162	42.54 S	171.34 E
Arthur's Pass National Park ♠	162	42.50 S	171.40 E
Arthurs Seat ∧[2]	159	38.21 S	144.57 E
Arthurs Town	228	24.38 N	75.42 W
Arthurton	158b	34.16 S	137.45 E
Arti	76	56.26 N	58.32 E
Artibonite ≃	228	19.15 N	72.47 W
Artico, Océano → Arctic Ocean ⊤[1]	16	85.00 N	170.00 E
Artigas	242	30.24 S	56.28 W
Artigas ◆[8]	276c	10.30 N	66.56 W
Artigas, Casa de ⊥	248	34.39 S	56.03 W
Artik	74	40.37 N	43.59 E
Artilleros	248	34.22 S	57.34 W
Artilleros, Punta ≻	248	34.28 S	57.32 W
Artillery Lake ⊜	166	63.09 N	107.52 W
Artlenburg	48	53.22 N	10.29 E
Artois □[9]	46	50.30 N	2.30 E
Art'om	79	43.22 N	132.13 E
Art'om-Ostrov	74	40.28 N	50.20 E
Art'omovka, S.S.S.R.	68	49.46 N	35.04 E
Art'omovka, S.S.S.R.	73	48.29 N	37.23 E
Art'omovka, S.S.S.R.	73	47.53 N	38.38 E
Art'omovo	73	48.22 N	37.53 E
Art'omovsk, S.S.S.R.	73	48.27 N	38.42 E
Art'omovsk, S.S.S.R.	73	48.35 N	38.00 E
Art'omovsk, S.S.S.R.	76	54.21 N	93.26 E
Art'omovskij, S.S.S.R.	76	57.21 N	61.54 E
Art'omovskij, S.S.S.R.	78	58.12 N	114.45 E
Art'omovskij, S.S.S.R.	79	43.27 N	132.22 E
Artova	120	40.03 N	36.19 E
Artuby ≃	56	43.44 N	6.22 E
Artur de Paiva	142	14.28 S	16.20 E
Artur Nogueira	246	22.35 S	47.09 W
Arturo Segui	248	34.51 S	58.09 W
Arturo Segui ◆[8]	248	34.51 S	58.09 W
Artvin	120	41.11 N	41.49 E
Artvin □[4]	120	41.05 N	42.00 E
Artybaš	76	51.48 N	87.16 E
Artyk	64	64.12 N	145.06 E
Aru, Kepulauan II	154	6.00 S	134.30 E
Aru, Tanjung ≻	102	2.10 S	116.34 E
Aru, Teluk C	104	4.09 N	98.12 E
Arua	144	3.01 N	30.55 E
Aruã ≃	240	2.39 S	55.38 W
Aruanã	245	14.54 S	51.05 W
Aruângua (Luangwa) ≃	144	15.36 S	30.25 E
Aruba I	231s	12.30 N	69.58 W
Aru Basin ⊤[1]	14	5.30 S	133.30 E
Arufu	140	7.50 N	9.14 E
Arujá	246	23.24 S	46.20 W
Arujá □[7]	277b	23.24 S	46.20 W
Arumanduba	240	1.29 S	52.29 W
Arume	164m	26.36 N	128.07 E
Arume-wan C	164m	26.35 N	128.08 E
Arumuganeri	112	8.34 N	78.07 E
Arun ≃, As.	114	26.49 N	87.09 E
Arun ≃, Eng., U.K.	44	50.48 N	0.33 W
Arunachal Pradesh □[8]	110	28.30 N	95.00 E
Arundel, Qué., Can.	196	45.58 N	74.37 W
Arundel, Eng., U.K.	44	50.51 N	0.34 W
Årup	41	55.23 N	10.04 E
Aru Passage ⋓	164r	6.57 N	158.20 E
Aruppukkottai	112	9.31 N	78.06 E
Arurandéua ≃	240	3.43 S	48.50 W
Arus, Tanjung ≻	102	1.20 N	120.48 E
Arusha	144	3.22 S	36.41 E
Arusha □[4]	144	4.00 S	36.15 E
Arusha Chini	144	3.35 S	37.20 E
Arusha National Park ♠	144	3.17 S	36.56 E
Arusi □[4]	134	8.00 N	39.40 E
Aruvi ≃	112	8.49 N	79.55 E
Aruwimi ≃	128	1.13 N	23.36 E
Arvada	190	39.50 N	105.05 W
Arvajcheer	80	46.15 N	102.45 E
Arve ≃	54	46.12 N	6.08 E
Arverne ◆[8]	266	40.35 N	73.48 W
Arves, Les Aiguilles d' ∧	56	45.08 N	6.21 E
Arvi	110	20.59 N	78.14 E
Arvida	176	48.25 N	71.11 W
Arvidsjaur	24	65.35 N	19.07 E
Arvier	56	45.42 N	7.11 E
Arvieux	56	44.46 N	6.44 E
Arvika	26	59.39 N	12.36 E
Arvillard	56	45.27 N	6.07 E
Arvin	218	35.12 N	118.50 W
Arvonia	182	37.41 N	78.20 W
Àrvorezinha	242	28.53 S	52.10 W
Arwadin	134	16.16 N	38.46 E
Arwal	114	25.15 N	84.41 E
Arwala	102	7.41 S	126.49 E
Aryamūn	132	31.11 N	30.54 E
Aryiroúpolis	257c	37.54 N	23.45 E
Arys → Orzysz, Pol.	30	53.49 N	21.56 E
Arys', S.S.S.R.	75	42.26 N	68.48 E
Arys' ≃	75	42.48 N	68.12 E
Arys, Ozero ⊜	76	45.50 N	66.20 E
Arzachena	36	41.05 N	9.22 E
Arzamas	70	55.23 N	43.50 E
Arzano	60	40.55 N	14.16 E
Arzew	138	35.51 N	0.19 W
Arzew, Golfe d' C	34	35.50 N	0.10 W
Arzew, Salines d' ⊜	34	35.40 N	0.15 W
Arzfeld	52	50.05 N	6.16 E
Arzignano	58	45.31 N	11.20 E
Arz Lubnān ◆[3]	120	34.14 N	36.03 E
Arzni	74	40.19 N	44.36 E
Arzo	154	2.56 S	140.47 E
Arzon ≃	56	45.11 N	3.54 E
Arzúa	34	42.56 N	8.09 W
As, Bel.	52	51.01 N	5.35 E
Aš, Česko.	50	50.10 N	12.10 E
Ås, Nor.	26	59.40 N	10.48 E
Asa, Nihon	86	34.33 N	132.26 E
Aša, S.S.S.R.	76	55.00 N	57.16 E
Asa ≃, Nihon	84	35.39 N	139.26 E
Asa ≃, Nihon	86	34.01 N	131.09 E
Asab	146	25.29 S	17.59 E
Asaba, Nig.	140	6.12 N	6.44 E
Asaba, Nihon	84	34.42 N	137.56 E
Asadābād, Afg.	110	34.52 N	71.09 E
Asadābād, Īrān	118	34.47 N	48.07 E
Asafo	140	6.11 N	0.28 W
Asagaya ◆[8]	258	35.42 N	139.38 E
Aşağıçığıl	120	38.03 N	31.52 E
Aşağı Dağ ∧	74	40.01 N	43.11 E
Aşağıhanik	120	37.43 N	39.59 E
Aşağı İhtik	120	39.38 N	38.49 E
Asagı Kuluşağı	120	38.39 N	38.39 E
Aşağılahan	120	38.50 N	39.59 E
Aşağı Mestikân	120	38.25 N	38.46 E
Ašagy-G'ojn'uk	74	41.18 N	47.00 E
Asahan	104	2.23 N	102.33 E
Asahan ≃	104	3.02 N	99.52 E
Asahi, Nihon	84	36.14 N	140.31 E
Asahi, Nihon	84	35.59 N	136.07 E
Asahi, Nihon	84	36.05 N	137.21 E
Asahi, Nihon	84	35.14 N	137.22 E
Asahi, Nihon	84	35.43 N	140.39 E
Asahi, Nihon	84	36.07 N	137.52 E
Asahi, Nihon	84	35.02 N	136.40 E
Asahi, Nihon	84	36.57 N	137.34 E
Asahi, Nihon	84	35.12 N	137.02 E
Asahi, Nihon	86	34.59 N	133.50 E
Asahi, Nihon	86	34.51 N	132.16 E
Asahi, Nihon	86	34.17 N	131.28 E
Asahi ◆[8]	260	34.44 N	135.34 E
Asahi ≃	86	34.36 N	133.58 E
Asahi-chosuichi ⊜[1]	84	36.04 N	137.25 E
Asahi-dake ∧, Nihon	82a	43.40 N	142.51 E
Asahi-dake ∧, Nihon	84	37.14 N	139.21 E
Asahigawa → Asahikawa	82a	43.46 N	142.22 E
Asahi-gawa-daiichi-dam ◆[6]	86	34.53 N	133.22 E
Asahikawa	82a	43.46 N	142.22 E
Asahi-ko ⊜[1]	86	34.56 N	133.51 E
Ašt	75	40.41 N	70.20 E
Asaka	84	35.48 N	139.36 E
Asaka, Camp (United States) ■	258	35.47 N	139.36 E
Asakanskij Golec, Gora ∧	78	50.18 N	109.55 E
Asakawa	84	37.05 N	140.25 E
Asake ≃	84	35.00 N	136.41 E
Asako	86	35.14 N	134.48 E
Asakura	86	33.23 N	130.44 E
Asālafpur ◆[8]	262a	28.38 N	77.05 E
Asale	134	14.22 N	40.32 E
Asale, Lake ⊜	134	14.19 N	40.18 E
Asamankese	140	5.52 N	0.42 W
Asama-yama ∧	84	36.24 N	138.31 E
Asambar ∧	113	36.29 N	73.38 E
Asanbāni, Bhārat	116	24.07 N	87.27 E
Asanbani, Bhārat	116	22.43 N	86.20 E
Asani	144	4.25 S	29.05 E
Asankrangwa	140	5.48 N	2.26 W
Asan-man C	88	36.56 N	126.51 E
Asanovo	70	52.19 N	47.24 E
Asansol, Bhārat	116	23.41 N	86.59 E
Asansol, Bhārat	116	24.14 N	87.17 E
Ašap	76	57.07 N	56.30 E
Åsarna	26	62.39 N	14.21 E
Asarum	26	56.12 N	14.50 E
'As'As, Qūr ∧[2]	132	28.43 N	30.12 E
Asashina	84	36.16 N	138.25 E
Āsāsuni	116	22.32 N	89.10 E
Asati	262b	22.29 N	88.14 E
Asa-yama ∧	86	34.47 N	132.23 E
Asayita	134	11.33 N	41.30 E
Asbeck	253	51.21 N	7.18 E
Asberg	253	51.26 N	6.40 E
Asbesberge ∧∧	148	28.55 S	23.15 E
Asbest	76	57.00 N	61.30 E
Asbestos	196	45.46 N	71.57 W
Asbe Teferi	134	9.02 N	40.58 E
Åsbro	40	59.00 N	15.03 E
Asbury	200	40.42 N	75.01 W
Asbury Park	198	40.13 N	74.01 W
Ascensión, Méx.	222	31.06 N	107.59 W
Ascensión, Méx.	222	24.20 N	99.55 W
Ascension I	10	7.57 S	14.22 W
Ascensión, Bahía de la C	222	19.40 N	87.30 W
Ascent	148	27.12 S	29.03 E
Aščerino	255b	55.36 N	37.46 E
Asch	54	47.57 N	10.49 E
Aščhabad	118	37.57 N	58.23 E
Aschaffenburg	52	49.59 N	9.09 E
Ascheberg, B.R.D.	48	51.47 N	7.37 E
Ascheberg, B.R.D.	50	54.08 N	10.20 E
Aschendorf	48	53.04 N	7.22 E
Aschersleben	50	51.45 N	11.27 E
Asciano	60	43.14 N	11.33 E
Aščikol', Ozero ⊜	76	45.05 N	67.15 E
Aščiozek ≃	70	49.12 N	48.06 E
Aščitastysor, Ozero ⊜	76	49.19 N	63.59 E
Ascoli Piceno	60	42.51 N	13.34 E
Ascoli Piceno □[4]	60	43.01 N	13.34 E
Ascoli Satriano	60	41.12 N	15.34 E
Ascona	54	46.09 N	8.46 E
Ascope	238	7.43 S	79.07 W
Ascot, Austl.	161a	27.26 S	153.04 E
Ascot, Eng., U.K.	44	51.25 N	0.41 W
Ascot ≃	196	45.21 N	71.51 W
Ascotán	242	21.44 S	68.18 W
Ascros	56	43.55 N	7.01 E
Aseb	134	13.00 N	42.45 E
Åseda	26	57.10 N	15.20 E
Asedjrad ∧∧[1]	138	24.28 N	1.52 E
Asekejevo	70	53.36 N	52.49 E
Asela	134	7.59 N	39.08 E
Åsele	26	64.10 N	17.20 E
Asem ≃	105a	6.14 S	107.42 E
Asembagus	105a	7.45 S	114.14 E
Asembourg	52	49.43 N	6.02 E
Åsen	26	63.36 N	11.03 E
Asendabo	134	9.50 N	37.33 E
Asendorf	48	52.46 N	9.00 E
Asenovgrad	38	42.01 N	24.52 E
Åsensbruk	26	58.48 N	12.25 E
Aseri	66	59.27 N	26.52 E
Aşfar, Jabal al- ∧	122	32.12 N	36.54 E
Aşfar al-Maḥaṭṭah	122	30.11 N	35.46 E
Aşfūn al-Maṭā'inah	130	25.23 N	32.32 E
Åsgårdstrand	26	59.21 N	10.28 E
Ash, Eng., U.K.	44	51.17 N	1.16 E
Ash, Eng., U.K.	44	51.15 N	0.44 W
Ash ≃	44	51.48 N	0.02 W
Åshammar	40	60.39 N	16.32 E
Ashanti □[4]	140	6.45 N	1.30 W
'Asharah, Wādī al- ∨	132	30.21 N	32.15 E
Asharoken	266	40.56 N	73.22 W
Ashaway	197	41.25 N	71.47 W
Ashbourne, Eire	42	53.31 N	6.24 W
Ashbourne, Eng., U.K.	44	53.02 N	1.44 W
Ash Brook Swamp Reservation ♠	266	40.37 N	74.21 W
Ashburn, Ga., U.S.	182	31.43 N	83.39 W
Ashburn, Mo., U.S.	209	39.33 N	91.10 W
Ashburn, Va., U.S.	198	39.03 N	77.29 W
Ashburnham	197	42.38 N	71.55 W
Ashburton, Austl.	264b	37.52 S	145.05 E
Ashburton, N.Z.	162	43.55 S	171.45 E
Ashburton, Eng., U.K.	44	50.31 N	3.45 W
Ashburton ≃, Austl.	152	21.40 S	114.56 E
Ashburton ≃, N.Z.	162	44.04 S	171.48 E
Ashburton, North Branch ≃	162	43.54 S	171.44 E
Ashburton, South Branch ≃	162	43.44 S	171.32 E
Ashburton Downs	152	23.24 S	117.04 E
Ashby	197	42.41 N	71.49 W
Ashby, Lake ⊜	210	28.56 N	81.07 W
Ashby-de-la-Zouch	44	52.46 N	1.28 W
Ash Creek ≃, Calif., U.S.	194	41.05 N	121.08 W
Ash Creek ≃, Conn., U.S.	266	41.08 N	73.14 W
Ashcroft	172	50.43 N	121.17 W
Ashdod, Mass., U.S.	273	42.04 N	70.45 W
Ashdod, Yis.	122	31.49 N	34.40 E
Ashdod ⊥	122	31.45 N	34.40 E
Ashdot Ya'aqov	122	32.40 N	35.35 E
Ashdown	184	33.41 N	94.08 W
Ashdown Forest ◆[3]	44	51.04 N	0.03 E
Asheboro	182	35.42 N	79.49 W
Ashern	174	51.11 N	98.21 W
Asherton	186	28.27 N	99.46 W
Asheville	182	35.34 N	82.33 W
Ashewat	110	31.22 N	68.32 E
Asheweig ≃	166	54.17 N	87.12 W
Ashfield, Austl.	264a	33.53 S	151.08 E
Ashfield, Mass., U.S.	197	42.32 N	72.48 W
Ashford, Austl.	156	29.20 S	151.06 E
Ashford, Eng., U.K.	44	51.08 N	0.53 E
Ashford, Eng., U.K.	250	51.26 N	0.27 W
Ashford, Ala., U.S.	184	31.11 N	85.14 W
Ashford, Wash., U.S.	214	46.46 N	122.02 W
Ashford Airport ⊠	44	51.04 N	1.01 E
Ash Fork	190	35.13 N	112.29 W
Ash Grove	184	37.19 N	93.35 W
Ashhurst	162	40.18 S	175.45 E
Ashibe	82	33.48 N	129.46 E
Ashibetsu	82a	43.31 N	142.11 E
Ashida	86	34.31 N	133.16 E
Ashida ≃	86	34.26 N	133.25 E
Ashikaga	84	36.20 N	139.27 E
Ashikagga-gakkō ⊥	84	36.22 N	139.30 E
Ashimori	86	34.43 N	133.48 E
Ashingdon	250	51.36 N	0.42 E
Ashington	42	55.12 N	1.35 W
Ashino-ko ⊜	84	35.13 N	139.00 E
Ashio	84	36.38 N	139.27 E
Ashio-sanchi ∧∧	84	36.35 N	139.30 E
Ashippun	206	43.14 N	88.31 W
Ashippun ≃	206	43.10 N	88.33 W
Ashitaka-yama ∧	84	35.12 N	138.49 E
Ashiya, Nihon	86	34.43 N	135.17 E
Ashiya, Nihon	86	33.53 N	130.40 E
Ashiya ≃	260	34.43 N	135.18 E
Ashiyasu	84	35.38 N	138.23 E
Ashiyoro	82a	43.15 N	143.30 E
Ashizuri-kokutei-kōen ♠	86	33.07 N	132.27 E
Ashizuri-zaki ≻	82	32.44 N	133.01 E
Ashkhabad → Aščhabad	118	37.57 N	58.23 E
Ashkum	206	40.53 N	87.57 W
Ashland, Ala., U.S.	184	33.16 N	85.50 W
Ashland, Calif., U.S.	216	37.42 N	122.07 W
Ashland, Ill., U.S.	209	39.53 N	90.01 W
Ashland, Kans., U.S.	188	37.11 N	99.46 W
Ashland, Ky., U.S.	178	38.28 N	82.38 W
Ashland, Maine, U.S.	176	46.38 N	68.24 W
Ashland, Mass., U.S.	197	42.16 N	71.28 W
Ashland, Miss., U.S.	184	34.50 N	89.11 W
Ashland, Mo., U.S.	209	38.47 N	92.16 W
Ashland, Mont., U.S.	192	45.35 N	106.16 W
Ashland, Nebr., U.S.	188	41.03 N	96.22 W
Ashland, N.H., U.S.	178	43.42 N	71.38 W
Ashland, N.Y., U.S.	200	42.18 N	74.20 W
Ashland, Ohio, U.S.	204	40.52 N	82.19 W
Ashland, Oreg., U.S.	192	42.12 N	122.42 W
Ashland, Pa., U.S.	200	40.47 N	76.21 W
Ashland, Va., U.S.	198	37.45 N	77.29 W
Ashland, Wis., U.S.	180	46.35 N	90.53 W
Ashland □[6]	204	40.52 N	82.19 W
Ashland, Mount ∧	192	42.05 N	122.43 W
Ashland City	184	36.16 N	87.04 W
Ashley, Austl.	156	29.19 S	149.49 E
Ashley, Eng., U.K.	252	53.21 N	2.20 W
Ashley, Ill., U.S.	209	38.20 N	89.11 W
Ashley, Ind., U.S.	206	41.32 N	85.04 W
Ashley, Mich., U.S.	180	43.11 N	84.29 W
Ashley, Mo., U.S.	209	39.15 N	91.14 W
Ashley, N. Dak., U.S.	188	46.02 N	99.22 W
Ashley, Ohio, U.S.	204	40.25 N	82.57 W
Ashley ≃	162	43.16 S	172.43 E
Ashley Creek ≃	190	40.21 N	109.22 W
Ashley Falls	197	42.03 N	73.20 W
Ashley Green	250	51.44 N	0.35 W
Ashmore	184	39.32 N	88.01 W
Ashmore Islands II	150	12.14 S	123.05 E
Ashmūn	132	30.18 N	30.58 E
Ashmura	122	33.03 N	35.39 E
Ashokan Reservoir ⊜[1]	200	41.58 N	74.10 W
Ashoknagar	110	24.34 N	77.43 E
Ashqelon	122	31.40 N	34.35 E
Ashridge Park ♠	250	51.48 N	0.34 W
Ash-Shabakah	118	30.49 N	43.39 E
Ash-Shabb ⊤[4]	130	22.19 N	29.46 E
Ash-Shāgūr	122	31.50 N	35.39 E
Ash-Shā'ib ∧[2]	132	29.50 N	30.56 E
Ash-Shajarah	122	32.39 N	35.56 E
Ash-Shallāl al-Khāmis (Fifth Cataract) ╰	130	18.23 N	33.47 E
Ash-Shallāl ar-Rābi' (Fourth Cataract) ╰	130	18.47 N	32.03 E
Ash-Shallāl as-Sablūkah (Sixth Cataract) ╰	130	16.20 N	32.42 E
Ash-Shallāl ath-Thālith (Third Cataract) ╰	130	19.49 N	30.19 E
Ash-Shallūfah	132	30.07 N	32.34 E
Ash-Shamāl □[4]	120	34.30 N	36.00 E
Ash-Shamālīyah □[4]	130	19.00 N	30.00 E
Ash-Shanāwīyah	132	29.08 N	31.08 E
Ash-Shaqrā'	118	25.15 N	45.15 E
Ash-Sharāh ◆[1]	122	30.20 N	35.30 E
Ash-Shāriqah	118	25.22 N	55.23 E
Ash-Sharmah	118	28.01 N	35.18 E
Ash-Sharqāṭ	118	35.27 N	43.16 E
Ash-Sharqīyah □[4]	132	30.48 N	31.48 E
Ash-Sharqīyah ◆[1]	118	27.00 N	49.00 E
Ash-Shaṭrah	118	31.25 N	46.10 E
Ash-Shawāshinah	132	29.22 N	30.36 E
Ash-Shawbak	122	30.32 N	35.34 E
Ash-Shaykh Faḍl	132	28.29 N	30.50 E
Ash-Shaykh 'Ibādah	132	27.48 N	30.52 E
Ash-Shaykh Miskīn	122	32.49 N	36.09 E
Ash-Shaykh Sa'd	122	32.50 N	36.02 E
Ash-Shaykh Timay	132	27.53 N	30.51 E
Ash-Shiḥr	134	14.44 N	49.35 E
Ash-Shīn	132	31.01 N	30.53 E
Ash-Shināfīyah	118	31.35 N	44.39 E
Ash-Shīyāḥ	122	33.51 N	35.30 E
Ash-Shufayyah	118	23.50 N	39.08 E
Ash-Shuhadā'	132	30.36 N	30.54 E
Ash-Shuqayq	134	17.43 N	42.01 E
Ash-Shurayf	118	25.43 N	39.14 E
Ash-Shurayk	130	18.48 N	33.34 E
Ash-Shuwayfāt	122	33.49 N	35.31 E
Ash-Shuwayr	122	33.55 N	35.43 E
Ash Slough ≃	216	37.02 N	120.32 W
Ashta, Bhārat	112	16.57 N	74.24 E
Ashta, Bhārat	114	23.01 N	76.43 E
Ashtabula	204	41.52 N	80.48 W
Ashtabula □[6]	204	41.44 N	80.46 W
Ashtabula ≃	204	41.55 N	80.47 W
Ashtabula, East Branch ≃	204	41.48 N	80.37 W
Ashtabula, Lake ⊜[1]	188	47.11 N	97.58 W
Ashtabula, West Branch ≃	204	41.48 N	80.37 W
Ashtead	44	51.19 N	0.18 W

Symbols in the index entries represent the broad categories identified in the key at the right. Symbols with superior numbers (∧∧[2]) identify subcategories (see complete key on page *I* · *26*).

Kartensymbole in dem Registerverzeichnis stellen die rechts in Schlüssel erklärten Kategorien dar. Symbole mit hochgestellten Ziffern (∧∧[2]) bezeichnen Unterabteilungen einer Kategorie (vgl. vollständiger Schlüssel auf Seite *I* · *26*).

Los símbolos incluídos en el texto del índice representan las grandes categorias identificadas con la clave a la derecha. Los símbolos con numeros en su parte superior (∧∧[2]) identifican las subcategorias (véase la clave completa en la página *I* · *26*).

Les symboles de l'index représentent les catégories indiquées dans la légende à droite. Les symboles suivis d'un indice (∧∧[2]) représentent des sous-catégories (voir légende complète à la page *I* · *26*).

Os símbolos incluídos no texto do índice representam as grandes categorias identificadas com a chave à direita. Os símbolos com números em sua parte superior (∧∧[2]) identificam as subcategorias (veja-se a chave completa à página *I* · *26*).

English	Deutsch	Español	Français	Português
∧ Mountain	Berg	Montaña	Montagne	Montanha
∧∧ Mountains	Berge	Montañas	Montagnes	Montanhas
)(Pass	Pass	Paso	Col	Passo
∨ Valley, Canyon	Tal, Cañon	Valle, Cañón	Vallée, Canyon	Vale, Canhão
⊻ Plain	Ebene	Llano	Plaine	Planície
≻ Cape	Kap	Cabo	Cap	Cabo
I Island	Insel	Isla	Île	Ilha
II Islands	Inseln	Islas	Îles	Ilhas
• Other Topographic Features	Andere Topographische Objekte	Otros Elementos Topográficos	Autres données topographiques	Outros Elementos Topográficos

ESPAÑOL — Nombre | Página | Lat.°′ | Long.°′ W=Oeste
FRANÇAIS — Nom | Page | Lat.°′ | Long.°′ W=Ouest
PORTUGUÊS — Nome | Página | Lat.°′ | Long.°′ W=Oeste

Ashton, S. Afr. 148 33.50 S 20.05 E
Ashton, Eng., U.K. 252 53.13 N 2.45 W
Ashton, Idaho, U.S. 192 44.04 N 111.27 W
Ashton, Ill., U.S. 180 41.52 N 89.13 W
Ashton, Iowa, U.S. 188 43.19 N 95.47 W
Ashton, Md., U.S. 198 39.09 N 77.00 W
Ashton, Nebr., U.S. 188 41.15 N 98.48 W
Ashton, R.I., U.S. 197 41.56 N 71.26 W
Ashton-in-Makerfield 42 53.29 N 2.39 W
Ashton-under-Lyne 42 53.29 N 2.06 W
Ashton upon Mersey 252 53.26 N 2.19 W
Ashuanipi Lake @ 166 52.35 N 66.10 W
Ashuelot ≃ 178 42.46 N 72.29 W
Ashurst's Beacon ∧[2] 252 53.34 N 2.45 W
Ashville, Ala., U.S. 184 33.50 N 86.15 W
Ashville, N.Y., U.S. 204 42.06 N 79.23 W
Ashville, Ohio, U.S. 208 39.43 N 82.57 W
Ashville, Pa., U.S. 204 40.34 N 78.33 W
Ashwater 44 50.44 N 4.16 W
Ashwaubenon 180 44.29 N 88.03 W
Ashworth Moor Reservoir @[1] 252 53.38 N 2.16 W
Asi (Nahr al-'Āṣī) ≃ 120 36.02 N 35.58 E
Asia •[1] 12 50.00 N 100.00 E
Asia, Kepulauan II 98 1.03 N 131.18 E
Asiago 58 45.52 N 11.30 E
Asia Menor → Asia Minor ◆[1] 22 39.00 N 32.00 E
Asia Minor ◆[1] 22 39.00 N 32.00 E
Asian Exhibition Area ♠ 257d 35.47 N 51.24 E
Asid Gulf C 106 12.07 N 123.30 E
Asie → Asia •[1] 12 50.00 N 100.00 E
Asie Mineure → Asia Minor ◆[1] 22 39.00 N 32.00 E
Asien → Asia •[1] 12 50.00 N 100.00 E
Asiga Point ≻ 164n 15.03 N 145.40 E
Asikuma 140 5.35 N 1.00 W
Asilah 138 35.32 N 6.00 W
Asilimiao 78 47.56 N 117.37 E
Asinara, Golfo dell' C 36 41.00 N 8.30 E
Asinara, Isola I 36 41.05 N 8.18 E
Asino 76 57.00 N 86.09 E
Asipoquobah Lake @ 174 53.40 N 91.15 W
'Asīr ◆[1] 134 19.00 N 42.00 E
Asir, Ras (Cape Guardafui) ≻ 134 11.48 N 51.22 E
Ašitkovo 72 55.26 N 38.36 E
Aska 110 19.36 N 84.39 E
Aşkale 120 39.55 N 40.42 E
Askanija-Nova 68 46.27 N 33.52 E
Askarovo 76 53.21 N 58.30 E
Asker 26 59.50 N 10.26 E
Askern 42 53.37 N 1.09 W
Askersund 40 58.53 N 14.54 E
Askham 148 26.59 S 20.47 E
Askim 26 59.35 N 11.10 E
Askino 76 56.05 N 56.34 E
Askira 136 10.39 N 12.55 E
Askiz 76 53.08 N 90.32 E
Askja ∧[1] 24a 65.00 N 16.48 W
Askø I 41 54.54 N 11.30 E
Äsköping 40 59.09 N 16.04 E
Askov 41 55.28 N 9.06 E
Askraal 148 34.09 S 20.52 E
Askrigg 42 54.19 N 2.04 W
Askvoll 26 61.21 N 5.04 E
Aslanapa 120 39.13 N 29.52 E
Aslan-Sara 74 39.02 N 48.16 E
Åsljunga 41 56.19 N 13.22 E
Ašlyk 76 57.33 N 68.40 E
Ašlyk ≃ 76 57.50 N 69.12 E
Asmaca 120 37.53 N 35.58 E
Āsmār 110 35.02 N 71.22 E
Asmara → Asmera 134 15.20 N 38.53 E
Asmera 134 15.20 N 38.53 E
Asmundtorp 41 55.53 N 12.56 E
Asnæs 41 55.49 N 11.31 E
Asnæs ≻[1] 41 55.40 N 11.00 E
Asnebumskit Hill ∧[2] 197 42.18 N 71.54 W
Åsnen @ 26 56.38 N 14.42 E
Asni 138 31.14 N 7.55 W
Asnières [-sur-Seine] 46 48.55 N 2.17 E
Asō, Nihon 84 35.59 N 140.29 E
Aso, Nihon 86 32.58 N 131.02 E
Aso ≃ 60 43.06 N 13.51 E
Asoc 142 1.26 N 11.18 E
Aso-kokuritsu-kōen ♠ 82 33.00 N 131.07 E
Asola 58 45.13 N 10.24 E
Asolo 58 45.48 N 11.54 E
Asomante 230m 18.23 N 66.36 W
Ason 263a 6.34 N 3.31 E
Asosa 134 10.03 N 34.32 E
Aso-san ∧ 82 32.53 N 131.06 E
Asoteriba, Jabal ∧ 130 21.51 N 36.30 E
Asotin 192 46.20 N 117.03 W
Asouf Mellene, Oued V 138 25.51 N 1.33 E
Asowsches Meer → Azovskoje More ⊤[2] 68 46.00 N 36.00 E
Aspach 58 48.11 N 13.18 E
Aspach-le-Bas 54 47.46 N 7.09 E
Aspang Markt 30 47.33 N 16.06 E
Aspara ≃ 75 43.17 N 73.28 E
Aspatria 42 54.46 N 3.20 W
Aspe 34 38.21 N 0.46 W
Aspeas 198 39.59 N 77.13 W
Aspen 190 39.11 N 106.49 W
Aspen Butte ∧ 192 42.19 N 122.05 W
Aspendale 264b 38.02 S 145.07 E
Aspendus ⊥ 120 37.08 N 31.12 E
Aspen Knolls 274c 39.05 N 77.05 W
Aspen Lake @ 192 42.18 N 122.00 W
Asperg 52 48.54 N 9.07 E
Aspermont 186 33.08 N 100.14 W
Aspern ◆[8] 254b 48.13 N 16.29 E
Aspern, Flugplatz ⊠ 254b 48.13 N 16.30 E
Asperup 41 55.29 N 9.55 E
Aspid, Mount ∧ 170 53.30 N 167.33 W
Aspindza 74 41.36 N 43.15 E
Aspinwall → Colón, Pan. 226 9.22 N 79.54 W
Aspinwall, Pa., U.S. 269b 40.30 N 79.55 W
Aspiring, Mount ∧ 162 44.23 S 168.44 E
Aspö 40 59.29 N 17.02 E
Aspres-sur-Buëch 56 44.31 N 5.45 E
Aspromonte ∧∧ 36 38.10 N 15.55 E
Asprópirgos 257c 38.04 N 23.35 E
Aspropótamos ≃ 38 40.52 N 21.41 E
Aspull 252 53.34 N 2.35 W
Aspy Bay C 176 46.55 N 60.25 W
Asquins 46 47.29 N 3.45 E
Asquith, Austl. 264a 33.41 S 151.06 E
Asquith, Sask., Can. 174 52.08 N 107.13 W
Asralt Chajrchan ∧∧ 78 48.29 N 107.24 E
Asrāni 113 29.31 N 72.07 E
Assa 138 28.34 N 9.27 W
Assa ≃, S.S.S.R. 74 43.13 N 45.25 E
Assa ≃, S.S.S.R. 75 43.55 N 70.25 E
As-Sa'ata 130 13.37 N 29.59 E
Assab → Aseb 134 13.00 N 42.45 E
'Assâba ∧∧[1] 140 16.00 N 12.00 W
Assabet ≃ 273 42.28 N 71.21 W
As-Sabkhah 120 35.48 N 39.15 E
Aş-Şabyā 134 17.09 N 42.37 E
Aş-Şadārah 134 14.30 N 48.04 E
As-Sa'dīyah 118 34.11 N 45.07 E
Aş-Şaff 130 29.34 N 31.17 E
Aş-Şāfī 122 31.02 N 35.28 E
As-Safīrah 120 36.04 N 37.22 E
Aş-Şāfiyah 130 15.31 N 30.07 E
Assag, Uad V 138 25.41 N 14.40 W
Assago 256b 45.24 N 9.08 E
Aş-Şaḥrā' al-Gharbīyah (Western Desert) ◆[2] 130 27.00 N 27.00 E
Aş-Şaḥrā' al-Lībīyah (Libyan Desert) ◆[2] 126 24.00 N 25.00 E
Aş-Şaḥrā' ash-Sharqīyah (Eastern Desert) ◆[2] 130 28.00 N 32.00 E
Assaí 245 23.22 S 50.49 W
Assaikwatamo ≃ 174 56.52 N 95.50 W
Assal, Lac @ 134 11.41 N 42.25 E
'Assāl al-Ward 122 33.52 N 36.24 E
As-Salamīyah 120 35.01 N 37.03 E
As-Salīf 134 15.18 N 42.40 E
Aş-Şāliḥīyah 132 30.47 N 31.59 E
As-Sallīmah 134 14.02 N 45.46 E
As-Sallūm 130 31.34 N 25.09 E
As-Salmān 118 30.30 N 44.32 E
As-Salṭ 122 32.03 N 35.44 E
Assam □[3] 110 26.00 N 92.00 E
As-Samāwah 118 31.18 N 45.17 E
As-Samū' 122 31.24 N 35.04 E
Assam Valley V 114 26.30 N 90.30 E
'Assān 120 36.05 N 37.14 E
Aş-Şanāfīn al-Qiblīyah 132 30.27 N 31.18 E
Aş-Şanamayn 122 33.05 N 36.10 E
As-Santah 132 30.45 N 31.08 E
Aş-Şaqlabīyah 120 35.22 N 36.23 E
Aş-Şarafand 122 33.27 N 35.18 E
Assaré 240 6.52 S 39.52 W
Aş-Şarīḥ 122 32.30 N 35.54 E
As-Sarīrīyah 132 28.20 N 30.45 E
Assateague Island I 198 38.05 N 75.10 W
Assawoman Bay C 198 38.25 N 75.05 W
Assawoman Canal ≍ 198 38.31 N 75.04 W
Assawompset Pond @ 197 41.50 N 70.55 W
Asse 46 50.55 N 4.12 E
Asse ≃ 56 43.53 N 5.53 E
Assean Lake @ 174 56.13 N 96.30 W
Assebroek 46 51.12 N 3.16 E
Assekaifaf 138 27.08 N 8.50 E
Assel 48 53.41 N 9.25 E
Asseln ◆[8] 253 51.32 N 7.35 E
Assembleia Nacional, Palacio da ♥ 256c 38.43 N 9.09 W
Assen 48 52.59 N 6.34 E
Assendelft 48 52.27 N 4.45 E
Assenede 46 51.14 N 3.45 E
Assens 41 55.16 N 9.55 E
Asserbo 41 56.01 N 12.01 E
Assergi 60 42.25 N 13.30 E
Asseria ⊥ 36 44.02 N 15.39 E
Ássia 120 35.09 N 33.36 E
As-Sīb 118 23.41 N 58.11 E
As-Sidr 118 23.27 N 39.45 E
As-Sijn 122 32.47 N 36.28 E
As-Simākīyah 122 31.18 N 35.48 E
As-Sinbillāwayn 132 30.53 N 31.27 E
Assiniboia 174 49.38 N 105.59 W
Assiniboine ≃ 174 49.53 N 97.08 W
Assiniboine, Mount ∧ 172 50.52 N 115.39 W
Assiniboine Indian Reserve ◆[4] 174 50.21 N 103.28 W
Assinika ≃ 174 52.37 N 96.10 W
Assinippi 273 42.09 N 70.51 W
Assis 245 22.40 S 50.25 W
Assiscunk Creek ≃ 198 40.05 N 74.51 W
Assisi 60 43.04 N 12.37 E
Asslar 52 50.35 N 8.28 E
Assling 58 48.00 N 12.00 E
Assmannshausen 52 49.59 N 7.52 E
Asso 56 45.52 N 9.16 E
Assodé 140 18.26 N 8.28 E
Assomada 140a 15.06 N 23.41 W
Assonet 197 41.48 N 71.04 W
As-Subū' ⊥ 130 22.45 N 32.34 E
As-Sūdān → Sudan □[1] 130 15.00 N 30.00 E
As-Sufāl 134 14.06 N 48.42 E
Aş-Şufayyah 130 15.30 N 34.42 E
Aş-Şūfīyah 132 30.55 N 31.46 E
As-Sukhnah, Sūrīy. 120 34.52 N 38.52 E
As-Sukhnah, Urd. 122 32.08 N 36.04 E
As-Sulaymānīyah, Ar. Sa. 118 24.09 N 47.19 E
As-Sulaymānīyah, 'Irāq 118 35.33 N 45.26 E
As-Sulaymānīyah □[4] 118 35.40 N 45.30 E
As-Sulaymī 118 26.17 N 41.21 E
As-Sulayyil 134 20.27 N 45.34 E
As-Sulṭān 136 31.07 N 17.10 E
As-Sumayḥ 130 9.49 N 27.39 E
Aş-Şummān ◆[1] 118 25.00 N 47.00 E
As-Summāqīyāt 122 32.26 N 36.24 E
Assumption, Ill., U.S. 209 39.31 N 89.03 W
Assumption, Ohio, U.S. 206 41.40 N 83.54 W
Assumption Island I 128 9.45 S 46.30 E
Assunpink Creek ≃ 275 40.13 N 74.46 W
As-Sūrīyah → Syria □[1] 118 35.00 N 38.00 E
As-Su'ūdīyah 132 29.33 N 31.14 E
Aş-Şuwār 120 35.30 N 40.39 E
As-Suwaydā' 122 32.42 N 36.34 E
As-Suwaydā' □[8] 122 32.45 N 36.45 E
As-Suways (Suez) 132 29.58 N 32.33 E
As-Suways □[4] 132 29.59 N 32.33 E
Asta, Cima d' ∧ 58 46.10 N 11.36 E
Astachovo 73 47.52 N 39.37 E
Astaffort 32 44.04 N 0.40 E
Astakós 38 38.32 N 21.05 E
Āstāneh, Īrān 118 33.53 N 49.22 E
Āstāneh, Īrān 118 37.17 N 49.59 E
Āstārā, Īrān 118 38.26 N 48.52 E
Astara, S.S.S.R. 74 38.28 N 48.52 E
Aštarak 74 40.18 N 44.22 E
Astaškovo 72 55.32 N 38.38 E
Astatula 210 28.43 N 81.44 W
Asten 48 51.24 N 5.45 E
Asti 56 44.54 N 8.12 E
Asti □[4] 56 44.55 N 8.10 E
Astica 242 30.56 S 67.23 W
Astico ≃ 58 45.37 N 11.37 E
Astillero 34 43.24 N 3.49 W
Astipálaia 38 36.30 N 26.30 E
Astipálaia I 38 36.35 N 26.25 E
Astley Bridge 252 53.36 N 2.26 W
Astley Green 252 53.29 N 2.27 W
Astley Hall ⊥ 252 53.39 N 2.38 W
Astola Island I 110 25.07 N 63.51 E
Astolfo Dutra 246 21.19 S 42.52 W
Aston, Eng., U.K. 252 53.18 N 2.40 W
Aston, Pa., U.S. 275 39.52 N 75.27 W
Aston Clinton 44 51.48 N 0.44 W
Astor 113 35.22 N 74.51 E
Astor ≃ 113 35.35 N 74.38 E
Astorga, Bra. 245 23.13 S 51.40 W
Astorga, Esp. 34 42.27 N 6.03 W
Astorga, Pil. 106 6.54 N 125.27 E
Astoria, Ill., U.S. 184 40.14 N 90.21 W
Astoria, Oreg., U.S. 214 46.11 N 123.50 W
Astoria ◆[8] 266 40.46 N 73.55 W
Astoria Column ⊥ 214 46.11 N 123.50 W
Åstorp 41 56.08 N 12.57 E
Astove Island I 128 10.06 S 47.45 E
Astra 244 45.44 S 67.30 W
Astrachan' 70 46.21 N 48.03 E
Astrachan Bazar 74 39.14 N 48.31 E
Astrachanka 76 51.33 N 69.47 E
Astrachanskij 70 46.12 N 47.16 E
Astrachanskij Zapovednik ◆[4] 70 46.00 N 48.32 E
Astrakhan → Astrachan' 70 46.21 N 48.03 E
Astrodome ♠ 212 29.41 N 95.25 W
Astrolabe, Cape ≻ 165e 8.20 S 160.34 E
Astrolabe, Récifs de l' ✢[2] 165f 19.48 S 165.37 E
Astrolabe Bay C 154 5.20 S 145.50 E
Astudillo 34 42.12 N 4.18 W
Asturias 106 10.34 N 123.43 E
Asturias □[9] 34 43.20 N 6.00 W
Asubulak 76 49.31 N 83.03 E
Asuisui, Cape ≻ 165a 13.47 S 172.29 W
Asuka 86 34.28 N 135.50 E
Asuke 84 35.08 N 137.19 E
Asunción 242 25.16 S 57.40 W
Asunción, Bahía C 222 27.06 N 114.11 W
Asunción, Cerro de la ∧ 222 24.15 N 99.56 W
Asuncion Island I 98 19.40 N 145.24 E
Asunción Mita 226 14.20 N 89.43 W
Åsunden @, Sve. 26 57.44 N 13.22 E
Åsunden @, Sve. 26 57.58 N 15.50 E
Asunga, Wādī V 136 13.21 N 22.17 E
'Āṣūr, Tall ∧ 122 31.59 N 35.17 E
Aşutka 120 39.09 N 38.37 E
Asuwa 84 36.01 N 136.16 E
Asuwa ≃ 84 36.04 N 136.11 E
Aswa ≃ 144 3.43 N 31.55 E
Aswān 130 24.05 N 32.53 E
Aswatthaberia 262b 22.26 N 88.32 E
Asy ≃ 75 43.31 N 78.20 E
Asyūṭ 132 27.11 N 31.11 E
Asyūṭ □[4] 132 27.20 N 30.50 E
Asyūṭī, Wādī al- V 132 27.11 N 31.16 E
Aszód 30 47.39 N 19.31 E
Ata I, Tonga 14 22.20 S 176.12 W
Ata I, Tonga 164w 21.03 S 175.00 W
Atabaj 75 43.30 N 68.20 E
Atabasca → Athabasca ≃ 166 58.40 N 110.50 W
Atabasca, Lago → Athabasca, Lake @ 166 59.07 N 110.00 W
Atabey 120 37.57 N 30.39 E
Atacama □[4] 242 27.30 S 70.00 W
Atacama, Desierto de ◆[2] 18 24.30 S 69.15 W
Atacama, Puna de ∧∧[1] 242 25.00 S 68.00 W
Atacama, Salar de ≡ 242 23.30 S 68.15 W
Atacama Trench ✢[1] 18 21.00 S 72.00 W
Ataco 236 3.35 N 75.23 W
Atacora, Chaîne de l' ∧∧ 140 10.45 N 1.30 E
Atacuari ≃ 236 3.47 S 70.44 W
Atafu I[1] 14 8.33 S 172.30 W
Atagaj 78 55.06 N 99.23 E
Atago-san ∧ 86 35.03 N 135.37 E
Atago-yama ∧ 84 35.18 N 140.03 E
Ātāi ≃[1] 116 22.51 N 89.33 E
'Aṭā'iṭah, Jabal al- ∧ 122 30.40 N 35.39 E
Atakakup Indian Reserve ◆[4] 174 53.24 N 106.55 W
Atakano-seki ⊥ 84 36.24 N 136.25 E
Ataki 68 48.25 N 27.47 E
Atakora □[5] 140 10.00 N 1.35 E
Atakora, Réserve d' ◆[4] 140 11.30 N 2.10 E
Atakpamé 140 7.32 N 1.08 E
Atalaia, Bra. 240 9.31 S 36.02 W
Atalaia, Port. 256c 38.42 N 8.55 W
Atalándi 38 38.39 N 23.00 E
Atalanka 78 54.50 N 103.05 E
Atalaya 248 35.02 S 57.32 W
Atalaya, Pan. 226 8.03 N 80.56 W
Atalaya, Perú 238 10.44 S 73.45 W
Atalaya, Cerro ∧, Chile 244 52.45 S 72.42 W
Atalaya, Cerro ∧, Perú 238 12.38 S 71.56 W
Atalaya, Punta ≻ 248 35.01 S 57.31 W
Atamanovka 78 51.56 N 113.37 E
Atamanovo 76 56.24 N 93.36 E
Atambua 102 9.07 S 124.54 E
Atami 84 35.05 N 139.04 E
Atapupu 102 9.00 S 124.51 E
'Atāq 134 14.33 N 46.48 E
'Atāqah, Jabal ∧∧ 132 29.58 N 32.20 E
Ataque 246 22.02 S 45.34 W
Atar 140 20.31 N 13.03 W
Ataram, Erg n' ◆[2] 138 23.46 N 1.44 E
Atarés, Castillo de ⊥ 276b 23.08 N 82.21 W
Atāri 113 31.36 N 74.35 E
Atary 70 57.32 N 49.18 E
Atas Bogd ∧∧ 92 43.18 N 96.36 E
Atascadero 216 35.29 N 120.40 W
At'aševo 70 54.36 N 46.06 E
Atasu 76 48.42 N 71.38 E
Atata I 164w 21.03 S 175.15 W
Atatžurk Heykeli ⊥ 257b 41.00 N 28.59 E
Ataur 262a 28.43 N 77.24 E
Ataúro, Ilaa de I 102 8.13 S 125.35 E
Atbara ('Aṭbarah) ≃ 130 17.40 N 33.56 E
'Aṭbarah 130 17.42 N 33.59 E
'Aṭbarah (Atbara) ≃ 130 17.40 N 33.56 E
Atbasar 76 51.48 N 68.20 E
Atbaši 75 41.10 N 75.48 E
Atbaši ≃ 75 41.24 N 75.38 E
Atbaši, Chrebet ∧∧ 75 40.55 N 75.40 E
Atchafalaya ≃ 184 29.53 N 91.28 W
Atchafalaya Bay C 184 29.25 N 91.20 W
Atchison 188 39.34 N 95.07 W
Atco 198 39.46 N 74.53 W
Atebubu 140 7.45 N 0.59 W
Ateca 34 41.20 N 1.47 W
Ateleta 60 41.51 N 14.12 E
Ateli 114 28.06 N 76.17 E
Atemajac de Brizuela 224 20.11 N 103.42 W
Atemajac del Valle 224 20.45 N 103.22 W
Atemar 70 54.11 N 45.24 E
Atemble 154 5.05 S 144.45 E
Atenango del Río 224 18.05 N 99.06 W
Atenas, C.R. 226 9.58 N 84.23 W
Atenas → Athínai, Ellás 38 37.58 N 23.43 E
Atencingo 224 18.30 N 98.36 W
Atenco □[7] 276a 19.34 N 99.00 W
Atengo ≃ 224 21.50 N 104.43 W
Atenguillo 224 20.25 N 104.31 W
Atenquique 224 19.31 N 103.30 W
Atepcevo 72 55.20 N 36.46 E
Aterno ≃ 60 42.11 N 13.51 E
Aterrado 240 4.15 S 45.38 W
Aterrado, Ribeirão do ≃ 246 22.09 S 45.03 W
Atessa 60 42.04 N 14.27 E
Aṭfīḥ 132 29.24 N 31.15 E
Aṭfīḥī, Wādī al- V 132 29.23 N 31.16 E
Atghara 262b 22.37 N 88.27 E
Ātgharia 116 24.06 N 89.14 E
Atglen 198 39.57 N 75.58 W
Ath 46 50.38 N 3.47 E
Athabasca 172 54.43 N 113.17 W
Athabasca ≃ 166 58.40 N 110.50 W
Athabasca, Lake @ 166 59.07 N 110.00 W
Athalmer 172 50.32 N 116.02 W
Athapapuskow Lake @ 174 54.33 N 101.40 W
Athārabānki ≃[1] 116 22.49 N 89.39 E
Athārān Hazāri 113 31.11 N 72.06 E
Athboy 28 53.37 N 6.55 W
Athel, Oued el- V 138 25.09 N 9.53 W
Athen → Athínai 38 37.58 N 23.43 E
Athena 192 45.49 N 118.30 W
Athènes → Athínai 38 37.58 N 23.43 E
Athenry 28 53.18 N 8.45 W
Athens, Ont., Can. 202 44.38 N 75.57 W
Athens → Athínai, Ellás 38 37.58 N 23.43 E
Athens, Ala., U.S. 184 34.48 N 86.58 W
Athens, Ga., U.S. 182 33.57 N 83.23 W
Athens, Ill., U.S. 209 39.58 N 89.44 W
Athens, La., U.S. 184 32.39 N 93.01 W
Athens, Maine, U.S. 178 44.55 N 69.41 W
Athens, Mich., U.S. 206 42.05 N 85.14 W
Athens, N.Y., U.S. 200 42.16 N 73.49 W
Athens, Ohio, U.S. 178 39.20 N 82.06 W
Athens, Pa., U.S. 200 41.57 N 76.31 W
Athens, Tenn., U.S. 182 35.27 N 84.36 W
Athens, Tex., U.S. 212 32.12 N 95.51 W
Athens, W. Va., U.S. 182 37.25 N 81.01 W
Athens, Wis., U.S. 180 45.02 N 90.05 W
Athenstedt 50 51.56 N 10.55 E
Atherley 202 44.36 N 79.22 W
Atherstone 44 52.35 N 1.31 W
Atherton, Austl. 156 17.16 S 145.29 E
Atherton, Eng., U.K. 42 53.31 N 2.31 W
Atherton, Calif., U.S. 216 37.28 N 122.12 W
Athi ≃ 144 2.59 S 38.31 E
Athiaínou 120 35.04 N 33.32 E
Athiémé 140 6.35 N 1.40 E
Athies-sur-Laon 46 49.34 N 3.41 E
Athínai (Athens) 38; 257c 37.58 N 23.43 E
Athinisin Panepistimion ♥[2] 257c 37.59 N 23.44 E
Äthiopien → Ethiopia □[1] 134 9.00 N 39.00 E
Athi River 144 1.27 S 36.59 E
Athis-Mons 251 48.43 N 2.24 E
Athlat al-Bāshā ∧[2] 132 27.31 N 32.20 E
Athlone 28 53.25 N 7.56 W
Áth Luain → Athlone 28 53.25 N 7.56 W
Athni 112 16.44 N 75.04 E
Athok 100 17.12 N 95.05 E
Athol, N.Z. 162 45.31 S 168.35 E
Athol, Mass., U.S. 197 42.36 N 72.14 W
Athol Bay C 202 43.53 N 77.15 W
Atholl Island I 230b 25.05 N 77.16 W
Athol Springs 200 42.46 N 78.52 W
Áthos ∧ 38 40.09 N 24.19 E
Ath-Tha'lah 122 32.42 N 36.26 E
Ath-Thamad 130 29.41 N 34.18 E
Ath-Thanīyah 122 31.10 N 35.43 E
Athus 52 49.34 N 5.50 E
Athy 28 53.00 N 7.00 W
Ati 136 13.13 N 18.20 E
Atiak 144 3.15 N 32.07 E
Atibaia 246 23.07 S 46.33 W
Atibaia ≃ 245 22.42 S 47.17 W
Atico 238 16.14 S 73.39 W
Aticonipi, Lac @ 176 51.52 N 59.22 W
Atienza 34 41.12 N 2.52 W
Atikokan 180 48.45 N 91.37 W
Atikonak Lake @ 166 52.40 N 64.30 W
Atil 190 30.50 N 111.35 W
Atimaono 164s 17.46 S 149.28 W
Atimonan 106 14.00 N 121.55 E
Atina 60 41.37 N 13.48 E
Atiquizaya 226 13.58 N 89.46 W
Atirāmpattinam 112 10.21 N 79.24 E
Atışalan 257b 41.03 N 28.52 E
Atışmektebi 257b 40.55 N 29.11 E
Atitlán, Lago de @ 226 14.42 N 91.12 W
Atitlán, Volcán ∧[1] 226 14.35 N 91.11 W
Atizapán de Zaragoza 276a 19.33 N 99.15 W
Atka, S.S.S.R. 64 60.50 N 151.48 E
Atka, Alaska, U.S. 170 52.12 N 174.12 W
Atka Island I 170 52.15 N 174.30 W
Atkaracalar 120 40.50 N 33.04 E
Atkarsk 70 51.52 N 45.00 E
Atkins 184 35.14 N 92.56 W
Atkinson, Ill., U.S. 180 41.25 N 90.01 W
Atkinson, Nebr., U.S. 188 42.32 N 98.59 W
Atkinson, N.H., U.S. 197 42.51 N 71.10 W
Atkinson, N.C., U.S. 182 34.28 N 78.06 W
Atkinson Island I 212 29.40 N 94.58 W
Atkinson Lake @ 174 55.59 N 94.48 W
Atkri 154 1.44 S 130.04 E
Atlacomulco de Fabela 224 19.48 N 99.53 W
Atlanta, Ga., U.S. 182 33.45 N 84.23 W
Atlanta, Ill., U.S. 184 40.16 N 89.14 W
Atlanta, Mich., U.S. 180 45.00 N 84.09 W
Atlanta, Mo., U.S. 184 39.54 N 92.29 W
Atlanta, N.Y., U.S. 200 42.33 N 77.28 W
Atlanta, Ohio, U.S. 208 39.34 N 83.11 W
Atlanta, Tex., U.S. 184 33.07 N 94.10 W
Atlantic, Iowa, U.S. 188 41.24 N 95.01 W
Atlantic, N.C., U.S. 182 34.54 N 76.20 W
Atlantic, Pa., U.S. 204 41.30 N 80.21 W
Atlantic, Va., U.S. 198 37.54 N 75.30 W
Atlantic □[6] 198 39.27 N 74.44 W
Atlantic Beach 266 40.35 N 73.44 W
Atlantic City 198 39.22 N 74.26 W
Atlantic Highlands 198 40.25 N 74.03 W
Atlantic-Indian Basin ✢[1] 9 60.00 S 15.00 E
Atlantic Indian Ridge ✢[3] 4 54.00 S 20.00 E
Atlántico □[5] 236 10.45 N 75.00 W
Atlántico, Océano → Atlantic Ocean ⊤[1] 8 0.00 25.00 W
Atlantic Ocean ⊤[1] 4; 8 0.00 25.00 W
Atlantic Peak ∧ 190 42.37 N 109.00 W
Atlántida 242 34.46 S 55.45 W
Atlántida □[5] 226 15.40 N 87.00 W
Atlantique 266 40.39 N 73.10 W
Atlantique □[5] 140 6.35 N 2.15 E
Atlantique, Océan → Atlantic Ocean ⊤[1] 8 0.00 25.00 W
Atlantischer Ozean → Atlantic Ocean ⊤[1] 8 0.00 25.00 W
Atlas, Mich., U.S. 206 42.56 N 83.32 W
Atlas, Pa., U.S. 198 40.48 N 76.26 W
Atlasburg 204 40.20 N 80.23 W
Atlas Mountains ∧∧ 138 33.00 N 2.00 W
Atlasova, Ostrov I 64 50.53 N 155.27 E
Atlas Saharien ∧∧ 138 33.25 N 1.20 E
Atlas Tellien ∧∧ 138 36.00 N 3.00 E
Atlin 170 59.35 N 133.42 W
Atlin Lake @ 170 59.20 N 133.45 W
'Atlit 122 32.41 N 34.56 E
Atlixco 224 18.54 N 98.26 W
Atmakūr 112 15.53 N 78.35 E
Atmanov Ugol 70 53.07 N 41.23 E
Atmis 70 53.28 N 43.57 E
Atmore 184 31.02 N 87.29 W
Ätna → Etna, Monte ∧[1] 36 37.46 N 15.00 E
Atna ≃ 26 61.44 N 10.49 E
Atna Peak ∧ 172 53.57 N 128.03 W
Atna Range ∧∧ 172 55.25 N 127.00 W
Atnis 76 58.48 N 69.38 E
Atnosen 26 61.44 N 10.49 E
Atō 86 34.24 N 131.43 E
Atocha 238 20.56 S 66.14 W
Atocha, Estación de ◆[5] 256a 40.24 N 3.41 W
Atocongo 276d 12.08 S 76.56 W
Atocongo ⊥ 276d 12.12 S 76.55 W
Atoka 186 34.23 N 96.08 W
Atomic Energy Commission Nevada Test Site ♥[3] 194 37.00 N 116.10 W
Atomic Energy Commission Oak Ridge Area ♥[3] 182 35.56 N 85.15 W
Atotonilco, Méx. 222 24.15 N 102.45 W
Atotonilco, Méx. 224 23.35 N 104.20 W
Atotonilco, Cerro ∧∧ 186 26.08 N 104.43 W
Atotonilco, Lago de @ 224 20.22 N 103.39 W
Atotonilco el Alto 224 20.33 N 102.31 W
Atotonilco [Tula] 224 20.00 N 99.13 W
Atoui, Khatt (Uad Atui) V 138 20.30 N 15.35 W
Atoyac 224 20.01 N 103.32 W
Atoyac ≃, Méx. 224 18.10 N 98.31 W
Atoyac ≃, Méx. 224 16.30 N 97.31 W
Atoyac ≃, Méx. 224 17.05 N 100.29 W
Atoyac de Alvarez 224 17.12 N 100.26 W
Atpur 262b 22.50 N 88.23 E
Atrå 26 59.59 N 8.45 E
'Aṭrah, Jabal ∧ 122 29.40 N 35.34 E
Atrai ≃ 114 24.29 N 89.03 E
Atrak (Atrek) ≃ 118 37.28 N 53.57 E
Ätran ≃ 26 56.53 N 12.30 E
Atrato ≃ 236 8.17 N 76.58 W
Atrauli 114 28.02 N 78.17 E
Atrek (Atrak) ≃ 118 37.28 N 53.57 E
Atri 60 42.35 N 13.58 E
Atripalda 60 40.55 N 14.50 E
Atrisco 190 34.59 N 106.41 W
Atrop 253 51.24 N 6.43 E
Atsion Lake @ 275 39.44 N 74.44 W
Atsugi 84 35.27 N 139.22 E
Atsugi Naval Air Station (United States) ■ 84 35.28 N 139.27 E
Atsumi, Nihon 82 38.37 N 139.35 E
Atsumi, Nihon 84 34.37 N 137.07 E
Atsumi-hantō ≻[1] 84 34.39 N 137.15 E
Atsumi-wan C 84 34.43 N 137.10 E
Atsuta 164m 26.17 N 127.49 E
Atta 262a 28.34 N 77.20 E
At-Tabbīn 132 29.47 N 31.18 E
Aṭ-Ṭafīlah 122 30.50 N 35.36 E
At-Taḥrīr □[4] 132 30.40 N 30.15 E
Aṭ-Ṭā'if 134 21.16 N 40.24 E
Attainville 251 49.03 N 2.21 E
At-Tāj 136 24.13 N 23.18 E
Aṭ-Ṭalibīyah 263c 30.00 N 31.11 E
At-Tall 122 33.36 N 36.18 E
Attalla 184 34.01 N 86.05 W
At-Tall al-Kabīr 132 30.34 N 31.47 E
At-Tamīmī 136 32.20 N 23.04 E
Attapu 100 14.48 N 106.50 E
Attar, Oued el V 138 33.27 N 5.26 E
Aṭ-Ṭāsah ∧[2] 132 30.34 N 32.37 E
At-Taṭālīyah 132 27.20 N 30.50 E
Attáviros ∧, Ellás 38 36.12 N 27.52 E
Attáviros ∧, Tür. 120 36.10 N 27.45 E
Attawapiskat 166 52.55 N 82.26 W
Attawapiskat ≃ 166 52.57 N 82.18 W
Attawapiskat Lake @ 166 52.18 N 87.54 W
Attawaugan 197 41.52 N 71.53 W
Aṭ-Ṭawd 132 30.47 N 30.37 E
Aṭ-Ṭawīl ∧∧ 118 29.20 N 39.35 E
Aṭ-Ṭayrīyah 132 30.39 N 30.46 E
At-Taysīyah ≡ 118 28.00 N 44.00 E
Aṭ-Ṭayyibah, Miṣr 132 28.16 N 30.39 E
Aṭ-Ṭayyibah, Sūrīy. 122 32.48 N 36.46 E
Aṭ-Ṭayyibah, Sūrīy. 122 32.33 N 36.14 E
Aṭ-Ṭayyibah, Urd. 122 32.33 N 35.43 E
Attel 58 48.01 N 12.10 E
Attel ≃ 58 48.01 N 12.11 E
Attendorn 52 51.07 N 7.54 E
Attenhausen 54 47.59 N 10.20 E
Atterberry 209 40.04 N 89.55 W
Attersee 58 47.55 N 13.33 E
Attersee @ 58 47.52 N 13.33 E
Attert ≃ 52 49.52 N 6.05 E
Attica, Ind., U.S. 206 40.17 N 87.15 W
Attica, Kans., U.S. 188 37.15 N 98.13 W
Attica, N.Y., U.S. 200 42.52 N 78.17 W
Attica, Ohio, U.S. 204 41.04 N 82.53 W
Attichy 46 49.25 N 3.03 E
Attigliano 60 42.31 N 12.17 E
Attigny 52 49.29 N 4.35 E
Attikí ◆[1] 38 38.00 N 23.30 E
'Attīl 122 32.22 N 35.04 E
Attimis 58 46.11 N 13.16 E
Aṭ-Ṭīnah 132 31.03 N 32.18 E
Attingal 112 8.41 N 76.50 E
Attir 130 6.04 N 30.50 E
Attleboro 197 41.56 N 71.17 W
Attleborough 44 52.31 N 1.01 E
Attnang 58 48.01 N 13.43 E
Attock 113 33.54 N 72.15 E
Attow, Ben ∧ 28 57.14 N 5.17 W
Attoyac Bayou ≃ 184 31.29 N 94.18 W
Attu 171a 52.56 N 174.45 E
Attu Island I 171a 52.55 N 173.00 E
At-Tulaymāt ∧[2] 132 29.04 N 32.20 E
Aṭ-Ṭunayb 122 31.48 N 35.57 E
Āttūr, Bhārat 112 11.36 N 78.37 E
Aṭ-Ṭūr, Miṣr 130 28.14 N 33.37 E
Aṭ-Ṭurayf 118 31.44 N 38.33 E
Aṭ-Ṭuwayshah 130 12.21 N 26.32 E
Aṭ-Ṭuwayyah 118 27.36 N 41.13 E
Atucatiquini ≃ 238 7.44 S 67.57 W
Atucha 248 33.58 S 59.18 W
Atuel ≃ 242 36.17 S 66.50 W
Atui, Uad (Khatt Atoui) V 138 2.03 N 15.35 W
Atuntagui 236 0.20 N 78.13 W
Atuona 164x 9.48 S 139.02 W
At'urjevo 70 54.21 N 43.19 E
Atushi 75 39.42 N 75.48 E
Åtvidaberg 26 58.12 N 16.00 E
Atwater, Sask., Can. 174 50.47 N 102.10 W
Atwater, Calif., U.S. 216 37.21 N 120.36 W
Atwater, Ill., U.S. 209 39.20 N 89.44 W
Atwater, Minn., U.S. 188 45.08 N 94.47 W
Atwater, Ohio, U.S. 204 41.01 N 81.10 W
Atwood, Ont., Can. 202 43.40 N 81.01 W
Atwood, Calif., U.S. 270 33.52 N 117.50 W
Atwood, Ill., U.S. 184 39.48 N 88.28 W
Atwood, Ind., U.S. 206 41.16 N 85.59 W
Atwood, Kans., U.S. 188 39.48 N 101.03 W
Atwood, Tenn., U.S. 184 35.59 N 88.41 W
Atwood Lake @[1] 204 40.33 N 81.13 W
Atzacán 224 18.54 N 97.05 W
Atzalpur 262a 28.43 N 77.21 E
Atzendorf 50 51.55 N 11.35 E
Atzgersdorf ◆[8] 254b 48.09 N 16.18 E
Au 54 47.19 N 9.59 E
Aua 164u 14.16 S 170.40 W
Auagrām 116 23.31 N 87.41 E
Aua Island I 154 1.27 S 143.04 E
Auak 164r 6.58 N 158.16 E
Aualá-Missu ≃ 240 10.51 S 53.08 W
Auari ≃ 236 3.33 N 63.48 W
Auasberge ∧∧ 146 22.45 S 17.22 E
Auati Paraná ≃[1] 236 1.51 S 65.37 W
Auau Channel U 219a 20.51 N 156.45 W
Aub, B.R.D. 52 49.33 N 10.04 E
Aub, Namibia 148 26.33 S 19.08 E
Aubagne 56 43.17 N 5.34 E
Aubange 52 49.35 N 5.48 E
Aube □[5] 46 48.15 N 4.05 E
Aube ≃ 46 48.34 N 3.43 E
Aubenas 56 44.37 N 4.23 E
Aubenton 46 49.50 N 4.12 E
Aubepierre 251 48.38 N 2.53 E
Aubergenville 251 48.58 N 1.51 E
Auberive 54 47.47 N 5.03 E
Auberry 216 37.05 N 119.29 W
Aubervilliers 46 48.55 N 2.23 E
Aubetin ≃ 46 48.49 N 3.01 E
Aubette ≃ 251 49.00 N 1.54 E
Aubigny-en-Artois 46 50.21 N 2.35 E
Aubigny-sur-Nère 46 47.29 N 2.26 E
Aubin 32 44.32 N 2.14 E
Aubinadong ≃ 180 46.51 N 83.22 W
Auboué 52 49.13 N 5.59 E
Aubrac ∧∧ 32 44.40 N 3.00 E
Aubrives 52 50.06 N 4.46 E
Aubry Lake @ 170 67.23 N 126.30 W
Auburn, Austl. 158b 34.01 S 138.41 E
Auburn, Austl. 264a 33.51 S 151.02 E
Auburn, Ala., U.S. 184 32.36 N 85.29 W
Auburn, Calif., U.S. 216 38.54 N 121.04 W
Auburn, Ill., U.S. 209 39.36 N 89.45 W
Auburn, Ind., U.S. 206 41.22 N 85.04 W
Auburn, Ky., U.S. 184 36.52 N 86.43 W
Auburn, Maine, U.S. 178 44.06 N 70.14 W
Auburn, Mass., U.S. 197 42.12 N 71.50 W
Auburn, Mich., U.S. 180 43.36 N 84.04 W
Auburn, Nebr., U.S. 188 40.23 N 95.51 W
Auburn, N.J., U.S. 275 39.43 N 75.22 W
Auburn, N.Y., U.S. 200 42.56 N 76.34 W
Auburn, Pa., U.S. 198 40.36 N 76.06 W
Auburn, Wash., U.S. 214 47.18 N 122.13 W
Auburn ≃ 156 25.38 S 151.12 E
Auburndale, Fla., U.S. 210 28.04 N 81.48 W
Auburndale, Mass., U.S. 273 42.21 N 71.22 W
Auburn Heights 206 42.41 N 83.15 W
Auburn Range ∧∧ 156 25.10 S 150.30 E
Auburn Ravine V 216 38.51 N 121.31 W
Auburn Southeast 200 42.54 N 76.32 W
Aubusson 32 45.57 N 2.11 E
Auby-sur-Semois 52 49.49 N 5.10 E
Auca Mahuída 242 37.53 S 68.31 W
Auca Mahuida, Sierra ∧∧ 242 37.45 S 68.55 W
Aucará 238 14.15 S 74.05 W
Auce 66 56.28 N 22.53 E
Auch 32 43.39 N 0.35 E
Auchel 46 50.30 N 2.28 E
Auchencairn 42 54.51 N 3.53 W
Auchi 140 7.02 N 6.14 E
Auchinleck 42 55.28 N 4.17 W
Auchterarder 28 56.18 N 3.43 W
Auchterderran 42 56.09 N 3.16 W
Auchtermuchty 28 56.17 N 3.15 W
Aucilla ≃ 182 30.05 N 83.59 W
Auckland 162 36.52 S 174.46 E
Auckland Islands II 9 50.40 S 166.30 E
Auckland Park ◆[8] 263d 26.11 S 28.00 E
Auckland Park Race Course ♠ 263d 26.11 S 28.00 E
Aude □[5] 32 43.05 N 2.30 E
Aude ≃ 32 43.13 N 3.14 E
Audenge 32 44.41 N 1.31 W
Audenshaw 252 53.28 N 2.08 W
Audenshaw Reservoirs @[1] 252 53.28 N 2.08 W
Auderghem 46 50.49 N 4.26 E
Audeux 54 47.16 N 5.53 E
Audierne 32 48.01 N 4.32 W
Audincourt 54 47.29 N 6.50 E
Audo Range ∧∧ 134 6.30 N 41.30 E
Audrain □[6] 209 39.12 N 91.50 W
Audresselles 46 50.49 N 1.36 E
Audruicq 46 50.53 N 2.05 E
Audubon, Iowa, U.S. 188 41.43 N 94.55 W
Audubon, N.J., U.S. 198 39.54 N 75.04 W
Audubon, Pa., U.S. 275 40.07 N 75.27 W
Audubon Park 208 38.12 N 85.43 W
Audun-le-Roman 52 49.22 N 5.53 E
Aue 50 50.35 N 12.42 E
Aue ≃ 48 53.05 N 8.04 E
Auer → Ora 58 46.21 N 11.18 E
Auerbach, D.D.R. 50 50.41 N 12.54 E
Auerbach, D.D.R. 50 50.30 N 12.23 E
Auersberg ∧ 50 50.27 N 12.39 E
Auerswalde 50 50.54 N 12.55 E
Auf dem Kreinberge 253 51.27 N 7.36 E
Auf dem Schnee ◆[8] 253 51.26 N 7.25 E
Auffargis 251 48.42 N 1.53 E
Auffay 46 49.43 N 1.06 E
Augarten ♠ 254b 48.14 N 16.23 E
Augathella 156 25.48 S 146.35 E
Aughnacloy 42 54.25 N 6.59 W
Aughton 252 53.32 N 2.56 W
Aughton Park 252 53.33 N 2.53 W
Aughwick Creek ≃ 204 40.22 N 77.50 W
Auglaize □[6] 206 40.34 N 84.12 W
Auglaize ≃ 178 41.17 N 84.21 W
Augrabies 148 28.37 S 20.20 E
Augrabies Falls National Park ♠ 148 28.35 S 20.19 E
Augrabiesvalle ∟ 148 28.35 S 20.19 E
Au Gres 180 44.03 N 83.42 W
Au Gres ≃ 180 44.02 N 83.40 W
Au Gres, East Branch ≃ 180 44.05 N 83.41 W
Augsburg 54 48.23 N 10.53 E
Augusta, Austl. 152 34.19 S 115.10 E
Augusta, It. 36 37.13 N 15.13 E
Augusta, Ark., U.S. 184 35.17 N 91.22 W
Augusta, Ga., U.S. 182 33.29 N 81.57 W
Augusta, Ill., U.S. 184 40.14 N 90.57 W
Augusta, Kans., U.S. 188 37.41 N 96.58 W
Augusta, Ky., U.S. 208 38.46 N 84.00 W
Augusta, Maine, U.S. 178 44.19 N 69.47 W
Augusta, Mich., U.S. 206 42.20 N 85.21 W
Augusta, Mo., U.S. 209 38.34 N 90.53 W
Augusta, Mont., U.S. 192 47.30 N 112.24 W
Augusta, N.J., U.S. 200 41.08 N 74.44 W
Augusta, Ohio, U.S. 204 40.41 N 81.01 W
Augusta, Wis., U.S. 180 44.41 N 91.07 W
Augusta, Golfo di C 36 37.10 N 15.20 E
Augustdorf 48 51.53 N 8.43 E
Augustenborg 41 54.57 N 9.53 E
Augustine Island I 170 59.22 N 153.28 W
Augustines, Lac des @ 180 47.37 N 76.05 W
Augusto Cardoso 144 12.44 S 34.50 E
Augusto Severo 240 5.52 S 37.19 W
Augustów 30 53.51 N 22.59 E
Augustowski, Kanał ≍ 66 53.54 N 23.26 E
Augustus, Mount ∧ 152 24.20 S 116.50 E
Augustusburg 50 50.49 N 13.06 E
Augustus Downs 156 18.33 S 139.52 E
Auiia, Ribeirão ≃ 245 12.09 S 53.20 W
Aujon ≃ 54 48.09 N 4.48 E
Auki 165e 8.46 S 160.42 E
Aulander 182 36.14 N 77.06 W
Aulanko 26 61.02 N 24.27 E
Auld, Lake @ 152 22.32 S 123.44 E
Aulendorf 54 47.57 N 9.38 E
Aulestad 26 61.13 N 10.17 E
Aulís ⊥ 38 38.27 N 23.35 E
Aulitivik Island I 166 69.32 N 67.50 W
Aulla 58 44.12 N 9.58 E
Aulnay 32 46.01 N 0.21 W
Aulnay-sous-Bois 46 48.57 N 2.31 E
Aulnay-sur-Mauldre 251 48.56 N 1.51 E
Aulne ≃ 32 48.17 N 4.16 W
Aulneau Peninsula ≻[1] 174 49.23 N 94.29 W
Aulnois-sur-Seille 52 48.52 N 6.19 E
Aulnoye-Aymeries 46 50.12 N 3.50 E
Ault, Fr. 46 50.06 N 1.27 E
Ault, Ky., U.S. 208 38.12 N 83.14 W
Aultman 204 40.34 N 79.16 W
Aultshire 206 40.13 N 85.19 W
Auly 68 48.33 N 34.28 E
Auma 50 50.42 N 11.54 E
Aumale 46 49.46 N 1.45 E
Auma Point ≻ 154 7.55 S 145.25 E
Aumar 164r 6.57 N 158.10 E
Aumetz 52 49.25 N 5.56 E
Aumont-Aubrac 32 44.43 N 3.17 E
Aumühle 48 53.31 N 10.19 E
Auna 140 10.12 N 4.45 E
Auneau 46 48.27 N 1.46 E
Auneuil 46 49.22 N 2.00 E
Auning 26 56.26 N 10.23 E
Auno 136 11.50 N 12.53 E
Aunuu I 164u 14.17 S 170.33 W
Auob ≃ 146 26.25 S 20.35 E
Auponhia 102 1.56 S 125.29 E
Aups 56 43.37 N 6.14 E
Aur, Pulau I 102 2.27 N 104.31 E
Aura 26 60.36 N 22.34 E
Aurach 52 49.15 N 10.25 E
Aurach ≃ 52 49.34 N 10.59 E
Aurachmat 75 41.34 N 70.07 E
Auraiya 114 26.28 N 79.31 E
Aurangābād, Bhārat 112 19.53 N 75.20 E
Aurangābād, Bhārat 114 24.45 N 84.22 E
Auray 32 47.40 N 2.59 W
Aurdal 26 60.56 N 9.24 E
Aure 26 63.16 N 8.32 E
Aure ≃ 154 7.05 S 145.19 E
Aurelius 206 42.31 N 84.31 W

Symbol	English	Deutsch	Español	Français	Português
≃	River	Fluss	Río	Rivière	Rio
≍	Canal	Kanal	Canal	Canal	Canal
∟	Waterfall, Rapids	Wasserfall, Stromschnellen	Cascada, Rápidos	Chute d'eau, Rapides	Cascata, Rápidos
U	Strait	Meeresstrasse	Estrecho	Détroit	Estreito
C	Bay, Gulf	Bucht, Golf	Bahía, Golfo	Baie, Golfe	Baía, Golfo
@	Lake, Lakes	See, Seen	Lago, Lagos	Lac, Lacs	Lago, Lagos
≡	Swamp	Sumpf	Pantano	Marais	Pântano
⊼	Ice Features, Glacier	Eis- und Gletscherformen	Accidentes Glaciales	Formes glaciaires	Acidentes Glaciares
⊤	Other Hydrographic Features	Andere Hydrographische Objekte	Otros Elementos Hidrográficos	Autres données hydrographiques	Outros Elementos Hidrográficos
✢	Submarine Features	Untermeerische Objekte	Accidentes Submarinos	Formes de relief sous-marin	Acidentes Submarinos
□	Political Unit	Politische Einheit	Unidad Política	Entité politique	Unidade Política
♥	Cultural Institution	Kulturelle Institution	Institución Cultural	Institution culturelle	Instituição Cultural
⊥	Historical Site	Historische Stätte	Sitio Histórico	Site historique	Sitio Histórico
♠	Recreational Site	Erholungs- und Ferienort	Sitio de Recreo	Centre de loisirs	Sítio de Lazer
⊠	Airport	Flughafen	Aeropuerto	Aéroport	Aeroporto
■	Military Installation	Militäranlage	Instalación Militar	Installation militaire	Instalação Militar
◆	Miscellaneous	Verschiedenes	Misceláneo	Divers	Miscelânea

Aurès, Massif de l' ▲▲ 138 35.08 N 6.30 E
Auri, Kepulauan II 154 1.59 S 134.42 E
Aurich • 48 53.28 N 7.29 E
Aurich □[6] 48 53.20 N 7.20 E
Auriesville Shrine ♁[1] 200 42.54 N 74.19 W
Auriflama 245 20.41 S 50.34 W
Aurigny → Alderney I 28 49.43 N 2.12 W
Aurilândia 245 16.44 S 50.28 W
Aurillac 32 44.56 N 2.26 E
Aurina, Valle V 58 47.00 N 12.00 E
Aurine, Alpi (Zillertaler Alpen) ▲▲ 58 47.00 N 11.55 E
Aurino ≃ 58 46.48 N 11.55 E
Auriol 56 43.23 N 5.38 E
Aurisina 58 45.45 N 13.41 E
Aurizona 240 1.17 S 45.46 W
Aurlandsfjorden C[2] 26 61.05 N 7.02 E
Aurlandsvangen 26 60.54 N 7.11 E
Auron 56 44.14 N 6.56 E
Auronzo di Cadore 58 46.33 N 12.26 E
Aurora, Bra. 240 6.57 S 38.58 W
Aurora, Bra. 277a 22.46 S 43.24 W
Aurora, Ont., Can. 202 44.00 N 79.28 W
Aurora, S. Afr. 148 32.42 S 18.29 E
Aurora, Alaska, U.S. 170 64.51 N 147.46 W
Aurora, Colo., U.S. 190 39.44 N 104.52 W
Aurora, Ill., U.S. 206 42.46 N 88.19 W
Aurora, Ind., U.S. 208 39.04 N 84.54 W
Aurora, Maine, U.S. 176 44.51 N 68.20 W
Aurora, Minn., U.S. 180 47.31 N 92.14 W
Aurora, Mo., U.S. 184 36.58 N 93.43 W
Aurora, Nebr., U.S. 188 40.52 N 98.00 W
Aurora, N.C., U.S. 182 35.18 N 76.47 W
Aurora, N.Y., U.S. 200 42.46 N 76.42 W
Aurora, Ohio, U.S. 204 41.19 N 81.21 W
Aurora, Oreg., U.S. 214 45.14 N 122.45 W
Aurora, Utah, U.S. 190 38.55 N 111.56 W
Aurora, W. Va., U.S. 178 39.19 N 79.33 W
Aurora Pond ◎ 269a 41.20 N 81.23 W
Auroux 56 44.45 N 3.44 E
Aursunden ◎ 26 62.40 N 11.40 E
Aurukun Mission 154 13.19 S 141.45 E
Aurunci, Monti ▲▲ 60 41.22 N 13.40 E
Aus 146 26.40 S 16.15 E
Ausable ≃, Ont., Can. 180 43.19 N 81.46 W
Au Sable ≃, Mich., U.S. 180 44.25 N 83.20 W
Au Sable, North Branch ≃ 180 44.40 N 84.23 W
Au Sable, South Branch ≃ 180 44.40 N 84.23 W
Au Sable Forks 178 44.27 N 73.41 W
Au Sable Point ≻ 180 44.20 N 83.20 W
Ausangate, Nevado ▲ 238 13.48 S 71.14 W
Auschwitz → Oświęcim 30 50.03 N 19.12 E
Ausevik ⊥ 26 61.32 N 5.16 E
Ausoni, Monti ▲▲ 60 41.25 N 13.20 E
Ausserferrera 54 46.33 N 9.26 E
Ausserfragant 58 46.56 N 13.06 E
Aussig → Ústí nad Labem 50 50.40 N 14.02 E
Aussois 56 45.14 N 6.45 E
Aust-Agder □[6] 26 58.50 N 8.00 E
Austerlitz, Ned. 48 52.05 N 5.19 E
Austerlitz, N.Y., U.S. 200 42.19 N 73.28 W
Austerlitz ◂[5] 251 48.50 N 2.22 E
Austin, Bra. 277a 22.43 S 43.32 W
Austin, Man., Can. 174 49.57 N 98.56 W
Austin, Ind., U.S. 208 38.45 N 85.48 W
Austin, Minn., U.S. 180 43.40 N 92.59 W
Austin, Nev., U.S. 194 39.30 N 117.04 W
Austin, Pa., U.S. 204 41.38 N 78.05 W
Austin, Tex., U.S. 212 30.16 N 97.45 W
Austin □[6] 212 29.53 N 96.15 W
Austin ◂[8] 268 41.54 N 87.45 W
Austin, Lake ◎ 152 27.40 S 118.00 E
Austin, Lake ◎[1] 212 30.19 N 97.46 W
Austin Bayou ≃ 212 29.07 N 95.18 W
Austinburg 204 41.46 N 80.51 W
Austin Channel ⊔ 166 75.35 N 103.25 W
Austin Lake ◎ 206 42.11 N 85.33 W
Austinmer 160 34.18 S 150.56 E
Austin's Post 148 29.32 S 25.49 E
Austintown 204 41.06 N 80.46 W
Austinville 182 36.51 N 80.55 W
Austnes 26 62.38 N 6.16 E
Austonio 212 31.11 N 95.38 W
Austonley 252 53.34 N 1.50 W
Australes, Îles II 14 23.00 S 150.00 W
Australia □[1] 150 25.00 S 135.00 E
Australia Mountain ▲ 170 63.36 N 138.08 W
Australian-Antarctic Rise ⊹[3] 9 50.00 S 130.00 E
Australian Capital Territory □[8] 161b 35.30 S 149.00 E
Australian War Memorial ⊥ 161b 35.17 S 149.09 E
Australia Plains 158b 34.06 S 139.09 E
Australie → Australia □[1] 150 25.00 S 135.00 E
Australien → Australia □[1] 150 25.00 S 135.00 E
Australind 158a 33.16 S 115.44 E
Austral Seamount Chain ⊹[3] 14 24.00 S 150.00 W
Austråt 26 63.43 N 9.45 E
Austria □[1] 22
30 47.20 N 13.20 E
Austvågøya I 24 68.20 N 14.36 E
Autazes 236 3.35 S 59.08 W
Auteuil, Fr. 46 49.21 N 2.05 E
Auteuil, Fr. 251 48.50 N 1.49 E
Auteuil, Lac d' ◎ 176 50.38 N 61.17 W
Autheuil 46 49.06 N 1.17 E
Authie ≃ 46 50.21 N 1.38 E
Authon 56 44.14 N 6.08 E
Authon-du-Perche 46 48.12 N 0.55 E
Authon-la-Plaine 46 48.27 N 1.57 E
Autlán de Navarro 224 19.46 N 104.22 W
Autore, Monte ▲ 60 41.58 N 13.12 E
Autoua 165f 16.21 S 167.45 E
Autrey-lès-Gray 54 47.29 N 5.30 E
Autriche → Austria □[1] 30 47.20 N 13.20 E
Autumn Hill 274b 39.16 N 76.48 W
Autun 32 46.57 N 4.18 E
Auve 52 49.02 N 4.42 E
Auvergne 154 15.41 S 130.01 E
Auvergne □[9] 32 45.25 N 2.30 E
Auvernaux 251 48.32 N 2.30 E
Auvers-sur-Oise 46 49.04 N 2.10 E
Auvézère ≃ 32 45.12 N 0.51 E
Aux Barques, Pointe ≻ 180 44.04 N 82.58 W
Aux Cayes → Les Cayes 228 18.12 N 73.45 W
Auxerre 46 47.48 N 3.34 E
Auxier 182 37.44 N 82.46 W
Auxi-le-Château 46 50.14 N 2.07 E
Auxon 46 48.06 N 3.55 E
Auxonne 54 47.12 N 5.23 E
Aux Sable Creek ≃ 206 41.23 N 88.20 W
Auxvasse 209 39.01 N 91.54 W
Auxvasse Creek ≃ 209 38.41 N 91.49 W
Auxy 54 46.57 N 4.24 E
Auyamita, Quebrada ≃ 276c 10.30 N 66.46 W
Auyán-Tepuí ▲ 236 5.55 N 62.32 W
Auzances 32 46.02 N 2.30 E
Auzon ≃ 56 44.02 N 4.54 E
Ava, Ill., U.S. 184 37.53 N 89.30 W
Ava, Mo., U.S. 184 36.57 N 92.40 W
Avaavaroa Passage ⊔ 164k 21.16 S 159.47 W
Avadchara 74 43.31 N 40.39 E
Avadh Plains ≚ 114 26.20 N 82.00 E
Avaí 245 22.08 S 49.22 W
Avakubi 144 1.20 N 27.34 E
Aval' 75 40.19 N 71.50 E
Avala ⊥ 38 44.45 N 20.35 E
Avaldsnes 26 59.21 N 5.16 E
Avallon 46 47.29 N 3.54 E
Avaloirs, Les ▲[2] 32 48.28 N 0.07 W
Avalon, Calif., U.S. 218 33.49 N 118.16 W
Avalon, N.J., U.S. 198 39.06 N 74.43 W
Avalon, Pa., U.S. 204 40.30 N 80.04 W
Avalon, Tex., U.S. 212 32.12 N 96.48 W
Avalon, Wis., U.S. 206 42.38 N 88.52 W
Avalon Peninsula ≻[1] 176 47.30 N 53.30 W
Avan ≃ 44 51.35 N 3.48 W
Avana ≃ 164k 21.14 S 159.43 W
Avanley 252 53.16 N 2.45 W
Avanos 120 38.43 N 34.51 E
Avant 186 36.29 N 96.04 W
Avante 276a 19.19 N 99.06 W
Avarapa, Passe ⊔ 164s 17.35 S 149.50 W
Avaray, Château d' ⊥ 46 47.43 N 1.34 E
Avaré 245 23.05 S 48.55 W
Avarskoje Kojsu ≃ 74 42.47 N 46.48 E
Avarua 164k 21.12 S 159.46 W
Avarua Harbour C 164k 21.11 S 159.46 W
Avatanak Island I 170 54.03 N 165.19 W
Avatele 164v 19.06 S 169.55 W
Avatele Bay C 164v 19.05 S 169.56 W
Avatiu 164k 21.12 S 159.47 W
Avatiu Harbour C 164k 21.11 S 159.47 W
Avčala 74 41.48 N 44.48 E
'Avdat ⊥ 122 30.48 N 34.46 E
Avdejevka 73 48.08 N 37.46 E
Avdotjino 73 47.55 N 37.51 E
Ave ≃ 34 41.20 N 8.45 W
Avebury 44 51.27 N 1.51 W
Avebury Stone Circle ⊥ 44 51.28 N 1.51 W
Avegadje ▲ 140 7.14 N 0.38 E
Aveiro, Bra. 240 3.15 S 55.10 W
Aveiro, Port. 34 40.38 N 8.39 W
Aveiro, Ria de ≃[1] 34 40.38 N 8.44 W
Āvej 118 35.34 N 49.13 E
Avelar 246 22.20 S 43.25 W
Avelengo 58 46.38 N 11.13 E
Aveley 250 51.30 N 0.16 E
Avelgem 46 50.46 N 3.26 E
Avella, It. 60 40.58 N 14.36 E
Avella, Pa., U.S. 204 40.17 N 80.28 W
Avellaneda, Arg. 242 29.07 S 59.40 W
Avellaneda, Arg. 248 34.39 S 58.23 W
Avellaneda □[5] 278 34.40 S 58.20 W
Avellaneda, Estacion ◂[5] 278 34.41 S 58.22 W
Avelle, Île I 265a 45.24 N 74.00 W
Avellino 60 40.54 N 14.47 E
Avellino □[4] 60 40.57 N 15.00 E
Avenal 216 36.00 N 120.08 W
Avenal Creek ≃ 216 35.47 N 120.04 W
Aven Armand •[5] 32 44.15 N 3.22 E
Avenas 54 46.12 N 4.37 E
Avenches 54 46.53 N 7.02 E
Avenel 266 40.35 N 74.17 W
Aventureiro 246 21.45 S 42.49 W
Aventureiro, Ribeirão do ≃ 246 21.52 S 42.39 W
Avenue 198 38.17 N 76.45 W
Avenwedde 48 51.55 N 8.27 E
Averbode 52 51.02 N 4.59 E
Averbode, Abbaye d' ♁[1] 52 51.02 N 4.59 E
Averill Park 200 42.38 N 73.33 W
Avern ◎ 40 58.54 N 15.32 E
Avernakø I 41 55.01 N 10.17 E
Avernes 251 49.05 N 1.52 E
Avernes, Rû des ≃ 251 49.04 N 2.51 E
Averøya I 26 63.01 N 7.34 E
Aversa 60 40.58 N 14.12 E
Avery, Calif., U.S. 216 38.13 N 120.22 W
Avery, Idaho, U.S. 192 47.15 N 115.49 W
Avery, Tex., U.S. 184 33.33 N 94.47 W
Avery Island 184 29.55 N 91.55 W
Avery Point ≻ 202 44.40 N 79.07 W
Aves, Islas de II 236 12.00 N 67.30 W
Avesnelles 46 50.07 N 3.57 E
Avesnes 32 50.07 N 3.56 E
Avesnes-le-Comte 46 50.17 N 2.32 E
Avesnes-lès-Aubert 46 50.12 N 3.23 E
Avesnes-sur-Helpe 46 50.07 N 3.56 E
Avesta 40 60.09 N 16.12 E
Aveto ≃ 56 44.42 N 9.23 E
Aveyron □[5] 32 44.15 N 2.40 E
Aveyron ≃ 32 44.05 N 1.16 E
Avezzano 60 42.02 N 13.25 E
Avgustovka 70 52.16 N 50.44 E
Aviano 58 46.04 N 12.36 E
Aviemore 28 57.12 N 3.50 W
Avigliana 56 45.05 N 7.23 E
Avigliano 36 40.44 N 15.44 E
Avignon 56 43.57 N 4.49 E
Ávila 34 40.39 N 4.42 W
Avila, Parque Nacional el ♠ 236 10.35 N 66.48 W
Ávila, Sierra de ▲▲ 34 40.35 N 5.08 W
Avila Beach 216 35.11 N 120.44 W
Avilés 34 43.33 N 5.55 W
Avilla 206 41.22 N 85.14 W
Avilley 54 47.26 N 6.16 E
Avinger 212 32.54 N 94.33 W
Avinurme 66 58.59 N 26.51 E
Avio 58 45.44 N 10.56 E
Avion 46 50.24 N 2.50 E
Avioth 52 49.34 N 5.24 E
Avis 200 41.11 N 77.19 W
Avisio ≃ 58 46.07 N 11.05 E
Aviston 209 38.36 N 89.36 W
Aviz 34 39.03 N 7.53 W
Avize 46 48.58 N 4.01 E
Avlan Gölü ◎ 120 36.34 N 29.57 E
Avlum 41 56.16 N 8.48 E
Avnbøl 41 54.58 N 9.39 E
Avnik 120 39.50 N 41.59 E
Avoca, Austl. 159 37.05 S 143.28 E
Avoca, Iowa, U.S. 188 41.29 N 95.20 W
Avoca, N.Y., U.S. 200 42.25 N 77.25 W
Avoca, Pa., U.S. 200 41.20 N 75.45 W
Avoca ≃ 159 36.41 S 143.28 E
Avoca, Mount ▲ 159 37.07 S 143.21 E
Avoca Beach 160 33.29 S 151.29 E
Avocado Heights 270 34.03 N 118.00 W
Avola, B.C., Can. 172 51.47 N 119.19 W
Avola, It. 36 36.54 N 15.09 E
Avon, Austl. 158b 34.17 S 138.20 E
Avon, Fr. 46 48.24 N 2.43 E
Avon, Conn., U.S. 197 41.49 N 72.50 W
Avon, Ill., U.S. 180 40.40 N 90.26 W
Avon, Mass., U.S. 197 42.08 N 71.02 W
Avon, Minn., U.S. 180 45.37 N 94.27 W
Avon, Mont., U.S. 192 46.36 N 112.36 W
Avon, N.C., U.S. 182 35.21 N 75.30 W
Avon, N.Y., U.S. 200 42.55 N 77.45 W
Avon, Ohio, U.S. 204 41.27 N 82.01 W
Avon, Pa., U.S. 198 40.22 N 76.23 W
Avon, S. Dak., U.S. 188 43.00 N 98.04 W
Avon □[6] 44 51.30 N 2.40 W
Avon ≃, Austl. 158a 31.40 S 116.07 E
Avon ≃, N.S., Can. 176 45.10 N 64.15 W
Avon ≃, Ont., Can. 202 43.18 N 81.11 W
Avon ≃, Eng., U.K. 44 51.59 N 2.10 W
Avon ≃, Eng., U.K. 44 50.43 N 1.46 W
Avon ≃, Eng., U.K. 44 50.17 N 3.52 W
Avon ≃, Eng., U.K. 44 51.30 N 2.43 W
Avon ≃, Scot., U.K. 42 56.01 N 3.40 W
Avon, Rû d' ≃ 251 48.39 N 2.46 E
Avon Basin C 269a 41.30 N 82.03 W
Avon by the Sea 198 40.12 N 74.01 W
Avondale, Rh. 144 17.43 S 30.58 E
Avondale, Ariz., U.S. 190 33.26 N 112.21 W
Avondale, Colo., U.S. 188 38.14 N 104.21 W
Avondale, Md., U.S. 274c 38.56 N 76.59 W
Avondale, Ohio, U.S. 204 40.53 N 81.26 W
Avondale Heights 264b 37.46 S 144.51 E
Avon Downs 156 20.05 S 137.30 E
Avondrust 148 34.21 S 21.51 E
Avon Lake 204 41.30 N 82.01 W
Avonlea 174 50.00 N 105.04 W
Avonmore, Ont., Can. 196 45.10 N 74.58 W
Avonmore, Pa., U.S. 204 40.32 N 79.28 W
Avonmouth 44 51.31 N 2.42 W
Avon Park 210 27.36 N 81.31 W
Avon Reservoir ◎[1] 160 34.24 S 150.40 E
Avontuur 148 33.44 S 23.11 E
Avon Water ≃ 42 55.47 N 4.01 W
Avoudrey 54 47.08 N 6.26 E
Avrainville 251 48.34 N 2.15 E
Avranches 32 48.41 N 1.22 W
Avranlo 74 41.39 N 43.52 E
Avre ≃, Fr. 46 48.47 N 1.22 E
Avre ≃, Fr. 46 49.53 N 2.20 E
Avrieux 56 45.13 N 6.43 E
Avrora ♁ 255a 59.57 N 30.21 E
Avroult 46 50.38 N 2.09 E
Avtatkujul ≃ 170 64.06 N 178.10 E
Avtovo ◂[8] 255a 59.52 N 30.15 E
Avu Avu 165e 9.50 S 160.23 E
Awa, Nihon 86 34.04 N 134.12 E
Awa, Nihon 164m 26.36 N 127.56 E
Awaba 160 33.01 S 151.33 E
A'waj, Nahr al- ≃ 122 33.20 N 36.34 E
Awaji 86 34.35 N 135.01 E
Awaji-shima I 86 34.21 N 134.51 E
Awakino 162 38.39 S 174.38 E
Awal Aw Ballou 134 1.29 N 43.02 E
Awal Edo 134 4.14 N 40.39 E
'awālī 118 26.05 N 50.33 E
Awang 105b 8.54 S 116.24 E
Awano 84 36.31 N 139.41 E
Awanui 162 35.03 S 173.15 E
Awara, Nihon 84 36.13 N 136.12 E
Awara, Yai. 134 5.30 N 40.00 E
Awarawar, Tanjung ≻ 105a 6.45 S 111.56 E
Aware 134 8.15 N 44.10 E
Awarua Point ≻ 162 44.15 S 168.03 E
Awasa 134 6.45 N 38.15 E
Awasa, Lake ◎ 134 7.05 N 38.25 E
Awasan Bay C 106 9.56 N 125.36 E
Awash 134 8.59 N 40.10 E
Awash ≃ 134 11.45 N 41.05 E
Awa-shima I, Nihon 82 38.27 N 139.14 E
Awa-shima I, Nihon 86 34.16 N 133.38 E
Awaso 140 6.14 N 2.16 W
Awatere ≃ 162 41.37 S 174.10 E
Awbārī 136 26.35 N 12.46 E
Awbārī □[4] 136 25.30 N 13.00 E
Awdeyle 134 2.00 N 44.51 E
Awe 140 8.09 N 9.07 E
Awe, Loch ◎ 28 56.15 N 5.15 W
Awegyun 100 12.44 N 98.44 E
Awīn 257d 35.48 N 51.24 E
Awīsh al-Ḥajar 132 31.01 N 31.19 E
Awjilah 136 29.09 N 21.15 E
Awka 140 6.12 N 7.05 E
Awlād Mūsā 132 30.48 N 31.44 E
Aworo Kit 130 10.59 N 32.38 E
Aworro 154 7.45 S 143.10 E
Awosting 266 41.09 N 74.20 W
Awsīm 132 30.07 N 31.08 E
Awul 154 6.00 S 151.00 E
Awuna ≃ 170 69.04 N 155.30 W
Axams 58 47.14 N 11.18 E
Axarfjördur C 24a 66.15 N 16.45 W
Axat 32 42.48 N 2.14 E
Axbridge 44 51.18 N 2.49 W
Axe ≃, Eng., U.K. 44 50.42 N 3.03 W
Axe ≃, Eng., U.K. 44 51.19 N 2.59 W
Axedale 159 36.47 S 144.30 E
Axe Edge ▲▲[2] 252 53.14 N 1.57 W
Axel 48 51.16 N 3.55 E
Axel Heiberg Island I 16 80.30 N 92.00 W
Axim 140 4.52 N 2.14 W
Axinim 236 4.02 S 59.22 W
Axiós (Vardar) ≃ 38 40.31 N 22.43 E
Axixá 240 2.51 S 44.04 W
Ax-les-Thermes 32 42.43 N 1.50 E
Axminster 44 50.47 N 3.00 W
Axmouth 44 50.42 N 3.02 W
Axochiapan 224 18.30 N 98.46 W
Axtell, Kans., U.S. 188 39.52 N 96.15 W
Axtell, Nebr., U.S. 188 40.29 N 99.08 W
Axtell, Tex., U.S. 212 31.39 N 96.58 W
Aÿ 46 49.03 N 4.00 E
Ayabaca 236 4.38 S 79.43 W
Ayabe 86 35.18 N 135.15 E
Ayachi, Ari n' ▲ 138 32.29 N 4.57 W
Ayacucho, Arg. 242 37.09 S 58.29 W
Ayacucho, Bol. 238 17.51 S 63.20 W
Ayacucho, Perú 238 13.07 S 74.13 W
Ayacucho □[5] 238 14.00 S 74.00 W
Ayamé 140 5.37 N 3.11 W
Ayamiken 142 2.07 N 10.01 E
Ayamonte 34 37.13 N 7.24 W
Āyān 262b 22.43 N 88.09 E
Ayancık 120 41.57 N 34.36 E
Ayangba 140 7.30 N 7.08 E
Ayapel 236 8.19 N 75.09 W
Ayarza, Laguna de ◎ 226 14.25 N 90.08 W
Ayas, It. 56 45.50 N 7.41 E
Ayaş, Tür. 120 40.01 N 32.21 E
Ayase 84 35.26 N 139.26 E
Ayase ≃ 258 35.45 N 139.49 E
Ayauta 86 33.14 N 133.53 E
Ayaviri 238 14.52 S 70.35 W
Ayaviri ≃ 238 15.01 S 70.22 W
Ayazağa 257b 41.06 N 28.59 E
Āybak 110 36.16 N 68.01 E
Ayden 182 35.25 N 77.20 W
Aydere 118 38.24 N 56.45 E
Aydın 120 37.51 N 27.51 E
Aydın □[4] 120 37.45 N 28.00 E
Aydıncık 120 36.08 N 33.19 E
Aydın Dağları ▲▲ 120 38.00 N 28.00 E
Aydin Ula ▲ 76 42.55 N 87.35 E
Aydos Dağı ▲ 257b 40.56 N 29.15 E
Ayelu ▲ 134 10.04 N 40.46 E
Ayémé 142 0.02 N 10.17 E
Ayer, Schw. 54 46.11 N 7.36 E
Ayer, Mass., U.S. 197 42.34 N 71.35 W
Ayer Baloi 104 1.35 N 103.20 E
Ayer Chawan, Pulau I 261c 1.17 N 103.42 E
Ayer Hitam, Malay. 104 2.56 N 102.24 E
Ayer Hitam, Malay. 104 1.55 N 103.11 E
Ayer Jerneh 104 4.24 N 103.24 E
Ayer Kuning Selatan 104 2.30 N 102.28 E
Ayer Merbau, Pulau I 261c 1.16 N 103.43 E
Ayers Cliff 196 45.10 N 72.03 W
Ayers Rock ▲ 152 25.23 S 131.05 E
Ayersville 206 41.14 N 84.17 W
Ayía Marína 38 37.09 N 26.52 E
Ayía Paraskeví 38 39.15 N 26.16 E
Ayiássos 38 39.05 N 26.23 E
Ayía Varvára 257c 37.59 N 23.39 E
Aying 58 47.58 N 11.46 E
Ayınkâf 120 37.34 N 41.10 E
Áyioi Anáryiroi 257c 38.02 N 23.43 E
Áyion Óros ≻[1] 38 40.15 N 24.15 E
Áyios Dhimítrios 257c 37.56 N 23.44 E
Áyios Ioánnis Réndis 257c 37.58 N 23.40 E
Áyios Kírikos 38 37.37 N 26.14 E
Áyios Nikólaos 38 35.11 N 25.42 E
Ayíou Nikoláou, Moní ♁[1] 257c 37.53 N 23.27 E
Ayíou Órous, Kólpos C 38 40.12 N 24.03 E
Aykota 134 15.12 N 37.05 E
Ayl 122 30.13 N 35.32 E
Aylesbury 44 51.50 N 0.50 W
Aylesford 44 51.18 N 0.29 E
Aylesham 44 51.13 N 1.13 E
Aylmer, Lake ◎ 196 45.50 N 71.22 W
Aylmer, Mount ▲ 172 51.19 N 115.26 W
Aylmer, Passage ⊔ 176 50.33 N 59.23 W
Aylmer East 178 45.24 N 75.51 W
Aylmer Lake ◎ 166 64.05 N 108.30 W
Aylmer West 202 42.46 N 80.59 W
Aylsham, Sask., Can. 174 53.11 N 103.49 W
Aylsham, Eng., U.K. 44 52.49 N 1.15 E
'Ayn, Jabal al- ▲[2] 122 30.49 N 34.26 E
'Ayn al-'Arab 120 36.54 N 38.21 E
'Ayn al-Ghazālah 136 32.10 N 23.20 E
'Ayn Dār 118 25.59 N 49.23 E
'Ayn Dīwār 120 37.17 N 42.11 E
Aynı 120 37.43 N 41.55 E
'Aynīn ⊤[4] 134 20.48 N 41.39 E
Aynor 182 34.00 N 79.12 W
'Aynūnah 118 28.05 N 35.08 E
Ayo 238 15.41 S 72.16 W
Ayo Ayo 238 17.05 S 68.00 W
Ayod 130 8.07 N 31.26 E
Ayodhya 114 26.48 N 82.12 E
Ayo el Chico 224 20.32 N 102.21 W
Ayom 130 7.52 N 28.23 E
Ayoquezco 224 16.41 N 96.50 W
Ayora 34 39.04 N 1.03 W
Ayorou 140 14.44 N 0.55 E
Ayos 142 3.54 N 12.31 E
Ayoulehaimiao 92 44.19 N 115.22 E
'Ayoûn el 'Atroûs 140 16.40 N 9.37 W
Ayr, Austl. 156 19.35 S 147.24 E
Ayr, Ont., Can. 202 43.17 N 80.27 W
Ayr, Scot., U.K. 42 55.28 N 4.38 W
Ayr ≃ 42 55.29 N 4.28 W
'Ayrah 122 32.37 N 36.32 E
Ayrancı 120 37.22 N 33.42 E
Ayre, Point of ≻ 42 54.26 N 4.22 W
Ayrolle, Étang de l' ◎ 32 43.05 N 3.03 E
Aysgarth 42 54.17 N 2.00 W
Aysha 134 10.46 N 42.37 E
'Aytā al-Fakhkhār 122 33.38 N 35.54 E
'Aytanīt 122 33.34 N 35.40 E
Ayton, Austl. 154 15.56 S 145.22 E
Ayton, Ont., Can. 202 44.03 N 80.56 W
Ayu, Kepulauan II 98 0.28 N 131.03 E
Ayun ≃ 100 13.24 N 108.28 E
Ayuñgon 106 9.51 N 123.08 E
Ayutla 224 20.07 N 104.22 W
Ayutla [de los Libres] 224 16.54 N 99.13 W
Ayvacık, Tür. 120 39.36 N 26.24 E
Ayvacık, Tür. 120 41.00 N 36.39 E
Ayvalı 120 38.44 N 37.38 E
Ayvalık 120 39.18 N 26.41 E
Aywaille 52 50.28 N 5.40 E
Azabarabān, Ra's ≻ 132 28.51 N 32.43 E
Azacualpa, Hond. 226 15.19 N 88.33 W
Azacualpa, Hond. 226 14.27 N 86.09 W
Azādpur ◂[8] 262a 28.43 N 77.11 E
Azai 84 35.26 N 136.18 E
Azaila 34 41.17 N 0.29 W
Azakpert 120 39.14 N 40.30 E
Azalea Park 210 28.32 N 81.15 W
Azama 164m 26.11 N 127.49 E
Azamatovo 70 53.18 N 53.28 E
Azambuja 34 39.04 N 8.52 W
Azamgarh 114 26.04 N 83.11 E
Azamgarh □[5] 114 26.00 N 83.00 E
Azamiga-dake ▲ 86 34.20 N 131.47 E
Azángaro 238 14.55 S 70.13 W
Azángaro ≃ 238 15.17 S 70.10 W
Azanka 76 58.02 N 64.48 E
Azanovo 70 56.43 N 48.13 E
Azao ▲ 138 25.12 N 8.08 E
Azaouâd ◂[1] 140 19.00 N 3.00 W
Azaouak, Vallée de l' V 140 15.30 N 3.18 E
Azapa, Quebrada de ≃ 238 18.30 S 70.17 W
Azar V 140 16.02 N 4.04 E
Azara 140 8.21 N 9.12 E
Āžarbāījān-e Bākhtarī □[4] 74 38.00 N 45.00 E
Āžarbāījān-e Khāvarī □[4] 74 38.00 N 47.00 E
Azare 140 11.40 N 10.11 E
Āžar Shahr 118 37.45 N 45.59 E
Azas ≃ 78 52.26 N 96.15 E
Azay-le-Rideau 46 47.16 N 0.28 E
Azay-sur-Cher 46 47.21 N 0.51 E
Azay-sur-Indre 46 47.12 N 0.57 E
A'zāz 120 36.35 N 37.03 E
Azazga 138 36.44 N 4.22 E
Azcapotzalco □[7] 276a 19.24 N 99.12 W
Azcuénaga 248 34.23 S 59.21 W
Aždaak, Gora ▲ 74 40.13 N 44.56 E
Azdavay 120 41.39 N 33.18 E
Azefal •[8] 138 21.00 N 14.45 W
Azeffoun 138 36.53 N 4.25 E
Azejevo 70 54.41 N 42.02 E
Azemmour 138 33.20 N 8.25 W
Azenhas do Mar 256c 38.50 N 9.28 W
Azerbaidzhan Soviet Socialist Republic → Azerbajdžanskaja Sovetskaja Socialističeskaja Respublika □[3] 74 40.30 N 47.30 E
Azerbajdžanskaja Sovetskaja Socialističeskaja Respublika □[3] 74 40.30 N 47.30 E
Azergues ≃ 54 45.56 N 4.44 E
Azezo 134 12.35 N 37.28 E
Azgir 70 47.50 N 47.54 E
Azhikode 112 11.59 N 75.21 E
Azile 144 3.32 N 29.52 E
Azimganj 116 24.14 N 88.15 E
Azincourt 46 50.28 N 2.08 E
Azizbekov 74 39.40 N 45.30 E
Azle 212 32.54 N 97.33 W
'az'ma ≃ 72 56.29 N 35.49 E
Aznakajevo 70 54.53 N 53.04 E
Aznapuquio 276d 11.59 S 77.04 W
Azogues 236 2.44 S 78.50 W
Azoia 256c 38.46 N 9.29 W
Azor 122 32.01 N 34.48 E
Azores → Açores, Arquipélago dos II 138a 38.30 N 28.00 W
Azores-Gibraltar Ridge ⊹[3] 10 38.00 N 19.00 W
Azores Plateau ⊹[3] 10 38.30 N 30.00 W
Azoum, Bahr (Wādī 'Azūm) V 136 10.53 N 20.15 E
Azov 73 47.07 N 39.25 E
Azov, Sea of → Azovskoje More ⊤[2] 68 46.00 N 36.00 E
Azovo-Sivašskij Zapovednik ◂[4] 68 46.08 N 35.08 E
Azovskij Kanal ≊ 73 47.07 N 39.27 E
Azovskoje 68 45.34 N 34.34 E
Azovskoje More ⊤[2] 68 46.00 N 36.00 E
Azoyú 224 16.43 N 98.44 W
Azpeitia 34 43.11 N 2.16 W
Azraq, Bahr ≃ 136 10.52 N 20.35 E
Azraq, Wādī al- V 130 10.33 N 28.40 E
Azrou 138 33.27 N 5.14 W
Azrou, Oued V 138 22.15 N 6.39 E
Aztalan State Park ♠ 206 43.04 N 88.51 W
Aztec 190 36.49 N 107.59 W
Azteca, Estadio ♠ 276a 19.18 N 99.09 W
Aztec Peak ▲ 190 33.48 N 110.55 W
Aztec Ruins National Monument ♠ 190 36.51 N 108.10 W
Azua 228 18.27 N 70.44 W
Azuaga 34 38.16 N 5.41 W
Azuay □[4] 236 3.00 S 79.00 W
Azucena 242 37.29 S 59.18 W
Azuchi 84 35.09 N 136.08 E
Azuchi-jō ⊥ 84 35.10 N 136.08 E
Azuer ≃ 34 39.08 N 3.36 W

ENGLISH Name	Page	Lat.°′	Long.°′

Azuero, Península de ≻[1] 236 7.40 N 80.35 W
Azuga 38 45.27 N 25.33 E
Azul 242 36.47 S 59.51 W
Azul, Cerro ▲, C.R. 226 9.54 N 85.14 W
Azul, Cerro ▲, Ec. 236a 0.54 S 91.21 W
Azul, Cerro ▲, Hond. 226 14.32 N 88.23 W
Azul, Cordillera ▲▲ 238 9.00 S 75.35 W
Azul, Serra ▲▲[1] 238 14.50 S 54.50 W
Azul, Sierra ▲▲ 224 23.15 N 98.20 W
'Azūm, Wādī (Bahr Azoum) V 136 10.53 N 20.15 E
Azuma, Nihon 84 35.56 N 140.30 E
Azuma, Nihon 84 36.36 N 138.20 E
Azumaya-san ▲ 84 36.32 N 138.25 E
Azumazaka 260 34.26 N 135.39 E
Azumi 84 36.11 N 137.47 E
Azur, Côte D' •[2] 56 43.30 N 7.00 E
Azurduy 238 19.59 S 64.29 W
Azure Lake ◎ 172 52.23 N 120.00 W
Azusa 218 34.08 N 117.55 W
Azusa ≃ 84 36.17 N 137.56 E
Ažu-Tajga, Gora ▲ 76 51.35 N 88.45 E
Az-Zabābidah 122 32.23 N 35.20 E
Az-Zāb al-Kabīr → Great Zab ≃ 118 36.00 N 43.21 E
Az-Zāb as-Ṣaghīr → Little Zab ≃ 118 35.12 N 43.25 E
Az-Zabdānī 122 33.43 N 36.05 E
Aẓ-Ẓāhirīyah 122 31.25 N 34.58 E
Aẓ-Ẓahrān (Dhahran) 118 26.18 N 50.08 E
Az-Zamālik ◂[8] 263c 30.04 N 31.13 E
Azzanello 58 45.18 N 9.55 E
Az-Zankalūn 132 30.33 N 31.27 E
Azzano Decimo 58 45.53 N 12.43 E
Az-Zaqāzīq 132 30.35 N 31.31 E
Az-Zarbah 120 36.04 N 36.59 E
Az-Zarqā' 122 32.05 N 36.06 E
Az-Zawāmil 132 30.21 N 31.26 E
Az-Zāwiyah 136 32.45 N 12.44 E
Az-Zāwiyah □[4] 136 32.50 N 12.15 E
Az-Zaydāb 130 17.26 N 33.53 E
Az-Zaydīyah 134 15.18 N 43.04 E
Az-Zaytīyah ◂[8] 132 29.58 N 32.31 E
Az-Zaytūn ◂[8] 263c 30.06 N 31.19 E
Azzel Matti, Sebkha ≃ 138 25.55 N 0.56 E
Az-Zilfī 118 26.18 N 44.48 E
Az-Zrārīyah 122 33.21 N 35.20 E
Az-Zubayr 118 30.23 N 47.43 E
'Azzūn 122 32.11 N 35.03 E
Azzurra, Grotta •[5] 60 40.35 N 14.14 E
Az-Zuwaytīnah 136 30.58 N 20.07 E

B

Ba ≃ 100 13.02 N 109.03 E
Baa 102 10.43 S 123.03 E
Baaba, Île I 165f 20.03 S 163.59 E
Baacagaan 92 45.35 N 99.27 E
Baad 54 47.19 N 10.07 E
Ba'adweyn 134 7.12 N 47.24 E
Baah 102 10.28 S 121.59 E
Baak 253 51.25 N 7.10 E
Baal 52 51.02 N 6.17 E
Baao 106 13.27 N 123.22 E
Baar 54 47.12 N 8.32 E
Baar ◂[1] 54 48.00 N 8.30 E
Baarbach ≃ 253 51.27 N 7.39 E
Baardskeerdersbos 148 34.34 S 19.35 E
Baarle-Hertog 52 51.27 N 4.56 E
Baarle-Nassau 48 51.27 N 4.53 E
Baarlo 48 51.20 N 6.05 E
Baarn 48 52.13 N 5.16 E
Baasrode 46 51.02 N 4.10 E
Baba 236 1.47 S 79.40 W
Baba ≃ 142 6.25 N 17.07 E
Baba Burnu ≻ 120 39.29 N 26.04 E
Babaçulândia 240 7.13 S 47.46 W
Babadag, Rom. 38 44.54 N 28.43 E
Babadağ, Tür. 120 37.48 N 28.52 E
Babadag, Gora ▲ 74 41.02 N 48.19 E
Babaeski 120 41.26 N 27.06 E
Babahoyo 236 1.49 S 79.31 W
Babai ≃ 114 28.01 N 81.28 E
Babaiqiao 90 32.26 N 118.57 E
Babajevo 66 59.23 N 35.56 E
Babajkovka 68 49.01 N 34.32 E
Babajurt 74 43.36 N 46.47 E
Babak 102 7.08 N 125.41 E
Babakin 152 32.07 S 118.01 E
Babana 140 10.26 N 3.50 E
Babanango 148 28.30 S 31.00 E
Babanka 68 48.43 N 30.26 E
Babanūsah 130 11.20 N 27.48 E
Babar, Kepulauan II 154 7.50 S 129.45 E
Babar, Pulau I 154 7.55 S 129.45 E
Bābarpur ◂[8] 262a 28.41 N 77.17 E
Babat, Indon. 102 2.45 S 103.38 E
Babat, Indon. 105a 7.06 S 112.10 E
Babatag, Chrebet ▲▲ 75 38.15 N 68.20 E
Babati 144 4.13 S 35.45 E
Bābā Valī Ṣāḥeb 110 31.40 N 65.40 E
Bābayn, Jabal ▲ 130 22.38 N 25.00 E
Babb 172 48.51 N 113.26 W
Babbacombe Bay C 44 50.30 N 3.25 W
Babb Creek ≃ 200 41.33 N 77.23 W
Babbitt, Minn., U.S. 180 47.43 N 91.57 W
Babbitt, Nev., U.S. 194 38.39 N 118.37 W
B'abdā 122 33.50 N 35.32 E
B'abdāt 122 33.53 N 35.40 E
Babel, Mont de ▲ 176 51.27 N 68.42 W
Babelijamun 154 2.04 S 137.43 E
Babelsberg ◂[8] 254a 52.24 N 13.05 E
Babelsberg, Schloss ⊥ 254a 52.24 N 13.05 E
Babelthuap I 165b 7.30 N 134.36 E
Babenhausen, B.R.D. 52 49.57 N 8.56 E
Babenhausen, B.R.D. 54 48.09 N 10.15 E
Babenki 72 55.21 N 37.11 E
Babenkovo 73 49.15 N 37.21 E
Babeyru 144 1.52 N 27.27 E
Babi, Pulau I 104 2.05 N 96.39 E
Babia, Arroyo de la ≃ 186 28.25 N 101.45 W
Babiči 66 52.17 N 30.00 E
Bābil 132 30.41 N 31.00 E
Babile 134 9.15 N 42.19 E
Babilônia 246 22.33 S 44.28 W
Babilônia ≃ 245 17.10 S 53.05 W
Babimost 30 52.10 N 15.51 E
Babīna 114 25.15 N 78.28 E
Babina Greda 38 45.07 N 18.33 E
Babinda 156 17.20 S 145.55 E
Babine 172 55.19 N 126.37 W
Babine ≃ 172 55.42 N 127.40 W
Babine Lake ◎ 172 54.45 N 126.00 W
Babine Range ▲▲ 172 55.00 N 126.25 W
Babino, S.S.S.R. 66 59.50 N 40.49 E
Babino, S.S.S.R. 66 56.44 N 34.17 E
Babino, S.S.S.R. 66 59.14 N 31.26 E
Babino, S.S.S.R. 70 57.22 N 48.45 E
Babiogórski Park Narodowy ♠ 30 49.35 N 19.30 E
Babo 154 2.33 S 133.25 E
Bābol 118 36.34 N 52.42 E
Bābol Sar 118 36.43 N 52.39 E
Babonã ≃ 238 6.35 S 66.27 W
Baboon Point ≻ 148 32.19 S 18.20 E
Baboquivari Mountains ▲▲ 190 31.45 N 111.35 W
Baboquivari Peak ▲ 190 31.46 N 111.35 W
Babor, Djebel ▲ 34 36.30 N 5.28 E
Baborów 30 50.09 N 17.59 E
Babošino 72 54.13 N 37.08 E
Baboua 142 5.48 N 14.49 E
Babrongan Tower ▲[2] 152 18.36 S 123.33 E

DEUTSCH Name	Seite	Breite°′	Länge°′ E = Ost

Babson Park, Fla., U.S. 210 27.50 N 81.32 W
Babson Park, Mass., U.S. 273 42.18 N 71.23 W
Babson Reservoir ◎[1] 273 42.38 N 70.40 W
Babstovo 79 48.07 N 132.27 E
Bab-Taza 138 35.03 N 5.14 W
Bābu Bheri 262b 22.51 N 88.14 E
Babungo 142 6.04 N 10.26 E
Bābupur, Bhārat 116 24.01 N 87.10 E
Bābūpur, Bhārat 262a 28.30 N 76.59 E
Babura 140 12.46 N 9.01 E
Babuškin 78 51.41 N 105.54 E
Babuškin ◂[8] 255b 55.52 N 37.42 E
Babuyan 106 10.00 N 118.54 E
Babuyan Channel ⊔ 106 18.44 N 121.40 E
Babuyan Island I 98 19.32 N 121.57 E
Babuyan Islands II 98 19.10 N 121.40 E
Baby 277a 22.42 S 43.23 W
Baby, Canal do ≊ 277a 22.42 S 43.21 W
Babylon 200 40.42 N 73.20 W
Babylon ⊥ 118 32.33 N 44.24 E
Babynino 66 54.23 N 35.43 E
Babyšmola ⊥ 76 44.23 N 63.10 E
Bača ≃ 58 46.09 N 13.48 E
Bacaba, Igarapé ≃ 236 3.35 S 68.45 W
Bacabal 240 4.14 S 44.47 W
Bacacay 106 13.18 N 123.47 E
Bacajá ≃ 240 3.25 S 51.50 W
Bacajaí ≃ 240 3.27 S 51.53 W
Bacalar, Laguna de ◎ 222 18.43 N 88.22 W
Bacalhau, Canal do ≊ 277a 23.03 S 43.35 W
Bacaligo 74 42.33 N 44.57 E
Bačalino 76 57.46 N 67.17 E
Bacan, Pulau I 154 0.35 S 127.30 E
Bacao 106 10.27 N 119.48 E
Bacarra 106 18.15 N 120.35 E
Bacatuba 240 5.40 S 43.42 W
Bacău 38 46.34 N 26.55 E
Bacău □[4] 38 46.30 N 26.45 E
Baccalieu Island I 176 48.08 N 52.48 W
Baccarat 54 48.27 N 6.45 E
Bacchiglione ≃ 58 45.11 N 12.14 E
Bacchus Marsh 159 37.41 S 144.27 E
Baceno 54 46.16 N 8.19 E
Bacerac 222 30.18 N 108.50 W
Bacevič̌i 66 53.24 N 29.14 E
Bac-giang 100 21.16 N 106.12 E
Bach 54 47.16 N 10.24 E
Bac-ha 92 22.32 N 104.17 E
Bachagou 88 40.36 N 122.54 E
Bachaquero 236 9.56 N 71.08 W
Bacharach 52 50.04 N 7.46 E
Bacharden 118 38.26 N 57.25 E
Bachardok 118 38.46 N 58.30 E
Bachawan 106 12.28 N 122.06 E
Bachčisaraj 68 44.45 N 33.51 E
Bacheli 112 18.40 N 81.16 E
Bacheng 96 31.27 N 120.52 E
Bachi, Zhg. 90 24.48 N 115.49 E
Bachi, Zhg. 96 31.04 N 120.39 E
Bachíniva 222 28.45 N 107.15 W
Bach-ma 100 16.12 N 107.52 E
Bachmač 68 51.13 N 32.46 E
Bachmetjevka 70 51.06 N 44.46 E
Bachmut ≃ 73 48.56 N 38.03 E
Bachmutovka 73 48.52 N 39.03 E
Bachmutovo 66 56.22 N 34.03 E
Bacho 104 6.37 N 101.39 E
Bachok 104 6.04 N 102.24 E
Bacht 75 40.43 N 68.42 E
Bachta, S.S.S.R. 64 62.28 N 89.00 E
Bachta, S.S.S.R. 76 55.45 N 92.26 E
Bachtemir ≃ 70 45.43 N 47.38 E
Bachten-Berg ▲[2] 254a 52.20 N 12.54 E
Bachty 76 46.39 N 82.42 E
Bachu 80 39.50 N 78.20 E
Bachuma 134 6.48 N 35.53 E
Back ≃, N.W. Ter., Can. 166 67.15 N 95.15 W
Back ≃, Va., U.S. 198 37.06 N 76.17 W
Bačka ◂[1] 38 45.50 N 19.30 E
Bac-kan 100 22.08 N 105.50 E
Bačka Palanka 38 45.15 N 19.24 E
Bačka Topola 38 45.49 N 19.38 E
Back Bay ◂[8] 273 42.21 N 71.05 W
Back Bay C, Bhārat 262c 18.56 N 72.49 E
Back Bay C, Va., U.S. 198 36.35 N 75.57 W
Backberg 40 60.37 N 16.37 E
Backbone Ranges ▲▲ 170 63.30 N 129.00 W
Back Branch ≃ 274c 38.50 N 76.48 W
Back Brook ≃ 266 40.26 N 74.39 W
Back Channel ≃[1] 269b 40.30 N 80.05 W
Back Creek ≃ 178 38.02 N 79.54 W
Backe 26 63.49 N 16.24 E
Bäckefors 26 58.48 N 12.10 E
Bäckehagen 40 60.39 N 15.34 E
Backford 252 53.15 N 2.54 W
Bäckhammar 40 59.10 N 14.11 E
Bački Petrovac 38 45.22 N 19.35 E
Backnang 52 48.56 N 9.25 E
Back River C 198 39.16 N 76.27 W
Backstairs Passage ⊔ 158b 35.42 S 138.05 E
Bac-lieu (Vinh-loi) 100 9.17 N 105.44 E
Bacliff 212 29.31 N 94.59 W
Bac-ninh 100 21.11 N 106.03 E
Baco, Mount ▲ 106 12.49 N 121.10 E
Bacoachi 222 30.38 N 109.56 W
Bacoli 60 40.48 N 14.05 E
Bacolod 106 10.40 N 122.57 E
Bacon 106 13.03 N 124.03 E
Bacongo 263b 4.18 S 15.16
Bacon Peak ▲ 214 48.39 N 121.31 W
Bacons Run ≃ 275 40.06 N 74.41 W
Baconton 182 31.23 N 84.10 W
Bacoor 106 14.28 N 120.56 E
Bacoor Bay C 259f 14.28 N 120.54 E
Bac-quang 100 22.29 N 104.52 E
Bacqueville-en-Caux 46 49.47 N 1.00 E
Bácsalmás 38 46.08 N 19.20 E
Bács-Kiskun □[6] 30 46.30 N 19.25 E
Bacton 44 52.52 N 1.28 E
Bacuag 106 9.37 N 125.38 E
Bacuit Bay C 106 11.07 N 119.23 E
Bácum 222 27.33 N 110.05 W
Bacümber 78 48.29 N 106.42 E
Bacungan 106 9.56 N 118.42 E
Bacup 42 53.43 N 2.12 W
Bacuranao ≃[8] 276b 23.10 N 82.14 W
Bacuri, Cachoeira ⌊ 240 5.29 S 54.18 W
Bacuri, Ilha do I 240 2.55 S 49.43 W
Bacurituba 240 2.43 S 44.43 W
Bačurka 24 68.32 N 56.57 E
Bacuyangan 106 9.39 N 122.27 E
Bād 118 33.41 N 52.01 E
Bad ≃, S. Dak., U.S. 188 44.22 N 100.22 W
Bad ≃, Wis., U.S. 180 46.38 N 90.40 W
Bad, South Fork ≃ 188 44.02 N 101.40 W
Bada 78 51.23 N 109.54 E
Badagara 112 11.36 N 75.35 E
Badagri 140 6.27 N 2.55 E
Badagri □[8] 263a 6.27 N 3.18 E
Badagri Creek C 263a 6.25 N 3.18 E
Badahl 132 28.56 N 30.54 E
Bad Aibling 58 47.52 N 12.00 E
Badajia 90 33.57 N 120.17 E
Badajós ≃ 236 3.15 S 63.02 W
Badajós, Lago ◎ 236 3.15 S 62.47 W
Badajoz 34 38.53 N 6.58 W
Badakani 142 4.46 S 14.52 E
Badakhshan □[4] 110 36.45 N 72.00 E
Badal Khān Goth 110 26.31 N 67.06 E
Badalona 34 41.27 N 2.15 E
Badalucco 56 43.55 N 7.51 E
Badam 75 42.23 N 69.15 E
Bādāmi 112 15.55 N 75.41 E

Symbols in the index entries represent the broad categories identified in the key at the right. Symbols with superior numbers (▲▲[2]) identify subcategories (see complete key on page I · 26).

Kartensymbole in dem Registerverzeichnis stellen die rechts in Schlüssel erklärten Kategorien dar. Symbole mit hochgestellten Ziffern (▲▲[2]) bezeichnen Unterabteilungen einer Kategorie (vgl. vollständiger Schlüssel auf Seite I · 26).

Los símbolos incluídos en el texto del índice representan las grandes categorias identificadas con la clave a la derecha. Los símbolos con numeros en su parte superior (▲▲[2]) identifican las subcategorías (véase la clave completa en la página I · 26).

Les symboles de l'index représentent les catégories indiquées dans la légende à droite. Les symboles suivis d'un indice (▲▲[2]) représentent des sous-catégories (voir légende complète à la page I · 26).

Os símbolos incluídos no texto do índice representam as grandes categorias identificadas com a chave à direita. Os símbolos com números em sua parte superior (▲▲[2]) identificam as subcategorias (veja-se a chave completa à página I · 26).

	English	Deutsch	Español	Français	Português
▲	Mountain	Berg	Montaña	Montagne	Montanha
▲▲	Mountains	Berge	Montañas	Montagnes	Montanhas
)(	Pass	Pass	Paso	Col	Passo
V	Valley, Canyon	Tal, Cañon	Valle, Cañón	Vallée, Canyon	Vale, Canhão
≚	Plain	Ebene	Llano	Plaine	Planície
≻	Cape	Kap	Cabo	Cap	Cabo
I	Island	Insel	Isla	Île	Ilha
II	Islands	Inseln	Islas	Îles	Ilhas
•	Other Topographic Features	Andere Topographische Objekte	Otros Elementos Topográficos	Autres données topographiques	Outros Elementos Topográficos

ESPAÑOL — Nombre | Página | Lat.°′ | Long.°′ W=Oeste
FRANÇAIS — Nom | Page | Lat.°′ | Long.°′ W=Ouest
PORTUGUÊS — Nome | Página | Lat.°′ | Long.°′ W=Oeste

Bādāmpahār 114 22.06 N 86.06 E
Badana, Lac ≃ 134 0.52 S 42.05 E
Badanah 118 30.59 N 41.02 E
Badanga 136 11.36 N 17.26 E
Badanganj 116 22.54 N 87.33 E
Badaohao 94 41.47 N 121.57 E
Badaohe, Zhg. 88 40.02 N 122.17 E
Badaohe, Zhg. 88 40.24 N 118.42 E
Badaojiang 88 41.56 N 126.24 E
Badarma 78 57.46 N 102.36 E
Badaryn Uul ⋀ 78 50.20 N 101.20 E
Badas 102 4.36 N 114.27 E
Badas, Kepulauan II 102 0.35 N 107.06 E
Badata, Gora Λ 78 51.55 N 111.35 E
Bad Aussee 58 47.36 N 13.47 E
Bad Axe 180 43.48 N 83.00 W
Badaying 88 41.22 N 117.28 E
Badazhou 92 24.36 N 105.04 E
Bad Bentheim 48 52.19 N 7.10 E
Bad Bergzabern 52 49.07 N 8.00 E
Bad Berka 50 50.54 N 11.17 E
Bad Bertrich 52 50.04 N 7.02 E
Bad Bibra 50 51.12 N 11.35 E
Bad Blankenburg 50 50.41 N 11.16 E
Bad Bramstedt 48 53.55 N 9.53 E
Bad Breisig 52 50.31 N 7.18 E
Bad Buchau 54 48.03 N 9.36 E
Bad Cannstatt ◆[8] 52 48.48 N 9.12 E
Badchyzskij Zapovednik ◆[4] 118 35.48 N 61.42 E
Bad Creek ≃ 206 41.25 N 83.57 W
Baddā 122 33.41 N 36.26 E
Baddeck 176 46.07 N 60.45 W
Bad Ditzenbach 52 48.35 N 9.41 E
Baddo ≃ 110 27.59 N 64.21 E
Bad Doberan 50 54.06 N 11.53 E
Baddomalhi 113 31.59 N 74.40 E
Bad Dreibergen 48 53.12 N 8.01 E
Bad Driburg 48 51.44 N 9.01 E
Bad Düben 50 51.36 N 12.34 E
Bad Dürkheim 52 49.28 N 8.10 E
Bad Dürrenberg 50 51.18 N 12.04 E
Bad Dürrheim 54 48.01 N 8.32 E
Bade, Centraf. 142 6.41 N 17.07 E
Bade, Indon. 154 7.10 S 139.35 E
Badé ≃ 142 4.26 N 18.16 E
Badeggi 140 9.05 N 6.08 E
Badéguichéri 140 14.31 N 5.22 E
Bad Eilsen 48 52.14 N 9.06 E
Badel 50 52.44 N 11.19 E
Bad Elster 50 50.17 N 12.14 E
Bademli 120 37.02 N 32.41 E
Bad Ems 52 50.20 N 7.43 E
Baden, B.R.D. 48 53.00 N 9.04 E
Baden, Ont., Can. 202 43.24 N 80.39 W
Baden, Öst. 254b 48.00 N 16.14 E
Baden, Schw. 54 47.29 N 8.18 E
Baden, Pa., U.S. 204 40.38 N 80.14 W
Baden, Yai. 134 17.00 N 38.00 E
Baden-Baden 52 48.46 N 8.14 E
Baden-Powell, Mount Λ 218 34.21 N 117.46 W
Badenweiler 54 47.48 N 7.40 E
Baden-Württemberg □[3] 30 48.30 N 9.00 E
Baderna 58 45.12 N 13.46 E
Badersleben 50 51.59 N 10.53 E
Bad Essen 48 52.19 N 8.20 E
Badfish Creek ≃ 206 42.50 N 89.10 W
Bad Frankenhausen 50 51.21 N 11.06 E
Bad Freienwalde 50 52.47 N 14.01 E
Bad Friedrichshall 52 49.14 N 9.11 E
Bad Fusch 58 47.12 N 12.51 E
Bad Gandersheim 48 51.52 N 10.01 E
Badgastein 58 47.07 N 13.08 E
Badger, Newf., Can. 176 48.59 N 56.02 W
Badger, Minn., U.S. 188 48.47 N 96.01 W
Badger Creek ≃, Colo., U.S. 188 40.17 N 103.42 W
Badger Creek ≃, Colo., U.S. 190 38.28 N 105.52 W
Badger Creek ≃, Oreg., U.S. 214 45.16 N 121.11 W
Badger Pass)(216 37.40 N 119.39 W
Badger's Mount 250 51.20 N 0.09 E
Badgery Creek ≃ 264a 33.51 S 150.46 E
Badgery's Creek 264a 33.53 S 150.44 E
Bādghīsāt □[4] 118 35.00 N 63.45 E
Bad Godesberg 52 50.41 N 7.10 E
Bad Goisern 58 47.38 N 13.37 E
Badgom 113 34.01 N 74.43 E
Bad Gottleuba 50 50.51 N 13.56 E
Bad Griesbach 54 48.27 N 8.14 E
Bad Grund 48 51.48 N 10.14 E
Bad Hall 30 48.02 N 14.13 E
Badhāna 113 31.28 N 74.37 E
Bad Harzburg 50 51.53 N 10.33 E
Bad Heilbrunn 58 47.45 N 11.28 E
Badhela ◆[8] 262a 28.38 N 77.04 E
Bad Helmstedt 50 52.14 N 11.03 E
Bad Hersfeld 52 50.52 N 9.42 E
Badhoevedorp 48 52.21 N 4.46 E
Bad Hofgastein 58 47.10 N 13.06 E
Bad Homburg vor der Höhe 52 50.13 N 8.37 E
Bad Honnef am Rhein 52 50.39 N 7.13 E
Bad Hönningen 52 50.31 N 7.19 E
Badia (Abtei) 58 46.37 N 11.54 E
Badia, Val V 58 46.40 N 11.53 E
Badia a Prataglia 60 43.47 N 11.52 E
Badia Calavena 58 45.34 N 11.09 E
Badia Polesine 58 45.05 N 11.29 E
Badia Tedalda 60 43.42 N 12.11 E
Badifa 140 13.12 N 3.47 E
Badile Camuno, Pizzo Λ 54 46.01 N 10.25 E
Badīn 110 24.39 N 68.50 E
Bādinan 262b 22.54 N 88.14 E
Badinko ≃ 140 13.42 N 9.35 W
Badin Lake ⊜[1] 182 35.27 N 80.06 W
Badiraguato 222 25.22 N 107.31 W
Bad Ischl 58 47.43 N 13.37 E
Bad Kissingen 52 50.12 N 10.04 E
Bad Kleinen 50 53.46 N 11.28 E
Bad Kleinkirchheim 58 46.49 N 13.49 E
Bad Klosterlausnitz 50 50.55 N 11.52 E
Bad Kohlgrub 58 47.40 N 11.03 E
Bad König 52 49.45 N 9.01 E
Bad Kösen 50 51.08 N 11.43 E
Bad Köstritz 50 50.56 N 12.01 E
Bad Kreuznach 52 49.52 N 7.51 E
Bad Krozingen 54 47.55 N 7.43 E
Bādkulla 116 23.17 N 88.32 E
Badlands ⋀ 188 46.45 N 103.30 W
Badlands ⋀[2] 188 43.30 N 102.20 W
Badlands National Monument ♠ 188 43.47 N 102.15 W
Bad Langensalza 52 51.06 N 10.38 E
Bad Lauchstädt 50 51.23 N 11.52 E
Bad Lausick 50 51.08 N 12.38 E
Bad Lauterberg [im Harz] 48 51.38 N 10.28 E
Bad Leonfelden 30 48.33 N 14.19 E
Bādli 262a 28.45 N 77.09 E
Bad Liebenstein 50 50.49 N 10.21 E
Bad Liebenwerda 50 51.31 N 13.23 E
Bad Liebenzell 52 48.46 N 8.44 E
Bad Lippspringe 48 51.46 N 8.49 E
Bad Meinberg 48 51.53 N 8.58 E
Bad Mergentheim 52 49.30 N 9.46 E
Bad Mingolsheim 52 49.14 N 8.39 E
Badminton Stadium ♠ 261c 1.18 N 103.53 E
Bad Mukran 50 54.26 N 13.35 E
Bad Münder 48 52.12 N 9.27 E
Bad Münster am Stein 52 49.49 N 7.51 E
Bad Münstereifel 52 50.33 N 6.46 E
Bad Muskau 50 51.32 N 14.43 E
Bad Nauheim 52 50.22 N 8.44 E
Bad Nenndorf 48 52.20 N 9.22 E
Badnera 112 20.52 N 77.44 E
Badner Lindkogel Λ 254b 48.01 N 16.11 E
Bad Neuenahr-Ahrweiler 52 50.33 N 7.08 E
Bad Neustadt an der Saale 52 50.19 N 10.13 E
Bad Niedernau 54 48.27 N 8.53 E
Bad Oeynhausen 48 52.12 N 8.48 E
Badogo 140 11.02 N 8.13 W
Bad Oldesloe 48 53.48 N 10.22 E
Ba-don 100 17.45 N 106.27 E
Ba-dong, Viet. 100 9.40 N 106.34 E
Badong, Zhg. 92 31.02 N 110.20 E
Badonviller 54 48.30 N 6.54 E
Bad Orb 52 50.14 N 9.20 E
Badou, Togo 140 7.35 N 0.36 E
Badou, Zhg. 88 36.27 N 117.55 E
Badouling 90 32.10 N 117.36 E
Badoumbé 140 13.38 N 10.13 W
Bad Peterstal 54 48.26 N 8.12 E
Badplaas 148 25.57 S 30.35 E
Bad Polzin → Połczyn Zdrój 30 53.46 N 16.06 E
Bad Pyrmont 48 51.59 N 9.15 E
Badr 132 30.33 N 30.43 E
Bad Ragaz 54 47.00 N 9.30 E
Bādrāh 110 27.20 N 68.01 E
Badrao 110 34.46 N 69.40 E
Bad Rappenau 52 49.14 N 9.06 E
Bad Rehburg 48 52.26 N 9.13 E
Bad Reichenhall 58 47.43 N 12.52 E
Badreïna ⍑[4] 140 17.44 N 11.05 W
Badr Ḥunayn 118 23.44 N 38.46 E
Badrīnāth 114 30.44 N 79.29 E
Bad Rippoldsau 54 48.26 N 8.19 E
Bad River Indian Reservation ◆[4] 180 46.33 N 90.40 W
Bad Rothenfelde 48 52.06 N 8.09 E
Bad Saarow-Pieskow 50 52.17 N 14.03 E
Bad Sachsa 50 51.36 N 10.32 E
Bad Salzdetfurth 48 52.03 N 10.01 E
Bad Salzig 52 50.12 N 7.38 E
Bad Salzschlierf 52 50.37 N 9.29 E
Bad Salzuflen 48 52.05 N 8.44 E
Bad Salzungen 52 50.48 N 10.13 E
Bad Sankt Leonhard im Lavanttal 30 46.58 N 14.48 E
Bad Sassendorf 48 51.35 N 8.10 E
Bad Schandau 50 50.55 N 14.10 E
Bad Schmiedeberg 50 51.41 N 12.44 E
Bad Schwalbach 52 50.08 N 8.04 E
Bad Schwartau 50 53.55 N 10.40 E
Bad Segeberg 48 53.56 N 10.17 E
Bādshāhpur 114 25.47 N 82.49 E
Bad Soden, B.R.D. 52 50.08 N 8.30 E
Bad Soden, B.R.D. 52 50.17 N 9.22 E
Bad Sooden-Allendorf 52 51.16 N 9.58 E
Bad Steben 50 50.22 N 11.38 E
Bad Stuer 50 53.22 N 12.19 E
Bad Suderode 50 51.44 N 11.07 E
Bad Sulza 50 51.05 N 11.37 E
Bad Sülze 50 54.06 N 12.38 E
Bad Teinach 52 48.41 N 8.41 E
Bad Tennstedt 50 51.09 N 10.50 E
Bad Tölz 58 47.46 N 11.34 E
Badu, Bra. 277a 22.54 S 43.04 W
Badu, Zhg. 90 26.51 N 119.35 E
Badu, Zhg. 90 27.38 N 118.57 E
Badu, Zhg. 92 24.15 N 105.41 E
Badu Island I 154 10.07 S 142.08 E
Badujie 90 28.32 N 117.57 E
Badulla 112 6.59 N 81.03 E
Badung, Selat Ɥ 105b 8.40 S 115.22 E
Badupi 110 21.36 N 93.25 E
Bādura 116 22.16 N 90.21 E
Bāduria 116 22.44 N 88.47 E
Badvel 112 14.45 N 79.03 E
Bad Vilbel 52 50.12 N 8.42 E
Bad Vöslau 30 47.57 N 16.16 E
Bad Waldsee 54 47.55 N 9.45 E
Bad Warmbrunn → Cieplice Śląskie Zdrój 30 50.52 N 15.41 E
Badwater Creek ≃ 192 43.17 N 108.08 W
Bad Westernkotten 48 51.38 N 8.21 E
Bad Wiessee 58 47.43 N 11.43 E
Bad Wildungen 52 51.07 N 9.07 E
Bad Wilsnack 50 52.57 N 11.57 E
Bad Wimpfen 52 49.14 N 9.09 E
Bad Wimsbach-Neydharting 58 48.04 N 13.54 E
Bad Windsheim 52 49.31 N 10.25 E
Bad Wörishofen 54 48.00 N 10.36 E
Bad Wurzach 54 47.54 N 9.54 E
Badžalskij Chrebet ⋀ 79 50.40 N 134.50 E
Baediam 140 15.03 N 11.51 W
Bække 41 55.34 N 9.09 E
Baena 34 37.37 N 4.19 W
Baependi 246 21.57 S 44.53 W
Baependi ≃ 246 21.52 S 45.04 W
Baerl 253 51.29 N 6.41 E
Baesweiler 52 50.54 N 6.11 E
Báez 230p 22.13 N 79.45 W
Baeza, Ec. 236 0.27 S 77.53 W
Baeza, Esp. 34 37.59 N 3.28 W
Baezaeko ≃ 172 53.09 N 123.48 W
Bafa Gölü ⊜ 120 37.30 N 27.25 E
Bafang 142 5.09 N 10.11 E
Bafatá 140 12.10 N 14.40 W
Bafelé 140 10.09 N 10.08 W
Baffa 113 34.26 N 73.13 E
Baffin Basin ✧[1] 16 73.00 N 68.00 W
Baffin Bay C, N.A. 16 73.00 N 66.00 W
Baffin Bay C, Tex., U.S. 186 27.15 N 97.33 W
Baffin Island I 166 68.00 N 70.00 W
Bafia 142 4.44 N 11.16 E
Bafilo 140 9.21 N 1.16 E
Bafing ≃ 140 13.49 N 10.50 W
Bafing Makana 140 12.33 N 10.15 W
Bafoulabé 140 13.48 N 10.50 W
Bafoussam 142 5.29 N 10.24 E
Bāfq 118 31.35 N 55.24 E
Bafra 120 41.34 N 35.56 E
Bafra Burnu ≻ 120 41.44 N 35.58 E
Bāft 118 29.14 N 56.38 E
Bafuku 144 4.15 N 27.54 E
Bafwabaka 144 2.07 N 27.40 E
Bafwabalinga 144 0.51 N 27.04 E
Bafwaboli 144 0.39 N 26.10 E
Bafwangbe 144 1.39 N 26.51 E
Bafwapada 144 0.56 N 26.57 E
Bafwasende 144 1.05 N 27.16 E
Bafwasomboli 144 1.27 N 27.01 E
Baga 116 22.26 N 90.28 E
Baga I 165e 7.49 S 156.33 E
Bagabag 106 16.37 N 121.15 E
Bagabag Island I 154 4.50 S 146.15 E
Baga-Burul 70 46.00 N 44.36 E
Bagac 106 14.36 N 120.23 E
Bagacay Point ≻ 106 8.58 N 124.48 E
Bagac Bay C 106 14.36 N 120.22 E
Bagaces 226 10.31 N 85.15 W
Baga Chentijn Nuruu ⋀ 78 48.30 N 107.30 E
Bagage Λ 144 3.23 N 40.12 E
Bagagem ≃, Bra. 240 11.37 S 48.12 W
Bagagem ≃, Bra. 245 13.58 S 48.21 W
Bagaha 114 27.06 N 84.05 E
Bagahak, Gunong Λ 106 5.03 N 118.44 E
Bagahu ⊜ 76 46.57 N 87.27 E
Bagajevskij 68 47.19 N 40.23 E
Bāgalkot 112 16.11 N 75.42 E
Bagamanoc 106 13.57 N 124.17 E
Bagamoyo 144 6.26 S 38.54 E
Bagan 76 54.06 N 77.40 E
Bagana 70 54.22 N 51.25 E
Bagana, Mount Λ 165e 6.09 S 155.12 E
Baganalin 92 38.57 N 94.08 E
Bagan Datoh 104 3.59 N 100.47 E
Bagañga 106 7.35 N 126.34 E
Bagan Serai 104 5.01 N 100.32 E
Bagansiapi-api 104 2.09 N 100.49 E
Bagansinembah 104 1.46 N 100.29 E
Bagansitukang 104 2.38 N 100.15 E
Baganza ≃ 58 44.47 N 10.19 E
Bagara 75 40.55 N 68.26 E
Bağarası 120 37.42 N 27.33 E
Bagasra 110 21.29 N 70.57 E
Bagata 142 3.44 S 17.57 E
Bāgātipāra 116 24.18 N 88.57 E
Bagawi 130 12.19 N 34.21 E
Bagbag Creek ≃ 259f 14.39 N 120.57 E
Bagband 48 53.21 N 7.36 E
Bagbe ≃ 140 8.42 N 11.15 W
Bagbele 144 4.21 N 29.17 E
Bāgda 116 23.13 N 86.41 E
Bagdad → Baghdād, 'Irāq 118 33.21 N 44.25 E
Bagdad, Ariz., U.S. 190 34.34 N 113.11 W
Bagdad, Fla., U.S. 184 30.36 N 87.02 W
Bagdad, Ky., U.S. 208 38.16 N 85.04 W
Bagdaha 116 23.13 N 88.53 E
Bagdanga 116 24.02 N 88.32 E
Bagdarin 78 54.26 N 113.36 E
Bagé 242 31.20 S 54.06 W
Bagehadu 110 35.25 N 85.50 E
Bâgé-le-Châtel 54 46.18 N 4.56 E
Bagenkop 41 54.45 N 10.41 E
Bagerovo 68 45.23 N 36.17 E
Bāgevādi 112 16.35 N 75.58 E
Baggao 106 17.56 N 121.46 E
Baggeryd 24 57.30 N 14.07 E
Baggetorp 40 59.01 N 16.04 E
Baggio ◆[8] 256b 45.27 N 9.06 E
Baggs 190 41.02 N 107.39 W
Baggy Point ≻ 44 51.09 N 4.16 W
Bāgh 113 33.59 N 73.47 E
Baghdād 118 33.21 N 44.25 E
Baghdād □[4] 118 34.00 N 43.46 E
Baghdobā 116 22.08 N 87.54 E
Baghelkhand Plateau ⋀[1] 114 23.45 N 82.20 E
Bāgh-e Malek 118 31.32 N 49.55 E
Bāgherhāt 114 22.40 N 89.48 E
Bagheria 36 38.05 N 13.30 E
Bāgherpāra 116 23.14 N 89.21 E
Bāghia 116 23.27 N 90.29 E
Baghia Bīl ☷ 116 23.07 N 90.03 E
Bāghīn 118 30.12 N 36.48 E
Baghlān 110 36.13 N 68.46 E
Baghlān □[4] 110 35.45 N 69.00 E
Baghlīn 110 36.14 N 65.55 E
Bāghmati ≃ 114 25.46 N 85.58 E
Bāghmundi 114 23.12 N 86.03 E
Bāghpat 114 28.57 N 77.13 E
Baghrān Khowleh 110 33.01 N 64.58 E
Bagillt 252 53.16 N 3.10 W
Bagilt Bank ✧[4] 252 53.17 N 3.09 W
Bağırpaşa Dağı Λ 120 39.30 N 40.06 E
Bagley 188 47.31 N 95.24 W
Bāgli 114 22.39 N 76.21 E
Bağlum 120 40.03 N 32.51 E
Bāglung 114 28.16 N 83.36 E
Bagmanl'ar 74 40.38 N 46.18 E
Bagn 26 60.49 N 9.34 E
Bagnacavallo 60 44.25 N 12.00 E
Bagnaia 60 42.25 N 12.09 E
Bāgnān 116 22.28 N 87.59 E
Bagnara Cálabra 36 38.18 N 15.49 E
Bagnara di Romagna 60 44.23 N 11.49 E
Bagnasco 56 44.18 N 8.02 E
Bagnell Dam ◆[6] 184 38.11 N 92.39 W
Bagnères-de-Bigorre 32 43.04 N 0.09 E
Bagnères-de-Luchon 32 42.47 N 0.36 E
Bagnes, Vallée de V 54 46.03 N 7.18 E
Bagneux 251 48.48 N 2.18 E
Bagni Acque Albule 60 41.57 N 12.43 E
Bagni del Masino 54 46.15 N 9.36 E
Bagni di Lucca 60 44.01 N 10.35 E
Bagni di Rabbi 58 46.24 N 10.48 E
Bagno a Ripoli 60 43.45 N 11.19 E
Bagno di Romagna 60 43.50 N 11.57 E
Bagnolet 251 48.52 N 2.25 E
Bagnoli del Trigno 60 41.42 N 14.27 E
Bagnoli di Sopra 58 45.11 N 11.53 E
Bagnoli Irpino 60 40.50 N 15.04 E
Bagnolo in Piano 58 44.46 N 10.40 E
Bagnolo Mella 58 45.26 N 10.10 E
Bagnols-en-Forêt 56 43.32 N 6.42 E
Bagnols-les-Bains 56 44.30 N 3.40 E
Bagnols-sur-Cèze 56 44.10 N 4.37 E
Bagnone 58 44.19 N 10.00 E
Bagnoregio 60 42.37 N 12.05 E
Bagno Vignoni 60 43.02 N 11.39 E
Bågø I 41 55.18 N 9.49 E
Bago ≃ 106 10.33 N 122.50 E
Bagodar 114 24.05 N 85.52 E
Bagodo 142 6.25 N 13.23 E
Bagoé ≃ 140 12.36 N 6.34 W
Bagolino 58 45.49 N 10.28 E
Bagoni 136 7.53 N 10.43 E
Bagot □[6] 196 45.40 N 72.45 W
Bagotville 176 48.21 N 70.53 W
Bagrationovsk 66 54.23 N 20.39 E
Bagraula ◆[8] 262a 28.34 N 77.04 E
Bagre 240 1.54 S 50.12 W
Bagrinovcy 68 49.17 N 27.56 E
Bagshot 44 51.22 N 0.42 W
Bagua 238 5.40 S 78.31 W
Baguazhou 96 32.11 N 118.46 E
Bāguiati 262b 22.36 N 88.26 E
Baguio 106 16.25 N 120.36 E
Bagula 116 23.19 N 88.39 E
Bagumbayan 259f 14.28 N 121.03 E
Bagur, Cabo ≻ 34 41.57 N 3.14 E
Bagyrlaj ≃ 70 48.08 N 51.14 E
Bagzane, Monts ⋀ 140 17.43 N 8.45 E
Bāh 114 26.53 N 78.36 E
Bahado 134 5.48 N 47.11 E
Bāhādurābād Ghāt 114 25.09 N 89.42 E
Bahādurganj 114 27.32 N 82.50 E
Bahādurgarh 114 28.41 N 76.56 E
Bāhādurpur 116 23.25 N 88.28 E
Bahaia, Mount Λ 134 11.13 N 49.43 E
Bahamas □[1] 220
228 24.15 N 76.00 W
Bahār 118 34.54 N 48.26 E
Baharāgora 116 22.17 N 86.43 E
Baharpur 116 23.41 N 89.34 E
Bahau 104 2.49 N 102.25 E
Bahau ≃ 102 2.34 N 116.20 E
Bahāwalnagar 113 29.59 N 73.16 E
Bahāwalpur 113 29.24 N 71.41 E
Bahce 120 37.14 N 36.34 E
Bahçeköy 257b 41.11 N 28.59 E
Bahçeköy su kemeri ≍[1] 257b 41.03 N 28.59 E
Bahechuan 88 40.59 N 124.49 E
Bahemdan 120 38.19 N 41.09 E
Baheri 114 28.47 N 79.30 E
Bahi, Pil. 106 13.53 N 123.38 E
Bahi, Tan. 144 5.59 S 35.19 E
Bahia → Salvador 245 12.59 S 38.31 W
Bahia □[3] 240 11.00 S 42.00 W
Bahía Blanca 242 38.43 S 62.17 W
Bahía Bustamante 244 45.08 S 66.32 W
Bahía de Caráquez 236 0.36 S 80.25 W
Bahía Honda 230p 22.54 N 83.10 W
Bahia Honda Key I 210 24.40 N 81.16 W
Bahia Honda Point ≻ 106 9.24 N 118.07 E
Bahía Kino 222 28.50 N 111.55 W
Bahía Laura 244 48.24 S 66.29 W
Bahía Negra 238 20.15 S 58.12 W
Bahīj 132 30.56 N 29.35 E
Bahir Dar 134 11.35 N 37.28 E
Bahi Swamp ☷ 144 6.05 S 35.10 E
Bah'i Temple ⛉[1] 268 42.05 N 87.41 W
Bahjoi 114 28.24 N 78.37 E
Bahl 113 28.38 N 75.38 E
Bahlolpur 262a 28.37 N 77.24 E
Bahn 140 7.05 N 8.45 W
Bahnāy 132 30.23 N 31.04 E
Bahnayā 132 30.41 N 31.23 E
Bahoruco, Sierra de Λ 228 18.10 N 71.25 W
Baḥrah 134 21.24 N 39.29 E
Bahraich 114 27.35 N 81.36 E
Bahraich □[5] 114 27.50 N 81.40 E
Bahrain □[1] 108
118 26.00 N 50.30 E
Baḥr al-Ghazāl □[4] 130 8.00 N 28.00 E
Bahrām Chāh 118 29.26 N 64.03 E
Baḥrānī, Ḥālat al- I 118 24.22 N 54.15 E
Bahrdorf 50 52.23 N 11.00 E
Bahrein → Bahrain □[1] 118 26.00 N 50.30 E
Bahser 120 37.57 N 39.18 E
Bahtīm 132 30.08 N 31.17 E
Bahṭīṭ 132 30.29 N 31.38 E
Bāhū Kalāt 118 25.43 N 61.25 E
Bahulu, Pulau I 102 3.33 S 122.18 E
Bahumbelu 102 2.13 S 121.41 E
Bahūt 132 31.10 N 31.19 E
Bahuta 79 43.20 N 122.16 E
Baï 140 13.38 N 3.22 W
Baia 60 40.49 N 14.04 E
Baia-de-Aramă 38 45.00 N 22.49 E
Baía dos Tigres 142 16.36 S 11.43 E
Baía Farta 142 12.40 S 13.11 E
Baía Formosa 240 6.22 S 35.00 W
Baia-Mare 38 47.40 N 23.35 E
Baiano 60 40.57 N 14.37 E
Baião 240 2.41 S 49.41 W
Baiardo 56 43.54 N 7.43 E
Baia Sprie 38 47.40 N 23.42 E
Baibao 95 39.04 N 115.31 E
Baibaoying 79 46.34 N 128.05 E
Baïbokoum 136 7.46 N 15.43 E
Baibuting 96 30.33 N 120.46 E
Baicaochang 92 32.08 N 103.59 E
Baicaoling ⋀ 92 26.10 N 101.20 E
Baicheng 79 45.38 N 122.46 E
Baidian 96 30.47 N 119.14 E
Baidiao 92 28.07 N 101.28 E
Baidoa 134 3.04 N 43.48 E
Baidunzi 92 43.11 N 95.19 E
Baidyabāti 116 22.47 N 88.20 E
Baidya Bāzār 116 23.39 N 90.37 E
Baidyanāth 114 24.29 N 86.42 E
Baie-Comeau 176 49.13 N 68.10 W
Baie-Comeau-Hauterive, Parc de ♠ 176 49.30 N 68.05 W
Baie-des-ha! Ha! 176 50.56 N 58.56 W
Baie-de-Shawinigan 196 46.34 N 72.45 W
Baie-du-Renard 176 49.17 N 61.50 W
Baie-d'Urfé 196 45.25 N 73.55 W
Baie-Johan-Beetz 176 50.17 N 62.48 W
Baie-Mahault 231o 16.16 N 61.35 W
Baienfurt 58 47.49 N 9.38 E
Baiersbronn 54 48.30 N 8.22 E
Baiersdorf 52 49.39 N 11.01 E
Baies, Lac des ⊜ 180 47.18 N 77.40 W
Baie-Saint-Claire 176 49.54 N 64.30 W
Baie-Saint-Paul 176 47.27 N 70.30 W
Baie-Trinité 176 49.25 N 67.18 W
Baie Verte 176 49.56 N 56.11 W
Baieville 196 46.08 N 72.43 W
Baifutu 88 35.01 N 116.07 E
Baigezhuang 95 39.54 N 118.09 E
Baigneux-les-Juifs 54 47.36 N 4.38 E
Baigong 90 24.18 N 116.14 E
Baigouhe, Zhg. 95 39.07 N 116.01 E
Baigouhe, Zhg. 95 39.42 N 115.58 E
Baiguoshu 96 30.45 N 119.07 E
Baigusi 92 33.10 N 103.52 E
Baihāli Jot Λ 113 32.51 N 76.32 E
Baihaojiang 96 31.16 N 121.08 E
Baihar 114 22.06 N 80.33 E
Baihe ≃ 95 40.22 N 116.19 E
Baihedian 90 29.12 N 120.55 E
Baihekou 92 31.46 N 110.13 E
Baihou 90 24.18 N 116.48 E
Baihu ⊜, Zhg. 90 30.17 N 113.15 E
Baihu ⊜, Zhg. 90 31.16 N 117.30 E
Baihuachang 97 29.07 N 104.37 E
Baihuashan Λ 95 39.50 N 115.35 E
Baijala 262b 22.51 N 88.16 E
Baijiagou 94 42.34 N 123.36 E
Baijiang 90 29.51 N 119.20 E
Baijiawu 95 39.30 N 116.28 E
Baijiechang 97 29.17 N 106.31 E
Baijietan 97 28.44 N 105.30 E
Baijnāth 114 29.55 N 79.37 E
Baiju 90 33.04 N 120.20 E
Baikal, Lago → Bajkal, Ozero ⊜ 78 53.00 N 107.40 E
Baikal-See → Bajkal, Ozero ⊜ 78 53.00 N 107.40 E
Baikeshu 96 30.26 N 118.55 E
Baikonur → Bajkonyr 76 47.50 N 66.03 E
Baikuerte 75 39.58 N 75.33 E
Baikunthapur, Bhārat 114 23.15 N 82.33 E
Baikunthapur, Bhārat 262b 22.59 N 88.13 E
Bailadores 236 8.15 N 71.50 W
Bailaiqiao 90 32.40 N 118.23 E
Bailang, Zhg. 79 46.57 N 120.05 E
Bailang, Zhg. 110 29.11 N 89.12 E
Baildon 42 53.52 N 1.46 W
Baile Átha Cliath → Dublin 28 53.20 N 6.15 W
Bailebao 95 39.55 N 114.51 E
Băile Govora 38 45.05 N 24.11 E
Băile Herculane 38 44.54 N 22.25 E
Bailén 34 38.06 N 3.46 W
Băile Olănești 38 45.11 N 24.16 E
Băilești 38 44.02 N 23.21 E
Bailey 182 35.47 N 78.07 W
Bailey Lakes 204 40.57 N 82.21 W
Bailey Run ≃ 269b 40.35 N 79.47 W
Baileys Crossroads 274c 38.51 N 77.08 W
Bail Hongal 112 15.49 N 74.52 E
Baili 92 25.45 N 110.33 E
Bailian 92 24.09 N 112.22 E
Bailin, Zhg. 90 27.12 N 120.10 E
Bailin, Zhg. 97 29.11 N 105.57 E
Bailinchang 97 28.45 N 106.26 E
Bailingmiao → Daerhanmaoming'anqi 92 41.42 N 110.23 E
Bailinshi 90 26.20 N 113.18 E
Bailique 240 0.58 N 50.04 W
Bailique, Ilha I 240 1.02 N 49.58 W
Bailleau-sous-Gallardon 251 48.32 N 1.39 E
Bailleul 46 50.44 N 2.44 E
Ba-Illi 136 10.30 N 16.34 E
Baillie ≃ 166 65.10 N 104.24 W
Bailieborough 28 53.54 N 6.59 W
Baillie-Hamilton Island I 166 75.53 N 94.35 W
Baillie Islands II 166 70.33 N 128.10 W
Baillies Bacolet 231k 12.02 N 61.41 W
Baillif 231o 16.01 N 61.45 W
Bailly-Romainvilliers 251 48.50 N 2.49 E
Bailonggang 96 31.15 N 121.44 E
Bailongjiang ≃ 92 32.18 N 105.42 E
Bailuchang 97 28.56 N 105.57 E
Bailugh 110 32.41 N 66.46 E
Bailuhe ≃ 90 32.25 N 115.34 E
Bailuhu ⊜ 90 30.03 N 113.06 E
Bailundo 142 12.12 S 15.52 E
Bailuo 90 29.37 N 113.15 E
Baima 97 30.03 N 103.44 E
Baimachang, Zhg. 92 29.18 N 107.30 E
Baimachang, Zhg. 94 41.59 N 122.30 E
Baimachang, Zhg. 97 29.11 N 104.37 E
Baimachang, Zhg. 97 29.09 N 104.16 E
Baimachang, Zhg. 97 29.39 N 103.57 E
Baimaguan 95 40.41 N 116.52 E
Baimahe ≃ 88 35.14 N 116.14 E
Baimakou 92 25.55 N 102.06 E
Baimamiao, Zhg. 92 36.58 N 108.08 E
Baimamiao, Zhg. 97 29.33 N 104.59 E
Baimao 96 31.39 N 120.52 E
Baimaokou C[1] 96 31.44 N 121.04 E
Baimaosha I 96 31.43 N 121.14 E
Baimaotang ≃ 96 31.44 N 121.04 E
Baimaoxinshi 96 31.35 N 120.54 E
Baimaqiao 96 31.35 N 119.10 E
Baimashan Λ 92 27.12 N 110.32 E
Baimashi 90 29.15 N 118.42 E
Baimazhai 90 28.06 N 115.50 E
Baimiaozi, Zhg. 79 46.18 N 123.35 E
Baimiaozi, Zhg. 88 40.34 N 120.36 E
Baimiaozi, Zhg. 94 41.55 N 122.12 E
Baimiaozi, Zhg. 97 29.47 N 106.29 E
Baimuqiao 96 32.01 N 120.19 E
Baimuru 154 7.30 S 144.49 E
Bain ≃ 44 53.05 N 0.12 W
Baïna Bondio 142 5.10 N 16.33 E
Bainbridge, Ga., U.S. 182 30.54 N 84.34 W
Bainbridge, N.Y., U.S. 200 42.18 N 75.29 W
Bainbridge, Ohio, U.S. 208 39.14 N 83.16 W
Bainbridge, Pa., U.S. 198 40.05 N 76.40 W
Bainbridge Island I 214 47.37 N 122.33 W
Bainchi 116 23.07 N 88.14 E
Bainchipota 262b 22.52 N 88.16 E
Bain-de-Bretagne 32 47.50 N 1.41 W
Baing 105b 10.14 S 120.34 E
Bainiqiao 90 29.35 N 114.09 E
Bains-les-Bains 54 48.00 N 6.16 E
Bainville 188 48.08 N 104.13 W
Bainyik 154 3.40 S 143.00 E
Baipeng 92 24.09 N 109.25 E
Baipi 90 27.45 N 115.52 E
Baipu 96 32.15 N 120.46 E
Baiqibao 94 41.48 N 122.30 E
Baiqipu 94 41.32 N 121.24 E
Baiqitun 79 44.23 N 126.32 E
Baiqiu 90 32.44 N 112.38 E
Baiquan, Zhg. 79 47.36 N 126.07 E
Baiquan, Zhg. 90 30.06 N 122.08 E
Baiqueyuan 90 31.48 N 115.05 E
Bair, Pa., U.S. 198 39.54 N 76.50 W
Bā'ir, Urd. 122 30.46 N 36.41 E
Bā'īr, Wādī V 122 30.58 N 37.09 E
Baird 186 32.24 N 99.24 W
Bairdford 204 40.38 N 79.53 W
Baird Inlet C 170 60.45 N 164.00 W
Baird Mountains ⋀ 170 67.35 N 161.30 W
Baird Peninsula ≻[1] 166 69.00 N 75.15 W
Baire 230p 20.19 N 76.20 W
Bairia 114 27.00 N 85.23 E
Bairiki 164t 1.20 N 173.01 E
Bair Island I 272 37.32 N 122.13 W
Bairkum 75 42.05 N 68.11 E
Bairnsdale 156 37.50 S 147.38 E
Bairoil 190 42.15 N 107.33 W
Bairrinho 246 22.36 S 47.06 W
Bairro Alto 246 23.29 S 45.21 W
Bairuopu 90 28.12 N 112.46 E
Bais, Fr. 32 48.15 N 0.22 W
Bais, Pil. 106 9.35 N 123.07 E
Baise 92 23.57 N 106.26 E
Baïse ≃ 32 44.07 N 0.17 E
Baisha, Zhg. 90 25.40 N 118.59 E
Baisha, Zhg. 90 24.39 N 113.31 E
Baisha, Zhg. 90 26.58 N 115.22 E
Baisha, Zhg. 90 25.24 N 117.16 E
Baisha, Zhg. 90 34.22 N 112.32 E
Baisha, Zhg. 90 29.26 N 119.16 E
Baisha, Zhg. 92 21.51 N 112.09 E
Baisha, Zhg. 97 28.47 N 104.41 E
Baisha, Zhg. 100 19.17 N 109.27 E
Baishaba 97 30.03 N 106.21 E
Baishachang 97 28.55 N 105.45 E
Baishan I 96 30.35 N 121.43 E
Baishanji 90 33.48 N 116.40 E
Baishantu 94 42.21 N 122.35 E
Baishapu 90 29.58 N 115.04 E
Baishatan 88 36.52 N 121.43 E
Baishazhen, Zhg. 90 34.20 N 113.14 E
Baishazhen, Zhg. 97 29.04 N 106.07 E
Baishe 90 27.02 N 116.20 E
Baishecun 95 40.10 N 116.18 E
Baishi, Zhg. 90 27.18 N 119.45 E
Baishi, Zhg. 90 26.48 N 119.46 E
Baishi, Zhg. 92 22.36 N 110.55 E
Baishidu 90 25.26 N 113.01 E
Baishilashan Λ 79 46.38 N 128.27 E
Baishiyi 97 29.29 N 106.22 E
Baishizhai 94 40.57 N 122.58 E
Baishui, Zhg. 90 28.42 N 113.04 E
Baishui, Zhg. 97 30.06 N 105.38 E
Baishuifan 90 30.17 N 115.43 E
Baishuijiang 92 33.29 N 106.01 E
Baishuijie 92 32.39 N 105.32 E
Baishuiwan 96 30.34 N 119.39 E
Baishun 90 25.12 N 114.01 E
Baishuxia 90 27.22 N 113.41 E
Baisingga 116 21.39 N 86.54 E
Baisley Pond ⊜ 266 40.41 N 73.47 W
Baisogala 66 55.38 N 23.43 E
Bāisrasi 116 23.27 N 90.02 E
Baita, Bhārat 262b 22.27 N 88.11 E
Baita, Zhg. 96 31.48 N 119.35 E
Baitadi 114 29.32 N 80.26 E
Baital 116 22.57 N 87.28 E
Baitazi 88 42.19 N 120.19 E
Baitazibeigou 94 42.17 N 120.48 E
Bai-thuong 100 19.54 N 105.23 E
Baitings Reservoir ⊜[1] 252 53.40 N 1.59 W
Baitoutan 92 32.30 N 106.56 E
Baitugang 90 33.28 N 112.22 E
Baituzhen 96 31.59 N 119.21 E
Baiwang 92 24.14 N 108.32 E
Baiwenzhen 92 38.15 N 111.06 E
Baixa Grande 245 11.57 S 40.11 W
Baixi, Zhg. 90 28.21 N 121.07 E
Baixi, Zhg. 97 29.39 N 106.28 E
Baixian 96 31.09 N 119.39 E
Baixio 240 6.44 S 38.43 W
Baixo Longa 142 15.42 S 18.50 E
Baiyan 90 28.04 N 120.02 E
Baiyangdian ⊜ 88 38.51 N 116.01 E
Baiyanghe 76 43.13 N 88.28 E
Baiyangzhen 90 34.25 N 112.12 E
Baiyanshan Λ 90 26.05 N 118.25 E
Baiyer River 154 5.35 S 144.10 E
Baiyinchang 92 36.47 N 104.07 E
Baiyinheshuo 79 44.31 N 119.51 E
Baiyinnuoletun 79 46.45 N 124.16 E
Baiyintaohai 79 43.12 N 120.23 E
Baiyu, Zhg. 92 31.18 N 98.49 E
Baiyu, Zhg. 95 40.01 N 115.37 E
Baiyunding 92 29.00 N 98.34 E
Baiyundu 90 26.10 N 118.47 E
Baiyunebo 92 41.58 N 110.02 E
Baiyunguan 261a 39.54 N 116.19 E
Baiyushan ⋀ 92 37.21 N 107.50 E
Baizha 90 29.11 N 115.37 E
Baizhongpu 90 33.22 N 114.50 E
Baizizhen 97 30.06 N 105.43 E
Baja 30 46.11 N 18.57 E
Baja, Punta ≻, Chile 164z 27.10 S 109.22 W
Baja, Punta ≻, Méx. 222 28.28 N 111.45 W
Baja, Punta ≻, Méx. 222 29.58 N 115.49 W
Baja California 190 32.18 N 115.12 W
Baja California ≻[1] 222 28.00 N 113.30 W
Baja California Norte □[3] 222 30.00 N 115.00 W
Baja California Seamount Province ✧ 16 26.00 N 124.00 W
Baja California Sur □[3] 222 26.00 N 112.00 W
Bajada del Agrio 242 38.23 S 70.02 W
Baján, Méx. 186 26.32 N 101.15 W
Bajan, S.S.S.R. 74 40.34 N 46.09 E
Bajan-Adraga 78 48.37 N 111.05 E
Bajan-Agt 78 49.02 N 102.05 E
Bajanaul 76 50.47 N 75.42 E
Bajancagaan 92 45.06 N 98.40 E
Bajanchajrchan 78 49.18 N 96.20 E
Bajanchongor 80 46.10 N 100.45 E
Bajanchongor □[4] 92 45.00 N 99.30 E
Bajancogt 78 45.54 N 106.10 E
Bajandaj 78 53.04 N 105.30 E
Bajandalaj 92 43.28 N 103.31 E
Bajande'ger 92 45.45 N 112.24 E
Bajandelger 78 47.44 N 108.07 E
Bajandun 78 49.15 N 113.20 E
Bajandžargalan 92 45.31 N 108.01 E
Bajandzürch 78 50.12 N 98.58 E
Bajan-Enger 76 48.25 N 90.50 E
Bajan Erchet Uul ⋀ 78 47.30 N 105.30 E
Bajango 78 48.55 N 106.06 E
Bajangol 78 50.44 N 103.27 E
Bajangov' 92 44.44 N 100.24 E
Bajanleg 92 44.33 N 100.35 E
Bajannuur 76 48.54 N 91.14 E
Bajanölgij □[4] 76 48.20 N 89.50 E
Bajan-Öndör 92 44.47 N 98.39 E
Bajan-Ovoo, Mong. 78 47.47 N 112.05 E
Bajan-Ovoo, Mong. 92 43.11 N 105.37 E
Bajánsenye 30 46.48 N 16.23 E
Bajan Tümen → Čojbalsan 78 48.04 N 114.30 E
Bajan-Uul, Mong. 78 49.41 N 96.20 E
Bajan-Uul, Mong. 78 47.40 N 101.30 E
Bajan-Uul, Mong. 78 49.07 N 112.45 E
Bājaur □[9] 113 34.50 N 71.25 E
Baja Verapaz □[5] 226 15.05 N 90.20 W
Bajawa 105b 8.47 S 120.59 E
Bajbičetau ⋀ 75 41.12 N 75.15 E
Baj-Chak 78 51.13 N 94.34 E
Bajčunas 70 47.14 N 52.55 E
Bajčurovo 70 51.20 N 42.41 E
Bajdonovo 78 54.17 N 104.38 E
Bajdrag Gol ≃ 92 45.38 N 99.15 E
Bājengdoba 114 25.54 N 90.31 E
Baje Phukura 116 23.09 N 89.45 E
Bajer 78 55.44 N 99.30 E
Bajevo 76 53.17 N 80.46 E
Bajgakum 76 44.18 N 66.28 E
Bajghera 262a 28.32 N 77.01 E
Bājgīrān 118 37.36 N 58.24 E
Bajgul 70 48.49 N 49.08 E
Bajiachaidamuhu ⊜ 92 37.30 N 95.12 E
Bajiaokou 88 37.38 N 121.05 E
Bajiazi, Zhg. 94 41.36 N 123.53 E
Bajiazi, Zhg. 94 42.17 N 122.37 E
Bajiazi, Zhg. 94 42.21 N 121.27 E
Bājil 134 15.04 N 43.16 E
Bajimba, Mount Λ 156 29.18 S 152.07 E
Bajina Bašta 38 43.58 N 19.34 E
Bajinghe ≃ 92 23.02 N 100.39 E
Bajkadam 75 43.44 N 69.55 E
Bajkal 78 51.53 N 104.47 E
Bajkal, Ozero ⊜ 78 53.00 N 107.40 E
Bajkalovo, S.S.S.R. 76 57.24 N 63.46 E
Bajkalovo, S.S.S.R. 76 57.45 N 67.40 E
Bajkal'sk 78 51.33 N 104.05 E
Bajkal'skij Chrebet ⋀ 78 55.00 N 108.40 E
Bajkal'skoje 78 55.21 N 109.12 E
Bajkit 64 61.41 N 96.25 E
Bajkonyr 76 47.50 N 66.03 E
Bajkovo 70 54.47 N 44.51 E
Bajmak 76 52.36 N 58.19 E
Bajmok 38 45.58 N 19.25 E
Bajnazar 76 48.32 N 73.42 E
Bajo, Indon. 102 0.27 N 120.48 E
Bajo, Indon. 105b 8.35 S 119.01 E
Bajo, Canal ≍ 256a 40.27 N 3.43 W
Bajool 156 23.39 S 150.39 E
Bajos de Haina 228 18.25 N 70.02 W
Bajos del Balsamar 224 17.34 N 100.48 W
Bajrački 73 48.22 N 38.32 E
Bajr'aki 70 54.43 N 53.24 E
Bajram-Ali 118 37.37 N 62.10 E
Bajsa 78 53.58 N 113.33 E
Bajseit 75 43.35 N 78.20 E
Bajsun 75 38.14 N 67.12 E
Bajsuntau, Gory ⋀ 75 38.35 N 67.28 E
Baj-S'ut 78 51.42 N 95.22 E
Bajtajlak 76 45.15 N 75.00 E
Bajtas 76 45.24 N 64.51 E
Bajulmati 105a 7.56 S 114.23 E
Bajžansaj 75 43.13 N 69.56 E
Bakal 76 54.56 N 58.48 E
Bakala, Centraf. 142 6.11 N 20.22 E
Bakala, Centraf. 142 3.46 N 17.33 E
Bakaldy 70 55.39 N 44.44 E
Bakalé, Kaga ⋀ 142 7.21 N 20.29 E
Bakali ≃ 142 4.34 S 17.06 E
Bakaly 70 55.10 N 53.48 E
Bakambe 142 5.39 S 23.37 E
Bakanas 76 44.50 N 76.15 E
Bakanas ≃ 76 47.05 N 79.18 E
Bakap 104 4.26 N 101.04 E
Bākarganj 114 22.33 N 90.21 E
Bakaruma 114 22.32 N 83.25 E
Bakau, Pulau I 261c 1.16 N 103.43 E
Bakbakty 76 44.35 N 76.40 E
Bakčar 76 57.01 N 82.05 E
Bakčar ≃ 76 57.37 N 82.18 E
Bake 102 3.03 S 100.16 E
Bakel 140 14.54 N 12.27 W
Bakem 102 1.58 S 105.54 E
Bakenberg Λ[2] 50 54.35 N 13.07 E
Bakenkop 148 28.01 S 23.02 E
Bakeoven Creek ≃ 214 45.12 N 121.05 W
Baker, Calif., U.S. 194 35.16 N 116.04 W
Baker, Fla., U.S. 184 30.48 N 86.40 W
Baker, La., U.S. 184 30.35 N 91.10 W
Baker, Mont., U.S. 188 46.22 N 104.17 W
Baker, Oreg., U.S. 192 44.47 N 117.50 W
Baker ≃ 214 48.38 N 121.41 W
Baker, Canal Ɥ 244 48.00 S 74.00 W
Baker, Mount Λ 214 48.47 N 121.49 W
Baker Butte Λ 190 34.27 N 111.22 W
Baker Canyon V 270 33.47 N 117.38 W
Baker Creek ≃, B.C., Can. 172 52.59 N 122.30 W
Baker Creek ≃, Ohio, U.S. 269a 41.21 N 81.54 W
Baker Creek ≃, Oreg., U.S. 214 45.15 N 123.14 W
Baker Island I, Oc. 14 0.15 N 176.27 W
Baker Island I, Alaska, U.S. 170 55.20 N 133.36 W
Baker Lake 166 64.15 N 96.00 W
Baker Lake ⊜, Austl. 152 26.54 S 126.05 E
Baker Lake ⊜, N.W. Ter., Can. 166 64.10 N 95.30 W
Baker Lake ⊜, Ill., U.S. 268 42.08 N 88.07 W
Baker Lake ⊜[1] 214 48.43 N 121.37 W
Bakersfield 216
218 35.23 N 119.01 W
Bakersfield South 218 35.20 N 119.03 W
Bakers Hill 158a 31.45 S 116.27 E
Bakers Island I 273 42.32 N 70.47 W
Bakerstown 204 40.39 N 79.56 W
Baker Street 250 51.30 N 0.21 E
Bakersville, N.C., U.S. 182 36.01 N 82.09 W
Bakersville, Ohio, U.S. 204 40.21 N 81.39 W
Bakerville 148 26.00 S 26.06 E
Bakeshu 88 42.26 N 124.37 E
Bâ Kêv 100 13.42 N 107.12 E
Bakewell 42 53.13 N 1.40 W
Bakhra 116 22.24 N 88.11 E
Bākhrābād 116 23.43 N 90.53 E
Bakhri 114 25.35 N 86.16 E
Bakhtegān, Daryācheh-ye ⊜ 118 29.20 N 54.05 E
Bakhtīarī va Chahār Maḥāll □[8] 118 32.00 N 51.00 E

Symbol	English	Deutsch	Español	Français	Português
≃	River	Fluss	Río	Rivière	Rio
≍	Canal	Kanal	Canal	Canal	Canal
ʟ	Waterfall, Rapids	Wasserfall, Stromschnellen	Cascada, Rápidos	Chute d'eau, Rapides	Cascata, Rápidos
Ɥ	Strait	Meeresstrasse	Estrecho	Détroit	Estreito
C	Bay, Gulf	Bucht, Golf	Bahía, Golfo	Baie, Golfe	Baía, Golfo
⊜	Lake, Lakes	See, Seen	Lago, Lagos	Lac, Lacs	Lago, Lagos
☷	Swamp	Sumpf	Pantano	Marais	Pântano
✱	Ice Features, Glacier	Eis- und Gletscherformen	Accidentes Glaciales	Formes glaciaires	Acidentes Glaciares
⍑	Other Hydrographic Features	Andere Hydrographische Objekte	Otros Elementos Hidrográficos	Autres données hydrographiques	Outros Elementos Hidrográficos
✧	Submarine Features	Untermeerische Objekte	Accidentes Submarinos	Formes de relief sous-marin	Acidentes Submarinos
□	Political Unit	Politische Einheit	Unidad Politica	Entité politique	Unidade Política
⛉	Cultural Institution	Kulturelle Institution	Institución Cultural	Institution culturelle	Instituição Cultural
⊥	Historical Site	Historische Stätte	Sitio Histórico	Site historique	Sitio Histórico
♠	Recreational Site	Erholungs- und Ferienort	Sitio de Recreo	Centre de loisirs	Sítio de Lazer
⊠	Airport	Flughafen	Aeropuerto	Aéroport	Aeroporto
▪	Military Installation	Militäranlage	Instalación Militar	Installation militaire	Instalação Militar
◆	Miscellaneous	Verschiedenes	Misceláneo	Divers	Miscelânea

ENGLISH — Name | Page | Lat.°′ | Long.°′

DEUTSCH — Name | Seite | Breite°′ | Länge°′ E=Ost

Symbols in the index entries represent the broad categories identified in the key at the right. Symbols with superior numbers (⛰[2]) identify subcategories (see complete key on page I · 26).

Kartensymbole in dem Registerverzeichnis stellen die rechts in Schlüssel erklärten Kategorien dar. Symbole mit hochgestellten Ziffern (⛰[2]) bezeichnen Unterabteilungen einer Kategorie (vgl. vollständiger Schlüssel auf Seite I · 26).

Los símbolos incluídos en el texto del índice representan las grandes categorias identificadas con la clave a la derecha. Los símbolos con numeros en su parte superior (⛰[2]) identifican las subcategorias (véase la clave completa en la página I · 26).

Les symboles de l'index représentent les catégories indiquées dans la légende à droite. Les symboles suivis d'un indice (⛰[2]) représentent des sous-catégories (voir légende complète à la page I · 26).

Os símbolos incluídos no texto do índice representam as grandes categorias identificadas com a chave à direita. Os símbolos com números em sua parte superior (⛰[2]) identificam as subcategorias (veja-se a chave completa à página I · 26).

∧ Mountain	Berg	Montaña	Montagne	Montanha
⛰ Mountains	Berge	Montañas	Montagnes	Montanhas
)(Pass	Pass	Paso	Col	Passo
∨ Valley, Canyon	Tal, Cañon	Valle, Cañón	Vallée, Canyon	Vale, Canhão
⌣ Plain	Ebene	Llano	Plaine	Planície
≻ Cape	Kap	Cabo	Cap	Cabo
I Island	Insel	Isla	Île	Ilha
II Islands	Inseln	Islas	Îles	Ilhas
• Other Topographic Features	Andere Topographische Objekte	Otros Elementos Topográficos	Autres données topographiques	Outros Elementos Topográficos

ESPAÑOL / FRANÇAIS / PORTUGUÊS

Nombre / Nom / Nome	Página / Page	Lat.° ′	Long.° ′ W=Oeste / W=Ouest
Bani, Jbel	138	29.30 N	8.00 W
Bania	142	4.00 N	16.07 E
Banī 'Adī al-Baḥrīyah	132	27.15 N	30.55 E
Banī 'Adī al-Qiblīyah	132	27.15 N	30.56 E
Banī Aḥmad	132	28.03 N	30.46 E
Banī 'Alī	132	28.29 N	30.43 E
Baniara, Indon.	104	2.31 N	98.39 E
Baniara, Pap. N. Gui.	154	9.46 S	149.53 E
Bānibāha	116	23.42 N	89.37 E
Bani Bangou	140	15.03 N	2.42 E
Banie	30	53.06 N	14.38 E
Banifing	140	12.27 N	7.07 W
Banihāl Pass	113	33.31 N	75.13 E
Banī Ḥasan ash-Shurūq	132	27.54 N	30.51 E
Banika I	165e	9.05 S	159.12 E
Banī Khālid	132	27.50 N	30.44 E
Banikoara	140	11.18 N	2.26 E
Banī Majdūl	263c	30.02 N	31.07 E
Banī Mazār	132	28.30 N	30.48 E
Banī Muḥammadīyāt	132	27.17 N	31.05 E
Banī Mūsā	132	29.08 N	31.03 E
Banīnah	136	32.05 N	20.16 E
Baniou	34	35.25 N	4.21 E
Banī Rāfi'	132	27.22 N	30.53 E
Banī Salāmah	132	30.19 N	30.51 E
Banī Sha'rān	132	27.19 N	30.51 E
Banī Shuqayr	132	27.23 N	30.59 E
Banister	182	36.42 N	78.48 W
Banī Suhaylah	122	31.20 N	34.20 E
Banī Suwayf	132	29.05 N	31.05 E
Banī Suwayf □[4]	132	29.03 N	31.02 E
Banī 'Ubayd, Miṣr	132	31.01 N	31.39 E
Banī 'Ubayd, Miṣr	132	27.57 N	30.46 E
Bāniyāchung	110	24.31 N	91.22 E
Bāniyās, Sūrīy.	120	35.11 N	35.57 E
Bāniyās, Sūrīy.	122	33.15 N	35.41 E
Banī Zayd	132	27.13 N	31.09 E
Banja Luka	36	44.46 N	17.11 E
Banjar	105a	7.22 S	108.32 E
Banjarmasin	102	3.20 S	114.35 E
Banjarnegara	105a	7.23 S	109.41 E
Banjing	96	32.19 N	120.24 E
Banjir Kanal	259e	6.11 S	106.49 E
Banjita	94	41.11 N	120.52 E
Banjšćice	58	46.04 N	13.42 E
Banjuangou	95	40.44 N	115.11 E
Banjul	140	13.28 N	16.39 W
Bank	74	39.25 N	49.15 E
Bānka	114	24.53 N	86.55 E
Ban'ka	255b	55.49 N	37.22 E
Banka Banka	152	18.48 S	134.01 E
Bānkādāba	116	22.58 N	87.21 E
Ban Kaeng Khoi	100	14.35 N	101.01 E
Ban Kai Kiang	100	14.57 N	99.12 E
Bankana	142	4.25 S	16.11 E
Bankas	140	14.04 N	3.31 W
Ban Katèp	100	16.48 N	105.52 E
Ban Kavak	100	17.18 N	105.37 E
Bankberg	148	32.22 S	25.26 E
Ban Kèngkabao	100	16.48 N	104.45 E
Ban Kèngkok	100	16.26 N	105.12 E
Ban Kèngtangan	100	16.05 N	105.22 E
Bankeryd	26	57.51 N	14.07 E
Ban Khan Na Yao	259a	13.47 N	100.41 E
Bankhari	116	23.44 N	90.03 E
Ban Kheun	100	20.13 N	101.07 E
Ban Khlong Bua Loi	259a	13.41 N	100.41 E
Ban Khlong Kua	100	6.57 N	100.08 E
Ban Khlong Samrong	259a	13.39 N	100.36 E
Ban Khlong Song	259a	13.51 N	100.43 E
Ban Khok Bao Sao	259a	13.52 N	100.39 E
Ban Khuan Mao	100	7.58 N	99.37 E
Bankilaré	140	14.35 N	0.44 E
Bankipur	262b	22.48 N	88.14 E
Ban Kota Baru	104	6.27 N	101.21 E
Ban Krang	100	12.52 N	99.18 E
Ban Kruat	100	14.25 N	103.07 E
Banks, Eng., U.K.	252	53.41 N	2.56 W
Banks, Ala., U.S.	184	31.44 N	85.50 W
Banks, Oreg., U.S.	174	45.37 N	123.07 W
Banks, Cape	264a	34.00 S	151.15 E
Banks, Point	170	58.36 N	152.18 W
Banksian	174	53.41 N	94.10 W
Banks Island I, B.C., Can.	172	53.25 N	130.10 W
Banks Island I, N.W. Ter., Can.	166	73.15 N	121.30 W
Banks Islands II	165f	13.50 S	167.30 E
Banks Lake [1]	174	47.45 N	119.15 W
Banksmeadow	264a	33.58 S	151.13 E
Banks Peninsula [1]	154	43.45 S	173.00 E
Banks Sands [4]	252	53.43 N	2.59 W
Banks Strait	156	40.40 S	148.07 E
Bankstown	160	33.55 S	151.02 E
Bankstown Aerodrome ⊠	264a	33.55 S	150.59 E
Banksville	266	41.09 N	73.38 W
Banksville	249	40.24 N	80.03 W
Ban Kum Daeng	259a	13.53 N	100.36 E
Bankumuna	142	4.28 S	19.57 E
Bānkura	116	23.15 N	87.04 E
Bānkura □[5]	116	23.15 N	87.15 E
Ban Laem Sing	259a	13.30 N	100.34 E
Banlamen	94	41.51 N	122.27 E
Banlashanzi	94	41.26 N	123.28 E
Ban Lat Phrao	259a	13.47 N	100.36 E
Ban Le Kathe	100	15.49 N	98.53 E
Banliyuan	96	30.50 N	118.58 E
Ban Luk Kho	259a	13.34 N	100.27 E
Ban Mae La Luang	100	18.32 N	97.56 E
Ban Mae Mo	100	18.15 N	99.42 E
Bānmankhi Bazar	114	25.53 N	87.11 E
Banmauk	100	24.24 N	95.51 E
Ban-m'diap	100	12.56 N	108.43 E
Ban-m'drack	100	12.42 N	108.47 E
Banmian	90	26.02 N	118.06 E
Ban Mit	100	18.51 N	101.55 E
Ban Muangngat	100	19.05 N	104.04 E
Ban Muang Yot	100	19.22 N	100.34 E
Bann	42	55.10 N	6.46 W
Banna	56	45.11 N	7.51 E
Ban Nadou	100	15.51 N	105.38 E
Ban Nagnom	100	17.02 N	105.44 E
Ban Nahin	100	18.14 N	104.13 E
Bannaja	78	57.05 N	108.12 E
Ban Nakala	100	16.17 N	105.11 E
Ban Na Kha	100	9.26 N	98.28 E
Ban Nalan	100	15.50 N	106.04 E
Ban Nalao	100	18.42 N	101.34 E
Ban Namcha	100	19.09 N	102.53 E
Ban Nam Chan	100	18.01 N	103.53 E
Ban Namnga	100	20.22 N	102.19 E
Ban Nam Tao	100	17.50 N	101.15 E
Ban Nam Thaeng	100	15.34 N	105.30 E
Ban Na San	100	8.48 N	99.22 E
Ban Naxon	100	18.22 N	101.38 E
Ban Naxouang	100	18.25 N	104.29 E
Bannay	46	47.23 N	2.53 E
Bannerman, Mount [2]	152	19.26 S	127.10 E
Bannesdorf	50	54.28 N	11.13 E
Bannewitz	54	51.00 N	13.43 E
Ban Ngam	100	20.11 N	104.52 E
Bannikovo	76	56.07 N	70.17 E
Banning	218	33.56 N	116.52 W
Banningville → Bandundu	142	3.18 S	17.20 E
Bannister	158a	32.40 S	116.33 E
Bannister	158a	32.33 S	116.23 E
Bannister Ditch	269a	41.18 N	82.01 W
Bannock	204	40.06 N	80.59 W
Bannockburn, Austl.	159	38.03 S	144.10 E
Bannockburn, Rh.	144	20.16 S	29.51 E
Bannockburn, Scot., U.K.	42	56.06 N	3.55 W
Bannockburn, Ill., U.S.	268	42.12 N	87.52 W
Bannockburn Battlesite (1314) I	42	56.06 N	3.54 W
Bannock Creek	192	42.53 N	112.40 W
Bannock Peak	192	42.36 N	112.42 W
Ban Nong Lumphuk	100	14.40 N	102.43 E
Ban Nong Takhian	100	13.08 N	101.24 E
Banno-saki	164m	26.33 N	128.09 E
Bannovka	76	53.45 N	62.57 E
Bannovskij	73	49.02 N	37.35 E
Bannu	113	32.59 N	70.36 E
Bañolas	34	42.07 N	2.46 E
Banon, Fr.	56	44.02 N	5.38 E
Bañón, Méx.	224	23.11 N	102.29 W
Ban O Pao	259a	13.50 N	100.38 E
Baños, Ec.	236	1.24 S	78.25 W
Baños, Perú	238	10.05 S	76.45 W
Baños de Cerrato	34	41.55 N	4.28 W
Bánovce nad Bebravou	30	48.43 N	18.14 E
Banow	110	35.38 N	69.15 E
Ban Pak Bong	100	18.32 N	98.56 E
Ban Pak Chan	100	10.32 N	98.51 E
Ban Pakha	100	14.38 N	107.24 E
Ban Pakkhop	100	18.49 N	101.32 E
Ban Pak Nam	100	10.26 N	99.15 E
Ban Pakneun	100	19.14 N	101.24 E
Ban Pak Phraek	100	8.13 N	100.12 E
Banpās	116	23.24 N	87.45 E
Ban Phai, Thai	100	16.04 N	102.44 E
Ban Phai, Thai	100	17.33 N	103.00 E
Ban Phe	100	12.38 N	101.26 E
Ban Pho	100	13.36 N	101.05 E
Ban Phon	100	15.25 N	106.42 E
Ban Phông Pho	100	14.36 N	105.52 E
Banphot Phisai	100	15.56 N	99.59 E
Ban Phraek Kasa	259a	13.34 N	100.38 E
Ban Phya	100	21.35 N	102.55 E
Ban Pong	100	13.49 N	99.53 E
Banpu	88	34.28 N	119.18 E
Banpura	116	22.27 N	87.22 E
Banqiao, Zhg.	90	30.06 N	120.27 E
Banqiao, Zhg.	96	31.55 N	118.39 E
Banqiao, Zhg.	97	29.31 N	105.59 E
Banqiaochang	97	29.54 N	104.21 E
Banqiaodian	90	31.46 N	112.31 E
Banqiaoji	90	32.19 N	116.37 E
Banqiaoxi	97	29.41 N	103.47 E
Ban Rai	100	15.05 N	99.31 E
Banreaba	164t	1.20 N	173.02 E
Ban Ron Phibun	100	8.09 N	99.51 E
Ban Sa-ang	100	17.26 N	105.44 E
Ban Saen To	100	16.05 N	99.51 E
Ban Sakhla	259a	13.32 N	100.30 E
Ban Salik	100	18.30 N	100.45 E
Ban Samang	100	19.43 N	102.36 E
Ban Sam Phan	100	8.33 N	99.09 E
Ban Sam Pong	100	18.32 N	102.47 E
Ban Samrong	100	14.23 N	102.50 E
Bansang	140	13.26 N	14.39 W
Ban San Xieng La	100	19.27 N	102.26 E
Bānsbāria	116	22.58 N	88.24 E
Bānsda	110	20.45 N	73.22 E
Banshanpu	90	27.42 N	113.24 E
Banshi	90	25.20 N	115.23 E
Banshigou	94	41.09 N	120.58 E
Bānsi	114	27.11 N	82.56 E
Bansi	116	23.50 N	90.15 E
Ban Signo	100	17.51 N	105.04 E
Banská Bystrica	30	48.44 N	19.07 E
Banská Štiavnica	30	48.28 N	18.56 E
Bansko	38	41.50 N	23.29 E
Bānskupi	116	24.10 N	86.41 E
Ban Songkhon	100	17.58 N	105.10 E
Ban Song Kong	259a	13.53 N	100.34 E
Ban Sop Huai Hai	100	19.33 N	98.05 E
Ban Söppheung	100	18.33 N	104.17 E
Banstala	262b	22.32 N	88.25 E
Banstead	44	51.19 N	0.12 W
Ban Sum Sui	100	14.28 N	99.05 E
Bānswāra	110	23.33 N	74.27 E
Banta, Calif., U.S.	216	37.45 N	121.22 W
Banta, Zhg.	90	32.41 N	118.35 E
Banta, Pulau I	105b	8.25 S	119.14 E
Bantaian	104	1.56 N	100.54 E
Ban Takhlo	100	15.27 N	100.44 E
Bantam	197	41.44 N	73.14 W
Bantam Lake	197	41.42 N	73.13 W
Ban Tamru	259a	13.31 N	100.41 E
Bantan	97	29.52 N	105.52 E
Ban Tao Pun	259a	13.53 N	100.41 E
Bantarkawung	105a	7.13 S	108.55 E
Bantayad	106	11.10 N	123.43 E
Bantayan Island I	106	11.13 N	123.44 E
Banteln	48	52.04 N	9.44 E
Banten	105a	6.03 S	106.09 E
Banten, Teluk	105a	6.00 S	106.10 E
Bantenan, Tanjung	105a	8.47 S	114.32 E
Ban Teung	100	17.54 N	105.29 E
Ban Thabôk	100	18.22 N	103.12 E
Ban Thanoun	100	19.50 N	101.29 E
Ban Thapayi	100	16.19 N	105.41 E
Bantheville	52	49.21 N	5.05 E
Ban Thieng	100	19.08 N	102.12 E
Ban Thuang	100	18.43 N	103.14 E
Ban Tian Sa	259a	13.35 N	100.34 E
Bantigui Point	106	13.41 N	121.28 E
Banting	104	2.49 N	101.30 E
Banton (Jones)	106	12.57 N	122.05 E
Ban Tong Khop	100	17.04 N	104.16 E
Banton Island I	106	12.56 N	122.04 E
Bāntra	262b	22.35 N	88.19 E
Bantry	28	51.41 N	9.27 W
Bantry Bay	28	51.38 N	9.48 W
Bantul	105a	7.54 S	110.20 E
Bāntva	110	21.29 N	70.05 E
Banūr	114	30.34 N	76.43 E
Ban Van Hom	100	18.44 N	104.01 E
Ban Vat	100	16.54 N	106.25 E
Banwell	44	51.20 N	2.52 W
Banwy	44	52.42 N	3.16 W
Ban Xènkhalôk	100	19.42 N	101.54 E
Banxiancun	90	30.33 N	119.42 E
Ban Xot	100	18.11 N	105.03 E
Banyak, Kepulauan II	104	2.10 N	97.15 E
Ban Ya Plong	100	8.53 N	98.35 E
Banyo	146	6.45 N	11.49 E
Banyumas	105a	7.31 S	109.17 E
Banyuwangi	105a	8.12 S	114.21 E
Banyuwedang	105b	8.08 S	114.36 E
Banz	50	50.08 N	10.57 E
Banzare Coast [2]	9	67.00 S	126.00 E
Banzhuyuan	97	28.44 N	106.18 E
Banzi	95	40.36 N	117.26 E
Banzyville	142	4.18 N	21.11 E
Bao, Ouadi	136	16.36 N	23.05 E
Baoan, Zhg.	90	30.11 N	114.43 E
Baoan, Zhg.	90	22.34 N	114.07 E
Baoan, Zhg.	96	31.46 N	121.26 E
Baoancun	89	48.13 N	125.52 E
Baochang → Taipusiqi, Zhg.	88	41.56 N	115.22 E
Baochang, Zhg.	96	32.04 N	121.25 E
Baocheng	92	33.08 N	107.09 E
Baode	92	39.06 N	111.11 E
Baodi	95	39.44 N	117.17 E
Baoding (Qingyuan)	92	38.52 N	115.29 E
Baofeng	92	33.54 N	113.02 E
Baofutan	90	30.31 N	119.29 E
Baoguosi	97	29.35 N	103.31 E
Baoguotu	88	42.20 N	120.43 E
Bao-ha	100	22.11 N	104.21 E
Baohe	95	39.02 N	115.39 E
Baohekou	90	30.32 N	118.15 E
Baoji, Zhg.	92	34.22 N	107.14 E
Baoji, Zhg.	96	31.43 N	121.16 E
Baojiagou	90	30.42 N	114.40 E
Baojiapu	94	40.51 N	122.14 E
Baojiatun	95	40.22 N	116.25 E
Baojiawazi	94	41.38 N	123.24 E
Baojing	92	28.43 N	109.25 E
Baokang → Keerqinzuozhongqi	79	44.11 N	123.18 E
Bao-lac	100	22.57 N	105.40 E
Baolinchang	92	30.25 N	105.02 E
Baolizhen	79	42.56 N	123.46 E
Bao-loc	100	11.32 N	107.48 E
Baolunyuan	92	32.22 N	105.40 E
Baoma	140	7.58 N	11.37 W
Baomachang	97	29.58 N	104.12 E
Baon	106	6.47 N	126.05 E
Baoning	92	23.31 N	106.24 E
Baoqing	79	46.21 N	132.14 E
Baoqiuhe	95	39.36 N	117.38 E
Baoquan	88	36.16 N	119.04 E
Baoro	142	5.40 N	15.58 E
Baoshan, Zhg.	90	32.39 N	113.54 E
Baoshan, Zhg.	92	26.19 N	104.27 E
Baoshan, Zhg.	92	25.09 N	99.09 E
Baoshan, Zhg.	96	31.25 N	121.29 E
Baoting	100	18.42 N	109.45 E
Baotou (Paotow)	92	40.40 N	109.59 E
Baotun	94	42.29 N	122.52 E
Baoulé, Afr.	140	12.36 N	6.34 W
Baoulé, Mali	140	13.33 N	9.54 W
Baowei	92	22.39 N	106.50 E
Baoxikou	90	23.16 N	115.14 E
Baoxingchang	97	29.38 N	105.41 E
Baoxinji	90	32.35 N	115.00 E
Baoyan	96	31.55 N	119.21 E
Baoyiji	90	32.13 N	116.42 E
Baoying	90	33.16 N	119.20 E
Baoyinghu	90	33.05 N	119.10 E
Baozhuchang	97	29.48 N	104.15 E
Baozidian	95	40.11 N	117.48 E
Baozixie	90	30.28 N	114.34 E
Bāp	110	27.23 N	72.21 E
Bapanling	94	40.58 N	123.08 E
Bāpatla	112	15.54 N	80.28 E
Bapaume	46	50.06 N	2.51 E
Bapchule	190	33.12 N	111.50 W
Bapsfontein	148	26.08 S	28.25 E
Baptiste Lake	202	45.07 N	78.02 W
Baptistown	198	40.31 N	75.00 W
Bāqa el Gharbiyya	122	32.25 N	35.03 E
Baqar, Maṣrif Baḥr al-	132	31.05 N	32.08 E
Baqar, Wādī al-	136	27.49 N	18.37 E
Baqing	110	32.15 N	93.30 E
B'aqlīn	122	33.41 N	35.33 E
Ba'qūbah	118	33.45 N	44.38 E
Baquedano	242	23.20 S	69.51 W
Ba-queo	259c	10.48 N	106.38 E
Bar, Jugo.	38	42.05 N	19.05 E
Bar, S.S.S.R.	68	49.04 N	27.40 E
Bar, S.S.S.R.	78	51.17 N	107.33 E
Bar	52	49.42 N	4.50 E
Bāra, Bhārat	114	25.13 N	87.22 E
Bara, Bhārat	262b	22.43 N	88.31 E
Bara, Bhārat	262b	22.46 N	88.17 E
Barabai	102	2.35 S	115.23 E
Bara Bāngurda	116	22.57 N	86.24 E
Bāra Banki	114	26.55 N	81.12 E
Bāra Banki □[5]	114	27.00 N	81.20 E
Barabanovo	72	54.43 N	38.10 E
Barābhūm	116	23.02 N	86.22 E
Barabinsk	76	55.21 N	78.21 E
Barabinskaja Step'	76	55.00 N	79.00 E
Baraboo	180	43.28 N	89.45 W
Baraboo Range [2]	180	43.25 N	89.40 W
Baraboulé	140	14.12 N	1.51 W
Barachois Pond Provincial Park	176	48.26 N	58.14 W
Baracoa, Cuba	230p	20.21 N	74.30 W
Baracoa, Hond.	226	15.43 N	87.52 W
Baradā	122	33.30 N	36.28 E
Baradero	248	33.48 S	59.30 W
Baradero	248	33.55 S	59.16 W
Baradine	156	30.56 S	149.04 E
Bara Doāni	116	22.06 N	89.59 E
Baraga	180	46.47 N	88.30 W
Baragaon → Nālanda	114	25.07 N	85.25 E
Baragoi	144	1.47 N	36.47 E
Baraguá	230p	21.41 N	78.38 W
Baragwanath	263d	26.16 S	27.59 E
Baragwanath Aerodrome ⊠	263d	26.15 S	27.59 E
Baragwanath Military Hospital	263d	26.16 S	27.56 E
Bārah	130	13.42 N	30.22 E
Barahānuddin	116	22.30 N	90.43 E
Barāigrām	116	24.19 N	89.10 E
Baraily	114	23.00 N	78.14 E
Bara Issa	140	16.09 N	3.28 W
Bāra Jamda	114	22.09 N	85.23 E
Barajas, Aeropuerto ⊠	256a	40.28 N	3.34 W
Barajas de Madrid [8]	256a	40.28 N	3.35 E
Bara Jorda	116	23.10 N	86.50 E
Barak	120	36.51 N	37.59 E
Baraka	144	4.06 S	29.06 E
Baraka, Khawr (Barka)	134	18.13 N	37.35 E
Barakah	130	10.58 N	27.59 E
Barākar	116	24.07 N	86.14 E
Barakār	116	23.42 N	86.48 E
Bara Khunta	116	21.43 N	86.38 E
Barakī Barak	110	33.56 N	68.55 E
Barakkol'skij	76	52.12 N	67.49 E
Bārākot	110	21.33 N	85.01 E
Bārākpur	116	22.55 N	89.32 E
Barakula	156	26.26 S	150.31 E
Barāl	262b	22.27 N	88.22 E
Baralaba	156	24.11 S	149.49 E
Barām	116	22.57 N	86.18 E
Baram	102	4.36 N	113.59 E
Baram, Tanjong	102	4.35 N	113.59 E
Barama	236	7.40 N	59.15 W
Barāmāria	116	21.42 N	87.04 E
Bārāmati	112	18.09 N	74.35 E
Bāramūla	113	34.12 N	74.21 E
Bārān, Bhārat	114	25.06 N	76.31 E
Baran', S.S.S.R.	66	54.29 N	30.18 E
Baran', S.S.S.R.	66	54.30 N	28.40 E
Baranagar	116	22.38 N	88.22 E
Baranakovo	76	58.08 N	82.58 E
Barancevo	72	55.04 N	37.38 E
Baranello	60	41.32 N	14.34 E
Barangbarang	102	6.24 S	120.28 E
Barangeon	46	47.12 N	2.10 E
Barani	140	13.10 N	3.53 W
Barania Góra	30	49.37 N	19.00 E
Baraniki	70	46.31 N	41.50 E
Baranikovka	73	49.10 N	39.50 E
Baranoa	236	10.48 N	74.55 W
Barano d'Ischia	60	40.42 N	13.55 E
Baranof	170	57.05 N	134.50 W
Baranof Island I	170	57.00 N	135.00 W
Baranoviči	66	53.08 N	26.02 E
Baranovka	68	50.18 N	27.40 E
Baranovskoje	72	55.25 N	38.45 E
Baranów Sandomierski	30	50.30 N	21.33 E
Barany, S.S.S.R.	66	57.20 N	29.09 E
Barany, S.S.S.R.	70	57.38 N	52.16 E
Baranya □[6]	30	46.05 N	18.15 E
Barão Ataliba Nogueira	246	22.24 S	46.45 W
Barão de Aquino	246	22.07 S	42.39 W
Barão de Bom Jardim	245	12.17 S	38.36 W
Barão de Cocais	245	19.56 S	43.28 W
Barão de Geraldo	246	22.49 S	47.06 W
Barão de Grajaú	240	6.45 S	43.01 W
Barão de Juparanã	246	22.21 S	43.41 W
Barão de Melgaço	238	16.13 S	55.58 W
Barão de Tromaí	240	1.29 S	45.36 W
Baraolt	38	46.05 N	25.36 E
Baraoltului, Munții	38	46.15 N	25.45 E
Barapasi	154	2.07 S	137.00 E
Baras	106	13.40 N	124.22 E
Barasāhi	116	21.43 N	86.44 E
Bārāsat, Bhārat	116	22.43 N	88.29 E
Bārasat, Bhārat	262b	22.51 N	88.22 E
Baraševo	70	54.32 N	42.53 E
Baraši	68	50.43 N	28.01 E
Baraški	24	65.40 N	52.10 E
Barat, Lintasan	105a	7.08 S	112.40 E
Baratã	256c	38.48 N	9.19 W
Baratang Island I	100	12.13 N	92.45 E
Barataria	184	29.44 N	90.08 W
Barataria Bay	184	29.22 N	89.57 W
Barat Daya, Kepulauan II	98	7.25 S	128.00 E
Barate	102	9.54 S	123.38 E
Bar'atino, S.S.S.R.	66	54.19 N	34.31 E
Bar'atino, S.S.S.R.	72	54.43 N	36.49 E
Baratolia	116	22.25 N	86.37 E
Baratta	156	31.59 S	139.06 E
Baraula	262a	28.34 N	77.22 E
Baraut	114	29.06 N	77.16 E
Baraya	236	3.10 N	75.04 W
Barba, Volcán [1]	226	10.08 N	84.06 W
Barbacena	246	21.14 S	43.46 W
Barbacoas	236	1.41 N	78.09 W
Barbades → Barbados □[1]	231g	13.10 N	59.32 W
Barbadillo	276d	12.02 S	76.56 W
Barbadillo del Mercado	34	42.02 N	3.21 W
Barbadoes Island I	275	40.07 N	75.22 W
Barbados □[1]	220		
	231g	13.10 N	59.32 W
Barbalha	240	7.19 S	39.17 W
Barbar	130	18.01 N	33.59 E
Bárbara	236	0.53 S	72.30 W
Barbarano Vicentino	58	45.24 N	11.32 E
Barbarasco	58	44.14 N	9.56 E
Barbareta, Isla I	226	16.26 N	86.09 W
Barbaros	120	40.54 N	27.27 E
Barbas, Cabo	138	22.18 N	16.41 W
Barbaši	66	57.42 N	28.24 E
Barbastro	34	42.02 N	0.08 E
Barbate	34	36.11 N	5.55 W
Barbate de Franco	34	36.12 N	5.55 W
Barbeau Peak	16	81.54 N	75.01 W
Barbentane	56	43.54 N	4.45 E
Barber Booth	252	53.22 N	1.50 W
Barberena	226	14.18 N	90.22 W
Barberena, Río de	224	22.34 N	97.52 W
Barberino di Mugello	60	44.00 N	11.15 E
Barberino Val d'Elsa	60	43.32 N	11.10 E
Barbers Point	219c	21.18 N	158.07 W
Barbers Point Naval Air Station	219c	21.19 N	158.04 W
Barberton, S. Afr.	146	25.48 S	31.03 E
Barberton, Ohio, U.S.	204	41.01 N	81.36 W
Barbezieux	32	45.28 N	0.09 W
Bar Bigha	114	25.13 N	85.44 E
Barbil	114	22.06 N	85.20 E
Barbis	50	51.37 N	10.25 E
Barbizon	46	48.27 N	2.36 E
Barbosa, Col.	236	6.26 N	75.20 W
Barbosa, Col.	236	5.57 N	73.37 W
Barboursville	178	38.24 N	82.18 W
Barbourville	182	36.52 N	83.53 W
Barbuda I	228	17.38 N	61.48 W
Barbuise	46	48.33 N	3.35 E
Barby	50	51.58 N	11.53 E
Barca	30	48.41 N	21.16 E
Barčadiv	75	38.19 N	72.29 E
Barcaldine	156	23.33 S	145.17 E
Barcarena	256c	38.44 N	9.17 W
Barcarena, Ribeira de	256c	38.42 N	9.27 W
Barcarrota	34	38.31 N	6.51 W
Barce → Al-Marj	136	32.30 N	20.54 E
Barcellona Pozzo di Gotto	36	38.09 N	15.13 E
Barcelona, Esp.	34		
	256d	41.23 N	2.11 E
Barcelona, Méx.	222	26.12 N	103.25 W
Barcelona, Pil.	106	12.52 N	124.09 E
Barcelona, Ven.	236	10.08 N	64.42 W
Barcelona [8]	256a	40.22 N	3.34 E
Barcelona, Aeropuerto Transoceánico de ⊠	256d	41.18 N	2.05 E
Barcelona, Campo Fútbol Club	256d	41.23 N	2.08 E
Barcelona, Universidad de [2]	256d	41.23 N	2.10 E
Barcelone → Barcelona	34	41.23 N	2.11 E
Barceloneta	230m	18.27 N	66.32 W
Barcelonnette	56	44.23 N	6.39 E
Barcelos, Bra.	236	0.58 S	62.57 W
Barcelos, Port.	34	41.32 N	8.37 W
Barchaticha	70	57.34 N	45.13 E
Barchyn	78	48.43 N	110.17 E
Barcillonnette	56	44.26 N	5.55 E
Barcin	30	52.52 N	17.57 E
Barcis	58	46.11 N	12.33 E
Barclay	198	39.08 N	75.51 W
Barclay Brook	266	40.19 N	74.22 W
Barcoo	156	25.30 S	142.50 E
Barcroft, Lake [1]	274c	38.51 N	77.09 W
Barcs	30	45.58 N	17.28 E
Barcy	251	49.01 N	2.53 E
Barczewo	30	53.50 N	20.42 E
Bard	56	45.36 N	7.45 E
Barda, S.S.S.R.	74	40.23 N	47.08 E
Barda, S.S.S.R.	76	56.54 N	55.38 E
Barda del Medio	242	38.43 S	68.10 W
Bardai, Sūd.	130	12.43 N	21.53 E
Bardaï, Tchad	136	21.22 N	16.59 E
Bardawīl, Sabkhat al-	130	31.10 N	33.10 E
Bardejov	30	49.18 N	21.16 E
Bárdenas Reales [1]	34	42.10 N	1.25 W
Bardera	134	2.21 N	42.20 E
Bardeskan	118	35.12 N	57.58 E
Bardi	56	44.38 N	9.44 E
Bardīa	114	28.18 N	81.22 E
Bardīyah	136	31.46 N	25.06 E
Bardız	120	40.26 N	42.20 E
Bardney	42	53.12 N	0.21 W
Bardoc	152	30.20 S	121.17 E
Bardoli	110	21.07 N	73.07 E
Bardolino	58	45.33 N	10.43 E
Bardonecchia	56	45.05 N	6.42 E
Bardonia	266	41.07 N	74.00 W
Bardoux, Lac	176	51.09 N	67.50 W
Bardowick	48	53.18 N	10.23 E
Bardsey Island I	44	52.45 N	4.45 W
Bardsey Sound	44	52.47 N	4.45 W
Bardstown	184	37.49 N	85.28 W
Bardswell Group II	172	52.10 N	128.20 W
Bardu	24	68.52 N	18.21 E
Bardufoss	24	69.04 N	18.30 E
Bardwell, Ky., U.S.	184	36.52 N	89.01 W
Bardwell, Tex., U.S.	212	32.16 N	96.42 W
Bardwell Lake [1]	212	32.16 N	96.39 W
Bare	134	4.42 N	42.47 E
Bareggio	256b	45.29 N	9.00 E
Barei, Wādī	130	13.27 N	23.57 E
Bareilly	114	28.21 N	79.25 E
Barenburg	48	52.37 N	8.47 E
Barenc'ovo More → Barents Sea [2]	12	74.00 N	36.00 E
Barendrecht	48	51.51 N	4.32 E
Barengapāra	114	25.14 N	90.14 E
Bärenklau	50	51.56 N	14.34 E
Bärenstein, D.D.R.	50	50.30 N	13.02 E
Bärenstein, D.D.R.	50	50.48 N	13.47 E
Barentin	46	49.33 N	0.57 E
Barentsøya I	10	78.27 N	21.15 E
Barents Sea [2]	12	74.00 N	36.00 E
Barents Trough [1]	10	74.00 N	28.00 E
Barentu	134	15.04 N	37.37 E
Bareo	102	3.45 N	115.27 E
Baresville	198	39.48 N	76.57 W
Bareta	113	29.52 N	75.42 E
Barfleur	32	49.40 N	1.15 W
Barfleur, Pointe de	32	49.42 N	1.16 W
Barga	58	44.04 N	10.29 E
Bargāchia, Bhārat	116	22.39 N	88.07 E
Bargāchia, Bhārat	262b	22.48 N	88.27 E
Bargagli	56	44.27 N	9.05 E
Bargaintown	198	39.22 N	70.35 W
Bargal	134	11.18 N	51.07 E
Bargara	156	24.49 S	152.27 E
Bargarh	110	21.20 N	83.37 E
Bargas	34	39.56 N	4.03 W
Barge	56	44.43 N	7.20 E
Barg-e Maṯāl	110	35.40 N	71.21 E
Bargemon	56	43.37 N	6.32 E
Bargen	54	47.48 N	8.37 E
Bargersville	208	39.31 N	86.10 W
Barghanak	118	33.56 N	62.26 E
Barghe	58	45.41 N	10.24 E
Bargnop	130	9.30 N	28.28 E
Bargo	160	34.18 S	150.35 E
Bargoed	44	51.43 N	3.15 W
Bargteheide	48	53.44 N	10.16 E
Bārguna	116	22.09 N	90.07 E
Barguzin	78	53.37 N	109.37 E
Barguzin	78	53.27 N	109.00 E
Barguzinskij Chrebet	78	54.30 N	110.20 E
Barguzinskij Zaliv	78	53.26 N	108.48 E
Barguzinskij Zapovednik	78	54.25 N	109.40 E
Bārh	114	25.29 N	85.43 E
Bar Harbor	178	44.23 N	68.13 W
Barharwa	114	24.52 N	87.47 E
Barhau	102	5.19 S	102.10 E
Barhi	114	24.18 N	85.25 E
Barhiya	114	25.17 N	86.02 E
Bāri, Bhārat	114	26.39 N	77.36 E
Bāri, Bhārat	114	23.03 N	78.05 E
Bari, It.	36	41.07 N	16.52 E
Bari, Zaïre	142	3.19 N	19.23 E
Bari	114	27.55 N	83.27 E
Baria	236	1.56 N	66.35 W
Baricella	58	44.39 N	11.32 E
Barichara	236	6.38 N	73.14 W
Barīdī, Ra's	118	24.17 N	37.31 E
Bāri Doāb [1]	113	30.25 N	73.00 E
Barī Gāv	110	33.52 N	67.49 E
Barigazzo	58	44.16 N	10.39 E
Barigua, Salina de	231s	12.08 N	69.59 W
Barika	34	35.23 N	5.22 E
Barika, Oued	34	35.22 N	5.18 E
Barikiwa	144	9.28 S	37.54 E
Barīkowṯ	110	35.18 N	71.32 E
Barillas	226	15.48 N	91.18 W
Bariloche → San Carlos de Bariloche	244	41.09 S	71.18 W
Barilo-Krepinskaja	73	47.45 N	39.32 E
Barīm I	134	12.40 N	43.25 E
Barima	236	8.33 N	60.25 W
Barin	74	39.13 N	44.28 E
Barinas, P.R.	230m	18.01 N	66.51 W
Barinas, Ven.	236	8.38 N	70.12 W
Barinas □[3]	236	8.10 N	69.50 W
Baring	214	47.46 N	121.29 W
Baring, Cape	166	70.05 N	117.20 W
Baringa, Zaïre	142	6.17 S	16.55 E
Baringa, Zaïre	142	0.45 N	20.52 E
Baring Channel	166	73.48 N	98.50 W
Baringo	144	0.28 N	35.58 E
Baringo, Lake	144	0.38 N	36.05 E
Båring Vig	41	55.32 N	9.56 E
Barinitas	236	8.45 N	70.25 W
Baripāda	116	21.56 N	86.43 E
Bariri	245	22.04 S	48.44 W
Bārīs	130	24.40 N	30.36 E
Barisacho	74	42.28 N	44.54 E
Bari Sādri	110	24.25 N	74.28 E
Barisāl	114	22.42 N	90.22 E
Barisan, Pegunungan	102	3.00 S	102.15 E
Barisciano	60	42.19 N	13.35 E
Bariti Bil	262b	22.48 N	88.26 E
Barit Island I	106	18.52 N	121.15 E
Barito	102	3.32 S	114.29 E
Barjā	122	33.39 N	35.26 E
Barjac	56	44.18 N	4.21 E
Barjols	56	43.33 N	6.00 E
Barjora	116	23.26 N	87.17 E
Barjūj, Wādī	136	25.57 N	13.12 E
Bark	206	42.55 N	88.50 W
Barka (Khawr Baraka)	134	18.13 N	37.35 E
Barka Kāna	114	23.37 N	85.29 E
Barkal	110	22.44 N	92.23 E
Barkava	66	56.43 N	26.36 E
Barkelsby	41	54.30 N	9.50 E
Barken	40	60.07 N	15.31 E
Barker, N.Y., U.S.	200	43.20 N	78.33 W
Barker, Ur.	248	34.16 S	57.27 W
Barker Point	266	40.51 N	73.44 W
Barker Reservoir [1]	212	29.44 N	95.44 W
Barkers Brook	275	40.03 N	74.45 W
Barkerville	172	53.04 N	121.31 W
Barkerville Historical Park	172	53.04 N	121.30 W
Barkeyville	204	41.12 N	79.58 W
Barkhamsted Reservoir [1]	197	41.57 N	72.57 W
Bārkhān	110	29.54 N	69.31 E
Barkhanpur	116	23.50 N	89.33 E
Barking [8]	44	51.33 N	0.06 E
Barkingside [8]	250	51.36 N	0.05 E
Barki Saraiya	114	24.10 N	85.53 E
Barkisland	252	53.41 N	1.55 W
Bark Lake, Ont., Can.	180	46.54 N	82.28 W
Bark Lake, Ont., Can.	202	45.27 N	77.51 W
Barkley, Lake [1]	184	36.40 N	87.55 W
Barkley Sound	172	48.53 N	125.20 W
Barkly, Mount [2]	152	21.34 S	132.28 E
Barkly East	148	30.58 S	27.33 E
Barkly Tableland [1]	152	18.00 S	136.00 E
Barkly West	148	28.05 S	24.31 E
Barksdale	186	29.44 N	100.02 W
Barkuhi	114	22.13 N	78.42 E
Barla	120	38.01 N	30.47 E
Bârlad → Bîrlad	38	46.14 N	27.40 E
Barlassina	256b	45.39 N	9.08 E
Barlby	42	53.48 N	1.03 W
Barleben	50	52.12 N	11.37 E
Bar-le-Duc	52	48.47 N	5.10 E
Barlee, Lake	152	29.10 S	119.30 E
Barlee, Mount [2]	152	24.37 S	128.06 E
Barlee Range	152	23.35 S	116.00 E
Barles	56	44.16 N	6.16 E
Barletta	36	41.19 N	16.17 E
Barlin	46	50.27 N	2.37 E
Barlinek	30	53.00 N	15.12 E
Barlow	184	37.03 N	89.03 W
Barluk	78	54.32 N	101.43 E
Barma	154	1.54 S	133.00 E
Barmancak, Ozero	70	48.02 N	44.40 E
Barmašovo	68	47.07 N	32.26 E
Barmedman	156	34.09 S	147.23 E
Barmen [8]	253	51.17 N	7.13 E
Barmer	110	25.45 N	71.23 E
Barmera	156	34.15 S	140.28 E
Barmer-Stausee [1]	253	51.14 N	7.16 E
Barmouth	44	52.43 N	4.03 W
Barmouth Bay	44	52.42 N	4.08 W
Barmstedt	48	53.47 N	9.46 E
Barnaby Manor Oaks	274c	38.50 N	76.58 W
Barnagar	110	23.03 N	75.22 E
Barnāla	113	30.23 N	75.33 E
Barnard Castle	42	54.33 N	1.55 W
Barnasht	132	29.41 N	31.15 E
Barnaul	76	53.22 N	83.45 E
Barn Bluff	156	41.43 S	145.56 E
Barneberg	50	52.08 N	11.03 E
Barnechea	276e	33.21 S	70.31 W
Barnegat	198	39.45 N	74.13 W
Barnegat Bay	198	39.52 N	74.07 W
Barnegat Light	198	39.46 N	74.06 W
Barne Inlet	9	80.15 S	160.15 E
Barnes	204	41.40 N	79.01 W
Barnes [8]	250	51.28 N	0.15 W
Barnesboro	204	40.40 N	78.47 W
Barnes Corners	202	43.49 N	75.49 W
Barnes Lake	174	56.23 N	98.06 W
Barnes Sound	210	25.14 N	80.23 W
Barnesville, Ga., U.S.	182	33.04 N	84.09 W
Barnesville, Minn., U.S.	188	46.39 N	96.25 W
Barnesville, Ohio, U.S.	178	39.59 N	81.11 W
Barnet [8]	44	51.40 N	0.13 W
Barnetby le Wold	42	53.35 N	0.25 W
Barnett	209	39.16 N	89.42 W
Barnetts	198	37.22 N	77.09 W
Barneveld, Ned.	48	52.08 N	5.35 E
Barneveld, N.Y., U.S.	200	43.16 N	75.12 W
Barneville-Carteret	32	49.23 N	1.47 W
Barnhart, Mo., U.S.	209	38.23 N	92.40 W
Barnhart, Tex., U.S.	186	31.08 N	101.10 W
Barnhill	204	40.27 N	81.21 W
Barnim □[9]	50	52.40 N	13.45 E
Barnoldswick	42	53.55 N	2.11 W
Barnówko	50	52.48 N	14.45 E
Barnsboro	275	39.46 N	75.09 W
Barnsdall	186	36.34 N	96.10 W
Barnsley	42	53.34 N	1.28 W
Barnstable	197	41.42 N	70.18 W
Barnstable □[6]	197	41.42 N	70.18 W
Barnstable Harbor	197	41.43 N	70.18 W
Barnstaple	44	51.05 N	4.04 W
Barnstaple Bay	44	51.05 N	4.20 W
Barnston	252	53.21 N	3.05 W
Barnstorf	48	52.42 N	8.30 E
Barnt Green	44	52.22 N	1.59 W
Barnton	252	53.16 N	2.33 W
Barntrup	48	51.59 N	9.06 E
Barnum Island	266	40.36 N	73.39 W
Barnwell, Alta., Can.	172	49.46 N	112.15 W
Barnwell, S.C., U.S.	182	33.15 N	81.23 W
Baro	140	8.37 N	6.25 E
Baro	134	8.26 N	33.13 E
Barobo	106	8.33 N	126.07 E
Baroda, Bhārat	112	22.18 N	73.12 E
Baroda, Bhārat	114	25.30 N	76.39 E
Baroda, Mich., U.S.	206	41.57 N	86.29 W
Baroe	148	33.13 S	24.33 E
Barola I	165e	7.30 S	158.20 E
Barometer	162	41.50 S	173.39 E
Baron Bluff [4]	231n	17.47 N	64.47 W
Baronissi	60	40.44 N	14.45 E
Barons	172	50.00 N	113.05 W
Barora Ite I	165e	7.35 S	158.24 E
Barossa Reservoir [1]	158b	34.39 S	138.51 E
Barotac Nuevo	106	10.54 N	122.42 E
Barotac Viejo	106	11.03 N	122.51 E
Barotseland □[9]	128	16.00 S	24.00 E
Barotse Plain	142	15.40 S	23.10 E
Barouéli	140	13.04 N	6.50 W
Barpathār	110	26.17 N	93.53 E
Barpeta	110	26.19 N	91.00 E
Bar Point	204	42.03 N	83.07 W
Barqah (Cyrenaica) [1]	136	31.00 N	22.30 E
Barqah, Jabal al-	122	30.25 N	34.18 E
Barq al-'Izz	132	31.01 N	31.26 E
Barquisimeto	236	10.04 N	69.19 W
Barr	54	48.24 N	7.27 E
Barra, Bra.	240	11.05 S	43.10 W
Barra, Gam.	140	13.20 N	16.36 W
Barra, Ponta da	146	23.45 S	35.30 E
Barraba	156	30.22 S	150.36 E
Barracão	242	26.15 S	53.38 W
Barracão do Barreto	238	8.48 S	58.24 W
Barracas [8]	278	34.38 S	58.22 W
Barrackpore	116	22.46 N	88.21 E
Barrackpore Airport ⊠	262b	22.47 N	88.22 E
Barrackpore Cantonment	262b	22.46 N	88.22 E
Barrackville	178	39.30 N	80.10 W
Barracouta, Cape	148	34.26 S	21.22 E
Barra da Estiva	245	13.38 S	41.19 W
Barra de Santa Rosa	240	6.43 S	36.04 W
Barra de Santo Antônio	240	9.24 S	35.30 W
Barra de São Francisco	246	21.58 S	42.42 W
Barra do Bugres	238	15.05 S	57.11 W
Barra do Corda	240	5.30 S	45.15 W
Barra do Cuanza	142	9.09 S	13.00 E
Barra do Dande	142	8.28 S	13.22 E
Barra do Garças	245	15.53 S	52.15 W
Barra do Mendes	245	11.43 S	42.04 W
Barra do Piraí	246	22.28 S	43.49 W
Barra do Ribeiro	242	30.18 S	51.18 W
Barra dos Coqueiros	240	10.54 S	37.03 W
Barra Falsa, Ponta da	146	22.55 S	35.37 E
Barrafranca	36	37.23 N	14.13 E
Barra Funda [8]	277b	23.31 S	46.39 W
Barra Mansa	246	22.32 S	44.11 W
Barranca, Perú	238	4.50 S	76.42 W
Barranca, Perú	238	10.45 S	77.46 W
Barrancabermeja	236	7.03 N	73.52 W
Barranca del Cobre, Parque Nacional	222	27.15 N	107.41 W
Barrancas, Chile	242	33.27 S	70.46 W
Barrancas, Col.	236	10.57 N	72.50 W
Barrancas, Ven.	236	8.42 N	62.11 W
Barrancas, Ven.	236	8.46 N	70.06 W
Barrancas	242	36.52 S	69.45 W
Barranco	276d	12.09 S	77.02 W
Barranco Azul	186	29.21 N	104.17 W
Barranco de Guadalupe	186	30.02 N	104.44 W
Barranco do Velho	34	37.14 N	7.56 W
Barrancos	34	38.08 N	6.59 W
Barrânia	246	21.33 S	46.32 W
Barranjoey Head	160	33.34 S	151.20 E
Barranqueras	242	27.29 S	58.56 W
Barranquilla	236	10.59 N	74.48 W
Barranquitas	230m	18.11 N	66.18 W
Barras	240	4.15 S	42.18 W
Barrax	34	39.03 N	2.12 W
Barraza	242	30.38 S	71.26 W
Barre, Mass., U.S.	197	42.26 N	72.06 W
Barre, Vt., U.S.	178	44.12 N	72.30 W
Barrea	60	41.45 N	13.59 E
Barreal	242	31.38 S	69.28 W
Barre-des-Cévennes	56	44.15 N	3.39 E
Barre des Écrins	56	44.55 N	6.22 E
Barree	204	40.35 N	78.06 W
Barre Falls Reservoir [1]	197	42.24 N	72.00 W
Barreira	246	22.37 S	43.25 W
Barreiras	245	12.08 S	45.00 W
Barreirinha	240	2.47 S	57.03 W
Barreirinhas	240	2.45 S	42.50 W
Barreiro	34	38.40 N	9.04 W
Barreiro	245	15.43 S	52.45 W
Barreiros	240	8.49 S	35.12 W
Barrême	56	43.57 N	6.22 E
Barren	184	37.11 N	86.37 W
Barren, Îles II	147b	18.25 S	43.40 E
Barren Island I	244	52.22 S	59.40 W
Barren Islands II	170	58.55 N	152.15 W
Barren River Lake [1]	184	36.45 N	86.02 W
Barren Run	269b	40.09 N	79.42 W
Barre Plains	197	42.23 N	72.07 W
Barret-le-Bas	56	44.16 N	5.44 E
Barretos	245	20.33 S	48.33 W
Barrett	212	29.53 N	95.04 W
Barrett, Mount	152	18.10 S	127.33 E

English	Deutsch	Español	Français	Português
River	Fluss	Río	Rivière	Rio
Canal	Kanal	Canal	Canal	Canal
Waterfall, Rapids	Wasserfall, Stromschnellen	Cascada, Rápidos	Chute d'eau, Rapides	Cascata, Rápidos
Strait	Meeresstrasse	Estrecho	Détroit	Estreito
Bay, Gulf	Bucht, Golf	Bahía, Golfo	Baie, Golfe	Baía, Golfo
Lake, Lakes	See, Seen	Lago, Lagos	Lac, Lacs	Lago, Lagos
Swamp	Sumpf	Pantano	Marais	Pântano
Ice Features, Glacier	Eis- und Gletscherformen	Accidentes Glaciales	Formes glaciaires	Acidentes Glaciares
Other Hydrographic Features	Andere Hydrographische Objekte	Otros Elementos Hidrográficos	Autres données hydrographiques	Outros Elementos Hidrográficos
Submarine Features	Untermeerische Objekte	Accidentes Submarinos	Formes de relief sous-marin	Acidentes Submarinos
Political Unit	Politische Einheit	Unidad Política	Entité politique	Unidade Política
Cultural Institution	Kulturelle Institution	Institución Cultural	Institution culturelle	Instituição Cultural
Historical Site	Historische Stätte	Sitio Histórico	Site historique	Sitio Histórico
Recreational Site	Erholungs- und Ferienort	Sitio de Recreo	Centre de loisirs	Sítio de Lazer
Airport	Flughafen	Aeropuerto	Aéroport	Aeroporto
Military Installation	Militäranlage	Instalación Militar	Installation militaire	Instalação Militar
Miscellaneous	Verschiedenes	Misceláneo	Divers	Miscelânea

ENGLISH — Name | Page | Lat.°′ | Long.°′
DEUTSCH — Name | Seite | Breite°′ | Länge°′ E=Ost

Barrhead, Alta., Can. 172 54.08 N 114.24 W
Barrhead, Scot., U.K. 42 55.48 N 4.24 W
Barrhill 42 55.07 N 4.46 W
Barriada Pomar Alto 256d 41.29 N 2.14 E
Barrie 202 44.24 N 79.40 W
Barriefield 202 44.14 N 76.28 W
Barrie Island I 180 45.55 N 82.40 W
Barrien 48 52.56 N 8.49 E
Barrier, Cape ≻ 162 36.21 S 175.31 E
Barrier Bay C 9 67.45 S 81.10 E
Barrier Range ⛰ 156 31.25 S 141.25 E
Barrigada 164p 13.28 N 144.48 E
Barrilla Draw ∨ 186 31.21 N 103.23 W
Barr Ilyās 122 33.46 N 35.54 E
Barrington, N.S., Can. 176 43.34 N 65.34 W
Barrington, Ill., U.S. 206 42.09 N 88.08 W
Barrington, N.J., U.S. 275 39.52 N 75.04 W
Barrington, R.I., U.S. 197 41.44 N 71.18 W
Barrington Hills 206 42.07 N 88.09 W
Barrington Lake ◎ 174 56.55 N 100.15 W
Barrington Tops ∧ 156 32.00 S 151.28 E
Barrington Woods 268 42.09 N 88.04 W
Barringun 156 29.01 S 145.43 E
Barrinho 246 23.07 S 45.22 W
Barrio Azul ⬩[8] 276b 23.04 N 82.23 W
Barrio Obrero Industrial 276d 12.04 S 77.04 W
Barrita Vieja 226 13.55 N 90.54 W
Barrīyat al-Uṣayfir 132 31.18 N 30.40 E
Barro, Bra. 240 7.11 S 38.47 W
Barro, Gui.-B. 140 12.24 N 15.30 W
Barro Alto 245 15.04 S 48.58 W
Barro Branco 246 22.23 S 44.30 W
Barro Duro 240 2.52 S 42.17 W
Barrois □[9] 52 48.40 N 5.15 E
Barron 180 45.24 N 91.51 W
Barron Creek ≃ 272 37.27 N 122.05 W
Barron Lake 206 41.51 N 86.11 W
Barros Arana, Cerro ∧ 244 43.53 S 72.12 W
Barrouallie 231h 13.14 N 61.17 W
Barrow, Arg. 242 38.18 S 60.14 W
Barrow, Alaska, U.S. 170 71.17 N 156.47 W
Barrow, Point ≻ 170 71.23 N 156.30 W
Barrow Bay C 202 44.58 N 81.13 W
Barrow Creek 152 21.33 S 133.53 E
Barrowford 42 53.52 N 2.13 W
Barrow-in-Furness 42 54.07 N 3.14 W
Barrow Island I 152 20.48 S 115.23 E
Barrow Range ⛰ 152 26.04 S 127.28 E
Barrows 174 52.49 N 101.27 W
Barrow Strait Ʊ 166 74.21 N 94.10 W
Barrowsville 197 41.57 N 71.12 W
Barry, Wales, U.K. 44 51.24 N 3.18 W
Barry, Ill., U.S. 209 39.42 N 91.02 W
Barry, Tex., U.S. 212 32.06 N 96.38 W
Barry □[6] 206 42.35 N 85.18 W
Barrydale 148 33.55 S 20.43 E
Barrys Bay 202 45.29 N 77.41 W
Barrys Bay C 202 45.28 N 77.42 W
Barryton 180 43.45 N 85.09 W
Barrytown 200 42.00 N 73.56 W
Barryville 200 41.29 N 74.55 W
Barsakel'mes, Ostrov I 76 45.40 N 59.58 E
Barsalogho 140 13.25 N 1.03 W
Baršatas 76 48.13 N 78.21 E
Bårse 41 55.07 N 11.58 E
Bārsi 112 18.14 N 75.42 E
Baršin 76 49.45 N 69.36 E
Barsinghausen 48 52.18 N 9.27 E
Barskaun 75 42.10 N 77.37 E
Barsø I 41 55.07 N 9.34 E
Barssel 48 53.10 N 7.44 E
Barst 52 49.04 N 6.50 E
Barstow, Calif., U.S. 218 34.54 N 117.01 W
Barstow, Tex., U.S. 186 31.28 N 103.24 W
Barsuki 72 54.15 N 37.30 E
Bar-sur-Aube 54 48.14 N 4.43 E
Bar-sur-Seine 46 48.07 N 4.22 E
Bart 198 39.56 N 76.05 W
Bārta ≃ 66 56.24 N 21.03 E
Bartala 262b 22.33 N 88.16 E
Bartang 110 38.05 N 71.51 E
Bartazuga, Jabal ∧ 130 21.44 N 33.33 E
Bartelso 209 38.32 N 89.28 W
Bartenheim 54 47.38 N 7.28 E
Bartenstein 52 49.21 N 9.53 E
Barter Island I 170 70.08 N 143.35 W
Barth 50 54.22 N 12.43 E
Barthe ≃ 50 54.22 N 12.41 E
Barthélemy, Deo)(100 19.26 N 104.06 E
Bārthi 116 23.02 N 90.12 E
Bartholomew □[6] 208 39.13 N 85.55 W
Bartholomew, Bayou ≃ 184 32.43 N 92.04 W
Bartibougou 140 12.52 N 0.48 E
Bartica 236 6.24 N 58.37 W
Bartın 120 41.38 N 32.21 E
Bartle Frere ∧ 156 17.23 S 145.49 E
Bartlesville 186 36.45 N 95.59 W
Bartlett, Ill., U.S. 206 41.59 N 88.11 W
Bartlett, Nebr., U.S. 188 41.53 N 98.33 W
Bartlett, N.H., U.S. 178 44.05 N 71.17 W
Bartlett, Tenn., U.S. 184 35.12 N 89.52 W
Bartlett, Tex., U.S. 212 30.48 N 97.26 W
Bartlett Brook ≃ 273 42.42 N 71.13 W
Bartlett Cove 170 58.27 N 135.55 W
Bartlett Reservoir ◎[1] 190 33.52 N 111.37 W
Bartletts Harbour 176 50.57 N 57.00 W
Bartley 188 40.15 N 100.18 W
Bartolomé Bavio → General Mansilla 248 35.05 S 57.45 W
Bartolomé de las Casas 242 25.24 S 59.34 W
Bartolomeu de Gusmão, Aeroporto ⊠ 246 22.56 S 43.43 W
Bartolomeu Dias 146 21.10 S 35.09 E
Barton, Austl. 152 30.31 S 132.39 E
Barton, N.Y., U.S. 200 42.03 N 76.27 W
Barton, Ohio, U.S. 204 40.06 N 80.51 W
Barton, Vt., U.S. 178 44.45 N 72.11 W
Barton Aerodrome ⊠ 252 53.28 N 2.23 W
Barton Lake 206 42.06 N 85.35 W
Barton Mills 44 52.20 N 0.31 E
Barton Park ♠ 264a 33.57 S 151.09 E
Barton Run ≃ 275 39.53 N 74.51 W
Barton-under-Needwood 44 52.45 N 1.43 W
Barton-upon-Humber 42 53.41 N 0.27 W
Bartonville 180 40.39 N 89.39 W
Barton Water Swing Bridge ⬩[5] 252 53.28 N 2.21 W
Bartoszyce 30 54.16 N 20.49 E
Bartow, Fla., U.S. 210 27.54 N 81.50 W
Bartow, Ga., U.S. 182 32.53 N 82.29 W
Baru, Kali ≋ 259e 6.10 S 106.51 E
Barueri 246 23.31 S 46.53 W
Barueri □[7] 277b 23.31 S 46.53 W
Barugo 106 11.20 N 124.44 E
Bāruipāra 262b 22.46 N 88.14 E
Bāruipur 116 22.21 N 88.27 E
Bārūk, Jabal al- ∧ 122 33.43 N 35.45 E
Barumun ≃ 104 2.30 N 100.09 E
Bāruni 114 25.29 N 85.59 E
Barun-Šibertuj, Gora ∧ 64 49.42 N 109.59 E
Barus 104 2.00 N 98.24 E
Baruta 276c 10.26 N 66.53 W
Baruth 50 52.03 N 13.30 E
Baruun Bajan-Ulaan 92 45.32 N 101.40 E
Baruun Urt 80 46.40 N 113.12 E
Barvas 28 58.22 N 6.32 W
Barvenkovo 68 48.54 N 37.02 E
Barver 48 52.37 N 8.35 E
Barvicha 255b 55.44 N 37.16 E
Barview 192 43.21 N 124.18 W
Barwa 116 23.51 N 86.26 E
Barwāh 110 22.16 N 76.03 E
Barwāla ⬩[8] 262a 28.46 N 77.04 E
Bärwalde → Mieszkowice 30 52.46 N 14.30 E
Barwāni 110 22.02 N 74.54 E
Barwa Sāgar 114 25.23 N 78.44 E
Barwell 44 52.32 N 1.21 W
Barwice 30 53.45 N 16.22 E
Barwick 182 30.54 N 83.44 W
Barwidgee 152 27.02 S 120.54 E
Barwon ≃, Austl. 156 30.00 S 148.05 E
Barwon ≃, Austl. 159 38.13 S 144.25 E
Barybino, S.S.S.R. 72 55.16 N 37.54 E
Barybino, S.S.S.R. 72 54.56 N 37.47 E
Barycz ≃ 30 51.42 N 16.15 E
Barykino 73 49.17 N 38.24 E
Barykova, Mys ≻ 170 63.02 N 179.29 E
Barykovo 72 54.38 N 38.48 E
Barynino 72 55.47 N 36.21 E
Baryš 70 53.39 N 47.08 E
Baryš ≃ 70 54.35 N 46.48 E
Baryševka 68 50.22 N 31.19 E
Baryševo 76 54.58 N 83.11 E
Baryšniki 70 56.57 N 46.33 E
Barzah 122 33.34 N 36.19 E
Barzas 76 55.43 N 86.19 E
Barzio 54 45.57 N 9.27 E
Basa 140 4.55 N 7.30 W
Bas'a ≃ 66 53.46 N 31.01 E
Basacato del Este 142 3.37 N 8.54 E
Basai Dārāpur ⬩[8] 262a 28.40 N 77.08 E
Bāsa'īdū 118 26.39 N 55.17 E
Basail, Arg. 242 27.52 S 59.18 W
Bāsāil, Bngl. 116 24.14 N 90.04 E
Basakin 70 48.11 N 42.18 E
Basāl 113 33.33 N 72.15 E
Basalt ≃ 156 19.38 S 145.52 E
Basalt Island I 261d 22.19 N 114.22 E
Basaluzzo 56 44.46 N 8.42 E
Basandīlah 132 31.12 N 31.26 E
Basankusu 142 1.14 N 19.48 E
Bašanta 70 46.05 N 41.56 E
Basanti 116 22.12 N 88.42 E
Basarabi 38 44.10 N 28.24 E
Basargečar 74 40.11 N 45.43 E
Basatongwulashan ∧ 110 33.05 N 91.30 E
Basavakalyān 112 17.52 N 76.57 E
Basavilbaso 242 32.22 S 58.53 W
Basbirin 120 37.19 N 41.38 E
Baščelakskij Chrebet ⛰ 76 51.15 N 84.30 E
Baschi 60 42.40 N 12.13 E
Basco 98 20.27 N 121.58 E
Bascom 204 41.08 N 83.17 W
Bascuñán, Cabo ≻ 242 28.51 S 71.30 W
Basdahl 48 53.26 N 8.59 E
Basdorf, B.R.D. 52 51.12 N 8.58 E
Basdorf, D.D.R. 50 52.44 N 13.26 E
Basekpio 144 4.44 N 24.40 E
Basel (Bâle) 54 47.33 N 7.35 E
Baselga di Pinè 58 46.08 N 11.14 E
Baselice 60 41.24 N 14.58 E
Basella 34 42.01 N 1.18 E
Basel-Land □[3] 54 47.30 N 7.50 E
Basel-Stadt □[3] 54 47.38 N 7.40 E
Basen ≃ 86 34.48 N 132.51 E
Bas-en-Basset 56 45.18 N 4.06 E
Basento ≃ 36 40.21 N 16.50 E
Başeu ≃ 38 47.44 N 27.15 E
Basey 106 11.17 N 125.04 E
Bashākerd, Kūhhā-ye ⛰ 118 26.42 N 59.00 E
Bashaw 172 52.35 N 112.58 W
Bashee ≃ 148 32.15 S 28.53 E
Basher Kill ≃ 200 41.27 N 74.35 W
Bashgah Airfield ⊠ 257d 35.40 N 51.16 E
Bashi Channel Ʊ 98 22.00 N 121.00 E
Bashikejike 110 37.30 N 85.50 E
Bashiqiao 96 31.40 N 120.22 E
Bashtīl 263c 30.05 N 31.11 E
Basi, Bhārat 113 30.36 N 76.50 E
Basi, Bhārat 113 30.41 N 76.24 E
Basiad Bay C 106 14.16 N 122.19 E
Basiano 102 1.16 S 122.50 E
Basibasy 147b 22.10 S 43.40 E
Başıbüyük 257b 40.57 N 29.08 E
Basid 75 38.07 N 72.09 E
Basilaki Island I 154 10.35 S 151.00 E
Basilan → Isabela 106 6.42 N 121.58 E
Basilan Island I 106 6.34 N 122.03 E
Basilan Peak ∧ 106 6.33 N 122.04 E
Basilan Strait Ʊ 106 6.49 N 122.05 E
Basildon 44 51.35 N 0.25 E
Basildon □[8] 250 51.35 N 0.29 E
Basile 184 30.29 N 92.36 W
Basiliano 58 46.01 N 13.06 E
Basilicata □[4] 36 40.30 N 16.10 E
Basílio 242 31.53 S 53.01 W
Basin, Mont., U.S. 192 46.16 N 112.16 W
Basin, Wyo., U.S. 192 44.23 N 108.02 W
Bäsingen ◎ 40 60.09 N 16.20 E
Basinger 210 27.23 N 81.02 W
Basingstoke 44 51.15 N 1.05 W
Basingstoke Canal ≋ 250 51.21 N 0.29 W
Basingwerk Abbey ♁[1] 252 53.17 N 3.12 W
Basin Lake ◎ 174 52.38 N 105.18 W
Basīrhāt 116 22.40 N 88.53 E
Basīrpur 113 30.35 N 73.50 E
Basīt, Ra's al- ≻ 120 35.51 N 35.48 E
Basiyingzi 94 42.05 N 121.37 E
Basjanovskij 76 58.19 N 60.44 E
Baška 36 44.58 N 14.46 E
Baskahegan Lake ◎ 178 45.30 N 67.48 W
Baskakovka 66 54.36 N 34.19 E
Başkale 118 38.02 N 44.00 E
Baskatong, Réservoir ◎[1] 180 46.48 N 75.50 W
Baškaus ≃ 76 51.09 N 87.43 E
Baškend 74 40.38 N 45.32 E
Basket Lake ◎ 174 49.43 N 92.00 W
Basking Ridge 266 40.42 N 74.33 W
Baškino 72 55.18 N 36.41 E
Baškirskaja Avtonomnaja Sovetskaja Socialističeskaja Respublika □[3] 76 54.00 N 56.00 E
Baškirskij, Zapovednik ♠ 76 53.30 N 57.58 E
Başköy 74 39.53 N 44.32 E
Baskuduk 76 49.43 N 61.32 E
Baš-Kugandy 75 42.00 N 74.39 E
Baskunčak, Ozero ◎ 70 48.12 N 46.54 E
Baslow 42 53.15 N 1.38 W
Başmakcı 120 37.54 N 30.01 E
Bašmakovo 70 53.12 N 43.02 E
Basmat 112 19.19 N 77.10 E
Bäsna 40 60.32 N 15.12 E
Başnık 120 38.07 N 40.44 E
Bāsoda 114 23.51 N 77.56 E
Basoko 142 1.14 N 23.36 E
Basoko ≃ 263b 4.19 S 15.16 E
Basoli 113 32.30 N 75.49 E
Basom 200 43.04 N 78.24 W
Basongo 142 4.20 S 20.24 E
Basora, Punt ≻ 231s 12.25 N 69.52 W
Basovizza 58 45.38 N 13.52 E
Başpınar 120 39.12 N 38.42 E
Basque Provinces → Vascongadas □[9] 34 43.00 N 2.45 W
Basra → Al-Başrah 118 30.30 N 47.47 E
Bas-Rhin □[5] 32 48.35 N 7.40 E
Bass, Îlots de II 14 27.55 S 143.26 W
Bassano 172 50.47 N 112.28 W
Bassano del Grappa 58 45.46 N 11.44 E
Bassari 140 9.15 N 0.47 E
Bassas da India ✣[2] 128 21.25 S 39.42 E
Bass Creek ≃ 206 42.37 N 89.04 W
Basse-Californie → Baja California ≻[1] 222 28.00 N 113.30 W
Bassecourt 54 47.20 N 7.15 E
Bassein 100 16.47 N 94.44 E
Bassein ≃[1] 100 15.56 N 94.18 E
Basse-Kotto □[5] 142 5.00 N 21.30 E
Bassen 48 53.04 N 9.04 E
Bassenheim 52 50.21 N 7.27 E
Bassenthwaite 42 54.41 N 3.12 W
Bassenthwaite Lake ◎ 42 54.38 N 3.13 W
Basse-Pointe 230e 14.52 N 61.07 W
Basses, Pointe des ≻ 231o 15.52 N 61.17 W
Basses-Alpes □[5] 56 44.10 N 6.00 E
Basse Santa Su 140 13.19 N 14.13 W
Basses-Pyrénées □[5] 32 43.15 N 0.50 W
Basse-Terre, Guad. 231o 16.00 N 61.44 W
Basseterre, St. K.-N. 228 17.18 N 62.43 W
Basse Terre, Trin. 231r 10.08 N 61.18 W
Basse-Terre I 231o 16.10 N 61.40 W
Bassett, Nebr., U.S. 188 42.35 N 99.32 W
Bassett, Va., U.S. 182 36.46 N 79.59 W
Bassett Creek ≃ 184 31.25 N 87.56 W
Bassetts Creek ≃ 184 31.27 N 87.55 W
Basse-Yutz 52 49.21 N 6.11 E
Bassfield 184 31.30 N 89.44 W
Bass Harbor 178 44.16 N 68.19 W
Bass Hill 264a 33.54 S 151.00 E
Bassignana 56 45.00 N 8.44 E
Bassikounou 140 15.52 N 5.57 W
Bassila 140 9.01 N 1.40 E
Bassin Des Aghlabites ⊥ 36 35.43 N 10.10 E
Bass Lake, Calif., U.S. 216 37.19 N 119.33 W
Bass Lake, Ind., U.S. 206 41.12 N 86.36 W
Bass Lake ◎, Ont., Can. 202 44.49 N 76.08 W
Bass Lake ◎, Ind., U.S. 206 41.13 N 86.36 W
Bass Lake ◎[1] 216 37.19 N 119.34 W
Bass Point ≻ 160 34.36 S 150.54 E
Bass River 176 45.25 N 63.47 W
Bass Strait Ʊ 156 39.20 S 145.30 E
Bassum 48 52.51 N 8.43 E
Basswood Lake ◎, Ont., Can. 180 46.20 N 83.23 W
Basswood Lake ◎, N.A. 180 48.06 N 91.40 W
Basta 116 21.41 N 87.03 E
Båstad 26 56.26 N 12.51 E
Basṭah 122 30.14 N 35.32 E
Bastak 118 27.14 N 54.22 E
Basṭām 118 36.29 N 55.04 E
Baštanka 68 47.24 N 32.25 E
Bastei ♠ 50 50.58 N 14.04 E
Bastelica 36 42.00 N 9.02 E
Basti 114 26.48 N 82.43 E
Bastia, Fr. 32 42.42 N 9.27 E
Bastia, It. 60 43.04 N 12.33 E
Bastian 182 37.09 N 81.09 W
Bastiglia 58 44.43 N 11.00 E
Bastimentos 226 9.21 N 82.12 W
Bastimentos, Isla I 226 9.18 N 82.08 W
Bastiões ≃ 240 6.33 S 39.29 W
Bastogne 52 50.00 N 5.43 E
Bastrop, La., U.S. 184 32.47 N 91.55 W
Bastrop, Tex., U.S. 212 30.07 N 97.19 W
Bastrop □[6] 212 33.00 N 97.18 W
Bastrop Bay C 212 29.06 N 95.11 W
Bastrop State Park ♠ 212 30.07 N 97.17 W
Bastuträsk 26 64.47 N 20.02 E
Basubāti 262b 22.47 N 88.12 E
Bāsudebpur, Bhārat 116 21.49 N 87.38 E
Bāsudebpur, Bhārat 262b 22.49 N 88.25 E
Basuo → Dongfang 100 19.05 N 108.39 E
Basuolaling ⛰ 92 38.44 N 98.20 E
Bāsūr, Jabal al- ∧[2] 132 30.34 N 30.35 E
Bāsūs 263c 30.08 N 31.13 E
Baswa 116 24.08 N 87.52 E
Basyūn 132 30.57 N 30.49 E
Bas-Zaïre □[4] 142 5.30 S 14.30 E
Bata 142 1.51 N 9.45 E
Bataan □[4] 106 14.40 N 120.25 E
Bataan, Mount ∧ 106 14.31 N 120.28 E
Bataan Peninsula ≻[1] 106 14.40 N 120.25 E
Batabanó 230p 22.43 N 82.17 W
Batabanó, Golfo de C 230p 22.15 N 82.30 W
Batac 106 18.05 N 120.35 E
Batad 106 11.25 N 123.06 E
Batagaj 64 67.38 N 134.38 E
Batagaj-Alyta 64 67.48 N 130.25 E
Batag Island I 106 12.38 N 125.04 E
Batagol 78 52.22 N 100.45 E
Bataguaçu 245 21.42 S 52.22 W
Batai Kandao)(110 33.23 N 70.19 E
Bataiporã 245 22.20 S 53.17 W
Batajsk 73 47.10 N 39.44 E
Batak 38 41.57 N 24.13 E
Batak, Jazovir ◎[1] 38 41.59 N 24.11 E
Batakan 102 4.05 S 114.38 E
Batāla 113 31.48 N 75.12 E
Batalha, Bra. 240 9.41 S 37.08 W
Batalha, Bra. 240 4.01 S 42.05 W
Batalha, Port. 34 39.39 N 8.50 W
Batalha ≃ 245 21.42 S 49.10 W
Bataly 76 52.52 N 62.00 E
Batam, Pulau I 102 1.05 N 104.03 E
Batama, S.S.S.R. 78 53.53 N 101.36 E
Batama, Zaïre 144 0.56 N 26.39 E
Batamaj 64 63.31 N 129.27 E
Batamšinskij 76 50.36 N 58.16 E
Batan, Pil. 106 11.35 N 122.30 E
Batan, Zhg. 88 34.10 N 120.04 E
Batanagar 116 22.31 N 88.15 E
Batanes □[4] 106 20.30 N 121.50 E
Batang, Indon. 105a 6.55 S 109.45 E
Batang, Zhg. 92 30.02 N 99.02 E
Batangafo 142 7.18 N 18.18 E
Batangas 106 13.45 N 121.03 E
Batangas □[4] 106 13.50 N 121.00 E
Batangas Bay C 106 13.43 N 121.00 E
Batangbatangdaya 105a 6.56 S 113.59 E
Batang Berjuntai 104 3.23 N 101.25 E
Batanghari ≃ 102 1.16 S 104.05 E
Batang Kali 104 3.28 N 101.38 E
Batangtoru 104 1.29 N 99.03 E
Batan Island I, Pil. 98 20.26 N 121.58 E
Batan Island I, Pil. 106 13.15 N 124.00 E
Batan Islands II 98 20.30 N 121.50 E
Batanta, Pulau I 154 0.50 S 130.40 E
Batas ≃ 277a 22.44 S 43.24 W
Batas Island I 106 11.10 N 119.36 E
Bátaszék 30 46.12 N 18.44 E
Batatais 245 20.53 S 47.37 W
Batatuba 246 23.04 S 46.25 W
Batavia, Arg. 242 34.47 S 65.41 W
Batavia, Ill., U.S. 206 41.51 N 88.19 W
Batavia, Iowa, U.S. 180 41.00 N 92.10 W
Batavia, Mich., U.S. 206 41.55 N 85.06 W
Batavia, N.Y., U.S. 200 43.00 N 78.11 W
Batavia, Ohio, U.S. 208 39.05 N 84.11 W
Batawa 202 44.10 N 77.36 W
Batbatan Island I 106 11.28 N 121.55 E
Batcengel 78 47.47 N 101.58 E
Batchawana ≃ 180 46.55 N 84.32 W
Batchawana Mountain ∧ 180 47.04 N 84.24 W
Batchelor 154 13.04 S 131.01 E
Bătdâmbâng 100 13.06 N 103.12 E
Bateau Channel Ʊ 202 44.10 N 76.31 W
Bate Bay C 264a 34.04 S 151.12 E
Bateckij 66 58.39 N 30.19 E
Bate Heath 252 53.19 N 2.28 W
Bateia 246 22.20 S 45.49 W
Batemans Bay 156 35.43 S 150.11 E
Batenbrock ⬩[8] 253 51.31 N 6.57 E
Batepito 222 30.49 N 109.12 W
Bates, Mount ∧ 164c 29.01 S 167.56 E
Batesburg 182 33.54 N 81.33 W
Bates Creek ≃ 190 42.41 N 106.37 W
Bates Range ⛰ 152 27.25 S 121.13 E
Batesville, Ark., U.S. 184 35.46 N 91.39 W
Batesville, Ind., U.S. 208 39.18 N 85.13 W
Batesville, Miss., U.S. 184 34.18 N 90.00 W
Batesville, Tex., U.S. 186 28.57 N 99.37 W
Bath, Ont., Can. 202 44.11 N 76.47 W
Bath, Eng., U.K. 44 51.23 N 2.22 W
Bath, Ill., U.S. 209 40.11 N 90.08 W
Bath, Maine, U.S. 178 43.55 N 69.49 W
Bath, Mich., U.S. 206 42.49 N 84.27 W
Bath, N.Y., U.S. 200 42.20 N 77.19 W
Bath, Ohio, U.S. 204 41.11 N 81.38 W
Bath, Pa., U.S. 198 40.44 N 75.24 W
Bath □[6] 208 38.14 N 83.48 W
Batha □[5] 136 14.00 N 19.00 E
Batha ≃ 136 12.47 N 17.34 E
Bath Addition 275 40.06 N 74.52 W
Bathgate, Scot., U.K. 42 55.55 N 3.39 W
Bathgate, N. Dak., U.S. 188 48.53 N 97.29 W
Bathsheba 231g 13.13 N 59.31 W
Bathurst, Austl. 156 33.25 S 149.35 E
Bathurst, N.B., Can. 176 47.36 N 65.39 W
Bathurst → Banjul, Gam. 140 13.28 N 16.39 W
Bathurst, S. Afr. 148 33.30 S 26.50 E
Bathurst, Cape ≻ 166 70.35 N 128.00 W
Bathurst, Lake ◎ 160 35.04 S 149.44 E
Bathurst Inlet 166 66.50 N 108.01 W
Bathurst Inlet C 166 68.10 N 108.50 W
Bathurst Island I, Austl. 154 11.37 S 130.23 E
Bathurst Island I, N.W. Ter., Can. 16 76.00 N 100.30 W
Bathurst Island Mission 154 11.45 S 130.38 E
Bati 134 11.10 N 40.02 E
Batia 140 10.54 N 1.29 E
Batiāgarh 114 24.07 N 79.21 E
Batibla 142 5.56 N 21.09 E
Batié 140 9.53 N 2.55 W
Bāṭin, Wādī al- ∨ 118 29.35 N 47.00 E
Batina 38 45.51 N 18.51 E
Batiquitos Lagoon C 218 33.05 N 117.18 W
Batīr 122 31.16 N 35.42 E
Batırga 120 36.24 N 36.11 E
Batiscan ≃ 196 46.31 N 72.15 W
Batiste Creek ≃ 212 30.04 N 94.28 W
Batkanu 140 9.05 N 12.25 W
Batken 75 40.03 N 70.50 E
Batlajsagyr, Peski ⬩[2] 70 47.20 N 48.40 E
Batley 42 53.44 N 1.37 W
Batlow 161b 35.31 S 148.09 E
Batman 120 37.52 N 41.07 E
Batna 138 35.34 N 6.11 E
Batna □[5] 138 35.00 N 6.00 E
Batnorov 78 47.57 N 111.27 E
Batō, Nihon 84 36.44 N 140.10 E
Bato, Pil. 106 10.20 N 124.47 E
Ba-to, Viet. 100 14.46 N 108.44 E
Bato, Lake ◎ 106 13.19 N 123.21 E
Batoala 142 0.48 N 13.27 E
Batoche Rectory National Historic Site ⊥ 174 52.41 N 106.02 W
Batoka 144 16.47 S 27.15 E
Baton Rouge 184 30.23 N 91.11 W
Batoque 240 4.24 S 40.22 W
Batorampon Point ≻ 106 7.07 N 121.54 E
Batoti 113 33.06 N 75.19 E
Batouri 142 4.26 N 14.22 E
Batovi 245 15.53 S 53.24 W
Batovi ≃ 245 11.56 S 53.36 W
Baṭrah 132 31.10 N 31.27 E
Ba-tri 100 10.02 N 106.36 E
Bātsawul 110 34.15 N 70.52 E
Batson 212 30.15 N 94.37 W
Batsto ≃ 275 39.39 N 74.39 W
Batsto, Skit Branch ≃ 275 39.46 N 74.41 W
Batsto Village ⊥ 198 39.39 N 74.39 W
Battaglia Terme 58 45.17 N 11.47 E
Battambang → Bătdâmbâng 100 13.06 N 103.12 E
Battenberg 52 51.01 N 8.38 E
Batten Kill ≃ 200 43.06 N 73.35 W
Batterie, Pointe de la ≻ 230e 14.44 N 60.54 W
Bätterkinden 54 47.08 N 7.32 E
Battersea ⬩[8] 250 51.28 N 0.10 W
Batticaloa 112 7.43 N 81.42 E
Battice 52 50.39 N 5.49 E
Battin 214 45.29 N 122.34 W
Battle 44 50.55 N 0.29 E
Battle ≃ 174 52.43 N 108.15 W
Battle Creek, Iowa, U.S. 188 42.19 N 95.36 W
Battle Creek, Mich., U.S. 206 42.19 N 85.11 W
Battle Creek, Nebr., U.S. 188 42.00 N 97.36 W
Battle Creek ≃, N.A. 192 48.36 N 109.11 W
Battle Creek ≃, Calif., U.S. 194 40.21 N 122.11 W
Battle Creek ≃, Idaho, U.S. 192 42.14 N 116.32 W
Battle Creek ≃, Mich., U.S. 206 42.19 N 85.12 W
Battle Creek ≃, Tex., U.S. 186 32.50 N 98.58 W
Battle Creek, North Fork ≃ 194 40.26 N 122.00 W
Battle Creek, South Fork ≃ 194 40.26 N 122.00 W
Battlefields 144 18.31 S 29.52 E
Battle Green ⊥ 273 42.27 N 71.14 W
Battle Ground, Ind., U.S. 206 40.31 N 86.50 W
Battle Ground, Wash., U.S. 214 45.47 N 122.32 W
Battle Harbour 166 52.16 N 55.35 W
Battle Lake 188 46.17 N 95.43 W
Battlement Mesa ∧ 190 39.20 N 108.00 W
Battlemount 148 26.57 S 23.46 E
Battle Mountain 194 40.38 N 116.56 W
Battle Mountain ∧ 190 41.02 N 107.16 W
Battlesbridge 250 51.37 N 0.34 E
Battonya 30 46.17 N 21.01 E
Battuello 256b 45.27 N 8.56 E
Batu 105a 7.52 S 112.31 E
Batu ∧ 134 6.55 N 39.46 E
Batu, Kepulauan II 100 0.18 S 98.28 E
Batuan 106 12.25 N 123.47 E
Batu Arang 104 3.19 N 101.28 E
Batuata, Pulau I 102 6.12 S 122.42 E
Batuata, Tanjung ≻ 105b 9.37 S 120.29 E
Batu-batu 102 4.09 S 119.52 E
Batu Berinchang, Gunong ∧ 104 4.31 N 101.23 E
Batubetumpang 102 2.53 S 106.09 E
Batubrok, Bukit ∧ 102 1.10 N 114.36 E
Batuc 222 29.15 N 109.44 W
Batu Caves 104 3.14 N 101.40 E
Batudaka, Pulau I 102 0.28 S 121.48 E
Batu Enam 104 2.35 N 102.43 E
Batu Gajah 104 4.28 N 101.03 E
Batui 102 1.17 S 122.33 E
Batui, Pegunungan ⛰ 102 1.15 S 122.10 E
Batuidu 102 10.38 S 123.25 E
Batukau, Bukit ∧ 105b 8.20 S 115.05 E
Batukelau 102 0.48 N 115.01 E
Batu Laut 104 2.41 N 101.31 E
Batulicin 102 3.27 S 116.00 E
Batumata Point ≻ 154 10.17 S 148.57 E
Batumelinggang 104 3.50 N 98.25 E
Batumi 74 41.38 N 41.38 E
Batu Pahat (Bandar Penggaram) 104 1.51 N 102.56 E
Batupanjang 104 1.43 N 101.31 E
Batu Puteh, Gunong ∧ 104 4.13 N 101.27 E
Batuputih 102 1.24 N 118.29 E
Batura ∧ 113 36.31 N 74.30 E
Baturaja 102 4.08 S 104.10 E
Batu Rakit 104 5.27 N 103.03 E
Baturetno 105a 7.59 S 110.56 E
Baturin 68 51.21 N 32.51 E
Baturino, S.S.S.R. 76 57.48 N 85.12 E
Baturino, S.S.S.R. 255b 55.35 N 37.31 E
Baturinskaja 68 45.47 N 39.22 E
Baturité 240 4.20 S 38.53 W
Baturité, Serra de ⛰ 240 4.15 S 39.05 W
Baturotok 105b 8.42 S 117.10 E
Baturusa 102 2.02 S 106.07 E
Batusangkar 102 0.27 S 100.35 E
Batutinggi 102 1.55 S 113.19 E
Bat Yam 122 32.01 N 34.45 E
Batyrevo 70 55.04 N 47.38 E
Batyr-Mala, Ozero ◎ 70 47.35 N 44.45 E
Bau 102 1.25 N 110.08 E
Baú, Igarapé ≃ 240 7.26 S 54.47 W
Bauang 106 16.31 N 120.20 E
Baubašata, Gory ⛰ 75 41.20 N 72.45 E
Baubau 102 5.28 S 122.38 E
Bauchi 140 10.19 N 9.50 E
Baud 32 47.52 N 3.01 W
Baudette 180 48.43 N 94.36 W
Baudh 110 20.50 N 84.19 E
Baudó ≃ 236 4.57 N 77.22 W
Baudó, Serranía de ⛰ 236 6.00 N 77.05 W
Baudouin Stadium ♠ 263b 4.20 S 15.20 E
Baudouinville 144 7.04 S 29.46 E
Baudour 46 50.29 N 3.49 E
Bauernschaft 253 51.34 N 6.33 E
Bauerstown 269b 40.30 N 79.59 W
Baugé 32 47.33 N 0.06 W
Baugo Creek ≃ 206 41.40 N 86.04 W
Baukau ⬩[8] 253 51.33 N 7.12 E
Baúl, Cerro ∧ 224 17.38 N 100.19 W
Bauld, Cape ≻ 176 51.38 N 55.25 W
Baulkham Hills 264a 33.46 S 151.00 E
Baulmes 54 46.48 N 6.32 E
Bauma 54 47.23 N 8.53 E
Baumann, Pic ∧ 140 6.52 N 0.46 E
Baumberg 253 51.07 N 6.54 E
Baume ≃ 56 44.26 N 4.20 E
Baume-les-Dames 54 47.21 N 6.22 E
Baumholder 52 49.37 N 7.20 E
Baumschulenweg ⬩[8] 254a 52.28 N 13.29 E
Baun 102 10.18 S 123.43 E
Baunach 52 49.59 N 10.50 E
Baunach ≃ 52 50.14 N 10.28 E
Baunatal 52 51.16 N 9.25 E
Baunei 36 40.02 N 9.40 E
Baunt 78 55.16 N 113.08 E
Baunt, Ozero ◎ 78 55.12 N 113.00 E
Bāuphal 116 22.25 N 90.33 E
Baure 140 12.50 N 8.45 E
Baures 238 13.35 S 63.35 W
Bāuria 116 22.29 N 88.10 E
Bauru 245 22.19 S 49.04 W
Baús 245 18.19 S 53.10 W
Bausendorf 52 50.01 N 6.59 E
Bausenhagen 253 51.31 N 7.48 E
Bauska 66 56.24 N 24.14 E
Bauta 230p 22.59 N 82.33 W
Bauta □[7] 276b 22.59 N 82.33 W
Bautino 74 44.33 N 50.15 E
Bautzen 50 51.11 N 14.26 E
Bauxite 184 34.33 N 92.30 W
Bauya 140 8.11 N 12.34 W
Bavans 54 47.29 N 6.44 E
Bavari 56 44.26 N 9.01 E
Bavaria → Bayern □[9] 30 49.00 N 11.30 E
Bavarian Alps → Bayerische Alpen ⛰ 58 47.30 N 11.00 E
Bavay 46 50.18 N 3.47 E
Båven ◎ 40 59.01 N 16.56 E
Baveno 54 45.55 N 8.30 E
Baviaanskloofberge ⛰ 148 33.35 S 24.10 E
Bavilliers 54 47.37 N 6.50 E
Bavispe 222 30.24 N 108.50 W
Bavispe, Río de ≃ 222 29.15 N 109.11 W
Bavleny 70 56.24 N 39.34 E
Bavly 70 54.25 N 53.17 E
Bavnhöj ∧[2] 41 55.55 N 10.07 E
Bavtugaj 74 43.11 N 46.49 E
Baw 100 23.19 N 95.50 E
Bāwal 114 28.05 N 76.35 E
Bawal, Pulau I 102 2.44 S 110.06 E
Bāwāli 262b 22.25 N 88.12 E
Bawang 105a 7.06 S 109.55 E
Baw Baw, Mount ∧ 159 37.50 S 146.17 E
Baw Beese Lake ◎ 206 41.54 N 84.36 W
Bawdeswell 44 52.45 N 1.01 E
Bawdwin 100 23.06 N 97.18 E
Bawean, Pulau I 105a 5.46 S 112.40 E
Baweigang 96 31.57 N 120.14 E
Bawku 140 11.05 N 0.14 W
Bawlake 100 19.11 N 97.21 E
Bawmi 100 17.19 N 94.35 E
Bawn 134 10.12 N 43.02 E
Bawtry 42 53.26 N 1.01 W
Baxenden 252 53.44 N 2.20 W
Baxian, Zhg. 95 39.06 N 116.23 E
Baxian, Zhg. 97 29.23 N 106.32 E
Baxiantong 79 43.08 N 121.03 E
Baxley 182 31.47 N 82.21 W
Baxter, Iowa, U.S. 180 41.49 N 93.09 W
Baxter, Minn., U.S. 180 46.20 N 94.16 W
Baxter, Tenn., U.S. 184 36.09 N 85.38 W
Baxter Estates 266 40.50 N 73.42 W
Baxter Springs 188 37.02 N 94.44 W
Baxter State Park ♠ 178 46.00 N 68.58 W
Baxterville 184 31.06 N 89.36 W
Bay 184 35.45 N 90.34 W
Bay, Laguna de ◎ 259f 14.28 N 121.07 E
Baya, Zaïre 142 4.57 N 19.43 E
Baya, Zaïre 144 11.52 S 27.27 E
Bayāḍah, Wādī al- ∨ 136 26.08 N 18.35 E
Bayāḍ an-Naṣārā 132 29.04 N 31.08 E
Bayag 106 18.16 N 121.02 E
Bay al-Kabīr, Wādī ∨ 136 31.15 N 15.57 E
Bayambang 106 15.49 N 120.27 E
Bayamo 230p 20.23 N 76.39 W
Bayamo ≃ 230p 20.34 N 76.44 W
Bayamón 230m 18.24 N 66.09 W
Bayan, Indon. 105b 8.16 S 116.26 E
Bayan, Zhg. 79 46.05 N 127.24 E
Bāyan, Band-e ⛰ 110 34.20 N 65.30 E
Bayāna 114 26.54 N 77.17 E
Bayanbayanan 259f 14.39 N 121.06 E
Bayanchagan 79 47.19 N 124.03 E
Bayanchaganmiao 79 48.35 N 119.49 E
Bayang 106 7.48 N 124.12 E
Bayanga 142 2.53 N 16.19 E
Bayange 92 39.19 N 107.31 E
Bayanhaote 92 38.50 N 105.41 E
Bayanheshuomiao 79 48.51 N 119.46 E
Bayanjie 79 49.36 N 124.37 E
Bayankalashanmai ⛰ 92 33.48 N 98.10 E
Bayanluke 79 50.52 N 119.33 E
Bayannaobao 92 39.44 N 107.40 E
Bayano ≃ 236 9.00 N 79.06 W
Bayantala 79 43.44 N 123.16 E
Bayard, Fla., U.S. 182 30.09 N 81.31 W
Bayard, Iowa, U.S. 188 41.51 N 94.33 W
Bayard, Nebr., U.S. 188 41.45 N 103.20 W
Bayard, N. Mex., U.S. 190 32.46 N 108.08 W
Bayard, Ohio, U.S. 204 40.46 N 81.04 W
Bayard, W. Va., U.S. 178 39.16 N 79.22 W
Bayard, Col)(56 44.37 N 6.05 E
Bayard Cutting Arboretum ♠ 266 40.45 N 73.10 W
Bayat, Indon. 102 2.06 S 103.38 E
Bayat, Tür. 120 40.39 N 34.15 E
Bayat, Tür. 120 38.59 N 30.56 E
Bayawan 106 9.22 N 122.48 E
Baybay 106 10.41 N 124.48 E
Bayberry 200 43.08 N 76.13 W
Bayboro 182 35.09 N 76.46 W
Bay Bulls 176 47.19 N 52.49 W
Bayburt 120 40.16 N 40.15 E
Bay Center 214 46.38 N 123.57 W
Bay City, Mich., U.S. 180 43.36 N 83.53 W
Bay City, Oreg., U.S. 214 45.31 N 123.53 W
Bay City, Tex., U.S. 212 28.59 N 95.58 W
Bay Creek ≃, Ill., U.S. 184 37.16 N 88.31 W
Bay Creek ≃, Ill., U.S. 209 39.20 N 90.46 W
Bayḍā', Bi'r ⊤[4] 132 29.45 N 32.13 E
Bay de Verde 176 48.05 N 52.54 W
Bay du Nord ≃ 176 47.44 N 55.25 W
Baye, Cap ≻ 165f 20.57 S 165.25 E
Bayel 54 48.12 N 4.47 E
Bayerische Alpen ⛰ 58 47.30 N 11.00 E
Bayern □[3] 30 49.00 N 11.30 E
Bayern □[9] 30 49.00 N 11.30 E
Bayers Creek ≃ 274a 43.00 N 79.02 W
Bayeuen 104 4.36 N 97.53 E
Bayeux, Bra. 240 7.08 S 34.56 W
Bayeux, Fr. 32 49.16 N 0.42 W
Bay Farm Island I 272 37.43 N 122.14 W
Bayfield, Colo., U.S. 190 37.14 N 107.36 W
Bayfield, Wis., U.S. 180 46.49 N 90.49 W
Bayfield, Île I 176 51.13 N 58.23 W
Bayfield Ridge ∧ 180 46.45 N 91.25 W
Bayford 250 51.46 N 0.06 W
'Bayh 122 33.44 N 35.31 E
Bayḥā al-Qiṣād 134 14.48 N 45.43 E
Bay Harbor Islands 210 25.53 N 80.08 W
Bay Head 198 40.04 N 74.03 W
Bayiji 88 34.18 N 117.41 E
Bayındır 120 38.13 N 27.40 E
Bayinguoleng Zizhiziou □[4] 76 42.30 N 85.00 E
Bayingzi 94 41.28 N 120.46 E
Baykal, Lake ◎ 78 53.00 N 107.40 E
Baykonur → Bajkonyr 76 47.50 N 66.03 E
Bay L'Argent 176 47.33 N 54.54 W
Bayley Point ≻ 154 16.56 S 139.02 E
Baylis 209 39.44 N 90.54 W
Bay Meadows Race Track ♠ 272 37.32 N 122.18 W
Bay Minette 184 30.53 N 87.47 W
Baynūnah ⬩[1] 118 23.50 N 52.45 E
Bayo 34 43.09 N 8.58 W
Bayombong 106 16.29 N 121.09 E
Bayon 54 48.29 N 6.19 E
Bayona 34 42.07 N 8.51 W
Bayonne, Fr. 32 43.29 N 1.29 W
Bayonne, N.J., U.S. 200 40.41 N 74.07 W
Bayonne ≃ 196 46.05 N 73.10 W
Bayonne Bridge ⬩[5] 266 40.38 N 74.09 W
Bayons 56 44.20 N 6.10 E
Bayou La Batre 184 30.24 N 88.15 W
Bayóvar 238 5.50 S 81.03 W
Bay Park 266 40.38 N 73.40 W
Bay Point ≻ 206 41.44 N 83.25 W
Bayport, Fla., U.S. 210 28.33 N 83.39 W
Bay Port, Mich., U.S. 180 43.51 N 83.23 W
Bayport, Minn., U.S. 180 45.01 N 92.47 W
Bayport, N.Y., U.S. 200 40.44 N 73.03 W
Bayraktar 74 39.41 N 42.08 E
Bayramiç 120 39.48 N 26.37 E
Bayramören 120 40.57 N 33.12 E
Bayreuth 30 49.57 N 11.35 E
Bay Ridge 198 38.56 N 76.28 W
Bay Ridge ⬩[8] 266 40.37 N 74.02 W
Bay Ridge Channel Ʊ 266 40.39 N 74.02 W
Bayrischzell 58 47.40 N 12.00 E
Bay Roberts 176 47.36 N 53.16 W
Bayrūt (Beirut) 120 33.53 N 35.30 E
Bayrūt □[4] 122 33.56 N 35.30 E
Bays, Lake of ◎ 202 45.15 N 79.04 W
Bay Saint Louis 184 30.19 N 89.20 W
Bay Shore 200 40.44 N 73.15 W
Bayshore Gardens 210 27.26 N 82.35 W
Bayside, Ont., Can. 202 44.07 N 77.30 W
Bayside, Mass., U.S. 273 42.18 N 70.53 W
Bayside, Wis., U.S. 206 43.11 N 87.54 W
Bayside ⬩[8] 266 40.46 N 73.46 W
Bay Springs 184 31.53 N 89.17 W
Bayswater 264b 37.51 S 145.16 E
Bayswater North 264b 37.49 S 145.17 E
Bayt ad-Dīn 122 33.42 N 35.35 E
Bayt ad-Din ⊥ 122 33.41 N 35.34 E
Bayt al-Faqīh 134 14.32 N 43.20 E
Bayt Ḥānūm 122 31.32 N 34.33 E
Bayt Jālā 122 31.43 N 35.11 E
Bayt Jinn 122 33.19 N 35.53 E
Bayt Laḥm (Bethlehem) 122 31.43 N 35.12 E
Bayt Mirī 122 33.52 N 35.36 E
Baytown 212 29.44 N 94.58 W
Bayt Sāḥūr 122 31.42 N 35.13 E
Bayt Sīrā 122 31.53 N 35.03 E
Bayuan ≃ 106 9.22 N 122.48 E
Bayunglencir 102 2.03 S 103.41 E
Bayview, Austl. 264a 33.40 S 151.18 E
Bay View, N.Z. 162 39.25 S 176.53 E
Bay View, N.Y., U.S. 200 42.47 N 78.51 W
Bay View, Ohio, U.S. 204 41.28 N 82.50 W
Bayview ⬩[8] 272 37.44 N 122.23 W
Bay Village 204 41.29 N 81.55 W
Bayville, N.J., U.S. 198 39.55 N 74.09 W
Bayville, N.Y., U.S. 200 40.54 N 73.33 W
Baywood Park 216 35.20 N 120.50 W
Bayyāḍah, Ra's al- ≻ 122 33.10 N 35.10 E
Bayyā'īyah al-Kabīrah 120 35.42 N 37.09 E
Bayyūḍah ⊤[4] 130 17.32 N 32.07 E
Bayzo 140 13.52 N 4.45 E
Baza 34 37.29 N 2.46 W
Baza, Sierra de ⛰ 34 37.15 N 2.45 W
Bazainville 251 48.48 N 1.40 E
Bazalija 68 49.43 N 26.27 E
Bazar 78 53.58 N 116.05 E
Bazarčaj 74 39.40 N 45.48 E
Bazar-d'uzi, Gora ∧ 74 41.13 N 47.51 E
Bāzār-e Panjvā'ī 110 31.32 N 65.28 E
Bazargic → Tolbuhin 38 43.34 N 27.50 E
Bazar-Kurgan 75 41.02 N 72.45 E
Bazarnyje Mataki 70 54.56 N 49.56 E
Bazarnyj Karabulak 70 52.16 N 46.25 E
Bazarnyj Syzgan 70 53.45 N 45.46 E
Bazarovo 72 54.47 N 38.10 E
Bazaršolan 70 49.04 N 51.56 E
Bazartobe 70 49.23 N 51.50 E
Bazaruto, Ilha do I 146 21.40 S 35.28 E
Bazas 32 44.26 N 0.13 W
Bazavluk ≃ 68 47.34 N 34.04 E
Bazdār 110 26.21 N 65.03 E
Bazeilles 52 49.40 N 4.59 E
Bazemont 251 48.56 N 1.52 E
Bazetta 204 41.20 N 80.47 W
Bazhong 92 31.51 N 106.39 E
Bazi, Zhg. 90 24.32 N 114.10 E
Bazi, Zhg. 90 24.46 N 113.10 E
Baziège 32 43.27 N 1.37 E
Bažigan 74 44.33 N 45.41 E
Bazine 188 38.27 N 99.42 W
Baziqiao 96 32.07 N 119.52 E

Symbols in the index entries represent the broad categories identified in the key at the right. Symbols with superior numbers (⛰[2]) identify subcategories (see complete key on page I · 26).

Kartensymbole in dem Registerverzeichnis stellen die rechts in Schlüssel erklärten Kategorien dar. Symbole mit hochgestellten Ziffern (⛰[2]) bezeichnen Unterabteilungen einer Kategorie (vgl. vollständiger Schlüssel auf Seite I · 26).

Los símbolos incluídos en el texto del índice representan las grandes categorias identificadas con la clave a la derecha. Los símbolos con numeros en su parte superior (⛰[2]) identifican las subcategorías (véase la clave completa en la página I · 26).

Les symboles de l'index représentent les catégories indiquées dans la légende à droite. Les symboles suivis d'un indice (⛰[2]) représentent des sous-catégories (voir légende complète à la page I · 26).

Os símbolos incluídos no texto do índice representam as grandes categorias identificadas com a chave à direita. Os símbolos com números em sua parte superior (⛰[2]) identificam as subcategorias (veja-se a chave completa à página I · 26).

∧ Mountain	Berg	Montaña	Montagne	Montanha
⛰ Mountains	Berge	Montañas	Montagnes	Montanhas
)(Pass	Pass	Paso	Col	Passo
∨ Valley, Canyon	Tal, Cañon	Valle, Cañón	Vallée, Canyon	Vale, Canhão
≚ Plain	Ebene	Llano	Plaine	Planície
≻ Cape	Kap	Cabo	Cap	Cabo
I Island	Insel	Isla	Île	Ilha
II Islands	Inseln	Islas	Îles	Ilhas
⊥ Other Topographic Features	Andere Topographische Objekte	Otros Elementos Topográficos	Autres données topographiques	Outros Elementos Topográficos

≃ River	Fluss	Río	Rivière	Rio
☰ Canal	Kanal	Canal	Canal	Canal
⌞ Waterfall, Rapids	Wasserfall, Stromschnellen	Cascada, Rápidos	Chute d'eau, Rapides	Cascata, Rápidos
⊔ Strait	Meeresstrasse	Estrecho	Détroit	Estreito
C Bay, Gulf	Bucht, Golf	Bahía, Golfo	Baie, Golfe	Baía, Golfo
⊜ Lake, Lakes	See, Seen	Lago, Lagos	Lac, Lacs	Lago, Lagos
⚌ Swamp	Sumpf	Pantano	Marais	Pântano
⊽ Ice Features, Glacier	Eis- und Gletscherformen	Accidentes Glaciales	Formes glaciaires	Acidentes Glaciares
⊸ Other Hydrographic Features	Andere Hydrographische Objekte	Otros Elementos Hidrográficos	Autres données hydrographiques	Outros Elementos Hidrográficos

⊹ Submarine Features	Untermeerische Objekte	Accidentes Submarinos	Formes de relief sous-marin	Acidentes Submarinos
□ Political Unit	Politische Einheit	Unidad Politica	Entité politique	Unidade Política
☗ Cultural Institution	Kulturelle Institution	Institución Cultural	Institution culturelle	Instituição Cultural
⊥ Historical Site	Historische Stätte	Sitio Histórico	Site historique	Sitio Histórico
♠ Recreational Site	Erholungs- und Ferienort	Sitio de Recreo	Centre de loisirs	Sítio de Lazer
⊠ Airport	Flughafen	Aeropuerto	Aéroport	Aeroporto
■ Military Installation	Militäranlage	Instalación Militar	Installation militaire	Instalação Militar
⊸ Miscellaneous	Verschiedenes	Misceláneo	Divers	Miscelânea

ENGLISH | DEUTSCH

Name / Name	Page / Seite	Lat. / Breite	Long. / Länge E = Ost

Symbols in the index entries represent the broad categories identified in the key at the right. Symbols with superior numbers (∧∧[2]) identify subcategories (see complete key on page I · 26).

Kartensymbole in dem Registerverzeichnis stellen die rechts in Schlüssel erklärten Kategorien dar. Symbole mit hochgestellten Ziffern (∧∧[2]) bezeichnen Unterabteilungen einer Kategorie (vgl. vollständiger Schlüssel auf Seite I · 26).

Los símbolos incluídos en el texto del índice representan las grandes categorias identificadas con la clave a la derecha. Los símbolos con numeros en su parte superior (∧∧[2]) identifican las subcategorías (véase la clave completa en la página I · 26).

Les symboles de l'index représentent les catégories indiquées dans la légende à droite. Les symboles suivis d'un indice (∧∧[2]) représentent des sous-catégories (voir légende complète à la page I · 26).

Os símbolos incluídos no texto do índice representam as grandes categorias identificadas com a chave à direita. Os símbolos com números em sua parte superior (∧∧[2]) identificam as subcategorias (veja-se a chave completa à página I · 26).

∧ Mountain	Berg	Montaña	Montagne	Montanha
∧∧ Mountains	Berge	Montañas	Montagnes	Montanhas
)(Pass	Pass	Paso	Col	Passo
∨ Valley, Canyon	Tal, Cañon	Valle, Cañón	Vallée, Canyon	Vale, Canhão
≃ Plain	Ebene	Llano	Plaine	Planície
› Cape	Kap	Cabo	Cap	Cabo
I Island	Insel	Isla	Île	Ilha
II Islands	Inseln	Islas	Îles	Ilhas
● Other Topographic Features	Andere Topographische Objekte	Otros Elementos Topográficos	Autres données topographiques	Outros Elementos Topográficos

ESPAÑOL

Nombre	Página	Lat.°′	Long.°′ W=Oeste
Beregovo	68	48.13 N	22.39 E
Beregovoj	76	55.12 N	73.12 E
Bereguardo	56	45.15 N	9.01 E
Bereka ≃	68	49.12 N	36.59 E
Bereketli	120	40.31 N	37.18 E
Bereku	144	4.27 S	35.44 E
Berekua	230d	15.14 N	61.19 W
Berekum	140	7.27 N	2.37 W
Bérem	142	7.33 N	13.55 E
Beren, Liman ⊜	70	46.52 N	44.55 E
Berenda Slough ≃	216	37.00 N	120.29 W
Berendejevo	72	56.36 N	39.01 E
Berendža	79	54.35 N	136.18 E
Berens ≃	174	52.21 N	97.02 W
Berens Island I	174	52.18 N	97.17 W
Berens River	174	52.22 N	97.02 W
Bere Regis	44	50.46 N	2.14 W
Beresford, Austl.	156	29.14 S	136.40 E
Beresford, N.B., Can.	176	47.42 N	65.42 W
Beresford, S. Dak., U.S.	188	43.05 N	96.47 W
Beresina → Berezina ≃	66	52.33 N	30.14 E
Berestečko	68	50.23 N	25.07 E
Bereşti	38	46.06 N	27.53 E
Beretăul (Berettyó) ≃	38	46.59 N	21.07 E
Berettyó (Beretăul) ≃	38	46.59 N	21.07 E
Berettyóújfalu	30	47.14 N	21.32 E
Berevo, Madag.	147b	19.44 S	44.58 E
Berevo, Madag.	147b	17.14 S	44.17 E
Berezajka	66	57.59 N	33.54 E
Berezan'	68	50.19 N	31.30 E
Berezanskaja	68	45.43 N	39.34 E
Berežany	68	49.27 N	24.56 E
Berezdov	68	50.27 N	27.05 E
Berezina ≃, S.S.S.R.	66	53.48 N	25.59 E
Berezina ≃, S.S.S.R.	66	52.33 N	30.14 E
Berezino, S.S.S.R.	66	53.49 N	28.59 E
Berezino, S.S.S.R.	66	54.54 N	28.12 E
Berezino, S.S.S.R.	68	46.14 N	29.12 E
Berezino, S.S.S.R.	70	50.06 N	48.52 E
Berezna	68	51.34 N	31.47 E
Berezn'agi	68	49.59 N	41.06 E
Berezn'aki, S.S.S.R.	68	49.09 N	31.57 E
Berezn'aki, S.S.S.R.	68	49.51 N	33.01 E
Bereznegovatoje	68	47.20 N	32.49 E
Berežnica	68	51.27 N	26.27 E
Bereznik	24	62.51 N	42.40 E
Berezniki	76	59.24 N	56.46 E
Berford Lake ⊜	202	44.48 N	81.11 W
Berg, B.R.D.	58	47.58 N	11.21 E
Berg, Lux.	52	49.49 N	6.05 E
Berg, Nor.	24	69.26 N	17.15 E
Berg, Öst.	58	46.45 N	13.09 E
Berga, D.D.R.	50	50.45 N	12.10 E
Berga, D.D.R.	50	51.27 N	11.00 E
Berga, Esp.	34	42.06 N	1.51 E
Berga, Sve.	40	59.21 N	16.26 E
Bergama	120	39.07 N	27.11 E
Bergambacht	48	51.56 N	4.46 E
Bergamo	56	45.41 N	9.43 E
Bergamo □[4]	58	45.50 N	9.48 E
Bergantín	236	10.01 N	64.22 W
Bergantino	58	45.05 N	11.15 E
Bergbaumuseum ⩡	253	51.29 N	7.13 E
Bergby	26	60.56 N	17.02 E
Berge, B.R.D.	48	52.37 N	7.44 E
Berge, B.R.D.	253	51.21 N	7.22 E
Berge, D.D.R.	50	53.15 N	11.50 E
Bergedorf ◆[8]	48	53.29 N	10.13 E
Bergei Λ[2]	253	51.13 N	7.46 E
Bergeijk	48	51.19 N	5.22 E
Bergen, B.R.D.	48	52.48 N	9.58 E
Bergen, B.R.D.	50	52.53 N	10.58 E
Bergen, B.R.D.	58	47.48 N	12.35 E
Bergen → Mons, Eur.	46	50.27 N	3.56 E
Bergen, Ned.	48	52.40 N	4.41 E
Bergen, Nor.	26	60.23 N	5.20 E
Bergen, N.Y., U.S.	200	43.05 N	77.57 W
Bergen □[6]	200	40.53 N	74.03 W
Bergen aan Zee	48	52.38 N	4.37 E
Bergen [auf Rügen]	50	54.25 N	13.26 E
Bergen Basin C	266	40.39 N	73.49 W
Bergen-Belsen-Denkmal ⊥	48	52.46 N	9.55 E
Berg en Dal	240	5.09 N	55.04 W
Bergenfield	200	40.55 N	74.00 W
Bergen Mall ◆[9]	266	40.55 N	74.04 W
Bergen op Zoom	48	51.30 N	4.17 E
Berger	209	38.40 N	91.21 W
Bergerac	32	44.51 N	0.29 E
Bergères-Lès-Vertus	46	48.53 N	4.00 E
Bergerhof	253	51.12 N	7.21 E
Bergfelde	50	52.40 N	13.19 E
Berggiesshübel	50	50.52 N	13.57 E
Berghausen, B.R.D.	253	51.18 N	7.17 E
Berghausen, B.R.D.	253	51.07 N	6.55 E
Bergheim, B.R.D.	52	50.55 N	6.38 E
Bergheim, Fr.	54	48.12 N	7.22 E
Bergheim, Öst.	58	47.50 N	13.02 E
Berghem	48	51.46 N	5.34 E
Berghofen ◆[8]	253	51.29 N	7.32 E
Bergholtz	200	43.06 N	78.53 W
Bergholtz Creek ≃	274a	43.05 N	78.57 W
Bergholz	204	40.31 N	80.53 W
Bergholz-Rehbrücke	50	52.20 N	13.05 E
Bergisch-Born	253	51.09 N	7.15 E
Bergisches Land ◆[1]	253	51.07 N	7.10 E
Bergisches Land, Naturpark ♠	253	51.07 N	7.29 E
Bergisch Gladbach	52	50.59 N	7.07 E
Bergkamen	48	51.38 N	7.38 E
Bergkvara	26	56.23 N	16.05 E
Bergland	180	46.35 N	89.34 W
Bergneustadt	52	51.01 N	7.39 E
Bergnicourt	46	49.25 N	4.15 E
Bergö I	26	62.58 N	21.11 E
Bergoo	178	38.29 N	80.18 W
Bergos	120	40.14 N	26.36 E
Bergplaas	148	33.54 S	22.40 E
Bergrheinfeld	52	50.00 N	10.10 E
Bergsäng	40	60.06 N	13.33 E
Bergsbrunna	40	59.49 N	17.43 E
Bergse Maas ≃	48	51.45 N	5.08 E
Bergshamra	40	59.38 N	18.37 E
Bergsjö	26	61.59 N	17.04 E
Bergslagen ◆[1]	40	59.55 N	15.00 E
Bergstrasse-Odenwald, Naturpark ♠	52	49.40 N	9.00 E
Bergstrom Air Force Base ■	212	30.12 N	97.40 W
Bergtheim	52	49.54 N	10.04 E
Berguent	138	34.03 N	2.02 W
Bergues	46	50.58 N	2.26 E
Bergum	48	53.11 N	5.59 E
Bergün	54	46.38 N	9.45 E
Bergville	148	28.52 S	29.18 E
Bergvreten	40	60.31 N	16.26 E
Bergwitz	50	51.48 N	12.35 E
Berhala, Selat Ʉ	102	0.48 S	104.25 E
Berhampore	116	24.06 N	88.15 E
Berhampur	112	19.19 N	84.47 E
Beri, Bhārat	114	28.42 N	76.35 E
Beri, Pil.	106	12.41 N	124.22 E
Berici, Monti ⋀	58	45.26 N	11.31 E
Berih ≃	261c	1.23 N	103.40 E
Berikul'skij	76	55.32 N	88.08 E
Beringa, Ostrov I	64	55.00 N	165.15 E
Beringen	52	51.03 N	5.13 E
Bering Glacier ⍓	170	60.15 N	143.30 W
Beringhausen	52	51.24 N	8.46 E
Beringil	130	12.10 N	25.41 E
Beringin	102	3.41 S	104.18 E
Beringovskij	170	63.03 N	179.19 E
Bering Sea ⊹[2]	16	60.00 N	175.00 W
Bering Strait Ʉ	170	65.30 N	169.00 W
Berislav	68	46.51 N	33.26 E
Berisso	248	34.52 S	57.53 W
Berisso □[5]	278	34.55 S	57.53 W

FRANÇAIS

Nom	Page	Lat.°′	Long.°′ W=Ouest
Berja	34	36.51 N	2.57 W
Berkåk	26	62.50 N	10.00 E
Berkane	138	34.59 N	2.20 W
Berkel ≃	48	52.09 N	6.12 E
Berkeley, Eng., U.K.	44	51.42 N	2.27 W
Berkeley, Calif., U.S.	216	37.57 N	122.18 W
Berkeley, Ill., U.S.	268	41.53 N	87.55 W
Berkeley, Mo., U.S.	209	38.45 N	90.20 W
Berkeley, R.I., U.S.	197	41.56 N	71.25 W
Berkeley, Vale of ∨	44	51.43 N	2.25 W
Berkeley Heights	200	40.41 N	74.27 W
Berkeley Hills	269b	40.32 N	80.00 W
Berkeley Hills ⋀[2]	272	37.54 N	122.16 W
Berkeley Springs	178	39.38 N	78.14 W
Berkhamsted	44	51.46 N	0.35 W
Berkheim	54	48.02 N	10.04 E
Berkley	197	41.51 N	71.05 W
Berkley Plantation ⊥	198	37.19 N	77.10 W
Berkner Island I	9	79.30 S	49.30 W
Berks □[6]	198	40.20 N	75.50 W
Berkshire, Mass., U.S.	197	42.30 N	73.12 W
Berkshire, N.Y., U.S.	200	42.18 N	76.11 W
Berkshire □[6], Eng., U.K.	44	51.30 N	1.20 W
Berkshire □[6], Mass., U.S.	197	42.27 N	73.15 W
Berkshire Downs ⋀[1]	44	51.33 N	1.24 W
Berkshire Hills ⋀[2]	197	42.20 N	73.10 W
Berlaar	52	51.07 N	4.39 E
Berlaimont	46	50.12 N	3.49 E
Berland ≃	172	54.01 N	116.50 W
Berlanga de Duero	34	41.28 N	2.51 W
Berlenga I	34	39.25 N	9.30 W
Berlengas ≃	240	5.39 S	42.19 W
Berlevåg	24	70.51 N	29.06 E
Berlicum	48	51.42 N	5.23 E
Berlikum	48	53.15 N	5.39 E
Berlin (West), B.R.D.	50 254a	 52.31 N	 13.24 E
Berlin (Ost), D.D.R.	50 254a	 52.30 N	 13.25 E
Berlin, S. Afr.	148	32.54 S	27.35 E
Berlin, Conn., U.S.	197	41.37 N	72.45 W
Berlin, Md., U.S.	198	38.20 N	75.13 W
Berlin, Mass., U.S.	197	42.23 N	71.38 W
Berlin, N.H., U.S.	178	44.29 N	71.10 W
Berlin, N.J., U.S.	198	39.48 N	74.57 W
Berlin, N.Y., U.S.	200	42.42 N	73.23 W
Berlin, Ohio, U.S.	204	40.34 N	81.48 W
Berlin, Pa., U.S.	178	39.55 N	78.57 W
Berlin, Wis., U.S.	180	43.58 N	88.55 W
Berlin □[5]	254a	52.33 N	13.30 E
Berlin, Mount Λ	9	76.03 S	135.52 W
Berlin Center	204	41.01 N	80.57 W
Berlinchen	50	53.13 N	12.34 E
Berliner Brücke ◆[5]	253	51.27 N	6.47 E
Berliner Forst Düppel ♠	254a	52.25 N	13.07 E
Berliner Forst Grunewald ♠	254a	52.28 N	13.13 E
Berliner Mauer (Berlin Wall) ⊥	254a	52.35 N	13.22 E
Berliner Stadtforst Spandau ♠	254a	52.35 N	13.10 E
Berlinguet Inlet C	166	71.10 N	85.35 W
Berlin Heights	204	41.20 N	82.30 W
Berlin-ichthyosaur State Park ♠	194	38.51 N	117.35 W
Berlin Lake ⊜[1]	204	41.00 N	81.00 W
Berlin Mountain Λ	200	42.42 N	73.17 W
Berlinsville	200	40.47 N	75.35 W
Berlin-Tegel, Flughafen ⊠	254a	52.34 N	13.18 E
Berlin-Tempelhof, Zentralflughafen ⊠	254a	52.29 N	13.25 E
Bermagui	156	36.25 S	150.04 E
Bermejillo	222	25.53 N	103.37 W
Bermejo	242	31.37 S	67.39 W
Bermejo ≃	242	26.51 S	58.23 W
Bermejo, Paso de)(	242	32.50 S	70.05 W
Bermen, Lac ⊜	166	53.35 N	68.55 W
Bermeo	34	43.26 N	2.43 W
Bermillo de Sayago	34	41.22 N	6.06 W
Bermo	114	23.47 N	85.57 E
Bermondsey ◆[8]	250	51.30 N	0.04 W
Bermuda □[2]	220 230a	 32.20 N	 64.45 W
Bermuda Rise ⊹[3]	16	33.00 N	65.00 W
Bermudes → Bermuda □[2]	230a	32.20 N	64.45 W
Bermudian Creek ≃	198	40.01 N	76.55 W
Bern (Berne)	54	46.57 N	7.26 E
Bern (Berne) □[3]	54	46.45 N	7.40 E
Berna → Bern	54	46.57 N	7.26 E
Bernabéu, Estadio ♠	256a	40.27 N	3.41 W
Bernal ◆[8]	248	34.42 S	58.17 W
Bernalda	36	40.24 N	16.41 E
Bernam ≃	104	3.48 N	100.57 E
Bernardston	197	42.40 N	72.33 W
Bernardsville	200	40.43 N	74.34 W
Bernasconi	242	37.54 S	63.43 W
Bernate	256b	45.29 N	8.49 E
Bernau am Chiemsee	58	47.48 N	12.22 E
Bernau bei Berlin	50	52.40 N	13.35 E
Bernaville	46	50.08 N	2.10 E
Bernay	46	49.06 N	0.36 E
Bern-Belp, Flughafen ⊠	54	46.55 N	7.30 E
Bernbeuren	54	47.44 N	10.46 E
Bernburg	50	51.48 N	11.44 E
Berndorf	30	47.57 N	16.08 E
Berne, B.R.D.	48	53.11 N	8.29 E
Berne → Bern, Schw.	54	46.57 N	7.26 E
Berne, Ind., U.S.	206	40.39 N	84.57 W
Berne, N.Y., U.S.	200	42.38 N	74.08 W
Berneburg	52	51.04 N	9.53 E
Berner Alpen ⋀	54	46.30 N	7.30 E
Berneray I	28	57.43 N	7.15 W
Berneval-le-Grand	46	49.57 N	1.12 E
Berngardovka	255a	60.01 N	30.36 E
Bernhardina	148	27.53 S	28.40 E
Bernhards Bay	200	43.15 N	75.56 W
Bernice	184	32.49 N	92.39 W
Bernie	184	36.40 N	89.58 W
Bernier Bay C	166	71.00 N	87.30 W
Bernier Island I	152	24.52 S	113.08 E
Bernina ⋀	54	46.22 N	9.50 E
Bernina, Passo del)(	54	46.24 N	10.03 E
Bernina, Piz Λ	54	46.21 N	9.51 E
Bernkastel-Kues	52	49.55 N	7.04 E
Bernried	58	47.52 N	11.17 E
Bernsbach	50	50.34 N	12.46 E
Bernsdorf	50	51.22 N	14.04 E
Bernsfelden	52	49.34 N	9.53 E
Bernstadt, D.D.R.	50	51.03 N	14.50 E
Bernstadt → Bierutów, Pol.	30	51.08 N	17.32 E
Bernstein → Pełczyce	30	53.03 N	15.18 E
Bernville	198	40.26 N	76.07 W
Bero ≃	142	15.10 S	12.09 E
Beroga	104	2.56 N	101.55 E
Beroldingen ⊥	54	46.55 N	8.36 E
Berolzheim	52	49.28 N	9.32 E
Beromünster	54	47.12 N	8.11 E
Berón de Astrada	242	27.33 S	57.32 W
Beror Hayil	122	31.33 N	34.38 E
Beroroha	147b	21.41 S	45.10 E
Ber'ostovica	66	53.07 N	23.58 E
Béroubouay	140	10.32 N	2.44 E
Beroun	30	49.58 N	14.04 E
Berounka ≃	30	50.00 N	14.24 E
Berovo	38	41.42 N	22.51 E
Berowra	160	33.37 S	151.09 E

PORTUGUÊS

Nome	Página	Lat.°′	Long.°′ W=Oeste
Ber'oza, S.S.S.R.	66	52.32 N	24.59 E
Ber'oza, S.S.S.R.	68	51.44 N	33.52 E
Ber'ozno	68	51.00 N	26.45 E
Ber'ožnoje	66	59.55 N	39.17 E
Ber'ozovaja ≃	70	48.31 N	41.03 E
Ber'ozovaja Rudka	68	50.19 N	32.14 E
Ber'ozovka, S.S.S.R.	24	65.00 N	56.26 E
Ber'ozovka, S.S.S.R.	24	59.35 N	56.02 E
Ber'ozovka, S.S.S.R.	66	53.26 N	38.53 E
Ber'ozovka, S.S.S.R.	66	53.43 N	25.30 E
Ber'ozovka, S.S.S.R.	68	47.49 N	32.28 E
Ber'ozovka, S.S.S.R.	68	47.12 N	30.55 E
Ber'ozovka, S.S.S.R.	68	45.35 N	33.20 E
Ber'ozovka, S.S.S.R.	70	52.06 N	45.07 E
Ber'ozovka, S.S.S.R.	70	51.11 N	53.16 E
Ber'ozovka, S.S.S.R.	76	54.02 N	76.35 E
Ber'ozovka, S.S.S.R.	76	59.39 N	56.04 E
Ber'ozovka, S.S.S.R.	76	57.37 N	57.18 E
Ber'ozovka, S.S.S.R.	76	51.51 N	82.58 E
Ber'ozovka, S.S.S.R.	76	56.03 N	93.07 E
Ber'ozovka, S.S.S.R.	76	59.24 N	82.38 E
Ber'ozovka, S.S.S.R.	78	56.03 N	93.07 E
Ber'ozovka, S.S.S.R.	78	57.46 N	116.09 E
Ber'ozovka, S.S.S.R.	79	50.35 N	127.52 E
Ber'ozovka, S.S.S.R.	255a	59.56 N	30.49 E
Ber'ozovo, S.S.S.R.	64	63.56 N	65.02 E
Ber'ozovo, S.S.S.R.	68	51.35 N	27.20 E
Ber'ozovo, S.S.S.R.	70	51.56 N	48.28 E
Ber'ozovo, S.S.S.R.	72	54.19 N	41.01 E
Ber'ozovo, S.S.S.R.	72	54.03 N	36.24 E
Ber'ozovskaja	70	50.16 N	43.59 E
Ber'ozovskij	76	55.39 N	86.16 E
Ber'ozovskij R'adok	66	58.06 N	34.29 E
Ber'ozovskoje	76	55.50 N	89.36 E
Ber'ozovyj, Ostrov I	66	60.18 N	28.38 E
Berra	58	44.59 N	11.58 E
Berras, Arroyo los ≃	278	34.34 S	58.40 W
Berre ≃	56	44.24 N	4.40 E
Berre, Étang de C	56	43.28 N	5.11 E
Berrechid	138	33.17 N	7.35 W
Berre-des-Alpes	56	43.50 N	7.19 E
Berre-l'Étang	56	43.28 N	5.11 E
Ber Remad, Oued ∨	138	31.45 N	1.10 E
Berri	156	34.17 S	140.36 E
Berriane	138	32.50 N	3.46 E
Berridale	161b	36.22 S	148.50 E
Berrien □[6]	206	41.59 N	86.30 W
Berrien Springs	206	41.57 N	86.20 W
Berrigan	156	35.40 S	145.49 E
Berrima	160	34.30 S	150.20 E
Berriozábal	224	16.48 N	93.16 W
Berrouaghia	34	36.08 N	2.55 E
Berrugosa Point >	106	10.23 N	125.33 E
Berry, Austl.	160	34.47 S	150.42 E
Berry, Ala., U.S.	184	33.39 N	87.36 W
Berry, Ky., U.S.	208	38.31 N	84.23 W
Berry □[9]	46	47.20 N	2.10 E
Berry, Canal du ≅	46	47.17 N	1.25 E
Berry-au-Bac	46	49.24 N	3.54 E
Berry Creek ≃, Alta., Can.	172	50.50 N	111.36 W
Berry Creek ≃, Tex., U.S.	212	30.40 N	97.36 W
Berryessa, Lake ⊜[1]	216	38.35 N	122.14 W
Berryessa Creek ≃	272	37.24 N	121.53 W
Berryessa Peak Λ	216	38.40 N	122.11 W
Berry Head >	44	50.24 N	3.29 W
Berry Islands II	228	25.34 S	77.45 W
Berry Mountain Λ	198	40.31 N	77.02 W
Berrysburg	198	40.36 N	76.49 W
Berrys Creek ≃	266	40.47 N	74.05 W
Berryville, Ark., U.S.	184	36.22 N	93.34 W
Berryville, Va., U.S.	178	39.09 N	77.59 W
Beršad'	68	48.23 N	29.30 E
Berseba	146	26.00 S	17.46 E
Bersenbrück	48	52.33 N	7.56 E
Bersimis 2 Dam ◆[6]	176	49.22 N	69.47 W
Bersimis Indian Reserve ◆[4]	176	49.05 N	68.37 W
Bersut	70	55.32 N	50.54 E
Bertam	104	5.09 N	102.03 E
Bertasuyu ≃	74	41.09 N	41.53 E
Berté, Lac ⊜	176	50.48 N	68.30 W
Bertha	188	46.16 N	95.04 W
Berthåga	40	59.52 N	17.35 E
Berthelsdorf	50	51.05 N	14.13 E
Berthier □[6]	196	46.30 N	73.45 W
Berthierville	196	46.05 N	73.10 W
Berthold	188	48.19 N	101.44 W
Berthoud	190	40.18 N	105.05 W
Berthoud Pass)(	190	39.45 N	105.45 W
Bertincourt	46	50.05 N	2.59 E
Bertinoro	60	44.09 N	12.08 E
Bertioga	246	23.51 S	46.09 W
Bertioga, Enseada da C	246	23.50 S	46.08 W
Bertkow	50	52.43 N	11.54 E
Bertlich	253	51.37 N	7.04 E
Bertogne	52	50.05 N	5.40 E
Bertolinia	240	7.38 S	43.57 W
Bertoua	142	4.35 N	13.41 E
Bertram	186	30.45 N	98.03 W
Bertrand, Mich., U.S.	206	41.46 N	86.16 W
Bertrand, Nebr., U.S.	188	40.32 N	99.38 W
Bertrix	52	49.51 N	5.15 E
Bertry	46	50.05 N	3.27 E
Beru I	14	1.20 S	176.00 E
Beruas	104	4.30 N	100.47 E
Beruri	236	3.54 S	61.22 W
Berville	204	42.55 N	82.53 W
Berville-sur-Mer	46	49.26 N	0.22 E
Berwang	54	47.24 N	10.45 E
Berwick, Austl.	159	38.02 S	145.21 E
Berwick, N.S., Can.	176	45.03 N	64.44 W
Berwick, La., U.S.	184	29.42 N	91.13 W
Berwick, Maine, U.S.	178	43.16 N	70.51 W
Berwick, Pa., U.S.	200	41.03 N	76.15 W
Berwick-upon-Tweed	42	55.46 N	2.00 W
Berwyn, Ill., U.S.	206	41.50 N	87.47 W
Berwyn, Pa., U.S.	198	40.03 N	75.27 W
Berwyn ⋀	44	52.53 N	3.24 W
Berwyn Heights	274c	38.59 N	76.54 W
Bērze ≃	66	56.41 N	23.37 E
Berzé-la-Ville	54	46.22 N	4.42 E
Berz-Macomb Airport ⊠	271	42.40 N	82.58 W
Bès ≃	56	44.08 N	6.14 E
Besalampy	147b	16.45 S	44.30 E
Besana in Brianza	56	45.42 N	9.17 E
Besançon	54	47.15 N	6.02 E
Besani	114	24.08 N	80.17 E
Besar, Gunong Λ, Malay.	104	5.10 N	101.18 E
Besar, Gunong Λ, Malay.	104	2.30 N	103.10 E
Besar, Pulau I	105b	8.28 S	122.22 E
Besar Hantu, Gunong Λ	104	3.12 N	102.02 E
Besaya ≃	34	43.21 N	4.04 W
Besbes	36	36.42 N	7.51 E
Besed' ≃	66	52.38 N	31.09 E
Besedino	68	51.42 N	36.28 E
Besedy	255b	55.37 N	37.47 E
Besenfeld	52	48.35 N	8.25 E
Bešenkoviči	66	55.03 N	29.27 E
Beserah	104	3.52 N	103.22 E
Besigheim	52	49.00 N	9.08 E
Besikama	102	9.36 S	124.57 E
Beşiktaş ◆[8]	257b	41.03 N	29.01 E
Beşiri	120	37.55 N	41.18 E
Besitang	104	4.02 N	98.12 E
Beškent	118	38.49 N	65.39 E
Beskid Mountains ⋀	30	49.40 N	20.00 E
Beškube	75	39.50 N	68.18 E
Beskudnikovo ◆[8]	255b	55.52 N	37.34 E
Beslan	74	43.12 N	44.33 E
Beslenej	74	44.14 N	41.44 E
Besnard Lake ⊜	174	55.24 N	106.05 W
Besni	120	37.41 N	37.52 E

Besor, Nahal ∨	122	31.28 N	34.22 E
Besós ≃	256d	41.25 N	2.04 E
Besozzo	56	45.51 N	8.39 E
Besp'atovo	72	54.45 N	38.54 E
Beşpınar	120	41.09 N	35.14 E
Besputa ≃	72	54.50 N	37.58 E
Bessa Monteiro	142	7.07 S	13.44 E
Bessancourt	251	49.02 N	2.13 E
Bessans	56	45.19 N	7.00 E
Bessarabia □[9]	38	47.00 N	28.30 E
Bessarabka, S.S.S.R.	68	46.20 N	28.58 E
Bessarabka, S.S.S.R.	76	53.37 N	73.17 E
Besse, B.R.D.	52	51.13 N	9.23 E
Besse, Nig.	140	11.15 N	4.30 E
Bessèges	56	44.17 N	4.06 E
Bessemer, Ala., U.S.	184	33.25 N	86.57 W
Bessemer, Mich., U.S.	180	46.27 N	89.24 W
Bessemer, Pa., U.S.	204	40.59 N	80.30 W
Bessemer City	182	35.17 N	81.17 W
Besser	41	55.52 N	10.39 E
Bessé-sur-Braye	46	47.50 N	0.45 E
Bessheim	26	61.31 N	8.51 E
Besshiyama	86	33.50 N	133.23 E
Bessho	260	34.27 N	135.31 E
Bessonovka	70	53.18 N	45.03 E
Best	48	51.31 N	5.24 E
Best'ach	64	61.52 N	129.55 E
Bestam ⊥	76	43.53 N	62.22 E
Bestamak, S.S.S.R.	76	49.43 N	55.07 E
Bestamak, S.S.S.R.	76	49.13 N	78.21 E
Beštau, Gora Λ	74	44.06 N	43.01 E
Besten	253	51.39 N	6.54 E
Bestensee	50	52.15 N	13.37 E
Bestobe	76	52.30 N	73.05 E
Beštor, Gora Λ	75	42.03 N	70.50 E
Bestuževo	24	61.37 N	43.58 E
Besuki	105a	7.45 S	113.41 E
Besut ≃	104	5.48 N	102.35 E
Beswick Aboriginal Reserve ◆[4]	154	14.30 S	133.10 E
Betā	262b	22.55 N	88.14 E
Betafo	147b	19.50 S	46.51 E
Betāgi	116	22.25 N	90.11 E
Bet Alfa	122	32.31 N	35.26 E
Beta Main Canal ≅	216	36.34 N	120.11 W
Betamba	142	2.13 S	21.23 E
Betang Melaka	104	2.28 N	102.25 E
Betano	102	9.10 S	125.43 E
Betanzos, Bol.	238	19.34 S	65.27 W
Betanzos, Esp.	34	43.17 N	8.12 W
Betanzos, Ría de C[1]	34	43.23 N	8.15 W
Bétaré Oya	142	5.36 N	14.05 E
Betarsjön ⊜	26	63.44 N	16.52 E
Bet Bet Creek ≃	159	36.52 S	143.52 E
Betbetti	130	15.06 N	24.12 E
Betchworth	250	51.14 N	0.16 W
Bet Dagan	122	32.00 N	34.50 E
Betém	246	22.52 S	44.17 W
Bétera	34	39.35 N	0.27 W
Bétérou	140	9.12 N	2.16 E
Bet Guvrin	122	31.36 N	34.54 E
Bet Ha'arava	122	31.48 N	35.32 E
Bethal	148	26.27 S	29.28 E
Bethalto	209	38.55 N	90.03 W
Bethanien	146	26.32 S	17.11 E
Bethanien □[5]	146	26.30 S	17.00 E
Bethany, Conn., U.S.	197	41.26 N	73.01 W
Bethany, Ill., U.S.	209	39.39 N	88.44 W
Bethany, Mo., U.S.	184	40.16 N	94.02 W
Bethany, N.Y., U.S.	200	42.55 N	78.08 W
Bethany, Okla., U.S.	186	35.31 N	97.38 W
Bethany, Pa., U.S.	200	41.37 N	75.21 W
Bethany, W. Va., U.S.	204	40.12 N	80.33 W
Bethany Reservoir ⊜[1]	216	37.47 N	121.37 W
Bet HaShitta	122	32.33 N	35.26 E
Bethel, Alaska, U.S.	170	60.48 N	161.46 W
Bethel, Conn., U.S.	197	41.22 N	73.25 W
Bethel, Del., U.S.	198	38.34 N	75.37 W
Bethel, Ky., U.S.	208	38.15 N	83.52 W
Bethel, Maine, U.S.	178	44.25 N	70.48 W
Bethel, Mo., U.S.	209	39.53 N	92.02 W
Bethel, N.C., U.S.	182	35.48 N	77.22 W
Bethel, N.Y., U.S.	200	41.41 N	74.52 W
Bethel, Ohio, U.S.	208	38.58 N	84.05 W
Bethel, Pa., U.S.	198	40.28 N	76.18 W
Bethel, Wash., U.S.	214	47.32 N	122.38 W
Bethel Island	216	38.01 N	121.39 W
Bethel Manor	198	37.06 N	76.25 W
Bethel Park	204	40.18 N	80.02 W
Bethelsdorp	148	33.52 S	25.34 E
Bethel Springs	184	35.14 N	88.36 W
Béthencourt-sur-Mer	46	50.05 N	1.30 E
Bethersden	44	51.08 N	0.48 E
Bethesda, Wales, U.K.	42	53.11 N	4.03 W
Bethesda, Md., U.S.	198	38.59 N	77.06 W
Bethesda, Ohio, U.S.	178	40.01 N	81.04 W
Bethesdaweg	148	31.55 S	24.45 E
Béthisy-Saint-Pierre	46	49.18 N	2.49 E
Bethlehem, S. Afr.	148	28.15 S	28.15 E
Bethlehem, Conn., U.S.	197	41.38 N	73.13 W
Bethlehem, Ind., U.S.	208	38.32 N	85.25 W
Bethlehem, Ky., U.S.	208	38.24 N	85.04 W
Bethlehem, Pa., U.S.	200	40.37 N	75.25 W
Bethlehem, W. Va., U.S.	178	40.02 N	80.40 W
Bethlehem → Bayt Lahm, Urd.	122	31.43 N	35.12 E
Bethlehem Center	200	42.40 N	73.42 W
Bethlehem Steel Corporation ⩡[3], Md., U.S.	274b	39.13 N	76.29 W
Bethlehem Steel Corporation (Lackawanna Plant) ⩡[3], N.Y., U.S.	274a	42.49 N	78.52 W
Bethnal Green ◆[8]	250	51.32 N	0.03 W
Bethoncourt	54	47.32 N	6.48 E
Bethpage	200	40.45 N	73.29 W
Bethpage State Park ♠	200	40.45 N	73.27 W
Bethulie	148	30.32 S	25.59 E
Bethune, Sask., Can.	174	50.43 N	105.08 W
Béthune, Fr.	46	50.32 N	2.38 E
Bethune, S.C., U.S.	182	34.25 N	80.21 W
Béthune ≃	46	49.53 N	1.09 E
Beticos, Sistemas ⋀	34	37.00 N	4.00 W
Betijoque	236	9.23 N	70.44 W
Betil	116	24.14 N	89.43 E
Betio	164t	1.21 N	172.56 E
Betio I	164t	1.20 N	172.56 E
Betioky, Madag.	147b	22.27 S	43.44 E
Betioky, Madag.	147b	23.42 S	44.22 E
Betis ≃	104	4.53 N	101.48 E
Betlica	66	54.01 N	33.57 E
Bet Netofa, Biq'at ⩦	122	32.49 N	35.19 E
Betnoti	116	21.44 N	86.51 E
Beton-Bazoches	46	48.42 N	3.15 E
Betong, Malay.	102	1.24 N	111.31 E
Betong, Thai	100	5.45 N	101.05 E
Betoota	156	25.42 S	140.44 E
Betor	134	11.40 N	39.00 E
Bétou	142	3.03 N	18.31 E
Betpak-Dala ◆[2]	76	46.00 N	70.00 E
Betroka	147b	23.16 S	46.06 E
Betsham	250	51.25 N	0.19 E
Bet Sh'ean	122	32.30 N	35.30 E
Bet She'arim, Horbat ⊥	122	32.42 N	35.08 E
Bet Shemesh	122	31.45 N	35.00 E
Betsiamites	176	48.56 N	68.38 W
Betsiamites ≃	176	48.56 N	68.38 W
Betsiamites, Pointe >	176	48.55 N	68.37 W
Betsiboka ≃	147b	16.03 S	46.36 E
Betsie, Point >	180	44.42 N	86.16 W
Betsioky	147b	21.31 S	44.28 E
Betsy Layne	182	37.33 N	82.38 W
Bette Λ	136	22.00 N	19.12 E
Bettembourg	52	49.32 N	6.02 E

Bettendorf	180	41.32 N	90.30 W
Betterton	198	39.52 N	76.04 W
Bettiah	114	26.48 N	84.30 E
Bettie	212	32.48 N	94.58 W
Bettles Field	170	66.55 N	151.30 W
Bettola	56	44.47 N	9.36 E
Bettona	60	43.01 N	12.29 E
Bettrath ◆[8]	253	51.13 N	6.26 E
Bettsville	204	41.15 N	83.14 W
Betty's Bay	148	34.22 S	18.52 E
Betūl	114	21.55 N	77.54 E
Betūl □[5]	114	22.00 N	78.00 E
Betumbe-Bongo	142	2.11 S	18.46 E
Betung, Indon.	102	1.52 S	103.16 E
Betung, Indon.	102	2.50 S	104.14 E
Betuwe ◆[1]	48	51.55 N	5.30 E
Betwa ≃	114	25.55 N	80.12 E
Betws-y-Coed	44	53.05 N	3.48 W
Betz	46	49.09 N	2.57 E
Betz ≃	46	48.09 N	2.45 E
Betzdorf	52	50.47 N	7.53 E
Béu	142	6.14 S	15.28 E
Beucha	50	51.19 N	12.34 E
Beuel	52	50.38 N	7.14 E
Beugneux	46	49.14 N	3.25 E
Beuil	56	44.06 N	6.59 E
Beulah, Austl.	156	35.56 S	142.26 E
Beulah, Colo., U.S.	190	38.05 N	104.59 W
Beulah, Mich., U.S.	180	44.38 N	86.06 W
Beulah, Miss., U.S.	184	33.42 N	90.59 W
Beulah, N. Dak., U.S.	188	47.16 N	101.47 W
Beulah, Lake ⊜	206	42.49 N	88.23 W
Beulah Beach	204	41.25 N	82.22 W
Beulah Reservoir ⊜[1]	192	43.56 N	118.09 W
Beulaville	182	34.55 N	77.46 W
Beult ≃	44	51.14 N	0.25 E
Beure	54	47.12 N	6.00 E
Beuron	54	48.03 N	8.58 E
Beuthen → Bytom	30	50.22 N	18.54 E
Beuvron ≃, Fr.	46	47.29 N	1.15 E
Beuvron ≃, Fr.	46	47.28 N	3.31 E
Beuvronne ≃	251	48.56 N	2.44 E
Beuvry	46	50.31 N	2.41 E
Beuzeville	46	49.20 N	0.21 E
Bevagna	60	42.56 N	12.36 E
Bevensen	48	53.05 N	10.34 E
Bever ≃	48	52.01 N	7.46 E
Bevera ≃	56	43.49 N	7.34 E
Beveren	46	51.13 N	4.15 E
Beverino	56	44.14 N	9.47 E
Beverley, Austl.	158a	32.06 S	116.56 E
Beverley, Eng., U.K.	42	53.52 N	0.26 W
Beverley Minster ⩡[1]	42	53.50 N	0.27 W
Beverlo	52	51.05 N	5.12 E
Beverly, Mass., U.S.	197	42.33 N	70.53 W
Beverly, N.J., U.S.	198	40.04 N	74.55 W
Beverly, Ohio, U.S.	178	39.33 N	81.38 W
Beverly, Tex., U.S.	212	31.30 N	97.10 W
Beverly ◆[8]	268	41.43 N	87.41 W
Beverly Farms, Md., U.S.	274c	39.04 N	77.11 W
Beverly Farms, Mass., U.S.	273	42.34 N	70.49 W
Beverly Harbor C	273	42.32 N	70.53 W
Beverly Hills, Austl.	264a	33.57 S	151.05 E
Beverly Hills, Calif., U.S.	218	34.03 N	118.26 W
Beverly Hills, Fla., U.S.	210	28.56 N	82.28 W
Beverly Hills, Mich., U.S.	206	42.32 N	83.15 W
Beverly Lake ⊜	166	64.36 N	100.30 W
Beverly Municipal Airport ⊠	273	42.35 N	70.55 W
Beverly Run ≃	198	37.55 N	77.11 W
Beverly Shores	206	41.41 N	87.00 W
Bevern	48	51.51 N	9.29 E
Beverstausee ⊜[1]	253	51.09 N	7.23 E
Beverstedt	48	53.26 N	8.49 E
Beverungen	48	51.39 N	9.22 E
Beverwijk	48	52.28 N	4.40 E
Bevier	184	39.45 N	92.34 W
Bevin, Lac ⊜	196	45.57 N	74.35 W
Bevoalavo	147b	25.13 S	45.26 E
Bewār	114	27.13 N	79.18 E
Bewdley, Ont., Can.	202	44.05 N	78.19 W
Bewdley, Eng., U.K.	44	52.22 N	2.19 W
Bex	54	46.15 N	7.01 E
Bexhill on Sea	44	50.50 N	0.29 E
Bexley, Austl.	264a	33.57 S	151.08 E
Bexley, Ohio, U.S.	208	39.58 N	82.56 W
Bexley ◆[8]	44	51.26 N	0.10 E
Beyazköy	120	41.21 N	27.42 E
Beybach ≃	52	50.13 N	7.23 E
Beyçayırı	120	40.15 N	26.55 E
Beyce	120	39.54 N	29.00 E
Beycuma	120	41.19 N	31.59 E
Bey Dağları ⋀	120	36.40 N	30.15 E
Beydili	120	40.10 N	31.01 E
Beyenburg ◆[8]	253	51.15 N	7.18 E
Beykoz	120	41.08 N	29.05 E
Beyla	140	8.41 N	8.37 W
Beyla □[4]	140	8.55 N	8.25 W
Beylerbeyi ◆[8]	257b	41.03 N	29.03 E
Beylikahır	120	39.42 N	31.13 E
Beylul	134	13.10 N	42.26 E
Beynes	251	48.51 N	1.53 E
Beynes-Thiverval, Aérodrome de ⊠	251	48.51 N	1.54 E
Beyoğlu ◆[8]	257b	41.02 N	28.59 E
Beypazarı	120	40.10 N	31.56 E
Beypınarı	120	39.31 N	37.44 E
Beypore	112	11.11 N	75.49 E
Beyrouth → Bayrūt	120	33.53 N	35.30 E
Beyşehir	120	37.41 N	31.43 E
Beyşehir Gölü ⊜	120	37.40 N	31.30 E
Bezaha	147b	23.30 S	44.31 E
Bežanickaja Vozvyšennost' ⋀[1]	66	56.54 N	29.20 E
Bežanicy	66	56.58 N	29.53 E
Bezau	54	47.23 N	9.54 E
Bezavona Λ	147b	15.02 S	49.52 E
Bezdež	66	52.19 N	25.18 E
Bezděz Λ	50	50.32 N	14.43 E
Bezděz ⊥	50	50.32 N	14.46 E
Bèze	54	47.28 N	5.16 E
Bežeck	66	57.47 N	36.39 E
Bežeckij Verch ⋀[1]	66	57.36 N	36.54 E
Bezenčuk	70	52.59 N	49.26 E
Bezerra ≃	245	13.16 S	47.31 W
Bezerros	240	8.14 S	35.45 W
Bezet	122	33.05 N	35.08 E
Béziers	32	43.21 N	3.15 E
Bezmein	118	38.05 N	58.12 E
Bezmenšur	70	56.29 N	51.17 E
Bezons	251	48.56 N	2.13 E
Bežta	74	42.08 N	46.08 E
Bezwada → Vijayawāda	112	16.31 N	80.37 E
Bezym'anka	70	49.56 N	43.15 E
Bezym'annaja	70	51.20 N	46.26 E
Bezymennoje	73	47.06 N	37.56 E
Bezzecca	58	45.55 N	10.43 E
Bezzubovo	72	55.27 N	38.55 E
Bhabānipur, Bhārat	262b	22.57 N	88.27 E
Bhabānipur, Bhārat	262b	22.56 N	88.13 E
Bhābta	116	23.59 N	88.15 E
Bhabua	114	25.03 N	83.37 E
Bhadarwah	113	32.59 N	75.43 E
Bhadaur	113	30.29 N	75.19 E
Bhādgāon → Bhaktapur	114	27.42 N	85.27 E
Bhadohi	114	25.25 N	82.34 E
Bhādra	113	29.07 N	75.10 E
Bhadra ⊜[1]	112	13.42 N	75.35 E
Bhadra ≃[1]	116	22.19 N	89.31 E
Bhadrāchalam	112	17.40 N	80.53 E
Bhadrakh	110	21.04 N	86.30 E
Bhadrāvati	112	13.52 N	75.43 E
Bhadreswar	116	22.50 N	88.21 E
Bhādua	262b	22.41 N	88.12 E

Bhāg	110	29.02 N	67.49 E
Bhagaiya	114	25.12 N	87.29 E
Bhāgalpur	114	25.15 N	87.00 E
Bhāgalpur □[5]	114	25.00 N	87.00 E
Bhāgirathi ≃, Bhārat	114	30.08 N	78.35 E
Bhāgīrathi ≃, Bhārat	116	23.25 N	88.23 E
Bhagirathpur	116	24.05 N	88.29 E
Bhagwānpur	116	22.07 N	87.45 E
Bhāi Pheru	113	31.12 N	73.57 E
Bhairab ≃[1]	116	22.51 N	89.34 E
Bhairab Bāzār	110	24.04 N	90.58 E
Bhairawa	114	27.31 N	83.24 E
Bhaironghāti	110	31.01 N	78.53 E
Bhaisa	112	19.06 N	77.58 E
Bhakkar	113	31.38 N	71.04 E
Bhākra Dam ◆[6]	113	31.24 N	76.30 E
Bhaktapur	114	27.42 N	85.27 E
Bhal	262c	19.11 N	73.08 E
Bhālki	112	18.02 N	77.13 E
Bhalswa ◆[8]	262a	28.44 N	77.10 E
Bhalwāl	113	32.16 N	72.54 E
Bhamo	100	24.16 N	97.14 E
Bhandāra	110	21.10 N	79.39 E
Bhandārdaha	262b	22.37 N	88.13 E
Bhandāria	116	22.29 N	90.04 E
Bhānder	114	25.44 N	78.45 E
Bhander Plateau ⋀[1]	114	24.10 N	80.20 E
Bhāndup ◆[8]	262c	19.09 N	72.57 E
Bhānga	116	23.22 N	89.59 E
Bhāngar	116	22.31 N	88.37 E
Bhānvad	110	21.56 N	69.47 E
Bhārat → India □[1]	108	20.00 N	77.00 E
Bharatpur, Bhārat	114	27.13 N	77.29 E
Bharatpur, Bhārat	116	23.53 N	88.05 E
Bharatpur □[5]	114	27.00 N	77.15 E
Bharthana	114	26.45 N	79.14 E
Bhātai	116	23.36 N	89.11 E
Bhātāpāra	110	21.44 N	81.56 E
Bhātār	116	23.25 N	87.54 E
Bhatewar	110	24.38 N	74.00 E
Bhatgaon → Bhaktapur	114	27.42 N	85.27 E
Bhātghar Lake ⊜[1]	112	18.12 N	73.49 E
Bhātiāpāra Ghāt	114	23.13 N	89.42 E
Bhatinda	113	30.12 N	74.57 E
Bhatkal	112	13.58 N	74.34 E
Bhātpāra	116	22.52 N	88.24 E
Bhātpur	262b	22.43 N	88.25 E
Bhātsāla	116	22.33 N	90.30 E
Bhattapratāp	116	22.45 N	89.48 E
Bhattiprolu	112	16.06 N	80.47 E
Bhātua	262b	22.57 N	88.22 E
Bhaun	113	32.52 N	72.45 E
Bhaunagar	112	21.46 N	72.09 E
Bhaunja	262a	28.40 N	77.25 E
Bhavāni	112	11.27 N	77.41 E
Bhawānīgarh	114	30.16 N	76.02 E
Bhawāni Mandi	110	24.25 N	75.50 E
Bhawānipatna	112	19.54 N	83.10 E
Bhedia	116	23.36 N	87.42 E
Bheigeir, Beinn Λ[2]	42	55.44 N	6.05 W
Bhendkhal	262c	18.53 N	72.59 E
Bhera	113	32.29 N	72.55 E
Bheramara	116	24.02 N	88.58 E
Bheri ≃	114	28.44 N	81.16 E
Bheula, Beinn Λ	42	56.08 N	4.58 W
Bhīkampur	262a	28.45 N	77.27 E
Bhikangaon	110	21.52 N	75.57 E
Bhilai	110	21.13 N	81.26 E
Bhilainagar → Bhilai	110	21.13 N	81.26 E
Bhīlsa □[5]	114	24.00 N	77.50 E
Bhīlwāra	110	25.21 N	74.38 E
Bhīma ≃	112	16.25 N	77.17 E
Bhīmavaram	112	16.32 N	81.32 E
Bhimbar	113	32.59 N	74.04 E
Bhīmphedi	114	27.32 N	85.07 E
Bhīmpur, Bhārat	116	22.37 N	87.08 E
Bhimpur, Bhārat	262b	22.46 N	88.08 E
Bhind	114	26.34 N	78.48 E
Bhind □[5]	114	26.30 N	78.35 E
Bhinga	114	27.43 N	81.56 E
Bhīnmāl	110	25.00 N	72.15 E
Bhiwandi	112	19.18 N	73.04 E
Bhiwāni	114	28.47 N	76.08 E
Bhoāgāchi	262b	22.57 N	88.20 E
Bhojpur	114	27.10 N	87.03 E
Bhojudih	116	23.38 N	86.27 E
Bhokardan	112	20.16 N	75.46 E
Bhola	114	22.41 N	90.39 E
Bhola ≃[1]	116	22.04 N	89.49 E
Bhongaon	114	27.15 N	79.11 E
Bhongīr	112	17.31 N	78.53 E
Bhonrāsa	114	22.59 N	76.12 E
Bhopāl	114	23.16 N	77.24 E
Bhopar	262c	19.12 N	73.05 E
Bhopura	262a	28.42 N	77.20 E
Bhoutan → Bhutan □[1]	110	27.30 N	90.30 E
Bhowali	114	29.23 N	79.31 E
Bhuāpur	262a	28.43 N	77.26 E
Bhuban	110	20.53 N	85.50 E
Bhubaneswar	110	20.14 N	85.50 E
Bhucho	113	30.13 N	75.06 E
Bhuj	110	23.16 N	69.40 E
Bhunarheri	114	30.13 N	76.27 E
Bhusāwal	110	21.03 N	75.46 E
Bhūshana	116	23.24 N	89.40 E
Bhutali	262c	19.07 N	73.04 E
Bhutan □[1]	108 110	 27.30 N	 90.30 E
Biá ≃	236	3.28 S	67.23 W
Bia, Phou Λ	100	18.59 N	103.09 E
Bībānak	118	32.11 N	64.11 E
Biabo ≃	238	6.58 S	76.23 W
Biacesa	58	45.56 N	10.47 E
Biache-Saint-Vaast	46	50.18 N	2.57 E
Biadene	58	45.47 N	12.04 E
Biafo Glacier ⍓	113	35.50 N	75.40 E
Biafra, Bight of C[3]	124	4.00 N	8.00 E
Biak I	154	1.00 S	136.00 E
Biała	30	50.23 N	17.40 E
Biała ≃	30	50.03 N	20.55 E
Biała Piska	30	53.37 N	22.04 E
Biała Podlaska	30	52.02 N	23.06 E
Biała Rawska	30	51.49 N	20.29 E
Białobrzegi	30	51.40 N	20.57 E
Białogard	30	54.01 N	16.00 E
Białowieski Park Narodowy ♠	30	52.40 N	23.50 E
Biały Bór	30	53.54 N	16.51 E
Białystok	30	53.09 N	23.09 E
Bian ≃	154	8.07 S	139.56 E
Bianba	110	30.49 N	94.59 E
Bianco, Canale ≅	58	45.02 N	11.30 E
Bianco, Monte (Mont Blanc) Λ	56	45.50 N	6.52 E
Bian'er	92	31.14 N	101.28 E
Bianga	142	4.51 N	20.25 E
Bian'gezhuang	95	39.28 N	115.53 E
Bianjiayuan	88	36.02 N	116.53 E
Biankouma	140	7.44 N	7.37 W
Biankouma □[5]	140	7.45 N	7.30 W
Bianlinpu	88	37.26 N	116.32 E
Bianminchang	97	29.41 N	105.04 E
Bianniulupucun	94	41.30 N	123.42 E
Bianquanwopu	94	41.21 N	120.48 E
Bianzè	56	45.18 N	8.07 E
Biaora	114	23.55 N	76.54 E
Biaro, Pulau I	102	2.05 N	125.20 E
Biarritz	32	43.29 N	1.34 W
Biasca	54	46.22 N	8.58 E
Bias Fortes	246	21.36 S	43.46 W
Biassono	56	45.37 N	9.16 E
Biaza	76	56.38 N	78.18 E
Bibā	132	28.55 N	30.59 E
Bibai	82a	43.19 N	141.52 E
Bībān	132.	30.47 N	30.40 E
Bibane, Bahiret el C	138	33.16 N	11.19 E
Bibanga	142	6.15 S	23.56 E
Bibban, Khawr ∨	130	11.00 N	32.41 E

≃ River	Fluss	Río	Rivière	Rio
≅ Canal	Kanal	Canal	Canal	Canal
⌊ Waterfall, Rapids	Wasserfall, Stromschnellen	Cascada, Rápidos	Chute d'eau, Rapides	Cascata, Rápidos
Ʉ Strait	Meeresstrasse	Estrecho	Détroit	Estreito
C Bay, Gulf	Bucht, Golf	Bahía, Golfo	Baie, Golfe	Baía, Golfo
⊜ Lake, Lakes	See, Seen	Lago, Lagos	Lac, Lacs	Lago, Lagos
⩦ Swamp	Sumpf	Pantano	Marais	Pântano
⍓ Ice Features, Glacier	Eis- und Gletscherformen	Accidentes Glaciales	Formes glaciaires	Acidentes Glaciares
⍑ Other Hydrographic Features	Andere Hydrographische Objekte	Otros Elementos Hidrográficos	Autres données hydrographiques	Outros Elementos Hidrográficos

⊹ Submarine Features	Untermeerische Objekte	Accidentes Submarinos	Formes de relief sous-marin	Acidentes Submarinos
□ Political Unit	Politische Einheit	Unidad Politica	Entité politique	Unidade Política
⩡ Cultural Institution	Kulturelle Institution	Institución Cultural	Institution culturelle	Instituição Cultural
⊥ Historical Site	Historische Stätte	Sitio Histórico	Site historique	Sítio Histórico
♠ Recreational Site	Erholungs- und Ferienort	Sitio de Recreo	Centre de loisirs	Sítio de Lazer
⊠ Airport	Flughafen	Aeropuerto	Aéroport	Aeroporto
■ Military Installation	Militäranlage	Instalación Militar	Installation militaire	Instalação Militar
◆ Miscellaneous	Verschiedenes	Misceláneo	Divers	Miscelânea

Name	Page	Lat.	Long.
Bibb City	182	32.30 N	84.59 W
Bibbiano	58	44.40 N	10.28 E
Bibbiena	60	43.42 N	11.49 E
Bibbona	60	43.16 N	10.35 E
Bibémi	136	9.19 N	13.53 E
Biberach	54	48.20 N	8.02 E
Biberach an der Riss	54	48.06 N	9.47 E
Biberbach	52	48.31 N	10.48 E
Bibert ≃	52	49.27 N	10.59 E
Bibey ≃	34	42.24 N	7.13 W
Bibiani	140	6.28 N	2.20 W
Bībi Chīni	116	22.28 N	90.12 E
Bībi Nāni	110	29.42 N	67.23 E
Bibione	58	45.38 N	13.00 E
Bibir'ovo	66	54.28 N	33.08 E
Biblián	236	2.42 S	78.52 W
Biblis	52	49.41 N	8.27 E
Bibo	92	29.02 N	99.20 E
Bic	176	48.22 N	68.42 W
Biča	76	57.53 N	70.37 E
Bicas	246	21.43 S	43.04 W
Bicas do Meio	246	22.31 S	45.21 W
Bicaz	38	46.54 N	26.05 E
Bicaz, Lacul ⊜[1]	38	47.00 N	26.00 E
Biccari	60	41.24 N	15.11 E
Bicester	44	51.54 N	1.09 W
Bičevinka	66	59.44 N	37.40 E
Biche, Lac la ⊜	172	54.50 N	112.03 W
Bichhia	114	22.27 N	80.42 E
Bichl	58	47.43 N	11.24 E
Bichlbach	54	47.25 N	10.47 E
Bichota Canyon ∨	270	34.16 N	117.48 W
Biči ≃	79	52.10 N	139.50 E
Bičigt	78	47.06 N	95.05 E
Bickenbach	52	49.45 N	8.37 E
Bickerstaffe	252	53.32 N	2.50 W
Bickerton, Cape ≻	9	66.20 S	136.56 E
Bickerton Island I	154	13.45 S	136.12 E
Bickle Knob ∧	178	38.56 N	79.44 W
Bickley •[8]	250	51.24 N	0.03 E
Bicknacre	250	51.42 N	0.35 E
Bicknell, Ind., U.S.	184	38.47 N	87.19 W
Bicknell, Utah, U.S.	190	38.20 N	111.33 W
Bicknor	250	51.18 N	0.40 E
Bicol ≃	106	13.44 N	123.07 E
Bicske	30	47.29 N	18.37 E
Bicudo ≃	245	18.04 S	44.33 W
Bičura	78	50.36 N	107.35 E
Bičurina	76	56.51 N	55.25 E
Bida, Nig.	136	12.20 N	13.25 E
Bida, Nig.	140	9.05 N	6.01 E
Bīdar	112	17.54 N	77.33 E
Biddeford	178	43.30 N	70.26 W
Biddenden	44	51.07 N	0.39 E
Biddiyā	122	32.07 N	35.05 E
Biddulph	44	53.08 N	2.10 W
Bideford	44	51.01 N	4.13 W
Bidente ≃	60	44.24 N	12.12 E
Bidford-on-Avon	44	52.10 N	1.51 W
Bidhūna	114	26.49 N	79.31 E
Bidi	134	1.00 N	42.40 E
Bidian	90	32.38 N	113.03 E
Bīdokht	118	34.21 N	58.46 E
Bidon Cinq → Post Maurice Cortier	138	22.18 N	1.05 E
Bidor	104	4.07 N	101.17 E
Bidston	252	53.24 N	3.05 W
Bidwell	178	38.55 N	82.18 W
Bidwell, Mount ∧	194	41.58 N	120.10 W
Bidya ≃[1]	116	21.56 N	88.42 E
Bidyādhari ≃	262b	22.23 N	88.35 E
Bidyādharpur	262b	22.50 N	88.24 E
Bidžan	79	47.58 N	131.58 E
Bidžan ≃	79	47.44 N	132.19 E
Bié, Ang.	142	12.22 S	16.56 E
Bie, Sve.	40	59.05 N	16.12 E
Bié □[5]	142	16.00 S	19.30 E
Biebelried	52	49.46 N	10.04 E
Bieber, B.R.D.	52	50.09 N	9.19 E
Bieber, Calif., U.S.	194	41.07 N	121.08 W
Biebrza ≃	30	53.37 N	22.56 E
Biecz	30	49.44 N	21.14 E
Biedenkopf	52	50.55 N	8.32 E
Biederitz	50	52.09 N	11.43 E
Biedermannsdorf	254b	48.05 N	16.21 E
Bieguzhuang	95	39.19 N	116.39 E
Biei	82a	43.35 N	142.28 E
Biel (Bienne)	54	47.10 N	7.12 E
Bielawa	30	50.41 N	16.38 E
Bielawski, Mount ∧	216	37.13 N	122.06 W
Bielefeld	48	52.01 N	8.31 E
Bieler Lake ⊜	166	70.20 N	73.00 W
Bielersee ⊜	54	47.05 N	7.10 E
Bielin	50	52.47 N	14.28 E
Biella	56	45.34 N	8.03 E
Bielsk	30	52.40 N	19.49 E
Bielsko-Biała	30	49.49 N	19.02 E
Bielsk Podlaski	30	52.47 N	23.12 E
Biemenhorst	48	51.49 N	6.36 E
Bienenbüttel	48	53.08 N	10.29 E
Bienfait	174	49.08 N	102.47 W
Bien-hoa	100	10.57 N	106.49 E
Bienne → Biel	54	47.10 N	7.12 E
Bienne ≃, Fr.	46	48.15 N	0.04 E
Bienne ≃, Fr.	54	46.20 N	5.38 E
Bienno	58	45.56 N	10.18 E
Bientina	60	43.42 N	10.37 E
Bienville	184	32.21 N	92.59 W
Bienville, Lac ⊜	166	55.05 N	72.40 W
Biere, D.D.R.	50	51.58 N	11.39 E
Bière, Schw.	54	46.33 N	6.20 E
Bierné	28	47.49 N	0.32 W
Bieruń Stary	30	50.06 N	19.06 E
Bierutów	30	51.08 N	17.32 E
Bierwart	52	50.34 N	5.01 E
Biesbos •[1]	48	51.45 N	4.50 E
Biesdorf •[8]	254a	52.31 N	13.33 E
Biese ≃	50	52.45 N	11.37 E
Biesel •[8]	253	51.10 N	6.29 E
Biesenthal	50	52.46 N	13.37 E
Bieshan	95	39.58 N	117.29 E
Biesiesvlei	148	26.22 S	25.55 E
Biesles	54	48.05 N	5.18 E
Bieszczadzki Park Narodowy ♣	30	49.05 N	22.45 E
Bieteluobaoluosika	79	48.35 N	119.56 E
Bietigheim, B.R.D.	52	48.54 N	8.14 E
Bietigheim, B.R.D.	52	48.58 N	9.07 E
Bietschhorn ∧	54	46.24 N	7.51 E
Bièvre	52	49.56 N	5.01 E
Bièvre ≃	251	48.47 N	2.20 E
Bièvres	251	48.45 N	2.13 E
Biferno ≃	60	41.59 N	15.02 E
Bifoum	142	0.22 S	10.23 E
Bifuka	82a	44.29 N	142.21 E
Bifurcación	248	34.19 S	56.48 W
Big ≃, Austl.	159	37.18 S	146.02 E
Big ≃, Alaska, U.S.	170	63.00 N	154.56 W
Big ≃, Mo., U.S.	209	38.28 N	90.37 W
Biga	120	40.13 N	27.14 E
Bigadiç	120	39.23 N	28.08 E
Big A Mountain ∧	182	37.03 N	82.02 W
Big Annemessex River C	198	38.03 N	75.50 W
Big Averill Lake ⊜	196	44.59 N	71.44 W
Big Bald ∧	182	34.45 N	84.19 W
Big Bald Mountain ∧	176	47.12 N	66.25 W
Big Baldy ∧	192	44.47 N	115.13 W
Big Baldy Mountain ∧	192	46.58 N	110.37 W
Big Bar Creek	172	51.12 N	122.06 W
Big Basin Redwoods State Park ♣	216	37.09 N	122.17 W
Big Bay	180	46.49 N	87.44 W
Big Bay C, N.Z.	162	44.18 S	168.05 E
Big Bay De Noc C	180	45.46 N	86.43 W
Big Bay Point ≻	202	44.24 N	79.31 W
Big Bear City	218	34.16 N	116.51 W
Big Bear Lake	218	34.15 N	116.53 W
Big Bear Lake ⊜	218	34.15 N	116.55 W
Big Beaver, Sask., Can.	174	49.08 N	105.10 W
Big Beaver, Pa., U.S.	204	40.50 N	80.20 W
Big Beaver Airport ⊠	271	42.33 N	83.06 W
Big Beaver Creek ≃, Mich., U.S.	271	42.32 N	83.01 W
Big Beaver Creek ≃, Ohio, U.S.	208	39.01 N	83.03 W
Big Beaver Creek ≃, Wash., U.S.	214	48.40 N	121.08 W
Big Bell	152	27.21 S	117.40 E
Big Belt Mountains ⛰	192	46.40 N	111.25 W
Big Bend, Swaz.	148	26.50 S	31.57 E
Big Bend, Wis., U.S.	206	42.53 N	88.12 W
Big Bend National Park ♣	186	29.12 N	103.12 W
Big Bend Reservoir ⊜[1]	172	52.57 N	115.37 W
Big Black ≃	184	32.00 N	91.05 W
Big Blue ≃, U.S.	188	39.11 N	96.32 W
Big Blue ≃, Ind., U.S.	208	39.20 N	85.59 W
Big Blue, West Fork ≃	188	40.42 N	96.59 W
Big Bone Lick State Park ♣	208	38.53 N	84.45 W
Big Bonito Creek ≃	190	33.34 N	109.56 W
Big Brady Creek ≃	186	31.07 N	98.59 W
Big Brook ≃	266	40.19 N	74.10 W
Big Brushy Creek ≃, Tex., U.S.	212	32.32 N	96.20 W
Big Brushy Creek ≃, Tex., U.S.	212	29.12 N	96.55 W
Big Bureau Creek ≃	184	41.17 N	89.21 W
Bigbury Bay C	44	50.16 N	3.48 W
Big Cabin Creek ≃	184	36.26 N	95.08 W
Big Canoe Creek ≃	184	33.52 N	86.04 W
Big Canyon ∨	186	30.05 N	101.55 W
Big Carlos Pass C	210	26.24 N	81.52 W
Big Cedar Lake ⊜	202	44.37 N	78.10 W
Big Chino Wash ∨	190	34.52 N	112.28 W
Big Clear Lake ⊜	202	44.43 N	76.55 W
Big Clifty	184	37.33 N	86.09 W
Big Coulee Creek ≃	192	46.17 N	108.56 W
Big Cow Creek ≃	184	30.34 N	93.44 W
Big Creek, B.C., Can.	172	51.44 N	123.03 W
Big Creek, Calif., U.S.	216	37.12 N	119.09 W
Big Creek ≃, B.C., Can.	172	51.40 N	122.50 W
Big Creek ≃, Ont., Can.	204	42.36 N	80.27 W
Big Creek ≃, Ont., Can.	204	42.19 N	82.27 W
Big Creek ≃, U.S.	184	40.16 N	94.03 W
Big Creek ≃, Ark., U.S.	184	34.21 N	91.03 W
Big Creek ≃, Calif., U.S.	216	36.53 N	119.15 W
Big Creek ≃, Calif., U.S.	216	37.12 N	119.19 W
Big Creek ≃, Idaho, U.S.	192	45.06 N	114.44 W
Big Creek ≃, Ill., U.S.	209	39.07 N	88.52 W
Big Creek ≃, Ind., U.S.	206	40.38 N	86.46 W
Big Creek ≃, Ind., U.S.	208	38.48 N	85.39 W
Big Creek ≃, Kans., U.S.	188	38.47 N	98.55 W
Big Creek ≃, La., U.S.	184	32.10 N	91.53 W
Big Creek ≃, Mo., U.S.	209	38.52 N	90.50 W
Big Creek ≃, Ohio, U.S.	269a	41.27 N	81.41 W
Big Creek ≃, Oreg., U.S.	214	46.11 N	123.35 W
Big Creek ≃, Tex., U.S.	212	31.09 N	96.52 W
Big Creek ≃, Tex., U.S.	212	29.22 N	95.34 W
Big Creek ≃, Wash., U.S.	214	47.15 N	121.10 W
Big Creek, East Fork ≃	184	40.16 N	94.03 W
Big Creek Parkway ♣	269a	41.24 N	81.45 W
Big Creek Peak ∧	192	44.28 N	113.32 W
Big Crow Island I	266	40.37 N	73.33 W
Big Cypress Creek ≃	212	33.00 N	94.51 W
Big Cypress Indian Reservation •[4]	210	26.14 N	80.49 W
Big Cypress National Preserve ♣	210	25.55 N	81.10 W
Big Cypress Swamp ≋	210	26.10 N	81.38 W
Big Dalton Canyon ∨	270	34.10 N	117.48 W
Big Dalton Wash ∨	270	34.04 N	117.58 W
Big Darby Creek ≃	208	39.37 N	82.58 W
Big Delta	170	64.09 N	145.50 W
Big Diomede Island → Ratmanova, Ostrov I	170	65.46 N	169.02 W
Big Ditch ☰	206	40.13 N	88.22 W
Big Dry Creek ≃	192	47.30 N	106.19 W
Big Eau Pleine ≃	180	44.48 N	90.00 W
Big Elk Creek ≃	198	39.35 N	75.52 W
Big Elkhart Creek ≃	212	31.22 N	95.41 W
Big Elm Creek ≃	212	30.53 N	96.56 W
Bigelow Bight C[3]	178	43.15 N	70.30 W
Bigéné	142	3.25 N	15.38 E
Big Escambia Creek ≃	184	30.58 N	87.14 W
Big Falls	180	48.12 N	93.48 W
Bigflat	184	36.00 N	92.24 W
Big Flat Creek ≃	184	31.33 N	87.31 W
Big Flats	200	42.08 N	76.56 W
Bigfork, Minn., U.S.	180	47.45 N	93.39 W
Bigfork, Mont., U.S.	192	48.04 N	114.04 W
Big Fork ≃	180	48.31 N	93.43 W
Big Four Ditch ☰	206	40.27 N	88.10 W
Big Frog Mountain ∧	182	35.00 N	84.32 W
Biggar, Sask., Can.	174	52.04 N	108.00 W
Biggar, Scot., U.K.	42	55.38 N	3.32 W
Biggarsberg ∧	148	28.12 S	29.48 E
Bigge	52	51.21 N	8.28 E
Biggers	184	36.20 N	90.48 W
Biggestausee ⊜[1]	52	51.05 N	7.55 E
Biggin Hill •[8]	44	51.18 N	0.04 E
Biggin Hill Aerodrome ⊠	250	51.19 N	0.03 E
Biggleswade	44	52.05 N	0.17 W
Biggs, Calif., U.S.	216	39.25 N	121.43 W
Biggs, Oreg., U.S.	214	45.40 N	120.50 W
Big Gull Lake ⊜	202	44.50 N	76.58 W
Big Gully Creek ≃	174	53.13 N	109.03 W
Bighāi ≃[1]	116	22.10 N	90.13 E
Big Hawk Lake ⊜	202	45.10 N	78.44 W
Bighead ≃	202	44.36 N	80.35 W
Big Hole ≃	192	45.34 N	112.20 W
Big Hole National Battlefield ⊥	192	45.35 N	113.35 W
Bighorn ≃	192	46.09 N	107.28 W
Big Horn Basin ≚[1]	192	44.15 N	108.10 W
Bighorn Canyon National Recreation Area ♣	192	45.00 N	108.15 W
Big Horn Lake ⊜[1]	192	45.06 N	108.08 W
Bighorn Mountains ⛰	192	44.00 N	107.30 W
Bight, Head of ≻	152	31.30 S	131.10 E
Big Huckleberry Mountain ∧	214	45.51 N	121.47 W
Big Island	182	37.32 N	79.22 W
Big Island I, N.W. Ter., Can.	166	62.43 N	70.43 W
Big Island I, Ont., Can.	174	49.10 N	94.40 W
Big Island I, Ont., Can.	202	44.33 N	78.30 W
Big Knob ∧	182	36.40 N	82.31 W
Big Koniuji Island I	170	55.06 N	159.33 W
Big Lake, Alaska, U.S.	170	61.33 N	149.52 W
Big Lake, Minn., U.S.	180	45.20 N	93.45 W
Big Lake, Tex., U.S.	186	31.12 N	101.28 W
Big Lake, Wash., U.S.	214	48.24 N	122.14 W
Big Lake ⊜, Maine, U.S.	176	45.10 N	67.40 W
Big Lake ⊜, Wash., U.S.	214	48.23 N	122.12 W
Bigler	204	40.59 N	78.19 W
Biglerville	198	39.56 N	77.15 W
Big Lick Creek ≃	206	40.22 N	85.27 W
Big Lookout Mountain ∧	192	44.37 N	117.17 W
Big Lost ≃	192	43.50 N	112.44 W
Big Monon Ditch ☰	206	40.52 N	86.46 W
Big Mossy Point ≻	174	53.42 N	98.03 W
Big Mountain ∧, B.C., Can.	170	56.53 N	131.31 W
Big Mountain ∧, Nev., U.S.	194	41.17 N	119.04 W
Big Mountain Creek ≃	172	55.04 N	118.39 W
Big Muddy ≃	184	37.35 N	89.31 W
Big Muddy, Casey Fork ≃	184	38.06 N	88.57 W
Big Muddy Creek ≃, Mont., U.S.	188	48.08 N	104.36 W
Big Muddy Creek ≃, N. Dak., U.S.	188	46.37 N	101.24 W
Big Muddy Lake ⊜	174	49.08 N	104.54 W
Big Muscamoot Bay C	271	42.33 N	82.40 W
Bignasco	54	46.20 N	8.36 E
Big Nasty Creek ≃	188	45.41 N	102.51 W
Bignona	140	12.49 N	16.14 W
Big Oak Flat	216	37.49 N	120.16 W
Bigosovo	66	55.49 N	27.43 E
Bigot, Morne ∧[2]	230e	14.31 N	61.04 W
Big Otter ≃	182	37.07 N	79.23 W
Big Otter Creek ≃	202	42.38 N	80.48 W
Big Ox Creek ≃	208	38.44 N	85.52 W
Big Pine	194	37.10 N	118.17 W
Big Pine Creek ≃	206	40.18 N	87.15 W
Big Pine Key	210	24.40 N	81.21 W
Big Pine Key I	210	24.42 N	81.23 W
Big Pine Mountain ∧	194	34.42 N	119.39 W
Big Piney	190	42.32 N	110.07 W
Big Piney ≃	184	37.53 N	92.04 W
Big Piney Creek ≃	184	35.20 N	93.20 W
Big Pipe Creek ≃	198	39.36 N	77.17 W
Big Plain	208	39.50 N	83.17 W
Big Pocono State Park ♣	200	41.03 N	75.19 W
Bigpoint	184	30.35 N	88.29 W
Big Pond	200	41.53 N	76.43 W
Big Porcupine Creek ≃	192	46.16 N	106.43 W
Big Porcupine Lake ⊜	202	45.27 N	78.36 W
Big Prairie	204	40.40 N	82.06 W
Big Prairie Creek ≃	184	32.35 N	87.45 W
Big Quilcene ≃	214	47.49 N	122.52 W
Big Quill Lake ⊜	174	51.55 N	104.22 W
Big Raccoon Creek ≃	184	39.46 N	87.22 W
Big Rapids	180	43.42 N	85.29 W
Bigras, Île I	265a	45.31 N	73.51 W
Big Rib ≃	180	44.56 N	89.41 W
Big Rideau Lake ⊜	202	44.45 N	76.14 W
Big River	174	53.50 N	107.01 W
Big River Indian Reserve •[4]	174	53.33 N	107.10 W
Big Rock	206	41.46 N	88.33 W
Big Rock Creek ≃	206	41.38 N	88.32 W
Big Rocky Creek ≃	212	29.34 N	96.50 W
Big Run	204	40.58 N	78.53 W
Big Sable ≃	180	44.02 N	86.31 W
Big Sable Point ≻	180	44.03 N	86.31 W
Big Salmon ≃	170	61.52 N	134.56 W
Big Salmon Range ⛰	170	60.20 N	132.40 W
Big Sand Lake ⊜	166	57.45 N	99.42 W
Big Sandy, Mont., U.S.	192	48.11 N	110.07 W
Big Sandy, Tenn., U.S.	184	36.15 N	88.05 W
Big Sandy, Tex., U.S.	212	32.35 N	95.07 W
Big Sandy ≃, U.S.	178	31.20 N	81.20 W
Big Sandy ≃, Ariz., U.S.	190	34.19 N	113.31 W
Big Sandy ≃, Tenn., U.S.	184	36.15 N	88.06 W
Big Sandy ≃, Wyo., U.S.	192	41.51 N	109.47 W
Big Sandy, Levisa Fork ≃	182	38.06 N	82.36 W
Big Sandy, Rolling Fork ≃	182	37.24 N	82.26 W
Big Sandy, Tug Fork ≃	182	38.06 N	82.36 W
Big Sandy Creek ≃, Calif., U.S.	216	35.47 N	120.43 W
Big Sandy Creek ≃, Colo., U.S.	188	38.06 N	102.29 W
Big Sandy Creek ≃, Ga., U.S.	182	32.42 N	82.57 W
Big Sandy Creek ≃, Mont., U.S.	192	48.34 N	109.48 W
Big Sandy Creek ≃, Nebr., U.S.	188	40.13 N	97.18 W
Big Sandy Creek ≃, Tex., U.S.	186	33.11 N	97.40 W
Big Sandy Creek ≃, Tex., U.S.	212	32.33 N	95.05 W
Big Sandy Creek ≃, Tex., U.S.	212	30.31 N	94.28 W
Big Sandy Lake ⊜, Sask., Can.	174	54.26 N	104.04 W
Big Sandy Lake ⊜, Minn., U.S.	180	46.45 N	93.17 W
Big Sandy Reservoir ⊜[1]	190	42.16 N	109.26 W
Big Satilla Creek ≃	182	31.27 N	82.03 W
Bigsby Island I	188	49.04 N	94.35 W
Big Sewickley Creek ≃	269b	40.35 N	80.13 W
Big Shawnee Creek ≃	206	40.15 N	87.18 W
Big Sheep Mountain ∧	192	47.03 N	105.43 W
Big Signal Peak ∧	194	39.31 N	123.06 W
Big Sioux ≃	188	42.30 N	96.25 W
Big Sky	192	45.17 N	111.17 W
Big Slough ≃	182	30.56 N	84.33 W
Big Smoky Valley ∨	194	38.30 N	117.15 W
Big Snowy Mountains ⛰	192	46.50 N	109.30 W
Big Southern Butte ∧	192	43.23 N	113.01 W
Big Spanish Channel ⊔	210	24.44 N	81.20 W
Bigspring, Mo., U.S.	209	38.38 N	91.28 W
Big Spring, Tex., U.S.	186	32.15 N	101.28 W
Big Springs	188	41.04 N	102.05 W
Big Spruce Knob ∧	178	38.16 N	80.12 W
Big Squaw Mountain ∧	178	45.30 N	69.45 W
Bigstick Lake ⊜	174	50.16 N	109.20 W
Bigstone ≃	174	55.55 N	94.36 W
Big Stone City	188	45.18 N	96.28 W
Big Stone Gap	182	36.52 N	82.47 W
Bigstone Lake ⊜, Man., Can.	174	53.42 N	95.44 W
Big Stone Lake ⊜, U.S.	188	45.25 N	96.40 W
Big Sur	216	36.15 N	121.48 W
Big Sur ≃	216	36.17 N	121.51 W
Big Swamp Creek ≃	184	32.19 N	86.49 W
Big Swan Creek ≃	184	35.46 N	87.24 W
Big Thicket National Preserve ♣	212	32.35 N	94.40 W
Big Thompson ≃	190	40.21 N	104.45 W
Big Timber	192	45.50 N	109.57 W
Big Timber Creek ≃	275	39.53 N	75.08 W
Big Timber Creek, South Branch ≃	275	39.50 N	75.05 W
Big Torch Key I	210	24.43 N	81.26 W
Big Tree	200	42.46 N	78.49 W
Big Trout Lake ⊜, Ont., Can.	166	53.45 N	90.00 W
Big Trout Lake ⊜, Ont., Can.	202	44.56 N	78.56 W
Big Tujunga Canyon ∨	218	34.16 N	118.18 W
Big Tujunga Dam •[6]	270	34.18 N	118.12 W
Biguaçu	242	27.30 S	48.40 W
Big Valley	172	52.02 N	112.46 W
Bigwa	144	7.13 S	39.09 E
Big Walnut Creek ≃, Ind., U.S.	184	39.30 N	86.57 W
Big Walnut Creek ≃, Ohio, U.S.	204	40.02 N	82.54 W
Big Warrambool ≃	156	30.05 S	147.33 E
Big Wells	186	28.34 N	99.34 W
Big White Mountain ∧	172	49.42 N	118.58 W
Big Wood ≃	192	42.52 N	114.54 W
Bihać	36	44.49 N	15.52 E
Bīhar	114	25.11 N	85.31 E
Bihār □[3]	114	25.00 N	86.00 E
Biharamulo	144	2.38 S	31.20 E
Bihārīganj	114	25.44 N	86.59 E
Bihen	134	10.38 N	48.24 E
Bihor □[5]	38	47.00 N	22.15 E
Bihoro	82a	43.49 N	144.07 E
Bihta	114	25.33 N	84.52 E
Bihu	90	28.21 N	119.48 E
Bija ≃	76	52.25 N	85.05 E
Bijagós, Arquipélago dos II	140	11.25 N	16.20 W
Bijainagar	110	25.56 N	74.38 E
Bijaipura	114	24.46 N	77.48 E
Bījāpur, Bhārat	112	18.48 N	80.49 E
Bijāpur, Bhārat	112	16.50 N	75.42 E
Bījār	118	35.52 N	47.36 E
Bijauri	114	28.06 N	82.20 E
Bijāwar	114	24.38 N	79.30 E
Bijbān Chāh	118	26.54 N	64.42 E
Bījbiāra	113	33.48 N	75.06 E
Bijeljina	38	44.45 N	19.13 E
Bijelo Polje	38	43.02 N	19.44 E
Bījenābād	118	27.55 N	58.03 E
Bijeypur	114	26.03 N	77.22 E
Bijiang	100	26.30 N	98.55 E
Bijianqiao	97	30.14 N	106.09 E
Bijiaqiao	96	31.02 N	119.02 E
Bijiashan ∧	95	40.17 N	116.50 E
Bijie	92	27.18 N	105.20 E
Bijlikol', •Ero ⊜	75	43.03 N	70.41 E
Bijna	262b	22.55 N	88.27 E
Bijni	114	26.31 N	90.40 E
Bijnor	114	29.22 N	78.08 E
Bijnor □[5]	114	29.30 N	78.25 E
Bijōki	258	35.49 N	139.39 E
Bijou	194	38.57 N	119.58 W
Bijou Creek ≃	188	40.17 N	103.52 W
Bijpur	116	22.56 N	88.26 E
Bijsk	76	52.34 N	85.15 E
Bijuk-Karasu ≃	68	45.27 N	34.47 E
Bijwāsan •[8]	262a	28.32 N	77.03 E
Bīkaner	110	28.01 N	73.18 E
Bīkaner □[5]	113	28.42 N	73.25 E
Bīkaner Canal ☰	113	30.08 N	73.57 E
Bikar I[1]	14	12.15 N	170.06 E
Bikbulovo	70	55.39 N	53.26 E
Bike	134	9.30 N	41.18 E
Bikeman Island I	164t	1.22 N	173.00 E
Bikenibeu	164t	1.21 N	173.07 E
Bikeqi	92	40.49 N	111.13 E
Bikeru	102	5.15 S	120.07 E
Bikfayyā	122	33.55 N	35.41 E
Bikié	142	3.06 S	13.52 E
Bikin	79	46.48 N	134.16 E
Bikin ≃	79	46.51 N	134.02 E
Bikini I[1]	14	11.35 N	165.23 E
Bikita	144	20.06 S	31.41 E
Bikl'an'	70	55.37 N	52.10 E
Bikoro	142	0.45 S	18.07 E
Bikova	66	56.45 N	27.04 E
Bikuar, Parque Nacional do ♣	142	15.12 S	14.42 W
Bila ≃	104	2.30 N	100.08 E
Bilaa Point ≻	106	9.49 N	125.26 E
Bilac	245	21.24 S	50.28 W
Bilād Ghāmid •[1]	134	20.00 N	41.30 E
Bilād Zahrān •[1]	134	20.16 N	41.14 E
Bílá hora ⊥	50	50.10 N	14.10 E
Bilanga	140	12.32 N	0.02 W
Bilāra	110	26.10 N	73.42 E
Bilāri	114	28.38 N	78.48 E
Bil'arsk	70	54.58 N	50.22 E
Bilāsipāra	114	26.14 N	90.14 E
Bilāspur, Bhārat	113	31.20 N	76.45 E
Bilāspur, Bhārat	114	22.05 N	82.09 E
Bilaspur, Bhārat	114	28.53 N	79.16 E
Bilāspur □[5]	114	22.30 N	82.10 E
Bil'asuvar	74	39.24 N	48.24 E
Bilatan Island I	106	4.59 N	120.00 E
Bilato	102	0.32 N	122.38 E
Bilauktaung Range ⛰	100	13.00 N	99.00 E
Bilauri	114	28.41 N	80.21 E
Bilbao	34	43.15 N	2.58 W
Bilbays	132	30.25 N	31.34 E
Bilbays Military Base ■	132	30.24 N	31.36 E
Bilbilis ⊥	34	41.25 N	1.39 W
Bil'čir	78	51.02 N	110.34 E
Bileća	38	42.53 N	18.26 E
Bilecik	120	40.09 N	29.59 E
Bilecik □[4]	120	40.10 N	30.10 E
Biles Island I	275	40.10 N	74.45 W
Biłgoraj	30	50.34 N	22.43 E
Bilgrām	114	27.11 N	80.02 E
Bili	144	4.09 N	25.10 E
Bili ≃	126	4.50 N	22.29 E
Bilian	90	28.21 N	120.33 E
Bilican Dağları ⛰	120	38.58 N	42.10 E
Bilifyā	132	29.07 N	31.03 E
Bilimora	110	20.45 N	72.57 E
Bilin	100	17.14 N	97.15 E
Bilin ≃	100	17.05 N	97.08 E
Bílina	50	50.35 N	13.45 E
Bílina ≃	50	50.40 N	14.02 E
Biliran Island I	106	11.35 N	124.28 E
Biliran Strait ⊔	106	11.30 N	124.28 E
Biliuhe ≃	88	39.30 N	122.36 E
Bilk •[8]	253	51.12 N	6.47 E
Bilkfontein	148	27.50 S	23.56 E
Billabong Creek ≃	156	35.06 S	144.02 E
Billeberga	41	55.53 N	13.00 E
Billerbeck	48	51.59 N	7.17 E
Billerica	197	42.34 N	71.16 W
Billericay	44	51.38 N	0.25 E
Billesdon	44	52.37 N	0.55 W
Billesholm	41	56.03 N	13.00 E
Billiat	54	46.04 N	5.47 E
Billiatt National Park ♣	156	35.00 S	140.30 E
Billigheim	52	49.21 N	9.15 E
Billiluna	152	19.37 S	127.41 E
Billinge, Sve.	41	55.58 N	13.21 E
Billinge, Eng., U.K.	252	53.30 N	2.42 W
Billingen ⛰[2]	26	58.24 N	13.45 E
Billingham	42	54.36 N	1.17 W
Billings, Mo., U.S.	184	37.04 N	93.33 W
Billings, Mont., U.S.	192	45.47 N	118.27 W
Billings, Okla., U.S.	186	36.32 N	97.27 W
Billingsfors	26	58.59 N	12.15 E
Billings Heights	192	45.50 N	108.33 W
Billingshurst	44	51.01 N	0.28 W
Billmerich	253	51.30 N	7.47 E
Billolo ≃	263b	4.07 S	15.19 E
Billom	32	45.44 N	3.21 E
Billund	41	55.44 N	9.07 E
Bill Williams ≃	190	34.17 N	114.03 W
Bill Williams Mountain ∧	190	35.17 N	112.12 W
Billy Chinook, Lake ⊜[1]	192	44.33 N	121.20 W
Billy-Montigny	46	50.25 N	2.52 E
Bilma	136	18.41 N	12.56 E
Biloela	156	24.24 S	150.30 E
Bilo Gora ⛰	36	46.06 N	16.46 E
Biloxi	184	30.24 N	88.53 W
Biloxi ≃	184	30.26 N	89.00 W
Biloxi Creek ≃	212	31.05 N	94.37 W
Bilpa Morea Claypan ≚	156	25.00 S	140.00 E
Bilpin	160	33.30 S	150.31 E
Bilqās Qism Awwal	132	31.13 N	31.21 E
Bilsārā	116	23.05 N	88.10 E
Bilshausen	48	51.37 N	10.10 E
Bilsi	114	28.08 N	78.55 E
Bilston	44	52.34 N	2.04 W
Biltāj	132	31.00 N	30.59 E
Biltān	132	30.23 N	31.10 E
Bilthoven	48	52.07 N	5.17 E
Biltine	136	14.32 N	20.55 E
Biltine □[5]	136	15.00 N	21.00 E
Biltmore Forest	182	35.32 N	82.32 W
Bilugyun Island I	100	16.24 N	97.32 E
Bilwascarma	226	14.45 N	83.53 W
Bilzen	52	50.52 N	5.31 E
Bima	105b	8.28 S	118.43 E
Bimbān	130	24.26 N	32.53 E
Bimbe	142	11.49 S	15.49 E
Bimbéréké	140	10.13 N	2.40 E
Bimberi Peak ∧	161b	35.40 S	148.47 E
Bimbila	140	8.51 N	0.04 E
Bimbo	142	4.18 N	18.33 E
Bimbowrie	156	32.03 S	140.09 E
Bimé	263b	4.09 S	15.11 E
Bimini Islands II	228	25.44 N	79.15 W
Bina	165e	8.55 S	160.46 E
Bīna-Etāwa	114	24.11 N	78.11 E
Binagadi	74	40.28 N	49.49 E
Binaiya, Gunung ∧	154	3.11 S	129.26 E
Binalbagan	106	10.12 N	122.50 E
Binalbagan ≃	106	10.12 N	122.51 E
Binalonan	106	16.03 N	120.36 E
Binanga	104	1.24 N	99.46 E
Binangonan	106	14.28 N	121.11 E
Bin'anzhen	79	45.50 N	127.45 E
Binas	46	47.54 N	1.28 E
Binasco	56	45.20 N	9.06 E
Binau	52	49.22 N	9.04 E
Binboğadağı ∧	120	38.21 N	36.32 E
Binche	46	50.24 N	4.10 E
Bindal	24	65.06 N	12.30 E
Bindebango	156	27.45 S	147.24 E
Binder	78	48.35 N	110.36 E
Binder Foulbé	136	9.58 N	14.28 E
Bindki	114	26.02 N	80.36 E
Bindloss	174	50.52 N	110.16 W
Bindow	254a	52.17 N	13.45 E
Bindura	144	17.19 S	31.20 E
Bine-el-Ouidane	138	32.07 N	6.26 W
Binéfar	34	41.51 N	0.18 E
Binford	188	47.34 N	98.21 W
Binga, Pil.	106	10.45 N	119.19 E
Binga, Zaïre	142	2.23 N	20.30 E
Binga, Monte ∧	146	19.45 S	33.04 E
Bingara	156	29.52 S	150.34 E
Bingaram Island I	112	10.56 N	72.17 E
Bingay Point ≻	106	13.04 N	124.11 E
Bingcha	90	32.30 N	120.52 E
Bingen, B.R.D.	52	49.57 N	7.54 E
Bingen, Wash., U.S.	214	45.43 N	121.28 W
Binger	186	35.18 N	98.21 W
Bingerbrück	52	49.58 N	7.53 E
Bingerville	140	5.21 N	3.54 W
Bingham, Eng., U.K.	44	52.57 N	0.57 W
Bingham, Maine, U.S.	178	45.03 N	69.53 W
Bingham Creek ≃	214	47.09 N	123.24 W
Bingham Farms	271	42.32 N	83.16 W
Binghamton	200	42.08 N	75.54 W
Bin Ghunaymah, Jabal ∧[2]	136	25.00 N	15.30 E
Bingi	144	0.24 S	29.05 E
Bingley	42	53.51 N	1.50 W
Bingöl	120	38.53 N	40.29 E
Bingöl □[4]	120	39.00 N	40.40 E
Bingöl Dağları ⛰	120	39.20 N	41.20 E
Binhai (Dongkan)	90	34.03 N	119.51 E
Binh-ca	100	21.48 N	105.18 E
Binh-chanh	259c	10.40 N	106.34 E
Binh-gia	100	21.59 N	106.21 E
Binh-hung-hoa	259c	10.49 N	106.37 E
Binh-khe	100	13.57 N	108.51 E
Binh-kieu	100	15.35 N	108.04 E
Binh-son	100	15.18 N	108.46 E
Binh-trung	259c	10.47 N	106.46 E
Binigsian Point ≻	106	9.50 N	122.23 E
Bining-lès-Rohrbach	52	49.02 N	7.15 E
Binit Point ≻	106	9.54 N	125.17 E
Binjai	104	3.36 N	98.30 E
Binjiang ≃	90	23.40 N	112.58 E
Binjohara	104	2.12 N	98.12 E
Binna Burra	161a	28.13 S	153.14 E
Binnah, Ras ≻	134	11.06 N	51.13 E
Binnaway	156	31.33 S	149.23 E
Binnian, Slieve ∧	42	54.08 N	5.58 W
Binningen	54	47.32 N	7.34 E
Binodepur	116	23.26 N	89.30 E
Binongko, Pulau I	102	5.57 S	124.02 E
Binpur	116	22.36 N	86.55 E
Binscarth	174	50.37 N	101.16 W
Binsheim	253	51.31 N	6.42 E
Bintan, Pulau I	102	1.05 N	104.30 E
Bintang	140	13.10 N	16.08 W
Bintauna	102	0.53 N	123.33 E
Bint Goda	130	13.17 N	31.33 E
Bintimani ∧	140	9.13 N	11.07 W
Bint Jubayl	122	33.07 N	35.26 E
Bintuhan	102	4.48 S	103.22 E
Bintulu	102	3.10 N	113.02 E
Bintuni, Teluk C	154	2.20 S	133.30 E
Binxian, Zhg.	79	45.44 N	127.29 E
Binxian, Zhg.	88	37.28 N	117.56 E
Binxian, Zhg.	92	35.00 N	108.08 E
Binyamina	122	32.31 N	34.57 E
Binyang	92	23.18 N	108.46 E
Bin Yauri	140	10.47 N	4.50 E
Bin Yumayn, Ghayl ⊤[4]	134	15.35 N	49.20 E
Binz	50	54.24 N	13.36 E
Binza	263b	4.21 S	15.14 E
Binza ≃	263b	4.21 S	15.14 E
Binzert (Bizerte)	138	37.17 N	9.52 E
Bio Addo	134	8.16 N	49.52 E
Bío-Bío □[4]	242	37.45 S	72.00 W
Bío-Bío ≃	242	36.49 S	73.10 W
Biodi	144	3.19 N	28.35 E
Bio Gorge ∨	140	8.20 N	2.20 W
Biograd	36	43.56 N	15.27 E
Biola	216	36.48 N	120.01 W
Bionaz	56	45.52 N	7.25 E
Biondo	144	0.23 S	25.13 E
Biondo Monument ⊥	136	31.25 N	10.15 E
Biot	56	43.38 N	7.06 E
Bipindi	142	3.05 N	10.25 E
Bippus	206	40.57 N	85.37 W
Bīr	112	18.59 N	75.46 E
Bir, Ras ≻	134	11.59 N	43.22 E
Bira, Bhārat	262b	22.47 N	88.34 E
Bira, S.S.S.R.	79	49.02 N	132.30 E
Bira, S.S.S.R.	79	49.15 N	137.16 E
Birab	154	6.12 S	138.25 E
Bīraba	116	23.51 N	90.34 E
Birakan	79	49.01 N	131.42 E
Bi'r 'Alī	134	14.01 N	48.19 E
Bi'r al-Uzam	136	31.54 N	23.58 E
Birao	136	10.17 N	22.47 E
Birati	262b	22.39 N	88.27 E
Birātnagar	114	26.29 N	87.17 E
Birava	144	2.21 S	28.54 E
Bīrbhūm □[5]	114	24.00 N	87.40 E
Bîrca	38	43.58 N	23.37 E
Bircao → Bur Gavo	134	1.10 S	41.50 E
Birch	252	53.34 N	2.13 W
Birch ≃, Alta., Can.	166	58.30 N	112.15 W
Birch ≃, W. Va., U.S.	178	38.35 N	80.53 W
Birch Bay	214	48.55 N	122.45 W
Birch Bay C	214	48.53 N	122.47 W
Birch Bay State Park ♣	214	49.54 N	123.47 W
Birch Cliff •[8]	265b	43.41 N	79.17 W
Birch Creek ≃, Alaska, U.S.	170	66.30 N	146.30 W
Birch Creek ≃, Idaho, U.S.	192	43.51 N	112.43 W
Birch Creek ≃, Mont., U.S.	192	47.45 N	109.34 W
Birch Hill Reservoir ⊜[1]	197	42.40 N	72.07 W
Birch Hills	174	52.59 N	105.25 W
Birchington	44	51.23 N	1.19 E
Birch Island	172	51.36 N	119.55 W
Birch Island I	174	52.25 N	99.55 W
Birch Lake ⊜, Ont., Can.	174	51.24 N	92.20 W
Birch Lake ⊜, Sask., Can.	174	53.28 N	108.07 W
Birch Mountains ⛰[2]	166	57.30 N	112.30 W
Bir Chouhada	34	35.53 N	6.18 E
Birch Pond ⊜	273	42.28 N	71.00 W
Birch River	174	52.23 N	101.06 W
Birch Run	180	43.15 N	83.48 W
Birch Run ≃	275	40.09 N	75.37 W
Birch Tree	184	37.00 N	91.30 W
Birch Vale	252	53.23 N	1.57 W
Birchwood, N.Z.	162	45.56 S	167.52 E
Birchwood, Alaska, U.S.	170	61.28 N	149.22 W
Birchwood, Wis., U.S.	180	45.40 N	91.33 W
Birchwood Park, Del., U.S.	275	39.40 N	75.41 W
Birchwood Park, N.J., U.S.	198	40.06 N	74.09 W
Birchy Bay	176	49.21 N	54.44 W
Bird City	188	39.45 N	101.32 W
Bird Creek ≃	186	36.13 N	95.44 W
Bird Hills Wildflower Sanctuary ♣	159	38.23 S	144.11 E
Bird Island	188	44.46 N	94.54 W
Bird Island I, Falk. Is.	234	54.00 S	38.05 W
Bird Island I, S. Afr.	148	33.51 S	26.18 E
Bird Islet I	150	22.10 S	155.28 E
Bird River C	274b	39.23 N	76.23 W
Birdsall	200	42.23 N	77.55 W
Birdsboro	198	40.16 N	75.48 W
Birds Landing	272	38.08 N	121.52 W
Birdsview	214	48.32 N	121.52 W
Birdsville	156	25.54 S	139.22 E
Birdtail Creek ≃	174	50.16 N	101.12 W
Birdum	154	15.39 S	133.13 E
Birdum Creek ≃	154	15.14 S	133.00 E
Birdwood	158b	34.49 S	138.57 E
Birecik	120	37.02 N	37.58 E
Bireuen	104	5.12 N	96.41 E
Bīrganj	114	27.00 N	84.52 E
Bir Gara	136	13.11 N	15.58 E
Bir Ghbalou	34	36.16 N	3.35 E
Birgi	116	22.42 N	86.41 E
Birigui	245	21.18 S	50.19 W
Biri Island I	106	12.40 N	124.22 E
Birik	120	39.01 N	38.15 E
Birikčul'	76	53.20 N	89.56 E
Biril'ussy	76	57.07 N	90.32 E
Birimbāl	132	31.21 N	30.30 E
Birimbāl al-Qadīmah	132	31.10 N	31.44 E
Birimşe	120	38.03 N	38.32 E
Biritiba-Mirim	246	23.35 S	46.02 W
Bīrjand	118	32.53 N	59.13 E
Birkat as-Sab'	132	30.38 N	31.05 E
Birkat Ghiṭās	132	31.07 N	30.16 E
Birkdale	252	53.37 N	3.02 W
Birkeland	26	58.20 N	8.14 E
Birken	172	50.29 N	122.36 W
Birkenfeld, B.R.D.	52	49.51 N	9.42 E
Birkenfeld, B.R.D.	52	49.39 N	7.10 E
Birkenfeld, B.R.D.	52	48.52 N	8.38 E
Birkenfeld, Oreg., U.S.	214	46.00 N	123.20 W
Birkenhead	42	53.24 N	3.02 W
Birkenhead Park ♣	252	53.24 N	3.02 W
Birkenwerder bei Berlin	50	52.41 N	13.16 E
Birkerød	41	55.50 N	12.26 E
Birkesdorf	52	50.49 N	6.28 E
Birket Fatimé	136	12.54 N	19.05 E
Birkfeld	30	47.21 N	15.42 E
Birkholz	254a	52.38 N	13.34 E
Birkkar-Spitze ∧	58	47.25 N	11.25 E
Birksgate Range ⛰	152	27.10 S	129.45 E
Bîrlad	38	46.14 N	27.40 E
Bîrlad ≃	38	45.36 N	27.31 E
Birla Museum ⊍	262b	22.32 N	88.22 E
Birlik, S.S.S.R.	70	47.28 N	50.32 E
Birlik, S.S.S.R.	76	44.05 N	73.31 E
Birling	250	51.19 N	0.25 E
Birling ∧[2]	264a	33.57 S	150.43 E
Birmā	132	30.51 N	30.54 E
Birmaj	74	39.46 N	47.56 E
Birmania → Burma □[1]	100	22.00 N	98.00 E
Birmanie → Burma □[1]	100	22.00 N	98.00 E
Birmingham, Eng., U.K.	44	52.30 N	1.50 W
Birmingham, Ala., U.S.	184	33.31 N	86.49 W
Birmingham, Iowa, U.S.	180	40.53 N	91.57 W
Birmingham, Mich., U.S.	206	42.33 N	83.15 W
Birmingham, N.J., U.S.	275	39.59 N	74.43 W
Birmingham, Ohio, U.S.	204	41.20 N	82.21 W
Birmingham, Pa., U.S.	204	40.38 N	78.13 W
Birmingham Airport ⊠	44	52.27 N	1.45 W
Birmitrapur	114	22.24 N	84.46 E
Bir Mogreïn (Fort-Trinquet)	138	25.14 N	11.35 W
Birnagar	116	23.14 N	88.33 E
Birnamwood	180	44.56 N	89.13 W
Bi'r Naṣīf	118	24.51 N	39.11 E
Birnbaum	58	46.41 N	12.54 E
Birni	140	10.00 N	1.31 E
Birnie I[1]	14	3.35 S	171.31 W
Birni Ngaouré	140	13.05 N	2.54 E
Birnin Gwari	140	11.01 N	6.48 E
Birnin Kebbi	140	12.32 N	4.12 E
Birni Nkonni	140	13.48 N	5.15 E
Birnin Kudu	140	11.27 N	9.30 E
Birobidžan	79	48.48 N	132.57 E
Birofel'd	79	48.26 N	132.47 E
Birome	212	31.49 N	96.58 W
Birqāsh	132	30.10 N	31.02 E
Birr	28	53.05 N	7.54 W
Birregurra	159	38.20 S	143.48 E
Birribi	154	9.31 S	147.27 E
Birrie ≃	156	29.43 S	146.37 E
Birrindudu	152	18.22 S	129.27 E
Birs ≃	54	47.22 N	7.22 E
Birsilpur	110	28.10 N	72.15 E

The columns headed ENGLISH / DEUTSCH read: Name, Page, Lat.°′, Long.°′ / Name, Seite, Breite°′, Länge°′ E=Ost.

Symbols in the index entries represent the broad categories identified in the key at the right. Symbols with superior numbers (⛰[2]) identify subcategories (see complete key on page *I* · 26).

Kartensymbole in dem Registerverzeichnis stellen die rechts in Schlüssel erklärten Kategorien dar. Symbole mit hochgestellten Ziffern (⛰[2]) bezeichnen Unterabteilungen einer Kategorie (vgl. vollständiger Schlüssel auf Seite *I* · 26).

Los símbolos incluídos en el texto del índice representan las grandes categorias identificadas con la clave a la derecha. Los símbolos con numeros en su parte superior (⛰[2]) identifican las subcategorías (véase la clave completa en la página *I* · 26).

Les symboles de l'index représentent les catégories indiquées dans la légende à droite. Les symboles suivis d'un indice (⛰[2]) représentent des sous-catégories (voir légende complète à la page *I* · 26).

Os símbolos incluídos no texto do índice representam as grandes categorias identificadas com a chave à direita. Os símbolos com números em sua parte superior (⛰[2]) identificam as subcategorias (veja-se a chave completa à página *I* · 26).

Symbol	English	Deutsch	Español	Français	Português
∧	Mountain	Berg	Montaña	Montagne	Montanha
⛰	Mountains	Berge	Montañas	Montagnes	Montanhas
)(	Pass	Pass	Paso	Col	Passo
∨	Valley, Canyon	Tal, Cañon	Valle, Cañón	Vallée, Canyon	Vale, Canhão
≚	Plain	Ebene	Llano	Plaine	Planície
≻	Cape	Kap	Cabo	Cap	Cabo
I	Island	Insel	Isla	Île	Ilha
II	Islands	Inseln	Islas	Îles	Ilhas
•	Other Topographic Features	Andere Topographische Objekte	Otros Elementos Topográficos	Autres données topographiques	Outros Elementos Topográficos

ESPAÑOL / FRANÇAIS / PORTUGUÊS

Nombre / Nom / Nome	Página / Page / Página	Lat.°′	Long.°′ W=Oeste / W=Ouest / W=Oeste
Birsk	76	55.25 N	55.32 E
Birstall	44	52.41 N	1.07 W
Birstein	52	50.21 N	9.19 E
Birštonas	66	54.37 N	24.02 E
Birten	253	51.38 N	6.29 E
Birtle	174	50.25 N	101.03 W
Birtley	42	54.54 N	1.34 W
Bir'učij	73	46.53 N	39.33 E
Bir'učij, Ostrov I	68	46.08 N	35.05 E
Bir'učja ≃	73	47.23 N	39.07 E
Birufu	154	5.52 S	138.24 E
Bir'ukovo	73	47.57 N	39.44 E
Bir'ul'ka	78	53.52 N	106.21 E
Bir'ul'ovo ◆[8]	255b	55.35 N	37.40 E
Birūr	112	13.37 N	75.58 E
Bir'usa ≃	78	57.43 N	95.24 E
Biržai	66	56.12 N	24.45 E
Bîrzava ≃	38	45.16 N	20.49 E
Birżebbuġa	36	35.49 N	14.32 E
Bisa, Pulau I	154	1.15 S	127.28 E
Bisaccia	60	41.01 N	15.22 E
Bisāi, Bhārat	116	22.10 N	86.24 E
Bisai, Nihon	84	35.16 N	136.44 E
Bīsalpur	114	28.18 N	79.48 E
Bisamberg	254b	48.20 N	16.22 E
Bisamberg ∧[2]	254b	48.19 N	16.22 E
Bisan-shotō II	86	34.24 N	133.50 E
Bisbee, Ariz., U.S.	190	31.27 N	109.55 W
Bisbee, N. Dak., U.S.	188	48.37 N	99.23 W
Biscarosse, Étang de C	32	44.20 N	1.10 E
Biscarrosse	32	44.24 N	1.10 W
Biscay, Bay of C	32	44.00 N	4.00 W
Biscayne Bay C	210	25.33 N	80.15 W
Biscayne National Monument ♠	210	25.25 N	80.12 W
Bisceglie	36	41.14 N	16.31 E
Bischheim	54	48.37 N	7.45 E
Bischofsburg → Biskupiec	30	53.52 N	20.58 E
Bischofsheim, B.R.D.	52	50.24 N	10.01 E
Bischofsheim, B.R.D.	52	49.59 N	8.22 E
Bischofshofen	58	47.25 N	13.13 E
Bischofstal → Ujazd	30	50.24 N	18.22 E
Bischofstein → Bisztynek	30	54.06 N	20.55 E
Bischofswerda	50	51.07 N	14.10 E
Bischofswiesen	58	47.39 N	12.57 E
Bischofszell	54	47.29 N	9.15 E
Bischwald, Étang de ⊛	52	49.00 N	6.42 E
Bischwiller	52	48.46 N	7.52 E
Biscoe, Ark., U.S.	184	34.49 N	91.24 W
Biscoe, N.C., U.S.	182	35.22 N	79.47 W
Biscoe Islands II	9	66.00 S	66.30 W
Biscotasi Lake ⊛	180	47.19 N	82.07 W
Biscucuy	236	9.22 N	69.59 W
Bise	164m	26.42 N	127.54 E
Bisei	86	34.41 N	133.33 E
Bisentina, Isola I	60	42.35 N	11.54 E
Bisenzio ≃	60	43.46 N	11.06 E
Biser	76	58.25 N	58.53 E
Biserovo	255b	55.47 N	38.07 E
Biserovskoje, Ozero ⊛	255b	55.46 N	38.07 E
Bisert'	76	56.52 N	59.03 E
Bisert' ≃	76	56.39 N	57.55 E
Bise-zaki >	164m	26.43 N	127.53 E
Bisha	134	15.28 N	37.34 E
Bīshah, Wādī V	134	21.24 N	43.26 E
Bishahari	116	23.10 N	89.01 E
Bishan	97	29.37 N	106.13 E
Bishanga	142	4.31 S	21.02 E
Bishārah, Ma'ṭan ⊤[4]	136	22.58 N	22.39 E
Bīshat Qā'id	132	30.38 N	31.32 E
Bishaykhāli	116	23.28 N	89.09 E
Bishenpur	110	24.38 N	93.46 E
Bishkhāli ≃[1]	116	21.59 N	89.59 E
Bishnāh	113	32.37 N	74.52 E
Bishnupur, Bhārat	116	23.05 N	87.19 E
Bishnupur, Bhārat	116	22.23 N	88.16 E
Bishnupur, Bhārat	262b	22.37 N	88.31 E
Bishop, Calif., U.S.	194	37.22 N	118.24 W
Bishop, Pa., U.S.	269b	40.19 N	80.12 W
Bishop, Tex., U.S.	186	27.35 N	97.48 W
Bishop Airport ⊠	206	42.58 N	83.44 W
Bishop Auckland	42	54.40 N	1.40 W
Bishop's Castle	44	52.29 N	3.00 W
Bishop's Cleeve	44	51.57 N	2.04 W
Bishop's Falls	176	49.01 N	55.30 W
Bishops Frome	44	52.08 N	2.29 W
Bishops Head	198	38.16 N	76.05 W
Bishops Lydeard	44	51.04 N	3.12 W
Bishop's Stortford	44	51.53 N	0.09 E
Bishopsteignton	44	50.34 N	3.31 W
Bishopstoke	44	50.59 N	1.19 W
Bishop's Waltham	44	50.58 N	1.12 W
Bishopton	196	45.35 N	71.35 W
Bishopville, Md., U.S.	198	38.22 N	75.12 W
Bishopville, S.C., U.S.	182	34.13 N	80.20 W
Bishrī, Jabal ⋀	120	35.26 N	39.32 E
Bisianumu	154	9.25 S	147.25 E
Bisina, Lake ⊛	144	1.38 N	33.56 E
Bisingen	54	48.18 N	8.55 E
Biskamža	76	53.30 N	89.30 E
Biskaya, Golf von → Biscay, Bay of C	32	44.00 N	4.00 W
Biskintā	122	33.57 N	35.48 E
Biškon' ≃	73	49.15 N	39.35 E
Biskra	138	34.51 N	5.44 E
Biskupiec	30	53.52 N	20.58 E
Bisley, Eng., U.K.	44	51.45 N	2.08 W
Bisley, Eng., U.K.	250	51.20 N	0.38 W
Bislich	253	51.41 N	6.29 E
Bislig	106	8.13 N	126.19 E
Bislig Bay C	106	8.14 N	126.22 E
Bismarck, Ill., U.S.	206	40.16 N	87.37 W
Bismarck, Mo., U.S.	184	37.46 N	90.38 W
Bismarck, N. Dak., U.S.	188	46.48 N	100.47 W
Bismarck Archipelago II	154	5.00 S	150.00 E
Bismarck Range ⋀	154	5.30 S	144.45 E
Bismarck Sea ⊤[2]	154	4.00 S	148.00 E
Bismark	50	52.39 N	11.32 E
Bismil	120	37.51 N	40.40 E
Bismo	26	61.53 N	8.16 E
Biso	144	1.46 N	31.25 E
Bison	188	45.31 N	102.28 W
Bison Peak ∧	190	39.14 N	105.30 W
Bispberg	40	60.22 N	15.47 E
Bispgården	26	63.02 N	16.37 E
Bispingen	48	53.05 N	10.00 E
Bisrakh	262a	28.34 N	77.26 E
Bisrāmpur	114	24.15 N	83.56 E
Bissa, Djebel ∧	34	36.26 N	1.28 E
Bissau	140	11.51 N	15.35 W
Bissaula	136	7.00 N	10.27 E
Bissegem	46	50.49 N	3.13 E
Bissendorf	48	52.31 N	9.45 E
Bissett	174	51.02 N	95.40 W
Bissigh, Lach ≃	134	0.34 N	42.08 E
Bissikrima	140	10.51 N	10.56 W
Bissingen	52	48.43 N	10.37 E
Bissingheim ◆[8], B.R.D.	253	51.21 N	7.31 E
Bissingheim ◆[8], B.R.D.	253	51.24 N	6.49 E
Bissorã	140	12.14 N	15.31 W
Bistcho Lake ⊛	166	59.40 N	118.40 W
Bisten	52	49.15 N	6.42 E
Bistineau, Lake ⊛[1]	184	32.25 N	93.22 W
Bistra ≃	38	45.29 N	22.11 E
Bistreț	38	43.54 N	23.30 E
Bistrița	38	47.08 N	24.30 E
Bistrița ≃	38	46.30 N	26.57 E
Bistrița-Năsăud □[4]	38	47.15 N	24.30 E
Biswān	114	27.30 N	81.00 E
Bisztynek	30	54.06 N	20.55 E
Bitadton	106	11.30 N	122.05 E
Bitam	142	2.05 N	11.29 E
Bitam, Oued ≃	34	35.15 N	5.11 E
Bitatolo	263b	4.09 S	15.14 E
Bitatolo ≃	263b	4.09 S	15.19 E
Bitburg	52	49.58 N	6.31 E
Bitca	255b	55.34 N	37.37 E
Bitca ≃	255b	55.34 N	37.37 E
Bitche	52	49.03 N	7.26 E
Bitchū	86	34.47 N	133.27 E
Bitéa, Ouadi V	136	13.11 N	20.10 E
Bithlo	210	28.33 N	81.06 W
Bitia, Wādī V	130	17.34 N	32.15 E
Bitik	70	50.09 N	50.30 E
Bitkin	136	11.59 N	18.13 E
Bitlis	120	38.22 N	42.06 E
Bitlis □[4]	120	38.30 N	42.10 E
Bitola	38	41.01 N	21.20 E
Bitolj → Bitola	38	41.01 N	21.20 E
Bitonto	36	41.06 N	16.42 E
Bitra Island I	112	11.33 N	72.09 E
Bitschwiller-lès-Thann	54	47.50 N	7.05 E
Bitter Creek ≃, Utah, U.S.	190	39.58 N	109.25 W
Bitter Creek ≃, Wyo., U.S.	190	41.31 N	109.27 W
Bitterfeld	50	51.37 N	12.20 E
Bitterfontein	148	31.00 S	18.32 E
Bitter Lake ⊛	174	50.08 N	109.48 W
Bittermark ◆[8]	253	51.27 N	7.28 E
Bitterness, Mount ∧	162	44.45 S	170.18 E
Bittern Lake ⊛	174	53.55 N	105.50 W
Bitterroot ≃	192	46.52 N	114.06 W
Bitterroot, East Fork ≃	192	45.57 N	114.08 W
Bitterroot, West Fork ≃	192	45.57 N	114.08 W
Bitterroot Range ⋀	192	47.06 N	115.10 W
Bitterwater Creek ≃	216	35.41 N	119.58 W
Bitti	36	40.29 N	9.23 E
Bittou	140	11.16 N	0.18 W
Bit'ug ≃	68	50.37 N	39.55 E
Bitung	102	1.27 N	125.11 E
Bitupitá	240	2.54 S	41.16 W
Bituruna	242	26.10 S	51.34 W
Biu	136	10.35 N	12.13 E
Bivalve	198	38.18 N	75.54 W
Bivins	184	33.01 N	94.12 W
Bivio	54	46.28 N	9.38 E
Biwabik	180	47.32 N	92.23 W
Biwa-ko ⊛	84	35.15 N	136.05 E
Biwako ◆[5]	84	35.07 N	135.56 E
Biwa-ko-kokutei-kōen ♠	84	35.15 N	136.05 E
Biwa-ko-ōhashi ◆[5]	84	35.08 N	135.56 E
Bixby	186	35.57 N	95.53 W
Biyalā	132	31.10 N	31.13 E
Biyang	90	32.44 N	113.20 E
Biyela	148	27.47 S	32.08 E
Biyo Keraba	134	10.22 N	42.37 E
Biyo Weraba	134	8.52 N	42.14 E
Biysk → Bijsk	76	52.34 N	85.15 E
Biyunsi (Temple of the Azure Clouds) ʊ[1]	95	40.00 N	116.11 E
Biz'aki	70	55.56 N	52.28 E
Bizana	148	30.58 S	29.52 E
Biz'ar	76	57.31 N	56.09 E
Bizard, Île I	265a	45.29 N	73.54 W
Bižbul'ak	70	53.43 N	54.16 E
Bizcocho, Cuchilla del ⋀[2]	248	33.45 S	57.30 W
Bizen	86	34.44 N	134.09 E
Bizerte □[8]	36	37.10 N	9.50 E
Bizerte, Lac de ⊛	36	37.12 N	9.52 E
Bjæverskov	41	55.27 N	12.02 E
Bjala	38	43.27 N	25.44 E
Bjala Slatina	38	43.28 N	23.56 E
Bjargtangar >	24a	65.31 N	24.32 W
Bjärnum	41	56.17 N	13.42 E
Bjärred	41	55.43 N	13.01 E
Bjärsjölagård	41	55.44 N	13.41 E
Bjästa	26	63.12 N	18.30 E
Bjelaja → Belaja ≃	62	56.00 N	54.32 E
Bjelovar	36	45.54 N	16.51 E
Bjernede	41	55.27 N	11.38 E
Bjerrelide ∧[2]	41	55.47 N	9.53 E
Bjerringbro	26	56.23 N	9.40 E
Björbo	40	60.28 N	14.42 E
Bjørkelangen	26	59.53 N	11.34 E
Björklinge	40	60.02 N	17.33 E
Björknäs	40	59.19 N	18.14 E
Björkö I	40	59.53 N	19.00 E
Björköby	26	63.21 N	21.19 E
Björköfjärden C	40	59.53 N	18.56 E
Björkvik	40	58.50 N	16.31 E
Björna	26	63.34 N	18.33 E
Bjørnafjorden C[2]	26	60.06 N	5.22 E
Björndammen	40	59.12 N	16.49 E
Björneborg → Pori, Suomi	26	61.29 N	21.47 E
Björneborg, Sve.	40	59.15 N	14.15 E
Bjornesfjorden ⊛	26	60.10 N	7.41 E
Björnlunda	40	59.04 N	17.09 E
Bjørnøya I	10	74.25 N	19.00 E
Bjurholm	26	63.56 N	19.13 E
Bjuv	41	56.05 N	12.54 E
Bkāsīn	122	33.34 N	35.35 E
Bla	140	12.57 N	5.46 W
Bla ≃	100	14.18 N	107.52 E
Blace	38	43.17 N	21.18 E
Black (Lixianjiang) (Da) ≃, As.	100	21.15 N	105.20 E
Black ≃, Man., Can.	174	50.49 N	96.20 W
Black ≃, Ont., Can.	180	48.42 N	80.38 W
Black ≃, Ont., Can.	180	48.36 N	86.16 W
Black ≃, Ont., Can.	202	44.32 N	77.22 W
Black ≃, Ont., Can.	202	44.42 N	79.19 W
Black ≃, Ont., Can.	202	44.20 N	79.20 W
Black ≃, U.S.	184	35.38 N	91.19 W
Black ≃, Alaska, U.S.	170	66.39 N	144.50 W
Black ≃, Ariz., U.S.	190	33.44 N	110.13 W
Black ≃, La., U.S.	184	31.16 N	91.50 W
Black ≃, Mich., U.S.	180	45.39 N	84.29 W
Black ≃, Mich., U.S.	180	46.40 N	90.03 W
Black ≃, Mich., U.S.	204	43.00 N	82.25 W
Black ≃, Mich., U.S.	206	42.24 N	86.17 W
Black ≃, N. Mex., U.S.	186	32.14 N	104.03 W
Black ≃, N.C., U.S.	182	34.35 N	78.16 W
Black ≃, N.Y., U.S.	202	43.59 N	76.04 W
Black ≃, Ohio, U.S.	204	41.28 N	82.11 W
Black ≃, S.C., U.S.	182	33.24 N	79.15 W
Black ≃, Vt., U.S.	178	44.55 N	72.13 W
Black ≃, Vt., U.S.	178	43.16 N	72.27 W
Black ≃, Wash., U.S.	214	46.49 N	123.13 W
Black ≃, Wis., U.S.	180	43.57 N	91.22 W
Black, East Branch ≃	204	41.22 N	82.07 W
Black, East Fork ≃	180	44.26 N	90.42 W
Black, Middle Fork ≃	206	42.25 N	86.14 W
Black, North Fork ≃	206	42.25 N	86.15 W
Black, West Branch ≃	204	41.22 N	82.07 W
Blackadder Water ≃	42	55.46 N	2.15 W
Blackall	156	24.25 S	145.28 E
Black Bay C	180	48.40 N	88.30 W
Black Bear Creek ≃	186	36.25 N	96.38 W
Blackberry Heights	206	41.45 N	88.23 W
Black Birch Lake ⊛	174	56.54 N	107.45 W
Black Brook ≃, Mass., U.S.	273	41.59 N	71.03 W
Black Brook ≃, Mass., U.S.	273	42.38 N	71.21 W
Black Brook ≃, N.J., U.S.	266	40.42 N	74.31 W
Blackburn, Austl.	264b	37.49 S	145.09 E
Blackburn, Eng., U.K.	42		
	252	53.45 N	2.29 W
Blackburn □[8]	252	53.42 N	2.28 W
Blackburn, Mount ∧	170	61.44 N	143.26 W
Blackbutt	161a	26.53 S	152.06 E
Black Butte ∧, Calif., U.S.	218	34.33 N	117.43 W
Black Butte ∧, Mont., U.S.	192	46.47 N	110.56 W
Black Butte ∧, Mont., U.S.	192	44.54 N	111.51 W
Black Butte Lake ⊛[1]	194	39.45 N	122.20 W
Blackbutt Range ⋀	161a	27.00 S	152.00 E
Black Canyon of the Gunnison National Monument ♠	190	38.32 N	107.42 W
Blackcraig Hill ∧	42	55.20 N	4.08 W
Black Creek, B.C., Can.	172	49.50 N	125.08 W
Black Creek, Ont., Can.	274a	43.00 N	79.01 W
Black Creek, N.Y., U.S.	200	42.17 N	78.14 W
Black Creek ≃, Ont., Can.	204	42.43 N	82.21 W
Black Creek ≃, Ont., Can.	265b	43.41 N	79.32 W
Black Creek ≃, Ont., Can.	274a	42.59 N	79.01 W
Black Creek ≃, Ariz., U.S.	190	35.16 N	109.14 W
Black Creek ≃, Fla., U.S.	182	30.03 N	81.42 W
Black Creek ≃, Mich., U.S.	206	41.49 N	83.54 W
Black Creek ≃, Mich., U.S.	206	43.11 N	86.14 W
Black Creek ≃, Miss., U.S.	184	33.01 N	90.21 W
Black Creek ≃, Miss., U.S.	184	30.39 N	88.39 W
Black Creek ≃, Mo., U.S.	209	39.41 N	91.55 W
Black Creek ≃, N.Y., U.S.	200	43.19 N	75.04 W
Black Creek ≃, N.Y., U.S.	200	43.06 N	77.41 W
Black Creek ≃, N.Y., U.S.	274a	43.05 N	78.57 W
Black Creek ≃, N.Y., U.S.	274a	43.03 N	78.42 W
Black Creek ≃, Pa., U.S.	200	41.00 N	76.10 W
Black Creek ≃, S.C., U.S.	182	34.18 N	79.37 W
Black Creek, North Fork ≃	182	30.05 N	81.51 W
Black Creek, South Fork ≃	182	30.05 N	81.51 W
Black Creek Park ♠	265b	43.46 N	79.31 W
Black Creek Pioneer Village ⊥	265b	43.47 N	79.32 W
Black Cypress Bayou ≃	184	32.42 N	93.55 W
Black Cypress Creek ≃	212	32.53 N	94.26 W
Blackden Heath	252	53.14 N	2.20 W
Black Devon ≃	42	56.06 N	3.47 W
Black Diamond, Alta., Can.	172	50.42 N	114.14 W
Black Diamond, Wash., U.S.	214	47.18 N	122.00 W
Black Donald Lake ⊛[1]	202	45.13 N	76.55 W
Blackduck	180	47.44 N	94.33 W
Black Duck ≃	166	56.51 N	89.02 W
Black Eagle	192	47.31 N	111.17 W
Black Esk ≃	42	55.12 N	5.10 W
Blackfalds	172	52.23 N	113.47 W
Blackfeet Indian Reservation ◆[4]	192	48.40 N	113.00 W
Blackfellow Creek ≃	161a	27.34 S	152.14 E
Blackfoot, Idaho, U.S.	192	43.11 N	112.20 W
Blackfoot, Mont., U.S.	172	48.34 N	112.52 W
Blackfoot ≃, Idaho, U.S.	192	43.08 N	112.30 W
Blackfoot ≃, Mont., U.S.	192	46.52 N	113.53 W
Blackfoot, North Fork ≃	192	46.59 N	113.07 W
Blackfoot Indian Reserve ◆[4]	172	50.45 N	113.00 W
Blackfoot Reservoir ⊛[1]	192	42.55 N	111.35 W
Blackford □[6]	206	40.27 N	85.22 W
Black Forest → Schwarzwald ⋀	54	48.00 N	8.15 E
Blackhall Colliery	42	54.44 N	1.14 W
Blackhall Mountain ∧	190	41.02 N	106.41 W
Black Hameldon ∧[2]	252	53.44 N	2.08 W
Black Hawk	174	48.48 N	93.59 W
Black Hawk Creek ≃	180	42.30 N	92.21 W
Blackhead Bay C	176	48.34 N	53.15 W
Blackheath, Austl.	160	33.38 S	150.17 E
Blackheath, S. Afr.	263d	26.08 S	27.58 E
Blackheath, Eng., U.K.	250	51.12 N	0.31 W
Black Hill ∧[2], Eng., U.K.	252	53.20 N	2.01 W
Black Hill ∧[2], Eng., U.K.	252	53.33 N	1.53 W
Black Hills ⋀	188	44.00 N	104.00 W
Black Hills ⋀[2]	272	37.50 N	121.52 W
Blackhope Star ∧	42	55.44 N	3.05 W
Black Horse, Ohio, U.S.	204	41.09 N	81.18 W
Black Horse, Pa., U.S.	275	39.55 N	75.25 W
Black Horse Creek ≃	275	40.05 N	75.43 W
Black Island I	174	51.10 N	96.30 W
Black Jack	209	38.49 N	90.18 W
Black Lake	196	46.03 N	71.21 W
Black Lake ⊛, Ont., Can.	202	44.46 N	76.18 W
Black Lake ⊛, Sask., Can.	166	59.10 N	105.20 W
Black Lake ⊛, Mich., U.S.	180	45.28 N	84.15 W
Black Lake ⊛, N.Y., U.S.	202	44.31 N	75.35 W
Black Lake ⊛, Wash., U.S.	214	47.00 N	122.58 W
Black Lake Bayou ≃	184	32.01 N	93.09 W
Blacklegs Creek ≃	204	40.30 N	79.27 W
Blackley ◆[8]	252	53.31 N	2.13 W
Black Lick	204	40.28 N	79.12 W
Blacklick Creek ≃	204	40.28 N	79.13 W
Blacklick Creek, North Branch ≃	204	40.29 N	78.55 W
Blacklick Estates	208	39.54 N	83.22 W
Black Mesa ∧, Ariz., U.S.	190	36.35 N	110.20 W
Black Mesa ∧, Okla., U.S.	186	36.57 N	102.59 W
Blackmoor ⋀[1]	44	50.24 N	4.46 W
Blackmoorfoot Reservoir ⊛[1]	252	53.37 N	1.51 W
Blackmoor Vale V	44	50.56 N	2.25 W
Blackmore	250	51.41 N	0.19 E
Blackmore, Mount ∧	192	45.27 N	111.01 W
Black Moshannon State Park ♠	204	40.54 N	78.03 W
Black Mountain	182	35.37 N	82.19 W
Black Mountain ∧, D.Y.	114	27.17 N	90.23 E
Black Mountain ∧, Wales, U.K.	44	51.52 N	3.46 W
Black Mountain ∧, Ariz., U.S.	190	32.46 N	110.57 W
Black Mountain ∧, Calif., U.S.	216	35.24 N	120.21 W
Black Mountain ∧, Calif., U.S.	218	35.08 N	117.14 W
Black Mountain ∧, Calif., U.S.	272	37.19 N	122.09 W
Black Mountain ∧, Idaho, U.S.	192	46.53 N	115.33 W
Black Mountain ∧, Ky., U.S.	182	36.54 N	82.54 W
Black Mountain ∧, Mont., U.S.	192	46.44 N	112.31 W
Black Mountain ∧, Oreg., U.S.	192	45.13 N	119.17 W
Black Mountain ∧, Wyo., U.S.	192	44.45 N	107.22 W
Black Mountain ∧[2], Calif., U.S.	218	32.59 N	117.07 W
Black Mountain ∧[2], Tex., U.S.	212	31.09 N	97.44 W
Black Mountains ⋀, Wales, U.K.	44	51.57 N	3.08 W
Black Mountains ⋀, Ariz., U.S.	190	35.30 N	114.30 W
Black Nossob ≃	146	23.05 S	18.45 E
Black Oak	206	41.35 N	87.25 W
Black Peak ∧	190	34.22 N	114.13 W
Black Pine Peak ∧	192	42.08 N	113.08 W
Black Pipe Creek ≃	188	43.47 N	101.14 W
Black Point	216	38.07 N	122.31 W
Black Point >, Austl.	158b	34.37 S	137.54 E
Black Point >, Austl.	160	34.47 S	150.50 E
Black Point >, Alaska, U.S.	170	57.00 N	153.18 W
Black Point >, Calif., U.S.	218	33.28 N	118.36 W
Blackpool	42		
	252	53.50 N	3.03 W
Blackpool □[8]	252	53.47 N	3.02 W
Blackpool (Squires Gate) Airport ⊠	42	53.47 N	3.02 W
Blackpool Football Ground ♠	252	53.49 N	3.03 W
Blackpool Tower ʊ	252	53.49 N	3.03 W
Black Range ⋀	190	33.20 N	107.50 W
Black River, Jam.	231q	18.01 N	77.51 W
Black River, N.Y., U.S.	202	44.01 N	75.48 W
Black River Bay C, Jam.	231q	18.00 N	77.51 W
Black River Bay C, N.Y., U.S.	202	43.58 N	76.07 W
Black River Falls	180	44.23 N	90.52 W
Black Rock, Austl.	264b	37.59 S	145.01 E
Black Rock, Ark., U.S.	184	36.06 N	91.06 W
Black Rock, Mass., U.S.	273	42.14 N	70.49 W
Black Rock I[2]	28	54.05 N	10.28 W
Black Rock II[1]	234	53.39 S	41.48 W
Black Rock Desert ◆[2]	194	41.10 N	119.00 W
Black Rock Harbor C	266	41.09 N	73.13 W
Blackrod	252	53.35 N	2.35 W
Blacksburg, S.C., U.S.	182	35.07 N	81.31 W
Blacksburg, Va., U.S.	182	37.14 N	80.25 W
Blacks Creek ≃	275	40.08 N	74.43 W
Black Sea ⊤[2]	22	43.00 N	35.00 E
Blacks Fork ≃	190	41.24 N	109.38 W
Blacks Harbour	176	45.03 N	66.47 W
Blackshear	182	31.18 N	82.14 W
Blackshear, Lake ⊛[1]	182	31.56 N	83.56 W
Blacksod Bay C	28	54.08 N	10.00 W
Black Springs	160	33.52 S	149.42 E
Black Springs Hill ∧[2]	264b	37.46 S	145.19 E
Black Star Canyon V	270	33.47 N	117.39 W
Blackstone, Mass., U.S.	197	42.01 N	71.30 W
Blackstone, Va., U.S.	182	37.04 N	78.00 W
Blackstone ≃, Alta., Can.	172	52.50 N	116.07 W
Blackstone ≃, Yukon, Can.	170	65.51 N	137.12 W
Blackstone Lake ⊛	202	45.14 N	79.53 W
Black Sugarloaf Mountain ∧	156	31.20 S	151.33 E
Black Thunder Creek ≃	188	43.33 N	104.41 W
Blacktown	160	33.46 S	150.55 E
Black Umbeluzi ≃	148	26.08 S	31.52 E
Black Umfolozi ≃	148	28.22 S	31.58 E
Blackville	182	33.22 N	81.16 W
Black Volta (Volta Noire) ≃	140	8.41 N	1.33 W
Blackwall Tunnel ◆[5]	250	51.30 N	0.01 E
Blackwalnut Point >	198	38.40 N	76.20 W
Black Warrior ≃	184	32.32 N	87.51 W
Blackwatch Hills	200	43.05 N	77.27 W
Blackwater	156	23.35 S	148.53 E
Blackwater ≃, Eire	28	51.51 N	7.50 W
Blackwater ≃, Eire	42	53.39 N	6.43 W
Blackwater ≃, Eur.	42	54.31 N	6.34 W
Blackwater ≃, Eng., U.K.	44	51.45 N	1.00 E
Blackwater ≃, U.S.	184	30.36 N	87.02 W
Blackwater ≃, Md., U.S.	198	38.21 N	76.01 W
Blackwater ≃, Mo., U.S.	184	38.56 N	92.51 W
Blackwater ≃, Va., U.S.	198	36.33 N	76.55 W
Blackwater Creek ≃, Austl.	156	25.56 S	144.20 E
Black Water Creek ≃, Fla., U.S.	210	28.51 N	81.24 W
Blackwater Draw V	186	33.35 N	101.50 W
Blackwater-foot	42	55.30 N	5.19 W
Blackwater Lake ⊛	170	64.00 N	123.05 W
Blackwater Sound Џ	210	25.10 N	80.25 W
Blackwell, Okla., U.S.	186	36.48 N	97.17 W
Blackwell, Tex., U.S.	186	32.05 N	100.19 W
Blackwood, Austl.	158b	35.02 S	138.37 E
Blackwood, Austl.	159	37.29 S	144.19 E
Blackwood, N.J., U.S.	275	39.48 N	75.04 W
Blackwood, Cape >	154	7.50 S	144.30 E
Blackwood Terrace	275	39.48 N	75.05 W
Bladel	48	51.23 N	5.13 E
Bladenboro	182	34.33 N	78.48 W
Bladensburg, Md., U.S.	274c	38.56 N	76.55 W
Bladensburg, Ohio, U.S.	204	40.17 N	82.17 W
Blades	198	38.38 N	75.36 W
Bladgrond	148	28.52 S	19.57 E
Bladworth	174	51.18 N	106.09 W
Blaenau Ffestiniog	44	52.59 N	3.56 W
Blaenavon	44	51.48 N	3.05 W
Bláfell ∧	24a	64.32 N	19.53 W
Blagaj	36	43.15 N	17.50 E
Blagdon	44	51.20 N	2.43 W
Blagodarnoje, S.S.S.R.	62	45.06 N	43.27 E
Blagodarnoje, S.S.S.R.	76	47.03 N	82.10 E
Blagodatnoje, S.S.S.R.	68	51.32 N	34.54 E
Blagodatnoje, S.S.S.R.	73	47.53 N	38.29 E
Blagodatnoje, S.S.S.R.	73	47.42 N	37.25 E
Blagodatnoje, S.S.S.R.	76	51.18 N	72.49 E
Blagodatovka	70	52.14 N	50.27 E
Blagoevgrad	38	42.01 N	23.06 E
Blagoveščenka, S.S.S.R.	70	51.19 N	44.03 E
Blagoveščenka, S.S.S.R.	76	54.22 N	66.58 E
Blagoveščenka, S.S.S.R.	76	52.50 N	79.52 E
Blagoveščensk, S.S.S.R.	76	55.01 N	55.59 E
Blagoveščensk, S.S.S.R.	79	50.17 N	127.32 E
Blagoveščenskoje, S.S.S.R.	75	43.18 N	74.12 E
Blagoveščenskoje, S.S.S.R.	76	58.08 N	62.58 E
Blåhø ∧	26	62.45 N	9.19 E
Blåhøj	41	55.51 N	9.01 E
Blaichach	54	47.34 N	10.15 E
Blain, Fr.	32	47.29 N	1.46 W
Blain, Pa., U.S.	198	40.20 N	77.31 W
Blaina	44	51.46 N	3.10 W
Blain City	204	40.40 N	78.34 W
Blaine, Minn., U.S.	180	45.11 N	93.14 W
Blaine, Wash., U.S.	214	48.59 N	122.44 W
Blaine Creek ≃	178	38.11 N	82.37 W
Blaine Hill	269b	40.16 N	79.53 W
Blaine Lake	174	52.50 N	106.54 W
Blaineys	214	48.53 N	123.47 W
Blainville-sur-l'Eau	54	48.33 N	6.24 E
Blair, Ont., Can.	202	43.23 N	80.23 W
Blair, Nebr., U.S.	188	41.33 N	96.08 W
Blair, Okla., U.S.	186	34.47 N	99.20 W
Blair, Wis., U.S.	180	44.18 N	91.14 W
Blair □[6]	204	40.30 N	78.25 W
Blair Athol	156	22.42 S	147.33 E
Blairgowrie	28	56.36 N	3.21 W
Blairmore	172	49.36 N	114.26 W
Blairs Mills	204	40.17 N	77.43 W
Blairstown, Iowa, U.S.	180	41.55 N	92.05 W
Blairstown, N.J., U.S.	200	40.59 N	74.57 W
Blairsville, Ga., U.S.	182	34.53 N	83.58 W
Blairsville, Pa., U.S.	204	40.26 N	79.16 W
Blaise ≃, Fr.	46	48.46 N	1.25 E
Blaise ≃, Fr.	54	48.38 N	4.43 E
Blaisy-Bas	54	47.22 N	4.44 E
Blaj	38	46.11 N	23.55 E
Blajkfjället ∧	26	64.33 N	16.12 E
Blakehurst	264a	33.59 S	151.07 E
Blakeley Canal Ξ	216	36.09 N	119.48 W
Blakely, Ga., U.S.	182	31.23 N	84.56 W
Blakely, Pa., U.S.	200	41.28 N	75.31 W
Blakely Island I	214	48.33 N	122.50 W
Blakeney, Eng., U.K.	44	51.46 N	2.29 W
Blakeney, Eng., U.K.	44	52.58 N	1.00 E
Blake Plateau ✧[4]	16	31.00 N	79.00 W
Blake Point >	180	48.12 N	88.25 W
Blakes	198	37.30 N	76.22 W
Blakesburg	180	40.58 N	92.38 W
Blakeslee, Ohio, U.S.	206	41.31 N	84.44 W
Blakeslee, Pa., U.S.	200	41.06 N	75.36 W
Blake Terrace ✧[4]	4	31.00 N	79.00 W
Blalock Island I	192	45.53 N	119.41 W
Blamont, Fr.	54	47.23 N	6.51 E
Blâmont, Fr.	54	48.35 N	6.51 E
Blanba	110	30.49 N	94.59 E
Blanc, Cap >, Afr.	138	20.46 N	17.03 W
Blanc, Cap >, Tun.	138	37.20 N	9.50 E
Blanc, Mont (Monte Bianco) ∧	56	45.50 N	6.52 E
Blanca	190	37.27 N	105.31 W
Blanca, Bahía C	242	38.55 S	62.10 W
Blanca, Cordillera ⋀	238	9.10 S	77.35 W
Blanca, Isla I	238	9.06 S	78.38 W
Blanca, Laguna ⊛	244	52.25 S	71.10 W
Blanca, Punta >, Arg.	248	34.57 S	57.40 W
Blanca, Punta >, C.R.	226	10.57 N	85.54 W
Blanca, Sierra ∧	190	31.15 N	105.26 W
Blanca Lake ⊛	214	47.53 N	121.21 W
Blanca Peak ∧	190	37.35 N	105.29 W
Blanc du Cheilon, Mont ∧	54	45.59 N	7.25 E
Blanchard, Okla., U.S.	186	35.08 N	97.39 W
Blanchard, Pa., U.S.	200	41.04 N	77.36 W
Blanchard, Wash., U.S.	214	48.36 N	122.26 W
Blanchard ≃	206	41.02 N	84.18 W
Blanchardville	180	42.49 N	89.52 W
Blanche ≃, Ont., Can.	180	47.34 N	79.32 W
Blanche ≃, Qué., Can.	196	46.40 N	72.08 W
Blanche, Cape >	152	33.01 S	134.09 E
Blanche, Dent ∧	54	46.03 N	7.36 E
Blanche, Lake ⊛, Austl.	152	22.25 S	123.17 E
Blanche, Lake ⊛, Austl.	156	29.15 S	139.39 E
Blanche, Mer → Beloje More ⊤[2]	24	65.30 N	38.00 E
Blanche Channel Џ	165e	8.30 S	157.30 E
Blancheface	251	48.32 N	2.06 E
Blanchester	178	39.17 N	83.55 W
Blanchisseuse	231r	10.47 N	61.18 W
Blanco, S. Afr.	148	33.57 S	22.24 E
Blanco, Tex., U.S.	186	30.06 N	98.25 W
Blanco ≃, Arg.	242	31.54 S	69.42 W
Blanco ≃, Arg.	244	47.22 S	71.12 W
Blanco ≃, Bol.	238	12.30 S	64.18 W
Blanco ≃, Perú	238	5.27 S	73.47 W
Blanco ≃, Tex., U.S.	186	29.51 N	97.55 W
Blanco, Cabo → Blanc. Cap >, Afr.	138	20.46 N	17.03 W
Blanco, Cabo >, C.R.	226	9.34 N	85.07 W
Blanco, Cañon V	190	35.20 N	105.05 W
Blanco, Cape >	192	42.50 N	124.34 W
Blanco, Lago ⊛	244	54.03 S	69.00 W
Blanco, Mar → Beloje More ⊤[2]	24	65.30 N	38.00 E
Blanco, Monte → Blanc, Mont ∧	56	45.50 N	6.52 E
Blanco, Rio ≃	190	37.07 N	107.03 W
Blanc-Sablon	176	51.25 N	57.07 W
Bland, Mo., U.S.	209	38.18 N	91.38 W
Bland, Va., U.S.	182	37.06 N	81.07 W
Blanda ≃	24a	65.39 N	20.18 W
Blandburg	204	40.41 N	78.25 W
Blandford	197	42.11 N	72.56 W
Blandford Forum	44	50.52 N	2.11 W
Blanding	190	37.37 N	109.29 W
Blandinsville	180	40.33 N	90.52 W
Blandon	198	40.26 N	75.53 W
Blandy	251	48.34 N	2.47 E
Blanes	34	41.41 N	2.48 E
Blangkejeren	104	3.59 N	97.20 E
Blangpidie	104	3.45 N	96.51 E
Blangy-le-Château	46	49.14 N	0.17 E
Blangy-sur-Bresle	46	49.56 N	1.38 E
Blankenberg	52	50.45 N	7.22 E
Blankenberge	46	51.19 N	3.08 E
Blankenburg	50	51.48 N	10.58 E
Blankenburg ◆[8]	254a	52.35 N	13.28 E
Blankenese ◆[8]	48	53.33 N	9.48 E
Blankenfelde	50	52.20 N	13.23 E
Blankenfelde ◆[8]	254a	52.37 N	13.23 E
Blankenhain	50	50.51 N	11.21 E
Blankenheim, B.R.D.	52	50.26 N	6.39 E
Blankenheim, D.D.R.	50	51.31 N	11.25 E
Blankensee	50	52.14 N	13.08 E
Blankenstein	253	51.24 N	7.14 E
Blanket	186	31.49 N	98.47 W
Blanquefort	32	44.53 N	0.39 W
Blansko	30	49.22 N	16.39 E
Blantyre	144	15.47 S	35.00 E
Blanzac	56	45.07 N	3.51 E
Blanzy	54	46.42 N	4.23 E
Blaricum	48	52.16 N	5.15 E
Blarney Castle ♠	28	51.56 N	8.34 W
Blasdell	200	42.47 N	78.49 W
Blasheim	48	52.18 N	8.34 E
Błaszki	30	51.39 N	18.27 E
Blatná	30	49.26 N	13.53 E
Blatnica	38	43.42 N	28.31 E
Blatten	54	46.25 N	7.50 E
Blatzheim	52	50.51 N	6.38 E
Blau ≃	54	48.23 N	9.49 E
Blaubeuren	54	48.24 N	9.47 E
Blauen ∧	54	47.47 N	7.42 E
Blauer Nil → Blue Nile ≃	130	15.38 N	32.31 E
Blaufelden	52	49.18 N	9.58 E
Blauvelt	266	41.04 N	73.58 W
Blauvelt State Park ♠	266	41.04 N	73.56 W
Blåvands Huk >	26	55.33 N	8.05 E
Blawenburg	266	40.24 N	74.42 W
Blawnox	269b	40.29 N	79.52 W
Blaxland	160	33.45 S	150.36 E
Blaxland Creek ≃	264a	33.48 S	150.46 E
Blaydon	42	54.58 N	1.42 W
Blaye-et-Sainte-Luce	32	45.08 N	0.39 W
Blayney	156	33.32 S	149.15 E
Blaze, Point >	154	12.56 S	130.12 E
Błażowa	30	49.54 N	22.05 E
Bleaklow Head ∧	252	53.28 N	1.50 W
Blean	44	51.19 N	1.02 E
Bleckede	50	53.17 N	10.44 E
Bled	36	46.22 N	14.06 E
Bledsoe	186	33.38 N	103.01 W
Bleecker	200	43.07 N	74.22 W
Blefjell ∧	26	59.48 N	9.10 E
Blega	105a	7.08 S	113.03 E
Bleibach	54	48.07 N	8.01 E
Bleiberg ob Villach	58	46.37 N	13.41 E
Bleiburg	30	46.35 N	14.48 E
Bleicherode	50	51.26 N	10.34 E
Bleidenstadt	52	50.08 N	8.08 E
Blekendorf	50	54.16 N	10.38 E
Blekinge □[9]	26	56.20 N	15.05 E
Blekinge Län □[6]	26	56.20 N	15.20 E
Blendecques	46	50.43 N	2.16 E
Bléneau	46	47.42 N	2.57 E
Blénestroff	52	48.54 N	6.45 E
Blenheim, Austl.	161a	27.39 S	152.20 E
Blenheim, Ont., Can.	204	42.20 N	82.00 W
Blenheim, N.Z.	162	41.31 S	173.57 E
Blenheim, N.J., U.S.	275	39.48 N	75.05 W
Blenheim Palace ʊ	44	51.47 N	1.21 W
Blenio, Val V	54	46.27 N	8.58 E
Blénod-lès-Pont-à-Mousson	52	48.53 N	6.03 E
Blénod-lès-Toul	54	48.36 N	5.50 E
Bléone ≃	56	44.03 N	6.00 E
Blérancourt	46	49.31 N	3.09 E
Bléré	46	47.20 N	1.00 E
Blerick	48	51.23 N	6.10 E
Blériot-Plage	46	50.57 N	1.50 E
Blesbokspruit ≃	263d	26.14 S	28.29 E
Blessing	212	28.52 N	96.13 W
Bletchingley	250	51.14 N	0.06 W
Bletchley	44	52.00 N	0.46 W
Bletterans	54	46.45 N	5.27 E
Bleu → Changjiang ≃	80	31.48 N	121.10 E
Bleury	251	48.31 N	1.45 E
Blevio	56	45.50 N	9.05 E
Blewett Falls Lake ⊛[1]	182	35.03 N	79.54 W
Blexen	48	53.32 N	8.32 E
Blida	138	36.28 N	2.50 E
Blidö I	40	59.37 N	18.54 E
Blidworth	44	53.06 N	1.07 W
Bliedinghausen ◆[8]	253	51.09 N	7.12 E
Bliersheim	253	51.23 N	6.43 E
Blies ≃	52	49.07 N	7.04 E
Blieskastel	52	49.14 N	7.16 E
Bligh Sound Џ	162	44.50 S	167.32 E
Bligh Water Џ	165g	17.00 S	178.00 E
Bligny	46	49.11 N	3.52 E
Bligny-sur-Ouche	54	47.06 N	4.40 E
Blik, Mount ∧	106	6.58 N	124.15 E
Blind ≃	266	40.57 N	73.42 W
Blind Creek ≃	264b	37.54 S	145.12 E
Blindley Heath	250	51.12 N	0.04 W
Blind River	180	46.10 N	82.58 W
Blinman	156	31.06 S	138.41 E
Blinnenhorn ∧	54	46.26 N	8.19 E
Blinovskij	70	49.23 N	42.19 E
Bliss	200	42.35 N	78.15 W
Blissfield, Mich., U.S.	206	41.50 N	83.52 W
Blissfield, Ohio, U.S.	204	40.24 N	81.58 W
Blitar	105a	8.06 S	112.09 E
Blithe ≃	44	52.45 N	1.50 W
Blithfield Reservoir ⊛[1]	44	52.48 N	1.53 W
Blitta	140	8.19 N	0.59 E
Blizn'uki	68	48.52 N	36.33 E
Blocher	208	38.43 N	85.39 W
Block Dam ◆[6]	202	45.12 N	76.54 W
Block Island	197	41.10 N	71.34 W
Block Island I	197	41.11 N	71.35 W
Block Island Sound Џ	197	41.10 N	71.45 W
Blockley	44	52.01 N	1.45 W
Blockton	188	40.37 N	94.29 W
Blodgett Mills	200	42.34 N	76.08 W
Bloedel	172	50.07 N	125.23 W
Bloedrivier, S. Afr.	148	28.06 S	30.33 E
Bloedrivier, S. Afr.	148	27.53 S	30.30 E
Bloekomspruit	148	26.45 S	28.21 E
Bloemendaal	48	52.24 N	4.37 E
Bloemfontein	148	29.12 S	26.07 E
Bloemhof	148	27.38 S	25.32 E
Blois	46	47.35 N	1.20 E
Blokhus	26	57.15 N	9.35 E
Blokzijl	48	52.44 N	5.57 E
Blombacher Bach ◆[8]	253	51.15 N	7.14 E
Blombacka	40	59.37 N	13.47 E
Blomberg	48	51.56 N	9.05 E
Blomstermåla	26	56.59 N	16.20 E
Blonay	54	46.28 N	6.54 E
Blönduós	24a	65.39 N	20.15 W
Blongas	105b	8.53 S	116.02 E
Blonville-sur-Mer	46	49.19 N	0.02 E
Blood Indian Creek ≃	174	50.55 N	111.03 W
Blood Indian Reserve ◆[4]	172	49.30 N	113.10 W
Blood Mountain ∧	182	34.44 N	83.56 W
Blood River ⊥	148	28.20 S	30.35 E
Bloods Creek	152	26.28 S	135.17 E
Bloodsworth Island I	198	38.10 N	76.03 W
Bloodvein ≃	174	51.45 N	96.44 W
Bloody Foreland >	28	55.09 N	8.17 W
Bloomdale	206	41.10 N	83.33 W
Bloomer	180	45.07 N	91.29 W
Bloomfield, Ont., Can.	202	43.59 N	77.14 W
Bloomfield, Conn., U.S.	197	41.50 N	72.44 W
Bloomfield, Ind., U.S.	184	39.01 N	86.56 W
Bloomfield, Iowa, U.S.	180	40.45 N	92.25 W
Bloomfield, Ky., U.S.	184	37.55 N	85.19 W
Bloomfield, Mo., U.S.	184	36.53 N	89.56 W
Bloomfield, Nebr., U.S.	188	42.36 N	97.39 W
Bloomfield, N.J., U.S.	200	40.48 N	74.12 W
Bloomfield, N. Mex., U.S.	190	36.43 N	107.59 W
Bloomfield, Ohio, U.S.	204	40.03 N	81.44 W
Bloomfield ◆[8]	269b	40.27 N	79.56 W
Bloomfield Glens	271	42.33 N	83.20 W
Bloomfield Highlands	271	42.36 N	83.16 W
Bloomfield Hills	206	42.35 N	83.15 W
Bloomfield Village	206	42.33 N	83.15 W

	English	Deutsch	Español	Français	Português
≃	River	Fluss	Río	Rivière	Rio
Ξ	Canal	Kanal	Canal	Canal	Canal
Ⅼ	Waterfall, Rapids	Wasserfall, Stromschnellen	Cascada, Rápidos	Chute d'eau, Rapides	Cascata, Rápidos
Џ	Strait	Meeresstrasse	Estrecho	Détroit	Estreito
C	Bay, Gulf	Bucht, Golf	Bahía, Golfo	Baie, Golfe	Baía, Golfo
⊛	Lake, Lakes	See, Seen	Lago, Lagos	Lac, Lacs	Lago, Lagos
☷	Swamp	Sumpf	Pantano	Marais	Pântano
⊼	Ice Features, Glacier	Eis- und Gletscherformen	Accidentes Glaciales	Formes glaciaires	Acidentes Glaciares
⊤	Other Hydrographic Features	Andere Hydrographische Objekte	Otros Elementos Hidrográficos	Autres données hydrographiques	Outros Elementos Hidrográficos
✧	Submarine Features	Untermeerische Objekte	Accidentes Submarinos	Formes de relief sous-marin	Acidentes Submarinos
□	Political Unit	Politische Einheit	Unidad Politica	Entité politique	Unidade Política
ʊ	Cultural Institution	Kulturelle Institution	Institución Cultural	Institution culturelle	Instituição Cultural
⊥	Historical Site	Historische Stätte	Sitio Histórico	Site historique	Sitio Histórico
♠	Recreational Site	Erholungs- und Ferienort	Sitio de Recreo	Centre de loisirs	Sítio de Lazer
⊠	Airport	Flughafen	Aeropuerto	Aéroport	Aeroporto
■	Military Installation	Militäranlage	Instalación Militar	Installation militaire	Instalação Militar
◆	Miscellaneous	Verschiedenes	Misceláneo	Divers	Miscelânea

ENGLISH | DEUTSCH

Name	Page	Lat.	Long.
Bloomingburg, N.Y., U.S.	200	41.33 N	74.26 W
Bloomingburg, Ohio, U.S.	208	39.36 N	83.24 W
Bloomingdale, Ill., U.S.	206	41.58 N	88.05 W
Bloomingdale, Mich., U.S.	206	42.23 N	85.57 W
Bloomingdale, N.J., U.S.	200	41.00 N	74.20 W
Bloomingdale, Ohio, U.S.	204	40.21 N	80.49 W
Blooming Glen	198	40.22 N	75.15 W
Blooming Grove, Ind., U.S.	208	39.30 N	85.04 W
Blooming Grove, N.Y., U.S.	200	41.25 N	74.11 W
Blooming Grove, Pa., U.S.	200	41.21 N	75.09 W
Blooming Grove, Tex., U.S.	212	32.06 N	96.43 W
Blooming Prairie	180	43.52 N	93.03 W
Bloomington, Calif., U.S.	218	34.04 N	117.24 W
Bloomington, Ill., U.S.	206	40.29 N	89.00 W
Bloomington, Ind., U.S.	208	39.10 N	86.32 W
Bloomington, Minn., U.S.	180	44.50 N	93.17 W
Bloomington, N.Y., U.S.	200	41.53 N	74.03 W
Bloomington, Tex., U.S.	186	28.39 N	96.54 W
Bloomington, Wis., U.S.	180	42.53 N	90.55 W
Bloomington, Lake ⊜[1]	206	40.37 N	88.55 W
Blooming Valley	204	41.40 N	80.03 W
Bloomsburg	200	41.00 N	76.27 W
Bloomsbury, Austl.	156	20.43 S	148.35 E
Bloomsbury, N.J., U.S.	200	40.39 N	75.05 W
Bloomsdale Gardens	275	40.07 N	74.52 W
Bloomville, N.Y., U.S.	200	42.20 N	74.48 W
Bloomville, Ohio, U.S.	204	41.03 N	83.01 W
Blora	105a	6.57 S	111.25 E
Bloserville	198	40.12 N	77.24 W
Blossburg	200	41.41 N	77.04 W
Blossom	186	33.40 N	95.23 W
Blossom Hill	198	40.05 N	76.19 W
Blötberget	40	60.07 N	15.04 E
Blotzheim	54	47.36 N	7.29 E
Blouberg	146	23.08 S	28.56 E
Blouberg Λ	146	23.01 S	28.59 E
Bloubergstrand	148	33.47 S	18.28 E
Blouin, Lac ⊜	180	48.10 N	77.44 W
Bloumet	138	23.27 N	6.06 E
Blountstown	182	30.27 N	85.03 W
Blountsville	184	34.05 N	86.35 W
Blovice	30	49.35 N	13.33 E
Blovstrød	41	55.52 N	12.24 E
Blowering Reservoir ⊜[1]	161b	35.30 S	148.15 E
Blowing Rock	182	36.08 N	81.41 W
Bloxham	44	52.02 N	1.22 W
Bloxom	198	37.50 N	75.38 W
Blšanka ≃	50	50.10 N	13.34 E
Blšany	50	50.10 N	13.29 E
Bludenz	54	47.09 N	9.49 E
Bludnaja ≃	78	51.24 N	110.39 E
Blue ≃, Ariz., U.S.	190	33.13 N	109.11 W
Blue ≃, Colo., U.S.	190	40.03 N	106.24 W
Blue ≃, Ind., U.S.	206	41.07 N	85.30 W
Blue ≃, Ind., U.S.	208	38.11 N	86.19 W
Blue ≃, Okla., U.S.	186	33.53 N	95.56 W
Blue, Middle Fork ≃	208	38.33 N	86.07 W
Blue, South Fork ≃	208	38.26 N	86.11 W
Blue, West Fork ≃	208	38.33 N	86.07 W
Blue Anchor	275	39.41 N	74.53 W
Blue Ash	208	39.14 N	84.22 W
Blue Ball	208	39.29 N	84.21 W
Blue Bell	198	40.09 N	75.16 W
Bluebell Hill	250	51.20 N	0.30 E
Blue Bonnets, Champ de Course ♠	265a	45.29 N	73.39 W
Blue Brook ≃	266	40.40 N	74.25 W
Blue Buck Knob Λ[2]	184	36.57 N	92.07 W
Blue Creek	208	38.47 N	83.20 W
Blue Creek ≃, Calif., U.S.	216	38.28 N	120.22 W
Blue Creek ≃, Idaho, U.S.	192	42.02 N	116.08 W
Blue Creek ≃, Nebr., U.S.	188	41.19 N	102.10 W
Blue Creek ≃, N. Mex., U.S.	190	32.50 N	105.00 W
Blue Creek ≃, Ohio, U.S.	206	41.07 N	84.26 W
Blue Cypress Lake ⊜	210	27.44 N	80.45 W
Blue Earth	180	43.38 N	94.06 W
Blue Earth ≃	180	44.09 N	94.02 W
Bluefield, Va., U.S.	182	37.15 N	81.17 W
Bluefield, W. Va., U.S.	182	37.16 N	81.13 W
Bluefields	226	12.00 N	83.45 W
Bluefields, Laguna de C	226	12.02 N	83.44 W
Bluefields Bay C	231q	18.10 N	78.03 W
Blue Grass Airport ⊠	208	38.02 N	84.36 W
Blue Grotto → Azzurra, Grotta ●[5]	60	40.35 N	14.14 E
Blue Gum Mine	144	18.25 S	29.25 E
Blue Hill, Maine, U.S.	178	44.25 N	68.36 W
Blue Hill, Nebr., U.S.	188	40.20 N	98.27 W
Blue Hill Bay C	178	44.15 N	68.30 W
Blue Hills	197	41.47 N	72.42 W
Blue Hills of Couteau ⋀[2]	176	47.59 N	57.43 W
Blue Hills Reservation ♠	273	42.13 N	71.05 W
Blue Island	206	41.40 N	87.41 W
Blue Jay	218	34.15 N	117.13 W
Bluejoint Lake ⊜	192	42.35 N	119.40 W
Blue Knob Λ	204	40.17 N	78.34 W
Blue Knob State Park ♠	204	40.16 N	78.35 W
Blue Licks Battlefield State Park ♠	208	38.26 N	84.00 W
Blue Mesa Reservoir ⊜[1]	190	38.27 N	107.10 W
Blue Mosque ᵾ[1]	263c	30.02 N	31.15 E
Blue Mound, Ill., U.S.	209	39.42 N	89.07 W
Blue Mound, Kans., U.S.	188	38.05 N	95.00 W
Blue Mound, Tex., U.S.	212	32.51 N	97.19 W
Blue Mountain, Miss., U.S.	184	34.40 N	89.02 W
Blue Mountain, N.Y., U.S.	200	42.07 N	74.01 W
Blue Mountain Λ, N.B., Can.	176	47.49 N	66.19 W
Blue Mountain Λ, Newf., Can.	176	50.24 N	57.10 W
Blue Mountain Λ, Ont., Can.	202	44.28 N	80.22 W
Blue Mountain Λ, Ark., U.S.	184	34.41 N	94.03 W
Blue Mountain Λ, Mont., U.S.	188	47.16 N	104.10 W
Blue Mountain Λ, N.H., U.S.	178	44.47 N	71.28 W
Blue Mountain Λ, Pa., U.S.	178	40.15 N	77.30 W
Blue Mountain Λ[2], Ont., Can.	180	48.15 N	80.07 W
Blue Mountain Λ[2], Ont., Can.	202	44.40 N	77.58 W
Blue Mountain Peak Λ	231q	18.03 N	76.35 W
Blue Mountains ⋀, Austl.	160	33.37 S	150.17 E
Blue Mountains ⋀, Jam.	231q	18.06 N	76.40 W
Blue Mountains ⋀, U.S.	192	45.30 N	118.15 W
Blue Mountains ⋀, Maine, U.S.	178	44.50 N	70.35 W
Blue Mud Bay C	154	13.26 S	135.56 E
Blue Nile (Al-Baḥr al-Azraq) (Abay) ≃	130	15.38 N	32.31 E
Bluenose Lake ⊜	166	68.30 N	119.35 W
Blue Point	266	40.45 N	73.02 W
Blue Point >	266	40.44 N	73.02 W
Blue Rapids	188	39.41 N	96.39 W
Blue Ridge, Alta., Can.	172	54.08 N	115.22 W
Blue Ridge, Ga., U.S.	182	34.52 N	84.20 W
Blue Ridge, Ill., U.S.	206	40.17 N	88.29 W
Blue Ridge ⋀	168	37.00 N	82.00 W
Blue Ridge Summit	198	39.43 N	77.28 W
Blue River	172	52.05 N	119.17 W
Blue Rock Springs Park ♠	272	38.08 N	122.12 W
Bluesky	172	56.04 N	118.14 W
Blue Springs	188	40.09 N	96.40 W
Bluestone ≃	182	37.34 N	80.59 W
Bluestone Dam ●[6]	182	37.36 N	80.53 W
Bluestone Lake ⊜[1]	182	37.30 N	80.50 W
Bluewater	190	35.15 N	107.59 W
Blue Water Bridge ●[5]	204	43.00 N	82.25 W
Bluff, N.Z.	162	46.36 S	168.20 E
Bluff, Utah, U.S.	190	37.17 N	109.33 W
Bluff Cape >	100	18.00 N	94.26 E
Bluff City, Ill., U.S.	209	40.11 N	90.14 W
Bluff City, Tenn., U.S.	182	36.28 N	82.16 W
Bluff Cove C	270	33.48 N	118.24 W
Bluff Creek ≃, U.S.	186	36.58 N	97.26 W
Bluff Creek ≃, Kans., U.S.	188	37.02 N	99.29 W
Bluff Dale	186	32.21 N	98.01 W
Bluff Island I	261d	22.19 N	114.21 E
Bluff Knoll Λ	152	34.23 S	118.20 E
Bluff Park	184	33.27 N	86.47 W
Bluff Point >, Austl.	152	27.50 S	114.06 E
Bluff Point >, H.K.	261d	22.11 N	114.12 E
Bluffs	209	39.45 N	90.32 W
Bluff Springs	209	39.59 N	90.21 W
Bluffton, Ind., U.S.	206	40.44 N	85.11 W
Bluffton, Ohio, U.S.	206	40.54 N	83.54 W
Bluffton, S.C., U.S.	182	32.14 N	80.52 W
Bluffy Lake ⊜	174	50.47 N	92.55 W
Bluford	209	38.20 N	88.45 W
Blum	212	32.09 N	97.24 W
Blumberg, B.R.D.	54	47.50 N	8.31 E
Blumberg, D.D.R.	50	52.36 N	13.37 E
Blumenau	242	26.56 S	49.03 W
Blumenhof	174	50.01 N	107.41 W
Blümlisalp Λ	54	46.30 N	7.47 E
Blunt	188	44.31 N	99.59 W
Blupblup Island I	154	3.30 S	144.37 E
Bly	192	42.24 N	121.02 W
Blying Sound U	170	59.50 N	149.15 W
Blyth, Austl.	158b	33.51 S	138.29 E
Blyth, Ont., Can.	180	43.44 N	81.26 W
Blyth, Eng., U.K.	42	55.07 N	1.30 W
Blyth ≃, Austl.	154	12.04 S	134.35 E
Blyth ≃, Eng., U.K.	42	55.08 N	1.31 W
Blyth ≃, Eng., U.K.	44	52.18 N	1.40 E
Blyth Bridge	42	55.42 N	3.24 W
Blythe	194	33.37 N	114.36 W
Blythe ≃	44	52.31 N	1.42 W
Blythedale	204	40.15 N	79.48 W
Blytheswood	204	42.07 N	82.36 W
Blytheville	184	35.56 N	89.55 W
Blytheville Air Force Base ■	184	35.57 N	89.57 W
Blyth Range ⋀	152	26.50 S	129.00 E
Bnei Braq → Bene Beraq	122	32.05 N	34.50 E
Bø, Nor.	24	68.37 N	14.33 E
Bø, Nor.	26	59.25 N	9.04 E
Bo, S.L.	140	7.56 N	11.21 W
Boa	144	10.32 S	28.06 E
Boa Barrinha	246	23.18 S	47.10 W
Boac	106	13.27 N	121.50 E
Boaco	226	12.28 N	85.40 W
Boaco □[5]	226	12.30 N	85.30 W
Boadilla del Monte	256a	40.24 N	3.53 W
Boa Esperança, Bra.	245	21.05 S	45.34 W
Boa Esperança, Bra.	246	22.48 S	42.34 W
Boai	92	35.10 N	113.04 E
Boa Jerubatuba	246	23.18 S	47.04 W
Boali	142	4.48 N	18.07 E
Boalia	116	23.35 N	88.57 E
Boalsburg	204	40.46 N	77.48 W
Boano, Pulau I	154	2.56 S	127.56 E
Boa Nova	245	14.22 S	40.10 W
Boara Pisani	58	45.08 N	11.47 E
Boara Polesine	58	45.07 N	11.48 E
Board Camp Mountain Λ	194	40.42 N	123.43 W
Boardman	204	41.02 N	80.40 W
Boardman ≃	180	44.46 N	85.38 W
Boario Terme	58	45.54 N	10.10 E
Boat Basin	172	49.29 N	126.25 W
Boat Harbour C	230b	24.59 N	77.25 W
Boat Lake ⊜	202	44.44 N	81.13 W
Boatman	156	27.16 S	146.55 E
Boa Vereda	246	22.27 S	46.14 W
Boa Viagem	240	5.07 S	39.44 W
Boa Vida	246	22.18 S	42.47 W
Boa Vista, Bra.	236	2.49 N	60.40 W
Boa Vista, Bra.	242	26.17 S	48.50 W
Boa Vista, Bra.	246	21.40 S	46.20 W
Boa Vista I	140a	16.05 N	22.50 W
Boa Vista, Morro Λ[2]	277a	22.53 S	43.06 W
Boa Vista, Serra da Λ	246	21.45 S	44.08 W
Boa Vista do Ramos	240	3.08 S	58.05 W
Boavita	236	6.20 N	72.35 W
Boawai	105b	8.46 S	121.10 E
Boayan Island I	106	10.34 N	119.09 E
Boaz	184	34.12 N	86.10 W
Boba	105b	8.57 S	121.04 E
Bobai	92	22.12 N	109.52 E
Bobbau	50	51.41 N	12.16 E
Bobbili	112	18.34 N	83.22 E
Bobbing	250	51.21 N	0.43 E
Bobbingworth	250	51.44 N	0.13 E
Bobbin Head	264a	33.39 S	151.08 E
Bobbio	56	44.46 N	9.23 E
Bobbio Pellice	56	44.48 N	7.07 E
Bobbys Run ≃	275	39.58 N	74.48 W
Bobcaygeon	202	44.33 N	78.33 W
Bobigny	46	48.54 N	2.27 E
Böbingen, B.R.D.	52	48.49 N	9.54 E
Bobingen, B.R.D.	54	48.16 N	10.50 E
Bobitz	50	53.47 N	11.20 E
Bob Lake ⊜	202	44.55 N	78.47 W
Böblingen	52	48.41 N	9.01 E
Bob-Lo Park ♠	271	42.06 N	83.07 W
Bobo Dioulasso	140	11.12 N	4.18 W
Boboiob, Gora Λ	75	40.52 N	70.21 E
Bobolice	30	53.57 N	16.36 E
Bobon	106	12.32 N	124.34 E
Bobonaza ≃	236	2.36 S	76.38 W
Bobonong	146	21.58 S	28.17 E
Bobotsari	105a	7.18 S	109.22 E
Boboye, Dallol V	140	14.00 N	3.00 E
Bobr	66	54.20 N	29.16 E
Bóbr ≃, Pol.	30	52.04 N	15.04 E
Bobr ≃, S.S.S.R.	66	54.03 N	28.51 E
Bobrik ≃	66	52.08 N	26.46 E
Bobrikovo	73	47.56 N	39.13 E
Bobrinec	68	48.03 N	32.09 E
Bobrka	68	49.38 N	24.18 E
Bobrov	68	51.06 N	40.02 E
Bobrovica	68	50.44 N	31.22 E
Bobrujsk	66	53.09 N	29.14 E
Bobs Creek ≃	209	38.57 N	90.42 W
Bobs Lake ⊜	202	44.40 N	76.35 W
Bobtown	178	39.46 N	79.59 W
Bobuk	130	11.30 N	34.05 E
Bobures	236	9.15 N	71.11 W
Boby, Pic Λ	147b	22.12 S	46.55 E
Boca ●[8]	278	34.38 S	58.21 W
Bôca, Cachoeira de L	240	5.27 S	54.24 W
Boca Brava, Isla I	226	8.13 N	82.16 W
Boca Chica	230m	17.59 N	66.32 W
Boca Chica Key I	210	24.34 N	81.42 W
Bôca da Mata	240	9.41 S	36.11 W
Boca del Monte	226	8.21 N	82.07 W
Boca del Pozo	236	11.00 N	64.23 W
Boca del Río	224	19.06 N	96.06 W
Boca del Rosario	248	34.26 S	57.17 W
Boca de Quadra U	172	55.08 N	130.50 W
Bôca do Acre	238	8.45 S	67.23 W
Bôca do Jari	240	1.07 S	51.58 W
Bocage, Cap >	165f	21.12 S	165.35 E
Boca Grande	210	26.45 N	82.16 W
Boca Grande Channel U	210	24.34 N	82.03 W
Boca Grande Key I	210	24.32 N	82.00 W
Bocaina, Rio da ≃	246	22.40 S	45.00 W
Bocaina, Serra da ⋀	246	22.43 S	44.40 W
Bocaina de Minas	246	22.10 S	44.24 W
Bocaiúva	245	17.07 S	43.49 W
Bocanda	140	7.04 N	4.30 W
Bocanegra	276d	12.01 S	77.07 W
Bocaranga	142	6.59 N	15.39 E
Boca Raton	210	26.21 N	80.05 W
Boca Reservoir ⊜[1]	216	39.24 N	120.06 W
Bocas del Toro	226	9.20 N	82.15 W
Bocas del Toro □[4]	226	8.50 N	82.10 W
Bocas del Toro, Archipiélago de II	226	9.20 N	82.10 W
Bocay	226	14.19 N	85.10 W
Bocay ≃	226	14.20 N	85.10 W
Boccaleone	60	44.39 N	11.48 E
Boccea ●[8]	257a	41.58 N	12.19 E
Boccon	58	45.19 N	11.39 E
Bocconi	58	44.01 N	11.46 E
Bočejkovo	66	55.01 N	29.09 E
Bochan	78	53.09 N	103.48 E
Bochil	224	16.59 N	92.55 W
Böchmörön	76	49.40 N	90.20 E
Bochnia	30	49.58 N	20.26 E
Bocholt, Bel.	52	51.10 N	5.35 E
Bocholt, B.R.D.	48	51.50 N	6.36 E
Bocholtz	52	50.49 N	6.00 E
Bochov	50	50.06 N	13.02 E
Bochum, B.R.D.	52		
	253	51.28 N	7.13 E
Bochum, S. Afr.	146	23.17 S	29.07 E
Bockel	48	53.12 N	9.17 E
Böckel ●[8]	253	51.13 N	7.12 E
Bockenem	48	52.00 N	10.07 E
Bockhorn	48	53.23 N	8.01 E
Böckstein	58	47.05 N	13.07 E
Bockum	253	51.20 N	6.44 E
Bockum ●[8]	253	51.21 N	6.38 E
Bockum-Hövel	48	51.42 N	7.46 E
Bocognano	36	42.05 N	9.03 E
Boconó	236	9.15 N	70.16 W
Bocq ≃	52	50.20 N	4.53 E
Boczów	50	52.19 N	14.58 E
Boda, Centraf.	142	4.19 N	17.28 E
Böda, Sve.	26	57.15 N	17.03 E
Boda, Sve.	26	61.01 N	15.13 E
Bodafors	26	57.30 N	14.42 E
Boda Glasbruk	26	56.44 N	15.40 E
Bodāi	262b	22.48 N	88.29 E
Bodajbo	78	57.51 N	114.10 E
Bodalangi	142	3.14 N	22.14 E
Bodalla	156	36.05 S	150.03 E
Bodallin	152	31.22 S	118.52 E
Bodanga Dawili	142	5.33 N	16.45 E
Bodåsgruvan	40	60.25 N	16.26 E
Bodcau Creek ≃	184	33.01 N	93.31 W
Boddington	158a	32.48 S	116.28 E
Bode	188	42.52 N	94.17 W
Bode ≃	50	52.01 N	11.12 E
Bodega Bay C	194	38.15 N	123.00 W
Bodegraven	48	52.05 N	4.45 E
Bodele ●[1]	136	16.30 N	16.30 E
Bodelschwingh ●[8]	253	51.33 N	7.22 E
Boden → Fleres, It.	58	46.58 N	11.21 E
Boden, Sve.	26	65.50 N	21.42 E
Bodenburg	48	52.01 N	10.01 E
Bodenfelde	48	51.38 N	9.33 E
Bodenheim	52	49.56 N	8.18 E
Bodensee (Lake Constance) ⊜	54	47.35 N	9.25 E
Bodenteich	50	52.50 N	10.41 E
Bodenwerder	48	51.59 N	9.31 E
Bode Sadu	140	9.00 N	4.47 E
Bodhan	112	18.40 N	77.54 E
Bodiam	44	51.00 N	0.33 E
Bodināyakkanūr	112	10.01 N	77.21 E
Bodine, Mount Λ	172	55.37 N	125.49 W
Bodjoki	142	2.59 N	22.18 E
Bodjokola	142	3.54 N	20.17 E
Bodmin	44	50.29 N	4.43 W
Bodmin Moor ●[3]	44	50.33 N	4.33 W
Bodø	24	67.17 N	14.23 E
Bodocó	240	7.47 S	39.55 W
Bodoquena, Serra da ⋀[1]	238	21.00 S	56.50 W
Bodoupa	142	5.43 N	17.36 E
Bodri ≃	105a	6.52 S	110.10 E
Bodrog ≃	38	48.07 N	21.25 E
Bodrum	120	37.02 N	27.26 E
Bodstedt	50	54.22 N	12.37 E
Bo-duc (Bu-dop)	100	11.58 N	106.48 E
Bodzentyn	30	50.56 N	20.57 E
Boè, Piz Λ	58	46.31 N	11.48 E
Boëge	54	46.13 N	6.25 E
Boegoebergdam ●[6]	148	29.02 S	22.12 E
Boekelo	48	52.13 N	6.47 E
Boele ●[8]	253	51.24 N	7.28 E
Boémbé	142	2.54 S	15.39 E
Boende	142	0.13 S	20.52 E
Bœng Lvea	100	12.36 N	105.34 E
Boeni	147a	12.55 S	45.06 E
Boën-sur-Lignon	56	45.44 N	3.59 E
Boeo, Capo >	36	37.48 N	12.26 E
Boer	88	35.42 N	119.45 E
Boerboonfontein	148	33.43 S	20.32 E
Boerne	186	29.47 N	98.44 W
Boertala Zizhizhou □[4]	76	45.00 N	83.00 E
Boeslunde	41	55.18 N	11.17 E
Boesmansriviermond	148	33.42 S	26.39 E
Boetsap	148	27.59 S	24.30 E
Boeuf Creek ≃	209	38.36 N	91.09 W
Boffa	140	10.10 N	14.02 W
Boffa □[4]	140	10.20 N	14.00 W
Boffalora	256b	45.28 N	8.50 E
Boffzen	48	51.45 N	9.23 E
Bofoku	142	0.57 S	20.53 E
Bofors	40	59.20 N	14.32 E
Bofosso	140	8.40 N	9.42 W
Bōfu → Hōfu	86	34.03 N	131.34 E
Boga	144	1.03 N	29.56 E
Bogachiel ≃	214	47.55 N	124.28 W
Bogadjim	154	5.25 S	145.45 E
Bogal, Lak ≃	144	0.45 N	40.50 E
Bogale	100	16.17 N	95.24 E
Bogalusa	184	30.47 N	89.52 W
Bogan ≃	156	32.45 S	148.08 E
Bogandé	140	12.59 N	0.08 W
Bog and Vly Meadows ☰	266	40.56 N	74.19 W
Bogan Gate	156	33.07 S	147.48 E
Bogangolo	142	5.34 N	18.15 E
Bogantungan	156	23.39 S	147.18 E
Bogastow Brook ≃	273	42.12 N	71.22 W
Bogata	186	33.28 N	95.13 W
Bogataja Černeščina	68	48.59 N	35.35 E
Bogatiščevo-Jepišino	72	54.47 N	38.25 E
Bogatyje Saby	70	56.01 N	50.27 E
Bogatynia	50	50.53 N	15.00 E
Bogatyr'	70	53.25 N	50.02 E
Bogatyrevo	70	50.22 N	48.46 E
Boğazkale	120	40.02 N	34.37 E
Boğazköy	257b	41.11 N	28.46 E
Boğazköy ≃	257b	41.10 N	28.49 E
Boğazlıyan	120	39.12 N	35.15 E
Bogbonga	142	1.35 N	19.25 E
Bogdanovič	76	56.47 N	62.01 E
Bogdanovka, S.S.S.R.	70	52.10 N	52.37 E
Bogdanovka, S.S.S.R.	70	52.42 N	50.46 E
Bogdanovka, S.S.S.R.	74	41.18 N	43.35 E
Bogdo Ula Λ	76	43.50 N	88.20 E
Bogd-Uul	92	45.09 N	100.43 E
Bogdyn ≃	78	47.20 N	95.50 E
Bogeduoshanmai ⋀	80	43.30 N	89.45 E
Bogel	52	50.11 N	7.48 E
Bogembaj	76	52.29 N	72.20 E
Bogen	30	48.55 N	12.43 E
Bogenfels	146	27.23 S	15.22 E
Bogense	41	55.34 N	10.06 E
Boger City	182	35.29 N	81.13 W
Boges	52	50.11 N	7.48 E
Bogess Creek ≃	272	37.18 N	122.19 W
Boget	70	49.40 N	47.59 E
Boggabilla	156	28.37 S	150.21 E
Boggabri	156	30.42 S	150.02 E
Boggola, Mount Λ	152	23.48 S	117.40 E
Boggs Run ≃	269b	40.32 N	80.14 W
Boggstown	208	39.34 N	85.55 W
Boggy Creek ≃	212	31.07 N	95.46 W
Boggy Peak Λ	230c	17.03 N	61.51 W
Bogia	154	4.15 S	144.55 E
Bogie Lake ⊜	271	42.37 N	83.31 W
Bogilima	142	3.34 N	19.16 E
Boğlan	120	38.58 N	41.03 E
Bogliasco	56	44.23 N	9.04 E
Bognanco Fonti	54	46.07 N	8.12 E
Bognes	24	68.10 N	16.00 E
Bognor Regis	44	50.47 N	0.41 W
Bogny-sur-Meuse	52	49.51 N	4.46 E
Bogo, Cam.	136	10.44 N	14.36 E
Bogo, Pil.	106	11.03 N	124.00 E
Bogø I	41	54.56 N	12.04 E
Bogo Bay C	106	11.05 N	124.01 E
Bogoduchov	68	50.10 N	35.30 E
Bogol Manya	134	4.32 N	41.32 E
Bogol'ubovo, S.S.S.R.	66	55.32 N	32.57 E
Bogol'ubovo, S.S.S.R.	70	56.13 N	40.31 E
Bogomila	38	41.36 N	21.28 E
Bogon	134	2.56 N	42.00 E
Bogong, Mount Λ	156	36.45 S	147.18 E
Bogong Peaks ⋀	161b	35.34 S	148.28 E
Bogor	105a	6.35 S	106.47 E
Bogoro	144	1.24 N	30.17 E
Bogorodčany	68	48.48 N	24.32 E
Bogorodick	66	53.46 N	38.08 E
Bogorodickoje	70	46.20 N	41.10 E
Bogorodičnoje	73	49.01 N	37.30 E
Bogorodsk, S.S.S.R.	24	62.16 N	52.28 E
Bogorodsk, S.S.S.R.	70	56.06 N	43.31 E
Bogorodskoje, S.S.S.R.	70	46.20 N	43.53 E
Bogorodskoje, S.S.S.R.	70	57.49 N	50.45 E
Bogorodskoje, S.S.S.R.	72	55.02 N	38.29 E
Bogorodskoje, S.S.S.R.	72	55.26 N	36.14 E
Bogorodskoje, S.S.S.R.	79	52.22 N	140.30 E
Bogorodskoje ●[8]	255b	55.49 N	37.44 E
Bogoso	140	5.34 N	2.01 W
Bogosskij Chrebet ⋀	74	42.15 N	46.05 E
Bogotá, Col.	236	4.36 N	74.05 W
Bogota, N.J., U.S.	266	40.53 N	74.02 W
Bogotá ≃	236	4.18 N	74.48 W
Bogotol	76	56.12 N	89.33 E
Bogou	140	10.39 N	0.11 E
Bogovarovo	24	58.59 N	47.01 E
Bogra	114	24.51 N	89.22 E
Bograd	76	54.13 N	90.51 E
Bogučany	78	58.23 N	97.29 E
Bogučar	68	49.57 N	40.33 E
Bogučar ≃	68	49.57 N	40.39 E
Bogué	140	16.35 N	14.16 W
Bogue Chitto ≃	184	30.35 N	89.49 W
Bogue Chitto Creek ≃	184	32.10 N	87.14 W
Bogues Bay C	198	37.52 N	75.29 W
Bogunaj	76	56.14 N	94.35 E
Böğürtlen	120	37.10 N	38.04 E
Boguslav	68	49.33 N	30.53 E
Bogušovsk	66	54.51 N	30.13 E
Bogustan	75	41.41 N	70.05 E
Bohai C	88	38.30 N	120.00 E
Bohain-en-Vermandois	46	49.59 N	3.27 E
Bohaiwan C	88	38.40 N	118.20 E
Bohan	52	49.52 N	4.53 E
Bohannon	198	37.24 N	76.22 W
Bohemia	200	40.46 N	73.07 W
Bohemia → Čechy □[9]	30	49.50 N	14.00 E
Bohemia ≃	198	39.29 N	75.55 W
Bohemia Downs	152	18.53 S	126.14 E
Bohemian Forest ⋀	30	49.15 N	12.45 E
Bohetai	94	42.01 N	123.13 E
Bohicon	140	7.12 N	2.04 E
Bohinjska Bistrica	36	46.17 N	13.57 E
Böhlen	50	51.12 N	12.23 E
Böhlitz-Ehrenberg ●[8]	50	51.21 N	12.17 E
Böhme ≃	48	52.46 N	9.28 E
Böhmen → Čechy □[9]	30	49.50 N	14.00 E
Böhmenkirch	52	48.41 N	9.55 E
Böhmerwald → Bohemian Forest ⋀	30	49.15 N	12.45 E
Bohmte	48	52.22 N	8.19 E
Bohners Lake	206	42.37 N	88.17 W
Böhnsdorf ●[8]	254a	52.24 N	13.33 E
Bohodou	140	9.46 N	9.04 W
Bohol	134	5.43 N	46.10 E
Bohol □[4]	106	9.50 N	124.10 E
Bohol I	106	9.50 N	124.10 E
Bohol Madagoi ≃	134	2.00 N	43.12 E
Bohol Strait U	106	9.45 N	123.40 E
Bohon	106	18.30 N	120.35 E
Bohongou	140	12.30 N	0.42 E
Bohorok	104	3.30 N	98.12 E
Bohotleh Wein	134	8.16 N	46.24 E
Bohsdorf	50	51.38 N	14.32 E
Bohuslän □[9]	26	58.15 N	11.50 E
Bohušovice nad Ohří	50	50.29 N	14.07 E
Boi	140	9.34 N	9.27 E
Boi, Ponta do >	246	23.58 S	45.15 W
Boiaçu	236	0.27 S	61.46 W
Boiano	60	41.29 N	14.29 E
Boiceville	200	41.59 N	74.15 W
Boiestown	176	46.27 N	66.25 W
Boigu Island I	154	9.16 S	142.12 E
Boila	144	16.10 S	39.50 E
Boiling Springs, N.C., U.S.	182	35.16 N	81.40 W
Boiling Springs, Pa., U.S.	198	40.09 N	77.08 W
Boinville-en-Mantois	251	48.56 N	1.46 E
Boinvilliers	251	48.55 N	1.40 E
Boipeba, Ilha de I	245	13.39 S	38.55 W
Boiro	34	42.39 N	8.54 W
Bois, Lac des ⊜, N.W. Ter., Can.	170	66.40 N	125.15 W
Bois, Lac des → Woods, Lake of the ⊜, N.A.	174	49.15 N	94.45 W
Bois, Ribeirão dos ≃	245	20.12 S	53.07 W
Bois, Rio dos ≃	245	18.35 S	50.02 W
Bois Blanc Island I	180	45.45 N	84.28 W
Bois Brule ≃	180	46.45 N	91.37 W
Boischâtel	196	46.54 N	71.08 W
Bois-Colombes	251	48.55 N	2.16 E
Bois d'Arc Creek ≃	186	33.50 N	95.50 W
Bois-d'Arcy	251	48.48 N	2.01 E
Bois-des-Filion	196	45.40 N	73.45 W
Bois de Sioux ≃	188	46.16 N	96.36 W
Bois du Roi Λ	32	47.00 N	4.02 E
Boise	192	43.37 N	116.13 W
Boise ≃	192	43.49 N	117.01 W
Boise, Middle Fork ≃	192	43.42 N	115.38 W
Boise, North Fork ≃	192	43.42 N	115.38 W
Boise, South Fork ≃	192	43.36 N	115.51 W
Boise City	186	36.44 N	102.31 W
Boisemont	251	49.01 N	2.00 E
Bois-Guillaume	46	49.28 N	1.08 E
Bois-le-Roi	46	48.28 N	2.42 E
Boissettes	251	48.31 N	2.37 E
Boissevain	174	49.14 N	100.03 W
Boissise-la-Bertrand	251	48.32 N	2.35 E
Boissy-l'Aillerie	251	49.05 N	2.02 E
Boissy-Saint-Léger	46	48.45 N	2.31 E
Boissy-sous-Saint-Yon	251	48.34 N	2.13 E
Boistfort Peak Λ	214	46.29 N	123.12 W
Boitzenburg	50	53.15 N	13.37 E
Boizenburg	50	53.22 N	10.43 E
Boja	105a	7.06 S	110.16 E
Bojadła	30	51.57 N	15.50 E
Bojador, Cabo >	138	26.08 N	14.30 W
Bojarka	68	50.19 N	30.19 E
Bojarkino	72	54.57 N	38.31 E
Bojarsk	78	56.19 N	106.04 E
Bojayá ≃	236	6.35 N	76.54 W
Bojeador, Cape >	106	18.30 N	120.34 E
Bojelebung	106	6.31 N	122.11 E
Bojevo	68	51.24 N	39.19 E
Boji Plain ≚	144	1.30 N	39.45 E
Bojizhang	88	41.49 N	117.46 E
Bojnūrd	118	37.28 N	57.19 E
Bojonegoro	105a	7.09 S	111.52 E
Boju	140	7.25 N	7.52 E
Boju Ega	140	7.24 N	8.04 E
B'ojuk-Kirs, Gora Λ	74	39.41 N	46.44 E
Bojuru	242	31.38 S	51.26 W
Bokad	262c	18.53 N	72.58 E
Bokada	142	4.08 N	19.23 E
Bokal	158a	33.29 S	116.54 E
Bokala, Zaïre	142	3.07 S	17.02 E
Bokala, Zaïre	142	2.03 N	18.59 E
Bokalike	110	36.47 N	91.41 E
Bokani	140	9.26 N	5.13 E
Bokāro	114	23.51 N	86.02 E
Bokatola	142	0.38 S	18.46 E
Bokchito	186	34.01 N	96.09 W
Boké	140	10.56 N	14.18 W
Boké □[4]	140	11.00 N	14.20 W
Bokeelia	210	26.42 N	82.09 W
Bokel	48	53.23 N	8.46 E
Bokela	142	1.08 S	21.56 E
Bokes Creek ≃	178	40.19 N	83.10 W
Boketu	79	48.46 N	121.57 E
Bokfontein	148	32.48 S	19.16 E
Bokhara	148	27.57 S	20.30 E
Bokhara ≃	156	29.55 S	146.42 E
Boki	136	8.48 N	13.32 E
Bokino	70	52.38 N	41.26 E
Bokkeveldberg ⋀	148	31.22 S	19.02 E
Bokkol Λ	144	1.50 N	37.02 E
Böklund	41	54.36 N	9.34 E
Boknafjorden C[2]	26	59.10 N	5.35 E
Boko, Congo	142	4.47 S	14.38 E
Boko, S.S.S.R.	76	49.05 N	81.38 E
Bokod	106	16.30 N	120.50 E
Bokode	142	3.58 N	19.29 E
Bokolako	140	13.36 N	12.33 W
Bokonbajevskoje	75	42.07 N	77.00 E
Bokondji	142	2.22 N	18.42 E
Bokondo	142	0.15 N	22.32 E
Bokong	102	9.58 S	124.04 E
Bokoro	136	12.23 N	17.03 E
Boko Songo	142	4.26 S	13.37 E
Bokota	142	0.51 S	22.18 E
Bokote	142	0.05 S	20.08 E
Bokovo-Antratsit → Antracit	73	48.06 N	39.06 E
Bokovo Platovo	73	48.07 N	39.01 E
Bokovskaja	70	49.15 N	41.49 E
Bokpunt >	148	33.34 S	18.19 E
Bokpyin	100	11.16 N	98.46 E
Boksburg	148	26.12 S	28.14 E
Boksburg North	263d	26.12 S	28.15 E
Boksburg South	263d	26.14 S	28.15 E
Boksburg West	263d	26.13 S	28.14 E
Boksitogorsk	66	59.28 N	33.51 E
Bokungu	142	0.41 S	22.19 E
Bol, Jugo.	36	43.16 N	16.40 E
Bol, Tchad	136	13.28 N	14.43 E
Bola	165e	9.37 S	160.39 E
Bolaang Mongondow	102	0.56 N	124.10 E
Bolaï I	142	4.20 N	17.21 E
Bolama, Gui.-B.	140	11.35 N	15.28 W
Bolama, Zaïre	142	1.57 N	22.58 E
Bolān ≃	110	28.38 N	67.42 E
Bolanda, Jabal Λ	130	7.44 N	25.28 E
Bol'andkiik ≃	75	39.11 N	72.17 E
Bolands	230c	17.02 N	61.53 W
Bolangum	156	36.46 S	142.53 E
Bolaños	224	21.41 N	103.47 W
Bolaños, Río de ≃	224	21.14 N	104.08 W
Bolaños de Calatrava	34	38.54 N	3.40 W
Bolayır	120	40.31 N	26.45 E
Bolbec	46	49.34 N	0.29 E
Bolčary	76	59.49 N	68.48 E
Bolchov	66	53.27 N	36.01 E
Bolchuny	70	47.59 N	46.25 E
Bolda ≃	70	46.10 N	48.14 E
Boldasevo	70	54.43 N	45.33 E
Boldekow	50	53.43 N	13.35 E
Bolderslev	41	54.59 N	9.18 E
Bold Heath	252	53.24 N	2.42 W
Boldon	42	54.57 N	1.27 W
Bol'džuan	75	38.19 N	69.40 E
Bole, Ghana	140	9.02 N	2.29 W
Bole, Zhg.	76	44.53 N	82.05 E
Bolechov	68	49.04 N	23.52 E
Boléko, Gabon	142	0.56 N	12.14 E
Boleko, Zaïre	142	1.31 S	19.53 E
Bolero	144	10.59 S	33.45 E
Boles	184	34.47 N	94.03 W
Bolesławiec	30	51.16 N	15.34 E
Boleszkowice	30	52.44 N	14.36 E
Boletice nad Labem	50	50.45 N	14.13 E
Boley	186	35.29 N	96.29 W
Bolgart	152	31.16 S	116.30 E
Bolgatanga	140	10.46 N	0.52 W
Bolgrad	68	45.41 N	28.36 E
Boli, Sūd.	130	6.01 N	28.43 E
Boli, Tchad	136	10.50 N	18.43 E
Boli, Zhg.	79	45.46 N	130.35 E
Bolia	142	1.36 S	18.23 E
Boliden	26	64.52 N	20.23 E
Boligee	184	32.45 N	88.02 W
Boligeqiu	94	42.14 N	121.40 E
Bolinao	106	16.23 N	119.54 E
Bolinas	216	37.54 N	122.42 W
Boling	212	29.16 N	95.57 W
Bolingbrook	206	41.42 N	88.03 W
Bolinger Creek ≃	272	37.47 N	122.00 W

Name	Seite	Breite	Länge E=Ost
Bolingo	142	3.30 S	21.43 E
Bolishan	79	43.50 N	123.31 E
Bolívar, Arg.	242	36.15 S	61.06 W
Bolivar, Austl.	158b	34.46 S	138.36 E
Bolívar, Col.	236	1.50 N	76.58 W
Bolívar, Col.	236	5.50 N	76.01 W
Bolívar, Col.	236	4.21 N	76.10 W
Bolívar, Perú	238	7.18 S	77.48 W
Bolivar, Mo., U.S.	184	37.37 N	93.25 W
Bolivar, N.Y., U.S.	200	42.04 N	78.10 W
Bolivar, Ohio, U.S.	204	40.39 N	81.27 W
Bolivar, Pa., U.S.	204	40.23 N	79.10 W
Bolivar, Tenn., U.S.	184	35.16 N	88.59 W
Bolívar □[3]	236	6.20 N	63.30 W
Bolívar □[4]	236	1.35 S	79.00 W
Bolívar □[5]	236	9.00 N	74.40 W
Bolívar, Cerro Λ	236	7.28 N	63.25 W
Bolívar, Pico Λ	236	8.30 N	71.02 W
Bolivar Peninsula >[1]	186	29.27 N	94.39 W
Bolivar Run	204	41.59 N	78.39 W
Bolivia □[1]	232		
	238	17.00 S	65.00 W
Bolivie → Bolivia □[1]	238	17.00 S	65.00 W
Bolivien → Bolivia □[1]	238	17.00 S	65.00 W
Boljarovo	38	42.09 N	26.49 E
Boljoon	106	9.38 N	123.29 E
Bolkar Dağları ⋀	120	37.15 N	34.20 E
Bölkenbusch	253	51.21 N	7.06 E
Boll	52	48.38 N	9.37 E
Bolladello	256b	45.41 N	8.50 E
Bollate	56	45.33 N	9.07 E
Böllberg Λ[2]	253	51.23 N	7.19 E
Bollendorf	52	49.51 N	6.22 E
Bollène	56	44.17 N	4.45 E
Bollensdorf	254a	52.31 N	13.43 E
Bolles Canal ≊	210	26.38 N	80.34 W
Bolles Harbor	206	41.51 N	83.24 W
Bollin ≃	42	53.23 N	2.28 W
Bolling Air Force Base ■	274c	38.51 N	77.02 W
Bollington, Eng., U.K.	42	53.18 N	2.06 W
Bollington, Eng., U.K.	252	53.22 N	2.25 W
Bollmora	40	59.15 N	18.13 E
Bollnäs	26	61.21 N	16.25 E
Bollon	156	28.05 S	147.15 E
Bollstabruk	26	63.00 N	17.39 E
Bollstanäs	40	59.30 N	17.56 E
Bollullos par del Condado	34	37.20 N	6.32 W
Bollwerk	253	51.10 N	7.35 E
Bolmen ⊜	26	56.55 N	13.40 E
Bolnisi	74	41.28 N	44.33 E
Bolobo	142	2.10 S	16.14 E
Bolochovo	72	54.05 N	37.50 E
Bologna	58	44.29 N	11.20 E
Bologna □[4]	58	44.28 N	11.26 E
Bologne, Fr.	54	48.12 N	5.08 E
Bologne → Bologna, It.	58	44.29 N	11.20 E
Bolognesi	238	6.35 S	73.10 W
Bolognola	60	42.59 N	13.14 E
Bologoje	66	57.54 N	34.02 E
Bologovo	66	56.54 N	31.42 E
Bololo	142	3.50 S	21.08 E
Bolomba	142	0.29 N	19.12 E
Bolombo	142	3.59 S	21.22 E
Bolombo ≃	142	1.32 N	21.14 E
Bolon'	79	49.55 N	136.07 E
Bolon', Ozero ⊜	79	49.51 N	136.22 E
Bolonchén de Rejón	222	20.00 N	89.49 W
Bolondo	142	0.27 N	20.01 E
Bolondrón	230p	22.46 N	81.27 W
Bolonia → Bologna	58	44.29 N	11.20 E
Bolo Silase	134	8.54 N	39.27 E
Bolotino	68	47.42 N	27.21 E
Bolotnoje	76	55.41 N	84.23 E
Boloto	72	54.10 N	36.20 E
Bolotovskoje	76	58.33 N	62.28 E
Bolovens, Plateau des ⋀[1]	100	15.20 N	106.20 E
Bolpur	116	23.40 N	87.43 E
Bol'šaja	66	59.36 N	41.48 E
Bol'šaja ≃	70	48.36 N	41.00 E
Bol'šaja Atn'a	70	56.15 N	49.27 E
Bol'šaja Balachn'a ≃	64	73.37 N	107.05 E
Bol'šaja Belaja ≃	78	52.52 N	103.05 E
Bol'šaja Ber'ostovica	66	53.11 N	24.01 E
Bol'šaja Bira ≃	79	48.07 N	133.21 E
Bol'šaja Blagoveščenka	68	46.52 N	33.04 E
Bol'šaja Brembola	72	56.45 N	38.55 E
Bol'šaja Čalykla ≃	70	51.51 N	49.34 E
Bol'šaja Černigovka	70	52.07 N	50.52 E
Bol'šaja Chalan'	68	50.56 N	37.26 E
Bol'šaja Cheta ≃	64	69.33 N	84.15 E
Bol'šaja Chobda ≃	76	50.56 N	54.34 E
Bol'šaja Chundala	66	60.04 N	34.18 E
Bol'šaja Čuja ≃	78	58.56 N	112.13 E
Bol'šaja Čurakovka	76	53.03 N	64.20 E
Bol'šaja Damba	70	46.57 N	51.47 E
Bol'šaja Dmitrijevka	70	51.21 N	45.15 E
Bol'šaja Dora	66	59.05 N	37.38 E
Bol'šaja Džalga	70	45.59 N	42.42 E
Bol'šaja Glušica	70	52.24 N	50.28 E
Bol'šaja Golova, Porog L	24	62.49 N	41.48 E
Bol'šaja Ižora	66	59.56 N	29.34 E
Bol'šaja Ižorka ≃	255a	59.48 N	30.36 E
Bol'šaja Kakša ≃	70	57.53 N	45.28 E
Bol'šaja Kamenka	70	53.39 N	50.31 E
Bol'šaja Kamenka ≃	73	48.22 N	40.04 E
Bol'šaja Kandala	70	54.32 N	49.22 E
Bol'šaja Karpunicha	70	57.42 N	45.20 E
Bol'šaja Kaskara	76	57.11 N	65.58 E
Bol'šaja Kemčug ≃	78	56.53 N	91.51 E
Bol'šaja Ket'	76	57.39 N	91.45 E
Bol'šaja Ket' ≃	78	57.57 N	91.13 E
Bol'šaja Kinel' ≃	70	53.14 N	50.30 E
Bol'šaja Kirsanovka	73	47.40 N	38.54 E
Bol'šaja Kokšaga ≃	70	56.08 N	47.47 E
Bol'šaja Konkudera ≃	78	57.34 N	112.30 E
Bol'šaja Kuberle ≃	70	47.20 N	42.02 E
Bol'šaja Kugul'ta ≃	70	45.45 N	41.57 E
Bol'šaja Kuonamka ≃	64	70.45 N	113.24 E
Bol'šaja Laba ≃	74	44.16 N	40.53 E
Bol'šaja Lipovica	70	52.33 N	41.20 E
Bol'šaja Log	73	48.12 N	39.06 E
Bol'šaja Martynovka	70	47.17 N	41.40 E
Bol'šaja Mošanica	66	53.58 N	29.37 E
Bol'šaja Murta	76	56.55 N	93.07 E
Bol'šaja Norja	70	56.41 N	52.43 E
Bol'šaja Ochta ●[8]	255a	59.57 N	30.25 E
Bol'šaja Ol'šanka	70	51.32 N	44.17 E
Bol'šaja Orlovka	70	47.20 N	41.16 E
Bol'šaja Osinovaja ≃	170	66.30 N	174.00 E
Bol'šaja Pas'ma	70	58.38 N	43.53 E
Bol'šaja Rečka	78	51.57 N	104.44 E
Bol'šaja Ržaksa	70	52.08 N	42.13 E
Bol'šaja Sestra ≃	72	56.16 N	35.56 E
Bol'šaja Smedva ≃	72	54.50 N	38.34 E
Bol'šaja Sosnova	70	57.40 N	54.36 E
Bol'šaja Talovaja	68	46.58 N	40.37 E
Bol'šaja Tarel'	78	53.45 N	106.40 E
Bol'šaja Tavolžka	70	52.07 N	49.04 E
Bol'šaja Uča	70	56.37 N	52.05 E
Bol'šaja Usa	76	56.44 N	55.06 E
Bol'šaja Višera	66	58.55 N	32.08 E
Bol'šaja Vladimirovka	76	50.53 N	79.31 E
Bol'šaja Vys' ≃	68	48.45 N	30.54 E
Bolsa Knolls	216	36.44 N	121.38 W
Bol'šakovo, S.S.S.R.	66	54.53 N	21.40 E
Bol'šakovo, S.S.S.R.	255b	55.54 N	37.17 E
Bol'šečernigovka	73	48.57 N	39.25 E
Bol'šekrepinskaja	73	47.36 N	39.22 E

Symbols in the index entries represent the broad categories identified in the key at the right. Symbols with superior numbers (⋀[2]) identify subcategories (see complete key on page *I* · *26*).

Kartensymbole in dem Registerverzeichnis stellen die rechts in Schlüssel erklärten Kategorien dar. Symbole mit hochgestellten Ziffern (⋀[2]) bezeichnen Unterabteilungen einer Kategorie (vgl. vollständiger Schlüssel auf Seite *I* · *26*).

Los símbolos incluídos en el texto del índice representan las grandes categorias identificadas con la clave a la derecha. Los símbolos con numeros en su parte superior (⋀[2]) identifican las subcategorías (véase la clave completa en la página *I* · *26*).

Les symboles de l'index représentent les catégories indiquées dans la légende à droite. Les symboles suivis d'un indice (⋀[2]) représentent des sous-catégories (voir légende complète à la page *I* · *26*).

Os símbolos incluídos no texto do índice representam as grandes categorias identificadas com a chave à direita. Os símbolos com números em sua parte superior (⋀[2]) identificam as subcategorias (veja-se a chave completa à página *I* · *26*).

	English	Deutsch	Español	Français	Português
Λ	Mountain	Berg	Montaña	Montagne	Montanha
⋀	Mountains	Berge	Montañas	Montagnes	Montanhas
)(	Pass	Pass	Paso	Col	Passo
V	Valley, Canyon	Tal, Cañon	Valle, Cañón	Vallée, Canyon	Vale, Canhão
≚	Plain	Ebene	Llano	Plaine	Planície
>	Cape	Kap	Cabo	Cap	Cabo
I	Island	Insel	Isla	Île	Ilha
II	Islands	Inseln	Islas	Îles	Ilhas
●	Other Topographic Features	Andere Topographische Objekte	Otros Elementos Topográficos	Autres données topographiques	Outros Elementos Topográficos

⁓ River | Fluss | Río | Rivière | Rio
≃ Canal | Kanal | Canal | Canal | Canal
L Waterfall, Rapids | Wasserfall, Stromschnellen | Cascada, Rápidos | Chute d'eau, Rapides | Cascata, Rápidos
⊔ Strait | Meeresstrasse | Estrecho | Détroit | Estreito
C Bay, Gulf | Bucht, Golf | Bahía, Golfo | Baie, Golfe | Baía, Golfo
@ Lake, Lakes | See, Seen | Lago, Lagos | Lac, Lacs | Lago, Lagos
≚ Swamp | Sumpf | Pantano | Marais | Pântano
☰ Ice Features, Glacier | Eis- und Gletscherformen | Accidentes Glaciales | Formes glaciaires | Acidentes Glaciares
⊤ Other Hydrographic Features | Andere Hydrographische Objekte | Otros Elementos Hidrográficos | Autres données hydrographiques | Outros Elementos Hidrográficos

✦ Submarine Features | Untermeerische Objekte | Accidentes Submarinos | Formes de relief sous-marin | Acidentes Submarinos
□ Political Unit | Politische Einheit | Unidad Politica | Entité politique | Unidade Política
✝ Cultural Institution | Kulturelle Institution | Institución Cultural | Institution culturelle | Instituição Cultural
⊥ Historical Site | Historische Stätte | Sitio Histórico | Site historique | Sitio Histórico
♠ Recreational Site | Erholungs- und Ferienort | Sitio de Recreo | Centre de loisirs | Sítio de Lazer
⊠ Airport | Flughafen | Aeropuerto | Aéroport | Aeroporto
■ Military Installation | Militäranlage | Instalación Militar | Installation militaire | Instalação Militar
◆ Miscellaneous | Verschiedenes | Misceláneo | Divers | Miscelânea

ENGLISH

DEUTSCH

Symbols in the index entries represent the broad categories identified in the key at the right. Symbols with superior numbers (⛰2) identify subcategories (see complete key on page *I* · *26*).

Kartensymbole in dem Registerverzeichnis stellen die rechts in Schlüssel erklärten Kategorien dar. Symbole mit hochgestellten Ziffern (⛰2) bezeichnen Unterabteilungen einer Kategorie (vgl. vollständiger Schlüssel auf Seite *I* · *26*).

Los símbolos incluídos en el texto del índice representan las grandes categorias identificadas con la clave a la derecha. Los símbolos con numeros en su parte superior (⛰2) identifican las subcategorías (véase la clave completa en la página *I* · *26*).

Les symboles de l'index représentent les catégories indiquées dans la légende à droite. Les symboles suivis d'un indice (⛰2) représentent des sous-catégories (voir légende complète à la page *I* · *26*).

Os símbolos incluídos no texto do índice representam as grandes categorias identificadas com a chave à direita. Os símbolos com números em sua parte superior (⛰2) identificam as subcategorias (veja-se a chave completa à página *I* · *26*).

Mountain	Berg	Montaña	Montagne	Montanha
Mountains	Berge	Montañas	Montagnes	Montanhas
Pass	Pass	Paso	Col	Passo
Valley, Canyon	Tal, Cañon	Valle, Cañón	Vallée, Canyon	Vale, Canhão
Plain	Ebene	Llano	Plaine	Planície
Cape	Kap	Cabo	Cap	Cabo
Island	Insel	Isla	Île	Ilha
Islands	Inseln	Islas	Îles	Ilhas
Other Topographic Features	Andere Topographische Objekte	Otros Elementos Topográficos	Autres données topographiques	Outros Elementos Topográficos

ESPAÑOL

Nombre	Página	Lat.°′	Long.°′ W=Oeste
Braunwald	54	46.56 N	9.00 E
Brava	134	1.05 N	44.02 E
Brava I	140a	14.52 N	24.43 W
Brava, Costa ◆[2]	34	41.45 N	3.04 E
Brava, Punta ≻	248	34.56 S	56.10 W
Brave	178	39.44 N	80.16 W
Bravića	68	47.22 N	28.26 E
Bråviken C	40	58.38 N	16.32 E
Bravo, Cerro ∧, Bol.	238	17.40 S	64.35 W
Bravo, Cerro ∧, Perú	238	5.32 S	79.15 W
Bravo del Norte (Rio Grande) ≃	168	25.55 N	97.09 W
Brawley	194	32.59 N	115.31 W
Brawley Peaks ∧∧	194	38.15 N	118.55 W
Brawley Wash ∨	190	32.34 N	111.26 W
Bray, Bel.	46	50.26 N	4.06 E
Bray, Eire	28	53.12 N	6.06 W
Bray ≃	44	50.59 N	3.53 W
Bray, Pays de ◆[1]	46	49.46 N	1.26 E
Braybrook	264b	37.47 S	144.51 E
Bray-Dunes	46	51.05 N	2.31 E
Braye ≃	46	47.45 N	0.42 E
Bray Island I	166	69.20 N	76.45 W
Braymer	184	39.35 N	93.48 W
Bray-sur-Seine	46	48.25 N	3.14 E
Bray-sur-Somme	46	49.56 N	2.43 E
Brazeau ≃	172	52.55 N	115.15 W
Brazeau, Mount ∧	172	52.33 N	117.21 W
Brazeau Dam ◆[6]	172	52.45 N	115.30 W
Brazen Head ≻	148	31.43 S	29.25 E
Brazey-en-Plaine	54	47.08 N	5.13 E
Brazil	184	39.32 N	87.08 W
Brazil □[1]	18	10.00 S	55.00 W
Brazil Basin ✢[1]	8	15.00 S	26.00 W
Brazo Chico, Arroyo ≃	248	33.45 S	58.32 W
Brazo Largo, Arroyo ≃	248	33.47 S	58.36 W
Brazópolis	246	22.28 S	45.37 W
Brazoria	212	29.03 N	95.34 W
Brazoria □[6]	212	29.12 N	95.25 W
Brazos □[6]	212	30.40 N	96.18 W
Brazos ≃	186	28.53 N	95.23 W
Brazos, Clear Fork ≃	186	33.01 N	98.40 W
Brazos, Double Mountain Fork ≃	186	33.15 N	100.00 W
Brazos, Salt Fork ≃	186	33.15 N	100.00 W
Brazo Sur [del Rio Coig] ≃	244	51.32 S	70.04 W
Brazzaville	142		
	263b	4.16 S	15.17 E
Brazzaville (Maya Maya) Airport ⊠	263b	4.15 S	15.15 E
Brčko	38	44.53 N	18.48 E
Brda ≃	30	53.07 N	18.08 E
Brea	218	33.55 N	117.54 W
Brea, Punta ≻	230m	17.56 N	66.55 W
Brea Canyon ∨	270	33.55 N	117.55 W
Brea Creek ≃	270	33.53 N	117.59 W
Breadalbane	156	23.49 S	139.35 E
Brea Dam ◆[6]	270	33.54 N	117.56 W
Bread and Cheese Creek ≃	274b	39.17 N	76.29 W
Breaden Bluff ∧[2]	152	26.56 S	124.32 E
Breadysville	275	40.13 N	75.04 W
Breakenridge, Mount ∧	172	49.43 N	121.56 W
Breakheart Reservation ♠	273	42.29 N	71.02 W
Breaksea Sound ⋓	162	45.35 S	166.40 E
Bream Bay C	162	35.55 S	174.30 E
Bream Head ≻	162	35.51 S	174.35 E
Breamish ≃	42	55.31 N	1.56 W
Bream's Eaves	44	51.45 N	2.34 W
Bream Tail ≻	162	36.03 S	174.35 E
Brea Pozo	242	28.15 S	63.57 W
Bréau	251	48.34 N	2.53 E
Breaux Bridge	184	30.16 N	91.54 W
Breaza	38	45.11 N	25.40 E
Brebes	105a	6.53 S	109.03 E
Brécey	32	48.44 N	1.10 W
Brechfa	44	51.54 N	4.36 W
Brechin	28	56.44 N	2.40 W
Brecht	52	51.21 N	4.38 E
Brechten ◆[8]	253	51.35 N	7.28 E
Breckenridge, Colo., U.S.	190	39.29 N	106.03 W
Breckenridge, Mich., U.S.	180	43.24 N	84.29 W
Breckenridge, Minn., U.S.	188	46.16 N	96.35 W
Breckenridge, Tex., U.S.	186	32.45 N	98.54 W
Breckerfeld	52	51.16 N	7.28 E
Breckland ◆[1]	44	52.28 N	0.37 E
Brecknock → Brecon	44	51.57 N	3.24 W
Brecknock, Península ≻[1]	244	54.35 S	71.50 W
Brecksville	269a	41.19 N	81.38 W
Břeclav	30	48.46 N	16.53 E
Brecon	44	51.57 N	3.24 W
Brecon Beacons ∧	44	51.53 N	3.31 W
Brecon Beacons National Park ♠	44	51.52 N	3.25 W
Bred	41	55.22 N	10.07 E
Breda, Ned.	48	51.35 N	4.46 E
Breda, Iowa, U.S.	188	42.11 N	94.59 W
Bredaryd	26	57.10 N	13.44 E
Bredasdorp	148	34.32 S	20.02 E
Bredbo	161b	35.57 S	149.10 E
Bredbo ≃	161b	35.58 S	149.08 E
Bredbury	252	53.25 N	2.06 W
Bredbyn	26	63.27 N	18.06 E
Breddin	50	52.52 N	12.13 E
Brede Å ≃	41	55.09 N	8.42 E
Bredebro	41	55.03 N	8.49 E
Bredell	263d	26.05 S	28.17 E
Bredenbeck	48	52.15 N	9.37 E
Bredenbruch	253	51.21 N	7.45 E
Bredenbury	174	50.57 N	102.03 W
Bredene	46	51.14 N	2.58 E
Bredeney ◆[8]	253	51.24 N	6.59 E
Bredenscheid-Stüter	253	51.22 N	7.11 E
Bredereiche	50	53.08 N	13.14 E
Bredgar	250	51.18 N	0.42 E
Bredhurst	250	51.20 N	0.35 E
Bredon Hill ∧[2]	44	52.06 N	2.03 W
Bredsjö	40	59.50 N	14.44 E
Bredsjön ⊛	40	60.13 N	13.55 E
Bredstedt	41	54.37 N	8.59 E
Bredsten	41	55.42 N	9.24 E
Bredy	76	52.26 N	60.21 E
Bree	52	51.08 N	5.36 E
Breë ≃	148	34.24 S	20.50 E
Breeches Lake ⊛	196	45.54 N	71.28 W
Breeds Pond ⊛	273	42.28 N	70.59 W
Breedsville	206	42.21 N	86.08 W
Breese	209	38.36 N	89.32 W
Breesport	200	42.10 N	76.44 W
Breeza Plains	154	14.50 S	144.07 E
Breezewood	269b	40.34 N	80.03 W
Breg ≃	54	47.57 N	8.31 E
Bregalnica ≃	38	41.43 N	22.09 E
Breganze	58	45.42 N	11.34 E
Bregenz	54	47.30 N	9.46 E
Bregenzer Wald ∧∧	54	47.20 N	10.00 E
Bregninge, Dan.	41	55.01 N	10.37 E
Bregninge, Dan.	41	55.41 N	11.19 E
Bregovo	38	44.09 N	22.39 E
Breguzzo	58	46.00 N	10.42 E
Brégy	251	49.05 N	2.52 E
Bréhal	32	48.54 N	1.31 W
Brehna	50	51.33 N	12.12 E
Breiðafjörður C	24a	65.15 N	23.15 W
Breidbach	148	32.54 S	27.27 E
Breid Bay C	9	70.15 S	24.15 E
Breidenbach	52	49.08 N	7.25 E
Breidenstein	52	50.55 N	8.28 E
Breil-sur-Roya	56	43.56 N	7.30 E
Breinizer	204	40.24 N	79.16 W
Breisach	54	48.01 N	7.40 E

FRANÇAIS

Nom	Page	Lat.°′	Long.°′ W=Ouest
Breisgau ◆[1]	54	47.45 N	7.45 E
Breitbrunn	58	48.02 N	11.08 E
Breitenbrunn	50	50.29 N	12.46 E
Breitenfelde	48	53.36 N	10.38 E
Breitengüssbach	52	49.58 N	10.53 E
Breitenlee ◆[8]	254b	48.15 N	16.30 E
Breitenstein	50	51.37 N	10.56 E
Breitenworbis	50	51.24 N	10.25 E
Breithorn ∧	54	45.56 N	7.45 E
Breitlingsee ⊛	50	52.23 N	12.28 E
Breitscheid, B.R.D.	52	51.22 N	6.52 E
Breitscheid, B.R.D.	52	50.41 N	8.11 E
Breitungen	50	50.45 N	10.20 E
Brejinho de Nazaré	240	11.01 S	48.34 W
Brejo	240	3.41 S	42.47 W
Brejo, Riacho do ≃	240	8.08 S	42.49 W
Brejo da Porta	240	8.28 S	45.45 W
Brejo de São Felix	240	5.24 S	43.24 W
Brejões	245	13.06 S	39.48 W
Brejo Grande	240	10.26 S	36.28 W
Brejo Santo	240	7.29 S	39.00 W
Brejtovo	66	58.18 N	37.52 E
Brekken	26	62.39 N	11.53 E
Brekstad	26	63.41 N	9.41 E
Breloh	48	53.01 N	10.04 E
Bremangerlandet I	26	61.51 N	5.02 E
Brembio	56	45.13 N	9.34 E
Brembo ≃	56	45.35 N	9.32 E
Brême → Bremen	48	53.04 N	8.49 E
Bremelau	54	48.20 N	9.32 E
Bremen, B.R.D.	48	53.04 N	8.49 E
Bremen, Ga., U.S.	182	33.43 N	85.09 W
Bremen, Ind., U.S.	206	41.27 N	86.09 W
Bremen, Ohio, U.S.	178	39.42 N	82.26 W
Bremen □[3]	48	53.05 N	8.50 E
Bremer ≃, Austl.	158b	35.23 S	139.02 E
Bremer ≃, Austl.	161a	27.39 S	152.45 E
Bremer Bay C	152	34.23 S	119.25 E
Bremerhaven	48	53.33 N	8.34 E
Bremerton	214	47.34 N	122.38 W
Bremerton East	214	47.35 N	122.38 W
Bremervörde	48	53.29 N	9.08 E
Bremgarten	54	47.21 N	8.21 E
Bremke, B.R.D.	48	52.07 N	9.06 E
Bremke, B.R.D.	52	51.15 N	8.12 E
Bremke ◆[8]	253	51.23 N	7.41 E
Bremner ≃	180	48.41 N	85.31 W
Bremond	212	31.10 N	96.41 W
Brem River	172	50.26 N	124.39 W
Breña	276d	12.04 S	77.04 W
Brendel Lake ⊛	271	42.38 N	83.30 W
Brenderup	41	55.29 N	9.59 E
Brendlorenzen	52	50.20 N	10.13 E
Brendon Hills ∧∧[2]	44	51.07 N	3.25 W
Brenes	34	37.33 N	5.52 W
Brenham	212	30.10 N	96.24 W
Bren Mar Park	274c	38.48 N	77.09 W
Brenne ≃	46	47.24 N	0.51 E
Brenne ◆[1]	32	46.45 N	1.10 E
Brennero (Brenner)	58	47.00 N	11.30 E
Brennero, Passo del → Brenner Pass ⋈	58	47.00 N	11.30 E
Brenner Pass ⋈	58	47.00 N	11.30 E
Breno, It.	58	45.57 N	10.18 E
Breno, Schw.	54	46.02 N	8.53 E
Brénod	54	46.04 N	5.36 E
Brent, Ala., U.S.	184	32.56 N	87.10 W
Brent, Fla., U.S.	184	30.27 N	87.15 W
Brent ◆[8]	44	51.34 N	0.17 W
Brent ≃	44	51.28 N	0.18 W
Brenta ≃	58	45.11 N	12.18 E
Brenta, Gruppo di ∧∧	58	46.11 N	10.54 E
Brentford ◆[8]	250	51.29 N	0.18 W
Brenthurst	263d	26.16 S	28.23 E
Brentino	58	45.40 N	10.55 E
Brentonico	58	45.49 N	10.57 E
Brentwood, Eng., U.K.	44	51.38 N	0.18 E
Brentwood, Calif., U.S.	216	37.56 N	121.42 W
Brentwood, Md., U.S.	198	38.56 N	76.57 W
Brentwood, N.Y., U.S.	200	40.47 N	73.14 W
Brentwood, Ohio, U.S.	208	39.13 N	84.32 W
Brentwood, Pa., U.S.	204	40.22 N	79.59 W
Brentwood □[8]	250	51.37 N	0.20 E
Brentwood Bay	214	48.35 N	123.28 W
Brentwood Estates	204	40.25 N	80.45 W
Brentwood Heights ◆[8]	270	34.04 N	118.30 W
Brentwood Lake	204	41.19 N	82.05 W
Brentwood Park	263d	26.08 S	28.18 E
Brenz	52	48.33 N	10.17 E
Brenz ≃	52	48.34 N	10.24 E
Bréon, Ruisseau du ≃	251	48.40 N	2.49 E
Brera, Palazzo di ⊎	256b	45.28 N	9.11 E
Brereton Park	148	26.55 S	30.30 E
Brescello	58	44.54 N	10.31 E
Brescia	58	45.33 N	13.15 E
Brescia □[4]	58	45.38 N	10.18 E
Bresewitz	50	54.24 N	12.40 E
Brésil → Brazil □[1]	18	10.00 S	55.00 W
Breskens	48	51.24 N	3.34 E
Breslau, Ont., Can.	202	43.28 N	80.25 W
Breslau → Wrocław, Pol.	30	51.06 N	17.00 E
Breslau, Tex., U.S.	212	29.31 N	97.00 W
Bresle ≃	46	50.04 N	1.22 E
Bresles	46	49.25 N	2.15 E
Bresnahan, Mount ∧	152	23.50 S	117.55 E
Bressanone (Brixen)	58	46.43 N	11.39 E
Bressay I	28	60.08 N	1.05 W
Bresse ◆[1]	54	46.30 N	5.15 E
Bresso	256b	45.32 N	9.11 E
Bressuire	32	46.51 N	0.30 W
Brest, Blg.	38	43.38 N	24.35 E
Brest, Fr.	32	48.24 N	4.29 W
Brest, S.S.S.R.	66	52.06 N	23.42 E
Brestanica	36	45.59 N	15.29 E
Bretagne □[9]	32	48.00 N	3.00 W
Bretenoux	32	44.55 N	1.50 E
Breteuil	46	49.38 N	2.18 E
Breteuil-sur-Iton	46	48.50 N	0.55 E
Bréthencourt	251	48.30 N	1.55 E
Bretherton	252	53.41 N	2.48 W
Brétigny, Aérodrome de ⊠	251	48.35 N	2.20 E
Brétigny-sur-Orge	46	48.37 N	2.19 E
Bretnig	50	51.08 N	14.04 E
Breton	172	53.07 N	114.28 W
Bretón, Canal de ⋓	230p	21.10 N	79.30 W
Breton, Pertuis ⋓	32	46.25 N	1.20 W
Breton Bay C	198	38.16 N	76.39 W
Breton Sound ⋓	184	29.30 N	89.30 W
Breton Woods	198	40.03 N	74.07 W
Brett ≃	44	51.58 N	0.58 E
Brett, Cape ≻	162	35.10 S	174.20 E
Bretten	52	49.02 N	8.42 E
Breu ≃	236	3.29 S	66.20 W
Breueh, Pulau I	100	5.41 N	95.05 E
Breuil-Bois-Robert	251	48.57 N	1.43 E
Breuil-Cervinia	54	45.56 N	7.38 E
Breuillet	251	48.34 N	2.10 E
Breuilpont	46	48.58 N	1.26 E
Breukelen	48	52.10 N	5.00 E
Breux	251	48.34 N	2.11 E
Brevard	182	35.09 N	82.44 W
Brevard □[6]	210	28.18 N	80.42 W
Brévenne ≃	56	45.51 N	4.40 E
Brevens bruk	40	59.01 N	15.35 E
Breves	240	1.40 S	50.29 W
Brevig Mission	170	65.20 N	166.29 W
Brevik, Nor.	26	59.04 N	9.42 E
Brevik, Sve.	40	59.21 N	18.12 E
Brevoort Island I	166	63.30 N	64.20 W
Brewarrina	156	29.57 S	146.52 E
Brewer	178	44.48 N	68.46 W

PORTUGUÊS

Nome	Página	Lat.°′	Long.°′ W=Oeste
Brewer Island I	272	37.33 N	122.16 W
Brewersville	208	39.05 N	85.37 W
Brewerton	200	43.14 N	76.08 W
Brewerville	140	6.26 N	10.47 W
Brewongle	160	33.29 S	149.43 E
Brewood	44	52.41 N	2.10 W
Brewster, Kans., U.S.	188	39.22 N	101.23 W
Brewster, Mass., U.S.	197	41.46 N	70.05 W
Brewster, Minn., U.S.	188	43.42 N	95.28 W
Brewster, Nebr., U.S.	188	41.56 N	99.52 W
Brewster, N.Y., U.S.	200	41.24 N	73.37 W
Brewster, Ohio, U.S.	204	40.43 N	81.36 W
Brewster, Wash., U.S.	192	48.06 N	119.47 W
Brewster, Kap ≻	16	70.19 N	22.05 W
Brewster, Lake ⊛	156	33.28 S	146.00 E
Brewster, Mount ∧	162	44.04 S	169.27 E
Brewton	184	31.07 N	87.04 W
Breyten	148	26.16 S	30.00 E
Brežice	36	45.54 N	15.36 E
Brézins	56	45.21 N	5.19 E
Březnice	30	49.33 N	13.57 E
Breznik	38	42.44 N	22.54 E
Brezno, Česko.	30	48.50 N	19.39 E
Březno, Česko.	50	50.24 N	13.26 E
Brézolles	46	48.41 N	1.04 E
Březová	50	50.06 N	12.39 E
Bria	142	6.32 N	21.59 E
Brian Boru Peak ∧	172	55.05 N	127.35 W
Briançon	56	44.54 N	6.39 E
Brian Head ∧	190	37.41 N	112.50 W
Brianza □[9]	56	45.40 N	9.10 E
Briar	212	33.00 N	97.34 W
Briarcliff Manor	200	41.09 N	73.50 W
Briar Creek	200	40.10 N	76.46 W
Briar Creek ≃	212	32.06 N	96.22 W
Briare	46	47.38 N	2.44 E
Briare, Canal de ≅	46	48.02 N	2.43 E
Briarres-sur-Essonne	46	48.14 N	2.25 E
Briarwood Beach	204	41.06 N	81.54 W
Briarwood Center ◆[9]	271	42.14 N	83.45 W
Bribano	58	46.06 N	12.05 E
Bribie Island I	161a	27.00 S	153.07 E
Bričany	68	48.22 N	27.04 E
Bricelyn	180	43.34 N	93.49 W
Brice Run ≃	274b	39.19 N	76.50 W
Brices Cross Roads National Battlefield Site ⊥	184	34.31 N	88.41 W
Briceville	182	36.11 N	84.11 W
Bricherasio	56	44.49 N	7.18 E
Bricht	253	51.41 N	6.51 E
Brí Chualann → Bray	28	53.12 N	6.06 W
Brickaville	147b	18.49 S	49.04 E
Brickebacken	40	59.15 N	15.15 E
Brick Lake ⊛	210	28.10 N	81.12 W
Brick Town	198	40.04 N	74.08 W
Briçonnet, Lac ⊛	176	51.27 N	60.11 W
Bricquebec	32	49.28 N	1.38 W
Bridal Veil	214	45.33 N	122.11 W
Bridalveil Fall ↳	216	37.43 N	119.39 W
Bride	42	54.22 N	4.22 W
Bridesburg ◆[8]	275	40.00 N	75.04 W
Bridge ≃	172	50.45 N	121.55 W
Bridge City	184	30.01 N	93.51 W
Bridge Creek ≃	214	48.26 N	120.52 W
Bridgehampton	197	40.56 N	72.18 W
Bridge Lake	172	51.29 N	120.43 W
Bridgend, Scot., U.K.	42	55.48 N	6.16 W
Bridgend, Wales, U.K.	44	51.31 N	3.35 W
Bridgenorth	202	44.23 N	78.23 W
Bridge of Weir	42	55.52 N	4.35 W
Bridge Point ≻	228	25.35 N	76.44 W
Bridgeport, Ont., Can.	202	43.29 N	80.29 W
Bridgeport, Ala., U.S.	184	34.57 N	85.43 W
Bridgeport, Calif., U.S.	216	38.10 N	119.13 W
Bridgeport, Conn., U.S.	197		
	266	41.11 N	73.11 W
Bridgeport, Ill., U.S.	184	38.43 N	87.46 W
Bridgeport, Mich., U.S.	180	43.22 N	83.53 W
Bridgeport, Nebr., U.S.	188	41.40 N	103.06 W
Bridgeport, N.J., U.S.	275	39.48 N	75.21 W
Bridgeport, N.Y., U.S.	200	43.09 N	75.58 W
Bridgeport, Ohio, U.S.	204	40.04 N	80.45 W
Bridgeport, Pa., U.S.	275	40.06 N	75.21 W
Bridgeport, Tex., U.S.	212	33.13 N	97.45 W
Bridgeport, Wash., U.S.	192	48.00 N	119.40 W
Bridgeport, W. Va., U.S.	178	39.17 N	80.15 W
Bridgeport, Lake ⊛[1]	212	33.13 N	97.48 W
Bridgeport, University of ⊎[2]	266	41.10 N	73.12 W
Bridgeport Airport ⊠	275	39.47 N	75.20 W
Bridgeport Harbor C	266	41.10 N	73.11 W
Bridgeport Municipal Airport ⊠	266	41.10 N	73.08 W
Bridgeport Reservoir ⊛[1]	216	38.22 N	119.14 W
Bridger	192	45.18 N	108.55 W
Bridge River Indian Reserve ◆[4]	172	50.45 N	122.00 W
Bridger Peak ∧	190	41.12 N	107.02 W
Bridges Point ≻	164o	1.58 N	157.28 W
Bridgeton, Mo., U.S.	209	38.47 N	90.28 W
Bridgeton, N.J., U.S.	198	39.26 N	75.14 W
Bridgetown, Austl.	152	33.57 S	116.08 E
Bridgetown, Barb.	231g	13.06 N	59.37 W
Bridgetown, N.S., Can.	176	44.51 N	65.18 W
Bridgetown, Ohio, U.S.	208	39.10 N	84.39 W
Bridge Trafford	252	53.14 N	2.49 W
Bridgeville, Del., U.S.	198	38.45 N	75.36 W
Bridgeville, Pa., U.S.	204	40.22 N	80.07 W
Bridgewater, N.S., Can.	176	44.23 N	64.31 W
Bridgewater, Conn., U.S.	200	41.32 N	73.22 W
Bridgewater, Maine, U.S.	176	46.25 N	67.51 W
Bridgewater, Mass., U.S.	197	41.59 N	70.58 W
Bridgewater, N.Y., U.S.	200	42.58 N	75.15 W
Bridgewater, Pa., U.S.	275	40.05 N	74.55 W
Bridgewater, S. Dak., U.S.	188	43.33 N	97.30 W
Bridgewater, Va., U.S.	178	38.18 N	78.59 W
Bridgewater Canal ≅	252	53.20 N	2.45 W
Bridgman	206	41.57 N	86.33 W
Bridgnorth	44	52.33 N	2.25 W
Bridgwater	44	51.08 N	3.00 W
Bridgwater Bay C	44	51.16 N	3.12 W
Bridlington	42	54.05 N	0.12 W
Bridlington Bay C	42	54.04 N	0.08 W
Bridport	44	50.44 N	2.46 W
Brie ◆[1]	46	48.40 N	3.20 E
Briec	32	48.06 N	4.00 W
Brie-Comte-Robert	46	48.41 N	2.37 E
Brie Français ◆[1]	251	48.40 N	2.50 E
Brieg → Brzeg	30	50.52 N	17.27 E
Brielle, Ned.	48	51.54 N	4.10 E
Brielle, N.J., U.S.	198	40.07 N	74.03 W
Brienne-le-Château	54	48.24 N	4.32 E
Brienne-sur-Aisne	46	49.26 N	4.03 E
Brienno	54	45.55 N	9.07 E
Brienon-sur-Armançon	46	48.00 N	3.37 E
Brien Run ≃	274b	39.20 N	76.28 W
Brienz	54	46.46 N	8.03 E
Brienzer Rothorn ∧	54	46.48 N	8.04 E

Name	Page	Lat.	Long.
Brienzersee ⊛	54	46.43 N	7.57 E
Brierfield	42	53.50 N	2.14 W
Brier Hill	202	44.32 N	75.40 W
Brierley Hill	44	52.29 N	2.07 W
Brier Mountain ∧	200	41.37 N	77.02 W
Briese	254a	52.42 N	13.18 E
Briese ≃	254a	52.41 N	13.15 E
Brieselang	50	52.35 N	13.00 E
Briesen	50	52.20 N	14.16 E
Brieske	50	51.29 N	13.57 E
Brieskow-Finkenheerd	50	52.16 N	14.35 E
Briest	50	52.31 N	12.08 E
Briey	52	49.15 N	5.56 E
Brig	54	46.19 N	8.00 E
Brigach ≃	54	47.58 N	8.30 E
Brigantine	198	39.24 N	74.22 W
Brig Bay	176	51.04 N	56.55 W
Brigden	204	42.49 N	82.17 W
Brigg	42	53.34 N	0.30 W
Briggs	186	30.53 N	97.56 W
Brigham City	190	41.31 N	112.01 W
Brighouse	42	53.42 N	1.47 W
Brighstone	44	50.38 N	1.24 W
Bright	156	36.44 S	146.58 E
Brightlingsea	44	51.49 N	1.02 E
Brightmoor ◆[8]	271	42.24 N	83.14 W
Brighton, Austl.	158b	35.01 S	138.31 E
Brighton, Austl.	159	37.55 S	145.00 E
Brighton, Ont., Can.	202	44.02 N	77.44 W
Brighton, N.Z.	162	45.57 S	170.20 E
Brighton, Eng., U.K.	44	50.50 N	0.08 W
Brighton, Colo., U.S.	190	39.59 N	104.49 W
Brighton, Fla., U.S.	210	28.52 N	82.20 W
Brighton, Ill., U.S.	209	39.02 N	90.08 W
Brighton, Iowa, U.S.	180	41.10 N	91.49 W
Brighton, Mich., U.S.	206	42.32 N	83.47 W
Brighton, N.Y., U.S.	200	43.08 N	77.34 W
Brighton ◆[8]	273	42.21 N	71.08 W
Brighton Downs	156	23.22 S	141.34 E
Brighton Indian Reservation ◆[4]	210	27.04 N	81.05 W
Brighton-Le-Sands	264a	33.58 S	151.09 E
Brighton Park ◆[8]	268	41.49 N	87.42 W
Brighton State Recreation Area ♠	206	42.30 N	83.48 W
Brightsand Lake ⊛	174	53.36 N	108.52 W
Brightwaters	266	40.43 N	73.16 W
Brightwood	214	45.23 N	122.01 W
Brightwood ◆[8]	274c	38.58 N	77.02 W
Brigittenau ◆[8]	254b	48.14 N	16.22 E
Brignoles	56	43.24 N	6.04 E
Brignoud	56	45.15 N	5.54 E
Brigus	176	47.32 N	53.13 W
Brihuega	34	40.48 N	2.52 W
Briis-sous-Forges	251	48.38 N	2.07 E
Brijuni I	58	44.55 N	13.46 E
Brikama	140	13.15 N	16.39 W
Brilhante ≃	245	21.58 S	54.18 W
Brill	44	51.49 N	1.03 W
Brilliant, B.C., Can.	172	49.19 N	117.38 W
Brilliant, Ala., U.S.	184	34.01 N	87.46 W
Brilliant, Ohio, U.S.	204	40.16 N	80.38 W
Brillion	180	44.11 N	88.04 W
Brilon	52	51.24 N	8.34 E
Brilyn Park	274c	38.54 N	77.10 W
Brimfield, Eng., U.K.	44	52.18 N	2.42 W
Brimfield, Ind., U.S.	206	41.27 N	85.24 W
Brimfield, Mass., U.S.	197	42.07 N	72.12 W
Brimfield, Ohio, U.S.	204	41.06 N	81.21 W
Brimington	42	53.16 N	1.23 W
Brindabella	161b	35.23 S	148.45 E
Brindisi	36	40.38 N	17.56 E
Brindle	252	53.43 N	2.36 W
Brindley Heath	250	51.12 N	0.03 W
Bringelly	160	33.56 S	150.44 E
Bringelly Creek ≃	264a	33.58 S	150.38 E
Brinje	36	45.00 N	15.08 E
Brinkerton	269b	40.13 N	79.32 W
Brinkhaven	204	40.28 N	82.12 W
Brinkleigh	274b	39.18 N	76.50 W
Brinkley, Austl.	158b	35.14 S	139.13 E
Brinkley, Ark., U.S.	184	34.53 N	91.12 W
Brinkum	48	53.00 N	8.47 E
Brinkworth	156	33.42 S	138.24 E
Brinnon	214	47.41 N	122.54 W
Brinon-sur-Beuvron	46	47.17 N	3.30 E
Brins, Ābār al- ⍑[4]	132	30.29 N	30.05 E
Brinscall	252	53.41 N	2.34 W
Brion, Île I	176	47.48 N	61.28 W
Brione	54	46.18 N	8.47 E
Briones Hills ∧∧[2]	272	37.56 N	122.08 W
Briones Regional Park ♠	272	37.56 N	122.08 W
Briones Reservoir ⊛[1]	272	37.55 N	122.12 W
Brioni	58	44.55 N	13.46 E
Brionne	46	49.12 N	0.43 E
Brion-sur-Ource	54	47.55 N	4.39 E
Brioso, Ribeirão ≃	245	20.21 S	52.05 W
Brioude	32	45.18 N	3.23 E
Briouze	32	48.42 N	0.22 W
Brisbane, Austl.	161a	27.28 S	153.02 E
Brisbane, Calif., U.S.	216	37.41 N	122.24 W
Brisbane ≃	161a	27.24 S	153.09 E
Brisbane, Mount ∧	161a	27.05 S	152.32 E
Brisbane Water National Park ♠	160	33.30 S	151.15 E
Brisben	200	42.22 N	75.41 W
Brisbin	204	40.50 N	78.21 W
Briseñas de Matamoros	224	20.16 N	102.33 W
Brisighella	60	44.13 N	11.46 E
Brissac	56	43.52 N	3.42 E
Brissago	54	46.07 N	8.43 E
Bristol, Eng., U.K.	44	51.27 N	2.35 W
Bristol, Conn., U.S.	197	41.41 N	72.57 W
Bristol, Fla., U.S.	182	30.26 N	84.58 W
Bristol, Ill., U.S.	206	41.39 N	88.27 W
Bristol, Ind., U.S.	206	41.43 N	85.49 W
Bristol, N.H., U.S.	178	43.36 N	71.45 W
Bristol, Pa., U.S.	198	40.06 N	74.52 W
Bristol, R.I., U.S.	197	41.40 N	71.16 W
Bristol, S. Dak., U.S.	188	45.21 N	97.45 W
Bristol, Tenn., U.S.	182	36.36 N	82.11 W
Bristol, Vt., U.S.	178	44.08 N	73.05 W
Bristol, Va., U.S.	182	36.36 N	82.11 W
Bristol, Wis., U.S.	206	42.34 N	88.03 W
Bristol □[6], Mass., U.S.	197	41.54 N	71.06 W
Bristol □[6], R.I., U.S.	197	41.42 N	71.18 W
Bristol (Lulsgate) Airport ⊠	44	51.23 N	2.43 W
Bristol Bay C	170	58.00 N	159.00 W
Bristol Center	200	42.49 N	77.23 W
Bristol Channel ⋓	44	51.20 N	4.00 W
Bristol Lake ⊛	194	34.28 N	115.41 W
Bristolville	204	41.23 N	80.52 W
Bristow	186	35.50 N	96.23 W
Bristow Island I	154	9.08 S	143.14 E
Britânia	245	15.14 S	51.09 W
Británicas, Islas → British Isles II	4	54.00 N	4.00 W
Britannia	265b	43.37 N	79.41 W
Britannia Beach	172	49.38 N	123.12 W
Britannia Range ∧∧	9	80.00 S	158.00 E
Britische Jungfern-Inseln → British Virgin Islands □[2]	230m	18.30 N	64.30 W
Britisches Antarktis-Territorium → British Antarctic Territory □[2]	9	60.00 S	45.00 W
British Antarctic Territory □[2]	9	60.00 S	45.00 W
British Columbia □[4]	166		
	172	54.00 N	125.00 W
British Honduras → Belize □[2]	222	17.15 N	88.45 W
British Indian Ocean Territory □[2]	12	10.00 S	72.00 E
British Isles II	4	54.00 N	4.00 W

Name	Page	Lat.	Long.
British Mountains ∧∧	170	69.00 N	140.20 W
British Museum ⊎	250	51.31 N	0.08 W
British Virgin Islands □[2]	230m	18.30 N	64.30 W
Britland Edge Hill ∧[2]	252	53.31 N	1.50 W
Brito Godins	142	8.57 S	16.32 E
Briton Ferry	44	51.38 N	3.49 W
Brits	148	25.42 S	27.45 E
Britstown	148	30.37 S	23.30 E
Britt	180	43.06 N	93.48 W
Brittany → Bretagne □[9]	32	48.00 N	3.00 W
Brittas	42	53.14 N	6.27 W
Britten	148	27.42 S	25.17 E
Brittingham	186	25.45 N	103.24 W
Britton, Mich., U.S.	206	41.59 N	83.50 W
Britton, S. Dak., U.S.	188	45.48 N	97.45 W
Britton, Tex., U.S.	212	32.33 N	97.04 W
Britton, Mount ∧[2]	152	26.31 S	134.43 E
Britz	50	52.53 N	13.49 E
Britz ◆[8]	254a	52.27 N	13.26 E
Brive-la-Gaillarde	32	45.10 N	1.32 E
Brives-Charensac	56	45.03 N	3.56 E
Briviesca	34	42.33 N	3.19 W
Brivio	56	45.44 N	9.27 E
Brixen im Thale	58	47.27 N	12.15 E
Brixham	44	50.24 N	3.30 W
Brixlegg	58	47.25 N	11.53 E
Brixton	156	23.32 S	144.57 E
Brixworth	44	52.20 N	0.54 W
Briziana	138	33.04 N	1.14 E
Brlik, S.S.S.R.	75	44.05 N	73.31 E
Brlik, S.S.S.R.	75	43.40 N	73.49 E
Brno	30	49.12 N	16.37 E
Bro	40	59.31 N	17.38 E
Broa, Ensenada de la C	230p	22.35 N	82.00 W
Broach	110	21.42 N	72.58 E
Broad ≃, U.S.	182	34.00 N	81.04 W
Broad ≃, Fla., U.S.	210	25.28 N	81.09 W
Broad ≃, Ga., U.S.	182	33.59 N	82.39 W
Broadalbin	200	43.03 N	74.12 W
Broad Arrow	152	30.20 S	121.27 E
Broad Axe	275	40.10 N	75.15 W
Broadback ≃	166	51.21 N	78.52 W
Broad Bay C	28	58.15 N	6.15 W
Broadbottom	252	53.26 N	2.01 W
Broad Brook	197	41.55 N	72.33 W
Broad Chalke	44	51.02 N	1.57 W
Broad Clyst	44	50.46 N	3.26 W
Broad Creek C	198	38.45 N	76.15 W
Broadford, Austl.	159	37.13 S	145.03 E
Broadford, Scot., U.K.	28	57.14 N	5.54 W
Broad Haven C	28	54.18 N	9.55 W
Broadheath	252	53.24 N	2.21 W
Broadhurst Range ∧∧	152	22.23 S	122.09 E
Broadkill ≃	198	38.47 N	75.10 W
Broad Law ∧	42	55.30 N	3.22 W
Broadley Common	250	51.45 N	0.04 E
Broadmeadows	159	37.40 S	144.54 E
Broad Meadow Water ≃	42	53.28 N	6.12 W
Broadmoor	216	37.41 N	122.29 W
Broad Pass ⋈	170	63.18 N	149.09 W
Broad Run ≃, Pa., U.S.	275	39.56 N	75.41 W
Broad Run ≃, Pa., U.S.	275	39.59 N	75.40 W
Broad Run ≃, Va., U.S.	198	38.41 N	77.29 W
Broad Sound ⋓, Austl.	156	22.10 S	149.45 E
Broad Sound ⋓, Mass., U.S.	273	42.25 N	70.58 W
Broad Sound Channel ⋓	156	22.05 S	150.20 E
Broadstairs	44	51.22 N	1.27 E
Broad Street	250	51.17 N	0.38 E
Broad Top	204	40.12 N	78.08 W
Broadus	188	45.27 N	105.25 W
Broadview, Sask., Can.	174	50.20 N	102.30 W
Broadview, Ill., U.S.	206	41.52 N	87.51 W
Broadview, Ind., U.S.	208	39.10 N	87.33 W
Broadview Heights	204	41.19 N	81.41 W
Broadwater	188	41.36 N	102.51 W
Broadway, Eng., U.K.	44	52.02 N	1.51 W
Broadway, Ohio, U.S.	204	40.21 N	83.25 W
Broadway, Va., U.S.	178	38.38 N	78.46 W
Broadwell	209	40.04 N	89.27 W
Broadwindsor	44	50.49 N	2.48 W
Broadwood	162	35.16 S	173.23 E
Broager	41	54.53 N	9.41 E
Brobo	140	7.43 N	4.42 W
Broby	26	56.15 N	14.05 E
Brobyværk	41	55.14 N	10.15 E
Broc	54	46.36 N	7.06 E
Brocēni	66	56.42 N	22.35 E
Brochet	166	57.53 N	101.40 W
Brochet, Lac du ⊛	176	49.40 N	69.37 W
Brochterbeck	48	52.13 N	7.44 E
Brock	174	51.27 N	108.42 W
Brock ≃	42	53.52 N	2.47 W
Brock Creek ≃	275	40.15 N	74.50 W
Brocken ∧	50	51.48 N	10.36 E
Brockenhurst	44	50.49 N	1.34 W
Brockenscheidt	253	51.38 N	7.25 E
Brockhagen	48	51.59 N	8.20 E
Brockham	250	51.14 N	0.17 W
Brockman, Mount ∧	152	22.28 S	117.18 E
Brock Monument ⊥	274a	43.09 N	79.04 W
Brockport, N.Y., U.S.	200	43.13 N	77.56 W
Brockport, Pa., U.S.	204	41.16 N	78.44 W
Brocks Beach	202	44.27 N	80.06 W
Brocks Creek	154	13.28 S	131.25 E
Brockton, Mass., U.S.	197		
	273	42.05 N	71.01 W
Brockton, Mont., U.S.	188	48.09 N	104.55 W
Brockton, Pa., U.S.	198	40.45 N	76.04 W
Brockton Reservoir ⊛[1]	273	42.07 N	71.03 W
Brockville	202	44.35 N	75.41 W
Brockway	204	41.15 N	78.47 W
Brockworth	44	51.51 N	2.09 W
Brocoió, Ilha do I	277a	22.45 S	43.07 W
Brocton	204	42.23 N	79.27 W
Brod	38	41.31 N	21.12 E
Broddbo	40	59.59 N	16.28 E
Brodenbach	52	50.14 N	7.26 E
Broderick	216	38.35 N	121.31 W
Brodeur Peninsula ≻[1]	166	73.00 N	88.00 W
Brodhead, Ky., U.S.	182	37.24 N	84.25 W
Brodhead, Wis., U.S.	180	42.37 N	89.22 W
Brodhead Creek ≃	200	40.59 N	75.08 W
Brodheadsville	200	40.55 N	75.24 W
Brodick	42	55.35 N	5.09 W
Brodnax	182	36.42 N	78.02 W
Brodnica	30	53.16 N	19.23 E
Brodokalmak	76	55.35 N	62.06 E
Brody, Pol.	30	51.45 N	14.45 E
Brody, S.S.S.R.	68	50.06 N	25.10 E
Broedersput	148	26.49 S	25.08 E
Broek [op Langendijk]	48	52.40 N	4.48 E
Brogan	192	44.15 N	117.31 W
Broglie	46	49.01 N	0.32 E
Brohlbach ≃	52	50.29 N	7.20 E
Broich ◆[8]	253	51.25 N	6.51 E
Broichweiden	52	50.49 N	6.09 E
Broitzem	48	52.14 N	10.29 E
Brok	30	52.43 N	21.52 E
Brok ∧	113	34.32 N	76.35 E
Brokdorf	48	53.52 N	9.19 E
Broke	160	32.45 S	151.06 E
Broke Inlet C	152	34.55 S	116.25 E
Broken ≃	159	36.41 S	146.00 E
Broken Arrow	186	36.03 N	95.48 W

Name	Page	Lat.	Long.
Broken Back Range ∧∧	160	32.47 S	151.13 E
Broken Bay C	160	33.34 S	151.18 E
Broken Bow, Nebr., U.S.	188	41.24 N	99.38 W
Broken Bow, Okla., U.S.	184	34.02 N	94.44 W
Broken Cross, Eng., U.K.	252	53.15 N	2.10 W
Broken Cross, Eng., U.K.	252	53.15 N	2.29 W
Brokenhead ≃	174	50.25 N	96.40 W
Broken Hill, Austl.	156	31.57 S	141.27 E
Broken Hill → Kabwe, Zam.	144	14.27 S	28.27 E
Brokenstraw Creek ≃	204	41.51 N	79.09 W
Broken Sword Creek ≃	204	40.46 N	83.11 W
Brokopondo	240	5.04 N	54.58 W
Brokopondo □[5]	240	4.20 N	55.20 W
Brölbach ≃	52	50.47 N	7.18 E
Bromberg → Bydgoszcz	30	53.08 N	18.00 E
Bromborough	42	53.19 N	2.59 W
Brome, B.R.D.	50	52.36 N	10.56 E
Brome, Qué., Can.	196	45.12 N	72.34 W
Brome □[6]	196	45.10 N	72.30 W
Brome, Lac ⊛	196	45.15 N	72.30 W
Brome Mountain ∧	196	45.17 N	72.38 W
Bromley ◆[8]	44	51.24 N	0.02 E
Bromley Common ◆[8]	250	51.22 N	0.03 E
Bromma ◆[8]	40	59.21 N	17.55 E
Bromma flygplats ⊠	40	59.21 N	17.55 E
Brommö I	40	58.50 N	13.41 E
Bromo, Gunung ∧	105a	7.57 S	112.57 E
Bromölla	26	56.04 N	14.28 E
Brompton, Eng., U.K.	42	54.22 N	1.25 W
Brompton, Eng., U.K.	250	51.23 N	0.33 E
Brompton Lake ⊛	196	45.27 N	72.09 W
Bromptonville	196	45.28 N	71.57 W
Bromsgrove	44	52.20 N	2.03 W
Bromyard	44	52.11 N	2.30 W
Bron	56	45.44 N	4.55 E
Bron, Aéroport de ⊠	56	45.43 N	4.56 E
Brønderslev	26	57.16 N	9.58 E
Bronevskaja	24	61.43 N	39.10 E
Brong-Ahafo □[4]	140	7.45 N	1.30 W
Broni	56	45.04 N	9.16 E
Bronickaja Guta	68	50.56 N	27.19 E
Bronkhorstspruit	148	25.50 S	28.43 E
Bronkhorstspruitdam ⊛[1]	148	25.55 S	28.42 E
Bronkow	50	51.40 N	13.55 E
Bronllys	44	52.01 N	3.16 W
Bronlund Peak ∧	166	57.26 N	126.38 W
Bronnicy	72	55.25 N	38.16 E
Bronnikovo	76	58.32 N	68.25 E
Bronnoje	66	52.19 N	30.29 E
Brønnøysund	24	65.30 N	12.10 E
Bronnzell	52	50.31 N	9.41 E
Brøns	41	55.11 N	8.44 E
Bronson, Fla., U.S.	182	29.27 N	82.38 W
Bronson, Kans., U.S.	188	37.54 N	95.04 W
Bronson, Mich., U.S.	206	41.52 N	85.12 W
Bronson, Tex., U.S.	184	31.21 N	94.01 W
Bronson Lake ⊛	174	53.52 N	109.43 W
Bronte, It.	36	37.48 N	14.50 E
Bronte, Tex., U.S.	186	31.53 N	100.18 W
Bronte Creek ≃	202	43.23 N	79.43 W
Bronte Park	156	42.08 S	146.30 E
Bronwood	182	31.50 N	84.22 W
Bronx	200	40.49 N	73.56 W
Bronx □[6]	200	40.49 N	73.56 W
Bronx ◆[8]	266	40.49 N	73.56 W
Bronx Park ♠	266	40.52 N	73.53 W
Bronxville	266	40.56 N	73.50 W
Bronx-Whitestone Bridge ◆[5]	266	40.48 N	73.50 W
Bronx Zoo ♠	266	40.51 N	73.53 W
Bronzolo (Branzoll)	58	46.24 N	11.19 E
Brooch, Lac ⊛	176	50.44 N	67.58 W
Broodsnyersplaas	148	26.03 S	29.29 E
Brook	206	40.52 N	87.22 W
Brookdale	216	37.06 N	122.06 W
Brooke	198	38.23 N	77.23 W
Brooke □[6]	204	40.18 N	80.33 W
Brookeland	184	31.09 N	94.00 W
Brooker	182	29.53 N	82.20 W
Brooke's Point	106	8.47 N	117.50 E
Brookfield, N.S., Can.	176	45.15 N	63.17 W
Brookfield, Conn., U.S.	197	41.29 N	73.25 W
Brookfield, Ill., U.S.	206	41.49 N	87.51 W
Brookfield, Mass., U.S.	197	42.13 N	72.06 W
Brookfield, Mich., U.S.	206	42.27 N	84.47 W
Brookfield, Mo., U.S.	184	39.47 N	93.04 W
Brookfield, N.Y., U.S.	200	42.49 N	75.19 W
Brookfield, Ohio, U.S.	204	41.14 N	80.34 W
Brookfield, Wis., U.S.	206	43.04 N	88.09 W
Brookfield Center	197	41.28 N	73.23 W
Brookfield Zoo ♠	268	41.50 N	87.50 W
Brookford	182	35.42 N	81.21 W
Brookhaven, Miss., U.S.	184	31.35 N	90.26 W
Brookhaven, Pa., U.S.	275	39.52 N	75.23 W
Brookhaven Manor	268	41.44 N	87.58 W
Brookhaven National Laboratory ⊎[3]	197	40.54 N	72.52 W
Brookings, Oreg., U.S.	192	42.03 N	124.17 W
Brookings, S. Dak., U.S.	188	44.19 N	96.48 W
Brookland	44	50.59 N	0.50 E
Brookland ◆[8]	274c	38.56 N	76.59 W
Brooklands	204	42.38 N	83.06 W
Brookland Terrace	275	39.44 N	75.37 W
Brooklandville	274b	39.26 N	76.41 W
Brooklawn	275	39.53 N	75.08 W
Brooklet	182	32.23 N	81.40 W
Brooklin	202	43.57 N	78.57 W
Brookline, Mass., U.S.	197	42.21 N	71.07 W
Brookline, N.H., U.S.	197	42.44 N	71.40 W
Brooklyn, N.S., Can.	176	44.03 N	64.42 W
Brooklyn, Conn., U.S.	197	41.47 N	71.57 W
Brooklyn, Ill., U.S.	209	40.14 N	90.46 W
Brooklyn, Ind., U.S.	208	39.32 N	86.22 W
Brooklyn, Iowa, U.S.	180	41.44 N	92.27 W
Brooklyn, Mich., U.S.	206	42.06 N	84.15 W
Brooklyn, Miss., U.S.	184	31.03 N	89.11 W
Brooklyn, Ohio, U.S.	204	41.25 N	81.49 W
Brooklyn, Pa., U.S.	200	41.45 N	75.48 W
Brooklyn, Wash., U.S.	214	46.47 N	123.31 W
Brooklyn, Wis., U.S.	206	42.51 N	89.22 W
Brooklyn ◆[8], Md., U.S.	274b	39.14 N	76.36 W
Brooklyn ◆[8], N.Y., U.S.	200	40.42 N	74.00 W
Brooklyn Battery Tunnel ◆[5]	266	40.42 N	74.01 W
Brooklyn Bridge ◆[5]	266	40.42 N	74.00 W
Brooklyn Center	180	45.05 N	93.20 W
Brooklyn College ⊎[2]	266	40.38 N	73.57 W
Brooklyn Heights	269a	41.24 N	81.40 W
Brooklyn Marine Park ♠	266	40.35 N	73.55 W
Brooklyn Museum ⊎	266	40.40 N	73.58 W
Brookmans Park	250	51.43 N	0.12 W
Brookmere	172	49.49 N	120.53 W
Brookmont	274c	38.57 N	77.07 W
Brookneal	182	37.03 N	78.57 W
Brook Park	204	41.24 N	81.48 W
Brookport	184	37.08 N	88.38 W
Brooks, Alta., Can.	172	50.35 N	111.53 W
Brooks, Calif., U.S.	216	38.45 N	122.09 W
Brooks, Maine, U.S.	178	44.33 N	69.07 W

Symbol	English	Deutsch	Español	Français	Português
≃	River	Fluss	Río	Rivière	Rio
≅	Canal	Kanal	Canal	Canal	Canal
↳	Waterfall, Rapids	Wasserfall, Stromschnellen	Cascada, Rápidos	Chute d'eau, Rapides	Cascata, Rápidos
⋓	Strait	Meeresstrasse	Estrecho	Détroit	Estreito
C	Bay, Gulf	Bucht, Golf	Bahía, Golfo	Baie, Golfe	Baía, Golfo
⊛	Lake, Lakes	See, Seen	Lago, Lagos	Lac, Lacs	Lago, Lagos
≋	Swamp	Sumpf	Pantano	Marais	Pântano
✲	Ice Features, Glacier	Eis- und Gletscherformen	Accidentes Glaciales	Formes glaciaires	Acidentes Glaciares
⍑	Other Hydrographic Features	Andere Hydrographische Objekte	Otros Elementos Hidrográficos	Autres données hydrographiques	Outros Elementos Hidrográficos

Symbol	English	Deutsch	Español	Français	Português
✢	Submarine Features	Untermeerische Objekte	Accidentes Submarinos	Formes de relief sous-marin	Acidentes Submarinos
□	Political Unit	Politische Einheit	Unidad Politica	Entité politique	Unidade Política
⊎	Cultural Institution	Kulturelle Institution	Institución Cultural	Institution culturelle	Instituição Cultural
⊥	Historical Site	Historische Stätte	Sitio Histórico	Site historique	Sítio Histórico
♠	Recreational Site	Erholungs- und Ferienort	Sitio de Recreo	Centre de loisirs	Sítio de Lazer
⊠	Airport	Flughafen	Aeropuerto	Aéroport	Aeroporto
■	Military Installation	Militäranlage	Instalación Militar	Installation militaire	Instalação Militar
◆	Miscellaneous	Verschiedenes	Misceláneo	Divers	Miscelânea

Brooks, Oreg., U.S. 214 45.03 N 122.58 W
Brooks, Mount ∧ 170 63.11 N 150.40 W
Brooks Bay C 172 50.13 N 127.55 W
Brooksburg 208 38.44 N 85.15 W
Brookshire 212 29.47 N 95.57 W
Brookside, Del., U.S. 275 39.40 N 75.44 W
Brookside, Pa., U.S. 204 42.08 N 80.00 W
Brookside, Tex., U.S. 212 29.35 N 95.18 W
Brookside Park ♠ 269a 41.27 N 81.43 W
Brooks Island I 272 37.54 N 122.21 W
Brooks Mountain ∧ 170 65.33 N 167.09 W
Brooks Place 273 42.02 N 71.01 W
Brooks Range ⩓ 170 68.00 N 154.00 W
Brookston 206 40.36 N 86.52 W
Brook Street 250 51.37 N 0.17 E
Brooksville, Fla., U.S. 210 28.33 N 82.23 W
Brooksville, Ky., U.S. 208 38.41 N 84.04 W
Brooksville, Miss., U.S. 184 33.14 N 88.35 W
Brookton 152 32.22 S 117.01 E
Brooktondale 200 42.23 N 76.24 W
Brookvale 264a 33.46 S 151.17 E
Brookview 200 42.32 N 73.43 W
Brookville, Ind., U.S. 208 39.25 N 85.01 W
Brookville, Mass., U.S. 197 42.08 N 71.01 W
Brookville, N.Y., U.S. 266 40.49 N 73.35 W
Brookville, Ohio, U.S. 208 39.50 N 84.25 W
Brookville, Pa., U.S. 204 41.09 N 79.05 W
Brookville Lake ⊜[1] 208 39.30 N 85.00 W
Brookwood, Eng., U.K. 250 51.18 N 0.38 W
Brookwood, Ind., U.S. 268 40.30 N 87.22 W
Brooloo 156 26.29 S 152.42 E
Broomall 275 39.59 N 75.22 W
Broome 152 17.58 S 122.14 E
Broome □[6] 200 42.08 N 75.54 W
Broome County Airport ⊠ 200 42.13 N 75.59 W
Broomes Island 198 38.25 N 76.33 W
Broomfield, Eng., U.K. 250 51.46 N 0.28 E
Broomfield, Eng., U.K. 250 51.14 N 0.38 E
Broomfield, Colo., U.S. 190 39.56 N 105.04 W
Broons 32 48.19 N 2.16 W
Brooten 188 45.30 N 95.07 W
Brophy, Mount ∧[2] 152 19.11 S 128.51 E
Brophy Lake ⊜ 271 42.39 N 83.46 W
Brora 28 58.01 N 3.51 W
Brora ≃ 28 58.01 N 3.51 W
Brørup 41 55.29 N 9.01 E
Broseley 44 52.37 N 2.29 W
Brosewere Bay C 266 40.37 N 73.42 W
Brošnev-Osada 68 49.00 N 24.13 E
Brossac 32 45.20 N 0.03 W
Brossard 196 45.26 N 73.29 W
Brossasco 56 44.34 N 7.21 E
Brosso 56 45.30 N 7.48 E
Brotas de Macaúbas 245 12.00 S 42.38 W
Broteni 148 29.38 S 29.42 E
Brothers Brook ≃ 266 41.02 N 73.36 W
Brötjärna 40 60.30 N 15.01 E
Broto 34 42.36 N 0.06 W
Brotterode 50 50.49 N 10.26 E
Brotton 42 54.34 N 0.56 W
Brou 46 48.13 N 1.11 E
Brough, Eng., U.K. 42 54.32 N 2.19 W
Brough, Eng., U.K. 42 53.44 N 0.35 W
Brougham 202 43.55 N 79.06 W
Broughshane 42 54.54 N 6.12 W
Broughton, Eng., U.K. 44 52.23 N 0.46 W
Broughton, Eng., U.K. 252 53.49 N 2.43 W
Broughton, Scot., U.K. 42 55.37 N 3.25 W
Broughton, Pa., U.S. 204 40.21 N 79.59 W
Broughton in Furness 42 54.17 N 3.12 W
Broughton Island I 166 67.35 N 63.50 W
Broughty Ferry 28 56.28 N 2.53 W
Broumov 30 50.35 N 16.20 E
Brousseval 54 48.29 N 4.58 E
Brou-sur-Chantereine 251 48.53 N 2.38 E
Brouvelieures 54 48.14 N 6.44 E
Brouwershaven 48 51.44 N 3.54 E
Brouwershavensche Gat Ш 48 51.45 N 3.50 E
Brovary 68 50.31 N 30.46 E
Brovst 26 57.06 N 9.32 E
Broward □[6] 210 26.09 N 80.29 W
Browerville 188 46.05 N 94.52 W
Brown □[6], Ill., U.S. 209 39.59 N 90.45 W
Brown □[6], Ind., U.S. 208 39.12 N 86.15 W
Brown □[6], Ohio, U.S. 208 38.52 N 83.54 W
Brown, Mount ∧ 174 48.52 N 111.09 W
Brown, Point ≻ 214 46.56 N 124.10 W
Brownbacks 275 40.11 N 75.37 W
Brown City 180 43.13 N 82.59 W
Brown Clee Hill ∧[2] 44 52.28 N 2.35 W
Brown County State Park ♠ 208 39.09 N 86.14 W
Brown Creek ≃ 266 40.43 N 73.04 W
Browndale 200 41.40 N 75.27 W
Brown Deer 206 43.10 N 87.59 W
Browne Bay C 166 73.08 N 97.30 W
Brownfield 186 33.11 N 102.16 W
Brown Gelly ∧[2] 44 50.32 N 4.32 W
Brownhills 44 52.39 N 1.55 W
Browning, Ill., U.S. 209 40.08 N 90.22 W
Browning, Mo., U.S. 184 40.02 N 93.10 W
Browning, Mont., U.S. 192 48.34 N 113.01 W
Browning Entrance C 172 53.41 N 130.30 W
Browning Island I 202 45.00 N 79.25 W
Brown Lake ⊜ 166 65.55 N 91.15 W
Brownlee Park 206 42.18 N 85.05 W
Brownlee Reservoir ⊜[1] 192 44.40 N 117.05 W
Brown Mountain ∧, Calif., U.S. 194 35.41 N 117.01 W
Brown Mountain ∧, Calif., U.S. 270 34.14 N 118.08 W
Brown Mountain ∧[2] 212 31.51 N 97.39 W
Brown Point ≻ 266 40.43 N 73.04 W
Brownsboro 212 32.18 N 95.37 W
Browns Brook ≃ 266 41.09 N 73.17 W
Brownsburg, Qué., Can. 196 45.41 N 74.25 W
Brownsburg, Ind., U.S. 208 39.51 N 86.24 W
Browns Canyon ∨ 270 34.18 N 118.35 W
Brownsdale 180 43.44 N 92.52 W
Browns Island I 272 38.02 N 121.52 W
Browns Lake 206 42.42 N 88.14 W
Brownsmead 214 46.13 N 123.32 W
Browns Mills 198 39.58 N 74.34 W
Browns Point 214 47.18 N 122.21 W
Browns Town, Jam. 231q 18.24 N 77.22 W
Brownstown, Ill., U.S. 209 39.00 N 88.57 W
Brownstown, Ind., U.S. 208 38.53 N 86.03 W
Brownstown, Pa., U.S. 198 40.08 N 76.13 W
Brownstown Creek ≃ 271 42.06 N 83.13 W
Browns Valley, Calif., U.S. 216 39.15 N 121.23 W
Browns Valley, Minn., U.S. 188 45.36 N 96.50 W
Brownsville, Ont., Can. 202 42.52 N 80.50 W
Brownsville, Calif., U.S. 216 39.28 N 121.16 W
Brownsville, Fla., U.S. 210 25.50 N 80.17 W
Brownsville, Ind., U.S. 208 39.40 N 85.00 W
Brownsville, Ky., U.S. 184 37.12 N 86.16 W
Brownsville, La., U.S. 184 32.30 N 92.10 W
Brownsville, Oreg., U.S. 192 44.24 N 122.59 W
Brownsville, Pa., U.S. 178 40.01 N 79.53 W
Brownsville, Tenn., U.S. 184 35.36 N 89.15 W
Brownsville, Tex., U.S. 186 25.54 N 97.30 W
Brownton 180 44.44 N 94.21 W
Browntown 266 40.24 N 74.19 W
Brownvale 172 56.08 N 117.53 W
Brownville, Ala., U.S. 184 33.24 N 87.52 W
Brownville, Maine, U.S. 178 45.18 N 69.02 W
Brownville, N.Y., U.S. 202 40.40 N 73.55 W
Brownville Junction 178 45.21 N 69.03 W
Brown Willy ∧[2] 44 50.35 N 4.36 W
Brownwood 186 31.43 N 98.59 W
Brownwood, Lake ⊜[1] 186 31.51 N 99.02 W
Browse Island I 150 14.07 S 123.33 E
Broxbourne 250 51.45 N 0.01 W
Broxbourne □[8] 250 51.44 N 0.04 W
Broxton 182 31.38 N 82.53 W
Broye ≃ 54 46.55 N 7.02 E
Broyhill Park 274c 38.52 N 77.12 W
Broża 66 52.57 N 29.07 E
Brozas 34 39.37 N 6.46 W
Brozzo 58 45.43 N 10.14 E
Brtonigla 58 45.23 N 13.38 E
Brû 54 48.21 N 6.41 E
Bruay-en-Artois 46 50.29 N 2.33 E
Bruay-sur-l'Escaut 46 50.23 N 3.32 E
Bruce, Miss., U.S. 184 33.59 N 89.21 W
Bruce, S. Dak., U.S. 188 44.26 N 96.54 W
Bruce, Wis., U.S. 180 45.28 N 91.20 W
Bruce □[6] 202 44.30 N 81.15 W
Bruce, Mount ∧ 152 22.36 S 118.08 E
Bruce Bay 162 43.35 S 169.41 E
Bruce Creek ≃ 265b 43.52 N 79.18 W
Bruce Lake ⊜ 174 50.49 N 93.20 W
Bruce Mines 180 46.18 N 83.48 W
Bruce Museum ♥ 266 41.01 N 73.37 W
Bruce Peninsula ≻[1] 180 44.50 N 81.20 W
Bruce Rock 152 31.53 S 118.09 E
Bruceville 212 31.19 N 97.14 W
Bruchberg ∧ 50 51.47 N 10.29 E
Bruchhausen 52 51.26 N 8.01 E
Bruchhausen-Vilsen 48 52.50 N 9.00 E
Bruchmühle 254a 52.33 N 13.47 E
Br'uchoveckaja 68 45.48 N 38.59 E
Bruchsal 52 49.07 N 8.35 E
Brück, D.D.R. 50 52.12 N 12.46 E
Bruck, Öst. 58 47.17 N 12.49 E
Bruck an der Leitha 30 47.57 N 16.44 E
Bruck an der Mur 30 47.25 N 15.16 E
Brückenau 52 50.18 N 9.47 E
Bruckhausen •[8] 253 51.29 N 6.44 E
Bruckmühl 58 47.53 N 11.54 E
Brudager 41 55.07 N 10.41 E
Bruderheim 172 53.47 N 112.56 W
Brue ≃ 44 51.13 N 3.00 W
Brue-Auriac 56 43.32 N 5.57 E
Brueil-en-Vexin 251 49.02 N 1.49 E
Brüel 50 53.44 N 11.43 E
Bruges → Brugge 46 51.13 N 3.14 E
Brugg 54 47.29 N 8.12 E
Brugge (Bruges), Bel. 46 51.13 N 3.14 E
Brügge, B.R.D. 253 51.13 N 7.34 E
Brüggen 52 51.14 N 6.11 E
Brugherio 56 45.33 N 9.18 E
Brugnato 56 44.14 N 9.43 E
Brühl 52 50.48 N 6.54 E
Bruin, Ky., U.S. 208 38.11 N 83.01 W
Bruin, Pa., U.S. 204 41.04 N 79.44 W
Bruinisse 48 51.40 N 4.06 E
Bruin Point ∧ 190 39.39 N 110.22 W
Bruja, Cerro ∧ 226 9.29 N 79.34 W
Brujo, Cerro ∧ 226 10.09 N 85.38 W
Brule 188 41.06 N 101.53 W
Brule ≃ 180 45.57 N 88.12 W
Brûlé, Lac ⊜ 166 52.17 N 63.52 W
Brule Lake ⊜ 202 45.03 N 77.04 W
Brûly 46 49.58 N 4.31 E
Brumadinho 245 20.08 S 44.13 W
Brumado 245 14.13 S 41.40 W
Brumath 52 48.44 N 7.43 E
Brumby Creek ≃ 152 24.09 S 118.39 E
Brummen 48 52.05 N 6.09 E
Brumunddal 26 60.53 N 10.56 E
Bruna ≃ 60 42.45 N 10.53 E
Brunate 56 45.49 N 9.06 E
Brunau 50 52.45 N 11.28 E
Brundby 41 55.49 N 10.37 E
Brundidge 184 31.43 N 85.49 W
Brune ≃ 46 49.45 N 3.47 E
Bruneau 192 42.53 N 115.48 W
Bruneau ≃ 192 42.57 N 115.58 W
Bruneau, East Fork ≃ 192 42.34 N 115.38 W
Brunei → Bandar Seri Begawan 102 4.56 N 114.55 E
Brunei □[1] 98
102 4.30 N 114.40 E
Brunei, Teluk C 102 5.05 N 115.18 E
Brünen 48 51.43 N 6.39 E
Brunette Creek ≃ 152 18.47 S 135.41 E
Brunette Downs 152 18.38 S 135.57 E
Brunette Island I 176 47.16 N 55.54 W
Brunflo 26 63.05 N 14.49 E
Brungle 161b 35.10 S 148.14 E
Brunico (Bruneck) 58 46.48 N 11.56 E
Brünigpass)(54 46.46 N 8.09 E
Brüninghausen 253 51.13 N 7.41 E
Brunkeberg 26 59.26 N 8.29 E
Brünn → Brno, Česko. 30 49.12 N 16.37 E
Brünn, D.D.R. 50 50.27 N 10.51 E
Brunn, D.D.R. 50 53.40 N 13.22 E
Brunna 40 59.51 N 17.26 E
Brunn am Gebirge 254b 48.07 N 16.17 E
Brunnen 54 47.00 N 8.36 E
Brunner 162 42.27 S 171.19 E
Brunner, Lake ⊜ 162 42.37 S 171.27 E
Brunnerville 198 40.11 N 76.17 W
Brunni 54 47.03 N 8.42 E
Brunnsvik 40 60.12 N 15.08 E
Bruno 174 52.15 N 105.30 W
Brunot Island I 269b 40.28 N 80.03 W
Brunow 254a 52.44 N 13.52 E
Brunoy 46 48.42 N 2.30 E
Brunsbüttel 48 53.54 N 9.07 E
Brunsbüttelkoog 48 53.54 N 9.08 E
Brunson 182 32.56 N 81.11 W
Brunssum 52 50.56 N 5.59 E
Brunswick, Austl. 264b 37.46 S 144.58 E
Brunswick → Braunschweig, B.R.D. 48 52.16 N 10.31 E
Brunswick, Ga., U.S. 182 31.10 N 81.29 W
Brunswick, Maine, U.S. 178 43.55 N 69.58 W
Brunswick, Md., U.S. 198 39.19 N 77.37 W
Brunswick, Mo., U.S. 184 39.26 N 93.08 W
Brunswick, Ohio, U.S. 204 41.14 N 81.50 W
Brunswick ≃ 158a 33.15 S 115.45 E
Brunswick, Península de ≻[1] 244 53.30 S 71.25 W
Brunswick Junction 158a 33.15 S 115.51 E
Brunswick Lake ⊜ 180 49.00 N 83.23 W
Brunswick Naval Air Station ■ 178 43.54 N 69.56 W
Brunswick Square •[9] 266 40.25 N 74.23 W
Bruntál 30 49.59 N 17.28 E
Brus, Laguna de C 226 15.50 N 84.35 W
Brus'any 70 53.13 N 49.24 E
Brusasco 56 45.09 N 8.04 E
Bruselas → Bruxelles 46 50.50 N 4.20 E
Brusendorf 254a 52.19 N 13.31 E
Brush 188 40.15 N 103.37 W
Brush Creek ≃, Ohio, U.S. 206 41.26 N 84.24 W
Brush Creek ≃, Pa., U.S. 269b 40.23 N 79.46 W
Brush Creek ≃, Utah, U.S. 190 40.25 N 109.20 W
Brush Run ≃ 269b 40.18 N 80.07 W
Brush Valley 204 40.32 N 79.04 W
Brushy Creek ≃, Okla., U.S. 186 34.55 N 95.34 W
Brushy Creek ≃, Tex., U.S. 212 30.48 N 95.09 W
Brushy Creek ≃, Tex., U.S. 212 30.43 N 97.03 W
Brushy Creek ≃, Tex., U.S. 212 31.55 N 95.26 W
Brushy Creek ≃, Tex., U.S. 212 32.59 N 96.12 W
Brushy Creek ≃, Tex., U.S. 212 29.04 N 96.34 W
Brusilov 68 50.17 N 29.32 E
Brusio 54 46.14 N 10.07 E
Brus Laguna 226 15.47 N 84.35 W
Brusovo 66 57.51 N 35.24 E
Brusque 242 27.06 S 48.56 W
Brussel → Bruxelles 46 50.50 N 4.20 E
Brussels → Bruxelles, Bel. 46 50.50 N 4.20 E
Brussels, Ont., Can. 202 43.44 N 81.15 W
Brussels, Ill., U.S. 209 38.57 N 90.36 W
Brusson 56 45.45 N 7.44 E
Brüssow 50 53.24 N 14.07 E
Brusy 30 53.53 N 17.45 E
Brutelles 46 50.08 N 1.31 E
Bruthen 156 37.43 S 147.48 E
Bruton 44 51.07 N 2.27 W
Brüx → Most 50 50.32 N 13.39 E
Bruxelles (Brussel) (Brussels) 46
52 50.50 N 4.20 E
Bruxelles National, Aéroport ⊠ 46 50.54 N 4.30 E
Bruyères 54 48.12 N 6.43 E
Bruyères-le-Châtel 251 48.36 N 2.11 E
Bruzual 236 8.03 N 69.19 W
Brwinów 30 52.09 N 20.43 E
Bryan, Ohio, U.S. 206 41.28 N 84.33 W
Bryan, Tex., U.S. 212 30.40 N 96.22 W
Bryan Coast •[2] 9 73.45 S 82.00 W
Bryansk → Br'ansk 66 53.15 N 34.22 E
Bryans Road 198 38.38 N 77.04 W
Bryant, Ind., U.S. 206 40.32 N 84.58 W
Bryant, S. Dak., U.S. 188 44.35 N 97.28 W
Bryant Creek ≃ 184 36.36 N 92.17 W
Bryant Mountain ∧ 197 42.28 N 72.58 W
Bryantville 197 42.03 N 70.51 W
Bryas, Lac ⊜ 196 46.44 N 73.05 W
Bryce Canyon National Park ♠ 190 37.29 N 112.12 W
Brykalansk 24 65.30 N 54.12 E
Brykovka 70 52.32 N 48.35 E
Bryli 66 53.54 N 30.33 E
Brymbo 44 53.06 N 3.04 W
Bryn 252 53.30 N 2.39 W
Brynamman 44 51.49 N 3.52 W
Bryn Athyn 275 40.08 N 75.04 W
Bryn Brawd ∧[2] 44 52.09 N 3.54 W
Bryncethin 44 51.33 N 3.34 W
Bryne 26 58.44 N 5.39 E
Brynford 252 53.16 N 3.14 W
Bryn Gates 252 53.30 N 2.37 W
Bryn'kovskaja 68 46.02 N 38.35 E
Brynmawr, Wales, U.K. 44 51.49 N 3.11 W
Bryn Mawr, Calif., U.S. 218 34.03 N 117.14 W
Bryn Mawr, Pa., U.S. 198 40.01 N 75.19 W
Bryn Mawr College ♥[2] 275 40.02 N 75.19 W
Bryrup 41 56.01 N 9.31 E
Bryson, Qué., Can. 178 45.41 N 76.37 W
Bryson, Tex., U.S. 186 33.10 N 98.23 W
Bryson City 182 35.26 N 83.27 W
Bryte 216 38.36 N 121.33 W
Brza Palanka 38 44.28 N 22.27 E
Brzeg 30 50.52 N 17.27 E
Brześć Kujawski 30 52.37 N 18.55 E
Brześć Nad Bugiem → Brest 66 52.06 N 23.42 E
Brzesko 30 49.59 N 20.36 E
Brzeszcze 30 49.59 N 19.08 E
Brzeziny 30 51.48 N 19.46 E
Brzozów 30 49.42 N 22.02 E
Bsharrī 120 34.15 N 36.01 E
Bua 154 6.45 S 147.35 E
Bua ≃ 144 12.42 S 34.13 E
Buada Lagoon C 164b 0.31 S 166.55 E
Buad Island I 106 11.40 N 124.51 E
Buagan ≃ 259e 6.17 S 106.55 E
Buakonikai 164d 0.52 S 169.36 E
Bū al-Ḥīḍān 136 28.10 N 19.18 E
Bū al-Ḥīḍān, Wādī ∨ 136 27.25 N 19.22 E
Buangor, Mount ∧ 159 37.18 S 143.13 E
Buapinang 102 4.46 S 121.34 E
Buariki 164t 1.36 N 172.58 E
Buariki I 164t 1.36 N 172.58 E
Buatan 104 0.44 N 101.51 E
Bua Yai 100 15.35 N 102.25 E
Buayan 106 6.07 N 125.15 E
Buayan ≃ 106 6.06 N 125.14 E
Buba 140 11.36 N 14.55 W
Bubai 258 35.40 N 139.29 E
Bubanza 144 3.06 S 29.23 E
Bubaque 140 11.17 N 15.50 W
Bubendorf 54 47.27 N 7.44 E
Bubia 154 6.40 S 146.55 E
Būbiyān I 118 29.47 N 48.10 E
Bublitz → Bobolice 30 53.57 N 16.36 E
Bubu ≃ 144 6.03 S 35.19 E
Bubu, Gunong ∧ 104 4.42 N 100.47 E
Bubuan Island I, Pil. 106 6.11 N 120.58 E
Bubuan Island I, Pil. 106 6.21 N 121.58 E
Bubuduo 110 30.06 N 84.38 E
Buburu 142 1.26 N 18.03 E
Bubus, Bukit (Buket Bubut) ∧ 104 6.12 N 101.06 E
Bubusar Pass)(113 35.09 N 74.02 E
Bubye ≃ 144 22.20 S 31.07 E
Buc 251 48.46 N 2.08 E
Bučač 68 49.04 N 25.23 E
Bucak 120 37.28 N 30.36 E
Bucakkışla 120 36.57 N 33.02 E
Bucaramanga 236 7.08 N 73.09 W
Bucarest → București 38 44.26 N 26.06 E
Bucas Grande Island I 106 9.40 N 125.57 E
Buccament Bay C 231h 13.11 N 61.16 W
Buccaneer Archipelago II 150 16.17 S 123.20 E
Bucchianico 60 42.18 N 14.11 E
Buccinasco 256b 45.24 N 9.07 E
Buccino 36 40.37 N 15.23 E
Bucelas 256c 38.54 N 9.07 W
Bucelas ∧[2] 256c 38.53 N 9.07 W
Buch •[8] 254a 52.38 N 13.30 E
Buchanan 248 34.58 S 58.13 W
Buchanan, Sask., Can. 174 51.43 N 102.45 W
Buchanan, Liber. 140 5.57 N 10.02 W
Buchanan, Ga., U.S. 182 33.48 N 85.11 W
Buchanan, Mich., U.S. 206 41.50 N 86.22 W
Buchanan, N.Y., U.S. 200 41.16 N 73.56 W
Buchanan, Va., U.S. 182 37.32 N 79.41 W
Buchanan, Lake ⊜ 156 21.28 S 145.52 E
Buchanan, Lake ⊜[1] 186 30.48 N 98.25 W
Buchanan Creek ≃ 152 19.11 S 136.16 E
Buchanan Field ⊠ 272 37.59 N 122.03 W
Buchanan Hills ⩓[2] 152 18.53 S 131.02 E
Buchan Gulf C 166 71.47 N 74.16 W
Buchan Ness ≻ 28 57.32 N 1.48 W
Buchans 176 48.49 N 56.52 W
Buchara 118 39.48 N 64.25 E
Buchara □[4] 76 43.30 N 64.00 E
Buchardo 242 34.43 S 63.31 W
Bucharest → București 38 44.26 N 26.06 E
Buchelay 251 48.59 N 1.40 E
Büchen, B.R.D. 48 53.29 N 10.36 E
Buchen, B.R.D. 52 49.32 N 9.17 E
Buchenberg 54 47.42 N 10.14 E
Büchenbeuren 52 49.55 N 7.16 E
Buchenwalddenkmal ⊥ 50 51.01 N 11.15 E
Buchholz, B.R.D. 253 51.23 N 7.15 E
Buchholz, D.D.R. 50 52.10 N 12.55 E
Buchholz, D.D.R. 254a 52.35 N 13.47 E
Buchholz •[8], B.R.D. 253 51.23 N 6.46 E
Buchholz •[8], D.D.R. 254a 52.36 N 13.26 E
Buchholz in der Nordheide 48 53.20 N 9.52 E
Buchloe 54 48.02 N 10.44 E
Bucholt 253 51.39 N 6.43 E
Buchon, Point ≻ 216 35.15 N 120.54 W
Buchow-Karpzow 254a 52.31 N 12.57 E
Buchs, Schw. 54 47.23 N 8.04 E
Buchs, Schw. 54 47.10 N 9.28 E
Buchufontein 148 30.18 S 19.36 E
Buchy 46 49.35 N 1.22 E
Bucine 60 43.29 N 11.37 E
Buck, Lake ⊜ 152 19.38 S 130.21 E
Buckatunna 184 31.27 N 88.32 W
Buckatunna Creek ≃ 184 31.30 N 88.32 W
Buck Branch ≃ 274b 39.01 N 77.10 W
Buck Creek 206 40.29 N 86.46 W
Buck Creek ≃, Ind., U.S. 208 39.37 N 85.56 W
Buck Creek ≃, Ind., U.S. 208 40.11 N 85.30 W
Buck Creek ≃, Ky., U.S. 182 36.59 N 84.29 W
Buck Creek ≃, Ohio, U.S. 208 39.56 N 83.51 W
Buck Creek ≃, Pa., U.S. 275 40.15 N 74.50 W
Buckden, Eng., U.K. 42 54.12 N 2.05 W
Buckden, Eng., U.K. 44 52.17 N 0.16 W
Bückeburg 48 52.16 N 9.02 E
Bücken 48 52.46 N 9.07 E
Buckeye 190 33.22 N 112.35 W
Buckeye Creek ≃ 216 38.54 N 121.55 W
Buckeye Lake 178 39.56 N 82.29 W
Buckeystown 198 39.20 N 77.26 W
Buckfastleigh 44 50.29 N 3.46 W
Buckhannon 178 38.59 N 80.14 W
Buckhaven 28 56.11 N 3.03 W
Buck Hill Falls 200 41.11 N 75.16 W
Buck Hollow ≃ 214 45.10 N 120.50 W
Buckholts 212 30.52 N 97.08 W
Buckhorn ≃ 170 66.13 N 161.10 W
Buckhorn Island State Park ♠ 274a 43.03 N 78.59 W
Buckhorn Lake ⊜, Ont., Can. 202 44.28 N 78.23 W
Buckhorn Lake ⊜, Calif., U.S. 218 34.50 N 117.59 W
Buckie 28 57.40 N 2.58 W
Buckingham, Austl. 158a 33.24 S 116.19 E
Buckingham, Qué., Can. 178 45.35 N 75.25 W
Buckingham, Eng., U.K. 44 52.00 N 1.00 W
Buckingham, Pa., U.S. 198 40.18 N 75.01 W
Buckingham, Va., U.S. 182 37.32 N 78.37 W
Buckingham Bay C 154 12.10 S 135.46 E
Buckingham Palace ♥ 250 51.30 N 0.08 W
Buckinghamshire □[6] 44 51.45 N 0.48 W
Buck Island I, Vir. Is., U.S. 230m 18.17 N 64.54 W
Buck Island I, Vir. Is., U.S. 231n 17.48 N 64.37 W
Buck Lake ⊜, Alta., Can. 172 53.00 N 114.45 W
Buck Lake ⊜, Ont., Can. 202 45.25 N 79.24 W
Buckland, Eng., U.K. 250 51.15 N 0.15 W
Buckland, Alaska, U.S. 170 66.16 N 161.20 W
Buckland, Mass., U.S. 197 42.36 N 72.48 W
Buckland, Ohio, U.S. 206 40.37 N 84.16 W
Buckland Brewer 44 50.57 N 4.14 W
Buckland Common 250 51.45 N 0.39 W
Buckleboo 156 32.55 S 136.12 E
Buckley, Wales, U.K. 44 53.09 N 3.04 W
Buckley, Ill., U.S. 206 40.36 N 88.02 W
Buckley, Wash., U.S. 214 47.10 N 122.02 W
Buckley ≃ 156 20.22 S 137.57 E
Buckley Bay C 9 68.16 S 148.12 E
Bucklin, Kans., U.S. 188 37.33 N 99.38 W
Bucklin, Mo., U.S. 184 39.47 N 92.53 W
Buck Mountain ∧, Va., U.S. 182 36.40 N 81.15 W
Buck Mountain ∧, Wash., U.S. 192 48.26 N 119.50 W
Bucknell Manor 198 38.46 N 77.04 W
Buckner 208 38.23 N 85.26 W
Buckner Creek ≃ 188 38.11 N 99.34 W
Buckners Creek ≃ 212 29.53 N 96.53 W
Buckow 50 52.34 N 14.04 E
Buckow •[8] 254a 52.25 N 13.26 E
Bucks □[6] 198 40.19 N 75.08 W
Buckshot Lake ⊜ 202 45.00 N 77.04 W
Buckskin Creek ≃ 208 39.14 N 83.17 W
Bucks Knob ∧ 214 46.41 N 123.20 W
Bucksport 178 44.34 N 68.48 W
Bucktown 275 40.10 N 75.43 W
Bückwitz 50 52.52 N 12.29 E
Buc-Louis-Blériot, Aérodrome de ⊠ 251 48.45 N 2.05 E
Bučmany 68 51.04 N 28.04 E
Bucoda 214 46.48 N 122.52 W
Buco Zau 142 4.46 S 12.33 E
Bucquoy 46 50.08 N 2.42 E
Buctouche 176 46.28 N 64.43 W
Bucun 88 36.37 N 117.27 E
București 38 44.26 N 26.06 E
Bucutua Island I 106 6.09 N 121.49 E
Bucy-lès-Pierrepont 46 49.39 N 3.54 E
Bucyrus 204 40.48 N 82.58 W
Bud 26 62.55 N 6.55 E
Buda 180 41.20 N 89.41 W
Buda •[8] 254c 47.30 N 19.02 E
Budafok •[8] 254c 47.26 N 19.02 E
Budagovo 78 54.38 N 100.08 E
Budakalász 254c 47.37 N 19.03 E
Budakeszi 254c 47.31 N 18.56 E
Buda-Kosel'ovo 66 52.43 N 30.34 E
Budalin 100 22.22 N 95.08 E
Budaörs 254c 47.27 N 18.58 E
Budapest 30
254c 47.30 N 19.05 E
Budapest □[7] 254c 47.30 N 19.05 E
Budapesti Műszaki Egyetem ♥[2] 254c 47.29 N 19.02 E
Búðardalur 24a 65.10 N 21.42 W
Budarin 70 47.54 N 42.36 E
Budarino 70 50.31 N 51.04 E
Budatétény •[8] 254c 47.25 N 19.01 E
Budaun 114 28.03 N 79.07 E
Budaun □[5] 114 28.10 N 79.00 E
Budawang Range ⩓ 160 35.16 S 150.10 E
Budayuan 88 40.56 N 125.19 E
Budberg 253 51.32 N 6.38 E
Bud Bud 134 4.15 N 46.30 E
Budd Coast •[2] 9 66.30 S 113.00 E
Buddh Gaya 114 24.42 N 84.59 E
Budd Inlet C 214 47.06 N 122.54 W
Budd Lake 200 40.52 N 74.44 W
Buddtown 275 39.58 N 74.42 W
Buddu 130 11.54 N 24.08 E
Buddusò 36 40.35 N 9.16 E
Bude, Eng., U.K. 44 50.50 N 4.33 W
Bude, Miss., U.S. 184 31.28 N 90.51 W
Bude Bay C 44 50.50 N 4.37 W
Budel 48 51.17 N 5.35 E
Budelikesihu ⊜ 110 33.00 N 86.25 E
Büdelsdorf 41 54.18 N 9.40 E
Büderich 48 51.37 N 6.34 E
Buderus 253 51.33 N 7.38 E
Budești 38 44.14 N 26.28 E
Budge Budge 116 22.27 N 88.10 E
Budhhāta 116 22.36 N 89.10 E
Budhlāda 113 29.56 N 75.34 E
Budi 142 3.04 S 23.56 E
Büdingen 52 50.17 N 9.07 E
Búdir 24a 64.56 N 13.58 W
Budišov nad Budišovkou 30 49.47 N 17.38 E
Budjala 142 2.39 N 19.42 E
Budleigh Salterton 44 50.38 N 3.20 W
Budogošč' 66 59.17 N 32.27 E
Budogovišči 66 53.36 N 36.18 E
Bud'onnovka 70 50.52 N 52.48 E
Bud'onnovskaja 70 46.56 N 41.33 E
Bud'onnyj 73 47.27 N 39.46 E
Bud'onnys 75 42.29 N 72.34 E
Budrio 58 44.32 N 11.32 E
Budslav 66 54.47 N 27.27 E
Budweis → České Budějovice 30 48.59 N 14.28 E
Budworth Mere ⊜ 252 53.17 N 2.31 W
Budy 68 49.53 N 36.02 E
Budylka 68 50.30 N 34.26 E
Budyně nad Ohří 50 50.22 N 14.09 E
Budžak ⩓[1] 68 46.10 N 29.00 E
Buea 142 4.09 N 9.14 E
Buëch ≃ 56 44.12 N 5.57 E
Buechel 208 38.12 N 85.39 W
Bueil 46 48.56 N 1.27 E
Buela 142 5.55 S 14.33 E
Buell 209 39.02 N 91.27 W
Buena 198 39.31 N 74.56 W
Buena Esperanza 242 34.45 S 65.15 W
Buena Esperanza, Cabo de → Good Hope, Cape of ≻ 148 34.24 S 18.30 E
Buena Park, Calif., U.S. 218 33.52 N 118.00 W
Buena Park, Wis., U.S. 206 42.48 N 88.14 W
Buenaventura, Col. 236 3.53 N 77.04 W
Buenaventura, Méx. 222 29.51 N 107.29 W
Buena Vista, Bol. 238 17.27 S 63.40 W
Buena Vista, Guat. 226 13.49 N 90.19 W
Buena Vista, Méx. 194 32.32 N 116.44 W
Buenavista, Méx. 224 22.30 N 103.10 W
Buena Vista, Para. 242 25.55 S 55.34 W
Buenavista, Pil. 106 13.15 N 121.57 E
Buenavista, Pil. 106 7.15 N 122.16 E
Buenavista, Pil. 106 10.04 N 118.49 E
Buenavista, Pil. 106 8.59 N 125.24 E
Buena Vista, Colo., U.S. 190 38.50 N 106.08 W
Buena Vista, Fla., U.S. 210 25.49 N 80.12 W
Buena Vista, Ga., U.S. 182 32.19 N 84.31 W
Buena Vista, Md., U.S. 274c 38.57 N 76.50 W
Buena Vista, Miss., U.S. 184 33.47 N 88.56 W
Buena Vista, Va., U.S. 182 37.44 N 79.21 W
Buenavista, Bahía de C 230p 22.30 N 79.08 W
Buenavista, Cerro ∧ 226 9.33 N 83.45 W
Buena Vista, Cordillera de ⩓ 236 10.40 N 70.10 W
Buena Vista Canal ≅ 218 35.21 N 119.06 W
Buenavista de Cuéllar 224 18.27 N 99.25 W
Buena Vista Lake Bed ⊜ 194 35.11 N 119.17 W
Buenavista Revolución Mexicana 224 16.03 N 93.04 W
Buenavista Tomatlán 224 19.12 N 102.36 W
Buen Día 186 26.21 N 104.32 W
Buendia, Embalse de ⊜[1] 34 40.25 N 2.43 W
Buenga ≃ 142 6.07 S 15.58 E
Bueno ≃ 244 40.13 S 73.43 W
Bueno Brandão 246 22.27 S 46.21 W
Buenolândia 245 15.48 S 50.17 W
Buenópolis 245 17.54 S 44.11 W
Buenos Aires, Arg. 248
278 34.36 S 58.27 W
Buenos Aires, Col. 236 3.02 N 76.38 W
Buenos Aires, C.R. 226 9.10 N 83.20 W
Buenos Aires □[4] 242 36.00 S 60.00 W
Buenos Aires, Lago (Lago General Carrera) ⊜ 244 46.35 S 72.00 W
Buen Pasto 244 45.05 S 69.28 W
Buer •[8] 253 51.36 N 7.03 E
Buerarema 245 14.57 S 39.19 W
Buerāt, Bi'r ⊤[4] 132 28.59 N 32.10 E
Buerhanbudashan ⩓ 92 36.00 N 96.00 E
Buerjin 76 47.43 N 86.53 E
Buertuokai 75 39.35 N 74.58 E
Buesaco 236 1.23 N 77.09 W
Buescher State Park ♠ 212 30.02 N 97.09 W
Buet, Le ∧ 54 46.02 N 6.52 E
Buey ≃ 230p 20.28 N 77.05 W
Bufa, Cerro ∧ 224 20.44 N 104.50 W
Bufalotta, Fosso della ≃ 257a 41.59 N 12.30 E
Buffalo, Ill., U.S. 209 39.51 N 89.25 W
Buffalo, Ind., U.S. 206 40.53 N 86.45 W
Buffalo, Iowa, U.S. 180 41.27 N 90.43 W
Buffalo, Kans., U.S. 188 37.42 N 95.42 W
Buffalo, Minn., U.S. 180 45.10 N 93.53 W
Buffalo, Mo., U.S. 184 37.39 N 93.06 W
Buffalo, N.Y., U.S. 200
274a 42.54 N 78.53 W
Buffalo, Ohio, U.S. 178 39.55 N 81.31 W
Buffalo, Okla., U.S. 186 36.50 N 99.38 W
Buffalo, S.C., U.S. 182 34.43 N 81.41 W
Buffalo, S. Dak., U.S. 188 45.35 N 103.33 W
Buffalo, Tex., U.S. 212 31.28 N 96.04 W
Buffalo, Wyo., U.S. 192 44.21 N 106.42 W
Buffalo ≃, Can. 166 60.55 N 115.00 W
Buffalo ≃, S. Afr. 148 28.43 S 30.37 E
Buffalo ≃, Ark., U.S. 184 36.10 N 92.26 W
Buffalo ≃, Minn., U.S. 188 47.06 N 96.49 W
Buffalo ≃, Miss., U.S. 184 31.04 N 91.34 W
Buffalo ≃, N.Y., U.S. 204 42.53 N 78.53 W
Buffalo ≃, Tenn., U.S. 184 36.00 N 87.50 W
Buffalo ≃, Wis., U.S. 180 44.22 N 91.55 W
Buffalo Airpark ⊠ 274a 42.52 N 78.43 W
Buffalo Bayou ≃ 212 29.46 N 95.05 W
Buffalo Bill Reservoir ⊜[1] 192 44.29 N 109.13 W
Buffalo Bill State Park ♠ 192 44.30 N 109.14 W
Buffalo Center 180 43.23 N 93.57 W
Buffalo Coast Guard Base ■ 274a 42.52 N 78.54 W
Buffalo Creek ≃, U.S. 188 45.57 N 102.56 W
Buffalo Creek ≃, U.S. 204 40.16 N 80.37 W
Buffalo Creek ≃, Ill., U.S. 268 42.08 N 87.55 W
Buffalo Creek ≃, Iowa, U.S. 180 42.06 N 91.18 W
Buffalo Creek ≃, Kans., U.S. 188 39.35 N 97.43 W
Buffalo Creek ≃, Ky., U.S. 208 38.28 N 83.03 W
Buffalo Creek ≃, Minn., U.S. 188 44.51 N 94.00 W
Buffalo Creek ≃, N.Y., U.S. 200 42.52 N 78.47 W
Buffalo Creek ≃, Okla., U.S. 186 36.47 N 99.15 W
Buffalo Creek ≃, Pa., U.S. 198 40.29 N 77.08 W
Buffalo Creek ≃, Pa., U.S. 200 40.58 N 76.53 W
Buffalo Grove 206 42.09 N 87.58 W
Buffalo Harbor C 202 42.51 N 78.52 W
Buffalo Lake 188 44.44 N 94.37 W
Buffalo Lake ⊜, Alta., Can. 172 52.27 N 112.54 W
Buffalo Lake ⊜, N.W. Ter., Can. 166 60.10 N 115.30 W
Buffalo Narrows 174 55.51 N 108.30 W
Buffalo Pound Provincial Park ♠ 174 50.36 N 105.30 W
Buffalo Run ≃ 269b 40.12 N 79.37 W
Buffalo Zoo ♠ 274a 42.56 N 78.51 W
Buffels ≃ 148 33.45 S 21.11 E
Buffington Harbor C 268 41.38 N 87.25 W
Buffum, Lake ⊜ 210 27.48 N 81.40 W
Buford, Ga., U.S. 182 34.07 N 84.00 W
Buford, Ohio, U.S. 208 39.04 N 83.50 W
Buford Dam •[6] 182 34.11 N 84.03 W
Bug ≃ 22 52.31 N 21.05 E
Buga, Col. 236 3.54 N 76.17 W
Buga, Nig. 140 8.30 N 7.21 E
Bugajevka, S.S.S.R. 73 48.25 N 38.53 E
Bugajevka, S.S.S.R. 73 49.39 N 39.42 E
Bugajevka, S.S.S.R. 73 49.28 N 37.23 E
Bugalagrande 236 4.11 N 76.09 W
Bugallon 106 15.57 N 120.13 E
Buganga 144 0.03 S 31.59 E
Bugasong 106 11.03 N 122.04 E
Bugat, Mong. 76 48.59 N 90.10 E
Bugat, Mong. 78 47.55 N 101.16 E
Bug Atoti 134 10.41 N 50.45 E
Bugeat 32 45.35 N 1.59 E
Bugel, Ujung ≻ 105a 6.26 S 111.03 E
Bugene 144 1.35 S 31.08 E
Bugey •[1] 54 45.55 N 5.30 E
Buggenhout 46 51.01 N 4.12 E
Bugio I 256c 38.39 N 9.18 W
Bugiri 144 0.34 N 33.45 E
Bugisu □[5] 144 1.03 N 34.10 E
Buğlan Geçidi)(120 38.56 N 41.10 E
Bugle 44 50.24 N 4.47 W
Bug Méridional → Južnyj Bug ≃ 68 46.59 N 31.58 E
Bugni Point ≻ 106 12.36 N 123.14 E
Bugojno 36 44.03 N 17.27 E
Bugøynes 24 69.58 N 29.39 E
Bugrino 24 68.48 N 49.09 E
Bugry, S.S.S.R. 66 58.46 N 35.15 E
Bugry, S.S.S.R. 255a 60.04 N 30.24 E
Bugsanga ≃ 106 12.26 N 120.59 E
Bugsuk Island I 106 8.15 N 117.18 E
Buguba 154 3.41 S 137.30 E
Buguey 106 18.17 N 121.50 E
Bugul'dejka 78 52.33 N 106.05 E
Bugul'ma 70 54.33 N 52.48 E
Bugul'minsko-Belebejevskaja Vozvyšennost' ⩓[1] 70 54.54 N 52.42 E
Bugun' ≃ 75 42.58 N 68.35 E
Bugun'skoje Vodochranilišče ⊜[1] 75 42.45 N 69.05 E
Buguruslan 70 53.39 N 52.26 E
Buhamanggenaishankou)(110 34.00 N 92.43 E
Buhanhua 94 42.39 N 122.46 E
Buḥayrah, Rayyāḥ al- ≅ 132 30.43 N 30.45 E
Buḥaythān, Jabal al- ∧ 122 30.55 N 35.53 E
Buhera 144 19.18 S 31.29 E
Buhi 106 13.26 N 123.31 E
Buhi, Lake ⊜ 106 13.26 N 123.31 E
Bühl, B.R.D. 52 48.42 N 8.08 E
Buhl, Fr. 54 47.56 N 7.11 E
Buhl, Idaho, U.S. 192 42.36 N 114.46 W
Buhl, Minn., U.S. 180 47.30 N 92.47 W
Buhler 188 38.08 N 97.46 W
Bühler ≃ 52 49.10 N 9.47 E
Bühlertal 52 48.41 N 8.10 E
Buhuai 110 33.22 N 80.36 E
Buhuși 38 46.43 N 26.41 E
Bui Dam •[6] 140 8.22 N 2.10 W
Buile Hill Park ♠ 252 53.29 N 2.18 W
Builth Wells 44 52.09 N 3.24 W
Buin, Chile 242 33.44 S 70.45 W
Buin, Pap. N. Gui. 165e 6.50 S 155.44 E
Buin, Piz ∧ 54 46.50 N 10.08 E
Buinen 48 52.55 N 6.50 E
Buinsk, S.S.S.R. 70 55.12 N 47.03 E
Buinsk, S.S.S.R. 70 54.57 N 48.17 E
Buíque 240 8.37 S 37.09 W
Buir Nuur ⊜ 78 47.48 N 117.42 E
Buis-les-Baronnies 56 44.16 N 5.16 E
Buitenpost 48 53.15 N 6.09 E
Buitepos 146 22.18 S 19.57 E
Buj 70 58.30 N 41.30 E
Buj ≃ 70 56.13 N 54.12 E
Bujaki 24 59.03 N 48.40 E
Bujalance 34 37.54 N 4.22 W
Bujant, Mong. 76 48.10 N 91.55 E
Bujant, Mong. 76 48.33 N 89.34 E
Bujant ≃ 78 47.08 N 97.38 E
Bujant-Ovoo 92 44.58 N 107.08 E
Bujaraloz 34 41.30 N 0.09 W
Bujaru 240 1.31 S 48.01 W
Buje 36 45.24 N 13.40 E
Buji 92 33.58 N 95.22 E
Bujiadong 96 30.55 N 119.31 E
Bujnaksk 74 42.49 N 47.07 E
Bujnoviči 68 51.52 N 28.33 E
Bujukly 79 49.30 N 142.47 E
Bujumbura 144 3.23 S 29.22 E
Buk 30 52.22 N 16.31 E
Buka 75 40.48 N 69.11 E
Bukačača 78 52.59 N 116.55 E
Bukačevcy 68 49.15 N 24.29 E
Bukaishan ∧ 79 46.38 N 133.28 E
Buka Island I 165e 5.15 S 154.35 E
Bukama 144 9.12 S 25.51 E
Bukan' 66 53.55 N 34.42 E
Bukanovskaja 70 49.42 N 42.18 E
Buka Passage Ш 165e 5.25 S 154.41 E
Bukarest → București 38 44.26 N 26.06 E
Bukarevo 72 55.57 N 36.44 E
Bukavu 144 2.30 S 28.52 E
Bukechi ⊜ 110 31.30 N 91.05 E
Bukedi □[5] 144 0.50 N 34.00 E
Bukene 144 4.14 S 32.53 E
Bukhara → Buchara 118 39.48 N 64.25 E
Bukhayt, Bi'r ⊤[4] 132 29.13 N 32.17 E
Bukide, Pulau I 102 3.47 N 125.36 E
Bukidnon □[4] 106 8.00 N 125.00 E
Bukima 144 1.48 S 33.25 E
Bukitbatu 104 1.27 N 102.00 E
Bukit Betong 104 4.15 N 101.56 E
Bukit Fraser 104 3.43 N 101.45 E
Bukit Kachi 104 6.24 N 100.32 E
Bukit Mertajam 104 5.22 N 100.28 E
Bukit Panjang 261c 1.23 N 103.46 E

Symbols in the index entries represent the broad categories identified in the key at the right. Symbols with superior numbers (⩓[2]) identify subcategories (see complete key on page I · 26).

Kartensymbole in dem Registerverzeichnis stellen die rechts in Schlüssel erklärten Kategorien dar. Symbole mit hochgestellten Ziffern (⩓[2]) bezeichnen Unterabteilungen einer Kategorie (vgl. vollständiger Schlüssel auf Seite I · 26).

Los símbolos incluídos en el texto del índice representan las grandes categorias identificadas con la clave a la derecha. Los símbolos con numeros en su parte superior (⩓[2]) identifican las subcategorías (véase la clave completa en la página I · 26).

Les symboles de l'index représentent les catégories indiquées dans la légende à droite. Les symboles suivis d'un indice (⩓[2]) représentent des sous-catégories (voir légende complète à la page I · 26).

Os símbolos incluídos no texto do índice representam as grandes categorias identificadas com a chave à direita. Os símbolos com números em sua parte superior (⩓[2]) identificam as subcategorias (veja-se a chave completa à página I · 26).

	English	Deutsch	Español	Français	Português
∧	Mountain	Berg	Montaña	Montagne	Montanha
⩓	Mountains	Berge	Montañas	Montagnes	Montanhas
)(	Pass	Pass	Paso	Col	Passo
∨	Valley, Canyon	Tal, Cañon	Valle, Cañón	Vallée, Canyon	Vale, Canhão
≚	Plain	Ebene	Llano	Plaine	Planície
≻	Cape	Kap	Cabo	Cap	Cabo
I	Island	Insel	Isla	Île	Ilha
II	Islands	Inseln	Islas	Îles	Ilhas
•	Other Topographic Features	Andere Topographische Objekte	Otros Elementos Topográficos	Autres données topographiques	Outros Elementos Topográficos

ESPAÑOL — Nombre | Página | Lat.°′ | Long.°′ W=Oeste
FRANÇAIS — Nom | Page | Lat.°′ | Long.°′ W=Ouest
PORTUGUÊS — Nome | Página | Lat.°′ | Long.°′ W=Oeste

Symbol	English	Deutsch	Español	Français	Português
≃	River	Fluss	Río	Rivière	Rio
≍	Canal	Kanal	Canal	Canal	Canal
↳	Waterfall, Rapids	Wasserfall, Stromschnellen	Cascada, Rápidos	Chute d'eau, Rapides	Cascata, Rápidos
⋈	Strait	Meeresstrasse	Estrecho	Détroit	Estreito
C	Bay, Gulf	Bucht, Golf	Bahía, Golfo	Baie, Golfe	Baía, Golfo
@	Lake, Lakes	See, Seen	Lago, Lagos	Lac, Lacs	Lago, Lagos
☷	Swamp	Sumpf	Pantano	Marais	Pântano
❄	Ice Features, Glacier	Eis- und Gletscherformen	Accidentes Glaciales	Formes glaciaires	Acidentes Glaciares
●	Other Hydrographic Features	Andere Hydrographische Objekte	Otros Elementos Hidrográficos	Autres données hydrographiques	Outros Elementos Hidrográficos
✣	Submarine Features	Untermeerische Objekte	Accidentes Submarinos	Formes de relief sous-marin	Acidentes Submarinos
□	Political Unit	Politische Einheit	Unidad Politica	Entité politique	Unidade Política
⊽	Cultural Institution	Kulturelle Institution	Institución Cultural	Institution culturelle	Instituição Cultural
⊥	Historical Site	Historische Stätte	Sitio Histórico	Site historique	Sítio Histórico
♣	Recreational Site	Erholungs- und Ferienort	Sitio de Recreo	Centre de loisirs	Sítio de Lazer
⊠	Airport	Flughafen	Aeropuerto	Aéroport	Aeroporto
■	Military Installation	Militäranlage	Instalación Militar	Installation militaire	Instalação Militar
◆	Miscellaneous	Verschiedenes	Misceláneo	Divers	Miscelânea

Butler, Ind., U.S. 206 41.26 N 84.52 W
Butler, Ky., U.S. 208 38.47 N 84.22 W
Butler, Mo., U.S. 184 38.16 N 94.20 W
Butler, N.J., U.S. 200 41.00 N 74.21 W
Butler, Ohio, U.S. 204 40.35 N 82.26 W
Butler, Okla., U.S. 186 35.38 N 99.11 W
Butler, Pa., U.S. 204 40.52 N 79.54 W
Butler, Tex., U.S. 212 30.19 N 97.18 W
Butler, Wis., U.S. 206 43.06 N 88.05 W
Butler □[6], Ohio, U.S. 208 39.26 N 84.30 W
Butler □[6], Pa., U.S. 204 40.52 N 79.54 W
Butler, Lake ⊜ 210 28.28 N 81.33 W
Butler Lake ⊜ 268 42.17 N 87.58 W
Butler Point ≻ 197 41.40 N 70.43 W
Butler Reservoir ⊜[1] 266 40.59 N 74.23 W
Butlerville 208 39.02 N 85.31 W
Buto 142 15.46 S 15.09 E
Butong 102 1.06 S 114.50 E
Bütow → Bytów 30 54.11 N 17.30 E
Butru 156 21.30 S 139.43 E
Butsha 144 0.57 N 29.13 E
Buttapietra 58 45.20 N 11.00 E
Butte, Mont., U.S. 192 46.00 N 112.32 W
Butte, Nebr., U.S. 188 42.58 N 98.51 W
Butte □[6] 216 39.27 N 121.30 W
Butte City 216 39.28 N 121.59 W
Butte Creek ≃, Calif., U.S. 216 39.12 N 121.56 W
Butte Creek ≃, Oreg., U.S. 214 45.09 N 122.46 W
Butte du Lion ◆ 46 50.40 N 4.24 E
Butte Falls 192 42.33 N 122.34 W
Buttelstedt 50 51.05 N 11.20 E
Butte Mountains ⋀ 194 39.50 N 115.05 W
Butten 52 48.58 N 7.13 E
Butter Brook ≃ 273 42.31 N 71.24 W
Butter Creek ≃ 192 45.52 N 119.19 W
Butterfield, Ill., U.S. 268 41.50 N 88.02 W
Butterfield, Minn., U.S. 188 43.58 N 94.48 W
Butterfield Creek ≃ 268 41.33 N 87.37 W
Butterfield Lake ⊜ 202 44.19 N 75.46 W
Butterley Reservoir ⊜[1] 252 53.35 N 1.56 W
Buttermere 42 54.33 N 3.17 W
Butternut 180 46.01 N 90.30 W
Butternut Creek ≃, N.Y., U.S. 200 42.25 N 75.22 W
Butternut Creek ≃, N.Y., U.S. 200 43.06 N 76.00 W
Butterwick 44 52.59 N 0.05 E
Butterworth, Malay. 104 5.25 N 100.24 E
Butterworth, S. Afr. 148 32.23 S 28.04 E
Büttgen 52 51.12 N 6.36 E
Buttlar 52 50.45 N 9.57 E
Buttle Lake ⊜ 172 49.46 N 125.36 W
Button Islands II 166 60.35 N 64.45 W
Buttonville 265b 43.52 N 79.22 W
Buttonville Airfield ⊠ 265b 43.52 N 79.23 W
Buttonwillow 216 35.24 N 119.28 W
Buttrio 58 46.01 N 13.20 E
Buttstädt 50 51.07 N 11.25 E
Butty Head ≻ 152 33.54 S 121.38 E
Buttzville 200 40.50 N 75.00 W
Butuan 106 8.57 N 125.33 E
Butuan Bay C 106 9.06 N 125.20 E
Butuj 78 53.27 N 112.22 E
Bū Tumayyim, Wādī ∨ 136 26.56 N 19.13 E
Butung, Pulau I 102 5.00 S 122.55 E
Buturlino, S.S.S.R. 70 55.34 N 44.55 E
Buturlino, S.S.S.R. 72 54.55 N 37.29 E
Buturlinovka 68 50.50 N 40.36 E
Butwal 114 27.42 N 83.27 E
Butylicy 70 55.32 N 41.31 E
Butzbach 52 50.26 N 8.40 E
Bützfleth 48 53.39 N 9.28 E
Bützow 50 53.50 N 11.59 E
Bützsee ⊜ 50 52.49 N 12.53 E
Butztown 198 40.39 N 75.22 W
Buwarah, Sabkhat al- ≚ 120 35.09 N 41.12 E
Buwaydān 122 33.12 N 36.26 E
Buxar 114 25.35 N 83.59 E
Buxtehude 48 53.28 N 9.41 E
Buxton, Guy. 236 6.47 N 58.02 W
Buxton, S. Afr. 148 27.38 S 24.42 E
Buxton, Eng., U.K. 42 53.15 N 1.55 W
Buxton, N.C., U.S. 182 35.16 N 75.32 W
Buxton, N. Dak., U.S. 188 47.36 N 97.06 W
Buxton, Oreg., U.S. 214 45.41 N 123.12 W
Buxton, Mount Λ 172 51.35 N 127.55 W
Buxy 54 46.43 N 4.41 E
Buye 144 4.38 N 27.30 E
Buyiqiao 96 31.47 N 119.48 E
Büyükada 120 40.52 N 29.07 E
Büyükada I 257b 40.52 N 29.07 E
Büyük Ağrı Dağı Λ 74 39.42 N 44.18 E
Büyükarmudan 120 39.35 N 38.26 E
Büyükbakkal 257b 40.59 N 29.11 E
Büyükçekmece 120 41.01 N 28.34 E
Büyükdere ◆[8] 257b 41.09 N 29.02 E
Büyük Doğanca 120 41.11 N 26.25 E
Büyükkale 120 38.01 N 27.34 E
Büyükkarıştıran 120 41.18 N 27.32 E
Büyükkemikli Burnu ≻ 120 40.18 N 26.14 E
Büyük Lâçin 120 40.47 N 34.54 E
Büyükmenderes ≃ 120 37.27 N 27.11 E
Büyükzap → Great Zab ≃ 118 36.00 N 43.21 E
Buyun Uzun 118 39.13 N 63.19 E
Buzan ≃ 70 46.18 N 49.06 E
Buzanaj, Peski ◆[2] 74 47.30 N 49.50 E
Buzançais 32 46.53 N 1.25 E
Buzancy 52 49.25 N 4.57 E
Bužaninovo 72 56.23 N 38.18 E
Bužarovo 72 55.59 N 36.47 E
Buzău 38 45.09 N 26.49 E
Buzău □[4] 38 45.00 N 26.30 E
Buzău ≃ 38 45.26 N 27.44 E
Buzăului, Munţii ⋀ 38 45.35 N 26.10 E
Buzaymah 136 24.55 N 22.02 E
Buzen 86 33.40 N 131.18 E
Búzī ≃ 146 19.50 S 34.43 E
Buziaş 38 45.39 N 21.36 E
Buziji 90 33.49 N 118.14 E
Buzinovka 70 48.32 N 43.53 E
Búzios, Cabo dos ≻ 245 22.44 S 41.53 W
Búzios, Ilha dos I 246 23.48 S 45.08 W
Buzlanovo 255b 55.46 N 37.13 E
Buzovna 74 40.31 N 50.04 E
Buzu 134 15.35 N 50.55 E
Buzuluk, S.S.S.R. 62
70 52.47 N 52.15 E
Buzuluk, S.S.S.R. 76 51.55 N 66.16 E
Buzuluk ≃, S.S.S.R. 70 52.47 N 52.16 E
Buzuluk ≃, S.S.S.R. 70 50.13 N 42.12 E
Buzzards Bay 197 41.45 N 70.37 W
Buzzards Bay C 197 41.33 N 70.47 W
Bwana Mkubwa 144 13.01 S 28.42 E
Bwandougou 140 8.13 N 5.40 W
Bwasa 142 3.53 S 18.25 E
Bwendi 144 4.01 N 26.41 E
Bwlch 44 51.54 N 3.15 W
By 40 60.12 N 16.28 E
Byadgi 112 14.41 N 75.29 E
Byam Channel ⋈ 166 75.20 N 105.20 W
Byam Martin Channel ⋈ 166 75.45 N 104.00 W
Byam Martin Island I 166 75.15 N 104.00 W
Byberry Creek ≃ 275 40.04 N 74.59 W
Byblos → Jubayl 120 34.07 N 35.39 E
Byček ≃ 73 48.26 N 37.48 E
Bychawa 30 51.01 N 22.32 E
Bychov 66 53.32 N 30.12 E
Byčicha 66 55.41 N 29.58 E
Byčki, S.S.S.R. 66 54.15 N 34.39 E
Byčki, S.S.S.R. 70 53.38 N 40.54 E
Byculla ◆[8] 262c 18.58 N 72.49 E
Byczyna 30 51.07 N 18.11 E
Bydalen 26 63.06 N 13.47 E
Bydgoski, Kanał ≅ 30 53.08 N 17.36 E
Bydgoszcz 30 53.08 N 18.00 E
Byelorussian Soviet Socialist Republic → Belorusskaja Socialističeskaja Respublika □[3] 66 53.30 N 28.00 E
Byers, Pa., U.S. 275 40.05 N 75.41 W
Byers, Tex., U.S. 186 34.04 N 98.11 W
Byersdale 269b 40.37 N 80.13 W
Byers Run ≃ 269b 40.24 N 79.42 W
Byesville 178 39.58 N 81.32 W
Byfang ◆[8] 253 51.24 N 7.06 E
Byfield, Eng., U.K. 44 52.11 N 1.14 W
Byfield, Mass., U.S. 197 42.46 N 70.57 W
Byfleet 44 51.20 N 0.29 W
Byford 158a 32.13 S 116.00 E
Bygdeå 26 64.04 N 20.51 E
Bygdeträsket ⊜ 26 64.26 N 20.32 E
Bygdin 26 61.20 N 8.48 E
Bygdin ⊜ 26 61.21 N 8.36 E
Bygi 70 57.13 N 53.44 E
Byglandsfjord 26 58.41 N 7.48 E
Byglandsfjorden ⊜ 26 58.48 N 7.50 E
Byhalia 184 34.52 N 89.41 W
Byk ≃ 68 46.55 N 29.28 E
Bykle 26 59.21 N 7.20 E
Bykov 79 47.21 N 142.32 E
Bykovec 68 47.13 N 28.27 E
Bykovka, S.S.S.R. 68 50.17 N 27.58 E
Bykovka, S.S.S.R. 72 55.29 N 37.40 E
Bykovka ≃ 255b 55.34 N 38.07 E
Bykovo, S.S.S.R. 70 49.47 N 45.22 E
Bykovo, S.S.S.R. 72 54.01 N 37.54 E
Bykovo, S.S.S.R. 72 55.37 N 38.04 E
Bykovo, Aeroport ⊠ 72 55.36 N 38.05 E
Bylas 190 33.08 N 110.07 W
Bylbasovka 73 48.51 N 37.30 E
Bylderup 41 54.57 N 9.07 E
Byley 252 53.13 N 2.25 W
Bylkyldak 76 48.38 N 75.16 E
Bylnice 30 49.04 N 18.01 E
Bylot Island I 166 73.13 N 78.34 W
Byng Inlet 180 45.46 N 80.33 W
Bynum, Mont., U.S. 172 47.59 N 112.19 W
Bynum, N.C., U.S. 182 35.47 N 79.08 W
Bynum, Tex., U.S. 212 31.58 N 97.00 W
Byodoin Temple ᵿ[1] 260 34.53 N 135.48 E
Byram ≃ 266 40.59 N 73.39 W
Byramgore Reef ✧[2] 112 11.54 N 71.49 E
Byram Lake Reservoir ⊜[1] 266 41.10 N 73.41 W
Byrd ᵿ[3] 9 80.00 S 120.00 W
Byrd, Lac ⊜ 180 47.01 N 76.56 W
Byrd Glacier ⊓ 9 80.15 S 160.20 E
Byrd International Airport ⊠ 198 37.30 N 77.19 W
Byrd Land ◆[1] 9 80.00 S 120.00 W
Byrdstown 184 36.34 N 85.08 W
Byrka 78 50.39 N 118.31 E
Byrnedale 204 41.17 N 78.30 W
Byro 152 26.05 S 116.09 E
Byrock 156 30.40 S 146.24 E
Byron, Calif., U.S. 216 37.52 N 121.38 W
Byron, Ga., U.S. 182 32.39 N 83.46 W
Byron, Ill., U.S. 180 42.08 N 89.15 W
Byron, Mich., U.S. 206 42.49 N 83.57 W
Byron, N.Y., U.S. 200 43.05 N 78.04 W
Byron, Wyo., U.S. 192 44.48 N 108.30 W
Byron, Cape ≻ 156 28.39 S 153.38 E
Byron, Isla I 244 47.47 S 75.12 W
Byron Bay 156 28.39 S 153.37 E
Byron Center 206 42.49 N 85.42 W
Byrranga, Gory ⋀ 64 75.00 N 104.00 E
Byšice-Liblice 50 50.19 N 14.38 E
Bysjön ⊜ 40 60.23 N 14.30 E
Byske 26 64.57 N 21.12 E
Byskeälven ≃ 26 64.57 N 21.13 E
Bystraja ≃ 70 47.58 N 41.00 E
Bystřany 50 50.38 N 13.51 E
Bystrica ≃ 70 58.38 N 49.05 E
Bystřice 30 49.45 N 14.41 E
Bystřice pod Hostýnem 30 49.24 N 17.40 E
Bystrovka 75 42.47 N 75.43 E
Bystryj 76 57.50 N 73.58 E
Bystrzyca ≃ 30 51.13 N 16.54 E
Bystrzyca Kłodzka 30 50.18 N 16.38 E
Bytantaj ≃ 64 68.46 N 134.20 E
Bytča, Česko. 30 49.14 N 18.36 E
Bytča, S.S.S.R. 66 54.18 N 28.24 E
Byten' 66 52.54 N 25.29 E
Bytkov 68 48.38 N 24.26 E
Bytom (Beuthen) 30 50.22 N 18.54 E
Bytoš' 66 53.50 N 34.06 E
Bytów 30 54.11 N 17.30 E
Byumba 144 1.35 S 30.04 E
Byvalki 68 51.51 N 30.37 E
Byxelkrok 26 57.20 N 17.00 E
Bzura ≃ 30 52.23 N 20.09 E

C

Caacupé 242 25.23 S 57.09 W
Čaadajevka 70 53.09 N 45.56 E
Čaadajevo 70 55.40 N 42.02 E
Caaguazú 242 25.26 S 56.02 W
Caaguazú □[5] 242 25.00 S 55.45 W
Caamaño Sound ⋈ 172 52.49 N 129.28 W
Caapiranga 236 3.18 S 61.13 W
Caapucú 242 26.13 S 57.12 W
Caazapá 242 26.09 S 56.24 W
Caazapá □[5] 242 26.10 S 56.00 W
Cabaçal ≃ 238 16.00 S 57.42 W
Cabaceiras 240 7.30 S 36.17 W
Cabadbaran 106 9.10 N 125.38 E
Cabadiangan Plateau ⋀[1] 106 9.50 N 122.36 E
Cabagan 106 17.26 N 121.46 E
Cabaiguán 230p 22.05 N 79.30 W
Cabalete Island I 106 14.17 N 121.50 E
Cabalian 106 10.16 N 125.10 E
Cabaliana, Lago ⊜ 236 3.20 S 60.50 W
Cabalian Bay C 106 10.13 N 125.10 E
Cabalian Point ≻ 106 12.06 N 122.01 E
Caballería, Cabo de ≻ 34 40.05 N 4.05 E
Caballero Creek ≃ 270 34.11 N 118.32 W
Caballito ◆[8] 278 34.37 S 58.27 W
Caballo, Caño ≃[1] 236 8.00 N 66.45 W
Caballocoha 236 3.54 S 70.32 W
Caballones, Cayo I 230p 20.52 N 79.00 W
Caballo Reservoir ⊜[1] 190 32.58 N 107.18 W
Caballos, Cerro de los Λ 224 23.04 N 102.55 W
Cabana 238 8.24 S 78.02 W
Cabanaconde 238 15.37 S 71.59 W
Cabañas 230p 22.58 N 82.55 W
Cabanatuan 106 15.29 N 120.58 E
Cabangan 106 15.10 N 120.03 E
Cabano 176 47.41 N 68.53 W
Čabanovka 73 49.02 N 38.46 E
Cabarruyan Island I 106 16.18 N 119.59 E
Cabaun Island I 106 12.34 N 124.30 E
Cabeceiras 245 15.48 S 46.59 W
Cabecera de Dupí 226 8.22 N 81.54 W
Cabeço de Montachique 256c 38.54 N 9.11 W
Cabedelo 240 6.58 S 34.50 W
Cabeleira ≃ 245 17.58 S 50.20 W
Cabellera, Sierra de la ⋀ 190 30.55 N 109.07 W
Cabery 206 41.00 N 88.12 W
Cabeza, Arrecife ✧[2] 224 19.04 N 95.51 W
Cabeza de Lagarto, Punta ≻ 238 10.07 S 78.12 W
Cabeza del Buey 34 38.43 N 5.13 W
Cabeza de Tigre 276c 10.28 N 66.46 W
Cabezas 238 18.46 S 63.24 W
Cabiao 106 15.15 N 120.51 E
Cabiate 256b 45.40 N 9.10 E
Cabildo, Arg. 242 38.29 S 61.54 W
Cabildo, Chile 242 32.26 S 71.05 W
Cabimas 236 10.23 N 71.28 W
Cabin Branch ≃, Md., U.S. 274b 39.13 N 76.35 W
Cabin Branch ≃, Md., U.S. 274c 38.51 N 76.48 W
Cabin Creek ≃ 188 46.55 N 104.52 W
Cabinda 142 5.33 S 12.12 E
Cabinda □[5] 142 5.00 S 12.30 E
Cabinet Mountains ⋀ 192 48.08 N 115.46 W
Cabingaan Island I 106 5.41 N 121.03 E
Cabin John 198 38.58 N 77.09 W
Cabin John Creek ≃ 274b 38.58 N 77.09 W
Cabin John Creek Park ◆ 274c 38.59 N 77.09 W
Cabin John Regional Park ◆ 274c 39.02 N 77.09 W
Cabiri 142 8.52 S 13.39 E
Cabirülensar 120 37.00 N 38.59 E
Cable 180 46.13 N 91.17 W
Cable Airport ⊠ 270 34.08 N 117.41 W
Cables 152 27.59 S 123.23 E
Cabo 240 8.17 S 35.02 W
Cabo, Ciudad del → Cape Town 148 33.55 S 18.22 E
Cabo Blanco 244 47.12 S 65.45 W
Cabo Delgado □[5] 144 12.35 S 39.00 E
Cabo Frio 245 22.53 S 42.01 W
Cabo Gracias a Dios 226 14.59 N 83.10 W
Cabo Ledo 142 9.39 S 13.17 E
Cabonga, Réservoir ⊜[1] 180 47.20 N 76.35 W
Cabool 184 37.07 N 92.06 W
Caboolture 156 27.05 S 152.57 E
Cabo Raso 244 44.21 S 65.14 W
Caborca 222 30.37 N 112.06 W
Cabo Rojo 230m 18.05 N 67.09 W
Cabot, Ark., U.S. 184 34.58 N 92.01 W
Cabot, Pa., U.S. 204 40.46 N 79.46 W
Cabot, Mount Λ 178 44.31 N 71.24 W
Cabot Head ≻ 202 45.14 N 81.17 W
Cabot Strait ⋈ 176 47.20 N 59.30 W
Cabourg 32 49.17 N 0.08 W
Cabo Verde 246 21.28 S 46.24 W
Cabo Verde → Cape Verde □[1] 140a 16.00 N 24.00 W
Cabo Verde ≃ 246 21.28 S 46.17 W
Cabo Verde, Ribeirão do ≃ 246 21.20 S 44.32 W
Cabra 34 37.28 N 4.27 W
Cabra Island I 106 13.53 N 120.02 E
Cabral 228 18.15 N 71.13 W
Cabramatta 264a 33.54 S 150.56 E
Cabramurra 161b 35.58 S 148.23 E
Cabras 36 39.56 N 8.32 E
Cabras Island I 164p 13.27 N 144.40 E
Cabrel 224 20.06 N 105.14 W
Cabrera I 34 39.09 N 2.56 E
Cabrera ≃, Col. 236 3.26 N 75.07 W
Cabrera ≃, Esp. 34 42.25 N 6.49 W
Cabrera, Sierra de la ⋀ 34 42.12 N 6.40 W
Cabrera de Mataró 256d 41.32 N 2.24 E
Cabreúva 246 23.18 S 47.08 W
Cabri 174 50.37 N 108.28 W
Cabriel ≃ 34 39.14 N 1.03 W
Cabrillo National Monument ◆ 218 32.41 N 117.15 W
Cabrils 256d 41.32 N 2.22 E
Cabrobó 240 8.31 S 39.19 W
Cabruta 236 7.38 N 66.15 W
Cabrutica ≃ 236 8.03 N 64.26 W
Cabucan Island I 106 6.09 N 120.55 E
Cabucgayan 106 11.29 N 124.34 E
Cabuçu, Bra. 246 22.50 S 42.55 W
Cabuçu, Bra. 277a 22.47 S 43.32 W
Cabuçu, Bra. 277b 23.25 S 46.32 W
Cabuçu ≃ 277a 22.59 S 43.37 W
Cabuçu de Cima ≃ 246 23.31 S 46.33 W
Cabugao 106 17.48 N 120.27 E
Cabulauan Island I 106 11.23 N 120.06 E
Cabullón, Punta ≻ 230m 17.58 N 66.35 W
Cabulo 142 10.15 S 16.40 E
Cabure 236 11.08 N 69.38 W
Cabusilan Mountains ⋀ 106 15.05 N 120.22 E
Cabuta 142 9.50 S 14.48 E
Cabuya 226 9.36 N 85.06 W
Cabuyal 226 10.40 N 85.40 W
Cabuyaro 236 4.18 N 72.49 W
Caca 70 48.11 N 44.11 E
Caca, Laguna ⊜ 276b 22.57 N 82.27 W
Caçador 242 26.47 S 51.00 W
Čacahoatán 226 14.59 N 92.10 W
Čačak 38 43.53 N 20.21 E
Cacaluta 224 20.03 N 104.52 W
Cacaoui, Lac ⊜ 176 50.53 N 66.58 W
Caçapava 246 23.06 S 45.42 W
Caçapava do Sul 242 30.30 S 53.30 W
Caçapava Velha 246 23.07 S 45.39 W
Cacapon ≃ 178 39.37 N 78.16 W
Cacapon State Park ◆ 178 39.32 N 78.23 W
Cacas 120 38.23 N 41.17 E
Caccamo 36 37.56 N 13.40 E
Caccia, Capo ≻ 36 40.34 N 8.09 E
Čačenka ≃ 255b 55.46 N 37.18 E
Cacequi 242 29.53 S 54.49 W
Cáceres, Bra. 238 16.04 S 57.41 W
Cáceres, Col. 236 7.35 N 75.20 W
Cáceres, Esp. 34 39.29 N 6.22 W
Cachan 251 48.48 N 2.20 E
Cachán ≃ 224 18.11 N 103.08 W
Cacharí 242 36.24 S 59.32 W
Cache 186 34.38 N 98.38 W
Cache ≃, Ark., U.S. 184 34.42 N 91.20 W
Cache ≃, Ill., U.S. 184 37.04 N 89.10 W
Caché, Lac ⊜ 196 46.21 N 74.39 W
Cache Creek 172 50.48 N 121.19 W
Cache Creek ≃, Calif., U.S. 216 38.42 N 121.42 W
Cache Creek ≃, Calif., U.S. 218 35.06 N 117.58 W
Cache Creek, North Fork ≃ 216 38.59 N 122.30 W
Cache la Poudre ≃ 190 40.25 N 104.36 W
Cache Mountain Λ 170 65.31 N 147.20 W
Cache Peak Λ, Calif., U.S. 218 35.13 N 118.15 W
Cache Peak Λ, Idaho, U.S. 192 42.11 N 113.40 W
Cache Slough ≃ 216 38.11 N 121.40 W
Cacheu 140 12.16 N 16.10 W
Cacheu C[1] 140 12.10 N 16.21 W
Cachi 242 25.06 S 66.11 W
Cachimbo, Serra do ⋀ 240 8.30 S 55.50 W
Cachimo 142 8.21 S 21.20 E
Cachingues 142 13.05 S 16.43 E
Cachir 78 48.06 N 98.52 E
Cáchira ≃ 236 7.52 N 73.40 W
Cachkadzor 74 40.33 N 44.43 E
Cachoeira 245 12.36 S 38.58 W
Cachoeira ≃ 246 23.06 S 46.29 W
Cachoeira, Ribeirão ≃ 277b 23.38 S 46.43 W
Cachoeira, Rio da ≃ 277a 23.00 S 43.18 W
Cachoeira Alta 245 18.48 S 50.58 W
Cachoeira de Goiás 245 16.44 S 50.38 W
Cachoeira de Minas 246 22.21 S 45.47 W
Cachoeira do Sul 242 30.02 S 52.54 W
Cachoeira Paulista 246 22.40 S 45.01 W
Cachoeiras 277a 22.39 S 43.28 W
Cachoeiras de Macacu 246 22.28 S 42.39 W
Cachoeirinha 240 8.29 S 36.14 W
Cachoeirinha ≃ 246 22.36 S 46.25 W
Cachoeiro de Itapemirim 245 20.51 S 41.06 W
Cachorros, Rio dos ≃ 277a 22.52 S 43.34 W
Cachos, Punta ≻ 242 27.39 S 71.02 W
Cachos, Rio dos ≃ 277b 23.36 S 46.26 W
Cachuela Esperanza 238 10.32 S 65.38 W
Cachuma, Lake ⊜[1] 194 34.35 N 119.55 W
Cacilhas 256c 38.41 N 9.09 W
Cacimbinhas 240 9.24 S 36.59 W
Cacine 140 11.08 N 14.57 W
Căciulaţi 38 44.38 N 26.10 E
Cacnipa Island I 106 10.30 N 119.04 E
Cacocum 230p 20.44 N 76.23 W
Cacólo 142 10.07 S 19.17 E
Caconda 142 13.43 S 15.06 E
Caconde 246 21.33 S 46.38 W
Caçorotiba 246 22.51 S 42.51 W
Cacra 238 12.48 S 75.48 W
Cactus Flat ≚ 194 37.45 N 116.45 W
Cactus Peak Λ 194 37.47 N 116.53 W
Caçu 245 18.37 S 51.04 W
Cacuaco 142 8.47 S 13.22 E
Cacula 142 14.29 S 14.10 E
Caculé 245 14.30 S 42.13 W
Caculuvar ≃ 142 16.46 S 14.36 E
Caçumba, Ilha I 245 17.46 S 39.17 W
Cacuri 142 8.14 S 18.20 E
Cacuso 142 9.26 S 15.43 E
Čadan 76 51.17 N 91.35 E
Cadaqués 34 42.17 N 3.17 E
Cadariri ≃ 240 6.20 S 57.46 W
Čadca 30 49.26 N 18.48 E
Caddo, Okla., U.S. 186 34.07 N 96.16 W
Caddo, Tex., U.S. 186 32.38 N 98.40 W
Caddo ≃ 184 34.10 N 93.03 W
Caddo Creek ≃ 186 34.14 N 96.59 W
Caddo Lake ⊜[1] 184 32.42 N 94.01 W
Caddo Mills 212 33.04 N 96.14 W
Caddo Peak Λ 212 32.29 N 97.24 W
Caddy Vista 206 42.50 N 87.54 W
Cadena, Arroyo de la ≃ 186 26.17 N 104.00 W
Cadena, Cerro Λ 186 25.50 N 104.04 W
Cadena, Punta ≻ 230m 18.18 N 67.14 W
Cadenberge 48 53.46 N 9.04 E
Cadenet 56 43.44 N 5.22 E
Cadeo 56 44.58 N 9.48 E
Cader Bronwyn Λ 44 52.54 N 3.22 W
Cadereyta Jiménez 222 25.36 N 100.00 W
Cader Idris Λ 44 52.42 N 3.54 W
Cadibarrawirracanna, Lake ⊜ 152 28.52 S 135.27 E
Cadig Mountains ⋀ 106 14.05 N 122.35 E
Cadillac, Sask., Can. 174 49.44 N 107.43 W
Cadillac, Fr. 32 44.38 N 0.19 W
Cadillac, Mich., U.S. 180 44.15 N 85.24 W
Cadipietra (Steinhaus) 58 46.59 N 11.59 E
Cadishead 252 53.25 N 2.26 W
Cadix → Cádiz 34 36.32 N 6.18 W
Cádiz, Esp. 34 36.32 N 6.18 W
Cadiz, Pil. 106 10.57 N 123.18 E
Cadiz, Ind., U.S. 208 39.57 N 85.30 W
Cadiz, Ohio, U.S. 204 40.16 N 81.00 W
Cádiz, Bahía de C 34 36.32 N 6.16 W
Cádiz, Golfo de C 34 36.50 N 7.10 W
Cadiz Lake ⊜ 194 34.18 N 115.24 W
Cadlao Island I 106 11.13 N 119.21 E
Cadnam 44 50.55 N 1.35 W
Čadobec 78 58.40 N 98.51 E
Čadobec ≃ 78 58.40 N 98.50 E
Cadogan 204 40.45 N 79.35 W
Cadomin 172 53.02 N 117.20 W
Cadoneghe 58 45.26 N 11.55 E
Cadore ◆[1] 58 46.30 N 12.20 E
Cadosia 200 41.58 N 75.16 W
Cadott 180 44.57 N 91.09 W
Cadoux 152 30.47 S 117.08 E
Cadron Creek, North Fork ≃ 184 35.17 N 92.29 W
Cadure, Fosso delle ≃ 257a 41.56 N 12.12 E
Caduruan Point ≻ 106 11.45 N 124.05 E
Cadwell 182 32.20 N 83.03 W
Cady Marsh Ditch ≅ 268 41.33 N 87.29 W
Cady Mountain Λ[2] 214 48.33 N 123.07 W
Čadyr-Lunga 68 46.03 N 28.47 E
Cadzand 48 51.22 N 3.25 E
Caen 32 49.11 N 0.21 W
Caengo (Kwenge) ≃ 142 4.50 S 18.42 E
Caerano di San Marco 58 45.47 N 12.00 E
Caere ⊥ 60 42.02 N 12.07 E
Caergwrle 44 53.07 N 3.03 W
Caerleon 44 51.37 N 2.57 W
Caernarvon 44 53.08 N 4.16 W
Caernarvon Bay C 28 53.05 N 4.30 W
Caernarvon Castle ⊥ 44 53.08 N 4.16 W
Caerphilly 44 51.35 N 3.14 W
Caerphilly Castle ⊥ 44 51.34 N 3.14 W
Caersws 44 52.31 N 3.25 W
Caesar Creek ≃ 208 39.29 N 84.06 W
Caesar Creek, Anderson Fork ≃ 208 39.33 N 83.58 W
Caetanópolis 245 19.18 S 44.24 W
Caeté 245 19.54 S 43.40 W
Caeté ≃ 238 9.03 S 68.39 W
Caetité 245 14.04 S 42.29 W
Cafayate 242 26.05 S 65.58 W
Cafelândia do Leste Matogrossense 245 16.40 S 53.25 W
Cafima 142 16.39 S 16.27 E
Cafu 142 16.27 S 15.14 E
Cafuini ≃ 236 1.17 N 57.11 W
Cafundó 246 22.31 S 46.25 W
Cagaanchajrchan 78 49.25 N 94.15 E
Cagaangol 76 48.57 N 89.07 E
Cagaannuur, Mong. 76 49.32 N 89.42 E
Cagaannuur, Mong. 78 50.20 N 105.03 E
Cagaan Nuur ⊜ 78 48.10 N 99.42 E
Cagaan-Ovoo 92 45.46 N 105.12 E
Cagaan-Uul 78 49.53 N 98.42 E
Cagaan-Üür 78 50.34 N 101.34 E
Çágado ≃ 246 22.02 S 43.09 W
Čagan ≃ 70 51.12 N 51.20 E
Cagan-Aman 70 47.34 N 46.43 E
Cagan-Churtej, Chrebet ⋀ 78 51.32 N 110.00 E
Cagarra, Ilhas II 277a 23.02 S 43.12 W
Cagayan □[4] 106 18.00 N 121.50 E
Cagayan ≃, Pil. 98
106 18.22 N 121.37 E
Cagayancillo 106 9.34 N 121.12 E
Cagayan de Oro 106 8.29 N 124.39 E
Cagayan de Sulu 106 7.01 N 118.30 E
Cagayan Island I 106 9.36 N 121.14 E
Cagayan Islands II 106 9.40 N 121.16 E
Cagayan Sulu Island I 106 7.01 N 118.30 E
Čagda 64 58.45 N 130.37 E
Cageri 74 42.39 N 42.45 E
Çağış 120 39.30 N 28.01 E
Çağlarca 120 39.05 N 39.10 E
Cagli 58 43.33 N 12.39 E
Cagliari 36 39.20 N 9.00 E
Cagliari, Golfo di C 36 39.05 N 9.10 E
Čaglinka ≃ 76 53.53 N 69.42 E
Cagnano Varano 60 41.49 N 15.47 E
Cagnes-sur-Mer 56 43.40 N 7.09 E
Čagoda 66 59.10 N 35.17 E
Čagoda ≃ 66 59.05 N 35.18 E
Čagodošča ≃ 66 58.57 N 36.35 E

ENGLISH

Name	Page	Lat.°′	Long.°′

Čagra ≃ 70 52.37 N 48.15 E
Cağrankaya 74 40.47 N 40.33 E
Cagraray Island I 106 13.18 N 123.52 E
Cagua 236 10.11 N 67.27 W
Caguán ≃ 236 0.08 S 74.18 W
Caguas 230m 18.14 N 66.02 W
Cagveri 74 41.48 N 43.29 E
Cagwait 106 8.55 N 126.18 E
Cahaba ≃ 184 32.20 N 87.05 W
Cahabón 226 15.34 N 89.49 W
Cahabón ≃ 226 15.25 N 89.36 W
Cahama 142 16.17 S 14.19 E
Caha Mountains ⋀ 28 51.45 N 9.45 W
Caher 28 52.21 N 7.56 W
Cahirciveen 28 51.57 N 10.13 W
Cahokia 209 38.33 N 90.10 W
Cahokia Creek ≃ 209 38.47 N 90.01 W
Cahokia Mounds State Park ◆ 209 38.39 N 90.03 W
Cahoon Creek ≃ 269a 41.29 N 81.55 W
Cahoon Park ◆ 269a 41.29 N 81.56 W
Cahoonzie 200 41.26 N 74.43 W
Cahore Point ≻ 28 52.34 N 6.11 W
Cahors 32 44.27 N 1.26 E
Cahto Peak Λ 194 39.41 N 123.35 W
Cahuilla Indian Reservation ◆[4] 194 33.30 N 116.43 W
Cahuinari ≃ 236 1.21 S 70.44 W
Cahuita, Punta ≻ 226 9.45 N 82.49 W
Caí ≃ 242 29.56 S 51.16 W
Caia ≃ 34 38.50 N 7.05 W
Caiabis, Serra dos ⋀[1] 238 11.30 S 56.30 W
Caianda 142 11.02 S 23.31 E
Caiapó ≃, Bra. 240 8.52 S 49.36 W
Caiapó ≃, Bra. 245 15.49 S 51.53 W
Caiapó, Serra ⋀ 245 17.00 S 52.00 W
Caiapônia 245 16.57 S 51.49 W
Caiazzo 60 41.11 N 14.22 E
Caibarién 230p 22.31 N 79.28 W
Cai-bau, Dao I 100 21.10 N 107.27 E
Caibiran 106 11.34 N 124.35 E
Caiçara, Bra. 240 6.36 S 35.29 W
Caiçara, Bra. 240 5.04 S 36.03 W
Caiçara, Bra. 245 15.34 S 50.12 W
Caicara, Ven. 236 7.37 N 66.10 W
Caiçara ≃, Bra. 236 3.11 S 64.49 W
Caicara ≃, Ven. 236 7.44 N 69.04 W
Caicara de Maturín 236 9.49 N 63.36 W
Caiçaras 246 22.40 S 43.51 W
Caicedonia 236 4.20 N 75.50 W
Caicó 240 6.27 S 37.06 W
Caicos Islands II 228 21.56 N 71.58 W
Caicos Passage ⋈ 228 22.00 N 72.30 W
Caicun 95 39.28 N 117.01 E
Caieiras 246 23.22 S 46.44 W
Caieiras □[7] 277b 23.23 S 46.41 W
Caigou 90 33.16 N 114.32 E
Caihuaping 90 26.54 N 113.23 E
Caijiachang, Zhg. 97 29.53 N 105.02 E
Caijiachang, Zhg. 97 29.44 N 106.29 E
Caijiagang 97 28.55 N 106.21 E
Caijialou 94 41.24 N 121.06 E
Caijiazhen 92 34.17 N 107.39 E
Caijiazhuang 95 40.48 N 114.44 E
Caille 56 43.46 N 6.44 E
Cailloma 238 15.12 S 71.46 W
Caillou Bay C 184 29.06 N 90.56 W
Caima Bay C 106 13.42 N 122.48 E
Caimán, Islas → Cayman Islands □[2] 228 19.30 N 80.40 W
Caimán, Laguna ⊜ 236 3.38 N 69.30 W
Caimanera 230p 19.59 N 75.09 W
Caïmanes → Cayman Islands □[2] 228 19.30 N 80.40 W
Caiman Point ≻ 106 15.55 N 119.46 E
Caimbambo 142 12.58 S 14.01 E
Cain ≃ 44 52.46 N 3.08 W
Caina 238 10.11 S 76.20 W
Cain Creek ≃ 188 44.17 N 98.10 W
Cainde 142 15.42 S 13.12 E
Caine ≃ 238 18.23 S 65.21 W
Caino 58 45.38 N 10.18 E
Cains ≃ 176 46.40 N 65.47 W
Cainsdorf 50 50.41 N 12.29 E
Cainsville 184 40.26 N 93.47 W
Cai-nuoc 100 8.56 N 105.01 E
Cairari 240 2.33 S 49.07 W
Caird Coast ●[2] 9 76.00 S 24.30 W
Caire, Le → Al-Qāhirah 132 30.03 N 31.15 E
Cairnbrook 204 40.07 N 78.49 W
Cairn Curran Reservoir ⊜[1] 159 37.04 S 143.59 E
Cairngorm Mountains ⋀ 28 57.06 N 3.30 W
Cairn Mountain Λ 170 61.10 N 155.20 W
Cairnryan 42 54.58 N 5.02 W
Cairns 156 16.55 S 145.46 E
Cairns Lake ⊜ 174 51.42 N 94.30 W
Cairnsmore of Carsphairn Λ 42 55.15 N 4.12 W
Cairnsmore of Fleet Λ 42 54.59 N 4.20 W
Cairn Table Λ 42 55.29 N 4.02 W
Cairn Water ≃ 42 55.07 N 3.45 W
Cairo → Al-Qāhirah, Miṣr 132 30.03 N 31.15 E
Cairo, Ga., U.S. 182 30.53 N 84.12 W
Cairo, Ill., U.S. 184 37.00 N 89.11 W
Cairo, Nebr., U.S. 188 41.00 N 98.36 W
Cairo, N.Y., U.S. 200 42.18 N 74.00 W
Cairo, Ohio, U.S. 206 40.50 N 84.05 W
Cairo, W. Va., U.S. 178 39.13 N 81.09 W
Cairo (Almaza) Airport ⊠, Miṣr 263c 30.06 N 31.22 E
Cairo (Imbābah) Airport ⊠, Miṣr 263c 30.04 N 31.12 E
Cairo, University of ᵿ[2] 263c 30.02 N 31.02 E
Cairoçu, Pico do Λ 246 23.18 S 44.36 W
Cairofa 142 14.05 S 12.54 E
Cairo International Airport ⊠ 132 30.08 N 31.24 E
Cairo Main Station ◆[5] 263c 30.04 N 31.15 E
Cairo Montenotte 56 44.24 N 8.16 E
Cairu 245 13.30 S 39.03 W
Caister-on-Sea 44 52.39 N 1.44 E
Caistor 42 53.30 N 0.20 W
Caitingqiao 95 39.54 N 117.39 E
Caitou 142 14.28 S 13.06 E
Caiundo 142 15.46 S 17.28 E
Caiwan 92 25.50 N 110.50 E
Caixa, Rio da ≃ 245 13.02 S 42.17 W
Caixi 90 25.15 N 116.28 E
Caiyu I 90 22.39 N 115.30 E
Caiyuzhen 95 39.39 N 116.37 E
Caiza 238 20.02 S 65.40 W
Caizhuang 88 34.17 N 114.08 E
Čaja ≃, S.S.S.R. 76 58.08 N 82.57 E
Čaja ≃, S.S.S.R. 78 58.15 N 109.35 E
Cajabamba, Ec. 236 1.42 S 78.45 W
Cajabamba, Perú 238 7.37 S 78.03 W
Cajacay 238 10.10 S 77.26 W
Caja de Muertos, Isla I 230m 17.54 N 66.32 W
Cajamar 246 23.21 S 46.53 W
Cajamar □[7] 277b 23.22 S 46.52 W
Cajamarca 238 7.10 S 78.31 W
Cajamarca □[5] 238 6.15 S 78.50 W
Čajan 75 43.02 N 69.23 E
Čajan ≃ 75 42.52 N 68.56 E
Cajapió 240 2.58 S 44.48 W
Cajarc 32 44.29 N 1.50 E
Cajari 240 3.20 S 45.01 W
Cajari ≃ 240 0.48 S 51.43 W
Cajatambo 238 10.29 S 77.02 W
Čajatyn, Chrebet ⋀ 79 52.25 N 138.25 E
Cajàzeiras 240 6.54 S 38.34 W
Čajek 75 41.56 N 74.30 E

DEUTSCH

Name	Seite	Breite°′	Länge°′ E=Ost

Čajkovskij 70 56.47 N 54.09 E
Čajniče 38 43.33 N 19.04 E
Cajones ≃ 224 17.45 N 95.55 W
Cajones, Cayos II 226 16.05 N 83.12 W
Cajon Mountain Λ 218 34.16 N 117.25 W
Cajon Pass)(218 34.19 N 117.26 W
Cajon Summit)(218 34.21 N 117.27 W
Caju ◆[8] 277a 22.53 S 43.13 W
Cajuapara ≃ 240 4.17 S 47.25 W
Cajueiro 240 9.25 S 36.08 W
Cajuru 245 21.17 S 47.18 W
Cakeni 142 17.48 S 19.27 E
Cakir 78 50.27 N 103.35 E
Çakıralan 120 41.10 N 35.47 E
Çakırgöl Dağı Λ 120 40.34 N 39.42 E
Çakmak 120 37.37 N 34.19 E
Çakmak Dağı Λ 120 39.46 N 42.12 E
Čakovec 36 46.23 N 16.26 E
Čakovice ◆[8] 50 50.08 N 14.31 E
Čakung ≃ 259e 6.11 S 106.55 E
Čakva 74 41.44 N 41.45 E
Çal 120 38.05 N 29.24 E
Cala, S. Afr. 148 31.30 S 27.37 E
Cala, Tür. 74 41.05 N 43.21 E
Cala, Embalse de ⊜[1] 34 37.50 N 6.00 W
Calabacillas 224 23.13 N 99.45 W
Calabanga 106 13.42 N 123.12 E
Calabar 140 4.57 N 8.19 E
Calabasas, Arroyo ≃ 270 34.12 N 118.36 W
Calabazar 276b 23.01 N 82.22 W
Calabazas Creek ≃ 272 37.25 N 121.58 W
Calabogie 202 45.18 N 76.43 W
Calabogie Lake ⊜ 202 45.16 N 76.45 W
Calabozo 236 8.56 N 67.26 W
Calabozo, Ensenada de C 236 11.30 N 71.45 W
Calabria □[4] 36 39.00 N 16.30 E
Calabugdong Island I 106 11.06 N 119.41 E
Calaca 106 13.56 N 120.49 E
Calacuccia 36 42.20 N 9.03 E
Caladang, Mount Λ 106 14.49 N 121.21 E
Caladesi Island I 210 28.02 N 82.49 W
Caladesi Island State Park ◆ 210 28.02 N 82.48 W
Calafat 38 43.59 N 22.56 E
Calafate 244 50.20 S 72.18 W
Calafquen, Lago ⊜ 244 39.31 S 72.10 W
Calagnaan Island I 106 11.29 N 123.13 E
Calaguas Islands II 106 14.27 N 122.55 E
Calahorra 34 42.18 N 1.58 W
Calais, Fr. 46 50.57 N 1.50 E
Calais, Maine, U.S. 178 45.11 N 67.17 W
Calais, Canal de ≅ 46 50.57 N 1.51 E
Calala 142 12.59 S 23.30 E
Calalaste, Sierra de ⋀ 242 25.30 S 67.30 W
Calalzo di Cadore 58 46.27 N 12.23 E
Calama, Bra. 238 8.03 S 62.53 W
Calama, Chile 242 22.28 S 68.56 W
Calamar, Col. 236 1.58 N 72.32 W
Calamar, Col. 236 10.15 N 74.55 W
Calamarca 238 16.55 S 68.09 W
Calamba, Pil. 106 10.11 N 123.17 E
Calamba, Pil. 106 8.35 N 123.39 E
Calamba, Pil. 106 14.13 N 121.10 E
Calamian Group II 106 12.00 N 120.00 E
Calamity Creek ≃ 186 29.41 N 103.42 W
Calamocha 34 40.55 N 1.18 W
Calamus ≃ 188 41.48 N 99.09 W
Calañas 34 37.39 N 6.53 W
Calanca, Val ∨ 54 46.22 N 9.07 E
Calanda 34 40.56 N 0.14 W
Calandagan Island I 106 10.39 N 120.15 E
Calang 104 4.38 N 95.34 E
Calangianus 36 40.56 N 9.12 E
Calapan 106 13.25 N 121.10 E
Calape 106 9.54 N 123.52 E
Calapooia ≃ 192 44.38 N 123.08 W
Calapooya Mountains ⋀ 192 43.30 N 122.50 W
Călăraşi 38 44.11 N 27.20 E
Cala Ratjada 34 39.42 N 3.25 E
Calarcá 236 4.31 N 75.38 W
Calatafimi 36 37.55 N 12.52 E
Calatagan 106 13.50 N 120.38 E
Calatayud 34 41.21 N 1.38 W
Calau 50 51.45 N 13.56 E
Calauag Bay ≃ 106 14.02 N 122.13 E
Calauan 106 14.09 N 121.19 E
Calauit Island I 106 12.18 N 119.54 E
Calaveras □[6] 216 38.12 N 120.41 W
Calaveras ≃ 216 37.58 N 121.22 W
Calaveras, North Fork ≃ 216 38.12 N 120.43 W
Calaveras Big Trees State Park ◆ 216 38.16 N 120.19 W
Calaveras Point ≻ 272 37.28 N 122.03 W
Calaveras Reservoir ⊜[1] 216 37.28 N 121.49 W
Calaveritas Creek ≃ 216 38.10 N 120.40 W
Calavino 58 46.03 N 10.59 E
Calavite, Cape ≻ 106 13.27 N 120.18 E
Calavite, Mount Λ 106 13.29 N 120.24 E
Calavite Passage ⋈ 106 13.36 N 120.25 E
Calavon ≃ 56 43.51 N 5.00 E
Calawah ≃ 214 47.56 N 124.27 W
Calawah, North Fork ≃ 214 47.58 N 124.20 W
Calawah, South Fork ≃ 214 47.58 N 124.20 W
Calayan 106 19.16 N 121.28 E
Calayan Island I 106 19.20 N 121.27 E
Čalba 79 52.43 N 131.27 E
Calbayog 106 12.04 N 124.36 E
Calbe 50 51.54 N 11.46 E
Calbiga 106 11.38 N 125.01 E
Calbuco 244 41.46 S 73.08 W
Calca 238 13.20 S 71.57 W
Calçado ≃ 246 22.05 S 43.04 W
Calcasieu ≃ 184 30.05 N 93.20 W
Calcasieu Lake ⊜ 184 29.50 N 93.17 W
Calceta 236 0.51 S 80.10 W
Calcha 238 21.06 S 67.31 W
Calchaquí → Luis D'Abreu 242 29.54 S 60.18 W
Calchaquí ≃ 242 26.03 S 65.50 W
Calcinaia 60 43.41 N 10.37 E
Calcinato 58 45.27 N 10.24 E
Calcio 56 45.30 N 9.50 E
Calcium 202 44.01 N 75.51 W
Calçoene 240 2.30 N 50.57 W
Calcutta 116
262b 22.32 N 88.22 E
Calcutta, Ohio, U.S. 204 40.41 N 80.34 W
Calcutta □[5] 116 22.30 N 88.30 E
Calcutta, University of ᵿ[2] 262b 22.35 N 88.22 E
Caldaro (Kaltern) 58 46.25 N 11.14 E
Caldarola 60 43.08 N 13.13 E
Caldas, Bra. 246 21.56 S 46.23 W
Caldas, Col. 236 6.05 N 75.38 W
Caldas □[5] 236 5.15 N 75.30 W
Caldas ≃ 256d 41.31 N 2.13 E
Caldas da Rainha 34 39.24 N 9.08 W
Caldas de Reyes 34 42.36 N 8.38 W
Caldas Novas 245 17.45 S 48.38 W
Caldè 54 45.57 N 8.38 E
Caldecott Tunnel ◆[5] 272 37.52 N 122.12 W
Caldeirão, Serra do ⋀ 34 37.42 N 8.21 W
Calder ≃ 42 53.44 N 1.21 W
Caldera 242 27.04 S 70.50 W
Caldera, Punta ≻ 226 9.54 N 84.44 W
Calder and Hebble Navigation Canal ≅ 252 53.43 N 1.54 W
Calder Bridge 42 54.27 N 3.29 W
Calderbrook 252 53.39 N 2.05 W
Calderdale □[8] 252 53.44 N 2.00 W

Symbols in the index entries represent the broad categories identified in the key at the right. Symbols with superior numbers (⋀[2]) identify subcategories (see complete key on page I · 26).

Kartensymbole in dem Registerverzeichnis stellen die rechts in Schlüssel erklärten Kategorien dar. Symbole mit hochgestellten Ziffern (⋀[2]) bezeichnen Unterabteilungen einer Kategorie (vgl. vollständiger Schlüssel auf Seite I · 26).

Los símbolos incluidos en el texto del índice representan las grandes categorías identificadas con la clave a la derecha. Los símbolos con números en su parte superior (⋀[2]) identifican las subcategorías (véase la clave completa en la página I · 26).

Les symboles de l'index représentent les catégories indiquées dans la légende à droite. Les symboles suivis d'un indice (⋀[2]) représentent des sous-catégories (voir légende complète à la page I · 26).

Os símbolos incluídos no texto do índice representam as grandes categorias identificadas com a chave à direita. Os símbolos com números em sua parte superior (⋀[2]) identificam as subcategorias (veja-se a chave completa à página I · 26).

Λ Mountain	Berg	Montaña	Montagne	Montanha
⋀ Mountains	Berge	Montañas	Montagnes	Montanhas
)(Pass	Pass	Paso	Col	Passo
∨ Valley, Canyon	Tal, Cañon	Valle, Cañón	Vallée, Canyon	Vale, Canhão
≚ Plain	Ebene	Llano	Plaine	Planície
≻ Cape	Kap	Cabo	Cap	Cabo
I Island	Insel	Isla	Île	Ilha
II Islands	Inseln	Islas	Îles	Ilhas
● Other Topographic Features	Andere Topographische Objekte	Otros Elementos Topográficos	Autres données topographiques	Outros Elementos Topográficos

ESPAÑOL: Nombre — Página — Lat.°′ — Long.°′ W=Oeste
FRANÇAIS: Nom — Page — Lat.°′ — Long.°′ W=Ouest
PORTUGUÊS: Nome — Página — Lat.°′ — Long.°′ W=Oeste

Nombre / Nom / Nome	Página / Page	Lat.°′	Long.°′
Caldere	120	40.49 N	37.01 E
Calderstones Park ♠	252	53.23 N	2.54 W
Caldes	58	46.22 N	10.56 E
Caldew ≃	42	54.54 N	2.56 W
Caldey Island I	44	51.38 N	4.40 W
Caldicot	44	51.36 N	2.45 W
Caldiero	58	45.22 N	11.11 E
Çaldıran	74	39.09 N	43.55 E
Caldonazzo	58	45.59 N	11.16 E
Caldonazzo, Lago di @	58	46.01 N	11.15 E
Čaldonka	78	53.47 N	119.12 E
Caldwell, Idaho, U.S.	192	43.40 N	116.41 W
Caldwell, Kans., U.S.	188	37.02 N	97.37 W
Caldwell, N.J., U.S.	266	40.51 N	74.17 W
Caldwell, Ohio, U.S.	178	39.45 N	81.31 W
Caldwell, Tex., U.S.	212	30.32 N	96.42 W
Caldwell □6	212	29.50 N	97.40 W
Caldwell Creek ≃	204	41.37 N	79.37 W
Caldwell-Wright Airport ⊠	266	40.53 N	74.17 W
Caldy	252	53.21 N	3.10 W
Caldy Island I	44	51.38 N	4.41 W
Cale ≃	44	50.59 N	2.20 W
Caledon, Ont., Can.	202	43.52 N	80.00 W
Caledon, S. Afr.	148	34.12 S	19.23 E
Caledon ≃	148	30.31 S	26.05 E
Caledon East	202	43.52 N	79.52 W
Caledonia, Belize	222	18.14 N	88.29 W
Caledonia, N.S., Can.	176	44.22 N	65.02 W
Caledonia, Ont., Can.	202	43.04 N	79.56 W
Caledonia, Ill., U.S.	206	42.22 N	88.53 W
Caledonia, Mich., U.S.	206	42.47 N	85.31 W
Caledonia, Minn., U.S.	180	43.38 N	91.29 W
Caledonia, Miss., U.S.	184	33.39 N	88.20 W
Caledonia, N.Y., U.S.	200	42.58 N	77.51 W
Caledonia, Ohio, U.S.	204	40.38 N	82.58 W
Caledonia, Pa., U.S.	204	41.17 N	78.27 W
Caledonian Canal ⌶	28	57.20 N	4.30 W
Caledonia State Park ♠	198	39.56 N	77.29 W
Calego	142	12.10 S	23.36 E
Calella	34	41.37 N	2.40 E
Calemba	142	16.04 S	15.44 E
Calen	156	20.54 S	148.46 E
Calendžicha	74	42.37 N	42.04 E
Calenzano	60	43.51 N	11.09 E
Calera	184	33.06 N	86.45 W
Calera Creek ≃	272	37.27 N	121.54 W
Caleta Victor Rosales	224	22.57 N	102.42 W
Caleta, Punta ≻	230p	20.04 N	74.18 W
Caleta Olivia	246	46.26 S	67.32 W
Caleufú	242	35.35 S	64.33 W
Calexico	194	32.40 N	115.30 W
Calf Island I	273	42.20 N	70.54 W
Calf Islands II	266	40.59 N	73.38 W
Calfkiller ≃	184	35.49 N	85.29 W
Calf of Man I	42	54.03 N	4.48 W
Calfpasture ≃	178	37.58 N	79.28 W
Calf Pasture Point ≻	266	41.05 N	73.24 W
Çalgan	120	37.35 N	38.19 E
Calgary	172	51.03 N	114.05 W
Calhan	188	39.02 N	104.18 W
Calhariz ✦8	256c	38.44 N	9.12 W
Calhoun, Ala., U.S.	184	32.03 N	86.33 W
Calhoun, Ga., U.S.	182	34.30 N	84.57 W
Calhoun, Ky., U.S.	184	37.32 N	87.16 W
Calhoun, Mo., U.S.	184	38.28 N	93.37 W
Calhoun, Tenn., U.S.	182	35.17 N	84.45 W
Calhoun □6, Ill., U.S.	209	39.09 N	90.37 W
Calhoun □6, Mich., U.S.	206	42.14 N	85.00 W
Calhoun City	184	33.51 N	89.19 W
Calhoun Falls	182	34.06 N	82.36 W
Cali, Col.	236	3.27 N	76.31 W
Çali, Tür.	120	40.10 N	28.54 E
Calian Point ≻	106	6.07 N	125.42 E
Calicoan Island I	106	10.59 N	125.48 E
Calico Ghost Town ⊥	218	34.57 N	116.52 W
Calico Rock	184	36.07 N	92.09 W
Calicut	112	11.15 N	75.46 E
Caliente, Calif., U.S.	218	35.17 N	118.38 W
Caliente, Nev., U.S.	194	37.37 N	114.31 W
Caliente Creek ≃	218	35.17 N	118.48 W
Califon	200	40.43 N	74.50 W
California, Mo., U.S.	184	38.38 N	92.34 W
California, Pa., U.S.	204	40.04 N	79.53 W
California □3	168 / 194	37.30 N	119.30 W
California, Golfo de C	222	28.00 N	112.00 W
California, University of (U.C.L.A.) ʋ2, Calif., U.S.	270	34.04 N	118.26 W
California, University of ʋ2, Calif., U.S.	272	37.52 N	122.15 W
California Aqueduct ⌶1	194	33.52 N	117.12 W
California City	218	35.08 N	117.58 W
California Creek ≃	186	33.05 N	99.33 W
California Institute of Technology ʋ2	270	34.08 N	118.08 W
California Institution for Men ʋ	270	33.59 N	117.40 W
California Institution for Women ʋ	270	33.57 N	117.38 W
California State College (Dominguez Hills) ʋ2	270	33.52 N	118.17 W
California State Polytechnic University ʋ2	270	34.04 N	117.49 W
California State University (Northridge) ʋ2, Calif., U.S.	270	34.14 N	118.32 W
California State University (Los Angeles) ʋ2, Calif., U.S.	270	34.04 N	118.10 W
California State University (Fullerton) ʋ2, Calif., U.S.	270	33.53 N	117.53 W
California State University (Long Beach) ʋ2, Calif., U.S.	270	33.47 N	118.06 W
California State University (Hayward) ʋ2, Calif., U.S.	272	37.39 N	122.04 W
Calihualá	224	17.35 N	98.10 W
Calilegua	242	23.47 S	64.47 W
Călimănești	38	45.14 N	24.20 E
Călimani, Munții ⋏	38	47.07 N	25.03 E
Calimere, Point ≻	112	10.18 N	79.52 E
Calimesa	218	34.00 N	117.03 W
Calindo ≃	245	14.26 S	43.51 W
Calingasta	242	31.19 S	69.25 W
Calingiri	152	31.06 S	116.27 E
Calinog	106	11.07 N	122.32 E
Calintaan	106	12.35 N	120.56 E
Calion	184	33.20 N	92.32 W
Calipatria	194	33.08 N	115.31 W
Calispell Peak Λ	192	48.26 N	117.30 W
Calistoga	216	38.35 N	122.35 W
Calitri	36	40.54 N	15.27 E
Calitzdorp	148	33.33 S	21.42 E
Calixtlahuaca ⊥	224	19.20 N	99.42 W
Calizzano	56	44.14 N	8.07 E
Calka	74	41.37 N	44.05 E
Calkinskoje, Vodochranilišče @1	74	41.38 N	44.03 E
Çalkojdy	75	40.44 N	73.39 E
Calla	216	37.46 N	121.11 W
Callabonna, Lake @	156	29.45 S	140.04 E
Callabonna Creek ≃	156	29.38 S	140.08 E
Callac	32	48.24 N	3.26 W
Callaghan, Mount Λ	194	39.42 N	116.57 W
Callahan	182	30.34 N	81.49 W
Callahans	266	40.58 N	74.37 W
Callan	28	52.33 N	7.23 W
Callander, Ont., Can.	180	46.13 N	79.23 W
Callander, Scot., U.K.	28	56.15 N	4.14 W
Callang	106	17.02 N	121.38 E
Callanmarca	238	12.52 S	74.38 W
Callanna	156	29.38 S	137.55 E
Callantsoog	48	52.49 N	4.41 E
Callao, Perú	238 / 276d	12.04 S	77.09 W
Callao, Va., U.S.	198	37.58 N	76.34 W
Callao □4	276d	12.04 S	77.09 W
Callas	56	43.35 N	6.32 E
Callaway	188	41.17 N	99.56 W
Callaway □6	209	38.50 N	91.52 W
Calle	52	51.20 N	8.13 E
Callensburg	204	41.08 N	79.33 W
Callery	204	40.45 N	80.02 W
Call Hill Λ2	200	42.13 N	77.40 W
Calliano, It.	56	45.00 N	8.15 E
Calliano, It.	58	45.56 N	11.05 E
Calliaqua	231h	13.08 N	61.12 W
Callicoon	200	41.46 N	75.03 W
Callicoon Center	200	41.50 N	74.57 W
Calliham	186	28.29 N	98.21 W
Calling Lake	172	55.15 N	113.12 W
Calling Lake @	172	55.13 N	113.15 W
Callington, Austl.	158b	35.07 S	139.02 E
Callington, Eng., U.K.	44	50.30 N	4.18 W
Calliope	156	24.00 S	151.12 E
Callosa de Ensarriá	34	38.39 N	0.07 W
Callosa de Segura	34	38.08 N	0.52 W
Calloway Canal ⌶	216	35.24 N	119.01 W
Calmar, Alta., Can.	172	53.16 N	113.49 W
Calmar → Kalmar, Sve.	26	56.40 N	16.22 E
Calmar, Iowa, U.S.	180	43.11 N	91.52 W
Călmățui ≃	38	44.50 N	27.50 E
Calmazzo	60	43.40 N	12.46 E
Calmbach	52	48.46 N	8.35 E
Çalm Lake @	180	48.46 N	92.04 W
Čal'mny-Varre	24	67.10 N	37.33 E
Calna	24	61.55 N	34.01 E
Calnali	224	20.55 N	98.35 W
Calne	44	51.27 N	2.00 W
Calobre	226	8.19 N	80.51 W
Calola	142	16.30 S	17.51 E
Calolbon	106	13.36 N	124.06 E
Calolziocorte	56	45.48 N	9.26 E
Calonne-Ricouart	46	50.29 N	2.29 E
Caloocan	259f	14.39 N	120.58 E
Caloosahatchee ≃	210	26.31 N	82.01 W
Caloosahatchee Canal ⌶	210	26.46 N	81.27 W
Caloote	158b	34.58 S	139.16 E
Calore ≃	36	41.11 N	14.28 E
Calotlán ≃	224	22.06 N	103.42 W
Caloundra	156	26.48 S	153.08 E
Calpan	224	19.06 N	98.27 W
Calpe	34	38.39 N	0.03 E
Calpulalpan	224	19.35 N	98.35 W
Calpy	70	55.05 N	53.06 E
Calshot	44	50.49 N	1.19 W
Calstock	44	50.30 N	4.12 W
Caltagirone	36	37.14 N	14.31 E
Caltanissetta	36	37.29 N	14.04 E
Çaltılıbük	120	39.57 N	28.36 E
Čaltyr'	73	47.17 N	39.30 E
Caluango	142	8.21 S	19.40 E
Calubian	106	11.27 N	124.26 E
Calucinga	142	11.18 S	16.12 E
Călugăreni	38	44.07 N	26.01 E
Caluire-et-Cuire	56	45.48 N	4.51 E
Calulo	142	10.00 S	14.53 E
Calumbolaca	142	9.09 S	13.48 E
Calumet, Mich., U.S.	180	47.14 N	88.27 W
Calumet, Minn., U.S.	180	47.19 N	93.17 W
Calumet, Pa., U.S.	204	40.13 N	79.28 W
Calumet ≃	268	41.44 N	87.32 W
Calumet, Lake @	268	41.41 N	87.35 W
Calumet City	206	41.37 N	87.31 W
Calumet Harbor C	268	41.44 N	87.32 W
Calumet Park	268	41.44 N	87.33 W
Calumet Park ♠	268	41.43 N	87.32 W
Calumet Sag Channel ⌶	268	41.42 N	87.57 W
Calunda	142	12.06 S	23.23 E
Caluquembe	142	13.47 S	14.44 E
Calusa Island I	106	9.37 N	121.01 E
Caluso	56	45.18 N	7.53 E
Caluya Island I	106	11.55 N	121.34 E
Calvados □5	32	49.10 N	0.30 W
Calvert, Ala., U.S.	184	31.09 N	88.01 W
Calvert, Tex., U.S.	212	30.59 N	96.40 W
Calvert □6	198	38.33 N	76.35 W
Calvert ≃	154	16.17 S	137.44 E
Calvert Hills	154	17.15 S	137.20 E
Calvert Island I	172	51.35 N	128.00 W
Calverton, Md., U.S.	274c	39.03 N	76.56 W
Calverton, N.Y., U.S.	197	40.55 N	72.45 W
Calvi	32	42.34 N	8.45 E
Calvi, Monte Λ	60	43.05 N	10.37 E
Calvi dell'Umbria	60	42.24 N	12.34 E
Calvillo	224	21.51 N	102.43 W
Calvin, Okla., U.S.	186	34.58 N	96.15 W
Calvin, Pa., U.S.	204	40.20 N	78.02 W
Calvinia	148	31.25 S	19.45 E
Calvisano	58	45.20 N	10.20 E
Calvo, Monte Λ	60	41.44 N	15.46 E
Calvörde	50	52.23 N	11.17 E
Calw	52	48.43 N	8.44 E
Calwa	216	36.42 N	119.46 W
Calypso	182	35.09 N	78.06 W
Calzada	238	6.02 S	77.02 W
Cam ≃	44	52.21 N	0.15 E
Camabatela	142	8.11 S	15.22 E
Camaçari	245	12.41 S	38.18 W
Camachigama, Lac @	180	47.50 N	76.19 W
Camacho	222	24.25 N	102.18 W
Camacosni	226	14.57 N	85.08 W
Camaguán	236	8.06 N	67.36 W
Camagüey	230p	21.23 N	77.55 W
Camagüey □4	230p	21.30 N	78.10 W
Camagüey, Archipiélago de II	230p	22.18 N	78.00 W
Camaiore	58	43.56 N	10.18 E
Camaiú ≃	238	5.30 S	59.42 W
Camajuani	230p	22.28 N	79.44 W
Camaldol, Eromo di ʋ1	60	43.46 N	11.47 E
Camaldoli ʋ1	58	43.48 N	11.46 E
Camamu	245	13.57 S	39.07 W
Camanà	238	16.37 S	72.42 W
Camanche	180	41.47 N	90.15 W
Camanche Reservoir @1	216	38.13 N	120.58 W
Camandag Island I	106	11.59 N	124.25 E
Camanducaia	246	22.46 S	46.09 W
Camanducaia ≃, Bra.	246	22.39 S	46.58 W
Camanducaia ≃, Bra.	246	22.55 S	46.25 W
Camano Island I	214	48.10 N	122.30 W
Camaoi ≃	240	3.12 S	48.04 W
Camapuã	245	19.30 S	54.05 W
Camaquã	242	30.51 S	51.49 W
Camaquã ≃	242	31.17 S	51.47 W
Camará	236	3.55 S	62.44 W
Camarajibe	240	8.01 S	34.58 W
Camararé ≃	238	12.15 S	58.55 W
Camarat, Cap ≻	56	43.12 N	6.41 E
Camarda	60	42.23 N	13.29 E
Çamardı	120	37.50 N	35.00 E
Camarès	32	43.49 N	2.53 E
Camargo	238	20.39 S	65.13 W
Camarillo	218	34.13 N	119.02 W
Camarillo Heights	218	34.14 N	119.02 W
Camariñas, Esp.	34	43.09 N	9.15 W
Camariñas, Esp.	34	43.07 N	9.10 W
Camarines Norte □4	106	14.10 N	122.40 E
Camarines Sur □4	106	13.35 N	123.20 E
Camarón, Arroyo ≃	186	27.08 N	100.00 W
Camarón, Cabo ≻	226	16.00 N	85.05 W
Camaronero, Laguna C	224	23.00 N	106.07 W
Camarones	244	44.48 S	65.42 W
Camarones ≃	238	19.11 S	70.17 W
Camarones, Bahía C	244	44.45 S	65.34 W
Camas, Esp.	34	37.24 N	6.02 W
Camas, Wash., U.S.	214	45.35 N	122.24 W
Camas Creek ≃, Idaho, U.S.	192	44.53 N	114.44 W
Camas Creek ≃, Idaho, U.S.	192	43.20 N	114.24 W
Camas Creek ≃, Idaho, U.S.	192	43.53 N	112.11 W
Camas Creek ≃, Oreg., U.S.	192	45.01 N	118.59 W
Camatá ≃	238	15.09 S	68.26 W
Camatambo	142	6.30 S	15.18 E
Ca-mau → Quan-long	100	9.11 N	105.08 E
Ca-mau, Mui ≻	100	8.38 N	104.44 E
Camaxilo	142	8.21 S	18.56 E
Camba	102	4.54 S	119.50 E
Camba Cassai	142	9.40 S	19.18 E
Cambados	34	42.30 N	8.48 W
Cambaquara	246	23.54 S	45.27 W
Cambará	245	23.03 S	50.05 W
Çambar Dağı Λ	120	40.21 N	42.26 E
Cambay	110	22.18 N	72.37 E
Camberg	52	50.18 N	8.16 E
Camberley	44	51.21 N	0.45 W
Camberwell	159	37.50 S	145.04 E
Camberwell ✦8	250	51.28 N	0.05 W
Cambiano	56	44.58 N	7.47 E
Camblaya ≃	238	20.57 S	64.45 W
Cambo	42	55.10 N	1.57 W
Cambo ≃	142	7.40 S	17.17 E
Cambodge → Cambodia □1	100	13.00 N	105.00 E
Cambodia □1	98 / 100	13.00 N	105.00 E
Cambois	42	55.10 N	1.31 W
Cambonda, Serra ⋏	142	12.06 S	14.00 E
Camboon	156	25.03 S	150.26 E
Cambooya	161a	27.42 S	151.52 E
Camboriú	242	27.01 S	48.38 W
Camboriú, Ponta do ≻	242	25.10 S	47.55 W
Camborne	28	50.12 N	5.19 W
Cambra	200	41.12 N	76.18 W
Cambrai, Austl.	158b	34.39 S	139.17 E
Cambrai, Fr.	46	50.10 N	3.14 E
Cambremer	46	49.09 N	0.03 E
Cambria, Calif., U.S.	216	35.34 N	121.05 W
Cambria, Ind., U.S.	206	40.22 N	86.33 W
Cambria, Mich., U.S.	206	41.49 N	84.40 W
Cambria, Wis., U.S.	180	43.33 N	89.06 W
Cambria □6	204	40.29 N	79.16 W
Cambria Ice Field ⊼	172	55.55 N	129.30 W
Cambrian Mountains ⋏	28	52.35 N	3.35 W
Cambrian Park	216	37.16 N	121.56 W
Cambridge (Galt), Ont., Can.	202	43.22 N	80.19 W
Cambridge, N.Z.	162	37.53 S	175.28 E
Cambridge, Eng., U.K.	44	52.13 N	0.08 E
Cambridge, Idaho, U.S.	192	44.34 N	116.41 W
Cambridge, Ill., U.S.	180	41.18 N	90.12 W
Cambridge, Iowa, U.S.	180	41.54 N	93.32 W
Cambridge, Md., U.S.	198	38.34 N	76.04 W
Cambridge, Mass., U.S.	197	42.22 N	71.06 W
Cambridge, Minn., U.S.	180	45.31 N	93.14 W
Cambridge, Nebr., U.S.	188	40.17 N	100.10 W
Cambridge, N.Y., U.S.	200	43.02 N	73.23 W
Cambridge, Ohio, U.S.	198	40.02 N	81.35 W
Cambridge, Wis., U.S.	206	43.00 N	89.01 W
Cambridge Bay	166	69.03 N	105.05 W
Cambridge City	208	39.49 N	85.10 W
Cambridge Fiord C2	172	71.20 N	74.44 W
Cambridge Gulf C	154	14.55 S	128.15 E
Cambridge Park	264a	33.45 S	150.43 E
Cambridge Reservoir @1	273	42.24 N	71.16 W
Cambridgeshire □6	44	52.20 N	0.05 E
Cambridge Springs	204	41.48 N	80.04 W
Cambrils	34	41.04 N	1.03 E
Cambuci	245	21.34 S	41.55 W
Cambuci ✦8	277b	23.34 S	46.37 W
Cambui	246	22.37 S	46.04 W
Cambulo	142	7.48 S	21.14 E
Cambuquira	246	21.51 S	45.18 W
Cambural	276c	10.26 N	66.59 W
Camburg	50	51.03 N	11.42 E
Camburu ≃	246	23.41 S	45.28 W
Çamby	208	39.40 N	86.19 W
Čamčakly	118	37.56 N	63.06 E
Camden, Austl.	160	34.03 S	150.42 E
Camden, S. Afr.	148	26.38 S	30.07 E
Camden, Ala., U.S.	184	31.59 N	87.17 W
Camden, Ark., U.S.	184	33.35 N	92.50 W
Camden, Del., U.S.	198	39.07 N	75.33 W
Camden, Ill., U.S.	209	40.09 N	90.46 W
Camden, Ind., U.S.	206	40.37 N	86.32 W
Camden, Maine, U.S.	178	44.12 N	69.04 W
Camden, Mich., U.S.	206	41.45 N	84.46 W
Camden, Miss., U.S.	184	32.47 N	89.50 W
Camden, N.J., U.S.	198	39.57 N	75.07 W
Camden, N.C., U.S.	182	36.20 N	76.10 W
Camden, N.Y., U.S.	200	43.20 N	75.45 W
Camden, Ohio, U.S.	208	39.38 N	84.39 W
Camden, S.C., U.S.	182	34.16 N	80.36 W
Camden, Tenn., U.S.	184	36.04 N	88.06 W
Camden, Tex., U.S.	212	30.55 N	94.44 W
Camden □6, N.J., U.S.	198	39.57 N	75.07 W
Camden □6, N.C., U.S.	198	36.28 N	76.21 W
Camden ✦8	44	51.33 N	0.10 W
Camden, Grupo II	244	54.40 S	71.58 W
Camden Aerodrome ⊠	264a	34.03 S	150.41 E
Camden Bay C	170	70.00 N	145.00 W
Camden Hills State Park ♠	178	44.17 N	69.05 W
Camden Lake @	208	44.25 N	76.52 W
Camden Station ✦5	274b	39.17 N	76.37 W
Camdenton	184	38.00 N	92.45 W
Camedo	54	46.09 N	8.37 E
Cameia, Parque Nacional da ♠	142	11.45 S	21.20 E
Camel ≃	44	50.33 N	4.55 W
Camel, Mount Λ	159	36.45 S	144.43 E
Camelback Mountain Λ, Alaska, U.S.	170	62.33 N	157.20 W
Camelback Mountain Λ	200	41.03 N	75.21 W
Camelford	44	50.37 N	4.41 W
Camels Back Λ	162	36.58 S	175.35 E
Camels Hump Λ	178	44.19 N	72.53 W
Cameo Acres	272	37.51 N	121.58 W
Camerano	56	43.32 N	13.33 E
Cameri	56	45.30 N	8.39 E
Cameri, Aeroporto ⊠	256b	45.32 N	8.40 E
Camerino	60	43.08 N	13.04 E
Cameron, La., U.S.	184	29.48 N	93.19 W
Cameron, Mo., U.S.	184	39.44 N	94.14 W
Cameron, N.Y., U.S.	200	42.12 N	77.24 W
Cameron, Pa., U.S.	204	41.27 N	78.10 W
Cameron, S.C., U.S.	182	33.33 N	80.43 W
Cameron, Tex., U.S.	212	30.51 N	96.59 W
Cameron, W. Va., U.S.	178	39.50 N	80.34 W
Cameron, Wis., U.S.	180	45.25 N	91.44 W
Cameron □6	204	41.31 N	78.14 W
Cameron ≃	214	49.17 N	124.38 W
Cameron, Lac @	196	46.06 N	74.50 W
Cameron Highlands	104	4.29 N	101.27 E
Cameron Hills ⋏2	166	59.48 N	118.00 W
Cameron Lake @, B.C., Can.	214	49.17 N	124.37 W
Cameron Lake @, Ont., Can.	202	44.34 N	78.45 W
Cameron Mills	200	42.11 N	77.22 W
Cameron Mountains ⋏	162	46.00 S	167.00 E
Cameron Run ≃	274c	38.48 N	77.04 W
Cameroon □1	124	6.00 N	12.00 E
Camerota	36	40.02 N	15.23 E
Cameroun → Cameroon □1	124	6.00 N	12.00 E
Cameroun, Mont Λ	140	4.12 N	9.11 E
Cameroun Occidental □4	142	5.30 N	9.30 E
Cameroun Oriental □4	142	6.00 N	13.00 E
Camerún → Cameroon □1	124	6.00 N	12.00 E
Cametá	240	2.15 S	49.30 W
Camfield	154	17.09 S	131.21 E
Camiçi	120	40.40 N	37.00 E
Camiguin □4	106	9.15 N	124.40 E
Camiguin Island I, Pil.	106	18.56 N	121.55 E
Camiguin Island I, Pil.	106	9.11 N	124.42 E
Camiling	106	15.42 N	120.24 E
Camilla	182	31.14 N	84.12 W
Camillus	200	43.02 N	76.19 W
Camin	50	53.27 N	10.58 E
Camiña	238	19.18 S	69.26 W
Caminha	34	41.52 N	8.50 W
Camino	216	38.44 N	120.41 W
Camiranga	240	1.48 S	46.17 W
Camiri	238	20.03 S	63.31 W
Camisano Vicentino	58	45.31 N	11.43 E
Camisea ≃	238	11.35 S	72.58 W
Camiyanı	120	40.52 N	38.38 E
Camlad ≃	44	52.36 N	3.10 W
Çamlıbel	120	40.05 N	36.29 E
Çamlıca	120	40.46 N	26.39 E
Çamlıdere	120	40.30 N	32.29 E
Cam-lo	100	16.49 N	106.59 E
Čamlyk ≃	74	44.46 N	40.45 E
Cammal	200	41.24 N	77.28 W
Cammin → Kamień Pomorski	30	53.58 N	14.46 E
Camoapa	226	12.23 N	85.31 W
Camocim	240	2.54 S	40.50 W
Camogli	56	44.21 N	9.09 E
Camonica, Val V	58	46.00 N	10.20 E
Camooweal	156	19.55 S	138.07 E
Camopi ≃	240	3.11 N	52.20 W
Camorim ≃	277a	22.59 S	43.25 W
Camorim, Reprêsa do @1	277a	22.58 S	43.27 W
Camorta Island I	100	8.08 N	93.30 E
Camotes Islands II	106	10.40 N	124.24 E
Camotes Sea ⊤2	106	10.30 N	124.15 E
Camp □6	212	33.00 N	94.58 W
Campagna	36	40.40 N	15.08 E
Campagna di Roma ✦1	60	41.50 N	12.35 E
Campagna Lupia	58	45.21 N	12.06 E
Campagnano di Roma	60	42.08 N	12.23 E
Campagnatico	60	42.53 N	11.16 E
Campagne-lès-Hesdin	46	50.24 N	1.52 E
Campaign	184	35.46 N	85.38 W
Campamento	226	14.33 N	86.42 W
Campamento, Cerro Λ	276a	19.18 N	99.17 W
Campamento Alianza	238	20.46 S	69.42 W
Campana	248	34.10 S	58.57 W
Campana, Isla I	244	48.20 S	75.15 W
Campanario	34	38.52 N	5.37 W
Campanario, Cerro de Λ	238	5.57 S	77.31 W
Campanella, Punta ≻	60	40.34 N	14.19 E
Campanha	246	21.50 S	45.24 W
Campania □4	36	41.00 N	14.30 E
Camparada	256b	45.39 N	9.19 E
Campaspe ≃, Austl.	156	21.00 S	146.24 E
Campaspe ≃, Austl.	159	36.41 S	144.31 E
Campbell, S. Afr.	148	28.48 S	23.44 E
Campbell, Calif., U.S.	216	37.17 N	121.57 W
Campbell, Mo., U.S.	184	36.30 N	90.04 W
Campbell, Nebr., U.S.	188	40.18 N	98.44 W
Campbell, N.Y., U.S.	200	42.14 N	77.12 W
Campbell, Ohio, U.S.	204	41.05 N	80.36 W
Campbell, Tex., U.S.	212	33.09 N	95.57 W
Campbell □6	208	38.55 N	84.20 W
Campbell, Cape ≻	162	41.44 S	174.17 E
Campbell Airport ⊠, Ill., U.S.	268	42.20 N	88.04 W
Campbell Airport ⊠, Pa., U.S.	269b	40.21 N	80.11 W
Campbellfield	264b	37.41 S	144.57 E
Campbellford	202	44.18 N	77.48 W
Campbell Hall	200	41.27 N	74.16 W
Campbell Hill Λ2	206	40.22 N	83.43 W
Campbell Island	172	52.10 N	128.09 W
Campbell Island I	9	52.30 S	169.05 E
Campbell Lake @	172	50.01 N	125.27 W
Campbell Plateau ⌘3	9	56.00 S	165.00 E
Campbellpore	113	33.46 N	72.22 E
Campbell Range ⋏	170	61.08 N	129.45 W
Campbell Rise ⌘3	4	56.00 S	165.00 E
Campbell River	172	50.01 N	125.15 W
Campbells ≃	160	33.42 S	149.37 E
Campbells Bay	178	45.44 N	76.36 W
Campbellsburg, Ind., U.S.	208	38.39 N	86.16 W
Campbellsburg, Ky., U.S.	208	38.31 N	85.12 W
Campbell Slough ≃	216	39.22 N	121.51 W
Campbellsport	180	43.36 N	88.17 W
Campbells River	160	33.54 S	149.37 E
Campbells Run ≃	269b	40.24 N	80.05 W
Campbellsville	184	37.21 N	85.20 W
Campbellton, N.B., Can.	176	48.00 N	66.40 W
Campbellton, Newf., Can.	176	49.17 N	54.56 W
Campbellton, P.E.I., Can.	176	46.47 N	64.18 W
Campbellton, Fla., U.S.	182	30.57 N	85.24 W
Campbell Town, Austl.	156	41.56 S	147.29 E
Campbelltown, Austl.	158b	34.53 S	138.40 E
Campbelltown, Austl.	160	34.04 S	150.49 E
Campbelltown, Pa., U.S.	198	40.17 N	76.35 W
Campbellville	202	43.29 N	79.59 W
Campbeltown	42	55.26 N	5.36 W
Camp Creek ≃, Calif., U.S.	216	38.38 N	120.40 W
Camp Creek ≃, Mo., U.S.	209	39.02 N	91.12 W
Camp Creek Lake @1	212	31.03 N	96.19 W
Camp David ʋ	198	39.38 N	77.28 W
Camp de Frileuse ■	251	48.52 N	1.55 E
Camp de Satory ■	251	48.47 N	2.06 E
Camp Dix	208	38.29 N	83.17 W
Camp Douglas	180	43.55 N	90.16 W
Campeche	222	19.51 N	90.32 W
Campeche, Bahía de C	222	20.00 N	94.00 W
Campechuela	230p	20.14 N	77.17 W
Campegine	58	44.45 N	10.32 E
Campello Monti	54	45.56 N	8.15 E
Camperdown, Austl.	159	38.14 S	143.09 E
Camperdown, S. Afr.	148	29.42 S	30.33 E
Camperville	174	51.59 N	100.09 W
Campestre, Bra.	246	21.16 S	42.56 W
Campestre, Bra.	246	21.43 S	46.15 W
Camp Fuchinobe (United States) ■	84	35.34 N	139.10 E
Cam-pha	100	21.01 N	107.19 E
Camp Hill, Ala., U.S.	184	32.43 N	85.39 W
Camp Hill, Pa., U.S.	178	40.14 N	76.55 W
Campi Bisenzio	60	43.49 N	11.08 E
Campidano ✦1	36	39.30 N	8.50 E
Campiglia dei Fosci	60	43.27 N	11.03 E
Campiglia Marittima	60	43.03 N	10.37 E
Campillo de Llerena	34	38.30 N	5.50 W
Campillos	34	37.03 N	4.51 W
Campina ✦1	34	37.45 N	4.45 W
Campina Grande	240	7.13 S	35.53 W
Campinas	246	22.54 S	47.05 W
Campina Verde	245	19.31 S	49.28 W
Campinho, Rio do ≃	277a	22.52 S	43.37 W
Campione del Garda	58	45.45 N	10.45 E
Campitello	58	46.28 N	11.44 E
Camp King	140	4.55 N	7.58 W
Camp Lake	206	42.32 N	88.09 W
Camp Lake @	202	45.27 N	78.54 W
Camp Leger de Melun ■	251	48.34 N	2.34 E
Camp Lejeune Marine Corps Base ■	182	34.40 N	77.21 W
Campli	60	42.43 N	13.41 E
Camplong	102	10.02 S	123.55 E
Campo, Cam.	142	2.22 N	9.49 E
Campo, Moç.	146	17.44 S	36.21 E
Campo, Colo., U.S.	188	37.06 N	102.35 W
Campo, Réserve de ✦4	142	2.35 N	9.57 E
Campo Alegre, Bra.	240	9.48 S	36.21 W
Campoalegre, Col.	236	2.41 N	75.20 W
Campo Alegre de Goiás	245	17.39 S	47.45 W
Campobasso	60	41.34 N	14.39 E
Campobasso □4	60	41.38 N	14.35 E
Campobello di Licata	36	37.15 N	13.55 E
Campobello di Mazara	36	37.38 N	12.45 E
Campobello Island I	176	44.53 N	66.55 W
Campo Belo	245	20.53 S	45.16 W
Campo Blenio	54	46.34 N	8.56 E
Campo Catino	60	41.48 N	13.20 E
Campocologno	54	46.13 N	10.08 E
Campo Cumbica ■	277b	23.27 S	46.28 W
Campo da Bocaina	246	22.17 S	46.06 W
Campodarsego	58	45.30 N	11.54 E
Campo de Criptana	34	39.24 N	3.07 W
Campo de la Cruz	236	10.23 N	74.53 W
Campo de Marte ♠	276d	12.04 S	77.03 W
Campo de Marte ■	277b	23.30 S	46.37 W
Campo de Mayo ■	278	34.32 S	58.38 W
Campo di Giove	60	42.01 N	14.03 E
Campo di Trens (Trens)	58	46.52 N	11.29 E
Campo do Coelho	246	22.15 S	42.39 W
Campodolcino	54	46.24 N	9.21 E
Campo Erê	242	26.23 S	53.03 W
Campo Florido	245	19.47 S	48.35 W
Campoformido	58	46.01 N	13.09 E
Campo Formoso	240	10.31 S	40.20 W
Campogalliano	58	44.41 N	10.50 E
Campo Gallo	242	26.35 S	62.51 W
Campo Grande, Arg.	242	27.13 S	54.58 W
Campo Grande, Bra.	245	20.27 S	54.37 W
Campo Grande ✦8, Bra.	246	22.54 S	43.34 W
Campo Grande ✦8, Port.	256c	38.45 N	9.09 W
Campo Indian Reservation ✦4	194	32.40 N	116.20 W
Cam Point ≻	154	8.55 S	152.30 E
Campo Largo, Arg.	242	26.48 S	60.50 W
Campo Largo, Bra.	242	25.26 S	49.32 W
Campolaro	58	45.55 N	10.20 E
Campolasta (Astfeld)	58	46.40 N	11.22 E
Campo Libertad ■	276b	23.05 N	82.26 W
Campolide	246	21.36 S	43.53 W
Campolieto	60	41.38 N	14.46 E
Campo Ligure	56	44.32 N	8.42 E
Campo Limpo	246	23.12 S	46.48 W
Campo Maior, Bra.	240	4.49 S	42.10 W
Campo Maior, Port.	34	39.01 N	7.04 W
Campomarino	60	41.57 N	15.02 E
Campo Militar Número Uno ■	276a	19.27 N	99.14 W
Campo Morado	224	17.35 N	100.05 W
Campomorone	56	44.30 N	8.53 E
Campo Mourão	245	24.03 S	52.22 W
Campo Nôvo	242	27.42 S	53.48 W
Campo Pequeno ♠	256c	38.44 N	9.08 W
Campo Quijano	242	24.55 S	65.39 W
Camporgiano	58	44.09 N	10.20 E
Camporredondo	238	6.07 S	78.21 W
Campos	245	21.45 S	41.18 W
Campos Altos	245	19.41 S	46.10 W
Camposampiero	58	45.34 N	11.56 E
Campo Santo, Arg.	242	24.40 S	65.06 W
Camposanto, It.	58	44.47 N	11.08 E
Campos Belos	245	13.03 S	46.53 W
Campos de Cunha	246	22.55 S	44.49 W
Campos do Jordão	246	22.44 S	45.35 W
Campos Elyseos	246	22.42 S	43.17 W
Campos Gerais	246	21.14 S	45.46 W
Campos Novos	242	27.24 S	51.12 W
Campos Sales	240	7.04 S	40.23 W
Campo Tencia, Pizzo Λ	54	46.26 N	8.43 E
Campotosto	60	42.33 N	13.22 E
Campotosto, Lago di @	60	42.32 N	13.22 E
Campo Tures (Sand in Taufers)	58	46.55 N	11.57 E
Campovalano	60	42.44 N	13.40 E
Campoyo Point ≻	106	9.38 N	123.09 E
Camp Pendleton Marine Corps Base ■	218	33.19 N	117.18 W
Camp Point	209	40.03 N	91.04 W
Camp Ruby	212	30.42 N	94.45 W
Camps-en-Amiénois	28	49.52 N	1.58 E
Campsie	264a	33.55 S	151.06 E
Campsie Fells ⋏2	42	56.02 N	4.12 W
Camp Springs	198	38.48 N	76.55 W
Campti	184	31.54 N	93.07 W
Campton	182	37.44 N	83.33 W
Camptonville	216	39.27 N	121.03 W
Camptown	200	41.44 N	76.14 W
Campus	206	41.01 N	88.18 W
Campuya ≃	236	1.43 S	73.30 W
Camp Verde	190	34.34 N	111.51 W
Campville	200	42.06 N	76.09 W
Camp Wood	186	29.40 N	100.01 W
Cam-ranh	100	11.54 N	109.09 E
Cam-ranh, Vinh C	100	11.53 N	109.10 E
Camrose, Alta., Can.	172	53.01 N	112.50 W
Camrose, Wales, U.K.	44	51.51 N	5.01 W
Camsell ≃	166	65.40 N	118.07 W
Camu ≃	240	1.15 N	57.09 W
Camucia	60	43.16 N	11.58 E
Camucuio	142	14.12 S	13.20 E
Camurí Chiquito, Quebrada ≃	276c	10.37 N	66.52 W
Camuy	230m	18.29 N	66.51 W
Çam-xuyen	100	18.15 N	106.00 E
Čamyndy	75	41.37 N	74.20 E
Čamzinka	70	54.24 N	45.47 E
Çan, Tür.	120	40.02 N	27.03 E
Çan, Tür.	120	39.09 N	40.13 E
Can ≃	44	51.48 N	0.25 E
Čaňa	30	48.37 N	21.18 E
Canaan, Conn., U.S.	197	42.02 N	73.20 W
Canaan, Fla., U.S.	210	28.48 N	81.14 W
Canaan, Ind., U.S.	208	38.52 N	85.25 W
Canaan, N.Y., U.S.	200	42.25 N	73.27 W
Canaan, Vt., U.S.	178	45.00 N	71.32 W
Canaan ≃	176	45.55 N	65.47 W
Canaan Lake @	266	40.47 N	73.01 W
Canaan Valley State Park ♠	178	39.02 N	79.32 W
Cana Brava ≃, Bra.	245	13.11 S	48.11 W
Cana Brava ≃, Bra.	245	12.12 S	48.40 W
Cana Brava, Córrego ≃	245	16.50 S	44.56 W
Cana Brava, Ribeirão ≃	245	16.35 S	46.34 W
Canaçari, Lago @	240	2.57 S	58.15 W
Canachí	222	24.04 N	107.05 W
Canada □1	166	60.00 N	95.00 W
Canada Bay C	176	50.43 N	56.10 W
Canada Dam ✦6	116	24.10 N	87.10 E
Cañada de Caracheo	224	20.22 N	100.57 W
Cañada de Gómez	242	32.49 S	61.24 W
Cañada Honda	242	31.59 S	68.33 W
Canada Lake @	200	43.10 N	74.32 W
Cañada Nieto	248	33.43 S	58.05 W
Canadarago Lake @	200	42.48 N	75.01 W
Cañada Verde → Villa Huidobro	242	34.50 S	64.35 W
Canadaway Creek ≃	204	42.28 N	79.22 W
Canadensis	200	41.12 N	75.15 W
Canadian	186	35.55 N	100.23 W
Canadian ≃	186	35.27 N	95.03 W
Canadian, Deep Fork ≃	186	35.28 N	95.50 W
Canadian Forces Base Borden ■	202	44.17 N	79.55 W
Canadian Forces Base Montreal ■	265a	45.31 N	73.25 W
Canadice Lake @	200	42.43 N	77.34 W
Cañadón Seco	244	46.33 S	67.35 W
Cana do Reino	246	21.47 S	45.50 W
Canaguá ≃	236	7.57 N	69.36 W
Canahuan Islands II	106	11.49 N	124.43 E
Canaima, Parque Nacional ♠	236	4.27 N	62.00 W
Canajoharie	178	42.54 N	74.35 W
Çanakkale	120	40.09 N	26.24 E
Çanakkale □4	120	40.10 N	26.45 E
Çanakkale Boğazı (Dardanelles) Ш	120	40.15 N	26.25 E
Canal, Anse du C	231o	16.23 N	61.30 W
Canal, Islas del → Channel Islands II	28	49.20 N	2.20 W
Canala	165f	21.32 S	165.57 E
Canale	56	44.48 N	8.00 E
Canale, Val V	58	46.29 N	13.30 E
Canale del Ferro ≃	58	46.21 N	13.07 E
Canalejas	224	19.57 N	99.39 W
Canal Flats	172	50.09 N	115.48 W
Canal Fulton	204	40.54 N	81.36 W
Canal Lake @	202	44.34 N	79.03 W
Canal Lewisville	204	40.18 N	81.50 W
Canal Point	210	26.52 N	80.38 W
Canals	242	33.33 S	62.53 W
Canal Winchester	178	39.51 N	82.48 W
Canandaigua	200	42.54 N	77.17 W
Canandaigua Lake @	200	42.49 N	77.16 W
Canandaigua Outlet ≃	200	43.04 N	77.00 W
Cananea	222	30.57 N	110.18 W
Cananéia	242	25.01 S	47.57 W
Cananguchal	236	0.51 N	75.47 W
Canan Station	204	40.28 N	78.26 W
Canapine, Forca)(	60	42.45 N	13.12 E
Canápolis	245	18.44 S	49.13 W
Canapville	46	49.19 N	0.08 E
Cañar	236	2.33 S	78.56 W
Cañar □4	236	2.30 S	79.00 W
Canard ≃	204	42.08 N	83.06 W
Canard, Lac au @	196	45.48 N	71.31 W
Canarias, Islas (Canary Islands) II	138	28.00 N	15.30 W
Canaries	231f	13.55 N	61.04 W
Canaro	58	44.56 N	11.40 E
Canarreos, Archipiélago de los II	230p	21.50 N	82.30 W
Canarsie ✦8	266	40.38 N	73.53 W
Canarsie Park ♠	266	40.38 N	73.53 W
Canarsie Pol I	266	40.37 N	73.52 W
Canary Basin ⌘1	8	27.00 N	25.00 W
Canary Islands → Canarias, Islas II	138	28.00 N	15.30 W
Cañas	226	10.25 N	85.07 W
Cañas, Río de las ≃	224	22.29 N	105.36 W
Canaseraga Creek ≃	200	42.45 N	77.50 W
Cañasgordas	236	6.45 N	76.01 W
Canastota	200	43.10 N	75.45 W
Canastra ≃	240	11.23 S	49.41 W
Canastra, Serra da ⋏2	245	20.00 S	46.20 W
Canatlán	222	24.31 N	104.47 W
Canaveral, Cape ≻	210	28.27 N	80.32 W
Canaveral Bight C3	210	28.26 N	80.33 W
Canaveral National Seashore ♠	210	28.45 N	80.45 W
Canaveral Peninsula ≻1	210	28.28 N	80.34 W
Cañaveras	34	40.22 N	2.24 W
Canavese ✦1	56	45.20 N	7.40 E
Canavieiras	245	15.39 S	38.57 W
Cañazas	226	8.19 N	81.13 W
Cañazas, Serranía de ⋏	236	8.52 N	78.22 W
Canazei	58	46.28 N	11.46 E
Canbelego	156	31.33 S	146.19 E
Canberra	161b	35.17 S	149.08 E
Canby, Calif., U.S.	194	41.27 N	120.52 W
Canby, Minn., U.S.	**188**	**44.43 N**	**96.16 W**
Canby, Oreg., U.S.	**214**	**45.16 N**	**122.42 W**
Cancajanang, Mount Λ	106	11.04 N	124.47 E
Cancale	32	48.41 N	1.51 W
Cancano, Lago di @	58	46.31 N	10.18 E
Cance ≃	56	45.12 N	4.48 E
Cancello e Arnone	60	41.04 N	14.03 E
Canchaque	238	5.24 S	79.36 W
Canche ≃	46	50.31 N	1.39 E
Canchyuaya, Cerros de ⋏	238	7.10 S	74.30 W
Cancon	32	44.32 N	0.38 E
Cancuén ≃	226	15.59 N	90.00 W
Cancún, Punta ≻	222	21.08 N	86.45 W
Čančur	78	53.49 N	106.59 E
Canda	58	45.03 N	11.30 E
Candala → Qandala	134	11.23 N	49.53 E
Candarave	238	17.16 S	70.15 W
Çandarlı	120	38.56 N	26.56 E
Çandarlı Körfezi C	120	38.52 N	26.55 E
Candás	34	43.35 N	5.46 W

≃ River — Fluss — Río — Rivière — Rio
⌶ Canal — Kanal — Canal — Canal — Canal
Waterfall, Rapids — Wasserfall, Stromschnellen — Cascada, Rápidos — Chute d'eau, Rapides — Cascata, Rápidos
Ш Strait — Meeresstrasse — Estrecho — Détroit — Estreito
C Bay, Gulf — Bucht, Golf — Bahía, Golfo — Baie, Golfe — Baía, Golfo
@ Lake, Lakes — See, Seen — Lago, Lagos — Lac, Lacs — Lago, Lagos
Swamp — Sumpf — Pantano — Marais — Pântano
⊼ Ice Features, Glacier — Eis- und Gletscherformen — Accidentes Glaciales — Formes glaciaires — Acidentes Glaciares
⊤ Other Hydrographic Features — Andere Hydrographische Objekte — Otros Elementos Hidrográficos — Autres données hydrographiques — Outros Elementos Hidrográficos

⌘ Submarine Features — Untermeerische Objekte — Accidentes Submarinos — Formes de relief sous-marin — Acidentes Submarinos
□ Political Unit — Politische Einheit — Unidad Politica — Entité politique — Unidade Política
ʋ Cultural Institution — Kulturelle Institution — Institución Cultural — Institution culturelle — Instituição Cultural
⊥ Historical Site — Historische Stätte — Sitio Histórico — Site historique — Sitio Histórico
♠ Recreational Site — Erholungs- und Ferienort — Sitio de Recreo — Centre de loisirs — Sítio de Lazer
⊠ Airport — Flughafen — Aeropuerto — Aéroport — Aeroporto
■ Military Installation — Militäranlage — Instalación Militar — Installation militaire — Instalação Militar
✦ Miscellaneous — Verschiedenes — Misceláneo — Divers — Miscelânea

Candé 32 47.34 N 1.02 W
Candeias, Bra. 245 12.40 S 38.33 W
Candeias, Bra. 245 20.47 S 45.16 W
Candeias ≃ 238 8.39 S 63.31 W
Candela, It. 60 41.08 N 15.31 E
Candela, Méx. 222 26.50 N 100.40 W
Candela, Rio de ≃ 222 27.16 N 100.18 W
Candelaria, Arg. 242 32.04 S 65.49 W
Candelaria, Arg. 242 27.28 S 55.44 W
Candelária, Bra. 242 29.40 S 52.48 W
Candelaria, Col. 236 3.25 N 76.20 W
Candelaria, Cuba 230p 22.44 N 82.58 W
Candelaria, Pil. 106 15.38 N 119.56 E
Candelaria ≃ 222 18.37 N 91.14 W
Candelaria, Cerro ∧ 224 23.25 N 103.43 W
Candelaria Loxicha 224 15.54 N 96.31 W
Candelaro ≃ 60 41.34 N 15.53 E
Candeleda 34 40.09 N 5.14 W
Candelo, Austl. 156 36.46 S 149.42 E
Candelo, It. 56 45.33 N 8.07 E
Candia → Iráklion 38 35.20 N 25.09 E
Candiac 196 45.23 N 73.31 W
Candia Canavese 56 45.20 N 7.53 E
Candia Lomellina 56 45.11 N 8.36 E
Cândido Aguilar 222 25.30 N 98.02 W
Cândido de Abreu 242 24.35 S 51.20 W
Cândido Mendes 240 1.27 S 45.43 W
Candies Creek ≃ 182 35.18 N 84.51 W
Candijay 106 9.49 N 124.30 E
Çandır, Tür. 120 39.15 N 35.32 E
Çandır, Tür. 120 40.16 N 33.29 E
Candle 170 65.55 N 161.56 W
Candle Lake ⊜ 174 53.50 N 105.18 W
Candlemas Islands II 18 57.03 S 26.40 W
Candlestick Park ♦ 272 37.43 N 122.23 W
Candlewood, Lake ⊜ 197 41.32 N 73.27 W
Candlewood Isle 197 41.29 N 73.27 W
Candlewood Knolls 197 41.29 N 73.28 W
Candlewood Shores 197 41.29 N 73.26 W
Candman' 92 45.20 N 97.59 E
Cando, Ang. 142 16.30 S 18.19 E
Cando, Sask., Can. 174 52.23 N 108.14 W
Cando, N. Dak., U.S. 188 48.32 N 99.12 W
Candombé ≃ 142 16.54 S 21.52 E
Candon 106 17.12 N 120.27 E
Candor, N.C., U.S. 182 35.18 N 79.45 W
Candor, N.Y., U.S. 200 42.14 N 76.21 W
Candover 148 27.28 S 31.57 E
Cane ≃, Austl. 152 21.33 S 115.23 E
Cane ≃, N.C., U.S. 182 36.00 N 82.16 W
Canea → Khaniá 38 35.31 N 24.02 E
Caneadea 200 42.23 N 78.09 W
Caneças 256c 38.49 N 9.14 W
Cane Creek ≃ 184 36.29 N 90.28 W
Canegrate 256b 45.34 N 8.56 E
Canela 242 29.22 S 50.50 W
Canelles, Embalse de ⊜¹ 34 42.10 N 0.30 E
Canelles Point ≻ 231f 13.47 N 60.54 W
Canelli 56 44.43 N 8.17 E
Canelón Chico, Arroyo ≃ 248 34.29 S 56.20 W
Canelones 248 34.32 S 56.17 W
Canelones □⁵ 248 34.35 S 56.15 W
Canelón Grande, Arroyo ≃ 248 34.30 S 56.24 W
Cane Run ≃ 208 38.13 N 84.37 W
Cañete, Chile 242 37.48 S 73.24 W
Cañete, Esp. 34 40.03 N 1.35 W
Cañete, Perú 238 13.05 S 76.24 W
Cañete ≃ 238 13.08 S 76.24 W
Caneva 58 45.58 N 12.26 E
Caney 188 37.01 N 95.56 W
Caney ≃ 186 36.39 N 95.42 W
Caney Brook ≃ 266 41.07 N 73.50 W
Caney Creek ≃, U.S. 186 36.50 N 95.58 W
Caney Creek ≃, Ark., U.S. 184 33.46 N 93.07 W
Caney Creek ≃, Tex., U.S. 186 28.46 N 95.39 W
Caney Creek ≃, Tex., U.S. 212 32.48 N 95.33 W
Caney Creek ≃, Tex., U.S. 212 31.52 N 96.13 W
Caney Creek ≃, Tex., U.S. 212 30.04 N 96.08 W
Caney Creek ≃, Tex., U.S. 212 30.28 N 95.38 W
Caney Creek ≃, Tex., U.S. 212 31.03 N 94.33 W
Caney Creek ≃, Tex., U.S. 212 30.07 N 95.10 W
Caney Creek ≃, Tex., U.S. 212 30.53 N 95.48 W
Canfield 204 41.06 N 80.46 W
Canfield Island I 266 41.06 N 73.23 W
Canfranc 34 42.43 N 0.31 W
Cangaiba ✦⁸ 277b 23.30 S 46.31 W
Cangallo 238 13.33 S 74.12 W
Cangamba 142 13.40 S 19.54 E
Cangandala 142 9.45 S 16.33 E
Cangas, Bra. 238 16.05 S 56.33 W
Cangas, Esp. 34 42.16 N 8.47 W
Cangas de Narcea 34 43.11 N 6.33 W
Cangas de Onís 34 43.21 N 5.07 W
Cangbu 90 30.49 N 114.35 E
Can-giuoc ≃ 259c 10.42 N 106.37 E
Cangkuang, Tanjung ≻ 105a 6.51 S 105.15 E
Cangniutun 95 39.23 N 115.54 E
Cangola 142 7.58 S 15.52 E
Cangombe 142 14.24 S 19.59 E
Cangongo 142 9.24 S 17.30 E
Cangqian, Zhg. 96 30.17 N 120.25 E
Cangqian, Zhg. 96 30.18 N 120.00 E
Cangreja, Cerros de ∧ 226 15.35 N 86.55 W
Cangshangtun 95 40.03 N 117.32 E
Canguaretama 240 6.24 S 35.08 W
Canguçu 242 31.24 S 52.41 W
Cangumbe 142 12.00 S 19.17 E
Cangwu (Longwei) 92 23.22 N 111.13 E
Cangxi 92 31.48 N 105.57 E
Cangyrtas 75 40.53 N 72.50 E
Cangyuan 92 23.12 N 99.16 E
Cangzhou 88 38.19 N 116.51 E
Canhoca 142 9.15 S 14.41 E
Canhotinho 240 8.53 S 36.12 W
Caniapiscau 166 57.40 N 69.30 W
Caniapiscau, Lac ⊜ 166 54.10 N 69.55 W
Canicanian 106 14.46 N 122.01 E
Canicattì 36 37.21 N 13.51 E
Canigao Channel ꓴ 106 10.15 N 124.42 E
Canillas ✦⁸ 256a 40.28 N 3.38 W
Canillejas ✦⁸ 256a 40.27 N 3.37 W
Canim Lake 172 51.46 N 120.54 W
Canim Lake ⊜ 172 51.52 N 120.45 W
Canim Lake Indian Reserve ✦⁴ 172 51.47 N 121.00 W
Canimo Island I 106 14.07 N 123.04 E
Canindé 240 4.22 S 39.19 W
Canindé ≃ 240 6.15 S 42.52 W
Canindé de São Francisco 240 9.39 S 37.48 W
Canino 60 42.28 N 11.45 E
Canipaan 106 8.35 N 117.16 E
Canipo Island I 106 10.59 N 120.57 E
Canisius College ✤² 274a 42.55 N 78.52 W
Canistear Reservoir ⊜¹ 266 41.08 N 74.29 W
Canisteo 200 42.16 N 77.36 W
Canisteo ≃ 200 42.07 N 77.08 W
Canistota 188 43.36 N 97.18 W
Cañitas 224 23.36 N 102.43 W
Canjáyar 34 37.00 N 2.44 W
Canjinge 142 12.12 S 21.17 E
Çankırı 120 40.36 N 33.37 E
Çankırı □⁴ 120 40.45 N 33.25 E
Canlaon 106 10.22 N 123.12 E
Canlaon Volcano ∧¹ 106 10.25 N 123.08 E
Canley Vale 264a 33.53 S 150.57 E
Canmore 172 51.05 N 115.21 W
Canna I 28 57.03 N 6.33 W
Cannanore 112 11.51 N 75.22 E
Cannara 60 43.00 N 12.35 E
Cannel City 182 37.47 N 83.17 W
Cannelton 184 37.55 N 86.45 W
Canner ≃ 52 49.24 N 6.16 E
Cannero-Riviera 54 46.01 N 8.41 E
Cannes 56 43.33 N 7.01 E
Canneto 60 43.12 N 10.44 E
Canneto sull'Oglio 58 45.09 N 10.25 E
Cannifton 202 44.12 N 77.23 W
Canning, Arg. 278 34.53 S 58.30 W
Canning, N.S., Can. 176 45.09 N 64.25 W
Canning ≃, Austl. 158a 32.01 S 115.51 E
Canning ≃, Alaska, U.S. 170 70.05 N 145.30 W
Canning Hill ∧² 152 28.50 S 117.49 E
Canning Lake ⊜ 202 44.57 N 78.48 W
Canning Reservoir ⊜¹ 158a 32.10 S 116.09 E
Cannington, Ont., Can. 202 44.21 N 79.02 W
Cannington, Eng., U.K. 44 51.09 N 3.04 W
Cannobio 54 46.04 N 8.42 E
Cannock 44 52.42 N 2.09 W
Cannock Chase ✦⁴ 44 52.43 N 2.00 W
Cannon ≃ 180 44.35 N 92.33 W
Cannon Air Force Base ■ 186 34.23 N 103.18 W
Cannonball ≃ 188 46.26 N 100.38 W
Cannon Beach 214 45.55 N 123.57 W
Cannondale 197 41.08 N 73.16 W
Cannon Falls 180 44.31 N 92.54 W
Cannonsburg 206 43.03 N 85.28 W
Cannonsville Reservoir ⊜¹ 200 42.08 N 75.19 W
Cann River 156 37.34 S 149.10 E
Caño, Isla del I 226 8.44 N 83.53 W
Caño Amarillo, Estación ✦⁵ 276c 10.31 N 66.55 W
Canoas 242 29.56 S 51.11 W
Canoas ≃, Bra. 242 27.36 S 51.25 W
Canoas ≃, Bra. 246 21.30 S 47.09 W
Canobie Lake 273 42.48 N 71.15 W
Canobie Lake ⊜ 273 42.49 N 71.15 W
Canoe 172 50.45 N 119.13 W
Canoe ≃, B.C., Can. 172 52.09 N 118.27 W
Canoe ≃, Mass., U.S. 273 41.58 N 71.08 W
Canoe Brook ≃ 266 40.45 N 74.22 W
Canoe Brook Reservoirs ⊜¹ 266 40.45 N 74.21 W
Canoe Creek Indian Reserve ✦⁴ 172 51.32 N 122.15 W
Canoe Lake ⊜ 174 55.11 N 108.15 W
Canoe Lake Indian Reserve ✦⁴ 174 55.08 N 108.12 W
Canoga Park ✦⁸ 270 34.12 N 118.35 W
Canoinhas 242 26.10 S 50.24 W
Canol 170 65.14 N 126.56 W
Canon 182 34.21 N 83.07 W
Canon ≃ 214 46.36 N 123.53 W
Canonbie 42 55.05 N 2.57 W
Canon City 190 38.27 N 105.14 W
Cañón de Río Blanco, Parque Nacional ♦ 224 18.38 N 97.06 W
Caño Negro 226 10.54 N 84.44 W
Canonsburg 204 40.16 N 80.11 W
Canonsburg Lake ⊜ 269b 40.16 N 80.07 W
Canoochee ≃ 182 31.59 N 81.18 W
Canopus ⊥ 132 31.18 N 30.03 E
Canora 174 51.37 N 102.26 W
Canosa [di Puglia] 36 41.13 N 16.04 E
Canossa ⊥ 58 44.35 N 10.27 E
Canot, Pointe ≻ 231o 16.12 N 61.28 W
Canouan I 228 12.43 N 61.20 W
Canova 188 43.53 N 97.30 W
Canova Beach 210 28.08 N 80.34 W
Cànoves ≃ 256d 41.37 N 2.22 E
Canow 50 53.12 N 12.54 E
Canowindra 156 33.34 S 148.38 E
Can Quer, Torrente de ≃ 256d 41.31 N 2.11 E
Can Rull 256d 41.33 N 2.05 E
Cansado 138 20.51 N 17.02 W
Cansanção 240 10.41 S 39.31 W
Canso 176 45.20 N 61.00 W
Canso, Strait of ꓴ 176 45.37 N 61.25 W
Canta 238 11.25 S 76.38 W
Cantabria 224 19.50 N 101.44 W
Cantábrica, Cordillera ✦ 34 43.00 N 5.00 W
Cantabriques → Cantábrica, Cordillera ✦ 34 43.00 N 5.00 W
Cantagalo 245 21.58 S 42.22 W
Cantagalo, Cachoeira ↳ 240 7.18 S 54.52 W
Cantal □⁵ 32 45.05 N 2.45 E
Cantal ✦ 32 45.10 N 2.40 E
Cantalejo 34 41.15 N 3.55 W
Cantalupo in Sabina 60 42.18 N 12.39 E
Cantalupo nel Sannio 60 41.31 N 14.24 E
Cantal'vejergyn ≃ 170 67.38 N 179.22 W
Cantanhede, Bra. 240 3.39 S 44.24 W
Cantanhede, Port. 34 40.21 N 8.36 W
Cantareira ✦⁸ 277b 23.27 S 46.37 W
Cantareira, Serra da ∧ 277b 23.25 S 46.39 W
Cantaura 236 9.19 N 64.21 W
Cant Clough Reservoir ⊜¹ 252 53.46 N 2.09 W
Canteleu 46 49.27 N 1.02 E
Canterbury, Austl. 264a 33.55 S 151.07 E
Canterbury, Austl. 264b 37.49 S 145.05 E
Canterbury, N.B., Can. 176 45.53 N 67.29 W
Canterbury, Eng., U.K. 44 51.17 N 1.05 E
Canterbury Bight C³ 162 44.15 S 171.38 E
Canterbury Cathedral ✤¹ 44 51.17 N 1.05 E
Canterbury Park Racecourse ♦ 264a 33.54 S 151.07 E
Canterbury Plains ═ 162 44.00 S 171.45 E
Canterbury Woods 274c 38.49 N 77.15 W
Can-tho 100 10.02 N 105.47 E
Cantiano 60 43.28 N 12.38 E
Cantil 218 35.18 N 117.58 W
Cantiles, Cayo I 230p 21.36 N 82.02 W
Cantin, Cap ≻ 138 32.34 N 9.19 W
Cantin Lake ⊜ 174 53.27 N 95.10 W
Canto do Buriti 240 8.07 S 42.58 W
Canto do Pontes 277a 22.58 S 43.04 W
Canto Grande 276d 11.59 S 77.01 W
Cantoira 56 45.21 N 7.23 E
Canton, Conn., U.S. 197 41.49 N 72.54 W
Canton, Ga., U.S. 182 34.14 N 84.29 W
Canton, Ill., U.S. 180 40.33 N 90.02 W
Canton, Kans., U.S. 188 38.23 N 97.26 W
Canton, Maine, U.S. 178 44.28 N 70.19 W
Canton, Mass., U.S. 197 42.09 N 71.09 W
Canton, Minn., U.S. 180 43.32 N 91.56 W
Canton, Miss., U.S. 184 32.37 N 90.02 W
Canton, Mo., U.S. 209 40.08 N 91.32 W
Canton, N.J., U.S. 208 39.28 N 75.25 W
Canton, N.Y., U.S. 178 44.36 N 75.10 W
Canton, Ohio, U.S. 204 40.48 N 81.22 W
Canton, Okla., U.S. 186 36.03 N 98.35 W
Canton, Pa., U.S. 200 41.39 N 76.51 W
Canton, S. Dak., U.S. 188 43.18 N 96.35 W
Canton, Tex., U.S. 212 32.33 N 95.52 W
Canton → Guangzhou, Zhg. 90 23.06 N 113.16 E
Canton I, Can. / End. 164h 2.50 S 171.40 W
Canton I, Oc. 14 2.50 S 171.43 W
Canton Airport ⊠ 164h 2.46 S 171.43 W
Canton and Enderbury □² 14 2.50 S 171.43 W
Canton Et Ederburg → Canton and Enderbury □² 14 2.50 S 171.40 W
Canton Lake ⊜¹ 186 36.08 N 98.36 W
Cantonment 184 30.38 N 87.19 W
Cantorbéry → Canterbury 44 51.17 N 1.05 E
Cantrall 209 39.56 N 89.41 W
Cantribana 256c 38.53 N 9.25 W
Cantù 56 45.44 N 9.08 E
Cantu ≃ 242 24.46 S 52.54 W
Cantua Creek 216 36.30 N 120.19 W
Cantua Creek ≃ 216 36.28 N 120.17 W
Cantwell 170 63.23 N 148.57 W
Cañuelas 248 35.03 S 58.44 W
Cañuelas □⁵ 278 34.56 S 58.41 W
Cañuelas, Arroyo ≃ 248 34.55 S 58.38 W
Canumã 236 4.02 S 59.04 W
Canumã ≃ 236 3.55 S 59.10 W
Canungra 161a 28.01 S 153.10 E
Canungra ≃ 161a 27.55 S 153.06 E
Canungra Jungle Training Ground ■ 161a 28.02 S 153.10 E
Canutama 238 6.32 S 64.20 W
Canutillo 190 31.55 N 106.36 W
Canvastown 162 41.18 S 173.40 E
Canvey 44 51.32 N 0.36 E
Canvey Island I 44 51.33 N 0.34 E
Čany 76 55.19 N 76.46 E
Čany, Ozero ⊜ 76 54.50 N 77.30 E
Cany-Barville 46 49.47 N 0.38 E
Canyon, Yukon, Can. 170 60.52 N 137.02 W
Canyon, Calif., U.S. 272 37.49 N 122.09 W
Canyon, Tex., U.S. 186 34.59 N 101.55 W
Canyon City 192 44.23 N 118.57 W
Canyon Creek 172 54.22 N 115.05 W
Canyon Creek ≃, Ariz., U.S. 190 33.49 N 110.40 W
Canyon Creek ≃, Calif., U.S. 216 39.22 N 120.45 W
Canyon Creek ≃, Idaho, U.S. 192 42.59 N 115.59 W
Canyon Creek ≃, Wash., U.S. 214 45.57 N 122.22 W
Canyon Creek ≃, Wash., U.S. 214 48.43 N 120.55 W
Canyon de Chelly National Monument ♦ 190 36.01 N 109.26 W
Canyon Ferry Lake ⊜¹ 192 46.33 N 111.37 W
Canyon Lake ⊜¹ 186 29.52 N 98.16 W
Canyonlands National Park ♦ 190 38.10 N 110.00 W
Canyonville 192 42.56 N 123.17 W
Canzar 142 7.38 S 21.32 E
Canzo 56 45.51 N 9.16 E
Caobanal 224 17.37 N 93.22 W
Cao-bang 100 22.40 N 106.15 E
Caochiyan 97 30.21 N 104.22 E
Caocun, Zhg. 88 34.02 N 117.08 E
Caocun, Zhg. 96 31.42 N 118.56 E
Caodian, Zhg. 90 28.39 N 120.23 E
Caodian, Zhg. 90 33.21 N 112.39 E
Caodian, Zhg. 92 32.32 N 111.11 E
Cao'e 90 30.01 N 120.52 E
Cao'ejiang ≃ 90 30.06 N 120.42 E
Caofang 90 26.04 N 116.35 E
Caogezhai 95 40.09 N 117.50 E
Caohe 95 38.57 N 115.32 E
Caohe ≃ 88 40.29 N 124.08 E
Caohecheng 94 40.46 N 124.02 E
Caohekou 94 40.54 N 123.53 E
Caohezhang 94 41.04 N 124.03 E
Caojiawopeng 94 42.00 N 122.20 E
Caojiawopu 94 42.37 N 122.19 E
Caojiawu 95 39.24 N 116.31 E
Caojiazhen 96 31.55 N 121.38 E
Caojiezi 97 29.53 N 106.24 E
Caojing 96 30.47 N 121.24 E
Caojun 88 33.40 N 114.40 E
Cao-lanh 100 10.27 N 105.38 E
Caolaoji 90 33.06 N 117.22 E
Caolisport, Loch C 42 55.54 N 5.37 W
Caomaji 88 34.52 N 116.17 E
Caombo 142 8.40 S 16.32 E
Caonillas, Lago ⊜ 230m 18.16 N 66.39 W
Caopeng 96 31.44 N 121.17 E
Caoping 90 28.48 N 118.22 E
Caopu 88 34.34 N 118.52 E
Caoqiao 96 31.32 N 119.59 E
Caorle 58 45.36 N 12.53 E
Caorso 56 45.03 N 9.52 E
Caoshi, Zhg. 88 42.17 N 125.16 E
Caoshi, Zhg. 90 33.32 N 116.29 E
Caota 90 29.42 N 120.08 E
Caotang 96 31.16 N 118.59 E
Caoxi 90 28.42 N 117.18 E
Caoxian 88 34.53 N 115.33 E
Caoyang 90 32.56 N 120.20 E
Caoyangxi 90 26.34 N 118.47 E
Cap, Le → Cape Town 148 33.55 S 18.22 E
Cap, Pointe du ≻ 231f 14.07 N 60.57 W
Capac 180 43.01 N 82.56 W
Capage 142 13.21 S 21.05 E
Čapajevka, S.S.S.R. 68 49.33 N 32.06 E
Čapajevka, S.S.S.R. 68 49.26 N 35.42 E
Čapajevka, S.S.S.R. 68 47.29 N 36.20 E
Čapajevka, S.S.S.R. 72 54.38 N 35.50 E
Čapajevka ≃ 70 53.08 N 49.37 E
Čapajevo, S.S.S.R. 68 49.21 N 35.54 E
Čapajevo, S.S.S.R. 70 50.12 N 51.10 E
Čapajevsk 70 52.58 N 49.41 E
Capala 142 13.37 S 14.04 E
Capalbio 60 42.27 N 11.25 E
Capalonga 106 14.20 N 122.30 E
Capanaparo ≃ 236 7.01 N 67.07 W
Capanema, Bra. 240 1.12 S 47.11 W
Capanema, Bra. 242 25.40 S 53.48 W
Capanema ≃ 242 25.35 S 53.48 W
Capangombe 142 15.05 S 13.08 E
Capanne, Monte ∧ 60 42.46 N 10.10 E
Capannoli 60 43.35 N 10.41 E
Capannori 60 43.50 N 10.34 E
Capão Bonito 245 24.01 S 48.20 W
Capão Doce, Morro do ∧ 242 26.43 S 51.25 W
Capão Redondo ✦⁸ 277b 23.40 S 46.46 W
Capaotigamau, Lac ⊜ 176 50.18 N 68.14 W
Caparica 256c 38.40 N 9.12 W
Caparo ≃ 236 7.30 N 64.02 W
Capas 106 15.20 N 120.35 E
Capatárida 236 11.11 N 70.37 W
Cap aux Meules, Île du I 176 47.23 N 61.54 W
Capay 216 38.32 N 122.03 W
Cap-Chat 176 49.06 N 66.42 W
Cap-Chat, Parc de ♦ 176 48.55 N 66.50 W
Cap-de-la-Madeleine 196 46.22 N 72.31 W
Capdevila ✦⁸ 276b 23.03 N 82.24 W
Cape ≃ 156 20.49 S 146.51 E
Cape Barren Island I 156 40.25 S 148.12 E
Cape Basin ✦¹ 10 35.00 S 5.00 E
Cape Breton Highlands National Park ♦ 176 46.45 N 60.45 W
Cape Breton Island I 176 46.00 N 60.30 W
Cape Broyle 176 47.06 N 52.57 W
Cape Canaveral 210 28.24 N 80.37 W
Cape Charles 198 37.16 N 76.01 W
Cape Coast 140 5.05 N 1.15 W
Cape Cod Bay C 197 41.52 N 70.22 W
Cape Cod Canal ⊼ 197 41.47 N 70.30 W
Cape Cod National Seashore ♦ 197 41.56 N 70.06 W
Cape Comorin → Kanniyākumāri 112 8.05 N 77.34 E
Cape Coral 210 26.33 N 81.57 W
Cape Croker Indian Reserve ✦⁴ 202 44.55 N 81.01 W
Cape Dorset 166 64.14 N 76.32 W
Cape Elizabeth 178 43.34 N 70.12 W
Cape Fear ≃ 182 33.53 N 78.00 W
Cape Girardeau 184 37.19 N 89.32 W
Cape Hatteras National Seashore ♦ 182 35.30 N 76.35 W
Cape Henlopen State Park ♦ 198 38.45 N 75.06 W
Cape Jervis 158b 35.36 S 138.06 E
Cape Johnson Seamount ✦³ 14 17.00 N 177.20 W
Capela, Bra. 240 10.30 S 37.04 W
Capela, Bra. 240 9.25 S 36.04 W
Cape la Hune 176 47.33 N 56.52 W
Capel Curig 44 53.06 N 3.54 W
Capelengue 142 9.12 S 19.43 E
Capelinha 245 17.42 S 42.31 W
Cape Lisburne 170 68.52 N 166.05 W
Capel'ka 66 58.03 N 28.59 E
Capella 156 23.05 S 148.02 E
Capella ∧ 154 5.00 S 141.05 E
Capelle [aan de IJssel] 48 51.55 N 4.35 E
Capellen 52 49.38 N 5.59 E
Cape Lookout State Park ♦ 214 45.21 N 123.59 W
Cape May 198 38.56 N 74.55 W
Cape May □⁶ 198 38.56 N 74.55 W
Cape May Court House 198 39.05 N 74.50 W
Cape May Point 198 38.56 N 74.58 W
Capembe ≃ 142 16.10 S 21.00 E
Capenda Camulemba 142 9.24 S 18.27 E
Capenga ≃ 277a 22.49 S 43.37 W
Capenhurst 252 53.15 N 2.57 W
Cape of Good Hope (Kaap) □⁴ 146 31.00 S 23.00 E
Cape of Good Hope Nature Reserve ✦⁴ 148 34.18 S 18.26 E
Cape Pole 170 55.58 N 133.48 W
Cape Pond ⊜ 273 42.38 N 70.38 W
Cape Porpoise 178 43.22 N 70.26 W
Cape Rise ✦³ 10 41.00 S 13.00 E
Capernaum ⊥ 122 32.53 N 35.34 E
Cape Romanzof 170 61.49 N 165.56 W
Capertee 160 33.09 S 149.59 E
Capertee ≃ 160 33.12 S 150.28 E
Cape Sable Island I 176 43.25 N 65.37 W
Capesterre, Guad. 231o 15.54 N 61.13 W
Capesterre, Guad. 231o 16.03 N 61.34 W
Capesterre, Pointe de la ≻ 231o 16.03 N 61.33 W
Capesthorne Hall ⊥ 252 53.15 N 2.14 W
Capestrano 60 42.16 N 13.46 E
Capetinga ≃ 246 22.04 S 47.14 W
Cape Tormentine 176 46.08 N 63.47 W
Cape Town (Kaapstad) 148 33.55 S 18.22 E
Cape Verde □¹ 124 140a 16.00 N 24.00 W
Cape Verde Basin ✦¹ 8 14.00 N 33.00 W
Cape Verde Islands → Cape Verde □¹ 140a 16.00 N 24.00 W
Cape Verde Terrace ✦³ 10 18.30 N 22.00 W
Capeville 198 37.12 N 75.57 W
Cape Vincent 202 44.08 N 76.20 W
Cape Yakataga 170 60.04 N 142.26 W
Cape York Peninsula ✦¹ 154 14.00 S 142.30 E
Cap-Haïtien 228 19.45 N 72.12 W
Capibary ≃ 242 24.06 S 56.26 W
Capilla de Farruco 242 32.53 S 55.25 W
Capilla del Monte 242 30.51 S 64.31 W
Capilla del Señor 248 34.18 S 59.06 W
Capim 240 1.41 S 47.47 W
Capim ≃ 240 1.40 S 47.47 W
Capim Melado, Morro do ∧ 277a 22.50 S 43.29 W
Capinas Point ≻ 106 11.05 N 125.14 E
Capinópolis 245 18.41 S 49.35 W
Capinota 238 17.43 S 66.14 W
Capinzal 242 27.20 S 51.36 W
Capinzal, Cachoeira ↳ 240 8.42 S 58.18 W
Capira 226 8.45 N 79.53 W
Cap Island I 106 5.57 N 120.06 E
Capistrano 240 4.28 S 38.55 W
Capistrano Beach 218 33.27 N 117.40 W
Capistrello 60 41.57 N 13.23 E
Capitachouane ≃ 176 47.36 N 76.54 W
Capital Airport ⊠ 209 39.51 N 89.41 W
Capital City Airport ⊠ 206 42.47 N 84.35 W
Capitan 190 33.35 N 105.35 W
Capitán Aracena, Isla I 244 54.10 S 71.20 W
Capitán Bado 245 23.16 S 55.32 W
Capitán Bermúdez 242 32.49 S 60.43 W
Capitán Meza 242 26.55 S 55.15 W
Capitan Peak ∧ 190 33.36 N 105.16 W
Capitán Sarmiento 242 34.10 S 59.48 W
Capitão, Igarapé ≃ 238 5.58 S 64.48 W
Capitão de Campos 240 4.28 S 41.57 W
Capitão Noronha, Ribeirão ≃ 245 13.19 S 54.36 W
Capitari 236 0.51 N 61.24 W
Capitola 216 36.58 N 121.57 W
Capitol Heights 198 38.53 N 76.55 W
Capitol Park 198 39.08 N 75.30 W
Capitol Peak ∧ 194 41.50 N 117.18 W
Capitol Reef National Park ♦ 190 38.11 N 111.20 W
Capitol View 182 33.57 N 80.56 W
Capivara, Lago ⊜ 246 22.35 S 50.18 W
Capivari 245 23.00 S 47.31 W
Capivari ≃, Bra. 238 19.16 S 57.10 W
Capivari ≃, Bra. 245 12.30 S 39.55 W
Capivari ≃, Bra. 246 21.30 S 44.20 W
Capivari ≃, Bra. 246 21.53 S 46.15 W
Capivari ≃, Bra. 246 22.56 S 47.16 W
Capivari ≃, Bra. 246 22.14 S 44.57 W
Capivari ≃, Bra. 246 22.26 S 45.47 W
Capivari ≃, Bra. 246 21.12 S 44.52 W
Capiz → Roxas 106 11.35 N 122.45 E
Capiz □⁴ 106 11.30 N 122.30 E
Caplan 176 48.06 N 65.41 W
Čaplejevka 68 51.43 N 33.12 E
Caplen 212 29.29 N 94.33 W
Caples Lake ⊜¹ 216 38.42 N 120.03 W
Caplina ≃ 238 18.14 S 70.33 W
Čaplinka 68 46.23 N 33.32 E
Čaplino, S.S.S.R. 68 48.09 N 36.14 E
Čaplino, S.S.S.R. 170 64.25 N 172.15 W
Čapljina 36 43.07 N 17.42 E
Caplone, Monte ∧ 58 45.48 N 10.38 E
Čaplygin 66 53.15 N 39.58 E
Cap Mountain ∧ 170 63.25 N 123.29 W
Capnoyan Island I 106 10.32 N 119.17 E
Capoche ≃ 144 15.23 S 32.53 E
Capodichino, Aeroporto di ⊠ 60 40.50 N 14.17 E
Capodimonte 60 42.33 N 11.55 E
Capo di Ponte 58 46.02 N 10.21 E
Capoeiras, Cachoeira das ↳ 240 6.48 S 58.21 W
Capolago 54 45.55 N 8.59 E
Capoliveri 60 42.45 N 10.22 E
Caporolo ≃ 142 12.56 S 13.00 E
Capostrada 60 43.57 N 10.54 E
Capot ≃ 230e 14.51 N 61.05 W
Capoti-an, Mount ∧ 106 11.45 N 125.15 E
Capotoan, Mount ∧ 106 12.09 N 124.57 E
Cap-Pelé 176 46.13 N 64.18 W
Cappelle 60 42.03 N 13.22 E
Cappelle sul Tavo 60 42.28 N 14.06 E
Cappeln 48 52.48 N 8.07 E
Cappenberg 253 51.39 N 7.32 E
Cappenberg, Schloss ⊥ 253 51.39 N 7.32 E
Cappercleuch 42 55.29 N 3.12 W
Capracotta 60 41.50 N 14.16 E
Capraia 60 43.03 N 9.50 E
Capraia, Isola di I 60 43.02 N 9.49 E
Capranica 60 42.15 N 12.11 E
Caprara, Isola I 60 42.08 N 15.31 E
Caprarola 60 42.19 N 12.14 E
Capreol 180 46.43 N 80.56 W
Caprese Michelangelo 60 43.39 N 11.59 E
Capri 60 40.33 N 14.14 E
Capri, Isola di I 60 40.33 N 14.13 E
Capriati a Volturno 60 41.28 N 14.08 E
Capricorn, Cape ≻ 156 23.30 S 151.13 E
Capricorn Group II 156 23.28 S 152.00 E
Caprino Veronese 58 45.36 N 10.47 E
Caprivi Strip (Caprivizipfel) □⁹ 146 17.59 S 23.00 E
Caprolace, Lago di ⊜ 60 41.21 N 12.58 E
Capron, Ill., U.S. 206 42.24 N 88.44 W
Capron, Va., U.S. 198 36.42 N 77.11 W
Cap-Saint-Jacques → Vung-tau 100 10.21 N 107.04 E
Cap-Santé 196 46.40 N 71.47 W
Capstone 250 51.21 N 0.34 E
Captain Anthony Meldahl Dam ✦⁶ 208 38.48 N 84.11 W
Captain Cook 219d 19.30 N 155.55 W
Captain Cook Bridge ✦⁵ 264a 34.00 S 151.08 E
Captain Cook Landing Place ⊥ 264a 34.00 S 151.14 E
Captain Cook Monument ⊥ 164c 29.00 S 167.56 E
Captain Cook's Monument ⊥ 164s 17.30 S 149.30 W
Captain Daniel Wright Woods ♦ 268 42.13 N 87.56 W
Captain Harbor C 266 41.00 N 73.36 W
Captain Pond ⊜ 273 42.48 N 71.10 W
Captains Flat 161b 35.35 S 149.27 E
Captieux 32 44.18 N 0.16 W
Captina Creek ≃ 178 39.52 N 80.48 W
Captiva 210 26.31 N 82.11 W
Captiva Island I 210 26.31 N 82.11 W
Captree Island I 266 40.39 N 73.16 W
Captree State Park ♦ 266 40.39 N 73.16 W
Capua 60 41.06 N 14.12 E
Capual Island I 106 6.02 N 121.24 E
Capuáva 277b 23.39 S 46.29 W
Capuça I 142 17.22 S 21.18 E
Capucapu ≃ 236 1.45 S 58.35 W
Capuchin, Cape ≻ 230d 15.38 N 61.28 W
Capul 106 12.25 N 124.11 E
Capulín, Río del ≃ 186 27.31 N 101.33 W
Capulin Mountain National Monument ♦ 186 36.48 N 103.55 W
Capul Island I 106 12.26 N 124.10 E
Capuna 142 15.38 S 19.43 E
Capurro 248 34.25 S 56.28 W
Caputh 50 52.21 N 13.00 E
Cap-Vert → Cape Verde □¹ 140a 16.00 N 24.00 W
Caquende 246 21.20 S 44.33 W
Caquetá □⁸ 236 1.00 N 74.00 W
Caquetá (Japurá) ≃ 236 3.08 S 64.46 W
Caquiaviri 238 17.03 S 68.36 W
Čar ≃ 76 50.22 N 80.55 E
Čara 78 56.54 N 118.12 E
Čara ≃ 64 60.22 N 120.50 E
Cará, Ilha I 240 0.01 S 50.50 W
Carabalbeda 276c 10.37 N 66.50 W
Carabanchel Alto ✦⁸ 256a 40.22 N 3.45 W
Carabanchel Bajo ✦⁸ 256a 40.23 N 3.47 W
Carabao Island I 106 12.04 N 121.56 E
Carabaya, Cordillera de ✦ 238 13.50 S 70.45 W
Carabinani ≃ 236 1.58 S 61.39 W
Carabobo □³ 228 10.10 N 68.05 W
Caraboost 161b 35.36 S 147.44 E
Caracal 38 44.07 N 24.21 E
Caracalla, Terme di ⊥ 257a 41.53 N 12.29 E
Caracaraí 236 1.50 N 61.08 W
Caracas 236 276c 10.30 N 66.56 W
Čarach 76 59.03 N 62.15 E
Carache 236 9.38 N 70.14 W
Caracol, Bra. 240 9.17 S 43.20 W
Caracol, Bra. 242 22.01 S 57.02 W
Caracol, Ribeirão ≃ 245 18.38 S 54.19 W
Caracollo 238 17.39 S 67.10 W
Caracorum → Karakoram Range ✦ 110 35.30 N 77.00 E
Caracuaro de Morelos 224 18.46 N 101.02 W
Caradoc Indian Reserve ✦⁴ 204 42.48 N 81.29 W
Caraga 106 7.20 N 126.34 E
Caraga ≃ 106 7.20 N 126.34 E
Caraghnan Mountain ∧ 156 31.20 S 149.03 E
Caraglio 56 44.25 N 7.26 E
Caraguatá, Arroyo ≃ 278 34.24 S 58.38 W
Caraguatatuba 246 23.37 S 45.25 W
Caraguatatuba, Enseada de C 246 23.40 S 45.20 W
Caraguatay 242 25.14 S 56.52 W
Caraí 245 17.12 S 41.42 W
Caraïbes, Mer des → Caribbean Sea ✦² 228 15.00 N 73.00 W
Caraigres, Cerro ∧ 226 9.43 N 84.05 W
Caraíva ≃ 245 16.48 S 39.08 W
Carajari ≃ 240 4.45 S 54.20 W
Carajás, Serra dos ✦ 240 6.00 S 51.20 W
Caramagna-Piemonte 56 44.46 N 7.44 E
Caramanico Terme 60 42.09 N 14.00 E
Caramay 106 10.11 N 119.14 E
Caramoan 106 13.46 N 123.52 E
Caramoan Peninsula ✦¹ 106 13.48 N 123.40 E
Caramoran 106 13.59 N 124.08 E
Caramy ≃ 62 43.25 N 6.13 E
Caraná ≃ 238 13.20 S 59.17 W
Caranavi 238 15.46 S 67.36 W
Carancahua Creek ≃ 212 28.51 N 96.19 W
Carandaí 245 20.57 S 43.48 W
Carandaiti 238 20.45 S 63.04 W
Carangola 245 20.44 S 42.02 W
Carano 58 46.16 N 11.27 E
Caransebeș 38 45.25 N 22.13 E
Carapá ≃ 242 24.30 S 54.20 W
Carapachay ✦¹ 278 34.25 S 58.35 W
Carapajó 240 2.16 S 49.22 W
Caraparaná ≃ 236 1.45 S 73.13 W
Carapari 238 21.49 S 63.44 W
Carapeguá 242 25.48 S 57.14 W
Carapeva 246 23.12 S 45.24 W
Carapicuíba 277b 23.31 S 46.50 W
Carapó 245 22.38 S 54.48 W
Carapo ≃ 236 7.46 N 70.23 W
Carappee Hill ∧² 158 33.26 S 136.16 E
Caraquet 176 47.48 N 64.57 W
Carare ≃ 236 6.48 N 74.06 W
Carasco 56 44.21 N 9.21 E
Caraș-Severin □⁴ 38 45.00 N 22.00 E
Carata, Laguna C 226 13.56 N 83.30 W
Caratasca, Laguna de C 226 15.23 N 83.55 W
Carate Brianza 56 45.41 N 9.14 E
Caratinga 245 19.47 S 42.08 W
Carauari 236 4.52 S 66.54 W
Caraúbas, Bra. 240 7.43 S 36.31 W
Caraúbas, Bra. 240 5.47 S 37.34 W
Caravaca 34 38.06 N 1.51 W
Caravaggio 56 45.30 N 9.38 E
Caravela, Ilha I 140 11.30 N 16.20 W
Caravelas 245 17.45 S 39.15 W
Caravelí 238 15.46 S 73.22 W
Caravelle, Presqu'île de la ≻¹ 230e 14.45 N 60.55 W
Caraway 184 35.46 N 90.19 W
Carayaó 242 25.10 S 56.26 W
Caraybamba 238 14.24 S 73.09 W
Caraz 238 9.03 S 77.45 W
Caraza ✦⁸ 278 34.42 S 58.26 W
Carazinho 242 28.18 S 52.48 W
Carazo □⁵ 226 11.45 N 86.15 W
Carballino 34 42.26 N 8.04 W
Carballo 34 43.13 N 8.41 W
Carberry 174 49.52 N 99.20 W
Carbet, Pitons du ∧ 230e 14.42 N 61.07 W
Carbó 222 29.42 N 110.58 W
Carbon, Alta., Can. 172 51.29 N 113.09 W
Carbon, Pa., U.S. 269b 40.17 N 79.34 W
Carbon, Tex., U.S. 186 32.16 N 98.50 W
Carbon □⁶ 200 40.52 N 75.45 W
Carbon ≃ 214 47.07 N 122.13 W
Carbon, Cap ≻ 34 36.47 N 5.06 E
Carbonado 214 47.05 N 122.03 W
Carbonara, Capo ≻ 36 39.06 N 9.31 E
Carbonare 58 45.56 N 11.13 E
Carbon-Blanc 32 44.53 N 0.31 W
Carbon Canyon Dam ✦⁶ 270 33.55 N 117.50 W
Carbon Creek ≃ 270 33.49 N 118.04 W
Carbondale, Colo., U.S. 190 39.24 N 107.13 W
Carbondale, Ill., U.S. 184 37.44 N 89.13 W
Carbondale, Kans., U.S. 188 38.49 N 95.41 W
Carbondale, Pa., U.S. 200 41.35 N 75.30 W
Carbonear 176 47.45 N 53.13 W
Carboneras de Guadazaon 34 39.53 N 1.48 W
Carbon Hill 184 33.48 N 87.32 W
Carbonia 36 39.11 N 8.32 E
Carbonin 58 46.37 N 12.13 E
Carcagente 34 39.08 N 0.27 W
Carcajou ≃ 170 65.37 N 128.43 W
Carcalgong Hill ∧ 160 32.52 S 149.41 E
Carcans, Étang de C 32 45.08 N 1.08 W
Carcar 106 10.06 N 123.38 E
Carcaraña 242 32.51 S 61.09 W
Carcarañá ≃ 242 32.27 S 60.48 W
Carcare 56 44.21 N 8.18 E
Carcar Point ≻ 106 10.05 N 123.41 E
Carcassonne 32 43.13 N 2.21 E
Carcastillo 34 42.23 N 1.26 W
Carcavelos, Port. 256c 38.53 N 9.14 W
Carcavelos, Port. 256c 38.41 N 9.20 W
Carceri, Eremo delle ⊥ 60 43.05 N 12.42 E
Carcès 62 43.28 N 6.11 E
Carchi □⁴ 236 0.45 N 78.00 W
Carcross 170 60.10 N 134.42 W
Cardabia 152 23.06 S 113.48 E
Çardak 120 38.06 N 36.49 E
Cardal 248 34.18 S 56.24 W
Cardamum Island I 112 11.14 N 72.47 E
Čardara 75 41.17 N 67.55 E
Čardara, Step' ✦¹ 75 42.00 N 68.00 E
Čardarinskoje Vodochranilišče ⊜¹ 75 41.10 N 68.15 E
Cardeña 34 38.13 N 4.19 W
Cárdenas, Cuba 230p 23.02 N 81.12 W
Cárdenas, Méx. 224 17.59 N 93.22 W
Cárdenas, Méx. 222 22.00 N 99.40 W
Cárdenas, Nic. 226 11.12 N 85.31 W
Cárdenas, Bahía de C 230p 23.05 N 81.10 W
Çardi 120 39.41 N 29.10 E
Cardiel, Lago ⊜ 244 48.55 S 71.15 W
Cardiff, Austl. 160 32.57 S 151.40 E
Cardiff, Wales, U.K. 44 51.29 N 3.13 W
Cardiff, Md., U.S. 198 39.42 N 76.20 W
Cardiff, N.J., U.S. 198 39.25 N 74.36 W
Cardiff-by-the-Sea 218 33.01 N 117.17 W
Cardigan, P.E.I., Can. 176 46.14 N 62.37 W
Cardigan, Wales, U.K. 44 52.06 N 4.40 W
Cardigan Bay C, P.E.I., Can. 176 46.10 N 62.30 W
Cardigan Bay C, Wales, U.K. 44 52.30 N 4.20 W
Cardigan Island I 44 52.08 N 4.41 W
Cardigan State Park ♦ 178 43.38 N 71.54 W
Cardinal 202 44.47 N 75.23 W
Cardinal Heights 202 45.27 N 75.37 W
Cardinal Lake ⊜ 172 56.14 N 117.44 W
Cardington, S. Afr. 148 27.11 S 23.30 E
Cardington, Ohio, U.S. 204 40.30 N 82.53 W
Cardinia Creek ≃ 264b 38.12 S 145.23 E
Cardito 60 40.57 N 14.18 E
Cardón, Punta ≻ 236 11.37 N 70.14 W
Cardona 248 33.53 S 57.23 W
Cardoner ≃ 34 41.41 N 1.51 E
Cardoso 245 20.04 S 49.54 W
Cardozo 248 32.38 S 56.21 W
Card Sound ꓴ 210 25.20 N 80.18 W
Cardston 172 49.12 N 113.18 W
Cardwell, Austl. 156 18.16 S 146.02 E
Cardwell, Mo., U.S. 184 36.03 N 90.17 W
Cardwell Mountain ∧ 184 35.41 N 85.41 W
Čardžou 126 39.06 N 63.34 E
Čardžou □⁴ 118 38.51 N 63.34 E
Careaçu 246 22.02 S 45.42 W
Careen Lake ⊜ 174 57.00 N 108.10 W
Carega, Cima ∧ 58 45.44 N 11.08 E
Carei 38 47.42 N 22.28 E
Careiro 236 3.12 S 59.45 W
Careiro, Ilha do I 236 3.10 S 59.48 W
Caren 242 30.51 S 70.47 W
Carencavan 74 40.24 N 44.38 E
Carencro 184 30.19 N 92.03 W
Carentan 32 49.18 N 1.14 W
Cares ≃ 34 43.19 N 4.36 W
Caresana 56 45.13 N 8.30 E
Caretta 182 37.20 N 81.41 W
Carevščina 72 52.26 N 46.43 E
Carey 204 40.57 N 83.23 W
Carey, Lake ⊜ 152 29.05 S 122.15 E
Carey Downs 152 25.38 S 115.27 E
Careysburg 140 6.30 N 10.32 W
Cargados Carajos Shoals II 12 16.38 S 59.38 E
Carhaix-Plouguer 32 48.17 N 3.35 W
Carhuamayo 238 10.55 S 76.02 W
Carhuanca 238 13.44 S 73.47 W
Carhuaz 238 9.16 S 77.38 W
Carhué 248 37.11 S 62.44 W
Caria □⁹ 120 37.30 N 28.00 E
Cariacica 245 20.16 S 40.25 W
Cariaco 236 10.29 N 63.33 W
Cariaco, Golfo de C 236 10.30 N 64.00 W
Cariamanga 238 4.20 S 79.35 W
Cariango 142 10.37 S 15.20 E
Cariati 36 39.30 N 16.57 E
Caribana, Punta ≻ 236 8.37 N 76.52 W
Caribbean Sea ✦² 228 15.00 N 73.00 W

Symbols in the index entries represent the broad categories identified in the key at the right. Symbols with superior numbers (✦²) identify subcategories (see complete key on page I · 26).

Kartensymbole in dem Registerverzeichnis stellen die rechts in Schlüssel erklärten Kategorien dar. Symbole mit hochgestellten Ziffern (✦²) bezeichnen Unterabteilungen einer Kategorie (vgl. vollständiger Schlüssel auf Seite I · 26).

Los símbolos incluidos en el texto del índice representan las grandes categorías identificadas con la clave a la derecha. Los símbolos con números en su parte superior (✦²) identifican las subcategorías (véase la clave completa en la página I · 26).

Les symboles de l'index représentent les catégories indiquées dans la légende à droite. Les symboles suivis d'un indice (✦²) représentent des sous-catégories (voir légende complète à la page I · 26).

Os símbolos incluídos no texto do índice representam as grandes categorias identificadas com a chave à direita. Os símbolos com números em sua parte superior (✦²) identificam as subcategorias (veja-se a chave completa à página I · 26).

	English	Deutsch	Español	Français	Português
∧	Mountain	Berg	Montaña	Montagne	Montanha
✦	Mountains	Berge	Montañas	Montagnes	Montanhas
)(	Pass	Pass	Paso	Col	Passo
∨	Valley, Canyon	Tal, Cañon	Valle, Cañón	Vallée, Canyon	Vale, Canhão
═	Plain	Ebene	Llano	Plaine	Planície
≻	Cape	Kap	Cabo	Cap	Cabo
I	Island	Insel	Isla	Île	Ilha
II	Islands	Inseln	Islas	Îles	Ilhas
✦	Other Topographic Features	Andere Topographische Objekte	Otros Elementos Topográficos	Autres données topographiques	Outros Elementos Topográficos

ESPAÑOL: Nombre — Página — Lat.°′ — Long.°′ W=Oeste
FRANÇAIS: Nom — Page — Lat.°′ — Long.°′ W=Ouest
PORTUGUÊS: Nome — Página — Lat.°′ — Long.°′ W=Oeste

Symbol	English	Deutsch	Español	Français	Português
≃	River	Fluss	Rio	Rivière	Rio
	Canal	Kanal	Canal	Canal	Canal
	Waterfall, Rapids	Wasserfall, Stromschnellen	Cascada, Rápidos	Chute d'eau, Rapides	Cascata, Rápidos
⊔	Strait	Meeresstrasse	Estrecho	Détroit	Estreito
C	Bay, Gulf	Bucht, Golf	Bahía, Golfo	Baie, Golfe	Baía, Golfo
◎	Lake, Lakes	See, Seen	Lago, Lagos	Lac, Lacs	Lago, Lagos
	Swamp	Sumpf	Pantano	Marais	Pântano
	Ice Features, Glacier	Eis- und Gletscherformen	Accidentes Glaciales	Formes glaciaires	Acidentes Glaciares
	Other Hydrographic Features	Andere Hydrographische Objekte	Otros Elementos Hidrográficos	Autres données hydrographiques	Outros Elementos Hidrográficos
✣	Submarine Features	Untermeerische Objekte	Accidentes Submarinos	Formes de relief sous-marin	Acidentes Submarinos
□	Political Unit	Politische Einheit	Unidad Politica	Entité politique	Unidade Política
ᐁ	Cultural Institution	Kulturelle Institution	Institución Cultural	Institution culturelle	Instituição Cultural
⊥	Historical Site	Historische Stätte	Sitio Histórico	Site historique	Sitio Histórico
♠	Recreational Site	Erholungs- und Ferienort	Sitio de Recreo	Centre de loisirs	Sítio de Lazer
⊠	Airport	Flughafen	Aeropuerto	Aéroport	Aeroporto
■	Military Installation	Militäranlage	Instalación Militar	Installation militaire	Instalação Militar
◆	Miscellaneous	Verschiedenes	Misceláneo	Divers	Miscelânea

Name / Name	Page / Seite	Lat.°′ / Breite°′	Long.°′ / Länge°′ E=Ost
Castillo, Pampa del ⌣	244	45.58 S	68.24 W
Castillo de San Marcos National Monument ♠	182	29.44 N	81.20 W
Castillo Incasico de Ingapirca ⊥	236	2.34 S	78.50 W
Castillon-la-Bataille	32	44.51 N	0.03 W
Castillos	242	34.12 S	53.50 W
Castillos, Laguna de ◎	242	34.20 S	53.54 W
Castillo Velasco	224	16.45 N	96.35 W
Castine	178	44.23 N	68.48 W
Castione della Presolana	58	45.54 N	10.04 E
Castions di Strada	58	45.54 N	13.11 E
Castle Acre	44	52.42 N	0.41 E
Castle Air Force Base ■	216	37.22 N	120.34 W
Castlebar	28	53.52 N	9.17 W
Castlebellingham	42	53.54 N	6.23 W
Castleberry	184	31.17 N	87.02 W
Castleblayney	28	54.07 N	6.44 W
Castle Bruce	230d	15.26 N	61.16 W
Castle Cape ≻	170	56.15 N	158.06 W
Castle Cary	44	51.06 N	2.31 W
Castlecliff	162	39.57 S	174.59 E
Castlecrag	264a	33.48 S	151.13 E
Castle Crags State Park ♠	194	41.10 N	122.20 W
Castle Creek	200	42.14 N	75.55 W
Castle Creek ≃, Austl.	159	36.41 S	145.29 E
Castle Creek ≃, Idaho, U.S.	192	43.06 N	116.16 W
Castle Dale	190	39.13 N	111.01 W
Castledawson	42	54.47 N	6.33 W
Castle Dome Peak ∧	190	33.05 N	114.08 W
Castle Donington	44	52.51 N	1.19 W
Castle Douglas	42	54.57 N	3.56 W
Castleford	42	53.44 N	1.21 W
Castlegar	172	49.19 N	117.40 W
Castle Harbour C	230a	32.21 N	64.40 W
Castle Hill	264a	33.44 S	151.00 E
Castle Hills, Del., U.S.	198	39.41 N	75.34 W
Castle Hills, Tex., U.S.	186	29.32 N	98.31 W
Castleisland	28	52.14 N	9.27 W
Castlemaine	159	37.04 S	144.13 E
Castlemore	265b	43.47 N	79.41 W
Castle Mountain ∧, Yukon, Can.	170	64.32 N	135.25 W
Castle Mountain ∧, Calif., U.S.	216	35.56 N	120.20 W
Castle Neck ≻[1]	273	42.41 N	70.45 W
Castle Neck ≃	273	42.40 N	70.44 W
Castle Park	218	32.37 N	117.04 W
Castle Peak ∧, Colo., U.S.	190	39.00 N	106.55 W
Castle Peak ∧, Idaho, U.S.	192	44.02 N	114.35 W
Castle Peak ∧, Wash., U.S.	214	48.58 N	120.51 W
Castlepoint	162	40.54 S	176.13 E
Castle Point □[8]	250	51.33 N	0.35 E
Castlerea	28	53.46 N	8.29 W
Castlereagh ≃	156	30.12 S	147.32 E
Castle Rock, Colo., U.S.	190	39.22 N	104.51 W
Castle Rock, Pa., U.S.	275	39.58 N	75.26 W
Castle Rock, Wash., U.S.	214	46.17 N	122.54 W
Castle Rock ∧, Oreg., U.S.	192	44.02 N	118.11 W
Castle Rock ∧, Va., U.S.	182	37.57 N	78.44 W
Castle Rock Butte ∧	188	45.00 N	103.27 W
Castle Rock Lake ◎[1]	180	43.56 N	89.58 W
Castle Shannon	269b	40.22 N	80.02 W
Castleshaw Moor •–[3]	252	53.36 N	2.00 W
Castleside	42	54.50 N	1.52 W
Castleton, Eng., U.K.	42	53.21 N	1.46 W
Castleton, Eng., U.K.	42	54.28 N	0.56 W
Castleton, Eng., U.K.	252	53.35 N	2.11 W
Castleton, Ind., U.S.	208	39.54 N	86.03 W
Castleton, Vt., U.S.	178	43.37 N	73.11 W
Castleton on Hudson	200	42.32 N	73.45 W
Castletown, I. of Man	42	54.04 N	4.40 W
Castletown, Scot., U.K.	28	58.35 N	3.23 W
Castletown Berehaven	28	51.39 N	9.55 W
Castlewellan	42	54.16 N	5.57 W
Castlewood, Ky., U.S.	208	38.04 N	84.27 W
Castlewood, S. Dak., U.S.	188	44.43 N	97.02 W
Castlewood, Va., U.S.	182	36.54 N	82.17 W
Častoje	72	54.11 N	37.47 E
Častooz'ornoje	76	55.34 N	67.53 E
Castor	172	52.13 N	111.53 W
Castor ≃, Ont., Can.	202	45.18 N	75.10 W
Castor ≃, Mo., U.S.	184	36.51 N	89.44 W
Castorano	60	42.54 N	13.43 E
Castor Creek ≃	184	31.47 N	92.22 W
Castorland	202	43.53 N	75.31 W
Castra Vetera ⊥	253	51.39 N	6.28 E
Castres	32	43.36 N	2.15 E
Castricum	48	52.33 N	4.39 E
Castries, Fr.	56	43.40 N	3.59 E
Castries, St. Luc.	231f	14.01 N	61.00 W
Castries, Port C	231f	14.01 N	61.01 W
Castro, Bra.	242	24.47 S	50.00 W
Castro, Chile	244	42.29 S	73.46 W
Castro, It.	58	45.48 N	10.04 E
Castro, Arroyo de ≃	248	33.37 S	56.10 W
Castro, Punta ≻	244	43.22 S	65.03 W
Castro Barros	242	30.35 S	65.44 W
Castrocaro	60	44.10 N	11.57 E
Castrocielo	60	41.32 N	13.42 E
Castro Daire	34	40.54 N	7.56 W
Castro dei Volsci	60	41.30 N	13.24 E
Castro del Río	34	37.41 N	4.28 W
Castrojeriz	34	42.17 N	4.08 W
Castro Marim	34	37.13 N	7.26 W
Castronuño	34	41.23 N	5.16 W
Castropignano	60	41.37 N	14.33 E
Castropol	34	43.32 N	7.02 W
Castrop-Rauxel	48	51.34 N	7.18 E
Castro-Urdiales	34	43.23 N	3.13 W
Castro Valley	216	37.42 N	122.04 W
Castro Verde	34	37.42 N	8.05 W
Castrovillari	36	39.49 N	16.13 E
Castroville, Calif., U.S.	216	36.46 N	121.45 W
Castroville, Tex., U.S.	186	29.21 N	98.53 W
Castrovirreyna	238	13.16 S	75.19 W
Castuera	34	38.43 N	5.33 W
Čast Uul ∧	76	48.40 N	90.55 E
Častyje	70	57.19 N	54.59 E
Casula	144	15.25 S	33.40 E
Casummit Lake	174	51.28 N	92.24 W
Casupá	242	34.07 S	55.39 W
Caswell Sound ᥙ	162	45.00 S	167.10 E
Çat	120	39.40 N	41.00 E
Cat ≃	174	51.07 N	91.25 W
Catacamas	226	14.54 N	85.56 W
Catacaos	238	5.16 S	80.41 W
Catacocha	236	4.04 S	79.38 W
Cataguarino	246	21.18 S	42.43 W
Cataguases	246	21.24 S	42.41 W
Catahoula Lake ◎	184	31.30 N	92.06 W
Çatak	118	38.01 N	43.07 E
Catalaban Island I	106	11.51 N	125.28 E
Çatalan	120	37.14 N	35.16 E
Catalão	245	18.10 S	47.57 W
Catalão, Ponta do ≻	277a	22.51 S	43.13 W
Çatalca	120	41.09 N	28.27 E
Catalina, Newf., Can.	176	48.31 N	53.05 W
Catalina, Chile	242	25.13 S	69.43 W
Catalina → Santa Catalina Island I	218	33.23 N	118.24 W
Catalina, Punta ≻	244	52.32 S	68.47 W
Catalina Point ≻	164p	13.31 N	144.55 E
Catalonia → Cataluña □[9]	34	42.00 N	2.00 E
Cataluña □[9]	34	42.00 N	2.00 E
Cataluña, Museo de Arte de ⚑	256d	41.23 N	2.09 E
Catalzeytin	120	41.57 N	34.13 E
Catamarca	242	28.28 S	65.47 W
Catamarca □[4]	242	27.00 S	67.00 W
Catamare	276c	10.36 N	67.02 W
Catamayo	236	3.59 S	79.21 W
Catamayo ≃	236	4.18 S	80.09 W
Catanauan	106	13.36 N	122.19 E
Catanduanes □[4]	106	13.47 N	124.16 E
Catanduanes Island I	106	13.45 N	124.15 E
Catanduva	245	21.08 S	48.58 W
Catane → Catania	36	37.30 N	15.06 E
Catania	36	37.30 N	15.06 E
Catania, Golfo di C	36	37.25 N	15.15 E
Cataño	230m	18.27 N	66.07 W
Catanzaro	36	38.54 N	16.36 E
Catára ≃	142	13.34 S	12.35 E
Cataract Creek ≃	190	36.03 N	112.35 W
Cataract Reservoir ◎[1]	160	34.16 S	150.48 E
Catarama	236	1.35 S	79.28 W
Cataraqui	202	44.16 N	76.32 W
Cataraqui ≃	202	44.13 N	76.28 W
Cataricahua	238	18.14 S	66.49 W
Catarina	240	6.12 S	39.54 W
Catarina, Raso da ∧∧[1]	240	9.40 S	38.40 W
Catarman, Pil.	106	9.08 N	124.40 E
Catarman, Pil.	106	12.30 N	124.38 E
Catarman ≃	106	12.31 N	124.39 E
Catarroja	34	39.24 N	0.24 W
Catasauqua	198	40.39 N	75.29 W
Catastrophe, Cape ≻	156	34.59 S	136.00 E
Catatumbo ≃	236	9.22 N	71.45 W
Catawba	208	40.00 N	83.37 W
Catawba ≃	182	34.36 N	80.54 W
Catawba Dam •–[6]	182	34.57 N	81.04 W
Catawba Island	204	41.35 N	82.50 W
Catawissa, Mo., U.S.	209	38.25 N	90.47 W
Catawissa, Pa., U.S.	200	40.57 N	76.28 W
Catawissa Creek ≃	200	40.57 N	76.28 W
Cataxa	144	15.58 S	33.12 E
Catbalogan	106	11.46 N	124.53 E
Catchabutan, Punta ≻	226	15.50 N	86.32 W
Catchacoma Lake ◎	202	44.45 N	78.20 W
Cateco Cangola	142	8.27 S	15.48 E
Cateel	106	7.48 N	126.27 E
Cateel ≃	106	7.47 N	126.27 E
Cateel Bay C	106	7.54 N	126.25 E
Catemaco	224	18.25 N	95.07 W
Catemaco, Lago ◎	224	18.25 N	95.05 W
Catembe	146	26.00 S	32.33 E
Catende, Ang.	142	11.14 S	21.30 E
Catende, Bra.	240	8.40 S	35.43 W
Caterham	44	51.17 N	0.04 W
Catete	142	9.06 S	13.43 E
Catete •–[8]	277a	22.55 S	43.10 W
Catete ≃	240	6.04 S	54.09 W
Catfish Creek ≃, Ont., Can.	202	42.39 N	81.01 W
Catfish Creek ≃, Tex., U.S.	212	31.47 N	95.56 W
Catford •–[8]	250	51.27 N	0.01 W
Catharine Creek ≃	200	42.21 N	76.51 W
Cathcart	148	32.18 S	27.09 E
Cathead Mountain ∧	200	43.17 N	74.17 W
Cathedral City	194	33.47 N	116.28 W
Cathedral Gorge State Park ♠	194	37.50 N	114.30 W
Cathedral Mountain ∧	186	30.10 N	103.40 W
Cathedral of the Pines ⚑[1]	197	42.47 N	71.58 W
Cathedral Pass)(	148	28.55 S	29.01 E
Cathedral Provincial Park ♠	192	49.05 N	120.10 W
Cathedral Range ∧∧	216	37.47 N	119.21 W
Catherines Peak ∧	231q	18.04 N	76.42 W
Catheys Valley	216	37.25 N	120.06 W
Cathkin Mountain Pass)(	148	29.08 S	29.20 E
Cathlamet	214	46.12 N	123.23 W
Catholic University ⚑[2]	274c	38.56 N	77.00 W
Catia •–[8]	276c	10.31 N	66.57 W
Catia La Mar	276c	10.36 N	67.02 W
Catignano	60	42.21 N	13.57 E
Catimbau Pequeno	246	22.46 S	42.38 W
Catingueira	240	7.08 S	37.37 W
Catingueiro	246	22.10 S	46.52 W
Catió	140	11.13 N	15.10 W
Cat Island I, Ba.	228	24.27 N	75.30 W
Cat Island I, Mass., U.S.	273	42.31 N	70.49 W
Cat Island I, Miss., U.S.	184	30.13 N	89.06 W
Čatkal ≃	75	41.38 N	70.01 E
Čatkal'skij Chrebet ∧∧	75	41.40 N	71.05 E
Cat Lake ◎	174	51.40 N	91.50 W
Catlettsburg	178	38.25 N	82.36 W
Catlin	184	40.04 N	87.42 W
Catlins ≃	162	46.29 S	169.43 E
Catnip Mountain ∧	194	41.52 N	119.23 W
Cato	200	43.10 N	76.34 W
Catoche, Cabo ≻	222	21.35 N	87.05 W
Catoctin Creek ≃	198	39.18 N	77.33 W
Catoctin Mountain ∧	198	39.26 N	77.31 W
Cato Island I	156	23.15 S	155.32 E
Catolé do Rocha	240	6.21 S	37.45 W
Católica, Universidad ⚑[2], Chile	276e	33.27 S	70.39 W
Católica, Universidad ⚑[2], Perú	276d	12.04 S	77.05 W
Catonsville	198	39.16 N	76.44 W
Catoosa	186	36.11 N	95.45 W
Catorce	224	23.42 N	100.54 W
Catorce, Sierra ∧∧	224	23.36 N	100.52 W
Catota	142	13.52 S	17.15 E
Catria, Monte ∧	60	43.28 N	12.42 E
Catriló	242	36.26 S	63.24 W
Catrimani	236	0.27 N	61.41 W
Catrimani ≃	236	0.28 N	61.44 W
Catrine	42	55.30 N	4.20 W
Cats, Mont des ∧[2]	46	50.47 N	2.40 E
Catskill	200	42.13 N	73.52 W
Catskill Aqueduct ≃	266	41.11 N	73.48 W
Catskill Creek ≃	200	42.12 N	73.51 W
Catskill Game Farm ♠	200	42.15 N	74.01 W
Catskill Mountains ∧∧	200	42.10 N	74.30 W
Catskill Park ♠	200	42.00 N	74.30 W
Cat Spring	212	29.51 N	96.20 W
Catt, Mount ∧	172	54.21 N	128.47 W
Cattaraugus	200	42.20 N	78.52 W
Cattaraugus □[6]	204	42.15 N	78.45 W
Cattaraugus Creek ≃	204	42.35 N	79.10 W
Cattaraugus Creek, South Branch ≃	204	42.26 N	78.53 W
Cattaraugus Indian Reservation •–[4]	200	42.33 N	78.56 W
Cattenom	52	49.25 N	6.15 E
Catterick	42	54.22 N	1.38 W
Catterick Camp	42	54.22 N	1.43 W
Cattle Canyon ∨	270	34.14 N	117.46 W
Cattolica	60	43.58 N	12.44 E
Cattolica del Sacro Cuore, Università ⚑[2]	256b	45.27 N	9.11 E
Catton	42	54.55 N	2.15 W
Catu	245	12.21 S	38.23 W
Catuala	142	16.29 S	19.03 E
Catuane	146	26.48 S	32.18 E
Catubig	106	12.24 N	125.03 E
Catubig ≃	106	12.34 N	125.01 E
Catuçaba	246	23.15 S	45.12 W
Catumbela	142	12.25 S	13.34 E
Catumbela ≃	142	12.27 S	13.29 E
Catur	144	13.45 S	35.30 E
Catus	32	44.34 N	1.20 E
Čatyrtaš	75	40.55 N	76.26 E
Cau ≃	100	21.07 N	106.18 E
Cau, Rach ≃	259c	10.51 N	106.49 E
Cauaburi ≃	236	0.17 S	65.56 W
Cauale ≃	142	7.18 S	16.39 E
Cauaxi ≃	240	3.50 S	48.10 W
Cauayan, Pil.	106	16.56 N	121.46 E
Cauayan, Pil.	106	9.58 N	122.37 E
Cauca □[5]	236	2.30 N	76.50 W
Cauca ≃	236	8.54 N	74.28 W
Caucaia	240	3.42 S	38.39 W
Caucaia do Alto	246	23.41 S	47.02 W
Caucase, Monts du → Bol'šoj Kavkaz ∧∧	74	42.30 N	45.00 E
Caucasia	236	8.00 N	75.12 W
Caucaso → Bol'šoj Kavkaz ∧∧	74	42.30 N	45.00 E
Caucasus → Bol'šoj Kavkaz ∧∧	74	42.30 N	45.00 E
Cauchon Lake ◎	174	55.25 N	96.30 W
Caudebec-en-Caux	46	49.32 N	0.44 E
Caudebec-lès-Elbeuf	46	49.17 N	1.02 E
Caudry	46	50.08 N	3.25 E
Caughdenoy	200	43.16 N	76.12 W
Caughnawaga	265a	45.25 N	73.41 W
Caughnawaga Indian Reserve •–[4]	196	45.23 N	73.41 W
Cauitan, Mount ∧	106	17.16 N	121.00 E
Cauit Point ≻	106	12.16 N	122.38 E
Cauldcleuch Head ∧	42	55.18 N	2.51 W
Caulfield	159	37.53 S	145.03 E
Caulfield Racecourse ♠	264b	37.53 S	145.02 E
Caulkerbush	42	54.54 N	3.40 W
Caulonia	36	38.23 N	16.25 E
Caumont-sur-Durance	56	43.54 N	4.57 E
Caumsett State Park ♠	266	40.55 N	73.28 W
Çaúngula	142	8.25 S	18.40 E
Čaunskaja Guba C	64	69.20 N	170.00 E
Cauquenes	242	35.58 S	72.21 W
Caura ≃	236	7.38 N	64.53 W
Caurés ≃	236	1.21 S	62.20 W
Caurimare ≃	276c	10.28 N	66.48 W
Caurio [de Guadalupe]	224	19.54 N	101.49 W
Causapscal	176	48.22 N	67.14 W
Causapscal, Parc de ♠	176	48.20 N	66.55 W
Čausovo	72	54.49 N	36.55 E
Çaussade	32	44.10 N	1.32 E
Čausy	66	53.48 N	30.58 E
Cautário ≃	238	12.13 S	64.34 W
Cautín □[4]	244	38.55 S	72.30 W
Caution, Cape ≻	172	51.10 N	127.47 W
Çauto ≃	230p	20.33 N	77.14 W
Čauvaj	75	40.08 N	72.13 E
Cauvery ≃	112	11.09 N	79.52 E
Cauvery Falls ⌊	112	12.18 N	77.17 E
Caux, Pays de •–[1]	46	49.40 N	0.40 E
Cava	246	22.41 S	43.26 W
Cava de'Tirreni	60	40.42 N	14.42 E
Cávado ≃	34	41.32 N	8.48 W
Cavaglià	56	45.24 N	8.05 E
Cavaillon	56	43.50 N	5.02 E
Cavalaire-sur-Mer	56	43.10 N	6.32 E
Cavalcante	245	13.48 S	47.30 W
Cavalese	58	46.17 N	11.27 E
Cavalheiro	245	17.15 S	48.02 W
Cavalier	188	48.48 N	97.37 W
Cavalière	56	43.09 N	6.26 E
Cavalla (Cavally) ≃	140	4.22 N	7.32 W
Cavallermaggiore	56	44.43 N	7.41 E
Cavalli Islands II	162	34.58 S	173.58 E
Cavallino, Litorale di ⊥[2]	58	45.27 N	12.30 E
Cavallo, Monte ∧	58	46.08 N	12.30 E
Cavalos, Ilha dos I	240	0.18 S	50.48 W
Cavalos, Ribeirão dos ≃	246	21.29 S	44.13 W
Cava Manara	56	45.08 N	9.07 E
Cavan	28	54.00 N	7.21 W
Cavan □[6]	28	53.55 N	7.30 W
Çavanaugh, Lake ◎	214	48.23 N	122.00 W
Čavan'ga	24	66.06 N	37.47 E
Cavarzere	58	45.08 N	12.05 E
Cavaso del Tomba	58	45.51 N	11.52 E
Çavdır	120	37.09 N	29.42 E
Cave, It.	60	41.49 N	12.56 E
Cave, N.Z.	162	44.19 S	170.57 E
Cave City, Ark., U.S.	184	35.57 N	91.33 W
Cave City, Ky., U.S.	184	37.08 N	85.58 W
Cave Creek ≃	190	33.34 N	112.07 W
Cave del Predil	58	46.26 N	13.34 E
Cavedine	58	45.59 N	10.59 E
Caveiras ≃	242	27.35 S	50.56 W
Cavelo	142	17.33 S	19.21 E
Cavendish	156	37.31 S	142.02 E
Cavernago	56	45.38 N	9.46 E
Cavertitz	50	51.23 N	13.08 E
Cave Spring	182	34.07 N	85.20 W
Cavettsville	269b	40.22 N	79.46 W
Cavezzo	58	44.50 N	11.02 E
Cavi	56	44.17 N	9.22 E
Caviana, Ilha I	240	0.10 N	50.10 W
Cavili Island I	106	9.17 N	120.50 E
Cavinzas, Isla I	276d	12.07 S	77.13 W
Cavite	106		
	259f	14.29 N	120.55 E
Çavite □[4]	106	14.15 N	120.50 E
Čavlisaj	75	41.08 N	69.44 E
Cavo, Monte ∧	257a	41.45 N	12.42 E
Cavour	56	44.47 N	7.22 E
Cavour, Canale ≅	56	45.11 N	7.54 E
Cavriago	58	44.42 N	10.31 E
Cavriana	58	45.21 N	10.36 E
Cavtat	38	42.35 N	18.13 E
Çavuş	120	37.36 N	31.56 E
Çavuşbaşı ≃	257b	40.58 N	28.51 E
Çavuşcu Gölü ◎	120	38.25 N	31.53 E
Çavuşlar	120	40.43 N	32.04 E
Cawatose, Lac ◎	180	47.20 N	77.07 W
Cawayan	106	11.56 N	123.46 E
Cawit Point ≻	106	9.18 N	126.12 E
Cawker City	188	39.30 N	98.26 W
Cawnpore → Kānpur	114	26.28 N	80.21 E
Cawood, Eng., U.K.	42	53.50 N	1.07 W
Cawood, Ky., U.S.	182	36.47 N	83.14 W
Cawston, B.C., Can.	172	49.11 N	119.45 W
Cawston, Eng., U.K.	44	52.46 N	1.10 E
Cawthon	212	30.25 N	96.14 W
Caxambu	246	21.59 S	44.56 W
Caxias, Bra.	240	4.50 S	43.21 W
Caxias, Port.	256c	38.42 N	9.16 W
Caxias do Sul	242	29.10 S	51.11 W
Caxito	142	8.33 S	13.36 E
Caxiuana, Baía de C	240	1.45 S	51.20 W
Caxopa	142	11.52 S	20.52 E
Çay	120	38.35 N	31.02 E
Cayambe	236	0.03 N	78.08 W
Cayambe ∧[1]	236	0.02 N	77.59 W
Cayapoñga	106	5.48 N	125.33 E
Cayce	182	33.59 N	81.04 W
Çaycuma	120	41.25 N	32.05 E
Caycuse	214	48.53 N	124.22 W
Caycuse ≃	214	48.48 N	124.41 W
Cay-duong, Vinh C	100	10.10 N	104.45 E
Cayenne	240	4.56 N	52.20 W
Cayenne □[8]	240	4.00 N	53.00 W
Cayes → Les Cayes	228	18.12 N	73.45 W
Cayeux-sur-Mer	46	50.11 N	1.29 E
Cayey	230m	18.07 N	66.10 W
Cayey, Sierra de ∧∧	230m	18.07 N	66.02 W
Çayırhan	120	40.06 N	31.37 E
Çayırlı	120	39.48 N	40.01 E
Çayırlıahmetçiler	120	40.58 N	31.27 E
Çayırşeyhi	120	39.18 N	35.40 E
Caylus	32	44.14 N	1.46 E
Cayman Brac I	228	19.43 N	79.49 W
Cayman Islands □[2]	220		
	228	19.30 N	80.30 W
Cayman Trench ⊹[1]	16	19.00 N	80.00 W
Cayo Agua, Isla I	226	9.09 N	82.02 W
Cayra	120	40.41 N	39.06 E
Cayres	56	44.55 N	3.48 E
Cay Sal Bank ⊹[4]	228	23.45 N	80.00 W
Cayucos	216	35.27 N	120.54 W
Cayuga, Ont., Can.	202	42.56 N	79.51 W
Cayuga, Ind., U.S.	184	39.57 N	87.28 W
Cayuga, N. Dak., U.S.	188	46.04 N	97.23 W
Cayuga, N.Y., U.S.	200	42.55 N	76.44 W
Cayuga, Tex., U.S.	212	31.57 N	95.57 W
Cayuga □[6]	200	42.56 N	76.34 W
Cayuga Creek ≃	200	42.52 N	78.47 W
Cayuga Heights	200	42.28 N	76.30 W
Cayuga Lake ◎	200	42.45 N	76.45 W
Cayuta	200	42.17 N	76.42 W
Cayuta Creek ≃	200	41.59 N	76.30 W
Cazage	142	11.02 S	20.45 E
Cazalla de la Sierra	34	37.56 N	5.45 W
Căzănești	38	44.37 N	27.01 E
Cazaux, Étang de C	32	44.30 N	1.10 W
Cazenovia	200	42.56 N	75.51 W
Cazenovia Creek ≃	200	42.52 N	78.50 W
Cazenovia Creek, East Branch ≃	200	42.46 N	78.38 W
Cazenovia Creek, West Branch ≃	200	42.46 N	78.39 W
Cazenovia Lake ◎	200	42.57 N	75.53 W
Cazenovia Park ♠	274a	42.51 N	78.48 W
Cazères	32	43.13 N	1.05 E
Cazhai	96	31.12 N	121.34 E
Cazin	36	44.58 N	15.57 E
Çazis	54	46.43 N	9.25 E
Čazma	36	45.45 N	16.37 E
Cazombo	142	11.54 S	22.52 E
Cazones ≃	224	20.44 N	97.12 W
Cazones, Ensenada de C	230p	22.06 N	81.32 W
Cazones, Golfo de C	230p	21.55 N	81.20 W
Cazorla, Esp.	34	37.55 N	3.00 W
Cazorla, Ven.	236	8.01 N	67.00 W
Cazorla, Sierra de ∧∧	34	37.55 N	2.55 W
Ccapi	238	13.52 S	72.05 W
Cchaltubo	74	42.20 N	42.35 E
Cchenis-Ckali ≃	74	42.07 N	42.18 E
Çchinvali	74	42.13 N	43.56 E
Čchorocku	74	42.32 N	42.07 E
Cchunkuri	74	42.23 N	42.34 E
Cea ≃	34	42.00 N	5.36 W
Ceanannus Mór	28	53.44 N	6.53 W
Ceará → Fortaleza	240	3.43 S	38.30 W
Ceará □[3]	240	5.00 S	40.00 W
Ceará-Mirim	240	5.38 S	35.26 W
Ceará Mirim ≃	240	5.40 S	35.13 W
Ceatharlach → Carlow	28	52.50 N	6.55 W
Cébaco, Isla I	236	7.32 N	81.09 W
Čebarkul'	76	54.58 N	60.25 E
Çebeciköy	257b	41.07 N	28.52 E
Čeboksary	70	56.09 N	47.15 E
Cebolla Creek ≃	190	38.29 N	107.13 W
Cebollar	242	29.06 S	66.33 W
Cebollatí	242	33.16 S	53.47 W
Cebollín	222	25.47 N	106.10 W
Cebollita Peak ∧	190	34.43 N	107.51 W
Céboruco, Volcán ∧[1]	224	21.09 N	104.30 W
Čebotovka, S.S.S.R.	73	48.41 N	40.00 E
Čebotovka, S.S.S.R.	73	48.42 N	39.51 E
Cebreros	34	40.27 N	4.28 W
Čebrikovo	68	47.09 N	30.06 E
Čebsara	66	59.12 N	38.50 E
Cebu	106	10.18 N	123.54 E
Cebu □[4]	106	10.20 N	123.45 E
Çebu I	106	10.20 N	123.40 E
Čeburgol'	68	45.34 N	38.07 E
Ceccano	60	41.34 N	13.20 E
Cecchignola •–[8]	257a	41.49 N	12.29 E
Ceceda	186	26.04 N	103.25 W
Çeceli	120	39.43 N	33.52 E
Čečel'nik	68	48.14 N	29.21 E
Čečen', Ostrov I	74	43.58 N	47.45 E
Čečeno-Ingušskaja Avtonomnaja Sovetskaja Socialističeskaja Respublika □[3]	74	43.15 N	45.40 E
Cecer Chaan → Öndörchaan	78	47.19 N	110.39 E
Cecerleg, Mong.	78	49.30 N	97.36 E
Cecerleg, Mong.	78	47.30 N	101.27 E
Çecerleg, Mong.	78	48.55 N	101.09 E
Čečeviči	66	53.31 N	29.51 E
Çecheng	95	39.06 N	116.48 E
Čechov, S.S.S.R.	72	55.09 N	37.27 E
Čechov, S.S.S.R.	79	47.28 N	141.59 E
Čechtice	30	49.37 N	15.03 E
Čechy □[9]	30	49.50 N	14.00 E
Cecil, Ga., U.S.	182	31.05 N	83.11 W
Cecil, Ohio, U.S.	206	41.13 N	84.35 W
Cecil, Pa., U.S.	204	40.20 N	80.11 W
Cecil □[6]	198	39.36 N	75.50 W
Cecilia	184	37.40 N	85.57 W
Cecilia, Mount ∧[2]	152	20.45 S	120.55 E
Cecilio Báez	242	25.03 S	56.19 W
Cecil Park	264a	33.52 S	150.51 E
Cecil Plains	156	27.32 S	151.12 E
Cecil Rhodes, Mount ∧	152	25.26 S	121.26 E
Cecilton	198	39.24 N	75.52 W
Cecina	60	43.19 N	10.31 E
Cecina ≃	60	43.18 N	10.29 E
Çecita, Lago di ◎	36	39.24 N	16.30 E
Čečorsk	66	52.55 N	30.55 E
Čečuj ≃	78	58.12 N	109.18 E
Čečujsk	78	58.05 N	108.42 E
Cedar ≃, Mich., U.S.	180	43.53 N	84.29 W
Cedar ≃, Mich., U.S.	180	45.25 N	87.21 W
Cedar ≃, Nebr., U.S.	188	41.22 N	97.57 W
Cedar ≃, N.Y., U.S.	178	43.51 N	74.11 W
Cedar ≃, Wash., U.S.	214	47.30 N	122.12 W
Cedar, Middle Branch ≃	206	42.38 N	84.05 W
Cedar, West Branch ≃	206	42.41 N	84.09 W
Cedar, West Fork ≃	180	42.37 N	92.29 W
Cedar Bayou ≃	212	29.41 N	94.56 W
Cedar Bluff Reservoir ◎[1]	188	38.47 N	99.47 W
Cedar Bluffs	188	41.24 N	96.37 W
Cedar Breaks National Monument ♠	190	37.29 N	112.53 W
Cedar Brook	198	39.43 N	74.54 W
Cedar Brook ≃, N.J., U.S.	266	40.23 N	74.23 W
Cedar Brook ≃, N.J., U.S.	266	40.19 N	74.33 W
Cedar Brook ≃, N.J., U.S.	275	39.40 N	74.43 W
Cedar Brook Park ♠	265b	43.45 N	79.14 W
Cedarburg	180	43.17 N	87.59 W
Cedar City, Mo., U.S.	209	38.36 N	92.11 W
Cedar City, Utah, U.S.	190	37.41 N	113.04 W
Cedar Creek	212	30.05 N	97.30 W
Cedar Creek ≃, U.S.	180	41.17 N	91.21 W
Cedar Creek ≃, Ala., U.S.	184	32.13 N	87.06 W
Cedar Creek ≃, Ariz., U.S.	190	33.48 N	110.18 W
Cedar Creek ≃, Conn., U.S.	266	41.09 N	73.13 W
Cedar Creek ≃, Del., U.S.	198	38.55 N	75.20 W
Cedar Creek ≃, Ga., U.S.	184	34.08 N	85.19 W
Cedar Creek ≃, Idaho, U.S.	192	42.24 N	114.49 W
Cedar Creek ≃, Ind., U.S.	206	41.12 N	85.02 W
Cedar Creek ≃, Iowa, U.S.	180	40.58 N	91.40 W
Cedar Creek ≃, Iowa, U.S.	188	42.24 N	94.59 W
Cedar Creek ≃, Iowa, U.S.	188	42.08 N	94.35 W
Cedar Creek ≃, Ky., U.S.	208	38.25 N	84.53 W
Cedar Creek ≃, Mo., U.S.	209	38.38 N	92.13 W
Cedar Creek ≃, N. Dak., U.S.	188	46.07 N	101.18 W
Cedar Creek ≃, Ohio, U.S.	204	41.38 N	83.17 W
Cedar Creek ≃, Pa., U.S.	269b	40.10 N	79.47 W
Cedar Creek ≃, Tex., U.S.	186	32.53 N	98.37 W
Cedar Creek ≃, Tex., U.S.	212	32.04 N	96.05 W
Cedar Creek ≃, Tex., U.S.	212	30.51 N	96.12 W
Cedar Creek ≃, Tex., U.S.	212	30.02 N	97.17 W
Cedar Creek ≃, Wash., U.S.	214	45.56 N	122.37 W
Cedar Creek Reservoir ◎[1]	212	32.20 N	96.10 W
Cedar Crest Manor	275	39.41 N	75.28 W
Cedaredge	190	38.54 N	107.56 W
Cedar Falls	180	42.32 N	92.27 W
Cedar Grove, Ont., Can.	265b	43.52 N	79.12 W
Cedar Grove, Ind., U.S.	208	39.21 N	84.56 W
Cedar Grove, W. Va., U.S.	178	38.13 N	81.26 W
Cedar Grove, Wis., U.S.	180	43.33 N	87.45 W
Cedar Grove Reservoir ◎[1]	266	40.52 N	74.13 W
Cedar Hammock	210	27.27 N	82.36 W
Cedar Heights	275	40.05 N	75.17 W
Cedar Hill, Mo., U.S.	209	38.21 N	90.39 W
Cedar Hill, N.Y., U.S.	200	42.33 N	73.47 W
Cedar Hill, Tenn., U.S.	184	36.33 N	87.01 W
Cedar Hill, Tex., U.S.	212	32.35 N	96.57 W
Cedar Hills, Fla., U.S.	182	30.16 N	81.45 W
Cedar Hills, Oreg., U.S.	214	45.31 N	122.46 W
Cedarhurst, Md., U.S.	198	39.07 N	76.41 W
Cedarhurst, N.Y., U.S.	266	40.38 N	73.44 W
Cedar Island I, Md., U.S.	198	37.56 N	75.52 W
Cedar Island I, N.Y., U.S.	266	40.38 N	73.21 W
Cedar Island I, Va., U.S.	198	37.39 N	75.36 W
Cedar Island Lake ◎	271	42.38 N	83.28 W
Cedar Key	182	29.08 N	83.02 W
Cedar Knolls	266	40.49 N	74.27 W
Cedar Lake, Ind., U.S.	206	41.22 N	87.26 W
Cedar Lake, Tex., U.S.	212	28.54 N	95.35 W
Cedar Lake ◎, Ont., Can.	180	46.02 N	78.30 W
Cedar Lake ◎, Ind., U.S.	206	41.22 N	87.26 W
Cedar Lake ◎, N.J., U.S.	266	40.55 N	74.28 W
Cedar Lake ◎, Tex., U.S.	186	32.49 N	102.17 W
Cedar Lake ◎[1]	174	53.15 N	100.10 W
Cedar Lake Creek ≃	212	28.50 N	95.35 W
Cedar Lane	212	28.54 N	95.38 W
Cedar Mill	214	45.32 N	122.51 W
Cedarmont	148	26.50 S	29.01 E
Cedar Mountain ∧	194	41.36 N	120.16 W
Cedar Point	206	41.16 N	89.08 W
Cedar Point ≻, Conn., U.S.	266	41.06 N	73.22 W
Cedar Point ≻, Ohio, U.S.	204	41.42 N	83.20 W
Cedar Pond ◎	266	41.07 N	74.06 W
Cedar Rapids, Iowa, U.S.	180	41.59 N	91.40 W
Cedar Rapids, Nebr., U.S.	188	41.34 N	98.09 W
Cedar Ridge	216	39.12 N	121.01 W
Cedar Run ≃	198	38.41 N	77.29 W
Cedars	275	40.13 N	75.22 W
Cedars of Lebanon → Arz Lubnān •–[3]	120	34.14 N	36.03 E
Cedar Springs, Ont., Can.	204	42.17 N	82.02 W
Cedar Springs, Mich., U.S.	180	43.13 N	85.33 W
Cedar Swamp ≡, Mass., U.S.	273	42.33 N	71.05 W
Cedar Swamp ≡, N.J., U.S.	275	39.48 N	75.20 W
Cedartown	182	34.01 N	85.15 W
Cedarvale, B.C., Can.	172	55.01 N	128.20 W
Cedar Vale, Kans., U.S.	188	37.06 N	96.30 W
Cedarville, S. Afr.	148	30.23 S	29.03 E
Cedarville, Calif., U.S.	194	41.32 N	120.10 W
Cedarville, Ind., U.S.	206	40.12 N	85.01 W
Cedarville, Mass., U.S.	197	41.49 N	70.32 W
Cedarville, Mich., U.S.	180	46.00 N	84.22 W
Cedarville, N.Y., U.S.	200	42.56 N	75.07 W
Cedarville, Ohio, U.S.	208	39.44 N	83.48 W
Cedarville, Pa., U.S.	275	40.14 N	75.40 W
Cedarville Reservoir ◎[1]	206	41.12 N	85.01 W
Cedar Wash ∨	190	35.53 N	111.25 W
Cedarwood Park	198	40.03 N	74.08 W
Cedegolo	58	46.05 N	10.21 E
Çedeira	34	43.39 N	8.03 W
Čeder	78	51.25 N	94.45 E
Cedillo, Embalse de ◎[1]	34	39.40 N	7.25 E
Cedral	224	23.48 N	100.44 W
Cedrino ≃	36	40.23 N	9.44 E
Cedro	240	6.36 S	39.03 W
Cedrón ≃	34	39.48 N	3.33 W
Cedros, Hond.	226	14.35 N	87.08 W
Cedros, Méx.	222	24.41 N	101.47 W
Cedros, Isla I	222	28.12 N	115.15 W
Ceduna	152	32.07 S	133.40 E
Cedynia	30	52.50 N	14.14 E
Ceel	92	45.47 N	95.32 E
Ceepeecee	172	49.52 N	126.43 W
Cefalonia → Kefallinía I	38	38.15 N	20.35 E
Cefalù	36	38.02 N	14.01 E
Cefni ≃	42	53.12 N	4.23 W
Çega ≃	34	41.33 N	4.46 W
Čeganly	70	53.54 N	53.34 E
Čegdomyn	79	51.07 N	133.05 E
Čegem ≃	74	43.38 N	43.48 E
Čegem Pervyj	74	43.34 N	43.35 E
Čegitun'	170	66.34 N	171.06 W
Cegléd	30	47.10 N	19.48 E
Ceglie Messapico	36	40.39 N	17.31 E
Cehegín	34	38.06 N	1.48 W
Ceheng	92	25.10 N	105.48 E
Cehu-Silvaniei	38	47.25 N	23.11 E
Ceiba	230m	18.16 N	65.39 W
Ceibo, Arroyo ≃	248	33.57 S	58.27 W
Ceilán → Sri Lanka □[1]	112	7.00 N	81.00 E
Čeil'dag	74	40.17 N	49.18 E
Ceiriog ≃	44	52.57 N	3.02 W
Çeirw ≃	44	52.59 N	3.27 W
Čekalin	72	54.06 N	36.15 E
Čekan	70	54.51 N	53.34 E
Čekanovskij	78	56.13 N	101.25 E
Ceke	92	42.18 N	100.59 E
Çekerek ≃	120	40.34 N	35.46 E
Çekhira	138	34.17 N	10.06 E
Čekmaguš	76	55.08 N	54.40 E
Çekmeköy	257b	41.03 N	29.10 E
Čekšino	66	59.39 N	40.33 E
Čekujevo	24	63.34 N	38.56 E
Čekunda	79	50.48 N	132.10 E
Çela	142	11.25 S	15.07 E
Čel'abinsk	76	55.10 N	61.24 E
Čelákovice	50	50.10 N	14.46 E
Celâlli	120	39.42 N	37.26 E
Celano	60	42.05 N	13.33 E
Celanova	34	42.09 N	7.58 W
Celaque, Montaña de ∧∧	226	14.32 N	88.43 W
Çelaya	224	20.31 N	100.49 W
Čelbas ≃	68	46.06 N	38.59 E
Čelbasskaja	68	45.59 N	39.22 E
Cele	110	37.00 N	80.47 E
Celebes → Sulawesi I	102	2.00 S	121.00 E
Celebes Basin ⊹[1]	12	4.00 N	122.00 E
Celebes Sea ⊤[2]	102	3.00 N	122.00 E
Çelebiler	120	41.26 N	32.57 E
Čeleken	118	39.26 N	53.07 E
Celendín	238	6.52 S	78.09 W
Celenza sul Trigno	60	41.52 N	14.35 E
Celenza Valfortore	60	41.34 N	14.58 E
Celerina	54	46.31 N	9.51 E
Celeryville	204	41.02 N	82.45 W
Celeste	186	33.18 N	96.12 W
Celestún	222	20.52 N	90.24 W
Celica	236	4.07 S	79.59 W
Çelikhân	120	38.02 N	38.15 E
Celina, S.S.S.R.	70	46.32 N	41.02 E
Celina, Ohio, U.S.	206	40.33 N	84.34 W
Celina, Tenn., U.S.	184	36.33 N	85.30 W
Celina, Tex., U.S.	186	33.19 N	96.47 W
Celinnoje, S.S.S.R.	76	54.31 N	63.39 E
Celinnoje, S.S.S.R.	76	53.04 N	85.40 E
Celinnyj	70	46.40 N	44.32 E
Celinograd	76	51.10 N	71.30 E
Çelje	36	46.14 N	15.16 E
Čelkar	76	47.50 N	59.36 E
Celldömölk	30	47.16 N	17.09 E
Celle	48	52.37 N	10.05 E
Celle, Ruisseau la ≃	251	48.35 N	2.01 E
Celle Ligure	56	44.20 N	8.33 E
Celles	52	50.14 N	5.01 E
Celles-sur-Plaine	54	48.28 N	6.57 E
Cellettes	46	47.32 N	1.23 E
Cellina ≃	58	46.02 N	12.47 E
Çellino Attanasio	60	42.36 N	13.52 E
Čelmozero	24	64.18 N	31.48 E
Čelno-Veršiny	70	54.26 N	51.06 E
Čelobitjevo	255b	55.55 N	37.40 E
Celone ≃	60	41.36 N	15.41 E
Celorico da Beira	34	40.38 N	7.23 W
Celoron	204	42.06 N	79.17 W
Çeltik	120	41.11 N	32.19 E
Çeltikçi, Tür.	120	40.20 N	32.28 E
Çeltikçi, Tür.	120	37.32 N	30.29 E
Čel'uš	76	51.32 N	87.46 E
Čel'uskin, Mys ≻	64	77.45 N	104.20 E
Čel'uskincev Park ♠	255a	60.01 N	30.19 E
Çemaes Head ≻	44	52.07 N	4.44 W
Čemal	76	51.25 N	86.01 E
Čembilej	70	55.19 N	45.43 E
Cembra	58	46.10 N	11.13 E
Cembra, Val di ∨	58	46.10 N	11.13 E
Cement City	206	42.04 N	84.20 W
Çementon, N.Y., U.S.	200	42.09 N	73.55 W
Çementon, Pa., U.S.	198	40.41 N	75.30 W
Çemer	68	51.07 N	31.13 E
Çemerisy	68	51.42 N	30.24 E
Čemerno	36	43.11 N	18.37 E
Čemerno)(	38	43.14 N	18.37 E
Čemerovcy	68	49.01 N	26.21 E
Cemesskaja Buchta C	68	44.40 N	37.50 E
Cemilbey	120	40.21 N	35.04 E
Çemişgezek	120	39.04 N	38.55 E
Çemmaes	44	52.37 N	3.42 W
Çemolgan	75	43.23 N	76.37 E
Čenča	78	55.57 N	110.59 E
Cencenighe	58	46.21 N	11.58 E
Çenchermandal	78	47.40 N	109.05 E
Čency	72	56.03 N	36.01 E
Cenderawasih, Teluk C	154	2.30 S	135.20 E
Cendras	56	44.09 N	4.04 E
Cene	56	45.47 N	9.49 E
Cenepa ≃	236	4.35 S	78.12 W
Ceneri, Monte)(	54	46.08 N	8.55 E
Çengel	76	48.56 N	89.10 E
Čengel'dy, S.S.S.R.	75	41.51 N	68.59 E
Čengel'dy, S.S.S.R.	75	43.59 N	77.26 E
Çengelköy •–[8]	257b	41.03 N	29.03 E
Cengles, Croda di ∧	58	46.34 N	10.38 E
Ceno ≃	36	44.41 N	10.05 E
Cenovo	38	43.32 N	25.39 E
Cenrana	102	3.18 S	118.50 E
Censeau	54	46.49 N	6.04 E
Centallo	56	44.30 N	7.35 E
Centenario	242	38.48 S	68.08 W
Centenário do Sul	245	22.48 S	51.37 W
Centennial Lake ◎	275	39.50 N	74.51 W
Centennial Lake ◎[1]	202	45.10 N	72.05 W
Centennial Mountains ∧∧	192	44.35 N	111.55 W
Centennial Park ♠, Austl.	264a	33.54 S	151.14 E
Centennial Park ♠, Ont., Can.	265b	43.39 N	79.35 W
Centennial Wash ∨	190	33.14 N	112.46 W
Centeno	60	42.48 N	11.49 E
Center, Colo., U.S.	190	37.45 N	106.06 W
Center, Ind., U.S.	206	40.26 N	86.04 W
Center, Mo., U.S.	209	39.30 N	91.32 W
Center, Nebr., U.S.	188	42.37 N	97.53 W
Center, N. Dak., U.S.	188	47.07 N	101.18 W
Center, Tex., U.S.	184	31.48 N	94.11 W
Centerbrook	197	41.21 N	72.25 W
Center Brunswick	200	42.45 N	73.37 W
Centerburg	204	40.18 N	82.42 W
Center City	180	45.24 N	92.49 W
Center Cross	198	37.48 N	76.47 W
Centereach	200	40.51 N	73.06 W
Centerfield	208	38.21 N	83.24 W
Center Hill	210	28.38 N	82.03 W
Center Hill Lake ◎[1]	184	36.00 N	85.45 W
Center Line	204	42.29 N	83.03 W
Center Moriches	178	40.48 N	72.48 W
Center Mountain ∧	192	45.06 N	115.13 W

Symbols in the index entries represent the broad categories identified in the key at the right. Symbols with superior numbers (∧∧[2]) identify subcategories (see complete key on page *I* · *26*).

Kartensymbole in dem Registerverzeichnis stellen die rechts in Schlüssel erklärten Kategorien dar. Symbole mit hochgestellten Ziffern (∧∧[2]) bezeichnen Unterabteilungen einer Kategorie (vgl. vollständiger Schlüssel auf Seite *I* · *26*).

Los símbolos incluídos en el texto del índice representan las grandes categorias identificadas con la clave a la derecha. Los símbolos con numeros en su parte superior (∧∧[2]) identifican las subcategorías (véase la clave completa en la página *I* · *26*).

Les symboles de l'index représentent les catégories indiquées dans la légende à droite. Les symboles suivis d'un indice (∧∧[2]) représentent des sous-catégories (voir légende complète à la page *I* · *26*).

Os símbolos incluídos no texto do índice representam as grandes categorias identificadas com a chave à direita. Os símbolos com números em sua parte superior (∧∧[2]) identificam as subcategorias (veja-se a chave completa à página *I* · *26*).

∧	Mountain	Berg	Montaña	Montagne	Montanha
∧∧	Mountains	Berge	Montañas	Montagnes	Montanhas
)(	Pass	Pass	Paso	Col	Passo
∨	Valley, Canyon	Tal, Cañon	Valle, Cañón	Vallée, Canyon	Vale, Canhão
⌣	Plain	Ebene	Llano	Plaine	Planície
≻	Cape	Kap	Cabo	Cap	Cabo
I	Island	Insel	Isla	Île	Ilha
II	Islands	Inseln	Islas	Îles	Ilhas
⊥	Other Topographic Features	Andere Topographische Objekte	Otros Elementos Topográficos	Autres données topographiques	Outros Elementos Topográficos

ESPAÑOL — Nombre / Página / Lat.°′ / Long.°′ W=Oeste
FRANÇAIS — Nom / Page / Lat.°′ / Long.°′ W=Ouest
PORTUGUÊS — Nome / Página / Lat.°′ / Long.°′ W=Oeste

Center Point, Ala., U.S. 184 33.38 N 86.41 W
Center Point, Iowa, U.S. 180 42.11 N 91.46 W
Center Point, Tex., U.S. 186 29.57 N 99.02 W
Centerport, N.Y., U.S. 200 40.54 N 73.22 W
Centerport, Pa., U.S. 198 40.29 N 76.01 W
Center Square, N.J., U.S. 275 39.46 N 75.23 W
Center Square, Pa., U.S. 198 40.10 N 75.18 W
Centerton, Ind., U.S. 208 39.31 N 86.24 W
Centerton, N.J., U.S. 275 40.00 N 74.57 W
Center Valley 198 40.32 N 75.24 W
Centerville, Del., U.S. 275 39.30 N 75.10 W
Centerville, Ind., U.S. 208 39.49 N 85.00 W
Centerville, Iowa, U.S. 180 40.43 N 92.52 W
Centerville, Mass., U.S. 197 41.39 N 70.21 W
Centerville, Mo., U.S. 184 37.26 N 90.58 W
Centerville, N.Y., U.S. 200 42.29 N 78.15 W
Centerville, Ohio, U.S. 208 39.38 N 84.10 W
Centerville, Pa., U.S. 204 41.44 N 79.46 W
Centerville, S. Dak., U.S. 188 43.07 N 96.58 W
Centerville, Tenn., U.S. 184 35.47 N 87.28 W
Centerville, Tex., U.S. 212 31.16 N 95.59 W
Centerville, Utah, U.S. 190 40.55 N 111.52 W
Centerville, Wash., U.S. 214 45.45 N 120.54 W
Centinela 186 28.47 N 100.34 W
Centinela, Cerro del ∧ 224 19.13 N 104.17 W
Cento 58 44.43 N 11.17 E
Centocelle ◂[8] 257a 41.53 N 12.34 E
Cento Croci, Passo di)(56 44.25 N 9.37 E
Central, Bra. 240 11.08 S 42.08 W
Central, Alaska, U.S. 170 65.34 N 144.48 W
Central, Ariz., U.S. 190 32.52 N 109.48 W
Central, N. Mex., U.S. 190 32.46 N 108.09 W
Central, S.C., U.S. 182 34.44 N 82.47 W
Central, Tex., U.S. 212 31.26 N 94.49 W
Central □[4], Ghana 140 5.30 N 1.00 W
Central □[4], Kenya 144 0.45 S 37.00 E
Central □[4], Malawi 144 13.00 S 34.00 E
Central □[4], Zam. 144 15.00 S 29.00 E
Central □[5], Bots. 146 21.30 S 26.00 E
Central □[5], Pap. N. Gui. 154 9.00 S 147.00 E
Central □[5], Para. 242 25.30 S 57.30 W
Central □[5], S. Lan. 112 7.30 N 80.50 E
Central, Cordillera ∧∧, Bol. 238 18.30 S 64.55 W
Central, Cordillera ∧∧, Col. 236 5.00 N 75.00 W
Central, Cordillera ∧∧, C.R. 226 10.10 N 84.05 W
Central, Cordillera ∧∧, Perú 238 8.00 S 77.00 W
Central, Cordillera ∧∧, Pil. 106 17.20 N 120.57 E
Central, Cordillera ∧∧, P.R. 230m 18.10 N 66.35 W
Central, Cordillera ∧∧, Rep. Dom. 228 18.45 N 70.30 W
Central, Macizo → Central, Massif ∧∧ 32 45.00 N 3.10 E
Central, Massif ∧∧ 32 45.00 N 3.10 E
Central, Planalto ∧∧[1] 232 18.00 S 47.00 W
Central, Sistema ∧∧ 34 40.30 N 5.00 W
Central African Empire □[1] 126 7.00 N 21.00 E
Central Aguirre 230m 17.57 N 66.13 W
Central Barren 208 38.22 N 86.06 W
Central Basin ⊹[1] 4 10.00 S 80.00 E
Central Brāhui Range ∧∧ 110 29.20 N 66.55 E
Central Bridge 200 42.43 N 74.20 W
Central Butte 174 50.47 N 106.30 W
Central City, Ill., U.S. 209 41.14 N 88.16 W
Central City, Iowa, U.S. 180 42.12 N 91.31 W
Central City, Ky., U.S. 184 37.18 N 87.07 W
Central City, Nebr., U.S. 188 41.07 N 98.00 W
Central City, Pa., U.S. 204 40.06 N 78.48 W
Central Division □[5], Fiji 165g 18.05 S 178.30 E
Central Division □[5], Sol.is. 165e 9.30 S 160.00 E
Central Falls 197 41.54 N 71.23 W
Central Heights 190 32.25 N 110.48 W
Central Highlands 269b 40.16 N 79.50 W
Centralia, Ill., U.S. 209 38.31 N 89.08 W
Centralia, Kans., U.S. 188 39.44 N 96.08 W
Centralia, Mo., U.S. 209 39.13 N 92.08 W
Centralia, Tex., U.S. 212 31.16 N 95.02 W
Centralia, Wash., U.S. 214 46.43 N 122.58 W
Centralia, Lake ⊜ 209 38.32 N 88.59 W
Centralia Draw ↳ 186 31.27 N 101.16 W
Centralina 245 18.34 S 49.13 W
Central Intelligence Agency ♥ 274c 38.57 N 77.09 W
Central Internacional, Aeropuerto ⊠ 276a 19.26 N 99.04 W
Central Island I 144 3.30 N 36.03 E
Central Islip 200 40.47 N 73.12 W
Central Lake 180 45.04 N 85.16 W
Central Makrān Range ∧∧ 118 26.40 N 64.30 E
Central Mount Stuart ∧ 152 21.54 S 133.27 E
Central Mount Wedge ∧ 152 22.51 S 131.50 E
Central No. 2 Division □[5] 165f 16.10 S 168.00 E
Central No. 2 Division □[8] 165f 16.30 S 167.30 E
Central'no-Bokovskoj 255b 55.53 N 37.51 E
◂[8]Ral'no-Bokovskoj 73 48.11 N 39.03
Central No. 1 Division □[5] 165f 17.30 S 169.00 E
Central'nolesnoj Zapovednik ◂[4] 66 56.32 N 32.50 E
Central Nyack 266 41.06 N 73.57 W
Central'nyj, S.S.S.R. 66 53.41 N 39.38 E
Central'nyj, S.S.S.R. 76 57.41 N 80.57 E
Central'nyj, S.S.S.R. 76 58.45 N 84.28 E
Central'nyj, S.S.S.R. 76 55.12 N 87.40 E
Central'nyje Karakumy ◂[2] 118 39.00 N 60.00 E
Centralnyj Park Imeni Gor'kogo ♠ 255b 55.44 N 37.46 E
Centralnyj Stadion Imeni V.I. Lenina ♠ 255b 55.43 N 37.33 E
Central Pacific Basin ⊹[1] 14 7.00 N 176.00 W
Central Park, N.J., U.S. 266 40.26 N 74.18 W
Central Park, Wash., U.S. 214 46.58 N 123.41 W
Central Park ♠ 266 40.47 N 73.58 W
Central Point 192 42.23 N 122.57 W
Central Railroad Station ◂[5] 262c 18.58 N 72.50 E
Central Range ∧∧ 154 5.00 S 142.30 E
Central Region □[6] 42 56.05 N 4.20 W
Central Square 200 43.17 N 76.09 W
Central Utah Canal ≡ 190 39.35 N 112.12 W
Central Valley, Calif., U.S. 194 40.41 N 122.22 W
Central Valley, N.Y., U.S. 200 41.20 N 74.07 W
Central Village 197 41.43 N 71.54 W
Centre 184 34.09 N 85.40 W
Centre □[5] 140 13.00 N 1.00 W
Centre □[6] 200 40.55 N 77.47 W
Centre, Canal du ≡ 32 46.27 N 4.07 E
Centre Atomique de Marcoule ♥[3] 56 44.08 N 4.42 E
Centre City 275 39.46 N 75.11 W
Centre d'Energie Atomique de Pierrelatte ♥[3] 56 44.21 N 4.44
Centre d'Études ♥[3] 251 48.33 N 2.21 E
Centre Hall 204 40.51 N 77.41 W
Centre Island 266 40.54 N 73.32 W
Centre Island I 162 46.28 S 167.51 E
Centre Island Park ♠ 265b 43.37 N 79.23 W
Centre Lake ⊜ 202 44.36 N 75.51 W
Centre Peak ∧ 172 55.41 N 126.26 W
Centreville, Ala., U.S. 184 32.56 N 87.08 W
Centreville, Ill., U.S. 209 38.33 N 90.06 W
Centreville, Ky., U.S. 208 38.13 N 84.24 W
Centreville, Md., U.S. 198 39.03 N 76.04 W
Centreville, Mich., U.S. 206 41.55 N 85.32 W
Centreville, Miss., U.S. 184 31.05 N 91.04 W
Centreville, Va., U.S. 198 38.50 N 77.26 W
Centro Puntas 230m 18.22 N 67.16 W
Centro Río Mayo 244 45.35 S 71.06 W
Centro Simón Bolívar ◂[9] 276c 10.30 N 66.55 W
Century, Fla., U.S. 184 30.58 N 87.16 W
Century, W. Va., U.S. 178 39.06 N 80.11 W
Century City ◂[8] 270 34.03 N 118.26 W
Cenxi 92 22.59 N 111.00 E
Čepca 70 57.54 N 53.25 E
Čepca ≃ 70 58.36 N 50.04 E
Čepeckij 70 58.29 N 51.12 E
Čepel' 68 49.19 N 36.55 E
Čepelare 38 41.44 N 24.41 E
Čepel'ovo 72 55.11 N 37.30 E
Čepovan 58 46.03 N 13.47 E
Cepoy 46 48.03 N 2.44 E
Ceprano 60 41.33 N 13.31 E
Ceptia 142 12.56 S 17.35 E
Cepu 105a 7.09 S 111.35 E
Ceraino 58 45.35 N 10.50 E
Ceram → Seram I 154 3.00 S 129.00 E
Ceram Sea → Seram, Laut ⊤[2] 154 2.30 S 128.00 E
Cerano, It. 56 45.25 N 8.47 E
Cerano, Méx. 224 20.07 N 101.23 W
Čerčany 30 49.51 N 14.43 E
Čerchov ∧ 30 49.23 N 12.47 E
Cercié 54 46.07 N 4.40 E
Cercola 60 40.51 N 14.21 E
Čerdakly 70 54.23 N 48.51 E
Cerdas 238 20.48 S 66.29 W
Cerdeña, Isla de → Sardegna I 36 40.00 N 9.00 E
Čerdojak 76 48.48 N 84.00 E
Cerdon, Fr. 46 47.38 N 2.22 E
Cerdon, Fr. 54 46.05 N 5.28 E
Čerdyn' 24 60.23 N 56.24 E
Cère ≃ 32 44.55 N 1.53 E
Cerea 58 45.12 N 11.13 E
Cereal 174 51.25 N 110.48 W
Cereales 242 36.49 S 63.51 W
Čerecha ≃ 66 57.46 N 28.21 E
Cereglio 58 44.18 N 11.04 E
Čereja 66 54.37 N 29.17 E
Čerek ≃ 74 43.42 N 44.03 E
Čeremchovo 78 53.09 N 103.05 E
Čeremisinovo 68 51.54 N 37.15 E
Čeremšan, S.S.S.R. 70 54.40 N 51.30 E
Čeremšan, S.S.S.R. 70 55.15 N 48.07 E
Čeremšanka, S.S.S.R. 76 59.10 N 76.51 E
Čeremšanka, S.S.S.R. 76 56.07 N 60.19 E
Čeremušskij 24 61.16 N 47.12 E
Cerenti 102 0.30 S 101.52 E
Čerepanovka 70 57.07 N 54.10 E
Čerepanovo 76 54.13 N 83.22 E
Čerepaška, Ostrov I 73 47.11 N 38.59 E
Čerepet' 72 54.07 N 36.23 E
Čerepkovo ◂[8] 255b 55.46 N 37.23 E
Čerepovec 66 59.08 N 37.54 E
Ceres, Arg. 242 29.53 S 61.57 W
Ceres, Bra. 245 15.17 S 49.35 W
Ceres, It. 56 45.19 N 7.23 E
Ceres, S. Afr. 148 33.21 S 19.18 E
Ceres, Calif., U.S. 216 37.35 N 120.57 W
Ceres, N.Y., U.S. 200 42.00 N 78.16 W
Ceresco, Mich., U.S. 206 42.16 N 85.04 W
Ceresco, Nebr., U.S. 188 41.03 N 96.39 W
Ceresole Reale 56 45.26 N 7.15 E
Céreste 56 43.51 N 5.35 E
Céret 32 42.29 N 2.45 E
Cereté 236 8.53 N 75.48 W
Čerevkovka 68 48.50 N 37.40 E
Čerevkovka ◂[8] 73 48.50 N 37.40 E
Čerevkovo 24 61.46 N 45.12 E
Cereweh 105b 8.52 S 116.51 E
Cerf Island I 128 9.32 S 50.59 E
Čerga 76 51.35 N 85.38 E
Cergy 251 49.02 N 2.04 E
Ceri ≃ 44 52.03 N 4.29 W
Ceriale 56 44.06 N 8.14 E
Ceriana 56 43.53 N 7.46 E
Ceriano 256b 45.38 N 9.05 E
Cerignola 36 41.16 N 15.54 E
Čerikov 66 53.34 N 31.23 E
Cérilly 32 46.37 N 2.49 E
Cerisiers 46 48.08 N 3.29 E
Čerkašina 78 58.37 N 108.30 E
Čerkasovo 72 54.33 N 36.48 E
Čerkasskoje, S.S.S.R. 68 48.35 N 38.56 E
Čerkasskoje, S.S.S.R. 70 52.26 N 47.13 E
Čerkasskoje, S.S.S.R. 73 48.50 N 37.23 E
Čerkassy, S.S.S.R. 66 52.41 N 38.43 E
Čerkassy, S.S.S.R. 68 49.26 N 32.04 E
Çerkeş 120 40.50 N 32.54 E
Čerkesovskij 70 50.41 N 42.34 E
Čerkessk 74 44.14 N 42.04 E
Çerkezköy 120 41.17 N 28.00 E
Čerkizovo, S.S.S.R. 72 55.12 N 38.45 E
Čerkizovo, S.S.S.R. 255b 55.58 N 37.48 E
Čerkizovo, S.S.S.R. 255b 55.57 N 37.22 E
Cerknica 36 45.48 N 14.22 E
Čerkovišče 66 55.54 N 30.51 E
Čerlak 76 54.09 N 74.48 E
Čerlakskij 76 53.47 N 74.31 E
Cermei 38 46.33 N 21.51 E
Čermen 74 43.11 N 44.42 E
Cermignano 60 42.35 N 13.47 E
Çermik 120 38.09 N 39.27 E
Čern' 66 53.27 N 36.55 E
Cerna, Jugo. 38 45.11 N 18.42 E
Cerna, Rom. 38 45.04 N 28.18 E
Čern'achov 68 50.27 N 28.39 E
Čern'achovsk (Insterburg) 66 54.38 N 21.49 E
Černá hora ∧ 30 48.58 N 13.48 E
Černaja 68 47.37 N 29.20 E
Čern'ajevo 79 52.45 N 126.00 E
Černak [illegible]
Čern'anka 68 50.55 N 37.49 E
Cernăuţi → Černovcy 68 48.18 N 25.56 E
Černava, S.S.S.R. 66 52.30 N 38.03 E
Černava, S.S.S.R. [illegible]
Černavčicy 66 52.13 N 23.44 E
Černavka, S.S.S.R. 70 52.18 N 47.24 E
Černavka, S.S.S.R. [illegible]
Cernavodă 54 44.20 N 28.02 E
Cernay 46 47.49 N 7.10 E
Cernay-la-Ville 46 48.40 N 1.58 E
Cerne Abbas 44 50.49 N 2.29 W
Černeckoje 72 55.15 N 37.20 E
Cernei, Munții ∧∧ 38 45.02 N 22.31 E
Černelica 68 48.48 N 25.26 E
Černevcy 68 48.33 N 28.09 E
Černigov 68 51.30 N 31.18 E
Černigov □[4] 66 52.13 N 32.45 E
Černigovka, S.S.S.R. 68 47.13 N 36.14 E
Černigovka, S.S.S.R. 76 50.28 N 71.27 E
Černigovka, S.S.S.R. 79 44.21 N 132.33 E
Černigovka, S.S.S.R. 79 49.37 N 129.57 E
Černigovskaja 68 44.41 N 39.40 E
Černigovskoje Polesje ◂[1] 68 51.30 N 31.20 E
Černi vrăh ∧ 38 42.34 N 23.17 E
Černobaj 68 49.41 N 32.19 E
Černobbio 56 45.50 N 9.04 E
Černogolovka 72 56.00 N 38.22 E
Černogorsk 76 53.49 N 91.18 E
Černokol'skaja 76 56.42 N 72.49 E
Černorečenskoje 75 43.00 N 74.55 E
Černorečje 74 43.15 N 45.41 E
Černovcy 68 48.18 N 25.56 E
Černovka, S.S.S.R. 76 56.47 N 76.28 E
Černovka, S.S.S.R. 79 51.43 N 128.12 E
Čern'ovo, S.S.S.R. 66 58.39 N 28.14 E
Čern'ovo, S.S.S.R. 72 54.43 N 38.36 E
Čern'ovo, S.S.S.R. 255b 55.50 N 37.18 E
Černovskije Kopi 78 52.00 N 113.15 E
Černovskoje, S.S.S.R. 70 57.29 N 54.36 E
Černovskoje, S.S.S.R. 70 58.42 N 47.24 E
Černucha 70 55.36 N 43.46 E
Černuchi 68 50.16 N 32.57 E
Černuchino 73 48.19 N 38.30 E
Cernusco sul Naviglio 56 45.31 N 9.19 E
Černuška, S.S.S.R. 76 56.29 N 56.03 E
Černuška, S.S.S.R. 78 52.58 N 101.55 E
Cerny-en-Laonnois 46 49.27 N 3.40 E
Černyševa, Kr'až ∧∧ 24 66.30 N 59.00 E
Černyševsk 78 52.35 N 117.00 E
Černyševskij 64 63.00 N 112.15 E
Černyškovskij 70 48.27 N 42.14 E
Čer'omošč ≃ 68 48.23 N 25.37 E
Čer'omuchova 70 54.57 N 51.09 E
Čer'omuski ◂[8] 255b 55.41 N 37.35 E
Cerralvo 222 26.06 N 99.37 W
Cerralvo, Isla I 222 24.17 N 109.52 W
Cerreto, Passo del)(58 44.18 N 10.13 E
Cerreto d'Esi 60 43.19 N 12.59 E
Cerreto Guidi 60 43.45 N 10.53 E
Cerreto Sannita 60 41.17 N 14.33 E
Cerrigydrudion 44 53.02 N 3.33 W
Cërrik 38 41.02 N 19.57 E
Cerrillos, Arg. 242 24.54 S 65.29 W
Cerrillos, N. Mex., U.S. 190 35.26 N 106.08 W
Cerrina 56 45.07 N 8.13 E
Cerritos, Méx. 224 22.26 N 100.17 W
Cerritos, Calif., U.S. 270 33.51 N 118.05 W
Cerro 54 45.54 N 8.36 E
Cerro, Forca di)(60 42.45 N 12.47 E
Cerro Azul, Arg. 242 27.38 S 55.29 W
Cêrro Azul, Bra. 242 24.50 S 49.15 W
Cerro Azul, Méx. 224 21.12 N 97.44 W
Cerro Azul, Perú 238 13.02 S 76.30 W
Cerro Chato 242 33.06 S 55.08 W
Cerro Colorado 242 33.52 S 55.33 W
Cêrro Corá 240 6.03 S 36.21 W
Cerro de Garnica, Parque Nacional ♠ 224 19.35 N 100.47 W
Cerro de las Campanas, Parque Nacional ♠ 224 20.40 N 100.30 W
Cerro de las Mesas ⊥ 224 18.47 N 96.05 W
Cerro de los Angeles ♥[1] 256a 40.19 N 3.41 W
Cerro de Pasco 238 10.41 S 76.16 W
Cerro Gordo 209 39.53 N 88.44 W
Cerro Grande ≃ 276c 10.37 N 66.49 W
Cêrro Largo 242 28.09 S 54.45 W
Cerro Moreno 242 23.28 S 70.25 W
Cerro Prieto 194 32.27 N 115.17 W
Cerro Vera 242 33.11 S 57.28 W
Čerskij 64 68.45 N 161.45 E
Čerskogo, Chrebet ∧∧ 78 52.00 N 114.00 E
Čerskogo, Gora ∧ 78 55.05 N 108.40 E
Certaldo 60 43.33 N 11.02 E
Čertanovka ≃ 255b 55.38 N 37.47 E
Čertanovo ◂[8] 255b 55.38 N 37.37 E
Čertkovo 73 49.23 N 40.10 E
Čertolino 66 56.12 N 33.54 E
Čertomlyk 68 47.37 N 34.09 E
Certosa (Karthaus) 58 46.42 N 10.54 E
Certosa di Pavia 56 45.15 N 9.09 E
Čerusti 66 55.33 N 40.01 E
Červ'anka 78 57.41 N 99.33 E
Cervantes 106 16.59 N 120.44 E
Cervarezza 58 44.23 N 10.20 E
Cervaro 60 41.29 N 13.54 E
Cervaro ≃ 60 41.30 N 15.52 E
Cervati, Monte ∧ 36 40.17 N 15.29 E
Cervelló 256d 41.24 N 1.57 E
Cervelló, Riera de ≃ 256d 41.24 N 2.01 E
Červen' 66 53.42 N 28.26 E
Červen Brjag 38 43.16 N 24.06 E
Červený Kostelec 30 50.29 N 16.06 E
Cervera 34 41.40 N 1.17 E
Cervera del Río Alhama 34 42.01 N 1.57 W
Cervera de Pisuerga 34 42.52 N 4.30 W
Cerveteri 60 42.00 N 12.06 E
Cervia 60 44.15 N 12.22 E
Cervialto, Monte ∧ 36 40.47 N 15.08 E
Cervignano del Friuli 58 45.49 N 13.20 E
Cervin, Mont → Matterhorn ∧ 54 45.59 N 7.43 E
Cervinara 60 41.01 N 14.37 E
Cervione 36 42.20 N 9.31 E
Červl'onnaja 74 43.30 N 45.54 E
Cervo, Esp. 34 43.40 N 7.25 W
Cervo, It. 56 43.55 N 8.07 E
Cervo ≃, Bra. 246 22.07 S 45.49 W
Cervo ≃, It. 56 45.22 N 8.24 E
Cervo, Capo ≻ 56 43.55 N 8.08 E
Cervo, Rio do ≃ 246 21.12 S 45.10 W
Červonaja Kamenka 68 48.38 N 33.26 E
Červonoarmejsk, S.S.S.R. 68 50.08 N 25.16 E
Červonoarmejsk, S.S.S.R. 68 50.28 N 28.14 E
Červonoarmejskoje, S.S.S.R. 68 45.47 N 28.44 E
Červonoarmejskoje, S.S.S.R. 68 47.57 N 35.27 E
Červonograd 68 50.24 N 24.14 E
Červonogranitnoje 68 50.34 N 28.33 E
Červonoje, S.S.S.R. 68 51.46 N 34.04 E
Červonoje, S.S.S.R. 68 49.57 N 28.53 E
Červonoje, Ozero ⊜ 66 52.24 N 27.57 E
Červonopartizansk 73 48.04 N 39.50 E
Červonyj Donec 68 49.29 N 36.34 E
Cesana Torinese 56 44.57 N 6.47 E
Cesano, It. [illegible]
Cesano, It. [illegible]
Cesano ≃ [illegible]
Cesano Boscone 256b 45.27 N 9.06 E
Cesano Maderno 56 45.38 N 9.08 E
César ≃ 236 9.00 N 73.58 W
Cesate 256b 45.36 N 9.05 E
Cesena 60 44.08 N 12.15 E
Cesenatico 60 44.12 N 12.24 E
Cesi, Poggio ∧ 257a 42.02 N 12.44 E
Cesiomaggiore 58 46.05 N 11.59 E
Cēsis 66 57.18 N 25.15 E
Česká Kamenice 50 50.48 N 14.25 E
Česká Lípa 50 50.42 N 14.32 E
Česká Socialistická Republika □[3] 30 49.40 N 15.10 E
Česká Třebová 30 49.54 N 16.27 E
České Budějovice 30 48.59 N 14.28 E
České středohoří ∧∧ 50 50.35 N 14.09 E
Českomoravská vrchovina ∧∧[1] 30 49.20 N 15.30 E
Československo → Czechoslovakia □[1] 30 49.30 N 17.00 E
Český Brod 50 50.02 N 14.58 E
Český Krumlov 30 48.49 N 14.19 E
Český Těšín 30 49.45 N 18.37 E
Česma 76 53.50 N 60.40 E
Çeşme 120 38.18 N 26.19 E
Céspedes 230p 21.35 N 78.17 W
Çessalto 58 45.42 N 12.36 E
Češskaja Guba C 24 67.30 N 46.30 E
Cessnock 160 32.50 S 151.21 E
Cesson 251 48.34 N 2.36 E
Cestos ≃ 140 5.40 N 9.10 W
Cesvaine 66 56.58 N 26.19 E
Čet' ≃ 76 53.41 N 94.28 E
Cetara 60 40.39 N 14.42 E
Cetate 38 44.06 N 23.03 E
Cetatea Albă → Belgorod-Dnestrovskij 68 46.12 N 30.20 E
Četbulak 75 41.17 N 73.58 E
Cetian 90 25.44 N 116.22 E
Cetina ≃ 36 43.26 N 16.42 E
Cetinje 38 42.23 N 18.55 E
Çetinkaya 120 39.15 N 37.38 E
Četlasskij Kamen', Gora ∧[2] 24 64.22 N 50.45 E
Cetona 60 42.58 N 11.54 E
Cetona, Monte ∧ 60 42.56 N 11.52 E
Cetronia 198 40.35 N 75.31 W
Cetti Bay C 164p 13.19 N 144.39 E
Četyrboki 68 50.02 N 27.01 E
Céüse, Montagne de ∧ 56 44.31 N 5.57 E
Ceuta 34 35.53 N 5.19 W
Ceva 56 44.23 N 8.02 E
Cevedale, Monte (Zufallspitze) ∧ 58 46.27 N 10.37 E
Cevennen → Cévennes ◂[1] 32 44.00 N 3.30 E
Cévennes ◂[1] 32 44.00 N 3.30 E
Cévennes, Parc National des ♠ 56 44.20 N 3.45 E
Cevins 56 45.35 N 6.28 E
Cevio 54 46.19 N 8.36 E
Cevizli 120 37.12 N 31.45 E
Cevizlik 74 40.48 N 39.38 E
Ceyhan 120 37.04 N 35.47 E
Ceyhan ≃ 120 36.45 N 35.42 E
Ceylânpınar 120 36.51 N 40.02 E
Ceylon, Sask., Can. 174 49.28 N 104.36 W
Ceylon, Minn., U.S. 188 43.32 N 94.38 W
Ceylon → Sri Lanka □[1] 112 7.00 N 81.00 E
Ceylon I 112 7.00 N 81.00 E
Ceyzériat 54 46.10 N 5.19 E
Cèze ≃ 56 44.06 N 4.42 E
Chaam, Ned. 48 51.31 N 4.52 E
Cha-am, Thai 100 12.48 N 99.58 E
Chaanling 90 29.39 N 113.49 E
Chaatl Island I 172 53.00 N 132.25 W
Chabanais 32 45.52 N 0.43 E
Chabang Tiga 104 5.19 N 103.08 E
Chabaricha 24 65.50 N 52.16 E
Chabařovice 50 50.40 N 13.56 E
Chabarovo 62 69.39 N 60.24 E
Chabarovsk 79 48.27 N 135.06 E
Chabarovsk □[4] 79 54.00 N 136.00 E
Chabarowsk → Chabarovsk 79 48.27 N 135.06 E
Chabary 76 53.37 N 79.33 E
Chabás 242 33.15 S 61.22 W
Chabeuil 56 44.54 N 5.01 E
Chabez 74 44.02 N 41.47 E
Chābi 114 22.49 N 80.41 E
Chabjuwardoo Bay C 152 22.57 S 113.48 E
Chablais ◂[1] 54 46.18 N 6.39 E
Chablis 46 47.49 N 3.48 E
Chabogongba 110 31.47 N 81.14 E
Chaboje 255a 59.53 N 30.46 E
Chabot, Lake ⊜, Calif., U.S. 272 37.43 N 122.07 W
Chabot, Lake ⊜, Calif., U.S. 272 38.08 N 122.14 W
Chabris 46 47.15 N 1.39 E
Chabuchaer, S.S.S.R. 76 43.42 N 81.04 E
Chabuchaer, Zhg. 76 43.42 N 81.04 E
Chabu-Rabot, Pereval)(75 38.40 N 70.43 E
Chacabuco 242 34.38 S 60.29 W
Chacaito, Quebrada ≃ 276c 10.29 N 66.52 W
Chacaltaya, Nevado ∧ 238 16.20 S 68.08 W
Chacaltianguis 224 18.20 N 95.50 W
Chacao 276c 10.30 N 66.51 W
Chácara 246 21.41 S 43.13 W
Chacarilla 276d 12.02 S 77.01 W
Chacarita, Cementerio de la ◂ 278 34.33 S 58.28 W
Chacayán 238 10.24 S 76.25 W
Chacewater 44 50.15 N 5.10 W
Chachalgi, Gora ∧ 74 42.48 N 45.09 E
Chachani, Nevado ∧ 238 16.12 S 71.33 W
Chachapoyas 238 6.13 S 77.51 W
Chachas 238 15.30 S 72.16 W
Chachoengsao 100 13.42 N 101.05 E
Chāchora 114 24.10 N 76.59 E
Chāchro 110 25.07 N 70.15 E
Chachu 110 33.16 N 81.41 E
Chačinčaj ≃ 74 40.13 N 47.18 E
Chačmas 74 41.28 N 48.48 E
Chaco □[4] 242 26.25 S 60.30 W
Chaco ≃ 190 36.46 N 108.39 W
Chaco Austral ◂[1] 242 26.30 S 61.30 W
Chaco Boreal ◂[1] 242 23.00 S 60.00 W
Chaco Canyon National Monument ♠ 190 36.06 N 108.00 W
Chaco Central ◂[1] 242 25.00 S 59.45 W
Chacón, Arroyo ≃ 278 34.53 S 58.39 W
Chacon, Cape ≻ 170 54.42 N 132.00 W
Chacorão, Cachoeira do ↳ 240 6.32 S 58.12 W
Chacra Cerro 276d 11.55 S 77.04 W
Chacra Ríos, Coliseo ♠ 276d 12.03 S 77.04 W
Chacuaco Creek ≃ 186 37.34 N 103.38 W
Chad □[1] 126 / 136 15.00 N 19.00 E
Chad, Lake (Lac Tchad) ⊜ 136 13.20 N 14.00 E
Chadabulak 78 50.38 N 116.18 E
Chadbourn 182 34.19 N 78.50 W
Chadderton 42 53.33 N 2.08 W
Chadds Ford 275 39.52 N 75.35 W
Chādegān 118 32.46 N 50.39 E
Chadian, Zhg. 92 26.48 N 105.48 E
Chadian, Zhg. 95 39.14 N 117.45 E
Chadianzi 97 30.31 N 104.22 E
Chadileuvú ≃ 238 37.46 S 66.00 W
Chadiza 144 14.05 S 32.28 E
Chadron 188 42.50 N 103.00 W
Chadstone 264b 37.53 S 145.05 E
Chadwell Saint Mary 250 51.29 N 0.22 E
Chadwick 180 42.01 N 89.53 W
Chadwick Pond ⊜ 273 42.44 N 71.05 W
Chadwicks 200 43.01 N 75.16 W
Chadžalmachi 74 42.26 N 47.13 E
Chadžibejskij Liman ⊜ 68 46.39 N 30.33 E
Chae Hom 100 18.43 N 99.35 E
Chaem ≃ 100 18.11 N 98.38 E
Chaersen 79 46.19 N 121.54 E
Chaeryŏng 88 38.24 N 125.36 E
Chafarinas, Islas II 34 35.11 N 2.26 W
Chafe 140 11.56 N 6.55 E
Chaffee 184 37.11 N 89.40 W
Chaffins 197 42.21 N 71.51 W
Chafurray 236 3.10 N 73.14 W
Chāgai 118 29.19 N 64.42 E
Chāgai Hills ∧∧[2] 118 29.30 N 64.15 E
Chagandianlisu 92 41.47 N 103.29 E
Chagang Do □[4] 88 40.50 N 126.30 E
'Chaghcharān 110 34.32 N 65.15 E
Chagny 54 46.55 N 4.45 E
Chagos Archipelago II 12 6.00 S 72.00 E
Chagrin ≃ 204 41.40 N 81.27 W
Chagrin, Aurora Branch ≃ 269a 41.25 N 81.25 W
Chagrin Falls 204 41.26 N 81.24 W
Chagrin Falls Park 204 41.21 N 81.32 W
Chagrin Valley Parkway ♠ 269a 41.26 N 81.25 W
Chaguanas 231r 10.31 N 61.25 W
Chaguaramas 236 9.20 N 66.16 W
Chaguaya 238 21.49 S 64.50 W
Chahaeryouhouqi 92 41.52 N 112.56 E
Chahaeryouzhongqi 92 41.09 N 112.38 E
Chahaignes 46 47.44 N 0.31 E
Chāhak 118 33.17 N 58.54 E
Chahal 226 15.45 N 89.34 W
Chahancheluo 88 41.39 N 114.22 E
Chahanhu ⊜ 88 41.23 N 113.55 E
Chahanwusu → Dulan 92 36.16 N 98.28 E
Chahār Bāgh, Afg. 110 35.58 N 69.38 E
Chahār Bāgh, Afg. 118 37.00 N 65.14 E
Chahār Borjak 118 30.17 N 62.03 E
Chahār Deh-ye Ghowrband 110 34.59 N 68.44 E
Chahayang 79 48.24 N 124.15 E
Chāh Bahār 118 25.18 N 60.37 E
Chahe, Zhg. 90 33.16 N 119.02 E
Chahe, Zhg. 92 33.48 N 97.22 E
Chahe, Zhg. 95 39.50 N 115.21 E
Chāh Gheybī, Hāmūn-e ☷ 118 28.06 N 60.50 E
Chahuamiao 90 33.00 N 115.56 E
Chahuites 224 16.17 N 94.11 W
Chai Badan 100 15.04 N 101.05 E
Chaibāsā 114 22.34 N 85.49 E
Chaidamuhe ≃ 92 36.39 N 96.20 E
Chaidamupendi ⊻[1] 110 37.00 N 95.00 E
Chaidamushan ∧∧ 92 38.00 N 95.40 E
Chaigou 88 36.15 N 119.36 E
Chaihe 79 44.47 N 129.42 E
Chaihe ≃ 94 42.20 N 123.52 E
Chaijiawan 90 29.10 N 113.06 E
Chaillé-les-Marais 32 46.24 N 1.01 W
Chailley 46 48.05 N 3.42 E
Chailly-en-Bière 46 48.28 N 2.35 E
Chainat 100 15.11 N 100.08 E
Chaîne Annamitique ∧∧ 100 17.00 N 106.00 E
Chainhurst 250 51.12 N 0.29 E
Chain O'Lakes State Park ♠, Ill., U.S. 206 42.27 N 88.11 W
Chain O'Lakes State Park ♠, Ind., U.S. 206 41.20 N 85.26 W
Chainpur 114 23.08 N 84.15 E
Chaiqiao 90 29.51 N 121.56 E
Chairel, Laguna de C 224 22.17 N 97.57 W
Chaishudian 95 40.46 N 116.30 E
Chaiši 74 42.57 N 42.12 E
Chait 75 39.11 N 70.53 E
Chaital 116 22.31 N 88.47 E
Chaiwobao 76 43.33 N 87.59 E
Chaiya 100 9.23 N 99.14 E
Chaiyaphum 100 15.48 N 102.02 E
Chajarí 242 30.46 S 57.59 W
Chajdarken 75 39.57 N 71.21 E
Chaj Doāb ∧∧[1] 113 32.15 N 73.00 E
Chajia 97 29.37 N 104.27 E
Chajian 90 32.40 N 118.46 E
Chajianling 88 39.14 N 114.36 E
Chajiaqiao, Zhg. 90 34.00 N 120.07 E
Chajiaqiao, Zhg. 97 29.39 N 104.48 E
Chajpudyrskaja Guba C 24 68.30 N 59.30 E
Chajrchan 78 48.37 N 101.53 E
Chajrchandulaan 92 45.57 N 102.03 E
Chajul 226 15.30 N 91.02 W
Chaka, Sūd. 144 4.49 N 31.14 E
Chaka, Zhg. 92 36.48 N 99.19 E
Chakachamna Lake ⊜ 170 61.13 N 152.35 W
Chakaer 110 36.32 N 80.43 E
Chakāltor 116 23.14 N 86.22 E
Chak Amru 113 32.22 N 75.11 E
Chakari 144 18.05 S 29.51 E
Chakaria 110 21.45 N 92.05 E
Chakarnaba 136 14.13 N 20.51 E
Chakasskaja Avtonomnaja Oblast' □[8] 76 53.00 N 90.00 E
Chakayanchi ⊜ 92 36.40 N 99.20 E
Chākdaha, Bhārat 116 23.05 N 88.31 E
Chakdaha, Bhārat 262b 22.20 N 88.20 E
Chake Chake 144 5.15 S 39.46 E
Chakhānsūr 118 31.10 N 62.04 E
Chakhānsūr □[4] 118 30.30 N 62.00 E
Chākia 114 26.25 N 85.03 E
Chak Jhumra 113 31.34 N 73.11 E
Chakkarat 100 15.00 N 102.16 E
Chakou, Zhg. 88 38.03 N 113.36 E
Chakou, Zhg. 95 38.53 N 116.41 E
Chakradharpur 114 22.42 N 85.38 E
Chakrāta 110 30.42 N 77.51 E
Chākulia 116 22.29 N 86.43 E
Chakwāl 113 32.56 N 72.52 E
Cha Kwo Ling 261d 22.18 N 114.13 E
Chal 262c 19.06 N 73.08 E
Chala 238 15.52 S 74.16 W
Chalabesa 144 11.22 S 31.01 E
Chalagou 92 34.10 N 97.44 E
Chalais 32 45.16 N 0.02 E
Chalamont 54 46.00 N 5.10 E
Chalampé 54 47.49 N 7.33 E
Chalatenango 226 14.03 N 88.56 W
Chalaua 144 16.06 S 39.11 E
Chalaux ≃ 46 47.23 N 3.54 E
Chalbi Desert ◂[2] 144 3.00 N 37.20 E
Chalcatongo de Hidalgo 224 17.02 N 97.35 W
Chalchgol 78 48.11 N 114.54 E
Chalchihuites 224 23.29 N 103.53 W
Chalchuapa 226 13.59 N 89.41 W
Chalcis → Khalkís 38 38.28 N 23.36 E
Chalco [de Díaz Covarrubias] 224 19.16 N 98.54 W
Chaldan 74 40.43 N 47.15 E
Chaldon 250 51.17 N 0.07 W
Chaleine 251 48.36 N 1.43 E
Chalengkou 110 37.57 N 93.40 E
Châlette-sur-Loing 46 48.01 N 2.44 E
Chaleur Bay C 176 48.00 N 65.45 W
Chalfant 269b 40.25 N 79.52 W
Chalfant Run ≃ 269b 40.25 N 79.48 W
Chalfont 198 40.17 N 75.13 W
Chalfont Common 250 51.38 N 0.33 W
Chalfont Saint Peter 44 51.37 N 0.33 W
Chalford 44 51.44 N 2.09 W
Chalhuanca 238 14.17 S 73.15 W
Chalía (Shehuen) ≃ 244 49.35 S 69.34 W
Chalifert 251 48.53 N 2.46 E
Chaligny 56 48.37 N 6.05 E
Chalihuey 224 22.43 N 104.04 W
Chalilovo 76 51.24 N 58.04 E
Chalindrey 54 47.48 N 5.26 E
Chaling 90 26.47 N 113.33 E
Chālisgaon 112 20.28 N 75.01 E
Chalisi 92 32.55 N 102.04 E
Chaliun 78 48.50 N 103.59 E
Chalk 250 51.26 N 0.25 E
Chalkabad 76 42.42 N 59.43 E
Chalk Draw ↳ 186 29.36 N 103.15 W
Chalk River 180 46.01 N 77.27 W
Chalkyitsik 170 66.39 N 143.43 W
Challakere 112 14.19 N 76.39 E
Challans 32 46.51 N 1.53 W
Challapata 238 18.54 S 66.47 W
Challenge 216 39.29 N 121.13 W
Challenger, Mount ∧ 214 48.50 N 121.20 W
Challes-les-Eaux 56 45.33 N 5.59 E
Challis 192 44.30 N 114.14 W
Chall Sar ∧ 113 34.46 N 73.04 E
Challviri, Salar de ⊻ 238 22.32 S 67.34 W
Chal'mer-Ju 24 67.58 N 64.50 E
Chalmers 206 40.40 N 86.52 W
Chalmette 184 29.56 N 89.58 W
Chalone Creek ≃ 216 36.21 N 121.14 W
Chalonnes-sur-Loire 32 47.21 N 0.46 W
Châlons-sur-Marne 46 48.57 N 4.22 E
Chalon-sur-Saône 54 46.47 N 4.51 E
Chalosse ◂[1] 32 43.45 N 0.30 W
Chalt 113 36.15 N 74.20 E
Chaltel, Cerro (Monte Fitzroy) ∧ 244 49.17 S 73.05 W
Chalturin 70 58.33 N 48.54 E
Chalturino 68 49.31 N 35.17 E
Chaluhe 79 43.43 N 126.00 E
Chaluolehu ⊜ 110 34.00 N 81.45 E
Châlus, Fr. 32 45.39 N 0.59 E
Chālūs, Īrān 118 36.38 N 51.26 E
Cham, B.R.D. 30 49.13 N 12.41 E
Cham, Schw. 54 47.11 N 8.28 E
Chama, Perú 276d 12.08 S 77.00 W
Chama, N. Mex., U.S. 190 36.54 N 106.35 W
Chama ≃ 236 9.03 N 71.40 W
Chama, Rio ≃ 190 36.03 N 106.05 W
Chamá, Sierra de ∧∧ 226 15.40 N 90.30 W
Chamah, Gunong ∧ 104 5.13 N 101.33 E
Chamaicó 242 35.03 S 64.58 W
Chamal, Sierra ∧∧ 224 22.45 N 99.15 W
Chamama 144 12.55 S 33.43 E
Chamamatjurt 74 43.36 N 46.30 E
Chaman 110 30.55 N 66.22 E
Chamangonge 142 11.16 S 20.24 E
Chamao, Khao ∧ 100 12.57 N 101.45 E
Chamarande 251 48.31 N 2.13 E
Chamar-Daban, Chrebet ∧∧ 78 51.15 N 105.00 E
Chāmārpāra 262b 22.35 N 88.08 E
Chamaya ≃ 238 5.44 S 78.39 W
Chamba, Bhārat 113 32.34 N 76.08 E
Chamba, Moç. 144 12.07 S 36.57 E
Chamba, Tan. 144 11.35 S 36.58 E
Chambal ≃ 114 26.29 N 79.15 E
Chambaran, Plateau de ∧∧[1] 56 45.15 N 5.15 E
Chambas 230p 22.12 N 78.55 W
Chambas ≃ 230p 22.24 N 78.54 W
Chamberlain, Sask., Can. 174 50.50 N 105.34 W
Chamberlain, S. Dak., U.S. 188 43.49 N 99.20 W
Chamberlain ≃ 154 15.08 S 128.06 E
Chamberlain Lake ⊜ 176 46.17 N 69.20 W
Chamberlin, Mount ∧ 170 69.16 N 144.55 W
Chamberry, Ruisseau ≃ 265a 45.20 N 73.58 W
Chambers, Ariz., U.S. 190 35.11 N 109.26 W
Chambers, Nebr., U.S. 188 42.12 N 98.45 W
Chambers, N.Y., U.S. 200 42.16 N 76.57 W
Chambers □[6] 212 29.42 N 94.40 W
Chambers Brook ≃ 266 40.35 N 74.41 W
Chambersburg, Ill., U.S. 209 39.49 N 90.39 W
Chambersburg, Ind., U.S. 208 38.31 N 86.24 W
Chambersburg, Pa., U.S. 198 39.56 N 77.39 W
Chambers Corner 275 40.01 N 74.44 W
Chambers Creek ≃ 212 31.58 N 96.10 W
Chambers Creek, North Fork ≃ 212 32.16 N 96.58 W
Chambers Creek, South Fork ≃ 212 32.16 N 96.58 W
Chambers Island I 180 45.11 N 87.12 W
Chambéry 56 45.34 N 5.56 E
Chambeshi ≃ 144 11.21 S 30.37 E
Chambi, Djebel ∧ 138 35.11 N 8.42 E
Chambira ≃, Perú 236 4.28 S 74.50 W
Chambira ≃, Perú 236 3.55 S 73.45 W
Chambishi 144 12.40 S 28.03 E
Chamblee 182 33.54 N 84.18 W
Chambley-Bussières 52 49.03 N 5.54 E
Chambly, Qué., Can. 265a 45.27 N 73.17 W
Chambly, Fr. 46 49.10 N 2.15 E
Chambly □[6] 196 45.30 N 73.20 W
Chambly, Bassin de ⊜ 196 45.27 N 73.17 W
Chambly, Canal de ≡ 265a 45.25 N 73.15 W
Chambois 46 48.48 N 0.07 E
Chambon-sur-Dolore 56 45.30 N 3.37 E
Chambon-sur-Voueize 32 46.11 N 2.25 E
Chambord, Château de ⊥ 46 47.37 N 1.31 E
Chambourcy 251 48.54 N 2.03 E
Chambri Lake ⊜ 154 4.16 S 143.08 E
Chambry 251 49.00 N 2.54 E
Chamburi Kalāt 118 26.08 N 64.43 E
Chamdo → Changdu 92 31.11 N 97.15 E
Chamdor 263d 26.08 S 27.48 E
Chame 226 8.35 N 79.53 W
Chame, Punta ≻ 226 8.39 N 79.42 W
Chamela 224 19.32 N 105.05 W
Chamela, Bahía C 224 19.33 N 105.07 W
Chamelecón 226 15.24 N 88.01 W
Chamelecón ≃ 226 15.51 N 87.49 W
Chamical (Gobernador Gordillo) 242 30.21 S 66.19 W
Chamizo 248 34.10 S 56.41 W
Chamizo, Arroyo ≃ 248 34.15 S 56.44 W
Chamkanī 110 33.48 N 69.49 E
Chamlia ≃ 114 29.38 N 80.24 E
Chamois, It. 56 45.50 N 7.37 E
Chamois, Mo., U.S. 209 38.41 N 91.46 W
Chamojie 79 49.25 N 124.45 E
Chamoli 114 30.24 N 79.21 E
Chamonix-Mont-Blanc 54 45.55 N 6.52 E
Chamousset 56 45.33 N 6.12 E
Chamoux-sur-Gelon 56 45.32 N 6.13 E
Chāmpa 114 22.03 N 82.39 E
Champādānga 116 22.50 N 87.58 E
Champagne, Yukon, Can. 170 60.47 N 136.29 W
Champagne, Fr. 56 45.16 N 4.48 E
Champagne □[9] 32 49.00 N 4.30 E
Champagne Castle ∧ 148 29.06 S 29.20 E
Champagne-en-Valromay 54 45.54 N 5.41 E
Champagner-Berge ∧[2] 254a 52.31 N 13.05 E
Champagne-sur-Seine 46 48.24 N 2.48 E
Champagney 54 47.42 N 6.41 E
Champagnole 54 46.45 N 5.55 E
Champ-agny 56 45.27 N 6.42 E
Champāhāti 116 22.23 N 88.29 E

Symbol	English	Deutsch	Español	Français	Português
≃	River	Fluss	Río	Rivière	Rio
≡	Canal	Kanal	Canal	Canal	Canal
↳	Waterfall, Rapids	Wasserfall, Stromschnellen	Cascada, Rápidos	Chute d'eau, Rapides	Cascata, Rápidos
)(	Strait	Meeresstrasse	Estrecho	Détroit	Estreito
C	Bay, Gulf	Bucht, Golf	Bahía, Golfo	Baie, Golfe	Baía, Golfo
⊜	Lake, Lakes	See, Seen	Lago, Lagos	Lac, Lacs	Lago, Lagos
☷	Swamp	Sumpf	Pantano	Marais	Pântano
⊞	Ice Features, Glacier	Eis- und Gletscherformen	Accidentes Glaciales	Formes glaciaires	Acidentes Glaciares
⊤	Other Hydrographic Features	Andere Hydrographische Objekte	Otros Elementos Hidrográficos	Autres données hydrographiques	Outros Elementos Hidrográficos

Symbol	English	Deutsch	Español	Français	Português
⊹	Submarine Features	Untermeerische Objekte	Accidentes Submarinos	Formes de relief sous-marin	Acidentes Submarinos
□	Political Unit	Politische Einheit	Unidad Política	Entité politique	Unidade Política
♥	Cultural Institution	Kulturelle Institution	Institución Cultural	Institution culturelle	Instituição Cultural
⊥	Historical Site	Historische Stätte	Sitio Histórico	Site historique	Sítio Histórico
♠	Recreational Site	Erholungs- und Ferienort	Sitio de Recreo	Centre de loisirs	Sítio de Lazer
⊠	Airport	Flughafen	Aeropuerto	Aéroport	Aeroporto
▪	Military Installation	Militäranlage	Instalación Militar	Installation militaire	Instalação Militar
◂	Miscellaneous	Verschiedenes	Misceláneo	Divers	Miscelânea

ENGLISH / DEUTSCH

Name	Page (Seite)	Lat. (Breite)	Long. (Länge E=Ost)
Champaign	184	40.07 N	88.14 W
Champaign □[6], Ill., U.S.	206	40.07 N	88.12 W
Champaign □[6], Ohio, U.S.	208	40.07 N	83.45 W
Champapur	116	24.02 N	86.31 E
Champaquí, Cerro ∧	242	31.59 S	64.56 W
Champaran □[5]	114	26.50 N	84.40 E
Champasak	100	14.53 N	105.52 E
Champaubert, Réservoir de ⊜[1]	54	48.35 N	4.50 E
Champāwat	114	29.20 N	80.06 E
Champcueil	251	48.31 N	2.27 E
Champdāni	116	22.48 N	88.21 E
Champdeniers	32	46.29 N	0.24 W
Champdepraz	56	45.41 N	7.39 E
Champdeuil	251	48.37 N	2.44 E
Champdor	54	46.01 N	5.36 E
Champdoré, Lac ⊜	166	55.55 N	65.49 W
Champeaux	46	48.35 N	2.48 E
Champeix	32	45.36 N	3.08 E
Champerico	226	14.18 N	91.55 W
Champéry	54	46.10 N	6.52 E
Champex	54	46.02 N	7.07 E
Champier	56	45.27 N	5.17 E
Champigneulles	52	48.44 N	6.10 E
Champigny-sur-Marne	251	48.49 N	2.31 E
Champion, Alta., Can.	172	50.14 N	113.09 W
Champion, Mich., U.S.	180	46.31 N	87.58 W
Champion, Ohio, U.S.	204	41.17 N	80.51 W
Champion, Pa., U.S.	204	40.05 N	79.21 W
Champlain	196	44.59 N	73.27 W
Champlain □[6]	196	46.45 N	72.35 W
Champlain ≃	196	46.27 N	72.17 W
Champlain, Lake ⊜	178	44.45 N	73.15 W
Champlain, Pont ◆[5]	196	45.28 N	73.32 W
Champlain Canal ≋	200	43.20 N	73.34 W
Champlan	251	48.43 N	2.16 E
Champlin Creek ≃	266	40.43 N	73.12 W
Champlitte-et-le-Prélot	54	47.37 N	5.31 E
Champlon	52	50.07 N	5.28 E
Champoluc	56	45.50 N	7.44 E
Champotón	222	19.21 N	90.43 W
Champrond-en-Gâtine	46	48.24 N	1.05 E
Champs	46	47.44 N	3.36 E
Champs-sur-Marne	251	48.51 N	2.36 E
Chāmpua	114	22.05 N	85.40 E
Champvans	54	47.06 N	5.26 E
Chāmrāil	262b	22.38 N	88.18 E
Chāmrājnagar Rāmasamudram	112	11.55 N	76.57 E
Chamrousse	56	45.08 N	5.52 E
Chamsara ≃	78	52.42 N	95.46 E
Chamusca	34	39.21 N	8.29 W
Chamza Chakimzada	75	40.26 N	71.30 E
Chana	100	6.55 N	100.44 E
Chanabadskij	75	40.49 N	72.58 E
Chanakyapuri □[9]	262a	28.36 N	77.11 E
Chānanwāla	113	30.22 N	73.57 E
Chañar	242	30.32 S	65.58 W
Chañaral	242	26.21 S	70.37 W
Chañaral, Isla I	242	29.02 S	71.35 W
Chanārān	118	36.39 N	59.06 E
Chanas	56	45.18 N	4.49 E
Chānasma	110	23.43 N	72.07 E
Chanbogd	92	43.12 N	107.10 E
Chancay	238	11.35 S	77.16 W
Chancay ≃	238	11.37 S	77.15 W
Chance	198	38.11 N	75.56 W
Chanceaux	54	47.31 N	4.42 E
Chanceaux-sur-Choisille	46	47.28 N	0.42 E
Chanch	78	51.30 N	100.40 E
Chan Chan ⊥	238	8.06 S	79.05 W
Chanchelulla Peak ∧	194	40.28 N	122.59 W
Chanchiang → Zhanjiang	92	21.16 N	110.28 E
Chanchöchij Uul ∧∧	78	49.30 N	94.30 E
Chanchongor	92	43.49 N	104.51 E
Chanco	242	35.44 S	72.32 W
Chancy	54	46.08 N	6.00 E
Chanda → Chandrapur, Bhārat	112	19.57 N	79.18 E
Chanda, S.S.S.R.	78	55.00 N	107.14 E
Chanda ≃	78	55.00 N	107.14 E
Chāndābila	116	22.05 N	87.00 E
Chandagajty	76	50.44 N	92.03 E
Chandalar	170	67.30 N	148.30 W
Chandalar ≃	170	66.36 N	145.48 W
Chandalar, East Fork ≃	170	67.05 N	147.16 W
Chandalar, Middle Fork ≃	170	67.10 N	148.19 W
Chandalar, North Fork ≃	170	67.10 N	148.19 W
Chandan Chauki	114	28.33 N	80.47 E
Chandankiāri	116	23.34 N	86.22 E
Chandannagar	116	22.51 N	88.21 E
Chandanpratap	116	23.33 N	89.24 E
Chandapāra	116	22.46 N	90.16 E
Chandar	116	23.54 N	89.58 E
Chandausi	114	28.27 N	78.46 E
Chandeleur Islands II	184	29.48 N	88.51 W
Chandeleur Sound U	184	29.55 N	89.10 W
Chanderi	114	24.43 N	78.08 E
Chandernagore → Chandannagar	116	22.51 N	88.21 E
Chandīgarh	113	30.44 N	76.55 E
Chandīgarh □[3]	113	30.45 N	76.45 E
Chāndil	114	22.58 N	86.03 E
Chandīpur	116	23.59 N	89.01 E
Chanditala	262b	22.41 N	88.16 E
Chandla	114	25.05 N	80.12 E
Chandler, Qué., Can.	176	48.21 N	64.41 W
Chandler, Ariz., U.S.	190	33.18 N	111.50 W
Chandler, Ind., U.S.	184	38.03 N	87.22 W
Chandler, Okla., U.S.	186	35.42 N	96.53 W
Chandler, Tex., U.S.	212	32.18 N	95.29 W
Chandler ≃	170	69.27 N	151.30 W
Chandler, Mount ∧[2]	152	27.00 S	133.20 E
Chandler Lake ⊜	170	68.15 N	152.43 W
Chandler Park ♠	271	42.24 N	82.58 W
Chandler's Cross	250	51.40 N	0.27 W
Chandler's Ford	44	50.59 N	1.23 W
Chandlers Valley	204	41.56 N	79.18 W
Chandlerville	209	40.03 N	90.09 W
Chandless ≃	238	9.08 S	69.51 W
Chandman'	76	50.02 N	92.03 E
Chāndor Hills ∧∧[2]	112	20.30 N	74.00 E
Chandos Lake ⊜	202	44.49 N	78.00 W
Chāndpara	116	22.58 N	88.47 E
Chāndpur, Bhārat	114	29.09 N	78.16 E
Chāndpur, Bngl.	110	22.08 N	91.55 E
Chāndpur, Bngl.	114	23.13 N	90.39 E
Chāndpur ◆[8]	262a	28.45 N	77.01 E
Chāndra	116	22.28 N	87.09 E
Chandra Dighalia	116	23.04 N	89.46 E
Chandrakona	116	22.44 N	87.31 E
Chandrakona Road	116	22.44 N	87.21 E
Chandrapur	112	19.57 N	79.18 E
Chāndvad	112	20.20 N	74.15 E
Chandyga	64	62.40 N	135.36 E
Chanfang	95	39.56 N	115.55 E
Chang, Ko I	100	12.05 N	102.20 E
Changa	74	44.27 N	50.36 E
Changācha	116	23.16 N	89.01 E
Changaj	78	47.51 N	99.26 E
Changajn Nuruu ∧∧	80	47.30 N	100.00 E
Changal	78	49.19 N	104.19 E
Changalane	146	26.16 S	32.13 E
Changan → Xi'an, Zhg.	92	34.15 N	108.52 E
Chang'an, Zhg.	92	26.00 N	109.34 E
Chang'an, Zhg.	96	30.28 N	120.27 E
Changanācheri	112	9.28 N	76.33 E
Changane ≃	146	24.43 S	33.32 E
Changara	144	16.54 S	33.14 E
Changarul'skij Chrebet ∧∧	78	51.10 N	103.00 E
Changbai	88	41.26 N	128.11 E
Changbaishan ∧∧	88	42.05 N	128.00 E
Changchaoling	96	31.00 N	119.40 E
Changcheng, Zhg.	90	31.49 N	116.54 E
Changcheng, Zhg.	100	19.24 N	108.42 E
Changcheng (Great Wall) ⊥	88	40.30 N	117.00 E
Chang Chenmo ≃	110	34.17 N	78.19 E
Changchiak'ou → Zhangjiakou	95	40.50 N	114.53 E
Ch'angchih → Changzhi	92	36.11 N	113.08 E
Changchou → Zhangzhou	90	24.33 N	117.39 E
Changchow → Changzhou	96	31.47 N	119.57 E
Changchun	79	43.53 N	125.19 E
Changchunling	79	45.22 N	125.28 E
Changdan	88	37.56 N	126.45 E
Changdanghu ⊜	96	31.35 N	119.35 E
Changde	92	28.55 N	111.38 E
Changdian	95	40.01 N	116.32 E
Ch'angdo	88	38.30 N	127.40 E
Ch'ang-dong	88	39.03 N	126.34 E
Changdu	92	31.11 N	97.15 E
Change Islands	176	49.40 N	54.25 W
Changgang	90	24.38 N	113.05 E
Changgangzi	94	41.26 N	122.41 E
Changgi-got ≻	88	36.05 N	129.34 E
Changgi-li	261b	37.35 N	126.44 E
Changgi-ri	261b	37.38 N	126.41 E
Changgou, Zhg.	90	34.15 N	113.50 E
Changgou, Zhg.	95	39.34 N	115.53 E
Changgouzhen	95	39.44 N	115.52 E
Changguandian	90	32.58 N	115.16 E
Changguowei	90	29.15 N	121.56 E
Changgye-ri	88	34.33 N	126.49 E
Changgyong Palace ♥	261b	37.36 N	127.00 E
Chang-hai → Shanghai	96	31.14 N	121.28 E
Changhang	88	36.01 N	126.40 E
Changhe	96	30.11 N	120.11 E
Changhowŏn	88	37.08 N	127.39 E
Ch'anghsü Shan I	90	26.14 N	119.58 E
Changhu ⊜	90	30.15 N	112.35 E
Changhua, T'aiwan	90	24.05 N	120.32 E
Changhua, Zhg.	90	30.11 N	119.13 E
Changhŭng	88	34.41 N	126.52 E
Changhŭng-ni	88	40.24 N	128.19 E
Changi	261c	1.23 N	103.59 E
Changi, Tanjong ≻	261c	1.23 N	104.00 E
Changi Airport ⊠	261c	1.22 N	103.59 E
Changi Prison ♥	261c	1.22 N	103.58 E
Changji	76	44.01 N	87.19 E
Changjiang, Zhg.	90	25.52 N	116.20 E
Changjiang, Zhg.	90	25.19 N	113.56 E
Changjiang, Zhg.	100	19.17 N	109.02 E
Changjiang (Yangtze) ≃	80	31.48 N	121.10 E
Changjiangbu	90	30.52 N	113.43 E
Changjiapuzi	94	40.51 N	123.43 E
Changjiazhuang	95	40.35 N	115.24 E
Changjie	90	29.16 N	121.40 E
Changjing	96	31.45 N	120.29 E
Changjin-ŭp	88	40.23 N	127.15 E
Changji Zizhizhou □[4]	76	42.30 N	85.00 E
Changkaiwei	90	28.04 N	116.18 E
Changkalajier	75	40.09 N	76.59 E
Changkeng	96	30.19 N	121.57 E
Changkiakow → Zhangjiakou	95	40.50 N	114.53 E
Changlai	96	31.58 N	121.17 E
Changlapod Pass)(	114	30.08 N	87.06 E
Changle, Zhg.	90	29.25 N	120.37 E
Changle, Zhg.	90	26.00 N	119.31 E
Changle, Zhg.	96	31.56 N	121.15 E
Changlejie	90	28.52 N	113.19 E
Changleqiao	96	30.21 N	119.51 E
Changli, Zhg.	88	36.57 N	119.45 E
Changli, Zhg.	88	39.43 N	119.11 E
Changling, Zhg.	79	44.15 N	123.58 E
Changling, Zhg.	88	39.47 N	122.43 E
Changlingfeng	95	40.11 N	118.24 E
Changlingji	90	32.30 N	114.54 E
Changlinhe	90	31.40 N	117.29 E
Changlun	104	6.26 N	100.26 E
Changlupu	96	31.04 N	119.17 E
Changmong-ni	88	34.58 N	128.41 E
Changning, Zhg.	92	26.19 N	112.21 E
Changning (Anningqiao), Zhg.	92	28.21 N	104.53 E
Changning, Zhg.	92	24.55 N	99.35 E
Changning, Zhg.	95	39.59 N	114.55 E
Ch'angnyŏng	88	35.33 N	128.29 E
Changnyŏn-ni	88	38.37 N	125.16 E
Changokurt	62	61.58 N	64.18 E
Ch'angpin	90	23.20 N	121.28 E
Changping, Zhg.	92	32.33 N	107.30 E
Changping, Zhg.	95	40.14 N	116.14 E
Changpingzhen	88	40.14 N	116.14 E
Changpu	90	23.48 N	115.26 E
Changputong	92	28.05 N	98.29 E
Ch'angp'yŏng-dong	88	41.27 N	127.31 E
Changqiao, Zhg.	90	26.49 N	118.50 E
Changqiao, Zhg.	90	24.15 N	117.39 E
Changqing	88	36.34 N	116.43 E
Changsa	92	19.51 N	110.53 E
Changsan-got ≻	88	38.08 N	124.39 E
Changsha, Zhg.	90	24.13 N	116.07 E
Changsha, Zhg.	90	28.11 N	113.01 E
Changshageng	97	29.58 N	104.38 E
Changshan	90	28.55 N	118.30 E
Changshanjiang ≃	90	28.57 N	118.50 E
Changshanqiao	97	29.30 N	104.13 E
Changshanqundao II	88	39.00 N	122.45 E
Changsheng	90	26.16 N	116.01 E
Changshengchang	97	29.31 N	106.39 E
Changshitai	94	42.33 N	120.43 E
Changshitou	92	35.03 N	99.11 E
Changshou	92	29.51 N	107.06 E
Changshoudian	90	31.26 N	112.35 E
Changshoujie	90	28.44 N	113.57 E
Changshu	96	31.39 N	120.45 E
Changshui	92	34.21 N	111.29 E
Changsŏng	88	35.20 N	126.49 E
Changsŏn-gang ≃	88	39.15 N	126.02 E
Changsu	88	35.40 N	127.32 E
Changtai, Zhg.	90	24.40 N	117.46 E
Changtai, Zhg.	94	41.34 N	122.00 E
Changtancun	94	41.33 N	123.02 E
Ch'angte → Changde	92	28.55 N	111.38 E
Changteh → Anyang	88	36.06 N	114.21 E
Changting	79	44.32 N	128.47 E
Changtumiao	92	43.30 N	114.34 E
Changuinola ≃	226	9.28 N	82.27 W
Changwu, Zhg.	79	46.00 N	125.36 E
Changwu, Zhg.	92	35.09 N	107.42 E
Changxi ≃	90	26.53 N	119.41 E
Changxindian	95	39.49 N	116.12 E
Changxing	96	31.01 N	119.54 E
Changxingdao I	88	39.34 N	121.23 E
Changxingdian, Zhg.	94	41.27 N	121.44 E
Changxingdian, Zhg.	94	41.33 N	123.29 E
Changxingmeikuang	96	31.06 N	119.43 E
Changxuanling	90	31.08 N	114.20 E
Changyi	88	36.51 N	119.23 E
Changyŏn	88	38.15 N	125.06 E
Changyuan	88	35.13 N	114.39 E
Changyukou	95	40.46 N	115.08 E
Changzhi	92	36.11 N	113.08 E
Changzhou (Changchow)	96	31.47 N	119.57 E
Chanhanga	142	16.04 S	14.07 E
Chanh-hung	259c	10.44 N	106.41 E
Chani	78	57.05 N	120.58 E
Chani ≃	78	57.02 N	120.59 E
Chanino	66	54.13 N	36.37 E
Chanka, Ozero (Xingkathu) ⊜	79	45.00 N	132.24 E
Chankiang → Zhanjiang	92	21.16 N	110.28 E
Chankou	92	35.52 N	104.27 E
Chanlar	74	40.34 N	46.20 E
Channagiri	112	14.02 N	75.56 E
Channahon	206	41.26 N	88.14 W
Channapatna	112	12.39 N	77.13 E
Channel Islands II, Eur.	28	49.20 N	2.20 W
Channel Islands II, Calif., U.S.	194	34.00 N	120.00 W
Channel Islands National Monument ♠	218	33.28 N	119.02 W
Channel Lake	206	42.29 N	88.08 W
Channel North Basin C	164h	2.49 S	171.43 W
Channel-Port-aux-Basques	176	47.34 N	59.09 W
Channelview	212	29.46 N	95.07 W
Channing, Mich., U.S.	180	46.09 N	88.05 W
Channing, Tex., U.S.	186	35.41 N	102.20 W
Chanshan	88	36.26 N	120.52 E
Chantada	34	42.37 N	7.46 W
Chantajskoje, Ozero ⊜	64	68.20 N	91.00 E
Chantang	90	33.41 N	117.37 E
Chantau	76	44.13 N	73.51 E
Chanteloup	251	48.51 N	2.44 E
Chanteloup-les-Vignes	251	48.59 N	2.02 E
Chantengo, Laguna C	224	16.37 N	99.07 W
Chanthaburi	100	12.36 N	102.09 E
Chantilly	46	49.12 N	2.28 E
Chantonnay	32	46.41 N	1.03 W
Chantraine	54	48.10 N	6.26 E
Chantrans	54	47.03 N	6.09 E
Chantrey Inlet C	166	67.48 N	96.20 W
Chanty-Mansijsk	64	61.00 N	69.06 E
Chanuj ≃	78	49.22 N	102.22 E
Chanumla	100	8.19 N	93.05 E
Chanute	188	37.41 N	95.27 W
Chanute Air Force Base ■	206	40.18 N	88.09 W
Chanuwāla	113	32.44 N	73.08 E
Chanž'onkovo	73	48.06 N	38.06 E
Chao, Isla I	238	8.45 S	78.47 W
Chaoan	90	23.41 N	116.38 E
Chaobaihe ≃	95	39.48 N	117.08 E
Chaobaixinhe ≃	95	39.37 N	117.26 E
Chaobeiyingzi	94	42.06 N	122.18 E
Chaocheng	88	36.05 N	115.35 E
Ch'aochou, T'aiwan	90	22.33 N	120.32 E
Ch'aochou → Chaoan, Zhg.	90	23.41 N	116.38 E
Chaogezhen	88	35.38 N	114.11 E
Chaohe ≃	95	38.52 N	115.46 E
Chaohu ⊜	90	31.31 N	117.33 E
Chaomidian	95	39.04 N	117.01 E
Chao Phraya ≃	100	13.32 N	100.36 E
Chaoshui	79	49.44 N	127.21 E
Chaoshuiji	88	37.42 N	120.55 E
Chaource	46	48.04 N	4.08 E
Chaoxian	90	31.36 N	117.52 E
Chaoyang, Zhg.	79	44.34 N	126.20 E
Chaoyang, Zhg.	90	23.17 N	116.37 E
Chaoyang, Zhg.	94	41.35 N	120.28 E
Chaoyangchuan	88	42.54 N	129.21 E
Chaoyangdian	79	50.02 N	124.16 E
Chaoyanggou	94	42.07 N	121.04 E
Chaoyangpo	79	43.37 N	124.42 E
Chaoyangshan	79	43.02 N	125.40 E
Chaoyangsi	94	41.37 N	120.59 E
Chaozhuang	88	34.18 N	114.56 E
Chapa	100	22.21 N	103.50 E
Chapada dos Guimarães	238	15.26 S	55.45 W
Chapadinha	240	3.44 S	43.21 W
Chapala	224	20.18 N	103.12 W
Chapala, Lago de ⊜	224	20.15 N	103.00 W
Chaparé ≃	238	15.58 S	64.42 W
Chapareillan	56	45.28 N	5.58 E
Chāparmukh	110	26.12 N	92.32 E
Chaparra	230p	21.10 N	76.29 W
Chaparra, Bahía de C	230p	21.13 N	76.31 W
Chaparral	236	3.43 N	75.28 W
Chapčeranga	78	49.42 N	112.24 E
Chapeauroux	56	44.50 N	3.44 E
Chapecó	242	27.06 S	52.36 W
Chapecó ≃	242	27.06 S	53.01 W
Chapel-en-le-Frith	42	53.20 N	1.54 W
Chapel Hill, N.C., U.S.	182	35.55 N	79.04 W
Chapel Hill, Tenn., U.S.	184	35.38 N	86.41 W
Chapel Hill Channel U	266	40.32 N	74.02 W
Chapelle Creek ≃	188	44.16 N	99.55 W
Chapel Oaks	274c	38.54 N	76.55 W
Chapel Point ≻	44	50.16 N	4.46 W
Chapelton	231q	18.05 N	77.16 W
Chapeltown	252	53.38 N	2.24 W
Chapet	251	48.58 N	1.56 E
Chapéu, Ribeirão do ≃	246	23.14 S	45.18 W
Chapicuy	242	31.39 S	57.54 W
Chapimarca	238	13.58 S	73.04 W
Chapin	209	39.46 N	90.24 W
Chapin, Lake ⊜	206	41.56 N	86.21 W
Chaplain, Lake ⊜[1]	214	47.57 N	121.51 W
Chapleau	180	47.50 N	83.24 W
Chapleau ≃	180	48.29 N	82.57 W
Chapleau, Lac ⊜	196	46.14 N	74.57 W
Chaplin, Sask., Can.	174	50.28 N	106.40 W
Chaplin, Conn., U.S.	197	41.48 N	72.08 W
Chaplin ≃	184	37.50 N	85.11 W
Chaplin Lake ⊜	174	50.18 N	106.35 W
Chapman, Kans., U.S.	188	38.58 N	97.01 W
Chapman, Nebr., U.S.	188	41.02 N	98.09 W
Chapman, Pa., U.S.	198	40.46 N	75.24 W
Chapman ≃	146	22.19 S	20.00 E
Chapman, Cape ≻	166	69.12 N	88.59 W
Chapman, Mount ∧	172	51.50 N	118.20 W
Chapman College ♥[2]	270	33.47 N	117.51 W
Chapman Creek ≃	188	38.58 N	97.00 W
Chapman Lake ⊜	174	56.58 N	98.12 W
Chapmanville	178	37.58 N	82.01 W
Chapman Woods	270	34.08 N	118.05 W
Chapo	186	29.17 N	104.20 W
Chaponval	251	49.04 N	2.09 E
Chappaqua	200	41.10 N	73.46 W
Chappel Hill	212	30.09 N	96.16 W
Chappell	188	41.06 N	102.28 W
Chāpra, Bhārat	114	25.46 N	84.45 E
Chāpra, Bhārat	116	23.32 N	88.33 E
Chapry	73	47.14 N	39.31 E
Chaptico Bay C	198	38.21 N	76.49 W
Chapultepec, Méx.	194	32.22 N	115.05 W
Chapultepec, Méx.	194	31.50 N	116.38 W
Chapultepec ∧	224	23.27 N	103.04 W
Chapultepec, Bosque de ♠	276a	19.25 N	99.12 W
Chapultepec, Castillo de ⊥	276a	19.25 N	99.11 W
Chá Pungana	142	13.44 S	18.39 E
Chaqui	238	19.36 S	65.32 W
Chaquiago	242	27.32 S	66.21 W
Char ≃	44	50.44 N	2.53 W
Chara ≃	79	49.48 N	130.45 E
Charaa ≃	78	49.38 N	105.49 E
Charabali	70	47.24 N	47.16 E
Charadai	242	27.38 S	59.54 W
Charagua	238	19.48 S	63.13 W
Charagun	78	51.36 N	111.05 E
Char-Ajrag	92	45.48 N	109.19 E
Charal	78	51.58 N	96.39 E
Charalá	236	6.17 N	73.10 W
Charām	118	30.45 N	50.44 E
Charaña	238	17.36 S	69.28 W
Charan Kanoa	164n	15.08 N	145.43 E
Charanor	78	50.05 N	116.40 E
Charanpur	116	23.45 N	87.02 E
Charapán	224	19.41 N	102.06 W
Charata	242	27.13 S	61.12 W
Charauz	78	52.16 N	106.17 E
Charavines-les-Bains	56	45.26 N	5.31 E
Charazani → Amarete	238	15.14 S	68.58 W
Charazargaj	78	52.57 N	104.41 E
Charbala	64	64.07 N	120.19 E
Char Bansi	116	22.59 N	90.43 E
Charbatovo	78	53.46 N	106.00 E
Charbon	160	32.54 S	149.58 E
Charbonnières-les-Bains	56	45.47 N	4.44 E
Charcana	238	15.15 S	73.04 W
Charcas	224	23.08 N	101.07 W
Charco Azul, Bahía de C	226	8.15 N	82.45 W
Charco Hondo	230m	18.25 N	66.43 W
Charcos de Figueroa	222	27.45 N	102.11 W
Charcos de Risa	222	26.15 N	103.10 W
Charcot Island I	9	69.45 S	75.15 W
Charcyzsk	73	48.02 N	38.09 E
Chard	44	50.53 N	2.58 W
Chardon	204	41.35 N	81.12 W
Charduār	110	26.52 N	92.46 E
Chardzhou → Čardžou	118	39.06 N	63.34 E
Charef, Oued ∨	138	34.07 N	2.05 W
Charente □[5]	32	45.40 N	0.10 E
Charente ≃	32	45.57 N	1.05 W
Charente-Maritime □[5]	32	45.30 N	0.45 W
Charenton-du-Cher	32	46.44 N	2.38 E
Charenton-le-Pont	251	48.49 N	2.25 E
Charentonne ≃	46	49.07 N	0.44 E
Charest ≃	196	46.36 N	72.14 W
Charga, Ozero ⊜	78	52.52 N	111.54 E
Chārghāt	116	24.17 N	88.45 E
Char Hāim	116	23.04 N	90.38 E
Chari ≃	136	12.58 N	14.31 E
Chariāl Canal ≋	262b	22.28 N	88.11 E
Chari-Baguirmi □[5]	136	11.00 N	17.00 E
Charik	78	54.15 N	101.39 E
Chārīkār	110	35.01 N	69.11 E
Charing	44	51.13 N	0.48 E
Charing Cross	204	42.20 N	82.06 W
Charino, S.S.S.R.	66	59.57 N	43.44 E
Charino, S.S.S.R.	72	54.33 N	37.52 E
Charistvala	74	42.26 N	43.02 E
Chariton	180	41.01 N	93.19 W
Chariton ≃	184	39.19 N	92.57 W
Chariton, Mussel Fork ≃	184	39.24 N	92.55 W
Chariton, South Fork ≃	184	40.52 N	93.00 W
Charitonovo, S.S.S.R.	24	61.27 N	47.28 E
Charitonovo, S.S.S.R.	72	56.52 N	36.44 E
Charity	236	7.24 N	58.36 W
Charkhāri	114	25.24 N	79.45 E
Charkhi Dādri	114	28.37 N	76.16 E
Char'kin	70	48.46 N	51.49 E
Charkop ◆[8]	262c	19.13 N	72.49 E
Char'kov (Kharkov)	68	50.00 N	36.15 E
Char'kov □[4]	73	49.42 N	37.10 E
Charkow → Char'kov	68	50.00 N	36.15 E
Char Lākhpur	116	24.04 N	90.40 E
Char Lālmohan	116	22.13 N	90.42 E
Charland, Lac ⊜	196	46.52 N	74.11 W
Charlbury	44	51.53 N	1.29 W
Charl Cilliers	148	26.39 S	29.12 E
Charlemagne	196	45.43 N	73.29 W
Charlemont	197	42.38 N	72.52 W
Charleroi, Bel.	46	50.25 N	4.26 E
Charleroi, Pa., U.S.	204	40.09 N	79.57 W
Charleroi à Bruxelles, Canal de ≋	46	50.51 N	4.19 E
Charles □[6]	198	38.32 N	76.59 W
Charles ≃	197	42.22 N	71.03 W
Charles, Cape ≻	198	37.08 N	75.58 W
Charles, Lake ⊜	268	42.15 N	87.58 W
Charles, Peak ∧	152	32.52 S	121.11 E
Charlesbourg	196	46.51 N	71.16 W
Charles Branch ≃	274c	38.47 N	76.48 W
Charles City, Iowa, U.S.	180	43.04 N	92.40 W
Charles City, Va., U.S.	198	37.20 N	77.04 W
Charles City □[6]	198	37.20 N	77.02 W
Charles De Gaulle, Aéroport ⊠	46	49.01 N	2.33 E
Charles Island I	166	62.40 N	74.15 W
Charles Lee Tilden Regional Park ♠	272	37.54 N	122.15 W
Charles Mill Lake ⊜[1]	204	40.45 N	82.22 W
Charles Mound ∧[2]	180	42.30 N	90.14 W
Charles Point ≻	154	12.23 S	130.36 E
Charles Sound U	162	45.02 S	167.04 E
Charleston, Austl.	158b	34.55 S	138.54 E
Charleston, N.Z.	162	41.54 S	171.26 E
Charleston, Ark., U.S.	184	35.18 N	94.02 W
Charleston, Ill., U.S.	184	39.30 N	88.10 W
Charleston, Miss., U.S.	184	34.00 N	90.04 W
Charleston, Mo., U.S.	184	36.55 N	89.21 W
Charleston, S.C., U.S.	182	32.48 N	79.57 W
Charleston, W. Va., U.S.	178	38.21 N	81.38 W
Charleston Lake ⊜	202	44.32 N	76.00 W
Charleston Peak ∧	194	36.16 N	115.42 W
Charleston Rise ✧[3]	16	30.00 N	75.00 W
Charlestown, Austl.	160	32.58 S	151.42 E
Charlestown, St. K.-N.	228	17.08 N	62.37 W
Charlestown, S. Afr.	148	27.30 S	29.55 E
Charlestown, Ind., U.S.	208	38.27 N	85.40 W
Charlestown, N.H., U.S.	178	43.14 N	72.26 W
Charlestown, Pa., U.S.	275	40.06 N	75.33 W
Charlestown, R.I., U.S.	197	41.23 N	71.45 W
Charles Town, W. Va., U.S.	178	39.17 N	77.52 W
Charlestown ◆[8]	273	42.23 N	71.04 W
Charlesville	142	5.27 S	20.58 E
Charlesworth	252	53.26 N	1.59 W
Charleville	156	26.24 S	146.15 E
Charleville-Mézières	52	49.46 N	4.43 E
Charlevoix	180	45.19 N	85.16 W
Charlevoix, Lake ⊜	180	45.15 N	85.08 W
Charley ≃	170	65.20 N	142.49 W
Charlie Bluff	206	42.50 N	88.58 W
Charlie Creek ≃	210	27.21 N	81.49 W
Charlie Lake	172	56.16 N	120.57 W
Charlieu	32	46.10 N	4.10 E
Charlotte, Mich., U.S.	206	42.36 N	84.50 W
Charlotte, N.C., U.S.	182	35.14 N	80.50 W
Charlotte, Tenn., U.S.	184	36.11 N	87.24 W
Charlotte, Tex., U.S.	186	28.52 N	98.43 W
Charlotte □[6]	210	26.54 N	81.58 W
Charlotte Amalie	230m	18.21 N	64.56 W
Charlotte Court House	182	37.03 N	78.39 W
Charlotte Creek ≃	200	42.27 N	75.01 W
Charlotte Harbor	210	26.58 N	82.04 W
Charlotte Harbor C	210	26.45 N	82.12 W
Charlotte Lake ⊜	172	52.11 N	125.20 W
Charlottenberg	26	59.53 N	12.17 E
Charlottenburg	240	5.51 N	54.46 W
Charlottenburg ◆[8]	254a	52.31 N	13.16 E
Charlottenburg, Schloss ⊥	254a	52.31 N	13.14 E
Charlottesburg Reservoir ⊜[1]	266	41.02 N	74.26 W
Charlottesville, Ind., U.S.	208	39.47 N	85.37 W
Charlottesville, Va., U.S.	182	38.02 N	78.29 W
Charlottetown, P.E.I., Can.	176	46.14 N	63.08 W
Charlotte Town (Gouyave), Gren.	231k	12.10 N	61.44 W
Charlotteville	200	42.33 N	74.40 W
Charlovka	24	68.47 N	37.15 E
Charlton, Austl.	156	36.16 S	143.21 E
Charlton, Mass., U.S.	197	42.08 N	71.58 W
Charlton ◆[8]	250	51.29 N	0.02 E
Charlton City	197	42.09 N	71.58 W
Charlton Island I	166	52.00 N	79.30 W
Charlton Kings	44	51.53 N	2.03 W
Charlu	24	61.48 N	30.52 E
Charly-sur Marne	46	48.58 N	3.17 E
Charm	204	40.30 N	81.47 W
Charmentray	251	48.57 N	2.47 E
Charmes	54	48.22 N	6.17 E
Charmes-sur-Rhône	56	44.52 N	4.50 E
Charmey	54	46.38 N	7.10 E
Charminster	44	50.43 N	2.28 W
Charmois-l'Orgueilleux	54	48.06 N	6.16 E
Charmont-en-Beauce	46	48.14 N	2.06 E
Charmouth	44	50.45 N	2.55 W
Charnay-lès-Mâcon	54	46.18 N	4.47 E
Charneca	256c	38.44 N	9.27 W
Charnock Richard	252	53.38 N	2.41 W
Char Nuur ⊜, Mong.	78	48.06 N	93.12 E
Char Nuur ⊜, Mong.	78	48.20 N	96.05 E
Charnwood Forest ◆[3]	44	52.43 N	1.15 W
Charny, Qué., Can.	196	46.43 N	71.16 W
Charny, Fr.	46	47.53 N	3.06 E
Charny, Fr.	251	48.58 N	2.46 E
Charny-sur-Meuse	52	49.12 N	5.22 E
Charo	224	19.45 N	101.03 W
Charolles	32	46.26 N	4.17 E
Charouine	138	29.01 N	0.16 W
Charovsk	66	59.59 N	40.11 E
Charpi ≃	79	49.40 N	136.10 E
Charquemont	54	47.13 N	6.49 E
Charrette Creek ≃	209	38.37 N	91.03 W
Charron Lake ⊜	174	52.45 N	95.15 W
Charroux	32	46.09 N	0.24 E
Chars	46	49.10 N	1.56 E
Chārsadda	113	34.09 N	71.44 E
Charter Oak, Calif., U.S.	270	34.06 N	117.52 W
Charter Oak, Iowa, U.S.	188	42.04 N	95.35 W
Charters Towers	156	20.05 S	146.16 E
Charterwood	269b	40.33 N	80.00 W
Chartiers Creek ≃	204	40.28 N	80.03 W
Chartiers Run ≃, Pa., U.S.	269b	40.36 N	79.43 W
Chartiers Run ≃, Pa., U.S.	269b	40.15 N	80.12 W
Chartley	197	41.57 N	71.14 W
Chartres	46	48.27 N	1.30 E
Chartrettes	46	48.29 N	2.42 E
Chartridge	250	51.44 N	0.39 W
Chart Sutton	250	51.13 N	0.35 E
Chartwell ⊥	250	51.14 N	0.05 E
Char Us Nuur ⊜	80	48.00 N	92.10 E
Charutajuvom	24	66.49 N	59.30 E
Chās	116	23.38 N	86.10 E
Chasavjurt	74	43.15 N	46.37 E
Chascomús	248	35.34 S	58.01 W
Chašdala	75	39.42 N	67.07 E
Chase, B.C., Can.	172	50.49 N	119.41 W
Chase, Alaska, U.S.	170	62.27 N	150.07 W
Chase, Kans., U.S.	188	38.21 N	98.21 W
Chase, Md., U.S.	198	39.22 N	76.22 W
Chase, Mount ∧	178	46.07 N	68.29 W
Chase Brook ≃	273	42.48 N	71.27 W
Chase City	182	36.48 N	78.28 W
Chasefu Mission	144	11.55 S	33.08 E
Chase Lake	202	43.46 N	75.19 W
Chase River	214	49.08 N	123.55 W
Chasetown	44	52.41 N	1.56 W
Chashui ≃	90	31.44 N	113.11 E
Chasicó	244	40.18 S	68.58 W
Chasidaba	94	42.19 N	121.19 E
Chaska	180	44.47 N	93.35 W
Chaslands Mistake ≻	162	46.38 S	169.22 E
Chasŏng	88	41.27 N	126.37 E
Chasŏngganggu	88	41.34 N	126.36 E
Chassahowitzka	210	28.43 N	82.34 W
Chassahowitzka Bay C	210	28.41 N	82.40 W
Chassahowitzka Swamp ≡	210	28.38 N	82.37 W
Chasseron, Mont ∧	54	46.51 N	6.33 E
Chasse-sur-Rhône	56	45.34 N	4.49 E
Chassezac ≃	56	44.26 N	4.19 E
Chašuri	74	42.00 N	43.36 E
Chasurta	78	52.17 N	108.52 E
Chasuta	238	6.35 S	76.11 W
Chāt	118	37.59 N	55.16 E
Chatanbulag	92	43.11 N	109.10 E
Chatanga	64	71.58 N	102.30 E
Chatanga ≃	64	72.55 N	106.00 E
Chatangskij Zaliv C	64	73.30 N	109.00 E
Chatanika	170	65.07 N	147.31 W
Chatanika ≃	170	65.04 N	149.18 W
Château-Arnoux	56	44.06 N	6.00 E
Chateaubelair	231h	13.17 N	61.15 W
Chateaubelair Bay C	231h	13.17 N	61.15 W
Châteaubriant	32	47.43 N	1.23 W
Château-Chinon	32	47.04 N	3.56 E
Château d'Oex	54	46.28 N	7.08 E
Château-du-Loir	46	47.42 N	0.25 E
Châteaudun	46	48.05 N	1.20 E
Châteaufort	251	48.44 N	2.06 E
Chateaugay	196	44.56 N	74.05 W
Château-Gontier	32	47.50 N	0.42 W
Châteauguay	196	45.23 N	73.45 W
Châteauguay □[6]	196	45.15 N	73.45 W
Châteauguay (Chateauguay) ≃	196	45.24 N	73.45 W
Châteauguay-Centre	196	45.21 N	73.45 W
Châteauguay Heights	265a	45.23 N	73.44 W
Château-Landon	46	48.09 N	2.42 E
Château-la-Vallière	46	47.33 N	0.19 E
Châteaulin	32	48.12 N	4.05 W
Châteaumeillant	32	46.34 N	2.12 E
Châteauneuf	56	43.23 N	5.10 E
Châteauneuf-de-Randon	56	44.39 N	3.40 E
Châteauneuf-du-Pape	56	44.03 N	4.50 E
Châteauneuf-du-Rhône	56	44.29 N	4.43 E
Châteauneuf-en-Thymerais	46	48.35 N	1.15 E
Châteauneuf-sur-Charente	32	45.36 N	0.03 W
Châteauneuf-sur-Loire	46	47.52 N	2.14 E
Châteauneuf-sur-Sarthe	32	47.41 N	0.30 W
Châteauneuf-Val-de-Bargis	46	47.17 N	3.14 E
Château-Porcien	46	49.32 N	4.15 E
Château-Queyras	56	44.45 N	6.47 E
Châteauredon	56	44.01 N	6.13 E
Châteaurenard	46	47.56 N	2.56 E
Châteaurenard-Provence	56	43.53 N	4.51 E
Château-Renault	46	47.35 N	0.55 E
Château-Richer	176	46.58 N	71.01 W
Châteauroux	32	46.49 N	1.42 E
Château-Salins	52	48.49 N	6.30 E
Château-Thierry	46	49.03 N	3.24 E
Châteauvillain	54	48.02 N	4.55 E
Châteaux, Pointe des ≻	231o	16.15 N	61.11 W
Châtel	54	46.17 N	6.50 E
Châtel-Censoir	46	47.31 N	3.38 E
Châtelet	46	50.24 N	4.31 E
Châtelineau	52	50.25 N	4.31 E
Châtellerault	32	46.49 N	0.33 E
Châtel-Saint-Denis	54	46.32 N	6.54 E
Châtel-sur-Moselle	54	48.18 N	6.24 E
Châtelus-Malvaleix	32	46.18 N	2.01 E
Châtenay-en-France	251	49.04 N	2.27 E
Châtenay-Malabry	251	48.46 N	2.17 E
Châtenois, Fr.	54	48.16 N	7.24 E
Châtenois, Fr.	54	48.18 N	5.50 E
Châtenois-les-Forges	54	47.34 N	6.51 E
Chatfield, Minn., U.S.	180	43.51 N	92.11 W
Chatfield, Ohio, U.S.	204	40.57 N	82.56 W
Chatgal	78	50.26 N	100.07 E
Chatham, N.B., Can.	176	47.02 N	65.28 W
Chatham, Ont., Can.	204	42.24 N	82.11 W
Chatham, Eng., U.K.	44		
	250	51.23 N	0.32 E
Chatham, Ill., U.S.	209	39.40 N	89.42 W
Chatham, La., U.S.	184	32.19 N	92.27 W
Chatham, Mass., U.S.	197	41.41 N	69.58 W
Chatham, N.J., U.S.	200	40.44 N	74.23 W
Chatham, N.Y., U.S.	200	42.22 N	73.36 W
Chatham, Ohio, U.S.	204	41.06 N	82.01 W
Chatham, Pa., U.S.	198	39.51 N	75.49 W
Chatham, Va., U.S.	182	36.50 N	79.24 W
Chatham ◆[8]	268	41.45 N	87.37 W
Chatham ≃	210	25.42 N	81.17 W
Chatham, Isla I	244	50.40 S	74.20 W
Chatham Head	176	47.00 N	65.33 W
Chatham Island I	14	43.55 S	176.30 W
Chatham Islands II	14	44.00 S	176.30 W
Chatham Rise ✧[3]	14	43.30 S	178.00 W
Chatham Sound U	172	54.32 N	130.35 W
Chatham Strait U	170	57.30 N	134.45 W
Chatian	90	27.54 N	118.58 E
Châtillon, Fr.	54	45.53 N	4.37 E
Châtillon, Fr.	251	48.48 N	2.17 E
Châtillon, It.	56	45.45 N	7.37 E
Châtillon-Coligny	46	47.50 N	2.51 E
Châtillon-en-Bazois	32	47.03 N	3.49 E
Châtillon-en-Diois	56	44.41 N	5.28 E
Châtillon-la-Borde	251	48.33 N	2.49 E
Châtillon-sur-Chalaronne	54	46.07 N	4.58 E
Châtillon-sur-Indre	32	46.59 N	1.11 E
Châtillon-sur-Loire	46	47.35 N	2.45 E
Châtillon-sur-Marne	46	49.06 N	3.45 E
Châtillon-sur-Seine	54	47.51 N	4.33 E
Chātmohar	116	24.13 N	89.15 E
Chat Moss ◆[3]	252	53.27 N	2.27 W
Chato, Cerro ∧	244	42.29 S	72.01 W
Chatom	184	31.28 N	88.16 W
Chatonville	251	48.33 N	1.52 E
Chatou	251	48.54 N	2.09 E
Chatra, Bhārat	114	24.13 N	84.52 E
Chatra, Bhārat	262b	22.46 N	88.20 E
Chatrapur	112	19.21 N	84.59 E
Châtres	251	48.43 N	2.49 E
Chats, Lac des ⊜	202	45.28 N	76.23 W
Chatsquot Mountain ∧	172	53.08 N	127.30 W
Chātsu	110	26.36 N	75.57 E
Chatswood	264a	33.48 S	151.12 E
Chatsworth, Austl.	156	21.58 S	140.19 E
Chatsworth, Ont., Can.	202	44.27 N	80.54 W
Chatsworth, Rh.	144	19.38 S	31.13 E
Chatsworth, Ga., U.S.	182	34.46 N	84.46 W
Chatsworth, Ill., U.S.	206	40.45 N	88.18 W
Chatsworth, N.J., U.S.	198	39.46 N	74.33 W
Chatsworth ◆[8]	270	34.15 N	118.36 W
Chatsworth Reservoir ⊜[1]	218	34.14 N	118.37 W
Chattahoochee	182	30.42 N	84.51 W
Chattahoochee ≃	182	30.52 N	84.57 W
Chattanooga, Ohio, U.S.	206	40.38 N	84.47 W
Chattanooga, Tenn., U.S.	184	35.03 N	85.19 W
Chattenden	250	51.25 N	0.32 E
Chatteris	44	52.27 N	0.03 E
Châttillon-de-Michaille	54	46.08 N	5.47 E
Chatton	42	55.33 N	1.55 W
Chatun'	72	55.00 N	37.50 E
Chaturat	100	15.34 N	101.51 E
Chatwood	198	39.58 N	75.35 W
Chatyrka	64	62.03 N	175.15 E
Chaubaria	116	22.59 N	88.40 E
Chaubourg, Mount ∧[2]	231f	14.02 N	60.57 W
Chauchaiñeu, Sierra ∧	244	41.57 S	68.18 W
Chauconin	251	48.58 N	2.51 E
Chaudes-Aigues	32	44.51 N	3.00 E
Chaudfontaine	52	50.35 N	5.38 E
Chaudière ≃	176	46.45 N	71.17 W
Chauekuktuli, Lake ⊜	170	60.03 N	158.45 W
Chauffayer	56	44.45 N	6.01 E
Chaugācha	116	23.16 N	89.01 E
Chauk	100	20.54 N	94.50 E
Chaukhandi	262a	28.37 N	77.24 E
Chaullay	238	12.57 S	72.39 W
Chaulnes	46	49.49 N	2.48 E
Chaumergy	54	46.51 N	5.29 E
Chaumes-en-Brie	251	48.40 N	2.51 E
Chaumont, Fr.	54	48.07 N	5.08 E
Chaumont, N.Y., U.S.	202	44.04 N	76.08 W
Chaumont ≃	202	44.04 N	76.08 W
Chaumont, Rû de ≃	251	48.31 N	2.40 E
Chaumont Bay C	202	44.02 N	76.13 W
Chaumont-en-Vexin	46	49.16 N	1.53 E
Chaumont-Porcien	46	49.39 N	4.15 E
Chaumont-sur-Aire	52	48.56 N	5.15 E
Chaumont-sur-Loire	46	47.29 N	1.11 E
Chaumont-sur-Tharonne	46	47.37 N	1.54 E
Chaumua	262b	22.39 N	88.33 E
Chaumuhāni	114	22.56 N	91.07 E
Chauncey	178	39.24 N	82.08 W
Chaungwabyin	100	13.41 N	98.22 E
Chaungzon	100	16.22 N	97.32 E
Chauny	46	49.37 N	3.13 E
Chaupāran	114	24.23 N	85.15 E
Chau-phu	100	10.42 N	105.07 E
Chaussin	54	46.58 N	5.25 E
Chausu-yama ∧	84	35.14 N	137.39 E
Chausuyama-kofun ⊥	84	36.25 N	139.50 E
Chautāra	114	27.46 N	85.42 E
Chautauqua	204	42.14 N	79.28 W
Chautauqua □[6]	204	42.15 N	79.30 W
Chautauqua Creek ≃	204	42.20 N	79.36 W
Chautauqua Lake ⊜	204	42.12 N	79.27 W
Chauvigny	32	46.34 N	0.39 E
Chauvin	174	52.42 N	110.07 W
Chauvirey-le-Châtel	54	47.47 N	5.45 E
Chauvry	251	49.03 N	2.16 E
Chavakkad	112	10.32 N	76.06 E
Chaval	240	3.02 S	41.15 W
Chavanges	54	48.31 N	4.34 E
Chavannes, Lac ⊜	180	46.51 N	77.10 W
Chavarría, Arg.	242	28.57 S	58.35 W
Chavarría, Perú	276d	12.01 S	77.05 W
Chavast	75	40.13 N	68.50 E
Chavenay	251	48.51 N	1.59 E
Chavenay-Villepreux, Aérodrome de ⊠	251	48.51 N	1.58 E
Chavertovo	72	54.17 N	39.12 E
Chaves, Bra.	240	0.10 S	49.55 W
Chaves, Port.	34	41.44 N	7.28 W
Chaville	251	48.48 N	2.10 E
Chaviña	238	14.59 S	73.50 W
Chavinda	224	20.01 N	102.27 W
Cháviva	236	4.22 N	72.20 W
Chavki	72	54.20 N	38.13 E
Chavornay	54	46.43 N	6.34 E
Chavuma	142	13.05 S	22.40 E

Symbols in the index entries represent the broad categories identified in the key at the right. Symbols with superior numbers (∧∧[2]) identify subcategories (see complete key on page *I · 26*).

Kartensymbole in dem Registerverzeichnis stellen die rechts in Schlüssel erklärten Kategorien dar. Symbole mit hochgestellten Ziffern (∧∧[2]) bezeichnen Unterabteilungen einer Kategorie (vgl. vollständiger Schlüssel auf Seite *I · 26*).

Los símbolos incluídos en el texto del índice representan las grandes categorias identificadas con la clave a la derecha. Los símbolos con numeros en su parte superior (∧∧[2]) identifican las subcategorías (véase la clave completa en la página *I · 26*).

Les symboles de l'index représentent les catégories indiquées dans la légende à droite. Les symboles suivis d'un indice (∧∧[2]) représentent des sous-catégories (voir légende complète à la page *I · 26*).

Os símbolos incluídos no texto do índice representam as grandes categorias identificadas com a chave à direita. Os símbolos com números em sua parte superior (∧∧[2]) identificam as subcategorias (veja-se a chave completa na página *I · 26*).

Symbol	English	Deutsch	Español	Français	Português
∧	Mountain	Berg	Montaña	Montagne	Montanha
∧∧	Mountains	Berge	Montañas	Montagnes	Montanhas
)(	Pass	Pass	Paso	Col	Passo
∨	Valley, Canyon	Tal, Cañon	Valle, Cañón	Vallée, Canyon	Vale, Canhão
≚	Plain	Ebene	Llano	Plaine	Planície
≻	Cape	Kap	Cabo	Cap	Cabo
I	Island	Insel	Isla	Île	Ilha
II	Islands	Inseln	Islas	Îles	Ilhas
⊥	Other Topographic Features	Andere Topographische Objekte	Otros Elementos Topográficos	Autres données topographiques	Outros Elementos Topográficos

ESPAÑOL

Nombre	Página	Lat.°′	Long.°′ W=Oeste
Chawa'nanake	110	31.36 N	89.41 E
Chawang	100	8.25 N	99.30 E
Chawinda	113	32.21 N	74.42 E
Chay ≃	100	21.39 N	105.12 E
Chaya, Nihon	86	34.34 N	133.49 E
Chaya, Zhg.	92	30.32 N	98.00 E
Chayanta	238	18.27 S	66.30 W
Chayuan	90	29.20 N	121.34 E
Chayuanpu	90	27.40 N	112.57 E
Chayue	96	30.49 N	119.21 E
Chazay-d'Azergues	56	45.53 N	4.37 E
Chazelles-sur-Lyon	56	45.38 N	4.23 E
Chazumba	224	18.12 N	97.40 W
Chazy	178	44.53 N	73.26 W
Chbar ≃	100	13.19 N	107.05 E
Cheadle, Eng., U.K.	42	53.24 N	2.13 W
Cheadle, Eng., U.K.	44	52.59 N	1.59 W
Cheadle Hulme	42	53.22 N	2.12 W
Cheaha Mountain ∧	184	33.30 N	85.47 W
Cheakamus Indian Reserve •[4]	172	49.48 N	123.11 W
Cheam •[8]	250	51.21 N	0.13 W
Cheam View	214	49.15 N	121.41 W
Cheapside	212	29.17 N	97.24 W
Cheat, Shavers Fork ≃	178	39.06 N	79.33 W
Cheb	50	50.01 N	12.25 E
Chebacco Lake ⊜	273	42.37 N	70.48 W
Chebanse	206	41.00 N	87.54 W
Chebba	138	35.14 N	10.02 E
Chebeigou	79	43.28 N	127.04 E
Chebogue Point ›	176	43.45 N	66.07 W
Cheboksary → Čeboksary	70	56.09 N	47.15 E
Cheboygan	180	45.39 N	84.29 W
Chech, Erg •[2]	138	25.00 N	2.15 W
Chechaouene	138	35.10 N	5.16 W
Ch'ech'eng	90	22.05 N	120.42 E
Chech'on	88	37.08 N	128.12 E
Chęciny	30	50.48 N	20.28 E
Checleset Bay ⊂	172	50.03 N	127.40 W
Checoslovaquia → Czechoslovakia □[1]	30	49.30 N	17.00 E
Checotah	186	35.28 N	95.31 W
Chedabucto Bay ⊂	176	45.23 N	61.10 W
Chedaoyu	95	40.22 N	117.57 E
Cheddar	44	51.17 N	2.46 W
Cheduba Island ❙	100	18.48 N	93.38 E
Cheduba Strait ⊍	100	18.56 N	93.45 E
Chedun	90	24.09 N	117.19 E
Chée ≃	52	48.45 N	4.39 E
Cheecham Hills ⩕[2]	174	56.20 N	111.10 W
Cheektowaga	200	42.55 N	78.46 W
Cheepie	156	26.39 S	145.01 E
Cheerchenghe ≃	80	39.25 N	88.20 E
Cheesequake	266	40.25 N	74.17 W
Cheesequake Creek ≃	266	40.28 N	74.16 W
Cheesequake State Park ♠	266	40.26 N	74.16 W
Cheetham Hill •[8]	252	53.31 N	2.15 W
Chefang, Zhg.	94	41.35 N	121.26 E
Chefang, Zhg.	96	31.15 N	120.45 E
Chef-Boutonne	32	46.07 N	0.04 W
Chefoo → Yantai	88	37.33 N	121.20 E
Chefornak	170	60.13 N	164.12 W
Chefumage ≃	142	12.15 S	22.19 E
Chefuzwe	146	17.38 S	24.30 E
Chegar Perah	104	4.25 N	101.56 E
Chegga ⊤[4]	138	25.30 N	5.46 W
Chehalis	214	46.40 N	122.58 W
Chehalis ≃	214	46.57 N	123.50 W
Chehalis, South Fork ≃	214	46.40 N	123.15 W
Chehalis Indian Reservation •[4]	214	46.49 N	123.13 W
Chehe	92	25.00 N	107.38 E
Chehel Dokhtarān	118	35.06 N	62.19 E
Cheil, Ras el- ›	134	7.45 N	49.48 E
Cheine	50	52.52 N	11.04 E
Cheiron, Cimedu ∧	32	43.49 N	6.58 E
Cheiron, Montagne du ∧	56	43.48 N	6.58 E
Chejiatun	94	41.57 N	123.01 E
Chejiawopeng	94	42.29 N	123.07 E
Cheju	80	33.31 N	126.32 E
Cheju-do ❙	80	33.20 N	126.30 E
Chekiang → Zhejiang □[4]	90	29.00 N	120.00 E
Chek Jawa, Tanjong ›	261c	1.24 N	104.00 E
Chela, Serra da ∧	142	16.00 S	13.10 E
Chelan	192	47.51 N	120.01 W
Chelan □[6]	214	47.56 N	120.52 W
Chelan, Lake ⊜	192	48.05 N	120.30 W
Chelas •[8]	256c	38.45 N	9.07 W
Cheleiros	256c	38.53 N	9.20 W
Cheleiros, Ribeira de ≃	256c	38.54 N	9.22 W
Chelford	252	53.16 N	2.16 W
Chelforó	242	39.04 S	66.32 W
Chelga	134	12.30 N	37.04 E
Chelghoum el Aïd	138	36.10 N	6.10 E
Chélia, Djebel ∧	138	35.19 N	6.42 E
Chéliff, Oued ≃	138	36.01 N	0.07 E
Chelīk-e Yās Khān	110	37.05 N	66.14 E
Chellaston	44	52.53 N	1.27 W
Chelles	46	48.53 N	2.36 E
Chelles-le-Pin, Aérodrome de ⊠	251	48.55 N	2.35 E
Chełm	30	51.10 N	23.28 E
Chelmer ≃	44	51.48 N	0.40 E
Chelmer and Blackwater Navigation ≅	250	51.44 N	0.43 E
Chełmno	30	53.22 N	18.26 E
Chelmorton	252	53.13 N	1.50 W
Chelmsford, Ont., Can.	180	46.35 N	81.12 W
Chelmsford, Eng., U.K.	44	51.44 N	0.28 E
Chelmsford, Mass., U.S.	197	42.36 N	71.21 W
Chelmsford □[8]	250	51.44 N	0.30 E
Chełmża	30	53.12 N	18.37 E
Chelsea, Austl.	159	38.03 S	145.07 E
Chelsea, Iowa, U.S.	180	41.55 N	92.24 W
Chelsea, Mass., U.S.	197	42.24 N	71.02 W
Chelsea, Mich., U.S.	206	42.19 N	84.01 W
Chelsea, Okla., U.S.	186	36.32 N	95.26 W
Chelsea, Vt., U.S.	178	43.59 N	72.27 W
Chelsea Estates	198	39.41 N	75.36 W
Chelsea Park	214	47.28 N	122.21 W
Chelsfield •[8]	250	51.21 N	0.08 E
Cheltenham, Austl.	264a	33.46 S	151.05 E
Cheltenham, Austl.	264b	37.58 S	145.03 E
Cheltenham, Eng., U.K.	44	51.54 N	2.04 W
Cheltenham, Md., U.S.	198	38.44 N	76.50 W
Cheltenham, Pa., U.S.	198	40.04 N	75.08 W
Chelva	34	39.45 N	0.59 W
Chelvand	118	38.18 N	48.50 E
Chelyabinsk → Čel'abinsk	76	55.10 N	61.24 E
Chelyāma	116	23.37 N	86.33 E
Chelyan	178	38.12 N	81.30 W
Chelyuskintsy Ice Tongue ⊓	9	66.20 S	82.00 E
Chemagal	144	0.41 S	35.07 E
Chemaïa	138	31.30 N	8.47 W
Chemainus	172	48.55 N	123.43 W
Chemainus ⊜	214	48.53 N	123.41 W
Chemaogang	96	31.33 N	121.52 E
Chemax	222	20.39 N	87.56 W
Chemba	144	17.08 S	34.52 E
Chembūr •[8]	262c	19.04 N	72.54 E
Chemčik ≃	76	51.47 N	92.00 E
Chemehuevi Indian Reservation •[4]	194	34.30 N	114.23 W

FRANÇAIS

Nom	Page	Lat.°′	Long.°′ W=Ouest
Chemillé	32	47.13 N	0.44 W
Chemin	54	46.59 N	5.19 E
Cheminis, Colline ∧[2]	180	48.08 N	79.31 W
Chemnitz → Karl-Marx-Stadt	50	50.50 N	12.55 E
Chemnitz ≃	50	50.59 N	12.47 E
Chemor	104	4.43 N	101.07 E
Chemulpo → Inch'ŏn	88	37.28 N	126.38 E
Chemult	192	43.13 N	121.47 W
Chemung, Ill., U.S.	206	42.25 N	88.40 W
Chemung, N.Y., U.S.	200	42.01 N	76.37 W
Chemung □[6]	200	42.06 N	76.49 W
Chemung ≃	200	41.55 N	76.31 W
Chemung County Airport ⊠	200	42.10 N	76.53 W
Chemung Lake ⊜	202	44.25 N	78.22 W
Chena ≃	170	64.48 N	147.55 W
Chena, Cerro de ∧	276e	33.36 N	70.45 W
Chenāb ≃	113	29.23 N	71.02 E
Chenachane	138	26.00 N	4.15 W
Chenango □[6]	200	42.32 N	75.31 W
Chenango ≃	200	42.05 N	75.55 W
Chenango Bridge	200	42.10 N	75.52 W
Chenango Forks	200	42.14 N	75.51 W
Chenango Valley State Park ♠	200	42.14 N	75.50 W
Chenaut	248	34.15 S	59.13 W
Chenbaerhuqi (Bayankuren)	79	49.21 N	119.31 E
Chenbofang	88	37.27 N	115.18 E
Chencaishi	90	29.37 N	120.22 E
Chenchiang → Zhenjiang	96	32.13 N	119.26 E
Chencun	90	22.58 N	113.13 E
Chencuntang	92	23.48 N	110.49 E
Chendai	90	23.48 N	117.24 E
Chendauli •[8]	262c	19.07 N	72.54 E
Chenderiang	104	4.16 N	101.14 E
Chenderoh, Tasek ⊜	104	4.58 N	100.57 E
Chêne, Rivière du ≃, Qué., Can.	196	45.33 N	73.54 W
Chêne, Rivière du ≃, Qué., Can.	196	46.34 N	72.00 W
Chêne-Bourg	54	46.12 N	6.12 E
Chenele	142	12.54 S	23.54 E
Chenequa	206	43.07 N	88.23 W
Chénéville	196	45.53 N	75.03 W
Cheney, Kans., U.S.	188	37.38 N	97.47 W
Cheney, Wash., U.S.	192	47.29 N	117.34 W
Cheney Reservoir ⊜[1]	188	37.45 N	97.50 W
Cheneys Point	204	42.08 N	79.24 W
Cheneyville	184	31.01 N	92.17 W
Chenfang	90	28.01 N	117.32 E
Cheng'an	88	36.27 N	114.41 E
Chengannur	112	9.20 N	76.38 E
Chengbu	92	26.18 N	110.13 E
Chengchow → Zhengzhou	92	34.48 N	113.39 E
Chengde	95	40.58 N	117.53 E
Chengdu (Chengtu)	97	30.39 N	104.04 E
Chengele	110	28.47 N	96.16 E
Chenggang	90	26.32 N	115.26 E
Chenghai	90	23.30 N	116.46 E
Chenghu ⊜	96	31.13 N	120.49 E
Chenghuang	92	22.32 N	109.39 E
Chengjia	90	24.50 N	112.50 E
Chengjiachang	97	29.24 N	104.36 E
Chengjiahe	90	32.18 N	112.27 E
Chengjiang	92	24.45 N	102.54 E
Chengjiangzhen	97	29.52 N	106.23 E
Chengkou	92	31.54 N	108.41 E
Chenglingji	90	29.26 N	113.09 E
Chenglong	90	24.51 N	114.41 E
Chengmai	100	19.48 N	110.02 E
Chengpu	90	25.46 N	118.48 E
Chengqian	88	35.21 N	117.21 E
Chengqianwei	90	28.09 N	116.13 E
Chengshanjiao ›	80	37.23 N	122.39 E
Chengteh → Chengde	95	40.58 N	117.53 E
Chengtu → Chengdu	97	30.39 N	104.04 E
Ch'engtzuliao	259d	25.06 N	121.27 E
Chengwu	88	34.58 N	115.52 E
Chengxian	92	33.43 N	105.41 E
Chengxihu ⊜	90	32.24 N	116.15 E
Chengyang	88	36.18 N	120.22 E
Chengzi	88	41.57 N	117.16 E
Chengzituan	88	39.30 N	122.30 E
Ch'enhsien → Chezhou	90	25.48 N	112.59 E
Chenhu ⊜	90	30.29 N	113.22 E
Chenies	250	51.41 N	0.32 W
Chenil, Lac ⊜	176	51.51 N	59.41 W
Cheniménil	54	48.08 N	6.36 E
Chenjiachang, Zhg.	97	30.04 N	105.15 E
Chenjiachang, Zhg.	97	29.35 N	104.52 E
Chenjiagang	88	34.25 N	119.49 E
Chenjiahe	92	29.28 N	109.59 E
Chenjiaji	90	30.42 N	114.21 E
Chenjiapang	96	31.14 N	119.42 E
Chenjiapu	95	40.31 N	115.37 E
Chenjiaqiao	96	31.27 N	121.16 E
Chenjiatun, Zhg.	94	42.20 N	124.06 E
Chenjiatun, Zhg.	94	40.57 N	121.01 E
Chenjiawan	96	31.02 N	120.35 E
Chenjiaxiang	90	31.29 N	113.45 E
Chenjiayang	90	33.47 N	120.10 E
Chenjiazhen	96	31.30 N	121.48 E
Chenjiazui	95	39.17 N	116.59 E
Chenkeng	90	25.06 N	116.15 E
Chenlingjiao	96	30.23 N	118.47 E
Chenliu	88	34.43 N	114.31 E
Chenlong	259b	31.17 N	121.25 E
Chenmu	96	31.10 N	120.53 E
Chennevières	251	49.00 N	2.07 E
Chennevières-lès-Louvres	251	49.03 N	2.33 E
Chenoa	206	40.45 N	88.43 W
Chenonceaux	46	47.20 N	1.04 E
Chenôve	54	47.17 N	5.00 E
Chenoweth	214	45.37 N	121.13 W
Chenqiao	88	34.58 N	114.32 E
Chenqing	79	49.08 N	127.16 E
Chenshanzhuang	95	39.43 N	117.30 E
Chenshian	90	33.50 N	119.11 E
Chenshichang	97	29.17 N	106.00 E
Chens-sur-Léman	54	46.20 N	6.16 E
Chentejn Nuur ⩕	78	48.30 N	108.30 E
Chentij	78	48.05 N	109.45 E
Chentij □[4]	78	48.00 N	110.30 E
Chentij Chan ∧	78	48.50 N	109.10 E
Chenxi	92	27.51 N	109.59 E
Chenyang → Shenyang	94	41.48 N	123.27 E
Cheonan → Ch'ŏnan	88	36.48 N	127.09 E
Cheongju → Ch'ŏngju	88	36.39 N	127.31 E
Chepachet	197	41.55 N	71.40 W
Chepaizi	76	44.55 N	84.30 E
Chepaúa	142	12.58 S	22.43 E
Chepén	238	7.13 S	79.27 W
Chépénéhé	165f	20.47 S	167.09 E
Chepes	242	31.21 S	66.36 W
Chépica	242	34.44 S	71.17 W
Chepo	236	9.10 N	79.06 W
Chepstow	44	51.39 N	2.41 W
Cheptainville	251	48.33 N	2.16 E
Cher □[5]	32	47.05 N	2.30 E
Cher ≃	32	47.21 N	0.29 E
Cherain	52	50.11 N	5.52 E
Cherán	224	19.41 N	101.57 W
Chéran ≃	56	45.53 N	5.56 E
Cheranchi	140	12.40 N	7.42 E
Cherangany Hills ⩕[2]	144	1.15 N	35.27 E
Cherasco	56	44.39 N	7.51 E
Cherāt	113	33.49 N	71.53 E
Cheraw	182	34.42 N	79.53 W

PORTUGUÊS

Nome	Página	Lat.°′	Long.°′ W=Oeste
Cheraw State Park ♠	182	34.36 N	79.55 W
Cherbaniani Reef ⊹[2]	112	12.18 N	71.53 E
Cherbourg	32	49.39 N	1.39 W
Cherchell	138	36.36 N	2.12 E
Cherelato	134	6.00 N	38.10 E
Cheremkhovo → Čeremchovo	78	53.09 N	103.05 E
Chérence	251	49.05 N	1.41 E
Chereponi	140	10.09 N	0.17 E
Cherepovets → Čerepovec	66	59.08 N	37.54 E
Chergui, Chott ech ⊜	138	34.21 N	0.30 E
Chergui, Île ❙	138	34.44 N	11.14 E
Chergui, Zahrez ⊜	138	35.12 N	3.32 E
Cheribon → Cirebon	105a	6.44 S	108.34 E
Cherio ≃	58	45.46 N	9.55 E
Cherita, Sebkret ⊜	36	35.21 N	10.19 E
Cheriton	198	37.17 N	75.58 W
Cheriyam Island ❙	112	10.09 N	73.40 E
Cherkassy → Čerkassy	68	49.26 N	32.04 E
Cherkessk → Čerkessk	74	44.14 N	42.04 E
Cherlen → Kerulen ≃	80	48.48 N	117.00 E
Chermside	161a	27.23 S	153.02 E
Chernigov → Černigov	68	51.30 N	31.18 E
Chernofski	170	53.24 N	167.33 W
Chernogorsk → Černogorsk	76	53.49 N	91.18 E
Chernovtsy → Černovcy	68	48.18 N	25.56 E
Chero ≃	56	44.58 N	9.51 E
Cherokee, Ala., U.S.	184	34.46 N	87.58 W
Cherokee, Iowa, U.S.	188	42.45 N	95.33 W
Cherokee, Kans., U.S.	188	37.21 N	94.49 W
Cherokee, Okla., U.S.	186	36.45 N	98.21 W
Cherokee, Tex., U.S.	186	30.59 N	98.43 W
Cherokee □[6]	212	31.48 N	95.10 W
Cherokee, Lake ⊜[1]	212	32.21 N	94.39 W
Cherokee Canal ≅	216	39.18 N	121.55 W
Cherokee Indian Reservation •[4]	182	35.25 N	83.24 W
Cherokee Lake ⊜[1]	182	36.16 N	83.20 W
Cherokee Point ›	182	26.16 N	77.03 W
Cherokee Ranch	198	40.25 N	75.55 W
Cherokees, Lake O' The ⊜[1]	184	36.39 N	94.49 W
Cherokee Sound	228	26.17 N	77.04 W
Chéroy	46	48.12 N	3.00 E
Cherpuči	79	53.01 N	138.52 E
Cherquenco	242	38.41 S	72.00 W
Cherrabun	152	18.29 S	125.19 E
Cherrapunji	110	25.18 N	91.42 E
Cherry Brook ≃, Mass., U.S.	273	42.23 N	71.17 W
Cherry Brook ≃, N.J., U.S.	266	41.01 N	74.00 W
Cherry City	269b	40.29 N	79.58 W
Cherry Creek, B.C., Can.	214	49.17 N	124.47 W
Cherry Creek, N.Y., U.S.	204	42.18 N	79.06 W
Cherry Creek ≃, Ariz., U.S.	190	33.41 N	110.49 W
Cherry Creek ≃, Calif., U.S.	216	37.53 N	119.58 W
Cherry Creek ≃, Colo., U.S.	188	39.45 N	105.01 W
Cherry Creek ≃, Mont., U.S.	188	46.48 N	105.15 W
Cherry Creek ≃, N. Dak., U.S.	188	47.41 N	103.02 W
Cherry Creek ≃, S. Dak., U.S.	188	44.36 N	101.30 W
Cherry Creek, East Fork ≃	216	38.06 N	119.47 W
Cherry Creek, West Fork ≃	216	38.04 N	119.54 W
Cherry Fork	208	38.53 N	83.37 W
Cherry Grove, N.Y., U.S.	200	40.39 N	73.06 W
Cherry Grove, Oreg., U.S.	214	45.27 N	123.15 W
Cherry Hill, Ill., U.S.	268	41.32 N	88.02 W
Cherry Hill, N.J., U.S.	198	39.55 N	75.01 W
Cherry Hill •[8]	274b	39.15 N	76.38 W
Cherry Hill Mall •[9]	275	39.56 N	75.02 W
Cherry Island ❙	275	39.43 N	75.31 W
Cherry Lake ⊜[1]	216	38.00 N	119.54 W
Cherryland	216	37.41 N	122.06 W
Cherry Lane	269b	40.34 N	79.33 W
Cherryplain	200	42.38 N	73.22 W
Cherry Point Marine Corps Air Station ■	182	34.54 N	76.54 W
Cherryvale	188	37.16 N	95.33 W
Cherry Valley, Ark., U.S.	184	35.24 N	90.45 W
Cherry Valley, Calif., U.S.	218	33.57 N	116.53 W
Cherry Valley, Ill., U.S.	206	42.13 N	88.59 W
Cherry Valley, Mass., U.S.	197	42.15 N	71.52 W
Cherry Valley, N.Y., U.S.	200	42.48 N	74.45 W
Cherry Valley, Pa., U.S.	204	41.10 N	79.48 W
Cherry Valley Creek ≃	200	42.35 N	74.56 W
Cherryville, N.C., U.S.	182	35.23 N	81.23 W
Cherryville, Pa., U.S.	198	40.45 N	75.33 W
Cherrywood	265b	43.52 N	79.08 W
Cherson	68	46.38 N	32.35 E
Chersonesskij, Mys ›	68	44.35 N	33.23 E
Chertsey	44	51.24 N	0.30 W
Cherwell ≃	44	51.44 N	1.15 W
Chesaning	180	43.11 N	84.07 W
Chesapeake	198	36.43 N	76.15 W
Chesapeake and Delaware Canal ≅	198	40.30 N	75.58 W
Chesapeake and Ohio Canal National Historical Park ♠	198	39.03 N	77.16 W
Chesapeake Bay ⊂	198	38.40 N	76.25 W
Chesapeake Bay Bridge-Tunnel •[5]	198	37.00 N	76.02 W
Chesapeake Beach	198	38.41 N	76.32 W
Chesapeake City	198	39.32 N	75.49 W
Chesdin, Lake ⊜[1]	198	37.15 N	77.33 W
Cheseaux	54	46.35 N	6.36 E
Chesham	44	51.43 N	0.38 W
Chesham Bois	250	51.41 N	0.37 W
Cheshire, Conn., U.S.	197	41.30 N	72.54 W
Cheshire, Mass., U.S.	197	42.34 N	73.10 W
Cheshire, N.Y., U.S.	200	42.49 N	77.20 W
Cheshire □[6], Eng., U.K.	42	53.23 N	2.30 W
Cheshire □[6], N.H., U.S.	197	42.50 N	72.15 W
Cheshire Plain ⊻	42	53.17 N	2.40 W
Cheshire Reservoir ⊜[1]	197	42.32 N	73.11 W
Chesht-e Sharīf	118	34.21 N	63.44 E
Cheshunt	44	51.43 N	0.02 W
Chesil Beach •[2]	44	50.38 N	2.33 W
Cheslatta Lake ⊜	172	53.44 N	125.18 W
Chesley	202	44.17 N	81.05 W
Chesnee	182	35.09 N	81.52 W
Chess ≃	250	51.38 N	0.27 W
Chessington •[8]	250	51.21 N	0.18 W
Chessy	251	48.53 N	2.46 E
Chest Creek ≃	204	40.53 N	78.44 W
Chester, Eng., U.K.	42	53.12 N	2.54 W
Chester, Calif., U.S.	194	40.19 N	121.14 W

Chester, Conn., U.S.	197	41.24 N	72.27 W
Chester, Ill., U.S.	184	37.55 N	89.49 W
Chester, Md., U.S.	198	38.58 N	76.17 W
Chester, Mass., U.S.	197	42.17 N	72.59 W
Chester, Mont., U.S.	192	48.31 N	110.58 W
Chester, Nebr., U.S.	188	40.01 N	97.37 W
Chester, N.J., U.S.	200	40.47 N	74.42 W
Chester, Okla., U.S.	186	36.13 N	98.55 W
Chester, Pa., U.S.	198	39.51 N	75.21 W
Chester, S.C., U.S.	182	34.43 N	81.12 W
Chester, Tex., U.S.	212	30.55 N	94.36 W
Chester, Vt., U.S.	178	43.16 N	72.36 W
Chester, Va., U.S.	198	37.21 N	77.27 W
Chester, W. Va., U.S.	204	40.37 N	80.34 W
Chester □[6]	198	39.58 N	75.36 W
Chester □[8]	252	53.16 N	2.52 W
Chester ≃	198	39.00 N	76.10 W
Chester Basin	176	44.34 N	64.19 W
Chesterbrook	274c	38.55 N	77.09 W
Chester Brook ≃	273	42.23 N	71.14 W
Chester Creek ≃	198	39.50 N	75.22 W
Chester Creek, East Branch ≃	275	39.56 N	75.32 W
Chester Creek, West Branch ≃	275	39.54 N	75.27 W
Chesterfield, Eng., U.K.	42	53.15 N	1.25 W
Chesterfield, Conn., U.S.	197	41.24 N	72.11 W
Chesterfield, Ill., U.S.	209	39.15 N	90.04 W
Chesterfield, Ind., U.S.	208	40.07 N	85.36 W
Chesterfield, Mass., U.S.	197	42.24 N	72.50 W
Chesterfield, S.C., U.S.	182	34.44 N	80.05 W
Chesterfield, Va., U.S.	182	37.23 N	77.31 W
Chesterfield □[6]	198	37.20 N	77.25 W
Chesterfield, Île ❙	128	16.20 S	43.58 E
Chesterfield, Îles ❙❙	150	19.30 S	158.00 E
Chesterfield Inlet	166	63.21 N	90.42 W
Chesterfield Inlet ⊂	166	63.25 N	90.45 W
Chester Heights	275	39.53 N	75.28 W
Chester Hill, Austl.	264a	33.53 S	151.00 E
Chesterhill, Ohio, U.S.	178	39.29 N	81.52 W
Chester Hill, Pa., U.S.	204	40.53 N	78.14 W
Chester Island ❙	275	39.50 N	75.21 W
Chesterland	204	41.31 N	81.21 W
Chester-le-Street	42	54.52 N	1.34 W
Chester Morse Lake ⊜[1]	214	47.23 N	121.42 W
Chester Octoraro Lake ⊜	198	39.48 N	76.02 W
Chester Springs	275	40.06 N	75.37 W
Chesterton	206	41.37 N	87.04 W
Chesterton Range ⩕	156	25.30 S	147.27 E
Chestertown	198	39.13 N	76.04 W
Chesterville, Ont., Can.	202	45.06 N	75.14 W
Chesterville, Ohio, U.S.	204	40.29 N	82.41 W
Chestnut	209	40.03 N	89.11 W
Chestnut Hill, Mass., U.S.	273	42.20 N	71.10 W
Chestnut Hill, Pa., U.S.	200	40.04 N	75.12 W
Chestnut Hill •[8]	275	40.04 N	75.13 W
Chestnut Hill ∧[2]	275	40.13 N	75.45 W
Chestnut Hill Reservoir ⊜[1]	273	42.20 N	71.10 W
Chestnut Ridge ∧	204	40.09 N	79.24 W
Chestnut Ridge Park ♠	274a	42.43 N	78.46 W
Chest Peak ∧	162	43.06 S	172.01 E
Chesu	110	30.31 N	82.37 E
Chesuncook Lake ⊜	178	46.00 N	69.20 W
Cheswick	204	40.32 N	79.47 W
Cheswold	198	39.13 N	75.35 W
Chet ≃	44	52.33 N	1.32 E
Cheta ≃	64	71.54 N	102.06 E
Chetaibi	36	37.04 N	7.23 E
Chetco ≃	192	42.03 N	124.16 W
Chetek	180	45.19 N	91.39 W
Chéticamp	176	46.38 N	61.01 W
Chetlat Island ❙	112	11.42 N	72.42 E
Chetopa	188	37.02 N	95.05 W
Chetput	112	12.28 N	79.21 E
Chetumal Bay ⊂	222	18.20 N	88.05 W
Chetwynd	172	55.42 N	121.40 W
Cheung Chau ❙	261d	22.12 N	114.01 E
Cheung Kwan O ⊂	261d	22.17 N	114.15 E
Cheung Shui Tan	261d	22.26 N	114.12 E
Chevak	170	61.39 N	165.17 W
Cheval-Blanc, Montagne du ⩕	56	44.07 N	6.26 E
Cheval Blanc, Pointe du ›	228	19.41 N	73.27 W
Chevannes	251	48.32 N	2.27 E
Chevelon Creek ≃	190	34.57 N	110.31 W
Chevening	250	51.18 N	0.08 E
Chevenoz	54	46.20 N	6.39 E
Cheverly	274c	38.55 N	76.55 W
Cheverny	46	47.30 N	1.28 E
Chevillon	54	48.32 N	5.08 E
Chevilly-Larue	251	48.46 N	2.21 E
Chevington Drift	42	55.17 N	1.36 W
Cheviot, N.Z.	162	42.49 S	173.16 E
Cheviot, Ohio, U.S.	208	39.11 N	84.35 W
Cheviot Hills ⩕[2]	42	55.24 N	2.20 W
Chevreuse	46	48.42 N	2.03 E
Chèvreville	251	49.07 N	2.51 E
Chevril, Lac du ⊜	56	45.29 N	6.56 E
Chevry-Cossigny	251	48.43 N	2.40 E
Chevy Chase	274c	38.58 N	77.05 W
Chevy Chase Heights	204	40.36 N	79.08 W
Chevy Chase View	274c	39.01 N	77.05 W
Chewaucan ≃	192	42.30 N	120.18 W
Chew Bahir (Lake Stefanie) ⊜	134	4.40 N	36.50 E
Chewelah	192	48.17 N	117.43 W
Chew Magna	44	51.22 N	2.35 W
Chew Reservoir ⊜[1]	252	53.31 N	1.56 W
Chews Landing	275	39.50 N	75.04 W
Chewton, Austl.	159	37.05 S	144.16 E
Chewton, Pa., U.S.	204	40.53 N	80.20 W
Chexbres	54	46.29 N	6.47 E
Cheyenne, Okla., U.S.	186	35.37 N	99.40 W
Cheyenne, Wyo., U.S.	190	41.08 N	104.49 W
Cheyenne ≃	188	44.40 N	101.15 W
Cheyenne, Dry Fork ≃	188	43.25 N	105.23 W
Cheyenne River Indian Reservation •[4]	188	45.05 N	101.20 W
Cheyenne Wells	188	38.51 N	102.11 W
Cheyne Bay ⊂	152	34.35 S	118.50 E
Cheyne Point ›	152	33.58 S	122.34 E
Cheyney	275	39.56 N	75.31 W
Chezhen	88	37.54 N	117.37 E
Chezhou	90	25.48 N	112.59 E
Chhab	113	33.14 N	71.54 E
Chhabra	114	24.40 N	76.50 E
Chhachhrauli	114	30.15 N	77.22 E
Chhajārsi	262a	28.38 N	77.23 E
Chhalera Bāngar	262a	28.33 N	77.20 E
Chhanka	116	23.59 N	89.55 E
Chhātak	110	25.02 N	91.40 E
Chhatarpur, Bhārat	114	24.23 N	84.11 E
Chhatarpur, Bhārat	114	24.54 N	79.36 E
Chhatarpur □[5]	114	24.55 N	79.35 E
Chhātna	116	23.18 N	86.58 E
Chhattīsgarh ⊻	112	21.15 N	82.00 E
Chhay Arêng ≃	100	11.31 N	103.25 E
Chhêb Kândal	100	13.45 N	105.24 E
Chheharta	113	31.38 N	74.48 E
Chhibrāmau	114	27.09 N	79.31 E
Chhināmor	262b	22.48 N	88.18 E
Chhindwāra	114	22.04 N	78.56 E
Chhindwāra □[5]	114	22.00 N	78.50 E
Chhiruti	116	24.01 N	88.11 E

Chhitauni	114	27.09 N	83.58 E
Chhlong ≃	100	12.15 N	105.58 E
Chhota Bāisdia	116	22.00 N	90.27 E
Chhota-Chhindwāra	114	23.03 N	79.29 E
Chhota Udepur	110	22.19 N	74.01 E
Ch'hsing Yen ❙	90	21.44 N	120.50 E
Chhukha Dzong	114	27.09 N	89.36 E
Chi ≃	100	15.11 N	104.43 E
Chía	236	4.52 N	74.04 W
Chiador	246	22.01 S	43.03 W
Chiador, Cachoeira do ⌞	246	22.03 S	43.02 W
Chiahsien	90	23.05 N	120.35 E
Chiahsing → Jiaxing	96	30.46 N	120.45 E
Chiai	90	23.29 N	120.27 E
Chialamberto	56	45.22 N	7.21 E
Chiali	90	23.10 N	120.11 E
Chiambala ≃	142	16.22 S	11.49 E
Chiamboni, Ras ›	134	1.38 S	41.36 E
Chiampo	58	45.33 N	11.17 E
Chiampo ≃	58	45.20 N	11.16 E
Chiamussu → Jiamusi	79	46.50 N	130.21 E
Chian → Ji'an	90	27.07 N	114.58 E
Chiana, Val di ∨	60	43.15 N	11.50 E
Chianciano Terme	60	43.03 N	11.50 E
Chiang Dao	100	19.22 N	98.58 E
Chiang Kham	100	19.32 N	100.18 E
Chiang Khan	100	17.52 N	101.36 E
Chiang Khian	100	19.37 N	100.00 E
Chiang Mai	100	18.47 N	98.59 E
Chiangmen → Jiangmen	90	22.35 N	113.05 E
Chiang Rai	100	19.54 N	99.50 E
Chiang Saen	100	20.16 N	100.05 E
Chiangtu → Yangzhou	90	32.24 N	119.26 E
Chiangyin → Jiangyin	96	31.55 N	120.16 E
Chiani ≃	60	42.52 N	12.14 E
Chianje	142	15.45 S	13.48 E
Chianni	60	43.29 N	10.38 E
Chianti □[4]	60	43.22 N	11.23 E
Chianti ⩕[1]	60	43.25 N	11.20 E
Chianti, Monti del ⩕	60	43.32 N	11.25 E
Chiaoch'i	90	24.49 N	121.46 E
Chiaohsien → Jiaoxian	88	36.18 N	119.58 E
Chiaopanshan	90	24.49 N	121.21 E
Chiaotso → Jiaozuo	92	35.15 N	113.18 E
Chiao-tung University ⊌[2]	259b	31.14 N	121.24 E
Chiapa	238	19.32 S	69.13 W
Chiapa de Corzo	224	16.42 N	93.00 W
Chiapaot'ai	90	24.11 N	121.01 E
Chiapas □[3]	222	16.30 N	92.30 W
Chiaramonte Gulfi	36	37.01 N	14.43 E
Chiaravalle	60	43.36 N	13.19 E
Chiaravalle Centrale	36	38.41 N	16.25 E
Chiareggio	58	46.19 N	9.47 E
Chiari	56	45.32 N	9.56 E
Chiasso	54	45.50 N	9.01 E
Chiautla de Tapia	224	18.17 N	98.36 W
Chiautzingo	224	19.12 N	98.28 W
Chiavari	56	44.19 N	9.19 E
Chiavenna	54	46.19 N	9.24 E
Chiba	84	35.36 N	140.07 E
Chiba □[5]	84	35.30 N	140.20 E
Chibabava	146	20.19 S	33.39 E
Chiba-kō ⊂	258	35.35 N	140.06 E
Chibakou	90	29.36 N	113.01 E
Chibango	142	13.38 S	21.56 E
Chiba University ⊌[2]	258	35.36 N	140.07 E
Chibemba	142	15.45 S	14.05 E
Chibi	144	20.19 S	30.30 E
Chibia	142	15.11 S	13.41 E
Chibiribira Falls ⌞	144	21.14 S	32.20 E
Chibouet ≃	196	45.47 N	72.52 W
Chibougamau	166	49.55 N	74.22 W
Chibuto	146	24.44 S	33.33 E
Chibuzhangchuhu ⊜	110	33.25 N	90.15 E
Chibwe	144	14.12 S	28.31 E
Chica, Laguna ⊜	224	20.06 N	96.40 W
Chicago	206		
	268	41.53 N	87.38 W
Chicago, North Branch ≃	206	41.53 N	87.38 W
Chicago, North Branch, West Fork ≃	268	42.03 N	87.54 W
Chicago, South Branch ≃	268	41.53 N	87.38 W
Chicago, University of ⊌[2]	268	41.47 N	87.36 W
Chicago-Hammond Airport ⊠	268	41.32 N	87.32 W
Chicago Harbor ⊂	268	41.53 N	87.37 W
Chicago Heights	206	41.30 N	87.38 W
Chicago-Hinsdale Airport ⊠	268	41.46 N	87.56 W
Chicagoland Airport ⊠	268	42.12 N	87.56 W
Chicago Lawn •[8]	268	41.47 N	87.41 W
Chicago-Midway Airport ⊠	206	41.47 N	87.45 W
Chicago-O'Hare International Airport ⊠	268	41.59 N	87.54 W
Chicago Park	216	39.09 N	120.58 W
Chicago Portage National Historic Site ⊥	268	41.48 N	87.49 W
Chicago Ridge	206	41.42 N	87.47 W
Chicago Sanitary and Ship Canal ≅	206	41.32 N	88.05 W
Chicago Stadium ♠	268	41.53 N	87.40 W
Chicama ≃	238	7.56 S	79.17 W
Chicamacomico ≃	198	38.26 N	75.59 W
Chicapa ≃	142	6.26 S	20.47 E
Chic-Chocs, Monts ⩕	176	48.55 N	66.00 W
Chic-Chocs, Parc des ♠	176	49.05 N	65.42 W
Chichagof Island ❙	170	57.30 N	135.30 W
Chichas, Cordillera de ⩕	238	20.30 S	66.30 W
Chīchāwatni	113	30.32 N	72.42 E
Chiché ≃	240	8.15 S	53.30 W
Chicheng	88	40.54 N	115.46 E
Chichén Itzá	222	20.40 N	88.34 W
Chichén Itzá ⊥	222	20.40 N	88.35 W
Chichester, Eng., U.K.	44	50.50 N	0.48 W
Chichester, N.Y., U.S.	200	42.06 N	74.19 W
Chichester Range ⩕	152	22.00 S	118.50 E
Chichi	90	23.50 N	120.46 E
Chichibu	84	35.59 N	139.05 E
Chichibu-tama-kokuritsu-kōen ♠	84	35.52 N	139.00 E
Chichica	226	8.22 N	81.40 W
Chichicastenango	226	14.56 N	91.07 W
Chichigalpa	226	12.34 N	87.02 W
Chichigapa	224	17.47 N	94.25 W
Ch'ich'ihaerh → Qiqihaer	79	47.19 N	123.55 E
Chichihualco	224	17.41 N	99.39 W
Chichimilá	222	20.37 N	88.13 W
Chichiriviche	236	10.56 N	68.16 W
Chichishima-rettō ❙❙	14	27.06 N	142.12 E
Chicholi	114	22.01 N	77.40 E
Chichra	116	22.19 N	86.53 E
Chicicatiapa ≃	224	18.18 N	96.19 W
Chickahominy ≃	198	37.14 N	76.53 W
Chickaloon	170	61.48 N	148.28 W
Chickamauga	182	34.52 N	85.18 W
Chickamauga Lake ⊜[1]	182	35.22 N	85.02 W

Chickamin ≃	172	55.47 N	130.58 W
Chickasaw, Ala., U.S.	184	30.46 N	88.05 W
Chickasaw, Ohio, U.S.	206	40.26 N	84.30 W
Chickasaw Bogue ≃	184	32.17 N	87.55 W
Chickasaw Creek ≃	184	30.44 N	88.03 W
Chickasawhatchie Creek ≃	182	31.19 N	84.29 W
Chickasawhay ≃	184	31.00 N	88.45 W
Chickasaw National Recreation Area ♠	186	34.25 N	96.59 W
Chickasha	186	35.02 N	97.58 W
Chicken	170	64.04 N	141.56 W
Chicken Brook ≃	273	42.08 N	71.25 W
Chickerell	44	50.37 N	2.30 W
Chickies Creek ≃	198	40.03 N	76.32 W
Chiclana de la Frontera	34	36.25 N	6.08 W
Chiclayo	238	6.46 S	79.51 W
Chico, Calif., U.S.	194	39.44 N	121.50 W
Chico, Tex., U.S.	186	33.18 N	97.48 W
Chico, Wash., U.S.	214	47.37 N	122.43 W
Chico ≃, Arg.	244	43.48 S	66.25 W
Chico ≃, Arg.	244	42.25 S	70.30 W
Chico ≃, Arg.	244	49.56 S	68.32 W
Chico ≃, Pan.	226	8.20 N	80.28 W
Chico ≃, Pil.	106	17.58 N	121.36 E
Chico ≃, S.A.	244	51.40 S	69.09 W
Chico, Arroyo ≃	276b	23.02 N	82.17 W
Chicoa	144	15.37 S	32.24 E
Chicobi, Lac ⊜	180	48.53 N	78.30 W
Chico Creek ≃	188	38.15 N	104.20 W
Chicolete Creek ≃	212	29.05 N	96.49 W
Chicomba	142	14.09 S	14.57 E
Chicomo	146	24.31 S	34.17 E
Chicomuselo	222	15.46 N	92.16 W
Chiconautla, Cerro ∧	276a	19.39 N	98.58 W
Chicontepec	224	20.58 N	98.10 W
Chicopee, Ga., U.S.	182	34.16 N	83.51 W
Chicopee, Mass., U.S.	197	42.10 N	72.36 W
Chicopee ≃	197	42.09 N	72.37 W
Chicora	204	40.57 N	79.45 W
Chicorato	222	26.02 N	107.54 W
Chicot ≃	265a	45.35 N	73.51 W
Chicot State Park ♠	184	30.47 N	92.19 W
Chicoutimi	176	48.26 N	71.04 W
Chicoutimi ≃	176	48.26 N	71.05 W
Chicoutimi, Parc de ♠	176	48.30 N	70.15 W
Chicualoque	224	20.23 N	97.39 W
Chicuma	142	13.23 S	14.51 E
Chicxulub	222	21.08 N	89.31 W
Chidambaram	112	11.24 N	79.42 E
Chiddingstone Causeway	250	51.12 N	0.10 E
Chidenguele	146	24.54 S	34.13 E
Chidley, Cape ›	166	60.23 N	64.26 W
Chidlow	158a	31.52 S	116.14 E
Chidu	110	30.35 N	94.50 E
Chief	212	32.33 N	96.10 W
Chief Justice William Cushing Memorial State Park ♠	273	42.10 N	70.45 W
Chiefland	182	29.29 N	82.52 W
Chiefs Point ›	202	44.42 N	81.18 W
Chief's Point Indian Reserve •[4]	202	44.41 N	81.17 W
Chiehyang → Jieyang	90	23.35 N	116.21 E
Chiemgauer Alpen ⩕	58	47.40 N	12.30 E
Chiemsee ⊜	58	47.54 N	12.29 E
Chien, Bayou de ≃	184	36.35 N	89.11 W
Chienchiao Airport ⊠	96	30.12 N	120.12 E
Chienes (Kiens)	58	46.48 N	11.50 E
Chiengi	144	8.39 S	29.10 E
Chiengo	142	13.20 S	21.55 E
Chiens, Rivière aux ≃	265a	45.39 N	73.46 W
Chienti ≃	60	43.18 N	13.45 E
Chieri	56	45.01 N	7.49 E
Chiers ≃	52	49.39 N	5.00 E
Chiesa in Valmalenco	58	46.16 N	9.51 E
Chiese ≃	58	45.08 N	10.25 E
Chieti	60	42.21 N	14.10 E
Chieti □[4]	60	42.07 N	14.21 E
Chietla	224	18.31 N	98.35 W
Chieuti	60	41.51 N	15.10 E
Chieveley	44	51.27 N	1.19 W
Chièvres	46	50.35 N	3.48 E
Chifeng	88	42.18 N	119.00 E
Chigasaki	84	35.19 N	139.24 E
Chiginagak, Mount ∧	170	57.08 N	156.59 W
Chigmit Mountains ⩕	170	60.00 N	153.00 W
Chignahuapan	224	19.50 N	98.02 W
Chignall Saint James	250	51.46 N	0.25 E
Chignall Smealy	250	51.47 N	0.25 E
Chignecto, Cape ›	176	45.20 N	64.57 W
Chignecto Bay ⊂	176	45.35 N	64.45 W
Chignik	170	56.18 N	158.23 W
Chignik Bay ⊂	170	56.22 N	158.15 W
Chignik Lagoon	170	56.14 N	158.44 W
Chignik Lake	170	56.20 N	158.29 W
Chignolo Po	56	45.09 N	9.29 E
Chigorodó	236	7.41 N	76.42 W
Chigu	90	27.34 N	114.40 E
Chigubo	146	22.50 S	33.34 E
Chigwell	44	51.38 N	0.05 E
Chigwell Row	250	51.37 N	0.07 E
Chigyŏng	88	39.51 N	127.26 E
Chihaya-akasaka	260	34.24 N	135.38 E
Chihaya Castle ⊥	260	34.24 N	135.40 E
Chihe	90	32.32 N	117.58 E
Ch'ihfeng → Chifeng	88	42.18 N	119.00 E
Chihli, Gulf of → Bohai ⊂	88	38.30 N	120.00 E
Chihpen	90	22.42 N	121.03 E
Ch'ihshang	90	23.07 N	121.12 E
Chihsi → Jixi	79	45.17 N	130.59 E
Ch'ihsing Shan ∧	259d	25.10 N	121.33 E
Ch'ihtung	90	22.46 N	120.16 E
Ch'ihu, T'aiwan	90	23.58 N	120.28 E
Chihu, Zhg.	90	24.07 N	117.51 E
Chihuahua	222	28.38 N	106.05 W
Chihuxi ≃	90	26.38 N	117.24 E
Chii-san ∧	88	35.20 N	127.44 E
Chiitola	24	61.16 N	29.38 E
Chijiantan	95	39.12 N	117.24 E
Chikaskia ≃	186	36.37 N	97.15 W
Chik Ballāpur	112	13.28 N	77.44 E
Chik Chu Wan ⊂	261d	22.12 N	114.12 E
Chikhli	112	20.21 N	76.15 E
Chikindzonot	222	20.20 N	88.29 W
Chik Kang	261d	22.26 N	114.21 E
Chikmagalūr	112	13.19 N	75.47 E
Chiknai ≃	116	24.06 N	89.17 E
Chiknāyakanhalli	112	13.26 N	76.37 E
Chikoa	144	13.24 S	32.07 E
Chikodi	112	16.26 N	74.36 E
Chikote	144	15.52 S	26.54 E
Chikou	90	30.44 N	117.32 E
Chikrêng ≃	100	12.51 N	104.14 E
Ch'iku	90	23.08 N	120.07 E
Chikugo	86	33.10 N	130.33 E
Chikugo ≃	82	33.09 N	130.21 E
Chikuma ≃	84	36.59 N	138.14 E
Chikuminuk Lake ⊜	170	60.14 N	159.00 W
Chikura	84	34.57 N	139.57 E
Chikusa	86	35.09 N	134.26 E
Chikusa ≃	86	34.44 N	134.24 E
Chikushino	86	33.17 N	130.38 E
Chikwawa	144	16.03 S	34.48 E
Chi-Kyaw	100	20.17 N	93.54 E
Chila, Ang.	142	12.04 S	14.29 E

English	Deutsch	Español	Français	Português
≃ River	Fluss	Río	Rivière	Rio
≅ Canal	Kanal	Canal	Canal	Canal
⌞ Waterfall, Rapids	Wasserfall, Stromschnellen	Cascada, Rápidos	Chute d'eau, Rapides	Cascata, Rápidos
⊍ Strait	Meeresstrasse	Estrecho	Détroit	Estreito
⊂ Bay, Gulf	Bucht, Golf	Bahía, Golfo	Baie, Golfe	Baía, Golfo
⊜ Lake, Lakes	See, Seen	Lago, Lagos	Lac, Lacs	Lago, Lagos
☷ Swamp	Sumpf	Pantano	Marais	Pântano
⊓ Ice Features, Glacier	Eis- und Gletscherformen	Accidentes Glaciales	Formes glaciaires	Acidentes Glaciares
⊤ Other Hydrographic Features	Andere Hydrographische Objekte	Otros Elementos Hidrográficos	Autres données hydrographiques	Outros Elementos Hidrográficos
⊹ Submarine Features	Untermeerische Objekte	Accidentes Submarinos	Formes de relief sous-marin	Acidentes Submarinos
□ Political Unit	Politische Einheit	Unidad Política	Entité politique	Unidade Política
⊌ Cultural Institution	Kulturelle Institution	Institución Cultural	Institution culturelle	Instituição Cultural
⊥ Historical Site	Historische Stätte	Sitio Histórico	Site historique	Sitio Histórico
♠ Recreational Site	Erholungs- und Ferienort	Sitio de Recreo	Centre de loisirs	Sítio de Lazer
⊠ Airport	Flughafen	Aeropuerto	Aéroport	Aeroporto
■ Military Installation	Militäranlage	Instalación Militar	Installation militaire	Instalação Militar
• Miscellaneous	Verschiedenes	Misceláneo	Divers	Miscelânea

Symbols in the index entries represent the broad categories identified in the key at the right. Symbols with superior numbers (∧²) identify subcategories (see complete key on page I · 26).

Kartensymbole in dem Registerverzeichnis stellen die rechts in Schlüssel erklärten Kategorien dar. Symbole mit hochgestellten Ziffern (∧²) bezeichnen Unterabteilungen einer Kategorie (vgl. vollständiger Schlüssel auf Seite I · 26).

Los símbolos incluidos en el texto del índice representan las grandes categorías identificadas con la clave a la derecha. Los símbolos con números en su parte superior (∧²) identifican las subcategorías (véase la clave completa en la página I · 26).

Les symboles de l'index représentent les catégories indiquées dans la légende à droite. Les symboles suivis d'un indice (∧²) représentent des sous-catégories (voir légende complète à la page I · 26).

Os símbolos incluídos no texto do índice representam as grandes categorias identificadas com a chave à direita. Os símbolos com números em sua parte superior (∧²) identificam as subcategorias (veja-se a chave completa à página I · 26).

Symbol	English	Deutsch	Español	Français	Português
∧	Mountain	Berg	Montaña	Montagne	Montanha
∧∧	Mountains	Berge	Montañas	Montagnes	Montanhas
)(	Pass	Pass	Paso	Col	Passo
V	Valley, Canyon	Tal, Cañon	Valle, Cañón	Vallée, Canyon	Vale, Canhão
≡	Plain	Ebene	Llano	Plaine	Planície
≻	Cape	Kap	Cabo	Cap	Cabo
I	Island	Insel	Isla	Île	Ilha
II	Islands	Inseln	Islas	Îles	Ilhas
⊥	Other Topographic Features	Andere Topographische Objekte	Otros Elementos Topográficos	Autres données topographiques	Outros Elementos Topográficos

ESPAÑOL — Nombre | Página | Lat.°′ | Long.°′ W=Oeste

FRANÇAIS — Nom | Page | Lat.°′ | Long.°′ W=Ouest

PORTUGUÊS — Nome | Página | Lat.°′ | Long.°′ W=Oeste

Christopher Lake ⊜	152	24.49 S	127.42 E
Christoval	186	31.12 N	100.30 W
Chroma ≃	64	71.36 N	144.49 E
Chromtau	76	50.17 N	58.27 E
Chrudim	30	49.57 N	15.48 E
Chrustal'noje	73	48.10 N	38.50 E
Chrustal'nyj	79	44.24 N	135.06 E
Chrysler Corporation (Hamtramck Plant) ʋ[3]	271	42.23 N	83.03 W
Chrzanów	30	50.09 N	19.24 E
Chuacús, Sierra de ⩘	226	15.05 N	90.45 W
Chuādānga	114	23.38 N	88.51 E
Chualar	216	36.34 N	121.31 W
Chuanbu	96	31.17 N	119.49 E
Chuanergu	95	39.20 N	117.43 E
Chuan'gang	96	31.57 N	121.04 E
Chuangjiapuzi	94	40.50 N	124.06 E
Chuanhongjiang	96	31.49 N	121.29 E
Chuanliao	90	28.17 N	120.13 E
Chuansha	96	31.12 N	121.42 E
Chuanshan	90	29.53 N	121.57 E
Chuanxindian, Zhg.	88	42.33 N	117.27 E
Chuanxindian, Zhg.	94	41.25 N	120.30 E
Chuanyanghe ☲	90	33.46 N	119.51 E
Chuathbaluk	170	61.40 N	159.15 W
Chubbuck	192	42.55 N	112.28 W
Chūbu-sangaku-kokuritsu-kōen ♠	84	36.30 N	137.41 E
Chubut □[4]	244	44.00 S	69.00 W
Chubut ≃	244	43.20 S	65.03 W
Ch'üchiang → Shaoguan	90	24.50 N	113.37 E
Chuchi Lake ⊜	172	55.10 N	124.33 W
Chuchou → Zhuzhou	90	27.50 N	113.09 E
Chuchra	68	50.13 N	34.49 E
Chu Chua	172	51.21 N	120.10 W
Chuchuwayha Indian Reserve ◆[4]	172	49.21 N	120.06 W
Chuckatuck	198	36.52 N	76.35 W
Chučni	74	41.57 N	47.55 E
Chucuito	238	15.53 S	69.53 W
Chucun	90	33.04 N	116.32 E
Chucunaque ≃	236	8.09 N	77.44 W
Chudan ≃	78	52.08 N	109.40 E
Chudat	74	41.38 N	48.42 E
Chuderhe ≃	79	46.48 N	123.37 E
Chudleigh	44	50.36 N	3.38 W
Chudojelan'	78	54.42 N	99.37 E
Chudunskij Chrebet ⩘	78	52.00 N	110.00 E
Chuen Lung	261d	22.24 N	114.06 E
Chugach Islands II	170	59.06 N	151.42 W
Chugach Mountains ⩘	170	61.00 N	145.00 W
Chugiak	170	61.25 N	149.30 W
Chuginadak Island I	170	52.49 N	169.50 W
Chūgoku-sanchi ⩘	86	34.58 N	132.57 E
Chugwater	190	41.46 N	104.49 W
Chugwater Creek ≃	188	42.07 N	104.51 W
Chugyo-ri	261b	37.39 N	126.50 E
Chūhar Kāna	113	31.45 N	73.48 E
Chuhe	90	34.03 N	113.35 E
Chuhuichupa	222	29.38 N	108.22 W
Chuí	242	33.41 S	53.27 W
Chuius Mountain ∧	172	54.51 N	124.30 W
Chukai	104	4.15 N	103.25 E
Chukchi Sea ⫧[2]	16	69.00 N	171.00 W
Chukehu ⊜	110	31.40 N	88.00 E
Chukou	90	25.44 N	113.22 E
Chulakeaganhe ≃	110	36.35 N	92.20 E
Chulalongkorn University ʋ[2]	259a	13.44 N	100.33 E
Chula Vista	218	32.39 N	117.05 W
Chuld	92	45.03 N	105.32 E
Chullora	264a	33.54 S	151.04 E
Chulmleigh	44	50.55 N	3.52 W
Chulo	74	41.41 N	42.18 E
Chulp'o	88	35.37 N	126.40 E
Chulucanas	238	5.06 S	80.10 W
Chulumani	238	16.24 S	67.31 W
Chuluota	210	28.38 N	81.10 W
Chuma	238	15.24 S	68.56 W
Chumaerhe ≃	110	34.39 N	95.00 E
Chumalag	74	43.14 N	44.28 E
Chumbicha	242	28.52 S	66.14 W
Chummi, Ozero ⊜	79	50.18 N	137.17 E
Chum Phae	100	16.32 N	102.06 E
Chumphon	100	10.30 N	99.10 E
Chumphon Buri	100	15.21 N	103.24 E
Chumpi	238	15.06 S	73.46 W
Chum Saeng	100	15.54 N	100.19 E
Chumunjin	88	37.54 N	128.49 E
Chunal	252	53.25 N	1.57 W
Chunan, T'aiwan	90	24.41 N	120.52 E
Chun'an, Zhg.	90	29.35 N	118.58 E
Chunār	114	25.08 N	82.54 E
Chuncheon → Ch'unch'ŏn	88	37.52 N	127.43 E
Chunchi, Ec.	236	2.17 S	78.55 W
Chunchi, Zhg.	90	27.22 N	119.20 E
Ch'unch'ŏn	88	37.52 N	127.43 E
Chunchula	184	30.55 N	88.12 W
Chūnd	113	31.26 N	72.17 E
Chungang University ʋ[2]	261b	37.30 N	126.58 E
Chungari	79	50.21 N	138.12 E
Chungari ≃	79	50.04 N	136.55 E
Ch'ungch'ŏng Namdo □[4]	88	36.30 N	127.00 E
Ch'ungch'ŏng Pukdo □[4]	88	36.45 N	128.00 E
Chunggang-ni	88	40.52 N	127.20 E
Chungho	259d	25.00 N	121.29 E
Chunghwa	88	38.52 N	125.47 E
Ch'ungju	88	36.58 N	127.58 E
Chungking → Chongqing	97	29.39 N	106.34 E
Chungli	90	24.57 N	121.13 E
Chungliao	90	22.40 N	121.30 E
Ch'ungmu	88	34.51 N	128.25 E
Chungp'u	90	23.25 N	120.31 E
Chungp'yŏngjang	88	41.11 N	128.03 E
Chungsam-ni	88	38.34 N	127.09 E
Chŭngsan	88	39.06 N	125.22 E
Chŭngsanha-ri ◆[8]	261b	37.35 N	126.54 E
Chungshan → Zhongshan	90	22.31 N	113.22 E
Chungshan Bridge ◆[5]	259d	25.05 N	121.31 E
Chunguj ≃	78	48.51 N	93.32 E
Chungyang Shanmo ⩘	90	23.30 N	121.00 E
Chunheji	90	32.12 N	115.22 E
Chunhua, Zhg.	92	34.50 N	108.31 E
Chunhua, Zhg.	96	31.56 N	118.56 E
Chunhuás	222	19.12 N	88.55 W
Chūniān	113	30.58 N	73.59 E
Chuntuquí	222	17.31 N	90.09 W
Chünüj ≃	78	48.48 N	102.00 E
Chunya	144	8.32 S	33.25 E
Ch'unyang, Taehan	88	36.56 N	128.54 E
Chunyang, Zhg.	79	43.24 N	129.24 E
Chunzach	74	42.33 N	46.43 E
Chunze	114	29.51 N	88.41 E
Chūō	86	35.00 N	133.58 E
Chūō ◆[8]	258	35.40 N	139.47 E
Chuŏr Phnum Krâvanh ⩘	100	12.00 N	103.15 E
Chuosijia	92	31.55 N	102.08 E
Chupaca	238	12.04 S	75.19 W
Chupadera Arroyo ∨	190	33.47 N	106.37 W
Chupadero, Cerro ∧	190	31.01 N	111.37 W
Chupaderos	224	23.50 N	102.20 W
Chupara Point ≻	231r	10.48 N	61.22 W
Chuquibamba	238	15.50 S	72.39 W
Chuquibambilla	238	14.07 S	72.43 W
Chuquicamata	242	22.19 S	68.56 W
Chuquisaca □[5]	238	20.00 S	64.20 W
Chuquitanta	276d	11.58 S	77.06 W
Chur	54	46.51 N	9.32 E
Churachandpur	110	24.20 N	93.40 E
Churāmankāti	116	23.14 N	89.09 E
Churcampa	238	12.42 S	74.24 W
Church	252	53.45 N	2.24 W
Churchdown	44	51.53 N	2.10 W
Church Hill	198	39.08 N	75.59 W
Churchill, Man., Can.	166	58.46 N	94.10 W
Churchill, Ohio, U.S.	204	41.09 N	80.39 W
Churchill, Pa., U.S.	269b	40.27 N	79.51 W
Churchill, Va., U.S.	274c	38.54 N	77.10 W
Churchill ≃, Can.	166	58.47 N	94.12 W
Churchill ≃, Newf., Can.	166	53.30 N	60.10 W
Churchill, Cape ≻	166	58.46 N	93.12 W
Churchill, Mount ∧, B.C., Can.	172	49.58 N	123.51 W
Churchill, Mount ∧, Alaska, U.S.	170	61.25 N	141.43 W
Churchill Downs ♠	208	38.12 N	85.46 W
Churchill Falls ⌞	166	53.35 N	64.27 W
Churchill Lake ⊜	174	55.55 N	108.20 W
Churchill National Park ♠	159	37.58 S	145.17 E
Church of the Nativity ʋ[1]	122	31.43 N	35.12 E
Church Point	184	30.24 N	92.13 W
Church Rock	190	35.46 N	108.35 W
Church Street	250	51.26 N	0.28 E
Church Stretton	44	52.32 N	2.49 W
Churchton	198	38.48 N	76.32 W
Churchtown, Eng., U.K.	252	53.40 N	2.58 W
Churchtown, Pa., U.S.	198	40.08 N	75.58 W
Church View	198	37.41 N	76.41 W
Churchville, Ont., Can.	265b	43.38 N	79.45 W
Churchville, Md., U.S.	198	39.34 N	76.15 W
Churchville, N.Y., U.S.	200	43.06 N	77.53 W
Churchville, Pa., U.S.	275	40.11 N	75.01 W
Churchyn ≃	78	48.37 N	110.42 E
Churdan	188	42.09 N	94.29 W
Churen Himāl ∧	114	28.44 N	83.12 E
Churfirsten ∧	54	47.08 N	9.17 E
Churia Range ⩘	114	27.40 N	83.40 E
Churintzio	224	20.09 N	102.04 W
Chürmen	92	43.20 N	104.10 E
Churmuli	79	51.00 N	136.50 E
Churn ≃	44	51.38 N	1.53 W
Churn Creek ≃	172	51.30 N	122.17 W
Churnet ≃	44	52.55 N	1.50 W
Churni ≃[1]	116	23.28 N	88.44 E
Chursdorf	50	50.46 N	12.15 E
Churu	110	28.18 N	74.57 E
Churu □[5]	113	28.45 N	74.50 E
Churubusco, Ind., U.S.	206	41.14 N	85.19 W
Churubusco, N.Y., U.S.	196	44.57 N	73.56 W
Churuguara	236	10.49 N	69.32 W
Churumuco	224	18.37 N	101.38 W
Churwalden	54	46.47 N	9.33 E
Chušenga	78	51.27 N	110.55 E
Chushālgarh	113	33.30 N	71.54 E
Chushan	90	23.46 N	120.41 E
Chushui ≃	90	26.02 N	113.09 E
Chushul	110	33.36 N	78.39 E
Chuska Mountains ⩘	190	36.15 N	108.50 W
Chuska Peak ∧	190	35.53 N	108.50 W
Chusovoy → Čusovoj	76	58.17 N	57.49 E
Chust	68	48.10 N	23.18 E
Chūta	164m	26.32 N	127.58 E
Chutag	78	49.23 N	102.43 E
Chutag-Uul	92	43.22 N	110.20 E
Chute-à-Blondeau	196	45.35 N	74.29 W
Chute-Panet	196	46.51 N	71.51 W
Chutor-Michajlovskij	68	52.03 N	33.56 E
Chutorskoj	70	46.52 N	42.59 E
Chutu ≃	79	49.27 N	140.02 E
Chutung	90	24.44 N	121.06 E
Chuwang	88	36.02 N	114.52 E
Chuwei	259d	25.08 N	121.27 E
Chuxian	90	32.19 N	118.17 E
Chuxiong	92	25.02 N	101.30 E
Chuy	242	33.41 S	53.27 W
Chužar	78	52.49 N	99.54 E
Chuzenji-ko ⊜	84	36.44 N	139.29 E
Chuzhai	90	33.22 N	113.37 E
Chužir	78	53.11 N	107.20 E
Chūzu	84	35.06 N	136.00 E
Chvalynsk	70	52.30 N	48.07 E
Chvančkara	74	42.34 N	43.01 E
Chvastoviči	66	53.28 N	35.06 E
Chvatovka	70	52.21 N	46.34 E
Chvojnaja	66	58.54 N	34.32 E
Chvorost'anka	70	52.36 N	48.59 E
Chwefru ≃	44	52.09 N	3.25 W
Ch'wiya-ri	88	38.03 N	125.32 E
Chypre → Cyprus □[1]	120	35.00 N	33.00 E
Chyrov	68	49.33 N	22.49 E
Ciago	58	46.12 N	12.46 E
Ciales	230m	18.20 N	66.28 W
Ciamis	105a	7.20 S	108.21 E
Ciampino	60	41.48 N	12.36 E
Ciampino, Aeroporto di ⊠	257a	41.48 N	12.36 E
Ciandur	105a	6.24 S	105.59 E
Cianjur	105a	6.49 S	107.08 E
Ciano d'Enza	58	44.36 N	10.24 E
Cianorte	245	23.37 S	52.37 W
Cians, Gorges du ∨	56	43.57 N	6.59 E
Čiatura	74	42.17 N	43.17 E
Ciawi, Indon.	105a	7.10 S	108.09 E
Ciawi, Indon.	105a	6.40 S	106.50 E
Ciawigebang	105a	6.58 S	108.34 E
Ciba	97	29.07 N	105.55 E
Cibadak	105a	6.53 S	106.46 E
Cibaliung	105a	6.46 S	105.51 E
Čibargata	75	41.08 N	69.48 E
Cibatu	105a	7.06 S	107.59 E
Cibeber	105a	6.56 S	107.07 E
Cibecue	190	34.03 N	110.29 W
Cibiana	58	46.23 N	12.17 E
Cibinong	105a	6.27 S	106.51 E
Čibisovka	68	50.47 N	40.05 E
Čibižek	76	54.27 N	93.40 E
Cibolo Creek ≃	186	29.34 N	104.24 W
Cibuta	190	31.04 N	110.54 W
Cicagna	56	44.25 N	9.14 E
Cicalengka	105a	6.59 S	107.50 E
Čičarija ⩘	36	45.30 N	13.54 E
Čičatka	79	54.03 N	121.18 E
Cicciano	60	40.58 N	14.32 E
Cicero, Ill., U.S.	206	41.51 N	87.45 W
Cicero, Ind., U.S.	208	40.08 N	86.01 W
Cicero, N.Y., U.S.	200	43.10 N	76.07 W
Cicero Creek ≃	184	40.01 N	86.01 W
Cícero Dantas	240	10.36 S	38.23 W
Čichačovo, S.S.S.R.	66	57.17 N	29.54 E
Čichačovo, S.S.S.R.	79	51.50 N	141.07 E
Čichareši	74	42.48 N	43.03 E
Cichengzhen	90	30.00 N	121.22 E
Čičikleja ≃	68	47.23 N	31.34 E
Cicladas, Islas de la → Kikládhes II	38	37.30 N	25.00 E
Cicolano ◆[1]	60	42.12 N	13.12 E
Cicurug	105a	6.47 S	106.47 E
Cidacos ≃	34	42.21 N	1.38 W
Cidade, Rio da ≃	246	22.25 S	43.09 W
Cidade Universitária ʋ[2], Bra.	277a	22.52 S	43.14 W
Cidade Universitária ʋ[2], Bra.	277b	23.33 S	46.43 W
Cide	120	41.54 N	33.00 E
Cidra	230m	18.11 N	66.10 W
Cidra, Lago de ⊜[1]	230m	18.12 N	66.08 W
Ciechanów	30	52.53 N	20.38 E
Ciechanowiec	30	52.42 N	22.31 E
Ciechocinek	30	52.52 N	18.49 E
Ciego de Avila	230p	21.51 N	78.46 W
Ciempozuelos	34	40.10 N	3.37 W
Ciénaga	236	11.01 N	74.15 W
Ciénaga de Oro	236	8.53 N	75.37 W
Ciénega de Flores	186	25.57 N	100.11 W
Cienfuegos	230p	22.09 N	80.27 W
Cienfuegos, Bahía de C	230p	22.07 N	80.29 W
Cieplice Śląskie-Zdrój	30	50.52 N	15.41 E
Čierna [nad Tisou]	30	48.25 N	22.05 E
Čierny Balog	30	48.45 N	19.40 E
Cíes, Islas II	34	42.13 N	8.54 W
Cieszanów	30	50.16 N	23.08 E
Cieszyn	30	49.45 N	18.38 E
Cieza	34	38.14 N	1.25 W
Çiftalan	257b	41.15 N	28.54 E
Çiftehan	120	37.31 N	34.46 E
Çifteler	120	39.22 N	31.03 E
Çiftlik, Tür.	120	38.11 N	34.30 E
Çiftlik, Tür.	120	40.08 N	39.27 E
Cifuentes, Cuba	230p	22.39 N	80.03 W
Cifuentes, Esp.	34	40.47 N	2.37 W
Čiganak, S.S.S.R.	70	51.47 N	43.18 E
Čiganak, S.S.S.R.	76	45.06 N	73.58 E
Čiganaki	70	47.57 N	43.05 E
Čigirin	68	49.04 N	32.40 E
Cigliano	56	45.18 N	8.01 E
Čigorak	70	51.26 N	42.09 E
Cigou	90	33.51 N	113.35 E
Cigüela ≃	34	39.08 N	3.44 W
Cihangir	120	40.03 N	29.07 E
Cihara	105a	6.52 S	106.06 E
Cihe ≃	90	33.27 N	115.31 E
Cihuatlán	224	19.14 N	104.35 W
Cihuatlán ≃	224	19.10 N	104.38 W
Čiili	76	44.10 N	66.45 E
Cijara, Embalse de ⊜[1]	34	39.18 N	4.52 W
Čijen	75	43.08 N	75.55 E
Čijirčik, Pereval)(	75	40.15 N	73.20 E
Čijli ≃	75	40.17 N	72.38 E
Cijulang	105a	7.44 S	108.27 E
Čik	76	55.01 N	82.27 E
Cikajang	105a	7.22 S	107.47 E
Cikalong-kulon	105a	6.42 S	107.12 E
Cikampek	105a	6.24 S	107.27 E
Čikan	78	54.54 N	105.39 E
Čikan ≃	78	54.54 N	105.40 E
Cikarang	105a	6.15 S	107.09 E
Cikatomas	105a	7.37 S	108.15 E
Čikišl'ar	118	37.34 N	53.55 E
Čikoj	78	50.16 N	106.54 E
Čikoj ≃	78	51.02 N	106.39 E
Čikola	74	43.12 N	43.55 E
Cikou	90	29.42 N	114.46 E
Ciksı	120	38.30 N	40.55 E
Cilacap	105a	7.44 S	109.00 E
Çilader	120	41.02 N	37.06 E
Cilamaya	105a	6.15 S	107.35 E
Cilavegna	56	45.19 N	8.44 E
Çıldır	74	41.08 N	43.07 E
Çıldır Gölü ⊜	74	41.04 N	43.15 E
Ciledug	105a	6.54 S	108.44 E
Cilegon	105a	6.01 S	106.03 E
Čilekovo	70	47.50 N	43.30 E
Cilento ◆[1]	36	40.15 N	15.10 E
Čil'gazi	75	40.10 N	70.39 E
Čili	92	29.17 N	111.00 E
Čilik, S.S.S.R.	75	43.36 N	78.15 E
Čilik, S.S.S.R.	76	51.07 N	54.07 E
Čilik ≃	75	43.05 N	78.28 E
Cililin	105a	6.56 S	107.26 E
Cilimus	105a	6.52 S	108.29 E
Cilincing ◆[8]	259e	6.06 S	106.56 E
Cill Áirne → Killarney	28	52.03 N	9.30 W
Cill Choinnigh → Kilkenny	28	52.39 N	7.15 W
Cilleruelo de Bezana	34	42.58 N	3.51 W
Cil'ma ≃	24	65.27 N	52.06 E
Cimabanche (Schluderbach)	58	46.37 N	12.11 E
Cima Gogna	58	46.31 N	12.28 E
Cimahi	105a	6.53 S	107.32 E
Cimalaka	105a	6.49 S	107.56 E
Cimalmotto	54	46.17 N	8.29 E
Cimarron, Kans., U.S.	188	37.48 N	100.21 W
Cimarron, N. Mex., U.S.	190	36.31 N	104.55 W
Cimarron ≃, U.S.	186	36.10 N	96.17 W
Cimarron ≃, N. Mex., U.S.	186	36.20 N	104.31 W
Cimarron, North Fork ≃	188	37.25 N	101.13 W
Čimbaj	76	42.57 N	59.47 E
Čimčinej, Gora ∧[2]	170	63.37 N	178.04 E
Cimetière, Pointe du ≻	231o	15.58 N	61.19 W
Cimini, Monti ⩘	60	42.20 N	12.10 E
Cimino, Monte ∧	60	42.24 N	12.12 E
Čimion	75	40.16 N	71.31 E
Čimišlija	68	46.32 N	28.44 E
Cimitile	60	40.56 N	14.31 E
Čimkent	75	42.18 N	69.36 E
Čimkent □[4]	75	42.30 N	68.00 E
Čimkorgon	75	42.50 N	75.30 E
Cimla ≃	70	48.01 N	42.24 E
Ciml'ansk	70	47.38 N	42.04 E
Ciml'anskoje Vodochranilišče ⊜[1]	70	48.00 N	43.00 E
Cimolais	58	46.17 N	12.26 E
Cimone, Monte ∧	58	44.12 N	10.42 E
Cîmpeni	38	46.22 N	23.03 E
Cîmpia Turzii	38	46.33 N	23.54 E
Cîmpina	38	45.08 N	25.44 E
Cimpu	102	3.25 S	120.22 E
Cîmpulung	38	45.16 N	25.03 E
Cîmpulung Moldovenesc	38	47.31 N	25.34 E
Čimtarga, Gora ∧	75	39.12 N	68.10 E
Čina ≃	78	54.20 N	112.24 E
Cina, Tanjung ≻	102	5.56 S	104.45 E
Činabad	75	40.52 N	71.58 E
Činadijevo	68	48.30 N	22.50 E
Cinandali	74	41.53 N	45.34 E
Çınar	120	37.44 N	40.25 E
Çınarcık	120	40.39 N	29.06 E
Cinaruco ≃	236	6.41 N	67.07 W
Činaz	75	40.56 N	68.45 E
Cinca ≃	34	41.26 N	0.21 E
Cincar ∧	36	43.54 N	17.04 E
Cincinnati, Iowa, U.S.	180	40.38 N	92.56 W
Cincinnati, Ohio, U.S.	208	39.06 N	84.31 W
Cincinnatus	200	42.33 N	75.54 W
Cinco Balas, Cayos II	230p	21.06 N	79.20 W
Cinco de Mayo	186	25.46 N	104.19 W
Cinco de Outubro	142	9.34 S	17.50 E
Cinco Palos, Sierra ⩘	224	22.40 N	99.36 W
Cinco Pinos	226	13.14 N	86.52 W
Cinco Saltos	242	38.49 S	68.04 W
Cinderella	263d	26.15 S	28.16 E
Cinderella Dam ◆[6]	263d	26.15 S	28.14 E
Cinderford	44	51.50 N	2.29 W
Cinder Island I	266	40.36 N	73.36 W
Çine	120	37.36 N	28.04 E
Cinebar	214	46.36 N	122.32 W
Cinema	172	53.11 N	122.30 W
Ciney	52	50.18 N	5.06 E
Cingaly	76	60.13 N	69.45 E
Çingife	120	37.20 N	37.33 E
Čingikan, Gora ∧	78	52.32 N	114.27 E
Čingis	76	54.08 N	81.41 E
Čingistaj	76	49.13 N	85.55 E
Cingoli	60	43.22 N	13.13 E
Cinigiano	60	42.53 N	11.24 E
Cinisello Balsamo	256b	45.33 N	9.13 E
Činiševcy	68	47.42 N	28.52 E
Činja-Voryk	24	63.13 N	52.38 E
Cinkota ◆[8]	254c	47.31 N	19.14 E
Cínovec	50	50.43 N	13.45 E
Cinq, Lac des ⊜	196	46.51 N	72.59 W
Cinq-Doigts, Lac ⊜	196	46.36 N	74.32 W
Cinquemiglia, Piano delle ⊻	60	41.50 N	14.00 E
Cinqueterre □[9]	56	44.10 N	9.45 E
Cintalapa ≃	224	16.41 N	93.36 W
Cintalapa de Figueroa	224	16.44 N	93.43 W
Cinto, Monte ∧	36	42.23 N	8.56 E
Cinto Euganeo	58	45.16 N	11.40 E
Cintra → Sintra	34	38.48 N	9.23 W
Cintra, Golfo de C	138	23.00 N	16.20 W
Cinzas, Rio das ≃	242	22.56 S	50.32 W
Ciocănești	38	44.12 N	27.04 E
Ciociaria ◆[1]	60	41.45 N	13.15 E
Çiomas	105a	6.12 S	106.01 E
Čiovo, Otok I	36	43.30 N	16.20 E
Cipa ≃	78	55.23 N	115.55 E
Ciparay	105a	7.03 S	107.43 E
Cipatujah	105a	7.45 S	108.00 E
Cipikan	78	54.55 N	113.21 E
Cipikan ≃	78	55.14 N	113.05 E
Cipó	240	11.06 S	38.31 W
Cipó ≃	245	18.40 S	43.59 W
Cipolândia	245	20.08 S	55.24 W
Cipolletti	242	38.56 S	67.59 W
Çiqikou	97	29.35 N	106.26 E
Čir	70	48.29 N	43.10 E
Čir ≃	70	48.35 N	42.51 E
Čirachčaj ≃	74	41.40 N	48.11 E
Čiragidzor	74	40.27 N	46.19 E
Ciranjang	105a	6.49 S	107.14 E
Circeo, Monte ∧	60	41.14 N	13.03 E
Circeo, Parco Nazionale del ♠	60	41.17 N	13.05 E
Čirčik	75	41.29 N	69.35 E
Čirčik ≃	75	40.54 N	68.41 E
Çırçır	120	40.04 N	36.48 E
Circle, Alaska, U.S.	170	65.50 N	144.04 W
Circle, Mont., U.S.	192	47.25 N	105.35 W
Circle Hot Springs	170	65.28 N	144.39 W
Circleville, N.Y., U.S.	200	41.31 N	75.23 W
Circleville, Ohio, U.S.	208	39.36 N	82.57 W
Circleville, Pa., U.S.	269b	40.20 N	79.44 W
Circleville, Utah, U.S.	190	38.10 N	112.16 W
Circular Reef ✣[2]	154	3.25 S	147.47 E
Circus World ♠	210	28.14 N	81.38 W
Cirebon	105a	6.44 S	108.34 E
Cireglio	60	43.59 N	10.51 E
Ciremay, Gunung ∧	105a	6.54 S	108.24 E
Cirencester	44	51.44 N	1.59 W
Cirey-sur-Vezouze	54	48.35 N	6.57 E
Čirgalandy	78	50.36 N	97.20 E
Ciriè	56	45.14 N	7.36 E
Čirikovo	72	55.23 N	37.14 E
Čirikrabat ⊥	76	44.07 N	62.35 E
Ciriquiri ≃	238	8.05 S	65.18 W
Cirk, Gora ∧	170	64.33 N	175.25 E
Cîrlibaba	38	47.35 N	25.07 E
Cirò Marina	36	39.22 N	17.08 E
Čirpan	38	42.12 N	25.20 E
Cirque, Cerro ∧	238	17.22 S	69.22 W
Ciruas	105a	6.06 S	106.13 E
Cisa, Passo della)(	58	44.28 N	9.55 E
Cisano	58	45.32 N	10.43 E
Cisarua	105a	6.40 S	106.59 E
Cisco, Ill., U.S.	209	40.01 N	88.43 W
Cisco, Tex., U.S.	186	32.23 N	98.59 W
Cishan	88	36.37 N	114.07 E
Cislago	56	45.39 N	8.58 E
Cisliano	256b	45.27 N	8.59 E
Çismar	50	54.11 N	10.59 E
Čismena	72	56.02 N	36.13 E
Cismon ≃	58	46.55 N	11.43 E
Cismon del Grappa	58	45.55 N	11.44 E
Čišmy	76	54.35 N	55.20 E
Cisnădie	38	45.43 N	24.09 E
Cisne	184	38.31 N	88.26 W
Cisneros	236	6.33 N	75.04 W
Cisnes ≃	244	44.45 S	72.42 W
Cisolok	105a	6.57 S	106.26 E
Cison di Valmarino	58	45.58 N	12.10 E
Cispus ≃	214	46.25 N	122.10 W
Cisse ≃	46	47.25 N	0.47 E
Cissna Park	206	40.34 N	87.54 W
Čistá	50	50.03 N	12.42 E
Cisterna di Latina	60	41.35 N	12.49 E
Cistierna	34	42.48 N	5.07 W
Čistoje	70	56.32 N	43.02 E
Čistooz'ornoje	76	54.43 N	76.33 E
Čistopol'	70	55.21 N	50.37 E
Čistopolje, S.S.S.R.	73	47.31 N	39.27 E
Čistopolje, S.S.S.R.	76	52.34 N	67.15 E
Čistovodovka	73	49.24 N	37.20 E
Čita	78	52.03 N	113.30 E
Čita □[4]	78	52.00 N	117.00 E
Citac, Nevado ∧	238	12.50 S	75.15 W
Citaré ≃	240	1.11 N	54.41 W
Citeli-Ckaro	74	41.28 N	46.07 E
Cité Universitaire ʋ[2]	251	48.49 N	2.20 E
Citlaltépetl, Volcán (Pico de Orizaba) ∧[1]	224	19.01 N	97.16 W
Citra	182	29.25 N	82.06 W
Citronelle	184	31.06 N	88.14 W
Citrus □[6]	210	28.52 N	82.28 W
Citrusdal	148	32.36 S	19.00 E
Citrus Heights	216	38.42 N	121.17 W
Citrus Springs	210	29.00 N	82.27 W
Citrus Tower ʋ	210	28.33 N	81.44 W
Cittadella	58	45.39 N	11.47 E
Città della Pieve	60	42.57 N	12.00 E
Città del Vaticano → Vatican City □[1]	257a	41.54 N	12.27 E
Città di Castello	60	43.27 N	12.14 E
Cittaducale	60	42.23 N	12.57 E
Cittanova	36	38.21 N	16.05 E
Cittareale	60	42.37 N	13.10 E
Città Sant'Angelo	60	42.31 N	14.03 E
Città Universitaria ʋ[2]	257a	41.55 N	12.31 E
City Beach	158a	31.56 S	115.45 E
City Bell ◆[8]	248	34.52 S	58.05 W
City College of New York ʋ[2]	266	40.49 N	73.57 W
City Island ◆[8]	266	40.51 N	73.47 W
City Mills	273	42.07 N	71.21 W
City of Commerce	270	33.59 N	118.08 W
City of Hope ʋ	270	34.08 N	117.58 W
City Of industry	270	34.01 N	117.57 W
City of London ◆[8]	250	51.31 N	0.05 W
City of Refuge National Historical Park ♠	219d	19.25 N	155.54 W
City of Westminster ◆[8]	250	51.30 N	0.09 W
City Point	210	28.24 N	80.45 W
Ciucaș ∧	38	45.31 N	25.55 E
Ciudad	224	23.44 N	105.42 W
Ciudad Acuña	222	29.18 N	100.55 W
Ciudad Allende	222	28.20 N	100.51 W
Ciudad Altamirano	224	18.20 N	100.40 W
Ciudad Anáhuac	222	27.14 N	100.09 W
Ciudad Barrios	226	13.46 N	88.16 W
Ciudad Bolívar	236	8.08 N	63.33 W
Ciudad Bolivia	236	8.21 N	70.34 W
Ciudad Camargo, Méx.	222	27.40 N	105.10 W
Ciudad Camargo, Méx.	222	26.19 N	98.50 W
Ciudad Chetumal	222	18.30 N	88.18 W
Ciudad Darío	226	12.43 N	86.08 W
Ciudad de Guayana → Ciudad Guayana	236	8.22 N	62.40 W
Ciudad del Cabo → Cape Town	148	33.55 S	18.22 E
Ciudad del Carmen	222	18.38 N	91.50 W
Ciudad del Maíz	224	22.24 N	99.36 W
Ciudad de los Deportes ♠	276a	19.23 N	99.11 W
Ciudad del Vaticano → Vatican City □[1]	257a	41.54 N	12.27 E
Ciudad de México (Mexico City)	224 / 276a	19.24 N	99.09 W
Ciudad de Naucalpan de Juárez	276a	19.28 N	99.14 W
Ciudad Deportiva ♠, Cuba	276b	23.07 N	82.22 W
Ciudad Deportiva ♠, Méx.	276a	19.24 N	99.06 W
Ciudad de Valles	224	21.59 N	99.01 W
Ciudad de Villaldama	222	26.30 N	100.26 W
Ciudadela	34	40.02 N	3.50 E
Ciudadela, Parque de la ♠	256d	41.23 N	2.11 E
Ciudad General Belgrano	278	34.43 S	58.32 W
Ciudad Guayana	236	8.22 N	62.40 W
Ciudad Guerrero	222	28.33 N	107.30 W
Ciudad Guzmán	224	19.41 N	103.29 W
Ciudad Hidalgo, Méx.	224	19.41 N	100.34 W
Ciudad Hidalgo, Méx.	226	14.41 N	92.09 W
Ciudad Ixtepec	224	16.34 N	95.06 W
Ciudad Jardín	276a	19.19 N	99.09 W
Ciudad Jiménez	222	27.08 N	104.55 W
Ciudad Juárez	222	31.44 N	106.29 W
Ciudad Lerdo	186	25.32 N	103.32 W
Ciudad Lineal ◆[8]	256a	40.27 N	3.40 W
Ciudad Madero	224	22.16 N	97.50 W
Ciudad Mante	224	22.44 N	98.57 W
Ciudad Manuel Doblado	224	20.44 N	101.56 W
Ciudad Melchor Múzquiz	222	27.53 N	101.31 W
Ciudad Mendoza	224	18.48 N	97.11 W
Ciudad Mier	222	26.26 N	99.09 W
Ciudad Miguel Alemán	222	26.23 N	99.01 W
Ciudad Obregón	222	27.29 N	109.56 W
Ciudad Ocampo	224	22.50 N	99.20 W
Ciudad Ojeda (Lagunillas)	236	10.12 N	71.19 W
Ciudad Piar	236	7.27 N	63.19 W
Ciudad Real	34	38.59 N	3.56 W
Ciudad Rodrigo	34	40.36 N	6.32 W
Ciudad Sahagún	224	19.47 N	98.33 W
Ciudad Santos	224	21.36 N	98.58 W
Ciudad Serdán	224	18.59 N	97.27 W
Ciudad Tecún Umán	226	14.40 N	92.09 W
Ciudad Trujillo → Santo Domingo	228	18.28 N	69.54 W
Ciudad Universitaria ◆[8]	256a	40.27 N	3.44 W
Ciudad Universitaria ʋ[2], Esp.	256a	40.27 N	3.43 W
Ciudad Universitaria ʋ[2], Méx.	276a	19.20 N	99.11 W
Ciudad Universitaria ʋ[2], Ven.	276c	10.29 N	66.53 W
Ciudad Victoria, Méx.	194	32.20 N	115.06 W
Ciudad Victoria, Méx.	224	23.44 N	99.08 W
Ciudad Vieja	226	14.31 N	90.46 W
Ciuma	142	13.14 S	15.40 E
Ciurana ≃	34	41.08 N	0.39 E
Civa Burnu ≻	120	41.22 N	36.35 E
Civate	56	45.50 N	9.21 E
Civenna	54	45.56 N	9.16 E
Civetta, Monte ∧	58	46.23 N	12.03 E
Civezzano	58	46.05 N	11.11 E
Cividale del Friuli	58	46.06 N	13.25 E
Cividate al Piano	56	45.33 N	9.50 E
Cividate Camuno	58	45.57 N	10.17 E
Civil' ≃	70	56.08 N	47.35 E
Civil'sk	70	55.53 N	47.29 E
Civitacampomarano	60	41.47 N	14.41 E
Civita Castellana	60	42.17 N	12.25 E
Civita di Bagno	60	42.18 N	13.26 E
Civitanova Alta	60	43.19 N	13.40 E
Civitanova del Sannio	60	41.40 N	14.24 E
Civitanova Marche	60	43.18 N	13.44 E
Civitaquana	60	42.19 N	13.54 E
Civitavecchia	60	42.06 N	11.48 E
Civitella del Tronto	60	42.46 N	13.40 E
Civitella di Romagna	60	44.00 N	11.56 E
Civitella in Val di Chiana	60	43.25 N	11.43 E
Civitella Marittima	60	43.00 N	11.17 E
Civitella Roveto	60	41.54 N	13.25 E
Civray	32	46.09 N	0.18 E
Çivril	120	38.18 N	29.45 E
Čivyrkujskij Zaliv C	78	53.45 N	109.10 E
Ciwidey	105a	7.06 S	107.27 E
Cixi	90	30.11 N	121.15 E
Çiyutuo	94	41.31 N	122.53 E
Čiža	24	67.06 N	44.19 E
Čiža Vtoraja	70	50.52 N	49.40 E
Cize	54	46.12 N	5.26 E
Çizhuping	97	29.11 N	103.36 E
Čižinskije Razlivy ≋	70	50.25 N	49.40 E
Çizre	120	37.20 N	42.12 E
Čkalov → Orenburg	76	51.54 N	55.06 E
Čkalovo, S.S.S.R.	68	46.28 N	34.11 E
Čkalovo, S.S.S.R.	76	53.38 N	70.24 E
Čkalovsk	70	56.46 N	43.16 E
Čkalovskij	255b	55.54 N	38.04 E
C K Creek ≃	192	47.36 N	108.29 W
Čl'a, Ozero ⊜	79	53.27 N	140.03 E
Clachan	42	55.45 N	5.34 W
Clackamas	214	45.25 N	122.34 W
Clackamas □[6]	214	45.10 N	122.16 W
Clackamas ≃	214	45.22 N	122.36 W
Clackamas, Oak Grove Fork ≃	214	45.05 N	122.03 W
Clackamas Heights	214	45.23 N	122.34 W
Clackline	158a	31.43 S	116.31 E
Clackmannan	42	56.06 N	3.46 W
Clacton-on-Sea	44	51.48 N	1.09 E
Claerwen ≃	44	52.44 N	3.37 W
Claerwen Reservoir ⊜[1]	44	52.17 N	3.43 W
Claflin	188	38.31 N	98.32 W
Claiborne	184	31.32 N	87.31 W
Clain ≃	32	46.47 N	0.32 E
Claire, Lake ⊜	166	58.30 N	112.00 W
Claire, Pointe ≻	265a	45.25 N	73.50 W
Clair Engle Lake ⊜[1]	194	40.52 N	122.43 W
Claireville	265b	43.45 N	79.38 W
Claireville Reservoir ⊜[1]	265b	43.44 N	79.39 W
Clairfontaine-en-Yvelines	46	48.37 N	1.55 E
Clairis ≃	46	48.07 N	2.45 E
Clairmarais	46	50.46 N	2.18 E
Clairmont	172	55.16 N	118.47 W
Clairton	204	40.18 N	79.53 W
Clairvaux-les-Lacs	54	46.34 N	5.45 E
Claix	56	45.07 N	5.40 E
Clallam □[6]	214	48.10 N	123.49 W
Clallam Bay	214	48.15 N	124.16 W
Clam ≃, Mich., U.S.	180	44.05 N	85.00 W
Clam ≃, Wis., U.S.	180	45.57 N	92.33 W
Clam, North Fork ≃	180	45.46 N	92.18 W
Clamart	251	48.48 N	2.16 E
Clamecy	46	47.27 N	3.31 E
Clam Gulch	170	60.15 N	151.22 W
Clam Lake ⊜	174	55.19 N	105.43 W
Clampton	152	29.56 S	119.06 E
Clan Alpine Mountains ⩘	194	39.40 N	117.55 W
Clandonald	172	53.34 N	110.44 W
Clandon Park ♠	250	51.15 N	0.30 W
Clandulla	160	32.55 S	149.57 E
Clane	42	53.18 N	6.41 W
Clans	56	44.00 N	7.09 E
Clanton	184	32.50 N	86.38 W
Clanwilliam	148	32.11 S	18.54 E
Claonaig	28	55.46 N	5.22 W
Clapperton Island I	180	46.02 N	82.13 W
Clapp Farm	204	41.24 N	79.32 W
Clara, Eire	28	53.20 N	7.36 W
Clara, Miss., U.S.	184	31.35 N	88.42 W
Clara ≃	156	18.30 S	141.18 E
Clara City	188	44.57 N	95.22 W
Clara Island I	100	10.54 N	97.55 E
Claraville	156	18.40 S	141.43 E
Claraz	242	37.54 S	59.17 W
Clare, Austl.	156	33.25 S	143.55 E
Clare, Austl.	158b	33.50 S	138.36 E
Clare, Eng., U.K.	44	52.25 N	0.35 E
Clare, Mich., U.S.	180	43.49 N	84.46 W
Clare □[6]	28	52.50 N	9.00 W
Clare ≃, Ont., Can.	202	44.28 N	77.17 W
Clare ≃, Eire	28	53.20 N	9.03 W
Clare Island I	28	53.48 N	10.00 W
Claremont, Ont., Can.	202	43.58 N	79.07 W
Claremont, Eng., U.K.	250	51.21 N	0.22 W
Claremont, Calif., U.S.	218	34.06 N	117.43 W
Claremont, N.H., U.S.	178	43.23 N	72.20 W
Claremont, S. Dak., U.S.	188	45.40 N	98.01 W
Claremont, Va., U.S.	198	37.14 N	76.58 W
Claremont ∧	194	39.53 N	120.57 W
Claremont Colleges ʋ[2]	270	34.06 N	117.44 W
Claremore	186	36.19 N	95.36 W
Claremorris	28	53.44 N	9.00 W
Clarence, N.Z.	162	42.10 S	173.56 E
Clarence, Ill., U.S.	206	40.28 N	87.58 W
Clarence, Iowa, U.S.	180	41.53 N	91.04 W
Clarence, Mo., U.S.	209	39.44 N	92.16 W
Clarence, N.Y., U.S.	200	42.59 N	78.35 W
Clarence, Pa., U.S.	204	41.03 N	77.56 W
Clarence ≃, Austl.	156	29.25 S	153.22 E
Clarence ≃, N.Z.	162	42.10 S	173.57 E
Clarence, Isla I	244	54.10 S	71.50 W
Clarence, Port C	170	65.15 N	166.40 W
Clarence Cannon Lake ⊜[1]	209	39.30 N	91.45 W
Clarence Center	200	43.00 N	78.35 W
Clarence Creek	196	45.30 N	75.13 W
Clarence E. Hancock Airport ⊠	202	43.07 N	76.07 W
Clarence Fahnestook Memorial State Park ♠	200	41.26 N	73.50 W
Clarence Island I	9	61.09 S	54.06 W
Clarence J. Brown Reservoir ⊜[1]	208	39.58 N	83.44 W
Clarence Strait ⋓, Austl.	154	12.00 S	131.00 E
Clarence Strait ⋓, Alaska, U.S.	170	55.25 N	132.00 W
Clarence Town, Austl.	160	32.35 S	151.47 E
Clarence Town, Ba.	228	23.06 N	74.59 W
Clarenceville, Qué., Can.	196	45.04 N	73.15 W
Clarenceville, Mich., U.S.	271	42.27 N	83.19 W
Clarendon, Austl.	158b	35.07 S	138.38 E
Clarendon, Ark., U.S.	184	34.42 N	91.18 W
Clarendon, N.Y., U.S.	200	43.11 N	78.04 W
Clarendon, Pa., U.S.	204	41.47 N	79.06 W
Clarendon, Tex., U.S.	186	34.56 N	100.53 W
Clarendon Hills	268	41.48 N	87.59 W
Clarens	148	28.30 S	28.29 E
Clarenville	176	48.10 N	53.58 W
Claresholm	172	50.02 N	113.35 W
Claret	56	43.52 N	3.54 E
Clarholz	48	51.54 N	8.11 E
Claridge	204	40.22 N	79.37 W
Clarie Coast ⌶[2]	9	66.30 S	133.00 E
Clarin	106	9.58 N	124.01 E
Clarinda	188	40.44 N	95.02 W
Clarines	236	9.56 N	65.10 W
Clarington	204	41.20 N	79.07 W
Clarion, Iowa, U.S.	180	42.44 N	93.44 W
Clarion, Pa., U.S.	204	41.13 N	79.24 W
Clarion □[6]	204	41.13 N	79.24 W
Clarion ≃	204	41.07 N	79.41 W
Clarión, Isla I	222	18.22 N	114.44 W
Clarion, West Branch ≃	204	41.29 N	78.41 W
Clarion Fracture Zone ✣	16	19.00 N	122.00 W
Clarissa	188	46.08 N	94.57 W
Clark, N.J., U.S.	266	40.38 N	74.19 W
Clark, Ohio, U.S.	204	40.27 N	81.54 W
Clark, S. Dak., U.S.	188	44.53 N	97.44 W
Clark, Tex., U.S.	212	30.23 N	94.46 W
Clark □[6], Ind., U.S.	208	38.17 N	85.44 W
Clark □[6], Ohio, U.S.	208	39.56 N	83.49 W
Clark □[6], Wash., U.S.	214	45.48 N	122.31 W
Clark, Lake ⊜	170	60.15 N	154.15 W
Clark, Mount ∧	170	64.25 N	124.12 W
Clark, Point ≻	180	44.04 N	81.45 W
Clark Air Base ■	106	15.11 N	120.32 E
Clark Branch ≃	275	39.43 N	74.45 W
Clark Creek ≃, Kans., U.S.	188	39.05 N	96.42 W
Clark Creek ≃, Pa., U.S.	198	40.22 N	76.58 W
Clarkdale	190	34.46 N	112.03 W
Clarke ≃	156	19.12 S	145.30 E
Clarke City	176	50.12 N	66.38 W
Clarke Island I	156	40.33 S	148.10 E
Clarke Lake ⊜	174	54.25 N	106.51 W
Clarke Range ⩘	156	20.50 S	148.33 E
Clarke River	156	19.13 S	145.27 E
Clarkfield	188	44.48 N	95.48 W
Clark Fork	192	48.08 N	116.11 W
Clark Fork ≃	192	48.09 N	116.15 W
Clark Hill	208	38.18 N	83.12 W
Clark Hill Lake ⊜[1]	182	33.50 N	82.20 W
Clarklake	206	42.04 N	84.21 W
Clark Lake ⊜	206	42.07 N	84.19 W
Clark Mills	200	43.06 N	75.22 W
Clark Mountain ∧, Calif., U.S.	194	35.32 N	115.35 W
Clark Mountain ∧, Wash., U.S.	214	48.03 N	120.57 W
Clarks, La., U.S.	184	32.02 N	92.08 W
Clarks, Nebr., U.S.	188	41.13 N	97.50 W
Clarks ≃	184	37.03 N	88.33 W
Clarks, West Fork ≃	184	36.59 N	88.31 W
Clarksboro	275	39.48 N	75.14 W
Clarksburg, Ont., Can.	202	44.43 N	80.27 W
Clarksburg, Calif., U.S.	216	38.25 N	121.32 W
Clarksburg, Ill., U.S.	209	39.20 N	88.44 W
Clarksburg, Ind., U.S.	208	39.26 N	85.21 W
Clarksburg, Md., U.S.	198	39.14 N	77.17 W
Clarksburg, N.J., U.S.	198	40.12 N	74.27 W
Clarksburg, Ohio, U.S.	208	39.30 N	83.09 W
Clarksburg, W. Va., U.S.	178	39.17 N	80.21 W
Clarksburg State Park ♠	197	42.43 N	73.06 W
Clarks Creek ≃, Ky., U.S.	208	38.40 N	84.44 W
Clarks Creek ≃, Tex., U.S.	212	29.11 N	96.53 W
Clarksdale	184	34.12 N	90.34 W
Clarks Green	200	41.30 N	75.42 W
Clark's Harbour	176	43.26 N	65.38 W
Clarks Hill	206	40.15 N	86.43 W
Clarks Island I	273	42.01 N	70.38 W
Clarks Mills	204	41.24 N	80.11 W
Clarkson, Ont., Can.	265b	43.31 N	79.37 W
Clarkson, Ky., U.S.	184	37.30 N	86.13 W
Clarkson, N.Y., U.S.	200	43.14 N	77.56 W
Clarks Point	170	58.51 N	158.30 W
Clarks Summit	200	41.30 N	75.42 W
Clarkston	206	42.44 N	83.25 W
Clark's Town	231q	18.25 N	77.34 W

≃ River	Fluss	Río	Rivière	Rio
☲ Canal	Kanal	Canal	Canal	Canal
⌞ Waterfall, Rapids	Wasserfall, Stromschnellen	Cascada, Rápidos	Chute d'eau, Rapides	Cascata, Rápidos
⋓ Strait	Meeresstrasse	Estrecho	Détroit	Estreito
C Bay, Gulf	Bucht, Golf	Bahía, Golfo	Baie, Golfe	Baía, Golfo
⊜ Lake, Lakes	See, Seen	Lago, Lagos	Lac, Lacs	Lago, Lagos
≋ Swamp	Sumpf	Pantano	Marais	Pântano
⍓ Ice Features, Glacier	Eis- und Gletscherformen	Accidentes Glaciales	Formes glaciaires	Acidentes Glaciares
⫧ Other Hydrographic Features	Andere Hydrographische Objekte	Otros Elementos Hidrográficos	Autres données hydrographiques	Outros Elementos Hidrográficos

✣ Submarine Features	Untermeerische Objekte	Accidentes Submarinos	Formes de relief sous-marin	Acidentes Submarinos
□ Political Unit	Politische Einheit	Unidad Politica	Entité politique	Unidade Política
ʋ Cultural Institution	Kulturelle Institution	Institución Cultural	Institution culturelle	Instituição Cultural
⊥ Historical Site	Historische Stätte	Sitio Histórico	Site historique	Sitio Histórico
♠ Recreational Site	Erholungs- und Ferienort	Sitio de Recreo	Centre de loisirs	Sítio de Lazer
⊠ Airport	Flughafen	Aeropuerto	Aéroport	Aeroporto
■ Military Installation	Militäranlage	Instalación Militar	Installation militaire	Instalação Militar
◆ Miscellaneous	Verschiedenes	Misceláneo	Divers	Miscelânea

ENGLISH — Name | Page | Lat.°′ | Long.°′
DEUTSCH — Name | Seite | Breite°′ | Länge°′ E=Ost

Clarksville, Ark., U.S. 184 35.28 N 93.28 W
Clarksville, Del., U.S. 198 38.33 N 75.09 W
Clarksville, Ind., U.S. 208 38.17 N 85.45 W
Clarksville, Iowa, U.S. 180 42.47 N 92.40 W
Clarksville, Md., U.S. 198 39.13 N 76.57 W
Clarksville, Mich., U.S. 206 42.50 N 85.15 W
Clarksville, Mo., U.S. 209 39.22 N 90.54 W
Clarksville, N.Y., U.S. 200 42.35 N 73.58 W
Clarksville, Ohio, U.S. 208 39.24 N 83.59 W
Clarksville, Tenn., U.S. 184 36.32 N 87.21 W
Clarksville, Tex., U.S. 186 33.37 N 95.03 W
Clarksville, Va., U.S. 182 36.37 N 78.34 W
Clarksville City 212 32.32 N 94.34 W
Clarkton, Mo., U.S. 184 36.27 N 89.58 W
Clarkton, N.C., U.S. 182 34.29 N 78.39 W
Claro ≃, Bra. 245 15.28 S 51.43 W
Claro ≃, Bra. 245 19.08 S 50.40 W
Claro ≃, Bra. 245 19.06 S 47.52 W
Claro ≃, Ven. 236 8.50 N 68.36 W
Claro, Arroyo ≃ 278 34.25 S 58.41 W
Claro, Ribeirão ≃, Bra. 245 17.37 S 46.47 W
Claro, Ribeirão ≃, Bra. 277b 23.40 S 46.17 W
Clary 46 50.05 N 3.24 E
Claryville 200 41.55 N 74.34 W
Clatskanie 214 46.06 N 123.12 W
Clatskanie ≃ 214 46.08 N 123.14 W
Clatsop ☐[6] 214 46.01 N 123.41 W
Claude 186 35.07 N 101.22 W
Claudy 42 54.54 N 7.09 W
Claughton 42 54.06 N 2.40 W
Claussnitz 50 50.56 N 12.53 E
Clausthal-Zellerfeld 48 51.48 N 10.20 E
Claver 106 9.35 N 125.44 E
Claverack 200 42.13 N 73.44 W
Claveria, Pil. 106 8.38 N 124.55 E
Claveria, Pil. 106 18.37 N 121.05 E
Clavet 174 52.00 N 106.23 W
Clavey ≃ 216 37.52 N 120.07 W
Clavos, Laguna de ⊛ 186 27.37 N 104.52 W
Clawit, Mount ∧ 106 16.58 N 120.58 E
Clawson 212 31.24 N 94.47 W
Claxton 182 32.10 N 81.55 W
Clay, Ky., U.S. 184 37.29 N 87.49 W
Clay, Tex., U.S. 212 30.23 N 96.21 W
Clay, W. Va., U.S. 178 38.28 N 81.05 W
Clay ☐[6] 209 38.45 N 88.40 W
Claybank Creek ≃ 184 31.10 N 85.44 W
Clay Center, Kans., U.S. 188 39.23 N 97.08 W
Clay Center, Nebr., U.S. 188 40.32 N 98.03 W
Clay Center, Ohio, U.S. 204 41.34 N 83.22 W
Clay City, Ill., U.S. 184 38.41 N 88.21 W
Clay City, Ind., U.S. 184 39.17 N 87.07 W
Clay City, Ky., U.S. 182 37.52 N 83.55 W
Clay Creek ≃ 188 38.06 N 102.31 W
Clay Cross 44 53.10 N 1.24 W
Claydon 44 52.06 N 1.07 E
Claye-Souilly 46 48.57 N 2.42 E
Claygate 250 51.22 N 0.20 W
Claygate Cross 250 51.16 N 0.19 E
Clayhole Wash ∨ 190 36.59 N 113.17 W
Clayhurst 172 56.15 N 120.01 W
Claymont 198 39.48 N 75.28 W
Clayoquot Sound U 172 49.11 N 126.08 W
Claypole 278 34.48 S 58.20 W
Claypool, Ariz., U.S. 190 33.25 N 110.51 W
Claypool, Ind., U.S. 206 41.08 N 85.53 W
Claysburg 204 40.18 N 78.27 W
Clay Springs 190 34.22 N 110.18 W
Claysville 204 40.07 N 80.25 W
Clayton, Austl. 264b 37.56 S 145.07 E
Clayton, Eng., U.K. 42 53.47 N 1.52 W
Clayton, Ala., U.S. 184 31.53 N 85.27 W
Clayton, Calif., U.S. 272 37.57 N 121.56 W
Clayton, Del., U.S. 198 39.17 N 75.38 W
Clayton, Ga., U.S. 182 34.53 N 83.23 W
Clayton, Ill., U.S. 209 40.02 N 90.57 W
Clayton, Ind., U.S. 208 39.41 N 86.31 W
Clayton, Mich., U.S. 206 41.52 N 84.14 W
Clayton, Mo., U.S. 209 38.39 N 90.20 W
Clayton, N.J., U.S. 198 39.39 N 75.06 W
Clayton, N. Mex., U.S. 186 36.27 N 103.11 W
Clayton, N.C., U.S. 182 35.39 N 78.28 W
Clayton, N.Y., U.S. 202 44.14 N 76.05 W
Clayton, Okla., U.S. 186 34.35 N 95.21 W
Clayton, Tex., U.S. 212 32.06 N 94.28 W
Clayton ≃ 156 29.06 S 138.05 E
Claytonia 204 41.00 N 79.58 W
Clayton-le-Moors 42 53.47 N 2.23 W
Clayton-le-Woods 252 53.41 N 2.38 W
Clayton Valley ∨ 272 37.58 N 121.58 W
Claytonville 206 40.34 N 87.49 W
Clay Village 208 38.11 N 85.07 W
Clayville 200 42.59 N 75.15 W
Clear ≃ 172 56.11 N 119.42 W
Clear, Cape › 170 59.48 N 147.54 W
Clear, Lake ⊛ 202 45.26 N 77.12 W
Clear, Mount ∧ 161b 35.52 S 149.04 E
Clear Boggy Creek ≃ 186 34.03 N 95.47 W
Clearbrook, B.C., Can. 214 49.08 N 122.26 W
Clearbrook, Minn., U.S. 188 47.42 N 95.26 W
Clear Creek 208 39.07 N 86.32 W
Clear Creek ≃, Ala., U.S. 184 34.00 N 87.19 W
Clear Creek ≃, Ariz., U.S. 190 34.59 N 110.38 W
Clear Creek ≃, Calif., U.S. 194 40.31 N 122.22 W
Clear Creek ≃, Calif., U.S. 270 34.17 N 118.12 W
Clear Creek ≃, Calif., U.S. 272 37.20 N 122.21 W
Clear Creek ≃, Colo., U.S. 190 39.50 N 104.57 W
Clear Creek ≃, Ky., U.S. 208 38.10 N 85.17 W
Clear Creek ≃, Mo., U.S. 184 38.00 N 93.56 W
Clear Creek ≃, Mont., U.S. 192 48.46 N 109.25 W
Clear Creek ≃, Nebr., U.S. 188 41.08 N 99.06 W
Clear Creek ≃, Ohio, U.S. 208 39.33 N 84.20 W
Clear Creek ≃, Oreg., U.S. 214 45.09 N 121.31 W
Clear Creek ≃, Oreg., U.S. 214 45.23 N 122.29 W
Clear Creek ≃, Tenn., U.S. 182 36.05 N 84.42 W
Clear Creek ≃, Tex., U.S. 186 33.16 N 97.03 W
Clear Creek ≃, Tex., U.S. 212 29.09 N 97.23 W
Clear Creek ≃, Tex., U.S. 212 29.33 N 95.05 W
Clear Creek ≃, Wash., U.S. 214 46.07 N 122.00 W
Clear Creek ≃, Wyo., U.S. 192 44.53 N 106.04 W
Clear Creek State Park ♠ 204 41.20 N 79.05 W
Clearfield, Iowa, U.S. 188 40.48 N 94.29 W
Clearfield, Ky., U.S. 208 38.10 N 83.26 W
Clearfield, Pa., U.S. 204 41.02 N 78.27 W
Clearfield, Utah, U.S. 190 41.07 N 112.01 W
Clearfield ☐[6] 204 41.02 N 78.27 W
Clearfield Creek ≃ 204 41.02 N 78.24 W
Clear Fork Reservoir ⊛[1] 204 40.42 N 82.38 W
Clearing ✈[8] 268 41.47 N 87.47 W
Clear Island I 28 51.26 N 9.30 W
Clear Lake, Iowa, U.S. 180 43.08 N 93.23 W
Clear Lake, S. Dak., U.S. 188 44.45 N 96.41 W
Clearlake, Wash., U.S. 214 48.28 N 122.14 W
Clear Lake, Wis., U.S. 180 45.15 N 92.16 W
Clear Lake ⊛, Man., Can. 174 50.42 N 100.00 W
Clear Lake ⊛, Ont., Can. 202 44.30 N 78.13 W
Clear Lake ⊛, Ont., Can. 202 45.14 N 79.57 W
Clear Lake ⊛, Ont., Can. 202 44.59 N 79.33 W
Clear Lake ⊛, Ind., U.S. 206 41.44 N 84.50 W
Clear Lake ⊛[1], Calif., U.S. 194 39.02 N 122.50 W
Clear Lake ⊛[1], La., U.S. 184 31.55 N 93.05 W
Clearlake Highlands 216 38.57 N 122.38 W
Clearlake Oaks 216 39.07 N 122.40 W
Clearlake Park 216 38.58 N 122.39 W
Clear Lake Reservoir ⊛[1] 194 41.52 N 121.08 W
Clear Lake Shores 212 29.33 N 95.02 W
Clearmont 192 44.38 N 106.23 W
Clear Run 204 41.08 N 78.45 W
Clear Site 170 64.19 N 149.11 W
Clearview, Ohio, U.S. 204 41.25 N 82.10 W
Clearview, Wash., U.S. 214 47.45 N 122.06 W
Clearview, W. Va., U.S. 204 40.09 N 80.41 W
Clearview Estates 269b 40.34 N 80.16 W
Clearwater, B.C., Can. 172 51.38 N 120.02 W
Clearwater, Man., Can. 174 49.08 N 99.01 W
Clearwater, Fla., U.S. 210 27.58 N 82.48 W
Clearwater, Kans., U.S. 188 37.30 N 97.30 W
Clearwater, Nebr., U.S. 188 42.10 N 98.11 W
Clearwater, Wash., U.S. 214 47.35 N 124.17 W
Clearwater ≃, Can. 174 56.44 N 111.23 W
Clearwater ≃, Alta., Can. 172 52.23 N 114.50 W
Clearwater ≃, B.C., Can. 172 51.42 N 120.00 W
Clearwater ≃, Idaho, U.S. 192 46.25 N 117.02 W
Clearwater ≃, Minn., U.S. 188 47.54 N 96.16 W
Clearwater ≃, Mont., U.S. 192 46.58 N 113.23 W
Clearwater ≃, Wash., U.S. 214 47.33 N 124.21 W
Clearwater, Middle Fork ≃ 192 46.09 N 115.59 W
Clearwater, North Fork ≃ 192 46.30 N 116.19 W
Clearwater, South Fork ≃ 192 46.09 N 115.59 W
Clear Water Bay C 261d 22.17 N 114.18 E
Clearwater Beach Island I 210 27.59 N 82.49 W
Clearwater Lake ⊛, B.C., Can. 172 52.15 N 120.13 W
Clearwater Lake ⊛, Man., Can. 174 54.05 N 101.00 W
Clearwater Mountains ∧∧ 192 46.00 N 115.30 W
Clearwater Provincial Park ♠ 174 54.03 N 101.10 W
Cleator Moor 42 54.31 N 3.30 W
Clebit 186 34.21 N 94.52 W
Cleburne 212 32.21 N 97.23 W
Clee Hills ∧∧[2] 44 52.25 N 2.35 W
Cle Elum 214 47.12 N 120.56 W
Cle Elum ≃ 214 47.11 N 121.01 W
Cle Elum Lake ⊛[1] 214 47.18 N 121.06 W
Cleethorpes 42 53.34 N 0.02 W
Cleeve Cloud ∧[2] 44 51.34 N 2.00 W
Clefmont 54 48.06 N 5.31 E
Clelles 56 44.50 N 5.37 E
Clementon 275 39.49 N 74.59 W
Clementsport 176 44.40 N 65.37 W
Clemson 182 34.41 N 82.50 W
Clemville 212 29.00 N 96.08 W
Clendenin 178 38.29 N 81.21 W
Clendening Lake ⊛[1] 204 40.16 N 81.13 W
Clenze 50 52.56 N 10.58 E
Cleobury Mortimer 44 52.23 N 2.29 W
Cleona 198 40.20 N 76.29 W
Cléon-d'Andran 56 44.37 N 4.56 E
Cleopatra Needle ∧ 106 10.07 N 118.58 E
Clères 46 49.36 N 1.07 E
Clerke Rocks II[1] 234 55.01 S 34.41 W
Clermont, Austl. 156 22.49 S 147.39 E
Clermont, Qué., Can. 176 47.41 N 70.14 W
Clermont, Fr. 46 49.23 N 2.24 E
Clermont, Fla., U.S. 210 28.33 N 81.46 W
Clermont, N.J., U.S. 275 39.59 N 74.48 W
Clermont, Pa., U.S. 204 41.41 N 78.29 W
Clermont ☐[6] 208 39.05 N 84.11 W
Clermont-en-Argonne 52 49.06 N 5.04 E
Clermont-Ferrand 32 45.47 N 3.05 E
Clermont State Park ♠ 200 42.05 N 73.55 W
Clerval 54 47.24 N 6.30 E
Clervaux 52 50.04 N 6.01 E
Cléry-Saint-André 46 47.49 N 1.45 E
Cles 58 46.22 N 11.02 E
Cleve 156 33.42 S 136.30 E
Clevedon 44 51.27 N 2.51 W
Cleveland, Austl. 161a 27.32 S 153.17 E
Cleveland, Ala., U.S. 184 33.59 N 86.35 W
Cleveland, Fla., U.S. 210 26.57 N 82.00 W
Cleveland, Ga., U.S. 182 34.36 N 83.46 W
Cleveland, Miss., U.S. 184 33.45 N 90.50 W
Cleveland, N.C., U.S. 182 35.44 N 80.40 W
Cleveland, N.Y., U.S. 200 43.14 N 75.53 W
Cleveland, Ohio, U.S. 204 / 269a 41.30 N 81.41 W
Cleveland, Okla., U.S. 186 36.19 N 96.28 W
Cleveland, Tenn., U.S. 184 35.10 N 84.53 W
Cleveland, Tex., U.S. 212 30.21 N 95.05 W
Cleveland, Va., U.S. 182 36.57 N 82.09 W
Cleveland ☐[6] 42 54.35 N 1.15 W
Cleveland, Cape › 156 19.11 S 147.01 E
Cleveland, Mount ∧, Austl. 156 41.25 S 145.23 E
Cleveland, Mount ∧, Mont., U.S. 192 48.56 N 113.51 W
Cleveland Heights 204 41.30 N 81.34 W
Cleveland Hills ∧∧[2] 42 54.23 N 1.05 W
Cleveland-Hopkins International Airport ⊠ 269a 41.25 N 81.51 W
Clevelândia 242 26.24 S 52.21 W
Clevelândia do Norte 240 3.49 N 51.52 W
Cleveland Museum of Art ʊ 269a 41.31 N 81.37 W
Cleveland National Forest ♠ 270 33.47 N 117.38 W
Cleveland Park ✈[8] 274c 38.56 N 77.04 W
Cleveland Peninsula ›[1] 172 55.45 N 132.00 W
Cleveland Pond ⊛ 273 42.07 N 70.58 W
Cleveland State University ʊ[2] 269a 41.30 N 81.40 W
Cleveland Zoo ♠ 269a 41.27 N 81.43 W
Cleveleys 42 53.53 N 3.03 W
Cleversburg 198 40.02 N 77.28 W
Cleves → Kleve, B.R.D. 48 51.48 N 6.09 E
Cleves, Ohio, U.S. 208 39.10 N 84.45 W
Clew Bay C 28 53.50 N 9.50 W
Clewiston 210 26.45 N 80.56 W
Cley next the Sea 44 52.58 N 1.03 E
Clichy 46 48.54 N 2.18 E
Clichy-sous-Bois 251 48.55 N 2.33 E
Clifden 28 53.29 N 10.01 W
Cliffdale Creek ≃ 156 16.56 S 138.48 E
Cliffdell 214 46.44 N 120.42 W
Cliffe 44 51.28 N 0.30 E
Cliffe Marshes ☵ 250 51.28 N 0.30 E
Cliffe Woods 250 51.26 N 0.30 E
Clifford, Ont., Can. 202 43.58 N 80.58 W
Clifford, S. Afr. 148 31.04 S 27.28 E
Clifford, Ind., U.S. 208 39.17 N 85.52 W
Clifford, Pa., U.S. 200 41.39 N 75.36 W
Clifford Park ♠ 264b 37.43 S 145.16 E
Cliffside 200 42.31 N 74.59 W
Cliffside Park 266 40.49 N 73.59 W
Cliffwood 266 40.26 N 74.14 W
Cliffwood Beach 266 40.27 N 74.14 W
Clifton, Austl. 161a 27.56 S 151.54 E
Clifton, Eng., U.K. 252 53.46 N 2.49 W
Clifton, Ariz., U.S. 190 33.03 N 109.18 W
Clifton, Ill., U.S. 206 40.56 N 87.56 W
Clifton, Kans., U.S. 188 39.34 N 97.17 W
Clifton, N.J., U.S. 200 40.53 N 74.08 W
Clifton, N.Y., U.S. 200 43.03 N 77.49 W
Clifton, Oreg., U.S. 214 46.12 N 123.27 W
Clifton, Tenn., U.S. 184 35.23 N 88.01 W
Clifton, Tex., U.S. 212 31.47 N 97.35 W
Clifton, Lake ⊛ 158a 32.49 S 115.41 E
Clifton Court Forebay ⊛[1] 216 37.50 N 121.35 W
Clifton Forge 182 37.49 N 79.49 W
Clifton Gorge ∨ 44 51.28 N 2.37 W
Clifton Heights 275 39.56 N 75.18 W
Clifton Hills 156 26.52 S 138.50 E
Clifton Knolls 200 42.52 N 73.46 W
Clifton Park ♠ 274b 39.19 N 76.35 W
Clifton Point › 230b 25.01 N 77.34 W
Clifton Springs 200 42.58 N 77.08 W
Clifty, Mount ∧ 214 47.07 N 121.10 W
Clifty Creek ≃ 208 39.09 N 85.54 W
Clifty Falls State Park ♠ 208 38.45 N 85.26 W
Clignon ≃ 46 49.07 N 3.04 E
Climax, Sask., Can. 174 49.13 N 108.23 W
Climax, Colo., U.S. 190 39.22 N 106.11 W
Climax, Ga., U.S. 182 30.53 N 84.26 W
Climax, Mich., U.S. 206 42.14 N 85.20 W
Climax, Pa., U.S. 204 40.59 N 79.23 W
Clinch ≃ 182 35.53 N 84.29 W
Clinchco 182 37.10 N 82.22 W
Clingen 50 51.14 N 10.55 E
Clingmans Dome ∧ 182 35.35 N 83.30 W
Clint 190 31.35 N 106.14 W
Clinton, B.C., Can. 172 51.05 N 121.35 W
Clinton, Ont., Can. 180 43.37 N 81.32 W
Clinton, N.Z. 162 46.12 S 169.22 E
Clinton, Ala., U.S. 184 32.55 N 88.00 W
Clinton, Ark., U.S. 184 35.36 N 92.28 W
Clinton, Conn., U.S. 197 41.17 N 72.32 W
Clinton, Ill., U.S. 209 40.09 N 88.57 W
Clinton, Ind., U.S. 184 39.40 N 87.24 W
Clinton, Iowa, U.S. 180 41.51 N 90.12 W
Clinton, Ky., U.S. 184 36.40 N 89.02 W
Clinton, La., U.S. 184 30.52 N 91.01 W
Clinton, Maine, U.S. 178 44.38 N 69.30 W
Clinton, Md., U.S. 198 38.46 N 76.54 W
Clinton, Mass., U.S. 197 42.25 N 71.41 W
Clinton, Mich., U.S. 206 42.04 N 83.58 W
Clinton, Minn., U.S. 188 45.28 N 96.26 W
Clinton, Miss., U.S. 184 32.20 N 90.20 W
Clinton, Mo., U.S. 184 38.22 N 93.46 W
Clinton, N.J., U.S. 200 40.38 N 74.55 W
Clinton, N.C., U.S. 182 35.00 N 78.20 W
Clinton, N.Y., U.S. 200 43.03 N 75.23 W
Clinton, Ohio, U.S. 204 40.56 N 81.42 W
Clinton, Okla., U.S. 186 35.31 N 98.59 W
Clinton, Pa., U.S. 204 40.29 N 80.18 W
Clinton, S.C., U.S. 182 34.29 N 81.53 W
Clinton, Tenn., U.S. 182 36.06 N 84.08 W
Clinton, Tex., U.S. 212 33.06 N 96.14 W
Clinton, Wash., U.S. 214 47.59 N 122.22 W
Clinton, Wis., U.S. 206 42.34 N 88.52 W
Clinton ☐[6], Ill., U.S. 209 38.37 N 89.22 W
Clinton ☐[6], Ind., U.S. 206 40.17 N 86.31 W
Clinton ☐[6], Mich., U.S. 206 42.56 N 84.36 W
Clinton ☐[6], N.Y., U.S. 196 44.57 N 73.42 W
Clinton ☐[6], Ohio, U.S. 208 39.27 N 83.50 W
Clinton ☐[6], Pa., U.S. 200 41.08 N 71.26 W
Clinton ≃ 204 42.36 N 82.48 W
Clinton, Cape › 156 22.32 S 150.47 E
Clinton, Middle Branch ≃ 271 42.36 N 82.54 W
Clinton, North Branch ≃ 204 42.36 N 82.54 W
Clinton-Colden Lake ⊛ 166 63.58 N 107.27 W
Clintondale 200 41.01 N 77.29 W
Clinton Park 200 42.36 N 73.43 W
Clinton Reservoir ⊛[1] 266 41.05 N 74.27 W
Clinton Township 204 42.33 N 82.53 W
Clintonville, Mich., U.S. 271 42.43 N 83.22 W
Clintonville, Pa., U.S. 204 41.12 N 79.53 W
Clintonville, Wis., U.S. 180 44.37 N 88.46 W
Clintwood 182 37.09 N 82.27 W
Clio, Ala., U.S. 184 31.43 N 85.36 W
Clio, Mich., U.S. 180 43.11 N 83.44 W
Clio, S.C., U.S. 182 34.35 N 79.33 W
Clipperton I[1] 220 10.17 N 109.13 W
Clipperton Fracture Zone ⊹ 16 10.00 N 112.00 W
Clisham ∧ 28 57.57 N 6.49 W
Clisson 32 47.05 N 1.17 W
Clitheroe 42 53.53 N 2.23 W
Clitunno ≃ 60 42.56 N 12.37 E
Clive, Austl. 156 22.46 S 149.18 E
Clive, N.Z. 162 39.35 S 176.55 E
Cliza 238 17.36 S 65.56 W
Cloates, Point › 152 22.43 S 113.40 E
Clock Face 252 53.25 N 2.43 W
Clocolan 148 29.00 S 27.30 E
Clodomira 242 27.35 S 64.08 W
Cloe 204 40.56 N 78.56 W
Cloete 186 27.55 N 101.10 W
Clogher Head › 28 53.48 N 6.12 W
Cloisters ʊ 266 40.52 N 73.56 W
Clonakilty 28 51.37 N 8.54 W
Clonakilty Bay C 28 51.35 N 8.50 W
Cloncurry 156 20.42 S 140.30 E
Cloncurry ≃ 156 18.37 S 140.40 E
Clondalkin 28 53.19 N 6.24 W
Clonee 42 53.25 N 6.26 W
Clonmel 28 52.21 N 7.42 W
Clontarf 264a 33.48 S 151.16 E
Clo-oose 172 48.40 N 124.49 W
Cloppenburg 48 52.50 N 8.02 E
Cloquallum Creek ≃ 214 46.58 N 123.24 W
Cloquet 180 46.43 N 92.28 W
Cloquet ≃ 180 46.52 N 92.35 W
Clorinda 242 25.17 S 57.43 W
Closter 266 40.59 N 73.58 W
Cloudcroft 190 32.58 N 105.45 W
Cloud Peak ∧ 192 44.25 N 107.10 W
Cloudy Bay C 162 41.27 S 174.10 E
Cloudy Mountain ∧ 170 63.11 N 156.05 W
Clough 42 54.18 N 5.50 W
Clough Foot 252 53.43 N 2.08 W
Clove Lakes Park ♠ 266 40.37 N 74.07 W
Clovelly, Austl. 264a 33.55 S 151.16 E
Clovelly, Eng., U.K. 44 51.00 N 4.24 W
Clover 182 35.07 N 81.14 W
Clover Bank 200 42.45 N 78.53 W
Clover Creek ≃ 192 43.00 N 115.11 W
Cloverdale, B.C., Can. 214 49.06 N 122.44 W
Cloverdale, Ala., U.S. 184 34.56 N 87.46 W
Cloverdale, Calif., U.S. 194 38.48 N 123.01 W
Cloverdale, Ill., U.S. 268 41.56 N 88.07 W
Cloverdale, Ind., U.S. 184 39.31 N 86.48 W
Cloverdale, Ky., U.S. 208 38.10 N 84.53 W
Cloverdale, Mich., U.S. 206 42.32 N 85.23 W
Cloverdale, Ohio, U.S. 206 41.01 N 84.18 W
Cloverdale, Oreg., U.S. 214 45.12 N 123.53 W
Cloverdale Mall ✈[9] 265b 43.38 N 79.34 W
Cloverdene 263d 26.09 S 28.22 E
Cloverleaf 212 29.47 N 95.13 W
Clover Pass 170 55.28 N 131.47 W
Cloverport 184 37.50 N 86.38 W
Cloverville 206 43.11 N 86.10 W
Clovis, Calif., U.S. 216 36.49 N 119.42 W
Clovis, N. Mex., U.S. 186 34.24 N 103.12 W
Clowbridge Reservoir ⊛[1] 252 53.45 N 2.16 W
Clowne 42 53.18 N 1.16 W
Cloyes-sur-le-Loir 46 48.00 N 1.14 E
Cluain Meala → Clonmel 28 52.21 N 7.42 W
Cluj 38 46.47 N 23.36 E
Cluj ☐[4] 38 46.45 N 23.45 E
Clun 44 52.26 N 3.00 W
Clun ≃ 44 52.22 N 2.53 W
Clune 204 40.34 N 79.18 W
Clunes 159 37.18 S 143.47 E
Clun Forest ✈[3] 44 52.28 N 3.07 W
Cluny, Austl. 156 24.31 S 139.35 E
Cluny, Fr. 54 46.26 N 4.39 E
Cluses 54 46.04 N 6.36 E
Clusone 58 45.53 N 9.57 E
Clute 212 29.01 N 95.24 W
Clutha ≃ 162 46.21 S 169.48 E
Clwyd ☐[6] 44 53.05 N 3.20 W
Clwyd ≃ 42 53.20 N 3.30 W
Clwyd, Vale of ∨ 42 53.12 N 3.24 W
Clwydian Range ∧∧ 42 53.10 N 3.20 W
Clydach 44 51.43 N 3.50 W
Clyde, Alta., Can. 172 54.09 N 113.39 W
Clyde, N.W. Ter., Can. 166 70.25 N 68.30 W
Clyde, N.Z. 162 45.11 S 169.19 E
Clyde, Calif., U.S. 216 38.02 N 122.02 W
Clyde, Kans., U.S. 188 39.36 N 97.24 W
Clyde, Mich., U.S. 271 42.41 N 83.37 W
Clyde, N.Y., U.S. 200 43.05 N 76.52 W
Clyde, Ohio, U.S. 204 41.18 N 82.59 W
Clyde, Tex., U.S. 186 32.24 N 99.30 W
Clyde ≃, Austl. 160 35.23 S 150.15 E
Clyde ≃, N.S., Can. 176 43.35 N 65.25 W
Clyde ≃, Ont., Can. 202 44.58 N 76.22 W
Clyde ≃, Dom. 230d 15.33 N 61.18 W
Clyde ≃, Scot., U.K. 42 55.56 N 4.29 W
Clyde ≃, N.Y., U.S. 200 43.04 N 77.00 W
Clyde ≃, Vt., U.S. 178 44.56 N 72.12 W
Clyde, Firth of C[1] 42 55.42 N 5.00 W
Clydebank 42 55.54 N 4.24 W
Clydegale Lake ⊛ 202 45.25 N 78.23 W
Clyde Lake ⊛ 172 55.18 N 111.28 W
Clyde No.3 204 39.59 N 80.03 W
Clyde Park 192 45.53 N 110.36 W
Clyde Potts Reservoir ⊛[1] 266 40.48 N 74.35 W
Clydesdale 148 26.54 S 27.55 E
Clydesdale ∨ 42 55.42 N 3.50 W
Clymer, N.Y., U.S. 204 42.03 N 79.35 W
Clymer, Pa., U.S. 204 40.40 N 79.01 W
Clynnog-fawr 44 53.01 N 4.23 W
Clywedog ≃, Wales, U.K. 44 53.02 N 2.52 W
Clywedog ≃, Wales, U.K. 44 52.27 N 3.32 W
Ćmielów 30 50.53 N 21.31 E
Cna ≃, S.S.S.R. 66 57.33 N 34.36 E
Cna ≃, S.S.S.R. 66 52.10 N 27.03 E
Cna ≃, S.S.S.R. 70 54.32 N 42.05 E
Cna ≃, S.S.S.R. 72 55.25 N 39.10 E
Cnoc Moy ∧[2] 42 55.23 N 5.46 W
Côa ≃ 34 41.05 N 7.06 W
Coacalco ☐[7] 276a 19.37 N 99.06 W
Coacalco de Berriozábal 276a 19.37 N 9.05 W
Coachella 194 33.41 N 116.10 W
Coachella Canal ☲ 194 33.34 N 116.00 W
Coacoyole 222 24.31 N 106.34 W
Coacuilco 224 21.07 N 98.35 W
Coahoma 186 32.18 N 101.18 W
Coahuayana 224 18.44 N 103.41 W
Coahuayana, Río de ≃ 224 18.41 N 103.45 W
Coahuayutla de Guerrero 224 18.19 N 101.49 W
Coahuila 190 32.12 N 114.59 W
Coahuila ☐[3] 222 27.20 N 102.00 W
Coal ≃ 170 59.39 N 126.57 W
Coalbrook 148 26.51 S 27.53 E
Coalbrookdale 44 52.38 N 2.30 W
Coalburg 204 41.11 N 80.36 W
Coalburn 42 55.36 N 3.54 W
Coal City 206 41.17 N 88.17 W
Coalcomán de Matamoros 224 18.47 N 103.09 W
Coal Creek 170 65.22 N 143.10 W
Coal Creek ≃, Colo., U.S. 188 40.30 N 104.26 W
Coal Creek ≃, Ind., U.S. 184 39.57 N 87.25 W
Coal Creek ≃, Wash., U.S. 192 47.19 N 118.36 W
Coal Creek Flat 162 45.29 S 169.18 E
Coaldale, Alta., Can. 172 49.43 N 112.37 W
Coaldale, Pa., U.S. 200 40.50 N 75.54 W
Coal Fire Creek ≃ 184 33.15 N 88.18 W
Coal Fork 178 38.19 N 81.32 W
Coalgate, N.Z. 162 43.29 S 171.58 E
Coalgate, Okla., U.S. 186 34.32 N 96.13 W
Coal Grove 178 38.30 N 82.39 W
Coal Harbour 172 50.36 N 127.35 W
Coal Hill 184 35.26 N 93.40 W
Coal Hill Park ♠ 261a 39.56 N 116.23 E
Coalhurst 172 49.45 N 112.56 W
Coalinga 216 36.09 N 120.21 W
Coalisland 42 54.33 N 6.42 W
Coal Island I 162 46.07 S 166.38 E
Coalmont 172 49.31 N 120.41 W
Coalpit Heath 44 51.32 N 2.28 W
Coalport 204 40.45 N 78.32 W
Coal River 170 59.45 N 126.55 W
Coal Run ≃ 269b 40.21 N 80.07 W
Coalspur 172 53.11 N 117.01 W
Coalton 209 39.17 N 89.19 W
Coaltown 204 41.02 N 80.20 W
Coal Valley ∨ 194 38.56 N 115.25 W
Coalville, S. Afr. 148 26.01 S 29.10 E
Coalville, Eng., U.K. 44 52.44 S 1.20 W
Coalville, Utah, U.S. 190 40.55 N 111.24 W
Coamo 230m 18.05 N 66.22 W
Coamo, Lago ⊛[1] 230m 18.01 N 66.23 W
Coan, Cerro ∧ 238 7.26 S 78.43 W
Coapilla 224 17.08 N 93.10 W
Coaraci 245 14.38 S 39.32 W
Coari 236 4.05 S 63.08 W
Coari ≃ 236 4.30 S 63.33 W
Coari, Lago de ⊛ 236 4.15 S 63.22 W
Coarsegold 216 37.16 N 119.42 W
Coast ☐[4], Kenya 144 3.00 N 39.30 E
Coast ☐[4], Tan. 144 7.00 S 39.00 E
Coast Mountains ∧∧ 166 55.00 N 129.00 W
Coast Ranges ∧∧ 168 41.00 N 123.30 W
Coatán ≃ 226 14.48 N 92.31 W
Coatbridge 42 55.52 N 4.01 W
Coatepec 224 19.27 N 96.58 W
Coatepec de Harinas 224 18.54 N 99.43 W
Coatepeque 226 14.42 N 91.52 W
Coatepeque, Lago de ⊛ 226 13.52 N 89.33 W
Coatepetl, Cerro ∧ 224 18.25 N 97.35 W
Coates Creek ≃ 202 44.24 N 79.54 W
Coatesville 198 39.59 N 75.49 W
Coatiçaba 245 13.59 S 46.31 W
Coaticook 196 45.08 N 71.48 W
Coaticook ≃ 196 45.20 N 71.53 W
Coatsburg 209 40.02 N 91.10 W
Coats Island I 166 62.30 N 83.00 W
Coats Land ✈[1] 9 77.00 S 28.00 W
Coatzacoalcos 224 18.09 N 94.25 W
Coatzacoalcos ≃ 224 18.10 N 94.27 W
Coatzacoalcos, Bahía C 224 18.10 N 94.27 W
Coatzintla 224 20.29 N 97.27 W
Coayllo 238 12.44 S 76.28 W
Coazze 56 45.03 N 7.18 E
Cobá ⊥ 222 20.36 N 87.35 W
Cobadin 38 44.04 N 28.13 E
Cobalt, Ont., Can. 180 47.24 N 79.41 W
Cobalt, Conn., U.S. 197 41.34 N 72.34 W
Cobán 226 15.29 N 90.19 W
Çobanlar 120 38.41 N 30.47 E
Cobar 156 31.30 S 145.49 E
Cobargo 156 36.23 S 149.53 E
Cobb 216 38.49 N 122.43 W
Cobb Creek ≃ 186 35.05 N 98.25 W
Cobberas, Mount ∧ 156 36.52 S 148.10 E
Cobbetts Lake ⊛ 273 42.48 N 71.17 W
Cobbin's Brook ≃ 250 51.41 N 0.01 W
Cobb Island 198 38.16 N 76.51 W
Cobb Island I, Md., U.S. 198 38.16 N 76.51 W
Cobb Island I, Va., U.S. 198 37.20 N 75.44 W
Cobbitty 264a 34.01 S 150.41 E
Cobbitty ∧[2] 264a 33.59 S 150.42 E
Cobble Hill 214 48.41 N 123.36 W
Cobble Mountain Reservoir ⊛[1] 197 42.08 N 72.55 W
Cobblers Reef ⊹[2] 231g 13.06 N 59.26 W
Cobblestone Mountain ∧ 218 34.37 N 118.52 W
Cobbs Creek ≃ 275 39.54 N 75.15 W
Cobbs Creek Park ♠ 275 39.58 N 75.16 W
Cobb Seamount ⊹[3] 16 46.45 N 130.50 W
Cobden, Austl. 159 38.20 S 143.05 E
Cobden, Ont., Can. 180 45.38 N 76.53 W
Cobden, Ill., U.S. 184 37.32 N 89.15 W
Cobeña 256a 40.34 N 3.30 W
Cobequid Bay C 176 45.21 N 63.45 W
Cobequid Mountains ∧∧ 176 45.30 N 63.30 W
Cobh 28 51.51 N 8.17 W
Cobham, Eng., U.K. 44 51.20 N 0.25 W
Cobham, Eng., U.K. 250 51.23 N 0.24 E
Cobham ≃ 174 53.15 N 93.58 W
Cobham Hall ⊥ 250 51.23 N 0.25 E
Cobija, Bol. 238 11.02 S 68.44 W
Cobija, Chile 242 22.33 S 70.16 W
Coblenz → Koblenz 52 50.21 N 7.35 E
Cobleskill 200 42.41 N 74.29 W
Cobleskill Creek ≃ 200 42.43 N 74.20 W
Coboconk 202 44.39 N 78.48 W
Cobo Hall ʊ 271 42.19 N 83.03 W
Cobolgo, Gora ∧ 74 42.50 N 46.23 E
Čoboto, Cerro ∧ 190 31.29 N 112.05 W
Čoboty 255b 55.39 N 37.21 E
Cobourg 202 43.58 N 78.10 W
Cobourg Peninsula ›[1] 154 11.20 S 132.15 E
Cobquecura 242 36.08 S 72.47 W
Cobram 156 35.55 S 145.39 E
Cobras, Ilha das I 277a 22.54 S 43.10 W
Cobras, Ribeirão das ≃ 246 23.08 S 46.05 W
Cobre ≃ 226 8.01 N 81.18 W
Cóbuè 144 12.04 S 34.50 E
Coburg, Austl. 159 37.45 S 144.58 E
Coburg, B.R.D. 52 50.15 N 10.58 E
Coburg Island I 166 76.00 N 79.25 W
Coburn 200 40.52 N 77.28 W
Coburn Mountain ∧ 178 45.28 N 70.06 W
Cobuya ≃ 236 2.20 S 70.50 W
Coca ≃ 236 0.29 S 76.58 W
Coca, Pizzo di ∧ 58 46.04 N 10.01 E
Coca, Punta › 226 12.28 N 83.30 W
Cocachacra 238 17.06 S 71.46 W
Cocais ∧ 246 21.51 S 42.53 W
Cocais, Ribeirão dos ≃ 246 21.59 S 47.15 W
Cocal 240 3.28 S 41.34 W
Cocalico Creek ≃ 198 40.07 N 76.14 W
Coccaglio 58 45.34 N 9.58 E
Cocconato 56 45.05 N 8.02 E
Cocentaina 34 38.45 N 0.26 W
Cochabamba 238 17.24 S 66.09 W
Cochabamba ☐[5] 238 17.30 S 65.40 W
Cochagual 242 31.54 S 68.23 W
Cochatauri 74 42.01 N 42.15 E
Cochato ≃ 273 42.10 N 71.01 W
Coche, Isla I 236 10.45 N 63.55 W
Cochem 52 50.11 N 7.09 E
Cochesett 273 42.14 N 70.48 W
Cochetopa Creek ≃ 190 38.31 N 106.47 W
Cochichewick, Lake ⊛ 273 42.42 N 71.06 W
Cochin 112 9.58 N 76.14 E
Cochinos (Bay of Pigs), Bahía de C 230p 22.07 N 81.10 W
Cochinos, Cayos II 226 15.57 N 86.33 W
Cochise Head ∧ 190 32.03 N 109.18 W
Cochituate 197 42.19 N 71.22 W
Cochituate, Lake ⊛ 273 42.17 N 71.22 W
Cochituate State Park ♠ 197 42.20 N 71.22 W
Cochran 182 32.23 N 83.21 W
Cochrane, Alta., Can. 172 51.11 N 114.28 W
Cochrane, Ont., Can. 166 49.04 N 81.01 W
Cochrane, Wis., U.S. 180 44.14 N 91.50 W
Cochrane ≃ 166 57.52 N 101.38 W
Cochrane, Lago (Lago Pueyrredón) ⊛ 244 47.20 S 72.00 W
Cochranton 204 41.31 N 80.03 W
Cochranville 198 39.53 N 75.55 W
Cochstedt 50 51.53 N 11.24 E
Cockatoo-Inseln → Buccaneer Archipelago II 150 16.17 S 123.20 E
Cockburn 156 32.05 S 141.00 E
Cockburn, Canal U 244 54.20 S 71.30 W
Cockburn, Cape › 154 11.20 S 132.52 E
Cockburn, Mount ∧ 152 22.46 S 130.36 E
Cockburn Island I 180 45.55 N 83.22 W
Cockburn Sound U 158a 32.12 S 115.42 E
Cockburnspath 42 55.56 N 2.21 W
Cock Clarks 250 51.42 N 0.37 E
Cockenoe Island I 266 41.05 N 73.21 W
Cockenzie 42 55.58 N 2.58 W
Cockerham 42 53.59 N 2.50 W
Cockermouth 42 54.40 N 3.21 W
Cockeysville 198 39.29 N 76.39 W
Cockfosters ✈[8] 250 51.39 N 0.09 W
Cockpit Country ✈[1] 231q 18.18 N 77.43 W
Cockrell Hill 212 32.45 N 96.54 W
Cockroach Island I 230m 18.24 N 65.04 W
Cockscomb Point › 164u 14.14 S 170.40 W
Coclé ☐[4] 226 8.30 N 80.15 W
Coclé del Norte ≃ 226 9.05 N 80.35 W
Coclois 46 48.28 N 4.20 E
Coco ≃ 226 15.00 N 83.10 W
Coco, Cayo I 230p 22.30 N 78.28 W
Coco, Isla del I 220 5.32 N 87.04 W
Côco, Rio do ≃ 240 9.27 S 50.02 W
Cocoa 210 28.21 N 80.44 W
Cocoa Beach 210 28.19 N 80.36 W
Cocobeach 142 0.59 N 9.36 E
Coco Channel U 100 13.45 N 93.00 E
Cococi 240 6.25 S 40.30 W
Cocodrie Lake ⊛[1] 184 30.58 N 92.25 W
Coco Islands II 100 14.05 N 93.18 E
Coconino Plateau ∧∧[1] 190 35.50 N 112.30 W
Cocorocuma, Cayos ⊹[2] 226 15.45 N 83.00 W
Côcos 245 14.10 S 44.33 W
Côcos, Vereda de ≃ 245 12.44 S 44.48 W
Cocos Basin ⊹[1] 12 7.00 S 95.00 E
Cocos Bay C 231r 10.27 N 61.00 W
Cocos Island I 164p 13.14 N 144.39 E
Cocos Islands ☐[2] 12 12.10 S 96.55 E
Cocos Islands II 4 12.10 S 96.55 E
Cocos Ridge ⊹[3] 16 5.30 N 87.30 W
Cocotá ✈[8] 277a 22.49 S 43.11 W
Coctitlán 224 19.14 N 98.52 W
Cocuiza ≃ 236 10.59 N 71.17 W
Cocula, Méx. 224 18.14 N 99.40 W
Cocula, Méx. 224 20.23 N 103.50 W
Cod ≃ 42 54.10 N 1.22 W
Cod, Cape › 197 41.42 N 70.15 W
Codăești 38 46.52 N 27.46 E
Codajás 236 3.50 S 62.05 W
Coddenham 44 52.09 N 1.07 E
Codera, Cabo › 236 10.35 N 66.05 W
Coderre 174 50.10 N 106.23 W
Coderre, Ruisseau ≃ 265a 45.43 N 73.19 W
Codesa 172 55.45 N 118.04 W
Codfish Island I 162 46.47 S 167.38 E
Codigoro 60 44.49 N 12.08 E
Cod Island I 166 57.45 N 61.50 W
Codlea 38 45.42 N 25.27 E
Codnor 44 53.03 N 1.23 W
Codó 240 4.29 S 43.53 W
Codogno 56 45.09 N 9.42 E
Codorus 198 39.48 N 76.52 W
Codorus Creek ≃ 198 40.03 N 76.38 W
Codorus State Park ♠ 198 39.48 N 76.54 W
Codòzinho 240 4.46 S 44.10 W
Çodpa 238 18.50 S 69.44 W
Čodro 76 50.50 N 88.34 E
Codroipo 58 45.58 N 12.59 E
Codroy 176 47.53 N 59.24 W
Codroy Pond 176 48.04 N 58.52 W
Codsall 44 52.38 N 2.12 W
Cody, Nebr., U.S. 188 42.56 N 101.15 W
Cody, Wyo., U.S. 192 44.32 N 109.03 W
Coeburn 182 36.57 N 82.28 W
Coelemu 242 36.29 S 72.42 W
Coelho da Rocha 246 22.47 S 43.23 W
Coelho Neto 240 4.15 S 43.00 W
Coemba 142 12.08 S 18.05 E
Coen 154 13.56 S 143.12 E
Coen ≃ 154 13.56 S 142.02 E
Coeneo [de la Libertad] 224 19.49 N 101.35 W
Coeroeni ≃ 240 3.21 N 57.31 W
Coesfeld 48 51.56 N 7.10 E
Coetivy Island I 128 7.08 S 56.16 E
Coeur d'Alene 192 47.41 N 116.46 W
Coeur d'Alene ≃ 192 47.28 N 116.48 W
Coeur d'Alene, South Fork ≃ 192 47.33 N 116.15 W
Coeur d'Alene Indian Reservation ✈[4] 192 47.18 N 116.45 W
Coeur d'Alene Lake ⊛[1] 192 47.32 N 116.48 W
Coeur d'Alene Mountains ∧∧ 192 47.50 N 116.05 W
Coevorden 48 52.40 N 6.45 E
Coeymans 200 42.28 N 73.48 W
Coffeen 209 39.05 N 89.24 W
Coffeen Lake ⊛[1] 209 39.03 N 89.20 W
Coffeeville 184 33.59 N 89.40 W
Coffeyville 188 37.02 N 95.37 W
Coffin, Île I 176 47.33 N 61.30 W
Coffin Bay C 152 34.27 S 135.19 E
Coffin Bay Peninsula ›[1] 152 34.32 S 135.15 E
Coffs Harbour 156 30.18 S 153.08 E
Cofimvaba 148 32.00 S 27.35 E
Cofradía 226 15.24 N 88.09 W
Cofre de Perote, Parque Nacional ♠ 224 19.32 N 97.10 W
Cofrentes 34 39.14 N 1.04 W
Coggeshall 44 51.52 N 0.41 E
Coggiola 56 45.41 N 8.11 E
Coggon 180 42.17 N 91.32 W
Coglians, Monte (Hohe Warte) ∧ 58 46.37 N 12.53 E
Cogliate 256b 45.39 N 9.05 E
Cognac 32 45.42 N 0.20 W
Cogne 56 45.37 N 7.21 E
Cognin 56 45.34 N 5.54 E
Cogoleto 56 44.23 N 8.39 E
Cogolin 56 43.15 N 6.32 E
Cogollo del Cengio 58 45.47 N 11.25 E
Cogolludo 34 40.57 N 3.05 W
Cogolo 58 46.21 N 10.41 E
Cogswell 188 46.07 N 97.47 W
Cogswell Reservoir ⊛[1] 270 34.14 N 117.58 W
Cogt 92 45.25 N 96.42 E
Cogtčandman' 92 45.42 N 104.22 E
Cogtong Bay C 106 9.51 N 124.33 E
Cogt-Ovoo 92 44.30 N 105.35 E
Çoğun 120 39.20 N 34.08 E
Cohansey ≃ 198 39.21 N 75.22 W
Cohasset 197 42.14 N 70.48 W
Cohasset Harbor C 273 42.15 N 70.47 W
Cohenga ≃ 238 10.17 S 73.57 W
Cohoctah 206 42.46 N 83.57 W
Cohocton 200 42.30 N 77.30 W
Cohocton ≃ 200 42.09 N 77.05 W
Cohoe 170 60.23 N 151.18 W
Cohoes 200 42.46 N 73.42 W
Cohoni 238 16.44 S 67.51 W
Cohoon, Lake ⊛[1] 198 36.45 N 76.38 W
Cohuna 156 35.49 S 144.13 E
Coiba, Isla de I 236 7.27 N 81.45 W
Coig (Coyle) ≃ 244 50.58 S 69.11 W
Coignières 251 48.45 N 1.55 E
Coils Creek ≃ 194 39.32 N 116.16 W
Coimbatore 112 11.00 N 76.58 E
Coimbra, Bra. 238 19.55 S 57.47 W
Coimbra, Bra. 245 20.52 S 42.48 W
Coimbra, Port. 34 40.12 N 8.25 W
Coín, Esp. 34 36.40 N 4.45 W
Coin, Iowa, U.S. 188 40.40 N 95.14 W
Coipasa, Lago de ⊛ 238 19.12 S 68.07 W
Coipasa, Salar de ⊻ 238 19.26 S 68.09 W
Coire → Chur 54 46.51 N 9.32 E
Çoixtlahuaca 224 17.43 N 97.19 W
Čojbalsan (Bajan Tümen), Mong. 78 48.04 N 114.30 E
Čojbalsan, Mong. 78 48.34 N 114.50 E
Čojbalsan Uul ∧ 78 47.49 N 107.00 E
Cojedes 236 9.37 N 68.55 W
Cojedes ☐[3] 236 9.20 N 68.20 W
Cojedes ≃ 236 8.34 N 68.05 W
Cojímar 276b 23.10 N 82.18 W
Cojímar ≃ 276b 23.10 N 82.17 W
Cojudo Blanco, Cerro ∧ 244 47.05 S 69.20 W
Cojumatlán de Régules 224 20.07 N 102.50 W
Cojutepeque 226 13.43 N 88.56 W
Çokak 120 37.45 N 36.19 E
Cokato 180 45.05 N 94.11 W
Cokeburg 204 40.06 N 80.04 W
Coker 263a 6.29 N 3.20 E
Cokeville 190 42.05 N 110.57 W
Çoki 140 15.30 N 15.59 W
Čoktal 75 42.36 N 76.44 E
Čokurdach 64 70.38 N 147.55 E
Colāba ✈[8] 262c 18.54 N 72.48 E
Colāba Point › 262c 18.53 N 72.48 E
Colac 159 38.20 S 143.35 E
Colac, Lake ⊛ 159 38.18 S 143.35 E
Çolaklı 120 38.22 N 38.33 E

Symbols in the index entries represent the broad categories identified in the key at the right. Symbols with superior numbers (∧∧[2]) identify subcategories (see complete key on page I · 26).

Kartensymbole in dem Registerverzeichnis stellen die rechts in Schlüssel erklärten Kategorien dar. Symbole mit hochgestellten Ziffern (∧∧[2]) bezeichnen Unterabteilungen einer Kategorie (vgl. vollständiger Schlüssel auf Seite I · 26).

Los símbolos incluídos en el texto del índice representan las grandes categorias identificadas con la clave a la derecha. Los símbolos con numeros en su parte superior (∧∧[2]) identifican las subcategorías (véase la clave completa en la página I · 26).

Les symboles de l'index représentent les catégories indiquées dans la légende à droite. Les symboles suivis d'un indice (∧∧[2]) représentent des sous-catégories (voir légende complète à la page I · 26).

Os símbolos incluídos no texto do índice representam as grandes categorias identificadas com a chave à direita. Os símbolos com números em sua parte superior (∧∧[2]) identificam as subcategorias (veja-se a chave completa à página I · 26).

	English	Deutsch	Español	Français	Português
∧	Mountain	Berg	Montaña	Montagne	Montanha
∧∧	Mountains	Berge	Montañas	Montagnes	Montanhas
)(	Pass	Pass	Paso	Col	Passo
∨	Valley, Canyon	Tal, Cañon	Valle, Cañón	Vallée, Canyon	Vale, Canhão
⊻	Plain	Ebene	Llano	Plaine	Planície
›	Cape	Kap	Cabo	Cap	Cabo
I	Island	Insel	Isla	Île	Ilha
II	Islands	Inseln	Islas	Îles	Ilhas
⊥	Other Topographic Features	Andere Topographische Objekte	Otros Elementos Topográficos	Autres données topographiques	Outros Elementos Topográficos

ESPAÑOL — Nombre | Página | Lat.°′ | Long.°′ W=Oeste
FRANÇAIS — Nom | Page | Lat.°′ | Long.°′ W=Ouest
PORTUGUÊS — Nome | Página | Lat.°′ | Long.°′ W=Oeste

Nombre / Nom / Nome	Página / Page	Lat.°′	Long.°′
Colalao del Valle	242	26.22 S	65.57 W
Colan-Conhué	244	43.16 S	69.51 W
Colapsin Point ≻	106	6.38 N	125.25 E
Colares, Bra.	240	0.56 S	48.17 W
Colares, Port.	34	38.48 N	9.27 W
Colares, Ribeira de ≃	256c	38.49 N	9.28 W
Colatina	245	19.32 S	40.37 W
Cölbe	52	50.51 N	8.48 E
Colbeck, Cape ≻	9	77.06 S	157.48 W
Colberry Park	271	42.36 N	83.16 W
Colbert	186	33.51 N	96.30 W
Colbinabbin	156	36.35 S	144.49 E
Colbitz	50	52.19 N	11.36 E
Colbitz-Letzlinger Heide ◆[3]	50	52.27 N	11.35 E
Colborne, Ont., Can.	202	44.00 N	77.53 W
Colborne, Ont., Can.	202	42.51 N	80.19 W
Colbún	242	35.42 S	71.25 W
Colburn	206	40.31 N	86.43 W
Colby, Kans., U.S.	188	39.24 N	101.03 W
Colby, Wis., U.S.	180	44.55 N	90.19 W
Colca	238	12.18 S	75.13 W
Colca ≃	238	15.51 S	72.26 W
Colcamar	238	6.16 S	77.55 W
Colcapirhua	238	17.25 S	66.15 W
Colchagua □[4]	242	34.30 S	71.15 W
Colchester, Ont., Can.	204	41.59 N	82.56 W
Colchester, Eng., U.K.	44	51.54 N	0.54 E
Colchester, Conn., U.S.	197	41.34 N	72.20 W
Colchester, Ill., U.S.	180	40.25 N	90.48 W
Cold Bay	170	55.11 N	162.30 W
Cold Bay C	170	55.13 N	162.33 W
Coldblow ◆[8]	250	51.26 N	0.10 E
Cold Brook	200	43.15 N	75.03 W
Cold Creek ≃	202	44.12 N	77.36 W
Colden	200	42.39 N	78.41 W
Cold Fell ∧	42	54.54 N	2.36 W
Cold Harbor Battlefield (1864) ⊥	198	37.36 N	77.20 W
Coldingham	42	55.53 N	2.10 W
Colditz	50	51.07 N	12.48 E
Cold Lake	174	54.27 N	110.10 W
Cold Lake ⊜	174	54.33 N	110.05 W
Cold Lake Indian Reserve ◆[4]	174	54.33 N	110.10 W
Cold Norton	250	51.40 N	0.40 E
Coldrano	58	46.38 N	10.50 E
Cold Spring, Ky., U.S.	208	39.01 N	84.27 W
Cold Spring, Minn., U.S.	180	45.27 N	94.26 W
Cold Spring, N.J., U.S.	198	38.59 N	74.57 W
Cold Spring, N.Y., U.S.	200	41.25 N	73.57 W
Coldspring, Tex., U.S.	212	30.36 N	95.08 W
Cold Spring Harbor	266	40.52 N	73.27 W
Cold Spring Harbor C	266	40.53 N	73.28 W
Coldsprings, Ont., Can.	202	44.17 N	78.18 W
Cold Springs, N.Y., U.S.	200	43.08 N	76.15 W
Cold Springs Creek ≃	188	44.32 N	104.06 W
Cold Spring Terrace	266	40.50 N	73.26 W
Coldstream, Austl.	264b	37.44 S	145.23 E
Coldstream, Scot., U.K.	42	55.39 N	2.15 W
Cold Stream ≃	216	39.35 N	120.22 W
Coldwater, Ont., Can.	202	44.42 N	79.40 W
Coldwater, Kans., U.S.	188	37.16 N	99.19 W
Coldwater, Mich., U.S.	206	41.57 N	85.00 W
Coldwater, Miss., U.S.	184	34.41 N	89.59 W
Coldwater, Ohio, U.S.	206	40.29 N	84.38 W
Coldwater ≃, Ont., Can.	202	44.44 N	79.39 W
Coldwater ≃, Mich., U.S.	206	42.04 N	85.08 W
Coldwater Canyon ∨	270	34.14 N	117.44 W
Coldwater Indian Reserve ◆[4]	172	50.04 N	120.48 W
Coldwater Lake ⊜	206	41.49 N	84.58 W
Cole □[6]	209	38.30 N	92.13 W
Cole ≃, Ang.	142	9.07 S	15.50 E
Cole ≃, Eng., U.K.	44	52.28 N	1.44 W
Cole ≃, Eng., U.K.	44	51.42 N	1.42 W
Colebrook, N.H., U.S.	178	44.54 N	71.30 W
Colebrook, Ohio, U.S.	204	41.32 N	80.46 W
Colebrook River Lake ⊜[1]	197	42.03 N	73.04 W
Cole Camp	184	38.28 N	93.12 W
Coledale	160	34.17 S	150.57 E
Coleen ≃	170	67.05 N	142.31 W
Coleford National Park ♠	148	29.53 S	29.28 E
Colégio, Morro do ∧	277b	23.38 S	46.21 W
Coleman, Alta., Can.	172	49.38 N	114.30 W
Coleman, Fla., U.S.	210	28.48 N	82.04 W
Coleman, Md., U.S.	198	39.21 N	76.05 W
Coleman, Mich., U.S.	180	43.46 N	84.35 W
Coleman, Tex., U.S.	186	31.50 N	99.26 W
Coleman, Wis., U.S.	180	45.04 N	88.02 W
Coleman ≃	154	15.06 S	141.38 E
Colembert	46	50.45 N	1.50 E
Colen Lakes ⊜	174	54.33 N	95.25 W
Colenso	148	28.50 S	29.44 E
Colerain	204	40.07 N	80.49 W
Coleraine, Austl.	156	37.36 S	141.42 E
Coleraine, N. Ire., U.K.	42	55.08 N	6.40 W
Coleraine, Minn., U.S.	180	47.17 N	93.27 W
Coleridge	188	42.30 N	97.13 W
Coleridge, Lake ⊜	162	43.17 S	171.30 E
Coleroon ≃	112	11.23 N	79.46 E
Coles	184	31.17 N	91.03 W
Colesberg	148	30.45 S	25.05 E
Coles Brook ≃	266	40.55 N	74.02 W
Coleshill, Eng., U.K.	44	52.30 N	1.42 W
Coleshill, Eng., U.K.	250	51.39 N	0.38 W
Coles Point	198	38.09 N	76.38 W
Colesville, Md., U.S.	274c	39.05 N	77.00 W
Colesville, N.J., U.S.	200	41.15 N	74.39 W
Coleto Creek ≃	186	28.41 N	97.01 W
Coleville, Sask., Can.	174	51.43 N	109.16 W
Coleville, Calif., U.S.	216	38.33 N	119.30 W
Colfax, Calif., U.S.	216	39.06 N	120.57 W
Colfax, Ill., U.S.	206	40.34 N	88.37 W
Colfax, Ind., U.S.	184	40.12 N	86.40 W
Colfax, Iowa, U.S.	180	41.41 N	93.14 W
Colfax, La., U.S.	184	31.31 N	92.42 W
Colfax, Wash., U.S.	192	46.53 N	117.22 W
Colfax, Wis., U.S.	180	45.00 N	91.44 W
Colfiorito	60	43.02 N	12.55 E
Colgate	206	43.12 N	88.12 W
Colgate Creek ≃	274b	39.15 N	76.32 W
Colgong	114	25.16 N	87.13 E
Colhué Huapi, Lago ⊜	244	45.30 S	68.48 W
Coliban ≃	159	36.56 S	144.33 E
Colibris, Pointe à ≻	231o	16.15 N	61.11 W
Colibris, Pointe des ≻	231o	16.17 N	61.06 W
Colico	54	46.08 N	9.22 E
Coligny, Fr.	54	46.23 N	5.21 E
Coligny, S. Afr.	148	26.17 S	26.15 E
Colijnsplaat	48	51.46 N	3.51 E
Colima, Méx.	190	32.25 N	115.05 W
Colima, Méx.	224	19.14 N	103.43 W
Colima □[3]	224	19.10 N	104.00 W
Colima, Nevado de ∧	224	19.33 N	103.38 W
Colimes ≃	236	1.32 S	80.00 W
Colin ≃	46	47.08 N	2.32 E
Colina	242	33.12 S	70.41 W
Colinas, Bra.	240	6.02 S	44.14 W
Colinas, Bra.	245	14.12 S	48.03 W
Colinet	176	47.13 N	53.33 W
Colinton, Austl.	161b	35.51 S	149.09 E
Colinton, Alta., Can.	172	54.37 N	113.15 W
Coll I	28	56.38 N	6.34 W
Colla	248	34.04 S	57.21 W
Colla, Arroyo ≃	248	34.19 S	57.20 W
Collagna	58	44.21 N	10.16 E
Collalbo (Klobenstein)	58	46.32 N	11.28 E
Collalto Sabino	60	42.08 N	13.02 E
Collamer	200	43.06 N	76.04 W
Collarenebri	156	29.33 S	148.35 E
Collarmele	60	42.03 N	13.38 E
Collaroy	264a	33.44 S	151.18 E
Collazzone	60	42.54 N	12.26 E
Collbran	190	39.14 N	107.57 W
Collecchio	58	44.45 N	10.13 E
Collecorvino	60	42.27 N	14.01 E
Colle di Tora	60	42.13 N	12.57 E
Colle di Val d'Elsa	60	43.25 N	11.07 E
Colleen Bawn	144	21.00 S	29.13 E
Colleferro	60	41.44 N	12.59 E
College	170	64.51 N	147.47 W
College City	216	39.00 N	122.00 W
College Corner	208	39.34 N	84.49 W
Collegedale	184	35.04 N	85.03 W
College Meadows	208	39.56 N	86.07 W
College Park, Ga., U.S.	182	33.39 N	84.27 W
College Park, Md., U.S.	198	39.00 N	76.55 W
College Park Airport ⊠	274c	38.58 N	76.55 W
College Place	192	46.03 N	118.23 W
College Point ◆[8]	266	40.47 N	73.51 W
College Station	212	30.37 N	96.21 W
Collegeville, Ind., U.S.	206	40.56 N	87.09 W
Collegeville, Pa., U.S.	198	40.11 N	75.27 W
Collégien	251	48.50 N	2.40 E
Collegno	56	45.05 N	7.34 E
Colle Isarco (Gossensass)	58	46.56 N	11.26 E
Collepardo	60	41.46 N	13.22 E
Collepietro	60	42.13 N	13.46 E
Collerina	156	29.41 S	146.38 E
Collesalvetti	60	43.35 N	10.28 E
Colle Sannita	60	41.22 N	14.50 E
Colletorto	60	41.40 N	14.58 E
Colleymount	172	54.01 N	126.09 W
Colleyville	212	32.53 N	97.09 W
Colli a Volturno	60	41.36 N	14.06 E
Colli del Tronto	60	42.52 N	13.44 E
Colli di Monte Bove	60	42.06 N	13.09 E
Collie	158a	33.21 S	116.09 E
Collie ≃	158a	33.18 S	115.44 E
Collier □[6]	210	26.10 N	81.22 W
Collier Bay C	150	16.10 S	124.15 E
Collier Bridge ◆[5]	210	26.57 N	82.04 W
Collier City	210	26.14 N	80.09 W
Collier Range ⩘	152	24.43 S	119.12 E
Collier Row ◆[8]	250	51.36 N	0.10 E
Colliers	204	40.22 N	80.33 W
Collier-Seminole State Park ♠	210	25.59 N	81.36 W
Colliersville	200	42.29 N	74.59 W
Collierville	184	35.03 N	89.40 W
Collin □[6]	212	33.07 N	96.35 W
Collina, Passo della)(	60	44.01 N	10.56 E
Collingbourne Kingston	44	51.18 N	1.13 W
Collingdale	198	39.55 N	75.17 W
Collings Pass)(	148	28.13 S	29.38 E
Collingswood	275	39.55 N	75.04 W
Collingwood, Austl.	264b	37.48 S	145.00 E
Collingwood, Ont., Can.	202	44.29 N	80.13 W
Collingwood, N.Z.	162	40.40 S	172.41 E
Collingwood Bay C	154	9.20 S	149.30 E
Collins, Ga., U.S.	182	32.11 N	82.07 W
Collins, Iowa, U.S.	180	41.54 N	93.18 W
Collins, Miss., U.S.	184	31.39 N	89.33 W
Collins, N.Y., U.S.	200	42.30 N	78.55 W
Collins, Ohio, U.S.	204	41.16 N	82.30 W
Collins ≃	184	35.48 N	85.37 W
Collins, Mount ∧[2]	180	47.51 N	80.59 W
Collins Bay	202	44.15 N	76.36 W
Collinsburg	204	40.13 N	79.46 W
Collins Center	200	42.30 N	78.51 W
Collins Lake ⊜	202	44.22 N	76.27 W
Collins Park	198	39.41 N	75.33 W
Collinston	184	32.41 N	91.52 W
Collinsville, Austl.	156	20.34 S	147.51 E
Collinsville, Ala., U.S.	184	34.16 N	85.52 W
Collinsville, Calif., U.S.	272	38.05 N	121.51 W
Collinsville, Conn., U.S.	197	41.49 N	72.55 W
Collinsville, Ill., U.S.	209	38.41 N	89.51 W
Collinsville, Miss., U.S.	184	32.30 N	88.51 W
Collinsville, N.J., U.S.	266	40.49 N	74.28 W
Collinsville, Okla., U.S.	186	36.22 N	95.51 W
Collinwood	184	35.10 N	87.44 W
Collio	58	45.48 N	10.20 E
Collipulli	242	37.57 S	72.26 W
Collique	276d	11.55 S	77.03 W
Collister	192	43.38 N	116.15 W
Collo	138	37.00 N	6.34 E
Collobrières	56	43.14 N	6.18 E
Collombey	54	46.16 N	6.57 E
Collomsville	200	41.09 N	77.09 W
Collon	42	53.47 N	6.29 W
Collonges	54	46.08 N	5.54 E
Collooney	28	54.11 N	8.29 W
Colma	216	37.41 N	122.28 W
Colma Creek ≃	272	37.38 N	122.23 W
Colman	188	43.59 N	96.49 W
Colmar	54	48.05 N	7.22 E
Colmar Manor	274c	38.56 N	76.57 W
Colmars	56	44.11 N	6.38 E
Colmenar	34	36.54 N	4.20 W
Colmenar de Oreja	34	40.06 N	3.23 W
Colmenar Viejo	34	40.40 N	3.46 W
Colmeneros	224	18.06 N	101.40 W
Colmesneil	184	30.54 N	94.25 W
Colmnitz	50	50.54 N	13.31 E
Colmonell	42	55.08 N	4.55 W
Coln ≃	44	51.42 N	1.42 W
Colnbrook	250	51.29 N	0.31 W
Colne	42	53.52 N	2.09 W
Colne ≃, Eng., U.K.	44	51.48 N	1.01 E
Colne ≃, Eng., U.K.	250	51.26 N	0.30 W
Colnett, Cabo ≻	222	30.58 N	116.19 W
Colney Heath	250	51.44 N	0.15 W
Colney Street	250	51.42 N	0.20 W
Colo	180	42.01 N	93.19 W
Colo ≃	160	33.26 S	150.53 E
Cologna Veneta	58	45.18 N	11.23 E
Cologne → Köln, B.R.D.	52	50.56 N	6.59 E
Cologne, Minn., U.S.	180	44.47 N	93.46 W
Cologne, N.J., U.S.	198	39.30 N	74.37 W
Cologno al Serio	56	45.37 N	9.42 E
Cologno Monzese	256b	45.32 N	9.17 E
Cololo, Nevado ∧	238	14.53 S	69.06 W
Coloma, Calif., U.S.	216	38.48 N	120.53 W
Coloma, Mich., U.S.	206	42.11 N	86.19 W
Coloma, Wis., U.S.	180	44.02 N	89.31 W
Coloma, Ensenada de C	230p	22.13 N	83.34 W
Colomb-Béchar → Béchar	138	31.37 N	2.13 W
Colombes	46	48.55 N	2.15 E
Colombey-les-Belles	54	48.32 N	5.54 E
Colombey-les-Deux-Eglises	54	48.13 N	4.53 E
Colombia, Col.	236	3.24 N	74.49 W
Colombia, Méx.	186	27.42 N	99.45 W
Colombia □[1]	232		
	236	4.00 N	72.00 W
Colombian Basin ✢[1]	16	13.00 N	75.00 W
Colombie → Colombia □[1]	236	4.00 N	72.00 W
Colombie britannique → British Columbia □[4]	172	54.00 N	125.00 W
Colombier	54	46.58 N	6.52 E
Colombo, Bra.	242	25.17 S	49.14 W
Colombo, S. Lan.	112	6.56 N	79.51 E
Colome	188	43.15 N	99.43 W
Colón, Arg.	242	33.53 S	61.07 W
Colón, Arg.	242	32.13 S	58.08 W
Colón, Cuba	230p	22.43 N	80.54 W
Colón, Pan.	226	9.22 N	79.54 W
Colon, Mich., U.S.	206	41.57 N	85.19 W
Colón, Ur.	242	33.53 S	54.43 W
Colón, Ur.	248	34.48 S	56.14 W
Colón □[4]	226	9.00 N	80.20 W
Colón □[5]	226	15.40 N	85.30 W
Colón, Archipiélago de → Galápagos □[4]	236a	0.30 S	90.30 W
Colón, Archipiélago de (Galapagos Islands) II	236a	0.30 S	90.30 W
Colón, Cementerio ◆	276b	23.08 N	82.23 W
Colón, Isla I	226	9.24 N	82.17 W
Colón, Montañas de ⩘	226	14.55 N	84.45 W
Colón, Teatro ♠	278	34.36 S	58.23 W
Colona	152	31.38 S	132.05 E
Colonard-Corubert	46	48.25 N	0.39 E
Colonarie ≃	231h	13.14 N	61.06 W
Colonarie Bay C	231h	13.14 N	61.07 W
Colonelganj	114	27.08 N	81.42 E
Colonet	194	31.05 N	116.10 W
Colongulac, Lake ⊜	159	38.10 S	143.11 E
Colonia → Köln, B.R.D.	52	50.56 N	6.59 E
Colonia, N.J., U.S.	200	40.35 N	74.18 W
Colonia □[5]	248	34.10 S	57.30 W
Colônia ≃	245	15.11 S	39.45 W
Colonia, Aeropuerto ⊠	248	34.28 S	57.49 W
Colonia, Cuchilla de la ⩘[2]	248	34.15 S	57.35 W
Colonia Agrícola Turén	236	9.15 N	69.05 W
Colonia Alvear Oeste	242	35.00 S	67.40 W
Colonia Anáhuac	222	28.25 N	106.40 W
Colonia Benjamín Aceval	242	24.58 S	57.34 W
Colonia Caroya	242	31.02 S	64.05 W
Colonia Cristóbal Obregón	224	16.20 N	93.30 W
Colonia del Sacramento	248	34.28 S	57.51 W
Colonia Dora	242	28.36 S	62.57 W
Colonia Elisa	242	26.56 S	59.32 W
Colonia Guadalupe	194	32.04 N	116.37 W
Colonia Hogar Ricardo Gutiérrez	278	34.51 S	58.51 W
Colonia José Mármol	242	26.59 S	60.44 W
Colonial Acres	198	39.31 N	76.20 W
Colonia Las Heras	244	46.33 S	68.57 W
Colonia Lavalleja	242	31.06 S	57.01 W
Colonial Beach	198	38.15 N	76.58 W
Colonial Crest	198	40.20 N	76.50 W
Colônia Leopoldina	240	8.57 S	35.39 W
Colonial Heights, Ill., U.S.	268	41.05 N	88.01 W
Colonial Heights, Va., U.S.	198	37.15 N	77.25 W
Colonial Manor	275	39.51 N	75.09 W
Colonial National Historical Park ♠	198	37.12 N	76.45 W
Colonial Park	198	40.18 N	76.49 W
Colonial Village, N.Y., U.S.	200	43.08 N	78.58 W
Colonial Village, Pa., U.S.	275	40.04 N	75.24 W
Colonial Williamsburg ⊥	198	37.16 N	76.42 W
Colonia Morelos	190	30.50 N	109.10 W
Colonia Nicolich	248	34.50 S	56.02 W
Colonia Progreso, Méx.	194	32.35 N	115.37 W
Colonia Progreso, Méx.	224	23.48 N	103.18 W
Colonia Providencia	230m	17.59 N	66.00 W
Colonias Unidas	242	26.42 S	59.38 W
Colonia Valdense	248	34.20 S	57.14 W
Colonia Vicente Guerrero	222	30.45 N	116.00 W
Colonia Villafañe	242	26.12 S	59.05 W
Colonie	200	42.43 N	73.50 W
Colon Koret	142	0.34 N	23.28 E
Colonna	257a	41.50 N	12.45 E
Colonna, Capo ≻	36	39.02 N	17.11 E
Colonnata	58	44.05 N	10.10 E
Colonsay	174	51.59 N	105.53 W
Colonsay I	28	56.05 N	6.10 W
Colony	188	38.04 N	95.22 W
Colora	198	39.40 N	76.06 W
Colorada, Punta ≻	278	34.45 S	58.06 W
Coloradas, Lomas ⩘[2]	244	43.24 S	67.24 W
Colorado, C.R.	226	10.46 N	83.35 W
Colorado, Hond.	226	15.47 N	87.19 W
Colorado, Alaska, U.S.	170	63.09 N	149.26 W
Colorado □[6]	212	29.40 N	96.30 W
Colorado □[3]	168	39.30 N	105.30 W
Colorado ≃, Arg.	234	39.50 S	62.08 W
Colorado ≃, Bra.	238	13.03 S	62.20 W
Colorado ≃, N.A.	190	31.54 N	114.57 W
Colorado ≃, Tex., U.S.	186	28.36 N	95.58 W
Colorado ≊	276a	19.24 N	98.59 W
Colorado, Arroyo ∨	190	34.58 N	107.13 W
Colorado, Cerro ∧, Arg.	244	45.02 S	69.38 W
Colorado, Cerro ∧, Chile	276e	33.24 S	70.45 W
Colorado, Cerro ∧, Méx.	222	31.31 N	115.31 W
Colorado, Cerro ∧, Perú	276d	12.07 S	76.55 W
Colorado, North Fork ≃	190	40.12 N	105.50 W
Colorado, Williams Fork ≃	190	40.03 N	106.11 W
Colorado City, Ariz., U.S.	190	36.58 N	112.58 W
Colorado City, Tex., U.S.	186	32.24 N	100.52 W
Colorado de Abajo	186	26.28 N	99.54 W
Colorado National Monument ♠	190	39.04 N	108.25 W
Colorado Plateau ⩘[1]	190	36.30 N	108.00 W
Colorado River Aqueduct ≊[1]	218	33.50 N	117.23 W
Colorado River Indian Reservation ◆[4]	190	34.00 N	114.25 W
Colorado Springs	190	38.50 N	104.49 W
Colorines	224	19.07 N	100.12 W
Colorno	58	44.56 N	10.23 E
Colosseo ⊥	257a	41.54 N	12.29 E
Colotepec ≃	224	15.47 N	97.03 W
Colotlán	224	22.06 N	103.16 W
Colotlipa	224	17.25 N	99.09 W
Colo Vale	160	34.24 S	150.29 E
Čolpon	75	42.12 N	75.28 E
Čolpon-Ata	75	42.40 N	77.06 E
Colpoy Bay C	202	44.47 N	81.05 W
Colquechaca	238	18.40 S	66.01 W
Colquencha	238	17.00 S	68.17 W
Colquiri	238	17.25 S	67.08 W
Colquitt	182	31.10 N	84.44 W
Colsterworth	44	52.48 N	0.37 W
Colstrip	192	45.53 N	106.38 W
Colt	184	35.08 N	90.49 W
Colta	238	15.10 S	73.18 W
Coltauco	242	34.18 S	71.06 W
Coltishall	44	52.44 N	1.22 E
Colton, Austl.	152	33.29 S	134.56 E
Colton, Calif., U.S.	218	34.04 N	117.20 W
Colton, Ohio, U.S.	206	41.28 N	83.57 W
Colton, Oreg., U.S.	214	45.10 N	12.26 W
Colton, S. Dak., U.S.	188	43.47 N	96.56 W
Coltons Point	198	38.14 N	76.45 W
Colts Neck	198	40.17 N	74.11 W
Coltsville Center	204	41.05 N	80.34 W
Columbia, Ala., U.S.	182	31.18 N	85.07 W
Columbia, Calif., U.S.	216	38.02 N	120.24 W
Columbia, Conn., U.S.	197	41.42 N	72.18 W
Columbia, Ill., U.S.	209	38.27 N	90.12 W
Columbia, Ind., U.S.	208	39.35 N	85.12 W
Columbia, Ky., U.S.	184	37.06 N	85.18 W
Columbia, La., U.S.	184	32.06 N	92.05 W
Columbia, Md., U.S.	198	39.13 N	76.52 W
Columbia, Miss., U.S.	184	31.15 N	89.56 W
Columbia, Mo., U.S.	209	38.57 N	92.20 W
Columbia, N.J., U.S.	200	40.56 N	75.06 W
Columbia, N.C., U.S.	182	35.55 N	76.15 W
Columbia, Pa., U.S.	198	40.02 N	76.30 W
Columbia, S.C., U.S.	182	34.00 N	81.03 W
Columbia, Tenn., U.S.	184	35.37 N	87.02 W
Columbia □[6], N.Y., U.S.	200	42.15 N	73.47 W
Columbia □[6], Oreg., U.S.	214	45.57 N	123.03 W
Columbia □[6], Pa., U.S.	200	41.00 N	76.28 W
Columbia ≃	166	46.15 N	124.05 W
Columbia, Cape ≻	16	83.08 N	70.35 W
Columbia, Mount ∧	172	52.09 N	117.25 W
Columbia Airport ⊠	269a	41.19 N	81.58 W
Columbia Basin ⌣[1]	192	46.45 N	119.05 W
Columbia Center	269a	41.19 N	81.56 W
Columbia City, Ind., U.S.	206	41.10 N	85.29 W
Columbia City, Oreg., U.S.	214	45.55 N	122.51 W
Columbia Cross Roads	200	41.50 N	76.48 W
Columbia Falls, Maine, U.S.	178	44.39 N	67.44 W
Columbia Falls, Mont., U.S.	192	48.23 N	114.11 W
Columbia Heights	214	46.09 N	122.58 W
Columbia Icefield ⊓	172	52.10 N	117.30 W
Columbia Lake ⊜	172	50.15 N	115.57 W
Columbia Lake Indian Reserve ◆[4]	172	50.25 N	115.57 W
Columbia Mountains ⩘	172	51.30 N	118.30 W
Columbiana, Ala., U.S.	184	33.11 N	86.36 W
Columbiana, Ohio, U.S.	204	40.53 N	80.42 W
Columbiana □[6]	204	40.47 N	80.46 W
Columbia Plateau ⩘[1]	192	44.00 N	117.30 W
Columbia Regional Airport ⊠	209	38.50 N	92.13 W
Columbia Road Reservoir ⊜[1]	188	45.45 N	98.15 W
Columbia State Historical Park ♠	216	38.02 N	120.25 W
Columbia Station	204	41.20 N	81.57 W
Columbia University ʊ[2]	266	40.48 N	73.58 W
Columbiaville, Mich., U.S.	180	43.09 N	83.25 W
Columbiaville, N.Y., U.S.	200	42.19 N	73.45 W
Columbine, Cape ≻	148	32.47 S	18.52 E
Columbretes, Islas II	34	39.52 N	0.40 E
Columbus, Ga., U.S.	182	32.29 N	84.59 W
Columbus, Ind., U.S.	208	39.13 N	85.55 W
Columbus, Kans., U.S.	188	37.10 N	94.50 W
Columbus, Miss., U.S.	184	33.30 N	88.25 W
Columbus, Mont., U.S.	192	45.38 N	109.15 W
Columbus, Nebr., U.S.	188	41.25 N	97.22 W
Columbus, N.J., U.S.	198	40.04 N	74.43 W
Columbus, N. Mex., U.S.	190	31.50 N	107.38 W
Columbus, N.C., U.S.	182	35.15 N	82.12 W
Columbus, N. Dak., U.S.	188	48.54 N	102.47 W
Columbus, Ohio, U.S.	204	39.57 N	83.00 W
Columbus, Pa., U.S.	204	41.56 N	79.35 W
Columbus, Tex., U.S.	212	29.42 N	96.33 W
Columbus, Wis., U.S.	180	43.21 N	89.01 W
Columbus Air Force Base ■	184	33.38 N	88.26 W
Columbus Grove	206	40.55 N	84.04 W
Columbus Junction	180	41.17 N	91.22 W
Columbus Park ♠	268	41.53 N	87.47 W
Columbus Point ≻, Ba.	228	24.08 N	75.16 W
Columbus Point ≻, Trin.	231r	11.08 N	60.48 W
Columbus Salt Marsh ☷	194	38.04 N	117.58 W
Coluna	245	18.14 S	42.50 W
Colusa	216	39.13 N	122.01 W
Colusa □[6]	216	39.13 N	122.01 W
Colusa Trough ≊	216	39.02 N	121.59 W
Colver	204	40.33 N	78.47 W
Colville, N.Z.	162	36.38 S	175.28 E
Colville, Wash., U.S.	192	48.33 N	117.54 W
Colville ≃, Alaska, U.S.	170	70.25 N	150.30 W
Colville ≃, Wash., U.S.	192	48.37 N	118.05 W
Colville, Cape ≻	162	36.28 S	175.21 E
Colville Indian Reservation ◆[4]	192	48.15 N	119.00 W
Colville Lake ⊜	170	67.10 N	126.00 W
Colwell	42	55.04 N	2.04 W
Colwood	214	48.26 N	123.29 W
Colwyn	275	39.55 N	75.15 W
Colwyn Bay	42	53.18 N	3.43 W
Colyton, Austl.	264a	33.47 S	150.48 E
Colyton, Eng., U.K.	44	50.44 N	3.04 W
Comacchio	60	44.42 N	12.11 E
Comacchio, Valli di C	60	44.38 N	12.06 E
Comacho	246	22.20 S	47.13 W
Comal	105a	6.55 S	109.31 E
Comala	224	19.19 N	103.45 W
Comalapa, Guat.	226	14.44 N	90.53 W
Comalapa, Nic.	226	12.17 N	85.31 W
Comalcalco	224	18.16 N	93.13 W
Comales	222	26.10 N	98.56 W
Comalito, Cerro ∧	224	20.30 N	104.36 W
Comallo	244	41.02 S	70.16 W
Comallo, Arroyo ≃	244	40.29 S	70.12 W
Coman, Mount ∧	9	74.02 S	65.04 W
Comanche, Okla., U.S.	186	34.22 N	97.58 W
Comanche, Tex., U.S.	186	31.54 N	98.36 W
Comanche Creek ≃	188	39.53 N	104.19 W
Comandante Fontana	242	25.20 S	59.41 W
Comandante Leal	242	30.53 S	65.47 W
Comandante Luis Piedrabuena	244	49.59 S	68.54 W
Comandante Nicanor Otamendi	242	38.07 S	57.51 W
Comănești	38	46.25 N	26.26 E
Comanja de Corona	224	21.19 N	101.42 W
Comarapa	238	17.54 S	64.29 W
Comas, Perú	238	11.46 S	75.02 W
Comas, Perú	276d	11.57 S	77.04 W
Comayagua	226	14.25 N	87.37 W
Comayagua □[5]	226	14.30 N	87.40 W
Comayagua, Montañas de ⩘	226	14.23 N	87.26 W
Combahee ≃	182	32.30 N	80.31 W
Combarbalá	242	31.11 S	71.02 W
Combé	240	5.30 N	55.10 W
Combeaufontaine	54	47.43 N	5.53 E
Combe Martin	44	51.13 N	4.02 W
Comber, Ont., Can.	204	42.14 N	82.33 W
Comber, N. Ire., U.K.	42	54.33 N	5.45 W
Comberbach	252	53.17 N	2.32 W
Combermere Bay C	100	19.37 N	93.34 E
Comberton	44	52.11 N	0.02 E
Combe Seamount ✢[3]	14	12.30 S	177.30 W
Comblain-au-Pont	52	50.28 N	5.35 E
Combles	46	50.01 N	2.52 E
Combloux	56	45.54 N	6.39 E
Combourg	32	48.25 N	1.45 W
Comboyne	156	31.36 S	152.29 E
Comboyuro Point ≻	161a	27.04 S	153.24 E
Combres	46	48.19 N	1.04 E
Combronde	32	45.59 N	3.05 E
Combs	252	53.18 N	1.57 W
Combs-la-Ville	46	48.40 N	2.34 E
Combs Reservoir ⊜[1]	252	53.19 N	1.57 W
Comburg ʊ[1]	52	49.06 N	9.44 E
Comb Wash ∨	190	37.13 N	109.42 W
Come by Chance	176	47.51 N	53.58 W
Comeglians	58	46.31 N	12.52 E
Comelico Superiore	58	46.35 N	12.30 E
Comemoração ≃	238	11.45 S	60.56 W
Comendador Gomes	245	19.41 S	49.05 W
Comer	182	34.04 N	83.08 W
Comercinho	245	16.19 S	41.47 W
Comerío	230m	18.13 N	66.14 W
Comet	156	23.37 S	148.33 E
Comet ≃	156	23.34 S	148.32 E
Cometela	146	21.51 S	34.29 E
Comfort, N.C., U.S.	182	35.00 N	77.30 W
Comfort, Tex., U.S.	186	29.58 N	98.49 W
Comfort, Cape ≻	166	65.08 N	83.21 W
Comfort, Point ≻	266	40.27 N	74.08 W
Comfrey	188	44.07 N	94.54 W
Comilla	114	23.27 N	91.12 E
Comines	46	50.46 N	3.01 E
Comino, Capo ≻	36	40.31 N	9.50 E
Comiskey Park ♠	268	41.50 N	87.38 W
Comiso	36	36.56 N	14.37 E
Comitán [de Domínguez]	222	16.15 N	92.08 W
Comloșu Mare	38	45.54 N	20.38 E
Commack	200	40.51 N	73.18 W
Commencement Bay C	214	47.17 N	122.28 W
Commentry	32	46.17 N	2.44 E
Commerce, Ga., U.S.	182	34.12 N	83.28 W
Commerce, Mich., U.S.	206	42.34 N	83.30 W
Commerce, Okla., U.S.	186	36.56 N	94.53 W
Commerce, Tex., U.S.	186	33.15 N	95.54 W
Commerce City	188	39.49 N	104.55 W
Commerce Lake ⊜	271	42.35 N	83.30 W
Commerciale Luigi Bocconi, Università ʊ[2]	256b	45.26 N	9.11 E
Commercial Point	208	39.46 N	83.04 W
Commercy	52	48.45 N	5.35 E
Commewijne □[5]	240	5.25 N	54.50 W
Comminges ◆[1]	32	43.15 N	0.45 E
Committee Bay C	166	68.30 N	86.30 W
Commodore	204	40.43 N	78.57 W
Commondale	148	27.20 S	30.56 E
Common Edge	252	53.47 N	3.02 W
Commonwealth Bay C	9	66.54 S	142.40 E
Commonwealth Range ⩘	9	84.15 S	172.20 E
Commoron Creek ≃	156	28.22 S	150.08 E
Community Center	218	34.16 N	118.44 W
Como, Austl.	264a	34.00 S	151.04 E
Como, It.	56	45.47 N	9.05 E
Como, Miss., U.S.	184	34.31 N	90.03 W
Como, N.C., U.S.	198	36.30 N	77.00 W
Como, Tex., U.S.	212	33.03 N	95.28 W
Como, Wis., U.S.	206	42.37 N	88.28 W
Como □[4]	54	45.59 N	9.13 E
Como ≃	142	0.09 N	9.50 E
Como, Lago di ⊜	54	46.00 N	9.20 E
Como, Lake ⊜	206	42.36 N	88.29 W
Como, Mount ∧	216	39.02 N	119.28 W
Comodoro Py	242	35.19 S	60.31 W
Comodoro Rivadavia	244	45.52 S	67.30 W
Como Lake ⊜	180	47.55 N	83.30 W
Comologno	54	46.12 N	8.34 E
Comondú	222	26.03 N	111.46 W
Comonfort	224	20.43 N	100.46 W
Comoras → Comoros □[1]	147a	12.10 S	44.15 E
Comores → Comoros □[1]	147a	12.10 S	44.15 E
Comorin, Cape ≻	112	8.04 N	77.34 E
Comoros □[1]	128		
	147a	12.10 S	44.10 E
Comox	172	49.40 N	124.55 W
Companhia Siderúrgica Nacional ʊ[3]	246	22.31 S	44.07 W
Compans	251	49.00 N	2.40 E
Compatsch	54	46.58 N	10.25 E
Compiègne	46	49.25 N	2.50 E
Compo Cove C	266	41.07 N	73.21 W
Compostela, Méx.	224	21.15 N	104.53 W
Compostela, Pil.	106	7.40 N	126.02 E
Comprida, Ilha I, Bra.	242	24.50 S	47.42 W
Comprida, Ilha I, Bra.	277a	23.02 S	43.12 W
Comps-sur-Artuby	56	43.43 N	6.30 E
Compstall	252	53.25 N	2.03 W
Compton, Eng., U.K.	250	51.13 N	0.38 W
Compton, Calif., U.S.	218	33.54 N	118.13 W
Compton, Ill., U.S.	206	41.42 N	89.05 W
Compton □[6]	196	45.20 N	71.25 W
Compton Airport ⊠	270	33.53 N	118.15 W
Compton Creek ≃, Calif., U.S.	270	33.50 N	118.12 W
Compton Creek ≃, N.J., U.S.	266	40.26 N	74.05 W
Comptonville	263d	26.17 S	27.58 E
Comstock, Mich., U.S.	206	42.16 N	85.31 W
Comstock, Nebr., U.S.	188	41.33 N	99.14 W
Comstock, Tex., U.S.	186	29.41 N	101.11 W
Comstock Park	206	43.02 N	85.40 W
Comunanza	60	42.57 N	13.25 E
Con ≃, S.S.S.R.	66	52.54 N	36.00 E
Con ≃, Viet.	100	19.04 N	105.00 E
Čona ≃	64	62.54 N	111.06 E
Conakry	140	9.31 N	13.43 W
Conambo ≃	236	2.07 S	76.03 W
Conanicut Island I	197	41.32 N	71.21 W
Cona Niyeu	244	41.53 S	67.00 W
Conara Junction	156	41.50 S	147.26 E
Conasauga ≃	182	34.33 N	84.55 W
Conaskonk Point ≻	266	40.27 N	74.11 W
Conca ≃	60	43.58 N	12.43 E
Concarán	242	32.34 S	65.15 W
Concarneau	32	47.52 N	3.55 W
Conceição, Bra.	238	7.24 S	58.05 W
Conceição, Bra.	240	7.33 S	38.31 W
Conceição, Bra.	246	22.25 S	47.11 W
Conceição, Moç.	146	18.45 S	36.10 E
Conceição ≃	245	12.24 S	46.57 W
Conceição, Cachoeira da ⌊	238	9.34 S	64.22 W
Conceição, Ilha da I	277a	22.52 S	43.07 W
Conceição, Riacho ≃	240	6.34 S	39.52 W
Conceição da Aparecida	245	21.06 S	46.12 W
Conceição da Barra	245	18.35 S	39.45 W
Conceição da Ibitipoca	246	21.43 S	43.55 W
Conceição da Pedra	246	22.09 S	45.27 W
Conceição das Alagoas	245	19.55 S	48.23 W
Conceição de Ipanema	245	19.55 S	41.41 W
Conceição de Jacareí	246	23.02 S	44.09 W
Conceição do Almeida	245	12.48 S	39.12 W
Conceição do Araguaia	240	8.15 S	49.17 W
Conceição do Canindé	240	7.54 S	41.34 W
Conceição do Coité	240	11.33 S	39.16 W
Conceição do Formoso	246	21.25 S	43.21 W
Conceição do Mato Dentro	245	19.01 S	43.25 W
Conceição do Maú	236	3.35 N	59.53 W
Conceição do Norte	245	12.13 S	47.18 W
Conceição do Rio Verde	246	21.53 S	45.05 W
Conceição dos Ouros	246	22.25 S	45.47 W
Concepción, Arg.	242	27.20 S	65.35 W
Concepción, Arg.	242	28.23 S	57.53 W
Concepción, Bol.	238	16.15 S	62.04 W
Concepción, Bol.	238	11.29 S	66.31 W
Concepción, Chile	242	36.50 S	73.03 W
Concepción, Col.	236	6.46 N	72.42 W
Concepción, Guat.	226	15.37 N	91.41 W
Concepción, Gui. Ecu.	142	3.23 N	8.46 E
Concepción, Pan.	226	8.31 N	82.37 W
Concepción, Para.	242	23.25 S	57.17 W
Concepción, Perú	238	11.55 S	75.17 W
Concepcion, Pil.	106	11.13 N	123.06 E
Concepcion, Pil.	106	10.42 N	123.03 E
Concepcion, Pil.	106	12.24 N	122.06 E
Concepcion, Pil.	106	15.19 N	120.39 E
Concepción □[4]	242	37.00 S	72.30 W
Concepción □[5]	242	23.00 S	57.00 W
Concepción, Bahía C	222	26.39 N	111.48 W
Concepción, Estrecho del ɯ	244	50.30 S	74.55 W
Concepción, Laguna ⊜	238	17.29 S	61.25 W
Concepción, Río de la ≃	222	30.32 N	113.02 W
Concepción, Volcán ∧[1]	226	11.34 N	85.37 W
Concepcion Bay C	106	11.15 N	123.07 E
Concepción de Ataco	226	13.52 N	89.51 W
Concepción de Buenos Aires	224	19.58 N	103.16 W
Concepción de la Sierra	242	27.59 S	55.31 W
Concepción de la Vega → La Vega	228	19.13 N	70.31 W
Concepcion del Oro	222	24.38 N	101.25 W
Concepción del Uruguay	242	32.29 S	58.14 W
Concepción Quezaltepeque	226	14.06 N	88.58 W
Conception, Point ≻	194	34.27 N	120.27 W
Conception Bay C, Newf., Can.	176	47.45 N	53.00 W
Conception Bay C, Namibia	146	23.53 S	14.28 E
Concession	144	17.22 S	30.57 E
Conchagua	226	13.19 N	87.52 W
Conchagua, Volcán de ∧[1]	226	13.14 N	87.46 W
Conchal	246	22.20 S	47.10 W
Conchal, Ribeirão do ≃	246	22.20 S	47.10 W
Conchalí	276e	33.24 S	70.39 W
Conchas ≃	186	35.23 N	104.18 W
Conchas Dam	186	35.22 N	104.11 W
Conchas Lake ⊜[1]	186	35.25 N	104.14 W
Conche	176	50.53 N	55.54 W
Conches	32	48.51 N	2.43 E
Conches-en-Ouche	46	48.58 N	0.56 E
Conchi	242	22.02 S	68.38 W
Conchillas	248	34.15 S	58.04 W
Conchitas, Arroyo ≃	278	34.45 S	58.09 W
Concho	190	34.28 N	109.36 W
Conchos ≃, Méx.	222	29.35 N	104.25 W
Conchos ≃, Méx.	222	25.07 N	98.32 W
Concise	54	46.51 N	6.43 E
Conco	58	45.48 N	11.36 E
Concón	242	32.55 S	71.31 W
Conconongon Point ≻	106	12.14 N	120.13 E
Concord, Austl.	264a	33.52 S	151.06 E
Concord, Ont., Can.	265b	43.48 N	79.29 W
Concord, Calif., U.S.	216	37.59 N	122.02 W
Concord, Ga., U.S.	182	33.05 N	84.26 W
Concord, Ill., U.S.	209	39.49 N	90.22 W
Concord, Ky., U.S.	208	38.41 N	83.30 W
Concord, Mass., U.S.	197	42.27 N	71.21 W
Concord, Mich., U.S.	206	42.10 N	84.38 W
Concord, Mo., U.S.	209	38.31 N	90.23 W
Concord, N.H., U.S.	178	43.12 N	71.32 W
Concord, N.C., U.S.	182	35.25 N	80.35 W
Concord, Pa., U.S.	204	40.15 N	77.42 W
Concord, Tex., U.S.	212	31.16 N	96.09 W
Concord ≃	273	42.39 N	71.18 W
Concord Battleground ⊥	273	42.28 N	71.21 W
Concordia, Arg.	242	31.24 S	58.02 W
Concórdia, Bra.	236	4.35 S	66.35 W
Concórdia, Bra.	242	27.14 S	52.01 W
Concordia, Méx.	222	25.47 N	103.07 W
Concordia, Méx.	224	23.17 N	106.04 W
Concordia, Kans., U.S.	188	39.34 N	97.39 W
Concordia, Mo., U.S.	184	38.59 N	93.34 W
Concordia Gardens	206	41.09 N	85.08 W
Concordia Sagitaria ⊥	58	45.45 N	12.51 E
Concordia sulla Secchia	58	44.55 N	10.59 E
Concord Naval Weapons Station ■	272	38.03 N	122.02 W
Concordville	275	39.53 N	75.31 W
Concord West	264a	33.51 S	151.05 E
Concorezzo	56	45.35 N	9.20 E
Concrete	214	48.32 N	121.45 W
Con-cuong	100	19.02 N	104.54 E
Conda	142	11.06 S	14.20 E
Condamine	156	26.56 S	150.08 E
Condat-en-Féniers	32	45.21 N	2.46 E
Condé, Ang.	142	10.50 S	14.37 E
Conde, Bra.	245	11.49 S	37.37 W
Condé, Fr.	32	48.51 N	0.33 W
Conde, S. Dak., U.S.	188	45.09 N	98.06 W
Condécourt	251	49.02 N	1.57 E
Condé-en-Brie	46	49.00 N	3.33 E
Condega	226	13.21 N	86.24 W
Condega, Punta ≻	226	13.06 N	87.25 W
Condeixa	240	0.54 S	48.36 W
Condé-sur-l'Escaut	46	50.27 N	3.35 E
Condè-sur-Vesgre	251	48.45 N	1.40 E
Condeúba	245	14.53 S	41.59 W
Conde Villa Señor	276d	12.02 S	77.05 W
Condino	58	45.53 N	10.36 E
Condobolin	156	33.05 S	147.09 E
Condom	32	43.58 N	0.22 E
Condon	192	45.14 N	120.11 W
Condoto, Col.	236	5.06 N	76.37 W
Condoto, Perú	236	4.30 S	74.55 W

English	Deutsch	Español	Français	Português
≃ River	Fluss	Río	Rivière	Rio
≊ Canal	Kanal	Canal	Canal	Canal
⌊ Waterfall, Rapids	Wasserfall, Stromschnellen	Cascada, Rápidos	Chute d'eau, Rapides	Cascata, Rápidos
ɯ Strait	Meeresstrasse	Estrecho	Détroit	Estreito
C Bay, Gulf	Bucht, Golf	Bahía, Golfo	Baie, Golfe	Baía, Golfo
⊜ Lake, Lakes	See, Seen	Lago, Lagos	Lac, Lacs	Lago, Lagos
☷ Swamp	Sumpf	Pantano	Marais	Pântano
⊓ Ice Features, Glacier	Eis- und Gletscherformen	Accidentes Glaciales	Formes glaciaires	Acidentes Glaciares
⫧ Other Hydrographic Features	Andere Hydrographische Objekte	Otros Elementos Hidrográficos	Autres données hydrographiques	Outros Elementos Hidrográficos
✢ Submarine Features	Untermeerische Objekte	Accidentes Submarinos	Formes de relief sous-marin	Acidentes Submarinos
□ Political Unit	Politische Einheit	Unidad Politica	Entité politique	Unidade Política
ʊ Cultural Institution	Kulturelle Institution	Institución Cultural	Institution culturelle	Instituição Cultural
⊥ Historical Site	Historische Stätte	Sitio Histórico	Site historique	Sitio Histórico
♠ Recreational Site	Erholungs- und Ferienort	Sitio de Recreo	Centre de loisirs	Sítio de Lazer
⊠ Airport	Flughafen	Aeropuerto	Aéroport	Aeroporto
■ Military Installation	Militäranlage	Instalación Militar	Installation militaire	Instalação Militar
◆ Miscellaneous	Verschiedenes	Misceláneo	Divers	Miscelânea

Condove 56 45.07 N 7.18 E
Condrieu 56 45.27 N 4.46 E
Condroz □[9] 52 50.25 N 5.00 E
Cone 186 33.48 N 101.23 W
Conecuh ≃ 184 30.58 N 87.14 W
Conegliano 58 45.53 N 12.18 E
Conejos 190 37.05 N 106.01 W
Conejos ≃ 190 37.18 N 105.44 W
Conemaugh 204 40.24 N 78.52 W
Conemaugh ≃ 204 40.28 N 79.27 W
Conemaugh River Lake ⊜[1] 204 40.28 N 79.17 W
Cone Mountain Λ 170 66.12 N 156.03 W
Conero, Monte Λ 60 43.33 N 13.36 E
Conestoga 198 39.57 N 76.21 W
Conestoga Creek ≃ 198 39.56 N 76.23 W
Conestogo 202 43.32 N 80.30 W
Conestogo ≃ 202 43.32 N 80.29 W
Conestogo Lake ⊜ 202 43.44 N 80.44 W
Conesus 200 42.43 N 77.41 W
Conesus Lake ⊜ 200 42.47 N 77.43 W
Conesville 204 40.11 N 81.54 W
Conewago Creek ≃ 198 40.07 N 76.42 W
Conewago Lake ⊜ 198 40.06 N 76.52 W
Conewango Creek ≃ 204 41.50 N 79.09 W
Coney Island •[8] 266 40.34 N 74.00 W
Confederation Lake ⊜ 174 51.05 N 92.44 W
Configni 60 42.25 N 12.38 E
Conflans-en-Jarnisy 52 49.10 N 5.51 E
Conflans-Sainte-Honorine 46 48.59 N 2.06 E
Conflict Group II 154 10.45 S 151.45 E
Confluence 178 39.49 N 79.21 W
Confolens 32 46.01 N 0.41 E
Confraternidad, Parque ♠ 276d 12.09 S 77.02 W
Confusion Bay C 176 49.58 N 55.47 W
Confuso ≃ 242 25.09 S 57.34 W
Congamond 197 42.01 N 72.46 W
Congaree ≃ 182 33.45 N 80.37 W
Congelin 158a 32.50 S 116.54 E
Congers 200 41.09 N 74.11 W
Congers Lake ⊜ 266 41.09 N 73.57 W
Cong Hoa Stadium ♠ 259c 10.45 N 106.40 E
Conghua 90 23.32 N 113.32 E
Congjiang 92 25.41 N 108.47 E
Congkou 88 36.12 N 120.23 E
Congleton 44 53.10 N 2.13 W
Congo 240 7.48 S 36.40 W
Congo □[1] 10 1.00 S 15.00 E
Congo (république du) → Congo □[1], Afr. 142 1.00 S 15.00 E
Congo □[1] 142 1.00 S 15.00 E
Congo (Zaire) (Zaïre) ≃ 128 6.04 S 12.24 E
Congo, Democratic Republic of the → Zaire □[1] 10 0.00 25.00 E
Congo, Serra do ⩘ 142 6.30 S 13.43 E
Congo Basin ≚[1] 10 0.00 20.00 E
Congonhal 246 22.09 S 46.02 W
Congonhas, Aeroporto de ⊠ 246 23.38 S 46.38 W
Congonhas, Ribeirão do ≃ 246 21.37 S 47.05 W
Congonhinhas 245 23.33 S 50.33 W
Congor Bay C 231g 13.11 N 59.29 W
Congost ≃ 256d 41.33 N 2.15 E
Congregación Cuauhtémoc 224 22.38 N 98.08 W
Congregación Ignacio Zaragoza 224 23.15 N 98.50 W
Congresbury 44 51.23 N 2.48 W
Congress, Sask., Can. 174 49.46 N 106.00 W
Congress, Ohio, U.S. 204 40.55 N 82.03 W
Congyang 90 30.42 N 117.12 E
Conie ≃ 46 48.06 N 1.30 E
Coningsby 44 53.07 N 0.10 W
Conisbrough 42 53.29 N 1.13 W
Coniston, Ont., Can. 180 46.29 N 80.51 W
Coniston, Eng., U.K. 42 54.22 N 3.05 W
Coniston Water ⊜ 42 54.20 N 3.04 W
Conitaca 222 24.10 N 106.43 W
Conjeeveram → Kānchipuram 112 12.50 N 79.43 E
Conjola 160 35.13 S 150.27 E
Conjola, Lake C 160 35.16 S 150.27 E
Çonjuror Bay C 166 65.45 N 118.07 W
Čon-Kemin ≃ 75 42.42 N 75.54 E
Conklin, Alta., Can. 172 55.38 N 111.05 W
Conklin, N.Y., U.S. 200 42.02 N 75.48 W
Conklingville Dam •[6] 200 43.17 N 74.02 W
Conklin Point ≻ 266 40.41 N 73.17 W
Conkouati 142 4.00 S 11.13 E
Conliège 54 46.39 N 5.36 E
Conlin, Lake ⊜ 210 28.14 N 81.07 W
Çonlu 120 40.13 N 28.06 E
Conn, Lough ⊜ 28 54.04 N 9.20 W
Connah's Quay 42 53.13 N 3.03 W
Connaught □[9] 28 53.45 N 9.00 W
Connaughton 275 40.05 N 75.19 W
Connaughton, Mount Λ[2] 152 22.42 S 122.40 E
Connaught Place ♠ 262a 28.38 N 77.12 E
Connaux 56 44.05 N 4.36 E
Conneaut 204 41.57 N 80.34 W
Conneaut Creek ≃ 204 41.58 N 80.33 W
Conneaut Lake 204 41.36 N 80.19 W
Conneaut Lake ⊜ 204 41.37 N 80.18 W
Conneaut Outlet ≃ 204 41.33 N 80.06 W
Conneautville 204 41.36 N 80.18 W
Connecticut □[3] 197 / 168 41.45 N 72.45 W
Connecticut ≃ 178 41.17 N 72.21 W
Connell 192 46.40 N 118.52 W
Connell, Mount Λ 172 49.18 N 115.38 W
Connellsville 178 40.01 N 79.35 W
Connelly 200 41.55 N 73.59 W
Connel Park 42 55.23 N 4.12 W
Connemara 156 24.13 S 142.17 E
Conner 106 17.48 N 121.19 E
Connerré 46 48.03 N 0.30 E
Connersville, Fla., U.S. 210 27.54 N 81.47 W
Connersville, Ind., U.S. 208 39.39 N 85.08 W
Connetquot ≃ 266 40.43 N 73.08 W
Connetquot Brook ≃ 266 40.45 N 73.09 W
Connetquot River State Park ♠ 200 40.46 N 73.09 W
Connewarre, Lake ⊜ 159 38.14 S 144.27 E
Conn Island I 274c 39.00 N 77.16 W
Conn Lake ⊜ 166 70.34 N 73.30 W
Connoquenessing 204 40.49 N 80.59 W
Connoquenessing Creek ≃ 204 40.51 N 80.19 W
Connors Range ⩘ 156 21.40 S 149.10 E
Conodoguinet Creek ≃ 198 40.17 N 76.55 W
Cononaco ≃ 236 1.32 S 75.35 W
Conotton Creek ≃ 204 40.34 N 81.23 W
Conover 182 35.42 N 81.12 W
Conowingo 198 39.40 N 76.09 W
Conowingo •[6] 198 39.33 N 76.04 W
Conowingo Creek ≃ 198 39.41 N 76.12 W
Conowingo Dam •[6] 198 39.39 N 76.10 W
Conquest 174 51.32 N 107.17 W
Conquista 245 19.56 S 47.33 W
Conquista, Ribeirão da ≃ 246 21.17 S 43.51 W
Conrad, Iowa, U.S. 180 42.14 N 92.52 W
Conrad, Mont., U.S. 192 48.10 N 111.57 W
Conrado 246 22.32 S 43.33 W
Conroe 212 30.19 N 95.27 W
Conroe, Lake ⊜[1] 212 30.25 N 95.37 W
Çonsandolo 60 44.39 N 11.46 E
Čon-Saryoj 75 42.37 N 76.53 E
Conscience Bay C 266 40.57 N 73.07 W
Consdorf 52 49.46 N 6.20 E
Consecon 202 44.00 N 77.31 W
Conselheiro Lafaiete 245 20.40 S 43.48 W
Conselheiro Paulino 246 22.13 S 42.31 W
Conselheiro Pena 245 19.10 S 41.30 W
Conselice 60 44.31 N 11.49 E
Conselve 58 45.14 N 11.52 E
Conservatória 246 22.18 S 43.57 W
Consett 42 54.51 N 1.49 W
Conshohocken 198 40.05 N 75.18 W
Consolação 246 22.33 S 45.55 W
Consolação •[8] 277b 23.33 S 46.39 W
Consolación del Norte 230p 22.45 N 83.33 W
Consolación del Sur 230p 22.30 N 83.31 W
Consolidated Main Reef Mines •[7] 263d 26.11 S 27.56 E
Con Son II 100 8.43 N 106.36 E
Consort 174 52.01 N 110.46 W
Constable 196 44.56 N 74.18 W
Constableville 202 43.34 N 75.26 W
Constance → Konstanz 54 47.40 N 9.10 E
Constance, Lake → Bodensee ⊜ 54 47.35 N 9.25 E
Constance Lake ⊜ 202 45.25 N 75.58 W
Constan Creek ≃ 202 45.17 N 76.46 W
Constan Lake ⊜ 202 45.24 N 77.00 W
Constanța 38 44.11 N 28.39 E
Constanța □[4] 38 44.20 N 28.20 E
Constantia 200 43.15 N 76.00 W
Constantina 34 37.52 N 5.37 W
Constantine, Alg. 138 36.22 N 6.37 E
Constantine, Mich., U.S. 206 41.50 N 85.40 W
Constantine □[8] 36 36.20 N 6.35 E
Constantine, Cape ≻ 170 58.25 N 158.50 W
Constantinople → İstanbul 120 41.01 N 28.58 E
Constânzia 34 39.28 N 8.20 W
Constitución, Chile 242 35.20 S 72.25 W
Constitución, Ur. 242 31.05 S 57.50 W
Constitución •[8] 278 34.37 S 58.23 W
Constitucíon de 1857, Parque Nacional ♠ 194 32.05 N 115.55 W
Constitution ≃ 231g 13.05 N 59.37 W
Constitution, Mount Λ 214 48.40 N 122.50 W
Consuegra 34 39.28 N 3.36 W
Consul 174 49.21 N 109.30 W
Consuma 60 43.47 N 11.35 E
Consuma, Passo della)(60 43.47 N 11.36 E
Contai 116 21.47 N 87.45 E
Contamana 238 7.15 S 74.54 W
Contarina 58 45.00 N 12.13 E
Contas, Rio de ≃ 245 14.17 S 39.01 W
Contee 198 39.05 N 76.52 W
Contenda 246 23.36 S 45.53 W
Contendas do Sincorá 245 13.45 S 41.02 W
Contentnea Creek ≃ 182 35.21 N 77.23 W
Contes 56 43.49 N 7.19 E
Contigliano 60 42.24 N 12.46 E
Continental 206 41.06 N 84.16 W
Continental Peak Λ 190 42.16 N 108.43 W
Contoocook ≃ 178 43.27 N 71.35 W
Contoocook Lake ⊜ 197 42.47 N 72.01 W
Contraalmirante Cordero 242 38.44 S 68.10 W
Contra Costa □[6] 216 37.55 N 121.55 W
Contra Costa Canal ≍ 272 38.02 N 121.58 W
Contra Loma Reservoir ⊜[1] 272 37.58 N 121.49 W
Contramaestre 230p 20.18 N 76.15 W
Contramaestre ≃ 230p 20.31 N 76.18 W
Contratación 236 6.18 N 73.29 W
Contrecoeur 196 45.51 N 73.14 W
Contre Island ≻[1] 266 40.54 N 73.32 W
Contreras, Embalse de ⊜[1] 34 39.32 N 1.30 W
Contres 46 47.25 N 1.26 E
Contrexéville 54 48.11 N 5.54 E
Contrisson 52 48.48 N 4.57 E
Controller Bay C 170 60.07 N 144.15 W
Contumaza 238 7.22 S 78.49 W
Contwoyto Lake ⊜ 166 65.42 N 110.50 W
Conty 46 49.44 N 2.09 E
Contz-les-Bains 52 49.27 N 6.21 E
Convención 236 8.28 N 73.21 W
Convent 184 30.06 N 90.50 W
Convento 226 9.21 N 83.30 W
Convent Station 266 40.47 N 74.26 W
Conversano 36 40.58 N 17.08 E
Converse 206 40.35 N 85.52 W
Converse Lake ⊜ 266 41.08 N 73.39 W
Converse Pond Brook ≃ 266 41.03 N 73.40 W
Convoy 206 40.55 N 84.42 W
Conway, P.E.I., Can. 176 46.40 N 63.59 W
Conway, S. Afr. 148 31.43 S 25.16 E
Conway, Wales, U.K. 42 53.17 N 3.50 W
Conway, Ark., U.S. 184 35.05 N 92.26 W
Conway, Fla., U.S. 210 28.31 N 81.20 W
Conway, Mass., U.S. 197 42.31 N 72.42 W
Conway, Mo., U.S. 184 37.30 N 92.49 W
Conway, N.H., U.S. 178 43.59 N 71.07 W
Conway, N.C., U.S. 182 36.26 N 77.20 W
Conway, Pa., U.S. 204 40.40 N 80.14 W
Conway, S.C., U.S. 182 33.50 N 79.03 W
Conway, Wash., U.S. 214 48.21 N 122.21 W
Conway ≃ 42 53.17 N 3.50 W
Conway, Cape ≻ 156 20.32 S 148.56 E
Conway, Lake ⊜ 152 28.17 S 135.35 E
Conway, Lake ⊜[1] 184 35.00 N 92.25 W
Conway, Mount Λ 152 23.45 S 133.25 E
Conway, Vale of V 42 53.12 N 3.48 W
Conway Bay C 42 53.18 N 3.55 W
Conway Springs 188 37.24 N 97.39 W
Conyers 182 33.40 N 84.01 W
Conyngham 200 40.59 N 76.03 W
Coo 52 50.24 N 5.52 E
Coober Pedy 152 29.01 S 134.43 E
Cooch Behār 114 26.19 N 89.26 E
Cooch Behār □[5] 114 26.20 N 89.20 E
Coogee, Austl. 158a 32.07 S 115.46 E
Coogee, Austl. 264a 33.55 S 151.16 E
Coogee Bay C 264a 33.55 S 151.16 E
Coogoon ≃ 156 27.19 S 148.50 E
Cook, Austl. 152 30.37 S 130.25 E
Cook, Ind., U.S. 206 41.22 N 87.26 W
Cook, Minn., U.S. 180 47.51 N 92.41 W
Cook, Nebr., U.S. 188 40.31 N 96.10 W
Cook, Wash., U.S. 214 45.43 N 121.40 W
Cook □[6] 206 41.53 N 87.38 W
Cook, Bahía C 244 55.10 S 70.10 W
Cook, Baie de C 164s 17.29 S 149.49 W
Cook, Cape ≻ 172 50.08 N 127.55 W
Cook, Mount Λ 162 43.36 S 170.10 E
Cook, Point ≻ 264b 37.55 S 144.48 E
Cookardinia 161b 35.34 S 147.14 E
Cook Bay C, Ont., Can. 202 44.15 N 79.30 W
Cook Bay C, N. Heb. 165f 18.45 S 169.10 E
Cookbundoon ≃ 160 34.28 S 150.04 E
Cook Creek ≃ 214 47.17 N 124.05 W
Cooke, Mount Λ 158a 32.25 S 116.18 E
Cookernup 158a 33.00 S 115.54 E
Cookes Peak Λ 190 32.32 N 107.44 W
Cookeville 184 36.10 N 85.31 W
Cook Forest State Park ♠ 204 41.22 N 79.12 W
Cookham 44 51.34 N 0.43 W
Cookhouse 148 32.44 S 25.48 E
Cook Ice Shelf ◸ 9 68.40 S 152.30 E
Cooking Lake ⊜ 172 53.25 N 113.02 W
Cook Inlet C 170 60.30 N 152.00 W
Cook-Inseln → Cook Islands □[2] 14 20.00 S 158.00 W
Cook Island I 164o 1.57 N 157.28 W
Cook Islands □[2] 14 20.00 S 158.00 W
Cook Islands II 14 20.00 S 158.00 W
Cooks ≃ 264a 33.56 S 151.10 E
Cooksburg 204 41.20 N 79.12 W
Cooks Falls 200 41.57 N 74.59 W
Cook's Harbour 176 51.36 N 55.52 W
Cookshire 196 45.25 N 71.38 W
Cooksmill Green 250 51.44 N 0.22 E
Cooks Mills 274a 43.00 N 79.11 W
Cookstown, Ont., Can. 202 44.11 N 79.42 W
Cookstown, N. Ire., U.K. 42 54.39 N 6.45 W
Cook Strait ʊ 162 41.15 S 174.30 E
Cooksville, Ill., U.S. 206 40.33 N 88.43 W
Cooksville, Md., U.S. 198 39.19 N 77.01 W
Cooksville, Wis., U.S. 206 42.50 N 89.14 W
Cooksville Creek ≃ 265b 43.34 N 79.34 W
Cooktown 154 15.28 S 145.15 E
Cookville 212 33.11 N 94.51 W
Coolabah 156 31.02 S 146.43 E
Cooladdi 156 26.39 S 145.28 E
Coolah 156 31.50 S 149.42 E
Coolamon 156 34.49 S 147.12 E
Coolangatta 161a 28.10 S 153.32 E
Coolawanyah 152 21.47 S 117.48 E
Coole ≃ 46 48.56 N 4.21 E
Cooleemee 182 35.49 N 80.33 W
Cooley Lake ⊜ 271 42.37 N 83.27 W
Coolgardie 152 30.57 S 121.10 E
Coolidge, Ariz., U.S. 190 32.59 N 111.31 W
Coolidge, Ga., U.S. 182 31.01 N 83.52 W
Coolidge, Tex., U.S. 212 31.45 N 96.39 W
Coolidge, Mount Λ 188 43.44 N 103.29 W
Coolidge Dam •[6] 190 33.00 N 110.20 W
Coolidge Field ⊠ 230c 17.09 N 61.47 W
Coolidge Point ≻ 273 42.34 N 70.44 W
Coolin 192 48.28 N 116.51 W
Cooling 250 51.27 N 0.32 E
Cooloongup, Lake ⊜ 158a 32.18 S 115.47 E
Coolspring 204 41.02 N 79.05 W
Coolumburra, Mount Λ 160 35.01 S 150.10 E
Coolup 158a 32.44 S 115.53 E
Cooma 161b 36.14 S 149.08 E
Coombe Cottage ⊥ 264b 37.43 S 145.23 E
Coomberdale 152 30.28 S 116.02 E
Coomera 161a 27.52 S 153.19 E
Coomera ≃ 161a 27.53 S 153.24 E
Coominya 161a 27.23 S 152.30 E
Coonabarabran 156 31.16 S 149.17 E
Coonalpyn 156 35.42 S 139.51 E
Coonamble 156 30.57 S 148.23 E
Coonana 152 31.01 S 123.07 E
Coon Creek ≃, Calif., U.S. 216 38.51 N 121.34 W
Coon Creek ≃, Ill., U.S. 206 42.15 N 88.48 W
Coon Creek ≃, Tex., U.S. 212 31.59 N 95.52 W
Coon Creek Lake ⊜[1] 212 32.04 N 95.52 W
Coondambo 156 31.04 S 135.52 E
Coondapoor 112 13.38 N 74.42 E
Coongan ≃ 152 20.53 S 119.47 E
Coongoola 156 27.39 S 145.54 E
Coonoor 112 11.21 N 76.49 E
Coon Rapids, Iowa, U.S. 188 41.52 N 94.41 W
Coon Rapids, Minn., U.S. 180 45.09 N 93.18 W
Coontown 266 40.37 N 74.31 W
Coon Valley 180 43.42 N 91.01 W
Cooper 186 33.23 N 95.35 W
Cooper ≃, N.J., U.S. 275 39.57 N 75.07 W
Cooper ≃, Wash., U.S. 214 47.23 N 121.23 W
Cooper, Mount Λ 152 26.11 S 127.56 E
Cooper, North Branch ≃ 275 39.55 N 75.02 W
Cooper Center 206 42.23 N 85.37 W
Cooper Creek ≃ 156 28.29 S 137.46 E
Cooper Island I 230m 18.22 N 64.30 W
Cooper Lake ⊜ 190 41.37 N 105.50 W
Cooper Landing 170 61.57 N 145.18 W
Cooper Mountain Λ 170 60.23 N 149.51 W
Cooper River Parkway ♠ 275 39.55 N 75.03 W
Cooper Road 184 32.35 N 93.48 W
Coopers 184 32.46 N 86.33 W
Coopersale Common 250 51.42 N 0.08 E
Coopersburg 198 40.31 N 75.23 W
Coopers Plains, Austl. 161a 27.34 S 153.02 E
Coopers Plains, N.Y., U.S. 200 42.11 N 77.08 W
Cooperstown, N. Dak., U.S. 188 47.27 N 98.07 W
Cooperstown, N.Y., U.S. 200 42.42 N 74.56 W
Cooperstown, Pa., U.S. 204 41.30 N 79.52 W
Cooperstown, Pa., U.S. 204 40.43 N 79.57 W
Coopersville 206 43.04 N 85.57 W
Coorabie 152 31.54 S 132.18 E
Cooranbong 160 33.04 S 151.27 E
Coorow 152 29.53 S 116.01 E
Cooroy 156 26.25 S 152.55 E
Coos □[6] 196 45.04 N 71.20 W
Coosa ≃ 184 32.30 N 86.16 W
Coosawhatchie ≃ 182 32.32 N 80.52 W
Coos Bay 192 43.22 N 124.13 W
Coos Bay C 192 43.23 N 124.16 W
Cootamundra 156 34.39 S 148.02 E
Cootehill 28 54.04 N 7.05 W
Coot-Tha, Mount Λ[2] 161a 27.29 S 152.58 E
Cooyar 161a 26.59 S 151.50 E
Cooyar Creek ≃ 161a 27.24 S 152.03 E
Çooyar Mountain Λ 161a 26.57 S 151.47 E
Çop 68 48.26 N 22.10 E
Copacabana, Arg. 242 28.12 S 67.29 W
Copacabana, Bol. 238 16.10 S 69.05 W
Copacabana •[8] 277a 22.58 S 43.11 W
Copacabana, Forte de ⊥ 277a 22.59 S 43.11 W
Copainalá 224 17.05 N 93.12 W
Copake 200 42.06 N 73.33 W
Copake Falls 200 42.07 N 73.31 W
Copala 224 16.37 N 98.58 W
Copalillo 224 18.02 N 99.07 W
Copalis ≃ 214 47.07 N 124.13 W
Copalis Beach 214 47.07 N 124.10 W
Copalita ≃ 224 15.46 N 96.03 W
Copalquín 222 25.29 N 107.00 W
Copán, Hond. 226 14.50 N 89.09 W
Copan, Okla., U.S. 186 36.54 N 95.56 W
Copán □[5] 226 14.50 N 89.00 W
Copán ⊥ 226 14.50 N 89.09 W
Copanatoyac 224 17.15 N 98.45 W
Copándaro de Galeana 224 19.53 N 101.13 W
Copano Bay C 186 28.05 N 97.05 W
Copatana 236 2.48 S 67.04 W
Cope 188 39.40 N 102.51 W
Copeá, Paraná ≃[1] 236 3.52 S 63.20 W
Copeau ≃ 174 52.45 N 103.00 W
Copeland 210 25.57 N 81.22 W
Copeland Island I 42 54.41 N 5.32 W
Copenhagen → København, Dan. 41 55.40 N 12.35 E
Copenhagen, N.Y., U.S. 202 43.54 N 75.41 W
Copenhague → København 41 55.40 N 12.35 E
Copertino 36 40.16 N 18.03 E
Copetonas 242 38.43 S 60.27 W
Copeville 212 33.05 N 96.25 W
Copiague 200 40.41 N 73.24 W
Copiague Neck ≻[1] 266 40.40 N 73.22 W
Copiapó 242 27.22 S 70.20 W
Copiapó ≃ 242 27.19 S 70.56 W
Coplay 198 40.44 N 75.29 W
Copley, Austl. 156 30.32 S 138.25 E
Copley, Ohio, U.S. 204 41.06 N 81.39 W
Copoas, Mount Λ 106 10.48 N 119.17 E
Copolo 142 10.22 S 14.07 E
Çoporito 236 8.56 N 62.00 W
Čopoviči 68 50.49 N 27.58 E
Copparo 58 44.54 N 11.49 E
Coppell 212 32.57 N 97.01 W
Coppename ≃ 240 5.48 N 55.55 W
Coppenbrügge 48 52.07 N 9.32 E
Copper ≃ 170 60.30 N 144.50 W
Copperas Cove 186 31.08 N 97.54 W
Copperas Mountain Λ 266 41.02 N 74.28 W
Copperbelt □[4] 144 13.00 S 28.00 E
Copper Butte Λ 192 48.42 N 118.28 W
Copper Center 170 61.58 N 145.19 W
Copper Cliff 180 46.28 N 81.04 W
Copper Creek ≃ 182 36.40 N 82.45 W
Copper Harbor 180 47.27 N 87.53 W
Coppermine 166 67.50 N 115.05 W
Coppermine ≃ 166 67.49 N 115.04 W
Copper Mine Point ≻, Br. Vir. Is. 230m 18.26 N 64.25 W
Coppermine Point ≻, Ont., Can. 180 46.59 N 84.47 W
Copper Mountain 172 49.20 N 120.33 W
Copper Mountain Λ, Alaska, U.S. 170 55.14 N 132.36 W
Copper Mountain Λ, Wyo., U.S. 190 43.27 N 107.57 W
Copperopolis 216 37.59 N 120.38 W
Coppet 54 46.19 N 6.12 E
Copplestone 44 50.49 N 3.45 W
Coppull 252 53.37 N 2.40 W
Copster Green 252 53.48 N 2.30 W
Copton Creek ≃ 172 54.16 N 119.15 W
Copton Point ≻ 106 10.00 N 123.22 E
Copulhué, Paso de)(242 37.35 S 71.08 W
Coqueiro Grande, Serra do Λ 246 21.40 S 42.55 W
Coquet ≃ 42 55.22 N 1.37 W
Coquet Dale V 42 55.16 N 1.50 W
Coquí 230m 17.59 N 66.14 W
Coquilhatville → Mbandaka 142 0.04 N 18.16 E
Coquille 192 43.11 N 124.11 W
Coquille ≃ 192 43.07 N 124.26 W
Coquille, East Fork ≃ 192 43.06 N 124.04 W
Coquille, Middle Fork ≃ 192 43.05 N 124.09 W
Coquille, South Fork ≃ 192 43.02 N 124.07 W
Coquimatlán 224 19.12 N 103.48 W
Coquimbana 242 28.21 S 70.56 W
Coquimbo 242 29.58 S 71.21 W
Coquimbo □[4] 242 31.00 S 71.00 W
Corabia 38 43.46 N 24.30 E
Coração de Jesus 245 16.42 S 44.22 W
Coração de Maria 245 12.14 S 38.45 W
Coracora 238 15.02 S 73.47 W
Corail, Mer de → Coral Sea ⊹[2] 14 20.00 S 158.00 E
Çorak Gölü ⊜ 120 37.40 N 29.46 E
Coral 204 40.30 N 79.11 W
Coralaque ≃ 238 16.26 S 70.45 W
Coral Bay C, Pil. 106 8.25 N 117.20 E
Coral Bay C, Vir. Is., U.S. 230m 18.20 N 64.41 W
Coral Gables 210 25.45 N 80.16 W
Coral Harbour 166 64.08 N 83.10 W
Coral Hills 274c 38.52 N 76.55 W
Coral Sea ⊹[2] 14 20.00 S 158.00 E
Coral Sea Basin ⊹[1] 14 14.00 S 152.00 E
Coral Sea Plateau ⊹[3] 14 17.00 S 149.00 E
Coral Springs 210 26.16 N 80.13 W
Coralville 180 41.40 N 91.35 W
Coralville Lake ⊜[1] 180 41.47 N 91.48 W
Coram, Mont., U.S. 192 48.36 N 114.02 W
Coram, N.Y., U.S. 200 40.52 N 73.00 W
Corangamite, Lake ⊜ 159 38.10 S 143.25 E
Corantijn (Courantyne) ≃ 240 5.55 N 57.05 W
Coraopolis 204 40.31 N 80.10 W
Coraopolis Heights 269b 40.29 N 80.10 W
Corato 36 41.09 N 16.25 E
Corbara, Lago di ⊜[1] 60 42.43 N 12.15 E
Corbeil-Essonnes 46 48.36 N 2.29 E
Corbenay 54 47.54 N 6.20 E
Corbeny 46 49.28 N 3.49 E
Corbeolona 56 45.10 N 9.22 E
Corbera, Riera de ≃ 256d 41.27 N 1.59 E
Corberon 54 47.01 N 4.59 E
Corbett 200 42.03 N 75.02 W
Corbetta 56 45.28 N 8.55 E
Corbettsville 200 42.01 N 75.48 W
Corbie 46 49.55 N 2.30 E
Corbières ⩘ 32 42.55 N 2.38 E
Corbigny 46 47.15 N 3.40 E
Corbin 182 36.57 N 84.05 W
Corbion 52 49.48 N 5.00 E
Corbola 58 45.00 N 12.05 E
Corbones ≃ 34 37.36 N 5.39 W
Corbu 38 44.29 N 24.43 E
Corby 44 52.29 N 0.40 W
Corcaigh → Cork 28 51.54 N 8.28 W
Córcega 230m 18.19 N 67.15 W
Córcega, Isla de → Corse I 36 42.00 N 9.00 E
Corciano 60 43.08 N 12.17 E
Corcieux 54 48.10 N 6.53 E
Corcolle •[8] 257a 41.55 N 12.46 E
Corcoran 216 36.06 N 119.33 W
Corcovado Λ 277a 22.57 S 43.13 W
Corcovado, Golfo C 244 43.30 S 73.30 W
Corcovado, Volcán Λ[1] 244 43.12 S 72.48 W
Corcubión 34 42.57 N 9.11 W
Cordâ, Ribeirão ≃ 240 6.26 S 48.17 W
Cordeaux Reservoir ⊜[1] 160 34.22 S 150.45 E
Cordeiro 245 22.02 S 42.22 W
Cordele, Ga., U.S. 182 31.58 N 83.47 W
Cordele, Tex., U.S. 212 29.08 N 96.38 W
Cordell 186 35.17 N 98.59 W
Cordell Hull Reservoir ⊜[1] 184 36.25 N 85.40 W
Cordenons 58 45.59 N 12.42 E
Corder 184 39.06 N 93.38 W
Cordes 32 44.04 N 1.57 E
Cordignano 58 45.57 N 12.25 E
Cordilheiras, Serra das ⩘[1] 240 7.30 S 48.30 W
Cordillera □[5] 242 25.15 S 57.00 W
Cordillo Downs 156 26.43 S 140.38 E
Cordisburgo 245 19.07 S 44.21 W
Córdoba, Arg. 242 31.24 S 64.11 W
Córdoba, Esp. 34 37.53 N 4.46 W
Córdoba, Méx. 224 18.53 N 96.56 W
Córdoba □[4] 242 32.00 S 64.00 W
Córdoba □[5] 236 8.20 N 75.40 W
Cordon 106 16.40 N 121.28 E
Cordova → Córdoba, Esp. 34 37.53 N 4.46 W
Córdova, Perú 238 14.04 S 75.03 W
Cordova, Ala., U.S. 184 33.46 N 87.11 W

ENGLISH

Name	Page	Lat.°′	Long.°′
Cordova, Alaska, U.S.	170	60.33 N	145.46 W
Cordova, Ill., U.S.	180	41.41 N	90.19 W
Cordova, Md., U.S.	198	38.52 N	76.00 W
Córdova, Península ≻[1]	244	53.20 S	72.50 W
Cordova Bay C	170	54.55 N	132.35 W
Cordova Lake ⊜	202	44.35 N	77.49 W
Cordova Peak Λ	170	60.51 N	145.16 W
Corea, Estrecho de → Korea Strait ʊ	80	34.00 N	129.00 E
Corea del Norte → Korea, North □[1]	88	40.00 N	127.00 E
Corea del Sur → Korea, South □[1]	88	36.30 N	128.00 E
Coreaú	240	3.33 S	40.39 W
Coreaú ≃	240	2.54 S	40.50 W
Core Creek ≃	275	40.11 N	74.55 W
Corée, Détroit de → Korea Strait ʊ	80	34.00 N	129.00 E
Coree, Mount Λ	161b	35.18 S	148.48 E
Corée du Nord → Korea, North □[1]	88	40.00 N	127.00 E
Corée du Sud → Korea, South □[1]	88	36.30 N	128.00 E
Coreglia Antelminelli	58	44.04 N	10.31 E
Coreinbob	161b	35.13 S	147.38 E
Coremas	240	7.01 S	37.58 W
Corerepe	222	25.40 N	108.40 W
Corese Terra	60	42.10 N	12.42 E
Corey Lake ⊜	206	41.55 N	85.45 W
Corfe Castle	44	50.38 N	2.04 W
Corfield	156	21.43 S	143.22 E
Corfu → Kérkira, Ellás	38	39.36 N	19.56 E
Corfu, N.Y., U.S.	200	42.58 N	78.24 W
Corfu → Kérkira I	38	39.40 N	19.42 E
Corhanwarrabul Creek ≃	264b	37.55 S	145.12 E
Cori	60	41.39 N	12.55 E
Coria	34	39.59 N	6.32 W
Coria del Río	34	37.16 N	6.03 W
Coriaí ≃	240	3.18 S	52.04 W
Coribe	245	13.50 S	44.28 W
Coricudgy, Mount Λ	160	32.50 S	150.22 E
Corigliano Calabro	36	39.36 N	16.31 E
Corinaldo	60	43.39 N	13.03 E
Corinda	156	17.53 S	138.35 E
Corinna	178	44.55 N	69.16 W
Corinne, Pa., U.S.	275	39.54 N	75.40 W
Corinne, Utah, U.S.	190	41.35 N	112.07 W
Corinne, W. Va., U.S.	182	37.34 N	81.22 W
Corinth → Kórinthos, Ellás	38	37.56 N	22.56 E
Corinth, Ky., U.S.	208	38.30 N	84.34 W
Corinth, Miss., U.S.	184	34.56 N	88.31 W
Corinth, N.Y., U.S.	200	43.15 N	73.49 W
Corinth, Gulf of → Korinthiakós Kólpos C	38	38.19 N	22.04 E
Corinth Canal → Korínthou, Dhiórix ≍	38	37.57 N	22.56 E
Corinto, Bra.	245	18.21 S	44.27 W
Corinto, El Sal.	226	13.49 N	87.58 W
Corinto, Nic.	226	12.29 N	87.10 W
Corio	159	38.04 S	144.23 E
Corio Bay C	159	38.07 S	144.24 E
Coripata	238	16.18 S	67.36 W
Corire	238	16.14 S	72.28 W
Coris	238	9.50 S	77.45 W
Corisco, Isla de I	142	0.53 N	9.20 E
Corixa Grande ≃	238	17.31 S	57.52 W
Corixao ≃	238	18.22 S	57.23 W
Cork	28	51.54 N	8.28 W
Cork □[6]	28	52.00 N	8.30 W
Cork Harbour C	28	51.45 N	8.15 W
Corkscrew	210	26.28 N	81.33 W
Corkscrew Swamp ≋	210	26.25 N	81.34 W
Corlay	32	48.19 N	3.03 W
Corleone	36	37.49 N	13.18 E
Corleto Perticara	36	40.23 N	16.03 E
Çorlu	120	41.09 N	27.48 E
Cormainville	46	48.08 N	1.36 E
Cormano	256b	45.33 N	9.10 E
Cormatin	54	46.33 N	4.41 E
Cormeilles	46	49.15 N	0.23 E
Cormeilles-en-Parisis	46	48.59 N	2.12 E
Cormery	46	47.16 N	0.51 E
Cormons	58	45.58 N	13.28 E
Cormoran Reef ⊹[2]	165b	7.50 N	134.32 E
Cormorant	174	54.14 N	100.35 W
Cormorant Lake ⊜	174	54.13 N	100.47 W
Čormoz	76	58.53 N	56.08 E
Çorna	58	45.53 N	10.10 E
Čornaja, S.S.S.R.	24	68.35 N	56.30 E
Čornaja, S.S.S.R.	72	55.45 N	38.04 E
Čornaja ≃, S.S.S.R.	255a	59.55 N	30.59 E
Čornaja ≃, S.S.S.R.	255a	59.47 N	30.10 E
Čornaja ≃, S.S.S.R.	255a	59.50 N	30.00 E
Čornaja ≃, S.S.S.R.	255a	60.01 N	30.10 E
Čornaja ≃, S.S.S.R.	255b	55.41 N	37.58 E
Čornaja Cholunica	76	58.51 N	51.42 E
Čornaja Gr'az', S.S.S.R.	72	54.31 N	35.52 E
Čornaja Gr'az', S.S.S.R.	72	54.58 N	36.48 E
Čornaja Gr'az', S.S.S.R.	255b	55.58 N	37.19 E
Čornaja Rečka	255a	59.56 N	30.58 E
Čornaja Rečka ≃, S.S.S.R.	255a	59.46 N	30.45 E
Čornaja Rečka ≃, S.S.S.R.	255a	59.55 N	30.22 E
Čornaja Sloboda	24	60.48 N	37.46 E
Cornaredo	256b	45.30 N	9.02 E
Cornas	56	44.58 N	4.51 E
Cornedo Vicentino	58	45.37 N	11.20 E
Cornelia, S. Afr.	148	27.13 S	28.52 E
Cornelia, Ga., U.S.	182	34.31 N	83.32 W
Cornélio Procópio	245	23.08 S	50.39 W
Cornelius, N.C., U.S.	182	35.29 N	80.52 W
Cornelius, Oreg., U.S.	214	45.31 N	123.04 W
Cornelius Grinnell Bay C	166	63.20 N	64.50 W
Cornell, Calif., U.S.	218	34.08 N	118.47 W
Cornell, Ill., U.S.	206	41.00 N	88.44 W
Cornell, Wis., U.S.	180	45.10 N	91.09 W
Cornellà	256d	41.21 N	2.04 E
Corner Brook	176	48.57 N	57.57 W
Corner Inlet C	159	38.43 S	146.20 E
Corner Store	275	40.07 N	75.30 W
Cornes, Lac des ⊜	196	46.43 N	75.09 W
Cornforth	42	54.42 N	1.31 W
Cornholme	252	53.44 N	2.08 W
Cornia ≃	60	42.57 N	10.33 E
Corniglia	56	44.07 N	9.42 E
Corning, Ark., U.S.	184	36.24 N	90.35 W
Corning, Calif., U.S.	194	39.56 N	122.11 W
Corning, Iowa, U.S.	188	40.59 N	94.44 W
Corning, Kans., U.S.	188	39.39 N	96.02 W
Corning, N.Y., U.S.	200	42.09 N	77.04 W
Corning, Ohio, U.S.	178	39.36 N	82.05 W
Cornish	178	43.48 N	70.48 W
Cornish, Mount Λ	152	20.13 S	126.28 E
Corn Islands II	226	12.15 N	83.00 W
Cornland	209	39.56 N	89.24 W
Çorno ≃	60	42.49 N	12.55 E
Čornobajevka	68	46.42 N	32.32 E
Çorno Grande Λ	60	42.28 N	13.34 E
Čornoje, S.S.S.R.	70	57.32 N	46.25 E
Čornoje, S.S.S.R.	76	51.44 N	77.34 E
Čornolesskoje	74	44.42 N	43.42 E
Čornomorskij	68	44.51 N	38.29 E
Čornomorskij Zapovednik •[4]	68	46.10 N	32.00 E

DEUTSCH

Name	Seite	Breite°′	Länge°′ E=Ost
Čornomorskoje, S.S.S.R.	68	45.03 N	35.58 E
Čornomorskoje, S.S.S.R.	68	45.30 N	32.42 E
Čornoreck	76	52.45 N	76.40 E
Cornuda	58	45.50 N	12.00 E
Cornwall, Ont., Can.	196	45.02 N	74.44 W
Cornwall, N.Y., U.S.	200	41.26 N	74.01 W
Cornwall, Pa., U.S.	198	40.14 N	76.31 W
Cornwall □[6]	44	50.30 N	4.40 W
Cornwall Bridge	197	41.49 N	73.22 W
Cornwallis Island I	166	75.15 N	94.30 W
Cornwall on the Hudson	200	41.27 N	74.00 W
Cornwell	210	27.23 N	81.05 W
Cornwells Heights	275	40.04 N	74.57 W
Čornyj Jar	70	48.04 N	46.08 E
Čornyj Mys, S.S.S.R.	24	68.20 N	38.37 E
Čornyj Mys, S.S.S.R.	76	55.33 N	80.04 E
Čornyj Ostrov	68	49.32 N	26.46 E
Čornyj Otrog	76	51.55 N	55.59 E
Čornyj Rynok	74	44.24 N	46.33 E
Čornyj Tašlyk ≃	68	48.11 N	30.51 E
Corny Point	156	34.55 S	137.03 E
Coro	236	11.25 N	69.41 W
Coro, Golfete de C	231s	11.30 N	69.55 W
Coro, Sierra del ⩘	224	23.25 N	100.30 W
Coroaci	245	18.35 S	42.17 W
Coroa Grande	246	22.54 S	43.52 W
Coroatá	240	4.08 S	44.08 W
Çoroca ≃	142	15.43 S	11.55 E
Čoroch (Çoruh) ≃	120	41.36 N	41.35 E
Corocoro	238	17.12 S	68.29 W
Corocoro Island I	236	8.30 N	60.10 W
Coroico	238	16.10 S	67.44 W
Coroico ≃	238	15.27 S	67.50 W
Coromandel, Bra.	245	18.28 S	47.13 W
Coromandel, N.Z.	162	36.46 S	175.30 E
Coromandel Coast ⊥[2]	112	14.00 N	80.10 E
Coromandel Peninsula ≻[1]	162	36.50 S	175.35 E
Coromandel Range ⩘	162	37.00 S	175.40 E
Coron	106	12.00 N	120.12 E
Corona, Calif., U.S.	218	33.52 N	117.34 W
Corona, N. Mex., U.S.	190	34.15 N	105.36 W
Corona •[8]	266	40.45 N	73.52 W
Coronación, Golfo de la → Coronation Gulf C	166	68.25 N	110.00 W
Coronación, Isla de la → Coronation Island I	9	60.37 S	45.30 W
Corona Del Mar •[8]	218	33.36 N	117.52
Coronado, Méx.	224	22.55 N	100.56 W
Coronado, Calif., U.S.	218	32.41 N	117.11 W
Coronado, Bahía de C	226	9.00 N	83.50 W
Coronado, Sierra ⩘	224	23.05 N	100.56 W
Coronado National Memorial ♠	190	31.10 N	110.29 W
Coronado Naval Amphibious Base ■	218	32.40 N	117.10 W
Coronados, Golfo de los C	244	41.40 S	74.00 W
Coronation	172	52.05 N	111.27 W
Coronation Gardens ♠	265b	43.41 N	79.29 W
Coronation Gulf C	166	68.25 N	110.00 W
Coronation Island I, B.A.T.	9	60.37 S	45.30 W
Coronation Island I, Alaska, U.S.	170	55.52 N	134.15 W
Coronation Park ♠	263d	26.06 S	27.47 E
Coron Bay C	106	11.54 N	120.08 E
Coronda	242	31.58 S	60.55 W
Coronel	242	37.01 S	73.08 W
Coronel Bogado	242	27.11 S	56.18 W
Coronel Brandsen	248	35.10 S	58.14 W
Coronel Dorrego	242	38.42 S	61.17 W
Coronel Du Graty	242	27.40 S	60.56 W
Coroneles Sánchez → Fortín Paredes	238	19.20 S	59.58 W
Coronel Eugenio del Busto	242	38.57 S	64.15 W
Coronel Fabriciano	245	19.31 S	42.38 W
Coronel Moldes	242	25.16 S	65.29 W
Coronel Murta	245	16.37 S	42.11 W
Coronel Oviedo	242	25.25 S	56.27 W
Coronel Pacheco	246	21.35 S	43.16 W
Coronel Ponce	245	15.34 S	55.01 W
Coronel Pringles	242	37.58 S	61.22 W
Coronel Suárez	242	37.28 S	61.55 W
Coronel Vidal	242	37.27 S	57.43 W
Coronel Vivida	242	25.58 S	52.34 W
Corongo	238	8.35 S	77.55 W
Corongoros	224	19.17 N	102.48 W
Coronie □[5]	240	5.50 N	56.20 W
Coron Island I	106	11.55 N	120.14 E
Coronita	218	33.52 N	117.36 W
Coropuna, Nevado Λ	238	15.31 S	72.42 W
Çorovodë	38	40.30 N	20.13 E
Corowa	156	36.02 S	146.23 E
Corozal, Belize	222	18.24 N	88.24 W
Corozal, Col.	236	9.19 N	75.18 W
Corozal, Hond.	226	15.48 N	86.43 W
Corozal, P.R.	230m	18.21 N	66.17 W
Corps	56	44.49 N	5.57 E
Corpus	242	27.07 S	55.31 W
Corpus Christi	186	27.48 N	97.24 W
Corpus Christi, Lake ⊜[1]	186	28.10 N	97.53 W
Corpus Christi Bay C	186	27.48 N	97.20 W
Corpus Christi Naval Air Station ■	186	27.42 N	97.16 W
Corque	238	18.21 S	67.42 W
Corquín	226	14.34 N	88.52 W
Corral	244	39.52 S	73.26 W
Corral de Almaguer	34	39.46 N	3.11 W
Corral de Bustos	242	33.17 S	62.12 W
Corralillo	230p	22.59 N	80.35 W
Corralito, Arroyo del ≃	248	33.39 S	58.03 W
Corralito, Cuchilla ⩘[2]	248	33.40 S	57.44 W
Corralitos, Méx.	186	26.57 N	104.39 W
Corralitos, Calif., U.S.	216	36.59 N	121.48 W
Correas, Arroyo ≃	278	34.24 S	58.32 W
Correctionville	188	42.28 N	95.47 W
Corredor	277b	23.27 S	46.19 W
Correggio	58	44.46 N	10.47 E
Corregidor Island I	106	14.23 N	120.35 E
Córrego do Bom Jesus	246	22.38 S	46.02 W
Córrego do Ouro, Bra.	245	16.18 S	50.32 W
Córrego do Ouro, Bra.	246	21.22 S	45.47 W
Córrego Rico	245	15.14 S	47.48 W
Correia de Almeida	246	21.17 S	43.38 W
Corrente	240	10.27 S	45.10 W
Corrente ≃, Bra.	240	4.18 S	42.11 W
Corrente ≃, Bra.	245	13.08 S	43.28 W
Corrente ≃, Bra.	245	19.19 S	50.50 W
Corrente Grande ≃	245	19.02 S	42.09 W
Correntes	240	9.08 S	36.19 W
Correntes ≃	245	17.38 S	55.08 W
Correntes, Cabo das ≻	146	24.11 S	35.34 E
Correntes, Riacho ≃	240	5.29 S	40.41 W
Correntezas	246	22.30 S	42.31 W
Correnti, Isola delle I	36	36.38 N	15.05 E
Correntina	245	13.20 S	44.39 W
Corrèze □[5]	32	45.20 N	1.50 E
Correzzana	256b	45.40 N	9.18 E
Corrib, Lough ⊜	28	53.05 N	9.10 W

Symbols in the index entries represent the broad categories identified in the key at the right. Symbols with superior numbers (⩘²) identify subcategories (see complete key on page *I* · 26).

Kartensymbole in dem Registerverzeichnis stellen die rechts in Schlüssel erklärten Kategorien dar. Symbole mit hochgestellten Ziffern (⩘²) bezeichnen Unterabteilungen einer Kategorie (vgl. vollständiger Schlüssel auf Seite *I* · 26).

Los símbolos incluídos en el texto del índice representan las grandes categorias identificadas con la clave a la derecha. Los símbolos con numeros en su parte superior (⩘²) identifican las subcategorias (véase la clave completa en la página *I* · 26).

Les symboles de l'index représentent les catégories indiquées dans la légende à droite. Les symboles suivis d'un indice (⩘²) représentent des sous-catégories (voir légende complète à la page *I* · 26).

Os símbolos incluídos no texto do índice representam as grandes categorias identificadas com a chave à direita. Os símbolos com números em sua parte superior (⩘²) identificam as subcategorias (veja-se a chave completa à página *I* · 26).

Symbol	English	Deutsch	Español	Français	Português
Λ	Mountain	Berg	Montaña	Montagne	Montanha
⩘	Mountains	Berge	Montañas	Montagnes	Montanhas
)(	Pass	Pass	Paso	Col	Passo
V	Valley, Canyon	Tal, Cañon	Valle, Cañón	Vallée, Canyon	Vale, Canhão
≚	Plain	Ebene	Llano	Plaine	Planície
≻	Cape	Kap	Cabo	Cap	Cabo
I	Island	Insel	Isla	Île	Ilha
II	Islands	Inseln	Islas	Îles	Ilhas
⊥	Other Topographic Features	Andere Topographische Objekte	Otros Elementos Topográficos	Autres données topographiques	Outros Elementos Topográficos

ESPAÑOL

Nombre	Página	Lat.°′	Long.°′ W=Oeste
Corridonia	60	43.15 N	13.30 E
Corrientes	242	27.28 S	58.50 W
Corrientes □[4]	242	29.00 S	58.00 W
Corrientes ≃, Arg.	242	30.21 S	59.33 W
Corrientes ≃, S.A.	236	3.43 S	74.35 W
Corrientes, Cabo >, Arg.	242	38.01 S	57.32 W
Corrientes, Cabo >, Col.	236	5.30 N	77.34 W
Corrientes, Cabo >, Cuba	230p	21.45 N	84.31 W
Corrientes, Cabo >, Méx.	224	20.25 N	105.42 W
Corrientes, Ensenada de C	230p	21.51 N	84.36 W
Corrigan	212	31.00 N	94.50 W
Corrigin	152	32.21 S	117.52 E
Corrimal	160	34.22 S	150.54 E
Corringham	250	51.31 N	0.28 E
Corroios	256c	38.38 N	9.09 W
Corropoli	60	42.49 N	13.50 E
Corrotoman ≃	198	37.40 N	76.29 W
Corry	204	41.56 N	73.39 W
Corryong	161b	36.12 S	147.54 E
Corryong Creek ≃	161b	36.06 S	147.59 E
Corse (Corsica) I	36	42.00 N	9.00 E
Corse, Cap >	56	43.00 N	9.25 E
Corserine Λ	42	55.09 N	4.22 W
Corsham	44	51.26 N	2.11 W
Corsica, Pa., U.S.	204	41.10 N	79.12 W
Corsica, S. Dak., U.S.	188	43.25 N	98.24 W
Corsica → Corse I	36	42.00 N	9.00 E
Corsicana	212	32.06 N	96.28 W
Corsica River C	198	39.05 N	76.08 W
Corsico	56	45.26 N	9.07 E
Corsock	42	55.04 N	3.57 W
Corson Inlet C	198	39.12 N	74.39 W
Cortaccia (Kurtatsch)	58	46.19 N	11.13 E
Cort Adelaer, Kap >	166	62.00 N	42.00 W
Cortaderas	242	32.30 S	65.00 W
Cortado, Rio do ≃	277a	23.00 S	43.25 W
Cortazar	224	20.29 N	100.56 W
Corte	36	42.18 N	9.08 E
Corte Alto	244	40.57 S	73.10 W
Cortegana	34	37.55 N	6.49 W
Corte Madera	216	37.55 N	122.31 W
Corte Madera Creek ≃	272	37.23 N	122.14 W
Cortemaggiore	58	44.59 N	9.56 E
Cortemilia	56	44.35 N	8.12 E
Cortes	106	9.17 N	126.11 E
Cortés □[5]	226	15.30 N	88.00 W
Cortés, Ensenada de C	230p	22.05 N	83.52 W
Cortez, Colo., U.S.	190	37.21 N	108.35 W
Cortez, Fla., U.S.	210	27.28 N	82.41 W
Cortez Mountains ⛰	194	40.20 N	116.20 W
Cortina Creek ≃	216	39.06 N	122.02 W
Cortina d'Ampezzo	58	46.32 N	12.08 E
Cortines	248	34.34 S	59.13 W
Čortkov	68	49.01 N	25.48 E
Cortland, Ill., U.S.	206	41.55 N	88.41 W
Cortland, Ind., U.S.	208	38.58 N	85.58 W
Cortland, Nebr., U.S.	188	40.30 N	96.42 W
Cortland, N.Y., U.S.	200	42.36 N	76.11 W
Cortland, Ohio, U.S.	204	41.20 N	80.44 W
Cortland □[6]	200	42.36 N	76.11 W
Corton	44	52.32 N	1.44 E
Cortona	60	43.16 N	11.59 E
Çorubal (Koliba) ≃	140	11.57 N	15.06 W
Čoruch-Dajron	75	40.24 N	69.40 E
Coruche	34	38.57 N	8.31 W
Çoruh (Čoroch) ≃	120	41.36 N	41.35 E
Çorum, Tür.	120	40.33 N	34.58 E
Çorum, Tür.	120	39.14 N	28.27 E
Çorum □[4]	120	40.30 N	34.40 E
Corumbá	238	19.01 S	57.39 W
Corumbá ≃	245	18.19 S	48.55 W
Corumbá de Goiás	245	15.55 S	48.48 W
Corumbaíba	245	18.09 S	48.34 W
Corumbataí ≃	242	23.55 S	51.57 W
Corumbaú, Ponta de >	245	16.53 S	39.06 W
Corumbiara Antigo ≃	238	13.13 S	62.06 W
Corumo ≃	236	6.49 N	60.52 W
Corund	38	46.28 N	25.11 E
Corunna, Ont., Can.	204	42.53 N	82.26 W
Corunna → La Coruña, Esp.	34	43.22 N	8.23 W
Corunna, Ind., U.S.	206	41.26 N	85.09 W
Corunna, Mich., U.S.	206	42.59 N	84.07 W
Corunna Downs	152	21.28 S	119.51 E
Coruripe	240	10.08 S	36.10 W
Corvallis, Mont., U.S.	192	46.19 N	114.07 W
Corvallis, Oreg., U.S.	192	44.34 N	123.16 W
Corvara in Badia	58	46.33 N	11.52 E
Corve ≃	44	52.22 N	2.43 W
Corve Dale V	44	52.30 N	2.40 W
Corvey, Kloster ʊ[1]	48	51.46 N	9.25 E
Corviale ✦[8]	257a	41.52 N	12.25 E
Corvo I	138a	39.42 N	31.06 W
Corwen	44	52.59 N	3.22 W
Corwin, Cape >	170	59.54 N	165.41 W
Corwith	180	42.59 N	93.57 W
Corydon, Ind., U.S.	208	38.13 N	86.07 W
Corydon, Iowa, U.S.	180	40.45 N	93.19 W
Corydon, Ky., U.S.	184	37.44 N	87.43 W
Coryell	212	31.33 N	97.37 W
Coryell □[6]	212	31.25 N	97.40 W
Coryell Creek ≃	212	31.23 N	97.35 W
Coryton	250	51.31 N	0.31 E
Coryville	204	41.53 N	78.24 W
Corzu	38	44.28 N	23.10 E
Corzuela	242	26.57 S	60.58 W
Cos → Kos I	38	36.50 N	27.10 E
Cosa (Ansedonia) ⊥	60	42.25 N	11.18 E
Cosamaloapan [de Carpio]	222	18.22 N	95.48 W
Cosapa	238	18.11 S	68.40 W
Cosby	44	52.33 N	1.11 W
Cos Cob	266	41.02 N	73.36 W
Cos Cob Harbor C	266	41.01 N	73.36 W
Coscomatepec [de Bravo]	224	19.04 N	97.02 W
Cosel → Koźle	30	50.20 N	18.08 E
Coseley	44	52.33 N	2.06 W
Cosenza	36	39.17 N	16.15 E
Cosgrove's Creek ≃	264a	33.50 S	150.46 E
Coshocton	204	40.16 N	81.51 W
Coshocton □[6]	204	40.16 N	81.51 W
Cosigüina, Punta >	226	12.54 N	87.41 W
Cosigüina, Volcán Λ[1]	226	12.59 N	87.34 W
Coslada	256a	40.25 N	3.34 W
Cosmo ✦[8]	246	22.54 S	43.37 W
Cosmoledo Group II	128	9.43 S	47.35 E
Cosmópolis, Bra.	246	22.38 S	47.12 W
Cosmopolis, Wash., U.S.	214	46.57 N	123.46 W
Cosmorama	245	20.28 S	49.47 W
Cosmos ✦[8]	277a	22.55 S	44.37 W
Cosne-sur-Loire	46	47.24 N	2.55 E
Cosoleacaque	224	18.00 N	94.37 W
Cospán	238	7.26 S	78.33 W
Cosquín	242	31.15 S	64.29 W
Cossato	56	45.34 N	8.10 E
Cossatot ≃	184	33.48 N	94.09 W
Cossayuna	200	43.11 N	73.26 W
Cossayuna Lake ⊜	200	43.12 N	73.25 W
Cossebaude	50	51.05 N	13.38 E
Cossé-le-Vivien	28	47.57 N	0.55 W
Čošskaja Guba C	24	67.30 N	46.30 E
Cosson ≃	46	47.30 N	1.15 E
Cossonay	54	46.37 N	6.31 E

FRANÇAIS

Nom	Page	Lat.°′	Long.°′ W=Ouest
Cost	212	29.26 N	97.32 W
Costa, Cayo I	210	26.41 N	82.15 W
Costa, Sierra de la → Coast Ranges ⛰	168	41.00 N	123.30 W
Costacciaro	60	43.21 N	12.42 E
Costa de Caparica	256c	38.38 N	9.14 W
Costa del Marfil → Ivory Coast □[1]	140	8.00 N	5.00 W
Costa de San José	248	33.51 S	56.53 W
Costa di Rovigo	58	45.03 N	11.42 E
Costa Mesa	218	33.39 N	117.55 W
Costanera, Cadena → Coast Mountains ⛰	166	55.00 N	129.00 W
Costanero, Canal de ☰	278	34.28 S	58.28 W
Costa Rica	222	28.55 N	111.36 W
Costa Rica □[1]	220		
	226	10.00 N	84.00 W
Costaros	56	44.54 N	3.50 E
Costas	246	22.39 S	45.56 W
Costello	204	41.36 N	78.03 W
Costermansville → Bukavu	144	2.30 S	28.52 E
Costessey	44	52.40 N	1.11 E
Costești	38	44.40 N	24.53 E
Costiera, Catena ⛰	36	39.20 N	16.05 E
Costigan Lake ⊜	174	56.56 N	105.55 W
Costigliole d'Asti	56	44.47 N	8.11 E
Costigliole Saluzzo	56	44.34 N	7.29 E
Costilla	190	36.59 N	105.32 W
Costilla Creek ≃	190	36.59 N	105.43 W
Cosumnes ≃	216	38.16 N	121.26 W
Cosumnes, Middle Fork ≃	216	38.33 N	120.51 W
Cosumnes, North Fork ≃	216	38.33 N	120.51 W
Cosumnes, South Fork ≃	216	38.33 N	120.49 W
Coswig, D.D.R.	50	51.53 N	12.26 E
Coswig, D.D.R.	50	51.07 N	13.34 E
Cotabambas	238	13.45 S	72.21 W
Cotabato	106	7.13 N	124.15 E
Cotabato □[4]	106	6.40 N	124.45 E
Cotacajes ≃	238	16.00 S	67.01 W
Cotagaita	238	20.50 S	65.41 W
Cotagaita ≃	238	21.01 S	65.23 W
Cotahuasi	238	15.12 S	72.56 W
Cotão Λ[2]	256c	38.45 N	9.18 W
Cotati	216	38.20 N	122.42 W
Cotaxtla ≃	224	19.02 N	96.08 W
Coteau-Landing	196	45.15 N	74.13 W
Coteau-Station	196	45.17 N	74.14 W
Coteaux	228	18.12 N	74.02 W
Côte d'Ivoire → Ivory Coast □[1]	140	8.00 N	5.00 W
Côte-d'Or □[5]	46	47.30 N	4.50 E
Cotegipe	245	12.02 S	44.15 W
Cote Indian Reserve ✦[4]	174	51.38 N	101.53 W
Cotentin >[1]	32	49.30 N	1.30 W
Côte-Saint-Luc	265a	45.28 N	73.40 W
Côtes-du-Nord □[5]	32	48.25 N	2.40 W
Côte Visitation ✦[8]	265a	45.33 N	73.36 W
Cotherstone	156	22.37 S	148.14 E
Cothi ≃	44	51.52 N	4.10 W
Coti ≃	238	8.36 S	65.33 W
Cotia	246	23.37 S	46.56 W
Cotia □[7]	277b	23.38 S	46.56 W
Cotia ≃	246	23.31 S	46.51 W
Cotia, Represa de ⊜[1]	277b	23.44 S	46.57 W
Cotignac	56	43.32 N	6.09 E
Cotignola	60	44.23 N	11.56 E
Cotija de la Paz	224	19.49 N	102.43 W
Cotingo ≃	236	3.55 N	60.30 W
Cotmeana ≃	38	44.24 N	24.45 E
Cotoca	238	17.49 S	63.03 W
Cotonou	140	6.21 N	2.26 E
Cotopaxi □[4]	236	0.55 S	78.55 W
Cotopaxi Λ[1]	236	0.40 S	78.26 W
Cotorra, Isla I	231r	10.02 N	62.16 W
Cotovêlo, Cachoeira do ʟ	238	7.08 S	58.43 W
Cotswold Hills ⛰[2]	44	51.45 N	2.10 W
Cottage Grove, Ind., U.S.	208	39.36 N	84.52 W
Cottage Grove, Oreg., U.S.	192	43.48 N	123.03 W
Cottage Grove, Wis., U.S.	206	43.05 N	89.12 W
Cottage Hills	209	38.55 N	90.04 W
Cottageville	182	32.56 N	80.29 W
Cottam, Ont., Can.	204	42.08 N	82.45 W
Cottam, Eng., U.K.	252	53.47 N	2.46 W
Cottanello	60	42.24 N	12.41 E
Cottbus	50	51.45 N	14.19 E
Cottbus □[5]	50	51.45 N	14.00 E
Cottekill	200	41.51 N	74.06 W
Cottel Island I	176	48.51 N	53.42 W
Cottenham	44	52.18 N	0.09 E
Cotter	184	36.16 N	92.32 W
Cotter ≃	161b	35.19 S	148.57 E
Cottesloe	158a	31.59 S	115.45 E
Cottiennes, Alpes (Alpi Cozie) ⛰	56	44.45 N	7.00 E
Cottingham (Haltemprice)	42	53.47 N	0.24 W
Cottleville	209	38.45 N	90.39 W
Cottondale, Ala., U.S.	184	33.11 N	87.27 W
Cottondale, Fla., U.S.	182	30.48 N	85.23 W
Cotton Lake ⊜, Man., Can.	174	55.05 N	96.50 W
Cotton Lake ⊜, Tex., U.S.	212	29.48 N	94.48 W
Cotton Plant	184	35.00 N	91.15 W
Cottonport	184	30.59 N	92.03 W
Cotton Valley	184	32.49 N	93.25 W
Cottonwood, Ariz., U.S.	190	34.45 N	112.01 W
Cottonwood, Calif., U.S.	194	40.23 N	122.17 W
Cottonwood, Idaho, U.S.	192	46.03 N	116.21 W
Cottonwood, Minn., U.S.	188	44.37 N	95.41 W
Cottonwood ≃, Kans., U.S.	188	38.23 N	96.03 W
Cottonwood ≃, Minn., U.S.	188	44.17 N	94.25 W
Cottonwood Creek ≃, Calif., U.S.	216	36.27 N	119.20 W
Cottonwood Creek ≃, Calif., U.S.	216	36.52 N	120.12 W
Cottonwood Creek ≃, Calif., U.S.	218	35.13 N	117.59 W
Cottonwood Creek ≃, Mont., U.S.	192	48.16 N	110.52 W
Cottonwood Creek ≃, Mont., U.S.	192	48.33 N	107.45 W
Cottonwood Creek ≃, N. Dak., U.S.	188	46.16 N	98.15 W
Cottonwood Creek ≃, Okla., U.S.	186	35.54 N	97.27 W
Cottonwood Creek ≃, Oreg., U.S.	192	43.53 N	117.43 W
Cottonwood Creek ≃, S. Dak., U.S.	188	43.59 N	101.46 W
Cottonwood Creek ≃, Tex., U.S.	186	31.23 N	103.46 W
Cottonwood Creek ≃, Tex., U.S.	186	32.48 N	100.21 W
Cottonwood Creek ≃, Utah, U.S.	190	39.09 N	110.55 W
Cottonwood Creek ≃, Wyo., U.S.	192	43.51 N	108.09 W
Cottonwood Creek, Middle Fork ≃	194	40.23 N	122.20 W
Cottonwood Creek, South Fork ≃	194	40.23 N	122.20 W
Cottonwood Falls	188	38.22 N	96.32 W

PORTUGUÊS

Nome	Página	Lat.°′	Long.°′ W=Oeste
Cottonwood Wash V, Ariz., U.S.	190	36.19 N	113.59 W
Cottonwood Wash V, Ariz., U.S.	190	35.00 N	110.39 W
Cotubandê	277a	22.51 S	43.01 W
Cotuhé ≃	236	2.53 S	69.44 W
Cotuí	228	19.03 N	70.09 W
Cotuit	197	41.37 N	70.26 W
Cotulla	186	28.26 N	99.14 W
Cotunduba, Ilha de I	277a	22.58 S	43.09 W
Coubert	251	48.40 N	2.42 E
Coubre, Pointe de la >	32	45.41 N	1.13 W
Coubron	251	48.55 N	2.35 E
Couches-les-Mines	54	46.52 N	4.34 E
Couchiching, Lake ⊜	202	44.40 N	79.23 W
Coucouron	56	44.48 N	3.58 E
Coucy-le-Château-Auffrique	46	49.31 N	3.19 E
Coudekerque-Branche	46	51.02 N	2.24 E
Coudersport	204	41.46 N	78.01 W
Coudres, Île aux I	176	47.24 N	70.23 W
Couer d'Alene Indian Reservation ✦[4]	192	47.18 N	116.45 W
Couesnon ≃	32	48.37 N	1.31 W
Couffo ≃	140	6.35 N	1.59 E
Cougar	214	46.03 N	122.18 W
Cougar Reservoir ⊜[1]	192	44.06 N	122.12 W
Couhé	32	46.18 N	0.11 E
Couillet	46	50.23 N	4.27 E
Couilly-Pont-aux-Dames	251	48.53 N	2.52 E
Coulanges-la-Vineuse	46	47.42 N	3.35 E
Coulanges-sur-Yonne	46	47.31 N	3.32 E
Coulee City	192	47.37 N	119.17 W
Coulee Dam	192	47.58 N	118.59 W
Coulee Dam National Recreation Area ♠	192	47.48 N	119.45 W
Coulihaut	230d	15.30 N	61.29 W
Coulman Island I	9	73.27 S	169.40 E
Coulmier-le-Sec	54	47.45 N	4.29 E
Coulogne	46	50.55 N	1.53 E
Coulomby	46	50.42 N	2.00 E
Coulommiers	46	48.49 N	3.05 E
Coulon ≃	56	43.51 N	5.00 E
Coulonge ≃	180	45.51 N	76.46 W
Coulonge-Est ≃	180	46.06 N	76.44 W
Coulsdon ✦[8]	250	51.19 N	0.08 W
Coulta	156	34.23 S	135.29 E
Coulters	269b	40.18 N	79.48 W
Coulterville, Calif., U.S.	216	37.43 N	120.12 W
Coulterville, Ill., U.S.	184	38.11 N	89.36 W
Council	192	44.44 N	116.26 W
Council Bluffs	188	41.16 N	95.52 W
Council Grove	188	38.40 N	96.29 W
Council Grove Lake ⊜[1]	188	38.42 N	96.31 W
Countegany	161b	36.11 S	149.27 E
Country Campus	212	30.49 N	95.26 W
Country Club Estates	210	28.03 N	81.57 W
Country Club Hills	268	41.34 N	87.44 W
Country Hills	269b	40.19 N	79.42 W
Country Homes	192	47.45 N	117.24 W
Country Ridge Estates	266	41.02 N	73.41 W
Countryside	268	41.47 N	87.52 W
Countryside Lake ⊜	268	42.15 N	88.03 W
Countryside Manor	268	42.18 N	87.56 W
County Park ♠	274a	43.06 N	78.54 W
Coupar Angus	28	56.33 N	3.17 W
Coupeville	214	48.13 N	122.41 W
Coupland	212	30.28 N	97.24 W
Coupon	204	40.32 N	78.31 W
Coupvray	251	48.54 N	2.48 E
Courantyne (Corantijn) ≃	240	5.55 N	57.05 W
Courbevoie	46	48.54 N	2.15 E
Courbons	56	44.06 N	6.12 E
Courçay	46	47.15 N	0.52 E
Courcelle	251	48.42 N	2.06 E
Courcelles, Bel.	46	50.28 N	4.22 E
Courcelles, Fr.	251	49.07 N	2.18 E
Courcelles-Chaussy	52	49.07 N	6.24 E
Courcelles-les-Lens	46	50.25 N	3.01 E
Courcelles-sur-Nied	52	49.04 N	6.18 E
Courchevel	56	45.25 N	6.38 E
Cour-Cheverny	46	47.30 N	1.27 E
Courcibo ≃	240	4.53 N	53.00 W
Courçon	32	46.15 N	0.49 W
Courcouronnes	251	48.37 N	2.24 E
Courdimanche	251	49.02 N	2.00 E
Cour-et-Buis	56	45.26 N	5.00 E
Courgent	251	48.54 N	1.40 E
Courland → Kurzeme □[9]	66	56.50 N	22.30 E
Courmayeur	56	45.47 N	6.58 E
Couronne, Cap >	56	43.19 N	5.03 E
Couronnement, Île du → Coronation Island I	9	60.37 S	45.30 W
Courpière	56	45.45 N	3.33 E
Courquetaine	251	48.41 N	2.45 E
Course Brook ≃	273	42.17 N	71.22 W
Courson-les-Carrières	46	47.36 N	3.30 E
Court	54	47.14 N	7.20 E
Courtacon	46	48.42 N	3.17 E
Courtalain	46	48.05 N	1.09 E
Courteilles	46	48.44 N	1.01 E
Courtenay, B.C., Can.	172	49.41 N	125.00 W
Courtenay, Fr.	46	48.02 N	3.03 E
Courthézon	56	44.05 N	4.53 E
Courtice	202	43.55 N	78.46 W
Courtisols	52	48.59 N	4.31 E
Courtland, Ont., Can.	202	42.51 N	80.38 W
Courtland, Ala., U.S.	184	34.40 N	87.18 W
Courtland, Calif., U.S.	216	38.20 N	121.34 W
Courtland, Va., U.S.	198	36.43 N	77.04 W
Courtleigh	274b	39.22 N	76.46 W
Courtney, Pa., U.S.	269b	40.13 N	79.58 W
Courtney, Tex., U.S.	212	30.16 N	96.04 W
Courtney Creek ≃	186	31.16 N	102.50 W
Courtomer, Fr.	46	48.38 N	0.22 E
Courtomer, Fr.	251	48.39 N	2.54 E
Courtrai → Kortrijk	46	50.50 N	3.16 E
Courtright	204	42.49 N	82.28 W
Courtry, Fr.	251	48.33 N	2.46 E
Courtry, Fr.	251	48.55 N	2.36 E
Court-Saint-Étienne	46	50.39 N	4.34 E
Courville	196	46.53 N	71.10 W
Courville-sur-Eure	46	48.27 N	1.15 E
Coushatta	184	32.00 N	93.21 W
Cousin ≃	46	47.15 N	4.04 E
Cousiño, Parque ♠	276e	33.28 S	70.40 W
Cousins Lake ⊜	174	56.49 N	98.32 W
Cousolre	46	50.15 N	4.09 E
Coussegrey	46	47.57 N	4.01 E
Coussey	54	48.25 N	5.41 E
Coustellet	56	43.53 N	5.11 E
Coutances	32	49.03 N	1.26 W
Coutevroult	251	48.52 N	2.51 E
Couto, Serra do ⛰	246	22.18 S	43.20 W
Couto de Magalhães ≃	245	13.37 S	53.09 W
Couto Magalhães	240	8.17 S	49.16 W
Coutras	32	45.02 N	0.08 W
Coutts	172	49.00 N	111.57 W
Couture, Lac ⊜	166	60.07 N	75.20 W
Couture-sur-Loir	46	47.45 N	0.41 E
Couves, Ilha das I	246	23.25 S	44.52 W
Couvet	54	46.56 N	6.38 E
Couvin	46	50.03 N	4.29 E
Cova da Piedade	256c	38.40 N	9.10 W
Covane	146	21.22 S	33.56 E

Covasna	38	45.51 N	26.11 E
Covasna □[4]	38	46.00 N	26.00 E
Cove	192	45.18 N	117.49 W
Covedale	208	39.07 N	84.37 W
Cove Harbor C	266	41.03 N	73.30 W
Cove Island I	180	45.17 N	81.44 W
Covelo, Ang.	142	12.06 S	13.55 E
Covelo, Calif., U.S.	194	39.48 N	123.15 W
Cove Neck	266	40.53 N	73.31 W
Cove Neck >[1]	266	40.53 N	73.30 W
Coventry, Eng., U.K.	44	52.25 N	1.30 W
Coventry, Conn., U.S.	197	41.48 N	72.23 W
Coventry, Del., U.S.	275	39.40 N	75.38 W
Coventry, R.I., U.S.	197	41.41 N	71.34 W
Coventry Cathedral ʊ[1]	44	52.25 N	1.30 W
Coventryville	275	40.10 N	75.41 W
Cove Point	198	38.23 N	76.24 W
Cove Point >	198	38.23 N	76.23 W
Cover ≃	42	54.17 N	1.46 W
Covered Wells	190	32.10 N	112.08 W
Covert	206	42.17 N	86.16 W
Covigliaio	60	44.08 N	11.18 E
Covilhã	34	40.17 N	7.30 W
Covina	218	34.05 N	117.53 W
Covington, Ind., U.S.	184	40.09 N	87.24 W
Covington, Ky., U.S.	208	39.05 N	84.30 W
Covington, La., U.S.	184	30.29 N	90.06 W
Covington, Ohio, U.S.	208	40.07 N	84.21 W
Covington, Okla., U.S.	186	36.18 N	97.35 W
Covington, Pa., U.S.	200	41.45 N	77.05 W
Covington, Tenn., U.S.	184	35.34 N	89.38 W
Covington, Tex., U.S.	212	32.11 N	97.16 W
Covington, Va., U.S.	182	37.47 N	79.59 W
Covões	256c	38.50 N	9.20 W
Covunco, Arroyo ≃	242	38.29 S	69.32 W
Cow ≃	180	47.23 N	83.59 W
Cowal ✦[1]	42	56.05 N	5.08 W
Cowal, Lake ⊜	156	33.35 S	147.25 E
Cowan, Ky., U.S.	208	38.24 N	83.54 W
Cowan, Tenn., U.S.	184	35.10 N	86.01 W
Cowan, Lake ⊜	152	31.50 S	121.50 E
Cowanesque	200	41.56 N	77.30 W
Cowanesque ≃	200	42.00 N	77.07 W
Cowan Heights	270	33.47 N	117.47 W
Cowan Lake ⊜, Sask., Can.	174	54.00 N	107.15 W
Cowan Lake ⊜, Ohio, U.S.	208	39.23 N	83.54 W
Cowan Lake State Park ♠	208	39.23 N	83.53 W
Cowansburg	269b	40.15 N	79.46 W
Cowanshannock Creek ≃	204	40.51 N	79.30 W
Cowansville, Qué., Can.	196	45.12 N	72.45 W
Cowansville, Pa., U.S.	204	40.53 N	79.36 W
Cowaramup	152	33.52 S	115.05 E
Coward	182	33.58 N	79.45 W
Coward Springs	156	29.24 S	136.49 E
Cowarie	156	27.43 S	138.20 E
Cow Bayou ≃	212	31.19 N	97.00 W
Cowbridge	44	51.28 N	3.27 W
Cowburn Tunnel ✦[5]	252	53.21 N	1.52 W
Cow Canyon V	270	34.01 N	120.06 W
Cowcowing Lakes ⊜	152	31.01 S	117.18 E
Cow Creek ≃, Kans., U.S.	188	38.02 N	97.56 W
Cow Creek ≃, Mont., U.S.	192	47.47 N	108.56 W
Cow Creek ≃, Okla., U.S.	186	34.10 N	98.00 W
Cow Creek ≃, Oreg., U.S.	192	42.57 N	123.20 W
Cow Creek ≃, Wash., U.S.	192	46.45 N	118.09 W
Cowden, Ill., U.S.	209	39.15 N	88.52 W
Cowden, Pa., U.S.	269b	40.19 N	80.13 W
Cowdenbeath	42	56.07 N	3.21 W
Cowell	156	33.41 S	136.55 E
Coweman ≃	214	46.06 N	122.52 W
Cowen	178	38.25 N	80.34 W
Cowen, Mount Λ	192	45.23 N	110.29 W
Cowes, Austl.	159	38.27 S	145.14 E
Cowes, Eng., U.K.	44	50.45 N	1.18 W
Cowessess Indian Reserve ✦[4]	174	50.31 N	102.42 W
Coweta	186	35.57 N	95.39 W
Cowgulch Creek ≃	192	46.02 N	107.52 W
Cow Head	176	49.55 N	57.48 W
Cowhouse Creek ≃	212	31.10 N	97.35 W
Cowichan ≃	214	48.46 N	123.38 W
Cowichan Bay	172	48.44 N	123.40 W
Cowichan Lake ⊜	172	48.54 N	124.20 W
Cowiche Creek, North Fork ≃	214	46.38 N	120.41 W
Cowiche Creek, South Fork ≃	214	46.38 N	120.41 W
Cowles Dam ✦[6]	263d	26.13 S	28.28 E
Cowlesville	200	42.51 N	78.28 W
Cowley, Austl.	156	26.54 S	144.49 E
Cowley, Alta., Can.	172	49.34 N	114.05 W
Cowley, Eng., U.K.	44	51.43 N	1.12 W
Cowley, Wyo., U.S.	192	44.53 N	108.28 W
Cowley ✦[8]	250	51.32 N	0.29 W
Cowlitz □[6]	214	46.07 N	122.43 W
Cowlitz ≃	214	46.05 N	122.53 W
Cowm Reservoir ⊜[1]	252	53.40 N	2.11 W
Cow Palace ʊ	272	37.42 N	122.25 W
Cowpasture ≃	178	37.48 N	79.45 W
Cowpens	182	35.01 N	81.48 W
Cowpens National Battlefield ♠	182	35.06 N	81.46 W
Cowplain	44	50.54 N	1.01 W
Cowra	156	33.50 S	148.41 E
Cox ≃	154	15.19 S	135.25 E
Cox, Mount Λ[2]	152	24.55 S	125.36 E
Coxá ≃	245	14.16 S	44.11 W
Cox Creek ≃	202	43.35 N	80.29 W
Coxheath	250	51.14 N	0.30 E
Coxim	245	18.30 S	54.45 W
Coxim ≃	245	18.34 S	54.46 W
Coxipi, Lac ⊜	176	51.33 N	58.25 W
Coxipó da Ponte	238	15.38 S	56.04 W
Coxquihui	224	20.11 N	97.35 W
Coxs ≃	160	33.57 S	150.25 E
Coxsackie	200	42.21 N	73.48 W
Cox's Bāzār	110	21.26 N	91.59 E
Cox's Cove	176	49.07 N	58.05 W
Coyah	140	9.43 N	13.23 W
Coyame	222	29.28 N	105.06 W
Coyanosa Draw V	186	31.18 N	103.06 W
Coya Sur	242	22.25 S	69.38 W
Coyhaique	244	45.34 S	72.04 W
Coyle, Water of ≃	42	55.28 N	4.32 W
Coyoacán	276a	19.20 N	99.10 W
Coyoacán □[7]	276a	19.19 N	99.11 W
Coyote	216	37.13 N	121.44 W
Coyote ≃	222	30.48 N	112.35 W
Coyote, Punta >	226	9.46 N	85.16 W
Coyote Creek ≃, Calif., U.S.	194	33.13 N	116.13 W
Coyote Creek ≃, Calif., U.S.	216	37.28 N	122.03 W
Coyote Creek ≃, Calif., U.S.	270	33.47 N	118.05 W
Coyote Creek, East Fork ≃	216	37.10 N	121.30 W
Coyote Creek, Middle Fork ≃	216	37.10 N	121.30 W
Coyote Hills ⛰[2]	272	37.33 N	122.05 W
Coyote Hills Regional Park ♠	272	37.33 N	122.06 W
Coyote Lake ⊜	194	35.04 N	116.45 W
Coyote Lake ⊜[1]	216	37.06 N	121.32 W
Coyotepec	224	19.46 N	99.12 W
Coyote Point >	272	37.35 N	122.19 W
Coyote Wash V	190	32.40 N	114.08 W
Coy Pond ⊜	273	42.36 N	70.49 W
Coyuca de Benítez	224	17.02 N	100.04 W

Coyuca de Catalán	224	18.20 N	100.39 W
Coyutla	224	20.15 N	97.39 W
Cozad	188	40.52 N	99.59 W
Cozes	32	45.35 N	0.50 W
Cozie, Alpi (Alpes Cottiennes) ⛰	56	44.45 N	7.00 E
Cozoyoapan	224	16.46 N	98.15 W
Cozumel	222	20.31 N	86.55 W
Cozumel, Isla de I	222	20.25 N	86.55 W
Cozy Lake	266	41.01 N	74.30 W
Crab Alley Bay C	198	38.55 N	76.17 W
Crab Creek ≃	192	46.49 N	119.55 W
Crab Hill	231g	13.19 N	59.38 W
Crab Meadow ≋	266	40.55 N	73.20 W
Crab Orchard, Ky., U.S.	182	37.28 N	84.30 W
Crab Orchard, Tenn., U.S.	182	35.55 N	84.53 W
Crab Orchard Lake ⊜[1]	184	37.43 N	89.05 W
Crabtree	204	40.22 N	79.35 W
Crabtree Creek ≃	269b	40.21 N	79.30 W
Crabtree Mills	196	45.58 N	73.28 W
Craches	251	48.34 N	1.49 E
Crackenback ≃	161b	36.21 S	148.36 E
Cracovie → Kraków	30	50.03 N	19.58 E
Cračovka	70	52.57 N	52.52 E
Cradle Mountain National Park ♠	156	42.00 S	146.00 E
Cradock, Austl.	156	32.04 S	138.30 E
Cradock, S. Afr.	148	32.08 S	25.36 E
Crafers-Bridgewater	158b	35.01 S	138.47 E
Crafthole	148	26.24 S	24.03 E
Crafton	204	40.26 N	80.04 W
Crafts Creek ≃	275	40.07 N	74.46 W
Cragg Vale	252	53.42 N	2.00 W
Cragsmoor	200	41.40 N	74.23 W
Craig, B.C., Can.	214	49.18 N	124.15 W
Craig, Alaska, U.S.	170	55.29 N	133.09 W
Craig, Colo., U.S.	190	40.31 N	107.33 W
Craig, Mo., U.S.	184	40.11 N	95.23 W
Craig, Nebr., U.S.	188	41.47 N	96.22 W
Craig, Point Λ	152	26.51 S	126.19 E
Craig Air Force Base ▪	184	32.21 N	86.59 W
Craig Beach	204	41.07 N	81.01 W
Craig Creek ≃	182	37.39 N	79.49 W
Craigellachie	172	50.59 N	118.43 W
Craighall ✦[8]	263d	26.07 S	28.02 E
Craighall Park ✦[8]	263d	26.08 S	28.01 E
Craighouse	42	55.51 N	5.57 W
Craigmont	192	46.15 N	116.28 W
Craigmore	144	20.28 S	32.50 E
Craigmyle	172	51.40 N	112.15 W
Craignure	28	56.28 N	5.42 W
Craigsville, Pa., U.S.	204	40.51 N	79.39 W
Craigsville, Va., U.S.	182	38.05 N	79.23 W
Craigville	206	40.47 N	85.06 W
Craik	174	51.03 N	105.49 W
Crailsheim	52	49.08 N	10.04 E
Craiova	38	44.19 N	23.48 E
Crake ≃	42	54.14 N	3.03 W
Craley	198	39.57 N	76.31 W
Cramant	46	48.59 N	3.59 E
Cramlington	42	55.05 N	1.36 W
Cranage	252	53.12 N	2.22 W
Cranberry	204	41.21 N	79.43 W
Cranberry Brook ≃	273	42.11 N	71.01 W
Cranberry Creek	200	43.09 N	74.14 W
Cranberry Island I	202	44.44 N	81.18 W
Cranberry Lake	200	40.57 N	74.45 W
Cranberry Lake ⊜, Ont., Can.	202	44.47 N	75.50 W
Cranberry Lake ⊜, Ont., Can.	202	44.26 N	76.19 W
Cranberry Lake ⊜, N.Y., U.S.	178	44.10 N	74.50 W
Cranberry Lake ⊜, Wash., U.S.	214	47.17 N	123.05 W
Cranberry Pond ⊜	266	41.08 N	74.12 W
Cranberry Portage	174	54.35 N	101.23 W
Cranborne Chase ✦[3]	44	50.55 N	2.05 W
Cranbourne	159	38.06 S	145.17 E
Cranbrook, Austl.	152	34.18 S	117.32 E
Cranbrook, B.C., Can.	172	49.31 N	115.46 W
Cranbrook, Eng., U.K.	44	51.06 N	0.33 E
Cranbrook ʊ[3]	271	42.34 N	83.14 W
Cranbury	266	40.19 N	74.31 W
Cranbury Brook ≃	266	40.19 N	74.37 W
Crandall	212	32.38 N	96.27 W
Crandon	180	45.34 N	88.54 W
Crandon Lakes	200	41.07 N	74.50 W
Crane, Ariz., U.S.	194	32.42 N	114.40 W
Crane, Ind., U.S.	184	38.54 N	86.54 W
Crane, Mo., U.S.	184	36.54 N	93.34 W
Crane, Tex., U.S.	186	31.24 N	102.21 W
Crane Beach ♠[2]	273	42.41 N	70.46 W
Cranebrook	264a	33.43 S	150.42 E
Crane Creek ≃	180	43.01 N	91.58 W
Crane Creek Reservoir ⊜[1]	192	44.22 N	116.35 W
⊜, Ont., Can.	202	45.13 N	79.57
Crane Lake ⊜, Sask., Can.	174	50.06 N	109.06 W
Crane Mountain Λ	192	42.04 N	120.13 W
Crane Neck Point >	266	40.58 N	73.10 W
Crane Prairie Reservoir ⊜	192	43.44 N	122.02 W
Crane River Indian Reserve ✦[4]	174	51.30 N	99.14 W
Cranesville	204	41.54 N	80.21 W
Cranfield	44	52.05 N	0.35 W
Cranfills Gap	212	31.46 N	97.50 W
Cranford	200	40.39 N	74.19 W
Crange ✦[8]	253	51.32 N	7.11 E
Cran-Gévrier	54	45.54 N	6.06 E
Crank	252	53.29 N	2.45 W
Cranleigh	44	51.09 N	0.30 W
Crans	54	46.19 N	7.28 E
Cranston	197	41.47 N	71.26 W
Cranston Heights	275	39.38 N	75.38 W
Craolândia	240	7.57 S	47.15 W
Craon	32	47.51 N	0.57 W
Craonne	46	49.26 N	3.47 E
Craponne, Fr.	56	45.20 N	3.51 E
Craponne, Fr.	56	45.44 N	4.43 E
Craponne, Canal de ☰	56	43.40 N	4.39 E
Crary Mountains ⛰	9	76.48 S	117.40 W
Craryville	200	42.11 N	73.35 W
Crasna	38	45.36 N	26.08 E
Crasna (Kraszna) ≃	38	48.09 N	22.20 E
Crassier	54	46.22 N	6.11 E
Crater Lake ⊜, St. Vin.	231h	13.20 N	61.11 W
Crater Lake ⊜, Oreg., U.S.	192	42.56 N	122.06 W
Crater Lake National Park ♠	192	42.49 N	122.08 W
Crater Mount Λ	154	6.30 S	145.10 E
Crater Point >	154	5.22 S	152.09 E
Craters of the Moon National Monument ♠	192	43.20 N	113.35 W
Cratéus	240	5.10 S	40.40 W
Crato	240	7.14 S	39.23 W
Crau ✦[1]	56	43.36 N	4.50 E
Crauford, Cape >	166	73.43 N	84.50 W
Cravant	46	47.41 N	3.41 E
Cravari ≃	238	12.06 S	58.03 W
Cravat	209	38.25 N	89.06 W
Craven	174	50.39 N	104.50 W
Craven Arms	44	52.26 N	2.50 W
Cravensville	161b	36.24 S	147.34 E
Cravo Norte	236	6.18 N	70.12 W
Cravo Norte ≃	236	6.18 N	70.12 W
Cravo Sur ≃	236	4.42 N	71.36 W
Crawfish ≃	206	43.00 N	88.49 W
Crawford, Scot., U.K.	42	55.28 N	3.40 W
Crawford, Colo., U.S.	190	38.42 N	107.37 W

Crawford, Miss., U.S.	184	33.18 N	88.37 W
Crawford, Nebr., U.S.	188	42.41 N	103.25 W
Crawford, Tex., U.S.	212	31.32 N	97.27 W
Crawford □[6], Ind., U.S.	208	38.20 N	86.28 W
Crawford □[6], Ohio, U.S.	204	40.48 N	82.58 W
Crawford □[6], Pa., U.S.	204	41.39 N	80.10 W
Crawford Bay	172	49.42 N	116.48 W
Crawford Countryside	268	41.32 N	87.43 W
Crawford Notch State Park ♠	178	44.13 N	71.25 W
Crawfordsville, Ark., U.S.	184	35.14 N	90.20 W
Crawfordsville, Ind., U.S.	184	40.02 N	86.54 W
Crawfordville, Fla., U.S.	182	30.11 N	84.23 W
Crawfordville, Ga., U.S.	182	33.33 N	82.54 W
Crawinkel	50	50.47 N	10.47 E
Crawley	44	51.07 N	0.12 W
Crawshawbooth	252	53.43 N	2.17 W
Cray	44	51.55 N	3.36 W
Crayford ✦[8]	250	51.27 N	0.11 E
Crays Hill	250	51.36 N	0.28 E
Crazy Mountains ⛰	192	46.08 N	110.20 W
Crazy Peak Λ	192	46.01 N	110.16 W
Crazy Woman Creek ≃	192	44.29 N	106.08 W
Creal Springs	184	37.37 N	88.50 W
Creamery	275	40.13 N	75.25 W
Crean Lake ⊜	174	54.05 N	106.10 W
Crêches-sur-Saône	54	46.15 N	4.47 E
Crécy, Forêt de ♠	251	48.48 N	2.53 E
Crécy-en-Brie	46	48.51 N	2.55 E
Crécy-en-Ponthieu	46	50.15 N	1.53 E
Crécy-sur-Serre	46	49.42 N	3.37 E
Credit ≃	202	43.33 N	79.35 W
Crediton	44	50.47 N	3.39 W
Cree ≃, Sask., Can.	166	59.00 N	105.47 W
Cree ≃, Scot., U.K.	42	54.52 N	4.20 W
Creede	190	37.51 N	106.56 W
Creedmoor	182	36.07 N	78.41 W
Creedmore	212	30.12 N	97.43 W
Creek Brook ≃	273	42.47 N	71.08 W
Creek Locks	200	41.52 N	74.03 W
Creekmouth ✦[8]	250	51.31 N	0.06 E
Creekside	204	40.41 N	79.12 W
Creekwood	268	41.39 N	87.59 W
Creel	222	27.45 N	107.38 W
Cree Lake ⊜	166	57.30 N	106.30 W
Creemore	202	44.19 N	80.06 W
Creetown	42	54.54 N	4.23 W
Creglingen	52	49.28 N	10.01 E
Crégy-lès-Meaux	251	48.58 N	2.52 E
Créhange	52	49.03 N	6.35 E
Creighton, Sask., Can.	174	54.45 N	101.54 W
Creighton, S. Afr.	148	30.01 S	29.51 E
Creighton, Nebr., U.S.	188	42.28 N	97.54 W
Creighton, Pa., U.S.	204	40.35 N	79.47 W
Creighton Mine	180	46.28 N	81.11 W
Creil, Fr.	46	49.16 N	2.29 E
Creil, Ned.	48	52.45 N	5.40 E
Crema	56	45.22 N	9.41 E
Cremia	54	46.05 N	9.16 E
Crémieu	56	45.43 N	5.15 E
Cremona, Alta., Can.	172	51.33 N	114.29 W
Cremona, It.	58	45.07 N	10.02 E
Cremona □[4]	58	45.12 N	10.00 E
Crenshaw, Miss., U.S.	184	34.30 N	90.12 W
Crenshaw, Pa., U.S.	204	41.15 N	78.46 W
Crépieux-la-Pape	56	45.48 N	4.52 E
Crep Nudo Λ	58	46.13 N	12.24 E
Crepori ≃	240	5.42 S	57.08 W
Crépy-en-Laonnois	46	49.36 N	3.31 E
Crépy-en-Valois	46	49.14 N	2.54 E
Créquy	46	50.29 N	2.03 E
Cres	36	44.58 N	14.25 E
Cres, Otok I	36	44.50 N	14.25 E
Cresaptown	178	39.36 N	78.50 W
Crescent, N.Y., U.S.	200	42.49 N	73.43 W
Crescent, Okla., U.S.	186	35.57 N	97.36 W
Crescent, Oreg., U.S.	192	43.29 N	121.41 W
Crescent, Lake ⊜	214	48.05 N	123.50 W
Crescent Beach, B.C., Can.	214	49.04 N	122.53 W
Crescent Beach, Fla., U.S.	210	27.15 N	82.32 W
Crescent City, Calif., U.S.	194	41.45 N	124.12 W
Crescent City, Fla., U.S.	182	29.26 N	81.30 W
Crescent City, Ill., U.S.	206	40.46 N	87.51 W
Crescent Ditch ☰	216	36.29 N	120.07 W
Crescent Group II	98	16.31 N	111.38 E
Crescent Heights	212	32.11 N	95.56 W
Crescentino	56	45.11 N	8.06 E
Crescent Lake ⊜, Fla., U.S.	182	29.28 N	81.30 W
Crescent Lake ⊜, Oreg., U.S.	192	43.29 N	121.59 W
Crescent Lake Estates	271	42.38 N	83.25 W
Crescent Spur	172	53.35 N	120.41 W
Crescentville ✦[8]	275	40.02 N	75.05 W
Crescenzago ✦[8]	256b	45.30 N	9.15 E
Cresco, Iowa, U.S.	180	43.22 N	92.07 W
Cresco, Pa., U.S.	200	41.09 N	75.17 W
Crespano del Grappa	58	45.49 N	11.50 E
Crespian	56	43.53 N	4.06 E
Crespières	251	48.53 N	1.55 E
Crespin	46	50.25 N	3.39 E
Crespino	58	44.59 N	11.53 E
Crespo	242	32.02 S	60.19 W
Cressbrook Creek ≃	161a	27.05 S	152.27 E
Cressely	251	48.43 N	2.05 E
Cressey	216	37.25 N	120.40 W
Cresskill	266	40.57 N	73.57 W
Cresskill Brook ≃	266	40.57 N	73.58 W
Cresson, Pa., U.S.	204	40.28 N	78.35 W
Cresson, Tex., U.S.	212	32.32 N	97.37 W
Cressona	198	40.38 N	76.12 W
Cressy	159	38.02 S	143.38 E
Crest	56	44.44 N	5.02 E
Cresta	54	46.28 N	9.31 E
Crested Butte	190	38.52 N	106.59 W
Cresthaven	210	26.19 N	80.05 W
Crest Hill	206	41.32 N	88.07 W
Crestline, Calif., U.S.	218	34.14 N	117.17 W
Crestline, Ohio, U.S.	204	40.47 N	82.44 W
Creston, B.C., Can.	172	49.06 N	116.31 W
Creston, Newf., Can.	176	47.09 N	55.11 W
Creston, Calif., U.S.	216	35.31 N	120.31 W
Creston, Ill., U.S.	206	41.56 N	88.58 W
Creston, Iowa, U.S.	188	41.04 N	94.22 W
Creston, Ohio, U.S.	204	40.59 N	81.54 W
Crestone Peak Λ	190	37.58 N	105.36 W
Crestview, Fla., U.S.	184	30.46 N	86.34 W
Crestview, Wis., U.S.	206	42.49 N	87.49 W
Crestview Heights	200	42.05 N	76.07 W
Crestwood, Ill., U.S.	268	41.39 N	87.44 W
Crestwood, Ky., U.S.	208	38.19 N	85.28 W
Crestwood, Mo., U.S.	209	38.33 N	90.23 W
Creswell, Eng., U.K.	42	53.16 N	1.12 W
Creswell, Oreg., U.S.	192	43.55 N	123.01 W
Creswell Bay C	166	72.35 N	93.25 W
Creswell Creek ≃	152	18.10 S	135.11 E
Creswell Downs	152	17.57 S	135.55 E
Creswick	159	37.26 S	143.54 E
Creta, Isla de → Kríti I	38	35.29 N	24.42 E
Crete, Ill., U.S.	206	41.27 N	87.38 W
Crete, Nebr., U.S.	188	40.38 N	96.58 W
Crete → Kríti I	38	35.29 N	24.42 E

≃ River	Fluss	Río	Rivière	Rio	
☰ Canal	Kanal	Canal	Canal	Canal	
ʟ Waterfall, Rapids	Wasserfall, Stromschnellen	Cascada, Rápidos	Chute d'eau, Rapides	Cascata, Rápidos	
⋃ Strait	Meeresstrasse	Estrecho	Détroit	Estreito	
C Bay, Gulf	Bucht, Golf	Bahía, Golfo	Baie, Golfe	Baía, Golfo	
⊜ Lake, Lakes	See, Seen	Lago, Lagos	Lac, Lacs	Lago, Lagos	
≋ Swamp	Sumpf	Pantano	Marais	Pântano	
⍓ Ice Features, Glacier	Eis- und Gletscherformen	Accidentes Glaciales	Formes glaciaires	Acidentes Glaciares	
⊤ Other Hydrographic Features	Andere Hydrographische Objekte	Otros Elementos Hidrográficos	Autres données hydrographiques	Outros Elementos Hidrográficos	

✣ Submarine Features	Untermeerische Objekte	Accidentes Submarinos	Formes de relief sous-marin	Acidentes Submarinos
□ Political Unit	Politische Einheit	Unidad Politica	Entité politique	Unidade Política
ʊ Cultural Institution	Kulturelle Institution	Institución Cultural	Institution culturelle	Instituição Cultural
⊥ Historical Site	Historische Stätte	Sitio Histórico	Site historique	Sitio Histórico
♠ Recreational Site	Erholungs- und Ferienort	Sitio de Recreo	Centre de loisirs	Sítio de Lazer
⊠ Airport	Flughafen	Aeropuerto	Aéroport	Aeroporto
▪ Military Installation	Militäranlage	Instalación Militar	Installation militaire	Instalação Militar
✦ Miscellaneous	Verschiedenes	Misceláneo	Divers	Miscelânea

ENGLISH: Name, Page, Lat.°′, Long.°′ — DEUTSCH: Name, Seite, Breite°′, Länge°′ E=Ost

Name	Page	Lat.	Long.
Crete, Sea of → Kritikón Pélagos ≂[2]	38	35.46 N	23.54 E
Créteil	46	48.48 N	2.28 E
Crétéville	36	36.40 N	10.20 E
Cretin, Cape >	154	6.40 S	147.52 E
Creus, Cabo de >	34	42.19 N	3.19 E
Creuse □[5]	32	46.05 N	2.00 E
Creuse ≃	32	47.00 N	0.34 E
Creussen	30	49.51 N	11.37 E
Creutzwald-la-Croix	52	49.12 N	6.41 E
Creuzburg	52	51.03 N	10.15 E
Crevacuore	56	45.41 N	8.15 E
Crevalcore	58	44.43 N	11.09 E
Creve Coeur, Ill., U.S.	180	40.39 N	89.35 W
Creve Coeur, Mo., U.S.	209	38.40 N	90.27 W
Crèvecœur-en-Auge	46	49.07 N	0.01 E
Crèvecœur-en-Brie	251	48.45 N	2.55 E
Creve Coeur Lake ⊜	209	38.43 N	90.29 W
Crèvecœur-le-Grand	46	49.36 N	2.05 E
Crevillente	34	38.15 N	0.48 W
Crevoladossola	54	46.09 N	8.18 E
Crewe, Eng., U.K.	44	53.05 N	2.27 W
Crewe, Va., U.S.	182	37.05 N	78.08 W
Crewkerne	44	50.53 N	2.48 W
Crews Lake ⊜	210	28.23 N	82.31 W
Crewsville	210	27.16 N	81.36 W
Crib Point	159	38.22 S	145.12 E
Cricamola ≃	226	8.59 N	81.54 W
Criccieth	44	52.55 N	4.14 W
Criciúma	242	28.40 S	49.23 W
Crick	44	52.21 N	1.07 W
Cricket	182	36.11 N	81.12 W
Crickhowell	44	51.53 N	3.07 W
Cricklade	44	51.39 N	1.51 W
Cridersville	206	40.39 N	84.09 W
Crieff	28	56.23 N	3.52 W
Criel-sur-Mer	46	50.01 N	1.19 E
Criffell ∧	42	54.57 N	3.38 W
Crikvenica	36	45.11 N	14.42 E
Crillon, Mount ∧	170	58.40 N	137.10 W
Crimea → Krymskij Poluostrov >[1]	68	45.00 N	34.00 E
Crimmitschau	50	50.49 N	12.23 E
Crîngeni	38	44.01 N	24.47 E
Cringila	160	34.28 S	150.53 E
Cripple Creek	190	38.45 N	105.11 W
Criques, Grande Île de I	263b	4.20 S	15.25 E
Criquetot l'Esneval	46	49.39 N	0.16 E
Crirninoso, Monte ∧	246	21.32 S	43.25 W
Crisenoy	251	48.36 N	2.45 E
Crisfield	198	37.59 N	75.51 W
Crisólia	246	22.15 S	46.25 W
Crisóstomo, Ribeirão ≃	240	10.19 S	50.26 W
Criss Creek	172	51.03 N	120.44 W
Crissiumal	242	27.30 S	54.07 W
Cristal, Monts de ∧∧	142	0.30 N	10.30 E
Cristal, Sierra del ∧∧	230p	20.33 N	75.31 W
Cristalândia	240	10.36 S	49.11 W
Cristalina	245	16.45 S	47.36 W
Cristalino ≃	245	12.38 S	50.40 W
Cristallo ∧	58	46.34 N	12.12 E
Cristianópolis	245	17.13 S	48.45 W
Cristina	246	22.13 S	45.16 W
Cristinápolis	240	11.29 S	37.46 W
Cristino Castro	240	8.49 S	44.13 W
Cristóbal	226	9.21 N	79.55 W
Cristóbal, Punta de >	230p	22.12 N	81.51 W
Cristóbal Colón, Pico ∧	236	10.50 N	73.41 W
Cristoforo Colombo, Aeroporto di ⊠	56	44.25 N	8.49 E
Cristo Redentor, Estatua do ◆[1]	277a	22.57 S	43.13 W
Cristuru-Secuiesc	38	46.17 N	25.02 E
Crişu Alb ≃	38	46.42 N	21.17 E
Crişu Negru ≃	38	46.42 N	21.16 E
Crişu Repede (Sebes Körös) ≃	38	46.55 N	20.59 E
Crittenden	208	38.47 N	84.36 W
Crivitz, D.D.R.	50	53.35 N	11.38 E
Crivitz, Wis., U.S.	180	45.14 N	88.01 W
Crixalândia	245	15.18 S	47.15 W
Crixás	245	14.27 S	49.58 W
Crixás ≃	240	11.02 S	48.34 W
Crixás Açu ≃	245	13.19 S	50.36 W
Crixás Mirim ≃	245	13.30 S	50.30 W
Crna ≃	38	41.35 N	21.59 E
Crna Gora □[3]	38	42.30 N	19.18 E
Črnomelj	36	45.34 N	15.11 E
Croal ≃	252	53.33 N	2.23 W
Croatia → Hrvatska □[3]	36	45.10 N	15.30 E
Croce Domini, Passo di)(	58	45.54 N	10.24 E
Crocefieschi	56	44.35 N	9.01 E
Crocetta del Montello	58	45.50 N	12.02 E
Crocheron	198	38.15 N	76.03 W
Crockenhill	250	51.23 N	0.10 E
Crocker	184	37.57 N	92.16 W
Crocker, Banjaran ∧∧	102	5.40 N	116.14 E
Crockery Creek ≃	206	43.02 N	86.05 W
Crocketford	42	55.02 N	3.50 W
Crockett, Calif., U.S.	216	38.03 N	122.13 W
Crockett, Tex., U.S.	212	31.19 N	95.28 W
Crockham Hill	250	51.14 N	0.04 E
Crocus Hill → The Valley	228	18.13 N	63.04 W
Croeira, Serra da ∧∧	240	6.45 S	46.00 W
Croft	252	53.26 N	2.33 W
Crofton, B.C., Can.	214	48.52 N	123.38 W
Crofton, Ky., U.S.	184	37.03 N	87.29 W
Crofton, Md., U.S.	198	39.01 N	76.42 W
Crofton, Nebr., U.S.	188	42.44 N	97.30 W
Croghan	202	43.54 N	75.24 W
Croglin	42	54.49 N	2.39 W
Croil Islands II	196	44.58 N	74.58 W
Croisette, Cap >	56	43.13 N	5.20 E
Croisilles	46	50.12 N	2.53 E
Croissy-Beaubourg	251	48.50 N	2.40 E
Croissy-sur-Seine	251	48.53 N	2.09 E
Croix	46	50.40 N	3.09 E
Croix, Lac à la ⊜	176	51.16 N	70.13 W
Croix, Lac la ⊜	180	48.21 N	92.05 W
Croker, Cape >, Austl.	154	10.58 S	132.35 E
Croker, Cape >, Ont., Can.	202	44.58 N	80.59 W
Croker Island I	154	11.12 S	132.32 E
Crolles	56	45.17 N	5.53 E
Cromarty	28	57.40 N	4.02 W
Cromby	275	40.09 N	75.32 W
Cromer, Austl.	264a	33.44 S	151.17 E
Cromer, Eng., U.K.	44	52.56 N	1.18 E
Cromínia	245	17.17 S	49.21 W
Cromwell, N.Z.	162	45.03 S	169.12 E
Cromwell, Ala., U.S.	184	32.14 N	88.17 W
Cromwell, Conn., U.S.	197	41.36 N	72.39 W
Cromwell, Ind., U.S.	206	41.24 N	85.37 W
Cromwell Park ♠	269a	41.28 N	82.08 W
Cronadun	162	42.02 S	171.52 E
Cronenberg ◆[8]	253	51.12 N	7.08 E
Cronin, Mount ∧	172	54.54 N	126.52 W
Cronton	252	53.23 N	2.46 W
Cronulla	160	34.03 S	151.09 E
Cronulla Beach •[2]	264a	34.02 S	151.11 E
Crook, Eng., U.K.	42	54.43 N	1.44 W
Crook, Colo., U.S.	188	40.51 N	102.48 W
Crooked ≃, B.C., Can.	172	54.50 N	122.54 W
Crooked ≃, Mo., U.S.	184	39.13 N	93.49 W
Crooked ≃, Oreg., U.S.	192	44.34 N	121.16 W
Crooked Creek	170	61.52 N	158.08 W
Crooked Creek ≃, U.S.	186	36.57 N	100.06 W
Crooked Creek ≃, Ark., U.S.	184	36.14 N	92.29 W
Crooked Creek ≃, Ill., U.S.	209	38.30 N	89.25 W
Crooked Creek ≃, Ind., U.S.	206	40.45 N	86.30 W
Crooked Creek ≃, Mo., U.S.	209	39.34 N	91.55 W
Crooked Creek ≃, Mont., U.S.	192	47.27 N	107.58 W
Crooked Creek ≃, Pa., U.S.	200	41.55 N	77.08 W
Crooked Creek ≃, Pa., U.S.	204	40.45 N	79.33 W
Crooked Creek Lake ⊜[1]	204	40.42 N	79.30 W
Crooked Creek State Park ♠	204	40.42 N	79.29 W
Crooked Island I	228	22.45 N	74.13 W
Crooked Island Passage ⊔	228	22.55 N	74.35 W
Crooked Lake, Ind., U.S.	206	41.41 N	85.02 W
Crooked Lake, Mich., U.S.	206	42.29 N	85.25 W
Crooked Lake ⊜, Newf., Can.	176	48.24 N	56.17 W
Crooked Lake ⊜, Sask., Can.	174	50.36 N	102.45 W
Crooked Lake ⊜, N.A.	180	48.13 N	91.50 W
Crooked Lake ⊜, Fla., U.S.	210	27.48 N	81.35 W
Crooked Lake ⊜, Ind., U.S.	206	41.40 N	85.03 W
Crooked River	174	52.51 N	103.44 W
Crookes Point >	266	40.32 N	74.08 W
Crookham	269b	40.12 N	79.59 W
Crookston	188	47.47 N	96.37 W
Crooksville	178	39.46 N	82.06 W
Crookwell	156	34.28 S	149.28 E
Cropper	208	38.19 N	85.07 W
Crosby, Eng., U.K.	42	53.30 N	3.02 W
Crosby, Minn., U.S.	180	46.28 N	93.57 W
Crosby, Miss., U.S.	184	31.17 N	91.04 W
Crosby, N. Dak., U.S.	188	48.55 N	103.18 W
Crosby, Pa., U.S.	204	41.45 N	78.24 W
Crosby, Tex., U.S.	212	29.55 N	95.04 W
Crosby ◆[8]	263d	26.12 S	27.59 E
Crosby, Mount ∧	192	43.53 N	109.20 W
Crosby Lake ⊜	202	44.45 N	76.26 W
Crosbyton	186	33.40 N	101.14 W
Crosne	251	48.43 N	2.28 E
Cross ≃	142	4.42 N	8.21 E
Cross, Cape >	146	21.49 S	13.57 E
Cross Banks II	273	42.43 N	70.49 W
Cross Bay C	174	53.15 N	99.25 W
Cross Bay Bridge ◆[5]	266	40.35 N	73.49 W
Cross City	182	29.39 N	83.07 W
Cross County Center ◆[9]	266	40.56 N	73.51 W
Cross Creek ≃, Calif., U.S.	216	36.08 N	119.38 W
Cross Creek ≃, Ohio, U.S.	204	40.18 N	80.36 W
Crossen, D.D.R.	50	50.45 N	12.29 E
Crossen → Krosno Odrzańskie, Pol.	30	52.04 N	15.05 E
Crossens	252	53.41 N	2.57 W
Crossett	184	33.08 N	91.58 W
Cross Fell ∧	42	54.42 N	2.29 W
Crossfield	172	51.26 N	114.02 W
Crossgar	42	54.24 N	5.45 W
Crosshill	42	55.19 N	4.39 W
Crossinsee ⊜	254a	52.22 N	13.41 E
Cross Island I	262c	18.57 N	72.51 E
Cross Keys	275	39.43 N	75.02 W
Cross Keys Airport ⊠	275	39.42 N	75.02 W
Cross Lake ⊜, Man., Can.	174	54.45 N	97.30 W
Cross Lake ⊜, Ont., Can.	180	46.53 N	79.57 W
Cross Lake ⊜, N.Y., U.S.	200	43.08 N	76.29 W
Crossley, Mount ∧	162	42.50 S	172.04 E
Crossmaglen	42	54.05 N	6.37 W
Crossman	158a	32.47 S	116.36 E
Crossman ≃	158a	32.47 S	116.32 E
Crossman Peak ∧	190	34.32 N	114.07 W
Cross Plains, Ind., U.S.	208	38.57 N	85.12 W
Cross Plains, Tex., U.S.	186	32.08 N	99.11 W
Cross Plains, Wis., U.S.	180	43.07 N	89.39 W
Cross Roads	212	32.03 N	95.58 W
Cross Sound ⊔	170	58.10 N	136.30 W
Crossville, Ill., U.S.	184	38.10 N	88.04 W
Crossville, Tenn., U.S.	184	35.58 N	85.02 W
Crosswicks	275	40.09 N	74.39 W
Crosswicks Creek ≃	198	40.09 N	74.43 W
Crostolo ≃	58	44.55 N	10.38 E
Croston	252	53.40 N	2.46 W
Croswell	180	43.16 N	82.37 W
Crotch Lake ⊜	202	44.55 N	76.48 W
Crotenay	54	46.45 N	5.49 E
Crothersville	208	38.48 N	85.50 W
Croton	204	40.14 N	82.41 W
Crotona Park ♠	266	40.50 N	73.54 W
Crotone	36	39.05 N	17.07 E
Croton Falls	200	41.21 N	73.40 W
Croton-on-Hudson	200	41.12 N	73.54 W
Croton Point >	266	41.10 N	73.54 W
Crottendorf	50	50.30 N	12.56 E
Crouch ≃	44	51.37 N	0.57 E
Croult ≃	251	48.57 N	2.25 E
Crouse Run ≃	269b	40.35 N	79.58 W
Crouy	46	49.24 N	3.22 E
Crow ≃	180	45.15 N	93.31 W
Crow, North Fork ≃	180	45.05 N	93.45 W
Crow, South Fork ≃	180	45.05 N	93.45 W
Crow Agency	192	45.36 N	107.27 W
Crowborough	44	51.03 N	0.09 E
Crow Creek ≃, U.S.	188	40.23 N	104.29 W
Crow Creek ≃, Calif., U.S.	272	37.42 N	122.03 W
Crow Creek ≃, Ill., U.S.	184	40.56 N	89.27 W
Crow Creek ≃, Mont., U.S.	188	45.45 N	105.06 W
Crow Creek ≃, Mont., U.S.	192	46.11 N	111.29 W
Crow Creek ≃, S. Dak., U.S.	188	43.57 N	99.15 W
Crow Creek ≃, Wyo., U.S.	192	43.19 N	109.09 W
Crow Creek Indian Reservation ◆[4]	188	44.11 N	99.30 W
Crowder	186	35.07 N	95.40 W
Crowduck Lake ⊜	174	50.08 N	95.15 W
Crowdy Head >	156	31.50 S	152.45 E
Crowe ≃	202	44.22 N	77.46 W
Crowe Lake ⊜	202	44.29 N	77.46 W
Crowell	186	33.59 N	99.43 W
Crow Hill ∧[2]	252	53.42 N	1.58 W
Crowhurst	250	51.12 N	0.01 W
Crow Indian Reservation ◆[4]	192	45.27 N	108.00 W
Crow Lake	174	49.12 N	93.57 W
Crow Lake ⊜	202	44.43 N	76.37 W
Crowland	44	52.41 N	0.11 W
Crowl Creek ≃	156	31.58 S	144.53 E
Crowle	42	53.37 N	0.49 W
Crowley, Calif., U.S.	216	36.21 N	119.17 W
Crowley, La., U.S.	184	30.13 N	92.22 W
Crowley, Tex., U.S.	212	32.35 N	97.22 W
Crowley, Lake ⊜[1]	194	37.37 N	118.44 W
Crowleys Ridge ∧	184	35.45 N	90.45 W
Crown	204	41.23 N	79.16 W
Crown Hill	202	44.26 N	79.39 W
Crown Island I	154	5.05 S	146.55 E
Crown Mines ◆[7]	263d	26.13 S	28.00 E
Crown Mountain ∧	230m	18.21 N	64.58 W
Crown Point, Ind., U.S.	206	41.25 N	87.22 W
Crown Point, N.Y., U.S.	178	43.57 N	73.25 W
Crown Point State Park ♠	214	45.32 N	122.15 W
Crown Prince Frederick Island I	166	70.02 N	86.50 W
Crown Prince Range ∧∧	165e	6.25 S	155.43 E
Crown Village	266	40.40 N	73.27 W
Crow Peak ∧	192	46.18 N	111.54 W
Crow Rock Creek ≃	192	47.06 N	106.15 W
Crows Landing	216	37.24 N	121.04 W
Crow's Nest, Austl.	161a	27.16 S	152.03 E
Crows Nest, Austl.	264a	33.50 S	151.12 E
Crowsnest, B.C., Can.	172	49.38 N	114.41 W
Crowsnest Pass)(	172	49.39 N	114.45 W
Crows Nest Peak ∧	188	44.03 N	103.58 W
Crowthorne	44	51.23 N	0.49 W
Crowton	252	53.16 N	2.38 W
Crow Wing ≃	188	46.19 N	94.20 W
Croxley Green	44	51.39 N	0.27 W
Croxteth Park ♠	252	53.26 N	2.53 W
Croyde	44	51.07 N	4.13 W
Croydon, Austl.	156	18.12 S	142.14 E
Croydon, Austl.	159	37.48 S	145.17 E
Croydon, Austl.	264a	33.53 S	151.07 E
Croydon, Pa., U.S.	198	40.05 N	74.54 W
Croydon ◆[8]	44	51.23 N	0.06 W
Croydon Park	264a	33.54 S	151.07 E
Croydon Peak ∧	178	43.28 N	72.13 W
Croydon Station	172	53.05 N	119.44 W
Crozet	182	38.04 N	78.42 W
Crozet Basin ✣[1]	6	40.00 S	60.00 E
Crozon	32	48.15 N	4.29 W
Cruas	56	44.39 N	4.46 E
Crucea	38	44.32 N	28.14 E
Crucero	238	14.21 S	70.00 W
Crucero, Cerro ∧	224	21.41 N	104.25 W
Cruces	230p	22.21 N	80.16 W
Crucible	178	39.57 N	79.58 W
Crucilândia	245	20.23 S	44.21 W
Crudgington	44	52.46 N	2.33 W
Cruger	184	33.14 N	90.14 W
Cruillas	222	24.45 N	98.31 W
Crum Creek ≃	275	39.51 N	75.19 W
Crumhorn Mountain ∧	200	42.33 N	74.55 W
Crumlin, Ont., Can.	202	43.01 N	81.09 W
Crumlin, N. Ire., U.K.	42	54.37 N	6.14 W
Crum Lynne	275	39.52 N	75.20 W
Crummock Water ⊜	42	54.34 N	3.18 W
Crump Lake ⊜	192	42.17 N	119.50 W
Crumpton	198	39.14 N	75.55 W
Crumpton Point >	230d	15.35 N	61.19 W
Crumstown	206	41.38 N	86.25 W
Crupet	52	50.21 N	4.48 E
Cruseilles	54	46.02 N	6.07 E
Cruser Brook ≃	266	40.27 N	74.39 W
Crusnes	52	49.26 N	5.25 E
Crusnes ≃	52	49.27 N	5.36 E
Cruz, Arroyo de la ≃, Calif., U.S.	216	35.42 N	121.09 W
Cruz, Arroyo de la ≃, Ur.	248	34.00 S	56.08 W
Cruz, Cabo >	230p	19.51 N	77.44 W
Cruz, Cañada de la ≃	248	34.09 S	58.58 W
Cruz, Cayo I	230p	22.15 N	77.49 W
Cruz Alta, Arg.	242	33.01 S	61.49 W
Cruz Alta, Bra.	242	28.39 S	53.36 W
Cruz Bay	230m	18.20 N	64.48 W
Cruz das Almas	246	22.44 S	46.51 W
Cruz de Elorza	224	23.49 N	100.29 W
Cruz del Eje	242	30.44 S	64.48 W
Cruz Descoberta	246	22.45 S	46.48 W
Cruzeiro	246	22.34 S	44.58 W
Cruzeiro do Oeste	245	23.46 S	53.04 W
Cruzeiro do Sul	238	7.38 S	72.36 W
Cruzeta	240	6.25 S	36.47 W
Cruz Grande, Chile	242	29.25 S	71.18 W
Cruz Grande, Méx.	224	16.44 N	99.08 W
Cruzília	246	21.50 S	44.48 W
Cruz Machado	242	26.01 S	51.21 W
Cruzy-le-Châtel	46	47.51 N	4.12 E
Crvenka	38	45.39 N	19.28 E
Crymmych	44	51.59 N	4.40 W
Crystal, Minn., U.S.	180	45.00 N	93.25 W
Crystal, N. Dak., U.S.	188	48.36 N	97.40 W
Crystal ≃	190	39.25 N	107.14 W
Crystal Bay	216	39.15 N	120.00 W
Crystal Bay C	210	28.55 N	82.43 W
Crystal Beach, Ont., Can.	274a	42.52 N	79.04 W
Crystal Beach, Fla., U.S.	210	28.06 N	82.47 W
Crystal Beach, Tex., U.S.	212	29.27 N	94.38 W
Crystal Brook	156	33.21 S	138.13 E
Crystal Cave •[5]	198	40.32 N	75.51 W
Crystal City, Man., Can.	174	49.09 N	98.56 W
Crystal City, Mo., U.S.	209	38.13 N	90.23 W
Crystal City, Tex., U.S.	186	28.41 N	99.50 W
Crystal Creek ≃	268	41.58 N	87.51 W
Crystal Falls	180	46.05 N	88.20 W
Crystal Gardens	206	42.14 N	88.23 W
Crystal Lake, Fla., U.S.	210	30.26 N	85.41 W
Crystal Lake, Ill., U.S.	206	42.14 N	88.19 W
Crystal Lake, N.Y., U.S.	200	42.31 N	74.12 W
Crystal Lake, N.Y., U.S.	200	42.28 N	78.20 W
Crystal Lake ⊜, Ont., Can.	202	44.45 N	78.30 W
Crystal Lake ⊜, Mass., U.S.	273	42.48 N	71.09 W
Crystal Lake ⊜, Mass., U.S.	273	42.29 N	71.05 W
Crystal Lake ⊜, Mich., U.S.	180	44.40 N	86.10 W
Crystal Lake ⊜, N.J., U.S.	266	41.02 N	74.15 W
Crystal Lakes	208	39.52 N	84.04 W
Crystal Lawns	206	41.34 N	88.09 W
Crystal Manor	206	42.14 N	88.17 W
Crystal Palace Stadium and Motor Race Track ♠	250	51.25 N	0.04 W
Crystal River	182	28.54 N	82.36 W
Crystal Spring Lake ⊜	275	39.43 N	75.01 W
Crystal Springs, Fla., U.S.	210	28.11 N	82.10 W
Crystal Springs, Miss., U.S.	184	31.59 N	90.21 W
Crystal Springs Dam ◆[6]	272	37.32 N	122.22 W
Crystal Vista	206	42.14 N	88.24 W
Csepel ◆[8]	254c	47.24 N	19.14 E
Csepel-sziget I	254c	47.24 N	19.03 E
Cserhát ∧∧	30	47.55 N	19.30 E
Csesznek ⊥	30	47.16 N	17.53 E
Csobánka	254c	47.38 N	18.58 E
Csomád	254c	47.40 N	19.15 E
Csömör	254c	47.33 N	19.14 E
Csömöri-patak ≃	254c	47.36 N	19.07 E
Csongrád	30	46.43 N	20.09 E
Csongrád □[6]	30	46.25 N	20.15 E
Csorna	30	47.37 N	17.16 E
Çsurgó	30	46.16 N	17.06 E
Ču	75	43.36 N	73.45 E
Ču ≃	76	45.00 N	67.44 E
Cúa	236	10.10 N	66.54 W
Cuacnopalan	224	18.49 N	97.30 W
Cuácua ≃	144	17.54 N	36.48 E
Cuadro Nacional	242	34.37 S	68.17 W
Cuajimalpa	276a	19.21 N	99.18 W
Cuajimalpa □[7]	276a	19.21 N	99.17 W
Cuajinicuilapa	224	16.28 N	98.25 W
Cuále	142	8.06 S	16.03 E
Cua-lo	100	18.49 N	105.43 E
Cuamato	142	17.05 S	15.09 E
Cuambog	106	7.20 N	125.52 E
Cuanavale ≃	142	15.07 S	19.14 E
Cuando	142	16.32 S	22.07 E
Cuando (Kwando) ≃	142	18.27 S	23.32 E
Cuando Cubango □[5]	142	16.00 S	20.00 E
Cuangar	142	17.36 S	18.39 E
Cuango, Ang.	142	9.10 S	17.58 E
Cuango, Ang.	142	6.17 S	16.41 E
Cuango, Ang.	142	14.30 S	18.59 E
Cuango (Kwango) ≃	142	3.14 S	17.23 E
Cuanza ≃	142	9.19 S	13.08 E
Cuanza-Norte □[5]	142	8.50 S	14.30 E
Cuanza-Sul □[5]	142	10.50 S	14.50 E
Cuao ≃	236	4.55 N	67.40 W
Cuapiaxtla	224	19.18 N	97.46 W
Cua-rao	100	19.16 N	104.27 E
Cuaró	242	30.37 S	56.54 W
Cuartillo, Arroyo ≃	248	33.45 S	59.06 W
Cuarto ≃	242	33.25 S	63.02 W
Cuatir ≃	142	17.01 S	18.09 E
Cuatro Caminos	276b	22.54 N	82.23 W
Cuatro Ciénegas [de Carranza]	186	26.59 N	102.05 W
Cuatro Islands II	106	10.31 N	124.39 E
Cuauhtémoc, Méx.	222	28.25 N	106.52 W
Cuauhtémoc, Méx.	224	19.20 N	103.36 W
Cuauhtémoc, Méx.	224	22.27 N	102.21 W
Cuautepec [de Hinojosa]	224	20.02 N	98.18 W
Cuautepec el Alto	276a	19.34 N	99.08 W
Cuautitlán	224	19.26 N	104.23 W
Cuautitlán □[7]	276a	19.39 N	99.13 W
Cuautitlán [de Romero Rubio]	224	19.40 N	99.11 W
Cuautla, Méx.	224	20.11 N	104.21 W
Cuautla, Méx.	224	18.48 N	98.57 W
Cuautzin, Cerro ∧	276a	19.09 N	99.06 W
Cuba, Port.	34	38.10 N	7.53 W
Cuba, Ala., U.S.	184	32.26 N	88.23 W
Cuba, Ill., U.S.	180	40.30 N	90.12 W
Cuba, Kans., U.S.	188	39.48 N	97.27 W
Cuba, Mo., U.S.	184	38.04 N	91.24 W
Cuba, N. Mex., U.S.	190	36.01 N	107.04 W
Cuba, N.Y., U.S.	200	42.13 N	78.17 W
Cuba □[1]	220		
	230p	21.30 N	80.00 W
Cubabi, Cerro ∧	190	31.42 N	112.46 W
Cubadak	102	0.19 N	100.00 E
Cubagua, Isla I	236	10.48 N	64.10 W
Cuba Island I	266	40.38 N	73.32 W
Cubal	142	13.02 S	14.19 E
Cubal ≃, Ang.	142	12.42 S	13.56 E
Cubal ≃, Ang.	142	12.13 S	13.39 E
Cubal ≃, Ang.	142	11.19 S	13.48 E
Cuba Lake ⊜	200	42.15 N	78.18 W
Cubanea	244	40.40 S	63.30 W
Cubango (Okavango) ≃	128	18.50 S	22.25 E
Çubangui ≃	142	14.22 S	19.58 E
Čubaricha	76	57.37 N	68.22 E
Čubarovo	72	55.12 N	36.56 E
Cubatão	246	23.53 S	46.25 W
Cubatão □[7]	277b	23.48 S	46.20 W
Cubatão, Serra do •[4]	246	23.52 S	46.28 W
Cubati	240	6.51 S	36.21 W
Cub Hills ∧∧[2]	174	54.20 N	104.30 W
Çubia ≃	142	16.01 S	21.50 E
Čublas	24	64.44 N	45.00 E
Cub Run ≃	198	38.48 N	77.28 W
Çubuk	120	40.15 N	33.02 E
Çubuklu ◆[8]	257b	41.06 N	29.04 E
Cuc ≃	240	1.22 N	53.33 W
Cucalaya ≃	226	13.39 N	83.37 W
Cucamonga	218	34.06 N	117.35 W
Cucamonga Creek ≃	270	33.57 N	117.37 W
Cucamonga Peak ∧	218	34.14 N	117.36 W
Çucco, Monte ∧	60	43.22 N	12.45 E
Čučeviči	66	52.35 N	26.52 E
Cuchara, Río de la ≃	224	16.37 N	97.41 W
Cucharas	224	22.52 N	105.19 W
Cucharas ≃	188	37.55 N	104.32 W
Cuchi	142	14.36 S	16.58 E
Cuchi ≃	142	15.28 S	17.21 E
Cuchibi ≃	142	15.00 S	20.45 E
Cuchilla Alta, Cerro ∧	226	15.10 N	88.12 W
Cuchilla Áquila, Cerro ∧	224	21.27 N	101.03 W
Cuchillo-Có	242	38.20 S	64.37 W
Cuchillo Negro Creek ≃	190	33.08 N	107.14 W
Çuchivero ≃	236	7.40 N	65.57 W
Čuchloma	66	58.45 N	42.41 E
Čuchlomskoje, Ozero ⊜	66	58.46 N	42.35 E
Cuchumatanes, Altos ∧∧	226	15.35 N	91.25 W
Cuckels Brook ≃	266	40.33 N	74.33 W
Cuckfield	44	51.00 N	0.09 W
Cuckney	42	53.15 N	1.08 W
Çuckold Point >	274b	39.14 N	76.24 W
Čučkovo, S.S.S.R.	66	59.36 N	41.14 E
Čučkovo, S.S.S.R.	70	54.17 N	41.26 E
Cucuí	236	1.12 N	66.50 W
Čučuleny	68	47.02 N	28.22 E
Cucumbi	142	10.17 S	19.05 E
Cucuron	56	43.47 N	5.26 E
Cucurpe	222	30.20 N	110.43 W
Cúcuta	236	7.54 N	72.31 W
Cudachar	74	42.21 N	47.11 E
Cudahy, Calif., U.S.	270	33.58 N	118.11 W
Cudahy, Wis., U.S.	206	42.57 N	87.52 W
Cuddalore	112	11.45 N	79.45 E
Cuddapah	112	14.28 N	78.49 E
Cuddeback Lake ⊜	218	35.18 N	117.28 W
Cuddebackville	200	41.28 N	74.36 W
Cuddington	252	53.14 N	2.36 W
Cuddle Lake ⊜	174	55.25 N	95.47 W
Cuddy	269b	40.21 N	80.09 W
Cuddy Mountain ∧	192	44.46 N	116.47 W
Cudgegong	160	32.48 S	149.49 E
Cudgegong ≃	160	32.37 S	149.43 E
Cudgewa	161b	36.12 S	147.46 E
Cudgewa Creek ≃	161b	36.03 S	147.55 E
Cudham ◆[8]	250	51.19 N	0.05 E
Çudia Park ♠	265b	43.43 N	79.13 W
Čudin	66	52.44 N	26.59 E
Çudjoe Key I	210	24.40 N	81.30 W
Čudnov	68	50.04 N	28.06 E
Čudovo	66	59.07 N	31.41 E
Čudskoje Ozero (Peipsi Järv) ⊜	66	58.45 N	27.30 E
Cudworth, Sask., Can.	174	52.30 N	105.45 W
Cudworth, Eng., U.K.	42	53.35 N	1.25 W
Cue	152	27.25 S	117.54 E
Cuebe ≃	142	15.48 S	17.30 E
Cueio ≃, Ang.	142	16.17 S	17.46 E
Cueio ≃, Ang.	142	15.27 S	21.21 E
Cuelei ≃	142	15.33 S	17.21 E
Cuéllar	34	41.25 N	4.19 W
Cuemaní ≃	236	0.20 S	73.06 W
Cuenca, Ec.	236	2.53 S	78.59 W
Cuenca, Esp.	34	40.04 N	2.08 W
Cuencamé [de Ceniceros]	222	24.53 N	103.42 W
Cuerámaro	224	20.37 N	101.43 W
Cuernavaca	224	18.55 N	99.15 W
Cuero	212	29.06 N	97.18 W
Cuers	56	43.14 N	6.04 E
Cuervo, Laguna del ⊜	222	29.17 N	105.57 W
Cuervos	222	32.38 N	114.52 W
Cuesmes	46	50.26 N	3.55 E
Cuesta Pass)(	216	35.21 N	120.38 W
Cueto	230p	20.39 N	75.56 W
Cuetzala del Progreso	224	18.07 N	99.50 W
Cuetzalan del Progreso	224	20.02 N	97.31 W
Cuevas, Cerro ∧	238	22.00 S	65.12 W
Cuevas del Almanzora	34	37.18 N	1.53 W
Çuevo	238	20.27 S	63.32 W
Čufarovo	70	54.06 N	47.19 E
Cuffley	44	51.47 N	0.07 W
Cufra → Al-Kufrah ◆[1]	136	24.20 N	23.15 E
Cufré	248	34.12 S	57.06 W
Cufré, Arroyo ≃	248	34.27 S	57.09 W
Cufré, Cuchilla ∧∧[2]	248	34.20 S	57.10 W
Cuggiono	56	45.31 N	8.49 E
Cugir	38	45.50 N	23.22 E
Çuglieri	36	40.11 N	8.34 E
Čugujev	68	49.50 N	36.41 E
Čugujevka	79	44.08 N	133.53 E
Čugunaš	76	52.52 N	87.46 E
Čuguš, Gora ∧	74	43.47 N	40.16 E
Cuiabá	238	15.35 S	56.05 W
Cuiabá ≃	238	17.05 S	56.36 W
Cuiari	236	1.30 N	68.11 W
Cuiari ≃	236	1.30 N	68.11 W
Cuicatlán	224	17.48 N	96.58 W
Cuichapa	224	17.59 N	94.15 W
Cuidado, Punta >	164z	27.08 S	109.19 W
Cuieiras ≃	236	2.50 S	60.31 W
Cuigezhuang, Zhg.	95	40.01 N	116.28 E
Cuigezhuang, Zhg.	95	40.02 N	117.54 E
Cuihengcun	90	22.28 N	113.33 E
Cuihuangkou	95	39.32 N	117.11 E
Cuijiatun	94	40.57 N	121.09 E
Cuijiazhuang	94	40.57 N	122.44 E
Cuilapa	226	14.17 N	90.18 W
Çuilco	226	15.24 N	91.58 W
Ču-Ilijskije Gory ∧∧	75	43.52 N	75.00 E
Cuilo (Kwilu) ≃	142	3.22 S	17.22 E
Cuilo Futa	142	6.25 S	15.44 E
Cuimba	142	6.08 S	14.38 E
Cuinarana	240	0.47 S	47.35 W
Cuio	142	12.58 S	12.58 E
Cuiqiao	88	34.12 N	114.36 E
Cuiseaux	54	46.30 N	5.24 E
Cuisery	54	47.22 N	5.19 E
Cuisy	251	49.01 N	2.46 E
Cuité	240	6.29 S	36.09 W
Cuité ≃	245	19.05 S	41.31 W
Cuitláhuac	224	18.49 N	96.43 W
Cuíto ≃	142	18.01 S	20.48 E
Cuíto-Cuanavale	142	15.10 S	19.10 E
Cuitzeo, Lago de ⊜	224	19.55 N	101.05 W
Cuitzeo del Porvenir	224	19.59 N	101.09 W
Cuitzmala	224	19.23 N	104.59 W
Cuiuni ≃	236	0.45 S	63.07 W
Cuivre ≃	209	38.56 N	90.42 W
Cuivre, North Fork ≃	209	39.02 N	90.59 W
Cuivre, West Fork ≃	209	39.02 N	90.59 W
Cuivre River State Park ♠	209	39.02 N	90.57 W
Çuixi	90	28.16 N	117.10 E
Čuja ≃, S.S.S.R.	76	50.24 N	86.39 E
Čuja ≃, S.S.S.R.	78	59.17 N	112.24 E
Cují	276c	10.28 N	67.02 W
Çukas	102	0.25 S	104.18 E
Čukčagirskoje Ozero ⊜	79	52.00 N	136.36 E
Čukotskij, Mys >	170	64.14 N	173.10 W
Čukotskij Poluostrov >[1]	170	66.00 N	175.00 W
Çukurca	118	37.15 N	43.37 E
Čukurčak	75	41.47 N	71.07 E
Čukurino	73	48.05 N	37.18 E
Çulaba	106	11.40 N	124.32 E
Čulak-Kurgan	75	43.46 N	69.12 E
Culaman	106	5.58 N	125.40 E
Culari ≃	240	1.27 N	53.42 W
Culasi, Pil.	106	10.43 N	125.43 E
Culasi, Pil.	106	11.26 N	122.03 E
Culasian	106	8.51 N	117.29 E
Culasi Point >	106	11.37 N	122.42 E
Culbertson, Mont., U.S.	188	48.09 N	104.31 W
Culbertson, Nebr., U.S.	188	40.14 N	100.50 W
Culbertson Run ≃	275	40.03 N	75.45 W
Culbin	158a	33.10 S	116.50 E
Culcairn	156	35.40 S	147.03 E
Culcheth	252	53.27 N	2.32 W
Culdaff	42	55.18 N	7.11 W
Culebra, Bahía de C	226	10.37 N	85.40 W
Culebra, Isla de I	230m	18.19 N	65.17 W
Culebra, Laguna de la ⊜	224	22.28 N	98.20 W
Culebra, Sierra de la ∧∧	34	41.54 N	6.20 W
Culebra Peak ∧	190	37.07 N	105.11 W
Culebrinos ≃	230m	18.24 N	67.11 W
Culebrita, Isla I	230m	18.19 N	65.14 W
Culemborg	48	51.56 N	5.13 E
Culgoa ≃	156	29.56 S	146.20 E
Culham Inlet C	152	33.55 S	120.04 E
Culiacán	222	24.48 N	107.24 W
Culiacán, Cerro ∧	224	20.20 N	100.58 W
Culiacancito	222	24.50 N	107.32 W
Culion	106	11.53 N	120.01 E
Culion Island I	106	11.50 N	119.55 E
Culiseu ≃	245	12.14 S	53.17 W
Cúllar de Baza	34	37.35 N	2.34 W
Cull Creek ≃	272	37.42 N	122.03 W
Cullen	184	32.58 N	93.27 W
Cullen Bullen	160	33.18 S	150.01 E
Cullen Point >	154	11.57 S	141.54 E
Culleoka, Tenn., U.S.	184	35.29 N	86.59 W
Culleoka, Tex., U.S.	212	33.08 N	96.29 W
Cullera	34	39.10 N	0.15 W
Cullinan	148	25.40 S	28.32 E
Cullman	184	34.11 N	86.51 W
Cullom	206	40.53 N	88.16 W
Cullompton	44	50.52 N	3.24 W
Cullowhee	182	35.19 N	83.11 W
Cully	54	46.29 N	6.44 E
Çulm ≃	44	50.46 N	3.31 W
Čul'man	64	56.52 N	124.52 E
Cülmen	120	37.19 N	38.48 E
Culmore	274c	38.51 N	77.08 W
Culoz	56	45.51 N	5.47 E
Culpeper	178	38.28 N	77.53 W
Culpina	238	20.50 S	64.58 W
Cultus Lake	214	49.04 N	121.58 W
Cultus Lake ⊜	214	49.03 N	121.58 W
Cultus Lake Provincial Park ♠	214	49.03 N	121.58 W
Culú Culú, Arroyo ≃	248	35.19 S	58.57 W
Culuene ≃	245	12.56 S	52.51 W
Çulukidze	74	42.20 N	42.25 E
Çuluunchoroot	78	49.45 N	114.20 E
Çuluut	92	45.49 N	107.02 E
Čuluut ≃	78	49.11 N	100.41 E
Culver, Ind., U.S.	206	41.13 N	86.25 W
Culver, Oreg., U.S.	192	44.32 N	121.13 W
Culver, Point >	152	32.54 S	124.43 E
Culver City	218	34.01 N	118.24 W
Culverden	162	42.46 S	172.51 E
Culvers Lake	200	41.10 N	74.48 W
Çulverstone Green	250	51.20 N	0.21 E
Čulym	76	55.06 N	80.58 E
Čulym ≃, S.S.S.R.	76	54.38 N	78.16 E
Čulym ≃, S.S.S.R.	76	57.43 N	83.51 E
Čulyšman ≃	76	51.20 N	87.45 E
Čum	24	67.06 N	63.07 E
Cuma	142	12.52 S	15.05 E
Çuma (Cumæ) ⊥	60	40.50 N	14.06 E
Čumakovo	76	55.41 N	79.02 E
Cumalı	120	36.42 N	27.27 E
Cuman'	68	50.49 N	25.53 E
Cumaná	236	10.28 N	64.10 W
Cumanacoa	236	10.15 N	63.55 W
Cumanayagua	230p	22.09 N	80.12 W
Cumaovası	120	38.15 N	27.09 E
Cumari	245	18.16 S	48.11 W
Cumbal	236	0.54 N	77.47 W
Cumbal, Volcán de ∧[1]	236	0.57 N	77.52 W
Cumbe	240	10.21 S	37.14 W
Cumbee	210	28.04 N	81.55 W
Cumberland, B.C., Can.	172	49.37 N	125.01 W
Cumberland, Iowa, U.S.	188	41.16 N	94.52 W
Cumberland, Ky., U.S.	182	36.59 N	82.59 W
Cumberland, Md., U.S.	178	39.39 N	78.46 W
Cumberland, Va., U.S.	182	37.30 N	78.15 W
Cumberland, Wash., U.S.	214	47.17 N	121.56 W
Cumberland, Wis., U.S.	180	45.32 N	92.01 W
Cumberland □[6], N.J., U.S.	198	39.26 N	75.14 W
Cumberland □[6], Pa., U.S.	198	40.12 N	77.12 W
Cumberland ≃	168	37.09 N	88.25 W
Cumberland, Caney Fork ≃	184	36.09 N	85.52 W
Cumberland, Cape >	165f	14.39 S	166.37 E
Cumberland, Lake ⊜[1]	184	36.57 N	84.55 W
Cumberland City	184	36.23 N	87.38 W
Cumberland Falls State Park ♠	182	36.50 N	84.20 W
Cumberland Gap)(	182	36.36 N	83.41 W
Cumberland Gap National Historical Park ♠	182	36.36 N	83.40 W
Cumberland Hill	197	41.59 N	71.28 W
Cumberland House	174	53.58 N	102.16 W
Cumberland Indian Reserve ◆[4]	174	53.04 N	104.50 W
Cumberland Islands II	156	20.40 S	149.09 E
Cumberland Lake ⊜	174	54.02 N	102.17 W
Cumberland Peninsula >[1]	166	66.50 N	64.00 W
Cumberland Plateau ∧∧[1]	168	36.00 N	85.00 W
Cumberland Sound ⊔	166	65.10 N	65.30 W
Cumbernauld	42	55.58 N	3.59 W
Cumborah	156	29.44 S	147.46 E
Cumbres de Monterrey, Parque Nacional ♠	222	25.31 N	100.18 W
Cumbria □[6]	42	54.30 N	3.00 W
Cumbrian Mountains ∧∧	42	54.30 N	3.05 W
Čumbur-Kosa	73	46.57 N	38.53 E
Cumby	212	33.08 N	95.50 W
Çumeral Nuevo	190	30.54 N	110.51 W
Čumerna ∧	38	42.47 N	25.58 E
Çumiana	56	44.59 N	7.22 E
Čumikan	79	54.42 N	135.19 E
Cuminá → Paru de Oeste ≃	240	1.30 S	56.00 W
Cuminapanema ≃	240	1.09 S	54.54 W
Cumming	182	34.13 N	84.08 W
Cummings Mountain ∧	218	35.03 N	118.34 W
Cummington	197	42.27 N	72.54 W
Cummins	156	34.16 S	135.44 E
Cummins, Mount ∧	172	52.03 N	118.15 W
Cummins Creek ≃	212	29.43 N	96.31 W
Cummins Range ∧∧	152	19.05 S	127.10 E
Cumnock	42	55.27 N	4.16 W
Cumnor	44	51.44 N	1.20 W
Cumpas	222	30.02 N	109.48 W
Çumra	120	37.34 N	32.48 E
Cumshewa Inlet C	172	53.03 N	131.45 W
Cumueté ≃	240	9.20 S	50.10 W
Cumuripa	222	28.08 N	109.53 W
Çumwhinton	42	54.52 N	2.51 W
Čumyš ≃	76	53.31 N	83.10 E
Č'un' ≃	70	55.44 N	54.16 E
Čun'a ≃, S.S.S.R.	64	61.36 N	96.30 E
Čuna ≃, S.S.S.R.	78	57.47 N	95.26 E
Cunani	240	2.52 N	51.06 W
Cunauaru ≃	236	3.10 S	63.01 W
Cunaviche	236	7.22 N	67.25 W
Cunco	242	38.55 S	72.02 W
Cuncumén	242	31.53 S	70.38 W
Cundanama ≃	236	3.30 N	65.06 W
Cunderdin	152	31.39 S	117.15 E
Çundinamarca □[5]	236	5.00 N	74.00 W
Čundža	76	43.32 N	79.28 E
Cunene (Kunene) ≃	142	17.20 S	11.50 E
Cuneo	56	44.23 N	7.32 E
Cuneo □[4]	56	44.31 N	7.34 E
Cunewalde	50	51.06 N	14.30 E
Cuney	212	32.02 N	95.25 W
Cung-hau, Cua ≃[1]	100	9.46 N	106.34 E
Çungüş	120	38.13 N	39.17 E
Cunha	246	23.05 S	44.58 W
Cunhambebe	246	23.00 S	44.20 W
Cunha Porã	242	26.54 S	53.09 W
Cunhinga ≃	142	10.38 S	16.48 E
Cunhuã, Igarapé ≃	238	5.46 S	64.36 W
Cunlhat	56	45.38 N	3.35 E
Cunliffe	158b	34.05 S	137.45 E
Cunnamulla	156	28.04 S	145.41 E
Cunningham, Austl.	161a	28.09 S	151.51 E
Cunningham, Kans., U.S.	188	37.39 N	98.26 W
Cunninghame □[9]	42	55.40 N	4.30 W
Cunningham Falls State Park ♠	198	39.35 N	77.27 W
Cunningham Lake ⊜	230b	25.04 N	77.26 W
Cunningham Park ♠, Mass., U.S.	273	42.15 N	71.03 W
Cunningham Park ♠, N.Y., U.S.	266	40.44 N	73.46 W
Cunninghams Gap National Park ♠	161a	28.01 S	152.22 E
Čunojar	78	57.27 N	97.18 E
Cunqian	90	28.30 N	115.10 E
Čunskij	78	56.05 N	99.41 E
Cuntan	97	29.37 N	106.36 E
Čuny	66	59.39 N	36.04 E
Cuogang	78	49.14 N	118.08 E
Čuokkaraš'ša ∧	24	69.57 N	24.32 E
Çuorgnè	56	45.23 N	7.39 E
Çupa	24	66.16 N	33.00 E
Çupachovka	68	50.23 N	34.36 E
Čupalejka	70	55.11 N	42.33 E
Cupar, Sask., Can.	174	50.57 N	104.12 W
Cupar, Scot., U.K.	28	56.19 N	3.01 W
Cupecê, Ribeirão ≃	277b	23.37 S	46.42 W
Cupello	60	42.04 N	14.40 E
Cuperly	46	49.04 N	4.26 E
Cupertino	216	37.19 N	122.02 W
Cupica, Golfo de C	236	6.35 N	77.25 W
Cupins	245	19.51 S	51.03 W

Symbols in the index entries represent the broad categories identified in the key at the right. Symbols with superior numbers (∧∧[2]) identify subcategories (see complete key on page *I* · 26).

Kartensymbole in dem Registerverzeichnis stellen die rechts in Schlüssel erklärten Kategorien dar. Symbole mit hochgestellten Ziffern (∧∧[2]) bezeichnen Unterabteilungen einer Kategorie (vgl. vollständiger Schlüssel auf Seite *I* · 26).

Los símbolos incluídos en el texto del índice representan las grandes categorias identificadas con la clave a la derecha. Los símbolos con numeros en su parte superior (∧∧[2]) identifican las subcategorías (véase la clave completa en la página *I* · 26).

Les symboles de l'index représentent les catégories indiquées dans la légende à droite. Les symboles suivis d'un indice (∧∧[2]) représentent des sous-catégories (voir légende complète à la page *I* · 26).

Os símbolos incluídos no texto do índice representam as grandes categorias identificadas com a chave à direita. Os símbolos com números em sua parte superior (∧∧[2]) identificam as subcategorias (veja-se a chave completa à página *I* · 26).

English	Deutsch	Español	Français	Português
∧ Mountain	Berg	Montaña	Montagne	Montanha
∧∧ Mountains	Berge	Montañas	Montagnes	Montanhas
)(Pass	Pass	Paso	Col	Passo
V Valley, Canyon	Tal, Cañon	Valle, Cañón	Vallée, Canyon	Vale, Canhão
≚ Plain	Ebene	Llano	Plaine	Planície
> Cape	Kap	Cabo	Cap	Cabo
I Island	Insel	Isla	Île	Ilha
II Islands	Inseln	Islas	Îles	Ilhas
• Other Topographic Features	Andere Topographische Objekte	Otros Elementos Topográficos	Autres données topographiques	Outros Elementos Topográficos

ESPAÑOL · FRANÇAIS · PORTUGUÊS

Nombre / Nom / Nome	Página / Page	Lat.°′	Long.°′ W=Oeste / W=Ouest
Cupra Marittima	60	43.01 N	13.51 E
Cupramontana	60	43.27 N	13.07 E
Ćuprija	38	43.56 N	21.23 E
Cupsaw Lake ⊜	266	41.07 N	74.15 W
Cuqiao	97	30.36 N	103.59 E
Cuquema ≃	142	12.03 S	17.40 E
Cuquenán ≃	236	4.45 N	61.30 W
Cuquío	224	20.55 N	103.02 W
Čur	70	57.07 N	52.58 E
Curaçá	240	8.59 S	39.54 W
Curaçao I	231s	12.11 N	69.00 W
Curacautín	242	38.26 S	71.53 W
Curacaví	242	33.24 S	71.09 W
Čuračiki	70	55.44 N	47.26 E
Curacó ≃	242	38.49 S	64.57 W
Curaglia	54	46.41 N	8.51 E
Curahuara	238	17.40 S	68.02 W
Curanga ≃	238	9.58 S	70.58 W
Curanilahue	242	37.28 S	73.21 W
Curanipe	242	35.50 S	72.38 W
Čurapča	64	62.00 N	132.24 E
Curapi ≃	240	1.25 N	53.49 W
Curaray ≃	236	2.20 S	74.05 W
Čurbek	75	39.59 N	69.56 E
Curcani	38	44.12 N	26.35 E
Curcubăta ∧	38	46.27 N	22.42 E
Curdies ≃	159	38.30 S	142.55 E
Cure ≃	46	47.40 N	3.41 E
Curecanti National Recreation Area ♠	190	38.24 N	107.25 W
Curepipe	147c	20.19 S	57.31 E
Curepto	242	35.05 S	72.01 W
Curiapo	236	8.33 N	61.00 W
Curib	74	42.14 N	46.49 E
Curicó	242	34.59 S	71.14 W
Curicuriari ≃	236	0.14 S	66.48 W
Curières, Lac ⊜	196	46.41 N	74.51 W
Curimatá	240	10.02 S	44.17 W
Curimeo	224	20.01 N	101.42 W
Curinhuás ≃	226	12.49 N	83.41 W
Curioso, Cabo ≻	244	49.10 S	67.37 W
Curious, Mount ∧	152	27.28 S	114.20 E
Curitiba	242	25.25 S	49.15 W
Curitibanos	242	27.18 S	50.36 W
Curiuaú ≃	236	1.51 S	61.14 W
Curiúva	245	24.02 S	50.27 W
Curl Curl	264a	33.46 S	151.18 E
Curlewis	156	31.07 S	150.16 E
Curnamona	156	31.39 S	139.32 E
Curoca Norte	142	16.18 S	12.58 E
Curone ≃	56	45.03 N	8.54 E
Curon Venosta (Graun)	58	46.49 N	10.32 E
Čuroviči	68	52.10 N	32.01 E
Currais Novos	240	6.15 S	36.31 W
Curralinho	240	1.48 S	49.47 W
Curramulka	158b	34.42 S	137.42 E
Curran	209	39.44 N	89.46 W
Currant Creek ≃, Colo., U.S.	190	38.29 N	105.24 W
Currant Creek ≃, Mont., U.S.	192	46.22 N	108.39 W
Currant Mountain ∧	194	38.55 N	115.25 W
Currarong	160	35.01 S	150.49 E
Currency Creek	158b	35.28 S	138.46 E
Current ≃	180	48.27 N	89.11 W
Current, Jacks Fork ≃	184	37.12 N	91.17 W
Current Islands II	182	25.22 N	76.49 W
Currie, Austl.	156	39.56 S	143.52 E
Currie, Scot., U.K.	42	55.54 N	3.20 W
Currie, Minn., U.S.	188	43.59 N	95.40 W
Currituck	182	36.27 N	76.01 W
Currituck □[6]	198	36.28 N	76.03 W
Currituck Sound ⋃	182	36.20 N	75.52 W
Currituok Seamount ✢[3]	14	30.05 S	173.25 W
Curry	170	62.37 N	150.01 W
Curry, Lake ⊜[1]	216	38.22 N	122.08 W
Curry Rivel	44	51.02 N	2.52 W
Curryville, Mo., U.S.	209	39.21 N	91.21 W
Curryville, Pa., U.S.	204	40.17 N	78.20 W
Curslack ←[8]	48	53.27 N	10.13 E
Curtarolo	58	45.31 N	11.50 E
Curtea-de-Argeș	38	45.08 N	24.41 E
Curtice	204	41.37 N	83.22 W
Curtina	242	32.09 S	56.07 W
Curtin Springs	152	25.20 S	131.45 E
Curtis, Esp.	34	43.07 N	8.03 W
Curtis, Ark., U.S.	184	34.00 N	93.06 W
Curtis, Nebr., U.S.	188	40.38 N	100.31 W
Curtis, Port ⍑[3]	156	24.00 S	151.30 E
Curtis Bay C	274b	39.13 N	76.35 W
Curtis Creek C	274b	39.12 N	76.35 W
Curtis Island I, Austl.	156	23.38 S	151.09 E
Curtis Island I, N.Z.	14	30.30 S	178.34 W
Curtis Lake ⊜	166	66.38 N	89.02 W
Curtisville	204	40.37 N	79.50 W
Curu ≃	240	3.22 S	39.04 W
Curuá ≃, Bra.	240	1.55 S	55.07 W
Curuá ≃, Bra.	240	5.23 S	54.22 W
Curuá, Ilha I	240	0.48 N	50.10 W
Curuá do Sul ≃	240	2.39 S	54.10 W
Curuaés ≃	240	7.30 S	54.45 W
Curuan	106	7.13 N	122.14 E
Curuá Una ≃	240	2.24 S	54.05 W
Curubandé	226	10.43 N	85.26 W
Curuçá	240	0.43 S	47.50 W
Curuçá ←[8]	277b	23.30 S	46.25 W
Curuçá ≃	236	4.27 S	71.23 W
Curuçambaba	240	2.08 S	49.18 W
Čurug, Indon.	105a	6.15 S	106.33 E
Čurug, Jugo.	38	45.29 N	20.04 E
Curuguaty	242	24.31 S	55.42 W
Curumo	276c	10.27 N	66.52 W
Curumu	240	1.01 S	51.03 W
Curunga	142	12.51 S	21.12 E
Curup	102	3.28 S	102.32 E
Curupá	240	9.54 S	45.54 W
C'urupinsk	68	46.37 N	32.43 E
Curupira, Sierra de ⋀	236	1.25 N	64.30 W
Curuquetê ≃	238	8.20 S	65.40 W
Cururu ≃, Bra.	238	7.12 S	58.03 W
Cururu ≃, Bra.	240	0.39 S	50.11 W
Cururu-Açu ≃	240	8.58 S	57.13 W
Cururupu	240	1.50 S	44.52 W
Curutú ≃	236	5.05 N	63.28 W
Curuzú-Cuatiá	242	29.47 S	58.03 W
Curva Grande	240	2.37 S	45.27 W
Curvelo	245	18.45 S	44.25 W
Curwensville	204	40.58 N	78.32 W
Curwensville Lake ⊜[1]	204	40.55 N	78.37 W
Curwensville State Park ♠	204	40.55 N	78.34 W
Curwood, Mount ∧[2]	180	46.42 N	88.14 W
Cusago	256b	45.27 N	9.02 E
Cusano Milanino	56	45.33 N	9.11 E
Cusano Mutri	60	41.20 N	14.30 E
Cusapin	226	9.11 N	81.54 W
Cusco → Cuzco	238	13.31 S	71.59 W
Cuscuzeiro, Pico do ∧	246	23.18 S	44.47 W
Cushabatay ≃	238	7.09 S	75.08 W
Cushendall	42	55.06 N	6.04 W
Cushendun	42	55.07 N	6.03 W
Cushing, Okla., U.S.	186	35.59 N	96.46 W
Cushing, Tex., U.S.	212	31.43 N	94.50 W
Cushman	184	35.53 N	91.45 W
Cushman, Lake ⊜[1]	214	47.28 N	123.14 W
Cusiana ≃	236	4.33 N	71.51 W
Cusick	192	48.20 N	117.18 W
Cusihuiriáchic	222	28.14 N	106.50 W
Cusna, Monte ∧	58	44.17 N	10.23 E
Čusovaja ≃	76	58.13 N	56.22 E
Čusovoj	76	58.17 N	57.49 E
Cusseta	182	32.18 N	84.47 W
Cussewago Creek ≃	204	41.38 N	80.11 W
Cussey-sur-l'Ognon	54	47.20 N	5.56 E
Cusso ≃	142	14.16 S	15.36 E
Cust, N.Z.	162	43.19 S	172.22 E
Čust, S.S.S.R.	75	41.00 N	71.15 E
Custar	206	41.17 N	83.51 W
Custer, Mich., U.S.	180	43.58 N	86.14 W
Custer, Mont., U.S.	192	46.08 N	107.33 W
Custer, Okla., U.S.	186	35.40 N	98.53 W
Custer, S. Dak., U.S.	188	43.46 N	103.36 W
Custer, Wash., U.S.	214	48.55 N	122.38 W
Custer Battlefield National Monument ♠	192	45.32 N	107.20 W
Custer City	204	41.54 N	78.39 W
Custer Creek ≃	188	46.42 N	105.29 W
Custer State Park ♠	188	43.43 N	103.23 W
Custines	52	48.48 N	6.09 E
Custódia	240	8.07 S	37.39 W
Cut and Shoot	212	30.19 N	95.25 W
Cutato ≃	142	10.33 S	16.48 E
Cut Bank	192	48.38 N	112.20 W
Cutbank ≃	172	54.44 N	118.31 W
Cut Bank Creek ≃, N.A.	188	48.35 N	100.52 W
Cut Bank Creek ≃, Mont., U.S.	192	48.29 N	112.14 W
Cut Beaver Lake ⊜	174	53.47 N	102.38 W
Čutejevo	70	55.16 N	47.47 E
Cutervo	238	6.22 S	78.51 W
Cuthand Creek ≃	184	33.23 N	94.57 W
Cuthbert	182	31.46 N	84.48 W
Cut Knife	174	52.44 N	109.01 W
Cutler, Calif., U.S.	216	36.31 N	119.17 W
Cutler, Maine, U.S.	178	44.40 N	67.12 W
Cutler Ridge	210	25.36 N	80.24 W
Cutlerville	206	42.51 N	85.40 W
Čutovo	68	49.43 N	35.10 E
Cutral-Có	242	38.56 S	69.14 W
Cutro	36	39.02 N	16.59 E
Cuttack	110	20.30 N	85.50 E
Cuttyhunk Island I	197	41.25 N	70.56 W
Čutyr'	70	57.24 N	53.17 E
Cutzamalá ≃	224	18.22 N	100.39 W
Cutzamala de Pinzón	224	18.28 N	100.34 W
Cutzio	224	18.39 N	100.54 W
Čuvašskaja Avtonomnaja Sovetskaja Socialističeskaja Respublika □[3]	70	55.30 N	47.00 E
Cuvette □[5]	142	0.30 S	16.00 E
Cuvier, Cape ≻	152	24.05 S	113.22 E
Cuvilly	46	49.33 N	2.42 E
Cuvo ≃	142	10.50 S	13.47 E
Cuxhaven	48	53.52 N	8.42 E
Cuxton	250	51.22 N	0.27 E
Cuyabá → Cuiabá	238	15.35 S	56.05 W
Cuyagnateje ≃	230p	22.05 N	83.58 W
Cuyahoga □[6]	204	41.30 N	81.41 W
Cuyahoga ≃	204	41.30 N	81.42 W
Cuyahoga County Airport ⊠	269a	41.34 N	81.29 W
Cuyahoga Falls	204	41.08 N	81.29 W
Cuyahoga Heights	269a	41.26 N	81.39 W
Cuyahoga Ohio Canal ⩧	269a	41.26 N	81.40 W
Cuyahoga Valley National Recreation Area ♠	204	41.20 N	81.35 W
Cuyama ≃	194	34.54 N	120.18 W
Cuyamaca Peak ∧	194	32.57 N	116.36 W
Cuyamaca Rancho State Park ♠	194	32.58 N	116.32 W
Cuyamel	226	15.38 N	88.12 W
Cuyapo	106	15.46 N	120.40 E
Cuyk	48	51.44 N	5.52 E
Cuyler	200	42.44 N	75.57 W
Cuylerville	200	42.47 N	77.52 W
Cuyo	106	10.51 N	121.00 E
Cuyo East Pass ⋃	106	11.00 N	121.28 E
Cuyo Island I	106	10.51 N	121.02 E
Cuyo Islands II	106	11.04 N	120.57 E
Cuyo West Pass ⋃	106	11.00 N	120.30 E
Cuyuni ≃	236	6.23 N	58.41 W
Cuyutlán, Laguna de C	224	19.00 N	104.10 W
Cuzco	238	13.31 S	71.59 W
Cuzco □[5]	238	12.30 S	72.30 W
Cuzcuz	242	31.39 S	71.14 W
Čuzik ≃	76	58.03 N	80.37 E
Cuzna ≃	34	38.04 N	4.41 W
Cuzzago	54	46.00 N	8.22 E
Cvetkovo	68	49.11 N	31.33 E
Cvetnogorsk	76	54.14 N	90.27 E
Cvetnoje	68	48.57 N	32.29 E
Cvikov	50	50.48 N	14.40 E
Cwmbran	44	51.39 N	3.00 W
Cyangugu	144	2.29 S	28.54 E
Cybinka	30	52.12 N	14.48 E
Cybulev	68	49.06 N	29.50 E
Cyčevsko-V'azemskije Gr'ady ∧	66	55.35 N	34.00 E
Cyclades → Kikládhes II	38	37.30 N	25.00 E
Cyclone	204	41.50 N	78.35 W
Cygnet	206	41.14 N	83.39 W
Cygnet Bay C	152	16.35 S	123.05 E
Cygnet Lake ⊜	174	56.47 N	94.54 W
Cygnet River	158b	35.42 S	137.31 E
Cylburn Park ♠	274b	39.21 N	76.39 W
Cynin ≃	44	51.48 N	4.29 W
Cynthiana, Ky., U.S.	208	38.23 N	84.18 W
Cynthiana, Ohio, U.S.	208	39.10 N	83.21 W
Cynwyl Elfed	44	51.55 N	4.22 W
Cypern → Cyprus □[1]	120	35.00 N	33.00 E
Cypress, Calif., U.S.	270	33.50 N	118.01 W
Cypress, La., U.S.	184	31.36 N	93.02 W
Cypress, Tex., U.S.	212	29.58 N	95.42 W
Cypress Bayou ≃	184	35.03 N	91.42 W
Cypress Creek ≃, Fla., U.S.	210	28.05 N	82.24 W
Cypress Creek ≃, Tex., U.S.	184	30.19 N	93.45 W
Cypress Creek ≃, Tex., U.S.	212	30.02 N	95.19 W
Cypress Gardens ♠	210	28.00 N	81.42 W
Cypress Hills ⋀[2]	174	49.40 N	109.30 W
Cypress Hills Provincial Park ♠, Alta., Can.	174	49.39 N	110.10 W
Cypress Hills Provincial Park ♠, Sask., Can.	174	49.39 N	109.30 W
Cypress Island I	214	48.35 N	122.42 W
Cypress Lake ⊜, Sask., Can.	174	49.28 N	109.29 W
Cypress Lake ⊜, Fla., U.S.	210	28.05 N	81.19 W
Cypress Point ≻	216	36.35 N	121.59 W
Cypress Quarters	210	27.16 N	80.48 W
Cypress River	174	49.34 N	99.05 W
Cypress Swamp ≃	198	37.02 N	76.53 W
Cypress Swamp ☷	198	38.30 N	75.17 W
Cyprus □[1]	22		
	120	35.00 N	33.00 E
Cyrenaica → Barqah ←[1]	136	31.00 N	22.30 E
Cyrene	209	39.17 N	91.06 W
Cyrene ⊥	136	32.49 N	21.52 E
Cyril	186	34.54 N	98.12 W
Czechoslovakia □[1]	263d	26.11 S	28.06 E
Cyrus Field Bay C	166	62.50 N	64.55 W
Cysoing	46	50.34 N	3.13 E
Cythera → Kíthira I	38	36.20 N	22.58 E
Czaplinek	30	53.34 N	16.14 E
Czarna Białostocka	30	53.19 N	23.16 E
Czarna Woda	30	53.51 N	18.06 E
Czarne	30	53.42 N	16.57 E
Czarnków	30	52.55 N	16.34 E
Czechoslovakia □[1], Eur.	22	49.30 N	17.00 E
Czechoslovakia □[1]	30	49.30 N	17.00 E
Czechowice-Dziedzice	30	49.54 N	19.00 E
Czempiń	30	52.10 N	16.47 E
Czerniejewo	30	52.26 N	17.30 E
Czernowitz → Černovcy	68	48.18 N	25.56 E
Czersk	30	53.48 N	18.00 E
Czerwieńsk	30	52.01 N	15.25 E
Częstochowa	30	50.49 N	19.06 E
Człopa	30	53.06 N	16.08 E
Człuchów	30	53.41 N	17.21 E
Czudec	30	49.57 N	21.50 E
D			
Da → Black ≃	100	21.15 N	105.20 E
Daaden	52	50.44 N	7.58 E
Daan, Zhg.	90	27.52 N	117.53 E
Daan, Zhg.	90	23.05 N	115.37 E
Daan, Zhg.	100	23.19 N	110.34 E
Daanbantayan	106	11.14 N	124.00 E
Daanchang	97	29.23 N	106.01 E
Daanping	94	41.10 N	123.25 E
Ḍabāb, Jabal aḍ- ∧	122	31.02 N	35.38 E
Ḍaba Gorayale	134	8.42 N	44.55 E
Dabagou	94	42.27 N	122.00 E
Ḍab'ah, Ra's aḍ- ≻	130	31.05 N	28.26 E
Ḍabai	140	11.31 N	5.11 E
Dabaiqipu	94	41.52 N	122.36 E
Dabaizhuang	95	39.27 N	117.23 E
Dabajuro	236	11.02 N	70.40 W
Dabakala	140	8.22 N	4.26 W
Dabali	94	41.51 N	120.37 E
Dabaling ∧	90	24.28 N	113.17 E
Dabancheng	76	43.21 N	88.19 E
Dabangdian	90	31.37 N	113.41 E
Dabanyingzi	94	42.11 N	121.55 E
Dabao	88	40.34 N	124.12 E
Dabaojiagangzi	94	42.09 N	123.33 E
Dabaozhuang	95	40.18 N	116.58 E
Dabaozi	95	40.11 N	115.10 E
Dabaro	134	6.11 N	48.22 E
Dabashan ⋀	92	31.55 N	109.05 E
Dabasi	97	28.55 N	105.09 E
Dabat	134	12.58 N	37.48 E
Dabayingzi	94	42.11 N	121.35 E
Dabbūrīya	122	32.41 N	35.22 E
Dabegabis	148	28.07 S	18.36 E
Dabeiba	236	7.01 N	76.16 W
Dabeiwa	95	40.48 N	117.31 E
Dabeiyingzi	94	42.05 N	122.08 E
Dabendorf	50	52.14 N	13.26 E
Daber → Dobra	30	53.35 N	15.18 E
Daberas	146	25.38 S	18.29 E
Daberg ←[8]	253	51.40 N	7.47 E
Dabhoi	110	22.11 N	73.26 E
Dābhol	112	17.36 N	73.10 E
Ḍab'ī, Wādī aḍ- ∨	122	31.42 N	36.42 E
Dąbie	30	52.06 N	18.49 E
Dąbie ←[8]	50	53.24 N	14.40 E
Dąbie, Jezioro ⊜	50	53.27 N	14.40 E
Dabieshan ⋀	90	31.00 N	115.40 E
Dabilda	136	12.46 N	14.34 E
Ḍablān	120	34.52 N	40.34 E
Ďáblice ←[8]	50	50.08 N	14.29 E
Dabnou	140	14.09 N	5.22 E
Dabo	54	48.39 N	7.14 E
Dabob Bay C	214	47.47 N	122.50 W
Dabobeizhuang	95	39.18 N	117.59 E
Dabola	140	10.45 N	11.07 W
Dabola □[4]	140	10.36 N	11.07 W
Dabong	104	5.23 N	102.01 E
Dabou	140	5.19 N	4.23 W
Daboya	140	9.32 N	1.23 W
Dabra	114	25.54 N	78.20 E
Dābri ←[8]	262a	28.37 N	77.05 E
Dabringhausen	52	51.05 N	7.11 E
Dąbrowa Białostocka	30	53.39 N	23.20 E
Dąbrowa Tarnowska	30	50.11 N	21.00 E
Dabu, Zhg.	90	23.52 N	116.54 E
Dabu, Zhg.	90	24.20 N	114.35 E
Dabus ≃	134	10.48 N	35.10 E
Dabusunhu ⊜	92	36.58 N	94.55 E
Dabusutu-Ula, Gora ∧	76	50.44 N	92.40 E
Dacaitun	94	41.38 N	121.18 E
Dacangzigou	94	40.59 N	121.01 E
Dacaocun	95	40.34 N	117.07 E
Dacata ≃	134	7.15 N	42.15 E
Dacca	114	23.43 N	90.25 E
Dacca □[8]	114	24.00 N	90.25 E
Dachaidan	92	37.53 N	95.07 E
Dachakou	90	29.38 N	118.18 E
Dachang, Zhg.	95	39.53 N	116.59 E
Dachang, Zhg.	96	31.18 N	121.25 E
Dachang, Zhg.	96	32.12 N	118.45 E
Dachang Airport ⊠	259b	31.18 N	121.25 E
Dachangshandao I	88	39.10 N	122.34 E
Dachau	30	48.15 N	11.27 E
Dachauer Moos ☷	58	48.12 N	11.25 E
Dacheng	90	28.34 N	115.31 E
Dachengji	90	33.52 N	119.26 E
Dachenjiabao	96	32.11 N	120.22 E
Dachenshan I	96	30.21 N	121.52 E
Dachenxiangtun	94	41.34 N	123.31 E
Dachi	90	25.10 N	116.46 E
Dachongyu	95	40.23 N	117.41 E
Dachsberg ∧[2]	253	51.30 N	6.30 E
Dačice	30	49.05 N	15.26 E
Dac-lac, Cao Nguyen ⋀[1]	100	12.50 N	108.05 E
Dačnoje ←[8]	255a	59.50 N	30.16 E
Dacoma	186	36.40 N	98.34 W
Dacorum □[8]	250	51.45 N	0.30 W
Dacun, Zhg.	92	27.55 N	101.08 E
Dacun, Zhg.	96	31.12 N	119.40 E
Dacura, Laguna C	226	14.24 N	83.15 W
Dadal	78	49.01 N	111.07 E
Dadali	165e	8.07 S	159.06 E
Dadanawa	236	2.50 N	59.30 W
Dadaolizhuang	95	39.59 N	116.59 E
Dadaotun	94	41.46 N	122.13 E
Dadar ←[8]	262c	19.01 N	72.50 E
Daday	120	41.28 N	33.28 E
Dadayungou	94	41.23 N	123.04 E
Daddys Creek ≃	182	36.05 N	84.47 W
Dade □[6]	210	25.33 N	80.32 W
Dade Battlefield State Historic Memorial ⊥	210	28.38 N	82.09 W
Dade Battlefield State Historic Site ⊥	210	28.38 N	82.09 W
Dade City	210	28.22 N	82.12 W
Dadeville	184	32.50 N	85.46 W
Dādhar	110	29.28 N	67.39 E
Dadian	90	33.36 N	117.16 E
Dadiangas → General Santos	106	6.07 N	125.11 E
Dadianzi	94	42.11 N	124.02 E
Dading	92	27.04 N	105.31 E
Dadingjiawopu	94	41.13 N	122.16 E
D'adino	78	55.44 N	105.45 E
Dadle	134	5.23 N	46.57 E
Ḍadnah	118	25.33 N	56.21 E
Dadon	114	27.57 N	78.28 E
Dadonggejiang	95	39.51 N	116.48 E
Dadongzhou	94	41.44 N	124.00 E
Dadou ≃	32	43.44 N	1.49 E
Dādpur, Bhārat	262b	22.42 N	88.33 E
Dādpur, Bhārat	262b	22.54 N	88.31 E
Dādra and Nagar Haveli □[8]	112	20.05 N	73.00 E
Dādri	114	28.34 N	77.33 E
Dādu	110	26.44 N	67.47 E
Dadugang	92	22.23 N	100.55 E
Daduhe ≃	92	29.33 N	103.45 E
Dadukou, Zhg.	90	25.44 N	119.05 E
Dadukou, Zhg.	92	26.40 N	101.39 E
Dadukou, Zhg.	97	28.45 N	105.13 E
Dadukou, Zhg.	97	29.28 N	106.29 E
Daegu → Taegu	88	35.52 N	128.35 E
Daejeon → Taejŏn	88	36.20 N	127.26 E
Daerhanmaoming'anqi (Bailingmiao)	92	41.42 N	110.23 E
Daerhanwangfu	79	44.19 N	122.15 E
Daerhao	88	41.42 N	115.54 E
Daet	106	14.05 N	122.55 E
Daf'	136	28.03 N	19.57 E
Dafan, Zhg.	90	29.41 N	114.40 E
Dafan, Zhg.	94	42.38 N	122.11 E
Dafangshen, Zhg.	94	42.34 N	123.28 E
Dafangshen, Zhg.	94	42.25 N	123.14 E
Dafangshen, Zhg.	94	42.36 N	123.04 E
Dafanpuzi	94	41.37 N	122.50 E
Dafeng (Dazhongji)	90	33.12 N	120.30 E
Dafna	122	33.14 N	35.38 E
Dafoe	174	51.46 N	104.32 W
Dafoe ≃	174	55.55 N	94.48 W
Dafoe Lake ⊜	174	55.43 N	96.15 W
Dafosi (Great Buddha Temple) υ[1]	96	30.16 N	120.09 E
Dafoutuo	95	40.24 N	115.58 E
Dafu	90	29.55 N	118.35 E
Dafushui ≃	90	30.52 N	113.32 E
Dagā ≃	100	16.56 N	94.45 E
Dagana	140	16.31 N	15.30 W
Dagana ←[1]	136	13.05 N	16.00 E
Dagang, Zhg.	90	33.12 N	120.07 E
Dagang, Zhg.	90	22.49 N	113.23 E
Dagang, Zhg.	96	32.12 N	119.39 E
Dagangtou	90	28.18 N	119.44 E
Daganwangzhai	94	40.49 N	122.33 E
Daganzo de Arriba	256a	40.33 N	3.27 W
Dagaokan	94	40.46 N	122.22 E
Dagaolifangcun	94	41.10 N	122.28 E
Dagaolitun	94	42.26 N	123.53 E
Dagaoyang	96	30.35 N	120.26 E
Daga Post	130	9.12 N	33.58 E
Dagash	130	19.22 N	33.24 E
Dagda	66	56.06 N	27.32 E
Dageløkke	41	55.04 N	10.53 E
Dagenham ←[8]	250	51.32 N	0.10 E
Dagestanskaja Avtonomnaja Sovetskaja Socialističeskaja Respublika □[3]	74	43.00 N	47.00 E
Dagestanskije Ogni	74	42.07 N	48.12 E
Daggafontein	263d	26.18 S	28.28 E
Daggafontein Mines ←[7]	263d	26.18 S	28.29 E
Daggett	218	34.52 N	116.53 W
Dagg Sound ⋃	162	45.23 S	166.46 E
Daghfalī	130	19.17 N	32.30 E
Dağkızılca	120	38.18 N	27.24 E
Dagmersellen	54	47.13 N	7.59 E
Dagö → Hiiumaa I	66	58.52 N	22.40 E
Dagomys	74	43.40 N	39.41 E
Dagongtun	79	42.48 N	121.58 E
Dagoretti	144	1.18 S	36.46 E
Dagsboro	198	38.33 N	75.15 W
Dagshai	113	30.53 N	77.03 E
Dagu	95	38.59 N	117.41 E
Dagua, Col.	236	3.40 N	76.41 W
Dagua, Pap. N. Gui.	154	3.25 S	143.20 E
Daguan, Zhg.	90	31.14 N	117.01 E
Daguan, Zhg.	92	27.44 N	104.16 E
Daguao	230m	18.14 N	65.41 W
Dagufen'gou	95	40.41 N	116.20 E
Daguhe ≃, Zhg.	88	37.34 N	121.17 E
Daguhe ≃, Zhg.	88	36.42 N	120.26 E
D'Aguilar, Mount ∧	161a	27.19 S	152.47 E
D'Aguilar Range ⋀	161a	27.10 S	152.45 E
Dagujia	88	42.22 N	124.52 E
Dagujiazi	94	42.20 N	123.20 E
Dagupan	106	16.03 N	120.20 E
Dagus Mines	204	41.21 N	78.37 W
Dagutang	90	29.38 N	116.06 E
Dagwin	100	18.04 N	97.41 E
Dahabān	134	21.55 N	39.04 E
Dahanchang	95	39.29 N	117.05 E
Dahaneh-ye Ghowrī	110	35.54 N	68.30 E
Dahaneh-ye Kāshār	110	35.09 N	66.14 E
Dahan-e Qowmghī	110	34.28 N	66.31 E
Dahantun	94	42.10 N	122.41 E
Dahasah, Wādī ∨	132	28.08 N	31.00 E
Daḥdāḥ, Tall ∧[2]	122	32.36 N	36.03 E
Dahe	96	31.42 N	120.37 E
Daheba	97	30.06 N	106.03 E
Dahebei	95	39.10 N	117.39 E
Daheiyugou	94	41.21 N	121.55 E
Dahekou	96	32.16 N	119.05 E
Dahengdu	90	29.03 N	121.30 E
Daheqiao	90	29.25 N	115.16 E
Dahijuri	116	22.31 N	86.59 E
Dahīrpur ←[8]	262a	28.43 N	77.12 E
Dahl	52	51.18 N	7.31 E
Dahl ←[8]	253	51.11 N	6.26 E
Dahlak Archipelago II	134	15.45 N	40.30 E
Dahlak Kebir Island I	134	15.38 N	40.11 E
Dahle	253	51.18 N	7.45 E
Dahlem	52	50.23 N	6.33 E
Dahlem ←[8]	254a	52.28 N	13.17 E
Dahlem, Museum υ	254a	52.27 N	13.18 E
Dahlen	50	51.22 N	12.59 E
Dahlenburg	50	53.11 N	10.44 E
Dahlerau	253	51.13 N	7.19 E
Dahlewitz	50	52.19 N	13.26 E
Dahlgren, Ill., U.S.	184	38.12 N	88.41 W
Dahlgren, Va., U.S.	198	38.20 N	77.03 W
Dahlhausen	50	53.03 N	12.20 E
Dahlia	144	18.35 S	27.08 E
Dahlonega	182	34.32 N	89.59 W
Dahlonega Plateau ⋀[1]	182	34.10 N	84.20 W
Dahlwitz-Hoppegarten	50	52.30 N	13.38 E
Dahmarū	132	28.41 N	30.49 E
Dahme, B.R.D.	50	54.13 N	11.04 E
Dahme, D.D.R.	50	51.52 N	13.25 E
Dahme ≃	50	52.25 N	13.35 E
Dahn	52	49.09 N	7.47 E
Dahomey → Benin □[1]	140	9.30 N	2.15 E
Dahong	96	31.53 N	121.17 E
Dahongmen	95	39.47 N	116.20 E
Dahongshan ⋀	90	31.30 N	113.00 E
Dahongtaizi	94	41.41 N	121.23 E
Dahoucun	95	38.51 N	115.37 E
Dahra, Lībīya	136	29.34 N	17.50 E
Dahra, Sén.	140	15.21 N	15.29 W
Dahra ⋀	138	36.20 N	1.21 E
Dähre	50	52.48 N	10.54 E
Dahsah, Wādī ad- ∨	132	27.19 N	31.26 E
Dahshūr	132	29.45 N	31.14 E
Dahu, Zhg.	90	26.22 N	119.06 E
Dahu, Zhg.	90	26.04 N	117.19 E
Dahu, Zhg.	90	26.10 N	114.57 E
Dahua	92	23.44 N	107.59 E
Dahuan	90	22.33 N	113.29 E
Dahuangdi	94	42.08 N	122.27 E
Dahuangji	88	35.06 N	115.15 E
Dahuangpu	95	39.26 N	117.16 E
Dahuangshanpu	94	41.16 N	121.23 E
Dahuashancun	95	40.17 N	117.04 E
Dahuasi	97	30.05 N	104.08 E
Dahūk	118	36.52 N	43.00 E
Dahuni	154	10.31 S	149.55 E
Dahushan	94	41.37 N	122.09 E
Dahy, Nafūd ad- ←[2]	126	22.20 N	45.35 E
Dai, Pulau I	154	7.33 S	129.41 E
Daia	38	44.00 N	25.59 E
Daian	84	35.05 N	136.33 E
Daibagnyahāti	116	22.33 N	89.52 E
Daibosatsu-rei ∧	84	35.45 N	138.51 E
Daibu	96	31.18 N	119.30 E
Daiei	86	35.29 N	133.45 E
Daifang	90	27.32 N	115.41 E
Daigo	84	36.46 N	140.21 E
Daigo ←[8]	260	34.57 N	135.50 E
Daiguantun	95	39.57 N	117.50 E
Daihaiyingzi	94	42.30 N	121.26 E
Daiji	90	33.48 N	115.03 E
Daijiagou	97	30.00 N	106.33 E
Daijiang ≃	90	26.14 N	119.40 E
Daijiasi	97	29.14 N	105.09 E
Daijiayao	90	32.56 N	120.44 E
Daikanbō ∧	86	33.00 N	131.04 E
Daik-U	100	17.47 N	96.40 E
Dā'īl	122	32.45 N	36.08 E
Dailekh	114	28.50 N	81.44 E
Daimanji-san ∧	82	36.15 N	133.19 E
Daimiel	34	39.04 N	3.37 W
Daimon, Nihon	84	36.44 N	137.03 E
Daimon, Nihon	258	35.53 N	139.44 E
Daimuken-zan ∧	84	35.15 N	138.10 E
Dainan	90	32.43 N	120.06 E
Daingean	28	53.18 N	7.17 W
Daingerfield	212	33.02 N	94.44 W
Dainhāt	116	23.37 N	88.04 E
Dainichiga-take ∧	84	36.00 N	136.50 E
Daintree	154	16.15 S	145.19 E
Daiō-zaki ≻	82	34.17 N	136.54 E
Daiqintala	79	45.16 N	121.44 E
Dāira Dīn Panāh	113	30.34 N	70.56 E
Dairago	256b	45.34 N	8.52 E
Daireaux	242	36.36 S	61.45 W
Dairen → Lüda	88	38.53 N	121.35 E
Dairy City → Cypress	270	33.50 N	118.01 W
Dairy Creek, East Fork ≃	214	45.34 N	123.09 W
Dairy Creek, West Fork ≃	214	45.34 N	123.09 W
Dairyland → La Palma, Calif., U.S.	270	33.51 N	118.02 W
Dairyland, N.Y., U.S.	200	41.45 N	74.33 W
Dairyland Reservoir ⊜[1]	180	45.30 N	91.00 W
Dairy Valley → Cerritos	270	33.51 N	118.05 W
Dai-sen ∧	86	35.22 N	133.33 E
Dai-sen-oki-kokuritsu-kōen ♠	86	35.20 N	133.35 E
Daisen-zan ∧	86	34.07 N	133.56 E
Daisetta	212	30.07 N	94.39 W
Daishin	84	37.12 N	140.15 E
Daishōji ≃	84	36.18 N	136.15 E
Daisongdao I	90	24.03 N	118.03 E
Daitō, Nihon	86	34.42 N	135.38 E
Daitō, Nihon	86	35.19 N	132.58 E
Daiwa, Nihon	86	34.32 N	132.57 E
Daiwa, Nihon	86	34.57 N	132.39 E
Daixi	96	30.40 N	120.01 E
Daixian	92	39.08 N	113.01 E
Daixiqiao	96	31.36 N	120.04 E
Daiya ≃	84	36.45 N	139.46 E
Daiyunshan ⋀	90	25.46 N	118.16 E
Dajabón	228	19.33 N	71.42 W
Dājal	110	29.33 N	70.23 E
Da'jānīyah, Jabal ad- ∧	122	30.34 N	35.43 E
Dajan Uul ⋀	92	45.20 N	95.30 E
Dajarra	156	21.41 S	139.31 E
Dajianshan ∧	92	26.42 N	103.34 E
Dajiao	96	31.51 N	121.13 E
Dajidian	95	38.50 N	115.26 E
Dajin I	90	21.52 N	113.02 E
Dajindian	90	34.24 N	113.01 E
Dajing	90	28.24 N	121.07 E
Dajingjie	90	28.59 N	113.19 E
Dajishan	90	24.38 N	114.26 E
Dajitai	94	42.20 N	121.11 E
Dajiuba	110	36.50 N	89.35 E
Dajiyang ⋃	90	30.54 N	122.18 E
Daju	95	39.12 N	115.31 E
Dak ⊜	118	32.48 N	61.14 E
Dakangpu	94	41.32 N	121.06 E
Dakanzi	94	40.52 N	122.53 E
Dakar	140	14.40 N	17.26 W
Dākātia ≃[1]	116	22.57 N	90.42 E
Dakecihu ⊜	110	31.55 N	87.35 E
Dakendabanshan ⋀	92	38.25 N	95.55 E
Dakengkou	90	24.33 N	113.37 E
Dak-gle	100	15.11 N	107.48 E
Dakhal, Bi'r ad- ⍑[4]	132	28.40 N	32.24 E
Dakhal, Wādī ad- ∨	132	28.49 N	32.45 E
Dakhla	138	23.43 N	15.57 W
Dakingari	140	11.37 N	4.01 E
Dakka → Dacca	114	23.43 N	90.25 E
Dākoānk	100	7.02 N	93.43 E
Dakongcheng	95	39.30 N	117.09 E
Dakongwan	94	40.51 N	122.19 E
Dakoro	140	14.31 N	6.46 E
Dakota City, Iowa, U.S.	180	42.43 N	94.12 W
Dakota City, Nebr., U.S.	188	42.25 N	96.25 W
Dakou	90	34.27 N	112.44 E
Dakouraoua	140	13.58 N	6.15 E
Dakoutun	95	39.35 N	117.14 E
Đakovica	38	42.23 N	20.25 E
Đakovo	38	45.19 N	18.25 E
Dakshingram	116	24.03 N	87.48 E
Dak-to	100	14.42 N	107.51 E
Dakumu	79	48.51 N	124.18 E
Dakunlun	88	36.34 N	117.52 E
Dakwa	144	4.00 N	26.26 E
Dakwah, Tall ad- ∧[2]	122	33.25 N	36.56 E
Dala, Ang.	142	8.05 S	15.50 E
Dala, Ang.	142	11.03 S	20.17 E
Dala, Sol.is.	165e	8.35 S	160.40 E
Dalaas	54	47.07 N	10.00 E
Dalaba	140	10.42 N	12.15 W
Dalaba □[4]	140	10.45 N	12.18 W
Dalabani	140	10.28 N	9.27 W
Dala Cachibo	142	10.28 S	14.39 E
Dala-Floda	40	60.31 N	14.47 E
Dalaguete	106	9.46 N	123.32 E
Dalahan (Shiqizhan)	79	52.06 N	125.46 E
Dala-Husby	40	60.21 N	16.00 E
Dalai	79	45.28 N	124.18 E
Dala-Järna	26	60.33 N	14.21 E
Dalajchöl	76	47.59 N	90.47 E
Dalaji	79	51.38 N	120.06 E
Dalälven ≃	40	60.38 N	17.27 E
Dalama	120	37.47 N	28.04 E
Dalaman ≃	120	36.40 N	28.45 E
Dalāmī	130	11.52 N	30.28 E
Dalan	90	23.19 N	114.47 E
Dalandzadgad	92	43.35 N	104.30 E
Dalandžargalan	92	45.58 N	108.59 E
Dalane ←[1]	26	58.35 N	6.20 E
Dalang	90	22.57 N	113.56 E
Dalantuozi	94	41.28 N	122.47 E
Dalao	140	11.29 N	13.40 W
Dalaodao I	90	25.47 N	119.43 E
Dalarna □[9]	26	61.01 N	14.04 E
Dalarö	40	59.08 N	18.24 E
Dalat, Malay.	102	2.44 N	111.56 E
Da-lat, Viet.	100	11.56 N	108.25 E
Dalatando	142	9.18 S	14.54 E
Dalatehouqi	92	41.09 N	107.58 E
Dalateqi	92	40.28 N	110.02 E
Dalavakasır	120	37.14 N	41.45 E
Dalayaozi	95	40.49 N	117.41 E
Dalbana ≃	240	4.48 N	57.27 W
Dālbandin	118	28.53 N	64.25 E
Dalbeattie	42	54.56 N	3.49 W
D'Albertis Dome ∧	154	5.00 S	142.05 E
Dalbosjön C	26	58.45 N	12.48 E
Dalby, Austl.	156	27.11 S	151.16 E
Dalby, Sve.	41	55.40 N	13.20 E
Dalcahue	244	42.23 S	73.40 W
Dalch ≃	44	50.52 N	3.47 W
Dale, Nor.	26	60.35 N	5.49 E
Dale, Wales, U.K.	44	51.43 N	5.11 W
Dale, Ind., U.S.	184	38.10 N	86.59 W
Dale, Pa., U.S.	204	40.18 N	78.54 W
Dale, Tex., U.S.	212	29.56 N	97.34 W
Dale ≃	158a	32.10 S	116.49 E
Dale Bridge	158a	32.05 S	116.49 E
Dalecarlia → Dalarna □[9]	26	61.01 N	14.04 E
Dale City	198	38.38 N	77.18 W
Dale Hollow Dam ←[6]	182	36.25 N	85.30 W
Dale Hollow Lake ⊜[1]	182	36.36 N	85.19 W
Dale Lake ⊜	194	34.08 N	115.42 W
Dalen	26	59.27 N	8.00 E
Dalengtu	88	41.11 N	113.45 E
Daleshankou)(	92	28.12 N	98.08 E
Daleside	148	26.30 S	28.04 E
Dalesville	196	45.42 N	74.24 W
Dalesville ≃	196	45.40 N	74.24 W
Daleszyce	30	50.48 N	20.48 E
Dalet	100	19.59 N	93.51 E
Daleville, Ind., U.S.	208	40.07 N	85.33 W
Daleville, Pa., U.S.	200	41.18 N	75.31 W
Dalfsen	48	52.30 N	6.16 E
Dalgaranga	152	27.46 S	117.02 E
Dalgaranger ∧	152	27.51 S	117.06 E
Dalgety	161b	36.30 S	148.50 E
Dalgety Brook ≃	152	25.07 S	115.47 E
Dalgety Downs	152	25.17 S	116.15 E
Dal Goble	134	9.52 N	49.50 E
Dalgomai	114	26.06 N	90.47 E
Dalhart	186	36.04 N	102.31 W
Dalhausen	48	51.37 N	9.17 E
Dalhousie, Bhārat	113	32.32 N	75.59 E
Dalhousie, N.B., Can.	176	48.04 N	66.23 W
Dalhousie, Cape ≻	170	70.14 N	129.42 W
Dalhousie Island I	116	21.35 N	88.45 E
Dalhousie Lake ⊜	202	44.58 N	76.35 W
Dalhousie Square ♠	262b	22.33 N	88.22 E
Dali, Zhg.	92	34.47 N	109.57 E
Dali, Zhg.	92	25.38 N	100.09 E
Daliandao I	90	25.40 N	119.42 E
Daliangdi	88	41.54 N	115.45 E
Daliangshan ⋀	92	28.00 N	103.00 E
Dalianhe	94	40.57 N	123.15 E
Daliankeng	95	40.54 N	117.45 E
Dalianwukou	96	30.17 N	119.00 E
Dalías	34	36.49 N	2.52 W
Dalihe ≃	92	37.05 N	110.20 E
Daliji	90	33.48 N	117.48 E
Dalikou	90	26.52 N	118.00 E
Dalin, Zhg.	79	43.43 N	122.45 E
Dalin, Zhg.	97	30.17 N	104.07 E
Daling	94	41.27 N	121.15 E
Dalingbeigou	94	40.42 N	123.08 E
Dalinghe	94	41.35 N	121.02 E
Dalinghe ≃	88	40.56 N	121.43 E
Dalinghekou ≃[1]	88	40.55 N	121.50 E
Dalipe Point ≻	106	10.46 N	121.55 E
Daliu	95	38.51 N	116.19 E
Daliushugou	94	40.46 N	122.14 E
Daliutai	94	41.25 N	121.55 E
Daliutun	94	42.14 N	122.46 E
Daliuzhen	88	37.44 N	116.50 E
Daliuzhuang, Zhg.	90	33.04 N	114.03 E
Daliuzhuang, Zhg.	95	39.52 N	118.00 E
Dāliyat el Karmel	122	32.42 N	35.03 E
Daliyya	122	32.35 N	35.04 E
Dalizi	88	41.45 N	126.49 E
Dalj	38	45.29 N	18.59 E
Daljā'	132	27.39 N	30.42 E
Dalkarlsberg	40	59.26 N	14.51 E
Dalkeith	42	55.54 N	3.04 W
Dālkola	114	25.52 N	87.51 E
Dall, Mount ∧	170	62.35 N	152.18 W
Dāllah, 'Ayn ⍑[4]	130	27.19 N	27.20 E
Dallardsville	212	30.38 N	94.38 W
Dallas, Ala., U.S.	184	33.50 N	86.40 W
Dallas, Ga., U.S.	182	33.55 N	84.51 W
Dallas, N.C., U.S.	182	35.19 N	81.11 W
Dallas, Oreg., U.S.	192	44.55 N	123.19 W
Dallas, Pa., U.S.	200	41.20 N	75.58 W
Dallas, Tex., U.S.	212	32.47 N	96.48 W
Dallas, Wis., U.S.	180	45.16 N	91.51 W
Dallas □[6]	212	32.17 N	96.47 W
Dallas Center	180	41.41 N	93.58 W
Dallas City	180	40.38 N	91.10 W
Dallas-Fort Worth Regional Airport ⊠	212	32.54 N	97.01 W
Dallas Naval Air Station ■	212	32.44 N	96.59 W
Dallastown	198	39.54 N	76.39 W
Dallau	52	49.23 N	9.11 E
Dallgow	50	52.32 N	13.05 E
Dalli Rajhāra	112	20.35 N	81.04 E
Dall Island I	170	54.50 N	132.55 W
Dall Lake ⊜	170	60.18 N	163.35 W
Dalmā' I	118	24.30 N	52.20 E
Dalmacija □[9]	36	43.00 N	17.00 E
Dalmacio Vélez Sarsfield	242	32.36 S	63.35 W
Dal'mamedli	74	40.42 N	46.34 E
Dalmatia	198	40.39 N	76.54 W
Dalmatia → Dalmacija □[9]	36	43.00 N	17.00 E
Dalmatovo	76	56.16 N	62.56 E
Dalmau	114	26.04 N	81.02 E
Dalmellington	42	55.19 N	4.24 W
Dalmeny	174	52.20 N	106.46 W
Dalmine	56	45.39 N	9.36 E
Dalmose	41	55.18 N	11.26 E
Dal'n'aja	79	45.56 N	142.04 E
Dal'n'aja Muja	78	54.21 N	103.37 E
Dal'neje-Konstantinovo	70	55.49 N	44.06 E
Dal'ne-Rusanovo	72	54.15 N	36.45 E
Dal'nik	68	46.28 N	30.34 E
Daloa	140	6.53 N	6.27 W
Daloa □[5]	140	7.00 N	6.45 W
Dalong	110	28.54 N	90.33 E
Dalongchang	95	39.50 N	116.06 E
Dalonghua	95	39.18 N	115.18 E
Dalongtian	90	24.14 N	115.44 E
Dalovice	50	50.11 N	12.55 E
Dalqū	130	20.07 N	30.37 E
Dalroy	172	51.07 N	113.39 W
Dalry, Scot., U.K.	42	55.07 N	4.10 W
Dalry, Scot., U.K.	42	55.43 N	4.44 W
Dalrymple, Mount ∧	156	21.02 S	148.38 E
Dalrymple Creek ≃	161a	27.59 S	151.46 E
Dalrymple Lake ⊜	202	44.38 N	79.07 W
Dalsbruk (Taalintehdas)	26	60.02 N	22.31 E
Dalsingh Sarai	114	25.40 N	85.50 E
Dalsingpara	114	26.47 N	89.22 E
Dalsjöfors	26	57.43 N	13.05 E
Dalsland □[9]	26	58.30 N	12.50 E
Dals-Långed	26	58.55 N	12.18 E
Dal'stroja	170	68.19 N	177.39 W
Dalton, S. Afr.	148	29.20 S	30.40 E
Dalton, Eng., U.K.	252	53.34 N	2.46 W
Dalton, Ga., U.S.	182	34.47 N	84.58 W
Dalton, Mass., U.S.	197	42.29 N	73.09 W
Dalton, Nebr., U.S.	188	41.25 N	102.58 W
Dalton, N.Y., U.S.	200	42.32 N	77.57 W
Dalton, Ohio, U.S.	204	40.48 N	81.42 W
Dalton, Pa., U.S.	200	41.32 N	75.45 W
Dalton City	209	39.43 N	88.48 W
Daltonganj	114	24.02 N	84.04 E
Dalton Gardens	192	47.44 N	116.46 W
Dalton Iceberg Tongue ⊓	9	66.15 S	121.30 E
Dalton-in-Furness	42	54.09 N	3.11 W
Dalu	94	41.27 N	123.19 E
Dalubeikou	95	38.59 N	117.12 E
Daludalu	104	1.05 N	100.15 E
Daluis, Gorges de ∨	56	44.04 N	6.49 E
Dalum, B.R.D.	48	52.35 N	7.14 E

Symbol	English	Deutsch	Español	Français	Português
≃	River	Fluss	Río	Rivière	Rio
⩧	Canal	Kanal	Canal	Canal	Canal
⌊	Waterfall, Rapids	Wasserfall, Stromschnellen	Cascada, Rápidos	Chute d'eau, Rapides	Cascata, Rápidos
⋃	Strait	Meeresstrasse	Estrecho	Détroit	Estreito
C	Bay, Gulf	Bucht, Golf	Bahía, Golfo	Baie, Golfe	Baía, Golfo
⊜	Lake, Lakes	See, Seen	Lago, Lagos	Lac, Lacs	Lago, Lagos
☷	Swamp	Sumpf	Pantano	Marais	Pântano
⊓	Ice Features, Glacier	Eis- und Gletscherformen	Accidentes Glaciales	Formes glaciaires	Acidentes Glaciares
⍑	Other Hydrographic Features	Andere Hydrographische Objekte	Otros Elementos Hidrográficos	Autres données hydrographiques	Outros Elementos Hidrográficos
✢	Submarine Features	Untermeerische Objekte	Accidentes Submarinos	Formes de relief sous-marin	Acidentes Submarinos
□	Political Unit	Politische Einheit	Unidad Política	Entité politique	Unidade Política
υ	Cultural Institution	Kulturelle Institution	Institución Cultural	Institution culturelle	Instituição Cultural
⊥	Historical Site	Historische Stätte	Sitio Histórico	Site historique	Sitio Histórico
♠	Recreational Site	Erholungs- und Ferienort	Sitio de Recreo	Centre de loisirs	Sítio de Lazer
⊠	Airport	Flughafen	Aeropuerto	Aéroport	Aeroporto
■	Military Installation	Militäranlage	Instalación Militar	Installation militaire	Instalação Militar
←	Miscellaneous	Verschiedenes	Misceláneo	Divers	Miscelânea

ENGLISH Name / DEUTSCH Name	Page / Seite	Lat.°′ / Breite°′	Long.°′ / Länge°′ E=Ost
Dalum, Dan.	41	55.22 N	10.22 E
Daluojiazhuang	96	32.09 N	120.08 E
Daluotaozi	94	41.17 N	122.52 E
Daluoxi	90	25.14 N	118.36 E
Daluping	90	26.11 N	114.30 E
Dalupiri Island I, Pil.	106	19.05 N	121.14 E
Dalupiri Island I, Pil.	106	12.25 N	124.16 E
Dalushan I	90	28.06 N	121.25 E
Daluxi	90	24.28 N	117.01 E
Daluzhuang	96	30.06 N	120.15 E
Dalview	263d	26.15 S	28.21 E
Dalvik	24a	65.59 N	18.32 W
Dalwallinu	152	30.17 S	116.40 E
Dalworthington Gardens	212	32.42 N	97.10 W
Daly ≃	154	13.20 S	130.19 E
Daly Bay C	166	64.00 N	89.40 W
Daly City	216	37.42 N	122.29 W
Daly Lake ⊜	174	56.33 N	105.40 W
Daly Point ≻	202	44.53 N	80.14 W
Daly River	154	13.45 S	130.50 E
Daly River Aboriginal Reserve ↢[4]	154	14.20 S	130.00 E
Daly Waters	154	16.15 S	133.22 E
Dāmā, Sūrīy.	122	32.57 N	36.25 E
Dama, Zhg.	90	24.21 N	116.32 E
Dama, Zhg.	90	32.03 N	118.02 E
Damaiyu I	90	25.13 N	119.35 E
Damān	112	20.25 N	72.51 E
Damān □[8]	112	20.10 N	73.00 E
Damang I	90	21.55 N	113.08 E
Damanhūr	132	31.02 N	30.28 E
Damanling	95	40.36 N	115.08 E
Damaopu	94	41.16 N	121.07 E
Damaoshan ∧∧	96	31.43 N	119.17 E
Damar	120	41.15 N	41.34 E
Damar, Pulau I, Indon.	154	7.09 S	128.40 E
Damar, Pulau I, Indon.	154	1.00 S	128.24 E
Damara	142	4.58 N	18.42 E
Damaraja	105a	6.55 S	108.05 E
Damaraland □[9]	146	22.34 S	17.06 E
Damariscotta	178	44.02 N	69.32 W
Damāş, Mişr	132	30.48 N	31.20 E
Damas → Dimashq, Sūrīy.	122	33.30 N	36.18 E
Damasco → Dimashq	122	33.30 N	36.18 E
Damascus → Dimashq, Sūrīy.	122	33.30 N	36.18 E
Damascus, Ark., U.S.	184	35.22 N	92.25 W
Damascus, Ga., U.S.	182	31.18 N	84.43 W
Damascus, Md., U.S.	198	39.17 N	77.12 W
Damascus, Ohio, U.S.	204	40.54 N	80.58 W
Damascus, Pa., U.S.	200	41.42 N	75.04 W
Damascus, Va., U.S.	182	36.37 N	81.46 W
Damascus International Airport ⊠	122	33.29 N	36.13 E
Damaskus → Dimashq	122	33.30 N	36.18 E
Damāţ	132	30.57 N	30.57 E
Damāvand	118	35.43 N	52.04 E
Damāvand, Qolleh-ye ∧	118	35.56 N	52.08 E
Damba	142	6.41 S	15.08 E
Dambach-la-Ville	54	48.20 N	7.26 E
Dambarta	140	12.26 N	8.31 E
Dambeck	50	52.48 N	11.09 E
Dambuki	79	54.20 N	121.35 E
Dam-doi	100	8.50 N	105.15 E
Damelevières	54	48.33 N	6.23 E
Damengjialazi	94	41.04 N	120.53 E
Damengzhuang	95	39.32 N	116.59 E
Damergou ↢[1]	140	15.00 N	8.55 E
Damerham	44	50.57 N	1.52 W
Dämeritzsee ⊜	254a	52.25 N	13.45 E
Damery	46	49.04 N	3.53 E
Dames Quarter	198	38.11 N	75.54 W
Dam Gamad	130	13.17 N	27.28 E
Dāmghān	118	39.09 N	54.22 E
Damianópolis	245	14.33 S	46.10 W
Damianpu	97	30.36 N	104.10 E
Damiao, Zhg.	88	42.26 N	118.22 E
Damiao, Zhg.	88	34.20 N	117.23 E
Damiao, Zhg.	92	37.18 N	104.39 E
Damiao, Zhg.	94	42.33 N	122.18 E
Damiaochang	97	29.39 N	106.05 E
Damiaogou	94	41.06 N	123.52 E
Damiaojiang	96	31.00 N	120.28 E
Damiaoshan	92	25.06 N	109.15 E
Damiaoshang	95	39.56 N	115.12 E
Damıar	74	41.15 N	41.34 E
Dămienești	38	46.44 N	26.59 E
Damietta → Dumyāţ	132	31.25 N	31.48 E
Damietta Mouth → Dumyāţ, Maşabb ≃[1]	132	31.32 N	31.51 E
Damin	90	28.56 N	120.29 E
Daming	88	36.19 N	115.06 E
Damintun	94	41.52 N	122.56 E
Dāmiyā	122	32.06 N	35.33 E
Damm	253	51.40 N	6.48 E
Dammai Island I	106	5.47 N	120.25 E
Dammarie	46	48.21 N	1.30 E
Dammarie-lès-Lys	46	48.31 N	2.39 E
Dammartin-en-Goële	46	49.03 N	2.41 E
Dammartin-en-Serve	46	48.54 N	1.37 E
Dammastock ∧	54	46.39 N	8.25 E
Damme, Bel.	46	51.15 N	3.17 E
Damme, B.R.D.	48	52.30 N	8.08 E
Damme, D.D.R.	50	53.17 N	14.01 E
Dāmodar ≃	114	22.17 N	88.05 E
Dāmodar Main Canal ☰	116	23.01 N	87.53 E
Damoh	114	23.50 N	79.27 E
Damolândia	245	16.16 S	49.22 W
Damon	212	29.17 N	95.45 W
Damongo	140	9.05 N	1.49 W
Damotapāda	262c	19.03 N	73.04 E
Damous	34	36.33 N	1.42 E
Damozhuang	95	39.53 N	115.40 E
Dampar, Tasek ⊜	104	3.02 N	102.43 E
Dampelas → Sabang	102	0.11 N	119.51 E
Dampier	152	20.39 S	116.45 E
Dampier, Cape ≻	154	6.02 S	151.02 E
Dampier, Selat ⊔	154	0.40 S	130.40 E
Dampier Archipelago II	152	20.35 S	116.35 E
Dampier Land ≻[1]	152	17.30 S	122.55 E
Dampierre, Fr.	46	48.42 N	1.59 E
Dampierre, Fr.	54	47.09 N	5.45 E
Dampierre, Château de ⊥	251	48.42 N	1.59 E
Dampierre-en-Burly	46	47.46 N	2.31 E
Dampierre-sur-Linotte	54	47.31 N	6.14 E
Dampierre-sur-Salon	54	47.33 N	5.41 E
Dampier Strait ⊔	154	5.36 S	148.12 E
Dampit	105a	8.13 S	112.45 E
Dampmart	251	48.53 N	2.44 E
Damprichard	54	47.15 N	6.53 E
Dâmrei, Chuŏr Phnum ∧∧	100	11.00 N	104.05 E
Damují ≃	230p	22.11 N	80.33 W
Damüls	54	47.17 N	9.53 E
Dāmurhuda	116	23.36 N	88.47 E
Damutougou	88	42.28 N	118.56 E
Damuyang C	90	29.20 N	122.06 E
Damville	46	48.52 N	1.04 E
Damvillers	52	49.20 N	5.24 E
Dan	122	33.14 N	35.39 E
Dan ≃	182	36.42 N	78.45 W
Dana, Cam.	136	10.14 N	15.18 E
Dana, Ind., U.S.	184	39.48 N	87.30 W
Dana, Mount ∧	216	37.54 N	119.13 W
Dana, Pulau I	102	10.50 S	121.16 E
Danai	102	0.29 N	103.26 E
Danajon Bank ↢[4]	106	10.16 N	124.17 E
Danakil Plain ≚	134	12.25 N	40.30 E
Dananè	140	7.16 N	8.09 W
Dananè □[5]	140	7.15 N	8.00 W
Da-nang	100	16.04 N	108.13 E
Danan'gou	95	40.32 N	117.49 E
Da'nanhu	92	42.28 N	93.32 E
Danao, Pil.	106	12.29 N	122.39 E
Danao, Pil.	106	10.32 N	124.02 E
Dana Point	218	33.29 N	117.44 W
Dana Point ≻	218	33.28 N	117.43 W
Dānāpur	114	25.38 N	85.03 E
Danba	92	31.00 N	101.50 E
Danboro	198	40.21 N	75.08 W
Danbury, Eng., U.K.	44	51.44 N	0.33 E
Danbury, Conn., U.S.	197	41.23 N	73.27 W
Danbury, Iowa, U.S.	188	42.14 N	95.43 W
Danbury, Nebr., U.S.	188	40.03 N	100.24 W
Danbury, N.C., U.S.	182	36.24 N	80.12 W
Danbury, Tex., U.S.	212	29.14 N	95.21 W
Danby Lake ⊜	194	34.14 N	115.07 W
Dancheng	90	33.39 N	115.11 E
Danchengji	90	33.47 N	116.17 E
Dand	110	31.37 N	65.41 E
Dandaragan	152	30.40 S	115.42 E
Dande ≃	142	8.28 S	13.21 E
Dandeldhura	114	29.18 N	80.35 E
Dandeli	112	15.15 N	74.37 E
Dandenong	159	37.59 S	145.12 E
Dandenong, Mount ∧	264b	37.50 S	145.21 E
Dandenong Creek ≃	264b	38.01 S	145.05 E
Danderyd	40	59.25 N	18.01 E
Dandīl	132	29.10 N	31.02 E
Dandot	113	32.39 N	72.58 E
Dandridge	182	36.01 N	83.25 W
Dan Dume	140	11.27 N	7.10 E
Dane □[6]	206	43.04 N	89.15 W
Dane ≃	42	53.15 N	2.31 W
Danea	140	11.27 N	13.12 W
Dane County Regional Airport-Truax Field ⊠	206	43.08 N	89.20 W
Dänemark → Denmark □[1]	26	56.00 N	10.00 E
Dänemark-Strasse → Denmark Strait ⊔	10	67.00 N	25.00 W
Danevang	212	29.03 N	96.13 W
Danewitz	254a	52.44 N	13.40 E
Danfeng	92	33.40 N	110.17 E
Danfengzhen	92	24.50 N	103.56 E
Danforth, Ill., U.S.	206	40.49 N	87.59 W
Danforth, Maine, U.S.	178	45.40 N	67.52 W
Danforth Hills ∧∧	190	40.15 N	108.00 W
Dānga, Bhārat	262b	22.47 N	88.28 E
Dānga, Bngl.	116	23.54 N	90.36 E
Danga ≃	261c	1.27 N	103.43 E
Dangādiha	116	21.30 N	86.19 E
Danganqundao I	90	22.06 N	113.30 E
Danganqundao II	90	22.00 N	114.14 E
Dan'ganshan I	90	22.03 N	114.16 E
Dangara, S.S.S.R.	75	38.06 N	69.22 E
Dangara, S.S.S.R.	75	40.35 N	70.54 E
Dangba	88	40.46 N	118.32 E
Dangchang	92	34.03 N	104.23 E
Dangcheng	88	38.46 N	114.34 E
Dange, Ang.	142	8.09 S	14.46 E
Dangé, Fr.	32	46.56 N	0.36 E
Dange, Nig.	140	12.52 N	5.21 E
Dange-lá-Menha	142	9.32 S	14.39 E
Danger, Point ≻	161a	28.10 S	153.33 E
Danger Point ≻	148	34.40 S	19.17 E
Dang-Haoussa	142	5.52 N	13.29 E
Danghui	95	40.03 N	117.04 E
Dangkou	96	31.32 N	120.34 E
Dangla	134	11.18 N	36.54 E
Dango	130	10.00 N	24.45 E
Dan Gora	140	11.30 N	8.09 E
Dangshan	88	34.26 N	116.21 E
Dangtu	90	31.34 N	118.30 E
Dan Gulbi	140	11.38 N	6.16 E
Dangxiong	110	30.31 N	91.08 E
Dangyang	92	30.50 N	111.38 E
Dangyu	95	40.00 N	118.01 E
Dani	140	13.43 N	0.10 W
Dania	210	26.03 N	80.09 W
Daniel	190	42.52 N	110.04 W
Daniel, Mount ∧	214	47.34 N	121.11 W
Daniel, Serra ∧∧[1]	245	13.40 S	54.55 W
Daniel Boone Home ⊥	209	38.39 N	90.52 W
Daniel Boone Homestead ⊥	198	40.21 N	75.49 W
Daniels	274b	39.26 N	77.03 W
Daniel's Harbour	176	50.14 N	57.35 W
Danielskuil	148	28.11 S	23.33 E
Danielson	197	41.48 N	71.53 W
Daniels Pass)(	190	40.18 N	111.15 W
Daniels Run ≃	274c	38.51 N	77.17 W
Danielsville, Ga., U.S.	182	34.07 N	83.13 W
Danielsville, Pa., U.S.	198	40.48 N	75.32 W
Danilov	70	58.12 N	40.12 E
Danilovka, S.S.S.R.	70	52.33 N	45.23 E
Danilovka, S.S.S.R.	70	50.21 N	44.06 E
Danilovo	72	55.40 N	38.46 E
Danilovskaja Vozvyšennost' ∧∧[1]	70	58.12 N	40.16 E
Danilovskoje	72	56.48 N	35.45 E
Daning, Zhg.	92	24.39 N	111.51 E
Daning, Zhg.	92	36.33 N	110.38 E
Daningbashi	75	38.45 N	75.04 E
Dänisch Nienhof	50	54.28 N	10.07 E
Danissa Hills ∧∧[2]	144	3.17 N	40.59 E
Daniupucun	94	41.23 N	122.37 E
Danja	140	11.21 N	7.31 E
Danjo-guntō II	82	32.02 N	128.23 E
Danjoutin	54	47.37 N	6.52 E
Ḍank	118	23.33 N	56.17 E
Dankama	140	13.20 N	7.44 E
Dankersen	48	52.17 N	8.58 E
Danki	72	54.55 N	37.34 E
Dankov	66	53.15 N	39.08 E
Dankova, Pik ∧	75	41.05 N	77.38 E
Dankug	134	11.00 N	49.02 E
Danleng, Zhg.	92	29.18 N	103.10 E
Danleng, Zhg.	97	30.01 N	103.30 E
Danlí	226	14.00 N	86.35 W
Danmark → Denmark □[1]	26	56.00 N	10.00 E
Dannebrog	188	41.07 N	98.33 W
Dannemare	41	54.45 N	11.12 E
Dannemarie	54	47.38 N	7.08 E
Dannemora, Sve.	40	60.11 N	17.49 E
Dannemora, N.Y., U.S.	178	44.43 N	73.43 W
Dannenberg	50	53.06 N	11.05 E
Dannenreich	254a	52.19 N	13.45 E
Dannenwalde	50	53.04 N	13.11 E
Dannevirke	162	40.12 S	176.07 E
Dannewerk	41	54.29 N	9.31 E
Dannhauser	148	28.04 S	30.04 E
Danno-ura ♠	86	34.23 N	134.08 E
Dano	140	11.09 N	3.04 W
Danompari	102	0.09 N	115.02 E
Dañoso, Cabo ≻	244	48.50 S	67.13 W
Dan Ryan Woods ♠	268	41.45 N	87.39 W
Dan Sai	100	17.17 N	101.09 E
Danshanzhen	97	30.06 N	104.54 E
Danshui	90	22.49 N	114.27 E
Dansville, Mich., U.S.	206	42.34 N	84.18 W
Dansville, N.Y., U.S.	200	42.34 N	77.42 W
Dāntan	116	21.57 N	87.16 E
Dante, Som.	134	10.25 N	51.16 E
Dante, Va., U.S.	182	36.53 N	82.18 W
Dantewāra	112	18.54 N	81.21 E
Dantuzhen	96	32.12 N	119.31 E
Danube ≃	22	45.20 N	29.40 E
Danube, Mouths of the ≃[1]	38	45.10 N	29.50 E
Danubio → Danube ≃	22	45.20 N	29.40 E
Danubyu	100	17.15 N	95.35 E
Danvers, Ill., U.S.	180	40.32 N	89.11 W
Danvers, Mass., U.S.	197	42.34 N	70.56 W
Danvers ≃	273	42.32 N	70.53 W
Danville, Qué., Can.	196	45.47 N	72.01 W
Danville, Ark., U.S.	184	35.03 N	93.24 W
Danville, Calif., U.S.	216	37.49 N	122.00 W
Danville, Ga., U.S.	182	32.37 N	83.15 W
Danville, Ill., U.S.	184	40.08 N	87.37 W
Danville, Ind., U.S.	208	39.46 N	86.32 W
Danville, Ky., U.S.	184	37.39 N	84.46 W
Danville, Mo., U.S.	209	38.54 N	91.32 W
Danville, Ohio, U.S.	204	40.27 N	82.16 W
Danville, Pa., U.S.	200	40.57 N	76.37 W
Danville, Vt., U.S.	178	44.25 N	66.09 W
Danville, Va., U.S.	182	36.35 N	79.24 W
Danxian, Zhg.	88	34.48 N	116.03 E
Danxian (Nada), Zhg.	100	19.35 N	109.17 E
Danyang, Zhg.	90	26.22 N	119.30 E
Danyang, Zhg.	96	32.00 N	119.35 E
Danyanghu ⊜	96	31.25 N	118.41 E
Danzig → Gdańsk	30	54.23 N	18.40 E
Danzig, Gulf of C	30	54.40 N	19.15 E
Dao	106	10.31 N	121.57 E
Dâo ≃	34	40.20 N	8.11 W
Daocheng	92	29.06 N	100.38 E
Daodemiao	79	43.41 N	120.19 E
Daodi	95	39.32 N	118.11 E
Daofu	92	31.07 N	101.08 E
Daoguanhe	90	30.54 N	114.57 E
Daohu	90	29.42 N	117.29 E
Daolazui	95	40.06 N	115.06 E
Daoliban	94	41.52 N	121.37 E
Daolin	90	27.59 N	112.42 E
Daolinggang	88	34.02 N	114.34 E
Daoliupu	97	30.12 N	105.09 E
Daomaguan	88	39.04 N	114.36 E
Daosa	114	26.53 N	76.20 E
Daoshiwu	96	30.18 N	118.57 E
Daoshui ≃	90	30.44 N	114.39 E
Daoshuqiao	96	31.51 N	119.41 E
Daotiancun	79	48.53 N	130.03 E
Daotou	88	37.14 N	120.20 E
Daoudi	140	14.08 N	13.58 W
Daoukro	140	7.03 N	3.58 W
Daoulas	32	48.22 N	4.15 W
Daoura, Oued ∨	138	29.03 N	4.33 W
Daoxian	92	25.35 N	111.27 E
Daozhen	92	28.42 N	107.56 E
Daozi	79	45.00 N	123.43 E
Dapa	106	9.46 N	126.03 E
Dapango	140	10.52 N	0.12 E
Dapanzhuang	88	37.20 N	115.28 E
Dapaozi	79	45.27 N	122.07 E
Dapdap	106	14.14 N	122.15 E
Dapeng	90	22.34 N	114.29 E
Daphne	184	30.36 N	87.54 W
Dapiak, Mount ∧	106	8.15 N	123.28 E
Daping, Zhg.	90	23.11 N	115.49 E
Daping, Zhg.	90	24.24 N	115.58 E
Dapingshan	92	25.30 N	109.39 E
Dapishi	90	26.30 N	112.54 E
Dapitan	106	8.39 N	123.25 E
Dapitan ≃	106	8.38 N	123.25 E
Dapitan Bay C	106	8.40 N	123.23 E
Dapto	160	34.30 S	150.47 E
Dapu, Zhg.	90	23.16 N	113.32 E
Dapu, Zhg.	90	24.32 N	116.42 E
Dapu, Zhg.	96	31.19 N	119.56 E
Dapujie	90	27.00 N	112.46 E
Daqian	96	30.55 N	120.11 E
Daqiangmen	96	31.29 N	120.27 E
Daqiangzi	94	42.21 N	120.29 E
Daqiao, Zhg.	90	28.11 N	114.16 E
Daqiao, Zhg.	90	32.21 N	119.41 E
Daqiao, Zhg.	90	24.56 N	113.09 E
Daqiao, Zhg.	90	29.39 N	121.26 E
Daqiao, Zhg.	90	26.38 N	118.54 E
Daqiao, Zhg.	96	30.59 N	121.14 E
Daqiaochang	97	28.52 N	105.40 E
Daqiaojie	96	30.46 N	119.14 E
Daqiaokou	90	27.06 N	113.38 E
Daqiaotou	95	30.47 N	120.52 E
Daqiaozhai	92	25.21 N	106.15 E
Daqinggou, Zhg.	88	41.16 N	114.10 E
Daqinggou, Zhg.	88	41.12 N	125.07 E
Daqinghe	88	39.13 N	118.51 E
Daqinghe ≃, Zhg.	88	42.26 N	123.50 E
Daqinghe ≃, Zhg.	95	39.04 N	116.55 E
Daqingshan ∧, Zhg.	79	45.35 N	127.51 E
Daqingshan ∧, Zhg.	94	42.03 N	123.45 E
Daqiu	90	25.24 N	119.39 E
Daqqāq	130	12.56 N	26.58 E
Daquan	92	41.21 N	95.17 E
Daquantou	95	39.31 N	114.46 E
Daquanyan	94	42.37 N	123.32 E
Dāqūf	132	28.24 N	30.38 E
Daqushan I	90	27.48 N	121.08 E
Dar'ā	122	32.37 N	36.06 E
Dar'ā □[8]	122	33.00 N	36.10 E
Dārāb	118	28.45 N	54.34 E
Dārāban	110	31.44 N	70.20 E
Darabani	38	48.11 N	26.35 E
Darāfisah	130	13.23 N	31.59 E
Daraga	106	11.54 N	123.52 E
Daragodleh	134	10.10 N	44.57 E
Daraina	147b	13.12 S	49.40 E
Daraj	136	30.09 N	10.26 E
Darājīl	132	30.39 N	30.52 E
Darakeh	257d	35.48 N	51.23 E
Darakht-e Yahyá	110	31.50 N	68.08 E
Daram Island I	106	11.38 N	124.47 E
Dārān	118	32.59 N	50.24 E
Daraoli ↢[8]	262c	19.11 N	72.48 E
Darap	102	1.13 S	112.03 E
Dār as-Salām	263c	29.59 N	31.13 E
Darasun	78	51.40 N	114.00 E
Daraut-Kurgan	75	39.33 N	72.13 E
Darave	262c	19.02 N	73.01 E
Darāw	130	24.25 N	32.56 E
Darawah	132	30.13 N	31.06 E
Dārayyā	122	33.27 N	36.15 E
Darb al-Ḥājj	132	30.10 N	31.33 E
Darb al-Ḥajj, Jabal ∧	122	30.05 N	35.26 E
Darband, Īrān	257d	35.49 N	51.26 E
Darband, Pāk.	113	34.20 N	72.52 E
Darbāsīyah	120	37.04 N	40.39 E
Darbaza	75	41.35 N	69.02 E
Darbėnai	66	56.01 N	21.15 E
Dar-Beni-Kriche-Bahri	34	35.30 N	5.20 W
Darbhanga	114	26.10 N	85.54 E
Darbhanga □[5]	114	26.00 N	86.00 E
Darboruk	134	9.52 N	44.30 E
Darby, Mont., U.S.	192	46.01 N	114.11 W
Darby, Pa., U.S.	198	39.54 N	75.15 W
Darby, Cape ≻	170	64.20 N	162.22 W
Darby Creek ≃	275	39.52 N	75.18 W
Darbydale	208	39.51 N	83.11 W
Darčeli	74	42.27 N	41.42 E
Darchan	78	49.28 N	105.56 E
D'Archiac, Mount ∧	162	43.28 S	170.35 E
D'Arcy	172	50.33 N	122.29 W
D'Arcy Island I	214	48.34 N	123.17 W
Darda	38	45.37 N	18.41 E
Dardadine	158a	33.14 S	116.50 E
Dardanelle, Ark., U.S.	184	35.13 N	93.09 W
Dardanelle, Calif., U.S.	216	38.20 N	119.50 W
Dardanelle Lake ⊜[1]	184	35.25 N	93.20 W
Dardanelles → Çanakkale Boğazı ⊔	120	40.15 N	26.25 E
Dardanup	158a	33.24 S	115.45 E
Dardara	34	35.08 N	5.15 W
Dardenelles Cone ∧	216	38.25 N	119.53 W
Dardenne Creek ≃	209	38.52 N	90.32 W
Dardenne Lake ⊜	209	38.52 N	90.38 W
Dardesheim	50	51.59 N	10.49 E
Dardistān □[9]	113	35.30 N	74.00 E
Dare	198	37.10 N	76.26 W
Dare ≃	134	7.18 N	42.15 E
Darebin Creek ≃	264b	37.47 S	145.02 E
Dareda	144	4.13 S	35.33 E
Dar-el-Beida → Casablanca	138	33.39 N	7.35 W
Darende	120	38.34 N	37.30 E
Darent ≃	44	51.28 N	0.13 E
Daresbury	252	53.21 N	2.38 W
Dar-es-Salaam	144	6.48 S	39.17 E
Daressalam → Dar-es-Salaam	144	6.48 S	39.17 E
Darfeld	48	52.01 N	7.16 E
Darfo	58	45.53 N	10.11 E
Dārfūr □[4]	130	13.00 N	25.00 E
Dargai	113	34.11 N	71.53 E
Dargan-Ata	64	40.29 N	62.10 E
Dargaville	162	35.56 S	173.53 E
Dargle ≃	42	53.12 N	6.06 W
Dargol	140	13.55 N	1.15 E
Dargun	50	53.54 N	12.51 E
Dari, Sūd.	130	5.48 N	30.21 E
Dari (Jimai), Zhg.	92	33.55 N	99.54 E
Dāriāpur	116	23.36 N	89.27 E
Darıca	120	40.45 N	29.23 E
Darie Hills ∧∧[2]	134	8.15 N	47.25 E
Darién, Col.	236	3.56 N	76.31 W
Darien, Conn., U.S.	197	41.05 N	73.28 W
Darien, Ga., U.S.	182	31.22 N	81.26 W
Darien, N.Y., U.S.	200	41.43 N	70.37 W
Darien, Wis., U.S.	206	42.36 N	88.42 W
Darién, Cordillera de ∧∧	226	12.55 N	85.30 W
Darién, Serranía del ∧∧	236	8.20 N	77.22 W
Darien Center	200	42.54 N	78.23 W
Darien Lakes State Park ♠, N.Y., U.S.	200	42.55 N	78.25 W
Darien Lakes State Park ♠, N.Y., U.S.	202	42.54 N	78.24 W
Dariganga	92	45.21 N	113.38 E
Darigayos Point ≻	106	16.50 N	120.20 E
Darjeeling	114	27.02 N	88.16 E
Darjeeling □[5]	114	26.50 N	88.20 E
Darjevka	73	47.42 N	39.41 E
Darjinskij	76	49.04 N	72.56 E
Darjinskoje	70	51.20 N	51.44 E
Darkan	158a	33.20 S	116.44 E
Darke □[6]	208	40.06 N	84.38 W
Darke Peak	156	33.28 S	136.12 E
Darkhāna	113	30.39 N	72.11 E
Darkhazīneh	118	31.54 N	48.59 E
Dark Head ≻	231h	13.17 N	61.16 W
Darkin ≃	158a	32.00 S	116.14 E
Darkūsh	120	35.59 N	36.23 E
Darlaston	44	52.34 N	2.02 W
Darling, S. Afr.	148	33.23 S	18.23 E
Darling, Miss., U.S.	184	34.22 N	90.23 W
Darling, Pa., U.S.	275	39.54 N	75.28 W
Darling ≃	156	34.07 S	141.55 E
Darling, Lake ⊜[1]	188	48.35 N	101.40 W
Darling Downs ↢[1]	156	27.30 S	150.30 E
Darlingford	174	49.12 N	98.22 W
Darling Range ∧∧	152	32.00 S	116.00 E
Darlington, Austl.	158a	31.55 S	116.05 E
Darlington, Austl.	159	38.00 S	143.03 E
Darlington, Eng., U.K.	42	54.31 N	1.34 W
Darlington, Md., U.S.	198	39.39 N	76.11 W
Darlington, Pa., U.S.	204	40.49 N	80.26 W
Darlington, S.C., U.S.	182	34.18 N	79.52 W
Darlington, Wis., U.S.	180	42.41 N	90.07 W
Darlington Brook ≃	266	41.05 N	74.11 W
Darlington Corners	275	39.55 N	75.34 W
Darlington Range ∧∧	161a	27.50 S	153.15 E
Darlot, Lake ⊜	152	27.48 S	121.35 E
Darłowo	30	54.26 N	16.23 E
Darma Pass)(	114	30.29 N	80.34 W
Darmstadt	52	49.53 N	8.40 E
Darmstadt □[5]	52	50.00 N	8.40 E
Darnah	136	32.46 N	22.39 E
Darnah □[4]	136	32.30 N	22.45 E
Darnall	148	29.23 S	31.18 E
Darnétal	46	49.27 N	1.09 E
Darney	54	48.05 N	6.03 E
Darnick	156	32.51 S	143.37 E
Darnley, Cape ≻	9	67.43 S	69.30 E
Darnley Bay C	170	69.35 N	123.30 W
Daroca	34	41.07 N	1.25 W
Darodih	116	23.14 N	86.27 E
Daror ⫪[4]	134	8.13 N	44.40 E
Dar-Ould-Zidouh	138	32.22 N	6.49 W
Darou Mousti	140	15.03 N	16.03 W
Darovoje	72	54.34 N	38.22 E
Darr ≃	156	23.39 S	143.50 E
Darra	161a	27.34 S	152.58 E
Darragh	269b	40.16 N	79.41 W
Darrah, Mount ∧	172	49.28 N	114.35 W
Darrang □[5]	114	25.30 N	89.30 E
Darregueira	242	37.42 S	63.10 W
Darreh Gaz	118	37.27 N	59.07 E
Darrington	214	48.15 N	121.36 W
Darrouzett	186	36.27 N	100.20 W
Darryl Gardens	274b	39.25 N	76.25 W
Dārsana	116	23.32 N	88.52 E
Darscheid	52	50.12 N	6.53 E
Darss ≻[1]	50	54.25 N	12.31 E
Darsser Ort ≻	50	54.29 N	12.31 E
Dart ≃	44	50.20 N	3.33 W
Dart, Cape ≻	9	73.06 S	126.20 W
Dār Ta'izzah	120	36.17 N	36.51 E
Dartford	44	51.27 N	0.14 E
Dartford □[8]	250	51.26 N	0.15 E
Dartford Tunnel ↢[5]	250	51.28 N	0.16 E
Dartmoor	156	37.55 S	141.17 E
Dartmoor ↢[3]	44	50.35 N	4.00 W
Dartmoor National Park ♠	44	50.37 N	3.52 W
Dartmouth, N.S., Can.	176	44.40 N	63.34 W
Dartmouth, Eng., U.K.	44	50.21 N	3.35 W
Dartmouth ≃	176	48.53 N	64.34 W
Dartmouth, Lake ⊜	156	26.04 S	145.18 E
Darton	42	53.36 N	1.32 W
Dartuch, Cabo ≻	34	39.56 N	3.48 E
Daru, Pap. N. Gui.	154	9.04 S	143.21 E
Daru, S.L.	140	7.59 N	10.50 W
Daruvar	36	45.36 N	17.13 E
Darvaza	118	40.11 N	58.24 E
Darvāzahgêy	110	31.48 N	67.44 E
Darvazskij Chrebet ∧∧	75	38.30 N	71.15 E
Darvel	42	55.37 N	4.18 W
Darvel, Teluk C	102	4.50 N	118.30 E
Darvi	78	47.02 N	93.35 E
Darvinskij Zapovednik ↢[4]	66	58.50 N	37.40 E
Darwen	42	53.42 N	2.28 W
Darwen ≃	42	53.45 N	2.41 W
Darwendale	144	17.43 S	30.33 E
Dārwha	112	20.19 N	77.46 E
Darwin, Arg.	244	39.12 S	65.46 W
Darwin, Austl.	154	12.28 S	130.50 E
Darwin, Bahía C	244	45.27 S	74.40 W
Darwin, Isla I	236a	1.39 N	92.00 W
Darwin, Volcán ∧[1]	236a	0.10 S	91.18 W
Darwin River	154	12.49 S	130.58 E
Daryābād	114	26.53 N	81.33 E
Darya Khān	113	31.48 N	71.06 E
Daryāpur	110	20.56 N	77.20 E
Darz Āb	110	35.58 N	65.22 E
Darzo	58	45.51 N	10.33 E
Dār Zubi	130	13.07 N	23.40 E
Dās	113	35.05 N	75.05 E
Dās I	118	25.09 N	52.53 E
Dasāda	110	23.19 N	71.50 E
Dasanjiazi, Zhg.	94	42.31 N	122.54 E
Dasanjiazi, Zhg.	94	42.05 N	122.32 E
Dašava	68	49.16 N	24.01 E
Dašbalbar	78	49.36 N	114.24 E
Dasburg	52	50.03 N	6.07 E
Dase → Dese	134	11.05 N	39.41 E
Dašev	68	49.00 N	29.26 E
Dashafa	95	39.19 N	116.19 E
Dashahu ⊜	90	30.11 N	113.46 E
Dashaling	94	41.20 N	123.01 E
Dashalitu	94	42.31 N	122.30 E
Dashankou	95	40.17 N	115.49 E
Dashanpu	97	29.25 N	104.49 E
Dashanzhuang	88	38.02 N	117.39 E
Dashaping	90	29.24 N	113.51 E
Dashazhai	79	46.16 N	121.25 E
Dashengfenchang	96	31.53 N	121.34 E
Dashengpu	94	41.13 N	121.02 E
Dashentang	95	39.13 N	117.56 E
Dashetai	92	40.58 N	109.19 E
Dashields Dam ↢[6]	204	40.33 N	80.12 W
Dashihe ≃	95	39.35 N	116.05 E
Dashiqiao, Zhg.	90	33.57 N	113.53 E
Dashiqiao, Zhg.	94	41.52 N	123.17 E
Dashiqiao, Zhg.	97	30.07 N	106.12 E
Dashiqiao, Zhg.	97	30.39 N	105.37 E
Dashiqiao, Zhg.	97	30.28 N	106.29 E
Dashitou, Zhg.	79	43.19 N	128.28 E
Dashitou, Zhg.	92	42.49 N	95.19 E
Dashlūţ	132	27.34 N	30.42 E
Dash Point	214	47.19 N	122.26 W
Dasht ≃	118	25.10 N	61.40 E
Dashtīārī ≃	118	25.09 N	61.32 E
Dashu	96	31.13 N	120.56 E
Dashun	90	28.06 N	119.52 E
Dashutang	92	23.00 N	103.55 E
Dashuwan	95	40.37 N	117.19 E
Dasi, Zhg.	90	33.48 N	115.55 E
Dasi (Huangfansi), Zhg.	92	38.15 N	100.22 E
Dašinčilen	78	47.51 N	104.03 E
Dasizhan	79	45.53 N	130.24 E
Daska	113	32.20 N	74.21 E
Daškesan	74	40.30 N	46.04 E
Daskop	148	33.44 S	22.43 E
Daškovka	66	53.44 N	30.13 E
Dasmina	116	22.17 N	90.35 E
Dasol	106	15.59 N	119.52 E
Dasol Bay C	106	15.53 N	119.51 E
Daspalla	110	20.21 N	84.51 E
Dassalan Island I	106	6.45 N	121.28 E
Dassel, B.R.D.	48	51.48 N	9.41 E
Dassel, Minn., U.S.	180	45.05 N	94.19 W
Dasseneiland I	148	33.26 S	18.04 E
Dasserat, Lac ⊜	180	48.16 N	79.25 W
Dassiefontein	148	31.35 S	24.25 E
Dassow	50	53.50 N	10.59 E
Dastakert	74	39.23 N	46.02 E
Dastgardān	118	34.19 N	56.51 E
Daštidžum	75	38.01 N	70.12 E
Daštioburdon	75	39.24 N	69.04 E
Dastjerd	118	34.33 N	50.15 E
Dāsuria	116	24.07 N	89.08 E
Dasūya	113	31.49 N	75.38 E
Datachang	97	28.55 N	104.21 E
Datagenoyang	102	2.03 N	115.10 E
Datai	95	39.58 N	115.54 E
Dataizi	94	41.17 N	121.46 E
Datan, Zhg.	88	41.31 N	115.54 E
Datan, Zhg.	88	39.31 N	122.11 E
Datang, Zhg.	90	24.47 N	113.43 E
Datang, Zhg.	92	22.23 N	108.23 E
Datang, Zhg.	92	24.11 N	109.00 E
Datangwei	90	25.17 N	114.56 E
Datça	120	36.45 N	27.40 E
Datchet	250	51.29 N	0.34 W
Date	82a	42.27 N	140.51 E
Date Creek ≃	190	34.13 N	113.29 W
Datia	114	25.40 N	78.28 E
Datia □[5]	114	25.50 N	78.30 E
Datian, Zhg.	90	24.06 N	116.19 E
Datian, Zhg.	90	25.42 N	117.49 E
Datianwei	90	25.54 N	115.10 E
Dativli	262c	19.11 N	73.03 E
D'at'kovo	66	53.36 N	34.20 E
D'atloviči	66	52.20 N	26.50 E
D'atlovo, S.S.S.R.	66	53.28 N	25.24 E
D'atlovo, S.S.S.R.	72	56.14 N	36.16 E
Datong, Zhg.	79	46.03 N	124.50 E
Datong, Zhg.	90	30.48 N	117.45 E
Datong, Zhg.	92	40.08 N	113.13 E
Datong, Zhg.	92	37.03 N	101.45 E
Datonghe ≃	92	36.20 N	102.55 E
Datongshan ∧∧	92	38.00 N	99.30 E
Datongzhen	90	32.50 N	118.52 E
Datoushan	88	41.50 N	117.08 E
Dātra	262b	22.58 N	88.16 E
Datta	79	49.18 N	140.22 E
Dattapāra	116	23.01 N	90.53 E
Dattapukur	116	22.45 N	88.33 E
Dattapulia	116	23.14 N	88.43 E
Datteln	48	51.40 N	7.23 E
Datteln-Hamm-Kanal ☰	253	51.39 N	7.21 E
Datu, Tanjung ≻	102	2.06 N	109.39 E
Datuan	96	30.58 N	121.44 E
Datumakuta	102	2.32 N	117.51 E
Datun, Zhg.	79	43.49 N	125.12 E
Datun, Zhg.	88	40.37 N	119.57 E
Datun, Zhg.	94	40.59 N	122.55 E
Datuopu	90	28.03 N	112.58 E
Datu Piang	106	7.01 N	124.30 E
Daua (Dawa) ≃	134	4.11 N	42.06 E
Daubiche ≃	79	44.54 N	133.35 E
Daudkāndi	116	23.32 N	90.43 E
Dāūd Khel	113	32.53 N	71.34 E
Daudnagar	114	25.02 N	84.24 E
Daugai	66	54.22 N	24.20 E
Daugård	41	55.44 N	9.43 E
Daugava (Zapadnaja Dvina) ≃	66	57.04 N	24.03 E
Daugavpils	66	55.53 N	26.32 E
Dauin	106	9.12 N	123.16 E
Daulatābād (Shirin Tagāo), Afg.	110	36.26 N	64.55 E
Daulatabad, Bhārat	116	24.08 N	88.22 E
Daulatkhan	116	22.38 N	90.49 E
Daulatpur, Bhārat	262b	22.26 N	88.18 E
Daulatpur (Ramchandrapur), Bngl.	116	23.58 N	89.50 E
Daulatpur, Bngl.	116	24.00 N	88.52 E
Daulatpur, Bngl.	116	22.53 N	89.31 E
Daulatpur, Pāk.	110	26.30 N	67.58 E
Daule, Bhārat	262c	19.10 N	73.03 E
Daule, Ec.	236	1.50 S	79.56 W
Daule, Ec.	236	0.24 N	80.00 W
Daule ≃	236	2.10 S	79.52 W
Daultāla	113	33.12 N	73.09 E
Daulton Creek ≃	216	37.04 N	119.59 W
Daun	52	50.11 N	6.50 E
Daund	112	18.28 N	74.36 E
Daung Kyun I	100	12.14 N	98.05 E
Daunia, Monti della ∧∧	60	41.27 N	15.06 E
Dauphin, Man., Can.	174	51.09 N	100.03 W
Dauphin, Pa., U.S.	198	40.22 N	76.56 W
Dauphin □[6]	198	40.15 N	76.52 W
Dauphin ≃	174	51.58 N	98.04 W
Dauphiné □[9]	32	44.50 N	6.00 E
Dauphin Island I	184	30.14 N	88.12 W
Dauphin Lake ⊜	174	51.17 N	99.48 W
Daura	140	13.02 N	8.21 E
Daurija	78	49.56 N	116.52 E
Daurskij Chrebet ∧∧	78	50.30 N	112.30 E
Daurskoje	76	55.14 N	92.05 E
Dausenau	52	50.20 N	7.45 E
Dāvangere	112	14.28 N	75.55 E
Davant	184	29.37 N	89.51 W
Davao	106	7.04 N	125.36 E
Davao ≃	106	7.04 N	125.37 E
Davao del Norte □[4]	106	7.10 N	125.50 E
Davao del Sur □[4]	106	6.15 N	125.40 E
Davao Gulf C	106	6.40 N	125.55 E
Davao Oriental □[4]	106	7.30 N	126.30 E
Dāvar Panāh	118	27.21 N	62.21 E
Dāvarzan	118	36.23 N	56.50 E
Davel	148	26.24 S	29.40 E
Daveluyville	196	46.12 N	72.08 W
Davenda	78	53.33 N	119.18 E
Davenham	42	53.14 N	2.31 W
Davenport, Calif., U.S.	216	37.01 N	122.12 W
Davenport, Fla., U.S.	210	28.10 N	81.36 W
Davenport, Iowa, U.S.	180	41.32 N	90.41 W
Davenport, Nebr., U.S.	188	40.19 N	97.49 W
Davenport, N.Y., U.S.	200	42.28 N	74.51 W
Davenport, Okla., U.S.	186	35.42 N	96.46 W
Davenport, Wash., U.S.	192	47.39 N	118.09 W
Davenport, Mount ∧	152	22.23 S	130.51 E
Davenport Downs	156	24.08 S	141.07 E
Davenport Range ∧∧	152	20.47 S	134.48 E
Daventry	44	52.16 N	1.09 W
Davey, Port C	156	43.19 S	145.55 E
Daveyton Location	263d	26.09 S	28.25 E
David	226	8.26 N	82.26 W
David City	188	41.15 N	97.08 W
David-Gorodok	68	52.03 N	27.14 E
Davido-Nikol'skoje	73	48.30 N	39.50 E
David Point ≻	231k	12.14 N	61.39 W
Davids Island I	266	40.53 N	73.46 W
Davidson, Sask., Can.	174	51.18 N	106.59 W
Davidson, N.C., U.S.	182	35.30 N	80.51 W
Davidson, Okla., U.S.	186	34.14 N	99.05 W
Davidson Creek ≃	212	30.21 N	96.27 W
Davidson Heights, Pa., U.S.	204	40.35 N	80.15 W
Davidson Heights, Pa., U.S.	269b	40.36 N	80.16 W
Davidson Lake ⊜	174	53.47 N	99.37 W
Davidson Mountains ∧∧	170	68.45 N	142.10 W
Davidson Park ♠	264a	33.45 S	151.12 E
Davidsville	204	40.14 N	78.56 W
Davie	210	26.05 N	80.14 W
Davies, Mount ∧	152	26.14 S	129.16 E
Davignab	148	27.32 S	19.48 E
Davila	106	18.29 N	120.35 E
Davilla	212	30.47 N	97.17 W
Davington	42	55.18 N	3.12 W
Davin Lake ⊜	174	56.50 N	103.40 W
Davinópolis	245	15.58 S	50.08 W
Davis, Calif., U.S.	216	38.33 N	121.44 W
Davis, N.C., U.S.	182	34.48 N	76.28 W
Davis, Okla., U.S.	186	34.30 N	97.03 W
Davis, W. Va., U.S.	178	39.08 N	79.28 W
Davis ≃	152	21.42 S	121.05 E
Davis, Mount ∧	178	39.47 N	79.10 W
Davis Bay C	9	66.08 S	134.05 E
Davisboro	182	32.59 N	82.36 W
Davisburg	206	42.45 N	83.33 W
Davis City	180	40.38 N	93.49 W
Davis Cove	176	47.40 N	54.18 W
Davis Creek ≃, Mich., U.S.	271	42.27 N	83.43 W
Davis Creek ≃, Mo., U.S.	209	39.12 N	91.53 W
Davis Dam	190	35.11 N	114.35 W
Davis Dam ↢[6]	190	35.11 N	114.21 W
Davis Island I	269b	40.29 N	80.05 W
Davis Lake ⊜, Ill., U.S.	268	42.16 N	88.05 W
Davis Lake ⊜, Oreg., U.S.	192	43.37 N	121.51 W
Davis-Monthan Air Force Base ▪	190	32.11 N	110.53 W
Davis Mountains ∧∧	186	30.35 N	104.00 W
Davison	206	43.02 N	83.31 W
Davis Park	200	40.42 N	72.59 W
Davis Point ≻	272	38.03 N	122.15 W
Davis Sea ⫪[2]	9	66.00 S	92.00 E
Davisson Lake ⊜	214	46.30 N	122.20 W
Davis Strait ⊔	166	67.00 N	57.00 W
Davisville	275	40.11 N	75.03 W
Davlekanovo	76	54.13 N	55.03 E
Davos	54	46.48 N	9.50 E
Davron	251	48.52 N	1.57 E
Davst	76	50.36 N	92.28 E
Davulga	120	38.58 N	31.23 E
Davutlar	120	37.43 N	27.17 E
Davy	182	37.29 N	81.39 W
Davydkovo, S.S.S.R.	72	56.17 N	36.49 E
Davydkovo, S.S.S.R.	255b	55.35 N	37.12 E
Davydov Brod	68	47.14 N	33.12 E
Davydovka	68	51.10 N	39.25 E
Davydovo	72	55.37 N	38.52 E
Davydovskoje	72	55.52 N	36.48 E
Davyhulme	252	53.27 N	2.22 W
Dawa, Zhg.	94	41.54 N	123.32 E
Dawa, Zhg.	94	41.00 N	122.03 E
Dawa (Daua) ≃	134	4.11 N	42.06 E
Dawaki	140	12.06 N	8.20 E
Dawan	92	23.52 N	109.29 E
Dawangcun	96	30.45 N	118.59 E
Dawangdian	95	39.04 N	115.26 E
Dawangdong	95	38.53 N	116.21 E
Dawangji	90	34.00 N	117.46 E
Dawangjiadao I	88	39.27 N	123.07 E
Dawangqiao	88	36.58 N	118.31 E
Dawangsangou	94	41.43 N	121.36 E
Dawangzhuang, Zhg.	95	38.59 N	115.56 E
Dawangzhuang, Zhg.	95	39.23 N	116.28 E
Dawanshan I	90	21.57 N	113.43 E
Dawāsir, Wādī ad- ∨	134	20.24 N	46.29 E
Dawatun	94	41.05 N	121.01 E
Dawei	92	25.09 N	110.21 E
Daweihe	88	36.42 N	118.57 E
Daweizhuang	95	39.34 N	116.53 E
Daweizigou	94	42.38 N	123.09 E
Dawenhe ≃	88	35.38 N	116.24 E
Dawenkou	88	35.59 N	117.07 E
Dawera, Pulau I	154	7.44 S	130.00 E
Dawlan	100	16.44 N	98.01 E
Dawley	44	52.40 N	2.28 W
Dawlish	44	50.35 N	3.28 W
Dawn	198	37.50 N	77.22 W
Dawna Range ∧∧	100	16.50 N	98.15 E
Dawrah	130	12.22 N	24.19 E
Daws Heath	250	51.34 N	0.37 E
Dawson, Yukon, Can.	170	64.04 N	139.25 W
Dawson, Ga., U.S.	182	31.47 N	84.26 W
Dawson, Ill., U.S.	209	39.51 N	89.28 W
Dawson, Minn., U.S.	188	44.56 N	96.03 W
Dawson, Nebr., U.S.	188	40.08 N	95.50 W
Dawson, Tex., U.S.	212	31.54 N	96.43 W
Dawson ≃	156	23.38 S	149.46 E
Dawson, Isla I	244	53.55 S	70.45 W
Dawson, Mount ∧	172	51.09 N	117.25 W
Dawson Bay C	174	52.55 N	100.50 W
Dawson Creek	172	55.46 N	120.14 W
Dawson Inlet C	166	61.50 N	93.25 W
Dawson-Lambton Glacier ⍓	9	76.15 S	27.30 W
Dawson Range ∧∧, Austl.	156	24.20 S	149.45 E
Dawson Range ∧∧, Yukon, Can.	170	62.40 N	139.00 W
Dawson Ridge	204	40.42 N	80.22 W
Dawson Springs	184	37.10 N	87.41 W
Dawsonville	182	34.25 N	84.07 W
Dawu	90	31.34 N	114.06 E
Dawudapu	94	41.36 N	123.03 E
Dawuji	95	39.51 N	116.30 E
Dawujiawopeng	94	41.55 N	122.29 E
Dawujiazi	94	42.16 N	121.52 E
Dawulancun	94	41.56 N	121.05 E
Dax	32	43.43 N	1.03 W
Daxi ≃	90	28.18 N	119.44 E
Daxian	92	31.18 N	107.30 E
Daxiaoqindao I	88	38.18 N	120.48 E
Daxin	92	22.50 N	107.26 E
Daxing, Zhg.	88	39.44 N	116.20 E
Daxing (Huangcun), Zhg.	95	39.41 N	116.29 E
Daxing, Zhg.	96	31.50 N	121.40 E
Daxing'anling-shanmai ∧∧	79	49.40 N	122.00 E
Daxingchang	97	30.17 N	103.26 E
Daxingcun	96	31.45 N	121.40 E

Symbols in the index entries represent the broad categories identified in the key at the right. Symbols with superior numbers (∧∧[2]) identify subcategories (see complete key on page *I* · *26*).

Kartensymbole in dem Registerverzeichnis stellen die rechts in Schlüssel erklärten Kategorien dar. Symbole mit hochgestellten Ziffern (∧∧[2]) bezeichnen Unterabteilungen einer Kategorie (vgl. vollständiger Schlüssel auf Seite *I* · *26*).

Los símbolos incluídos en el texto del índice representan las grandes categorias identificadas con la clave a la derecha. Los símbolos con numeros en su parte superior (∧∧[2]) identifican las subcategorías (véase la clave completa en la página *I* · *26*).

Les symboles de l'index représentent les catégories indiquées dans la légende à droite. Les symboles suivis d'un indice (∧∧[2]) représentent des sous-catégories (voir légende complète à la page *I* · *26*).

Os símbolos incluídos no texto do índice representam as grandes categorias identificadas com a chave à direita. Os símbolos com números em sua parte superior (∧∧[2]) identificam as subcategorias (veja-se a chave completa à página *I* · *26*).

Symbol	English	Deutsch	Español	Français	Português
∧	Mountain	Berg	Montaña	Montagne	Montanha
∧∧	Mountains	Berge	Montañas	Montagnes	Montanhas
)(	Pass	Pass	Paso	Col	Passo
∨	Valley, Canyon	Tal, Cañon	Valle, Cañón	Vallée, Canyon	Vale, Canhão
≚	Plain	Ebene	Llano	Plaine	Planície
≻	Cape	Kap	Cabo	Cap	Cabo
I	Island	Insel	Isla	Île	Ilha
II	Islands	Inseln	Islas	Îles	Ilhas
⊥	Other Topographic Features	Andere Topographische Objekte	Otros Elementos Topográficos	Autres données topographiques	Outros Elementos Topográficos

ESPAÑOL

Nombre	Página	Lat.°′	Long.°′ W=Oeste
Daxingji	90	33.55 N	118.29 E
Daxingzhai	92	23.13 N	102.21 E
Daxinji	90	34.03 N	119.28 E
Daxinzhuang, Zhg.	95	39.26 N	118.20 E
Daxinzhuang, Zhg.	95	40.23 N	116.44 E
Daxiyang	96	30.21 N	121.58 E
Daxueshan ⩕	92	30.10 N	101.50 E
Daxujia	88	34.18 N	117.34 E
Daxujie	90	29.32 N	121.52 E
Daya	90	25.24 N	114.22 E
Dayakou	92	22.46 N	100.18 E
Dayanchi	92	27.41 N	101.55 E
Dayang	90	25.56 N	118.48 E
Dayangcha	88	42.04 N	126.43 E
Dayanggou	94	41.14 N	123.51 E
Dayanghe ≃	88	39.54 N	123.40 E
Dayangji	88	36.04 N	116.31 E
Dayangquanzi	94	41.17 N	121.39 E
Dayaniguas, Ensenada de C	230p	22.20 N	83.15 W
Dayao	92	25.43 N	101.13 E
Dayaopu	90	27.59 N	113.42 E
Dayaoshan	92	24.05 N	110.17 E
Dayboro	161a	27.11 S	152.50 E
Daye	90	30.06 N	114.57 E
Dayghar	262c	19.09 N	73.03 E
Day Heights	208	39.11 N	84.14 W
Dayi	97	30.37 N	103.31 E
Dayiji	90	32.32 N	119.14 E
Daying, Zhg.	88	39.19 N	113.46 E
Daying, Zhg.	88	39.53 N	123.07 E
Daying, Zhg.	88	34.27 N	113.59 E
Daying, Zhg.	88	37.19 N	115.43 E
Daying, Zhg.	90	33.59 N	112.51 E
Dayingzhen	95	39.05 N	116.06 E
Dayingzi, Zhg.	88	41.28 N	120.21 E
Dayingzi, Zhg.	88	41.19 N	118.19 E
Dayingzi, Zhg.	94	41.08 N	122.50 E
Day Island	214	47.15 N	122.33 W
Day Lake ◎	214	48.23 N	121.58 W
Daylesford	159	37.21 S	144.09 E
Daym Zubayr	130	7.43 N	26.13 E
Dayong, Zhg.	90	22.28 N	113.16 E
Dayong, Zhg.	92	28.59 N	110.15 E
Dayr, Jabal ad- ∧	130	12.27 N	30.42 E
Dayr Abū Sa'īd	122	32.30 N	35.41 E
Dayr al-'Ashā'ir	122	33.32 N	36.01 E
Dayr al-Balaḥ	122	31.25 N	34.21 E
Dayr al-Ghuṣūn	122	32.21 N	35.05 E
Dayr 'Alī	122	33.17 N	36.18 E
Dayr 'Allā	122	32.12 N	35.37 E
Dayr 'Aṭīyah	120	34.06 N	36.46 E
Dayr az-Zawr	120	35.20 N	40.09 E
Dayr az-Zawr □[8]	120	35.30 N	39.00 E
Dayr Dibwān	122	31.55 N	35.16 E
Dayr Ḥāfir	120	36.09 N	37.42 E
Dayrīk	120	37.10 N	42.08 E
Dayr Jabal aṭ-Ṭayr	132	28.17 N	30.45 E
Dayr Mawās	132	27.38 N	30.51 E
Dayr Qānūn	122	33.36 N	36.08 E
Dayr Sharaf	122	32.15 N	35.11 E
Dayrūṭ, Miṣr	132	31.13 N	30.30 E
Dayrūṭ, Miṣr	132	27.33 N	30.49 E
Dayrūṭ ash-Sharīf	132	27.35 N	30.49 E
Days Island I	274b	39.24 N	76.22 W
Daysland	172	52.52 N	112.15 W
Day Star Indian Reserve ◆[4]	174	51.43 N	104.14 W
Dayton, Ill., U.S.	206	41.23 N	88.47 W
Dayton, Ind., U.S.	206	40.23 N	86.46 W
Dayton, Iowa, U.S.	180	42.16 N	94.04 W
Dayton, Ky., U.S.	208	39.07 N	84.28 W
Dayton, Mich., U.S.	206	41.48 N	86.26 W
Dayton, Nev., U.S.	216	39.14 N	119.36 W
Dayton, N.J., U.S.	266	40.22 N	74.31 W
Dayton, N.Y., U.S.	200	42.25 N	78.58 W
Dayton, Ohio, U.S.	208	39.45 N	84.15 W
Dayton, Oreg., U.S.	214	45.13 N	123.05 W
Dayton, Pa., U.S.	200	40.35 N	76.39 W
Dayton, Pa., U.S.	204	40.53 N	79.16 W
Dayton, Tenn., U.S.	184	35.30 N	85.00 W
Dayton, Tex., U.S.	212	30.03 N	94.54 W
Dayton, Va., U.S.	178	38.25 N	78.56 W
Dayton, Wash., U.S.	192	46.19 N	117.59 W
Dayton, Wyo., U.S.	192	44.53 N	107.16 W
Daytona Beach	182	29.12 N	81.00 W
Dayu	102	1.59 S	115.04 E
Dayuba	97	29.15 N	103.34 E
Dayudao I	90	22.16 N	113.56 E
Dayuling ⩕	90	25.20 N	114.16 E
Dayushan I	96	30.19 N	121.58 E
Dayville, Conn., U.S.	197	41.51 N	71.53 W
Dayville, Oreg., U.S.	192	44.28 N	119.32 W
Dazaifu	86	33.25 N	130.30 E
Dazaifu ⊥	86	33.31 N	130.31 E
Dazaohuo	92	36.40 N	94.04 E
Dazaoliyingzi	94	42.07 N	121.20 E
Dazaomiao	96	32.06 N	121.29 E
Dazhangzi	88	40.46 N	118.07 E
Dazhaotai	94	41.14 N	123.03 E
Dazhengjiatun	88	39.37 N	122.52 E
Dazhengzhuangzi	95	39.16 N	116.46 E
Dazhi	90	34.29 N	113.17 E
Dazhiba	92	27.09 N	99.52 E
Dazhifang	94	41.21 N	123.12 E
Dazhou	90	28.53 N	118.58 E
Dazhu	92	30.48 N	107.12 E
Dazhuangke	95	40.32 N	115.42 E
Dazhubao	97	28.59 N	103.38 E
Dazhuge	88	35.58 N	118.37 E
Dazhuyuan	90	23.43 N	115.57 E
Dazifangshen	94	42.27 N	124.12 E
Daziling	94	41.21 N	121.26 E
Dazixi ≃	90	25.45 N	118.27 E
Daziying	94	41.42 N	123.36 E
Dazkırı	120	37.55 N	29.52 E
Dazu	97	29.43 N	105.42 E
Dazui	90	30.16 N	114.02 E
Dazuojiao ≻	90	24.54 N	118.58 E
De Aar	148	30.39 S	24.00 E
Dead ≃, Mich., U.S.	180	46.34 N	87.24 W
Dead ≃, N.J., U.S.	266	40.39 N	74.31 W
Deadhorse	170	70.11 N	148.27 W
Dead Horse Point State Park ♠	190	38.28 N	109.44 W
Dead Lake ◎	174	55.40 N	105.01 W
Deadman ≃	172	50.45 N	120.55 W
Deadman Brook ≃	266	41.08 N	73.22 W
Deadman Creek ≃	216	37.12 N	120.42 W
Deadman Hill ∧	152	23.48 S	119.25 E
Deadmans Cay	228	23.14 N	75.14 W
Deadman's Creek Indian Reserve ◆[4]	172	50.49 N	121.00 W
Dead Run ≃	274c	38.57 N	77.11 W
Dead Sea (Al-Baḥr al-Mayyit) (Yam HaMelaḥ) ◎	122	31.30 N	35.30 E
Deadwood	188	44.23 N	103.44 W
Deadwood ≃	192	44.05 N	115.40 W
Deadwood Reservoir ◎[1]	192	44.19 N	115.40 W
Deagan Island I	106	12.15 N	123.51 E
Deakin	152	30.46 S	128.58 E
Deakin, Mount ∧[2]	152	17.38 S	130.48 E
Deakin Bay C	9	68.23 S	150.10 E
Deal, Eng., U.K.	44	51.14 N	1.24 E
Deal, N.J., U.S.	198	40.15 N	74.00 W
Deale	198	38.47 N	76.33 W
Dealesville	148	28.40 S	25.37 E
Deal Island	198	38.09 N	75.56 W
Deal Island I	198	38.09 N	75.56 W
Deam Lake ◎[1]	208	38.28 N	85.51 W
Dean	90	29.20 N	115.46 E
Dean ≃, B.C., Can.	172	52.50 N	126.57 W
Dean ≃, Eng., U.K.	42	53.20 N	2.14 W
Dean, Forest of ◆[3]	44	51.48 N	2.30 W
Dean Channel ⋓	172	52.33 N	127.13 W
Deane	252	53.34 N	2.28 W
Deán Funes	242	30.26 S	64.21 W
Dean Row	252	53.20 N	2.11 W
Deans	266	40.24 N	74.31 W
Deansboro	200	42.60 N	75.26 W

FRANÇAIS

Nom	Page	Lat.°′	Long.°′ W=Ouest
Deans Dundas Bay C	166	72.15 N	118.25 W
Deanville	212	30.26 N	96.46 W
Dearborn	206	42.18 N	83.10 W
Dearborn □[6]	208	39.06 N	84.51 W
Dearborn ≃	192	47.07 N	111.55 W
Dearborn Heights, Ill., U.S.	268	41.43 N	87.48 W
Dearborn Heights, Mich., U.S.	206	42.19 N	83.14 W
Dearg, Beinn ∧	28	57.48 N	4.57 W
Dear Reservoir ◎[1]	42	55.20 N	3.37 W
Dease ≃	170	59.54 N	128.30 W
Dease Arm C	170	66.52 N	119.37 W
Dease Lake ◎	170	58.35 N	130.02 W
Dease Strait ⋓	166	68.40 N	108.00 W
Death Valley	194	36.18 N	116.25 W
Death Valley V	194	36.30 N	117.00 W
Death Valley National Monument ♠	194	36.30 N	117.00 W
Deatsville	184	32.37 N	86.24 W
Deauville	46	49.22 N	0.04 E
Debagrām	116	23.41 N	88.18 E
Debal'cevo	73	48.20 N	38.24 E
Debānāndapur	262b	22.56 N	88.22 E
Debao	92	23.21 N	106.31 E
Debar	38	41.31 N	20.30 E
De Bary	210	28.52 N	81.15 W
Debauch Mountain ∧	170	64.31 N	159.52 W
Débé	231r	10.12 N	61.27 W
Deben ≃	44	51.58 N	1.24 E
Debenham	44	52.13 N	1.11 E
De Beque	190	39.20 N	108.13 W
De Berry	184	32.18 N	94.10 W
Debesy	70	57.39 N	53.49 E
Debet ≃	74	41.22 N	44.58 E
Debhāta	114	22.33 N	88.58 E
Dębica	30	50.04 N	21.24 E
De Bilt	48	52.06 N	5.10 E
Debipur	116	24.14 N	88.38 E
Debīr Char	116	22.24 N	90.41 E
Dęblin	30	51.35 N	21.50 E
Dębno	30	52.45 N	14.40 E
Debo, Lac ◎	140	15.18 N	4.09 W
Deborah, Mount ∧	170	63.38 N	147.15 W
Deborah West, Lake ◎	152	30.45 S	119.07 E
Deboyne Islands II	154	10.45 S	152.25 E
Debra	116	22.24 N	87.33 E
Debre Birhan	134	9.40 N	39.33 E
Debrecen	30	47.32 N	21.38 E
Debre Markos	134	10.20 N	37.45 E
Debre May	134	11.19 N	37.30 E
Debre Tabor	134	11.50 N	38.05 E
Debre Zebit	134	11.50 N	38.40 E
Debre Zeyt	134	8.47 N	39.00 E
Debrzno	30	53.33 N	17.14 E
Debstedt	48	53.37 N	8.38 E
Decatur, Ala., U.S.	184	34.36 N	86.59 W
Decatur, Ga., U.S.	182	33.46 N	84.18 W
Decatur, Ill., U.S.	209	39.51 N	89.32 W
Decatur, Ind., U.S.	206	40.50 N	84.56 W
Decatur, Mich., U.S.	206	42.17 N	85.58 W
Decatur, Miss., U.S.	184	32.26 N	89.07 W
Decatur, Nebr., U.S.	188	42.00 N	96.15 W
Decatur, Ohio, U.S.	208	38.49 N	83.42 W
Decatur, Tenn., U.S.	182	35.31 N	84.47 W
Decatur, Tex., U.S.	212	33.14 N	97.35 W
Decatur □[6]	208	39.20 N	85.29 W
Decatur, Lake ◎[1]	209	39.51 N	88.52 W
Decatur Island I	214	48.31 N	122.50 W
Decatur Municipal Airport ⊠	209	39.50 N	88.52 W
Decaturville	184	35.35 N	88.07 W
Decazeville	32	44.34 N	2.15 E
Deccan ⩕[1]	112	14.00 N	77.00 E
Decelles, Réservoir ◎[1]	180	47.42 N	78.08 W
Deception, Mount ∧	214	47.49 N	123.14 W
Deception Bay C	161a	27.07 S	153.05 E
Deception Lake ◎	174	56.33 N	104.15 W
Deception Pass ☲	214	48.24 N	122.38 W
Deception Pass State Park ♠	214	48.24 N	122.39 W
Dechang	92	27.24 N	102.10 E
Dechêne, Lac ◎	176	51.15 N	67.51 W
Dechenhöhle •[5]	253	51.22 N	7.39 E
Decherd	184	35.13 N	86.05 W
Dechu	110	26.47 N	72.20 E
Déchy	46	50.21 N	3.07 E
Decimomannu	36	39.19 N	8.58 E
Děčín	50	50.48 N	14.13 E
Děčínské stěny ⩕	50	50.50 N	14.12 E
Decize	32	46.50 N	3.27 E
Decker Lake	172	54.17 N	125.50 W
Decker Lake ◎[1]	212	30.18 N	97.36 W
Deckers Point	204	40.46 N	78.59 W
Deckerville	180	43.32 N	82.44 W
De Cocksdorp	48	53.08 N	4.52 E
Decorah	180	43.18 N	91.48 W
Decs	30	46.17 N	18.46 E
Deda	38	46.57 N	24.53 E
Dedaye	100	16.24 N	95.53 E
Deddington	44	51.59 N	1.19 W
Dededo	164p	13.31 N	144.49 E
Dedegöl Dağı ∧	120	37.39 N	31.17 E
Dedeköy	120	37.58 N	29.36 E
Dedeleben	50	52.03 N	10.25 E
Dedeli	74	39.11 N	43.05 E
Dedelow	50	53.22 N	13.48 E
Dedemsvaart	48	52.36 N	6.28 E
Dedenevo	72	56.15 N	37.31 E
Dedesdorf	48	53.27 N	8.30 E
Dedham	197	42.15 N	71.10 W
Dediāpāda	110	21.38 N	73.35 E
Dedilovskije Vyselki	72	54.20 N	38.03 E
Dedinovo	72	55.03 N	39.07 E
Dedo, Cerro ∧	244	44.49 S	71.52 W
Dedo de Deus ∧	246	22.30 S	43.03 W
De Doorns	148	33.28 S	19.41 E
Dédougou	140	12.28 N	3.28 W
Dedoviči	66	57.32 N	29.56 E
Dedovsk	72	55.52 N	37.07 E
Dedu	79	48.31 N	126.14 E
Deduru ≃	112	7.36 N	79.48 E
Dedza	144	14.22 S	34.20 E
Dee ≃, Eire	42	53.52 N	6.20 W
Dee ≃, U.K.	42	53.19 N	3.11 W
Dee ≃, U.K.	44	53.11 N	2.53 W
Dee ≃, Eng., U.K.	42	54.18 N	2.32 W
Dee ≃, Scot., U.K.	28	57.08 N	2.04 W
Dee ≃, Scot., U.K.	42	54.50 N	4.03 W
Dee, Loch ◎	42	55.05 N	4.24 W
Deedsville	206	40.55 N	86.06 W
De Efteling ♠	48	51.39 N	5.02 E
Deeg	114	27.28 N	77.20 E
Deelfontein	148	30.59 S	23.48 E
Deelpan	148	26.19 S	25.36 E
Deenwood	182	31.14 N	82.23 W
Deep ≃, Ind., U.S.	206	41.34 N	87.17 W
Deep ≃, N.C., U.S.	182	35.36 N	79.03 W
Deepavaal Brook ≃	266	40.53 N	74.16 W
Deep Bay C	174	56.25 N	103.00 W
Deep Brook ≃, Mass., U.S.	273	42.38 N	71.22 W
Deep Brook ≃, N.J., U.S.	266	40.58 N	74.09 W
Deep Creek ≃, U.S.	190	41.44 N	113.00 W
Deep Creek ≃, Calif., U.S.	218	34.20 N	117.14 W
Deep Creek ≃, Del., U.S.	198	38.38 N	75.37 W
Deep Creek ≃, Idaho, U.S.	192	42.15 N	116.40 W
Deep Creek ≃, Md., U.S.	274b	39.17 N	76.28 W
Deep Creek ≃, Oreg., U.S.	214	45.23 N	122.26 W
Deep Creek ≃, Tex., U.S.	186	32.31 N	100.55 W

PORTUGUÊS

Nome	Página	Lat.°′	Long.°′ W=Oeste
Deep Creek ≃, Tex., U.S.	186	32.45 N	99.10 W
Deep Creek ≃, Utah, U.S.	190	40.10 N	113.50 W
Deep Creek Indian Reserve ◆[4]	172	52.16 N	122.07 W
Deeping Fen ☵	44	52.44 N	0.13 W
Deep Red Creek ≃	186	34.17 N	98.39 W
Deep River, Ont., Can.	180	46.06 N	77.30 W
Deep River, Conn., U.S.	197	41.23 N	72.26 W
Deep River, Iowa, U.S.	180	41.35 N	92.22 W
Deep River, Wash., U.S.	214	46.21 N	123.41 W
Deep Run ≃, Md., U.S.	274b	39.13 N	76.42 W
Deep Run ≃, Md., U.S.	274b	39.25 N	76.40 W
Deep Run ≃, N.J., U.S.	266	40.26 N	74.22 W
Deep Run ≃, N.J., U.S.	275	39.44 N	74.41 W
Deepwater, Austl.	156	29.27 S	151.51 E
Deepwater, Mo., U.S.	184	38.16 N	93.47 W
Deep Water, N.J., U.S.	198	39.41 N	75.29 W
Deep Well	152	24.25 S	134.05 E
Deer ≃	202	43.56 N	75.34 W
Deer Creek, Ind., U.S.	206	40.37 N	86.23 W
Deer Creek, Minn., U.S.	188	46.24 N	95.19 W
Deer Creek ≃, U.S.	198	39.37 N	76.09 W
Deer Creek ≃, Calif., U.S.	216	35.56 N	119.28 W
Deer Creek ≃, Calif., U.S.	216	39.13 N	121.17 W
Deer Creek ≃, Calif., U.S.	216	38.22 N	121.21 W
Deer Creek ≃, Calif., U.S.	272	37.24 N	122.09 W
Deer Creek ≃, Ill., U.S.	268	41.32 N	87.37 W
Deer Creek ≃, Ind., U.S.	206	40.34 N	86.41 W
Deer Creek ≃, Kans., U.S.	188	39.40 N	99.06 W
Deer Creek ≃, Miss., U.S.	184	32.33 N	90.47 W
Deer Creek ≃, Nebr., U.S.	188	40.28 N	100.00 W
Deer Creek ≃, Ohio, U.S.	208	39.27 N	83.00 W
Deer Creek ≃, Okla., U.S.	186	35.38 N	98.28 W
Deer Creek ≃, Oreg., U.S.	214	45.08 N	123.15 W
Deer Creek ≃, Pa., U.S.	269b	40.32 N	79.51 W
Deer Creek ≃, Wash., U.S.	214	48.16 N	121.55 W
Deer Creek ≃, Wyo., U.S.	190	42.52 N	105.52 W
Deer Creek ≃, Wyo., U.S.	192	43.09 N	107.42 W
Deer Creek Indian Reservation ◆[4]	180	47.50 N	93.25 W
Deer Creek Lake ◎[1]	208	39.40 N	83.15 W
Deerfield, Ill., U.S.	206	42.10 N	87.51 W
Deerfield, Ind., U.S.	206	40.17 N	84.59 W
Deerfield, Kans., U.S.	188	37.59 N	101.08 W
Deerfield, Mass., U.S.	197	42.33 N	72.36 W
Deerfield, Mich., U.S.	206	41.53 N	83.47 W
Deerfield, Ohio, U.S.	204	41.02 N	81.03 W
Deerfield, Wis., U.S.	206	43.03 N	89.05 W
Deerfield ≃	197	42.35 N	72.35 W
Deerfield Beach	210	26.19 N	80.06 W
Deerfield Manor	268	42.10 N	87.55 W
Deerfield Street	198	39.31 N	75.14 W
Deer Grove ♠	268	42.09 N	88.04 W
Deer Harbor	214	48.37 N	123.00 W
Deering	170	66.05 N	162.43 W
Deering, Mount ∧[2]	152	24.53 S	129.04 E
Deer Island ≻[1]	273	42.21 N	70.58 W
Deer Island I, N.B., Can.	176	45.00 N	66.57 W
Deer Island I, Alaska, U.S.	170	54.53 N	162.25 W
Deer Island I, Oreg., U.S.	214	45.58 N	122.50 W
Deer Isle	178	44.13 N	68.41 W
Deer Lake, Newf., Can.	176	49.10 N	57.26 W
Deer Lake, Pa., U.S.	198	40.37 N	76.03 W
Deer Lake ◎, Newf., Can.	176	49.07 N	57.35 W
Deer Lake ◎, Ont., Can.	174	52.40 N	94.30 W
Deer Lakes Regional Park ♠	269b	40.38 N	79.49 W
Deerlijk	46	50.51 N	3.21 E
Deer Lodge	192	46.24 N	112.44 W
Deer Mountain ∧	178	45.01 N	70.56 W
Deer Park, Austl.	264b	37.47 S	144.47 E
Deer Park, Ala., U.S.	184	31.13 N	88.19 W
Deer Park, Calif., U.S.	216	38.32 N	122.28 W
Deer Park, Fla., U.S.	210	28.05 N	80.54 W
Deer Park, Ill., U.S.	268	42.09 N	88.04 W
Deer Park, N.Y., U.S.	200	40.46 N	73.20 W
Deer Park, Ohio, U.S.	208	39.13 N	84.24 W
Deer Park, Tex., U.S.	212	29.43 N	95.08 W
Deer Park, Wash., U.S.	192	47.57 N	117.28 W
Deer Park Airport ⊠	266	40.46 N	73.19 W
Deerpass Bay C	166	65.56 N	122.25 W
Deer Pond ◎, Newf., Can.	176	48.30 N	54.45 W
Deer Pond ◎, N.J., U.S.	266	40.57 N	74.24 W
Deer River, Minn., U.S.	180	47.20 N	93.48 W
Deer River, N.Y., U.S.	202	43.56 N	75.36 W
Deersville	204	40.19 N	81.11 W
Deer Trail	188	39.37 N	104.02 W
Deerwood	180	46.28 N	93.54 W
Deesa	110	24.15 N	72.10 E
Dee Why	160	33.45 S	151.17 E
Dee Why Head ≻	264a	33.46 S	151.19 E
Dee Why Lagoon C	264a	33.45 S	151.18 E
Defengzhuang	88	41.02 N	113.16 E
Defereggen V	58	46.55 N	12.25 E
Defereggen Alpen ⩕	58	46.52 N	12.20 E
Deferiet	202	44.02 N	75.41 W
Defiance, Iowa, U.S.	188	41.49 N	95.20 W
Defiance, Ohio, U.S.	206	41.17 N	84.22 W
Defiance, Pa., U.S.	204	40.10 N	78.14 W
Defiance □[6]	206	41.19 N	84.30 W
Defiance, Mount ∧	214	45.38 N	121.43 W
Defiance Plateau ⩕[1]	190	36.00 N	109.15 W
Deflotte, Cap ≻	165f	21.10 S	167.25 E
De Forest	180	43.15 N	89.20 W
De Forest Lake ◎	266	41.08 N	73.58 W
De Funiak Springs	184	30.43 N	86.07 W
Dega Ahmedo	134	8.00 N	43.00 E
Deganga	116	22.40 N	88.39 E
Deganwy	42	53.18 N	3.47 W
Deganya	122	32.42 N	35.35 E
Dega Werabe	134	8.08 N	45.22 E
Dege	92	31.50 N	98.40 E
Degeberga	26	55.50 N	14.05 E
Degeh-Bur	134	8.14 N	43.35 E
Dégelis (Saint-Rose-du-Dégelis)	176	47.33 N	68.39 W
Degema	140	4.45 N	6.47 E
Degerby	26	60.02 N	20.23 E
Degeres	75	43.14 N	75.49 E
Degerfors	40	59.14 N	14.26 E
Degerhamn	26	56.21 N	16.24 E
Degerndorf	58	47.44 N	12.06 E
Deggendorf	30	48.51 N	12.59 E
Deggingen	52	48.36 N	9.43 E
Degh ≃	113	31.25 N	74.04 E
Değirmendere	120	38.07 N	27.09 E
Degla Reidab	134	2.51 N	42.18 E
Deglunden ◎	40	60.05 N	13.49 E
Dego	56	44.27 N	8.19 E
Degollado	224	20.28 N	102.09 W
Degoma	134	12.28 N	37.37 E
Degong	104	4.05 N	101.08 E
De Graafschap ◆[1]	48	52.00 N	6.30 E
De Graff	206	40.19 N	83.55 W
De Gray Lake ◎[1]	184	34.15 N	93.15 W
De Grey	152	20.10 S	119.12 E
De Grey ≃	152	20.12 S	119.11 E
Degt'ari	68	50.35 N	32.45 E
Degt'arka ≃	255a	59.57 N	30.52 E
Degt'arsk	76	56.42 N	60.06 E
Degtevo	70	49.11 N	40.39 E
Degunino ◆[8]	255b	55.52 N	37.33 E
De Haan	46	51.16 N	3.02 E
Deharda	116	21.40 N	87.25 E
Deh Bālā	113	34.04 N	70.29 E
Deh Bārez	118	27.26 N	57.12 E
Deh Bīd	118	30.38 N	53.13 E
Dehdez	118	31.43 N	50.17 E
Dehej	110	21.42 N	72.35 E
Dehgolān	118	35.17 N	47.25 E
Dehibat	138	32.01 N	10.42 E
Dehiwala-Mount Lavinia	112	6.51 N	79.52 E
Deh Kord	118	33.49 N	48.53 E
Dehlorān	118	32.41 N	47.16 E
De Hoek	148	32.57 S	18.46 E
De Hoge Veluwe, Nationale Park ♠	48	52.02 N	5.55 E
Dehra Dūn	114	30.19 N	78.02 E
Dehri	114	24.52 N	84.11 E
Dehrn	52	50.25 N	8.05 E
Deh Salm	118	31.12 N	59.19 E
Dehu	112	18.35 N	73.51 W
Dehua	90	25.32 N	118.15 E
Dehuang	88	35.12 N	114.25 E
Dehui	79	44.34 N	125.43 E
Deidesheim	52	49.24 N	8.11 E
Deilbach ≃	253	51.23 N	7.05 E
Deilinghofen	52	51.22 N	7.47 E
Dein	154	5.30 S	146.10 E
Deinze	46	50.59 N	3.32 E
Deir el Asad	122	32.56 N	35.16 E
Deister ⩕	48	52.15 N	9.30 E
Deiva Marina	56	44.13 N	9.30 E
Dej	38	47.09 N	23.52 E
Deje	40	59.36 N	13.28 E
Dejima	84	36.05 N	140.10 E
Dejnau	118	39.15 N	63.11 E
De Jongs, Tanjong ≻	154	6.56 S	138.32 E
Deka ≃, Afr.	146	18.03 S	26.44 E
Deka ≃, Rh.	144	18.03 S	26.44 E
De Kalb, Ill., U.S.	206	41.56 N	88.45 W
De Kalb, Miss., U.S.	184	32.46 N	88.39 W
De Kalb, Tex., U.S.	184	33.31 N	94.37 W
De Kalb □[6], Ill., U.S.	206	41.59 N	88.41 W
De Kalb □[6], Ind., U.S.	206	41.22 N	85.04 W
De Kalb Junction	202	44.30 N	75.16 W
Dekan, Hochland von → Deccan ⩕[1]	112	14.00 N	77.00 E
De-Kastri	79	51.28 N	140.47 E
Dekemhare	134	15.05 N	39.02 E
Dekese	142	3.27 S	21.24 E
Dekhgila Military Base ■	132	31.08 N	29.48 E
Dekina	140	7.39 N	7.02 E
Dekoa	142	6.19 N	19.04 E
De Koog	48	53.05 N	4.45 E
De Krim	48	52.38 N	6.38 E
De La Blache, Lac ◎	176	50.05 N	69.29 W
Delabole	44	50.37 N	4.42 W
Delafield	206	43.04 N	88.24 W
Delai	92	30.54 N	98.56 E
Del Aire	270	33.55 N	118.21 W
Delamere, Austl.	158b	35.35 S	138.11 E
Delamere, Eng., U.K.	252	53.13 N	2.39 W
Delamere Forest ◆[3]	42	53.14 N	2.38 W
Delami Mayal, Jabal ∧	130	11.38 N	30.23 E
Del Amo Center ◆[9]	270	33.50 N	118.21 W
De Lancey, N.Y., U.S.	200	42.12 N	74.58 W
De Lancey, Pa., U.S.	204	40.59 N	78.58 W
Delanco	198	40.03 N	74.57 W
De Land	210	29.02 N	81.18 W
Delanggu	105a	7.37 S	110.41 E
Delano, Calif., U.S.	216	35.41 N	119.15 W
Delano, Minn., U.S.	180	45.02 N	93.47 W
Delano, Pa., U.S.	200	40.50 N	76.04 W
Delano Peak ∧	190	38.22 N	112.23 W
Delanson	200	42.45 N	74.11 W
Delaport Point ≻	230b	25.05 N	77.27 W
Delapu	110	31.35 N	91.35 E
Delārām	118	32.11 N	63.25 E
Delareyville	148	26.44 S	25.29 E
Delarof Islands II	171a	51.30 N	178.45 W
Delaronde Lake ◎	174	54.05 N	107.05 W
Del'atiči	66	53.47 N	25.59 E
Del'atin	68	48.32 N	24.37 E
Delatite ≃	159	37.10 S	146.00 E
Delavan, Ill., U.S.	184	40.22 N	89.33 W
Delavan, Wis., U.S.	206	42.38 N	88.39 W
Delavan Lake	206	42.38 N	88.35 W
Delavan Lake ◎	206	42.37 N	88.38 W
Delaware, Ont., Can.	204	42.55 N	81.25 W
Delaware, N.J., U.S.	200	40.53 N	75.04 W
Delaware, Ohio, U.S.	204	40.18 N	83.04 W
Delaware, Okla., U.S.	186	36.47 N	95.38 W
Delaware □[3]	198	39.10 N	75.30 W
Delaware □[6], Ind., U.S.	206	40.18 N	85.23 W
Delaware □[6], N.Y., U.S.	200	42.17 N	74.55 W
Delaware □[6], Ohio, U.S.	204	40.18 N	83.04 W
Delaware □[6], Pa., U.S.	198	39.55 N	75.23 W
Delaware □[3]	168	39.10 N	75.30 W
Delaware ≃, U.S.	178	39.20 N	75.25 W
Delaware ≃, Kans., U.S.	188	39.03 N	95.24 W
Delaware, East Branch ≃	200	41.55 N	75.17 W
Delaware, University of ʋ[2]	275	39.41 N	75.45 W
Delaware, West Branch ≃	200	41.56 N	75.17 W
Delaware and Raritan Canal ☲	198	40.29 N	74.26 W
Delaware Aqueduct ☲[1]	200	42.05 N	74.54 W
Delaware Bay C	198	39.05 N	75.15 W
Delaware City	198	39.34 N	75.36 W
Delaware Lake ◎[1]	204	40.20 N	83.00 W
Delaware Memorial Bridge ◆[5]	198	39.41 N	75.31 W
Delaware Mountains ⩕	186	31.35 N	104.40 W
Delaware Park	200	40.43 N	75.11 W
Delaware Park ♠	274a	42.56 N	78.52 W
Delaware Park Race Track ♠	275	39.42 N	75.40 W
Delaware Seashore State Park ♠	198	38.38 N	75.04 W
Delaware State Park ♠	204	40.23 N	83.04 W
Delaware Water Gap	200	40.59 N	75.09 W
Delaware Water Gap National Recreation Area ♠	200	41.08 N	74.55 W
Delbrück	48	51.46 N	8.33 E
Delburne	172	52.12 N	113.14 W
Del Campillo	242	34.22 S	64.29 W
Del Carril	248	35.31 S	59.30 W
Del City	186	35.27 N	97.27 W
Del Dios	218	33.04 N	117.08 W
Delegate	156	37.03 S	148.58 E
Delémont	54	47.22 N	7.21 E
De Leon	186	32.07 N	98.32 W
De Leon Springs	182	29.07 N	81.21 W
de Lesquin, Aéroport ⊠	46	50.35 N	3.07 E
Delet ⋓	26	60.15 N	20.35 E
Delevan	200	42.29 N	78.29 W
Delfim Moreira	246	22.30 S	45.17 W
Delfinópolis	245	20.20 S	46.51 W
Delft	48	52.00 N	4.21 E
Delft Island I	112	9.30 N	79.42 E
Delfzijl	48	53.19 N	6.46 E
Delgada, Punta ≻	244	42.46 S	63.38 W
Delgado, Cabo ≻	144	10.40 S	40.35 E
Del Gallego	106	13.56 N	122.36 E
Delger ≃	78	49.17 N	100.40 E
Delgerchaan Uul ∧	78	49.58 N	106.23 E
Delgerchangaj	92	45.14 N	104.50 E
Delgerchet	92	45.49 N	110.28 E
Delgercogt	92	46.08 N	106.29 E
Delgerech	92	45.49 N	111.12 E
Del Haven	198	39.03 N	74.56 W
Delhi, Bhārat	114		
	262a	28.40 N	77.13 E
Delhi, Ont., Can.	202	42.51 N	80.30 W
Delhi, Calif., U.S.	216	37.26 N	120.46 W
Delhi, Iowa, U.S.	180	42.26 N	91.20 W
Delhi, La., U.S.	184	32.27 N	91.30 W
Delhi, N.Y., U.S.	200	42.17 N	74.55 W
Delhi □[3]	113	28.37 N	77.10 E
Delhi, University of ʋ[2]	262a	28.42 N	77.13 E
Delhi Cantonment	262a	28.36 N	77.08 E
Delhi Hills	208	39.05 N	84.07 W
Delhi Railroad Station ◆[5]	262a	28.40 N	77.13 E
Delhi Tail Distributary ☲	262a	28.41 N	77.10 E
Deli, Pulau I	105a	7.00 S	105.32 E
Delia	172	51.38 N	112.23 W
Deliblato	38	44.50 N	21.03 E
Delice	120	39.58 N	34.02 E
Delice ≃	120	40.28 N	34.10 E
Delices	230d	15.17 N	61.16 W
Deliceto	60	41.13 N	15.23 E
Delicias, Cuba	230p	21.11 N	76.34 W
Delicias, Méx.	222	28.13 N	105.28 W
Delicias, Laguna ◎	222	28.07 N	105.40 W
De Lier	48	51.57 N	4.15 E
Delight	184	34.02 N	93.30 W
Delightful	204	41.18 N	80.57 W
Deliilyas	120	39.20 N	36.48 E
Delījān	118	33.59 N	50.40 E
Deliklıkaya ≻	120	41.12 N	30.20 E
Deliktaş	120	39.21 N	37.13 E
Délimbé	136	9.53 N	22.37 E
Delingha	92	37.14 N	97.11 E
Dēliņkalns ∧	66	57.30 N	27.25 E
Déli Pályaudvar ◆[5]	254c	47.30 N	19.01 E
Delisle	174	51.55 N	107.08 W
Delisle ≃	196	45.23 N	74.10 W
Delitua	104	3.30 N	98.41 E
Delitzsch	50	51.31 N	12.20 E
Delkern	218	35.21 N	119.01 W
Dellach	58	46.40 N	13.05 E
Dell City	190	31.56 N	105.12 W
Delle	54	47.30 N	7.00 E
Dellenbaugh, Mount ∧	190	36.07 N	113.32 W
Dellensjöarna ◎	26	61.54 N	16.41 E
Delligsen	48	51.57 N	9.48 E
Dello	58	45.25 N	10.04 E
Dell Rapids	188	43.50 N	96.43 W
Dellroy	204	40.33 N	81.12 W
Dellwig	253	51.29 N	7.41 E
Dellwig ◆[8]	253	51.29 N	6.56 E
Dellwood	209	38.44 N	90.16 W
Dellwood Highlands	268	41.34 N	88.03 W
Dellys	138	36.55 N	3.55 E
Del Mar, Calif., U.S.	218	32.58 N	117.16 W
Delmar, Del., U.S.	198	38.27 N	75.34 W
Delmar, Iowa, U.S.	180	42.00 N	90.37 W
Delmar, Md., U.S.	198	38.27 N	75.34 W
Delmar, N.Y., U.S.	197	42.38 N	73.52 W
Delmar, N.Y., U.S.	200	42.37 N	73.50 W
Del Mar Heights	216	35.26 N	120.52 W
Del Mar Woods	268	42.12 N	87.51 W
Delmas, Sask., Can.	174	52.55 N	108.36 W
Delmas, S. Afr.	148	26.08 S	28.43 E
Delme	52	48.53 N	6.24 E
Delme ≃	48	53.05 N	8.40 E
Delmenhorst	48	53.03 N	8.38 E
Delmiro Gouveia	240	9.23 S	37.59 W
Delmont, N.J., U.S.	198	39.13 N	74.57 W
Delmont, Pa., U.S.	204	40.25 N	79.34 W
Delmont, S. Dak., U.S.	188	43.16 N	98.10 W
Del Monte Heights	216	36.36 N	121.50 W
Del Monte Park	216	36.36 N	121.56 W
Delnice	36	45.24 N	14.48 E
Del Norte	190	37.41 N	106.21 W
De-Longa, Ostrova II	64	76.30 N	153.00 E
De Long Mountains ⩕	170	68.20 N	162.00 W
De-Long-Strasse → Longa, Proliv ⋓	64	70.20 N	178.00 E
Deloraine, Austl.	156	41.31 S	146.39 E
Deloraine, Man., Can.	174	49.12 N	100.29 W
Delorme, Lac ◎	166	54.31 N	69.52 W
Deloro	202	44.31 N	77.37 W
Delos → Dhílos ⊥	38	37.26 N	25.16 E
Delph	252	53.34 N	2.01 W
Delphi	206	40.36 N	86.41 W
Delphi → Dhelfoí ⊥	38	38.30 N	22.29 E
Delphi Falls	200	42.53 N	75.55 W
Delphos, Kans., U.S.	188	39.16 N	97.46 W
Delphos, Ohio, U.S.	206	40.50 N	84.20 W
Delph Reservoir ◎[1]	252	53.38 N	2.27 W
Delportshoop	148	28.22 S	24.20 E
Del Puerto Creek ≃	216	37.32 N	121.07 W
Delran	275	40.02 N	74.58 W
Delrath	253	51.08 N	6.47 E
Delray ◆[8]	271	42.18 N	83.08 W
Delray Beach	210	26.28 N	80.04 W
Del Rey	216	36.40 N	119.36 W
Del Rey Oaks	216	36.36 N	121.50 W
Del Rio	186	29.22 N	100.54 W
Del Rosa	218	34.08 N	117.15 W
Delsbo	26	61.48 N	16.35 E
Delson	196	45.22 N	73.33 W
Delstern ◆[8]	253	51.20 N	7.31 E
Delta, Ont., Can.	202	44.37 N	76.08 W
Delta, Méx.	190	32.22 N	115.12 W
Delta, Colo., U.S.	190	38.44 N	108.04 W
Delta, Mo., U.S.	184	37.12 N	89.44 W
Delta, Ohio, U.S.	206	41.34 N	84.00 W
Delta, Pa., U.S.	198	39.44 N	76.19 W
Delta, Utah, U.S.	190	39.21 N	112.35 W
Delta ≃	170	64.09 N	146.18 W
Delta Amacuro □[8]	236	8.30 N	61.30 W
Delta Barrage ◆[6]	132	30.11 N	31.07 E
Delta Beach	174	50.11 N	98.19 W
Delta City	184	33.04 N	90.48 W
Delta Downs	156	17.00 S	141.18 E
Delta Junction	170	64.02 N	145.41 W
Delta Mendota Canal ☲	216	37.49 N	121.34 W
Delta Peak ∧	170	56.39 N	129.34 W
Delta Reservoir ◎[1]	200	43.17 N	75.26 W
Deltaville	198	37.33 N	76.20 W
Delton	206	42.30 N	85.24 W
Deltona	210	28.54 N	81.16 W
Delungra	156	29.39 S	150.50 E
Del'un-Uranskij Chrebet ⩕	78	56.30 N	114.00 E
Delüün	76	47.42 N	90.59 E
De Luz Creek ≃	218	33.22 N	117.19 W
Del Valle	212	30.12 N	97.40 W
Delvinë	38	39.57 N	20.06 E
Del Viso	248	34.27 S	58.48 W
Delyn □[8]	252	53.16 N	3.11 W
Demak	105a	6.53 S	110.38 E
Demaki	70	58.26 N	54.41 E
Demarcation Point ≻	170	69.40 N	141.15 W
Demarest	266	40.57 N	73.58 W
Demarest Brook ≃	266	40.57 N	73.58 W
Demavend, Mount → Damāvand, Qolleh-ye ∧	118	35.56 N	52.08 E
Demba	142	5.30 S	22.16 E
Demba Chio	142	9.41 S	13.41 E
Dembecha	134	10.35 N	37.30 E
Dembi	134	8.05 N	36.27 E
Dembia, Centraf.	144	5.07 N	24.25 E
Dembia, Zaïre	144	3.31 N	25.50 E
Dembidolo	134	8.30 N	34.48 E
Dembo	142	3.56 S	12.35 E
Dême ≃	46	47.43 N	0.29 E
Demerara ≃	236	6.48 N	58.10 W
Demerthin	50	52.58 N	12.17 E
Demidov	66	55.16 N	31.31 E
Demidovka	68	50.25 N	25.20 E
Demidovo	66	59.17 N	38.17 E
Deming, N. Mex., U.S.	190	32.16 N	107.45 W
Deming, Wash., U.S.	214	48.49 N	122.13 W
Demini ≃	236	0.46 S	62.56 W
Demirci	120	39.03 N	28.40 E
Demircidere	120	37.33 N	27.50 E
Demir Kapija V	38	41.24 N	22.15 E
Demirköy	120	41.49 N	27.45 E
Demirtaş	120	40.16 N	29.06 E
Demitz-Thumitz	50	51.09 N	14.14 E
Demjanka ≃	76	59.34 N	69.20 E
Demjanovka	76	54.04 N	65.22 E
Demjanovo	24	60.22 N	47.03 E
Demjansk	66	57.38 N	32.28 E
Demjanskoje	76	59.36 N	69.18 E
Demjas	70	51.13 N	49.08 E
Demmeltrath ◆[8]	253	51.11 N	7.03 E
Demmin	50	53.54 N	13.02 E
Demmitt	172	55.26 N	119.54 W
Demnat	138	31.44 N	6.59 W
Democracy, Monument of ⊥	259a	13.45 N	100.30 E
Democrat Point ≻	266	40.37 N	73.18 W
Demoiselles, Grotte des •[5]	56	43.55 N	3.45 E
Demonte	56	44.19 N	7.17 E
De Montigny, Lac ◎	180	48.08 N	77.54 W
Demopolis	184	32.31 N	87.50 W
Demorest	182	34.31 N	83.32 W
De Mossville	208	38.48 N	84.25 W
Demotte	206	41.12 N	87.12 W
Dempo, Gunung ∧	102	4.02 S	103.09 E
Dempster, Point ≻	152	33.39 S	123.52 E
Demsa	136	9.32 N	13.14 E
Demta	154	2.20 S	140.08 E
Demurino	68	48.10 N	36.29 E
De Naauwte	148	30.08 S	21.42 E
Denain	46	50.20 N	3.23 E
Denair	216	37.32 N	120.47 W
Denali	170	63.11 N	147.28 W
Denan	134	6.30 N	43.30 E
Denare Beach	174	54.40 N	102.05 W
Denau	75	38.16 N	67.54 E
Denbigh, Ont., Can.	202	45.08 N	77.16 W
Denbigh, Wales, U.K.	42	53.11 N	3.25 W
Denbigh, Cape ≻	170	64.23 N	161.31 W
Den Burg	48	53.03 N	4.48 E
Denby Dale	42	53.35 N	1.38 W
Den Chai	100	17.59 N	100.04 E
Dendang	102	3.05 S	107.54 E
Dendé	142	3.46 S	11.09 E
Dender (Dendre) ≃	46	51.02 N	4.06 E
Denderleeuw	46	50.53 N	4.04 E
Dendermonde	46	51.02 N	4.07 E
Dendron	198	37.03 N	76.56 W
Dendy Park ♠	264b	37.56 S	145.00 E
Deneba	134	9.50 N	39.09 E
Denekamp	48	52.23 N	7.00 E
Denenchōfu ◆[8]	258	35.35 N	139.41 E
Deneysville	148	26.53 S	28.06 E
Denežnikovo, S.S.S.R.	72	55.26 N	38.07 E
Denežnikovo, S.S.S.R.	73	49.02 N	38.57 E
Dengcheng	90	33.41 N	114.27 E
Deng Deng	142	5.12 N	13.31 E
Denge	144	3.34 N	28.14 E
Denge Marsh ☵	44	50.57 N	0.55 E
Dengfeng	90	34.29 N	113.04 E
Denggongchang	97	30.24 N	103.49 E
Dengjingguan	97	29.10 N	104.56 E
Dengke	92	32.31 N	97.59 E
Dengkou	92	40.20 N	106.59 E
Denglongshu	88	41.20 N	115.15 E
Dengmingsi	88	37.53 N	116.42 E
Dengshahe	88	39.13 N	122.04 E
Dengshipuzi	94	42.17 N	123.08 E
Dengta	90	24.01 N	114.49 E
Denguiro	142	5.38 N	23.02 E
Dengxian	92	32.42 N	112.01 E
Dengyoufang	88	41.34 N	114.32 E
Den Haag → 's-Gravenhage	48	52.06 N	4.18 E
Denham, Austl.	152	25.55 S	113.32 E
Denham, Eng., U.K.	250	51.34 N	0.30 W
Denham, Ind., U.S.	206	41.09 N	86.43 W
Denham, Mount ∧	231q	18.13 N	77.32 W
Denham Aerodrome ⊠	250	51.36 N	0.31 W
Denham Island I	156	16.43 S	139.09 E
Denham Place ʋ	250	51.34 N	0.30 W
Denham Range ⩕	156	21.55 S	147.46 E
Denham Sound ⋓	152	25.40 S	113.15 E
Denham Springs	184	30.29 N	90.57 W
Den Helder	48	52.54 N	4.45 E
Denholme	252	53.48 N	1.54 W
Denia	34	38.51 N	0.07 E
Denial Bay	152	32.06 S	133.32 E
Dénié	140	11.14 N	7.29 W
Deniliquin	156	35.32 S	144.58 E
Deniskoviči, S.S.S.R.	66	52.44 N	26.41 E
Deniskoviči, S.S.S.R.	66	52.19 N	31.43 E
Denison, Iowa, U.S.	188	42.01 N	95.21 W
Denison, Tex., U.S.	186	33.45 N	96.33 W
Denison, Mount ∧	170	58.25 N	154.27 W
Denison Dam ◆[6]	186	33.36 N	96.18 W
Denisovka, S.S.S.R.	24	66.14 N	55.20 E
Denisovka, S.S.S.R.	76	52.28 N	61.46 E
Denisovo	72	54.28 N	37.51 E
Denisy	251	48.33 N	1.56 E
Denizli	120	37.46 N	29.06 E
Denizli □[4]	120	37.40 N	29.15 E
Denkanikota	112	12.32 N	77.48 E
Denkendorf	52	48.41 N	9.19 E
Denkingen	54	47.53 N	9.19 E
Denklingen, B.R.D.	52	50.55 N	7.39 E
Denklingen, B.R.D.	54	47.55 N	10.51 E
Den'kovo	72	56.01 N	36.21 E
Denman Glacier ⛆	9	66.45 S	99.25 E
Denmark, Austl.	152	34.57 S	117.21 E
Denmark, S.C., U.S.	182	33.19 N	81.09 W
Denmark, Wis., U.S.	180	44.21 N	87.50 W
Denmark □[1]	22		
	26	56.00 N	10.00 E
Denmark, Lake ◎	266	40.58 N	74.31 W
Denmark Bay C	166	70.33 N	103.20 W
Denmark Strait ⋓	10	67.00 N	25.00 W
Dennemont	251	49.01 N	1.42 E
Dennery	231f	13.55 N	60.54 W
Dennis	197	41.44 N	70.12 W
Dennison	204	40.24 N	81.19 W
Dennis Port	197	41.39 N	70.08 W
Denniston	162	41.44 S	171.48 E
Denniston Creek ≃	272	37.30 N	122.28 W
Dennisville	198	39.12 N	74.49 W
Denny	42	56.02 N	3.55 W
Den Oever	48	52.56 N	5.02 E
Denouval	251	48.58 N	2.03 E
Denpasar	105b	8.39 S	115.13 E
Denshaw	252	53.35 N	2.02 W

Symbol	English	Deutsch	Español	Français	Português
≃	River	Fluss	Río	Rivière	Rio
☲	Canal	Kanal	Canal	Canal	Canal
⌞	Waterfall, Rapids	Wasserfall, Stromschnellen	Cascada, Rápidos	Chute d'eau, Rapides	Cascata, Rápidos
⋓	Strait	Meeresstrasse	Estrecho	Détroit	Estreito
C	Bay, Gulf	Bucht, Golf	Bahía, Golfo	Baie, Golfe	Baía, Golfo
◎	Lake, Lakes	See, Seen	Lago, Lagos	Lac, Lacs	Lago, Lagos
☵	Swamp	Sumpf	Pantano	Marais	Pântano
⛆	Ice Features, Glacier	Eis- und Gletscherformen	Accidentes Glaciales	Formes glaciaires	Acidentes Glaciares
⫪	Other Hydrographic Features	Andere Hydrographische Objekte	Otros Elementos Hidrográficos	Autres données hydrographiques	Outros Elementos Hidrográficos
✧	Submarine Features	Untermeerische Objekte	Accidentes Submarinos	Formes de relief sous-marin	Acidentes Submarinos
□	Political Unit	Politische Einheit	Unidad Politica	Entité politique	Unidade Política
ʋ	Cultural Institution	Kulturelle Institution	Institución Cultural	Institution culturelle	Instituição Cultural
⊥	Historical Site	Historische Stätte	Sitio Histórico	Site historique	Sitio Histórico
♠	Recreational Site	Erholungs- und Ferienort	Sitio de Recreo	Centre de loisirs	Sítio de Lazer
⊠	Airport	Flughafen	Aeropuerto	Aéroport	Aeroporto
■	Military Installation	Militäranlage	Instalación Militar	Installation militaire	Instalação Militar
◆	Miscellaneous	Verschiedenes	Misceláneo	Divers	Miscelânea

Dent Ditch ⩨ 269a 41.18 N 82.08 W
Denton, Eng., U.K. 42 53.27 N 2.07 W
Denton, Md., U.S. 198 38.53 N 75.50 W
Denton, Mich., U.S. 271 42.16 N 83.31 W
Denton, Mont., U.S. 192 47.19 N 109.57 W
Denton, Tex., U.S. 212 33.13 N 97.08 W
Denton □6 212 33.07 N 97.10 W
Denton Creek ≃ 186 32.58 N 96.57 W
Dentonia Park ♦ 265b 43.42 N 79.17 W
D'Entrecasteaux, Point ≻ 152 34.50 S 116.00 E
D'Entrecasteaux Islands II 154 9.30 S 150.40 E
Dents du Midi ⩕ 54 46.10 N 6.56 E
Denver, Colo., U.S. 190 39.43 N 105.01 W
Denver, Ind., U.S. 206 40.52 N 86.05 W
Denver, Iowa, U.S. 180 42.40 N 92.20 W
Denver, Pa., U.S. 198 40.14 N 76.08 W
Denver City 186 32.58 N 102.50 W
Denville 200 40.53 N 74.29 W
Denzlingen 54 48.04 N 7.52 E
Deoband 114 29.42 N 77.41 E
Deocha 116 24.03 N 87.35 E
Deogarh, Bhārat 110 25.32 N 73.54 E
Deogarh, Bhārat 112 21.32 N 84.44 E
Deogarh, Bhārat 114 24.33 N 78.15 E
Deogarh ∧ 114 23.32 N 82.16 E
Deogarh Hills ⩕2 114 23.35 N 82.30 E
Deoghar 114 24.29 N 86.42 E
Deolāli 112 19.57 N 73.50 E
Deoli, Bhārat 110 25.45 N 75.23 E
Deoli, Bhārat 116 22.03 N 86.49 E
Deoli -•8 262a 28.30 N 77.14 E
Deopāra 116 22.55 N 90.15 E
Deori 114 23.08 N 78.41 E
Deoria 114 26.31 N 83.47 E
Deoria □5 114 26.50 N 83.50 E
Deori Khās 114 23.24 N 79.01 E
Deosai Mountains ⩕ 113 35.20 N 75.12 E
Deosil 114 23.42 N 82.15 E
Dep ≃ 79 52.54 N 127.45 E
Depāl 116 21.44 N 87.33 E
De Panne 46 51.06 N 2.35 E
Depāra 262b 22.53 N 88.34 E
Departure Bay 214 49.12 N 123.58 W
DePaul University ⩔2 268 41.56 N 87.39 W
Depauville 202 44.08 N 76.04 W
Depauw 208 38.20 N 86.13 W
De Peel ⩨ 48 51.25 N 6.00 E
De Pere 180 44.27 N 88.04 W
Depew, N.Y., U.S. 200 42.54 N 78.42 W
Depew, Okla., U.S. 186 35.48 N 96.31 W
Deping 88 37.28 N 116.57 E
De Pinte 46 51.00 N 3.39 E
Depoe Bay 192 44.49 N 124.04 W
Depok 105a 6.24 S 106.50 E
Deport 186 33.32 N 95.19 W
Deposit 200 42.04 N 75.25 W
Depósito 236 3.12 N 60.35 W
Deptford -•8 250 51.28 N 0.02 W
Deptford Terrace 275 39.48 N 75.09 W
Depuch Island I 152 20.38 S 117.43 E
Depue 180 41.19 N 89.19 W
Deputy 208 38.48 N 85.39 W
Deqin 92 28.38 N 98.52 E
Deqing, Zhg. 92 23.09 N 111.45 E
Deqing, Zhg. 96 30.33 N 120.05 E
De Queen 184 34.02 N 94.21 W
De Quincy 184 30.27 N 93.26 W
Dera, Lak (Lach Dera) ≃ 134 0.15 N 42.17 E
Dera Bugti 110 29.02 N 69.09 E
Derac 228 19.39 N 71.49 W
Dera Ghāzi Khān 113 30.03 N 70.38 E
Dera Gopipur 113 31.54 N 76.13 E
Dera Ismāīl Khān 113 31.50 N 70.54 E
Dera Nānak 113 32.02 N 75.01 E
Dera Nawāb 113 29.06 N 71.06 E
Dera-patak ≃ 254c 47.39 N 19.05 E
Derāwar Fort 113 28.46 N 71.20 E
Deražn'a 68 49.16 N 27.26 E
Derbent 74 42.03 N 48.18 E
Derbesiye 120 37.06 N 40.40 E
Derbeškinskij 70 55.52 N 53.30 E
Derbetovka 70 45.48 N 43.05 E
Der Bodden ⊔ 50 54.16 N 13.12 E
Derby, Austl. 152 17.18 S 123.38 E
Derby, Austl. 156 41.09 S 147.47 E
Derby, S. Afr. 148 25.55 S 27.02 E
Derby, Eng., U.K. 44 52.55 N 1.29 W
Derby, Conn., U.S. 197 41.19 N 73.05 W
Derby, Kans., U.S. 188 37.33 N 97.16 W
Derby, Maine, U.S. 178 45.14 N 68.59 W
Derby, N.Y., U.S. 200 42.41 N 78.58 W
Derby, Ohio, U.S. 208 39.46 N 83.12 W
Derby, Vt., U.S. 196 44.57 N 72.08 W
Derby Acres 216 35.15 N 119.35 W
Derby Line 178 45.00 N 72.06 W
Derbyshire □6 44 53.00 N 1.33 W
Derdepoort 146 24.42 S 26.20 E
Derecho ≃ 236 2.38 S 69.54 W
Derečin 66 53.15 N 24.55 E
Derecske 30 47.21 N 21.34 E
Dereishaklı 120 41.03 N 39.08 E
Dereköy, Tür. 120 40.08 N 37.47 E
Dereköy, Tür. 120 39.16 N 27.19 E
Dereköy, Tür. 120 41.56 N 27.21 E
Dereli 120 40.45 N 38.27 E
Derenburg 50 51.52 N 10.54 E
Derendorf -•8 253 51.15 N 6.48 E
Derenwu 95 39.40 N 116.46 E
Dereseki 257b 41.08 N 29.08 E
Derev'anka 24 61.34 N 34.27 E
Derewa ≃ 154 2.48 S 136.10 E
Derg, Lough @ 28 53.00 N 8.20 W
Dergači, S.S.S.R. 68 50.07 N 36.07 E
Dergači, S.S.S.R. 70 51.14 N 48.46 E
Dergaon 110 26.42 N 93.58 E
Der Grabow C 50 54.23 N 12.50 E
De Ridder 184 30.51 N 93.17 W
De Rijp 48 52.34 N 4.50 E
Derik 120 37.22 N 40.17 E
Derinkuyu 120 38.23 N 34.45 E
Der Kanal → English Channel ⊔ 28 50.20 N 1.00 W
Derkul 70 51.16 N 51.18 E
Derkul ≃ 73 48.35 N 39.41 E
Dermbach 52 50.43 N 10.06 E
Dermott 184 33.32 N 91.26 W
Dermulo 58 46.20 N 11.04 E
Derne 253 51.35 N 7.41 E
Derne -•8 253 51.34 N 7.31 E
Dernieres, Isles II 184 29.02 N 90.47 W
Dernoviči 68 51.36 N 29.43 E
Deroche 214 49.11 N 122.04 W
Dero Eri 134 9.02 N 46.48 E
Derong 92 28.47 N 99.14 E
Derrame 186 26.19 N 104.23 W
Derre 144 16.56 S 36.11 E
Derrick City 204 41.58 N 78.34 W
Derrinallum 159 37.57 S 143.13 E
Derry → Londonderry, N. Ire., U.K. 42 55.00 N 7.19 W
Derry, N.H., U.S. 178 42.53 N 71.19 W
Derry, Pa., U.S. 204 40.20 N 79.18 W
Derrykeevan 42 55.08 N 6.29 W
Derry West 265b 43.39 N 79.42 W
Der Sārāi -•8 262a 28.33 N 77.11 E
Dersau 50 54.07 N 10.20 E
Derschlag 52 51.00 N 7.37 E
Dersingham 44 52.51 N 0.30 E
Derudeb 130 17.32 N 36.06 E
De Rust 148 33.30 S 22.32 E
Deruta 60 42.59 N 12.25 E
De Ruyter 200 42.46 N 75.53 W
De Ruyter Reservoir @1 200 42.49 N 75.53 W
Der'uzino 72 56.18 N 38.16 E
Derval 32 47.40 N 1.40 W
Derventa 38 44.58 N 17.55 E
Derwent 172 53.39 N 110.58 W
Derwent ≃, Austl. 156 43.03 S 147.22 E
Derwent ≃, Eng., U.K. 42 54.38 N 3.34 W
Derwent ≃, Eng., U.K. 42 53.45 N 0.57 W
Derwent ≃, Eng., U.K. 42 54.57 N 1.41 W
Derwent ≃, Eng., U.K. 44 52.50 N 1.15 W
Derwent Bridge 156 42.08 S 146.13 E
Derwent Water @ 42 54.34 N 3.08 W
Deržavino 70 53.13 N 52.22 E
Deržavinskij 76 51.03 N 66.19 E
Desaguadero ≃, Arg. 242 34.13 S 66.47 W
Desaguadero ≃, Bol. 238 18.24 S 67.05 W
Deşt 120 39.10 N 39.49 E
Des Allemands 184 29.50 N 90.28 W
Désappointement, Îles du II 14 14.10 S 141.20 W
Des Arc 184 34.58 N 91.30 W
Desborough 44 52.27 N 0.49 W
Descabezado Grande, Volcán ∧1 242 35.36 S 70.45 W
Descanso, Bra. 242 26.50 S 53.35 W
Descanso, Calif., U.S. 194 32.51 N 116.37 W
Descanso, Punta ≻ 194 32.16 N 117.03 W
Descanso Gardens ♦ 270 34.12 N 118.13 W
Descartes 32 46.58 N 0.42 E
Deschaillons 196 46.32 N 72.07 W
Deschambault 196 46.39 N 71.56 W
Deschambault Lake 174 54.55 N 103.22 W
Deschambault Lake @ 174 54.40 N 103.35 W
Descharme Lake @ 174 57.05 N 109.13 W
Deschênes 178 45.23 N 75.48 W
Deschenes, Lake @ 202 45.22 N 75.51 W
Deschutes ≃, Oreg., U.S. 192 45.38 N 120.54 W
Deschutes ≃, Wash., U.S. 214 47.02 N 122.54 W
Deschutes-Umatilla Plateau ⩕1 192 45.00 N 119.40 W
Descoberto 246 21.27 S 42.58 W
Descoberto, Serra do ∧ 246 21.24 S 42.57 W
Dese 134 11.05 N 39.41 E
Deseado ≃ 244 47.45 S 65.54 W
Deseado, Cabo ≻ 244 52.44 S 74.44 W
Desembarco de los 33 Orientales, Monumento ⊥ 248 33.48 S 58.25 W
Desengaño, Punta ≻ 244 49.15 S 67.37 W
Desenzano del Garda 58 45.28 N 10.32 E
Deseret Peak ∧ 190 40.28 N 112.38 W
Deseronto 202 44.12 N 77.03 W
Désert ≃ 180 46.23 N 75.58 W
Désert, Lac @ 180 46.35 N 76.19 W
Desertas, Ilhas I 138 32.30 N 16.30 W
Desert Creek ≃ 216 38.48 N 119.19 W
Desert Hot Springs 194 33.58 N 116.30 W
Desert Lake @, Ont., Can. 202 44.32 N 76.35 W
Desert Lake @, Nev., U.S. 194 37.58 N 115.15 W
Desert Mountains ⩕ 216 39.16 N 119.00 W
Desertores, Grupo II 244 42.43 S 73.00 W
Desert Peak ∧ 190 41.11 N 113.22 W
Desert Valley ∨ 194 41.15 N 118.20 W
Desert View Highlands 218 34.37 N 118.13 W
Desfogue del Lago, Canal de ⩨ 276a 19.26 N 99.03 W
Desford 44 52.39 N 1.17 W
Deshaies 231o 16.18 N 61.48 W
Desheng 92 24.45 N 108.28 E
Deshengbo 92 26.58 N 103.59 E
Deshengchang 97 29.06 N 105.25 E
Deshengtai 94 42.14 N 123.45 E
Deshengyingzi 94 41.44 N 123.14 E
Deshler, Nebr., U.S. 188 40.08 N 97.44 W
Deshler, Ohio, U.S. 206 41.12 N 83.54 W
Deshnoke 110 27.48 N 73.21 E
Deshon Manor 204 40.52 N 79.57 W
Deshu 118 30.26 N 63.19 E
Deshun 96 31.58 N 120.29 E
Desiderio Tello 242 31.13 S 66.19 W
Desio 56 45.37 N 9.13 E
Des Lacs ≃ 188 48.17 N 101.25 W
Deslinde, Arroyo ≃ 248 33.44 S 58.52 W
Desmarais 172 55.56 N 113.49 W
De Smet 188 44.23 N 97.33 W
De Smet, Lake @1 192 44.29 N 106.45 W
Des Moines, Iowa, U.S. 180 41.35 N 93.37 W
Des Moines, N. Mex., U.S. 186 36.46 N 103.50 W
Des Moines, Wash., U.S. 214 47.24 N 122.19 W
Des Moines ≃ 180 40.22 N 91.26 W
Des Moines, East Fork ≃ 188 42.41 N 94.12 W
Desmoronado, Cerro ∧ 224 20.21 N 104.59 W
Desna 68 50.56 N 30.46 E
Desna ≃, S.S.S.R. 68 50.33 N 30.32 E
Desna ≃, S.S.S.R. 72 55.26 N 37.30 E
Desolación, Isla I 244 53.00 S 74.10 W
Désolation, Cap de la → Disappointment, Cape ≻ 234 54.53 S 36.07 W
Desolation Point ≻ 106 10.28 N 125.39 E
Desor, Mount ∧2 180 47.58 N 89.01 W
De Soto, Ill., U.S. 184 37.49 N 89.14 W
De Soto, Ind., U.S. 206 40.15 N 85.17 W
De Soto, Mo., U.S. 184 38.08 N 90.33 W
De Soto, Tex., U.S. 212 32.35 N 96.51 W
De Soto □6 210 27.11 N 81.48 W
De Soto City 210 27.27 N 81.24 W
De Soto National Memorial ⊥ 210 27.31 N 82.40 W
De Soto State Park ♦ 184 34.28 N 85.36 W
Despatch 148 33.46 S 25.30 E
Despeñaperros, Desfiladero de)(34 38.24 N 3.30 W
Des Plaines 206 42.02 N 87.54 W
Des Plaines ≃ 206 41.24 N 88.16 W
Despotovac 38 44.05 N 21.33 E
Despujols 106 12.31 N 122.01 E
Desruisseaux 231f 13.47 N 60.56 W
Dessau 50 51.50 N 12.14 E
Dessel 52 51.14 N 5.07 E
Destacado Island I 106 12.16 N 124.06 E
De Steeg 48 52.02 N 6.04 E
Destek 120 40.51 N 36.12 E
Destelbergen 46 51.03 N 3.48 E
Destêrro 240 7.17 S 37.06 W
Destin 184 30.24 N 86.30 W
D'Estrées, Passe du ⊔ 165f 19.38 S 163.23 E
Destruction, Mount ∧2 152 24.35 S 127.59 E
Destruction Bay 170 61.15 N 138.48 W
Destruction Island I 214 47.40 N 124.30 W
Desvres 46 50.40 N 1.50 E
Deta 38 45.24 N 21.13 E
Detčino 72 54.49 N 36.19 E
Dethlingen 48 52.57 N 10.07 E
Detling 250 51.18 N 0.34 E
Detmold 48 51.56 N 8.52 E
Detmold □6 48 51.48 N 8.00 E
Detour, Point ≻ 180 45.36 N 86.37 W
Detrital Wash ∨ 190 36.02 N 114.28 W
Detroit, Ill., U.S. 209 39.37 N 90.40 W
Detroit, Mich., U.S. 206
271 42.20 N 83.03 W
Detroit, Tex., U.S. 186 33.40 N 95.16 W
Detroit ≃ 204 42.06 N 83.08 W
Detroit, University of ⩔2 271 42.25 N 83.08 W
Detroit Beach 206 41.55 N 83.20 W
Detroit City Airport ⊠ 271 42.25 N 83.01 W
Detroit Institute of Arts ⩔ 271 42.22 N 83.04 W
Detroit Lake @1 192 44.42 N 122.10 W
Detroit Lakes 188 46.49 N 95.51 W
Detroit Metropolitan-Wayne County Airport ⊠ 271 42.13 N 83.22 W
Detroit Race Course ♦ 271 42.23 N 83.19 W
Detroit-Windsor Tunnel -•5 271 42.20 N 83.02 W
Detroit Zoological Park ♦ 271 42.29 N 83.09 W
Detskosel'skij 255a 59.44 N 30.28 E
Dett 144 18.38 S 26.50 E
Dettelbach 52 49.48 N 10.09 E
Dettifoss ⌊ 24a 65.50 N 16.20 W
Dettingen an der Erms 52 48.32 N 9.20 E
Dettwiller 52 48.45 N 7.28 E
Det Udom 100 14.54 N 105.05 E
Detva 30 48.31 N 19.28 E
Deuben 50 51.06 N 12.04 E
Deuels Corners 274a 42.45 N 78.45 W
Deuil-la-Barre 251 48.59 N 2.20 E
Deūlgaon Rāja 112 20.01 N 76.02 E
Deulpur 262b 22.36 N 88.10 E
Deulti 116 22.26 N 87.56 E
Deurne, Bel. 46 51.13 N 4.28 E
Deurne, Ned. 48 51.28 N 5.47 E
Deusen -•8 253 51.33 N 7.26 E
Deutsche Bucht C 30 54.30 N 7.30 E
Deutsche Demokratische Republik → German Democratic Republic □1 30 52.00 N 12.30 E
Deutsch Eylau → Iława 30 53.37 N 19.33 E
Deutsch Krone → Wałcz 30 53.17 N 16.28 E
Deutschlandsberg 30 46.49 N 15.13 E
Deutsch-Luxemburger-Naturpark ♦ 52 49.55 N 6.15 E
Deutsch-Neudorf 50 50.38 N 13.27 E
Deutsch Wagram 254b 48.18 N 16.34 E
Deutsch Wusterhausen 254a 52.18 N 13.35 E
Deutzen 50 51.06 N 12.26 E
Deux-Montagnes 196 45.32 N 73.53 W
Deux-Montagnes □6 196 45.35 N 74.05 W
Deux-Montagnes, Lac des @ 265a 45.28 N 73.59 W
Deux-Sèvres □5 32 46.30 N 0.20 W
Deva 38 45.53 N 22.55 E
Devakottai 112 9.57 N 78.49 E
De Valls Bluff 184 34.47 N 91.28 W
Devaprayāg 114 30.09 N 78.37 E
Dev'atern'a 70 56.12 N 53.24 E
Dev'atiny 24 60.56 N 36.46 E
Devault 275 40.05 N 75.32 W
Dévaványa 30 47.02 N 20.58 E
Devecikonağı 120 39.55 N 28.34 E
Devecser 30 47.06 N 17.26 E
Deve Dağı ∧ 120 40.34 N 41.21 E
Develi 120 38.23 N 35.30 E
Deventer 48 52.15 N 6.10 E
Devers 212 30.02 N 94.36 W
Devers Canal, West Branch ⩨ 212 29.57 N 94.46 W
Deversoir Military Base ■ 132 30.25 N 32.20 E
Devès, Monts du ⩕ 32 45.00 N 3.45 E
Devět Skal ∧ 30 49.40 N 16.02 E
Devgad Bāria 110 22.42 N 73.54 E
De View, Bayou ≃ 184 34.48 N 91.18 W
Devīkot 110 26.42 N 71.12 E
Devil Lake @ 202 44.35 N 76.27 W
Deville 52 49.53 N 4.42 E
Déville-lès-Rouen 46 49.28 N 1.02 E
Devil Peak ∧ 216 37.32 N 119.44 W
Devil River Peak ∧ 162 40.58 S 172.39 E
Devils ≃ 186 29.39 N 100.58 W
Devils Brook ≃ 266 40.20 N 74.37 W
Devils Canyon ∨ 270 34.16 N 117.58 W
Devil's Den State Park ♦ 184 35.46 N 94.16 W
Devils Hole Rapids ⌊ 274a 43.08 N 79.03 W
Devil's Hopyard State Park ♦ 197 41.28 N 72.22 W
Devil's Island → Diable, Île du I 240 5.17 N 52.35 W
Devils Lake 188 48.07 N 98.59 W
Devils Lake @, Mich., U.S. 206 41.58 N 84.17 W
Devils Lake @, N. Dak., U.S. 188 48.01 N 98.52 W
Devil's Lake State Park ♦ 180 43.24 N 89.44 W
Devils Paw ∧ 170 58.44 N 133.50 W
Devils Postpile National Monument ♦ 216 37.37 N 119.05 W
Devils Tower National Monument ♦ 188 44.31 N 104.57 W
Devil's Water ≃ 42 54.58 N 2.02 W
Devin 38 41.45 N 24.24 E
Devine, B.C., Can. 172 50.32 N 122.30 W
Devine, Tex., U.S. 186 29.08 N 98.54 W
Devizes 44 51.22 N 1.59 W
Devladovo 68 48.07 N 33.45 E
De Voe Lake @ 266 40.23 N 74.23 W
Devoll ≃ 38 40.49 N 19.51 E
Dévoluy ⩕ 56 44.39 N 5.53 E
Devon, Alta., Can. 172 53.22 N 113.44 W
Devon, S. Afr. 148 26.21 S 28.48 E
Devon, Pa., U.S. 275 40.03 N 75.25 W
Devon □6 44 50.45 N 3.50 W
Devon ≃ 44 53.04 N 0.43 W
Devon Island I 16 75.00 N 87.00 W
Devonport, Austl. 156 41.11 S 146.21 E
Devonport, N.Z. 162 36.49 S 174.48 E
Devonport, Eng., U.K. 44 50.22 N 4.10 W
Devonshire Plaza -•9 271 42.17 N 83.00 W
Devore 218 34.13 N 117.25 W
Devoto 242 31.24 S 62.19 W
Devrek 120 41.13 N 31.57 E
Devrekâni 120 41.36 N 33.51 E
Devres ≃ 120 41.06 N 34.25 E
Devure ≃ 144 19.50 S 31.45 E
Dewa, Ujung ≻ 104 2.55 N 95.48 E
Dewakang-lompo, Pulau I 102 5.24 S 118.25 E
Dewa-kyūryō ⩕2 82 39.05 N 140.10 E
Dewart 200 41.07 N 76.53 W
Dewart Lake @ 206 41.22 N 85.47 W
Dewās 110 22.58 N 76.04 E
Dewas □5 114 22.30 N 76.30 E
Dewdney 172 49.10 N 122.12 W
Dewetsdorp 148 29.33 S 26.34 E
Dewey, P.R. 230m 18.18 N 65.18 W
Dewey, Ill., U.S. 206 40.19 N 88.17 W
Dewey, Okla., U.S. 186 36.48 N 95.56 W
Dewey, Wash., U.S. 214 48.25 N 122.37 W
Dewey Beach 198 38.42 N 75.05 W
Deweyville 184 30.18 N 93.45 W
De Witt, Ark., U.S. 184 34.18 N 91.20 W
Dewitt, Ill., U.S. 209 40.11 N 88.47 W
De Witt, Iowa, U.S. 180 41.49 N 90.33 W
De Witt, Mich., U.S. 206 42.51 N 84.34 W
De Witt, Nebr., U.S. 188 40.24 N 96.55 W
De Witt, N.Y., U.S. 200 43.02 N 76.04 W
De Witt □6, Ill., U.S. 206 40.12 N 88.55 W
De Witt □6, Tex., U.S. 212 29.07 N 97.20 W
Dewittville 204 42.14 N 79.27 W
Dewsbury 42 53.42 N 1.37 W
Dexing 90 28.54 N 117.36 E
Dexingjie 88 39.54 N 122.50 E
Dexter, Maine, U.S. 178 45.01 N 69.18 W
Dexter, Mich., U.S. 206 42.20 N 83.53 W
Dexter, Mo., U.S. 184 36.48 N 89.57 W
Dexter, N. Mex., U.S. 186 33.12 N 104.22 W
Dexter, N.Y., U.S. 202 44.01 N 76.03 W
Dexterity Fiord C2 166 71.11 N 73.03 W
Deyang 92 31.14 N 104.22 E
Dey-Dey, Lake @ 152 29.12 S 131.04 E
Deyhūk 118 33.17 N 57.30 E
Deyyer 118 27.50 N 51.55 E
Dez ≃ 118 31.39 N 48.52 E
Dezadeash Lake @ 170 60.28 N 136.58 W
Dezfūl 118 32.23 N 48.24 E
Dez Gerd 118 30.45 N 51.57 E
Dezhou 88 37.27 N 116.18 E
Dezh Shāhpūr 118 35.31 N 46.10 E
Dežneva, Mys ≻ 170 66.06 N 169.45 W
Dezong 110 32.09 N 90.20 E
Dezzo di Scalve 58 45.59 N 10.05 E
Dhabān Singh 113 31.45 N 73.35 E
Dhāding 114 27.52 N 84.55 E
Dhādkā 116 22.47 N 86.30 E
Dháfna ∧ 257c 38.07 N 23.38 E
Dháfni 38 37.48 N 22.01 E
Dhafníon, Moní ⩔1 257c 38.01 N 23.38 E
Dhahab 130 28.29 N 34.32 E
Dhahran → Aẓ-Ẓahrān 118 26.18 N 50.08 E
Dhāka 114 26.41 N 85.10 E
Dhākauli 114 24.45 N 77.51 E
Dhakuria Lake @ 262b 22.31 N 88.22 E
Dhaleswari ≃ 116 23.32 N 90.34 E
Dháli 120 35.01 N 33.25 E
Dhamār 134 14.46 N 44.23 E
Dhampur 114 29.19 N 78.31 E
Dhāmrai 116 23.55 N 90.13 E
Dhamtari 112 20.41 N 81.34 E
Dhāmura 116 22.53 N 90.12 E
Dhanaula 113 30.17 N 75.35 E
Dhanaura 114 28.58 N 78.15 E
Dhānbād 116 23.48 N 86.27 E
Dhānbād □5 114 23.47 N 86.26 E
Dhandhuka 110 22.22 N 71.59 E
Dhanera 116 23.25 N 86.39 E
Dhaneswargāti 116 23.25 N 89.20 E
Dhangarhi 114 28.41 N 80.36 E
Dhaniakhāli 116 22.58 N 88.06 E
D'hanis 186 29.20 N 99.17 W
Dhankuta 114 26.59 N 87.20 E
Dhansar 262c 19.07 N 73.05 E
Dhanushkodi 112 9.11 N 79.24 E
Dhānyahānā 262b 22.48 N 88.11 E
Dhār 110 22.36 N 75.18 E
Dharampur 112 20.32 N 73.11 E
Dharān Bāzār 114 26.49 N 87.17 E
Dharangaon 110 21.01 N 75.16 E
Dhārāpuram 112 10.44 N 77.31 E
Dhāri 110 21.20 N 71.01 E
Dhārīwāl 113 31.57 N 75.19 E
Dharmābād 112 18.54 N 77.51 E
Dharmapuri 112 12.08 N 78.10 E
Dharmavaram 112 14.26 N 77.43 E
Dharmjaygarh 114 22.28 N 83.13 E
Dharmkot 113 30.57 N 75.14 E
Dharmsāla 113 32.13 N 76.19 E
Dhārni 110 21.33 N 76.53 E
Dhārwār 112 15.28 N 75.01 E
Dhasān ≃ 114 25.48 N 79.24 E
Dhātrigrām 116 23.15 N 88.20 E
Dhaulāgiri ∧ 114 28.42 N 83.30 E
Dhebar Lake @ 110 24.16 N 74.00 E
Dhelfoí ⊥ 38 38.30 N 22.29 E
Dhenkānāl 110 20.40 N 85.36 E
Dherínia 120 35.03 N 33.57 E
Dhërmiu ⩔1 38 40.08 N 19.42 E
Dheskáti 38 39.55 N 21.49 E
Dheune ≃ 54 46.54 N 5.00 E
Dhiavolítsion 38 37.18 N 21.58 E
Dhībān 122 31.30 N 35.47 E
Dhidhimótikhon 38 41.21 N 26.30 E
Dhíkti ⩕ 38 35.08 N 25.22 E
Dhílos ⊥ 38 37.26 N 25.16 E
Dhimitsána 38 37.37 N 22.03 E
Dhiónisos 257c 38.06 N 23.53 E
Dhirāsrām 116 23.57 N 90.25 E
Dhirwah, Wādī adh- ∨ 122 31.18 N 36.56 E
Dhodhekánisos (Dodecanese) II 38 36.30 N 27.00 E
Dhodhóni ⊥ 38 39.34 N 20.47 E
Dhokra 262b 22.40 N 88.34 E
Dholka 110 22.43 N 72.28 E
Dholpur 114 26.42 N 77.54 E
Dhone 112 15.25 N 77.53 E
Dhopākholai 116 23.08 N 89.10 E
Dhorāji 110 21.44 N 70.27 E
Dhosha 116 22.15 N 88.33 E
Dhowa 116 24.03 N 86.54 E
Dhoxáton 38 41.05 N 24.14 E
Dhrāngadhra 110 22.59 N 71.28 E
Dhrapetsóna 257c 37.57 N 23.37 E
Dhrol 110 22.34 N 70.25 E
Dhron ≃ 52 49.52 N 6.54 E
Dhubāb 134 12.56 N 43.25 E
Dhubri 114 26.02 N 89.58 E
Dhudiāl 113 33.04 N 72.58 E
Dhulāgarh 262b 22.35 N 88.11 E
Dhulāsār 116 21.52 N 90.14 E
Dhule 110 20.54 N 74.47 E
Dhulia → Dhule 110 20.54 N 74.47 E
Dhuliān 114 24.41 N 87.58 E
Dhulikhel 114 27.37 N 85.33 E
Dhūlsīrās -•8 262a 28.33 N 77.02 E
Dhünn 52 51.06 N 7.16 E
Dhünn-Stausee @1 253 51.05 N 7.16 E
Dhupgāri 114 26.36 N 89.01 E
Dhūri 114 30.22 N 75.52 E
Dhutumkhar ≃ 262c 18.54 N 73.00 E
Diabakania 140 10.38 N 10.58 W
Diable, Île du (Devil's Island) I 240 5.17 N 52.35 W
Diable, Lac du @ 196 46.31 N 74.20 W
Diable, Morne au ∧ 230d 15.37 N 61.27 W
Diable, Pointe du ≻ 230e 14.47 N 60.54 W
Diable, Rivière du ≃ 196 46.03 N 74.38 W
Diablo, Calif., U.S. 216 37.50 N 121.58 W
Diablo, Wash., U.S. 214 48.43 N 121.09 W
Diablo, Canyon ∨ 190 35.18 N 110.59 W
Diablo, Isla del → Diable, Île du I 240 5.17 N 52.35 W
Diablo, Mount ∧ 216 37.53 N 121.55 W
Diablo, Sierra del ⩕ 186 27.20 N 104.05 W
Diablo Lake @1 214 48.43 N 121.08 W
Diablo Plateau ⩕1 190 31.30 N 105.30 W
Diablo Range ⩕ 216 37.00 N 121.20 W
Diablotin, Morne ∧ 230d 15.30 N 61.24 W
Diabo 140 7.47 N 5.11 W
Diaca 144 11.30 S 39.59 E
Diadema 246 23.42 S 46.37 W
Diadema □7 277b 23.42 S 46.36 W
Diadema Argentina 244 45.46 S 67.40 W
Diafarabé 140 14.09 N 5.01 W
Diagonal 188 40.48 N 94.20 W
Diaka ≃1 140 15.13 N 4.14 W
Dialakoto 140 13.19 N 13.18 W
Dialassagou 140 13.45 N 3.37 W
Diamant, Pointe du ≻ 230e 14.27 N 61.03 W
Diamante 242 32.04 S 60.39 W
Diamante ≃ 242 34.31 S 66.56 W
Diamante, Punta del ≻ 224 16.47 N 99.52 W
Diamante de Ubá 246 21.12 S 42.55 W
Diamantina 245 18.15 S 43.36 W
Diamantina ≃ 156 26.45 S 139.10 E
Diamantina, Chapada ⩕1, Bra. 240 11.30 S 41.10 W
Diamantina, Chapada ⩕1, Bra. 245 13.00 S 41.50 W
Diamantina Lakes 156 23.46 S 141.09 E
Diamantina Trough ⩪1 14 37.00 S 105.00 E
Diamantino 238 14.25 S 56.27 W
Diamond, Ill., U.S. 206 41.17 N 88.15 W
Diamond, Mo., U.S. 184 37.00 N 94.19 W
Diamond, Ohio, U.S. 204 41.06 N 81.01 W
Diamond Bar 218 33.58 N 117.51 W
Diamond Brook ≃ 266 40.56 N 74.08 W
Diamond Creek 264b 37.41 S 145.09 E
Diamond Creek ≃ 159 37.44 S 145.09 E
Diamond Harbour 116 22.12 N 88.12 E
Diamond Head ⊥6 219c 21.16 N 157.49 W
Diamond Hill 197 41.59 N 71.25 W
Diamond Hill Reservoir @1 273 42.00 N 71.24 W
Diamond Hill State Park ♦ 273 42.00 N 71.26 W
Diamond Islets II 156 17.25 S 150.58 E
Diamond Lake 206 42.15 N 88.00 W
Diamond Lake @, Ont., Can. 202 45.04 N 78.13 W
Diamond Lake @, Ill., U.S. 268 42.15 N 88.00 W
Diamond Lake @, Mich., U.S. 206 41.54 N 85.59 W
Diamond Lake @, Oreg., U.S. 192 43.10 N 122.09 W
Diamond Peak ∧, Idaho, U.S. 192 44.09 N 113.05 W
Diamond Peak ∧, Oreg., U.S. 192 43.33 N 122.09 W
Diamond Peak ∧, Wash., U.S. 192 46.07 N 117.32 W
Diamond Springs 216 38.42 N 120.49 W
Diamondville 190 41.47 N 110.32 W
Diamounguel 140 15.06 N 12.55 W
Diana 212 32.43 N 94.45 W
Diana, Baie C 166 60.50 N 69.50 W
Dianalund 41 55.32 N 11.30 E
Dianbai (Shuidong) 92 21.33 N 111.16 E
Dianchi @ 92 24.50 N 102.42 E
Diancun 95 39.55 N 116.14 E
Dianfangba 92 32.54 N 103.35 E
Diangounté Kamara 140 14.33 N 9.31 W
Dianhu 90 33.58 N 119.38 E
Dianji 88 36.32 N 120.27 E
Dianjiang 92 30.21 N 107.23 E
Diano Marina 56 43.54 N 8.05 E
Dianópolis 240 11.38 S 46.50 W
Dianqianhe 90 30.44 N 116.02 E
Dianra 140 8.45 N 6.14 W
Dianshang 96 31.10 N 118.51 E
Dianshanhu @ 96 31.08 N 120.55 E
Diantou 90 27.18 N 120.11 E
Dianxia 90 27.58 N 115.40 E
Dianzi 94 41.37 N 122.05 E
Diaobingshan 94 42.28 N 123.33 E
Diaoebao 95 40.43 N 115.49 E
Diaohetou 95 39.17 N 116.41 E
Diaojiapu 90 32.22 N 119.54 E
Diaoshuilouzi 94 40.59 N 122.22 E
Diaotai 90 29.40 N 119.39 E
Diaouala 140 10.07 N 5.28 W
Diaowo 95 39.30 N 116.04 E
Diapaga 140 12.04 N 1.47 E
Diapangou 140 12.07 N 0.11 E
Dias 246 22.28 S 45.34 W
Diascund Creek Reservoir @1 198 37.27 N 76.54 W
Diavolo, Mount ∧ 100 12.42 N 92.55 E
Dibai 114 28.13 N 78.15 E
Dibāng ≃ 110 27.50 N 95.32 E
Dibay → Dubayy 118 25.18 N 55.18 E
Dibaya 142 6.30 S 22.57 E
Dibbersen 48 53.22 N 9.52 E
Dibbīn 122 32.26 N 36.34 E
Dibble Iceberg Tongue ⩓ 9 65.40 S 135.10 E
Dibeng 148 27.35 S 22.54 E
D'Iberville 184 30.26 N 88.54 W
Dibete 146 23.45 S 26.26 E
Dibi 134 4.12 N 41.58 E
Dibo 134 6.31 N 41.52 E
Diboll 212 31.11 N 94.47 W
Dibrugarh 110 27.29 N 94.54 E
Dibs 130 12.34 N 24.14 E
Dibs, Bi'r ⩒4 130 22.12 N 29.32 E
Dichāon Kalān -•8 262a 28.39 N 76.59 E
Dickelsbach ≃ 253 51.24 N 6.45 E
Dickens 186 33.37 N 100.50 W
Dickerson 198 39.13 N 77.25 W
Dickey, Lake @ 214 48.06 N 124.31 W
Dickey, West Fork ≃ 214 47.55 N 124.42 W
Dickey Lake @ 202 44.47 N 77.44 W
Dickinson, N. Dak., U.S. 188 46.53 N 102.47 W
Dickinson, Pa., U.S. 198 40.07 N 77.20 W
Dickinson, Tex., U.S. 212 29.28 N 95.03 W
Dickinson Bayou ≃ 212 29.28 N 94.58 W
Dickinson Island I 271 42.37 N 82.38 W
Dicks 148 27.43 S 30.10 E
Dickson 184 36.05 N 87.23 W
Dickson City 200 41.27 N 75.37 W
Dicle → Tigris ≃ 118 31.00 N 47.25 E
Dicomano 60 43.53 N 11.31 E
Diculom 106 7.54 N 122.14 E
Dicun 90 33.46 N 117.32 E
Didam 48 51.56 N 6.08 E
Didao 79 45.22 N 130.51 E
Didbiran 79 51.58 N 139.20 E
Didcot 44 51.37 N 1.15 W
Didesa ≃ 134 9.56 N 35.45 E
Didiéni 140 13.53 N 8.06 W
Didimbo 142 17.30 S 21.45 E
Didinga Hills ⩕ 144 4.20 N 33.35 E
Didsbury 172 51.40 N 114.08 W
Didsbury -•8 252 53.25 N 2.14 W
Dīdwāna 110 27.24 N 74.34 E
Didy 147b 18.07 S 48.32 E
Didyma ⊥ 120 37.25 N 27.15 E
Die 56 44.45 N 5.22 E
Die Aue -•1 253 51.40 N 6.35 E
Die Berg ∧ 146 25.12 S 30.09 E
Die Boss 148 31.59 S 19.44 E
Diébougou 140 10.58 N 3.15 W
Dieburg 52 49.54 N 8.50 E
Dieciocho de Julio 242 33.41 S 53.33 W
Dieciocho de Marzo 222 25.38 N 97.50 W
Diecke 140 7.21 N 8.58 W
Diedenhofen → Thionville 52 49.22 N 6.10 E
Diedersdorf 254a 52.20 N 13.21 E
Die Erpe ≃ 254a 52.27 N 13.38 E
Diefenbaker, Lake @1 174 51.00 N 106.55 W
Diego de Almagro, Isla I 244 51.25 S 75.10 W
Diego de Ocampo, Pico ∧ 228 19.35 N 70.45 W
Diego Garcia I 12 7.20 S 72.25 E
Diego Gaynor 248 34.17 S 59.14 W
Diego Ramírez, Islas II 234 56.30 S 68.44 W
Diégo-Suarez 147b 12.16 S 49.17 E
Diégo-Suarez □4 147b 13.30 S 49.10 E
Die Haard -•1 253 51.41 N 7.15 E
Diekirch 52 49.53 N 6.10 E
Dieksee @ 50 54.10 N 10.30 E
Dieleemu 76 46.22 N 88.43 E
Dielingen 48 52.26 N 8.20 E
Dielsdorf 54 47.29 N 8.27 E
Diéma 140 14.32 N 9.12 W
Diemansputs 148 29.54 S 21.33 E
Diembéring 140 12.28 N 16.47 W
Diemel ≃ 48 51.39 N 9.27 E
Diemelsee, Naturpark ♦ 52 51.20 N 8.45 E
Diemel-Talsperre -•6 52 51.22 N 8.43 E
Diemen 48 52.20 N 4.58 E
Diemuchuoke 110 32.42 N 79.29 E
Dien-bien-phu 100 21.23 N 103.01 E
Diepenau 48 52.25 N 8.44 E
Diepenheim 48 52.12 N 6.33 E
Diepensee 254a 52.22 N 13.31 E
Diepenveen 48 52.18 N 6.08 E
Diepholz 48 52.35 N 8.21 E
Diepoldsau 54 47.23 N 9.38 E
Dieppe, N.B., Can. 176 46.06 N 64.45 W
Dieppe, Fr. 46 49.56 N 1.05 E
Dierbao 88 40.20 N 114.32 E
Dierdorf 52 50.33 N 7.39 E
Dieren 48 52.03 N 6.06 E
Dierhagen 50 45.18 N 12.21 E
Dieringhausen 52 50.59 N 7.31 E
Dierks 184 34.07 N 94.01 W
Diersfordt 253 51.42 N 6.33 E
Diesdorf 50 52.45 N 10.52 E
Dieskau 50 51.26 N 12.02 E
Diessem -•8 253 51.20 N 6.35 E
Diessen 58 47.56 N 11.06 E
Diessenhofen 54 47.41 N 8.45 E
Diest 52 50.59 N 5.03 E
Dietenheim 54 48.12 N 10.04 E
Dietersdorf 52 50.13 N 10.49 E
Dietfurt 52 48.57 N 10.56 E
Dietikon 54 47.24 N 8.24 E
Dietkorom 136 13.41 N 12.03 E
Dietmannsried 54 47.49 N 10.17 E
Dietrich 192 42.55 N 114.16 W
Dietzenbach 52 50.01 N 8.47 E
Dieulefit 56 44.31 N 5.04 E
Dieulouard 52 48.51 N 6.04 E
Dieu-sur-Meuse 52 49.04 N 5.25 E
Dieuze 52 48.49 N 6.43 E
Dieveniškės 66 54.12 N 25.37 E
Dievenow → Dziwnów 30 54.03 N 14.45 E
Diever 48 52.52 N 6.19 E
Die Ville ⩕2 52 50.40 N 6.55 E
Diez 52 50.22 N 8.01 E
Dif 134 1.00 N 41.00 E
Difang 88 35.23 N 117.52 E
Diffa 136 13.19 N 12.37 E
Diffa □5 136 16.00 N 13.30 E
Differdange 52 49.32 N 5.52 E
Difficult Run ≃ 274c 38.58 N 77.14 W
Diffun 106 16.34 N 121.33 E
Difuri I 112 5.24 N 73.38 E
Dīg 108 27.28 N 77.20 E
Digambarpur 116 21.57 N 88.22 E
Digba 144 4.24 N 25.47 E
Digboi 110 27.23 N 95.38 E
Digby Neck ≻1 176 44.30 N 66.10 W
Dige 88 34.22 N 114.28 E
Digerberget ∧2 40 60.35 N 13.25 E
Digges Islands II 166 62.35 N 77.50 W
Diggle 252 53.34 N 1.59 W
Dīghalia 116 23.07 N 89.39 E
Dighipāra 116 21.58 N 88.17 E
Dighode 262c 18.54 N 73.02 E
Dighra 262b 22.47 N 88.32 E
Dighton, Kans., U.S. 188 38.29 N 100.28 W
Dighton, Mass., U.S. 197 41.49 N 71.07 W
Di Giorgio 218 35.15 N 118.51 W
Dīglūr 112 18.33 N 77.36 E
Digmoor 252 53.32 N 2.45 W
Dīgnagar 116 23.27 N 87.41 E
Dignano 58 46.05 N 12.56 E
Digne 56 44.06 N 6.14 E
Digoin 32 46.29 N 3.59 E
Digomi 74 41.47 N 44.44 E
Digong 94 42.11 N 122.03 E
Digor 74 40.23 N 43.24 E
Digora 74 43.10 N 44.09 E
Digos 106 6.45 N 125.20 E
Digra 262b 22.50 N 88.20 E
Digras 112 20.07 N 77.43 E
Digri 110 25.10 N 69.07 E
Digul ≃ 154 7.07 S 138.42 E
Dih 120 37.46 N 42.11 E
Dihaer 76 42.35 N 89.49 E
Dih Dahot ≃ 134 10.40 N 49.25 E
Dihun 134 7.18 N 42.42 E
Diirmentobe 76 45.44 N 63.37 E
Dijag 24 65.48 N 57.39 E
Dijlah → Tigris ≃ 118 31.00 N 47.25 E
Dijlah, Wādī ∨ 132 29.58 N 31.18 E
Dijle (Dyle) ≃ 52 50.53 N 4.42 E
Dijle Kanaal ⩨ 52 50.53 N 4.42 E
Dijohan Point ≻ 106 16.19 N 122.14 E
Dijon 54 47.19 N 5.01 E
Dik 136 9.58 N 17.31 E
Dikaja 66 59.15 N 39.30 E
Dikala 144 4.41 N 31.23 E
Dikan'ka 68 49.49 N 34.32 E
Dikbıyık 120 41.13 N 36.38 E
Dike 180 42.28 N 92.38 W
Dikhil 134 11.06 N 42.22 E
Dikili 120 39.04 N 26.53 E
Dikirnis 132 31.05 N 31.35 E
Dikli 66 57.35 N 25.06 E
Diklosmta, Gora ∧ 74 42.29 N 45.47 E
Dikmen 120 39.53 N 32.50 E
Dikodougou 140 9.04 N 5.46 W
Dikomu Di Kai ∧ 146 24.58 S 24.31 E
Diksmuide (Dixmude) 46 51.02 N 2.52 E
Dikson 64 73.30 N 80.35 E
Dikumbiya 134 14.42 N 37.30 E
Dikwa 136 12.02 N 13.56 E
Dila 134 6.21 N 38.17 E
Ḍil' al-'Ifrīt ∧2 132 28.23 N 31.09 E
Dilbeek 46 50.51 N 4.16 E
Dile Point ≻ 106 17.34 N 120.20 E
Dilerpur 262b 22.51 N 88.10 E
Dili 102 8.33 S 125.35 E
Diligent Strait ⊔ 100 12.11 N 92.57 E
Di-linh 100 11.35 N 108.04 E
Diližan 74 40.45 N 44.52 E
Diližanskij Zapovednik ♦ 74 40.40 N 45.00 E
Dill ≃ 52 50.33 N 8.29 E
Dill City 186 35.17 N 99.08 W
Dillenburg 52 50.44 N 8.17 E
Diller 188 40.07 N 96.56 W
Dilley, Oreg., U.S. 214 45.29 N 123.07 W
Dilley, Tex., U.S. 186 28.40 N 99.10 W
Dillia ∨ 136 16.53 N 11.00 E
Dillia Téfidinga 136 15.16 N 12.06 E
Dilling 130 12.03 N 29.39 E
Dillingen 52 49.21 N 6.44 E
Dillingen an der Donau 52 48.34 N 10.29 E
Dillingham 170 59.02 N 158.29 W
Dillon, Colo., U.S. 190 39.37 N 106.04 W
Dillon, Mont., U.S. 192 45.13 N 112.38 W
Dillon, S.C., U.S. 182 34.25 N 79.22 W
Dillon ≃ 174 55.56 N 108.57 W
Dillon Bay C 165f 18.48 S 168.58 E
Dillon Cone ∧ 162 42.16 S 173.13 E
Dillon Lake @ 174 55.45 N 109.30 W
Dillon Lake @1 178 40.02 N 82.10 W
Dillon Reservoir @1 190 39.35 N 106.02 W
Dillon State Park ♦ 178 40.03 N 82.08 W
Dillonvale 204 40.12 N 80.47 W
Dillsboro 208 39.01 N 85.04 W
Dillsburg 198 40.07 N 77.02 W
Dilltown 204 40.29 N 79.00 W
Dillwyn 182 37.32 N 78.27 W
Dilly 140 15.01 N 7.40 W
Dilolo 142 10.42 S 22.20 E
Dilworth 188 46.53 N 96.42 W
Dilworthtown 275 39.54 N 75.34 W
Dima, Ang. 142 15.27 S 20.10 E
Dima, Yai. 134 6.16 N 36.22 E
Dimāpur 110 25.54 N 93.44 E
Dimaro 58 46.20 N 10.52 E

Symbols in the index entries represent the broad categories identified in the key at the right. Symbols with superior numbers (⩕2) identify subcategories (see complete key on page *I* · 26).

Kartensymbole in dem Registerverzeichnis stellen die rechts in Schlüssel erklärten Kategorien dar. Symbole mit hochgestellten Ziffern (⩕2) bezeichnen Unterabteilungen einer Kategorie (vgl. vollständiger Schlüssel auf Seite *I* · 26).

Los símbolos incluídos en el texto del índice representan las grandes categorías identificadas con la clave a la derecha. Los símbolos con numeros en su parte superior (⩕2) identifican las subcategorías (véase la clave completa en la página *I* · 26).

Les symboles de l'index représentent les catégories indiquées dans la légende à droite. Les symboles suivis d'un indice (⩕2) représentent des sous-catégories (voir légende complète à la page *I* · 26).

Os símbolos incluídos no texto do índice representam as grandes categorias identificadas com a chave à direita. Os símbolos com números em sua parte superior (⩕2) identificam as subcategorias (veja-se a chave completa à página *I* · 26).

∧	Mountain	Berg	Montaña	Montagne	Montanha
⩕	Mountains	Berge	Montañas	Montagnes	Montanhas
)(	Pass	Pass	Paso	Col	Passo
∨	Valley, Canyon	Tal, Cañon	Valle, Cañón	Vallée, Canyon	Vale, Canhão
≚	Plain	Ebene	Llano	Plaine	Planície
≻	Cape	Kap	Cabo	Cap	Cabo
I	Island	Insel	Isla	Île	Ilha
II	Islands	Inseln	Islas	Îles	Ilhas
⊥	Other Topographic Features	Andere Topographische Objekte	Otros Elementos Topográficos	Autres données topographiques	Outros Elementos Topográficos

ESPAÑOL

Nombre	Página	Lat.°′	Long.°′ W=Oeste
Dimasalang	106	12.12 N	123.51 E
Dimashq (Damascus)	122	33.30 N	36.18 E
Dimashq ☐[8]	120	34.00 N	36.45 E
Dimasse, Rass ≻	36	35.37 N	11.03 E
Dimataling	106	7.32 N	123.22 E
Dimbelenge	142	5.33 S	23.07 E
Dimbokro	140	6.39 N	4.42 W
Dimbokro ☐[5]	140	6.45 N	4.15 W
Dimboola	156	36.27 S	142.02 E
Dimbou	142	1.29 S	11.52 E
Dîmbovița ☐[4]	38	45.00 N	25.30 E
Dîmbovița ≃	38	44.14 N	26.27 E
Dimbulah	156	17.09 S	145.07 E
Dime Box	212	30.21 N	96.50 W
Dimetoka	120	40.16 N	27.17 E
Dimitrov	73	48.15 N	37.18 E
Dimitrovgrad, Blg.	38	42.03 N	25.36 E
Dimitrovgrad, Jugo.	38	43.01 N	22.47 E
Dimitrovgrad, S.S.S.R.	24	54.14 N	49.39 E
Dimitrovo → Pernik	38	42.36 N	23.02 W
Dimitrovskoje	75	40.16 N	69.03 E
Dimlang ∧	136	8.24 N	11.47 E
Dimmitt	186	34.33 N	102.19 W
Dimo	144	5.19 N	29.10 E
Dimock	200	41.45 N	75.32 W
Dimona	122	31.04 N	35.02 E
Dimondale	206	42.39 N	84.39 W
Dinach	134	9.12 N	50.40 E
Dinagat	106	9.59 N	125.35 E
Dinagat Island I	106	10.12 N	125.35 E
Dinagat Sound Џ	106	9.59 N	125.50 E
Dinahican Point ≻	106	14.42 N	121.44 E
Dinājpur	114	25.38 N	88.38 E
Dinalupihan	106	14.52 N	120.28 E
Dinamarca → Denmark ☐[1]	26	56.00 N	10.00 E
Dinamarca, Estrecho de → Denmark Strait Џ	10	67.00 N	25.00 W
Dinamita	186	25.43 N	103.38 W
Dinamo	70	50.15 N	41.38 E
Dinamo, Stadion ♠	255b	55.48 N	37.34 E
Dinan	32	48.27 N	2.02 W
Dīnānagar	113	32.09 N	75.28 E
Dinant	52	50.16 N	4.55 E
Dinar	120	38.04 N	30.10 E
Dinara ⋀	36	43.50 N	16.35 E
Dinard	32	48.38 N	2.04 W
Dinaric Alps → Dinara ⋀	36	43.50 N	16.35 E
Dinarische Alpen → Dinara ⋀	36	43.50 N	16.35 E
Dinas, Pil.	106	7.38 N	123.20 E
Dinas, Wales, U.K.	44	52.00 N	4.54 W
Dinas Head ≻	44	52.02 N	4.55 W
Dinas Powis	44	51.26 N	3.14 W
Dindanko	140	14.08 N	9.30 W
Dindar, Nahr ad- (Dinder) ≃	130	14.06 N	33.40 E
Dindar National Park ♠	130	12.40 N	35.20 E
Dīndārpur ⊸[8]	262a	28.36 N	76.59 E
Dinde	142	14.12 S	13.44 E
Dinder (Nahr ad-Dindar) ≃	130	14.06 N	33.40 E
Dindi ≃	112	16.21 N	79.13 E
Dindigul	112	10.21 N	77.57 E
Dindima	140	10.18 N	10.12 E
Dindori	114	22.57 N	81.05 E
Dineksaray	120	37.23 N	32.37 E
Dinga, Pāk.	110	25.26 N	67.10 E
Dinga, Pāk.	113	32.38 N	73.43 E
Dinga, Zaïre	142	5.19 S	16.34 E
Dingalan Bay C	106	15.18 N	121.25 E
Dingan	100	19.44 N	110.21 E
Dingba	144	3.24 N	27.55 E
Dingbian	92	37.40 N	107.41 E
Dingbianji	92	36.37 N	108.41 E
Dingden	48	51.46 N	6.37 E
Dinge	142	4.58 S	12.22 E
Dingelsdorf	54	47.44 N	9.09 E
Dingelstädt	50	51.18 N	10.19 E
Dingelstedt	50	51.58 N	10.58 E
Dingeryu	95	39.37 N	114.55 E
Dingfeng	96	31.20 N	121.45 E
Dingfou	96	31.18 N	119.10 E
Dinggou	90	32.34 N	119.39 E
Dingila	144	3.39 N	26.22 E
Dingjiaao	97	29.24 N	106.09 E
Dingjiagou	94	40.40 N	122.35 E
Dingjiandian	96	32.06 N	120.52 E
Dingjiasuo	90	32.32 N	120.40 E
Dingjiazhuang	96	32.11 N	120.16 E
Dingjie	114	28.29 N	88.06 E
Dingkouzhen	92	39.55 N	106.40 E
Dingla	114	27.21 N	87.08 E
Dingle	28	52.08 N	10.15 W
Dingle ⊸[8]	252	53.23 N	2.57 W
Dingle Bay C	28	52.05 N	10.15 W
Dingley	264b	37.58 S	145.07 E
Dinglingen	54	48.20 N	7.50 E
Dingman Creek ≃	202	42.55 N	81.25 W
Dingmans Ferry	200	41.14 N	74.53 W
Dingnan	90	24.48 N	114.59 E
Dingnanshui ≃	90	24.28 N	115.26 E
Dingo	156	23.39 S	149.20 E
Dingolfing	30	48.38 N	12.31 E
Dingqing	92	31.32 N	95.27 E
Dingras	106	18.06 N	120.42 E
Dingri	110	28.35 N	86.38 E
Dingshan	96	31.17 N	119.50 E
Dingshanqiao	96	31.21 N	119.23 E
Dingtao	88	35.04 N	115.34 E
Dingtuna	40	59.34 N	16.22 E
Dinguira	140	14.11 N	11.16 W
Dinguiraye	140	11.18 N	10.43 W
Dinguiraye ☐[4]	140	11.30 N	10.55 W
Dingwall, N.S., Can.	176	46.54 N	60.28 W
Dingwall, Scot., U.K.	28	57.35 N	4.29 W
Dingxi	92	35.38 N	104.29 E
Dingxian	88	38.32 N	114.59 E
Dingxiang	92	38.30 N	113.00 E
Dingxiao	92	25.13 N	105.07 E
Dingxing	95	39.17 N	115.46 E
Dingyan	90	32.23 N	120.45 E
Dingyuan	90	32.32 N	117.40 E
Dingzhouying	95	40.20 N	115.43 E
Dingzichang	97	28.54 N	106.08 E
Dingzigang C	88	36.37 N	120.50 E
Dinh, Mui ≻	100	11.22 N	109.01 E
Dīnhāta	114	26.08 N	89.28 E
Dinh-ca	100	21.45 N	106.03 E
Dinh-lap	100	21.33 N	107.06 E
Dinkel ≃	48	52.30 N	6.58 E
Dinkelsbühl	52	49.04 N	10.19 E
Dinkelscherben	54	48.21 N	10.35 E
Dinkey Creek ≃	216	36.54 N	119.07 W
Dinklage	48	52.40 N	8.07 E
Dinnebito Wash ∨	190	35.29 N	111.14 W
Dinner Point ≻	210	28.28 N	82.41 W
Dinnington	42	53.22 N	1.12 W
Dinokwe	146	23.24 S	26.40 E
Dinorwic	174	49.41 N	92.30 W
Dinorwic Lake ◎	174	49.37 N	92.33 W
Dinosaur	190	40.15 N	109.01 W
Dinosaur National Monument ♠	190	40.32 N	108.58 W
Dinosaur Provincial Park ♠	172	50.45 N	111.30 W
Dinskaja	68	45.13 N	39.14 E
Dinslaken	48	51.34 N	6.44 E
Dinslaken ☐[8]	253	51.36 N	6.43 E
Dinslakener Bruch	253	51.35 N	6.43 E
Dinslaken-Schwarze Heide, Flughafen ⊠	253	51.37 N	6.51 E
Dinsmore, Sask., Can.	174	51.20 N	107.26 W
Dinsmore, Fla., U.S.	182	30.26 N	81.46 W
Dinsor	134	2.28 N	43.00 E
Dinteloord	48	51.37 N	4.22 E

FRANÇAIS

Nom	Page	Lat.°′	Long.°′ W=Ouest
Dinuba	216	36.32 N	119.23 W
Dinwiddie	198	37.05 N	77.35 W
Dinwiddie ☐[6]	198	37.10 N	77.20 W
Dinxperlo	48	51.52 N	6.29 E
Diö	26	56.38 N	14.13 E
Diobo	142	2.16 N	20.29 E
Diodār	110	24.06 N	71.47 E
Dioïla	140	12.29 N	6.48 W
Diois ☐[9]	56	44.40 N	5.20 E
Diomede	170	65.47 N	169.00 W
Dion ≃	140	10.12 N	8.39 W
Dionísio	245	19.49 S	42.45 W
Dionísio Cerqueira	242	26.15 S	53.38 W
Dionne, Lac ◎	176	49.26 N	67.55 W
Dions	56	43.56 N	4.19 E
Diorama	245	16.21 S	51.14 W
Dios	165e	5.33 S	154.58 E
Diósd	254c	47.25 N	18.57 E
Diouloulou	140	13.03 N	16.36 W
Dioumanténé	140	10.32 N	5.55 W
Dioundiou	140	12.37 N	3.33 E
Dioungani	140	14.19 N	2.44 W
Dioura	140	14.50 N	5.15 W
Diourbel	140	14.40 N	16.15 W
Diourbel ☐[4]	140	15.30 N	15.30 W
Dipaculao	106	15.51 N	121.32 E
Dipai	90	23.50 N	114.06 E
Dīpālpur	113	30.40 N	73.39 E
Diplo	110	24.28 N	69.35 E
Dipolog	106	8.35 N	123.20 E
Dippoldiswalde	50	50.54 N	13.40 E
Dipton	162	45.54 S	168.22 E
Dipu	96	30.38 N	119.41 E
Diqiyingzi	94	42.11 N	121.29 E
Dique Florentino Ameghino	244	43.40 S	66.25 W
Dīr	113	35.12 N	71.53 E
Dira, Djebel ∧	34	36.05 N	3.38 E
Diré	140	16.16 N	3.24 W
Direction, Cape ≻	154	12.51 S	143.32 E
Dire Dawa	134	9.37 N	41.52 E
Direkli	120	39.43 N	36.40 E
Diriamba	226	11.51 N	86.14 W
Dirico	142	17.58 S	20.47 E
Diriomo	226	11.52 N	86.03 W
Dirk Hartog Island I	152	25.48 S	113.00 E
Dirkiesdorp	148	27.10 S	30.25 E
Dirkiesrus	148	26.20 S	24.44 E
Dirkou	136	19.01 N	12.53 E
Dirkshorn	48	52.45 N	4.45 E
Dirksland	48	51.44 N	4.06 E
Dirrah	130	13.37 N	26.06 E
Dirranbandi	156	28.35 S	148.14 E
Dirri	134	4.22 N	46.38 E
Dirs	134	18.32 N	42.05 E
Dirschau → Tczew	30	54.06 N	18.47 E
Dirty Devil ≃	190	37.53 N	110.24 W
Dīsah	130	12.02 N	34.19 E
Disappointment, Cape ≻, Falk. Is.	234	54.53 S	36.07 W
Disappointment, Cape ≻, Wash., U.S.	214	46.18 N	124.03 W
Disappointment, Lake ◎	152	23.30 S	122.50 E
Disappointment, Mount ∧	159	37.25 S	145.18 E
Disappointment Creek ≃	190	38.01 N	108.51 W
Disaster Bay C	156	37.17 S	150.00 E
Disbrow Drain ≡	271	42.06 N	83.27 W
Disco	204	42.41 N	83.02 W
Discovery	263d	26.10 S	27.54 E
Discovery, Port C	214	48.05 N	122.52 W
Discovery Bay C	156	38.12 S	141.07 E
Discovery Island I	214	48.25 N	123.15 W
Discovery Passage Џ	172	50.00 N	125.15 W
Discovery Tablemount ✢[3]	8	42.00 S	0.05 E
Disentis	54	46.43 N	8.51 E
Dishāshah	132	28.59 N	30.51 E
Dishergarh	116	23.41 N	86.50 E
Dishman	192	47.39 N	117.17 W
Dishnā	130	26.07 N	32.28 E
Dishna ≃	170	63.37 N	157.18 W
Dişidi	120	38.47 N	39.00 E
Disihao	79	50.28 N	124.35 E
Disko	206	41.00 N	85.57 W
Disko I	166	69.50 N	53.30 W
Disko Bugt C	166	69.15 N	52.00 W
Disley	252	53.21 N	2.02 W
Disley Tunnel ⊸[5]	252	53.22 N	2.03 W
Dismal ≃	188	41.50 N	100.05 W
Dismal Lakes ◎	166	67.26 N	117.07 W
Dismal Swamp Canal ≡	198	36.45 N	76.20 W
Disna	66	55.33 N	28.10 E
Disna ≃	66	55.34 N	28.12 E
Disney	186	36.29 N	95.01 W
Disneyland ♠	218	33.48 N	117.55 W
Disneyworld ♠	210	28.27 N	81.28 W
Disputanta	198	37.08 N	77.14 W
Disraëli	196	45.54 N	71.21 W
Dissen	48	52.07 N	8.12 E
Dissimieux, Lac ◎	176	49.51 N	69.48 W
Distant	204	40.59 N	79.22 W
Disteghil Sār ∧	113	36.19 N	75.12 E
Disteln	253	51.36 N	7.09 E
Distington	42	54.36 N	3.32 W
District Heights	274c	38.51 N	76.53 W
District of Columbia ☐[5]	168		
	274c	38.54 N	77.01 W
Distrito Federal ☐[5], Arg.	248	34.36 S	58.26 W
Distrito Federal ☐[5], Bra.	245	15.45 S	47.45 W
Distrito Federal ☐[5], Méx.	224	19.15 N	99.10 W
Distrito Federal ☐[5], Ven.	236	10.30 N	66.55 W
Distroff	52	49.20 N	6.16 E
Disūq	132	31.08 N	30.39 E
Ditfurt	50	51.50 N	11.11 E
Dithmarschen ⊸[1]	30	54.05 N	9.00 E
Dit Island I	106	11.15 N	120.56 E
Ditton, Eng., U.K.	250	51.18 N	0.27 E
Ditton, Eng., U.K.	252	53.22 N	2.45 W
Ditton ≃	196	45.23 N	71.12 W
Ditton Priors	44	52.30 N	2.35 W
Ditzingen	52	48.49 N	9.03 E
Ditzum	48	53.18 N	7.16 E
Diu	110	20.42 N	70.59 E
Diuata Mountains ⋀	106	9.10 N	125.47 E
Diuata Point ≻	106	9.05 N	125.12 E
Dīva	262c	19.09 N	72.59 E
Divalá	226	8.25 N	82.43 W
Dīvāndarreh	118	35.55 N	47.02 E
Dive	262c	19.11 N	73.02 E
Divejevo	70	55.03 N	43.15 E
Divenié	142	2.41 S	12.05 E
Divenskaja	66	59.12 N	30.01 E
Diveria ≃	54	46.09 N	8.19 E
Dives ≃, Fr.	32	49.19 N	0.05 W
Dives ≃, Fr.	46	48.50 N	0.01 E
Diviči	74	41.12 N	48.59 E
Dividing Creek	198	39.16 N	75.06 W
Dividing Creek ≃	198	38.05 N	75.32 W
Dividing Ridge ∧	209	39.07 N	90.39 W
Divignano	256b	45.40 N	8.36 E
Divilican Bay C	106	17.25 N	122.19 E
Divin	68	51.58 N	24.35 E
Divine Corners	200	41.48 N	74.40 W
Divinhe	146	20.40 S	34.49 E
Divino	245	20.37 S	42.09 W
Divino de Virginópolis	245	18.48 S	42.38 W
Divinolândia	246	21.40 S	46.45 W
Divinópolis	245	20.09 S	44.54 W

PORTUGUÊS

Nome	Página	Lat.°′	Long.°′ W=Oeste
Divion	46	50.28 N	2.30 E
Divis ∧[2]	42	54.37 N	6.01 W
Divisa Nova	246	21.31 S	46.12 W
Divisões, Serra das ⋀[2]	245	17.00 S	51.00 W
Divisor, Serra do (Cordillera Ultraoriental) ⋀[1]	238	8.20 S	73.30 W
Divizija	68	45.57 N	29.59 E
Divnogorsk	76	55.58 N	92.22 E
Divnoje	70	45.55 N	43.22 E
Divo	140	5.50 N	5.22 W
Divo ☐[5]	140	5.40 N	5.30 W
Divonne-les-Bains	54	46.22 N	6.08 E
Divriği	120	39.23 N	38.07 E
Dīwāl Qol	110	34.19 N	67.54 E
Dix, Ill., U.S.	209	38.27 N	88.56 W
Dix, Nebr., U.S.	188	41.14 N	103.29 W
Dix ≃	182	37.49 N	84.43 W
Dix, Lac des ◎	54	46.03 N	7.24 E
Dixboro	206	42.19 N	83.39 W
Dixfield	178	44.32 N	70.27 W
Dix Hills	197	40.49 N	73.22 W
Dixie	265b	43.36 N	79.36 W
Dixie Square ⊸[9]	268	41.37 N	87.40 W
Dixie Valley ∨	194	39.50 N	117.55 W
Dix-Milles, Lac ◎	180	46.46 N	77.45 W
Dixmoor	268	41.38 N	87.40 W
Dixmude → Diksmuide	46	51.02 N	2.52 E
Dixon, Calif., U.S.	216	38.27 N	121.49 W
Dixon, Ill., U.S.	180	41.50 N	89.29 W
Dixon, Ky., U.S.	184	37.31 N	87.41 W
Dixon, Mo., U.S.	184	37.60 N	92.06 W
Dixon, N. Mex., U.S.	190	36.12 N	105.53 W
Dixon, Ohio, U.S.	206	40.57 N	84.48 W
Dixon Entrance Џ	170	54.25 N	132.30 W
Dixons Mills	184	32.04 N	87.47 W
Dixons Pond ◎	266	40.56 N	74.27 W
Dixonville	204	40.43 N	79.01 W
Dixville	196	45.04 N	71.46 W
Diyadin	74	39.33 N	43.41 E
Diyālā ☐[4]	118	34.00 N	45.00 E
Diyālā (Sīrvān) ≃	118	33.14 N	44.31 E
Diyarbakır	120	37.55 N	40.14 E
Diyarbakır ☐[4]	120	38.05 N	40.15 E
Diyarb Najm	132	30.45 N	31.26 E
Diyu al-Wasta	132	30.54 N	31.30 E
Dizangsi	94	41.26 N	120.57 E
Dizhou	92	23.00 N	106.20 E
Dizy	46	49.04 N	3.58 E
Dizzard Point ≻	44	50.45 N	4.38 W
Dja ≃	142	2.02 N	15.12 E
Dja, Réserve de ⊸[4]	142	3.05 N	13.00 E
Djabalpur → Jabalpur	114	23.10 N	79.57 E
Djabir	142	0.32 N	24.05 E
Djadié ≃	142	0.46 N	12.58 E
Djado	136	21.01 N	12.18 E
Djado, Plateau du ⋀[1]	136	21.45 N	12.50 E
Djaipur → Jaipur	110	26.55 N	75.49 E
Djakarta → Jakarta	259e	6.10 S	106.48 E
Djakonovo	72	54.34 N	38.20 E
Djakovka	70	50.43 N	46.46 E
Djakovo	73	47.57 N	39.09 E
Djakovo ⊸[8]	255b	55.39 N	37.40 E
Djamaa	138	33.32 N	6.00 E
Djamba, Ang.	142	16.46 S	13.59 E
Djamba, Zaïre	142	9.49 S	22.07 E
Djambala	142	2.33 S	14.45 E
Djamschedpur → Jamshedpur	116	22.48 N	86.11 E
Djanet	138	24.34 N	9.29 E
Djangatiti Dafana	136	11.46 N	21.19 E
Djaposten	142	3.25 N	13.32 E
Djaret, Oued ∨	138	26.32 N	1.30 E
Djaul Island I	154	2.56 S	150.55 E
Djebel Abiod	36	36.58 N	9.05 E
Djebeniana	138	35.02 N	10.55 E
Djebibina	36	36.07 N	10.06 E
Djebobo ∧	140	8.20 N	0.35 E
Djébren	136	11.14 N	19.01 E
Djédaa	136	13.31 N	18.34 E
Djedda → Juddah	134	21.30 N	39.12 E
Djedi, Oued ∨	138	34.28 N	6.05 E
Djeffara (Gefara) ⊻	136	32.30 N	11.45 E
Djéké Djéké	136	8.25 N	18.12 E
Djelfa	138	34.40 N	3.15 E
Djelo-Binza	263b	4.23 S	15.16 E
Djema	130	6.03 N	25.19 E
Djember	136	10.25 N	17.50 E
Djemila ⊥	34	36.25 N	5.44 E
Djemmal	138	35.38 N	10.46 E
Djenein	138	31.44 N	10.09 E
Djénné	140	13.54 N	4.33 W
Djenoun, Garet el ∧	138	25.05 N	5.25 E
Djeradou	36	36.15 N	10.23 E
Djerba, Île de I	138	33.48 N	10.54 E
Djerem ≃	142	5.20 N	13.24 E
Djerid, Chott ≋	138	33.42 N	8.26 E
Dji ≃	142	6.47 N	22.14 E
Djiba	142	1.21 S	13.09 E
Djibasso	140	13.07 N	4.10 W
Djibo	140	14.06 N	1.38 W
Djibouti	134	11.36 N	43.09 E
Djibouti ☐[1]	126		
	134	11.30 N	43.00 E
Djibrouïa	140	13.13 N	11.14 W
Djidjelli	138	36.48 N	5.46 E
Djilbabo Plain ⊻	134	4.00 N	39.10 E
Djohong	142	6.50 N	14.42 E
Djokjakarta → Yogyakarta	105a	7.48 S	110.22 E
Djokoumatombi	142	0.47 N	15.22 E
Djolu	142	0.37 N	22.21 E
Djombo	142	1.21 N	20.22 E
Djoua ≃	142	1.13 N	13.12 E
Djoué ≃	263b	4.19 S	15.14 E
Djougou	140	9.42 N	1.40 E
Djouho Battinga	142	6.38 N	20.34 E
Djoum	142	2.40 N	12.40 E
Djouna	136	10.27 N	20.04 E
Djugu	144	1.55 N	30.30 E
Djúpivogur	24a	64.40 N	14.10 W
Djura	40	60.37 N	15.00 E
Djurås	40	60.33 N	15.08 E
Djurmo	40	60.33 N	15.10 E
Djurö	40	59.19 N	18.41 E
Djurö I	26	58.52 N	13.28 E
Djursholm	40	59.24 N	18.05 E
Dmanisi	74	41.22 N	44.12 E
Dmitr'ašovka	66	52.09 N	39.04 E
Dmitrija Lapteva, Proliv Џ	64	73.00 N	142.00 E
Dmitrijevka, S.S.S.R.	73	48.55 N	39.10 E
Dmitrijevka, S.S.S.R.	73	47.56 N	38.56 E
Dmitrijevka, S.S.S.R.	75	43.30 N	77.02 E
Dmitrijevka, S.S.S.R.	76	55.10 N	75.36 E
Dmitrijev-L'govskij	68	52.08 N	35.05 E
Dmitrijevskij	76	49.08 N	57.50 E
Dmitrijevskoje, S.S.S.R.	70	45.48 N	41.54 E
Dmitrijevskoje, S.S.S.R.	72	54.40 N	37.38 E
Dmitrijev Usad, S.S.S.R.	66	54.08 N	43.08 E
Dmitrijev Usad, S.S.S.R.	70	54.14 N	43.18 E
Dmitrijevy Gory	70	55.12 N	41.47 E
Dmitrov	72	56.21 N	37.31 E
Dmitrova Gora	72	56.40 N	36.59 E
Dmitrovcy	72	55.16 N	38.55 E
Dmitroviči	66	53.59 N	29.06 E
Dmitrovka, S.S.S.R.	68	45.29 N	35.04 E
Dmitrovka, S.S.S.R.	68	46.51 N	36.35 E
Dmitrovka, S.S.S.R.	68	48.48 N	32.44 E
Dmitrovskij Pogost	66	55.19 N	39.49 E
Dmitrovsk-Orlovskij	66	52.30 N	35.09 E
Dmuchajlovka	68	49.03 N	34.46 E
Dnepr ≃	68	46.30 N	32.18 E
Dnepr'any	68	46.44 N	33.16 E
Dneprodzeržinsk	68	48.30 N	34.37 E
Dneprodzeržinskoje Vodochranilšče ◎[1]	68	48.45 N	34.00 E
Dnepropetrovsk	68	48.27 N	34.59 E
Dneprovka	68	47.26 N	34.38 E
Dneprovskij Liman C[1]	68	46.35 N	31.55 E
Dneprovsko-Bugskij Kanal ≡	68	52.03 N	25.35 E
Dneprovskoje	66	55.40 N	33.55 E
Dnestr ≃	68	46.18 N	30.17 E
Dnestrovskij Liman ◎	68	46.15 N	30.17 E
Dnieper → Dnepr ≃	68	46.30 N	32.18 E
Dniepropetrovsk → Dnepropetrovsk	68	48.27 N	34.59 E
Dniester → Dnestr ≃	68	46.18 N	30.17 E
Dno	66	57.50 N	29.59 E
Do, Lac ◎	140	15.54 N	2.45 W
Doa	144	16.44 S	34.32 E
Do Āb-e Mīkh-e Zarrīn	110	35.16 N	68.00 E
Doaktown	176	46.33 N	66.08 W
Doangdoangan-besar, Pulau I	102	5.24 S	117.55 E
Doany	147b	14.22 S	49.31 E
Doba	136	8.39 N	16.51 E
Dobane	130	6.24 N	24.42 E
Dobbertin	50	53.37 N	12.04 E
Dobbiaco (Toblach)	58	46.44 N	12.14 E
Dobbin	212	30.22 N	95.46 W
Dobbins	216	39.22 N	121.12 W
Dobbs Ferry	200	41.01 N	73.52 W
Dobbyn	156	19.48 S	140.00 E
Dobczyce	30	49.54 N	20.06 E
Dobel	52	48.48 N	8.29 E
Dobele	66	56.37 N	23.16 E
Döbeln	50	51.07 N	13.07 E
Doberai, Jazirah (Vogelkop) ≻[1]	154	1.30 S	132.30 E
Döberitz	254a	52.33 N	13.03 E
Doberlug-Kirchhain	50	51.38 N	13.34 E
Döbern	50	51.37 N	14.36 E
Dobiegniew	30	52.59 N	15.47 E
Döbling ⊸[8]	254b	48.15 N	16.22 E
Dobo	154	5.46 S	134.13 E
Doboj	38	44.44 N	18.06 E
Dobra, Pol.	30	51.54 N	18.37 E
Dobra, Pol.	30	53.35 N	15.18 E
Dobra ≃	36	45.33 N	15.31 E
Dobr'anka, S.S.S.R.	68	52.04 N	31.11 E
Dobr'anka, S.S.S.R.	76	58.27 N	56.24 E
Dobr'ankka	68	48.21 N	30.54 E
Dobre Miasto	30	53.59 N	20.25 E
Döbriach	58	46.47 N	13.39 E
Dobrich → Tolbuhin	38	43.34 N	27.50 E
Dobrinka, S.S.S.R.	70	48.49 N	42.58 E
Dobrinka, S.S.S.R.	70	50.49 N	41.51 E
Dobrinka, S.S.S.R.	70	52.09 N	40.29 E
Dobříš	30	49.47 N	14.11 E
Dobritz	50	52.01 N	12.13 E
Dobrodzień	30	50.44 N	18.27 E
Dobroje, S.S.S.R.	66	52.52 N	39.48 E
Dobroje, S.S.S.R.	66	57.06 N	32.02 E
Dobroměřice	50	50.23 N	13.46 E
Dobromil'	68	49.34 N	22.47 E
Dobropolje	68	48.28 N	37.05 E
Dobroslavka	66	52.24 N	26.15 E
Dobroteasa	38	44.47 N	24.23 E
Dobrotvor	68	50.14 N	24.22 E
Dobroveličkovka	68	48.23 N	31.11 E
Dobrovol' (Schlossberg in Ostpreussen)	66	54.46 N	22.31 E
Dobrovolje	68	48.41 N	36.37 E
Dobrudžansko plato ⋀[1]	38	43.32 N	27.50 E
Dobruš	66	52.25 N	31.19 E
Dobruška	30	50.17 N	16.10 E
Dobryn'	68	51.46 N	29.12 E
Dobrzany	30	53.22 N	15.25 E
Dobrzyń nad Wisłą	30	52.38 N	19.20 E
Dobšiná	30	48.49 N	20.23 E
Dobson	182	36.24 N	80.43 W
Döč ≃	78	49.39 N	114.48 E
Doce ≃, Bra.	245	19.37 S	39.49 W
Doce ≃, Bra.	245	18.28 S	51.05 W
Doce de Octubre	186	25.38 N	97.47 W
Doce Leguas, Cayos de las II	230p	20.55 N	79.05 W
Docking	44	52.55 N	0.38 E
Dockton	214	47.22 N	122.28 W
Dockweiler	52	50.15 N	6.46 E
Dockweiler State Beach ♠	270	33.55 N	118.26 W
Doctor Arroyo	224	23.40 N	100.11 W
Doctor Coss	186	25.55 N	99.11 W
Doctor Edmund A. Babler Memorial State Park ♠	209	38.36 N	90.43 W
Doctor González	222	25.52 N	99.57 W
Doctor Hicks Range ⋀	152	28.40 S	124.20 E
Doctors Creek ≃	198	40.11 N	74.41 W
Doda	113	33.08 N	75.34 E
Doda Betta ∧	112	11.24 N	76.44 E
Dod Ballāpur	112	13.18 N	77.32 E
Doddinghurst	250	51.40 N	0.18 E
Doddo ≃	136	7.05 N	19.10 E
Doddridge	184	33.06 N	93.54 W
Doddsville	184	33.39 N	90.31 W
Dodecanese → Dhodhekánisos II	38	36.30 N	27.00 E
Dodéo	142	7.29 N	12.04 E
Dodge, Nebr., U.S.	188	41.43 N	96.52 W
Dodge, Tex., U.S.	212	30.45 N	95.24 W
Dodge ☐[6]	206	43.14 N	88.40 W
Dodge Brothers State Park Number 8 ♠, Mich., U.S.	271	42.36 N	83.01 W
Dodge Brothers State Park Number 4 ♠, Mich., U.S.	271	42.37 N	83.22 W
Dodge Center	180	44.02 N	92.51 W
Dodge City	188	37.45 N	100.01 W
Dodge Park	274c	38.56 N	76.53 W
Dodger Stadium ♠	270	34.04 N	118.14 W
Dodgeville	180	42.58 N	90.08 W
Dodman Point ≻	44	50.13 N	4.48 W
Dodo	146	18.45 S	25.20 E
Dodo Goei	130	5.57 N	27.26 E
Dodola	134	7.02 N	39.07 E
Dodoma	144	6.11 S	35.45 E
Dodoma ☐[4]	144	6.00 S	36.00 E
Dodori ≃	144	1.52 S	41.02 E
Dodsland	174	51.48 N	108.49 W
Dodson, La., U.S.	184	32.05 N	92.39 W
Dodson, Mont., U.S.	192	48.24 N	108.15 W
Dodson, Tex., U.S.	186	34.46 N	100.02 W
Dodson Peninsula ≻[1]	9	75.46 S	62.50 W
Dodurga	120	39.48 N	29.55 E
Doe Lake ◎	202	45.32 N	79.25 W
Doe River	172	56.00 N	120.05 W
Doerun	182	31.19 N	83.55 W
Doesburg	48	52.01 N	6.09 E
Doetinchem	48	51.58 N	6.17 E
Dog ≃	180	48.51 N	89.37 W
Dogāchia	262b	22.58 N	88.31 E
Dogadda	114	29.48 N	78.37 E
Dō ga-mori ∧	86	33.09 N	132.53 E
Doğanbey, Tür.	120	38.04 N	26.53 E
Doğanbey, Tür.	120	37.48 N	31.54 E
Doğanbey, Tür.	120	37.37 N	27.11 E
Doğançay	120	40.37 N	30.20 E
Doganella	60	41.34 N	12.56 E
Doğanhisar	120	38.09 N	31.41 E
Doğanşehir	120	38.06 N	37.53 E
Dog Creek	172	51.35 N	122.15 W
Dog Creek ≃, Mont., U.S.	192	47.44 N	109.36 W
Dog Creek ≃, Ohio, U.S.	206	41.03 N	84.23 W
Dog Ear Creek ≃	188	43.42 N	99.59 W
Dog Islands II	230m	18.29 N	64.28 W
Dog Lake ◎, Man., Can.	174	51.02 N	98.30 W
Dog Lake ◎, Ont., Can.	180	48.18 N	84.10 W
Dog Lake ◎, Ont., Can.	180	48.46 N	89.32 W
Dog Lake ◎, Ont., Can.	202	44.27 N	76.20 W
Dogliani	56	44.32 N	7.56 E
Dogna	58	46.27 N	13.19 E
Dōgo II	82	36.15 N	133.16 E
Dogondoutchi	140	13.38 N	4.02 E
Dōgo-yama ∧	86	35.04 N	133.14 E
Dogpound Creek ≃	172	51.50 N	114.24 W
Dogs, Isle of I	250	51.29 N	0.01 W
D'ogtevo	68	49.10 N	40.39 E
Doğubayazıt	74	39.32 N	44.08 E
Doguéraoua	140	13.58 N	5.35 E
Dogura	154	10.05 S	150.05 E
Doha → Ad-Dawḥah	118	25.17 N	51.32 E
Dohad	110	22.50 N	74.16 E
Dohār	116	23.35 N	90.09 E
Dohhi	114	24.32 N	84.54 E
Dohna	50	50.57 N	13.51 E
Dohrgaul	253	51.06 N	7.27 E
Dohrīghāt	114	26.16 N	83.31 E
Doi	86	33.57 N	133.30 E
Doi, Kinh ≡	259c	10.43 N	106.37 E
Doigab	134	0.59 N	43.38 E
Doiran, Lake ◎	38	41.13 N	22.44 E
Dois de Novembro, Cachoeira ⌊	238	8.52 S	62.16 W
Dois Irmãos	240	9.16 S	49.05 W
Dois Irmãos, Pico ∧	277a	22.59 S	43.14 W
Dois Riachos	240	9.23 S	37.05 W
Dōjō	258	35.51 N	139.32 E
Dōjō ⊸[8]	260	34.52 N	135.14 E
Doka, Indon.	154	6.39 S	134.15 E
Doka, Sūd.	130	13.31 N	35.46 E
Doki ≃	86	34.18 N	133.48 E
Dokka	26	60.50 N	10.05 E
Dokkane, Djebel ∧	138	35.23 N	8.00 E
Dokkum	48	53.19 N	6.00 E
Dokmetepe	120	40.19 N	36.18 E
Dokri	110	27.23 N	68.06 E
Dokšicy	66	54.54 N	27.46 E
Dokská pahorkatina ⋀[2]	50	50.30 N	14.45 E
Dokšukino	74	43.33 N	43.50 E
Doksy	50	50.35 N	14.38 E
Dokučajevsk	73	47.44 N	37.40 E
Dol'a, S.S.S.R.	73	47.53 N	37.41 E
Dola, Ohio, U.S.	206	40.47 N	83.42 W
Dolak ≃	154	8.20 S	138.30 E
Doland	188	44.54 N	98.06 W
Dolavón	244	43.18 S	65.42 W
Dolaybaköy	257b	40.54 N	29.15 E
Dolbeau	166	48.53 N	72.14 W
Dolberg	48	51.42 N	7.55 E
Dolceacqua	56	43.51 N	7.37 E
Dol-de-Bretagne	32	48.33 N	1.45 W
Dole	54	47.06 N	5.30 E
Dolega	226	8.34 N	82.25 W
Dolen	212	30.26 N	94.54 W
Dolgaja	76	55.49 N	64.15 E
Dolgaja, Kosa ≻[2]	68	46.43 N	37.41 E
Dolgarrog	42	53.11 N	3.51 W
Dolgelin	50	52.29 N	14.24 E
Dolgellau	44	52.44 N	3.53 W
Dolgen'koje	73	49.01 N	37.19 E
Dolgeville	200	43.06 N	74.46 W
Dolgij, Ostrov I	24	69.15 N	59.04 E
Dolgij Most	78	56.45 N	96.48 E
Dolginovo	66	54.39 N	27.29 E
Dolgoi Island I	170	55.10 N	161.45 W
Dolgoje	68	52.04 N	37.34 E
Dolgoprudnyj	72	55.56 N	37.31 E
Dolgorukovo	66	52.19 N	38.21 E
Dolgoščelje	24	66.03 N	43.24 E
Dolianova	36	39.23 N	9.11 E
Dolina	73	48.59 N	37.27 E
Dolinnyj	70	51.16 N	52.11 E
Dolinovskoje	73	48.36 N	38.33 E
Dolinsk	79	47.21 N	142.48 E
Dolinskaja	68	48.07 N	32.44 E
Dolisie	142	4.12 S	12.41 E
Dolj ☐[4]	38	44.15 N	23.45 E
Döllach	58	46.58 N	12.54 E
Dollard-des-Ormeaux	196	45.29 N	73.49 W
Dollar Law ∧	42	55.33 N	3.17 W
Döllbach	52	50.26 N	9.44 E
Dolle	50	52.25 N	11.37 E
Dollern	48	53.32 N	9.32 E
Dollerup	41	54.46 N	9.40 E
Döllnitz	50	51.24 N	12.01 E
Dollnstein	52	48.52 N	11.04 E
Döllstädt	50	51.05 N	10.49 E
Dolmabahçe Sarayı ⊍	257b	41.02 N	29.00 E
Dolmatovka	68	46.13 N	32.26 E
Dolmatovskij	70	57.29 N	42.18 E
Dolni Dâbnik	38	43.24 N	24.26 E
Dolní Jiřetín	50	50.35 N	13.33 E
Dolni Lom	38	43.31 N	22.47 E
Dolnomoravský úval ∨	30	49.00 N	17.15 E
Dolný Kubín	30	49.12 N	19.17 E
Dolo, It.	58	45.25 N	12.05 E
Dolo, Som.	134	4.13 N	42.08 E
Dolo Bay	134	4.12 N	42.09 E
Dolokparibuan	104	3.01 N	98.39 E
Dolomites → Dolomiti ⋀	58	46.25 N	11.50 E
Dolomiti (Dolomiten) ⋀	58	46.25 N	11.50 E
Dolon'	76	50.40 N	79.18 E
Dolon ≃	56	45.18 N	4.46 E
Dolon, Pereval)(	75	41.52 N	75.45 E
Dolores, Arg.	242	36.20 S	57.40 W
Dolores, Col.	236	3.33 N	74.54 W
Dolores, Esp.	34	38.08 N	0.46 W
Dolores, Guat.	222	16.31 N	89.25 W
Dolores, Méx.	186	26.20 N	101.29 W
Dolores, Méx.	222	28.53 N	108.27 W
Dolores, Colo., U.S.	190	37.28 N	108.30 W
Dolores, Ur.	242	33.33 S	58.13 W
Dolores, Ven.	236	8.18 N	69.34 W
Dolores ≃, Pil.	106	12.02 N	125.29 E
Dolores ≃, U.S.	190	38.49 N	109.17 W
Dolores, Mission ⊍[1]	272	37.46 N	122.26 W
Dolores Hidalgo	224	21.10 N	100.56 W
Dolphin, Cape ≻	244	51.15 S	58.57 W
Dolphin and Union Strait Џ	166	69.05 N	114.45 W
Dolphin Head ∧	231q	18.22 N	78.10 W
Dölsach	58	46.49 N	12.51 E
Dolsk	30	52.00 N	17.03 E
Dol'skoje	72	54.47 N	36.26 E
Dolton, Eng., U.K.	44	50.53 N	4.01 W
Dolton, Ill., U.S.	206	41.39 N	87.37 W
Dolwyddelan	44	53.03 N	3.53 W
Dolžak	68	48.41 N	26.32 E
Dolžanskaja, S.S.S.R.	68	46.37 N	37.48 E
Dolžanskaja, S.S.S.R.	73	48.03 N	39.39 E
Dolžicy, S.S.S.R.	66	58.31 N	29.08 E
Dolžicy, S.S.S.R.	66	58.00 N	29.51 E
Dolžik	68	50.13 N	35.55 E
Dom ∧, Indon.	154	2.40 S	136.53 E
Dom ∧, Schw.	54	46.06 N	7.50 E
D'oma ≃	76	54.42 N	55.57 E
Domacha	66	52.28 N	34.58 E
Domačovo	68	51.44 N	23.37 E
Domadare	134	1.48 N	41.13 E
Domaine, Pointe du ≻	265a	45.23 N	73.54 W
Domanevka	68	47.37 N	30.58 E
Domaniç	120	39.48 N	29.37 E
Domaniči	66	53.02 N	33.25 E
Domar, Enneri ∨	136	18.11 N	18.04 E
Domariāganj	114	27.13 N	82.40 E
Domart-en-Ponthieu	46	50.04 N	2.07 E
Domasi	144	15.18 S	35.20 E
Domaška	70	53.00 N	50.47 E
Domaso	54	46.09 N	9.19 E
Domat/Ems	54	46.50 N	9.28 E
Domažlice	30	49.27 N	12.56 E
Dombaj	74	43.17 N	41.37 E
Dombarovskij	76	50.46 N	59.32 E
Dombås	26	62.05 N	9.08 E
Dombasle-sur-Meurthe	54	48.38 N	6.21 E
Dombe	146	19.59 S	33.25 E
Dombe Grande	142	12.58 S	13.11 E
Dombes ⊸[1]	54	46.00 N	5.03 E
Domboj-Ul'gan, Gora ∧	74	43.14 N	41.41 E
Dombóvár	30	46.23 N	18.08 E
Dombrád	30	48.14 N	21.56 E
Dombresson	54	47.04 N	6.58 E
Domburg	48	51.34 N	3.30 E
Dom Cavati	245	19.23 S	42.06 W
Dome à Collenias	138	27.15 N	9.42 E
Dome Creek	172	53.44 N	121.01 W
Domegge di Cadore	58	46.27 N	12.25 E
Domène	56	45.12 N	5.50 E
Dome of the Rock, The (Mosque of Omar) ⊍[1]	122	31.47 N	35.13 E
Dome Peak ∧, Pil.	106	5.37 N	125.20 E
Dome Peak ∧, Wash., U.S.	214	48.18 N	121.02 W
Domett	162	42.51 S	173.13 E
Domèvre-en-Haye	52	48.49 N	5.55 E
Domeyko	242	28.57 S	70.54 W
Domeyko, Cordillera ⋀	242	24.30 S	69.00 W
Domfront	32	48.36 N	0.39 W
Domiciano Ribeiro	245	16.56 S	47.46 W
Dominal, Parc ♠	56	44.52 N	6.32 E
Domingos Martins	245	20.22 S	40.40 W
Dominguez	270	33.50 N	118.13 W
Dominguez Channel Џ	270	38.47 N	118.15 W
Dominguez Hills ⋀[2]	270	33.52 N	118.14 W
Dominica ☐[1]	220		
	230d	15.30 N	61.20 W
Dominica Channel Џ	228	15.10 N	61.15 W
Dominicain (république) → Dominican Republic ☐[1]	228	19.00 N	70.40 W
Dominical	226	9.13 N	83.51 W
Dominical, Punta ≻	226	9.13 N	83.50 W
Dominicana, República → Dominican Republic ☐[1]	228	19.00 N	70.40 W
Dominican Republic ☐[1]	220		
	228	19.00 N	70.40 W
Dominikanische Republik → Dominican Republic ☐[1]	228	19.00 N	70.40 W
Dominion	176	46.13 N	60.01 W
Dominion, Cape ≻	166	66.13 N	74.28 W
Dominion Astrophysical Observatory ⊍[3]	214	48.31 N	123.25 W
Dominique → Dominica ☐[1]	230d	15.30 N	61.20 W
Domiongo	142	4.37 S	21.15 E
Domitilla, Catacombe di ⊥	257a	41.52 N	12.31 E
Dömitz	50	53.08 N	11.14 E
Dom Joaquim	245	18.57 S	43.16 W
Domleschg ∨	54	46.44 N	9.28 E
Dommartin-lès-Toul	54	48.40 N	5.54 E
Dommartin-Varimont	52	48.58 N	4.46 E
Dommary-Baroncourt	52	49.17 N	5.42 E
Dommel ≃	48	51.40 N	5.20 E
Dommitzsch	50	51.38 N	12.53 E
Domnarvet	40	60.30 N	15.27 E
Domnești	38	44.25 N	25.56 E
Domnino	72	54.10 N	38.11 E
Dom Noi ≃	100	15.17 N	105.28 E
Domo	134	7.54 N	46.52 E
Domodedovo	72	55.26 N	37.46 E
Domodedovo, Aeroport ⊠	72	55.25 N	37.53 E
Domodossola	54	46.07 N	8.17 E
Domohani	114	26.35 N	88.48 E
Domoni	147a	12.15 S	44.32 E
Domont	251	49.02 N	2.20 E
Dompaire	54	48.13 N	6.13 E
Dom Pedrito	242	30.59 S	54.40 W
Dom Pedro	240	4.29 S	44.27 W
Dom Pedro II, Estação ⊸[5]	277a	23.54 S	43.12 W
Dompierre-sur-Besbre	32	46.31 N	3.41 E
Dompu	105b	8.32 S	118.28 E
Domremy	174	52.47 N	105.44 W
Domrémy-la-Pucelle	54	48.27 N	5.41 E
Domselaar	248	35.04 S	58.18 W
Dom Silvério	245	20.09 S	42.58 W
Domsjö	26	63.15 N	18.43 E
Domuyo, Volcán ∧[1]	242	36.38 S	70.26 W
Domvast	46	50.12 N	1.55 E
Dom Viçoso	246	22.13 S	45.09 W
Dom Yai ≃	100	15.18 N	105.10 E
Domzāle	36	46.08 N	14.36 E
Don ≃, Bhārat	112	16.17 N	76.27 E
Don ≃, Ont., Can.	202	43.39 N	79.21 W
Don ≃, Lao	100	15.07 N	105.48 E
Don ≃, S.S.S.R.	62	47.04 N	39.18 E
Don ≃, Eng., U.K.	42	53.39 N	0.59 W
Don ≃, Eng., U.K.	252	53.47 N	2.14 W
Don ≃, Scot., U.K.	28	57.10 N	2.04 W
Dona Ana, Moç.	144	17.25 S	35.07 E
Dona Ana, N. Mex., U.S.	190	32.23 N	106.49 W
Donada	58	45.02 N	12.12 E
Donadeu	242	26.43 S	62.44 W
Dona Eusébia	246	21.18 S	42.48 W
Donaghadee	42	54.39 N	5.33 W
Donaghmore	42	54.32 N	6.49 W
Donahoe Creek ≃	212	30.49 N	97.12 W
Donald	156	36.22 S	143.00 E
Donalda	172	52.35 N	112.34 W
Donaldson, Ark., U.S.	184	34.14 N	92.55 W
Donaldson, Ind., U.S.	206	41.22 N	86.27 W
Donaldson, Pa., U.S.	198	40.38 N	76.24 W
Donaldson Crossroads	269b	40.16 N	80.07 W
Donaldsonville	184	30.06 N	90.59 W
Donalsonville	182	31.03 N	84.53 W
Donard, Slieve ∧	42	54.11 N	5.55 W
Donau → Danube ≃	22	45.20 N	29.40 E
Donaueschingen	54	47.57 N	8.29 E
Donaufeld ⊸[8]	254b	48.15 N	16.25 E
Donau Kanal ≡	254b	48.10 N	16.30 E
Donaumoos ≋	54	48.30 N	10.15 E
Donaupark ♠	254b	48.14 N	16.25 E
Donauried ⊸[1]	52	48.35 N	10.40 E
Donaustadt ⊸[8]	254b	48.13 N	16.30 E
Donauturm ⊍	254b	48.14 N	16.25 E
Donauwörth	52	48.43 N	10.46 E
Don Benito	34	38.57 N	5.52 W
Dönberg	253	51.18 N	7.10 E
Don Bosco ⊸[8]	248	34.42 S	58.18 W
Doncaster, Austl.	264b	37.47 S	145.08 E
Doncaster, Eng., U.K.	42	53.32 N	1.07 W
Doncaster ≃	196	45.58 N	74.06 W

≃	River	Fluss	Río	Rivière	Rio
≡	Canal	Kanal	Canal	Canal	Canal
⌊	Waterfall, Rapids	Wasserfall, Stromschnellen	Cascada, Rápidos	Chute d'eau, Rapides	Cascata, Rápidos
Џ	Strait	Meeresstrasse	Estrecho	Détroit	Estreito
C	Bay, Gulf	Bucht, Golf	Bahía, Golfo	Baie, Golfe	Baía, Golfo
◎	Lake, Lakes	See, Seen	Lago, Lagos	Lac, Lacs	Lago, Lagos
≋	Swamp	Sumpf	Pantano	Marais	Pântano
⊼	Ice Features, Glacier	Eis- und Gletscherformen	Accidentes Glaciales	Formes glaciaires	Acidentes Glaciares
⊤	Other Hydrographic Features	Andere Hydrographische Objekte	Otros Elementos Hidrográficos	Autres données hydrographiques	Outros Elementos Hidrográficos

✢	Submarine Features	Untermeerische Objekte	Accidentes Submarinos	Formes de relief sous-marin	Acidentes Submarinos
☐	Political Unit	Politische Einheit	Unidad Politica	Entité politique	Unidade Política
⊍	Cultural Institution	Kulturelle Institution	Institución Cultural	Institution culturelle	Instituição Cultural
⊥	Historical Site	Historische Stätte	Sitio Histórico	Site historique	Sitio Histórico
♠	Recreational Site	Erholungs- und Ferienort	Sitio de Recreo	Centre de loisirs	Sítio de Lazer
⊠	Airport	Flughafen	Aeropuerto	Aéroport	Aeroporto
■	Military Installation	Militäranlage	Instalación Militar	Installation militaire	Instalação Militar
⊸	Miscellaneous	Verschiedenes	Misceláneo	Divers	Miscelânea

Name	Page	Lat.°′	Long.°′
Doncaster East	264b	37.47 S	145.10 E
Donchêry	52	49.42 N	4.52 E
Doncovka	73	49.35 N	39.16 E
Dondaicha	110	21.20 N	74.34 E
Dondo, Ang.	142	9.38 S	14.25 E
Dondo, Moç.	146	19.36 S	34.44 E
Dondo, Teluk C	102	0.55 N	120.30 E
Dondra Head ≻	112	5.55 N	80.35 E
Don-duong	100	11.51 N	108.35 E
Dond'ušany	68	48.15 N	27.37 E
Doneck, S.S.S.R.	73	48.00 N	37.48 E
Doneck, S.S.S.R.	73	48.21 N	40.02 E
Doneck □[4]	73	48.00 N	37.30 E
Doneck, Aeroport ⊠	73	48.08 N	37.45 E
Doneckij Kr'až ∧	73	48.15 N	38.45 E
Donegal, Eire	28	54.39 N	8.07 W
Donegal, S. Afr.	148	26.10 S	23.58 E
Donegal, Pa., U.S.	204	40.07 N	79.23 W
Donegal □[6]	28	54.50 N	8.00 W
Donegal Bay C	28	54.30 N	8.30 W
Donetsk → Doneck	73	48.00 N	37.48 E
Donga ≃	136	8.19 N	9.58 E
Dongan → Mishan, Zhg.	79	45.33 N	131.52 E
Dongan, Zhg.	90	33.24 N	114.24 E
Dongan, Zhg.	92	26.17 N	111.07 E
Dongan, Zhg.	96	31.35 N	119.44 E
Dongan, Zhg.	96	30.30 N	118.48 E
Dongao	90	29.12 N	121.25 E
Dongao I	90	22.01 N	113.43 E
Dongara	152	29.15 S	114.56 E
Dongargarh	110	21.12 N	80.44 E
Dongazhen	88	36.11 N	116.16 E
Dongba, Zhg.	95	39.58 N	116.32 E
Dongba, Zhg.	96	31.18 N	119.03 E
Dongbahe	95	39.58 N	116.27 E
Dongbaimiao	95	40.34 N	116.05 E
Dongbeibao	88	36.06 N	117.08 E
Dongbeicha	88	41.43 N	127.23 E
Dongbulizhadamu	110	34.27 N	93.12 E
Dongchang	96	31.52 N	121.38 E
Dongchangjie	96	32.04 N	119.18 E
Dongchansi	97	30.20 N	105.20 E
Dongcheng	90	28.56 N	121.16 E
Dongchong	90	26.35 N	119.52 E
Dongchuan	92	26.10 N	103.01 E
Dongcun	96	30.57 N	121.46 E
Dongdaban	94	41.43 N	120.49 E
Dongdaoan	88	38.21 N	117.12 E
Dongdu	88	35.50 N	117.42 E
Dongduluo	95	39.04 N	115.15 E
Dongen	48	51.37 N	4.56 E
Dongfang (Basuo)	100	19.05 N	108.39 E
Dongfeng, Zhg.	88	42.40 N	125.28 E
Dongfeng, Zhg.	90	27.20 N	118.53 E
Dongfeng, Zhg.	97	29.59 N	104.48 E
Dongfengtai	95	39.34 N	117.45 E
Donggala	102	0.40 S	119.44 E
Donggang	90	22.58 N	115.57 E
Donggangzi	79	45.53 N	129.49 E
Dongge	114	29.38 N	90.59 E
Donggi	102	1.33 S	122.15 E
Donggongshan ⩕	90	27.36 N	119.26 E
Donggongsuo	96	32.07 N	121.25 E
Donggou, Zhg.	90	32.16 N	119.00 E
Donggou, Zhg.	90	33.38 N	119.40 E
Donggou, Zhg.	96	32.17 N	118.59 E
Donggu	90	26.46 N	115.22 E
Dongguan, Zhg.	90	23.03 N	113.46 E
Dongguan, Zhg.	90	27.49 N	116.25 E
Dongguan, Zhg.	96	30.22 N	119.28 E
Dongguanchang	97	30.47 N	106.16 E
Dongguang	88	37.53 N	116.30 E
Dongguanpu	96	31.13 N	120.43 E
Dongguanyingzi	94	41.56 N	120.38 E
Dongguayu I	90	27.38 N	121.07 E
Donggugang	95	39.10 N	116.49 E
Donggui ⊜	96	31.21 N	119.52 E
Dong-hai, Viet.	100	12.34 N	109.14 E
Donghai (Haizhou), Zhg.	88	34.34 N	119.11 E
Donghai → East China Sea •[2]	80	30.00 N	126.00 E
Donghaidao I	92	21.02 N	110.25 E
Donghenghe ☰	96	31.54 N	120.17 E
Dong-hoi	100	17.29 N	106.36 E
Donghu ⊜	110	32.10 N	84.40 E
Donghuanggou	94	40.43 N	123.29 E
Donghuwei	90	26.28 N	113.07 E
Dongi	102	2.02 S	121.28 E
Dongio	54	46.27 N	8.58 E
Dongjia	88	37.18 N	118.24 E
Dongjiadao I	90	25.19 N	119.46 E
Dongjiang	90	25.57 N	113.15 E
Dongjiang ≃	90	23.06 N	114.00 E
Dongjiangkou	92	33.37 N	108.49 E
Dongjidao I	90	28.43 N	121.55 E
Dongjie	90	25.53 N	116.22 E
Dongjielang	90	31.03 N	115.57 E
Dongjingcheng	79	44.07 N	129.09 E
Dongjinghe ≃	90	30.31 N	112.50 E
Dongjingji	88	40.06 N	114.00 E
Dongjiu	110	29.58 N	94.53 E
Dongkaihecheng	94	41.04 N	122.38 E
Dongkalang	102	0.10 N	120.06 E
Dongkeng	90	27.48 N	119.42 E
Dong-khe	100	22.26 N	106.27 E
Dongkou	88	35.29 N	115.20 E
Dongkun	90	25.26 N	119.44 E
Donglan	92	24.40 N	107.18 E
Donglaohuyu	94	42.28 N	124.17 E
Donglaojunpu	94	41.24 N	121.22 E
Dongli	92	20.50 N	110.20 E
Dongliang	94	42.00 N	121.25 E
Dongliangjia	95	40.52 N	118.17 E
Donglidian	88	36.02 N	118.23 E
Donglinchang	97	29.39 N	104.07 E
Dongling	94	41.50 N	123.35 E
Dongling ʊ[1]	94	41.49 N	123.29 E
Dongliu, Zhg.	90	30.14 N	116.53 E
Dongliu, Zhg.	96	32.06 N	118.58 E
Dongliujiazi	94	42.21 N	122.44 E
Donglizhuang	95	39.21 N	116.47 E
Donglong	90	23.36 N	116.50 E
Donglucun	79	49.28 N	128.50 E
Dongmenshi	90	28.29 N	114.02 E
Dongming	88	35.18 N	115.08 E
Dong-nai ≃	100	10.45 N	106.46 E
Dongnangou	94	41.25 N	122.02 E
Dong-nhien, Rach ≃	259c	10.49 N	106.46 E
Dongning	79	44.04 N	131.07 E
Dongo, Ang.	142	14.36 S	15.48 E
Dongo, It.	54	46.07 N	9.17 E
Dongo, Zaïre	142	2.43 N	18.24 E
Dongobe	142	4.37 N	23.12 E
Dongobesh	144	4.04 S	35.23 E
Dongola → Dungulah	130	19.10 N	30.29 E
Dongon Point ≻	106	12.44 N	120.48 E
Dongou	142	2.02 N	18.04 E
Dongpi	90	27.15 N	116.06 E
Dongping, Zhg.	88	35.55 N	116.18 E
Dongping, Zhg.	90	27.24 N	118.39 E
Dongpinghu ⊜	88	35.59 N	116.22 E
Dongpushi	90	30.03 N	120.34 E
Dongqi ≃	90	25.00 N	118.27 E
Dongqian	96	30.52 N	120.23 E
Dongqiao	90	31.12 N	112.48 E
Dongqing	96	31.49 N	120.03 E
Dongqingduizi	94	41.02 N	122.08 E
Dongsanjiazi	94	41.54 N	122.48 E
Dongsanlintang	96	31.09 N	121.31 E
Dongshaer	110	28.41 N	89.09 E
Dongshahe ≃	94	41.07 N	121.50 E
Dongshajiao	90	30.19 N	122.09 E
Dongshan, Zhg.	90	23.46 N	117.31 E
Dongshan, Zhg.	92	19.50 N	110.14 E
Dongshankou	94	41.31 N	123.28 E
Dongshanqiao	96	31.52 N	118.46 E
Dongshaqundao (Pratas Islands) II	80	20.42 N	116.43 E
Dongshe	96	32.07 N	121.12 E
Dongsheng	92	39.57 N	110.00 E
Dongsheshanzi	94	42.15 N	123.09 E
Dongshi, Zhg.	90	24.43 N	115.59 E
Dongshi, Zhg.	90	24.42 N	118.27 E
Dongshi, Zhg.	95	39.49 N	116.34 E
Dongshuangzhai	88	40.18 N	113.56 E
Dongshuiyan	95	39.15 N	115.23 E
Dongtai	90	32.51 N	120.20 E
Dongtaihu C	96	31.05 N	120.30 E
Dongtaipingzhen	79	45.18 N	122.05 E
Dongtangou	95	39.23 N	118.22 E
Dongtangshu	96	31.33 N	120.51 E
Dongtianmushan ∧	96	30.22 N	119.31 E
Dongtinghu	96	30.53 N	119.30 E
Dongtinghu ⊜	90	29.20 N	112.54 E
Dongtingwei	90	24.59 N	114.54 E
Dongtingxi	92	28.34 N	110.36 E
Dongtingxishan ∧	96	31.07 N	120.16 E
Dongtingzhen	88	38.29 N	115.08 E
Dongtou	90	27.50 N	121.09 E
Dongtoushan I	90	27.50 N	121.08 E
Dong-trieu	100	21.05 N	106.31 E
Dongtuhulu	94	41.55 N	121.33 E
Dongtuoshanzi	94	42.10 N	123.08 E
Dongtuozi	94	41.17 N	121.53 E
Dong-van	100	23.16 N	105.22 E
Dongwangfu	79	44.47 N	120.53 E
Dongwangzhuang	96	32.16 N	120.32 E
Dongwe ≃	142	13.58 S	23.53 E
Dongwenhe ≃	88	35.28 N	118.32 E
Dongwuquan	95	39.20 N	115.43 E
Dongxi, Zhg.	90	28.35 N	120.02 E
Dongxi, Zhg.	92	28.47 N	106.39 E
Dongxi, Zhg.	97	30.24 N	104.33 E
Dongxi, Zhg.	97	28.46 N	104.41 E
Dongxi ≃, Zhg.	90	27.02 N	118.18 E
Dongxi ≃, Zhg.	90	24.36 N	117.37 E
Dongxiacun	96	31.11 N	119.05 E
Dongxiagaogao	94	42.36 N	122.30 E
Dongxiang	90	28.13 N	116.35 E
Dongxiangdao I	90	25.36 N	119.48 E
Dongxiaofangshen	94	40.50 N	122.22 E
Dongxin	96	31.24 N	121.41 E
Dongxing	79	46.23 N	127.52 E
Dongxingchang, Zhg.	97	29.36 N	105.04 E
Dongxingchang, Zhg.	97	29.16 N	103.55 E
Dongxinghe	95	39.46 N	114.49 E
Dongxingsha I	96	31.23 N	121.44 E
Dongxinpu	94	41.00 N	123.18 E
Dongxinzhen	96	31.57 N	121.42 E
Dongyang	90	29.16 N	120.14 E
Dongyangqiao	96	30.52 N	120.34 E
Dongyangzhen	79	48.03 N	124.17 E
Dongyaoji	88	35.56 N	113.58 E
Dongyian	95	39.22 N	115.46 E
Dongyinhe ≃	95	39.09 N	117.43 E
Dongyou	90	27.11 N	118.42 E
Dongyuezhen	97	30.24 N	103.32 E
Dongzhang	90	25.44 N	119.17 E
Dongzhaocun	95	40.02 N	116.46 E
Dongzhaozhuang	95	39.57 N	118.24 E
Dongzhenbeng	96	30.59 N	121.01 E
Dongzhizhuang	95	40.25 N	116.50 E
Dongzhuangpu	95	40.34 N	115.42 E
Dongziya	95	38.50 N	116.44 E
Donie	212	31.29 N	96.13 W
Doninga	140	10.37 N	1.26 W
Donington	44	52.55 N	0.12 W
Doniphan, Mo., U.S.	184	36.37 N	90.50 W
Doniphan, Nebr., U.S.	188	40.46 N	98.22 W
Don Islands II	106	11.05 N	123.38 E
Donja Stubica	36	45.59 N	15.58 E
Donjek ≃	170	62.35 N	140.00 W
Donjezk → Doneck	73	48.00 N	37.48 E
Donji Vakuf	36	44.09 N	17.25 E
Donk	48	51.33 N	5.37 E
Donkerpoort	148	30.32 S	25.30 E
Donkey Creek ≃	188	44.12 N	104.58 W
Donkey Town	250	51.20 N	0.39 W
Don Martín	186	27.32 N	100.37 W
Don Matías	236	6.30 N	75.22 W
Don Mills •[8]	265b	43.44 N	79.20 W
Don Mills Centre •[9]	265b	43.44 N	79.21 W
Don Muang Airport ⊠	259a	13.56 N	100.37 E
Donna Buang, Mount ∧	159	37.43 S	145.40 E
Donnacona	196	46.40 N	71.47 W
Donnaz	56	45.36 N	7.46 E
Donnellson	209	39.02 N	89.29 W
Donnells Reservoir ⊜[1]	216	38.20 N	119.56 W
Donnelly, Alta., Can.	172	55.44 N	117.06 W
Donnelly, Alaska, U.S.	170	63.41 N	145.53 W
Donnelly, Idaho, U.S.	192	44.44 N	116.05 W
Donnellys Crossing	162	35.43 S	173.37 E
Donnemarie-Dontilly	46	48.29 N	3.08 E
Donner	184	29.42 N	90.58 W
Donner Lake ⊜[1]	216	39.20 N	120.16 W
Donner Memorial State Park ♠	216	39.18 N	120.16 W
Donner Pass)(	216	39.19 N	120.20 W
Donnersberg ∧	52	50.23 N	8.32 E
Donner und Blitzen ≃	192	43.17 N	118.49 W
Donnybrook, Austl.	152	33.35 S	115.49 E
Donnybrook, S. Afr.	148	30.00 S	29.48 E
Donora	204	40.11 N	79.52 W
Donors Hills	156	18.42 S	140.33 E
Donovan	206	40.53 N	87.37 W
Don Peninsula ≻[1]	172	52.30 N	128.10 W
Donque	142	15.28 S	14.06 E
Donskoj, S.S.S.R.	66	53.58 N	38.20 E
Donskoj, S.S.S.R.	73	47.25 N	40.14 E
Donskoje, S.S.S.R.	66	52.37 N	39.00 E
Donskoje, S.S.S.R.	70	45.21 N	41.59 E
Donskoje, S.S.S.R.	73	47.31 N	37.33 E
Donskoje Belogorje ⩕[1]	68	50.30 N	39.45 E
Donsol	106	12.54 N	123.36 E
Don Torcuato	278	34.30 S	58.38 W
Don Torcuato, Aeródromo ⊠	278	34.30 S	58.36 W
Donuzlav, Ozero ⊜	68	45.23 N	33.05 E
Donyztau ⩕	76	46.25 N	57.00 E
Donzdorf	52	48.41 N	9.48 E
Donzère	56	44.27 N	4.43 E
Donzy	46	47.22 N	3.08 E
Dood Nuur ⊜	78	51.20 N	99.20 E
Doomadgee Aborginal Reserve •[4]	156	17.43 S	138.36 E
Doomadgee Mission	156	17.56 S	138.49 E
Doon, Ont., Can.	202	43.23 N	80.26 W
Doon, Iowa, U.S.	188	43.17 N	96.14 W
Doon ≃	42	55.26 N	4.38 W
Doon, Loch ⊜	42	55.15 N	4.22 W
Doondi	156	28.15 S	148.28 E
Doonerak, Mount ∧	170	67.56 N	150.37 W
Doongalla Forest Reserve ♠	264b	37.51 S	145.20 E
Doonside	264a	33.46 S	150.52 E
Dooralong	160	33.12 S	151.22 E
Doorn	48	52.03 N	5.21 E
Doorndam	148	28.03 S	21.03 E
Doornik → Tournai	46	50.36 N	3.23 E
Door Peninsula ≻[1]	188	44.55 N	87.20 W
Dopping Brook ≃	273	42.12 N	71.23 W
Dor	122	32.37 N	34.55 E
Dora	184	33.44 N	87.05 W
Dora, Lake ⊜, Austl.	152	22.05 S	122.55 E
Dora, Lake ⊜, Fla., U.S.	210	29.00 N	81.37 W
Dora Baltea ≃	56	45.11 N	8.05 E
Dora di Rhêmes ≃	56	45.42 N	7.11 E
Dorado	230m	18.28 N	66.15 W
Doraha	113	30.49 N	76.01 E
Dorāh Ān)(	113	36.07 N	71.15 E
Dorândia	246	22.27 S	43.57 W
Dora Riparia ≃	56	45.05 N	7.44 E
Doratama ∧	113	34.54 N	76.00 E
Doraville	182	33.54 N	84.17 W
Dorchester, N.B., Can.	176	45.54 N	64.31 W
Dorchester, Ont., Can.	202	42.59 N	81.04 W
Dorchester, Eng., U.K.	44	51.39 N	1.10 W
Dorchester, Eng., U.K.	44	50.43 N	2.26 W
Dorchester, Ill., U.S.	209	39.05 N	89.53 W
Dorchester, Nebr., U.S.	188	40.39 N	97.07 W
Dorchester, N.J., U.S.	198	39.17 N	74.58 W
Dorchester, Wis., U.S.	180	45.00 N	90.20 W
Dorchester □[6]	198	38.34 N	76.04 W
Dorchester •[8]	273	42.17 N	71.04 W
Dorchester, Cape ≻	166	65.29 N	77.30 W
Dorchester Bay C	273	42.19 N	71.02 W
Dorchester Crossing	176	46.10 N	64.34 W
Dorchester Heights National Historic Site ⊥	273	42.20 N	71.03 W
Dorchheim	52	50.30 N	8.04 E
Dordabis	146	22.52 S	17.38 E
Dordives	46	48.09 N	2.46 E
Dordogne □[5]	32	45.10 N	0.45 E
Dordogne ≃	32	45.02 N	0.35 W
Dordon	44	52.36 N	1.37 W
Dordrecht, Ned.	48	51.49 N	4.40 E
Dordrecht, S. Afr.	148	31.20 S	27.03 E
Doré ≃, Sask., Can.	174	54.56 N	107.45 W
Dore ≃, Fr.	56	45.50 N	3.35 E
Dore ≃, Eng., U.K.	44	51.57 N	2.52 W
Dore, Monts ⩕	32	45.30 N	2.45 E
Doreissou	136	10.33 N	15.08 E
Doré Lake	174	54.31 N	107.06 W
Doré Lake ⊜	174	54.46 N	107.17 W
Dorena	192	43.47 N	122.55 W
Dorena Lake ⊜[1]	192	43.46 N	122.55 W
Dores do Indaiá	245	19.27 S	45.36 W
Dores do Paraibuna	246	21.31 S	43.39 W
Dorf Dienten	58	47.22 N	13.00 E
Dorfen	30	48.17 N	12.08 E
Dorfgastein	58	47.15 N	13.06 E
Dorfmark	48	52.54 N	9.46 E
Dorgali	36	40.17 N	9.35 E
Dori	140	14.02 N	0.02 W
Doring ≃	148	31.54 S	18.39 E
Doringbaai	148	31.48 S	18.15 E
Doringkop ∧	263d	26.15 S	27.50 E
Dorino	72	56.28 N	36.09 E
Dorion-Vaudreuil	196	45.23 N	74.01 W
Dorje Lāpka ∧	114	28.11 N	85.47 E
Dorking	44	51.14 N	0.20 W
Dorloo	200	42.43 N	74.37 W
Dormaa Ahenkro	140	7.17 N	2.53 W
Dormagen	52	51.05 N	6.50 E
Dormans	46	49.04 N	3.38 E
Dormidontovka	79	47.45 N	134.57 E
Dornach	54	47.29 N	7.37 E
Dornap	253	51.15 N	7.04 E
Dornbach •[8]	254b	48.14 N	16.18 E
Dornbirn	54	47.25 N	9.44 E
Dorndorf, D.D.R.	50	51.00 N	11.40 E
Dorndorf, D.D.R.	52	50.50 N	10.05 E
Dornecy	46	47.26 N	3.35 E
Dorney	250	51.30 N	0.40 W
Dornhan	54	48.21 N	8.30 E
Dorno	56	45.09 N	8.57 E
Dornoch	28	57.52 N	4.02 W
Dornoch Firth C[2]	28	57.52 N	4.02 W
Dornod □[4]	78	48.00 N	115.00 E
Dornogov' □[4]	92	44.30 N	110.00 E
Dornsife	198	40.45 N	76.47 W
Dornstadt	54	48.28 N	9.56 E
Dornstetten	54	48.28 N	8.30 E
Dornumersiel	48	53.40 N	7.28 E
Doro, Indon.	105a	7.02 S	109.41 E
Doro, Mali	140	16.09 N	0.51 W
Dorochovo	72	55.33 N	36.23 E
Dorog	30	47.43 N	18.44 E
Dorogobuž	66	54.55 N	33.18 E
Dorohoi	38	47.57 N	26.24 E
Dorokempo	105b	8.33 S	118.15 E
Doromata	105b	8.46 S	118.13 E
Doromo	144	3.49 N	26.17 E
Döröö Nuur ⊜	78	47.40 N	93.30 E
Dorošata	70	57.21 N	51.08 E
Dorošicha	72	56.52 N	35.50 E
Dorotea	26	64.16 N	16.24 E
Dorothy	198	39.24 N	74.49 W
Dorothy, Lake ⊜	214	47.34 N	121.22 W
Dorotockeys Run ≃	266	40.59 N	73.58 W
Dorpat → Tartu	66	58.23 N	26.43 E
Dörpen	48	52.57 N	7.20 E
Dorr	206	42.43 N	85.43 W
Dorrance	188	38.51 N	98.35 W
Dorre Island I	152	25.09 S	113.07 E
Dorridge	44	52.22 N	1.45 W
Dorrigo	156	30.21 S	152.43 E
Dorris	194	41.58 N	121.55 W
Dorset, Ohio, U.S.	204	41.41 N	80.40 W
Dorset, Vt., U.S.	200	43.15 N	73.06 W
Dorset □[6]	44	50.47 N	2.20 W
Dorset Peak ∧	178	43.19 N	73.02 W
Dorsey Run ≃	274b	39.11 N	76.48 W
Dorseyville	269b	40.35 N	79.53 W
Dorsten	48	51.39 N	6.58 E
Dorstfeld •[8]	253	51.31 N	7.25 E
Dort → Dordrecht	48	51.49 N	4.40 E
Dortan	54	46.19 N	5.40 E
Dortmund	48		
	253	51.31 N	7.28 E
Dortmund-Ems-Kanal ☰	48	51.32 N	7.27 E
Dortmunder Rieselfelder •[1]	253	51.39 N	7.25 E
Dortmund-Wickede, Flughafen ⊠	253	51.32 N	7.35 E
Dorton	182	37.17 N	82.35 W
Dörtyol	120	36.52 N	36.12 E
Dorum	48	53.41 N	8.34 E
Doruma	144	4.44 N	27.42 E
Dorval	196	45.27 N	73.44 W
Dorval, Île I	265a	45.26 N	73.45 W
Dorval Gardens Centre •[9]	265a	45.27 N	73.44 W
Dörverden	48	52.51 N	9.13 E
Dörvöldžin	78	48.11 N	93.54 E
Dörzbach	52	49.23 N	9.42 E
Dosara	140	12.32 N	6.09 E
Dosara ∧	113	34.38 N	72.30 E
Dos Arroyos	224	17.02 N	99.40 W
Dosatuj	78	50.23 N	118.38 E
Dos Bahías, Cabo ≻	244	44.55 S	65.32 W
Dos Bocas	230m	18.20 N	66.40 W
Dos Bocas, Lago ⊜[1]	230m	18.19 N	66.40 W
Doscatoje	70	55.23 N	42.07 E
Dosewallips ≃	214	47.42 N	122.53 W
Doshan Tappeh Airfield ⊠	257d	35.42 N	51.28 E
Dos Hermanas	34	37.17 N	5.55 W
Dos Hermanas, Islas II	248	34.05 S	58.17 W
Dōshi	84	35.32 N	139.02 E
Dōshi ≃	84	35.30 N	139.14 E
Doshisha University ʊ	260	35.02 N	135.46 E
Dosi	154	5.56 S	134.34 E
Dosjebro	41	55.49 N	13.01 E
Do-son	100	20.42 N	106.47 E
Dosoris Island ≻[1]	266	40.53 N	73.38 W
Dosoris Pond ⊜	266	40.54 N	73.38 W
Dos Palos	216	36.59 N	120.37 W
Dos Reyes, Punta ≻	242	24.23 S	70.35 W
Dosse ≃	50	53.13 N	12.20 E
Dossin Great Lakes Museum ʊ	271	42.20 N	82.59 W
Dosso	140	13.03 N	3.12 E
Dosso □[5]	140	13.00 N	3.00 E
Dossor	70	47.32 N	53.01 E
Doster	206	42.27 N	85.33 W
Doswell	198	37.52 N	77.27 W
Dothan	184	31.13 N	85.24 W
Doting Cove	176	49.27 N	53.57 W
Dot Lake	170	63.40 N	194.04 W
Dotnuva	66	55.21 N	23.54 E
Dotson	212	32.01 N	94.31 W
Döttingen	54	47.34 N	8.16 E
Doty	214	46.38 N	123.17 W
Douai	46	50.22 N	3.04 E
Douala	142	4.03 N	9.42 E
Douarnenez	32	48.06 N	4.20 W
Doubabougou	140	14.13 N	7.59 W
Double, Lac ⊜	176	50.46 N	70.23 W
Doublé, Pointe ≻	231o	16.20 N	61.00 W
Double Bayou	212	29.41 N	94.39 W
Double Cone ∧	162	45.04 S	168.48 E
Double Island Point ≻	156	25.56 S	153.11 E
Double Mountain ∧	218	35.02 N	118.29 W
Double Point ≻	156	17.39 S	146.09 E
Double Springs	184	34.09 N	87.24 W
Doubletop Peak ∧	190	43.21 N	110.17 W
Doubs	54	46.56 N	6.21 E
Doubs ≃, Eur.	32	47.10 N	6.25 E
Doubs ≃, Eur.	54	46.54 N	5.02 E
Doubtful Sound ɰ	162	45.17 S	166.51 E
Doubtless Bay C	162	34.55 S	173.25 E
Douchy	46	47.57 N	3.03 E
Douchy-les-Mines	46	50.18 N	3.23 E
Doudeville	46	49.43 N	0.48 E
Doudian	95	39.39 N	116.03 E
Doué ≃[1]	140	16.38 N	15.02 W
Douentza	140	15.00 N	2.57 W
Dougga ⊥	138	36.25 N	9.13 E
Doughboy	160	35.15 S	149.39 E
Doughboy Bay C	162	47.02 S	167.41 E
Douglas, Ont., Can.	202	45.31 N	76.56 W
Douglas, I. of Man	42	54.09 N	4.28 W
Douglas, S. Afr.	148	29.04 S	23.46 E
Douglas, Scot., U.K.	42	55.33 N	3.51 W
Douglas, Alaska, U.S.	170	58.16 N	134.22 W
Douglas, Ariz., U.S.	190	31.21 N	109.33 W
Douglas, Ga., U.S.	182	31.31 N	82.51 W
Douglas, Mich., U.S.	206	42.38 N	86.12 W
Douglas, N. Dak., U.S.	188	47.51 N	101.30 W
Douglas, Wyo., U.S.	190	42.45 N	105.24 W
Douglas □[6]	216	38.55 N	119.39 W
Douglas ≃	42	53.43 N	2.50 W
Douglas, Cape ≻	170	58.52 N	153.18 W
Douglas, Mount ∧	170	58.52 N	153.31 W
Douglas, Mount ∧[2]	152	28.39 S	123.53 E
Douglas Aircraft Company ʊ[3]	270	33.50 N	118.09 W
Douglas Channel ɰ	172	53.30 N	129.12 W
Douglas Creek ≃	190	40.06 N	108.46 W
Douglas Lake	172	50.10 N	120.12 W
Douglas Lake ⊜[1]	182	36.00 N	83.22 W
Douglas Lake Indian Reserve •[4]	172	50.10 N	120.49 W
Douglas Park	160	34.11 S	150.43 E
Douglas Park ♠	268	41.52 N	87.42 W
Douglass, Kans., U.S.	188	37.31 N	97.01 W
Douglass, Tex., U.S.	212	31.40 N	94.53 W
Douglass Run ≃	269b	40.15 N	79.48 W
Douglas Station	174	49.53 N	99.46 W
Douglassville	198	40.15 N	75.44 W
Douglasville	182	33.45 N	84.45 W
Douglas Water ≃	42	55.38 N	3.46 W
Dougouro, Ouadi ∨	136	17.53 N	21.31 E
Dougouzi, Zhg.	79	49.57 N	127.01 E
Dougouzi, Zhg.	94	41.16 N	122.34 E
Douhe ≃	95	39.13 N	118.03 E
Doujiapu	94	41.05 N	122.12 E
Doujiazhuang	95	40.22 N	116.59 E
Doulaincourt	54	48.19 N	5.12 E
Doulevant-le-Château	54	48.23 N	4.55 E
Doullens	46	50.09 N	2.21 E
Doumanaba	140	11.40 N	5.56 W
Doumanga	142	2.41 S	12.40 E
Doumba	142	5.05 N	14.18 E
Doumdégué	142	7.29 N	18.58 E
Doumé	142	4.14 N	13.27 E
Doumé ≃	142	4.06 N	14.34 E
Doumen, Zhg.	90	22.14 N	113.11 E
Doumen, Zhg.	95	39.18 N	115.53 E
Douna	140	14.39 N	1.44 W
Dounguila	142	2.53 S	11.58 E
Doupov	50	50.10 N	13.08 E
Doupovské hory ⩕	50	50.13 N	13.08 E
Dour	46	50.24 N	3.47 E
Doura	140	13.14 N	5.55 W
Dourada, Serra ⩕[1]	245	13.10 S	48.45 W
Douradinho	246	21.45 S	45.46 W
Dourado ≃, Bra.	245	21.22 S	49.41 W
Dourado ≃, Bra.	246	21.43 S	45.44 W
Dourados	245	22.13 S	54.48 W
Dourados ≃	245	21.58 S	54.18 W
Dourados, Serra dos ⩕[1]	242	23.30 S	53.30 W
Dourbali	136	11.49 N	15.52 E
Dourdan	46	48.32 N	2.01 E
Dourdou ≃	32	44.00 N	2.41 E
Dourges	46	50.26 N	2.59 E
Dourkoulé	136	14.27 N	22.13 E
Douro (Duero) ≃	34	41.08 N	8.40 W
Doushanhe	90	31.38 N	114.42 E
Dousman	206	43.01 N	88.28 W
Douthat State Park ♠	182	37.55 N	79.50 W
Douvaine	54	46.19 N	6.18 E
Douvres, Fr.	32	49.17 N	0.23 W
Douvres → Dover, Eng., U.K.	44	51.08 N	1.19 E
Douvres, Falaises de •[4]	263b	4.06 S	15.25 E
Douvrin	46	50.31 N	2.50 E
Doux ≃	56	45.04 N	4.50 E
Douy-la-Ramée	251	49.04 N	2.53 E
Douyu	88	37.53 N	114.30 E
Douz	138	33.28 N	9.01 E
Douze ≃	32	43.54 N	0.30 W
Douzhangzhuang	95	39.23 N	116.55 E
Douzishan	97	29.04 N	104.57 E
Douzy	52	49.40 N	5.03 E
Dovadola	60	44.07 N	11.53 E
Dovbyš	68	50.22 N	27.59 E
Dove ≃	44	52.50 N	1.35 W
Dove Creek	190	37.46 N	108.54 W
Dove Creek ≃, Tex., U.S.	186	31.20 N	100.36 W
Dove Creek ≃, Utah, U.S.	190	41.37 N	113.15 W
Dove Holes	252	53.18 N	1.53 W
Dove Holes Tunnel •[5]	252	53.18 N	1.53 W
Dover, Austl.	156	43.19 S	147.01 E
Dover, S. Afr.	148	27.02 S	27.46 E
Dover, Eng., U.K.	44	51.08 N	1.19 E
Dover, Ark., U.S.	194	35.24 N	93.07 W
Dover, Del., U.S.	186	39.10 N	75.32 W
Dover, Fla., U.S.	210	28.00 N	82.13 W
Dover, Idaho, U.S.	214	48.15 N	116.36 W
Dover, Ky., U.S.	208	38.45 N	83.53 W
Dover, Mass., U.S.	273	42.15 N	71.17 W
Dover, N.H., U.S.	178	43.12 N	70.56 W
Dover, N.J., U.S.	198	40.53 N	74.34 W
Dover, N.C., U.S.	182	35.13 N	77.26 W
Dover, Ohio, U.S.	204	40.32 N	81.29 W
Dover, Okla., U.S.	196	35.59 N	97.55 W
Dover, Pa., U.S.	198	40.00 N	76.51 W
Dover, Tenn., U.S.	184	36.29 N	87.50 W
Dover, Point ≻	152	32.32 S	125.32 E
Dover, Strait of (Pas de Calais) ɰ	46	51.00 N	1.30 E
Dover Air Force Base ■	198	39.08 N	75.28 W
Dovercourt	44	51.56 N	1.16 E
Dover-Foxcroft	178	45.11 N	69.13 W
Dover Heights	264a	33.53 S	151.17 E
Dover Hills	266	40.52 N	74.33 W
Dover Plains	200	41.44 N	73.35 W
Dovers Hills ⩕[2]	152	23.10 S	128.45 E
Dove Stone Reservoir ⊜[1]	252	53.32 N	1.58 W
Doveton	264b	38.00 S	145.14 E
Dovey Valley ∨	44	52.35 N	3.50 W
Dovol'noje	76	54.30 N	79.40 E
Dovre	26	61.59 N	9.15 E
Dovrefjell ⩕	26	62.06 N	9.25 E
Dovsk	66	53.09 N	30.28 E
Dowa	144	13.40 S	33.58 E
Dowagiac	206	41.59 N	86.06 W
Dowagiac ≃	206	41.51 N	86.16 W
Dowagiac Creek ≃	206	41.49 N	86.10 W
Dow City	188	41.56 N	95.30 W
Dowell	198	38.21 N	76.27 W
Dowerin	152	31.12 S	117.02 E
Dowker, Île I	265a	45.24 N	73.54 W
Dowlatābād, Afg.	110	36.26 N	64.55 E
Dowlatābād, Afg.	110	36.59 N	66.50 E
Dowlatābād, Īrān	118	28.18 N	56.40 E
Dowlatābād, Īrān	257d	35.37 N	51.27 E
Dowlat Yār	110	34.33 N	65.47 E
Dowling Lake ⊜	172	51.44 N	112.00 W
Downe •[8]	250	51.20 N	0.03 E
Down East	275	40.03 N	75.32 W
Downers Grove	206	41.48 N	88.01 W
Downey, Calif., U.S.	218	33.56 N	118.08 W
Downey, Idaho, U.S.	192	42.26 N	112.07 W
Downey, Ill., U.S.	268	42.18 N	87.51 W
Downey Creek ≃	214	48.16 N	121.14 W
Downham, Eng., U.K.	44	52.26 N	0.15 E
Downham, Eng., U.K.	250	51.38 N	0.30 E
Downham Market	44	52.36 N	0.23 E
Down House ⊥	250	51.20 N	0.03 E
Downieville	216	39.34 N	120.50 W
Downing	184	40.29 N	92.22 W
Downingtown	198	40.00 N	75.42 W
Downingtown Airport ⊠	275	39.59 N	75.45 W
Downpatrick	42	54.20 N	5.43 W
Downpatrick Head ≻	28	54.20 N	9.20 W
Downs, Ill., U.S.	206	40.24 N	88.52 W
Downs, Kans., U.S.	188	39.30 N	98.33 W
Downs Mountain ∧	190	43.18 N	109.40 W
Downsview Dells Park ♠	265b	43.44 N	79.30 W
Downsville	200	42.05 N	75.00 W
Downsville Dam •[6]	200	42.05 N	74.58 W
Downton	44	51.00 N	1.44 W
Downton, Mount ∧	172	52.42 N	124.51 W
Downton Lake ⊜	172	50.51 N	123.00 W
Downwind Acres Airfield ⊠	271	42.09 N	83.34 W
Dow Rūd	118	33.28 N	49.04 E
Dows	180	42.39 N	93.30 W
Dowsārī	118	28.25 N	57.59 E
Dowshī	110	35.37 N	68.41 E
Doyle	194	40.02 N	120.06 W
Doyles	176	47.50 N	59.12 W
Doylesburg	204	40.13 N	77.42 W
Doylestown, Ohio, U.S.	204	40.58 N	81.42 W
Doylestown, Pa., U.S.	198	40.19 N	75.08 W
Doyline	184	32.32 N	93.25 W
Dōzan ≃	86	33.58 N	133.47 E
Dozier	184	31.30 N	86.28 W
Dozois, Réservoir ⊜[1]	180	47.30 N	77.05 W
Dozza	60	44.22 N	11.37 E
Dra, Hamada du •[2]	138	29.00 N	6.45 W
Drâa, Cap ≻	138	28.44 N	11.08 W
Drâa, Oued ∨	138	28.43 N	11.09 W
Draa el Mizan	34	36.32 N	3.50 E
Drabble → José Enrique Rodó	248	33.41 S	57.34 W
Drabenderhöhe	52	50.57 N	7.27 E
Drabov	68	49.58 N	32.08 E
Drac ≃	56	45.13 N	5.41 E
Dracena	245	21.32 S	51.29 W
Drachenfels ⊥	52	50.40 N	7.12 E
Drachten	48	53.06 N	6.05 E
Dračie Jaskyně •[5]	30	49.05 N	19.35 E
Dracut	197	42.40 N	71.18 W
Dragalina	38	44.26 N	27.20 E
Drăgănești-Olt	38	44.10 N	24.32 E
Drăgănești-Vlașca	38	44.06 N	25.36 E
Drăgășani	38	44.40 N	24.16 E
Drag Lake ⊜	202	45.05 N	78.24 W
Dragone ≃	58	44.23 N	10.37 E
Dragonera, Isla I	34	39.35 N	2.19 E
Dragoni	60	41.16 N	14.18 E
Dragonja ≃	58	45.28 N	13.37 E
Dragons Mouth ɰ	231r	10.45 N	61.46 W
Dragon Swamp ≃	198	37.33 N	76.34 W
Dragoon	190	32.02 N	110.02 W
Dragør	41	55.36 N	12.41 E
Draguignan	56	43.32 N	6.28 E
Drain	192	43.40 N	123.19 W
Drake, Mo., U.S.	209	38.28 N	91.28 W
Drake, N. Dak., U.S.	188	47.55 N	100.23 W
Drakenburg	48	52.41 N	9.13 E
Drakensberg ⩕	146	27.00 S	30.00 E
Drake Passage ɰ	18	58.00 S	70.00 W
Drake Peak ∧	192	42.19 N	120.07 W
Drakesboro	184	37.13 N	87.03 W
Drakes Branch	182	37.00 N	78.36 W
Drakes Brook ≃	266	40.49 N	74.43 W
Drake Well Museum ʊ	204	41.36 N	79.39 W
Drakino	72	54.52 N	37.17 E
Dráma	38	41.09 N	24.08 E
Dramburg → Drawsko Pomorskie	30	53.32 N	15.48 E
Drammen	26	59.44 N	10.15 E
Drancy	46	48.56 N	2.27 E
Dranda	74	42.53 N	41.09 E
Drang ≃	100	13.19 N	107.21 E
Drangajökull ⍓	24a	66.11 N	22.15 W
Drangstedt	48	53.36 N	8.44 E
Dranov, Ostrovul I	38	44.52 N	29.15 E
Dransfeld	48	51.30 N	9.45 E
Dranske	50	54.38 N	13.14 E
Drap	56	43.45 N	7.19 E
Draper, N.C., U.S.	182	36.31 N	79.41 W
Draper, Utah, U.S.	190	40.32 N	111.52 W
Draperstown	42	54.48 N	6.47 W
Drās	113	34.27 N	75.46 E
Drau (Drava) (Dráva) ≃	36	45.33 N	18.55 E
Drava (Drau) (Dráva) ≃	36	45.33 N	18.55 E
Draveil	46	48.41 N	2.25 E
Dravinja ≃	36	46.22 N	15.57 E
Dravograd	36	46.35 N	15.02 E
Dravosburg	269b	40.21 N	79.51 W
Drawa ≃	30	52.52 N	15.59 E
Drawno	30	53.13 N	15.45 E
Drawsko Pomorskie	30	53.32 N	15.48 E
Drayton, Ont., Can.	202	43.46 N	80.40 W
Drayton, N. Dak., U.S.	188	48.38 N	97.11 W
Drayton, S.C., U.S.	182	34.58 N	81.54 W
Drayton Plains	206	42.41 N	83.23 W
Drayton Valley	172	53.13 N	114.59 W
Drean	36	36.41 N	7.46 E
Drebach	50	50.40 N	13.01 E
Drebkau	50	51.39 N	14.13 E
Dreifelder Weiher ⊜	52	50.36 N	7.49 E
Dreihausen	52	50.43 N	8.50 E
Dreiherrnspitze (Picco dei Tre Signori) ∧	58	47.04 N	12.15 E
Dreikikir	154	3.35 S	142.45 E
Drejø I	41	54.58 N	10.25 E
Dremsel, Mount ∧	154	2.10 S	146.55 E
Drena	58	45.58 N	10.56 E
Drenovec	38	43.42 N	22.59 E
Drensteinfurt	48	51.48 N	7.44 E
Drenthe □[4]	48	52.45 N	6.30 E
Dresde → Dresden	50	51.03 N	13.44 E
Dresden, Ont., Can.	204	42.35 N	82.11 W
Dresden, D.D.R.	50	51.03 N	13.44 E
Dresden, N.Y., U.S.	200	42.41 N	76.58 W
Dresden, Ohio, U.S.	204	40.07 N	82.01 W
Dresden, Tenn., U.S.	184	36.18 N	88.42 W
Dresden □[5]	50	51.10 N	14.00 E
Dresher	275	40.08 N	75.10 W
Dretun'	66	55.41 N	29.13 E
Dreux	46	48.44 N	1.22 E
Drevenack	253	51.40 N	6.45 E
Drew	184	33.49 N	90.32 W
Drewer	253	51.40 N	7.07 E
Drewitz, D.D.R.	50	52.12 N	12.10 E
Drewitz, D.D.R.	50	52.22 N	13.07 E
Drewitz •[8]	254a	52.22 N	13.08 E
Drewryville	198	36.43 N	77.18 W
Drews Reservoir ⊜[1]	192	42.10 N	120.40 W
Drew University ʊ[2]	266	40.46 N	74.25 W
Drexel	208	39.45 N	84.16 W
Drexel Gardens	208	39.44 N	86.15 W
Drexel Hill	275	39.57 N	75.19 W
Drexel University ʊ[2]	275	39.57 N	75.11 W
Drezdenko	30	52.51 N	15.50 E
Drezna	72	55.44 N	38.51 E
Dribin	66	54.08 N	31.06 E
Driebergen	48	52.03 N	5.16 E
Drienov	30	48.53 N	21.17 E
Driesen → Drezdenko	30	52.51 N	15.50 E
Driffield	42	54.00 N	0.27 W
Drifton	200	41.00 N	75.54 W
Driftpile ≃	172	55.23 N	115.40 W
Drift Pile River Indian Reserve •[4]	172	55.18 N	115.45 W
Driftwood	204	41.20 N	78.08 W
Driftwood ≃, B.C., Can.	172	55.43 N	126.15 W
Driftwood ≃, Ind., U.S.	208	39.12 N	85.56 W
Driftwood Creek ≃	188	40.11 N	100.39 W
Driggs	192	43.44 N	111.14 W
Drin ≃	38	41.17 N	20.02 E
Drina ≃	38	44.53 N	19.21 E
Dringenberg	48	51.40 N	9.02 E
Drinit, Pellg i C	38	41.45 N	19.28 E
Driorejo	105a	7.21 S	112.37 E
Driscoll	186	27.40 N	97.45 W
Driskill Mountain ∧[2]	184	32.25 N	92.54 W
Drissa ≃	66	55.47 N	27.55 E
Drisv'aty, Ozero ⊜	66	55.38 N	26.35 E
Driver	198	36.49 N	76.30 W
Drizzle Lake ⊜	202	45.20 N	78.10 W
Drjanovo	38	42.58 N	25.27 E
Drniš	36	43.51 N	16.09 E
Dro	58	45.58 N	10.54 E
Drøbak	26	59.39 N	10.39 E
Drobeta-Turnu-Severin	38	44.38 N	22.39 E
Drobylevo	72	55.44 N	35.53 E
Drobyš'ovo, S.S.S.R.	73	49.02 N	37.44 E
Drobyšovo, S.S.S.R.	76	53.58 N	74.40 E
Drochtersen	48	53.42 N	9.23 E
Drocourt	251	49.03 N	1.46 E
Drogheda	28	53.43 N	6.21 W
Drogičin	66	52.11 N	25.09 E
Drogobyč	68	49.21 N	23.30 E
Drohiczyn	30	52.24 N	22.41 E
Drohobycz → Drogobyč	68	49.21 N	23.30 E
Droichead Átha → Drogheda	28	53.43 N	6.21 W
Droichead Nua	28	53.11 N	6.48 W
Droitwich	44	52.16 N	2.09 W
Drokija	68	48.03 N	27.48 E
Drolshagen	52	51.01 N	7.46 E
Dromana	159	38.21 S	144.58 E
Dromara	42	54.23 N	6.01 W
Drôme □[5]	56	44.35 N	5.10 E
Drôme ≃	56	44.46 N	4.46 E
Drömling •[1]	50	52.29 N	11.04 E
Dromore	42	54.25 N	6.09 W
Dronero	56	44.28 N	7.22 E
Dronfield	42	53.19 N	1.27 W
Drongen	46	51.03 N	3.40 E
Dronne ≃	32	45.02 N	0.09 W
Dronninglund	26	57.09 N	10.18 E
Dronrijp	48	53.11 N	5.38 E
Dröschede	253	51.22 N	7.39 E
Drosiá	257c	38.07 N	23.52 E
Droskovo	66	52.31 N	37.05 E
Drossen → Ośno	30	52.28 N	14.50 E
Drottningholms slott ⊥	40	59.19 N	17.53 E
Droué	46	48.02 N	1.05 E
Droue-sur-Drouette	251	48.36 N	1.42 E
Drouette ≃	251	48.37 N	1.37 E
Drouin	159	38.08 S	145.51 E
Drov'anaja	78	51.35 N	113.02 E
Droylsden	252	53.29 N	2.10 W
Droyssig	50	51.02 N	12.01 E
Drožžanoje	70	54.44 N	47.34 E
Dr. Petru Groza	38	46.32 N	22.28 E
Druid Hill Park ♠	274b	39.19 N	76.39 W
Druja	66	55.47 N	27.27 E
Druk-Yul → Bhutan □[1]	110	27.30 N	90.30 E
Drulingen	52	48.52 N	7.11 E
Drum, Mount ∧	170	62.07 N	144.35 W
Drumbo	202	43.14 N	80.33 W
Drumheller	172	51.28 N	112.42 W
Drummond, N.Z.	162	46.09 S	168.09 E
Drummond, Mont., U.S.	192	46.40 N	113.09 W
Drummond, Wis., U.S.	180	46.20 N	91.15 W
Drummond □[6]	196	45.50 N	72.20 W
Drummond, Lake ⊜	198	36.36 N	76.28 W
Drummond Island I	180	46.00 N	83.40 W
Drummond Range ⩕	156	23.30 S	147.15 E
Drummondville	196	45.53 N	72.29 W
Drummore	42	54.42 N	4.54 W
Drummoyne	264a	33.51 S	151.09 E
Drumright	186	35.59 N	96.36 W
Drunen	48	51.42 N	5.08 E
Drusenheim	52	48.46 N	7.57 E
Druskininkai	66	54.01 N	23.58 E
Drut' ≃	66	53.03 N	30.42 E
Druten	48	51.54 N	5.36 E
Druyes-les-Belles-Fontaines	46	47.33 N	3.25 E
Družba, S.S.S.R.	76	45.15 N	82.26 E
Družba, S.S.S.R.	255b	55.53 N	37.45 E
Družina	64	68.14 N	145.18 E
Družkovka	78	48.37 N	37.33 E
Družnaja Gorka	66	59.17 N	30.08 E
Drvar	36	44.22 N	16.24 E
Drwęca ≃	30	53.00 N	18.42 E
Dry ≃	154	14.54 S	132.24 E
Dry Arm C	192	47.45 N	106.20 W
Dry Bay C	170	59.08 N	138.25 W
Dryberry Lake ⊜	174	49.33 N	93.53 W
Dryburgh Abbey ʊ[1]	42	55.34 N	2.39 W
Dry Cimarron ≃	186	36.54 N	102.59 W
Dry Creek ≃, Calif., U.S.	194	38.35 N	122.51 W
Dry Creek ≃, Calif., U.S.	216	39.13 N	121.25 W
Dry Creek ≃, Calif., U.S.	216	38.39 N	121.28 W
Dry Creek ≃, Calif., U.S.	216	38.22 N	122.18 W
Dry Creek ≃, Calif., U.S.	216	36.47 N	119.46 W
Dry Creek ≃, Calif., U.S.	216	37.27 N	120.37 W

Symbols in the index entries represent the broad categories identified in the key at the right. Symbols with superior numbers (⩕[2]) identify subcategories (see complete key on page *I* · 26).

Kartensymbole in dem Registerverzeichnis stellen die rechts in Schlüssel erklärten Kategorien dar. Symbole mit hochgestellten Ziffern (⩕[2]) bezeichnen Unterabteilungen einer Kategorie (vgl. vollständiger Schlüssel auf Seite *I* · 26).

Los símbolos incluídos en el texto del índice representan las grandes categorías identificadas con la clave a la derecha. Los símbolos con numeros en su parte superior (⩕[2]) identifican las subcategorías (véase la clave completa en la página *I* · 26).

Les symboles de l'index représentent les catégories indiquées dans la légende à droite. Les symboles suivis d'un indice (⩕[2]) représentent des sous-catégories (voir légende complète à la page *I* · 26).

Os símbolos incluídos no texto do índice representam as grandes categorias identificadas com a chave à direita. Os símbolos com números em sua parte superior (⩕[2]) identificam as subcategorias (veja-se a chave completa à página *I* · 26).

∧ Mountain	Berg	Montaña	Montagne	Montanha
⩕ Mountains	Berge	Montañas	Montagnes	Montanhas
)(Pass	Pass	Paso	Col	Passo
∨ Valley, Canyon	Tal, Cañon	Valle, Cañón	Vallée, Canyon	Vale, Canhão
≈ Plain	Ebene	Llano	Plaine	Planície
≻ Cape	Kap	Cabo	Cap	Cabo
I Island	Insel	Isla	Île	Ilha
II Islands	Inseln	Islas	Îles	Ilhas
• Other Topographic Features	Andere Topographische Objekte	Otros Elementos Topográficos	Autres données topographiques	Outros Elementos Topográficos

ESPAÑOL Nombre / FRANÇAIS Nom / PORTUGUÊS Nome	Página / Page	Lat.°′	Long.°′ W=Oeste / W=Ouest
Dry Creek ≃, Calif., U.S.	216	36.58 N	120.13 W
Dry Creek ≃, Calif., U.S.	216	38.14 N	121.24 W
Dry Creek ≃, Calif., U.S.	216	38.58 N	121.32 W
Dry Creek ≃, Calif., U.S.	272	37.22 N	122.23 W
Dry Creek ≃, Oreg., U.S.	192	43.34 N	117.21 W
Dry Creek ≃, Oreg., U.S.	214	45.30 N	121.03 W
Dry Creek ≃, Tex., U.S.	212	32.46 N	95.28 W
Dry Creek ≃, Wyo., U.S.	190	41.23 N	109.38 W
Dry Creek ≃, Wyo., U.S.	192	44.30 N	108.03 W
Dry Creek ≃, Wyo., U.S.	192	43.13 N	108.54 W
Dry Creek Mountain Λ	194	41.22 N	116.22 W
Dryden, Ont., Can.	174	49.47 N	92.50 W
Dryden, N.Y., U.S.	200	42.29 N	76.18 W
Dryden, Wash., U.S.	214	47.33 N	120.34 W
Dry Devils ≃	186	29.47 N	100.59 W
Dryfe Water ≃	42	55.08 N	3.26 W
Dry Frio ≃	186	29.17 N	99.39 W
Drygalski Island I	9	65.45 S	92.30 E
Dry Lake ⊜	188	48.15 N	98.58 W
Drymen	42	56.04 N	4.27 W
Dry Prong	184	31.35 N	92.32 W
Dry Ridge	208	38.41 N	84.35 W
Dry Run	204	40.10 N	77.45 W
Drysdale	159	38.11 S	144.34 E
Drysdale ≃	154	13.59 S	126.51 E
Dry Tortugas II	210	24.38 N	82.55 W
Drzewica	30	51.27 N	20.28 E
Drzewice	50	52.38 N	14.38 E
Dschang	142	5.27 N	10.04 E
Dschidda → Juddah	134	21.30 N	39.12 E
Dscuba → Juba ≃	134	0.12 S	42.40 E
Du	140	10.30 N	0.59 W
Dua ≃	142	3.20 N	20.53 E
Duabo	140	5.40 N	8.05 W
Duāigaon	116	24.14 N	90.51 E
Duala → Douala	142	4.03 N	9.42 E
Duan	92	24.06 N	108.10 E
Duancun	95	38.52 N	115.56 E
Duane L. Bliss State Park ♠	216	38.59 N	120.06 W
Duanesburg	200	42.46 N	74.08 W
Duanjialing	95	39.59 N	117.09 E
Duaringa	156	23.43 S	149.40 E
Duarte	218	34.08 N	117.58 W
Duarte, Pico Λ	228	19.02 N	70.59 W
Duartina	245	22.24 S	49.25 W
Duas Barras	246	22.02 S	42.32 W
Duayaw Nkwanta	140	7.10 N	2.06 W
Dubá	50	50.34 N	14.33 E
Dubach	184	32.42 N	92.39 W
Dubai → Dubayy	118	25.18 N	55.18 E
Dubawnt ≃	166	64.33 N	100.06 W
Dubawnt Lake ⊜	166	63.08 N	101.30 W
Dubayy	118	25.18 N	55.18 E
Dubbah, Jabal ad- Λ[2]	132	30.26 N	30.38 E
Dubbeldam	48	51.47 N	4.42 E
Dubbo	156	32.15 S	148.36 E
Dubbo Hill Λ	161b	35.25 S	148.36 E
Dubele	144	2.54 N	29.33 E
Dübendorf	54	47.25 N	8.38 E
Dübener Heide ◆[3]	50	51.40 N	12.40 E
Dubenskij	76	51.27 N	56.38 E
Dubh Artach II[1]	28	56.08 N	6.40 W
Dubí	50	50.42 N	13.45 E
Dubi Bheri	262b	22.53 N	88.17 E
Dubica	36	45.11 N	16.48 E
Dubie	144	8.33 S	28.32 E
Dubinino	72	56.09 N	37.01 E
Dubino	54	46.09 N	9.27 E
Dubjazy	70	56.08 N	49.13 E
Dubki, S.S.S.R.	255a	60.00 N	30.00 E
Dubki, S.S.S.R.	255b	55.41 N	37.14 E
Dublin, Austl.	158b	34.27 S	138.21 E
Dublin, Ont., Can.	202	43.31 N	81.17 W
Dublin (Baile Átha Cliath), Eire	24	53.20 N	6.15 E
Dublin (Baile Átha Cliath), Eire	28	53.20 N	6.15 W
Dublin, Calif., U.S.	216	37.42 N	121.56 W
Dublin, Ga., U.S.	182	32.32 N	82.54 W
Dublin, Ind., U.S.	208	39.49 N	85.13 W
Dublin, Md., U.S.	198	39.39 N	76.15 W
Dublin, Ohio, U.S.	204	40.06 N	83.07 W
Dublin, Pa., U.S.	198	40.22 N	75.12 W
Dublin, Tex., U.S.	186	32.05 N	98.21 W
Dublin, Va., U.S.	182	37.06 N	80.41 W
Dublin □[6]	42	53.20 N	6.15 W
Dublin (Collinstown) Airport ⊠	42	53.26 N	6.15 W
Dublin Bay C	42	53.20 N	6.06 W
Dublin Canyon V	272	37.42 N	121.59 W
Dublon I	165c	7.23 N	151.53 E
Dubna, S.S.S.R.	72	54.09 N	36.58 E
Dubna, S.S.S.R.	72	56.44 N	37.10 E
Dubna ≃, S.S.S.R.	66	56.22 N	26.10 E
Dubna ≃, S.S.S.R.	72	56.47 N	37.15 E
Dubňany	30	48.55 N	17.06 E
Dubnevo	72	55.06 N	38.08 E
Dubnica nad Váhom	30	48.58 N	18.09 E
Dubno	68	50.26 N	25.44 E
Dubois, Idaho, U.S.	192	44.10 N	112.14 W
Dubois, Ill., U.S.	209	38.13 N	89.13 W
Dubois, Ind., U.S.	184	38.27 N	86.48 W
Du Bois, Nebr., U.S.	188	40.02 N	96.04 W
Du Bois, Pa., U.S.	204	41.07 N	78.46 W
Dubois, Wyo., U.S.	190	43.33 N	109.38 W
Du Bois Reservoir ⊜[1]	204	41.06 N	78.38 W
Duboistown	200	41.13 N	77.04 W
Dub'onki	70	54.27 N	46.18 E
Dubossarskoje Vodochranilišče ⊜[1]	38	48.02 N	28.42 E
Dubossary, S.S.S.R.	68	47.16 N	29.08 E
Dubossary, S.S.S.R.	68	47.07 N	29.10 E
Dubovaja Rošča	66	53.11 N	36.04 E
Dubov'azovka	68	51.08 N	33.22 E
Duboviči	68	51.38 N	33.35 E
Dubovka, S.S.S.R.	68	51.26 N	41.25 E
Dubovka, S.S.S.R.	70	49.03 N	44.50 E
Dubovoje	66	53.08 N	40.05 E
Dubovskij	70	56.21 N	46.48 E
Dubovskoje	70	47.25 N	42.46 E
Dubovyj Ovrag	70	48.20 N	44.37 E
Dubovyj Umet	70	52.59 N	50.17 E
Duboweitun	79	50.42 N	120.14 E
Dubra	116	23.32 N	86.31 E
Dubrājpur	116	23.48 N	87.23 E
Dubréka	140	9.48 N	13.31 W
Dubreka □[4]	140	10.00 N	13.40 W
Dubrova, S.S.S.R.	66	52.25 N	29.58 E
Dubrova, S.S.S.R.	68	51.47 N	28.13 E
Dubrova, S.S.S.R.	70	57.42 N	55.01 E
Dubrova, S.S.S.R.	70	56.59 N	54.33 E
Dubrovica	68	51.34 N	26.34 E
Dubroviči	70	54.39 N	39.56 E
Dubrovicy	72	56.46 N	39.10 E
Dubrovino	76	55.28 N	83.17 E
Dubrovka, S.S.S.R.	66	59.51 N	30.56 E
Dubrovka, S.S.S.R.	66	53.42 N	33.30 E
Dubrovka, S.S.S.R.	66	59.13 N	36.13 E
Dubrovka, S.S.S.R.	72	54.44 N	36.21 E
Dubrovka, S.S.S.R.	73	47.54 N	39.02 E
Dubrovki	70	53.49 N	43.19 E
Dubrovnik	38	42.38 N	18.07 E
Dubrovno	66	54.35 N	30.41 E
Dubrovnoje, S.S.S.R.	76	54.49 N	68.06 E
Dubrovnoje, S.S.S.R.	76	57.58 N	69.25 E
Dubrovo	66	59.51 N	33.34 E
Dubrovskoje	78	58.45 N	111.10 E
Dubunskaja	76	43.46 N	80.13 E
Dubuque	180	42.30 N	90.41 W
Dubysa ≃	66	55.05 N	23.26 E
Duchana	75	38.02 N	68.13 E
Duchang	90	29.15 N	116.13 E
Duchcov	50	50.37 N	13.45 E
Ducherow	50	53.46 N	13.46 E
Duchesne	190	40.10 N	110.24 W
Duchesne ≃	190	40.05 N	109.41 W
Duchess	156	21.22 S	139.52 E
Duchess Hill	144	18.18 S	30.13 E
Duchovnickoje	70	52.28 N	48.15 E
Duchovščina	66	55.12 N	32.25 E
Duck ≃	184	36.02 N	87.52 W
Duckabush ≃	214	47.38 N	122.56 W
Duck Bay	174	52.10 N	100.09 W
Duck Creek ≃, Ont., Can.	271	42.18 N	82.41 W
Duck Creek ≃, Calif., U.S.	216	37.55 N	121.16 W
Duck Creek ≃, Ind., U.S.	208	40.08 N	85.57 W
Duck Creek ≃, Nev., U.S.	194	40.06 N	114.43 W
Duck Creek ≃, N. Dak., U.S.	188	46.03 N	102.14 W
Duck Creek ≃, Tex., U.S.	186	33.14 N	100.42 W
Duck Creek ≃, Tex., U.S.	212	32.48 N	96.31 W
Duck Creek ≃, Tex., U.S.	212	31.06 N	96.17 W
Duck Creek ≃, Wis., U.S.	180	44.33 N	88.02 W
Duck Hill	184	33.38 N	89.43 W
Duck Island Harbor C	266	40.55 N	73.23 W
Duck Key I	210	24.46 N	80.56 W
Duck Lake, Sask., Can.	174	52.47 N	106.13 W
Duck Lake, Mich., U.S.	206	42.24 N	84.47 W
Duck Lake ⊜, Man., Can.	174	54.52 N	98.11 W
Duck Lake ⊜, Mich., U.S.	206	42.23 N	84.47 W
Duck Lake ⊜, Mich., U.S.	271	42.40 N	83.35 W
Duck Mountain Λ	174	51.35 N	101.00 W
Duck Mountain Provincial Park ♠, Man., Can.	174	51.36 N	100.55 W
Duck Mountain Provincial Park ♠, Sask., Can.	174	51.38 N	101.53 W
Ducktown	182	35.03 N	84.23 W
Duck Valley Indian Reservation ◆[4]	194	42.00 N	116.10 W
Duckwall Mountain Λ	216	37.58 N	120.07 W
Duclair	46	49.29 N	0.53 E
Ducos	230e	14.34 N	60.58 W
Du Couedic, Cape ≻	156	36.04 S	136.42 E
Ducun	96	31.07 N	120.27 E
Duda ≃	236	2.33 N	74.02 W
Dudačkino	66	59.57 N	32.53 E
Dudčany	68	47.12 N	33.46 E
Duddington	44	52.36 N	0.32 W
Duddon ≃	42	54.15 N	3.13 W
Dudelange	52	49.28 N	6.05 E
Dudergofka ≃	255a	59.52 N	30.12 E
Duderstadt	48	51.31 N	10.16 E
Dūdhi	114	24.13 N	83.15 E
Dudh Kosi ≃	114	27.08 N	86.26 E
Dudhnai	114	25.59 N	90.44 E
Dudinka	64	69.25 N	86.15 E
Dudkin	68	47.53 N	40.32 E
Dudley, Eng., U.K.	44	52.30 N	2.05 W
Dudley, Mass., U.S.	197	42.03 N	71.56 W
Dudley, Pa., U.S.	204	40.12 N	78.10 W
Dudley Pond ⊜	273	42.20 N	71.22 W
Dudna ≃	112	19.07 N	76.54 E
Dudo	134	9.20 N	50.14 E
Dudo ≃	134	9.12 N	50.42 E
Dudorovskij	66	53.40 N	35.22 E
Dudullu	257b	41.02 N	29.09 E
Dudweiler	52	49.17 N	7.02 E
Dudzele	46	51.17 N	3.14 E
Due	79	50.50 N	142.06 E
Duékoué	140	6.45 N	7.21 W
Duerbote (Taikang)	79	46.52 N	124.27 E
Dueré	240	11.20 S	49.17 W
Dueré ≃	240	10.59 S	49.48 W
Duerji	79	45.39 N	121.49 E
Duerna ≃	34	42.19 N	5.54 W
Duero (Douro) ≃	34	41.08 N	8.40 W
Dueville	58	45.38 N	11.32 E
Due West	182	34.20 N	82.23 W
Dufault, Lac ⊜	180	48.19 N	79.00 W
Duff Dunbar	113	32.15 N	77.12 E
Duffel	46	51.06 N	4.31 E
Dufferin □[6]	202	44.05 N	80.15 W
Duffer Peak Λ	194	41.40 N	118.44 W
Duffield	152	25.50 S	134.40 E
Duffin Creek ≃	202	43.49 N	79.02 W
Dufourspitze Λ	54	45.55 N	7.52 E
Dufresne ≃	196	46.16 N	73.59 W
Dufur	214	45.27 N	121.08 W
Duga Resa	36	45.27 N	15.30 E
Dugdemona ≃	184	31.47 N	92.22 W
Dugede	110	30.54 N	90.48 E
Dugger	184	39.04 N	87.16 W
Dugino	73	47.09 N	39.27 E
Dugi Otok I	36	44.00 N	15.04 E
Dugna	72	54.25 N	36.51 E
Dugny	251	48.57 N	2.25 E
Dugny-sur-Meuse	52	49.06 N	5.23 E
Dug Pond ⊜	273	42.17 N	71.22 W
Du Gué ≃	166	57.21 N	70.45 W
Duğur	120	41.31 N	42.42 E
Duhernal Lake ⊜	266	40.24 N	74.22 W
Duhi	130	7.07 N	28.45 E
Duhnen	48	53.53 N	8.38 E
Duhu	90	22.04 N	112.56 E
Duida, Cerro Λ	236	3.25 N	65.40 W
Duifken Point ≻	154	12.33 S	141.38 E
Duilongdeqing	114	29.56 N	90.42 E
Duimianshan Λ	79	47.58 N	129.07 E
Duin Dui	165f	15.24 S	167.46 E
Duingen	48	52.00 N	9.42 E
Duingt	56	45.50 N	6.12 E
Duino	58	45.46 N	13.36 E
Duisburg	52		
	253	51.25 N	6.46 E
Duissern ◆[8]	253	51.26 N	6.47 E
Duitama	236	5.50 N	73.02 W
Duiveland I	48	51.38 N	4.00 E
Duiwelskloof	146	23.42 S	30.06 E
Duji	88	34.11 N	115.48 E
Dujiadao I	88	36.44 N	121.27 E
Dujiahang	96	31.03 N	121.29 E
Dujuma	134	1.14 N	42.37 E
Dukana ⍑[4]	144	3.59 N	37.16 E
Dukazi	110	30.54 N	92.52 E
Duke	186	34.40 N	99.34 W
Duke Center	204	41.57 N	78.29 W
Duke Island I	170	54.56 N	131.20 W
Dukelský priesmyk)(	68	49.25 N	21.43 E
Duke of York Bay C	166	65.25 N	84.50 W
Duke of York Island I	154	4.10 S	152.26 E
Dukes □[6]	197	41.23 N	70.31 W
Dukes Brook ≃	266	40.33 N	74.37 W
Duk Fadiat	130	7.45 N	31.25 E
Duk Faiwil	130	7.30 N	31.29 E
Dukhān	118	25.25 N	50.48 E
Dukhmays	132	31.07 N	31.04 E
Duki	110	30.09 N	68.34 E
Dukinfield	252	53.29 N	2.05 W
Dukla	30	49.34 N	21.41 E
Dūkštas	66	55.32 N	26.20 E
Duku, Nig.	136	10.49 N	10.46 E
Duku, Nig.	140	11.10 N	4.55 E
Dula	142	4.41 N	20.22 E
Dūlāb	257d	35.37 N	51.27 E
Dulag	106	10.57 N	125.02 E
Dulāi	114	23.57 N	89.31 E
Dulais ≃	44	51.41 N	3.47 W
Dulan (Chahanwusu)	92	36.16 N	98.28 E
Dulanhu ⊜	92	36.50 N	98.42 E
Dul'apino	70	57.15 N	40.49 E
Dulas ≃, Wales, U.K.	44	52.16 N	3.22 W
Dulas ≃, Wales, U.K.	44	52.36 N	3.50 W
Dulas Bay C	42	53.23 N	4.15 W
Dulata	76	43.26 N	80.50 E
Dulayb, Khawr V	130	11.45 N	32.47 E
Dulaym	136	25.58 N	14.03 E
Dulce	190	36.56 N	107.00 W
Dulce ≃	242	30.31 S	62.32 W
Dulce, Arroyo ≃	248	35.28 S	57.41 W
Dulce, Bahía C	224	16.33 N	98.50 W
Dulce, Golfo C	226	8.32 N	83.14 W
Dulce Grande	224	22.59 N	102.14 W
Dulce Nombre de Culmí	226	15.09 N	85.37 W
Dul'durga	78	50.41 N	113.36 E
Dulebino	72	55.47 N	38.32 E
Duleek	42	53.39 N	6.25 W
Dulgalach ≃	64	67.44 N	133.12 E
Dulin	88	38.22 N	116.43 E
Duliu	95	39.13 N	116.16 E
Duliujianhe ≃	95	38.51 N	117.20 E
Duliuzhen	95	39.01 N	116.54 E
Duljo Point ≻	106	9.35 N	123.43 E
Dulkaninna	156	29.01 S	138.27 E
Dülken	52	51.15 N	6.20 E
Dulles International Airport ⊠	198	38.58 N	77.28 W
Dullstroom	146	25.27 S	30.07 E
Dul Madoba	134	9.08 N	45.58 E
Dülmen	48	51.51 N	7.16 E
Dulovka	66	57.32 N	28.20 E
Dulovo	38	43.49 N	27.09 E
Dulq Maghār	120	36.22 N	38.39 E
D'ul'tydag, Gora Λ	74	41.58 N	46.56 E
Dulung ≃	116	22.08 N	87.05 E
Duluquin Point ≻	106	7.45 N	122.05 E
Duluth, Ga., U.S.	182	34.00 N	84.09 W
Duluth, Minn., U.S.	180	46.47 N	92.06 W
Dulverton	44	51.03 N	3.33 W
Dulwich ◆[8]	250	51.26 N	0.05 W
Duma, Bots.	146	18.45 S	22.46 E
Dūmā, Lubnān	120	34.12 N	35.50 E
Dūmā, Sūrīy.	122	33.35 N	36.24 E
Duma, Zaïre	144	4.57 N	27.19 E
Dumaguete	106	9.18 N	123.18 E
Dumai	104	1.41 N	101.27 E
Dumalag	106	11.18 N	122.37 E
Dumalinao	106	7.49 N	123.23 E
Dumali Point ≻	106	13.07 N	121.33 E
Dumanjug	106	10.04 N	123.26 E
Dumanquilas Bay C	106	7.34 N	123.04 E
Dumaran Channel Џ	106	10.25 N	119.45 E
Dumaran Island I	106	10.33 N	119.51 E
Dumaresq ≃	156	28.40 S	150.28 E
Dumaring	102	1.36 N	118.12 E
Dumas, Ark., U.S.	184	33.53 N	91.29 W
Dumas, Tex., U.S.	186	35.52 N	101.58 W
Dumayr	122	33.38 N	36.40 E
Dumayrah	132	31.08 N	31.22 E
Dumbarton	42	55.57 N	4.35 W
Dumbarton Bridge ◆[5]	272	37.31 N	122.07 W
Dumbarton Point ≻	272	37.30 N	122.06 W
Dumbier Λ	30	48.57 N	19.37 E
Dumbleyung	152	33.19 S	117.44 E
Dumbo	142	14.06 S	17.24 E
Dumbrăveni	38	46.14 N	24.35 E
Dum-Dum	116	22.35 N	88.24 E
Dum-Dum International Airport ⊠	116	22.38 N	88.25 E
Dume, Point ≻	218	34.00 N	118.48 W
Dumei	90	24.47 N	117.21 E
Dümeli	120	40.32 N	33.31 E
Dumfries, Scot., U.K.	42	55.04 N	3.37 W
Dumfries, Va., U.S.	198	38.34 N	77.20 W
Dumfries and Galloway □[4]	28	55.00 N	4.00 W
Duminiči	66	53.55 N	35.06 E
Dumjor	262b	22.38 N	88.13 E
Dumka	116	24.16 N	87.15 E
Dumlupınar	120	38.52 N	30.00 E
Dummar	122	33.32 N	36.14 E
Dümmer ⊜	48	52.31 N	8.19 E
Dummer Range ⩘	152	20.11 S	125.59 E
Dumoga-kecil	102	0.31 N	123.55 E
Dumoine ≃	180	46.13 N	77.51 W
Dumoine, Lac ⊜	180	46.53 N	77.54 W
Dumont, Iowa, U.S.	180	42.45 N	92.58 W
Dumont, N.J., U.S.	200	40.56 N	74.00 W
Dumont, Lac ⊜	180	46.04 N	76.27 W
Dumont d'urville ♉[3]	9	66.35 S	140.00 E
Dümpelfeld	52	50.27 N	6.56 E
Dümpten ◆[8]	253	51.27 N	6.54 E
Dumpu	154	5.50 S	145.45 E
Dumra	114	26.34 N	85.31 E
Dumraon	114	25.33 N	84.09 E
Dumria	116	22.47 N	89.26 E
Dumuriā	116	22.11 N	86.20 E
Dumyāṭ (Damietta)	132	31.25 N	31.48 E
Dumyāṭ □[4]	132	31.20 N	31.45 E
Dumyāṭ, Far' ≃	132	31.32 N	31.51 E
Dumyāṭ, Maṣabb ≃[1]	132	31.32 N	31.51 E
Dün Λ	50	51.21 N	10.30 E
Duna → Danube ≃	22	45.20 N	29.40 E
Dünaburg → Daugavpils	66	55.53 N	26.32 E
Dunaföldvár	30	46.48 N	18.55 E
Dunaharaszti	30	47.21 N	19.05 E
Dunaj	255a	59.58 N	30.56 E
Dunaj → Danube ≃	22	45.20 N	29.40 E
Dunaj, Ostrova II	64	73.52 N	124.29 E
Dunajec ≃	30	50.15 N	20.44 E
Dunajevcy	68	48.54 N	26.51 E
Dunajevo	78	52.05 N	117.02 E
Dunajská Streda	30	48.01 N	17.35 E
Dunakeszi	30	47.38 N	19.08 E
Dunany Point ≻	42	53.52 N	6.14 W
Dunărea → Danube ≃	22	45.20 N	29.40 E
Dunărea Veche ≃	38	45.17 N	28.02 E
Dunas	242	31.45 S	52.17 W
Duna-Tisza-csatorna Ξ	254c	47.21 N	19.05 E
Dunaújváros	30	46.58 N	18.57 E
Dunav → Danube ≃	22	45.20 N	29.40 E
Dunavățu-de-Sus	38	44.59 N	29.13 E
Duna-völgyi-főcsatorna Ξ	30	46.12 N	18.56 E
Dunback	162	45.23 S	170.38 E
Dunbar, Scot., U.K.	42	56.00 N	2.31 W
Dunbar, W. Va., U.S.	178	38.22 N	81.45 W
Dunbarton	265b	43.49 N	79.06 W
Dunblane, Sask., Can.	174	51.11 N	106.52 W
Dunblane, Scot., U.K.	28	56.12 N	3.59 W
Duncan, B.C., Can.	172	48.47 N	123.42 W
Duncan, Ariz., U.S.	190	32.43 N	109.06 W
Duncan, Miss., U.S.	184	34.03 N	90.45 W
Duncan, Okla., U.S.	186	34.30 N	97.57 W
Duncan ≃	172	50.11 N	116.57 W
Duncan Dam ◆[6]	172	50.15 N	116.55 W
Duncan Lake ⊜	172	50.20 N	117.00 W
Duncannon	198	40.23 N	77.02 W
Duncan Passage Џ	100	11.00 N	92.30 E
Duncans	231q	18.28 N	77.32 W
Duncansby Head ≻	28	58.39 N	3.01 W
Duncan's Creek ≃	264a	33.53 S	150.39 E
Duncanville	212	32.39 N	96.55 W
Dunchurch	44	52.20 N	1.16 W
Dundaga	66	57.31 N	22.21 E
Dundāhera	262a	28.38 N	77.26 E
Dundalk, Ont., Can.	202	44.10 N	80.24 W
Dundalk, Eire	28	54.01 N	6.25 W
Dundalk, Md., U.S.	198	39.15 N	76.31 W
Dundalk Bay C	28	53.57 N	6.17 W
Dundas, Austl.	264a	33.48 S	151.02 E
Dundas, Ont., Can.	202	43.16 N	79.58 W
Dundas, Minn., U.S.	180	44.26 N	93.12 W
Dundas □[6]	202	45.00 N	75.20 W
Dundas, Cape ≻	202	44.57 N	81.07 W
Dundas, Lake ⊜	152	32.35 S	121.50 E
Dundas Island I	172	54.33 N	130.55 W
Dundas Peninsula ≻[1]	166	74.50 N	111.30 W
Dundas Strait Џ	154	11.20 S	131.35 E
Dún Dealgan → Dundalk	28	54.01 N	6.25 W
Dundee, S. Afr.	148	28.12 S	30.16 E
Dundee, Scot., U.K.	28	56.28 N	3.00 W
Dundee, Fla., U.S.	210	28.07 N	81.37 W
Dundee, Ill., U.S.	206	42.06 N	88.17 W
Dundee, Mich., U.S.	206	41.57 N	83.40 W
Dundee, Miss., U.S.	184	34.32 N	90.27 W
Dundee, N.Y., U.S.	200	42.31 N	76.59 W
Dundee, Ohio, U.S.	204	40.35 N	81.37 W
Dundee, Oreg., U.S.	214	45.17 N	123.01 W
Dundee Creek C	274b	39.21 N	76.22 W
Dundgov' □[4]	92	45.30 N	106.30 E
Dundīṭ	132	30.41 N	31.18 E
Dundoo	156	27.39 S	144.39 E
Dundrum, Eire	42	53.17 N	6.15 W
Dundrum, N. Ire., U.K.	42	54.16 N	5.51 W
Dundrum Bay C	42	54.13 N	5.45 W
Dundurn	174	51.49 N	106.30 W
Dundwa Range ⩘	114	27.45 N	82.30 E
Duneaton Water ≃	42	55.32 N	3.42 W
Dunedin, N.Z.	162	45.52 S	170.30 E
Dunedin, Fla., U.S.	210	28.00 N	82.47 W
Dunedoo	156	32.01 S	149.24 E
Duneland Beach	206	41.45 N	86.50 W
Dunellen	266	40.35 N	74.28 W
Dunewood	266	40.38 N	73.11 W
Dunfermline	42	56.04 N	3.29 W
Du Ngae, Khao Λ	100	15.10 N	98.47 E
Dungannon, N. Ire., U.K.	42	54.31 N	6.46 W
Dungannon, Va., U.S.	182	36.50 N	82.28 W
Dūngarpur	110	23.50 N	73.43 E
Dungarvan	28	52.05 N	7.37 W
Dungarvan Harbour C	28	52.10 N	7.35 W
Dungas	140	13.04 N	9.20 E
Dungeness ≻	44	50.55 N	0.58 E
Dungeness ≃	214	48.08 N	123.06 W
Dungeness Spit ≻[2]	214	48.10 N	123.09 W
Dungiven	42	54.55 N	6.55 W
Dungo, Lagoa do ⊜	142	17.20 S	18.58 E
Dungog	156	32.24 S	151.46 E
Dungu	144	3.37 N	28.34 E
Dungun ≃	104	4.47 N	103.23 E
Dunham	196	45.08 N	72.48 W
Dunham Lake ⊜	271	42.39 N	83.41 W
Dunham-on-the-Hill	252	53.15 N	2.47 W
Dunham Town	252	53.23 N	2.24 W
Dunhe ≃	90	30.27 N	114.11 E
Dunheved, Austl.	264a	33.45 S	150.47 E
Dunheved → Launceston, Eng., U.K.	44	50.38 N	4.21 W
Dunhoucun	90	27.02 N	114.58 E
Dunhua	79	43.21 N	128.13 E
Dunhuang	92	40.12 N	94.41 E
Dunières	56	45.13 N	4.20 E
Dunilovo, S.S.S.R.	66	57.46 N	38.55 E
Dunilovo, S.S.S.R.	70	57.00 N	41.27 E
Dunkeld ◆[8]	263d	26.09 S	28.03 E
Dunkern ⊜	40	59.09 N	16.52 E
Dunker Pond ⊜	266	41.05 N	74.28 W
Dunkerque	46	51.03 N	2.22 E
Dunkery Hill Λ[2]	44	51.11 N	3.35 W
Dunkinsvilie	208	38.51 N	83.30 W
Dunkirk → Dunkerque, Fr.	46	51.03 N	2.22 E
Dunkirk, Ind., U.S.	206	40.23 N	85.13 W
Dunkirk, N.Y., U.S.	204	42.29 N	79.20 W
Dunkirk, Ohio, U.S.	206	40.48 N	83.39 W
Dunk's Green	250	51.15 N	0.19 E
Dunkuj	130	12.50 N	32.49 E
Dunkwa, Ghana	140	5.22 N	1.12 W
Dunkwa, Ghana	140	5.58 N	1.46 W
Dún Laoghaire	28	53.17 N	6.08 W
Dunlap, Iowa, U.S.	188	41.51 N	95.36 W
Dunlap, Tenn., U.S.	184	35.23 N	85.23 W
Dunlap Acres	218	34.03 N	117.06 W
Dunleary → Dún Laoghaire	28	53.17 N	6.08 W
Dunleer	42	53.50 N	6.24 W
Dun-le-Palestel	32	46.17 N	1.48 E
Dunlop	42	55.43 N	4.32 W
Dunloy	42	55.01 N	6.25 W
Dunmarra	154	16.42 S	133.25 E
Dunmore	200	41.25 N	75.38 W
Dunmore Town	228	25.30 N	76.39 W
Dunmurry	42	54.33 N	6.00 W
Dunn	182	35.19 N	78.37 W
Dünnbach ≃	52	50.10 N	7.18 E
Dunnellon	210	29.03 N	82.28 W
Dunnet Head ≻	28	58.39 N	3.23 W
Dunnigan	216	38.53 N	121.58 W
Dunning	188	41.50 N	100.06 W
Dunning Creek ≃	204	40.02 N	78.28 W
Dunningtown	269b	40.25 N	79.35 W
Dunn Loring	274c	38.53 N	77.14 W
Dunnockshaw	252	53.45 N	2.17 W
Dunns Bridge	206	41.13 N	86.59 W
Dunnville	202	42.54 N	79.36 W
Dunolly	159	36.52 S	143.44 E
Dunoon	42	55.57 N	4.56 W
Dunqul ⍑[4]	130	23.26 N	31.37 E
Dunqulah	130	19.10 N	30.29 E
Dunqulah al-Qadīmah	130	18.13 N	30.45 E
Dunqunāb	130	21.06 N	37.05 E
Dunqunāb, Khalīj C	130	21.05 N	37.08 E
Dunrea	174	49.25 N	99.44 W
Dun Rig Λ	42	55.34 N	3.10 W
Duns	42	55.47 N	2.20 W
Dunsandel	162	43.40 S	172.11 E
Dunseith	188	48.50 N	100.02 W
Dunsford	44	50.41 N	3.40 W
Dunsmuir	194	41.13 N	122.16 W
Dunstable, Eng., U.K.	44	51.53 N	0.32 W
Dunstable, Mass., U.S.	197	42.40 N	71.29 W
Dunstan Mountains ⩘	162	44.57 S	169.32 E
Dunster, B.C., Can.	172	53.08 N	119.50 W
Dunster, Eng., U.K.	44	51.12 N	3.27 W
Dun-sur-Auron	32	46.53 N	2.34 E
Dun-sur-Meuse	52	49.23 N	5.11 E
Dunton Green	44	51.18 N	0.11 E
Dunton Wayletts	250	51.35 N	0.24 E
Duntou	90	29.21 N	119.46 E
Duntroon	162	44.52 S	170.41 E
Duntroon Royal Military College ■	161b	35.18 S	149.12 E
Dunvegan	263d	26.09 S	28.09 E
Dunville	176	47.16 N	53.54 W
Dunwich	161a	27.31 S	153.23 E
Dunyāpur	113	29.48 N	71.44 E
Duobe ≃	140	5.45 N	8.00 W
Duobukulehe ≃	79	49.56 N	125.12 E
Duogu'nao	92	31.32 N	103.14 E
Duojundian	95	39.22 N	117.31 E
Duolun	88	42.15 N	116.18 E
Duolundabohuer	110	33.25 N	93.54 E
Duomaer	110	34.15 N	79.45 E
Duomo ♉[1]	256b	45.27 N	9.11 E
Duomula	110	34.07 N	82.30 E
Duong-dong	100	10.13 N	103.58 E
Duopatela	110	28.28 N	88.14 E
Duoyue	97	30.11 N	103.42 E
Duozhuang	88	35.35 N	118.12 E
Du Page □[6]	206	41.52 N	88.06 W
Du Page ≃	206	41.25 N	88.14 W
Du Page, East Branch ≃	268	41.42 N	88.09 W
Dupangling ⩘	92	25.32 N	111.11 E
Duparquet, Lac ⊜	180	48.28 N	79.16 W
Dupax	106	16.17 N	121.05 E
Duping	92	27.11 N	108.20 E
Dupl'atka	70	51.07 N	42.20 E
Dupli	72	54.21 N	36.54 E
Dupo	209	38.31 N	90.13 W
Dupont, Ind., U.S.	208	38.53 N	85.31 W
Dupont, Ohio, U.S.	206	41.03 N	84.18 W
Dupont, Pa., U.S.	200	41.20 N	75.45 W
Du Pont, Wash., U.S.	214	47.06 N	122.38 W
Dupree	188	45.03 N	101.36 W
Duque Bacelar	240	4.09 S	42.57 W
Duque de Bragança	142	9.06 S	15.57 E
Duque de Caxias	246	22.47 S	43.18 W
Duque de Caxias □[7]	277a	22.45 S	43.16 W
Duque de York, Isla I	244	50.40 S	75.20 W
Duquesne	204	40.21 N	79.51 W
Duquesne University ♉[2]	269b	40.26 N	79.59 W
DuQuoin	184	38.01 N	89.14 W
Dūrā	122	31.30 N	35.02 E
Durack ≃	154	15.33 S	127.52 E
Durack Range ⩘	150	17.00 S	128.00 E
Durağan	120	41.25 N	35.04 E
Durak	120	39.42 N	28.17 E
Dural	160	33.41 S	151.02 E
Duran	190	34.28 N	105.24 W
Durance ≃	56	43.55 N	4.44 E
Durand, Ill., U.S.	180	42.26 N	89.20 W
Durand, Mich., U.S.	206	42.55 N	83.59 W
Durand, Wis., U.S.	180	44.38 N	91.58 W
Durand, Récif ✢[2]	165f	22.03 S	168.39 E
Durango, Esp.	34	43.10 N	2.37 W
Durango, Méx.	224	24.02 N	104.40 W
Durango, Colo., U.S.	190	37.16 N	107.53 W
Durango □[3]	224	23.30 N	104.45 W
Duranillin	158a	33.31 S	116.48 E
Durant, Iowa, U.S.	180	41.36 N	90.54 W
Durant, Miss., U.S.	184	33.04 N	89.51 W
Durant, Okla., U.S.	186	34.00 N	96.23 W
Duras	32	44.41 N	0.11 E
Durasovka	70	51.41 N	44.55 E
Duraton ≃	34	41.37 N	4.07 W
Duraur ≃	134	10.40 N	49.25 E
Durazno	242	33.22 S	56.31 W
Durazno, Arroyo ≃	248	34.41 S	58.52 W
Durazzo → Durrës	38	41.19 N	19.26 E
Durbādānga	116	22.57 N	89.15 E
Durban	148	29.55 S	30.56 E
Durban Roodepoort Deep Gold Mines ◆[7]	263d	26.10 S	27.51 E
Durbanville	148	33.50 S	18.39 E
Durbe	66	56.35 N	21.21 E
D'urbel'džin	75	41.16 N	74.57 E
Durbet-Daba, Pereval)(	76	49.37 N	89.25 E
Durbin	178	38.33 N	79.50 W
Durbo	134	11.30 N	50.18 E
Durbuy	52	50.21 N	5.28 E
Durchholz	253	51.23 N	7.17 E
Durdent ≃	46	49.51 N	0.36 E
Đurđevac	36	46.03 N	17.04 E
Durdur ≃	134	10.38 N	44.02 E
Dureji	110	25.53 N	67.18 E
Düren	52	50.48 N	6.28 E
Durg	110	21.11 N	81.17 E
Durg □[5]	114	22.00 N	81.10 E
Durgāpur	116	23.29 N	87.20 E
Durham, Ont., Can.	202	44.10 N	80.49 W
Durham, Eng., U.K.	42	54.47 N	1.34 W
Durham, Calif., U.S.	194	39.44 N	121.48 W
Durham, Conn., U.S.	197	41.29 N	72.41 W
Durham, Mo., U.S.	209	39.58 N	91.40 W
Durham, N.H., U.S.	178	43.08 N	70.56 W
Durham, N.C., U.S.	182	35.59 N	78.54 W
Durham, Oreg., U.S.	214	45.25 N	122.46 W
Durham □[6], Ont., Can.	202	44.05 N	78.35 W
Durham □[6], Eng., U.K.	42	54.45 N	1.45 W
Durham Cathedral ♉[1]	42	54.46 N	1.36 W
Durham Downs	156	27.05 S	141.54 E
Durham Heights Λ	166	71.08 N	122.56 W
Durham Pond ⊜	266	41.00 N	74.27 W
Durhamville	200	43.07 N	75.40 W
Durian ≃	105a	6.01 S	106.24 E
Durian, Selat Џ	104	0.42 N	103.42 E
Duriansebatang	102	0.47 S	109.56 E
Durian Tipus	104	3.07 N	102.13 E
D'urinskije Razlivy ☷	70	50.25 N	50.20 E
Durlabhpur	262b	22.47 N	88.29 E
Durlach ◆[8]	52	49.00 N	8.28 E
Durlešty	68	47.02 N	28.45 E
Durmersheim	52	48.56 N	8.16 E
Durmitor Λ	38	43.08 N	19.01 E
Durness	28	58.33 N	4.45 W
Durnikino	70	51.39 N	42.49 E
Dürnkrut	30	48.28 N	16.51 E
Durón	34	40.38 N	2.43 W
Duross Heights	275	39.41 N	75.37 W
Dürre Liesing ≃	254b	48.08 N	16.16 E
Durrell	176	49.40 N	54.44 W
Dürrenboden	54	46.57 N	8.50 E
Durrës	38	41.19 N	19.26 E
Durrie	156	25.38 S	140.16 E
Durrington	44	51.13 N	1.45 W
Dürröhrsdorf	50	51.01 N	14.00 E
Dursey Head ≻	28	51.35 N	10.14 W
Dursley	44	51.42 N	2.21 W
Dursunbey	120	39.35 N	28.38 E
D'urt'uli	76	55.29 N	54.52 E
Duru	144	4.14 N	28.45 E
Duru Λ	134	5.30 N	37.10 E
Dūruḥ	118	32.17 N	60.30 E
Durunkah	132	27.08 N	31.10 E
Durūz, Jabal ad- ⩘	122	32.40 N	36.44 E
D'Urville Island I	162	40.50 S	173.52 E
Duryea	200	41.21 N	75.45 W
Dušak	118	37.13 N	60.02 E
Dušanbe	75	38.35 N	68.48 E
Dušanbe □[4]	75	38.40 N	69.40 E
Dušekan	64	60.39 N	109.03 E
Dušeti	74	42.06 N	44.42 E
Dusetos	66	55.45 N	25.51 E
Dushai ≃	92	32.48 N	110.38 E
Dushan, Zhg.	90	31.36 N	116.14 E
Dushan, Zhg.	92	25.53 N	107.30 E
Dushanbe → Dušanbe	75	38.35 N	68.48 E
Dushanhu ⊜	88	35.06 N	116.52 E
Dushantou	96	30.46 N	119.47 E
Dushanzi	76	44.20 N	84.51 E
Dusheng	88	38.23 N	116.33 E
Dushichang	97	29.10 N	106.31 E
Dushikou	88	41.17 N	115.38 E
Dushore	200	41.31 N	76.24 W
Düshorn	48	52.49 N	9.37 E
Dushu	90	33.21 N	113.09 E
Dushuhu ⊜	96	31.17 N	120.42 E
Dusios Ežeras ⊜	66	54.18 N	23.42 E
Dusky Sound Џ	162	45.47 S	166.28 E
Dušocha, Gora Λ	75	39.10 N	70.01 E
Duson	184	30.12 N	92.11 W
Dušonovo	72	56.04 N	38.18 E
Düssel	253	51.16 N	7.03 E
Düsselbach ≃	253	51.13 N	6.45 E
Düsseldorf	52		
	253	51.12 N	6.47 E
Düsseldorf □[5]	48	51.15 N	7.00 E
Düsseldorf, Flughafen ⊠	52	51.17 N	6.45 E
Düsseldorf, Universität ♉[2]	253	51.12 N	6.48 E
Düsseldorf-Mettmann □[8]	253	51.16 N	6.58 E
Dusslingen	54	48.27 N	9.03 E
Dussnang	54	47.26 N	8.58 E
Duston	44	52.14 N	0.56 W
Dutaliutexingsishan ⩘	110	34.15 N	87.00 E
Dutch Creek ≃	184	35.03 N	93.24 W
Dutchess □[6]	200	41.42 N	73.56 W
Dutch Harbor	170	53.53 N	166.32 W
Dutch John	190	40.55 N	109.24 W
Dutchman Creek ≃	216	37.11 N	120.28 W
Dutchman Draw V	190	37.00 N	113.29 W
Dutianjie	92	24.38 N	101.31 E
Dutlhe	146	23.55 S	23.47 E
Dutoitspiek Λ	148	33.46 S	19.12 E
Dutou	96	31.19 N	120.54 E
Dutovlje	58	45.46 N	13.50 E
Dutovo	24	63.47 N	56.35 E
Dutsen Wai	140	10.50 N	8.12 E
Dutton, Ont., Can.	204	42.39 N	81.30 W
Dutton, Eng., U.K.	252	53.19 N	2.38 W
Dutton, Mich., U.S.	206	42.50 N	85.35 W
Dutton, Mont., U.S.	192	47.51 N	111.43 W
Dutton ≃	156	20.45 S	143.12 E
Dutton, Mount Λ, Alaska, U.S.	170	55.10 N	162.15 W
Dutton, Mount Λ, Utah, U.S.	190	38.01 N	112.13 W
Dutun	95	39.46 N	117.02 E
Dutzow	209	38.37 N	90.59 W
Duut	76	47.30 N	91.40 E
Duval, Lac ⊜	180	46.19 N	76.55 W
Duvall	214	47.44 N	121.59 W
Duvan	76	55.42 N	57.54 E
Duvanka ≃	73	49.35 N	38.10 E
Duvannyj	74	40.06 N	49.24 E
Duved	26	63.24 N	12.52 E
Duvernay ◆[8]	265a	45.35 N	73.40 W
Duvno	36	43.43 N	17.14 E
Duwamish	214	47.32 N	122.19 W
Duwaydār, Bi'r ad- ⍑[4]	132	30.55 N	32.31 E
Duxbury	197	42.02 N	70.40 W
Duxbury Bay C	197	42.02 N	70.39 W
Duxun	90	23.55 N	117.37 E
Duyagan Point ≻	106	12.36 N	121.33 E
Duyang	92	23.59 N	107.47 E
Duyun	92	26.12 N	107.31 E
Düzce	120	40.50 N	31.10 E
Duze	90	29.07 N	118.56 E
Dve Mogili	38	43.36 N	25.52 E
Dvina Occidental → Zapadnaja Dvina ≃	66	57.04 N	24.03 E
Dvina Setentrional → Severnaja Dvina ≃	24	64.32 N	40.30 E
Dvinje, Ozero ⊜	66	56.08 N	31.12 E
Dvinsk → Daugavpils	66	55.53 N	26.32 E
Dvinskaja Guba C	24	65.00 N	39.45 E
Dvojnovskij	70	51.03 N	42.27 E
Dvorcy	72	54.37 N	36.00 E
Dvorec	78	58.23 N	101.55 E
Dvoriši	66	58.12 N	35.13 E
Dvornikovo	72	55.30 N	38.38 E
Dvuch Cirkoje, Gora Λ	64	67.35 N	168.07 E
Dvugorbaja, Gora Λ	170	68.30 N	179.20 E
Dvulučnoje	68	50.02 N	38.02 E
Dvůr Králové [nad Labem]	30	50.26 N	15.48 E
Dwangwa ≃	144	12.33 S	34.12 E
Dwarbasini	262b	22.59 N	88.14 E
Dwārka	110	22.14 N	68.58 E
Dwārka ≃	116	23.44 N	88.11 E
Dwārkeswar ≃	116	23.06 N	87.21 E
Dwarli	262c	19.12 N	73.08 E
Dwars Kill ≃	266	40.58 N	73.58 W
Dwellingup	158a	32.43 S	116.02 E
Dwight	206	41.05 N	88.26 W
Dwight D. Eisenhower Lock ◆[5]	196	45.00 N	74.45 W
Dwina-Bucht → Dvinskaja Guba C	24	65.00 N	39.45 E
Dwingeloo	48	52.50 N	6.21 E
Dwyfor ≃	44	52.55 N	4.17 W
Dwyka	148	33.02 S	21.30 E
Dwyka ≃	148	33.18 S	21.39 E
Dyam ≃	76	46.00 N	85.50 E
Dybbøl	41	54.55 N	9.45 E
Dyberry Creek ≃	200	41.35 N	75.15 W
Dyche Stadium ♠	268	42.04 N	87.41 W
Dych-Tau, Gora Λ	74	43.03 N	43.08 E
Dyck, Schloss ⊥	253	51.09 N	6.34 E
Dyer, Ind., U.S.	206	41.30 N	87.31 W
Dyer, Tenn., U.S.	184	36.04 N	88.59 W
Dyer, Cape ≻	166	66.37 N	61.18 W
Dyer Bay C	202	45.10 N	81.18 W
Dyer Island I	148	34.41 S	19.25 E
Dyero	140	12.50 N	6.30 W
Dyersburg	184	36.03 N	89.23 W
Dyersville	180	42.29 N	91.08 W
Dyess Air Force Base ■	186	32.25 N	99.51 W
Dyfed □[6]	44	52.00 N	4.30 W
Dyfi ≃	44	52.32 N	4.03 W
Dyje (Thaya) ≃	30	48.37 N	16.56 E
Dyke Ackland Bay C	154	9.00 S	148.45 E
Dyken Pond ⊜	200	42.43 N	73.26 W
Dykes Pond ⊜	273	42.36 N	70.44 W
Dyle (Dijle) ≃	52	51.04 N	4.25 E
Dylym	74	43.04 N	46.38 E
Dymchurch	44	51.02 N	1.00 E
Dyment	174	49.37 N	92.19 W
Dymer	68	50.47 N	30.18 E
Dymock	44	51.59 N	2.26 W
Dynów	30	49.49 N	22.14 E
Dyreborg	41	55.04 N	10.13 E
Dyrnesvågen	26	63.26 N	7.51 E
Dyrotz	254a	52.33 N	12.58 E
Dysart, Sask., Can.	174	50.56 N	104.02 W
Dysart, Scot., U.K.	42	56.08 N	3.08 W
Dysart, Iowa, U.S.	180	42.10 N	92.18 W
Dysart, Pa., U.S.	204	40.36 N	78.31 W
Dysnų Ežeras ⊜	66	55.29 N	26.20 E
Dysse-Alin', Chrebet ⩘	79	52.05 N	135.00 E
Dysselsdorp	148	33.34 S	22.28 E
Dysynni ≃	44	52.36 N	4.05 W
Dzaamar	78	48.10 N	104.50 E
Dzaamaryn Uul ⩘	78	48.20 N	104.40 E
Džabžur	74	40.54 N	43.58 E
Dzachuj	92	45.00 N	96.32 E
Džagdy, Chrebet ⩘	79	53.40 N	131.00 E
Džalagaš	76	45.05 N	64.40 E
Džalal-Abad	75	40.56 N	73.00 E
Džalinda	79	53.29 N	123.54 E
Džamantau, Gory ⩘	75	40.55 N	74.40 E
Džamašuj	75	40.52 N	71.28 E
Džambejty	70	50.16 N	52.35 E
Džambul, S.S.S.R.	70	47.34 N	50.12 E
Džambul, S.S.S.R.	75	42.54 N	71.22 E
Džambul, S.S.S.R.	76	47.12 N	71.42 E
Džambul □[4]	76	44.00 N	72.00 E
Džanga	118	40.00 N	53.03 E
Džangi-Džol	75	41.36 N	72.08 E
Džankoj	68	45.43 N	34.24 E
Džansugurov	76	45.24 N	79.29 E
Džanybek	70	49.25 N	46.51 E
Dzaoudzi	147a	12.47 S	45.17 E

English	Deutsch	Español	Français	Português
≃ River	Fluss	Río	Rivière	Rio
Ξ Canal	Kanal	Canal	Canal	Canal
ʟ Waterfall, Rapids	Wasserfall, Stromschnellen	Cascada, Rápidos	Chute d'eau, Rapides	Cascata, Rápidos
Џ Strait	Meeresstrasse	Estrecho	Détroit	Estreito
C Bay, Gulf	Bucht, Golf	Bahía, Golfo	Baie, Golfe	Baía, Golfo
⊜ Lake, Lakes	See, Seen	Lago, Lagos	Lac, Lacs	Lago, Lagos
☷ Swamp	Sumpf	Pantano	Marais	Pântano
⊼ Ice Features, Glacier	Eis- und Gletscherformen	Accidentes Glaciales	Formes glaciaires	Acidentes Glaciares
⍑ Other Hydrographic Features	Andere Hydrographische Objekte	Otros Elementos Hidrográficos	Autres données hydrographiques	Outros Elementos Hidrográficos
✢ Submarine Features	Untermeerische Objekte	Accidentes Submarinos	Formes de relief sous-marin	Acidentes Submarinos
□ Political Unit	Politische Einheit	Unidad Política	Entité politique	Unidade Política
♉ Cultural Institution	Kulturelle Institution	Institución Cultural	Institution culturelle	Instituição Cultural
⊥ Historical Site	Historische Stätte	Sitio Histórico	Site historique	Sitio Histórico
♠ Recreational Site	Erholungs- und Ferienort	Sitio de Recreo	Centre de loisirs	Sítio de Lazer
⊠ Airport	Flughafen	Aeropuerto	Aéroport	Aeroporto
■ Military Installation	Militäranlage	Instalación Militar	Installation militaire	Instalação Militar
◆ Miscellaneous	Verschiedenes	Misceláneo	Divers	Miscelânea

ENGLISH — Name | Page | Lat. °′ | Long. °′
DEUTSCH — Name | Seite | Breite °′ | Länge °′ E = Ost

Džardžan 64 68.43 N 124.02 E
Džargalant → Chovd, Mong. 76 48.01 N 91.39 E
Džargalant, Mong. 78 48.47 N 100.43 E
Džargalant, Mong. 78 48.37 N 99.17 E
Džargalant, Mong. 78 47.19 N 99.39 E
Džargalant, Mong. 78 46.57 N 115.15 E
Džargaltchaan 78 47.32 N 109.28 E
Džarylgač, Ostrov I 68 46.02 N 32.55 E
Džarylgačskij Zaliv C 68 46.05 N 32.50 E
Dzaudzhikau → Ordžonikidze 74 43.03 N 44.40 E
Džaur 79 50.02 N 138.30 E
Džava 74 42.24 N 43.54 E
Dzavchan 78 48.48 N 93.07 E
Dzavchan □[4] 78 48.00 N 96.00 E
Dzavchan ≃ 78 48.54 N 93.23 E
Dzavchanmandal 78 48.22 N 95.03 E
Džavchlant → Uliastaj 78 47.45 N 96.49 E
Džazator 76 49.45 N 87.23 E
Džbán ∧ 50 50.12 N 13.45 E
Džebel 118 39.38 N 54.14 E
Džebrail 74 39.23 N 47.02 E
Dzegamčaj ≃ 74 41.00 N 45.59 E
Dželinda 64 70.08 N 114.00 E
Dzemul 222 21.12 N 89.18 W
Dzeng 142 3.45 N 12.00 E
Dženretlen, Mys ≻ 170 67.07 N 173.45 W
Dzenzik, Mys ≻ 68 46.30 N 36.07 E
Džergetal 75 41.30 N 75.47 E
Džermuk 74 39.51 N 45.41 E
Dzerzhinsk → Dzeržinsk 70 56.15 N 43.24 E
Dzeržinsk, S.S.S.R. 66 53.41 N 27.08 E
Dzeržinsk, S.S.S.R. 68 50.09 N 27.56 E
Dzeržinsk, S.S.S.R. 70 56.15 N 43.24 E
Dzeržinsk, S.S.S.R. 73 48.26 N 37.50 E
Dzeržinskaja, Gora ∧ 66 53.51 N 27.03 E
Dzeržinskij, S.S.S.R. 68 48.02 N 39.26 E
Dzeržinskij, S.S.S.R. 72 55.38 N 37.50 E
Dzeržinskij, S.S.S.R. 76 54.01 N 90.12 E
Dzeržinskij •[8] 73 48.02 N 39.26 E
Dzeržinskoje, S.S.S.R. 76 56.49 N 95.18 E
Dzeržinskoje, S.S.S.R. 76 45.50 N 81.07 E
Džetim, Chrebet ⋀ 75 41.35 N 77.05 E
Džetygara 76 52.11 N 61.12 E
Džetyoguz 75 42.27 N 78.14 E
Džezdy 76 48.04 N 67.05 E
Džezkazgan, S.S.S.R. 76 47.53 N 67.27 E
Džezkazgan, S.S.S.R. 76 47.47 N 67.46 E
Dzhambul → Džambul 75 42.54 N 71.22 E
Działdowo 30 53.15 N 20.10 E
Działoszyce 30 50.22 N 20.21 E
Dzibalchén 222 19.31 N 89.45 W
Dzibilchaltun ⊥ 222 21.05 N 89.36 W
Džida ≃ 78 50.37 N 106.14 E
Džidinskij, Chrebet ⋀ 78 50.10 N 102.00 E
Dzierzgoń 30 53.56 N 19.21 E
Dzierżoniów (Reichenbach) 30 50.44 N 16.39 E
Dzilam González 222 21.17 N 88.56 W
Džilav 75 39.19 N 67.45 E
Džilga 75 41.43 N 69.01 E
Džinst 92 45.22 N 100.35 E
Dzioua 138 33.14 N 5.14 E
Džirgatal' 75 39.13 N 71.12 E
Dzitás 222 20.51 N 88.31 W
Dzitbalché 222 20.19 N 90.03 W
Dziwna ≃[1] 50 54.01 N 14.44 E
Dziwnów 30 54.03 N 14.45 E
Džizak 75 40.06 N 67.50 E
Dzodze 140 6.14 N 1.00 E
Džubga 68 44.20 N 38.43 E
Džugdžur, Chrebet ⋀ 64 58.00 N 136.00 E
Džūkste 66 56.47 N 23.15 E
Džul'fa 74 38.58 N 45.38 E
Džumabazar 75 39.31 N 67.13 E
Džumgoltau, Chrebet ⋀ 75 42.18 N 74.32 E
Dzungarian Basin → Zhuangaerpendi ≚[1] 76 45.00 N 88.00 E
Dzungarian Gate (Džungarskije Vorota))(76 45.25 N 82.25 E
Džungarskij Alatau, Chrebet ⋀ 76 45.00 N 81.00 E
Džungarskije Vorota → Dzungarian Gate)(76 45.25 N 82.25 E
Džurak-Sal ≃ 70 47.18 N 43.36 E
Džurch 78 48.55 N 100.10 E
Džurin 68 48.41 N 28.18 E
Džurun 76 49.15 N 57.37 E
Džusaly 76 45.28 N 64.05 E
Dzüünchangaj 78 49.19 N 95.20 E
Dzüüncharaa 78 48.52 N 106.28 E
Dzüüngovy 78 49.55 N 93.52 E
Dzuunmod 78 47.45 N 106.58 E
Dzygovka 68 48.22 N 28.19 E

E

Eads 188 38.29 N 102.47 W
Eagar 190 34.06 N 109.11 W
Eagle, Alaska, U.S. 170 64.46 N 141.16 W
Eagle, Colo., U.S. 190 39.39 N 106.50 W
Eagle, N.Y., U.S. 200 42.33 N 78.18 W
Eagle, Wis., U.S. 206 42.53 N 88.28 W
Eagle ≃, Newf., Can. 166 53.35 N 57.25 W
Eagle ≃, Yukon, Can. 170 67.20 N 137.10 W
Eagle ≃, Colo., U.S. 190 39.39 N 107.04 W
Eagle, Mount ∧ 231n 17.46 N 64.49 W
Eagle Bay 172 50.56 N 119.12 W
Eagle Bend 188 44.10 N 93.53 W
Eagle Bridge 200 42.57 N 73.24 W
Eagle Butte 188 45.00 N 101.14 W
Eagle Chief Creek ≃ 186 36.22 N 98.27 W
Eagle Creek 214 45.21 N 122.21 W
Eagle Creek ≃, Sask., Can. 174 52.22 N 107.24 W
Eagle Creek ≃, Ariz., U.S. 190 32.58 N 109.25 W
Eagle Creek ≃, Ind., U.S. 208 39.43 N 86.12 W
Eagle Creek ≃, Ky., U.S. 208 38.36 N 85.04 W
Eagle Creek ≃, Mont., U.S. 192 48.12 N 111.11 W
Eagle Creek ≃, N. Mex., U.S. 186 32.47 N 104.20 W
Eagle Creek ≃, Ohio, U.S. 204 41.18 N 80.53 W
Eagle Creek ≃, Ohio, U.S. 208 38.43 N 83.51 W
Eagle Creek ≃, Oreg., U.S. 192 44.45 N 117.10 W
Eagle Creek ≃, Oreg., U.S. 214 45.21 N 122.23 W
Eagle Creek, East Fork ≃ 208 38.47 N 83.43 W
Eagle Creek, West Fork ≃ 208 38.47 N 83.43 W
Eagle Creek Reservoir @[1] 208 39.50 N 86.18 W
Eagledale 214 47.37 N 122.32 W
Eagle Farm Airport ⊠ 161a 27.27 S 153.11 E
Eagle Grove 180 42.40 N 93.54 W
Eagle Harbor 200 43.15 N 78.15 W
Eaglehawk 159 36.43 S 144.15 E
Eagle Hill ≃ 273 42.42 N 70.49 W
Eagle Key I 210 25.09 N 80.36 W
Eagle Lake, Fla., U.S. 210 27.59 N 81.45 W
Eagle Lake, Maine, U.S. 176 47.02 N 68.36 W
Eagle Lake, Mich., U.S. 206 41.48 N 86.02 W
Eagle Lake, Tex., U.S. 212 29.35 N 96.20 W
Eagle Lake @, B.C., Can. 172 51.55 N 124.25 W
Eagle Lake @, Ont., Can. 174 50.39 N 94.54 W
Eagle Lake @, Ont., Can. 174 49.42 N 93.13 W
Eagle Lake @, Ont., Can. 202 44.41 N 76.43 W
Eagle Lake @, Ont., Can. 202 45.08 N 78.29 W
Eagle Lake @, Calif., U.S. 194 40.39 N 120.44 W
Eagle Lake @, Maine, U.S. 176 46.20 N 69.20 W
Eagle Lake @, Mich., U.S. 206 41.48 N 86.02 W
Eagle Lake @, Tex., U.S. 212 29.34 N 96.21 W
Eagle Lake @, Wis., U.S. 206 42.42 N 88.07 W
Eagle Mountain, Calif., U.S. 194 33.49 N 115.27 W
Eagle Mountain, Tex., U.S. 212 32.52 N 97.30 W
Eagle Mountain ∧ 192 46.20 N 115.07 W
Eagle Mountain ∧[2] 180 47.54 N 90.33 W
Eagle Mountain Lake @[1] 212 32.55 N 97.30 W
Eagle Nest Butte ∧ 188 43.27 N 101.39 W
Eagle Nest Lake @ 212 29.13 N 95.37 W
Eagle Pass 186 28.43 N 100.30 W
Eagle Peak ∧, Calif., U.S. 194 41.17 N 120.12 W
Eagle Peak ∧, Calif., U.S. 218 35.15 N 118.28 W
Eagle Peak ∧, Calif., U.S. 272 37.54 N 121.54 W
Eagle River, Alaska, U.S. 170 61.19 N 149.34 W
Eagle River, Mich., U.S. 180 47.24 N 88.18 W
Eagle River, Wis., U.S. 180 45.55 N 89.15 W
Eagle Rock 182 37.38 N 79.48 W
Eagle Rock •[8] 270 34.09 N 118.12 W
Eagle Rock Reservation ♠ 266 40.49 N 74.14 W
Eaglesfield 42 55.03 N 3.12 W
Eaglesham, Alta., Can. 172 55.47 N 117.53 W
Eaglesham, Scot., U.K. 42 55.44 N 4.18 W
Eagles Mere 200 41.25 N 76.35 W
Eagle Village 170 64.47 N 141.07 W
Eagleville, Conn., U.S. 197 41.47 N 72.17 W
Eagleville, Pa., U.S. 275 40.10 N 75.24 W
Eagleville, Wis., U.S. 206 42.52 N 88.26 W
Ealing •[8] 44 51.31 N 0.20 W
Eamont ≃ 42 54.40 N 2.39 W
Earaheedy 152 25.34 S 121.39 E
Earby 42 53.56 N 2.08 W
Earcroft 252 53.43 N 2.29 W
Eardisley 44 52.08 N 2.59 W
Eardley Lake @ 174 52.32 N 96.05 W
Ear Falls 174 50.38 N 93.13 W
Earle 184 35.16 N 90.28 W
Earlestown 252 53.27 N 2.39 W
Earl Grey 174 50.56 N 104.45 W
Earlham 184 41.30 N 94.07 W
Earlimart 216 35.53 N 119.16 W
Earlington 184 37.16 N 87.30 W
Earl Park 206 40.42 N 87.25 W
Earls Colne 44 51.56 N 0.42 E
Earl Shilton 44 52.35 N 1.20 W
Earl Soham 44 52.14 N 1.16 E
Earlston 42 55.39 N 2.40 W
Earlton 200 42.21 N 73.54 W
Earlville, Ill., U.S. 206 41.35 N 88.55 W
Earlville, N.Y., U.S. 200 42.44 N 75.33 W
Earlville, Pa., U.S. 198 40.19 N 75.44 W
Earlwood 264a 33.56 S 151.08 E
Early 188 42.28 N 95.09 W
Early Winters Creek ≃ 214 48.35 N 120.35 W
Earn ≃ 28 56.21 N 3.19 W
Earnslaw, Mount ∧ 162 44.37 S 168.24 E
Earsdon 42 55.03 N 1.29 W
Earth 186 34.14 N 102.24 W
Easington 42 54.47 N 1.19 W
Easingwold 42 54.07 N 1.11 W
Easley 182 34.50 N 82.36 W
East ≃, Ont., Can. 202 45.20 N 79.17 W
East ≃, Colo., U.S. 190 38.40 N 106.51 W
East ≃, N.Y., U.S. 266 40.48 N 73.48 W
East, University of the ʋ[2] 259f 14.36 N 120.59 E
East Aberthaw 44 51.23 N 3.22 W
East Acton 273 42.29 N 71.25 W
East Allen ≃ 42 54.55 N 2.19 W
East Alliance 204 40.55 N 81.04 W
East Alligator ≃ 154 12.08 S 132.42 E
East Alton 209 38.53 N 90.06 W
East Amherst 200 43.01 N 78.42 W
East Angus 196 45.29 N 71.40 W
East Arlington 200 43.04 N 73.09 W
East Atlantic Beach 266 40.35 N 73.43 W
East Aurora 200 42.46 N 78.37 W
East Avon 200 42.55 N 77.42 W
East Bangor 200 40.53 N 75.11 W
East Barming 250 51.16 N 0.28 E
East Barnet •[8] 250 51.38 N 0.09 W
East Basin C 269a 41.32 N 81.40 W
East Bay C, Fla., U.S. 182 30.05 N 85.32 W
East Bay C, N.Y., U.S. 200 40.38 N 73.32 W
East Bay C, Tex., U.S. 212 29.30 N 94.35 W
East Bedfont •[8] 250 51.27 N 0.26 W
East Bend 182 36.13 N 80.31 W
East Berbice □[5] 236 5.20 N 57.50 W
East Berkshire 196 44.56 N 72.42 W
East-Berlin → Berlin (Ost), D.D.R. 254a 52.30 N 13.25 E
East Berlin, Conn., U.S. 197 41.37 N 72.43 W
East Berlin, Pa., U.S. 198 39.56 N 76.59 W
East Bernard 212 29.32 N 96.04 W
East Bernstadt 182 37.11 N 84.07 W
East Berwick 200 41.03 N 76.13 W
East Bethany 200 42.56 N 78.06 W
East Bhāgīrath Plain ≚ 116 23.30 N 88.30 E
East Billerica 273 42.35 N 71.14 W
East Blackstone 197 42.02 N 71.31 W
East Bloomfield 200 42.54 N 77.26 W
East Boston •[8] 273 42.23 N 71.02 W
Eastbourne, N.Z. 162 41.18 S 174.54 E
Eastbourne, Eng., U.K. 44 50.46 N 0.17 E
East Brady 204 40.59 N 79.37 W
East Braintree 174 49.37 N 95.38 W
East Branch 200 41.59 N 75.08 W
East Branch Clarion River Lake @[1] 204 41.35 N 78.35 W
East Brewster 197 41.46 N 70.04 W
East Brewton 184 31.05 N 87.04 W
East Bridgewater 197 42.02 N 70.58 W
East Brimfield Lake @[1] 197 42.06 N 72.10 W
East Brookfield 197 42.14 N 72.03 W
East Brooklyn 197 41.48 N 71.54 W
East Brother I 261d 22.20 N 113.58 E
East Brunswick 198 40.25 N 74.23 W
East Bucas Island I 106 9.43 N 126.02 E
East Burwood 264b 37.51 S 145.09 E
Eastbury 250 51.37 N 0.25 W
East Butler 204 40.53 N 79.51 W
East Butte ∧ 192 48.52 N 111.09 W
East Cache Creek ≃ 186 34.08 N 98.16 W
East Caicos I 228 21.41 N 71.30 W
East Calder 42 55.54 N 3.27 W
East Canaan 197 42.01 N 73.17 W
East Canada Creek ≃ 200 43.00 N 74.45 W
East Canton 204 40.47 N 81.17 W
East Cape ≻, N.Z. 162 37.41 S 178.33 E
East Cape ≻, Alaska, U.S. 171a 51.21 N 179.29 E
East Cape ≻, Fla., U.S. 210 25.07 N 81.05 W
East Carbon 190 39.33 N 110.25 W
East Carlisle 204 41.19 N 82.05 W
East Caroline Basin ✢[1] 14 3.00 N 147.00 E
East Castor ≃ 202 45.16 N 75.17 W
East Catfish Creek ≃ 202 42.47 N 81.04 W
East-Central □[3] 140 6.00 N 7.30 E
East Channel ≃[1] 170 69.20 N 134.00 W
East Chatham 200 42.25 N 73.32 W
East Chelmsford 197 42.36 N 71.18 W
Eastchester 200 40.57 N 73.49 W
Eastchester Bay C 266 40.51 N 73.48 W
East Chicago 206 41.38 N 87.27 W
East Chicago Heights 268 40.31 N 87.35 W
East China Sea ⊤[2] 80 30.00 N 126.00 E
Eastchurch 44 51.25 N 0.52 E
East Clandon 250 51.15 N 0.29 W
East Claridon 204 41.32 N 81.07 W
East Cleddau ≃ 44 51.46 N 4.52 W
East Cleveland 204 41.32 N 81.35 W
East Coast Bays 162 36.45 S 174.46 E
East Concord 200 42.33 N 78.38 W
East Corinth 178 45.00 N 69.01 W
Eastcote •[8] 250 51.35 N 0.24 W
East Cote Blanche Bay C 184 29.35 N 91.40 W
East Coulée 172 51.20 N 112.19 W
East Creek ≃ 266 40.27 N 74.09 W
East Cross Creek ≃ 202 44.17 N 78.44 W
East Demerara □[5] 236 6.20 N 58.00 W
East Dennis 197 41.45 N 70.10 W
East Dereham 44 52.41 N 0.56 E
East Detroit 204 42.28 N 82.56 W
East Dismal Swamp ≡ 182 35.45 N 76.35 W
East Ditch ≍ 266 40.56 N 74.19 W
East Don ≃ 265b 43.43 N 79.20 W
East Douglas 197 42.04 N 71.43 W
East Dublin 182 32.32 N 82.52 W
East Dubuque 180 42.30 N 90.39 W
East Dundee 206 42.06 N 88.16 W
East Durham 200 42.22 N 74.06 W
East Ely 194 39.15 N 114.53 W
Eastend, Sask., Can. 174 49.31 N 108.48 W
East End, Vir. Is., U.S. 230m 18.21 N 64.40 W
East End Point ≻ 230b 25.03 N 77.16 W
East Enterprise 208 38.52 N 84.59 W
Easter Island → Pascua, Isla de I 164z 27.07 S 109.22 W
Easterly 212 31.06 N 96.23 W
Eastern □[4], Ghana 140 6.30 N 0.30 W
Eastern □[4], Kenya 144 0.05 N 38.00 E
Eastern □[4], S.L. 140 8.15 N 11.00 W
Eastern □[4], Zam. 144 13.00 S 32.15 E
Eastern Bay C 198 38.51 N 76.19 W
Eastern Caprivi Strip □[5] 146 17.45 S 24.00 E
Eastern Channel → Tsushima-kaikyō ⊔ 82 34.00 N 129.00 E
Eastern Cove C 158b 35.46 S 137.50 E
Eastern Creek ≃, Austl. 156 20.10 S 141.08 E
Eastern Creek ≃, Austl. 264a 33.39 S 150.51 E
Eastern Desert → Aṣ-Ṣaḥrā'ash-Sharqīyah •[2] 130 28.00 N 32.00 E
Eastern Division □[5], Fiji 165g 19.00 S 180.00 E
Eastern Division □[5], Sol.is. 165e 10.30 S 162.00 E
Eastern Fields ✢[2] 154 10.20 S 145.45 E
Eastern Ghāts ⋀ 112 14.00 N 78.50 E
Eastern Highlands □[5] 154 6.30 S 145.15 E
Eastern Island I 164g 28.12 N 177.20 W
Eastern Michigan University ʋ[2] 271 42.15 N 83.37 W
Eastern Native •[8] 263d 26.13 S 28.05 E
Eastern Neck Island I 198 39.02 N 76.13 W
Eastern Point ≻ 273 42.35 N 70.40 W
Eastern Sayans → Vostočnyj Sajan ⋀ 78 53.00 N 97.00 E
Eastern Shore •[1] 198 38.40 N 75.50 W
Eastern Yamuna Canal ≍ 262a 28.40 N 77.15 E
East Falkland I 244 51.55 S 59.00 W
East Falls •[8] 275 40.01 N 75.11 W
East Falmouth 197 41.35 N 70.34 W
East Farleigh 250 51.15 N 0.29 E
East Farmingdale 266 40.44 N 73.26 W
East Faxon 200 41.15 N 76.58 W
East Fayetteville 182 35.05 N 78.51 W
East Flat Rock 182 35.17 N 82.32 W
Eastford 197 41.54 N 72.05 W
East Fork Lake @[1] 208 39.02 N 84.07 W
East Foxboro 273 42.04 N 71.12 W
East Freedom 204 40.21 N 78.26 W
East Freetown 197 41.46 N 70.58 W
East Frisian Islands → Ostfriesische Inseln II 48 53.44 N 7.25 E
East Gaffney 182 35.05 N 81.42 W
East Gallatin ≃ 192 45.53 N 111.20 W
Eastgate 214 47.34 N 122.08 W
East Germany → German Democratic Republic □[1] 30 52.00 N 12.30 E
East Ghor Canal → Ghawr ash-Sharqīyah, Qanāt al- ≍ 122 32.41 N 35.38 E
East Glacier Park 192 48.27 N 113.13 W
East Glenville 200 42.51 N 73.57 W
East Granby 197 41.57 N 72.44 W
East Grand Forks 188 47.56 N 97.01 W
East Grand Rapids 206 42.56 N 85.35 W
East Greenbush 200 42.35 N 73.42 W
East Greenville, Ohio, U.S. 204 40.48 N 81.36 W
East Greenville, Pa., U.S. 198 40.24 N 75.30 W
East Greenwich, N.Y., U.S. 200 43.09 N 73.24 W
East Greenwich, R.I., U.S. 197 41.40 N 71.27 W
East Grinstead 44 51.08 N 0.01 W
East Haddam 197 41.27 N 72.28 W
East Half Hollow Hills 266 40.48 N 73.19 W
Eastham, Eng., U.K. 252 53.19 N 2.58 W
Eastham, Mass., U.S. 197 41.50 N 69.58 W
East Ham •[8] 250 51.32 N 0.03 E
East Hampton, Conn., U.S. 197 41.35 N 72.31 W
Easthampton, Mass., U.S. 197 42.16 N 72.40 W
East Hampton, N.Y., U.S. 197 40.58 N 72.11 W
East Hanningfield 250 51.41 N 0.34 E
East Hanover 266 40.49 N 74.22 W
East Harbor State Park ♠ 204 41.32 N 82.49 W
East Harling 44 52.26 N 0.55 E
East Hartford 197 41.46 N 72.39 W
East Hartland 197 42.00 N 72.55 W
East Harwich 197 41.43 N 70.02 W
East Haven 197 41.17 N 72.52 W
East Hazel Crest 268 41.35 N 87.39 W
East Helena 192 46.35 N 111.56 W
East Herkimer 200 43.02 N 74.58 W
East Hertfordshire □[8] 250 51.46 N 0.02 W
East Hickory 204 41.35 N 79.24 W
East Highland Park 198 37.36 N 77.25 W
East Hills, Austl. 264a 33.58 S 150.59 E
East Hills, N.Y., U.S. 266 40.47 N 73.38 W
East Hoathly 44 50.55 N 0.10 E
East Horsley 44 51.15 N 0.26 W
East Humber ≃ 202 43.47 N 79.35 W
East Huntington 266 40.52 N 73.24 W
East Ilsley 44 51.32 N 1.17 W
East-Indian Ridge ✢[3] 4 15.00 S 88.00 E
East Irvington 266 41.03 N 73.51 W
East Island ≻[1] 266 40.54 N 73.38 W
East Islip 266 40.44 N 73.11 W
East Jewett 200 42.14 N 74.09 W
East Jordan 180 45.10 N 85.07 W
East Keansburg 266 40.26 N 74.07 W
East Kelowna 172 49.51 N 119.25 W
East Kilbride 42 55.46 N 4.10 W
East Killingly 197 41.51 N 71.49 W
East Kingston 200 41.57 N 73.58 W
Eastlake, Mich., U.S. 180 44.15 N 86.18 W
Eastlake, Ohio, U.S. 204 41.34 N 81.35 W
East Lake @, Ont., Can. 202 43.55 N 77.12 W
East Lake @, N.J., U.S. 266 40.58 N 74.21 W
East Lake Tohopekaliga @ 210 28.18 N 81.17 W
East Lamma Channel ⊔ 261d 22.15 N 114.07 E
Eastland 186 32.24 N 98.49 W
Eastland •[9], Mich., U.S. 271 42.27 N 82.56 W
Eastland •[9], Pa., U.S. 269b 40.22 N 79.50 W
East Lansdowne 275 39.56 N 75.16 W
East Lansing 206 42.44 N 84.29 W
East Laurinburg 182 34.46 N 79.27 W
Eastleigh 44 50.58 N 1.22 W
East Lewistown 204 40.57 N 80.42 W
East Liberty 206 40.20 N 83.35 W
East Liberty •[8] 269b 40.27 N 79.55 W
East Lindfield 264a 33.46 S 151.11 E
East Linton 42 55.59 N 2.39 W
East Liverpool 204 40.38 N 80.35 W
East London (Oos-Londen) 148 33.00 S 27.55 E
East Longmeadow 197 42.04 N 72.31 W
East Looe 44 50.22 N 4.27 W
East Los Angeles 218 34.01 N 118.09 W
East Lyme 197 41.22 N 72.13 W
East Lynn 206 40.28 N 87.48 W
East Lynn Lake @[1] 178 38.05 N 82.20 W
East Machias 178 44.44 N 67.24 W
Eastmain 166 52.15 N 78.30 W
Eastmain ≃ 166 52.15 N 78.35 W
East Malling 250 51.17 N 0.26 E
Eastman, Qué., Can. 196 45.18 N 72.19 W
Eastman, Ga., U.S. 182 32.12 N 83.11 W
East Mansfield 273 42.01 N 71.11 W
East Marin Island I 272 37.58 N 122.27 W
East Markham 42 53.15 N 0.54 W
East McKeesport 269b 40.23 N 79.48 W
East Meadow 200 40.43 N 73.34 W
East Meadow ≃ 273 42.47 N 71.02 W
East Meadow Brook ≃ 266 40.39 N 73.34 W
East Mecca 204 41.24 N 80.45 W
East Mengo □[5] 144 1.00 N 32.30 E
East Meredith 200 42.25 N 74.53 W
East Midlands Airport ⊠ 44 52.50 N 1.20 W
East Millbury 197 42.13 N 71.45 W
East Millinocket 178 45.37 N 68.35 W
East Millstone 266 40.30 N 74.35 W
East Missoula 192 46.52 N 113.58 W
East Molesey 250 51.24 N 0.21 W
East Moline 180 41.31 N 90.25 W
East Monongahela 269b 40.12 N 79.55 W
East Mountain 212 32.35 N 94.51 W
East Mustang Creek ≃ 212 29.03 N 96.27 W
East Naples 210 26.08 N 81.46 W
East Nassau 200 42.30 N 73.30 W
East Neck 266 40.54 N 73.26 W
East Newark 266 40.45 N 74.10 W
East New Britain □[5] 154 6.00 S 152.00 E
East New Market 198 38.36 N 75.56 W
East New York •[8] 266 40.40 N 73.53 W
East Nimār □[5] 114 22.00 N 76.30 E
East Nishnabotna ≃ 188 40.39 N 95.37 W
East Nodaway ≃ 184 40.38 N 95.01 W
East Norriton 198 40.09 N 75.18 W
East Northfield 197 42.43 N 72.27 W
East Northport 200 40.52 N 73.19 W
East Norwich 200 40.50 N 73.32 W
East Novaya Zemlya Trough ✢[1] 10 74.00 N 62.00 E
East Oakville Creek ≃ 265b 43.28 N 79.48 W
East Olympia 214 46.58 N 122.50 W
Easton, Eng., U.K. 44 50.32 N 2.26 W
Easton, Calif., U.S. 216 36.39 N 119.47 W
Easton, Conn., U.S. 197 41.15 N 73.18 W
Easton, Ill., U.S. 209 40.14 N 89.50 W
Easton, Md., U.S. 198 38.46 N 76.04 W
Easton, Mass., U.S. 273 42.02 N 71.06 W
Easton, Pa., U.S. 198 40.42 N 75.12 W
Easton, Tex., U.S. 212 32.23 N 94.35 W
Easton, Wash., U.S. 214 47.14 N 121.11 W
Eastondale 273 42.02 N 71.04 W
Easton Reservoir @[1] 197 41.16 N 73.16 W
East Orange 200 40.46 N 74.13 W
East Orleans 197 41.47 N 69.58 W
East Orne Bank ✢[4] 14 27.45 S 157.25 W
East Otto 200 42.23 N 78.45 W
Eastover 182 33.52 N 80.41 W
East Pacific Basin ✢[1] 14 12.00 N 150.00 W
East Palatka 182 29.40 N 81.35 W
East Palestine 204 40.50 N 80.33 W
East Palo Alto 216 37.27 N 122.07 W
East Park Reservoir @[1] 216 39.21 N 122.30 W
East Parkrose 214 45.33 N 122.32 W
East Peak ∧ 106 11.13 N 119.29 E
East Peckham 44 51.15 N 0.23 E
East Pembroke, Mass., U.S. 273 42.05 N 70.46 W
East Pembroke, N.Y., U.S. 200 42.60 N 78.18 W
East Peoria 180 40.40 N 89.34 W
East Pepperell 197 42.40 N 71.34 W
East Petersburg 198 40.06 N 76.21 W
East Pharsalia 200 42.34 N 75.43 W
East Pine 172 55.43 N 121.13 W
East Pines 274c 38.57 N 76.55 W
East Pittsburgh 269b 40.24 N 79.48 W
East Point 182 33.40 N 84.27 W
East Point ≻, P.E.I., Can. 176 46.27 N 61.58 W
East Point ≻, Mass., U.S. 197 42.25 N 70.54 W
East Point ≻, Vir. Is., U.S. 231n 17.45 N 64.34 W
Eastpoint •[9] 274b 39.18 N 76.31 W
Eastport, Newf., Can. 176 48.39 N 53.45 W
Eastport, Idaho, U.S. 192 48.59 N 116.11 W
Eastport, Maine, U.S. 178 44.54 N 67.00 W
Eastport, N.Y., U.S. 197 40.49 N 72.44 W
East Porterville 194 36.04 N 118.56 W
East Potomac Park ♠ 274c 38.52 N 77.01 W
East Prairie 184 36.47 N 89.23 W
East Prairie ≃ 172 55.34 N 116.25 W
East Prospect 198 39.58 N 76.31 W
East Providence 197 41.49 N 71.23 W
East Pryor Mountain ∧ 192 45.11 N 108.20 W
East Quogue 197 40.51 N 72.35 W
East Rājasthān Uplands ⋀[1] 114 26.40 N 76.35 E
East Randolph 200 42.10 N 78.57 W
East Retford 42 53.19 N 0.56 W
East Richmond 216 37.57 N 122.19 W
Eastridge Center •[9] 272 37.20 N 121.49 W
East Rigaud ≃ 196 45.27 N 74.22 W
Eastriggs 42 54.59 N 3.10 W
East River C 198 37.24 N 76.21 W
East Rochester, N.Y., U.S. 200 43.07 N 77.29 W
East Rochester, Ohio, U.S. 204 40.45 N 81.02 W
East Rockaway 266 40.39 N 73.40 W
East Rockingham 182 34.57 N 79.45 W
East Rockwood 206 42.03 N 83.13 W
East Rosebud Creek ≃ 192 45.29 N 109.27 W
East Rutherford 266 40.51 N 74.06 W
Eastry 44 51.15 N 1.18 E
East Saint Louis 209 38.38 N 90.09 W
East Salem 198 40.37 N 77.14 W
East Salt Creek ≃ 190 39.13 N 108.54 W
East Sandwich 197 41.45 N 70.27 W
East Sandy Creek ≃ 204 41.22 N 79.51 W
East Schodack 200 42.34 N 73.38 W
East Scotia Basin ✢[1] 9 57.00 S 35.00 W
East Sepik □[5] 154 4.00 S 143.30 E
East Setauket 200 40.57 N 73.06 W
East Shoal Lake @ 174 50.23 N 97.37 W
East Siberian Sea → Vostočno-Sibirskoje More ⊤[2] 12 74.00 N 166.00 E
East Side 200 41.04 N 75.46 W
East Side Canal ≍, Calif., U.S. 216 35.33 N 119.33 W
East Side Canal ≍, Calif., U.S. 216 37.21 N 120.55 W
East Sister Island I 156 39.39 S 148.00 E
East Smethport 204 41.49 N 78.26 W
East Smithfield 200 41.52 N 76.38 W
East Sooke 214 48.22 N 123.43 W
Eastsound 214 48.42 N 122.55 W
East Sound ⊔ 214 48.39 N 122.53 W
East Sparta 204 40.40 N 81.21 W
East Spencer 182 35.41 N 80.26 W
East Springfield, Ohio, U.S. 204 40.27 N 80.52 W
East Springfield, Pa., U.S. 204 41.57 N 80.28 W
East Stony Creek ≃ 200 43.15 N 74.12 W
East Stour ≃ 44 51.08 N 0.53 E
East Stroudsburg 200 41.00 N 75.11 W
East Sudbury 273 42.24 N 71.24 W
East Sullivan 178 44.30 N 68.09 W
East Sydenham ≃ 204 42.35 N 82.23 W
East Syracuse 200 43.04 N 76.05 W
East Tasmania Rise ✢[3] 14 43.00 S 152.00 E
East Tawas 180 44.17 N 83.29 W
East Templeton 197 42.34 N 78.02 W
East Texas 200 40.33 N 75.33 W
East Thompson 197 42.00 N 71.48 W
East Tilbury 250 51.28 N 0.26 E
East Troy 206 42.47 N 88.24 W
East Tulare 216 36.12 N 119.20 W
East Tustin 270 33.46 N 117.49 W
East Twin ≃ 180 44.08 N 87,34 W
Eastvale 204 40.46 N 80.19 W
East Vandergrift 204 40.36 N 79.34 W
Eastview 208 40.19 N 80.38 W
Eastville 198 37.21 N 75.57 W
East Walker ≃ 194 38.53 N 119.10 W
East Walpole 197 42.10 N 71.13 W
East Wareham 197 41.46 N 70.40 W
East Washington 204 40.10 N 80.14 W
East Waterford 198 40.22 N 77.36 W
East Wenatchee 192 47.25 N 120.16 W
East Wenonah 275 39.47 N 75.08 W
East White Plains 266 41.03 N 73.47 W
Eastwick •[8] 275 39.55 N 75.14 W
East Wickham •[8] 250 51.28 N 0.07 E
East Williamson 200 43.14 N 77.09 W
East Williston 266 40.46 N 73.38 W
East Wilmington 182 34.13 N 77.53 W
East Wittering 44 50.41 N 0.53 W
Eastwood, Austl. 264a 33.48 S 151.05 E
Eastwood, Eng., U.K. 44 53.01 N 1.18 W
Eastwood, Eng., U.K. 250 51.34 N 0.40 E
Eastwood, Eng., U.K. 252 53.43 N 2.03 W
Eastwood, Mich., U.S. 206 42.19 N 85.32 W
Eastwood, Pa., U.S. 269b 40.17 N 79.31 W
East Worcester 200 42.37 N 74.40 W
East Yegua Creek ≃ 212 30.19 N 96.45 W
East Yellow Creek ≃ 184 39.38 N 93.04 W
East York, Ont., Can. 202 43.41 N 79.20 W
East York, Pa., U.S. 198 39.58 N 76.43 W
Eaton, Austl. 158a 33.19 S 115.43 E
Eaton, Colo., U.S. 190 40.32 N 104.42 W
Eaton, Ind., U.S. 206 40.21 N 85.21 W
Eaton, N.Y., U.S. 200 42.51 N 75.37 W
Eaton, Ohio, U.S. 208 39.45 N 84.38 W
Eaton ≃ 196 45.28 N 71.39 W
Eaton Estates 204 41.19 N 81.59 W
Eatonia 174 51.13 N 109.23 W
Eaton-Nord ≃ 196 45.24 N 71.35 W
Eaton Park 210 28.00 N 81.54 W
Eaton Rapids 206 42.36 N 84.39 W
Eatons Neck 266 40.56 N 73.24 W
Eatons Neck ≻[1] 266 40.57 N 73.23 W
Eatons Neck Point ≻ 200 40.57 N 73.24 W
Eaton Socon 44 52.13 N 0.18 W
Eatonton 182 33.20 N 83.23 W
Eatontown 198 40.18 N 74.07 W
Eatonville 214 46.52 N 122.16 W
Eaton Wash V 270 34.04 N 118.03 W
Eaton Wash Dam •[6] 270 34.10 N 118.06 W
Eau ≃ 42 53.31 N 0.44 W
Eaubonne 251 49.00 N 2.17 E
Eau Claire, Mich., U.S. 206 41.59 N 86.18 W
Eau Claire, Pa., U.S. 204 41.08 N 79.48 W
Eau Claire, Wis., U.S. 180 44.49 N 91.31 W
Eau Claire ≃, Wis., U.S. 180 44.55 N 89.37 W
Eau Claire ≃, Wis., U.S. 180 44.49 N 91.31 W
Eau-Claire, Lac à l' @, Qué., Can. 166 56.10 N 74.25 W
Eau-Claire, Lac à l' @, Qué., Can. 196 46.33 N 73.04 W
Eau d'Heure ≃ 52 50.18 N 4.24 E
Eau Galle ≃ 180 44.37 N 92.00 W
Eau Gallie 210 28.08 N 80.38 W
Eaulne ≃ 46 49.54 N 1.07 E
Eauripik I[1] 98 6.42 N 143.03 E
Eauze 32 43.52 N 0.06 E
Ebabaka 142 2.30 S 18.19 E
Eban 140 9.44 N 4.56 E
Ebanga 142 12.44 S 14.44 E
Ebangalakata 142 0.29 S 21.29 E
Ebano 224 22.13 N 98.22 W
Ébano, Laguna C 226 15.53 N 84.52 W
Ebba Ksour 138 35.57 N 8.50 E
Ebb and Flow Indian Reserve •[4] 174 51.05 N 99.05 W
Ebb and Flow Lake @ 174 51.05 N 98.56 W
Ebbegebirge ⋀ 52 51.10 N 7.45 E
Ebbegebirge, Naturpark ♠ 253 51.08 N 7.40 E
Ebben Creek ≃ 273 42.38 N 70.45 W
Ebberup 41 55.15 N 9.59 E
Ebbetts Pass)(216 38.33 N 119.48 W
Ebbs 58 47.38 N 12.13 E
Ebbw ≃ 44 51.33 N 2.59 W
Ebbw Vale 44 51.47 N 3.12 W
Ebebiyín 142 2.09 N 11.20 E
Ebejty, Ozero @ 76 54.38 N 71.44 E
Ebel 142 0.07 N 11.05 E
Ebeleben 50 51.17 N 10.43 E
Ebeltoft 41 56.12 N 10.41 E
Ebeltoft Vig C 41 56.10 N 10.36 E
Ebenau 58 47.47 N 13.11 E
Ebendorf 50 52.11 N 11.34 E
Ebene Reichenau 58 46.51 N 13.54 E
Ebenezer 265b 43.46 N 79.40 W
Ebenezer Ridge ∧ 208 39.06 N 84.55 W
Eben Junction 180 46.21 N 86.58 W
Ebenrode → Nesterov 66 54.38 N 22.34 E
Ebensburg 204 40.29 N 78.44 W
Ebensee 58 47.48 N 13.46 E
Ebensfeld 52 50.04 N 10.58 E
Eberbach 52 49.28 N 8.59 E
Ebergassing 254b 48.03 N 16.31 E
Eber Gölü @ 120 38.38 N 31.12 E
Ebergötzen 48 51.34 N 10.06 E
Ebermannstadt 52 49.23 N 11.13 E
Ebern 52 50.05 N 10.47 E
Eberndorf 30 46.35 N 14.38 E
Ebersbach, B.R.D. 52 48.43 N 9.31 E
Ebersbach, D.D.R. 50 51.00 N 14.35 E
Eberschwang 58 48.09 N 13.34 E
Ebersdorf 48 53.31 N 9.03 E
Ebersdorf bei Coburg 52 50.13 N 11.04 E
Eberstein 30 46.48 N 14.34 E
Eberswalde 50 52.50 N 13.49 E
Ebetsu 82a 43.07 N 141.34 E
Ebian 92 29.10 N 103.20 E
Ebina 84 35.26 N 139.25 E
Ebingen 54 48.13 N 9.01 E
Ebnat 54 47.15 N 9.08 E
Ebo 142 11.02 S 14.41 E
Ebola ≃ 142 3.20 N 20.57 E
Eboli 36 40.37 N 15.04 E
Ebolowa 142 2.54 N 11.09 E
Ebon I[1] 14 4.35 N 168.44 E
Ebony 146 22.05 S 15.15 E
Eboshi-yama ∧ 86 35.04 N 133.04 E
Éboué Stadium ♠ 263b 4.16 S 15.16 E
Ebrach 52 49.50 N 10.29 E
Ébrié, Lagune C 140 5.14 N 4.26 W
Ebro ≃ 34 40.43 N 0.54 E
Ebro, Delta del ≚[2] 34 40.43 N 0.54 E
Ebro, Embalse del @[1] 34 43.00 N 3.58 W
Ebstorf 48 53.01 N 10.25 E
Ebute-ikorodu 263a 6.37 N 3.30 E
Ebute-Metta •[8] 263a 6.29 N 3.23 E
Ecarté, Chenal ≃[1] 204 42.28 N 82.29 W
Ecatepec □[7] 276a 19.36 N 99.04 W
Ecatepec de Morelos 276a 19.35 N 99.04 W
Écaussinnes-d'Enghen 46 50.34 N 4.10 E
Ecclefechan 42 55.03 N 3.17 W
Eccles, Eng., U.K. 42 53.29 N 2.21 W
Eccles, Eng., U.K. 250 51.19 N 0.29 E
Eccles, W. Va., U.S. 182 37.47 N 81.16 W
Ecclesfield 42 53.27 N 1.27 W
Eccleshall 44 52.52 N 2.15 W
Eccleston, Eng., U.K. 252 53.27 N 2.47 W
Eccleston, Eng., U.K. 252 53.39 N 2.44 W
Eccleston, Md., U.S. 274b 39.24 N 76.44 W
Eceabat 120 40.11 N 26.21 E
Echabi 79 53.30 N 142.59 E
Echague 106 16.42 N 121.40 E
Echallens 54 46.38 N 6.38 E
Echaporã 245 22.26 S 50.12 W
Echarcon 251 48.34 N 2.24 E
Échauffour 46 48.44 N 0.23 E
Echeconnee Creek ≃ 182 32.39 N 83.36 W
Echeng 90 30.24 N 114.51 E
Échenoz-la-Méline 54 47.36 N 6.08 E
Echi ≃ 84 35.13 N 136.07 E
Echigawa 84 35.10 N 136.12 E
Echigo-sammyaku ⋀ 82 37.50 N 139.50 E
Echimamish ≃ 174 54.20 N 97.27 W
Echizen 84 35.54 N 136.00 E
Echizen-kaga-kaigan-kokutei-kōen ♠ 84 36.08 N 136.05 E
Echizen-misaki ≻ 84 35.59 N 135.57 E
Echo 188 44.37 N 95.25 W
Echo Bay C 266 40.54 N 73.46 W
Echoing ≃ 174 55.51 N 92.05 W
Echoing Lake @ 174 54.31 N 92.15 W
Echo Lake @, Ill., U.S. 268 42.13 N 88.05 W
Echo Lake @, N.J., U.S. 266 41.04 N 74.25 W
Echo Summit ∧ 216 38.50 N 120.02 W
Echt 48 51.06 N 5.52 E
Echterdingen 52 48.41 N 9.10 E
Echternach 52 49.48 N 6.26 E
Echternacherbrück 52 49.49 N 6.25 E
Echuca 156 36.08 S 144.46 E
Echunga 158b 35.07 S 138.48 E
Écija 34 37.32 N 5.05 W
Ecilda Paullier 248 34.22 S 57.04 W
Eck, Loch @ 42 56.05 N 5.00 W
Eckartsberga 50 51.07 N 11.34 E
Eckbolsheim 54 48.35 N 7.41 E
Eckenhagen 52 50.59 N 7.41 E
Eckernförde 41 54.28 N 9.50 E
Eckernförder Bucht C 41 54.30 N 10.02 E
Eckerö I 26 60.14 N 19.35 E
Eckington 42 53.19 N 1.21 W
Eckley 200 40.59 N 75.51 W
Eckville 172 52.21 N 114.22 W
Eckwarderhörne 48 53.31 N 8.14 E
Ecleto 212 29.03 N 97.45 W
Ecleto Creek ≃ 186 28.52 N 97.45 W
Eclipse Sound ⊔ 166 72.38 N 79.00 W
Ećmiadzin 74 40.10 N 44.18 E
Ecola State Park ♠ 214 45.57 N 123.58 W
École ≃ 251 48.32 N 2.33 E
Écommoy 46 47.50 N 0.16 E
Econfina ≃ 182 30.02 N 83.55 W
Econlockhatchee ≃ 210 28.42 N 81.02 W
Economy, Ind., U.S. 208 39.59 N 85.05 W
Economy, Pa., U.S. 204 40.39 N 80.14 W
Economy Park ♠ 269b 40.37 N 80.12 W
Écorce, Lac de l' @[1] 180 47.05 N 76.24 W
Écorces, Lac des @ 196 46.00 N 74.32 W
Ecorse 206 42.15 N 83.09 W
Ecorse ≃ 271 42.14 N 83.09 W
Ecorse, South Branch ≃ 271 42.14 N 83.09 W
Écos 46 49.10 N 1.39 E
Écosse → Scotland □[8] 28 57.00 N 4.00 W
Écouen 46 49.01 N 2.23 E
Écouen, Château d' ⊥ 251 49.01 N 2.23 E
Écouis 46 49.19 N 1.26 E
Ecoute, Rû d' ≃ 251 48.39 N 2.26 E
Ecquevilly 251 48.57 N 1.55 E
Écrosnes 251 48.33 N 1.44 E
Ecru 184 34.21 N 89.01 W
Ecser 254c 47.27 N 19.20 E
Ecstall ≃ 172 54.09 N 129.56 W
Ecuador □[1] 232 / 236 2.00 S 77.30 W
Ecuandureo 224 20.10 N 102.11 W
Écueillé 32 47.05 N 1.21 E

Symbols in the index entries represent the broad categories identified in the key at the right. Symbols with superior numbers (⋀[2]) identify subcategories (see complete key on page *I* · 26).

Kartensymbole in dem Registerverzeichnis stellen die rechts in Schlüssel erklärten Kategorien dar. Symbole mit hochgestellten Ziffern (⋀[2]) bezeichnen Unterabteilungen einer Kategorie (vgl. vollständiger Schlüssel auf Seite *I* · 26).

Los símbolos incluídos en el texto del índice representan las grandes categorias identificadas con la clave a la derecha. Los símbolos con numeros en su parte superior (⋀[2]) identifican las subcategorías (véase la clave completa en la página *I* · 26).

Les symboles de l'index représentent les catégories indiquées dans la légende à droite. Les symboles suivis d'un indice (⋀[2]) représentent des sous-catégories (voir légende complète à la page *I* · 26).

Os símbolos incluídos no texto do índice representam as grandes categorias identificadas com a chave à direita. Os símbolos com números em sua parte superior (⋀[2]) identificam as subcategorias (veja-se a chave completa à página *I* · 26).

	English	Deutsch	Español	Français	Português
∧	Mountain	Berg	Montaña	Montagne	Montanha
⋀	Mountains	Berge	Montañas	Montagnes	Montanhas
)(	Pass	Pass	Paso	Col	Passo
V	Valley, Canyon	Tal, Cañon	Valle, Cañón	Vallée, Canyon	Vale, Canhão
≚	Plain	Ebene	Llano	Plaine	Planície
≻	Cape	Kap	Cabo	Cap	Cabo
I	Island	Insel	Isla	Île	Ilha
II	Islands	Inseln	Islas	Îles	Ilhas
•	Other Topographic Features	Andere Topographische Objekte	Otros Elementos Topográficos	Autres données topographiques	Outros Elementos Topográficos

ESPAÑOL

Nombre	Página	Lat.°′	Long.°′ W=Oeste
Écuises	54	46.45 N	4.32 E
Ecum Secum	176	44.58 N	62.08 W
Écury-sur-Coole	46	48.54 N	4.20 E
Ed, Sve.	26	58.55 N	11.55 E
Ed, Yai.	134	13.52 N	41.40 E
Eda ←[8]	258	35.34 N	139.34 E
Edah	152	28.17 S	117.10 E
Edam, Sask., Can.	174	53.12 N	108.46 W
Edam, Ned.	48	52.31 N	5.03 E
Edarene	138	25.27 N	8.22 E
Eday I	28	59.11 N	2.47 W
Eddington Gardens	275	40.06 N	74.57 W
Eddleston	42	55.43 N	3.13 W
Eddrachillis Bay C	28	58.19 N	5.15 W
Eddy	212	31.18 N	97.15 W
Eddystone	198	39.51 N	75.21 W
Eddystone Point ≻	156	41.00 S	148.21 E
Eddystone Rocks II[1]	44	50.12 N	4.15 W
Eddyville, Iowa, U.S.	180	41.09 N	92.38 W
Eddyville, Ky., U.S.	184	37.03 N	88.04 W
Eddyville, N.Y., U.S.	200	41.54 N	74.02 W
Ede, Ned.	48	52.03 N	5.40 E
Ede, Nig.	140	7.44 N	4.27 E
Edéa	142	3.48 N	10.08 E
Edebäck	40	60.04 N	13.33 E
Edebo	40	60.01 N	18.34 E
Edegem	48	51.09 N	4.27 E
Edehon Lake ⊜	166	60.25 N	97.15 W
Edéia	245	17.18 S	49.55 W
Edelény	30	48.18 N	20.44 E
Edelweiss Spitze ∧	58	47.07 N	12.50 E
Edemissen	48	52.23 N	10.16 E
Eden, Austl.	156	37.04 S	149.54 E
Éden, Bra.	277a	22.48 S	43.24 W
Eden, N. Ire., U.K.	42	54.44 N	5.47 W
Eden, Mich., U.S.	206	42.32 N	84.26 W
Eden, Miss., U.S.	184	32.59 N	90.20 W
Eden, N.Y., U.S.	200	42.39 N	78.54 W
Eden, Tex., U.S.	186	31.13 N	99.51 W
Eden, Wyo., U.S.	190	42.03 N	109.26 W
Eden ≃, Eng., U.K.	42	54.57 N	3.01 W
Eden ≃, Eng., U.K.	44	51.10 N	0.11 E
Eden ≃, Wales, U.K.	44	52.48 N	3.53 W
Edenbridge	44	51.12 N	0.04 E
Edenburg	148	29.45 S	25.56 E
Eden Canyon ∨	272	37.42 N	122.01 W
Edendale, N.Z.	162	46.19 S	168.47 E
Edendale, S. Afr.	148	29.39 S	30.18 E
Edenderry	28	53.21 N	7.35 W
Edenfield	252	53.40 N	2.18 W
Eden Hill ∧[2]	197	41.20 N	73.19 W
Edenkoben	52	49.17 N	8.07 E
Eden Lake ⊜	174	56.38 N	100.15 W
Eden Mills	202	43.35 N	80.09 W
Eden Park ←[8]	250	51.23 N	0.02 W
Edenside ∨	42	54.40 N	2.35 W
Edenton	182	36.04 N	76.39 W
Edenvale	263d	26.08 S	28.09 E
Edenvale Location	263d	26.08 S	28.11 E
Eden Valley, Austl.	158b	34.39 S	139.06 E
Eden Valley, Minn., U.S.	180	45.19 N	94.33 W
Edenville	148	27.37 S	27.34 E
Edeowie	156	31.27 S	138.27 E
Eder ≃	52	51.13 N	9.27 E
Ederkopf ∧	52	50.56 N	8.12 E
Ederstausee ⊜[1]	52	51.11 N	9.00 E
Eder-Talsperre ←[6]	52	51.11 N	9.02 E
Edesheim	52	49.16 N	8.08 E
Edessa → Édhessa	38	40.48 N	22.03 E
Edewecht	48	53.07 N	8.02 E
Edfu → Idfū	130	24.58 N	32.52 E
Edgar, Nebr., U.S.	188	40.22 N	97.58 W
Edgar, Wis., U.S.	180	44.55 N	90.00 W
Edgard	184	30.03 N	90.34 W
Edgar Ranges ⋀	152	18.43 S	123.25 E
Edgars Creek ≃	264b	37.44 S	144.58 E
Edgartown	197	41.23 N	70.31 W
Edgartown Harbor C	197	41.24 N	70.30 W
Edgecliff	212	32.39 N	97.22 W
Edgecumbe	162	37.59 S	176.50 E
Edgefield	182	33.47 N	81.56 W
Edge Hill ←[8]	252	53.24 N	2.57 W
Edge Hill ∧[2]	44	52.08 N	1.27 W
Edgeley, Ont., Can.	265b	43.48 N	79.31 W
Edgeley, N. Dak., U.S.	188	46.22 N	98.43 W
Edgely	275	40.07 N	74.50 W
Edgemere	198	39.14 N	76.27 W
Edgemont, Calif., U.S.	218	33.53 N	117.18 W
Edgemont, Pa., U.S.	275	39.57 N	75.27 W
Edgemont, S. Dak., U.S.	188	43.18 N	103.50 W
Edgemont Park	206	42.44 N	84.36 W
Edge Mountain ∧	170	58.12 N	152.06 W
Edgeroi	156	30.07 S	149.48 E
Edgerton, Alta., Can.	174	52.45 N	110.27 W
Edgerton, Ind., U.S.	206	41.05 N	84.49 W
Edgerton, Minn., U.S.	188	43.53 N	96.08 W
Edgerton, Ohio, U.S.	206	41.27 N	84.45 W
Edgerton, Wis., U.S.	206	42.50 N	89.04 W
Edgerton, Wyo., U.S.	190	43.25 N	106.15 W
Edgewater, Ala., U.S.	184	33.32 N	86.57 W
Edgewater, Fla., U.S.	210	28.60 N	80.54 W
Edgewater, N.J., U.S.	266	40.50 N	73.58 W
Edgewater Heights	271	42.12 N	83.31 W
Edgewater Park	275	40.04 N	74.54 W
Edgewater Park ♠	269a	41.29 N	81.43 W
Edgewater Point ≻	266	40.55 N	73.44 W
Edgewood, B.C., Can.	172	49.47 N	118.08 W
Edgewood, Fla., U.S.	210	28.29 N	81.32 W
Edgewood, Ill., U.S.	184	38.55 N	88.40 W
Edgewood, Ind., U.S.	208	39.41 N	86.09 W
Edgewood, Ind., U.S.	208	40.06 N	85.44 W
Edgewood, Iowa, U.S.	180	42.39 N	91.24 W
Edgewood, Md., U.S.	178	39.25 N	76.18 W
Edgewood, Ohio, U.S.	204	41.52 N	80.46 W
Edgewood, Pa., U.S.	200	40.47 N	76.35 W
Edgewood, Pa., U.S.	269b	40.26 N	79.53 W
Edgewood, Tex., U.S.	212	32.42 N	95.53 W
Edgewood Arsenal ■	198	39.20 N	76.17 W
Edgeworth	204	40.33 N	80.11 W
Edgware ←[8]	250	51.37 N	0.17 W
Edgworth	252	53.39 N	2.24 W
Édhessa	38	40.48 N	22.03 E
Edievale	162	45.48 S	169.22 E
Ediger	52	50.06 N	7.09 E
Edimbourg → Edinburgh	42	55.57 N	3.13 W
Edimburgo → Edinburgh	42	55.57 N	3.13 W
Edina, Liber.	140	6.01 N	10.10 W
Edina, Minn., U.S.	180	44.55 N	93.20 W
Edina, Mo., U.S.	209	40.10 N	92.11 W
Edinboro	204	41.52 N	80.08 W
Edinboro Lake ⊜	204	41.53 N	80.08 W
Edinburg, Ill., U.S.	209	39.39 N	89.23 W
Edinburg, Ind., U.S.	208	39.21 N	85.58 W
Edinburg, Miss., U.S.	184	32.48 N	89.20 W
Edinburg, N. Dak., U.S.	188	48.30 N	97.52 W
Edinburg, N.Y., U.S.	200	43.13 N	74.07 W
Edinburg, Ohio, U.S.	204	41.06 N	81.09 W
Edinburg, Tex., U.S.	186	26.18 N	98.10 W
Edinburg, Va., U.S.	178	38.49 N	78.34 W
Edinburgh	42	55.57 N	3.13 W
Edinburgh (Turnhouse) Airport ⊠	42	55.57 N	3.21 W
Edinburgh Castle ⊥	42	55.56 N	3.14 W
Edinburgh Channel Ʊ	226	14.45 N	82.40 W
Edinburgh Mountain ∧	214	48.38 N	124.24 W
Edinburgh Reef ⇝[2]	226	14.50 N	82.39 W
Edincik	120	40.20 N	27.51 E
Edingen → Enghien	46	50.42 N	4.02 E

FRANÇAIS

Nom	Page	Lat.°′	Long.°′ W=Ouest
Edirne	120	41.40 N	26.34 E
Edirne □[4]	120	41.20 N	26.40 E
Edison, Ga., U.S.	182	31.33 N	84.44 W
Edison, N.J., U.S.	200	40.31 N	74.24 W
Edison, Ohio, U.S.	204	40.33 N	82.52 W
Edison, Pa., U.S.	198	40.17 N	75.07 W
Edison Bridge ←[5]	204	41.27 N	82.49 W
Edison National Historic Site ⊥	266	40.47 N	74.14 W
Edison Park ←[8]	268	42.01 N	87.49 W
Edisseja	74	44.03 N	44.33 E
Edisto ≃	182	32.39 N	80.24 W
Edisto, North Fork ≃	182	33.16 N	80.53 W
Edisto, South Fork ≃	182	33.16 N	80.53 W
Edith	160	33.48 S	149.55 E
Edith, Mount ∧	192	46.26 N	111.11 W
Edithburgh	158b	35.06 S	137.44 E
Edith River	154	14.11 S	132.02 E
Edithvale	264b	38.02 S	145.07 E
Edjeleh	138	27.38 N	9.50 E
Edjudina	152	29.48 S	122.23 E
Edmeston	200	42.42 N	75.15 W
Edmond	186	35.39 N	97.29 W
Edmondbyers	42	54.51 N	1.58 W
Edmonds	214	47.48 N	122.22 W
Edmonston	274c	38.57 N	76.56 W
Edmonton, Austl.	156	17.01 S	145.45 E
Edmonton, Alta., Can.	172	53.33 N	113.28 W
Edmonton, Ky., U.S.	184	36.59 N	85.37 W
Edmonton ←[8]	250	51.37 N	0.04 W
Edmore, Mich., U.S.	180	43.25 N	85.03 W
Edmore, N. Dak., U.S.	188	48.25 N	98.27 W
Edmund	152	23.46 S	116.02 E
Edmund Lake ⊜	174	54.45 N	93.15 W
Edmundson Acres	218	35.14 N	118.49 W
Edmundston	176	47.22 N	68.20 W
Edna, Kans., U.S.	188	37.04 N	95.22 W
Edna, Pa., U.S.	269b	40.19 N	79.39 W
Edna, Tex., U.S.	212	28.59 N	96.39 W
Edna Bay	170	55.57 N	133.40 W
Ednor	198	39.09 N	76.59 W
Edo ≃	84	35.37 N	139.53 E
Edogawa ←[8]	258	35.42 N	139.52 E
Edolo	58	46.11 N	10.20 E
Edom	212	32.22 N	95.37 W
Edon	206	41.33 N	84.46 W
Edosaki	84	35.57 N	140.19 E
Edremit	120	39.35 N	27.01 E
Edremit Körfezi C	120	39.30 N	26.45 E
Edrengijn Nuruu ⋀	92	44.15 N	97.45 E
Edsbro	40	59.54 N	18.29 E
Edsbruk	26	58.02 N	16.28 E
Edsbyn	26	61.23 N	15.49 E
Edsgatan	40	59.26 N	13.33 E
Edson	172	53.35 N	116.26 W
Edson Butte ∧	192	42.52 N	124.20 W
Eduardo Castex	242	35.54 S	64.18 W
Eduardo VII, Península → Edward VII Peninsula ≻[1]	9	77.40 S	155.00 W
Educación	276a	19.14 N	99.03 W
Eduni, Mount ∧	170	64.15 N	128.04 W
Edward, Lake ⊜	144	0.25 S	29.30 E
Edward, Mount ∧	152	23.22 S	131.55 E
Edwardes Park ♠	264b	37.43 S	145.00 E
Edward Island I	180	48.24 N	88.36 W
Edwards, Calif., U.S.	218	34.54 N	117.53 W
Edwards, Miss., U.S.	184	32.20 N	90.36 W
Edwards, N.Y., U.S.	202	44.20 N	75.15 W
Edwards ≃	180	41.09 N	90.59 W
Edwards Air Force Base ■	218	34.54 N	117.52 W
Edwards Airport ⊠	266	40.45 N	73.03 W
Edwardsburg	206	41.48 N	86.05 W
Edwards Butte ∧	214	45.23 N	123.41 W
Edwards Creek	156	28.21 S	135.51 E
Edwards Gardens ♠	265b	43.44 N	79.22 W
Edwards Plateau ⋀[1]	186	31.20 N	101.00 W
Edwards Run ≃	275	39.48 N	75.12 W
Edwardsville, Ill., U.S.	209	38.49 N	89.58 W
Edwardsville, Ind., U.S.	208	38.16 N	85.55 W
Edwardsville, Pa., U.S.	200	41.17 N	75.53 W
Edward VIII Bay C	9	66.50 S	57.00 E
Edward VII Peninsula ≻[1]	9	77.40 S	155.00 W
Edwinstowe	42	53.12 N	1.04 W
Edziza Peak ∧	170	57.40 N	130.36 W
Eede	48	51.15 N	3.28 E
Eefde	48	52.10 N	6.14 E
Eek	170	60.12 N	162.15 W
Eek ≃	170	60.12 N	162.15 W
Eeklo	46	51.11 N	3.34 E
Eel ≃, Calif., U.S.	194	40.40 N	124.20 W
Eel ≃, Ind., U.S.	184	39.07 N	86.57 W
Eel ≃, Ind., U.S.	206	40.45 N	86.22 W
Eel, Middle Fork ≃	194	39.42 N	123.21 W
Eel, North Fork ≃	194	39.57 N	123.26 W
Eel, South Fork ≃	194	40.22 N	123.55 W
Eel Bay C	202	44.19 N	76.02 W
Eelde	48	53.07 N	6.35 E
Eels Creek ≃	202	44.35 N	78.03 W
Eels Lake ⊜	202	44.54 N	78.08 W
Eemskanaal Ξ	48	53.15 N	6.45 E
Eerbeek	48	52.07 N	6.04 E
Eergetu	79	46.12 N	122.43 E
Eergu'nahe (Argun') ≃	64	53.20 N	121.28 E
Eergunaqi	79	50.54 N	121.57 E
Eersel	48	51.22 N	5.19 E
Eexta	48	53.10 N	6.59 E
Efate I	165f	17.40 S	168.25 E
Eferding	30	48.18 N	14.02 E
Eféri	138	24.22 N	9.30 E
Effiakuma	140	5.06 N	1.39 W
Effigy Mounds National Monument ♠	180	43.06 N	91.13 W
Effingham, Eng., U.K.	250	51.16 N	0.24 W
Effingham, Ill., U.S.	184	39.07 N	88.33 W
Effingham, Kans., U.S.	188	39.31 N	95.24 W
Effingham □[6]	209	39.07 N	88.33 W
Effingham Lake ⊜	202	44.59 N	77.22 W
Effon-Alaiye	140	7.40 N	4.56 E
Effort	200	40.56 N	75.26 W
Efiduasi	140	6.51 N	1.24 W
Efkere	120	38.47 N	35.40 E
Eforie	38	44.06 N	28.38 E
Efrikemer Ξ[1]	257b	41.03 N	28.58 E
Efringen-Kirchen	54	47.49 N	7.35 E
Ega ≃	34	42.19 N	1.55 W
Egadi, Isole II	36	37.56 N	12.16 E
Egan	212	32.28 N	97.17 W
Egaña	242	36.59 S	59.06 W
Egan Range ⋀	194	39.00 N	115.00 W
Eganville	180	45.32 N	77.06 W
Egau ≃	54	48.36 N	10.34 E
Egba □[8]	263a	6.41 N	3.23 E
Egbe, Nig.	140	8.16 N	5.31 E
Egbe, Nig.	263a	6.33 N	3.17 E
Egbunda	144	2.44 N	27.12 E
Egede og Rothes Fjord C[2]	166	66.00 N	38.00 W
Egedesminde	166	68.42 N	52.45 W
Égée, Mer → Aegean Sea ⊤[2]	38	38.30 N	25.00 E
Egegik	170	58.13 N	157.22 W
Egeln	50	51.56 N	11.25 E
Egeo, Mar → Aegean Sea ⊤[2]	38	38.30 N	25.00 E
Eger → Cheb, Česko.	50	50.01 N	12.25 E
Eger, Magy.	30	47.54 N	20.23 E
Eger (Ohře) ≃	50	50.32 N	14.08 E
Egeria Mountain ∧	172	53.55 N	130.22 W
Egernsund	41	54.54 N	9.37 E

PORTUGUÊS

Nome	Página	Lat.°′	Long.°′ W=Oeste
Egerpohl	253	51.07 N	7.27 E
Egersund	26	58.27 N	6.00 E
Egerta	134	2.10 N	43.14 E
Egerton	252	53.38 N	2.26 W
Egerton, Mount ∧	9	80.50 S	158.50 E
Egeskov ⊥	41	55.10 N	10.30 E
Egestorf	48	53.11 N	10.04 E
Egestorf [am Süntel]	48	52.17 N	9.31 E
Egg	54	47.26 N	9.54 E
Egge ⋀	48	51.40 N	8.55 E
Eggebek	41	54.37 N	9.22 E
Eggelsberg	58	48.05 N	13.00 E
Eggenburg	30	48.39 N	15.50 E
Eggenfelden	30	48.25 N	12.46 E
Eggenstein	52	49.04 N	8.23 E
Eggerscheid	253	51.19 N	6.53 E
Eggersdorf	50	52.32 N	13.49 E
Eggesin	50	53.41 N	14.05 E
Egg Harbor City	198	39.32 N	74.39 W
Egg Island Point ≻	198	39.11 N	75.08 W
Egg Lagoon	156	39.39 S	143.58 E
Egg Lake ⊜, Man., Can.	174	54.21 N	101.26 W
Egg Lake ⊜, Sask., Can.	174	55.05 N	105.30 W
Egglestone Abbey ʋ[1]	42	54.32 N	1.54 W
Egham	44	51.26 N	0.34 W
Éghezée	52	50.36 N	4.54 E
Egijn ≃	78	49.24 N	103.36 E
Eğil	120	38.15 N	40.05 E
Egilsstaðir	24a	65.16 N	14.18 W
Egipto → Egypt □[1]	130	27.00 N	30.00 E
Égletons	32	45.24 N	2.03 E
Eglin Air Force Base ■	184	30.29 N	86.30 W
Eglinton	42	55.02 N	7.11 W
Eglisau	54	47.34 N	8.32 E
Egloskerry	44	50.39 N	4.27 W
Égly	251	48.35 N	2.13 E
Egmond aan Zee	48	52.36 N	4.37 E
Egmond-Binnen	48	52.35 N	4.39 E
Egmont, Cape ≻, N.S., Can.	176	46.51 N	60.18 W
Egmont, Cape ≻, N.Z.	162	39.17 S	173.45 E
Egmont, Mount ∧	162	39.18 S	174.04 E
Egmont Bay C	176	46.35 N	64.12 W
Egmont Channel Ʊ	210	27.36 N	82.45 W
Egmont Key I	210	27.35 N	82.46 W
Egmont National Park ♠	162	39.15 S	174.05 E
Egna (Neumarkt)	58	46.19 N	11.16 E
Egnach	54	47.33 N	9.23 E
Egoryevsk → Jegorjevsk	72	55.23 N	39.02 E
Egota ←[8]	258	35.43 N	139.40 E
Egra	116	21.54 N	87.32 E
Egremont, Alta., Can.	172	54.02 N	113.08 W
Egremont, Eng., U.K.	42	54.29 N	3.33 W
Eğret	120	38.57 N	30.18 E
Égreville	46	48.10 N	2.52 E
Eğridir	120	37.52 N	30.51 E
Eğridir Gölü ⊜	120	38.02 N	30.53 E
Eğriköy	120	38.44 N	27.21 E
Egton	42	54.26 N	0.45 W
Egtved	41	55.37 N	9.18 E
Éguas, Rio das ≃	245	13.26 S	44.14 W
Éguilles	56	43.34 N	5.22 E
Eguisheim	54	48.03 N	7.18 E
Egum Atoll I[1]	154	9.25 S	151.55 E
Egvekinot	170	66.19 N	179.10 W
Egypt, Mass., U.S.	197	42.13 N	70.46 W
Egypt, Pa., U.S.	198	40.41 N	75.32 W
Egypt, Tex., U.S.	212	29.24 N	96.14 W
Egypt □[1]	126		
	130	27.00 N	30.00 E
Egypt, Lake of ⊜[1]	184	37.35 N	88.55 W
Égypte → Egypt □[1]	130	27.00 N	30.00 E
Egyptian Museum ʋ	263c	30.03 N	31.04 E
Eha-Amufu	140	6.40 N	7.46 E
Ehen ≃	42	54.25 N	3.30 W
Ehime □[5]	86	33.40 N	132.50 E
Ehingen	54	48.17 N	9.43 E
Ehingen ←[8]	253	51.22 N	6.42 E
Ehle ≃	50	52.12 N	11.44 E
Ehmen	50	52.24 N	10.41 E
Ehra-Lessien	50	52.34 N	10.46 E
Ehrang	52	49.49 N	6.41 E
Ehrenberg	190	33.36 N	114.31 W
Ehrenberg Range ⋀	152	23.18 S	130.20 E
Ehrenbreitstein, Feste ⊥	52	50.21 N	7.37 E
Ehrenburg ⊥	52	50.12 N	7.27 E
Ehrenfeld	204	40.22 N	78.47 W
Ehrenfriedersdorf	50	50.38 N	12.58 E
Ehreshoven	52	50.58 N	7.20 E
Ehrhardt	182	33.06 N	81.01 W
Ehrhorn	48	53.10 N	9.53 E
Ehringhausen	253	51.11 N	7.33 E
Ehringhausen ←[8]	253	51.09 N	7.11 E
Ehrwald	54	47.24 N	10.55 E
Ehwa Women's University ʋ[2]	261b	37.34 N	126.56 E
Éibar	34	43.11 N	2.28 W
Eibau	50	50.58 N	14.40 E
Eibelshausen	52	50.49 N	8.20 E
Eibelstadt	52	49.43 N	10.00 E
Eibenstock	50	50.29 N	12.35 E
Eibergen	48	52.06 N	6.39 E
Eibiswald	30	46.41 N	15.15 E
Eibsee ⊜	58	47.27 N	10.58 E
Eicha	50	50.21 N	10.34 E
Eich-Berg ∧[2]	254a	52.39 N	13.50 E
Eiche, D.D.R.	254a	52.34 N	13.36 E
Eiche, D.D.R.	254a	52.25 N	12.58 E
Eichenbarleben	50	52.10 N	11.24 E
Eichenbrandt	254a	52.38 N	13.51 E
Eichlinghofen ←[8]	253	51.29 N	7.24 E
Eichsfeld ←[1]	52	51.25 N	10.20 E
Eichstädt	254a	52.42 N	13.07 E
Eichstätt	30	48.54 N	11.12 E
Eichstetten	54	48.05 N	7.44 E
Eichtersheim	52	49.14 N	8.46 E
Eichwalde	50	52.22 N	13.37 E
Eickelborn	48	51.39 N	8.13 E
Eicken ←[8]	253	51.13 N	6.26 E
Eickerend	253	51.13 N	6.34 E
Eickerkopf ∧[2]	253	51.21 N	7.42 E
Eicklingen	48	52.33 N	10.10 E
Eide	26	62.55 N	7.26 E
Eidelstedt ←[8]	48	53.36 N	9.53 E
Eider ≃	41	54.19 N	8.58 E
Eiderstedt ≻[1]	41	54.22 N	8.50 E
Eidfjord	26	60.28 N	7.05 E
Eidsvåg, Nor.	26	60.27 N	5.21 E
Eidsvåg, Nor.	26	62.47 N	8.03 E
Eidsvold	156	25.22 S	151.07 E
Eidsvoll	26	60.19 N	11.14 E
Eifa	52	50.58 N	8.34 E
Eifel ⋀	52	50.15 N	6.45 E
Eiffel, Tour ⊥	251	48.51 N	2.18 E
Eiffel Flats	144	18.15 S	29.59 E
Eifgenbach ≃	253	51.05 N	7.09 E
Eigen ←[8]	253	51.33 N	6.57 E
Eigenji	84	35.04 N	136.18 E
Eigenrieden	50	51.11 N	10.22 E
Eiger ∧	54	46.35 N	8.00 E
Eigg I	28	56.54 N	6.10 W
Eight Degree Channel Ʊ	112	8.00 N	73.00 E
Eighteenmile Creek ≃, N.Y., U.S.	200	42.43 N	78.58 W
Eighteenmile Creek ≃, N.Y., U.S.	200	43.21 N	78.43 W
Eight Mile Creek ≃, Ont., Can.	274a	43.14 N	79.11 W
Eightmile Creek ≃, Ind., U.S.	206	40.57 N	85.22 W

Eightmile Creek ≃, Oreg., U.S.	214	45.36 N	121.05 W
Eights Coast •[2]	9	73.30 S	93.00 W
Eighty Mile Beach •[2]	152	19.45 S	121.00 E
Eiheiji	84	36.05 N	136.20 E
Eijerlandsche Gat C	48	53.12 N	4.50 E
Eijsden	52	50.47 N	5.43 E
Eik	134	8.58 N	45.09 E
Eikeren ⊜	26	59.38 N	9.58 E
Eikesdalsvatnet ⊜	26	62.34 N	8.11 E
Eil	134	8.00 N	49.51 E
Eildon	159	37.14 S	145.56 E
Eildon, Lake ⊜[1]	159	37.11 S	145.55 E
Eilean Gowan Island I	202	45.02 N	79.25 W
Eileen	206	41.17 N	88.15 W
Eilenburg	50	51.27 N	12.37 E
Eil Malk I	165b	7.09 N	134.22 E
Eilpe ←[8]	253	51.21 N	7.29 E
Eilsleben	50	52.09 N	11.13 E
Eimbeckhausen	48	52.14 N	9.25 E
Eimke	48	52.58 N	10.19 E
Eina	26	60.38 N	10.36 E
Einasleigh	156	18.31 S	144.05 E
Einasleigh ≃	156	17.30 S	142.17 E
Einbeck	48	51.49 N	9.52 E
Eindhoven	48	51.26 N	5.28 E
Eine	46	50.52 N	3.37 E
Einme	100	16.54 N	95.11 E
Einöd	52	49.16 N	7.19 E
Einruhr	52	50.35 N	6.22 E
Einsiedel	50	50.46 N	12.58 E
Einsiedeln	54	47.08 N	8.45 E
Einville-au-Jard	54	48.39 N	6.30 E
Eirauli	262c	19.10 N	72.59 E
Eire → Ireland □[1]	28	53.00 N	8.00 W
Eiru ≃	238	6.42 S	69.52 W
Eirunepé	238	6.40 S	69.52 W
Eisbach ≃	52	49.38 N	8.22 E
Eisch ≃	52	49.45 N	6.07 E
Eiseb ≃	146	20.26 S	20.05 E
Eisenach	50	50.59 N	10.19 E
Eisenberg, B.R.D.	52	49.38 N	8.05 E
Eisenberg, D.D.R.	50	50.58 N	11.53 E
Eisenerz	30	47.33 N	14.53 E
Eisenerzer Alpen ⋀	30	47.28 N	14.45 E
Eisenhower, Mount ∧	172	51.18 N	115.55 W
Eisenhower Memorial Park ♠	266	40.44 N	73.34 W
Eisenhüttenstadt	50	52.10 N	14.39 E
Eisenkappel	38	46.29 N	14.36 E
Eisenschmitt	52	50.03 N	6.43 E
Eisenstadt	30	47.51 N	16.32 E
Eiserfeld	52	50.50 N	7.59 E
Eisern	52	50.50 N	8.02 E
Eisfeld	50	50.26 N	10.54 E
Eišiškės	66	54.10 N	25.00 E
Eisk → Jejsk	68	46.42 N	38.16 E
Eisleben	50	51.31 N	11.32 E
Eislingen	52	48.42 N	9.42 E
Eita	164t	1.21 N	173.05 E
Eithon ≃	44	52.12 N	3.27 W
Eitorf	52	50.46 N	7.26 E
Ejasi → Eyasi, Lake ⊜	144	3.40 S	35.05 E
Ejby, Dan.	41	55.26 N	9.57 E
Ejby, Dan.	41	55.30 N	12.07 E
Ejea de los Caballeros	34	42.08 N	1.08 W
Ejeda	147b	24.20 S	44.31 E
Ejido	236	8.33 N	71.14 W
Ejigbo, Nig.	140	7.55 N	4.19 E
Ejigbo, Nig.	263a	6.33 N	3.18 E
Ejinaqi	92	41.50 N	100.50 E
Ejstrup	41	55.59 N	9.17 E
Ejura	140	7.23 N	1.22 W
Ejutla de Crespo	224	16.34 N	96.44 W
Ekalaka	188	45.53 N	104.33 W
Ekáli	257c	38.07 N	23.50 E
Ekalla	142	1.27 S	14.00 E
Ekanga	142	2.23 S	23.14 E
Ekas	105b	8.53 S	116.27 E
Ekaterinburg → Sverdlovsk	76	56.51 N	60.36 E
Ekaterinodar → Krasnodar	68	45.02 N	39.00 E
Ekaterinoslav → Dnepropetrovsk	68	48.27 N	34.59 E
Ekeby	41	56.00 N	12.58 E
Ekenäs (Taamisaari)	26	59.58 N	23.26 E
Ekenässjön	26	57.30 N	15.00 E
Ekeren	46	51.17 N	4.25 E
Ekerö I	40	59.18 N	17.43 E
Eket, Nig.	140	4.39 N	7.56 E
Eket, Sve.	41	56.15 N	13.11 E
Eketahuna	162	40.39 S	175.42 E
Ekhínos	38	41.17 N	24.59 E
Ekiatap ≃	170	68.46 N	179.00 W
Ekiatapskij Chrebet ⋀, S.S.S.R.	64	68.30 N	179.00 E
Ekiatapskij Chrebet ⋀, S.S.S.R.	170	69.00 N	177.00 E
Ekibastuz	76	51.42 N	75.22 E
Ekimčan	79	53.04 N	132.58 E
Ekityki, Ozero ⊜	170	67.30 N	179.30 E
Ekitykskij Chrebet ⋀	170	67.45 N	179.00 E
Ekiya	86	34.30 N	133.26 E
Eko → Lagos	140	6.27 N	3.24 E
Ekoli	142	0.23 S	24.16 E
Ekoln ⊜	40	59.45 N	17.37 E
Ekolsund	40	59.37 N	17.22 E
Ekolsundsviken C	40	59.35 N	17.24 E
Ekombe	142	1.16 N	21.36 E
Ekonda	64	65.47 N	105.17 E
Ekoungounou	142	0.33 S	15.38 E
Ekovamou	142	0.07 N	16.31 E
Ekpoma	140	6.46 N	6.08 E
Eksāra	262b	22.38 N	88.17 E
Eksel	52	51.09 N	5.23 E
Eksere	120	36.48 N	32.01 E
Eksjö	26	57.40 N	14.57 E
Ekuk	170	58.49 N	158.34 W
Ekuku	142	0.42 S	21.38 E
Ekuta	142	2.59 N	18.42 E
Ekwan ≃	166	53.14 N	82.13 W
Ekwendeni	144	11.23 S	33.50 E
Ekwok	170	59.22 N	157.30 W
El- → Ad-, Al-, An-, Ar-, As-, Ash-, At-, Az-			
Ela	100	19.37 N	96.13 E
El Aaiún	138	27.09 N	13.12 W
El Abiodh Sidi Cheikh	138	32.56 N	0.42 E
El-Adde	134	2.35 N	46.13 E
El Adeb Larache	138	27.22 N	8.52 E
El Adelanto	226	14.10 N	89.50 W
El-Aden Hindi	134	2.18 N	42.00 E
El Affroun	138	36.30 N	2.38 E
El-Afwein	134	9.55 N	47.14 E
El Aguacate	276c	10.28 N	66.59 W
El Aguilar	242	23.12 S	65.42 W
Elaía	38	39.35 N	20.20 E
Elaine	184	34.18 N	90.51 W
El Alamein → Al-'Alamayn	130	30.49 N	28.57 E
El Álamo, Méx.	186	27.32 N	100.52 W
El Álamo, Méx.	186	26.29 N	99.46 W
El Álamo, Méx.	194	31.34 N	116.02 W
El Alia	36	37.10 N	10.03 E
El Alto, Chile	276e	33.30 S	70.43 W
El Alto, Perú	236	4.18 S	81.07 W
Elamanchili	112	17.33 N	82.52 E
El Amparo de Apure	236	7.06 N	70.45 W
Elan ≃, Rom.	38	46.07 N	28.04 E
Elan' ≃, S.S.S.R.	68	51.07 N	41.25 E
Elancourt	251	48.47 N	1.58 E

Elands ≃	146	25.10 S	29.10 E
Elandsbaai	148	32.19 S	18.21 E
Elandsfontein	263d	26.10 S	28.12 E
Elandskraal	148	28.28 S	30.32 E
Elandsvlei	148	32.19 S	19.33 E
El Angel	236	0.37 N	77.56 W
Elanora Heights	264a	33.42 S	151.17 E
El Aouinet	36	35.52 N	7.54 E
El Arahal	34	37.16 N	5.33 W
El Arba	138	36.37 N	3.13 E
El Arco	222	28.00 N	113.25 W
El Arenal	224	20.47 N	103.42 W
El Aricha	138	34.09 N	1.10 W
El Aroussa	36	36.22 N	9.28 E
El Arrabal Torrelletas	256d	41.21 N	1.57 E
El Arrayán	276e	33.21 S	70.28 W
El Asnam (Orléansville)	138	36.10 N	1.20 E
Elassón	38	39.54 N	22.11 E
Elat	122	29.33 N	34.57 E
Elat, Gulf of → Aqaba, Gulf of C	118	29.00 N	34.40 E
Elat Landing Ground ⊠	122	29.34 N	34.55 W
El-Avaji	134	3.37 N	47.00 E
El Avila, Cerro ∧	276c	10.33 N	66.52 W
El Avión	222	24.08 N	106.59 W
Elayu	134	11.13 N	49.00 E
Elâzığ	120	38.41 N	39.14 E
Elâzığ □[4]	120	38.35 N	39.30 E
El Azúcar, Presa de ⊜[1]	222	26.10 N	99.00 W
Elba, Ala., U.S.	184	31.25 N	86.04 W
Elba, Mich., U.S.	206	43.03 N	83.27 W
Elba, N.Y., U.S.	200	43.05 N	78.11 W
Elba → Elbe ≃	30	53.50 N	9.00 E
Elba, Isola d' I	60	42.46 N	10.17 E
El'ban	79	50.06 N	136.31 E
El Banco	236	9.00 N	73.58 W
El Barco de Avila	34	40.21 N	5.31 W
El Barco de Valdeorras	34	42.25 N	6.59 W
El Barreal	190	31.17 N	107.10 W
El Barril	224	23.02 N	102.08 W
El Barrio	224	16.48 N	95.15 W
Elbasan	38	41.06 N	20.05 E
Elbaşı	120	38.41 N	35.59 E
El Baúl	236	8.57 N	68.17 W
El Bayadh	138	33.40 N	1.01 E
Elbe	214	46.45 N	121.49 W
Elbe (Labe) ≃	30	53.50 N	9.00 E
Elbe-Havel-Kanal Ξ	50	52.24 N	12.23 E
El-Beida → Zāwiyat al-Bayḍā'	136	32.46 N	21.43 E
Elbe-Lübeck-Kanal Ξ	50	53.50 N	10.36 E
El Beni □[5]	238	14.00 S	65.30 W
El-Berde	134	4.52 N	43.40 E
Elberfeld ←[8]	253	51.16 N	7.08 E
Elbert	188	39.13 N	104.32 W
Elbert, Mount ∧	190	39.07 N	106.27 W
Elberta	180	44.37 N	86.14 W
Elberton	182	34.07 N	82.52 W
Elbeuf	46	49.17 N	1.00 E
Elbeyli	120	36.41 N	37.26 E
Elbing → Elbląg	30	54.10 N	19.25 E
Elbingerode	50	51.45 N	10.46 E
Elbistan	120	38.13 N	37.12 E
Elbląg (Elbing)	30	54.10 N	19.25 E
Elbląski, Kanał Ξ	30	53.43 N	19.53 E
El Bluff	226	11.59 N	83.40 W
El Bolsón	244	41.58 S	71.31 W
El Bonillo	34	38.57 N	2.32 W
El Bordo	236	2.06 N	76.58 W
El-Borj	34	35.43 N	5.40 W
El-Borouj	138	32.30 N	7.10 W
El Bosque	224	17.04 N	92.44 W
El Bosque, Aeropuerto ⊠	276e	33.34 S	70.42 W
Elbow	174	51.07 N	106.35 W
Elbow ≃	172	51.03 N	114.02 W
Elbow Cay I	228	23.57 N	80.29 W
Elbow Lake	188	45.59 N	95.58 W
Elbow Lake ⊜	174	54.50 N	100.53 W
Elbridge	200	43.02 N	76.27 W
El'brus, Gora ∧, S.S.S.R.	74	43.21 N	42.26 E
El'brus, Gora ∧, S.S.S.R.	76	53.50 N	69.42 E
Elbrus, Mount → El'brus, Gora ∧	74	43.21 N	42.26 E
El'brusskij	74	43.38 N	42.10 E
Elbsandsteingebirge ⋀	50	50.50 N	14.20 E
El-Bur	134	4.40 N	46.40 E
Elburg	48	52.26 N	5.50 E
El Burgo de Osma	34	41.35 N	3.04 W
Elburn	206	41.54 N	88.28 W
Elburz Mountains → Alborz, Reshteh-ye Kūhhā-ye ⋀	118	36.00 N	53.00 E
El'buzd ≃	73	46.53 N	39.43 E
El'buzo	73	46.53 N	39.41 E
El Caburé	242	26.01 S	62.22 W
El Cajon	218	32.48 N	116.58 W
El Callao	236	7.21 N	61.49 W
El Calvario	236	4.22 N	73.40 W
El Calvario ←[8]	276b	23.05 N	82.20 W
El Calverio	236	8.59 N	67.00 W
El Camarón	226	12.48 N	85.28 W
El Campamento	230m	18.22 N	66.28 W
El Campamento ←[8]	256a	40.24 N	3.46 W
El Campo	212	29.12 N	96.16 W
El Cano	276b	23.02 N	82.28 W
El Capitan ∧, Calif., U.S.	216	37.43 N	119.38 W
El Capitan ∧, Mont., U.S.	192	46.01 N	114.23 W
El Capomo	224	21.17 N	105.13 W
El Caribe	276c	10.37 N	66.50 W
El Carmen, Arg.	242	24.23 S	65.16 W
El Carmen, Bol.	238	18.49 S	58.33 W
El Carmen, Chile	276e	33.21 S	70.43 W
El Carmen, Col.	236	8.30 N	73.27 W
El Carmen, Méx.	224	19.19 N	97.40 W
El Carmen, Méx.	224	15.35 N	93.05 W
El Carmen, Nic.	226	11.59 N	86.31 W
El Carmen, Perú	238	13.30 S	76.04 W
El Carmen, Ven.	276c	10.24 N	67.01 W
El Carmen, Ven.	276c	10.24 N	66.50 W
El Carmen, Canal Ξ	276e	33.18 S	70.41 W
El Carmen de Bolívar	236	9.43 N	75.08 W
El Carricito	222	28.24 N	103.23 W
El Carril	242	25.05 S	65.28 W
El Carrizal	224	23.00 N	97.50 W
El Carrizo	222	29.58 N	105.16 W
El Casco	186	25.34 N	104.35 W
El Castillo	226	11.01 N	84.24 W
El Cedral	226	16.26 N	90.03 W
El Cedrito	222	29.11 N	101.59 W
El Cenajo, Embalse de ⊜[1]	34	38.25 N	2.00 W
El Centinela	194	32.38 N	115.40 W
El Centro	194	32.48 N	115.34 W
El Cerrito, Col.	236	3.42 N	76.19 W
El Cerrito, Calif., U.S.	216	37.55 N	122.18 W
El Cerrito, Calif., U.S.	218	33.49 N	117.31 W
El Cerro, Bol.	238	17.31 S	61.34 W
El Cerro, Ur.	248	34.00 S	58.15 W
El Cerro del Aripo ∧	231r	10.43 N	61.15 W
El Cesar □[5]	236	9.20 N	73.30 W
El Chamal	224	23.56 N	97.54 W
El Chante	224	19.41 N	104.10 W
El Charco Largo	222	24.10 N	97.58 W
Elche	34	38.15 N	0.42 W
Elche de la Sierra	34	38.27 N	2.03 W

El Chimborazo, Cerro ∧	226	13.05 N	85.58 W
El'chkakvun ≃	170	68.42 N	171.00 E
Elcho	180	45.26 N	89.11 W
Elcho Island I	154	11.55 S	135.45 E
El Cholar	242	37.25 S	70.39 W
El Chorrillo	242	33.18 S	66.16 W
El Ciprés	194	31.50 N	116.38 W
El Coacoyul	224	17.37 N	101.26 W
El Cobre	230p	20.03 N	75.57 W
El Cobre ←[8]	276b	23.02 N	82.19 W
El Cocuy	236	6.25 N	72.27 W
El Cojo	276c	10.37 N	66.53 W
El Cojo, Quebrada ≃	276c	10.37 N	66.53 W
El Colorado	242	26.18 S	59.22 W
El Colorado, Canal de Ξ	276e	33.34 S	70.32 W
El Cóndor, Cerro ∧	242	26.38 S	68.22 W
El Congo	226	13.54 N	89.30 W
El Consuelo	222	31.02 N	111.53 W
El Corazón	236	1.12 S	79.06 W
El Corcovado	244	43.32 S	71.36 W
El Corozo	276c	10.35 N	66.58 W
El Corpus	226	13.16 N	87.03 W
El Corte de Madera Creek ≃	272	37.19 N	122.20 W
El Cortijo	276e	33.22 S	70.42 W
El Coto	230m	18.28 N	66.44 W
El Cotorro	276b	23.03 N	82.16 W
El Coyote	190	30.50 N	112.40 W
El Cozón	222	31.18 N	112.29 W
El Cristo	230p	20.07 N	75.45 W
El Cubo → Casigua	236	8.46 N	72.30 W
El Cuco	226	13.10 N	88.07 W
El Cuidado	224	22.20 N	103.07 W
El Cuy	244	39.56 S	68.20 W
Elda	34	38.29 N	0.47 W
El Dab	134	8.58 N	46.38 E
Eldagsen	48	52.10 N	9.40 E
El-Dambahaddo	134	3.14 N	46.45 E
El Dátil	222	30.07 N	112.15 W
Elde ≃	50	53.17 N	12.40 E
Eldekanal Ξ	50	53.24 N	11.36 E
Eldena, D.D.R.	50	54.05 N	13.26 E
Eldena, D.D.R.	50	53.13 N	11.25 E
El Depósito	224	17.44 N	94.23 W
El Der	134	5.08 N	43.08 E
El-Der ≃	134	9.00 N	47.30 E
Elder Island I	266	40.38 N	73.23 W
Elder Mills	265b	43.49 N	79.38 W
Eldersville	204	40.21 N	80.29 W
Elderton	204	40.42 N	79.21 W
El Descanso	194	32.12 N	116.55 W
El Desemboque, Méx.	222	29.30 N	112.27 W
El Desemboque, Méx.	222	30.30 N	112.59 W
Eldforsen	40	60.26 N	14.13 E
El'dikan	64	60.48 N	135.11 E
Eldingen	48	52.41 N	10.21 E
Eld Inlet C	214	47.04 N	123.01 W
El Diviso	236	1.22 N	78.14 W
El Djem	138	35.18 N	10.43 E
El Djouf ←[2]	124	20.30 N	8.00 W
Eldon, Iowa, U.S.	180	40.55 N	92.13 W
Eldon, Mo., U.S.	184	38.21 N	92.35 W
El-Don Far	134	10.35 N	49.02 E
Eldon Hazlett State Park ♠	209	38.39 N	89.22 W
Eldora, Iowa, U.S.	180	42.19 N	93.26 W
Eldora, Pa., U.S.	269b	40.10 N	79.53 W
Eldorado, Arg.	242	26.24 S	54.38 W
Eldorado, Bra.	242	24.32 S	48.06 W
Eldorado, Méx.	222	24.17 N	107.21 W
El Dorado, Ark., U.S.	184	33.13 N	92.40 W
El Dorado, Calif., U.S.	216	38.41 N	120.51 W
Eldorado, Ill., U.S.	184	37.49 N	88.26 W
El Dorado, Kans., U.S.	188	37.49 N	96.52 W
Eldorado, Ohio, U.S.	208	39.54 N	84.41 W
Eldorado, Okla., U.S.	186	34.28 N	99.39 W
Eldorado, Tex., U.S.	186	30.52 N	100.36 W
El Dorado, Ven.	236	6.44 N	61.38 W
El Dorado □[6]	216	38.43 N	120.48 W
Eldorado Hills	216	38.37 N	120.27 W
El Dorado Park ♠	270	33.49 N	118.05 W
Eldorado Peak ∧	214	48.32 N	121.08 W
El Dorado Springs	184	37.52 N	94.01 W
Eldoret	144	0.31 N	35.17 E
Eldred, Ill., U.S.	209	39.17 N	90.33 W
Eldred, N.Y., U.S.	200	41.32 N	74.53 W
Eldred, Pa., U.S.	204	41.57 N	78.23 W
Eldridge	180	41.39 N	90.35 W
Eldridge, Mount ∧	170	64.46 N	141.48 W
Eldridges Hill	275	39.40 N	75.18 W
Eleanor	178	38.32 N	81.56 W
Eleanor, Lake ⊜[1]	216	37.59 N	119.51 W
Eleazer	148	26.40 S	26.53 E
Electra	186	34.02 N	98.55 W
Electric City	192	47.56 N	119.02 W
Eleele	219b	21.55 N	159.35 W
Elefante, Isla del → Elephant Island I	9	61.10 S	55.14 W
Elefantes, Rio dos (Olifants) ≃	146	24.10 S	32.40 E
Elegest ≃	78	51.32 N	94.05 E
El Eglab ←[2]	138	26.25 N	5.00 W
Elei, Wādī ∨	130	22.04 N	34.27 E
Eleja	66	56.26 N	23.42 E
Elektrogorsk	72	55.53 N	38.47 E
Elektrostal'	72	55.47 N	38.28 E
Elektrougli	72	55.43 N	38.13 E
Elektrozavod	70	52.34 N	54.01 E
Elele	140	5.07 N	6.48 E
Elemi	120	41.04 N	35.30 E
Elena	38	42.56 N	25.53 E
El Encantado	276c	10.27 N	66.47 W
El Encanto, Col.	236	1.37 S	73.14 W
El Encanto, Guat.	222	17.17 N	89.34 W
Elend	50	51.44 N	10.41 E
Elepete	263a	6.41 N	3.28 E
Elephanta Caves •[5]	262c	18.58 N	72.56 E
Elephanta Island (Ghārāpuri) I	262c	18.57 N	72.55 E
Elephant Butte Reservoir ⊜[1]	190	33.19 N	107.10 W
Elephant Island I	9	61.10 S	55.14 W
Elephant Lake ⊜	202	45.08 N	78.07 W
Elephant Mountain ∧	178	44.46 N	70.46 W
Elesbão Veloso	240	6.13 S	42.08 W
Eleşkirt	120	39.48 N	42.42 E
El Estor	226	15.32 N	89.21 W
El Estribo	224	22.26 N	99.17 W
Elets → Jelec	66	52.37 N	38.30 E
El Eulma	138	36.08 N	5.40 E
Eleusis → Elevsís	38	38.02 N	23.32 E
Eleutério	246	22.19 S	46.43 W
Eleuthera I	228	25.10 N	76.14 W
Eleuthera Point ≻	228	24.40 N	76.11 W
Eleva	180	44.35 N	91.28 W
Eleven Point ≃	184	36.09 N	91.05 W
Elevsínos, Kólpos C	257c	38.02 N	23.34 E
Elevsís	38	38.02 N	23.32 E
Elevtheroúpolis	38	40.55 N	24.16 E
El Fahs	36	36.22 N	9.55 E
El Faro	230m	18.00 N	66.47 W
Elfenbeinküste → Ivory Coast □[1]	140	8.00 N	5.00 W
El Ferrol del Caudillo	34	43.29 N	8.14 W
Elfers	210	28.13 N	82.43 W
Elfgen	253	51.05 N	6.32 E
Elfin Cove	170	58.12 N	136.20 W
Elfros	174	51.43 N	103.52 W
El Fud	134	7.20 N	42.50 E
El Fuerte	222	26.25 N	108.39 W
El Galpón	242	25.23 S	64.38 W
El Garrobo	226	13.35 N	85.29 W
Elgershausen	52	51.16 N	9.22 E
Elgin, Austl.	158a	33.31 S	115.37 E

≃ River	Fluss	Río	Rivière	Rio
Ξ Canal	Kanal	Canal	Canal	Canal
Waterfall, Rapids	Wasserfall, Stromschnellen	Cascada, Rápidos	Chute d'eau, Rapides	Cascata, Rápidos
Ʊ Strait	Meeresstrasse	Estrecho	Détroit	Estreito
C Bay, Gulf	Bucht, Golf	Bahía, Golfo	Baie, Golfe	Baía, Golfo
⊜ Lake, Lakes	See, Seen	Lago, Lagos	Lac, Lacs	Lago, Lagos
Swamp	Sumpf	Pantano	Marais	Pântano
Ice Features, Glacier	Eis- und Gletscherformen	Accidentes Glaciales	Formes glaciaires	Acidentes Glaciares
⊤ Other Hydrographic Features	Andere Hydrographische Objekte	Otros Elementos Hidrográficos	Autres données hydrographiques	Outros Elementos Hidrográficos

⇝ Submarine Features	Untermeerische Objekte	Accidentes Submarinos	Formes de relief sous-marin	Acidentes Submarinos
□ Political Unit	Politische Einheit	Unidad Politica	Entité politique	Unidade Política
ʋ Cultural Institution	Kulturelle Institution	Institución Cultural	Institution culturelle	Instituição Cultural
⊥ Historical Site	Historische Stätte	Sitio Histórico	Site historique	Sitio Histórico
♠ Recreational Site	Erholungs- und Ferienort	Sitio de Recreo	Centre de loisirs	Sítio de Lazer
⊠ Airport	Flughafen	Aeropuerto	Aéroport	Aeroporto
■ Military Installation	Militäranlage	Instalación Militar	Installation militaire	Instalação Militar
← Miscellaneous	Verschiedenes	Misceláneo	Divers	Miscelânea

Name	Page	Lat.	Long.
Elgin, Ont., Can.	202	44.36 N	76.13 W
Elgin, Scot., U.K.	28	57.39 N	3.20 W
Elgin, Ill., U.S.	206	42.02 N	88.17 W
Elgin, Iowa, U.S.	180	42.57 N	91.38 W
Elgin, Minn., U.S.	180	44.08 N	92.15 W
Elgin, Nebr., U.S.	188	41.59 N	98.05 W
Elgin, N. Dak., U.S.	188	46.24 N	101.51 W
Elgin, Ohio, U.S.	206	40.44 N	84.28 W
Elgin, Oreg., U.S.	192	45.34 N	117.55 W
Elgin, Pa., U.S.	204	41.54 N	79.45 W
Elgin, Tex., U.S.	212	30.21 N	97.22 W
Elgin □[6]	204	42.42 N	81.15 W
Elgin, Lake ⊜	196	45.45 N	71.20 W
El Gogorrón, Parque Nacional ♠	224	21.48 N	100.48 W
El Goléa	138	30.30 N	2.50 E
El Golfete ⊜	226	15.44 N	88.53 W
El Golfo de Santa Clara	222	31.42 N	114.30 W
El Goloso •[8]	256a	40.33 N	3.42 W
Elgon, Mount Λ	144	1.08 N	34.33 E
Elgoras, Gora Λ	24	68.06 N	31.30 E
El Granada	216	37.30 N	122.28 W
El Grove	34	42.30 N	8.52 W
El Grullo	224	19.48 N	104.13 W
El Guaje	222	27.52 N	103.18 W
El Guamo	236	10.02 N	74.59 W
El Guanábano	276c	10.24 N	67.01 W
El Guapo	236	10.09 N	65.58 W
El Guarapo	276c	10.36 N	66.58 W
El Guarda	276a	19.09 N	99.11 W
El Guayabo	236	8.37 N	72.20 W
El Guettâra •[4]	138	22.01 N	2.59 W
El'gygytgyn, Ozero ⊜	170	67.30 N	172.00 E
El Hadjar	36	36.48 N	7.45 E
El-Hajeb	138	33.43 N	5.13 W
Elham	44	51.10 N	1.07 E
El-Hamurre	134	7.11 N	48.55 E
El Hank •[4]	138	24.30 N	7.00 W
El Haouaria	36	37.03 N	11.02 E
El Hatillo	276c	10.26 N	66.49 W
El Hatillo, Quebrada ≃	276c	10.27 N	66.47 W
El Havre → Le Havre	46	49.30 N	0.08 E
El Her	134	5.40 N	42.26 E
El Higo	224	21.46 N	98.28 W
Elhovo	38	42.10 N	26.34 E
El Huecu	242	37.37 S	70.36 W
Eliase	154	8.21 S	130.47 E
Elías Piña	228	18.53 N	71.42 W
Elías Romero	248	34.46 S	58.52 W
Eliasville	186	32.57 N	98.46 W
Elida, N. Mex., U.S.	186	33.57 N	103.39 W
Elida, Ohio, U.S.	206	40.47 N	84.12 W
El Idrissia	138	34.30 N	2.37 E
Elila	144	2.43 S	25.53 E
Elila ≃	144	2.45 S	25.53 E
Elim, Namibia	146	17.48 S	15.31 E
Elim, S. Afr.	148	34.35 S	19.45 E
Elim, Alaska, U.S.	170	64.37 N	162.15 W
Elimsport	200	41.08 N	77.02 W
Elingampangu	142	2.03 S	24.02 E
Elinghu ⊜	92	34.50 N	97.35 E
Elin Pelin	38	42.40 N	23.36 E
Eliot	178	43.09 N	70.48 W
Elipa	142	0.53 S	24.34 E
Elisabeth-Sophien-Koog	41	54.30 N	8.53 E
Élisabethville, Fr.	251	48.58 N	1.51 E
Élisabethville → Lubumbashi, Zaïre	144	11.40 S	27.28 E
Elisenvaara	24	61.25 N	29.46 E
Eliseu Martins	240	8.13 S	43.42 W
Elista	70	46.16 N	44.14 E
Elizabeth, Austl.	158b	34.43 S	138.40 E
Elizabeth, Colo., U.S.	190	39.22 N	104.36 W
Elizabeth, Ill., U.S.	180	42.19 N	90.13 W
Elizabeth, La., U.S.	184	30.52 N	92.48 W
Elizabeth, N.J., U.S.	200	40.40 N	74.11 W
Elizabeth, Pa., U.S.	204	40.16 N	79.53 W
Elizabeth, W. Va., U.S.	178	39.04 N	81.24 W
Elizabeth ≃, N.J., U.S.	266	40.38 N	74.12 W
Elizabeth ≃, Va., U.S.	198	36.54 N	76.20 W
Elizabeth, Cape ≻	214	47.22 N	124.22 W
Elizabeth, West Branch ≃	266	40.42 N	74.14 W
Elizabeth Bay C	146	27.04 S	15.11 E
Elizabeth City	182	36.18 N	76.14 W
Elizabeth Creek ≃	212	33.02 N	97.14 W
Elizabeth Islands II	197	41.27 N	70.47 W
Elizabeth Lake ⊜	271	42.38 N	83.23 W
Elizabeth Lake Estates	271	42.38 N	83.22 W
Elizabeth Park ♠	271	42.07 N	83.11 W
Elizabeth Port C	266	40.41 N	74.09 W
Elizabeth Reef I[1]	150	29.56 S	159.04 E
Elizabethton	182	36.21 N	82.13 W
Elizabethtown, Ill., U.S.	184	37.27 N	88.18 W
Elizabethtown, Ind., U.S.	208	39.08 N	85.49 W
Elizabethtown, Ky., U.S.	184	37.42 N	85.52 W
Elizabethtown, N.C., U.S.	182	34.38 N	78.37 W
Elizabethtown, N.Y., U.S.	178	44.13 N	73.36 W
Elizabethtown, Pa., U.S.	198	40.09 N	76.36 W
Elizabethville	198	40.33 N	76.49 W
Eliza Howell Park ♠	271	42.24 N	83.16 W
Elizaville, Ind., U.S.	208	40.08 N	86.24 W
Elizaville, N.Y., U.S.	200	42.03 N	73.48 W
El-Jadida (Mazagan)	138	33.16 N	8.30 W
El Jaralito	222	26.07 N	104.10 W
El Jebel	190	39.22 N	107.02 W
El-Jebha	34	35.13 N	4.38 W
El Jícaro	226	13.43 N	86.08 W
El Jobean	210	26.58 N	82.13 W
Ełk	30	53.50 N	22.22 E
Elk □[6]	204	41.26 N	78.43 W
Elk ≃, Alta., Can.	172	52.55 N	115.40 W
Elk ≃, B.C., Can.	172	49.10 N	115.14 W
Ełk ≃, Pol.	30	53.31 N	22.47 E
Elk ≃, Colo., U.S.	190	40.29 N	106.58 W
Elk ≃, Kans., U.S.	188	37.15 N	95.41 W
Elk ≃, Minn., U.S.	180	45.18 N	93.34 W
Elk ≃, Mo., U.S.	184	36.38 N	94.38 W
Elk ≃, W. Va., U.S.	178	38.21 N	81.38 W
Elk ≃, Wis., U.S.	180	45.42 N	90.37 W
Elkader	180	42.51 N	91.24 W
El Kairouan	138	35.41 N	10.07 E
El Kala	138	36.50 N	8.30 E
El Kantara	138	33.41 N	10.55 E
El-Karafab	130	18.10 N	31.36 E
El Kasserine	138	35.11 N	8.48 E
Elk Bayou ≃	216	36.06 N	119.24 W
Elk City	186	35.25 N	99.25 W
Elk City Lake ⊜[1]	188	37.25 N	95.55 W
Elk Creek	194	39.36 N	122.32 W
Elk Creek ≃, Okla., U.S.	186	34.48 N	99.09 W
Elk Creek ≃, Oreg., U.S.	192	43.38 N	123.34 W
Elk Creek ≃, Pa., U.S.	204	42.01 N	80.22 W
Elk Creek ≃, S. Dak., U.S.	188	44.15 N	102.22 W
Elk Creek ≃, Wash., U.S.	214	46.38 N	123.17 W
Elkedra ≃	152	21.08 S	136.22 E
El Kef	138	36.11 N	8.43 E
El Kef □[8]	36	36.00 N	9.00 E
El-Kelâa-des-Srarhna	138	32.02 N	7.23 W
El Kere	134	5.48 N	42.10 E
El Kerma	34	35.36 N	0.35 W
Elk Grove	216	38.25 N	121.22 W
Elk Grove Village	268	42.01 N	87.59 W
Elkhart, Ill., U.S.	209	40.01 N	89.29 W
Elkhart, Ind., U.S.	206	41.41 N	85.58 W
Elkhart, Kans., U.S.	188	37.00 N	101.54 W
Elkhart, Tex., U.S.	212	31.38 N	95.35 W
Elkhart □[6]	206	41.35 N	85.50 W
Elkhart ≃	206	41.41 N	85.58 W
Elkhart Lake	180	43.50 N	88.01 W
El Khatt •[4]	138	22.40 N	10.05 W
Elkhead Creek ≃	190	40.31 N	107.26 W
Elkhead Mountains ⩕	190	40.50 N	107.05 W
El Khnâchîch •[4]	138	21.50 N	3.45 W
Elkhorn, Man., Can.	174	49.58 N	101.14 W
Elk Horn, Iowa, U.S.	188	41.36 N	95.03 W
Elkhorn, Wis., U.S.	206	42.40 N	88.33 W
Elkhorn ≃	188	41.07 N	96.19 W
Elkhorn, North Fork ≃	188	42.00 N	97.21 W
Elkhorn City	182	37.18 N	82.21 W
Elkhorn Creek ≃, Ky., U.S.	208	38.19 N	84.52 W
Elkhorn Creek ≃, Mo., U.S.	209	39.05 N	91.20 W
Elkhorn Peaks ⩕	192	43.22 N	111.06 W
Elki	118	37.34 N	43.10 E
Elkin	182	36.16 N	80.51 W
Elkins	178	38.55 N	79.51 W
Elkins Park	198	40.05 N	75.08 W
Elk Island I	174	50.45 N	96.32 W
Elk Island National Park ♠	172	53.37 N	112.45 W
Elkland	200	41.59 N	77.21 W
Elk Mills	198	39.39 N	75.50 W
Elk Mountain	190	41.41 N	106.25 W
Elk Mountain Λ, Wash., U.S.	214	46.08 N	122.28 W
Elk Mountain Λ, Wyo., U.S.	190	41.38 N	106.32 W
Elk Neck State Park ♠	198	39.30 N	75.58 W
Elko, B.C., Can.	172	49.18 N	115.07 W
Elko, Nev., U.S.	194	40.50 N	115.46 W
El Kouif	36	35.29 N	8.19 E
Elk Peak Λ	192	46.27 N	110.46 W
Elk Plain	214	47.04 N	122.24 W
Elk Point, Alta., Can.	172	53.34 N	110.54 W
Elk Point, S. Dak., U.S.	188	42.41 N	96.41 W
Elk Rapids	180	44.54 N	85.25 W
El Krib	36	36.19 N	9.09 E
Elkridge	198	39.13 N	76.42 W
Elk River, Idaho, U.S.	192	46.47 N	116.11 W
Elk River, Minn., U.S.	180	45.18 N	93.35 W
Elk River C	198	39.31 N	75.55 W
El Kseur	138	36.46 N	4.49 E
Elk State Park ♠	204	41.38 N	78.34 W
Elkton, Ky., U.S.	184	36.49 N	87.09 W
Elkton, Md., U.S.	198	39.36 N	75.50 W
Elkton, Mich., U.S.	180	43.49 N	83.11 W
Elkton, Ohio, U.S.	204	40.46 N	80.42 W
Elkton, S. Dak., U.S.	188	44.14 N	96.29 W
Elkton, Va., U.S.	178	38.25 N	78.38 W
Elkville	184	37.55 N	89.14 W
Ell, Lake ⊜	152	29.13 S	127.46 E
Elland	42	53.41 N	1.50 W
Ellard Lake ⊜	174	54.33 N	91.55 W
Ellás → Greece □[1]	38	39.00 N	22.00 E
Ellavalla	152	25.05 S	114.22 E
Ellaville	182	32.15 N	84.18 W
Ellefeld	50	50.29 N	12.23 E
Ellef Ringnes Island I	16	78.30 N	104.00 W
El Leh	134	3.48 N	39.48 E
Elleker	152	35.00 S	117.43 E
Ellemandsbjerg Λ[2]	41	56.07 N	10.32 E
Ellen ≃	42	54.43 N	3.30 W
Ellen, Mount Λ	190	38.07 N	110.49 W
Ellendale, Austl.	152	17.56 S	124.48 E
Ellendale, Del., U.S.	198	38.47 N	75.25 W
Ellendale, Minn., U.S.	180	43.52 N	93.18 W
Ellendale, N. Dak., U.S.	188	46.06 N	98.32 W
Ellensburg	192	47.00 N	120.32 W
Ellenton, Fla., U.S.	210	29.47 N	81.26 W
Ellenton, Ga., U.S.	182	31.11 N	83.35 W
Ellenville	200	41.43 N	74.24 W
Eller •[8]	253	51.12 N	6.51 E
Ellerbee	182	35.04 N	79.46 W
Ellero ≃	56	44.27 N	7.54 E
Ellès	36	35.57 N	9.06 E
Ellesmere	44	52.54 N	2.54 W
Ellesmere, Lake C	162	43.48 S	172.25 E
Ellesmere Island I	16	81.00 N	80.00 W
Ellesmere Park	252	53.29 N	2.20 W
Ellesmere Port	42	53.17 N	2.54 W
Ellesmere Port □[8]	252	53.18 N	2.47 W
Ellettsville	184	39.14 N	86.37 W
Ellewoutsdijk	48	51.24 N	3.49 E
Ellezelles	46	50.44 N	3.41 E
Ellice ≃	166	68.02 N	103.26 W
Ellice Islands → Tuvalu □[1]	14	8.00 S	178.00 E
Ellice Islands II	6	8.00 S	178.00 E
Ellichpur → Achalpur	110	21.16 N	77.31 E
Ellicott City	198	39.16 N	76.48 W
Ellicott Creek ≃	200	43.01 N	78.53 W
Ellicott Creek Park ♠	274a	43.01 N	78.50 W
Ellicottville	200	42.17 N	78.40 W
Ellijay	182	34.42 N	84.28 W
El Limón, Méx.	222	24.16 N	107.04 W
El Limón, Méx.	224	18.05 N	101.59 W
El Limón, Méx.	224	19.49 N	104.11 W
El Limón, Nic.	226	12.45 N	86.44 W
El Limoncito	276c	10.29 N	66.47 W
Ellingen	52	49.04 N	10.58 E
Ellinger	212	29.50 N	96.44 W
Ellinghorst •[8]	253	51.34 N	6.57 E
Ellington, Eng., U.K.	42	55.13 N	1.34 W
Ellington, Conn., U.S.	197	41.54 N	72.28 W
Ellington, Mo., U.S.	184	37.14 N	90.58 W
Ellington, N.Y., U.S.	204	42.13 N	79.07 W
Ellinikón	257c	37.53 N	23.44 E
Ellinikón, Aerolimín ⊠	257c	37.54 N	23.44 E
Ellinwood	188	38.21 N	98.35 W
Elliot	148	31.18 S	27.50 E
Elliot, Mount Λ	156	19.29 S	146.58 E
Elliotdale	148	31.55 S	28.38 E
Elliotganj	116	23.31 N	90.52 E
Elliot Lake	180	46.23 N	82.39 W
Elliot Lake ⊜	174	52.55 N	95.20 W
Elliott, Austl.	152	17.33 S	133.32 E
Elliott, Ill., U.S.	206	40.28 N	88.16 W
Elliott, Iowa, U.S.	188	41.09 N	95.10 W
Elliott □[6]	208	38.13 N	83.10 W
Elliott, Mount Λ	152	20.29 S	126.37 E
Elliott Bay C	214	47.36 N	122.22 W
Elliott Key I	210	25.27 N	80.11 W
Elliottville	208	38.11 N	83.16 W
Ellis	188	38.56 N	99.34 W
Ellis □[6]	212	32.20 N	96.48 W
Ellisburg	202	43.44 N	76.08 W
Ellis Island I	266	40.42 N	74.02 W
Ellis Mountain Λ	214	48.10 N	124.19 W
Ellison Creek Reservoir ⊜[1]	212	32.56 N	94.43 W
Ellisport	214	47.25 N	122.26 W
Ellisras	146	23.40 S	27.46 E
Elliston, Austl.	152	33.39 S	134.55 E
Elliston, Newf., Can.	176	48.38 N	53.03 W
Elliston, Mont., U.S.	192	46.33 N	112.26 W
Ellisville, Miss., U.S.	184	31.36 N	89.12 W
Ellisville, Mo., U.S.	209	38.35 N	90.35 W
Ellmau	58	47.31 N	12.18 E
Ellmauer Halt Λ	58	47.34 N	12.18 E
Ellon	28	57.22 N	2.05 W
Ellora	112	20.01 N	75.10 E
Ellore → Elūru	112	16.42 N	81.06 E
Elloree	182	33.32 N	80.34 W
Ellport	204	40.52 N	80.16 W
Ellrich	50	51.35 N	10.40 E
Ellsworth, Ill., U.S.	206	40.27 N	88.43 W
Ellsworth, Kans., U.S.	188	38.44 N	98.14 W
Ellsworth, Maine, U.S.	178	44.33 N	68.26 W
Ellsworth, Mich., U.S.	180	45.10 N	85.15 W
Ellsworth, Minn., U.S.	188	43.31 N	96.01 W
Ellsworth, Ohio, U.S.	204	41.01 N	80.52 W
Ellsworth, Pa., U.S.	204	40.07 N	80.01 W
Ellsworth, Wash., U.S.	214	45.37 N	122.36 W
Ellsworth, Wis., U.S.	180	44.44 N	92.29 W
Ellsworth Air Force Base ■	188	44.08 N	103.05 W
Ellsworth Land •[1]	9	75.30 S	80.00 W
Ellsworth Mountains ⩕	9	79.00 S	85.00 W
El Lucero	186	25.53 N	103.25 W
Ellwangen	52	48.57 N	10.07 E
Ellwanger Berge ⩕[2]	52	49.00 N	10.15 E
Ellwood City	204	40.50 N	80.17 W
Elm, B.R.D.	48	53.31 N	9.12 E
Elm, Schw.	54	46.55 N	9.11 E
Elm, Eng., U.K.	44	52.38 N	0.10 E
Elm ⩕[2]	50	52.09 N	10.53 E
Elm ≃, U.S.	188	45.36 N	98.19 W
Elm ≃, Ill., U.S.	184	38.24 N	88.14 W
Elm ≃, N. Dak., U.S.	188	47.15 N	96.50 W
Elma, Iowa, U.S.	180	43.15 N	92.26 W
Elma, N.Y., U.S.	200	42.51 N	78.38 W
Elma, Wash., U.S.	214	47.00 N	123.25 W
El Macero	216	38.33 N	121.41 W
Elmadağ (Küçükyozgat)	120	39.55 N	33.15 E
Elma Dağı Λ	120	39.49 N	33.00 E
El Maharès	138	34.32 N	10.30 E
El Mahdia	138	35.30 N	11.04 E
El Mahia •[1]	138	22.30 N	2.30 W
El Malah	34	35.24 N	1.05 W
Elmalı	120	36.44 N	29.56 E
El Manchón	226	14.23 N	92.02 W
El Maneadero	222	31.45 N	116.35 W
El Manteco	236	7.27 N	62.32 W
Elmas Burnu ≻	257b	41.13 N	29.13 E
Elmaton	212	28.53 N	96.09 W
El Mayoco	244	42.39 S	70.59 W
Elmberg Λ	58	47.40 N	13.57 E
Elmbridge □[8]	250	51.22 N	0.23 W
Elm Brook ≃	273	42.29 N	71.16 W
Elm City	182	35.48 N	77.52 W
Elm Creek, Man., Can.	174	49.41 N	98.00 W
Elm Creek, Nebr., U.S.	188	40.43 N	99.22 W
Elm Creek ≃, Minn., U.S.	188	43.45 N	94.11 W
Elm Creek ≃, S. Dak., U.S.	188	44.21 N	102.42 W
Elm Creek ≃, Tex., U.S.	186	33.12 N	98.50 W
Elm Creek ≃, Tex., U.S.	186	32.40 N	99.41 W
Elm Creek ≃, Tex., U.S.	186	28.54 N	100.12 W
Elm Creek ≃, Tex., U.S.	212	29.15 N	97.32 W
El Meco	224	22.35 N	99.20 W
El Médano	222	24.25 N	111.30 W
El Meghaïer	138	33.55 N	5.58 E
El Melón, Sierra ⩕	224	23.56 N	99.39 W
Elmen	54	47.20 N	10.32 E
Elmer	198	39.36 N	75.10 W
El Mesón	224	18.35 N	95.26 W
El Metlaoui	138	34.20 N	8.24 E
Elm Grove	206	43.03 N	88.04 W
Elmhurst, Austl.	159	37.11 S	143.15 E
Elmhurst, Ill., U.S.	206	41.53 N	87.56 W
Elmhurst, Pa., U.S.	200	41.22 N	75.33 W
Elmhurst •[8]	266	40.44 N	73.53 W
El Mijao	276c	10.23 N	66.48 W
El Milia	138	36.48 N	6.14 E
El Mimbre	186	25.40 N	102.20 W
Elmina	140	5.05 N	1.21 W
El Minao	230m	18.22 N	66.05 W
Elmira, Ont., Can.	202	43.36 N	80.33 W
Elmira, P.E.I., Can.	176	46.27 N	62.04 W
Elmira, Calif., U.S.	216	38.21 N	121.55 W
Elmira, N.Y., U.S.	200	42.06 N	76.49 W
El Mirador	224	21.01 N	97.57 W
El Mirage	190	33.36 N	112.19 W
El Mirage Lake ⊜	218	34.38 N	117.35 W
Elmira Heights	200	42.08 N	76.49 W
Elm Mott	212	31.40 N	97.06 W
Elmo, Mont., U.S.	172	47.50 N	114.21 W
Elmo, Tex., U.S.	212	32.43 N	96.10 W
El Moknine	138	35.38 N	10.54 E
El Molinillo	34	39.28 N	4.13 W
El Molinito	276a	19.27 N	99.15 W
Elmont, N.Y., U.S.	266	40.42 N	73.42 W
Elmont, Va., U.S.	198	37.43 N	77.30 W
El Monte, Chile	242	33.41 S	71.01 W
El Monte, Calif., U.S.	218	34.04 N	118.02 W
El Monte Airport ⊠	270	34.06 N	118.02 W
Elmora	204	40.36 N	78.45 W
El Moral	186	28.51 N	100.39 W
Elmore, Austl.	156	36.30 S	144.37 E
Elmore, Minn., U.S.	180	43.30 N	94.05 W
Elmore, Ohio, U.S.	204	41.29 N	83.18 W
Elmore City	186	34.37 N	97.24 W
El Morro ⊥	230m	18.28 N	66.07 W
El Morro National Monument ♠	190	35.05 N	108.22 W
Elm Point ≻	266	40.49 N	73.46 W
Elmpt	52	51.13 N	6.10 E
El Mreiti •[4]	138	23.29 N	7.52 W
El Mreyyé •[1]	140	19.30 N	7.00 W
Elmschenhagen •[8]	50	54.18 N	10.12 E
Elmsdale	176	44.58 N	63.30 W
Elmsford	200	41.03 N	73.49 W
Elmshorn	48	53.45 N	9.39 E
Elmstein	52	49.21 N	7.56 E
Elmswell	44	52.15 N	0.53 E
El Mulato	186	29.22 N	104.10 W
Elmvale	202	44.35 N	79.52 W
Elmville	208	38.20 N	84.46 W
Elmwood, Ont., Can.	202	44.14 N	81.03 W
Elmwood, Ill., U.S.	180	40.47 N	89.58 W
Elmwood, Mass., U.S.	273	42.01 N	70.58 W
Elmwood, Nebr., U.S.	188	40.50 N	96.18 W
Elmwood, Wis., U.S.	180	44.47 N	92.09 W
Elmwood •[8]	275	39.56 N	75.14 W
Elmwood Park, Ill., U.S.	206	41.55 N	87.49 W
Elmwood Park, N.J., U.S.	266	40.54 N	74.07 W
Elmwood Park, Wis., U.S.	206	42.41 N	87.50 W
El Naranjo, Arg.	242	25.44 S	64.59 W
El Naranjo, Méx.	224	22.30 N	98.38 W
Elne	32	42.36 N	2.58 E
El Negralejo	256a	40.24 N	3.31 W
El Negrito	226	15.16 N	87.41 W
El Nevado, Cerro Λ	236	3.59 N	74.04 W
El Nido, Pil.	106	11.11 N	119.23 E
El Nido, Calif., U.S.	216	37.08 N	120.29 W
El Nihuil	242	35.02 S	68.40 W
El Niybo	134	4.32 N	39.59 E
Elnora, Alta., Can.	172	51.59 N	113.12 W
Elnora, Ind., U.S.	184	38.53 N	87.05 W
El Oasis	276c	10.35 N	66.59 W
El-Obeid → Al-Ubayyiḍ	130	13.11 N	30.13 E
Elobey, Islas II	142	0.59 N	9.30 E
Eloida, Lake ⊜	202	44.40 N	75.58 W
Eloi Mendes	246	21.37 S	45.34 W
Eloise	210	27.60 N	81.44 W
Elokobatindi	142	3.27 N	10.08 E
Elora, Ont., Can.	202	43.41 N	80.26 W
Elora, Tenn., U.S.	184	35.01 N	86.21 W
El Oro □[4]	236	3.30 S	79.50 W
Elortondo	242	33.42 S	61.37 W
Elorza	236	7.03 N	69.31 W
El Oso	236	4.59 N	65.25 W
El Otro Lado	276c	10.24 N	66.49 W
El Oued	138	33.20 N	6.58 E
Eloy	190	32.45 N	111.33 W
Éloyes	54	48.06 N	6.37 E
El Pacayal	222	15.37 N	92.02 W
El Palmar, Bol.	238	21.54 S	63.39 W
El Palmar, Ven.	236	7.58 N	61.53 W
El Palmar, Ven.	276c	10.38 N	66.52 W
El Palomar	278	34.36 S	58.36 W
El Palomar, Base Aérea Militar ■	278	34.37 S	58.37 W
El Palqui	242	30.45 S	70.59 W
El Pantanoso, Arroyo ≃	278	34.47 S	58.40 W
El Pao, Ven.	236	9.38 N	68.08 W
El Pao, Ven.	236	8.01 N	62.38 W
El Paradero	236	10.38 N	69.32 W
El Paraíso, Hond.	226	13.51 N	86.34 W
El Paraíso, Méx.	224	17.25 N	100.15 W
El Paraíso □[5]	226	14.10 N	86.30 W
El Pardo •[8]	256a	40.31 N	3.47 W
El Pardo, Monte de ⩕[2]	256a	40.33 N	3.48 W
El Paso, Nic.	226	12.07 N	85.53 W
El Paso, Ill., U.S.	206	40.44 N	89.01 W
El Paso, Tex., U.S.	190	31.45 N	106.29 W
El Paso Creek ≃	218	35.02 N	118.51 W
El Paso de Robles → Paso Robles	216	35.38 N	120.41 W
El Paso Peaks ⩕	194	35.28 N	117.43 W
El Pato	236	2.50 N	74.48 W
El Paují	276c	10.26 N	66.49 W
El Pedregal •[8]	276c	10.30 N	66.51 W
El Peñuelo	222	24.34 N	100.46 W
El Peral	276e	33.35 S	70.34 W
El Perú	236	7.19 N	61.49 W
El Pescado, Arroyo ≃	248	34.54 S	57.47 W
El Petén □[5]	226	16.15 N	89.50 W
Elphinstone	174	50.33 N	100.19 W
El Pilar	236	10.32 N	63.09 W
El Pinar, Parque Nacional ♠	276c	10.29 N	66.56 W
El Piñón	236	10.24 N	74.50 W
El Pintado	242	24.38 S	61.27 W
El Piojo, Arroyo ≃	278	34.50 S	58.45 W
El Piquete	242	24.13 S	64.39 W
El Placer	224	23.33 N	106.10 W
El Plantío •[8]	256a	40.28 N	3.49 W
El Platanillo	224	18.28 N	101.52 W
El Plomo	190	31.15 N	112.04 W
El Polvorín	230m	18.26 N	66.17 W
El Porcal	256a	40.18 N	3.32 W
El Portal, Calif., U.S.	216	37.41 N	119.47 W
El Portal, Fla., U.S.	210	25.52 N	80.11 W
El Porvenir, Méx.	186	27.33 N	104.57 W
El Porvenir, Méx.	194	32.05 N	116.38 W
El Porvenir, Méx.	222	31.15 N	105.51 W
El Porvenir, Méx.	224	15.44 N	93.22 W
El Potosí	222	24.51 N	100.19 W
El Potosí, Parque Nacional ♠	224	22.00 N	99.58 W
El Potrero	186	26.23 N	100.27 W
El Potro, Cerro Λ	242	28.24 S	69.39 W
El Progreso, Ec.	236a	0.54 S	89.33 W
El Progreso, Guat.	226	14.51 N	90.04 W
El Progreso, Guat.	226	14.21 N	89.51 W
El Progreso, Hond.	226	15.21 N	87.49 W
El Progreso □[5]	226	14.50 N	90.00 W
El Puente del Arzobispo	34	39.48 N	5.10 W
El Puerto de Santa María	34	36.36 N	6.13 W
El Puesto	242	27.57 S	67.38 W
El Quebrachal	242	25.17 S	64.04 W
El Quelite	224	23.32 N	106.28 W
Elquera Bushland ♠	264a	33.42 S	150.04 E
Elqui ≃	242	29.54 S	71.17 W
El Quiché □[5]	226	15.30 N	90.55 W
Elrama	204	40.15 N	79.56 W
El Ranchito	224	18.40 N	103.41 W
El Rastro	236	9.03 N	67.27 W
El Real	236	8.08 N	77.43 W
El Recreo •[8]	276c	10.30 N	66.53 W
El Reloj	276a	19.18 N	99.08 W
El Remolino, Méx.	186	28.44 N	101.07 W
El Remolino, Méx.	224	17.39 N	94.13 W
El Reno	186	35.32 N	97.57 W
El Rio	218	34.14 N	119.10 W
El Rito	190	36.21 N	106.11 W
El Rito ≃	190	36.12 N	106.14 W
El Roba	144	3.57 N	40.01 E
El Roble	224	23.32 N	106.14 W
Elrose	174	51.13 N	108.01 W
Elroy	180	43.45 N	90.16 W
El Rucio	224	23.23 N	102.05 W
Elsa, Yukon, Can.	170	63.55 N	135.28 W
Elsa, Tex., U.S.	186	26.18 N	97.59 W
Elsa ≃	60	43.43 N	10.52 E
Elsah	209	38.57 N	90.22 W
El Sahuaro	190	31.05 N	112.55 W
El Salto, Chile	276e	33.23 S	70.38 W
El Salto, Méx.	224	20.32 N	103.11 W
El Salto, Méx.	224	23.47 N	105.22 W
El Salvador	106	8.34 N	124.32 E
El Salvador □[1]	220		
	226	13.50 N	88.55 W
El Samán de Apure	236	7.55 N	68.44 W
El Santo	230p	22.42 N	79.41 W
Elsass → Alsace □[9]	32	48.30 N	7.30 E
El Sauce	226	12.53 N	86.32 W
El Sauz	222	29.02 N	106.16 W
El Sauzal	222	31.54 N	116.41 W
Elsberry	209	39.10 N	90.47 W
Elsbethen	58	47.45 N	13.05 E
Elsburg	263d	26.15 S	28.12 E
Elsdorf, B.R.D.	48	53.14 N	9.20 E
Elsdorf, B.R.D.	52	50.54 N	6.34 E
El Segundo	218	33.55 N	118.24 W
El Seibo	228	18.46 N	69.02 W
Elsen	48	51.44 N	8.39 E
Elsey	253	51.22 N	7.34 E
Elsfleth	48	53.14 N	8.28 E
El Siasgo, Arroyo ≃	248	35.33 S	58.33 W
Elsie, Mich., U.S.	206	43.05 N	84.23 W
Elsie, Oreg., U.S.	214	45.52 N	123.35 W
Elsinore → Helsingør, Dan.	41	56.02 N	12.37 E
Elsinore, Utah, U.S.	190	38.41 N	112.09 W
Elsinore, Lake ⊜[1]	218	33.39 N	117.21 W
El Sitio	276c	10.28 N	66.46 W
Elsloo	52	50.56 N	5.46 E
Elsmere, Del., U.S.	198	39.44 N	75.36 W
Elsmere, Ky., U.S.	208	39.00 N	84.36 W
Elsmere, N.Y., U.S.	200	42.38 N	73.49 W
El Sobrante	216	37.58 N	122.19 W
El Socorro	236	8.59 N	65.44 W
El Sombrero	236	9.23 N	67.03 W
Elspe	52	51.09 N	8.04 E
Elspeet	48	52.17 N	5.46 E
Elst	48	51.55 N	5.50 E
Elstal	50	52.32 N	12.59 E
Elstead	44	51.11 N	0.43 W
Elster	50	51.50 N	12.49 E
Elsterberg	50	50.36 N	12.10 E
Elstergebirge ⩕	50	50.15 N	12.20 E
Elsterwerda	50	51.28 N	13.31 E
Elston, Ind., U.S.	206	40.22 N	86.55 W
Elston, Mo., U.S.	209	38.37 N	92.19 W
Elstow	44	52.07 N	0.28 W
Elstra	50	51.13 N	14.08 E
Elstree	44	51.39 N	0.16 W
Elstree Aerodrome ⊠	250	51.39 N	0.19 W
El Sueco	222	29.54 N	106.24 W
El Tajín ⊥	224	20.27 N	97.23 W
El Talar	248	34.27 S	58.39 W
El Tamarindo	226	13.11 N	87.54 W
El Tambo	236	1.26 N	77.23 W
El Tanque	186	26.28 N	99.38 W
El Tapextle	224	23.52 N	105.33 W
El Tarf	36	36.45 N	8.20 E
Elten	48	51.52 N	6.10 E
El Tepozteco, Parque Nacional ♠	224	19.00 N	99.00 W
El Terrero	224	18.58 N	102.28 W
Eltham, Austl.	159	37.44 S	145.09 E
Eltham, N.Z.	162	39.26 S	174.18 E
Eltham •[8]	250	51.27 N	0.04 E
El Tigre, Col.	236	2.28 N	68.15 W
El Tigre, Ven.	236	8.55 N	64.15 W
El Tigrito → San José de Guanipa	236	8.54 N	64.09 W
El Timbiriche	224	18.38 N	101.31 W
El Tisey, Cerro Λ	226	12.59 N	86.22 W
Eltmann	52	49.58 N	10.40 E
El Tocuyo	236	9.47 N	69.48 W
El Tofo	242	29.27 S	71.15 W
El'ton, S.S.S.R.	70	49.08 N	46.50 E
Elton, Eng., U.K.	252	53.16 N	2.49 W
Elton, La., U.S.	184	30.29 N	92.42 W
Elton, Pa., U.S.	204	40.17 N	78.48 W
El'ton, Ozero ⊜	70	49.16 N	46.35 E
El Toreo ♠	276a	19.27 N	99.13 W
El Toro	218	33.38 N	117.42 W
El Toro Λ	230m	18.16 N	65.49 W
El Toro I	224	21.26 N	97.31 W
El Toro, Cerro Λ	224	20.40 N	100.43 W
El Toro Marine Corps Air Station ■	218	33.41 N	117.44 W
El Tranco, Embalse de ⊜[1]	34	38.10 N	2.45 W
El Tránsito, Chile	242	28.52 S	70.17 W
El Tránsito, El Sal.	226	13.22 N	88.21 W
El Trapiche	236	3.03 N	77.33 W
El Trébol	242	32.12 S	61.42 W
El Triunfo, Hond.	226	13.06 N	87.00 W
El Triunfo, Hond.	226	15.46 N	87.26 W
El Triunfo, Méx.	222	23.47 N	110.08 W
El Tuito	224	20.19 N	105.22 W
El Tunal	242	24.48 S	65.45 W
El Turbio	244	51.41 S	72.05 W
Eltville	52	50.02 N	8.07 E
Eltz, Burg ⊥	52	50.12 N	7.20 E
Elunchanzizhiqi (Alihe)	79	50.34 N	123.40 E
Elunchunzizhiqi (Xiaoergou)	79	49.30 N	123.47 E
Elura → Ellora	112	20.01 N	75.10 E
Elūru	112	16.42 N	81.06 E
Elva	66	58.13 N	26.25 E
El Valle	226	8.36 N	80.08 W
El Valle •[8]	276c	10.27 N	66.55 W
Elvas	34	38.53 N	7.10 W
Elvas ≃	246	21.12 S	44.08 W
Elven	32	47.44 N	2.35 W
El Verano	216	38.18 N	122.29 W
El Verde	224	23.21 N	106.09 W
Elverdissen	48	52.05 N	8.38 E
Elverlingsen	253	51.17 N	7.42 E
Elverta	216	38.43 N	121.28 W
Elverum	26	60.53 N	11.34 E
El Viejo	226	12.40 N	87.10 W
El Vigía	236	8.38 N	71.39 W
Elvira	248	35.14 S	59.29 W
Elvo ≃	56	45.23 N	8.21 E
El Volcán, Arg.	242	33.15 S	66.12 W
El Volcán, Chile	242	33.49 S	70.11 W
El Wak, Kenya	144	2.49 N	40.56 E
El-Wak, Som.	134	2.50 N	41.03 E
El-Wanot	134	4.07 N	47.07 E
El-Warre	134	3.39 N	45.18 E
Elwha ≃	214	48.10 N	123.35 W
Elwood, Austl.	264b	37.53 S	144.59 E
Elwood, Ill., U.S.	206	41.24 N	88.07 W
Elwood, Ind., U.S.	206	40.17 N	85.50 W
Elwood, Kans., U.S.	188	39.45 N	94.52 W
Elwood, Nebr., U.S.	188	40.36 N	99.52 W
Elwood, N.J., U.S.	198	39.35 N	74.43 W
Elwood, N.Y., U.S.	197	40.51 N	73.20 W
Elwood Park, Fla., U.S.	210	27.28 N	82.30 W
Elwood Park, Pa., U.S.	269b	40.10 N	80.17 W
Elwy ≃	42	53.16 N	3.26 W
Elwyn	275	39.54 N	75.24 W
Elxleben	50	51.02 N	10.56 E
Ely, Eng., U.K.	44	52.24 N	0.16 E
Ely, Minn., U.S.	180	47.54 N	91.51 W
Ely, Mo., U.S.	209	39.41 N	91.39 W
Ely, Nev., U.S.	194	39.15 N	114.53 W
Ely, Isle of •[1]	44	52.24 N	0.10 E
El Yagual	236	7.29 N	68.25 W
Ely Cathedral ⊥[1]	44	52.24 N	0.16 E
El Yopal	236	5.21 N	72.23 W
Elyria	204	41.22 N	82.06 W
Elyria Airport ⊠	269a	41.20 N	82.06 W
Elysburg	200	40.52 N	76.33 W
Elysian Park ♠	270	34.05 N	118.14 W
El Yunque Λ	230m	18.19 N	65.48 W
Elywood Park ♠	269a	41.23 N	82.06 W
Elz	52	50.25 N	8.02 E
Elz ≃	54	48.21 N	7.45 E
Elzach	54	48.10 N	8.04 E
El Zamural	276c	10.27 N	67.00 W
El Zapotal	224	15.27 N	93.10 W
El Zapotán	224	18.41 N	103.39 W
El Zapote de Calabacillas	222	25.42 N	106.32 W
Elzbach ≃	52	50.12 N	7.22 E
Elze, B.R.D.	48	52.07 N	9.44 E
Elze, B.R.D.	48	52.35 N	9.44 E
El Zig-Zag	276c	10.33 N	66.58 W
Emadle	134	5.13 N	46.56 E
Emae I	165f	17.04 S	168.24 E
Emajõgi ≃	66	58.26 N	27.15 E
Emali	144	2.05 S	37.38 E
Emalı Bendi •[6]	257b	41.04 N	29.06 E
Emån ≃	26	57.08 N	16.30 E
Émancé	251	48.35 N	1.44 E
Emau I	165f	17.28 S	168.30 E
Emba	76	48.50 N	58.08 E
Emba ≃	70	46.38 N	53.14 E
Embarcación	242	23.13 S	64.06 W
Embarras ≃, Alta., Can.	172	53.27 N	116.37 W
Embarras ≃, Ill., U.S.	184	38.39 N	87.37 W
Embarras, North Fork ≃	184	38.55 N	87.59 W
Embarrass	180	44.40 N	88.42 W
Embarrass ≃, Minn., U.S.	180	47.24 N	92.25 W
Embarrass ≃, Wis., U.S.	180	44.23 N	88.45 W
Embarrass, Middle Branch ≃	180	44.43 N	88.55 W
Embetsu	82a	44.44 N	141.47 E
Embid	34	40.58 N	1.43 W
Embira ≃	238	7.19 S	70.15 W
Embleton	42	55.30 N	1.37 W
Emboabas	246	21.18 S	44.08 W
Embondo	142	0.15 N	19.38 E
Embrach	54	47.30 N	8.36 E
Embreeville, Pa., U.S.	275	39.56 N	75.44 W
Embreeville, Tenn., U.S.	182	36.11 N	82.28 W
Embro	202	43.09 N	80.54 W
Embrun, Ont., Can.	202	45.16 N	75.17 W
Embrun, Fr.	56	44.34 N	6.30 E
Embry	46	50.29 N	1.58 E
Embu, Bra.	246	23.39 S	46.51 W
Embu, Kenya	144	0.32 S	37.27 E
Embu □[7]	277b	23.40 S	46.50 W
Embu-Guaçu	246	23.49 S	46.48 W
Embu-Mirim ≃	277b	23.39 S	46.51 W
Emden, B.R.D.	48	53.22 N	7.12 E
Emden, Ill., U.S.	184	40.18 N	89.29 W
Emden, Mo., U.S.	209	39.48 N	91.52 W
Emei	97	29.36 N	103.31 E
Emeigh	204	40.42 N	78.47 W
Emel' ≃	76	46.20 N	81.46 E
Emelle	184	32.44 N	88.19 W
Emerado	188	47.55 N	97.22 W
Émerainville	251	48.49 N	2.37 E
Emerald, Austl.	156	23.32 S	148.10 E
Emerald, Austl.	159	37.56 S	145.26 E
Emerald Basin •[1]	6	57.00 S	161.00 E
Emerald Bay State Park ♠	216	38.57 N	120.05 W
Emerald Lake	216	37.28 N	122.16 W
Emero ≃	238	13.19 S	67.17 W
Emerson, Man., Can.	174	49.00 N	97.12 W
Emerson, Ark., U.S.	184	33.06 N	93.11 W
Emerson, Ga., U.S.	182	34.08 N	84.45 W
Emerson, Iowa, U.S.	188	41.01 N	95.24 W
Emerson, Mo., U.S.	209	39.53 N	91.42 W
Emerson, Nebr., U.S.	188	42.17 N	96.44 W
Emerson, N.J., U.S.	266	40.58 N	74.02 W
Emery, S. Dak., U.S.	188	43.36 N	97.37 W
Emery, Utah, U.S.	190	38.55 N	111.15 W
Emeryville, Ont., Can.	204	42.18 N	82.45 W
Emeryville, Calif., U.S.	216	37.50 N	122.17 W
Emet	120	39.20 N	29.15 E
Emgayet	136	29.04 N	12.58 E
Emhouse	212	32.09 N	96.35 W
Emi	78	50.36 N	97.49 E
Emigrant Gap	216	39.19 N	120.38 W
Emigrant Gap)(	216	39.18 N	120.40 W
Emigsville	198	40.01 N	76.44 W
Emiliano Zapata, Méx.	222	17.45 N	91.46 W
Emiliano Zapata, Méx.	224	16.10 N	94.01 W
Emilia-Romagna □[4]	36	44.35 N	11.00 E
Emílio de Carvalho	142	5.55 S	12.57 E
Emin	76	46.27 N	83.23 E
Eminābād	113	32.02 N	74.16 E
Emine, nos ≻	38	42.42 N	27.51 E
Eminence, Ky., U.S.	208	38.22 N	85.11 W
Eminence, Mo., U.S.	184	37.09 N	91.22 W
Emira Island I	154	1.40 S	150.00 E
Emiralem	120	38.36 N	27.09 E
Emiratos Arabes Unidos → United Arab Emirates □[1]	118	24.00 N	54.00 E
Emirdağ	120	39.01 N	31.10 E
Emır Dağları ⩕	120	38.50 N	31.15 E
Emirhan	120	39.42 N	37.46 E
Emisou, Tarso Λ	136	21.13 N	18.32 E
Emita	156	40.00 S	147.54 E
Emlembe Λ	148	25.57 S	31.11 E
Emlenton	204	41.11 N	79.43 W
Emlichheim	48	52.36 N	6.50 E
Emma ≃	240	3.51 N	54.32 W
Emmaån ≃	40	58.44 N	15.35 E
Emmaboda	26	56.38 N	15.32 E
Emmarentia •[8]	263d	26.10 S	28.01 E
Emmaste	66	58.42 N	22.36 E
Emmaus, S.S.S.R.	72	56.47 N	36.07 E
Emmaus, Pa., U.S.	198	40.32 N	75.30 W
Emmaville	156	29.26 S	151.36 E
Emme ≃	54	47.13 N	7.34 E
Emmeline Lake ⊜	174	55.00 N	106.22 W
Emmeloord	48	52.43 N	5.45 E
Emmen	48	52.47 N	7.00 E
Emmenbrücke	54	47.04 N	8.17 E
Emmendingen	54	48.07 N	7.50 E
Emmental V	54	46.56 N	7.45 E
Emmer ≃	48	52.03 N	9.23 E
Emmer-Compascuum	48	52.48 N	7.02 E
Emmer-Erfscheidenveen	48	52.48 N	7.01 E
Emmerich	48	51.50 N	6.15 E
Emmerstedt	50	52.15 N	10.58 E
Emmet, Austl.	156	24.40 S	144.28 E
Emmet, Ark., U.S.	184	33.44 N	93.28 W
Emmetsburg	188	43.07 N	94.41 W
Emmett, Idaho, U.S.	192	43.52 N	116.30 W
Emmett, Mich., U.S.	204	42.59 N	82.46 W
Emmiganūru	112	15.44 N	77.29 E
Emmitsburg	198	39.42 N	77.20 W
Emmonak	170	62.46 N	164.30 W
Emneth	44	52.38 N	0.11 E
Emo	180	48.38 N	93.50 W
Emőd	30	47.56 N	20.49 E
Emory	212	32.52 N	95.46 W
Emory ≃	182	35.56 N	84.29 W
Emory Peak Λ	186	29.13 N	103.17 W
Empalme	222	27.58 N	110.51 W
Empalme Escobedo	224	20.41 N	100.44 W
Empalme Purísima	224	23.55 N	105.05 W
Empalme San Vicente	248	34.58 S	58.22 W
Empangeni	148	28.50 S	31.48 E
Empedrado, Arg.	242	27.57 S	58.48 W
Empedrado, Chile	242	35.36 S	72.17 W
Emperor Jimmu, Tomb Of ⊥	260	34.29 N	135.47 E
Emperor Nintoku, Tomb of ⊥	260	34.34 N	135.29 E
Emperor Range ⩕	165e	5.45 S	154.55 E
Emperor Seamount Chain •[3]	6	45.00 N	170.00 E
Emperor Tenchi, Tomb of ⊥	260	34.59 N	135.48 E
Empfingen	54	48.24 N	8.42 E
Empire, Calif., U.S.	216	37.38 N	120.54 W
Empire, Nev., U.S.	216	40.37 N	119.21 W
Empire, Ohio, U.S.	204	40.31 N	80.37 W
Empire, Oreg., U.S.	192	43.23 N	124.17 W
Empire Centrafricaine → Central African Empire □[1]	126	7.00 N	21.00 E
Empoli	60	43.43 N	10.57 E
Emporia, Kans., U.S.	188	38.24 N	96.11 W
Emporia, Va., U.S.	198	36.41 N	77.32 W
Emporium	204	41.31 N	78.14 W
Empress	174	50.57 N	110.00 W
Empress Augusta Bay C	165e	6.25 S	155.05 E
Emptinne	52	50.19 N	5.07 E
Emrekom	74	39.58 N	41.57 E
Ems ≃	48	53.30 N	7.00 E
Emscher ≃	253	51.34 N	6.42 E
Emscher Bruch •[1]	253	51.34 N	7.09 E
Emsdetten	48	52.10 N	7.31 E
Ems-Jade-Kanal ≍	48	53.19 N	7.10 E
Emskirchen	52	49.33 N	10.43 E
Emsland •[1]	48	52.50 N	7.20 E
Emst •[8]	253	51.21 N	7.30 E
Emstek	48	52.50 N	8.09 E
Emsworth, Eng., U.K.	44	50.51 N	0.56 W
Emsworth, Pa., U.S.	204	40.30 N	80.04 W
Emu Creek ≃	161a	26.56 S	152.19 E
Emu Downs	158b	33.54 S	138.59 E
Emuerhe ≃	79	53.24 N	124.00 E
Emukae	82	33.18 N	129.38 E
Emu Park	156	23.15 S	150.50 E
Emu Plains	264a	33.45 S	150.41 E
Emuren	263a	6.40 N	3.31 E
Emusuo	79	43.45 N	128.10 E
En (Inn) ≃	32	48.35 N	13.28 E
Ena	84	35.29 N	137.40 E
Enana	146	17.29 S	16.19 E
Enånger	26	61.32 N	17.00 E
Enaratoli	154	3.55 S	136.21 E
Enard Bay C	28	58.06 N	5.20 W
Ena-san Λ	84	35.26 N	137.36 E
Enbacka	40	60.25 N	15.36 E
Enborne ≃	44	51.24 N	1.06 W
Encampment	190	41.12 N	106.47 W
Encampment ≃	190	41.18 N	106.43 W
Encantado	242	29.15 S	51.53 W
Encantado •[8]	277a	22.54 S	43.18 W
Encanto, Cape ≻	106	15.44 N	121.37 E
Encarnação	256c	38.47 N	9.06
Encarnación	242	27.20 S	55.54 W
Encarnación ≃	224	21.19 N	102.36 W
Encarnación de Díaz	224	21.31 N	102.14 W
Encha	88	37.25 N	115.42 E
Enchenberg	52	49.01 N	7.20 E

Symbols in the index entries represent the broad categories identified in the key at the right. Symbols with superior numbers (⩕[2]) identify subcategories (see complete key on page *I* · 26).

Kartensymbole in dem Registerverzeichnis stellen die rechts in Schlüssel erklärten Kategorien dar. Symbole mit hochgestellten Ziffern (⩕[2]) bezeichnen Unterabteilungen einer Kategorie (vgl. vollständiger Schlüssel auf Seite *I* · 26).

Los símbolos incluidos en el texto del índice representan las grandes categorías identificadas con la clave a la derecha. Los símbolos con números en su parte superior (⩕[2]) identifican las subcategorías (véase la clave completa en la página *I* · 26).

Les symboles de l'index représentent les catégories indiquées dans la légende à droite. Les symboles suivis d'un indice (⩕[2]) représentent des sous-catégories (voir légende complète à la page *I* · 26).

Os símbolos incluídos no texto do índice representam as grandes categorias identificadas com a chave à direita. Os símbolos com números em sua parte superior (⩕[2]) identificam as subcategorias (veja-se a chave completa à página *I* · 26).

Λ	Mountain	Berg	Montaña	Montagne	Montanha
⩕	Mountains	Berge	Montañas	Montagnes	Montanhas
)(	Pass	Pass	Paso	Col	Passo
V	Valley, Canyon	Tal, Cañon	Valle, Cañón	Vallée, Canyon	Vale, Canhão
≐	Plain	Ebene	Llano	Plaine	Planície
≻	Cape	Kap	Cabo	Cap	Cabo
I	Island	Insel	Isla	Île	Ilha
II	Islands	Inseln	Islas	Îles	Ilhas
•	Other Topographic Features	Andere Topographische Objekte	Otros Elementos Topográficos	Autres données topographiques	Outros Elementos Topográficos

ESPAÑOL

Nombre	Página	Lat. °′	Long. °′ W=Oeste
Enchi	140	5.49 N	2.49 W
Enchilayas	190	30.50 N	112.50 W
Enchovas, Enseada das C	246	23.57 S	45.18 W
Enciastraia, Monte ∧	56	44.22 N	6.53 E
Encinal	186	28.02 N	99.21 W
Encinas	186	25.40 N	101.08 W
Encinitas	218	33.03 N	117.17 W
Encino, N. Mex., U.S.	190	34.39 N	105.28 W
Encino, Tex., U.S.	186	26.57 N	98.08 W
Encino ◂[8]	270	34.09 N	118.30 W
Encino Reservoir ⊜[1]	270	34.05 N	118.31 W
Encontrados	236	9.03 N	72.14 W
Encounter Bay C	158b	35.35 S	138.44 E
Encrucijada, Cuba	230p	22.37 N	79.52 W
Encrucijada, Méx.	224	18.18 N	93.29 W
Encruzilhada	245	15.31 S	40.54 W
Encruzilhada do Sul	242	30.32 S	52.31 W
Encs	30	48.20 N	21.08 E
Endako	172	54.05 N	125.02 W
Endako ≃	172	54.05 N	124.55 W
Endau ≃	104	2.39 N	103.38 E
Ende	105b	8.50 S	121.39 E
Ende, Teluk C	105b	8.52 S	121.30 E
Endeavor, Pa., U.S.	204	41.35 N	79.23 W
Endeavor, Wis., U.S.	180	43.43 N	89.29 W
Endeavour	174	52.08 N	102.40 W
Endeavour Strait ⊔	154	10.50 S	142.15 E
Endelave I	41	55.46 N	10.17 E
Enderbury I[1]	14	3.08 S	171.05 W
Enderby, B.C., Can.	172	50.33 N	119.08 W
Enderby, Eng., U.K.	44	52.36 N	1.12 W
Enderby Land ◂[1]	9	67.30 S	53.00 E
Enderlin	188	46.37 N	97.36 W
Endicott, N.Y., U.S.	200	42.06 N	76.03 W
Endicott, Wash., U.S.	192	46.56 N	117.41 W
Endicott Mountains ⩕	170	67.50 N	152.00 W
Endimari ≃	238	8.46 S	66.07 W
Endine	58	45.46 N	9.59 E
Endine Gaiano	58	45.48 N	9.59 E
Endingen	54	48.09 N	7.42 E
Endja, Oued ≃	34	36.31 N	6.15 E
Endō	258	35.23 N	139.27 E
Endola	146	17.37 S	15.50 E
'En Dor	122	32.39 N	35.25 E
Endorf in Oberbayern	58	47.54 N	12.18 E
Endre ≃	56	43.28 N	6.36 E
Endrick ∧	160	35.12 S	150.12 E
Endwell	200	42.07 N	76.02 W
Ene ≃	238	11.09 S	74.19 W
Enemonzo	58	46.25 N	12.53 E
Enez	120	40.44 N	26.04 E
Enfer, Pointe d' ≻	230e	14.24 N	60.52 W
Enfida	36	36.07 N	10.23 E
Enfield, Austl.	158b	34.53 S	138.35 E
Enfield, Austl.	264a	33.53 S	151.06 E
Enfield, N.Z.	162	45.03 S	170.52 E
Enfield, Conn., U.S.	197	41.58 N	72.36 W
Enfield, N.H., U.S.	178	43.34 N	71.57 W
Enfield, N.C., U.S.	182	36.11 N	77.47 W
Enfield, Va., U.S.	198	37.43 N	77.12 W
Enfield ◂[8]	44	51.40 N	0.05 W
Engadine	160	34.04 S	151.01 E
Engaño, Cabo ≻	228	18.37 N	68.20 W
Engaru	82a	44.03 N	143.31 E
Engažimo	78	57.51 N	114.56 E
Engcobo	148	31.37 S	28.00 E
'En Gedi	122	31.27 N	35.23 E
Engelberg	54	46.49 N	8.25 E
Engelhard	182	35.31 N	76.02 W
Engel's	70	51.30 N	46.07 E
Engelschmanplaat I	48	53.28 N	6.02 E
Engelsdorf	50	51.20 N	12.29 E
Engelskirchen	52	50.59 N	7.24 E
Engel's'ovo	73	48.22 N	39.23 E
Engen	54	47.51 N	8.46 E
Engenheiro Passos	246	22.30 S	44.41 W
Engenheiro Paulo de Frontin	246	22.33 S	43.41 W
Engenho	238	15.10 S	56.25 W
Engenho, Ilha do I	277a	22.50 S	43.07 W
Engenho de Dentro ◂[8]	277a	22.54 S	43.18 W
Engenho do Mato	277a	22.52 S	43.01 W
Engenho Nôvo	246	21.49 S	43.00 W
Engenho Nôvo ◂[8]	277a	22.55 S	43.17 W
Enger	48	52.08 N	8.34 E
Engestofte	41	54.46 N	11.34 E
Engesvang	41	56.10 N	9.21 E
'En Gev	122	32.47 N	35.38 E
Enggano, Pulau I	102	5.24 S	102.16 E
Enghershatu ∧	134	16.40 N	38.20 E
Enghien (Edingen), Bel.	46	50.42 N	4.02 E
Enghien (Les-Bains), Fr.	46	48.58 N	2.19 E
Enghien-Moisselles, Aéroport d' ⊠	251	49.02 N	2.21 E
Engiadina Bassa ∨	54	46.50 N	10.20 E
Engis	52	50.35 N	5.25 E
Engizek Dağı ∧	120	37.50 N	37.10 E
Engjan	26	63.09 N	8.32 E
England	184	34.33 N	91.58 W
England □[8]	28	52.30 N	1.30 W
England Air Force Base ■	184	31.20 N	92.33 W
Englebright Lake ⊜[1]	216	39.15 N	121.15 W
Englee	176	50.44 N	56.06 W
Englefield, Cape ≻	166	69.51 N	85.39 W
Englefield Green	250	51.26 N	0.35 W
Englefontaine	46	50.11 N	3.39 E
Englehart	180	47.49 N	79.52 W
Englehart ≃	180	47.51 N	79.50 W
Englewood, B.C., Can.	172	50.33 N	126.53 W
Englewood, Colo., U.S.	190	39.39 N	104.59 W
Englewood, Fla., U.S.	210	26.58 N	82.21 W
Englewood, Ind., U.S.	208	38.50 N	86.31 W
Englewood, Kans., U.S.	188	37.02 N	100.01 W
Englewood, N.J., U.S.	200	40.54 N	73.59 W
Englewood, Ohio, U.S.	208	39.53 N	84.18 W
Englewood, Tenn., U.S.	182	35.26 N	84.29 W
Englewood ◂[8]	268	41.47 N	87.39 W
Englewood Cliffs	266	40.53 N	73.57 W
Englewood Reservoir ⊜[1]	208	39.58 N	84.18 W
English, Ind., U.S.	208	38.20 N	86.28 W
English, Ky., U.S.	208	38.37 N	85.08 W
English ≃, Ont., Can.	166	50.12 N	95.00 W
English ≃, N.A.	196	45.13 N	73.50 W
English ≃, Iowa, U.S.	180	41.29 N	91.30 W
English Bay	170	59.22 N	151.55 W
English Bāzār	114	25.00 N	88.09 E
English Center	200	41.26 N	77.17 W
English Channel (La Manche) ⊔	28	50.20 N	1.00 W
English Coast ◂[2]	9	73.45 S	73.00 W
English Harbour C	230c	17.00 N	61.46 W
English Harbour West	176	47.28 N	55.29 W
Englishman ≃	214	49.22 N	124.18 W
Englishtown	198	40.18 N	74.22 W
Engong	142	0.36 N	10.06 E
Engter	48	52.23 N	8.04 E
Enguera	34	38.59 N	0.41 W
Engum	41	55.44 N	9.40 E
Engure	66	57.10 N	23.13 E
Engures Ezers ⊜	66	57.16 N	23.06 E
Engwilen	54	47.37 N	9.05 E
'En Harod	122	32.33 N	35.23 E
'En HaShofet	122	32.35 N	35.06 E
Enid	186	36.19 N	97.48 W
Enid Lake ⊜[1]	184	34.10 N	89.50 W
Enilda	172	55.25 N	116.18 W
Eningen unter Achalm	54	48.29 N	9.16 E
Eninogorsk	76	54.36 N	52.30 E

FRANÇAIS

Nom	Page	Lat. °′	Long. °′ W=Ouest
Eniwa	82a	42.45 N	141.33 E
Eniwetok I[1]	14	11.30 N	162.15 E
Enka	182	35.32 N	82.38 W
Enkeldoorn	144	19.01 S	30.53 E
Enkenbach	52	49.29 N	7.54 E
Enkhuizen	48	52.42 N	5.17 E
Enkirch	52	49.59 N	7.07 E
Enköping	40	59.38 N	17.04 E
Enle	92	24.02 N	101.09 E
Enmedio	186	29.04 N	103.29 W
Enmelen	170	65.01 N	175.54 W
Enmore	236	6.46 N	57.59 W
Enna	36	37.34 N	14.17 E
Ennadai Lake ⊜	166	60.53 N	101.15 W
Enné, Ouadi ∨	136	14.24 N	18.45 E
Ennedi ⩕[1]	136	17.15 N	22.00 E
Ennenda	54	47.01 N	9.05 E
Ennepe ≃	253	51.22 N	7.27 E
Ennepe-Ruhr-Kreis □[8]	253	51.21 N	7.15 E
Ennepestausee ⊜[1]	253	51.14 N	7.25 E
Ennepetal	52	51.18 N	7.22 E
Ennerdale Water ⊜	42	54.31 N	3.23 W
Ennery	251	49.05 N	2.06 E
'En Netafim	122	29.35 N	34.53 E
Enngonia	156	29.19 S	145.51 E
Enniger	48	51.50 N	7.56 E
Ennigerloh	48	51.50 N	8.02 E
Ennigloh	48	52.12 N	8.34 E
Ennis, Eire	28	52.50 N	8.59 W
Ennis, Mont., U.S.	192	45.21 N	111.44 W
Ennis, Tex., U.S.	212	32.20 N	96.38 W
Enniscorthy	28	52.30 N	6.34 W
Enniskillen	28	54.21 N	7.38 W
Ennis Lake ⊜[1]	192	45.26 N	111.41 W
Ennistymon	28	52.57 N	9.13 W
Enns	30	48.13 N	14.29 E
Enns ≃	30	48.14 N	14.32 E
Eno	26	62.48 N	30.09 E
Enø I	41	55.10 N	11.40 E
Eno ≃	86	34.53 N	132.41 E
Enochs	186	33.52 N	102.46 W
Enoggera Army Base ■	161a	27.25 S	152.58 E
Enola	198	40.17 N	76.56 W
Enon	208	39.53 N	83.56 W
Enontekiö	24	68.23 N	23.38 E
Enon Valley	204	40.51 N	80.28 W
Enoree ≃	182	34.26 N	81.25 W
Enosburg Falls	178	44.55 N	72.48 W
Eno-shima I	84	35.18 N	139.29 E
Enping	92	22.11 N	112.17 E
Enragé, Point ≻	176	44.16 N	64.15 W
Enrekang	102	3.34 S	119.47 E
Enrile	106	17.34 N	121.42 E
Enrique Fynn	248	34.50 S	59.08 W
Enrique Urien	242	27.34 S	60.32 W
Enriquillo	228	17.54 N	71.14 W
Enriquillo, Lago ⊜	228	18.27 N	71.39 W
Ens	48	52.38 N	5.50 E
Ensay	156	37.23 S	147.50 E
Enschede	48	52.12 N	6.53 E
Enseada	246	23.29 S	45.05 W
Ensenada, Arg.	248	34.51 S	57.55 W
Ensenada, Méx.	222	31.52 N	116.37 W
Ensenada, P.R.	230m	17.58 N	66.56 W
Ensenada □[5]	278	34.50 S	58.00 W
Enshi	92	30.17 N	109.19 E
Enshū-nada ⍑[2]	82	34.27 N	137.38 E
Ensisheim	54	47.52 N	7.21 E
Enstaberga	40	58.45 N	16.51 E
Entebbe	144	0.04 N	32.28 E
Entenbühl ∧	30	49.46 N	12.24 E
Enter	48	52.18 N	6.34 E
Enterprise, Guy.	236	6.56 N	58.24 W
Enterprise, Ala., U.S.	184	31.19 N	85.51 W
Enterprise, Calif., U.S.	194	39.32 N	121.22 W
Enterprise, Kans., U.S.	188	38.54 N	97.07 W
Enterprise, Miss., U.S.	184	32.10 N	88.49 W
Enterprise, Oreg., U.S.	192	45.25 N	117.17 W
Enterprise, Utah, U.S.	190	37.34 N	113.43 W
Entiat ≃	192	47.40 N	120.14 W
Entiat, Lake ⊜	192	47.40 N	120.12 W
Entiat Mountains ⩕	214	48.00 N	120.42 W
Entinas, Punta ≻	34	36.41 N	2.46 W
Entlebuch	54	47.00 N	8.04 E
Entlebuch ∨	54	46.58 N	8.00 E
Entracque	56	44.14 N	7.24 E
Entraigues-sur-Sorgue	56	44.00 N	4.55 E
Entrains-sur-Nohain	46	47.27 N	3.15 E
Entrance, Cape ≻	154	2.21 S	150.12 E
Entraunes	56	44.11 N	6.45 E
Entraygues	32	44.39 N	2.34 E
Entrechaux	56	44.13 N	5.08 E
Entrée, Île d' I	176	47.17 N	61.42 W
Entremont-le-Vieux	56	45.26 N	5.53 E
Entrepeñas, Embalse de ⊜[1]	34	40.34 N	2.42 W
Entre Rios, Bol.	238	21.32 S	64.12 W
Entre Rios, Bra.	245	11.56 S	38.05 W
Entre-Rios, Moç.	144	14.57 S	37.20 E
Entre Ríos □[4]	242	32.00 S	59.00 W
Entre Rios de Minas	245	20.41 S	44.04 W
Entrevaux	56	43.57 N	6.49 E
Entrèves	56	45.49 N	6.57 E
Entriken	204	40.20 N	78.12 W
Entringen	52	48.33 N	8.58 E
Entroncamento	34	39.28 N	8.28 W
Entupido	246	22.30 S	44.51 W
Entwistle	172	53.36 N	115.00 W
Entzheim, Aéroport d' ⊠	54	48.32 N	7.38 E
Enu, Pulau I	154	7.05 S	134.30 E
Enugu	140	6.27 N	7.27 E
Enumclaw	214	47.12 N	121.59 W
Enurmino	170	66.57 N	171.49 W
Envalira, Port d')(	34	42.35 N	1.45 E
Envermeu	46	49.54 N	1.16 E
Envies, Rivière des ≃	196	46.37 N	72.24 W
Envigado	236	6.10 N	75.35 W
Envira	238	7.18 S	70.13 W
'En Yahav	122	30.38 N	35.11 E
Enyamba	144	3.40 S	24.58 E
Enyanghe	92	31.48 N	106.31 E
Enyellé	142	2.49 N	18.06 E
Enys, Mount ∧	162	43.14 S	171.38 E
Enz ≃	52	49.01 N	9.07 E
Enza ≃	58	44.54 N	10.31 E
Enzan	84	35.42 N	138.44 E
Enzaran, Bir ⍑[4]	138	23.56 N	14.33 W
Enzbach ≃	52	49.54 N	6.25 E
Enzklösterle	52	48.40 N	8.28 E
Enzweihingen	52	48.55 N	8.58 E
Eo ≃	34	43.28 N	7.03 W
Eola	214	44.55 N	123.07 W
Eolia	209	39.14 N	91.01 W
Eolie, Isole II	36	38.30 N	15.00 E
Epanomí	38	40.26 N	22.56 E
Épars, Bois de l' ♠	251	48.45 N	1.45 E
Epazote, Cerro ∧	222	24.35 N	105.07 W
Epe, B.R.D.	48	52.11 N	7.02 E
Epe, Ned.	48	52.21 N	6.00 E
Epe, Nig.	140	6.37 N	3.59 E
Epecuén, Lago ⊜	242	37.10 S	62.54 W
Epéna	142	1.22 N	17.29 E
Épernay	46	49.03 N	3.57 E
Épernon	46	48.37 N	1.41 E
Épernon, Les Taillis d' ♠	251	48.40 N	1.45 E
Epes	184	32.42 N	88.07 W
Ephesus ⊥	120	37.55 N	27.17 E
Ephraim	190	39.22 N	111.35 W
Ephrata, Pa., U.S.	198	40.11 N	76.10 W
Ephrata, Wash., U.S.	192	47.19 N	119.33 W
Ephrata Cloister ⊥	198	40.12 N	76.09 W
Ephratah	200	43.00 N	74.32 W
Epi I	165f	16.43 S	168.15 E

PORTUGUÊS

Nome	Página	Lat. °′	Long. °′ W=Oeste
Épiais-lès-Louvres	251	49.02 N	2.33 E
Épila	34	41.36 N	1.17 W
Épinac-les-Mines	54	46.59 N	4.31 E
Épinal	54	48.11 N	6.27 E
Épinay-sous-Sénart	251	48.42 N	2.31 E
Épinay-sur-Orge	251	48.40 N	2.20 E
Épinay-sur-Seine	251	48.57 N	2.19 E
Episkopí	120	34.40 N	32.54 E
Epo	154	8.40 S	146.30 E
Époisses	46	47.30 N	4.10 E
Epomeo, Monte ∧	60	40.44 N	13.54 E
Épône	251	48.57 N	1.49 E
Eppalock, Lake ⊜[1]	159	36.52 S	144.31 E
Eppendorf	50	50.48 N	13.14 E
Eppendorf ◂[8]	253	51.27 N	7.11 E
Eppenhausen ◂[8]	253	51.21 N	7.31 E
Eppeville	46	49.44 N	3.03 E
Epping, Austl.	159	37.39 S	145.02 E
Epping, Austl.	264a	33.46 S	151.05 E
Epping, Eng., U.K.	44	51.43 N	0.07 E
Epping, N.H., U.S.	178	43.02 N	71.04 W
Eppingen	52	49.08 N	8.54 E
Epping Forest □[8]	250	51.43 N	0.10 E
Epping Forest ◂[3]	44	51.40 N	0.03 E
Epping Forest ♠	250	51.40 N	0.03 E
Epping Green, Eng., U.K.	250	51.45 N	0.07 W
Epping Green, Eng., U.K.	250	51.44 N	0.05 E
Epping Upland	250	51.43 N	0.06 E
Epsom	44	51.20 N	0.16 W
Epsom and Ewell □[8]	250	51.20 N	0.16 W
Epsom Downs Race Course ♠	250	51.19 N	0.15 W
Epte ≃, Fr.	46	49.04 N	1.37 E
Epte ≃, Zhg.	76	44.55 N	83.37 E
Épuisay	46	47.54 N	0.56 E
Epukiro	146	21.41 S	19.08 E
Epukiro ≃	146	20.45 S	21.05 E
Epupa Falls ᒪ	142	16.55 S	13.10 E
Epuyén	244	42.14 S	71.21 W
Epworth	42	53.32 N	0.49 W
Eqlīd	118	30.55 N	52.39 E
Equality	184	37.44 N	88.20 W
Equata	142	0.13 S	9.18 E
Équateur □[4]	142	1.00 N	20.30 E
Équateur → Ecuador □[1]	236	2.00 S	77.30 W
Equatorial Guinea □[1]	10		
	142	2.00 N	9.00 E
Équihen-Plage	46	50.41 N	1.34 E
Equimina ≃	142	13.11 S	12.47 E
Equinunk	200	41.51 N	75.14 W
Equi Terme	58	44.09 N	10.10 E
Era ≃, It.	60	43.40 N	10.38 E
Era ≃, Pap. N. Gui.	154	7.35 S	144.41 E
Erac Creek ≃	156	26.56 S	145.48 E
Eraclea	58	45.35 N	12.40 E
Eradu	152	28.41 S	115.02 E
Éragny	251	49.01 N	2.06 E
Eramosa ≃	202	43.32 N	80.14 W
Eran Bay C	106	9.06 N	117.43 E
Eranga	142	1.52 S	18.56 E
Erangal ◂[8]	262c	19.10 N	72.47 E
Erap	154	6.35 S	146.40 E
Erath	184	29.58 N	92.02 W
Erave	154	6.40 S	143.50 E
Erave ≃	154	6.40 S	143.55 E
Erba	56	45.48 N	9.15 E
Erba, Jabal ∧, Sūd.	130	20.45 N	36.50 E
Erba, Jabal ∧, Sūd.	130	19.04 N	36.46 E
Erbaa	120	40.42 N	36.36 E
Erbach, B.R.D.	52	49.40 N	8.59 E
Erbach, B.R.D.	54	48.20 N	9.53 E
Erbenheim	52	50.03 N	8.18 E
Erbeskopf ∧	52	49.44 N	7.05 E
Erčimijn Nuruu ⩕	78	49.24 N	100.00 E
Erciş	74	39.02 N	43.22 E
Erciyeş Dağı ∧	120	38.32 N	35.28 E
Ercolano	60	40.48 N	14.21 E
Ercolano (Herculaneum) ⊥	60	40.46 N	14.20 E
Érd	30	47.23 N	18.56 E
Erdaobaihe ≃	88	42.34 N	128.08 E
Erdaofang, Zhg.	94	41.54 N	123.57 E
Erdaofang, Zhg.	94	41.37 N	122.34 E
Erdaofangshen	94	42.09 N	123.17 E
Erdaogangzi, Zhg.	94	41.57 N	122.09 E
Erdaogangzi, Zhg.	94	42.04 N	123.06 E
Erdaohe	79	43.37 N	127.35 E
Erdaohezi, Zhg.	79	45.07 N	127.16 E
Erdaohezi, Zhg.	79	45.08 N	129.39 E
Erdaohuayuantun	88	42.17 N	127.07 E
Erdaojingzi	94	41.49 N	122.20 E
Erdaoliangzi, Zhg.	88	40.50 N	119.04 E
Erdaoliangzi, Zhg.	95	40.31 N	118.03 E
Erdaowan	79	47.58 N	124.33 E
Erdek	120	40.24 N	27.48 E
Erdemli	120	36.37 N	34.18 E
Erdene, Mong.	78	47.48 N	107.55 E
Erdene, Mong.	92	45.08 N	97.40 E
Erdene, Mong.	92	44.40 N	111.05 E
Erdenebulgan	78	50.07 N	101.35 E
Erdenebüren	76	48.26 N	91.27 E
Erdenedalaj	92	46.02 N	104.58 E
Erdenemandal	78	48.32 N	101.19 E
Erdenheim	275	40.05 N	75.13 W
Erdevik	38	45.07 N	19.25 E
Erdhausen	52	50.45 N	8.34 E
Erdiao	96	32.12 N	121.12 E
Erding	30	48.18 N	11.54 E
Erdnijevskij	70	46.52 N	46.17 E
Erebato ≃	236	5.54 N	64.16 W
Erebus, Mount ∧	9	77.32 S	167.09 E
Erechim	242	27.38 S	52.17 W
Ereğli, Tür.	120	41.17 N	31.25 E
Ereğli, Tür.	120	37.31 N	34.04 E
Eregun	263a	6.36 N	3.22 E
Erei, Monti ⩕	36	37.20 N	14.20 E
Eremita	246	21.35 S	45.04 W
Erenas	106	12.25 N	124.19 E
Erenköy	120	40.58 N	38.08 E
Erenköy ◂[8]	257b	40.58 N	29.04 E
Erepecu, Lago do ⊜	240	1.20 S	56.35 W
Eresma ≃	34	41.26 N	4.45 W
Eressós	38	39.18 N	25.51 E
Erétria	38	38.24 N	23.48 E
Erez	122	31.34 N	34.34 E
Érezée	52	50.18 N	5.33 E
Erfa ≃	52	49.40 N	9.23 E
Erfde	41	54.19 N	9.19 E
Erfenisdam ◂[6]	148	28.33 S	26.50 E
Erfoud	138	31.28 N	4.10 W
Erft ≃	52	51.11 N	6.44 E
Erftstadt	52	50.48 N	6.46 E
Erfurt	50	50.58 N	11.01 E
Erfurt □[5]	50	51.10 N	10.45 E
Ergani	120	38.17 N	39.46 E
Erg el Agreb	138	30.48 N	5.30 E
Ergene ≃	120	41.01 N	26.22 E
Ergenzingen	54	48.29 N	8.48 E
Erges (Erjas) ≃	34	39.40 N	7.01 E
Ergig ≃	136	11.22 N	15.24 E
Ergļi	66	56.54 N	25.38 E
Ergste	52	51.25 N	7.34 E
Erguvejem ≃	170	65.20 N	176.00 W
Erhai ⊜	92	25.48 N	100.11 E
Érherhi, Ahzar ∨	140	14.56 N	3.24 E
Erhlin	90	23.54 N	120.22 E
Erhshui	90	23.49 N	120.36 E
Erhulai	88	41.23 N	125.08 E
Eria ≃	34	42.03 N	5.44 W
Erial	198	39.46 N	75.01 W
Eriba	130	16.37 N	36.04 E
Erica, Austl.	159	37.59 S	146.22 E
Erica, Ned.	48	52.43 N	6.55 E
Erice	36	38.02 N	12.36 E
Ericeira	34	38.59 N	9.25 W
Erichsen Lake ⊜	166	70.38 N	80.21 W
Erichshagen	48	52.40 N	9.14 E
Ericht, Loch ⊜	28	56.50 N	4.25 W
Erick	186	35.13 N	99.52 W
Erickson, B.C., Can.	172	49.05 N	116.28 W
Erickson, Man., Can.	174	50.30 N	99.55 W
Ericson	188	41.47 N	98.41 W
Erie, Colo., U.S.	190	40.03 N	105.03 W
Erie, Ill., U.S.	180	41.39 N	90.05 W
Erie, Kans., U.S.	188	37.34 N	95.15 W
Erie, Mich., U.S.	206	41.48 N	83.30 W
Erie, Pa., U.S.	204	42.08 N	80.04 W
Erie □[6], N.Y., U.S.	200	42.54 N	78.53 W
Erie □[6], Ohio, U.S.	204	41.27 N	82.42 W
Erie □[6], Pa., U.S.	204	42.08 N	80.04 W
Erie, Lake ⊜	180	42.15 N	81.00 W
Erieau	204	42.16 N	81.56 W
Erie Basin C	266	40.40 N	74.01 W
Erie Beach, Ont., Can.	204	42.16 N	82.00 W
Erie Beach, Ont., Can.	274a	42.53 N	78.57 W
Erie Canal → New York State Barge Canal ≅	200	43.05 N	78.43 W
Erie International Airport ⊠	204	42.05 N	80.11 W
Erigavo	134	10.37 N	47.24 E
Eriksberg ⊥	40	58.56 N	16.22 E
Eriksdale	174	50.52 N	98.06 W
Erímanthos ∧	38	37.59 N	21.51 E
Erimo-misaki ≻	82a	41.55 N	143.15 E
Erin, Ont., Can.	202	43.45 N	80.07 W
Erin, N.Y., U.S.	200	42.11 N	76.40 W
Erindale	265b	43.32 N	79.39 W
Eriskay I	28	57.04 N	7.13 W
Eriswil	54	47.05 N	7.51 E
Erith ◂[8]	250	51.29 N	0.10 E
Erithraí	38	38.13 N	23.19 E
Eritrea □[4]	134	15.20 N	39.00 E
Erivan → Jerevan	74	40.11 N	44.30 E
Erjas (Erges) ≃	34	39.40 N	7.01 W
Erjia	96	32.02 N	121.13 E
Erkelenz	52	51.05 N	6.19 E
Erken ⊜	40	59.51 N	18.34 E
Erken-Jurt	74	44.27 N	41.54 E
Erkheim	54	48.02 N	10.20 E
Erkilet	120	38.49 N	35.27 E
Erkner	50	52.25 N	13.45 E
Erkner, Forst ◂[3]	254a	52.22 N	13.47 E
Erkowit	130	18.46 N	37.07 E
Erkrath	52	51.13 N	6.55 E
Erl	58	47.41 N	12.11 E
Erlach	54	47.03 N	7.06 E
Erlands Point	214	47.36 N	122.42 W
Erlangchang	97	30.18 N	106.00 E
Erlangen	52	49.36 N	11.01 E
Erlanger	208	39.01 N	84.37 W
Erlanghe	90	30.19 N	116.04 E
Erlangmiao	90	33.46 N	112.23 E
Erlbach	50	50.18 N	12.22 E
Erldunda	152	25.14 S	133.12 E
Erle ◂[8]	253	51.33 N	7.05 E
Erli	56	44.08 N	8.06 E
Erlian	92	43.46 N	112.05 E
Erling	96	31.53 N	119.36 E
Erling, Lake ⊜[1]	184	33.05 N	93.35 W
Erlistoun	152	28.20 S	122.08 E
Erlongshan, Zhg.	79	50.04 N	126.47 E
Erlongshan, Zhg.	79	48.28 N	126.31 E
Erlongshan, Zhg.	79	47.20 N	132.28 E
Erlsbach	58	46.55 N	12.15 E
Erma	198	38.59 N	74.54 W
Ermana, Chrebet ⩕	78	50.00 N	113.30 E
Ermatingen	54	47.41 N	9.06 E
Erme ≃	44	50.18 N	3.56 W
Ermelik	120	39.42 N	39.02 E
Ermelindo Matarazo ◂[8]	277b	23.29 S	46.29 W
Ermelo, Ned.	48	52.17 N	5.37 E
Ermelo, S. Afr.	148	26.34 S	29.58 E
Ermenak	120	36.38 N	32.54 E
Ermendegou	94	42.02 N	121.56 E
Ermenonville	46	49.08 N	2.42 E
Ermidas	34	38.00 N	8.23 W
Ermil Post	130	13.37 N	27.36 E
Ermineskin Indian Reserve ◂[4]	172	52.52 N	113.30 W
Ermington	264a	33.48 S	151.04 E
Ermita de los Correa	224	22.54 N	103.01 W
Ermitaž ʊ	255a	59.56 N	30.20 E
Ermont	46	48.59 N	2.16 E
Ermoúpolis	38	37.26 N	24.56 E
Ermsleben	50	51.44 N	11.21 E
Ernaballa Mission	152	26.17 S	132.07 E
Ernākulam	112	9.59 N	76.17 E
Erndtebrück	52	50.59 N	8.15 E
Erne, Lower Lough ⊜	28	54.10 N	7.30 W
Erne, Upper Lough ⊜	28	54.20 N	7.30 W
Ernée	32	48.18 N	0.56 W
Ernest	204	40.41 N	79.10 W
Ernestina	248	35.16 S	59.34 W
Ernest Legouve Reef ⌖[2]	14	35.10 S	150.40 W
Ernest Sound ⊔	172	55.52 N	132.10 W
Erni, Uad ∨	138	26.45 N	10.47 W
Ernici, Monti ⩕	60	41.48 N	13.22 E
Ernst-Thälman, Pioneerpark ♠	254a	52.28 N	13.33 E
Ernst-Thälmann-Stadion ♠	254a	52.23 N	13.05 E
Erode	112	11.21 N	77.44 E
Eromanga	156	26.40 S	143.16 E
Eromanga I	165f	18.45 S	169.05 E
Erongo	146	21.44 S	15.53 E
Erongoberge ⩕	146	21.45 S	15.37 E
Eroto	134	16.13 N	37.57 E
Erp	52	50.46 N	6.43 E
Erpfendorf	58	47.35 N	12.28 E
Erpuzi	95	40.29 N	115.33 E
Erquelinnes	46	50.18 N	4.07 E
Err, Piz d' ∧	54	46.33 N	9.41 E
Errabiddy	152	25.28 S	117.07 E
Erramala Range ⩕	112	15.30 N	78.10 E
Errego	144	16.02 S	37.14 E
Errer ≃	134	7.32 N	42.05 E
Er-Riad → Ar-Riyāḍ	118	24.38 N	46.43 E
Errigal ∧	28	55.02 N	8.07 W
Errington	214	49.17 N	124.22 W
Erris Head ≻	28	54.19 N	10.00 W
Errol Heights	214	45.29 N	122.33 W
Ersekë	38	40.20 N	20.41 E
Ershijiazi	94	41.17 N	120.32 E
Ershilipu	95	40.07 N	117.24 E
Ershiqizhan	79	53.23 N	123.16 E
Ershiwuzhan	79	53.22 N	123.55 E
Erskine	188	47.40 N	96.00 W
Erskine, Lake ⊜	266	41.06 N	74.15 W
Erskine Inlet C	166	76.15 N	102.20 W
Erskine Park	264a	33.49 S	150.47 E
Erstein	54	48.26 N	7.40 E
Erstfeld	54	46.49 N	8.39 E
Ertai, Zhg.	76	44.14 N	80.52 E
Ertai, Zhg.	76	46.07 N	90.06 E
Ertaizi, Zhg.	94	40.47 N	120.54 E
Ertaizi, Zhg.	94	41.52 N	121.56 E
Ertaizi, Zhg.	94	42.05 N	123.35 E
Ertaizi, Zhg.	94	42.35 N	124.00 E
Ertil'	68	51.51 N	40.49 E
Ertingen	54	48.06 N	9.28 E
Erto	58	46.16 N	12.22 E
Ertuğrul	120	39.34 N	27.43 E
Ertvelde	46	51.11 N	3.45 E
Erua	162	39.14 S	175.24 E
Eruar	116	23.28 N	87.52 E
Erudina	156	31.28 S	139.23 E
Erundu	146	20.36 S	16.25 E
Erunkan	263a	6.37 N	3.24 E
Erva, Ponta da ≻	256c	38.50 N	8.58 W
Erval	242	32.02 S	53.24 W
Erval d'Oeste	242	27.13 S	51.34 W
Ervalla	40	59.22 N	15.15 E
Erving	197	42.36 N	72.24 W
Ervy-le-Châtel	46	48.02 N	3.55 E
Erwin, N.C., U.S.	182	35.20 N	78.41 W
Erwin, Tenn., U.S.	182	36.09 N	82.25 W
Erwitte	48	51.37 N	8.20 E
Erwood	174	52.50 N	102.10 W
Erxleben	50	52.13 N	11.14 E
Érythrée → Eritrea □[4]	134	15.20 N	39.00 E
Eryuan	92	26.06 N	99.55 E
Erzaohang	96	31.05 N	121.49 E
Erzgebirge (Krušné hory) ⩕	50	50.30 N	13.10 E
Erzhan	79	43.58 N	128.44 E
Erzhou I	90	22.00 N	114.11 E
Erzhuang	95	39.24 N	117.22 E
Erzin	78	50.15 N	95.10 E
Erzincan	120	39.44 N	39.29 E
Erzincan □[4]	120	39.40 N	39.30 E
Erzingen	54	47.39 N	8.25 E
Erzurum	120	39.55 N	41.17 E
Erzurum □[4]	120	40.00 N	41.30 E
Esa-Ala	154	9.44 S	150.49 E
Esambo	142	3.40 S	23.24 E
Esan-saki ≻	82a	41.49 N	141.11 E
Esashi, Nihon	82	39.12 N	141.09 E
Esashi, Nihon	82	41.52 N	140.07 E
Esashi, Nihon	82a	44.56 N	142.35 E
Esbiye	120	40.57 N	38.44 E
Esbjerg	26	55.28 N	8.27 E
Esbly	251	48.54 N	2.49 E
Esbo → Espoo	26	60.13 N	24.40 E
Esborn	253	51.23 N	7.20 E
Esca ≃	34	42.37 N	1.03 W
Escada	240	8.22 S	35.14 W
Escalada	248	34.10 S	59.07 W
Escalante, Pil.	106	10.50 N	123.33 E
Escalante, Utah, U.S.	190	37.47 N	111.36 W
Escalante ≃, Utah, U.S.	190	37.17 N	110.53 W
Escalante ≃, Ven.	236	9.15 N	71.50 W
Escalante Desert ◂[2]	190	37.50 N	113.30 W
Escalón, Méx.	222	26.45 N	104.20 W
Escalon, Calif., U.S.	216	37.48 N	121.00 W
Escalona	34	40.10 N	4.24 W
Escambia ≃	184	30.32 N	87.11 W
Escanaba	180	45.45 N	87.04 W
Escanaba ≃	180	45.47 N	87.04 W
Escanaba, East Branch ≃	180	46.16 N	87.27 W
Escanaba, Middle Branch ≃	180	46.16 N	87.27 W
Escandón, Puerto de)(	34	40.17 N	1.00 W
Escárcega de Matamoros	222	18.37 N	90.43 W
Escarpada Point ≻	106	18.31 N	122.13 E
Escarpado Peak ∧	106	8.36 N	117.22 E
Escatawpa ≃	184	30.25 N	88.35 W
Escaudain	46	50.20 N	3.21 E
Escaut (Schelde) ≃	46	51.22 N	4.15 E
Esch ≃	52	48.54 N	6.04 E
Eschach	54	47.44 N	9.36 E
Eschau	54	48.29 N	7.43 E
Eschebrügge	48	52.37 N	6.46 E
Eschede	48	52.44 N	10.14 E
Eschen	54	47.13 N	9.31 E
Eschenlohe	58	47.36 N	11.11 E
Eschershausen	48	51.56 N	9.38 E
Escholzmatt	54	46.55 N	7.56 E
Eschscholtz Bay C	170	66.18 N	161.25 W
Esch-sur-Alzette	52	49.30 N	5.59 E
Esch-sur-Sûre	52	49.55 N	5.55 E
Eschwege	52	51.11 N	10.04 E
Eschweiler	52	50.49 N	6.16 E
Esclave, Grand Lac de l' → Great Slave Lake ⊜	166	61.30 N	114.00 W
Esclavo, Gran Lago del → Great Slave Lake ⊜	166	61.30 N	114.00 W
Escobal	226	9.09 N	79.58 W
Escobar □[5]	278	34.23 S	58.46 W
Escobar, Arroyo ≃	278	34.21 S	58.44 W
Escobedo	186	27.13 N	101.21 W
Escocesa, Bahía C	228	19.25 N	69.45 W
Escoheag	197	41.35 N	71.32 W
Escondido, Bra.	245	17.05 S	39.31 W
Escondido, Calif., U.S.	218	33.07 N	117.05 W
Escondido ≃, Méx.	186	28.39 N	100.34 W
Escondido ≃, Nic.	226	12.04 N	83.45 W
Escondido Canal ≅	218	33.11 N	116.58 W
Escondido Creek ≃	218	33.01 N	117.15 W
Escorial → San Lorenzo de El Escorial	34	40.35 N	4.09 W
Escoutay ≃	56	44.29 N	4.42 E
Escravos ≃[1]	140	5.35 N	5.10 E
Escrick	42	53.53 N	1.02 W
Escuadrón 201	276a	19.22 N	99.06 W
Escudero, Arroyo ≃	248	34.20 S	57.05 W
Escudo de Veraguas, Isla I	226	9.06 N	81.33 W
Escuinapa [de Hidalgo]	224	22.51 N	105.48 W
Escuintla, Guat.	226	14.18 N	90.47 W
Escuintla, Méx.	222	15.20 N	92.38 W
Escuintla □[5]	226	14.10 N	91.00 W
Escuminac, Point ≻	176	47.04 N	64.46 W
Escurial, Serra do ∧	240	10.04 S	41.05 W
Esebi	144	2.57 N	30.39 E
Eséka	142	3.39 N	10.46 E
Esenler	257b	41.02 N	28.51 E
Esenli	120	40.41 N	37.24 E
Esens	48	53.39 N	7.37 E
Ésera ≃	34	42.06 N	0.15 E
Esesi	120	39.49 N	39.19 E
Eşfahān (Isfahan)	118	32.40 N	51.38 E
Eşfahān □[4]	118	32.30 N	53.00 E
Esfí ≃	226	8.28 N	82.16 W
Esgueva ≃	34	41.40 N	4.43 W
Eshan	92	24.11 N	102.22 E
Esher	44	51.23 N	0.22 W
Eshkāshem	113	36.42 N	71.34 E
Eshowe	148	28.58 S	31.29 E
Esh-Sham → Dimashq	122	33.30 N	36.18 E
Eshta'ol	122	31.47 N	35.00 E
Esiama	140	4.56 N	2.21 W
Esine	58	45.55 N	10.15 E
Esino ≃	60	43.39 N	13.22 E
Esira	147b	24.20 S	46.42 E
Esirgâh	120	39.48 N	38.52 E
Esk	161a	27.15 S	152.25 E
Esk ≃, N.Z.	162	43.06 S	171.57 E
Esk ≃, U.K.	42	54.58 N	3.04 W
Esk ≃, Eng., U.K.	42	54.29 N	0.37 W
Esk ≃, Eng., U.K.	42	54.21 N	3.23 W
Eskdale, N.Z.	162	39.24 S	176.50 E
Eskdale, W. Va., U.S.	178	38.05 N	81.27 W
Eskdale ∨	42	55.10 N	3.00 W
Eski Dzhumaya → Târgovište	38	43.15 N	26.34 E
Eskifjördur	24a	65.04 N	13.59 W
Eskiikan	75	43.12 N	68.31 E
Eskiköy	120	36.36 N	30.34 E
Eskilstrup	41	54.51 N	11.54 E
Eskilstuna	40	59.22 N	16.30 E
Eski Malatya	120	38.26 N	38.23 E
Eskimo Lakes ⊜	170	69.15 N	132.17 W
Eskimo Point	166	61.07 N	94.03 W
Eskipazar	120	40.58 N	32.33 E
Eskişehir	120	39.46 N	30.32 E
Eskişehir □[4]	120	39.35 N	31.10 E
Eskridge	188	38.52 N	96.06 W
Esla ≃	34	41.29 N	6.03 W
Eslām Qal'eh	118	34.40 N	61.04 E
Eslohe	52	51.15 N	8.09 E
Eslöv	41	55.50 N	13.20 E
Esmā'īlābād	118	28.48 N	56.39 E
Eşme	120	38.24 N	28.59 E
Esmeralda, Austl.	156	18.50 S	142.34 E
Esmeralda, Cuba	230p	21.51 N	78.07 W
Esmeralda, Méx.	186	25.40 N	103.30 W
Esmeralda, Ven.	236	3.10 N	65.33 W
Esmeralda, Isla I	244	48.57 S	75.25 W
Esmeraldas	236	0.59 N	79.42 W
Esmeraldas □[4]	236	0.40 N	79.30 W
Esmeraldas ≃	236	0.58 N	79.38 W
Esmirna → İzmir	120	38.25 N	27.09 E
Esmond, N. Dak., U.S.	188	48.02 N	99.46 W
Esmond, R.I., U.S.	197	41.53 N	71.30 W
Esnagi Lake ⊜	180	48.38 N	84.32 W
Esneux	52	50.32 N	5.34 E
Esong	142	2.09 N	10.58 E
Esopus Creek ≃	200	42.04 N	73.56 W
Espada, Punta ≻	236	12.05 N	71.07 W
Espagne → Spain □[1]	34	40.00 N	4.00 W
Espalion	32	44.31 N	2.46 E
Espaly-Saint-Marcel	56	45.03 N	3.52 E
España → Spain □[1]	34	40.00 N	4.00 W
Espanola, Ont., Can.	180	46.15 N	81.46 W
Espanola, N. Mex., U.S.	190	36.06 N	106.02 W
Española, Isla I	236a	1.25 S	89.42 W
Esparta	226	9.59 N	84.40 W
Esparto	216	38.42 N	122.01 W
Espasingen	54	47.49 N	9.00 E
Espe, Dan.	41	55.12 N	10.25 E
Espe, S.S.S.R.	75	43.52 N	74.10 E
Espejo	34	37.41 N	4.33 W
Espejo, Canal de ≅	276e	33.32 S	70.43 W
Espelkamp	48	52.25 N	8.36 E
Espenberg, Cape ≻	170	66.33 N	163.36 W
Espenhain	50	51.11 N	12.29 E
Espera, Arroyo ≃[1]	278	34.24 S	58.36 W
Espera Feliz	245	20.39 S	41.55 W
Esperança, Bra.	236	4.24 S	69.52 W
Esperança, Bra.	240	7.01 S	35.51 W
Esperance, Austl.	152	33.51 S	121.53 E
Esperance, N.Y., U.S.	200	42.46 N	74.15 W
Esperance Bay C	152	33.51 S	121.53 E
Esperantina	240	3.54 S	42.14 W
Esperantinópolis	240	4.53 S	44.53 W
Esperanza, Arg.	242	31.27 S	60.56 W
Esperanza, Méx.	222	27.35 N	109.56 W
Esperanza, Méx.	224	18.52 N	97.24 W
Esperanza, Pil.	106	11.44 N	124.03 E
Esperanza, Pil.	106	8.43 N	125.36 E
Esperanza, P.R.	230m	18.06 N	65.28 W
Esperanza, S. Afr.	148	30.21 S	30.40 E
Esperanza, Sierra de la ⩕	226	15.40 N	85.45 W
Esperanza Inlet C	172	49.48 N	127.10 W
Espergærde	41	56.00 N	12.34 E
Esperia	60	41.23 N	13.41 E
Esperito, Arroyo ≃[1]	278	34.23 S	58.36 W
Espevær	26	59.36 N	5.10 E
Espichel, Cabo ≻	34	38.25 N	9.13 W
Espinal, Col.	236	4.09 N	74.53 W
Espinal, Méx.	224	16.29 N	95.03 W
Espinazo	186	26.16 N	101.06 W
Espinazo, Sierra del → Espinhaço, Serra do ⩕	245	17.30 S	43.30 W
Espinazo del Diablo, Sierra ⩕	224	23.55 N	106.00 W
Espingarda ≃	240	10.03 S	47.13 W
Espinhaço, Serra do ⩕	245	17.30 S	43.30 W
Espinho	34	41.00 N	8.39 W
Espinillo	242	24.58 S	58.34 W
Espinillo, Arroyo ≃	248	34.59 S	57.36 W
Espinillo, Punta ≻	248	34.50 S	56.26 W
Espino	236	8.34 N	66.01 W
Espinosa	245	14.56 S	42.50 W
Espinos de Judio	224	19.52 N	104.35 W
Espírito Santo → Vila Velha	240	3.13 N	51.13 W
Espírito Santo □[3]	245	19.30 S	40.30 W
Espírito Santo do Dourado	246	22.03 S	45.58 W
Espíritu Santo I	165f	15.50 S	166.50 E
Espíritu Santo, Bahía del C	222	19.20 N	87.35 W
Espíritu Santo, Isla del I	222	24.30 N	110.22 W
Espita	222	21.01 N	88.19 W
Esplanada	245	11.47 S	37.57 W
Esplugas	256d	41.23 N	2.06 E
Espoir, Bay d' C	176	47.50 N	55.51 W
Espoo (Esbo)	26	60.13 N	24.40 E
Esposende	34	41.32 N	8.47 W
Esposizione Universale di Roma ♠	257a	41.50 N	12.28 E
Espumoso	242	28.44 S	52.51 W
Espungabera	146	20.29 S	32.48 E
Espy	200	41.01 N	76.25 W
Espyville Station	204	41.36 N	80.29 W
Esquatzel Coulee ∨	192	46.17 N	119.07 W
Esquel	244	42.54 S	71.19 W
Esquimalt	172	48.26 N	123.24 W
Esquina	242	30.01 S	59.32 W
Esquina Negra	248	35.02 S	58.03 W
Esquipulas, Guat.	226	14.34 N	89.21 W
Esquipulas, Nic.	226	12.40 N	85.47 W
Esquiú	242	29.23 S	65.17 W
Esrum Sø ⊜	41	56.00 N	12.24 E
Essa ≃	66	54.53 N	28.40 E
Essaoui Mellene, Oued ∨	138	27.26 N	6.40 E
Essaouira (Mogador)	138	31.30 N	9.47 W
Essarts	251	48.30 N	1.46 E
Essé	142	4.05 N	11.53 E
Esse ≃	60	43.16 N	11.54 E
Esseg → Osijek	38	45.33 N	18.41 E
Essel ◂[8]	253	51.37 N	7.15 E
Essen, Bel.	46	51.28 N	4.28 E
Essen, B.R.D.	48	52.43 N	7.57 E
Essen, B.R.D.	52		
	253	51.28 N	7.01 E
Essenberg	253	51.26 N	6.42 E
Essendon, Austl.	159	37.46 S	144.55 E
Essendon, Eng., U.K.	250	51.46 N	0.09 W
Essendon, Mount ∧	152	24.59 S	120.28 E
Essendon Airport ⊠	159	37.43 S	144.53 E
Essen-Mülheim, Flughafen ⊠	253	51.24 N	6.58 E
Essentuki → Jessentuki	74	44.03 N	42.51 E
Essequibo □[5]	236	7.15 N	58.45 W
Essequibo ≃	236	6.59 N	58.23 W
Essequibo Islands □[5]	236	6.45 N	58.35 W
Es Sers	36	36.04 N	9.02 E
Essex, Ont., Can.	204	42.10 N	82.49 W
Essex, Conn., U.S.	197	41.21 N	72.24 W
Essex, Ill., U.S.	206	41.11 N	88.11 W
Essex, Iowa, U.S.	188	40.50 N	95.18 W
Essex, Md., U.S.	198	39.18 N	76.29 W
Essex, Mass., U.S.	197	42.38 N	70.47 W
Essex, Mo., U.S.	184	36.49 N	95.52 W
Essex, Mont., U.S.	172	48.17 N	113.37 W
Essex □[6], Ont., Can.	204	42.10 N	82.50 W
Essex □[6], Eng., U.K.	44	51.48 N	0.40 E
Essex □[6], Mass., U.S.	197	42.31 N	70.55 W
Essex □[6], N.J., U.S.	200	40.48 N	74.12 W
Essex □[6], Vt., U.S.	196	44.57 N	71.43 W
Essex □[6], Va., U.S.	198	37.55 N	76.55 W
Essex ≃	273	42.39 N	70.46 W
Essex Bay C	273	42.39 N	70.44 W
Essex Fells	266	40.50 N	74.17 W
Essex Junction	178	44.29 N	73.07 W
Essex Skypark ⊠	274b	39.18 N	76.28 W
Essexvale	144	20.18 S	28.56 E
Essexville	180	43.37 N	83.50 W

≃ River	Fluss	Río	Rivière	Rio
≅ Canal	Kanal	Canal	Canal	Canal
ᒪ Waterfall, Rapids	Wasserfall, Stromschnellen	Cascada, Rápidos	Chute d'eau, Rapides	Cascata, Rápidos
⊔ Strait	Meeresstrasse	Estrecho	Détroit	Estreito
C Bay, Gulf	Bucht, Golf	Bahía, Golfo	Baie, Golfe	Baía, Golfo
⊜ Lake, Lakes	See, Seen	Lago, Lagos	Lac, Lacs	Lago, Lagos
☷ Swamp	Sumpf	Pantano	Marais	Pântano
⍓ Ice Features, Glacier	Eis- und Gletscherformen	Accidentes Glaciales	Formes glaciaires	Acidentes Glaciares
⍑ Other Hydrographic Features	Andere Hydrographische Objekte	Otros Elementos Hidrográficos	Autres données hydrographiques	Outros Elementos Hidrográficos

⌖ Submarine Features	Untermeerische Objekte	Accidentes Submarinos	Formes de relief sous-marin	Acidentes Submarinos
□ Political Unit	Politische Einheit	Unidad Política	Entité politique	Unidade Política
ʊ Cultural Institution	Kulturelle Institution	Institución Cultural	Institution culturelle	Instituição Cultural
⊥ Historical Site	Historische Stätte	Sitio Histórico	Site historique	Sitio Histórico
♠ Recreational Site	Erholungs- und Ferienort	Sitio de Recreo	Centre de loisirs	Sítio de Lazer
⊠ Airport	Flughafen	Aeropuerto	Aéroport	Aeroporto
■ Military Installation	Militäranlage	Instalación Militar	Installation militaire	Instalação Militar
◂ Miscellaneous	Verschiedenes	Misceláneo	Divers	Miscelânea

ENGLISH

Name	Page	Lat.	Long.
Essig	52	50.40 N	6.54 E
Essington	275	39.52 N	75.18 W
Essling	254b	48.13 N	16.32 E
Esslingen	52	48.45 N	9.16 E
Es Smala es Souassi	36	35.21 N	10.33 E
Esson Lake	202	45.02 N	78.16 W
Essonne □5	46	48.36 N	2.20 E
Essonne	46	48.37 N	2.29 E
Essoyes	54	48.04 N	4.32 E
Es-Suki	130	13.20 N	33.54 E
Essvik	26	62.19 N	17.24 E
Est □5	140	12.00 N	1.00 E
Est	251	48.53 N	2.22 E
Est, Canal de l'	54	48.45 N	5.35 E
Est, Cap	147b	15.16 S	50.29 E
Est, Île de l'	176	47.37 N	61.26 W
Est, Pointe de l'	176	49.08 N	61.41 W
Estacada	214	45.17 N	122.20 W
Estaca de Bares, Punta de la	34	43.46 N	7.42 W
Estacado, Llano	186	33.30 N	102.40 W
Estados, Isla de los (Staten Island)	244	54.47 S	64.15 W
Estados Unidos → United States □1	168	38.00 N	97.00 W
Eşţahbānāt	118	29.08 N	54.04 E
Estaires	46	50.38 N	2.43 E
Estambul → İstanbul	120	41.01 N	28.58 E
Estância, Bra.	240	11.16 S	37.26 W
Estancia, Pil.	106	11.28 N	123.09 E
Estancia, S. Afr.	148	26.17 S	29.52 E
Estancia, N. Mex., U.S.	190	34.45 N	106.04 W
Estancia de los López	224	20.53 N	104.31 W
Estandarte	240	1.26 S	45.32 W
Estanislao del Campo	242	25.03 S	60.06 W
Estanzuelas	226	13.38 N	88.30 W
Estarreja	34	40.45 N	8.34 W
Estats, Pique d'	34	42.40 N	1.24 E
Estavayer-le-Lac	54	46.51 N	6.50 E
Estcourt	148	29.01 S	29.52 E
Este	58	45.14 N	11.39 E
Este	48	53.32 N	9.47 E
Este, Parque Nacional del	276c	10.30 N	66.50 W
Este, Punta	230m	18.08 N	65.16 W
Esteban Echeverría	248	34.50 S	58.28 W
Esteban Echeverría □5	278	34.51 S	58.32 W
Estefanía, Lago → Stefanie, Lake	134	4.40 N	36.50 E
Esteio	242	29.51 S	51.10 W
Estelí	226	13.05 N	86.23 W
Estelí □5	226	13.10 N	86.20 W
Estella	34	42.40 N	2.02 W
Estelline, S. Dak., U.S.	188	44.35 N	96.54 W
Estelline, Tex., U.S.	186	34.33 N	100.26 W
Estell Manor	198	39.23 N	74.48 W
Estèng	56	44.14 N	6.45 E
Estepa	34	37.18 N	4.54 W
Estepona	34	36.26 N	5.08 W
Ester	170	64.51 N	148.01 W
Esterel	56	43.30 N	6.50 E
Esterháza	30	47.37 N	16.53 E
Esterhazy	174	50.40 N	102.08 W
Esterias, Cap	142	0.37 N	9.20 E
Esternay	46	48.44 N	3.34 E
Estero	210	26.26 N	81.49 W
Estero Bay, Calif., U.S.	216	35.24 N	120.53 W
Estero Bay, Fla., U.S.	210	26.25 N	81.52 W
Estero Island	210	26.26 N	81.56 W
Estéron	56	43.49 N	7.11 E
Esteros	242	26.37 S	63.39 W
Esterwegen	48	52.59 N	7.38 E
Estes Park	190	40.23 N	105.31 W
Este Sudeste, Cayos del	226	12.26 N	81.27 W
Estevan	174	49.07 N	103.05 W
Estevan Group	172	53.05 N	129.40 W
Estevan Point	172	49.23 N	126.33 W
Esther Island	170	60.50 N	148.05 W
Estherville	188	43.24 N	94.50 W
Estill	182	32.45 N	81.14 W
Estissac	46	48.16 N	3.49 E
Estiva	246	22.28 S	46.02 W
Estiva, Ribeirão da	277b	23.44 S	46.23 W
Estling, Lake	266	40.53 N	74.30 W
Estocolmo → Stockholm	40	59.20 N	18.03 E
Eston, Sask., Can.	174	51.10 N	108.46 W
Eston, Eng., U.K.	42	54.34 N	1.07 W
Estonian Soviet Socialist Republic → Estonskaja Sovetskaja Socialističeskija Respublika □3	66	59.00 N	26.00 E
Estonskaja Sovetskaja Socialističeskaja Respublika □3	66	59.00 N	26.00 E
Estonskaja Sovetskaja Socialističeskaj Respublika □3	62	59.00 N	26.00 E
Estoril	256c	38.42 N	9.23 W
Estrasburgo → Strasbourg	54	48.35 N	7.45 E
Estrées-Saint-Denis	46	49.26 N	2.39 E
Estreito, Serra do	240	11.00 S	43.25 W
Estrêla	242	29.29 S	51.58 W
Estrela	34	40.19 N	7.37 W
Estrêla	277a	22.43 S	43.13 W
Estrela, Serra da	34	40.20 N	7.38 W
Estrêla do Indaiá	245	19.31 S	45.47 W
Estrêla do Leste	245	16.17 S	53.34 W
Estrêla do Norte	245	13.49 S	49.04 W
Estrêla dos Anapurus	240	3.40 S	43.06 W
Estrêla do Sul	245	18.46 S	47.42 W
Estrella	216	35.45 N	120.41 W
Estrella, Cerro de la	276a	19.20 N	99.05 W
Estrella, Punta	222	30.55 N	114.43 W
Estremadura □9	34	39.15 N	9.10 W
Estremoz	34	38.51 N	7.35 W
Estrondo, Serra do	240	9.00 S	48.45 W
Estuaire □4	142	0.10 S	10.00 E
Estuary	174	50.56 N	109.46 W
Esumba, Île	142	2.00 N	21.12 E
Eszék → Osijek	38	45.33 N	18.41 E
Esztergom	30	47.48 N	18.45 E
Étables	32	48.38 N	2.50 W
Etadunna	156	28.43 S	138.38 E
Etah, Bhārat	114	27.38 N	78.40 E
Etah, Grn.	16	78.19 N	72.38 W
Etah □5	114	27.40 N	78.50 E
Étain	52	49.13 N	5.38 E
Etajima	86	34.15 N	132.30 E
Eta-jima	86	34.15 N	132.28 E
Étalle	52	49.41 N	5.36 E
Étampes	46	48.26 N	2.09 E
Etamunbanie, Lake	156	26.15 S	139.44 E
Étaples	46	50.31 N	1.39 E
États-Unis → United States □1	168	38.00 N	97.00 W
Etāwah, Bhārat	114	25.32 N	76.22 E
Etāwah, Bhārat	114	26.46 N	79.02 E
Etāwah □5	114	26.40 N	79.20 E
Etchemin	176	46.46 N	71.14 W
Etchojoa	222	26.55 N	109.38 W
Etchoropo	222	26.41 N	109.40 W
Etéké	142	1.29 S	11.35 E
Etembue	142	1.17 N	9.25 E
Eten	238	6.54 S	79.52 W
Etendard, Pic de l'	56	45.09 N	6.09 E
Eternity Range	9	69.46 S	64.34 W
Ethan	188	43.33 N	103.59 W
Ethel	184	33.07 N	89.34 W
Ethel	152	24.09 S	118.26 E
Ethelbert	174	51.31 N	100.22 W
Ethel Creek	152	22.54 S	120.09 E
Ethel Lake	170	63.21 N	136.00 W
Ethiopia □1	126		
	134	9.00 N	39.00 E
Ethiopie → Ethiopia □1	134	9.00 N	39.00 E
Ethnikón Mousíon	257c	37.59 N	23.44 E
Ethridge, Mont., U.S.	172	48.34 N	112.07 W
Ethridge, Tenn., U.S.	184	35.19 N	87.18 W
Eticoga	140	11.09 N	16.08 W
Eticuera Creek	216	38.41 N	122.16 W
Etili	120	39.59 N	26.54 E
Etimesğut	120	39.57 N	32.40 E
Étiolles	251	48.38 N	2.29 E
Etiopía → Ethiopia □1	134	9.00 N	39.00 E
Etiwanda	218	34.08 N	117.31 W
Etjo	146	21.09 S	16.30 E
Etna, Calif., U.S.	194	41.27 N	122.54 W
Etna, N.Y., U.S.	200	42.29 N	76.23 W
Etna, Pa., U.S.	204	40.30 N	79.57 W
Etna, Wyo., U.S.	190	43.02 N	111.00 W
Etna, Monte	36	37.46 N	15.00 E
Etna Green	206	41.17 N	86.03 W
Etne	26	59.40 N	5.56 E
Etobicoke	202	43.39 N	79.34 W
Etobicoke Creek	202	43.35 N	79.32 W
Etoile	144	11.38 S	27.34 E
Étoile, Chaîne de l'	56	43.22 N	5.30 E
Etoka	142	0.10 N	23.23 E
Etolin Island	170	56.08 N	132.26 W
Etolin Strait	170	60.20 N	165.15 W
Etomami	174	52.48 N	102.33 W
Eton, Austl.	156	21.16 S	148.58 E
Eton, Eng., U.K.	44	51.31 N	0.37 W
Eton College	250	51.30 N	0.36 W
Etondo	142	7.46 S	23.36 E
Etonia Creek	182	29.42 N	81.39 W
Etorofu-tō → Iturup, Ostrov	82a	44.54 N	147.30 E
Etosha National Park	146	18.45 S	15.00 E
Etoshapan	146	18.45 S	16.15 E
Etoumbi	142	0.01 S	14.57 E
Etowah	182	35.20 N	84.32 W
Etowah	182	34.15 N	85.11 W
Étréchy	46	48.30 N	2.12 E
Étrépagny	46	49.18 N	1.37 E
Étretat	46	49.42 N	0.12 E
Etrotroka	147b	22.53 S	47.36 E
Etroubles	56	45.49 N	7.14 E
Etsch → Adige	58	45.10 N	12.20 E
Eṭ Ṭaiyiba	122	32.16 N	35.01 E
Ettal	58	47.34 N	11.05 E
Ettalong	160	33.31 S	151.21 E
Ettelbruck	52	49.52 N	6.05 E
Ettenheim	54	48.15 N	7.49 E
Etten-Leur	48	51.34 N	4.38 E
Etterbeek	46	50.50 N	4.23 E
Etters	198	40.09 N	76.45 W
Ettington	44	52.09 N	1.36 W
Eṭ Ṭīra	122	32.14 N	34.57 E
Ettlingen	52	48.56 N	8.24 E
Ettrema Creek	160	34.50 S	150.22 E
Ettrick	198	37.14 N	77.25 W
Ettrick Forest	42	55.30 N	3.00 W
Ettrick Pen	42	55.22 N	3.16 W
Ettrick Water	42	55.31 N	2.55 W
Ettringen, B.R.D.	52	50.21 N	7.13 E
Ettringen, B.R.D.	54	48.06 N	10.39 E
Etuku	144	3.43 S	25.44 E
Etuokeqi	92	39.08 N	108.00 E
Etyka	78	51.00 N	116.50 E
Etzatlán	224	20.46 N	104.05 W
Etzikom Coulee	174	49.25 N	111.10 W
Etzná-Tixmucuy	222	19.35 N	90.15 W
Eu	46	50.03 N	1.25 E
Eua	14	21.22 S	174.56 W
Eua Iki	164w	21.07 S	174.59 W
Eubank Acres	212	30.23 N	97.42 W
Eubanque	246	21.33 S	43.30 W
Euboea → Évvoia	38	38.34 N	23.50 E
Eucalyptus Hills	218	32.56 N	116.56 W
Euchiniko	172	53.20 N	123.50 W
Eucla	152	31.43 S	128.52 E
Euclid, Ohio, U.S.	204	41.34 N	81.32 W
Euclid, Pa., U.S.	204	41.00 N	79.56 W
Euclid Center	206	42.08 N	86.24 W
Euclid Creek	269a	41.35 N	81.35 W
Euclid Creek Reservation	269a	41.33 N	81.32 W
Euclides da Cunha	240	10.31 S	39.01 W
Eucumbene	161b	36.07 S	148.38 E
Eucumbene	161b	36.21 S	148.38 E
Eucumbene, Lake	161b	36.05 S	148.45 E
Eucumbene Dam	161b	36.07 S	148.40 E
Eudistes, Lac des	176	50.30 N	65.15 W
Eudora, Ark., U.S.	184	33.07 N	91.16 W
Eudora, Kans., U.S.	188	38.57 N	95.06 W
Eudunda	158b	34.11 S	139.04 E
Eufaula, Ala., U.S.	184	31.54 N	85.09 W
Eufaula, Okla., U.S.	186	35.17 N	95.35 W
Eufaula Lake	186	35.17 N	95.31 W
Eufrates → Euphrates	118	31.00 N	47.25 E
Euganei, Colli	58	45.19 N	11.40 E
Eugendorf	58	47.52 N	13.07 E
Eugene	192	44.02 N	123.05 W
Eugenia, Punta	222	27.50 N	115.05 W
Eugenia Lake	202	44.20 N	80.30 W
Eugenio Bustos	242	33.46 S	69.04 W
Eugênio de Melo	246	23.09 S	45.47 W
Eugênio Penzo	242	22.13 S	55.53 W
Eugenópolis	245	21.06 S	42.11 W
Eugmo	26	63.49 N	22.45 E
Eugowra	156	33.26 S	148.23 E
Euijeongbu → Ŭijŏngbu	88	37.44 N	127.03 E
Euless	212	32.50 N	97.05 W
Eulo	156	28.10 S	145.03 E
Eulogio Sánchez Errázuriz, Aeropuerto	276e	33.27 S	70.33 W
Eume	34	43.25 N	8.08 W
Eumemmerring Creek	264b	38.03 S	145.10 E
Eumungerie	156	31.57 S	148.37 E
Eungela National Park	156	21.00 S	148.30 E
Eunice, La., U.S.	184	30.30 N	92.25 W
Eunice, N. Mex., U.S.	186	32.26 N	103.09 W
Eupen	52	50.38 N	6.02 E
Euphrat → Euphrates	118	31.00 N	47.25 E
Euphrates (Fırat) (Al-Furāt)	118	31.00 N	47.25 E
Eupora	184	33.32 N	89.16 W
Eure	198	36.26 N	76.51 W
Eure □5	46	49.10 N	1.00 E
Eure	46	49.18 N	1.12 E
Eure-et-Loir □5	46	48.30 N	1.30 E
Eureka, Alaska, U.S.	170	65.11 N	150.13 W
Eureka, Calif., U.S.	194	40.47 N	124.09 W
Eureka, Ill., U.S.	180	40.43 N	89.16 W
Eureka, Kans., U.S.	188	37.49 N	96.17 W
Eureka, Mo., U.S.	209	38.30 N	90.38 W
Eureka, Mont., U.S.	192	48.53 N	115.03 W
Eureka, Nev., U.S.	194	39.31 N	115.58 W
Eureka, Pa., U.S.	204	40.15 N	78.46 W
Eureka, Pa., U.S.	275	40.15 N	75.11 W
Eureka, S. Dak., U.S.	188	45.46 N	99.38 W
Eureka, Tex., U.S.	212	32.01 N	96.18 W
Eureka, Utah, U.S.	190	39.57 N	112.07 W
Eureka, Mount	152	26.34 S	121.32 E
Eureka Springs	184	36.24 N	93.44 W
Eurinilla Creek	156	30.50 S	140.01 E
Euroa	159	36.45 S	145.35 E
Europa, Île	128	22.20 S	40.22 E
Europa, Picos de	34	43.12 N	4.48 W
Europabrücke	58	47.11 N	11.23 E
Europa Point	34	36.10 N	5.22 W
Europe	4	50.00 N	28.00 E
Europe	10	50.00 N	20.00 E
Europoort	48	51.58 N	4.00 E
Eursinge	48	52.46 N	6.28 E
Eurville	54	48.35 N	5.02 E
Euseigne	54	46.10 N	7.25 E
Euskirchen	52	50.39 N	6.47 E
Eustace	212	32.18 N	96.01 W
Eustis, Fla., U.S.	210	28.51 N	81.41 W
Eustis, Nebr., U.S.	188	40.40 N	100.02 W
Eustis, Lake	210	28.50 N	81.44 W
Euston	156	34.35 S	142.44 E
Euston Station	250	51.32 N	0.08 W
Eutaw	184	32.50 N	87.53 W
Eutin	50	54.08 N	10.37 E
Eutingen	52	48.28 N	8.44 E
Eutsuk Lake	172	53.20 N	126.44 W
Eutzsch	50	51.49 N	12.38 E
Euxton	252	53.40 N	2.41 W
Euzet-les-Bains	56	44.04 N	4.14 E
Eva, Bra.	236	3.00 S	59.18 W
Eva, Ala., U.S.	184	34.20 N	86.46 W
Evadale	184	30.21 N	94.04 W
Eva Downs	152	18.01 S	134.52 E
Evale	142	16.33 S	15.44 E
Evällen	40	60.03 N	18.20 E
Evançon	56	45.40 N	7.41 E
Evandale	156	41.34 S	147.14 E
Evans, Lac	166	50.55 N	77.00 W
Evans, Mount	190	39.35 N	105.38 W
Evansburg, Alta., Can.	172	53.36 N	115.01 W
Evansburg, Pa., U.S.	275	40.11 N	75.26 W
Evans Center	200	42.39 N	79.02 W
Evans City	204	40.45 N	80.03 W
Evans Creek	192	42.25 N	123.11 W
Evansdale	180	42.30 N	92.17 W
Evans Head	156	29.07 S	153.26 E
Evans Mills	202	44.05 N	75.48 W
Evansport	206	41.25 N	84.24 W
Evans Strait	166	63.15 N	82.00 W
Evanston, Ill., U.S.	206	42.03 N	87.42 W
Evanston, Pa., U.S.	269b	40.16 N	79.41 W
Evanston, Wyo., U.S.	190	41.16 N	110.58 W
Evansville, Ill., U.S.	184	38.05 N	89.56 W
Evansville, Ind., U.S.	184	37.58 N	87.35 W
Evansville, Wis., U.S.	206	42.47 N	89.18 W
Evansville, Wyo., U.S.	190	42.52 N	106.16 W
Evant	186	31.29 N	98.09 W
Eva Perón → La Plata	248	34.55 S	57.57 W
Evart	180	43.54 N	85.08 W
Evarts	182	36.52 N	83.12 W
Evaton	148	26.31 S	27.54 E
Evaz	118	27.46 N	53.59 E
Ève	251	49.05 N	2.42 E
Evecquemont	251	49.02 N	1.57 E
Eveking	253	51.14 N	7.44 E
Eveleth	180	47.28 N	92.32 W
Evelyn, Mount	154	13.36 S	132.53 E
Evening Shade	184	36.04 N	91.37 W
Evenkamp	253	51.40 N	7.39 E
Evenkijskij Nacionalnyj Okrug □8	78	59.15 N	104.00 E
Evenlode	44	51.47 N	1.21 W
Evensk	64	61.57 N	159.14 E
Even Yehuda	122	32.16 N	34.53 E
Everard, Lake	152	31.25 S	135.05 E
Everard, Mount, Austl.	152	26.16 S	132.04 E
Everard, Mount, B.C., Can.	172	51.05 N	125.45 W
Everard Ranges	152	27.05 S	132.28 E
Evercreech	44	51.09 N	2.30 W
Evere	52	50.52 N	4.24 E
Everek	118	38.23 N	35.30 E
Everest	188	39.41 N	95.26 W
Everest, Mount (Zhumulangmafeng)	114	27.59 N	86.56 E
Everett, Ont., Can.	202	44.11 N	79.57 W
Everett, Mass., U.S.	197	42.24 N	71.03 W
Everett, N.J., U.S.	266	40.21 N	74.09 W
Everett, Pa., U.S.	178	40.01 N	78.23 W
Everett, Wash., U.S.	214	47.59 N	122.13 W
Everett, Mount	197	42.06 N	73.25 W
Everett Mountains	166	62.45 N	67.12 W
Evergem	46	51.07 N	3.42 E
Everglades City	210	25.52 N	81.23 W
Everglades National Park	210	25.27 N	80.53 W
Evergreen, Ala., U.S.	184	31.26 N	86.57 W
Evergreen, Calif., U.S.	194	35.54 N	120.26 W
Evergreen, Mont., U.S.	192	48.13 N	114.18 W
Evergreen, Tex., U.S.	212	30.33 N	95.14 W
Evergreen Lake	206	40.40 N	89.02 W
Evergreen Park	206	41.43 N	87.42 W
Evergreen Plaza	268	41.43 N	87.41 W
Everly	188	43.10 N	95.20 W
Everman	212	32.38 N	97.17 W
Everöd	26	55.54 N	14.06 E
Eversael	253	51.33 N	6.39 E
Eversberg	52	51.21 N	8.20 E
Eversen	48	52.45 N	10.02 E
Everson, Pa., U.S.	204	40.06 N	79.35 W
Everson, Wash., U.S.	214	48.55 N	122.21 W
Everswinkel	48	51.55 N	7.50 E
Everton	208	39.34 N	85.05 W
Everton	252	53.25 N	2.58 W
Everton Football Ground	252	53.26 N	2.58 W
Evesen	48	52.17 N	8.59 E
Evesham, Sask., Can.	174	52.24 N	109.50 W
Evesham, Eng., U.K.	44	52.06 N	1.56 W
Evesham, Vale of	44	52.06 N	1.50 W
Évian-les-Bains	54	46.23 N	6.35 E
Evijärvi	26	63.22 N	23.29 E
Evinayong	142	1.27 N	10.34 E
Eving	253	51.33 N	7.29 E
Evingsen	253	51.18 N	7.44 E
Evionnaz	54	46.11 N	7.01 E
Evisa	36	42.15 N	8.47 E
Evje	26	58.36 N	7.51 E
Evolène	54	46.07 N	7.30 E
Évora	34	38.34 N	7.54 W
Evoron, Ozero	79	51.28 N	136.30 E
Evpatoria → Jevpatorija	68	45.12 N	33.22 E
Évrange	52	49.30 N	6.12 E
Évreux	46	49.01 N	1.09 E
Evrieu	56	45.35 N	5.34 E
'Evron	122	32.59 N	35.06 E
Évros (Marica) (Meriç)	38	40.52 N	26.12 E
Evrótas	38	36.48 N	22.40 E
Évry	46	48.38 N	2.27 E
Évry-les-Châteaux	251	48.39 N	2.38 E
Evungu	144	4.27 S	25.12 E
Évvoia	38	38.34 N	23.50 E
Évzonos	257c	37.57 N	23.49 E
Ewa	219c	21.21 N	158.02 W
Ewa Beach	219c	21.20 N	158.04 W
Ewan	275	39.42 N	75.11 W
Ewaninga	152	23.58 S	133.58 E
Ewan Lake	275	39.42 N	75.11 W
Ewansville	275	39.59 N	74.44 W
Ewarton	231q	18.11 N	77.05 W
Ewbank	148	26.14 S	23.35 E
Ewell, Eng., U.K.	250	51.21 N	0.15 W
Ewell, Md., U.S.	198	37.59 N	76.02 W
Ewen	180	46.32 N	89.17 W
Ewersbach	52	50.50 N	8.19 E
Ewes Water	42	55.08 N	3.00 W
Ewing, Ky., U.S.	208	38.26 N	83.52 W
Ewing, Mo., U.S.	209	40.00 N	91.43 W
Ewing, Nebr., U.S.	188	42.16 N	98.21 W
Ewing, Va., U.S.	182	36.38 N	83.26 W
Ewingsville	269b	40.24 N	80.06 W
Ewing Township	198	40.16 N	74.44 W
Ewo	142	0.53 S	14.49 E
Ewu	263a	6.33 N	3.19 E
Exaltación	238	13.16 S	65.15 W
Excelda	148	32.16 S	22.08 E
Excello	208	39.29 N	84.25 W
Excelsior	148	28.56 S	27.06 E
Excelsior Mountain	216	38.02 N	119.18 W
Excelsior Park	264a	33.45 S	151.01 E
Excelsior Springs	184	39.20 N	94.13 W
Excenevex	54	46.21 N	6.21 E
Exchange	200	41.07 N	76.41 W
Exchange Station	252	53.29 N	2.15 W
Excursion Inlet	170	58.25 N	135.27 W
Exe	44	50.37 N	3.25 W
Executive Committee Range	9	76.50 S	126.00 W
Exeter, Austl.	160	34.38 S	150.19 E
Exeter, Ont., Can.	180	43.21 N	81.29 W
Exeter, Eng., U.K.	44	50.43 N	3.31 W
Exeter, Calif., U.S.	216	36.18 N	119.09 W
Exeter, Nebr., U.S.	188	40.39 N	97.27 W
Exeter, N.H., U.S.	178	42.59 N	70.57 W
Exeter, Pa., U.S.	200	41.20 N	75.49 W
Exeter, R.I., U.S.	197	41.35 N	71.32 W
Exeter	178	43.02 N	70.55 W
Exeter Sound	166	66.14 N	62.00 W
Exford	44	51.08 N	3.38 W
Exhibition Park	265b	43.38 N	79.25 W
Exhibition Stadium	265b	43.38 N	79.25 W
Exincourt	54	47.30 N	6.50 E
Exira	188	41.35 N	94.52 W
Exline Slough	206	41.05 N	87.47 W
Exloërmond	48	52.54 N	6.57 E
Exmes	46	48.46 N	0.11 E
Exminster	44	50.41 N	3.29 W
Exmoor	44	51.10 N	3.45 W
Exmoor National Park	44	51.12 N	3.46 W
Exmore	198	37.32 N	75.50 W
Exmouth	44	50.37 N	3.25 W
Exmouth Gulf	152	22.23 S	114.07 E
Exmouth Gulf	152	22.00 S	114.20 E
Expedition Range	156	24.30 S	149.05 E
Experiment	182	33.16 N	84.17 W
Exploits	176	49.05 N	55.20 W
Exploits, Bay of	176	49.24 N	55.00 W
Exploits Dam	176	48.45 N	56.30 W
Export	204	40.25 N	79.37 W
Exshaw	172	51.03 N	115.09 W
Extension	214	49.06 N	123.57 W
Exter	48	52.08 N	8.46 E
Externsteine	48	51.52 N	8.55 E
Extertal	48	52.04 N	9.07 E
Exton	198	40.02 N	75.37 W
Extorás	224	21.06 N	99.23 W
Extrema	246	22.51 S	46.19 W
Extremadura □9	34	39.00 N	6.00 W
Exu	240	7.31 S	39.43 W
Exuma Sound	228	24.15 N	76.00 W
Eyak	170	60.32 N	145.36 W
Eyam	42	53.17 N	1.41 W
Eyasi, Lake	144	3.40 S	35.05 E
Eydehavn	26	58.31 N	8.53 E
Eye, Eng., U.K.	44	52.19 N	1.09 E
Eye, Eng., U.K.	44	52.35 N	0.10 W
Eyebrow	174	50.47 N	106.09 W
Eyemouth	42	55.52 N	2.06 W
Eye Peninsula	28	58.13 N	6.05 W
Eyers Grove	200	41.05 N	76.31 W
Eye Water	42	55.53 N	2.06 W
Eygalières	56	43.45 N	4.57 E
Eyguières	56	43.42 N	5.02 E
Eyhorne Street	250	51.16 N	0.38 E
Eyjafjördur	24a	65.54 N	18.15 W
Eylar Mountain	194	37.28 N	121.33 W
Eymet	32	44.40 N	0.24 E
Eymir	120	40.02 N	35.14 E
Eymoutiers	32	45.44 N	1.44 E
Eynsford	250	51.22 N	0.13 E
Eynsham	44	51.48 N	1.22 W
Eyota	180	43.59 N	92.14 W
Eyrarbakki	24a	63.53 N	21.05 W
Eyre	152	32.15 S	126.18 E
Eyre Creek	156	26.40 S	139.00 E
Eyre Mountains	162	45.20 S	168.30 E
Eyre North, Lake	156	28.40 S	137.10 E
Eyre Peninsula	152	34.00 S	135.45 E
Eyre South, Lake	156	29.30 S	137.20 E
Eyrieux	56	44.48 N	4.48 E
Eystrup	48	52.46 N	9.13 E
Eythorne	44	51.11 N	1.17 E
Eythra	50	51.14 N	12.17 E
Eyüp	257b	41.03 N	28.55 E
Eyvānakī	118	35.20 N	52.04 E
Ézanville	251	49.02 N	2.22 E
Ezbekīyah	263c	30.03 N	31.15 E
Èze	56	43.43 N	7.22 E
Ezeiza	248	34.51 S	58.32 W
Ezeiza, Aeropuerto Internacional de	278	34.49 S	58.32 W
Ezere	66	56.26 N	22.22 E
Ežerėlis	66	54.53 N	23.37 E
Ezeriş	38	45.24 N	21.53 E
Ezine	120	39.47 N	26.20 E
Ezinepazarı	120	40.34 N	36.09 E
Ezop, Chrebet	79	52.36 N	133.37 E
Ezpeleta	248	34.46 S	58.15 W
Ežva	24	61.47 N	50.40 E
Ézy-sur-Eure	46	48.52 N	1.25 E
Ezzell	212	29.17 N	96.58 W
F			
Faaa Airport	164s	17.33 S	149.36 W
Faaone	164s	17.40 S	149.18 W
Fabala	140	9.44 N	9.05 W
Fabbrico	58	44.52 N	10.50 E
Fabens	190	31.30 N	106.10 W
Fåberg	26	61.10 N	10.24 E
Faber Lake	166	63.56 N	117.15 W
Fabert Shoal	14	24.30 S	158.05 W
Fabius	200	42.50 N	75.59 W
Fåborg	41	55.06 N	10.15 E
Fábrega, Cerro	226	9.07 N	82.52 W
Fabrègues	56	43.33 N	3.46 E
Fabreville	265a	45.34 N	73.50 W
Fabriano	60	43.20 N	12.54 E
Fabrica	106	10.54 N	123.23 E
Fabrica di Roma	60	42.20 N	12.18 E
Fabričnyj	75	43.11 N	76.24 E
Facatativá	236	4.49 N	74.22 W
Facha	136	29.27 N	17.18 E
Faches-Thumesnil	46	50.35 N	3.04 E
Fachi	136	18.06 N	11.34 E
Facpi Point	164p	13.20 N	144.38 E
Factoryville	200	41.34 N	75.47 W
Facundo	244	45.18 S	69.58 W
Fada	136	17.14 N	21.33 E
Fadalto	58	46.05 N	12.20 E
Fada Ngourma	140	12.04 N	0.21 E
Fadd	30	46.28 N	18.50 E
Faddeja, Zaliv	64	76.40 N	107.20 E
Faddejevskij, Ostrov	64	75.30 N	144.00 E
Faddoi	130	8.07 N	32.07 E
Fadian Point	164p	13.26 N	144.49 E
Fadiffolu Atoll	112	5.25 N	73.30 E
Fadit	130	9.58 N	32.13 E
Faedis	58	46.10 N	13.20 E
Fænø	41	55.29 N	9.42 E
Faenza	60	44.17 N	11.53 E
Faeroe Islands □2	22	62.00 N	7.00 W
Faeröerne → Faeroe Islands □2	22	62.00 N	7.00 W
Faete, Monte	257a	41.45 N	12.44 E
Fafa	140	15.20 N	0.43 E
Fafadur	134	2.11 N	41.32 E
Fafakourou	140	13.04 N	14.34 W
Fafalog	164p	13.37 N	144.51 E
Fafe	34	41.27 N	8.10 W
Fafen	134	6.07 N	44.20 E
Faga	140	13.15 N	0.55 E
Fagaitua	164u	14.16 S	170.37 W
Fagaloa Bay	165a	13.54 S	171.28 W
Fagamalo	165a	13.25 S	172.21 W
Făgăraş	38	45.51 N	24.58 E
Făgăraş, Munţii	38	45.35 N	25.00 E
Fagasa	164u	14.17 S	170.43 W
Fagel	41	54.27 N	9.31 E
Fagernes	26	60.59 N	9.15 E
Fagersta	40	60.00 N	15.47 E
Fagertärn	40	58.46 N	14.42 E
Fagerviken	40	60.33 N	17.45 E
Făget	38	45.51 N	22.10 E
Faggen Bach	58	47.05 N	10.40 E
Faggo	140	11.23 N	9.57 E
Fagnano, Lago	244	54.35 S	68.00 W
Fagnano Olona	56	45.40 N	8.52 E
Fagnières	46	48.58 N	4.19 E
Faguibine, Lac	140	16.45 N	3.54 W
Fagundes	246	22.12 S	43.11 W
Fagurhólsmýri	24a	63.54 N	16.38 W
Fagwir	130	9.33 N	30.25 E
Fahl, Oued el	138	31.15 N	4.41 E
Fahraj	118	28.58 N	58.52 E
Fährdorf	50	53.58 N	11.28 E
Fahrland	50	52.28 N	13.01 E
Fahrlander See	254a	52.27 N	13.01 E
Fahrn → Varna	58	46.44 N	11.38 E
Fahrnau	54	47.39 N	7.50 E
Fahuaqiao	96	30.52 N	121.25 E
Faial	138a	38.34 N	28.42 W
Fā'id	132	30.19 N	32.19 E
Fā'id Military Base	132	30.20 N	32.16 E
Faido	54	46.29 N	8.48 E
Faillon, Lac	180	48.21 N	76.38 W
Failsworth	42	53.31 N	2.09 W
Fains-les-Sources	52	48.47 N	5.08 E
Fairbairn Park	264b	37.47 S	144.55 E
Fairbank	180	42.38 N	92.03 W
Fairbanks, Alaska, U.S.	170	64.51 N	147.43 W
Fairbanks, La., U.S.	184	30.00 N	92.02 W
Fair Bluff	182	34.19 N	79.02 W
Fairborn	208	39.49 N	84.02 W
Fairbourne	44	52.41 N	4.03 W
Fairburn	182	33.34 N	84.35 W
Fairbury, Ill., U.S.	206	40.45 N	88.31 W
Fairbury, Nebr., U.S.	188	40.08 N	97.11 W
Fairchance	178	39.49 N	79.45 W
Fairchild	180	44.36 N	90.58 W
Fairchild Air Force Base	192	47.38 N	117.38 W
Fairchild Creek	202	43.07 N	80.07 W
Fairdale	206	42.06 N	88.56 W
Faire	106	17.53 N	121.34 E
Fairfax, Ala., U.S.	184	32.48 N	85.11 W
Fairfax, Calif., U.S.	216	37.59 N	122.35 W
Fairfax, Del., U.S.	275	39.47 N	75.32 W
Fairfax, Minn., U.S.	188	44.32 N	94.31 W
Fairfax, Okla., U.S.	186	36.34 N	96.42 W
Fairfax, S.C., U.S.	182	33.01 N	81.18 W
Fairfax, S. Dak., U.S.	188	43.02 N	98.54 W
Fairfax, Vt., U.S.	178	44.40 N	73.01 W
Fairfax, Va., U.S.	198	38.51 N	77.18 W
Fairfax □6	198	38.45 N	77.15 W
Fairfax State Recreation Area	208	39.02 N	86.29 W
Fairfax Station	274c	38.48 N	77.20 W
Fairfield, Austl.	160	33.52 S	150.57 E
Fairfield, Ala., U.S.	184	33.29 N	86.55 W
Fairfield, Calif., U.S.	216	38.15 N	122.03 W
Fairfield, Conn., U.S.	200	41.09 N	73.15 W
Fairfield, Idaho, U.S.	192	43.21 N	114.48 W
Fairfield, Ill., U.S.	184	38.23 N	88.22 W
Fairfield, Iowa, U.S.	180	40.56 N	91.57 W
Fairfield, Maine, U.S.	178	44.35 N	69.36 W
Fairfield, Mont., U.S.	192	47.37 N	111.59 W
Fairfield, Nebr., U.S.	188	40.26 N	98.06 W
Fairfield, N.J., U.S.	266	40.53 N	74.17 W
Fairfield, N.Y., U.S.	200	43.08 N	74.55 W
Fairfield, Ohio, U.S.	208	39.20 N	84.33 W
Fairfield, Pa., U.S.	204	39.47 N	77.22 W
Fairfield, Tex., U.S.	212	31.44 N	96.10 W
Fairfield □6	197	41.11 N	73.11 W
Fairfield University	266	41.09 N	73.15 W
Fairford	44	51.44 N	1.47 W
Fairgrove	180	43.31 N	83.33 W
Fair Harbor	200	40.38 N	73.11 W
Fairhaven, Mass., U.S.	197	41.39 N	70.54 W
Fair Haven, Mich., U.S.	204	42.41 N	82.39 W
Fair Haven, N.J., U.S.	198	40.23 N	74.03 W
Fair Haven, N.Y., U.S.	200	43.19 N	76.42 W
Fairhaven, Ohio, U.S.	208	39.38 N	84.47 W
Fair Haven, Vt., U.S.	178	43.36 N	73.16 W
Fair Haven, Va., U.S.	274c	38.47 N	77.05 W
Fairhaven Bay	273	42.26 N	71.21 W
Fair Head	42	55.13 N	6.09 W
Fairhope, Ala., U.S.	184	30.31 N	87.54 W
Fairhope, Ohio, U.S.	204	40.51 N	81.19 W
Fairhope, Pa., U.S.	204	40.07 N	79.50 W
Fair Isle	28	59.30 N	1.40 W
Fairland, Ind., U.S.	208	39.35 N	85.52 W
Fairland, Md., U.S.	274c	39.05 N	76.58 W
Fairland, Okla., U.S.	186	36.45 N	94.51 W
Fairlane Town	271	42.19 N	83.13 W
Fair Lawn, N.J., U.S.	200	40.56 N	74.07 W
Fairlawn, Ohio, U.S.	204	41.08 N	81.36 W
Fairlee	274c	38.52 N	77.16 W
Fairleigh Dickinson University (Madison), N.J., U.S.	266	40.46 N	74.26 W
Fairleigh Dickinson University, N.J., U.S.	266	40.50 N	74.07 W
Fairleigh Dickinson University (Teaneck), N.J., U.S.	266	40.53 N	74.02 W
Fairless Hills	198	40.11 N	74.50 W
Fairlie, N.Z.	162	44.06 S	170.50 E
Fairlie, Scot., U.K.	42	55.46 N	4.51 W
Fairlight	44	50.53 N	0.40 E
Fairmont, Ill., U.S.	206	41.34 N	88.04 W
Fairmont, Minn., U.S.	188	43.39 N	94.28 W
Fairmont, Nebr., U.S.	188	40.38 N	97.35 W
Fairmont, N.C., U.S.	182	34.30 N	79.07 W
Fairmont, Pa., U.S.	269b	40.19 N	79.43 W
Fairmont, Wash., U.S.	214	48.54 N	122.16 W
Fairmont, W. Va., U.S.	178	39.29 N	80.09 W
Fairmont City	209	38.40 N	90.06 W
Fairmont Hot Springs	172	50.19 N	115.53 W
Fairmont Reservoir	218	34.43 N	118.26 W
Fairmont Terrace	272	37.43 N	122.07 W
Fairmount, Ga., U.S.	182	34.26 N	84.42 W
Fairmount, Ill., U.S.	184	40.03 N	87.56 W
Fairmount, Ind., U.S.	206	40.25 N	85.39 W
Fairmount, N. Dak., U.S.	188	46.03 N	96.36 W

DEUTSCH

Name	Seite	Breite	Länge E=Ost
Fairmount, N.Y., U.S.	200	43.04 N	76.15 W
Fairmount City	204	41.01 N	79.19 W
Fairmount Heights	198	38.54 N	76.55 W
Fairmount Park	275	40.00 N	75.12 W
Fair Ness	166	63.24 N	72.05 W
Fair Oaks, Calif., U.S.	216	38.39 N	121.16 W
Fair Oaks, Ga., U.S.	182	33.55 N	84.32 W
Fair Oaks, Ind., U.S.	206	41.05 N	87.16 W
Fairoaks, Pa., U.S.	269b	40.35 N	80.13 W
Fairoaks Airport	250	51.21 N	0.32 W
Fair Plain	206	42.05 N	86.28 W
Fairplay	190	39.19 N	105.60 W
Fairpoint	204	40.07 N	80.56 W
Fairport, Ont., Can.	265b	43.49 N	79.05 W
Fairport, N.Y., U.S.	200	43.06 N	77.27 W
Fairport Beach	265b	43.48 N	79.06 W
Fairport Harbor	204	41.45 N	81.17 W
Fairseat	250	51.20 N	0.20 E
Fairton	198	39.23 N	75.13 W
Fairview, Austl.	154	15.33 S	144.19 E
Fairview, Alta., Can.	172	56.04 N	118.23 W
Fairview, Ga., U.S.	182	34.58 N	85.16 W
Fairview, Ill., U.S.	180	40.38 N	90.10 W
Fairview, Ind., U.S.	206	40.18 N	85.11 W
Fairview, Kans., U.S.	188	39.50 N	95.44 W
Fairview, Md., U.S.	198	39.09 N	76.29 W
Fairview, Mich., U.S.	180	44.44 N	84.03 W
Fairview, Mont., U.S.	188	47.51 N	104.03 W
Fairview, N.J., U.S.	266	40.49 N	74.00 W
Fairview, N.J., U.S.	275	39.53 N	74.49 W
Fairview, N.Y., U.S.	200	41.44 N	73.56 W
Fairview, N.Y., U.S.	266	41.03 N	73.48 W
Fairview, Ohio, U.S.	204	40.03 N	81.14 W
Fairview, Okla., U.S.	186	36.16 N	98.29 W
Fairview, Pa., U.S.	204	42.03 N	80.13 W
Fairview, Pa., U.S.	204	41.01 N	79.44 W
Fairview, Tenn., U.S.	184	35.59 N	87.07 W
Fairview, Utah, U.S.	190	39.38 N	111.26 W
Fairview, W. Va., U.S.	178	39.36 N	80.15 W
Fairview Heights	209	38.36 N	90.00 W
Fairview Lanes	204	41.23 N	82.40 W
Fairview Mall	265b	43.47 N	79.21 W
Fairview Park, Ind., U.S.	184	39.41 N	87.25 W
Fairview Park, Ohio, U.S.	204	41.27 N	81.51 W
Fairview Park, Pa., U.S.	200	41.10 N	75.53 W
Fairview Peak, Nev., U.S.	194	39.14 N	118.08 W
Fairview Peak, Oreg., U.S.	192	43.35 N	122.39 W
Fairview Pointe Claire Centre	265a	45.28 N	73.50 W
Fairview Shores	210	28.36 N	81.23 W
Fairview Village	275	40.10 N	75.23 W
Fairvilla	210	28.35 N	81.24 W
Fairville	275	39.51 N	75.38 W
Fairweather, Mount	170	58.54 N	137.32 W
Fairy Lake	202	45.20 N	79.11 W
Fairy Meadow	160	34.23 S	150.54 E
Fairy Stone State Park	182	36.48 N	80.06 W
Fais	98	9.46 N	140.31 E
Faison	182	35.07 N	78.08 W
Faistós	38	35.01 N	24.48 E
Faith	188	45.02 N	102.02 W
Faiyum → Al-Fayyūm	132	29.19 N	30.50 E
Faizābād	114	26.47 N	82.08 E
Faizābād □5	114	26.30 N	82.30 E
Fajansovyj	66	54.04 N	34.24 E
Fajardo	230m	18.20 N	65.39 W
Fajou, Îlet à	231o	16.21 N	61.35 W
Fajr, Wādī	118	30.06 N	38.18 E
Fajzabad	75	38.34 N	69.19 E
Fak	120	37.51 N	39.05 E
Fakahatchee Strand	210	39.35 N	89.25 W
Fakaofo	14	9.22 S	171.14 W
Fakarava	14	16.20 S	145.37 W
Fakejev	70	48.57 N	49.56 E
Fakel	70	57.38 N	53.02 E
Fakenham	44	52.50 N	0.51 E
Fakfak	154	2.55 S	132.18 E
Fakılı	120	39.13 N	35.00 E
Fakirganj	114	25.58 N	90.02 E
Fakī Şādiq	130	12.08 N	23.55 E
Fakrinkotti	130	18.01 N	31.20 E
Fakse	41	55.15 N	12.08 E
Fakse Bugt	41	55.10 N	12.15 E
Fakse Ladeplads	41	55.13 N	12.11 E
Faku	94	42.30 N	123.24 E
Fal	44	50.08 N	5.02 W
Falaba	140	9.51 N	11.19 W
Faladyé	140	13.08 N	8.20 W
Falaise	32	48.54 N	0.12 W
Fālākāta	114	26.32 N	89.12 E
Falalu	14	7.38 N	151.41 E
Falam	100	22.55 N	93.40 E
Falāvarjān	118	32.33 N	51.30 E
Falcade	58	46.21 N	11.51 E
Falcão	246	22.17 S	44.16 W
Fălciu	38	46.18 N	28.08 E
Falck	52	49.14 N	6.38 E
Falcognana di Sotto	257a	41.45 N	12.33 E
Falcón □3	236	11.00 N	69.50 W
Falcon, Cap	138	35.46 N	0.48 W
Falcon, Cape	214	45.46 N	123.59 W
Falconara Alta	60	43.37 N	13.24 E
Falconara Marittima	60	43.37 N	13.24 E
Falconbridge	180	46.35 N	80.48 W
Falconer	204	42.07 N	79.12 W
Falcon Heights	192	42.08 N	121.45 W
Falcon Reservoir (Presa Falcón)	186	26.37 N	99.11 W
Falconwood	200	43.00 N	78.57 W
Faldsled	41	55.09 N	10.09 E
Faléa	140	12.16 N	11.17 W
Faleasao	164y	14.13 S	169.32 W
Falelima	165a	13.32 S	172.41 W
Falémé	140	14.46 N	12.14 W
Falenki	70	58.22 N	51.35 E
Falerii Novi	60	42.16 N	12.20 E
Falerone	60	43.06 N	13.28 E
Faleşty	68	47.34 N	27.43 E
Falevai	165a	13.55 S	171.59 W
Falfurrias	186	27.14 N	98.09 W
Falher	172	55.44 N	117.12 W
Falicon	56	43.45 N	7.17 E
Fálirou, Órmos	257c	37.56 N	23.40 E
Falkenau	50	50.51 N	13.07 E
Falkenberg, D.D.R.	50	52.48 N	13.58 E
Falkenberg, D.D.R.	50	51.35 N	13.14 E
Falkenberg → Niemodlin, Pol.	30	50.39 N	17.37 E
Falkenberg, Sve.	26	56.54 N	12.28 E
Falkenberg	254a	52.34 N	13.33 E
Falkenburg → Złocieniec	30	53.33 N	16.01 E
Falkenhagen, D.D.R.	50	52.26 N	14.19 E
Falkenhagen, D.D.R.	50	53.12 N	12.12 E
Falkenhagener See	254a	52.34 N	13.08 E
Falkenrehde	254a	52.30 N	12.56 E
Falkensee	50	52.33 N	13.04 E
Falkenstein, B.R.D.	30	49.06 N	12.30 E
Falkenstein, D.D.R.	50	50.29 N	12.22 E
Falkenthal	50	52.54 N	13.17 E
Falkirk	42	56.00 N	3.48 W
Falkland	172	50.30 N	119.33 W
Falkland-Inseln → Falkland Islands (Islas Malvinas) □2	244	51.45 S	59.00 W
Falkland Islands □2	234		
	244	51.45 S	59.00 W
Falkland Rise	4	52.00 S	50.00 W
Falkland Sound	244	51.45 S	59.25 W
Falköping	26	58.10 N	13.31 E
Fall, Ont., Can.	202	44.59 N	76.22 W
Fall, Kans., U.S.	188	37.24 N	95.40 W

Symbols in the index entries represent the broad categories identified in the key at the right. Symbols with superior numbers (²) identify subcategories (see complete key on page I · 26).

Kartensymbole in dem Registerverzeichnis stellen die rechts in Schlüssel erklärten Kategorien dar. Symbole mit hochgestellten Ziffern (²) bezeichnen Unterabteilungen einer Kategorie (vgl. vollständiger Schlüssel auf Seite I · 26).

Los símbolos incluídos en el texto del índice representan las grandes categorias identificadas con la clave a la derecha. Los símbolos con numeros en su parte superior (²) identifican las subcategorías (véase la clave completa en la página I · 26).

Les symboles de l'index représentent les catégories indiquées dans la légende à droite. Les symboles suivis d'un indice (²) représentent des sous-catégories (voir légende complète à la page I · 26).

Os símbolos incluídos no texto do índice representam as grandes categorias identificadas com a chave à direita. Os símbolos com números em sua parte superior (²) identificam as subcategorias (veja-se a chave completa à página I · 26).

Mountain	Berg	Montaña	Montagne	Montanha
Mountains	Berge	Montañas	Montagnes	Montanhas
Pass	Pass	Paso	Col	Passo
Valley, Canyon	Tal, Cañon	Valle, Cañón	Vallée, Canyon	Vale, Canhão
Plain	Ebene	Llano	Plaine	Planície
Cape	Kap	Cabo	Cap	Cabo
Island	Insel	Isla	Île	Ilha
Islands	Inseln	Islas	Îles	Ilhas
Other Topographic Features	Andere Topographische Objekte	Otros Elementos Topográficos	Autres données topographiques	Outros Elementos Topográficos

≃ River	Fluss	Río	Rivière	Rio
≊ Canal	Kanal	Canal	Canal	Canal
L Waterfall, Rapids	Wasserfall, Stromschnellen	Cascada, Rápidos	Chute d'eau, Rapides	Cascata, Rápidos
U Strait	Meeresstrasse	Estrecho	Détroit	Estreito
C Bay, Gulf	Bucht, Golf	Bahía, Golfo	Baie, Golfe	Baía, Golfo
⊜ Lake, Lakes	See, Seen	Lago, Lagos	Lac, Lacs	Lago, Lagos
≛ Swamp	Sumpf	Pantano	Marais	Pântano
⊓ Ice Features, Glacier	Eis- und Gletscherformen	Accidentes Glaciales	Formes glaciaires	Acidentes Glaciares
☷ Other Hydrographic Features	Andere Hydrographische Objekte	Otros Elementos Hidrográficos	Autres données hydrographiques	Outros Elementos Hidrográficos
✦ Submarine Features	Untermeerische Objekte	Accidentes Submarinos	Formes de relief sous-marin	Acidentes Submarinos
□ Political Unit	Politische Einheit	Unidad Politica	Entité politique	Unidade Política
⊎ Cultural Institution	Kulturelle Institution	Institución Cultural	Institution culturelle	Instituição Cultural
⊥ Historical Site	Historische Stätte	Sitio Histórico	Site historique	Sítio Histórico
♠ Recreational Site	Erholungs- und Ferienort	Sitio de Recreo	Centre de loisirs	Sítio de Lazer
⊠ Airport	Flughafen	Aeropuerto	Aéroport	Aeroporto
■ Military Installation	Militäranlage	Instalación Militar	Installation militaire	Instalação Militar
◆ Miscellaneous	Verschiedenes	Misceláneo	Divers	Miscelânea

Ferryland 176 47.02 N 52.53 W
Ferry Point Park ♠ 266 40.49 N 73.50 W
Ferrysburg 206 43.05 N 86.11 W
Ferry Village 274a 43.58 N 78.57 W
Ferryville
→ Menzel Bourguiba 138 37.10 N 9.48 E
Feršampenuaz 76 53.32 N 59.51 E
Fertile 188 47.32 N 96.17 W
Ferzikovo 72 54.32 N 36.45 E
Fès 138 34.05 N 4.57 W
Feshi 142 6.07 S 18.10 E
Fessenden 188 47.39 N 99.38 W
Festenberg
→ Twardogóra 30 51.22 N 17.28 E
Festus 209 38.13 N 90.24 W
Fetcham 44 51.17 N 0.22 W
Fet Dom, Tanjung ≻ 154 1.53 S 129.43 E
Fété Bowé 140 14.56 N 13.30 W
Feteşti 38 44.23 N 27.50 E
Fethiye 120 36.37 N 29.07 E
Fethiye Körfezi C 120 36.40 N 29.00 E
Fetisovo 62 42.46 N 52.38 E
Fetlar I 28 60.37 N 0.52 W
Fetsund 26 59.56 N 11.10 E
Fetzara, Lac ◎ 138 36.52 N 7.22 E
Feucherolles 251 48.52 N 1.58 E
Feucht 30 49.22 N 11.13 E
Feuchtwangen 52 49.10 N 10.20 E
Feudingen 52 50.56 N 8.19 E
Feuerland
→ Tierra del Fuego, Isla Grande de I 244 54.00 S 69.00 W
Feuet 136 24.57 N 10.04 E
Feuilles, Baie aux C 166 58.55 N 69.20 W
Feuilles, Rivière aux ≃ 166 58.47 N 70.04 W
Feuquières-en-Vimeu 46 50.04 N 1.36 E
Feura Bush 200 42.35 N 73.53 W
Feurs 56 45.45 N 4.14 E
Fevik 26 58.23 N 8.42 E
Fevzipaşa 120 37.07 N 36.37 E
Fey 52 49.02 N 6.06 E
Feyen 52 49.44 N 6.38 E
Feyẕābād, Afg. 110 37.06 N 70.34 E
Feyẕābād, Īrān 118 35.01 N 58.46 E
Feyzin 56 45.40 N 4.51 E
Fez
→ Fès 138 34.05 N 4.57 W
Fezzan
→ Fazzān ⁻¹ 136 26.00 N 14.00 E
Ffestiniog 44 52.58 N 3.55 W
Fforest Fawr ⁻¹ 44 51.52 N 3.36 W
F. Gilbert Hills State Forest ♠ 273 42.03 N 71.17 W
Fiambalá 242 27.41 S 67.38 W
Fiamignano 60 42.16 N 13.07 E
Fian 140 10.23 N 2.29 W
Fianarantsoa 147b 21.26 S 47.05 E
Fianarantsoa □⁴ 147b 22.00 S 47.00 E
Fianga 136 9.55 N 15.09 E
Fiano 56 45.13 N 7.31 E
Fiantsonana 147b 19.09 S 46.12 E
Fiastra, Abbazia di ᵛ¹ 60 43.13 N 13.25 E
Fiavè 58 46.00 N 10.50 E
Ficarolo 58 44.57 N 11.26 E
Fiche 134 9.52 N 38.46 E
Fichtelberg ∧ 50 50.26 N 12.57 E
Fichtenau 254a 52.27 N 13.42 E
Ficksburg 148 28.57 S 27.50 E
Ficulle 60 42.50 N 12.04 E
Fidalgo ≃ 240 7.28 S 42.32 W
Fiddlers Hamlet 250 51.41 N 0.08 E
Fiddletown 226 38.30 N 120.46 W
Fiddyment Creek ≃ 268 41.36 N 88.03 W
Fidelity 209 39.09 N 90.10 W
Fidenza 58 44.52 N 10.03 E
Fidīmīn 132 29.23 N 30.46 E
Fiditi 140 7.45 N 3.53 E
Fidji
→ Fiji □¹ 165g 18.00 S 175.00 E
Fidler Lake ◎ 174 57.11 N 96.57 W
Fidschi
→ Fiji □¹ 165g 18.00 S 175.00 E
Fiè (Völs) 58 46.31 N 11.30 E
Fieberbrunn 58 47.29 N 12.33 E
Field 172 51.24 N 116.29 W
Fieldale 182 36.42 N 79.57 W
Field Museum ᵛ 268 41.53 N 87.37 W
Fieldon 209 39.07 N 90.30 W
Fieldsboro 275 40.08 N 74.44 W
Fieldstone 266 40.44 N 74.33 W
Fiemme, Val di ∨ 58 46.24 N 11.25 E
Fiener Bruch ☷ 50 52.19 N 12.10 E
Fienvillers 46 50.07 N 2.14 E
Fier 38 40.43 N 19.34 E
Fier ≃ 54 45.56 N 5.50 E
Fiera Campionaria ♠ 256b 45.28 N 9.09 E
Fiera di Primiero 58 46.10 N 11.49 E
Fierenana 147b 18.29 S 48.24 E
Fiery Creek ≃, Austl. 156 18.23 S 139.52 E
Fiery Creek ≃, Austl. 159 37.44 S 142.56 E
Fiesch 54 46.20 N 8.10 E
Fiesole 60 43.48 N 11.17 E
Fiesso d'Artico 58 45.24 N 12.02 E
Fiesso Umbertiano 58 44.56 N 11.36 E
Fife 214 47.14 N 122.22 W
Fife □⁴ 28 56.13 N 3.02 W
Fife Lake, Sask., Can. 174 49.12 N 105.43 W
Fife Lake, Mich., U.S. 180 44.35 N 85.21 W
Fife Lake ◎ 174 49.14 N 105.53 W
Fife Ness ≻ 28 56.17 N 2.36 W
Fifield 180 45.53 N 90.25 W
Fifteenmile Creek ≃, Oreg., U.S. 214 45.37 N 121.07 W
Fifteenmile Creek ≃, Wyo., U.S. 192 44.01 N 108.01 W
Fifth Cataract
→ Ash-Shallāl al-Khāmis ↳ 130 18.23 N 33.47 E
Fifth Depot Lake ◎ 202 44.36 N 76.52 W
Figeac 32 44.37 N 2.02 E
Figeholm 26 57.22 N 16.33 E
Fig Garden 226 36.48 N 119.47 W
Fighting Island I 271 42.13 N 83.07 W
Figline Valdarno 60 43.37 N 11.28 E
Figtree 144 20.24 S 28.21 E
Figueira
→ Governador Valadares, Bra. 245 18.51 S 41.56 W
Figueira, Bra. 246 23.15 S 46.03 W
Figueira, Bra. 277a 22.42 S 43.27 W
Figueira, Cachoeira ↳ 240 9.49 S 58.13 W
Figueira da Foz 34 40.09 N 8.52 W
Figueras 34 42.16 N 2.58 E
Figuig 138 32.10 N 1.15 W
Figuras, Serra das ⩕ 240 11.25 S 45.30 W
Fihaonana 147b 18.36 S 47.12 E
Fiherenana ≃ 147b 23.19 S 43.37 E
Fiji □¹ 14
165g 18.00 S 175.00 E
Fiji Islands II 14 18.00 S 175.00 E
Fijnaart 48 51.37 N 4.31 E
Fik 134 8.10 N 42.18 E
Fiktūriyā, Bi'r ᵀ⁴ 132 30.24 N 30.36 E
Filabusi 144 20.34 S 29.20 E
Filadélfia, Bra. 240 7.21 S 47.30 W
Filadelfia, C.R. 226 10.26 N 85.34 W
Filadelfia, It. 36 38.48 N 16.18 E
Filadelfia
→ Philadelphia, Pa., U.S. 198 39.57 N 75.07 W
Fil'akovo 30 48.17 N 19.51 E
Filatova Gora 66 57.40 N 28.10 E
Filchner Ice Shelf ⊠ 9 79.00 S 40.00 W
File Lake ◎ 174 54.53 N 100.20 W
Filettino 60 41.53 N 13.19 E
Filey 42 54.12 N 0.17 W
Filey Bay C 42 54.12 N 0.16 W
Fili ⁻⁸ 255b 55.45 N 37.31 E
Fili ⊥ 38 38.10 N 23.40 E
Filiaşi 38 44.33 N 23.31 E
Filiatrá 38 37.10 N 21.35 E
Filicudi, Isola I 36 38.35 N 14.34 E
Filimonki 72 55.33 N 37.21 E
Filimonovo 76 56.12 N 95.28 E
Filingué 140 14.21 N 3.19 E
Filipinas
→ Philippines □¹ 106 13.00 N 122.00 E
Filipinas, Mar de
→ Philippine Sea ᵀ² 14 20.00 N 135.00 E
Filippiás 38 41.00 N 24.16 E
Filippoi ⊥ 38 41.00 N 24.16 E
Filippo Reef ᵀ² 14 5.30 S 151.50 W
Filippovka 70 53.59 N 49.46 E
Filippovo 70 58.18 N 50.30 E
Filippovskoje, S.S.S.R. 72 56.06 N 38.37 E
Filippovskoje, S.S.S.R. 72 56.48 N 39.07 E
Filipstad 40 59.43 N 14.10 E
Filisola 224 17.50 N 94.19 W
Fillmore, Sask., Can. 174 49.50 N 103.25 W
Fillmore, Calif., U.S. 218 34.24 N 118.55 W
Fillmore, Ill., U.S. 209 39.07 N 89.17 W
Fillmore, N.Y., U.S. 200 42.28 N 78.07 W
Fillmore, Utah, U.S. 190 38.58 N 112.20 W
Fillmore Glen State Park ♠ 200 42.42 N 76.20 W
Filomeno Mata 224 20.12 N 97.42 W
Filonovskaja 70 50.34 N 42.46 E
Filottrano 60 43.26 N 13.21 E
Filskov 41 55.48 N 9.02 E
Filton 44 51.31 N 2.35 W
Filzbach 54 47.07 N 9.08 E
Fimi ≃ 142 3.01 S 16.58 E
Fina, Réserve de ⁻⁴ 140 12.50 N 8.30 W
Finaalspan 263d 26.17 S 28.15 E
Finale Emilia 58 44.50 N 11.17 E
Finale Ligure 56 44.10 N 8.20 E
Finca El Rey, Parque Nacional ♠ 242 25.00 S 64.40 W
Fincastle 182 37.30 N 79.53 W
Finch 196 45.11 N 75.07 W
Fincham 42 52.37 N 0.30 E
Finch Lake ◎ 174 56.34 N 100.57 W
Finchley ⁻⁸ 250 51.36 N 0.10 W
Findel, Aéroport de ⊠ 52 49.37 N 6.10 E
Finderne 266 40.34 N 74.35 W
Findlay, Ill., U.S. 209 39.31 N 88.45 W
Findlay, Ohio, U.S. 206 41.02 N 83.39 W
Findlay, Mount ∧ 172 50.04 N 116.28 W
Findlay Creek ≃ 172 50.20 N 115.52 W
Findley Lake 204 42.07 N 79.44 W
Findley Lake ◎ 204 42.06 N 79.43 W
Finedon 44 52.20 N 0.39 W
Finejevo 72 56.02 N 38.53 E
Finesville 200 40.36 N 75.10 W
Fingal, Austl. 156 41.39 S 147.58 E
Fingal, Ont., Can. 204 42.43 N 81.19 W
Fingal, N. Dak., U.S. 188 46.46 N 97.47 W
Finger Lake ◎ 174 53.09 N 93.30 W
Fingoè 144 15.12 S 31.50 E
Finike 120 36.18 N 30.09 E
Finike Körfezi C 120 36.17 N 30.16 E
Finistère □⁵ 32 48.20 N 4.00 W
Finisterre 186 25.59 N 103.15 W
Finisterre
→ Land's End ≻ 28 50.03 N 5.44 W
Finisterre, Cabo de ≻ 34 42.53 N 9.16 W
Finisterre Range ⩕ 154 5.50 S 146.05 E
Finja 41 56.10 N 13.41 E
Finjasjön ◎ 41 56.08 N 13.42 E
Finke 152 25.34 S 134.35 E
Finke ≃ 152 26.20 S 136.00 E
Finke, Mount ∧² 152 30.55 S 134.02 E
Finkenkrug 254a 52.34 N 13.03 E
Finkenwerder ⁻⁸ 48 53.31 N 9.52 E
Finksburg 198 39.30 N 76.54 W
Finland □¹ 18
24 64.00 N 26.00 E
Finland, Gulf of (Suomenlahti) (Finskij Zaliv) C 26 60.00 N 27.00 E
Finlande
→ Finland □¹ 24 64.00 N 26.00 E
Finlandia
→ Finland □¹ 24 64.00 N 26.00 E
Finlandia, Golfo de
→ Finland, Gulf of C 66 60.00 N 27.00 E
Finl'andskij Vokzal ⁻⁵ 255a 59.57 N 30.22 E
Finlas, Loch ◎ 42 55.15 N 4.25 W
Finlay ≃ 166 57.00 N 125.05 W
Finley, Austl. 156 35.39 S 145.35 E
Finley, N. Dak., U.S. 188 47.31 N 97.50 W
Finley Creek ≃ 184 36.58 N 93.22 W
Finleyville, Pa., U.S. 204 40.09 N 78.11 W
Finleyville, Pa., U.S. 204 40.15 N 80.00 W
Finleyville Airport ⊠ 269b 40.15 N 80.01 W
Finmoore 172 53.59 N 123.37 W
Finn ≃ 28 54.50 N 7.29 W
Finne ⁻¹ 50 51.13 N 11.19 E
Finnegan 172 51.07 N 112.05 W
Finnentrop 52 51.09 N 7.58 E
Finnerödja 40 58.56 N 14.26 E
Finney Creek ≃ 214 48.31 N 121.51 W
Finnhamn 40 59.28 N 18.50 E
Finnie Bay C 166 65.13 N 77.30 W
Finnis, Cape ≻ 152 33.38 S 134.51 E
Finnischer Meerbusen
→ Finland, Gulf of C 66 60.00 N 27.00 E
Finniss 158b 35.24 S 138.49 E
Finniss ≃ 158b 35.30 S 138.53 E
Finnland
→ Finland □¹ 24 64.00 N 26.00 E
Finnmark □⁶ 24 70.00 N 25.00 E
Finn Mountain ∧ 170 60.37 N 157.11 W
Finno ∧² 144 3.27 N 41.32 E
Finnskogen ⁻³ 26 60.40 N 12.40 E
Finnsnes 24 69.14 N 17.59 E
Finocchio ⁻⁸ 257a 41.53 N 12.41 E
Finow 50 52.50 N 13.43 E
Finowfurt 50 52.51 N 13.41 E
Finowkanal ≅ 50 52.51 N 13.24 E
Fins, Fr. 46 50.02 N 3.03 E
Fins, 'Umān 118 22.56 N 59.13 E
Finsbury 263d 26.11 S 27.56 E
Finschhafen 154 6.35 S 147.50 E
Finse 26 60.36 N 7.30 E
Finskij Zaliv
→ Finland, Gulf of C 66 60.00 N 27.00 E
Finspång 40 58.43 N 15.47 E
Finsta 40 59.44 N 18.30 E
Finsteraarhorn ∧ 54 46.32 N 8.08 E
Finsterwalde 50 51.38 N 13.42 E
Finsterwolde 48 53.12 N 7.04 E
Fintel 48 53.10 N 9.40 E
Finvoy 42 55.00 N 6.30 W
Finzeg ≃ 58 46.12 N 11.26 E
Fiorano Modenese 58 44.32 N 10.49 E
Fiordland National Park ♠ 162 45.30 S 167.20 E
Fiorenzuola d'Arda 56 44.56 N 9.55 E
Fiorenzuola di Focara 60 43.57 N 12.48 E
Fiorito ⁻⁸ 278 34.42 S 58.27 W
Fiq 122 32.47 N 35.42 E
Firat
→ Euphrates ≃ 118 31.00 N 47.25 E
Firavitoba 236 5.40 N 73.00 W
Fircrest 214 47.14 N 122.31 W
Fire ≃ 180 48.52 N 83.21 W
Firebaugh 216 36.52 N 120.27 W
Firebrick 208 38.41 N 83.03 W
Fire Island Inlet C 266 40.38 N 73.16 W
Fire Island National Seashore ♠ 200 40.38 N 73.08 W
Fire Island Pines 266 40.40 N 73.04 W
Fire Islands II 266 40.40 N 73.11 W
Firenze (Florence) 58
60 43.46 N 11.15 E
Firenze □⁴ 60 43.50 N 11.20 E
Firenzuola 60 44.07 N 11.23 E
Firesteel Creek ≃ 188 43.43 N 97.58 W
Firgrove 252 53.37 N 2.08 W
Firmat 242 33.27 S 61.29 W
Firminópolis 245 16.40 S 50.19 W
Firminy 56 45.23 N 4.18 E
Firovo 66 57.29 N 33.40 E
Fīrozābād 114 27.09 N 78.25 E
Fīrozpur 113 30.55 N 74.36 E
Fīrozpur Jhirka 114 27.48 N 76.57 E
Firsanovka 255b 55.57 N 37.15 E
Firsovo 78 52.20 N 118.06 E
First Broad ≃ 182 35.11 N 81.37 W
First Cataract ↳ 130 24.01 N 32.52 E
First Cliff ⁻⁴ 273 42.12 N 70.43 W
First Connecticut Lake ◎ 196 45.05 N 71.15 W
First Herring Brook ≃ 273 42.11 N 70.45 W
First King 152 31.49 S 124.21 E
First Watchung Mountain ∧ 266 40.55 N 74.10 W
Firth 188 40.33 N 96.37 W
Firth ≃ 170 69.32 N 139.22 W
Fir'uza 118 37.56 N 58.04 E
Fīrūzābād 118 28.50 N 52.36 E
Fīrūz Bahram 257d 35.38 N 51.15 E
Fīrūz Kūh 118 35.45 N 52.47 E
Fischa ≃ 254b 48.04 N 16.35 E
Fischbach 52 49.44 N 7.23 E
Fischbachau 58 47.43 N 11.57 E
Fischbacher Alpen ⩕ 30 47.28 N 15.30 E
Fischbeck, B.R.D. 48 52.09 N 9.17 E
Fischbeck, D.D.R. 50 52.32 N 12.01 E
Fischeln ⁻⁸ 253 51.18 N 6.35 E
Fischen 54 47.28 N 10.16 E
Fischhausen
→ Primorsk 66 54.44 N 20.01 E
Fischland ⁻² 50 54.22 N 12.25 E
Fish ≃, Austl. 160 33.29 S 149.37 E
Fish ≃, Namibia 146 28.07 S 17.45 E
Fish ≃, Ala., U.S. 184 30.25 N 87.50 W
Fishbourne 44 50.44 N 1.12 W
Fish Brook ≃, Mass., U.S. 273 42.42 N 71.13 W
Fish Brook ≃, Mass., U.S. 273 42.38 N 70.58 W
Fish Camp 216 37.29 N 119.38 W
Fish Canyon ∨ 220 34.11 N 117.55 W
Fish Creek ≃, Ont., Can. 202 43.13 N 81.13 W
Fish Creek ≃, U.S. 206 41.28 N 84.45 W
Fish Creek ≃, Mont., U.S. 192 46.17 N 109.13 W
Fish Creek ≃, N.Y., U.S. 202 43.12 N 75.43 W
Fish Creek ≃, Oreg., U.S. 214 45.09 N 122.09 W
Fish Creek, East Branch ≃ 202 43.16 N 75.38 W
Fish Creek, West Branch ≃ 202 43.16 N 75.38 W
Fish Creek Mountain ∧ 214 45.05 N 122.08 W
Fisheating Creek ≃ 210 26.57 N 81.07 W
Fisher, Austl. 152 30.33 S 130.58 E
Fisher, Ark., U.S. 184 35.30 N 90.58 W
Fisher, Ill., U.S. 206 40.19 N 88.21 W
Fisher, La., U.S. 184 31.30 N 93.28 W
Fisher, Pa., U.S. 204 41.16 N 79.15 W
Fisher ≃, Man., Can. 174 51.26 N 97.18 W
Fisher ≃, Mont., U.S. 182 48.22 N 115.19 W
Fisher Bay C, Man., Can. 174 51.30 N 97.16 W
Fisher Bay C, Mich., U.S. 271 42.36 N 82.39 W
Fisher Branch 174 51.05 N 97.37 W
Fisher Channel ⊔ 172 52.10 N 127.42 W
Fisher Glacier ⊠ 9 73.15 S 66.00 E
Fisher Heights 269b 40.10 N 79.54 W
Fishermans Island I 198 37.06 N 75.58 W
Fisherman's Wharf ᵛ 272 37.48 N 122.25 W
Fishermens Bend Airfield ⊠ 264b 37.50 S 144.55 E
Fisher Peak ∧ 182 36.33 N 80.50 W
Fisher River Indian Reserve ⁻⁴ 174 51.26 N 97.20 W
Fishers, Ind., U.S. 208 39.57 N 86.01 W
Fishers, N.Y., U.S. 200 43.00 N 77.28 W
Fishers Island I 197 41.16 N 72.02 W
Fishers Peak ∧ 186 37.06 N 104.28 W
Fisher Strait ⊔ 166 63.15 N 83.30 W
Fishertown 200 40.08 N 78.35 W
Fisherville, Ont., Can. 265b 43.47 N 79.28 W
Fisherville, Pa., U.S. 275 40.01 N 75.45 W
Fishguard 44 51.59 N 4.59 W
Fishhook 209 39.48 N 90.53 W
Fish House 200 43.08 N 74.09 W
Fishing Bay C 198 38.18 N 76.01 W
Fishing Creek 198 38.20 N 76.14 W
Fishing Creek ≃, Ky., U.S. 182 37.06 N 84.41 W
Fishing Creek ≃, N.C., U.S. 182 35.57 N 77.31 W
Fishing Creek ≃, Pa., U.S. 200 41.07 N 77.29 W
Fishing Creek ≃, S.C., U.S. 182 34.36 N 80.54 W
Fishing Islands II 202 44.45 N 81.20 W
Fishing Lake ◎, Man., Can. 174 52.07 N 95.25 W
Fishing Lake ◎, Sask., Can. 174 51.50 N 103.32 W
Fishkill 200 41.32 N 73.53 W
Fishkill Creek ≃ 200 41.29 N 73.59 W
Fish Lake 206 41.34 N 86.33 W
Fish Lake ◎, Ont., Can. 202 44.06 N 77.11 W
Fish Lake ◎, Mich., U.S. 206 42.03 N 85.52 W
Fish Lake ◎, Wash., U.S. 214 47.50 N 120.42 W
Fishmoor Reservoir ◎ 252 53.44 N 2.28 W
Fish Point ≻ 204 43.43 N 82.40 W
Fishpool 252 53.35 N 2.17 W
Fish River 156 17.55 S 137.45 E
Fishs Eddy 200 41.58 N 75.10 W
Fisk 184 36.47 N 90.12 W
Fiskårdhon 38 38.27 N 20.35 E
Fiskdale 197 42.07 N 72.07 W
Fiskebäckskil 26 58.15 N 11.27 E
Fismes 46 49.18 N 3.41 E
Fišt, Gora ∧ 84 43.58 N 39.54 E
Fitchburg 197 42.35 N 71.48 W
Fitchville, Conn., U.S. 197 41.34 N 72.09 W
Fitchville, Ohio, U.S. 204 41.06 N 82.29 W
Fitiuta 164y 14.13 S 169.27 W
Fitri, Lac ◎ 136 12.50 N 17.28 E
Fittja 40 59.15 N 17.52 E
Fittleworth 44 50.58 N 0.35 W
Fitu 134 5.05 N 40.42 E
Fitzcarrald 238 11.45 S 72.25 W
Fitzgerald 182 31.43 N 83.15 W
Fitz Henry 269b 40.10 N 79.45 W
Fitz Hugh Sound ⊔ 172 51.40 N 127.57 W
Fitzmaurice ≃ 154 14.50 S 129.44 E
Fitz Roy, Arg. 244 47.02 S 67.15 W
Fitzroy, Austl. 264b 37.48 S 144.59 E
Fitzroy ≃, Austl. 152 17.31 S 123.35 E
Fitzroy ≃, Austl. 156 23.32 S 150.52 E
Fitzroy, Monte (Cerro Chaltel) ∧ 244 49.17 S 73.05 W
Fitzroy Crossing 152 18.11 S 125.35 E
Fitzwilliam 197 42.47 N 72.08 W
Fitzwilliam Island I 180 45.30 N 81.45 W
Fiuggi 60 41.48 N 13.13 E
Fiumalbo 58 44.11 N 10.39 E
Fiume
→ Rijeka 36 45.20 N 14.27 E
Fiumesino 60 43.38 N 13.22 E
Fiume Veneto 58 45.56 N 12.44 E
Fiumicino 36 41.46 N 12.14 E
Fiumicino ⁻⁸ 60 41.46 N 12.14 E
Five Corners 273 42.01 N 71.07 W
Five Dock 264a 33.52 S 151.08 E
Five Islands Harbour C 230c 17.06 N 61.54 W
Five Islands 176 45.25 N 64.02 W
Fivemile ≃ 266 41.03 N 73.27 W
Fivemile Creek ≃, N.Y., U.S. 200 42.22 N 77.22 W
Fivemile Creek ≃, Oreg., U.S. 214 45.36 N 121.05 W
Fivemile Creek ≃, Wyo., U.S. 192 43.14 N 108.12 W
Fivemile Point 200 42.06 N 75.48 W
Five Points, Calif., U.S. 216 36.26 N 120.06 W
Five Points, Ind., U.S. 208 39.35 N 86.20 W
Five Points, N. Mex., U.S. 190 35.04 N 106.41 W
Five Points, Ohio, U.S. 208 39.41 N 83.12 W
Five Points, Pa., U.S. 204 40.34 N 80.15 W
Five Points, Pa., U.S. 275 39.50 N 75.42 W
Fivizzano 58 44.14 N 10.08 E
Fiwila Mission 144 13.58 S 29.36 E
Fixin 54 47.15 N 4.58 E
Fix-Saint-Geneys 56 45.08 N 3.40 E
Fizi 144 4.18 S 28.57 E
Fizuli 74 39.37 N 47.08 E
Fjællebroen 41 55.03 N 10.24 E
Fjærlandsfjorden C² 26 61.17 N 6.40 E
Fjällåsen 24 67.29 N 20.10 E
Fjällbacka 26 58.36 N 11.17 E
Fjällsjöälven ≃ 26 63.29 N 16.50 E
Fjärdhundra 40 59.47 N 16.56 E
Fjärdhundra □⁹ 40 59.47 N 16.55 E
Fjenneslev 41 55.26 N 11.40 E
Fjerritslev 26 57.05 N 9.16 E
Fjugesta 40 59.10 N 14.52 E
Fkih-ben-Salah 138 32.32 N 6.40 W
Flachsmeer 48 53.07 N 7.28 E
Flacksta 40 59.23 N 16.27 E
Fladså ≃ 41 55.19 N 8.54 E
Fladungen 52 50.31 N 10.08 E
Flag Creek ≃ 268 41.43 N 87.55 W
Flagler 188 39.18 N 103.04 W
Flagler Beach 182 29.29 N 81.07 W
Flagstaff, S. Afr. 148 31.05 S 29.29 E
Flagstaff, Ariz., U.S. 190 35.12 N 111.39 W
Flagstaff Lake ◎ 178 45.10 N 70.15 W
Flagtown 266 40.31 N 74.41 W
Flaken-See ◎ 254a 52.25 N 13.46 E
Flåm 26 60.50 N 7.07 E
Flambeau ≃ 180 45.18 N 91.15 W
Flambeau, South Fork ≃ 180 45.39 N 90.48 W
Flamborough Head ≻ 42 54.07 N 0.04 W
Fläming ⁻¹ 50 52.00 N 12.30 E
Flaming Gorge National Recreation Area ♠ 190 41.30 N 109.30 W
Flaming Gorge Reservoir ◎¹ 190 41.15 N 109.30 W
Flamingo 210 25.09 N 80.56 W
Flamingo, Teluk C 154 5.33 S 138.00 E
Flammersfeld 52 50.38 N 7.32 E
Flanagan 206 40.53 N 88.52 W
Flanagan ≃ 174 52.50 N 93.28 W
Flanagan Passage ⊔ 230m 18.18 N 64.39 W
Flanders, Ont., Can. 180 48.44 N 92.05 W
Flanders, N.J., U.S. 266 40.51 N 74.42 W
Flanders, N.Y., U.S. 197 40.49 N 72.36 W
Flanders (Flandre) (Vlaanderen) □⁹ 46 51.00 N 3.00 E
Flanders Airport ⊠ 266 40.50 N 74.41 W
Flandes 236 4.18 N 74.49 W
Flandorf 254b 48.21 N 16.23 E
Flandre
→ Flanders □⁹ 46 51.00 N 3.00 E
Flandreau 188 44.03 N 96.36 W
Fläner ◎ 26 57.02 N 14.06 E
Flasher 188 46.27 N 101.14 W
Fläsjön ◎ 26 64.06 N 15.51 E
Flat, Alaska, U.S. 170 62.27 N 158.01 W
Flat, Tex., U.S. 212 31.19 N 97.38 W
Flat ≃, N.W. Ter., Can. 170 61.33 N 125.18 W
Flat ≃, Mich., U.S. 180 42.56 N 85.20 W
Flat ≃, N.C., U.S. 182 36.05 N 78.49 W
Flat Bay 176 48.24 N 58.36 W
Flatbush ⁻⁸ 266 40.39 N 73.56 W
Flat Creek ≃, Ky., U.S. 208 38.17 N 83.48 W
Flat Creek ≃, Mo., U.S. 184 36.45 N 93.31 W
Flat Creek ≃, Mont., U.S. 192 47.43 N 109.50 W
Flat Creek ≃, N.J., U.S. 266 40.27 N 74.10 W
Flat Creek ≃, Va., U.S. 182 37.24 N 77.53 W
Flat Creek Reservoir ◎¹ 212 32.14 N 95.45 W
Flatey 24a 65.19 N 23.07 W
Flateyri 24a 65.59 N 23.42 W
Flathead ≃ 192 47.22 N 114.47 W
Flathead, North Fork ≃ 192 48.28 N 114.04 W
Flathead, South Fork ≃ 192 48.23 N 114.04 W
Flathead Indian Reservation ⁻⁴ 192 47.30 N 114.25 W
Flathead Lake ◎ 192 47.52 N 114.08 W
Flat Holm I 44 51.23 N 3.08 W
Flat Island I 147c 19.52 S 57.40 E
Flat Lake ◎ 172 54.39 N 112.55 W
Flat Lick 182 36.50 N 83.46 W
Flatonia 212 29.47 N 97.06 W
Flatow, D.D.R. 254a 52.44 N 12.57 E
Flatow
→ Złotów, Pol. 30 53.22 N 17.02 E
Flat River, P.E.I., Can. 176 46.01 N 62.52 W
Flat River, Mo., U.S. 184 37.51 N 90.31 W
Flat River Reservoir ◎¹ 197 41.42 N 71.37 W
Flat Rock, Ala., U.S. 182 34.46 N 85.42 W
Flat Rock, Ill., U.S. 184 38.54 N 87.40 W
Flat Rock, Ind., U.S. 208 39.22 N 85.50 W
Flat Rock, Mich., U.S. 206 42.05 N 83.18 W
Flat Rock, Ohio, U.S. 204 41.14 N 82.52 W
Flatrock ≃ 208 39.12 N 85.56 W
Flatrock Creek ≃ 206 41.10 N 84.27 W
Flatrock Lake ◎ 174 55.37 N 100.47 W
Flatruet ⩕² 26 62.45 N 12.50 E
Flats 212 32.50 N 95.53 W
Flattery, Cape ≻, Austl. 156 14.58 S 145.21 E
Flattery, Cape ≻, Wash., U.S. 214 48.23 N 124.43 W
Flatts 230a 32.19 N 64.44 W
Flatwillow Creek ≃ 192 46.56 N 107.55 W
Flatwood 184 32.09 N 87.31 W
Flatwoods 178 38.31 N 82.43 W
Flaugherty Run ≃ 269b 40.33 N 80.13 W
Flaunden 250 51.42 N 0.32 W
Flavigny-sur-Moselle 54 48.34 N 6.11 E
Flavigny-sur-Ozerain 54 47.30 N 4.32 E
Flavy-le-Martel 46 49.43 N 3.12 E
Flawil 54 47.24 N 9.12 E
Flaxcombe 174 51.29 N 109.36 W
Flaxman Island I 170 70.13 N 146.00 W
Flax Pond ◎, Mass., U.S. 273 42.29 N 70.57 W
Flax Pond ◎, N.Y., U.S. 266 40.58 N 73.08 W
Flaxton 188 48.54 N 102.24 W
Flaxville 188 48.49 N 105.10 W
Flechas Point ≻ 106 10.22 N 119.34 E
Flechtingen 50 52.20 N 11.14 E
Fleckeby 41 54.29 N 9.41 E
Flecken Zechlin 50 53.09 N 12.46 E
Fleesensee ◎ 50 53.30 N 12.29 E
Fleet 44 51.16 N 0.50 W
Fleet Point ≻ 266 40.40 N 73.20 W
Fleets Bay C 198 37.40 N 76.19 W
Fleetville 200 41.36 N 75.43 W
Fleetwing Estates 275 40.07 N 74.51 W
Fleetwood, Eng., U.K. 42 53.56 N 3.01 W
Fleetwood, Pa., U.S. 198 40.27 N 75.49 W
Flehe ⁻⁸ 253 51.12 N 6.47 E
Flehingen 52 49.05 N 8.46 E
Fleischhacker Zoo ♠ 272 37.44 N 122.30 W
Fleischmanns 200 42.09 N 74.32 W
Flekkefjord 26 58.17 N 6.41 E
Fleming, Colo., U.S. 188 40.41 N 102.50 W
Fleming, Pa., U.S. 204 40.55 N 77.52 W
Fleming □⁶ 208 38.21 N 83.42 W
Fleming Creek ≃, Ont., Can. 204 42.26 N 81.43 W
Fleming Creek ≃, Ky., U.S. 208 38.22 N 83.57 W
Fleming Creek ≃, Mich., U.S. 271 42.16 N 83.40 W
Flemingsburg 208 38.25 N 83.44 W
Flemington, N.J., U.S. 200 40.31 N 74.52 W
Flemington, Pa., U.S. 200 41.07 N 77.28 W
Flemington Racecourse ♠ 264b 37.47 S 144.55 E
Flemish Cap ⁻³ 16 48.00 N 45.00 W
Flemsdorf 50 53.02 N 14.10 E
Flen 40 59.04 N 16.35 E
Flensburg 41 54.47 N 9.26 E
Flensburger Förde C 41 54.49 N 9.45 E
Fleres (Boden) 58 46.58 N 11.21 E
Flers 32 48.45 N 0.34 W
Flers-sur-Noye 46 49.44 N 2.15 E
Flesherton 202 44.16 N 80.33 W
Flesko, Tanjung ≻ 102 0.29 N 124.30 E
Fletcher, Ont., Can. 204 42.18 N 82.18 W
Fletcher, N.C., U.S. 182 35.26 N 82.30 W
Fletcher, Ohio, U.S. 208 40.09 N 84.07 W
Fletcher, Okla., U.S. 186 34.52 N 98.17 W
Fletcher Islands II 9 72.40 S 94.10 W
Fletcher Moss Museum ᵛ 252 53.25 N 2.14 W
Fletcher Pond ◎¹ 180 44.58 N 83.52 W
Fletchers Creek ≃ 265b 43.43 N 79.42 W
Fleurance 32 43.50 N 0.40 E
Fleur-de-Lys 176 50.07 N 56.08 W
Fleurier 54 46.54 N 6.35 E
Fleurus 52 50.29 N 4.33 E
Fleurville 54 46.27 N 4.53 E
Fleury-les-Aubrais 46 47.56 N 1.55 E
Fleury-Mérogis 251 48.38 N 2.22 E
Fleury-sur-Andelle 46 49.22 N 1.22 E
Fleuth ≃ 253 51.32 N 6.26 E
Fleuve □⁴ 140 16.00 N 14.30 W
Flexanville 251 48.51 N 1.44 E
Flexenpass)(54 47.09 N 10.10 E
Fley ⁻⁸ 253 51.23 N 7.30 E
Flieden 52 50.25 N 9.33 E
Flierich 253 51.35 N 7.48 E
Flight Locks ᵛ³ 274a 43.08 N 79.12 W
Flimby 42 54.41 N 3.31 W
Flims 54 46.50 N 9.17 E
Flinders ≃ 156 17.36 S 140.36 E
Flinders Bay C 152 34.23 S 115.19 E
Flinders Chase ♠ 152 35.54 S 136.40 E
Flinders Island I 156 40.00 S 148.00 E
Flinders Passage ⊔ 161a 27.49 S 152.49 E
Flinders Peak ∧² 159 37.51 S 144.24 E
Flinders Range ⩕ 14 31.25 S 138.45 E
Flinders Reefs ᵀ² 156 17.37 S 148.31 E
Flinders Street Station ⁻⁵ 264b 37.49 S 144.58 E
Flinesjön ◎ 40 60.23 N 16.06 E
Flines-lèz-Râches 46 50.25 N 3.11 E
Flin Flon 174 54.46 N 101.53 W
Flingern ⁻⁸ 253 51.14 N 6.49 E
Flins-sur-Seine 251 48.58 N 1.52 E
Flint, Wales, U.K. 42 53.15 N 3.07 W
Flint, Mich., U.S. 206 43.01 N 83.41 W
Flint, Tex., U.S. 212 32.12 N 95.21 W
Flint I 14 11.26 S 151.48 W
Flint ≃, Ga., U.S. 182 30.52 N 84.38 W
Flint ≃, Mich., U.S. 180 43.21 N 84.03 W
Flint, South Branch ≃ 206 43.10 N 83.23 W
Flint Castle ⊥ 252 53.16 N 3.07 W
Flint Creek ≃, Ala., U.S. 184 34.30 N 86.57 W
Flint Creek ≃, Mont., U.S. 192 46.39 N 113.08 W
Flint Creek ≃, N.Y., U.S. 200 42.57 N 77.03 W
Flint Creek Range ⩕ 192 46.20 N 113.05 W
Flint Hill 209 38.52 N 90.52 W
Flint Hills ∧² 188 38.50 N 100.00 W
Flint Lake ◎, N.W. Ter., Can. 166 69.10 N 74.20 W
Flint Lake ◎, Ind., U.S. 206 41.31 N 87.03 W
Flinton, Austl. 156 27.54 S 149.34 E
Flinton, Pa., U.S. 200 40.43 N 78.31 W
Flint Peak ∧ 270 34.10 N 118.12 W
Flint Pond ◎ 273 42.40 N 71.26 W
Flintrännan ⊔ 41 55.34 N 12.50 E
Flintridge 218 34.11 N 118.11 W
Flintville 184 34.59 N 86.25 W
Flipper Point ≻ 164a 19.18 N 166.35 E
Flirey 52 48.53 N 5.50 E
Flirsch 54 47.09 N 10.24 E
Flisa 26 60.34 N 12.06 E
Flitwick 44 52.00 N 0.29 W
Flixecourt 46 50.01 N 2.05 E
Flize 52 49.42 N 4.46 E
Flobecq (Vloesberg) 46 50.44 N 3.44 E
Floby 26 58.08 N 13.20 E
Floda, Sve. 26 57.48 N 12.22 E
Floda, Sve. 40 59.04 N 16.21 E
Flodden 42 55.38 N 2.10 W
Flodden Field Battlesite (1513) ⊥ 42 55.38 N 2.13 W
Flogny 46 47.57 N 3.52 E
Flöha 50 50.51 N 13.04 E
Flöha ≃ 50 50.51 N 13.04 E
Floing 52 49.43 N 4.56 E
Flomaton 184 31.00 N 87.16 W
Flomborn 52 49.41 N 8.09 E
Flomot 186 34.14 N 100.59 W
Floodwood 180 46.55 N 92.56 W
Flora, Ill., U.S. 184 38.40 N 88.29 W
Flora, Ind., U.S. 206 40.33 N 86.31 W
Flora, Miss., U.S. 184 32.33 N 90.19 W
Florac 32 44.19 N 3.36 E
Florala 184 31.00 N 86.20 W
Floral City 210 28.45 N 82.18 W
Floral Park, Mont., U.S. 192 45.57 N 112.26 W
Floral Park, N.Y., U.S. 266 40.43 N 73.42 W
Florange 52 49.20 N 6.07 E
Florânia 240 6.08 S 36.49 W
Flora Vista 190 36.48 N 108.02 W
Flor de Chile 242 25.19 S 69.50 W
Flore, Piton ∧ 231f 13.58 N 60.57 W
Floreffe 52 50.26 N 4.45 E
Florence
→ Firenze, It. 60 43.46 N 11.15 E
Florence, Ala., U.S. 184 34.49 N 87.40 W
Florence, Ariz., U.S. 190 33.02 N 111.23 W
Florence, Calif., U.S. 218 33.58 N 118.15 W
Florence, Colo., U.S. 190 38.23 N 105.08 W
Florence, Kans., U.S. 188 38.15 N 96.56 W
Florence, Ky., U.S. 208 39.00 N 84.38 W
Florence, N.J., U.S. 275 40.07 N 74.49 W
Florence, N.J., U.S. 275 39.44 N 74.55 W
Florence, Oreg., U.S. 192 43.58 N 124.07 W
Florence, Pa., U.S. 204 40.26 N 80.26 W
Florence, S.C., U.S. 182 34.12 N 79.46 W
Florence, Tex., U.S. 212 30.51 N 97.48 W
Florence, Wis., U.S. 180 45.56 N 88.07 W
Florencia, Col. 236 1.36 N 75.36 W
Florencia
→ Firenze, It. 60 43.46 N 11.15 E
Florencio Sánchez 248 33.53 S 57.24 W
Florencio Varela 248 34.49 S 58.17 W
Florencio Varela □⁵ 278 34.52 S 58.15 W
Florennes 52 50.15 N 4.37 E
Florentia 263d 26.16 S 28.08 E
Florenville 52 49.42 N 5.18 E
Florenz
→ Firenze 60 43.46 N 11.15 E
Flores, Bra. 240 7.51 S 37.59 W
Flores, Perú 276d 12.01 S 77.01 W
Flores, Ur. 248 33.35 S 57.00 W
Flores □⁵ 248 33.48 S 56.50 W
Flores ≃ 278 34.38 S 58.28 W
Flores ⁻⁸ 278 34.38 S 58.28 W
Flores I, Indon. 105b 8.30 S 121.00 E
Flores I, Port. 138a 39.26 N 31.13 W
Flores, Cachoeira das ↳ 245 14.19 S 53.32 W
Flores, Laut (Flores Sea) ᵀ² 102 8.00 S 120.00 E
Flores, Rio das ≃ 246 22.05 S 43.34 W
Flores, Selat ⊔ 105b 8.25 S 122.55 E
Flores da Cunha 242 29.02 S 51.11 W
Flores Island I 172 49.20 N 126.10 W
Flores Sea
→ Flores, Laut ᵀ² 102 8.00 S 120.00 E
Floresta 240 8.36 S 38.34 W
Floresta ⁻⁸ 278 34.38 S 58.29 W
Floresta Azul 245 14.51 S 39.41 W
Florestina 245 18.29 S 48.01 W
Florešty 68 47.53 N 28.17 E
Floresville 186 29.08 N 98.10 W
Florham Park 200 40.47 N 74.23 W
Floriano, Bra. 240 6.47 S 43.01 W
Floriano, Bra. 246 22.27 S 44.18 W
Floriano Peixoto, Bra. 238 9.03 S 67.24 W
Floriano Peixoto, Bra. 240 9.32 S 35.36 W
Florianópolis 242 27.35 S 48.34 W
Florida, Col. 236 3.21 N 76.15 W
Florida, Cuba 230p 21.32 N 78.14 W
Florida, Hond. 226 15.01 N 88.50 W
Florida, P.R. 230m 18.22 N 66.34 W
Florida, P.R. 230m 18.14 N 65.47 W
Florida, S. Afr. 263d 26.11 S 27.55 E
Florida, Ind., U.S. 208 40.10 N 85.42 W
Florida, N.Y., U.S. 200 41.20 N 74.22 W
Florida, Ohio, U.S. 206 41.20 N 84.12 W
Florida, Ur. 248 34.06 S 56.13 W
Florida ⁻⁸ 278 34.31 S 58.30 W
Florida □³ 168
182 28.00 N 82.00 W
Florida □⁵ 190 37.03 N 107.52 W
Florida, Cape ≻ 210 25.40 N 80.09 W
Florida, Cerro la ∧ 224 23.13 N 99.15 W
Florida, Straits of ⊔ 228 25.00 N 79.45 W
Florida Bay C 210 25.00 N 80.45 W
Floridablanca 236 7.04 N 73.06 W
Florida City 210 25.27 N 80.29 W
Florida Island I 165e 9.05 S 160.15 E
Florida Keys II 210 24.45 N 81.00 W
Florida Ridge 210 27.35 N 80.23 W
Florida State Indian Reservation ⁻⁴ 210 26.10 N 80.50 W
Floridia 36 37.04 N 15.10 E
Florido ≃ 222 27.43 N 105.10 W
Floridsdorf ⁻⁸ 254b 48.16 N 16.24 E
Floridsdorfer Brücke ⁻⁵ 254b 48.14 N 16.23 E
Florien 184 31.27 N 93.27 W
Florin 216 38.30 N 121.24 W
Flórina 38 40.47 N 21.24 E
Floriśbad 148 28.46 S 26.06 E
Florissant 209 38.48 N 90.20 W
Floriston 216 39.24 N 120.01 W
Florø 26 61.36 N 5.00 E
Flörsheim 52 50.01 N 8.26 E
Florvåg 26 60.25 N 5.14 E
Flosaille 56 45.39 N 5.18 E
Flossach ≃, B.R.D. 54 48.24 N 10.25 E
Flossach ≃, B.R.D. 58 48.13 N 10.30 E
Flossmoor 268 41.33 N 87.40 W
Flotantes, Jardínes ♠ 276a 19.16 N 99.06 W
Flöthbach ≃ 253 51.17 N 6.26 E
Flotten Lake ◎ 174 54.38 N 108.30 W
Flourtown 275 40.07 N 75.13 W
Flowerfield 268 41.52 N 88.02 W
Flower Hill 266 40.49 N 73.41 W
Flower Mound 212 33.02 N 97.04 W
Flower's Cove 176 51.18 N 56.44 W
Flowery Branch 182 34.11 N 83.55 W
Floyd, N. Mex., U.S. 186 34.13 N 103.35 W
Floyd, Tex., U.S. 212 33.09 N 96.15 W
Floyd, Va., U.S. 182 36.55 N 80.19 W
Floyd □⁶ 208 38.18 N 85.49 W
Floyd ≃ 188 42.29 N 96.23 W
Floydada 186 33.59 N 101.20 W
Floyds Fork ≃ 184 38.00 N 85.41 W
Fluchthorn ∧ 54 46.53 N 10.13 E
Flüela Pass)(54 46.45 N 9.57 E
Flüelen 54 46.54 N 8.38 E
Fluessen ◎ 52 52.57 N 5.32 E
Flühli 54 46.53 N 8.01 E
Flumen ≃ 34 41.43 N 0.09 W
Flumendosa ≃ 36 39.26 N 9.38 E
Flumeri 60 41.05 N 15.09 E
Flumet 56 45.49 N 6.31 E
Fluminimaggiore 36 39.26 N 8.30 E
Flums 54 47.05 N 9.20 E
Flüren 253 51.41 N 6.33 E
Flushing
→ Vlissingen, Ned. 48 51.26 N 3.35 E
Flushing, Mich., U.S. 206 43.04 N 83.51 W
Flushing, Ohio, U.S. 204 40.09 N 81.04 W
Flushing ⁻⁸ 266 40.45 N 73.49 W
Flushing Airport ⊠ 266 40.47 N 73.50 W
Flushing Bay C 266 40.47 N 73.51 W
Flushing Meadow-Corona Park ♠ 266 40.45 N 73.51 W
Fluvanna, N.Y., U.S. 204 42.07 N 79.17 W
Fluvanna, Tex., U.S. 186 32.53 N 101.09 W
Fluvia ≃ 34 42.12 N 3.07 E
Fly ≃ 154 8.30 S 143.41 E
Fly Creek 200 42.43 N 74.59 W
Fly Creek ≃ 192 45.59 N 107.59 W
Flyinge 41 55.45 N 13.21 E
Flying Fish Cove 102 10.25 S 105.43 E
Flying "w" Ranch Airport ⊠ 275 39.56 N 74.48 W
Flynn 212 31.09 N 96.08 W
Foam Lake 174 51.39 N 103.33 W
Fobaochang 97 28.47 N 106.05 E
Fobbing 250 51.32 N 0.29 E
Fobello 56 45.53 N 8.10 E
Foča, Jugo. 38 43.31 N 18.46 E
Foça, Tür. 120 38.39 N 26.46 E
Focene ⁻⁸ 257a 41.48 N 12.14 E
Fochville 148 26.30 S 27.30 E
Fockbek 41 54.18 N 9.36 E
Focşani 38 45.41 N 27.11 E
Fodda, Oued ≃ 34 35.14 N 1.28 E
Fodé 142 5.29 N 23.18 E
Fodécontea 140 10.50 N 14.22 W
Fodingshan ∧ 92 27.08 N 108.02 E
F'odorovka, S.S.S.R. 68 47.33 N 36.33 E

Symbols in the index entries represent the broad categories identified in the key at the right. Symbols with superior numbers (⩕²) identify subcategories (see complete key on page I · 26).

Kartensymbole in dem Registerverzeichnis stellen die rechts in Schlüssel erklärten Kategorien dar. Symbole mit hochgestellten Ziffern (⩕²) bezeichnen Unterabteilungen einer Kategorie (vgl. vollständiger Schlüssel auf Seite I · 26).

Los símbolos incluídos en el texto del índice representan las grandes categorías identificadas con la clave a la derecha. Los símbolos con numeros en su parte superior (⩕²) identifican las subcategorías (véase la clave completa en la página I · 26).

Les symboles de l'index représentent les catégories indiquées dans la légende à droite. Les symboles suivis d'un indice (⩕²) représentent des sous-catégories (voir légende complète à la page I · 26).

Os símbolos incluídos no texto do índice representam as grandes categorias identificadas com a chave à direita. Os símbolos com números em sua parte superior (⩕²) identificam as subcategorias (veja-se a chave completa à página I · 26).

∧ Mountain	Berg	Montaña	Montagne	Montanha
⩕ Mountains	Berge	Montañas	Montagnes	Montanhas
)(Pass	Pass	Paso	Col	Passo
∨ Valley, Canyon	Tal, Cañon	Valle, Cañón	Vallée, Canyon	Vale, Canhão
☷ Plain	Ebene	Llano	Plaine	Planície
≻ Cape	Kap	Cabo	Cap	Cabo
I Island	Insel	Isla	Île	Ilha
II Islands	Inseln	Islas	Îles	Ilhas
⁻ Other Topographic Features	Andere Topographische Objekte	Otros Elementos Topográficos	Autres données topographiques	Outros Elementos Topográficos

ESPAÑOL

Nombre	Página	Lat.°′	Long.°′ W=Oeste
F'odorovka, S.S.S.R.	68	49.23 N	35.07 E
F'odorovka, S.S.S.R.	70	52.21 N	52.55 E
F'odorovka, S.S.S.R.	70	53.28 N	49.38 E
F'odorovka, S.S.S.R.	70	51.09 N	51.59 E
F'odorovka, S.S.S.R.	72	56.15 N	37.14 E
F'odorovka, S.S.S.R.	73	47.20 N	38.23 E
F'odorovka, S.S.S.R.	76	53.22 N	76.18 E
F'odorovka, S.S.S.R.	76	53.11 N	55.11 E
F'odorovka, S.S.S.R.	76	56.05 N	78.49 E
F'odorovka, S.S.S.R.	76	53.38 N	62.42 E
F'odorovskoje, S.S.S.R.	72	56.44 N	36.58 E
F'odorovskoje, S.S.S.R.	72	56.08 N	38.04 E
F'odorovskoje, S.S.S.R.	72	56.07 N	38.52 E
F'odorovskoje, S.S.S.R.	72	56.19 N	37.40 E
Foëcy	46	47.10 N	2.10 E
Foeni	38	45.30 N	20.53 E
Fogang (Shijiao)	90	23.52 N	113.32 E
Fogdön ≻[1]	40	59.25 N	16.52 E
Fogelevo	75	42.03 N	69.32 E
Fogelsville	198	40.35 N	75.38 W
Foggaret el Arab	138	27.03 N	2.59 E
Foggaret ez Zoua	138	27.20 N	3.00 E
Foggia	60	41.27 N	15.34 E
Foggia □[4]	60	41.30 N	15.30 E
Foggy Island Bay C	170	70.15 N	147.30 W
Foglia ≃	60	43.55 N	12.54 E
Foglianise	60	41.10 N	14.40 E
Fogliano, Lago di C	60	41.24 N	12.54 E
Foglizzo	56	45.16 N	7.49 E
Fogo	176	49.43 N	54.17 W
Fogo I	140a	14.55 N	24.25 W
Fogo, Cape ≻	176	49.39 N	54.00 W
Fogo Island I	176	49.40 N	54.13 W
Fogolawa	140	12.19 N	8.41 E
Fogueteiro	256c	38.37 N	9.07 W
Fohnsdorf	30	47.13 N	14.41 E
Föhr I	30	54.43 N	8.30 E
Foia ∧	34	37.19 N	8.36 W
Foiano della Chiana	60	43.15 N	11.49 E
Foiano di Val Fortore	60	41.21 N	14.59 E
Foins, Lac aux @	180	47.05 N	78.11 W
Foivre ≃	52	49.30 N	4.32 E
Foix	32	42.58 N	1.36 E
Foix ⤙[1]	32	43.00 N	1.40 E
Fojnica	36	43.58 N	17.54 E
Foki	70	56.42 N	54.21 E
Fokino	66	53.27 N	34.24 E
Fokku	140	11.40 N	4.31 E
Folakara	147b	18.20 S	45.02 E
Folamasi	94	41.56 N	121.27 E
Folarskardhuten ∧	26	60.37 N	7.45 E
Folcroft	275	39.54 N	75.17 W
Folda C[2]	24	67.36 N	14.50 E
Foldingbro	41	55.26 N	9.01 E
Folembray	46	49.33 N	3.17 E
Foley, Ala., U.S.	184	30.25 N	87.41 W
Foley, Minn., U.S.	180	45.40 N	93.55 W
Foley, Mo., U.S.	209	39.03 N	90.44 W
Foleyet	180	48.16 N	82.30 W
Foley Island I	166	68.35 N	75.10 W
Folgares	142	14.54 S	15.08 E
Folgaria	58	45.55 N	11.10 E
Folgefonni ⊼	26	60.00 N	6.20 E
Folger Hill ∧[2]	197	41.17 N	70.01 W
Foligno	60	42.57 N	12.42 E
Folk	209	38.26 N	92.06 W
Folkärna	40	60.09 N	16.19 E
Folkestone	44	51.05 N	1.11 E
Folkingham	44	52.54 N	0.24 W
Folkston	182	30.50 N	82.01 W
Folkwangmuseum ʊ	253	51.27 N	7.00 E
Follafoss	26	63.59 N	11.06 E
Follainville-Dennemont	251	49.01 N	1.43 E
Follansbee	204	40.20 N	80.36 W
Folldal	26	62.08 N	10.03 E
Folle Anse, Pointe ≻	231o	15.57 N	61.20 W
Follebu	26	61.14 N	10.17 E
Follets Island I	212	29.02 N	95.10 W
Follett	186	36.26 N	100.08 W
Follina	58	45.57 N	12.07 E
Föllinge	26	63.40 N	14.37 E
Follonica	60	42.55 N	10.45 E
Follonica, Golfo di C	60	42.54 N	10.43 E
Folly Branch ≃	274b	38.56 N	76.49 W
Folmhusen	48	53.10 N	7.28 E
Folschviller	52	49.04 N	6.41 E
Folsom, Calif., U.S.	216	38.41 N	121.15 W
Folsom, N.J., U.S.	198	39.38 N	74.51 W
Folsom, Pa., U.S.	275	39.54 N	75.19 W
Folsom Lake @[1]	216	38.43 N	121.08 W
Folsom Lake State Recreation Area ▲	216	38.46 N	121.06 W
Fomboni	147a	12.16 S	43.45 E
Fomento, Cuba	230p	22.06 N	79.43 W
Fomento, Ur.	248	34.26 S	57.14 W
Fomin	70	46.58 N	43.38 E
Fominiči	66	54.07 N	34.41 E
Fominki	70	55.57 N	42.22 E
Fominskaja	24	61.17 N	48.40 E
Fominskoje, S.S.S.R.	66	58.59 N	39.06 E
Fominskoje, S.S.S.R.	66	59.43 N	42.05 E
Fomkino	70	54.25 N	50.30 E
Foncine-le-Bas	54	46.38 N	6.03 E
Fonda, Iowa, U.S.	188	42.35 N	94.51 W
Fonda, N.Y., U.S.	200	42.57 N	74.22 W
Fond d'Or Bay C	231f	13.56 N	60.54 W
Fond du Lac, Sask., Can.	166	59.19 N	107.10 W
Fond du Lac, Wis., U.S.	180	43.47 N	88.27 W
Fond du Lac ≃	166	59.17 N	106.00 W
Fond du Lac Indian Reservation ⤙[4]	180	46.45 N	92.37 W
Fondi	60	41.21 N	13.25 E
Fondi, Lago di C	60	41.19 N	13.20 E
Fondo	58	46.26 N	11.08 E
Fondouk el Aouareb	36	35.34 N	9.46 E
Fongfong	130	12.56 N	23.14 E
Fonni	36	40.07 N	9.15 E
Fonsagrada	34	43.08 N	7.04 W
Fonseca	236	10.54 N	72.51 W
Fonseca, Golfo de C	226	13.10 N	87.40 W
Fons-outre-Gardon	56	43.54 N	4.11 E
Font ≃	42	55.10 N	1.44 W
Fontaine, Fr.	54	47.40 N	7.00 E
Fontaine, Fr.	56	45.11 N	5.40 E
Fontainebleau, Fr.	46	48.24 N	2.42 E
Fontainebleau, S. Afr.	263d	26.07 S	27.59 E
Fontaine-Française	54	47.31 N	5.22 E
Fontaine-le-Dun	46	49.49 N	0.51 E
Fontaine-lès-Dijon	54	47.21 N	5.01 E
Fontaine-lès-Grès	46	48.25 N	3.54 E
Fontaine-lès-Luxeuil	54	47.51 N	6.20 E
Fontaines	54	46.51 N	4.46 E
Fontaines-sur-Saône	56	45.50 N	4.51 E
Fontan	56	44.00 N	7.33 E
Fontana, Arg.	242	27.25 S	59.02 W
Fontana, Calif., U.S.	218	34.06 N	117.26 W
Fontana, Wis., U.S.	206	42.33 N	88.35 W
Fontana, Lago @	244	44.56 S	71.30 W
Fontanafredda	58	45.58 N	12.34 E
Fontana Lake @[1]	182	35.26 N	83.38 W
Fontanarosa	60	41.01 N	15.01 E
Fontanelas	256c	38.51 N	9.26 W
Fontanelice	60	44.15 N	11.33 E
Fontanella	58	45.27 N	9.48 E
Fontanellato	58	44.53 N	10.10 E
Fontanelle	188	41.17 N	94.34 W
Fontanetto Po	56	45.12 N	8.11 E
Fontanigorda	56	44.33 N	9.19 E
Fontarabie, Lac @	176	51.10 N	66.25 W
Fontas ≃	166	58.20 N	121.50 W
Fonte, Bra.	277b	23.25 S	46.21 W

FRANÇAIS

Nom	Page	Lat.°′	Long.°′ W=Ouest
Fonte, It.	58	45.47 N	11.53 E
Fonte, It.	60	41.46 N	13.13 E
Fonte Avellana, Monastero di ʊ[1]	60	43.29 N	12.45 E
Fonte Blanda	60	42.34 N	11.10 E
Fonte Boa	236	2.32 S	66.01 W
Fonte Colombo, Convento di ʊ[1]	60	42.23 N	12.50 E
Fontenay, Abbaye de ʊ[1]	46	47.39 N	4.24 E
Fontenay-aux-Roses	251	48.47 N	2.17 E
Fontenay-en-Parisis	251	49.03 N	2.27 E
Fontenay-le-Comte	32	46.28 N	0.48 W
Fontenay-le-Fleury	251	48.49 N	2.03 E
Fontenay-lès-Briis	251	48.37 N	2.09 E
Fontenay-le-Vicomte	251	48.33 N	2.24 E
Fontenay-Saint-Père	251	49.02 N	1.45 E
Fontenay-sous-Bois	251	48.51 N	2.29 E
Fontenay-Trésigny	46	48.42 N	2.52 E
Fontenelle	176	48.52 N	64.52 W
Fontenelle Creek ≃	190	42.05 N	110.08 W
Fontenelle Reservoir @[1]	190	42.05 N	110.06 W
Fontespina	60	43.17 N	13.45 E
Fontevivo	58	44.51 N	10.10 E
Font Hill Manor	274b	39.17 N	76.52 W
Fontibón	236	4.40 N	74.09 W
Fonti del Clitunno ⍑[4]	60	42.49 N	12.46 E
Fontoy	52	49.21 N	6.00 E
Fontur ≻	24a	66.23 N	14.30 W
Fontvieille	56	43.43 N	4.43 E
Fonzaso	58	46.01 N	11.48 E
Foochow → Fuzhou	90	26.06 N	119.17 E
Foot Creek ≃	188	45.26 N	98.29 W
Foothill Farms	216	38.40 N	121.21 W
Foothills	172	53.04 N	116.48 W
Footprint Lake @	174	55.47 N	98.53 W
Footscray	159	37.48 S	144.54 E
Footville	206	42.40 N	89.12 W
Foping	92	33.22 N	108.19 E
Foppolo	58	46.03 N	9.45 E
Fora, Ponta de ≻	277a	22.57 S	43.07 W
Foraker, Mount ∧	170	62.56 N	151.26 W
Forbach, B.R.D.	52	48.41 N	8.21 E
Forbach, Fr.	52	49.11 N	6.54 E
Forbes	156	33.23 S	148.01 E
Forbes, Lac @	196	46.31 N	74.12 W
Forbes, Mount ∧	172	51.52 N	116.56 W
Forbes Field ▲	269b	40.27 N	79.57 W
Forbesganj	114	26.18 N	87.15 E
Forbes Reef	148	26.10 S	31.05 E
Forbes Road	204	40.21 N	79.32 W
Forbestown	216	39.31 N	121.16 W
Forbidden City ▲	261a	39.55 N	116.23 E
Forcados	140	5.22 N	5.24 E
Forcados ≃[1]	140	5.25 N	5.19 E
Forcalquier	56	43.58 N	5.47 E
Force	204	41.15 N	78.30 W
Forchheim, B.R.D.	52	49.43 N	11.04 E
Forchheim, D.D.R.	50	50.43 N	13.16 E
Forclaz, Col de la)(	54	46.04 N	7.00 E
Ford	188	37.38 N	99.45 W
Ford □[6]	206	40.27 N	88.06 W
Ford ≃	180	45.40 N	87.09 W
Ford, Cape ≻	154	13.26 S	129.52 E
Ford City, Calif., U.S.	216	35.09 N	119.27 W
Ford City, Pa., U.S.	204	40.46 N	79.32 W
Ford City ⤙[9]	268	41.46 N	87.44 W
Ford Cliff	204	40.45 N	79.32 W
Ford Dam ⤙[6]	271	42.13 N	83.33 W
Ford Dry Lake @	194	33.38 N	115.00 W
Førde, Nor.	26	59.36 N	5.29 E
Førde, Nor.	26	61.27 N	5.52 E
Førdefjorden C[2]	26	61.28 N	5.39 E
Forden	44	52.36 N	3.08 W
Förderstedt	50	51.54 N	11.38 E
Fordham University ʊ[2]	266	40.51 N	73.53 W
Fordingbridge	44	50.56 N	1.47 W
Ford Lake @	271	42.13 N	83.36 W
Ford Mansion ⊥	266	40.48 N	74.28 W
Ford Motor Company (River Rouge Plant) ʊ[3]	271	42.18 N	83.10 W
Ford Museum ʊ	271	42.18 N	83.14 W
Ford Ranges ∧∧	9	77.00 S	145.00 W
Fords	266	40.32 N	74.19 W
Fords Bridge	156	29.45 S	145.26 E
Fordsburg ⤙[8]	263d	26.13 S	28.02 E
Fords Prairie	214	46.47 N	123.05 W
Fordsville	184	37.38 N	86.43 W
Fordville	188	48.13 N	97.47 W
Fordyce	184	33.49 N	92.25 W
Fordyce Lake @[1]	216	39.23 N	120.28 W
Foré	140	13.08 N	10.42 W
Forécariah	140	9.26 N	13.06 W
Forécariah □[4]	140	9.30 N	13.15 W
Forel, Mont ∧	166	67.00 N	37.00 W
Foreland Point ≻	44	51.16 N	3.47 W
Foreman	184	33.43 N	94.24 W
Foremost	174	49.29 N	111.25 W
Forepaugh Airport ⊠	269a	41.21 N	81.30 W
Foresman	206	40.52 N	87.18 W
Forest, Bel.	46	50.48 N	4.19 E
Forest, Ont., Can.	180	43.06 N	82.00 W
Forest, Ind., U.S.	206	40.22 N	86.20 W
Forest, Miss., U.S.	184	32.22 N	89.28 W
Forest, Ohio, U.S.	206	40.48 N	83.31 W
Forest □[6]	204	41.29 N	79.27 W
Forest ≃	188	48.21 N	97.09 W
Forest, Middle Branch ≃	188	48.13 N	97.48 W
Forest Acres	182	34.01 N	80.58 W
Forestburg	172	52.35 N	112.04 W
Forest City, Iowa, U.S.	180	43.16 N	93.39 W
Forest City, N.C., U.S.	182	35.20 N	81.52 W
Forest City, Pa., U.S.	200	41.39 N	75.28 W
Forest Creek ≃	216	38.23 N	120.28 W
Forest Gate ⤙[8]	250	51.33 N	0.02 E
Forest Glade	212	31.39 N	96.31 W
Forest Grove, B.C., Can.	172	51.46 N	121.06 W
Forest Grove, Oreg., U.S.	214	45.31 N	123.07 W
Forest Grove, Pa., U.S.	269b	40.18 N	75.04 W
Forest Heights	274c	38.49 N	77.00 W
Forest Hill, Austl.	161a	27.35 S	152.22 E
Forest Hill, Austl.	161b	35.09 S	147.27 E
Forest Hill, Austl.	264b	37.50 S	145.11 E
Foresthill, Calif., U.S.	216	39.01 N	120.49 W
Forest Hill, Md., U.S.	198	39.35 N	76.23 W
Forest Hill, Tex., U.S.	212	32.40 N	97.16 W
Forest Hill ⤙[8]	265b	43.42 N	79.24 W
Forest Hill Park ▲	269a	41.31 N	81.35 W
Forest Hill Parkway ▲	269a	41.33 N	81.36 W
Forest Hills	269b	40.26 N	79.52 W
Forest Hills ⤙[8]	266	40.42 N	73.51 W
Forest Home	184	31.52 N	86.50 W
Forestier Peninsula ≻[1]	156	42.57 S	147.55 E
Forest Lake, Ill., U.S.	206	42.13 N	88.03 W
Forest Lake, Minn., U.S.	180	45.17 N	92.59 W
Forest Lake @, Ill., U.S.	268	42.13 N	88.03 W
Forest Lake @, Mass., U.S.	273	42.43 N	71.15 W
Forest Lawn Memorial Park ⤙	270	34.09 N	118.19 W
Forest Park, Ga., U.S.	182	33.37 N	84.22 W
Forest Park, Ill., U.S.	268	41.53 N	87.50 W
Forest Park, Ohio, U.S.	208	39.16 N	84.34 W
Forest Park ⤙[8]	274b	39.19 N	76.41 W
Forest Park ▲	266	40.42 N	73.51 W
Forest River	268	42.05 N	87.54 W
Forest Row	44	51.06 N	0.02 E

PORTUGUÊS

Nome	Página	Lat.°′	Long.°′ W=Oeste
Forest View	268	41.49 N	87.47 W
Forestville, Austl.	264a	33.46 S	151.13 E
Forestville, Qué., Can.	176	48.45 N	69.06 W
Forestville, Md., U.S.	274c	38.50 N	76.52 W
Forestville, N.Y., U.S.	204	42.26 N	79.10 W
Forestville, Pa., U.S.	204	41.06 N	80.00 W
Forestville, Wis., U.S.	180	44.41 N	87.29 W
Forêt l'Orient, Lac de la @[1]	46	48.17 N	4.20 E
Forêt-Noire → Schwarzwald ∧∧	54	48.00 N	8.15 E
Forez, Monts du ∧∧	32	45.35 N	3.48 E
Forfar	28	56.38 N	2.54 W
Forfry	251	49.03 N	2.51 E
Forgan	186	36.54 N	100.32 W
Forgaria	58	46.13 N	12.58 E
Forge Acres	274b	39.25 N	76.27 W
Forges-les-Bains	251	48.38 N	2.06 E
Forges-les-Eaux	46	49.37 N	1.33 E
Forget, Pointe ≻	265a	45.27 N	73.58 W
Forge Village	197	42.35 N	71.29 W
Forggensee @	54	47.36 N	10.44 E
Forillon, Parc National (Forillon National Park) ▲	176	48.55 N	64.25 W
Forino	60	40.52 N	14.44 E
Foristell	209	38.49 N	90.57 W
Fork	198	39.28 N	76.27 W
Forked Creek ≃	206	41.19 N	88.09 W
Forked Deer ≃	184	35.56 N	89.35 W
Forked Deer, Middle Fork ≃	184	36.01 N	89.13 W
Forked Deer, North Fork ≃	184	36.00 N	89.26 W
Forked Deer, South Fork ≃	184	36.00 N	89.26 W
Forked River	198	39.51 N	74.12 W
Forks	214	47.57 N	124.23 W
Forkston	200	41.31 N	76.07 W
Forksville	200	41.29 N	76.36 W
Forleti, Arroyo ≃	278	34.35 S	58.41 W
Forlì	60	44.13 N	12.03 E
Forlì □[4]	58	44.05 N	12.02 E
Forlimpopoli	60	44.11 N	12.07 E
Forman	188	46.07 N	97.38 W
Formazza	54	46.22 N	8.26 E
Formby	42	53.34 N	3.05 W
Formby Hills ∧∧[2]	252	53.34 N	3.06 W
Formby Point ≻	42	53.33 N	3.06 W
Formentera I	34	38.42 N	1.28 E
Formentor, Cabo de ≻	34	39.58 N	3.12 E
Formerie	46	49.39 N	1.44 E
Former Imperial Palace ʊ	260	35.01 N	135.46 E
Formia	60	41.15 N	13.37 E
Formiga	245	20.27 S	45.25 W
Formiga ≃	246	22.18 S	42.52 W
Formigine	58	44.34 N	10.51 E
Formignana	58	44.50 N	11.51 E
Forminha, Ribeirão ≃	245	18.01 S	53.38 W
Formosa, Arg.	242	26.11 S	58.11 W
Formosa, Bra.	245	15.32 S	47.20 W
Formosa □[4]	242	25.00 S	60.00 W
Formosa → Taiwan I, As.	90	23.30 N	121.00 E
Formosa I, T'aiwan	90	23.30 N	121.00 E
Formosa, Serra ∧∧[1]	240	12.00 S	55.00 W
Formosa Bay C	144	2.45 S	40.20 E
Formosa Strait U	90	24.00 N	119.00 E
Formoso ≃, Bra.	240	10.34 S	49.56 W
Formoso ≃, Bra.	245	17.25 S	44.57 W
Formoso ≃, Bra.	245	13.26 S	44.14 W
Formoso ≃, Bra.	245	18.25 S	52.28 W
Formoso ≃, Bra.	246	21.20 S	43.10 W
Forney	212	32.45 N	96.28 W
Forni Avoltri	58	46.35 N	12.46 E
Forni di sopra	58	46.25 N	12.35 E
Forni di sotto	58	46.23 N	12.40 E
Forni di Val d'Astico	58	45.51 N	11.22 E
Forno	58	46.21 N	11.37 E
Forno Alpi Graie	56	45.22 N	7.13 E
Forno di Zoldo	58	46.21 N	12.11 E
Fornosovo	66	59.35 N	30.35 E
Fornovo di Taro	58	44.42 N	10.06 E
Foro Romano ⊥	257a	41.54 N	12.29 E
Føroyar → Faeroe Islands □[2]	22	62.00 N	7.00 W
Forpost	76	56.47 N	72.10 E
Forres, Arg.	242	27.53 S	63.58 W
Forres, Scot., U.K.	28	57.37 N	3.38 W
Forrest, Austl.	152	30.51 S	128.06 E
Forrest, Ill., U.S.	206	40.45 N	88.25 W
Forrest ≃	154	15.18 S	128.04 E
Forrest, Mount ∧	152	24.48 S	127.45 E
Forrestal Research Center ʊ[3]	266	40.21 N	74.37 W
Forrest City	184	35.01 N	90.47 W
Forrester Island I	170	54.48 N	133.32 W
Forrest Lakes @	152	29.12 S	128.46 E
Forreston, Ill., U.S.	180	42.08 N	89.35 W
Forreston, Tex., U.S.	212	32.16 N	96.52 W
Fors	40	60.13 N	16.18 E
Forsan	186	32.07 N	101.22 W
Forsayth	156	18.35 S	143.36 E
Forsbacka	40	60.37 N	16.53 E
Forsby	26	60.30 N	25.56 E
Forserum	26	57.42 N	14.28 E
Forshaga	40	59.32 N	13.28 E
Forsmark	40	60.22 N	18.09 E
Forssa	26	60.49 N	23.38 E
Forst	50	51.44 N	14.39 E
Förste	48	51.44 N	10.10 E
Forster	156	32.11 S	152.31 E
Forstwald ⤙[8]	253	51.18 N	6.30 E
Forsyth, Ga., U.S.	182	33.02 N	83.56 W
Forsyth, Ill., U.S.	209	39.56 N	88.57 W
Forsyth, Mo., U.S.	184	36.41 N	93.06 W
Forsyth, Mont., U.S.	192	46.16 N	106.41 W
Forsyth Island I	154	16.50 S	139.06 E
Fort ⤙[8]	262c	18.56 N	72.50 E
Fort Abbās	113	29.12 N	72.52 E
Fort Adams	184	31.05 N	91.33 W
Fort Albany	166	52.15 N	81.37 W
Fort Alexander Indian Reserve ⤙[4]	174	50.27 N	96.15 W
Fortaleza	240	3.43 S	38.30 W
Fortaleza de Santa Teresa ▲	242	33.59 S	53.32 W
Fortaleza do Ituxi	238	7.29 S	66.20 W
Fortaleza dos Nogueiras	240	6.54 S	46.09 W
Fort Allen ■	230m	18.01 N	66.30 W
Fort Amherst National Historic Park ▲	176	46.15 N	63.06 W
Fort Ancient State Memorial ⊥	208	39.24 N	84.06 W
Fort Anne National Historic Park ▲	176	44.44 N	65.26 W
Fort Apache Indian Reservation ⤙[4]	190	34.01 N	110.28 W
Fort-Archambault → Sarh	136	9.09 N	18.23 E
Fort Assiniboine	172	54.20 N	114.46 W
Fort Atkinson	206	42.56 N	88.50 W
Fort Augusta ⊥	200	40.53 N	76.46 W
Fort Augustus	28	57.09 N	4.41 W
Fort Baker ■	272	37.50 N	122.29 W
Fort Battleford National Historic Park ▲	174	52.42 N	108.15 W
Fort Bayard → Zhanjiang	92	21.16 N	110.28 E
Fort Beaufort	148	32.46 S	26.40 E
Fort Beauséjour National Historic Park ▲	176	45.53 N	64.10 W
Fort Belknap Agency	192	48.30 N	108.46 W

Fort Belknap Indian Reservation ⤙[4]	192	48.16 N	108.38 W
Fort Belvoir ■	198	38.44 N	77.10 W
Fort Bend □[6]	212	29.32 N	95.47 W
Fort Benjamin Harrison ■	208	39.52 N	86.01 W
Fort Benning ■	182	32.22 N	84.50 W
Fort Benton	192	47.49 N	110.40 W
Fort Berthold Indian Reservation ⤙[4]	188	47.40 N	102.25 W
Fort Bidwell	194	41.52 N	120.09 W
Fort Bragg	194	39.26 N	123.48 W
Fort Bragg ■	182	35.09 N	78.59 W
Fort Branch	184	38.15 N	87.35 W
Fort Bridger	190	41.19 N	110.23 W
Fort Campbell ■	184	36.39 N	87.29 W
Fort Canby State Park ▲	214	46.17 N	124.04 W
Fort Canning ■	261c	1.18 N	103.51 E
Fort-Carnot	147b	21.53 S	47.28 E
Fort Caroline National Memorial ⊥	182	30.20 N	81.30 W
Fort Carson ■	190	38.44 N	104.48 W
Fort Casey Historical State Park ▲	214	48.10 N	122.40 W
Fort Chambly National Historic Park ▲	196	45.27 N	73.17 W
Fort-Chimo	166	58.06 N	68.25 W
Fort Chipewyan	166	58.42 N	111.08 W
Fort Churchill Historic State Monument ⊥	216	39.18 N	119.17 W
Fort Clatsop National Memorial ⊥	214	46.08 N	123.54 W
Fort Cobb	186	35.06 N	98.26 W
Fort Cobb Reservoir @[1]	186	35.12 N	98.29 W
Fort Collins	190	40.35 N	105.05 W
Fort Columbia Historical State Park ▲	214	46.15 N	123.56 W
Fort Constantine	156	20.28 S	140.37 E
Fort-Coulonge	178	45.51 N	76.44 W
Fort Covington	178	44.59 N	74.30 W
Fort-Crampel	142	6.59 N	19.11 E
Fort Custer State Recreation Area ▲	206	42.18 N	85.20 W
Fort-Dauphin	147b	25.02 S	47.00 E
Fort Davis, Ala., U.S.	184	32.15 N	85.43 W
Fort Davis, Tex., U.S.	186	30.35 N	103.54 W
Fort Davis National Historic Site ⊥	186	30.33 N	103.53 W
Fort de Douaumont ⊥	52	49.13 N	5.25 E
Fort Defiance	190	35.45 N	109.05 W
Fort-de-France	230e	14.36 N	61.05 W
Fort-de-France, Baie de C	230e	14.34 N	61.04 W
Fort-de-France-Lamentin, Aérodrome de ⊠	230e	14.35 N	61.00 W
Fort Deposit	184	31.59 N	86.35 W
Fort de Possel	142	5.01 N	19.15 E
Fort Detrick ■	198	39.27 N	77.26 W
Fort de Vaux ⊥	52	49.12 N	5.28 E
Fort Devens ■	197	42.32 N	71.37 W
Fort Dix ■	198	40.00 N	74.33 W
Fort Dodge	180	42.30 N	94.10 W
Fort Donelson National Military Park ▲	184	36.26 N	87.49 W
Fort Duchesne	190	40.17 N	109.52 W
Fort Dupont Park ▲	274c	38.53 N	76.57 W
Forteau	176	51.28 N	56.58 W
Forte dei Marmi	58	43.57 N	10.10 E
Forte de Magoito	256c	38.52 N	9.27 W
Fort Edward	200	43.16 N	73.35 W
Forte República	142	7.45 S	16.23 E
Fort Erie	202	42.54 N	78.56 W
Fort Erie Race Track ▲	274a	42.55 N	78.56 W
Fortescue ≃	152	21.00 S	116.06 E
Fort Eustis ■	198	37.09 N	76.35 W
Fortezza (Franzensfeste)	58	46.47 N	11.37 E
Fort Fairfield	176	46.46 N	67.50 W
Fort Fitzgerald	166	59.53 N	111.37 W
Fort Flatters → Zaouia el Kahla	138	28.09 N	6.43 E
Fort Foote Village	274c	38.46 N	77.01 W
Fort-Foureau	136	12.05 N	15.02 E
Fort Frances	180	48.36 N	93.24 W
Fort Franklin	170	65.11 N	123.46 W
Fort Fraser	172	54.04 N	124.33 W
Fort Frederica National Monument ▲	182	31.12 N	81.26 W
Fort Gaines	182	31.37 N	85.03 W
Fort Gardel	138	24.52 N	8.21 E
Fort Garland	190	37.26 N	105.26 W
Fort Gay	178	38.07 N	82.36 W
Fort-George	166	53.50 N	79.00 W
Fort George ⊥	274a	43.15 N	79.04 W
Fort George G. Meade ■	198	39.05 N	76.50 W
Fort Gibson	186	35.48 N	95.15 W
Fort Gibson Lake @[1]	186	36.00 N	95.18 W
Fort Good Hope	170	66.15 N	128.38 W
Fort Gordon ■	182	33.25 N	82.11 W
Fort-Gourand → Fdérik	138	22.41 N	12.43 W
Fort Green	210	27.36 N	81.57 W
Forth	42	55.47 N	3.41 W
Forth ≃	42	56.04 N	3.42 W
Forth, Carse of V	42	56.08 N	4.05 W
Forth, Firth of C[1]	42	56.05 N	2.55 W
Förtha	52	50.56 N	10.14 E
Fort Hall, Kenya	144	0.43 S	37.09 E
Fort Hall, Idaho, U.S.	192	43.02 N	112.26 W
Fort Hall Indian Reservation ⤙[4]	192	43.10 N	112.10 W
Fort Hamilton ■	266	40.37 N	74.02 W
Forth Bridge ⤙[5]	42	56.00 N	3.25 W
Fort Hertz → Putao	92	27.21 N	97.24 E
Fort Hill → Chitipa	144	9.43 S	33.16 E
Fort Hill State Memorial ⊥	208	39.07 N	83.25 W
Fort Hood ■	212	31.08 N	97.46 W
Fort Howard	198	39.12 N	76.27 W
Fort Huachuca ■	190	31.33 N	110.20 W
Fort Hunter	200	42.57 N	74.17 W
Fortierville	196	46.29 N	72.02 W
Fortin, Lac @	176	50.50 N	67.46 W
Fortín Ayacucho	238	19.58 S	59.47 W
Fortín Coronel Eugenio Garay	238	20.31 S	62.08 W
Fortín de las Flores	224	18.54 N	97.00 W
Fortín Florida	238	20.45 S	59.17 W
Fortín Garrapatal	238	21.27 S	61.30 W
Fortín Ingavi	238	19.55 S	60.47 W
Fortín Paredes (Coroneles Sánchez)	238	19.20 S	59.58 W
Fortín Teniente Montanía	242	22.04 S	59.57 W
Fortín Uno	242	38.51 S	65.17 W
Fort Jackson ■	182	34.01 N	80.57 W
Fort Jameson → Chipata	144	13.39 S	32.40 E
Fort Jefferson National Monument ▲	210	24.37 N	82.54 W
Fort Jennings	206	40.54 N	84.18 W
Fort Jeudy, Point of ≻	231k	12.00 N	61.42 W
Fort Johnson	200	42.57 N	74.14 W
Fort Johnston → Mangoche	144	14.28 S	35.16 E

Fort Jones	194	41.36 N	122.51 W
Fort Kent	176	47.15 N	68.36 W
Fort Klamath	192	42.42 N	122.00 W
Fort Knox ■	184	37.54 N	85.57 W
Fort Lallemand	138	31.13 N	6.17 E
Fort-Lamy → Ndjamena	136	12.07 N	15.03 E
Fort Langley	214	49.10 N	122.35 W
Fort Langley National Historic Park ▲	214	49.10 N	122.35 W
Fort Laramie	190	42.13 N	104.31 W
Fort Laramie National Historic Site ▲	188	42.09 N	104.41 W
Fort Lauderdale	210	26.07 N	80.08 W
Fort Lauderdale-Hollywood International Airport ⊠	210	26.04 N	80.09 W
Fort Laurens State Memorial ⊥	204	40.38 N	81.27 W
Fort Leavenworth ■	188	39.21 N	94.55 W
Fort Le Boeuf ⊥	204	41.56 N	79.59 W
Fort Lee	200	40.51 N	73.58 W
Fort Lee ■	198	37.14 N	77.20 W
Fort Lennox National Historic Park ▲	196	45.06 N	73.16 W
Fort Leonard Wood ■	184	37.45 N	92.07 W
Fort Lewis ■	214	47.05 N	122.37 W
Fort Liard	166	60.15 N	123.28 W
Fort Ligonier ⊥	204	40.15 N	79.14 W
Fort Lincoln State Park ▲	188	46.45 N	100.52 W
Fort Littleton	204	40.04 N	77.58 W
Fort Loramie	206	40.21 N	84.22 W
Fort Loudoun Lake @[1]	182	35.45 N	84.10 W
Fort Lupton	190	40.05 N	104.49 W
Fort Macleod	172	49.43 N	113.25 W
Fort Mac Mahon	138	29.51 N	1.45 E
Fort Madison	180	40.38 N	91.27 W
Fort Maguire	144	13.08 S	34.52 E
Fort-Mahon-Plage	46	50.21 N	1.34 E
Fort Malden National Historic Park ▲	271	42.06 N	83.07 W
Fort Matanzas National Monument ▲	182	29.40 N	81.18 W
Fort McClellan ■	184	34.43 N	85.47 W
Fort McDermitt Indian Reservation ⤙[4]	192	42.00 N	117.32 W
Fort McDowell Indian Reservation ⤙[4]	190	33.38 N	111.41 W
Fort McHenry National Monument ▲	198	39.16 N	76.35 W
Fort Mckinley	208	39.48 N	84.17 W
Fort McMurray	174	56.44 N	111.23 W
Fort McNair ■	274c	38.52 N	77.04 W
Fort McPherson	170	67.27 N	134.53 W
Fort Meade	210	27.45 N	81.48 W
Fort Mill	182	35.01 N	80.57 W
Fort Miller	200	43.10 N	73.35 W
Fort Miribel	138	29.31 N	2.55 E
Fort Mitchell	208	39.03 N	84.33 W
Fort Mojave Indian Reservation ⤙[4]	190	34.55 N	114.35 W
Fort Monmouth ■	198	40.19 N	74.02 W
Fort Monroe ■	198	37.00 N	76.18 W
Fort Montgomery	200	41.20 N	73.59 W
Fort Morgan	188	40.15 N	103.48 W
Fort Myer ■	274c	38.53 N	77.05 W
Fort Myers	210	26.37 N	81.54 W
Fort Myers Beach	210	26.27 N	81.57 W
Fort Myers Shores	210	26.43 N	81.45 W
Fort Myers Villas	210	26.34 N	81.52 W
Fort Necessity National Battlefield ⊥	178	39.47 N	79.39 W
Fort Neck ≻[1]	266	40.39 N	73.28 W
Fort Nelson	166	58.49 N	122.39 W
Fort Nelson ≃	166	59.30 N	124.00 W
Fort Niagara Beach	274a	43.16 N	79.03 W
Fort Niagara State Park ▲	274a	43.16 N	79.03 W
Fort Nonsense ⊥	266	40.48 N	74.29 W
Fort Norman	170	64.54 N	125.34 W
Fort Nottingham	148	29.25 S	29.55 E
Fort Ogden	210	27.05 N	81.57 W
Fort Ord ■	216	36.40 N	121.48 W
Fortore ≃	60	41.55 N	15.17 E
Fort Parker State Park ▲	212	31.36 N	96.33 W
Fort Payne	184	34.27 N	85.43 W
Fort Peck	192	48.01 N	106.27 W
Fort Peck Dam ⤙[6]	192	47.52 N	106.38 W
Fort Peck Indian Reservation ⤙[4]	192	48.22 N	105.40 W
Fort Peck Lake @[1]	192	47.45 N	106.50 W
Fort Pierce	210	27.27 N	80.20 W
Fort Pierce Inlet C	210	27.28 N	80.18 W
Fort Pierre	188	44.21 N	100.22 W
Fort Pitt Tunnel ⤙[5]	269b	40.25 N	80.00 W
Fort Plain	200	42.56 N	74.38 W
Fort Point National Historical Site ⊥	272	37.48 N	122.28 W
Fort Polk ■	184	31.04 N	93.11 W
Fort Portal	144	0.40 N	30.17 E
Fort Providence	166	61.21 N	117.39 W
Fort Pulaski National Monument ▲	182	32.01 N	80.59 W
Fort Qu'Appelle	174	50.56 N	103.09 W
Fort Raleigh National Historic Site ⊥	182	35.55 N	75.40 W
Fort Randall Dam ⤙[6]	188	42.48 N	98.35 W
Fort Recovery	206	40.25 N	84.47 W
Fort Reliance	166	62.42 N	109.08 W
Fort Resolution	166	61.10 N	113.40 W
Fortress Mountain ∧	192	44.20 N	109.47 W
Fortress of Louisburg National Historic Park ▲	176	45.56 N	59.57 W
Fort Riley ■	188	39.04 N	96.47 W
Fort Ritchie ■	198	39.43 N	77.30 W
Fort Rixon	144	20.01 S	29.18 E
Fort Rodd Hill National Historic Park ▲	214	48.26 N	123.28 W
Fortrose, N.Z.	162	46.34 S	168.48 E
Fortrose, Scot., U.K.	28	57.34 N	4.09 W
Fort Rosebery → Mansa	144	11.12 S	28.53 E
Fort-Rousset	142	0.29 S	15.55 E
Fort Rucker ■	184	31.20 N	85.42 W
Fort Saint	138	30.19 N	9.30 E
Fort Saint James	172	54.26 N	124.15 W
Fort Saint John	172	56.15 N	120.51 W
Fort Salonga	266	40.55 N	73.18 W
Fort Sandeman	110	31.20 N	69.27 E
Fort Saskatchewan	172	53.43 N	113.13 W
Fort Scott	188	37.50 N	94.42 W
Fort Seneca	204	41.13 N	83.10 W
Fort-Ševčenko	74	44.31 N	50.16 E
Fort Severn	166	56.00 N	87.38 W
Fort Shawnee	206	40.42 N	84.07 W
Fort Sheridan ■	206	42.13 N	87.48 W
Fort-Sibut	142	5.44 N	19.05 E
Fort Sill ■	186	34.40 N	98.25 W
Fort Simcoe Historical State Park ▲	214	46.21 N	120.50 W
Fort Simpson	166	61.52 N	121.23 W
Fort Smith, N.W. Ter., Can.	166	60.00 N	111.53 W
Fort Smith, Ark., U.S.	184	35.23 N	94.25 W
Fort Steele	172	49.37 N	115.38 W
Fort Stevens State Park ▲	214	46.10 N	124.00 W
Fort Stewart ■	182	31.52 N	81.37 W

Fort Stockton	186	30.53 N	102.53 W
Fort Sumner	186	34.28 N	104.15 W
Fort Sumter National Monument ▲	182	32.44 N	79.46 W
Fort Supply	186	36.35 N	99.35 W
Fort Tejon State Historical Park ▲	218	34.52 N	118.53 W
Fort Thomas, Ariz., U.S.	190	33.02 N	109.58 W
Fort Thomas, Ky., U.S.	208	39.04 N	84.26 W
Fort Thompson	188	44.03 N	99.26 W
Fort Tilden ■	266	40.33 N	73.53 W
Fort Totten Indian Reservation ⤙[4]	188	47.53 N	98.50 W
Fort Totten Park ▲	274c	38.57 N	77.00 W
Fort Towson	186	34.01 N	95.16 W
Fort-Trinquet → Bir Mogreïn	138	25.14 N	11.35 W
Fortuna, Arg.	242	35.07 S	65.23 W
Fortuna, Calif., U.S.	194	40.36 N	124.09 W
Fortuna, Río de la ≃	238	16.36 S	58.46 W
Fortuna Ledge (Marshall)	170	61.53 N	162.05 W
Fortune	176	47.04 N	55.50 W
Fortune Bay C	176	47.25 N	55.25 W
Fortune Ditch ≡	269a	41.20 N	82.03 W
Fortune Harbour	176	49.31 N	55.15 W
Fort Union National Monument ▲	190	35.55 N	105.01 W
Fort Valley	182	32.33 N	83.53 W
Fort Vancouver National Historic Site ⊥	214	45.38 N	122.37 W
Fort Vermilion	166	58.24 N	116.00 W
Fort Victoria	144	20.05 S	30.50 E
Fortville	208	39.56 N	85.51 W
Fort Wadsworth ■	266	40.36 N	74.04 W
Fort Walton Beach	184	30.25 N	86.36 W
Fort Washakie	190	43.00 N	108.53 W
Fort Washington	198	40.09 N	75.13 W
Fort Washington Forest	198	38.43 N	76.59 W
Fort Washington State Historical Park ▲	275	40.07 N	75.14 W
Fort Wayne	206	41.04 N	85.09 W
Fort Wayne Military Museum ʊ	271	42.18 N	83.06 W
Fort Wayne Municipal Airport (Baer Field) ⊠	206	40.59 N	85.11 W
Fort Wellington	236	6.24 N	57.36 W
Fort Wellington National Historic Park ▲	202	44.44 N	75.31 W
Fort White	182	29.55 N	82.43 W
Fort William → Thunder Bay, Ont., Can.	180	48.23 N	89.15 W
Fort William, Scot., U.K.	28	56.49 N	5.07 W
Fort William ⊥	262b	22.33 N	88.20 E
Fort Worth	212	32.45 N	97.20 W
Fort Yates	188	46.05 N	100.38 W
Forty Foot Drain ≡	44	52.28 N	0.05 W
Forty Fort	200	41.17 N	75.53 W
Fort Yukon	170	66.34 N	145.17 W
Fort Yuma Indian Reservation ⤙[4]	194	32.48 N	114.34 W
Forum ▲, Qué., Can.	265a	45.29 N	73.35 W
Forum ▲, Calif., U.S.	270	33.57 N	118.20 W
Forūr, Jazīreh-ye I	118	26.17 N	54.32 E
Foscagno, Passo di)(	58	46.30 N	10.08 E
Fosdinovo	58	44.08 N	10.01 E
Fosforitnyj	72	55.19 N	38.54 E
Foshan	90	23.03 N	113.09 E
Fosna ≻[1]	24	64.00 N	10.30 E
Fosnavåg	26	62.21 N	5.39 E
Foso	140	5.42 N	1.17 W
Foss ≃, Eng., U.K.	42	53.57 N	1.06 W
Foss ≃, Wash., U.S.	214	47.43 N	121.18 W
Fossacesia	60	42.15 N	14.29 E
Fossacesia Marina	60	42.15 N	14.30 E
Fossa Eugeniana ≡	253	51.33 N	6.36 E
Fossano	56	44.33 N	7.43 E
Fossanova, Abbazia di ʊ[1]	60	41.29 N	13.13 E
Fossato, Colle di)(	60	43.19 N	12.47 E
Fossato di Vico	60	43.18 N	12.46 E
Fossé	52	49.27 N	5.00 E
Fosse-Martin	251	49.05 N	2.54 E
Fosses	251	49.06 N	2.29 E
Fosses-la-Ville	52	50.24 N	4.42 E
Fossil	192	45.00 N	120.13 W
Fossil Butte National Monument ▲	192	41.50 N	110.40 W
Fossil Downs	152	18.08 S	125.38 E
Fossil Lake @	192	43.18 N	120.15 W
Fossombrone	60	43.41 N	12.48 E
Fosston	188	47.35 N	95.45 W
Fos-sur-Mer	56	43.26 N	4.57 E
Foster, Austl.	159	38.39 S	146.12 E
Foster, Ky., U.S.	208	38.48 N	84.13 W
Foster, R.I., U.S.	197	41.47 N	71.44 W
Foster ≃	174	55.47 N	105.49 W
Foster, Mount ∧	170	59.48 N	135.29 W
Foster Brook	204	41.59 N	78.37 W
Foster City	216	37.34 N	122.16 W
Foster Creek ≃	188	44.34 N	98.12 W
Fosterdale	200	41.42 N	74.58 W
Foster Joseph Sayers Reservoir @[1]	204	41.02 N	77.40 W
Foster Park	218	34.21 N	119.18 W
Fosters	184	33.06 N	87.41 W
Fosters Pond @	273	42.37 N	71.08 W
Foster Street	250	51.46 N	0.09 E
Foster Village	219c	21.22 N	157.56 W
Fostoria	204	41.09 N	83.25 W
Fót	254c	47.37 N	19.12 E
Fotadrevo	147b	24.03 S	45.01 E
Fotan	90	24.12 N	117.53 E
Fothergill	42	54.42 N	3.30 W
Fóti-Somlyó ∧[2]	254c	47.38 N	19.13 E
Foucarmont	46	49.51 N	1.34 E
Fou-Chouen → Fushun	94	41.52 N	123.53 E
Fouesnant	32	47.54 N	4.01 W
Foug	52	48.41 N	5.47 E
Fougamou	142	1.13 S	10.36 E
Fougères	32	48.21 N	1.12 W
Fougères-sur-Bièvre	46	47.27 N	1.21 E
Fougerolles	54	47.53 N	6.24 E
Fouhsin → Fuxinshi	94	42.03 N	121.46 E
Fouju	251	48.35 N	2.47 E
Fouke	184	33.16 N	93.53 W
Foula I	28	60.10 N	2.05 W
Foulain	54	48.02 N	5.13 E
Foulalaba	140	10.41 N	7.22 W
Foula Mori	140	12.10 N	13.51 W
Foul Bay C	130	23.30 N	35.39 E
Foulertons Brook ≃	266	40.50 N	74.20 W
Fouling → Fuling	92	29.42 N	107.21 E
Foulness ≃	42	53.47 N	0.43 W
Foulness Island I	44	51.36 N	0.55 E
Foulness Point ≻	44	51.38 N	0.57 E
Foulpointe	147b	17.41 S	49.31 E
Foulsham	44	52.48 N	1.01 E
Foulwind, Cape ≻	162	41.45 S	171.28 E
Foumban	142	5.43 N	10.55 E
Foumbot	142	5.30 N	10.38 E
Foumbouni	147a	11.50 S	43.30 E
Foum el Alba, Passe de)(	138	20.27 N	3.36 W
Foum-el-Hassane	138	28.59 N	8.55 W
Foum-Zguid	138	30.04 N	6.54 W
Foundiougne	140	14.08 N	16.28 W
Fountain	188	38.41 N	104.42 W

Symbol	English	Deutsch	Español	Français	Português
≃	River	Fluss	Río	Rivière	Rio
≡	Canal	Kanal	Canal	Canal	Canal
⌊	Waterfall, Rapids	Wasserfall, Stromschnellen	Cascada, Rápidos	Chute d'eau, Rapides	Cascata, Rápidos
U	Strait	Meeresstrasse	Estrecho	Détroit	Estreito
C	Bay, Gulf	Bucht, Golf	Bahía, Golfo	Baie, Golfe	Baía, Golfo
@	Lake, Lakes	See, Seen	Lago, Lagos	Lac, Lacs	Lago, Lagos
≋	Swamp	Sumpf	Pantano	Marais	Pântano
⊼	Ice Features, Glacier	Eis- und Gletscherformen	Accidentes Glaciales	Formes glaciaires	Acidentes Glaciares
⍑	Other Hydrographic Features	Andere Hydrographische Objekte	Otros Elementos Hidrográficos	Autres données hydrographiques	Outros Elementos Hidrográficos
✣	Submarine Features	Untermeerische Objekte	Accidentes Submarinos	Formes de relief sous-marin	Acidentes Submarinos
□	Political Unit	Politische Einheit	Unidad Politica	Entité politique	Unidade Política
ʊ	Cultural Institution	Kulturelle Institution	Institución Cultural	Institution culturelle	Instituição Cultural
⊥	Historical Site	Historische Stätte	Sitio Histórico	Site historique	Sitio Histórico
▲	Recreational Site	Erholungs- und Ferienort	Sitio de Recreo	Centre de loisirs	Sítio de Lazer
⊠	Airport	Flughafen	Aeropuerto	Aéroport	Aeroporto
■	Military Installation	Militäranlage	Instalación Militar	Installation militaire	Instalação Militar
⤙	Miscellaneous	Verschiedenes	Misceláneo	Divers	Miscelânea

ENGLISH: Name · Page · Lat.°′ · Long.°′
DEUTSCH: Name · Seite · Breite°′ · Länge°′ E=Ost

Fountain □6 206 40.17 N 87.13 W
Fountain City, Ind., U.S. 208 39.57 N 84.55 W
Fountain City, Wis., U.S. 180 44.08 N 91.43 W
Fountain Creek ≃ 209 38.20 N 90.22 W
Fountain Green 190 39.38 N 111.38 W
Fountain Hill 198 40.36 N 75.24 W
Fountain Inn 182 34.42 N 82.12 W
Fountain Park 206 41.50 N 84.32 W
Fountain Peak ∧ 194 34.57 N 115.32 W
Fountain Place 184 30.31 N 91.09 W
Fountains Abbey ⚲1 42 54.07 N 1.34 W
Fountaintown 208 39.42 N 85.47 W
Fountain Valley 218 33.43 N 117.57 W
Fouquières-lès-Béthune 46 50.31 N 2.37 E
Fourche LaFave ≃ 184 34.58 N 92.35 W
Fourche Maline ≃ 184 34.55 N 94.55 W
Fourchu 176 45.43 N 60.15 W
Four Elms 250 51.13 N 0.06 E
Four Hole Swamp ≃ 182 33.03 N 80.24 W
Fouriesburg 148 28.38 S 28.14 E
Fourmies 46 50.00 N 4.03 E
Four Mile Creek ≃, Ont., Can. 274a 43.15 N 79.08 W
Fourmile Creek ≃, N.Y., U.S. 274a 43.17 N 79.00 W
Four Mile Creek ≃, Ohio, U.S. 208 39.26 N 84.32 W
Four Mile Creek State Campsite ♠ 274a 43.16 N 79.00 W
Fourmile Draw ∨ 186 32.40 N 104.18 W
Four Mile Lake ⊜ 202 44.40 N 78.44 W
Four Mile Run ≃ 274c 38.50 N 77.02 W
Four Mountains, Islands of the II 170 52.50 N 170.00 W
Fournaise, Piton de la ∧ 147c 21.14 S 55.43 E
Fourneau, Pointe à ᐳ 265a 45.22 N 73.51 W
Fourneaux, Fr. 46 47.53 N 1.48 E
Fourneaux, Fr. 56 45.11 N 6.39 E
Fournier, Lac ⊜ 176 51.33 N 65.25 W
Fournière, Lac ⊜ 180 48.04 N 78.03 W
Foúrnoi I 130 37.34 N 26.30 E
Four Oaks 182 35.27 N 78.26 W
Fourqueux 251 48.53 N 2.04 E
Fours 32 46.49 N 3.43 E
Fourteenmile Creek ≃ 208 38.26 N 85.37 W
Fourteen Streams 148 28.04 S 24.53 E
Fourth Cataract → Ash-Shallāl ar-Rābi' ⚡ 130 18.47 N 32.03 E
Fourth Cliff ⚲4 273 42.09 N 70.42 W
Four Towns 271 42.37 N 83.25 W
Fous, Pointe des ᐳ 230d 15.12 N 61.20 W
Foussard ≃ 46 48.16 N 1.17 E
Fouta Djallon ⚲1 140 11.30 N 12.30 W
Fou-Tcheou → Fuzhou 90 26.06 N 119.17 E
Fouyang → Fuyang 90 32.52 N 115.42 E
Fouzon ≃ 46 47.16 N 1.27 E
Foveaux Strait Ц 162 46.35 S 168.00 E
Fowey 44 50.20 N 4.38 W
Fowler, Calif., U.S. 226 36.38 N 119.41 W
Fowler, Colo., U.S. 188 38.08 N 104.01 W
Fowler, Ind., U.S. 206 40.37 N 87.19 W
Fowler, Kans., U.S. 188 37.23 N 100.12 W
Fowler, Mich., U.S. 206 43.00 N 84.44 W
Fowler, Ohio, U.S. 204 41.19 N 80.40 W
Fowler, Point ᐳ 152 32.02 S 132.29 E
Fowler Creek ≃ 271 42.17 N 83.30 W
Fowlers Bay 152 31.59 S 132.27 E
Fowlerton 186 28.28 N 98.48 W
Fowlerville 206 42.40 N 84.04 W
Fowliang → Jingdezhen 90 29.16 N 117.11 E
Fowman 118 37.13 N 49.19 E
Fox ≃, Man., Can. 174 56.03 N 93.18 W
Fox ≃, U.S. 184 40.18 N 91.30 W
Fox ≃, U.S. 206 41.21 N 88.50 W
Fox ≃, Ill., U.S. 184 38.32 N 88.08 W
Fox ≃, Wis., U.S. 180 44.32 N 88.01 W
Fox, Cape ᐳ 172 54.47 N 130.51 W
Foxboro, Ont., Can. 202 44.15 N 77.26 W
Foxboro, Mass., U.S. 207 42.04 N 71.16 W
Fox Brook ≃ 266 41.03 N 74.17 W
Foxburg 204 41.09 N 79.41 W
Fox Chapel 269b 40.30 N 79.55 W
Fox Chase ⚲8 275 40.04 N 75.05 W
Fox Chase Manor 275 40.05 N 75.06 W
Fox Creek ≃, Ky., U.S. 208 38.16 N 83.41 W
Fox Creek ≃, N.Y., U.S. 200 42.41 N 74.18 W
Foxe Basin C 166 68.25 N 77.00 W
Foxe-Becken → Foxe Basin C 166 68.25 N 77.00 W
Foxe Channel Ц 166 64.30 N 80.00 W
Foxen ⊜ 26 59.23 N 11.52 E
Foxe Peninsula ᐳ1 166 65.00 N 76.00 W
Fox Glacier 162 43.28 S 170.00 E
Fox Harbour 176 52.22 N 55.41 W
Foxholes 42 54.08 N 0.28 W
Fox Hollow Lake ⊜ 266 41.02 N 74.40 W
Fox Island I, Ont., Can. 202 44.28 N 78.24 W
Fox Island I, Wash., U.S. 214 47.16 N 122.37 W
Fox Islands II 170 54.00 N 168.00 W
Fox Lake, Ill., U.S. 206 42.24 N 88.11 W
Fox Lake, Wis., U.S. 180 43.34 N 88.55 W
Fox Lake ⊜ 206 42.25 N 88.09 W
Fox Mountain ∧ 170 61.55 N 133.22 W
Foxpark 190 41.05 N 106.09 W
Fox Point 206 43.09 N 87.54 W
Fox Point ᐳ 266 40.54 N 73.35 W
Fox River Estates 206 41.58 N 88.20 W
Fox River Grove 206 42.12 N 88.13 W
Foxton 162 40.28 S 175.18 E
Foxton Beach 162 40.28 S 175.13 E
Foxvale 273 42.03 N 71.14 W
Fox Valley, Austl. 264a 33.45 S 151.06 E
Fox Valley, Sask., Can. 174 50.29 N 109.28 W
Foxwells 198 37.38 N 76.18 W
Foxwist Green 252 53.12 N 2.34 W
Foxworth 184 31.14 N 89.52 W
Foyedong 88 40.41 N 119.12 E
Foyle ≃ 42 55.04 N 7.15 W
Foyle, Lough ⊜ 40 55.07 N 7.08 W
Foynes 28 52.37 N 9.06 W
Foza 58 45.54 N 11.38 E
Foz do Cunene 142 17.16 S 11.50 E
Foz do Iguaçu 242 25.33 S 54.35 W
Foz do Jordão 238 9.23 S 71.56 W
Foz Giraldo 34 40.00 N 7.43 W
Fozhiling 90 31.20 N 116.17 E
Frabosa Soprana 56 44.17 N 7.48 E
Fracción del Refugio 224 21.57 N 100.02 W
Frackville 198 40.47 N 76.14 W
Fraction Run ≃ 268 41.34 N 88.04 W
Frade, Rio do ≃ 246 16.51 S 39.06 W
Fraga, Arg. 242 33.30 S 65.48 W
Fraga, Esp. 34 41.31 N 0.21 E
Fragneto Monforte 60 41.15 N 14.46 E
Fragoso, Cayo I 230p 22.44 N 79.30 W
Fragua, Sierra de la ∧ 186 26.41 N 102.13 W
Fraile Muerto 242 32.31 S 54.32 W
Fraïn, Chott el ⊜ 34 35.57 N 5.38 E
Fraire 46 50.16 N 4.30 E
Fraisans 54 47.09 N 5.46 E
Fraisse 56 45.23 N 4.15 E
Fraize 54 48.11 N 7.00 E
Frameries 46 50.24 N 3.54 E
Framingham 197 42.17 N 71.25 W
Framlingham 44 52.13 N 1.21 E
Frammersbach 52 50.04 N 9.28 E
Framnes Mountains ⋀ 9 67.50 S 62.35 E
Frampol 30 50.41 N 22.40 E
Frampton on Severn 44 51.46 N 2.22 W
França, Bra. 240 11.34 S 40.36 W
Franca, Bra. 245 20.32 S 47.24 W
Français, Récif de ⚲2 165f 19.40 S 163.20 E
Francavilla al Mare 60 42.25 N 14.17 E
Francavilla d'Ete 60 43.11 N 13.32 E
Francavilla Fontana 36 40.31 N 17.35 E
France □1 22
France 32 46.00 N 2.00 E
Frances ≃ 170 60.12 N 129.02 W
Francés, Cabo ᐳ 230p 21.54 N 84.02 W
Francés, Punta ᐳ 230p 21.38 N 83.12 W
Francês dos Carvalhos 246 22.05 S 44.29 W
Frances Lake ⊜ 170 61.25 N 129.30 W
Francés Viejo, Cabo ᐳ 228 19.39 N 69.55 W
Francesville 206 40.59 N 86.53 W
Franceville 142 1.38 S 13.35 E
Francfort-sur-Main → Frankfurt am Main 52 50.07 N 8.40 E
Franche-Comté □9 54 47.00 N 6.00 E
Francia 242 32.33 S 56.37 W
Francia → France □1 22 46.00 N 2.00 E
Francia, Estación de ⚲5 256d 41.23 N 2.11 E
Francia, Peña de ∧ 34 42.35 N 8.02 W
Francis 174 50.05 N 103.55 W
Francis, Lake ⊜ 196 45.02 N 71.20 W
Francisca, Punta ᐳ 222 21.34 N 87.21 W
Francis Case, Lake ⊜1 188 43.15 N 99.00 W
Francisco A. Berra 248 35.23 S 58.51 W
Francisco Alvarez 248 34.38 S 58.52 W
Francisco Beltrão 242 26.05 S 53.04 W
Francisco de Orellana 236 0.28 S 76.58 W
Francisco González Villarreal 222 25.22 N 97.53 W
Francisco Horta Barbosa ≃ 245 14.50 S 52.34 W
Francisco I. Madero, Méx. 222 25.45 N 103.21 W
Francisco I. Madero, Méx. 222 24.32 N 104.22 W
Francisco I. Madero, Méx. 224 21.36 N 104.49 W
Francisco I. Madero, Méx. 224 16.50 N 93.50 W
Francisco José, Tierra → Zeml'a Franca-Iosifa II 12 81.00 N 55.00 E
Francisco Morato 246 23.16 S 46.45 W
Francisco Morazán □5 226 14.15 N 87.15 W
Francisco Perito Moreno, Parque Nacional ♠ 244 47.50 S 72.08 W
Francisco Primo Verdad 224 21.48 N 101.55 W
Francisco Sá 245 16.28 S 43.30 W
Francisco Zarco 194 32.06 N 116.30 W
Francistown 146 21.11 S 27.32 E
Francitas 212 28.52 N 96.20 W
Franco da Rocha 246 23.20 S 46.43 W
Francofonte 36 37.13 N 14.53 E
François 176 47.35 N 56.45 W
François, Lacs à ⊜ 176 51.40 N 65.49 W
François-Joseph, Chutes ⚡ 142 7.34 S 17.17 E
François-Joseph, Îles du → Zeml' Franca-Iosifa II 12 81.00 N 55.00 E
François Lake 172 54.04 N 125.44 W
François Lake ⊜ 172 54.00 N 125.40 W
Francolise 60 41.11 N 14.03 E
Franconia Notch State Park ♠ 178 44.06 N 71.43 W
Franconville 261 48.59 N 2.14 E
Francs Peak ∧ 192 43.58 N 109.20 W
Francueil 46 47.19 N 1.05 E
Franeker 48 53.11 N 5.32 E
Frangy 54 46.01 N 5.56 E
Frank 269b 40.16 N 79.48 W
Frank and Poet Drain ≃ 271 42.06 N 83.12 W
Frankby 252 53.22 N 3.08 W
Frankel City 186 32.23 N 102.47 W
Frankenau 52 51.05 N 8.56 E
Frankenbach 52 50.40 N 8.34 E
Frankenberg 50 50.54 N 13.01 E
Frankenberg-Eder 52 51.03 N 8.48 E
Frankenburg 58 48.05 N 13.30 E
Frankenheim 52 50.32 N 10.04 E
Frankenhöhe ⋀ 52 49.15 N 10.15 E
Frankenmarkt 58 47.59 N 13.25 E
Frankenmuth 180 43.20 N 83.44 W
Frankenstein, B.R.D. 52 49.26 N 7.58 E
Frankenstein → Ząbkowice Śląskie, Pol. 30 50.36 N 16.53 E
Frankenthal 52 49.32 N 8.21 E
Frankenwald ⋀ 50 50.18 N 11.36 E
Frankfield 231q 18.09 N 77.22 W
Frankford, Ont., Can. 202 44.12 N 77.36 W
Frankford, Del., U.S. 198 38.31 N 75.14 W
Frankford, Mo., U.S. 209 39.29 N 91.19 W
Frankford ⚲8 275 40.01 N 75.05 W
Frankfort, S. Afr. 148 27.17 S 28.30 E
Frankfort, S. Afr. 148 32.44 S 27.26 E
Frankfort, Ill., U.S. 206 41.30 N 87.51 W
Frankfort, Ind., U.S. 206 40.17 N 86.31 W
Frankfort, Kans., U.S. 188 39.42 N 96.25 W
Frankfort, Ky., U.S. 208 38.12 N 84.52 W
Frankfort, Maine, U.S. 178 44.36 N 68.53 W
Frankfort, Mich., U.S. 180 44.38 N 86.14 W
Frankfort, N.Y., U.S. 200 43.02 N 75.04 W
Frankfort, Ohio, U.S. 208 39.24 N 83.11 W
Frankfort, S. Dak., U.S. 188 44.53 N 98.18 W
Frankfort Springs 204 40.30 N 80.25 W
Frankfurt □5 50 52.30 N 14.00 E
Frankfurt am Main 52 50.07 N 8.40 E
Frankfurt am Main, Flughafen ⊠ 52 50.02 N 8.33 E
Frankfurt an der Oder 50 52.20 N 14.33 E
Fränkische Alb ⋀ 52 49.20 N 11.00 E
Fränkische Rezat ≃ 52 49.11 N 11.01 E
Fränkische Saale ≃ 52 50.03 N 9.42 E
Frank Key I 210 25.07 N 80.54 W
Frankland ≃ 152 34.58 S 116.49 E
Franklin, S. Afr. 148 30.18 S 29.30 E
Franklin, Ariz., U.S. 190 32.42 N 109.05 W
Franklin, Ga., U.S. 182 33.17 N 85.08 W
Franklin, Idaho, U.S. 190 42.01 N 111.48 W
Franklin, Ill., U.S. 209 39.37 N 90.03 W
Franklin, Ind., U.S. 208 39.29 N 86.03 W
Franklin, Ky., U.S. 184 36.43 N 86.35 W
Franklin, La., U.S. 184 29.48 N 91.30 W
Franklin, Maine, U.S. 178 44.35 N 68.14 W
Franklin, Mass., U.S. 197 42.05 N 71.24 W
Franklin, Minn., U.S. 180 44.32 N 94.53 W
Franklin, Nebr., U.S. 188 40.06 N 98.57 W
Franklin, N.H., U.S. 178 43.27 N 71.39 W
Franklin, N.J., U.S. 200 41.07 N 74.35 W
Franklin, N.C., U.S. 182 35.11 N 83.23 W
Franklin, N.Y., U.S. 200 42.20 N 75.10 W
Franklin, Ohio, U.S. 208 39.34 N 84.18 W
Franklin, Pa., U.S. 204 41.24 N 79.50 W
Franklin, Tenn., U.S. 184 35.55 N 86.52 W
Franklin, Tex., U.S. 212 31.02 N 96.29 W
Franklin, Vt., U.S. 196 44.59 N 72.55 W
Franklin, Va., U.S. 198 36.41 N 76.55 W
Franklin, W. Va., U.S. 188 38.39 N 79.20 W
Franklin, Wis., U.S. 206 42.54 N 88.03 W
Franklin □5 166 72.00 N 100.00 W
Franklin □6, Ind., U.S. 208 39.25 N 85.01 W
Franklin □6, Ky., U.S. 208 38.14 N 84.52 W
Franklin □6, Mass., U.S. 197 42.36 N 72.36 W
Franklin □6, Mo., U.S. 209 38.25 N 91.03 W
Franklin □6, N.Y., U.S. 196 44.57 N 74.18 W
Franklin □6, Ohio, U.S. 208 39.57 N 83.00 W
Franklin □6, Pa., U.S. 198 39.56 N 77.40 W
Franklin □6, Tex., U.S. 212 33.07 N 95.13 W
Franklin □6, Vt., U.S. 196 44.57 N 72.52 W
Franklin, Mount ∧ 161b 35.29 S 148.47 E
Franklin, Point ᐳ 170 70.54 N 158.48 W
Franklin Canyon Reservoir ⊜1 270 34.06 N 118.25 W
Franklin Delano Roosevelt, Parque Nacional ♠ 248 34.52 S 56.03 W
Franklin Delano Roosevelt Lake ⊜1 192 48.20 N 118.10 W
Franklin Delano Roosevelt Park ♠ 275 39.54 N 75.11 W
Franklin Farms 269b 40.10 N 80.16 W
Franklin Grove 180 41.50 N 89.18 W
Franklin Harbor C 156 33.42 S 136.56 E
Franklin Island I 202 45.24 N 80.20 W
Franklin Lake ⊜, N.W. Ter., Can. 166 66.56 N 96.03 W
Franklin Lake ⊜, Nev., U.S. 194 40.24 N 115.12 W
Franklin Lake ⊜, N.J., U.S. 266 40.59 N 74.13 W
Franklin Lakes 266 41.01 N 74.12 W
Franklin Mountains ⋀, N.W. Ter., Can. 166 63.15 N 123.30 W
Franklin Mountains ⋀, N.Z. 162 44.55 S 167.45 E
Franklin Park, Ill., U.S. 206 41.56 N 87.49 W
Franklin Park, N.J., U.S. 266 40.26 N 74.32 W
Franklin Park, N.Y., U.S. 200 43.05 N 76.05 W
Franklin Park, Pa., U.S. 269b 40.35 N 80.06 W
Franklin Park, Va., U.S. 274c 38.55 N 77.09 W
Franklin Park ♠ 273 42.18 N 71.06 W
Franklin Pond ⊜ 266 41.06 N 74.35 W
Franklin Ridge ∧ 272 38.00 N 122.10 W
Franklin River 172 49.06 N 124.49 W
Franklin Roosevelt Park ⚲8 263d 26.09 S 27.59 E
Franklin Springs 200 43.02 N 75.24 W
Franklin Square 200 40.43 N 73.40 W
Franklin State Forest ♠ 273 42.04 N 71.26 W
Franklin Strait Ц 166 72.00 N 96.00 W
Franklinton, La., U.S. 184 30.51 N 90.09 W
Franklinton, N.C., U.S. 182 36.06 N 78.27 W
Franklintown 198 40.05 N 77.02 W
Franklinville, N.J., U.S. 198 39.37 N 75.05 W
Franklinville, N.Y., U.S. 200 42.20 N 78.28 W
Frankreich → France □1 22 46.00 N 2.00 E
Frankston, Austl. 159 38.08 S 145.07 E
Frankston, Tex., U.S. 212 32.03 N 95.30 W
Franksville 206 42.46 N 87.55 W
Frankton 206 40.13 N 85.46 W
Franktown 184 31.39 N 88.09 W
Frånö 26 62.54 N 17.50 E
Fr'anovo 72 56.08 N 38.27 E
Franschhoek 148 33.55 S 19.09 E
Fransfontein 146 20.12 S 15.01 E
Fränsta 26 62.30 N 16.09 E
Františkovy Lázně 50 50.04 N 12.21 E
Franvillers 46 49.58 N 2.30 E
Franzburg 50 54.11 N 12.52 E
Franzensburg ⊥ 254b 48.04 N 16.22 E
Franzensfeste → Fortezza 58 46.47 N 11.37 E
Franz Josef Glacier 162 43.24 S 170.11 E
Franz Josef Land → Zeml'a Franca-Iosifa II 12 81.00 N 55.00 E
Franz-Josefs-Bahnhof ⚲5 254b 48.13 N 16.21 E
Franz-Josefs-Höhe ∧ 58 47.04 N 12.45 E
Französische Süd- und Antarktis-Gebiete → French Southern and Antarctic Territories □2 6 49.30 S 69.30 E
Französisch-Polynesien → French Polynesia □2 14 15.00 S 140.00 W
Frascati 60 41.48 N 12.41 E
Frasdorf 58 47.48 N 12.16 E
Fraser 190 39.57 N 105.49 W
Fraser ≃, B.C., Can. 172 49.09 N 123.12 W
Fraser ≃, Newf., Can. 166 56.35 N 61.55 W
Fraser ≃, Colo., U.S. 190 40.06 N 105.58 W
Fraser, Mount ∧ 152 25.39 S 118.23 E
Fraserburg 148 31.55 S 21.30 E
Fraserburgh 28 57.42 N 2.00 W
Fraser Island I 156 25.15 S 153.10 E
Fraser Lake 172 54.04 N 124.51 W
Fraser Lake ⊜ 172 54.05 N 124.35 W
Fraser Mills 214 49.14 N 122.52 W
Fraser National Park ♠ 159 37.10 S 145.50 E
Fraser Plateau ⚲1 172 51.30 N 122.00 W
Fraser Range 152 32.03 S 122.48 E
Frasertown 162 38.58 S 177.24 E
Frasne 54 46.51 N 6.10 E
Frasnes-lez-Buissenal 46 50.40 N 3.36 E
Frassine ≃ 58 45.18 N 11.37 E
Frassinoro 58 44.18 N 10.34 E
Frati, Monte dei ∧ 60 43.40 N 12.10 E
Frattamaggiore 60 40.57 N 14.16 E
Frattòcchie 257a 41.46 N 12.37 E
Frauenberg → Frombork 30 54.22 N 19.41 E
Frauenfeld 54 47.34 N 8.54 E
Frauenstein 50 50.48 N 13.32 E
Frauenwald 50 50.35 N 10.51 E
Fraulautern 52 49.19 N 6.46 E
Fraureuth 50 50.42 N 12.20 E
Fray Bentos 242 33.08 S 58.18 W
Fray Marcos 242 34.11 S 55.44 W
Frazee 188 46.44 N 95.42 W
Frazer, Mont., U.S. 192 48.03 N 106.02 W
Frazer, Pa., U.S. 208 40.02 N 75.33 W
Frazeysburg 204 40.07 N 82.07 W
Frazier Mountain ∧ 218 34.47 N 118.58 W
Frazier Park 218 34.49 N 118.56 W
Fr'azino 72 55.58 N 38.04 E
Frecheiras 240 2.51 S 42.05 W
Frecheirinha 240 3.46 S 40.48 W
Frechen 52 50.54 N 6.49 E
Frechilla 34 42.08 N 4.50 W
Freckenhorst 48 51.55 N 7.58 E
Freckleton 252 53.45 N 2.52 W
Fredeburg 52 51.11 N 8.18 E
Freden 48 51.56 N 9.54 E
Fredensborg 41 55.58 N 12.24 E
Fredensborg Slot ⊥ 41 55.58 N 12.24 E
Frederic 180 45.40 N 92.28 W
Frederica 198 39.01 N 75.28 W
Fredericia 41 55.35 N 9.46 E
Frederick, Ill., U.S. 209 40.04 N 90.26 W
Frederick, Md., U.S. 198 39.25 N 77.25 W
Frederick, Okla., U.S. 186 34.23 N 99.01 W
Frederick, S. Dak., U.S. 188 45.50 N 98.30 W
Frederick □6 198 39.25 N 77.25 W
Frederick Hills ⋀2 154 12.41 S 136.00 E
Frederick House ≃ 180 49.19 N 81.16 W
Frederick House Lake ⊜ 180 48.40 N 80.55 W
Frederick Island I 152 34.04 S 122.00 E
Frederick Reef ⚲2 156 20.58 S 154.23 E
Fredericksburg, Ind., U.S. 208 38.26 N 86.11 W
Fredericksburg, Iowa, U.S. 180 42.58 N 92.12 W
Fredericksburg, Ohio, U.S. 204 40.41 N 81.52 W
Fredericksburg, Pa., U.S. 204 40.27 N 76.26 W
Fredericksburg, Tex., U.S. 186 30.17 N 98.52 W
Fredericksburg, Va., U.S. 198 38.18 N 77.29 W
Fredericksburg Battlefield (1862) ⊥ 198 38.17 N 77.28 W
Frederick Sound Ц 170 57.00 N 133.00 W
Fredericktown, Mo., U.S. 184 37.33 N 90.18 W
Fredericktown, Ohio, U.S. 204 40.29 N 82.33 W
Frederico Westphalen 242 27.22 S 53.24 W
Fredericton 176 45.58 N 66.39 W
Fredericton Junction 176 45.40 N 66.37 W
Frederik Hendrik-Eiland → Yos Sudarsa, Pulau I 154 7.50 S 138.30 E
Frederiksberg, Dan. 41 55.41 N 12.32 E
Frederiksberg, Dan. 41 55.25 N 11.34 E
Frederiksborg □6 41 55.56 N 12.18 E
Frederiksborg Slot ⊥ 41 55.56 N 12.19 E
Frederikshåb 166 62.00 N 49.43 W
Frederikshavn 26 57.26 N 10.32 E
Frederikssund 41 55.50 N 12.04 E
Frederiksted 231n 17.43 N 64.53 W
Frederiksværk 41 55.58 N 12.02 E
Frederik Willem IV Vallen ⚡ 240 3.28 N 57.37 W
Fredersdorf bei Berlin 50 52.31 N 13.44 E
Fredonia, Col. 236 5.55 N 75.41 W
Fredonia, Ariz., U.S. 190 36.57 N 112.32 W
Fredonia, Kans., U.S. 188 37.32 N 95.49 W
Fredonia, N. Dak., U.S. 188 46.20 N 99.06 W
Fredonia, N.Y., U.S. 204 42.27 N 79.20 W
Fredonia, Pa., U.S. 204 41.20 N 80.14 W
Fredrika 26 64.05 N 18.24 E
Fredriksberg 40 60.08 N 14.23 E
Fredrikstad 26 59.13 N 10.57 E
Freeburg, Ill., U.S. 209 38.26 N 89.55 W
Freeburg, Mo., U.S. 209 38.19 N 91.55 W
Freeburg, Pa., U.S. 198 40.46 N 76.57 W
Freedom, Calif., U.S. 216 36.55 N 121.48 W
Freedom, Pa., U.S. 204 40.41 N 80.15 W
Freehold, N.J., U.S. 198 40.16 N 74.17 W
Freehold, N.Y., U.S. 200 42.22 N 74.03 W
Freeland, Mich., U.S. 180 43.32 N 84.07 W
Freeland, Pa., U.S. 200 41.01 N 75.47 W
Freeland, Wash., U.S. 214 48.01 N 122.32 W
Freeland Park 206 40.37 N 87.30 W
Freeling, Mount ∧ 152 22.35 S 133.06 E
Freel Peak ∧ 216 38.52 N 119.54 W
Freels, Cape ᐳ, Newf., Can. 176 46.37 N 53.33 W
Freels, Cape ᐳ, Newf., Can. 176 49.15 N 53.28 W
Freeman 188 43.21 N 97.26 W
Freeman ≃ 172 54.20 N 114.47 W
Freeman, Lake ⊜ 206 40.42 N 86.45 W
Freemansburg 200 40.39 N 75.22 W
Freeport, Ba. 228 26.30 N 78.45 W
Freeport, N.S., Can. 176 44.17 N 66.19 W
Freeport, Ont., Can. 202 43.25 N 80.25 W
Freeport, Fla., U.S. 184 30.30 N 86.08 W
Freeport, Ill., U.S. 180 42.17 N 89.36 W
Freeport, Maine, U.S. 178 43.51 N 70.06 W
Freeport, Mich., U.S. 206 42.45 N 85.19 W
Freeport, N.Y., U.S. 200 40.39 N 73.35 W
Freeport, Ohio, U.S. 204 40.13 N 81.16 W
Freeport, Pa., U.S. 178 40.40 N 79.41 W
Freeport, Tex., U.S. 212 28.58 N 95.22 W
Freer 186 27.53 N 98.37 W
Freest 50 54.08 N 13.43 E
Freeston 212 31.32 N 96.15 W
Freestone 161a 28.08 S 152.08 E
Freestone □6 212 31.44 N 96.10 W
Freetown, Antig. 230c 17.03 N 61.42 W
Freetown, S.L. 140 8.30 N 13.15 W
Freetown, Ind., U.S. 208 38.58 N 86.08 W
Freetown, N.Y., U.S. 197 40.58 N 72.11 W
Freeville 200 42.31 N 76.21 W
Freewood Acres 198 40.10 N 74.15 W
Freezeout Lake ⊜ 192 47.40 N 112.03 W
Fregenal de la Sierra 34 38.10 N 6.39 W
Fregene ⚲8 60 41.51 N 12.12 E
Freiberg 50 50.54 N 13.20 E
Freiberger Mulde ≃ 50 51.10 N 12.48 E
Freiburg → Świebodzice, Pol. 30 50.52 N 16.19 E
Freiburg → Fribourg, Schw. 54 46.48 N 7.09 E
Freiburg □5 54 48.00 N 8.25 E
Freiburg an der Elbe 48 53.49 N 9.17 E
Freiburger Mulde ≃ 50 51.10 N 12.48 E
Freiburg im Breisgau 54 47.59 N 7.51 E
Freiendiez 52 50.23 N 8.02 E
Freienhufen 50 51.35 N 13.58 E
Freienwalde in Pommern → Chociwel 30 53.28 N 15.19 E
Freie Universität ⚲2 254a 52.26 N 13.16 E
Freilassing 58 47.50 N 12.59 E
Freilingen 52 50.33 N 7.50 E
Freinsheim 52 49.30 N 8.13 E
Freire 246 23.34 S 45.52 W
Freirina 242 28.30 S 71.06 W
Freisen 52 49.33 N 7.14 E
Freisenbruch ⚲8 253 51.27 N 7.06 E
Freising 30 48.23 N 11.44 E
Freistadt, Öst. 30 48.31 N 14.31 E
Freistadt → Kożuchów, Pol. 30 51.45 N 15.35 E
Freistett 52 48.41 N 7.56 E
Freital 50 51.00 N 13.39 E
Freiwaldau → Gozdnica 30 51.26 N 15.06 E
Freiwalde 50 51.58 N 13.44 E
Freixial 256c 38.54 N 9.09 W
Fréjorgues, Aéroport de ⊠ 56 43.33 N 4.00 E
Fréjus 56 43.26 N 6.44 E
Fréjus, Tunnel du ⚲5 56 45.13 N 6.42 E
Frémainville 251 49.04 N 1.52 E
Fremantle 158a 32.03 S 115.45 E
Fremdingen 52 48.58 N 10.27 E
Fremington 44 51.04 N 4.07 W
Fremont, Calif., U.S. 216 37.34 N 122.01 W
Fremont, Ind., U.S. 206 41.44 N 84.56 W
Fremont, Iowa, U.S. 180 41.13 N 92.26 W
Fremont, Mich., U.S. 180 43.28 N 85.57 W
Fremont, Nebr., U.S. 188 41.26 N 96.30 W
Fremont, N.C., U.S. 182 35.33 N 77.58 W
Fremont, Ohio, U.S. 204 41.21 N 83.07 W
Fremont, Wis., U.S. 180 44.16 N 88.52 W
Fremont ≃ 190 38.24 N 110.42 W
Fremont Airport ⊠ 272 37.28 N 121.56 W
Fremont Canyon ∨ 270 33.48 N 117.42 W
Fremont Island I 190 41.09 N 112.20 W
Fremont Lake ⊜ 192 42.57 N 109.48 W
Fremont Peak ∧, Calif., U.S. 216 36.46 N 121.30 W
Fremont Peak ∧, Calif., U.S. 218 35.12 N 117.27 W
Fremont Valley ∨ 218 35.10 N 118.00 W
French ≃ 180 45.56 N 80.54 W
French Broad ≃ 182 35.57 N 83.51 W
Frenchburg 182 37.57 N 83.37 W
French Camp 216 37.53 N 121.16 W
Frenchcap Cay I 230m 18.14 N 64.51 W
French Creek ≃, Man., Can. 174 57.02 N 92.12 W
French Creek ≃, U.S. 204 41.25 N 79.50 W
French Creek ≃, Ohio, U.S. 269a 41.27 N 82.07 W
French Creek ≃, Pa., U.S. 198 40.08 N 75.31 W
French Creek ≃, S. Dak., U.S. 188 43.38 N 102.55 W
French Creek, South Branch ≃, Pa., U.S. 204 41.54 N 79.54 W
French Creek, South Branch ≃, Pa., U.S. 275 40.10 N 75.42 W
French Creek, West Branch ≃ 204 41.58 N 79.52 W
French Creek State Park ♠ 198 40.13 N 75.47 W
French Frigate Shoals ⚲2 14 23.45 N 166.10 W
French Guiana □2 232
240 4.00 N 53.00 W
French Island I 159 38.21 S 145.21 E
French Lick 184 38.33 N 86.37 W
Frenchman Bay C, Ont., Can. 202 43.49 N 79.05 W
Frenchman Bay C, Maine, U.S. 178 44.25 N 68.10 W
Frenchman Butte 174 53.35 N 109.38 W
Frenchman Creek ≃, Ont., Can. 274a 42.56 N 78.59 W
Frenchman Creek ≃, N.A. 192 48.24 N 107.05 W
Frenchman Creek ≃, U.S. 188 40.13 N 100.50 W
Frenchman Flat ∨ 194 36.50 N 115.55 W
Frenchman Lake ⊜ 194 36.48 N 116.56 W
Frenchman Point ᐳ 202 44.35 N 81.18 W
Frenchmans Cap ∧ 156 42.16 S 145.50 E
Frenchmans Creek ≃ 272 37.29 N 122.27 W
French Pass 162 40.56 S 173.50 E
French Polynesia □2 14 15.00 S 140.00 W
Frenchs Forest 264a 33.45 S 151.14 E
French Southern and Antarctic Territories □2 6 49.30 S 69.30 E
French Stream ≃ 273 42.07 N 70.53 W
Frenchtown 200 40.32 N 75.04 W
Frenda 138 35.02 N 1.01 E
Freneuse 251 49.03 N 1.36 E
Frensdorferhaar 48 52.25 N 7.03 E
Frenštát pod Radhoštěm 30 49.33 N 18.14 E
Frentani, Monti dei ⋀ 60 41.54 N 14.37 E
Frépillon 251 49.03 N 2.12 E
Frere 148 28.52 S 29.47 E
Freren 48 52.29 N 7.32 E
Fresco 140 5.05 N 5.34 W
Fresco ≃ 240 6.39 S 51.59 W
Freshfield 252 53.34 N 3.04 W
Freshfield, Mount ∧ 172 51.44 N 116.57 W
Fresh Meadows ⚲8 266 40.44 N 73.48 W
Fresh Pond ⊜, Mass., U.S. 273 42.23 N 71.09 W
Fresh Pond ⊜, N.Y., U.S. 266 40.55 N 73.18 W
Freshwater 44 50.40 N 1.30 W
Freshwater Creek ≃ 216 39.12 N 122.04 W
Fresia 244 41.09 S 73.27 W
Fresnes 261 48.45 N 2.19 E
Fresnes-Saint-Mamès 54 47.33 N 5.52 E
Fresnes-en-Woëvre 52 49.08 N 5.39 E
Fresnes-sur-Escaut 46 50.26 N 3.35 E
Fresnes-sur-Marne 251 48.56 N 2.45 E
Fresnillo 224 23.10 N 102.53 W
Fresno, Col. 236 5.09 N 75.01 W
Fresno, Calif., U.S. 216 36.45 N 119.45 W
Fresno, Ohio, U.S. 204 40.20 N 81.44 W
Fresno, Tex., U.S. 212 29.32 N 95.27 W
Fresno □6 216 36.38 N 119.45 W
Fresno ≃ 216 37.05 N 120.33 W
Fresno, Lewis Fork ≃ 216 37.20 N 119.39 W
Fresno, Portillo del ⚲ 34 42.38 N 3.46 W
Fresno Air Terminal ⊠ 216 36.46 N 119.43 W
Fresno Reservoir ⊜1 192 48.41 N 109.57 W
Fresno Slough ≃ 216 36.47 N 120.22 W
Fresnoy-Folny 46 49.53 N 1.26 E
Fresnoy-le-Grand 46 49.57 N 3.25 E
Fressenneville 46 50.04 N 1.34 E
Fressin 46 50.27 N 2.03 E
Fréteval 46 47.53 N 1.13 E
Frétigney-et-Velloreille 54 47.29 N 5.56 E
Fretin 46 50.33 N 3.08 E
Frettes 54 47.41 N 5.34 E
Freu, Cabo del ᐳ 34 39.45 N 3.27 E
Freudenberg, B.R.D. 52 49.44 N 9.19 E
Freudenberg, B.R.D. 52 50.54 N 7.52 E
Freudenberg, D.D.R. 254a 52.42 N 13.49 E
Freudenstadt 54 48.28 N 8.25 E
Frévent 46 50.16 N 2.17 E
Frew ≃ 152 20.00 S 135.38 E
Frewash ≃ 44 52.53 N 1.14 W
Frewena 152 19.25 S 135.25 E
Frewsburg 204 42.03 N 79.10 W
Freyburg 50 51.13 N 11.46 E
Freycinet, Cape ᐳ 152 34.06 S 114.59 E
Freycinet Estuary C1 152 26.25 S 113.46 E
Freycinet Peninsula ᐳ1 156 42.13 S 148.18 E
Freyenstein 50 53.17 N 12.20 E
Freyre 242 31.10 S 62.06 W
Fria 140 10.27 N 13.32 W
Fria □4 140 10.30 N 13.40 W
Fria, Cape ᐳ 146 18.30 S 12.01 E
Friant 216 36.59 N 119.43 W
Friant Dam ⚲6 216 37.00 N 119.43 W
Friant-Kern Canal ≃ 216 35.22 N 119.06 W
Friars Point 184 34.22 N 90.38 W
Frías, Arg. 242 28.39 S 65.09 W
Frías, Perú 238 4.52 S 79.57 W
Fribourg (Freiburg) 54 46.48 N 7.09 E
Fribourg (Freiburg) □3 54 46.45 N 7.05 E
Frick 54 47.31 N 8.01 E
Frickhofen 52 50.30 N 8.07 E
Frick Park ♠ 269b 40.26 N 79.54 W
Friday 212 31.07 N 95.15 W
Friday Harbor 214 48.32 N 123.01 W
Fridaythorpe 42 54.01 N 0.40 W
Fridingen an der Donau 54 48.01 N 8.56 E
Fridley 180 45.05 N 93.15 W
Fridolfing 58 48.00 N 12.49 E
Fridtjof Nansen, Mount ∧ 9 85.21 S 167.33 W
Friedberg, B.R.D. 52 50.20 N 8.45 E
Friedberg, B.R.D. 58 48.21 N 10.58 E
Friedberg, Öst. 30 47.27 N 16.03 E
Friedburg 58 48.01 N 13.15 E
Friedeberg in der Neumark → Strzelce Krajeńskie 30 52.53 N 15.32 E
Friedeburg [/Saale] 50 51.37 N 11.44 E
Friedenau ⚲8 254a 52.28 N 13.20 E
Friedens 204 40.03 N 79.00 W
Friedensburg 198 40.36 N 76.14 W
Friedersdorf, D.D.R. 50 52.17 N 13.47 E
Friedersdorf, D.D.R. 50 51.01 N 14.34 E
Friedersdorf, D.D.R. 50 51.39 N 12.21 E
Friedesheim 148 27.55 S 26.43 E
Friedland, B.R.D. 52 51.25 N 9.55 E
Friedland, D.D.R. 50 53.40 N 13.33 E
Friedland, D.D.R. 50 52.06 N 14.16 E
Friedland → Mieroszów, Pol. 30 50.41 N 16.10 E
Friedrich-Ebert-Brücke ⚲5 253 51.28 N 6.43 E
Friedrich Krupp-Aktiengesellschaft ⚲3 253 51.28 N 7.00 E
Friedrichroda 50 50.52 N 10.34 E
Friedrichsbrunn 50 51.41 N 11.02 E
Friedrichsdorf 52 50.15 N 8.38 E
Friedrichsfeld 253 51.38 N 6.39 E
Friedrichsfelde ⚲8 254a 52.31 N 13.31 E
Friedrichshafen 54 47.39 N 9.28 E
Friedrichshagen ⚲8 254a 52.27 N 13.38 E
Friedrichshain ⚲8 254a 52.31 N 13.27 E
Friedrichshof 254a 52.19 N 13.46 E
Friedrichsort ⚲8 50 54.24 N 10.11 E
Friedrichsruh, Schloss ⊥ 48 53.32 N 10.20 E
Friedrichsruhe 50 53.31 N 11.45 E
Friedrichstadt 41 54.22 N 9.05 E
Friedrichsthal 50 52.48 N 13.16 E
Friedrichstrasse, Bahnhof ⚲5 254a 52.31 N 13.24 E
Friedrichswalde 50 53.02 N 13.42 E
Frielas 256c 38.49 N 9.09 W
Frielendorf 52 50.58 N 9.19 E
Friemersheim 253 51.23 N 6.42 E
Friend, Nebr., U.S. 188 40.38 N 97.17 W
Friend, Oreg., U.S. 214 45.21 N 121.16 W
Friends Colony ⚲8 262a 28.34 N 77.16 E
Friendship, N.Y., U.S. 200 42.12 N 78.08 W
Friendship, Tenn., U.S. 184 35.55 N 89.14 W
Friendship, Wis., U.S. 180 43.58 N 89.49 W
Friendship Creek ≃ 275 39.55 N 74.43 W
Friendship Shoal ⚲2 102 5.58 N 112.38 E
Friends Meeting House State Memorial ⊥ 204 40.09 N 80.47 W
Friendswood 212 29.32 N 95.12 W
Friern Barnet ⚲8 260 51.37 N 0.10 W
Fries 182 36.43 N 80.59 W
Friesach 30 46.57 N 14.24 E
Friesack 50 52.44 N 12.34 E
Friesenheim 54 48.22 N 7.53 E
Friesenhofen 54 47.45 N 10.04 E
Friesenried 54 47.52 N 10.31 E
Friesland □4 48 53.01 N 5.45 E
Fries Mills 275 39.39 N 75.03 W
Friesoythe 48 53.01 N 7.51 E
Frigento 60 41.01 N 15.06 E
Frignano 60 41.00 N 14.10 E
Frignano ⚲1 58 44.20 N 10.51 E
Friguia 140 12.03 N 10.56 W
Friitala 26 61.26 N 21.52 E
Frillendorf ⚲8 253 51.28 N 7.05 E
Frindsbury 260 51.24 N 0.30 E
Frinsted 250 51.17 N 0.43 E
Frinton-on-Sea 44 51.50 N 1.14 E
Fritrop ⚲8 253 51.29 N 6.55 E
Frio ≃, N.A. 226 11.08 N 84.46 W
Frio ≃, Tex., U.S. 212 28.30 N 98.10 W
Frio, Cabo ᐳ 245 22.53 S 42.00 W
Frio Draw ∨ 186 34.50 N 102.19 W
Friona 186 34.38 N 102.43 W
Frisange 52 49.32 N 6.12 E
Frisches Haff → Vislinskij Zaliv C 30 54.27 N 19.40 E
Frisco, Pa., U.S. 204 40.51 N 80.16 W
Frisco, Tex., U.S. 212 33.09 N 96.49 W
Frisco City 184 31.26 N 87.24 W
Frisco Creek ≃ 186 36.34 N 101.23 W
Frisian Islands II 22 53.35 N 6.40 E
Fritch 186 35.38 N 101.36 W
Fritsla 26 57.33 N 12.47 E
Fritzlar 52 51.08 N 9.16 E
Friuli □9 58 46.00 N 13.00 E
Friuli-Venezia Giulia □4 58 46.00 N 13.00 E
Friza, Proliv Ц 64 45.30 N 149.10 E
Frizington 42 54.32 N 3.30 W
Frobisher 174 49.12 N 102.26 W
Frobisher Bay 166 63.44 N 68.28 W
Frobisher Bay C 166 62.30 N 66.00 W
Frobisher Lake ⊜ 174 56.25 N 108.20 W
Frodsham 42 53.18 N 2.44 W
Frog Lake ⊜ 174 53.55 N 110.18 W
Frohavet Ц 26 63.52 N 9.26 E
Frohburg 50 51.03 N 12.33 E
Frohlinde ⚲8 253 51.32 N 7.21 E
Frohnau ⚲8 254a 52.38 N 13.18 E
Frohnhausen 253 51.29 N 7.48 E
Frohnhausen ⚲8 253 51.27 N 6.58 E
Frohnleiten 30 47.16 N 15.20 E
Frohse 50 52.02 N 11.43 E
Froid 188 48.20 N 104.30 W
Froid, Ruisseau ≃ 196 46.23 N 74.46 W
Froidmont-Cohartille 46 49.41 N 3.42 E
Froidos 52 49.03 N 5.07 E
Froissy 46 49.34 N 2.13 E
Froitzheim 52 50.42 N 6.34 E
Frolišči, S.S.S.R. 70 56.25 N 42.39 E
Frolišči, S.S.S.R. 72 56.18 N 39.13 E
Frolovo 70 49.47 N 43.39 E
Froman Run ≃ 269b 40.12 N 80.00 W
Fromberg 192 45.23 N 108.54 W
Frombork 30 54.22 N 19.41 E
Frome 44 51.14 N 2.20 W
Frome ≃, Austl. 156 29.06 S 137.52 E
Frome ≃, Eng., U.K. 44 50.41 N 2.04 W
Frome ≃, Eng., U.K. 44 52.03 N 2.38 W
Frome, Lake ⊜ 156 30.48 S 139.48 E
Frome Downs 156 31.13 S 139.46 E
Fromelennes 52 50.08 N 4.52 E
Fromentières 46 48.54 N 3.43 E
Frömern 253 51.30 N 7.44 E
Frommern 54 48.15 N 8.52 E
Fröndenberg 52 51.28 N 7.46 E
Frönsberg 253 51.21 N 7.46 E
Fronteiras 240 7.05 S 40.37 W
Frontenac 210 28.27 N 80.46 W
Frontenac □6, Ont., Can. 202 44.40 N 76.45 W
Frontenac □6, Qué., Can. 196 45.42 N 71.15 W
Frontenard 54 46.55 N 5.10 E
Frontenex-Villard-Rosset 56 45.38 N 6.19 E
Frontera 224 18.32 N 92.38 W
Frontera, Punta ᐳ 224 18.36 N 92.42 W
Fronteras 190 30.56 N 109.31 W
Frontier, Sask., Can. 174 49.12 N 108.34 W
Frontier, Mich., U.S. 206 41.47 N 84.36 W
Frontier, Wyo., U.S. 190 41.49 N 110.32 W
Frontignan 56 43.27 N 3.45 E
Frontino 236 6.46 N 76.08 W
Frontino, Páramo ∧ 236 6.28 N 76.04 W
Frontón, Isla I 276d 12.07 S 77.11 W
Front Range ⋀ 190 39.45 N 105.45 W
Front Royal 178 38.55 N 78.11 W
Frose 50 51.48 N 11.23 E
Frosinone 60 41.38 N 13.19 E
Frosinone □4 60 41.37 N 13.27 E
Frosna ᐳ1 26 63.45 N 10.25 E
Frosolone 60 41.36 N 14.27 E
Frösön 26 63.11 N 14.32 E
Frost 212 32.05 N 96.48 W
Frostavallen 41 55.58 N 13.30 E
Frostburg 178 39.39 N 78.56 W

Symbols in the index entries represent the broad categories identified in the key at the right. Symbols with superior numbers (⋀²) identify subcategories (see complete key on page I · 26).

Kartensymbole in dem Registerverzeichnis stellen die rechts in Schlüssel erklärten Kategorien dar. Symbole mit hochgestellten Ziffern (⋀²) bezeichnen Unterabteilungen einer Kategorie (vgl. vollständiger Schlüssel auf Seite I · 26).

Los símbolos incluidos en el texto del índice representan las grandes categorías identificadas con la clave a la derecha. Los símbolos con numeros en su parte superior (⋀²) identifican las subcategorías (véase la clave completa en la página I · 26).

Les symboles de l'index représentent les catégories indiquées dans la légende à droite. Les symboles suivis d'un indice (⋀²) représentent des sous-catégories (voir légende complète à la page I · 26).

Os símbolos incluídos no texto do índice representam as grandes categorias identificadas com a chave à direita. Os símbolos com números em sua parte superior (⋀²) identificam as subcategorias (veja-se a chave completa à página I · 26).

	English	Deutsch	Español	Français	Português
∧	Mountain	Berg	Montaña	Montagne	Montanha
⋀	Mountains	Berge	Montañas	Montagnes	Montanhas
⚲	Pass	Pass	Paso	Col	Passo
∨	Valley, Canyon	Tal, Cañon	Valle, Cañón	Vallée, Canyon	Vale, Canhão
═	Plain	Ebene	Llano	Plaine	Planície
ᐳ	Cape	Kap	Cabo	Cap	Cabo
I	Island	Insel	Isla	Île	Ilha
II	Islands	Inseln	Islas	Îles	Ilhas
⚲	Other Topographic Features	Andere Topographische Objekte	Otros Elementos Topográficos	Autres données topographiques	Outros Elementos Topográficos

≃ River	Fluss	Río	Rivière	Rio	
≚ Canal	Kanal	Canal	Canal	Canal	
⌊ Waterfall, Rapids	Wasserfall, Stromschnellen	Cascada, Rápidos	Chute d'eau, Rapides	Cascata, Rápidos	
⋃ Strait	Meeresstrasse	Estrecho	Détroit	Estreito	
C Bay, Gulf	Bucht, Golf	Bahía, Golfo	Baie, Golfe	Baía, Golfo	
⊜ Lake, Lakes	See, Seen	Lago, Lagos	Lac, Lacs	Lago, Lagos	
≣ Swamp	Sumpf	Pantano	Marais	Pântano	
⊼ Ice Features, Glacier	Eis- und Gletscherformen	Accidentes Glaciales	Formes glaciaires	Acidentes Glaciares	
⊤ Other Hydrographic Features	Andere Hydrographische Objekte	Otros Elementos Hidrográficos	Autres données hydrographiques	Outros Elementos Hidrográficos	
✣ Submarine Features	Untermeerische Objekte	Accidentes Submarinos	Formes de relief sous-marin	Acidentes Submarinos	
□ Political Unit	Politische Einheit	Unidad Política	Entité politique	Unidade Política	
▾ Cultural Institution	Kulturelle Institution	Institución Cultural	Institution culturelle	Instituição Cultural	
⊥ Historical Site	Historische Stätte	Sitio Histórico	Site historique	Sitio Histórico	
♠ Recreational Site	Erholungs- und Ferienort	Sitio de Recreo	Centre de loisirs	Sítio de Lazer	
⊠ Airport	Flughafen	Aeropuerto	Aéroport	Aeroporto	
■ Military Installation	Militäranlage	Instalación Militar	Installation militaire	Instalação Militar	
◆ Miscellaneous	Verschiedenes	Misceláneo	Divers	Miscelânea	

ENGLISH

DEUTSCH

Symbols in the index entries represent the broad categories identified in the key at the right. Symbols with superior numbers ([2]) identify subcategories (see complete key on page I · 26).

Kartensymbole in dem Registerverzeichnis stellen die rechts in Schlüssel erklärten Kategorien dar. Symbole mit hochgestellten Ziffern ([2]) bezeichnen Unterabteilungen einer Kategorie (vgl. vollständiger Schlüssel auf Seite I · 26).

Los símbolos incluídos en el texto del índice representan las grandes categorias identificadas con la clave a la derecha. Los símbolos con numeros en su parte superior ([2]) identifican las subcategorías (véase la clave completa en la página I · 26).

Les symboles de l'index représentent les catégories indiquées dans la légende à droite. Les symboles suivis d'un indice ([2]) représentent des sous-catégories (voir légende complète à la page I · 26).

Os símbolos incluídos no texto do índice representam as grandes categorias identificadas com a chave à direita. Os símbolos com números em sua parte superior ([2]) identificam as subcategorias (veja-se a chave completa à página I · 26).

English	Deutsch	Español	Français	Português
Mountain	Berg	Montaña	Montagne	Montanha
Mountains	Berge	Montañas	Montagnes	Montanhas
Pass	Pass	Paso	Col	Passo
Valley, Canyon	Tal, Cañon	Valle, Cañón	Vallée, Canyon	Vale, Canhão
Plain	Ebene	Llano	Plaine	Planície
Cape	Kap	Cabo	Cap	Cabo
Island	Insel	Isla	Île	Ilha
Islands	Inseln	Islas	Îles	Ilhas
Other Topographic Features	Andere Topographische Objekte	Otros Elementos Topográficos	Autres données topographiques	Outros Elementos Topográficos

ESPAÑOL

Nombre	Página	Lat.°′	Long.°′ W=Oeste
Gelbes Meer → Yellow Sea ⊤[2]	80	36.00 N	123.00 E
Gelderland □[4]	48	52.10 N	5.50 E
Geldermalsen	48	51.53 N	5.17 E
Geldern	48	51.31 N	6.20 E
Geldern □[8]	253	51.25 N	6.27 E
Geldrop	48	51.25 N	5.33 E
Geleen	52	50.58 N	5.52 E
Gelegra	120	40.01 N	31.50 E
Gelemso	134	8.48 N	40.35 E
Gelenau	50	50.42 N	12.58 E
Gelenbe	120	39.10 N	27.50 E
Gelendost	120	38.07 N	31.01 E
Gelendžik	68	44.33 N	38.06 E
Gélengdeng	136	10.56 N	15.32 E
Gelfingen	54	47.13 N	8.16 E
Gelgaudiškis	66	55.05 N	23.00 E
Gelib → Jilib	134	0.28 N	42.50 E
Gelibolu	120	40.24 N	26.40 E
Gelibolu Yarımadası (Gallipoli Peninsula) ≻[1]	120	40.20 N	26.30 E
Gelidonya Burnu ≻	120	36.13 N	30.25 E
Gelinden	52	50.46 N	5.15 E
Gélise ≃	32	44.11 N	0.17 E
Geliting	105b	8.39 S	122.18 E
Geliting, Teluk C	105b	8.36 S	122.17 E
Gellenstrom ⋃	50	54.28 N	13.03 E
Gellep-Stratum ◆[8]	253	51.20 N	6.41 E
Gellibrand	159	38.32 S	143.32 E
Gellibrand ≃	159	38.41 S	143.09 E
Gellibrand, Point ≻	264b	37.52 S	144.54 E
Gellinsor	134	6.24 N	46.46 E
Gel'm'azov	68	49.49 N	31.49 E
Gelnhausen	52	50.11 N	9.11 E
Gelså ≃	41	55.19 N	8.54 E
Gelsdorf	52	50.35 N	7.02 E
Gelsenkirchen	48	51.31 N	7.07 E
Gelsenkirchen-Horst, Galopprennbahn ♠	253	51.32 N	7.02 E
Gelsted	41	55.24 N	9.59 E
Gelt ≃	42	54.56 N	2.47 W
Geltendorf	58	48.07 N	11.01 E
Gelterkinden	54	47.28 N	7.51 E
Gelting	41	54.45 N	9.53 E
Geltow	50	52.22 N	12.58 E
Gel Turfo	134	3.05 N	45.58 E
Geluk	148	27.01 S	24.18 E
Geluksburg	148	28.30 S	29.33 E
Geluwe	46	50.48 N	3.04 E
Gelveri	120	38.17 N	34.23 E
Gemas	104	2.35 N	102.37 E
Gem Beach	204	41.35 N	82.50 W
Gembloux	52	50.34 N	4.41 E
Gembrook	159	37.57 S	145.33 E
Gemen	48	51.51 N	6.52 E
Gemena	142	3.15 N	19.46 E
Gemengchi ⊜	110	31.15 N	89.15 E
Gémenos	56	43.18 N	5.38 E
Gemerek	120	39.11 N	36.05 E
Gemert	48	51.34 N	5.40 E
Gemla	26	56.52 N	14.38 E
Gemlik	120	40.26 N	29.09 E
Gemlik Körfezi C	120	40.25 N	28.55 E
Gemolong	105a	7.24 S	110.50 E
Gemona del Friuli	58	46.16 N	13.09 E
Gemonio	56	45.53 N	8.40 E
Gemu Gofa □[4]	134	4.45 N	37.00 E
Gemünd	52	50.34 N	6.30 E
Gemünden, B.R.D.	52	50.03 N	9.41 E
Gemünden, B.R.D.	52	50.58 N	8.58 E
Gemünden, B.R.D.	52	49.54 N	7.28 E
Gemuzhakechi ⊜	110	33.47 N	85.30 E
Genadendal	148	34.02 S	19.33 E
Genale ≃	134	5.43 N	40.53 E
Genappe	46	50.36 N	4.27 E
Genarp	41	55.36 N	13.23 E
Genazzano	60	41.50 N	12.58 E
Genç	120	38.46 N	40.35 E
Gençay	32	46.23 N	0.24 E
Gencek	120	37.27 N	31.33 E
Gending	105a	7.48 S	113.18 E
Gendrey	54	47.12 N	5.41 E
Gendringen	48	51.52 N	6.22 E
Gendt	48	51.53 N	5.59 E
Genegantslet Creek ≃	200	42.18 N	75.48 W
Genemuiden	48	52.37 N	6.07 E
General Acha	242	37.23 S	64.36 W
General Alvear, Arg.	242	36.03 S	60.01 W
General Alvear, Arg.	242	34.58 S	67.42 W
General Aquino	242	24.26 S	56.42 W
General Arenales	242	34.18 S	61.18 W
General Artigas	242	26.53 S	56.17 W
General Belgrano	242	35.46 S	58.30 W
General Bravo	222	25.48 N	99.10 W
General Butler State Park ♠	208	38.40 N	85.10 W
General Cabrera	242	32.48 S	63.52 W
General Câmara	242	29.54 S	51.46 W
General Campos	242	31.32 S	58.24 W
General Carneiro	245	15.42 S	52.45 W
General Carrera, Lago (Lago Buenos Aires) ⊜	244	46.35 S	72.00 W
General Cepeda	222	25.23 N	101.27 W
General Conesa, Arg.	242	36.30 S	57.20 W
General Conesa, Arg.	244	40.06 S	64.26 W
General Daniel Cerri	242	38.42 S	62.24 W
General del Sur, Cementerio ◆	276c	10.28 N	66.55 W
General Enrique Martínez	242	33.12 S	53.48 W
General Enrique Mosconi	242	22.36 S	63.49 W
General Escobedo, Méx.	186	25.49 N	100.20 W
General Escobedo, Méx.	222	25.30 N	105.15 W
General Eugenio A. Garay	242	25.55 S	56.11 W
General Galarza	242	32.43 S	59.24 W
General Guido	242	36.40 S	57.46 W
General Gutiérrez	242	32.57 S	68.48 W
General Hornos	248	34.53 S	58.56 W
General Island I	106	9.25 N	126.00 E
General José de San Martín	242	26.33 S	59.21 W
General Juan Madariaga	242	37.00 S	57.09 W
General La Madrid	242	37.16 S	61.17 W
General Las Heras	248	34.56 S	58.57 W
General Las Heras □[5]	278	34.56 S	58.51 W
General Lavalle	242	36.24 S	56.58 W
General Levalle	242	34.01 S	63.56 W
General Lorenzo Vintter	244	40.44 S	64.29 W
General Luna	106	9.47 N	126.09 E
General MacArthur (Pambuhan Sur)	106	11.15 N	125.32 E
General Machado	142	12.03 S	17.30 E
General Mansilla (Bartolomé Bavio)	248	35.05 S	57.45 W
General Manuel Belgrano, Cerro ∧	242	29.01 S	67.49 W
General Martín Miguel de Güemes	242	24.40 S	65.03 W
General Mitchell Field ⊠	206	42.57 N	87.54 W
General Motors Corporation (Pontiac Division) ʊ[3]	271	42.49 N	83.17 W
General Motors Proving Grounds ʊ[3]	271	42.35 N	83.41 W
General Motors Technical Center ʊ[3]	271	42.31 N	83.02 W

FRANÇAIS

Nom	Page	Lat.°′	Long.°′ W=Ouest
General'nyj ≃	255a	60.00 N	30.32 E
General O'Brien	242	34.54 S	60.45 W
General Pacheco	278	34.28 S	58.38 W
General Paz, Arg.	242	27.45 S	57.37 W
General Paz, Arg.	248	35.31 S	58.19 W
General Pico	242	35.40 S	63.44 W
General Pinedo	242	27.19 S	61.17 W
General Pinto	242	34.46 S	61.53 W
General Pizarro	242	24.13 S	64.01 W
General Plaza (Limón)	236	2.58 S	78.25 W
General Racedo, Valle V	244	43.15 S	68.35 W
General Roca	242	39.02 S	67.35 W
General Rodríguez	248	34.36 S	58.57 W
General Rojo	242	33.28 S	60.17 W
General Rondon	242	24.34 S	54.04 W
General Saavedra	238	17.15 S	63.10 W
General Sampaio	240	4.02 S	39.29 W
General San Martín, Arg.	242	37.59 S	63.34 W
General San Martín, Arg.	248	34.34 S	58.32 W
General San Martín □[5]	278	34.34 S	58.34 W
General Santos (Dadiangas)	106	6.07 N	125.11 E
General Sarmiento	248	34.33 S	58.43 W
General Sarmiento □[5]	278	34.32 S	58.43 W
General'skoje	73	47.28 N	39.35 E
General Terán	222	25.16 N	99.41 W
General Tinio	106	15.21 N	121.03 E
General Toševo	38	43.42 N	28.02 E
General Treviño	186	26.14 N	99.29 W
General Urquiza ◆[8]	278	34.34 S	58.29 W
General Vargas	242	29.42 S	54.40 W
General Viamonte (Los Toldos)	242	35.01 S	61.01 W
General Villegas	242	35.02 S	63.01 W
General Vintter, Lago (Lago Palena) ⊜	244	43.55 S	71.40 W
General Warren Village	275	40.02 N	75.32 W
General Zuazua	186	25.54 N	100.07 W
Gênes → Genova	56	44.25 N	8.57 E
Genesee, Idaho, U.S.	192	46.33 N	116.56 W
Genesee, Pa., U.S.	204	41.59 N	77.52 W
Genesee, Wis., U.S.	206	42.58 N	88.21 W
Genesee □[6], Mich., U.S.	206	42.56 N	83.41 W
Genesee □[6], N.Y., U.S.	200	43.00 N	78.11 W
Genesee ≃	200	43.16 N	77.36 W
Geneseo, Ill., U.S.	180	41.27 N	90.09 W
Geneseo, Kans., U.S.	188	38.31 N	98.09 W
Geneseo, N.Y., U.S.	200	42.48 N	77.49 W
Geneva → Genève, Schw.	54	46.12 N	6.09 E
Geneva, S. Afr.	148	27.50 S	27.08 E
Geneva, Ala., U.S.	184	31.02 N	85.52 W
Geneva, Fla., U.S.	210	28.44 N	81.07 W
Geneva, Ill., U.S.	206	41.53 N	88.18 W
Geneva, Ind., U.S.	206	40.36 N	84.58 W
Geneva, Nebr., U.S.	188	40.32 N	97.36 W
Geneva, N.Y., U.S.	200	42.52 N	77.00 W
Geneva, Ohio, U.S.	204	41.48 N	80.57 W
Geneva, Pa., U.S.	204	41.35 N	80.14 W
Geneva, Wash., U.S.	214	48.45 N	122.24 W
Geneva, Lake (Lac Léman) (Lac de Genève) ⊜, Eur.	54	46.25 N	6.30 E
Geneva, Lake ⊜, Wis., U.S.	206	42.34 N	88.30 W
Geneva-on-the-lake	204	41.52 N	80.57 W
Genève (Geneva)	54	46.12 N	6.09 E
Genève □[3]	54	46.15 N	6.10 E
Genève, Lac de → Geneva, Lake ⊜	54	46.25 N	6.30 E
Genève-Cointrin, Aéroport ⊠	54	46.14 N	6.06 E
Genevia	184	34.43 N	92.13 W
Genevois ◆[1]	54	46.03 N	6.14 E
Genévriers, Île des I	176	51.15 N	58.26 W
Genf → Genève	54	46.12 N	6.09 E
Genga	60	43.26 N	12.56 E
Gengenbach	54	48.24 N	8.01 E
Genghis Khan, Wall of ⊥	78	49.00 N	116.00 E
Gengji	90	33.47 N	112.47 E
Gengkou	90	29.12 N	113.19 E
Gengma	92	23.34 N	99.06 E
Gengputou	96	31.12 N	119.55 E
Gengzhuangzi	94	40.59 N	122.42 E
Genhe ≃	79	50.16 N	119.22 E
Geničesk	68	46.11 N	34.48 E
Génicourt	251	49.05 N	2.04 E
Génicourt-sur-Meuse	52	49.02 N	5.26 E
Genil ≃	34	37.42 N	5.19 W
Génissiat	54	46.03 N	5.47 E
Genk	52	50.58 N	5.30 E
Genkai	86	33.51 N	130.30 E
Genkai-kokutei-kōen ♠	86	33.54 N	130.31 E
Genkai-nada ⊤[2]	82	34.00 N	130.00 E
Genkanyj, Chrebet ∧∧	170	66.15 N	172.20 W
Genlis	54	47.14 N	5.13 E
Gennach ≃	54	48.10 N	10.43 E
Gennargentu, Monti del ∧∧	36	39.59 N	9.19 E
Gennebreck	253	51.19 N	7.12 E
Gennep	48	51.42 N	5.58 E
Genner	41	55.07 N	9.26 E
Gennes	32	47.20 N	0.14 W
Gennevilliers	251	48.56 N	2.18 E
Genoa, Austl.	156	37.29 S	149.35 E
Genoa → Genova, It.	56	44.25 N	8.57 E
Genoa, Ill., U.S.	206	42.06 N	88.42 W
Genoa, Nebr., U.S.	188	41.27 N	97.44 W
Genoa, Nev., U.S.	216	39.00 N	119.51 W
Genoa, N.Y., U.S.	200	42.40 N	76.32 W
Genoa, Ohio, U.S.	204	41.31 N	83.22 W
Genoa, Wis., U.S.	180	43.35 N	91.13 W
Genoa, Arroyo ≃	244	44.58 S	70.06 W
Genoa City	206	42.30 N	88.20 W
Genoa Peak ∧	216	39.03 N	119.53 W
Genola	56	44.35 N	7.39 E
Génolhac	56	44.21 N	3.57 E
Genova (Genoa)	56	44.25 N	8.57 E
Genova □[4]	56	44.30 N	9.04 E
Genova, Golfo di C	56	44.10 N	8.55 E
Genova, Val V	58	46.11 N	10.40 E
Genovesa, Isla I	236a	0.20 N	89.58 W
Genrijetty, Ostrov I	64	77.06 N	156.30 E
Gensan → Wŏnsan	88	39.09 N	127.25 E
Gens de Terre ≃	180	46.53 N	76.00 W
Genshagen	254a	52.19 N	13.19 E
Genshagener Heide ◆[3]	254a	52.20 N	13.18 E
Genshiryoku-kenkyūsho ʊ[3]	84	36.27 N	140.36 E
Gensingen	52	49.53 N	7.55 E
Gensungen	52	51.08 N	9.26 E
Gent (Gand)	46	51.03 N	3.43 E
Gentbrugge	46	51.03 N	3.45 E
Gent-Brugge, Kanaal ≊	46	51.03 N	3.43 E
Genteng	105a	8.22 S	114.09 E
Genteng, Gili I	105a	7.12 S	113.54 E
Genteng, Tanjung ≻	105a	7.23 S	106.24 E
Genthin	50	52.24 N	12.09 E
Gentilly	251	48.49 N	2.21 E
Gentilly ≃	196	46.24 N	72.21 W
Genting	104	3.42 N	98.10 E

PORTUGUÊS

Nome	Página	Lat.°′	Long.°′ W=Oeste
Gentio do Ouro	240	11.25 S	42.30 W
Gentioux	32	45.47 N	1.59 E
Gent naar Terneuzen, Kanaal van ≊	46	51.04 N	3.44 E
Gentofte	41	55.45 N	12.33 E
Gentry, Lake ⊜	210	28.08 N	81.15 W
Genua → Genova	56	44.25 N	8.57 E
Genuang	104	2.29 N	102.53 E
Genval	46	50.43 N	4.29 E
Genyem	154	2.46 S	140.12 E
Genzano di Roma	60	41.42 N	12.41 E
Geographe Bay C	152	33.35 S	115.15 E
Geographe Channel ⋃	152	24.40 S	113.20 E
Geokčaj	74	40.39 N	47.44 E
Geokčaj ≃	74	40.39 N	47.45 E
Geok-Tepe	118	38.09 N	57.58 E
Geonkhāli	116	22.12 N	88.03 E
George, S. Afr.	148	33.58 S	22.24 E
George, Iowa, U.S.	188	43.21 N	96.00 W
George, Tex., U.S.	212	30.59 N	96.07 W
George ≃, Austl.	152	20.50 S	117.28 E
George ≃, Qué., Can.	166	58.49 N	66.10 W
George, Cape ≻	176	45.53 N	61.53 W
George, Lake ⊜, Austl.	152	22.37 S	123.38 E
George, Lake ⊜, Austl.	156	35.05 S	149.25 E
George, Lake ⊜, N.A.	180	46.28 N	84.10 W
George, Lake ⊜, Ug.	144	0.02 N	30.12 E
George, Lake ⊜, U.S.	206	41.45 N	85.00 W
George, Lake ⊜, Fla., U.S.	182	29.17 N	81.36 W
George, Lake ⊜, Ind., U.S.	206	41.40 N	87.30 W
George, Lake ⊜, N.Y., U.S.	178	43.35 N	73.35 W
George, Lake ⊜[1]	212	29.29 N	95.38 W
George Air Force Base ■	218	34.35 N	117.22 W
George B. Stevenson Dam ◆[6]	204	41.25 N	78.01 W
George Gill Range ∧∧	152	24.15 S	131.36 E
George H. Crosby-Manitou State Park ♠	180	47.29 N	91.10 W
George Mason University ʊ[2]	274c	38.50 N	77.17 W
Georgensgmünd	52	49.11 N	11.00 E
Georgenthal	50	50.49 N	10.40 E
Georges ≃	160	33.57 S	150.58 E
Georges Bank ⊹[4]	16	41.00 N	67.00 W
Georges Hall	264a	33.55 S	150.59 E
Georges Island I	273	42.19 N	70.56 W
George Sound ⋃	162	44.50 S	167.23 E
Georges River Bridge ◆[5]	264a	34.00 S	151.07 E
Georges Run	204	40.21 N	80.37 W
Georges Run ≃	269b	40.23 N	80.06 W
George Town, Austl.	156	41.06 S	146.50 E
Georgetown, Austl.	156	18.18 S	143.33 E
Georgetown, Ont., Can.	202	43.39 N	79.55 W
Georgetown, P.E.I., Can.	176	46.11 N	62.32 W
Georgetown, Cay. Is.	228	19.18 N	81.23 W
Georgetown, Gam.	140	13.30 N	14.47 W
Georgetown, Guy.	236	6.48 N	58.10 W
George Town → Pinang, Malay.	104	5.25 N	100.20 E
Georgetown, St. Vin.	231h	13.16 N	61.08 W
Georgetown, Calif., U.S.	216	38.54 N	120.50 W
Georgetown, Conn., U.S.	197	41.16 N	73.26 W
Georgetown, Del., U.S.	198	38.42 N	75.23 W
Georgetown, Fla., U.S.	182	29.23 N	81.38 W
Georgetown, Ga., U.S.	182	31.53 N	85.06 W
Georgetown, Idaho, U.S.	192	42.29 N	111.22 W
Georgetown, Ill., U.S.	184	39.59 N	87.38 W
Georgetown, Ind., U.S.	208	38.18 N	85.58 W
Georgetown, Ky., U.S.	208	38.13 N	84.33 W
Georgetown, Mass., U.S.	197	42.43 N	71.00 W
Georgetown, Miss., U.S.	184	31.52 N	90.10 W
Georgetown, N.J., U.S.	275	40.05 N	74.39 W
Georgetown, N.Y., U.S.	200	42.46 N	75.44 W
Georgetown, Ohio, U.S.	208	38.52 N	83.54 W
Georgetown, Pa., U.S.	204	40.39 N	80.30 W
Georgetown, S.C., U.S.	182	33.23 N	79.17 W
Georgetown, Tex., U.S.	212	30.38 N	97.41 W
Georgetown ◆[8]	274c	38.54 N	77.03 W
Georgetown Lake ⊜	192	46.11 N	113.17 W
Georgetown Rowley State Forest ♠	273	42.42 N	70.58 W
Georgetown University ʊ[2]	274c	38.54 N	77.04 W
George V Coast ⌓[2]	9	68.30 S	147.30 E
George VI Sound ⋃	9	71.00 S	68.00 W
George Washington Birthplace National Monument ♠	198	38.11 N	76.56 W
George Washington Bridge ◆[5]	266	40.51 N	73.57 W
George Washington Carver National Monument ♠	184	37.00 N	94.19 W
George Washington University ʊ[2]	274c	38.54 N	77.03 W
George West	186	28.20 N	98.07 W
Georgia □[3]	168		
	182	32.50 N	83.15 W
Georgia, Strait of ⋃	172	49.20 N	124.00 W
Georgia del Sur, Isla de → South Georgia I	234	54.15 S	36.45 W
Georgia Heights	268	41.32 N	87.20 W
Georgiana	184	31.33 N	86.44 W
Georgian Bay C	180	45.15 N	80.50 W
Georgian Bay Islands National Park ♠	180	44.54 N	79.52 W
Georgian Soviet Socialist Republic → Gruzinskaja Sovetskaja Socialističeskaja Respublika □[3]	74	42.00 N	44.00 E
Géorgie du Sud → South Georgia I	234	54.15 S	36.45 W
Georgijevka, S.S.S.R.	70	53.18 N	51.01 E
Georgijevka, S.S.S.R.	73	48.26 N	39.17 E
Georgijevka, S.S.S.R.	75	42.11 N	70.00 E
Georgijevka, S.S.S.R.	75	43.03 N	74.43 E
Georgijevka, S.S.S.R.	76	49.19 N	81.35 E
Georgijevsk	74	44.09 N	43.28 E
Georgina ≃	156	23.30 S	139.47 E
Georgina Island I	202	44.23 N	79.17 W
Georgina Islands Indian Reserve ◆[4]	202	44.22 N	79.19 W
Georgiu-Dež (Liski)	68	50.59 N	39.30 E
Georgsmarienhütte	48	52.12 N	8.02 E
Gera	50	50.52 N	12.04 E
Gera □[5]	50	50.45 N	11.45 E
Gera ≃	50	51.08 N	10.56 E
Geraardsbergen	46	50.46 N	3.52 E
Geraberg	50	50.43 N	10.50 E
Gerabronn	52	49.15 N	9.55 E
Gerais, Chapada dos ∧∧[1]	245	17.40 S	45.20 W
Gerais, Serra dos ∧	246	21.54 S	44.06 W
Geral, Serra ∧∧	245	14.00 S	41.00 W
Geral, Serra (Serra Grande) ⌓[4], Bra.	240	11.15 S	46.30 W
Geral, Serra ⌓[4], Bra.	242	26.30 S	50.30 W
Gerald	209	38.24 N	91.20 W
Geral de Goiás, Serra ⌓[4]	245	13.00 S	46.15 W
Geraldine, N.Z.	162	44.05 S	171.14 E
Geraldine, Mont., U.S.	192	47.36 N	110.16 W
Geral do Paranã, Serra ∧∧[2]	245	14.45 S	47.30 W
Geraldton, Austl.	152	28.46 S	114.36 E
Geraldton, Ont., Can.	166	49.44 N	86.57 W
Gerale	134	6.20 N	42.32 E
Gerard, Lake ⊜	266	41.06 N	74.33 W
Gerard, Mount ∧	152	27.13 S	122.41 E
Gérardmer	54	48.04 N	6.53 E
Gerasa ⊥	122	32.17 N	35.53 E
Gerasdorf	254b	48.18 N	16.28 E
Gerasimovka	76	58.37 N	71.53 E
Gerber	194	40.03 N	122.09 W
Gerber Reservoir ⊜[1]	192	42.12 N	121.06 W
Gerbéviller	54	48.30 N	6.31 E
Gerblingerode	48	51.29 N	10.15 E
Gerbstedt	50	51.38 N	11.37 E
Gerca	68	48.09 N	26.16 E
Gerchsheim	52	49.42 N	9.47 E
Gercüş	120	37.34 N	41.23 E
Gerdau	148	26.28 S	26.06 E
Gerdine, Mount ∧	170	61.35 N	152.26 W
Gerdview	263d	26.10 S	28.11 E
Gère ≃	56	45.32 N	4.54 E
Gerede	120	40.48 N	32.12 E
Gerenzano	256b	45.38 N	9.00 E
Gereshk	110	31.48 N	64.34 E
Geretsried	58	47.51 N	11.28 E
Gérgal	34	37.07 N	2.33 W
Gergebil'	74	42.31 N	47.05 E
Gerger	120	38.02 N	39.02 E
Geria Nij	116	23.56 N	86.55 E
Gerik	104	5.25 N	101.08 E
Gering	188	41.50 N	103.40 W
Geringswalde	50	51.04 N	12.54 E
Geriş	120	36.58 N	31.44 E
Gerlachovský štít ∧	30	49.12 N	20.08 E
Gerlafingen	54	47.10 N	7.34 E
Gerli ◆[8]	278	34.41 S	58.23 W
Gerlingen	52	48.48 N	9.03 E
Gerlogubi	134	6.51 N	45.05 E
Gerlos	58	47.14 N	12.02 E
Gerlos Pass)(	58	47.14 N	12.08 E
Germa (Jarmah) ⊥	136	26.33 N	13.04 E
Germagnano	56	45.15 N	7.28 E
Germaine Bank ⊹[4]	16	5.05 N	107.35 W
Germán	222	25.10 N	97.54 W
German Democratic Republic □[1]	22		
	30	52.00 N	12.30 E
Germania	204	41.39 N	77.40 W
Germano	204	40.25 N	80.57 W
Germanoviči	66	55.25 N	27.44 E
Germansen, Mount ∧	172	55.37 N	124.50 W
Germansen Lake ⊜	172	55.41 N	124.53 W
Germansen Landing	172	55.47 N	124.43 W
Germansville	198	40.42 N	75.42 W
Germantown, Ill., U.S.	209	38.33 N	89.32 W
Germantown, Ky., U.S.	208	38.39 N	83.58 W
Germantown, N.Y., U.S.	200	42.08 N	73.54 W
Germantown, Ohio, U.S.	208	39.38 N	84.22 W
Germantown, Tenn., U.S.	184	35.05 N	89.49 W
Germantown, Wis., U.S.	206	43.14 N	88.06 W
Germantown ◆[8]	275	40.03 N	75.11 W
Germantown Reservoir ⊜[1]	208	39.40 N	84.30 W
Germany, Federal of □[1]	22		
	30	51.00 N	9.00 E
Germany Flats ≚	266	41.05 N	74.39 W
Germay	54	48.25 N	5.21 E
Germencik	120	37.51 N	27.37 E
Germendorf	50	52.45 N	13.10 E
Germersheim	52	49.13 N	8.22 E
Germfask	180	46.15 N	85.55 W
Germī	118	39.01 N	48.03 E
Germili	120	39.06 N	38.49 E
Germiston	148		
	263d	26.15 S	28.05 E
Germiter	120	38.28 N	37.36 E
Gernrode	50	51.43 N	11.08 E
Gernsbach	52	48.46 N	8.19 E
Gernsheim	52	49.44 N	8.29 E
Gero	84	35.48 N	137.14 E
Geroda	52	50.17 N	9.53 E
Gerola Alta	54	46.03 N	9.32 E
Geroldsgrün	50	50.20 N	11.35 E
Geroldstein	52	50.06 N	7.56 E
Gerolstein	52	50.13 N	6.40 E
Gerolzhofen	52	49.54 N	10.21 E
Gerona, Esp.	34	41.59 N	2.49 E
Gerona, Pil.	106	15.36 N	120.36 E
Gerpinnes	46	50.20 N	4.31 E
Gerrards Cross	250	51.35 N	0.34 W
Gerrei ◆[1]	36	39.28 N	9.20 E
Gerresheim ◆[8]	253	51.14 N	6.52 E
Gerringong	160	34.45 S	150.50 E
Gerry	204	42.12 N	79.15 W
Gers □[5]	32	43.40 N	0.30 E
Gers ≃	32	44.09 N	0.39 E
Gersau	54	47.00 N	8.32 E
Gersdorf	50	50.45 N	12.42 E
Gersfeld	52	50.27 N	9.55 E
Gershøj	41	55.43 N	11.59 E
Gersprenz ≃	52	49.59 N	9.04 E
Gerstetten	52	48.37 N	10.01 E
Gersthofen	54	48.25 N	10.53 E
Gerstungen	52	50.58 N	10.04 E
Gertak Sanggul, Tanjong ≻	104	5.15 N	100.11 E
Gerthe ◆[8]	253	51.31 N	7.17 E
Gerufa	146	19.17 S	26.02 E
Gervais	214	45.07 N	122.54 W
Gerwisch	50	52.10 N	11.44 E
Gerza	132	29.26 N	31.11 E
Gerze	120	41.48 N	35.12 E
Gerzensee	54	46.51 N	7.33 E
Gescher	48	51.57 N	6.59 E
Geschwenda	50	50.44 N	10.49 E
Geseke	48	51.38 N	8.31 E
Geser	154	3.53 S	130.54 E
Gesher HaZiw	122	33.02 N	35.06 E
Gesi	105a	7.20 S	111.01 E
Gesoa	154	8.25 S	143.35 E
Gespunsart	52	49.49 N	4.50 E
Gessertshausen	54	48.20 N	10.44 E
Gesso ≃	56	44.24 N	7.33 E
Gessopalena	60	42.03 N	14.16 E
Gesten	41	55.31 N	9.12 E
Gesualdo	60	41.00 N	15.04 E
Geta	26	60.23 N	19.50 E
Getafe	34	40.18 N	3.43 W
Getafe, Aeropuerto ⊠	256a	40.18 N	3.43 W
Gethaoli	262c	19.08 N	73.01 E
Gethsémani	176	50.13 N	60.40 W
Geti	144	1.13 N	30.12 E
Getinge	26	56.49 N	12.44 E
Gettorf	41	54.24 N	9.58 E
Gettysburg, Ohio, U.S.	208	40.07 N	84.30 W
Gettysburg, Pa., U.S.	198	39.50 N	77.14 W
Gettysburg, S. Dak., U.S.	188	45.01 N	99.57 W
Gettysburg National Military Park ♠	198	39.49 N	77.15 W
Getulândia	246	22.40 S	44.06 W
Getulina	245	21.49 S	49.55 W
Getulio	106	10.45 N	122.40 E
Getúlio Vargas	242	27.50 S	52.16 W
Getz Ice Shelf ⊼	9	75.00 S	129.00 W
Getzville	200	43.01 N	78.46 W
Geudubang	104	4.54 N	97.23 E
Geumpang	104	4.48 N	96.09 E
Geureudong, Gunung ∧	104	4.48 N	96.48 E
Gevān	118	26.03 N	57.17 E
Gevaş	118	38.16 N	43.07 E
Gevelsberg	52	51.19 N	7.20 E
Gevgelija	38	41.08 N	22.30 E
Gévora ≃	34	38.53 N	6.57 W
Gevrey-Chambertin	54	47.14 N	4.57 E
Gewani	134	10.16 N	40.44 E
Geweke ◆[8]	253	51.22 N	7.25 E
Gex	54	46.20 N	6.04 E
Geyer	50	50.37 N	12.55 E
Geyer Ditch ≊	206	41.36 N	86.25 W
Geyikli	120	39.48 N	26.12 E
Geysdorp	148	26.32 S	25.18 E
Geyser	192	47.16 N	110.30 W
Geyser, Banc du ⊹[2]	128	12.25 S	46.25 E
Geyserville	194	38.42 N	122.54 W
Geyuan	90	28.31 N	117.44 E
Geyve	120	40.30 N	30.18 E
Gézenti	136	21.41 N	18.18 E
Gezer	122	31.52 N	34.55 E
Gez Gölü ⊜	120	38.35 N	33.06 E
Gezihu ⊜	110	38.10 N	90.42 E
Ghabāghib	122	33.10 N	36.13 E
Ghābat al-'Arab	130	9.02 N	29.29 E
Ghadaf, Wādī al- V	122	31.46 N	36.50 E
Ghafe	262c	19.05 N	73.07 E
Ghaggar ≃	113	29.30 N	74.53 E
Ghaghar Reservoir ⊜[1]	114	24.38 N	83.11 E
Ghāghra ≃	114	25.47 N	84.37 E
Ghāgra	114	23.17 N	84.33 E
Ghairatganj	114	23.24 N	78.13 E
Ghakhar	113	32.18 N	74.09 E
Ghallah, Wādī al- V	130	10.25 N	27.32 E
Ghammāzah al-Kubrā	132	29.43 N	31.18 E
Ghamrīn	132	30.30 N	30.55 E
Ghana □[1]	124		
	140	8.00 N	2.00 W
Ghansoli	262c	19.08 N	72.59 E
Ghanzi	146	21.38 S	21.45 E
Ghanzi □[5]	146	22.00 S	23.00 E
Ghārāpuri	262c	18.54 N	72.56 E
Gharaunda	114	29.33 N	76.58 E
Gharbah, Wādī V	132	29.40 N	31.58 E
Gharbi, Île I	138	34.39 N	11.03 E
Ghardaïa	138	32.31 N	3.37 E
Ghardimaou	36	36.26 N	8.27 E
Gharghoda	114	22.10 N	83.21 E
Gharībwāl	113	32.41 N	73.10 E
Gharīfah	122	33.38 N	35.33 E
Gharig	130	10.47 N	27.33 E
Ghārīyat al-Gharbīyah	122	32.41 N	36.13 E
Ghārīyat ash-Sharqīyah	122	32.40 N	36.16 E
Gharo	110	24.44 N	67.35 E
Gharrāf, Shaṭṭ al- ≃	118	32.30 N	45.48 E
Gharrah, Jabal ∧[2]	132	30.12 N	32.15 E
Gharroli ◆[8]	262a	28.37 N	77.20 E
Gharw, Jazīrat I	132	31.21 N	30.06 E
Gharyān	136	32.10 N	13.01 E
Gharyān □[4]	136	30.50 N	12.00 E
Ghaṣm	122	32.33 N	36.22 E
Ghāt	136	24.58 N	10.11 E
Ghātākhān	116	23.02 N	90.26 E
Ghātāl	116	22.40 N	87.43 E
Ghatampur	262b	22.54 N	88.10 E
Ghātkopar ◆[8]	262c	19.05 N	72.54 E
Ghātprabha ≃	112	16.20 N	75.48 E
Ghātsīla	116	22.36 N	86.29 E
Ghats Occidentales → Western Ghāts ∧∧	112	14.00 N	75.00 E
Ghats Orientales → Eastern Ghāts ∧∧	112	14.00 N	78.50 E
Ghawdex I	36	36.03 N	14.15 E
Ghawr ash-Sharqīyah, Qanāt al- ≊	122	32.41 N	35.38 E
Ghaylah ∧[1]	122	33.11 N	37.05 E
Ghayl Bā Wazīr	134	14.48 N	49.21 E
Ghayth, Wādī V	122	30.59 N	36.00 E
Ghazāl, Baḥr al- ≃	130	9.31 N	30.25 E
Ghazal, Bahr el V	136	13.01 N	15.28 E
Ghazālat al-Khīs	132	30.34 N	31.34 E
Ghazaouet	138	35.06 N	1.51 W
Ghāziābād	113	28.40 N	77.26 E
Ghāzīpur, Bhārat	114	25.35 N	83.34 E
Ghazipur, Bhārat	262b	22.36 N	88.34 E
Ghāzīpur □[5]	114	25.40 N	83.20 E
Ghāzipur ◆[8]	262a	28.38 N	77.19 E
Ghazīr	120	34.01 N	35.40 E
Ghazlūna	110	31.33 N	68.48 E
Ghaznī	110	33.33 N	68.26 E
Ghaznī □[4]	110	33.00 N	68.00 E
Ghaznī ≃	110	32.35 N	67.58 E
Ghazni Khel	113	32.33 N	70.44 E
Ghazzah (Gaza), Gaza	122	31.30 N	34.28 E
Ghazzah, Lubnān	122	33.40 N	35.49 E
Gheā ≃	262b	22.52 N	88.19 E
Ghedi	58	45.24 N	10.16 E
Ghemme	56	45.37 N	8.25 E
Ghennes Heights	269b	40.09 N	79.56 W
Ghent → Gent, Bel.	46	51.03 N	3.43 E
Ghent, Ky., U.S.	208	38.44 N	85.04 W
Ghent, N.Y., U.S.	200	42.20 N	73.37 W
Ghent, Ohio, U.S.	204	41.09 N	81.38 W
Gheora ◆[8]	262a	28.42 N	77.01 E
Gheorghe Gheorghiu-Dej	38	46.14 N	26.44 E
Gheorgheni	38	46.43 N	25.36 E
Gherla	38	47.02 N	23.55 E
Ghesar	262c	19.09 N	73.05 E
Ghigo	56	44.53 N	7.03 E
Ghīn, Tall ∧	122	32.39 N	36.43 E
Ghior	116	23.54 N	89.53 E
Ghisonàccia	36	42.00 N	9.25 E
Ghizar ≃	113	36.15 N	73.25 E
Ghlin	46	50.28 N	3.53 E
Gholson	212	31.43 N	97.12 W
Ghonda ◆[8]	262a	28.41 N	77.16 E
Ghondi ◆[8]	262a	28.42 N	77.16 E
Ghorāsahan	114	26.50 N	85.08 E
Ghorāsāl	116	23.56 N	90.38 E
Ghoshpur, Bhārat	262b	22.23 N	88.29 E
Ghoshpur, Bngl.	116	23.27 N	89.39 E
Ghotki	110	28.01 N	69.19 E
Ghowr □[4]	118	34.00 N	65.00 E
Ghubaysh	130	12.09 N	27.21 E
Ghubbet Raguda C	134	10.55 N	46.35 E
Ghudāf, Wādī al- V	118	32.56 N	43.30 E
Ghudāmis	136	30.08 N	9.30 E
Ghunthur	120	34.23 N	37.09 E
Ghurāb, Jabal ∧[2]	132	28.58 N	31.16 E
Ghurayrah	134	18.37 N	42.41 E
Ghūrīān	118	34.21 N	61.30 E
Ghurrān, Farsh al- ∧∧[1]	132	29.38 N	31.38 E
Ghushuri	262b	22.37 N	88.22 E
Ghuwaybah, Wādī V	132	29.36 N	32.20 E
Ghuwayr, 'Ayn al- ⊤[4]	122	31.37 N	35.25 E
Ghuzzayil, Sabkhat ⊜	136	29.50 N	19.35 E
Gia-dinh	100	10.48 N	106.42 E
Giaginskaja	68	44.53 N	40.05 E
Giang ≃	100	17.40 N	106.30 E
Giannutri, Isola di I	60	42.15 N	11.06 E
Giano, Monte ∧	60	42.25 N	13.06 E
Giano dell'Umbria	60	42.50 N	12.35 E
Giant City State Park ♠	184	37.39 N	89.12 W
Giant Mountain ∧	178	44.10 N	73.44 W
Giant's Castle ∧	148	29.21 S	29.27 E
Giants Castle Game Reserve ◆[4]	148	29.16 S	29.30 E
Giant's Causeway ♠	42	55.14 N	6.30 W
Giants Neck	197	41.18 N	72.11 W
Giants Tomb Island I	202	44.55 N	80.00 W
Gianyar	105b	8.32 S	115.20 E
Gia-rai	100	9.14 N	105.28 E
Giardinetto	60	41.19 N	15.24 E
Giarre	36	37.43 N	15.11 E
Giaveno	56	45.02 N	7.21 E
Giazza	58	45.39 N	11.07 E
Gibara	230p	21.07 N	76.08 W
Gibbon, Minn., U.S.	180	44.32 N	94.31 W
Gibbon, Nebr., U.S.	188	40.45 N	98.51 W
Gibbons	172	53.50 N	113.20 W
Gibbonsville	192	45.33 N	113.55 W
Gibb River	154	15.39 S	126.38 E
Gibbs, Mount ∧	152	32.55 S	120.00 E
Gibbsboro	275	39.50 N	74.58 W
Gibbstown	198	39.50 N	75.17 W
Gibeon	146	25.09 S	17.43 E
Gibeon □[5]	146	25.00 S	19.00 E
Gibraleón	34	37.23 N	6.58 W
Gibraltar, Gib.	34	36.09 N	5.21 W
Gibraltar, Mich., U.S.	206	42.06 N	83.12 W
Gibraltar, Pa., U.S.	198	40.17 N	75.52 W
Gibraltar □[2]	22		
	34	36.11 N	5.22 W
Gibraltar, Strait of (Estrecho de Gibraltar) ⋃	34	35.57 N	5.36 W
Gibraltar Point ≻, Ont., Can.	265b	43.36 N	79.23 W
Gibraltar Point ≻, Eng., U.K.	44	53.05 N	0.19 E
Gibsland	184	32.33 N	93.03 W
Gibson, Austl.	152	33.39 S	121.48 E
Gibson, Ga., U.S.	182	33.14 N	82.36 W
Gibson, N.Y., U.S.	200	42.08 N	76.59 W
Gibson, Pa., U.S.	200	41.44 N	75.38 W
Gibson ≃	202	44.58 N	79.51 W
Gibsonburg	204	41.23 N	83.19 W
Gibson City	206	40.28 N	88.22 W
Gibson Desert ◆[2]	152	24.30 S	126.00 E
Gibson Hill ∧[2]	204	41.51 N	80.10 W
Gibsonia	204	40.38 N	79.59 W
Gibson Indian Reserve ◆[4]	202	45.01 N	79.44 W
Gibson Island I	198	39.05 N	76.26 W
Gibsons	172	49.24 N	123.30 W
Gibsonton	210	27.51 N	82.23 W
Gidajevo	24	59.57 N	52.22 E
Gidami	134	9.58 N	34.37 E
Gidari	136	9.17 N	16.40 E
Giddalūr	112	15.21 N	78.55 E
Giddarbāha	113	30.12 N	74.40 E
Giddings	212	30.11 N	96.56 W
Gide	134	9.40 N	35.16 E
Gideälven ≃	26	63.20 N	19.08 E
Gidea Park ◆[8]	250	51.35 N	0.12 E
Gideåvallen	26	63.29 N	18.58 E
Gideon	184	36.27 N	89.55 W
Gidgee	152	27.16 S	119.22 E
Gidgi, Lake ⊜	152	29.16 S	126.03 E
Gidhni	116	22.29 N	86.51 E
Gidole	134	5.38 N	37.30 E
Gidrotorf	70	56.28 N	43.33 E
Gidžaki, Gora ∧	74	40.25 N	49.01 E
Giebelstadt	52	49.39 N	9.56 E
Gieboldehausen	48	51.36 N	10.13 E
Giedraičiai	66	55.05 N	25.15 E
Gielow	50	53.42 N	12.44 E
Gielsdorf	254a	52.36 N	13.52 E
Gien	46	47.42 N	2.38 E
Giengen	52	48.37 N	10.14 E
Giens	56	43.02 N	6.08 E
Gier ≃	56	45.35 N	4.46 E
Gierath	253	51.07 N	6.33 E
Gierle	52	51.16 N	4.51 E
Giesebitz → Izbica	30	54.42 N	17.26 E
Gieselwerder	48	51.36 N	9.33 E
Giesenkirchen ◆[8]	253	51.09 N	6.30 E
Giesing ◆[8]	58	48.06 N	11.35 E
Giessen	52	50.35 N	8.40 E
Gieten	48	53.00 N	6.46 E
Giethoorn	48	52.43 N	6.05 E
Gièvres	46	47.16 N	1.40 E
Giez	56	45.45 N	6.15 E
Giffard	196	46.51 N	71.12 W
Gifford, Scot., U.K.	42	55.54 N	2.45 W
Gifford, Fla., U.S.	210	27.41 N	80.25 W
Gifford, Ill., U.S.	206	40.18 N	88.01 W
Gifford, Ind., U.S.	206	41.06 N	87.01 W
Gifford, Pa., U.S.	204	41.51 N	78.36 W
Gifford ≃	166	70.21 N	83.05 W
Gifford Creek	152	24.05 S	116.11 E
Gifford Fjord C[2]	166	69.57 N	81.55 W
Gifford Pinchot State Park ♠	198	40.04 N	76.53 W
Giffre ≃	54	46.05 N	6.30 E
Gifhorn	48	52.29 N	10.33 E
Giflitz	52	51.09 N	9.07 E
Gif-sur-Yvette	251	48.42 N	2.08 E
Gifu	84	35.25 N	136.45 E
Gifu □[5]	84	35.45 N	137.00 E
Gigant	70	46.30 N	41.20 E
Giganta, Cerro ∧	222	26.07 N	111.36 W
Giganta, Sierra de la ∧∧	222	25.30 N	111.15 W
Gigante	236	2.23 N	75.33 W
Gigante Islands II	106	11.36 N	123.20 E
Gigatangan Island I	106	11.34 N	124.16 E
Gigen	38	43.42 N	24.29 E
Gigena → Alcira	242	32.45 S	64.20 W
Giggleswick	42	54.04 N	2.17 W
Gigha, Sound of ⋃	42	55.40 N	5.42 W
Gigha Island I	42	55.41 N	5.44 W
Gig Harbor	214	47.20 N	122.35 W
Giglio, Isola del I	60	42.21 N	10.54 E
Giglio Castello	60	42.22 N	10.54 E
Gigliola	60	44.51 N	12.14 E
Giglio Porto	60	42.22 N	10.55 E
Gigmoto	106	13.47 N	124.23 E
Gignod	56	45.46 N	7.17 E
Gihu → Gifu	84	35.25 N	136.45 E
Gijón	34	43.32 N	5.40 W
Gijunabena Islands II	165e	7.31 S	158.42 E
Gikongoro	144	2.29 S	29.34 E
Gila ≃	190	32.43 N	114.33 W
Gila, Middle Fork ≃	190	33.14 N	108.14 W
Gila Bend	190	32.57 N	112.43 W
Gila Bend Mountains ∧∧	190	33.10 N	113.10 W
Gila Cliff Dwellings National Monument ♠	190	33.02 N	108.16 W
Gila Mountains ∧∧	190	33.05 N	109.50 W
Gīlān □[4]	118	37.00 N	49.00 E
Gīlān-e Gharb	118	34.08 N	45.55 E
Gila River Indian Reservation ◆[4]	190	33.12 N	112.00 W
Gilātala	116	22.36 N	89.41 E
Gilbert, La., U.S.	184	32.03 N	91.39 W
Gilbert, Minn., U.S.	180	47.29 N	92.28 W
Gilbert ≃, Austl.	156	16.35 S	141.15 E
Gilbert ≃, Austl.	158b	34.22 S	138.40 E

≃ River	Fluss	Río	Rivière	Rio
≊ Canal	Kanal	Canal	Canal	Canal
↳ Waterfall, Rapids	Wasserfall, Stromschnellen	Cascada, Rápidos	Chute d'eau, Rapides	Cascata, Rápidos
⋃ Strait	Meeresstrasse	Estrecho	Détroit	Estreito
C Bay, Gulf	Bucht, Golf	Bahía, Golfo	Baie, Golfe	Baía, Golfo
⊜ Lake, Lakes	See, Seen	Lago, Lagos	Lac, Lacs	Lago, Lagos
≋ Swamp	Sumpf	Pantano	Marais	Pântano
⊼ Ice Features, Glacier	Eis- und Gletscherformen	Accidentes Glaciales	Formes glaciaires	Acidentes Glaciares
⊤ Other Hydrographic Features	Andere Hydrographische Objekte	Otros Elementos Hidrográficos	Autres données hydrographiques	Outros Elementos Hidrográficos

⊹ Submarine Features	Untermeerische Objekte	Accidentes Submarinos	Formes de relief sous-marin	Acidentes Submarinos
□ Political Unit	Politische Einheit	Unidad Politica	Entité politique	Unidade Política
ʊ Cultural Institution	Kulturelle Institution	Institución Cultural	Institution culturelle	Instituição Cultural
⊥ Historical Site	Historische Stätte	Sitio Histórico	Site historique	Sitio Histórico
♠ Recreational Site	Erholungs- und Ferienort	Sitio de Recreo	Centre de loisirs	Sítio de Lazer
⊠ Airport	Flughafen	Aeropuerto	Aéroport	Aeroporto
■ Military Installation	Militäranlage	Instalación Militar	Installation militaire	Instalação Militar
◆ Miscellaneous	Verschiedenes	Misceláneo	Divers	Miscelânea

Gilbert, Mount ∧ 172 50.51 N 124.20 W
Gilbert Airport ⊠ 269a 41.22 N 81.58 W
Gilbert Island I 209 39.35 N 91.11 W
Gilbert Islands
→ **Kiribati** □[1] 14 0.00 174.00 E
Gilbert Lake ⊜ 271 42.34 N 83.17 W
Gilbert Lake State Park ♠ 200 42.36 N 75.08 W
Gilberton 200 40.48 N 76.13 W
Gilbertown 184 31.53 N 88.19 W
Gilbert Peak ∧ 214 46.30 N 121.25 W
Gilbert Plains 174 51.09 N 100.29 W
Gilbert River 156 18.09 S 142.52 E
Gilberts 206 42.06 N 88.23 W
Gilbert Seamount ✢[3] 16 52.50 N 150.05 W
Gilbertsville, N.Y., U.S. 200 42.28 N 75.20 W
Gilbertsville, Pa., U.S. 198 40.19 N 75.37 W
Gilbertville 197 42.19 N 72.12 W
Gilbjerg Hoved ≻ 41 56.08 N 12.17 E
Gilboa 206 41.01 N 83.55 W
Gilboa, Hare ⩘[2] 122 32.30 N 35.23 E
Gilbués 240 9.50 S 45.21 W
Gilching 58 48.07 N 11.17 E
Gildehaus 48 52.18 N 7.06 E
Gildford 192 48.34 N 110.18 W
Gilead 206 41.48 N 85.09 W
Giles, Arroyo de ≃ 248 34.20 S 59.23 W
Giles Creek ≃ 152 17.25 S 130.50 E
Giles Point ≻ 158b 35.03 S 137.45 E
Gilette 56 43.51 N 7.10 E
Gilford 42 54.23 N 6.22 W
Gilford Island I 172 50.45 N 126.25 W
Gilford Park 198 39.58 N 74.08 W
Gilgai 152 31.15 S 119.56 E
Gilgandra 156 31.42 S 148.39 E
Gilgil 144 0.30 S 36.19 E
Gil Gil Creek ≃ 156 29.10 S 148.51 E
Gilgit 113 35.55 N 74.18 E
Gilgit ≃ 113 35.44 N 74.38 E
Gilgit Wazārat □[8] 113 35.10 N 74.55 E
Gilgo Island I 266 40.38 N 73.25 W
Gilgo State Park ♠ 266 40.38 N 73.22 W
Gilima 144 3.55 N 28.22 E
Gilimanuk 105a 8.10 S 114.26 E
Gil Island I 172 53.13 N 129.15 W
Gillam 174 56.21 N 94.43 W
Gilleland Creek ≃ 212 30.13 N 97.32 W
Gilleleje 41 56.07 N 12.19 E
Gillen, Lake ⊜ 152 26.11 S 124.38 E
Gilles, Lake ⊜ 156 32.50 S 136.45 E
Gillespie 209 39.07 N 89.49 W
Gillespie Point ≻ 162 43.24 S 169.50 E
Gillett, Ark., U.S. 184 34.07 N 91.22 W
Gillett, Pa., U.S. 200 41.57 N 76.48 W
Gillett, Wis., U.S. 180 44.54 N 88.18 W
Gillette, N.J., U.S. 266 40.41 N 74.28 W
Gillette, Wyo., U.S. 188 44.18 N 105.30 W
Gillette Castle State Park ♠ 197 41.26 N 72.25 W
Gillian, Lake ⊜ 166 69.32 N 75.23 W
Gillingham, Eng., U.K. 44 51.02 N 2.17 W
Gillingham, Eng., U.K. 44 51.24 N 0.33 E
Gillingham □[8] 250 51.22 N 0.35 E
Gilman, Conn., U.S. 197 41.34 N 72.16 W
Gilman, Ill., U.S. 206 40.46 N 87.59 W
Gilman, Iowa, U.S. 180 41.53 N 92.47 W
Gilman, Wis., U.S. 180 45.10 N 90.48 W
Gilman Hot Springs 218 33.50 N 116.59 W
Gilmer, Ill., U.S. 268 42.14 N 88.02 W
Gilmer, Tex., U.S. 212 32.44 N 94.57 W
Gilmer Park 206 41.36 N 86.15 W
Gilmore 161b 35.20 S 148.11 E
Gilmore City 188 42.44 N 94.27 W
Gilmore Creek ≃ 161b 35.18 S 148.13 E
Gilo ≃ 134 8.10 N 33.15 E
Gilroy 216 37.00 N 121.34 W
Gilserberg 52 50.57 N 9.04 E
Gilsizer Slough ≃ 216 38.58 N 121.44 W
Gilston Park ♠ 250 51.48 N 0.04 E
Giltner 188 40.47 N 98.09 W
Gil'uj ≃ 79 53.58 N 127.30 E
Giluwe, Mount ∧ 154 6.05 S 143.50 E
Gilwern 44 51.51 N 3.06 W
Gilze 48 51.33 N 4.57 E
Gimån ≃ 26 62.28 N 16.20 E
Gimbi 134 9.10 N 35.42 E
Gimborn 52 51.03 N 7.28 E
Gimcheon → Kimch'ŏn 88 36.07 N 128.05 E
Gimie, Mount ∧ 231f 13.52 N 61.01 W
Gimlet 208 38.13 N 83.09 W
Gimli 174 50.38 N 96.59 W
Gimo 40 60.11 N 18.11 E
Gimoly 24 63.03 N 32.19 E
Gimone ≃ 32 44.00 N 1.06 E
Gimont 32 43.38 N 0.53 E
Gimpu 102 1.36 S 120.02 E
Ginaldag, Gora ∧ 74 40.20 N 45.57 E
Ginderich 253 51.39 N 6.32 E
Ginebra → Genève 54 46.12 N 6.09 E
Gineste, Col de la)(56 43.15 N 5.27 E
Gingell 206 42.43 N 83.17 W
Gingera, Mount ∧ 161b 35.35 S 148.47 E
Ginger Hill 269b 40.12 N 80.00 W
Ginger Island I 230m 18.24 N 64.28 W
Gingin, Austl. 152 31.21 S 115.42 E
Gin Gin, Austl. 156 25.00 S 151.58 E
Gingindlovu 148 29.02 S 31.30 E
Gingoog 106 8.50 N 125.07 E
Gingoog Bay ⊂ 106 8.59 N 125.05 E
Gingst 50 54.27 N 13.16 E
Ginir 134 7.07 N 40.46 E
Ginkakuji Temple ♁[1] 260 35.03 N 135.47 E
Ginkgo State Park ♠ 192 46.59 N 120.01 W
Ginnosar 122 32.51 N 35.31 E
Ginosa 36 40.34 N 16.46 E
Ginowan 164m 26.17 N 127.46 E
Ginter 204 40.46 N 78.23 W
Ginza ⬥[8] 258 35.40 N 139.47 E
Ginzo de Limia 34 42.03 N 7.43 W
Gioia dei Marsi 60 41.57 N 13.42 E
Gioia del Colle 36 40.48 N 16.56 E
Gioia Tauro 36 38.26 N 15.54 E
Gioia Vecchio 60 41.54 N 13.44 E
Gioiosa Ionica 36 38.20 N 16.18 E
Gion 86 34.26 N 132.28 E
Giornico 54 46.24 N 8.52 E
Giovi, Passo dei)(56 44.33 N 8.57 E
Giporlos 106 11.07 N 125.27 E
Gipping ≃ 44 52.04 N 1.10 E
Gipsy 204 40.48 N 78.53 W
Giraglia, Île de la I 56 43.02 N 9.24 E
Giralia 152 22.41 S 114.21 E
Giraltovce 30 49.07 N 21.31 E
Girard, Ill., U.S. 209 39.27 N 89.47 W
Girard, Kans., U.S. 188 37.31 N 94.51 W
Girard, Mich., U.S. 206 42.02 N 85.00 W
Girard, Ohio, U.S. 204 41.10 N 80.42 W
Girard, Pa., U.S. 204 42.00 N 80.19 W
Girard, Tex., U.S. 186 33.22 N 100.40 W
Girardot 236 4.18 N 74.48 W
Girardville 198 40.47 N 76.17 W
Giraud, Pointe ≻ 230d 15.19 N 61.15 W
Giraul ≃ 142 15.04 S 12.08 E
Giraumont 52 49.10 N 5.55 E
Girbovu 38 44.44 N 23.21 E
Gird Gwalior □[5] 114 26.00 N 78.00 E
Girdletree 198 38.06 N 75.24 W
Girdwood 170 60.57 N 149.10 W
Giresun 120 40.55 N 38.24 E
Giresun □[4] 120 40.30 N 38.30 E
Girgarre 156 36.24 S 144.59 E
Girgaum ⬥[8] 262c 18.57 N 72.48 E
Girgenti → Agrigento 36 37.18 N 13.35 E
Girgir, Cape ≻ 154 3.50 S 144.34 E
Gīr Hills ⩘[2] 110 21.18 N 71.00 E
Giri ≃ 142 0.28 N 17.59 E
Giridih 116 24.11 N 86.18 E
Girifalco 36 38.49 N 16.25 E
Girilambone 156 31.15 S 146.54 E
Girimira 120 37.07 N 41.26 E
Girna ≃ 112 21.08 N 75.19 E
Giro, Nig. 140 11.06 N 4.46 E
Giro, Zaïre 144 3.08 N 29.15 E
Giromagny 54 47.45 N 6.50 E
Girón, Ec. 236 3.10 S 79.08 W
Giron, Fr. 54 46.14 N 5.46 E
Gironde □[5] 32 44.45 N 0.35 W
Gironde ⊂[1] 32 45.20 N 0.45 W
Gironville-sous-les-Côtes 52 48.48 N 5.40 E
Girou ≃ 32 43.46 N 1.23 E
Girouxville 172 55.45 N 117.20 W
Girtys Run ≃ 269b 40.28 N 79.58 W
Giru 156 19.31 S 147.06 E
Giruá 242 28.02 S 54.21 W
Girvan 42 55.15 N 4.51 W
Girvan, Water of ≃ 42 55.15 N 4.51 W
Girvas 24 62.30 N 33.40 E
Girvas, Vodopad ⌊ 24 62.27 N 33.40 E
Girwa ≃ 114 28.15 N 81.05 E
Gisborne, Austl. 159 37.29 S 144.35 E
Gisborne, N.Z. 162 38.40 S 178.01 E
Gisborne Lake ⊜ 176 47.48 N 54.50 W
Giscome 172 54.04 N 122.22 W
Gisenyi 144 1.42 S 29.15 E
Gislaved 26 57.18 N 13.32 E
Gislev 41 55.13 N 10.37 E
Gislinge 41 55.44 N 11.33 E
Gislövs läge 41 55.21 N 13.14 E
Gisors 46 49.17 N 1.47 E
Gissar 75 38.33 N 68.35 E
Gissarskij Chrebet ⩘ 75 39.00 N 68.40 E
Gisselfeld 41 55.18 N 11.59 E
Gissi 60 42.01 N 14.33 E
Gisslarbo 40 59.38 N 15.49 E
Gistel 46 51.10 N 2.57 E
Giswil 54 46.50 N 8.11 E
Gitambo 144 4.21 N 24.45 E
Gitarama 144 2.07 S 29.45 E
Gitega 144 3.26 S 29.56 E
Gittelde 48 51.48 N 10.10 E
Giuba, Isole II 134 0.50 S 42.15 E
Giudicarie, Valli ∨ 58 45.58 N 10.45 E
Giugliano in Campania 60 40.56 N 14.12 E
Giulianova 60 42.45 N 13.57 E
Giulie, Alpi → Julian Alps ⩘ 36 46.00 N 14.00 E
Giulietti, Lake ⊜ 134 13.15 N 40.55 E
Giumbo → Jumbo 134 0.12 S 42.38 E
Giurgiu 38 43.53 N 25.57 E
Giussano 56 45.42 N 9.14 E
Giv'atayim 122 32.04 N 34.48 E
Giv'at Brenner 122 31.52 N 34.48 E
Give 41 55.51 N 9.15 E
Giverny 46 49.04 N 1.32 E
Givet 52 50.08 N 4.50 E
Givors 56 45.35 N 4.46 E
Givrine, Col de la)(54 46.27 N 6.05 E
Givry 54 46.47 N 4.45 E
Givry-en-Argonne 52 48.57 N 4.53 E
Givry Island I 165c 7.07 N 151.53 E
Giyon 134 8.30 N 38.00 E
Giza → Al-Jīzah 132 30.01 N 31.13 E
Gīzāb 110 33.23 N 66.16 E
Gižduvan 118 40.06 N 64.41 E
Gizen 130 10.49 N 34.48 E
Gizeux 46 47.24 N 0.12 E
Gižiga 64 62.03 N 160.30 E
Gižiginskaja Guba ⊂ 64 61.30 N 158.00 E
Gizo 165e 8.06 S 156.51 E
Gizo Island I 165e 8.04 S 156.48 E
Giżycko 30 54.03 N 21.47 E
Gjedved 41 55.56 N 9.51 E
Gjern 41 56.14 N 9.45 E
Gjirokastër 38 40.05 N 20.10 E
Gjoa Haven 166 68.38 N 95.57 W
Gjøvik 26 60.48 N 10.42 E
Gjuesevo 38 42.14 N 22.28 E
Gjuhëzës, Kep i ≻ 38 40.25 N 19.18 E
Glace Bay 176 46.12 N 59.57 W
Glacier, B.C., Can. 172 51.16 N 117.31 W
Glacier, Wash., U.S. 214 48.53 N 121.57 W
Glacier Bay ⊂ 170 58.40 N 136.00 W
Glacier Bay National Monument ♠ 170 58.45 N 136.30 W
Glacier Hills 266 40.51 N 74.28 W
Glacier National Park ♠, B.C., Can. 172 51.15 N 117.35 W
Glacier National Park ♠, Mont., U.S. 192 48.35 N 113.40 W
Glacier Peak ∧ 214 48.07 N 121.07 W
Glad' 66 59.07 N 32.06 E
Gl'ad'anskoje 76 54.54 N 65.06 E
Gladbach → Mönchengladbach 52 51.12 N 6.28 E
Gladbeck 48 51.34 N 6.59 E
Gladbrook 180 42.11 N 92.43 W
Gladden 269b 40.21 N 80.11 W
Gladden Heights 269b 40.22 N 80.15 W
Glade Creek ≃ 192 45.54 N 119.42 W
Gladenbach 52 50.46 N 8.34 E
Glades □[6] 210 26.59 N 81.12 W
Glade Spring 182 36.47 N 81.47 W
Gladesville 264a 33.50 S 151.08 E
Gladewater 212 32.33 N 94.56 W
Gladewater, Lake ⊜[1] 212 32.35 N 94.57 W
Gladkovka 68 46.23 N 32.36 E
Gladsakse 41 55.44 N 12.29 E
Gladstone, Austl. 156 23.51 S 151.16 E
Gladstone, Austl. 156 33.17 S 138.22 E
Gladstone, Man., Can. 174 50.13 N 98.57 W
Gladstone, Mich., U.S. 180 45.50 N 87.03 W
Gladstone, Mo., U.S. 184 39.13 N 94.34 W
Gladstone, N.J., U.S. 200 40.43 N 74.40 W
Gladstone, Oreg., U.S. 214 45.23 N 122.36 W
Gladstone Brook ≃ 266 40.43 N 74.40 W
Gladwin 180 43.59 N 84.29 W
Gladwyne 275 40.02 N 75.17 W
Gladys Lake ⊜ 170 59.55 N 132.55 W
Glænø I 41 55.12 N 11.28 E
Glafsfjorden ⊜ 26 59.34 N 12.37 E
Gláma ∧ 24a 65.47 N 23.00 W
Glåma ≃ 26 59.12 N 10.57 E
Glamoč 36 44.03 N 16.51 E
Glamor Lake ⊜ 202 44.58 N 78.23 W
Glamsbjerg 41 55.16 N 10.07 E
Glan 106 5.49 N 125.10 E
Glan ⊜ 40 58.37 N 15.58 E
Glan ≃, B.R.D. 52 49.47 N 7.43 E
Glan ≃, Pil. 106 5.50 N 125.12 E
Glanamman 44 51.48 N 3.54 W
Gland 54 46.26 N 6.16 E
Gland ≃ 46 49.55 N 4.05 E
Glandon, Col du)(56 45.14 N 6.11 E
Glandorf, B.R.D. 48 52.05 N 7.59 E
Glandorf, Ohio, U.S. 206 41.07 N 84.05 W
Glâne ≃ 54 46.47 N 7.08 E
Glanerbrug 48 52.13 N 6.58 E
Glanshammar 40 59.19 N 15.24 E
Glanum ⊥ 56 43.49 N 4.47 E
Glan-y-don 252 53.19 N 3.15 W
Glaris → Glarus 54 47.02 N 9.04 E
Glarner Alpen ⩘ 54 46.55 N 9.00 E
Glärnisch ∧ 54 47.00 N 9.00 E
Glarus 54 47.02 N 9.04 E
Glarus □[3] 54 47.00 N 9.03 E
Glasco, Kans., U.S. 188 39.22 N 97.50 W
Glasco, N.Y., U.S. 200 42.03 N 73.57 W
Glasgow, Scot., U.K. 42 55.53 N 4.15 W
Glasgow, Ill., U.S. 209 39.33 N 90.29 W
Glasgow, Ky., U.S. 184 37.00 N 85.55 W
Glasgow, Mo., U.S. 184 39.14 N 92.50 W
Glasgow, Mont., U.S. 192 48.12 N 106.38 W
Glasgow, Pa., U.S. 204 40.42 N 78.27 W
Glasgow, Va., U.S. 182 37.38 N 79.27 W
Glasgow (Abbotsinch) Airport ⊠ 42 55.52 N 4.26 W
Glashütte, B.R.D. 48 53.41 N 10.02 E
Glashütte, D.D.R. 50 50.51 N 13.47 E
Glashütte ⬥[8] 253 51.13 N 6.52 E
Glaslyn 174 53.21 N 108.22 W
Glaslyn ≃ 44 52.56 N 4.06 W
Glas Maol ∧ 28 56.52 N .3.22 W
Glasow 50 52.20 N 13.28 E
Glassboro 198 39.42 N 75.07 W
Glassboro State College ♁[2] 275 39.42 N 75.07 W
Glass House Mountains 161a 26.53 S 152.58 E
Glassmanor 274c 38.49 N 76.59 W
Glass Mountains ⩘ 186 30.25 N 103.15 W
Glassport 204 40.19 N 79.54 W
Glastonbury, Eng., U.K. 44 51.06 N 2.43 W
Glastonbury, Conn., U.S. 197 41.43 N 72.37 W
Glatt ≃ 54 47.34 N 8.28 E
Glatten 54 48.26 N 8.31 E
Glattfelden 54 47.33 N 8.30 E
Glatz → Kłodzko 30 50.27 N 16.39 E
Glaubitz 50 51.19 N 13.22 E
Glauchau 50 50.49 N 12.32 E
Glaven ≃ 44 52.58 N 1.03 E
Glaze Brook ≃ 252 53.25 N 2.27 W
Glazebury 252 53.28 N 2.30 W
Glaževo 66 59.41 N 32.05 E
Glazok 70 53.06 N 40.42 E
Glazov 70 58.09 N 52.40 E
Glazovo, S.S.S.R. 72 54.57 N 37.22 E
Glazovo, S.S.S.R. 72 55.38 N 35.46 E
Glazovo, S.S.S.R. 72 54.47 N 37.34 E
Glazunovka 66 52.30 N 36.19 E
Glazunovskaja 70 49.50 N 42.51 E
Gleason 184 36.13 N 88.37 W
Glebovka 68 46.38 N 39.59 E
Glebovo, S.S.S.R. 72 56.54 N 37.43 E
Glebovo, S.S.S.R. 72 56.39 N 38.42 E
Gleed 214 46.40 N 120.37 W
Glehn 253 51.10 N 6.35 E
Gleichen 172 50.52 N 113.03 W
Gleidingen 48 52.16 N 9.50 E
Gleinalpe ⩘ 30 47.15 N 15.03 E
Gleisdorf 30 47.06 N 15.44 E
Gleiwitz → Gliwice 30 50.17 N 18.40 E
Glejbjerg 41 55.33 N 8.50 E
Glemsford 44 52.06 N 0.41 E
Glen ≃ 44 52.51 N 0.06 W
Glen Afton 162 37.37 S 175.02 E
Glen Alice 160 33.02 S 150.13 E
Glen Allen 198 37.40 N 77.30 W
Glen Alpine 182 35.44 N 81.47 W
Glenarchy 265b 43.29 N 79.46 W
Glenarden 198 38.56 N 76.52 W
Glenarm, N. Ire., U.K. 42 54.58 N 5.57 W
Glen Arm, Md., U.S. 274b 39.27 N 76.30 W
Glen Aubrey 200 42.15 N 76.01 W
Glenavon, Sask., Can. 174 50.10 N 103.10 W
Glen Avon, S. Afr. 148 31.43 S 26.12 E
Glen Avon Heights 218 34.01 N 117.29 W
Glenavy, N.Z. 162 44.55 S 171.06 E
Glenavy, N. Ire., U.K. 42 54.36 N 6.13 W
Glenboro 174 49.32 N 99.15 W
Glenbrook 160 33.46 S 150.37 E
Glenbrook Heights 216 39.15 N 121.02 W
Glenburn, N. Dak., U.S. 188 48.31 N 101.13 W
Glenburn, Pa., U.S. 200 41.31 N 75.44 W
Glen Burnie 198 39.10 N 76.37 W
Glen Burnie Park 198 39.09 N 76.38 W
Glen Campbell 204 40.49 N 78.50 W
Glen Canyon 190 37.05 N 111.41 W
Glen Canyon ∨ 190 37.10 N 110.50 W
Glen Canyon Dam ⬥[6] 190 36.48 N 111.13 W
Glen Canyon National Recreation Area ♠ 190 37.00 N 111.20 W
Glen Carbon 209 38.45 N 89.59 W
Glenclova 144 19.59 S 31.26 E
Glencoe, Austl. 156 37.42 S 140.37 E
Glencoe, Ont., Can. 204 42.45 N 81.43 W
Glencoe, S. Afr. 148 28.12 S 30.07 E
Glencoe, Ala., U.S. 184 33.57 N 85.56 W
Glencoe, Ill., U.S. 206 42.08 N 87.45 W
Glencoe, Ky., U.S. 208 38.43 N 84.49 W
Glencoe, Md., U.S. 198 39.33 N 76.38 W
Glencoe, Minn., U.S. 180 44.46 N 94.09 W
Glen Cove 200 40.52 N 73.37 W
Glendale, Rh. 144 17.21 S 31.04 E
Glendale, Ariz., U.S. 190 33.32 N 112.11 W
Glendale, Calif., U.S. 218 34.10 N 118.17 W
Glendale, Mass., U.S. 197 42.17 N 73.21 W
Glendale, Mo., U.S. 209 38.33 N 90.22 W
Glendale, Oreg., U.S. 192 42.44 N 123.26 W
Glendale, R.I., U.S. 197 41.58 N 71.38 W
Glendale, Tex., U.S. 212 31.01 N 95.18 W
Glendale, Utah, U.S. 190 37.19 N 112.36 W
Glendale, Wis., U.S. 206 43.07 N 87.57 W
Glendale Heights 268 41.55 N 88.03 W
Glendale Lake ⊜ 204 40.41 N 78.32 W
Glen Davis 160 33.08 S 150.17 E
Glendive 188 47.06 N 104.43 W
Glendive Creek ≃ 188 47.08 N 104.41 W
Glendo 190 42.30 N 105.02 W
Glendon, Alta., Can. 172 54.15 N 111.10 W
Glendon, Pa., U.S. 198 40.40 N 75.14 W
Glendora, Calif., U.S. 218 34.08 N 117.52 W
Glendora, N.J., U.S. 275 39.50 N 75.04 W
Glendo Reservoir ⊜[1] 188 42.31 N 104.58 W
Glendo State Park ♠ 188 42.33 N 104.58 W
Glen Eagle, Austl. 158a 32.17 S 116.11 E
Gleneagle, Austl. 161a 27.57 S 152.59 E
Glen Echo 274c 38.58 N 77.08 W
Glen Echo Amusement Park ♠ 274c 38.58 N 77.08 W
Gleneden Beach 192 44.53 N 124.02 W
Glen Elder 188 39.30 N 98.18 W
Glenelg 158b 34.59 S 138.31 E
Glenelg ≃ 156 38.03 S 141.00 E
Glen Ellen 216 38.22 N 122.31 W
Glen Ellyn 268 41.52 N 88.03 W
Glen Ellyn Countryside 268 41.55 N 88.04 W
Glenfield, Austl. 264a 33.58 S 150.54 E
Glenfield, Eng., U.K. 44 52.39 N 1.12 W
Glenfield, N.Y., U.S. 202 43.43 N 75.24 W
Glenfield, Pa., U.S. 269b 40.31 N 80.08 W
Glen Flora 212 29.21 N 96.12 W
Glen Florrie 152 22.55 S 115.59 E
Glenford 200 42.00 N 74.07 W
Glen Forest 158a 31.54 S 116.06 E
Glengallan Creek ≃ 161a 28.09 S 151.53 E
Glen Gardner 200 40.42 N 74.56 W
Glengarriff 28 51.45 N 9.33 W
Glengarry □[6] 196 45.15 N 74.40 W
Glengarry Range ⩘ 152 26.13 S 118.59 E
Glengyle 156 24.48 S 139.37 E
Glenham 200 41.31 N 73.56 W
Glenhaven 264a 33.42 S 151.00 E
Glen Head 266 40.50 N 73.37 W
Glen Hills 198 39.04 N 77.12 W
Glenhope 162 41.39 S 172.39 E
Glenhuntly 264b 37.54 S 145.03 E
Glen Innes 156 29.44 S 151.44 E
Glen Island I 266 40.53 N 73.47 W
Glen Lake 214 48.26 N 123.31 W
Glenluce 42 54.53 N 4.49 W
Glenluce Abbey ♁[1] 42 54.53 N 4.50 W
Glen Lyon 200 41.10 N 76.05 W
Glen Miller 202 44.08 N 77.35 W
Glen Mills 275 39.55 N 75.30 W
Glenmont, N.Y., U.S. 200 42.36 N 73.46 W
Glenmont, Ohio, U.S. 204 40.31 N 82.06 W
Glenmoor 204 40.40 N 80.37 W
Glenmoore, Pa., U.S. 198 40.05 N 75.46 W
Glen Moore, Pa., U.S. 198 40.03 N 76.18 W
Glenmora 184 30.59 N 92.35 W
Glenmore 274b 39.11 N 76.36 W
Glenmorgan 156 27.15 S 149.41 E
Glenn, Calif., U.S. 216 39.31 N 122.01 W
Glenn, Mich., U.S. 206 42.31 N 86.14 W
Glenn □[6] 216 39.29 N 122.18 W
Glennallen 170 62.07 N 145.33 W
Glenn-Colusa Canal ⌶ 216 39.07 N 122.08 W
Glenn Dale 274c 38.59 N 76.49 W
Glenns Creek ≃ 208 38.09 N 84.52 W
Glenns Ferry 192 42.57 N 115.18 W
Glennville 182 31.56 N 81.56 W
Glen Oak 268 41.53 N 88.02 W
Glenolden 275 39.54 N 75.17 W
Glenoma 214 46.31 N 122.09 W
Glenorchy 162 44.51 S 168.23 E
Glenore Grove 161a 27.32 S 152.24 E
Glenorie 160 33.33 S 151.00 E
Glenormiston 156 22.55 S 138.48 E
Glen Park 202 44.00 N 75.57 W
Glenreagh 156 30.03 S 152.59 E
Glen Richey 204 40.57 N 78.29 W
Glen Riddle 275 39.54 N 75.26 W
Glenridge, Mass., U.S. 273 42.15 N 71.20 W
Glen Ridge, N.J., U.S. 266 40.49 N 74.13 W
Glen Robertson 196 45.21 N 74.30 W
Glen Rock, N.J., U.S. 266 40.58 N 74.08 W
Glen Rock, Pa., U.S. 198 39.48 N 76.44 W
Glenrock, Wyo., U.S. 190 42.52 N 105.52 W
Glen Rose 212 32.14 N 97.45 W
Glen Ross 202 44.16 N 77.36 W
Glenroy, Austl. 152 17.22 S 126.06 E
Glenroy, Austl. 152 21.46 S 114.49 E
Glenroy, Austl. 264b 37.42 S 144.55 E
Glenroy ≃ 162 42.00 S 172.20 E
Glens Falls 200 43.19 N 73.39 W
Glenshaw 204 40.31 N 79.57 W
Glenside, S. Afr. 148 29.25 S 30.47 E
Glenside, N.J., U.S. 198 39.40 N 75.29 W
Glenside, Pa., U.S. 198 40.06 N 75.09 W
Glen Spey 200 41.29 N 74.49 W
Glen Stewart Park ♠ 265b 43.41 N 79.18 W
Glenties 28 54.47 N 8.17 W
Glen Ullin 188 46.49 N 101.50 W
Glenview 206 42.04 N 87.48 W
Glenview Countryside 268 42.04 N 87.50 W
Glenview Naval Air Station ■ 206 42.05 N 87.50 W
Glenville, Minn., U.S. 180 43.34 N 93.17 W
Glenville, N.Y., U.S. 266 41.04 N 73.50 W
Glenville, W. Va., U.S. 178 38.56 N 80.50 W
Glen Waverley 264b 37.53 S 145.10 E
Glen White 182 37.44 N 81.17 W
Glen Wild 200 41.29 N 74.49 W
Glen Wild Lake ⊜ 266 41.02 N 74.20 W
Glenwillard 204 40.34 N 80.13 W
Glen Williams 202 43.40 N 79.55 W
Glenwillow 204 41.22 N 81.28 W
Glenwood, N.B., Can. 176 48.59 N 54.52 W
Glenwood, Ala., U.S. 184 31.40 N 86.10 W
Glenwood, Ark., U.S. 184 34.20 N 93.33 W
Glenwood, Ga., U.S. 182 32.11 N 82.40 W
Glenwood, Ill., U.S. 268 41.33 N 87.37 W
Glenwood, Ind., U.S. 208 39.37 N 85.18 W
Glenwood, Iowa, U.S. 188 41.03 N 95.45 W
Glenwood, Minn., U.S. 188 45.39 N 95.23 W
Glenwood, N.J., U.S. 200 41.15 N 74.29 W
Glenwood, N. Mex., U.S. 190 33.19 N 108.53 W
Glenwood, N.Y., U.S. 200 42.37 N 78.39 W
Glenwood, Oreg., U.S. 214 45.39 N 123.16 W
Glenwood, Tex., U.S. 212 32.39 N 94.51 W
Glenwood, Utah, U.S. 190 38.46 N 111.59 W
Glenwood, Va., U.S. 182 36.35 N 79.22 W
Glenwood, Wash., U.S. 214 46.01 N 121.17 W
Glenwood City 180 45.04 N 92.10 W
Glenwood Landing 266 40.50 N 73.39 W
Glenwood Park 274c 38.58 N 76.50 W
Glenwood Springs 190 39.33 N 107.19 W
Glenwoodville 172 49.22 N 113.21 W
Gleschendorf 50 54.02 N 10.40 E
Glesien 50 51.27 N 12.13 E
Gletsch 54 46.34 N 8.22 E
Gleussen 52 50.08 N 10.53 E
Glew 248 34.53 S 58.23 W
Glidden, Iowa, U.S. 188 42.04 N 94.44 W
Glidden, Tex., U.S. 212 29.42 N 96.35 W
Glidden, Wis., U.S. 180 46.09 N 90.34 W
Glide 192 43.18 N 123.06 W
Gliener Berg ∧[2] 254a 52.42 N 13.00 E
Glienicke, D.D.R. 50 52.37 N 13.19 E
Glienicke, D.D.R. 50 52.13 N 14.05 E
Glífa 38 38.57 N 22.58 E
Glifádha 257c 37.52 N 23.45 E
Glimåkra 26 56.18 N 14.08 E
Glimmingehus 26 55.30 N 14.13 E
Glina 36 45.20 N 16.06 E
Glina ≃ 36 45.26 N 16.07 E
Glin'any 68 49.49 N 24.30 E
Glinde 48 53.32 N 10.13 E
Glindow 50 52.21 N 12.54 E
Glindowsee ⊜ 254a 52.21 N 12.56 E
Glinka 66 54.39 N 32.52 E
Glinkovo 75 42.55 N 69.40 E
Glittertinden ∧ 26 61.39 N 8.33 E
Gliwice (Gleiwitz) 30 50.17 N 18.40 E
Gliwicki, Kanał ⌶ 30 50.22 N 18.05 E
Globe, Ariz., U.S. 190 33.24 N 110.47 W
Globe, Ky., U.S. 208 38.17 N 83.14 W
Globino 68 49.23 N 33.17 E
Glod'any 68 47.47 N 27.31 E
Glodeanu-Siliştea 38 44.50 N 26.48 E
Glodok ⬥[8] 259e 6.08 S 106.48 E
Glogau → Głogów 30 51.40 N 16.05 E
Gloggnitz 30 47.40 N 15.57 E
Glogn ≃ 54 46.46 N 9.12 E
Głogów, Pol. 30 50.10 N 21.58 E
Głogów, Pol. 30 51.40 N 16.05 E
Głogówek 30 50.22 N 17.51 E
Glommersträsk 26 65.16 N 19.38 E
Glonn 58 47.59 N 11.52 E
Glorenza (Glurns) 58 46.40 N 10.33 E
Glória 240 9.11 S 38.18 W
Gloria, Sierra de la ⩘ 186 26.45 N 101.10 W
Gloria Glens Park 204 41.03 N 81.54 W
Glorieta 190 35.35 N 105.46 W
Glorieuses, Îles II 128 11.30 S 47.20 E
Glörstausee ⊜[1] 253 51.14 N 7.29 E
Glos-la-Ferrière 46 48.51 N 0.36 E
Glossop 42 53.27 N 1.57 W
Glossopteris, Mount ∧ 9 84.44 S 113.51 W
Gloster 184 31.12 N 91.01 W

ENGLISH

Name	Page	Lat.°′	Long.°′

Glostrup 41 55.40 N 12.24 E
Glotovka 70 53.57 N 46.42 E
Glotovo 24 63.30 N 49.23 E
Gloucester, Austl. 156 31.59 S 151.58 E
Gloucester, Eng., U.K. 44 51.53 N 2.14 W
Gloucester, Mass., U.S. 197 42.41 N 70.39 W
Gloucester, Va., U.S. 198 37.25 N 76.32 W
Gloucester □[6], N.J., U.S. 198 39.50 N 75.10 W
Gloucester □[6], Va., U.S. 198 37.25 N 76.30 W
Gloucester, Cabo ≻ 244 54.04 S 73.29 W
Gloucester, Cape ≻ 154 5.27 S 148.25 E
Gloucester, Vale of ∨ 44 51.55 N 2.10 W
Gloucester City 275 39.54 N 75.07 W
Gloucester Fisherman ⊥ 273 42.36 N 70.40 W
Gloucester Harbor ⊂ 197 42.36 N 70.40 W
Gloucester Island I 156 20.01 S 148.27 E
Gloucester Point 198 37.16 N 76.30 W
Gloucester Pool ⊜ 202 44.51 N 79.43 W
Gloucestershire □[6] 44 51.47 N 2.15 W
Glouster 178 39.30 N 82.05 W
Glover-Archbold Park ♠ 274c 38.55 N 77.05 W
Glover Creek ≃ 184 34.02 N 94.56 W
Glover Island I 176 48.44 N 57.45 W
Glover Reef ✢[2] 222 16.49 N 87.48 W
Gloversville 200 43.03 N 74.20 W
Glovertown 176 48.41 N 54.02 W
Glowe 50 54.35 N 13.28 E
Glöwen 50 52.55 N 12.05 E
Głowno 30 51.58 N 19.44 E
Głubczyce 30 50.13 N 17.49 E
Glubokij, S.S.S.R. 68 48.31 N 40.19 E
Glubokij, S.S.S.R. 70 47.01 N 42.47 E
Glubokij, S.S.S.R. 79 52.53 N 129.44 E
Glubokoje, S.S.S.R. 66 55.08 N 27.41 E
Glubokoje, S.S.S.R. 72 54.32 N 38.32 E
Glubokoje, S.S.S.R. 76 50.06 N 82.19 E
Głuchołazy 30 50.20 N 17.22 E
Gluchov 68 51.41 N 33.53 E
Gluchovo 255b 55.46 N 37.16 E
Glückauf-Kampfbahn ♠ 253 51.32 N 7.05 E
Glücksburg 41 54.50 N 9.33 E
Glückstadt, B.R.D. 48 53.47 N 9.25 E
Gluckstadt, S. Afr. 148 27.57 S 31.02 E
Glud 41 55.49 N 10.00 E
Glumslöv 41 55.56 N 12.48 E
Glumsø 41 55.21 N 11.42 E
Gluša 66 53.05 N 28.52 E
Glusk 66 52.54 N 28.41 E
Gluškeviči 68 51.34 N 27.47 E
Gluškovo 68 51.22 N 34.38 E
Glybokaja 68 48.07 N 25.56 E
Glyde ≃ 42 53.52 N 6.20 W
Glyder Fawr ∧ 44 53.06 N 4.01 W
Glyme ≃ 44 51.49 N 1.22 W
Glyndebourne 46 50.52 N 0.04 E
Glyndon, Md., U.S. 198 39.29 N 76.49 W
Glyndon, Minn., U.S. 188 46.52 N 96.35 W
Glyngøre 26 56.46 N 8.52 E
Glynneath 44 51.46 N 3.38 W
Gmelinka 70 50.24 N 46.54 E
Gmünd, Öst. 30 48.47 N 15.00 E
Gmünd, Öst. 58 46.54 N 13.32 E
Gmund am Tegernsee 58 47.45 N 11.44 E
Gmunden 58 47.55 N 13.48 E
Gnadenhutten 204 40.22 N 81.26 W
Gnadenhutten Monument ⊥ 204 40.21 N 81.25 W
Gnalta 156 31.03 S 142.20 E
Gnaraloo 152 23.51 S 113.31 E
Gnarp 26 62.03 N 17.16 E
Gnarpurt, Lake ⊜ 159 38.03 S 143.24 E
Gnarrenburg 48 53.22 N 9.00 E
Gnaw Bone 208 39.12 N 86.09 W
Gnesen → Gniezno 30 52.31 N 17.37 E
Gnesta 40 59.03 N 17.18 E
Gnezdovo 66 54.47 N 31.47 E
Gniben ≻ 41 56.01 N 11.18 E
Gniew 30 53.51 N 18.49 E
Gniewkowo 30 52.54 N 18.25 E
Gniezno 30 52.31 N 17.37 E
Gnilaja Lipa ≃ 68 49.07 N 24.44 E
Gnilec 66 52.22 N 36.01 E
Gniloj Jelanec ≃ 68 47.20 N 31.44 E
Gniloj Tikič ≃ 68 48.47 N 30.53 E
Gnivan' 68 49.06 N 28.20 E
Gnjilane 38 42.28 N 21.29 E
Gnoien 50 53.58 N 12.42 E
Gnosjö 26 57.22 N 13.44 E
Gnowangerup 152 33.56 S 117.59 E
Gō ≃ 86 35.02 N 132.13 E
Goa 106 13.42 N 123.29 E
Goa □[8] 112 14.20 N 74.00 E
Goageb 146 26.44 S 17.15 E
Goalen Head ≻ 156 36.40 S 150.05 E
Goāliar ≃ 116 24.07 N 90.18 E
Goālpāra 114 26.10 N 90.37 E
Goāltor 116 22.43 N 87.10 E
Goalundo Ghāt 116 23.43 N 89.46 E
Goan 140 13.14 N 5.09 W
Goangoa ≃ 130 5.48 N 25.09 E
Goascorán 226 13.36 N 87.45 W
Goascorán ≃ 226 13.25 N 87.48 W
Goat Fell ∧ 42 55.38 N 5.12 W
Goathland 42 54.23 N 0.44 W
Goat Island I 274a 43.05 N 79.04 W
Goat Mountain ∧ 192 47.21 N 113.21 W
Goat Peak ∧ 214 46.56 N 121.16 W
Goba 134 7.02 N 40.00 E
Gobabis 146 22.30 S 18.58 E
Gobabis □[5] 146 22.00 S 19.00 E
Gobai ≃ 116 23.37 N 86.28 E
Gobardānga 116 22.53 N 88.45 E
Göbel 120 40.00 N 28.09 E
Göbelsberg ∧ 58 48.06 N 13.32 E
Gobernador Andonaegui 248 34.10 S 59.19 W
Gobernador Costa 244 44.04 S 70.35 W
Gobernador Gregores 244 48.46 S 70.15 W
Gobernador Ingeniero Valentín Virasoro 242 28.03 S 56.02 W
Gobernador Juan E. Martínez 242 28.55 S 58.56 W
Gobernador Monteverde 278 34.48 S 58.16 W
Gobernador Racedo 242 31.34 S 60.04 W
Gobernador Udaondo 248 35.18 S 58.36 W
Gobi Desert ⬥[2] 92 43.00 N 106.00 E
Gobindapur, Bhārat 116 23.16 N 87.58 E
Gobindapur, Bhārat 262b 22.23 N 88.25 E
Gobindapur, Bhārat 262b 22.55 N 88.12 E
Gobindgarh 113 30.41 N 76.18 E
Gobindpur 116 23.50 N 86.31 E
Gobles 206 42.21 N 85.53 W
Gobō 86 33.53 N 135.10 E
Gobra 116 23.45 N 89.12 E
Gobur 144 4.20 N 31.04 E
Gobza ≃ 66 55.16 N 31.31 E
Göçbeyli 120 39.13 N 27.25 E
Goce Delčev 38 41.34 N 23.44 E
Goch 48 51.41 N 6.10 E
Gochas 146 24.55 S 18.55 E
Gochsheim 52 50.01 N 10.16 E
Go-cong 259c 10.50 N 106.50 E
Goðafoss ⌊ 24a 65.40 N 17.30 W
Godāgāri 114 24.28 N 88.20 E
Godalming 44 51.11 N 0.37 W
Godalo 134 4.36 N 43.27 E
Godar 118 28.12 N 63.14 E
Godāvari ≃ 112 17.00 N 81.45 E

DEUTSCH

Name	Seite	Breite°′	Länge°′ E=Ost

Godāvari, Mouths of the ≃[1] 112 16.25 N 82.00 E
Godbout 176 49.19 N 67.37 W
Godda 114 24.50 N 87.13 E
Goddard 208 38.22 N 83.37 W
Goddard Space Flight Center ♁ 274c 39.00 N 76.52 W
Goddelau 52 49.50 N 8.30 E
Goddua 136 26.26 N 14.18 E
Godeffroy 200 41.27 N 74.37 W
Godega di Sant'Urbano 58 45.56 N 12.24 E
Godegård 40 58.44 N 15.09 E
Godelheim 48 51.44 N 9.22 E
Gödene 120 36.34 N 30.21 E
Godere 134 5.05 N 43.50 E
Goderich 180 43.45 N 81.43 W
Goderville 46 49.39 N 0.22 E
Godfrey 209 38.57 N 90.11 W
Godhavn 166 69.15 N 53.33 W
Godhra 110 22.45 N 73.38 E
Godinlave 134 5.54 N 46.40 E
Godinne 52 50.21 N 4.52 E
Godley 212 32.27 N 97.32 W
Godmanchester 44 52.19 N 0.11 W
Godo, Indon. 105b 8.33 S 118.40 E
Gōdo, Nihon 84 35.25 N 136.36 E
Gōdo, Nihon 258 35.51 N 139.44 E
Gödöllő 254c 47.36 N 19.22 E
Gödöllői Dombvidék ⩘[2] 254c 47.37 N 19.16 E
Godong 105a 7.02 S 110.46 E
Godoy Cruz 242 32.55 S 68.50 W
Godramstein 52 49.12 N 8.05 E
Gods ≃ 174 56.22 N 92.51 W
Godshill 44 50.38 N 1.14 W
Godshorn 48 52.26 N 9.43 E
Gods Lake 174 54.40 N 94.09 W
Gods Lake ⊜ 174 54.40 N 94.20 W
Gods Mercy, Bay of ⊂ 166 63.30 N 86.10 W
Godstone 44 51.15 N 0.04 W
Godthåb 166 64.11 N 51.44 W
Godunovo 72 56.29 N 39.02 E
Godwin Austen (K2) ∧ 113 35.53 N 76.30 E
Goedemoed 148 30.33 S 26.26 E
Goedgegun 148 27.06 S 31.12 E
Goéland, Lac au ⊜ 166 49.47 N 76.48 W
Goélands, Lac aux ⊜ 166 55.27 N 64.17 W
Goeree I 48 51.50 N 3.55 E
Goes 48 51.30 N 3.54 E
Goetzenbruck 52 48.59 N 7.23 E
Goff, Som. 134 2.42 N 41.03 E
Goff, Kans., U.S. 188 39.40 N 95.56 W
Goff Creek ≃ 186 36.43 N 101.29 W
Goffle Brook ≃ 266 40.56 N 74.08 W
Goff's Oak 250 51.43 N 0.05 W
Goffstown 178 43.01 N 71.36 W
Gofoundurei 134 4.31 N 46.46 E
Gogama 180 47.40 N 81.43 W
Gogeb ≃ 134 7.10 N 37.27 E
Gogebic, Lake ⊜ 180 46.30 N 89.35 W
Gogebic Range ⩘[2] 180 46.45 N 89.25 W
Gogeh 134 8.12 N 38.27 E
Göggingen 54 48.20 N 10.52 E
Gogha 110 21.41 N 72.17 E
Gogland, Ostrov I 66 60.04 N 27.00 E
Goglio 54 46.18 N 8.16 E
Gogoi 146 20.17 S 33.08 E
Gogolevka 66 54.17 N 31.58 E
Gogolevo 68 49.56 N 33.48 E
Gogolin 30 50.30 N 18.02 E
Gogonou 140 10.50 N 2.50 E
Gogo-shima I 86 33.54 N 132.41 E
Gogrial 130 8.32 N 28.07 E
Gohad 114 26.26 N 78.27 E
Gohāla 116 23.15 N 89.59 E
Gohāla ≃ 116 24.08 N 89.35 E
Gohāna 114 29.08 N 76.42 E
Gohfeld 48 52.12 N 8.45 E
Gohitafla 140 7.30 N 5.53 W
Göhl 50 54.17 N 10.56 E
Gohoku 86 33.39 N 133.21 E
Go Home Lake ⊜ 202 45.00 N 79.51 W
Gohpur 110 26.53 N 93.38 E
Gohr 253 51.06 N 6.43 E
Göhrde 50 53.08 N 10.52 E
Göhren 50 54.20 N 13.44 E
Goiana, Bra. 240 7.33 S 34.59 W
Goianá, Bra. 246 21.32 S 43.12 W
Goianápolis 245 16.30 S 49.01 W
Goiandira 245 18.08 S 48.06 W
Goianésia 245 15.18 S 49.07 W
Goiânia 245 16.40 S 49.16 W
Goianinha 240 6.16 S 35.12 W
Goianira 245 16.30 S 49.26 W
Goianorte 240 8.35 S 48.56 W
Goiás 245 15.56 S 50.08 W
Goiás □[3] 245 15.00 S 49.00 W
Goiatuba 245 18.01 S 49.22 W
Goichran 110 31.04 N 78.07 E
Goikul 165b 7.22 N 134.36 E
Goil, Loch ⊂ 42 56.08 N 4.52 W
Goio-Erê 242 24.12 S 53.01 W
Goio-Erê ≃ 242 24.14 S 53.21 W
Goirle 48 51.32 N 5.04 E
Góis, Bra. 246 22.33 S 46.18 W
Góis, Port. 34 40.09 N 8.07 W
Goito 58 45.15 N 10.40 E
Gojam □[4] 134 11.00 N 37.00 E
Gojō 86 34.21 N 135.42 E
Gojōme 82 39.56 N 140.07 E
Gojra 113 31.09 N 72.41 E
Gojtchskij, Pereval)(74 44.18 N 39.18 E
Gokāk 112 16.10 N 74.50 E
Gokarna 116 24.03 N 88.07 E
Gokase ≃ 82 32.35 N 131.42 E
Gökçe 120 40.11 N 25.55 E
Gökçeada I, Tür. 38
120 40.10 N 25.50 E
Gökçen 120 38.07 N 27.53 E
Gökdere, Tür. 120 38.44 N 40.13 E
Gökdere, Tür. 120 40.29 N 36.47 E
Gōkōmutsumi 258 35.48 N 139.59 E
Göksholm 40 59.16 N 15.33 E
Göksu ≃, Tür. 74 39.19 N 42.17 E
Göksu ≃, Tür. 120 37.37 N 35.35 E
Göksu ≃, Tür. 120 36.20 N 34.05 E
Göksu Deresi ≃ 257b 41.06 N 29.03 E
Göksun 120 38.03 N 36.30 E
Göktepe 120 37.15 N 28.36 E
Gök Tepe ∧ 120 36.53 N 29.17 E
Gokwe 144 18.07 S 28.58 E
Gol 26 60.42 N 8.57 E
Gol, Khawr ∨ 130 6.55 N 30.16 E
Golabāri 262b 22.36 N 88.20 E
Golāghāt 110 26.31 N 93.58 E
Gola Gokaran Nath 114 28.05 N 80.28 E
Golaja Pristan' 68 46.31 N 32.31 E
Gołańcz 30 52.57 N 17.18 E
Golan Heights ⊥[4] 122 32.55 N 35.42 E
Golāshkerd 118 27.59 N 57.16 E
Gölbaşı, Tür. 120 39.48 N 32.49 E
Gölbası, Tür. 120 37.50 N 37.40 E
Golborne 252 53.29 N 2.36 W
Golcar 252 53.39 N 1.51 W
Gol'čicha 64 71.43 N 83.36 E
Golconda, Ill., U.S. 184 37.22 N 88.29 W
Golconda, Nev., U.S. 194 40.57 N 117.30 W
Gölcük, Tür. 120 40.44 N 29.48 E
Gölcuk, Tür. 120 39.18 N 27.59 E
Golczewo 50 53.49 N 14.59 E
Gołdap 30 54.19 N 22.19 E
Goldau 54 47.03 N 8.33 E
Gold Bar 214 47.51 N 121.42 W
Gold Beach 192 42.25 N 124.25 W
Goldbeck 50 52.43 N 11.52 E
Goldberg, D.D.R. 50 53.35 N 12.05 E
Goldberg → Złotoryja, Pol. 30 51.08 N 15.55 E

Symbols in the index entries represent the broad categories identified in the key at the right. Symbols with superior numbers (⩘[2]) identify subcategories (see complete key on page *I* · 26).

Kartensymbole in dem Registerverzeichnis stellen die rechts in Schlüssel erklärten Kategorien dar. Symbole mit hochgestellten Ziffern (⩘[2]) bezeichnen Unterabteilungen einer Kategorie (vgl. vollständiger Schlüssel auf Seite *I* · 26).

Los símbolos incluídos en el texto del índice representan las grandes categorias identificadas con la clave a la derecha. Los símbolos con numeros en su parte superior (⩘[2]) identifican las subcategorías (véase la clave completa en la página *I* · 26).

Les symboles de l'index représentent les catégories indiquées dans la légende à droite. Les symboles suivis d'un indice (⩘[2]) représentent des sous-catégories (voir légende complète à la page *I* · 26).

Os símbolos incluídos no texto do índice representam as grandes categorias identificadas com a chave à direita. Os símbolos com números em sua parte superior (⩘[2]) identificam as subcategorias (veja-se a chave completa à página *I* · 26).

∧ Mountain	Berg	Montaña	Montagne	Montanha
⩘ Mountains	Berge	Montañas	Montagnes	Montanhas
)(Pass	Pass	Paso	Col	Passo
∨ Valley, Canyon	Tal, Cañon	Valle, Cañón	Vallée, Canyon	Vale, Canhão
≚ Plain	Ebene	Llano	Plaine	Planície
≻ Cape	Kap	Cabo	Cap	Cabo
I Island	Insel	Isla	Île	Ilha
II Islands	Inseln	Islas	Îles	Ilhas
⊥ Other Topographic Features	Andere Topographische Objekte	Otros Elementos Topográficos	Autres données topographiques	Outros Elementos Topográficos

≃ River	Fluss	Río	Rivière	Rio	
≊ Canal	Kanal	Canal	Canal	Canal	
⅃ Waterfall, Rapids	Wasserfall, Stromschnellen	Cascada, Rápidos	Chute d'eau, Rapides	Cascata, Rápidos	
Ц Strait	Meeresstrasse	Estrecho	Détroit	Estreito	
C Bay, Gulf	Bucht, Golf	Bahía, Golfo	Baie, Golfe	Baía, Golfo	
⊜ Lake, Lakes	See, Seen	Lago, Lagos	Lac, Lacs	Lago, Lagos	
≋ Swamp	Sumpf	Pantano	Marais	Pântano	
⊼ Ice Features, Glacier	Eis- und Gletscherformen	Accidentes Glaciales	Formes glaciaires	Acidentes Glaciares	
╤ Other Hydrographic Features	Andere Hydrographische Objekte	Otros Elementos Hidrográficos	Autres données hydrographiques	Outros Elementos Hidrográficos	

✢ Submarine Features	Untermeerische Objekte	Accidentes Submarinos	Formes de relief sous-marin	Acidentes Submarinos
□ Political Unit	Politische Einheit	Unidad Politica	Entité politique	Unidade Política
♥ Cultural Institution	Kulturelle Institution	Institución Cultural	Institution culturelle	Instituição Cultural
⊥ Historical Site	Historische Stätte	Sitio Histórico	Site historique	Sitio Histórico
♠ Recreational Site	Erholungs- und Ferienort	Sitio de Recreo	Centre de loisirs	Sítio de Lazer
⊠ Airport	Flughafen	Aeropuerto	Aéroport	Aeroporto
■ Military Installation	Militäranlage	Instalación Militar	Installation militaire	Instalação Militar
◆ Miscellaneous	Verschiedenes	Misceláneo	Divers	Miscelânea

ENGLISH — Name / Page / Lat.°′ / Long.°′
DEUTSCH — Name / Seite / Breite°′ / Länge°′ E=Ost

Göynücek 120 40.24 N 35.32 E
Göynük 120 40.24 N 30.47 E
Goz Beïda 136 12.13 N 21.25 E
Gozdnica 30 51.26 N 15.06 E
Gozdowice 50 52.45 N 14.18 E
Gozenyama 84 36.32 N 140.20 E
Gözne 120 36.59 N 34.34 E
Gozo → Ghawdex I 36 36.03 N 14.15 E
Göz Tepe ∧[2] 257b 41.06 N 29.06 E
Gozzano 56 45.45 N 8.26 E
Graaff-Reinet 148 32.14 S 24.32 E
Graafwater 148 32.00 S 18.37 E
Graauw 48 51.20 N 4.05 E
Grabc'ovo 72 54.34 N 36.22 E
Graben 52 49.09 N 8.29 E
Grabenstätt 58 47.51 N 12.32 E
Grabill 206 41.13 N 84.58 W
Grabo 140 4.55 N 7.30 W
Grabouw 148 34.09 S 19.02 E
Grabovaja Balka, Les ♠ 73 48.09 N 38.37 E
Grabovo 76 53.07 N 74.52 E
Grabow 50 53.16 N 11.34 E
Grabowiec 30 50.50 N 23.33 E
Grabów nad Prosną 30 51.31 N 18.06 E
Gračac 36 44.18 N 15.51 E
Gračanica 38 44.42 N 18.19 E
Gračanica, Manastir ♰[1] 38 42.36 N 21.09 E
Graçay 46 47.08 N 1.51 E
Grace 192 42.35 N 111.44 W
Gracefield 178 46.06 N 76.03 W
Graceham 198 39.37 N 77.24 W
Graceton 204 40.30 N 79.10 W
Graceville, Fla., U.S. 182 30.58 N 85.31 W
Graceville, Minn., U.S. 188 45.34 N 96.26 W
Gračevka 72 55.06 N 36.49 E
Gračev Kust 70 51.59 N 49.50 E
Grächen 54 46.12 N 7.50 E
Grachovo 70 56.04 N 51.58 E
Gračí 70 49.49 N 43.33 E
Gracia ⬩[8] 256d 41.23 N 2.09 E
Gracias 226 14.35 N 88.35 W
Gracias a Dios □[5] 226 15.10 N 84.20 W
Gracias a Dios, Cabo ≻ 226 15.00 N 83.10 W
Gračiki ≃ 73 48.30 N 39.52 E
Graciosa I 138a 39.04 N 28.00 W
Graciosa, Isla I 138 29.15 N 13.30 W
Gračov 70 49.26 N 41.32 E
Gračovka 70 52.07 N 40.01 E
Gradačac 38 44.53 N 18.26 E
Gradara 60 43.57 N 12.46 E
Gradaús 240 7.43 S 51.11 W
Gradaús, Serra dos ∧[1] 240 8.00 S 50.45 W
Gr'adcy 66 56.24 N 31.55 E
Gräddö 40 59.46 N 19.02 E
Gradisca d'Isonzo 58 45.53 N 13.30 E
Gradižsk 68 49.13 N 33.07 E
Grado, Esp. 34 43.23 N 6.04 W
Grado, It. 58 45.40 N 13.23 E
Grado, Laguna di C 58 45.43 N 13.20 E
Gradoli 60 42.39 N 11.51 E
Grady, Ark., U.S. 184 34.05 N 91.42 W
Grady, N. Mex., U.S. 186 34.49 N 103.19 W
Gradyville 275 39.57 N 75.28 W
Græsted 41 56.04 N 12.17 E
Graettinger 188 43.14 N 94.45 W
Gräfelfing 58 48.07 N 11.25 E
Grafenau 30 48.52 N 13.25 E
Grafenberg ⬩[8] 253 51.14 N 6.50 E
Gräfenhainichen 50 51.44 N 12.27 E
Gräfenroda 50 50.45 N 10.48 E
Gräfenthal 50 50.31 N 11.18 E
Gräfentonna 50 51.05 N 10.44 E
Graffignano 60 42.34 N 12.12 E
Grafham Water ⊜ 44 52.17 N 0.20 W
Gräfinau-Angstedt 50 50.42 N 11.01 E
Grafing bei München 58 48.02 N 11.59 E
Gråfjell ∧ 26 60.16 N 9.29 E
Graford 186 32.56 N 98.14 W
Gräfrath ⬩[8] 253 51.13 N 7.04 E
Grafschaft Bentheim □[9] 48 52.30 N 7.00 E
Grafton, Austl. 156 29.41 S 152.56 E
Grafton, Ont., Can. 202 44.00 N 78.01 W
Grafton, Ill., U.S. 209 38.58 N 90.26 W
Grafton, Mass., U.S. 197 42.12 N 71.41 W
Grafton, N. Dak., U.S. 188 48.25 N 97.25 W
Grafton, N.Y., U.S. 200 42.46 N 73.27 W
Grafton, Ohio, U.S. 204 41.16 N 82.04 W
Grafton, W. Va., U.S. 178 39.20 N 80.01 W
Grafton, Wis., U.S. 180 43.19 N 87.56 W
Grafton, Cape ≻ 156 16.52 S 145.55 E
Grafton, Islas I 244 54.06 S 73.12 W
Grafton Lakes State Park ♠ 200 42.48 N 73.28 W
Grafty Green 250 51.12 N 0.41 E
Graglia 56 45.33 N 7.59 E
Gragnano 60 40.41 N 14.31 E
Gragnano Trebbiense 56 45.01 N 9.34 E
Graham, Calif., U.S. 270 33.58 N 118.15 W
Graham, N.C., U.S. 182 36.05 N 79.25 W
Graham, Tex., U.S. 186 33.06 N 98.35 W
Graham, Wash., U.S. 214 47.03 N 122.15 W
Graham, Mount ∧ 190 32.42 N 109.52 W
Graham Cave State Park ♠ 209 38.55 N 91.32 W
Graham Creek ≃ 208 38.49 N 85.39 W
Graham Island I 172 53.40 N 132.30 W
Graham Lake ⊜, Ont., Can. 202 44.34 N 75.53 W
Graham Lake ⊜, Maine, U.S. 176 44.40 N 68.25 W
Graham Land ⬩[1] 9 66.00 S 63.30 W
Graham Memorial Park ♠ 274b 39.25 N 76.30 W
Graham Moore, Cape ≻ 166 72.52 N 76.04 W
Graham Moore Bay C 166 75.26 N 101.25 W
Grahamstad → Grahamstown 148 33.19 S 26.31 E
Grahamstown 148 33.19 S 26.31 E
Grahamsville 200 41.51 N 74.33 W
Grahn 208 38.17 N 83.05 W
Graïba 138 34.30 N 10.13 E
Graie, Alpi (Alpes Grées) ∧ 56 45.30 N 7.10 E
Grain 44 51.28 N 0.43 E
Grain, Isle of I 44 51.27 N 0.41 E
Grain Coast ⬩[2] 140 5.00 N 9.00 W
Grainfield 188 39.07 N 100.28 W
Grajagan 105a 8.35 S 114.13 E
Grajagan, Teluk C 105a 8.40 S 114.18 E
Grajaú 240 5.49 S 46.08 W
Grajaú ≃ 240 3.41 S 44.48 W
Grajewo 30 53.39 N 22.27 E
Grajvoron 68 50.29 N 35.39 E
Gram 41 55.17 N 9.04 E
Gramacho 277a 22.44 S 43.18 W
Gramada 38 43.50 N 22.39 E
Gramado 242 29.24 S 50.54 W
Gramalote 236 7.53 N 72.48 W
Gramat 32 44.47 N 1.43 E
Gramatneusiedl 254b 48.02 N 16.29 E
Grambling 184 32.32 N 92.43 W
Gramilla 242 26.12 S 64.29 W
Graminea 246 22.10 S 46.38 W
Grammer 208 39.09 N 85.43 W
Grammichele 36 37.13 N 14.38 E
Grammont → Geraardsbergen 46 50.46 N 3.52 E
Gramoteino 76 54.31 N 86.22 E
Grampian 204 40.58 N 78.37 W
Grampian □[4] 28 57.15 N 2.45 W
Grampian Mountains ∧ 28 56.45 N 4.00 W
Gramschatz 52 49.56 N 9.58 E
Gramsh 38 40.52 N 20.11 E
Gramzow 50 53.12 N 14.00 E
Gran → Esztergom 30 47.48 N 18.45 E
Grana ≃ 56 44.25 N 7.27 E
Granaatboskolk 148 30.02 S 19.51 E
Granada, Col. 236 3.34 N 73.45 W
Granada, Esp. 34 37.13 N 3.41 W
Granada, Nic. 226 11.56 N 85.57 W
Granada, Pil. 106 10.40 N 123.02 E
Granada, Colo., U.S. 188 38.04 N 102.19 W
Granada, Minn., U.S. 180 43.42 N 94.21 W
Granada □[5] 226 11.50 N 86.00 W
Granada → Grenada □[1] 231k 12.07 N 61.40 W
Granada Hills ⬩[8] 270 34.16 N 118.31 W
Granadella 34 41.21 N 0.40 E
Granado 276d 12.04 S 76.57 W
Granaglione 60 44.07 N 10.58 E
Gran Altiplanicie Central ∧[1] 244 48.55 S 69.25 W
Granard 28 53.47 N 7.30 W
Granarolo dell'Emilia 58 44.33 N 11.27 E
Gran Bahía Australiana → Great Australian Bight C[3] 152 35.00 S 135.00 E
Gran Bajo de San Julián ∨ 244 49.30 S 68.30 W
Gran Barrera de Arrecifes → Great Barrier Reef ⬩[2] 150 18.00 S 145.50 E
Granbergsdal 40 59.24 N 14.35 E
Granbury 186 32.27 N 97.47 W
Granbury, Lake ⊜[1] 212 32.25 N 97.45 W
Granby, Qué., Can. 196 45.24 N 72.44 W
Granby, Colo., U.S. 190 40.05 N 105.56 W
Granby, Conn., U.S. 197 41.57 N 72.47 W
Granby, Mass., U.S. 197 42.15 N 72.31 W
Granby, Mo., U.S. 184 36.55 N 94.15 W
Granby ≃ 172 49.03 N 118.25 W
Granby, Lake ⊜[1] 190 40.09 N 105.50 W
Gran Canal del Desagüe ≍ 276a 19.29 N 99.05 W
Gran Canaria I 138 28.00 N 15.36 W
Grancey-le-Château 54 47.40 N 5.02 E
Gran Chaco ≍ 18 23.00 S 60.00 W
Grand 54 48.23 N 5.29 E
Grand ≃, Ont., Can. 202 42.51 N 79.34 W
Grand ≃, U.S. 184 39.23 N 93.06 W
Grand ≃, Mich., U.S. 206 43.04 N 86.15 W
Grand ≃, Ohio, U.S. 204 41.46 N 81.17 W
Grand ≃, S. Dak., U.S. 188 45.40 N 100.32 W
Grand ≃, Wis., U.S. 180 43.45 N 89.16 W
Grand, East Fork ≃ 184 40.12 N 94.21 W
Grand, Lac ⊜ 180 47.10 N 76.57 W
Grand, North Fork ≃ 188 45.47 N 102.16 W
Grand, South Fork ≃ 188 45.43 N 102.17 W
Grand Aféri 140 6.19 N 3.57 W
Grand Anse Bay C 231k 12.02 N 61.45 W
Grandas 34 43.13 N 6.52 W
Grandas de Salime, Embalse de ⊜[1] 34 43.10 N 6.45 W
Grand Bahama I 228 26.38 N 78.25 W
Grand Ballon ∧ 54 47.55 N 7.08 E
Grand Bank 176 47.06 N 55.46 W
Grand Bank ⬩[4] 16 47.00 N 52.00 W
Grand Bassa □[6] 140 6.00 N 9.30 W
Grand-Bassam 140 5.12 N 3.44 W
Grand Bay, N.B., Can. 176 45.18 N 66.12 W
Grand Bay, Ala., U.S. 184 30.29 N 88.21 W
Grand Bay C 230d 15.14 N 61.19 W
Grand Beach 174 50.35 N 96.40 W
Grand Bend 180 43.15 N 81.45 W
Grand Blanc 206 42.56 N 83.38 W
Grand-Bourg 231o 15.53 N 61.19 W
Grand Bruit 176 47.41 N 58.13 W
Grand Caicos I 228 21.47 N 71.43 W
Grand Caille Point ≻ 231f 13.52 N 61.05 W
Grand Calumet ≃ 268 41.38 N 87.34 W
Grand-Calumet, Île du I 178 45.44 N 76.41 W
Grand Canal ≍, Éire 28 53.21 N 6.14 W
Grand Canal → Yunhe ≍, Zhg. 80 32.12 N 119.31 E
Grand Cane 184 32.05 N 93.49 W
Grand Cañon du Verdon ∨ 56 43.47 N 6.27 E
Grand Canyon 190 36.03 N 112.09 W
Grand Canyon ∨ 190 36.10 N 112.45 W
Grand Canyon National Park ♠ 190 36.15 N 112.58 W
Grand Canyon of Pennsylvania ∨ 200 41.43 N 77.28 W
Grand Cape Mount □[6] 140 7.00 N 11.00 W
Grand Cayman I 228 19.20 N 81.15 W
Grand Central Terminal ⬩[5] 266 40.45 N 73.59 W
Grand Centre 174 54.25 N 110.13 W
Grand Cess 140 4.36 N 8.10 W
Grandchamp, Fr. 54 47.43 N 5.27 E
Grandchamp, Fr. 251 48.43 N 1.37 E
Grand-Charmont 54 47.32 N 6.50 E
Grand Chenier 184 29.46 N 92.58 W
Grand Combin ∧ 54 45.56 N 7.18 E
Grand Coulee 192 47.56 N 119.00 W
Grand Coulee ∨ 192 47.45 N 119.15 W
Grand Coulee Dam ⬩[6] 192 47.57 N 118.59 W
Grand-Couronne 46 49.21 N 1.00 E
Grand Cul-de-Sac Marin C 231o 16.20 N 61.35 W
Grande ≃, Arg. 242 36.52 S 69.45 W
Grande ≃, Arg. 242 24.12 S 64.42 W
Grande ≃, Bol. 238 15.51 S 64.39 W
Grande ≃, Bra. 232 11.05 S 43.09 W
Grande ≃, Bra. 245 19.52 S 50.20 W
Grande ≃, Bra. 277a 22.55 S 43.25 W
Grande ≃, Bra. 277b 23.45 S 46.22 W
Grande ≃, Qué., Can. 176 48.24 N 64.30 W
Grande ≃, Chile 242 30.35 S 71.11 W
Grande ≃, Esp. 34 39.07 N 0.44 W
Grande ≃, Méx. 224 17.13 N 100.55 W
Grande ≃, Méx. 224 17.43 N 96.56 W
Grande ≃, Méx. 224 16.47 N 95.52 W
Grande ≃, Pan. 226 8.18 N 80.24 W
Grande ≃, Perú 238 14.59 S 75.29 W
Grande ≃, S.A. 244 53.48 S 67.40 W
Grande, Arroyo ≃, Arg. 248 34.37 S 59.25 W
Grande, Arroyo ≃, Arg. 278 34.45 S 58.08 W
Grande, Arroyo ≃, Méx. 224 23.55 N 98.44 W
Grande, Arroyo ≃, Ur. 248 33.37 S 57.09 W
Grande, Bahía C[3] 244 50.45 S 68.45 W
Grande, Boca C 210 26.43 N 82.16 W
Grande, Boca ≃[1] 236 8.38 N 60.30 W
Grande, Cañada ≃, Arg. 248 35.19 S 57.48 W
Grande, Cañada ≃, Arg. 248 35.15 S 59.23 W
Grande, Cayo I 230p 20.59 N 79.09 W
Grande, Cuchilla ∧ 242 33.15 S 55.07 W
Grande, Igarapé ≃ 240 3.37 S 48.53 W
Grande, Ilha I, Bra. 242 23.45 S 54.03 W
Grande, Ilha I, Bra. 246 23.09 S 44.14 W
Grande, Lago ⊜, Arg. 244 46.48 S 69.09 W
Grande, Lago ⊜, Bra. 240 2.16 S 54.17 W
Grande, Laguna C 276b 23.05 N 82.30 W
Grande, Laguna ⊜ 248 34.14 S 58.53 W
Grande, Naviglio ≍ 256b 45.35 N 8.42 E
Grande, Ponta ≻ 245 16.22 S 39.01 W
Grande, Praia ⬩[2] 246 24.05 S 46.30 W
Grande, Punta ≻ 242 25.06 S 70.30 W
Grande, Riacho ≃ 240 9.25 S 41.08 W
Grande, Ribeirão ≃ 246 22.11 S 43.19 W
Grande, Rio (Bravo del Norte) ≃ 168 25.55 N 97.09 W
Grande, Serra ∧ 240 6.00 S 40.52 W
Grande, Serra → Geral, Serra ⬩[4] 240 11.15 S 46.30 W
Grande, Sierra ∧, Arg. 242 31.29 S 64.50 W
Grande, Sierra ∧, Méx. 186 29.40 N 104.55 W
Grande-Anse, N.B., Can. 176 47.48 N 65.11 W
Grande Anse, Guad. 231o 16.18 N 61.04 W
Grande Anse C 265a 45.23 N 73.53 W
Grande Anse du Diamant C 230e 14.28 N 61.02 W
Grande Casse, Pointe de la ∧ 56 45.24 N 6.50 E
Grande Cayemite I 228 18.37 N 73.45 W
Grande-Chartreuse, Couvent de la ♰[1] 56 45.22 N 5.50 E
Grande Comore I 147a 11.35 S 43.20 E
Grande da Botija, Ilha I 236 3.58 S 62.53 W
Grande de Añasco ≃ 230m 18.16 N 67.11 W
Grande de Arecibo ≃ 230m 18.29 N 66.42 W
Grande de Jutaí, Ilha I 240 3.15 S 49.37 W
Grande de Lipez ≃ 238 20.47 S 67.14 W
Grande de Loíza ≃ 230m 18.27 N 65.53 W
Grande de Manacapuru, Lago ⊜ 236 3.04 S 61.25 W
Grande de Manatí ≃ 230m 18.29 N 66.32 W
Grande de Matagalpa ≃ 226 12.54 N 83.32 W
Grande de San Miguel ≃ 226 13.14 N 88.22 W
Grande de Santa Marta, Ciénaga C 236 10.50 N 74.25 W
Grande de Santiago, Río ≃ 224 21.36 N 105.26 W
Grande de Tarija ≃ 238 22.53 S 64.21 W
Grande de Térraba ≃ 226 9.03 N 83.40 W
Grande do Curuaí, Lago ⊜ 240 2.15 S 55.20 W
Grande do Gurupá, Ilha I 240 1.00 S 51.30 W
Grande do Tapará, Ilha I 240 2.14 S 54.39 W
Grande Fausse Passe ≍ 165f 19.15 S 163.59 E
Grande Île I 265a 45.29 N 73.17 W
Grande Île de la Ndjili I 263b 4.19 S 15.24 E
Grande Inferior, Cuchilla ∧[2] 248 33.50 S 56.27 W
Grande-Entrée 176 47.33 N 61.34 W
Grande Pointe ≻ 231o 15.58 N 61.38 W
Grande-Prairie 172 55.10 N 118.48 W
Grand Erg de Bilma ⬩[2] 136 18.30 N 14.00 E
Grand Erg Occidental ⬩[2] 138 30.30 N 0.30 E
Grand Erg Oriental ⬩[2] 138 30.30 N 7.00 E
Grande-Rivière 176 48.24 N 64.30 W
Grande Rivière, Pointe de la ≻ 231o 16.18 N 61.37 W
Grande Rivière à Goyaves ≃ 231o 16.18 N 61.37 W
Grande Rivière de la Baleine ≃ 166 55.16 N 77.47 W
Grande Ronde ≃ 192 46.05 N 116.59 W
Grandes, Salinas ≃ 242 29.37 S 64.56 W
Grandes Antillas, Islas → Greater Antilles II 228 20.00 N 74.00 W
Grandes Antilles, Îles → Greater Antilles II 228 20.00 N 74.00 W
Grande Sassière, Aiguille de la ∧ 56 45.30 N 7.00 E
Grande Sauldre ≃ 46 47.22 N 1.55 E
Gran Desierto de Arena → Great Sandy Desert ⬩[2] 152 21.30 S 125.00 E
Gran Desierto Victoria → Great Victoria Desert ⬩[2] 152 28.30 S 127.45 E
Grandes-Piles 196 46.41 N 72.44 W
Grande-Étang 176 46.33 N 61.02 W
Grand Étang ⊜ 231k 12.06 N 61.42 W
Grande-Terre I 231o 16.20 N 61.25 W
Grande Vigie, Pointe de la ≻ 231o 16.31 N 61.28 W
Grand Eyvia ≃ 56 45.42 N 7.14 E
Grand Falls, N.B., Can. 176 47.03 N 67.44 W
Grand Falls, Newf., Can. 176 48.56 N 55.40 W
Grandfalls, Tex., U.S. 186 31.20 N 102.51 W
Grandfather Mountain ∧ 182 36.07 N 81.48 W
Grandfield 186 34.13 N 98.41 W
Grand Forks, B.C., Can. 172 49.02 N 118.27 W
Grand Forks, N. Dak., U.S. 188 47.55 N 97.03 W
Grand Forks Air Force Base ■ 188 47.57 N 97.25 W
Grand-Fort-Philippe 46 50.00 N 2.06 E
Grand Fougeray 32 47.44 N 1.44 W
Grand-Gallargues 56 43.43 N 4.10 E
Grand Gedeh □[6] 140 6.00 N 8.00 W
Grand Gorge 200 42.22 N 74.30 W
Grand-Halleux 52 50.19 N 5.54 E
Grand Haven 206 43.04 N 86.13 W
Grand Haven State Park ♠ 206 43.02 N 86.13 W
Grand Hers ≃ 32 43.47 N 1.20 E
Grandiči 66 53.43 N 23.49 E
Grandin, Lac ⊜ 166 63.59 N 119.30 W
Grandioznyj, Pik ∧ 78 53.50 N 96.11 E
Grand Island, Fla., U.S. 210 28.53 N 81.44 W
Grand Island, Nebr., U.S. 188 40.55 N 98.21 W
Grand Island, N.Y., U.S. 202 43.01 N 78.58 W
Grand Island I, Ont., Can. 202 44.34 N 78.50 W
Grand Island I, Mich., U.S. 180 46.30 N 86.40 W
Grand Island I, N.Y., U.S. 200 43.02 N 78.58 W
Grand Isle 184 29.14 N 90.00 W
Grand Isle □[6] 196 44.57 N 73.17 W
Grand Junction, Colo., U.S. 190 39.05 N 108.33 W
Grand Junction, Iowa, U.S. 188 42.02 N 94.14 W
Grand Junction, Mich., U.S. 206 42.24 N 86.04 W
Grand Junction, Tenn., U.S. 184 35.03 N 89.10 W
Grand lac des Îles ⊜ 196 46.43 N 73.30 W
Grand Lac du Nord ⊜ 176 50.54 N 67.06 W
Grand lac Germain ⊜ 176 51.12 N 66.41 W
Grand Lac Salé → Great Salt Lake ⊜ 190 41.10 N 112.30 W
Grand lac Victoria ⊜ 180 47.31 N 77.30 W
Grand-Lahou 140 5.08 N 5.01 W
Grand Lake 190 40.15 N 105.49 W
Grand Lake ⊜, N.B., Can. 176 45.42 N 66.05 W
Grand Lake ⊜, Newf., Can. 176 49.00 N 57.25 W
Grand Lake ⊜, N.A. 176 45.43 N 67.50 W
Grand Lake ⊜, La., U.S. 184 29.55 N 92.47 W
Grand Lake ⊜, Maine, U.S. 178 45.15 N 67.50 W
Grand Lake ⊜, Mich., U.S. 180 45.18 N 83.30 W
Grand Lake ⊜, Ohio, U.S. 206 40.30 N 84.32 W
Grand Lake-Saint Marys State Park ♠ 206 40.33 N 84.27 W
Grand Ledge 206 42.45 N 84.45 W
Grand Lieu, Lac de ⊜ 32 47.06 N 1.40 W
Grand Manan Channel ⊔ 176 44.45 N 66.52 W
Grand Manan Island I 176 44.40 N 66.50 W
Grand Marais, Mich., U.S. 180 46.40 N 85.59 W
Grand Marais, Minn., U.S. 180 47.45 N 90.20 W
Grand Meadow 180 43.42 N 92.34 W
Grand'Mère 196 46.37 N 72.41 W
Grand Mesa ∧ 190 39.00 N 108.00 W
Grandmesnil, Lac ⊜ 176 51.19 N 67.33 W
Grand Morié 140 5.59 N 4.08 W
Grand Morin ≃ 46 48.54 N 2.50 E
Grandola, It. 54 46.02 N 9.13 E
Grândola, Port. 34 38.10 N 8.34 W
Grand-Pabos, Rivière du ≃ 176 48.21 N 64.43 W
Grand Palace ⬩ 259a 13.45 N 100.30 E
Grand Passage ⊔ 165f 18.45 S 163.10 E
Grand-Popo 140 6.17 N 1.50 E
Grand Portage 180 47.58 N 89.41 W
Grand Portage Indian Reservation ⬩[4] 180 47.55 N 89.45 W
Grand Portage National Monument ♠ 180 48.02 N 89.57 W
Grand Prairie 212 32.45 N 96.59 W
Grandpré 52 49.20 N 4.52 E
Grand Pré National Historic Park ♠ 176 45.08 N 64.18 W
Grand Prix Airport ⊠ 271 42.33 N 83.11 W
Grand Rapids, Man., Can. 174 53.08 N 99.20 W
Grand Rapids, Mich., U.S. 206 42.58 N 85.40 W
Grand Rapids, Minn., U.S. 180 47.14 N 93.31 W
Grand Rapids, Ohio, U.S. 206 41.25 N 83.52 W
Grand Récif de Cook ⬩[2] 165f 19.25 S 163.50 E
Grand Récif Mathieu ⬩[2] 165f 20.51 S 164.20 E
Grand Rhône ≃ 56 43.20 N 4.50 E
Grand Ridge 206 41.14 N 88.50 W
Grandrieu, Bel. 46 50.12 N 4.10 E
Grandrieu, Fr. 56 44.47 N 3.38 E
Grand River 204 41.44 N 81.17 W
Grand' Rivière 230e 14.52 N 61.11 W
Grand Ronde 214 45.04 N 123.37 W
Grand Roy 231k 12.08 N 61.45 W
Grand Ruisseau ≃ 265a 45.39 N 73.12 W
Grand-Saint-Bernard, Col du ⊔ 54 45.50 N 7.10 E
Grand-Saint-Bernard, Tunnel du ⬩[5] 54 45.51 N 7.11 E
Grand Saline 212 32.41 N 95.43 W
Grand Saline Creek ≃ 212 32.41 N 95.36 W
Grandson 54 46.49 N 6.38 E
Grand Terrace 218 34.03 N 117.20 W
Grand Teton ∧ 192 43.44 N 110.48 W
Grand Teton National Park ♠ 192 43.30 N 43.57 W
Grand Tower 184 37.38 N 89.30 W
Grand Traverse Bay C 180 45.02 N 85.30 W
Grand Traverse Bay, East Arm C 180 44.52 N 85.28 W
Grand Traverse Bay, West Arm C 180 44.52 N 85.35 W
Grand Turk 228 21.28 N 71.08 W
Grand Union Canal ≍ 250 51.30 N 0.02 W
Grand Valley, Ont., Can. 202 43.54 N 80.19 W
Grand Valley, Colo., U.S. 190 39.27 N 108.03 W
Grand Valley, Pa., U.S. 204 41.43 N 79.32 W
Grandview, Man., Can. 174 51.10 N 100.45 W
Grandview, Ill., U.S. 209 39.49 N 89.37 W
Grandview, Mo., U.S. 184 38.53 N 94.32 W
Grandview, Pa., U.S. 269b 40.10 N 79.52 W
Grandview, Tex., U.S. 212 32.16 N 97.11 W
Grandview, Wash., U.S. 192 46.15 N 119.54 W
Grand View, Wis., U.S. 180 46.22 N 91.06 W
Grandview Beach 206 41.50 N 83.24 W
Grandview Heights, Ohio, U.S. 208 40.01 N 83.03 W
Grandview Heights, Pa., U.S. 198 40.03 N 76.17 W
Grandview Homes 206 40.44 N 84.04 W
Grand View-on-Hudson 266 41.44 N 73.55 W
Grandvillars 54 47.33 N 6.58 E
Grandville 206 42.54 N 85.46 W
Grandvilliers 46 49.40 N 1.56 E
Grand Wash Cliffs ⬩[4] 190 35.40 N 113.50 W
Grand Winterberg ∧ 52 48.59 N 7.37 E
Grandyle Village 202 43.01 N 78.57 W
Grâne 56 44.44 N 4.55 E
Grañén 34 41.56 N 0.22 W
Graneros 242 34.04 S 70.44 W
Grangärde 40 60.16 N 14.59 E
Grange, Austl. 158b 34.54 S 138.30 E
Grange, Eng., U.K. 252 53.23 N 3.09 W
Grange, Bois de la ♠ 251 48.45 N 2.30 E
Grange-Bléneau, Château de la ⊥ 46 48.41 N 2.55 E
Grange Hill 250 51.37 N 0.05 E
Grangemouth 42 56.02 N 3.45 W
Grängen ⊜ 40 59.45 N 14.47 E
Grangent, Lac de ⊜[1] 56 45.25 N 4.15 E
Grange-over-Sands 42 54.12 N 2.55 W
Granger, Tex., U.S. 212 30.43 N 97.27 W
Granger, Utah, U.S. 190 40.42 N 111.57 W
Granger, Wash., U.S. 192 46.21 N 120.11 W
Granger, Wyo., U.S. 190 41.35 N 109.58 W
Granges → Grenchen 54 47.11 N 7.24 E
Grängesberg 40 60.05 N 14.59 E
Granges-sur-Vologne 54 48.09 N 6.47 E
Grangeville, Idaho, U.S. 192 45.56 N 116.07 W
Grangeville, Pa., U.S. 198 39.47 N 76.58 W
Grangousier Hill ∧[2] 180 47.35 N 84.56 W
Gran Guardia 242 25.52 S 58.53 W
Granite, Md., U.S. 274b 39.21 N 76.51 W
Granite, Okla., U.S. 186 34.58 N 99.23 W
Granite City 209 38.42 N 90.09 W
Granite Creek ≃ 214 48.43 N 120.55 W
Granite Dam ⬩[6] 176 48.06 N 57.20 W
Granite Dome ∧ 216 38.13 N 119.44 W
Granite Downs 152 26.57 S 133.30 E
Granite Falls, Minn., U.S. 188 44.49 N 95.33 W
Granite Falls, N.C., U.S. 182 35.48 N 81.26 W
Granite Falls, Wash., U.S. 214 48.05 N 121.58 W
Granite Lake ⊜[1] 176 48.08 N 57.05 W
Granite Mountain ∧, Austl. 161b 35.44 S 148.13 E
Granite Mountain ∧, Alaska, U.S. 170 65.26 N 161.14 W
Granite Mountain ∧, Alaska, U.S. 172 55.30 N 132.35 W
Granite Mountains ∧ 192 42.35 N 107.30 W
Granite Pass)(192 44.38 N 107.30 W
Granite Peak ∧ 152 25.38 S 121.21 E
Granite Peak ∧, Mont., U.S. 192 45.34 N 112.02 W
Granite Peak ∧, Mont., U.S. 192 45.10 N 109.48 W
Granite Peak ∧, Nev., U.S. 194 40.48 N 119.25 W
Granite Peak ∧, Nev., U.S. 194 41.40 N 117.35 W
Granite Range ∧ 194 41.00 N 119.35 W
Graniteville, Mass., U.S. 197 42.36 N 71.28 W
Graniteville, S.C., U.S. 182 33.34 N 81.48 W
Graniteville, Vt., U.S. 178 44.08 N 72.29 W
Granitnoje 73 47.27 N 37.52 E
Granito 240 7.43 S 39.36 W
Granitogorsk 75 42.44 N 73.27 E
Granitola, Capo ≻ 36 37.33 N 12.40 E
Granity 162 41.38 S 171.51 E
Granja, Bra. 240 3.06 S 40.50 W
Granja, Port. 256c 38.51 N 9.06 W
Gran Khingan → Daxing'anlingshan mai ∧ 79 49.40 N 122.00 E
Granki 66 54.51 N 31.27 E
Grankulla (Kauniainen) 26 60.13 N 24.45 E
Gran Lago Salado → Great Salt Lake ⊜ 190 41.10 N 112.30 W
Gran Laguna Salada ⊜ 244 44.24 S 67.23 W
Gränna 26 58.01 N 14.28 E
Grannoch, Loch ⊜ 42 55.00 N 4.17 W
Granollers 34 41.37 N 2.18 E
Granön 26 64.15 N 19.19 E
Granov 68 48.52 N 29.34 E
Gran Pajonal ∧[1] 238 10.45 S 74.30 W
Gran Paradiso ∧ 56 45.32 N 7.16 E
Gran Paradiso, Parco Nazionale del ♠ 56 45.34 N 7.18 E
Gran Piedra ∧ 230p 20.01 N 75.38 W
Gran Pilastro (Hochfeiler) ∧ 58 46.58 N 11.44 E
Gran Quivira National Monument ♠ 190 34.05 N 106.14 W
Gran Rio ≃ 240 4.01 N 55.31 W
Gran Sasso d'Italia ∧ 60 42.27 N 13.42 E
Gransee 50 53.00 N 13.09 E
Grant, Fla., U.S. 210 27.56 N 80.32 W
Grant, Mich., U.S. 180 43.20 N 85.49 W
Grant, Nebr., U.S. 188 40.50 N 101.56 W
Grant □[6], Ind., U.S. 206 40.33 N 85.40 W
Grant □[6], Ky., U.S. 208 38.39 N 84.39 W
Grant ≃ 180 42.40 N 90.45 W
Grant, Lake ⊜ 208 39.00 N 83.53 W
Grant, Mount ∧ 198 38.34 N 118.48 W
Grant, Point ≻ 159 38.31 S 145.07 E
Granta 44 52.10 N 0.06 E
Grant Birthplace State Memorial ⊥ 208 38.54 N 84.14 W
Grant City 184 40.29 N 94.25 W
Grantham, Austl. 161a 27.34 S 152.12 E
Grantham, Eng., U.K. 44 52.55 N 0.39 W
Grantham, Pa., U.S. 198 40.09 N 77.00 W
Grant-Kohrs Ranch National Historic Site ⊥ 192 46.25 N 112.40 W
Grant Lake ⊜[1] 216 37.50 N 119.07 W
Grant Mills 273 41.57 N 71.26 W
Granton 42 55.59 N 3.14 W
Grantorto 58 45.36 N 11.43 E
Grantown-on-Spey 28 57.20 N 3.58 W
Grant Park 206 41.14 N 87.39 W
Grant Park ♠ 268 41.52 N 87.37 W
Grant Point ≻[1] 166 68.19 N 98.53 W
Grant Range ∧ 194 38.25 N 115.30 W
Grants 190 35.09 N 107.52 W
Grantsburg, Ind., U.S. 208 38.17 N 86.28 W
Grantsburg, Wis., U.S. 180 45.47 N 92.41 W
Grantshouse 42 55.53 N 2.19 W
Grants Pass 192 42.26 N 123.19 W
Grants Patch 152 30.27 S 121.07 E
Grant-Suttie Bay C 166 69.47 N 77.15 W
Grantsville, Utah, U.S. 190 40.36 N 112.28 W
Grantsville, W. Va., U.S. 188 38.55 N 81.06 W
Grantville, Ga., U.S. 182 33.14 N 84.50 W
Grantville, Pa., U.S. 198 40.23 N 76.39 W
Granum 172 49.52 N 113.30 W
Granville, Austl. 264a 33.50 S 151.01 E
Granville, Fr. 32 48.50 N 1.36 W
Granville, Ill., U.S. 180 41.16 N 89.14 W
Granville, Mass., U.S. 197 42.04 N 72.52 W
Granville, Mo., U.S. 209 39.34 N 92.06 W
Granville, N. Dak., U.S. 188 48.16 N 100.47 W
Granville, N.Y., U.S. 178 43.24 N 73.16 W
Granville, Ohio, U.S. 204 40.04 N 82.31 W
Granville, Pa., U.S. 198 40.33 N 77.38 W
Granville, W. Va., U.S. 178 39.39 N 79.59 W
Granville Lake ⊜ 174 56.18 N 100.30 W
Granvin 26 60.33 N 6.43 E
Granzin, D.D.R. 50 53.30 N 11.56 E
Granzin, D.D.R. 50 53.25 N 12.53 E
Grão Mogol 245 16.34 S 42.54 W
Grape Creek ≃ 190 38.26 N 105.16 W
Grape Island I 273 42.16 N 70.55 W
Grapeland 212 31.29 N 95.29 W
Grapeview 214 47.20 N 122.50 W
Grapeville 204 40.19 N 79.36 W
Grapevine 212 32.56 N 97.05 W
Grapevine Lake ⊜[1] 212 32.59 N 97.06 W
Grapevine Peak ∧ 194 36.57 N 117.09 W
Grappa, Monte ∧ 58 45.52 N 11.48 E
Grappenhall 252 53.22 N 2.32 W
Gras, Lac de ⊜ 166 64.30 N 110.30 W
Grasbult 148 30.52 S 21.47 E
Grasdorf 52 52.09 N 9.51 E
Graskop 146 24.58 S 30.49 E
Grasleben 50 52.18 N 11.01 E
Grasmere, S. Afr. 148 26.26 S 27.52 E
Grasmere, Eng., U.K. 42 54.28 N 3.02 W
Grasmere Lake ⊜ 266 40.36 N 74.05 W
Gräsö 40 60.21 N 18.28 E
Gräsö I 40 60.24 N 18.25 E
Grasonville 198 38.57 N 76.13 W
Grass ≃, Man., Can. 174 56.03 N 96.33 W
Grass ≃, N.Y., U.S. 178 44.59 N 74.46 W
Grass, North Branch ≃ 178 44.25 N 75.06 W
Grass, South Branch ≃ 178 44.22 N 75.05 W
Grassano 36 40.38 N 16.18 E
Grassau 58 47.47 N 12.27 E
Grass Cay I 226 16.08 N 88.15 W
Grass Creek 192 43.56 N 108.39 W
Grasscroft 252 53.32 N 2.02 W
Grasse 56 43.40 N 6.55 E
Grassendale ⬩[8] 252 53.21 N 2.54 W
Grassflat 204 41.00 N 78.07 W
Grass Hassock Channel ⊔ 266 40.36 N 73.48 W
Grasshopper Creek ≃ 192 45.06 N 112.47 W
Grassi Lagoon C 165e 8.12 S 157.40 E
Grassington 42 54.04 N 4.59 W
Grass Island I 266 40.39 N 73.18 W
Grässjön ⊜ 40 59.52 N 13.43 E
Grass Lake 206 42.15 N 84.13 W
Grass Lake ⊜ 206 42.27 N 88.10 W
Grass Patch 152 33.14 S 121.43 E
Grassrange 192 47.01 N 108.48 W
Grassridge Dam ⬩[6] 148 31.45 S 25.29 E
Grass River Provincial Park ♠ 174 54.40 N 100.50 W
Grass Valley, Austl. 158a 31.38 S 116.48 E
Grass Valley, Calif., U.S. 216 39.13 N 121.04 W
Grass Valley, Oreg., U.S. 214 45.22 N 120.47 W
Grassy 156 40.03 S 144.04 E
Grassy ≃ 180 48.42 N 81.27 W
Grassy Bay C 266 40.38 N 73.48 W
Grassy Brook ≃ 274a 43.03 N 79.07 W
Grassy Creek ≃ 206 40.55 N 86.30 W
Grassy Hill ∧ 261d 22.25 N 114.09 E
Grassy Island I 266 41.04 N 73.23 W
Grassy Island Lake ⊜ 174 51.50 N 110.50 W
Grassy Key I 210 24.46 N 80.57 W
Grassy Lake 172 49.49 N 111.43 W
Grassy Lake ⊜ 210 27.13 N 81.20 W
Grassy Plains 172 53.57 N 125.54 W
Grassy Sprain Reservoir ⊜[1] 266 40.58 N 73.51 W
Gråsten 41 54.55 N 9.36 E
Grästorp 26 58.20 N 12.40 E
Graterford 275 40.13 N 75.27 W
Graterford State Correctional Institution ⬩ 275 40.14 N 75.26 W
Gratens Point ≻ 176 48.09 N 52.57 W
Gratis 208 39.39 N 84.32 W
Gratitunon 105a 7.43 S 113.00 E
Gratz, Ky., U.S. 208 38.28 N 84.57 W
Gratz, Pa., U.S. 198 40.37 N 76.43 W
Gratztown 269b 40.14 N 79.47 W
Graubünden (Grischun) □[3] 54 46.45 N 9.30 E
Graudenz → Grudziądz 30 53.29 N 18.45 E
Graue Hörner ∧ 54 46.57 N 9.23 E
Graukogel ∧ 58 47.06 N 13.10 E
Graulinster 52 49.45 N 6.18 E
Graun → Curon Venosta 58 46.49 N 10.32 E
Graupa 50 51.00 N 13.54 E
Gravatá 240 8.12 S 35.34 W
Gravata ≃ 245 16.53 S 42.10 W
Grave 48 51.45 N 5.44 E
Gravedona 54 46.09 N 9.18 E
Gravelbourg 174 49.53 N 106.34 W
Gravel Creek ≃ 192 42.39 N 123.35 W
Gravelines 46 50.59 N 2.07 E
Gravellona-Toce 54 45.55 N 8.26 E
Gravell Point ≻ 166 67.10 N 76.43 W
Gravelly Bay C 274a 42.52 N 79.15 W
Gravelly Brook ≃ 266 40.25 N 74.13 W
Gravelly Pond ⊜ 273 42.36 N 70.48 W
Gravelotte, Fr. 52 49.07 N 6.01 E
Gravelotte, S. Afr. 146 23.56 S 30.34 E
Gravenhurst 202 44.55 N 79.22 W
Grävenwiesbach 52 50.23 N 8.27 E
Grave Peak ∧ 192 46.24 N 114.44 W
Gravesend, Austl. 156 29.35 S 150.19 E
Gravesend, Eng., U.K. 44 51.27 N 0.24 E
Gravesend Bay C 266 40.36 N 74.01 W
Gravesham □[8] 250 51.25 N 0.24 E
Gravette 184 36.26 N 94.27 W
Gravigny 46 49.03 N 1.10 E
Gravina in Puglia 36 40.49 N 16.25 E
Gravina Island I 172 55.17 N 131.45 W
Gray, Fr. 54 47.27 N 5.35 E
Gray, Ga., U.S. 182 33.01 N 83.32 W
Gray, Ky., U.S. 182 36.57 N 84.00 W
Gray, Maine, U.S. 178 43.53 N 70.20 W
Gray, Pa., U.S. 204 40.08 N 79.05 W
Grayback Mountain ∧, Alaska, U.S. 170 57.08 N 153.54 W
Grayback Mountain ∧, Oreg., U.S. 214 42.07 N 123.18 W
Grayland 214 46.48 N 124.06 W
Grayling, Alaska, U.S. 170 62.57 N 160.03 W
Grayling, Mich., U.S. 180 44.40 N 84.43 W
Grays ≃ 214 46.18 N 123.41 W
Grays Harbor □[6] 214 47.09 N 123.45 W
Grays Harbor C 214 46.56 N 124.05 W
Grayshott 44 51.11 N 0.45 W
Grayslake 206 42.21 N 88.03 W
Grays Lake ⊜ 268 42.21 N 88.03 W
Grays Lake ≍ 192 43.04 N 111.26 W
Grays Lake Outlet ≃ 192 43.22 N 111.46 W
Grayson, Sask., Can. 174 50.44 N 102.40 W
Grayson, Ala., U.S. 184 34.15 N 87.24 W
Grayson, Calif., U.S. 216 37.33 N 121.10 W
Grayson, Ky., U.S. 208 38.20 N 82.57 W
Grayson Lake ⊜[1] 208 38.13 N 83.00 W
Grayson Lake State Park ♠ 208 38.13 N 83.02 W
Grays Peak ∧ 190 39.37 N 105.45 W
Grays Point 264a 34.04 S 151.05 E
Grays River 214 46.21 N 123.37 W
Grays Thurrock 44 51.29 N 0.20 E
Gray Summit 209 38.29 N 90.49 W
Graysville 184 35.27 N 85.05 W
Graytown 204 41.33 N 83.16 W
Grayville 184 38.16 N 87.59 W
Gray Wolf ≃ 214 47.55 N 123.07 W
Graz 30 47.05 N 15.27 E
Grazalema 34 36.46 N 5.22 W
Graždanka ⬩[8] 255a 60.00 N 30.24 E
Gr'azeva ≃ 255b 55.34 N 37.21 E
Gr'azi 70 52.29 N 39.57 E
Grazierville 204 40.40 N 78.16 W
Gr'aznoje 72 54.02 N 39.07 E
Gr'aznovo, S.S.S.R. 72 54.18 N 36.49 E
Gr'aznovo, S.S.S.R. 255b 55.57 N 37.34 E
Gr'aznyj Irtek 70 51.56 N 53.11 E
Gr'azovec 66 58.53 N 40.14 E
Grdelica 38 42.54 N 22.04 E
Greaca, Lacul ⊜ 38 44.05 N 26.23 E
Greåker 26 59.16 N 11.02 E
Greasby 252 53.23 N 3.07 W
Great ≃ 231k 12.08 N 61.36 W
Great Abaco I 228 26.28 N 77.05 W
Great Adventure ♠ 198 40.09 N 74.27 W
Great Altcar 252 53.33 N 3.01 W
Great America ♠ 206 42.21 N 87.55 W
Great Amwell 250 51.48 N 0.01 W
Great Artesian Basin ⊔ 150 25.00 S 143.00 E
Great Astrolabe Reef ⬩[2] 165g 18.52 S 178.31 E
Great Australian Bight C[3] 152 35.00 S 135.00 E
Great Bacolet Point ≻ 231k 12.04 N 61.37 W
Great Baddow 44 51.43 N 0.29 E
Great Bahama Bank ⬩[4] 228 23.15 N 78.00 W
Great Barrier Island I 162 36.10 S 175.25 E
Great Barrier Reef ⬩[2] 150 18.00 S 145.50 E
Great Barrington 197 42.12 N 73.22 W
Great Barrow 252 53.12 N 2.48 W
Great Basin ⊔[1] 194 40.00 N 117.00 W
Great Bay C 170 39.30 N 74.23 W
Great Bear ≃ 170 64.54 N 125.35 W
Great Bear Lake ⊜ 166 66.00 N 120.00 W
Great Beaver Lake ⊜ 172 54.25 N 123.45 W

Symbols in the index entries represent the broad categories identified in the key at the right. Symbols with superior numbers (∧[2]) identify subcategories (see complete key on page I · 26).

Kartensymbole in dem Registerverzeichnis stellen die rechts in Schlüssel erklärten Kategorien dar. Symbole mit hochgestellten Ziffern (∧[2]) bezeichnen Unterabteilungen einer Kategorie (vgl. vollständiger Schlüssel auf Seite I · 26).

Los símbolos incluídos en el texto del índice representan las grandes categorías identificadas con la clave a la derecha. Los símbolos con numeros en su parte superior (∧[2]) identifican las subcategorías (véase la clave completa en la página I · 26).

Les symboles de l'index représentent les catégories indiquées dans la légende à droite. Les symboles suivis d'un indice (∧[2]) représentent des sous-catégories (voir légende complète à la page I · 26).

Os símbolos incluídos no texto do índice representam as grandes categorias identificadas com a chave à direita. Os símbolos com números em sua parte superior (∧[2]) identificam as subcategorias (veja-se a chave completa à página I · 26).

Symbol	English	Deutsch	Español	Français	Português
∧	Mountain	Berg	Montaña	Montagne	Montanha
∧∧	Mountains	Berge	Montañas	Montagnes	Montanhas
)(	Pass	Pass	Paso	Col	Passo
∨	Valley, Canyon	Tal, Cañon	Valle, Cañón	Vallée, Canyon	Vale, Canhão
≚	Plain	Ebene	Llano	Plaine	Planície
≻	Cape	Kap	Cabo	Cap	Cabo
I	Island	Insel	Isla	Île	Ilha
II	Islands	Inseln	Islas	Îles	Ilhas
⊥	Other Topographic Features	Andere Topographische Objekte	Otros Elementos Topográficos	Autres données topographiques	Outros Elementos Topográficos

ESPAÑOL

Nombre	Página	Lat.°′	Long.°′ W=Oeste
Great Bend, Kans., U.S.	188	38.22 N	98.46 W
Great Bend, N.Y., U.S.	202	44.02 N	75.43 W
Great Bend, Pa., U.S.	200	41.58 N	75.45 W
al-Murrah al-Kubra, Al-Buḥayrah (Great Bitter Lake) @	132	30.20 N	32.23 E
Great Blasket Island I	28	52.05 N	10.32 W
Great Blue Hill Λ[2]	197	42.13 N	71.07 W
Great Bookham	250	51.16 N	0.22 W
Great Braxted	250	51.48 N	0.42 E
Great Brewster Island I	273	42.20 N	70.53 W
Great Brook ≃	266	40.42 N	74.31 W
Great Budworth	252	53.18 N	2.30 W
Great Burnt Lake @	176	48.20 N	56.13 W
Great Burso Bank ✢[4]	252	53.29 N	3.06 W
Great Burstead	250	51.36 N	0.25 E
Great Camanoe Island I	230m	18.29 N	64.32 W
Great Captain Island I	266	40.59 N	73.38 W
Great Central Lake @	172	49.27 N	125.12 W
Great Channel U	100	6.25 N	94.20 E
Great Chazy ≃	196	44.56 N	73.23 W
Great Chazy, North Branch ≃	196	44.57 N	73.38 W
Great Clifton	42	54.31 N	3.29 W
Great Coco Island I	100	14.05 N	93.24 E
Great Coharie Creek ≃	182	34.50 N	78.22 W
Great Cove C	266	40.43 N	73.14 W
Great Crosby	252	53.29 N	3.01 W
Great Crossing	208	38.08 N	84.38 W
Great Cumbrae Island I	42	55.46 N	4.55 W
Great Dismal Swamp ≋	182	36.30 N	76.30 W
Great Ditch ≡	266	40.24 N	74.31 W
Great Divide Basin ⌣[1]	192	42.00 N	108.10 W
Great Dividing Range ⛰	150	25.00 S	147.00 E
Great Duck Island I	180	45.40 N	82.58 W
Great Dunmow	44	51.53 N	0.22 E
Great Eau ≃	42	53.25 N	0.13 E
Great Egg Harbor ≃	198	39.18 N	74.40 W
Great Egg Harbor Bay C	198	39.18 N	74.37 W
Great Egg Harbor Inlet C	198	39.20 N	74.34 W
Greater Antilles II	228	20.00 N	74.00 W
Greater Bombay □[5]	262c	19.08 N	72.51 E
Greater Buffalo International Airport ⊠	200	42.56 N	78.44 W
Greater Cincinnati Airport ⊠	208	39.03 N	84.40 W
Greater Khingan Mountains → Daxing'anling-shanmai ⛰	79	49.40 N	122.00 E
Greater London □[6]	44	51.30 N	0.10 W
Greater Manchester □[6]	42	53.30 N	2.20 W
Greater Pittsburgh International Airport ⊠	204	40.29 N	80.14 W
Greater Sunda Islands II	98	2.00 S	110.00 E
Greater Wilmington Airport ⊠	198	39.41 N	75.36 W
Greater Wollongong → Wollongong	160	34.25 S	150.54 E
Great Exuma I	228	23.32 N	75.50 W
Great Falls, Man., Can.	174	50.27 N	96.02 W
Great Falls, Mont., U.S.	192	47.30 N	111.17 W
Great Falls, S.C., U.S.	182	34.34 N	80.54 W
Great Falls, Va., U.S.	274c	39.00 N	77.17 W
Great Falls ⌊	274c	39.00 N	77.16 W
Great Falls Park ♠	274c	39.00 N	77.15 W
Great Fish Point ≻	148	33.30 S	27.10 E
Great Gable Λ	42	54.28 N	3.12 W
Great Gaddesden	250	51.47 N	0.30 W
Great Grimsby → Grimsby	42	53.35 N	0.05 W
Great Guana Cay I	228	24.00 N	76.20 W
Great Hameldon Λ[2]	252	53.45 N	2.19 W
Great Harwood	42	53.48 N	2.24 W
Greathead Bay C	231h	13.08 N	61.14 W
Great Himalaya Range ⛰	110	29.00 N	83.00 E
Greathouse Peak Λ	192	46.46 N	109.21 W
Great Inagua I	228	21.05 N	73.18 W
Great Indian Desert (Thar Desert) ◆[2]	110	28.00 N	72.00 E
Great Island I, N.Y., U.S.	266	41.05 N	73.44 W
Great Island I, N.Y., U.S.	266	40.38 N	73.30 W
Great Karroo (Groot Karroo) ⛰[1]	148	32.25 S	22.40 E
Great Kills ◆[8]	266	40.33 N	74.10 W
Great Kills Harbor C	266	40.32 N	74.08 W
Great Kills Park ♠	266	40.33 N	74.08 W
Great La Cloche Island I	180	46.01 N	81.52 W
Great Lake @	156	41.52 S	146.45 E
Great Lakes Naval Training Center ■	206	42.18 N	87.50 W
Great Lakes Steel Works ʊ[3]	271	42.15 N	83.08 W
Great Machipongo Inlet C	198	37.22 N	75.43 W
Great Malvern (Malvern)	44	52.07 N	2.19 W
Great Marsh ≋	198	36.32 N	75.57 W
Great Marton	252	53.48 N	3.02 W
Great Massingham	44	52.46 N	0.40 E
Great Meadows	200	40.52 N	74.55 W
Great Meadows National Wildlife Refuge ◆[4]	273	42.29 N	71.20 W
Great Mercury Island I	162	36.37 S	175.48 E
Great Meteor Tablemount ✢[3]	10	30.00 N	28.30 W
Great Miami ≃	178	39.06 N	84.49 W
Great Mills	198	38.14 N	76.30 W
Great Misery Island I	273	42.33 N	70.48 W
Great Missenden	44	51.43 N	0.43 W
Great Mis Tor Λ	44	50.34 N	4.01 W
Great Mosque ʊ[1]	136	32.46 N	22.40 E
Great Namaland □[9]	146	25.00 S	17.00 E
Great Neck	266	40.47 N	73.44 W
Great Neck ≻[1], Mass., U.S.	273	42.42 N	70.48 W
Great Neck ≻[1], N.Y., U.S.	266	40.50 N	73.45 W
Great Neck Estates	266	40.47 N	73.44 W
Great Nicobar I	100	7.00 N	93.50 E
Great North East Channel U	154	9.30 S	143.25 E
Great Notch Reservoir @[1]	266	40.53 N	74.12 W
Great Ormes Head ≻	42	53.21 N	3.52 W
Great Ouse ≃	44	52.47 N	0.22 E
Great Oxney Green	250	51.44 N	0.25 E
Great Palm Island I	156	18.43 S	146.37 E

FRANÇAIS

Nom	Page	Lat.°′	Long.°′ W=Ouest
Great Parndon	250	51.45 N	0.05 E
Great Patchogue Lake @	266	40.46 N	73.01 W
Great Peconic Bay C	197	40.56 N	72.30 W
Great Piece Meadows ≋	266	40.54 N	74.19 W
Great Plain of the Koukdjuak ⌣	166	66.00 N	73.00 W
Great Point ≻	197	41.23 N	70.03 W
Great Pubnico Lake @	176	43.42 N	65.43 W
Great Quittacas Pond @	197	41.48 N	70.54 W
Great River	266	40.45 N	73.10 W
Great River Bay C	231k	12.08 N	61.36 W
Great Ruaha ≃	144	7.56 S	37.52 E
Great Sacandaga Lake @	200	43.08 N	74.10 W
Great Saint Bernard Pass → Grand-Saint-Bernard, Col du)(	54	45.50 N	7.10 E
Great Sale Cay I	182	27.00 N	78.12 W
Great Salt Lake @	190	41.10 N	112.30 W
Great Salt Lake Desert ◆[2]	190	40.40 N	113.30 W
Great Salt Plains Lake @[1]	186	36.44 N	98.12 W
Great Sand Dunes National Monument ♠	190	37.43 N	105.36 W
Great Sand Hills ⛰[2]	174	50.35 N	109.05 W
Great Sandy Desert ◆[2], Austl.	152	21.30 S	125.00 E
Great Sandy Desert ◆[2], Oreg., U.S.	192	43.35 N	120.15 W
Great Sankey	252	53.23 N	2.39 W
Great Santa Cruz Island I	106	6.52 N	122.03 E
Great Scarcies (Kolenté) ≃	140	8.55 N	13.08 W
Great Sea Reef ✢[2]	165g	16.15 S	179.00 E
Great Seneca Creek ≃	198	39.08 N	77.20 W
Great Shelford	44	52.09 N	0.09 E
Great Sitkin Island I	170	52.03 N	176.07 W
Great Slave Lake @	166	61.30 N	114.00 W
Great Smoky Mountains ⛰	182	35.35 N	83.30 W
Great Smoky Mountains National Park ♠	182	35.39 N	83.30 W
Great Sound U, Ber.	230a	32.17 N	64.51 W
Great Sound U, N.J., U.S.	198	39.06 N	74.47 W
Great South Bay C	200	40.40 N	73.17 W
Great Stour ≃	44	51.19 N	1.15 E
Great Sutton	252	53.17 N	2.56 W
Great Swamp National Wildlife Refuge ◆[4]	266	40.43 N	74.28 W
Great Tenasserim ≃	100	12.24 N	98.37 E
Great Thatch Island I	230m	18.23 N	64.43 W
Great Torrington	44	50.57 N	4.08 W
Great Totham	250	51.47 N	0.43 E
Great Tsau Λ	146	21.14 S	22.45 E
Great Usutu (Maputo) ≃	148	26.11 S	32.42 E
Great Valley	200	42.13 N	78.38 W
Great Victoria Desert ◆[2]	152	28.30 S	127.45 E
Great Wall → Changcheng ⊥	88	40.30 N	117.00 E
Great Waltham	250	51.48 N	0.28 E
Great Warley	250	51.35 N	0.17 E
Great Whernside Λ	42	54.09 N	1.59 W
Great Wicomico ≃	198	37.48 N	76.18 W
Great World ʊ	259b	31.14 N	121.23 E
Great Yarmouth	44	52.37 N	1.44 E
Great Zab (Büyükzap) (Az-Zāb al-Kabīr) ≃	118	36.00 N	43.21 E
Grebbestad	26	58.42 N	11.15 E
Grebenhain	52	50.29 N	9.19 E
Grebenka	68	50.07 N	32.25 E
Grebenstein	52	51.26 N	9.24 E
Grebnevo	255b	55.58 N	38.05 E
Greb'onki	68	49.57 N	30.12 E
Gréboun, Mont Λ	140	20.00 N	8.35 E
Grèce → Greece □[1]	38	39.00 N	22.00 E
Grecia	226	10.05 N	84.18 W
Grecia → Greece □[1]	38	39.00 N	22.00 E
Grečiškino	73	48.52 N	38.54 E
Grecken @	40	59.35 N	14.44 E
Greco	242	32.48 S	57.03 W
Greco ◆[8]	256b	45.30 N	9.13 E
Greco, Monte Λ	60	41.48 N	14.00 E
Greco Island I	272	37.31 N	122.11 W
Gredos, Sierra de ⛰	34	40.18 N	5.05 W
Gredstedbro	41	55.24 N	8.45 E
Greece	200	43.14 N	77.38 W
Greece □[1]	22		
	38	39.00 N	22.00 E
Greeley, Colo., U.S.	190	40.25 N	104.42 W
Greeley, Kans., U.S.	188	38.22 N	95.08 W
Greeley, Nebr., U.S.	188	41.33 N	98.32 W
Greeley, Pa., U.S.	200	41.25 N	75.00 W
Greeleyville	182	33.35 N	79.58 W
Green □[6]	206	42.48 N	89.25 W
Green ≃, N.B., Can.	176	47.18 N	68.09 W
Green ≃, S. Afr.	148	30.40 S	23.17 E
Green ≃, U.S.	190	38.11 N	109.53 W
Green ≃, U.S.	197	42.35 N	72.36 W
Green ≃, Ill., U.S.	180	41.28 N	90.23 W
Green ≃, Ill., U.S.	206	41.46 N	89.10 W
Green ≃, Ky., U.S.	184	37.55 N	87.30 W
Green ≃, N. Dak., U.S.	188	46.52 N	102.35 W
Green ≃, Vt., U.S.	200	43.06 N	73.13 W
Green ≃, Wash., U.S.	214	46.20 N	122.34 W
Green ≃, Wash., U.S.	214	47.33 N	122.20 W
Greenacres	192	47.39 N	117.06 W
Green Acres ◆[9]	266	40.40 N	73.43 W
Greenacres City	210	26.37 N	80.07 W
Greenbackville	198	38.01 N	75.23 W
Greenbank	214	48.06 N	122.34 W
Green Bay	180	44.30 N	88.01 W
Green Bay C, Newf., Can.	176	49.43 N	55.58 W
Green Bay C, Ont., Can.	202	44.38 N	76.36 W
Green Bay C, U.S.	180	45.00 N	87.30 W
Greenbelt	274c	39.01 N	76.53 W
Greenbelt Park ♠	274c	38.59 N	76.54 W
Greenbo Lake @	208	38.29 N	82.54 W
Greenbo Lake State Park ♠	208	38.29 N	82.54 W
Greenbrae	216	37.57 N	122.31 W
Greenbrier, Ark., U.S.	184	35.14 N	92.23 W
Green Brier, Tenn., U.S.	184	36.27 N	86.49 W
Greenbrier ≃	178	37.49 N	80.30 W
Greenbrier State Park ♠	198	39.33 N	77.38 W
Green Brook	266	40.36 N	74.29 W
Green Brook ≃	266	40.33 N	74.32 W
Greenburg	184	30.51 N	90.40 W
Greenbush, Mass., U.S.	197	42.11 N	70.45 W
Greenbush, Minn., U.S.	188	48.42 N	96.11 W
Greenbush, Va., U.S.	198	37.45 N	75.41 W
Greenbushes	152	33.51 S	116.03 E
Green Camp	204	40.32 N	83.13 W
Green Cape ≻	156	37.15 S	150.03 E
Greencastle, Eire	42	55.12 N	6.59 W

PORTUGUÊS

Nome	Página	Lat.°′	Long.°′ W=Oeste
Greencastle, Ind., U.S.	184	39.38 N	86.52 W
Greencastle, Pa., U.S.	178	39.47 N	77.44 W
Green City	184	40.16 N	92.57 W
Green Cove Springs	182	30.00 N	81.41 W
Green Creek	198	39.03 N	74.54 W
Green Creek ≃, Ohio, U.S.	204	41.26 N	83.01 W
Green Creek ≃, Pa., U.S.	275	39.53 N	75.28 W
Greencrest Park	204	41.23 N	80.24 W
Greendale, Austl.	264a	33.55 S	150.39 E
Greendale, Ind., U.S.	208	39.07 N	84.52 W
Greendale, Wis., U.S.	206	42.57 N	88.00 W
Greendale, Wis., U.S.	206	42.39 N	88.25 W
Greene, B.R.D.	48	51.52 N	9.56 E
Greene, Iowa, U.S.	180	42.54 N	92.48 W
Greene, Maine, U.S.	178	44.11 N	70.08 W
Greene, N.Y., U.S.	200	42.20 N	75.46 W
Greene, R.I., U.S.	197	41.41 N	71.44 W
Greene □[6], Ill., U.S.	209	39.18 N	90.24 W
Greene □[6], N.Y., U.S.	200	42.13 N	73.52 W
Greene □[6], Ohio, U.S.	208	39.41 N	83.56 W
Greeneville	182	36.10 N	82.50 W
Green Farms	266	41.07 N	73.19 W
Greenfield, Eng., U.K.	252	53.32 N	2.01 W
Greenfield, Wales, U.K.	42	53.18 N	3.13 W
Greenfield, Calif., U.S.	216	36.19 N	121.15 W
Greenfield, Ill., U.S.	209	39.21 N	90.12 W
Greenfield, Ind., U.S.	208	39.47 N	85.46 W
Greenfield, Iowa, U.S.	188	41.18 N	94.28 W
Greenfield, Mass., U.S.	197	42.36 N	72.36 W
Greenfield, Mo., U.S.	184	37.25 N	93.51 W
Greenfield, Ohio, U.S.	208	39.21 N	83.23 W
Greenfield, Tenn., U.S.	184	36.09 N	88.48 W
Greenfield, Wis., U.S.	206	42.58 N	88.02 W
Greenfield Park, Qué., Can.	265a	45.29 N	73.29 W
Greenfield Park, N.Y., U.S.	200	41.44 N	74.29 W
Greenfields Village	275	75.10 N	39.49 W
Greenfield Village ⊥	271	42.18 N	83.14 W
Greenford ◆[8]	250	51.32 N	0.21 W
Green Forest	184	36.20 N	93.26 W
Green Harbor	197	42.05 N	70.39 W
Green Harbor ≃	273	42.05 N	70.39 W
Green Head ≻	152	30.05 S	114.58 E
Green Hill	275	39.59 N	75.36 W
Greenhill ◆[8]	250	51.35 N	0.20 W
Greenhills	208	39.16 N	84.31 W
Greenhithe	250	51.27 N	0.17 E
Greenhorn Creek ≃	188	38.08 N	104.38 W
Greenhurst	204	42.07 N	79.19 W
Green Hut Park	266	40.50 N	74.39 W
Green Island, N.Z.	162	45.54 S	170.26 E
Green Island, N.Y., U.S.	200	42.45 N	73.41 W
Green Island I, Antig.	230c	17.03 N	61.40 W
Green Island I, Gren.	231k	12.14 N	61.35 W
Green Island Bay C	106	10.12 N	119.22 E
Green Islands II	14	4.30 S	154.10 E
Green Knoll	266	40.36 N	74.36 W
Green Lake, Sask., Can.	174	54.17 N	107.47 W
Green Lake, Wis., U.S.	180	43.51 N	88.57 W
Green Lake @, B.C., Can.	172	51.24 N	121.15 W
Green Lake @, Sask., Can.	174	54.10 N	107.43 W
Green Lake @, Mich., U.S.	271	42.36 N	83.25 W
Green Lake @, N.Y., U.S.	274a	42.45 N	78.45 W
Green Lake @, Wis., U.S.	180	43.41 N	88.57 W
Green Lakes State Park ♠	202	43.03 N	75.58 W
Greenlal (Saint-Grégoire-de-Greenlay)	196	45.34 N	72.01 W
Greenland	180	46.46 N	89.06 W
Greenland □[2]	16	70.00 N	40.00 W
Greenland Basin ✢[1]	16	77.00 N	0.00 W
Greenland-Iceland Rise ✢[3]	10	67.00 N	27.00 W
Greenlands	148	27.07 S	27.40 E
Greenland Sea ⊤[2]	16	77.00 N	1.00 W
Green Lane	198	40.20 N	75.28 W
Green Lane Reservoir @[1]	198	40.22 N	75.29 W
Greenlaw	42	55.43 N	2.28 W
Greenlawn	266	40.52 N	73.22 W
Greenleaf	188	39.44 N	96.59 W
Green Lookout Mountain Λ	214	45.52 N	122.08 W
Green Manorville	197	42.00 N	72.32 W
Green Meadows	274c	38.58 N	76.57 W
Greenmount, Austl.	158a	31.54 S	116.03 E
Greenmount, Austl.	161a	27.47 S	151.54 E
Greenmount, Eng., U.K.	252	53.37 N	2.20 W
Greenmount, Md., U.S.	198	39.38 N	76.52 W
Green Mountain Reservoir @[1]	190	39.52 N	106.17 W
Green Mountains ⛰	178	43.45 N	72.45 W
Green Oak Lake @	271	42.27 N	83.43 W
Green Oaks	268	42.18 N	87.55 W
Greenock, Austl.	158b	34.27 S	138.55 E
Greenock, Scot., U.K.	42	55.57 N	4.45 W
Greenock, Pa., U.S.	269b	40.19 N	79.48 W
Greenodd	42	54.14 N	3.04 W
Greenore Point ≻	28	52.15 N	6.18 W
Greenough	152	28.57 S	114.44 E
Greenough ≃	152	28.51 S	114.38 E
Greenough, Mount Λ	170	69.10 N	141.35 W
Green Park	198	40.23 N	77.19 W
Green Peter Lake @[1]	192	44.28 N	122.30 W
Green Point ≻	266	40.43 N	73.06 W
Green Pond	266	41.01 N	74.29 W
Green Pond @	266	41.00 N	74.30 W
Green Pond Brook ≃	266	40.53 N	74.34 W
Green Pond Mountain Λ	266	40.58 N	74.33 W
Greenport	197	41.06 N	72.22 W
Green Ridge	275	39.51 N	75.25 W
Green River, Pap. N. Gui.	154	3.55 S	141.10 E
Green River, Utah, U.S.	190	38.59 N	110.10 W
Green River, Wyo., U.S.	190	41.32 N	109.28 W
Green River Gorge V	214	47.19 N	121.54 W
Green River Lake @[1]	184	37.15 N	85.15 W
Greensboro, Ala., U.S.	184	32.42 N	87.36 W
Greensboro, Fla., U.S.	182	30.34 N	84.45 W
Greensboro, Ga., U.S.	182	33.35 N	83.11 W
Greensboro, Md., U.S.	178	38.59 N	75.48 W
Greensboro, N.C., U.S.	182	36.04 N	79.47 W
Greensburg, Ind., U.S.	208	39.20 N	85.29 W
Greensburg, Kans., U.S.	188	37.36 N	99.18 W
Greensburg, Ky., U.S.	184	37.16 N	85.30 W
Greensburg, Ohio, U.S.	204	40.56 N	81.28 W
Greensburg, Pa., U.S.	204	40.18 N	79.33 W
Greens Fork	208	39.54 N	85.02 W
Greenside ◆[8]	263d	26.09 S	28.01 E

Greens Lake C	212	29.16 N	94.59 W
Greens Peak Λ	190	34.07 N	109.35 W
Greenspond	176	49.04 N	53.34 W
Green Springs	204	41.15 N	83.03 W
Greenstead	250	51.42 N	0.14 E
Greenstone	198	39.45 N	77.27 W
Green Street	250	51.40 N	0.16 W
Green Street Green ◆[8]	250	51.21 N	0.04 E
Greensville □[6]	198	36.40 N	77.30 W
Green Swamp ≋, Fla., U.S.	210	28.20 N	81.48 W
Green Swamp ≋, N.C., U.S.	182	34.10 N	78.20 W
Greentown, Ind., U.S.	206	40.29 N	85.58 W
Greentown, Ohio, U.S.	204	40.56 N	81.28 W
Greentown, Pa., U.S.	200	41.19 N	75.18 W
Green Tree, Pa., U.S.	269b	40.25 N	80.05 W
Green Tree, Pa., U.S.	275	40.02 N	75.30 W
Greenup, Ill., U.S.	184	39.15 N	88.10 W
Greenup, Ky., U.S.	208	38.34 N	82.50 W
Greenup □[6]	208	38.33 N	83.00 W
Greenvale	266	40.49 N	73.38 W
Green Valley, Ont., Can.	196	45.16 N	74.36 W
Green Valley, Ill., U.S.	180	40.24 N	89.38 W
Green Valley Creek ≃	216	38.13 N	122.08 W
Greenview	209	40.05 N	89.44 W
Green Village, N.J., U.S.	266	40.44 N	74.27 W
Greenvillage, Pa., U.S.	198	40.00 N	77.36 W
Greenville, Liber.	140	5.01 N	9.03 W
Greenville, Ala., U.S.	184	31.50 N	86.38 W
Greenville, Calif., U.S.	194	40.08 N	120.57 W
Greenville, Fla., U.S.	182	30.28 N	83.38 W
Greenville, Ill., U.S.	209	38.53 N	89.25 W
Greenville, Ind., U.S.	208	38.23 N	85.59 W
Greenville, Ky., U.S.	184	37.12 N	87.11 W
Greenville, Maine, U.S.	178	45.28 N	69.35 W
Greenville, Mich., U.S.	180	43.11 N	85.15 W
Greenville, Miss., U.S.	184	33.25 N	91.05 W
Greenville, Mo., U.S.	184	37.08 N	90.27 W
Greenville, N.H., U.S.	178	42.46 N	71.49 W
Greenville, N.C., U.S.	182	35.37 N	77.23 W
Greenville, N.Y., U.S.	200	42.25 N	74.01 W
Greenville, N.Y., U.S.	266	41.00 N	73.49 W
Greenville, Ohio, U.S.	208	40.06 N	84.38 W
Greenville, Pa., U.S.	204	41.24 N	80.23 W
Greenville, R.I., U.S.	197	41.52 N	71.33 W
Greenville, S.C., U.S.	182	34.51 N	82.23 W
Greenville, Tex., U.S.	212	33.08 N	96.07 W
Greenville Creek ≃	208	40.07 N	84.22 W
Green Water ≃, S. Afr.	148	29.00 S	22.10 E
Greenwater ≃, Wash., U.S.	214	47.09 N	121.39 W
Greenwater Lake Provincial Park ♠	174	52.33 N	103.33 W
Greenwell Point	160	34.55 S	150.44 E
Greenwich, Austl.	264a	33.50 S	151.11 E
Greenwich, Conn., U.S.	197	41.01 N	73.38 W
Greenwich, N.J., U.S.	198	39.24 N	75.21 W
Greenwich, N.Y., U.S.	200	43.05 N	73.30 W
Greenwich, Ohio, U.S.	204	41.02 N	82.31 W
Greenwich ◆[8]	44	51.28 N	0.02 E
Greenwich Cove C	266	41.01 N	73.35 W
Greenwich Creek ≃	266	41.02 N	73.37 W
Greenwich Point ≻	266	41.00 N	73.34 W
Greenwich Village ◆[8]	266	40.44 N	74.00 W
Greenwood, B.C., Can.	172	49.05 N	118.41 W
Greenwood, Ark., U.S.	184	35.13 N	94.15 W
Greenwood, Calif., U.S.	216	38.54 N	120.55 W
Greenwood, Del., U.S.	198	38.49 N	75.35 W
Greenwood, Ind., U.S.	208	39.37 N	86.07 W
Greenwood, Mass., U.S.	273	42.29 N	71.04 W
Greenwood, Miss., U.S.	184	33.31 N	90.11 W
Greenwood, Nebr., U.S.	188	40.58 N	96.27 W
Greenwood, N.Y., U.S.	200	42.08 N	77.39 W
Greenwood, Pa., U.S.	204	40.32 N	78.21 W
Greenwood, S.C., U.S.	182	34.12 N	82.10 W
Greenwood, Wis., U.S.	180	44.46 N	90.36 W
Greenwood, Lake @[1]	182	34.15 N	82.02 W
Greenwood Cemetery ◆	266	40.39 N	73.59 W
Greenwood Lake	200	41.14 N	74.18 W
Greenwood Lake @, U.S.	200	41.11 N	74.19 W
Greenwood Lake @, Mass., U.S.	273	42.00 N	71.17 W
Greenwood Race Track ♠	265b	43.40 N	79.19 W
Greer, Ohio, U.S.	204	40.31 N	82.13 W
Greer, S.C., U.S.	182	34.56 N	82.14 W
Greers Ferry Lake @[1]	184	35.30 N	92.10 W
Greerton	162	37.43 S	176.08 E
Grées, Alpes (Alpi Graie) ⛰	56	45.30 N	7.10 E
Greeson, Lake @[1]	184	34.10 N	93.45 W
Greetland	252	53.41 N	1.52 W
Greetsiel	48	53.30 N	7.05 E
Greffiers	251	48.37 N	1.51 E
Gréfodé	142	5.43 N	21.33 E
Grefrath, B.R.D.	52	51.20 N	6.20 E
Grefrath, B.R.D.	253	51.10 N	6.38 E
Gregadoo	161b	35.14 S	147.27 E
Gregbe	140	6.48 N	6.43 W
Gregg	269b	40.24 N	80.10 W
Gregg □[6]	212	32.30 N	94.50 W
Greggio	56	45.27 N	8.23 E
Greg Greg	161b	36.03 S	148.02 E
Gregoire Lake Indian Reserve ◆[4]	174	56.28 N	111.10 W
Gregório ≃	238	6.50 S	70.46 W
Gregory, Mich., U.S.	206	42.28 N	84.05 W
Gregory, S. Dak., U.S.	188	43.14 N	99.26 W
Gregory, Tex., U.S.	186	27.55 N	97.17 W
Gregory ≃	156	17.53 S	139.17 E
Gregory, Lake @, Austl.	152	25.38 S	119.58 E
Gregory, Lake @, Austl.	156	28.55 S	139.00 E
Gregory, Port ⊤[3]	152	28.10 S	114.14 E
Gregory Lake @	152	20.10 S	127.20 E
Gregory Range ⛰	156	19.00 S	143.05 E
Grégy-sur-Yerre	251	48.40 N	2.37 E
Greifenberg → Gryfice	30	53.56 N	15.12 E
Greifenburg	58	46.45 N	13.11 E
Greifendorf	50	51.01 N	13.06 E
Greifenhagen → Gryfino	30	53.12 N	14.30 E
Greifensee	54	47.22 N	8.41 E
Greifensee @	54	47.21 N	8.41 E
Greifenstein	254b	48.21 N	16.25 E
Greiffenberg	50	53.05 N	13.58 E
Greiffenburg ⊥	253	51.20 N	6.38 E
Greifswald	50	54.05 N	13.23 E
Greifswalder Bodden C	50	54.15 N	13.35 E
Greifswalder Oie I	50	54.14 N	13.55 E

Grein	30	48.14 N	14.51 E
Greinsheim	52	49.18 N	8.16 E
Greiz	50	50.39 N	12.12 E
Grejdernoje	70	46.53 N	45.01 E
Grejsdal	41	55.45 N	9.32 E
Grekov	70	47.24 N	43.41 E
Grekovo	73	48.54 N	40.14 E
Grem'ačij	78	57.01 N	108.12 E
Grem'ačinsk, S.S.S.R.	76	58.34 N	57.51 E
Grem'ačinsk, S.S.S.R.	78	52.48 N	107.57 E
Grem'ačje	68	51.29 N	39.00 E
Grem'aščevo	72	54.14 N	36.15 E
Gremersdorf	50	54.20 N	10.55 E
Gremicha	24	68.03 N	39.27 E
Grenå	26	56.25 N	10.53 E
Grenada	184	33.47 N	89.55 W
Grenada □[1]	220		
	231k	12.07 N	61.40 W
Grenada Lake @[1]	184	33.50 N	89.40 W
Grenade → Grenada □[1]	231k	12.07 N	61.40 W
Grenadier Island I	202	44.03 N	76.22 W
Grenadier Pond @	265b	43.38 N	79.28 W
Grenadine Islands II	228	12.40 N	61.15 W
Grenay	46	50.27 N	2.44 E
Grenchen	54	47.11 N	7.24 E
Grenell	202	44.16 N	76.04 W
Grenfell, Austl.	156	33.54 S	148.10 E
Grenfell, Sask., Can.	174	50.25 N	102.56 W
Grenoble	56	45.10 N	5.43 E
Grenola	188	37.21 N	96.27 W
Grenora	188	48.37 N	103.56 W
Grenoside	42	53.27 N	1.30 W
Grenville, Qué., Can.	196	45.37 N	74.36 W
Grenville, Gren.	231k	12.07 N	61.37 W
Grenville □[6]	202	44.50 N	75.40 W
Grenville, Cape ≻	154	11.58 S	143.14 E
Grenville Bay	196	45.38 N	74.36 W
Grenville Bay C	231k	12.07 N	61.36 W
Grenville Channel U	172	53.40 N	129.40 W
Grenzaa ≃	48	52.39 N	6.45 E
Grenz-Berg Λ[2]	254a	52.27 N	13.44 E
Grenzlandring ♠	52	51.11 N	6.17 E
Gréolières	56	43.48 N	6.57 E
Gréoux-les-Bains	56	43.45 N	5.53 E
Greppin	50	51.39 N	12.18 E
Gresenhorst	50	54.09 N	12.26 E
Gresham	214	45.30 N	122.26 W
Gresham Park	182	33.42 N	84.19 W
Gresik, Indon.	102	2.18 S	103.57 E
Gresik, Indon.	105a	7.09 S	112.38 E
Gressåmoen Nasjonalpark ♠	26	64.15 N	13.08 E
Gresse-en-Vercors	56	44.54 N	5.34 E
Gressey	251	48.50 N	1.37 E
Gressitt	198	37.29 N	76.43 W
Gressk	66	53.10 N	27.29 E
Gressoney, Val di V	56	45.47 N	7.49 E
Gressoney-la-Trinité	56	45.50 N	7.49 E
Gressoney-Saint-Jean	56	45.47 N	7.49 E
Gressy	251	48.58 N	2.41 E
Gresten	30	48.00 N	15.02 E
Grésy-sur-Aix	56	45.43 N	5.57 E
Grésy-sur-Isère	56	45.36 N	6.15 E
Greta	160	32.41 S	151.24 E
Greta ≃, Eng., U.K.	42	54.36 N	3.10 W
Greta ≃, Eng., U.K.	42	54.09 N	2.36 W
Greta ≃, Eng., U.K.	42	54.32 N	1.53 W
Gretna, Man., Can.	174	49.02 N	97.35 W
Gretna, La., U.S.	184	29.55 N	90.03 W
Gretna, Va., U.S.	182	36.57 N	79.22 W
Gretna Green	42	54.59 N	3.04 W
Gretz-Armainvilliers	46	48.44 N	2.44 E
Greussen	50	51.14 N	10.57 E
Greve, Dan.	41	55.36 N	12.15 E
Greve, It.	60	43.35 N	11.19 E
Greve ≃	60	43.46 N	11.13 E
Grevel ◆[8]	253	51.34 N	7.33 E
Grevelingen U	48	51.45 N	4.00 E
Grevelingendam ◆[5]	48	51.40 N	4.10 E
Greven	48	52.05 N	7.36 E
Grevená	38	40.05 N	21.25 E
Grevenbroich	52	51.05 N	6.35 E
Grevenbroich □[8]	253	51.08 N	6.38 E
Greven-Granzin	50	53.29 N	10.48 E
Grevenmacher	52	49.42 N	6.20 E
Grevesmühlen	50	53.51 N	11.10 E
Greve Strand	41	55.35 N	12.14 E
Greville Bay C	176	45.22 N	64.38 W
Grevinge	41	55.48 N	11.34 E
Grey □[6]	202	44.20 N	80.45 W
Grey ≃, Newf., Can.	176	47.38 N	57.05 W
Grey ≃, N.Z.	162	42.27 S	171.12 E
Grey, Cape ≻	154	13.00 S	136.40 E
Grey, Point ≻, Austl.	159	38.34 S	143.59 E
Grey, Point ≻, B.C., Can.	214	49.16 N	123.16 W
Greyabbey	42	54.32 N	5.33 W
Greybull	192	44.30 N	108.03 W
Greybull ≃	192	44.28 N	108.03 W
Grey Eagle	180	45.50 N	94.45 W
Grey Islands II	176	50.50 N	55.37 W
Greylingstad	148	26.44 S	28.45 E
Greylock, Mount Λ	197	42.38 N	73.10 W
Greymont ◆[8]	263d	26.10 S	27.58 E
Greymouth	162	42.28 S	171.12 E
Grey Range ⛰	156	27.00 S	143.35 E
Greys ≃	192	43.10 N	111.00 W
Greystanes	264a	33.49 S	150.55 E
Greystoke	42	54.40 N	2.52 W
Greystones	42	53.09 N	6.04 W
Greyton	148	34.04 S	19.38 E
Greytown, N.Z.	162	41.05 S	175.27 E
Greytown → San Juan del Norte, Nic.	226	10.55 N	83.42 W
Greytown, S. Afr.	148	29.07 S	30.30 E
Grez-Doiceau	52	50.44 N	4.42 E
Grez-sur-Loing	46	48.19 N	2.42 E
Grezzana	58	45.31 N	11.01 E
Gribanovskij	70	51.27 N	41.58 E
Gribb Bank ✢[4]	9	61.30 S	88.00 E
Gribbel Island I	172	53.25 N	129.00 W
Gribbin Head ≻	44	50.19 N	4.40 W
Gribingui ≃	136	8.33 N	19.05 E
Gribovka	72	54.19 N	38.27 E
Gricev	68	49.58 N	27.14 E
Gridley, Calif., U.S.	216	39.22 N	121.42 W
Gridley, Ill., U.S.	206	40.45 N	88.53 W
Griebnitz See @	254a	52.24 N	13.06 E
Griechenland → Greece □[1]	38	39.00 N	22.00 E
Griekwastad	148	28.49 S	23.15 E
Grier City	200	40.50 N	76.04 W
Gries am Brenner	58	47.03 N	11.29 E
Griesbach	30	48.28 N	13.11 E
Griesen	58	47.29 N	10.56 E
Griesheim	52	49.50 N	8.34 E
Gries im Sellrain	58	47.12 N	11.09 E
Griessem	48	52.00 N	9.12 E
Griesspitzen Λ	58	47.22 N	10.58 E
Griffin, Sask., Can.	174	49.40 N	103.26 W
Griffin, Ga., U.S.	182	33.15 N	84.16 W
Griffin, Lake @	210	28.52 N	81.51 W
Griffin Bay C	214	48.30 N	122.58 W
Griffiss Air Force Base ■	200	43.14 N	75.26 W
Griffith, Austl.	156	34.17 S	146.03 E
Griffith, Ind., U.S.	206	41.32 N	87.25 W
Griffith Airport ⊠	268	41.31 N	87.23 W
Griffith Island I, N.W. Ter., Can.	166	74.35 N	95.30 W
Griffith Island I, Ont., Can.	202	44.51 N	80.54 W
Griffith Park ♠	270	34.09 N	118.17 W
Grifton	182	35.23 N	77.26 W
Griggs Drain ≡	271	42.11 N	83.26 W
Griggs Reservoir @[1]	204	40.03 N	83.06 W

Griggstown	266	40.26 N	74.37 W
Griggsville	209	39.42 N	90.43 W
Grignan	56	44.25 N	4.54 E
Grignano	58	45.42 N	13.43 E
Grignasco	56	45.41 N	8.20 E
Grigno	58	46.01 N	11.38 E
Grignols	32	44.23 N	0.03 W
Grignon	251	48.51 N	1.51 E
Grigny	56	45.37 N	4.47 E
Grigoriopol'	68	47.10 N	29.18 E
Grigorjevka, S.S.S.R.	68	46.17 N	33.44 E
Grigorjevka, S.S.S.R.	73	47.27 N	38.23 E
Grigorjevka, S.S.S.R.	75	42.43 N	77.30 E
Grigorjevskoje, S.S.S.R.	72	54.49 N	37.59 E
Grigorjevskoje, S.S.S.R.	72	54.48 N	39.15 E
Grigorovka, S.S.S.R.	68	50.05 N	30.39 E
Grigorovka, S.S.S.R.	68	51.03 N	32.51 E
Grigorovka, S.S.S.R.	72	54.38 N	36.20 E
Grigorovo	72	56.42 N	37.35 E
Grigorovskoje	72	54.17 N	36.21 E
Grijalva ≃	222	18.36 N	92.39 W
Grijpskerk	48	53.15 N	6.18 E
Grillbach ≃	253	51.11 N	6.44 E
Grillby	40	59.37 N	17.15 E
Grillenburg	50	50.57 N	13.31 E
Grim, Cape ≻	156	40.41 S	144.41 E
Grima	142	3.59 N	17.06 E
Grimajlov	68	49.20 N	26.01 E
Grimari	142	5.44 N	20.03 E
Grimaud	56	43.16 N	6.31 E
Grimbergen	46	50.56 N	4.23 E
Grimeford Village	252	53.36 N	2.34 W
Grimes	216	39.04 N	121.54 W
Grimes □[6]	212	30.35 N	96.00 W
Grimlinghausen ◆[8]	253	51.10 N	6.44 E
Grimma	50	51.14 N	12.43 E
Grimmen	50	54.07 N	13.02 E
Grimmialp	54	46.34 N	7.29 E
Grimnitzsee @	50	52.58 N	13.47 E
Grimsargh	252	53.48 N	2.38 W
Grimsby, Ont., Can.	202	43.12 N	79.34 W
Grimsby, Eng., U.K.	42	53.35 N	0.05 W
Grimselpass)(	54	46.34 N	8.21 E
Grimselsee @	54	46.34 N	8.18 E
Grímsey I	24a	66.34 N	18.00 W
Grimshaw	172	56.11 N	117.36 W
Grímsstadir	24a	65.40 N	16.01 W
Grimstad	26	58.20 N	8.36 E
Grimstead	198	37.30 N	76.18 W
Grin'ava	68	47.59 N	24.49 E
Grindavík	24a	63.52 N	22.27 W
Grindelwald	54	46.37 N	8.02 E
Grindsted	41	55.45 N	8.56 E
Grindstone Island (Cap-aux-Meules)	176	47.23 N	61.52 W
Grindstone Island I	202	44.16 N	76.07 W
Grinnell	180	41.45 N	92.43 W
Grinnell, Lake @	266	41.06 N	74.38 W
Grinnell Peninsula ≻[1]	166	76.40 N	95.00 W
Grin'ovo	66	52.35 N	33.04 E
Grintavec Λ	36	46.21 N	14.32 E
Grinzing ◆[8]	254b	48.15 N	16.21 E
Grip	26	63.14 N	7.37 E
Gripsholms slott ⊥	40	59.15 N	17.13 E
Gripsholmsviken C	40	59.17 N	17.20 E
Griqualand East ◆[1]	148	30.30 S	29.00 E
Griqualand West ◆[1]	148	28.20 S	23.30 E
Grisdale	214	47.22 N	123.37 W
Grisee → Gresik	105a	7.09 S	112.38 E
Grišino	72	56.13 N	37.40 E
Griškovcy	68	49.56 N	28.36 E
Gris-Nez, Cap ≻	46	50.52 N	1.35 E
Grisons → Graubünden □[3]	54	46.45 N	9.30 E
Grisslehamn	40	60.06 N	18.50 E
Grissom Air Force Base ■	206	40.40 N	86.08 W
Gristow	50	54.10 N	13.20 E
Griswold, Man., Can.	174	49.45 N	100.25 W
Griswold, Iowa, U.S.	188	41.14 N	95.08 W
Griswold Creek ≃	269a	41.27 N	81.23 W
Griswoldville	197	42.39 N	72.49 W
Grisy-Suisnes	251	48.41 N	2.40 E
Grivai Pamia	142	7.03 N	19.26 E
Grivenskaja	68	45.38 N	38.09 E
Grizzana	58	44.15 N	11.09 E
Grizzly Bay C	216	38.07 N	122.01 W
Grizzly Bear Mountain Λ	166	65.22 N	121.00 W
Grizzly Creek ≃	272	37.52 N	122.06 W
Grizzly Flats	216	38.38 N	120.31 W
Grizzly Island I	272	38.08 N	121.58 W
Grizzly Mountain Λ, Idaho, U.S.	192	47.43 N	116.06 W
Grizzly Mountain Λ, Oreg., U.S.	192	44.26 N	120.57 W
Grizzly Mountain Λ, Wash., U.S.	192	48.25 N	118.30 W
Grizzly Slough ≃	272	38.06 N	121.53 W
Grmeč ⛰	36	44.40 N	16.30 E
Groaíras	240	3.53 S	40.23 W
Groais Island I	176	50.57 N	55.35 W
Grobbendonk	52	51.12 N	4.43 E
Gröben	254a	52.17 N	13.10 E
Gröbener-See @	254a	52.17 N	13.11 E
Gröbenzell	58	48.11 N	11.22 E
Grobina	66	56.33 N	21.10 E
Groblersdal	146	25.15 S	29.25 E
Groblershoop	148	28.55 S	20.59 E
Gröbming	58	47.26 N	13.54 E
Grobogan	105a	7.01 S	110.55 E
Gröbzig	50	51.41 N	11.52 E
Grodekovo	75	42.49 N	71.29 E
Grödig	58	47.44 N	13.02 E
Gröditsch	50	52.03 N	13.59 E
Gröditz	50	51.24 N	13.27 E
Grodków	30	50.43 N	17.22 E
Grodno	66	53.41 N	23.50 E
Grodno □[4]	24	54.45 N	26.00 E
Grodovka	73	48.15 N	37.23 E
Grodz'anka	66	53.33 N	28.45 E
Grodzisk Mazowiecki	30	52.07 N	20.37 E
Grodzisk [wielkopolski]	30	52.14 N	16.22 E
Groede	48	51.23 N	3.30 E
Groen ≃	146	30.40 S	23.17 E
Groënland → Greenland □[2]	16	70.00 N	40.00 W
Groenlandia → Greenland □[2]	16	70.00 N	40.00 W
Groenlo	48	52.03 N	6.38 E
Groenvlei	148	27.27 S	30.13 E
Groesbeck, Ohio, U.S.	208	39.13 N	84.35 W
Groesbeck, Tex., U.S.	212	31.31 N	96.32 W
Groesbeek	48	51.47 N	5.55 E
Grofa, Gora Λ	68	48.37 N	23.56 E
Grogol, Kali ≃	259e	6.10 S	106.47 E
Grogol-hilir ◆[8]	259e	6.13 S	106.47 E
Grohnde	48	52.01 N	9.25 E
Groitzsch	50	51.09 N	12.16 E
Groix	32	47.38 N	3.28 W
Groix, Île de I	32	47.38 N	3.27 W
Grójec	30	51.52 N	20.52 E
Grokgak	105a	8.11 S	114.47 E
Grolley	54	46.50 N	7.05 E
Grombalia	138	36.36 N	10.30 E
Grömitz	50	54.09 N	10.58 E
Gromo	58	45.58 N	9.56 E
Gromokleja ≃	68	47.21 N	32.14 E
Gromoslavka	70	48.12 N	43.37 E
Gromovka	68	46.19 N	34.06 E
Gronau, B.R.D.	48	52.13 N	7.00 E
Gronau, B.R.D.	48	52.05 N	9.46 E
Grondines (Saint-Charles-des-Grondines)	196	46.36 N	72.03 W

Symbol	English	Deutsch	Español	Français	Português
≃	River	Fluss	Río	Rivière	Rio
≡	Canal	Kanal	Canal	Canal	Canal
⌊	Waterfall, Rapids	Wasserfall, Stromschnellen	Cascada, Rápidos	Chute d'eau, Rapides	Cascata, Rápidos
U	Strait	Meeresstrasse	Estrecho	Détroit	Estreito
C	Bay, Gulf	Bucht, Golf	Bahía, Golfo	Baie, Golfe	Baía, Golfo
@	Lake, Lakes	See, Seen	Lago, Lagos	Lac, Lacs	Lago, Lagos
≋	Swamp	Sumpf	Pantano	Marais	Pântano
⊓	Ice Features, Glacier	Eis- und Gletscherformen	Accidentes Glaciales	Formes glaciaires	Acidentes Glaciares
⊤	Other Hydrographic Features	Andere Hydrographische Objekte	Otros Elementos Hidrográficos	Autres données hydrographiques	Outros Elementos Hidrográficos
✢	Submarine Features	Untermeerische Objekte	Accidentes Submarinos	Formes de relief sous-marin	Acidentes Submarinos
□	Political Unit	Politische Einheit	Unidad Politica	Entité politique	Unidade Política
ʊ	Cultural Institution	Kulturelle Institution	Institución Cultural	Institution culturelle	Instituição Cultural
⊥	Historical Site	Historische Stätte	Sitio Histórico	Site historique	Sitio Histórico
♠	Recreational Site	Erholungs- und Ferienort	Sitio de Recreo	Centre de loisirs	Sítio de Lazer
⊠	Airport	Flughafen	Aeropuerto	Aéroport	Aeroporto
■	Military Installation	Militäranlage	Instalación Militar	Installation militaire	Instalação Militar
◆	Miscellaneous	Verschiedenes	Misceláneo	Divers	Miscelânea

Name	Page	Lat.°′	Long.°′
Grondneus	148	28.06 S	20.48 E
Grone	48	51.32 N	9.53 E
Grönenbach	54	47.52 N	10.13 E
Grong	24	64.28 N	12.18 E
Grongemouth	42	56.01 N	3.44 W
Gröningen, D.D.R.	50	51.56 N	11.13 E
Groningen, Ned.	48	53.13 N	6.33 E
Groningen, Sur.	240	5.48 N	55.28 W
Groningen □[4]	48	53.15 N	6.45 E
Grønland → Greenland □[2]	16	70.00 N	40.00 W
Gronlid	174	53.06 N	104.28 W
Grønsund ⋓	41	54.53 N	12.08 E
Grönwohld	48	53.39 N	10.25 E
Groom	186	35.12 N	101.06 W
Groom Lake ⊜	194	37.15 N	115.48 W
Groot ≃, S. Afr.	148	33.45 S	24.36 E
Groot ≃, S. Afr.	148	33.54 S	21.39 E
Groot-Berg ≃	148	32.47 S	18.08 E
Groot-Brakrivier	148	34.01 S	21.46 E
Grootbruintjieshoogte ⛰	148	32.32 S	25.20 E
Grootebroek	48	52.43 N	5.13 E
Groote Eylandt I	154	14.00 S	136.40 E
Groot Elandsvlei	263d	26.08 S	27.40 E
Grootfontein	146	19.32 S	18.05 E
Grootfontein □[5]	146	19.00 S	20.00 E
Groot-Karasberge ⛰	148	27.20 S	18.40 E
Groot Karroo → Great Karroo ⛰[1]	148	32.25 S	22.40 E
Groot-Kei ≃	148	32.41 S	28.22 E
Groot Laagte ≃	146	20.37 S	21.37 E
Groot Letaba ≃	146	23.58 S	31.50 E
Groot-marico	146	25.37 S	26.26 E
Grootpan	148	25.58 S	26.33 E
Grootrivierhoogte ⛰	148	33.15 S	24.22 E
Groot Shingwidzi (Singuédeze) ≃	146	23.53 S	32.17 E
Groot-Swartberge ⛰	148	33.22 S	22.20 E
Groot-Vis ≃	148	33.30 S	27.08 E
Grootvlei	148	26.44 S	28.32 E
Grootvloer ⊜	148	30.00 S	20.40 E
Groot Winterhoekbergé ⛰	148	33.36 S	24.58 E
Gröpelingen ◆[8]	48	53.07 N	8.46 E
Gropello Cairoli	56	45.11 N	9.00 E
Gros Bois, Parc de ♠	251	48.44 N	2.32 E
Groscavallo	56	45.22 N	7.15 E
Grose ≃	160	33.36 S	150.41 E
Grosio	58	46.18 N	10.16 E
Gros Islet	231f	14.05 N	60.58 W
Gros Islet Bay C	231f	14.05 N	60.58 W
Groslay	251	48.59 N	2.21 E
Gros Mécatina, Cap du ≻	176	50.45 N	59.00 W
Gros-Morne	230e	14.43 N	61.01 W
Gros Morne ∧	176	49.36 N	57.48 W
Gros Morne National Park ♠	176	49.40 N	57.45 W
Grosne ≃	54	46.42 N	4.56 E
Grosotto	58	46.17 N	10.15 E
Gros Piton ∧	231f	13.49 N	61.04 W
Grosrouvre	251	48.47 N	1.46 E
Grossa, Ponta ≻, Bra.	246	23.35 S	45.13 W
Grossa, Ponta ≻, Bra.	277a	22.47 S	43.11 W
Grossaitingen	54	48.14 N	10.47 E
Grossalmerode	52	51.15 N	9.46 E
Grossalsleben	50	51.59 N	11.13 E
Gross Ammensleben	50	52.14 N	11.31 E
Grossarl	58	47.14 N	13.12 E
Grossauheim	52	50.06 N	8.56 E
Gross-Beeren	50	52.21 N	13.18 E
Gross Berkel	48	52.04 N	9.19 E
Gross-Bieberau	52	49.48 N	8.49 E
Grossbodungen	50	51.28 N	10.28 E
Gross Börnecke	50	51.50 N	11.29 E
Grossbothen	50	51.11 N	12.44 E
Grossbottwar	52	49.00 N	9.17 E
Grossbreitenbach	50	50.35 N	11.02 E
Grossburgwedel	48	52.29 N	9.51 E
Grossdeuben	50	51.14 N	12.23 E
Grossdubrau	50	51.15 N	14.28 E
Gross Düngen	48	52.06 N	10.01 E
Grosse Antillen → Greater Antilles II	228	20.00 N	74.00 W
Grosse Australische Bucht → Great Australian Bight C[3]	152	35.00 S	135.00 E
Grossebersdorf	50	50.47 N	11.57 E
Grosse Herrenwiese ⌅	254a	52.17 N	13.20 E
Grosse Ile	206	42.08 N	83.09 W
Grosse Île I, Qué., Can.	176	47.37 N	61.31 W
Grosse Ile I	206	42.08 N	83.09 W
Grossenbaum ◆[8]	253	51.22 N	6.47 E
Grossenbrode	50	54.22 N	11.05 E
Grossen-Buseck	52	50.36 N	8.47 E
Grossengottern	50	51.09 N	10.34 E
Grossengstingen	54	48.23 N	9.17 E
Grossenhain	50	51.17 N	13.31 E
Grossenheidorn	48	52.27 N	9.23 E
Grossenkneten	48	52.56 N	8.16 E
Grossen-Linden	52	50.31 N	8.39 E
Grossenlüder	52	50.35 N	9.32 E
Grossenritte	52	51.15 N	9.23 E
Grossenwiehe	41	54.43 N	9.15 E
Gross-Enzersdorf	254b	48.12 N	16.33 E
Grosse Pointe	204	42.24 N	82.55 W
Grosse Pointe ≻	231o	16.01 N	61.16 W
Grosse Pointe Farms	204	42.25 N	82.53 W
Grosse Pointe Park	204	42.23 N	82.56 W
Grosse Pointe Shores	204	42.26 N	82.53 W
Grosse Pointe Woods	204	42.27 N	82.55 W
Grosser Arber ∧	30	49.07 N	13.07 E
Grosser Bären-See → Great Bear Lake ⊜	166	66.00 N	120.00 W
Grosser Beerberg ∧	50	50.37 N	10.44 E
Grosser Chingan → Daxing'anling-shanmai ⛰	79	49.40 N	122.00 E
Grosser Feldberg ∧	52	50.14 N	8.26 E
Grosser Galtenberg ∧	58	47.20 N	11.58 E
Grosser Gleichberg ∧	50	50.23 N	10.35 E
Grosser Graben ⌅	254a	52.28 N	13.03 E
Grosser Heuberg ⛰[1]	54	48.06 N	8.55 E
Grosser Inselsberg ∧	50	50.52 N	10.28 E
Grosser Jasmunder Bodden C	50	54.31 N	13.29 E
Grosser Königstuhl ∧	58	46.57 N	13.47 E
Grosser Müggelsee ⊜	50	52.26 N	13.39 E
Grosse Röder ≃	50	51.30 N	13.25 E
Grosser oder Kaiser-Kanal → Yunhe ⌅	80	32.12 N	119.31 E
Grosser Plessower See ⊜	254a	52.23 N	12.54 E
Grosser Plöner See ⊜	50	54.06 N	10.25 E
Grosser Priel ∧	30	47.43 N	14.04 E
Grosser Rachel ∧	30	48.59 N	13.24 E
Grosser Ravens-Berg ∧[2]	254a	52.21 N	13.04 E
Grosser Salz-See → Great Salt Lake ⊜	190	41.10 N	112.30 W
Grosser Seddiner See ⊜	254a	52.17 N	13.02 E
Grosser Selchower See ⊜	50	52.14 N	13.53 E
Grosser Sklaven-See → Great Slave Lake ⊜	166	61.30 N	114.00 W
Grosser Walfisch-Fluss → Grande Rivière de la Baleine ≃	166	55.16 N	77.47 W
Grosser Wannsee ⊜	254a	52.26 N	13.11 E
Grosser Winterberg ∧[2]	50	50.54 N	14.16 E
Grosser Zern-See ⊜	254a	52.24 N	12.56 E
Grosse Sandspitze ∧	58	46.46 N	12.49 E
Grosse Sandwüste → Great Sandy Desert ◆[2]	152	21.30 S	125.00 E
Grosses Barrier-Riff → Great Barrier Reef ✣[2]	150	18.00 S	145.50 E
Grosses Meer ⊜	48	53.25 N	7.17 E
Grosses Moor ◆[3], B.R.D.	48	52.35 N	8.45 E
Grosses Moor ◆[3], B.R.D.	48	52.40 N	8.20 E
Grosse Sundainseln → Greater Sunda Islands II	98	2.00 S	110.00 E
Grosses Walsertal ∨	54	47.14 N	9.56 E
Grosse Syrte → Surt, Khalīj C	136	31.30 N	18.00 E
Grosseto	60	42.46 N	11.08 E
Grosseto □[4]	60	42.50 N	11.15 E
Grosseviči	79	47.59 N	139.30 E
Gross-Gerau	52	49.55 N	8.29 E
Gross Gleidingen	50	52.14 N	10.25 E
Gross Glienicke	254a	52.28 N	13.07 E
Gross-Glienicker See ⊜	254a	52.28 N	13.06 E
Grossglockner ∧	58	47.04 N	12.42 E
Grossgmain	58	47.43 N	12.55 E
Grossgörschen	50	51.13 N	12.11 E
Gross Grönau	50	53.46 N	10.44 E
Grosshansdorf	48	53.40 N	10.17 E
Grosshartmannsdorf	50	50.48 N	13.19 E
Gross-Hehlen	48	52.39 N	10.03 E
Grossheide	48	53.35 N	7.20 E
Grosshennersdorf	50	50.59 N	14.47 E
Grosshöchstetten	54	46.55 N	7.38 E
Grossholzleute	54	47.41 N	10.05 E
Grossjedlersdorf ◆[8]	254b	48.17 N	16.25 E
Grosskayna	50	51.17 N	11.56 E
Gross Kienitz	254a	52.19 N	13.28 E
Gross-Kollmar	48	53.44 N	9.30 E
Grosskorbetha	50	51.16 N	12.01 E
Gross Kreutz	50	52.24 N	12.46 E
Grosslehna	50	51.18 N	12.10 E
Gross Leine	50	52.00 N	14.03 E
Grosslittgen	52	50.02 N	6.47 E
Grossmachnow	50	52.16 N	13.28 E
Gross Möllen → Mielno	30	54.16 N	16.01 E
Grossmont	218	32.47 N	116.59 W
Gross Muckrow	50	52.04 N	14.26 E
Gross Oesingen	48	52.38 N	10.29 E
Grossörner	50	51.37 N	11.29 E
Grossos	240	4.59 S	37.09 W
Grossostheim	52	49.55 N	9.04 E
Grosspostwitz	50	51.07 N	14.26 E
Grossquenstedt	50	51.56 N	11.07 E
Grossräschen	50	51.35 N	14.00 E
Gross Rhüden	48	51.56 N	10.07 E
Grossrinderfeld	52	49.39 N	9.44 E
Gross Rodensleben	50	52.08 N	11.25 E
Grossröhrsdorf	50	51.08 N	14.01 E
Gross Rosenburg	50	51.55 N	11.53 E
Grossrückerswalde	50	50.38 N	13.07 E
Grossrudestedt	50	51.05 N	11.06 E
Grosssachsenheim	52	48.58 N	9.04 E
Gross-Sarau	50	53.45 N	10.44 E
Grossschirma	50	50.58 N	13.17 E
Grossschönau	50	50.54 N	14.40 E
Gross Schönebeck	50	52.54 N	13.32 E
Gross-Schulzendorf	254a	52.16 N	13.21 E
Grosssölk	58	47.25 N	13.58 E
Gross Strehlitz → Strzelce Opolskie	30	50.31 N	18.19 E
Grosstimmern	52	49.52 N	8.50 E
Gross-Umstadt	52	49.52 N	8.55 E
Grossvenediger ∧	58	47.06 N	12.21 E
Grosswardein → Oradea	38	47.03 N	21.57 E
Gross Wartenberg → Syców	30	51.19 N	17.43 E
Grossweil	58	47.41 N	11.18 E
Gross Windgällen ∧	54	46.49 N	8.44 E
Gross Wittensee	41	54.24 N	9.46 E
Gross Ziethen, D.D.R.	254a	52.44 N	13.01 E
Gross Ziethen, D.D.R.	254a	52.24 N	13.27 E
Grosszimmern	52	49.52 N	8.50 E
Grostenquin	52	48.59 N	6.44 E
Grosvenor, Lake ⊜	170	58.40 N	155.15 W
Grosvenor Dale	197	41.58 N	71.54 W
Gros Ventre ≃	192	43.33 N	110.46 W
Groswater Bay C	166	54.20 N	57.30 W
Grote Nete ≃	52	51.07 N	4.34 E
Groton, Conn., U.S.	197	41.19 N	72.12 W
Groton, Mass., U.S.	197	42.37 N	71.34 W
Groton, N.Y., U.S.	200	42.35 N	76.22 W
Groton, S. Dak., U.S.	188	45.27 N	98.06 W
Grottaferrata	60	41.47 N	12.40 E
Grottaglie	36	40.32 N	17.26 E
Grottaminarda	60	41.04 N	15.02 E
Grottammare	60	42.59 N	13.52 E
Grotte di Castro	60	42.40 N	11.52 E
Grottkau → Grodków	30	50.43 N	17.22 E
Grottoes	178	38.16 N	78.56 W
Grouard Mission	172	55.31 N	116.09 W
Groundbirch	172	55.47 N	120.55 W
Groundhog ≃	166	49.43 N	81.58 W
Grouse Creek	190	41.42 N	113.53 W
Grouse Creek ≃, Kans., U.S.	188	37.00 N	96.55 W
Grouse Creek ≃, Utah, U.S.	190	41.22 N	113.55 W
Grouse Creek Mountain ∧	192	44.22 N	113.54 W
Grouw	48	53.05 N	5.45 E
Grove, Okla., U.S.	186	36.36 N	94.46 W
Grove, Pa., U.S.	275	40.01 N	75.38 W
Grove City, Fla., U.S.	210	26.56 N	82.20 W
Grove City, Minn., U.S.	188	45.09 N	94.41 W
Grove City, Ohio, U.S.	208	39.53 N	83.06 W
Grove City, Pa., U.S.	204	41.10 N	80.05 W
Grove Hill	184	31.42 N	87.47 W
Groveland, Calif., U.S.	216	37.50 N	120.14 W
Groveland, Fla., U.S.	210	28.34 N	81.51 W
Groveland, Mass., U.S.	197	42.46 N	71.02 W
Groveland, N.Y., U.S.	200	42.40 N	77.46 W
Grovely Ridge ∧	44	51.08 N	2.04 W
Grove Mountains ⛰	9	72.53 S	74.53 E
Grove Park ◆[8]	250	51.26 N	0.01 E
Groveport	208	39.51 N	82.53 W
Grover	200	41.37 N	76.52 W
Grover City	194	35.07 N	120.37 W
Grover Cleveland Birthplace ⊥	266	40.50 N	74.16 W
Grover Cleveland Park ♠	274a	42.57 N	78.49 W
Grover Hill	206	41.01 N	84.29 W
Grovers Mills	266	40.19 N	74.37 W
Groves	184	29.57 N	93.55 W
Groveton, N.H., U.S.	178	44.36 N	71.31 W
Groveton, Pa., U.S.	269b	40.30 N	80.06 W
Groveton, Tex., U.S.	212	31.03 N	95.08 W
Groveton, Va., U.S.	274c	38.46 N	77.05 W
Grovetown	182	33.27 N	82.12 W
Groveville	198	40.11 N	74.40 W
Growler Peak ∧	190	32.24 N	113.07 W
Growler Wash ∨	190	32.35 N	113.30 W
Groznoje	75	42.36 N	71.12 E
Groznyj	74	43.20 N	45.42 E
Groznyy → Groznyj	74	43.20 N	45.42 E
Grube, B.R.D.	50	54.14 N	11.01 E
Grube, D.D.R.	254a	52.26 N	12.57 E
Grubišno Polje	36	45.42 N	17.10 E
Grudovo	38	42.21 N	27.10 E
Grudziądz	30	53.29 N	18.45 E
Gruesa, Punta ≻	238	20.22 S	70.11 W
Gruetli	184	35.22 N	85.40 W
Grugapark ♠	253	51.26 N	7.00 E
Grugliasco	56	45.04 N	7.35 E
Gruia	38	44.16 N	22.42 E
Gruinart, Loch C	42	55.52 N	6.20 W
Gruiten	52	51.14 N	7.01 E
Gruitrode	52	51.05 N	5.35 E
Grulla	186	26.16 N	98.39 W
Grumello del Monte	56	45.38 N	9.52 E
Grumman-Bethpage Airport ⊠	266	40.45 N	73.29 W
Grumman Corporation ʊ[3]	266	40.45 N	73.30 W
Grumme ◆[8]	253	51.30 N	7.14 E
Grumo Appula	36	41.01 N	16.43 E
Grums	26	59.21 N	13.06 E
Grun'	68	50.16 N	34.36 E
Grüna	50	50.49 N	12.47 E
Grünau	146	27.47 S	18.23 E
Grünau ◆[8]	254a	52.25 N	13.34 E
Grünau im Almtal	58	47.51 N	13.57 E
Grünbach	50	50.26 N	12.22 E
Grünberg, B.R.D.	52	50.35 N	8.58 E
Grünberg → Zielona Góra, Pol.	30	51.56 N	15.31 E
Grundlsee ⊜	58	47.38 N	13.52 E
Grundy	182	37.17 N	82.06 W
Grundy □[6]	206	41.22 N	88.26 W
Grundy Center	180	42.22 N	92.47 W
Grundy Lake Provincial Park ♠	180	45.48 N	80.34 W
Grünefeld	254a	52.41 N	12.58 E
Grünenplan	48	51.57 N	9.44 E
Grünewald, B.R.D.	253	51.13 N	7.37 E
Grünewald, D.D.R.	50	51.24 N	14.00 E
Grunewald ◆[8]	254a	52.30 N	13.17 E
Grunewald, Jagdschloss ⊥	254a	52.28 N	13.16 E
Grünhain	50	50.35 N	12.48 E
Grünhainichen	50	50.46 N	13.08 E
Grünheide	50	52.25 N	13.49 E
Grünsfeld	52	49.36 N	9.44 E
Grünstadt	52	49.34 N	8.10 E
Grüntal	254a	52.45 N	13.44 E
Grunthal	174	49.25 N	96.52 W
Grünwald	58	48.02 N	11.31 E
Gruševka	68	47.55 N	40.40 E
Gruševka ≃	73	47.26 N	40.00 E
Gruševskaja	73	47.26 N	39.57 E
Grušino	66	59.27 N	44.09 E
Gruver	186	36.16 N	101.24 W
Gruyère, Lac de la ⊜	54	46.38 N	7.06 E
Gruyères	54	46.35 N	7.05 E
Gruzdžiai	66	56.06 N	23.16 E
Gruzinskaja Sovetskaja Socialističeskaja Respublika ∧	74	42.00 N	44.00 E
Gruznovka	78	55.09 N	105.12 E
Gruzskaja Balka	68	46.25 N	40.19 E
Gruzskij Jelančik ≃	73	47.07 N	38.04 E
Gruzskoje	73	48.33 N	37.18 E
Gruzsko-Zor'anskoje	73	47.56 N	38.06 E
Grybów	30	49.38 N	20.56 E
Grycken ⊜	40	60.27 N	16.13 E
Gryfice	30	53.56 N	15.12 E
Gryfino	30	53.12 N	14.30 E
Grytdalen Nasjonalpark ♠	26	63.25 N	9.45 E
Grytgöl	40	58.48 N	15.33 E
Grythyttan	40	59.42 N	14.32 E
Gschnitz	58	47.03 N	11.22 E
Gschütt, Pass)(	58	47.35 N	13.30 E
Gschwend	52	48.56 N	9.44 E
Gstaad	54	46.28 N	7.17 E
Gsteig	54	46.23 N	7.16 E
Gua	114	22.12 N	85.23 E
Guabaria ≃[1]	116	22.10 N	90.30 E
Guabito	226	9.30 N	82.37 W
Guabu	96	32.16 N	118.53 E
Guacanayabo, Golfo de C	230p	20.28 N	77.30 W
Guacara	236	10.14 N	67.53 W
Guacarí	236	3.46 N	76.20 W
Guacayá ≃	236	0.36 S	70.30 W
Gu Achi	190	32.20 N	112.02 W
Guachinango	224	20.32 N	104.24 W
Guachiría ≃	236	5.27 N	70.36 W
Guachochic	222	26.51 N	107.05 W
Guaçuí	245	20.46 S	41.41 W
Guadajira ≃	34	38.52 N	6.41 W
Guadajoz ≃	34	37.50 N	4.51 W
Guadalajara, Esp.	34	40.38 N	3.10 W
Guadalajara, Méx.	224	20.40 N	103.20 W
Guadalamar ≃	34	38.05 N	3.06 W
Guadalaviar ≃	34	40.21 N	1.08 W
Guadalcanal	34	38.06 N	5.49 W
Guadalcanal I	165e	9.32 S	160.12 E
Guadalcázar	224	22.37 N	100.24 W
Guadalén ≃	34	38.05 N	3.32 W
Guadalén, Embalse de ⊜[1]	34	38.25 N	3.15 W
Guadalentin ≃	34	37.59 N	1.04 W
Guadalete ≃	34	36.35 N	6.13 W
Guadalhorce ≃	34	36.41 N	4.27 W
Guadalmena ≃	34	38.19 N	2.56 W
Guadalmez ≃	34	38.46 N	5.04 W
Guadalope ≃	34	41.15 N	0.03 W
Guadalquivir ≃	34	36.47 N	6.22 W
Guadalupe, Bol.	238	18.33 S	64.05 W
Guadalupe, Bra.	240	6.44 S	43.47 W
Guadalupe, Col.	236	2.01 N	75.45 W
Guadalupe, C.R.	226	9.57 N	84.03 W
Guadalupe, Méx.	186	28.09 N	100.36 W
Guadalupe, Méx.	222	16.16 N	91.27 W
Guadalupe, Méx.	222	25.41 N	100.15 W
Guadalupe, Méx.	224	22.45 N	102.31 W
Guadalupe, Perú	238	7.15 S	79.29 W
Guadalupe, Calif., U.S.	194	34.58 N	120.34 W
Guadalupe □[6]	212	29.37 N	97.45 W
Guadalupe ◆[8]	277a	22.50 S	43.23 W
Guadalupe → Guadeloupe □[2]	231o	16.15 N	61.35 W
Guadalupe ≃, Méx.	194	32.05 N	116.53 W
Guadalupe ≃, Calif., U.S.	272	37.25 N	121.58 W
Guadalupe ≃, Tex., U.S.	186	28.30 N	96.53 W
Guadalupe, Basílica de ʊ[1]	276a	19.29 N	99.07 W
Guadalupe, Isla de I	168	29.00 N	118.16 W
Guadalupe, Presa de ⊜[1]	276a	19.37 N	99.16 W
Guadalupe, Sierra de ⛰, Esp.	34	39.26 N	5.25 W
Guadalupe, Sierra de ⛰, Méx.	276a	19.35 N	99.08 W
Guadalupe [Bravos]	222	31.23 N	106.07 W
Guadalupe del Norte ⌅	276a	19.34 N	99.01 W
Guadalupe de Ramírez	224	17.45 N	98.10 W
Guadalupe Garzarón	222	24.35 N	101.15 W
Guadalupe Mountains ⛰	186	32.20 N	105.00 W
Guadalupe Peak ∧	186	31.50 N	104.52 W
Guadalupe Seamount ✣[3]	14	27.55 N	168.50 W
Guadalupe Slough ≃	272	37.27 N	122.02 W
Guadalupe Victoria, Méx.	186	27.47 N	101.04 W
Guadalupe Victoria, Méx.	222	24.27 N	104.07 W
Guadalupe Victoria, Méx.	224	19.17 N	97.21 W
Guadalupita	190	36.08 N	105.14 W
Guadarrama ≃	34	39.53 N	4.10 W
Guadarrama, Puerto de)(	34	40.43 N	4.10 W
Guadarrama, Sierra de ⛰	34	40.55 N	4.00 W
Guadazaón ≃	34	39.42 N	1.36 W
Guadeloupe □[2]	220		
	231o	16.15 N	61.35 W
Guadeloupe Passage ⋓	228	16.45 N	61.30 W
Guadiana ≃	34	37.14 N	7.22 W
Guadiana, Bahía de C	230p	22.05 N	84.24 W
Guadiana Menor ≃	34	37.56 N	3.15 W
Guadiaro ≃	34	36.17 N	5.17 W
Guadiela ≃	34	40.22 N	2.49 W
Guadix	34	37.18 N	3.08 W
Guafo, Boca del ⋓	244	43.40 S	74.15 W
Guafo, Isla I	244	43.36 S	74.43 W
Guagua	106	14.58 N	120.38 E
Guahe	95	39.12 N	115.00 E
Guaianazes ◆[8]	277b	23.33 S	46.25 W
Guaíba	242	30.06 S	51.19 W
Guaíba C[1]	242	30.15 S	51.12 W
Guaicaipuro □[5]	276c	10.25 N	66.57 W
Guaihezhen	90	33.28 N	112.59 E
Guaimaca	226	14.32 N	86.51 W
Guáimaro	230p	21.03 N	77.21 W
Guaimbé-Piriú ≃	242	22.55 S	55.03 W
Guaimozi	88	41.31 N	125.26 E
Guainía □[5]	236	2.30 N	69.00 W
Guainía ≃	236	2.01 N	67.07 W
Guaió ≃	277b	23.31 S	46.19 W
Guaipava	246	21.40 S	45.43 W
Guaiquica	246	22.25 S	47.14 W
Guaiquinima, Cerro ∧	236	5.49 N	63.40 W
Guaíra, Bra.	242	24.04 S	54.15 W
Guaíra, Bra.	245	20.19 S	48.18 W
Guairá □[5]	242	25.45 S	56.30 W
Guairá, Salto del (Salto das Sete Quedas) L	242	24.02 S	54.16 W
Guaire ≃	276c	10.25 N	66.46 W
Guáitara ≃	236	1.34 N	77.27 W
Guaitecas, Islas II	244	43.57 S	73.50 W
Guaiúba	240	4.02 S	38.38 W
Guajaba, Cayo I	230p	21.50 N	77.30 W
Guajará ≃	240	1.48 S	53.02 W
Guajará-Açu	240	1.38 S	48.07 W
Guajará-Miri	240	1.29 S	48.17 W
Guajará Mirim	238	10.48 S	65.22 W
Guajataca, Lago de ⊜[1]	230m	18.23 N	66.55 W
Guajiasi	94	41.15 N	120.54 E
Gualaca	226	8.32 N	82.18 W
Gualaceo	236	2.54 S	78.47 W
Gualala	194	38.46 N	123.32 W
Gualán	226	15.08 N	89.22 W
Gualaquiza	236	3.24 S	78.33 W
Gualdo Tadino	60	43.14 N	12.47 E
Gualeguay	242	33.09 S	59.20 W
Gualeguay ≃	242	33.19 S	59.39 W
Gualeguaychú	242	33.01 S	58.31 W
Gualicho, Salina ≌	244	40.24 S	65.15 W
Gualjaina	244	42.42 S	70.30 W
Gualtieri	58	44.54 N	10.38 E
Guam □[2]	14		
	164p	13.28 N	144.47 E
Guamá	240	1.37 S	47.27 W
Guamá ≃, Bra.	240	1.29 S	48.30 W
Guamá ≃, Cuba	230p	22.11 N	83.41 W
Guamal, Col.	236	9.09 N	74.14 W
Guamal, Col.	236	3.52 N	73.44 W
Guamal, Quebrada ≃	276c	10.31 N	66.59 W
Guamblin, Isla I	244	44.51 S	75.05 W
Guaminí	242	37.02 S	62.25 W
Guamo	236	4.02 N	74.58 W
Guamo Embarcadero	230p	20.37 N	76.58 W
Guamote	236	1.56 S	78.43 W
Guampí, Sierra de ⛰	236	6.00 N	65.35 W
Guampú ≃	226	14.59 N	85.03 W
Guamúchil	224	23.55 N	106.05 W
Guamués ≃	236	0.32 N	76.33 W
Gua Musang	104	4.53 N	101.58 E
Gu'an	95	39.26 N	116.18 E
Guanabacoa	230p	23.07 N	82.18 W
Guanabacoa □[7]	276b	23.07 N	82.18 W
Guanábana	230m	18.01 N	67.07 W
Guanabara, Baía de C	277a	22.50 S	43.10 W
Guanabara, Palácio de ʊ	277a	22.56 S	43.11 W
Guanacaste □[4]	226	10.30 N	85.15 W
Guanacaste, Cordillera de ⛰	226	10.45 N	85.05 W
Guanacaure, Cerro ∧	226	13.14 N	87.07 W
Guanaceví	222	25.56 N	105.57 W
Guanahacabibes, Golfo de C	230p	22.08 N	84.35 W
Guanahacabibes, Península de ≻[1]	230p	21.57 N	84.35 W
Guana Island I, Antig.	230c	17.07 N	61.44 W
Guana Island I, Br. Vir. Is.	230m	18.29 N	64.34 W
Guanaja	226	16.27 N	85.54 W
Guanaja, Isla de I	226	16.30 N	85.55 W
Guanajay	230p	22.55 N	82.42 W
Guanajibo ≃	230m	18.10 N	67.11 W
Guanajibo, Punta ≻	230m	18.10 N	67.11 W
Guanajuato	224	21.01 N	101.15 W
Guanajuato □[3]	224	21.00 N	101.00 W
Guanambi	245	14.13 S	42.47 W
Guañape, Isla I	238	8.33 S	78.57 W
Guanare	236	9.03 N	69.45 W
Guanare ≃	236	8.13 N	67.46 W
Guanare Viejo ≃	236	8.19 N	68.10 W
Guanarito	236	8.42 N	69.12 W
Guanay	238	15.28 S	67.52 W
Guanbuqiao	90	29.56 N	114.21 E
Guanchao	90	26.41 N	114.58 E
Guancheng	97	30.01 N	103.54 E
Guancun	96	31.30 N	119.43 E
Guandacol	242	29.31 S	68.32 W
Guandanghu	90	30.06 N	113.37 E
Guandi, Zhg.	88	41.48 N	116.52 E
Guandi, Zhg.	88	42.37 N	118.27 E
Guandian	90	32.40 N	118.04 E
Guandu	90	24.17 N	113.53 E
Guanduchang	97	30.04 N	106.25 E
Guane	230p	22.12 N	84.05 W
Guang'an	97	30.28 N	106.39 E
Guangchang	90	26.50 N	116.14 E
Guangde	96	30.54 N	119.26 E
Guangdeguan	92	27.23 N	104.29 E
Guangdong □[4]	80	23.00 N	113.00 E
Guangfeng	90	28.25 N	118.11 E
Guangfu, Zhg.	96	31.18 N	120.23 E
Guangfu, Zhg.	97	30.13 N	104.41 E
Guangfuyingzi	94	42.14 N	120.58 E
Guanghan	92	31.00 N	104.18 E
Guanghua	92	32.25 N	111.36 E
Guangji	90	29.52 N	115.34 E
Guangling, Zhg.	88	39.47 N	114.17 E
Guangling, Zhg.	96	32.06 N	120.13 E
Guangludao I	88	39.09 N	122.21 E
Guangmaoshan ∧	92	27.02 N	100.58 E
Guangnan	92	24.10 N	105.06 E
Guangningsi	88	39.08 N	121.45 E
Guangping	88	36.30 N	114.57 E
Guangrao	88	37.02 N	118.25 E
Guangshan	90	32.02 N	114.52 E
Guangshui	90	31.40 N	114.00 E
Guangxing	97	29.04 N	106.33 E
Guangxi Zhuang Zizhiqu □[4]	92	24.00 N	109.00 E
Guangyuan	92	32.23 N	105.58 E
Guangze	90	27.32 N	117.20 E
Guangzhen	96	30.45 N	121.07 E
Guangzhou (Canton)	90	23.06 N	113.16 E
Guangzong	88	37.06 N	115.08 E
Guanhães ≃	245	19.04 S	42.56 W
Guanhaiwei	90	30.11 N	121.25 E
Guanhe ≃, Zhg.	90	34.29 N	119.49 E
Guanhe ≃, Zhg.	90	32.16 N	115.42 E
Guanhekou ≃[1]	90	34.29 N	119.50 E
Guanhu	88	34.26 N	117.59 E
Guánica	230m	17.58 N	66.55 W
Guánica, Laguna de ⊜	230m	18.00 N	66.56 W
Guanipa ≃	236	9.56 N	62.26 W
Guanjianhe ≃	97	30.00 N	106.01 E
Guankou, Zhg.	90	30.35 N	115.20 E
Guankou, Zhg.	97	30.40 N	103.28 E
Guanlin	96	31.32 N	119.42 E
Guanling	92	25.57 N	105.29 E
Guanlipu	94	41.37 N	123.18 E
Guanmenshan	79	47.23 N	122.20 E
Guannan	88	34.07 N	119.23 E
Guano	236	1.35 S	78.38 W
Guano Creek ≃	192	42.12 N	119.31 W
Guanpata	226	15.01 N	85.02 W
Guanputou	95	38.58 N	117.04 E
Guanqian, Zhg.	90	26.12 N	117.57 E
Guanqian, Zhg.	90	27.48 N	118.31 E
Guanqian, Zhg.	90	30.42 N	117.39 E
Guanqian, Zhg.	90	25.57 N	116.33 E
Guanqiao, Zhg.	88	34.58 N	117.14 E
Guanqiao, Zhg.	90	25.03 N	118.06 E
Guanqiaopu	90	31.08 N	112.54 E
Guanshan I	90	27.21 N	120.36 E
Guanshanchang	97	28.46 N	103.42 E
Guanshi	90	26.43 N	112.53 E
Guanshui	88	40.55 N	124.33 E
Guanta	236	10.14 N	64.36 W
Guantánamo	230p	20.08 N	75.12 W
Guantánamo ≃	230p	19.55 N	75.12 W
Guantánamo, Bahía de C	230p	20.00 N	75.08 W
Guantanamo Bay Naval Station ■	230p	19.55 N	75.10 W
Guantang	96	31.37 N	119.06 E
Guantangqiao	96	32.09 N	119.27 E
Guantao	88	36.35 N	115.19 E
Guanting, Zhg.	90	34.19 N	113.47 E
Guanting, Zhg.	95	40.13 N	115.37 E
Guantingshuiku ⊜[1]	95	40.20 N	115.38 E
Guantou, Zhg.	90	26.08 N	119.33 E
Guantou, Zhg.	90	27.58 N	120.46 E
Guantunbao	88	40.28 N	113.24 E
Guanxian, Zhg.	88	36.30 N	115.27 E
Guanxian, Zhg.	92	31.00 N	103.40 E
Guanxun	90	24.19 N	117.45 E
Guanyin	97	29.50 N	105.57 E
Guanyinao	90	26.18 N	115.32 E
Guanyinchang, Zhg.	97	30.28 N	105.16 E
Guanyinchang, Zhg.	97	29.06 N	104.24 E
Guanyinchang, Zhg.	97	29.15 N	104.02 E
Guanyingzicun	94	41.52 N	121.53 E
Guanyinpu, Zhg.	97	28.58 N	104.53 E
Guanyinpu, Zhg.	97	30.16 N	103.51 E
Guanyinqiao, Zhg.	90	26.42 N	112.44 E
Guanyinqiao, Zhg.	97	29.46 N	104.12 E
Guanyinqiao, Zhg.	97	29.05 N	104.46 E
Guanyinshan	96	32.01 N	120.58 E
Guanyinsi, Zhg.	96	31.48 N	118.57 E
Guanyinsi, Zhg.	97	30.33 N	104.11 E
Guanyintan	97	29.35 N	105.14 E
Guanyintang, Zhg.	88	34.26 N	115.27 E
Guanyintang, Zhg.	90	31.01 N	112.35 E
Guanyintang, Zhg.	95	39.52 N	116.31 E
Guanyintang, Zhg.	96	32.09 N	121.09 E
Guanyinzhou	90	29.30 N	113.09 E
Guanyun (Dayishan)	88	34.20 N	119.17 E
Guanzhuang, Zhg.	88	37.12 N	114.30 E
Guanzhuang, Zhg.	90	28.58 N	117.24 E
Guanzhuang, Zhg.	90	32.49 N	114.16 E
Guaotou	90	27.37 N	120.33 E
Guapí	236	2.36 N	77.54 W
Guapiaçu ≃	246	22.40 S	42.55 W
Guapiara	245	24.10 S	48.32 W
Guápiles	226	10.13 N	83.46 W
Guapimirim	246	22.32 S	42.59 W
Guapimirim ≃	246	22.40 S	42.58 W
Guapó	245	16.49 S	49.32 W
Guapo Bay C	231r	10.12 N	61.40 W
Guaporé	242	28.51 S	51.54 W
Guaporé ≃, Bra.	242	29.10 S	51.54 W
Guaporé (Iténez) ≃, S.A.	238	11.54 S	65.01 W
Guaqui	238	16.35 S	68.51 W
Guará ≃	245	12.59 S	44.49 W
Guara, Sierra de ⛰	34	42.17 N	0.10 W
Guarabira	240	6.51 S	35.29 W
Guarabo	230m	18.16 N	65.58 W
Guaraçaí	245	21.02 S	51.11 W
Guaracarumbo	276c	10.34 N	66.59 W
Guaracha ≃	238	5.53 S	74.21 W
Guaraci, Bra.	245	22.57 S	51.40 W
Guaraci, Bra.	245	20.29 S	48.57 W
Guaraciaba do Norte	240	4.10 S	40.46 W
Guaraciama	245	17.03 S	43.41 W
Guaraguara, Punta ≻	231r	10.31 N	62.19 W
Guaraí ≃	277a	22.42 S	43.02 W
Guaramirim	242	26.27 S	49.00 W
Guaranda	236	1.36 S	79.00 W
Guaranésia	246	21.18 S	46.48 W
Guarani	246	21.22 S	43.03 W
Guaraniaçu	242	25.06 S	52.52 W
Guarani das Missões	242	28.08 S	54.34 W
Guarapari	245	20.40 S	40.30 W
Guarapiranga, Barragem do ◆[6]	277b	23.41 S	46.43 W
Guarapiranga, Reservatório de ⊜[1]	246	23.44 S	46.44 W
Guarapuava	242	25.23 S	51.27 W
Guaraqueçaba	242	25.17 S	48.21 W
Guarará	246	21.43 S	43.02 W
Guarará ≃	277b	23.39 S	46.30 W
Guararé	236	7.49 N	80.17 W
Guararema	246	23.25 S	46.02 W
Guaratiba, Morro de ∧	277a	23.04 S	43.33 W
Guaratinguetá	246	22.49 S	45.13 W
Guaratinguetá, Ribeirão de ≃	246	22.49 S	45.13 W
Guaratuba	242	25.54 S	48.34 W
Guar Chempedak	104	5.52 N	100.28 E
Guarcino	60	41.48 N	13.19 E
Guarda	34	40.32 N	7.16 W
Guardado de Abajo	186	26.22 N	98.57 W
Guardafui, Cape → Asir,ras ≻	134	11.48 N	51.22 E
Guardavalle	36	38.30 N	16.30 E
Guardea	60	42.37 N	12.18 E
Guardia Escolta	242	28.59 S	62.08 W
Guardiagrele	60	42.11 N	14.13 E
Guardia Lombardi	60	40.57 N	15.12 E
Guardia Mitre	244	40.26 S	63.41 W
Guardia Sanframondi	60	41.15 N	14.36 E
Guardiato ≃	34	38.20 N	5.22 W
Guardia Vieja, Arroyo de la ≃	248	33.37 S	57.07 W
Guardo	34	42.47 N	4.50 W
Guareí ≃	245	22.40 S	53.34 W

Name	Seite	Breite°′	Länge°′ E=Ost
Guareim (Quaraí) ≃	242	30.12 S	57.36 W
Guareña	34	38.51 N	6.06 W
Guareña ≃	34	41.29 N	5.23 W
Guarenas	236	10.28 N	66.37 W
Guaribe ≃, Bra.	238	7.41 S	60.18 W
Guaribe ≃, Ven.	236	9.53 N	65.11 W
Guarichapo ≃	236	7.27 N	62.03 W
Guarico	236	9.32 N	69.48 W
Guárico □[3]	236	8.40 N	66.35 W
Guárico ≃	236	7.55 N	67.23 W
Guárico, Embalse de ⊜[1]	236	9.05 N	67.25 W
Guarico, Punta ≻	230p	20.37 N	74.44 W
Guarizama	226	14.55 N	86.20 W
Guarujá	246	24.00 S	46.16 W
Guarulhos	246	23.28 S	46.32 W
Guarulhos □[7]	277b	23.26 S	46.29 W
Guarunta, Laguna ⊜	226	15.22 N	84.09 W
Guarus	245	21.44 S	41.20 W
Guasare ≃	236	11.03 N	72.02 W
Guasave	222	25.34 N	108.27 W
Guascama, Punta ≻	236	2.32 N	78.24 W
Guasdualito	236	7.15 N	70.44 W
Guasipati	236	7.28 N	61.54 W
Guastalla	58	44.55 N	10.39 E
Guāsuba ≃[1]	116	21.38 N	88.53 E
Guatajiagua	226	13.40 N	88.13 W
Guatemala	226	14.38 N	90.31 W
Guatemala □[5]	226	14.40 N	90.30 W
Guatemala □[1]	220		
	222	15.30 N	90.15 W
Guateque	236	5.00 N	73.28 W
Guatimozín	242	33.27 S	62.27 W
Guatire	236	10.28 N	66.32 W
Guatopo, Parque Nacional ♠	236	10.05 N	66.25 W
Guatraché	242	37.40 S	63.32 W
Guaugurina	154	10.37 S	150.28 E
Guaviare ≃	236	4.03 N	67.44 W
Guavio ≃	236	4.44 N	73.03 W
Guaxindiba ≃	277a	22.44 S	43.02 W
Guaxupé	246	21.18 S	46.42 W
Guayabal, Cuba	230p	20.42 N	77.36 W
Guayabal, Ven.	236	8.00 N	67.24 W
Guayabero ≃	236	2.36 N	72.47 W
Guayabo	222	26.00 N	107.26 W
Guayabo Colorado	224	19.02 N	101.35 W
Guayacán	242	29.58 S	71.22 W
Guayaguayare	231r	10.08 N	61.02 W
Guayama	230m	17.59 N	66.07 W
Guayambre ≃	226	14.26 N	86.02 W
Guayameo	224	18.12 N	101.19 W
Guayana → Ciudad Guayana	236	8.22 N	62.40 W
Guayana → Guyana □[1]	236	5.00 N	59.00 W
Guayana Francesa → French Guiana □[2]	240	4.00 N	53.00 W
Guayaneco, Archipiélago II	244	47.45 S	75.10 W
Guayanés, Punta ≻	230m	18.04 N	65.48 W
Guayanilla	230m	18.01 N	66.47 W
Guayanilla, Bahía de C	230m	18.00 N	66.46 W
Guayape	226	14.45 N	86.52 W
Guayape ≃	226	14.26 N	86.02 W
Guayapo ≃	236	4.30 N	67.35 W
Guayaquil	236	2.10 S	79.50 W
Guayas □[4]	236	2.00 S	80.00 W
Guayas ≃, Col.	236	1.23 N	74.50 W
Guayas ≃, Ec.	236	2.36 S	79.52 W
Guaybal, Lago ⊜[1]	230m	18.06 N	66.30 W
Guaycora	222	28.50 N	109.21 W
Guaycurú, Arroyo ≃	248	34.00 S	56.50 W
Guaymallén	242	32.54 S	68.47 W
Guaymas	222	27.56 N	110.54 W
Guaymoreto, Laguna de C	226	15.58 N	85.55 W
Guaynabo	230m	18.22 N	66.07 W
Guayquiraró ≃	242	30.10 S	58.34 W
Guayuriba ≃	236	3.55 N	73.05 W
Guazacapán	226	14.04 N	90.25 W
Guazapares	222	27.22 N	108.15 W
Guazárachic	222	26.57 N	106.43 W
Guazhou	96	32.15 N	119.23 E
Guazunamby, Arroyo ≃	278	34.24 S	58.38 W
Guba, Yai.	134	10.16 N	35.17 E
Guba, Zaïre	144	10.40 S	26.26 E
Gubacha	76	58.52 N	57.36 E
Gubam	154	8.40 S	141.55 E
Gubany	66	56.37 N	30.40 E
Gubari	70	51.32 N	42.33 E
Gubat	106	12.55 N	124.07 E
Gubbi	112	13.19 N	76.56 E
Gubbio	60	43.21 N	12.35 E
Gubeikou	95	40.42 N	117.09 E
Gubentaoligai	94	42.16 N	122.13 E
Gubin	30	51.56 N	14.45 E
Gubinicha	68	48.48 N	35.15 E
Gubino, S.S.S.R.	70	53.19 N	48.44 E
Gubino, S.S.S.R.	72	55.42 N	39.07 E
Gubio	136	12.29 N	12.48 E
Gubkin	68	51.18 N	37.32 E
Gubug	105a	7.03 S	110.40 E
Gucheng, Zhg.	88	37.22 N	115.56 E
Gucheng, Zhg.	90	25.53 N	116.11 E
Gucheng, Zhg.	90	32.46 N	118.32 E
Gucheng, Zhg.	90	33.59 N	117.29 E
Gucheng, Zhg.	92	32.18 N	111.35 E
Gucheng, Zhg.	95	39.08 N	115.42 E
Gucheng, Zhg.	95	40.32 N	116.02 E
Gucheng, Zhg.	96	30.29 N	119.46 E
Guchengcang	90	32.34 N	115.20 E
Guchenghu ⊜	96	31.17 N	118.54 E
Guchengzi, Zhg.	94	40.58 N	122.36 E
Guchengzi, Zhg.	94	40.40 N	120.31 E
Guchengzi, Zhg.	94	42.33 N	123.45 E
Guchengzi, Zhg.	94	41.44 N	123.35 E
Gučin-Us	92	45.30 N	102.28 E
Gücük	120	38.12 N	37.29 E
Gūdalūr, Bhārat	112	11.30 N	76.30 E
Gūdalūr, Bhārat	112	9.41 N	77.16 E
Gúdar, Sierra de ⛰	34	40.27 N	0.42 W
Gudauta	74	43.06 N	40.37 E
Gudbrandsdalen ∨	26	61.30 N	10.00 E
Gudensberg	52	51.10 N	9.22 E
Gudermes	74	43.20 N	46.08 E
Guderup	41	54.59 N	9.53 E
Gudhjem	26	55.13 N	14.59 E
Gudianzi	90	31.49 N	116.05 E
Gudivāda	112	16.27 N	80.59 E
Gudiyāttam	112	12.57 N	78.52 E
Gudme	41	55.09 N	10.43 E
Gudow	50	53.33 N	10.46 E
Güdül	120	40.13 N	32.15 E
Gūdūr	112	14.08 N	79.51 E
Gudvangen	26	60.52 N	6.50 E
Guebwiller (Gebweiler)	54	47.55 N	7.12 E
Guéckédou	140	8.33 N	10.09 W
Guéckédou □[4]	140	8.40 N	10.15 W
Gué-de-Longroi	251	48.30 N	1.43 E
Gué-d'Hossus	46	49.57 N	4.32 E
Guédi, Mont ∧	136	12.14 N	18.58 E
Guéguen, Lac ⊜	180	48.06 N	77.13 W
Guéhenno, Calvaire de ʊ[1]	32	47.56 N	2.42 W
Guéherville	251	48.32 N	1.53 E
Güejar ≃	236	2.55 N	73.14 W
Guelma	138	36.28 N	7.26 E
Guelph	202	43.33 N	80.15 W
Guelta Zemmur	138	25.15 N	12.20 W
Guéméné-sur-Scorff	32	48.04 N	3.12 W
Güemes	224	23.56 N	99.00 W
Guemes Island I	214	48.33 N	122.37 W
Guené	140	11.44 N	3.13 E
Guenguel ≃	244	45.41 S	70.20 W
Guer	28	47.54 N	2.07 W
Güera	138	20.48 N	17.08 W

Symbols in the index entries represent the broad categories identified in the key at the right. Symbols with superior numbers (⛰[2]) identify subcategories (see complete key on page *I* · *26*).

Kartensymbole in dem Registerverzeichnis stellen die rechts in Schlüssel erklärten Kategorien dar. Symbole mit hochgestellten Ziffern (⛰[2]) bezeichnen Unterabteilungen einer Kategorie (vgl. vollständiger Schlüssel auf Seite *I* · *26*).

Los símbolos incluídos en el texto del índice representan las grandes categorias identificadas con la clave a la derecha. Los símbolos con numeros en su parte superior (⛰[2]) identifican las subcategorías (véase la clave completa en la página *I* · *26*).

Les symboles de l'index représentent les catégories indiquées dans la légende à droite. Les symboles suivis d'un indice (⛰[2]) représentent des sous-catégories (voir légende complète à la page *I* · *26*).

Os símbolos incluídos no texto do índice representam as grandes categorias identificadas com a chave à direita. Os símbolos com números em sua parte superior (⛰[2]) identificam as subcategorias (veja-se a chave completa à página *I* · *26*).

Symbol	English	Deutsch	Español	Français	Português
∧	Mountain	Berg	Montaña	Montagne	Montanha
⛰	Mountains	Berge	Montañas	Montagnes	Montanhas
)(	Pass	Pass	Paso	Col	Passo
∨	Valley, Canyon	Tal, Cañon	Valle, Cañón	Vallée, Canyon	Vale, Canhão
≌	Plain	Ebene	Llano	Plaine	Planície
≻	Cape	Kap	Cabo	Cap	Cabo
I	Island	Insel	Isla	Île	Ilha
II	Islands	Inseln	Islas	Îles	Ilhas
✣	Other Topographic Features	Andere Topographische Objekte	Otros Elementos Topográficos	Autres données topographiques	Outros Elementos Topográficos

ESPAÑOL

Nombre	Página	Lat.°′	Long.°′ W=Oeste
Guera □[5]	136	11.30 N	18.30 E
Guéra, Massif de ⛰	136	11.55 N	18.12 E
Guérande	32	47.20 N	2.26 W
Guerara	138	32.46 N	4.34 E
Guerban'angeer	92	37.45 N	97.30 E
Guercif	138	34.15 N	3.21 W
Guerdjoumane, Djebel ∧	34	36.25 N	2.51 E
Gueré	136	9.12 N	18.10 E
Güere ≃	236	9.50 N	65.08 W
Guéréda	136	14.31 N	22.05 E
Guéret	32	46.10 N	1.52 E
Guérin Kouka	140	9.41 N	0.37 E
Guerla Mandatashan ∧	110	30.26 N	81.20 E
Guermantes	251	48.51 N	2.42 E
Guerne	204	40.46 N	81.54 W
Guernes	251	49.01 N	1.38 E
Guerneville	194	38.30 N	123.00 W
Guernica	248	34.56 S	58.25 W
Guernica y Luno	34	43.19 N	2.41 W
Guernsey	190	42.16 N	104.45 W
Guernsey □[6]	204	40.08 N	81.30 W
Guernsey □[2]	22		
	28	49.28 N	2.35 W
Guernsey I	32	49.27 N	2.35 W
Guernsey Reservoir ⊜[1]	188	42.19 N	104.48 W
Guernsey State Park ♠	188	42.20 N	104.50 W
Guerrero	186	28.20 N	100.23 W
Guerrero □[3]	224	17.40 N	100.00 W
Guerville	251	48.57 N	1.44 E
Guerzim	138	29.45 N	1.47 W
Guesle ≃	251	48.36 N	1.40 E
Guessou-Sud	140	10.03 N	2.38 E
Guest Peninsula ≻[1]	9	76.18 S	148.00 W
Gueydan	184	30.02 N	92.30 W
Guéyo	140	5.49 N	6.36 W
Gufang	90	29.04 N	119.32 E
Guffin Bay C	202	44.01 N	76.09 W
Guga	79	52.43 N	137.35 E
Gugang	90	28.17 N	113.46 E
Guge ∧	134	6.10 N	37.26 E
Gugera	113	30.58 N	73.19 E
Gugging	254b	48.19 N	16.15 E
Güglia, Pass dal)(	54	46.28 N	9.44 E
Güglingen	52	49.04 N	9.00 E
Guglionesi	60	41.55 N	14.55 E
Guguan	92	40.27 N	99.13 E
Guguan I	98	17.19 N	145.51 E
Guhe	90	31.54 N	117.58 E
Guhrau → Góra	30	51.40 N	16.33 E
Guia	238	15.22 S	56.14 W
Guia de Pacobaíba	246	22.43 S	43.10 W
Guialana, Cerro ∧	224	16.52 N	96.30 W
Guia Lopes	245	20.15 S	46.22 W
Guia Lopes da Laguna	238	21.26 S	56.07 W
Guiana Basin ✣[1]	18	10.00 N	50.00 W
Guibéroua	140	6.14 N	6.10 W
Guibes	146	26.41 S	16.42 E
Güicán	236	6.28 N	72.25 W
Guichen	32	47.58 N	1.48 W
Guichi	90	30.40 N	117.28 E
Guichicovi	224	16.58 N	95.06 W
Guichón	242	32.21 S	57.12 W
Guicun	90	33.37 N	114.11 E
Guide (Heyin)	92	36.03 N	101.28 E
Guider	136	9.56 N	13.57 E
Guide Rock	188	40.04 N	98.20 W
Guidexiang	97	29.51 N	104.47 E
Guidigri	140	13.40 N	9.51 E
Guidimouni	140	13.42 N	9.30 E
Guiding	92	26.28 N	107.07 E
Guidizzolo	58	45.19 N	10.35 E
Guidong	90	26.05 N	113.57 E
Guidonia	60	42.01 N	12.45 E
Guidouma	142	1.37 S	10.41 E
Guiers ≃	56	45.37 N	5.37 E
Guiers, Lac de ⊜	140	16.12 N	15.50 W
Guifujie	90	27.20 N	120.01 E
Guiglia	58	44.26 N	10.58 E
Guiglo	140	6.33 N	7.29 W
Guiglo □[5]	140	6.20 N	7.45 W
Guignes-Rabutin	46	48.38 N	2.48 E
Guihuayuan	97	30.37 N	105.25 E
Guihulngan	106	10.07 N	123.16 E
Güija, Lago de ⊜	226	14.17 N	89.31 W
Guijalo	106	13.44 N	123.52 E
Guijingqiao	96	31.21 N	119.40 E
Guijuelo	34	40.33 N	5.40 W
Guil ≃	56	44.40 N	6.36 E
Guilarte, Monte ∧	230m	18.09 N	66.46 W
Guilderland	200	42.42 N	73.54 W
Guildford, Austl.	264a	33.51 S	150.59 E
Guildford, Eng., U.K.	44	51.14 N	0.35 W
Guildford □[8]	250	51.16 N	0.32 W
Guildford Cathedral ψ[1]	250	51.14 N	0.35 W
Guildhall	178	44.34 N	71.34 W
Guilford, Conn., U.S.	197	41.17 N	72.41 W
Guilford, Ind., U.S.	208	39.10 N	84.55 W
Guilford, Maine, U.S.	178	45.14 N	69.29 W
Guilford, N.Y., U.S.	200	42.24 N	75.29 W
Guilford Courthouse National Military Park ♠	182	36.01 N	79.45 W
Guilherand	56	44.56 N	4.52 E
Guilherme Capelo	142	5.13 S	12.08 E
Guilin (Kweilin)	92	25.11 N	110.09 E
Guilinchang	97	30.13 N	105.50 E
Guilinzhen	97	30.15 N	104.53 E
Guiliuhe	79	46.11 N	121.45 E
Guillaume-Delisle, Lac ⊜	166	56.15 N	76.17 W
Guillaumes	56	44.05 N	6.51 E
Guillermo E. Hudson	278	34.47 S	58.10 W
Guillestre	56	44.40 N	6.39 E
Guillon	46	47.31 N	4.06 E
Guilsfield	44	52.42 N	3.09 W
Guilvinec	32	47.47 N	4.17 W
Guimarães, Bra.	240	2.08 S	44.36 W
Guimarães, Port.	34	41.27 N	8.18 W
Guimaras Island I	106	10.35 N	122.37 E
Guimaras Strait Ц	106	10.30 N	122.44 E
Guimba	106	15.40 N	120.46 E
Guimbal	106	10.40 N	122.19 E
Guimeishan	90	24.44 N	114.52 E
Guimuzhang ∧	90	24.40 N	116.48 E
Guin	184	33.58 N	87.55 W
Güina	226	14.04 N	85.18 W
Guina-Bissau → Guinea-Bissau □[1]	140	12.00 N	15.00 W
Guinan	92	35.24 N	100.57 E
Guinayang	259f	14.42 N	121.08 E
Guinayangan	106	13.54 N	122.27 E
Guinda	216	38.50 N	122.12 W
Guindulman	106	9.46 N	124.29 E
Guindulman Bay C	106	9.44 N	124.29 E
Guiné → Guinea-Bissau □[1]	140	12.00 N	15.00 W
Guinea	198	38.08 N	77.26 W
Guinea □[1]	124		
	140	11.00 N	10.00 W
Guinea, Gulf of C	10	2.00 N	2.30 E
Guinea Basin ✣[1]	10	0.30 N	5.00 W
Guinea-Bissau □[1]	124		
	140	12.00 N	15.00 W
Guineacor Creek ≃	160	34.21 S	150.05 E
Guinea Ecuatorial → Equatorial Guinea □[1]	142	2.00 N	9.00 E
Guinea Rise ✣[3]	10	3.00 S	0.30 W
Guinecourt, Lac ⊜	176	50.55 N	69.16 W
Guinée → Guinea □[1]	140	11.00 N	10.00 W
Guinée-Bissau → Guinea-Bissau □[1]	140	12.00 N	15.00 W

FRANÇAIS

Nom	Page	Lat.°′	Long.°′ W=Ouest
Guinée équitoriale → Equatorial Guinea □[1]	142	2.00 N	9.00 E
Güines, Cuba	230p	22.50 N	82.02 W
Guînes, Fr.	46	50.52 N	1.52 E
Guingamp	32	48.33 N	3.11 W
Guinguinéo	140	14.16 N	15.57 W
Guinobatan	106	13.11 N	123.36 E
Güinope	226	13.51 N	86.55 W
Guintacan Island I	106	11.19 N	123.54 E
Guintinguintin, Mount ∧	106	12.25 N	122.24 E
Guintinua Island I	106	14.26 N	122.51 E
Guiones, Punta ≻	226	9.54 N	85.41 W
Guiong	106	6.25 N	122.01 E
Guiperreux	251	48.40 N	1.42 E
Guiperreux, Étang de ⊜	251	48.40 N	1.43 E
Guiping	92	23.20 N	110.09 E
Guipúzcoa □[4]	34	43.10 N	2.10 W
Guir, Hamada du ◆[2]	138	30.45 N	3.15 W
Guir, Oued ∨	138	30.29 N	2.17 W
Güira de Melena	230p	22.48 N	82.30 W
Guiratinga	245	16.21 S	53.45 W
Guirenji	90	33.42 N	118.12 E
Güiria	236	10.34 N	62.18 W
Guiricema	245	21.00 S	42.43 W
Guisanbourg	240	4.25 N	51.56 W
Guisborough	42	54.32 N	1.04 W
Guiscard	46	49.39 N	3.03 E
Guise	46	49.54 N	3.38 E
Guiseley	42	53.53 N	1.42 W
Guishui ≃	90	28.27 N	112.47 E
Guisijan	106	11.05 N	122.03 E
Güisisil, Cerro ∧	226	12.37 N	86.13 W
Guist Creek ≃	208	38.09 N	85.13 W
Guita Koulouba	142	5.56 N	23.19 E
Guitiriz	34	43.11 N	7.54 W
Guitou	90	24.58 N	113.25 E
Guitrancourt	251	49.01 N	1.47 E
Guîtres	32	45.03 N	0.11 W
Guitri	140	5.31 N	5.14 W
Guiuan	106	11.02 N	125.43 E
Guixian	92	23.06 N	109.39 E
Guiyang, Zhg.	90	25.46 N	112.43 E
Guiyang (Kweiyang), Zhg.	92	26.35 N	106.43 E
Güiza ≃	236	1.22 N	78.36 W
Guizhou □[4]	92	27.00 N	107.00 E
Gujarat □[3]	110	22.00 N	72.00 E
Gūjar Khān	113	33.16 N	73.19 E
Gujiabeng	96	30.45 N	120.59 E
Gujiang	90	27.11 N	114.49 E
Gujiaqiao	90	32.51 N	116.33 E
Gujiatun	94	40.39 N	124.08 E
Gujiatuo	97	29.14 N	106.12 E
Gujiazi, Zhg.	94	42.02 N	123.01 E
Gujiazi, Zhg.	94	41.44 N	124.11 E
Gujrānwāla	113	32.26 N	74.33 E
Gujrāt	113	32.34 N	74.05 E
Gukas'an	74	41.03 N	43.52 E
Gukou	90	26.27 N	118.38 E
Gukovo	73	48.03 N	39.56 E
Gul, Tanjong ≻	261c	1.17 N	103.39 E
Gul'a	78	54.41 N	121.01 E
Gul'aj-Borisovka	68	46.38 N	40.13 E
Gul'ajevskije Koški, Ostrova II	24	68.55 N	55.10 E
Gul'ajpole	68	47.38 N	36.16 E
Gulang	92	37.36 N	102.58 E
Gulangyu I	90	24.28 N	118.04 E
Gulaothi	114	28.36 N	77.47 E
Gulargambone	156	31.20 S	148.28 E
Gulbarga	112	17.20 N	76.50 E
Gulbene	66	57.11 N	26.45 E
Gul'ča	75	40.19 N	73.26 E
Gul'ča ≃	75	40.20 N	73.26 E
Gulch	134	14.43 N	36.45 E
Guldborg	41	54.52 N	11.45 E
Guldborg Sund Ц	41	54.48 N	11.48 E
Guldsmedshyttan	40	59.42 N	15.06 E
Gülebağdı	120	39.52 N	39.50 E
Guledagudda	112	16.03 N	75.48 E
Guleicheng	90	23.47 N	117.36 E
Guleta	134	6.21 N	37.10 E
Gulf □[5]	154	7.00 S	145.00 E
Gulf Gate Estates	210	27.15 N	82.31 W
Gulf Hammock	182	29.15 N	82.43 W
Gulf Harbors	210	28.14 N	82.45 W
Gulf of Alaska Seamount Province ✣	16	55.00 N	144.00 W
Gulfport, Fla., U.S.	210	27.44 N	82.43 W
Gulfport, Miss., U.S.	184	30.22 N	89.06 W
Gulf Shores	184	30.17 N	87.41 W
Gulf Stream ≃	202	43.51 N	75.56 W
Gulgong	156	32.22 S	149.32 E
Gulicun, Zhg.	96	31.38 N	120.50 E
Gulicun, Zhg.	96	31.52 N	118.41 E
Gul Imām	113	32.16 N	70.32 E
Guling	90	23.45 N	114.26 E
Gulistān, Pāk.	110	30.36 N	66.35 E
Gulistan, S.S.S.R.	75	40.30 N	68.46 E
Gulistan Palace ψ	257d	35.41 N	51.25 E
Guljanci	38	43.38 N	24.42 E
Gulkana	170	62.16 N	145.23 W
Gull ≃	202	44.37 N	78.49 W
Gullande	42	56.02 N	2.50 W
Gulland Rock II[1]	44	50.34 N	4.59 W
Gullfoss ⌊	24a	64.24 N	20.08 W
Gullholmen	26	58.11 N	11.24 E
Gull Island I	271	42.32 N	82.41 W
Gullivan Bay C	210	25.52 N	81.38 W
Gull Lake	174	50.08 N	108.27 W
Gull Lake ⊜, Alta., Can.	172	52.35 N	114.00 W
Gull Lake ⊜, Ont., Can.	174	51.18 N	91.58 W
Gull Lake ⊜, Ont., Can.	202	44.51 N	78.47 W
Gull Lake ⊜, Mich., U.S.	206	42.24 N	85.25 W
Gull Lake ⊜, Minn., U.S.	180	46.25 N	94.20 W
Gullrock Lake ⊜	174	50.58 N	93.40 W
Gullspång	40	58.59 N	14.06 E
Güllü Dağı ∧	120	41.21 N	42.10 E
Güllük	120	37.14 N	27.36 E
Gulmarg	113	34.03 N	74.23 E
Gulnam	130	6.55 N	29.30 E
Gülnar	120	36.20 N	33.25 E
Gulong	79	45.51 N	124.14 E
Gulpen	52	50.48 N	5.54 E
Gülper See ⊜	50	52.44 N	12.14 E
Gulph Mills	275	40.04 N	75.21 W
Gülpınar	120	39.32 N	26.07 E
Gul'ripši	74	42.57 N	41.06 E
Gul'šad	76	46.39 N	74.24 E
Gülşehir	120	38.45 N	34.38 E
Gulsvik	26	60.23 N	9.35 E
Gulu, Ug.	144	2.47 N	32.18 E
Gulu, Zhg.	110	28.06 N	89.17 E
Gulukguluk	105a	7.04 S	113.40 E
Guluogongba	110	34.20 N	84.50 E
Gulwe	144	6.30 S	36.29 E
Gumaca	106	13.55 N	122.06 E
Gumahang	106	12.35 N	123.16 E
Gumal (Gowmal) ≃	110	31.56 N	70.22 E
Gumare	146	19.21 S	22.12 E
Gumba, Ang.	142	11.40 S	16.34 E
Gumba, Zaïre	142	2.57 N	21.26 E
Gumbinnen → Gusev	66	54.36 N	22.12 E
Gumbiro	144	10.16 S	35.39 E
Gumel	140	12.39 N	9.22 E
Gumeracha	158b	34.49 S	138.53 E
Gümgüm	74	39.10 N	41.28 E
Gumiao	90	32.26 N	113.16 E
Gumieńce ◆[8]	50	53.51 N	14.30 E
Gumla	114	23.03 N	84.33 E
Gumma □[5]	84	36.30 N	139.00 E
Gummersbach	52	51.02 N	7.34 E
Gummi	140	12.09 N	5.09 E

PORTUGUÊS

Nome	Página	Lat.°′	Long.°′ W=Oeste
Gumpas Pond ⊜	273	42.44 N	71.22 W
Gumpas Pond Brook ≃	273	42.42 N	71.21 W
Gumpoldskirchen	254b	48.03 N	16.17 E
Gumrak	70	48.47 N	44.22 E
Gum Swamp Creek ≃	182	32.08 N	82.55 W
Gumti ≃	116	23.32 N	90.43 E
Gümüşhacıköy	120	40.53 N	35.14 E
Gümüşhane	120	40.27 N	39.29 E
Gümüshane □[4]	120	40.15 N	39.45 E
Gümüşköy	257b	41.14 N	28.58 E
Gun ≃	206	42.28 N	85.40 W
Guna, Bhārat	114	24.39 N	77.19 E
Guna, Yai.	134	8.19 N	39.51 E
Guna □[5]	114	24.30 N	77.30 E
Guna ∧	134	11.42 N	38.12 E
Gunbar	156	34.01 S	145.25 E
Gun Barrel City	212	32.20 N	96.10 W
Gun Creek ≃	274a	43.03 N	78.55 W
Gunda	78	52.47 N	111.44 E
Gundagai	156	35.04 S	148.07 E
Gundelfingen, B.R.D.	52	48.33 N	10.22 E
Gundelfingen, B.R.D.	54	48.03 N	7.52 E
Gundelsheim	52	49.17 N	9.09 E
Gundertshausen	58	48.05 N	12.59 E
Gundik	105a	7.12 S	110.54 E
Gundji	142	2.05 N	21.27 E
Gundlakamma ≃	112	15.32 N	80.14 E
Gundlupet	112	11.48 N	76.41 E
Gündüzlü	120	40.53 N	37.43 E
Guneh Ghar ∧	113	35.19 N	71.47 E
Güney	120	38.09 N	29.05 E
Gungartan ∧	161b	36.18 S	148.24 E
Gungi	142	6.21 S	19.15 E
Gungo	142	11.48 S	14.08 E
Güngören	257b	41.01 N	28.53 E
Gungu	142	5.44 S	19.19 E
Gunib	74	42.25 N	46.57 E
Gunisao ≃	174	53.54 N	97.58 W
Gunisao Lake ⊜	174	53.33 N	96.15 W
Gunjrauliya	114	26.35 N	84.34 E
Gun Lake ⊜	206	42.37 N	85.32 W
Gunma	84	36.24 N	139.00 E
Gunnar	166	59.23 N	108.53 W
Günnarijn	92	45.38 N	102.01 E
Gunnarn	26	65.00 N	17.40 E
Gunnbjørns Fjeld ∧	16	68.55 N	29.53 W
Gunnebo	26	57.43 N	16.32 E
Gunnedah	156	30.59 S	150.15 E
Gunning Island I	266	40.22 N	73.59 W
Gunnislake	44	50.31 N	4.12 W
Gunnison, Colo., U.S.	190	38.33 N	106.56 W
Gunnison, Utah, U.S.	190	39.09 N	111.49 W
Gunnison ≃	190	39.03 N	108.35 W
Gunnison, Lake Fork ≃	190	38.28 N	107.19 W
Gunnison, North Fork ≃	190	38.47 N	107.50 W
Gunn Peak ∧	214	47.49 N	121.27 W
Gunpowder Creek ≃, Austl.	156	19.14 S	139.58 E
Gunpowder Creek ≃, Ky., U.S.	208	38.53 N	84.47 W
Gunpowder Falls ≃	198	39.24 N	76.22 W
Gunpowder River C	198	39.22 N	76.22 W
Gunpowder State Park ♠	198	39.37 N	76.40 W
Gunsan → Kunsan	88	35.58 N	126.41 E
Gunskirchen	58	48.08 N	13.57 E
Gunston Cove C	198	38.40 N	77.09 W
Guntakal	112	15.10 N	77.23 E
Güntersberge	50	51.38 N	10.59 E
Guntersblum	52	49.47 N	8.21 E
Guntersville	184	34.21 N	86.18 W
Guntersville Dam ◆[6]	184	34.13 N	86.23 W
Guntersville Lake ⊜[1]	184	34.45 N	86.03 W
Guntingsaga	104	2.33 N	99.39 E
Guntramsdorf	254b	48.03 N	16.19 E
Guntung	104	1.38 N	101.34 E
Guntūr	112	16.18 N	80.27 E
Gunungkencana	105a	6.34 S	106.04 E
Gunungmegang	102	3.27 S	103.52 E
Gunungsahilan	102	0.06 N	101.18 E
Gunungsitoli	104	1.17 N	97.37 E
Gunungtua	104	1.30 N	99.37 E
Gunupur	112	19.05 N	83.49 E
Gunyidi	152	30.08 S	116.04 E
Günz ≃	54	48.27 N	10.16 E
Gunza ≃	142	11.10 S	13.50 E
Günzburg	54	48.27 N	10.16 E
Gunzenhausen	52	49.07 N	10.45 E
Gunzigou	94	41.31 N	123.58 E
Guodian	96	30.27 N	120.33 E
Guoerbenaobao	92	43.14 N	112.28 E
Guoguantun	88	35.29 N	115.54 E
Gu Oidak Wash ∨	190	31.57 N	112.21 W
Guoji	90	32.59 N	113.06 E
Guojiadian	94	41.51 N	121.30 E
Guojiajiang	96	32.17 N	120.50 E
Guojiatun, Zhg.	88	41.31 N	117.02 E
Guojiatun, Zhg.	94	40.52 N	122.04 E
Guojiatun, Zhg.	94	42.00 N	122.51 E
Guojiawopeng	94	42.03 N	122.46 E
Guojiayao	95	40.37 N	115.39 E
Guojiayuan	96	32.10 N	120.35 E
Guojiga	76	43.47 N	80.48 E
Guokuishan ∧	79	45.17 N	129.30 E
Guoleizhuang	88	40.44 N	114.36 E
Guoluoshan ⛰	92	33.14 N	99.50 E
Guolutan	90	32.04 N	115.40 E
Guosu	88	38.24 N	114.00 E
Guoxian	92	38.54 N	112.50 E
Guoyang	90	33.32 N	116.12 E
Guozhangzi	88	40.43 N	118.47 E
Guozhuang	88	35.25 N	117.10 E
Guozhuangmiao	96	31.49 N	119.01 E
Gupeizhou	88	34.09 N	117.54 E
Gupis	113	36.14 N	73.26 E
Gura	70	57.18 N	51.25 E
Gura, Wādī ∨	130	17.28 N	35.10 E
Guraferdo	134	6.50 N	35.06 E
Gurag ∧	134	8.15 N	38.21 E
Gura-Galbena	68	46.43 N	28.42 E
Gurahonţ	38	46.16 N	22.21 E
Gura Humorului	38	47.33 N	25.54 E
Gurais	113	34.38 N	74.50 E
Guran	78	54.46 N	100.38 E
Gurara ≃	140	8.12 N	6.41 E
Gurdāspur	113	32.02 N	75.31 E
Gurdon	184	33.55 N	93.09 W
Gurdžaani	74	41.43 N	45.48 E
Güre	120	38.39 N	29.10 E
Gurejev	70	47.21 N	43.16 E
G'urg'an	74	40.23 N	50.19 E
Gurgaon	114	28.28 N	77.02 E
Gurgaon □[5]	114	28.20 N	77.00 E
Gurgei, Jabal ∧	130	13.50 N	24.19 E
Gurghiului, Munţii ⛰	38	46.41 N	25.12 E
Gurguan Point ≻	164n	15.00 N	145.35 E
Gurguéia ≃	240	6.50 S	43.24 W
Gurgura	134	7.50 N	41.30 E
Gūrha	110	14.14 N	74.50 E
Gurjev	70	47.07 N	51.56 E
Gurjev □[4]	76	45.00 N	53.00 E
Gurjevo	72	54.42 N	36.28 E
Gurjevsk, S.S.S.R.	66	54.47 N	20.38 E
Gurjevsk, S.S.S.R.	76	54.17 N	85.56 E
Gurk ≃	30	46.36 N	14.31 E
Gurkha	114	28.00 N	84.37 E
Gurktaler Alpen ⛰	58	46.55 N	14.00 E
Gurla Mandhata → Guerla Mandatashan ∧	110	30.26 N	81.20 E
Gurlevo	66	59.28 N	28.54 E
Gurnee	206	42.22 N	87.55 W
Gurnet Point ≻	273	42.01 N	70.34 W
Gurnley Football Ground ♠	252	53.47 N	2.14 W
Gursarai	114	25.37 N	79.11 E
Gurskøy I	26	62.15 N	5.41 E
Gürsu	120	40.13 N	29.12 E
Guru	110	29.34 N	66.43 E
Guru Har Sahāi	113	30.43 N	74.25 E
Gurun, Malay.	104	5.49 N	100.29 E
Gürün, Tür.	120	38.43 N	37.17 E
Gurupá	240	1.25 S	51.39 W
Gurupi	240	11.43 S	49.04 W
Gurupi ≃	240	1.13 S	46.06 W
Gurupi, Serra do ⛰[1]	240	5.00 S	47.30 W
Guru Sikhar ∧	110	24.39 N	72.46 E
Gurvanbulag	78	47.38 N	103.31 E
Gurvansajchan	92	45.22 N	107.00 E
Gurvan Sajchan Uul ⛰	92	43.50 N	103.30 E
Gurvan-Tes	92	43.28 N	101.21 E
Gurzuf	68	44.33 N	34.17 E
Gus' ≃	70	55.00 N	41.11 E
Gusar	75	39.28 N	67.50 E
Gušari	75	38.55 N	68.51 E
Gusarka	68	47.23 N	36.31 E
Gusasale	134	6.30 N	43.00 E
Gus'atin	68	49.05 N	26.11 E
Gusau	140	12.12 N	6.40 E
Gus'-Chrustal'nyj	70	55.37 N	40.40 E
Guselka	70	50.27 N	45.09 E
Güsen	50	52.21 N	11.59 E
Gusev, S.S.S.R.	66	54.36 N	22.12 E
Gusev, S.S.S.R.	68	48.27 N	40.32 E
Gusevo	66	56.06 N	33.21 E
Gusevskij	70	55.40 N	40.34 E
Gushan, Zhg.	88	39.53 N	123.36 E
Gushan, Zhg.	88	36.30 N	116.53 E
Gushan, Zhg.	96	31.44 N	120.33 E
Gushan ∧, Zhg.	90	26.05 N	119.22 E
Gushan ∧, Zhg.	94	41.18 N	120.35 E
Gushanbeizifu	94	42.10 N	120.30 E
Gushankou	95	39.38 N	115.49 E
Gushantun	79	48.18 N	123.47 E
Gushanzi, Zhg.	88	40.22 N	120.03 E
Gushanzi, Zhg.	94	41.03 N	123.03 E
Gushi, Zhg.	90	28.34 N	119.24 E
Gushi, Zhg.	90	32.12 N	115.41 E
Gushiago	140	9.55 N	0.12 W
Gushichan	164m	26.07 N	127.45 E
Gushikawa	164m	26.21 N	127.52 E
Gushu, Zhg.	88	34.15 N	115.48 E
Gushu, Zhg.	94	42.36 N	123.26 E
Gusi	102	6.07 N	117.08 E
Gusino	66	54.44 N	31.22 E
Gusinoje, Ozero ⊜	78	51.12 N	106.24 E
Gusinoje Ozero	78	51.09 N	106.10 E
Gusinoozersk	78	51.17 N	106.30 E
Guskef	75	39.02 N	69.20 E
Guskhara	116	23.30 N	87.45 E
Gus'-Khrustal'nyy → Gus'-Chrustal'nyj	70	55.37 N	40.40 E
Gusong	92	28.18 N	105.14 E
Guspini	36	39.32 N	8.38 E
Gussago	58	45.35 N	10.09 E
Gusselby	40	59.39 N	15.14 E
Güssing	30	47.04 N	16.20 E
Gussola	58	45.00 N	10.20 E
Gustav Holm, Kap ≻	166	67.00 N	34.00 W
Gustavo A. Madero	224	19.29 N	99.07 W
Gustavo A. Madero □[7]	276a	19.29 N	99.08 W
Gustavsberg	40	59.19 N	18.23 E
Gustavus	170	58.25 N	135.44 W
Güsten	50	51.49 N	11.35 E
Gustia	262b	22.59 N	88.26 E
Gustine, Calif., U.S.	216	37.16 N	121.00 E
Gustine, Tex., U.S.	186	31.51 N	98.24 W
Gustorf	52	51.04 N	6.34 E
Güstrow	50	53.48 N	12.10 E
Gusum	26	58.16 N	16.29 E
Gus'-Železnyj	70	55.03 N	41.10 E
Gutach	54	48.15 N	8.13 E
Gutaj	78	49.59 N	108.12 E
Gutara ≃	78	54.50 N	97.23 E
Gutarskij Chrebet ⛰	78	54.30 N	97.40 E
Gutenfels, Burg ⊥	52	50.07 N	7.46 E
Guten Hoffnung, Kap der → Good Hope, Cape of ≻	148	34.24 S	18.30 E
Güterfelde	254a	52.22 N	13.12 E
Gütersloh	48	51.54 N	8.23 E
Guthrie, Ind., U.S.	208	38.59 N	86.31 W
Guthrie, Ky., U.S.	184	36.39 N	87.10 W
Guthrie, Okla., U.S.	186	35.53 N	97.25 W
Guthrie, Tex., U.S.	186	33.37 N	100.19 W
Guthrie Center	188	41.41 N	94.30 W
Guthrie Lake ⊜	174	55.17 N	100.38 W
Gutian, Zhg.	90	26.36 N	118.46 E
Gutian, Zhg.	90	25.43 N	116.57 E
Gutian, Zhg.	90	25.15 N	116.46 E
Gutianxi ≃	90	26.22 N	118.42 E
Gutiérrez	238	19.25 S	63.34 W
Gutiérrez Zamora	224	20.27 N	97.05 W
Gutland □[9]	52	49.40 N	6.10 E
Gutland ◆[1]	52	49.40 N	6.10 E
Guton, Gora ∧	74	41.51 N	46.45 E
Guttannen	54	46.39 N	8.18 E
Guttau	50	51.15 N	14.34 E
Guttenberg, Iowa, U.S.	180	42.47 N	91.06 W
Guttenberg, N.J., U.S.	266	40.48 N	74.01 W
Guttentag → Dobrodzień	30	50.44 N	18.27 E
Guttstadt → Dobre Miasto	30	53.59 N	20.25 E
Gutu	144	19.38 S	31.10 E
Gutujevskij, Ostrov I	255a	59.54 N	30.14 E
Gutulia Nasjonalpark ♠	26	62.02 N	12.12 E
Guty	68	50.08 N	35.21 E
Gützkow	50	53.56 N	13.24 E
Güvem	120	40.36 N	32.40 E
Guwen	97	29.11 N	104.26 E
Guxhagen	52	51.12 N	9.28 E
Guxian, Zhg.	90	27.09 N	115.31 E
Guxian, Zhg.	90	32.26 N	113.37 E
Guxiandu	90	29.06 N	116.50 E
Guxianji	90	31.57 N	116.15 E
Guxihe	97	30.18 N	105.52 E
Guxiong	96	31.55 N	118.38 E
Guy	212	29.21 N	95.47 W
Guyana □[1]	232		
	236	5.00 N	59.00 W
Guyancourt	251	48.46 N	2.04 E
Guyancourt, Aéroport de ⊠	251	48.45 N	2.05 E
Guyane → Guyana □[1]	236	5.00 N	59.00 W
Guyane française → French Guiana □[2]	240	4.00 N	53.00 W
Guyang, Zhg.	88	34.58 N	114.58 E
Guyang, Zhg.	92	41.10 N	110.02 E
Guye	95	39.44 N	118.25 E
Guyenne □[9]	32	44.30 N	1.00 E
Guyi	90	25.38 N	118.47 E
Guyin	92	23.58 N	105.47 E
Guyizhen	97	30.22 N	103.33 E
Guymon	186	36.41 N	101.29 W
Guyonne, Ruisseau la ≃	251	48.49 N	1.52 E
Guyot, Mount ∧	182	35.42 N	83.15 W
Guyra	156	30.14 S	151.40 E
Guysborough	176	45.23 N	61.30 W
Guys Mills	204	41.38 N	79.59 W
Guyton	182	32.20 N	81.24 W
Guyuan, Zhg.	88	41.30 N	115.35 E
Guyuan, Zhg.	92	35.58 N	106.45 E
Guzar	62	38.36 N	66.15 E
Güzel ≃	74	39.44 N	43.01 E
Güzelbahçe	120	38.21 N	26.54 E
Güzelsu	120	36.54 N	31.53 E
Guzhang	92	28.31 N	109.57 E
Guzhen	90	33.19 N	117.21 E
Guzishan	88	41.42 N	118.06 E
Guzmán, Méx.	222	31.13 N	107.27 W
Guzmán → Ciudad Guzmán, Méx.	224	19.41 N	103.29 W
Guzmán, Laguna de ⊜	222	31.20 N	107.30 W
Gvardejsk	66	54.39 N	21.05 E
Gvardejskoje, S.S.S.R.	68	48.44 N	35.19 E
Gvardejskoje, S.S.S.R.	68	45.07 N	34.01 E
Gvardejskoje, S.S.S.R.	68	49.20 N	26.42 E
Gvardejsk [Tapiau]	66	54.39 N	21.05 E
Gvazda	68	50.44 N	40.30 E
Gvozdec	68	48.34 N	25.17 E
Gwa	100	17.36 N	94.35 E
Gwabegar	156	30.36 S	148.58 E
Gwadabawa	140	13.20 N	5.15 E
Gwādar	118	25.07 N	62.19 E
Gwagwada	140	10.14 N	7.14 E
Gwai	144	19.15 S	27.42 E
Gwai ≃	144	17.59 S	26.52 E
Gwalangu	142	2.19 N	18.11 E
Gwalchmai	42	53.15 N	4.25 W
Gwāl Haidarzai	110	30.45 N	68.53 E
Gwalia	152	28.55 S	121.20 E
Gwalior	114	26.13 N	78.10 E
Gwambygine	158a	31.59 S	116.48 E
Gwanara	140	8.55 N	3.09 E
Gwanda	144	20.57 S	29.01 E
Gwandu	140	12.30 N	4.41 E
Gwane	144	4.43 N	25.50 E
Gwangju → Kwangju	88	35.09 N	126.54 E
Gwarzo	140	11.56 N	7.56 E
Gwasero	140	9.29 N	3.30 E
Gwash ≃	44	52.39 N	0.27 W
Gwātar Bay C	118	25.04 N	61.36 E
Gwatt	54	46.43 N	7.38 E
Gwaun ≃	44	52.00 N	4.58 W
Gwda ≃	30	53.04 N	16.44 E
Gweebarra Bay C	28	54.52 N	8.20 W
Gweedore	28	55.03 N	8.14 W
Gwelo	144	19.27 S	29.49 E
Gwelo ≃	144	18.45 S	28.36 E
Gwembe	144	16.30 S	27.35 E
Gwendraeth Fâch ≃	44	51.44 N	4.18 W
Gwendraeth Fawr ≃	44	51.43 N	4.18 W
Gwent □[6]	44	51.43 N	2.57 W
Gwinn	180	46.17 N	87.26 W
Gwobu	144	2.37 N	26.13 E
Gwydir ≃	156	29.27 S	149.48 E
Gwynedd	275	40.12 N	75.15 W
Gwynedd □[6], Wales, U.K.	28		
	44	53.00 N	4.00 W
Gwynedd Square	275	40.13 N	75.18 W
Gwynedd Valley	275	40.11 N	75.15 W
Gwynn	198	37.30 N	76.17 W
Gwynneville	208	39.40 N	85.39 W
Gwynn Island I	198	37.30 N	76.17 W
Gwynn Oak Amusement Park ♠	274b	39.20 N	76.43 W
Gwynns Falls ≃	274b	39.16 N	76.37 W
Gwynns Falls Park ♠	274b	39.18 N	76.41 W
Gyál	254c	47.23 N	19.14 E
Gya La)(	114	28.44 N	84.40 E
Gyáli-patak ≃	254c	47.24 N	19.07 E
Gyangtse → Jiangzi	110	28.57 N	89.35 E
Gybdan	70	56.33 N	51.39 E
Gyda	64	70.52 N	78.30 E
Gydanskaja Guba C	64	71.20 N	76.30 E
Gydanskij Poluostrov ≻[1]	64	70.50 N	79.00 E
Gyebu	154	3.03 S	133.51 E
Gyemo Chen ∧	114	27.20 N	88.52 E
Gyeongju → Kyŏngju	88	35.51 N	129.14 E
Gyldenløves Fjord C[2]	166	64.30 N	41.30 W
Gyldenløveshøj ∧[2]	41	55.33 N	11.52 E
Gy [les-Nonains]	54	47.24 N	5.49 E
Gylling	41	55.53 N	10.11 E
Gymea Bay	264a	34.02 S	151.05 E
Gympie	156	26.11 S	152.40 E
Gyobingauk	100	18.13 N	95.39 E
Gyōda	84	36.08 N	139.28 E
Gyoma	30	46.56 N	20.50 E
Gyöngyös	30	47.47 N	19.56 E
Győr	30	47.42 N	17.38 E
Győr-Sopron □[6]	30	47.35 N	17.15 E
Gypsey Race ≃	42	54.05 N	0.12 W
Gypsum, Colo., U.S.	190	39.39 N	106.57 W
Gypsum, Kans., U.S.	188	38.42 N	97.26 W
Gypsum, Ohio, U.S.	204	41.30 N	82.52 W
Gypsum Creek ≃, U.S.	190	37.09 N	109.52 W
Gypsum Creek ≃, Kans., U.S.	188	38.51 N	97.25 W
Gypsum Hills ⛰[2]	186	36.25 N	99.20 W
Gypsum Point ≻	166	61.53 N	114.35 W
Gypsumville	174	51.45 N	98.35 W
Gyrbovec	68	46.50 N	29.21 E
Gysinge	40	60.17 N	16.53 E
Gyttorp	40	59.31 N	14.58 E
Gyula	30	46.39 N	21.17 E
Gyulafehérvár → Alba-Iulia	38	46.04 N	23.35 E
Gžat' ≃	66	55.56 N	34.33 E
Gžatsk	76	55.42 N	78.11 E
Gžel'	72	55.36 N	38.24 E
Gzhatsk → Gagarin	66	55.33 N	35.00 E

H

Haag → 's-Gravenhage	48	52.06 N	4.18 E
Haag am Hausruck	58	48.11 N	13.38 E
Haagen	54	47.38 N	7.40 E
Haag in Oberbayern	58	48.10 N	12.11 E
Haaksbergen	48	52.09 N	6.44 E
Haalenberg	146	26.52 S	15.30 E
Haaltert	46	50.54 N	4.00 E
Haamstede	48	51.43 N	3.45 E
Haan	52	51.11 N	7.00 E
Haapajärvi	26	63.45 N	25.20 E
Haapajärvi ⊜	26	63.33 N	27.00 E
Haapamäki	26	62.15 N	24.28 E
Haapavesi	26	64.08 N	25.22 E
Haapsalu	66	58.56 N	23.33 E
Haar	58	48.06 N	11.44 E
Haar ◆[8]	253	51.26 N	7.13 E
Ha'Arava (Wādī al-Jayb) ∨	122	31.04 N	35.27 E
Haardt ⛰	52	49.15 N	8.00 E
Haaren, B.R.D.	48	51.34 N	8.44 E
Haaren, Ned.	48	51.36 N	5.12 E
Haarlem, Ned.	48	52.23 N	4.38 E
Haarlem, S. Afr.	148	33.44 S	23.20 E
Haarlemmermeer ◆[1]	48	52.15 N	4.38 E
Haarzopf ◆[8]	253	51.25 N	6.58 E
Haast	162	43.53 S	169.03 E
Haast ≃	162	43.50 S	169.02 E
Haast Bluff	152	23.30 S	131.50 E
Haast Pass)(	162	44.06 S	169.21 E
Haatinao, Pointe ≻	164x	9.47 S	138.51 W
Haava, Canal Ц	164x	9.53 S	139.04 W
Habahe	76	47.53 N	86.12 E
Habana □[7]	276b	23.08 N	82.22 W
Habaqi, Zhg.	94	42.38 N	122.02 E
Habaqi, Zhg.	94	42.36 N	122.52 E
Habaqila	92	42.01 N	106.02 E
Habartov	50	50.08 N	12.33 E
Habaswein	144	1.01 N	39.29 E
Ḥabawna, Wādī ∨	134	17.51 N	44.59 E
Habay-la-Neuve	52	49.44 N	5.39 E
Ḥabbān	134	14.21 N	47.05 E
Ḥabbānīyah, Hawr al- ⊜	118	33.17 N	43.29 E
Ḥabbūsh	122	33.24 N	35.29 E
Habelschwerdt → Bystrzyca Kłodzka	30	50.18 N	16.38 E
Habère-Poche	54	46.15 N	6.29 E
Haberfield	264a	33.53 S	151.08 E
Habermehl Peak ∧	9	71.49 S	6.38 E
Ḥabīb, Wādī ∨	132	27.20 N	31.30 E
Habichtswald, Naturpark ♠	52	51.20 N	9.15 E
Habiganj	110	24.23 N	91.25 E
Habikino	86	34.33 N	135.37 E
Habīlah	130	12.41 N	22.33 E
Habinghorst ◆[8]	253	51.35 N	7.18 E
Hab Nadi Chowki	110	25.01 N	66.53 E
Habo	26	57.55 N	14.04 E
Habob, Wādī ∨	130	18.07 N	35.01 E
Habomai-shoto II, S.S.S.R.	64	43.30 N	146.10 E
Habomai-shotō → Malaja Kuril'skaja Gr'ada II, S.S.S.R.	82a	43.30 N	146.10 E
Haboro	82a	44.22 N	141.42 E
Hābra	116	22.50 N	88.38 E
Habsburg ⊥	54	47.28 N	8.13 E
Habsheim	54	47.44 N	7.25 E
Habshīyah, Jabal ⛰	134	16.40 N	49.40 E
Habu	260	34.27 N	135.24 E
Habutaki	260	34.25 N	135.26 E
Hache, Lac la ⊜	172	51.50 N	121.30 W
Hachen	52	51.22 N	7.59 E
Hachenburg	52	50.39 N	7.50 E
Hachi	110	27.46 N	94.01 E
Hachijō	260	34.37 N	135.48 E
Hachijō-jima I	80	33.05 N	139.48 E
Hachiman, Nihon	84	35.45 N	136.57 E
Hachiman → Ōmi-hachiman, Nihon	84	35.08 N	136.06 E
Hachiman-misaki ≻	84	35.08 N	140.19 E
Hachinohe	82	40.30 N	141.29 E
Hachiōji	84	35.39 N	139.20 E
Hachmühlen	48	52.10 N	9.28 E
Hacıbektaş	120	38.57 N	34.35 E
Hacienda Heights	218	33.58 N	117.58 W
Hacienda Miravalles	226	10.41 N	85.14 W
Hacihamza	120	41.05 N	34.28 E
Hacıishaklı	120	36.11 N	33.40 E
Hacıköy	120	40.04 N	35.31 E
Hacılar	120	38.39 N	35.27 E
Hackås	26	62.55 N	14.31 E
Hackberry, Ariz., U.S.	190	35.22 N	113.44 W
Hackberry, La., U.S.	184	29.59 N	93.21 W
Hackberry Creek ≃, Kans., U.S.	188	38.48 N	100.03 W
Hackberry Creek ≃, Tex., U.S.	212	31.53 N	97.12 W
Hackensack	200	40.53 N	74.03 W
Hackensack ≃	266	40.43 N	74.06 W
Hackett, Ark., U.S.	184	35.11 N	94.25 W
Hackett, Pa., U.S.	269b	40.15 N	80.01 W
Hacketts	250	51.45 N	0.05 W
Hackettstown	200	40.51 N	74.50 W
Hacking ≃	264a	34.04 S	151.06 E
Hacking, Port C	264a	34.05 S	151.09 E
Hackleburg	184	34.17 N	87.50 W
Hackletons Cliff ⌂[4]	231g	13.12 N	59.31 W
Hackney ◆[8]	44	51.33 N	0.03 W
Hack Point	198	39.28 N	75.53 W
Håckren ⊜	26	63.11 N	13.35 E
Haçlı Gölü ⊜	120	39.00 N	42.18 E
Haco	142	10.12 S	15.44 E
Hacreş Dağları ⛰	120	38.38 N	41.37 E
Hadāli	113	32.18 N	72.12 E
Hadalīya	130	16.10 N	36.06 E
Hadamar	52	50.27 N	8.02 E
Hadano	84	35.22 N	139.14 E
Ḥadāribah, Ra's al- ≻	130	22.04 N	36.54 E
HaDarom □[5]	122	30.40 N	34.50 E
Hadayingzi	94	42.22 N	121.40 E
Ḥadd, Ra's al- ≻	108	22.32 N	59.48 E
Haddad, Ouadi ∨	136	14.40 N	18.46 E
Ḥaddādīn, Qārat al- ∧[2]	132	30.04 N	30.58 E
Haddam, Conn., U.S.	197	41.29 N	72.31 W
Haddam, Kans., U.S.	188	39.51 N	97.18 W
Haddenham, Eng., U.K.	44	51.46 N	0.56 W
Haddenham, Eng., U.K.	44	52.22 N	0.09 E
Haddington	42	55.58 N	2.47 W
Haddock	182	33.02 N	83.26 W
Haddon Downs	156	26.21 S	140.50 E
Haddonfield	198	39.54 N	75.02 W
Haddon Heights	198	39.52 N	75.02 W
Hadejia	140	12.30 N	9.59 E
Hadejia ≃	136	12.50 N	10.51 E
Hadeln, Land ◆[1]	48	53.45 N	8.45 E
Haden	161a	27.14 S	151.53 E
Hadera	122	32.26 N	34.55 E
Ḥadera ≃	122	32.27 N	34.53 E
Hadersdorf ◆[8]	254b	48.13 N	16.14 E
Hadersfeld	254b	48.20 N	16.15 E
Haderslev	41	55.15 N	9.30 E
Haderslev Fjord C	41	55.17 N	9.40 E
Hadfield, Austl.	264b	37.42 S	144.56 E
Hadfield, Eng., U.K.	252	53.28 N	1.58 W
Hadībū	108	12.38 N	54.02 E
Ḥadīd, Jabal ∧[2]	132	30.20 N	30.06 E
Ḥadīd, Jabal al- ∧[2]	132	28.47 N	31.04 E
Hadım	120	36.59 N	32.28 E
Hadīyah	118	25.34 N	38.41 E
Hadjeb el Aïoun	36	35.24 N	9.33 E
Hadjout	34	36.31 N	2.25 E
Hadleigh, Eng., U.K.	44	52.03 N	0.58 E
Hadleigh, Eng., U.K.	250	51.33 N	0.37 E
Hadley, Mass., U.S.	197	42.21 N	72.35 W
Hadley, Mich., U.S.	206	42.57 N	83.24 W
Hadley, N.Y., U.S.	200	43.19 N	73.51 W
Hadley, Pa., U.S.	204	41.25 N	80.14 W
Hadley Bay C	166	72.30 N	107.45 W
Hadley Creek ≃	209	39.37 N	91.12 W
Hadlock	192	48.02 N	122.46 W
Hadlow	44	51.14 N	0.20 E
Hadlyme	197	41.25 N	72.25 W
Hadmersleben	50	51.59 N	11.18 E
Hadong, Taehan	88	35.05 N	127.44 E
Ha-dong, Viet.	100	20.58 N	105.46 E
Ḥaḍramawt ◆[1]	134	15.00 N	50.00 E
Ḥaḍramawt, Wādī ∨	134	15.55 N	50.00 E
Hadrian's Wall ⊥	42	54.59 N	2.26 W
Hadsten	41	56.20 N	10.03 E
Hadsund	26	56.43 N	10.07 E
Ḥaḍūr Shu'ayb ∧	134	15.18 N	43.59 E
Hadyai → Hat Yai	100	7.01 N	100.28 E
Haeju	88	38.02 N	125.42 E
Haemgon-ni ◆[8]	261b	37.35 N	126.49 E
Haena	219b	22.14 N	159.34 W
Haenam	88	34.34 N	126.35 E
Haena Point ≻	219b	22.14 N	159.34 W
Haenertsburg	146	24.00 S	29.50 E
Haengyŏng-ni	88	42.33 N	129.56 E
Haerbin (Harbin)	79	45.45 N	126.41 E
Haerhonghe ≃	92	42.40 N	110.42 E
Haerlikeshan ∧	92	43.08 N	94.20 E
Haernao	94	41.46 N	120.28 E
Haertao	94	42.21 N	122.04 E
Hafeïra, Oued el- ∨	138	25.18 N	10.48 W
Hafelekar Spitze ∧	58	47.19 N	11.23 E
Haffen-Mehr	48	51.44 N	6.28 E
Haffkrug-Scharbeutz	50	54.03 N	10.44 E
Hafford	174	52.48 N	107.20 W

≃	River	Fluss	Río	Rivière	Rio
Ξ	Canal	Kanal	Canal	Canal	Canal
⌊	Waterfall, Rapids	Wasserfall, Stromschnellen	Cascada, Rápidos	Chute d'eau, Rapides	Cascata, Rápidos
Ц	Strait	Meeresstrasse	Estrecho	Détroit	Estreito
C	Bay, Gulf	Bucht, Golf	Bahía, Golfo	Baie, Golfe	Baía, Golfo
⊜	Lake, Lakes	See, Seen	Lago, Lagos	Lac, Lacs	Lago, Lagos
☷	Swamp	Sumpf	Pantano	Marais	Pântano
⍓	Ice Features, Glacier	Eis- und Gletscherformen	Accidentes Glaciales	Formes glaciaires	Acidentes Glaciares
⊤	Other Hydrographic Features	Andere Hydrographische Objekte	Otros Elementos Hidrográficos	Autres données hydrographiques	Outros Elementos Hidrográficos

✣	Submarine Features	Untermeerische Objekte	Accidentes Submarinos	Formes de relief sous-marin	Acidentes Submarinos
□	Political Unit	Politische Einheit	Unidad Politica	Entité politique	Unidade Política
ψ	Cultural Institution	Kulturelle Institution	Institución Cultural	Institution culturelle	Instituição Cultural
⊥	Historical Site	Historische Stätte	Sitio Histórico	Site historique	Sitio Histórico
♠	Recreational Site	Erholungs- und Ferienort	Sitio de Recreo	Centre de loisirs	Sítio de Lazer
⊠	Airport	Flughafen	Aeropuerto	Aéroport	Aeroporto
■	Military Installation	Militäranlage	Instalación Militar	Installation militaire	Instalação Militar
◆	Miscellaneous	Verschiedenes	Misceláneo	Divers	Miscelânea

ENGLISH / DEUTSCH

Name	Page	Lat.°′	Long.°′
Haffouz	36	35.38 N	9.41 E
Hafik	120	39.52 N	37.24 E
Ḥafīra, Qā' al- ≚	122	31.06 N	36.14 E
Ḥafīrat al-'Aydā	118	26.26 N	39.10 E
Ḥafīt, Jabal ∧	118	24.03 N	55.46 E
Ḥāfiẓ, Bi'r ▾[4]	132	30.51 N	31.40 E
Hāfizābād	113	32.04 N	73.41 E
Hafızbey	120	37.12 N	30.31 E
Hāflong	110	25.11 N	93.02 E
Hafnarfjörður	24a	64.03 N	21.56 W
Haft Gel	118	31.27 N	49.27 E
Hafun, Ras ≻	126	10.27 N	51.26 E
Hafun Bay North C	134	10.45 N	51.15 E
Hafun Bay South C	134	10.10 N	51.05 E
Haga, Nihon	84	36.32 N	140.04 E
Haga, Nihon	86	35.09 N	134.33 E
HaGadol, HaMakhtesh •[7]	122	30.56 N	34.59 E
Haga-Haga	148	32.46 S	28.14 E
Hagal	88	40.23 N	127.15 E
HaGalil (Galilee) •[1]	122	32.54 N	35.20 E
Hagaman	200	42.59 N	74.09 W
Hagan	182	32.09 N	81.56 W
Hagari ≃	112	15.45 N	76.56 E
Hagar Shores	206	42.13 N	86.22 W
Hagarstown	209	38.57 N	89.10 W
Hage	48	53.36 N	7.17 E
Hagelberg ∧[2]	50	52.08 N	12.32 E
Hagemeister Island I	170	58.40 N	161.00 W
Hagen, B.R.D.	48	52.34 N	9.26 E
Hagen, B.R.D.	48	52.12 N	7.59 E
Hagen, B.R.D.	52	51.22 N	7.28 E
Hagenbrunn	254b	48.20 N	16.25 E
Hagen-Gebirge ∧∧	58	47.32 N	13.07 E
Hagenow	50	53.26 N	11.11 E
Hagensborg	172	52.23 N	126.33 W
Hagenwerder	50	51.04 N	14.58 E
Hagerman, Idaho, U.S.	192	42.49 N	114.54 W
Hagerman, N. Mex., U.S.	186	33.07 N	104.20 W
Hagerman Corners	265b	43.50 N	79.18 W
Hagerstown, Ind., U.S.	208	39.55 N	85.10 W
Hagerstown, Md., U.S.	178	39.39 N	77.43 W
Hagersville	202	42.58 N	80.03 W
Hagetmau	32	43.40 N	0.35 W
Hagfors	40	60.02 N	13.42 E
Haggen ◎	40	60.06 N	15.13 E
Haggetts Pond ◎	273	42.39 N	71.12 W
Haggin, Mount ∧	192	46.05 N	113.05 W
Hagi	86	34.24 N	131.25 E
Ha-giang	100	22.50 N	104.59 E
Hagitani	260	34.54 N	135.35 E
Hagiwara	84	35.52 N	137.12 E
Hagley	44	52.26 N	2.08 W
Hagondange	52	49.15 N	6.10 E
HaGosherim	122	33.13 N	35.37 E
Hags Head ≻	28	52.57 N	9.30 W
Hague, Sask., Can.	174	52.30 N	106.25 W
Hague, N. Dak., U.S.	188	46.02 N	99.59 W
Hague, Cap de la ≻	32	49.43 N	1.57 W
Haguenau	52	48.49 N	7.47 E
Hagues Peak ∧	190	40.29 N	105.38 W
Hahaia	147a	11.33 S	43.17 E
Hahajima-rettō II	14	26.37 N	142.10 E
Hāhipur	262b	22.47 N	88.10 E
Hahira	182	30.57 N	83.22 W
Hahlen	48	52.18 N	8.50 E
Hahn	52	50.31 N	7.53 E
Hahnenberg	253	51.12 N	7.24 E
Hahnenkamm ∧	58	47.25 N	12.22 E
Hahnenklee-Bockswiese	48	51.51 N	10.20 E
Hahnerberg •[8]	253	51.13 N	7.09 E
Hahnstätten	52	50.18 N	8.04 E
Hahntown	269b	40.19 N	79.44 W
Haho ≃	140	6.17 N	1.23 E
Hahyŏn-ni	88	38.33 N	127.57 E
Haian	90	32.34 N	120.28 E
Haianshan ∧∧	90	22.40 N	114.20 E
Haian Shanmo ∧∧	90	23.25 N	121.25 E
Haiba	96	32.04 N	120.38 E
Haibara, Nihon	84	34.32 N	135.57 E
Haibara, Nihon	84	34.44 N	138.13 E
Haibatpur	262a	28.37 N	77.26 E
Haibei	79	47.39 N	126.51 E
Haicheng, Zhg.	90	24.25 N	117.51 E
Haicheng, Zhg.	94	40.52 N	122.45 E
Haichenghe ≃	94	40.56 N	122.21 E
Haidargarh	114	26.37 N	81.22 E
Haidārpur •[8]	262a	28.43 N	77.09 E
Haiderabad → Hyderābād, Bhārat	112	17.23 N	78.29 E
Haiderabad → Hyderābād, Pāk.	110	25.22 N	68.22 E
Haidian	95	39.59 N	116.18 E
Haïdra	36	35.34 N	8.27 E
Haidun	90	29.36 N	121.49 E
Hai-duong	100	20.56 N	106.19 E
Haifa → Ḥefa	122	32.50 N	35.00 E
Haifa, Bay of → Ḥefa, Mifraẓ C	122	32.52 N	36.03 E
Haifeng	90	22.59 N	115.21 E
Haifengzheng	96	31.53 N	121.46 E
Haifuzhen	96	31.59 N	121.42 E
Haig	152	31.01 S	126.05 E
Haig, Mount ∧	172	49.17 N	114.29 W
Haiger	52	50.44 N	8.13 E
Haigerloch	54	48.22 N	8.48 E
Haigh	252	53.35 N	2.36 W
Haigler	188	40.01 N	101.56 W
Haihezhen	90	33.44 N	120.02 E
Haijima	258	35.42 N	139.21 E
Haik, Lake ◎	134	11.19 N	39.41 E
Haikang (Leizhou)	92	20.56 N	110.04 E
Haikou, Zhg.	90	28.20 N	120.06 E
Haikou, Zhg.	90	25.43 N	119.28 E
Haikou, Zhg.	90	29.04 N	117.46 E
Haikou, Zhg.	92	20.06 N	110.21 E
Haiku	219a	20.55 N	156.20 W
Ḥā'il	118	27.33 N	41.42 E
Hailaer	79	49.12 N	119.42 E
Hailaerhe ≃	80	49.35 N	117.55 E
Hailākāndi	110	24.41 N	92.34 E
Hailar → Hailaer	79	49.12 N	119.42 E
Hailasen	79	46.13 N	121.00 E
Hailesboro	202	44.18 N	75.27 W
Hailey, Eng., U.K.	250	51.46 N	0.01 W
Hailey, Idaho, U.S.	192	43.31 N	114.19 W
Haileybury	180	47.27 N	79.38 W
Hailin	79	44.35 N	129.22 E
Haillicourt	46	50.28 N	2.35 E
Hailsham	44	50.52 N	0.16 E
Hailun	79	47.28 N	126.58 E
Hailuoto	26	65.00 N	24.43 E
Hailuoto I	26	65.02 N	24.42 E
Haiman Tepesi ∧[2]	257b	41.12 N	29.15 E
Haimen, Zhg.	90	28.41 N	121.27 E
Haimen, Zhg.	90	23.14 N	116.38 E
Haimen, Zhg.	96	31.55 N	121.10 E
Haimenwan C	90	23.09 N	116.34 E
Haimi	165d	24.15 N	123.52 E
Haimiao	88	37.13 N	119.51 E
Haiming	54	47.15 N	10.53 E
Haina	52	51.02 N	8.58 E
Hainan → Hainandao I	100	19.00 N	109.30 E
Hainandao I	100	19.00 N	109.30 E
Hainault •[8]	250	51.36 N	0.06 E
Hainaut □[4]	46	50.30 N	3.50 E
Hainburg an der Donau	30	48.09 N	16.57 E
Hainchen	52	50.51 N	8.12 E
Haines, Alaska, U.S.	170	59.15 N	135.25 W
Haines, Oreg., U.S.	192	44.55 N	117.56 W
Haines City	210	28.07 N	81.37 W
Haines Falls	200	42.12 N	74.06 W
Haines Junction	170	60.45 N	137.30 W
Hainesport	198	39.59 N	74.50 W
Hainesville	268	42.21 N	88.04 W
Hainewalde	50	50.54 N	14.41 E
Hainfeld	30	48.02 N	15.46 E
Hainich ∧∧	50	51.05 N	10.27 E
Hainichen	50	50.58 N	13.07 E
Haining	96	30.25 N	120.32 E
Hainleite ∧∧	50	51.20 N	10.48 E
Hainsberg	50	50.59 N	13.38 E
Hainzenberg	58	47.13 N	11.54 E
Hai-phong	100	20.52 N	106.41 E
Haiqiao	96	31.47 N	121.19 E
Haiqing	79	47.53 N	134.40 E
Haitandao I	90	25.33 N	119.48 E
Haitangxi	97	29.33 N	106.35 E
Haitanxia ⋓	90	25.27 N	119.38 E
Haiti □[1]	220		
	228	19.00 N	72.25 W
Haitou, Zhg.	88	35.00 N	119.12 E
Haitou, Zhg.	100	19.34 N	108.58 E
Haitouji	88	35.23 N	115.19 E
Haitun	92	38.50 N	96.41 E
Haiwee Reservoir ◎[1]	194	36.10 N	117.57 W
Haiyan, Zhg.	92	36.54 N	101.12 E
Haiyan, Zhg.	96	30.31 N	120.57 E
Haiyang (Dongcun)	88	36.46 N	121.10 E
Haiyangdao I	88	39.02 N	123.14 E
Haiyingzi	88	41.22 N	115.05 E
Haiyuan	92	36.32 N	105.52 E
Haizhou	90	22.40 N	113.10 E
Haizhoumiao	94	42.00 N	121.39 E
Haizhouyingzi	94	42.07 N	121.46 E
Ḥajar, Tall al- ∧[2]	122	33.21 N	37.03 E
Ḥajar Banga	130	11.30 N	23.00 E
Hajdú-Bihar □[6]	30	47.25 N	21.30 E
Hajdúböszörmény	30	47.41 N	21.30 E
Hajdúnánás	30	47.51 N	21.26 E
Hajdúszoboszló	30	47.27 N	21.24 E
Hajiadian	88	41.32 N	117.10 E
Hājīganj	116	23.15 N	90.50 E
Hajiki-saki ≻	82	38.19 N	138.31 E
Hājīpur, Bhārat	114	25.41 N	85.13 E
Hājīpur, Bhārat	116	22.49 N	87.38 E
Hajipur, Bhārat	262b	22.57 N	88.19 E
Ḥājj, Wādī al- ∨	132	30.03 N	32.45 E
Hajnówka	30	52.45 N	23.36 E
Ḥajūl, Wādī ∨	132	29.42 N	32.22 E
Haka	100	22.39 N	93.37 E
Hakachi-zaki ≻	84	34.41 N	138.45 E
HaKarmel, Har (Mount Carmel) ∧	122	32.44 N	35.02 E
Hakata	86	34.07 N	132.57 E
Hakata-jima I	86	34.13 N	133.05 E
Hakataramea ≃	162	44.44 S	170.29 E
Hakendover	52	50.48 N	4.59 E
Haki	86	33.20 N	130.50 E
Hakkâri	118	37.34 N	43.45 E
Hakken-san ∧	82	34.10 N	135.54 E
Hakkōda-san ∧	82	40.40 N	140.53 E
Hak Kok Tau ≻	261d	22.16 N	114.15 E
Hako-dake ∧	82a	44.40 N	142.25 E
Hakodate	82a	41.45 N	140.43 E
Hakone	84	35.12 N	139.06 E
Hakoneno-seki ⊥	84	35.10 N	139.02 E
Hakone-tōge)(	84	35.11 N	139.01 E
Hakone-yama ∧	84	35.14 N	139.02 E
Håksberg	40	60.11 N	15.12 E
Hakskeenpan ◎	148	26.48 S	20.12 E
Hakuba	84	36.42 N	137.52 E
Hakui	84	36.53 N	136.47 E
Hakupu	164v	19.06 S	169.50 W
Hakusan	84	34.38 N	136.21 E
Haku-san ∧	84	36.09 N	136.46 E
Haku-san-kokuritsu-kōen ♠	84	36.12 N	136.47 E
Hakushū	84	35.48 N	138.20 E
Hakuta	86	35.21 N	133.17 E
Hakuta ≃	86	35.26 N	133.15 E
Hāla	110	25.49 N	68.25 E
Halaaobao	92	42.11 N	107.20 E
Ḥalab (Aleppo)	120	36.12 N	37.10 E
Ḥalab □[8]	120	36.00 N	37.00 E
Ḥalabjah	118	35.10 N	45.59 E
Halachó	222	20.29 N	90.05 W
Halaerjige	94	42.24 N	122.11 E
Halagetu	94	42.34 N	122.40 E
Halagigie Point ≻	164v	19.03 S	169.57 W
Halahai	79	44.39 N	125.07 E
Halahu (Heihai) ◎	92	38.15 N	97.40 E
Halahushao	94	42.11 N	121.44 E
Ḥalā'ib	130	22.13 N	36.38 E
Halalii Lake ◎	219b	21.52 N	160.11 W
Halamutai	76	46.10 N	84.52 E
Halasa	130	14.26 N	30.39 E
Halas-patak ≃	254c	47.24 N	19.20 E
Halasu	79	48.09 N	122.25 E
Halataojie	94	42.30 N	122.06 E
Halatiekeshan ∧∧	75	40.30 N	77.05 E
Halaula	219d	20.14 N	155.46 W
Hålaveden ∧∧[2]	26	58.05 N	14.45 E
Halawa, Cape ≻	219a	21.10 N	156.43 W
Halawa Bay C	219a	21.10 N	156.44 W
Halawa Heights	219c	21.23 N	157.55 W
Halawotelake	110	37.17 N	90.20 E
Ḥalbā	120	34.33 N	36.05 E
Halbach •[8]	253	51.12 N	7.12 E
Halbau → Iłowa	30	51.30 N	15.12 E
Halbe	50	52.06 N	13.42 E
Halberstadt	50	51.54 N	11.02 E
Halbert, Lake ◎[1]	212	32.04 N	96.25 W
Halberton	44	50.55 N	3.25 W
Halbrite	174	49.20 N	103.32 W
Ḥalbūn	122	33.40 N	36.15 E
Halbury	158b	34.05 S	138.31 E
Halcombe	162	40.09 S	175.30 E
Halcon, Mount ∧	106	13.16 N	121.00 E
Halcottsville	200	42.12 N	74.36 W
Haldeman	208	38.15 N	83.19 W
Halden	26	59.09 N	11.23 E
Halden •[8]	253	51.23 N	7.31 E
Haldensleben	50	52.18 N	11.26 E
Haldern	48	51.46 N	6.27 E
Haldi ≃	116	22.01 N	88.03 E
Haldībāri	114	26.20 N	88.46 E
Haldībunia	116	22.26 N	89.38 E
Haldimand □[6]	202	42.57 N	79.50 W
Haldwāni	114	29.13 N	79.31 E
Hale, Eng., U.K.	252	53.20 N	2.48 W
Hale, Eng., U.K.	252	53.23 N	2.21 W
Hale, Mo., U.S.	184	39.36 N	93.20 W
Hale ≃	152	24.56 S	135.53 E
Haleakala Crater •[6]	219a	20.43 N	156.13 W
Haleakala National Park ♠	219a	20.44 N	156.13 W
Haleb → Ḥalab	120	36.12 N	37.10 E
Halebarns	252	53.22 N	2.19 W
Haleb Island I	134	12.55 N	42.59 E
Hale Center	186	34.04 N	101.51 W
Hale Creek ≃	272	37.23 N	122.06 W
Haledon	266	40.56 N	74.11 W
Haledon Reservoir ◎[1]	266	40.59 N	74.12 W
Hale Eddy	200	42.00 N	75.23 W
Haleiwa	219c	21.35 N	158.07 W
Halekii-Pihana Heiaus State Monument ⊥	219a	20.54 N	156.29 W
Halenkov	30	49.19 N	18.08 E
Hales Corners	206	42.55 N	88.03 W
Halesite	197	40.52 N	73.25 W
Halesowen	44	52.26 N	2.05 W
Hale Street	250	51.13 N	0.24 E
Halesworth	44	52.21 N	1.30 E
Halethorpe	274b	39.15 N	76.41 W
Halewood	252	53.22 N	2.49 W
Haleyville	184	34.14 N	87.37 W
Half Assini	140	5.03 N	2.53 W
Ḥalfāyah, Naqb al- (Halfaya Pass))(	130	31.30 N	25.11 E
Halfaya Pass → Ḥalfāyah, Naqb al-)(	130	31.30 N	25.11 E
Half Day	268	42.12 N	87.56 W
Halfeti	120	37.15 N	37.52 E
Half Hollow Hills	266	40.48 N	73.21 W
Halfing	58	47.57 N	12.16 E
Halfmoon Bay, B.C., Can.	172	49.31 N	123.54 W
Half-Moon Bay, N.Z.	162	46.54 S	168.08 E
Half Moon Bay, Calif., U.S.	216	37.28 N	122.26 W
Halfmoon Bay C, Austl.	264b	37.58 S	145.00 E
Half Moon Bay C, Calif., U.S.	272	37.29 N	122.28 W
Half Moon Bay Airport ⊠	272	37.31 N	122.30 W
Half Moon Bay Beaches ♠	272	37.29 N	122.27 W
Halfway, Md., U.S.	178	39.37 N	77.46 W
Halfway, Oreg., U.S.	192	44.53 N	117.07 W
Halfway Lake ◎	174	55.03 N	98.24 W
Halgån ≃	40	60.16 N	13.27 E
Ḥalḥūl	122	31.35 N	35.07 E
Ḥalī ▾[4]	134	18.42 N	41.20 E
Haliburton	202	45.03 N	78.03 W
Haliburton □[6]	202	44.10 N	78.30 W
Haliburton Lake ◎	202	45.12 N	78.24 W
Halibut Point ≻	273	42.42 N	70.38 W
Haliç C	257b	41.02 N	28.58 E
Halicarnassus ⊥	120	37.03 N	27.23 E
Halicz ∧	68	49.05 N	22.48 E
Halifax, Austl.	156	18.35 S	146.18 E
Halifax, N.S., Can.	176	44.39 N	63.36 W
Halifax, Eng., U.K.	42		
	252	53.44 N	1.52 W
Halifax, Mass., U.S.	197	41.59 N	70.52 W
Halifax, N.C., U.S.	182	36.20 N	77.35 W
Halifax, Pa., U.S.	198	40.28 N	76.56 W
Halifax, Va., U.S.	182	36.46 N	78.56 W
Halifax Bay C	156	18.50 S	146.30 E
Halifax Citadel National Historic Park ♠	176	44.40 N	63.36 W
Halifax Harbour C	176	44.35 N	63.31 W
Haliimaile	219a	20.52 N	156.20 W
Halīl ≃	118	27.28 N	58.44 E
Halimatazi	94	42.37 N	122.35 E
Halimiye	120	36.40 N	32.45 E
Halim Perdanakusuma Airfield ▪	259e	6.16 S	106.54 E
Halimun, Gunung ∧	105a	6.42 S	106.26 E
Halin	134	9.08 N	48.47 E
Halingen	253	51.27 N	7.44 E
Hālisahar	116	22.56 N	88.25 E
Haliyāl	112	15.20 N	74.46 E
Haljala	66	59.26 N	26.16 E
Halkalı	257b	41.02 N	28.47 E
Halkett, Cape ≻	170	70.49 N	152.12 W
Halkirk	28	58.30 N	3.30 W
Halkyn	252	53.14 N	3.11 W
Halkyn Mountain ∧	252	53.14 N	3.13 W
Hall, Austl.	161b	35.10 S	149.04 E
Hall, Ind., U.S.	208	39.33 N	86.32 W
Hall, N.Y., U.S.	200	42.48 N	77.04 W
Hällabrottet	40	59.07 N	15.12 E
Hallam	264b	38.01 S	145.06 E
Hallam Peak ∧	172	52.11 N	118.46 W
Halland □[9]	26	57.00 N	12.40 E
Hallandale	210	25.60 N	80.09 W
Hallandsås ∧∧[2]	26	56.23 N	13.00 E
Hallands Län □[6]	26	56.45 N	13.00 E
Hallands Väderö I	26	56.26 N	12.33 E
Halla-san ∧	80	33.22 N	126.32 E
Hallau	54	47.42 N	8.27 E
Hällberga	40	59.19 N	16.36 E
Hällbybrunn	40	59.24 N	16.25 E
Halle, Bel.	46	50.44 N	4.13 E
Halle, B.R.D.	48	52.04 N	8.22 E
Halle, B.R.D.	48	51.59 N	9.33 E
Halle, D.D.R.	50	51.29 N	11.58 E
Halle □[5]	50	51.30 N	11.45 E
Halleberg ∧[2]	26	58.23 N	12.27 E
Hällefors	40	59.47 N	14.30 E
Hälleforsnäs	40	59.10 N	16.30 E
Hallein	58	47.41 N	13.06 E
Hällekis	26	58.38 N	13.25 E
Hallen	26	63.11 N	14.05 E
Hallenberg	52	51.06 N	8.37 E
Hallencourt	46	49.59 N	1.53 E
Hällestad	40	58.44 N	15.34 E
Hallett, Cape ≻	9	72.19 S	170.18 E
Hallettsville	212	29.27 N	96.56 W
Halliday	188	47.21 N	102.20 W
Halligen II	30	54.35 N	8.35 E
Halling	250	51.21 N	0.27 E
Hallingdalselvi ≃	26	60.24 N	9.35 E
Hällingsåfallet ⱶ	26	64.20 N	14.20 E
Hall Island I	170	60.40 N	173.05 W
Hall Islands II	14	8.37 N	152.00 E
Halliste ≃	66	58.31 N	25.03 E
Hall Lake ◎	166	68.41 N	82.17 W
Hall Meadow Brook Reservoir ◎[1]	197	41.52 N	73.10 W
Hall Mountain ∧	192	48.49 N	117.15 W
Hällnäs	26	64.19 N	19.38 E
Hallock	188	48.47 N	96.57 W
Hallowell	178	44.17 N	69.48 W
Hall Peninsula ≻[1]	166	63.30 N	66.00 W
Halls	184	35.53 N	89.24 W
Halls Bayou ≃	212	29.12 N	95.07 W
Hallsberg	40	59.04 N	15.07 E
Halls Brook ≃	273	42.00 N	70.43 W
Halls Creek	152	18.16 S	127.46 E
Halls Creek ≃	190	37.18 N	110.45 W
Hållsfjärden C[2]	40	59.08 N	17.40 E
Halls Lake ◎	202	45.07 N	78.45 W
Halls Stream ≃	196	45.01 N	71.30 W
Hållsta	40	59.18 N	16.27 E
Hallstadt	52	49.55 N	10.52 E
Hallstahammar	40	59.37 N	16.13 E
Hallstatt	58	47.33 N	13.39 E
Hallstätter See ◎	58	47.35 N	13.39 E
Hallstavik	40	60.03 N	18.36 E
Hallstead	200	41.58 N	75.45 W
Hallsville, Mo., U.S.	209	39.07 N	92.13 W
Hallsville, Tex., U.S.	212	32.30 N	94.34 W
Halluin	46	50.47 N	3.08 E
Hallwiler See ◎	54	47.18 N	8.13 E
Hallwood	198	37.53 N	75.35 W
Halma	52	50.05 N	5.08 E
Halmahera I	98	1.00 N	128.00 E
Halmahera, Laut (Halmahera Sea) ▾[2]	98	1.00 S	129.00 E
Halmstad	26	56.39 N	12.50 E
Hals	26	57.00 N	10.19 E
Halsafjorden C[2]	26	63.03 N	8.11 E
Halsall	252	53.35 N	2.57 W
Halsbrücke	50	50.57 N	13.21 E
Halsey, Nebr., U.S.	188	41.54 N	100.16 W
Halsey, Oreg., U.S.	192	44.23 N	123.07 W
Halsey Harbor C	106	11.45 N	119.56 E
Halsey Valley	200	42.08 N	76.27 W
Hälsingborg → Helsingborg	41	56.03 N	12.42 E
Hälsingland □[9]	26	61.30 N	17.00 E
Halstad	188	47.21 N	96.50 W
Halstead, Eng., U.K.	44	51.57 N	0.38 E
Halstead, Eng., U.K.	250	51.20 N	0.08 E
Halstead, Kans., U.S.	188	38.00 N	97.30 W
Halstenbek	48	53.38 N	9.50 E
Halsteren	48	51.32 N	4.16 E
Halstow Marshes ≡	250	51.29 N	0.33 E
Haltern	48	51.46 N	7.10 E
Haltiatunturi ∧	24	69.18 N	21.16 E
Haltom City	212	32.48 N	97.16 W
Halton	252	53.20 N	2.42 W
Halton □[6]	202	43.30 N	79.53 W
Halton □[8]	252	53.20 N	2.44 W
Haltwhistle	42	54.58 N	2.27 W
Halura, Pulau I	105b	10.19 S	120.07 E
Halūzonī, Wādī al- ∨	263c	30.05 N	31.24 E
Halvarsgårdarna	40	60.24 N	15.23 E
Halvarsnoren ◎	40	59.35 N	14.36 E
Halver	52	51.11 N	7.30 E
Halvorson, Mount ∧	172	53.15 N	120.33 W
Halwell	44	50.22 N	3.43 W
Ham, Fr.	46	49.45 N	3.04 E
Ham, Tchad	136	10.00 N	15.41 E
Ham •[8]	250	51.26 N	0.19 W
Ham, Oued el ≃	34	35.42 N	4.52 E
Hamaca ≃	226	14.14 N	85.07 W
Ḥamad	130	15.19 N	33.43 E
Hamada	86	34.53 N	132.05 E
Hamada •[1]	138	27.30 N	9.00 W
Hamadān	118	34.48 N	48.30 E
Hamadān □[8]	118	35.00 N	48.40 E
Ḥamāh	120	35.08 N	36.45 E
Ḥamāh □[8]	120	35.10 N	37.00 E
Hamahika-jima I	164m	26.19 N	127.57 E
Hamakeza	79	47.05 N	120.52 E
Hamakita	84	34.48 N	137.47 E
Hamale	140	10.59 N	2.44 W
Hamam	120	39.30 N	35.24 E
Hamamatsu	84	34.42 N	137.44 E
Hamamözü	120	40.48 N	35.02 E
Haman	88	35.15 N	128.24 E
Hamanaka	82a	43.05 N	145.10 E
Hamana-ko ◎	84	34.45 N	137.34 E
Hamano	258	35.33 N	140.08 E
Hamaoka	84	34.39 N	138.08 E
Hamar	26	60.48 N	11.06 E
Hamasaka	86	35.37 N	134.27 E
Ḥamāṭah, Jabal ∧	130	24.12 N	35.00 E
Hamatang	88	40.12 N	124.20 E
Hama-tombetsu	82a	45.07 N	142.23 E
Hambach	52	49.04 N	7.02 E
Hambaek-san ∧	88	37.09 N	128.55 E
Hambantota	112	6.07 N	81.07 E
Hamberg	263d	26.11 S	27.53 E
Hambergen	48	53.18 N	8.49 E
Hamber Provincial Park ♠	172	52.25 N	117.40 W
Hamble	44	50.52 N	1.19 W
Hambledon	44	50.56 N	1.04 W
Hambleton Hills ∧∧[2]	42	54.16 N	1.12 W
Hambly Lake ◎	202	44.28 N	76.41 W
Hamborn •[8]	253	51.29 N	6.46 E
Hambourg → Hamburg	48	53.33 N	9.59 E
Hambridge National Park ♠	156	33.25 S	136.00 E
Hamburg, B.R.D.	48	53.33 N	9.59 E
Hamburg, S. Afr.	148	33.17 S	27.28 E
Hamburg, Ark., U.S.	184	33.14 N	91.48 W
Hamburg, Conn., U.S.	197	41.23 N	72.21 W
Hamburg, Ill., U.S.	209	39.14 N	90.43 W
Hamburg, Iowa, U.S.	188	40.36 N	95.39 W
Hamburg, Mich., U.S.	206	42.27 N	83.48 W
Hamburg, N.J., U.S.	200	41.09 N	74.35 W
Hamburg, N.Y., U.S.	200	42.43 N	78.50 W
Hamburg, Pa., U.S.	198	40.34 N	75.59 W
Hamburg □[3]	48	53.35 N	10.00 E
Hamburg Airport ⊠	274a	42.42 N	78.55 W
Hamburg Ditch ≡	198	36.31 N	76.33 W
Hamburger Hallig ≻[1]	41	54.36 N	8.49 E
Hamburg Mountains ∧∧	266	41.08 N	74.32 W
Hamburgo → Hamburg	48	53.33 N	9.59 E
Hamburgsund	26	58.33 N	11.16 E
Ḥamḍ, Wādī al- ∨	118	25.54 N	36.38 E
Ḥamḍah	134	19.02 N	43.36 E
Hamdallay Timbou	140	12.03 N	10.37 W
Hamdam Āb, Dasht-e ≚	118	34.45 N	61.30 E
Ḥamdānah ▾[4]	134	19.58 N	40.35 E
Hamden, Conn., U.S.	197	41.21 N	72.56 W
Hamden, N.Y., U.S.	200	42.12 N	75.00 W
Hamden, Ohio, U.S.	178	39.10 N	82.32 W
Hamdilaye	140	13.34 N	2.24 E
Häme •[1]	26	61.30 N	24.30 E
Hämeenkangas •[3]	26	61.45 N	22.40 E
Hämeenkylä	26	60.16 N	24.47 E
Hämeen lääni □[4]	26	61.30 N	24.30 E
Hämeenlinna	26	61.00 N	24.27 E
Hameiershan ∧∧	92	37.34 N	96.15 E
Hamel	158a	32.52 S	115.55 E
HaMelah, Yam → Dead Sea ◎	122	31.30 N	35.30 E
Hämelerwald	48	52.22 N	10.05 E
Hamelin Pool	152	26.26 S	114.11 E
Hamelin Pool C	152	26.15 S	114.05 E
Hameln	48	52.06 N	9.21 E
HaMerkaz □[5]	122	32.05 N	34.55 E
Hamer Koke	134	5.12 N	36.45 E
Hamero Hadad	134	7.34 N	42.18 E
Hamersleben	50	52.04 N	11.05 E
Hamersley Range ∧∧	152	21.53 S	116.46 E
Hamersville	208	38.55 N	83.59 W
Hames Creek ≃	216	35.53 N	120.50 W
Hamgyŏng Namdo □[4]	88	40.00 N	127.30 E
Hamgyŏng-pukdo □[4]	88	41.45 N	129.50 E
Hamgyŏng-sanmaek ∧∧	88	41.50 N	128.30 E
Ham House ⊥	250	51.27 N	0.19 W
Hamhŭng	88	39.54 N	127.32 E
Hami	92	42.47 N	93.32 E
Hamidiye	120	41.09 N	26.40 E
Hamiguitan, Mount ∧	106	6.44 N	126.11 E
Hamilton, Austl.	156	37.45 S	142.02 E
Hamilton, Ber.	230a	32.17 N	64.46 W
Hamilton, Ont., Can.	202	43.15 N	79.51 W
Hamilton, N.Z.	162	37.47 S	175.17 E
Hamilton, Scot., U.K.	42	55.47 N	4.03 W
Hamilton, Ala., U.S.	184	34.09 N	88.06 W
Hamilton, Alaska, U.S.	170	62.54 N	163.53 W
Hamilton, Ga., U.S.	182	32.45 N	84.53 W
Hamilton, Ill., U.S.	180	40.24 N	91.21 W
Hamilton, Ind., U.S.	206	41.32 N	84.55 W
Hamilton, Kans., U.S.	188	37.59 N	96.10 W
Hamilton, Mass., U.S.	197	42.37 N	70.52 W
Hamilton, Mich., U.S.	206	42.41 N	86.00 W
Hamilton, Mo., U.S.	184	39.45 N	94.01 W
Hamilton, Mont., U.S.	192	46.15 N	114.09 W
Hamilton, N.C., U.S.	182	35.57 N	77.12 W
Hamilton, N.Y., U.S.	200	42.50 N	75.33 W
Hamilton, Ohio, U.S.	208	39.26 N	84.30 W
Hamilton, R.I., U.S.	197	41.33 N	71.26 W
Hamilton, Tex., U.S.	186	31.42 N	98.07 W
Hamilton, Wash., U.S.	214	48.31 N	121.59 W
Hamilton □[6], Ind., U.S.	208	40.03 N	86.01 W
Hamilton □[6], N.Y., U.S.	200	43.24 N	74.25 W
Hamilton □[6], Ohio, U.S.	208	39.06 N	84.31 W
Hamilton •[8]	274b	39.21 N	76.33 W
Hamilton ≃	156	23.30 S	139.47 E
Hamilton, Lake ◎	210	28.03 N	81.39 W
Hamilton, Lake ◎[1]	184	34.30 N	93.05 W
Hamilton, Mount ∧, Alaska, U.S.	170	61.10 N	159.46 W
Hamilton, Mount ∧, Calif., U.S.	216	37.21 N	121.38 W
Hamilton, Mount ∧, Nev., U.S.	194	39.14 N	115.32 W
Hamilton Acres	170	64.51 N	147.40 W
Hamilton Air Force Base ▪	272	38.03 N	122.31 W
Hamilton City	194	39.45 N	122.01 W
Hamilton Creek ≃	152	26.40 S	135.19 E
Hamilton Creek Indian Reserve •[4]	172	50.11 N	120.30 W
Hamilton Dome	190	43.46 N	108.34 W
Hamilton Harbour C	202	43.17 N	79.50 W
Hamilton Hill	158a	32.05 S	115.46 E
Hamilton Hotel	156	22.50 S	140.35 E
Hamilton Inlet C	166	54.00 N	57.30 W
Hamilton Lake ◎	206	41.33 N	84.55 W
Hamilton Mountain ∧	178	43.25 N	74.22 W
Hamilton Park, Ind., U.S.	206	40.17 N	85.19 W
Hamilton Park, Pa., U.S.	198	40.02 N	76.20 W
Hamilton Sound ⋓	176	49.30 N	54.30 W
Hamilton Square	275	40.14 N	74.40 W
Ḥamīm, Wādī al- ∨	136	30.10 N	21.32 E
Hamina	26	60.34 N	27.12 E
Hamiota	174	50.11 N	100.36 W
Ḥamir, Wādī ∨	118	31.37 N	42.12 E
Hamīrpur, Bhārat	113	31.41 N	76.31 E
Hamīrpur, Bhārat	114	25.57 N	80.09 E
Hamīrpur □[5]	114	25.30 N	26.40 E
Hamjong-ni	88	38.59 N	125.17 E
Hamler	206	41.14 N	84.02 W
Hamlet, Ind., U.S.	206	41.23 N	86.35 W
Hamlet, N.C., U.S.	182	34.53 N	79.42 W
Hamlet, Ohio, U.S.	208	39.01 N	84.12 W
Hamlet, Mount ∧	170	68.47 N	165.57 W
Hamley Bridge	158b	34.21 S	138.41 E
Hamlin, N.Y., U.S.	200	43.18 N	77.55 W
Hamlin, Pa., U.S.	200	41.24 N	75.24 W
Hamlin, Tex., U.S.	186	32.53 N	100.08 W
Hamlin, W. Va., U.S.	178	38.17 N	82.06 W
Hamlin Beach State Park ♠	200	43.22 N	77.58 W
Hamlin Lake ◎	180	44.03 N	86.27 W
Hamlin Valley Wash ∨	190	38.53 N	114.01 W
Hamm, B.R.D.	48	51.43 N	7.10 E
Hamm, B.R.D.	48		
	253	51.41 N	7.49 E
Hamm •[8], B.R.D.	253	51.12 N	6.44 E
Hamm •[8], B.R.D.	253	51.23 N	7.03 E
Hamm •[8], B.R.D.	253	51.15 N	6.25 E
Ḥammād, Wādī ∨	132	29.45 N	32.24 E
Hamma Hamma ≃	214	47.33 N	123.03 W
Ḥammām at-Turkumān	120	36.32 N	39.03 E
Hammamet, Alg.	36	35.27 N	7.58 E
Hammamet, Tun.	138	36.24 N	10.37 E
Hammamet, Golfe de C	138	36.05 N	10.40 E
Hammami •[1]	138	23.03 N	11.30 W
Hammam Lif	138	36.44 N	10.20 E
Ḥammānā	122	33.49 N	35.44 E
Hammar	40	58.49 N	14.57 E
Ḥammār, Hawr al- ◎	118	30.50 N	47.10 E
Hammarby	40	60.33 N	16.34 E
Hammarn	40	59.45 N	14.30 E
Hammarö	40	59.20 N	13.31 E
Hammarön I	40	59.19 N	13.31 E
Hammarstrand	26	63.06 N	16.21 E
Hamme	46	51.06 N	4.08 E
Hamme ≃	48	53.10 N	8.44 E
Hammel	41	56.15 N	9.52 E
Hammelburg	52	50.07 N	9.53 E
Hamme-Mille	52	50.47 N	4.43 E
Hammerbrücke	50	50.26 N	12.25 E
Hammerdal	26	63.36 N	15.21 E
Hammerfest	24	70.40 N	23.42 E
Hammermühle → Kępice	30	54.15 N	16.52 E
Hämmern	253	51.08 N	7.21 E
Hammershus ⊥	26	55.16 N	14.45 E
Hammersley Inlet C	214	47.12 N	123.00 W
Hammersmith •[8]	44	51.30 N	0.14 W
Hammerstein → Czarne	30	53.42 N	16.57 E
Hammerum	41	56.08 N	9.04 E
Hamminkeln	48	51.44 N	6.35 E
Hammon	186	35.38 N	99.23 W
Hammonasset ≃	197	41.16 N	72.33 W
Hammond, Ind., U.S.	206	41.36 N	87.30 W
Hammond, La., U.S.	184	30.30 N	90.28 W
Hammond, N.Y., U.S.	202	44.27 N	75.42 W
Hammond, Oreg., U.S.	214	46.12 N	123.57 W
Hammond, Wis., U.S.	180	44.59 N	92.26 W
Hammond Island I, Austl.	154	10.35 S	142.13 E
Hammond Island I, Calif., U.S.	272	38.06 N	121.57 W
Hammond Pond Park ♠	273	42.19 N	71.11 W
Hammondsport	200	42.25 N	77.13 W
Hammondsville	204	40.33 N	80.43 W
Hammondville	264a	33.57 S	150.57 E
Hammonia	148	28.43 S	27.49 E
Hammonton	198	39.38 N	74.48 W
Hamningberg	24	70.31 N	30.37 E
Ham-Nord	196	45.54 N	71.39 W
Hamo	120	39.36 N	38.11 E
Hamoir	52	50.26 N	5.32 E
Hamont	52	51.15 N	5.33 E
HaMore, Giv'at ∧	122	32.37 N	35.21 E
Hamorton	275	39.52 N	75.39 W
Hamoyet, Jabal ∧	134	17.33 N	38.02 E
Hampden, Austl.	158b	34.09 S	139.03 E
Hampden, Newf., Can.	176	49.33 N	56.51 W
Hampden, N.Z.	162	45.19 S	170.49 E
Hampden, Maine, U.S.	178	44.45 N	68.50 W
Hampden, Mass., U.S.	197	42.04 N	72.25 W
Hampden, N. Dak., U.S.	188	48.32 N	98.40 W
Hampden □[6]	197	42.07 N	72.36 W
Hampetorp	40	59.09 N	15.40 E
Hampshire	206	42.06 N	88.32 W
Hampshire □[6], Eng., U.K.	44	51.05 N	1.15 W
Hampshire □[6], Mass., U.S.	197	42.19 N	72.38 W
Hampshire Downs ∧∧[1]	44	51.15 N	1.17 W
Hampshire Heights	269b	40.20 N	79.33 W
Hampstead, Qué., Can.	265a	45.29 N	73.38 W
Hampstead, N.C., U.S.	182	34.22 N	77.49 W
Hampstead •[8]	250	51.33 N	0.11 W
Hampstead Heath ♠	250	51.34 N	0.10 W
Hampton, Austl.	264b	37.56 S	145.00 E
Hampton, N.B., Can.	176	45.32 N	65.51 W
Hampton, Ont., Can.	202	43.58 N	78.45 W
Hampton, Ark., U.S.	184	33.32 N	92.28 W
Hampton, Conn., U.S.	197	41.47 N	72.03 W
Hampton, Fla., U.S.	182	29.52 N	82.07 W
Hampton, Ga., U.S.	182	33.23 N	84.17 W
Hampton, Iowa, U.S.	180	42.45 N	93.12 W
Hampton, Nebr., U.S.	188	40.53 N	97.53 W
Hampton, N.H., U.S.	178	42.56 N	70.50 W
Hampton, N.J., U.S.	200	40.42 N	74.58 W
Hampton, Pa., U.S.	198	39.56 N	77.04 W
Hampton, S.C., U.S.	182	32.52 N	81.07 W
Hampton, Va., U.S.	198	37.01 N	76.22 W
Hampton •[8]	250	51.25 N	0.22 W
Hampton Bays	197	40.53 N	72.31 W
Hampton Butte ∧	192	43.46 N	120.17 W
Hampton Court Palace ⊌	250	51.24 N	0.20 W
Hampton Harbour C	152	20.40 S	116.30 E
Hampton National Historic Site ⊥	274b	39.25 N	76.35 W
Hampton Park	264b	38.02 S	145.15 E
Hampton Roads ▾[3]	198	36.58 N	76.20 W
Hampton Roads Bridge-Tunnel •[5]	198	37.00 N	76.18 W
Hampton Tableland ∧∧[1]	152	32.10 S	126.10 E
Hamp'yŏng	88	35.05 N	126.30 E
Hamr	50	50.35 N	13.35 E
Hamra	26	61.39 N	15.00 E
Hamra, Ouadi ∨	136	12.52 N	21.15 E
Hamra, Saguia el ∨	138	27.15 N	13.21 W
Ḥamrah, Jabal al- ∧	122	29.39 N	34.47 E
Ḥamran, Har ∧	122	30.41 N	34.34 E
Hamra Nationalpark ♠	26	61.45 N	14.55 E
Ḥamrat ash-Shaykh	130	14.35 N	27.58 E
Hamrivier	148	28.08 S	19.18 E
Hams Bluff •[4]	231n	17.46 N	64.52 W
Hams Fork ≃	190	41.35 N	109.59 W
Ham-Sud	196	45.46 N	71.36 W
Ham-tan	100	10.40 N	107.46 E
Hamtramck	206	42.24 N	83.03 W
Hamur	74	39.36 N	42.59 E
Hamura	84	35.45 N	139.19 E
Hamyang	88	35.32 N	127.42 E
Ḥamzah, Jabal al- ∧[2]	132	30.14 N	31.38 E
Han	140	10.41 N	2.27 W
Han, Grottes de •[5]	52	50.08 N	5.15 E
Han, Nong ◎	100	17.12 N	104.11 E
Hana	219a	20.45 N	155.59 W
Hanábana ≃	230p	22.23 N	80.58 W
Hanahan	182	32.55 N	80.00 W
Hanailike	75	39.16 N	76.26 E
Ḥanak	118	25.33 N	36.56 E
Hanakaoo Point ≻	219a	20.55 N	156.42 W
Hanalei	219b	22.07 N	159.30 W
Hanalei Bay C	219b	22.13 N	159.31 W
Hanamaki	82	39.23 N	141.07 E
Hanamaulu	219b	21.59 N	159.22 W
Hanamenu, Baie C	164x	9.46 S	139.08 W
Hanam-ni	88	38.23 N	126.43 E
Hanang ∧	144	4.26 S	35.24 E
Hanapepe	219b	21.55 N	159.35 W
Hanapepe ≃	219b	21.54 N	159.36 W
Hanapepe Bay C	219b	21.54 N	159.35 W
Hānār Char	116	23.08 N	90.38 E
Hanataka-sen ∧	86	35.24 N	132.45 E
Hana Teio	164x	9.59 S	139.06 W
Hanatetena	164x	9.58 S	139.04 W
Hana Tuuna	164x	10.00 S	139.07 W
Hanau	52	50.08 N	8.55 E
Hanaui	164x	9.45 S	139.05 W
Hanawa, Nihon	82	40.11 N	140.47 E
Hanawa, Nihon	84	36.57 N	140.25 E
Hanawa, Nihon	258	35.13 N	139.53 E
Hanbury ≃	166	63.37 N	104.33 W
Hanceville, B.C., Can.	172	51.55 N	123.03 W
Hanceville, Ala., U.S.	184	34.04 N	86.46 W
Hanchang	97	30.26 N	103.43 E
Hancheng, Zhg.	92	35.29 N	110.25 E
Hancheng, Zhg.	95	39.39 N	118.02 E
Hanches	251	48.36 N	1.39 E
Hanchō	260	34.47 N	135.27 E
Han-ch'ŏn C	261b	37.33 N	127.02 E
Hanchuan	90	30.39 N	113.48 E
Hanchung → Hanzhong	92	32.59 N	107.11 E
Hancock, Md., U.S.	178	39.42 N	78.11 W
Hancock, Mich., U.S.	180	47.07 N	88.35 W
Hancock, Minn., U.S.	188	45.30 N	95.48 W
Hancock, N.Y., U.S.	200	41.57 N	75.17 W
Hancock, Wis., U.S.	180	44.08 N	89.31 W
Hancock □[6], Ind., U.S.	208	39.47 N	85.46 W
Hancock □[6], Ohio, U.S.	206	41.02 N	83.39 W
Hancock □[6], W. Va., U.S.	204	40.30 N	80.33 W
Hancock, Lake ◎	210	27.58 N	81.50 W
Hancock International Airport ⊠	200	43.07 N	76.07 W
Hancocks Bridge	198	39.31 N	75.28 W
Hancun	95	39.24 N	116.36 E
Handa, Nihon	84	34.53 N	136.56 E
Handa, Nihon	86	34.02 N	134.02 E
Handan	88	36.37 N	114.29 E
Handaokou	88	34.16 N	116.24 E
Handawor	113	34.24 N	74.17 E
Handen	40	59.10 N	18.08 E
Handeni	144	5.26 S	38.01 E
Handforth	252	53.21 N	2.13 W
Handig Point ≻	106	10.49 N	125.42 E
Handlová	30	48.44 N	18.46 E
Hando	134	10.39 N	51.08 E
Handöl	26	63.16 N	12.26 E
Handorf	48	51.59 N	7.41 E
Handsworth	174	49.48 N	103.00 W
Handub	130	19.14 N	37.16 E
Handzame	46	51.02 N	3.00 E
HaNegev •[1]	122	30.30 N	34.55 E
Haney	172	49.13 N	122.36 W
Hane-yama ∧	86	33.14 N	131.08 E
Hane-zaki ≻	86	33.22 N	134.02 E
Hanford	216	36.20 N	119.39 W
Han'gang	88	34.39 N	114.38 E
Han-gang ≃	88	37.45 N	126.11 E
Hangang, First Bridge •[5]	261b	37.32 N	126.56 E
Hangang, Second Bridge •[5]	261b	37.34 N	126.54 E
Hangang, Third Bridge •[5]	261b	37.32 N	127.00 E
Hanga Roa	164z	27.09 S	109.26 W
Hangatiki	162	38.15 S	175.10 E
Hangbu	90	28.53 N	118.49 E
Hangchow → Hangzhou	96	30.15 N	120.10 E
Hangchow Bay → Hangzhouwan C	90	30.20 N	121.00 E
Hang Hau Town	261d	22.19 N	114.16 E
Hanging Gardens ♠	262c	18.58 N	72.48 E
Hanging Rock State Park ♠	182	36.25 N	80.15 W
Hangingstone Hill ∧[2]	44	50.39 N	3.57 W
Hanging Woman Creek ≃	192	45.19 N	106.31 W
Hangjinhouqi	92	40.41 N	106.59 E
Hangjinqi	92	39.59 N	108.57 E
Hangklip, Kaap ≻	148	34.26 S	18.48 E
Hangkou	90	29.03 N	114.27 E
Hangö (Hanko)	26	59.50 N	22.57 E
Hang-Tcheou → Hangzhou	96	30.15 N	120.10 E
Hangtou	96	31.01 N	121.35 E
Hangtschou → Hangzhou	96	30.15 N	120.10 E
Hangu, Pāk.	113	33.32 N	71.04 E
Hangu, Zhg.	95	39.15 N	117.47 E
Hanguang	90	24.16 N	113.08 E
Hanguchang	97	29.32 N	106.21 E
Hangugang	95	39.15 N	116.56 E
Hangxian (Linping)	96	30.25 N	120.18 E
Hangyu	96	30.35 N	119.23 E
Hangzhou (Hangchow)	96	30.15 N	120.10 E
Hangzhouwan C	90	30.20 N	121.00 E
Hani	120	38.24 N	40.24 E
Hänigsen	48	52.29 N	10.05 E
Hanimadu I	112	6.45 N	73.09 E
Hanīn	134	15.50 N	48.19 E
Ḥanīsh, Jazā'ir II	134	13.45 N	42.45 E
Ḥanita	122	33.05 N	35.10 E
Hanjalipan	102	2.15 S	112.47 E
Hanjiagou	94	40.42 N	120.47 E
Hanjiang, Zhg.	90	25.30 N	119.06 E
Hanjiang, Zhg.	90	24.48 N	118.38 E
Hanjiang ≃	90	23.41 N	116.38 E
Hanjiapuzi	94	40.48 N	123.14 E
Hanjiashu	95	39.11 N	117.04 E
Hanjiawa	96	31.16 N	119.18 E
Hankamer	212	29.51 N	94.38 W
Hankasalmi	26	62.23 N	26.26 E

Symbols in the index entries represent the broad categories identified in the key at the right. Symbols with superior numbers (∧∧[2]) identify subcategories (see complete key on page *I* · 26).

Kartensymbole in dem Registerverzeichnis stellen die rechts in Schlüssel erklärten Kategorien dar. Symbole mit hochgestellten Ziffern (∧∧[2]) bezeichnen Unterabteilungen einer Kategorie (vgl. vollständiger Schlüssel auf Seite *I* · 26).

Los símbolos incluídos en el texto del índice representan las grandes categorias identificadas con la clave a la derecha. Los símbolos con numeros en su parte superior (∧∧[2]) identifican las subcategorías (véase la clave completa en la página *I* · 26).

Les symboles de l'index représentent les catégories indiquées dans la légende à droite. Les symboles suivis d'un indice (∧∧[2]) représentent des sous-catégories (voir légende complète à la page *I* · 26).

Os símbolos incluídos no texto do índice representam as grandes categorias identificadas com a chave à direita. Os símbolos com números em sua parte superior (∧∧[2]) identificam as subcategorias (veja-se a chave completa à página *I* · 26).

∧ Mountain	Berg	Montaña	Montagne	Montanha
∧∧ Mountains	Berge	Montañas	Montagnes	Montanhas
)(Pass	Pass	Paso	Col	Passo
∨ Valley, Canyon	Tal, Cañon	Valle, Cañón	Vallée, Canyon	Vale, Canhão
≚ Plain	Ebene	Llano	Plaine	Planície
≻ Cape	Kap	Cabo	Cap	Cabo
I Island	Insel	Isla	Île	Ilha
II Islands	Inseln	Islas	Îles	Ilhas
• Other Topographic Features	Andere Topographische Objekte	Otros Elementos Topográficos	Autres données topographiques	Outros Elementos Topográficos

ESPAÑOL — Nombre, Página, Lat.°′, Long.°′ W=Oeste
FRANÇAIS — Nom, Page, Lat.°′, Long.°′ W=Ouest
PORTUGUÊS — Nome, Página, Lat.°′, Long.°′ W=Oeste

≃ River	Fluss	Río	Rivière	Rio
⩧ Canal	Kanal	Canal	Canal	Canal
∟ Waterfall, Rapids	Wasserfall, Stromschnellen	Cascada, Rápidos	Chute d'eau, Rapides	Cascata, Rápidos
Ⴎ Strait	Meeresstrasse	Estrecho	Détroit	Estreito
C Bay, Gulf	Bucht, Golf	Bahía, Golfo	Baie, Golfe	Baía, Golfo
⊜ Lake, Lakes	See, Seen	Lago, Lagos	Lac, Lacs	Lago, Lagos
☳ Swamp	Sumpf	Pantano	Marais	Pântano
⛉ Ice Features, Glacier	Eis- und Gletscherformen	Accidentes Glaciales	Formes glaciaires	Acidentes Glaciares
⍑ Other Hydrographic Features	Andere Hydrographische Objekte	Otros Elementos Hidrográficos	Autres données hydrographiques	Outros Elementos Hidrográficos
✧ Submarine Features	Untermeerische Objekte	Accidentes Submarinos	Formes de relief sous-marin	Acidentes Submarinos
□ Political Unit	Politische Einheit	Unidad Politica	Entité politique	Unidade Política
ɤ Cultural Institution	Kulturelle Institution	Institución Cultural	Institution culturelle	Instituição Cultural
⊥ Historical Site	Historische Stätte	Sitio Histórico	Site historique	Sitio Histórico
♠ Recreational Site	Erholungs- und Ferienort	Sitio de Recreo	Centre de loisirs	Sítio de Lazer
⊠ Airport	Flughafen	Aeropuerto	Aéroport	Aeroporto
■ Military Installation	Militäranlage	Instalación Militar	Installation militaire	Instalação Militar
◆ Miscellaneous	Verschiedenes	Misceláneo	Divers	Miscelânea

Symbols in the index entries represent the broad categories identified in the key at the right. Symbols with superior numbers ([2]) identify subcategories (see complete key on page I · 26).

Kartensymbole in dem Registerverzeichnis stellen die rechts in Schlüssel erklärten Kategorien dar. Symbole mit hochgestellten Ziffern ([2]) bezeichnen Unterabteilungen einer Kategorie (vgl. vollständiger Schlüssel auf Seite I · 26).

Los símbolos incluidos en el texto del índice representan las grandes categorías identificadas con la clave a la derecha. Los símbolos con numeros en su parte superior ([2]) identifican las subcategorías (véase la clave completa en la página I · 26).

Les symboles de l'index représentent les catégories indiquées dans la légende à droite. Les symboles suivis d'un indice ([2]) représentent des sous-catégories (voir légende complète à la page I · 26).

Os símbolos incluídos no texto do índice representam as grandes categorias identificadas com a chave à direita. Os símbolos com números em sua parte superior ([2]) identificam as subcategorias (veja-se a chave completa à página I · 26).

English	Deutsch	Español	Français	Português
Mountain	Berg	Montaña	Montagne	Montanha
Mountains	Berge	Montañas	Montagnes	Montanhas
Pass	Pass	Paso	Col	Passo
Valley, Canyon	Tal, Cañon	Valle, Cañón	Vallée, Canyon	Vale, Canhão
Plain	Ebene	Llano	Plaine	Planície
Cape	Kap	Cabo	Cap	Cabo
Island	Insel	Isla	Île	Ilha
Islands	Inseln	Islas	Îles	Ilhas
Other Topographic Features	Andere Topographische Objekte	Otros Elementos Topográficos	Autres données topographiques	Outros Elementos Topográficos

ESPAÑOL

Nombre · Página · Lat.°′ · Long.°′ W=Oeste

Hengdaochuan 88 41.15 N 125.31 E
Hengdaohe 79 43.18 N 127.18 E
Hengdaohezi, Zhg. 79 43.13 N 126.44 E
Hengdaohezi, Zhg. 94 42.07 N 123.49 E
Hengelo 48 52.15 N 6.45 E
Hengfan 96 30.20 N 119.45 E
Hengfeng 90 28.24 N 117.34 E
Henggang 90 29.32 N 115.27 E
Henggong 96 31.52 N 120.03 E
Henggouzi 79 43.12 N 124.47 E
Henghutou 94 42.05 N 124.00 E
Hengjie 96 31.13 N 119.30 E
Hengjing 96 31.11 N 120.32 E
Hengjinghong 96 30.34 N 120.59 E
Hengli 90 23.12 N 114.37 E
Henglin 96 31.42 N 120.06 E
Henglu 88 41.26 N 126.04 E
Henglutou 96 30.19 N 119.19 E
Hengmian 96 31.09 N 121.38 E
Hengoed 44 51.39 N 3.10 W
Hengsen 253 51.29 N 7.38 E
Hengsha ❙ 96 31.20 N 121.50 E
Hengshan, Zhg. 90 27.15 N 112.51 E
Hengshan, Zhg. 92 37.56 N 108.53 E
Hengshan, Zhg. 96 31.01 N 120.32 E
Hengshan ∧ 90 27.16 N 112.35 E
Hengshan ∧∧ 92 39.30 N 113.45 E
Hengshanchang 97 30.33 N 105.24 E
Hengshanqiao 96 31.46 N 120.07 E
Hengshanxia 96 30.18 N 118.44 E
Hengshi, Zhg. 90 26.05 N 114.38 E
Hengshi, Zhg. 90 23.52 N 113.15 E
Hengshitan 90 29.32 N 114.41 E
Hengshui 88 37.43 N 115.40 E
Hengshui ≃ 97 28.57 N 105.22 E
Hengsteysee ⊜[1] 253 51.25 N 7.28 E
Hengtangshi 96 31.41 N 121.02 E
Hengtianchi 97 29.07 N 105.01 E
Hengtianxi 97 29.05 N 105.03 E
Hengxi, Zhg. 90 29.42 N 121.35 E
Hengxi, Zhg. 90 28.46 N 120.29 E
Hengxi, Zhg. 96 31.43 N 118.46 E
Hengxian 92 22.42 N 109.13 E
Hengxiang 96 32.12 N 120.15 E
Hengxikou 90 29.26 N 121.26 E
Hengyan 90 29.25 N 118.34 E
Hengyang 92 26.51 N 112.30 E
Hénin-Beaumont 46 50.25 N 2.56 E
Henley Beach 158b 34.55 S 138.30 E
Henley-in-Arden 44 52.17 N 1.46 W
Henley-on-Thames 44 51.32 N 0.56 W
Henlopen, Cape ≻ 198 38.48 N 75.05 W
Henlow 44 52.02 N 0.18 W
Hennan ⊜ 26 62.06 N 15.46 E
Hennaya 34 34.58 N 1.22 W
Henneberg 50 50.29 N 10.21 E
Hennebont 32 47.48 N 3.17 W
Hennef 52 50.46 N 7.16 E
Hennen 52 51.27 N 7.39 E
Hennenman 148 27.59 S 27.01 E
Hennepin 180 41.15 N 89.21 W
Hennepin, Point ≻ 271 42.12 N 83.09 W
Hennersdorf 254b 48.07 N 16.22 E
Hennessey 186 36.06 N 97.54 W
Hennessey, Lake ⊜[1] 216 38.29 N 122.22 W
Hennickendorf 50 52.30 N 13.51 E
Henniez 54 46.44 N 6.54 E
Hennigsdorf 50 52.38 N 13.12 E
Henniker 178 43.11 N 71.49 W
Henning, Ill., U.S. 206 40.18 N 87.42 W
Henning, Minn., U.S. 188 46.19 N 95.27 W
Henning, Tenn., U.S. 184 35.41 N 89.34 W
Henri ≃ 196 46.30 N 71.47 W
Henri, Cap ≻ 176 49.48 N 64.23 W
Henri-Chapelle 52 50.40 N 5.56 E
Henrichemont 46 47.18 N 2.32 E
Henrichenburg 253 51.35 N 7.19 E
Henrico □[6] 198 37.30 N 77.20 W
Henrietta, N.Y., U.S. 200 43.03 N 77.37 W
Henrietta, Tex., U.S. 186 33.49 N 98.12 W
Henrietta Maria, Cape ≻ 166 55.09 N 82.20 W
Henry, Ill., U.S. 180 41.47 N 89.41 W
Henry, S. Dak., U.S. 188 44.53 N 97.28 W
Henry □[6], Ind., U.S. 208 39.55 N 85.22 W
Henry □[6], Ky., U.S. 208 38.26 N 85.09 W
Henry □[6], Ohio, U.S. 206 41.20 N 84.04 W
Henry ≃ 152 22.40 S 115.40 E
Henry, Cape ≻ 198 36.55 N 76.01 W
Henry, Mount ∧ 192 48.53 N 115.31 W
Henry, Mount ∧[2] 264a 33.50 S 150.38 E
Henry, Point ≻ 152 34.29 S 119.23 E
Henry Cowell Redwoods State Park ♠ 216 37.02 N 122.03 W
Henryetta 186 35.27 N 95.59 W
Henry Island ❙ 214 48.35 N 123.11 W
Henry Kater, Cape ≻ 166 69.05 N 66.44 W
Henry Mountains ∧∧ 190 38.00 N 110.50 W
Henry Pittier, Parque Nacional ♠ 236 10.25 N 67.43 W
Henrys Bend 204 41.28 N 79.37 W
Henrys Fork ≃, U.S. 190 41.00 N 109.39 W
Henrys Fork ≃, Idaho, U.S. 192 43.45 N 111.56 W
Henryville, Qué., Can. 196 45.08 N 73.11 W
Henryville, Ind., U.S. 208 38.32 N 85.46 W
Henry W. Coe State Park ♠ 216 37.12 N 121.30 W
Hensall 180 43.26 N 81.30 W
Henshaw, Lake ⊜[1] 194 33.15 N 116.45 W
Hensley 184 34.30 N 92.12 W
Henslow, Cape ≻ 165e 9.56 S 160.38 E
Henson Creek ≃ 274b 38.46 N 77.00 W
Hensonville 200 42.17 N 74.13 W
Henstedt-Ulzburg 48 53.47 N 9.58 E
Henstridge 44 50.59 N 2.24 W
Hentiesbaai 146 22.08 S 14.18 E
Hentona 164m 26.45 N 128.10 E
Henty 156 35.31 S 147.02 E
Henzada 100 17.38 N 95.28 E
Hepburn 174 52.31 N 106.43 W
Hepburn Springs 159 37.19 S 144.09 E
Hephzibah 182 33.19 N 82.06 W
Heping (Yangmingzhen), Zhg. 90 24.28 N 114.58 E
Heping, Zhg. 90 23.17 N 116.29 E
Heping, Zhg. 90 27.10 N 117.18 E
Heping, Zhg. 90 22.01 N 112.59 E
Heping, Zhg. 90 23.54 N 114.38 E
Hepo 90 23.28 N 115.56 E
Heppenheim an der Bergstrasse 52 49.39 N 8.38 E
Heppner 192 45.21 N 119.33 W
Heptonstall 252 53.45 N 2.01 W
Heptonstall Moor ≃ 252 53.46 N 2.05 W
Hepu (Lianzhou) 92 21.39 N 109.11 E
Hepworth 202 44.37 N 81.09 W
Heqi 96 31.03 N 119.49 E
Heqiao 96 31.30 N 119.53 E
Heqing 92 26.30 N 100.20 E
Hequ 92 39.29 N 111.19 E
Héraðsflói C 24a 65.45 N 14.10 W
Herāt 118 34.20 N 62.12 E
Herāt □[4] 118 34.30 N 62.00 E
Hérault □[5] 32 43.40 N 3.30 E
Hérault ≃ 32 43.17 N 3.26 E
Herbasse ≃ 56 45.02 N 4.57 E
Herbault 46 47.36 N 1.08 E
Herbede 52 51.25 N 7.16 E
Herbern 48 51.44 N 7.39 E
Herbert, Sask., Can. 174 50.26 N 107.12 W
Herbert, N.Z. 162 45.14 S 170.47 E
Herbert ≃ 156 18.32 S 146.17 E
Herbertabad 100 11.43 N 92.37 E
Herbert Hoover National Historic Site ⊥ 180 41.38 N 91.23 W
Herbertingen 54 48.04 N 9.26 E
Herbert Island ❙ 170 52.45 N 170.10 W
Herberton 156 17.23 S 145.23 E

FRANÇAIS

Nom · Page · Lat.°′ · Long.°′ W=Ouest

Herbert Peak ∧ 162 43.41 S 172.44 E
Herbertsdale 148 34.01 S 21.46 E
Herbeumont 52 49.47 N 5.14 E
Herbignac 32 47.27 N 2.19 W
Herb Lake 174 54.47 N 99.47 W
Herblay 46 49.00 N 2.10 E
Herblet Lake ⊜ 174 54.56 N 99.54 W
Herbolzheim 54 48.13 N 7.47 E
Herborn 52 50.40 N 8.17 E
Herbrechtingen 52 48.37 N 10.10 E
Herbsleben 50 51.07 N 10.50 E
Herbstein 52 50.34 N 9.20 E
Herceg-Novi 38 42.27 N 18.32 E
Herculaneum 209 38.16 N 90.23 W
Hercules 272 38.01 N 122.17 W
Herdecke 52 51.24 N 7.26 E
Herdorf 52 50.46 N 7.56 E
Herdringen 52 51.25 N 7.58 E
Herdubreid ∧ 24a 65.13 N 16.18 W
Heredia 226 10.00 N 84.07 W
Heredia □[4] 226 10.30 N 84.00 W
Hereford, Eng., U.K. 44 52.04 N 2.43 W
Hereford, Ariz., U.S. 190 31.26 N 110.06 W
Hereford, Md., U.S. 198 39.35 N 76.40 W
Hereford, Tex., U.S. 186 34.49 N 102.24 W
Hereford and Worcester □[6] 44 52.10 N 2.30 W
Hereford Cathedral ʊ[1] 44 52.04 N 2.43 W
Hereford Mountain ∧ 196 45.05 N 71.36 W
Hereke 120 40.48 N 29.39 E
Herekino 162 35.15 S 173.13 E
Herencia 34 39.21 N 3.22 W
Herentals 52 51.11 N 4.50 E
Herfølge 41 55.25 N 12.10 E
Herford 48 52.06 N 8.40 E
Hergatz 54 47.39 N 9.50 E
Hergisdorf 50 51.32 N 11.28 E
Hergla 36 36.02 N 10.31 E
Herhahn 52 50.33 N 6.26 E
Herheri 120 37.41 N 39.00 E
Héricourt 54 47.35 N 6.45 E
Hérimoncourt 54 47.26 N 6.53 E
Heringen 50 51.27 N 10.52 E
Heringsdorf 50 54.18 N 11.00 E
Herington 188 38.40 N 96.57 W
Heriot 162 45.50 S 169.16 E
Herisau 54 47.23 N 9.17 E
Heritage Range ∧∧ 9 79.30 S 84.00 W
Herk ≃ 52 50.58 N 5.07 E
Herk-de-Stad 52 50.56 N 5.10 E
Herkimer 200 43.02 N 74.59 W
Herkimer □[6] 200 43.02 N 74.59 W
Herleshausen 52 51.00 N 10.09 E
Herlev 41 55.43 N 12.27 E
Herlong 194 40.09 N 120.08 W
Herlufmagle 41 55.19 N 11.46 E
Herlufsholm 41 55.15 N 11.46 E
Hermagor 58 46.37 N 13.22 E
Herman, Minn., U.S. 188 45.49 N 96.08 W
Herman, Nebr., U.S. 188 41.40 N 96.13 W
Herman, Pa., U.S. 204 40.50 N 79.49 W
Herman, Lake ⊜ 272 38.05 N 122.09 W
Hermana Mayor Island ❙ 106 15.48 N 119.48 E
Hermanas 186 27.13 N 101.14 W
Hermann 209 38.42 N 91.27 W
Hermann Eckstein Park ♠ 263d 26.10 S 28.02 E
Hermannsburg, Austl. 152 23.57 S 132.45 E
Hermannsburg, B.R.D. 48 52.50 N 10.05 E
Hermannsdenkmal ⊥ 48 51.55 N 8.50 E
Hermannskogel ∧ 254b 48.16 N 16.18 E
Hermannstadt → Sibiu 38 45.48 N 24.09 E
Hermannstein 52 50.35 N 8.29 E
Hermano Peak ∧ 190 37.13 N 108.48 W
Hermansverk 26 61.11 N 6.51 E
Hermansville 180 45.42 N 87.37 W
Hermanus 148 34.25 S 19.16 E
Hermanville 184 31.58 N 90.50 W
Hermeray 251 48.38 N 1.41 E
Hermes 46 49.22 N 2.15 E
Hermeskeil 52 49.39 N 6.56 E
Hermidale 156 31.33 S 146.43 E
Hermies 46 50.07 N 3.02 E
Herminie 204 40.16 N 79.43 W
Hermiston 192 45.51 N 119.17 W
Hermitage, Newf., Can. 176 47.33 N 55.56 W
Hermitage, N.Z. 162 43.44 S 170.06 E
Hermitage, Ark., U.S. 184 33.27 N 92.10 W
Hermitage, Mo., U.S. 184 37.56 N 93.19 W
Hermitage Bay C 176 47.35 N 56.05 W
Hermitage Park 274c 39.05 N 77.04 W
Hermite, Islas ❙❙ 244 55.52 S 67.20 W
Hermit Islands ❙❙ 154 1.30 S 145.05 E
Hermleigh 186 32.38 N 100.46 W
Hermon, S. Afr. 148 33.27 S 18.59 E
Hermon, N.Y., U.S. 202 44.28 N 75.14 W
Hermon,, Mount → Shaykh, Jabal ash- ∧ 122 33.26 N 35.51 E
Hermosa Beach 270 33.52 N 118.24 W
Hermosillo, Méx. 190 32.30 N 114.59 W
Hermosillo, Méx. 222 29.04 N 110.58 W
Hermoso, Cerro ∧ 236 1.10 S 78.12 W
Hermsdorf 50 50.54 N 11.52 E
Hermsdorf ◂[8] 254a 52.37 N 13.18 E
Hermyingyi 100 14.15 N 98.21 E
Hernád (Hornád) ≃ 30 47.56 N 21.08 E
Hernals ◂[8] 254b 48.13 N 16.20 E
Hernandarias 242 25.22 S 54.45 W
Hernández 224 23.01 N 102.01 W
Hernandez Reservoir ⊜[1] 216 36.22 N 120.49 W
Hernando, Arg. 242 32.25 S 63.44 W
Hernando, Fla., U.S. 210 28.54 N 82.22 W
Hernando, Miss., U.S. 184 34.49 N 89.59 W
Hernando □[6] 210 28.34 N 82.22 W
Hernani 106 11.20 N 125.37 E
Herndon, Calif., U.S. 216 36.49 N 119.54 W
Herndon, Kans., U.S. 188 39.55 N 100.47 W
Herndon, Va., U.S. 198 38.58 N 77.23 W
Herndon Canal Ξ 216 36.46 N 119.46 W
Herne 48 51.32 N 7.13 E
Herne Bay 44 51.23 N 1.08 E
Herne Hill 158a 31.50 S 116.01 E
Herning 41 56.08 N 8.59 E
Hernwood Heights 274b 39.22 N 77.50 W
Héroes Chapultepec 276a 19.28 N 99.04 W
Héroes de Churubusco 276a 19.22 N 99.06 W
Herongate 250 51.36 N 0.21 E
Herongen 52 51.24 N 6.15 E
Heron Lake 188 43.47 N 95.19 W
Hérons, Île aux ❙ 265a 45.25 N 73.35 W
Heronsgate 250 51.38 N 0.31 W
Hérouville 251 49.06 N 2.08 E
Herowābād 118 37.37 N 48.32 E
Herpf 50 50.34 N 10.20 E
Herradura 242 26.29 S 58.18 W
Herräng 40 60.08 N 18.39 E
Herreid 188 45.50 N 100.04 W
Herrenalb 52 48.48 N 8.26 E
Herrenberg 52 48.35 N 8.52 E
Herrenchiemsee, Schloss ⊥ 58 47.52 N 12.23 E
Herrera 242 28.29 S 63.04 W
Herrera □[4] 226 7.54 N 80.38 W
Herrera del Duque 34 39.10 N 5.03 W
Herrera de Pisuerga 34 42.36 N 4.20 W
Herreras 222 25.10 N 105.31 W
Herrick, Austl. 156 41.06 S 147.52 E
Herrick, Ill., U.S. 209 39.13 N 88.59 W
Herrick Creek ≃ 172 54.20 N 121.30 W
Herrick Grove 202 44.04 N 76.12 W
Herricks 266 40.45 N 73.40 W
Herrieden 52 49.14 N 10.30 E

PORTUGUÊS

Nome · Página · Lat.°′ · Long.°′ W=Oeste

Herrin 184 37.48 N 89.02 W
Herring ≃ 273 42.10 N 70.44 W
Herring Bay C 198 38.44 N 76.33 W
Herring Cove, N.S., Can. 176 44.34 N 63.34 W
Herring Cove, Alaska, U.S. 170 55.21 N 131.41 W
Herring Creek ≃ 198 37.49 N 77.07 W
Herringen 48 51.40 N 7.44 E
Herring Run ≃ 274b 39.18 N 76.31 W
Herring Run Park ♠ 274b 39.19 N 76.33 W
Herritslev 41 54.42 N 11.41 E
Herrlingen 54 48.25 N 9.53 E
Herrljunga 26 58.05 N 13.02 E
Herrnburg 50 53.47 N 10.45 E
Herrnhut 50 51.01 N 14.44 E
Herrnstadt → Wąsosz 30 51.34 N 16.42 E
Herrsching am Ammersee 58 48.00 N 11.10 E
Herrs Island ❙ 269b 40.28 N 79.58 W
Herrskogen 40 59.32 N 16.15 E
Herry 46 47.13 N 2.57 E
Hersbruck 30 49.30 N 11.26 E
Herschbach 52 50.34 N 7.44 E
Herscheid 52 51.10 N 7.44 E
Herschel 174 51.38 N 108.21 W
Herschel Island ❙ 170 69.35 N 139.05 W
Herscher 206 41.03 N 88.06 W
Herselt 52 51.03 N 4.53 E
Herserange 52 49.31 N 5.47 E
Hersham 44 51.22 N 0.23 W
Hershey, Nebr., U.S. 188 41.10 N 101.00 W
Hershey, Pa., U.S. 198 40.17 N 76.39 W
Hersman 209 39.57 N 90.44 W
Herstadberg 40 58.38 N 16.10 E
Herstal 52 50.40 N 5.38 E
Herstmonceux 44 50.53 N 0.20 E
Herten 48 51.35 N 7.07 E
Hertford, Eng., U.K. 44 51.48 N 0.05 W
Hertford, N.C., U.S. 182 36.11 N 76.28 W
Hertford □[6] 198 36.28 N 77.01 W
Hertfordshire □[6] 44 51.50 N 0.10 W
Hertingfordbury 250 51.48 N 0.06 W
Hertsmere □[8] 250 51.41 N 0.17 W
Hertzogville 148 28.08 S 25.33 E
Heruncun 94 40.58 N 123.27 E
Hervás 34 40.16 N 5.51 W
Herve 52 50.38 N 5.48 E
Hervest 253 51.40 N 7.01 E
Hervey Bay C 156 25.00 S 153.00 E
Herxheim 52 49.09 N 8.13 E
Héry 46 47.54 N 3.38 E
Héry-sur-Ugines 56 45.46 N 6.28 E
Herzberg, D.D.R. 50 51.41 N 13.14 E
Herzberg, D.D.R. 50 52.54 N 12.58 E
Herzberg am Harz 48 51.39 N 10.20 E
Herzebrock 48 51.53 N 8.14 E
Herzfeld 48 51.40 N 8.08 E
Herzfelde 50 52.29 N 13.50 E
Herzhausen 52 51.11 N 8.53 E
Herzliyya 122 32.10 N 34.51 E
Herznach 54 47.28 N 8.03 E
Herzogenaurach 52 49.34 N 10.53 E
Herzogenbuchsee 54 47.12 N 7.41 E
Herzogenburg 30 48.17 N 15.42 E
Herzsprung 50 53.04 N 12.28 E
Heṣār, Kūh-e ∧∧ 110 34.50 N 66.35 E
Hesarak 257d 35.47 N 51.19 E
Hesdin 46 50.22 N 2.02 E
Heseerhe ≃ 75 39.29 N 76.29 E
Hesel 48 53.18 N 7.35 E
Hesepe 48 52.26 N 7.58 E
Heshachang 97 30.37 N 105.40 E
Heshangqiao 90 34.15 N 113.47 E
Heshaoqiao 90 32.55 N 118.22 E
Heshe 100 19.41 N 109.42 E
Heshengqiao 90 30.00 N 114.22 E
Heshi 90 25.04 N 118.37 E
Heshituoluogai 76 46.35 N 86.01 E
Heshui, Zhg. 90 24.24 N 114.56 E
Heshui, Zhg. 92 22.48 N 112.29 E
Heshui, Zhg. 92 22.18 N 111.52 E
Heshuijian 90 30.33 N 116.05 E
Heshun, Zhg. 90 27.30 N 117.24 E
Heshun, Zhg. 92 37.21 N 113.35 E
Heshuo 76 42.15 N 86.53 E
Hesketh Out Marsh ☷ 252 53.43 N 2.55 W
Heskin Green 252 53.38 N 2.42 W
Hesler 208 38.28 N 84.47 W
Hesperange 52 49.34 N 6.09 E
Hesperia, Calif., U.S. 218 34.25 N 117.18 W
Hesperia, Mich., U.S. 180 43.34 N 86.04 W
Hesperus Mountain ∧ 190 37.27 N 108.05 W
Hess ≃ 170 63.34 N 133.57 W
Hesselager 41 55.10 N 10.45 E
Hesselø ❙ 41 56.12 N 11.43 E
Hesselte 48 52.25 N 7.22 E
Hessen 50 52.02 N 10.15 E
Hessen □[3] 30 50.30 N 9.15 E
Hessen Cassal 206 41.00 N 85.05 W
Hessenthal 52 49.55 N 9.17 E
Hessische Rhön, Naturpark ♠ 52 50.35 N 9.50 E
Hessisch Lichtenau 52 51.12 N 9.43 E
Hessisch Oldendorf 48 52.10 N 9.15 E
Hessle 42 53.44 N 0.26 W
Hesso 156 32.08 S 137.27 E
Hess Tablemount ✢[3] 14 18.30 N 174.30 W
Hesston, Kans., U.S. 188 38.08 N 97.26 W
Hesston, Pa., U.S. 204 40.26 N 78.07 W
Heston ◂[8] 250 51.29 N 0.22 W
Heswall 42 53.20 N 3.06 W
Het ≃ 100 20.49 N 104.01 E
Hetai 92 23.22 N 112.19 E
Hetanbu 90 28.21 N 117.11 E
Hetang, Zhg. 90 26.40 N 119.09 E
Hetang, Zhg. 96 31.43 N 120.27 E
Hetang, Zhg. 97 28.58 N 106.03 E
Hetch Hetchy Aqueduct Ξ[1] 216 37.29 N 122.19 W
Hetch Hetchy Reservoir ⊜[1] 216 37.57 N 119.43 W
Hetian, Zhg. 90 23.19 N 115.38 E
Hetian, Zhg. 90 25.41 N 116.26 E
Hetian, Zhg. 110 37.08 N 79.54 E
Hetianhe ≃ 80 40.30 N 80.45 E
Het Loo, Paleis ʊ 48 52.14 N 5.56 E
Hetou 90 24.18 N 113.29 E
Hetoudian 88 37.02 N 120.35 E
Hetoupu 90 30.50 N 116.03 E
Hetouxi ≃ 90 23.58 N 117.24 E
Hettange-Grande 52 49.24 N 6.09 E
Hettenleidelheim 52 49.32 N 8.04 E
Hettick 209 39.21 N 90.02 W
Hettingen 54 48.13 N 9.14 E
Hettinger 188 46.00 N 102.39 W
Hetton-le-Hole 42 54.50 N 1.27 W
Hettstedt 50 51.38 N 11.30 E
Hetzendorf ◂[8] 254b 48.10 N 16.18 E
Hetzerath 52 49.52 N 6.49 E
Het Zoute 46 51.21 N 3.18 E
Heuchin 46 50.28 N 2.16 E
Heudeber 50 51.54 N 10.50 E
Heule 46 50.50 N 3.14 E
Heuningspruit 148 27.26 S 27.28 E
Heusden 46 51.02 N 5.16 E
Heustreu 52 50.21 N 10.15 E
Heusweiler 52 49.20 N 6.55 E
Heuvelton 202 44.37 N 75.25 W
Hève, Cap de la ≻ 46 49.31 N 0.04 E
Heven ◂[8] 253 51.26 N 7.17 E
Heverlee 52 50.52 N 4.42 E
Heves 30 47.36 N 20.17 E
Heves □[6] 30 47.50 N 20.15 E
Hewitt, N.J., U.S. 200 41.08 N 74.18 W
Hewitt, Tex., U.S. 212 31.28 N 97.12 W
Hewlett, N.Y., U.S. 266 40.38 N 73.42 W
Hewlett, Va., U.S. 198 37.55 N 77.35 W
Hewlett Bay Park 266 40.38 N 73.42 W
Hewlett Harbor 266 40.38 N 73.41 W
Hewlett Neck 266 40.37 N 73.42 W
Hewlett Point ≻ 266 40.50 N 73.45 W
Hewopu 94 41.14 N 122.24 E
Hewu 90 26.41 N 113.40 E
Hexen Kopf ∧ 54 47.01 N 10.28 E
Hexham 42 54.58 N 2.06 W
Hexi, Zhg. 90 24.52 N 117.15 E
Hexi, Zhg. 90 31.21 N 114.02 E
Hexi, Zhg. 95 40.35 N 117.52 E
Hexian, Zhg. 90 31.43 N 118.22 E
Hexian, Zhg. 92 24.15 N 111.43 E
Hexibao 92 38.34 N 102.11 E
Hexingchang 97 30.05 N 104.35 E
Hexingjie 96 31.55 N 120.36 E
Hexiwu 95 39.38 N 116.58 E
Hex-Rivierberge ∧∧ 148 33.25 S 19.37 E
Hextable 250 51.25 N 0.11 E
Hexton 162 38.37 S 177.58 E
Hexue 92 30.00 N 112.20 E
Heyan 94 42.30 N 120.29 E
Heyang, Zhg. 88 35.27 N 118.33 E
Heyang, Zhg. 92 35.15 N 110.06 E
Heybeli ◂[8] 257b 40.53 N 29.05 E
Heybeliada ❙ 257b 40.53 N 29.05 E
Heybridge 250 51.44 N 0.41 E
Heyburn 192 42.34 N 113.46 W
Heyburn State Recreation Area ♠ 192 47.20 N 116.49 W
Heyderbreck → Kędzierzyn 30 50.20 N 18.12 E
Heyerode 50 51.10 N 10.25 E
Heyrieux 56 45.38 N 5.03 E
Heysham 42 54.02 N 2.54 W
Heyuan 90 23.44 N 114.41 E
Heywood, Austl. 156 38.08 S 141.38 E
Heywood, Eng., U.K. 42 53.36 N 2.13 W
Heyworth 206 40.19 N 88.59 W
Hezan 120 38.21 N 40.38 E
Heze 88 35.17 N 115.27 E
Hezhang 92 27.00 N 104.37 E
Hezhao 88 37.08 N 115.17 E
Hezhen 90 29.56 N 120.10 E
Hezheng 92 35.25 N 103.10 E
Hezijian 95 40.13 N 116.03 E
Heziwei 90 24.54 N 115.14 E
Hiale 100 15.55 N 107.34 E
Hialeah 210 25.49 N 80.17 W
Hialeah Park Race Track ♠ 210 25.51 N 80.17 W
Hiawassee 182 34.58 N 83.46 W
Hiawatha, Kans., U.S. 188 39.51 N 95.32 W
Hiawatha, Utah, U.S. 190 39.29 N 111.01 W
Hiba-dōgo-taishaku-kokutei-kōen ♠ 86 35.07 N 133.08 E
Hibaiyo 106 10.16 N 123.20 E
Hibaldstow 42 53.31 N 0.32 W
Hibbing 180 47.25 N 92.56 W
Hibbs, Point ≻ 156 42.38 S 145.15 E
Hibernia 266 40.57 N 74.30 W
Hibernia Reef ✢[2] 150 12.00 S 123.23 E
Hibiki-nada ⊤[2] 86 34.00 N 130.30 E
Hiburi-shima ❙ 86 33.10 N 132.17 E
Hibuson Island ❙ 106 10.27 N 125.29 E
Hickam Air Force Base ■ 219c 21.20 N 157.57 W
Hickman, Calif., U.S. 216 37.37 N 120.45 W
Hickman, Ky., U.S. 184 36.34 N 89.11 W
Hickman, Nebr., U.S. 188 40.37 N 96.38 W
Hickman, Pa., U.S. 269b 40.23 N 80.09 W
Hickman's Harbour 176 48.06 N 53.44 W
Hickory, Miss., U.S. 184 32.19 N 89.01 W
Hickory, N.C., U.S. 182 35.44 N 81.21 W
Hickory, Pa., U.S. 204 40.18 N 80.18 W
Hickory Corners. 206 42.27 N 85.22 W
Hickory Creek ≃, Mich., U.S. 206 42.05 N 86.29 W
Hickory Creek ≃, Tex., U.S. 212 31.29 N 95.07 W
Hickory Hills 206 41.43 N 87.49 W
Hickory Run State Park ♠ 200 41.02 N 75.41 W
Hickory Township 204 41.15 N 80.27 W
Hicks, Point ≻ 156 37.48 S 149.17 E
Hicks Bay 162 37.36 S 178.18 E
Hickson Lake ⊜ 174 56.17 N 104.25 W
Hicksville, N.Y., U.S. 200 40.46 N 73.32 W
Hicksville, Ohio, U.S. 206 41.18 N 84.46 W
Hico 186 31.59 N 98.02 W
Hicpochee, Lake ⊜ 210 26.50 N 81.10 W
Hida → Hita 86 33.19 N 130.56 E
Hidaka, Nihon 84 35.54 N 139.21 E
Hidaka, Nihon 86 35.28 N 134.47 E
Hidaka, Nihon 86 33.55 N 135.09 E
Hidaka ≃ 86 33.52 N 135.09 E
Hidaka-sammyaku ∧∧ 82a 42.35 N 142.45 E
Hida-kiso-gawa-kokutei-kōen ♠ 84 35.37 N 137.15 E
Hida-kōchi ∧∧[1] 84 36.16 N 137.05 E
Hidalgo, Méx. 222 27.47 N 99.52 W
Hidalgo, Méx. 222 24.15 N 99.26 W
Hidalgo, Méx. 222 25.59 N 100.27 W
Hidalgo, Méx. 224 23.10 N 103.13 W
Hidalgo □[3] 224 20.30 N 99.00 W
Hidalgo, Presa ⊜[1] 222 26.30 N 108.35 W
Hidalgo del Parral 222 26.56 N 105.40 W
Hidalgo Yalalag 224 17.11 N 96.11 W
Hida-sammyaku ∧∧ 84 36.25 N 137.40 E
Hiddenhausen 48 52.08 N 8.38 E
Hidden Hills 218 34.09 N 118.43 W
Hiddensee ❙ 50 54.33 N 13.07 E
Hidden Valley, Calif., U.S. 216 38.46 N 121.09 W
Hidden Valley, Tex., U.S. 212 29.54 N 95.25 W
Hiddesen 48 51.55 N 8.50 E
Hiddinghausen 253 51.22 N 7.17 E
Hidilola 134 5.52 N 43.42 E
Hidrolândia 245 16.58 S 49.14 W
Hidrolina 245 14.37 S 49.25 W
Hieflau 30 47.36 N 14.44 E
Hienghène 165f 20.41 S 164.56 E
Hierapolis ⊥ 120 37.58 N 29.19 E
Hierges 52 50.06 N 4.44 E
Hierro (Ferro) ❙ 138 27.45 N 18.00 W
Hiesfeld 253 51.33 N 6.46 E
Hietzing ◂[8] 254b 48.11 N 16.18 E
Higashi ◂[8] 260 34.41 N 135.31 E
Higashibetsuin 260 34.58 N 135.34 E
Higashifuji-enshūjō ■ 84 35.17 N 138.51 E
Higashiichiki 82 31.40 N 130.20 E
Higashiiyayama 86 33.52 N 133.54 E
Higashiizu 84 34.48 N 139.04 E
Higashi-jima ❙ 164f 24.47 N 141.23 E
Higashimatsuyama 84 36.02 N 139.24 E
Higashimonzen 258 35.56 N 139.40 E
Higashimurayama 84 35.46 N 139.29 E
Higashinada ◂[8] 260 34.43 N 135.16 E
Higashinakano 258 35.38 N 139.25 E
Higashinari ◂[8] 260 34.40 N 135.33 E
Higashine 82 38.26 N 140.24 E
Higashinose 260 34.55 N 135.30 E
Higashiōizumi ◂[8] 258 35.45 N 139.36 E
Higashiōsaka 86 34.39 N 135.35 E
Higashishirakawa 84 35.39 N 137.19 E
Higashisumiyoshi ◂[8] 260 34.37 N 135.32 E
Higashitokonoo-san ∧ 86 35.25 N 134.55 E
Higashitsuno 86 33.23 N 133.02 E
Higashiura 84 34.59 N 136.58 E
Higashiyama ◂[8] 260 34.52 N 135.48 E
Higashiyodogawa ◂[8] 260 34.44 N 135.29 E
Higashiyoshino 84 34.24 N 135.58 E
Higbee 184 39.19 N 92.31 W
Higganum 197 41.30 N 72.34 W
Higgins 186 36.07 N 100.02 W
Higgins, Mount ∧ 214 48.19 N 121.45 W
Higgins Lake ⊜ 180 44.30 N 84.45 W
Higginsport 208 38.47 N 83.58 W
Higginsville, Austl. 152 31.45 S 121.43 E
Higginsville, Mo., U.S. 184 39.04 N 93.43 W
Higgs' Hope 148 29.19 S 23.16 E
Higham Ferrers 44 52.18 N 0.36 W
Higham Upshire 44 51.26 N 0.28 E
Highbank 212 31.10 N 96.50 W
High Bank Creek ≃ 206 42.37 N 85.11 W
High Bar Indian Reserve ◂[4] 172 51.06 N 122.00 W
High Beach 250 51.39 N 0.02 E
High Bentham 42 54.08 N 2.30 W
Highbridge, Eng., U.K. 44 51.13 N 2.49 W
High Bridge, N.J., U.S. 200 40.40 N 74.54 W
Highbury 154 16.25 S 143.09 E
Highcliff 269b 40.32 N 80.03 W
Higher Ballam 252 53.46 N 2.59 W
Higher Broughton ◂[8] 252 53.30 N 2.15 W
Higher Hogshead ∧[2] 252 53.42 N 2.09 W
Higher Penwortham 252 53.45 N 2.44 W
Higher Walton, Eng., U.K. 252 53.45 N 2.38 W
Higher Walton, Eng., U.K. 252 53.22 N 2.37 W
Higher Whitley 252 53.19 N 2.35 W
Highett 264b 37.57 S 145.03 E
High Falls 200 41.50 N 74.08 W
High Falls ⌊ 202 43.56 N 75.23 W
Highfield 144 17.50 S 31.00 E
High Force ⌊ 42 54.38 N 2.13 W
Highgate 204 42.30 N 81.49 W
Highgate Center 196 44.58 N 73.03 W
Highgate Springs 196 44.58 N 72.59 W
Highgrove 218 34.01 N 117.20 W
High Halstow 250 51.27 N 0.34 E
High Hesket 42 54.48 N 2.48 W
High Hill 209 38.53 N 91.23 W
High Hill ∧[2] 266 40.49 N 73.25 W
High Hill ≃, Can. 174 56.45 N 110.30 W
High Hill ≃, Man., Can. 174 55.52 N 94.42 W
High Hill Lake ⊜ 174 55.34 N 95.40 W
High Island ❙ 180 45.42 N 85.40 W
High Island Creek ≃ 180 44.35 N 93.54 W
High Knob ∧ 178 39.08 N 78.26 W
Highland, Calif., U.S. 218 34.08 N 117.12 W
Highland, Ill., U.S. 209 38.44 N 89.41 W
Highland, Ind., U.S. 206 41.33 N 87.27 W
Highland, Kans., U.S. 188 39.52 N 95.16 W
Highland, Md., U.S. 198 39.11 N 76.57 W
Highland, Mich., U.S. 271 42.38 N 83.37 W
Highland, N.Y., U.S. 200 41.43 N 73.58 W
Highland, Ohio, U.S. 208 39.21 N 83.36 W
Highland, Pa., U.S. 269b 40.33 N 80.04 W
Highland □[4] 28 57.40 N 5.00 W
Highland □[6] 208 39.12 N 83.37 W
Highland Beach 210 26.25 N 80.04 W
Highland City 210 27.58 N 81.53 W
Highland Creek ≃ 216 38.24 N 121.14 W
Highland Creek Park ♠ 265b 43.47 N 79.12 W
Highland Falls 200 41.22 N 73.58 W
Highland Heights, Ky., U.S. 208 39.04 N 84.27 W
Highland Heights, Ohio, U.S. 204 41.32 N 81.29 W
Highland Hills 268 41.52 N 88.01 W
Highland Home 184 31.57 N 86.19 W
Highland Lake, Ill., U.S. 268 42.21 N 88.04 W
Highland Lake, Mass., U.S. 273 42.41 N 72.37 W
Highland Lake, N.Y., U.S. 200 41.32 N 74.51 W
Highland Lake ⊜, Conn., U.S. 197 41.54 N 73.06 W
Highland Lake ⊜, Ill., U.S. 268 42.22 N 88.04 W
Highland Lake ⊜, N.J., U.S. 266 41.10 N 74.28 W
Highland Lakes 200 41.10 N 74.28 W
Highland Park, Ill., U.S. 206 42.11 N 87.48 W
Highland Park, Md., U.S. 274c 38.54 N 76.54 W
Highland Park, Mich., U.S. 206 42.24 N 83.06 W
Highland Park, N.J., U.S. 200 40.30 N 74.26 W
Highland Park, Pa., U.S. 200 40.38 N 77.35 W
Highland Park, Tex., U.S. 212 32.50 N 96.48 W
Highland Park ◂[8] 270 34.07 N 118.13 W
Highland Park ♠, Mass., U.S. 273 42.30 N 70.55 W
Highland Park ♠, Pa., U.S. 269b 40.29 N 79.55 W
Highland Peak ∧ 216 38.33 N 119.45 W
Highland Point ≻ 210 25.30 N 81.12 W
Highlands, N.J., U.S. 198 40.24 N 73.59 W
Highlands, N.C., U.S. 182 35.03 N 83.12 W
Highlands, Tex., U.S. 212 29.49 N 95.04 W
Highlands □[6] 210 27.20 N 81.16 W
Highlands Hammock State Park ♠ 210 27.28 N 81.33 W
Highland Silver Lake ⊜[1] 209 38.47 N 89.39 W
Highlands North ◂[8] 263d 26.09 S 28.05 E
Highland Springs 198 37.33 N 77.20 W
Highlands Reservoir ⊜[1] 212 29.50 N 95.02 W
Highland State Recreation Area ♠ 206 42.39 N 83.33 W
Highlandtown ◂[8] 274b 39.17 N 76.33 W
Highland Village 212 29.45 N 95.27 W
High Laver 250 51.45 N 0.13 E
High Legh 252 53.21 N 2.27 W
Highmore 188 44.31 N 99.27 W
High Ongar 250 51.43 N 0.16 E
High Park ♠ 265b 43.39 N 79.28 W
High Peak □[8] 252 53.23 N 1.55 W
High Peak ∧, Pil. 106 15.29 N 120.07 E
High Peak ∧, N.Y., U.S. 200 42.09 N 74.05 W
High Peak ◂[1] 42 53.22 N 1.50 W
High Plains ≍ 168 38.30 N 103.00 W
High Point, Fla., U.S. 210 27.55 N 82.42 W
High Point, N.C., U.S. 182 35.58 N 80.01 W
Highpoint, Ohio, U.S. 208 39.14 N 84.24 W
High Point ∧, N.J., U.S. 200 41.19 N 74.40 W
High Point ∧, Wyo., U.S. 192 41.37 N 107.47 W
High Point State Park ♠ 200 41.18 N 74.41 W
High Prairie 172 55.26 N 116.29 W
High Ridge 209 38.27 N 90.32 W
High River 172 50.35 N 113.52 W
High Rock 182 26.36 N 76.18 W
High Rock ∧ 178 39.33 N 79.06 W
Highrock Indian Reserve ◂[4] 174 55.54 N 100.30 W
Highrock Lake ⊜, Man., Can. 174 55.45 N 100.30 W
Highrock Lake ⊜, Sask., Can. 174 57.04 N 105.30 W
High Rock Lake ⊜[1] 182 35.40 N 80.17 W
High Seat ∧ 42 54.24 N 2.18 W
High Spire 198 40.13 N 76.48 W
High Springs 182 29.50 N 82.36 W
High Street ∧ 42 54.29 N 2.52 W
Hightown 252 53.32 N 3.04 W
Hightstown 198 40.16 N 74.31 W
High View 200 41.33 N 74.27 W
Highwater 196 45.01 N 72.26 W
Highway City 216 36.49 N 119.54 W
High Willhays ∧ 44 50.41 N 3.59 W
Highwood, Ill., U.S. 206 42.13 N 87.48 W
Highwood, Mont., U.S. 192 47.35 N 110.47 W
Highwood ≃ 172 50.49 N 113.47 W
Highwood Baldy ∧ 192 47.27 N 110.37 W
Highwood Creek ≃ 192 47.40 N 111.00 W
Highwood Mountains ∧∧ 192 47.25 N 110.30 W
Highworth 44 51.38 N 1.43 W
High Wycombe 44 51.38 N 0.46 W
Higlet 144 1.04 S 40.19 E
Higuera Blanca 224 19.42 N 105.10 W
Higuera de Zaragoza 222 25.59 N 109.16 W
Higuera Gorda 224 22.04 N 104.29 W
Higueras 186 25.58 N 100.01 W
Higüero, Punta ≻ 230m 18.22 N 67.16 W
Higuerote 236 10.29 N 66.06 W
Higüey 228 18.37 N 68.42 W
Hihyā 132 30.40 N 31.36 E
Hii ≃ 86 35.26 N 132.54 E
Hiiumaa ❙ 66 58.52 N 22.40 E
Hījānah, Buḥayrat al- ⊜ 122 33.18 N 36.36 E
Híjar 34 41.10 N 0.27 W
Ḥijāz, Jabal al- ∧∧ 134 19.45 N 41.55 E
Hiji 86 33.22 N 131.32 E
Hiji ≃ 86 33.36 N 132.29 E
Hijikawa 86 33.27 N 132.41 E
Hikami 86 35.10 N 135.02 E
Hikari, Nihon 84 35.39 N 140.30 E
Hikari, Nihon 86 33.58 N 131.56 E
Hikarigaoka 258 35.50 N 139.58 E
Hikawa 86 35.25 N 132.50 E
Hikawa Shrine ʊ[1] 258 35.54 N 139.38 E
Hiketa 86 34.13 N 134.24 E
Hiki ≃ 86 33.33 N 135.27 E
Hikigawa 86 33.34 N 135.27 E
Hikimi 86 34.34 N 132.01 E
Hikimi ≃ 86 34.37 N 131.48 E
Hikiura 260 34.33 N 134.58 E
Hikone 84 35.15 N 136.15 E
Hikone-jō ⊥ 84 35.15 N 136.14 E
Hiko-san ∧ 86 33.27 N 130.54 E
Hikueru ❙[1] 14 17.36 S 142.37 W
Hikurangi 162 35.36 S 174.18 E
Hikurangi ∧ 162 38.21 S 176.51 E
Hikutaia 162 37.17 S 175.39 E
Hikutivake 164v 18.56 S 169.53 W
Hila 102 7.35 S 127.24 E
Hilaban Island ❙ 106 12.03 N 125.34 E
Hilāl, Jabal ∧∧ 122 34.40 N 31.00 E
Hilāl, Ra's al- ≻ 136 32.57 N 22.10 E
Hilbersdorf 50 50.55 N 13.23 E
Hilbert 180 44.09 N 88.10 W
Hilchenbach 52 51.00 N 8.06 E
Hilda 174 50.28 N 110.03 W
Hildburghausen 50 50.25 N 10.44 E
Hilden 52 51.10 N 6.56 E
Hildenborough 250 51.13 N 0.15 E
Hilders 52 50.34 N 10.00 E
Hildesheim 48 52.09 N 9.57 E
Hildesheim □[6] 48 51.40 N 10.00 E
Hildreth 188 40.20 N 99.03 W
Hilgen 253 51.06 N 7.09 E
Hiligeo 104 1.22 N 97.10 E
Hiliotaluwa 104 0.44 N 97.53 E
Hill □[6] 212 32.02 N 97.10 W
Hillaby, Mount ∧ 231g 13.12 N 59.35 W
Hill Air Force Base ■ 192 41.05 N 111.58 W
Hillandale, S. Afr. 148 33.06 S 20.36 E
Hillandale, Md., U.S. 274c 39.01 N 76.58 W
Hill Bank 222 17.35 N 88.42 W
Hillbrow ◂[8] 263d 26.11 S 28.03 E
Hillburn 200 41.08 N 74.10 W
Hill City, Kans., U.S. 188 39.22 N 99.51 W
Hill City, Minn., U.S. 180 46.59 N 93.36 W
Hill City, S. Dak., U.S. 188 43.56 N 103.35 W
Hill Creek ≃ 190 39.55 N 109.40 W
Hillcrest, Ill., U.S. 206 41.57 N 89.04 W
Hillcrest, N.Y., U.S. 200 42.09 N 75.53 W
Hillcrest, N.Y., U.S. 200 41.09 N 74.02 W
Hillcrest Center 218 35.23 N 118.57 W
Hillcrest Heights 274c 38.52 N 76.57 W
Hillcrest Mines 172 49.34 N 114.23 W
Hillcrest Orchard 206 41.51 N 83.29 W
Hillcrest Park 216 38.07 N 122.16 W
Hill Cumorah ⊥ 200 43.01 N 77.15 W
Hille, B.R.D. 48 52.20 N 8.44 E
Hille, Sve. 40 60.44 N 17.11 E
Hillegom 48 52.18 N 4.35 E
Hillegossen 48 51.59 N 8.37 E
Hillen ◂[8] 253 51.37 N 7.13 E
Hillerød 41 55.56 N 12.19 E
Hillers Creek ≃ 209 38.38 N 91.54 W
Hillesheim 52 50.18 N 6.38 E
Hilli 114 25.17 N 89.01 E
Hilliard, Fla., U.S. 182 30.41 N 81.55 W
Hilliard, Ohio, U.S. 204 40.02 N 83.10 W
Hilliards 204 41.05 N 79.50 W
Hillingdon ◂[8] 44 51.32 N 0.27 W
Hillisburg 206 40.17 N 86.20 W
Hill Island Lake ⊜ 166 60.29 N 109.50 W
Hillister 184 30.40 N 94.23 W
Hillman 180 45.04 N 83.54 W
Hillmersdorf 50 51.42 N 13.29 E
Hills 188 43.32 N 96.21 W
Hills and Dales 204 39.42 N 84.13 W
Hillsboro, Ill., U.S. 209 39.09 N 89.29 W
Hillsboro, Kans., U.S. 188 38.21 N 97.12 W
Hillsboro, Ky., U.S. 208 38.18 N 83.40 W
Hillsboro, Md., U.S. 198 38.55 N 75.50 W
Hillsboro, Mo., U.S. 209 38.14 N 90.34 W
Hillsboro, N.H., U.S. 178 43.07 N 71.54 W
Hillsboro, N. Mex., U.S. 190 32.55 N 107.34 W
Hillsboro, N. Dak., U.S. 188 47.26 N 97.03 W
Hillsboro, Ohio, U.S. 208 39.12 N 83.37 W
Hillsboro, Oreg., U.S. 214 45.31 N 122.59 W
Hillsboro, Tex., U.S. 212 32.01 N 97.08 W
Hillsboro, Wis., U.S. 180 43.39 N 90.21 W
Hillsboro Beach 210 26.18 N 80.05 W
Hillsboro Canal Ξ 210 26.19 N 80.05 W
Hillsborough, N.B., Can. 176 45.56 N 64.39 W
Hillsborough, N. Ire., U.K. 42 54.28 N 6.05 W
Hillsborough, Calif., U.S. 216 37.34 N 122.20 W
Hillsborough, N.C., U.S. 182 36.05 N 79.07 W
Hillsborough □[6], Fla., U.S. 210 27.55 N 82.15 W
Hillsborough □[6], N.H., U.S. 197 42.49 N 71.41 W
Hillsborough ≃ 210 27.56 N 82.27 W
Hillsborough, Cape ≻ 156 20.54 S 149.03 E
Hillsborough Bay C, P.E.I., Can. 176 46.10 N 63.05 W
Hillsborough Bay C, Fla., U.S. 210 27.52 N 82.27 W
Hillsborough River State Park ♠ 210 28.09 N 82.14 W
Hillsburgh 202 43.47 N 80.09 W
Hills Creek Lake ⊜[1] 192 43.40 N 122.26 W
Hillsdale, Mich., U.S. 206 41.55 N 84.38 W
Hillsdale, N.J., U.S. 266 41.00 N 74.02 W
Hillsdale, N.Y., U.S. 200 42.11 N 73.31 W
Hillsdale, Pa., U.S. 204 40.45 N 78.53 W
Hillsdale □[6] 206 41.53 N 84.36 W
Hillsdale ◂[9] 272 37.32 N 122.18 W
Hillsdale Park ♠ 274b 39.19 N 76.42 W
Hills Flat 216 39.14 N 121.03 W
Hillsgrove 200 41.27 N 76.42 W
Hillside, Austl. 152 21.44 S 119.23 E
Hillside, Ill., U.S. 268 41.52 N 87.54 W
Hillside, Md., U.S. 274c 38.52 N 76.55 W
Hillside, N.J., U.S. 266 40.42 N 74.13 W
Hillside ◂[8] 266 40.42 N 73.47 W

Symbol	English	Deutsch	Español	Français	Português
≃	River	Fluss	Río	Rivière	Rio
Ξ	Canal	Kanal	Canal	Canal	Canal
⌊	Waterfall, Rapids	Wasserfall, Stromschnellen	Cascada, Rápidos	Chute d'eau, Rapides	Cascata, Rápidos
⋈	Strait	Meeresstrasse	Estrecho	Détroit	Estreito
C	Bay, Gulf	Bucht, Golf	Bahía, Golfo	Baie, Golfe	Baía, Golfo
⊜	Lake, Lakes	See, Seen	Lago, Lagos	Lac, Lacs	Lago, Lagos
☷	Swamp	Sumpf	Pantano	Marais	Pântano
◫	Ice Features, Glacier	Eis- und Gletscherformen	Accidentes Glaciales	Formes glaciaires	Acidentes Glaciares
⊤	Other Hydrographic Features	Andere Hydrographische Objekte	Otros Elementos Hidrográficos	Autres données hydrographiques	Outros Elementos Hidrográficos
✢	Submarine Features	Untermeerische Objekte	Accidentes Submarinos	Formes de relief sous-marin	Acidentes Submarinos
□	Political Unit	Politische Einheit	Unidad Politica	Entité politique	Unidade Política
ʊ	Cultural Institution	Kulturelle Institution	Institución Cultural	Institution culturelle	Instituição Cultural
⊥	Historical Site	Historische Stätte	Sitio Histórico	Site historique	Sitio Histórico
♠	Recreational Site	Erholungs- und Ferienort	Sitio de Recreo	Centre de loisirs	Sítio de Lazer
⊠	Airport	Flughafen	Aeropuerto	Aéroport	Aeroporto
■	Military Installation	Militäranlage	Instalación Militar	Installation militaire	Instalação Militar
◂	Miscellaneous	Verschiedenes	Misceláneo	Divers	Miscelânea

Name	Page	Lat.	Long.
Hillside Gardens	206	42.16 N	84.27 W
Hillside Heights	275	39.41 N	75.41 W
Hillston	156	33.29 S	145.32 E
Hillsville, Pa., U.S.	204	41.01 N	80.30 W
Hillsville, Va., U.S.	182	36.46 N	80.44 W
Hilltop	198	39.49 N	75.04 W
Hilltop Center ◆[9]	272	37.59 N	122.19 W
Hilltown, N. Ire., U.K.	42	54.12 N	6.09 W
Hilltown, Pa., U.S.	198	40.20 N	75.14 W
Hillview	209	39.27 N	90.33 W
Hillview Reservoir ⊜[1]	266	40.55 N	73.52 W
Hillwood	274c	38.52 N	77.10 W
Hilmar	216	37.25 N	120.51 W
Hilo	219d	19.43 N	155.05 W
Hilo Bay C	219d	19.44 N	155.05 W
Hilonghilong, Mount ∧	106	9.06 N	125.44 E
Hilongos	106	10.23 N	124.45 E
Hilo Point >	164n	15.02 N	145.36 E
Hilpsford Point >	42	54.03 N	3.12 W
Hils ∧	48	51.55 N	9.40 E
Hilshire Village	212	29.49 N	95.26 W
Hiltaba, Mount ∧	152	32.09 S	135.03 E
Hilter	48	52.08 N	8.08 E
Hilton, N.Y., U.S.	200	43.17 N	77.48 W
Hilton, Pa., U.S.	198	40.00 N	76.49 W
Hilton Head Island I	182	32.12 N	80.45 W
Hiltrop ◆[8]	253	51.30 N	7.15 E
Hiltrup	48	51.54 N	7.38 E
Hilvarenbeek	48	51.29 N	5.09 E
Hilversum	48	52.14 N	5.10 E
Hima	182	37.07 N	83.47 W
Himachal Pradesh □[8]	110	32.00 N	77.00 E
Himalayas ∧∧	110	28.00 N	84.00 E
Himalchuli ∧	114	28.25 N	84.39 E
Himamaylan	106	10.06 N	122.52 E
Himanka	26	64.04 N	23.39 E
Himarë	38	40.07 N	19.44 E
Himatnagar	110	23.36 N	72.57 E
Himberg	254b	48.05 N	16.26 E
Hime ≃	84	37.02 N	137.49 E
Himeji	86	34.49 N	134.42 E
Hime-shima I	86	33.43 N	131.40 E
Himeville	148	29.44 S	29.31 E
Himi	84	36.51 N	136.59 E
Himmelbjerget ∧∧[2]	41	56.06 N	9.42 E
Himmelgeist ◆[8]	253	51.10 N	6.49 E
Himmelpforten	48	53.36 N	9.18 E
Himmelsthür	48	52.09 N	9.55 E
Himmerfjärden C[2]	40	59.00 N	17.43 E
Himmerland ◆[1]	26	56.50 N	9.45 E
Himmetdede	120	38.55 N	35.07 E
Himrod	200	42.35 N	76.57 W
Ḥimṣ (Homs)	120	34.44 N	36.43 E
Ḥimṣ □[8]	120	34.15 N	38.00 E
Ḥimṣ, Baḥrat ⊜[1]	120	34.39 N	36.34 E
Hinabangan	106	11.42 N	125.04 E
Ḥīnah	122	33.21 N	35.56 E
Hinako, Kepulauan II	104	0.52 N	97.21 E
Hinase	86	34.44 N	134.16 E
Hinatuan	106	8.23 N	126.20 E
Hinatuan Island I	106	9.47 N	125.43 E
Hinatuan Passage ⋓	106	9.45 N	125.47 E
Hinche	228	19.09 N	72.01 W
Hinchinbrook Entrance ⋓	170	60.25 N	146.50 W
Hinchinbrook Island I, Austl.	156	18.23 S	146.17 E
Hinchinbrook Island I, Alaska, U.S.	170	60.22 N	146.30 W
Hinckley, Eng., U.K.	44	52.33 N	1.21 W
Hinckley, Ill., U.S.	206	41.46 N	88.38 W
Hinckley, Minn., U.S.	180	46.01 N	92.56 W
Hinckley, Ohio, U.S.	204	41.14 N	81.45 W
Hinckley, Utah, U.S.	190	39.20 N	112.40 W
Hinckley Reservoir ⊜[1]	200	43.20 N	75.05 W
Hincks, Murlong, and Nicholls National Park ♠	156	33.50 S	136.00 E
Hindan ≃	262a	28.30 N	77.27 E
Hindang	106	10.26 N	124.44 E
Hindaun	114	26.43 N	77.01 E
Hindelang	54	47.30 N	10.22 E
Hindelbank	54	47.03 N	7.32 E
Hindeloopen	48	52.56 N	5.24 E
Hindenburg → Zabrze	30	50.18 N	18.46 E
Hindhead	44	51.07 N	0.44 W
Hindley	42	53.32 N	2.35 W
Hindley Green	252	53.31 N	2.32 W
Hindman	182	37.20 N	82.59 W
Hindmarsh, Lake ⊜	156	36.03 S	141.55 E
Hindmarsh Island I	158b	35.32 S	138.52 E
Hindmarsh Valley	158b	35.30 S	138.38 E
Hindon	44	51.06 N	2.08 W
Hinds	162	44.00 S	171.34 E
Hindsholm I	41	55.33 N	10.40 E
Hinds Lake ⊜	176	48.57 N	57.00 W
Hindubāgh	110	30.49 N	67.45 E
Hindu Kush ∧∧	110	36.00 N	71.30 E
Hindu Malkot	113	30.09 N	73.55 E
Hindupur	112	13.49 N	77.29 E
Hines	192	43.34 N	119.05 W
Hines Creek	172	56.15 N	118.36 W
Hines Creek ≃	172	55.54 N	118.37 W
Hines Peak ∧	218	34.31 N	119.05 W
Hinesville	182	31.51 N	81.36 W
Hinganghāt	112	20.34 N	78.50 E
Hingatungan	106	10.35 N	125.11 E
Hingham	197	42.14 N	70.53 W
Hingham Bay C	197	42.17 N	70.55 W
Hingham Harbor C	273	42.15 N	70.53 W
Hingol ≃	118	25.23 N	65.28 E
Hingoli	112	19.43 N	77.09 E
Hinigaran	106	10.17 N	122.51 E
Hınıs	120	39.22 N	41.44 E
Hınıs ≃	74	39.18 N	42.12 E
Hinkley	218	34.56 N	117.12 W
Hinkson Creek ≃	209	38.56 N	92.23 W
Hinkston Creek ≃	208	38.18 N	84.14 W
Hinnerjoki	26	61.00 N	22.00 E
Hinnerup	41	56.16 N	10.04 E
Hinnøya I	24	68.30 N	16.00 E
Hino, Nihon	84	35.41 N	139.24 E
Hino, Nihon	84	35.00 N	136.15 E
Hino, Nihon	86	35.14 N	133.27 E
Hino ≃, Nihon	84	36.04 N	136.11 E
Hino ≃, Nihon	84	35.09 N	136.02 E
Hino ≃, Nihon	86	35.27 N	133.23 E
Hinoba-an	106	9.35 N	122.28 E
Hinode	84	35.45 N	139.14 E
Hinoemata	84	37.01 N	139.23 E
Hinohara	84	35.43 N	139.09 E
Hinojosa del Duque	34	38.30 N	5.09 W
Hinokage	82	32.39 N	131.24 E
Hino-misaki >, Nihon	86	33.53 N	135.04 E
Hinomi-saki >, Nihon	86	35.26 N	132.38 E
Hinsbeck	52	51.21 N	6.17 E
Hinsdale, Ill., U.S.	206	41.48 N	87.56 W
Hinsdale, Mass., U.S.	197	42.26 N	73.08 W
Hinsdale, Mont., U.S.	192	48.24 N	107.05 W
Hinsdale, N.H., U.S.	178	42.47 N	72.29 W
Hinsdale, N.Y., U.S.	200	42.10 N	78.23 W
Hinsel ◆[8]	253	51.26 N	7.05 E
Hinsen ⊜	40	60.39 N	16.05 E
Hinte	48	53.25 N	7.11 E
Hinterbichl	58	47.01 N	12.20 E
Hinterbrühl	254b	48.05 N	16.15 E
Hinterhermsdorf	50	50.55 N	14.22 E
Hinterrhein	54	46.32 N	9.12 E
Hinterrhein ≃	54	46.49 N	9.25 E
Hinterriss	58	47.28 N	11.28 E
Hintersdorf	254b	48.18 N	16.13 E
Hintersee, B.R.D.	58	47.36 N	12.50 E
Hintersee, D.D.R.	50	53.37 N	14.16 E
Hintersee, Öst.	58	47.42 N	13.17 E
Hintertux	58	47.07 N	11.41 E
Hinterweidenthal	52	49.12 N	7.45 E
Hinterzarten	54	47.54 N	8.06 E
Hinton, Alta., Can.	172	53.25 N	117.34 W
Hinton, Mo., U.S.	209	39.03 N	92.21 W
Hinton, Okla., U.S.	186	35.28 N	98.21 W
Hinton, W. Va., U.S.	182	37.41 N	80.53 W
Hi-numa ⊜	84	36.16 N	140.30 E
Hinuma ≃	84	36.16 N	140.28 E
Hinundayan	106	10.21 N	125.15 E
Hinwil	54	47.18 N	8.51 E
Hinzik	74	40.08 N	40.58 E
Hípico, Club ♠	276e	33.28 S	70.41 W
Hipólito	222	25.41 N	101.26 W
Hipólito Yrigoyen	242	32.55 S	66.20 W
Hippolytushoef	48	52.54 N	4.57 E
Hirado	82	33.22 N	129.33 E
Hirado-shima I	82	33.20 N	129.30 E
Hiraiwa-hana >	164f	24.48 N	141.18 E
Hiraizumi	82	38.59 N	141.07 E
Hirakata, Nihon	86	34.48 N	135.38 E
Hirakata, Nihon	258	35.56 N	139.33 E
Hirakawa, Nihon	258	35.23 N	140.03 E
Hirakawa, Nihon	260	34.52 N	135.47 E
Hirakubo	165d	24.35 N	124.19 E
Hīrākud	112	21.31 N	83.57 E
Hīrākud ⊜[1]	110	21.31 N	83.52 E
Hiram, Maine, U.S.	178	43.53 N	70.49 W
Hiram, Ohio, U.S.	204	41.19 N	81.09 W
Hiraman ≃	144	1.07 S	39.55 E
Hiran □[4]	134	4.10 N	45.20 E
Hirane-zaki >	86	33.43 N	132.08 E
Hirao	86	33.56 N	132.04 E
Hirao-dai ♠	86	33.48 N	130.51 E
Hiraoka → Higashiōsaka	86	34.39 N	135.35 E
Hīrāpur	114	24.22 N	79.13 E
Hirara	165d	24.48 N	125.17 E
Hirata, Nihon	84	35.15 N	136.38 E
Hirata, Nihon	86	35.26 N	132.49 E
Hiratsuka	84	35.19 N	139.21 E
Hiraya	84	35.19 N	137.37 E
Hirfanlı Barajı ◆[6]	120	39.18 N	33.29 E
Hirhafok	138	23.49 N	5.45 E
Hiriyūr	112	13.58 N	76.36 E
Ḥirjillah	122	33.22 N	36.18 E
Hîrlău	38	47.25 N	26.54 E
Hīrmand, Hāmūn-e ⊜	118	30.45 N	61.10 E
Hirokawa, Nihon	86	34.01 N	135.11 E
Hirokawa, Nihon	86	33.15 N	130.32 E
Hirok Sāmi	118	26.02 N	63.25 E
Hiromi	86	32.50 N	132.43 E
Hiroo	82a	42.17 N	143.19 E
Hirooka	258	35.15 N	140.04 E
Hirosaki	82	40.35 N	140.28 E
Hiroschima → Hiroshima	86	34.24 N	132.27 E
Hirose	86	35.22 N	133.10 E
Hiroshima	86	34.24 N	132.27 E
Hiroshima □[5]	86	34.30 N	133.00 E
Hiro-shima I	86	34.22 N	133.43 E
Hiroshima-wan C	86	34.06 N	132.20 E
Hirosima → Hiroshima	86	34.24 N	132.27 E
Hirota	260	34.45 N	135.21 E
Hirsau	52	48.44 N	8.44 E
Hirschaid	52	49.49 N	10.59 E
Hirschbach	50	50.33 N	10.44 E
Hirschberg, D.D.R.	50	50.24 N	11.49 E
Hirschberg → Jelenia Góra, Pol.	30	50.55 N	15.46 E
Hirschfeld	50	51.23 N	13.37 E
Hirschfelde, D.D.R.	50	50.57 N	14.53 E
Hirschfelde, D.D.R.	254a	52.38 N	13.48 E
Hirschhorn	52	49.27 N	8.53 E
Hirschstetten ◆[8]	254b	48.14 N	16.29 E
Hirshfeld Brook ≃	266	40.57 N	74.02 W
Hirsingue	54	47.35 N	7.15 E
Hirson	46	49.55 N	4.05 E
Hîrşova	38	44.41 N	27.57 E
Hirtshals	26	57.35 N	9.58 E
Hirtzfelden	54	47.55 N	7.27 E
Hirukawa	84	35.31 N	137.23 E
Hiru-zen ∧	86	35.19 N	133.40 E
Hirwaun	44	51.45 N	3.30 W
Hisābpur	262b	22.51 N	88.32 E
Hisai, Nihon	84	34.40 N	136.28 E
Hisai, Nihon	260	34.25 N	135.28 E
Hisār	113	29.10 N	75.43 E
Hisarköy	120	39.48 N	29.37 E
Hisarönu	120	41.33 N	32.02 E
Ḥisbān	122	31.48 N	35.48 E
Hisiu	154	9.05 S	146.45 E
Ḥismā ≚	118	29.00 N	35.40 E
Ḥiṣn al-'Abr	134	16.05 N	47.22 E
Ḥiṣn al-Qarn	134	15.11 N	49.05 E
Hispaniola I	228	19.00 N	71.00 W
Histon	44	52.15 N	0.06 E
Hisua	114	24.50 N	85.25 E
Ḥisyah	120	34.24 N	36.45 E
Hīt	118	33.38 N	42.49 E
Hita	86	33.19 N	130.56 E
Hitachi	84	36.36 N	140.39 E
Hitachi-ōta	84	36.32 N	140.31 E
Hitati → Hitachi	84	36.36 N	140.39 E
Hitchcock	212	29.21 N	95.01 W
Hitchin	44	51.57 N	0.17 W
Hitchins	208	38.17 N	82.55 W
Hither Green ◆[8]	250	51.27 N	0.01 W
Hither Hills State Park ♠	197	41.01 N	72.01 W
Hitiaa	164s	17.36 S	149.18 W
Hitokura	260	34.55 N	135.25 E
Hitotsubashi University ⊍[2]	258	35.42 N	139.27 E
Hitoyoshi	82	32.13 N	130.45 E
Hitra I	26	63.33 N	8.45 E
Hittarp	41	56.06 N	12.38 E
Hittisau	54	47.27 N	9.57 E
Hitzacker	50	53.09 N	11.02 E
Hitze-Berge ∧∧[2]	254a	52.35 N	13.07 E
Hiuchiga-take ∧	84	36.57 N	139.17 E
Hiuchi-nada ⟡[2]	86	34.05 N	133.20 E
Hiūnchuli Pātan ∧	114	28.50 N	82.37 E
Hiva Oa I	164x	9.45 S	139.00 W
Hi Vista	218	34.44 N	117.47 W
Hivris	120	38.18 N	42.10 E
Hiw I	165f	13.10 S	166.35 E
Hiwa	86	34.59 N	132.59 E
Hiwannee	184	31.43 N	88.48 W
Hiwasa	86	33.44 N	134.32 E
Hiwassee ≃	182	35.19 N	84.47 W
Hiwassee Lake ⊜[1]	182	35.10 N	84.05 W
Hixon	172	53.27 N	122.36 W
Hixson	182	35.09 N	85.14 W
Hiyoshi, Nihon	84	35.53 N	137.45 E
Hiyoshi, Nihon	86	35.09 N	135.31 E
Hiyoshi, Nihon	86	33.20 N	132.48 E
Hiyoshi ◆[8]	258	35.33 N	139.39 E
Hiyyon, Naḥal ∨	122	30.12 N	35.07 E
Hizaonna	164m	26.24 N	127.50 E
Hjälmare kanal ≊	40	59.24 N	15.56 E
Hjälmaren ⊜	40	59.15 N	15.45 E
Hjälmaresund ⋓	40	59.15 N	16.06 E
Hjarnø I	41	55.50 N	10.05 E
Hjelm I	41	56.08 N	10.48 E
Hjelmelandsvågen	26	59.14 N	6.11 E
Hjeltefjorden C[2]	26	60.40 N	4.55 E
Hjembæk	41	55.42 N	11.25 E
Hjo	26	58.18 N	14.17 E
Hjøllund	41	56.05 N	9.25 E
Hjordkær	41	55.01 N	9.19 E
Hjørring	26	57.28 N	9.59 E
Hjort Basin ⟡[1]	9	59.00 S	158.00 E
Hjortkvarn	40	58.53 N	15.25 E
Hjørundfjorden C[2]	26	62.21 N	6.23 E
Hlabisa	148	28.08 S	31.52 E
Hlaingbwe	100	17.08 N	97.50 E
Hlatikulu	148	27.00 S	31.25 E
Hlegu	100	17.06 N	96.14 E
Hlinsko	30	49.45 N	15.55 E
Hlobane	148	27.42 S	31.00 E
Hlohovec	30	48.25 N	17.47 E
Hluboká nad Vltavou	30	49.03 N	14.27 E
Hlučín	30	49.54 N	18.12 E
Hluhluwe	148	28.01 S	32.15 E
Hluhluwe Game Reserve ◆[4]	148	28.05 S	32.04 E
Hluti	148	27.13 S	31.35 E
Hmawbi	100	17.06 N	96.02 E
Hnilec ≃	30	48.53 N	21.01 E
Ho	140	6.35 N	0.30 E
Hoa-binh	100	20.50 N	105.20 E
Hoa-da	100	11.11 N	108.33 E
Hoagland	206	40.57 N	85.00 W
Hoagland Ditch ≊	206	40.48 N	86.48 W
Hoai-nhon	100	14.26 N	109.01 E
Hoanib ≃	146	19.27 S	12.46 E
Hoare Bay C	166	65.20 N	62.30 W
Hoarusib ≃	146	19.03 S	12.36 E
Hoa-thoi	259c	10.44 N	106.35 E
Hoback ≃	192	43.19 N	110.44 W
Hobart, Austl.	156	42.53 S	147.19 E
Hobart, Ind., U.S.	206	41.32 N	87.15 W
Hobart, N.Y., U.S.	200	42.22 N	74.40 W
Hobart, Okla., U.S.	186	35.01 N	99.06 W
Hobart, Wash., U.S.	214	47.25 N	121.58 W
Hobbs, Ind., U.S.	206	40.17 N	85.57 W
Hobbs, N. Mex., U.S.	186	32.42 N	103.08 W
Hobbs Coast ●[2]	9	74.45 S	131.00 W
Hobe Sound	210	27.04 N	80.08 W
Hobgood	182	36.02 N	77.24 W
Hobhole Drain ≊	44	52.59 N	0.02 E
Hobo	236	2.35 N	75.27 W
Hoboken, Bel.	46	51.10 N	4.21 E
Hoboken, N.J., U.S.	200	40.45 N	74.03 W
Hobro	26	56.38 N	9.48 E
Hobson	192	47.00 N	109.52 W
Hobson Lake ⊜	172	52.30 N	120.20 W
Hobsons Bay C	264b	37.51 S	144.56 E
Hoburgen >	26	56.55 N	18.07 E
Hocaköy, Tür.	120	37.08 N	32.16 E
Hocaköy, Tür.	120	41.03 N	30.17 E
Hocalar	120	38.34 N	30.00 E
Hocalı	120	38.41 N	27.41 E
Hochalmspitze ∧	58	47.01 N	13.19 E
Hochandochtla Mountain ∧	170	65.32 N	154.50 W
Höchberg	52	49.49 N	9.51 E
Hochburg	58	48.07 N	12.52 E
Hochdahl	52	51.13 N	6.56 E
Hochdorf	54	47.10 N	8.17 E
Höchenschwand	54	47.44 N	8.10 E
Hochfeiler (Gran Pilastro) ∧	58	46.58 N	11.44 E
Hochfeld	146	21.28 S	17.58 E
Hochfeld ◆[8]	253	51.25 N	6.46 E
Hochfelden	52	48.45 N	7.34 E
Hochfilzen	58	47.28 N	12.37 E
Hochfinstermünz	54	46.56 N	10.29 E
Hochgern ∧	58	47.45 N	12.30 E
Hochgolling ∧	58	47.16 N	13.45 E
Hochheide	253	51.27 N	6.41 E
Hochheim, B.R.D.	52	50.01 N	8.20 E
Hochheim, Tex., U.S.	212	29.19 N	97.17 W
Hochkirch	50	51.09 N	14.34 E
Hochkönig ∧	58	47.25 N	13.04 E
Hochkreuz ∧	58	46.49 N	13.04 E
Hochlar ◆[8]	253	51.36 N	7.10 E
Hochlarmark ◆[8]	253	51.34 N	7.11 E
Hochneukirch	52	51.06 N	6.26 E
Hochries ∧	58	47.45 N	12.14 E
Hochschwab ∧	30	47.37 N	15.09 E
Hochsimmer ∧	52	50.21 N	7.12 E
Hochspeyer	52	49.26 N	7.54 E
Höchst, B.R.D.	52	49.48 N	8.59 E
Höchst, Öst.	54	47.28 N	9.38 E
Höchst ◆[8]	52	50.07 N	8.33 E
Höchstadt an der Aisch	52	49.42 N	10.44 E
Höchstädt an der Donau	52	48.36 N	10.34 E
Höchsten	253	51.27 N	7.29 E
Höchstenbach	52	50.38 N	7.44 E
Hochtaunus, Naturpark ♠	52	50.20 N	8.20 E
Hochtor)(	58	47.05 N	12.51 E
Hoch'uan → Hechuan	97	30.00 N	106.16 E
Ho Chung	261d	22.22 N	114.14 E
Hochvogel ∧	54	47.23 N	10.26 E
Hockanum ≃	197	41.45 N	72.39 W
Hockenheim	52	49.19 N	8.33 E
Hockeroda	50	50.35 N	11.26 E
Hockessin	275	39.47 N	75.42 W
Hocking ≃	178	39.12 N	81.45 W
Hockley, Eng., U.K.	44	51.37 N	0.40 E
Hockley, Tex., U.S.	212	30.02 N	95.51 W
Hockomock Swamp ≋	273	41.59 N	71.05 W
Hodal	114	27.54 N	77.22 E
Hōdatsu-san ∧	84	36.47 N	136.49 E
Hodder ≃	42	51.37 N	0.40 E
Hoddesdon	44	51.46 N	0.01 W
Hoddlesden	252	53.42 N	2.26 W
Hodeida → Al-Ḥudaydah	134	14.48 N	42.57 E
Hodenhagen	48	52.46 N	9.35 E
Hodge	184	32.17 N	92.43 W
Hodgenville	184	37.34 N	85.44 W
Hodges, Lake ⊜[1]	218	33.03 N	117.05 W
Hodges Brook ≃	273	41.58 N	71.14 W
Hodges Creek ≃	209	39.15 N	90.13 W
Hodges Hill ∧[2]	176	49.04 N	55.53 W
Hodgeville	174	50.08 N	106.58 W
Hodgkins	268	41.46 N	87.51 W
Hodgkins Seamount ⟡[3]	16	53.20 N	135.45 W
Hodgson	174	51.13 N	97.34 W
Hodgson ≃	154	14.48 S	134.35 E
Hodgson, Mount ∧[2]	152	22.26 S	121.10 E
Hodh ◆[1]	140	16.10 N	8.40 W
Hod HaSharon	122	32.09 N	34.53 E
Hódmezővásárhely	30	46.25 N	20.20 E
Hodmo ≃	134	10.45 N	46.23 E
Hodna, Chott el ⊜	138	35.25 N	4.45 E
Hodna, Monts du ∧∧	138	35.50 N	4.50 E
Hodna, Plaine du ≚	34	35.38 N	4.30 E
Hodnet	44	52.51 N	2.35 W
Hodogaya ◆[8]	258	35.27 N	139.36 E
Hodogaya Baseball Ground ♠	258	35.27 N	139.35 E
Hodonín	30	48.51 N	17.08 E
Hodzana ≃	170	66.15 N	147.48 W
Hoed	41	56.19 N	10.49 E
Hoedekenskerke	48	51.25 N	3.55 E
Hoehne	188	37.17 N	104.23 W
Hoek van Holland	48	51.59 N	4.09 E
Hoeningen	253	51.05 N	6.41 E
Hoensbroek	52	50.55 N	5.55 E
Hœrdt	54	48.42 N	7.47 E
Hoerstgen	253	51.30 N	6.27 E
Hoeryŏng	88	42.27 N	129.44 E
Hoeyang	88	38.43 N	127.36 E
Hof, B.R.D.	50	50.18 N	11.55 E
Hof, Ísland	24a	64.34 N	14.39 W
Hofburg ⊍	254b	48.12 N	16.22 E
Höfðakaupstaður	24a	65.50 N	20.19 W
Hofei → Hefei	90	31.51 N	117.17 E
Hofeld	52	49.30 N	7.09 E
Höfen	52	50.32 N	6.15 E
Hoffman, Ill., U.S.	209	38.32 N	89.16 W
Hoffman, Minn., U.S.	188	45.50 N	95.48 W
Hoffman Estates	206	42.03 N	88.05 W
Hoffman Island I	266	40.35 N	74.03 W
Hoffmans	200	42.54 N	74.05 W
Hoffman Station	274a	43.04 N	78.50 W
Hoffnung	253	51.07 N	7.13 E
Hofgeismar	48	51.30 N	9.22 E
Hofheim	52	50.07 N	8.26 E
Hofheim in Unterfranken, B.R.D.	50		
	52	50.08 N	10.31 E
Höflein an der Donau	254b	48.21 N	16.17 E
Hofmeyr	148	31.39 S	25.50 E
Höfn	24a	64.17 N	15.10 W
Hofors	40	60.33 N	16.17 E
Hofsjökull ◸	24a	64.48 N	18.50 W
Hofstade	46	50.58 N	4.02 E
Hofstede ◆[8]	253	51.30 N	7.12 E
Hofstra University ⊍[2]	266	40.43 N	73.36 W
Hōfu	86	34.03 N	131.34 E
Hofuf → Al-Hufūf	118	25.22 N	49.34 E
Hofweier	54	48.25 N	7.55 E
Hogalbāria	116	23.53 N	88.51 E
Höganäs	41	56.12 N	12.33 E
Hogan Lake ⊜	180	45.52 N	78.30 W
Hogansburg	196	44.59 N	74.40 W
Hogansville	182	33.11 N	84.55 W
Hogarth, Mount ∧[2]	156	21.48 S	136.58 E
Hogar y Redención	276a	19.22 N	99.13 W
Hogatza ≃	170	66.00 N	155.29 W
Hogback Mountain ∧, U.S.	197	42.43 N	72.25 W
Hogback Mountain ∧, Mont., U.S.	192	44.54 N	112.07 W
Hogback Mountain ∧, S.C., U.S.	182	35.10 N	82.17 W
Högbo	40	60.40 N	16.48 E
Hog Canyon ∨	216	35.42 N	120.35 W
Hog Creek ≃	212	31.32 N	97.18 W
Högfors	40	59.59 N	15.01 E
Hoggar → Ahaggar ∧∧	138	23.00 N	6.30 E
Hoghton	252	53.44 N	2.35 W
Hoghton Tower ⊥	252	53.44 N	2.34 W
Hog Island I, Mass., U.S.	273	42.40 N	70.46 W
Hog Island I, Mich., U.S.	180	45.48 N	85.22 W
Hog Island I, Vt., U.S.	196	44.57 N	73.13 W
Hog Island I, Va., U.S.	198	37.25 N	75.41 W
Hog Island Bay C	198	37.27 N	75.46 W
Hogoro	144	5.57 S	36.27 E
Hog Point >	106	5.18 N	119.15 E
Hogs Back ●[4]	44	51.13 N	0.40 W
Högsby	26	57.10 N	16.02 E
Högsjö	40	59.02 N	15.41 E
Hoh ≃	214	47.45 N	124.29 W
Hoh, South Fork ≃	214	47.46 N	124.01 W
Hohe Acht ∧	52	50.23 N	7.00 E
Hohebach	52	49.22 N	9.44 E
Hohegeiss	50	51.40 N	10.40 E
Hohelimburg, Schloss ⊥	253	51.21 N	7.34 E
Hohe Mark, Naturpark ♠	253	51.38 N	6.49 E
Hohenaschau	58	47.45 N	12.19 E
Hohenau	242	27.05 S	55.45 W
Hohenau an der March	30	48.36 N	16.55 E
Hohenbrunn	58	48.03 N	11.42 E
Hohenbucko	50	51.46 N	13.28 E
Hohenbudberg ◆[8]	253	51.23 N	6.40 E
Hohendorf	50	54.01 N	13.44 E
Hohenebra	50	51.18 N	10.49 E
Hoheneggelsen	48	52.13 N	10.10 E
Hohenems	54	47.22 N	9.41 E
Hohenfurch	54	47.51 N	10.54 E
Hohengüstow	50	53.14 N	13.59 E
Hohenhameln	48	52.15 N	10.03 E
Hohenheide	253	51.29 N	7.47 E
Hohenkirchen, B.R.D.	48	53.39 N	7.55 E
Hohenkirchen, B.R.D.	52	51.23 N	9.29 E
Hohenkirchen, D.D.R.	50	53.51 N	11.17 E
Hohenkirchen, D.D.R.	50	50.51 N	10.41 E
Hohenleipisch	50	51.30 N	13.34 E
Hohenleuben	50	50.43 N	12.03 E
Hohenlimburg	52	51.21 N	7.35 E
Hohenlimburg, Schloss ⊥	253	51.21 N	7.34 E
Hohenlinden	58	48.09 N	12.00 E
Hohenmölsen	50	51.09 N	12.06 E
Hohen Neuendorf	50	52.40 N	13.16 E
Hohensalza → Inowrocław	30	52.48 N	18.15 E
Hohenschönhausen ◆[8]	254a	52.33 N	13.30 E
Hohenseeden	50	52.19 N	12.01 E
Hohenseefeld	50	51.53 N	13.18 E
Hohenstaufen	52	48.44 N	9.43 E
Hohenstein → Olsztynek	30	53.36 N	20.17 E
Hohenstein-Ernstthal	50	50.48 N	12.42 E
Hohensyburg ⊥	52	51.25 N	7.29 E
Hohenthurm	50	51.31 N	12.05 E
Hohenthurn	58	46.33 N	13.40 E
Hohentwiel ∧	54	47.46 N	8.49 E
Hohenwald	184	35.33 N	87.33 W
Hohenwarte-Stausee ⊜[1]	50	50.32 N	11.30 E
Hohenwarthe	50	52.13 N	11.42 E
Hohenwutzen	50	52.51 N	14.07 E
Hohenzethen	50	53.03 N	10.49 E
Hohenzollern, Burg ⊥	54	48.19 N	8.58 E
Hohenzollernkanal ≊	254a	52.32 N	13.20 E
Hoher Dachstein ∧	58	47.28 N	13.35 E
Hoher Freschen ∧	54	47.18 N	9.46 E
Hohe Rhön ∧∧	52	50.30 N	10.00 E
Hoher Ifen ∧	54	47.21 N	10.05 E
Hoherlehme	254a	52.19 N	13.37 E
Hoher Mechtin ∧[2]	50	53.03 N	10.55 E
Hoher Meissner ∧	48	51.12 N	9.50 E
Hoher Riffler ∧	54	47.07 N	10.22 E
Hoher Sonnblick ∧	58	47.03 N	12.57 E
Hoher Zinken ∧	58	47.40 N	13.20 E
Hohe Tauern ∧∧	58	47.10 N	12.30 E
Hohe Warte (Monte Coglians) ∧	58	46.37 N	12.53 E
Hoh Head >	214	47.46 N	124.29 W
Höhn	52	50.37 N	8.00 E
Hohndorf	50	50.45 N	12.40 E
Hohne	48	52.35 N	10.22 E
Hohneck, Le ∧	54	48.02 N	7.01 E
Hohnstein	50	50.59 N	14.10 E
Hohoe	140	7.09 N	0.28 E
Hōhoku	86	34.17 N	130.57 E
Ho-Ho-Kus	266	41.00 N	74.07 W
Hohokus Brook ≃	266	40.57 N	74.06 W
Hoholitna ≃	170	61.31 N	157.00 W
Höhscheid ◆[8]	253	51.09 N	7.04 E
Hohultslätt	26	56.58 N	15.39 E
Hohwacht	50	54.19 N	10.41 E
Hohwachter Bucht C	41	54.20 N	10.45 E
Hoi-an	100	15.52 N	108.19 E
Hoihow → Haikou	92	20.06 N	110.21 E
Hoima	144	1.26 N	31.21 E
Hoisdorf	48	53.39 N	10.20 E
Hoisington	188	38.31 N	98.47 W
Hoisten	253	51.08 N	6.42 E
Hoi-xuan	100	20.22 N	105.07 E
Hojāi	110	26.00 N	92.51 E
Højby, Dan.	41	55.55 N	11.37 E
Højby, Dan.	41	55.20 N	10.27 E
Höje	40	59.54 N	13.33 E
Højer	26	54.58 N	8.43 E
Højerup	41	55.17 N	12.27 E
Hōjō → Kasai, Nihon	86	34.56 N	134.50 E
Hōjō, Nihon	86	33.58 N	132.46 E
Hoka	120	40.21 N	40.55 E
Hokah	180	43.45 N	91.21 W
Hokang → Hegang	79	47.24 N	130.17 E
Hökåsen	40	59.40 N	16.35 E

ENGLISH

Name	Page	Lat.°′	Long.°′
Hokendauqua	198	40.39 N	75.29 W
Hökensås ∧∧[2]	26	58.11 N	14.08 E
Hokes Bluff	184	34.00 N	85.52 W
Hoketçe	120	38.16 N	36.13 E
Hōki ≃	84	36.47 N	140.08 E
Hokianga Harbour C	162	35.32 S	173.22 E
Hokitika	162	42.43 S	170.58 E
Hokkaidō □[5]	82a	44.00 N	143.00 E
Hokkaidō I	82a	44.00 N	143.00 E
Hokksund	26	59.47 N	9.59 E
Hoko ≃	214	48.17 N	124.22 W
Hōkōji	260	34.52 N	135.07 E
Hököpinge	41	55.30 N	13.00 E
Hokota	84	36.09 N	140.31 E
Hok So Wan	261d	22.13 N	114.14 E
Hokubo	86	34.57 N	133.38 E
Hokudan	86	34.32 N	134.56 E
Hokura ≃	84	37.10 N	138.16 E
Hokuriku-tunnel ◆[5]	84	35.42 N	136.10 E
Hokusei	84	35.09 N	136.31 E
Hola	144	1.29 S	40.02 E
Holalkere	112	14.02 N	76.11 E
Holanda → Netherlands □[1]	30	52.15 N	5.30 E
Holbæk	41	55.43 N	11.43 E
Holbeach	44	52.49 N	0.01 E
Holbeach Marsh ≋	44	52.52 N	0.05 E
Holberg	172	50.31 N	128.01 W
Holborn ◆[8]	250	51.31 N	0.07 W
Holbrook, Austl.	161b	35.44 S	147.19 E
Holbrook, Ariz., U.S.	190	34.54 N	110.10 W
Holbrook, Ill., U.S.	268	41.32 N	87.38 W
Holbrook, Md., U.S.	274b	39.24 N	76.51 W
Holbrook, Mass., U.S.	197	42.09 N	71.01 W
Holbrook, Nebr., U.S.	188	40.18 N	100.01 W
Holbrook, N.Y., U.S.	200	40.48 N	73.05 W
Holbrook Mountain ∧[2]	202	44.25 N	77.51 W
Holckenhavn	41	55.17 N	10.47 E
Holcomb, Ill., U.S.	206	42.04 N	89.06 W
Holcomb, N.Y., U.S.	200	42.54 N	77.25 W
Holcomb Creek ≃	218	34.17 N	117.08 W
Holden, Alta., Can.	172	53.14 N	112.14 W
Holden, Mass., U.S.	197	42.21 N	71.52 W
Holden, Mo., U.S.	184	38.43 N	94.01 W
Holden, Utah, U.S.	190	39.06 N	112.16 W
Holden, W. Va., U.S.	178	37.50 N	82.04 W
Holden, Mount ∧[2]	206	41.40 N	87.03 W
Holdenstedt	48	52.55 N	10.31 E
Holden Village	214	48.12 N	120.47 W
Holdenville	186	35.05 N	96.24 W
Holder	210	28.58 N	82.25 W
Holderness >[1]	42	53.47 N	0.10 W
Holdfast	174	50.58 N	105.25 W
Holdich	244	45.57 S	68.13 W
Holdingford	180	45.44 N	94.26 W
Holdorf	48	52.35 N	8.07 E
Holdrege	188	40.26 N	99.22 W
Holeby	41	54.43 N	11.28 E
Hole in the Mountain Peak ∧	194	40.55 N	115.05 W
Hole Narsipur	112	12.47 N	76.15 E
Holešov	30	49.20 N	17.35 E
Holetown	231g	13.11 N	59.39 W
Holgate, S. Afr.	148	33.59 S	22.21 E
Holgate, Ohio, U.S.	206	41.15 N	84.08 W
Holguín	230p	20.53 N	76.15 W
Hol-Hol, Djibouti	134	11.19 N	42.57 E
Holhol, Tür.	120	39.14 N	40.03 E
Holíč	30	48.49 N	17.10 E
Holice	30	50.04 N	15.59 E
Holiday Beach Provincial Park ♠	204	42.02 N	83.05 W
Holiday Hills	206	42.18 N	88.13 W
Holiday Lake Amusement Park ♠	275	40.02 N	74.56 W
Holiday Shores	209	38.55 N	89.56 W
Holitna ≃	170	61.40 N	157.12 W
Höljes	26	60.54 N	12.36 E
Hollabrunn	30	48.34 N	16.05 E
Holladay	190	40.40 N	111.49 W
Hollage	48	52.20 N	7.58 E
Hollam's Bird Island I	146	24.45 S	14.34 E
Holland, Man., Can.	174	49.32 N	98.55 W
Holland, Mich., U.S.	206	42.47 N	86.07 W
Holland, N.Y., U.S.	200	42.38 N	78.33 W
Holland, Ohio, U.S.	206	41.37 N	83.43 W
Holland, Pa., U.S.	275	40.10 N	74.59 W
Holland, Tex., U.S.	212	30.53 N	97.24 W
Holland, Va., U.S.	198	36.41 N	76.47 W
Holland □[9]	48	52.20 N	4.45 E
Holland → Netherlands □[1]	30	52.15 N	5.30 E
Holland ≃	202	44.12 N	79.31 W
Holland, Mount ∧	152	32.12 S	119.44 E
Hollandale	184	33.10 N	90.58 W
Hollande, Étang de ⊜	251	48.44 N	1.48 E
Holland Fen ≋	44	53.00 N	0.10 W
Hollandia → Jayapura	154	2.32 S	140.42 E
Holland Landing	202	44.06 N	79.29 W
Holland-on-Sea	44	51.48 N	1.13 E
Holland Park	161a	27.31 S	153.03 E
Holland Patent	200	43.14 N	75.15 W
Holland Point >	198	38.43 N	76.32 W
Holland Pond State Park ♠	197	42.04 N	72.09 W
Hollands Diep ⋓	48	51.42 N	4.30 E
Holland Straits ⋓	198	38.08 N	76.02 W
Holland Tunnel ◆[5]	266	40.44 N	74.02 W
Hollansburg	208	39.59 N	84.48 W
Holleben	50	51.26 N	11.53 E
Hollenfels, Château ⊥	52	49.43 N	6.03 E
Höllengebirge ∧∧	58	47.48 N	13.39 E
Hollenstedt	48	53.22 N	9.43 E
Höllenstein Berg ∧	254b	48.06 N	16.11 E
Hollern	48	53.36 N	9.32 E
Holleton	152	31.57 S	119.02 E
Holley	200	43.14 N	78.02 W
Hollick-Kenyon Plateau ∧∧[1]	9	79.00 S	97.00 W
Holliday, Mo., U.S.	209	39.29 N	92.08 W
Holliday, Tex., U.S.	186	33.49 N	98.42 W
Holliday Creek ≃	186	33.55 N	98.28 W
Holliday Park ♠	271	42.21 N	83.24 W
Hollidaysburg	204	40.26 N	78.23 W
Hollingbourne	250	51.16 N	0.38 E
Hollingstedt	41	54.27 N	9.19 E
Hollingworth	252	53.28 N	1.59 W
Hollingworth Lake ⊜	252	53.38 N	2.06 W
Hollins	252	53.34 N	2.17 W
Hollins Green	252	53.25 N	2.27 W
Hollinswood	274c	38.55 N	77.13 W
Hollis, N.H., U.S.	197	42.44 N	71.35 W
Hollis, Okla., U.S.	186	34.41 N	99.55 W
Hollis ◆[8]	266	40.43 N	73.46 W
Hollister	216	36.51 N	121.24 W
Holliston	197	42.12 N	71.26 W
Hollman, Cape >	154	4.59 S	150.06 E
Holloman Air Force Base ⊠	190	32.51 N	106.05 W
Holloway	204	40.10 N	81.08 W
Holloway Terrace	275	39.42 N	75.33 W
Hollow Rock	184	36.02 N	88.16 W
Hollowville	200	42.12 N	73.42 W
Hollsopple	204	40.13 N	78.56 W
Hollum	48	53.26 N	5.37 E
Höllviken C	41	55.26 N	12.54 E
Höllviksnäs	41	55.25 N	12.57 E
Holly, Colo., U.S.	188	38.03 N	102.07 W
Holly, Mich., U.S.	206	42.48 N	83.38 W
Holly, Wash., U.S.	214	47.34 N	122.58 W
Holly, Mount ∧[2]	275	40.00 N	74.47 W
Holly Grove	184	34.36 N	91.12 W
Holly Hill, Fla., U.S.	182	29.14 N	81.02 W
Holly Hill, S.C., U.S.	182	33.19 N	80.25 W
Holly Park	198	39.53 N	74.10 W

DEUTSCH

Name	Seite	Breite°′	Länge°′ E=Ost
Holly Pond ⊜	266	41.03 N	73.30 W
Holly River State Park ♠	178	38.40 N	80.21 W
Holly Run ≃	275	39.47 N	75.03 W
Holly Springs	184	34.41 N	89.26 W
Holly State Recreation Area ♠	206	42.49 N	83.32 W
Hollywood, Eire	42	53.06 N	6.35 W
Hollywood, Fla., U.S.	210	26.00 N	80.09 W
Hollywood, Md., U.S.	198	38.21 N	76.34 W
Hollywood, Pa., U.S.	275	40.05 N	75.06 W
Hollywood ◆[8]	218	34.06 N	118.21 W
Hollywood, Mount ∧	270	34.08 N	118.18 W
Hollywood Bowl ♠	270	34.07 N	118.20 W
Hollywood-Burbank Airport ⊠	218	34.12 N	118.21 W
Hollywood Heights	209	38.39 N	89.59 W
Hollywood Indian Reservation ◆[4]	210	26.02 N	80.13 W
Hollywood Park Race Track ♠	270	33.57 N	118.20 W
Hollywood Reservoir ⊜[1]	270	34.07 N	118.20 W
Holman Island	166	70.43 N	117.43 W
Hólmavík	24a	65.43 N	21.43 W
Holmdel	198	40.21 N	74.11 W
Holme, Dan.	41	56.07 N	10.11 E
Holme, Eng., U.K.	252	53.33 N	1.50 W
Holme ≃	42	53.41 N	1.43 W
Holme Chapel	252	53.45 N	2.11 W
Holmen, Nor.	26	60.40 N	10.22 E
Holmen, Wis., U.S.	180	43.58 N	91.15 W
Holmenkollen	26	59.58 N	10.40 E
Holmes, N.Y., U.S.	200	41.31 N	73.39 W
Holmes, Pa., U.S.	275	39.54 N	75.19 W
Holmes □[6]	204	40.33 N	81.55 W
Holmes, Mount ∧	192	44.49 N	110.51 W
Holmes Beach	210	27.31 N	82.43 W
Holmesburg ◆[8]	275	40.02 N	75.03 W
Holmes Creek ≃	184	30.30 N	85.47 W
Holmesglen	264b	37.53 S	145.06 E
Holmes Harbor C	214	48.04 N	122.32 W
Holmes Lake ⊜	174	57.05 N	96.45 W
Holmes Reefs ⟡[2]	154	16.27 S	148.00 E
Holmes Run ≃	274c	38.48 N	77.07 W
Holmes Run Acres	274c	38.51 N	77.13 W
Holmestrand	26	59.29 N	10.18 E
Holmesville, N.Y., U.S.	200	42.31 N	75.24 W
Holmesville, Ohio, U.S.	204	40.38 N	81.55 W
Holmeswood	252	53.39 N	2.52 W
Holmfirth	42	53.35 N	1.46 W
Holmia	236	4.58 N	59.35 W
Holmön I	26	63.47 N	20.53 E
Holmsbu	26	59.33 N	10.27 E
Holmsjön ⊜, Sve.	26	62.25 N	15.20 E
Holmsjön ⊜, Sve.	26	62.41 N	16.33 E
Holmsund	26	63.42 N	20.21 E
Hölö	40	59.01 N	17.35 E
Holod	38	46.47 N	22.08 E
Holoit, Punta >	222	21.37 N	88.08 W
Ḥolon	122	32.01 N	34.46 E
Holoog	146	27.22 S	17.55 E
Holopaw	210	28.08 N	81.04 W
Holroyd	264a	33.50 S	150.58 E
Holroyd ≃	154	14.10 S	141.36 E
Holsloot	48	52.44 N	6.48 E
Holstebro	26	56.21 N	8.38 E
Holsted	41	55.30 N	8.55 E
Holstein	188	42.29 N	95.33 W
Holsteinborg ⊥	41	55.13 N	11.28 E
Holsteinische Schweiz ◆[1]	50	54.11 N	10.36 E
Holsteinsborg	166	66.55 N	53.40 W
Holsterhausen	253	51.41 N	6.57 E
Holston ≃	182	35.57 N	83.51 W
Holston High Knob ∧	182	36.27 N	82.05 W
Holsworthy	44	50.49 N	4.21 W
Holt, Eng., U.K.	44	52.55 N	1.05 E
Holt, Wales, U.K.	44	53.05 N	2.53 W
Holt, Ala., U.S.	184	33.15 N	87.29 W
Holt, Calif., U.S.	216	37.56 N	121.26 W
Holt, Fla., U.S.	184	30.43 N	86.45 W
Holt, Mich., U.S.	206	42.39 N	84.31 W
Holt Creek ≃	188	42.28 N	98.50 W
Holte	41	55.49 N	12.28 E
Holtemme ≃	50	51.57 N	11.10 E
Holten	48	52.17 N	6.25 E
Holten ◆[8]	253	51.31 N	6.48 E
Holtenau ◆[8]	50	54.22 N	10.08 E
Holter Lake ⊜[1]	192	46.55 N	111.57 W
Holthausen, B.R.D.	48	52.33 N	7.17 E
Holthausen, B.R.D.	253	51.23 N	7.13 E
Holthausen ◆[8]	253	51.34 N	7.26 E
Holthusen	48	53.08 N	7.18 E
Holton, Ind., U.S.	208	39.04 N	85.23 W
Holton, Kans., U.S.	188	39.28 N	95.44 W
Holtorf	48	52.40 N	9.13 E
Holts Summit	209	38.39 N	92.07 W
Holtsville	200	40.49 N	73.02 W
Holtug	41	55.21 N	12.25 E
Holtville	194	32.49 N	115.23 W
Holtwick	48	52.00 N	7.05 E
Holtwood	198	39.50 N	76.19 W
Holwerd	48	53.22 N	5.54 E
Holy Cross	170	62.12 N	159.47 W
Holy Cross Mountain ∧	172	53.47 N	120.47 W
Holyhead	42	53.19 N	4.38 W
Holyhead Bay C	42	53.23 N	4.37 W
Holy Island I, Eng., U.K.	42	55.41 N	1.48 W
Holy Island I, Scot., U.K.	42	55.32 N	5.04 W
Holy Island I, Wales, U.K.	42	53.18 N	4.37 W
Holy Island I, Mass., U.S.	273	42.43 N	70.50 W
Holyoke, Colo., U.S.	188	40.35 N	102.18 W
Holyoke, Mass., U.S.	197	42.12 N	72.37 W
Holyrood	188	38.35 N	98.25 W
Holyrood Palace ⊍	42	55.56 N	3.12 W
Holy Sepulchre, The Church of the ⊍[1]	122	31.46 N	35.14 E
Holýšov	30	49.36 N	13.05 E
Holywell	42	53.17 N	3.13 W
Holywell Green	252	53.41 N	1.52 W
Holywood	42	54.38 N	5.50 W
Holzbüttgen	253	51.12 N	6.37 E
Holzen	52	51.26 N	7.31 E
Holzgau	54	47.16 N	10.21 E
Holzgerlingen	52	48.38 N	9.00 E
Holzhausen, B.R.D.	48	52.17 N	8.32 E
Holzhausen, B.R.D.	48	52.01 N	8.44 E
Holzhausen, B.R.D.	48	52.13 N	8.01 E
Holzhausen, D.D.R.	50	51.18 N	12.28 E
Holzhausen an der Haide	52	50.13 N	7.55 E
Holzheim	52	51.09 N	6.39 E
Holzkirchen	58	47.52 N	11.42 E
Holzminden	48	51.50 N	9.27 E
Holzweissig	50	51.36 N	12.18 E
Holzwickede	48	51.30 N	7.36 E
Homa	120	38.14 N	30.01 E
Homa Bay	144	0.31 S	34.27 E
Homalin	100	24.52 N	94.55 E
Homathko ≃	172	50.55 N	124.50 W
Homathko Snowfield ◸	172	51.05 N	124.30 W
Homāyūnshahr	118	32.41 N	51.31 E
Homberg, B.R.D.	52	50.43 N	8.59 E
Homberg, B.R.D.	52	51.02 N	9.24 E
Homberg, B.R.D.	52	51.28 N	6.38 E
Homberg, B.R.D.	253	51.18 N	6.56 E
Hombori	140	15.17 N	1.42 W
Hombori Tondo ∧	140	15.16 N	1.40 W
Hombourg-haut	52	49.08 N	6.46 E
Hombre Muerto, Salar de ≚	242	25.23 S	67.06 W

Symbols in the index entries represent the broad categories identified in the key at the right. Symbols with superior numbers (∧∧[2]) identify subcategories (see complete key on page *I* · 26).

Kartensymbole in dem Registerverzeichnis stellen die rechts in Schlüssel erklärten Kategorien dar. Symbole mit hochgestellten Ziffern (∧∧[2]) bezeichnen Unterabteilungen einer Kategorie (vgl. vollständiger Schlüssel auf Seite *I* · 26).

Los símbolos incluídos en el texto del indice representan las grandes categorias identificadas con la clave a la derecha. Los símbolos con numeros en su parte superior (∧∧[2]) identifican las subcategorías (véase la clave completa en la página *I* · 26).

Les symboles de l'index représentent les catégories indiquées dans la légende à droite. Les symboles suivis d'un indice (∧∧[2]) représentent des sous-catégories (voir légende complète à la page *I* · 26).

Os símbolos incluídos no texto do índice representam as grandes categorias identificadas com a chave à direita. Os símbolos com números em sua parte superior (∧∧[2]) identificam as subcategorias (veja-se a chave completa à página *I* · 26).

∧ Mountain	Berg	Montaña	Montagne	Montanha
∧∧ Mountains	Berge	Montañas	Montagnes	Montanhas
)(Pass	Pass	Paso	Col	Passo
∨ Valley, Canyon	Tal, Cañon	Valle, Cañón	Vallée, Canyon	Vale, Canhão
≚ Plain	Ebene	Llano	Plaine	Planície
> Cape	Kap	Cabo	Cap	Cabo
I Island	Insel	Isla	Île	Ilha
II Islands	Inseln	Islas	Îles	Ilhas
● Other Topographic Features	Andere Topographische Objekte	Otros Elementos Topográficos	Autres données topographiques	Outros Elementos Topográficos

ESPAÑOL / FRANÇAIS / PORTUGUÊS

Nombre / Nom / Nome	Página / Page	Lat.°′	Long.°′ W=Oeste / W=Ouest
Hombruch ◆[8]	253	51.29 N	7.26 E
Homburg, B.R.D.	52	49.19 N	7.20 E
Homburg → Bad Homburg vor der Höhe, B.R.D.	52	50.13 N	8.37 E
Home, Pa., U.S.	204	40.44 N	79.06 W
Home, Wash., U.S.	214	47.17 N	122.46 W
Homeacre	204	40.51 N	79.55 W
Home Bay C, N.W. Ter., Can.	166	68.45 N	67.10 W
Home Bay C, Gilb. Is.	164d	0.53 S	169.35 E
Homebush Bay C	264a	33.50 S	151.05 E
Home Corner	206	40.32 N	85.40 W
Homécourt	52	49.14 N	5.59 E
Home Creek ≃	186	31.29 N	99.14 W
Homedale, Idaho, U.S.	192	43.37 N	116.56 W
Homedale, Ohio, U.S.	204	40.04 N	83.02 W
Home Gardens	218	33.53 N	117.30 W
Home Hill	156	19.40 S	147.25 E
Homeland, Calif., U.S.	218	33.44 N	117.07 W
Homeland, Fla., U.S.	210	27.49 N	81.49 W
Homeland Canal ≊	216	35.57 N	119.27 W
Home of Franklin Delano Roosevelt National Historic Site ⊥	200	41.46 N	73.56 W
Home Place	208	39.55 N	86.07 W
Homer, Alaska, U.S.	170	59.39 N	151.33 W
Homer, Ga., U.S.	182	34.20 N	83.30 W
Homer, La., U.S.	184	32.48 N	93.04 W
Homer, Mich., U.S.	206	42.09 N	84.49 W
Homer, Nebr., U.S.	188	42.19 N	96.29 W
Homer, N.Y., U.S.	200	42.38 N	76.11 W
Homer, Ohio, U.S.	204	40.15 N	82.31 W
Homer, Tex., U.S.	212	31.18 N	94.36 W
Homer City	204	40.32 N	79.10 W
Homert ΛΛ[2]	253	51.11 N	7.39 E
Homert, Naturpark ♠, B.R.D.	52	51.15 N	8.10 E
Homert, Naturpark ♠, B.R.D.	253	51.17 N	7.49 E
Homer Tunnel ◆[5]	162	44.45 S	168.00 E
Homerville, Ga., U.S.	182	31.02 N	82.45 W
Homerville, Ohio, U.S.	204	41.02 N	82.08 W
Homer Wash V	194	34.20 N	115.02 W
Homer Youngs Peak Λ	192	45.19 N	113.41 W
Home Seamount ✢[3]	14	12.30 S	176.40 W
Homestead, Austl.	156	20.22 S	145.39 E
Homestead, Fla., U.S.	210	25.29 N	80.29 W
Homestead Air Force Base ■	210	25.29 N	80.23 W
Homestead National Monument of America ♠	188	40.14 N	96.54 W
Homestead Valley	272	37.54 N	122.32 W
Hometown, Ill., U.S.	268	41.44 N	87.44 W
Hometown, Pa., U.S.	200	40.49 N	75.59 W
Homewood, Ala., U.S.	184	33.29 N	86.48 W
Homewood, Calif., U.S.	216	39.05 N	120.10 W
Homewood, Ill., U.S.	206	41.34 N	87.40 W
Homewood, Ohio, U.S.	208	39.23 N	84.33 W
Homewood ◆[8]	269b	40.27 N	79.54 W
Homewood Acres	268	41.34 N	87.43 W
Homeworth	204	40.50 N	81.04 W
Hominy	186	36.25 N	96.24 W
Hominy Creek ≃	186	36.20 N	96.00 W
Hommersåk	26	58.58 N	5.42 E
Hommura	82	34.22 N	139.15 E
Homnābād	112	17.46 N	77.08 E
Homo Bay C	165f	15.57 S	168.11 E
Homochitto ≃	184	31.09 N	91.31 W
Homoíne	146	23.52 S	35.09 E
Homonhon Island I	106	10.44 N	125.43 E
Homosassa	210	28.47 N	82.37 W
Homosassa Bay C	210	28.45 N	82.43 W
Homosassa Springs	210	28.48 N	82.35 W
Homs → Al-Khums, Lībīya	136	32.39 N	14.16 E
Homs → Ḥimṣ, Sūrīy.	120	34.44 N	36.43 E
Honai	86	33.30 N	132.25 E
Honaker	182	37.01 N	81.59 W
Honami	86	33.36 N	130.42 E
Honan → Luoyang	92	34.41 N	112.28 E
Honan → Henan □[4]	80	34.00 N	114.00 E
Honāvar	112	14.17 N	74.27 E
Honaz	120	37.45 N	29.17 E
Honbetsu	82a	43.07 N	143.37 E
Hon-chong	100	10.10 N	104.37 E
Honda	236	5.12 N	74.45 W
Honda, Bahía C, Col.	236	12.21 N	71.47 W
Honda, Bahía C, Cuba	230p	22.57 N	83.10 W
Honda, Cañada ≃	248	33.57 S	59.21 W
Honda Bay C	106	9.53 N	118.49 E
Honddu ≃, Wales, U.K.	44	51.54 N	2.58 W
Honddu ≃, Wales, U.K.	44	51.57 N	3.23 W
Hondeklipbaai	146	30.20 S	17.18 E
Honderfontein	148	32.12 S	21.22 E
Hon-dien, Nui Λ	100	11.33 N	108.38 E
Hondo, Alta., Can.	172	55.04 N	114.02 W
Hondo, Nihon	82	32.27 N	130.12 E
Hondo, N. Mex., U.S.	190	33.23 N	105.16 W
Hondo, Tex., U.S.	186	29.21 N	99.09 W
Hondo ≃, Cuba	276b	22.55 N	82.16 W
Hondo ≃, Méx.	276a	19.26 N	99.15 W
Hondo ≃, N.A.	222	18.29 N	88.19 W
Hondo, Arroyo ≃	216	37.28 N	121.47 W
Hondo, Rio ≃, Calif., U.S.	270	33.55 N	118.10 W
Hondo, Rio ≃, N. Mex., U.S.	186	33.22 N	104.24 W
Hondo Creek ≃	186	28.45 N	99.11 W
Hondoji Temple ⚘[1]	258	35.51 N	139.56 E
Hondschoote	46	50.59 N	2.35 E
Hondsrug ΛΛ[2]	48	52.55 N	6.50 E
Honduras □[1]	220		
	226	15.00 N	86.30 W
Honduras, Cabo de ≻	226	16.01 N	86.02 W
Honduras, Gulf of C	220	16.10 N	87.50 W
Honduras, Port C	226	16.13 N	88.41 W
Honea Path	182	34.27 N	82.24 W
Hönebach	52	50.56 N	9.56 E
Hønefoss	26	60.10 N	10.18 E
Honeoye	200	42.47 N	77.31 W
Honeoye Creek ≃	200	42.58 N	77.43 W
Honeoye Falls	200	42.57 N	77.36 W
Honeoye Lake ⊜	200	42.45 N	77.31 W
Honesdale	200	41.34 N	75.16 W
Honey Brook	198	40.06 N	75.55 W
Honey Creek	206	42.45 N	88.19 W
Honey Creek ≃, Iowa, U.S.	180	42.09 N	93.03 W
Honey Creek ≃, Mo., U.S.	184	39.53 N	93.34 W
Honey Creek ≃, Ohio, U.S.	204	41.05 N	83.12 W
Honey Creek ≃, Pa., U.S.	198	40.36 N	77.35 W
Honey Creek ≃, Wis., U.S.	206	42.41 N	88.17 W
Honeydew	263d	26.05 S	27.55 E
Honeygo Run ≃	274b	39.22 N	76.25 W
Honey Grove	186	33.35 N	95.55 W
Honey Lake ⊜	194	40.16 N	120.19 W
Honeymoon Bay	172	48.49 N	124.10 W
Honeyville	190	41.38 N	112.04 W
Honfleur	46	49.25 N	0.14 E
Høng	41	55.31 N	11.18 E
Honga	142	15.09 S	15.12 E
Hon-gai	100	20.57 N	107.05 E
Hongan	90	31.18 N	114.37 E
Honga River C	198	38.19 N	76.10 W
Hongawa	86	33.43 N	133.19 E
Hongchang	90	34.05 N	113.20 E
Hongch'ŏn	88	37.42 N	127.52 E
Hongchoudai	90	29.03 N	121.11 E
Hongcun	96	31.01 N	119.15 E
Hongdong	92	36.19 N	111.39 E
Honge ≃	90	32.25 N	115.35 E
Höngen	52	51.02 N	5.56 E
Honggun	88	40.46 N	128.27 E
Hong-ha → Red ≃	100	20.17 N	106.34 E
Honghaiwan C	90	22.40 N	115.10 E
Honghe	92	23.23 N	102.35 E
Hongheercun	79	48.09 N	119.19 E
Honghu	90	29.48 N	113.27 E
Honghu ⊜	90	29.52 N	113.23 E
Honghuaerji	79	48.15 N	120.01 E
Honghuaji	90	33.52 N	114.26 E
Honghualiangzi	79	48.06 N	123.12 E
Honghuamu	79	48.33 N	125.39 E
Hongjiang, Zhg.	90	26.49 N	120.03 E
Hongjiang, Zhg.	92	27.00 N	109.51 E
Hong Kong → Victoria	261d	22.17 N	114.09 E
Hong Kong □[2]	80		
	261d	22.15 N	114.10 E
Hong Kong I	261d	22.15 N	114.11 E
Hong Kong, University of ⚘[2]	261d	22.17 N	114.08 E
Hongkou Park ♠	259b	31.16 N	121.28 E
Hongkou Stadium ♠	259b	31.16 N	121.28 E
Honglai	90	25.08 N	118.32 E
Honglanbu	96	31.37 N	118.57 E
Honglinqiao	96	30.59 N	118.59 E
Hongliutai	75	39.48 N	77.26 E
Hongliuyuan	92	41.04 N	95.26 E
Honglongdian	96	30.30 N	119.00 E
Honglu	90	25.44 N	119.20 E
Hongluan	90	28.31 N	117.01 E
Hongluoshan Λ	94	40.56 N	120.42 E
Hongluoxian	94	41.01 N	120.53 E
Hongmeichang	95	39.50 N	115.51 E
Hongmendu	92	26.10 N	102.37 E
Hongmenkou	92	27.22 N	100.30 E
Hongmenpu	97	30.37 N	104.08 E
Hongmiaozi	97	28.47 N	104.02 E
Hong-ngu	100	10.48 N	105.21 E
Hongō, Nihon	84	36.15 N	137.59 E
Hongō, Nihon	86	34.17 N	132.02 E
Hongō, Nihon	86	34.24 N	132.59 E
Hongpailou	97	30.38 N	104.01 E
Hongqiao, Zhg.	90	32.16 N	119.26 E
Hongqiao, Zhg.	90	28.14 N	121.01 E
Hongqiao, Zhg.	95	39.50 N	117.44 E
Hongqiao, Zhg.	96	31.29 N	121.49 E
Hongqiao, Zhg.	259b	31.12 N	121.22 E
Hongqiao Airport ⊠	259b	31.12 N	121.23 E
Hongrie → Hungary □[1]	30	47.00 N	20.00 E
Hongrui	88	35.08 N	118.38 E
Hongshan, Zhg.	79	48.02 N	129.00 E
Hongshan, Zhg.	88	36.37 N	118.00 E
Hongshi	88	41.21 N	119.32 E
Hongshidou	94	41.52 N	122.11 E
Hongshilazi	79	43.00 N	127.04 E
Hongshili	88	40.41 N	125.03 E
Hongshuibao	92	37.24 N	104.00 E
Hongshuichuan	95	40.06 N	117.55 E
Hongshuihe ≃	92	23.45 N	109.30 E
Hongshuyangzi	95	40.36 N	116.36 E
Hongsibao	92	37.18 N	106.02 E
Hongsŏng	88	36.36 N	126.39 E
Hongtang	90	26.06 N	119.14 E
Hongtian	90	25.52 N	117.15 E
Hongtugou	110	38.08 N	91.10 E
Hongtuwan	88	41.03 N	113.39 E
Hongtuzhang Λ	90	23.46 N	115.56 E
Honguedo, Détroit d' ⋓	176	49.15 N	64.00 W
Hongwŏn	88	40.02 N	127.57 E
Hongxingqiao	96	30.55 N	119.52 E
Hongxinpu	90	32.43 N	117.47 E
Hongya	92	29.58 N	103.31 E
Hongyang, Zhg.	90	26.32 N	119.27 E
Hongyang, Zhg.	90	23.28 N	116.13 E
Hongyanzi	94	40.38 N	120.31 E
Hongyōtoku	258	35.41 N	139.55 E
Hongze	90	33.19 N	118.53 E
Hongzehu ⊜	90	33.16 N	118.34 E
Honiara	165e	9.26 S	159.57 E
Honiton	44	50.48 N	3.13 W
Honjō, Nihon	82	39.23 N	140.03 E
Honjō, Nihon	84	36.24 N	138.01 E
Honjō, Nihon	84	36.14 N	139.11 E
Honkamäki ΛΛ[2]	26	62.58 N	27.05 E
Hon-kawane	84	35.07 N	138.09 E
Honker Bay C	272	38.04 N	121.56 W
Hönne ≃	253	51.28 N	7.46 E
Honnecourt-sur-Escaut	46	50.02 N	3.12 E
Honningsvåg	24	70.59 N	25.59 E
Honnō	84	35.29 N	140.18 E
Hönö	26	57.42 N	11.39 E
Honokaa	219d	20.05 N	155.28 W
Honokahua	219a	21.00 N	156.39 W
Honokawai	219a	20.57 N	156.41 W
Honolulu	219c	21.19 N	157.52 W
Honolulu □[6]	219c	21.19 N	157.52 W
Honolulu International Airport ⊠	219c	21.20 N	157.55 W
Honomu	219d	19.52 N	155.07 W
Honouliuli	219c	21.22 N	158.02 W
Hönow	50	52.32 N	13.38 E
Hon-shima I	86	34.23 N	133.47 E
Honshū I	82	36.00 N	138.00 E
Hontoon Island State Park ♠	210	28.59 N	81.22 W
Höntrop ◆[8]	253	51.27 N	7.08 E
Honuapo Bay C	219d	19.05 N	155.33 W
Honyakushiji Temple ⚘[1]	260	34.26 N	135.47 E
Hoo	250	51.25 N	0.34 E
Hood	216	38.22 N	121.31 W
Hood □[6]	212	32.25 N	97.45 W
Hood ≃, N.W. Ter., Can.	166	67.26 N	108.53 W
Hood ≃, Oreg., U.S.	214	45.42 N	121.30 W
Hood, East Fork ≃	214	45.36 N	121.38 W
Hood, Mount Λ	214	45.23 N	121.41 W
Hood Canal C	214	47.35 N	123.00 W
Hood Canal Floating Bridge ◆[5]	214	47.52 N	122.38 W
Hoodoo Peak Λ	192	48.15 N	120.19 W
Hood Point ≻, Austl.	152	34.23 S	119.34 E
Hood Point ≻, Pap. N. Gui.	154	10.05 S	147.45 E
Hood Pond ⊜	273	42.40 N	70.57 W
Hood River	214	45.43 N	121.31 W
Hood River □[6]	214	45.30 N	121.40 W
Hoodsport	214	47.24 N	123.09 W
Hoods Range ΛΛ	156	28.35 S	144.30 E
Hoof	52	51.17 N	9.20 E
Hoogerheide	48	51.25 N	4.20 E
Hoogeveen	48	52.43 N	6.29 E
Hoogeveense Vaart ≃	48	52.42 N	6.11 E
Hoogezand	48	53.09 N	6.47 E
Hooghly □[5]	116	22.50 N	88.15 E
Hooghly ≃[1]	116	21.55 N	88.05 E
Hooghly-Chinsura	116	22.54 N	88.24 E
Hoogkerk	48	53.13 N	6.30 E
Hooglede	46	50.59 N	3.05 E
Hoogstede	48	52.34 N	6.56 E
Hoogstraten	52	51.24 N	4.46 E
Hoogte	148	27.28 S	28.03 E
Hoogvliet	48	51.52 N	4.21 E
Hook	44	51.17 N	0.58 W
Hook ◆[8]	250	51.22 N	0.18 W
Hooker	186	36.52 N	101.13 W
Hooker, Bi'r ⍑[4]	132	30.23 N	30.20 E
Hooker Creek	152	18.20 S	130.40 E
Hook Head ≻	28	52.07 N	6.55 W
Hookina	156	31.45 S	138.20 E
Hook Island I	156	20.08 S	148.55 E
Hook Mountain State Park ♠	266	41.09 N	73.55 W
Hook Point ≻	156	25.48 S	153.05 E
Hooks	184	33.28 N	94.15 W
Hooksiel	48	53.38 N	8.01 E
Hoolehua	219a	21.10 N	157.06 W
Hoonah	170	58.07 N	135.26 W
Hoopa	194	41.03 N	123.40 W
Hoopa Valley Indian Reservation ◆[4]	194	41.08 N	123.40 W
Hooper	188	41.37 N	96.33 W
Hooper Bay	170	61.31 N	166.06 W
Hooper Islands II	198	38.20 N	76.13 W
Hooper Strait ⋓	198	38.12 N	76.03 W
Hoopersville	198	38.16 N	76.11 W
Hoopes Reservoir ⊜[1]	275	39.47 N	75.37 W
Hoopeston	206	40.28 N	87.40 W
Hooping Harbour	176	50.37 N	56.17 W
Hoople	188	48.32 N	97.38 W
Hoopstad	148	27.54 S	25.58 E
Hoopstick Brook ≃	266	40.39 N	74.41 W
Höör	41	55.56 N	13.32 E
Hoorn	48	52.38 N	5.04 E
Hoorn, Kap → Hornos, Cabo de ≻	244	55.59 S	67.16 W
Hoosac Range ΛΛ	197	42.45 N	73.02 W
Hoosac Tunnel ◆[5]	197	42.41 N	73.03 W
Hoosic ≃	200	42.54 N	73.39 W
Hoosick	200	42.52 N	73.20 W
Hoosick Falls	200	42.54 N	73.21 W
Hooton	252	53.18 N	2.57 W
Hoover Dam ◆[6]	190	36.00 N	114.27 W
Hoover Reservoir ⊜[1]	204	40.08 N	82.53 W
Hooversville	204	40.09 N	78.55 W
Hopa	120	41.25 N	41.24 E
Hopatcong	200	40.56 N	74.39 W
Hopatcong, Lake ⊜	200	40.57 N	74.38 W
Hopatcong State Park ♠	266	40.55 N	74.40 W
Hop Bottom	200	41.42 N	75.46 W
Hop Brook ≃	266	40.19 N	74.08 W
Hope, B.C., Can.	172	49.23 N	121.26 W
Hope, Alaska, U.S.	170	60.55 N	149.38 W
Hope, Ark., U.S.	184	33.40 N	93.36 W
Hope, Ind., U.S.	208	39.18 N	85.46 W
Hope, N.J., U.S.	200	40.55 N	74.58 W
Hope, N. Dak., U.S.	188	47.19 N	97.43 W
Hope, R.I., U.S.	197	41.44 N	71.34 W
Hope, Ben Λ	28	58.24 N	4.36 W
Hope, Point ≻	170	68.21 N	166.50 W
Hope Bay C	202	44.55 N	81.08 W
Hopedale, Newf., Can.	166	55.28 N	60.13 W
Hopedale, Ill., U.S.	184	40.25 N	89.25 W
Hopedale, La., U.S.	184	29.51 N	89.41 W
Hopedale, Mass., U.S.	197	42.08 N	71.33 W
Hopedale, Ohio, U.S.	204	40.20 N	80.54 W
Hope Farm	200	41.44 N	73.40 W
Hopefield	148	33.04 S	18.22 E
Hopeh → Hebei □[4]	88	38.00 N	116.00 E
Hope Island I, B.C., Can.	172	50.55 N	127.53 W
Hope Island I, Ont., Can.	202	44.55 N	80.12 W
Hopeland	198	40.14 N	76.16 W
Hopelawn	266	40.32 N	74.18 W
Hopelchén	222	19.46 N	89.51 W
Hope Mills	182	34.59 N	78.57 W
Hopen I	10	76.35 N	25.10 E
Hopes Advance, Baie C	166	59.25 N	69.40 W
Hopes Advance, Cap ≻	166	61.04 N	69.34 W
Hopetoun, Austl.	152	33.57 S	120.07 E
Hopetoun, Austl.	156	35.44 S	142.22 E
Hopetown	148	29.34 S	24.03 E
Hope Valley, Austl.	158b	34.50 S	138.44 E
Hope Valley, R.I., U.S.	197	41.30 N	71.43 W
Hopewell, N.J., U.S.	198	40.23 N	74.46 W
Hopewell, Pa., U.S.	204	40.08 N	78.16 W
Hopewell, Va., U.S.	198	37.18 N	77.17 W
Hopewell Islands II	166	58.25 N	78.00 W
Hopewell Junction	200	41.35 N	73.48 W
Hopewell Village National Historic Site ⊥	198	40.12 N	75.46 W
Hopfgarten	58	47.27 N	12.10 E
Hopfgarten in Defereggen	58	46.55 N	12.31 E
Hopi → Hebi	88	35.59 N	114.11 E
Hopi Buttes Λ	190	35.20 N	110.15 W
Hopi Indian Reservation ◆[4]	190	35.45 N	110.35 W
Hopingzhen	96	30.50 N	119.54 E
Hopkins, Mich., U.S.	206	42.37 N	85.45 W
Hopkins, Mo., U.S.	184	40.33 N	94.49 W
Hopkins □[6]	212	33.07 N	95.35 W
Hopkins, Lake ⊜	152	24.15 S	128.50 E
Hopkins Creek ≃	274a	43.17 N	78.46 W
Hopkinsville	184	36.52 N	87.29 W
Hopkinton, Iowa, U.S.	180	42.21 N	91.15 W
Hopkinton, Mass., U.S.	197	42.13 N	71.31 W
Hopkinton, R.I., U.S.	197	41.28 N	71.47 W
Hopland	194	38.58 N	123.07 W
Hopohoponga, Mui ≻	164w	21.09 S	175.02 W
Ho Poi	261d	22.25 N	114.03 E
Hoppegarten	254a	52.31 N	13.40 E
Hoppenrade	254a	52.32 N	12.56 E
Hopper Canyon V	218	34.22 N	118.51 W
Hoppo → Hepu	92	21.39 N	109.11 E
Hopsten	48	52.23 N	7.36 E
Hoptrup	41	55.11 N	9.28 E
Hopwood, Mount Λ	156	21.49 S	144.26 E
Hoque	142	14.39 S	13.54 E
Hoquiam	214	46.59 N	123.53 W
Hoquiam ≃	214	46.58 N	123.54 W
Horace Mountain Λ	170	67.40 N	149.06 W
Horado	84	35.36 N	136.50 E
Hōrai	84	34.56 N	137.34 E
Horakelifo	134	8.50 N	43.10 E
Horanchia	134	6.35 N	38.46 E
Horasan	120	40.03 N	42.11 E
Horatio	184	33.56 N	94.21 W
Horatio Gardens	268	42.10 N	87.57 W
Horažd'ovice	30	49.20 N	13.43 E
Horb am Neckar	54	48.26 N	8.41 E
Horbelev	41	54.49 N	12.04 E
Horbourg	54	48.05 N	7.23 E
Hörby	41	55.51 N	13.39 E
Horconcitos	226	8.19 N	82.10 W
Hordaland □[6]	26	60.15 N	6.30 E
Hörde ◆[8]	253	51.29 N	7.30 E
Horden	42	54.46 N	1.18 W
Horden ≃	154	3.50 S	141.25 E
Hordio	134	10.32 N	51.08 E
Horezu	38	45.08 N	23.59 E
Horgen	54	47.15 N	8.36 E
Hořice	30	50.22 N	15.38 E
Horicon	180	43.27 N	88.38 W
Horigane	258	35.50 N	139.27 E
Horine	209	38.16 N	90.26 W
Horinouchi	84	37.14 N	138.56 E
Horinouchi ◆[8]	258	35.41 N	139.40 E
Horio	134	5.00 N	47.26 E
Horizon Tablemount ✢[3]	14	19.30 N	169.00 W
Horizontina	242	27.37 S	54.19 W
Horka	50	51.16 N	14.56 E
Hörken	40	60.02 N	14.56 E
Horley	44	51.11 N	0.11 W
Horlick Mountains ΛΛ	9	85.23 S	121.00 W
Hormigueros	230m	18.09 N	67.08 W
Hormoz, Jazīreh-ye I	118	27.04 N	56.28 E
Hormuz, Strait of ⋓	118	26.34 N	56.15 E
Horn, B.R.D.	48	51.52 N	8.56 E
Horn, Öst.	30	48.40 N	15.40 E
Horn ◆[8]	48	53.38 N	10.05 E
Horn ≻	24a	66.28 N	22.28 W
Horn ≃, N.W. Ter., Can.	166	61.30 N	118.01 W
Horn ≃, Eur.	52	49.15 N	7.20 E
Horn, Cape → Hornos, Cabo de ≻	244	55.59 S	67.16 W
Hornád (Hernád) ≃	30	47.56 N	21.08 E
Hornaday ≃	170	69.22 N	123.50 W
Hornafjördur C	24a	64.17 N	15.16 W
Hornavan ⊜	24	66.10 N	17.30 E
Hornbach	52	49.11 N	7.22 E
Hornbæk	41	56.05 N	12.28 E
Hornbeak	184	36.20 N	89.18 W
Hornbeck	184	31.20 N	93.24 W
Hornberg	54	48.13 N	8.13 E
Hornbrook	194	41.55 N	122.33 W
Hornburg	50	52.01 N	10.36 E
Hornby, Ont., Can.	265b	43.34 N	79.50 W
Hornby, N.Z.	162	43.33 S	172.32 E
Hornby Bay C	166	66.35 N	117.50 W
Horncastle	42	53.13 N	0.07 W
Hornchurch ◆[8]	250	51.34 N	0.12 E
Horndal	40	60.18 N	16.25 E
Horndean	44	50.55 N	1.00 W
Horndon on the Hill	250	51.31 N	0.25 E
Horne	41	55.06 N	10.11 E
Horne, Îles de II	14	14.16 S	178.05 W
Hornebach ≃	253	51.39 N	7.38 E
Horneburg, B.R.D.	48	53.30 N	9.34 E
Horneburg, B.R.D.	253	51.38 N	7.18 E
Hörnefors	26	63.38 N	19.54 E
Hornell	200	42.19 N	77.40 W
Hornepayne	166	49.13 N	84.47 W
Hornerstown	198	40.06 N	74.31 W
Hornhausen	50	52.02 N	11.10 E
Horn Hill	250	51.37 N	0.32 W
Horní Jiřetín	50	50.35 N	13.32 E
Hornindal	26	61.58 N	6.31 E
Hornindalsvatnet ⊜	26	61.56 N	6.22 E
Hørning	41	56.05 N	10.03 E
Hörningsholm	40	59.03 N	17.40 E
Horní Počernice	50	50.06 N	14.38 E
Hornisgrinde Λ	52	48.36 N	8.12 E
Horn Island I, Austl.	154	10.37 S	142.17 E
Horn Island I, Miss., U.S.	184	30.13 N	88.38 W
Horní Slavkov	50	50.07 N	12.46 E
Hornitos	216	37.30 N	120.14 W
Horn Lake	184	34.58 N	90.02 W
Horn Lake ⊜	202	45.24 N	79.36 W
Hornomoravský úval V	30	49.25 N	17.20 E
Hornos, Cabo de (Cape Horn) ≻	244	55.59 S	67.16 W
Hornos, Isla I	244	55.57 S	67.17 W
Hornos, Islas de II	278	34.25 S	57.55 W
Hornow	50	51.38 N	14.31 E
Hornoy	46	49.51 N	1.54 E
Horn Plateau ΛΛ[1]	166	62.15 N	119.15 W
Horn Pond ⊜	273	42.28 N	71.09 W
Hornsby, Austl.	160	33.42 S	150.06 E
Hornsby, Ill., U.S.	209	39.10 N	89.45 W
Hornsbyville	198	37.12 N	76.28 W
Hornsea	42	53.55 N	0.10 W
Hornsey ◆[8]	250	51.35 N	0.07 W
Hornslet	41	56.19 N	10.20 E
Hornstorf	50	53.54 N	11.32 E
Hornsyld	41	55.45 N	9.51 E
Horntown	198	37.58 N	75.28 W
Hornu	46	50.26 N	3.49 E
Horoizumi	82a	42.01 N	143.09 E
Horoshiri-dake Λ	82a	42.43 N	142.41 E
Horotiu	162	37.43 S	175.12 E
Hořovice	30	49.50 N	13.54 E
Horqueta	242	23.24 S	56.53 W
Horrabridge	44	50.31 N	4.05 W
Horrelville	162	43.20 S	172.20 E
Horrem	253	51.06 N	6.48 E
Horseback Knob Λ[2]	208	39.14 N	83.06 W
Horse Cave	184	37.11 N	85.54 W
Horse Creek	190	41.25 N	105.11 W
Horse Creek ≃, Colo., U.S.	188	38.05 N	103.19 W
Horse Creek ≃, Fla., U.S.	210	27.06 N	81.58 W
Horse Creek ≃, Ill., U.S.	209	39.45 N	89.34 W
Horse Creek ≃, Mo., U.S.	184	37.46 N	93.53 W
Horse Creek ≃, Wyo., U.S.	188	41.57 N	103.58 W
Horse Creek ≃, Wyo., U.S.	190	42.52 N	110.03 W
Horsefly	172	52.20 N	121.24 W
Horsefly Lake ⊜	172	52.25 N	121.00 W
Horsehead Branch ≃	274b	39.23 N	76.46 W
Horsehead Creek ≃	188	43.17 N	103.22 W
Horsehead Lake ⊜	188	47.02 N	99.47 W
Horseheads	200	42.10 N	76.50 W
Horse Heaven Hills ΛΛ[2]	192	46.10 N	119.45 W
Horse Islands II	176	50.13 N	55.45 W
Horsell	250	51.19 N	0.34 W
Horseneck Brook ≃	266	41.01 N	73.38 W
Horsens	41	55.52 N	9.52 E
Horsens Fjord C	41	55.50 N	10.05 E
Horse Prairie Creek ≃	192	44.59 N	112.52 W
Horse Shoe Bend	192	43.55 N	116.12 W
Horseshoe Bend National Military Park ♠	184	33.00 N	85.46 W
Horseshoe Cove C	266	40.27 N	74.00 W
Horseshoe Creek ≃	188	42.27 N	104.58 W
Horseshoe Falls ⌊	274a	43.05 N	79.04 W
Horseshoe Lake ⊜, Man., Can.	174	52.12 N	95.50 W
Horseshoe Lake ⊜, N.J., U.S.	266	40.52 N	74.38 W
Horse Shoe Reef ✢[2]	230m	18.40 N	64.12 W
Horsfjärden C	40	59.04 N	18.09 E
Horsforth	42	53.51 N	1.39 W
Horsham, Austl.	156	36.43 S	142.13 E
Horsham, Eng., U.K.	44	51.04 N	0.21 W
Horsham, Pa., U.S.	198	40.11 N	75.06 W
Horsham Saint Faith	44	52.41 N	1.16 E
Hørsholm	41	55.53 N	12.30 E
Hörsingen	50	52.16 N	11.09 E
Horsley, Austl.	264a	33.51 S	150.51 E
Horsley, Eng., U.K.	250	51.16 N	0.26 W
Horslunde	41	54.54 N	11.14 E
Horšovský Týn	30	49.32 N	12.56 E
Horst, B.R.D.	48	53.48 N	9.37 E
Horst, D.D.R.	50	53.22 N	10.37 E
Horst, Ned.	48	51.27 N	6.04 E
Horst ◆[8]	253	51.32 N	7.02 E
Horsted Keynes	44	51.02 N	0.01 W
Hörstel	48	52.18 N	7.35 E
Horsthausen ◆[8]	253	51.33 N	7.13 E
Horstmar	48	52.05 N	7.17 E
Horstmar ◆[8]	253	51.36 N	7.33 E
Horsunlu	120	37.55 N	28.36 E
Horta	138a	38.32 N	28.38 W
Horta ◆[8]	256d	41.26 N	2.00 E
Horta, Ouadi V	136	17.51 N	21.52 E
Hortaleza ◆[8]	256a	40.28 N	3.39 W
Horten	26	59.25 N	10.30 E
Hortobágy □[9]	30	47.35 N	21.00 E
Horton, Eng., U.K.	250	51.28 N	0.32 W
Horton, Ind., U.S.	208	40.05 N	86.09 W
Horton, Kans., U.S.	188	39.40 N	95.32 W
Horton, Mich., U.S.	206	42.09 N	84.31 W
Horton ≃	170	70.00 N	126.53 W
Horton in Ribblesdale	42	54.09 N	2.17 W
Horton Kirby	250	51.23 N	0.15 E
Horton Lake ⊜	166	67.30 N	122.28 W
Hortonville, N.Y., U.S.	200	41.46 N	75.02 W
Hortonville, Wis., U.S.	180	44.20 N	88.38 W
Horumersiel	48	53.41 N	8.00 E
Hørup	41	54.56 N	9.55 E
Hørve	41	55.45 N	11.28 E
Horw	54	47.01 N	8.18 E
Horwich	42	53.37 N	2.33 W
Horwood Lake ⊜	180	48.03 N	82.20 W
Horzum	120	37.10 N	29.30 E
Hosaina	134	7.38 N	37.52 E
Hoşalay	120	42.00 N	33.27 E
Hösbach	52	50.00 N	9.12 E
Hosei University ⚘[2]	258	35.42 N	139.44 E
Hösel	52	51.19 N	6.54 E
Hosena	50	51.27 N	14.01 E
Hoséré Vokré Λ	136	8.20 N	13.15 E
Ḥoseynābād	118	35.33 N	47.08 E
Ḥoseynīyeh-ye Khodā-Dād	118	32.42 N	48.14 E
Hosford	182	30.23 N	84.48 W
Hoshāb	118	26.01 N	63.56 E
Hoshangābād	114	22.45 N	77.43 E
Hoshangābād □[5]	114	22.30 N	77.30 E
Hoshangābād Plain ⌣	114	22.35 N	77.25 E
Hoshiārpur, Bhārat	113	31.32 N	75.54 E
Hoshiarpur, Bhārat	262a	28.35 N	77.22 E
Hoshigajō Λ	86	34.31 N	134.19 E
Hosingen	52	50.01 N	6.05 E
Hosjö	40	60.35 N	15.46 E
Hoskins	154	5.27 S	150.30 E
Hosmer, B.C., Can.	172	49.35 N	114.57 W
Hosmer, S. Dak., U.S.	188	45.34 N	99.28 W
Hosoe	84	34.49 N	137.39 E
Hospental	54	46.37 N	8.34 E
Hospers	188	43.04 N	95.54 W
Hospet	112	15.16 N	76.24 E
Hospital de Orbigo	34	42.28 N	5.53 W
Hospitalet	34	41.22 N	2.08 E
Hossegor	32	43.40 N	1.27 W
Hosston	184	32.53 N	93.53 W
Hosta Butte Λ	190	35.35 N	108.12 W
Hoste, Isla I	244	55.15 S	69.00 W
Hostetter	204	40.16 N	79.24 W
Hostigrām	262b	22.26 N	88.31 E
Hostivař ◆[8]	50	50.01 N	14.32 E
Hostivice	50	50.04 N	14.15 E
Hošt'ka	50	50.30 N	14.20 E
Hostomice	50	50.35 N	13.46 E
Hostotipaquillo	224	21.04 N	104.04 W
Hosūr	112	12.43 N	77.49 E
Hot	100	18.06 N	98.36 E
Hota	258	35.08 N	139.51 E
Hotagen	26	63.59 N	14.15 E
Hotagen ⊜	26	63.53 N	14.29 E
Hotagsfjällen ΛΛ	26	64.20 N	14.30 E
Hotaka	84	36.20 N	137.53 E
Hotaka-dake Λ	84	36.17 N	137.39 E
Hotamış	120	37.36 N	33.13 E
Hotarele	38	44.10 N	26.22 E
Hotazel	148	27.15 S	23.00 E
Hotchkiss	190	38.48 N	107.43 W
Hotchkissville	197	41.46 N	73.13 W
Hot Creek Range ΛΛ	194	38.30 N	116.25 W
Hötensleben	50	52.08 N	11.01 E
Hotevilla	190	35.56 N	110.41 W
Hotham ≃	158a	32.58 S	116.22 E
Hotham Inlet C	170	66.45 N	162.00 W
Hotham Peak Λ	170	66.48 N	160.42 W
Hoting	26	64.07 N	16.10 E
Hot Springs, Mont., U.S.	192	47.37 N	114.40 W
Hot Springs → Truth or Consequences, N. Mex., U.S.	190	33.08 N	107.15 W
Hot Springs, N.C., U.S.	182	35.54 N	82.50 W
Hot Springs, S. Dak., U.S.	188	43.26 N	103.29 W
Hot Springs, Va., U.S.	182	38.00 N	79.50 W
Hot Springs National Park	184	34.30 N	93.03 W
Hot Springs Peak Λ, Calif., U.S.	194	40.22 N	120.07 W
Hot Springs Peak Λ, Nev., U.S.	194	41.22 N	117.26 W
Hot Sulphur Springs	190	40.04 N	106.06 W
Hottah Lake ⊜	166	65.04 N	118.29 W
Hottentot Bay C	146	26.05 S	14.58 E
Hottentotskloof	148	33.15 S	19.40 E
Hotton	52	50.16 N	5.27 E
Hötzum	50	52.13 N	10.37 E
Houaïlou	165f	21.17 S	165.38 E
Houa Khong □[4]	92	21.00 N	101.00 E
Houamuang	100	20.09 N	103.38 E
Houa Phan □[4]	92	20.30 N	104.00 E
Houbaishu	96	31.49 N	119.10 E
Houbao	88	41.54 N	125.14 E
Houcheng	96	31.55 N	120.26 E
Houdahepao	94	41.49 N	123.01 E
Houdain	46	50.27 N	2.32 E
Houdan	46	48.47 N	1.36 E
Houdelaincourt	54	48.33 N	5.28 E
Houdeng-Aimeries	46	50.29 N	4.08 E
Houeillès	32	44.12 N	0.02 E
Houffalize	52	50.08 N	5.47 E
Hough Green	252	53.23 N	2.47 W
Houghton, Mich., U.S.	180	47.06 N	88.34 W
Houghton, N.Y., U.S.	200	42.25 N	78.10 W
Houghton, Wash., U.S.	214	47.40 N	122.12 W
Houghton ◆[8]	263d	26.10 S	28.04 E
Houghton Green	252	53.25 N	2.34 W
Houghton Lake	180	44.18 N	84.45 W
Houghton Lake ⊜	180	44.20 N	84.45 W
Houghton-le-Spring	42	54.51 N	1.28 W
Houghton Regis	44	51.55 N	0.31 W
Houguangzhengtai	94	41.13 N	122.07 E
Hougujiazi	94	42.21 N	123.22 E
Houhai ⊜	261a	39.57 N	116.22 E
Hou Hoi Wan C	90	22.28 N	113.56 E
Houhuangtukan	94	41.02 N	122.29 E
Houillères de la Sarre, Canal des ≊	52	48.42 N	6.55 E
Houilles	251	48.56 N	2.11 E
Houjia	88	37.02 N	122.06 E
Houjiangfushan	95	40.03 N	117.09 E
Houjie	90	22.58 N	113.39 E
Houjiumen	94	42.38 N	123.18 E
Houkou	88	37.34 N	115.09 E
Houliujia	94	40.47 N	122.19 E
Houlka	184	34.02 N	89.01 W
Houlton	178	46.08 N	67.51 W
Houluan	95	39.13 N	116.32 E
Houlung	90	24.39 N	120.47 E
Houma, Tonga	164w	21.09 S	175.19 W
Houma, La., U.S.	184	29.36 N	90.43 W
Houma, Zhg.	92	35.40 N	111.29 E
Houmanzhoutun	94	42.29 N	123.14 E
Houmen	90	22.51 N	115.09 E
Houmont Park	212	29.50 N	95.13 W
Hound Creek ≃	192	47.13 N	111.23 W
Houndé	140	11.30 N	3.31 W
Hounslow ◆[8]	44	51.29 N	0.22 W
Houplines	46	50.42 N	2.55 E
Houqianjiayu	94	40.50 N	120.41 E
Houqiao	95	40.04 N	116.39 E
Housatonic	197	42.16 N	73.22 W
Housatonic ≃	197	41.10 N	73.07 W
House	186	34.39 N	103.54 W
House ≃	174	56.13 N	112.31 W
Houserville	204	40.50 N	77.50 W
House Springs	209	38.24 N	90.34 W
Houshan	96	31.03 N	120.21 E
Houshenfou	96	30.49 N	120.00 E
Houston, B.C., Can.	172	54.24 N	126.38 W
Houston, Del., U.S.	198	38.55 N	75.30 W
Houston, Minn., U.S.	180	43.45 N	91.34 W
Houston, Miss., U.S.	184	33.54 N	89.00 W
Houston, Mo., U.S.	184	37.22 N	91.58 W
Houston, Ohio, U.S.	206	40.15 N	84.20 W
Houston, Pa., U.S.	204	40.15 N	80.13 W
Houston, Tex., U.S.	212	29.46 N	95.22 W
Houston □[6]	212	31.20 N	95.20 W
Houston ≃	184	30.16 N	93.13 W
Houston, Lake ⊜[1]	212	29.58 N	95.07 W
Houston Creek ≃	208	38.13 N	84.15 W
Houston Intercontinental Airport ⊠	212	29.59 N	95.27 W
Houston Ship Channel ≊	212	29.21 N	94.47 W
Hout ≃	146	23.04 S	29.36 E
Houthalen	52	51.02 N	5.22 E
Houthulst	46	50.59 N	2.57 E
Houtkop	148	26.36 S	27.52 E
Houtkraal	148	30.23 S	24.05 E
Houtskär I	26	60.12 N	21.22 E
Houtzdale	204	40.49 N	78.21 W
Houwaterdam ◆[6]	148	30.20 S	23.39 E
Houwuliangdian	94	41.31 N	121.55 E
Houwutaigou	94	41.46 N	121.42 E
Houx	251	48.34 N	1.37 E
Houxi	90	28.46 N	118.49 E
Houxinlitun	94	41.05 N	122.33 E
Houxinqiu	94	42.34 N	122.43 E
Houyatai	94	41.26 N	121.49 E
Houying, Zhg.	88	40.24 N	123.50 E
Houying, Zhg.	95	39.42 N	118.18 E
Houying, Zhg.	95	39.51 N	117.15 E
Houyouzha	96	32.02 N	121.05 E
Houzhangcun	95	40.08 N	116.11 E
Houzhou	96	31.35 N	119.22 E
Houzitun	94	41.04 N	121.18 E
Hov	41	55.55 N	10.16 E
Hova	40	58.52 N	14.13 E
Hovborg	41	55.36 N	8.57 E
Høve, Dan.	41	55.50 N	11.30 E
Hove, Eng., U.K.	44	50.49 N	0.10 W
Hovedgård	41	55.57 N	9.58 E
Hövelhof	48	51.49 N	8.40 E
Hoven, Dan.	41	55.51 N	8.46 E
Hoven, S. Dak., U.S.	188	45.15 N	99.47 W
Hovenweep National Monument ♠	190	37.24 N	108.59 W
Hoveyzeh	118	31.27 N	48.04 E
Hovmantorp	26	56.47 N	15.08 E
Hovran ⊜	40	60.16 N	16.03 E
Hovsta	40	59.21 N	15.13 E
Howa, Ouadi (Wādī Howar) ⌊	130	17.30 N	27.08 E
Howar, Wādī (Ouadi Howa) ⌊	130	17.30 N	27.08 E
Howard, Austl.	156	25.19 S	152.34 E
Howard, Kans., U.S.	188	37.28 N	96.16 W
Howard, Ohio, U.S.	204	40.25 N	82.20 W
Howard, Pa., U.S.	204	41.01 N	77.40 W
Howard, S. Dak., U.S.	188	44.01 N	97.32 W
Howard, Wis., U.S.	180	44.33 N	88.04 W
Howard □[6], Ind., U.S.	206	40.29 N	86.08 W
Howard □[6], Md., U.S.	198	39.16 N	76.48 W
Howard Beach ◆[8]	266	40.40 N	73.51 W
Howard City	180	43.24 N	85.28 W
Howard Draw V	186	30.08 N	101.35 W
Howard Hanson Reservoir ⊜[1]	214	47.15 N	121.45 W
Howard Heights	274b	39.17 N	76.50 W
Howardian Hills ΛΛ[2]	42	54.07 N	1.00 W
Howard Island I	154	12.10 S	135.24 E
Howard Lake	180	45.04 N	94.04 W
Howard Pass)(	170	68.13 N	156.55 W
Howard Prairie Lake ⊜[1]	192	42.15 N	122.20 W
Howard University ⚘[2]	274c	38.55 N	77.01 W
Howden	42	53.45 N	0.52 W
Howe	206	41.43 N	85.25 W
Howe, Cape ≻	156	37.31 S	149.59 E
Howe Caverns ◆[5]	200	42.42 N	74.25 W
Howe Green	250	51.42 N	0.32 E
Howe Island I	202	44.17 N	76.15 W
Howeke	140	4.50 N	7.45 W
Howell	206	42.36 N	83.55 W
Howell Airport ⊠	268	41.39 N	87.45 W
Howell Island I	209	38.40 N	90.42 W
Howells	188	41.43 N	97.00 W
Howells Pond ⊜	266	41.03 N	74.42 W
Howes Cave	200	42.41 N	74.23 W
Howe Sound ⋓	172	49.22 N	123.18 W
Howe's Range ΛΛ	160	33.08 S	150.47 E
Howes Valley	160	32.50 S	150.51 E
Howey In The Hills	210	28.43 N	81.47 W
Howick, Qué., Can.	196	45.11 N	73.51 W
Howick, S. Afr.	148	29.28 S	30.14 E
Howitt, Mount Λ	156	37.10 S	146.40 E
Howland	178	45.14 N	68.40 W
Howland Island I	14	0.48 N	176.38 W
Howley	176	49.10 N	57.07 W
Howley, Mount Λ	176	48.17 N	58.26 W
Howqua ≃	159	37.14 S	146.08 E
Howrah	116	22.35 N	88.20 E
Howrah □[5]	116	22.36 N	88.10 E
Howrah Bridge ◆[5]	262b	22.35 N	88.21 E
Howrah Railroad Station ◆[5]	262b	22.35 N	88.21 E
Howse Peak Λ	172	51.49 N	116.41 W
Howser	172	50.18 N	116.57 W
Howson Peak Λ	172	54.25 N	127.44 W
Howth, Eire	42	53.23 N	6.04 W
Howth, Tex., U.S.	212	30.10 N	96.04 W
Howth Head ≻	42	53.22 N	6.03 W
Hoxie, Ark., U.S.	184	36.03 N	90.58 W
Hoxie, Kans., U.S.	188	39.21 N	100.26 W
Höxter	48	51.46 N	9.23 E
Hoxton Park	264a	33.55 S	150.51 E
Hoxton Park Aerodrome ⊠	264a	33.54 S	150.50 E
Hoy I	28	58.52 N	3.18 W
Hoya, B.R.D.	48	52.48 N	9.08 E
Hōya, Nihon	84	35.43 N	139.34 E
Høyanger	26	61.13 N	6.05 E
Hoyerswerda	50	51.26 N	14.14 E
Hoylake	42	53.23 N	3.11 W
Hoyleton, Austl.	158b	34.01 S	138.33 E
Hoyleton, Ill., U.S.	209	38.27 N	89.16 W
Hoym	50	51.47 N	11.19 E
Hōyo-kaikyō ⋓	86	33.18 N	131.59 E
Hoyos	34	40.10 N	6.43 W
Hōyō-shotō II	86	33.52 N	132.18 E
Hoyran	120	38.19 N	30.59 E
Hoyran Gölü ⊜	120	38.12 N	30.50 E
Höytiäinen ⊜	26	62.48 N	29.39 E
Hoyt Lakes	180	47.31 N	92.08 W
Hoytville, Mich., U.S.	206	42.45 N	84.53 W
Hoytville, Ohio, U.S.	206	41.11 N	83.47 W
Hozain ≃	46	48.16 N	4.06 E
Hozat	120	39.07 N	39.14 E
Hozumi	84	35.24 N	136.41 E
Hpru-so	100	19.25 N	97.08 E
Hradec Králové	30	50.12 N	15.50 E
Hrádek nad Nisou	50	50.48 N	14.51 E
Hradiště Λ	50	50.13 N	13.08 E
Hranice, Česko.	30	49.33 N	17.44 E
Hranice, Česko.	50	50.15 N	12.10 E
Hrdlovka	50	50.36 N	13.40 E
Hřensko	50	50.50 N	14.14 E
Hriňová	30	48.36 N	19.31 E
Hrob	50	50.39 N	13.44 E
Hron ≃	30	47.49 N	18.45 E
Hronov	30	50.29 N	16.12 E
Hrubieszów	30	50.49 N	23.55 E
Hrubý Jeseník ΛΛ	30	50.00 N	17.20 E
Hrvatska (Croatia) □[3]	36	45.10 N	15.30 E
Hsenwi	100	23.18 N	97.58 E
Hsiakuan → Xiaguan	92	25.34 N	100.14 E

≃ River	Fluss	Río	Rivière	Rio
≊ Canal	Kanal	Canal	Canal	Canal
⌊ Waterfall, Rapids	Wasserfall, Stromschnellen	Cascada, Rápidos	Chute d'eau, Rapides	Cascata, Rápidos
⋓ Strait	Meeresstrasse	Estrecho	Détroit	Estreito
C Bay, Gulf	Bucht, Golf	Bahía, Golfo	Baie, Golfe	Baía, Golfo
⊜ Lake, Lakes	See, Seen	Lago, Lagos	Lac, Lacs	Lago, Lagos
≣ Swamp	Sumpf	Pantano	Marais	Pântano
⩍ Ice Features, Glacier	Eis- und Gletscherformen	Accidentes Glaciales	Formes glaciaires	Acidentes Glaciares
⍑ Other Hydrographic Features	Andere Hydrographische Objekte	Otros Elementos Hidrográficos	Autres données hydrographiques	Outros Elementos Hidrográficos

✢ Submarine Features	Untermeerische Objekte	Accidentes Submarinos	Formes de relief sous-marin	Acidentes Submarinos
□ Political Unit	Politische Einheit	Unidad Política	Entité politique	Unidade Política
⚘ Cultural Institution	Kulturelle Institution	Institución Cultural	Institution culturelle	Instituição Cultural
⊥ Historical Site	Historische Stätte	Sitio Histórico	Site historique	Sitio Histórico
♠ Recreational Site	Erholungs- und Ferienort	Sitio de Recreo	Centre de loisirs	Sítio de Lazer
⊠ Airport	Flughafen	Aeropuerto	Aéroport	Aeroporto
■ Military Installation	Militäranlage	Instalación Militar	Installation militaire	Instalação Militar
◆ Miscellaneous	Verschiedenes	Misceláneo	Divers	Miscelânea

Hsiamen → Xiamen 90 24.28 N 118.07 E
Hsian → Xi'an 92 34.15 N 108.52 E
Hsiangt'an → Xiangtan 90 27.51 N 112.54 E
Hsiangyang → Xiangfan 92 32.03 N 112.01 E
Hsiaohungt'ou Hsü I 90 21.57 N 121.35 E
Hsichih 259d 25.04 N 121.39 E
Hsichi Hsü I 90 23.15 N 119.37 E
Hsich'üan Tao I 90 25.59 N 119.57 E
Hsientung 259d 25.09 N 121.44 E
Hsienyang → Xianyang 92 34.22 N 108.42 E
Hsi-hseng 100 20.09 N 97.15 E
Hsilo 90 23.49 N 120.27 E
Hsilo Ch'i ≃ 90 23.47 N 120.15 E
Hsinch'eng 90 24.08 N 121.39 E
Hsinchu 90 24.48 N 120.58 E
Hsinchuang 90 25.02 N 121.26 E
Hsinghua → Xinghua 90 32.57 N 119.50 E
Hsingt'ai → Xingtai 88 37.04 N 114.29 E
Hsinhailien → Xinhailian 88 34.39 N 119.16 E
Hsinhsiang → Xinxiang 88 35.20 N 113.51 E
Hsinhua 90 23.01 N 120.20 E
Hsining → Xining 92 36.38 N 101.55 E
Hsinkao Shan ∧ 90 23.28 N 120.57 E
Hsinking → Changchun 79 43.53 N 125.19 E
Hsinpeit'ou 259d 25.08 N 121.30 E
Hsinp'u → Xinhailian 88 34.39 N 119.16 E
Hsinshih 90 23.05 N 120.17 E
Hsintien 90 24.58 N 121.33 E
Hsintien Hsi ≃ 259d 25.00 N 121.32 E
Hsinyang → Xinyang 90 32.19 N 114.01 E
Hsipaw 100 22.37 N 97.18 E
Hsip'ing Hsü I 90 23.14 N 119.36 E
Hsiukuluan Ch'i ≃ 90 23.28 N 121.29 E
Hsiyü 90 23.36 N 119.30 E
Hsüanhua → Xuanhua 95 40.37 N 115.03 E
Hsüch'ang → Xuchang 90 34.03 N 113.49 E
Hsüchou → Xuzhou 88 34.16 N 117.11 E
Hsüehchia 90 23.14 N 120.11 E
Hsüehweng Shan ∧ 90 24.24 N 121.12 E
Hsuphãng 100 20.18 N 98.42 E
Huaan 90 25.02 N 117.34 E
Huab ≃ 146 20.52 S 13.25 E
Huabu 90 29.00 N 118.20 E
Huaca Juliana ⊥ 276d 12.07 S 77.02 W
Huacaña 238 14.02 S 74.02 W
Huacapistea ≃ 238 9.46 S 72.45 W
Huacaraje 238 13.33 S 63.45 W
Huacaybamba 238 9.05 S 76.50 W
Huachacalla 238 18.45 S 68.17 W
Huacheng 90 24.04 N 115.38 E
Huachi, Lago ◎ 238 14.11 S 63.30 W
Huachipa 276d 12.00 S 76.56 W
Huacho 238 11.07 S 77.37 W
Huachón 238 10.40 S 75.57 W
Huachos 238 13.12 S 75.31 W
Huachuan (Hunanying) 79 46.13 N 130.32 E
Huachuca City 190 31.34 N 110.21 W
Huaco 242 30.09 S 68.31 W
Huacrachuco 238 8.39 S 77.05 W
Huade 88 41.46 N 114.16 E
Huadian 79 42.58 N 126.43 E
Huadingshan ∧ 90 29.15 N 121.05 E
Huafeng 96 32.14 N 121.16 E
Huagaruancha, Cerro ∧ 238 10.32 S 75.58 W
Huaguchang 97 28.58 N 104.30 E
Huagutang 96 30.55 N 119.18 E
Hua Hin 100 12.34 N 99.58 E
Hua Hsü I 90 23.24 N 119.20 E
Huahua ≃ 226 13.53 N 83.28 W
Huaiá-Missu ≃ 240 10.52 S 53.15 W
Huaian, Zhg. 88 40.39 N 114.27 E
Huaian, Zhg. 90 33.32 N 119.10 E
Huaibin (Wulongji) 90 32.28 N 115.24 E
Huaide, Zhg. 79 43.32 N 124.50 E
Huaide, Zhg. 97 28.59 N 105.15 E
Huaidezhen 79 43.54 N 124.47 E
Huaihe ≃, Zhg. 88 37.28 N 114.55 E
Huaihe ≃, Zhg. 90 32.58 N 118.17 E
Huaihuazhenshi 96 31.05 N 119.41 E
Huaiji 92 24.01 N 112.18 E
Huailai 95 40.23 N 115.33 E
Huailinzhen 90 31.26 N 117.36 E
Huaillati 238 14.05 S 72.31 W
Huaillay 238 11.01 S 76.21 W
Huainan 90 32.40 N 117.00 E
Huaining 90 30.25 N 116.38 E
Huairou 95 40.19 N 116.37 E
Huaite → Huaide 79 43.32 N 124.50 E
Huaiyang 90 33.44 N 114.53 E
Huaiyin 90 33.35 N 119.02 E
Huai Yot 100 7.45 N 99.37 E
Huaiyuan 90 32.57 N 117.12 E
Huaiyushan ⛰ 90 28.50 N 117.50 E
Huaji 90 32.46 N 115.20 E
Huajiang 92 25.50 N 110.21 E
Huajianzi 94 40.48 N 122.12 E
Huajiaodao I 88 39.26 N 121.17 E
Huajiapuzi 94 40.52 N 123.14 E
Huajiayingzi 94 42.20 N 121.00 E
Huajimic 224 21.42 N 104.20 W
Huajintepec 224 16.36 N 98.14 W
Huajuapan de León 224 17.48 N 97.46 W
Huakou 90 25.13 N 117.35 E
Hualahuises 222 24.53 N 99.41 W
Hualalai ∧[1] 219d 19.42 N 155.52 W
Hualañé 242 34.59 S 71.49 W
Hualapai Indian Reservation ⇝[4] 190 35.38 N 113.30 W
Hualapai Mountains ⛰ 190 34.50 N 113.55 W
Hualapai Peak ∧ 190 35.04 N 113.54 W
Hualfín 242 27.14 S 66.50 W
Hualgayoc 238 6.46 S 78.37 W
Hualien 90 23.58 N 121.36 E
Hualin 79 44.35 N 129.35 E
Hualingpuzi 94 41.31 N 123.54 E
Hualjaina ≃ 244 42.37 S 70.25 W
Hualla 238 13.44 S 73.55 W
Huallaga ≃ 238 5.10 S 75.32 W
Huallanca, Perú 238 9.51 S 76.56 W
Huallanca, Perú 238 8.49 S 77.52 W
Hualong 92 36.05 N 102.36 E
Huamachuco 238 7.48 S 78.04 W
Huamanquiquia 238 13.44 S 74.15 W
Huamantla 224 19.19 N 97.56 W
Huambo (Nova Lisboa), Ang. 142 12.44 S 15.47 E
Huambo, Perú 238 15.44 S 72.07 W
Huambo □[5] 142 12.30 S 15.40 E
Huambo ≃ 238 7.04 S 77.10 W
Huambos 238 6.28 S 78.58 W
Huameiao 90 26.32 N 115.47 E
Huameishan ∧ 90 25.28 N 113.58 E
Huamugou 88 42.34 N 117.14 E
Huamuxtitlán 224 17.49 N 98.34 W
Huancabamba, Perú 238 5.14 S 79.28 W
Huancabamba, Perú 238 10.21 S 75.32 W
Huancané 238 15.12 S 69.46 W
Huancapi 238 13.41 S 74.04 W
Huancarama 238 13.39 S 73.05 W
Huancarqui 238 16.06 S 72.29 W
Huancavelica 238 12.46 S 75.02 W
Huancavelica □[5] 238 13.00 S 75.00 W
Huancayo 238 12.04 S 75.14 W
Huanchaca 238 20.20 S 66.39 W
Huanchaca, Serranía de ⛰ 238 14.30 S 60.39 W
Huandacareo 224 19.59 N 101.17 W
Huando 238 12.29 S 74.58 W
Huang'aicun 96 31.43 N 118.40 E
Huang'anshi 90 29.06 N 113.34 E
Huangbai 88 41.17 N 126.21 E
Huangbaozi 92 39.54 N 99.26 E
Huangbeipu 94 42.21 N 123.25 E
Huangbi 90 28.48 N 120.06 E
Huangcaoping 90 25.42 N 113.27 E
Huang Chi ≃ 259d 25.14 N 121.43 E
Huangchong 90 22.18 N 113.03 E
Huangchuan 90 32.09 N 115.03 E
Huangcun 95 39.56 N 116.11 E
Huangdai 96 31.26 N 120.33 E
Huangdan 97 29.10 N 103.44 E
Huangdao I 90 27.58 N 121.06 E
Huangdayang)(90 30.03 N 122.26 E
Huangdi, Zhg. 88 40.14 N 120.15 E
Huangdi, Zhg. 95 40.57 N 118.24 E
Huangdu, Zhg. 96 31.16 N 121.13 E
Huangdu, Zhg. 96 30.47 N 118.51 E
Huangduqiao 90 29.18 N 120.55 E
Huanggaihu ◎ 90 29.44 N 113.23 E
Huanggang, Zhg. 80 30.27 N 114.52 E
Huanggang, Zhg. 88 34.39 N 116.03 E
Huanggang, Zhg. 90 28.32 N 114.33 E
Huanggang, Zhg. 90 30.27 N 114.52 E
Huanggangshi 90 33.09 N 115.55 E
Huanggu'an 88 35.28 N 115.42 E
Huangguayingzi 94 41.46 N 120.46 E
Huangguoshu 92 26.02 N 105.32 E
Huanghai → Yellow Sea ⊤[2] 80 36.00 N 123.00 E
Huanghe ≃, Zhg. 80 37.32 N 118.19 E
Huanghe ≃, Zhg. 90 32.19 N 115.02 E
Huangheya 88 37.19 N 116.19 E
Huangho → Huanghe ≃ 90 32.19 N 115.02 E
Huang Hsi ≃ 90 23.57 N 121.36 E
Huanghu 96 30.27 N 119.48 E
Huanghua, Zhg. 88 38.22 N 117.21 E
Huanghua, Zhg. 90 28.14 N 113.14 E
Huanghuadianzi, Zhg. 88 42.15 N 126.26 E
Huanghuadianzi, Zhg. 94 41.44 N 122.48 E
Huangji 88 34.26 N 116.59 E
Huangjiadao I 88 36.43 N 121.37 E
Huangjialing 94 42.12 N 122.55 E
Huangjialu 96 31.00 N 121.45 E
Huangjiangshui ≃ 90 22.54 N 115.18 E
Huangjiatun 94 41.11 N 122.54 E
Huangjiazhai 96 32.01 N 121.36 E
Huangjinbu 90 28.27 N 116.47 E
Huangjing 96 31.39 N 121.06 E
Huangjinjing 97 29.44 N 104.38 E
Huangjinzi 79 50.02 N 127.20 E
Huangjueshu 97 29.50 N 106.27 E
Huangkan 95 40.22 N 116.28 E
Huangkeng 90 27.35 N 117.39 E
Huangkou 92 42.46 N 93.58 E
Huanglaomen 90 29.30 N 115.49 E
Huangli 96 31.39 N 119.42 E
Huanglian 97 29.17 N 106.18 E
Huangling 92 35.41 N 109.09 E
Huanglingji 90 30.25 N 114.03 E
Huanglong, Zhg. 90 23.34 N 116.58 E
Huanglong, Zhg. 92 35.45 N 109.42 E
Huanglongdang 90 31.58 N 112.28 E
Huanglongxi 97 30.19 N 103.58 E
Huangmao 90 28.07 N 114.04 E
Huangmapi 90 23.30 N 114.33 E
Huangmei 90 30.04 N 115.56 E
Huangnihe, Zhg. 79 43.32 N 127.59 E
Huangnihe, Zhg. 90 31.06 N 117.22 E
Huangnixi ≃ 90 24.48 N 116.31 E
Huangpi, Zhg. 90 30.53 N 114.22 E
Huangpi, Zhg. 90 26.39 N 115.51 E
Huangpujiang ≃ 96 31.24 N 121.31 E
Huangqi 90 26.21 N 119.54 E
Huangqiao 96 32.15 N 120.13 E
Huangshabao 90 25.08 N 112.44 E
Huangshahe 92 26.03 N 110.58 E
Huangshajie 90 29.03 N 113.08 E
Huangshan 88 36.57 N 122.18 E
Huangshan ∧ 90 30.07 N 118.10 E
Huangshanguan 88 37.32 N 120.16 E
Huangshapu 90 26.50 N 113.26 E
Huangshaqiao 90 28.56 N 114.40 E
Huangshatuo 94 41.12 N 122.31 E
Huangshi, Zhg. 90 30.13 N 115.05 E
Huangshi, Zhg. 90 26.15 N 115.54 E
Huangshi, Zhg. 90 25.23 N 119.04 E
Huangshi, Zhg. 92 29.00 N 111.02 E
Huangshidu 90 27.44 N 116.44 E
Huangshuihe 97 30.32 N 103.55 E
Huangsonggang 90 22.49 N 113.51 E
Huangtan, Zhg. 90 26.41 N 117.17 E
Huangtan, Zhg. 90 27.44 N 119.58 E
Huangtang, Zhg. 90 23.44 N 114.58 E
Huangtang, Zhg. 96 31.46 N 120.21 E
Huangtang, Zhg. 96 31.47 N 119.40 E
Huangtanghu ◎ 90 30.00 N 114.12 E
Huangtankou 90 28.50 N 118.53 E
Huangtantuan 90 30.53 N 113.33 E
Huangtian 90 23.52 N 114.58 E
Huangtianfan 90 29.10 N 120.08 E
Huangtu 90 27.36 N 118.00 E
Huangtuchang 97 30.41 N 104.18 E
Huangtugang 90 31.25 N 115.05 E
Huangtukan 94 41.21 N 122.45 E
Huangtuliangzi 88 41.14 N 118.39 E
Huangtuling 90 27.18 N 113.30 E
Huangtupo 95 39.47 N 116.16 E
Huanguelén 242 37.02 S 61.57 W
Huangxian 88 37.38 N 120.29 E
Huangxu 96 32.06 N 119.37 E
Huangyaguan 95 40.14 N 117.26 E
Huangyan 90 28.39 N 121.15 E
Huangyanzhuang 95 40.01 N 118.21 E
Huangyuan 92 36.42 N 101.25 E
Huangyuzeng 94 42.05 N 124.11 E
Huangze 90 29.35 N 120.55 E
Huangzeshan I 90 30.31 N 122.16 E
Huangzeyang)(90 30.36 N 122.28 E
Huangzhai 90 29.27 N 120.00 E
Huangzhawan 92 40.36 N 96.55 E
Huangzhong 92 36.31 N 101.40 E
Huangzhu 100 19.29 N 110.24 E
Huangzhuang, Zhg. 90 34.05 N 112.15 E
Huangzhuang, Zhg. 95 39.29 N 117.31 E
Huangzhuangwa ◎ 95 39.33 N 117.33 E
Huangzhuangzhen 95 39.53 N 117.05 E
Huani, Laguna C 226 14.45 N 83.20 W
Huaning 92 24.14 N 102.56 E
Huaniqueo [de Morales] 224 19.54 N 101.26 W
Huaniugouzi 94 41.34 N 122.35 E
Huaniupuzi 94 41.23 N 123.31 E
Huanjiang 92 24.54 N 108.21 E
Huanren 88 41.14 N 125.21 E
Huanshan 90 28.10 N 121.12 E
Huanshui ≃ 90 30.40 N 114.05 E
Huanta 238 12.56 S 74.15 W
Huantai 88 36.59 N 118.06 E
Huantan 90 31.49 N 113.04 E
Huantar 238 9.26 S 77.15 W
Huánuco 238 9.55 S 76.14 W
Huánuco □[5] 238 9.30 S 75.50 W
Huanuni 238 18.16 S 66.51 W
Huanxi 90 26.34 N 113.36 E
Huanxian 92 36.39 N 107.18 E
Huanxianghe ≃ 95 39.34 N 117.45 E
Huanxiling 94 41.17 N 123.54 E
Huanzo, Cordillera de ⛰ 238 14.30 S 73.20 W
Huapí, Montañas de ⛰ 226 12.30 N 85.00 W
Huap'ing Hsü I 90 25.24 N 121.58 E
Huaqiao, Zhg. 90 28.56 N 121.27 E
Huaqiao, Zhg. 90 29.32 N 117.11 E
Huaqiao, Zhg. 90 27.54 N 118.48 E
Huaqiao, Zhg. 92 27.28 N 110.02 E
Huaqiao, Zhg. 97 30.47 N 106.41 E
Huaqiaozi 97 30.30 N 103.53 E
Huara 238 19.59 S 69.47 W
Huaral 238 11.30 S 77.12 W
Huaraz 238 9.32 S 77.32 W
Huari, Bol. 238 19.00 S 66.48 W
Huari, Perú 238 9.20 S 77.14 W
Huariaca 238 10.27 S 76.07 W
Huaribamba 238 12.16 S 74.57 W
Huarina 238 16.12 S 68.38 W
Huarmey 238 10.04 S 78.10 W
Huarochirí 238 12.09 S 76.14 W
Huarocondo 238 13.25 S 72.13 W
Huarong 90 29.30 N 112.34 E
Huásabas 222 29.47 N 109.18 W
Huasaga ≃ 236 3.42 S 76.26 W
Hua Sai 100 8.02 N 100.18 E
Huasamota 224 22.30 N 104.30 W
Huascarán, Nevado ∧ 238 9.07 S 77.37 W
Huasco 242 28.28 S 71.14 W
Huasco ≃ 242 28.27 S 71.13 W
Huashan 88 34.39 N 116.44 E
Huashaoying 88 40.12 N 114.36 E
Huashishan ⛰ 90 24.24 N 113.38 E
Huashu 96 31.50 N 120.28 E
Huaspuc ≃ 226 14.38 N 84.26 W
Huatabampo 222 26.50 N 109.38 W
Huatangpu 90 25.48 N 112.52 E
Huating 92 35.09 N 107.10 E
Huatong 92 23.01 N 106.36 E
Huatunas, Laguna ◎ 238 13.06 S 66.15 W
Huatusco de Chicuellar 224 19.09 N 96.57 W
Huauchinango 224 20.11 N 98.03 W
Huaunta 226 13.33 N 83.32 W
Huaunta, Laguna C 226 13.38 N 83.34 W
Huaura 238 11.04 S 77.36 W
Huaura ≃ 238 11.06 S 77.39 W
Huautla 224 21.02 N 98.17 W
Huautla de Jiménez 224 18.08 N 96.51 W
Huaxian, Zhg. 88 35.37 N 114.32 E
Huaxian, Zhg. 90 23.22 N 113.12 E
Huaxian, Zhg. 92 34.30 N 109.40 E
Huayan 97 30.01 N 105.02 E
Huayang, Zhg. 92 33.25 N 107.44 E
Huayang, Zhg. 97 30.32 N 104.04 E
Huayingtai 94 40.43 N 122.19 E
Huaynamota, Río de ≃ 224 21.51 N 104.42 W
Huayna Potosí, Nevado ∧ 238 16.16 S 68.11 W
Huaytará 238 13.36 S 75.22 W
Huayuan, Zhg. 90 31.16 N 113.58 E
Huayuan, Zhg. 90 33.00 N 118.16 E
Huayuan, Zhg. 92 28.34 N 109.13 E
Huayuri, Pampa de ⊻ 238 14.30 S 75.30 W
Huazhou 92 21.40 N 110.33 E
Huazi 94 41.25 N 123.29 E
Huazigou 94 41.50 N 121.01 E
Huazikou 96 32.13 N 118.57 E
Huazolotitlán 224 16.17 N 97.56 W
Ḥubārah, Wādī ∨ 132 27.21 N 31.39 E
Ḥubayṭah, Bi'r ⊤[4] 132 30.27 N 32.27 E
Hubbard, Iowa, U.S. 180 42.18 N 93.18 W
Hubbard, Ohio, U.S. 204 41.10 N 80.34 W
Hubbard, Oreg., U.S. 214 45.11 N 122.48 W
Hubbard, Tex., U.S. 212 31.51 N 96.48 W
Hubbard Creek ≃ 186 32.54 N 98.53 W
Hubbard Creek Reservoir ◎[1] 186 32.45 N 99.00 W
Hubbard Lake ◎ 180 44.49 N 83.34 W
Hubbards 176 44.38 N 64.04 W
Hubbardston 197 42.29 N 72.01 W
Hubbard Woods 268 42.06 N 87.44 W
Hubbell 180 47.11 N 88.26 W
Hubbelrath 253 51.16 N 6.55 E
Hubei □[4] 80 31.00 N 112.00 E
Huben, Öst. 58 47.03 N 10.58 E
Huben, Öst. 58 46.56 N 12.34 E
Huberdeau 196 45.58 N 74.38 W
Huber Heights 208 39.50 N 84.07 W
Hublersburg 200 40.58 N 77.37 W
Hubli 112 15.21 N 75.10 E
Hubuleng 92 41.19 N 111.08 E
Hucaogang 96 32.00 N 120.29 E
Hucclecote 44 51.51 N 2.11 W
Hucha 96 31.16 N 119.47 E
Huch'ang 88 41.25 N 127.03 E
Huchi 90 31.08 N 117.40 E
Huchow → Huzhou 96 30.52 N 120.06 E
Huckarde ⇝[8] 253 51.32 N 7.24 E
Hückelhoven 48 51.03 N 6.13 E
Hückelhoven-Ratheim 52 51.04 N 6.10 E
Hückeswagen 52 51.08 N 7.20 E
Hucking 250 51.18 N 0.39 E
Huckingen ⇝[8] 253 51.22 N 6.43 E
Huckitta Creek ≃ 152 22.38 S 135.30 E
Huckleberry Island I 266 40.53 N 73.45 W
Huckleberry Mountain ∧ 192 43.51 N 122.19 W
Huckleberry Mountain ∧[2] 202 44.28 N 75.28 W
Hucknall 44 53.02 N 1.11 W
Hucqueliers 46 50.34 N 1.54 E
Hucun 95 39.02 N 115.56 E
Hudangtou 96 30.48 N 121.22 E
Huddart Park ♠ 272 37.26 N 122.19 W
Hudderfield Narrow Canal (disused) ≋ 252 53.29 N 2.06 W
Huddersfield 42 53.39 N 1.47 W
Huddinge 40 59.14 N 17.59 E
Huddle Park Golf Course ♠ 263d 26.09 S 28.07 E
Huddunge 40 60.03 N 16.59 E
Hude 48 53.07 N 8.27 E
Hudgin Creek ≃ 184 33.40 N 91.59 W
Hūdī 130 17.42 N 34.17 E
Hudiksvall 26 61.44 N 17.07 E
Hudingshan 90 33.45 N 113.17 E
Hudong 90 22.51 N 115.56 E
Hudoutun 88 42.06 N 124.50 E
Hudson, Qué., Can. 196 45.27 N 74.09 W
Hudson, Fla., U.S. 210 28.22 N 82.42 W
Hudson, Ill., U.S. 206 40.36 N 88.59 W
Hudson, Ind., U.S. 206 41.32 N 85.05 W
Hudson, Iowa, U.S. 180 42.24 N 92.28 W
Hudson, Md., U.S. 198 38.35 N 76.15 W
Hudson, Mass., U.S. 197 42.24 N 71.35 W
Hudson, Mich., U.S. 206 41.51 N 84.21 W
Hudson, N.H., U.S. 178 42.46 N 71.26 W
Hudson, N.C., U.S. 182 35.51 N 81.30 W
Hudson, N.Y., U.S. 200 42.15 N 73.47 W
Hudson, Ohio, U.S. 204 41.15 N 81.26 W
Hudson, S. Dak., U.S. 188 43.08 N 96.27 W
Hudson, Tex., U.S. 212 31.19 N 94.50 W
Hudson, Wis., U.S. 180 44.53 N 92.45 W
Hudson, Wyo., U.S. 190 42.54 N 108.35 W
Hudson □[6] 266 40.44 N 74.02 W
Hudson ≃, U.S. 178 40.42 N 74.02 W
Hudson ≃, Ga., U.S. 182 34.14 N 83.10 W
Hudson, Lake ◎[1] 184 36.20 N 95.05 W
Hudson Bay 174 52.52 N 102.25 W
Hudson Bay C 166 60.00 N 86.00 W
Hudson Falls 200 43.18 N 73.35 W
Hudson Highlands State Park ♠ 200 41.26 N 73.58 W
Hudson Hope 172 56.02 N 121.55 W
Hudson Lake 206 41.43 N 86.32 W
Hudson Mountains ⛰ 9 74.32 S 99.20 W
Hudsons Peak ∧ 161b 36.26 S 149.10 E
Hudson Strait)(166 62.30 N 72.00 W
Hudsonville 206 42.52 N 85.52 W
Hudun 134 9.08 N 47.32 E
Hudwin Lake ◎ 174 53.12 N 95.42 W
Hudžirt 76 47.05 N 91.10 E
Hue 100 16.28 N 107.36 E
Huebra ≃ 34 41.02 N 6.48 W
Huechucuicui, Punta ≻ 244 41.47 S 74.02 W
Huechulafquén, Lago ◎ 244 39.46 S 71.28 W
Huedin 38 46.52 N 23.02 E
Huehuetán 226 15.01 N 92.22 W
Huehuetenango 226 15.20 N 91.28 W
Huehuetenango □[5] 226 15.40 N 91.35 W
Huehuetlán el Chico 224 18.21 N 98.42 W
Huejúcar 224 22.21 N 103.13 W
Huejuquilla el Alto 224 22.36 N 103.52 W
Huejutla de Reyes 224 21.08 N 98.25 W
Huelgoat 32 48.22 N 3.45 W
Huelma 34 37.39 N 3.27 W
Huelva 34 37.16 N 6.57 W
Huelva, Río de ≃ 34 37.27 N 6.00 W
Huenque ≃ 238 16.12 S 69.44 W
Huentelauquén 242 31.35 S 71.32 W
Huércal-Overa 34 37.23 N 1.57 W
Huerfano ≃ 188 38.14 N 104.15 W
Huerhuero Creek ≃ 216 35.40 N 120.42 W
Huerhuero Creek, East Branch ≃ 216 35.31 N 120.32 W
Huerhuero Creek, Middle Branch ≃ 216 35.31 N 120.32 W
Huerlumada 110 32.45 N 90.00 E
Huerta, Sierra de la ⛰ 242 31.10 S 67.27 W
Huerva ≃ 34 41.39 N 0.52 W
Huesca 34 42.08 N 0.25 W
Huesca □[4] 34 42.05 N 0.00
Huéscar 34 37.49 N 2.32 W
Hueston Woods State Park ♠ 208 39.34 N 84.44 W
Huetamo de Núñez 224 18.35 N 100.53 W
Huete 34 40.08 N 2.41 W
Huey 209 38.36 N 89.17 W
Hueyapan 224 18.52 N 98.40 W
Hueyapan de Ocampo 224 18.07 N 95.09 W
Hueytown 184 33.27 N 86.59 W
Hufengchang 97 29.43 N 106.07 E
Hüffenhardt 52 49.18 N 9.04 E
Huffman 212 30.01 N 95.05 W
Huffman Dam ⇝[6] 208 39.48 N 84.05 W
Hüfingen 54 47.55 N 8.29 E
Ḥufrat an-Naḥās 130 9.45 N 24.19 E
Hügel, Villa ☼ 253 51.25 N 7.01 E
Huggins, Mount ∧ 9 78.17 S 162.28 E
Hugh ≃ 152 25.01 S 134.01 E
Hugh Butler Lake ◎[1] 188 40.22 N 100.42 W
Hughenden 156 20.51 S 144.12 E
Hughes, Austl. 152 30.42 S 129.31 E
Hughes, Alaska, U.S. 170 66.03 N 154.16 W
Hughes, Ark., U.S. 184 34.57 N 90.28 W
Hughes ≃ 174 56.46 N 100.01 W
Hughes, South Fork ≃ 178 39.08 N 81.20 W
Hughes Airport ⊠ 270 33.58 N 118.25 W
Hughes Creek ≃ 159 36.53 S 145.08 E
Hughes Springs 212 33.05 N 94.38 W
Hughesville 200 41.14 N 76.44 W
Hughson 216 37.36 N 120.52 W
Hughsonville 200 41.35 N 73.56 W
Hugh Town 28 49.55 N 6.17 W
Hugo, Colo., U.S. 188 39.08 N 103.28 W
Hugo, Okla., U.S. 186 34.01 N 95.31 W
Hugoton 188 37.11 N 101.21 W
Hugouji 90 33.23 N 117.08 E
Huguenot 200 41.25 N 74.38 W
Huguenot Lake ◎ 266 40.56 N 73.47 W
Huguf 134 9.59 N 45.50 E
Huhehaote (Huhehot) 92 40.51 N 111.40 E
Huhehot → Huhehaote 92 40.51 N 111.40 E
Huhsi 90 23.32 N 119.38 E
Huian, Zhg. 90 25.04 N 118.47 E
Huian, Zhg. 96 31.47 N 121.45 E
Huiarau Range ⛰ 162 38.45 S 177.00 E
Huib-Hochplato ⛰[1] 146 27.00 S 16.45 E
Huibieyang)(90 30.08 N 121.44 E
Huibu 90 28.18 N 115.15 E
Huichang, Zhg. 90 25.34 N 115.49 E
Huichang, Zhg. 95 39.04 N 115.04 E
Huichapan 224 20.23 N 99.39 W
Huicholes, Sierra de los ⛰ 224 22.00 N 104.00 W
Hŭich'ŏn 88 40.10 N 126.17 E
Huichou → Huiyang 90 23.05 N 114.24 E
Huichuan (Guanbao) 92 35.11 N 104.02 E
Huicungo 238 7.17 S 76.48 W
Huidong 92 26.41 N 102.36 E
Huidui 95 39.04 N 117.16 E
Huihe 96 31.45 N 121.43 E
Huijihe ≃ 90 33.53 N 115.36 E
Huila 142 15.04 S 13.32 E
Huila □[5], Ang. 142 15.20 S 15.00 E
Huila □[5], Col. 236 2.30 N 75.45 W
Huila, Nevado del ∧ 236 3.00 N 76.00 W
Huilai 90 23.04 N 116.18 E
Huili 92 26.43 N 102.10 E
Huiliuji 90 32.50 N 115.58 E
Huillapima 242 28.44 S 65.59 W
Huilong, Zhg. 90 27.30 N 118.24 E
Huilong, Zhg. 90 25.22 N 116.24 E
Huilong, Zhg. 90 24.09 N 113.58 E
Huilong, Zhg. 90 23.46 N 114.34 E
Huilong, Zhg. 97 30.28 N 105.26 E
Huilong, Zhg. 97 30.35 N 105.49 E
Huilongchang, Zhg. 97 30.41 N 106.34 E
Huilongchang, Zhg. 97 30.18 N 103.39 E
Huilongchang, Zhg. 97 29.41 N 104.17 E
Huilongchang, Zhg. 97 29.17 N 105.01 E
Huilotas, Sierra de las ⛰ 186 28.08 N 102.03 W
Huimanguillo 224 17.51 N 93.23 W
Huimin 88 37.29 N 117.29 E
Huinan 88 42.40 N 126.00 E
Huinca Renancó 242 34.50 S 64.23 W
Hüinghausen 253 51.11 N 7.48 E
Huining 92 35.41 N 105.08 E
Huipulco 276a 19.17 N 99.09 W
Huisachal 186 26.47 N 101.07 W
Huisduinen 48 52.56 N 4.44 E
Huishan 96 31.35 N 120.16 E
Huishui 92 26.07 N 106.24 E
Huismes 46 47.14 N 0.15 E
Huisne ≃ 46 47.59 N 0.11 E
Huissen 48 51.57 N 5.56 E
Huistepec 224 16.39 N 98.20 W
Huiting 88 34.05 N 116.04 E
Huitiupan 224 17.13 N 92.39 W
Huitong 92 26.54 N 109.31 E
Huitongqiao 92 24.43 N 98.56 E
Huittinen (Lauttakylä) 26 61.11 N 22.42 E
Huitzilán 224 19.58 N 97.41 W
Huitzuco de los Figueroa 224 18.18 N 99.21 W
Huixian 92 33.47 N 106.16 E
Huixquilucan □[7] 276a 19.24 N 99.18 W
Huixtla 222 15.09 N 92.28 W
Huiyang (Huizhou) 90 23.05 N 114.24 E
Huiyao 90 27.16 N 118.05 E
Huizache 224 22.55 N 100.25 W
Huize 92 26.27 N 103.09 E
Huizen 48 52.17 N 5.14 E
Huizhou → Huiyang 90 23.05 N 114.24 E
Hujia, Zhg. 94 41.20 N 121.52 E
Hujia, Zhg. 96 31.25 N 121.37 E
Hujiadian 97 29.41 N 104.07 E
Hujiajie 94 41.06 N 122.10 E
Hujiasi 97 29.16 N 105.13 E
Hujiawopu 94 42.34 N 122.11 E
Hujiayu 95 39.28 N 115.27 E
Hujiazhuang 95 39.51 N 117.07 E
Hujie 92 24.56 N 100.32 E
Ḥukayyim, Bi'r al- ⊤[4] 136 31.36 N 23.29 E
Hukeng 90 27.29 N 114.18 E
Hukou 90 29.45 N 116.13 E
Hŭksan-chedo II 88 34.30 N 125.20 E
Hukui → Fukui 84 36.04 N 136.13 E
Ḥukūmah 130 13.52 N 36.07 E
Hukuntsi 146 24.02 S 21.48 E
Hukuoka → Fukuoka 86 33.35 N 130.24 E
Hukusima → Fukushima 82 37.45 N 140.28 E
Hukuyama → Fukuyama 86 34.29 N 133.22 E
Hula 134 6.29 N 38.34 E
Ḥula, 'Emeq ⊻[1] 122 33.08 N 35.37 E
Hulahula ≃ 170 70.00 N 144.01 W
Hulan 79 46.00 N 126.38 E
Hulanhe ≃ 79 45.55 N 126.41 E
Hulbert, Mich., U.S. 180 46.21 N 85.09 W
Hulbert, Okla., U.S. 184 35.56 N 95.09 W
Hulberton 200 43.15 N 78.04 W
Ḥulda 122 31.50 N 34.53 E
Huldrefossen ⌊ 26 61.28 N 5.58 E
Hulei 90 24.50 N 116.48 E
Huleia Stream ≃ 219b 21.57 N 159.22 W
Hulett 188 44.41 N 104.36 W
Hulim 104 1.12 N 99.31 E
Hulín 30 49.19 N 17.28 E
Huliuhe ≃ 88 40.10 N 114.33 E
Hull, Qué., Can. 202 45.26 N 75.43 W
Hull → Kingston upon Hull, Eng., U.K. 42 53.45 N 0.20 W
Hull, Ill., U.S. 209 39.43 N 91.13 W
Hull, Iowa, U.S. 188 43.11 N 96.08 W
Hull, Mass., U.S. 197 42.17 N 70.53 W
Hull, Tex., U.S. 212 30.09 N 94.39 W
Hull □[6] 202 45.40 N 75.35 W
Hull I[1] 14 4.29 S 172.10 W
Hull ≃ 42 53.44 N 0.19 W
Hullavington 44 51.33 N 2.09 W
Hull Bay C 273 42.18 N 70.53 W
Hullbridge 44 51.37 N 0.38 E
Hull Glacier ⛉ 9 75.05 S 137.15 W
Hullo 66 59.00 N 23.14 E
Hulmeville 275 40.08 N 74.55 W
Hulot, Lac ◎ 176 50.14 N 69.18 W
Hüls, B.R.D. 52 51.22 N 6.30 E
Hüls, B.R.D. 253 51.40 N 7.08 E
Hülscheid 52 51.16 N 7.34 E
Hülser Berg ⇝[8] 253 51.24 N 6.31 E
Hülser Berg ∧[2] 253 51.23 N 6.33 E
Hulst 48 51.17 N 4.03 E
Hult 40 58.40 N 16.07 E
Hultsfred 26 57.29 N 15.50 E
Huludao 94 40.43 N 121.00 E
Hulufa 95 39.42 N 116.12 E
Hulun → Hailaer 79 49.12 N 119.42 E
Hulunchi ◎ 78 49.01 N 117.32 E
Huluyu 95 40.14 N 116.53 E
Ḥulwān 132 29.51 N 31.20 E
Ḥulwān Military Installation ■ 132 29.50 N 31.19 E
Ḥulwān Observatory ☼[3] 132 29.52 N 31.21 E
Huma 79 51.43 N 126.38 E
Humacao 230m 18.09 N 65.50 W
Humaerhe ≃ 79 51.40 N 126.44 E
Humahuaca 242 23.12 S 65.21 W
Humaitá, Bra. 238 7.31 S 63.02 W
Humaitá, Para. 242 27.03 S 58.33 W
Humaitá ≃ 238 8.16 S 72.44 W
Humansdorp 148 34.02 S 24.46 E
Humansville 184 37.48 N 93.35 W
Humara, Jabal al- ∧ 130 16.16 N 30.59 E
Humarock 273 42.08 N 70.41 W
Ḥumaydah 130 14.22 N 22.31 E
Humayingzi 88 41.06 N 116.48 E
Humayun's Tomb ⊥ 262a 28.36 N 77.15 E
Humbe 142 16.40 S 14.55 E
Humbe, Serra do ⛰ 142 12.13 S 15.25 E
Humbeek 46 50.58 N 4.23 E
Humber ≃, Ont., Can. 202 43.38 N 79.28 W
Humber ≃, Eng., U.K. 42 53.40 N 0.10 W
Humber, Mouth of the ≃[1] 42 53.32 N 0.08 E
Humber Bay C 265b 43.38 N 79.29 W
Humberside □[6] 42 53.55 N 0.40 W
Humberto de Campos 240 2.37 S 43.27 W
Humberto Primo 242 30.52 S 61.22 W
Humber Valley Park ♠ 265b 43.39 N 79.30 W
Humbird 180 44.32 N 90.53 W
Humble, Dan. 41 54.50 N 10.42 E
Humble, Tex., U.S. 212 30.00 N 95.16 W
Humboldt, Sask., Can. 174 52.12 N 105.07 W
Humboldt, Ariz., U.S. 190 34.30 N 112.14 W
Humboldt, Ill., U.S. 184 39.36 N 88.19 W
Humboldt, Iowa, U.S. 180 42.44 N 94.13 W
Humboldt, Kans., U.S. 188 37.49 N 95.26 W
Humboldt, Nebr., U.S. 188 40.10 N 95.57 W
Humboldt, S. Dak., U.S. 188 43.39 N 97.04 W
Humboldt, Tenn., U.S. 184 35.49 N 88.55 W
Humboldt ≃ 194 40.02 N 118.31 W
Humboldt, Mont ∧ 165f 21.53 S 166.25 E
Humboldt, North Fork ≃ 194 40.56 N 115.32 W
Humboldt, Parque ♠ 276c 10.28 N 66.54 W
Humboldt, Planetario ☼ 276c 10.30 N 66.50 W
Humboldt, South Fork ≃ 194 40.47 N 115.53 W
Humboldt Bay C 194 40.47 N 124.11 W
Humboldt Lake ◎ 194 39.58 N 118.38 W
Humboldt Mountains ⛰ 9 71.45 S 11.30 E
Humboldt Park ♠ 268 41.54 N 87.42 W
Humboldt Redwoods State Park ♠ 194 40.19 N 124.00 W
Humboldt Salt Marsh ☷ 194 39.50 N 117.55 W
Humboldt-Universität ☼[2] 254a 52.31 N 13.24 E
Hume, Calif., U.S. 194 36.47 N 118.55 W
Hume, N.Y., U.S. 200 42.29 N 78.08 W
Hume, Lake ◎[1] 156 36.06 S 147.05 E
Hume and Hovell Lookout ♠ 159 37.15 S 144.59 E
Hume and Hovell Memorial ⊥ 160 34.10 S 150.47 E
Humeburn 156 27.24 S 145.14 E
Hūmedān 118 25.24 N 59.39 E
Humen 90 22.49 N 113.41 E
Humen C[1] 90 22.44 N 113.40 E
Humenné 30 48.56 N 21.55 E
Húmera 256a 40.26 N 3.47 W
Humeston 180 40.52 N 93.30 W
Humla Karnāli ≃ 114 29.38 N 81.52 E
Humlebæk 41 55.58 N 12.33 E
Hummelfjell ∧ 26 62.27 N 11.17 E
Hummelo 48 52.00 N 6.14 E
Hummelstown 198 40.16 N 76.43 W
Hummels Wharf 200 40.50 N 76.50 W
Hümmling ⛰ 48 52.52 N 7.31 E
Humos, Isla I 244 45.38 S 73.59 W
Humpata 142 15.02 S 13.24 E
Hümpfershausen 52 50.40 N 10.13 E
Humphrey, Ark., U.S. 184 34.25 N 91.42 W
Humphrey, Nebr., U.S. 188 41.41 N 97.29 W
Humphrey Creek ≃ 274b 39.14 N 76.30 W
Humphreys, Mount ∧ 194 37.17 N 118.40 W
Humphreys Peak ∧ 190 35.20 N 111.40 W
Humpolec 30 49.32 N 15.22 E
Humppila 26 60.56 N 23.22 E
Humptulips 214 47.14 N 123.57 W
Humptulips ≃ 214 47.03 N 124.03 W
Humptulips, East Fork ≃ 214 47.15 N 123.54 W
Humptulips, West Fork ≃ 214 47.15 N 123.54 W
Humptulips Ridge ∧ 214 47.20 N 123.45 W
Ḥumrat Shaybūn, Jabal ⛰[2] 132 29.06 N 31.16 E
Humula 161b 35.29 S 147.45 E
Humuqiao 96 31.09 N 121.14 E
Humuya ≃ 226 15.13 N 87.57 W
Hūn 136 29.07 N 15.56 E
Hunabasi → Funabashi 84 35.42 N 139.59 E
Húnaflói C 24a 65.50 N 20.50 W
Hunan □[4] 92 28.00 N 111.00 E
Ḥunayshāt, Ghurd al- ⊥[8] 132 30.07 N 29.47 E
Hunchun 88 42.54 N 130.22 E
Huncoat 252 53.46 N 2.20 W
Hundeluft 50 51.58 N 12.20 E
Hundested 41 55.58 N 11.52 E
Hundewāli 113 31.55 N 72.38 E
Hundezler 120 40.45 N 40.15 E
Hundorp 26 61.33 N 9.54 E
Hundred 178 39.41 N 80.28 W
Hundred End 252 53.42 N 2.53 W
Hundred Island National Park ♠ 106 16.13 N 120.01 E
Hundred Islands II 106 16.13 N 120.03 E
Hundslund 41 55.55 N 10.04 E
Hundstein ∧ 58 47.20 N 12.54 E
Hundwil 54 47.22 N 9.19 E
Hunedoara 38 45.45 N 22.54 E
Hunedoara □[4] 38 45.45 N 23.00 E
Hünfeld 52 50.40 N 9.46 E
Hungary □[1] 22 47.00 N 20.00 E
Hungary □[1] 30 47.00 N 20.00 W
Hungary (Magyarország) □[1], Eur. 30 47.00 N 20.00 E
Hungchiang → Hongjiang 92 27.00 N 109.51 E
Hungen 52 50.28 N 8.54 E
Hungerford, Austl. 156 29.00 S 144.25 E
Hungerford, Eng., U.K. 44 51.26 N 1.30 W
Hungerford, Tex., U.S. 212 29.24 N 96.05 W
Hungf'ou Hsü I 90 22.03 N 121.33 E
Hŭngho-ri 88 37.14 N 127.44 E
Hŭngin-ni 88 39.03 N 126.26 E
Hung-long 259c 10.40 N 106.39 E
Hungmao 90 24.55 N 120.58 E
Hŭngnam 88 39.50 N 127.38 E
Hungría → Hungary □[1] 30 47.00 N 20.00 E
Hungry Horse 192 48.23 N 114.04 W
Hungry Horse Dam ⇝[6] 192 48.14 N 114.04 W
Hungry Horse Reservoir ◎[1] 192 48.15 N 113.50 W
Hungry Lake ◎ 202 44.48 N 76.53 W
Hung-yen 100 20.39 N 106.04 E
Hunhe 94 41.43 N 123.26 E
Hunhe ≃ 88 41.01 N 122.27 E
Huningue 54 47.36 N 7.35 E
Huni Valley 140 5.28 N 1.55 W
Hunjiang 88 41.56 N 126.29 E
Hunker 269b 40.12 N 79.38 W
Ḥunkurāb, Ra's ≻ 130 24.34 N 35.10 E
Hunn ◎ 40 58.51 N 15.57 E
Hunneberg ∧[2] 26 58.20 N 12.27 E
Hunnebostrand 26 58.27 N 11.18 E
Hunnewell 209 39.40 N 91.52 W
Hunnewell Lake ◎ 209 39.42 N 91.52 W
Hunsberge ⛰ 146 27.45 S 17.12 E
Hunseby 41 54.48 N 11.32 E
Hunshuitang 92 25.12 N 102.58 E
Hunspach 52 48.57 N 7.57 E
Hunsrück ⛰ 52 49.50 N 6.40 E
Hunstanton 44 52.57 N 0.30 E
Hunstein Range ⛰ 154 4.30 S 142.40 E
Hunsūr 112 12.18 N 76.17 E
Hunswinkel 253 51.05 N 7.48 E
Hunt □[6] 212 33.03 N 96.05 W
Hunte ≃ 48 52.30 N 8.19 E
Hunter, N. Dak., U.S. 188 47.12 N 97.13 W
Hunter, N.Y., U.S. 200 42.13 N 74.13 W
Hunter ≃, Austl. 160 32.50 S 151.42 E
Hunter ≃, N.Z. 162 44.22 S 169.25 E
Hunter, Mount ∧ 170 62.57 N 151.05 W
Hunter, Port C 160 32.55 S 151.48 E
Hunterdon □[6] 198 40.31 N 74.52 W
Hunter Island I, Austl. 156 40.32 S 144.45 E
Hunter Island I, B.C., Can. 172 51.55 N 128.05 W
Hunter Island I, N. Cal. 14 22.24 S 172.03 E
Hunter Island I, N.Y., U.S. 266 40.53 N 73.47 W
Hunter Island Ridge ⌒[3] 14 21.30 S 175.00 E
Hunter Liggett Military Reservation ■ 216 35.55 N 121.15 W
Hunter Mountain ∧ 200 42.10 N 74.14 W
Hunter Mountains ⛰ 162 45.42 S 167.25 E
Hunter River 176 46.21 N 63.21 W
Hunters Bay C 100 19.57 N 93.19 E
Hunters Creek Village 212 29.46 N 95.24 W
Huntersfield Mountain ∧ 200 42.21 N 74.21 W
Hunters Hill 264a 33.50 S 151.09 E
Hunters Point ≻ 272 37.43 N 122.22 W
Hunter's Quay 42 55.58 N 4.55 W
Hunters Road 144 19.09 S 29.48 E
Hunters Run 198 40.05 N 77.11 W
Huntersville 182 35.25 N 80.50 W
Huntertown 206 41.14 N 85.10 W
Hunterville 162 39.56 S 175.34 E
Hunter Wash ∨ 190 36.17 N 108.34 W
Huntingburg 184 38.18 N 86.57 W
Hunting Creek ≃ 198 39.33 N 77.20 W
Huntingdon, B.C., Can. 214 49.00 N 122.16 W
Huntingdon, Qué., Can. 196 45.05 N 74.10 W
Huntingdon, Eng., U.K. 44 52.20 N 0.12 W
Huntingdon, Pa., U.S. 204 40.29 N 78.01 W
Huntingdon, Tenn., U.S. 184 36.00 N 88.26 W
Huntingdon □[6], Qué., Can. 196 45.05 N 74.00 W
Huntingdon □[6], Pa., U.S. 204 40.29 N 78.01 W
Huntingdon Valley Creek ≃ 275 40.07 N 75.04 W
Hunting Island State Park ♠ 182 32.20 N 80.30 W
Huntington, Eng., U.K. 42 54.01 N 1.04 W
Huntington, Ind., U.S. 206 40.53 N 85.30 W
Huntington, Mass., U.S. 197 42.14 N 72.53 W
Huntington, N.Y., U.S. 200 40.51 N 73.25 W
Huntington, Oreg., U.S. 192 44.21 N 117.16 W
Huntington, Tex., U.S. 212 31.17 N 94.34 W

Symbols in the index entries represent the broad categories identified in the key at the right. Symbols with superior numbers (⛰[2]) identify subcategories (see complete key on page I · 26).

Kartensymbole in dem Registerverzeichnis stellen die rechts in Schlüssel erklärten Kategorien dar. Symbole mit hochgestellten Ziffern (⛰[2]) bezeichnen Unterabteilungen einer Kategorie (vgl. vollständiger Schlüssel auf Seite I · 26).

Los símbolos incluídos en el texto del índice representan las grandes categorias identificadas con la clave a la derecha. Los símbolos con numeros en su parte superior (⛰[2]) identifican las subcategorías (véase la clave completa en la página I · 26).

Les symboles de l'index représentent les catégories indiquées dans la légende à droite. Les symboles suivis d'un indice (⛰[2]) représentent des sous-catégories (voir légende complète à la page I · 26).

Os símbolos incluídos no texto do índice representam as grandes categorias identificadas com a chave à direita. Os símbolos com números em sua parte superior (⛰[2]) identificam as subcategorias (veja-se a chave completa à página I · 26).

	English	Deutsch	Español	Français	Português
∧	Mountain	Berg	Montaña	Montagne	Montanha
⛰	Mountains	Berge	Montañas	Montagnes	Montanhas
)(	Pass	Pass	Paso	Col	Passo
∨	Valley, Canyon	Tal, Cañon	Valle, Cañón	Vallée, Canyon	Vale, Canhão
⊻	Plain	Ebene	Llano	Plaine	Planície
≻	Cape	Kap	Cabo	Cap	Cabo
I	Island	Insel	Isla	Île	Ilha
II	Islands	Inseln	Islas	Îles	Ilhas
⊥	Other Topographic Features	Andere Topographische Objekte	Otros Elementos Topográficos	Autres données topographiques	Outros Elementos Topográficos

ESPAÑOL — Nombre | Página | Lat.°′ | Long.°′ W=Oeste
FRANÇAIS — Nom | Page | Lat.°′ | Long.°′ W=Ouest
PORTUGUÊS — Nome | Página | Lat.°′ | Long.°′ W=Oeste

Huntington, Utah, U.S. 190 39.20 N 110.58 W
Huntington, Va., U.S. 274c 38.48 N 77.15 W
Huntington, W. Va., U.S. 178 38.25 N 82.26 W
Huntington □[6] 206 40.53 N 85.30 W
Huntington Bay 266 40.54 N 73.25 W
Huntington Bay C 266 40.55 N 73.25 W
Huntington Beach, Calif., U.S. 218 33.39 N 118.01 W
Huntington Beach, N.Y., U.S. 266 40.54 N 73.23 W
Huntington Creek ≃, Nev., U.S. 194 40.37 N 115.43 W
Huntington Creek ≃, Pa., U.S. 200 41.06 N 76.22 W
Huntington Creek ≃, Utah, U.S. 190 39.09 N 110.55 W
Huntington Harbor C 266 40.54 N 73.26 W
Huntington Lake 216 37.15 N 119.14 W
Huntington Lake ⊜[1], Calif., U.S. 216 37.14 N 119.12 W
Huntington Lake ⊜[1], Ind., U.S. 206 40.50 N 85.25 W
Huntington Library Ʊ[3] 270 34.08 N 118.07 W
Huntington Mills 200 41.11 N 76.14 W
Huntington Park 218 33.59 N 118.13 W
Huntington Park ♠ 269a 41.29 N 81.56 W
Huntington Station 200 40.51 N 73.25 W
Huntington Woods 271 42.29 N 83.10 W
Huntingtown 198 38.37 N 76.37 W
Hunting Valley 269a 41.31 N 81.23 W
Huntingville 196 45.20 N 71.51 W
Huntley, Ill., U.S. 206 42.10 N 88.26 W
Huntley, Mont., U.S. 192 45.54 N 108.19 W
Huntly, N.Z. 162 37.33 S 175.10 E
Huntly, Scot., U.K. 28 57.27 N 2.47 W
Hunt Mountain ∧ 192 44.44 N 107.45 W
Hunton 250 51.13 N 0.28 E
Huntsburg 204 41.32 N 81.03 W
Hunt's Cross ◆[8] 252 53.21 N 2.51 W
Hunts Point 214 47.39 N 122.14 W
Huntsville, Ont., Can. 202 45.20 N 79.13 W
Huntsville, Ala., U.S. 184 34.44 N 86.35 W
Huntsville, Ark., U.S. 184 36.05 N 93.44 W
Huntsville, Ill., U.S. 209 40.11 N 90.52 W
Huntsville, Ind., U.S. 208 40.01 N 85.44 W
Huntsville, Mo., U.S. 184 39.26 N 92.33 W
Huntsville, Ohio, U.S. 206 40.26 N 83.49 W
Huntsville, Tenn., U.S. 182 36.25 N 84.29 W
Huntsville, Tex., U.S. 212 30.43 N 95.33 W
Huntsville, Utah, U.S. 190 41.16 N 111.46 W
Huntsville State Park ♠ 212 30.37 N 95.32 W
Hunū, Kathīb al- •[8] 132 30.37 N 32.49 E
Hunucmá 222 21.01 N 89.52 W
Hunut 120 40.39 N 41.09 E
Hünxe 48 51.38 N 6.46 E
Hünxer Wald ♠ 253 51.40 N 6.50 E
Hunyani (Panhame) ≃ 144 15.37 S 30.39 E
Hunyuan 88 39.48 N 113.41 E
Hun-yung 88 42.53 N 130.12 E
Hunza ≃ 113 35.55 N 74.22 E
Huobuxunhu ⊜ 92 36.39 N 96.20 E
Huocheng 76 44.12 N 80.26 E
Huoergeluo 79 45.35 N 120.56 E
Huoerpahu ⊜ 110 34.32 N 81.03 E
Huokou 90 26.28 N 119.16 E
Huolehe ≃ 79 44.55 N 122.35 E
Huolong 96 32.04 N 121.17 E
Huolongmen 79 49.48 N 125.47 E
Huolu 88 38.05 N 114.18 E
Huong-hoa 100 16.37 N 106.45 E
Huong-khe 100 18.13 N 105.41 E
Huong-thuy 100 16.25 N 107.40 E
Huon Gulf C 154 7.10 S 147.25 E
Huon Peninsula ≻[1] 154 6.25 S 147.25 E
Huonville 156 43.01 S 147.02 E
Huoqiu 90 32.20 N 116.16 E
Huorili 79 49.00 N 124.41 E
Huoshan 90 31.25 N 116.20 E
Huoshan ⋏ 92 36.40 N 111.50 E
Huoshaoliao 90 25.00 N 121.45 E
Huoshao Tao I 90 22.40 N 121.30 E
Huotong 90 26.53 N 119.25 E
Huotongxi ≃ 90 26.50 N 119.32 E
Huotuolaihuduke 92 40.19 N 104.18 E
Huoxi ≃ 90 25.20 N 117.21 E
Huoxian, Zhg. 92 36.37 N 111.40 E
Huoxian, Zhg. 95 39.46 N 116.46 E
Huoyan 90 33.42 N 113.40 E
Hupeh → Hubei □[4] 80 31.00 N 112.00 E
Hupu 96 31.45 N 120.54 E
Huqiao 96 31.26 N 119.26 E
Hura 116 23.18 N 86.39 E
Hūrand 74 38.51 N 47.22 E
Hurao (Hulin) 79 45.46 N 132.59 E
Hurāsāgar ≃ 116 24.04 N 89.40 E
Ḥuraydīn, Wādī V 122 30.59 N 33.53 E
Ḥuraymilā 118 25.08 N 46.08 E
Ḥūrayn 132 30.39 N 31.08 E
Hurd, Cape ≻ 180 45.13 N 81.44 W
Hurdalssjøen ⊜ 26 60.20 N 11.05 E
Hurdland 209 40.08 N 92.18 W
Hurdsfield 252 53.16 N 2.06 W
Hurepoix ◆[1] 251 48.40 N 2.10 E
Hurffville 275 39.46 N 75.07 W
Huriel 32 46.23 N 2.29 E
Hurley, Miss., U.S. 184 30.40 N 88.30 W
Hurley, N. Mex., U.S. 190 32.42 N 108.08 W
Hurley, N.Y., U.S. 200 41.55 N 74.04 W
Hurley, S. Dak., U.S. 188 43.17 N 97.05 W
Hurley, Wis., U.S. 180 46.28 N 90.08 W
Hurleyville 200 41.44 N 74.40 W
Hurlford 42 55.36 N 4.28 W
Hurlingham 248 34.36 S 58.38 W
Hurlock 178 38.38 N 75.52 W
Hurmāgai 118 28.18 N 64.26 E
Huron, Calif., U.S. 216 36.12 N 120.06 W
Huron, Ohio, U.S. 204 41.24 N 82.33 W
Huron, S. Dak., U.S. 188 44.22 N 98.13 W
Huron □[6], Ont., Can. 202 43.45 N 81.10 W
Huron □[6], Ohio, U.S. 204 41.15 N 82.37 W
Huron ≃ 206 42.03 N 83.14 W
Huron, East Branch ≃ 204 41.17 N 82.38 W
Huron, Lake ⊜ 180 44.30 N 82.15 W
Huron, Point ≻ 204 42.34 N 82.47 W
Huron, West Branch ≃ 204 41.17 N 82.38 W
Huron Gardens 206 42.38 N 83.20 W
Huron Mountains ⋏[2] 180 46.45 N 87.45 W
Hurons, Rivière des ≃ 196 45.28 N 73.16 W
Hurricane, Alaska, U.S. 170 62.59 N 149.38 W
Hurricane, Utah, U.S. 190 37.11 N 113.17 W
Hurricane, W. Va., U.S. 178 38.26 N 82.01 W
Hurricane Bayou ≃ 212 31.21 N 95.35 W
Hurricane Creek ≃, Ark., U.S. 184 34.05 N 92.23 W
Hurricane Creek ≃, Ga., U.S. 182 31.23 N 82.19 W
Hurricane Creek ≃, Ill., U.S. 209 38.53 N 89.13 W
Hurricane Wash V 190 37.00 N 113.23 W
Hurshi 116 24.17 N 88.28 E
Hursley 44 51.02 N 1.24 W
Hurso 134 9.38 N 41.38 E
Hurst 212 32.49 N 97.09 W
Hurstbourne Tarrant 44 51.17 N 1.23 W
Hurstbridge 159 37.38 S 145.12 E
Hurstpierpoint 44 50.56 N 0.11 W
Hurstville 160 33.58 S 151.06 E
Hurstwood Reservoir ⊜[1] 252 53.47 N 2.10 W
Hurtado ≃ 242 30.35 S 71.11 W

Hürth 52 50.52 N 6.51 E
Hurtsboro 184 32.14 N 85.25 W
Hurunui ≃ 162 42.55 S 173.17 E
Hurup 26 56.45 N 8.25 E
Husainābād 114 24.32 N 84.01 E
Husainīwāla 113 30.59 N 74.34 E
Husainpur 114 24.25 N 90.40 E
Húsavík 24a 66.04 N 17.18 W
Husby-Långhundra 40 59.45 N 18.01 E
Huse → Higashiōsaka 86 34.39 N 135.35 E
Husen ◆[8] 253 51.33 N 7.36 E
Hüseyinli 120 40.21 N 33.59 E
Hushan, Zhg. 79 45.35 N 130.35 E
Hushan, Zhg. 90 22.09 N 113.10 E
Hushan, Zhg. 90 28.36 N 118.59 E
Husheib 130 14.54 N 35.07 E
Hushi 97 28.57 N 105.22 E
Hushiha 95 40.52 N 116.59 E
Hushitai 94 41.57 N 123.30 E
Hushu, Zhg. 96 30.18 N 120.08 E
Hushu, Zhg. 96 31.52 N 118.59 E
Hushuguan 96 31.23 N 120.30 E
Huşi 38 46.40 N 28.04 E
Huskisson 160 35.02 S 150.40 E
Huskvarna 26 57.48 N 14.16 E
Huslia 170 65.42 N 156.25 W
Hussar 172 51.03 N 112.41 W
Hussigny-Godbrange 52 49.29 N 5.52 E
Hustisford 180 43.21 N 88.36 W
Huston ≃ 210 25.42 N 81.17 W
Hustontown 204 40.03 N 78.02 W
Husum, B.R.D. 41 54.28 N 9.03 E
Husum, Sve. 26 63.20 N 19.10 E
Husum, Wash., U.S. 214 45.49 N 121.29 W
Hutangqiao 96 31.46 N 119.57 E
Hutan Melintang 104 3.53 N 100.56 E
Hutanopan 104 0.41 N 99.42 E
Hutaym, Ḥarrat •[9] 118 26.15 N 40.20 E
Hutberg ∧[2] 50 52.09 N 14.33 E
Hutchins 212 32.39 N 96.43 W
Hutchinson, S. Afr. 148 31.30 S 23.09 E
Hutchinson, Kans., U.S. 188 38.05 N 97.56 W
Hutchinson, Minn., U.S. 180 44.54 N 94.22 W
Hutchinson, Pa., U.S. 204 40.13 N 79.44 W
Hutchinson ≃ 266 40.52 N 73.50 W
Hutchinson Island I 210 27.25 N 80.17 W
Hutch Mountain ∧ 190 34.47 N 111.22 W
Huthwaite 44 53.09 N 1.17 W
Hutou, Zhg. 90 25.15 N 118.03 E
Hutou, Zhg. 90 26.04 N 118.46 E
Hutou, Zhg. 96 31.37 N 119.37 E
Hutou, Zhg. 96 32.14 N 120.17 E
Hutouxi ≃ 90 25.57 N 118.02 E
Hutouya 88 37.13 N 119.46 E
Hutsonville 184 39.07 N 87.39 W
Hüttau 58 47.25 N 13.18 E
Hütteldorf ◆[8] 254b 48.12 N 16.16 E
Hüttener Berge ⋏[2] 41 54.26 N 9.40 E
Hüttenheim ◆[8] 253 51.22 N 6.43 E
Hüttental 52 50.54 N 8.02 E
Hutte Sauvage, Lac de la ⊜ 166 56.15 N 64.45 W
Huttig 184 33.02 N 92.11 W
Hutto 212 30.33 N 97.33 W
Hutton, Eng., U.K. 250 51.38 N 0.22 E
Hutton, Eng., U.K. 252 53.44 N 2.46 W
Hutton, Mount ∧ 156 25.51 S 148.20 E
Huttonsville 202 43.38 N 79.48 W
Huttrop ◆[8] 253 51.27 N 7.03 E
Hüttschlag 58 47.10 N 13.14 E
Huttwil 54 47.07 N 7.51 E
Hutubi 76 44.07 N 86.57 E
Hutuohe ≃ 88 38.14 N 116.05 E
Huu 105b 8.48 S 118.25 E
Huvalu Forest ◆[3] 164v 19.03 S 169.51 W
Huveaune ≃ 56 43.15 N 5.23 E
Hüvek 120 37.22 N 38.31 E
Huvudskär I 40 58.57 N 18.34 E
Huwan, Zhg. 90 31.41 N 114.53 E
Huwan, Zhg. 90 27.55 N 116.31 E
Huwei 90 23.42 N 120.24 E
Huwun 134 4.23 N 40.08 E
Ḥuwwārah 122 32.09 N 35.15 E
Huxford 184 31.13 N 87.28 W
Huxi 90 26.12 N 114.44 E
Huxian 92 34.09 N 108.32 E
Huxley 172 51.56 N 113.14 W
Huy 52 50.31 N 5.14 E
Huy ∧ 50 51.57 N 10.57 E
Huyang 90 25.26 N 118.27 E
Huyangzhen 90 32.25 N 112.45 E
Huyton-with-Roby 42 53.25 N 2.52 W
Huyuesi 96 30.23 N 118.45 E
Hüyük 120 37.57 N 31.37 E
Huyutou 90 26.44 N 119.49 E
Huzhen 90 28.50 N 120.15 E
Huzhou 96 30.52 N 120.06 E
Huzhu 92 37.00 N 102.00 E
Huzhuangtun 94 40.43 N 122.33 E
Huzi 90 30.56 N 113.42 E
Huzisawa → Fujisawa 84 35.21 N 139.29 E
Hvalsø 41 55.36 N 11.50 E
Hvannadalshnúkur ∧ 24a 64.01 N 16.41 W
Hvar 36 43.10 N 16.27 E
Hvar, Otok I 36 43.09 N 16.45 E
Hvarski Kanal ⊔ 36 43.15 N 16.37 E
Hveragerði 24a 64.03 N 21.10 W
Hvide Sande 26 55.59 N 8.08 E
Hvidovre 41 55.39 N 12.29 E
Hvittingfoss 26 59.29 N 10.01 E
Hvolsvöllur 24a 63.45 N 20.10 W
Hwach'ŏn 88 38.06 N 127.41 E
Hwach'ŏn-chŏsuji ⊜ 88 38.07 N 127.52 E
Hwach'ŏn-ni 88 39.01 N 126.02 E
Hwainan → Huainan 90 32.40 N 117.00 E
Hwaining → Anqing 90 30.31 N 117.02 E
Hwanggong-ni 88 40.03 N 129.27 E
Hwanghae Namdo □[4] 88 38.15 N 125.30 E
Hwanghae Pukdo □[4] 88 38.30 N 126.25 E
Hwang Ho → Huanghe ≃ 80 37.32 N 118.19 E
Hwangju 88 38.42 N 125.46 E
Hwangshih → Huangshi 90 30.13 N 115.05 E
Hyak 214 47.24 N 121.24 W
Hyakuna 164m 26.08 N 127.48 E
Hyakuri-ga-take ∧ 84 35.23 N 135.49 E
Hyannis, Mass., U.S. 197 41.39 N 70.17 W
Hyannis, Nebr., U.S. 188 41.59 N 101.44 W
Hyannis Port 197 41.38 N 70.18 W
Hyattsville 274c 38.56 N 76.56 W
Hyattville 192 44.15 N 107.36 W
Hybla Valley 198 38.45 N 77.05 W
Hyco Lake ⊜[1] 182 36.30 N 79.05 W
Hydaburg 170 55.12 N 132.49 W
Hyde, N.Z. 162 45.18 S 170.15 E
Hyde, Eng., U.K. 42 53.27 N 2.04 W
Hyde, Pa., U.S. 204 41.00 N 78.28 W
Hyden, Austl. 152 32.27 S 118.53 E
Hyden, Ky., U.S. 182 37.10 N 83.22 W
Hyde Park, Guy. 236 6.30 N 58.16 W
Hyde Park, N.Y., U.S. 200 41.47 N 73.56 W
Hyde Park, Vt., U.S. 178 44.36 N 72.37 W
Hyde Park ◆[8], Ill., U.S. 268 41.48 N 87.36 W
Hyde Park ◆[8], Mass., U.S. 273 42.15 N 71.08 W
Hyde Park ♠, Austl. 264a 33.53 S 151.13 E
Hyde Park ♠, Eng., U.K. 250 51.20 N 0.10 W
Hyde Park ♠, N.Y., U.S. 274a 43.06 N 79.01 W

Hyder 170 55.55 N 130.01 W
Hyderābād, Bhārat 112 17.23 N 78.29 E
Hyderābād, Pāk. 110 25.22 N 68.22 E
Hydetown 204 41.40 N 79.44 W
Hydra → Ídhra I 38 37.20 N 23.32 E
Hydraulic 172 52.36 N 121.42 W
Hyen ⊜ 40 60.36 N 16.12 E
Hyères 56 43.07 N 6.07 E
Hyères, Îles d' II 56 43.00 N 6.20 E
Hyères-Plage 56 43.06 N 6.10 E
Hyesan 88 41.23 N 128.12 E
Hyland ≃ 170 59.50 N 128.10 W
Hylestad 26 59.05 N 7.32 E
Hyllekrog I 41 54.36 N 11.30 E
Hyllinge, Dan. 41 55.16 N 11.37 E
Hyllinge, Sve. 41 56.06 N 12.51 E
Hyllstofta 41 56.08 N 13.16 E
Hyltebruk 26 57.00 N 13.14 E
Hymera 184 39.11 N 87.18 W
Hyndburn □[8] 252 53.45 N 2.23 W
Hyndman 178 39.49 N 78.44 W
Hyndman Peak ∧ 192 43.50 N 114.10 W
Hyne Field ⊠ 271 42.34 N 83.47 W
Hyōgo □[5] 86 35.00 N 135.00 E
Hyōgo ◆[8] 260 34.47 N 135.10 E
Hyŏn-ni 88 37.57 N 128.20 E
Hyōno-sen ∧ 86 35.21 N 134.31 E
Hyŏpch'ŏn 88 35.35 N 128.08 E
Hyrra Banda 142 5.57 N 22.04 E
Hyrum 190 41.38 N 111.51 W
Hyrynsalmi 26 64.40 N 28.32 E
Hysham 192 46.18 N 107.14 W
Hythe, Austl. 156 43.25 S 146.59 E
Hythe, Alta., Can. 172 55.20 N 119.33 W
Hythe, Eng., U.K. 44 51.05 N 1.05 E
Hythe, Eng., U.K. 44 50.51 N 1.24 W
Hythe End 250 51.27 N 0.32 W
Hyūga 82 32.25 N 131.38 E
Hyūga-nada ⊤[2] 82 32.00 N 131.35 E
Hyvinge → Hyvinkää 26 60.38 N 24.52 E
Hyvinkää 26 60.38 N 24.52 E

I

I □[4] 140 17.00 N 7.15 W
Iacanga 245 21.54 S 49.01 W
Iaciara 245 14.09 S 46.40 W
Iaco (Yaco) ≃ 238 9.03 S 68.34 W
Iaçu 245 12.45 S 40.13 W
Iaeger 182 37.28 N 81.49 W
Iago 212 29.17 N 95.58 W
Iakora 147b 23.06 S 46.40 E
Ialomiţa □[4] 38 44.30 N 27.20 E
Ialomiţa ≃ 38 44.42 N 27.51 E
Ialomiţei, Balta ☷ 38 44.30 N 28.00 E
Iamonia, Lake ⊜ 182 30.38 N 84.14 W
Iango 142 9.11 S 17.39 E
Iano, Monte ∧ 257a 41.46 N 12.44 E
Iapó ≃ 242 24.30 S 50.24 W
Iapu 245 19.26 S 42.13 W
Iaşi 38 47.10 N 27.35 E
Iaşi □[4] 38 47.15 N 27.15 E
Iatt, Lake ⊜[1] 184 31.35 N 92.40 W
Iauaretê 236 0.36 N 69.12 W
Iau Iabu ≃ 240 3.06 S 51.46 W
Iazu 38 44.44 N 27.25 E
Ib ≃ 110 21.34 N 83.48 E
Iba, Pil. 106 15.20 N 119.58 E
Iba, Zaïre 142 3.05 S 17.38 E
'Ibādah, Wādī V 132 27.49 N 30.54 E
Ibadan 140 7.17 N 3.30 E
Ibagaçaba ≃ 246 22.34 S 44.56 W
Ibagué 236 4.27 N 75.14 W
Ibaiti 245 23.50 S 50.10 W
Ibajay 106 11.49 N 122.10 E
Ibajay ≃ 106 11.49 N 122.10 E
Ibaka 142 4.16 S 23.12 E
Ibambi 144 2.22 N 27.37 E
Ibanda 144 0.08 S 30.29 E
Ibăneşti 38 48.04 N 26.22 E
Ibanshe 142 4.58 S 21.30 E
Ibapah Peak ∧ 190 39.50 N 113.55 W
Ibar ≃ 38 43.44 N 20.45 E
Ibara 86 34.36 N 133.28 E
Ibaraki, Nihon 84 36.17 N 140.26 E
Ibaraki, Nihon 86 34.49 N 135.34 E
Ibaraki □[5] 84 36.30 N 140.30 E
Ibarra 236 0.21 N 78.07 W
Ibarreta 242 25.13 S 59.51 W
Ibaruma 165d 24.30 N 124.17 E
Ibb 134 14.01 N 44.10 E
Ibba 144 4.48 N 29.06 E
Ibba ≃ 130 7.09 N 28.41 E
Ibbenbüren 48 52.16 N 7.43 E
Ibeke Gembo 142 1.24 S 18.51 E
Ibembo 142 2.38 N 23.37 E
Ibenga ≃ 142 2.20 N 18.08 E
Iberia, Mo., U.S. 184 38.05 N 92.18 W
Iberia, Ohio, U.S. 204 40.40 N 82.51 W
Iberian Basin ✢[1] 10 40.00 N 16.00 W
Ibérica, Peninsula ≻[1] 4 40.00 N 5.00 W
Ibérico, Sistema ⋏ 34 41.00 N 2.30 W
Íberoamericana, Universidad Ʊ[2] 276a 19.21 N 99.08 W
Ibertioga 246 21.25 S 43.58 W
Iberville 196 45.18 N 73.14 W
Iberville □[6] 196 45.15 N 73.10 W
Iberville, Lac d' ⊜ 166 55.55 N 73.15 W
Iberville, Mont d' ∧ 166 58.53 N 63.43 W
Ibese 263a 6.33 N 3.29 E
Ibeto 140 10.29 N 5.09 E
Ibi 140 8.12 N 9.45 E
Ibi ≃ 84 35.03 N 136.42 E
Ibiá 245 19.29 S 46.32 W
Ibiapaba, Serra da ⋏ 240 4.00 S 41.00 W
Ibiapina 240 3.55 S 40.54 W
Ibiara 240 7.30 S 38.25 W
Ibicaraí 245 14.51 S 39.36 W
Ibicuí 245 14.51 S 39.59 W
Ibicuí ≃ 242 29.25 S 56.47 W
Ibicuicito, Arroyo ≃ 248 33.49 S 58.49 W
Ibicuí da Armada ≃ 242 30.16 S 54.54 W
Ibicuy 248 33.44 S 59.10 W
Ibigawa 84 35.29 N 136.34 E
Ibipetuba 240 11.00 S 44.32 W
Ibipira 240 6.31 S 44.38 W
Ibiquera 245 12.38 S 40.57 W
Ibiraci 245 20.28 S 47.08 W
Ibiraçu 245 19.50 S 40.22 W
Ibirama 242 27.04 S 49.31 W
Ibirapuã 245 17.39 S 40.07 W
Ibirapuera ◆[8] 277b 23.37 S 46.40 W
Ibirapuera, Parque ♠ 277b 23.35 S 46.39 W
Ibirapuitã ≃ 242 29.22 S 55.57 W
Ibirataia 245 14.04 S 39.38 W
Ibiri 144 4.56 S 32.33 E
Ibirubá 242 28.38 S 53.06 W
Ibitiara 245 12.39 S 42.13 W
Ibitiguaia 246 21.57 S 43.25 W
Ibitinga 245 21.45 S 48.49 W
Ibitipoca 246 21.33 S 43.55 W
Ibitiúra 246 22.04 S 46.26 W
Ibituporanga 246 22.45 S 43.47 W
Ibiúna 246 23.39 S 47.13 W
Ibiza 34 38.54 N 1.26 E
Ibiza I 34 39.00 N 1.25 E
Iblei, Monti ⋏ 36 37.10 N 14.50 E
Ibnahs 132 30.34 N 31.07 E
Ibn Hāni', Ra's ≻ 120 35.35 N 35.43 E
Ibn Şirār, Bi'r ⊤[4] 134 19.30 N 42.41 E
Ibo 144 12.20 S 40.35 E
Ibo ≃ 86 34.46 N 134.35 E
Ibo, Ilha do I 144 12.20 S 40.36 E
Ibondo 144 2.38 S 32.40 E
Ibonma 154 3.28 S 133.28 E
Ibor ≃ 34 39.49 N 5.33 W
Ibotirama 245 12.11 S 43.13 W
Iboundji, Mont ∧ 142 1.08 S 11.48 E

İbradı 120 37.06 N 31.36 E
Ibrah, Wādī V 130 10.36 N 24.58 E
İbrala 120 37.09 N 33.31 E
Ibresi 70 55.18 N 47.03 E
'Ibrī 118 23.14 N 56.30 E
İbriktepe 120 41.00 N 26.30 E
Ibshān 132 31.10 N 31.10 E
Ibshawāy 132 29.22 N 30.41 E
Ibstock 44 52.42 N 1.23 W
Ibta' 122 32.47 N 36.09 E
Ibu 164m 26.45 N 128.19 E
Ibuki 84 35.24 N 136.23 E
Ibuki-jima I 86 34.08 N 133.32 E
Ibuki-sanchi ⋏ 84 35.35 N 136.18 E
Ibuki-yama ∧ 84 35.25 N 136.24 E
Iburg 48 52.09 N 8.02 E
Ibusuki 83b 31.16 N 130.39 E
Ibwe Munyama 144 16.09 S 28.34 E
Ibychen, Gora ∧ 78 51.36 N 109.45 E
Ica 238 14.04 S 75.42 W
Ica □[5] 238 14.20 S 75.30 W
Ica ≃, Perú 238 14.54 S 75.34 W
Içá (Putumayo) ≃, S.A. 236 3.07 S 67.58 W
Ica ≃, S.S.S.R. 66 56.52 N 26.59 E
Icabarú ≃ 236 4.45 N 62.15 W
Icadambanauan Island I 106 10.49 N 119.38 E
Icamaquã ≃ 242 28.34 S 56.00 W
Icamole 186 25.55 N 100.43 W
Içana 236 0.21 N 67.19 W
Içana (Isana) ≃ 236 0.26 N 67.19 W
Icaño, Arg. 242 28.41 S 62.54 W
Icaño, Arg. 242 28.54 S 65.19 W
Icatu 240 2.46 S 44.04 W
Icatuaçu 246 23.44 S 46.24 W
Icayché 222 18.05 N 89.10 W
Iceberg Pass)(190 40.25 N 105.45 W
Ice House Reservoir ⊜[1] 216 38.49 N 120.23 W
İçel □[4] 120 36.45 N 34.00 E
Iceland □[1] 22
24a 65.00 N 18.00 W
Icém 245 20.21 S 49.12 W
Ice Mountain ∧ 172 54.25 N 121.08 W
Ičera 78 58.32 N 109.47 E
İçerenköy ◆[8] 257b 40.58 N 29.06 E
Ichalkaranji 112 16.42 N 74.28 E
Ichāmāti ≃, Bhārat 116 22.35 N 88.57 E
Ichāmati ≃, Pāk. 116 24.00 N 89.15 E
Ichang → Yichang 92 30.42 N 111.11 E
Ichāpur 116 22.50 N 88.24 E
Ichawaynochaway Creek ≃ 182 31.10 N 84.28 W
Ich Bajan Ajrag ∧ 78 47.55 N 95.02 E
Ich Bogd Uul ⋏, Mong. 80
80 44.55 N 100.20 E
Ichbulag 92 45.26 N 113.10 E
Ich Buural Uul ∧ 78 48.00 N 94.30 E
Ichchāpuram 112 19.07 N 84.42 E
Ichdžargalan 92 45.31 N 108.50 E
Ichenhausen 54 48.22 N 10.18 E
Ichenheim 54 48.26 N 7.49 E
Ichhāwar 114 23.01 N 77.01 E
Ichi ≃ 86 34.46 N 134.41 E
Ichiba 86 34.05 N 134.17 E
Ichigaya, Camp ■ 258 35.44 N 139.41 E
Ichihara 84 35.31 N 140.05 E
Ichikai 84 36.32 N 140.06 E
Ichikawa, Nihon 84 35.44 N 139.55 E
Ichikawa, Nihon 86 34.59 N 134.46 E
Ichikawa-daimon 84 35.34 N 138.30 E
Ichilo ≃ 238 15.57 S 64.42 W
Ichinohe 82 40.13 N 141.17 E
Ichinomiya, Nihon 84 35.39 N 138.41 E
Ichinomiya, Nihon 84 35.18 N 136.48 E
Ichinomiya, Nihon 84 35.22 N 140.22 E
Ichinomiya, Nihon 86 34.28 N 134.51 E
Ichinomiya, Nihon 86 32.57 N 131.07 E
Ichinomiya, Nihon 86 35.06 N 134.35 E
Ichinomoto 260 34.37 N 135.50 E
Ichinose 260 35.53 N 135.10 E
Ichinoseki 82 38.55 N 141.08 E
Ichino-tani ⊥ 86 34.39 N 135.07 E
Ichino-tani Battlefield ⊥ 260 34.39 N 135.07 E
Ichiu 86 33.57 N 134.04 E
Ichkeul, Garaet ⊜ 36 37.10 N 9.40 E
Ichoca 238 17.12 S 67.17 W
Ich'on, C.M.I.K. 88 38.30 N 126.50 E
Ich'ŏn, Taehan 88 37.17 N 127.27 E
Ichtamir 78 47.30 N 100.52 E
Ichtegem 46 51.06 N 3.00 E
Ichtershausen 50 50.52 N 10.58 E
Ich-Uul, Mong. 78 48.33 N 98.40 E
Ich-Uul, Mong. 78 49.27 N 101.27 E
Icicle Creek ≃ 214 47.34 N 120.40 W
Ička, Gora ∧[2] 70 51.13 N 50.15 E
Ickenham ◆[8] 250 51.34 N 0.27 W
Ickern ◆[8] 253 51.36 N 7.21 E
Ickesburg 198 40.27 N 77.21 W
Icking 58 47.57 N 11.25 E
İçme 120 38.37 N 39.34 E
Ičn'a 68 50.52 N 32.24 E
Icó 240 6.24 S 38.51 W
Icoca 142 6.11 S 16.19 E
Iconha 245 20.48 S 40.48 W
Icoraci 240 1.18 S 48.28 W
Icy Bay C 170 60.00 N 141.15 W
Icy Cape ≻ 170 70.20 N 161.52 W
Icy Strait ⊔ 170 58.18 N 135.30 W
Ida, Som. 134 0.14 N 42.15 E
Ida, Mich., U.S. 206 41.55 N 83.34 W
Ida ≃ 78 53.10 N 103.20 E
Ida, Mount ∧, Austl. 152 29.14 S 120.25 E
Ida, Mount ∧, Jam. 231q 17.58 N 77.43 W
Idabel 184 33.54 N 94.50 W
Idaga Hamus 134 14.12 N 39.48 E
Ida Grove 188 42.21 N 95.28 W
Idah 140 7.07 N 6.43 E
Idaho □[3] 168
192 45.00 N 115.00 W
Idaho City 192 43.50 N 115.50 W
Idaho Falls 192 43.30 N 112.02 W
Idaho Springs 190 39.45 N 105.31 W
Idalou 186 33.40 N 101.41 W
Idanha-a-Nova 34 39.55 N 7.14 W
Idāppādi 112 11.35 N 77.51 E
Idar 110 23.50 N 73.00 E
Idarkopf ∧ 52 49.51 N 7.16 E
Idar-Oberstein 52 49.42 N 7.19 E
Idarwald ◆[3] 52 49.20 N 7.15 E
Idaville, Ind., U.S. 206 40.46 N 86.39 W
Idaville, Oreg., U.S. 214 45.31 N 123.53 W
Iddan 134 6.03 N 49.01 E
Iddo ◆[8] 263a 6.28 N 3.23 E
Ide 86 34.47 N 135.49 E
Idehan •[8] 136 28.00 N 11.30 E
Idehan ◆[2] 136 28.00 N 11.00 E
Idel' 24 64.08 N 34.14 E
Idelès 138 23.58 N 5.53 E
Idemba 142 2.38 S 11.38 E
Iden 50 52.46 N 11.55 E
Ider 78 48.13 N 97.23 E
Iderijn ≃ 78 49.16 N 100.41 E
Idermeg 78 47.36 N 111.15 E
Idfīnā 132 31.18 N 30.31 E
Idfū 130 24.58 N 32.52 E
Ídhi Óros ∧ 38 35.18 N 24.43 E
Ídhra 38 37.20 N 23.29 E
Ídhra I 38 37.20 N 23.32 E
Idi 104 4.57 N 97.46 E
Idice ≃ 58 44.35 N 11.49 E
Idi-cut 104 4.59 N 97.42 E
Idifina Barrage ◆[6] 132 31.17 N 30.31 E
Idimu 263a 6.35 N 3.17 E
Idio 106 11.37 N 122.06 E
Idiofa 142 5.02 S 19.36 E
Iditarod ≃ 170 63.02 N 158.58 W
Idkerberget 40 60.23 N 15.14 E
Idkū 132 31.18 N 30.18 E

Idkū, Buḥayrat ⊜ 132 31.16 N 30.17 E
Idle Hill 250 51.15 N 0.08 E
Idlib 120 35.55 N 36.38 E
Idlib □[8] 120 35.50 N 36.40 E
Idmū 132 28.09 N 30.41 E
Idnah 122 31.34 N 34.59 E
Idodi 144 7.47 S 35.11 E
Ídolo, Isla del I 224 21.25 N 97.27 W
Idomogu 263a 6.43 N 3.30 E
Idre 26 61.52 N 12.43 E
Idria 216 36.25 N 120.40 W
Idrica 66 56.21 N 28.53 E
Idrija 36 46.00 N 14.01 E
Idrijca ≃ 58 46.09 N 13.45 E
Idrinskoje 76 54.21 N 92.07 E
Idro 58 45.44 N 10.29 E
Idro, Lago d' ⊜ 58 45.47 N 10.30 E
Idroscalo ⊜ 256b 45.28 N 9.18 E
Idstedt 41 54.35 N 9.31 E
Idstein 52 50.13 N 8.16 E
Iduburojo, Isla I 236 9.05 N 60.42 W
Idutywa 148 32.02 S 28.16 E
Idyllwild 194 33.45 N 116.43 W
Idylside 206 41.31 N 88.07 W
Idylwood 274c 38.54 N 77.12 W
Idževan 74 40.53 N 45.07 E
Iecava 66 56.36 N 24.12 E
Iecava ≃ 66 56.41 N 23.42 E
Ielsi 60 41.30 N 14.48 E
Ienne 60 41.53 N 13.10 E
Iepê 245 22.40 S 51.05 W
Ieper (Ypres) 46 50.51 N 2.53 E
Ierápetra 38 35.00 N 25.45 E
Ierisós 38 40.24 N 23.52 E
Ierón Asklipioú ⊥ 38 37.37 N 23.02 E
Ieshima 86 34.40 N 134.32 E
Ieshima-shotō II 86 34.40 N 134.32 E
Iesi 60 43.31 N 13.14 E
Iesolo 58 45.32 N 12.38 E
If, Château d' ⊥ 56 43.17 N 5.19 E
Ifakara 144 8.08 S 36.41 E
Ifako 263a 6.39 N 3.20 E
Ifalik I[1] 98 7.15 N 144.27 E
Ifanadiana 147b 21.19 S 47.39 E
Ifata 138 25.29 N 7.58 E
Ife 140 7.30 N 4.30 E
Iferouâne 140 19.04 N 8.24 E
Iferten → Yverdon 54 46.47 N 6.39 E
Iffezheim 52 48.49 N 8.08 E
Ifni □[9] 138 29.20 N 10.00 W
Ifon 140 6.58 N 5.45 E
Iforas, Adrar des ⋏ 140 20.00 N 2.00 E
Ifould Lake ⊜ 152 30.53 S 132.09 E
Ifta 52 51.04 N 10.11 E
Ifugao □[4] 106 16.45 N 121.15 E
Iga 84 34.49 N 136.13 E
Iga ≃ 84 34.45 N 136.01 E
Igaci 240 9.33 S 36.38 W
Igal 30 46.31 N 17.55 E
Igalula, Tan. 144 5.14 S 33.00 E
Igalula, Tan. 144 5.38 S 32.38 E
Igan 102 2.49 N 111.43 E
Igan ≃ 102 2.51 N 111.39 E
Igana 140 7.59 N 3.14 E
Iganga 144 0.37 N 33.29 E
Iganmu ◆[8] 263a 6.29 N 3.22 E
Igaporã 245 13.46 S 42.43 W
Igara 240 10.24 S 40.07 W
Igaraí 246 21.25 S 46.49 W
Igara Paraná ≃ 236 2.09 S 71.47 W
Igarapé-Açu 240 1.07 S 47.37 W
Igarapé Grande 240 4.41 S 44.58 W
Igarapé-Mirí 240 1.59 S 48.58 W
Igaratá 246 23.12 S 46.07 W
Igarka 64 67.28 N 86.35 E
Igarra 140 7.18 N 6.07 E
Igarukiro 144 3.08 S 33.31 E
Igatimí 242 24.05 S 55.30 W
Igatpuri 112 19.42 N 73.33 E
Igaun 263a 6.42 N 3.23 E
Igawa 144 8.35 S 34.28 E
Igbaja 140 8.23 N 4.52 E
Igbobi 263a 6.32 N 3.22 E
Igboho 140 8.51 N 3.45 E
Igbologun 263a 6.25 N 3.20 E
Igbo-Ora 140 7.26 N 3.17 E
Igbor 140 7.27 N 8.34 E
Igdir, Īrān 74 39.20 N 47.30 E
ıġdır, Tür. 74 39.55 N 44.02 E
ıġdır, Tür. 120 40.16 N 35.38 E
Igdy 118 39.54 N 56.54 E
Igea Marina 60 44.08 N 12.29 E
Igel 52 49.42 N 6.32 E
Igelfors 40 58.51 N 15.41 E
Igelsberg 54 48.32 N 8.26 E
Igel'vejem ≃ 170 65.40 N 172.50 W
Igersheim 52 49.29 N 9.49 E
Iggesund 26 61.38 N 17.04 E
Ighil Izane 138 35.44 N 0.30 E
Ightham 250 51.17 N 0.17 E
Igirma 78 56.59 N 103.37 E
Igiugig 170 59.20 N 155.55 W
Iglau → Jihlava 30 49.24 N 15.36 E
Iglesia 242 30.24 S 69.13 W
Iglesias 36 39.19 N 8.32 E
Iglesiente ◆[1] 36 39.20 N 8.40 E
Igli 138 30.25 N 2.12 W
Iglino 76 54.50 N 56.26 E
Igloolik 166 69.24 N 81.49 W
Iglovo 72 55.47 N 36.40 E
Igls 58 47.14 N 11.25 E
Ignacej 68 47.41 N 28.40 E
Ignacio, Calif., U.S. 216 38.05 N 122.32 W
Ignacio, Colo., U.S. 190 37.07 N 107.38 W
Ignacio de la Llave 224 18.43 N 95.59 W
Ignacio Zaragoza, Méx. 222 29.35 N 107.30 W
Ignacio Zaragoza, Méx. 224 23.55 N 103.42 W
Ignalina 66 55.21 N 26.10 E
Ignašino 79 53.28 N 122.23 E
Ignatjevcy 70 57.32 N 51.39 E
Ignatovka 70 53.57 N 47.38 E
Ignatovo 72 56.10 N 37.32 E
İğneada 120 41.52 N 27.58 E
İğneada Burnu ≻ 120 41.54 N 28.03 E
Igney 54 48.17 N 6.24 E
Ignon ≃ 54 47.31 N 5.10 E
Igny 251 48.45 N 2.14 E
Igodovo 70 58.01 N 42.21 E
Igoumenítsa 38 39.30 N 20.16 E
Igra 70 57.33 N 53.04 E
Igreja Nova 240 10.07 S 36.39 W
Iguaçu ≃, Bra. 277a 22.45 S 43.14 W
Iguaçu ≃, S.A. 242 25.36 S 54.36 W
Iguaçu, Saltos do (Iguassu Falls) L 242 25.41 S 54.26 W
Iguaí 245 14.45 S 40.04 W
Iguala 224 18.21 N 99.32 W
Igualada 34 41.35 N 1.38 E
Iguana ≃ 236 7.54 N 65.46 W
Iguana, Sierra de la ⋏ 186 26.45 N 100.20 W
Iguape 242 24.43 S 47.33 W
Iguará ≃ 240 3.28 S 43.55 W
Iguaraçu 245 23.11 S 51.50 W
Iguassu Falls → Iguaçu, Saltos do L 242 25.41 S 54.26 W
Iguatemi 245 23.40 S 54.34 W
Iguatemi ≃ 245 23.55 S 54.10 W
Iguatu 240 6.22 S 39.18 W
Iguazú (Iguaçu), Parque Nacional ♠ 242 25.35 S 54.20 W
Iguéla 142 1.55 S 9.19 E
Iguetti, Sebkhet ☷ 138 25.05 N 9.50 W
Iguidi, Erg •[8] 138 26.35 N 5.40 W
Iguig 106 17.45 N 121.44 E
Igumale 140 6.49 N 7.59 E
Igumnovo 72 55.37 N 38.18 E

Igvak, Cape ≻ 170 57.26 N 156.00 W
Igżej 78 53.59 N 103.10 E
Ihavandiffulu Atoll I[1] 112 7.00 N 72.55 E
Iheya-shima I 83b 27.00 N 127.56 E
Ihiala 140 5.51 N 6.51 E
Ihirène, Oued V 138 20.25 N 4.35 E
Ihle ≃ 50 52.17 N 11.52 E
Ihlienworth 48 53.44 N 8.55 E
Ihmert 52 51.20 N 7.44 E
Ihnāsiyat al-Madīnah 132 29.05 N 30.56 E
Ihorombe 147b 23.00 S 47.33 E
Ihosy 147b 22.24 S 46.08 E
Ihosy ≃ 147b 21.58 S 43.38 E
Ihotry, Lac ⊜ 147b 21.56 S 43.41 E
Ihringen 54 48.02 N 7.39 E
Ihringshausen 52 51.21 N 9.31 E
İhsangazi 120 41.11 N 33.33 E
Ihtiman 38 42.26 N 23.49 E
Ihu 154 7.55 S 145.25 E
Ihugh 140 7.02 N 9.00 E
Ihwah 132 29.03 N 31.00 E
Ii 26 65.19 N 25.22 E
II □[4] 140 16.30 N 10.00 W
Iida 84 35.31 N 137.50 E
III □[4] 140 16.15 N 11.45 W
III Internacional 70 49.49 N 47.06 E
Iijima 84 35.40 N 137.56 E
Iijoki ≃ 24 65.20 N 25.17 E
Iiktu, Gora ∧ 76 49.51 N 87.40 E
Iinan 84 34.27 N 136.24 E
Iinashi ≃ 86 35.27 N 133.13 E
Iioka 84 35.42 N 140.43 E
Iisaku 66 59.06 N 27.19 E
Iisalmi 26 63.34 N 27.11 E
Ii-shima I 164m 26.43 N 127.47 E
Ii-suido ⊔ 164m 26.42 N 127.51 E
Iisvesi 26 62.40 N 27.02 E
Iitaka 84 34.26 N 136.21 E
Iittala 26 61.04 N 24.10 E
Iivaara ∧[2] 26 65.47 N 29.40 E
Iiyama 84 36.51 N 138.22 E
Iizuka 86 33.38 N 130.41 E
Ij ≃ 78 52.34 N 96.10 E
Ija ≃ 78 55.05 N 101.05 E
Ijaiye 263a 6.40 N 3.18 E
Ijaji 134 8.59 N 37.13 E
Ijara 144 1.36 S 40.31 E
Ijebu-Igbo 140 6.56 N 4.01 E
Ijebu-Ode 140 6.50 N 3.56 E
Ijesa-Tedo 263a 6.30 N 3.19 E
Ijill, Kediet ∧ 138 22.38 N 12.33 W
Ijill, Sebkhet ⊜ 138 22.47 N 12.53 W
Ijin 88 42.05 N 130.08 E
Ijira 84 35.31 N 136.44 E
IJmuiden 48 52.27 N 4.36 E
IJssel ≃ 48 52.30 N 6.00 E
IJsselmeer (Zuiderzee) ⊤[2] 48 52.45 N 5.25 E
IJsselmuiden 48 52.34 N 5.56 E
IJsselstein 48 52.02 N 5.03 E
Ijuh 164b 0.30 S 166.57 E
Ijuí 242 28.23 S 53.55 W
Ijuí ≃ 242 27.58 S 55.20 W
Iju Junction 263a 6.40 N 3.19 E
Iju Water Works Ʊ[3] 263a 6.40 N 3.20 E
IJzendijke 48 51.19 N 3.38 E
IJzer (Yser) ≃ 46 51.09 N 2.43 E
Ik ≃ 70 55.55 N 52.36 E
Ik, Ozero ⊜ 76 56.03 N 71.33 E
Ika 78 59.18 N 106.12 E
Ikaalinen 26 61.46 N 23.03 E
Ikahavo, Plateau de l' ⋏[1] 147b 17.25 S 45.50 E
Ikaho 84 36.30 N 138.55 E
Ikalamavony 147b 21.09 S 46.35 E
Ikali 142 2.02 S 21.02 E
Ikalou 142 4.03 S 11.48 E
Ikamatua 162 42.16 S 171.41 E
Ikang 140 4.50 N 8.32 E
Ikara 140 11.12 N 8.15 E
Ikare 140 7.32 N 5.45 E
Ikaría I 38 37.41 N 26.20 E
Ikari-dam ◆[6] 84 36.52 N 139.42 E
Ikari-ko ⊜ 84 36.56 N 139.41 E
Ikaruga 86 34.36 N 135.44 E
Ikast 41 56.08 N 9.10 E
Ikatan 170 54.45 N 163.19 W
Ikatskij Chrebet ⋏ 78 54.00 N 111.00 E
Ikawa 84 35.13 N 138.15 E
Ikawa-dam ◆[6] 84 35.12 N 138.13 E
Ikawhenua Range ⋏ 162 38.20 S 176.56 E
Ikazaki 86 33.32 N 132.39 E
Ikeda, Nihon 82a 42.55 N 143.27 E
Ikeda, Nihon 84 35.26 N 136.34 E
Ikeda, Nihon 84 35.53 N 136.21 E
Ikeda, Nihon 84 36.25 N 137.53 E
Ikeda, Nihon 86 34.01 N 133.48 E
Ikeda, Nihon 86 34.49 N 135.25 E
Ikegawa 86 33.36 N 133.11 E
Ikej 78 54.12 N 100.04 E
Ikeja 140 6.36 N 3.21 E
Ikeja □[8] 263a 6.30 N 3.25 E
Ikela 142 1.11 S 23.16 E
Ikélemba 142 1.14 N 16.31 E
Ikelemba ≃ 142 0.07 N 18.17 E
Ikema-shima I 165d 24.56 N 125.16 E
Ikepa ≃ 147b 17.01 S 46.45 E
Ikerre 140 7.31 N 5.14 E
Ike-shima I 164m 26.23 N 128.00 E
Ikeura 260 34.30 N 135.25 E
Iki I 82 33.47 N 129.43 E
Iki-Burul 70 45.49 N 44.39 E
Ikimba, Lake ⊜ 144 1.28 S 31.30 E
Īkinjī Maryūt 132 31.00 N 29.45 E
Ikire 140 7.23 N 4.12 E
Ikirun 140 7.55 N 4.41 E
İkitelli 257b 41.04 N 28.47 E
İkizce 120 39.36 N 32.40 E
İkizdere 120 40.47 N 40.33 E
Iko 142 0.35 S 16.01 E
Ikole 140 7.49 N 5.30 E
Ikolik, Cape ≻ 170 57.17 N 154.48 W
Ikom 140 5.58 N 8.42 E
Ikoma, Nihon 86 34.41 N 135.42 E
Ikoma, Tan. 144 2.04 S 34.37 E
Ikoma-sanchi ⋏ 260 34.40 N 135.40 E
Ikoma-tunnel ◆[5] 260 34.41 N 135.41 E
Ikoma-yama ∧ 260 34.40 N 135.41 E
Ikon-Chal' 74 44.18 N 41.55 E
Ikorec ≃ 68 50.58 N 39.45 E
Ikorodu 140 6.37 N 3.31 E
Ikot Ekpene 140 5.12 N 7.40 E
Ikoy ≃ 142 0.53 S 10.36 E
Ikoyi ◆[8] 263a 6.27 N 3.26 E
Ikoyi Prison Ʊ 263a 6.25 N 3.25 E
Ikozi 144 2.32 S 27.37 E
Ikpikpuk ≃ 170 70.50 N 154.25 W
Ikra 116 23.42 N 87.07 E
Ikr'anoje 70 46.06 N 47.45 E
Ikrāsh 132 30.45 N 31.30 E
Ikśa 72 56.10 N 37.31 E
Iksa ≃ 76 57.48 N 82.36 E
Iksāl 122 32.41 N 35.19 E
Ikti, Cape ≻ 170 56.00 N 158.30 W
Ikuata 263a 6.25 N 3.22 E
Ikuchi-shima I 86 34.17 N 133.07 E
Ikuji-hana ≻ 84 36.54 N 137.25 E
Ikuktlitlig Mountain ∧ 170 59.16 N 161.27 W
Ikungu 144 1.34 S 33.40 E
Ikuno 86 35.10 N 134.48 E
Ikuno ◆[8] 260 34.39 N 135.33 E
Ikurangi, Mount ∧ 164k 21.13 S 159.45 W
Ikusaka 84 36.25 N 137.56 E
Ikusu ≃ 263b 4.24 S 15.14 E
Ikuta 258 35.37 N 139.33 E
Ikuta ◆[8] 260 34.42 N 135.11 E
Ikva ≃ 68 50.33 N 25.24 E
Ikwah 132 30.41 N 31.28 E
Ila, Nig. 140 8.01 N 4.55 E
Ila, Zaïre 142 2.53 S 21.05 E

Symbol	English	Deutsch	Español	Français	Português
≃	River	Fluss	Río	Rivière	Rio
☰	Canal	Kanal	Canal	Canal	Canal
L	Waterfall, Rapids	Wasserfall, Stromschnellen	Cascada, Rápidos	Chute d'eau, Rapides	Cascata, Rápidos
⊔	Strait	Meeresstrasse	Estrecho	Détroit	Estreito
C	Bay, Gulf	Bucht, Golf	Bahía, Golfo	Baie, Golfe	Baía, Golfo
⊜	Lake, Lakes	See, Seen	Lago, Lagos	Lac, Lacs	Lago, Lagos
☷	Swamp	Sumpf	Pantano	Marais	Pântano
☷	Ice Features, Glacier	Eis- und Gletscherformen	Accidentes Glaciales	Formes glaciaires	Acidentes Glaciares
⊤	Other Hydrographic Features	Andere Hydrographische Objekte	Otros Elementos Hidrográficos	Autres données hydrographiques	Outros Elementos Hidrográficos
✢	Submarine Features	Untermeerische Objekte	Accidentes Submarinos	Formes de relief sous-marin	Acidentes Submarinos
□	Political Unit	Politische Einheit	Unidad Política	Entité politique	Unidade Política
Ʊ	Cultural Institution	Kulturelle Institution	Institución Cultural	Institution culturelle	Instituição Cultural
⊥	Historical Site	Historische Stätte	Sitio Histórico	Site historique	Sítio Histórico
♠	Recreational Site	Erholungs- und Ferienort	Sitio de Recreo	Centre de loisirs	Sítio de Lazer
⊠	Airport	Flughafen	Aeropuerto	Aéroport	Aeroporto
■	Military Installation	Militäranlage	Instalación Militar	Installation militaire	Instalação Militar
◆	Miscellaneous	Verschiedenes	Misceláneo	Divers	Miscelânea

Ilabaya 238 17.25 S 70.31 W
Ilacaon Point ➤ 106 11.00 N 123.12 E
Ilad 134 10.09 N 47.52 E
Ilagala 144 5.12 S 29.50 E
Ilagan 106 17.10 N 121.54 E
Ilagan ≃ 106 17.09 N 121.54 E
Ilaiyānkudi 112 9.38 N 78.38 E
Ilaka, Madag. 147b 20.20 S 47.09 E
Ilaka, Madag. 147b 19.33 S 48.52 E
Ilām, Īrān 118 33.38 N 46.26 E
Ilām, Nepāl 114 26.55 N 87.56 E
Ilam
→ Sri Lanka ☐[1] 112 7.00 N 81.00 E
Ilam Bāzār 116 23.38 N 87.32 E
Ilan 90 24.45 N 121.44 E
Ilan Ch'uan ≃ 90 24.42 N 121.48 E
Ilanskij 78 56.14 N 96.03 E
Ilanz 54 46.46 N 9.12 E
Ilara 263a 6.42 N 3.27 E
Ilaro 140 6.53 N 3.03 E
Ilasco 209 39.40 N 91.19 W
Iława 30 53.37 N 19.33 E
Ilawe 140 7.37 N 5.06 E
Ilay 54 46.37 N 5.53 E
Ilbenge 64 62.49 N 124.24 E
Ilberstedt 50 51.48 N 11.40 E
Ilbunga 152 26.25 S 135.03 E
Ilchester, Eng., U.K. 44 51.01 N 2.41 W
Ilchester, Md., U.S. 274b 39.15 N 76.46 W
Ildefonso, Islas II 244 55.44 S 69.26 W
Île-à-la-Crosse 174 55.27 N 107.53 W
Île-à-la-Crosse, Lac ⊜ 174 55.40 N 107.45 W
Île-aux-Tourtes, Pont ➤[5] 265a 45.25 N 73.59 W
Ilebo (Port-Francqui) 142 4.19 S 20.35 E
Île-Cadieux 265a 45.25 N 74.01 W
Île-de-France ☐[9] 46 49.00 N 2.20 E
Île de la Camargue ☐[9] 56 43.34 N 4.34 E
Ilek 70 51.30 N 53.22 E
Ilek ≃ 62 51.30 N 53.20 E
Île-Perrot 196 45.23 N 73.57 W
Ileret 144 4.19 N 36.13 E
Îles, Lac des ⊜, Qué., Can. 196 46.06 N 74.02 W
Îles, Lac des ⊜, Sask., Can. 174 54.26 N 109.25 W
Ilesha, Nig. 140 8.56 N 3.25 E
Ilesha, Nig. 140 7.38 N 4.45 E
Ilet' ≃ 70 55.56 N 48.14 E
Ilevskij Pogost 24 60.41 N 43.46 E
Ileza 24 60.43 N 43.54 E
Ilfeld 50 51.34 N 10.47 E
Ilford, Austl. 160 32.58 S 149.51 E
Ilford, Man., Can. 174 56.04 N 95.35 W
Ilford ➤[8] 250 51.33 N 0.05 E
Ilfov ☐[4] 38 44.30 N 26.00 E
Ilfracombe, Austl. 156 23.30 S 144.30 E
Ilfracombe, Eng., U.K. 44 51.13 N 4.08 W
Il Fuorn 54 46.40 N 10.12 E
Ilga ≃ 78 55.00 N 105.04 E
Ilgaz 120 40.56 N 33.38 E
Ilgaz Dağları ⋀ 120 41.00 N 33.35 E
Ilgın 120 38.17 N 31.55 E
Ilha ➤[8] 246 23.00 S 43.33 W
Ilhabela 246 23.47 S 45.21 W
Ilha das Flôres 240 10.27 S 36.33 W
Ilha Grande 236 0.27 S 65.02 W
Ilha Grande, Baía da ⊂ 246 23.09 S 44.30 W
Ilhas, Cachoeira das ⌊ 240 1.03 S 57.33 W
Ilhavo 34 40.36 N 8.40 W
Ilhéos
→ Ilhéus 245 14.49 S 39.02 W
Ilhéus 245 14.49 S 39.02 W
Ili 75 43.53 N 77.12 E
Ili ≃ 76 45.24 N 74.02 E
Ilia 38 45.56 N 22.39 E
Iliamna 170 59.45 N 154.54 W
Iliamna Lake ⊜ 170 59.30 N 155.00 W
Ilian, Mount ⋀ 106 10.26 N 119.33 E
Iliatenco 224 16.58 N 98.40 W
Iliç 120 39.28 N 38.34 E
Ilıca, Tür. 120 39.52 N 27.46 E
Ilıca, Tür. 120 39.57 N 41.07 E
Ilicínea 245 20.56 S 45.50 W
Iliff 188 40.45 N 103.04 W
Iliff, Lake ⊜ 266 41.02 N 74.43 W
Iligan 106 8.14 N 124.14 E
Iligan Bay ⊂ 106 8.25 N 124.05 E
Ilijan 106 13.38 N 121.04 E
Ilim ≃ 78 57.38 N 102.34 E
Ilimsk 78 56.46 N 103.52 E
Ilin 106 12.15 N 121.02 E
Ilin Island I 106 12.14 N 121.05 E
Ilinka 72 54.04 N 38.12 E
Ilinta ≃ 147b 25.02 S 44.05 E
Ilion 200 43.01 N 75.02 W
Ilio Point ➤ 219a 21.13 N 157.15 W
Ilioupolis 257c 37.56 N 23.45 E
Ilir 78 55.13 N 100.40 E
Ilirska Bistrica 36 45.34 N 14.15 E
Ilisira 120 37.12 N 33.02 E
Ilisós ≃ 257c 37.57 N 23.41 E
Ilja 66 54.25 N 27.18 E
Iljak 76 60.11 N 77.59 E
Iljičevsk 74 39.33 N 44.58 E
Iljičovsk 68 46.18 N 30.39 E
Iljincy 68 49.07 N 29.12 E
Iljinka, S.S.S.R. 70 48.32 N 41.05 E
Iljinka, S.S.S.R. 78 52.08 N 101.17 E
Iljino 66 55.57 N 31.40 E
Iljinskij, S.S.S.R. 24 61.02 N 32.41 E
Iljinskij, S.S.S.R. 76 58.35 N 55.41 E
Iljinskij, S.S.S.R. 78 52.05 N 114.10 E
Iljinskij, S.S.S.R. 79 47.58 N 142.12 E
Iljinskij, S.S.S.R. 255b 55.37 N 38.06 E
Iljinskij Pogost 72 55.28 N 38.54 E
Iljinskoje, S.S.S.R. 66 57.19 N 38.32 E
Iljinskoje, S.S.S.R. 66 53.14 N 35.26 E
Iljinskoje, S.S.S.R. 66 58.47 N 44.36 E
Iljinskoje, S.S.S.R. 66 56.58 N 37.11 E
Iljinskoje, S.S.S.R. 70 56.29 N 52.49 E
Iljinskoje, S.S.S.R. 72 56.34 N 35.57 E
Iljinskoje, S.S.S.R. 72 54.59 N 36.11 E
Iljinskoje, S.S.S.R. 255b 55.46 N 37.15 E
Iljinskoje-Chovanskoje 70 56.58 N 39.46 E
Iljinsko-Podomskoje 24 61.08 N 47.56 E
Iljinsko-Zaborskoje 70 57.16 N 44.23 E
Iljiny Gory ⋀[2] 66 56.34 N 34.12 E
Il'ka 78 51.43 N 108.32 E
Ilkal 112 15.58 N 76.08 E
Ilkeston 44 52.59 N 1.18 W
Il'kino 70 55.13 N 41.36 E
Ilkley 42 53.55 N 1.50 W
Ill ≃, Fr. 54 48.40 N 7.53 E
Ill ≃, Öst. 54 47.17 N 9.33 E
Illabot Creek ≃ 214 48.29 N 121.30 W
Illampu, Nevado ⋀ 248 15.50 S 68.34 W
Illana Bay ⊂ 106 7.25 N 123.45 E
Illapel 242 31.38 S 71.10 W
Illapel ≃ 242 31.37 S 71.09 W
Illarionovo 68 48.25 N 35.16 E
Illasi 58 45.28 N 11.10 E
Illawarra, Lake ⊂ 160 34.32 S 150.50 E
Illbillee, Mount ⋀ 152 27.02 S 132.30 E
Ille-et-Vilaine ☐[5] 32 48.10 N 1.30 W
Illéla 140 14.28 N 5.15 E
Iller ≃ 54 48.23 N 9.58 E
Illertissen 54 48.13 N 10.06 E
Illescas, Esp. 34 40.07 N 3.50 W
Illescas, Méx. 224 23.13 N 102.07 W
Illfurth 54 47.40 N 7.16 E
Illhaeusern 54 48.11 N 7.26 E
Illi, Ba ≃ 136 10.44 N 15.21 E
Illiers 46 48.18 N 1.15 E
Illimani, Nevado ⋀ 238 16.39 S 67.48 W
Illimo 238 6.28 S 79.51 W
Illingen 52 48.57 N 8.55 E
Illingworth 252 53.45 N 1.54 W
Illinois ☐[3] 168 40.00 N 89.00 W
Illinois ≃, Ill., U.S. 184 38.58 N 90.27 W
Illinois ≃, Oreg., U.S. 192 42.33 N 124.03 W
Illinois, University of (Circle Campus) ᵾ[2] 268 41.52 N 87.39 W
Illinois and Michigan Canal ≍ 268 41.32 N 88.05 W
Illinois Beach State Park ♠ 206 42.26 N 87.48 W
Illinois Institute of Technology ᵾ[2] 268 41.50 N 87.38 W
Illinois Peak ⋀ 192 47.02 N 115.04 W
Illiopolis 209 39.51 N 89.15 W
Illiwa ≃ 236 3.53 N 58.45 W
Illizi 138 26.29 N 8.28 E
Illkirch-Graffenstaden 54 48.32 N 7.43 E
Illminster 44 50.56 N 2.55 W
Illovo 148 30.05 S 30.50 E
Illzach 54 47.47 N 7.20 E
Ilm ≃ 50 51.07 N 11.40 E
Ilmajoki 26 62.44 N 22.34 E
Il'men', Ozero ⊜ 66 58.17 N 31.20 E
Ilmenau 50 50.41 N 10.55 E
Ilmenau ≃ 50 53.23 N 10.10 E
Il'menskij, Zapovednik ♠ 76 55.16 N 60.17 E
Il'mino 70 53.47 N 45.40 E
Ilo 238 17.38 S 71.20 W
Ilobasco 226 13.51 N 88.51 W
Ilobu 140 7.51 N 4.30 E
Iloc Island I 106 11.18 N 119.41 E
Ilocos Norte ☐[4] 106 18.10 N 120.45 E
Ilocos Sur ☐[4] 106 17.05 N 120.35 E
Iloilo 106 10.42 N 122.34 E
Iloilo ☐[4] 106 11.00 N 122.35 E
Iloilo Strait ꓤ 106 10.43 N 122.36 E
Ilomantsi 26 62.40 N 30.55 E
Ilondola Mission 144 10.42 S 31.47 E
Ilongero 144 4.40 S 34.52 E
Ilop 154 2.54 S 141.13 E
Ilopango, Lago de ⊜ 226 13.40 N 89.03 W
Ilora 140 7.45 N 3.50 E
Ilorin 140 8.30 N 4.32 E
Iloron, Cerro ⋀ 224 20.57 N 104.22 W
Ilovajsk 73 47.56 N 38.13 E
Ilovatka 70 50.31 N 45.55 E
Ilovka 68 50.43 N 38.38 E
Ilovl'a 70 49.18 N 43.59 E
Ilovl'a ≃ 70 49.14 N 43.54 E
Iłowa 30 51.30 N 15.12 E
Il Palone ⋀ 58 46.02 N 11.04 E
Il'pyrskij 64 59.56 N 164.10 E
Ilsan-ni 261b 37.41 N 126.46 E
Ilse ≃ 50 52.06 N 10.35 E
Ilsenburg 50 51.52 N 10.40 E
Ilshofen 52 49.10 N 9.55 E
Il'skij 68 44.51 N 38.35 E
Ilskov 41 56.14 N 9.06 E
Il Telegrafo ⋀ 60 42.22 N 11.10 E
Ilten 48 52.21 N 9.55 E
Ilu 142 4.12 S 23.02 E
Ilubabor ☐[4] 134 6.50 N 35.20 E
Iluhār 116 22.48 N 90.06 E
Ilūkste 66 55.58 N 26.18 E
Ilverich 253 51.17 N 6.42 E
Ilwaco 214 46.19 N 124.03 W
Ilwaki 102 7.56 S 126.26 E
İlyasbey 120 40.13 N 29.52 E
Iłża 30 51.11 N 21.14 E
Ima 78 55.13 N 115.55 E
Imabari 86 34.03 N 133.00 E
Imadomi 258 35.28 N 140.06 E
Imaichi 84 36.43 N 139.41 E
Imajō 84 35.46 N 136.12 E
Imajuku 258 35.58 N 139.21 E
Imajuku ➤[8] 258 35.29 N 139.32 E
Imaki 260 34.24 N 135.46 E
Imaloto ≃ 147b 23.27 S 45.13 E
Imambara ᵾ[1] 262b 22.54 N 88.25 E
İmamlar 120 40.47 N 30.59 E
Iman 79 45.55 N 133.43 E
Iman ≃ 79 45.57 N 133.42 E
Imanbaj ⊥ 76 43.13 N 60.25 E
Imandan-Makit, Gora ⋀ 78 54.15 N 117.38 E
Imandra, Ozero ⊜ 24 67.30 N 33.00 E
Imanombo 147b 24.26 S 45.49 E
Imantau 76 52.58 N 68.22 E
Imari 82 33.16 N 129.53 E
Imaruí 242 28.21 S 48.49 W
Imaruí, Lagoa ⊂ 242 28.21 S 48.52 W
Imasa 130 18.01 N 36.12 E
Imatra 26 61.10 N 28.46 E
Imavere 66 58.44 N 25.48 E
Imazu 84 35.24 N 136.02 E
Imbābah 132 30.04 N 31.13 E
Imbabura ☐[4] 236 0.22 N 78.25 W
Imbariê 246 22.39 S 43.13 W
Imbituba 242 28.14 S 48.40 W
Imbituva 242 25.12 S 50.35 W
Imboassu, Canal ≍ 277a 22.48 S 43.04 W
Imboden 184 36.12 N 91.10 W
Imbonga 142 0.43 S 19.46 E
Imbundi 142 5.44 S 16.16 E
Imeni Abaja 76 50.44 N 69.30 E
Imeni Babuškina 66 59.45 N 43.07 E
Imeni Čapajeva 75 43.28 N 76.50 E
Imeni C'urupy 72 55.30 N 38.39 E
Imeni Džambula, S.S.S.R. 76 45.26 N 74.24 E
Imeni Džambula, S.S.S.R. 76 47.43 N 74.09 E
Imeni Frunze 76 46.23 N 77.20 E
Imeni Il-go Okt'abr'a 78 55.54 N 119.36 E
Imeni Kalinina, S.S.S.R. 70 51.51 N 52.43 E
Imeni Kalinina, S.S.S.R. 75 41.28 N 76.22 E
Imeni Kalinina, S.S.S.R. 75 43.16 N 74.03 E
Imeni Kalinina, S.S.S.R. 76 43.40 N 59.07 E
Imeni Karla Libknechta 68 51.37 N 35.27 E
Imeni Kirova, S.S.S.R. 76 51.27 N 77.32 E
Imeni Kirova, S.S.S.R. 76 46.27 N 77.13 E
Imeni Leninskogo Komsomola 76 50.45 N 66.44 E
Imeni Marta 76 46.57 N 58.58 E
Imeni Michajla Ivanoviča Kalinina 70 57.59 N 45.07 E
Imeni Morozova 255a 59.59 N 31.02 E
Imeni Moskvy, Kanal ≍ 72 56.43 N 37.08 E
Imeni M.V. Lomonosova, Universitet ᵾ[2] 255b 55.43 N 37.32 E
Imeni Panfilova 75 43.23 N 77.07 E
Imeni Poliny Osipenko 79 52.25 N 136.28 E
Imeni Sardarova Karachana 75 38.26 N 68.46 E
Imeni Şeredy 73 46.52 N 40.03 E
Imeni Ševčenko 76 45.58 N 61.04 E
Imeni S.M. Kirova, Stadion ♠ 255a 59.58 N 30.14 E
Imeni Stepana Razina 70 54.54 N 44.18 E
Imeni Tel'mana 79 48.36 N 134.59 E
Imeni Timir'azeva 76 53.39 N 65.31 E
Imeni Vladimira Iljiča Lenina 70 53.36 N 46.58 E
Imeni Vorovskogo, S.S.S.R. 70 55.43 N 41.06 E
Imeni Vorovskogo, S.S.S.R. 72 55.43 N 38.20 E
Imeni XXI Partsjezda 76 50.43 N 67.50 E
Imeni Žel'abova 66 58.57 N 36.36 E
İmerhav 74 41.25 N 42.14 E
Imerimandroso 147b 17.23 S 48.38 E
Imese 142 2.07 N 18.06 E
Imgenbroich 52 50.34 N 6.16 E
Imi 134 6.28 N 42.18 E
Imías 230p 20.04 N 74.38 W
Imilac 242 24.14 S 68.53 W
Imilili ⌄[4] 138 23.18 N 15.54 W
Imi-n'tanout 138 31.10 N 8.50 W
Imišli 74 39.52 N 48.04 E
Imittós 257c 37.57 N 23.45 E
Imittós Óros ⋀ 257c 37.55 N 23.47 E
Imjin-gang ≃ 88 37.47 N 126.40 E
Imlay 194 40.39 N 118.09 W
Imlay City 180 43.02 N 83.05 W
Imlaystown 198 40.10 N 74.31 W
Imler 204 40.12 N 78.31 W
Immarna 152 30.30 S 132.09 E
Immendingen 54 47.56 N 8.44 E
Immenhausen 52 51.25 N 9.28 E
Immensen 48 52.23 N 10.04 E
Immenstaad 54 47.40 N 9.22 E
Immenstadt 54 47.33 N 10.13 E
Immigrath 253 51.06 N 6.57 E
Immingham Dock 42 53.37 N 0.12 W
Immokalee 210 26.25 N 81.25 W
Imnaha ≃ 192 45.49 N 116.46 W
Imo ≃ 140 4.36 N 7.35 E
Imogiri 105a 7.55 S 110.23 E
Imokt'an 88 38.50 N 126.41 E
Imola 60 44.21 N 11.42 E
Imono ≃ 263a 6.26 N 3.17 E
Imoro 263a 6.43 N 3.30 E
Im Ostholz ➤[8] 253 51.26 N 7.12 E
Imotski 36 43.27 N 17.13 E
Imp'a 88 35.59 N 126.49 E
Impasugong 106 8.19 N 125.00 E
Impe 142 2.44 S 15.17 E
Impendle 148 29.37 S 29.55 E
Impenekuim, Gora ⋀ 170 65.42 N 176.30 E
Imperatore, Campo ≚ 60 42.25 N 13.40 E
Imperatriz 240 5.32 S 47.29 W
Imperia 56 43.53 N 8.03 E
Imperia ☐[4] 58 43.58 N 7.47 E
Imperial, Sask., Can. 174 51.22 N 105.27 W
Imperial, Perú 238 13.04 S 76.21 W
Imperial, Calif., U.S. 194 32.51 N 115.34 W
Imperial, Mo., U.S. 208 38.22 N 90.23 W
Imperial, Nebr., U.S. 188 40.31 N 101.39 W
Imperial, Pa., U.S. 204 40.27 N 80.15 W
Imperial, Tex., U.S. 186 31.16 N 102.41 W
Imperial Beach 218 32.35 N 117.08 W
Imperial Dam ➤[6] 194 32.55 N 114.30 W
Imperial de Aragón, Canal ≍ 34 42.02 N 1.33 W
Imperial Mills 172 55.00 N 111.44 W
Imperial Palace ᵾ 258 35.41 N 139.45 E
Imperial Valley ⋁ 194 32.50 N 115.30 W
Imperio Centroafricana → Central African Empire ☐[1] 126 7.00 N 21.00 E
Impflingen 52 49.10 N 8.07 E
Impfondo 142 1.37 N 18.04 E
Imphāl 110 24.49 N 93.57 E
Impilachti 24 61.40 N 31.04 E
Imprensa, Gruta da •[6] 277a 23.00 S 43.15 W
Impruneta 60 43.41 N 11.15 E
Impulo 142 13.53 S 13.39 E
İmralı I 120 40.32 N 28.32 E
İmranlı 120 39.54 N 38.07 E
İmron 120 38.12 N 38.53 E
Imsil 88 35.37 N 127.15 E
Imst 54 47.14 N 10.44 E
Imtān 122 32.24 N 36.49 E
Imuris 222 30.47 N 110.52 W
Imuruan Bay ⊂ 106 10.40 N 119.16 E
Imuruk Basin ⊜ 170 65.06 N 165.36 W
Imuruk Lake ⊜ 170 65.36 N 163.10 W
Imute 263a 6.42 N 3.29 E
Imwŏn-ni 88 37.15 N 129.20 E
Ina, Nihon 84 37.10 N 139.32 E
Ina, Nihon 84 35.59 N 140.03 E
Ina, Nihon 84 35.50 N 137.57 E
Ina, Nihon 258 35.59 N 139.38 E
In'a, S.S.S.R. 64 59.24 N 144.48 E
In'a, S.S.S.R. 76 53.31 N 82.40 E
In'a, S.S.S.R. 76 50.48 N 86.37 E
Ina, Ill., U.S. 184 38.09 N 88.54 W
Ina ≃, Nihon 86 34.43 N 135.28 E
Ina ≃, Pol. 50 53.32 N 14.38 E
In'a ≃, S.S.S.R. 76 54.59 N 82.59 E
Inaba 260 34.26 N 135.27 E
Inabe 84 35.07 N 136.33 E
Ina-bonchi ≚[1] 84 35.45 N 137.57 E
Inabu 84 35.13 N 137.30 E
Inaccessible Island I 10 37.17 S 12.45 W
Inácios 246 21.22 S 46.59 W
Inada 260 34.54 N 135.08 E
Inagawa 86 34.53 N 135.22 E
Inagawan 106 9.33 N 118.39 E
Inage 258 35.38 N 140.05 E
Inagi 84 35.38 N 139.30 E
Inajá 240 8.54 S 37.49 W
Inajá ≃ 240 8.53 S 49.44 W
Inajá, Igarapé ≃ 236 3.22 N 63.46 W
In'akino 70 54.26 N 41.07 E
Inakona 165e 9.49 S 160.02 E
Inala 161a 27.35 S 152.58 E
Inamangando ≃ 142 14.03 S 12.23 E
Inambari ≃ 238 12.41 S 69.44 W
In Aménas 138 28.05 N 9.30 E
In Amguel 138 23.40 N 5.10 E
Inami, Nihon 84 36.33 N 136.58 E
Inami, Nihon 86 34.45 N 134.54 E
Inami, Nihon 86 33.48 N 135.13 E
Inamuragasaki Point ⊥ 258 35.18 N 139.32 E
Inanda 263d 26.07 S 28.03 E
Inangahua Junction 162 41.51 S 171.57 E
Inanwatan 154 2.08 S 132.10 E
Inaouene, Oued ≃ 138 34.12 N 4.54 W
Iñapari 238 10.57 S 69.35 W
Inaporok 154 8.15 S 141.55 E
Inarajan 164p 13.16 N 144.45 E
Inari 24 68.54 N 27.01 E
Inari ⊜ 24 69.00 N 28.00 E
Inarigda 64 63.14 N 107.27 E
Inas, Gunong ⋀ 104 5.15 N 100.56 E
Inasa 84 34.50 N 137.40 E
Inatsuke ➤[8] 258 35.46 N 139.43 E
Inatsuki 86 33.36 N 130.43 E
Inauaia 154 8.40 S 146.35 E
Inauini ≃ 238 8.30 S 67.24 W
Inawasiro-ko ⊜ 82 37.29 N 140.06 E
Inazawa 84 35.15 N 136.47 E
Inba 84 35.46 N 140.14 E
Inba-numa ⊜ 84 35.46 N 140.12 E
In Belbel 138 27.54 N 1.10 E
Inca 34 39.43 N 2.54 E
Inca de Oro 242 26.45 S 69.54 W
Incaguasi 242 29.13 S 71.03 W
Ince 252 53.17 N 2.49 W
Ince Blundell 252 53.31 N 3.02 W
İnce Burun ➤ 120 42.07 N 34.56 E
Ince-in-Makerfield 252 53.32 N 2.37 W
İncekum Burnu ➤ 120 36.13 N 33.58 E
İncesu 120 38.38 N 35.11 E
Inchas Military Base ■ 132 30.20 N 31.27 E
Inchcape II[1] 28 56.55 N 2.50 W
Inchini 134 8.48 N 37.43 E
Inchmarnock I 42 55.47 N 5.09 W
Inch'ŏn 88
261b 37.28 N 126.38 E
Inchwagh Lake ⊜ 271 42.27 N 83.41 W
İncirliova 120 37.50 N 27.43 E
Incisa in Val d'Arno 60 43.40 N 11.27 E
Incline Village 216 39.16 N 119.56 W
Incomati (Komati) ≃ 146 25.46 S 32.43 E
Inconfidência 246 22.16 S 43.13 W
Inconfidentes 246 22.20 S 46.20 W
Inčoun 170 66.18 N 170.17 W
Incudine 58 46.14 N 10.22 E
Incudine, l' ⋀ 36 41.51 N 9.12 E
Incy 24 65.48 N 40.26 E
Indaal, Loch ⊂ 42 55.44 N 6.20 W
Indaiá ≃ 245 18.27 S 45.22 W
Indaiá Grande ≃ 245 19.31 S 52.29 W
Indaiatuba 246 23.05 S 47.14 W
Indalsälven ≃ 26 62.31 N 17.27 E
Indanan 106 5.58 N 120.59 E
Indaparapeo 224 19.47 N 100.58 W
Inda Silase 134 14.05 N 38.20 E
Indaw 100 23.40 N 94.46 E
Indawgyi Lake ⊜ 100 25.10 N 96.19 E
Indé 222 25.54 N 105.13 W
Inde
→ India ☐[1] 108 20.00 N 77.00 E
Inde ≃ 52 50.54 N 6.21 E
Indemini 54 46.06 N 8.50 E
Independence, Calif., U.S. 194 36.48 N 118.12 W
Independence, Ind., U.S. 206 40.20 N 87.10 W
Independence, Iowa, U.S. 180 42.28 N 91.54 W
Independence, Kans., U.S. 188 37.13 N 95.42 W
Independence, Ky., U.S. 208 38.57 N 84.32 W
Independence, La., U.S. 184 30.38 N 90.30 W
Independence, Mo., U.S. 184 39.05 N 94.24 W
Independence, Ohio, U.S. 269a 41.23 N 81.39 W
Independence, Oreg., U.S. 192 44.51 N 123.11 W
Independence, Pa., U.S. 204 40.15 N 80.31 W
Independence, Tex., U.S. 212 30.19 N 96.21 W
Independence, Va., U.S. 182 36.37 N 81.09 W
Independence, Wis., U.S. 180 44.21 N 91.25 W
Independence ≃ 178 43.45 N 75.20 W
Independence Creek ≃ 186 30.27 N 101.44 W
Independence Hall ⊥ 275 39.57 N 75.09 W
Independence Lake ⊜[1] 216 39.26 N 120.18 W
Independence Mountains ⋀⋀ 194 41.15 N 116.05 W
Independencia, Bol. 238 17.07 S 66.53 W
Independência, Bra. 240 5.23 S 40.19 W
Independencia, Bahía de la ⊂ 238 14.15 S 76.10 W
Independencia, Isla I 238 14.15 S 76.12 W
Independența 38 43.58 N 28.05 E
Inder, Ozero ⊜ 70 48.27 N 51.54 E
Inderborskij 70 48.33 N 51.44 E
In der Bredde 253 51.20 N 7.23 E
İnderesi 120 37.50 N 35.40 E
Index 214 47.50 N 121.33 W
Index, Mount ⋀ 214 47.46 N 121.35 W
Indi 112 17.10 N 75.58 E
India ☐[1] 108 20.00 N 77.00 E
India Brook ≃ 266 40.47 N 74.37 W
India Gate ⊥ 262a 28.37 N 77.18 E
Indialantic 210 28.05 N 80.34 W
Indian ≃, Ont., Can. 202 45.16 N 76.14 W
Indian ≃, Ont., Can. 202 44.13 N 78.08 W
Indian ≃, Del., U.S. 198 38.36 N 75.10 W
Indian ≃, Mass., U.S. 273 42.47 N 70.58 W
Indian ≃, Mich., U.S. 180 45.59 N 86.15 W
Indian ≃, N.Y., U.S. 202 43.58 N 75.17 W
Indiana 204 40.37 N 79.09 W
Indiana ☐[6] 204 40.37 N 79.09 W
Indiana ☐[3] 168
184 40.00 N 86.15 W
Indiana Dunes National Lakeshore ♠ 206 41.40 N 87.00 W
Indiana Dunes State Park ♠ 206 41.40 N 87.02 W
Indian Agricultural Research Institute ᵾ[3] 262a 28.38 N 77.10 E
Indiana Harbor ⊂ 268 41.40 N 87.27 W
Indiana Harbor Canal ≍ 268 41.40 N 87.27 W
Indianapolis 208 39.46 N 86.09 W
Indianapolis (Weir Cook) Municipal Airport ⊠ 208 39.43 N 86.16 W
Indianapolis Motor Speedway ♠ 208 39.48 N 86.14 W
Indian Bayou ≃ 184 34.14 N 91.52 W
Indian Brook 176 46.23 N 60.32 W
Indian Caverns •[5] 204 40.38 N 78.05 W
Indian Church 222 17.45 N 88.40 W
Indian Creek 268 42.14 N 87.59 W
Indian Creek ≃, U.S. 208 39.19 N 84.38 W
Indian Creek ≃, Calif., U.S. 218 35.18 N 118.26 W
Indian Creek ≃, Ill., U.S. 206 41.26 N 88.46 W
Indian Creek ≃, Ill., U.S. 209 39.56 N 90.32 W
Indian Creek ≃, Ill., U.S. 268 42.11 N 87.55 W
Indian Creek ≃, Ind., U.S. 206 40.55 N 86.42 W
Indian Creek ≃, Ind., U.S. 208 39.23 N 86.29 W
Indian Creek ≃, Ind., U.S. 208 38.43 N 85.06 W
Indian Creek ≃, Ind., U.S. 208 38.10 N 86.14 W
Indian Creek ≃, Md., U.S. 274c 38.59 N 76.55 W
Indian Creek ≃, Mo., U.S. 184 36.33 N 94.29 W
Indian Creek ≃, N. Mex., U.S. 190 36.11 N 108.23 W
Indian Creek ≃, N.Y., U.S. 266 40.43 N 73.06 W
Indian Creek ≃, Ohio, U.S. 269a 41.17 N 81.31 W
Indian Creek ≃, S. Dak., U.S. 188 44.39 N 103.19 W
Indian Creek ≃, Tenn., U.S. 184 35.13 N 88.08 W
Indian Creek Lake ⊜[1] 212 31.44 N 95.58 W
Indianford 206 42.49 N 88.35 W
Indian Grave Mountain ⋀[2] 182 32.59 N 84.21 W
Indian Grove Brook ≃ 266 40.44 N 74.33 W
Indian Harbour Beach 210 28.10 N 80.35 W
Indian Head 174 50.32 N 103.40 W
Indian Head Brook ≃ 273 42.04 N 70.52 W
Indian Head Park 268 41.47 N 87.54 W
Indian Head Pond ⊜ 273 42.03 N 70.51 W
Indian Heights 206 40.25 N 86.08 W
Indian Island I 214 48.04 N 122.43 W
Indian Kentuck Creek ≃ 208 38.43 N 85.16 W
Indian Lake, Mich., U.S. 206 41.59 N 86.12 W
Indian Lake, N.Y., U.S. 178 43.47 N 74.16 W
Indian Lake ⊜, Ont., Can. 180 47.08 N 82.08 W
Indian Lake ⊜, Mich., U.S. 180 45.59 N 86.20 W
Indian Lake ⊜, Mich., U.S. 206 42.00 N 86.13 W
Indian Lake ⊜, Mich., U.S. 206 42.09 N 85.29 W
Indian Lake ⊜, N.J., U.S. 266 40.53 N 74.29 W
Indian Lake ⊜, Ohio, U.S. 206 40.29 N 83.53 W
Indian Lake Estates 210 27.48 N 81.19 W
Indian Lakes ⊜ 206 41.33 N 85.25 W
Indian Lake State Park ♠ 206 40.29 N 83.52 W
Indian Mills Brook ≃ 275 39.47 N 74.44 W
Indian Mills Lake ⊜ 275 39.48 N 74.44 W
Indian Neck 197 41.15 N 72.46 W
Indian Ocean ⊤[1] 4
6 10.00 S 70.00 E
Indianola, Iowa, U.S. 180 41.22 N 93.34 W
Indianola, Miss., U.S. 184 33.27 N 90.39 W
Indianola, Nebr., U.S. 188 40.14 N 100.25 W
Indianola, Pa., U.S. 269b 40.34 N 79.51 W
Indianola, Wash., U.S. 214 47.45 N 122.31 W
Indianópolis 245 19.02 S 47.55 W
Indianópolis ➤[8] 277b 23.36 S 46.38 W
Indian Peak ⋀, Utah, U.S. 190 38.16 N 113.53 W
Indian Peak ⋀, Wyo., U.S. 192 44.47 N 109.51 W
Indian Point ➤ 202 44.37 N 78.49 W
Indian Prairie Canal ≍ 210 27.02 N 80.57 W
Indian River 180 45.25 N 84.37 W
Indian River ☐[6] 210 27.43 N 80.36 W
Indian River ⊂ 210 28.00 N 80.30 W
Indian River Bay ⊂ 198 38.36 N 75.05 W
Indian River Inlet ⊂ 198 38.37 N 75.03 W
Indian Rock ⋀ 214 45.59 N 120.49 W
Indian Rock Paintings ⊥ 214 46.38 N 120.31 W
Indian Rocks Beach 210 27.53 N 82.51 W
Indian Springs, Nev., U.S. 194 36.34 N 115.40 W
Indian Springs, Va., U.S. 274c 38.49 N 77.10 W
Indian Stream ≃ 196 45.03 N 71.26 W
Indiantown 210 27.01 N 80.28 W
Indian Town Point ➤ 230c 17.06 N 61.40 W
Indian Village, Ind., U.S. 208 40.10 N 85.22 W
Indian Village, N.Y., U.S. 200 42.57 N 76.10 W
Indiaporã 245 19.57 S 50.17 W
Indiaroba 240 11.32 S 37.31 W
Indico, Océano
→ Indian Ocean ⊤[1] 6 10.00 S 70.00 E
Indien
→ India ☐[1] 108 20.00 N 77.00 E
Indien, Océan
→ Indian Ocean ⊤[1] 6 10.00 S 70.00 E
Indien, territoires britanniques de l'Ocen → British Indian Ocean Territory ☐[2] 12 10.00 S 72.00 E
Indiera Alta 230m 18.09 N 66.53 W
Indiga 24 67.41 N 49.00 E
Indigirka ≃ 64 70.48 N 148.54 E
Inđija 38 45.03 N 20.05 E
Indin 110 20.16 N 92.57 E
Indio 194 33.43 N 116.13 W
Indio ≃, Nic. 226 10.57 N 83.44 W
Indio ≃, Pan. 226 9.12 N 80.11 W
Indio, Punta ➤ 248 35.16 S 57.13 W
Indios, Canal de los ꓤ 230p 21.56 N 83.16 W
Indischer Ozean
→ Indian Ocean ⊤[1] 6 10.00 S 70.00 E
Indispensable Reefs ✣[2] 150 12.40 S 160.25 E
Indispensable Strait ꓤ 165e 9.00 S 160.30 E
Indo
→ Indus ≃ 110 24.20 N 67.47 E
Indochina ➤[1] 12 16.00 N 107.00 E
Indom 24 64.36 N 55.22 E
Indonesia ☐[1] 98 5.00 S 120.00 E
Indonesia, University of ᵾ[2] 259e 6.12 S 106.51 E
Indonesian Culture, Museum of ᵾ[3] 259e 6.09 N 106.49 E
Indonésie
→ Indonesia ☐[1] 98 5.00 S 120.00 E
Indonesien
→ Indonesia ☐[1] 98 5.00 S 120.00 E
Indooroopilly 161a 27.30 S 152.58 E
Indore 110 22.43 N 75.50 E
Indpur 116 23.10 N 86.56 E
Indragiri ≃ 102 0.22 S 103.26 E
Indramayu 105a 6.20 S 108.19 E
Indramayu, Tanjung ➤ 105a 6.14 S 108.17 E
Indrapuri 104 5.26 N 95.27 E
Indrāvati ≃ 112 18.44 N 80.16 E
Indre ☐[5] 32 46.45 N 1.30 E
Indre ≃ 32 47.16 N 0.19 E
Indre-et-Loire ☐[5] 32 47.15 N 0.45 E
Indrois ≃ 46 47.13 N 0.56 E
Indungo 142 14.48 S 16.17 E
Induno Olona 56 45.52 N 8.51 E
Indur
→ Indore 110 22.43 N 75.50 E
Indura 66 53.27 N 23.53 E
Indus ≃ 110 24.20 N 67.47 E
Industria ➤[8] 263d 26.12 S 27.59 E
Industry, Ill., U.S. 184 40.20 N 90.36 W
Industry, Pa., U.S. 204 40.39 N 80.25 W
Industry, Tex., U.S. 212 29.58 N 96.30 W
Indwe 148 31.27 S 27.23 E
Ine 86 35.39 N 135.17 E
İnebolu 120 41.58 N 33.46 E
İnece 120 41.41 N 27.04 E
İnecik 120 40.56 N 27.16 E
In Ecker 138 24.09 N 5.03 E
In Edjejou, Oued ⋁ 138 22.46 N 4.05 E
İnegöl 120 40.05 N 29.31 E
İnekollar 120 39.33 N 28.56 E
Inerie, Gunung ⋀ 105b 8.52 S 120.56 E
Inés, Monte ⋀ 244 48.29 S 69.40 W
Ineu 38 46.26 N 21.49 E
İnevi 120 38.40 N 32.56 E
Inez, Ky., U.S. 182 37.52 N 82.32 W
Inez, Tex., U.S. 212 28.54 N 96.47 W
Inez, Lake ⊜ 266 41.01 N 74.17 W
In Ezzane 138 23.28 N 11.12 E
Infanta, Pil. 106 15.50 N 119.55 E
Infanta, Pil. 106 14.45 N 121.39 E
Infantas 276d 11.57 S 77.04 W
Infante, Kaap ➤ 148 34.29 S 20.51 E
Inferior, Laguna ⊂ 224 16.20 N 94.40 W
Infermo, Cachoeira do ⌊ 240 1.00 S 56.04 W
Infiernillo, Canal del ꓤ 222 29.09 N 112.15 W
Infiernillo, Presa del ⊜[1] 224 18.35 N 101.45 W
Infiesto 34 43.21 N 5.22 W
Ing ≃ 100 20.13 N 100.27 E
Ingá 240 7.17 S 35.36 W
Ingabu 100 17.49 N 95.16 E
Ingaí 246 21.24 S 44.55 W
Ingaí ≃ 246 21.23 S 44.52 W
I-n-Gall 140 16.47 N 6.56 E
Ingalls 208 39.58 N 85.48 W
Ingalls Creek ≃ 214 47.28 N 120.39 W
Ingalls Park 206 41.32 N 88.03 W
Inganda 142 0.05 S 20.57 E
Ingarö I 40 59.16 N 18.28 E
Ingatestone 44 51.41 N 0.22 E
Ingatestone Hall ⊥ 250 51.39 N 0.23 E
Ingelfingen 52 49.18 N 9.39 E
Ingelheim 52 49.59 N 8.05 E
Ingelmunster 46 50.55 N 3.15 E
Ingelstad 26 56.45 N 14.55 E
Ingende 142 0.15 S 18.57 E
Ingeniero Budge ➤[8] 278 34.43 S 58.28 W
Ingeniero Jacobacci 244 41.18 S 69.35 W
Ingeniero Juan Allan 248 34.53 S 58.11 W
Ingeniero Luiggi 242 35.25 S 64.29 W
Ingeniero Maschwitz 248 34.23 S 58.44 W
Ingeniero Romulo Otamendi, Arg. 248 34.13 S 58.54 W
Ingeniero White 242 38.47 S 62.16 W
Ingeniero Williams 248 34.54 S 59.22 W
Ingenio, Río del ≃ 238 14.39 S 75.15 W
Ingenio La Esperanza 242 24.13 S 64.51 W
Ingenio Santa Ana 242 27.28 S 65.41 W
Ingersheim 54 48.06 N 7.18 E
Ingersoll 202 43.02 N 80.53 W
Ingham 156 18.39 S 146.10 E
Ingham ☐[6] 206 42.37 N 84.22 W
Ingička 75 39.52 N 67.20 E
Ingleborough ⋀ 42 54.11 N 2.23 W
Ingleburn 160 34.00 S 150.52 E
Inglesa, Costa
→ English Coast •[2] 9 73.45 S 73.00 W
Inglesby Lake ⊜ 202 44.27 N 77.03 W
Ingleside, Austl. 264a 33.41 S 151.13 E
Ingleside, Ont., Can. 196 45.00 N 75.00 W
Ingleside, Ill., U.S. 206 42.23 N 88.09 W
Ingleside, Tex., U.S. 186 27.53 N 97.13 W
Ingleside ➤[8] 272 37.43 N 122.28 W
Ingleton 42 54.10 N 2.27 W
Inglewood, Austl. 156 28.25 S 151.05 E
Inglewood, Austl. 156 36.34 S 143.52 E
Inglewood, Ont., Can. 202 43.47 N 79.56 W
Inglewood, N.Z. 162 39.09 S 174.12 E
Inglewood, Calif., U.S. 218 33.58 N 118.21 W
Inglewood, Wash., U.S. 214 47.44 N 122.15 W
Inglewood Forest ➤[3] 42 54.45 N 2.50 W
Inglis, Man., Can. 174 50.57 N 101.15 W
Inglis, Fla., U.S. 210 29.02 N 82.40 W
Inglis Lock ➤[5] 210 29.02 N 82.37 W
Ingoda ≃ 78 51.42 N 115.48 E
Ingogo 148 27.32 S 29.56 E
Ingolstadt 30 48.46 N 11.27 E
Ingonish 176 46.42 N 60.22 W
Ingornachoix Bay ⊂ 176 50.38 N 57.20 W
Ingraham, Lake ⊜ 210 25.09 N 81.08 W
Ingram, Pa., U.S. 269b 40.26 N 80.04 W
Ingram, Tex., U.S. 186 30.04 N 99.14 W
Ingram Bay ⊂ 198 37.48 N 76.17 W
Ingrave 250 51.36 N 0.21 E
Ingrid Christensen Coast •[2] 9 69.30 S 76.00 E
In Guezzam 140 19.32 N 5.42 E
Ingul ≃ 68 47.00 N 31.59 E
Ingulec 68 47.43 N 33.14 E
Ingulec ≃ 68 46.41 N 32.48 E
Ingulo-Kamenka 68 48.17 N 32.30 E
Inguri ≃ 74 42.24 N 41.33 E
Inguzet 76 58.50 N 83.52 E
Ingvallsbenning 40 60.15 N 15.53 E
Ingwavuma 148 27.09 S 32.00 E
Ingwavuma ≃ 148 26.58 S 32.17 E
Ingwe 144 13.02 S 26.25 E
Ingwiller 52 48.52 N 7.29 E
Inhaca 146 26.01 S 32.58 E
Inhaca, Ilha da I 148 26.03 S 32.57 E
Inhafenga 146 20.35 S 33.53 E
Inhambane 146 23.51 S 35.29 E
Inhambane ☐[5] 146 23.00 S 34.30 E
Inhambane, Baía de ⊂ 146 23.58 S 35.51 E
Inhambupe 245 11.47 S 38.21 W
Inhaminga 146 18.24 S 35.00 E
Inhapim 245 19.33 S 42.07 W
Inharrime 146 24.29 S 35.01 E
Inharrime ≃ 146 24.29 S 35.01 E
Inhassoro 146 21.33 S 35.11 E
Inhaúma 245 19.29 S 44.22 W
Inhaúma ➤[8] 277a 22.52 S 43.17 W
İnhisar 120 40.03 N 30.23 E
Inhoaíba ➤[8] 246 22.54 S 43.36 W
Inhobi ≃ 245 23.45 S 54.40 W
Inhomirim 246 22.35 S 43.10 W
Inhuma 240 6.40 S 41.42 W
Inhumas 245 16.22 S 49.30 W
Ini ≃ 136 9.30 N 12.20 E
Iniesta 34 39.26 N 1.45 W
Inimutaba 245 18.45 S 44.22 W
Ining
→ Yining 76 43.55 N 81.14 E
Inini ☐[8] 240 5.00 N 53.00 W
Inini ≃ 240 3.39 N 54.00 W
Inírida ≃ 236 3.55 N 67.52 W
Inisa 140 7.52 N 4.20 E
Inishbofin I 28 53.37 N 10.15 W
Inisheer I 28 53.02 N 9.26 W
Inishmaan I 28 53.05 N 9.32 W
Inishmore I 28 53.07 N 9.45 W
Inishowen Head ➤ 42 55.14 N 6.56 W
Inishtrahull ✣[2], Eire 28 55.26 N 7.14 W
Inishtrahull ✣[2], N. Ire., U.K. 28 55.26 N 7.14 W
Inishturk I 28 53.43 N 10.08 W
Initao 106 8.30 N 124.18 E
Injasuti ⋀ 146 29.09 S 29.23 E
Inje 88 38.05 N 128.09 E
Injibara 134 11.00 N 36.59 E
Injune 156 25.51 S 148.34 E
Inkeroinen 26 60.42 N 26.51 E
Inketete 142 2.37 S 21.53 E
Inkisi (Zadi) ≃ 142 4.46 S 14.52 E
Inkom 192 42.48 N 112.15 W
Inkster, Mich., U.S. 206 42.17 N 83.17 W
Inkster, N. Dak., U.S. 188 48.09 N 97.39 W
Inland Kaikoura Range ⋀⋀ 162 42.00 S 173.40 E
Inland Lake ⊜, Man., Can. 174 52.17 N 99.42 W
Inland Lake ⊜, Alaska, U.S. 170 66.27 N 159.47 W
Inland Sea
→ Seto-naikai ⊤[2] 82 34.20 N 133.30 E
Inle Lake ⊜ 100 20.32 N 96.55 E
Inmaculadita 222 29.55 N 111.48 W
Inman, Kans., U.S. 188 38.14 N 97.47 W
Inman, S.C., U.S. 182 35.03 N 82.05 W
Inman Mills 182 35.02 N 82.06 W
Inman Valley 158b 35.30 S 138.28 E
Inn (En) ≃ 32 48.35 N 13.28 E
Innamincka 156 27.45 S 140.44 E
Innellan 42 55.54 N 4.57 W
Inner Bay ⊂ 204 42.37 N 80.24 W
Innerbraz 54 47.09 N 9.55 E
Innerferrera 54 46.31 N 9.28 E
Innerfragant 58 46.58 N 13.04 E
Inner Harbor ⊂ 266 40.52 N 73.28 W
Inner Hebrides II 28 57.00 N 6.45 W
Innerkip 202 43.13 N 80.42 W
Innerleithen 42 55.38 N 3.05 W
Inner Mongolia
→ Neimenggu Zizhiqu ☐[4] 80 43.00 N 115.00 E
Inner Sound ꓤ 28 57.30 N 5.55 W
Innerste ≃ 48 52.15 N 9.50 E
Innerste-Talsperre ➤[6] 48 51.55 N 10.17 E
Innerthal 54 47.06 N 8.56 E
Innertkirchen 54 46.42 N 8.14 E
Innervillgraten 58 46.48 N 12.23 E
Innichen
→ San Candido 58 46.44 N 12.17 E
Inning 58 48.05 N 11.09 E
Innisfail, Austl. 156 17.32 S 146.02 E
Innisfail, Alta., Can. 172 52.02 N 113.57 W

ENGLISH: Name, Page, Lat.°′, Long.°′ — DEUTSCH: Name, Seite, Breite°′, Länge°′ E=Ost

Symbols in the index entries represent the broad categories identified in the key at the right. Symbols with superior numbers (⋀⋀[2]) identify subcategories (see complete key on page I · 26).

Kartensymbole in dem Registerverzeichnis stellen die rechts in Schlüssel erklärten Kategorien dar. Symbole mit hochgestellten Ziffern (⋀⋀[2]) bezeichnen Unterabteilungen einer Kategorie (vgl. vollständiger Schlüssel auf Seite I · 26).

Los símbolos incluidos en el texto del índice representan las grandes categorías identificadas con la clave a la derecha. Los símbolos con numeros en su parte superior (⋀⋀[2]) identifican las subcategorías (véase la clave completa en la página I · 26).

Les symboles de l'index représentent les catégories indiquées dans la légende à droite. Les symboles suivis d'un indice (⋀⋀[2]) représentent des sous-catégories (voir légende complète à la page I · 26).

Os símbolos incluídos no texto do índice representam as grandes categorias identificadas com a chave à direita. Os símbolos com números em sua parte superior (⋀⋀[2]) identificam as subcategorias (veja-se a chave completa à página I · 26).

⋀ Mountain	Berg	Montaña	Montagne	Montanha
⋀⋀ Mountains	Berge	Montañas	Montagnes	Montanhas
⋊ Pass	Pass	Paso	Col	Passo
⋁ Valley, Canyon	Tal, Cañon	Valle, Cañón	Vallée, Canyon	Vale, Canhão
≚ Plain	Ebene	Llano	Plaine	Planície
➤ Cape	Kap	Cabo	Cap	Cabo
I Island	Insel	Isla	Île	Ilha
II Islands	Inseln	Islas	Îles	Ilhas
• Other Topographic Features	Andere Topographische Objekte	Otros Elementos Topográficos	Autres données topographiques	Outros Elementos Topográficos

ESPAÑOL

Nombre	Página	Lat.°′	Long.°′ W=Oeste
Innisfil Creek ≃	202	44.07 N	79.59 W
Innisfree	172	53.22 N	111.32 W
Innisplain	161a	28.10 S	152.55 E
Innokentjevka	79	49.42 N	136.57 E
Innokentjevskij	79	48.37 N	140.10 E
Innoko ≃	170	62.14 N	159.45 W
Innolovo	255a	59.47 N	29.59 E
Innoshima	86	34.20 N	133.10 E
Inno-shima I	86	34.19 N	133.10 E
Innsbruck	58	47.16 N	11.24 E
Innviertel ◆[1]	58	48.10 N	13.15 E
Inny ≃	44	50.35 N	4.17 W
Ino, Nihon	86	33.33 N	133.26 E
Ino, Va., U.S.	198	37.46 N	76.48 W
Inoã	246	22.55 S	42.57 W
Inobonto	102	0.52 N	123.57 E
Inocência	245	19.47 S	51.48 W
Inokashira Park ♠	258	35.42 N	139.34 E
Inokovka	70	52.33 N	42.34 E
Inola	186	36.09 N	95.31 W
Ino-misaki ≻	86	33.01 N	133.06 E
Inongo	142	1.57 S	18.16 E
Inoni	142	3.04 S	15.39 E
İnönü	120	39.48 N	30.09 E
Inoue	260	34.48 N	135.08 E
In Ouzzal, Oued V	138	21.35 N	2.00 E
Inowrocław	30	52.48 N	18.15 E
Inozemcevo	74	44.06 N	43.06 E
Inp'ung-dong	88	41.25 N	126.34 E
Inrath ◆[8]	253	51.21 N	6.32 E
In Rhar	138	27.10 N	1.59 E
Ins	54	47.00 N	7.06 E
In Salah	138	27.12 N	2.28 E
Insan-ni	88	41.01 N	127.21 E
Insar	70	53.52 N	44.21 E
Insar ≃	70	54.43 N	45.18 E
Insch	28	57.21 N	2.37 W
Inscription, Cape ≻	152	25.29 S	112.59 E
Inscription Point ≻	264a	34.00 S	151.13 E
Insein	100	16.53 N	96.07 E
Insel Man → Isle of Man □[2]	42	54.15 N	4.30 W
Inshar	140	8.49 N	9.40 E
Inshāş ar-Raml	132	30.23 N	31.27 E
Insjön	26	60.41 N	15.05 E
Ińsko	30	53.27 N	15.33 E
In Sokki, Oued V	138	29.37 N	4.13 E
Inspiration	190	33.25 N	110.53 W
Insterburg → Černʼachovsk	66	54.38 N	21.49 E
Instow	174	49.44 N	108.16 W
Insurgente José María Morelos, Parque Nacional ♠	224	19.51 N	101.18 W
Inta	24	66.02 N	60.08 E
I-n-Tebezas ▾[4]	140	17.49 N	1.53 E
Intendente Alvear	242	35.14 S	63.35 W
İntepe	120	40.00 N	26.20 E
Intercession City	210	28.16 N	81.30 W
Intercourse	198	40.02 N	76.06 W
Interlagos ◆[8]	277b	23.42 S	46.42 W
Interlaken, Schw.	54	46.41 N	7.51 E
Interlaken, Mass., U.S.	200	42.19 N	73.20 W
Interlaken, N.J., U.S.	198	40.14 N	74.01 W
Interlaken, N.Y., U.S.	200	42.37 N	76.44 W
Interlândia	245	16.12 S	49.02 W
International Amphitheatre ♥	268	41.49 N	87.39 W
International Falls	180	48.36 N	93.25 W
International Peace Garden ♠	188	49.00 N	100.04 W
Interstate Park ♠	180	45.23 N	92.40 W
Inthanon, Doi ∧	100	18.35 N	98.29 E
Intibucá	226	14.16 N	88.10 W
Intibucá □[5]	226	14.20 N	88.15 W
Intipucá	226	13.12 N	88.04 W
Intiyaco	242	28.39 S	60.05 W
Intracoastal Waterway Ξ, U.S.	182	33.40 N	79.00 W
Intracoastal Waterway Ξ, U.S.	186	28.45 N	95.40 W
Intragna	54	46.10 N	8.42 E
Intrånget	40	60.20 N	16.09 E
Introbio	54	45.57 N	9.27 E
Introdacqua	60	42.00 N	13.54 E
Intschön → Inch'ŏn	88	37.28 N	126.38 E
Intu	102	0.15 S	115.21 E
Intutu	236	3.39 S	74.44 W
Inubō-saki ≻	84	35.42 N	140.53 E
Inukai	86	33.04 N	131.38 E
Inútil, Bahía C	244	53.30 S	69.50 W
Inuvik	170	68.25 N	133.30 W
Inuya ≃	238	10.41 S	73.30 W
Inuyama	84	35.23 N	136.56 E
In'va ≃	76	58.59 N	55.40 E
Inveralochy	160	34.57 S	149.39 E
Inveraray	28	56.13 N	5.05 W
Inverbervie	28	56.51 N	2.17 W
Invercargill	162	46.24 S	168.21 E
Inverell	156	29.47 S	151.07 E
Invergordon	28	57.42 N	4.10 W
Inverkeithing	42	56.02 N	3.25 W
Inverleigh	159	38.06 S	144.03 E
Inverloch	159	38.38 S	145.43 E
Invermay	174	51.48 N	103.09 W
Invermere	172	50.30 N	116.02 W
Inverness, N.S., Can.	176	46.14 N	61.18 W
Inverness, Qué., Can.	196	46.15 N	71.31 W
Inverness, Scot., U.K.	28	57.27 N	4.15 W
Inverness, Calif., U.S.	194	38.06 N	122.51 W
Inverness, Fla., U.S.	210	28.51 N	82.20 W
Inverness, Ill., U.S.	206	42.07 N	88.05 W
Inverness, Miss., U.S.	184	33.21 N	90.35 W
Inveruno	56	45.31 N	8.51 E
Inverurie	28	57.17 N	2.23 W
Inverway	152	17.50 S	129.38 E
Investigator Group II	152	33.45 S	134.30 E
Investigator Strait Џ	156	35.25 S	137.10 E
Inwood, Man., Can.	174	50.34 N	97.32 W
Inwood, Ont., Can.	204	42.49 N	81.59 W
Inwood, Fla., U.S.	210	28.02 N	81.46 W
Inwood, Ind., U.S.	206	41.19 N	86.12 W
Inwood, Iowa, U.S.	188	43.18 N	96.26 W
Inwood, N.Y., U.S.	266	40.37 N	73.45 W
Inwood Hill Park ♠	266	40.52 N	73.56 W
Inyanga	144	18.13 S	32.46 E
Inyanga Mountains ⋏	144	18.00 S	33.00 E
Inyangani ∧	144	18.20 S	32.50 E
Inyan Kara Mountain ∧	188	44.13 N	104.21 W
Inyantue	144	18.32 S	26.41 E
Inyati	144	19.39 S	28.54 E
Inyazura	144	18.43 S	32.10 E
Inyo, Mount ∧	194	36.44 N	117.59 W
Inyokern	194	35.39 N	117.49 W
Inyo Mountains ⋏	194	36.40 N	118.10 W
Inyonga	144	6.43 S	32.04 E
Inywa	100	23.56 N	96.17 E
Inza	70	53.51 N	46.21 E
Inza ≃	70	53.54 N	45.44 E
Inzago	56	45.32 N	9.29 E
Inzai	84	35.50 N	140.09 E
Inzana Lake ⊜	172	54.58 N	124.40 W
Inžavino	70	52.19 N	42.30 E
Inzell	58	47.46 N	12.44 E
Inzer	76	54.14 N	57.34 E
Inzer ≃	76	54.30 N	56.28 E
Inzersdorf ◆[8]	254b	48.09 N	16.21 E
Inzia ≃	142	3.45 S	17.57 E
Ioanna, Gora ∧	170	64.50 N	178.08 E
Ioánnina	38	39.40 N	20.50 E
Ioco	214	49.18 N	122.52 W
Iō-jima I, Nihon	83b	30.48 N	130.18 E
Iō-jima I, Nihon	164f	24.47 N	141.20 E
Iokanga	24	68.00 N	39.37 E
Iokanga ≃	24	68.00 N	39.43 E
Iola, Kans., U.S.	188	37.55 N	95.24 W

FRANÇAIS

Nom	Page	Lat.°′	Long.°′ W=Ouest
Iola, Pa., U.S.	200	45.08 N	76.32 W
Iola, Tex., U.S.	212	30.46 N	96.05 W
Iola, Wis., U.S.	180	44.36 N	89.08 W
Iolgo, Chrebet ⋏	76	51.30 N	86.25 E
Iolotan'	62	37.18 N	62.21 E
Ioma	154	8.20 S	147.50 E
Iôna, Ang.	142	16.50 S	12.20 E
Iona, N.S., Can.	176	45.58 N	60.48 W
Iona, Idaho, U.S.	192	43.32 N	111.56 W
Iona I	28	56.19 N	6.25 W
Iôna, Parque Nacional do ♠	142	16.30 S	12.00 E
Iona College ♥[2]	266	40.56 N	73.47 W
Ionaivo ≃	147b	22.56 S	46.54 E
Ione, Calif., U.S.	216	38.21 N	120.56 W
Ione, Oreg., U.S.	192	45.30 N	119.50 W
Ione, Wash., U.S.	192	48.45 N	117.25 W
Ionia, Mich., U.S.	206	42.59 N	85.04 W
Ionia, N.Y., U.S.	200	42.56 N	77.30 W
Ionia □[6]	206	42.56 N	85.04 W
Ionian Islands → Iónioi Nísoi II	38	38.30 N	20.30 E
Ionian Sea ▾[2]	22	39.00 N	19.00 E
Ionia State Park ♠	206	42.58 N	85.36 W
Ionico, Mare → Ionian Sea ▾[2]	22	39.00 N	19.00 E
Ionienne, Mer → Ionian Sea ▾[2]	22	39.00 N	19.00 E
Iónioi Nísoi II	38	38.30 N	20.30 E
Ionisches Meer → Ionian Sea ▾[2]	22	39.00 N	19.00 E
Ionivejem ≃	170	66.12 N	174.00 W
Iony, Ostrov I	64	56.26 N	143.25 E
Iordan	75	39.58 N	71.46 E
Iori ≃	74	41.03 N	46.17 E
Iory	75	39.30 N	67.53 E
Íos	38	36.44 N	25.17 E
Íos I	38	36.42 N	25.24 E
Ioscoe, Lake ⊜	266	41.02 N	74.19 W
Iosegun ≃	172	54.44 N	117.11 W
Iosegun Lake	172	54.29 N	116.50 W
Iovlevo	72	56.10 N	38.20 E
Iowa	184	30.14 N	93.01 W
Iowa □[3]	168	42.15 N	93.15 W
Iowa ≃	180	41.10 N	91.02 W
Iowa, South Fork ≃	180	42.18 N	93.04 W
Iowa City	180	41.40 N	91.32 W
Iowa Falls	180	42.31 N	93.16 W
Iowa Park	186	33.57 N	98.40 W
Iō-zan ∧	84	36.31 N	136.48 E
I Pak	261d	22.19 N	114.00 E
Ipala	144	4.30 S	32.53 E
Ipameri	245	17.43 S	48.09 W
Ipanema ◆[8]	246	22.59 S	43.12 W
Ipanema ≃	240	9.53 S	37.15 W
Ipanguaçu	240	5.30 S	36.52 W
Ipat, P.I.T.T.	164r	6.58 N	158.12 E
Ipat, S.S.S.R.	24	66.13 N	56.33 E
Ipatinga	245	19.30 S	42.32 W
Ipatovo	70	45.43 N	42.53 E
Ipaumirim	240	6.47 S	38.43 W
Ipava	184	40.21 N	90.19 W
Ípeiros ◆[1]	38	39.40 N	20.50 E
Ipel'(Ipoly) ≃	30	47.49 N	18.52 E
Iperu	140	6.52 N	3.38 E
Iphigenia Bay C	170	55.40 N	133.55 W
Iphofen	52	49.42 N	10.15 E
Ipiabas	246	22.23 S	43.53 W
Ipiales	236	0.50 N	77.37 W
Ipiaú	245	14.08 S	39.44 W
Ipiíba	246	22.52 S	42.57 W
Ipil	106	7.47 N	122.35 E
Ipin → Yibin	97	28.47 N	104.38 E
Ipirá	245	12.10 S	39.44 W
Ipiranga, Bra.	236	3.12 S	66.01 W
Ipiranga, Bra.	242	25.01 S	50.35 W
Ipiranga, Bra.	277a	22.43 S	43.12 W
Ipiranga ◆[8]	277b	23.36 S	46.35 W
Ipiranga ≃, Bra.	246	23.21 S	45.10 W
Ipiranga ≃, Bra.	277a	22.48 S	43.37 W
Ipiranga, Canal Ξ	277a	22.46 S	43.37 W
Ipiranga, Museu do ♥	277b	23.35 S	46.36 W
Ipitá	238	19.20 S	63.32 W
Ipitinga ≃	240	0.02 N	53.01 W
Ipixuna	240	4.22 S	44.34 W
Ipixuna ≃, Bra.	238	7.11 S	71.51 W
Ipixuna ≃, Bra.	238	5.45 S	63.02 W
Ipixuna ≃, Bra.	238	6.16 S	61.52 W
Ipixuna, Igarapé ≃	240	4.32 S	52.40 W
İpkaiye	120	40.12 N	27.06 E
Ipoh	104	4.35 N	101.05 E
Ipojuca	240	8.24 S	35.04 W
Ipojuca ≃	240	8.25 S	34.58 W
Ipokera	144	8.03 S	35.41 E
Ipole	144	5.47 S	32.44 E
Ipoly (Ipel') ≃	30	47.49 N	18.52 E
Iporá, Bra.	245	16.28 S	51.07 W
Iporã, Bra.	245	23.59 S	53.37 W
Ippa ≃	66	52.13 N	29.08 E
Ippinghausen	52	51.17 N	9.08 E
Ippy	142	6.15 N	21.12 E
İpsala	120	40.55 N	26.23 E
İpsile	120	40.14 N	37.33 E
Ipswich, Austl.	161a	27.36 S	152.46 E
Ipswich, Eng., U.K.	44	52.04 N	1.10 E
Ipswich, Mass., U.S.	197	42.41 N	70.50 W
Ipswich, S. Dak., U.S.	188	45.27 N	99.02 W
Ipswich ≃	197	42.42 N	70.48 W
Ipswich Bay C	197	42.41 N	70.42 W
Ipu	240	4.20 S	40.42 W
Ipubi	240	7.39 S	40.07 W
Ipueiras	240	4.33 S	40.43 W
Ipuh	102	3.00 S	101.30 E
Ipuiúna	246	22.06 S	46.11 W
Ipun, Isla I	244	44.37 S	74.46 W
Ipupiara	245	11.49 S	42.37 W
Iput' ≃	66	52.26 N	31.02 E
Iqfahș	132	28.47 N	30.49 E
Iquique	238	20.13 S	70.10 W
Iquitos	236	3.46 S	73.15 W
Ira	186	32.35 N	101.00 W
Iraan, Pil.	106	9.04 N	117.42 E
Iraan, Tex., U.S.	186	30.54 N	101.54 W
Irabu-jima I	165d	24.50 N	125.10 E
Iracema	240	5.48 S	38.18 W
Iracoubo	240	5.29 N	53.13 W
Irago-misaki ≻	84	34.35 N	137.01 E
Irago-suidō Џ	84	34.35 N	137.00 E
Iraí	242	27.11 S	53.15 W
Irajá ◆[8]	277a	22.51 S	43.19 W
Irajá ≃	277a	22.49 S	43.17 W
Irajol'	24	64.27 N	55.08 E
Irak → Iraq □[1]	118	33.00 N	44.00 E
Iráklion, Ellás	38	35.20 N	25.09 E
Iráklion, Ellás	257c	38.04 N	23.46 E
Irala	242	25.54 S	54.43 W
Irámuco	224	19.57 N	100.55 W
Iran (Īrān) □[1]	108		
	118	32.00 N	53.00 E
Iran, Pegunungan ⋏	102	2.05 N	114.55 E
Īrānshahr	118	27.13 N	60.41 E
Irapa	236	10.34 N	62.35 W
Irapuato	224	20.41 N	101.21 W
Iraq □[1]	108		
	118	33.00 N	44.00 E
Irará	245	12.02 S	38.46 W
Iratapuru ≃	240	0.36 S	52.35 W
Irati	242	25.27 S	50.39 W
Irati ≃	34	42.35 N	1.16 W
Irauçuba	240	3.45 S	39.47 W
Irāwan, Wādī V	136	26.35 N	12.45 E
Irazú, Volcán ∧[1]	226	9.58 N	83.53 W
Irba	78	58.07 N	99.00 E
Irbejskoje	78	55.39 N	95.28 E
Irbeni Väin (Irves Šaurums) Џ	66	57.48 N	22.05 E
Irbid	122	32.33 N	35.51 E
Irbid □[8]	122	32.33 N	35.51 E
Irbīl	118	36.11 N	44.01 E

PORTUGUÊS

Nome	Página	Lat.°′	Long.°′ W=Oeste
Irbīl □[4]	118	36.10 N	44.00 E
Irbit	76	57.41 N	63.03 E
Irby	252	53.21 N	3.07 W
Irdning	30	47.33 N	14.01 E
Irdyn'	68	49.23 N	31.44 E
Irebu	142	0.37 S	17.45 E
Irecê	240	11.18 S	41.52 W
Iredame	134	10.29 N	49.21 E
Iregua ≃	34	42.27 N	2.24 W
Ireland □[1]	22		
	28	53.00 N	8.00 W
Ireland Brook ≃	266	40.25 N	74.29 W
Ireland Island I	230a	32.19 N	64.50 W
Iren' ≃	76	57.27 N	56.56 E
Irene, S. Afr.	148	25.51 S	28.13 E
Irene, S. Dak., U.S.	188	43.05 N	97.10 W
Irene, Tex., U.S.	212	31.59 N	96.52 W
Ireng (Maú) ≃	236	3.33 N	59.51 W
İresi	120	39.09 N	39.53 E
Iresick Brook ≃	266	40.24 N	74.22 W
Ireton	188	42.58 N	96.19 W
Irfon ≃	44	52.09 N	3.24 W
Irgakly	74	44.22 N	44.45 E
Irgiz	76	48.37 N	61.16 E
Irgiz ≃	76	48.13 N	62.08 E
Irharhar, Oued V, Alg.	138	28.03 N	6.15 E
Irharrhar, Oued V, Alg.	138	20.25 N	6.10 E
Iri	88	35.56 N	126.57 E
Irian Jaya □[4]	154	5.00 S	138.00 E
Iriba	136	15.07 N	22.15 E
Irié	140	8.17 N	9.11 W
Iriga	106	13.25 N	123.25 E
Irigny	56	45.40 N	4.49 E
Irîgui ◆[1]	140	16.43 N	5.30 W
Iriklinskij	76	51.39 N	58.38 E
Iringa	144	7.46 S	35.42 E
Iringa □[4]	144	9.00 S	35.00 E
Irinjālakuda	112	10.20 N	76.14 E
Iriomote-jima I	165d	24.20 N	123.50 E
Iriona	226	15.57 N	85.11 W
Iriri ≃, Bra.	240	3.52 S	52.37 W
Iriri ≃, Bra.	277a	22.41 S	43.05 W
Iriri Novo ≃	240	8.46 S	53.22 W
Irische See → Irish Sea ▾[2]	28	53.30 N	5.20 W
Irish, Mount ∧	194	37.38 N	115.24 W
Irish Sea ▾[2]	28	53.30 N	5.20 W
Irishtown	156	40.55 S	145.08 E
Irituia	240	1.46 S	47.26 W
Irituia ≃	240	1.38 S	47.28 W
Iriyamazu	258	35.16 N	139.39 E
Irkās, Wādī V	132	28.57 N	32.00 E
Irkeštam	75	39.41 N	73.55 E
Irkinejeva ≃	78	58.30 N	96.48 E
Irkinejevo	78	58.30 N	96.49 E
Irklijev	68	49.32 N	32.18 E
Irklijevskaja	68	45.51 N	39.39 E
Irkoutsk → Irkutsk	78	52.16 N	104.20 E
Irkut ≃	78	52.18 N	104.15 E
Irkutsk	78	52.16 N	104.20 E
Irkutsk □[4]	78	56.00 N	106.00 E
Irlam	42	53.28 N	2.25 W
Irland → Ireland □[1]	28	53.00 N	8.00 W
Irlanda → Ireland □[1]	28	53.00 N	8.00 W
Irlanda, Marde → Irish Sea ▾[2]	28	53.30 N	5.20 W
Irlande → Ireland □[1]	28	53.00 N	8.00 W
Irlande,, Mer d' → Irish Sea ▾[2]	28	53.30 N	5.20 W
Irma	172	52.55 N	111.14 W
Irmauw	154	7.25 S	131.42 E
Irmino	73	48.36 N	38.36 E
Irnijärvi ⊜	26	65.36 N	29.05 E
Irnsum	48	53.05 N	5.47 E
Iro, Lac ⊜	136	10.06 N	19.25 E
Iroise C	32	48.15 N	4.55 W
Iron Baron	156	32.59 S	137.09 E
Iron Belt	180	46.25 N	90.19 W
Iron Bottom Sound Џ	165e	9.15 S	160.00 E
Iron Bridge, Ont., Can.	180	46.17 N	83.14 W
Iron Bridge, Eng., U.K.	44	52.38 N	2.29 W
Iron Bridge Dam ◆[6]	212	32.50 N	95.54 W
Iron City	184	35.01 N	87.35 W
Iron Cove C	264a	33.52 S	151.10 E
Iron Creek ≃	172	52.43 N	111.14 W
Irondale, Ala., U.S.	184	33.32 N	86.42 W
Irondale, Mo., U.S.	184	37.50 N	90.41 W
Irondale, Ohio, U.S.	204	40.34 N	80.44 W
Irondale ≃	202	44.49 N	78.37 W
Irondequoit	200	43.12 N	77.36 W
Irondequoit Bay C	200	43.12 N	77.32 W
Iron Gate V	38	44.41 N	22.31 E
Iron Gate Reservoir ⊜[1]	38	44.30 N	22.00 E
Ironia	266	40.50 N	74.38 W
Iron Knob	156	32.44 S	137.08 E
Iron Mountain	180	45.49 N	88.04 W
Iron Mountain ∧, Ariz., U.S.	190	33.27 N	111.10 W
Iron Mountain ∧, Calif., U.S.	270	34.17 N	117.43 W
Iron Mountains ⋏	182	36.30 N	81.50 W
Iron Range	154	12.42 S	143.18 E
Iron River, Mich., U.S.	180	46.05 N	88.39 W
Iron River, Wis., U.S.	180	46.34 N	91.24 W
Iron Springs	198	39.46 N	77.25 W
Ironstone Kopje ∧	146	25.08 S	24.05 E
Ironton, Minn., U.S.	180	46.28 N	93.59 W
Ironton, Mo., U.S.	184	37.36 N	90.38 W
Ironton, Ohio, U.S.	178	38.31 N	82.40 W
Ironwood	180	46.27 N	90.10 W
Ironworks Creek ≃	275	40.10 N	74.59 W
Iroquois, Ont., Can.	202	44.51 N	75.19 W
Iroquois, Ill., U.S.	206	40.50 N	87.35 W
Iroquois, S. Dak., U.S.	188	44.22 N	97.51 W
Iroquois □[6]	206	40.47 N	87.44 W
Iroquois ≃	206	41.05 N	87.49 W
Iroquois Falls	180	48.46 N	80.41 W
Iroquois Lock and Dam ◆[5]	202	44.45 N	75.23 W
Irō-zaki ≻	84	34.36 N	138.51 E
Irpen'	68	50.31 N	30.15 E
Irpen' ≃	68	50.34 N	30.16 E
Irrawaddy □[8]	100	17.00 N	95.00 E
Irrawaddy ≃	100	15.50 N	95.06 E
Irregully Creek ≃	152	23.06 S	116.21 E
Irrel	52	49.51 N	6.28 E
Irricana	172	51.19 N	113.37 W
Irrigon	192	45.54 N	119.30 W
Irrua	140	6.46 N	6.14 E
Irša ≃	68	50.45 N	29.30 E
Iršava	68	48.20 N	23.03 E
Irschenberg	58	47.50 N	11.55 E
Irsee	54	47.54 N	10.34 E
Irsina	36	40.45 N	16.15 E
Irt ≃	42	54.22 N	3.26 W
Irt'aš, Ozero ⊜	76	55.50 N	60.45 E
Irtek ≃	70	51.28 N	52.39 E
Irthing ≃	42	54.55 N	2.50 W
Irthlingborough	44	52.20 N	0.37 W
Irtyš	76	54.29 N	74.22 E
Irtyš ≃	64	61.04 N	68.52 E
Irtysch → Irtyš ≃	62	61.04 N	68.52 E
Irtysh → Irtyš ≃	62	61.04 N	68.52 E
Irtyšsk	76	53.21 N	75.27 E
Irubaj	70	50.11 N	51.21 E
Iruma	84	35.50 N	139.28 E
Iruma ≃	84	35.57 N	139.30 E
Iruma Air Base ■	258	35.50 N	139.24 E
Irumu	144	1.27 N	29.52 E
Irún	34	43.21 N	1.47 W
Irupana	238	16.28 S	67.28 W

Irurzun	34	42.55 N	1.50 W
Irves Šaurums (Irbeni Väin) Џ	66	57.48 N	22.05 E
Irvine, Alta., Can.	174	49.57 N	110.16 W
Irvine, Scot., U.K.	42	55.37 N	4.40 W
Irvine, Calif., U.S.	218	33.41 N	117.46 W
Irvine, Ky., U.S.	182	37.42 N	83.58 W
Irvine, Pa., U.S.	204	41.50 N	79.17 W
Irvine ≃	42	55.37 N	4.41 W
Irvine, Mount ∧	200	42.03 N	78.40 W
Irvine Creek ≃	202	43.41 N	80.25 W
Irvine Park ♠	270	33.48 N	117.45 W
Irvines Landing	172	49.38 N	124.03 W
Irvinestown	28	54.29 N	7.38 W
Irving, Ill., U.S.	209	39.12 N	89.24 W
Irving, N.Y., U.S.	204	42.34 N	79.07 W
Irving, Tex., U.S.	212	32.49 N	96.56 W
Irving Park ◆[8]	268	41.57 N	87.43 W
Irvington, Ill., U.S.	209	38.26 N	89.10 W
Irvington, Ky., U.S.	184	37.53 N	86.17 W
Irvington, N.J., U.S.	200	40.44 N	74.14 W
Irvington, N.Y., U.S.	200	41.02 N	73.52 W
Irvington, Ohio, U.S.	208	39.51 N	84.15 W
Irvington, Va., U.S.	198	37.40 N	76.25 W
Irvington ◆[8]	274b	39.17 N	76.41 W
Irvona	204	40.46 N	78.33 W
Irwell ≃	42	53.27 N	2.17 W
Irwin, Austl.	152	29.12 S	115.04 E
Irwin, Ohio, U.S.	208	40.07 N	83.29 W
Irwin, Pa., U.S.	269b	40.20 N	79.42 W
Irwin ≃	152	29.15 S	114.56 E
Irwin, Point ≻	152	35.04 S	116.56 E
Irwindale	270	34.06 N	117.56 W
Irwinton	182	32.49 N	83.10 W
Irwŏl-san ∧	88	36.50 N	129.06 E
Is	76	58.48 N	59.43 E
Is, Jabal ∧	130	21.49 N	35.39 E
Isa	140	13.14 N	6.24 E
'Īsā, Ra's ≻	134	15.11 N	42.39 E
Isaac ≃	156	22.52 S	149.20 E
Isaac Lake ⊜, B.C., Can.	172	53.10 N	120.50 W
Isaac Lake ⊜, Ont., Can.	202	44.47 N	81.14 W
Isaba	34	42.52 N	0.55 W
Isabel, Pil.	106	10.56 N	124.26 E
Isabel, S. Dak., U.S.	188	45.24 N	101.26 W
Isabel, Bahía C	236a	0.38 S	91.27 W
Isabela (Basilan), Pil.	106	6.42 N	121.58 E
Isabela, Pil.	106	10.12 N	122.59 E
Isabela, P.R.	230m	18.30 N	67.01 W
Isabela □[4]	106	17.00 N	122.00 E
Isabela, Cabo ≻	228	19.56 N	71.01 W
Isabela, Canal Џ	236a	0.20 S	90.55 W
Isabela, Isla I, Ec.	236a	0.30 S	91.06 W
Isabela, Isla I, Méx.	224	21.51 N	105.55 W
Isabella, Cordillera ⋏	226	13.45 N	85.15 W
Isabella Lake ⊜	202	45.24 N	79.49 W
Isabella Lake ⊜[1]	194	35.40 N	118.26 W
Isabelle ≃	180	47.50 N	91.41 W
Isabel Segunda	230m	18.09 N	65.27 W
Isábena ≃	34	42.11 N	0.21 E
Isaccea	38	45.16 N	28.28 E
Ísafjarđardjúp C[2]	24a	66.10 N	23.00 W
Ísafjörđur	24a	66.08 N	23.13 W
Isāgarh	114	24.50 N	77.53 E
Isagatedo	263a	6.32 N	3.20 E
Isahaya	82	32.50 N	130.03 E
Isak	104	4.28 N	96.55 E
Isaka, Tan.	144	3.54 S	32.56 E
Isaka, Zaïre	142	2.35 S	18.48 E
Isaka-Buku	142	3.55 S	22.03 E
Īsa Khel	113	32.42 N	71.16 E
Isakly	70	54.08 N	51.32 E
Isakovka	76	55.45 N	74.24 E
Isakovo, S.S.S.R.	66	55.11 N	34.40 E
Isakovo, S.S.S.R.	66	60.30 N	41.13 E
Isakovo, S.S.S.R.	72	54.36 N	37.02 E
Isakovo, S.S.S.R.	255b	55.59 N	37.23 E
Işalnița	38	44.24 N	23.44 E
Isalo, Parc National de l' ♠	147b	22.45 S	45.15 E
Isana (Içana) ≃	236	0.26 N	67.19 W
Īsānagar	114	27.54 N	81.13 E
Isandhlwana ⊥	148	28.21 S	30.39 E
Isandja Etat	142	2.59 S	22.00 E
Isando	263d	26.09 S	28.12 E
Isanga	142	1.26 S	22.18 E
Isangano Game Reserve ◆[4]	144	11.10 S	30.40 E
Isangi	142	0.46 N	24.15 E
Is'angulovo	76	52.12 N	56.36 E
Isanlu Makutu	140	8.17 N	5.46 E
Isan-ni	88	40.46 N	128.55 E
Isanti	180	45.29 N	93.15 W
Isar ≃	30	48.49 N	12.58 E
Isara	140	6.59 N	3.41 E
Isarco (Eisack) ≃	58	46.27 N	11.18 E
Isarco, Valle V	58	46.45 N	11.37 E
Isarog, Mount ∧	106	13.39 N	123.23 E
Isasi	263a	6.40 N	3.23 E
Isawa	84	35.39 N	138.38 E
Isbergues	46	50.37 N	2.27 E
İşçehisar	120	38.51 N	30.45 E
Iščerskaja	74	43.43 N	45.08 E
Ischgl	54	47.01 N	10.17 E
Ischia	60	40.44 N	13.57 E
Ischia, Isola d' I	60	40.43 N	13.54 E
Ischia di Castro	60	42.33 N	11.45 E
Ischim → Išim ≃	76	57.45 N	71.12 E
Ischitella	60	41.54 N	15.54 E
Ischma → Ižma ≃	24	65.19 N	52.54 E
Ischodnaja, Gora ∧	170	64.50 N	173.26 W
Ischua	200	42.15 N	78.24 W
Ischua Creek ≃	200	42.10 N	78.23 W
Iscuandé ≃	236	2.38 N	78.04 W
Isdes	46	47.40 N	2.15 E
Ise (Uji-yamada)	84	34.29 N	136.42 E
Ise ≃	50	52.30 N	10.33 E
Isebania	144	1.15 S	34.33 E
Isefjord C	41	55.52 N	11.49 E
Isehara	84	35.24 N	139.18 E
Išejevka	70	54.25 N	48.16 E
Iseke	144	6.25 S	35.01 E
Isel ≃	58	46.50 N	12.47 E
Iselin, N.J., U.S.	200	40.34 N	74.19 W
Iselin, Pa., U.S.	204	40.34 N	79.24 W
Iselle	54	46.12 N	8.12 E
Iseltwald	54	46.43 N	7.58 E
Isenbajevo	70	56.03 N	53.25 E
Isenbüttel	48	52.26 N	10.34 E
Isenyela	144	8.36 S	33.30 E
Iseo	58	45.39 N	10.03 E
Iseo, Lago d' ⊜	58	45.43 N	10.04 E
Iseramagazi	144	4.40 S	32.09 E
Iseran, Col de l')(	56	45.25 N	7.02 E
Isère □[5]	56	45.10 N	5.50 E
Isère ≃	56	44.59 N	4.51 E
Iseri	263a	6.39 N	3.23 E
Iseri-Oke	263a	6.38 N	3.23 E
Iseri-Osun	263a	6.31 N	3.17 E
Iserlohn	52	51.22 N	7.41 E
Iserlohn □[8]	253	51.24 N	7.36 E
Iserlohnerheide ◆[8]	253	51.24 N	7.42 E
Isernia	60	41.36 N	14.14 E
Isernia □[4]	60	41.40 N	14.15 E
Isesaki	84	36.19 N	139.12 E
Ise-shima-kokuritsu-kōen ♠	82	34.23 N	136.48 E
Iset' ≃	76	56.36 N	66.24 E
Isetskoje	76	56.29 N	65.21 E
Ise-wan C	84	34.43 N	136.43 E
Iseyin	140	7.58 N	3.36 E
Isezaki → Isesaki	82	36.19 N	139.12 E
Isfahan → Eşfahān	118	32.40 N	51.38 E
Isfana	75	39.50 N	69.31 E
Isfana ≃	75	40.13 N	69.26 E
Isfara	75	40.07 N	70.38 E

'Isfiyā	122	32.43 N	35.04 E
Ishenga Oswe	142	3.46 S	22.34 E
Isheri-Olofin	263a	6.35 N	3.17 E
Isherton	236	2.19 N	59.22 W
Ishi ≃	260	34.35 N	135.38 E
Ishibashi	84	36.26 N	139.52 E
Ishibe	84	35.00 N	136.04 E
Ishigaki	165d	24.20 N	124.09 E
Ishigaki-shima I	165d	24.24 N	124.12 E
Ishige	84	36.07 N	139.58 E
Ishii	86	34.04 N	134.26 E
Ishikari ≃	80	43.15 N	141.23 E
Ishikari-dake ∧	82a	44.33 N	143.02 E
Ishikari-heiya ⊻	82a	43.15 N	141.23 E
Ishikari-wan C	82a	43.25 N	141.01 E
Ishikawa, Nihon	84	37.09 N	140.27 E
Ishikawa, Nihon	164m	26.25 N	127.50 E
Ishikawa □[5]	84	36.45 N	136.45 E
Ishiki	84	34.48 N	137.01 E
Ishikiri	260	34.41 N	135.39 E
I-shima I	86	33.51 N	134.49 E
Ishinomaki	82	38.25 N	141.18 E
Ishioka	84	36.11 N	140.16 E
Ishiyama	260	34.58 N	135.55 E
Ishizuchi-kokutei-kōen ♠	86	33.45 N	133.08 E
Ishizuchi-san ∧	86	33.46 N	133.07 E
Ishkumān	113	36.32 N	73.49 E
Ishmant	132	29.12 N	31.11 E
Ishpeming	180	46.30 N	87.40 W
Ishua	140	7.24 N	5.57 E
Ishuizu ≃	260	34.33 N	135.27 E
Ishurdi	114	24.08 N	89.05 E
Isiboro ≃	238	15.28 S	65.05 W
Isidro Casanova	278	34.42 S	58.35 W
Isigny	32	49.19 N	1.06 W
ışıklı	120	38.19 N	29.51 E
Isil'kul'	76	54.55 N	71.16 E
Išim	76	56.09 N	69.27 E
Išim ≃	76	57.45 N	71.12 E
Išimbaj	76	53.28 N	56.02 E
Išimka	76	51.24 N	67.08 E
Išimskaja Step' ⊻	76	55.00 N	70.00 E
Isimu	102	0.40 N	122.51 E
Isinga	78	52.55 N	112.00 E
Isinga, Ozero ⊜	78	52.55 N	111.57 E
Isiolo	144	0.21 N	37.35 E
Isipingo Beach	148	29.59 S	30.57 E
Isiro (Paulis)	144	2.47 N	27.37 E
Isis	156	25.12 S	152.13 E
Isisford	156	24.16 S	144.26 E
Iskander	75	41.36 N	69.43 E
Iskâr, Jazovir ⊜[1]	38	43.23 N	27.29 E
Iskaten', Chrebet ⋏	170	66.30 N	179.00 W
Iškejevo	70	55.51 N	50.56 E
İskenderun	120	36.37 N	36.07 E
İskenderun Körfezi C	120	36.30 N	35.40 E
Iske R'az'ap	70	54.36 N	49.42 E
İskilip	120	40.45 N	34.29 E
Iski-Naukat	75	40.16 N	72.36 E
Iskininskij	70	47.13 N	52.41 E
Iskitim	76	54.38 N	83.18 E
Iskona ≃	72	55.34 N	36.05 E
Iskushuban	134	10.13 N	50.14 E
Iskut ≃	170	56.42 N	131.45 W
Isla	224	18.01 N	95.30 W
Isla Cristina	34	37.12 N	7.19 W
Isla de Maipo	242	33.45 S	70.54 W
İslâhiye	120	37.03 N	36.36 E
Islāmābād → Anantnāg, Bhārat	113	33.44 N	75.09 E
Islāmābād, Pāk.	113	33.42 N	73.10 E
Isla Mala	248	34.12 S	56.21 W
Islāmkot	110	24.42 N	70.11 E
Islamorada	210	24.56 N	80.37 W
Islāmpur, Bhārat	114	25.09 N	85.12 E
Islāmpur, Bhārat	114	26.16 N	88.12 E
Islāmpur, Bhārat	116	24.09 N	88.28 E
Islāmpur, Bhārat	116	21.43 N	87.39 E
Isla Mujeres	222	21.12 N	86.43 W
Island	184	37.27 N	87.09 W
Island □[6]	214	48.07 N	122.36 W
Island → Iceland □[1]	24a	65.00 N	18.00 W
Island Bay C	106	9.06 N	118.10 E
Island Beach State Park ♠	198	39.50 N	74.06 W
Island Bend	161b	36.19 S	148.29 E
Island Channel Џ	266	40.36 N	73.53 W
Island Creek	273	42.01 N	70.43 W
Island Falls, Sask., Can.	174	55.32 N	102.21 W
Island Falls, Maine, U.S.	178	46.00 N	68.16 W
Island Heights	198	39.57 N	74.09 W
Islandia → Iceland □[1]	24a	65.00 N	18.00 W
Island Lagoon ⊜	156	31.30 S	136.40 E
Island Lake, Man., Can.	174	53.58 N	94.47 W
Island Lake, Ill., U.S.	206	42.17 N	88.12 W
Island Lake, Mich., U.S.	206	42.31 N	83.44 W
Island Lake ⊜	174	53.47 N	94.25 W
Island Lake State Recreation Area ♠	206	42.30 N	83.43 W
Island Park, Idaho, U.S.	192	44.24 N	111.19 W
Island Park, N.Y., U.S.	266	40.36 N	73.40 W
Island Park, R.I., U.S.	197	41.37 N	71.14 W
Island Park Reservoir ⊜[1]	192	44.25 N	111.29 W
Island Point ≻	152	30.20 S	115.02 E
Island Pond	178	44.49 N	71.53 W
Island Pond ⊜	176	48.25 N	56.23 W
Islands, Bay of C, Newf., Can.	176	49.10 N	58.15 W
Islands, Bay Of C, N.Z.	162	35.12 S	174.10 E
Island View	206	40.31 N	83.53 W
Isla Patrulla	242	32.59 S	54.35 W
Islas de la Bahía □[5]	226	16.20 N	86.30 W
Islas Malvinas → Falkland Islands □[2]	244	51.45 S	59.00 W
Isla Verde	242	33.14 S	62.24 W
Isla Vista	194	34.25 N	119.53 W
Islay I	42	55.46 N	6.10 W
Islay, Punta ≻	238	17.01 S	72.07 W
Islay, Sound of Џ	42	55.50 N	6.01 W
Islay Creek ≃	216	35.17 N	120.53 W
Isle	180	46.08 N	93.29 W
Isle ≃, Fr.	32	44.55 N	0.15 W
Isle ≃, Eng., U.K.	44	50.59 N	2.53 W
Isle-Adam, Forêt de l' ♠	251	49.05 N	2.15 E
Isleat, Sound of Џ	28	57.05 N	5.50 W
Isle-aux-Morts	176	47.35 N	58.59 W
Isle of Hope	182	31.58 N	81.05 W
Isle of Man □[2]	22		
	42	54.15 N	4.30 W
Isle of Man (Ronaldsway) Airport ⊠	42	54.06 N	4.36 W
Isle of Palms	182	32.47 N	79.48 W
Isle of Wight	198	36.54 N	76.43 W
Isle of Wight □[6], Eng., U.K.	44	50.40 N	1.20 W
Isle of Wight □[6], Va., U.S.	198	36.50 N	76.42 W
Isle of Wight Bay C	198	38.22 N	75.06 W
Isle Royale National Park ♠	180	48.00 N	89.00 W
Isles, Lake of the ⊜	202	44.19 N	75.59 W
Isle Saint George	204	41.43 N	82.49 W
Islesboro Island I	178	44.20 N	68.53 W
Isleta	190	34.55 N	106.42 W
Isleta Indian Reservation ◆[4]	190	34.55 N	106.45 W
Isleton	216	38.10 N	121.37 W

Islets Caribou	176	49.30 N	67.14 W
Isleworth ◆[8]	250	51.28 N	0.20 W
Islington	197	42.13 N	71.11 W
Islington ◆[8], Ont., Can.	265b	43.39 N	79.32 W
Islington ◆[8], Eng., U.K.	44	51.34 N	0.06 W
Islip, Eng., U.K.	44	51.50 N	1.14 W
Islip, N.Y., U.S.	266	40.44 N	73.13 W
Islip-MacArthur Airport ⊠	200	40.48 N	73.06 W
Islip Terrace	266	40.46 N	73.13 W
Isloč' ≃	66	53.55 N	26.13 E
Islón	242	29.54 S	71.12 W
Ismael Cortinas (Arroyo Grande)	248	33.58 S	57.06 W
Ismailia → Al-Ismā'īlīyah	132	30.35 N	32.16 E
Ismā'īlīyah ◆[8]	263c	30.03 N	31.14 E
Ismā'īlīyah, Tur'at al- Ξ	132	30.04 N	31.16 E
İsmailli	120	38.56 N	27.13 E
Ismailly	74	40.47 N	48.09 E
Ismailovo	70	55.34 N	54.39 E
Ismaning	30	48.14 N	11.41 E
Isnā	130	25.18 N	32.33 E
Isny	54	47.41 N	10.02 E
Isoanala	147b	23.50 S	45.44 E
Isobe	84	34.22 N	136.49 E
Isogo ◆[8]	258	35.23 N	139.37 E
Isojoki	26	62.07 N	21.58 E
Isoka	144	10.10 S	32.35 E
Isokyrö	26	63.00 N	22.19 E
Isola, Fr.	56	44.11 N	7.03 E
Isola, Miss., U.S.	184	33.16 N	90.36 W
Isola, Monte ∧	58	45.42 N	10.05 E
Isola d'Asti	56	44.50 N	8.11 E
Isola del Cantone	56	44.39 N	8.57 E
Isola del Gran Sasso d'Italia	60	42.30 N	13.40 E
Isola della Scala	58	45.16 N	11.00 E
Isola del Liri	60	41.41 N	13.34 E
Isola di Capo Rizzuto	36	38.58 N	17.06 E
Isola Dovarese	58	45.10 N	10.18 E
Isola Farnese ◆[8]	60	42.01 N	12.23 E
Isola Vicentina	58	45.38 N	11.25 E
Isoletta	60	41.30 N	13.34 E
Isolillock Peak ∧	214	49.18 N	121.27 W
Isolo	263a	6.32 N	3.19 E
Isone	54	46.08 N	8.59 E
Isonzo (Soča) ≃	58	45.47 N	13.32 E
Isorella	58	45.18 N	10.19 E
Isosyöte ∧[2]	26	65.37 N	27.35 E
Iso-zaki ≻	84	36.23 N	140.38 E
İspanak	120	36.52 N	37.07 E
ısparta	120	37.46 N	30.33 E
ısparta □[4]	120	38.00 N	31.00 E
Isperih	38	43.43 N	26.50 E
Ispica	36	36.46 N	14.55 E
Ispikān	118	26.14 N	62.12 E
İspir	120	40.29 N	41.00 E
Ispra	56	45.49 N	8.37 E
Ispringen	52	48.55 N	8.40 E
Israel □[1]	108		
	122	31.30 N	35.00 E
Israel ≃	178	44.29 N	71.35 W
Issa	70	53.52 N	44.51 E
Issa ≃	66	56.58 N	28.47 E
Issano	236	5.49 N	59.25 W
Issaquah	214	47.32 N	122.02 W
Issaran, Ra's ≻	132	28.48 N	32.47 E
Issel (Oude IJssel) ≃	48	52.00 N	6.10 E
Isselburg	48	51.51 N	6.28 E
Isselhorst	48	51.57 N	8.24 E
Issen, Oued ≃	34	36.52 N	3.48 E
Isser, Oued ≃	34	35.08 N	1.28 W
Issia	140	6.29 N	6.35 W
Issigeac	32	44.44 N	0.36 E
Issime	56	45.41 N	7.51 E
Issogne	56	45.39 N	7.41 E
Issoire	32	45.33 N	3.15 E
Issole ≃	56	43.27 N	6.12 E
Issou	251	48.59 N	1.48 E
Issoudun	32	46.57 N	2.00 E
Issum	48	51.32 N	6.25 E
Issuna	144	5.23 S	34.46 E
Is-sur-Tille	54	47.31 N	5.06 E
Issy	46	48.50 N	2.18 E
Issyk	75	43.22 N	77.28 E
Issyk-Kul', Ozero ⊜	75	42.25 N	77.15 E
Issy-les-Moulineaux	251	48.49 N	2.17 E
Īstādeh-ye Moqor, Āb-e ⊜	110	32.32 N	67.57 E
İstanbul	120		
	257b	41.01 N	28.58 E
İstanbul □[4]	38	41.25 N	29.00 E
İstanbul (Yeşilköy) hava alani ⊠	257b	40.58 N	28.49 E
İstanbul Boğazı (Bosporus) Џ	120b	41.06 N	29.04 E
İstanbul Üniversitesi ♥[2]	257b	41.00 N	28.58 E
Isṭanhā	132	30.28 N	31.07 E
Istead Rise	250	51.24 N	0.22 E
Isteren ⊜	26	61.58 N	11.48 E
Isthmus Bay C	202	45.00 N	81.15 W
Istiaía	38	38.57 N	23.09 E
İstilil	120	37.14 N	41.04 E
İstinye ◆[8]	257b	41.06 N	29.03 E
Istisu	74	39.57 N	45.59 E
Istmina	236	5.10 N	76.39 W
Isto, Mount ∧	170	69.12 N	143.48 W
Istobensk	70	58.25 N	48.48 E
Istobnoje, S.S.S.R.	68	51.16 N	38.39 E
Istobnoje, S.S.S.R.	68	51.08 N	37.21 E
Istok	38	42.47 N	20.29 E
Istokpoga, Lake ⊜	210	27.22 N	81.17 W
Istra	72	55.55 N	36.52 E
Istra ≻[1]	36	45.15 N	14.00 E
Istra ≃	72	55.44 N	37.08 E
Istrana	58	45.41 N	12.07 E
ıstranca Dağları ⋏	120	41.50 N	27.30 E
Istres	56	43.31 N	4.59 E
Istria → Istra ≻[1]	36	45.15 N	14.00 E
Istrinskoje Vodochranilišče ⊜[1]	72	56.04 N	36.49 E
Isumi	84	35.17 N	140.19 E
Isumi ≃	84	35.18 N	140.29 E
Isumrud Strait Џ	154	4.45 S	145.50 E
Isunba	263a	6.27 N	3.17 E
Iswarīpur	116	22.19 N	89.07 E
Iswepe	148	26.50 S	30.31 E
Itá	242	25.29 S	57.21 W
Itabaiana, Bra.	240	10.41 S	37.26 W
Itabaiana, Bra.	240	7.20 S	35.20 W
Itabaianinha	240	11.16 S	37.47 W
Itabapoana	245	21.18 S	40.58 W
Itabashi ◆[8]	258	35.45 N	139.43 E
Itaberá	245	23.51 S	49.09 W
Itaberaba	245	12.32 S	40.18 W
Itaberaí	245	16.02 S	49.48 W
Itabi	240	10.08 S	37.06 W
Itabira	245	19.37 S	43.13 W
Itaboca	246	22.03 S	44.05 W
Itabocal ≃	240	1.48 S	47.26 W
Itaboraí	246	22.45 S	42.52 W
Itaboraí □[7]	277a	22.43 S	43.00 W
Itabuna	245	14.48 S	39.16 W
Itacaiúna ≃	240	5.21 S	49.08 W
Itacajá	240	8.19 S	47.46 W
Itacambiruçu ≃	245	16.44 S	42.45 W
Itacaré	245	14.18 S	39.00 W
Itacoatiara	240	3.08 S	58.25 W
Itacoatiara, Ponta de ≻	277a	22.59 S	43.02 W
Itacuaí ≃	236	4.20 S	70.12 W
Itacurubí del Rosario	242	24.29 S	56.41 W
Itacurussá	246	22.55 S	43.55 W
Itacurussá, Ilha de I	246	22.56 S	43.53 W

Symbol	English	Deutsch	Español	Français	Português
≃	River	Fluss	Río	Rivière	Rio
Ξ	Canal	Kanal	Canal	Canal	Canal
ᒪ	Waterfall, Rapids	Wasserfall, Stromschnellen	Cascada, Rápidos	Chute d'eau, Rapides	Cascata, Rápidos
Џ	Strait	Meeresstrasse	Estrecho	Détroit	Estreito
C	Bay, Gulf	Bucht, Golf	Bahía, Golfo	Baie, Golfe	Baía, Golfo
⊜	Lake, Lakes	See, Seen	Lago, Lagos	Lac, Lacs	Lago, Lagos
☷	Swamp	Sumpf	Pantano	Marais	Pântano
⊼	Ice Features, Glacier	Eis- und Gletscherformen	Accidentes Glaciales	Formes glaciaires	Acidentes Glaciares
▾	Other Hydrographic Features	Andere Hydrographische Objekte	Otros Elementos Hidrográficos	Autres données hydrographiques	Outros Elementos Hidrográficos
✦	Submarine Features	Untermeerische Objekte	Accidentes Submarinos	Formes de relief sous-marin	Acidentes Submarinos
□	Political Unit	Politische Einheit	Unidad Politica	Entité politique	Unidade Política
♥	Cultural Institution	Kulturelle Institution	Institución Cultural	Institution culturelle	Instituição Cultural
⊥	Historical Site	Historische Stätte	Sitio Histórico	Site historique	Sitio Histórico
♠	Recreational Site	Erholungs- und Ferienort	Sitio de Recreo	Centre de loisirs	Sítio de Lazer
⊠	Airport	Flughafen	Aeropuerto	Aéroport	Aeroporto
■	Military Installation	Militäranlage	Instalación Militar	Installation militaire	Instalação Militar
◆	Miscellaneous	Verschiedenes	Misceláneo	Divers	Miscelânea

Itaetê	245	12.59 S	40.58 W
Itagi	245	14.10 S	40.01 W
Itaguá	246	23.16 S	47.10 W
Itaguaçu	245	19.48 S	40.51 W
Itaguaí	246	22.52 S	43.47 W
Itaguajé	245	22.37 S	51.59 W
Itaguara	245	20.23 S	44.29 W
Itaguaré, Pico do ∧	246	22.30 S	45.10 W
Itaguari ≃	245	14.11 S	44.40 W
Itaguaru	245	15.44 S	49.37 W
Itaguatins	240	5.47 S	47.29 W
Itagüí	236	6.10 N	75.36 W
Itaguira	245	15.09 S	39.44 W
Itaí	245	23.24 S	49.06 W
Itá-Ibaté	242	27.26 S	57.20 W
Itaiçaba	240	4.40 S	37.51 W
Itaim	246	22.24 S	45.53 W
Itaim ≃, Bra.	240	7.02 S	42.02 W
Itaim ≃, Bra.	246	23.07 S	45.08 W
Itaim ≃, Bra.	246	22.19 S	45.51 W
Itaimbey ≃	242	24.46 S	54.24 W
Itainópolis	240	7.24 S	41.31 W
Itaiópolis	242	26.20 S	49.56 W
Itaipava	246	22.23 S	43.08 W
Itaipu, Bra.	246	22.58 S	43.02 W
Itaipu, Bra.	277a	22.44 S	43.26 W
Itaipu, Lagoa de C	277a	22.58 S	43.02 W
Itaipu, Ponta de ≻	277a	22.59 S	43.03 W
Itaituba	240	4.17 S	55.59 W
Itajá	245	19.07 S	51.37 W
Itajaí	242	26.53 S	48.39 W
Itajaí do Norte ≃	242	27.05 S	49.30 W
Itajaí do Sul ≃	242	27.12 S	49.39 W
Itajubá	246	22.26 S	45.27 W
Itajuípe	245	14.41 S	39.22 W
Itaka, S.S.S.R.	78	53.53 N	118.42 E
Itaka, Tan.	144	8.52 S	32.47 E
Itaki	263a	6.43 N	3.17 E
Itako	84	35.56 N	140.33 E
Itakura, Nihon	84	36.13 N	139.36 E
Itakura, Nihon	84	37.03 N	138.18 E
Itakyry	242	24.56 S	55.13 W
Italia → Italy □[1]	36	42.50 N	12.50 E
Itálica ⊥	34	37.30 N	6.05 W
Italie → Italy □[1]	36	42.50 N	12.50 E
Italien → Italy □[1]	36	42.50 N	12.50 E
Italy	212	32.11 N	96.53 W
Italy □[1]	22		
	36	42.50 N	12.50 E
Itamarandiba	245	17.51 S	42.51 W
Itamarandiba ≃	245	17.18 S	42.48 W
Itamarati	246	21.25 S	42.49 W
Itamari	245	13.47 S	39.37 W
Itamataré	240	2.16 S	46.24 W
Itambacuri	245	18.01 S	41.42 W
Itambé	245	15.15 S	40.37 W
Itambi	246	22.44 S	42.58 W
Itami	86	34.46 N	135.25 E
Itami, Camp ■	260	34.47 N	135.24 E
Itamonte	246	22.17 S	44.53 W
Itampolo	147b	24.41 S	43.57 E
Itandéua, Lago ⊜	240	2.01 S	55.10 W
Itandrano	147b	21.47 S	45.17 E
Itanhaém	245	24.11 S	46.47 W
Itanhandu	246	22.18 S	44.57 W
Itanhauã ≃	238	4.45 S	63.48 W
Itanhém	245	17.09 S	40.20 W
Itanhém ≃	245	17.32 S	39.12 W
Itanhomi	245	19.10 S	41.52 W
Itano	86	34.07 N	134.28 E
Itany (Litani) ≃	240	3.40 N	54.00 W
Itaobim	245	16.34 S	41.30 W
Itaocaia	277a	22.58 S	43.01 W
Itapaci	245	14.57 S	49.34 W
Itapagé	240	3.41 S	39.34 W
Itapagipe	245	19.54 S	49.22 W
Itapanhaú ≃	246	23.51 S	46.10 W
Itaparaná ≃	238	5.47 S	63.03 W
Itapaya	238	17.34 S	66.21 W
Itapé	245	14.54 S	39.26 W
Itapebi	245	15.56 S	39.32 W
Itapecerica	245	20.28 S	45.07 W
Itapecerica da Serra	246	23.43 S	46.50 W
Itapecerica da Serra □[7]	277b	23.44 S	46.52 W
Itapechinga	246	22.58 S	46.35 W
Itapecuru-Mirim	240	3.24 S	44.20 W
Itapemirim	245	21.01 S	40.50 W
Itapera	240	2.32 S	43.47 W
Itaperina, Pointe ≻	147b	24.59 S	47.06 E
Itaperuna	245	21.12 S	41.54 W
Itapeteiú	246	22.54 S	42.47 W
Itapetim	240	7.22 S	37.11 W
Itapetinga	245	15.15 S	40.15 W
Itapetininga	245	23.36 S	48.03 W
Itapetininga ≃	245	23.35 S	48.27 W
Itapeva, Bra.	245	23.58 S	48.52 W
Itapeva, Bra.	246	22.46 S	46.13 W
Itapevi	246	23.33 S	46.56 W
Itapevi □[7]	277b	23.31 S	46.55 W
Itapi ≃	240	0.47 S	57.16 W
Itapicuru	240	11.19 S	38.15 W
Itapicuru ≃, Bra.	240	11.47 S	37.32 W
Itapicuru ≃, Bra.	240	2.52 S	44.12 W
Itapicuru, Serra de ⛰[1]	240	6.35 S	45.25 W
Itapipoca	240	3.30 S	39.35 W
Itapira	246	22.26 S	46.50 W
Itapiranga, Bra.	240	2.45 S	58.01 W
Itapiranga, Bra.	242	27.08 S	53.43 W
Itapirapuã	245	15.52 S	50.36 W
Itapitanga	245	14.26 S	39.34 W
Itapiúna	240	4.33 S	38.57 W
Itápolis	245	21.35 S	48.46 W
Itaporã, Bra.	240	8.02 S	48.39 W
Itaporã, Bra.	245	22.01 S	54.54 W
Itaporanga, Bra.	240	7.18 S	38.10 W
Itaporanga, Bra.	245	23.42 S	49.29 W
Itaporanga d'Ajuda	240	10.59 S	37.18 W
Itapúa □[5]	242	26.50 S	55.50 W
Itapuranga	245	15.35 S	49.59 W
Itaquaciara	277b	23.47 S	46.51 W
Itaquaquecetuba	246	23.29 S	46.21 W
Itaquaquecetuba □[7]	277b	23.28 S	46.20 W
Itaquara	245	13.27 S	39.57 W
Itaquari	245	20.20 S	40.22 W
Itaquera •[8]	246	23.32 S	46.27 W
Itaquera, Ribeirão ≃	277b	23.28 S	46.26 W
Itaqui	242	29.08 S	56.33 W
Itaqui, Serra do ∧	277b	23.28 S	46.55 W
Itarantim	245	15.39 S	40.03 W
Itararé	245	24.07 S	49.20 W
Itararé ≃	242	23.10 S	49.42 W
Itārsi	114	22.37 N	77.45 E
Itarumã	245	18.42 S	51.25 W
Itasca, Ill., U.S.	268	41.58 N	87.59 W
Itasca, Tex., U.S.	212	32.10 N	97.09 W
Itasca State Park ♠	188	47.18 N	95.18 W
Itatá ≃, Bra.	240	3.28 S	51.57 W
Itata ≃, Chile	242	36.23 S	72.52 W
Itatí	242	27.16 S	58.15 W
Itatiaia	246	22.30 S	44.34 W
Itatiaia, Parque Nacional do ♠	246	22.28 S	44.37 W
Itatiba	246	23.00 S	46.51 W
Itatinga	245	23.07 S	48.36 W
Itatira	240	4.30 S	39.37 W
Itatka	76	56.49 N	85.37 E
Itatori	84	35.42 N	136.38 E
Itatskij	76	56.04 N	89.05 E
Itatupã	240	0.37 S	51.12 W
Itaú	240	5.50 S	37.59 W
Itauaiuri, Serra ∧[2]	240	1.47 S	54.06 W
Itauçu	245	16.13 S	49.37 W
Itaueira	240	7.36 S	43.02 W
Itaueira ≃	240	6.41 S	42.55 W
Itaúna	245	20.04 S	44.34 W
Itaúna, Morro do ∧[2]	277a	22.46 S	43.02 W
Itaúnas ≃	245	18.25 S	39.42 W
Itazuke-kūkō ⊠	86	33.52 N	130.28 E
Itbayat Island I	98	20.46 N	121.50 E
Itchen Lake ⊜	166	65.33 N	112.50 W
Ité ≃	236	7.00 N	74.15 W
Itéa	38	38.26 N	22.24 E
Iténez (Guaporé) ≃	238	11.54 S	65.01 W
Ith ∧	48	52.05 N	9.35 E
Ithaca, Mich., U.S.	180	43.18 N	84.36 W
Ithaca, N.Y., U.S.	200	42.27 N	76.30 W
Itháki	38	38.23 N	20.42 E
Itháki I	38	38.24 N	20.42 E
Ithan Creek ≃	275	40.00 N	75.21 W
Ithnayn	132	30.41 N	32.21 E
Itigi	144	5.42 S	34.29 E
Itikawa → Ichikawa	84	35.44 N	139.55 E
Itimādpur	114	27.15 N	78.12 E
Itimbiri ≃	142	2.02 N	22.44 E
Itinga	245	16.36 S	41.47 W
Itinga ≃	245	16.35 S	41.45 W
Itinomiya → Ichinomiya	84	35.18 N	136.48 E
Itipo	142	0.50 S	18.35 E
Itiquira	245	17.12 S	54.07 W
Itiquira ≃	238	17.18 S	56.44 W
Itirapina	245	22.15 S	47.49 W
Itire	263a	6.31 N	3.21 E
Itiruçu	245	13.31 S	40.09 W
Itiúba	240	10.43 S	39.51 W
Itiúba, Serra da ⛰	240	10.20 S	39.50 W
Itkillik ≃	170	70.08 N	150.57 W
Itlar'	72	56.51 N	39.17 E
Itlīdim	132	27.52 N	30.48 E
Itmīdah	132	30.46 N	31.20 E
Itmurynkol', Ozero ⊜	70	49.30 N	52.22 E
Itō	84	34.58 N	139.05 E
Itobi	246	21.44 S	46.58 W
Itobo	144	4.10 S	33.01 E
Itóca, Ilha de I	277a	22.46 S	43.04 W
Itóculo	144	14.42 S	40.18 E
Itoigawa	84	37.02 N	137.51 E
Itoko	142	1.00 S	21.45 E
Itomamo, Lac ⊜	176	49.11 N	70.28 W
Itoman	164m	26.08 N	127.40 E
Iton ≃	46	49.09 N	1.12 E
Itonamas ≃	238	12.28 S	64.24 W
Itororó	245	15.07 S	40.06 W
Itri	60	41.17 N	13.32 E
Iṭsā	132	29.15 N	30.48 E
Itsukaichi, Nihon	84	35.44 N	139.13 E
Itsukaichi, Nihon	86	34.24 N	132.22 E
Itsuki	82	32.24 N	130.50 E
Itsuku-shima I	86	34.16 N	132.19 E
Itsuwa	82	32.30 N	130.10 E
Itta Bena	184	33.30 N	90.20 W
Ittel, Oued ∨	138	34.19 N	6.01 E
Itter ≃	253	51.09 N	6.52 E
Ittersum	48	52.28 N	6.07 E
Itteville	251	48.31 N	2.21 E
Ittiḥād al-Imārāt al-'Arabīyah → United Arab Emirates □[1]	118	24.00 N	54.00 E
Ittiri	36	40.36 N	8.33 E
Ittygran, Ostrov I	170	64.36 N	172.40 W
Itu	245	23.16 S	47.19 W
Itu ≃	242	29.25 S	55.51 W
Ituaçu	245	13.49 S	41.18 W
Ituango	236	7.04 N	75.45 W
Ituberá	245	13.44 S	39.09 W
Itucumã ≃	238	6.59 S	69.48 W
Itueta	245	19.23 S	41.11 W
Ituí	246	21.32 S	42.55 W
Ituí ≃	236	4.38 S	70.19 W
Ituim ≃	242	28.35 S	51.20 W
Ituiutaba	245	18.58 S	49.28 W
Itula	144	3.29 S	27.52 E
Itumbiara	245	18.25 S	49.13 W
Itumirim	246	21.19 S	44.53 W
Itum-Kale	74	42.43 N	45.35 E
Ituna	174	51.10 N	103.30 W
Itungi Port	144	9.35 S	33.56 E
Itupeva	246	23.09 S	47.04 W
Itupeva ≃	246	22.03 S	47.15 W
Itupiranga	240	5.09 S	49.20 W
Ituporanga	242	27.25 S	49.36 W
Iturama	245	19.44 S	50.11 W
Iturbe	242	26.01 S	56.30 W
Iturbide	222	19.40 N	89.37 W
Ituri ≃	144	1.40 N	27.01 E
Iturup, Ostrov (Etorofu-tō) I	82a	44.54 N	147.30 E
Itutinga	246	21.18 S	44.40 W
Ituverava	245	20.20 S	47.47 W
Ituxi ≃	238	7.18 S	64.51 W
Ituzaingó, Arg.	242	27.36 S	56.41 W
Ituzaingó, Arg.	248	34.40 S	58.40 W
Ituzaingó, Ur.	248	34.25 S	56.26 W
Itwa	114	27.20 N	82.42 E
Ityāy al-Bārūd	132	30.53 N	30.40 E
Itz ≃	52	49.58 N	10.52 E
Itzehoe	48	53.55 N	9.31 E
I'udkovo	24	54.36 N	34.43 E
Iuka, Ill., U.S.	209	38.37 N	88.47 W
Iuka, Miss., U.S.	184	34.49 N	88.11 W
Iul'tin	170	67.50 N	178.48 W
Iul'tin, Gora ∧	170	67.50 N	178.25 W
Iúna	245	20.21 S	41.32 W
Iupeba	246	23.41 S	46.22 W
IV □[4]	140	15.45 N	13.00 W
Iva	182	34.19 N	82.40 W
Ivacevići	66	52.43 N	25.21 E
Ivačovo	66	60.32 N	36.22 E
Ivahona	147b	23.27 S	46.10 E
Ivaí ≃	245	23.18 S	53.42 W
Ivaiporã	242	24.15 S	51.45 W
Ivajlovgrad	38	41.32 N	26.08 E
Ivakoany, Massif de l' ⛰	147b	23.50 S	46.25 E
Ivalo	24	68.42 N	27.30 E
Ivalojoki ≃	24	68.43 N	27.36 E
Ivancevo	72	55.58 N	36.07 E
Ivančice	30	49.06 N	16.23 E
Ivancovo	72	56.39 N	35.50 E
Ivanec	36	46.13 N	16.08 E
Ivane-Puste	68	48.39 N	26.11 E
Ivangorod	66	59.24 N	28.10 E
Ivangrad	38	42.50 N	19.52 E
Ivanhoe, Austl.	156	32.54 S	144.18 E
Ivanhoe, Austl.	264b	37.46 S	145.03 E
Ivanhoe, Calif., U.S.	216	36.23 N	119.13 W
Ivanhoe, Ill., U.S.	268	42.17 N	88.02 W
Ivanhoe, Minn., U.S.	188	44.28 N	96.15 W
Ivanhoe, Va., U.S.	182	36.50 N	80.58 W
Ivanhoe ≃	180	48.40 N	82.11 W
Ivanhoe Lake ⊜	180	48.05 N	82.38 W
Ivanica	68	50.47 N	32.36 E
Ivanić Grad	36	45.42 N	16.24 E
Ivaniči	68	50.39 N	24.20 E
Ivanišči, S.S.S.R.	66	56.36 N	35.13 E
Ivanišči, S.S.S.R.	70	55.46 N	40.26 E
Ivanjica	38	43.35 N	20.14 E
Ivankov	68	50.56 N	29.54 E
Ivankovcy	79	49.06 N	134.28 E
Ivan'kovo	72	54.44 N	37.57 E
Ivan'kovskij	70	56.39 N	40.05 E
Ivan'kovskoje Vodochranilišče ⊜[1]	72	56.37 N	36.32 E
Ivanof Bay	170	55.54 N	159.29 W
Ivano-Frankovo	68	49.55 N	23.43 E
Ivano-Frankovsk	68	48.55 N	24.43 E
Ivanopol'	68	49.52 N	28.12 E
Ivanopolje	73	48.28 N	37.46 E
Ivano-šamševo	73	46.52 N	39.54 E
Ivanovka, S.S.S.R.	68	46.58 N	30.28 E
Ivanovka, S.S.S.R.	68	46.43 N	34.33 E
Ivanovka, S.S.S.R.	70	52.15 N	41.35 E
Ivanovka, S.S.S.R.	70	52.51 N	53.48 E
Ivanovka, S.S.S.R.	70	51.54 N	43.46 E
Ivanovka, S.S.S.R.	73	48.14 N	38.58 E
Ivanovka, S.S.S.R.	73	47.35 N	37.19 E
Ivanovka, S.S.S.R.	75	42.54 N	75.05 E
Ivanovka, S.S.S.R.	79	50.22 N	128.02 E
Ivanovka, S.S.S.R.	79	43.58 N	132.30 E
Ivanovo, S.S.S.R.	68	52.09 N	25.32 E
Ivanovo, S.S.S.R.	70	57.00 N	40.59 E
Ivanovo-Voznesensk → Ivanovo	70	57.00 N	40.59 E
Ivanovskaja, S.S.S.R.	24	60.48 N	55.52 E
Ivanovskaja, S.S.S.R.	68	45.17 N	38.29 E
Ivanovskoje, S.S.S.R.	66	59.17 N	28.49 E
Ivanovskoje, S.S.S.R.	68	51.37 N	34.57 E
Ivanovskoje, S.S.S.R.	72	55.52 N	36.55 E
Ivanovskoje, S.S.S.R.	72	54.55 N	36.50 E
Ivanovskoje, S.S.S.R.	72	55.05 N	37.50 E
Ivanovskoje, S.S.S.R.	72	56.23 N	37.07 E
Ivanovskoje, S.S.S.R.	255a	59.46 N	30.47 E
Ivan-Ozero	72	54.04 N	38.20 E
Ivan-Ozero, Ozero ⊜	72	54.07 N	38.17 E
Ivanpah Lake ⊜	194	35.35 N	115.25 W
Ivantejevka, S.S.S.R.	70	52.16 N	49.07 E
Ivantejevka, S.S.S.R.	72	55.58 N	37.55 E
Ivantejevo	66	57.48 N	33.09 E
Ivato	147b	20.37 S	47.12 E
Ivatuba	245	23.37 S	52.13 W
Ivdel'	62	60.42 N	60.24 E
Ivenec	66	53.53 N	26.45 E
Iver	250	51.31 N	0.30 W
Iver Heath	250	51.32 N	0.31 W
Iverny	251	49.00 N	2.47 E
Ivigtut	166	61.12 N	48.10 W
Ivindo ≃	142	0.09 S	12.09 E
Ivinheima ≃	245	23.14 S	53.42 W
Ivje	66	53.56 N	25.46 E
Ivn'a	68	51.04 N	36.08 E
Ivnica	68	50.09 N	29.03 E
Ivo	238	20.27 S	63.26 W
Ivohibe	147b	22.29 S	46.52 E
Ivolginsk	78	51.45 N	107.14 E
Ivón ≃	238	11.06 S	66.08 W
Ivondro	147b	24.47 S	46.52 E
Ivor	198	36.54 N	76.54 W
Ivorogbo	140	5.30 N	6.21 E
Ivory Coast □[1]	124		
	140	8.00 N	5.00 W
Ivory Coast •[2]	140	5.10 N	5.00 W
Ivoryton	197	41.21 N	72.27 W
Ivösjön ⊜	26	56.06 N	14.27 E
Ivot, S.S.S.R.	66	53.42 N	34.12 E
Ivot, S.S.S.R.	68	51.58 N	33.28 E
Ivotka ≃	68	51.57 N	33.22 E
Ivrea	56	45.28 N	7.52 E
İvrindi	120	39.34 N	27.29 E
Ivry-la-Bataille	46	48.53 N	1.28 E
Ivry[-sur-Seine]	46	48.49 N	2.23 E
Ivujivik	166	62.24 N	77.55 W
Ivybridge	44	50.23 N	3.56 W
Ivy Hatch	250	51.16 N	0.16 E
Ivyland	275	40.12 N	75.04 W
Ivywild	188	39.49 N	104.51 W
Iwade	86	34.15 N	135.19 E
Iwafune, Nihon	84	36.19 N	139.40 E
Iwafune, Nihon	260	34.44 N	135.54 E
Iwagi	86	34.15 N	133.09 E
Iwai	84	36.03 N	139.54 E
Iwai-shima I	86	33.47 N	131.58 E
Iwaizumi	82	39.50 N	141.48 E
Iwaki (Taira)	84	37.03 N	140.55 E
Iwaki-san ∧	82	40.39 N	140.18 E
Iwakuni	86	34.09 N	132.11 E
Iwakuni Marine Corps Air Station (United States) ■	86	34.08 N	132.14 E
Iwakura	84	35.17 N	136.52 E
Iwama	84	36.18 N	140.16 E
Iwami, Nihon	86	34.53 N	132.26 E
Iwami, Nihon	86	35.35 N	134.20 E
Iwami-kōgen ⛰[1]	86	35.00 N	132.30 E
Iwami-kokubun-ji ψ[1]	86	34.59 N	132.13 E
Iwamizawa	82a	43.12 N	141.46 E
Iwamura	84	35.22 N	137.26 E
Iwanai	82a	42.58 N	140.30 E
Iwanowo → Ivanovo	70	57.00 N	40.59 E
Iwanuma	82	38.06 N	140.52 E
Iwaoka •[8]	260	34.44 N	134.58 E
Iwase, Nihon	84	36.21 N	140.06 E
Iwase, Nihon	258	35.17 N	139.52 E
Iwata	84	34.42 N	137.48 E
Iwataki	86	35.34 N	135.09 E
Iwate □[5]	82	39.37 N	141.22 E
Iwate-san ∧	82	39.51 N	141.00 E
Iwatsuki	84	35.57 N	139.42 E
Iwaya → Awaji, Nihon	86	34.35 N	135.01 E
Iwaya, Nihon	260	34.35 N	135.02 E
Iwayama	260	34.52 N	135.52 E
Iwazono	260	34.45 N	135.19 E
Iwo	140	7.38 N	4.11 E
Iwo Jima → Iō-jima I	164f	24.47 N	141.20 E
Iwo Jima Air Base ■	164f	24.47 N	141.19 E
Iwŏn	88	40.19 N	128.39 E
Iwuy	46	50.14 N	3.19 E
Ixcán ≃	226	16.07 N	91.05 W
Ixchiguán	226	15.12 N	91.53 W
Ixcuintepec ≃	224	17.21 N	95.24 W
Ixelles	46	50.50 N	4.22 E
Ixhuatlán del Café	224	19.04 N	96.59 W
Ixiamas	238	13.45 S	68.09 W
Iximché ⊥	226	14.44 N	90.59 W
Ixmiquilpan	224	20.29 N	99.14 W
Ixonia	206	43.09 N	88.36 W
Ixopo	148	30.08 S	30.00 E
Ixtacalco	276a	19.23 N	99.07 W
Ixtacalco □[7]	276a	19.24 N	99.06 W
Ixtacihuatl ∧[1]	224	19.11 N	98.39 W
Ixtacihuatl y Popocatépetl, Parques Nacionales ♠	224	19.10 N	98.38 W
Ixtaltepec	224	16.30 N	95.03 W
Ixtapa, Punta ≻	224	17.39 N	101.40 W
Ixtapalapa	276a	19.21 N	99.06 W
Ixtapalapa □[7]	276a	19.21 N	99.04 W
Ixtapan de la Sal	224	18.50 N	99.41 W
Ixtlahuacán del Río	224	20.52 N	103.15 W
Ixtlán	224	20.11 N	102.24 W
Ixtlán de Juárez	224	17.20 N	96.29 W
Ixtlán del Río	224	21.02 N	104.22 W
Ixworth	44	52.18 N	0.50 E
Iya ≃	86	33.58 N	133.47 E
'Iyādh	134	14.59 N	46.51 E
'Iyāl Bakhīt	130	13.25 N	28.41 E
Iyang, Taehan	88	34.53 N	127.01 E
Iyang → Yiyang, Zhg.	92	28.36 N	112.20 E
Iyang, Gili I	105a	6.59 S	114.10 E
Iyo	86	33.46 N	132.42 E
Iyo-mishima	86	33.58 N	133.33 E
Iyo-nada ⊤[2]	86	33.40 N	132.20 E
Iž ≃	70	55.58 N	52.38 E
Iza ≃	38	47.54 N	23.57 E
Izabal	226	15.24 N	89.08 W
Izabal □[5]	226	15.30 N	89.00 W
Izabal, Lago de ⊜	226	15.30 N	89.10 W
'Izab al-Başāriṭah	132	31.23 N	31.47 E
Īzad Khvāst	118	31.31 N	52.07 E
Izalco	226	13.45 N	89.40 W
'Izam, Jabal al- ∧	122	30.51 N	35.46 E
Izapa ⊥	222	14.55 N	92.10 W
Izasa-misaki ≻	86	35.40 N	134.32 E
Iz'aslav	68	50.07 N	26.51 E
'Izbat Abū Şuql	122	31.09 N	33.49 E
Izberbaš	74	42.33 N	47.52 E
Izbica, Pol.	30	54.42 N	17.26 E
Izbica, Pol.	30	50.54 N	23.09 E
Izd'oškovo	66	55.08 N	33.37 E
Izegem	46	50.55 N	3.12 E
Īzeh	118	31.50 N	49.50 E
Izena-shima I	164m	26.56 N	127.56 E
Izendy	76	45.48 N	59.28 E
Izernore	54	46.13 N	5.33 E
Iževsk	70	56.51 N	53.14 E
Iževskoje	70	54.34 N	40.53 E
Izhevsk → Iževsk	70	56.51 N	53.14 E
Izkī	118	22.56 N	57.46 E
Ižma	24	65.02 N	53.55 E
Ižma ≃	24	65.19 N	52.54 E
Izmail	68	45.21 N	28.50 E
Izmajlovo	70	53.43 N	47.14 E
Izmajlovo •[8]	255b	55.48 N	37.46 E
Izmajlovskij Park ♠	255b	55.46 N	37.47 E
Izmalkovo	66	52.41 N	37.58 E
İzmir	120	38.25 N	27.09 E
İzmir □[4]	120	38.30 N	27.15 E
İzmir Körfezi C	120	38.30 N	26.50 E
İzmit (Kocaeli)	120	40.46 N	29.55 E
İzmit Körfezi C	120	40.45 N	29.35 E
Ižmorskij	76	56.11 N	86.38 E
Iznajar, Embalse de ⊜[1]	34	37.15 N	4.30 W
Iznalloz	34	37.23 N	3.31 W
İznik	120	40.26 N	29.43 E
İznik Gölü ⊜	120	40.26 N	29.30 E
Iznoski	66	54.59 N	35.19 E
Izola	58	45.32 N	13.40 E
Izoplit	72	56.38 N	36.12 E
Ižora ≃	255a	59.48 N	30.36 E
Izozog, Bañados de ☰	238	18.48 S	62.10 W
Izra'	122	32.51 N	36.15 E
Izsák	30	46.48 N	19.22 E
Iztapa	226	13.56 N	90.43 W
Izúcar de Matamoros	224	18.36 N	98.28 W
Izu-hantō ≻[1]	84	34.45 N	139.00 E
Izuhara	82	34.12 N	129.17 E
Iz'um	73	49.12 N	37.19 E
Izumi, Nihon	82	32.05 N	130.22 E
Izumi, Nihon	84	35.54 N	136.40 E
Izumi, Nihon	86	34.29 N	135.26 E
Izumi •[8]	258	35.25 N	139.30 E
Izumi-ōtsu	86	34.30 N	135.24 E
Izumi-sano	86	34.25 N	135.19 E
Izumizaki	84	37.09 N	140.17 E
Izumo	86	35.22 N	132.46 E
Izumo ≃	84	34.38 N	136.33 E
Izumrud	76	57.05 N	61.23 E
Izu-nagaoka	84	35.02 N	138.56 E
Izushi	86	35.28 N	134.52 E
Izu-shotō II	80	32.00 N	140.00 E
Izuwara	260	34.53 N	135.32 E
Izvarino	73	48.17 N	39.52 E
Izvestij CIK, Ostrova II	64	75.55 N	82.30 E
Izvestkovyj	79	48.59 N	131.33 E
J			
Ja'ār, Birkat al- ⊜	132	30.28 N	30.10 E
Jääsjärvi ⊜	26	61.36 N	26.07 E
Jabā, Sūrīy.	122	33.10 N	35.56 E
Jaba, Yai.	134	6.17 N	35.12 E
Jabābīn, Tallāt al- ⛰[2]	132	30.31 N	30.07 E
Jabal	136	28.36 N	19.58 E
Jabal,, Baḥr al- → Mountain Nile ≃	126	9.30 N	30.30 E
Jabal Abyad Plateau ⛰[1]	130	19.00 N	29.00 E
Jabal al-Awliyā'	130	15.14 N	32.30 E
Jabal an-Nūr	132	28.57 N	31.02 E
Jabal aṭ-Ṭayr	132	28.14 N	30.45 E
Jabal Dūd	130	13.25 N	33.09 E
Jabal Lubnān □[4]	122	33.50 N	35.40 E
Jabalón ≃	34	38.53 N	4.05 W
Jabal Os Sarāj	110	35.07 N	69.14 E
Jabalpur	114	23.10 N	79.57 E
Jabal Qerri	130	16.15 N	32.48 E
Jabal Şabāyā I	134	18.35 N	41.03 E
Jabal 'Uwaybid	132	30.09 N	32.12 E
Jabālyah	122	31.32 N	34.29 E
Jabavu	263d	26.15 S	27.53 E
Jabbān, Arḍ al- •[1]	122	32.08 N	36.35 E
Jabbeke	46	51.11 N	3.05 E
Jabbi	113	33.08 N	72.38 E
Jabbūl, Sabkhat al- ⊜	120	36.03 N	37.39 E
Jabel	50	53.32 N	12.32 E
Jabi	104	2.32 N	102.48 E
Jabjabah, Wādī ∨	130	22.37 N	33.17 E
Jablah	120	35.21 N	35.55 E
Jablanac	36	44.42 N	14.54 E
Jablanica	36	43.39 N	17.45 E
Jablanica ≃	38	43.07 N	21.57 E
Jablaničko Jezero ⊜[1]	36	43.40 N	17.50 E
Jablines	251	48.55 N	2.46 E
Jabločnoje	68	50.18 N	35.14 E
Jabločnyj	79	47.10 N	142.04 E
Jablonec nad Nisou	30	50.44 N	15.10 E
Jablonica	30	48.37 N	17.25 E
Jabłonka	30	49.29 N	19.41 E
Jablonné v Podještědí	50	50.48 N	14.47 E
Jablonoj → Jablonovyj Chrebet ⛰	78	53.30 N	115.00 E
Jablonov	68	48.24 N	24.57 E
Jablonovo	78	51.51 N	112.49 E
Jablonovyj Chrebet ⛰	78	53.30 N	115.00 E
Jabłonowo	30	53.24 N	19.09 E
Jablonowy-Gebirge → Jablonovyj Chrebet ⛰	78	53.30 N	115.00 W
Jablunkov	30	49.35 N	18.47 E
Jablunkovský průsmyk)(	30	49.32 N	18.45 E
Jaboatão	240	8.07 S	35.01 W
Jaboncillos	222	28.57 N	102.39 W
Jaboncillos Creek ≃	186	27.23 N	97.45 W
Jabonga	106	9.20 N	125.32 E
Jaborandi	245	20.40 S	48.25 W
Jabori	113	34.36 N	73.16 E
Jaboticabal	245	21.16 S	48.19 W
Jabrat Sa'īd ⊤[4]	130	16.06 N	31.50 E
Jabrīn ⊤[4]	108	23.17 N	48.58 E
Jabron ≃	56	44.33 N	4.45 E
Jabron, Torrent le ≃	56	44.09 N	5.57 E
Jabung	105a	5.29 S	105.40 E
Jabung, Tanjung ≻	102	1.01 S	104.22 E
Jaca	34	42.34 N	0.33 W
Jacala de Ledesma	224	21.01 N	99.11 W
Jacaleapa	226	14.00 N	86.40 W
Jacaltenango	226	15.40 N	91.44 W
Jacana	264b	37.42 S	144.55 E
Jacaraci	245	14.51 S	42.26 W
Jacaré ≃, Bra.	238	5.49 S	63.35 W
Jacaré ≃, Bra.	240	10.03 S	42.13 W
Jacaré ≃, Bra.	245	13.50 S	40.42 W
Jacaré ≃, Bra.	277a	22.56 S	43.04 W
Jacaré, Riacho ≃	240	8.28 S	39.39 W
Jacaré Guaçu ≃	242	21.50 S	48.56 W
Jacareí	246	23.19 S	45.58 W
Jacareí ≃	246	22.54 S	46.28 W
Jacarepaguá •[8]	246	22.56 S	43.20 W
Jacarepaguá, Lagoa de C	246	22.59 S	43.24 W
Jacaré Pepira ≃	242	21.54 S	48.52 W
Jacaré Velho	246	21.20 S	42.51 W
Jacarèzinho	245	23.09 S	49.59 W
Jaceruba	246	22.35 S	43.34 W
Jáchal	242	30.14 S	68.45 W
Jáchal ≃	242	30.44 S	68.08 W
Jachenau	58	47.36 N	11.25 E
Jachniki	68	50.26 N	33.10 E
Jachroma	72	56.17 N	37.30 E
Jachroma ≃	72	56.31 N	37.07 E
Jáchymov	50	50.20 N	12.55 E
Jaciara	245	15.59 S	54.57 W

ENGLISH

Name	Page	Lat.°′	Long.°′
Jacinto	245	16.10 S	40.17 W
Jacinto Aráuz	242	38.04 S	63.26 W
Jacinto City	212	29.46 N	95.16 W
Jacinto Machado	242	29.00 S	49.46 W
Jaci Paraná	238	9.15 S	64.23 W
Jaciparaná ≃	238	9.22 S	64.22 W
Jackass Creek ≃	216	37.22 N	119.23 W
Jack Creek ≃	192	42.59 N	121.32 W
Jackfish Lake ⊜	174	53.05 N	108.25 W
Jackhead Harbour	174	51.52 N	97.16 W
Jack Lake ⊜	202	44.42 N	78.03 W
Jack London State Historical Park ♠	216	38.21 N	122.32 W
Jackman	178	45.38 N	70.16 W
Jackman Creek ≃	214	48.30 N	121.43 W
Jackman Station	178	45.37 N	70.15 W
Jack Mountain ∧, Mont., U.S.	192	46.21 N	112.18 W
Jack Mountain ∧, Wash., U.S.	214	48.47 N	120.57 W
Jackpot	194	41.59 N	114.40 W
Jacksboro, Tenn., U.S.	182	36.20 N	84.11 W
Jacksboro, Tex., U.S.	186	33.13 N	98.10 W
Jacks Creek ≃	198	40.35 N	77.33 W
Jacks Island I	269b	40.37 N	79.43 W
Jacks Mountain ∧	200	40.45 N	77.30 W
Jackson, Ala., U.S.	184	31.31 N	87.53 W
Jackson, Calif., U.S.	216	38.21 N	120.46 W
Jackson, Ga., U.S.	182	33.18 N	83.58 W
Jackson, Ky., U.S.	182	37.33 N	83.23 W
Jackson, La., U.S.	184	30.50 N	91.13 W
Jackson, Mich., U.S.	206	42.15 N	84.24 W
Jackson, Minn., U.S.	188	43.37 N	95.01 W
Jackson, Miss., U.S.	184	32.18 N	90.12 W
Jackson, Mo., U.S.	184	37.23 N	89.40 W
Jackson, N.J., U.S.	198	40.06 N	74.23 W
Jackson, N.C., U.S.	182	36.23 N	77.25 W
Jackson, Ohio, U.S.	178	39.03 N	82.39 W
Jackson, Pa., U.S.	200	41.50 N	75.36 W
Jackson, S.C., U.S.	182	33.20 N	81.47 W
Jackson, Tenn., U.S.	184	35.37 N	88.49 W
Jackson, Wyo., U.S.	190	43.29 N	110.38 W
Jackson □[6], Ind., U.S.	208	38.53 N	86.03 W
Jackson □[6], Mich., U.S.	206	42.15 N	84.24 W
Jackson □[6], Tex., U.S.	212	29.00 N	96.35 W
Jackson ≃	178	37.47 N	79.46 W
Jackson, Cape ≻	162	41.00 S	174.18 E
Jackson, Lake ⊜, Fla., U.S.	210	27.55 N	81.10 W
Jackson, Lake ⊜, Fla., U.S.	210	27.29 N	81.28 W
Jackson, Mount ∧, Ant.	9	71.23 S	63.22 W
Jackson, Mount ∧, Austl.	152	30.15 S	119.16 E
Jackson, Port C	264a	33.50 S	151.16 E
Jackson Bay C	162	43.58 S	168.42 E
Jackson Brook ≃	266	40.53 N	74.34 W
Jackson Butte ∧	216	38.20 N	120.43 W
Jackson Center, Ohio, U.S.	206	40.27 N	84.02 W
Jackson Center, Pa., U.S.	204	41.16 N	80.09 W
Jackson Creek ≃, Can.	174	49.18 N	100.50 W
Jackson Creek ≃, Calif., U.S.	216	38.18 N	121.01 W
Jackson Creek ≃, Ill., U.S.	206	41.26 N	88.10 W
Jackson Heights •[8]	266	40.45 N	73.53 W
Jackson Lake ⊜[1], Ga., U.S.	182	33.22 N	83.52 W
Jackson Lake ⊜[1], Wyo., U.S.	192	43.55 N	110.40 W
Jackson Mountain ∧	178	44.46 N	70.32 W
Jackson Park ♠, Ont., Can.	271	42.17 N	83.01 W
Jackson Park ♠, Ill., U.S.	268	41.47 N	87.35 W
Jackson's Arm	176	49.52 N	56.47 W
Jacksons Creek ≃	159	37.40 S	144.48 E
Jacksons Head ≻	162	43.58 S	168.37 E
Jacksonville, Ala., U.S.	184	33.49 N	85.46 W
Jacksonville, Ark., U.S.	184	34.52 N	92.07 W
Jacksonville, Fla., U.S.	182	30.20 N	81.40 W
Jacksonville, Ill., U.S.	209	39.44 N	90.14 W
Jacksonville, N.C., U.S.	182	34.45 N	77.26 W
Jacksonville, N.Y., U.S.	200	42.31 N	76.37 W
Jacksonville, Oreg., U.S.	192	42.19 N	122.57 W
Jacksonville, Tex., U.S.	212	31.58 N	95.17 W
Jacksonville, Vt., U.S.	197	42.47 N	72.49 W
Jacksonville, Lake ⊜[1]	212	31.55 N	95.17 W
Jacksonville Beach	182	30.18 N	81.24 W
Jacks Reef	200	43.06 N	76.25 W
Jacks Run ≃	269b	40.13 N	79.35 W
Jacktown Acres	269b	40.19 N	79.45 W
Jacmel	228	18.14 N	72.32 W
Jacob, Morne ∧	230e	14.46 N	61.06 W
Jacobābād	110	28.17 N	68.26 E
Jacobina	240	11.11 S	40.31 W
Jacob Island I	202	44.28 N	78.28 W
Jacob Riis Park ♠	266	40.34 N	73.52 W
Jacobs Creek ≃	204	40.07 N	79.44 W
Jacobsdal	148	29.13 S	24.41 E
Jacobus	198	39.53 N	76.43 W
Jacomino	276b	23.06 N	82.20 W
Jacona de Plancarte	224	19.57 N	102.16 W
Jacques, Lac à ⊜	170	66.10 N	127.25 W
Jacques-Cartier ≃	196	46.40 N	71.45 W
Jacques-Cartier, Détroit de)(	176	50.00 N	63.30 W
Jacques-Cartier, Mont ∧	176	48.59 N	65.57 W
Jacques-Cartier, Pont •[5]	265a	45.31 N	73.32 W
Jacquet River	176	47.55 N	66.00 W
Jacqueville	140	5.12 N	4.25 W
Jacquinot Bay C	154	5.35 S	151.30 E
Jacu ≃	240	6.13 S	35.09 W
Jacu, Rio do ≃	277b	23.29 S	46.27 W
Jacuba ≃	245	18.25 S	52.28 W
Jacuecanga	246	23.01 S	44.13 W
Jacuí ≃, Bra.	242	30.02 S	51.15 W
Jacuí ≃, Bra.	246	23.05 S	45.08 W
Jacuípe	245	12.29 S	38.38 W
Jacuípe ≃	245	12.30 S	39.05 W
Jacumba	194	32.37 N	116.11 W
Jacundá	240	4.33 S	49.28 W
Jacundá ≃	240	1.57 S	50.26 W
Jacupiranga	242	24.42 S	48.00 W
Jacurici ≃	240	10.57 S	39.35 W
Jacutinga	246	22.17 S	46.37 W
Jada	136	8.46 N	12.09 E
Jada'ah, Jabal ∧[2]	132	29.58 N	30.40 E
Jadal •[1]	140	19.00 N	4.15 E
Jaddi, Rās ≻	118	25.14 N	63.31 E
Jade	48	53.20 N	8.14 E
Jade Buddha, Temple of the (Yufosi) ψ[1]	259b	31.14 N	121.26 E
Jadebusen C	48	53.30 N	8.10 E
Jäder	40	59.25 N	16.41 E
Jäderfors	40	60.41 N	16.40 E
Jade Run ≃	275	39.56 N	74.45 W
Jadīdah	118	34.01 N	42.28 E
Jadito Wash ∨	190	35.22 N	110.50 W
J.A.D. Jensens Nunatakker ∧	166	62.45 N	48.00 W
Jadotville → Likasi	144	10.59 S	26.44 E
Jadraque	34	40.55 N	2.55 W

DEUTSCH

Name	Seite	Breite°′	Länge°′ E=Ost
Jadrin	70	55.56 N	46.12 E
Jadromino	72	55.57 N	36.36 E
Jādū	136	31.57 N	12.01 E
Jaduty	68	51.22 N	32.19 E
Jægerspris	41	55.51 N	11.59 E
Jaeger Summit ∧	144	2.52 S	35.47 E
Ja'el ≃	134	10.56 N	51.09 E
Jaén, Esp.	34	37.46 N	3.47 W
Jaén, Perú	238	5.42 S	78.47 W
Jæren •[1]	26	58.45 N	5.45 E
Jāfarābād, Bhārat	110	20.52 N	71.22 E
Ja'farābād, Īrān	118	35.43 N	50.43 E
Jāfarpur	116	22.29 N	89.06 E
Jāfarpur •[8]	262a	28.40 N	77.01 E
Jaffa, Cape ≻	156	36.58 S	139.40 E
Jaffa, Tel Aviv- → Tel Aviv-Yafo	122	32.04 N	34.46 E
Jaffārah, Qūr al- ∧[2]	132	30.25 N	29.35 E
Jaffna	112	9.40 N	80.00 E
Jaffna Lagoon C	112	9.35 N	80.15 E
Jaffrey	178	42.50 N	72.04 W
Jafjaf aş-Şaghīr ⛰[2]	136	20.50 N	21.35 E
Jafr, Qā' al- •[7]	122	30.17 N	36.20 E
Jagādhri	114	30.10 N	77.18 E
Jägala ≃	66	59.29 N	25.09 E
Jagalūr	112	14.32 N	76.21 E
Jāgan	110	28.05 N	68.30 E
Jagannāthganj Ghāt	114	24.45 N	89.49 E
Jagannāthpūr	262b	22.43 N	88.19 E
Jagati	116	23.54 N	89.06 E
Jagatnagar	262b	22.47 N	88.13 E
Jagatpur •[8]	262a	28.44 N	77.14 E
Jagatsingpur	110	20.16 N	86.10 E
Jagdalpur	112	19.04 N	82.02 E
Jagdīspur	114	25.29 N	84.25 E
Jagel	41	54.27 N	9.32 E
Jägerndorf → Krnov	30	50.05 N	17.41 E
Jagersfontein	148	29.44 S	25.29 E
Jaggayyapeta	112	16.54 N	80.06 E
Jagged Mountain ∧	170	58.38 N	162.02 W
Jaghbūb ⊤[4]	136	29.40 N	24.43 E
Jagnob ≃	75	39.15 N	68.35 E
Jagny-sous-Bois	251	49.05 N	2.27 E
Jagodnoje, S.S.S.R.	64	62.33 N	149.40 E
Jagodnoje, S.S.S.R.	70	53.36 N	49.04 E
Jagodnyj	76	59.44 N	65.04 E
Jagorlyckij Liman C	68	46.24 N	31.50 E
Jagotin	68	50.17 N	31.46 E
Jagraon	113	30.47 N	75.29 E
Jagst ≃	52	49.14 N	9.11 E
Jagsthausen	52	49.19 N	9.28 E
Jagstzell	52	49.02 N	10.05 E
Jagtiāl	112	18.48 N	78.56 E
Jaguaquara	245	13.32 S	39.58 W
Jaguarão	242	32.34 S	53.23 W
Jaguarão (Yaguarón) ≃	242	32.39 S	53.12 W
Jaguarari	240	10.16 S	40.12 W
Jaguaretama	240	5.37 S	38.46 W
Jaguari	242	29.30 S	54.41 W
Jaguari ≃, Bra.	242	29.42 S	55.07 W
Jaguari ≃, Bra.	245	22.41 S	47.17 W
Jaguari ≃, Bra.	246	23.10 S	45.55 W
Jaguariaíva	242	24.15 S	49.42 W
Jaguaribara	240	5.40 S	38.37 W
Jaguaribe	240	5.53 S	38.37 W
Jaguaribe ≃	240	4.25 S	37.45 W
Jaguari-Mirim ≃	246	21.59 S	47.17 W
Jaguaripe	245	13.06 S	38.53 W
Jaguariúna	246	22.41 S	46.59 W
Jaguaruana	240	4.50 S	37.47 W
Jaguaruna	242	28.36 S	49.02 W
Jagüé	242	28.38 S	68.24 W
Jagüey Grande	230p	22.32 N	81.08 W
Jāguli	116	22.56 N	88.32 E
Jāgulia	262b	22.44 N	88.32 E
Jagungal, Mount ∧	161b	36.09 S	148.23 E
Jagunovskij	76	55.17 N	85.59 E
Jahānābād, Bhārat	114	25.13 N	84.59 E
Jahānābād, Pāk.	113	32.11 N	72.29 E
Jahāngīra	113	33.55 N	72.13 E
Jahāngīrābād	114	28.25 N	78.06 E
Jahangirpur •[8]	262a	28.44 N	77.13 E
Jahānia	113	30.02 N	71.49 E
Jahannam, Qārat ∧[2]	132	29.19 N	30.09 E
Jahnsdorf	50	50.44 N	12.51 E
Jahrom	118	28.31 N	53.33 E
Jahú → Jaú	245	22.18 S	48.33 W
Jai ≃	240	3.58 N	54.49 W
Jaicós	240	7.21 S	41.08 W
Jaidak	110	31.58 N	66.43 E
Jaihti ≃	116	24.08 N	86.48 E
Jaijōn	113	31.21 N	76.09 E
Jailolo	98	1.05 N	127.30 E
Jaimanitas ≃	276b	23.05 N	82.29 W
Jainti	114	26.42 N	89.36 E
Jaintiāpur	110	25.08 N	92.07 E
Jaipur	110	26.55 N	75.49 E
Jaipur □[5]	114	27.00 N	76.10 E
Jāis	114	26.15 N	81.32 E
Jaisalmer	110	26.55 N	70.54 E
Jaisan	76	50.51 N	56.14 E
Jaito	113	30.28 N	74.53 E
Jaja	76	56.12 N	86.26 E
Jaja ≃	76	56.58 N	86.23 E
Jājarkot	114	28.42 N	82.12 E
Jājarm	118	36.58 N	56.27 E
Jajce	36	44.21 N	17.16 E
Jajichi	164m	26.47 N	128.13 E
Jajjha	113	28.45 N	70.34 E
Jajl'u	76	51.48 N	87.36 E
Jajpan	75	40.23 N	70.48 E
Jājpur	110	20.51 N	86.20 E
Jajva	76	59.20 N	57.15 E
Jajva ≃	76	59.13 N	56.40 E
Jakarta	105a		
	259e	6.10 S	106.48 E
Jakarta, Teluk C	105a	6.05 S	106.48 E
Jakarta Kota Station •[5]	259e	6.08 S	106.49 E
Jakarta Raya □[4]	105a	6.10 S	106.45 E
Jakdūl ⊜	130	17.39 N	32.59 E
Jake Creek Mountain ∧	194	41.13 N	116.54 W
Jakenan	105a	6.45 S	111.11 E
Jākhal	113	29.48 N	75.50 E
Jakhāu	110	23.13 N	68.43 E
Jakkonen	24	66.33 N	29.52 E
Jakobsberg	40	59.26 N	17.50 E
Jakobsdalsberget ∧[2]	40	58.41 N	16.07 E
Jakobshagen → Dobrzany	30	53.22 N	15.25 E
Jakobshavn	166	69.13 N	51.06 W
Jakobstad (Pietarsaari)	26	63.40 N	22.42 E
Jakovlevići	66	54.20 N	30.31 E
Jakovlevka	79	44.26 N	133.28 E
Jakovlevo	72	54.48 N	37.26 E
Jakša	24	61.48 N	56.49 E
Jakšanga	70	58.23 N	45.56 E
Jakšur-Bodja	70	57.11 N	53.09 E
Jakupica ⛰	38	41.43 N	21.26 E
Jakutsk	64	62.13 N	129.49 E
Jakutskaja □[8]	78	58.00 N	121.00 E
Jal	186	32.07 N	103.12 W
Jala	224	21.05 N	104.26 W
Jalacingo	224	19.48 N	97.18 W
Jalajala	106	14.21 N	121.19 E
Jalājil	118	25.41 N	45.28 E
Jalālābād, Afg.	110	34.26 N	70.28 E
Jalālābād, Bhārat	113	30.37 N	74.15 E
Jalālābād, Bhārat	114	27.43 N	79.40 E
Jalālah al-Baḥrīyah, Jabal ⛰[1]	132	29.20 N	32.00 E
Jalālat al-Qiblīyah, Jabal al- ⛰	132	28.42 N	32.22 E
Jalaliyeh Race Track ♠	257d	35.43 N	51.24 E
Jalālpur, Bhārat	114	26.19 N	82.44 E

Symbols in the index entries represent the broad categories identified in the key at the right. Symbols with superior numbers (⛰[2]) identify subcategories (see complete key on page *I · 26*).

Kartensymbole in dem Registerverzeichnis stellen die rechts in Schlüssel erklärten Kategorien dar. Symbole mit hochgestellten Ziffern (⛰[2]) bezeichnen Unterabteilungen einer Kategorie (vgl. vollständiger Schlüssel auf Seite *I · 26*).

Los símbolos incluídos en el texto del índice representan las grandes categorias identificadas con la clave a la derecha. Los símbolos con numeros en su parte superior (⛰[2]) identifican las subcategorías (véase la clave completa en la página *I · 26*).

Les symboles de l'index représentent les catégories indiquées dans la légende à droite. Les symboles suivis d'un indice (⛰[2]) représentent des sous-catégories (voir légende complète à la page *I · 26*).

Os símbolos incluídos no texto do índice representam as grandes categorias identificadas com a chave à direita. Os símbolos com números em sua parte superior (⛰[2]) identificam as subcategorias (veja-se a chave completa à página *I · 26*).

∧ Mountain	Berg	Montaña	Montagne	Montanha
⛰ Mountains	Berge	Montañas	Montagnes	Montanhas
)(Pass	Pass	Paso	Col	Passo
∨ Valley, Canyon	Tal, Cañon	Valle, Cañón	Vallée, Canyon	Vale, Canhão
≚ Plain	Ebene	Llano	Plaine	Planície
≻ Cape	Kap	Cabo	Cap	Cabo
I Island	Insel	Isla	Île	Ilha
II Islands	Inseln	Islas	Îles	Ilhas
• Other Topographic Features	Andere Topographische Objekte	Otros Elementos Topográficos	Autres données topographiques	Outros Elementos Topográficos

ESPAÑOL Nombre	Página	Lat.°′	Long.°′ W=Oeste
Jalālpur, Pāk.	113	32.38 N	74.12 E
Jalālpur Pīrwāla	113	29.30 N	71.13 E
Jalama	74	41.44 N	48.34 E
Jalan'	76	58.21 N	91.53 E
Jalán ≃	226	14.39 N	86.12 W
Jalan Besar Stadium ♠	261c	1.18 N	103.52 E
Jalangi	116	24.08 N	88.42 E
Jalangi ≃	116	23.25 N	88.22 E
Jalan Kayu	261c	1.24 N	103.52 E
Jalapa, Guat.	226	14.38 N	89.59 W
Jalapa, Méx.	224	17.43 N	92.49 W
Jalapa, Nic.	226	13.55 N	86.08 W
Jalapa □[5]	226	14.35 N	89.55 W
Jalapa de Díaz	224	18.04 N	96.32 W
Jalapa Enríquez	224	19.32 N	96.55 W
Jalasjärvi	26	62.30 N	22.45 E
Jalaud ≃	106	10.45 N	122.40 E
Jālaun	114	26.09 N	79.21 E
Jal'čiki	70	55.09 N	48.01 E
Jalcocotán	224	21.28 N	105.07 W
Jalcomulco ≃	224	19.20 N	96.33 W
Jalda	116	21.56 N	87.30 E
Jalea de Catalán	224	17.26 N	99.51 W
Jalesar	114	27.29 N	78.19 E
Jaleshwar	114	26.38 N	85.48 E
Jaleswar	116	21.49 N	87.13 E
Jālgaon, Bhārat	112	21.01 N	75.34 E
Jālgaon, Bhārat	112	21.03 N	76.32 E
Jal'gelevo	255a	59.44 N	29.57 E
Jalhay	52	50.34 N	5.58 E
Jalirpār	116	23.13 N	89.58 E
Jalisco	224	21.27 N	104.54 W
Jalisco □[3]	224	20.20 N	103.40 W
Jallas ≃	34	42.54 N	9.08 W
Jallieu	56	45.35 N	5.16 E
Jālna	112	19.50 N	75.53 E
Jalón ≃	34	41.47 N	1.04 W
Jālor	110	25.21 N	72.37 E
Jalostotitlán	224	21.12 N	102.28 W
Jalpa	224	21.38 N	102.58 W
Jalpa de Méndez	224	18.08 N	93.05 W
Jalpaiguri	114	26.31 N	88.44 E
Jalpaiguri □[5]	114	26.40 N	89.00 E
Jalpan	224	21.14 N	99.29 W
Jalpug ≃	68	45.41 N	28.35 E
Jalpug, Ozero ◎	38	45.25 N	28.37 E
Jalta (Yalta), S.S.S.R.	68	44.30 N	34.10 E
Jalta, S.S.S.R.	73	46.58 N	37.16 E
Jaltemba, Bahía C	224	21.05 N	105.16 W
Jaltepec ≃	224	17.26 N	94.59 W
Jáltipan	224	17.58 N	94.42 W
Jaltocán	224	21.09 N	98.32 W
Jaltuškov	68	48.58 N	27.30 E
Jālū	136	29.02 N	21.32 E
Jālū, Wāḥat ⊤[4]	136	29.02 N	21.32 E
Jaluit I[1]	14	6.00 N	169.35 E
Jalutorovsk	76	56.40 N	66.18 E
Jam, S.S.S.R.	72	55.29 N	37.45 E
Jam, S.S.S.R.	75	40.07 N	68.11 E
Jama	73	48.52 N	38.06 E
Jamaare ≃	140	12.06 N	10.14 E
Jāmāibāti	262b	22.51 N	88.08 E
Jamaica	230p	20.12 N	75.09 W
Jamaica ⊸[8]	266	40.42 N	73.47 W
Jamaica □[1]	220		
	231q	18.15 N	77.30 W
Jamaica Bay C	200	40.36 N	73.51 W
Jamaica Channel ⋓	228	18.00 N	75.30 W
Jamaica Plain ⊸[8]	273	42.19 N	71.06 W
Jamaika → Jamaica □[1]	231q	18.15 N	77.30 W
Jamaïque → Jamaica □[1]	231q	18.15 N	77.30 W
Jamal, Poluostrov >[1]	64	70.00 N	70.00 E
Jam-Alin', Chrebet ⋀	79	53.00 N	134.36 E
Jamālīyah ⊸[8]	263c	30.03 N	31.16 E
Jamalo-Neneckij Nacionalnyj Okrug □[8]	24	66.30 N	64.00 E
Jamālpur, Bhārat	114	25.18 N	86.30 E
Jamālpur, Bngl.	114	24.55 N	89.56 E
Jamālpurganj	116	23.04 N	87.59 E
Jamame	134	0.04 N	42.46 E
Jamanari ≃	236	2.58 S	68.53 W
Jamanchalinka	70	47.40 N	51.35 E
Jamantau, Gora ∧	62	54.15 N	58.06 E
Jamanxim ≃	240	4.43 S	56.18 W
Jamapará	246	21.55 S	42.43 W
Jamari ≃	238	8.27 S	63.30 W
Jamari, Lago ◎	240	1.26 S	56.35 W
Jamarovka	78	50.38 N	110.16 E
Jamašurma	70	55.58 N	49.36 E
Jamay	224	20.18 N	102.43 W
Jamba	142	13.50 S	15.30 E
Jāmbād	116	22.42 N	86.35 E
Jambeiro	246	23.16 S	45.41 W
Jambeiro, Serra do ⋀[2]	246	23.13 S	45.38 W
Jambelí, Canal de ⋓	236	3.00 S	80.00 W
Jamberoo	160	34.39 S	150.47 E
Jambes	52	50.28 N	4.52 E
Jambi □[4]	102	1.30 S	103.00 E
Jambin	156	24.12 S	150.22 E
Jamboeye ≃	104	5.16 N	97.29 E
Jambol	38	42.29 N	26.30 E
Jambol □[4]	120	42.10 N	26.30 E
Jambongan, Pulau I	102	6.40 N	117.27 E
Jambuair, Tanjung >	104	5.16 N	97.30 E
Jambusar	110	22.03 N	72.48 E
James ≃, Austl.	156	20.36 S	137.41 E
James ≃, Alta., Can.	172	51.55 N	114.34 W
James ≃, U.S.	188	42.52 N	97.18 W
James ≃, Mo., U.S.	184	36.45 N	93.30 W
James ≃, Va., U.S.	182	36.57 N	76.26 W
James, Isla I	244	44.57 S	74.07 W
James, Lake ◎	206	41.42 N	85.02 W
James, Lake ◎[1]	182	35.45 N	81.55 W
Jamesābād	110	25.17 N	69.15 E
James Bay C	166	53.30 N	80.30 W
Jamesburg	198	40.21 N	74.26 W
James Bypass ≊	216	36.41 N	120.16 W
James City, N.C., U.S.	182	35.05 N	77.02 W
James City, Pa., U.S.	204	41.37 N	78.50 W
James City □[6]	198	37.17 N	76.48 W
James Craik	242	32.09 S	63.28 W
James Creek	204	40.23 N	78.10 W
James Gardens ♠	265b	43.40 N	79.31 W
James Island	214	48.37 N	123.22 W
James Island I	198	38.31 N	76.20 W
James M. Cox Dayton Municipal Airport ⊠	208	39.54 N	84.13 W
Jameson Raid Memorial ⊥	263d	26.11 S	27.49 E
James Point >	182	25.21 N	76.24 W
Jamesport	184	39.58 N	93.48 W
James Price Point >	152	17.30 S	122.08 E
James Ranges ⋀	152	24.06 S	132.30 E
James River Bridge ⊸[5]	198	37.00 N	76.30 W
James Ross, Cape >	166	74.40 N	114.25 W
James Ross Island I	9	64.15 S	57.45 W
James Ross Strait ⋓	166	69.40 N	95.30 W
James Smith Indian Reserve ⊸[4]	174	53.08 N	104.52 W
Jamestown, Austl.	156	33.12 S	138.36 E
Jamestown, S. Afr.	148	31.06 S	26.45 E
Jamestown, Calif., U.S.	216	37.57 N	120.25 W
Jamestown, Kans., U.S.	188	39.36 N	97.52 W
Jamestown, Ky., U.S.	184	36.59 N	85.04 W
FRANÇAIS Nom	**Page**	**Lat.°′**	**Long.°′ W=Ouest**
Jamestown, Mich., U.S.	206	42.50 N	85.51 W
Jamestown, N.C., U.S.	182	35.59 N	79.56 W
Jamestown, N. Dak., U.S.	188	46.54 N	98.42 W
Jamestown, N.Y., U.S.	204	42.06 N	79.14 W
Jamestown, Ohio, U.S.	208	39.39 N	83.44 W
Jamestown, Pa., U.S.	204	41.29 N	80.27 W
Jamestown, R.I., U.S.	197	41.30 N	71.22 W
Jamestown, Tenn., U.S.	184	36.26 N	84.57 W
Jamestown ⊥	198	37.12 N	76.46 W
Jamestown Festival Park ♠	198	37.14 N	76.48 W
Jamestown Reservoir ◎[1]	188	47.15 N	98.40 W
Jamesville, N.Y., U.S.	200	42.59 N	76.04 W
Jamesville, Va., U.S.	198	37.31 N	75.56 W
Jamet, Lac ◎	196	46.34 N	74.30 W
Jametz	52	49.26 N	5.23 E
Jamgarh ∧	113	34.35 N	73.37 E
Jamieson ≃	159	37.18 S	146.08 E
Jamiltepec	224	16.17 N	97.49 W
Jaminauá ≃	238	9.20 S	70.59 W
Jaminsk	66	52.46 N	28.16 E
Jaminskij	70	50.21 N	42.14 E
Jāmira ≃	116	21.45 N	87.02 E
Jamira ≃[1]	116	21.35 N	88.28 E
Jamison	198	40.16 N	75.05 W
Jamison City	200	41.18 N	76.22 W
Jamison Town	264a	33.46 S	150.41 E
Jam-Ižora	255a	59.42 N	30.36 E
Jamjodhpur	110	21.54 N	70.01 E
Jamkhandi	112	16.31 N	75.18 E
Jamki	76	59.33 N	66.47 E
Jamkino	72	55.55 N	38.24 E
Jamm	66	58.26 N	28.03 E
Jammalamadugu	112	14.50 N	78.24 E
Jammerbugten C	26	57.20 N	9.30 E
Jammerland Bugt C	41	55.35 N	11.05 E
Jammu	113	32.42 N	74.52 E
Jammu Airport ⊠	113	32.42 N	74.51 E
Jammu and Kashmir □[2]	110	34.00 N	76.00 E
Jāmnagar	110	22.28 N	70.04 E
Jamnotri	110	31.01 N	78.27 E
Jamoigne	52	49.42 N	5.25 E
Jamor ≃	256c	38.42 N	9.15 W
Jampang-kulon	105a	7.16 S	106.37 E
Jampol', S.S.S.R.	68	49.58 N	26.14 E
Jampol', S.S.S.R.	68	51.57 N	33.46 E
Jampol', S.S.S.R.	68	48.16 N	28.17 E
Jampol', S.S.S.R.	73	48.56 N	37.58 E
Jāmpur, Bhārat	262b	22.56 N	88.12 E
Jāmpur, Pāk.	113	29.39 N	70.36 E
Jämsä	26	61.52 N	25.12 E
Jamsah	130	27.38 N	33.35 E
Jämsänkoski	26	61.55 N	25.11 E
Jamshedpur	116	22.48 N	86.11 E
Jamsk	64	59.35 N	154.10 E
Jamskaja Sloboda	72	55.29 N	36.01 E
Jāmtāra	116	23.57 N	86.48 E
Jämtland □[9]	26	63.30 N	14.00 E
Jämtlands Län □[6]	24	63.00 N	14.40 E
Jamuāni	116	21.57 N	86.14 E
Jamuga	72	56.24 N	36.40 E
Jamūi	114	24.55 N	86.13 E
Jamuna ≃	114	23.51 N	89.45 E
Jamundí	236	3.15 N	76.32 W
Jāmuria	116	23.44 N	87.02 E
Jāmurki	116	24.09 N	90.02 E
Jana ≃	64	71.31 N	136.32 E
Janāi	262b	22.43 N	88.16 E
Janāj	132	31.00 N	30.46 E
Janajkino	70	50.43 N	51.06 E
Janas	256c	38.49 N	9.26 W
Janauacá, Lago ◎	236	3.28 S	60.17 W
Janaúba	245	15.48 S	43.19 W
Janaucu, Ilha I	240	0.30 N	50.10 W
Janaul	76	56.16 N	54.56 E
Jand	113	33.26 N	72.01 E
Janda, Laguna de la ◎	34	36.15 N	5.51 W
Jandaia	245	17.06 S	50.07 W
Jandaia do Sul	245	23.36 S	51.39 W
Jandaíra	240	11.34 S	37.47 W
Jandalī, Wādī al- ∨	132	30.05 N	31.52 E
Jandaq	118	34.02 N	54.26 E
Jandiāla	113	31.36 N	75.03 E
Jandiatuba ≃	236	3.28 S	68.42 W
Jandira	246	23.31 S	46.54 W
Jandowae	156	26.47 S	151.06 E
Jandrakinot	170	64.54 N	172.32 W
Jándula ≃	34	38.03 N	4.06 W
Jándula, Embalse de ◎[1]	34	38.30 N	4.00 W
Janeiro ≃	240	11.51 S	45.09 W
Jane Peak ∧	162	45.20 S	168.19 E
Janes Island I	198	38.00 N	75.52 W
Janes Island State Park ♠	198	38.00 N	75.52 W
Janesville, Calif., U.S.	194	40.18 N	120.32 W
Janesville, Minn., U.S.	180	44.07 N	93.42 W
Janesville, Wis., U.S.	206	42.41 N	89.01 W
Jangal Bādhāl	116	23.07 N	89.21 E
Jangamo	146	24.06 S	35.21 E
Jangany	147b	23.14 S	45.27 E
Jangaon	112	17.43 N	79.11 E
Jangarej	24	68.46 N	61.25 E
Jangel'skij	76	53.08 N	58.59 E
Jangel'urta, Gora ∧[2]	24	67.33 N	38.02 E
Jangeru	102	2.20 S	116.29 E
Jangiabad	75	41.08 N	70.05 E
Jangi-Bazar	75	41.40 N	70.53 E
Jangijer	75	40.17 N	68.50 E
Jangijul'	75	41.07 N	69.03 E
Jangikišlak	75	40.25 N	67.10 E
Jangikurgan, S.S.S.R.	75	40.34 N	71.09 E
Jangikurgan, S.S.S.R.	75	41.12 N	71.44 E
Jangipāra	116	22.45 N	88.04 E
Jangipur	114	24.28 N	88.04 E
Jangong	104	4.23 N	96.48 E
Jangulovo	70	56.26 N	50.25 E
Janikowo	30	52.45 N	18.07 E
Janīn	122	32.28 N	35.18 E
Janīn, Sabkhat al- ◎	136	30.30 N	21.00 E
Janina → Ioánnina	38	39.40 N	20.50 E
Janino	255a	59.56 N	30.36 E
Janisjarvi, Ozero ◎	24	61.59 N	30.57 E
Janiuay	106	10.58 N	122.30 E
Janja	38	44.40 N	19.15 E
Janjina, Jugo.	36	42.56 N	17.26 E
Janjina, Madag.	147b	20.30 S	45.50 E
Janka	116	21.52 N	87.56 E
Janka ≃	66	55.22 N	27.31 E
Jankan, Chrebet ⋀	78	55.45 N	118.00 E
Jankāpur	116	21.54 N	87.23 E
Jan Kempdorp (Andalusia)	148	27.55 S	24.51 E
Jan Lake ◎	174	54.55 N	102.55 W
Janlohong	102	2.15 N	117.03 E
Jan Mayen I	10	71.00 N	8.20 W
Jannale	134	1.50 N	44.42 E
Jannali	264a	34.01 S	151.04 E
Jannali Park ♠	264a	34.01 S	151.03 E
Janos	222	30.54 N	108.10 W
Janos, Río de ≃	222	30.56 N	108.08 W
Jánoshalma	30	46.18 N	19.20 E
Jánosháza	30	47.08 N	17.10 E
János-hegy ∧	254c	47.31 N	18.58 E
Janov	68	49.28 N	28.21 E
Janoviči	66	55.17 N	30.42 E
Janowiec Wielkopolski	30	52.46 N	17.31 E
PORTUGUÊS Nome	**Página**	**Lat.°′**	**Long.°′ W=Oeste**
Janów Lubelski	30	50.43 N	22.24 E
Jānsath	114	29.20 N	77.51 E
Jansen	174	51.47 N	104.43 W
Jansenville	148	32.57 S	24.40 E
Janskij	64	68.28 N	134.48 E
Janskij Zaliv C	64	71.50 N	136.00 E
Jantarnyj	66	54.52 N	19.57 E
Jantetelco	224	18.42 N	98.46 W
Jantikovo	70	55.32 N	47.48 E
Jantra ≃	38	43.38 N	25.34 E
Januária	245	15.29 S	44.22 W
Januário Cicco	240	6.09 S	35.35 W
Jan Van Riebeeck Park ♠	263d	26.10 S	27.59 E
Janvarcevo	70	51.26 N	52.15 E
Janville	46	48.12 N	1.53 E
Janville-sur-Juine	251	48.31 N	2.16 E
Janvry	251	48.39 N	2.09 E
Jany-Kurgan	75	43.55 N	67.15 E
Janzé	32	47.58 N	1.30 W
Janzūr	132	30.41 N	31.02 E
Jaora	110	23.38 N	75.08 E
Japan □[1]	80		
	82	36.00 N	138.00 E
Japan, Sea of ⊤[2]	80	40.00 N	135.00 E
Japan Basin ✣[1]	12	40.00 N	135.00 E
Japanisches Meer → Japan, Sea of ⊤[2]	80	40.00 N	135.00 E
Japaratinga	240	9.05 S	35.15 W
Japaratuba	240	10.35 S	36.57 W
Japeri	246	22.39 S	43.40 W
Japi	240	6.27 S	35.56 W
Japiim	238	7.37 S	72.54 W
Japla	114	24.33 N	84.01 E
Japoatã	240	10.20 S	36.48 W
Japon → Japan □[1]	82	36.00 N	138.00 E
Japón, Mar del → Japan, Sea of ⊤[2]	80	40.00 N	135.00 E
Japtiksal'a	64	69.21 N	72.32 E
Japuíba	246	22.35 S	42.42 W
Japurá	236	1.48 S	66.30 W
Japurá (Caquetá) ≃	236	3.08 S	64.46 W
Jaqué	236	7.31 N	78.10 W
Jaqui	238	15.30 S	74.26 W
Jar	70	58.15 N	52.06 E
Jarābulus	120	36.49 N	38.01 E
Jarad	134	18.59 N	41.24 E
Jaradū	132	29.18 N	30.42 E
Jaraguá	245	15.45 S	49.20 W
Jaraguá ⊸[8]	277b	23.27 S	46.44 W
Jaraguá, Pico do ∧	277b	23.26 S	46.46 W
Jaraguá do Sul	242	26.29 S	49.04 W
Jaraicejo	34	39.40 N	5.49 W
Jaraiz de la Vera	34	40.04 N	5.45 W
Jaral del Progreso	224	20.22 N	101.04 W
Jarales	190	34.37 N	106.46 W
Jarama ≃	34	40.02 N	3.39 W
Jarama, Canal del ≊	256a	40.18 N	3.32 W
Jaramānah	122	33.29 N	36.21 E
Jaramillo	244	47.11 S	67.09 W
Jaramor	70	56.07 N	48.44 E
Jaran' ≃	70	57.35 N	48.14 E
Jarandilla	34	40.08 N	5.39 W
Jaransk	70	57.19 N	47.54 E
Jarānwāla	113	31.20 N	73.26 E
Jarash	122	32.17 N	35.54 E
Jarawī, Wādī ∨	132	29.47 N	31.19 E
Jarbah, Jabal al- ∧	132	30.16 N	32.03 E
Jarbah, Wāḥat ⊤[4]	130	29.21 N	25.20 E
Jarbidge ≃	192	42.19 N	115.39 W
Järbo	40	60.43 N	16.36 E
Jarcevo	66	55.04 N	32.41 E
Jardas al-'Abīd	136	32.19 N	20.56 E
Jardim, Bra.	238	21.28 S	56.09 W
Jardim, Bra.	240	7.35 S	39.16 W
Jardim América ⊸[8]	277b	23.34 S	46.41 W
Jardim de Angicos	240	5.39 S	35.59 W
Jardim de Piranhas	240	6.22 S	37.20 W
Jardim do Seridó	240	6.35 S	36.46 W
Jardim Paulista ⊸[8]	277b	23.35 S	46.40 W
Jardín América	242	27.03 S	55.14 W
Jardines de la Reina II	230p	20.50 N	78.55 W
Jardines del Pedregal de San Angel	276a	19.18 N	99.13 W
Jardinópolis	245	21.02 S	47.46 W
Jardymly	74	38.55 N	48.15 E
Jaredi	140	12.46 N	5.05 E
Jarega	24	63.27 N	53.26 E
Jaremča	68	48.27 N	24.33 E
Jarenga	24	62.43 N	49.30 E
Jarensk	24	62.11 N	49.02 E
Järfälla	40	59.24 N	17.50 E
Jargara	68	46.27 N	28.27 E
Jargeau	46	47.52 N	2.07 E
Jari ≃, Bra.	238	5.07 S	62.21 W
Jari ≃, Bra.	240	1.09 S	51.54 W
Jari, Lago ◎	236	5.00 S	62.19 W
Jāria Jhānjail	114	25.02 N	90.39 E
Jaridih	114	23.38 N	86.04 E
Jarinu	246	23.06 S	46.44 W
Jarkino	78	59.08 N	99.23 E
Jarkovo	76	57.24 N	67.05 E
Jarkul'-Mat'uškino	76	55.51 N	76.06 E
Järlåsa	40	59.53 N	17.12 E
Jarmah	136	26.33 N	13.04 E
Jarmen	50	53.55 N	13.20 E
Jarmolincy	68	49.12 N	26.50 E
Järna	40	59.06 N	17.34 E
Jarnac	32	45.41 N	0.10 W
Jarny	52	49.09 N	5.53 E
Jaro	106	11.11 N	124.47 E
Jarochta	78	58.58 N	98.58 E
Jarocin	30	51.59 N	17.31 E
Jaroměř	30	50.21 N	15.55 E
Jaropolec	72	56.08 N	35.49 E
Jaroslavec	68	51.33 N	33.40 E
Jaroslavl'	70	57.37 N	39.52 E
Jaroslavl' □[4]	72	56.45 N	38.45 E
Jaroslavskaja	74	44.36 N	40.27 E
Jaroslavskij	79	44.10 N	132.13 E
Jaroslavskij Vokzal ⊸[5]	255b	55.47 N	37.39 E
Jarosław	30	50.02 N	22.42 E
Jarovaja	73	49.03 N	37.37 E
Järpen	26	63.21 N	13.29 E
Jarrahdale	158a	32.20 S	116.04 E
Jarratt	198	36.48 N	77.28 W
Jarrell	212	30.49 N	97.36 W
Jarrettsville	198	39.36 N	76.29 W
Jarrīs	132	27.55 N	30.46 E
Jarrow	42	54.59 N	1.29 W
Jarry, Parc ♠	265a	45.32 N	73.38 W
Jar-Sale	64	66.50 N	70.50 E
Jarsomovy	76	60.15 N	73.38 E
Jaru	238	10.26 S	62.27 W
Jaruco	230p	23.03 N	82.01 W
Jaruu	78	48.08 N	96.45 E
Järva-Jaani	66	59.02 N	25.53 E
Järvakandi	66	58.47 N	24.49 E
Järvelä	26	60.52 N	25.17 E
Järvenpää	26	60.28 N	25.06 E
Jarvie	172	54.27 N	113.59 W
Jarville-la-Malgrange	54	48.40 N	6.13 E
Jarvis	202	42.53 N	80.06 W
Jarvisburg	182	36.09 N	75.52 W
Jarvis Island I	14	0.23 S	160.02 W
Järvsö	26	61.43 N	16.10 E
Jarw, Tallat al- ∧[2]	132	30.36 N	30.13 E
Jarwa	114	27.39 N	82.31 E
Jasaan	106	8.39 N	124.45 E
Jasai	262c	18.56 N	73.01 E
Jašalta	70	46.20 N	42.17 E
Jasašnaja Tašla	70	53.55 N	48.16 E
Jaša Tomić	38	45.27 N	20.51 E
Jasdan	110	22.02 N	71.12 E
Jasel'da ≃	66	52.07 N	26.28 E
Jasenevo ⊸[8]	255b	55.36 N	37.33 E
Jasenki	68	51.32 N	38.12 E
Jasenovoje	72	54.10 N	36.47 E
Jasenovskij	73	48.10 N	39.10 E
Jasenskaja	68	46.22 N	38.16 E
Jashpurnagar	114	22.54 N	84.09 E
Jāshpur Pāts ⊸[1]	114	22.55 N	84.00 E
Jasidih	114	24.31 N	86.39 E
Jasień	30	51.46 N	15.01 E
Jasienica	50	53.37 N	14.32 E
Jasikan	140	7.24 N	0.28 E
Jašil'kul', Ozero ◎	110	37.45 N	72.55 E
Jasin	104	2.19 N	102.26 E
Jasin'a	68	48.16 N	24.20 E
Jasinga	105a	6.29 S	106.27 E
Jasinovataja	73	48.08 N	37.51 E
Jasinovka	73	48.08 N	37.57 E
Jāsk	118	25.38 N	57.46 E
Jaskhar	262c	18.54 N	72.59 E
Jaškino	76	55.54 N	85.26 E
Jaškul'	70	46.11 N	45.21 E
Jasło	30	49.45 N	21.29 E
Jasmine Estates	210	28.17 N	82.42 W
Jasmund >[1]	50	54.32 N	13.35 E
Jasnogorka	73	48.47 N	37.33 E
Jasnogorsk	72	54.29 N	37.42 E
Jasnomorskij	79	46.45 N	141.54 E
Jasnyj, S.S.S.R.	76	51.04 N	59.58 E
Jasnyj, S.S.S.R.	79	53.17 N	127.59 E
Jason Islands II	244	51.05 S	61.00 W
Jason Peninsula >[1]	9	66.10 S	61.00 W
Jasonville	184	39.10 N	87.12 W
Jasper, Alta., Can.	172	52.53 N	118.05 W
Jasper, Ala., U.S.	184	33.50 N	87.17 W
Jasper, Ark., U.S.	184	36.00 N	93.11 W
Jasper, Fla., U.S.	182	30.31 N	82.57 W
Jasper, Ga., U.S.	182	34.28 N	84.26 W
Jasper, Ind., U.S.	184	38.24 N	86.56 W
Jasper, Mich., U.S.	206	41.48 N	84.02 W
Jasper, Minn., U.S.	188	43.51 N	96.24 W
Jasper, Mo., U.S.	184	37.20 N	94.18 W
Jasper, N.Y., U.S.	200	42.07 N	77.30 W
Jasper, Tenn., U.S.	184	35.04 N	85.38 W
Jasper, Tex., U.S.	184	30.55 N	94.01 W
Jasper □[6]	206	40.57 N	87.09 W
Jasper Lake ◎	172	53.07 N	118.00 W
Jasper National Park ♠	172	52.53 N	118.03 W
Jaspur	114	29.17 N	78.49 E
Jasra	114	25.17 N	81.48 E
Jassans-Riottier	54	45.59 N	4.45 E
Jassar	113	32.06 N	74.57 E
Jassy → Iaşi	38	47.10 N	27.35 E
Jastarnia	30	54.43 N	18.40 E
Jastrebarsko	36	45.40 N	15.39 E
Jastrebovka, S.S.S.R.	68	51.27 N	37.32 E
Jastrebovka, S.S.S.R.	72	54.36 N	36.24 E
Jastrow → Jastrowie	30	53.26 N	16.49 E
Jastrowie	30	53.26 N	16.49 E
Jaswantnagar	114	26.53 N	78.55 E
Jászapáti	30	47.31 N	20.09 E
Jászberény	30	47.30 N	19.55 E
Jat, Uad el ∨	138	26.45 N	13.03 W
Jataí	245	17.53 S	51.43 W
Jatapu ≃	236	2.13 S	58.17 W
Jatate ≃	226	16.15 N	91.17 W
Jati, Bra.	240	7.41 S	39.01 W
Jāti, Pāk.	110	24.21 N	68.16 E
Jatibarang	105a	6.28 S	108.17 E
Jatibonico	230p	21.56 N	79.10 W
Jatibonico del Sur ≃	230p	21.33 N	79.09 W
Jatilawang	105a	7.32 S	109.06 E
Jatinegara ⊸[8]	259e	6.13 S	106.52 E
Jatiroto	105a	8.07 S	113.21 E
Jatisrono	105a	7.49 S	111.07 E
Játiva	34	38.59 N	0.31 W
Jatiwangi	105a	6.44 S	108.15 E
Jatni	110	20.10 N	85.42 E
Jatobá ≃	245	12.23 S	54.07 W
Jatoi Janūbi	113	29.31 N	70.51 E
Jātrāpur	116	22.44 N	89.45 E
Jatt (Tel Gat)	122	32.24 N	35.02 E
Jatung	114	27.29 N	88.55 E
Jatznick	50	53.35 N	13.56 E
Jáu, Ang.	142	15.12 S	13.31 E
Jaú, Bra.	245	22.18 S	48.33 W
Jaú ≃	236	1.54 S	61.26 W
Jauaperi ≃	236	1.26 S	61.35 W
Jauer → Jawor	30	51.03 N	16.11 E
Jaugrām	116	23.06 N	88.05 E
Jauja	238	11.48 S	75.30 W
Jauli	262a	28.44 N	77.21 E
Jaumave	224	23.25 N	99.23 W
Jaúna ≃	238	6.24 S	59.57 W
Jaunde → Yaoundé	142	3.52 N	11.31 E
Jaune, Mer → Yellow Sea ⊤[2]	80	36.00 N	123.00 E
Jaungulbene	66	57.04 N	26.36 E
Jaunjelgava	66	56.37 N	25.05 E
Jaunpass)(	54	46.36 N	7.20 E
Jaunpiebalga	66	57.11 N	26.03 E
Jaunpils	66	56.44 N	23.01 E
Jaunpur	114	25.44 N	82.41 E
Jaunpur □[5]	114	25.40 N	82.40 E
Jaupaci	245	16.18 S	50.54 W
Jauquara ≃	238	15.06 S	57.06 W
Jáuregui	248	34.36 S	59.10 W
Jauru ≃, Bra.	238	16.22 S	57.46 W
Jauru ≃, Bra.	245	18.40 S	54.36 W
Jausiers	56	44.25 N	6.44 E
Jauza ≃	255b	55.45 N	37.38 E
Java	188	45.30 N	99.53 W
Java → Jawa I	105a	7.30 S	110.00 E
Java Center	200	42.39 N	78.23 W
Javādi Hills ⋀[2]	112	12.35 N	78.50 E
Javalambre ∧	34	40.06 N	1.03 W
Javan	75	38.19 N	69.02 E
Javari (Yavarí) ≃	232	4.21 S	70.02 W
Javas	70	54.26 N	42.51 E
Java Sea → Jawa, Laut ⊤[2]	102	5.00 S	110.00 E
Java Trench ✣[1]	12	10.00 S	110.00 E
Java Village	200	42.40 N	78.26 W
Jávea	34	38.47 N	0.10 E
Jävenitz	50	52.31 N	11.30 E
Javier, Isla I	244	47.06 S	74.24 W
Javkino	68	47.16 N	32.37 E
Javlenka	76	54.21 N	68.27 E
Javor ⋀	38	44.05 N	18.55 E
Javorie ∧	30	48.27 N	19.18 E
Javorník	30	50.23 N	17.00 E
Javorníky ⋀	30	49.20 N	18.20 E
Javorov	68	49.56 N	23.23 E
Javorová skála ∧	30	49.31 N	14.30 E
Javr ≃	24	68.09 N	30.06 E
Jävre	26	65.09 N	21.59 E
Jawa (Java) I	105a	7.30 S	110.00 E
Jawa, Laut (Java Sea) ⊤[2]	102	5.00 S	110.00 E
Jawa Barat □[4]	105a	7.00 S	107.00 E
Jawāla Mukhi	113	31.53 N	76.19 E
Jaw'alīyāt, Jabal al- ∧	122	31.26 N	36.26 E
Jawa Tengah □[4]	105a	7.30 S	110.00 E
Jawa Timur □[4]	105a	8.00 S	113.00 E
Jawbar	122	33.31 N	36.19 E
Jawf, Wādī al- ∨	134	15.50 N	45.35 E
Jawi	102	0.48 S	109.16 E
Jawor	30	51.03 N	16.11 E
Jaworzno	30	50.13 N	19.15 E
Jay, Fla., U.S.	184	30.57 N	87.09 W
Jay, Okla., U.S.	186	36.25 N	94.48 W
Jay □[6]	206	40.26 N	84.59 W
Jaya, Puncak ∧	154	4.05 S	137.11 E
Jayamkondacholapuram	112	11.13 N	79.22 E
Jayanca	238	6.24 S	79.50 W
Jayapura (Sukarnapura)	154	2.32 S	140.42 E
Jay Cooke State Park ♠	180	46.41 N	92.23 W
Jaydebpur	114	24.00 N	90.26 E
Jaynagar	116	22.36 N	90.42 E
Jaynagar Majilpur	116	22.11 N	88.25 E
Jaynes	190	32.16 N	111.01 W
Jay Peak ∧	178	44.55 N	72.32 W
Jaypur	116	23.03 N	87.27 E
Jayrūd	120	33.49 N	36.44 E
Jayton	186	33.15 N	100.34 W
Jayuya	230m	18.13 N	66.36 W
Jaywick	44	51.47 N	1.08 E
Jaz	70	54.54 N	45.13 E
Jažełbicy	66	58.02 N	32.58 E
Jazevec	24	65.43 N	46.30 E
Jazgulem ≃	75	38.12 N	71.21 E
Jazīrat Muḥammad	263c	30.07 N	31.12 E
Jazjavan	75	40.39 N	71.44 E
Jažma	24	66.56 N	44.29 E
Jaz Mūrīān, Hāmūn-e ◎	118	27.20 N	58.55 E
Jazovaja	76	49.27 N	85.20 E
Jazykovo	70	54.18 N	47.24 E
Jazzīn	122	33.32 N	35.34 E
Jbā'	122	33.29 N	35.31 E
J B Thomas, Lake ◎[1]	186	32.35 N	101.10 W
J. C. Murphey Lake ◎	206	40.58 N	87.30 W
Jdiouia	34	35.57 N	0.50 E
Jeanerette	184	29.55 N	91.40 W
Jeanesville	200	40.56 N	75.58 W
Jeannette	204	40.20 N	79.35 W
Jebāl Bārez, Kūh-e ⋀	118	28.30 N	58.20 E
Jebba	140	9.08 N	4.50 E
Jebel	38	45.33 N	21.14 E
Jeber-Bergfrieden	50	51.59 N	12.20 E
Jeberos	238	5.17 S	76.13 W
Jebri	110	27.18 N	65.44 E
Jebus	102	1.44 S	105.29 E
Jechegnadzor	74	39.46 N	45.21 E
Jedarma	78	58.44 N	102.36 E
Jedburgh	42	55.29 N	2.34 W
Jedburgh Abbey ⊍[1]	42	55.27 N	2.34 W
Jeddore Lake ◎[1]	176	48.03 N	55.55 W
Jedelevo	70	53.24 N	47.45 E
Jedepo	140	5.16 N	8.20 W
Jedincy	68	48.10 N	27.19 E
Jedisa	74	42.31 N	44.16 E
Jedlesee ⊸[8]	254b	48.16 N	16.23 E
Jednevo	72	56.06 N	36.14 E
Jedogon	78	54.15 N	100.15 E
Jedrovo	66	57.55 N	33.38 E
Jędrzejów	30	50.39 N	20.18 E
Jedwabne	30	53.17 N	22.19 E
Jed Water ≃	42	55.32 N	2.33 W
Jeetzel (Jeetze) ≃	50	53.09 N	11.04 E
Jefawa	130	10.57 N	23.48 E
Jeffers	188	44.03 N	95.12 W
Jefferson, Ga., U.S.	182	34.07 N	83.35 W
Jefferson, Ind., U.S.	206	40.17 N	86.36 W
Jefferson, Iowa, U.S.	188	42.01 N	94.23 W
Jefferson, Md., U.S.	198	39.22 N	77.32 W
Jefferson, Mass., U.S.	197	42.22 N	71.53 W
Jefferson, N.J., U.S.	275	39.45 N	75.13 W
Jefferson, N.C., U.S.	182	36.26 N	81.28 W
Jefferson, N.Y., U.S.	200	42.14 N	73.54 W
Jefferson, N.Y., U.S.	200	42.29 N	74.37 W
Jefferson, Ohio, U.S.	204	41.44 N	80.46 W
Jefferson, Oreg., U.S.	192	44.43 N	123.01 W
Jefferson, Pa., U.S.	269b	39.56 N	80.04 W
Jefferson, S.C., U.S.	182	34.39 N	80.23 W
Jefferson, S. Dak., U.S.	188	42.36 N	96.34 W
Jefferson, Tex., U.S.	184	32.46 N	94.21 W
Jefferson, Wis., U.S.	206	43.00 N	88.48 W
Jefferson □[6], Ill., U.S.	209	38.19 N	88.55 W
Jefferson □[6], Ind., U.S.	208	38.44 N	85.23 W
Jefferson □[6], Ky., U.S.	208	38.14 N	85.10 W
Jefferson □[6], Mo., U.S.	209	38.20 N	90.34 W
Jefferson □[6], N.Y., U.S.	202	43.59 N	75.55 W
Jefferson □[6], Ohio, U.S.	204	40.22 N	80.37 W
Jefferson □[6], Pa., U.S.	204	41.09 N	79.05 W
Jefferson □[6], Wash., U.S.	214	47.50 N	122.36 W
Jefferson □[6], Wis., U.S.	206	43.02 N	88.46 W
Jefferson ≃	192	45.56 N	111.30 W
Jefferson, Mount ∧, U.S.	192	44.34 N	111.30 W
Jefferson, Mount ∧, Idaho, U.S.	192	44.34 N	111.30 W
Jefferson, Mount ∧, Nev., U.S.	194	38.46 N	116.55 W
Jefferson, Mount ∧, Oreg., U.S.	192	44.40 N	121.47 W
Jefferson City, Mo., U.S.	209	38.34 N	92.10 W
Jefferson City, Tenn., U.S.	182	36.07 N	83.30 W
Jefferson Park ⊸[8]	268	41.59 N	87.46 W
Jefferson Proving Ground ■	208	38.50 N	85.25 W
Jeffersonton	178	38.38 N	77.55 W
Jeffersontown	208	38.12 N	85.35 W
Jefferson Village	274c	38.52 N	77.10 W
Jeffersonville, Ga., U.S.	182	32.41 N	83.20 W
Jeffersonville, Ind., U.S.	208	38.17 N	85.44 W
Jeffersonville, N.Y., U.S.	200	41.20 N	73.47 W
Jeffersonville, Ohio, U.S.	208	39.39 N	83.34 W
Jeffrey City	190	42.29 N	107.49 W
Jefimovka	70	52.13 N	52.03 E
Jefimovskij	66	59.30 N	35.02 E
Jefremov	66	53.09 N	38.07 E
Jefremova	72	56.13 N	38.59 E
Jefremovka	73	47.19 N	38.29 E
Jefremovo-Stepanovka	68	48.43 N	40.50 E
Jefremovskaja	72	55.25 N	38.59 E
Jega	140	12.15 N	4.23 E
Jegenstorf	54	47.03 N	7.30 E
Jegindybulak, S.S.S.R.	76	49.45 N	76.23 E
Jegindybulak, S.S.S.R.	76	48.42 N	81.48 E
Jegorjevka	79	50.42 N	127.42 E
Jegorjevsk	72	55.23 N	39.02 E
Jegorlyk ≃	70	46.33 N	41.52 E
Jeguitinhonha	245	16.26 S	41.00 W
Jehol → Chengde	95	40.58 N	117.53 E
Jeinemeni, Cerro ∧	244	46.52 S	72.14 W
Jeja ≃	68	46.41 N	38.36 E
Jejsk	68	46.42 N	38.16 E
Jejskij Liman C	68	46.42 N	38.25 E
Jeju → Cheju	80	33.31 N	126.32 E
Jejui Guazú ≃	242	24.13 S	57.09 W
Jejur	262b	22.53 N	88.08 E
Jēkabpils	66	56.29 N	25.51 E
Jekaterinburg → Sverdlovsk	76	56.51 N	60.36 E
Jekaterinino	66	55.49 N	33.58 E
Jekaterininskoje	76	56.53 N	74.34 E
Jekaterinoslav → Dnepropetrovsk	68	48.27 N	34.59 E
Jekaterinoslavka	79	50.23 N	129.08 E
Jekaterinovka, S.S.S.R.	68	46.42 N	38.46 E
Jekaterinovka, S.S.S.R.	70	53.04 N	49.28 E
Jekaterinovka, S.S.S.R.	70	52.03 N	44.21 E
Jekaterinovka, S.S.S.R.	70	46.32 N	41.42 E
Jekaterinovka, S.S.S.R.	73	47.33 N	38.23 E
Jekaterinovka, S.S.S.R.	76	54.36 N	70.58 E
Jekaterinovka ⊸[8]	255b	55.46 N	37.23 E
Jekaterinovskaja	68	46.20 N	39.58 E
Jekateriny, Proliv ⋓	64	53.53 N	140.25 E
Jekimoviči	66	54.07 N	33.18 E
Jekpindykurylys	70	47.49 N	47.17 E
Jekyll Island I	182	31.04 N	81.25 W
Jekyll Island State Park ♠	182	31.02 N	81.25 W
Jelabuga	70	55.47 N	52.04 E
Jelai ≃, Indon.	102	2.59 S	110.45 E
Jelai ≃, Malay.	104	4.04 N	102.20 E
Jelan', S.S.S.R.	70	50.57 N	43.44 E
Jelan', S.S.S.R.	70	52.13 N	44.11 E
Jelan', S.S.S.R.	73	48.41 N	39.47 E
Jelan', S.S.S.R.	76	57.39 N	63.42 E
Jelan' ≃, S.S.S.R.	70	50.56 N	43.45 E
Jelan' ≃, S.S.S.R.	70	51.07 N	41.26 E
Jelancy	78	52.49 N	106.25 E
Jelanec	68	47.42 N	31.51 E
Jelanka	76	55.37 N	75.18 E
Jelan'-Koleno	68	51.09 N	41.14 E
Jelan'-Kolenovskij	68	51.10 N	41.10 E
Jelatak	164r	6.56 N	158.17 E
Jelat'ma	70	54.58 N	41.45 E
Jelaur, S.S.S.R.	70	54.34 N	50.21 E
Jelaur, S.S.S.R.	70	53.50 N	48.48 E
Jelchovka	70	53.51 N	50.18 E
Jel'covka	76	53.15 N	86.15 E
Jel'cy, S.S.S.R.	66	56.40 N	33.51 E
Jel'cy, S.S.S.R.	72	56.11 N	38.46 E
Jelec	66	52.37 N	38.30 E
Jeleckij	24	67.03 N	64.10 E
Jelenia Góra (Hirschberg)	30	50.55 N	15.46 E
Jelenskij	66	53.29 N	35.23 E
Jelgava	66	56.39 N	23.42 E
Jelgavkrasti	66	57.28 N	24.26 E
Jelisejevka	68	47.02 N	36.24 E
Jelizarovo, S.S.S.R.	68	48.12 N	34.33 E
Jelizarovo, S.S.S.R.	70	58.33 N	44.50 E
Jelizavetgradka	68	48.48 N	32.24 E
Jelizavetinka, S.S.S.R.	76	51.28 N	71.12 E
Jelizavetinka, S.S.S.R.	76	51.46 N	59.45 E
Jelizavetopol'skoje	76	52.51 N	60.36 E
Jelizavetovka	68	46.39 N	38.53 E
Jelizavety, Mys >	79	54.27 N	142.42 E
Jelizovo	66	53.24 N	29.01 E
Jelli	144	5.22 N	31.48 E
Jellico	132	36.35 N	84.08 W
Jelling	41	55.45 N	9.26 E
Jelloway	204	40.33 N	82.18 W
Jelm Mountain ∧	190	41.06 N	105.58 W
Jel'n'a	66	54.35 N	33.11 E
Jelnat'	70	57.20 N	42.49 E
Jel'niki	70	54.37 N	43.53 E
Jeloguj ≃	64	63.13 N	87.45 E
Jel'onovka, S.S.S.R.	73	47.50 N	37.40 E
Jel'onovka, S.S.S.R.	73	48.39 N	38.01 E
Jelošnoje	76	55.27 N	66.44 E
Jelovo	70	57.03 N	54.54 E
Jels	41	55.21 N	9.12 E
Jelšanka, S.S.S.R.	70	51.49 N	46.23 E
Jelšanka, S.S.S.R.	70	52.35 N	47.59 E
Jelšanka Pervaja	70	52.53 N	52.02 E
Jelšava	30	48.39 N	20.14 E
Jel'sk	68	51.48 N	29.09 E
Jemaa	140	9.27 N	8.23 E
Jemaja, Pulau I	102	2.55 N	105.45 E
Jemaluang	104	2.17 N	103.52 E
Jemantajevo	70	53.34 N	53.50 E
Jemanželinsk	76	54.45 N	61.20 E
Jemappes	46	50.27 N	3.53 E
Jember	105a	8.10 S	113.42 E
Jemca	24	63.04 N	40.20 E
Jemca ≃	24	63.15 N	41.20 E
Jemeljanovka	68	45.32 N	34.53 E
Jemeljanovo	76	56.11 N	92.40 E
Jemel'stan	24	61.13 N	52.29 E
Jemen → Yemen □[1]	134	15.00 N	44.00 E
Jemen, Volksrepublik → Yemen, People's Democratic Republic of □[1]	134	15.00 N	48.00 E
Jemeppe	52	50.37 N	5.30 E
Jemez ≃	190	35.22 N	106.31 W
Jemez Springs	190	35.46 N	106.42 W
Jemgum	48	53.16 N	7.23 E
Jemil'čino	68	50.52 N	27.48 E
Jemnice	30	49.01 N	15.35 E
Jemniště ⊥	30	49.45 N	14.48 E
Jempang, Danau ◎	102	0.26 S	116.12 E
Jena, D.D.R.	50	50.56 N	11.35 E
Jena, La., U.S.	184	31.41 N	92.08 W
Jenakijevo	73	48.14 N	38.13 E
Jenašimskij Polkan, Gora ∧	64	59.50 N	92.52 E
Jenaz	54	46.55 N	9.45 E
Jenbach	58	47.24 N	11.47 E
Jenbek	76	48.53 N	77.12 E
Jendarata	104	3.55 N	100.57 E
Jendongin	78	53.27 N	113.01 E
Jendouba (Souk el Arba)	138	36.30 N	8.47 E
Jendouba □[8]	36	36.30 N	8.45 E
Jeneponto	102	5.41 S	119.42 E
Jenera	206	40.54 N	83.44 W
Jeniang	104	5.49 N	100.38 E
Jenisej ≃	62	71.50 N	82.40 E
Jenisejsk	76	58.27 N	92.10 E
Jenisejskij Kr'až ⋀	64	59.00 N	93.00 E
Jenisejskij Zaliv C	64	72.30 N	80.00 E
Jenison	206	42.54 N	85.47 W
Jenkins	212	32.59 N	94.44 W
Jenkins, Mount ∧	152	25.36 S	129.41 E
Jenkinson Lake ◎[1]	216	38.44 N	120.33 W
Jenkinsville	182	34.16 N	81.17 W
Jenkintown	198	40.06 N	75.08 W
Jenks	186	36.01 N	95.58 W
Jenli	90	23.15 N	120.08 E
Jenners	204	40.09 N	79.03 W
Jennersdorf	30	46.57 N	16.08 E
Jennerstown	204	40.10 N	79.04 W
Jennifer Branch ≃	274b	39.25 N	76.30 W
Jennings, Fla., U.S.	182	30.36 N	83.06 W
Jennings, La., U.S.	184	30.13 N	92.39 W
Jennings, Mo., U.S.	209	38.44 N	90.17 W
Jennings □[6]	208	38.59 N	85.36 W
Jennings Creek ≃	206	40.53 N	84.17 W
Jennings Lodge	214	45.24 N	122.38 W
Jenotajevka	70	47.15 N	47.03 E
Jensen	190	40.22 N	109.17 W
Jensen Beach	210	27.15 N	80.14 W
Jens Munk Island I	166	69.42 N	79.30 W
Jenu	102	0.36 S	109.52 E
Jen'uka	78	57.58 N	121.42 E
Jenya	134	4.12 N	37.32 E
Jeonju → Chŏnju	88	35.49 N	127.08 E
Jepač	24	66.58 N	61.22 E
Jepara	105a	6.35 S	110.39 E
Jeparit	156	36.09 S	141.59 E
Jepelacio	238	6.07 S	76.57 W
Jepichin	70	48.16 N	45.14 E
Jepifan'	66	53.49 N	38.33 E
Jeppener	248	35.17 S	58.12 W
Jeptha Knob ∧[2]	208	38.11 N	85.07 W
Jepua (Jeppo)	26	63.24 N	22.37 E
Jequeri	245	20.27 S	42.40 W
Jequetepeque ≃	238	7.21 S	79.36 W
Jequié	245	13.51 S	40.05 W
Jequitaí	245	17.15 S	44.28 W
Jequitinhonha ≃	245	15.51 S	38.53 W

English	Deutsch	Español	Français	Português
≃ River	Fluss	Río	Rivière	Rio
≊ Canal	Kanal	Canal	Canal	Canal
⌞ Waterfall, Rapids	Wasserfall, Stromschnellen	Cascada, Rápidos	Chute d'eau, Rapides	Cascata, Rápidos
⋓ Strait	Meeresstrasse	Estrecho	Détroit	Estreito
C Bay, Gulf	Bucht, Golf	Bahía, Golfo	Baie, Golfe	Baía, Golfo
◎ Lake, Lakes	See, Seen	Lago, Lagos	Lac, Lacs	Lago, Lagos
≡ Swamp	Sumpf	Pantano	Marais	Pântano
⊼ Ice Features, Glacier	Eis- und Gletscherformen	Accidentes Glaciales	Formes glaciaires	Acidentes Glaciares
⊤ Other Hydrographic Features	Andere Hydrographische Objekte	Otros Elementos Hidrográficos	Autres données hydrographiques	Outros Elementos Hidrográficos
✣ Submarine Features	Untermeerische Objekte	Accidentes Submarinos	Formes de relief sous-marin	Acidentes Submarinos
□ Political Unit	Politische Einheit	Unidad Politica	Entité politique	Unidade Política
⊍ Cultural Institution	Kulturelle Institution	Institución Cultural	Institution culturelle	Instituição Cultural
⊥ Historical Site	Historische Stätte	Sitio Histórico	Site historique	Sitio Histórico
♠ Recreational Site	Erholungs- und Ferienort	Sitio de Recreo	Centre de loisirs	Sítio de Lazer
⊠ Airport	Flughafen	Aeropuerto	Aéroport	Aeroporto
■ Military Installation	Militäranlage	Instalación Militar	Installation militaire	Instalação Militar
⊸ Miscellaneous	Verschiedenes	Misceláneo	Divers	Miscelânea

Symbols in the index entries represent the broad categories identified in the key at the right. Symbols with superior numbers (∧[2]) identify subcategories (see complete key on page I · 26).

Kartensymbole in dem Registerverzeichnis stellen die rechts in Schlüssel erklärten Kategorien dar. Symbole mit hochgestellten Ziffern (∧[2]) bezeichnen Unterabteilungen einer Kategorie (vgl. vollständiger Schlüssel auf Seite I · 26).

Los símbolos incluidos en el texto del índice representan las grandes categorías identificadas con la clave a la derecha. Los símbolos con números en su parte superior (∧[2]) identifican las subcategorías (véase la clave completa en la página I · 26).

Les symboles de l'index représentent les catégories indiquées dans la légende à droite. Les symboles suivis d'un indice (∧[2]) représentent des sous-catégories (voir légende complète à la page I · 26).

Os símbolos incluídos no texto do índice representam as grandes categorias identificadas com a chave à direita. Os símbolos com números em sua parte superior (∧[2]) identificam as subcategorias (veja-se a chave completa à página I · 26).

	English	Deutsch	Español	Français	Português
∧	Mountain	Berg	Montaña	Montagne	Montanha
∧	Mountains	Berge	Montañas	Montagnes	Montanhas
)(	Pass	Pass	Paso	Col	Passo
∨	Valley, Canyon	Tal, Cañon	Valle, Cañón	Vallée, Canyon	Vale, Canhão
≃	Plain	Ebene	Llano	Plaine	Planície
>	Cape	Kap	Cabo	Cap	Cabo
I	Island	Insel	Isla	Île	Ilha
II	Islands	Inseln	Islas	Îles	Ilhas
⊛	Other Topographic Features	Andere Topographische Objekte	Otros Elementos Topográficos	Autres données topographiques	Outros Elementos Topográficos

ESPAÑOL — Nombre · Página · Lat. · Long. W=Oeste
FRANÇAIS — Nom · Page · Lat. · Long. W=Ouest
PORTUGUÊS — Nome · Página · Lat. · Long. W=Oeste

Nombre / Nom / Nome	Página / Page	Lat.	Long.
Johannesburg, Calif., U.S.	218	35.22 N	117.38 W
Johannesburg (Jan Smuts) Airport ⊠	263d	26.08 S	28.14 E
Johanngeorgenstadt	50	50.26 N	12.43 E
Johannisburg → Pisz	30	53.38 N	21.49 E
Johanniskreuz	52	49.20 N	7.49 E
Johannisthal ✦[8]	254a	52.26 N	13.30 E
Johar	134	2.48 N	45.33 E
Jōhen	82	32.57 N	132.35 E
Johi	110	26.41 N	67.37 E
Johilla ≃	114	23.37 N	81.14 E
John ≃	170	66.55 N	151.35 W
John Boyd Thacher State Park ♠	200	42.38 N	74.01 W
John Carroll University ⊍[2]	269a	41.29 N	81.32 W
John Day	192	44.25 N	118.57 W
John Day ≃	192	45.44 N	120.39 W
John Day, Middle Fork ≃	192	44.55 N	119.18 W
John Day, North Fork ≃	192	44.45 N	119.38 W
John Day, South Fork ≃	192	44.28 N	119.31 W
John Day Dam ✦[6]	214	45.43 N	120.41 W
John Day Fossil Beds National Monument ♠	192	44.34 N	119.39 W
Johney Creek ≃	186	28.27 N	98.54 W
John Fitzgerald Kennedy International Airport ⊠	200	40.38 N	73.47 W
John Fitzgerald Kennedy Space Center ⊍[3]	210	28.40 N	80.40 W
John Fitzgerald Kennedy Stadium ♠	275	39.54 N	75.10 W
John Forrest National Park ♠	158a	31.53 S	116.06 E
John Hancock Center ⊍	268	41.55 N	87.37 W
John J. Duffy Preserve ♠	268	41.39 N	87.55 W
John Martin Reservoir ⊜[1]	188	38.05 N	103.02 W
John McLaren Park ♠	272	37.43 N	122.25 W
John Muir National Historical Site ⊥	272	37.59 N	122.08 W
Johnny Run ≃	206	41.17 N	88.21 W
John O'Groats	28	58.38 N	3.05 W
John Pennekamp Coral Reef State Park ♠	210	25.11 N	80.15 W
John Redmond Reservoir ⊜[1]	188	38.18 N	95.55 W
Johns ≃	214	46.54 N	124.01 W
Johns Creek ≃	182	37.30 N	80.06 W
Johns Hopkins University ⊍[2]	274b	39.20 N	76.37 W
Johnson, Kans., U.S.	188	37.34 N	101.45 W
Johnson, Nebr., U.S.	188	40.24 N	96.01 W
Johnson, N.Y., U.S.	200	41.22 N	74.30 W
Johnson, Vt., U.S.	178	44.38 N	72.41 W
Johnson □[6], Ind., U.S.	208	39.29 N	86.03 W
Johnson □[6], Tex., U.S.	212	32.20 N	97.20 W
Johnson, Mount ∧	216	36.37 N	121.19 W
Johnson Bay C	198	38.03 N	75.20 W
Johnsonburg, N.J., U.S.	200	40.58 N	74.53 W
Johnsonburg, N.Y., U.S.	200	42.44 N	78.18 W
Johnsonburg, Pa., U.S.	204	41.29 N	78.41 W
Johnson City, N.Y., U.S.	200	42.07 N	75.57 W
Johnson City, Tenn., U.S.	182	36.19 N	82.21 W
Johnson City, Tex., U.S.	186	30.17 N	98.25 W
Johnson Creek, N.Y., U.S.	200	43.15 N	78.31 W
Johnson Creek, Wis., U.S.	206	43.05 N	88.47 W
Johnson Creek ≃, Idaho, U.S.	192	44.58 N	115.30 W
Johnson Creek ≃, Ky., U.S.	208	38.27 N	84.04 W
Johnson Creek ≃, N.Y., U.S.	200	43.22 N	78.16 W
Johnson Creek ≃, Tex., U.S.	212	32.02 N	94.59 W
Johnson Creek ≃, Wash., U.S.	214	46.35 N	121.42 W
Johnsondale	194	35.58 N	118.32 W
Johnson Drain ☰	271	42.26 N	83.28 W
Johnson Draw ∨, Tex., U.S.	186	31.58 N	101.41 W
Johnson Draw ∨, Tex., U.S.	186	30.08 N	101.07 W
Johnson Hall ⊥	200	43.01 N	74.23 W
Johnson Park ♠	266	40.30 N	74.27 W
Johnson Point ≻	231h	13.07 N	61.12 W
Johnsons Crossing	170	60.29 N	133.16 W
Johnsons Pond ⊜	273	42.44 N	71.03 W
Johnsons Station	212	32.42 N	97.08 W
Johnsonville, N.Z.	162	41.14 S	174.47 E
Johnsonville, N.Y., U.S.	200	42.55 N	73.31 W
Johnsonville, S.C., U.S.	182	33.49 N	79.27 W
Johnston, Wales, U.K.	44	51.46 N	5.00 W
Johnston, Iowa, U.S.	180	41.40 N	93.42 W
Johnston, R.I., U.S.	197	41.50 N	71.30 W
Johnston, S.C., U.S.	182	33.50 N	81.48 W
Johnston, Lake ⊜	152	32.25 S	120.30 E
Johnston City	184	37.49 N	88.56 W
Johnstone	42	55.50 N	4.31 W
Johnstone Peak ∧	270	34.10 N	117.48 W
Johnstone Strait ⊔	172	50.25 N	126.00 W
Johnston Falls ⊾	144	10.35 S	28.40 E
Johnston Island I	14	17.00 N	168.30 W
Johnstown, Colo., U.S.	190	40.20 N	104.54 W
Johnstown, N.Y., U.S.	200	43.00 N	74.22 W
Johnstown, Ohio, U.S.	204	40.09 N	82.41 W
Johnstown, Pa., U.S.	204	40.20 N	78.55 W
Johnstown Center	206	42.42 N	88.50 W
Johnstown Flood National Memorial ⊥	204	40.21 N	78.47 W
John Tyler Arboretum ♠	275	39.56 N	75.26 W
Jōhoku	84	36.28 N	140.22 E
Johol	104	2.36 N	102.16 E
Johor □[3]	104	2.00 N	103.30 E
Johor ≃	104	1.27 N	104.02 E
Johor, Selat ⊔	261c	1.28 N	103.48 E
Johor Baharu	104		
	261c	1.28 N	103.45 E
Jöhstadt	50	50.30 N	13.05 E
Joice Island I	272	38.08 N	122.02 W
Joigny	46	47.59 N	3.24 E
Joiner	184	35.31 N	90.09 W
Joinerville	212	32.11 N	94.55 W
Joinvile	242	26.18 S	48.50 W
Joinville	54	48.27 N	5.08 E
Joinville, Lac ⊜	196	46.18 N	75.12 W
Joinville Island I	9	63.15 S	55.45 W
Joinville-le-Pont	251	48.49 N	2.28 E
Jojogan	105a	6.58 S	111.46 E
Jojutla	224	18.37 N	99.11 W
Joka	262b	22.27 N	88.18 E
Jokaj I	164r	6.59 N	158.11 E
Jokaj Passage ⊔	164r	7.01 N	158.11 E
Jokau	130	8.24 N	33.49 E
Jokau ≃	134	8.22 N	33.47 E
Jokela	26	60.44 N	25.02 E
Jokioinen	26	60.49 N	23.28 E
Jokkmokk	24	66.37 N	19.50 E
Jökulsá á Brú ≃	24a	65.41 N	14.13 W
Jolārpettai	112	12.34 N	78.35 E
Jolfā	74	38.57 N	45.38 E
Joliet, Ill., U.S.	206	41.32 N	88.05 W
Joliet, Mont., U.S.	192	45.29 N	108.58 W
Joliett	198	40.37 N	76.27 W
Joliette	196	46.01 N	73.27 W
Joliette □[6]	196	46.25 N	74.00 W
Jolietville	208	40.03 N	86.15 W
Jöllenbeck	48	52.11 N	8.45 E
Jolly's Lookout National Park ♠	161a	27.25 S	152.45 E
Jollyville	212	30.27 N	97.47 W
Jolo	106	6.03 N	121.00 E
Jolo Group II	106	6.00 N	121.09 E
Jolo Island I	106	5.58 N	121.06 E
Jølstravatnet ⊜	26	61.32 N	6.13 E
Jomalig Island I	106	14.42 N	122.22 E
Jombang	105a	7.33 S	112.14 E
Jombo ≃	142	10.36 S	17.32 E
Jonacatepec	224	18.41 N	98.48 W
Jonah	212	30.38 N	97.32 W
Jonåker	40	58.44 N	16.40 E
Jonathan Dickinson State Park ♠	210	27.01 N	80.08 W
Jonava	66	55.05 N	24.17 E
Jones, Pil.	106	16.33 N	121.42 E
Jones, Mich., U.S.	206	41.54 N	85.48 W
Jones, Okla., U.S.	186	35.34 N	97.17 W
Jones ≃	273	42.00 N	70.42 W
Jones and Laughlin Steel Corporation ⊍[3], Pa., U.S.	269b	40.26 N	79.58 W
Jones and Laughlin Steel Corporation ⊍[3], Pa., U.S.	269b	40.37 N	80.14 W
Jones Beach State Park ♠	200	40.35 N	73.31 W
Jonesboro, Ark., U.S.	184	35.50 N	90.42 W
Jonesboro, Ga., U.S.	182	33.32 N	84.21 W
Jonesboro, Ill., U.S.	184	37.27 N	89.16 W
Jonesboro, Ind., U.S.	206	40.29 N	85.38 W
Jonesboro, La., U.S.	184	32.15 N	92.43 W
Jonesboro, Maine, U.S.	178	44.40 N	67.35 W
Jonesboro, Tenn., U.S.	182	36.18 N	82.28 W
Jonesburg	209	38.51 N	91.18 W
Jones Creek	212	28.58 N	95.27 W
Jones Creek ≃, Ont., Can.	202	44.30 N	75.49 W
Jones Creek ≃, Tex., U.S.	212	29.08 N	96.03 W
Jones Falls ≃	274b	39.18 N	76.37 W
Jones Falls, Moores Branch ≃	274b	39.23 N	76.40 W
Jones Falls, North Branch ≃	274b	39.25 N	76.42 W
Jones Falls, Slaughterhouse Branch ≃	274b	39.24 N	76.40 W
Jones Inlet C	200	40.35 N	73.34 W
Jones Mill	184	34.27 N	92.50 W
Jones Mountains ⩕	9	73.32 S	94.00 W
Jonesport	178	44.32 N	67.36 W
Jones Sound ⊔	166	76.00 N	85.00 W
Jonestown	184	34.14 N	90.28 W
Jonesville, Ind., U.S.	208	39.04 N	85.53 W
Jonesville, La., U.S.	184	31.38 N	91.49 W
Jonesville, Mich., U.S.	206	41.59 N	84.40 W
Jonesville, N.C., U.S.	182	36.15 N	80.51 W
Jonesville, N.Y., U.S.	200	42.55 N	73.49 W
Jonesville, S.C., U.S.	182	34.50 N	81.41 W
Jonesville, Va., U.S.	182	36.41 N	83.07 W
Jong ≃	140	7.32 N	12.23 W
Jonggol	105a	6.28 S	107.03 E
Jongkha	110	28.57 N	85.15 E
Jongunjärvi ⊜	26	65.17 N	27.15 E
Jónico, Mar → Ionian Sea ⊤[2]	22	39.00 N	19.00 E
Joniškėlis	66	56.02 N	24.10 E
Joniškis	66	56.14 N	23.37 E
Jonkersberg	148	33.55 S	22.15 E
Jönköping	26	57.47 N	14.11 E
Jönköpings Län □[6]	26	57.30 N	14.30 E
Jonquière	176	48.24 N	71.15 W
Jonquières	56	44.07 N	4.54 E
Jonsdorf	50	50.51 N	14.43 E
Jonstorp	41	56.14 N	12.40 E
Jontoy	134	0.05 S	42.35 E
Jonuta	222	18.05 N	92.08 W
Jonvilliers	251	48.34 N	1.42 E
Jonzac	32	45.27 N	0.26 W
Joplin, Mo., U.S.	184	37.06 N	94.31 W
Joplin, Mont., U.S.	192	48.34 N	110.46 W
Joppa, Ill., U.S.	184	37.12 N	88.51 W
Joppa, Md., U.S.	198	39.26 N	76.22 W
Jóquei Clube ♠	277b	23.35 S	46.41 W
Joquicingo	224	19.03 N	99.33 W
Jora	114	26.20 N	77.49 E
Jordan, Pil.	106	10.40 N	122.35 E
Jordan, Minn., U.S.	180	44.40 N	93.37 W
Jordan, Mont., U.S.	192	47.19 N	106.55 W
Jordan, N.Y., U.S.	200	43.04 N	76.28 W
Jordan □[1]	108	31.00 N	36.00 E
Jordan □[1]	118	31.00 N	38.00 E
Jordan (Nahr al-Urdunn) (HaYarden) ≃	122	31.46 N	35.33 E
Jordan ≃, B.C., Can.	214	48.26 N	124.08 W
Jordan ≃, Utah, U.S.	190	40.49 N	112.08 W
Jordan Bay C	176	43.45 N	65.12 W
Jordan Creek ≃	192	42.52 N	117.38 W
Jordânia	245	15.54 S	40.11 W
Jordania → Jordan □[1]	118	31.00 N	36.00 E
Jordanie → Jordan □[1]	118	31.00 N	36.00 E
Jordanien → Jordan □[1]	118	31.00 N	36.00 E
Jordan Lake ⊜	206	42.46 N	85.09 W
Jordanów	30	49.40 N	19.50 E
Jordans	250	51.37 N	0.36 W
Jordan Valley	192	42.58 N	117.03 W
Jordanville	200	42.55 N	74.57 W
Jordão ≃	242	25.46 S	52.07 W
Jordbro	40	59.09 N	18.07 E
Jördenstorf	50	53.52 N	12.37 E
Jordet	26	61.25 N	12.09 E
Jorge, Cabo ≻	244	51.39 S	75.17 W
Jorge Grego, Ilha I	246	23.13 S	44.09 W
Jorge Montt, Isla I	244	51.20 S	74.45 W
Jorge Montt, Ventisquero ⊼	244	48.17 S	73.30 W
Jorge V, Costade → George V Coast ⊤[2]	9	68.30 S	147.30 E
Jorge VI, Estrecho de → George VI Sound ⊔	9	71.00 S	68.00 W
Jorhāt	110	26.45 N	94.13 E
Jörlfeld	41	54.38 N	9.15 E
Jorm	110	36.52 N	70.51 E
Jörn	26	65.04 N	20.02 E
Jornado del Muerto ✦[2]	190	33.20 N	106.50 W
Joroinen	26	62.11 N	27.50 E
Jorong	102	3.58 S	114.56 E
Jöröö	78	49.43 N	106.42 E
Jöröö ≃	78	49.54 N	106.08 E
Jørpeland	26	59.01 N	6.03 E
J'orzovka	70	48.56 N	44.38 E
Jos	140	9.55 N	8.53 E
Jose Abad Santos	106	5.38 N	125.27 E
José Batlle y Ordóñez	242	33.28 S	55.07 W
José Bonifácio	245	21.03 S	49.41 W
José Cardel	224	19.22 N	96.22 W
José C. Paz	248	34.30 S	58.45 W
José de Freitas	240	4.45 S	42.35 W
José de San Martín	244	44.02 S	70.29 W
José Enrique Rodó (Drabble)	248	33.41 S	57.34 W
Joselândia	238	16.32 S	56.12 W
José María Blanco (Tres Lomas)	242	36.27 S	62.51 W
José Martí, Aeropuerto Internacional ⊠	276b	23.00 N	82.24 W
Jose Panganiban	106	14.17 N	122.41 E
José Pedro ≃	245	19.32 S	41.25 W
José Pedro Varela	242	33.27 S	54.32 W
Joseph	192	45.21 N	117.14 W
Joseph, Lac ⊜	166	52.45 N	65.15 W
Joseph, Lake ⊜	202	45.14 N	79.45 W
Joseph Bonaparte Gulf C	154	14.15 S	128.30 E
Joseph City	190	34.57 N	110.20 W
Joseph Creek ≃	192	46.03 N	117.01 W
Josephine, Pa., U.S.	204	40.29 N	79.11 W
Josephine, Tex., U.S.	212	33.04 N	96.19 W
Josephine, Lake ⊜	210	27.24 N	81.26 W
Josephine Peak ∧	270	34.17 N	118.09 W
Josephstaal	154	4.44 S	145.01 E
José Santos Arévalo	248	35.10 S	59.14 W
Jōshima	86	33.15 N	130.26 E
Joshīmath	110	30.34 N	79.34 E
Jōshin'etsu-kōgen-kokuritsu-kōen ♠	84	36.46 N	138.40 E
Joshua	212	32.28 N	97.23 W
Joshua Creek ≃	265b	43.29 N	79.37 W
Joshua Tree	194	34.08 N	116.19 W
Joshua Tree National Monument ♠	194	33.55 N	116.00 W
Joshua Trees State Park ♠	218	34.41 N	117.47 W
Joškar-Ola	70	56.38 N	47.52 E
Jos Plateau ⩕[1]	140	9.30 N	9.00 E
Jossa	52	50.14 N	9.35 E
Josselin	32	47.57 N	2.33 W
Jossigny	46	48.50 N	2.45 E
Jostedalsbreen ⊼	26	61.40 N	7.00 E
Jost Van Dyke Island I	230m	18.28 N	64.45 W
Jōtō, Nihon	86	34.42 N	134.04 E
Jōtō, Nihon	86	35.03 N	135.17 E
Jōtō ✦[8]	260	34.42 N	135.34 E
Jotunheimen ⩕	26	61.38 N	8.18 E
Jotunheimen Nasjonalpark ♠	26	61.35 N	8.30 E
Jouan, Récif ✣[2]	165f	20.39 S	167.01 E
Jouarre	46	48.56 N	3.08 E
Jouars-Pontchartrain	251	48.47 N	1.54 E
Joubertina	148	33.50 S	23.51 E
Joué-lès-Tours	46	47.21 N	0.40 E
Jougne	54	46.46 N	6.24 E
Jouques	56	43.38 N	5.38 E
Jourdanton	186	28.55 N	98.33 W
Joure	48	52.57 N	5.47 E
Joutsa	26	61.44 N	26.07 E
Joutseno	26	61.06 N	28.30 E
Joutsijärvi	24	66.40 N	28.00 E
Joux, Lac de ⊜	54	46.38 N	6.18 E
Joux, Vallée de ∨	54	46.35 N	6.15 E
Jouy	46	48.31 N	1.33 E
Jouy-en-Josas	251	48.46 N	2.10 E
Jouy-le-Moutier	251	49.01 N	2.03 E
Jouy-le-Potier	46	47.45 N	1.49 E
Jovellanos	230p	22.48 N	81.12 W
Jovellar	106	13.04 N	123.36 E
Jovet, Mont ∧	56	45.30 N	6.39 E
Joviânia	245	17.49 S	49.30 W
Jovita	242	34.30 S	63.56 W
Jowai	110	25.27 N	92.12 E
Jowlaenga, Mount ∧	152	17.21 S	122.56 E
Jowzjān □[4]	110	36.30 N	66.00 E
Joy	180	41.12 N	90.55 W
Joy, Mount ∧	170	63.46 N	132.55 W
Joya, Laguna de la C	224	15.55 N	93.40 W
Joyeuse	56	44.29 N	4.14 E
Jōyō	86	34.51 N	135.47 E
Joyous Pavilion Park ♠	261a	39.52 N	116.22 E
Joyuda	230m	18.07 N	67.11 W
Józefów	30	52.09 N	21.12 E
Jozini Dam ✦[6]	148	27.25 S	32.05 E
Juaba	240	2.23 S	49.33 W
Juagdan	106	10.00 N	124.35 E
Juami ≃	236	1.45 S	67.30 W
Ju'an	90	31.45 N	113.11 E
Juanacatlán	224	20.31 N	103.10 W
Juana Díaz	230m	18.03 N	66.31 W
Juan Aldama	222	24.19 N	103.21 W
Juan Anchorena ✦[8]	278	34.29 S	58.30 W
Juana Ramírez, Isla I	224	21.50 N	97.40 W
Juan Atucha	248	35.32 S	59.21 W
Juan B. Arruabarrena	242	30.20 S	58.19 W
Juan Blanco, Arroyo ≃	248	35.05 S	57.26 W
Juancheng	88	35.35 N	115.29 E
Juan de Fuca, Strait of ⊔	214	48.18 N	124.00 W
Juan de Garay	244	38.52 S	64.34 W
Juan de Mena	242	24.55 S	56.44 W
Juan de Nova, Île I	128	17.03 S	42.45 E
Juan Díaz Covarrubias	224	18.07 N	95.09 W
Juan E. Barra	242	37.48 S	60.29 W
Juan Eugenio	222	25.10 N	103.20 W
Juan Fernández, Islas II	234	33.00 S	80.00 W
Juan González Grande, Arroyo ≃	248	34.00 S	58.14 W
Juan González Romero	276a	19.30 N	99.04 W
Juangriego	236	11.05 N	63.57 W
Juan Gualberto Gómez	230p	22.52 N	81.33 W
Juan Guerra	238	6.35 S	76.21 W
Juanita, Méx.	224	17.47 N	95.09 W
Juanita, Wash., U.S.	214	47.42 N	122.13 W
Juan Jorba	242	33.37 S	65.16 W
Juan José Castelli	242	25.57 S	60.37 W
Juanjuí	238	7.11 S	76.45 W
Juankoski	26	63.04 N	28.21 E
Juan-les-Pins	56	43.34 N	7.06 E
Juan L. Lacaze	248	34.26 S	57.27 W
Juan N. Fernández	242	38.00 S	59.16 W
Juan Perez Sound ⊔	172	52.30 N	131.18 W
Juan Rodríguez Clara	224	18.00 N	95.25 W
Juan Tronconi	248	35.30 S	59.15 W
Juan Viñas	226	9.54 N	83.45 W
Juanziba	97	30.32 N	104.59 E
Juárez, Arg.	242	37.40 S	59.48 W
Juárez → Ciudad Juárez, Méx.	222	31.44 N	106.29 W
Juárez, Méx.	222	27.37 N	100.44 W
Juárez, Méx.	224	17.39 N	93.10 W
Juárez, Cerro ∧	224	20.37 N	99.17 W
Juárez, Sierra de ⩕	222	32.00 N	115.50 W
Juarzon	140	5.20 N	8.52 W
Juatinga, Ponta de ≻	246	23.17 S	44.30 W
Juàzeirinho	240	7.04 S	36.35 W
Juàzeiro	240	9.25 S	40.30 W
Juàzeiro do Norte	240	7.12 S	39.20 W
Jūbā	144	4.51 N	31.37 E
Juba ≃, Afr.	134	0.12 S	42.40 E
Juba ≃, Bra.	238	14.59 S	57.44 W
Jubachstausee ⊜[1]	253	51.10 N	7.37 E
Jūbāl, Madīq (Strait of Jubal) ⊔	130	27.40 N	33.55 E
Jubal, Strait of → Jūbāl, Madīq ⊔	130	27.40 N	33.55 E
Jubayl (Byblos)	120	34.07 N	35.39 E
Jubayl, Jabal ∧[2]	132	27.25 N	30.32 E
Jubayt	130	18.57 N	36.50 E
Jubbah	118	28.02 N	40.56 E
Jubb al-Jarrāḥ	120	34.49 N	37.19 E
Jubbātā al-Khashab	122	33.13 N	35.49 E
Jubb Jannīn	122	33.37 N	35.47 E
Jubbulpore → Jabalpur	114	23.10 N	79.57 E
Jubbulpore □[5]	114	23.30 N	80.10 E
Jubilee Downs	152	18.22 S	125.17 E
Jubilee Lake ⊜, Austl.	152	29.12 S	126.38 E
Jubilee Lake ⊜, Newf., Can.	176	48.04 N	55.11 W
Jubones ≃	236	3.13 S	79.57 W
Jubundha ≃	116	24.06 N	90.20 E
Jūbu-san ∧	260	34.50 N	135.55 E
Juby, Cap ≻	138	27.58 N	12.55 W
Jucá ≃	240	6.22 S	40.08 W
Júcar ≃	34	39.09 N	0.14 W
Juçara	245	15.53 S	50.51 W
Júcaro	230p	21.37 N	78.51 W
Jucás	240	6.32 S	39.32 W
Jüchen	52	51.06 N	6.30 E
Juchhöh	50	50.24 N	11.52 E
Juchipila	224	21.25 N	103.07 W
Juchipila ≃	224	21.03 N	103.25 W
Juchitán [de Zaragoza]	224	16.26 N	95.01 W
Juchitepec	224	19.06 N	98.53 W
Juchitlán	224	20.05 N	104.07 W
Juchnov	66	54.45 N	35.14 E
Juchoviči	66	56.02 N	28.39 E
Jucu ≃	245	20.24 S	40.19 W
Jucuapa	226	13.31 N	88.24 W
Jucurucu ≃	245	17.21 S	39.13 W
Jucurutu	240	6.02 S	37.01 W
Judaea ✦[1]	122	31.35 N	35.00 E
Judas, Punta ≻	226	9.31 N	84.32 W
Judaydat al-Khās	122	33.24 N	36.33 E
Judaydat 'Arṭūz	122	33.26 N	36.10 E
Juddah (Jidda)	134	21.30 N	39.12 E
Jude Island I	176	47.15 N	54.59 W
Judenburg	30	47.10 N	14.40 E
Judian	92	27.20 N	99.36 E
Judinki, S.S.S.R.	72	54.37 N	37.17 E
Judinki, S.S.S.R.	72	55.27 N	35.48 E
Judino, S.S.S.R.	66	58.43 N	39.17 E
Judino, S.S.S.R.	70	55.51 N	48.55 E
Judino, S.S.S.R.	72	54.09 N	38.19 E
Judino, S.S.S.R.	255b	55.40 N	37.12 E
Judío, Rambla del ≃	34	38.15 N	1.27 W
Judique	176	45.52 N	61.30 W
Judith ≃	192	47.44 N	109.38 W
Judith, Point ≻	197	41.22 N	71.29 W
Judith Gap	192	46.41 N	109.45 W
Judith Mountains ⩕	192	47.12 N	109.15 W
Judith Peak ∧	192	47.13 N	109.13 W
Judoma ≃	64	59.08 N	135.06 E
Judson, S.C., U.S.	182	34.50 N	82.27 W
Judson, Tex., U.S.	212	32.35 N	94.45 W
Judsonia	184	35.16 N	91.38 W
Juehedian	95	39.26 N	117.06 E
Juelsminde	41	55.43 N	10.01 E
Jueshui ≃	90	31.42 N	113.20 E
Juexi, Zhg.	90	29.27 N	121.57 E
Juexi, Zhg.	97	28.55 N	104.16 E
Jufari ≃	236	1.13 S	62.00 W
Jufayr, Bi'r al- ⊤[4]	132	30.49 N	32.40 E
Jufiang ≃	97	28.58 N	106.16 E
Jufrah, Jabal al- ∧	132	30.09 N	31.55 E
Jufrah, Wādī al- ∨	132	30.24 N	31.35 E
Jug	76	57.43 N	56.10 E
Jug ≃	24	60.45 N	46.20 E
Jughna	130	12.24 N	25.06 E
Jugo-Kamskij	76	57.42 N	55.35 E
Jugon	32	48.25 N	2.20 W
Jugo-Osetinskaja Avtonomnaja Oblast' □[8]	74	42.20 N	44.00 E
Jugorskij Šar, Proliv ⊔	62	69.45 N	60.35 E
Jugoslavija → Yugoslavia □[1]	22	44.00 N	19.00 E
Jugoslawien → Yugoslavia □[1]	22	44.00 N	19.00 E
Jugo-Zapad ✦[8]	255b	55.40 N	37.32 E
Juḥā	134	16.41 N	42.54 E
Juhe ≃	95	39.45 N	117.35 E
Jühnsdorf	254a	52.18 N	13.23 E
Jühnsdorfer Heide ✦[3]	254a	52.19 N	13.24 E
Juhu ✦[8]	262c	19.07 N	72.49 E
Juhuadao I	88	40.29 N	120.47 E
Juhu Airport ⊠	262c	19.06 N	72.50 E
Jui	262c	19.01 N	73.05 E
Juigalpa	226	12.05 N	85.24 W
Juile	224	17.45 N	94.59 W
Juillac	32	45.19 N	1.19 E
Juilly	251	49.01 N	2.42 E
Juiná ≃	238	12.36 S	58.57 W
Juine ≃	46	48.32 N	2.23 E
Juist	48	53.40 N	6.59 E
Juist I	48	53.40 N	7.00 E
Juisui	90	23.29 N	121.23 E
Juiz de Fora	246	21.45 S	43.20 W
Jujurieux	54	46.02 N	5.25 E
Jujū-san ∧	86	33.05 N	131.15 E
Jujuy → San Salvador de Jujuy	242	24.11 S	65.18 W
Jujuy □[4]	242	23.00 S	66.00 W
Jukagirskoje Ploskogorje ⩕[1]	64	66.00 N	155.00 E
Jukamenskoje	70	57.53 N	52.15 E
Jukonda ≃	76	59.38 N	67.26 E
Juksa	76	56.55 N	85.10 E
Juksejevo	24	59.52 N	54.19 E
Jukskei ≃	263d	26.06 S	28.06 E
Jukte	64	63.23 N	105.41 E
Jula ≃	24	63.49 N	44.44 E
Julāna	114	29.08 N	76.25 E
Julayfah, Bi'r al- ⊤[4]	132	30.43 N	29.35 E
Juldybajevo	76	52.20 N	57.52 E
Julebao	88	40.09 N	113.36 E
Julesburg	188	40.59 N	102.16 W
Juli	238	16.13 S	69.27 W
Juliaca	238	15.30 S	70.08 W
Julia Creek	156	20.39 S	141.45 E
Julia Creek ≃	156	20.00 S	141.11 E
Julian	204	40.52 N	77.56 W
Juliana, Lake ⊜	210	28.07 N	81.48 W
Julianakanaal ☰	52	51.05 N	5.50 E
Julian Alps ⩕	36	46.00 N	14.00 E
Julianatop ∧	240	3.41 N	56.32 W
Julianehåb	166	60.43 N	46.01 W
Julia Pfeiffer Burns State Park ♠	216	36.10 N	120.40 W
Jülich	52	50.55 N	6.21 E
Juliénas	54	46.14 N	4.43 E
Julijske Alpe → Julian Alps ⩕	36	46.00 N	14.00 E
Julimes	222	28.25 N	105.27 W
Júlio de Castilhos	242	29.14 S	53.41 W
Julio Prestes, Estação ✦[5]	277b	23.32 S	46.38 W
Julita ⊍	40	59.09 N	16.02 E
Juliuhe	94	42.03 N	122.55 E
Juliustown	275	40.01 N	74.40 W
Jullundur	113	31.19 N	75.34 E
Julu	88	37.13 N	115.01 E
Juma	24	65.07 N	33.16 E
Juma ≃	238	4.57 S	64.31 W
Jumaguzino	76	52.54 N	56.23 E
Jumahe ≃	88	39.14 N	115.45 E
Jumapolo	105a	7.42 S	111.00 E
Jumaševo	70	54.59 N	54.25 E
Jumay, Volcán ∧[1]	226	14.41 N	89.59 W
Jumbilla	238	5.54 S	77.45 W
Jumbo, Rh.	144	17.28 S	30.55 E
Jumbo, Som.	134	0.12 S	42.38 E
Jumbo Peak ∧	194	36.12 N	114.11 W
Jumeauville	251	48.55 N	1.47 E
Jumentos Cays II	228	22.42 N	75.55 W
Jumet	46	50.26 N	4.25 E
Jumièges	46	49.26 N	0.49 E
Jumilla	34	38.29 N	1.17 W
Jumla	114	29.17 N	82.10 E
Jummayzat Banī 'Amr	132	30.48 N	31.32 E
Jump ≃	180	45.17 N	91.05 W
Jump, North Fork ≃	180	45.25 N	90.40 W
Jump, South Fork ≃	180	45.25 N	90.40 W
Jūn	122	33.35 N	35.27 E
Junāgadh	110	21.31 N	70.28 E
Ju'nan	88	35.11 N	118.51 E
Junaynah, Ra's al- ∧, Miṣr	122	29.28 N	34.02 E
Junaynah, Ra's al- ∧, Miṣr	130	29.01 N	33.58 E
Junaynat al-'Aṭash ∧[2]	132	28.51 N	31.47 E
Juncal, Isla I	248	33.58 S	58.24 W
Juncal, Serra do ∧	246	22.45 S	45.55 W
Juncal do Norte ☵	256c	38.52 N	8.59 W
Juncal do Sul ☵	256c	38.51 N	8.58 W
Juncheng	88	38.57 N	114.41 E
Juncos	230m	18.14 N	65.55 W
Junction, Tex., U.S.	186	30.29 N	99.46 W
Junction, Utah, U.S.	190	38.14 N	112.13 W
Junction City, Ark., U.S.	184	33.01 N	92.43 W
Junction City, Ill., U.S.	209	40.45 N	89.36 W
Junction City, Kans., U.S.	188	39.02 N	96.50 W
Junction City, Ky., U.S.	184	37.35 N	84.48 W
Junction City, Oreg., U.S.	192	44.13 N	123.12 W
Junction City, Wash., U.S.	214	46.58 N	123.46 W
Jundī, Qārat al- ∧[2]	132	29.39 N	30.58 E
Jundiaí	246	23.11 S	46.52 W
Jundiaí ≃, Bra.	246	23.11 S	47.16 W
Jundiaí ≃, Bra.	246	23.32 S	46.15 W
Jundiaí do Sul	245	23.27 S	50.17 W
Jundiaí-Mirim ≃	246	23.10 S	46.56 W
Jundiapeba	246	23.33 S	46.15 W
Jundushan ⩕	95	40.30 N	116.05 E
Juneau, Alaska, U.S.	170	58.20 N	134.27 W
Juneau, Wis., U.S.	180	43.24 N	88.42 W
Junee	156	34.52 S	147.35 E
June in Winter, Lake ⊜	210	27.18 N	81.24 W
June Lake	216	37.47 N	119.04 W
June Park	210	28.04 N	80.41 W
Jungapeo	224	19.27 N	100.29 W
Jungbluth Ditch ☰	269a	41.27 N	82.07 W
Jungfernheide ♠	254a	52.34 N	13.17 E
Jungfern-Inseln → Virgin Islands □[2]	228	18.00 N	64.40 W
Jungfern-See ⊜	254a	52.25 N	13.05 E
Jungfrau ∧	54	46.32 N	7.58 E
Jungfraujoch ✦[5]	54	46.33 N	7.58 E
Jungle Habitat ♠	266	41.08 N	74.21 W
Junglinster	52	49.43 N	6.15 E
Jungshāhi	110	24.51 N	67.46 E
Juniata	188	40.36 N	98.30 W
Juniata □[6]	198	40.34 N	77.24 W
Juniata ✦[8]	275	40.01 N	75.07 W
Juniata ≃	178	40.24 N	77.01 W
Juniata, Frankstown Branch ≃	204	40.34 N	78.03 W
Juniata, Raystown Branch ≃	204	40.25 N	77.58 W
Juniata Gap	204	40.33 N	78.26 W
Juniata Terrace	198	40.35 N	77.34 W
Junín, Arg.	242	34.35 S	60.57 W
Junín, Ec.	236	0.56 S	80.13 W
Junín, Perú	238	11.10 S	76.00 W
Junín □[5]	238	11.30 S	75.00 W
Junín, Lago de ⊜	238	11.02 S	76.06 W
Junín de los Andes	244	39.56 S	71.05 W
Junior	178	38.59 N	79.57 W
Juniper	176	46.33 N	67.13 W
Junipero Serra Peak ∧	216	36.08 N	121.25 W
Juniville	46	49.24 N	4.23 E
Jūniyah	120	33.59 N	35.38 E
Jun Kharchanai	113	36.52 N	75.01 E
Junkou	90	26.42 N	116.49 E
Junliangcheng	95	39.04 N	117.27 E
Junnar	112	19.12 N	73.53 E
Juno Beach	210	26.52 N	80.04 W
Junokommunarskoje ✦[8]	73	48.13 N	38.18 E
Junqueiro	240	9.56 S	36.29 W
Junqueirópolis	245	21.32 S	51.26 W
Junsele	26	63.41 N	16.54 E
Junxian, Zhg.	88	35.43 N	114.31 E
Junxian, Zhg.	92	32.42 N	111.13 E
Junzhuang	95	40.00 N	116.06 E
Jūō	84	36.40 N	140.41 E
Juodkrantė	66	55.33 N	21.08 E
Juodupė	66	56.05 N	25.37 E
Juojärvi ⊜	26	62.43 N	28.33 E
Juparanã, Lagoa ⊜	245	19.35 S	40.18 W
Jupariteua	240	1.43 S	48.23 W
Jupiá	245	20.47 S	51.39 W
Jupille	52	50.39 N	5.38 E
Jupiter	210	26.56 N	80.06 W
Jupiter ≃	176	49.29 N	63.37 W
Jupiter Inlet C	210	26.57 N	80.04 W
Jupiter Island I	210	27.04 N	80.07 W
Juqueri ≃	246	23.24 S	46.52 W
Juqueri-Mirim	246	23.21 S	46.37 W
Juqueriquerê, Serra do ⩕	246	23.43 S	45.37 W
Juquiá	242	24.19 S	47.38 W
Juquiá-Guaçu ≃	246	24.00 S	47.16 W
Juquila	224	16.14 N	97.18 W
Juquitiba	246	23.57 S	47.03 W
Jur, Česko.	30	48.15 N	17.13 E
Jur, S.S.S.R.	64	59.52 N	137.39 E
Jura □[5]	54	46.50 N	5.50 E
Jura ⩕	54	46.45 N	6.30 E
Jura I	28	56.00 N	5.50 W
Jūra ≃	66	55.03 N	29.09 E
Jura, Sound of ⊔	28	55.55 N	5.22 W
Juramento	245	16.50 S	43.35 W
Juratiški	66	54.02 N	25.54 E
Jurays wa 'Izbatuhā	132	30.19 N	30.55 E
Jurbarkas	66	55.05 N	22.48 E
Jurcevo	66	60.02 N	32.36 E
Juréia	246	21.17 S	46.22 W
Jurenino	66	59.24 N	42.47 E
Jureviči	68	51.57 N	29.32 E
Jurga	76	55.42 N	84.51 E
Jurgamyš	76	55.21 N	64.28 E
Jurgenson Woods ♠	268	41.34 N	87.36 W
Juriesfontein	148	31.40 S	22.08 E
Juring	154	6.26 S	134.20 E
Jurino	70	56.18 N	46.18 E
Jurja	24	59.03 N	49.14 E
Jurjev → Tartu	66	58.23 N	26.43 E
Jurjevec	70	57.18 N	43.06 E
Jurjevka, S.S.S.R.	68	48.44 N	36.02 E
Jurjevka, S.S.S.R.	73	48.30 N	39.00 E
Jurjev-Pol'skij	70	56.30 N	39.41 E
Jurjevskoje	72	55.05 N	36.13 E
Jurla	76	59.17 N	54.19 E
Jurlovo, S.S.S.R.	72	55.54 N	37.16 E
Jurlovo, S.S.S.R.	72	55.19 N	35.52 E
Jūrmala	66	56.58 N	23.42 E
Jurong, Sing.	261c	1.21 N	103.42 E
Jurong, Zhg.	96	31.57 N	119.10 E
Jurong ≃	261c	1.18 N	103.44 E
Jurovo, S.S.S.R.	68	51.22 N	27.50 E
Jurovo, S.S.S.R.	70	57.30 N	43.50 E
Jurovo, S.S.S.R.	72	55.30 N	38.22 E
Jurovskoje	76	59.29 N	69.02 E
Jursla	40	58.40 N	16.11 E
Jurty	78	56.03 N	97.37 E
Juruá	236	3.27 S	66.03 W
Juruá ≃	232	2.37 S	65.44 W
Juruaia	246	21.15 S	46.35 W
Juruá Mirim ≃	238	8.08 S	72.48 W
Juruàzinho ≃	238	6.01 S	69.30 W
Juruena ≃	238	7.20 S	58.03 W
Jurujuba, Enseada de C	277a	22.56 S	43.07 W
Jurupari ≃	238	7.45 S	70.10 W
Jurupari, Arquipélago do II	240	0.07 N	50.30 W
Jurupari, Ilha I	240	0.20 N	50.07 W
Juruti	240	2.09 S	56.04 W
Jur'uzan'	76	54.52 N	58.26 E
Jur'uzan' ≃	76	55.42 N	57.00 E
Jurva	26	62.41 N	21.59 E
Jušala	76	57.04 N	64.17 E
Juscelândia	245	15.20 S	51.19 W
Jusepín	236	9.45 N	63.31 W
Jushiguan	92	24.47 N	97.38 E
Jūshiyama	84	35.06 N	136.46 E
Jushui ≃	90	30.38 N	114.51 E
Juskatla	172	53.37 N	132.18 W
Jus'ki	70	56.39 N	53.05 E
Juškovo	66	59.46 N	45.11 E
Juškozero	24	64.44 N	32.06 E
Jussey	54	47.49 N	5.54 E
Justa	70	47.07 N	46.18 E
Justice	268	41.45 N	87.50 W
Justin	212	33.05 N	97.18 W
Justineberg ∧[2]	40	58.43 N	15.04 E
Justiniano Posse	242	32.53 S	62.40 W
Justino Solari	242	29.22 S	58.12 W
Justo Daract	242	33.52 S	65.11 W
Justus	204	40.42 N	81.35 W
Jusut ≃	70	56.12 N	48.23 E
Jus'va	24	58.56 N	54.57 E
Jutaí	238	5.11 S	68.54 W
Jutaí ≃	232	2.43 S	66.57 W
Jutaza	70	54.35 N	53.16 E
Jütchendorf	254a	52.16 N	13.10 E
Jüterbog	50	51.59 N	13.04 E
Juththah, Jabal al- ∧	122	30.12 N	35.36 E
Juti	245	22.52 S	54.37 W
Jutiapa	226	14.17 N	89.54 W
Jutiapa □[5]	226	14.10 N	89.50 W
Juticalpa	226	14.42 N	86.15 W
Jutiquile	226	14.45 N	86.08 W
Jutland → Jylland ≻[1]	26	56.00 N	9.15 E
Jutogh	113	31.06 N	77.07 E
Jutphaas	48	52.03 N	5.05 E
Jutrosin	30	51.40 N	17.10 E
Juupajoki	26	61.47 N	24.27 E
Juuru	66	59.04 N	24.59 E
Juva	26	61.54 N	27.51 E
Juvisy-sur-Orge	46	48.41 N	2.23 E
Juvuln ⊜	26	63.43 N	13.09 E
Juwana	105a	6.42 S	111.09 E
Juwangi	105a	7.10 S	110.45 E
Juwayzah	122	33.02 N	35.51 E
Juxi	90	27.30 N	119.08 E
Juxian	88	35.37 N	118.54 E
Juxing	96	31.56 N	121.33 E
Juxtlahuaca	224	17.20 N	98.01 W
Juyanhai → Gashunhu ⊜	92	42.22 N	100.34 E
Juye	88	35.23 N	116.06 E
Jūyom	118	28.10 N	53.52 E
Juyongguan	95	40.18 N	116.04 E
Juža	70	56.35 N	42.01 E
Juzennecourt	54	48.11 N	4.59 E
Juziers	251	49.00 N	1.51 E
Juzihe ≃	88	40.18 N	123.35 E
Južno-Aleksandrovka	78	55.51 N	96.10 E
Južno-Aličurskij Chrebet ⩕	110	37.30 N	73.20 E
Južno-Jenisejskij	76	58.48 N	94.39 E
Južno-Mujskij Chrebet ⩕	78	55.40 N	114.00 E
Južno-Sachalinsk	79	46.58 N	142.42 E
Južno-Suchokumsk	74	44.37 N	45.34 E
Južno-Ural'sk	76	54.26 N	61.15 E
Južnyj, S.S.S.R.	70	56.08 N	44.09 E
Južnyj, S.S.S.R.	70	47.20 N	41.51 E
Južnyj, S.S.S.R.	76	49.21 N	73.01 E
Južnyj, S.S.S.R.	76	53.14 N	83.42 E
Južnyj, S.S.S.R.	76	53.33 N	60.02 E
Južnyj, Mys ≻	64	57.45 N	156.45 E
Južnyj-Alamyšik	75	40.46 N	72.38 E
Južnyj Bug ≃	68	46.59 N	31.58 E
Južnyj Golodnostepskij Kanal ☰	75	40.15 N	69.08 E
Južnyj Prijut	74	43.12 N	41.55 E
Južnyj Ural ⩕	76	54.00 N	58.30 E
Juzovka → Doneck	73	48.00 N	37.48 E
Jwālahari ✦[8]	262a	28.40 N	77.06 E
Jwayyā	122	33.14 N	35.19 E
Jyderup	41	55.40 N	11.26 E
Jylland ≻[1]	26	56.00 N	9.15 E
Jyllinge	41	55.45 N	12.07 E
Jyväskylä	26	62.14 N	25.44 E
K			
K2 → Godwin Austen ∧	113	35.53 N	76.30 E
Ka ≃	140	11.40 N	4.10 E
Kaaawa	219c	21.33 N	157.51 W
Kaabong	144	3.31 N	34.08 E
Kaachka	118	37.21 N	59.36 E
Kaala ∧	219c	21.31 N	158.09 W
Kaala Djerda	36	35.40 N	8.36 E
Kaalaea	219c	21.28 N	157.51 W
Kaala-Gomen	165f	20.40 S	164.25 E
Kaalspruit	148	29.15 S	26.10 E
Kaalualu Bay C	219d	18.58 N	155.37 W
Kaapahu Bay C	219a	20.39 N	156.05 W
Kaapmuiden	146	25.33 S	31.20 E
Kaap Plato ⩕[1]	148	28.20 S	23.57 E
Kaappunt ≻	148	34.21 S	18.30 E
Kaapstad → Cape Town	148	33.55 S	18.22 E
Kaariye Camii ⊍[1]	257b	41.01 N	28.55 E
Kaarli	66	59.24 N	26.27 E
Kaarssen	50	53.12 N	11.02 E
Kaarst	52	51.14 N	6.37 E
Kaaterskill Creek ≃	200	42.13 N	73.53 W
Kaatoan, Mount ∧	106	8.07 N	124.55 E
Kaatsheuvel	48	51.40 N	5.02 E
Kaavi	26	62.59 N	28.30 E
Kaba	140	10.09 N	11.40 W
Kaba, Goulbin ∨	140	13.42 N	6.19 E
Kabacan	106	7.08 N	124.49 E
Kabacan ≃	106	7.08 N	124.50 E
Kabadak	116	22.13 N	89.19 E
Kabadak ≃[1]	116	22.13 N	89.18 E
Kabadüz	120	40.53 N	37.56 E
Kabaena, Pulau I	102	5.15 S	121.55 E
Kabaena, Selat ⊔	102	5.00 S	122.00 E
Kabah ⊥	222	20.07 N	89.29 W
Kabala	140	9.35 N	11.33 W
Kabale	144	1.15 S	29.59 E
Kabali, Indon.	102	1.42 S	121.54 E
Kabalı, Tür.	120	41.52 N	35.05 E
Kabalo	144	6.03 S	26.55 E
Kabambare	144	4.42 S	27.43 E
Kaban'	76	54.39 N	66.28 E
Kabanjahe	104	3.06 N	98.30 E
Kabanje	73	49.13 N	38.12 E
Kabanjifa	134	3.34 N	43.30 E
Kabankalan	106	9.59 N	122.49 E
Kabanovka	70	53.39 N	51.18 E
Kabanovo	76	55.20 N	70.52 E
Kabansk	78	52.03 N	106.39 E
Kabardinka	68	44.39 N	37.57 E

Symbol	English	Deutsch	Español	Français	Português
≃	River	Fluss	Rio	Rivière	Rio
☰	Canal	Kanal	Canal	Canal	Canal
⊾	Waterfall, Rapids	Wasserfall, Stromschnellen	Cascada, Rápidos	Chute d'eau, Rapides	Cascata, Rápidos
⊔	Strait	Meerestrasse	Estrecho	Détroit	Estreito
C	Bay, Gulf	Bucht, Golf	Bahía, Golfo	Baie, Golfe	Baía, Golfo
⊜	Lake, Lakes	See, Seen	Lago, Lagos	Lac, Lacs	Lago, Lagos
☵	Swamp	Sumpf	Pantano	Marais	Pântano
⊼	Ice Features, Glacier	Eis- und Gletscherformen	Accidentes Glaciales	Formes glaciaires	Acidentes Glaciares
⊤	Other Hydrographic Features	Andere Hydrographische Objekte	Otros Elementos Hidrográficos	Autres données hydrographiques	Outros Elementos Hidrográficos
✣	Submarine Features	Untermeerische Objekte	Accidentes Submarinos	Formes de relief sous-marin	Acidentes Submarinos
□	Political Unit	Politische Einheit	Unidad Politica	Entité politique	Unidade Politica
⊍	Cultural Institution	Kulturelle Institution	Institución Cultural	Institution culturelle	Instituição Cultural
⊥	Historical Site	Historische Stätte	Sitio Histórico	Site historique	Sitio Histórico
♠	Recreational Site	Erholungs- und Ferienort	Sitio de Recreo	Centre de loisirs	Sitio de Lazer
⊠	Airport	Flughafen	Aeropuerto	Aéroport	Aeroporto
■	Military Installation	Militäranlage	Instalación Militar	Installation militaire	Instalação Militar
✦	Miscellaneous	Verschiedenes	Misceláneo	Divers	Miscelânea

ENGLISH Name	Page	Lat.°′	Long.°′

DEUTSCH Name	Seite	Breite°′	Länge°′ E=Ost

Symbols in the index entries represent the broad categories identified in the key at the right. Symbols with superior numbers (⛰[2]) identify subcategories (see complete key on page I · 26).

Kartensymbole in dem Registerverzeichnis stellen die rechts in Schlüssel erklärten Kategorien dar. Symbole mit hochgestellten Ziffern (⛰[2]) bezeichnen Unterabteilungen einer Kategorie (vgl. vollständiger Schlüssel auf Seite I · 26).

Los símbolos incluídos en el texto del índice representan las grandes categorias identificadas con la clave a la derecha. Los símbolos con numeros en su parte superior (⛰[2]) identifican las subcategorías (véase la clave completa en la página I · 26).

Les symboles de l'index représentent les catégories indiquées dans la légende à droite. Les symboles suivis d'un indice (⛰[2]) représentent des sous-catégories (voir légende complète à la page I · 26).

Os símbolos incluídos no texto do índice representam as grandes categorias identificadas com a chave à direita. Os símbolos com números em sua parte superior (⛰[2]) identificam as subcategorias (veja-se a chave completa à página I · 26).

∧ Mountain	Berg	Montaña	Montagne	Montanha
⛰ Mountains	Berge	Montañas	Montagnes	Montanhas
)(Pass	Pass	Paso	Col	Passo
∨ Valley, Canyon	Tal, Cañon	Valle, Cañón	Vallée, Canyon	Vale, Canhão
⌣ Plain	Ebene	Llano	Plaine	Planície
≻ Cape	Kap	Cabo	Cap	Cabo
I Island	Insel	Isla	Île	Ilha
II Islands	Inseln	Islas	Îles	Ilhas
◆ Other Topographic Features	Andere Topographische Objekte	Otros Elementos Topográficos	Autres données topographiques	Outros Elementos Topográficos

ESPAÑOL

Nombre	Página	Lat.°′	Long.°′ W=Oeste
Kamenec	66	52.24 N	23.49 E
Kamenec-Podol'skij	68	48.41 N	26.36 E
Kamenický Šenov	50	50.45 N	14.29 E
Kamen' Ignatija, Ostrov I	74	39.38 N	49.43 E
Kamenjak, Rt ≻	36	44.46 N	13.55 E
Kamenka, S.S.S.R.	24	65.54 N	44.05 E
Kamenka, S.S.S.R.	68	50.43 N	39.25 E
Kamenka, S.S.S.R.	68	49.02 N	32.06 E
Kamenka, S.S.S.R.	68	48.03 N	28.42 E
Kamenka, S.S.S.R.	70	57.23 N	41.49 E
Kamenka, S.S.S.R.	70	56.11 N	45.35 E
Kamenka, S.S.S.R.	70	53.13 N	44.03 E
Kamenka, S.S.S.R.	70	52.04 N	41.49 E
Kamenka, S.S.S.R.	70	51.07 N	50.19 E
Kamenka, S.S.S.R.	72	55.13 N	36.59 E
Kamenka, S.S.S.R.	72	56.11 N	37.18 E
Kamenka, S.S.S.R.	72	54.43 N	38.19 E
Kamenka, S.S.S.R.	73	47.25 N	37.42 E
Kamenka, S.S.S.R.	73	49.38 N	39.22 E
Kamenka, S.S.S.R.	73	49.07 N	37.18 E
Kamenka, S.S.S.R.	75	42.55 N	72.50 E
Kamenka, S.S.S.R.	76	58.33 N	95.51 E
Kamenka, S.S.S.R.	76	52.22 N	69.04 E
Kamenka, S.S.S.R.	79	44.28 N	136.01 E
Kamenka, S.S.S.R.	255a	59.59 N	30.53 E
Kamenka ◆[8]	255a	60.03 N	30.11 E
Kamenka ≃, S.S.S.R.	68	47.39 N	34.02 E
Kamenka ≃, S.S.S.R.	68	49.47 N	30.01 E
Kamenka ≃, S.S.S.R.	73	49.35 N	39.05 E
Kamenka ≃, S.S.S.R.	73	47.30 N	38.54 E
Kamenka ≃, S.S.S.R.	78	58.33 N	95.51 E
Kamenka ≃, S.S.S.R.	255a	60.01 N	30.12 E
Kamenka-Bugskaja	68	50.07 N	24.20 E
Kamenka-Dneprovskaja	68	47.29 N	34.25 E
Kamen'-Kaširskij	68	51.38 N	24.58 E
Kamen'-na-Obi	76	53.47 N	81.20 E
Kamennogorsk	24	60.58 N	29.07 E
Kamennoje, S.S.S.R.	68	47.53 N	35.25 E
Kamennoje, S.S.S.R.	68	51.31 N	27.38 E
Kamennomostskij	74	44.18 N	40.12 E
Kamennougol'naja Gr'ada ⩘	24	65.30 N	51.00 E
Kamennyj Brod, S.S.S.R.	68	50.25 N	27.49 E
Kamennyj Brod, S.S.S.R.	73	47.26 N	39.51 E
Kamennyj Jar	70	48.27 N	45.34 E
Kamenolomni	73	47.40 N	40.13 E
Kamen'-Rybolov	79	44.46 N	132.02 E
Kamensk	78	51.58 N	106.36 E
Kamenskij	70	50.53 N	45.29 E
Kamenskoje, S.S.S.R.	64	62.30 N	166.12 E
Kamenskoje, S.S.S.R.	68	45.49 N	29.16 E
Kamenskoje, S.S.S.R.	72	55.16 N	36.50 E
Kamensk-Šachtinskij	73	48.21 N	40.19 E
Kamensk-Ural'skij	76	56.28 N	61.54 E
Kamenz	50	51.16 N	14.06 E
Kameoka	86	35.00 N	135.35 E
Kamerik	48	52.06 N	4.54 E
Kamerun → Cameroon □[1]	124	6.00 N	12.00 E
Kamerunberg → Cameroun, Mont Λ	140	4.12 N	9.11 E
Kames	42	55.54 N	5.15 W
Kameškovo	70	56.21 N	41.00 E
Kāmet Λ	110	30.54 N	79.37 E
Kameur, Bahr ≃	136	9.26 N	20.50 E
Kameyama	84	34.51 N	136.27 E
Kami	86	35.05 N	134.53 E
Kamiah	192	46.14 N	116.02 W
Kamiakatsuka ◆[8]	258	35.46 N	139.39 E
Kamiak Butte Λ	192	46.52 N	117.10 W
Kamiasao	258	35.35 N	139.30 E
Kamień Krajeńskie	30	53.33 N	17.32 E
Kamienna ≃	30	51.06 N	21.47 E
Kamienna Góra	30	50.47 N	16.01 E
Kamień Pomorski	30	53.58 N	14.46 E
Kamieńsk	30	51.12 N	19.30 E
Kamieskroon	146	30.09 S	17.56 E
Kamifukuoka	258	35.52 N	139.31 E
Kamigōri	86	34.52 N	134.22 E
Kamigyō ◆[8]	260	35.02 N	135.45 E
Kamiichi	84	36.42 N	137.22 E
Kamiigusa Stadium ♠	258	35.43 N	139.37 E
Kamiishihara	258	35.39 N	139.32 E
Kamiiso	82a	41.49 N	140.39 E
Kamiita	86	34.07 N	134.24 E
Kamikamagari-jima I	86	34.11 N	132.44 E
Kamikatsu	86	33.53 N	134.24 E
Kamikawa, Nihon	82a	43.49 N	142.45 E
Kamikawa, Nihon	84	36.13 N	139.07 E
Kamikitazawa ◆[8]	258	35.40 N	139.38 E
Kamikume	260	34.55 N	135.03 E
Kâmil	120	41.07 N	34.47 E
Kamilukuak Lake ⊜	166	62.22 N	101.40 W
Kamimaki	260	34.34 N	135.43 E
Kamimanbata	258	35.51 N	139.34 E
Kamimizo	258	35.33 N	139.22 E
Kamina	144	8.44 S	25.00 E
Kaminaka, Nihon	84	35.28 N	135.51 E
Kaminaka, Nihon	86	33.48 N	134.22 E
Kaminak Lake ⊜	166	62.10 N	95.00 W
Kaminaljuyú ⊥	226	14.38 N	90.33 W
Kaminoho	84	35.37 N	137.03 E
Kaminokawa	84	36.26 N	139.55 E
Kaminokuni	82a	41.48 N	140.06 E
Kaminoseki	86	33.49 N	132.07 E
Kaminoyama	82	38.09 N	140.17 E
Kaminskij	70	57.10 N	41.28 E
Kaminuriak Lake ⊜	166	63.00 N	95.40 W
Kamioka	84	36.16 N	137.18 E
Kamioyamada	258	35.35 N	139.24 E
Kámiros ⊥	38	36.19 N	27.57 E
Kamiryūzu-zaki ≻	86	33.30 N	133.34 E
Kamisato	84	36.15 N	139.09 E
Kamishak Bay C	170	59.15 N	153.45 W
Kamishii	84	36.04 N	136.24 E
Kami-shima I	84	34.33 N	136.59 E
Kamishinden	260	34.49 N	135.30 E
Kamiš-Samarskich Ozer, Razlivy ☷	70	48.50 N	50.50 E
Kamisunagawa	82a	43.30 N	142.00 E
Kamitaira	84	36.24 N	136.54 E
Kamitakara	84	36.17 N	137.22 E
Kamitakino	260	34.57 N	134.59 E
Kamitomi	258	35.49 N	139.31 E
Kamitonda	86	33.43 N	135.27 E
Kamitsuruma	258	35.31 N	139.25 E
Kamitsushima	82	34.50 N	129.28 E
Kamituga	144	3.04 S	28.11 E
Kamiura	86	33.03 N	131.55 E
Kamiyahagi	84	35.18 N	137.29 E
Kamiyama	86	33.58 N	134.23 E
Kamiyamada	84	36.28 N	138.09 E
Kamiyama-shima I	164m	26.15 N	127.35 E
Kamiyugi	258	35.37 N	139.23 E
Kamīzgān	74	38.58 N	47.44 E
Kamkhat Muḥaywir Λ[2]	122	31.08 N	36.30 E
Kamku	110	27.30 N	96.30 E
Kamla ≃	114	26.22 N	85.53 E
Kamlach ≃	54	48.30 N	10.22 E
Kamloops	172	50.40 N	120.20 W
Kamloops Indian Reserve ◆[4]	172	50.42 N	120.20 W
Kamloops Lake ⊜	172	50.43 N	120.33 W
Kammanassieberg ⩘	148	33.39 S	22.43 E
Kammon-kaitei-tunnel ◆[5]	86	33.56 N	130.55 E
Kammuri-yama Λ	82	34.28 N	132.05 E
Kamnik	36	46.13 N	14.37 E
Kamniokan	78	56.17 N	111.57 E
Kamo, N.Z.	162	35.41 S	174.19 E
Kamo, Nihon	82	37.39 N	139.03 E
Kamo, Nihon	84	34.50 N	138.46 E
Kamo, Nihon	86	34.45 N	135.52 E
Kamo, Nihon	86	35.10 N	134.04 E

FRANÇAIS

Nom	Page	Lat.°′	Long.°′ W=Ouest
Kamo, Nihon	86	35.20 N	132.55 E
Kamo, Nihon	260	34.55 N	135.13 E
Kamo, S.S.S.R.	74	40.22 N	45.08 E
Kamo ≃, Nihon	84	35.06 N	140.06 E
Kamo ≃, Nihon	86	33.56 N	133.09 E
Kamoa Mountains ⩘	236	1.37 N	59.00 W
Kamoda-misaki ≻	86	33.50 N	134.45 E
Kamogata	86	34.32 N	133.35 E
Kamogawa, Nihon	84	35.06 N	140.06 E
Kamogawa, Nihon	86	34.51 N	133.49 E
Kamohio Bay C	219a	20.31 N	156.36 W
Kamojima	86	34.04 N	134.21 E
Kāmoke	113	31.58 N	74.13 E
Kamoshida ◆[8]	258	35.34 N	139.30 E
Kamoto	86	33.00 N	130.45 E
Kamp	52	50.14 N	7.37 E
Kāmpa	262b	22.56 N	88.28 E
Kampala	144	0.19 N	32.25 E
Kampar	104	4.18 N	101.09 E
Kampar ≃	102	0.32 N	103.08 E
Kamparkalns Λ[2]	66	57.18 N	22.47 E
Kampar-kanan ≃	102	0.16 N	101.41 E
Kampen	48	52.33 N	5.54 E
Kampene	144	3.36 S	26.40 E
Kampfe, Lake ⊜	266	41.02 N	74.21 W
Kamphaeng, Khao Λ	100	14.37 N	99.18 E
Kamphaeng Phet	100	16.28 N	99.30 E
Kampil	114	27.37 N	79.17 E
Kampinoska, Puszcza ◆[3]	30	52.20 N	20.30 E
Kampinoski Park Narodowy ♠	30	52.20 N	20.35 E
Kampire Dior Λ	113	36.43 N	74.17 E
Kampli	112	15.24 N	76.37 E
Kamp-Lintfort	48	51.30 N	6.31 E
Kamp'o	88	35.48 N	129.29 E
Kampolombo, Lake ⊜	144	11.37 S	29.42 E
Kampong Ayer Puteh	104	4.16 N	103.12 E
Kampong Baharu	104	3.43 N	103.17 E
Kampong Benta	104	3.32 N	103.22 E
Kampong Buloh	104	5.32 N	102.45 E
Kâmpóng Cham	100	12.00 N	105.27 E
Kampong Chenor	104	3.29 N	102.36 E
Kâmpóng Chhnăng	100	12.15 N	104.40 E
Kampong Dong	104	3.54 N	101.54 E
Kampong Guchil	104	5.33 N	102.14 E
Kampong Jabor	104	3.57 N	103.20 E
Kampong Jerangau	104	4.51 N	103.12 E
Kampong Kandang	104	2.11 N	102.18 E
Kâmpóng Kântuŏt	100	11.26 N	104.49 E
Kampong Kenyam	104	4.31 N	102.28 E
Kampong Kranji	261c	1.26 N	103.46 E
Kampong Kuala Kemaman	104	4.14 N	103.27 E
Kampong Lamir	104	3.36 N	103.21 E
Kampong Lawa	104	5.40 N	101.42 E
Kampong Loyang	261c	1.22 N	103.58 E
Kampong Mengkarak	104	3.19 N	102.27 E
Kampong Merang	104	5.32 N	102.57 E
Kampong Nuri	104	5.02 N	102.23 E
Kampong Penarek	104	5.37 N	102.48 E
Kampong Raja	104	5.48 N	102.35 E
Kampong Renggong	104	4.33 N	102.35 E
Kâmpóng Saôm	100	10.38 N	103.30 E
Kâmpóng Saôm, Chhâk C	100	10.50 N	103.32 E
Kampong Sebuyau	102	1.31 N	110.56 E
Kampong Sekendi	104	3.43 N	100.56 E
Kampong Surau	104	5.49 N	100.54 E
Kampong Tanjong Batu	104	3.12 N	103.27 E
Kampong Tanjong Keling	261c	1.18 N	103.42 E
Kampong Tebing Runtoh	261c	1.26 N	103.40 E
Kâmpóng Thum	100	12.42 N	104.54 E
Kâmpóng Trâlach	100	11.54 N	104.47 E
Kampong Ulu	100	10.03 N	98.33 E
Kampong Ulu Chalok	104	5.26 N	102.50 E
Kâmpôt	100	10.37 N	104.11 E
Kampsville	184	39.18 N	90.37 W
Kampti	140	10.08 N	3.27 W
Kampuchea → Cambodia □[1]	100	13.00 N	105.00 E
Kampung ≃	154	5.44 S	138.24 E
Kampungbaru	102	1.12 S	102.57 E
Kampung Sailolof	154	1.15 S	130.46 E
Kampville	209	38.51 N	90.33 W
Kāmrānga	116	23.14 N	90.47 E
Kamrau, Teluk C	154	3.32 S	133.37 E
Kamrup □[5]	114	26.30 N	90.00 E
Kamsack	174	51.34 N	101.54 W
Kamsdorf	50	50.38 N	11.28 E
Kamskij	24	60.04 N	53.13 E
Kamskoje Ustje	70	55.13 N	49.16 E
Kamskoje Vodochranilišče ⊜[1]	76	58.52 N	56.15 E
Kam Summa	134	0.18 N	42.48 E
Kamsu-ri	88	38.03 N	125.54 E
Kāmthi	110	21.14 N	79.12 E
Kam Tin	261d	22.27 N	114.03 E
Kamuchawie Lake ⊜	174	56.18 N	101.59 W
Kamudilo	144	7.42 S	27.18 E
Kamuela (Waimea)	219d	20.01 N	155.41 W
Kamui-misaki ≻	82a	43.20 N	140.21 E
Kámuk, Cerro Λ	226	9.17 N	83.04 W
Kamuli	144	0.57 N	33.07 E
Kamundan ≃	154	2.17 S	132.39 E
Kamutambaie ≃	142	7.17 S	23.41 E
Kamwandu	142	6.04 S	22.42 E
Kamyšet	78	55.12 N	98.42 E
Kamyšev, S.S.S.R.	70	46.39 N	42.38 E
Kamyšev, S.S.S.R.	70	46.53 N	42.31 E
Kamyševacha, S.S.S.R.	68	47.43 N	35.32 E
Kamyševacha, S.S.S.R.	73	48.42 N	38.23 E
Kamyševaja ≃	70	46.15 N	45.05 E
Kamyševatskaja	68	46.25 N	37.57 E
Kamyševskaja	70	47.37 N	41.49 E
Kamyšin	70	50.06 N	45.24 E
Kamyškurgon	75	40.34 N	70.24 E
Kamyšla	70	54.07 N	52.10 E
Kamyšlov	76	56.52 N	62.43 E
Kamyšlovskij Log ∨	76	55.00 N	71.00 E
Kamyslybas	76	46.11 N	61.57 E
Kamyslybas, Ozero ⊜	76	46.12 N	61.48 E
Kamyšnaja ≃	73	48.55 N	39.55 E
Kamyšnoje	76	51.58 N	61.47 E
Kamyšovyj	70	46.26 N	45.12 E
Kamyš-Zar'a	68	47.19 N	36.42 E
Kamyz'ak	70	46.07 N	48.05 E
Kamyz'ak ≃	70	46.00 N	48.06 E
Kan, Īrān	118	35.45 N	51.16 E
Kan, Sūd.	130	9.01 N	31.47 E
Kan ≃	76	56.31 N	93.47 E
Kana ≃	144	18.30 S	27.22 E
Kanaaupscow ≃	166	53.39 N	77.09 W
Kanab	190	37.03 N	112.32 W
Kanab Creek ≃	190	36.24 N	112.38 W
Kanada	86	33.41 N	130.47 E
Kanada → Canada □[1]	166	60.00 N	95.00 W
Kanadej	70	53.10 N	47.30 E
Kanae	84	35.30 N	137.49 E
Kanafis	130	9.48 N	25.40 E
Kanaga Island I	170	51.45 N	177.10 W
Kanaga Volcano Λ[1]	170	51.50 N	177.09 W
Kanagawa	258	35.28 N	139.38 E
Kanagawa □[5]	84	35.30 N	139.30 E
Kanagi	86	34.53 N	132.11 E
Kanai	258	35.35 N	139.28 E
Kānāipur	116	23.33 N	89.47 E
Kanairiktok ≃	166	55.05 N	60.20 W
Kanā'is, Ra's al- ≻	130	31.15 N	27.51 E
Kanajevka, S.S.S.R.	70	53.07 N	45.35 E
Kanajevka, S.S.S.R.	70	52.12 N	49.40 E

PORTUGUÊS

Nome	Página	Lat.°′	Long.°′ W=Oeste
Kanaka Creek ≃	216	39.25 N	120.57 W
Kanakapura	112	12.33 N	77.25 E
Kanakeswar	116	23.09 N	90.25 E
Kanákia I	257c	37.55 N	23.24 E
Kanākir	122	33.15 N	36.05 E
Kanal	58	46.05 N	13.38 E
Kanal-Inseln → Channel Islands II	28	49.20 N	2.20 W
Kanam	154	3.25 S	152.10 E
Kanamachi ◆[8]	258	35.56 N	139.53 E
Kanamori	258	35.32 N	139.28 E
Kanan	260	34.29 N	135.38 E
Kananaskis ≃	172	51.05 N	115.03 W
Kananga (Luluabourg)	142	5.54 S	22.25 E
Kananggar	105b	10.03 S	120.22 E
Kanangra Walls ♠[4]	160	34.00 S	150.07 E
Kananikol'skoje	76	52.47 N	57.29 E
Kanaoka	260	34.33 N	135.32 E
Kanapou Bay C	219a	20.33 N	156.33 W
Kanarase-yama Λ	86	33.26 N	131.15 E
Kanarraville	190	37.32 N	113.11 W
Kanaš	70	55.31 N	47.30 E
Kanasagō	84	36.33 N	140.28 E
Kanathea I	165g	17.16 S	179.09 W
Kanaudi	114	23.36 N	81.23 E
Kanava, S.S.S.R.	24	61.07 N	54.58 E
Kanava, S.S.S.R.	70	47.13 N	45.24 E
Kanavka	70	50.19 N	48.33 E
Kanawha	180	42.56 N	93.48 W
Kanawha ≃	178	38.50 N	82.08 W
Kanaya, Nihon	84	34.49 N	138.08 E
Kanaya, Nihon	86	34.04 N	135.15 E
Kanaya, Nihon	258	35.10 N	139.50 E
Kanayama	84	35.39 N	137.09 E
Kanazawa	84	36.34 N	136.39 E
Kanazawa ◆[8]	258	35.20 N	139.38 E
Kanazu	84	36.13 N	136.14 E
Kanbalu	100	23.12 N	95.31 E
Kanbauk	100	14.36 N	98.02 E
Kanbe	100	16.42 N	96.01 E
Kančalan ≃	170	65.08 N	176.25 E
Kanchanaburi	100	14.01 N	99.32 E
Kanchanadit	100	9.10 N	99.28 E
Kānchenjunga Λ	114	27.42 N	88.08 E
Kānchipuram	112	12.50 N	79.43 E
Kanchow → Ganzhou	90	25.54 N	114.55 E
Kānchrāpāra	116	22.57 N	88.28 E
Kańczuga	30	49.59 N	22.24 E
Kanda	86	33.47 N	130.59 E
Kandabulak	70	53.58 N	50.44 E
Kandagač	76	49.28 N	57.25 E
Kandāghat	113	30.59 N	77.07 E
Kandahar	174	51.46 N	104.21 W
Kandāhu	110	27.33 N	69.24 E
Kanda-Kanda	142	6.56 S	23.36 E
Kandala	142	6.02 S	19.24 E
Kandalakša	24	67.09 N	32.21 E
Kandalakšskaja Guba C	24	66.55 N	32.45 E
Kandang	104	3.03 N	97.20 E
Kandangan	102	2.47 S	115.16 E
Kandanghaur	105a	6.21 S	108.06 E
Kandat	76	57.08 N	89.02 E
Kandava	66	57.05 N	22.49 E
Kandavu I	165g	19.03 S	178.13 E
Kandavu Passage Ц	165g	18.45 S	178.00 E
Kandé	140	9.57 N	1.03 E
Kandel	52	49.05 N	8.11 E
Kandel Λ	54	48.04 N	8.01 E
Kander ≃	54	46.43 N	7.38 E
Kandern	54	47.43 N	7.40 E
Kandersteg	54	46.30 N	7.40 E
Kandhkot	110	28.14 N	69.11 E
Kāndhla	114	29.19 N	77.16 E
Kandi, Benin	140	11.08 N	2.56 E
Kāndi, Bhārat	116	23.57 N	88.02 E
Kandi, Tanjung ≻	102	1.19 N	121.28 E
Kandia ≃	113	35.30 N	73.17 E
Kandiāro	110	27.04 N	68.13 E
Kandik ≃	170	65.24 N	142.34 W
Kandilli ◆[8]	257b	41.04 N	29.03 E
Kandıra	120	41.04 N	30.09 E
Kandivli ◆[8]	262c	19.12 N	72.51 E
Kando ≃	86	35.22 N	132.40 E
Kandor, Ouadi ∨	136	17.13 N	20.52 E
Kandos	160	32.52 S	149.58 E
Kāndra	116	23.44 N	87.58 E
Kandrāch	110	25.29 N	65.29 E
Kāndrāng Garhi	114	27.43 N	84.47 E
Kandreho	147b	17.29 S	46.06 E
Kandrian	154	6.15 S	149.35 E
Kandry	70	54.34 N	54.07 E
Kandufuri I	112	7.05 N	72.48 E
Kandukūr	112	15.13 N	79.55 E
Kandute I	112	6.20 N	72.57 E
Kandy	112	7.18 N	80.38 E
Kane, Ill., U.S.	209	39.11 N	90.21 W
Kane, Pa., U.S.	204	41.40 N	78.49 W
Kane □[6]	206	41.53 N	88.18 W
Kaneda	258	35.28 N	139.22 E
Kanegasaku	258	35.48 N	139.57 E
Kaneilio Point ≻	219c	21.27 N	158.12 W
Kanektok ≃	170	59.45 N	161.55 W
Kanem □[5]	136	15.00 N	16.00 E
Kanemi	106	6.55 N	123.58 E
Kanenmyvejem ≃	170	66.04 N	178.40 W
Kaneohe	219c	21.25 N	157.48 W
Kaneohe Bay C	219c	21.28 N	157.49 W
Kaneohe Bay Marine Corps Air Station ■	219c	21.27 N	157.46 W
Kaneville	206	41.50 N	88.31 W
Kanevskaja	68	46.05 N	38.57 E
Kaneyama	84	35.28 N	137.06 E
Kanfanar	58	45.07 N	13.51 E
Kang	146	23.41 S	22.50 E
Kangaba	140	11.56 N	8.25 W
Kangal	120	39.15 N	37.24 E
Kangalassy	64	62.23 N	129.59 E
Kangān	118	27.50 N	52.03 E
Kānganheri ◆[8]	262a	28.33 N	76.59 E
Kanganpur	113	30.46 N	74.08 E
Kangar	104	6.26 N	100.12 E
Kangaré	140	11.35 N	8.10 W
Kangarilla	158b	35.09 S	138.40 E
Kangaroo ≃	160	34.46 S	150.18 E
Kangaroo Flat	158b	34.33 S	138.40 E
Kangaroo Ground	264b	37.41 S	145.13 E
Kangaroo Island I	156	35.50 S	137.06 E
Kangaroo Range National Park ♠	156	29.35 S	152.10 E
Kangaroo Valley	160	34.44 S	150.32 E
Kangasala	26	61.28 N	24.05 E
Kangasniemi	26	61.59 N	26.38 E
Kangāvar	118	34.30 N	47.58 E
Kangaz	68	46.07 N	28.33 E
Kangbao	88	41.53 N	114.40 E
Kangdarenshan	94	41.32 N	123.41 E
Kangding	92	30.03 N	102.02 E
Kangdong	88	39.09 N	126.05 E
Kangdu	90	27.00 N	116.36 E
Kangean, Kepulauan II	102	6.55 S	115.30 E
Kangean, Pulau I	102	6.54 S	115.20 E
Kangen ≃	130	6.47 N	33.09 E
Kanggezhuang	95	40.26 N	116.44 E
Kanggup'o	88	41.07 N	127.31 E
Kanggye	88	40.58 N	126.34 E
Kanggyŏng	88	36.10 N	127.00 E
Kanghwa	88	37.45 N	126.30 E
Kanghwa-do I	88	37.40 N	126.27 E
Kanghwa-man C	88	37.20 N	126.35 E
Kangil	78	52.15 N	116.20 E
Kangjin	88	34.39 N	126.45 E
Kangjinjing	79	46.12 N	126.48 E
Kangkar Lenggor	104	2.16 N	103.44 E
Kangkar Teberau	104	1.32 N	103.45 E
Kangley	206	41.09 N	88.53 W
Kangly	75	40.07 N	67.54 E

Kangma	110	28.34 N	89.51 E
Kangmaer	114	30.45 N	85.34 E
Kangnichumike	110	33.10 N	80.59 E
Kangnŭng	88	37.45 N	128.54 E
Kango	142	0.09 N	10.08 E
Kango Caves ♠[5]	148	33.23 S	22.14 E
Kangoku-iwa I	164f	24.48 N	141.17 E
Kangombe	142	14.03 S	23.40 E
Kangongo	142	17.57 S	21.02 E
Kangowa	142	9.55 S	22.48 E
Kangping	88	42.44 N	123.21 E
Kāngpokpi	110	25.08 N	93.58 E
Kangpu	92	27.43 N	99.00 E
Kāngra	113	32.06 N	76.16 E
Kāngra □[5]	113	32.00 N	76.15 E
Kangshan	90	22.51 N	120.17 E
Kangsŏ	88	38.58 N	125.26 E
Kangsŏ-ri	88	38.06 N	126.58 E
Kangsu	75	39.45 N	75.02 E
Kangto Λ	110	27.52 N	92.30 E
Kangtuyingzi	94	41.47 N	121.31 E
Känguruh-Insel → Kangaroo Island I	156	35.50 S	137.06 E
Kangwŏn Do □[4], C.M.I.K.	88	38.45 N	127.35 E
Kangwŏn Do □[4], Taehan	88	37.45 N	128.15 E
Kangxianzhuang	95	39.06 N	116.27 E
Kangyidaung	100	16.56 N	94.54 E
Kangzhuang	95	40.23 N	115.53 E
Kanhangad	112	12.19 N	75.04 E
Kanhar ≃	114	24.28 N	83.08 E
Kanheri Caves ♠[5]	262c	19.13 N	72.52 E
Kanholmsfjärden Ц	40	59.20 N	18.47 E
Kanhsien → Ganzhou	90	25.54 N	114.55 E
Kani, C. Iv.	140	8.29 N	6.36 W
Kani, Mya.	100	22.26 N	94.50 E
Kani, Nihon	84	35.22 N	137.04 E
Kaniama	142	7.31 S	24.11 E
Kaniamba	144	7.27 S	26.57 E
Kanibadam	75	40.17 N	70.25 E
Kanie	84	35.08 N	136.48 E
Kaniepa	144	9.00 S	27.21 E
Kaniere	162	42.45 S	171.00 E
Kaniere, Lake ⊜	162	42.50 S	171.09 E
Kaniet Islands II	154	0.53 S	145.30 E
Kanif	164q	9.31 N	138.05 E
Kanigiri	112	15.24 N	79.31 E
Kanihāula ◆[8]	262a	28.44 N	77.01 E
Kanin	50	52.17 N	12.50 E
Kanin, Poluostrov ≻[1]	24	68.00 N	45.00 E
Kanina	114	28.20 N	76.19 E
Kaningo	144	0.49 S	38.32 E
Kanin Kamen' Λ	24	68.18 N	45.00 E
Kanin Nos	24	68.39 N	43.14 E
Kanin Nos, Mys ≻	24	68.39 N	43.16 E
Kânireş	120	39.18 N	41.01 E
Kaniva	156	36.23 S	141.15 E
Kanjiža	38	46.04 N	20.04 E
Kānjur ◆[8]	262c	19.08 N	72.56 E
Kanjut Sār Λ	113	36.14 N	75.22 E
Kankaanpää	26	61.48 N	22.25 E
Kankakee	206	41.07 N	87.52 W
Kankakee □[6]	206	41.07 N	87.52 W
Kankakee ≃	206	41.23 N	88.16 W
Kankakee River State Park ♠	206	41.12 N	87.59 W
Kankan	140	10.23 N	9.18 W
Kankan □[4]	140	10.10 N	9.15 W
Kankar ◆[8]	262a	28.46 N	77.06 E
Kankéla	140	10.50 N	6.40 W
Kānker	112	20.17 N	81.29 E
Kankō → Hamhŭng	88	39.54 N	127.32 E
Kankossa	140	15.56 N	11.31 W
Kankunskij	64	57.37 N	126.08 E
Kanlıavşar	120	37.13 N	38.16 E
Kanlıca ◆[8]	257b	41.06 N	29.04 E
Kanmaw Kyun I	100	11.40 N	98.28 E
Kanmen	90	28.06 N	121.16 E
Kanmon-kaikyō Ц	86	33.56 N	130.56 E
Kanmuri-shima I	86	35.41 N	135.25 E
Kanmuri-yama Λ	86	34.28 N	132.05 E
Kanna	164m	26.28 N	127.57 E
Kanna ≃	84	36.17 N	139.09 E
Kannabe	86	34.32 N	133.23 E
Kannabe-yama Λ[2]	260	34.48 N	135.44 E
Kannack	100	14.07 N	108.37 E
Kannad	112	20.16 N	75.08 E
Kanna-kō C	164m	26.28 N	127.58 E
Kannami	84	35.05 N	138.57 E
Kannapolis	182	35.30 N	80.37 W
Kannauj	114	27.04 N	79.55 E
Kanniyākumāri	112	8.05 N	77.34 E
Kannod	114	22.40 N	76.44 E
Kannonkoski	26	62.58 N	25.15 E
Kannon-zaki ≻	258	35.15 N	139.45 E
Kannose ≃	86	34.54 N	132.49 E
Kannus	26	63.54 N	23.54 E
Kano, Nig.	140	12.00 N	8.30 E
Kano, Nihon	86	34.14 N	131.49 E
Kano □[3]	140	11.45 N	9.00 E
Kano ≃	84	35.05 N	138.52 E
Kanon, Punt ≻	231s	12.02 N	68.45 W
Kanona, N.Y., U.S.	200	42.22 N	77.22 W
Kanona, Zam.	144	13.04 S	30.38 E
Kanoneiland	148	28.39 S	21.05 E
Kanonerskij, Ostrov I	255a	59.54 N	30.13 E
Kanonji	86	34.07 N	133.39 E
Kanopolis	188	38.43 N	98.09 W
Kanopolis Lake ⊜[1]	188	38.38 N	98.00 W
Kanorado	188	39.20 N	102.02 W
Kanosh	190	38.48 N	112.26 W
Kanouse Brook ≃	266	41.02 N	74.26 W
Kanouse Mountain Λ	266	41.04 N	74.25 W
Kan'ov	68	49.44 N	31.28 E
Kan'ovka	24	67.08 N	39.40 E
Kanowit	102	2.06 N	112.09 E
Kanowna	152	30.36 S	121.36 E
Kanoya	82	31.23 N	130.51 E
Kanō-zan Λ	258	35.15 N	139.57 E
Kanpetlet	100	21.12 N	94.02 E
Kanpoli	262c	19.04 N	73.09 E
Kānpur	114	26.28 N	80.21 E
Kānpur □[5]	114	26.30 N	80.00 E
Kanra	84	36.13 N	138.55 E
Kansa ≃	84	34.55 N	137.34 E
Kansai University ▼[2]	260	34.46 N	135.31 E
Kansaj	75	40.30 N	69.41 E
Kansanshi	144	12.05 S	26.26 E
Kānsāripāra	262b	22.56 N	88.14 E
Kansas, Ill., U.S.	184	39.33 N	87.56 W
Kansas, Ohio, U.S.	204	41.15 N	83.17 W
Kansas □[3]	168		
	188	38.45 N	98.15 W
Kansas ≃	188	39.07 N	94.36 W
Kansas City, Kans., U.S.	188	39.07 N	94.39 W
Kansas City, Mo., U.S.	184	39.05 N	94.35 W
Kansau	100	23.50 N	93.35 E
Kansenia	144	10.19 S	26.02 E
Kanshan	96	30.12 N	120.25 E
Kanshi	90	24.56 N	116.54 E
Kansk	76	56.13 N	95.41 E
Kansŏng	88	38.22 N	128.29 E
Kansu → Gansu □[4]	92	37.00 N	103.00 E
Kansyat	154	2.15 S	138.51 E
Kant	75	42.55 N	74.55 E
Kantābānji	112	20.29 N	82.55 E
Kantabrisches Gebirge → Cantábrica, Cordillera ⩘	34	43.00 N	5.00 W
Kantalvi	262c	18.54 N	73.03 E
Kantang	100	7.25 N	99.31 E
Kāntāphor	114	22.35 N	76.34 E
Kantchari	140	12.29 N	1.31 E

Kantché	140	13.33 N	8.28 E
Kantemirovka, S.S.S.R.	73	49.41 N	39.51 E
Kantemirovka, S.S.S.R.	75	42.51 N	70.20 E
Kānth, Bhārat	114	29.04 N	78.38 E
Kanth → Kąty Wrocławskie, Pol.	30	51.02 N	16.46 E
Kantharalak	100	14.39 N	104.39 E
Kānthi Coastal Plain ⚌	116	21.45 N	87.45 E
Kantishna ≃	170	64.45 N	149.58 W
Kantner	204	40.06 N	78.56 W
Kantō-heiya ⚌	84	36.00 N	139.30 E
Kanton → Guangzhou	90	23.06 N	113.16 E
Kantong	90	32.59 N	116.19 E
Kantorp	40	59.01 N	16.28 E
Kantō-sammyaku ⩘	82	35.50 N	138.50 E
Kantō-sanchi ⩘	84	35.59 N	138.43 E
Kantubek	76	45.07 N	59.16 E
Kantu-long	100	19.57 N	97.36 E
Kantunilkín	222	21.06 N	87.29 W
Kanturk	28	52.10 N	8.55 W
Kanuku Mountains ⩘	236	3.12 N	59.30 W
Kanuma	84	36.33 N	139.44 E
Kanus	146	27.54 S	18.40 E
Kanuti ≃	170	66.26 N	153.02 W
Kan'utino	66	55.33 N	33.14 E
Kanye	146	24.59 S	25.19 E
Kanygtokynmankyn, Laguna C	170	69.20 N	178.45 E
Kanyu	146	20.05 S	24.39 E
Kanyutkwin	100	18.21 N	96.30 E
Kanzaki ≃	260	34.42 N	135.25 E
Kanzanavolok	24	62.23 N	36.58 E
Kanzenze	144	10.31 S	25.12 E
Kanzi	88	39.34 N	122.39 E
Kaohiung → Kaohsiung	90	22.38 N	120.17 E
Kaohsiung	90	22.38 N	120.17 E
Kaohsiung Ch'uan C	90	22.37 N	120.12 E
Kaohsiunghsien	90	22.38 N	120.21 E
Kaoje	140	11.14 N	4.07 E
Kaoko Otavi	146	18.14 S	13.40 E
Kaokoveld □[5]	146	18.00 S	13.30 E
Kaokoveld ⩘[1]	146	21.00 S	14.20 E
Kaolack	140	14.09 N	16.04 W
Kaolun → Kowloon	261d	22.18 N	114.10 E
Kaonga	263b	4.09 S	15.12 E
Kaongweshi ≃	142	7.53 S	22.20 E
Kaoping → Changzhi	92	36.11 N	113.08 E
Kaoshandian	90	30.54 N	114.32 E
Kaoshanji	95	40.11 N	117.17 E
Kaouar ◆[1]	136	19.00 N	12.40 E
Kapaa	219b	22.05 N	159.19 W
Kapadvanj	110	23.01 N	73.04 E
Kapal	76	45.08 N	79.03 E
Kapalong	106	7.35 N	125.42 E
Kapan	102	9.44 S	124.17 E
Kapanga, Zaïre	142	5.04 S	16.58 E
Kapanga, Zaïre	142	8.21 S	22.35 E
Kapangan	106	16.35 N	120.35 E
Kapaonik ⩘	38	43.20 N	20.50 E
Kāpāsia	116	24.07 N	90.32 E
Kapatagan	106	7.52 N	123.44 E
Kapatu	144	9.43 S	30.42 E
Kapcagajtuj	78	49.57 N	118.37 E
Kapchorwa	144	1.24 N	34.27 E
Kapelle	48	51.28 N	3.58 E
Kapellen, Bel.	46	51.19 N	4.26 E
Kapellen, B.R.D.	48	51.34 N	6.22 E
Kapellen, B.R.D.	52	51.25 N	6.35 E
Kapellen, B.R.D.	253	51.08 N	6.38 E
Kapelle-op-den-Bos	46	51.01 N	4.22 E
Kapellerfeld	254b	48.19 N	16.30 E
Kapellskär	40	59.43 N	19.04 E
Kapema	144	10.42 S	28.24 E
Kapenguria	144	1.04 N	35.07 E
Kapfenberg	30	47.26 N	15.18 E
Kapia	142	4.17 S	19.46 E
Kapıdağı Yarımadası ≻[1]	120	40.28 N	27.50 E
Kapikik Lake ⊜	174	51.32 N	91.57 W
Kapikog Lake ⊜	202	45.09 N	79.53 W
Kapilavastu	114	27.28 N	83.16 E
Kapilmuni	116	22.42 N	89.20 E
Kapingamarangi I[1]	14	1.04 N	154.46 E
Kapiri Mposhi	144	13.58 S	28.41 E
Kāpīsā □[4]	110	34.45 N	69.30 E
Kapiskau ≃	166	52.47 N	81.55 W
Kapit	102	2.01 N	112.56 E
Kapitanovka	68	48.54 N	31.42 E
Kapiti Island I	162	40.52 S	174.54 E
Kapiura ≃	154	5.45 S	150.35 E
Kapka, Massif du ⩘	136	15.07 N	21.45 E
Kapkataš	75	40.23 N	74.20 E
Kapkatas, Chrebet ⩘	75	41.50 N	76.10 E
Kapkinka	70	48.08 N	43.51 E
Kaplan	184	30.00 N	92.17 W
Kaplice	30	48.45 N	14.30 E
Kapoe	100	9.35 N	98.40 E
Kapoeta	144	4.47 N	33.35 E
Kapogere	154	9.50 S	147.45 E
Kapona	144	7.11 S	29.09 E
Kaponga	162	39.26 S	174.09 E
Kaporskoje	255a	59.45 N	29.58 E
Kapos ≃	30	46.44 N	18.30 E
Kaposvár	30	46.22 N	17.47 E
Kaposvar Creek ≃	174	50.31 N	101.55 W
Kapotn'a ◆[8]	255b	55.38 N	37.48 E
Kapowsin	214	46.59 N	122.13 W
Kapowsin, Lake ⊜	214	46.58 N	122.13 W
Kapp	26	60.42 N	10.52 E
Kappar	118	25.19 N	62.42 E
Kappel	52	50.00 N	7.21 E
Kappeln	41	54.40 N	9.56 E
Kappelshamn	26	57.51 N	18.47 E
Kapps	146	22.22 S	17.52 E
Kapralicha	76	56.11 N	67.15 E
Kaprijke	46	51.13 N	3.36 E
Kaprun	58	47.16 N	12.46 E
Kapsabet	144	0.12 N	35.06 E
Kapsan	88	41.04 N	128.19 E
Kap Shui Mun Ц	261d	22.19 N	114.04 E
Kapstadt → Cape Town	148	33.55 S	18.22 E
Kapsukas	66	54.33 N	23.21 E
Kaptai	110	22.21 N	92.17 E
Kaptipada	116	21.31 N	86.32 E
Kaptol	38	45.26 N	17.44 E
Kapuas ≃, Indon.	102	3.01 S	114.20 E
Kapuas ≃, Indon.	102	0.25 S	109.40 E
Kapuas Hulu, Pegunungan ⩘	102	1.25 N	113.30 E
Kapulo	144	8.18 S	29.15 E
Kapunda	158b	34.21 S	138.54 E
Kapūrthala	113	31.23 N	75.23 E
Kapur Utara, Pegunungan ⩘	105a	6.52 S	111.30 E
Kapuskasing	166	49.25 N	82.26 W
Kapuskasing ≃	166	49.49 N	82.00 W
Kapuskasing Lake ⊜	180	48.30 N	82.55 W
Kapustin Jar	70	48.36 N	45.45 E
Kapustino	68	48.57 N	31.14 E
Kapuvár	30	47.36 N	17.02 E
Kap Verde → Cape Verde □[1]	140a	16.00 N	24.00 W
Kapyrevščina	66	55.15 N	32.53 E
Kapytdžuch, Gora Λ	74	39.13 N	46.00 E
Kara, Mali	140	12.56 N	6.15 W
Kara	64	69.14 N	65.00 E
Kara, Yai.	134	5.50 N	37.08 E
Kara ≃	140	10.01 N	0.25 E
Karaali	120	39.40 N	32.57 E

Karaaul	76	48.57 N	79.15 E
Karabachskij Chrebet ⩘	74	39.42 N	46.36 E
Karabagl'ar	74	39.26 N	45.12 E
Kara-Balty	75	42.50 N	73.52 E
Karabanovo	72	56.19 N	38.42 E
Karabaš, S.S.S.R.	70	54.42 N	52.36 E
Karabaš, S.S.S.R.	76	55.29 N	60.14 E
Karabau	70	48.26 N	52.54 E
Karabekaul	118	38.30 N	64.08 E
Karabiğa	120	40.24 N	27.18 E
Karabil', Vozvyšennost' ⩘[1]	118	36.25 N	64.00 E
Kara-Bogaz-Gol, Zaliv C	62	41.00 N	53.15 E
Karabudachkent	74	42.41 N	47.34 E
Karabük	120	41.12 N	32.37 E
Karabula	78	58.08 N	97.23 E
Karabula ≃	78	58.22 N	97.02 E
Karabulak, S.S.S.R.	75	39.51 N	69.38 E
Karabulak, S.S.S.R.	75	42.32 N	69.46 E
Karabulak, S.S.S.R.	76	44.54 N	78.30 E
Karabulak, S.S.S.R.	76	47.34 N	84.41 E
Karabulduk	120	40.50 N	38.34 E
Karabutak	76	49.59 N	60.10 E
Karaca	120	40.12 N	39.08 E
Karacabey	120	40.13 N	28.21 E
Karacadağ	120	41.57 N	27.40 E
Karaca Dağ Λ	120	37.40 N	39.50 E
Karačaj ≃	74	41.28 N	49.00 E
Karačajevo-Čerkesskaja Avtonomnaja Oblast' □[4]	74	44.00 N	42.00 E
Karačajevsk	74	43.45 N	41.54 E
Karacaköy	120	41.24 N	28.22 E
Karačala	74	39.48 N	48.57 E
Karacali	120	40.53 N	37.17 E
Karacasu	120	37.43 N	28.37 E
Karacaviran, Tür.	120	39.44 N	38.08 E
Karacaviran, Tür.	120	37.33 N	39.22 E
Karaçayır	120	39.55 N	37.01 E
Karačev	66	53.07 N	35.00 E
Karāchi	110	24.52 N	67.03 E
Karachtaj	75	40.55 N	69.46 E
Karači	70	57.59 N	50.28 E
Karaçürun	120	37.35 N	38.57 E
Karād	112	17.17 N	74.12 E
Karadarja ≃	75	40.54 N	71.45 E
Karadeniz → Black Sea ⊤[2]	22	43.00 N	35.00 E
Karadere	120	40.59 N	30.50 E
Karadoğan	120	40.25 N	31.51 E
Karadoruk	120	38.53 N	37.22 E
Karaftit	78	54.12 N	111.54 E
Karagaj, S.S.S.R.	70	48.39 N	47.38 E
Karagaj, S.S.S.R.	70	58.16 N	54.56 E
Karagajly	76	49.20 N	75.48 E
Karaganda	76	49.50 N	73.10 E
Karagel	118	39.23 N	53.11 E
Karagičevskij	70	50.11 N	42.55 E
Karaginskij, Ostrov I	64	58.50 N	164.00 E
Karaginskij Zaliv C	64	58.50 N	164.00 E
Karagola Road	114	25.29 N	87.23 E
Karagölü ⊜	120	36.42 N	29.50 E
Karagoš, Gora Λ	76	51.44 N	89.24 E
Karagužicha	76	50.47 N	83.00 E
Karahallı	120	38.20 N	29.32 E
Karaia	114	25.54 N	78.01 E
Karaičev	70	48.37 N	42.13 E
Karaidel'	76	55.50 N	56.53 E
Karaidel'skij	76	55.49 N	57.05 E
Kāraikkudi	112	10.04 N	78.47 E
Karaisalı	120	37.16 N	35.03 E
Karaitivu I	112	8.23 N	79.47 E
Karaj	118	35.48 N	50.59 E
Karaj, Rūdkhāneh-ye ≃	257d	35.35 N	51.11 E
Karajantak	75	40.03 N	67.54 E
Karak	104	3.24 N	102.02 E
Karakabak	76	50.33 N	75.09 E
Karakain	75	41.26 N	74.19 E
Kara-Kala	118	38.26 N	56.18 E
Karakalpakskaja Avtonomnaja Sovetskaja Socialističeskaja Respublika □[3]	76	43.00 N	59.00 E
Karakastek	75	43.08 N	76.06 E
Karakavak	75	39.41 N	72.43 E
Karakecili	120	39.36 N	33.23 E
Karakelong, Pulau I	98	4.15 N	126.48 E
Karakendža	75	39.14 N	71.31 E
Karakišlak	75	39.44 N	67.40 E
Karakitang, Pulau I	102	3.11 N	125.32 E
Karakoin, Ozero ⊜	76	46.10 N	68.45 E
Karakojsu ≃	74	42.33 N	46.58 E
Karakojun ≃	75	41.10 N	75.45 E
Karakol', Ozero ⊜	76	45.35 N	64.22 E
Karakolka	75	41.32 N	77.23 E
Karakoram Range ⩘	110	35.30 N	77.00 E
Karakoro ≃	140	14.43 N	12.03 W
Karaköse	74	39.44 N	43.03 E
Karaksar	78	51.16 N	115.58 E
Karakudžur ≃	75	41.59 N	75.42 E
Karakul', S.S.S.R.	75	39.02 N	73.33 E
Karakul', S.S.S.R.	76	57.26 N	70.51 E
Karakul', S.S.S.R.	118	39.32 N	63.50 E
Karakul', Ozero ⊜	75	39.05 N	73.25 E
Karakulak	120	39.59 N	40.01 E
Kara-Kul'dža	75	40.37 N	73.35 E
Karakulino	70	56.01 N	53.43 E
Karakul'skoje	76	54.04 N	62.26 E
Karakum	76	46.49 N	79.33 E
Karakumskij Kanal ☲	118	37.35 N	61.50 E
Karakumy ◆[2]	62	39.00 N	60.00 E
Karakuni	260	34.28 N	135.28 E
Karakurt	120	40.10 N	42.36 E
Karakuwisa	146	18.56 S	19.40 E
Karala	262a	28.44 N	77.02 E
Karalat	70	45.55 N	48.18 E
Karalon	78	57.02 N	115.52 E
Karam	78	55.09 N	107.37 E
Karama ≃	102	2.18 S	119.06 E
Karamağara	120	39.42 N	35.31 E
Karamai → Kelamayi	76	45.37 N	84.53 E
Karaman, Tür.	120	37.05 N	29.20 E
Karaman, Tür.	120	37.11 N	33.14 E
Karamanlı	120	37.22 N	29.49 E
Karambu	102	3.51 S	116.04 E
Karamea	162	41.15 S	172.07 E
Karamea ≃	162	41.16 S	172.06 E
Karamea Bight C[3]	162	41.30 S	171.40 E
Karamıkbataklığı ☷	120	38.25 N	30.50 E
Karamoja □[5]	144	2.50 N	34.15 E
Karamürsel	120	40.42 N	29.36 E
Karamurt	75	42.19 N	69.58 E
Karamyš ≃	70	51.20 N	45.00 E
Karamyševo, S.S.S.R.	66	57.45 N	28.45 E
Karamyševo, S.S.S.R.	72	54.46 N	36.07 E
Karamyševo, S.S.S.R.	78	57.34 N	100.55 E
Karamzino	66	56.00 N	34.33 E
Karang, Gunung Λ	105a	6.16 S	106.03 E
Karang, Tanjung ≻	102	0.38 S	119.44 E
Karangagung	102	2.22 S	104.27 E
Karangampel	105a	6.28 S	108.27 E
Karangana	140	12.13 N	5.02 W
Karangasem	105b	8.27 S	115.37 E
Karangbinangun	105a	7.01 S	112.30 E
Karangbolong	105a	7.45 S	109.28 E
Karangbolong, Tanjung ≻	105a	7.46 S	109.03 E
Karanggede	105a	7.22 S	110.37 E
Karangkobar	105a	7.16 S	109.44 E
Karangnunggal	105a	7.38 S	108.06 E
Karangpandan	105a	7.37 S	111.04 E
Karangsembung	105a	6.51 S	108.39 E

English	Deutsch	Español	Français	Português
≃ River	Fluss	Río	Rivière	Rio
☲ Canal	Kanal	Canal	Canal	Canal
⌊ Waterfall, Rapids	Wasserfall, Stromschnellen	Cascada, Rápidos	Chute d'eau, Rapides	Cascata, Rápidos
Ц Strait	Meeresstrasse	Estrecho	Détroit	Estreito
C Bay, Gulf	Bucht, Golf	Bahía, Golfo	Baie, Golfe	Baía, Golfo
⊜ Lake, Lakes	See, Seen	Lago, Lagos	Lac, Lacs	Lago, Lagos
☷ Swamp	Sumpf	Pantano	Marais	Pântano
◿ Ice Features, Glacier	Eis- und Gletscherformen	Accidentes Glaciales	Formes glaciaires	Acidentes Glaciares
⊤ Other Hydrographic Features	Andere Hydrographische Objekte	Otros Elementos Hidrográficos	Autres données hydrographiques	Outros Elementos Hidrográficos
⊹ Submarine Features	Untermeerische Objekte	Accidentes Submarinos	Formes de relief sous-marin	Acidentes Submarinos
□ Political Unit	Politische Einheit	Unidad Politica	Entité politique	Unidade Política
▼ Cultural Institution	Kulturelle Institution	Institución Cultural	Institution culturelle	Instituição Cultural
⊥ Historical Site	Historische Stätte	Sitio Histórico	Site historique	Sitio Histórico
♠ Recreational Site	Erholungs- und Ferienort	Sitio de Recreo	Centre de loisirs	Sítio de Lazer
⊠ Airport	Flughafen	Aeropuerto	Aéroport	Aeroporto
■ Military Installation	Militäranlage	Instalación Militar	Installation militaire	Instalação Militar
◆ Miscellaneous	Verschiedenes	Misceláneo	Divers	Miscelânea

ENGLISH / DEUTSCH

Symbols in the index entries represent the broad categories identified in the key at the right. Symbols with superior numbers (∧∧[2]) identify subcategories (see complete key on page *I* · 26).

Kartensymbole in dem Registerverzeichnis stellen die rechts in Schlüssel erklärten Kategorien dar. Symbole mit hochgestellten Ziffern (∧∧[2]) bezeichnen Unterabteilungen einer Kategorie (vgl. vollständiger Schlüssel auf Seite *I* · 26).

Los símbolos incluídos en el texto del índice representan las grandes categorias identificadas con la clave a la derecha. Los símbolos con numeros en su parte superior (∧∧[2]) identifican las subcategorías (véase la clave completa en la página *I* · 26).

Les symboles de l'index représentent les catégories indiquées dans la légende à droite. Les symboles suivis d'un indice (∧∧[2]) représentent des sous-catégories (voir légende complète à la page *I* · 26).

Os símbolos incluídos no texto do índice representam as grandes categorias identificadas com a chave à direita. Os símbolos com números em sua parte superior (∧∧[2]) identificam as subcategorias (veja-se a chave completa à página *I* · 26).

∧	Mountain	Berg	Montaña	Montagne	Montanha
∧∧	Mountains	Berge	Montañas	Montagnes	Montanhas
)(	Pass	Pass	Paso	Col	Passo
∨	Valley, Canyon	Tal, Cañon	Valle, Cañón	Vallée, Canyon	Vale, Canhão
≍	Plain	Ebene	Llano	Plaine	Planície
≻	Cape	Kap	Cabo	Cap	Cabo
I	Island	Insel	Isla	Île	Ilha
II	Islands	Inseln	Islas	Îles	Ilhas
⊥	Other Topographic Features	Andere Topographische Objekte	Otros Elementos Topográficos	Autres données topographiques	Outros Elementos Topográficos

ESPAÑOL

Nombre	Página	Lat. °′	Long. °′ W=Oeste
Kawm ar-Rāhib	132	28.20 N	30.37 E
Kawm Birah	263c	30.05 N	31.08 E
Kawm Dafanah (Daphnæ) ⊥	132	30.52 N	32.11 E
Kawm Ḥamādah	132	30.46 N	30.42 E
Kawm Ishfīn	263c	30.11 N	31.15 E
Kawm Ishū	132	31.07 N	30.00 E
Kawm Ju'ayf (Naucratis) ⊥	132	30.54 N	30.36 E
Kawm Umbū	130	24.28 N	32.57 E
Kawnipi Lake ⊜	180	48.24 N	91.14 W
Kawthule □[3]	100	17.30 N	97.45 E
Kaya, H. Vol.	140	13.05 N	1.05 W
Kaya, Nihon	86	35.30 N	135.06 E
Kayaapu	102	5.26 S	102.24 E
Kayadibi, Tür.	120	39.55 N	34.15 E
Kayadibi, Tür.	120	39.29 N	36.43 E
Kayah □[3]	100	19.15 N	97.30 E
Kayak Island I	170	59.52 N	144.30 W
Kāyalpattinam	112	8.34 N	78.07 E
Kāyamba	262b	22.41 N	88.32 E
Kayambi	144	9.27 S	31.58 E
Kayan	100	16.54 N	96.34 E
Kayan ≃	102	2.55 N	117.35 E
Kayangel Islands II	98	8.04 N	134.43 E
Kayankulam	112	9.11 N	76.30 E
Kayapa	106	16.22 N	120.53 E
Kayaş	120	39.56 N	32.58 E
Kaya-san ▲	88	35.49 N	128.07 E
Kaycee	190	43.43 N	106.38 W
Kayeli	154	3.23 S	127.06 E
Kayembe-Mukulu	142	9.03 S	23.57 E
Kayen	105a	6.54 S	110.59 E
Kayes, Congo	142	4.25 S	11.41 E
Kayes, Mali	140	14.27 N	11.26 W
Kayes □[4]	140	14.00 N	11.00 W
Kayima	140	8.53 N	11.10 W
Kayış Dağı ▲	257b	40.59 N	29.09 E
Kaymakçı	120	38.10 N	28.08 E
Kaymaz	120	39.31 N	31.11 E
Kayna	50	50.59 N	12.14 E
Kaynak	120	37.43 N	39.37 E
Kayō, Nihon	86	34.51 N	133.42 E
Kayō, Nihon	164m	26.33 N	128.07 E
Kayoa, Pulau I	154	0.05 S	127.25 E
Kayombo	144	9.36 S	25.37 E
Kay Point ≻	170	69.18 N	138.22 W
Kāyser Gebergte ▲▲	240	3.03 N	56.35 W
Kayseri	120	38.43 N	35.30 E
Kayseri □[4]	120	38.30 N	35.55 E
Kaysersberg	54	48.08 N	7.15 E
Kaysville	190	41.02 N	111.56 W
Kayuadi, Pulau I	102	6.49 S	120.47 E
Kayuagung	102	3.24 S	104.50 E
Kayumas	105a	7.50 S	114.08 E
Kayuta Lake ⊜	200	43.25 N	75.12 W
Kayuyu	144	3.39 S	26.21 E
Kazach	74	41.06 N	45.22 E
Kazachskaja Sovetskaja Socialističeskaja Respublika □[3]	62	48.00 N	68.00 E
Kazachskij Melkosopočnik ▲▲[2]	76	49.00 N	72.00 E
Kazachstan	70	51.09 N	53.00 E
Kazačij	73	46.58 N	40.03 E
Kazačinskoje, S.S.S.R.	76	57.49 N	93.17 E
Kazačinskoje, S.S.S.R.	78	56.16 N	107.36 E
Kazačja Lopan'	68	50.21 N	36.11 E
Kazačje	64	70.44 N	136.13 E
Kazačji Lageri	68	46.42 N	32.59 E
Kazačka	70	51.28 N	43.56 E
Kazackij	76	49.20 N	58.31 E
Kazackoje	68	51.18 N	33.29 E
Kazakdarja	76	43.27 N	59.46 E
Kazakevičevo	79	48.17 N	134.46 E
Kazakh Soviet Socialist Republic → Kazachskaja Sovetskaja Socialističeskija Respublika □[3]	62	48.00 N	68.00 E
Kazaki	66	52.38 N	38.16 E
Kazaklija	68	46.00 N	28.37 E
Kazal'cevo	76	59.18 N	80.30 E
Kazalinsk	76	45.46 N	62.07 E
Kazan'	70	55.45 N	49.08 E
Kazan ≃	166	64.02 N	95.30 W
Kazanbulak	74	40.38 N	46.41 E
Kazancı	120	36.30 N	32.53 E
Kazandžik	118	39.16 N	55.32 E
Kazanga	142	5.10 S	23.06 E
Kazanka, S.S.S.R.	68	47.50 N	32.49 E
Kazanka, S.S.S.R.	76	53.20 N	67.27 E
Kazanka ≃	70	55.48 N	49.01 E
Kazanlâk	38	42.38 N	25.21 E
Kazan Lake ⊜	174	55.33 N	108.21 W
Kazanlı	120	36.50 N	34.45 E
Kazanovka	66	53.46 N	38.34 E
Kazan-rettō II	14	25.00 N	141.00 E
Kazanskaja	68	49.48 N	41.09 E
Kazanskij Vokzal ◆[5]	255b	55.46 N	37.40 E
Kazanskoje, S.S.S.R.	72	54.59 N	37.39 E
Kazanskoje, S.S.S.R.	76	55.38 N	69.14 E
Kazantip, Mys ≻	68	45.28 N	35.51 E
Kazarman	75	41.24 N	74.03 E
Kazatin	68	49.43 N	28.50 E
Kazatkul'	76	55.02 N	76.03 E
Kazbegi	74	42.39 N	44.39 E
Kazbek, Gora ▲	74	42.42 N	44.31 E
Kaz Dağı ▲	120	39.42 N	26.50 E
Kazembe	144	12.11 S	32.37 E
Kāzerūn	118	29.37 N	51.38 E
Kazgorodok, S.S.S.R.	76	52.53 N	70.42 E
Kazgorodok, S.S.S.R.	76	49.56 N	71.36 E
Kažim	24	60.20 N	51.30 E
Kazima	144	5.16 N	26.11 E
Kazi-Magomed	74	40.03 N	48.56 E
Kazimierza Wielka	30	50.16 N	20.30 E
Kazimierz Dolny	30	51.20 N	21.58 E
Kazincbarcika	30	48.16 N	20.37 E
Kazinga Channel ≃	144	0.13 S	29.53 E
Kazinka, S.S.S.R.	66	52.32 N	39.42 E
Kazinka, S.S.S.R.	68	50.14 N	37.50 E
Kāzipāra	262b	22.43 N	88.31 E
Kāzīr Char	116	22.46 N	90.33 E
Kaziza	142	10.42 S	23.52 E
Kazlų Rūda	66	54.46 N	23.30 E
Kaz'minskoje	74	44.35 N	41.41 E
Kaznačejevo	72	54.31 N	37.16 E
Kazo	84	36.07 N	139.36 E
Kaz'onnyj Torec ≃	73	48.54 N	37.46 E
Kaztalovka	70	49.46 N	48.42 E
Kazumba	142	6.25 S	22.02 E
Kazungula	144	17.45 S	25.20 E
Kazusa	84	35.17 N	140.05 E
Kazvin → Qazvīn	118	36.16 N	50.00 E
Kazy	118	39.13 N	57.30 E
Kazym ≃	64	63.54 N	65.50 E
Kazymskaja Kul'tbaza	64	63.40 N	67.14 E
Kazyr ≃	76	53.47 N	92.53 E
Kazzī, Qārat ▲[2]	136	21.26 N	24.30 E
Kbal Dâmrei	100	14.07 N	105.21 E
Kbely ◆[8]	50	50.07 N	14.32 E
Kchucin	79	46.04 N	137.51 E
Kcynia	30	53.00 N	17.30 E
Kdyně	30	49.23 N	13.02 E
Kéa	38	37.38 N	24.21 E
Kéa I	38	37.34 N	24.22 E
Keaau	219d	19.37 N	155.02 W
Keady	42	54.15 N	6.42 W
Keahole Point ≻	219d	19.44 N	156.03 W
Kealaikahiki Channel Ш	219a	20.37 N	156.50 W
Kealaikahiki Point ≻	219a	20.32 N	156.42 W
Kealakekua Bay C	219d	19.28 N	155.56 W
Kealia	219b	22.06 N	159.19 W
Keams Canyon	190	35.49 N	110.12 W
Keanae	219a	20.52 N	156.09 W

FRANÇAIS

Nom	Page	Lat. °′	Long. °′ W=Ouest
Keanapapa Point ≻	219a	20.54 N	157.04 W
Kean College of New Jersey ʊ[2]	266	40.41 N	74.14 W
Keansburg	198	40.27 N	74.08 W
Kearney, Mo., U.S.	184	39.22 N	94.22 W
Kearney, Nebr., U.S.	188	40.42 N	99.05 W
Kearney, Pa., U.S.	204	40.08 N	78.12 W
Kearns	190	40.39 N	111.59 W
Kearny, Ariz., U.S.	190	33.03 N	110.55 W
Kearny, N.J., U.S.	200	40.46 N	74.09 W
Kearsley	252	53.32 N	2.23 W
Kearsley Creek ≃	206	43.04 N	83.40 W
Keasbey	266	40.31 N	74.19 W
Keb' ≃	66	57.44 N	28.28 E
Kebajoran ◆[8]	259e	6.13 S	106.46 E
Keban	120	38.48 N	38.45 E
Keban Gölü ⊜[1]	120	38.50 N	39.15 E
Kebanyartimur	105a	7.09 S	112.52 E
Kébara	142	2.27 S	14.25 E
Kebbe	140	12.08 N	4.44 E
Kebeiti	110	36.47 N	79.29 E
Kébémer	140	15.22 N	16.27 W
Kébi, Mayo ≃	136	9.18 N	13.33 E
Kebili	138	33.42 N	8.58 E
Kebîr, Oued el ≃	34	36.50 N	6.07 E
Kebnekaise ▲	24	67.53 N	18.33 E
Kebri Dehar	134	6.47 N	44.17 E
Kebumen	105a	7.40 S	109.39 E
Keb'uty	70	45.50 N	44.14 E
Keče	75	43.14 N	71.22 E
Kecel	30	46.32 N	19.16 E
Kech ≃	118	26.00 N	62.44 E
Kechika ≃	166	59.36 N	127.05 W
Keçiborlu	120	37.57 N	30.18 E
Kecksburg	204	40.11 N	79.28 W
Kecskemét	30	46.54 N	19.42 E
Kedabek	74	40.34 N	45.49 E
Kedada	134	5.20 N	36.00 E
Kedah □[3]	104	6.00 N	100.40 E
Kėdainiai	66	55.17 N	24.00 E
Kédange-sur-Canner	52	49.19 N	6.20 E
Kedarnath	114	30.44 N	79.04 E
Kedārpur	116	23.18 N	90.27 E
Kedawung	105a	6.42 S	108.31 E
Kedges Straits Ш	198	38.03 N	76.02 W
Kedgwick	176	47.39 N	67.21 W
Kédhron	38	39.13 N	22.03 E
Kedianpo	90	31.23 N	112.51 E
Kediri	105a	7.49 S	112.01 E
Kedjebi	140	8.12 N	0.25 E
Kedon	64	64.08 N	159.14 E
Kedong	79	48.02 N	126.15 E
Kédougou	140	12.33 N	12.11 W
Kedrasju	24	64.36 N	60.24 E
Kedrovka	76	55.32 N	86.03 E
Kedu	92	26.33 N	104.21 E
Kedungdung	105a	7.06 S	113.15 E
Kedungjati	105a	7.10 S	110.37 E
Kedungwuni	105a	6.58 S	109.39 E
Kedvavom	24	64.15 N	53.27 E
Kędzierzyn	30	50.20 N	18.12 E
Keecheus Lake ⊜	214	47.22 N	121.22 W
Keefer	208	38.32 N	84.38 W
Keefers	172	50.02 N	121.33 W
Keego Harbor	206	42.37 N	83.21 W
Keele	44	53.00 N	2.17 W
Keele ≃	170	64.24 N	124.50 W
Keele Peak ▲	170	63.26 N	130.19 W
Keeley Lake ⊜	174	54.54 N	108.08 W
Keels	176	48.36 N	53.24 W
Keelung → Chilung	90	25.08 N	121.44 E
Keene, Ont., Can.	202	44.15 N	78.10 W
Keene, Calif., U.S.	218	35.13 N	118.33 W
Keene, Ky., U.S.	182	37.57 N	84.38 W
Keene, N.H., U.S.	178	42.56 N	72.17 W
Keene, Ohio, U.S.	204	40.21 N	81.52 W
Keene, Tex., U.S.	212	32.24 N	97.20 W
Keenesburg	190	40.07 N	104.31 W
Keeney Knob ▲	182	37.47 N	80.42 W
Keeneyville	268	41.59 N	88.07 W
Keeper Hill ▲[2]	28	52.45 N	8.16 W
Keerbergen	52	51.00 N	4.37 E
Keerqinyouzhongqi (Gaoliban)	79	44.53 N	121.58 E
Keerqinzuohouqi	79	42.58 N	122.20 E
Keerqinzuozhongqi (Baokang)	79	44.07 N	123.18 E
Keer-weer, Cape ≻	154	13.58 S	141.30 E
Keerzong	110	32.11 N	79.59 E
Keeseg ▲	58	46.58 N	12.14 E
Keeseville	178	44.30 N	73.29 W
Keetmanshoop	146	26.36 S	18.08 E
Keetmanshoop □[5]	146	26.30 S	19.00 E
Keewatin, Ont., Can.	174	49.46 N	94.34 W
Keewatin, Minn., U.S.	180	47.24 N	93.05 W
Keewatin □[5]	166	65.00 N	95.00 W
Kefa □[4]	134	6.50 N	36.00 E
Kefallinía I	38	38.15 N	20.35 E
Kéfalos	38	36.45 N	27.00 E
Kefamenanu	102	9.27 S	124.29 E
Kefar 'Azza	122	31.29 N	34.32 E
Kefar Blum	122	33.10 N	35.36 E
Kefar 'Eqron	122	31.51 N	34.49 E
Kefar Sava	122	32.10 N	34.54 E
Kefar Shammay	122	32.57 N	35.27 E
Kefar Syrkin	122	32.04 N	34.56 E
Kefar Szold	122	33.11 N	35.39 E
Kefar Vitkin	122	34.23 N	34.53 E
Kefar Warburg	122	31.43 N	34.44 E
Keferdiz	120	38.19 N	39.03 E
Keffi	140	8.51 N	7.52 E
Keffin Hausa	140	12.15 N	9.58 E
Keflavík	24a	64.02 N	22.36 W
Kega	24	65.10 N	36.54 E
Ke-ga, Mui ≻, Viet.	100	10.42 N	107.58 E
Ke-ga, Mui ≻, Viet.	100	12.53 N	109.28 E
Kegalla	112	7.15 N	80.21 E
Kégashka, Lac ⊜	176	50.20 N	61.25 W
Kegaska	176	50.12 N	61.17 W
Kegejli	76	42.45 N	59.35 E
Kegičovka	68	49.17 N	35.46 E
Keglo, Baie C	166	59.10 N	65.50 W
Kegnæs I	41	54.52 N	9.59 E
Kegon-no-taki ᒪ	84	36.44 N	139.31 E
Kegonsa, Lake ⊜	206	42.58 N	89.15 W
Kegonzhake	110	33.00 N	87.53 E
Keg River	166	57.48 N	117.52 W
Kegums	66	56.46 N	24.45 E
Kegworth	44	52.50 N	1.16 W
Kehdingen, Land ◆[1]	48	53.45 N	9.15 E
Kehe	79	50.38 N	122.08 E
Kehiwin Indian Reserve ◆[4]	172	54.07 N	110.48 W
Kehl	52	48.35 N	7.50 E
Kehlen	54	47.41 N	9.33 E
Kehoe	208	38.28 N	83.03 W
Kehra	66	59.20 N	25.20 E
Kehrigk	50	52.09 N	13.55 E
Ke-hsi Mānsām	100	21.56 N	97.50 E
Keighley	42	53.52 N	1.54 W
Keihoku	86	35.09 N	135.38 E
Keijō → Sŏul	88	37.33 N	126.58 E
Keila	66	59.18 N	24.25 E
Keilor	159	37.43 S	144.50 E
Keimoes	148	28.41 S	21.00 E
Kei Mouth	148	32.41 S	28.22 E
Keio University ʊ[2]	258	35.38 N	139.45 E
Kei Road	148	32.42 S	27.32 E
Keiser	184	35.41 N	90.06 W
Keiskammahoek	148	32.41 S	27.09 E
Keiskammapunt ≻	148	32.40 S	27.10 E
Keïta	140	14.46 N	5.46 E
Kéita, Bahr ≃	136	9.14 N	18.21 E
Keitele	26	63.11 N	26.22 E
Keitele ⊜	26	62.55 N	26.00 E
Keith, Austl.	156	36.06 S	140.21 E
Keith, Scot., U.K.	28	57.32 N	2.57 W
Keith Arm C	166	65.20 N	122.15 W
Keithley Creek	172	52.45 N	121.24 W
Keithsburg	180	41.06 N	90.56 W
Keiyasi	165g	17.54 S	177.45 E

PORTUGUÊS

Nome	Página	Lat. °′	Long. °′ W=Oeste
Keizer	214	44.57 N	123.01 W
Kejaman	102	2.39 N	113.45 E
Kejimkujik National Park ♠	176	44.21 N	65.18 W
Kejni, Gora ▲	170	64.30 N	174.54 W
Kejvy ▲▲	24	67.35 N	38.00 E
Kekaha	219b	21.58 N	159.43 W
Kekek ≃	180	48.24 N	75.48 W
Kekerengu	162	42.00 S	174.01 E
Kekertaluk Island I	166	68.10 N	66.30 W
Kékes ▲	30	47.55 N	20.02 E
Kekexili	110	35.11 N	93.35 E
Kekexilishanmai ▲▲	110	35.20 N	90.00 E
Kekeyaer	75	38.02 N	75.05 E
Keklau	165b	7.35 N	134.39 E
Kek Lok Si ʊ[1]	104	5.23 N	100.14 E
Kekpāra	116	22.27 N	86.35 E
Kekri	110	25.58 N	75.09 E
Kekurnoi, Cape ≻	170	57.44 N	155.15 W
Kelafo	134	5.40 N	44.20 E
Kelai ≃	102	2.10 N	117.29 E
Kelalihu ⊜	110	34.36 N	87.16 E
Kelam	134	4.48 N	36.06 E
Kelamayi	76	45.37 N	84.53 E
Kela Met	134	16.04 N	38.43 E
Kelan	92	39.48 N	111.39 E
Kelanang	104	2.48 N	101.26 E
Kelang	104	3.02 N	101.27 E
Kelang, Pulau I, Indon.	154	3.12 S	127.44 E
Kelang, Pulau I, Malay.	104	3.00 N	101.18 E
Kelani ≃	112	6.58 N	79.52 E
Kelantan	104	0.51 N	101.40 E
Kelantan □[3]	104	5.20 N	102.00 E
Kelantan ≃	104	6.11 N	102.15 E
Kelapa	102	1.52 S	105.42 E
Kelaqinzuoqi	88	41.08 N	119.38 E
Kelasuri	74	43.08 N	41.13 E
Kelat	208	38.32 N	84.19 W
Kelayres	200	40.54 N	76.00 W
Kelb, Ouadi V	136	15.19 N	18.51 E
Kel'badžar	74	40.07 N	46.02 E
Kelberg	52	50.17 N	6.55 E
Kelbia, Sebkra ⊜	36	35.51 N	10.16 E
Kelbra	50	51.26 N	11.02 E
Keld Ula ▲	76	43.20 N	85.25 E
Kel'd'ušovo	70	55.01 N	44.59 E
Kélékélé	263b	4.20 S	15.08 E
Kelenföld ◆[8]	254c	47.28 N	19.03 E
Kelenken', Gora ▲	170	66.07 N	170.52 W
Keles, S.S.S.R.	75	41.24 N	69.12 E
Keles, Tür.	120	39.55 N	29.14 E
Keles ≃	75	41.02 N	68.37 E
Kéléso	140	10.57 N	3.59 W
Keleti-főcsatorna Ξ	30	48.01 N	21.20 E
Keleti Pályaudvar ◆[5]	254c	47.30 N	19.06 E
Kelheim	30	48.55 N	11.52 E
Kelibia	138	36.51 N	11.06 E
Kelif	118	37.21 N	66.15 E
Keliyahe ≃	110	39.00 N	81.40 E
Kelkheim	52	50.08 N	8.26 E
Kelkit ≃	120	40.46 N	36.32 E
Kell	209	38.30 N	88.54 W
Kellé	142	0.06 S	14.33 E
Kellen	48	51.48 N	6.10 E
Kellenhusen	50	54.11 N	11.03 E
Keller, Tex., U.S.	212	32.56 N	97.15 W
Keller, Va., U.S.	198	37.37 N	75.46 W
Kellerberg	58	46.40 N	13.42 E
Kellerberrin	152	31.38 S	117.43 E
Keller Joch ▲	58	47.19 N	11.46 E
Keller Lake ⊜, N.W. Ter., Can.	166	64.00 N	121.30 W
Keller Lake ⊜, Sask., Can.	174	56.04 N	106.46 W
Kellerovka	76	53.50 N	69.17 E
Keller Peak ▲	218	34.12 N	117.03 W
Kellett, Cape ≻	166	71.59 N	125.34 W
Kellettville	204	41.33 N	79.16 W
Kelleys Island	204	41.36 N	82.42 W
Kelleys Island I	204	41.36 N	82.42 W
Kelliher	174	51.15 N	103.44 W
Kellinghusen	48	53.57 N	9.43 E
Kellmünz	54	48.07 N	10.08 E
Kellogg, Idaho, U.S.	192	47.32 N	116.07 W
Kellogg, Iowa, U.S.	180	41.43 N	92.54 W
Kellogg, Minn., U.S.	180	44.18 N	91.59 W
Kellogg Marsh	214	48.05 N	122.07 W
Kelloggsville	204	41.52 N	80.36 W
Kellojärvi ⊜	26	64.16 N	29.03 E
Kelloselkä	24	66.56 N	28.50 E
Kells → Ceanannus Mór	28	53.44 N	6.53 W
Kelly Lake ⊜	170	65.30 N	126.10 W
Kelly Run ≃, Pa., U.S.	269b	40.15 N	79.55 W
Kelly Run ≃, Pa., U.S.	269b	40.13 N	79.45 W
Kellyville, Austl.	264a	33.43 S	150.57 E
Kellyville, Okla., U.S.	186	35.57 N	96.13 W
Kelmė	66	55.38 N	22.56 E
Kel'mency	68	48.27 N	26.50 E
Kelmscott	158a	32.07 S	116.01 E
Kélo	136	9.19 N	15.48 E
Kelolokan	102	1.08 N	117.54 E
Kelottijärvi	24	68.31 N	22.04 E
Kelowna	172	49.53 N	119.29 W
Kelsall	42	53.13 N	2.43 W
Kelsey Bay	172	50.24 N	125.57 W
Kelsey Head ≻	44	50.24 N	5.08 W
Kelsey Lake ⊜	174	53.37 N	101.02 W
Kelseyville	194	38.59 N	122.50 W
Kelso, Scot., U.K.	42	55.36 N	2.25 W
Kelso, Wash., U.S.	214	46.09 N	122.54 W
Kelsterbach	52	50.04 N	8.32 E
Kel'temašat	75	42.30 N	70.17 E
Keltie Inlet C	166	64.28 N	73.28 W
Keluang	104	2.02 N	103.19 E
Keluang, Tanjung ≻	102	3.02 S	110.39 E
Kelud, Gunung ▲	105a	7.56 S	112.18 E
Kelulunhe → Kerulen ≃	80	48.48 N	117.00 E
Keluocun	79	49.16 N	125.44 E
Keluohe ≃	79	49.22 N	125.15 E
Kelvedon	44	51.51 N	0.42 E
Kelvedon Hatch	250	51.40 N	0.16 E
Kelvington	174	52.10 N	103.30 W
Kelvin Seamount ✢[3]	16	39.00 N	64.00 W
Kelyehed	134	8.44 N	49.10 E
Kelzenberg	253	51.07 N	6.30 E
Kem'	24	64.57 N	34.36 E
Kem' ≃, S.S.S.R.	24	64.57 N	34.41 E
Kem' ≃, S.S.S.R.	76	58.31 N	92.04 E
Kéma, Congo	263b	4.11 S	15.13 E
Kema, Indon.	102	1.23 N	125.04 E
Kema ≃, S.S.S.R.	66	59.21 N	44.29 E
Kema ≃, S.S.S.R.	66	60.16 N	37.20 E
Ké Macina	140	13.58 N	5.22 W
Kemah, Tür.	120	39.36 N	39.02 E
Kemah, Tex., U.S.	212	29.32 N	95.01 W
Kemaliye	120	39.16 N	38.29 E
Kemalpaşa, Tür.	120	41.30 N	41.30 E
Kemalpaşa, Tür.	120	38.25 N	27.26 E
Kemano	172	53.34 N	127.56 W
Kemasik	104	4.25 N	103.27 E
Kemayan	104	3.08 N	102.22 E
Kemayoran Airport ⊠	259e	6.09 S	106.51 E
Kembani	102	1.34 S	122.54 E
Kembé	142	4.36 N	21.54 E
Kemberg	50	51.46 N	12.38 E
Kemblesville	198	39.45 N	75.50 W
Kembolcha	134	11.02 N	39.43 E
Kembs	54	47.41 N	7.30 E
Kembul	154	5.55 S	150.40 E
Kemčug ≃	76	57.14 N	90.31 E
Kemena ≃	102	3.10 N	113.03 E
Kemer	120	36.38 N	29.21 E
Kemer ≃	257b	41.04 N	29.07 E
Kemer Barajı ◆[6]	120	37.34 N	28.31 E
Kemerburgaz	257b	41.09 N	28.54 E

Kemerhisar	120	37.49 N	34.36 E
Kemerovo	76	55.20 N	86.05 E
Kemi	24	65.49 N	24.32 E
Kemie	26	62.14 N	30.20 E
Kemijärvi	24	66.40 N	27.25 E
Kemijärvi ⊜	24	66.36 N	27.24 E
Kemijoki ≃	26	65.47 N	24.30 E
Kemiö → Kimito	26	60.10 N	22.45 E
Keml'a	70	54.42 N	45.15 E
Kemmel	46	50.47 N	2.49 E
Kemmelberg ▲[2]	46	50.47 N	2.50 E
Kemmerer	190	41.48 N	110.32 W
Kemminghausen ◆[8]	253	51.34 N	7.29 E
Kemmuna I	36	36.00 N	14.20 E
Kemnath	30	49.52 N	11.54 E
Kemnitz	50	54.04 N	13.31 E
Kemo-Gribingui □[5]	142	7.00 N	19.00 E
Kemp	212	32.26 N	96.14 W
Kemp, Lake ⊜[1]	186	33.45 N	99.13 W
Kemparana	140	12.50 N	4.56 W
Kemp Coast ◆[2]	9	67.10 S	58.00 E
Kempele	26	64.55 N	25.30 E
Kempen	52	51.22 N	6.25 E
Kempen □[9]	52	51.10 N	5.20 E
Kempener Land ◆[1]	253	51.19 N	6.29 E
Kempenfelt Bay C	202	44.23 N	79.36 W
Kempenich	52	50.25 N	7.07 E
Kempen-Krefeld □[8]	253	51.17 N	6.31 E
Kemper → Quimper	32	48.00 N	4.06 W
Kempisch Kanaal Ξ	52	51.10 N	4.49 E
Kempner	186	31.05 N	98.00 W
Kemp Peninsula ≻[1]	9	73.08 S	60.15 W
Kemps Bay	228	24.02 N	77.33 W
Kemps Creek ≃	264a	33.51 S	150.46 E
Kempsey	156	31.05 S	152.50 E
Kempston	44	52.07 N	0.30 W
Kempt, Lac ⊜	166	47.25 N	74.22 W
Kempten (Allgäu)	54	47.43 N	10.19 E
Kempton, Ill., U.S.	206	40.56 N	88.14 W
Kempton, Ind., U.S.	206	40.17 N	86.14 W
Kempton Park	148	26.06 S	28.14 E
Kempton Park Race Course ♠	250	51.25 N	0.23 W
Kemptville	202	45.01 N	75.38 W
Kemptville Creek ≃	202	45.03 N	75.39 W
Kemsing	250	51.18 N	0.14 E
Kemubu	104	5.18 N	102.01 E
Kemujan, Pulau I	105a	5.48 S	110.28 E
Kemul, Kong ▲	102	1.52 N	116.11 E
Ken ≃	114	25.46 N	80.31 E
Ken, Loch ⊜	42	55.02 N	4.02 W
Ken, Water of ≃	42	55.04 N	4.08 W
Kena ≃	24	62.05 N	39.06 E
Kenadsa	138	31.48 N	2.26 W
Kenaf	134	1.37 N	41.36 E
Kenai	170	60.33 N	151.15 W
Kenai Mountains ▲▲	170	60.00 N	150.00 W
Kenai Peninsula ≻[1]	170	60.10 N	150.00 W
Kenamuke Swamp ≋	130	5.55 N	33.48 E
Kenansville, Fla., U.S.	210	27.53 N	80.59 W
Kenansville, N.C., U.S.	182	34.58 N	77.58 W
Kenaral	75	42.32 N	72.08 E
Kenašči	70	50.32 N	53.20 E
Kenashiga-sen ▲	86	35.14 N	133.31 E
Kenaston	174	51.30 N	106.18 W
Kenberma	273	42.17 N	70.52 W
Kenbridge	182	36.58 N	78.08 W
Kenda	116	23.12 N	86.32 E
Kendai	114	22.45 N	82.37 E
Kendal, Sask., Can.	174	50.15 N	103.37 W
Kendal, Indon.	105a	6.55 S	110.12 E
Kendal, S. Afr.	148	26.04 S	28.58 E
Kendal, Eng., U.K.	42	54.20 N	2.45 W
Kendall, Austl.	156	31.38 S	152.43 E
Kendall, Fla., U.S.	210	25.41 N	80.19 W
Kendall, Mich., U.S.	206	42.22 N	85.49 W
Kendall, N.Y., U.S.	200	43.20 N	78.02 W
Kendall, Wis., U.S.	180	43.48 N	90.21 W
Kendall □[6]	206	41.38 N	88.27 W
Kendall, Cape ≻	166	63.36 N	87.09 W
Kendall, Mount ▲	162	41.22 S	172.24 E
Kendall Park	198	40.25 N	74.34 W
Kendallville	206	41.27 N	85.16 W
Kendari	102	3.57 S	122.35 E
Kendari, Teluk C	102	3.57 S	122.38 E
Kendawangan	102	2.32 S	110.12 E
Kende	140	11.30 N	4.12 E
Kendenup	152	34.29 S	117.39 E
Kendghāta	116	24.05 N	87.10 E
Kendikolu I	112	5.57 N	73.24 E
Kendiktas ▲▲	75	43.35 N	74.45 E
Kendleton	212	29.27 N	96.00 W
Kendrāpāra	110	20.30 N	86.25 E
Kendrew	148	32.32 S	24.30 E
Kendrick, Fla., U.S.	182	29.22 N	82.12 W
Kendrick, Idaho, U.S.	192	46.37 N	116.39 W
Kendrick Creek ≃	216	38.00 N	119.50 W
Kendua	262b	22.34 N	88.10 E
Kendu Bay	144	0.22 S	34.39 E
Kendyrlik	76	47.30 N	85.12 E
Kendyrlisor, Solončak ≋	76	42.50 N	54.30 E
Kenedy	186	28.49 N	97.51 W
Kenefick	212	30.07 N	94.51 W
Kenema	140	7.52 N	11.12 W
Kenes, S.S.S.R.	75	43.59 N	73.35 E
Kenes, S.S.S.R.	75	43.41 N	67.49 E
Kenga	76	57.27 N	80.57 E
Kenga ≃	76	58.05 N	80.37 E
Kenge	142	4.52 S	16.59 E
Kengeja	144	5.25 S	39.44 E
Kēng Hkam, Mya.	100	21.01 N	98.29 E
Keng Hkam, Mya.	100	21.27 N	97.03 E
Kengkou, Zhg.	90	28.27 N	120.26 E
Kengkou, Zhg.	90	29.48 N	117.22 E
Kengtian	90	25.54 N	119.26 E
Kēng Tung	100	21.17 N	99.36 E
Kenhardt	148	29.19 S	21.12 E
Kenhorst	198	40.18 N	75.57 W
Kenia	142	2.43 S	17.04 E
Kenia → Kenya □[1]	144	1.00 N	38.00 E
Kenia → Kenya, Mount ▲	144	0.10 S	37.20 E
Kéniéba	140	12.50 N	11.14 W
Kenilworth, Eng., U.K.	44	52.21 N	1.34 W
Kenilworth, Ill., U.S.	268	42.05 N	87.43 W
Kenilworth, N.J., U.S.	266	40.41 N	74.18 W
Kenilworth, Pa., U.S.	198	40.14 N	75.38 W
Kenilworth Castle ⊥	44	52.21 N	1.34 W
Keningau	102	5.20 N	116.10 E
Kenitra	138	34.16 N	6.40 W
Kenley ◆[8]	250	51.19 N	0.06 W
Kenly	182	35.36 N	78.07 W
Kenmare, Eire	28	51.53 N	9.35 W
Kenmare, N. Dak., U.S.	188	48.40 N	102.05 W
Kenmawr	269b	40.29 N	80.07 W
Kenmore, N.Y., U.S.	200	42.58 N	78.53 W
Kenmore, Wash., U.S.	214	47.46 N	122.14 W
Kennard, Ind., U.S.	208	39.54 N	85.31 W
Kennard, Pa., U.S.	204	41.28 N	80.20 W
Kennard, Tex., U.S.	212	31.22 N	95.11 W
Kennebec	188	43.54 N	99.52 W
Kennebec ≃	178	44.00 N	69.50 W
Kennebecasis Bay C	176	45.25 N	66.00 W
Kennebec Lake ⊜	202	44.43 N	77.00 W
Kennebunk	178	43.23 N	70.33 W
Kennedale	212	32.39 N	97.13 W
Kennedy, Rh.	144	18.52 S	27.10 E
Kennedy, Ala., U.S.	184	33.35 N	87.59 W
Kennedy, N.Y., U.S.	204	42.10 N	79.06 W
Kennedy, Cape → Canaveral, Cape ≻	210	28.27 N	80.32 W
Kennedy, Mount ▲	170	60.30 N	139.00 W

Kennedy Entrance Ш	170	59.00 N	152.00 W
Kennedy Lake ⊜	172	49.05 N	125.40 W
Kennedy Peak ▲	100	23.19 N	93.45 E
Kennedy Range ▲▲	152	24.30 S	115.00 E
Kennedyville	198	39.18 N	76.00 W
Kenner	184	29.59 N	90.15 W
Kennerdell	204	41.16 N	79.51 W
Kennet ≃, Eng., U.K.	44	52.26 N	0.28 E
Kennet ≃, Eng., U.K.	44	51.28 N	0.57 W
Kennetcook	176	45.11 N	63.44 W
Kenneth City	210	27.49 N	82.44 W
Kennett	184	36.14 N	90.03 W
Kennett Square	198	39.51 N	75.43 W
Kennewick	192	46.12 N	119.07 W
Kenney	209	40.06 N	89.05 W
Kenney Dam ◆[6]	172	53.37 N	124.58 W
Kennington	44	51.10 N	0.54 E
Kennisis Lake ⊜	202	45.13 N	78.39 W
Kenn Reef ✢[2]	150	21.12 S	155.46 E
Kenny	212	30.03 N	96.20 W
Kennydale	214	47.31 N	122.12 W
Kennywood Amusement Park ♠	269b	40.23 N	79.52 W
Kénogami	176	48.26 N	71.14 W
Kenogami ≃	166	51.06 N	84.28 W
Kenogamissi Lake ⊜	180	48.15 N	81.31 W
Keno Hill	170	63.55 N	135.18 W
Kenora	174	49.47 N	94.29 W
Kenosha	206	42.35 N	87.49 W
Kenosha □[6]	206	42.06 N	88.04 W
Kenova	178	38.24 N	82.35 W
Kenoza Lake	200	41.44 N	74.57 W
Kenoza Lake ⊜	273	42.47 N	71.03 W
Kenozero, Ozero ⊜	24	62.03 N	38.14 E
Ken Rock	206	42.15 N	89.03 W
Kensal	188	47.18 N	98.44 W
Kense	76	46.49 N	68.20 E
Kensico Reservoir ⊜[1]	200	41.05 N	73.46 W
Kensington, Austl.	264a	33.55 S	151.14 E
Kensington, P.E.I., Can.	176	46.26 N	63.38 W
Kensington, Calif., U.S.	216	37.54 N	122.16 W
Kensington, Conn., U.S.	197	41.38 N	72.46 W
Kensington, Kans., U.S.	188	39.46 N	99.02 W
Kensington, Md., U.S.	274c	39.02 N	77.03 W
Kensington, Ohio, U.S.	204	40.44 N	80.57 W
Kensington ◆[8], S. Afr.	263d	26.12 S	28.06 E
Kensington ◆[8], N.Y., U.S.	266	40.39 N	73.58 W
Kensington ◆[8], Pa., U.S.	275	39.58 N	75.08 W
Kensington and Chelsea ◆[8]	250	51.29 N	0.11 W
Kensington Metropolitan Park ♠	271	42.32 N	83.39 W
Kensington Park	210	27.22 N	82.31 W
Kent, S.L.	140	8.10 N	13.10 W
Kent, Conn., U.S.	197	41.43 N	73.29 W
Kent, N.Y., U.S.	200	43.20 N	78.08 W
Kent, Ohio, U.S.	204	41.09 N	81.22 W
Kent, Oreg., U.S.	214	45.12 N	120.42 W
Kent, Wash., U.S.	214	47.23 N	122.14 W
Kent □[6], Ont., Can.	204	42.25 N	82.10 W
Kent □[6], Eng., U.K.	44	51.15 N	0.40 E
Kent □[6], Del., U.S.	198	39.10 N	75.32 W
Kent □[6], Md., U.S.	198	39.13 N	76.04 W
Kent □[6], Mich., U.S.	206	42.56 N	85.33 W
Kent □[6], R.I., U.S.	197	41.40 N	71.38 W
Kent ≃	42	54.15 N	2.48 W
Kent, Vale of V	44	51.10 N	0.30 E
Kent Acres	198	39.08 N	75.31 W
Kentani	148	32.31 S	28.19 E
Kentau	75	43.36 N	68.36 E
Kent Bay C	166	69.59 N	96.02 W
Kent Bridge	204	42.31 N	82.04 W
Kent County Airport ⊠	206	42.54 N	85.39 W
Kentfield	272	37.57 N	122.33 W
Kent Group II	156	39.27 S	147.20 E
Kenthurst	264a	33.40 S	151.00 E
Kent Island I	198	38.55 N	76.20 W
Kent Lake ⊜	206	42.32 N	83.40 W
Kentland, Ind., U.S.	206	40.46 N	87.27 W
Kentland, Md., U.S.	274c	38.55 N	76.53 W
Kenton, Eng., U.K.	44	50.38 N	3.28 W
Kenton, Del., U.S.	198	39.14 N	75.40 W
Kenton, Mich., U.S.	180	46.28 N	88.54 W
Kenton, Ohio, U.S.	206	40.39 N	83.36 W
Kenton, Tenn., U.S.	184	36.12 N	89.01 W
Kenton □[6]	208	38.56 N	84.33 W
Kent Park	273	42.06 N	70.41 W
Kent Park Golf Course ♠	263d	26.08 S	28.04 E
Kent Peninsula ≻[1]	166	68.30 N	107.00 W
Kent Point ≻	198	38.50 N	76.22 W
Kentucky □[3]	168	37.30 N	85.15 W
Kentucky ≃	208	38.41 N	85.11 W
Kentucky, Middle Fork ≃	182	37.35 N	83.40 W
Kentucky, North Fork ≃	182	37.34 N	83.42 W
Kentucky, South Fork ≃	182	37.34 N	83.42 W
Kentucky Lake ⊜[1]	184	36.25 N	88.05 W
Kentucky State Horse Park ♠	208	38.08 N	84.31 W
Kentville	176	45.05 N	64.30 W
Kentwood, La., U.S.	184	30.56 N	90.31 W
Kentwood, Mich., U.S.	206	42.53 N	85.35 W
Kent Woodlands	272	37.57 N	122.34 W
Kenvil	266	40.53 N	74.38 W
Kenwick	158a	32.02 S	115.58 E
Kenwood, Calif., U.S.	216	38.25 N	122.33 W
Kenwood, Ohio, U.S.	208	39.12 N	84.23 W
Kenwood ◆[8]	268	41.49 N	87.36 W
Kenwood ⊥	250	51.34 N	0.10 W
Kenya □[1]	10		
	144	1.00 N	38.00 E
Kenya, Mount ▲	144	0.10 S	37.20 E
Kenyon, Eng., U.K.	252	53.27 N	2.34 W
Kenyon, Minn., U.S.	180	44.16 N	92.59 W
Kenyon, R.I., U.S.	197	41.27 N	71.38 W
Kenzingen	54	48.11 N	7.46 E
Kenzou	142	4.10 N	15.02 E
Keokea	219a	20.24 N	156.21 W
Keokuk	180	40.24 N	91.24 W
Keonchi	114	22.38 N	81.47 E
Keo Neua, Col de)(	100	18.23 N	105.09 E
Keonjhar □[5]	114	22.00 N	85.30 E
Keonjhargarh	110	21.38 N	85.35 E
Keon Park	264b	37.42 S	145.01 E
Keosauqua	180	40.44 N	91.58 W
Keota, Iowa, U.S.	180	41.21 N	91.57 W
Keota, Okla., U.S.	186	35.15 N	94.55 W
Kepahiang	102	3.39 S	102.34 E
Kepala Batas	104	5.31 N	100.26 E
Kepanjen	105a	8.07 S	112.34 E
Kepi	154	6.32 S	139.19 E
Kępice	30	54.15 N	16.52 E
Kepina	24	65.24 N	41.50 E
Kepingshan ▲▲	75	40.00 N	77.10 E
Kępno	30	51.17 N	17.59 E
Kepo	102	2.56 S	106.33 E
Keppel Bay C	156	23.21 S	150.55 E
Keppel Harbour C	261c	1.16 N	103.50 E
Kepsut	120	39.41 N	28.09 E
Keptown	209	39.05 N	88.40 W
Kequan	88	36.04 N	114.00 E
Kerala □[3]	112	10.00 N	76.30 E
Keramian, Pulau I	102	5.04 S	114.36 E
Kerandin	102	0.12 S	104.46 E
Kerang	156	35.44 S	143.55 E

Keranyo	134	5.04 N	38.18 E
Keratéa	38	37.48 N	23.59 E
Keratsínion	257c	37.58 N	23.37 E
Keraudren, Cape ≻	152	19.57 S	119.45 E
Kerava	26	60.24 N	25.07 E
Keravat	154	4.19 S	152.01 E
Kerbat ≃	104	5.01 N	102.51 E
Kerbela → Karbalā'	118	32.36 N	44.02 E
Kerbi ≃	79	52.28 N	136.25 E
Kerburan	120	37.33 N	41.44 E
Kerby	192	42.12 N	123.39 W
Kerč'	68	45.22 N	36.27 E
Kerčel'	76	59.18 N	64.46 E
Kerčemja	24	61.28 N	53.50 E
Kerčenskij Poluostrov ≻[1]	68	45.15 N	36.00 E
Kerčenskij Proliv Ш	68	45.22 N	36.38 E
Kerčevskij	24	59.55 N	56.17 E
Kerch → Kerč'	68	45.22 N	36.27 E
Kerckhoff Lake ⊜[1]	216	37.09 N	119.31 W
Kerec, Mys ≻	24	65.20 N	39.40 E
Kerej, Ozero ⊜	76	50.08 N	68.45 E
Kerema	154	8.00 S	145.45 E
Keremeos	172	49.12 N	119.50 W
Kerem Maharal	122	32.39 N	34.59 E
Kerempe Burnu ≻	120	42.01 N	33.21 E
Keren	134	15.46 N	38.28 E
Kerend	118	34.16 N	46.15 E
Kerens	212	32.08 N	96.14 W
Kerepes	254c	47.34 N	19.18 E
Keret'	24	66.16 N	33.34 E
Keret', Ozero ⊜	24	65.55 N	32.56 E
Kerewan	140	13.29 N	16.10 W
Kerga	24	62.39 N	46.00 E
Kergez	74	40.18 N	49.38 E
Kerguélen, Îles II	6	49.15 S	69.10 E
Kerguelen-Gaussberg Ridge ✢[3]	6	55.00 S	75.00 E
Kerhonkson	200	41.46 N	74.11 W
Kerian ≃	104	5.10 N	100.26 E
Kericho	144	0.22 S	35.17 E
Keri Kera	130	12.21 N	32.46 E
Kerikeri	162	35.13 S	173.58 E
Kerimäki	26	61.55 N	29.17 E
Kerinci, Gunung ▲	102	1.42 S	101.16 E
Kerio ≃	144	2.59 N	36.07 E
Keríon	38	37.40 N	20.48 E
Keritang	102	0.51 S	102.39 E
Kerkdriel	48	51.46 N	5.20 E
Kerken	52	51.27 N	6.22 E
Kerkenna, Îles II	138	34.44 N	11.12 E
Kerkhove	46	50.48 N	3.30 E
Kerkhoven	188	45.12 N	95.19 W
Kerki, S.S.S.R.	24	63.43 N	54.05 E
Kerki, S.S.S.R.	118	37.50 N	65.12 E
Kérkira (Corfu)	38	39.36 N	19.56 E
Kérkira I	38	39.40 N	19.42 E
Kerkrade [-Holz]	52	50.52 N	6.04 E
Kerling	104	3.35 N	101.36 E
Kermadec Islands II	14	29.16 S	177.55 W
Kermadec Ridge ✢[3]	14	31.00 S	177.30 W
Kermadec Trench ✢[1]	14	30.30 S	176.00 W
Kermajärvi ⊜	26	62.28 N	28.40 E
Kermān, Īrān	118	30.17 N	57.05 E
Kerman, Calif., U.S.	216	36.43 N	120.04 W
Kermān □[4]	118	29.00 N	57.30 E
Kermānshāh	118	34.19 N	47.04 E
Kermānshāhān □[4]	118	34.30 N	47.00 E
Kerme Körfezi C	120	36.50 N	28.00 E
Kermit	186	31.51 N	103.06 W
Kermit Roosevelt Seamount ✢[3]	16	39.45 N	145.50 W
Kermode, Mount ▲	172	52.57 N	131.51 W
Kern □[6]	218	35.20 N	118.55 W
Kern ≃	194	35.13 N	119.17 W
Kern, South Fork ≃	194	35.40 N	118.27 W
Kern City	218	35.18 N	119.05 W
Kernersville	182	36.07 N	80.04 W
Kernforschungs-zentrum ʊ[3]	52	49.07 N	8.26 E
Kern Island Canal Ξ	218	35.22 N	119.01 W
Kern River Channel ≃[1]	216	35.49 N	119.40 W
Kernville	194	35.43 N	118.26 W
Keroh	104	5.43 N	101.00 E
Keros	24	60.44 N	52.50 E
Kérou	140	10.50 N	2.06 E
Kérouané	140	9.16 N	9.01 W
Kérouané □[4]	140	9.10 N	8.50 W
Kerowagi	154	5.50 S	144.50 E
Kerpe Burnu ≻	120	41.10 N	30.11 E
Kerpen	52	50.52 N	6.41 E
Kerpinen'	68	46.47 N	28.22 E
Kerr	204	41.03 N	78.25 W
Kerre ≃	130	5.19 N	25.40 E
Kerrera I	28	56.24 N	5.33 W
Kerridge	252	53.17 N	2.06 W
Kerridge Hill ▲[2]	252	53.17 N	2.06 W
Kerrobert	174	51.55 N	109.08 W
Kerr Reservoir ⊜[1]	182	36.35 N	70.28 W
Kerrtown	204	41.38 N	80.10 W
Kerruish Park ♠	269a	41.26 N	81.34 W
Kerrville	186	30.03 N	99.08 W
Kerry	44	52.30 N	3.16 W
Kerry □[6]	28	52.10 N	9.30 W
Kerry Head ≻	28	52.25 N	9.57 W
Kersa	134	9.28 N	41.53 E
Kersbrook	158b	34.47 S	138.51 E
Kersey	204	41.22 N	78.36 W
Kershaw	182	34.33 N	80.35 W
Kersinyane	140	15.24 N	10.10 W
Kersley	172	52.49 N	122.25 W
Kerspestausee ⊜[1]	253	51.08 N	7.30 E
Kerstenhausen	52	51.04 N	9.13 E
Kert, Oued ≃	34	35.15 N	3.15 W
Kertamulia	102	0.23 S	109.09 E
Kerteh	104	4.31 N	103.27 E
Kerteminde	41	55.27 N	10.40 E
Kertosono	105a	7.35 S	112.06 E
Kerulen (Cherlen) (Kelulunhe) ≃	80	48.48 N	117.00 E
Kerva	70	55.37 N	39.35 E
Kerzaz	138	29.30 N	1.37 W
Kerzendorf	254a	52.16 N	13.17 E
Kerženec	70	56.28 N	44.26 E
Kerženec ≃	70	56.05 N	45.03 E
Kerzers	54	46.58 N	7.12 E
Kesabpur	116	22.55 N	89.13 E
Ke-sach	100	9.46 N	105.59 E
Kesagami Lake ⊜	166	50.23 N	80.15 W
Kesälahti	26	61.54 N	29.50 E
Keşan	120	40.51 N	26.37 E
Keşap	120	40.55 N	38.31 E
Kesbern	253	51.20 N	7.42 E
Kesch, Piz ▲	54	46.38 N	9.52 E
Kesennuma	82	38.54 N	141.35 E
Keshan	79	48.02 N	125.51 E
Keshena	180	44.52 N	88.38 W
Keshequa Creek ≃	200	42.43 N	77.50 W
Keshitage	110	37.23 N	78.05 E
Keshod	110	21.18 N	70.15 E
Keşirlik	120	41.58 N	27.12 E
Keşiş Dağları ▲▲	120	39.50 N	39.45 E
Keskastel	52	48.58 N	7.02 E
Keskin	120	39.41 N	33.37 E
Keski-Suomen lääni □[4]	26	62.30 N	25.30 E
Keskozero	24	61.24 N	33.12 E
Keskuvejem, Gora ▲	170	66.12 N	177.40 W
Kes'ma	66	58.27 N	37.04 E
Kesova Gora	66	57.35 N	37.17 E
Kespur	116	22.35 N	87.29 E
Kesra	36	35.49 N	9.22 E
Kessebüren	253	51.31 N	7.43 E
Kessel	52	51.08 N	4.37 E
Kesselsdorf	50	51.02 N	13.35 E

≃ River	Fluss	Río	Rivière	Rio	
Ξ Canal	Kanal	Canal	Canal	Canal	
ᒪ Waterfall, Rapids	Wasserfall, Stromschnellen	Cascada, Rápidos	Chute d'eau, Rapides	Cascata, Rápidos	
Ш Strait	Meeresstrasse	Estrecho	Détroit	Estreito	
C Bay, Gulf	Bucht, Golf	Bahía, Golfo	Baie, Golfe	Baía, Golfo	
⊜ Lake, Lakes	See, Seen	Lago, Lagos	Lac, Lacs	Lago, Lagos	
≋ Swamp	Sumpf	Pantano	Marais	Pântano	
Ice Features, Glacier	Eis- und Gletscherformen	Accidentes Glaciales	Formes glaciaires	Acidentes Glaciares	
Other Hydrographic Features	Andere Hydrographische Objekte	Otros Elementos Hidrográficos	Autres données hydrographiques	Outros Elementos Hidrográficos	

✢ Submarine Features	Untermeerische Objekte	Accidentes Submarinos	Formes de relief sous-marin	Acidentes Submarinos
□ Political Unit	Politische Einheit	Unidad Política	Entité politique	Unidade Política
ʊ Cultural Institution	Kulturelle Institution	Institución Cultural	Institution culturelle	Instituição Cultural
⊥ Historical Site	Historische Stätte	Sitio Histórico	Site historique	Sitio Histórico
♠ Recreational Site	Erholungs- und Ferienort	Sitio de Recreo	Centre de loisirs	Sítio de Lazer
⊠ Airport	Flughafen	Aeropuerto	Aéroport	Aeroporto
■ Military Installation	Militäranlage	Instalación Militar	Installation militaire	Instalação Militar
◆ Miscellaneous	Verschiedenes	Misceláneo	Divers	Miscelânea

ENGLISH | DEUTSCH
Name Page Lat.°′ Long.°′ | Name Seite Breite°′ Länge°′ E=Ost

Kessingland 44 52.25 N 1.42 E
Kesswil 54 47.36 N 9.20 E
Kestel Gölü @ 120 37.26 N 30.28 E
Kestell 148 28.19 S 28.38 E
Kesten'ga 24 65.55 N 31.47 E
Kestep 120 36.27 N 29.16 E
Kestilä 26 64.21 N 26.17 E
Keston ⁸ 250 51.22 N 0.02 E
Keswick, Ont., Can. 202 44.15 N 79.28 W
Keswick, Eng., U.K. 42 54.37 N 3.08 W
Keszthely 30 46.46 N 17.15 E
Ket' ≃ 76 58.55 N 81.32 E
Keta 140 5.55 N 1.00 E
Keta ≃ 84 34.56 N 137.50 E
Keta, Ozero @ 64 68.44 N 90.00 E
Ketaka 86 35.30 N 134.03 E
Keta Lagoon C 140 5.54 N 0.56 E
Ketam, Pulau I 261c 1.24 N 103.57 E
Ketama 34 34.50 N 4.37 W
Ketang 90 22.58 N 115.28 E
Ketapang, Indon. 102 1.52 S 109.59 E
Ketapang, Indon. 105a 5.44 S 105.48 E
Ketapang, Indon. 105a 6.54 S 113.17 E
Ketaun 102 3.23 S 101.49 E
Ketchikan 170 55.21 N 131.35 W
Ketchum 192 43.41 N 114.22 W
Kete Krachi 140 7.46 N 0.03 W
Ketelmeer @ 48 52.35 N 5.45 E
Keti Bandar 110 24.08 N 67.27 E
Ketinowan ▲ 144 0.40 N 35.50 E
Ketoj, Ostrov I 64 47.20 N 152.28 E
Kétou 140 7.22 N 2.36 E
Ketovo 76 55.21 N 65.18 E
Kętrzyn (Rastenburg) 30 54.06 N 21.23 E
Ketsch 52 49.22 N 8.31 E
Ketta 142 1.28 N 15.56 E
Kettering, Eng., U.K. 44 52.24 N 0.44 W
Kettering, Ohio, U.S. 208 39.41 N 84.10 W
Kettinge 41 54.42 N 11.45 E
Kettle ≃, N.A. 172 48.42 N 118.07 W
Kettle ≃, Minn., U.S. 180 45.52 N 46.45 W
Kettle Creek ≃, Ont., Can. 202 42.40 N 81.13 W
Kettle Creek ≃, Pa., U.S. 200 41.18 N 77.51 W
Kettle Creek Lake @ 204 41.20 N 78.08 W
Kettle Creek State Park ♠ 204 41.23 N 77.56 W
Kettle Falls 192 48.36 N 118.03 W
Kettleman City 216 36.06 N 119.58 W
Kettleman Hills ² 216 36.00 N 120.00 W
Kettle River Range 192 48.30 N 118.40 W
Kettlersville 206 40.22 N 84.16 W
Kettleshulme 252 53.19 N 2.01 W
Kettlewell 42 54.09 N 2.02 W
Kettwig 52 51.22 N 6.56 E
Kety 30 49.53 N 19.13 E
Ketzin 50 52.28 N 12.50 E
Keudemane 104 5.15 N 96.55 E
Keudepasi 104 4.18 N 95.56 E
Keudeteunom 104 4.27 N 95.48 E
Keudeunga 104 5.01 N 95.22 E
Keuka Lake @ 200 42.27 N 77.10 W
Keuka Lake, West Branch C 200 42.33 N 77.09 W
Keuka Park 200 42.37 N 77.06 W
Keukenhof ♠ 48 52.16 N 4.33 E
Keul' 78 58.25 N 102.49 E
Keula 50 51.20 N 10.31 E
Keum ≃ 76 59.32 N 70.35 E
Keurboomsrivier 148 34.00 S 23.24 E
Keurusselkä @ 26 62.10 N 24.40 E
Keuruu 26 62.16 N 24.42 E
Kevdo-Mel'sitovo 70 53.09 N 43.54 E
Kevelaer 48 51.35 N 6.15 E
Kevin 192 48.45 N 111.58 W
Kevsala 70 45.48 N 42.41 E
Kevuaieli, Ribeirão ≃ 245 13.00 S 53.27 W
Kew, Austl. 159 37.49 S 145.02 E
Kew, S. Afr. 263d 26.08 S 28.06 E
Kew, T./C. Is. 228 21.54 N 72.02 W
Kewanee 180 41.14 N 89.56 W
Kewanna 206 41.01 N 86.25 W
Kewäre 114 27.57 N 83.47 E
Kewaunee 180 44.27 N 87.30 W
Keweenaw Bay C 180 46.56 N 88.23 W
Keweenaw Peninsula ≻¹ 180 47.12 N 88.25 W
Keweenaw Point ≻ 180 47.30 N 87.50 W
Kew Gardens ♠, Ont., Can. 265b 43.40 N 79.18 W
Kew Gardens ♠, Eng., U.K. 250 51.28 N 0.18 W
Keyala 144 4.27 N 32.52 E
Keyangkeershan ▲ 110 31.20 N 87.13 E
Keya Paha ≃ 188 42.54 N 99.00 W
Key Biscayne 210 25.42 N 80.10 W
Keyes, Calif., U.S. 216 37.33 N 120.54 W
Keyes, Okla., U.S. 188 36.49 N 102.15 W
Keyesport 209 38.44 N 89.17 W
Keyhole Reservoir @¹ 188 44.21 N 104.51 W
Keyhole State Park ♠ 188 44.19 N 104.48 W
Key Indian Reserve ⁴ 174 51.45 N 102.08 W
Key Largo 210 25.04 N 80.28 W
Key Largo I 210 25.16 N 80.19 W
Keymer 44 50.55 N 0.08 W
Keyneton 158b 34.34 S 139.08 E
Keynsham 44 51.26 N 2.30 W
Keynshamburg 144 19.15 S 29.39 E
Keyport, N.J., U.S. 266 40.26 N 74.12 W
Keyport, Wash., U.S. 214 47.42 N 122.38 W
Keyport Harbor C 266 40.26 N 74.12 W
Keysborough 264b 38.00 S 145.10 E
Keysbrook 158a 32.26 S 115.59 E
Keyser 178 39.26 N 78.59 W
Keystone, Ind., U.S. 206 40.36 N 85.16 W
Keystone, Iowa, U.S. 180 42.00 N 92.12 W
Keystone, S. Dak., U.S. 188 43.54 N 103.25 W
Keystone, W. Va., U.S. 182 37.25 N 81.27 W
Keystone Lake @¹, Okla., U.S. 186 36.15 N 96.25 W
Keystone Lake @¹, Pa., U.S. 204 40.45 N 79.15 W
Keystone Peak ▲ 190 31.53 N 111.13 W
Keystone State Park ♠ 204 40.23 N 79.24 W
Keysun 120 37.34 N 37.50 E
Keysville, Fla., U.S. 210 27.52 N 82.06 W
Keysville, Va., U.S. 182 37.04 N 78.29 W
Keytesville 184 39.26 N 92.56 W
Key West 210 24.33 N 81.48 W
Key West Island I 210 24.33 N 81.47 W
Key West Naval Air Station ■ 210 24.34 N 81.41 W
Kez 70 57.53 N 53.43 E
Kezar Stadium ♠ 272 37.46 N 122.27 W
Kezhen 88 41.57 N 118.03 E
Kezi 144 20.58 S 28.32 E
Kežma 78 58.59 N 101.09 E
Kežmarok 30 49.08 N 20.25 E
Kgalagadi ☐⁵ 146 25.00 S 22.00 E
Kgatleng ☐⁵ 146 24.28 S 26.05 E
Kgun Lake @ 170 61.32 N 163.45 W
Khabab 122 33.00 N 36.16 E
Khabrat Umm Judhām ⁻¹ 132 30.24 N 31.58 E
Khābūr, Nahr al- ≃ 120 35.08 N 40.26 E
Khadar 262a 28.33 N 77.22 E
Khadari, Wādī al- V 130 10.29 N 26.15 E
Khadbūng Taung ▲ 100 18.57 N 94.37 E
Khadki (Kirkee) 112 18.34 N 73.52 E
Khadra 34 36.15 N 0.35 E
Khafūr, Wādī V 132 29.37 N 32.04 E
Khagaria 114 25.30 N 86.29 E
Khagdon ≃¹ 116 22.09 N 90.05 E
Khāgrāmuri 262b 22.26 N 88.14 E
Khaïdhárion 257c 37.33 N 22.53 E
Khaidik Gol ≃ 76 42.55 N 84.01 E
Khair 114 27.57 N 77.50 E
Khairābād 114 27.32 N 80.45 E
Khairāgarh 110 21.25 N 80.58 E
Khairbani 116 24.14 N 87.05 E
Khairna 262c 19.06 N 73.01 E
Khairpur, Pāk. 110 27.32 N 68.46 E
Khairpur, Pāk. 113 29.35 N 72.14 E
Khajrāho 110 24.50 N 79.58 E
Khājuri 116 21.52 N 87.58 E
Khajuri ⁸ 262a 28.43 N 77.16 E
Kha Khaeng ≃ 100 14.55 N 99.07 E
Khakhea 146 24.51 S 23.20 E
Khalándrion 257c 38.01 N 23.48 E
Khalatse 113 34.20 N 76.49 E
Khālidī, Khirbat al- ⊥ 122 29.39 N 35.14 E
Khālid Ibn al-Walīd ⁶ 122 32.43 N 35.41 E
Khalkhalah 122 33.04 N 36.32 E
Khálki I 120 36.17 N 27.35 E
Khalkidhikí ☐⁹ 38 40.25 N 23.27 E
Khalkís 38 38.28 N 23.36 E
Khālsar 110 34.31 N 77.41 E
Khambhāliya 110 22.12 N 69.39 E
Khambhāt, Gulf of C 112 21.00 N 72.30 E
Khāmgaon 112 20.41 N 76.34 E
Khamir 134 16.05 N 43.55 E
Khamīs Mushayṭ 134 18.18 N 42.44 E
Khamkeut 100 18.15 N 104.43 E
Khammam 112 17.15 N 80.09 E
Khan ≃ 146 22.37 S 14.56 E
Khāna 116 23.20 N 87.44 E
Khānābād 116 23.04 N 69.07 E
Khān Abū Shāmāt 122 33.40 N 36.54 E
Khānākul 116 22.43 N 87.51 E
Khān al-Baghdādī 118 33.51 N 42.33 E
Khānaqīn 118 34.21 N 45.22 E
Khān Arnabah 122 33.11 N 35.53 E
Khancoban 161b 36.12 S 148.05 E
Khandaghosh 116 23.13 N 87.41 E
Khandela 110 27.36 N 75.30 E
Khandla 148 28.37 S 31.05 E
Khandwa 114 21.50 N 76.20 E
Khāneh Khvodī 118 36.05 N 56.04 E
Khānewāl 110 30.18 N 71.56 E
Khāngāh Dogrān 113 31.50 N 73.37 E
Khāngarh, Pāk. 110 28.22 N 71.43 E
Khāngarh, Pāk. 113 29.55 N 71.10 E
Khangkhai 100 19.28 N 103.15 E
Khanh-hoa 100 12.15 N 109.06 E
Khanh-hung 100 9.36 N 105.58 E
Khaniá 38 35.31 N 24.02 E
Khanion, Kólpos C 38 35.34 N 23.48 E
Khānkurda 116 22.00 N 87.25 E
Khanna 113 30.42 N 76.13 E
Khannā, Qā' ≃ 122 32.04 N 36.26 E
Khānozai 110 30.37 N 67.19 E
Khānpur, Bhārat 262b 22.40 N 88.16 E
Khānpur, Pāk. 118 28.39 N 70.39 E
Khānpur ⁸, Bhārat 262a 28.31 N 77.14 E
Khānpur ⁸, Bhārat 262a 28.34 N 77.01 E
Khān Shaykhūn 120 35.26 N 36.38 E
Khanty-Mansijsk → Chanty-Mansijsk 62 61.00 N 69.06 E
Khān Yūnus 122 31.21 N 34.19 E
Khanzira, Ras ≻ 134 10.55 N 45.47 E
Khao Saming 100 12.21 N 102.27 E
Khao Yoi 100 13.14 N 99.50 E
Khapalu 113 35.10 N 76.20 E
Kharabā 122 32.34 N 36.27 E
Kharagdiha 114 24.25 N 86.10 E
Kharagpur, Bhārat 114 25.07 N 86.33 E
Kharagpur, Bhārat 116 22.20 N 87.20 E
Kharak 113 33.07 N 71.06 E
Kharān 110 28.35 N 65.25 E
Kharār 110 30.45 N 76.39 E
Kharar, Bhārat 113 30.45 N 76.39 E
Kharar, Bhārat 116 22.42 N 87.41 E
Khārāvli ² 262c 18.54 N 72.55 E
Kharāyij, Sabkhat al- @ 120 35.40 N 37.20 E
Kharaz, Jabal ▲ 134 12.44 N 44.09 E
Kharbatā 122 31.57 N 35.04 E
Kharbine → Haerbin 79 45.45 N 126.41 E
Khardah 116 22.44 N 88.22 E
Khārghar 262c 19.03 N 73.04 E
Khargon 110 21.49 N 75.36 E
Khariān 113 32.49 N 73.52 E
Kharian Road 113 32.50 N 73.54 E
Kharīm, Jabal ▲ 132 30.17 N 33.58 E
Khariṭ, Wādī al- V 130 24.26 N 33.03 E
Khārk, Jazīreh-ye I 118 29.15 N 50.20 E
Kharkov → Char'kov 68 50.00 N 36.15 E
Kharkurī, Jabal al- ▲² 132 13.57 N 47.09 E
Kharmān, Kūh-e ▲ 118 29.13 N 53.35 E
Kharri 262b 22.55 N 88.14 E
Kharsāwān 114 22.48 N 85.50 E
Kharsia 114 21.58 N 83.07 E
Khartoum → Al-Khurṭūm 130 15.36 N 32.32 E
Khartoum North → Al-Khurṭūm Baḥrī 130 15.38 N 32.33 E
Khartum → Al-Khurṭūm 130 15.36 N 32.32 E
Kharumwa 144 3.12 S 32.39 E
Khasbāti 262b 22.55 N 88.25 E
Khasebake 146 20.41 S 24.29 E
Khāsh, Afg. 118 31.31 N 62.52 E
Khāsh, Īrān 118 28.14 N 61.14 E
Khāsh ≃ 118 31.11 N 62.05 E
Khāsh, Dasht-e ⁻² 118 31.50 N 62.30 E
Khashab, Jabal al- ▲² 132 29.56 N 31.01 E
Khashm al-Qirbah 130 14.58 N 35.55 E
Khashm al-Qirbah, Khazzān @¹ 130 14.40 N 35.55 E
Khashshab, Tur'at al- ≃ 263c 29.53 N 31.17 E
Khashum 130 12.27 N 28.02 E
Khaskovo → Haskovo 38 41.56 N 25.33 E
Khatauli 114 29.17 N 77.43 E
Khātegaon 114 22.36 N 76.55 E
Khātra 116 22.59 N 86.51 E
Khaur 113 33.16 N 72.28 E
Khavda 110 23.51 N 69.43 E
Khawrah 134 14.26 N 46.09 E
Khawsa 100 15.03 N 97.50 E
Khayāla ⁸ 262a 28.40 N 77.06 E
Khaybar 134 25.42 N 39.31 E
Khaybar, Ḥarrat ⁹ 118 25.30 N 39.45 E
Khayerpur 262b 22.35 N 88.33 E
Khayrā Bil @ 262b 22.52 N 88.29 E
Khayrasole 116 23.48 N 87.16 E
Khayung ≃ 100 15.07 N 104.42 E
Khazar, Baḥr-e → Caspian Sea ⁻² 62 42.00 N 50.30 E
Kheardaha 262b 22.29 N 88.28 E
Khe-bo 100 19.08 N 104.41 E
Khed 112 17.43 N 73.23 E
Khefapur 262a 28.30 N 77.05 E
Khejurdaha 262b 22.59 N 88.10 E
Khemis el Khechna 34 36.39 N 3.20 E
Khemis Miliana 138 36.16 N 2.13 E
Khemisset 138 33.50 N 6.03 W
Khem Karan 113 31.09 N 74.34 E
Khemmarat 100 16.03 N 105.13 E
Khenchela 138 35.28 N 7.11 E
Khenifra 138 33.00 N 5.40 W
Khenjān 110 35.36 N 68.55 E
Khenyen 262b 22.59 N 88.19 E
Khera ⁸ 262a 28.46 N 77.08 E
Kheri 114 27.54 N 80.48 E
Kheri ☐⁵ 114 28.10 N 80.40 E
Kherli 114 27.12 N 77.02 E
Kherrata 138 36.31 N 5.26 E
Khersan ≃ 118 31.33 N 50.22 E
Kherson → Cherson 66 46.38 N 32.35 E
Kherwāra 110 23.59 N 73.35 E
Khetia 110 21.40 N 74.35 E
Khevāj 110 38.13 N 71.02 E
Khewāri 110 26.36 N 68.52 E
Khewra 113 32.39 N 73.01 E
Kheyr Khāneh 118 34.57 N 63.37 E
Khichīwāra Plateau ⁴¹ 114 24.25 N 77.30 E
Khichripur ⁸ 262a 28.37 N 77.19 E
Khilchipur 114 24.02 N 76.34 E
Khilkāpur 262b 22.46 N 88.29 E
Khimki → Chimki 72 55.54 N 37.26 E
Khíos 38 38.22 N 26.08 E
Khíos I 38 38.22 N 26.00 E
Khipro 110 25.50 N 69.22 E
Khirbat Abū Qashṭah 122 31.16 N 34.16 E
Khirbat al-Ghazālah 122 32.44 N 36.12 E
Khirbat 'Awwād 122 32.19 N 36.43 E
Khirbat Qanāfār 122 33.38 N 35.43 E
Khirbat Umm as-Surab 122 32.26 N 36.19 E
Khirbitā 132 30.45 N 30.40 E
Khiri Mat 100 16.59 N 99.48 E
Khirpai 116 22.42 N 87.37 E
Khisfīn 122 32.51 N 35.49 E
Khiuri Khala ▲ 114 29.58 N 81.18 E
Khiva → Chiva 62 41.24 N 60.22 E
Khivach 75 38.13 N 71.02 E
Khīyāv 118 38.24 N 47.40 E
Khlong Khlung 100 16.12 N 99.43 E
Khlong Thom 100 7.56 N 99.09 E
Khlong Yai 100 11.46 N 102.54 E
Khlung 100 12.27 N 102.14 E
Khmel'nitskiy → Chmel'nickij 68 49.25 N 27.00 E
Khoai, Hon I 100 8.26 N 104.50 E
Khogali 130 6.08 N 27.47 E
Khojāng ≃ 114 28.41 N 85.09 E
Khok Kloi 100 8.17 N 98.19 E
Khok Pho 100 6.43 N 101.06 E
Khoksa 116 23.48 N 89.17 E
Khok Samrong 100 15.04 N 100.44 E
Kholargós 257c 38.00 N 23.48 E
Kholm 110 36.42 N 67.41 E
Khomām 118 37.22 N 49.40 E
Khomas Highland ⁴¹ 146 22.30 S 16.30 E
Khombole 140 14.46 N 16.42 W
Khomeyn 118 33.38 N 50.04 E
Khomodimo 146 22.46 S 23.52 E
Khondmāl Hills ² 112 20.20 N 84.00 E
Khoni 262c 19.10 N 73.07 E
Khon Kaen 100 16.26 N 102.50 E
Khóra 38 37.04 N 21.43 E
Khorāsān ☐⁴ 118 35.00 N 58.00 E
Khora Sfakion 38 35.12 N 24.09 E
Khorel 262b 22.42 N 88.19 E
Khorramābād 118 33.30 N 48.20 E
Khorram Daraq 118 36.26 N 48.36 E
Khorramshahr 118 30.25 N 48.11 E
Khoru 262b 22.51 N 88.31 E
Khouribga 138 32.54 N 6.57 W
Khoutsiri 146 21.22 S 20.08 E
Khowai 116 24.06 N 91.38 E
Khowāng 116 27.16 N 94.53 E
Khowst 110 33.22 N 69.57 E
Khrisokhoús, Kólpos C 120 35.06 N 32.25 E
Khrisoúpolis 38 40.58 N 24.42 E
Khudiān 113 30.59 N 74.17 E
Khuff, Ar. Sa. 118 24.57 N 44.42 E
Khuff, Lībīya 136 28.20 N 18.48 E
Khugaung 100 26.07 N 98.16 E
Khūgīānī Sāni 110 31.31 N 66.12 E
Khuis 146 26.37 S 21.45 E
Khu Khan 100 14.42 N 104.12 E
Khulna 114 22.48 N 89.33 E
Khulna ☐⁸ 114 22.30 N 89.45 E
Khūm Bathéay 100 11.59 N 104.57 E
Khumbur Khūlē Ghar ▲ 110 32.49 N 68.47 E
Khungdungang ▲ 114 27.31 N 89.02 E
Khunjerab Pass)(113 36.52 N 75.27 E
Khun Tan, Doi ▲ 100 18.30 N 99.20 E
Khunti 114 23.05 N 85.17 E
Khun Yuam 100 18.49 N 97.57 E
Khūr 118 32.57 N 58.26 E
Khurai 114 24.03 N 78.19 E
Khuralji Khās ⁸ 262a 28.39 N 77.17 E
Khurayyif, Minqār ⁴ 132 28.55 N 30.26 E
Khurda 110 20.11 N 85.37 E
Khuria Tank @¹ 114 22.25 N 81.36 E
Khurigāchi 262b 22.49 N 88.20 E
Khurja 114 28.15 N 77.51 E
Khurli 110 28.19 N 65.52 E
Khurramshahr → Khorramshahr 118 30.25 N 48.11 E
Khūryān Mūryān II 108 17.30 N 56.00 E
Khūsf 118 32.46 N 58.53 E
Khushāb 113 32.18 N 72.21 E
Khushk Khurd ⁸ 262a 28.46 N 77.10 E
Khutshwe 146 23.19 S 24.29 E
Khutubi ≃ 76 44.45 N 86.25 E
Khuwayy 130 13.05 N 29.14 E
Khuzdār 110 27.48 N 66.37 E
Khūzestān ☐⁴ 118 31.00 N 49.00 E
Khvāf 118 34.33 N 60.08 E
Khvājeh Moḥammad, Kūh-e ▲ 110 36.22 N 70.17 E
Khvājeh Ra'ūf 110 33.19 N 64.43 E
Khvor 118 33.47 N 55.03 E
Khvormūj 118 28.39 N 51.23 E
Khvoy 118 38.33 N 44.58 E
Khwae Noi ≃ 100 14.01 N 99.32 E
Khyber ☐⁸ 113 34.00 N 71.00 E
Khyber Pass)(113 34.05 N 71.10 E
Kia 165e 7.33 S 158.26 E
Kialwe 144 9.22 S 27.08 E
Kiama, Austl. 160 34.41 S 150.51 E
Kiama, Zaïre 142 7.15 S 17.44 E
Kiamba 106 5.59 N 124.37 E
Kiambi 144 7.20 S 28.01 E
Kiamboni, Kap → Chiamboni, Ras ≻ 134 1.38 S 41.36 E
Kiambu 144 1.10 S 36.50 E
Kiamesha Lake 200 41.41 N 74.40 W
Kiamichi ≃ 184 33.57 N 95.14 W
Kiamika ≃ 196 46.38 N 75.15 W
Kiamika, Barrage ⁻⁶ 196 46.37 N 75.08 W
Kiamika, Réservoir @¹ 196 46.40 N 75.05 W
Kiamusze → Jiamusi 79 46.50 N 130.21 E
Kian → Ji'an 90 27.07 N 114.58 E
Kiana 170 66.59 N 160.25 W
Kiandra 161b 35.53 S 148.30 E
Kiangara 147b 17.58 S 47.02 E
Kiangarow, Mount ▲ 156 26.49 S 151.33 E
Kiangsi → Jiangxi ☐⁴ 90 28.00 N 116.00 E
Kiangsu → Jiangsu ☐⁴ 80 33.00 N 120.00 E
Kiantajärvi @ 26 65.03 N 29.07 E
Kiaohsien → Jiaoxian 88 36.18 N 119.58 E
Kibaek 41 56.02 N 8.51 E
Kibali ≃ 144 3.37 N 28.34 E
Kibamba 144 4.53 S 26.33 E
Kibanga Port 144 0.11 N 32.52 E
Kibangou 142 3.27 S 12.21 E
Kibanseke I 263b 4.26 S 15.23 E
Kibar 110 32.20 N 78.01 E
Kibara 144 2.09 S 33.27 E
Kibāsī 118 30.34 N 47.50 E
Kibau Iyayi 144 8.52 S 34.32 E
Kibawe 106 7.34 N 125.00 E
Kibaya 144 5.18 S 36.34 E
Kibbie 206 42.25 N 86.12 W
Kibenga 142 7.55 S 17.35 E
Kiberashi 144 5.23 S 37.26 E
Kiberege 144 7.57 S 36.52 E
Kiberi 154 7.25 S 143.48 E
Kibi, Ghana 140 6.10 N 0.33 W
Kibi, Nihon 86 34.39 N 133.51 E
Kibi-kōgen ⁴¹ 86 34.45 N 133.15 E
Kibila 144 8.14 S 26.23 E
Kibiti 144 7.44 S 38.57 E
Kiboga 144 1.02 N 30.58 E
Kiboko 144 2.15 S 37.42 E
Kibombo 144 3.54 S 25.55 E
Kibondo 144 3.35 S 30.42 E
Kibouendé, Congo 263b 4.17 S 15.09 E
Kibouendé, Congo 263b 4.19 S 15.11 E
Kibouendé I 263b 4.11 S 15.09 E
Kibouendé II 263b 4.12 S 15.09 E
Kibre Mengist 134 5.52 N 39.00 E
Kıbrıs → Cyprus ☐¹ 120 35.00 N 33.00 E
Kibumbu 144 3.32 S 29.45 E
Kibungo 144 2.10 S 30.32 E
Kibuye, Bdi. 144 3.40 S 29.59 E
Kibuye, Rw. 144 2.03 S 29.21 E
Kibwesa 144 6.28 S 29.57 E
Kibwezi 144 2.25 S 37.58 E
Kibworth Beauchamp 44 52.32 N 1.00 W
Kičevo 38 41.31 N 20.57 E
Kichčik 64 53.24 N 156.03 E
Kichijōji 258 35.42 N 139.35 E
Kickapoo 180 46.47 N 29.36 E
Kickapoo ≃ 180 43.05 N 90.53 W
Kickapoo Creek ≃, Ill., U.S. 184 40.08 N 89.27 W
Kickapoo Creek ≃, Tex., U.S. 186 31.31 N 99.58 W
Kickapoo Creek ≃, Tex., U.S. 212 32.16 N 95.28 W
Kickapoo Creek ≃, Tex., U.S. 212 30.47 N 95.08 W
Kicking Horse Pass)(172 51.27 N 116.18 W
Kičkino 70 47.05 N 44.02 E
Kičma 70 57.12 N 48.55 E
Kicman' 68 48.27 N 25.44 E
Kičmengskij Gorodok 24 59.59 N 45.48 E
Kičuj ≃ 70 55.13 N 51.16 E
Kidal 140 18.26 N 1.24 E
Kidapawan 106 7.01 N 125.03 E
Kidatu 144 7.42 S 36.57 E
Kidbrooke ⁸ 250 51.28 N 0.02 E
Kidderminster 44 52.23 N 2.14 W
Kidderpore ⁸ 262b 22.31 N 88.19 E
Kidderpore Docks ⁵ 262b 22.33 N 88.19 E
Kidd's Beach 148 33.09 S 27.42 E
Kidepo National Park ♠ 144 3.50 N 33.40 E
Kidete 144 6.25 S 37.16 E
Kidira 140 14.28 N 12.13 W
Kidlington 44 51.50 N 1.17 W
Kidnappers, Cape ≻ 162 39.39 S 177.07 E
Kido 154 9.15 S 146.55 E
Kidron 204 40.44 N 81.45 W
Kidsgrove 44 53.06 N 2.15 W
Kidugallo 144 6.47 S 38.12 E
Kidul, Pegunungan ▲ 105a 8.13 S 112.00 E
Kidwelly 44 51.45 N 4.18 W
Kiefersfelden 58 47.37 N 12.11 E
Kiekebusch 254a 52.21 N 13.33 E
Kiel, B.R.D. 41 54.20 N 10.08 E
Kiel, Wis., U.S. 180 43.55 N 88.02 W
Kiel Canal → Nord-Ostsee-Kanal ≅ 30 53.53 N 9.08 E
Kielce 30 50.52 N 20.37 E
Kielder 42 55.14 N 2.35 W
Kieler Bucht (Kiel Bay) C 41 54.35 N 10.35 E
Kieler Förde C 41 54.24 N 10.12 E
Kiembara 140 13.15 N 2.44 W
Kienberg 254a 52.40 N 12.54 E
Kien-binh 100 9.55 N 105.19 E
Kienge 144 10.34 S 27.33 E
Kien-hung 100 9.43 N 105.17 E
Kienitz 50 52.40 N 14.26 E
Kiens → Chienes 58 46.48 N 11.50 E
Kiental 54 46.35 N 7.43 E
Kierling 254b 48.19 N 16.17 E
Kierspe 52 51.08 N 7.35 E
Kierspe-Bahnhof 253 51.08 N 7.37 E
Kiester 180 43.32 N 93.43 W
Kieta 165e 6.13 S 155.38 E
Kietrz 30 50.05 N 18.01 E
Kietz 50 52.34 N 14.38 E
Kiev → Kijev 68 50.26 N 30.31 E
Kiewa 161b 36.16 S 147.01 E
Kiev → Kijev 68 50.26 N 30.31 E
Kifār 'Aṣyūn 122 31.39 N 35.08 E
Kifaya 140 12.10 N 13.04 W
Kiffa 140 16.37 N 11.24 W
Kifisiá 38 38.04 N 23.48 E
Kifisós ≃ 257c 38.06 N 23.45 E
Kifrī 118 34.42 N 45.58 E
Kifrī, Jabal ▲ 132 27.48 N 32.50 E
Kigač ≃ 70 46.28 N 49.12 E
Kigali 144 1.57 S 30.04 E
Kigezi ☐⁵ 144 1.00 S 29.45 E
Kiġi 120 39.19 N 40.21 E
Kigille 130 8.40 N 34.02 E
Kigoma 144 4.52 S 29.38 E
Kigoma ☐⁴ 144 4.50 S 30.00 E
Kigun, Cape ≻ 170 52.00 N 175.21 W
Kigwa 144 5.10 S 33.08 E
Kigzı 118 38.18 N 43.25 E
Kihei 219a 20.47 N 156.28 W
Kihikihi 162 38.02 S 175.21 E
Kihniö 26 62.12 N 23.11 E
Kihnu I 66 58.08 N 24.00 E
Kiholo Bay C 219d 19.52 N 155.56 W
Kihundo 144 9.25 S 38.59 E
Kihurio 144 4.28 S 38.04 E
Kii-hantō ≻¹ 86 34.00 N 135.45 E
Kiik 76 47.31 N 72.55 E
Kiikkaškan 76 49.28 N 77.04 E
Kiiminkinjoki ≃ 26 65.12 N 25.18 E
Kiirun → Chilung 90 25.08 N 121.44 E
Kii-sanchi ⁴ 82 34.00 N 135.50 E
Kii-suidō 88 33.55 N 134.55 E
Kija ≃ 64 56.22 N 86.39 E
Kijabe 144 0.56 S 36.34 E
Kijakty, Ozero @ 76 50.00 N 69.15 E
Kijal 104 4.21 N 103.29 E
Kijasovo 70 56.21 N 53.07 E
Kijev (Kiev) 68 50.26 N 30.31 E
Kijevka, S.S.S.R. 70 46.05 N 42.57 E
Kijevka, S.S.S.R. 76 50.16 N 71.33 E
Kijevka, S.S.S.R. 76 47.31 N 70.44 E
Kijevskij Vokzal ⁵ 255b 55.45 N 37.34 E
Kijevskoje 68 45.03 N 37.52 E
Kijevskoje Polesje ⁴¹ 68 51.00 N 30.00 E
Kijevskoje Vodochranilišče @¹ 68 51.00 N 30.25 E
Kijima-chosuichi @ 86 35.04 N 132.44 E
Kijimadaira 84 36.51 N 138.24 E
Kijima-dam ⁻⁶ 86 35.02 N 132.34 E
Kijkašor 70 64.06 N 49.46 E
Kijma 76 51.35 N 67.34 E
Kijoka 164m 26.42 N 128.09 E
Kikagati 144 1.02 S 30.40 E
Kikai-shima I 83b 28.19 N 129.59 E
Kikale 144 7.50 S 39.12 E
Kikati ≃ 142 14.48 S 12.28 E
Kikenka ≃ 255a 59.52 N 30.04 E
Kikerino 66 59.28 N 29.35 E
Kikerk Lake @ 166 67.20 N 113.20 W
Kikimi 263b 4.26 S 15.25 E
Kikimorka 70 58.10 N 49.27 E
Kikinda 38 45.50 N 20.28 E
Kikládhes II 38 37.30 N 25.00 E
Kiklah 136 32.05 N 12.41 E
Kiknur 70 57.19 N 47.14 E
Kikombo, Zaïre 142 5.59 S 18.09 E
Kikombo, Zaïre 142 5.40 S 18.48 E
Kikongo 142 4.16 S 17.11 E
Kikori 154 7.25 S 144.15 E
Kikori ≃ 154 7.10 S 144.05 E
Kikorze 50 53.39 N 15.01 E
Kiku ≃ 84 34.39 N 138.04 E
Kikuchi 86 32.59 N 130.45 E
Kikuchi ≃ 86 32.56 N 130.35 E
Kikugawa, Nihon 84 34.45 N 138.05 E
Kikugawa, Nihon 86 34.07 N 131.02 E
Kikuka 86 33.02 N 130.46 E
Kikuma 86 34.03 N 132.53 E
Kikuna 258 35.10 N 139.40 E
Kikusui 86 32.58 N 130.36 E
Kikvidze, S.S.S.R. 70 50.53 N 42.46 E
Kikvidze, S.S.S.R. 70 50.44 N 43.03 E
Kikvorsberg ⁴ 148 31.17 S 25.20 E
Kikwit 142 5.02 S 18.49 E
Kil 26 59.30 N 13.19 E
Kilaån ≃ 40 58.44 N 17.01 E
Kilaban 118 37.27 N 42.51 E
Kilafors 26 61.14 N 16.34 E
Kilakarai 112 9.14 N 78.47 E
Kila Kila 154 9.30 S 147.10 E
Kilambé, Cerro ▲ 226 13.34 N 85.42 W
Kilandras 120 38.34 N 30.11 E
Kilauea 219b 22.13 N 159.25 W
Kilauea Crater ⁶ 219d 19.25 N 155.17 W
Kilauea Point ≻ 219b 22.14 N 159.24 W
Kilbarchan 42 55.50 N 4.33 W
Kilbasan 120 37.20 N 33.12 E
Kilbirnie 42 55.46 N 4.41 W
Kilbourne, Ill., U.S. 209 40.09 N 90.01 W
Kilbourne, Ohio, U.S. 204 40.20 N 82.58 W
Kilbrannan Sound 42 55.40 N 5.25 W
Kilbuck Mountains ▲ 170 60.30 N 159.45 W
Kilbuck Run ≃ 269b 40.31 N 80.08 W
Kilchberg 54 47.19 N 8.33 E
Kilchis ≃ 214 45.30 N 123.52 W
Kilchu 88 40.58 N 129.20 E
Kilcoy 161a 26.57 S 152.33 E
Kilcullen 42 53.08 N 6.45 W
Kildare (Saint-Ambroise-de-Kildare), Qué., Can. 196 46.05 N 73.32 W
Kildare, Eire 28 53.10 N 6.55 W
Kildare ☐⁶ 28 53.15 N 6.45 W
Kildare, Cape ≻ 176 46.52 N 63.58 W
Kildeer 268 42.10 N 88.03 W
Kil'dinstroj 24 68.48 N 33.06 E
Kildonan, B.C., Can. 172 49.00 N 125.00 W
Kildonan, Rh. 144 17.21 S 30.37 E
Kildurk 154 16.26 S 129.37 E
Kilemary 70 56.47 N 46.52 E
Kilembe, Ug. 144 0.12 N 30.00 E
Kilembe, Zaïre 142 5.42 S 19.55 E
Kilgard 214 49.03 N 122.12 W
Kilgore, Ohio, U.S. 204 40.28 N 81.00 W
Kilgore, Tex., U.S. 212 32.23 N 94.53 W
Kilham 42 54.04 N 0.23 W
Kili I 14 5.39 N 169.04 E
Kilian Island I 166 73.35 N 107.53 W
Kilibo 140 8.34 N 2.36 E
Kilifi 144 3.38 S 39.51 E
Kilija 68 45.27 N 29.16 E
Kilijskoje Girlo ≃¹ 68 45.18 N 29.40 E
Kilikoiiūr 112 8.54 N 76.39 E
Kilima 144 0.59 S 29.12 E
Kilimanjaro ☐⁴ 144 3.45 S 37.45 E
Kilimanjaro ▲ 144 3.04 S 37.22 E
Kilimatinde 144 5.51 S 34.57 E
Kilimavony 147b 23.48 S 43.41 E
Kilimli 120 41.28 N 31.50 E
Kilinç 120 40.38 N 29.23 E
Kilinç Tepesi ▲ 120 40.32 N 38.10 E
Kilindoni 144 7.55 S 39.39 E
Kilingi-Nõmme 66 58.09 N 24.58 E
Kilis 120 36.44 N 37.05 E
Kilkare Woods 272 37.38 N 121.57 W
Kilkee 28 52.41 N 9.38 W
Kilkeel 42 54.04 N 6.00 W
Kilkenny 28 52.39 N 7.15 W
Kilkenny ☐⁶ 28 52.40 N 7.20 W
Kilkhampton 44 50.53 N 4.29 W
Kilkieran Bay C 28 53.15 N 9.45 W
Kilkis 38 41.00 N 22.53 E
Killala 28 54.13 N 9.13 W
Killala Bay C 28 54.15 N 9.10 W
Killaloe 28 52.48 N 8.27 W
Killaloe Station 180 45.33 N 77.25 W
Killam 172 52.47 N 111.51 W
Killara 264a 33.46 S 151.09 E
Killarney, Austl. 160 28.20 S 152.18 E
Killarney, Man., Can. 174 49.12 N 99.42 W
Killarney, Ont., Can. 180 45.58 N 81.31 W
Killarney, Eire 28 52.03 N 9.30 W
Killarney, Lake @ 230b 25.03 N 77.27 W
Killarney, Lakes of @ 28 52.01 N 9.30 W
Killarney Heights 264a 33.46 S 151.13 E
Killarney Provincial Park ♠ 180 46.05 N 81.30 W
Killawog 200 42.24 N 76.01 W
Killbear Point Provincial Park ♠ 202 45.21 N 80.12 W
Killbuck, N.Y., U.S. 204 42.10 N 78.41 W
Killbuck, Ohio, U.S. 204 40.30 N 81.59 W
Killbuck Creek ≃, Ill., U.S. 206 41.10 N 89.06 W
Killbuck Creek ≃, Ind., U.S. 208 40.07 N 85.41 W
Killbuck Creek ≃, Ohio, U.S. 204 40.20 N 82.47 W
Killdeer 188 47.22 N 102.45 W
Killean 42 55.39 N 5.40 W
Killearn 42 56.03 N 4.22 W
Killen 212 31.08 N 97.44 W
Killeen 84 34.52 N 87.32 W
Killi Dağ ▲ 74 40.21 N 42.10 E
Killik ≃ 170 69.00 N 153.58 W
Killington Mountain ▲ 178 43.36 N 72.49 W
Killingworth 197 41.21 N 72.30 W
Killini 38 37.55 N 21.09 E
Killini ▲ 38 37.57 N 22.23 E
Killinkoski 26 62.24 N 23.52 E
Killorglin 28 52.06 N 9.47 W
Killough 42 54.16 N 5.39 W
Kill Van Kull ⊔ 266 40.39 N 74.05 W
Killybegs 28 54.38 N 8.27 W
Killyleagh 42 54.24 N 5.39 W
Kilmacolm 42 55.54 N 4.38 W
Kilmarnock, Scot., U.K. 42 55.36 N 4.30 W
Kilmarnock, Va., U.S. 198 37.43 N 76.23 W
Kilmar Tor ▲² 44 50.33 N 4.29 W
Kilmaurs 42 55.39 N 4.32 W
Kil'mez' 70 57.01 N 51.22 E
Kil'mez' ≃ 70 56.58 N 50.28 E
Kilmichael 184 33.27 N 89.34 W
Kilmore 159 37.18 S 144.57 E
Kilmore Creek ≃ 206 40.20 N 86.38 W
Kilo 105b 8.21 S 118.24 E
Kilokri ⁸ 262a 28.35 N 77.16 E
Kiloli 144 6.50 S 33.59 E
Kilombero ≃ 144 8.31 S 37.22 E
Kilómetro Cincuenta 222 19.45 N 88.45 W
Kilomines 144 1.48 N 30.14 E
Kilondo 144 9.46 S 34.21 E
Kilosa 144 6.50 S 36.59 E
Kilpisjärvi 24 69.03 N 20.48 E
Kilrush 28 52.39 N 9.30 W
Kilsbergen ⁴² 40 59.20 N 14.47 E
Kilsmo 40 59.04 N 15.31 E
Kilsyth, Austl. 264b 37.48 S 145.19 E
Kilsyth, Scot., U.K. 42 55.59 N 4.04 W
Kiltān I 112 11.29 N 73.00 E
Kiltu-ri 88 34.35 N 127.20 E
Kilwa 144 9.18 S 28.25 E
Kilwa Island I 144 9.20 S 28.33 E
Kilwa Kisiwani 144 8.58 S 39.30 E
Kilwa Kivinje 144 8.45 S 39.24 E
Kilwa Masoko 144 8.56 S 39.31 E
Kilwinning 42 55.40 N 4.42 W
Kim 188 37.15 N 103.21 W
Kim ≃ 142 5.28 N 11.07 E
Kima 144 1.26 S 26.43 E
Kimaam 154 7.58 S 138.53 E
Kimamba 144 6.47 S 37.08 E
Kimande 144 7.22 S 35.30 E
Kīmān Fāris (Crocodilopolis) (Arsinoe) ⊥ 132 29.19 N 30.50 E
Kimba 156 33.09 S 136.25 E
Kimball, Minn., U.S. 180 45.19 N 94.18 W
Kimball, Nebr., U.S. 188 41.14 N 103.40 W
Kimball, S. Dak., U.S. 188 43.45 N 98.57 W
Kimball, Mount ▲ 170 63.14 N 144.39 W
Kimbanda 142 4.07 S 17.59 E
Kimbe Bay C 154 5.30 S 150.30 E
Kimberley, B.C., Can. 172 49.41 N 115.59 W
Kimberley, S. Afr. 148 28.43 S 24.46 E
Kimberley Downs 152 17.24 S 124.22 E
Kimberley Plateau ⁴¹ 150 17.00 S 127.00 E
Kimberly, Idaho, U.S. 192 42.32 N 114.22 W
Kimberly, Wis., U.S. 180 44.17 N 88.20 W
Kimberton 198 40.08 N 75.34 W
Kimbolton, N.Z. 162 40.03 S 175.47 E
Kimbolton, Eng., U.K. 44 52.18 N 0.24 W
Kimbolton, Ohio, U.S. 204 40.09 N 81.34 W
Kimbongo 142 6.08 S 18.01 E
Kimbwala 263b 4.22 S 15.12 E
Kimch'aek (Sŏngjin) 88 40.41 N 129.12 E
Kimch'ŏn 88 36.07 N 128.05 E
Kimerka ≃ 72 56.52 N 37.22 E
Kimhae 88 35.14 N 128.52 E
Kimhwa 88 38.26 N 127.36 E
Kimi, Cam. 142 6.05 N 11.30 E
Kími, Ellás 38 38.37 N 24.06 E
Kimil'tej 78 54.08 N 101.59 E
Kimito (Kemiö) 26 60.10 N 22.45 E
Kimi-tōge ▲² 260 34.43 N 135.06 E
Kimi-tōge)(86 34.23 N 135.37 E
Kimitsu 84 35.20 N 139.54 E
Kimiwan Lake @ 172 55.45 N 116.54 W
Kim Kim 261c 1.26 N 103.58 E
Kimmell 206 41.24 N 85.33 W
Kim-me-ni-oli Wash V 190 36.07 N 108.11 W
Kimolos I 38 36.48 N 24.34 E
Kimongo 142 4.29 S 12.58 E
Kimovsk 66 53.58 N 38.32 E
Kimpangu 142 5.51 S 15.01 E
Kim Plan 100 20.40 N 79.44 W
Kimp'o 261b 37.37 N 126.43 E
Kimp'o Airport ⊠ 261b 37.33 N 126.48 E
Kimpombo 263b 4.17 S 15.10 E
Kimpŏ-san ▲ 84 35.53 N 138.38 E
Kimry 72 56.52 N 37.21 E
Kimsquit 172 52.50 N 126.58 W
Kimstad 40 58.32 N 15.58 E
Kimu ≃ 84 34.39 N 138.04 E
Kimuenza 263b 4.27 S 15.17 E
Kimvula 142 5.44 S 15.58 E
Kimwanga 144 7.08 S 28.42 E
Kinabalian, Mount ▲ 106 8.14 N 125.25 E
Kinabalu, Gunong ▲ 102 6.05 N 116.33 E
Kinabatangan ⊥ 102 5.42 N 118.23 E
Kınalı ⁸ 257b 40.55 N 29.03 E
Kınalıada I 257b 40.55 N 29.03 E
Kinangaly ▲ 147b 19.12 S 45.40 E
Kinango 144 4.08 S 39.19 E
Kinapusan Island I 106 5.13 N 120.40 E
Kinara 154 2.16 S 132.44 E
Kinaros I 38 36.59 N 26.17 E
Kinasa 84 36.42 N 138.01 E
Kinauni 262a 28.39 N 77.23 E
Kinbasket Lake @ 172 51.58 N 118.03 W
Kincaid, Sask., Can. 172 49.39 N 107.00 W
Kincaid, Ill., U.S. 209 39.35 N 89.25 W
Kincaid, Lake @¹, Ill., U.S. 184 39.35 N 89.30 W
Kincardine, Ont., Can. 180 44.11 N 81.38 W
Kincardine, Scot., U.K. 42 56.04 N 3.44 W
Kinchafoonee Creek ≃ 182 31.38 N 84.10 W
Kinchang 100 26.32 N 98.02 E
Kinchara 262b 22.53 N 88.36 E
Kincheloe Air Force Base ■ 180 46.15 N 84.28 W
Kincolith 172 55.00 N 129.57 W
Kinda, Zaïre 142 4.47 S 21.48 E
Kinda, Zaïre 144 9.18 S 25.04 E
Kindadal 102 1.35 S 123.11 E
Kindanba 142 3.44 S 14.31 E
Kindarun Mountain ▲ 160 32.49 S 150.41 E
Kindberg 30 47.31 N 15.27 E
Kinde 180 43.56 N 83.00 W
Kindel'a 70 51.36 N 52.58 E
Kindel'a ≃ 70 52.31 N 52.41 E
Kindelbrück 50 51.16 N 11.05 E
Kindele 142 8.39 S 24.20 E
Kinder 194 30.29 N 92.51 W
Kinderhook, Ill., U.S. 209 39.42 N 91.09 W
Kinderhook, Mich., U.S. 206 41.48 N 85.00 W
Kinderhook, N.Y., U.S. 200 42.24 N 73.42 W
Kinderhook Creek ≃ 200 42.19 N 73.45 W
Kinder Reservoir @¹ 252 53.23 N 1.55 W
Kinder Scout ▲ 42 53.23 N 1.52 W
Kindersley 174 51.27 N 109.10 W
Kindia 140 10.04 N 12.51 W
Kindia ☐⁴ 140 10.00 N 12.45 W
Kindiikan 78 56.02 N 111.15 E
Kindley Field ⊠ 230a 32.22 N 64.40 W
Kindred 188 46.39 N 97.01 W
Kindu-Port-Empain 144 2.57 S 25.56 E
Kindykty, Ozero @ 76 51.15 N 62.14 E
Kinel' 70 53.14 N 50.39 E
Kinel'-Čerkassy 70 53.28 N 51.29 E
Kinel'skije Gory ⁴¹ 70 53.29 N 51.29 E
Kineo, Mount ▲ 178 45.42 N 69.44 W
Kinesi 144 1.28 S 33.52 E
Kinešma 70 57.26 N 42.09 E
Kineton 44 52.10 N 1.30 W
King 182 36.17 N 80.22 W
King ☐⁶ 214 47.28 N 121.42 W
King ≃, Austl. 154 14.14 S 131.59 E
King ≃, Austl. 159 36.41 S 146.25 E
King, Lake @ 152 25.38 S 120.08 E
King, Mount ▲ 156 25.10 S 147.31 E
Kingabwa ⁸ 263b 4.19 S 15.20 E
King and Queen ☐⁶ 198 37.42 N 76.50 W
King and Queen Court House 198 37.40 N 76.53 W
Kingarth 156 26.33 S 151.50 E
Kingarry 44 55.46 N 5.03 W
King City, Ont., Can. 202 43.56 N 79.32 W
King City, Calif., U.S. 216 36.13 N 121.08 W
King City, Mo., U.S. 184 40.03 N 94.31 W

Symbols in the index entries represent the broad categories identified in the key at the right. Symbols with superior numbers (⁴²) identify subcategories (see complete key on page I · 26).

Kartensymbole in dem Registerverzeichnis stellen die rechts in Schlüssel erklärten Kategorien dar. Symbole mit hochgestellten Ziffern (⁴²) bezeichnen Unterabteilungen einer Kategorie (vgl. vollständiger Schlüssel auf Seite I · 26).

Los símbolos incluidos en el texto del índice representan las grandes categorías identificadas con la clave a la derecha. Los símbolos con números en su parte superior (⁴²) identifican las subcategorías (véase la clave completa en la página I · 26).

Les symboles de l'index représentent les catégories indiquées dans la légende à droite. Les symboles suivis d'un indice (⁴²) représentent des sous-catégories (voir légende complète à la page I · 26).

Os símbolos incluídos no texto do índice representam as grandes categorias identificadas com a chave à direita. Os símbolos com números em sua parte superior (⁴²) identificam as subcategorias (veja-se a chave completa à página I · 26).

▲ Mountain	Berg	Montaña	Montagne	Montanha
▲ Mountains	Berge	Montañas	Montagnes	Montanhas
)(Pass	Pass	Paso	Col	Passo
V Valley, Canyon	Tal, Cañon	Valle, Cañón	Vallée, Canyon	Vale, Canhão
⁻ Plain	Ebene	Llano	Plaine	Planície
≻ Cape	Kap	Cabo	Cap	Cabo
I Island	Insel	Isla	Île	Ilha
II Islands	Inseln	Islas	Îles	Ilhas
⊥ Other Topographic Features	Andere Topographische Objekte	Otros Elementos Topográficos	Autres données topographiques	Outros Elementos Topográficos

ESPAÑOL — Nombre / Página / Lat.°′ / Long.°′ W=Oeste; FRANÇAIS — Nom / Page / Lat.°′ / Long.°′ W=Ouest; PORTUGUÊS — Nome / Página / Lat.°′ / Long.°′ W=Oeste

Nombre / Nom / Nome	Página / Page	Lat.°′	Long.°′ W=Oeste / W=Ouest
Kingcome Inlet C	172	50.50 N	126.10 W
King Cove	170	55.04 N	162.19 W
King Ditch ☰	269a	41.17 N	82.07 W
Kingdom City	209	38.58 N	91.56 W
King Edward ≃	154	14.14 S	126.35 E
Kingersheim	54	47.48 N	7.20 E
King Ferry	200	42.40 N	76.37 W
Kingfield	178	44.57 N	70.09 W
Kingfisher	186	35.52 N	97.56 W
King George	198	38.16 N	77.11 W
King George ☐[6]	198	38.15 N	77.10 W
King George, Mount ∧	172	50.35 N	115.24 W
King George Bay C	244	51.33 S	60.37 W
King George Island I	9	62.00 S	58.15 W
King George Islands II	166	57.20 N	78.25 W
King George's Dock ◆[5]	262b	22.32 N	88.18 E
King George Sound ⋓	152	35.03 S	117.57 E
King George's Reservoir ⊜[1]	250	51.39 N	0.01 W
King Hill	192	43.00 N	115.12 W
Kingisepp	66	59.22 N	28.36 E
King Island I, Austl.	156	39.50 S	144.00 E
King Island I, B.C., Can.	172	52.12 N	127.42 W
King Island I, Alaska, U.S.	170	64.58 N	168.05 W
Kinglake National Park ♠	159	37.35 S	145.25 E
King Lear Peak ∧	194	41.12 N	118.34 W
King Leopold Ranges ∧∧	150	17.30 S	125.45 E
Kingman, Ariz., U.S.	190	35.12 N	114.04 W
Kingman, Kans., U.S.	188	37.39 N	98.07 W
Kingman, Maine, U.S.	178	45.33 N	68.12 W
Kingman Reef ✧[2]	14	6.24 N	162.22 W
King Mountain ∧, B.C., Can.	170	58.17 N	128.54 W
King Mountain ∧, Qué., Can.	202	45.29 N	75.52 W
King Mountain ∧, Oreg., U.S.	192	43.49 N	118.52 W
King Mountain ∧, Oreg., U.S.	192	42.42 N	123.14 W
King of Prussia	198	40.05 N	75.23 W
King of Prussia Plaza ◆[9]	275	40.05 N	75.25 W
Kingoma, Congo	263b	4.09 S	15.15 E
Kingoma, Zaïre	142	5.11 S	13.34 E
Kingoma-Ngoma	142	5.50 S	16.49 E
Kingombe, Zaïre	144	3.56 S	26.35 E
Kingombe, Zaïre	144	7.24 S	26.11 E
Kingoonya	152	30.54 S	135.18 E
Kingoué	142	3.43 S	14.09 E
King Peak ∧	194	40.10 N	124.08 W
Kingri	110	30.27 N	69.49 E
Kings	206	42.00 N	89.06 W
Kings ☐[6], Calif., U.S.	216	36.20 N	119.39 W
Kings ☐[6], N.Y., U.S.	200	40.42 N	74.00 W
Kings ≃, Ark., U.S.	184	36.29 N	93.35 W
Kings ≃, Calif., U.S.	216	36.03 N	119.49 W
Kings ≃, Nev., U.S.	194	41.31 N	118.08 W
Kings, Middle Fork ≃	194	36.50 N	118.52 W
Kings, North Fork ≃	216	36.18 N	119.52 W
Kings, South Fork ≃	216	36.18 N	119.52 W
King Salmon	170	58.14 N	157.24 W
King Salmon ≃	170	58.15 N	157.30 W
Kings Beach	216	39.14 N	120.01 W
Kingsbridge	44	50.17 N	3.46 W
Kingsburg	216	36.31 N	119.33 W
Kingsbury, Eng., U.K.	44	52.35 N	1.40 W
Kingsbury, Ind., U.S.	206	41.31 N	86.42 W
Kingsbury ◆[8]	250	51.35 N	0.17 W
Kings Canyon National Park ♠	194	36.48 N	118.30 W
Kingsclere	44	51.20 N	1.14 W
Kingscote	158b	35.40 S	137.38 E
Kingscourt	42	53.55 N	6.48 W
Kings Creek	208	40.10 N	83.44 W
King's Creek ≃, Austl.	161a	27.57 S	151.42 E
Kings Creek ≃, Tex., U.S.	212	32.25 N	96.15 W
King's Cross Station ◆[5]	250	51.32 N	0.07 W
Kings Dominion ♠	198	37.51 N	77.27 W
Kingsdown	44	51.11 N	1.25 E
Kings Falls ↲	202	43.55 N	75.38 W
Kingsford, Austl.	264a	33.56 S	151.14 E
Kingsford, Mich., U.S.	180	45.48 N	88.04 W
Kingsford Heights	206	41.29 N	86.42 W
Kingsford Smith Airport ⊠	160	33.57 S	151.11 E
Kingsgate	172	49.00 N	116.11 W
Kingsgrove	264a	33.57 S	151.06 E
Kingshill	231n	17.44 N	64.48 W
Kings Island ♠	208	39.21 N	84.16 W
Kingskerswell	44	50.30 N	3.33 W
Kingsland, Eng., U.K.	44	52.15 N	2.47 W
Kingsland, Ark., U.S.	184	33.52 N	92.18 W
Kingsland, Ga., U.S.	182	30.48 N	81.41 W
Kingsland, Va., U.S.	198	37.24 N	77.26 W
Kings Langley	44	51.43 N	0.28 W
Kingsley, S. Afr.	148	27.55 S	30.33 E
Kingsley, Eng., U.K.	44	53.01 N	1.59 W
Kingsley, Eng., U.K.	252	53.16 N	2.40 W
Kingsley, Iowa, U.S.	188	42.35 N	95.58 W
Kingsley, Mich., U.S.	180	44.35 N	85.32 W
Kingsley, Pa., U.S.	200	41.46 N	75.45 W
Kingsley Dam ◆[6]	188	41.11 N	101.39 W
King's Lynn	44	52.45 N	0.24 E
Kings Mills	208	39.21 N	84.15 W
Kings Mountain	182	35.15 N	81.20 W
Kings Mountain National Military Park ♠	182	35.07 N	81.33 W
King Solomon's Mines ⊥	122	29.45 N	34.56 E
King Sound ⋓	152	17.00 S	123.30 E
Kings Park, N.Y., U.S.	200	40.53 N	73.16 W
Kings Park, Va., U.S.	274c	38.48 N	77.15 W
Kings Park ♠, Austl.	158a	31.57 S	116.49 E
King's Park ♠, H.K.	261d	22.19 N	114.10 E
Kings Peak ∧	190	40.46 N	110.22 W
Kings Plaza ◆[9]	266	40.37 N	73.55 W
King's Point, Newf., Can.	176	49.35 N	56.11 W
Kings Point, N.Y., U.S.	200	40.49 N	73.45 W
Kingsport	182	36.32 N	82.33 W
King's Sutton	44	52.01 N	1.16 W
Kingsteignton	44	50.33 N	3.35 W
King Sterndale	252	53.15 N	1.52 W
Kingsthorpe	161a	27.29 S	151.49 E
Kingston, Austl.	161a	27.40 S	153.07 E
Kingston, N.S., Can.	176	44.59 N	64.57 W
Kingston, Ont., Can.	202	44.14 N	76.30 W
Kingston, Jam.	231q	18.00 N	76.48 W
Kingston, N.Z.	162	45.20 S	168.42 E
Kingston, Norf. I.	164c	29.03 S	167.58 E
Kingston, Eng., U.K.	28	51.25 N	0.19 W
Kingston, Ga., U.S.	182	34.15 N	84.57 W
Kingston, Ill., U.S.	206	42.06 N	88.46 W
Kingston, Mass., U.S.	197	41.59 N	70.43 W
Kingston, Mo., U.S.	184	39.39 N	94.02 W
Kingston, N.J., U.S.	266	40.23 N	74.37 W
Kingston, N.Y., U.S.	200	41.56 N	74.00 W
Kingston, Ohio, U.S.	208	39.28 N	82.55 W
Kingston, Okla., U.S.	186	34.00 N	96.43 W
Kingston, Pa., U.S.	200	41.16 N	75.54 W
Kingston, R.I., U.S.	197	41.29 N	71.31 W
Kingston, Tenn., U.S.	182	35.52 N	84.31 W
Kingston, Wash., U.S.	214	47.48 N	122.30 W
Kingston ◆[8]	44	51.25 N	0.19 W
Kingston Bay C	273	42.00 N	70.42 W
Kingston Mills	202	44.17 N	76.27 W
Kingston Southeast	156	36.50 S	139.51 E
Kingston upon Hull (Hull)	42	53.45 N	0.20 W
Kingstown → Dún Laoghaire, Eire	28	53.17 N	6.08 W
Kingstown, St. Vin.	231h	13.09 N	61.14 W
Kingstown Bay C	231h	13.09 N	61.15 W
Kingstree	182	33.40 N	79.50 W
Kingsville, Austl.	264b	37.49 S	144.52 E
Kingsville, Ont., Can.	204	42.02 N	82.45 W
Kingsville, Md., U.S.	274b	39.27 N	76.25 W
Kingsville, Ohio, U.S.	204	41.53 N	80.41 W
Kingsville, Tex., U.S.	186	27.31 N	97.52 W
Kingswear	44	50.21 N	3.34 W
Kingswinford	44	52.29 N	2.10 W
Kingswood, Austl.	264a	33.46 S	150.43 E
Kingswood, S. Afr.	148	27.29 S	25.46 E
Kingswood, Eng., U.K.	44	51.27 N	2.22 W
Kingswood, Eng., U.K.	250	51.17 N	0.13 W
Kingswood Park	275	40.07 N	74.51 W
King's Worthy	44	51.06 N	1.18 W
Kingtechen → Jingdezhen	90	29.16 N	117.11 E
Kington	44	52.12 N	3.01 W
Kingunda	142	6.34 S	16.58 E
Kingungi	142	5.24 S	17.56 E
King William	198	37.41 N	77.01 W
King William ☐[6]	198	37.42 N	77.05 W
King William Island I	166	69.00 N	97.30 W
King William's Town	148	32.51 S	27.22 E
Kingwood	178	39.28 N	79.41 W
Kinh-duc	100	11.49 N	107.58 E
Kinhwa → Jinhua	90	29.07 N	119.39 E
Kınık	120	39.05 N	27.23 E
Kinira ≃	148	31.12 S	29.17 E
Kinistino	174	52.57 N	105.00 W
Kinjar Khās	113	29.55 N	70.58 E
Kinkala	142	4.22 S	14.46 E
Kinker Creek ≃	272	38.02 N	121.52 W
Kinkony, Lac ⊜	147b	16.08 S	45.50 E
Kinkora	275	40.07 N	74.45 W
Kinleith	162	38.16 S	175.54 E
Kinmount	202	44.47 N	78.39 W
Kinmundy	209	38.46 N	88.51 W
Kinn	26	61.36 N	4.45 E
Kinna	26	57.30 N	12.41 E
Kinnaird	172	49.17 N	117.39 W
Kinnairds Head ≻	28	57.42 N	2.00 W
Kinnekulle ∧[2]	26	58.35 N	13.23 E
Kinnelon	200	40.59 N	74.23 W
Kinnel Water ≃	42	55.08 N	3.25 W
Kinneret	122	32.43 N	35.33 E
Kinneret, Yam (Sea of Galilee) ⊜	122	32.48 N	35.35 E
Kinnerley	44	52.47 N	2.59 W
Kinniconick Creek ≃	208	38.37 N	83.09 W
Kinnula	26	63.22 N	24.58 E
Kino ≃	86	34.13 N	135.09 E
Kino, Bahía C	222	28.47 N	111.58 W
Kinoe	86	34.14 N	132.55 E
Kinogitan	106	9.00 N	124.48 E
Kinojévis ≃	180	48.23 N	78.21 W
Kinomoto	84	35.30 N	136.13 E
Kinonge ≃	196	45.39 N	74.55 W
Kinoni	144	0.39 S	30.27 E
Kinosaki	86	35.37 N	134.49 E
Kinpoku-san ∧	82	38.05 N	138.22 E
Kinross, S. Afr.	148	26.22 S	29.03 E
Kinross, Scot., U.K.	28	56.13 N	3.27 W
Kinsale, Eire	28	51.42 N	8.32 W
Kinsale, Va., U.S.	198	38.02 N	76.35 W
Kinsale, Old Head of ≻	28	51.36 N	8.32 W
Kinsarvik	26	60.23 N	6.43 E
Kinschasa → Kinshasa	142	4.18 S	15.18 E
Kinshasa (Léopoldville)	142	4.18 S	15.18 E
Kinshasa (Léopoldville), Zaïre	263b	4.18 S	15.18 E
Kinshasa ☐[4]	142	4.18 S	15.18 E
Kinshasa (Ndolo) Airport ⊠, Zaïre	263b	4.20 S	15.19 E
Kinshasa (Ndjili) Airport ⊠, Zaïre	263b	4.23 S	15.27 E
Kinshasa-Est ◆[8]	263b	4.18 S	15.18 E
Kinshasa-Quest ◆[8]	263b	4.20 S	15.15 E
Kinsley	188	37.55 N	99.25 W
Kinsman, Ill., U.S.	206	41.11 N	88.34 W
Kinsman, Ohio, U.S.	204	41.27 N	80.36 W
Kinsoundi	263b	4.10 S	15.15 E
Kinston	182	35.16 N	77.35 W
Kintamani	105b	8.14 S	115.19 E
Kintamo, Rapides de ↲	263b	4.19 S	15.15 E
Kintampo	140	8.03 N	1.43 W
Kintap	102	3.51 S	115.13 E
Kintari, Mont ∧[2]	263b	4.08 S	15.23 E
Kintélé	263b	4.09 S	15.21 E
Kintinian	140	11.36 N	9.23 W
Kintinku	144	5.53 S	35.14 E
Kintobongo-Bunge	144	8.54 S	26.23 E
Kintore, Mount ∧	152	26.34 S	130.30 E
Kintore Range ∧∧	152	23.25 S	129.20 E
Kintsana	263b	4.19 S	15.10 E
Kintus	76	60.09 N	71.25 E
Kintyre ≻[1]	28	55.32 N	5.35 W
Kintyre, Mull of ≻	42	55.17 N	5.55 W
Kinu ≃	84	35.56 N	139.57 E
Kinuseo Falls ↲	172	54.47 N	121.12 W
Kinuso	172	55.20 N	115.25 W
Kinver	44	52.27 N	2.14 W
Kinwood	212	29.56 N	95.23 W
Kinyangiri	144	4.27 S	34.37 E
Kinyeti ∧	144	3.57 N	32.54 E
Kinzia	142	3.36 S	18.26 E
Kinzig ≃, B.R.D.	52	50.08 N	8.54 E
Kinzig ≃, B.R.D.	54	48.37 N	7.49 E
Kinzua	192	44.59 N	120.03 W
Kinzua Creek ≃	204	41.47 N	78.50 W
Kinzua Dam ◆[6]	204	41.50 N	79.01 W
Kioa I	165g	16.39 S	179.55 E
Kioga-See → Kyoga, Lake ⊜	144	1.30 N	33.00 E
Kioshkokwi Lake ⊜	180	46.05 N	78.52 W
Kioto → Kyōto	84	35.00 N	135.45 E
Kiowa, Colo., U.S.	188	39.21 N	104.28 W
Kiowa, Kans., U.S.	188	37.01 N	98.29 W
Kiowa, Okla., U.S.	186	34.43 N	95.54 W
Kiowa Creek ≃, U.S.	186	36.46 N	99.55 W
Kiowa Creek ≃, Colo., U.S.	188	40.20 N	104.05 W
Kipahigan Lake ⊜	174	55.20 N	101.55 W
Kipandi	142	5.19 S	16.46 E
Kipanga	144	6.14 S	35.21 E
Kiparissía	38	37.14 N	21.40 E
Kiparissiakós Kólpos C	38	37.37 N	21.24 E
Kipatimu	144	8.29 S	38.56 E
Kipawa ≃	180	47.03 N	79.23 W
Kipawa, Lac ⊜	180	46.55 N	79.00 W
Kipawa, Parc de ♠	180	47.15 N	78.15 W
Kipembawe	144	7.39 S	33.24 E
Kipengere Range ∧∧	144	9.10 S	34.15 E
Kiperčeny	68	47.32 N	28.50 E
Kipijevo	24	65.40 N	54.23 E
Kipili	144	7.26 S	30.36 E
Kipini	144	2.32 S	40.31 E
Kipling	174	50.10 N	102.38 W
Kipnuk	170	59.56 N	164.03 W
Kippen	42	56.08 N	4.11 W
Kippenheim	54	48.17 N	7.49 E
Kippure ∧	42	53.11 N	6.20 W
Kípros → Cyprus ☐[1]	120	35.00 N	33.00 E
Kipsdorf	50	50.47 N	13.32 E
Kipton	204	41.16 N	82.18 W
Kipushi	144	11.46 N	27.14 E
Kipushia, Zaïre	144	12.58 S	29.30 E
Kipushia, Zaïre	144	6.10 S	25.12 E
Kira, Nihon	84	34.49 N	137.05 E
Kir'a, S.S.S.R.	70	55.04 N	46.53 E
Kira Kira	165e	10.27 S	161.55 E
Kirane	140	15.25 N	10.14 W
Kiranlık	120	39.07 N	41.41 E
Kiranomena	147b	18.17 S	46.03 E
Kīratpur	114	29.31 N	78.12 E
Kiraz	120	38.13 N	28.13 E
Kirazlı	120	40.02 N	26.41 E
Kırbaçbayırı ∧	257b	40.56 N	29.10 E
Kirbla	66	58.44 N	23.57 E
Kirbymoorside	42	54.16 N	0.55 W
Kirby Muxloe	44	52.38 N	1.13 W
Kirbyville	184	30.40 N	93.54 W
Kırçal	120	41.39 N	35.16 E
Kırcasalih	120	41.23 N	26.48 E
Kirchardt	52	49.12 N	8.59 E
Kirchbach in Steiermark	30	46.54 N	15.44 E
Kirchberg, B.R.D.	52	49.12 N	9.58 E
Kirchberg, B.R.D.	52	49.56 N	7.24 E
Kirchberg, D.D.R.	50	50.37 N	12.32 E
Kirchberg, Schw.	54	47.05 N	7.35 E
Kirchberg, Schw.	54	47.25 N	9.03 E
Kirch-Berg ∧[2]	254a	52.27 N	13.02 E
Kirchberg in Tirol	58	47.27 N	12.19 E
Kirchbichl	58	47.31 N	12.05 E
Kirchderne ◆[8]	253	51.33 N	7.30 E
Kirchdorf, B.R.D.	48	52.36 N	8.49 E
Kirchdorf, D.D.R.	50	54.00 N	11.26 E
Kirchdorf an der Krems	30	47.56 N	14.07 E
Kircheib	52	50.42 N	7.28 E
Kirchende	253	51.25 N	7.26 E
Kirchenlamitz	50	50.09 N	11.56 E
Kirchen-Wehbach	52	50.48 N	7.53 E
Kirchhain	52	50.49 N	8.55 E
Kirchheiligen	50	51.11 N	10.42 E
Kirchheimbolanden	52	49.40 N	8.00 E
Kirchheim in Schwaben	54	48.10 N	10.30 E
Kirchheim unter Teck	52	48.39 N	9.27 E
Kirchhellen	48	51.36 N	6.55 E
Kirchhellen Heide ◆[3]	253	51.36 N	6.53 E
Kirchhofen	254a	52.22 N	13.53 E
Kirchhörde ◆[8]	253	51.27 N	7.27 E
Kirchhundem	52	51.05 N	8.05 E
Kirchlinde ◆[8]	253	51.32 N	7.22 E
Kirchlinteln	48	52.56 N	9.19 E
Kirchmöser	50	52.22 N	12.25 E
Kirchohsen	48	52.03 N	9.23 E
Kirchschlag in der Buckligen Welt	30	47.31 N	16.18 E
Kirchveischede	52	51.05 N	7.59 E
Kirchwalsede	48	53.01 N	9.23 E
Kirchwerder ◆[8]	48	53.25 N	10.11 E
Kirchweyhe	48	52.59 N	8.52 E
Kirchzarten	54	47.58 N	7.56 E
Kircubbin	42	54.30 N	5.32 W
Kirda	75	41.06 N	69.00 E
Kirdāsah	132	30.02 N	31.07 E
Kireç, Tür.	120	39.33 N	28.22 E
Kirec, Tür.	120	40.59 N	39.10 E
Kirej ≃	78	54.12 N	100.40 E
Kirejevo	70	50.01 N	44.29 E
Kirejevsk	66	53.56 N	37.56 E
Kirejkovo	66	53.38 N	35.49 E
Kirenga ≃	78	57.47 N	108.07 E
Kirensk	78	57.46 N	108.08 E
Kirgali	120	37.55 N	40.00 E
Kirghiz Soviet Socialist Republic → Kirgizskaja Sovetskaja Socialističeskija Respublika ☐[3]	75	41.30 N	75.00 E
Kirgiz-Mijaki	76	53.38 N	54.47 E
Kirgizskaja Sovetskaja Socialističeskaja Respublika ☐[3]	75	41.30 N	75.00 E
Kirgizskij Chrebet ∧∧	75	42.30 N	74.00 E
Kirguises,, Estepas de → Kirgizskij Chrebet ∧∧	75	42.30 N	74.00 E
Kiri	142	1.27 S	19.00 E
Kiribati ☐[1]	14	0.00	174.00 E
Kiribati II	4	0.00	174.00 E
Kirigalpotta Mountain ∧	112	6.48 N	80.46 E
Kiriga-mine ∧	84	36.06 N	138.12 E
Kiriis West	148	26.34 S	19.00 E
Kırıkhan, Tür.	120	39.32 N	41.20 E
Kırıkhan, Tür.	120	36.32 N	36.19 E
Kirikiri Prisons ✪	263a	6.27 N	3.19 E
Kırıkkale	120	39.50 N	33.31 E
Kirikovka	68	50.22 N	35.07 E
Kirillov	66	59.52 N	38.23 E
Kirillovka	255b	55.57 N	37.20 E
Kirillovo, S.S.S.R.	70	57.07 N	45.27 E
Kirillovo, S.S.S.R.	70	53.47 N	42.40 E
Kirillovskoje	66	60.28 N	29.17 E
Kirin → Jilin	79	43.51 N	126.33 E
Kirin → Jilin ☐[4]	80	44.00 N	126.00 E
Kirínia (Kyrenia)	120	35.20 N	33.19 E
Kirishima-yaku-kokuritsu-kōen ♠	82	31.55 N	130.51 E
Kirishima-yama ∧	82	31.56 N	130.52 E
Kiriši	66	59.27 N	32.02 E
Kirizume-tōge ∧[2]	260	34.56 N	135.16 E
Kırka	120	39.17 N	30.33 E
Kırkağaç	120	39.06 N	27.40 E
Kirkbride	42	54.54 N	3.12 W
Kirkburton	42	53.37 N	1.42 W
Kirkby	42	53.29 N	2.54 W
Kirkby in Ashfield	44	53.06 N	1.15 W
Kirkby Lonsdale	42	54.13 N	2.36 W
Kirkby Malzeard	42	54.11 N	1.38 W
Kirkby Stephen	42	54.28 N	2.20 W
Kirkcaldy	42	56.07 N	3.10 W
Kirkcolm	42	54.58 N	5.05 W
Kirkconnel	42	55.23 N	4.00 W
Kirkcudbright	42	54.50 N	4.03 W
Kirkcudbright Bay C	42	54.48 N	4.04 W
Kirkdale ◆[8]	252	53.26 N	2.59 W
Kirkeby	41	56.09 N	9.27 E
Kirkee → Khadki	112	18.34 N	73.52 E
Kirkenær	26	60.28 N	12.03 E
Kirkenes	24	69.40 N	30.03 E
Kirke Stillinge	41	55.26 N	11.15 E
Kirkham	42	53.47 N	2.53 W
Kirkintilloch	42	55.57 N	4.10 W
Kirkjubæjarklaustur	24a	63.47 N	18.04 W
Kirkkonummi → Kyrkslätt	26	60.07 N	24.26 E
Kirkland, Qué., Can.	265a	45.27 N	73.52 W
Kirkland, Ill., U.S.	206	42.06 N	88.51 W
Kirkland, Tex., U.S.	186	34.23 N	100.04 W
Kirkland, Wash., U.S.	214	47.41 N	122.12 W
Kirkland Creek ≃	190	34.32 N	113.00 W
Kirkland Lake	180	48.09 N	80.02 W
Kırklar Dağı ∧	74	40.34 N	40.35 E
Kırklareli	120	41.44 N	27.12 E
Kırklareli ☐[4]	120	41.40 N	27.30 E
Kirklees ☐[8]	252	53.36 N	1.52 W
Kirkleydtch	252	53.18 N	2.12 W
Kirklin	184	40.12 N	86.22 W
Kirkliston	42	55.58 N	3.25 W
Kirk Michael	42	54.17 N	4.35 W
Kirkness Lake ⊜	174	51.32 N	93.56 W
Kirkpatrick, Mount ∧	9	84.20 S	166.19 E
Kirkpatrick Lake ⊜	172	51.52 N	111.18 W
Kirkstile	42	55.12 N	3.00 W
Kirksville, Ill., U.S.	209	39.34 N	88.40 W
Kirksville, Mo., U.S.	184	40.12 N	92.35 W
Kirkūk	118	35.28 N	44.28 E
Kirkūk ☐[4]	118	35.00 N	44.35 E
Kirkville	200	43.05 N	75.57 W
Kirkwall	28	58.59 N	2.58 W
Kirkwood, S. Afr.	148	33.22 S	25.15 E
Kirkwood, Del., U.S.	198	39.34 N	75.42 W
Kirkwood, Ill., U.S.	180	40.52 N	90.45 W
Kirkwood, Mo., U.S.	209	38.35 N	90.24 W
Kirkwood, N.J., U.S.	275	39.50 N	75.01 W
Kirkwood, N.Y., U.S.	200	42.02 N	75.48 W
Kırmıt	120	37.11 N	35.41 E
Kirn	52	49.47 N	7.28 E
Kirnāhar	116	23.45 N	87.52 E
Kirotshe	144	1.37 S	29.02 E
Kirov, S.S.S.R.	66	54.05 N	34.20 E
Kirov, S.S.S.R.	70	58.38 N	49.42 E
Kirova, Zaliv C	74	39.09 N	49.03 E
Kirovabad	74	40.40 N	46.22 E
Kirovakan	74	40.48 N	44.30 E
Kirovgrad	76	57.26 N	60.04 E
Kirovka	76	47.07 N	82.00 E
Kirovo, S.S.S.R.	68	47.41 N	35.46 E
Kirovo, S.S.S.R.	68	51.29 N	29.24 E
Kirovo, S.S.S.R.	73	48.50 N	38.03 E
Kirovo, S.S.S.R.	75	40.26 N	70.34 E
Kirovo, S.S.S.R.	76	55.33 N	63.46 E
Kirovo-Čepeck	70	58.33 N	50.01 E
Kirovograd	68	48.30 N	32.18 E
Kirovograd ☐[4]	38	48.10 N	30.20 E
Kirovsk, S.S.S.R.	24	67.37 N	33.35 E
Kirovsk, S.S.S.R.	66	53.16 N	29.29 E
Kirovsk, S.S.S.R.	73	48.38 N	38.39 E
Kirovsk, S.S.S.R.	73	49.01 N	37.56 E
Kirovsk, S.S.S.R.	74	38.48 N	48.43 E
Kirovsk, S.S.S.R.	118	37.42 N	60.23 E
Kirovsk, S.S.S.R.	255a	59.52 N	31.00 E
Kirovskij, S.S.S.R.	64	54.18 N	155.47 E
Kirovskij, S.S.S.R.	76	44.52 N	78.12 E
Kirovskij, S.S.S.R.	79	45.07 N	133.30 E
Kirovskij, S.S.S.R.	79	54.26 N	126.55 E
Kirovskije Ostrova II	255a	59.58 N	30.15 E
Kirovskoje, S.S.S.R.	68	48.33 N	34.53 E
Kirovskoje, S.S.S.R.	68	45.14 N	35.13 E
Kirovskoje, S.S.S.R.	73	48.10 N	38.28 E
Kirovskoje, S.S.S.R.	75	42.39 N	71.35 E
Kirpičnyj Zavod	255a	60.01 N	30.48 E
Kirpil'skaja	68	45.23 N	39.43 E
Kirriemuir	28	56.41 N	3.01 W
Kirs	76	59.21 N	52.14 E
Kirsanov	70	52.38 N	42.43 E
Kirsanovka	70	52.30 N	52.53 E
Kirschau	50	51.04 N	14.27 E
Kırşehir	120	39.09 N	34.10 E
Kırşehir ☐[4]	120	39.20 N	34.10 E
Kirtachi Seybou	140	12.48 N	2.29 E
Kīrthar Range ∧∧	110	27.00 N	67.10 E
Kirtland, N. Mex., U.S.	190	36.44 N	108.21 W
Kirtland, Ohio, U.S.	204	41.34 N	81.18 W
Kirtland Air Force Base ■	190	35.02 N	106.37 W
Kirtland Hills	204	41.37 N	81.24 W
Kirtle Water ≃	42	54.58 N	3.05 W
Kirton	44	52.56 N	0.04 W
Kirtorf	52	50.46 N	9.06 E
Kiruna	24	67.51 N	20.16 E
Kirundu	144	0.44 S	25.32 E
Kirurumo	144	5.53 S	34.11 E
Kirvin	212	31.46 N	96.20 W
Kirwan Heights	269b	40.22 N	80.06 W
Kirwee	162	43.30 S	172.13 E
Kirwin	188	39.40 N	99.07 W
Kirwin Reservoir ⊜[1]	188	39.39 N	99.50 W
Kiryandongo	144	1.53 N	32.03 E
Kiryū	84	36.24 N	139.20 E
Kirza	76	54.14 N	81.40 E
Kiržač	72	56.09 N	38.52 E
Kisa, Nihon	86	34.43 N	132.59 E
Kisa, Sve.	26	57.59 N	15.37 E
Kisabe	260	34.47 N	135.41 E
Kisai	84	36.06 N	139.35 E
Kisaichi	260	34.46 N	135.42 E
Kisakata	82	39.13 N	139.54 E
Kisaki	144	7.28 S	37.36 E
Kišaly	66	54.23 N	43.12 E
Kisambo	142	6.25 S	18.14 E
Kisanga	144	2.29 N	26.35 E
Kisangani (Stanleyville)	144	0.30 S	25.12 E
Kisantu	142	5.07 S	15.05 E
Kisar, Pulau I	102	8.05 S	127.10 E
Kisaralik ≃	170	60.51 N	161.16 W
Kisaran	104	2.59 N	99.37 E
Kisarawe	144	6.54 S	39.04 E
Kisarazu	84	35.23 N	139.55 E
Kisarazu Air Base ■	258	35.24 N	139.55 E
Kisawa	86	33.49 N	134.18 E
K.I. Sawyer Air Force Base ■	180	46.21 N	87.25 W
Kisbér	30	47.30 N	18.02 E
Kisbey	174	49.38 N	102.41 W
Kise ≃	84	35.06 N	138.53 E
Kiselevsk → Kisel'ovsk	76	54.00 N	86.39 E
Kisel'ovka	70	47.18 N	44.07 E
Kisel'ovsk	76	54.00 N	86.39 E
Kisengwa	144	6.00 S	25.50 E
Kisen-yama ∧[2]	260	34.54 N	135.51 E
Kiser Lake ⊜	208	40.11 N	83.58 W
Kisha	120	40.28 N	41.28 E
Kishanda	144	1.42 S	31.34 E
Kishanganga ≃	113	34.18 N	73.28 E
Kishanganj	114	26.07 N	87.56 E
Kishangarh, Bhārat	110	26.34 N	74.52 E
Kishangarh, Bhārat	110	27.52 N	70.34 E
Kishangarh ◆[8]	262a	28.31 N	77.08 E
Kishar Bāla	257d	35.49 N	51.13 E
Kishb, Ḥarrat al- •[9]	134	23.00 N	41.25 E
Kishi, Nig.	140	9.05 N	3.52 E
Kishi, Zaïre	144	10.04 S	26.26 E
Kishida ≃	86	35.08 N	134.27 E
Kishigawa	86	34.13 N	135.20 E
Kishikas ≃	174	52.45 N	91.43 W
Kishimoto	86	35.23 N	133.25 E
Kishinev → Kišin'ov	68	47.00 N	28.50 E
Kishiwada	86	34.28 N	135.22 E
Kishorganj	114	24.26 N	90.46 E
Kishtwār	113	33.19 N	75.46 E
Kishwaukee ≃	206	42.11 N	89.08 W
Kishwaukee, South Branch ≃	206	42.12 N	88.59 W
Kisia	142	4.35 S	18.22 E
Kisigo ≃	144	7.03 S	35.50 E
Kisii	144	0.41 S	34.46 E
Kisiju	144	7.24 S	39.20 E
Kiši-Karoj, Ozero ⊜	76	54.03 N	71.20 E
Kısıklı ◆[8]	257b	41.01 N	29.03 E
Kišin	68	51.08 N	27.41 E
Kišin'ov	68	47.00 N	28.50 E
Kısır Dağı ∧	74	40.58 N	43.06 E
Kısırkaya	257b	41.14 N	28.58 E
Kısırmandıra	257b	41.14 N	28.49 E
Kisiwada → Kishiwada	86	34.28 N	135.22 E
Kisiwani	144	4.08 S	37.57 E
Kisizi	144	1.00 S	29.56 E
Kiska Island I	171a	52.00 N	178.30 E
Kıskanlı	74	39.32 N	41.58 E
Kiskatinaw ≃	172	56.06 N	120.08 W
Kiska Volcano ∧[1]	171a	52.07 N	177.36 E
Kis-Kevély ∧[2]	254c	47.38 N	18.59 E
Kiski Lake ⊜	174	54.46 N	98.55 W
Kiskimere	269b	40.37 N	79.35 W
Kiskiminetas ≃	204	40.41 N	79.40 W
Kiskittogisu Lake ⊜	174	54.13 N	98.20 W
Kiskitto Lake ⊜	174	54.16 N	98.34 W
Kiskőrös	30	46.38 N	19.17 E
Kiskunfélegyháza	30	46.43 N	19.52 E
Kiskunhalas	30	46.26 N	19.30 E
Kiskunmajsa	30	46.30 N	19.45 E
Kışla	120	40.51 N	30.57 E
Kisl'akovka	68	46.44 N	31.59 E
Kisl'akovskaja	68	46.27 N	39.40 E
Kislovka	73	49.38 N	37.53 E
Kislovo	70	49.54 N	45.25 E
Kislovodsk	74	43.55 N	42.44 E
Kismayu	134	0.23 S	42.30 E
Kismet	266	40.38 N	73.12 W
Kisnema	66	60.20 N	37.39 E
Kiso, Nihon	84	35.56 N	137.47 E
Kiso, Nihon	258	35.34 N	139.26 E
Kiso ≃	84	35.02 N	136.45 E
Kisofukushima	84	35.51 N	137.42 E
Kisogawa	84	35.20 N	136.47 E
Kisoripur	116	22.05 N	88.34 E
Kisoro	144	1.17 S	29.41 E
Kiso-sammyaku ∧∧	84	35.43 N	137.50 E
Kisozaki	84	35.04 N	136.44 E
Kispest ◆[8]	254c	47.27 N	19.08 E
Kispiox	172	55.21 N	127.41 W
Kispiox ≃	172	55.16 N	127.41 W
Kispiox Mountain ∧	172	55.25 N	127.57 W
Kissamos	38	35.30 N	23.38 E
Kissena Park ♠	266	40.45 N	73.49 W
Kisseynew Lake ⊜	174	54.58 N	101.35 W
Kissidougou	140	9.11 N	10.06 W
Kissidougou ☐[4]	140	9.15 N	9.55 W
Kissimmee	210	28.18 N	81.24 W
Kissimmee ≃	210	27.10 N	80.53 W
Kissimmee, Lake ⊜	210	27.55 N	81.16 W
Kississing	174	55.07 N	101.07 W
Kississing Lake ⊜	174	55.10 N	101.20 W
Kisslegg	54	47.47 N	9.53 E
Kissū, Jabal ∧	130	21.35 N	25.09 E
Kista	70	46.05 N	43.06 E
Kistanje	36	43.59 N	15.58 E
Kistarcsa	254c	47.33 N	19.16 E
Kistendej	70	52.08 N	43.39 E
Kistigan Lake ⊜	174	54.38 N	92.37 W
Kistler	204	40.22 N	77.51 W
Kistruss	70	54.28 N	40.34 E
Kisújszállás	30	47.13 N	20.46 E
Kisuki	86	35.17 N	132.54 E
Kisumu	144	0.06 S	34.45 E
Kisvárda	30	48.13 N	22.05 E
Kiswere	144	9.26 S	39.33 E
Kita	140	13.03 N	9.29 W
Kita ◆[8], Nihon	258	35.45 N	139.44 E
Kita ◆[8], Nihon	260	34.42 N	135.30 E
Kita ◆[8], Nihon	260	35.03 N	135.45 E
Kitaaiki	84	36.04 N	138.34 E
Kita-daitō-jima I	80	25.57 N	131.18 E
Kitafuji-enshūjō ■	84	35.25 N	138.48 E
Kitagata	84	35.26 N	136.41 E
Kitagawa	86	33.27 N	134.03 E
Kitagi-shima I	86	34.23 N	133.32 E
Kitaibaraki	84	36.48 N	140.45 E
Kitain Temple ✪[1]	258	35.54 N	139.30 E
Kita-iō-jima I	14	25.26 N	141.17 E
Kitairiso	258	35.50 N	139.26 E
Kitajima	86	34.05 N	134.35 E
Kitakami	82	39.18 N	141.07 E
Kitakami ≃	82	38.25 N	141.19 E
Kitakami-sanchi ∧∧	82	39.30 N	141.30 E
Kitakata	82	37.39 N	139.52 E
Kitakyuschu → Kitakyūshū	86	33.53 N	130.50 E
Kitakyūshū	86	33.53 N	130.50 E
Kitale	144	1.01 N	35.00 E
Kitamachi ◆[8]	258	35.46 N	139.39 E
Kitamba ◆[8]	263b	4.19 S	15.14 E
Kitami	82a	43.48 N	143.54 E
Kitami-sanchi ∧∧	82a	44.22 N	142.43 E
Kitamoto	84	36.02 N	139.32 E
Kitanagato-kaigan-kokutei-kōen ♠	86	34.24 N	131.16 E
Kitanda, Zaïre	144	6.36 S	26.27 E
Kitanda, Zaïre	144	9.59 S	27.28 E
Kitangari	144	10.39 S	39.20 E
Kitangiri, Lake ⊜	144	4.05 S	34.19 E
Kitangua	142	6.17 S	20.22 E
Kitan-kaikō ⋓	86	34.17 N	135.00 E
Kitano, Nihon	86	33.20 N	130.35 E
Kitano, Nihon	258	35.47 N	139.26 E
Kitanoshinden	258	35.48 N	139.26 E
Kitatachibana	84	36.29 N	139.03 E
Kitatajima	258	35.56 N	139.30 E
Kitatawara	260	34.44 N	135.42 E
Kitaura	84	36.04 N	140.32 E
Kita-ura ⊜	84	36.00 N	140.34 E
Kitava Island I	154	8.40 S	151.20 E
Kitaya	144	10.39 S	40.10 E
Kit Carson, Calif., U.S.	216	38.41 N	120.07 W
Kit Carson, Colo., U.S.	188	38.46 N	102.48 W
Kitchener, Austl.	152	31.02 S	124.11 E
Kitchener, Ont., Can.	202	43.27 N	80.29 W
Kitee	26	62.06 N	30.09 E
Kitega → Gitega	144	3.26 S	39.56 E
Kiteiyab	134	17.12 N	33.43 E
Kitenda	142	6.53 S	17.21 E
Kitenevo	72	56.21 N	36.13 E
Kitengo	142	7.26 S	24.08 E
Kitgum	144	3.18 N	32.53 E
Kíthira	38	36.09 N	23.00 E
Kíthira I	38	36.20 N	22.58 E
Kíthnos	38	37.26 N	24.26 E
Kíthnos I	38	37.25 N	24.28 E
Kithraía	120	35.15 N	33.29 E
Kitimat	172	54.03 N	128.33 W
Kitimat ≃	172	54.06 N	128.38 W
Kitimat Ranges ∧∧	172	53.30 N	128.50 W
Kitinen ≃	24	67.08 N	27.29 E
Kitíou, Akrotírion ≻	120	34.48 N	33.36 E
Kiti Point ≻	164r	6.51 N	158.09 E
Kitlope ≃	172	53.10 N	127.45 W
Kitlope Lake ⊜	172	53.07 N	127.47 W
Kitō, Nihon	84	34.42 N	138.03 E
Kitō, Nihon	86	33.46 N	134.12 E
Kitoj	78	52.36 N	103.50 E
Kitoj ≃	78	52.39 N	103.56 E
Kitojskije Gol'cy ∧∧	78	52.10 N	101.20 E
Kitsap ☐[6]	214	47.41 N	122.44 W
Kitscoty	174	53.20 N	110.20 W
Kitshua-Nseke	142	4.26 S	19.36 E
Kitsuki	82	33.25 N	131.37 E
Kitsuregawa	84	36.43 N	140.01 E
Kittanning	204	40.49 N	79.32 W
Kittatinny Mountain ∧	113	34.18 N	73.28 E
Kittatinny Tunnel ◆[5]	204	40.09 N	77.41 W
Kittendorf	50	53.37 N	12.54 E
Kittery	178	43.05 N	70.45 W
Kittery Point	178	43.05 N	70.41 W
Kitt Green	252	53.33 N	2.41 W
Kittilä	24	67.40 N	24.54 E
Kittitas	192	46.59 N	120.25 W
Kittitas ☐[6]	214	47.13 N	121.01 W
Kitu	144	7.38 S	27.42 E
Kitui	144	1.22 S	38.01 E
Kitumbeine ∧[1]	144	2.44 S	36.16 E
Kitunda	144	6.48 S	33.13 E
Kitutu	144	3.17 S	28.05 E
Kitwanga	172	55.06 N	128.03 W
Kitwangar Indian Reserve ◆[4]	172	55.06 N	128.04 W
Kitwe	144	12.49 S	28.13 E
Kityang → Jieyang	90	23.35 N	116.21 E
Kitzbühel	58	47.27 N	12.23 E
Kitzbüheler Alpen ∧∧	58	47.20 N	12.20 E
Kitzingen	52	49.44 N	10.09 E
Kitzscher	50	51.09 N	12.33 E
Kiukiang → Jiujiang	90	29.44 N	115.59 E
Kiukiu, Pointe ≻	164x	9.47 S	139.09 W
Kiul	114	25.09 N	86.06 E
Kiunga, Kenya	144	1.45 S	41.29 E
Kiunga, Pap. N. Gui.	154	6.10 S	141.15 E
Kiuruvesi	26	63.39 N	26.37 E
Kiuschu → Kyūshū I	82	33.00 N	131.00 E
Kiu Tsui Chau I	261d	22.22 N	114.17 E
Kivač, Vodopad ↲	24	62.16 N	33.59 E
Kivak	170	64.16 N	172.57 W
Kivalina	170	67.59 N	164.33 W
Kivercy	68	50.50 N	25.27 E
Kiveriči	65	57.22 N	36.36 E
Kivijärvi	26	63.04 N	25.03 E
Kivijärvi ⊜	26	63.10 N	25.09 E
Kivik	26	55.41 N	14.15 E
Kiviõli	66	59.21 N	26.57 E
Kivu ☐[4]	144	2.30 S	27.00 E
Kivu, Lac ⊜	144	2.00 S	29.10 E
Kiwai Island I	154	8.30 S	143.25 E
Kiwalik	170	66.02 N	161.50 W
Kiwanis Lake	204	41.28 N	81.09 W
Kiyama	86	33.25 N	130.32 E
Kīyāmakī Dāgh ∧	74	38.47 N	45.53 E
Kiyan	164m	26.05 N	127.40 E
Kiyan-saki ≻	164m	26.05 N	127.39 E
Kıyıköy	120	41.38 N	28.05 E
Kiyiu Lake ⊜	174	51.38 N	108.55 W
Kiyokawa	84	35.29 N	139.17 E
Kiyomi	84	36.07 N	137.11 E
Kiyosawa	84	35.03 N	138.15 E
Kiyose	84	35.47 N	139.32 E
Kiyosu	84	35.13 N	136.50 E
Kiyosumi-yama ∧	84	35.09 N	140.09 E
Kiyotani	260	34.52 N	134.59 E
Kiyotsu ≃	84	37.03 N	138.41 E
Kizel	76	59.03 N	57.40 E
Kizhake Chālakudi	112	10.18 N	76.20 E
Kiziguro	144	1.46 S	30.23 E
Kızıl ≃	120	41.44 N	35.58 E
Kızıl Adalar II	120	40.52 N	29.05 E
Kızılcabölük	120	37.37 N	29.01 E
Kızılcahamam	120	40.28 N	32.39 E
Kızılçakçak	74	40.46 N	43.37 E
Kızıldağ ∧	120	36.25 N	32.42 E
Kızıldikme	120	39.05 N	37.01 E
Kızılhisar	120	37.33 N	29.18 E
Kiziljurt	74	43.12 N	46.53 E
Kızıloğlan	120	41.20 N	34.52 E
Kizil'skoje	76	52.44 N	58.54 E
Kızıltepe	120	37.12 N	40.36 E
Kızıltoprak ◆[8]	257b	40.58 N	29.03 E
Kızılveran	120	40.27 N	34.28 E
Kızılviran	120	37.52 N	32.07 E
Kızılyaka	120	37.09 N	32.54 E
Kizimkazi	144	6.27 S	39.28 E
Kižinga	78	51.51 N	109.55 E
Kizir ≃	76	53.51 N	93.06 E
Kızkalesi ⊥	120	36.28 N	34.04 E
Kızkulesi ◆[5]	257b	41.01 N	29.00 E
Kizl'ar	74	43.50 N	46.40 E
Kizl'arskij Zaliv C	74	44.33 N	46.55 E
Kizner	70	56.17 N	51.31 E
Kiz'oma	24	61.08 N	44.50 E
Kizu	86	34.44 N	135.49 E
Kizu ≃	84	34.53 N	135.42 E
Kizuki	258	35.34 N	139.40 E
Kizuri	260	34.39 N	135.34 E
Kizyl-Ajak	118	37.40 N	65.23 E
Kizyl-Arvat	118	38.58 N	56.15 E
Kizyl-Atrek	118	37.36 N	54.46 E
Kizyl-Su	118	39.48 N	53.01 E
Kjellerup	41	56.17 N	9.26 E
Kjøbenhavn → København	41	55.40 N	12.35 E
Kjustendil	38	42.17 N	22.41 E
Klaarstroom	148	33.20 S	22.32 E
Klaaswaal	48	51.46 N	4.26 E
Klabat, Gunung ∧	102	1.28 N	125.02 E
Kladanj	38	44.13 N	18.41 E
Kladbišči	70	55.32 N	45.33 E
Kläden	50	52.38 N	11.39 E
Kladkovo	72	55.24 N	38.51 E
Kladno	50	50.08 N	14.05 E
Kladovo	38	44.37 N	22.37 E
Kladow ◆[8]	254a	52.27 N	13.09 E
Klaeng	100	12.47 N	101.39 E
Klaffenbach	50	50.45 N	12.54 E
Klagan	102	5.58 N	117.27 E
Klagenfurt	30	46.38 N	14.18 E
Klågerup	41	55.36 N	13.15 E
Klagshamn	41	55.32 N	12.55 E
Klagstorp	41	55.24 N	13.22 E
Klahoose Indian Reserve ◆[4]	172	50.31 N	124.19 W
Klaipėda (Memel)	66	55.43 N	21.07 E
Klais	58	47.29 N	11.14 E
Klakah	105a	7.59 S	113.15 E
Klamath	194	41.32 N	124.02 W
Klamath ≃	194	41.33 N	124.04 W
Klamath Falls	192	42.13 N	121.46 W
Klamath Marsh ≋	192	42.54 N	121.44 W
Klamath Mountains ∧∧	194	41.40 N	123.20 W
Klämmingen ⊜	40	59.07 N	17.15 E
Klamm Pass)(	58	47.17 N	13.05 E
Klamono	154	1.08 S	131.30 E
Klang → Kelang	104	3.02 N	101.27 E
Klangpi	100	22.59 N	93.20 E
Klarälven (Trysilelva) ≃	26	59.23 N	13.32 E
Kl'as'ma	255b	55.59 N	37.50 E
Klášterec	50	50.24 N	13.10 E
Kl'asticy	66	55.53 N	28.36 E
Klaten	105a	7.42 S	110.35 E
Klatovy	30	49.24 N	13.18 E
Klatt Road	170	61.05 N	149.48 W
Klausdorf, B.R.D.	50	54.18 N	10.15 E
Klausdorf, D.D.R.	50	54.20 N	13.01 E
Klausenburg → Cluj	38	46.47 N	23.36 E
Klausenpass)(	54	46.52 N	8.51 E
Kl'avlino	70	54.17 N	52.01 E
Klawer	148	31.44 S	18.36 E
Klawock	170	55.33 N	133.06 W
Klazienaveen	48	52.44 N	7.00 E
Kl'az'ma	72	55.58 N	37.27 E
Kl'az'ma ≃	70	56.10 N	42.58 E
Kl'az'minskoje Vodochranilišče ⊜[1]	255b	55.59 N	37.35 E
Kleberg	212	32.40 N	96.37 W
Kleck	66	53.04 N	26.38 E
Kłecko	30	52.38 N	17.26 E
Kleczew	30	52.23 N	18.10 E
Kledering ◆[8]	254b	48.08 N	16.26 E
Kleef	253	51.11 N	6.56 E
Kleena Kleene	172	51.58 N	124.59 W
Kleinasien → Asia Minor ◆[1]	22	39.00 N	32.00 E
Kleinbeeren	254a	52.22 N	13.20 E
Kleinbegin	148	28.50 S	21.36 E
Klein Blesbokspruit ≃	263d	26.16 S	28.29 E
Kleinbodungen	50	51.28 N	10.32 E
Klein Bonaire I	231s	12.10 N	68.18 W
Klein Bünzow	50	53.53 N	13.48 E
Kleinburg	265b	43.50 N	79.38 W
Klein Curaçao I	231s	12.00 N	68.40 W
Kleine Elster ≃	50	51.32 N	13.23 E
Kleine Emme ≃	54	47.04 N	8.17 E
Kleine Emscher ≃	253	51.31 N	6.43 E
Kleineichen	253	51.08 N	7.21 E
Klein Elandsvlei	263d	26.09 S	27.39 E
Kleinenberg	48	51.35 N	8.58 E
Kleinenbroich	253	51.12 N	6.35 E
Kleiner Jasmunder Bodden C	50	54.28 N	13.32 E
Kleiner Ravens-Berg ∧[2]	254a	52.22 N	13.04 E
Kleiner Wannsee ⊜	254a	52.25 N	13.10 E
Kleiner Zern-See ⊜	254a	52.26 N	12.55 E
Kleine Spree ≃	50	51.31 N	14.24 E
Kleines Walsertal ∨	58	47.23 N	10.12 E

≃ River	Fluss	Río	Rivière	Rio
☰ Canal	Kanal	Canal	Canal	Canal
↲ Waterfall, Rapids	Wasserfall, Stromschnellen	Cascada, Rápidos	Chute d'eau, Rapides	Cascata, Rápidos
⋓ Strait	Meeresstrasse	Estrecho	Détroit	Estreito
C Bay, Gulf	Bucht, Golf	Bahía, Golfo	Baie, Golfe	Baía, Golfo
⊜ Lake, Lakes	See, Seen	Lago, Lagos	Lac, Lacs	Lago, Lagos
≋ Swamp	Sumpf	Pantano	Marais	Pântano
Ice Features, Glacier	Eis- und Gletscherformen	Accidentes Glaciares	Formes glaciaires	Acidentes Glaciares
Other Hydrographic Features	Andere Hydrographische Objekte	Otros Elementos Hidrográficos	Autres données hydrographiques	Outros Elementos Hidrográficos

✧ Submarine Features	Untermeerische Objekte	Accidentes Submarinos	Formes de relief sous-marin	Acidentes Submarinos
☐ Political Unit	Politische Einheit	Unidad Política	Entité politique	Unidade Política
✪ Cultural Institution	Kulturelle Institution	Institución Cultural	Institution culturelle	Instituição Cultural
⊥ Historical Site	Historische Stätte	Sitio Histórico	Site historique	Sitio Histórico
♠ Recreational Site	Erholungs- und Ferienort	Sitio de Recreo	Centre de loisirs	Sitio de Lazer
⊠ Airport	Flughafen	Aeropuerto	Aéroport	Aeroporto
■ Military Installation	Militäranlage	Instalación Militar	Installation militaire	Instalação Militar
◆ Miscellaneous	Verschiedenes	Misceláneo	Divers	Miscelânea

ENGLISH

Name Page Lat. Long.

DEUTSCH

Name Seite Breite Länge E=Ost

Symbols in the index entries represent the broad categories identified in the key at the right. Symbols with superior numbers (⛰[2]) identify subcategories (see complete key on page I · 26).

Kartensymbole in dem Registerverzeichnis stellen die rechts in Schlüssel erklärten Kategorien dar. Symbole mit hochgestellten Ziffern (⛰[2]) bezeichnen Unterabteilungen einer Kategorie (vgl. vollständiger Schlüssel auf Seite I · 26).

Los símbolos incluídos en el texto del índice representan las grandes categorias identificadas con la clave a la derecha. Los símbolos con numeros en su parte superior (⛰[2]) identifican las subcategorías (véase la clave completa en la página I · 26).

Les symboles de l'index représentent les catégories indiquées dans la légende à droite. Les symboles suivis d'un indice (⛰[2]) représentent des sous-catégories (voir légende complète à la page I · 26).

Os símbolos incluídos no texto do índice representam as grandes categorias identificadas com a chave à direita. Os símbolos com números em sua parte superior (⛰[2]) identificam as subcategorias (veja-se a chave completa à página I · 26).

	English	Deutsch	Español	Français	Português
∧	Mountain	Berg	Montaña	Montagne	Montanha
⛰	Mountains	Berge	Montañas	Montagnes	Montanhas
)(	Pass	Pass	Paso	Col	Passo
∨	Valley, Canyon	Tal, Cañon	Valle, Cañón	Vallée, Canyon	Vale, Canhão
≚	Plain	Ebene	Llano	Plaine	Planície
≻	Cape	Kap	Cabo	Cap	Cabo
I	Island	Insel	Isla	Île	Ilha
II	Islands	Inseln	Islas	Îles	Ilhas
•	Other Topographic Features	Andere Topographische Objekte	Otros Elementos Topográficos	Autres données topographiques	Outros Elementos Topográficos

ESPAÑOL · **FRANÇAIS** · **PORTUGUÊS**

Nombre / Nom / Nome	Página / Page / Página	Lat.°′	Long.°′ W=Oeste / W=Ouest / W=Oeste
Kondol'	70	52.49 N	45.03 E
Kondolole	144	1.20 N	25.58 E
Kondopoga	24	62.12 N	34.17 E
Kondratjevo, S.S.S.R.	66	60.38 N	28.08 E
Kondratjevo, S.S.S.R.	78	57.21 N	98.11 E
Kondrovka	70	54.36 N	43.17 E
Kondrovo	72	54.48 N	35.56 E
Konduga	136	11.39 N	13.24 E
Kondurča ≃	70	53.31 N	50.24 E
Koné	165f	21.04 S	164.52 E
Koné, Passe de Ш	165f	21.08 S	164.41 E
Konecbor	24	64.52 N	57.44 E
Konergino	170	65.54 N	178.50 W
Konevskij, Ostrov I	70	45.43 N	48.30 E
Konfara	140	11.55 N	8.50 W
Kong, C. Iv.	140	9.09 N	4.37 W
Køng, Dan.	41	55.07 N	11.50 E
Kŏng, Kaôh I	100	11.20 N	103.00 E
Kongakut ≃	170	69.48 N	141.50 W
Kongbo	142	4.44 N	21.23 E
Kongcheng	90	31.02 N	117.05 E
Kongeå ≃	41	55.23 N	8.40 E
Kongens Lyngby	41	55.46 N	12.31 E
Kongfang	90	27.58 N	116.53 E
Kongiganak	170	59.58 N	162.45 W
Konginkangas	26	62.46 N	25.48 E
Kongjiamatou	95	39.07 N	116.10 E
Kongjiatun	94	40.42 N	124.04 E
Kongjiawopeng	79	43.58 N	122.41 E
Kongjiazhuang	95	40.47 N	114.48 E
Kongjisihe ≃	76	43.55 N	80.55 E
Kongju	88	36.27 N	127.07 E
Konglong	90	29.56 N	115.54 E
Konglongshan	95	40.33 N	117.17 E
Kongmoon → Jiangmen	90	22.35 N	113.05 E
Kongo → Congo ≃	128	6.04 S	12.24 E
Kongō-ikoma-kokutei-kōen ♠	86	34.28 N	135.40 E
Kongolo, Zaïre	144	5.23 S	27.00 E
Kongolo, Zaïre	144	5.26 S	24.49 E
Kongor	130	7.10 N	31.21 E
Kongō-sanchi ⩘	260	34.27 N	135.41 E
Kongoussi	140	13.19 N	1.32 W
Kongō-zan ∧	86	34.25 N	135.41 E
Kongquehe ≃	80	40.40 N	90.10 E
Kongsberg	26	59.39 N	9.39 E
Kongsvinger	26	60.12 N	12.00 E
Kongsvoll	26	62.18 N	9.37 E
Kongsvoll-Hjerkinn Nasjonalpark ♠	26	62.15 N	9.35 E
Kongtongdao I	88	37.33 N	121.27 E
Kongwa	144	6.12 S	36.25 E
Kongyangcun	96	31.23 N	118.54 E
Kongzhen	96	31.29 N	119.00 E
Koni	144	10.42 S	27.15 E
Koniakari	140	14.34 N	10.54 W
Konice	30	49.35 N	16.53 E
Koniecpol	30	50.48 N	19.41 E
Königgrätz → Hradec Králové	30	50.12 N	15.50 E
Königheim	52	49.37 N	9.35 E
Königin Alexandra-Kette → Queen Alexandra Range ⩘	9	84.00 S	168.00 E
Königin Fabiola-Gebirge → Queen Fabiola Mountains ⩘	9	71.30 S	35.40 E
Königin Mary-Küste → Queen Mary Coast •[2]	9	67.00 S	96.00 E
Königin Maud-Land → Queen Maud Land ◆[1]	9	72.30 S	12.00 E
Königsbach	52	48.58 N	8.36 E
Königsberg, B.R.D.	52	50.05 N	10.34 E
Königsberg → Chojna, Pol.	30	52.58 N	14.28 E
Königsberg → Kaliningrad, S.S.S.R.	66	54.43 N	20.30 E
Königsborn	253	51.33 N	7.41 E
Königsbrück	50	51.16 N	13.54 E
Königsbrunn, B.R.D.	54	48.16 N	10.53 E
Königsbrunn, Öst.	254b	48.21 N	16.25 E
Königsdorf	58	47.49 N	11.28 E
Königsee	50	50.39 N	11.05 E
Königsfelden ʊ[1]	54	47.29 N	8.14 E
Königsfeld im Schwarzwald	54	48.08 N	8.25 E
Königshain	50	51.11 N	14.52 E
Königshardt ◆[8]	253	51.33 N	6.51 E
Königshofen	52	49.32 N	9.44 E
Königshofen im Grabfeld	52	50.18 N	10.29 E
Königslutter	50	52.15 N	10.49 E
Königsmoor ◆[3]	48	53.15 N	9.40 E
Königssee	58	47.33 N	12.58 E
Königsstuhl •[4]	50	54.34 N	13.40 E
Königstein, B.R.D.	52	50.11 N	8.29 E
Königstein, D.D.R.	50	50.55 N	14.04 E
Königstetten	254b	48.18 N	16.09 E
Königswalde	50	50.33 N	13.02 E
Königswartha	50	51.18 N	14.20 E
Königswinter	52	50.40 N	7.11 E
Königs Wusterhausen	50	52.18 N	13.37 E
Konin	30	52.13 N	18.16 E
Konispol	38	39.39 N	20.10 E
Kónitsa	38	40.02 N	20.45 E
Köniz	54	46.56 N	7.25 E
Konjic	38	43.39 N	17.57 E
Konka ≃	68	47.40 N	35.22 E
Könkämäälv ≃	24	68.29 N	22.17 E
Konkapot ≃	200	42.03 N	73.20 W
Konkiep ≃	146	28.03 S	17.21 E
Konkō	86	34.32 N	133.37 E
Kon'-Kolodez'	66	52.08 N	39.11 E
Konkouré ≃	140	9.58 N	13.42 W
Kon'kovo	73	47.20 N	38.10 E
Konkudera	78	57.33 N	112.30 E
Kon-Kuk University ʊ[2]	261b	37.32 N	127.05 E
Konnagar	116	22.42 N	88.22 E
Könnern	50	51.40 N	11.46 E
Konnevesi @	26	62.40 N	26.35 E
Konnur	112	16.12 N	74.45 E
Kōno	84	35.49 N	136.04 E
Konobejevo	72	55.24 N	38.40 E
Konohana ◆[8]	260	34.41 N	135.16 E
Kōnoike	260	34.42 N	135.37 E
Konolfingen	54	46.53 N	7.38 E
Konongo	140	6.37 N	1.11 W
Konoša	24	60.58 N	40.15 E
Kōno-shima I	86	34.28 N	133.31 E
Kōnosu	84	36.03 N	139.31 E
Konotop	68	51.14 N	33.12 E
Konovalovka	70	53.06 N	51.34 E
Kon'ovo, S.S.S.R.	24	62.08 N	39.16 E
Kon'ovo, S.S.S.R.	76	56.18 N	70.43 E
Konpienga ≃	140	10.52 N	0.51 E
Konradshöhe ◆[8]	254a	52.35 N	13.14 E
Konradsreuth	50	50.16 N	11.50 E
Konsankoro	140	9.02 N	9.00 W
Konsen-daichi ⩘	82a	63.25 N	144.52 E
Końskie	30	51.12 N	20.26 E
Konstadt → Wołczyn	30	51.01 N	18.03 E
Konstantinopel → İstanbul	120	41.01 N	28.58 E
Konstantinovka, S.S.S.R.	68	49.57 N	35.07 E
Konstantinovka, S.S.S.R.	68	47.51 N	31.09 E
Konstantinovka, S.S.S.R.	70	56.41 N	50.53 E
Konstantinovka, S.S.S.R.	73	48.32 N	37.43 E
Konstantinovka, S.S.S.R.	73	47.52 N	37.24 E
Konstantinovka, S.S.S.R.	255a	59.47 N	30.08 E
Konstantinovo	72	56.33 N	38.02 E
Konstantinovskij, S.S.S.R.	66	57.50 N	39.36 E
Konstantinovskij, S.S.S.R.	70	47.35 N	41.06 E
Konstantinovskije Porogi	66	60.34 N	37.04 E
Konstantynów Łódzki	30	51.45 N	19.20 E
Konstanz	54	47.40 N	9.10 E
Kontagora	140	10.24 N	5.28 E
Kontcha	142	7.58 N	12.14 E
Kontejevo	70	58.26 N	41.21 E
Kontha	100	19.30 N	96.03 E
Kontich	46	51.08 N	4.27 E
Kontiolahti	26	62.46 N	29.51 E
Kontiomäki	26	64.21 N	28.09 E
Konto	105a	7.46 S	112.19 E
Kontum	100	14.21 N	108.00 E
Kontum, Plateau du ⩘[1]	100	13.55 N	108.05 E
Kōnu	86	34.42 N	133.05 E
Kon'uchovo	76	55.08 N	70.38 E
Konus, Gora ∧	170	67.34 N	178.10 E
Konya	120	37.52 N	32.31 E
Konya □[4]	120	38.00 N	33.00 E
Konyr	70	50.25 N	53.25 E
Konyrat	70	49.36 N	47.01 E
Konyrolen	76	44.16 N	79.19 E
Konyševka	68	51.51 N	35.18 E
Konystanu	70	48.51 N	53.20 E
Konz	52	49.42 N	6.34 E
Konza	144	1.45 S	37.07 E
Konžakovskij Kamen', Gora ∧	76	59.38 N	59.08 E
Koocanusa, Lake @[1]	192	49.00 N	115.10 W
Koog [aan de Zaan]	48	52.27 N	4.49 E
Kookynie	152	29.20 S	121.29 E
Koolamarra	156	20.12 S	140.14 E
Koolatah	154	15.53 S	142.27 E
Koolau Range ⩘	219c	21.35 N	158.00 W
Kooloonong	156	34.53 S	143.09 E
Koolskamp	46	51.00 N	3.12 E
Koolyanobbing	152	30.50 S	119.35 E
Koolywurtie	158b	34.38 S	137.37 E
Koombana Bay C	158a	33.18 S	115.36 E
Koondrook	156	35.39 S	144.08 E
Koonga	66	58.35 N	24.12 E
Koonibba	152	31.58 S	133.27 E
Koontz Lake	206	41.25 N	86.29 W
Koontz Lake @	206	41.25 N	86.28 W
Koopan-Noord	148	26.53 S	20.41 E
Koopan-Suid	148	27.15 S	20.22 E
Koopmansfontein	148	28.14 S	24.01 E
Koorawatha	156	34.02 S	148.33 E
Koorda	152	30.50 S	117.29 E
Koosa	66	58.33 N	27.07 E
Koosfontein	148	27.22 S	25.27 E
Koosharem	190	38.31 N	111.53 W
Kooskia	192	46.09 N	115.59 W
Koossa	140	9.32 N	8.32 W
Kootenai (Kootenay) ≃	172	49.15 N	117.39 W
Kootenay (Kootenai) ≃	172	49.15 N	117.39 W
Kootenay Indian Reserve ◆[4]	172	49.37 N	115.45 W
Kootenay Lake @	172	49.35 N	116.50 W
Kootenay National Park ♠	172	51.00 N	116.00 W
Kootjieskolk	148	31.15 S	20.21 E
Kootwijk	48	52.12 N	5.45 E
Koo-wee-rup	159	38.12 S	145.30 E
Kooyong	264b	37.50 S	145.02 E
Kopa	75	43.32 N	75.50 E
Kopa ≃	75	43.40 N	76.15 E
Kopāganj	114	26.01 N	83.34 E
Kopāi ≃	116	23.48 N	87.47 E
Kopajgorod	68	48.51 N	27.48 E
Kopanbulak	76	48.56 N	80.52 E
Kopang	105b	8.39 S	116.21 E
Kopanovka	70	47.27 N	46.48 E
Kopanskaja	68	46.17 N	38.29 E
Kopapan	70	50.20 N	50.26 E
Kopargaon	112	19.53 N	74.29 E
Koparkhairna	262c	19.06 N	72.59 E
Koparpāda	262c	19.02 N	73.04 E
Kópasker	24a	66.20 N	16.24 W
Kopatkeviči	66	52.19 N	28.49 E
Kópavogur	24a	64.06 N	21.50 W
Kopceviči	68	52.14 N	28.19 E
Kop Dağı ∧	74	40.01 N	40.28 E
Kopdağı Geçidi)(	120	40.03 N	40.33 E
Kopejsk	76	55.07 N	61.37 E
Kopenhagen → København	41	55.40 N	12.35 E
Köpenick ◆[8]	50	52.27 N	13.34 E
Köpenick, Schloss ʊ	254a	52.27 N	13.34 E
Koper	36	45.33 N	13.44 E
Köpernitz	50	53.04 N	12.56 E
Kopervik	26	59.17 N	5.18 E
Kopeysk → Kopejsk	76	55.07 N	61.37 E
Kopice	50	53.44 N	14.32 E
Köping	40	59.31 N	16.00 E
Kopisty	50	50.34 N	13.35 E
Kopjevo	76	55.03 N	89.50 E
Koplik	38	42.13 N	19.26 E
Köpmanholmen	26	63.10 N	18.34 E
Kopnino	72	56.53 N	38.29 E
Kopondei, Tanjung ≻	105b	8.04 S	122.52 E
Koporje	66	59.44 N	29.01 E
Koporskij Zaliv C	66	59.52 N	28.55 E
Koppal	112	15.21 N	76.09 E
Koppang	26	61.34 N	11.04 E
Koppány ≃	30	46.35 N	18.26 E
Kopparberg	40	59.52 N	14.59 E
Kopparbergs Län □[6]	26	61.00 N	14.30 E
Koppeh Dāgh ⩘	118	37.50 N	58.00 E
Koppel	204	40.50 N	80.20 W
Kopperå	26	63.24 N	11.51 E
Kopperby	41	54.38 N	9.56 E
Kopperl	212	32.04 N	97.30 W
Koppi	79	48.32 N	140.07 E
Koppi ≃	79	48.33 N	140.08 E
Koppies	148	27.20 S	27.30 E
Koppom	26	59.43 N	12.09 E
Kopri	262c	19.11 N	72.58 E
Koprivnica	36	46.10 N	16.50 E
Köprü ≃	120	36.49 N	31.10 E
Köprüören	120	39.30 N	29.47 E
Kopt'ovo	70	56.43 N	40.31 E
Kopyčincy	68	49.06 N	25.55 E
Kopyl'	66	53.09 N	27.05 E
Kopylovka	76	58.40 N	82.22 E
Kopylovo, S.S.S.R.	24	60.35 N	45.02 E
Kopylovo, S.S.S.R.	72	56.26 N	36.25 E
Kopys'	66	54.19 N	30.18 E
Kor ≃	118	29.36 N	53.18 E
Kōra	84	35.12 N	136.15 E
Korab ⩘	38	41.47 N	20.34 E
Kor Aban	134	3.53 N	42.40 E
Korablino	70	53.55 N	40.01 E
Korahe	134	6.35 N	44.23 E
Kor'akovka	76	52.24 N	77.08 E
Kor'akskoje Nagorje ⩘	64	62.30 N	172.00 E
Kōraku-en ♠	86	34.38 N	133.53 E
Korakuen Stadium ♠	258	35.43 N	139.45 E
Korallenmeer → Coral Sea ⍑[2]	14	20.00 S	158.00 E
Koralpe ⩘	30	46.50 N	14.58 E
Korannaberg ⩘	148	27.25 S	22.32 E
Korapun	154	5.25 S	152.00 E
Koraput	112	18.49 N	82.43 E
Koraraika, Baie de C	147b	17.45 S	43.57 E
Korarou, Lac @	140	15.15 N	3.16 W
Korashir	134	3.20 N	46.22 E
Korat → Nakhon Ratchasima	100	14.58 N	102.07 E
Koratla	112	18.49 N	78.43 E
Kor'ažma	24	61.18 N	47.06 E
Korba, Bhārat	114	22.21 N	82.41 E
Korba, Tun.	36	36.35 N	10.52 E
Korbach	52	51.16 N	8.52 E
Korbeta	134	13.03 N	39.43 E
Korbol	136	10.01 N	17.43 E
Korbous	36	36.49 N	10.35 E
Korbu, Gunong ∧	104	4.43 N	101.17 E
Korçë	38	40.37 N	20.46 E
Korcevo	66	58.52 N	42.13 E
Korčula	36	42.58 N	17.08 E
Korčula, Otok I	36	42.57 N	16.50 E
Korčulanski Kanal Ш	36	43.03 N	16.40 E
Kordestān □[4]	118	35.30 N	47.00 E
Kord Kūy	118	36.48 N	54.07 E
Kordovo	76	54.06 N	93.17 E
Korea □[1]	4	38.00 N	127.00 E
Korea, North □[1]	80		
	88	40.00 N	127.00 E
Korea, South □[1]	80		
	88	36.30 N	128.00 E
Korea Bay C	88	39.00 N	124.00 E
Korea Strait Ш	80	34.00 N	129.00 E
Korea University ʊ[2]	261b	37.36 N	127.02 E
Korec	68	50.37 N	27.09 E
Korekozevo	72	54.20 N	36.11 E
Korelakša	24	65.33 N	32.22 E
Koreliči	66	53.34 N	26.08 E
Korem	134	12.30 N	39.30 E
Koré Mayroua	140	13.18 N	3.55 E
Koren (Die Wurzen))(	58	46.31 N	13.45 E
Korenkovo	68	45.07 N	36.24 E
Koren'ovo	68	51.25 N	34.55 E
Korenovsk	68	45.29 N	39.28 E
Korf	64	60.19 N	165.50 E
Korfovskij	79	48.14 N	135.02 E
Korga	148	30.12 S	20.28 E
Korgan	120	40.44 N	37.13 E
Korgašino	72	54.45 N	37.41 E
Kõrgessaare	66	58.59 N	22.28 E
Korgonskij Chrebet ⩘	76	50.45 N	84.30 E
Korgus	130	19.13 N	33.29 E
Korhogo	140	9.27 N	5.38 W
Korhogo □[5]	140	9.30 N	5.45 W
Kōri	260	34.47 N	135.39 E
Koridhallós	257c	37.59 N	23.39 E
Korido	154	0.50 S	135.35 E
Koriella	159	37.10 S	145.39 E
Korienzé	140	15.24 N	3.47 W
Korim	154	0.54 S	136.02 E
Korima, Oued el ∨	138	33.51 N	0.23 W
Koringberg	148	33.01 S	18.40 E
Koringplaas	148	32.48 S	20.58 E
Korinth	41	55.08 N	10.21 E
Korinthiakós Kólpos C	38	38.19 N	22.04 E
Kórinthos (Corinth)	38	37.56 N	22.56 E
Korínthou, Dhiórix ☰	38	37.57 N	22.56 E
Kőris-hegy ∧	30	47.18 N	17.45 E
Koritsa → Korçë	38	40.37 N	20.46 E
Köritz	50	52.51 N	12.27 E
Kōriyama, Nihon	82	37.24 N	140.23 E
Kōriyama → Yamato-Kōriyama, Nihon	86	34.38 N	135.47 E
Korizo, Passe de)(	136	22.28 N	15.27 E
Korkino, S.S.S.R.	76	54.54 N	61.23 E
Korkino, S.S.S.R.	78	54.23 N	105.14 E
Korkinskoje, Ozero @	255a	59.55 N	30.44 E
Korkuteli	120	37.04 N	30.13 E
Korla → Kuerle	80	41.44 N	86.09 E
Korl'aki	70	57.06 N	46.57 E
Korliki	64	61.31 N	82.22 E
Körlin → Karlino	30	54.03 N	15.51 E
Korma, S.S.S.R.	66	52.21 N	31.31 E
Korma, S.S.S.R.	66	53.08 N	30.48 E
Kormakíti, Akrotírion ≻	120	35.24 N	32.56 E
Körmend	30	47.01 N	16.37 E
Kormilovka	76	55.00 N	74.06 E
Kormovoje	70	46.17 N	43.30 E
Kornat, Otok I	36	43.50 N	15.16 E
Körnebach ≃	253	51.35 N	7.38 E
Kornejevka, S.S.S.R.	70	51.45 N	48.46 E
Kornejevka, S.S.S.R.	76	50.12 N	74.19 E
Kornejevka, S.S.S.R.	76	54.01 N	68.27 E
Kornelimünster	52	50.43 N	6.11 E
Körner	50	51.13 N	10.35 E
Kornešty	68	47.22 N	27.59 E
Korneuburg	254b	48.21 N	16.20 E
Kórnik	30	52.17 N	17.04 E
Kornilovo	76	53.32 N	81.05 E
Kornin	68	50.06 N	29.32 E
Kornouchovo	70	55.33 N	49.53 E
Korn'ovo	255a	60.03 N	30.45 E
Kornsjø	26	58.57 N	11.39 E
Kornwestheim	52	48.52 N	9.11 E
Koro, C. Iv.	140	8.34 N	7.28 W
Koro, Mali	140	14.04 N	3.05 W
Koro I	165g	17.19 S	179.23 E
Koroba	154	5.40 S	142.45 E
Koroča	68	50.48 N	37.11 E
Korodougou	140	12.26 N	6.17 W
Köroglu Tepesi ∧	120	40.31 N	31.53 E
Korogwe	144	5.09 S	38.29 E
Koroit	156	38.17 S	142.22 E
Korolevskij Belok, Gora ∧	76	51.00 N	83.43 E
Korolevu	165g	18.13 S	177.44 E
Korol'ovo	68	48.09 N	23.08 E
Korol'ovščina	66	55.49 N	31.45 E
Korom, Bahr ≃	136	10.35 N	19.45 E
Koromba ∧	165g	17.53 S	177.34 E
Koromiri I	164k	21.15 S	159.43 W
Koromo → Toyota	84	35.05 N	137.09 E
Koronadal	106	6.30 N	124.51 E
Kor'onevo	255b	55.40 N	38.00 E
Koróni	38	36.48 N	21.56 E
Korónia, Límni @	38	40.41 N	23.05 E
Koronowo	30	53.19 N	17.57 E
Korop	68	51.34 N	32.56 E
Koropele	142	4.44 N	17.11 E
Koropíon	38	37.54 N	23.53 E
Koror	165b	7.20 N	134.29 E
Koror I	165b	7.20 N	134.30 E
Kororoit Creek ≃	264b	37.52 S	144.52 E
Körös ≃	30	46.43 N	20.12 E
Koro Sea ⍑[2]	165g	18.00 S	179.50 E
Korosten'	68	50.57 N	28.39 E
Korostyšev	68	50.19 N	29.03 E
Korotkova	78	56.43 N	107.55 E
Korotojak	68	50.59 N	39.10 E
Koro Toro	136	16.05 N	18.30 E
Korotovo	66	58.57 N	37.28 E
Korotyš	66	52.22 N	37.27 E
Korovincy	68	50.48 N	33.45 E
Korovin Island I	170	55.25 N	160.15 W
Korovino, S.S.S.R.	68	51.25 N	36.45 E
Korovino, S.S.S.R.	70	53.49 N	53.03 E
Korovin Volcano ∧[1]	170	52.22 N	174.10 W
Korovou	165g	17.57 S	178.21 E
Koroyanitu, Mount ∧	165g	17.40 S	177.35 E
Korožečna ≃	66	57.32 N	38.18 E
Korpela	24	66.15 N	30.01 E
Korpilahti	26	62.01 N	25.33 E
Korpo (Korppoo)	26	60.10 N	21.34 E
Korså	40	60.38 N	16.08 E
Korsakov	79	46.38 N	142.46 E
Korsakovo	66	53.16 N	37.21 E
Korschen → Korsze	30	54.10 N	21.09 E
Korschenbroich	52	51.11 N	6.31 E
Korselbränna	26	64.27 N	15.35 E
Korševo	68	51.11 N	40.07 E
Korsika → Corse I	36	42.00 N	9.00 E
Korsnäs, Suomi	26	62.47 N	21.12 E
Korsnäs, Sve.	40	60.35 N	15.43 E
Korso	26	60.21 N	25.06 E
Korsør	41	55.20 N	11.09 E
Körsüleymanlı	120	38.17 N	38.01 E
Korsun'	73	48.12 N	38.05 E
Koršunovo	78	58.37 N	110.10 E
Korsun'-Ševčenkovskij	68	49.26 N	31.16 E
Korsze	30	54.10 N	21.09 E
Kortelisy	68	51.51 N	24.25 E
Kortemark	46	51.02 N	3.02 E
Kortgene	48	51.34 N	3.48 E
Kortkeros	24	61.49 N	51.28 E
Kortrijk (Courtrai)	46	50.50 N	3.16 E
Kortuz, Gora ∧	76	54.33 N	91.56 E
Korucu	120	39.28 N	27.22 E
Kor'ukovka	68	51.46 N	32.14 E
Korumburra	159	38.26 S	145.49 E
Korwai	114	24.08 N	78.03 E
Kōryō	86	34.33 N	135.45 E
Koryŏng	88	35.44 N	128.15 E
Koryst'	68	50.35 N	27.01 E
Korženevskoj, Pik ∧	75	39.04 N	72.00 E
Koržeuc'	68	48.13 N	27.02 E
Korževka	70	54.12 N	46.22 E
Kos	38	36.53 N	27.18 E
Kos I	38	36.50 N	27.10 E
Kosa, S.S.S.R.	24	59.56 N	54.55 E
Kosa, S.S.S.R.	78	54.47 N	108.52 E
Kosa, Yai.	134	7.51 N	36.51 E
Kosa ≃, S.S.S.R.	24	60.11 N	55.10 E
Kosa ≃, S.S.S.R.	70	58.26 N	51.15 E
Kosa ⊥	140	15.50 N	7.00 W
Koš-Agač	76	50.00 N	88.40 E
Kosai	84	34.43 N	137.33 E
Kosaja, Šivera ⅃	78	58.24 N	97.48 E
Kosaja Gora	72	54.07 N	37.33 E
Kosaka	82	40.19 N	140.44 E
Kosa-Meečkyn, Ostrov I	170	65.26 N	178.00 W
Kosan	88	38.52 N	127.24 E
Košankol'	70	49.56 N	48.11 E
Koščagyl	76	46.51 N	53.48 E
Kościan	30	52.06 N	16.38 E
Kościerzyna	30	54.08 N	18.00 E
Kosciusko	184	32.58 N	89.35 W
Kosciusko □[6]	206	41.14 N	85.51 W
Kosciusko, Mount ∧	161b	36.27 S	148.16 E
Kosciusko National Park ♠	161b	36.10 S	148.15 E
Kösdağı ∧	120	40.59 N	34.25 E
Kosdaulet, Peski ◆[2]	70	47.45 N	49.30 E
Kose, Nihon	260	34.25 N	135.46 E
Kose, S.S.S.R.	66	59.11 N	25.10 E
Köse, Tür.	120	40.13 N	39.39 E
Kösefakılı	120	39.36 N	34.09 E
Košelevka	72	55.09 N	38.05 E
Košelicha	70	55.02 N	43.33 E
Košerovo	72	55.38 N	38.22 E
Koserow	50	54.03 N	13.59 E
Kosha	130	20.49 N	30.32 E
Koshien Stadium ♠	260	34.42 N	135.22 E
Koshigaya	84	35.54 N	139.48 E
Koshigoe	258	35.18 N	139.30 E
Koshikijima-rettō II	82	31.45 N	129.49 E
Koshino	84	36.02 N	136.01 E
Koshk-e Kohneh	118	34.52 N	62.31 E
Koshkonong	184	36.36 N	91.39 W
Koshkonong, Lake @	206	42.52 N	88.58 W
Koshkonong Creek ≃	206	42.53 N	88.59 W
Koshlong Lake @	202	44.58 N	78.29 W
Kōshoku	84	36.38 N	138.06 E
Koshu → Kwangju	88	35.09 N	126.54 E
Kosi	114	27.48 N	77.26 E
Kosi, Lake @	148	26.55 S	32.52 E
Košice	30	48.43 N	21.15 E
Kosigi	112	15.51 N	77.16 E
Kosikovo	66	59.52 N	43.23 E
Kosino, S.S.S.R.	70	58.23 N	51.17 E
Kosino, S.S.S.R.	72	55.43 N	37.52 E
Kosju	24	65.38 N	59.03 E
Kosju ≃	24	66.18 N	59.53 E
Kosjuvom	24	66.17 N	59.50 E
Köşk	120	37.51 N	28.03 E
Koskaecodde Lake @	176	48.00 N	55.20 W
Koškar	76	47.27 N	53.29 E
Koški, S.S.S.R.	70	54.12 N	50.28 E
Koski, Suomi	26	60.39 N	23.09 E
Koškino	70	56.20 N	50.49 E
Koskol'	76	49.31 N	67.05 E
Koskuduk	76	44.06 N	77.22 E
Koskullskulle	24	67.12 N	20.50 E
Koslan	24	63.28 N	48.52 E
Köslin → Koszalin	30	54.12 N	16.09 E
Kosmonosy	50	50.26 N	15.00 E
Kosmosa, Monument ⊥	255b	55.49 N	37.38 E
Kosmynino	70	57.35 N	40.46 E
Kosoba, Gora ∧	76	48.15 N	79.40 E
Kosogor	70	57.07 N	47.34 E
Kosoj, Porog ⅃, S.S.S.R.	76	57.30 N	95.30 E
Kosoj, Porog ⅃, S.S.S.R.	78	57.44 N	96.20 E
Kosolapovo	70	56.57 N	49.37 E
Kosŏng	88	34.58 N	128.18 E
Kosor	120	40.39 N	42.39 E
Kosov	68	48.19 N	25.05 E
Kosovska Mitrovica	38	42.53 N	20.52 E
Kösreli	120	37.11 N	35.59 E
Kossanto	140	13.08 N	11.58 W
Kossdorf	50	51.29 N	13.14 E
Kosse	212	31.18 N	96.38 W
Kössen	58	47.40 N	12.24 E
Kossol Passage Ш	165b	7.52 N	134.36 E
Kossol Reef ✢[2]	165b	7.57 N	134.41 E
Kossovo	66	52.45 N	25.09 E
Kossuth	204	41.17 N	79.35 W
Kosta	26	56.51 N	15.23 E
Košt'ahy	50	50.39 N	13.45 E
Kostajnica	36	45.14 N	16.33 E
Koš-Tegirmen	75	42.47 N	73.53 E
Kostelec nad Labem	50	50.11 N	14.35 E
Kostenec	38	42.16 N	23.49 E
Koster	148	25.57 S	26.42 E
Kosterevo	70	55.56 N	39.37 E
Kosteröarna I	26	58.54 N	11.02 E
Kostešty	68	46.52 N	28.44 E
Koštice	50	50.24 N	13.55 E
Kostino, S.S.S.R.	70	52.24 N	51.39 E
Kostino, S.S.S.R.	70	52.11 N	51.20 E
Kostino, S.S.S.R.	72	56.18 N	37.43 E
Kostino, S.S.S.R.	255b	55.55 N	37.51 E
Kostino-Otdelec	68	51.33 N	41.26 E
Kost'kovo	66	60.02 N	33.14 E
Košt'ob'o	75	41.06 N	74.15 E
Kostonjärvi @	26	65.47 N	28.27 E
Kostopol'	68	50.53 N	26.26 E
Kostriževka	68	48.38 N	25.41 E
Kostroma	66	57.46 N	40.55 E
Kostroma ≃	24	57.47 N	40.55 E
Kostrovo	72	55.53 N	36.42 E
Kostrzyn	30	52.37 N	14.39 E
Kost'ukoviči	66	53.20 N	32.03 E
Kost'ukovka	66	52.32 N	30.56 E
Kosugaya ◆[8]	258	35.22 N	139.33 E
Kosuge	84	35.45 N	138.57 E
Kosugi	84	36.43 N	137.06 E
Kosum Phisai	100	16.13 N	103.01 E
Koszalin (Köslin)	30	54.12 N	16.09 E
Kőszeg	30	47.23 N	16.33 E
Koszyce	30	50.11 N	20.35 E
Kota, Bhārat	110	25.11 N	75.50 E
Kota, Bhārat	114	22.18 N	82.02 E
Kota, Malay.	104	2.31 N	102.10 E
Kota, Malay.	104	5.35 N	100.23 E
Kota □[5]	114	25.00 N	76.30 E
Kotaagung	102	5.30 S	104.38 E
Kotabaharu, Indon.	102	0.48 S	111.33 E
Kota Baharu, Malay.	104	6.08 N	102.15 E
Kotabangun	102	0.16 S	116.35 E
Kotabaru, Indon.	102	3.14 S	116.13 E
Kotabaru, Indon.	102	1.08 S	101.43 E
Kotabaru → Jayapura, Indon.	154	2.32 S	140.42 E
Kotabumi	102	4.50 S	104.54 E
Kotabunan	102	0.49 N	124.38 E
Kotadabok	102	0.30 S	104.33 E
Kot Addu	113	30.28 N	70.58 E
Kotagiri	112	11.26 N	76.53 E
Kot'ajevka	70	46.33 N	48.46 E
Kotake	86	33.30 N	130.40 E
Kota Kinabalu (Jesselton)	102	5.59 N	116.04 E
Kota Kota → Nkhota Kota	144	12.57 S	34.17 E
Kotālpur	116	23.02 N	87.36 E
Kotamobagu	102	0.46 N	124.19 E
Kotanemel', Gora ∧	76	47.43 N	77.18 E
Kotapinang	104	1.53 N	100.05 E
Kotari ⩘	36	44.05 N	15.30 E
Kota Sarang Semut	104	5.59 N	100.24 E
Kotatengah	104	1.05 N	100.33 E
Kota Tinggi	104	1.44 N	103.54 E
Kotawaringin	102	2.29 S	111.25 E
Kotchāndpur	114	23.24 N	89.01 E
Kotcho Lake @	166	59.05 N	121.10 W
Kot Chutta	113	29.53 N	70.39 E
Kotdwāra	114	29.45 N	78.32 E
Kotel	38	42.53 N	26.27 E
Kotel'nič	70	58.18 N	48.20 E
Kotel'niki	72	55.39 N	37.52 E
Kotel'nikovo	70	47.38 N	43.09 E
Kotel'nyj, Ostrov I	64	75.45 N	138.44 E
Kotel'va	68	50.05 N	34.45 E
Kot Fateh	113	30.07 N	75.05 E
Köthen	50	51.45 N	11.58 E
Koti → Kōchi	86	33.33 N	133.33 E
Kotido	144	3.00 N	34.06 E
Kotikovo	79	49.08 N	144.13 E
Kotka	26	60.28 N	26.55 E
Kot Kapūra	113	30.35 N	74.54 E
Kotkino	24	67.02 N	51.03 E
Kotla, Bhārat	113	32.15 N	76.02 E
Kotla, Lībīya	136	28.33 N	18.58 E
Kotl'akovo	72	56.17 N	35.49 E
Kotlas	24	61.16 N	46.35 E
Kotlenski prohod)(	38	42.53 N	26.27 E
Kotli	113	33.31 N	73.55 E
Kotlik	170	63.02 N	163.33 W
Kotlin, Ostrov I	255a	60.00 N	29.46 E
Kotly	66	59.36 N	28.45 E
Kot Mūmin	113	32.11 N	73.02 E
Kotō	84	35.08 N	136.14 E
Kōtō ◆[8]	258	35.41 N	139.48 E
Koto ≃, Nihon	86	33.58 N	131.13 E
Koto ≃, Nihon	86	34.21 N	134.02 E
Kotobiki-san ∧	86	35.03 N	132.47 E
Kotohira	86	34.11 N	133.49 E
Kotohira ʊ[1]	86	34.11 N	133.49 E
Kotohira-yama ∧	86	34.11 N	133.48 E
Kotonami	86	34.10 N	133.56 E
Koton-Karifi	140	8.08 N	6.48 E
Kotonkoro	140	11.02 N	5.58 E
Kotor	38	42.25 N	18.46 E
Kotoriba	36	46.21 N	16.49 E
Kotorovo	70	54.54 N	41.35 E
Kotor Varoš	36	44.37 N	17.23 E
Kotovka	68	49.08 N	34.57 E
Kotovo	70	50.18 N	44.50 E
Kotovsk, S.S.S.R.	68	47.45 N	29.33 E
Kotovsk, S.S.S.R.	68	46.49 N	28.34 E
Kotovsk, S.S.S.R.	70	52.36 N	41.32 E
Kot Pūtli	114	27.43 N	76.12 E
Kotra, Bhārat	110	24.22 N	73.10 E
Kotra, Bhārat	262b	22.46 N	88.34 E
Kot Rādha Kishan	113	31.10 N	74.06 E
Kotri	110	25.22 N	68.18 E
Kotri Allahrakhio	110	24.24 N	67.50 E
Kotrung → Uttarpara-Kotrung	262b	22.40 N	88.21 E
Kötschach	58	46.40 N	13.00 E
Kot Sultān	113	30.46 N	70.56 E
Kōtsu-zan ∧	86	34.01 N	134.12 E
Kottagūdem	112	17.33 N	80.38 E
Kottai Malai ∧	112	9.30 N	77.24 E
Kottas Mountains ⩘	9	74.20 S	12.00 W
Kottayam	112	9.35 N	76.31 E
Kotte	112	6.54 N	79.54 E
Kottenforst, Naturpark ♠	52	50.20 N	6.55 E
Kotto ≃	142	4.14 N	22.02 E
Kotton	134	9.37 N	50.32 E
Kottūr	112	10.32 N	76.59 E
Kottūru	112	14.49 N	76.13 E
Kotuj ≃	64	71.55 N	102.05 E
Kotum	120	38.25 N	42.18 E
Kot'užen'	68	47.51 N	28.36 E
Kotwālīpāra	116	22.59 N	89.59 E
Kotzebue	170	66.53 N	162.39 W
Kotzebue Sound Ш	170	66.20 N	163.00 W
Kotzenau → Chocianów	30	51.25 N	15.55 E
Kötzting	30	49.11 N	12.52 E
Koualé	140	11.24 N	7.01 W
Kouan	96	32.19 N	119.52 E
Kouandé	140	10.20 N	1.42 E
Kouango	142	4.58 N	19.59 E
Koubansaki	263b	4.22 S	15.09 E
Koubia	140	11.35 N	11.54 W
Kouchibouguac Bay C	176	46.50 N	64.50 W
Kouchibouguac National Park ♠	176	46.50 N	65.00 W
Koudougou	140	12.15 N	2.22 W
Kouéré	140	10.27 N	3.59 W
Koueveldberge ⩘	148	32.10 S	24.08 E
Kouga	136	9.56 N	21.03 E
Kougaberge ⩘	148	33.40 S	23.50 E
Kougarok Mountain ∧	170	65.41 N	165.13 W
K'ouhu	90	23.35 N	120.10 E
Kouilou □[5]	142	4.00 S	12.00 E
Kouilou ≃	142	4.28 S	11.41 E
Koukdjuak ≃	166	66.45 N	73.09 W
Kouki	142	7.10 N	17.18 E
Koúklia	120	34.42 N	32.34 E
Koukourou ≃	142	7.32 N	19.42 E
Koula-Moutou	142	1.08 S	12.29 E
Koulia Ba	140	14.11 N	14.28 W
Koulikoro	140	12.53 N	7.33 W
Koulouguidi	140	13.27 N	11.03 W
Koulountou ≃	140	13.15 N	13.37 W
Koumac	165f	20.33 S	164.17 E
Koumala	156	21.37 S	149.15 E
Koumameyong	142	0.11 N	11.51 E
Koumankou Markala	140	12.06 N	6.08 W
Koumbakara	140	12.42 N	14.29 W
Koumbal	136	9.26 N	22.39 E
Koumbala ≃	136	9.14 N	20.42 E
Koumban	142	7.43 N	15.12 E
Koumbia, Guinée	140	11.48 N	13.30 W
Koumbia, H. Vol.	140	11.14 N	3.42 W
Koumbisaleh ⊥	140	15.55 N	8.05 W
Koumbouma	140	10.24 N	12.56 W
Koumi	84	36.05 N	138.29 E
Koumou ∧	130	9.34 N	23.38 E
Koumpenntoum	140	13.59 N	14.34 W
Koumra	136	8.55 N	17.33 E
Koun	140	7.29 N	3.15 W
Kounda Ko ≃	140	12.13 N	11.03 W
Koundara	140	12.29 N	13.18 W
Koundara □[4]	140	12.25 N	13.10 W
Koundé	142	6.07 N	14.38 E
Koundougou	140	11.44 N	4.31 W
Koungheul	140	13.59 N	14.48 W
Koungoulou	142	3.32 S	13.20 E
Kouniohou	140	7.40 N	0.48 E
Kounradskij	76	46.59 N	75.00 E
Kountze	184	30.23 N	94.19 W
Koupé, Mont ∧	142	4.47 N	9.43 E
Koupéla	140	12.11 N	0.21 W
Kouqian	79	43.40 N	126.30 E
Kour, Oued n' ≃	34	35.14 N	3.45 W
Kouragué	140	12.18 N	10.02 W
Kourak	76	54.50 N	84.40 E
Kouriles,, Détroit des → Pervyj Kuril'skij Proliv Ш	64	50.50 N	156.36 E
Kouri-shima I	164m	26.42 N	128.01 E
Kourou	240	5.09 N	52.39 W
Kouroukoto	140	12.35 N	10.05 W
Kourouma	140	11.37 N	4.48 W
Kourouninkoto	140	13.52 N	9.35 W
Kouroussa	140	10.39 N	9.53 W
Kouroussa □[4]	140	10.40 N	9.55 W
Kourtiagou, Réserve de ◆[4]	140	11.35 N	1.30 E
Koury	140	12.11 N	4.48 W
Koussanar	140	13.52 N	14.05 W
Koussané, Mali	140	14.53 N	11.14 W
Koussane, Sén.	140	14.08 N	12.26 W
Kousser, Massif ∧	138	32.02 N	5.59 W
Koussi, Emi ∧	136	19.50 N	18.30 E
Koussili	140	13.30 N	11.38 W
Koutiala	140	12.23 N	5.28 W
Kouto	140	9.53 N	6.25 W
Koutomo I	165f	22.40 S	167.33 E
Koutou	88	38.35 N	114.24 E
Koutouba	140	8.41 N	3.12 W
Kouts	206	41.19 N	87.02 W
Kouvola	26	60.52 N	26.42 E
Kouya ≃	140	10.09 N	9.45 W
Kouyou ≃	142	0.45 S	16.38 E
Kova	78	58.18 N	100.21 E
Kova ≃	78	58.18 N	100.18 E
Kovaksa	70	55.31 N	43.30 E
Koval'ovka	68	47.16 N	31.43 E
Kovarskas	66	55.26 N	24.55 E
Kovarzino	66	60.09 N	38.33 E
Kovdor	24	67.34 N	30.22 E
Kovdozero, Ozero @	24	66.47 N	32.00 E
Kovel'	68	51.14 N	24.41 E
Kovernino	70	57.07 N	43.49 E
Kovilpatti	112	9.10 N	77.52 E
Kovin	38	44.45 N	20.59 E
Kovno → Kaunas	66	54.54 N	23.54 E
Kovpyta	68	51.23 N	30.50 E
Kovrina Vtoraja	70	47.01 N	41.44 E
Kovrov	70	56.22 N	41.18 E
Kovševata	68	49.29 N	30.38 E
Kovsug ≃	73	48.48 N	39.17 E
Kovūr	112	14.29 N	79.59 E
Kovvur	112	17.01 N	81.44 E
Kovylkin	70	48.16 N	41.28 E
Kovylkino	70	54.02 N	43.56 E
Kovža	24	61.09 N	38.58 E
Kovžinskij Zavod	66	60.24 N	37.04 E
Kowa	154	7.53 S	140.32 E
Kowal	30	52.32 N	19.09 E
Kowalewo Pomorskie	30	53.10 N	18.53 E
Kowangge	105b	8.16 S	118.32 E
Kowār	116	24.13 N	86.11 E
Koweït → Kuwait □[1]	118	29.30 N	47.45 E
Kowel → Kovel'	68	51.14 N	24.41 E
Kowhitirangi	162	42.52 S	171.01 E
Kowie → Port Alfred	148	33.36 S	26.55 E
Kowkcheh ≃	110	37.10 N	69.23 E
Kowloon (Jiulong)	261d	22.18 N	114.10 E
Kowloon City	261d	22.19 N	114.11 E
Kowmung ≃	160	33.52 S	150.16 E
Kowŏn	88	39.26 N	127.14 E
Kowt-e 'Ashrow	110	34.27 N	68.48 E
Kōya	86	34.12 N	135.35 E
Koyadaira	86	33.56 N	134.13 E
Kōyaguchi	86	34.18 N	135.33 E
Koyama ◆[8]	258	35.37 N	139.43 E
Koyama-ike @	86	35.30 N	134.09 E
Kōyama-misaki ≻	86	34.40 N	131.36 E
Koyambattur → Coimbatore	112	11.00 N	76.58 E
Koyang-ni	88	37.42 N	126.56 E
Köyceğiz	120	36.57 N	28.41 E
Köyceğiz Gölü @	120	36.55 N	28.40 E
Koyna Reservoir @[1]	112	17.25 N	73.45 E
Koyra ≃[1]	116	22.27 N	89.16 E
Koyuk	170	64.56 N	161.08 W
Koyuk ≃	170	64.55 N	161.12 W
Koyukuk	170	64.53 N	157.43 W
Koyukuk ≃	170	64.56 N	157.30 W
Koyukuk, Middle Fork ≃	170	67.03 N	151.04 W
Koyukuk, North Fork ≃	170	67.03 N	151.04 W
Koyukuk, South Fork ≃	170	66.35 N	151.57 W
Koyulhisar	120	40.18 N	37.51 E
Koyuneli	120	39.50 N	27.15 E
Köyyeri	120	38.30 N	36.30 E
Koza, Nihon	164m	26.20 N	127.50 E
Koža, S.S.S.R.	70	57.47 N	48.57 E
Kozağacı	120	39.24 N	31.50 E
Kozakai	84	34.48 N	137.22 E
Kōzaki	84	35.54 N	140.24 E
Kō-zaki ≻	82	34.05 N	129.13 E
Kozaklı	120	39.14 N	34.49 E
Kōzan, Nihon	86	34.35 N	133.03 E
Kozan, Tür.	120	37.27 N	35.49 E
Kozáni	38	40.18 N	21.47 E
Kožanka	68	49.58 N	29.46 E
Koz'any, S.S.S.R.	66	55.18 N	26.52 E
Kožany, S.S.S.R.	66	52.48 N	31.44 E
Kozara ⩘	36	45.00 N	16.50 E
Kozarac	36	44.58 N	16.51 E
Kozdinga	24	63.43 N	47.32 E
Kozelec	68	50.55 N	31.08 E
Kozel'ščina	68	49.13 N	33.51 E
Kozel'sk	72	54.02 N	35.48 E
Koževnikovo	76	56.16 N	84.00 E
Kozhikode → Calicut	112	11.15 N	75.46 E
Koziegłowy	30	50.36 N	19.09 E
Kozienice	30	51.35 N	21.33 E
Kožim	24	65.48 N	59.28 E
Kožimiz, Gora ∧	24	63.12 N	58.48 E
Kozin	68	50.14 N	30.39 E
Kozino	255b	55.54 N	37.11 E
Koźle	30	50.20 N	18.08 E
Kozlov	68	49.33 N	25.20 E
Kozlov Bereg	66	58.57 N	27.44 E
Kozlovka, S.S.S.R.	68	51.39 N	41.16 E
Kozlovka, S.S.S.R.	68	50.52 N	40.27 E
Kozlovka, S.S.S.R.	70	55.52 N	48.14 E
Kozlovka, S.S.S.R.	70	52.33 N	45.41 E
Kozlovo, S.S.S.R.	66	57.34 N	35.29 E
Kozlovo, S.S.S.R.	72	56.31 N	36.16 E
Kozlovščina	66	53.19 N	25.18 E
Kozlu, Tür.	120	41.26 N	31.46 E
Kozlu, Tür.	120	40.37 N	36.30 E
Koźmin	30	51.50 N	17.28 E
Koz'mino	24	61.56 N	48.19 E
Koz'modemjansk	70	56.20 N	46.36 E
Koz'mogorodskoje	24	65.32 N	44.55 E
Kozova	68	49.26 N	25.09 E
Kožpos'olok	24	63.10 N	38.06 E
Kožuchovo	255b	55.43 N	37.54 E

≃ River	Fluss	Río	Rivière	Rio
☰ Canal	Kanal	Canal	Canal	Canal
⅃ Waterfall, Rapids	Wasserfall, Stromschnellen	Cascada, Rápidos	Chute d'eau, Rapides	Cascata, Rápidos
Ш Strait	Meeresstrasse	Estrecho	Détroit	Estreito
C Bay, Gulf	Bucht, Golf	Bahía, Golfo	Baie, Golfe	Baía, Golfo
@ Lake, Lakes	See, Seen	Lago, Lagos	Lac, Lacs	Lago, Lagos
≋ Swamp	Sumpf	Pantano	Marais	Pântano
⍓ Ice Features, Glacier	Eis- und Gletscherformen	Accidentes Glaciales	Formes glaciaires	Acidentes Glaciares
⍑ Other Hydrographic Features	Andere Hydrographische Objekte	Otros Elementos Hidrográficos	Autres données hydrographiques	Outros Elementos Hidrográficos

✢ Submarine Features	Untermeerische Objekte	Accidentes Submarinos	Formes de relief sous-marin	Acidentes Submarinos
□ Political Unit	Politische Einheit	Unidad Politica	Entité politique	Unidade Política
ʊ Cultural Institution	Kulturelle Institution	Institución Cultural	Institution culturelle	Instituição Cultural
⊥ Historical Site	Historische Stätte	Sitio Histórico	Site historique	Sitio Histórico
♠ Recreational Site	Erholungs- und Ferienort	Sitio de Recreo	Centre de loisirs	Sítio de Lazer
⊠ Airport	Flughafen	Aeropuerto	Aéroport	Aeroporto
▪ Military Installation	Militäranlage	Instalación Militar	Installation militaire	Instalação Militar
◆ Miscellaneous	Verschiedenes	Misceláneo	Divers	Miscelânea

ENGLISH — Name, Page, Lat.°', Long.°'
DEUTSCH — Name, Seite, Breite°', Länge°' E=Ost

Name	Page	Lat.	Long.
Kożuchów	30	51.45 N	15.35 E
Kozuka	258	35.09 N	139.57 E
Kōzuki	86	34.59 N	134.20 E
Kozukue ◆[8]	258	35.30 N	139.36 E
Kozul'ka	76	56.10 N	91.24 E
Kożurla	76	55.21 N	79.02 E
Kōzu-shima I	82	34.13 N	139.10 E
Kozuya	260	34.52 N	135.45 E
Kożva	24	65.07 N	56.57 E
Kpandae	140	8.28 N	0.01 W
Kpandu	140	7.00 N	0.18 E
Kpong	140	6.09 N	0.04 E
Kra, Isthmus of •̲[3]	100	10.20 N	99.00 E
Kraai ≃	148	30.40 S	26.45 E
Kraaifontein	148	33.50 S	18.43 E
Kraal	148	26.34 S	28.26 E
Kraankuil	148	29.52 S	24.10 E
Krabbendijke	48	51.26 N	4.07 E
Krabi	100	8.04 N	98.55 E
Krâchéh	100	12.29 N	106.01 E
Krackow	50	53.20 N	14.16 E
Kraftsdorf	50	50.52 N	11.55 E
Kragan	105a	6.42 S	111.37 E
Kragenæs	41	54.55 N	11.22 E
Kragerø	26	58.52 N	9.25 E
Kraghave	41	54.48 N	11.53 E
Kragujevac	38	44.01 N	20.55 E
Krahenhöhe ◆[8]	253	51.10 N	7.06 E
Kraiburg	58	48.10 N	12.26 E
Kraichgau □[9]	52	49.10 N	8.50 E
Krainburg → Kranj	36	46.15 N	14.21 E
Krainka	72	54.07 N	36.21 E
Krai-Russkije	70	57.23 N	46.50 E
Krajčikovo	76	56.16 N	73.20 E
Krajenka	30	53.19 N	17.00 E
Krajeva	79	44.54 N	131.08 E
Krajneje	70	47.29 N	46.01 E
Krajnik Dolny	50	53.05 N	14.25 E
Krajnovka	74	43.57 N	47.24 E
Krakatau ∧[1]	105a	6.07 S	105.24 E
Krakatoa → Krakatau ∧[1]	105a	6.07 S	105.24 E
Krakau → Kraków	30	50.03 N	19.58 E
Krâkôr	100	12.32 N	104.12 E
Krakovec	68	49.57 N	23.07 E
Krakovo	70	53.36 N	50.51 E
Krakow, D.D.R.	50	53.39 N	12.16 E
Kraków, Pol.	30	50.03 N	19.58 E
Krakower See ⊜	50	53.37 N	12.17 E
Kraksaan	105a	7.46 S	113.25 E
Kraksdorf	50	54.18 N	11.04 E
Kralendijk	231s	12.10 N	68.17 W
Kraljevica	36	45.16 N	14.34 E
Kraljevo	38	43.43 N	20.41 E
Kralovice	30	49.59 N	13.29 E
Královské Vinohrady ◆[8]	50	50.01 N	14.29 E
Kralupy nad Vltavou	50	50.11 N	14.18 E
Kralupy u Chomutova	50	50.25 N	13.20 E
Kramatorsk	73	48.43 N	37.32 E
Kramer	206	40.20 N	87.17 W
Kramfors	26	62.56 N	17.47 E
Krammer ⋃	48	51.38 N	4.15 E
Krampnitz	254a	52.28 N	13.04 E
Krampnitzsee ⊜	254a	52.27 N	13.03 E
Kramsach	58	47.27 N	11.52 E
Kranebitten, Flughafen ⊠	58	47.16 N	11.20 E
Kranenburg	48	51.47 N	6.03 E
Krångede	26	63.09 N	16.05 E
Kranichfeld	50	50.51 N	11.12 E
Kranidhion	38	37.22 N	23.10 E
Kranj	36	46.15 N	14.21 E
Kranji	261c	1.26 N	103.45 E
Kranji ≃	261c	1.26 N	103.45 E
Kranji War Memorial ⊥	261c	1.26 N	103.45 E
Kranjska Gora	58	46.29 N	13.47 E
Kranskop	148	29.00 S	30.47 E
Kranskop ∧	148	27.43 S	29.41 E
Kranzberg	146	21.55 S	15.43 E
Krapina	36	46.10 N	15.52 E
Krapivinskij	76	55.00 N	86.49 E
Krapivna	66	53.38 N	35.31 E
Krapkowice	30	50.29 N	17.56 E
Krapperup	41	56.16 N	12.31 E
Krappitz → Krapkowice	30	50.29 N	17.56 E
Krapuh	104	3.39 N	98.10 E
Kras ∧∧[1]	58	45.48 N	14.00 E
Krasavino	24	60.58 N	46.26 E
Krasavka	70	51.11 N	43.24 E
Krasieo ≃	100	14.49 N	100.05 E
Krasilov	68	49.39 N	26.59 E
Krasino	62	70.45 N	54.27 E
Krasivaja Meča ≃	66	52.55 N	39.03 E
Krasivka	70	52.16 N	42.31 E
Krasivoje	76	51.54 N	66.46 E
Kraskino	79	42.44 N	130.48 E
Kraskovo	255b	55.39 N	37.59 E
Krāslava	66	55.54 N	27.10 E
Kraslice	50	50.18 N	12.31 E
Krasnaja ≃	73	49.01 N	38.15 E
Krasnaja Gora, S.S.S.R.	66	60.16 N	35.42 E
Krasnaja Gora, S.S.S.R.	66	53.01 N	31.37 E
Krasnaja Gorbatka	70	55.52 N	41.46 E
Krasnaja Gorka	70	56.12 N	43.04 E
Krasnaja Jaranga	170	65.40 N	172.50 W
Krasnaja Jaruga	68	50.48 N	35.39 E
Krasnaja Pachra	72	55.27 N	37.17 E
Krasnaja Pol'ana, S.S.S.R.	68	47.33 N	37.05 E
Krasnaja Pol'ana, S.S.S.R.	70	56.15 N	51.09 E
Krasnaja Pol'ana, S.S.S.R.	70	46.06 N	41.30 E
Krasnaja Pol'ana, S.S.S.R.	70	52.13 N	53.38 E
Krasnaja Poljana	74	43.41 N	40.13 E
Krasnaja Popovka	73	49.08 N	38.09 E
Krasnaja Sloboda, S.S.S.R.	66	52.51 N	27.10 E
Krasnaja Sloboda, S.S.S.R.	74	41.24 N	48.31 E
Krasnaja Talovka	73	48.51 N	39.51 E
Krasnaja Vol'a	66	52.23 N	27.04 E
Krasnaja Zar'a	66	52.47 N	37.41 E
Krásná Lípa	50	50.54 N	14.31 E
Krasn'anka	70	51.04 N	47.56 E
Krasneno	170	64.38 N	174.48 E
Kraśnik	30	50.56 N	22.13 E
Kraśnik Fabryczny	30	50.58 N	22.12 E
Krasnoarmejsk, S.S.S.R.	70	48.31 N	44.30 E
Krasnoarmejsk, S.S.S.R.	70	51.02 N	45.42 E
Krasnoarmejsk, S.S.S.R.	72	56.08 N	38.08 E
Krasnoarmejsk, S.S.S.R.	73	48.17 N	37.11 E
Krasnoarmejskaja	68	45.23 N	38.12 E
Krasnoarmejskij, S.S.S.R.	64	69.35 N	172.00 E
Krasnoarmejskij, S.S.S.R.	70	47.01 N	42.12 E
Krasnoarmejskoje, S.S.S.R.	70	55.46 N	47.11 E
Krasnoarmejskoje, S.S.S.R.	70	52.44 N	50.02 E
Krasnoarmejskoje, S.S.S.R.	73	47.14 N	37.56 E
Krasnoborsk, S.S.S.R.	24	61.34 N	45.53 E
Krasnoborsk, S.S.S.R.	70	53.46 N	48.04 E
Krasnobród	30	50.33 N	23.13 E
Krasnobrodskij	76	54.10 N	86.28 E
Krasnodar	68	45.02 N	39.00 E
Krasnodar □[8]	70	44.10 N	40.30 E
Krasnodarskij	73	48.15 N	39.51 E
Krasnodon	73	48.17 N	39.48 E
Krasnofarfornyj	66	59.08 N	31.51 E
Krasnoflotskoje	70	50.04 N	41.14 E
Krasnogorka	75	43.15 N	75.10 E
Krasnogorodskoje	66	56.50 N	28.17 E
Krasnogorovka	73	48.00 N	37.31 E
Krasnogorsk, S.S.S.R.	72	55.50 N	37.20 E
Krasnogorsk, S.S.S.R.	79	48.24 N	142.06 E
Krasnogorskij, S.S.S.R.	70	56.09 N	48.20 E
Krasnogorskij, S.S.S.R.	75	41.09 N	69.39 E
Krasnogorskij, S.S.S.R.	76	54.36 N	61.15 E
Krasnogorskoje, S.S.S.R.	70	57.42 N	52.30 E
Krasnogorskoje, S.S.S.R.	76	52.18 N	86.12 E
Krasnogovardejskij	76	57.22 N	62.20 E
Krasnograd	68	49.22 N	35.27 E
Krasnogvardejsk	75	39.46 N	67.16 E
Krasnogvardejskij, S.S.S.R.	72	54.04 N	37.46 E
Krasnogvardejskij, S.S.S.R.	76	51.24 N	69.18 E
Krasnogvardejskoje, S.S.S.R.	68	50.39 N	38.24 E
Krasnogvardejskoje, S.S.S.R.	68	45.29 N	34.17 E
Krasnogvardejskoje, S.S.S.R.	70	45.51 N	41.31 E
Krasnoil'sk	68	48.01 N	25.34 E
Krasnojar	70	48.54 N	51.46 E
Krasnojarka, S.S.S.R.	76	55.20 N	73.04 E
Krasnojarka, S.S.S.R.	76	59.26 N	60.30 E
Krasnoj Armii, Proliv ⋃	64	80.00 N	94.35 E
Krasnojarovo	79	51.27 N	128.28 E
Krasnojarsk	76	56.01 N	92.50 E
Krasnojarsk □[7]	78	56.00 N	94.00 E
Krasnojarskij	76	51.58 N	59.55 E
Krasnoje, S.S.S.R.	24	59.12 N	47.49 E
Krasnoje, S.S.S.R.	66	53.06 N	33.55 E
Krasnoje, S.S.S.R.	66	52.51 N	38.47 E
Krasnoje, S.S.S.R.	66	54.14 N	27.05 E
Krasnoje, S.S.S.R.	68	50.56 N	38.41 E
Krasnoje, S.S.S.R.	68	46.44 N	39.34 E
Krasnoje, S.S.S.R.	68	50.21 N	38.50 E
Krasnoje, S.S.S.R.	68	46.38 N	29.50 E
Krasnoje, S.S.S.R.	72	54.26 N	38.38 E
Krasnoje, S.S.S.R.	73	48.23 N	39.31 E
Krasnoje, S.S.S.R.	73	48.25 N	37.19 E
Krasnoje, S.S.S.R.	76	54.37 N	85.23 E
Krasnoje, Ozero ⊜	64	64.30 N	174.24 E
Krasnoje Echo	70	55.48 N	40.42 E
Krasnoje Gorodišče	72	54.04 N	38.44 E
Krasnoje-na-Volge	70	57.31 N	41.14 E
Krasnoje Selo, S.S.S.R.	70	48.02 N	45.13 E
Krasnoje Selo, S.S.S.R.	70	48.46 N	42.20 E
Krasnoje Selo, S.S.S.R.	255a	59.44 N	30.05 E
Krasnoje Znam'a, S.S.S.R.	66	57.26 N	35.13 E
Krasnoje Znam'a, S.S.S.R.	118	36.58 N	62.30 E
Krasnokamsk	76	58.04 N	55.48 E
Krasnokutsk	68	50.06 N	35.09 E
Krasnokutskoje	76	53.01 N	75.59 E
Krasnolesje	66	54.24 N	22.23 E
Krasnolesnyj	68	51.53 N	39.35 E
Krasnoluki	66	54.37 N	28.50 E
Krasnomajskij	66	57.37 N	34.22 E
Krasnookt'abr'skij, S.S.S.R.	70	56.40 N	47.45 E
Krasnookt'abr'skij, S.S.S.R.	70	48.53 N	44.45 E
Krasnookt'abr'skij, S.S.S.R.	75	42.50 N	74.18 E
Krasnooskol'koje Vodochranilišče ⊜[1]	73	49.17 N	37.37 E
Krasnoostrovskij	66	60.18 N	28.40 E
Krasnopavlovka	68	49.08 N	36.19 E
Krasnoperekopsk	68	45.57 N	33.47 E
Krasnopolje, S.S.S.R.	66	53.20 N	31.24 E
Krasnopolje, S.S.S.R.	68	50.46 N	35.16 E
Krasnorečenskij	79	44.41 N	135.14 E
Krasnoščelje	24	67.21 N	37.02 E
Krasnoščokovo	76	51.40 N	82.45 E
Krasnosel'kup	64	65.41 N	82.28 E
Krasnosel'sk	74	40.36 N	45.21 E
Krasnosel'skij	66	53.15 N	24.25 E
Krasnosel'skoje	68	45.25 N	32.42 E
Krasnosielc	30	53.03 N	21.10 E
Krasnoslobodsk, S.S.S.R.	70	48.42 N	44.34 E
Krasnoslobodsk, S.S.S.R.	70	54.26 N	43.48 E
Krasnotorka	73	48.41 N	37.31 E
Krasnoturansk	76	54.16 N	91.29 E
Krasnoturjinsk	76	59.46 N	60.12 E
Krasnoufimsk	76	56.37 N	57.46 E
Krasnoural'sk	76	58.21 N	60.03 E
Krasnousol'skij	76	53.54 N	56.27 E
Krasnovidovo	70	55.21 N	49.04 E
Krasnovišersk	24	60.23 N	56.59 E
Krasnovka, S.S.S.R.	73	47.24 N	37.26 E
Krasnovka, S.S.S.R.	73	48.47 N	40.07 E
Krasnovodsk	118	40.00 N	53.00 E
Krasnovodskij Poluostrov ≻[1]	118	40.30 N	53.15 E
Krasnovodskij Zaliv ⊂	118	39.55 N	53.15 E
Krasnoyarsk → Krasnojarsk	76	56.01 N	92.50 E
Krasnozatonskij	24	61.41 N	50.58 E
Krasnozavodsk	72	56.27 N	38.25 E
Krasnoznamensk	66	54.57 N	22.30 E
Krasnoznamenskij	76	51.03 N	69.30 E
Krasnoz'orskoje	76	53.59 N	79.14 E
Krásný Dvůr	50	50.10 N	13.24 E
Krasnyj	66	54.34 N	31.26 E
Krasnyj Aul	76	51.03 N	81.02 E
Krasnyj Bazar	74	39.41 N	46.58 E
Krasnyj Bogatyr'	70	56.02 N	41.08 E
Krasnyj Bor, S.S.S.R.	70	55.53 N	53.06 E
Krasnyj Bor, S.S.S.R.	70	55.17 N	43.59 E
Krasnyj Bor, S.S.S.R.	255a	59.41 N	30.41 E
Krasnyj Cholm, S.S.S.R.	66	58.03 N	37.07 E
Krasnyj Cholm, S.S.S.R.	70	54.11 N	40.42 E
Krasnyj Cholm, S.S.S.R.	76	51.35 N	54.09 E
Krasnyj Čhuduk	70	46.18 N	46.56 E
Krasnyj Čikoj	78	50.22 N	108.15 E
Krasnyje Baki	70	57.08 N	45.10 E
Krasnyje Barrikady	70	46.14 N	47.53 E
Krasnyje Četai	70	55.42 N	46.09 E
Krasnyje Gory	66	58.57 N	29.29 E
Krasnyje Okny	68	47.32 N	29.27 E
Krasnyje Partizany	68	50.57 N	31.47 E
Krasnyje Tkač	66	55.28 N	39.05 E
Krasnyje Tkači	70	57.30 N	39.45 E
Krasnyj Gul'aj	70	54.01 N	48.22 E
Krasnyj Jar, S.S.S.R.	70	50.42 N	44.46 E
Krasnyj Jar, S.S.S.R.	70	50.37 N	45.47 E
Krasnyj Jar, S.S.S.R.	70	51.38 N	46.25 E
Krasnyj Jar, S.S.S.R.	70	46.33 N	48.21 E
Krasnyj Jar, S.S.S.R.	70	53.30 N	50.22 E
Krasnyj Jar, S.S.S.R.	76	55.54 N	86.57 E
Krasnyj Jar, S.S.S.R.	76	55.14 N	72.56 E
Krasnyj Jar, S.S.S.R.	76	53.20 N	69.14 E
Krasnyj Jar, S.S.S.R.	76	57.07 N	84.33 E
Krasnyj Kl'uč	76	55.26 N	56.12 E
Krasnyj Kut, S.S.S.R.	70	50.57 N	46.58 E
Krasnyj Kut, S.S.S.R.	73	48.12 N	38.48 E
Krasnyj Liman, S.S.S.R.	68	51.32 N	39.50 E
Krasnyj Liman, S.S.S.R.	73	48.59 N	37.49 E
Krasnyj Log	68	51.23 N	39.46 E
Krasnyj Luč, S.S.S.R.	66	57.04 N	30.05 E
Krasnyj Luč, S.S.S.R.	73	48.08 N	38.56 E
Krasnyj Majak	70	56.03 N	41.23 E
Krasnyj Manyč, S.S.S.R.	70	45.31 N	44.42 E
Krasnyj Manyč, S.S.S.R.	70	46.59 N	41.07 E
Krasnyj Manyč, S.S.S.R.	70	46.33 N	42.10 E
Krasnyj Meliorator	70	50.02 N	46.06 E
Krasnyj Okt'abr', S.S.S.R.	70	56.06 N	41.23 E
Krasnyj Okt'abr', S.S.S.R.	70	51.33 N	45.42 E
Krasnyj Okt'abr', S.S.S.R.	72	55.37 N	36.30 E
Krasnyj Okt'abr', S.S.S.R.	72	56.07 N	38.53 E
Krasnyj Okt'abr', S.S.S.R.	73	48.56 N	39.23 E
Krasnyj Okt'abr', S.S.S.R.	73	48.15 N	38.12 E
Krasnyj Okt'abr', S.S.S.R.	76	55.37 N	64.48 E
Krasnyj Okt'abr', S.S.S.R.	76	46.50 N	75.59 E
Krasnyj Oskol	73	49.11 N	37.26 E
Krasnyj Partizan	70	46.20 N	43.10 E
Krasnyj Perekop	68	46.41 N	33.46 E
Krasnyj Profintern	70	57.45 N	40.27 E
Krasnyj Rog	66	52.57 N	33.45 E
Krasnyj Steklovar	70	56.13 N	48.47 E
Krasnyj Stroitel' ◆[8]	255b	55.35 N	37.37 E
Krasnyj Sulin	73	47.54 N	40.03 E
Krasnyj Tekstil'ščik	70	51.23 N	45.50 E
Krasnyj Tkač	72	55.28 N	39.05 E
Krasnystaw	30	50.59 N	23.10 E
Krasnyy Luch → Krasnyj Luč	73	48.08 N	38.56 E
Krasucha	66	57.23 N	33.12 E
Kras'ukovskaja	73	47.31 N	40.06 E
Kraszna (Crasna) ≃	38	48.09 N	22.20 E
Kratke Range ∧∧	154	6.25 S	145.35 E
Kratovo	38	42.05 N	22.11 E
Krauchenwies	54	48.01 N	9.14 E
Kraul Mountains ∧∧	9	73.10 S	14.10 W
Krauschwitz	50	51.31 N	14.41 E
Krautheim	52	49.23 N	9.38 E
Kravaře	50	50.38 N	14.23 E
Krawang	105a	6.19 S	107.17 E
Kray ◆[8]	253	51.28 N	7.05 E
Kražiai	66	55.36 N	22.40 E
Krbava ◆[1]	36	44.40 N	15.35 E
Kreamer Island I	210	26.46 N	80.44 W
Kreba	50	51.20 N	14.40 E
Krebs	186	34.56 N	95.43 W
Krečetovo	24	60.56 N	38.30 E
Krečevicy	66	58.37 N	31.21 E
Krefeld	52		
	253	51.20 N	6.34 E
Kregme	41	55.57 N	12.04 E
Kreiensen	48	51.51 N	9.58 E
Kreischa	50	50.56 N	13.45 E
Kreitzer Glacier ⛉	9	70.25 S	72.30 E
Kremastón, Tekhnití Límni ⊜[1]	38	38.55 N	21.30 E
Kremenčug	68	49.04 N	33.25 E
Kremenčugskoje Vodochranilišče ⊜[1]	68	49.20 N	32.30 E
Kremenec	68	50.07 N	25.45 E
Kremeneckaja Vozvyšennost' ∧∧[1]	68	50.15 N	26.00 E
Kremennaja	73	49.03 N	38.14 E
Kremen'ovka	73	47.20 N	37.29 E
Kremenskoj	70	47.49 N	41.08 E
Kremenskoje	72	55.06 N	35.57 E
Kremges	68	49.04 N	33.15 E
Kreml' ʋ	255b	55.45 N	37.37 E
Kremmen	50	52.45 N	13.01 E
Kremmling	190	40.03 N	106.24 W
Kremnica	30	48.43 N	18.54 E
Krempe	48	53.50 N	9.29 E
Krems an der Donau	30	48.25 N	15.36 E
Kremsbrücke	58	46.57 N	13.37 E
Kremsmünster	30	48.03 N	14.08 E
Krenitzin Islands II	170	54.08 N	166.00 W
Krensitz	50	51.29 N	12.27 E
Krepenskij	73	48.06 N	39.03 E
Krepkaja ≃	73	47.35 N	39.23 E
Krepoljin	38	44.16 N	21.37 E
Kresgeville	200	40.54 N	75.30 W
Kress	186	34.22 N	101.45 W
Kressbronn	54	47.35 N	9.36 E
Kressey Lake ⊜	275	39.44 N	75.07 W
Kresta, Zaliv ⊂	170	66.00 N	180.00 E
Krestcy, S.S.S.R.	66	58.15 N	32.31 E
Krestcy, S.S.S.R.	66	58.23 N	39.00 E
Krestjanskoje, S.S.S.R.	70	45.34 N	42.56 E
Krestjanskoje, S.S.S.R.	75	40.32 N	69.02 E
Krest-Major	64	67.37 N	144.45 E
Krestovaja Guba	62	74.07 N	55.33 E
Krestovo-Gorodišče	70	54.10 N	48.36 E
Krestovyj, Pereval)(	74	42.32 N	44.28 E
Kresty	72	55.16 N	37.06 E
Kreta → Kriti I	38	35.29 N	24.42 E
Kretek	105a	7.59 S	110.19 E
Kretinga	66	55.53 N	21.13 E
Kreuth	58	47.38 N	11.44 E
Kreuz an der Ostbahn → Krzyż	30	52.54 N	16.01 E
Kreuzberg	253	51.09 N	7.27 E
Kreuzberg ◆[8]	254a	52.30 N	13.23 E
Kreuzberg ∧	52	50.22 N	9.58 E
Kreuzburg → Kluczbork	30	50.59 N	18.13 E
Kreuzeck-Gruppe ∧∧	58	46.51 N	13.06 E
Kreuzen	58	46.40 N	13.35 E
Kreuzlingen	54	47.39 N	9.11 E
Kreuznach → Bad Kreuznach	52	49.52 N	7.51 E
Kreuztal	52	50.58 N	7.59 E
Krevo	66	54.19 N	26.17 E
Kreyenhagen	50	52.55 N	10.52 E
Krian	105a	7.24 S	112.35 E
Kria Vrísi	38	40.41 N	22.18 E
Kribi	142	2.57 N	9.55 E
Kričov	66	53.42 N	31.43 E
Kriebstein, Burg ⊥	50	51.02 N	13.00 E
Kriel	148	26.16 S	29.14 E
Kriens	54	47.02 N	8.17 E
Krigujgun, Mys ≻	170	65.30 N	171.05 W
Kriljon, Mys ≻	79	45.53 N	142.05 E
Krim → Krymskij Poluostrov ≻[1]	68	45.00 N	34.00 E
Křimice	30	49.46 N	13.15 E
Krim Krim	136	8.58 N	15.48 E
Krimml	58	47.13 N	12.11 E
Krimnicksee ⊜	254a	52.18 N	13.39 E
Krimpen aan de IJssel	48	51.54 N	4.35 E
Krinicčno-Lugskoje	73	47.45 N	39.12 E
Kriničkí	68	48.22 N	34.27 E
Kriničnaja	73	48.08 N	38.02 E
Kriničnoje	68	45.32 N	28.40 E
Krishna ≃	112	15.57 N	80.59 E
Krishna, Mouths of the ≃[1]	112	15.43 N	80.55 E
Krishnachaadrapur	116	21.50 N	86.49 E
Krishnagiri	112	12.32 N	78.14 E
Krishnamāti	262b	22.40 N	88.32 E
Krishnanagar, Bhārat	116	23.24 N	88.30 E
Krishnanagar, Bhārat	116	23.13 N	87.33 E
Krishnapur, Bhārat	262b	22.36 N	88.26 E
Krishnapur, Bngl.	116	23.30 N	89.56 E
Krishnarāja Sāgara ⊜[1]	112	12.30 N	76.26 E
Krishnarāmpur	116	22.43 N	88.14 E
Kristdala	26	57.24 N	16.11 E
Kristiania → Oslo	26	59.55 N	10.45 E
Kristianopel	26	56.15 N	16.02 E
Kristiansand	26	58.10 N	8.00 E
Kristianstad	26	56.02 N	14.08 E
Kristianstads Län □[6]	26	56.15 N	14.00 E
Kristiansund	26	63.07 N	7.45 E
Kristiinankaupunki → Kristinestad	26	62.17 N	21.23 E
Kristineberg	26	65.04 N	18.35 E
Kristinehamn	40	59.20 N	14.07 E
Kristinestad (Kristiinankaupunki)	26	62.17 N	21.23 E
Kriti I	38	35.29 N	24.42 E
Kritikón Pélagos •̲[2]	38	35.46 N	23.54 E
Kritzendorf	254b	48.20 N	16.18 E
Kriul'any	68	47.13 N	29.09 E
Kriuša	72	54.28 N	36.24 E
Kriv'ačka	70	58.40 N	45.27 E
Krivaja ≃	38	44.27 N	18.09 E
Krivaja, Kosa ≻[2]	73	47.02 N	38.06 E
Krivaja Ruda	68	49.31 N	32.59 E
Kriv'anskaja	73	47.24 N	40.10 E
Kriva Palanka	38	42.12 N	22.20 E
Krivcy	72	55.28 N	38.12 E
Kriviči	66	54.43 N	27.17 E
Krivinka	76	51.08 N	78.10 E
Krivodol	38	43.23 N	23.29 E
Krivoj Buzan	70	46.31 N	48.33 E
Krivoje Ozero	68	47.56 N	30.21 E
Krivoj Rog	68	47.55 N	33.21 E
Krivoj Torec ≃	73	48.39 N	37.32 E
Krivonosovo	68	49.55 N	39.16 E
Krivorožje, S.S.S.R.	68	48.51 N	40.45 E
Krivorožje, S.S.S.R.	68	48.31 N	38.40 E
Krivošeino	76	57.20 N	83.57 E
Krivošin	66	52.52 N	26.08 E
Krivoy Rog → Krivoj Rog	68	47.55 N	33.21 E
Kriwoi-Rog → Krivoj Rog	68	47.55 N	33.21 E
Križevci	36	46.02 N	16.33 E
Krizskoje	73	49.28 N	39.38 E
Krk, Otok I	36	45.05 N	14.35 E
Krn ∧	58	46.16 N	13.40 E
Krnov	30	50.05 N	17.41 E
Krobia	30	51.47 N	16.58 E
Krøderen ⊜	26	60.15 N	9.38 E
Krogager	41	55.42 N	8.51 E
Krögis	50	51.07 N	13.22 E
Krojanke → Krajenka	30	53.19 N	17.00 E
Krokek	40	58.40 N	16.24 E
Kroken	24	65.22 N	14.20 E
Krokodil ≃, S. Afr.	146	25.26 S	31.58 E
Krokodil ≃, S. Afr.	146	24.12 S	26.52 E
Krokom	26	63.19 N	14.30 E
Krokowa	30	54.48 N	18.11 E
Krolevec	68	51.33 N	33.23 E
Kröller-Müller, Rijksmuseum ʋ	48	52.05 N	5.50 E
Krölpa	50	50.41 N	11.32 E
Krombi Pits	146	19.30 S	25.02 E
Kroměříž	30	49.18 N	17.24 E
Krommenie	48	52.29 N	4.45 E
Krompachy	30	48.56 N	20.52 E
Kromy	66	52.43 N	35.46 E
Kron ≃	76	47.37 N	87.25 E
Kronach	50	50.14 N	11.20 E
Kronberg	52	50.10 N	8.30 E
Kronborg Slot ⊥	41	56.02 N	12.38 E
Krone ◆[8]	253	51.27 N	7.20 E
Krŏng Kaôh Kŏng	100	11.37 N	102.59 E
Krŏng Kêb	100	10.29 N	104.19 E
Kronobergs Län □[6]	26	56.40 N	14.40 E
Kronoby (Kruunupyy)	26	63.43 N	23.02 E
Kronockij Zaliv ⊂	64	54.12 N	160.36 E
Kronoki	64	54.36 N	161.10 E
Kronshagen	41	54.20 N	10.05 E
Kronstadt → Braşov, Rom.	38	45.39 N	25.37 E
Kronštadt, S.S.S.R.	66	59.59 N	29.45 E
Kronwa	100	15.25 N	98.26 E
Kroondal	148	25.45 S	27.19 E
Kroonstad	148	27.46 S	27.12 E
Kröpelin	50	54.04 N	11.48 E
Kropotkin, S.S.S.R.	62	45.26 N	40.34 E
Kropotkin, S.S.S.R.	78	58.30 N	115.17 E
Kropotkina, Gora ∧	78	53.43 N	117.32 E
Kropp	41	54.24 N	9.31 E
Kroppefjäll ∧[2]	26	58.40 N	12.13 E
Kroppenstedt	50	51.56 N	11.18 E
Kropstädt	50	51.58 N	12.44 E
Kropufino	66	60.23 N	39.10 E
Krościenko	30	49.27 N	20.26 E
Kröslin	50	54.07 N	13.45 E
Krošn'a	68	50.18 N	28.39 E
Krośniewice	30	52.16 N	19.10 E
Krosno	30	49.42 N	21.46 E
Krosno Odrzańskie	30	52.04 N	15.05 E
Krossen	50	50.58 N	11.59 E
Krostitz	50	51.28 N	12.27 E
Krotoszyn	30	51.42 N	17.26 E
Krotovka	70	53.18 N	51.12 E
Krotovo	76	56.57 N	69.20 E
Krotz Springs	184	30.32 N	91.45 W
Kröv	52	49.59 N	7.05 E
Kroya	105a	7.38 S	109.14 E
Krško	36	45.58 N	15.29 E
Kr'učkov	70	48.01 N	45.40 E
Kr'učkovo	66	57.03 N	35.34 E
Kruckow	50	53.54 N	13.14 E
Krudenburg	253	51.39 N	6.45 E
Kruenggeukueh	104	5.15 N	97.02 E
Kruengluak	104	2.50 N	97.45 E
Kruft	52	50.23 N	7.20 E
Kruger National Park ♠	146	24.00 S	31.40 E
Krugersdorp	148	26.05 S	27.35 E
Krugersdorp Race Course ♠	263d	26.08 S	27.45 E
Krugersdorp West	263d	26.06 S	27.45 E
Krugloje, S.S.S.R.	66	54.15 N	29.48 E
Krugloje, S.S.S.R.	73	47.01 N	39.15 E
Krugloozernyj	70	51.06 N	51.17 E
Kruglooz'ornoje	76	55.13 N	79.01 E
Kruglyži	70	58.31 N	47.42 E
Krugzell	54	47.47 N	10.16 E
Krui	102	5.11 S	103.56 E
Kruidfontein	148	32.51 S	21.57 E
Kruiningen	48	51.27 N	4.02 E
Kruisfontein	148	34.00 S	24.43 E
Kruishoutem	46	50.54 N	3.31 E
Kruisland	48	51.34 N	4.24 E
Kruisrivier	148	33.26 S	21.55 E
Kruisvallei	148	33.53 S	23.10 E
Krujë	38	41.30 N	19.48 E
Kr'ukov	70	47.24 N	42.28 E
Kr'ukovo, S.S.S.R.	64	66.30 N	159.31 E
Kr'ukovo, S.S.S.R.	72	55.28 N	36.32 E
Kr'ukovo, S.S.S.R.	72	55.59 N	37.10 E
Kr'ukovo, S.S.S.R.	73	47.40 N	39.13 E
Krukut, Kali ≃	259e	6.12 S	106.48 E
Krulevščina	66	55.02 N	27.45 E
Krumasye	154	1.40 S	133.09 E
Krumbach, B.R.D.	54	47.58 N	9.02 E
Krumbach, B.R.D.	54	48.14 N	10.22 E
Krumme Lanke ⊜	254a	52.27 N	13.14 E
Krummendammer Heide ◆[3]	254a	52.28 N	13.39 E
Krummenerl	253	51.05 N	7.45 E
Krummensee	254a	52.36 N	13.42 E
Krummhörn ◆[1]	48	53.25 N	7.10 E
Krumovgrad	38	41.28 N	25.39 E
Krumroy	204	39.58 N	81.24 W
Krün	58	47.30 N	11.16 E
Krung Thep (Bangok)	100		
	259a	13.45 N	100.31 E
Krung Thep Mahanakhon □[4]	259a	13.47 N	100.43 E
Krung Thon Bridge ◆[5]	259a	13.47 N	100.30 E
Krupá	50	50.08 N	13.41 E
Krupec	68	51.38 N	34.21 E
Krüpel-See ⊜	254a	52.18 N	13.42 E
Krupka	50	50.43 N	13.46 E
Krupki	66	54.19 N	29.08 E
Kruså	41	54.50 N	9.25 E
Krusenstern, Cape ≻	170	67.07 N	163.43 W
Kruševac	38	43.35 N	21.20 E
Kruševo	38	41.22 N	21.14 E
Krušinovka	66	53.14 N	29.50 E
Krušné hory (Erzgebirge) ∧∧	50	50.30 N	13.15 E
Kruszwica	30	52.41 N	18.19 E
Krutaja, S.S.S.R.	24	63.02 N	54.38 E
Krutaja, S.S.S.R.	76	57.24 N	76.27 E
Krutaja Gorka	76	55.25 N	73.15 E
Krutcy	66	57.10 N	29.23 E
Krutec, S.S.S.R.	66	60.17 N	39.25 E
Krutec, S.S.S.R.	72	56.10 N	38.33 E
Kruticha, S.S.S.R.	76	56.49 N	77.10 E
Kruticha, S.S.S.R.	76	53.58 N	81.14 E
Krutinka	76	56.01 N	71.31 E
Krutoje	66	52.26 N	37.28 E
Krutoj Log	76	57.53 N	58.14 E
Krutoj Majdan	70	55.35 N	44.04 E
Krutyje Verchi	72	54.19 N	36.26 E
Kruunupyy → Kronoby	26	63.43 N	23.02 E
Kruzenšterna, Proliv ⋃	64	48.30 N	153.50 E
Kruzof Island I	170	57.10 N	135.40 W
Krydor	174	52.47 N	107.03 W
Krylbo	40	60.08 N	16.13 E
Krylovskaja	68	46.07 N	39.19 E
Krym	73	47.19 N	39.31 E
Krymsk	68	44.56 N	37.59 E
Krymskaja Oblast' □[4]	68	45.00 N	34.00 E
Krymskij	68	47.40 N	40.46 E
Krymskije Gory ∧∧	68	44.45 N	34.25 E
Krymskij Poluostrov ≻[1]	68	45.00 N	34.00 E
Krymskij Zapovednik ◆[4]	68	44.42 N	34.12 E
Krymskoje	73	48.45 N	38.48 E
Krynica	30	49.25 N	20.56 E
Krynka ≃	73	47.36 N	38.47 E
Kryžina, Chrebet ∧∧	78	54.00 N	95.00 E
Kryžopol'	68	48.23 N	28.52 E
Krzepice	30	50.58 N	18.44 E
Krzeszowice	30	50.09 N	19.39 E
Krzeszyce	50	52.36 N	15.01 E
Krzna ≃	30	52.08 N	23.31 E
Krzywiń	30	51.58 N	16.49 E
Krzyż	30	52.54 N	16.01 E
Ksar Chellala	138	35.13 N	2.18 E
Ksar el Barka	140	18.24 N	12.13 W
Ksar el Boukhari	138	35.51 N	2.52 E
Ksar-el-Kebir	138	35.01 N	5.54 W
Ksar-es-Seghir	34	35.50 N	5.32 W
Ksar-es-Souk	138	31.58 N	4.25 W
Ksar Hellal	36	35.39 N	10.54 E
Ksar Rhilane	138	33.00 N	9.38 E
Ksaverovka	68	50.03 N	30.12 E
Ksel, Djebel ∧	138	33.44 N	1.10 E
Kšen' ≃	66	52.23 N	37.44 E
Ksenjevka	78	53.34 N	118.44 E
Ksenofontova	24	60.58 N	56.12 E
Kšenskij	68	51.52 N	37.43 E
Książ Wielkopolski	30	52.05 N	17.14 E
Ksob, Oued ≃, Alg.	34	35.46 N	4.34 E
Ksob, Oued ≃, Alg.	36	35.49 N	7.53 E
Ksour, Monts des ∧∧	138	32.45 N	0.30 W
Ksour Essaf	138	35.25 N	11.00 E
Kstovo	70	56.11 N	44.11 E
Kū', Wādī al- ∨	130	13.37 N	25.15 E
Kuah	104	6.19 N	99.51 E
Kuaidamaozi	88	41.40 N	125.44 E
Kuaijishan ∧∧	90	29.32 N	120.30 E
Kuala, Indon.	102	2.55 N	105.48 E
Kuala, Indon.	104	3.32 N	98.24 E
Kuala ≃	104	2.45 N	100.00 E
Kualabee	104	4.24 N	96.03 E
Kuala Berang	104	5.04 N	103.01 E
Kualacenako	102	0.28 S	102.40 E
Kuala Dungun	104	4.47 N	103.26 E
Kuala Kangsar	104	4.46 N	100.56 E
Kualakapuas	102	3.01 S	114.21 E
Kuala Kedah	104	6.06 N	100.18 E
Kuala Kelawang	104	2.56 N	102.05 E
Kuala Kerai	104	5.32 N	102.12 E
Kuala Kerau	104	3.43 N	102.22 E
Kualakeriau	102	0.50 N	113.20 E
Kuala Ketil	104	5.36 N	100.39 E
Kuala Kubu Baharu	104	3.34 N	101.39 E
Kuala Kurau	104	5.01 N	100.26 E
Kualakurun	102	1.07 S	113.53 E
Kualalangsa	104	4.32 N	98.01 E
Kuala Lipis	104	4.11 N	102.03 E
Kuala Lumpur	104	3.10 N	101.42 E
Kualamanjual	102	1.25 S	112.00 E
Kuala Nerang	104	6.15 N	100.36 E
Kualapesaguan	102	2.01 S	110.08 E
Kuala Pilah	104	2.44 N	102.15 E
Kualapuu	219a	21.09 N	157.01 W
Kuala Selangor	104	3.21 N	101.15 E
Kualasimpang	104	4.17 N	98.03 E
Kuala Terengganu	104	5.20 N	103.08 E
Kualu ≃	104	2.45 N	100.00 E
Kuamut	102	5.13 N	117.30 E
Kuamut ≃	102	5.13 N	117.32 E
Kuanbang	88	40.29 N	120.04 E
Kuancheng	95	40.38 N	118.27 E
Kuandang	102	0.52 N	122.55 E
Kuandian	88	40.43 N	124.44 E
Kuando → Cuando ≃	142	18.27 S	23.32 E
Kuanhsi	90	24.48 N	121.10 E
Kuanmiao	90	22.58 N	120.19 E
Kuanshan	90	23.03 N	121.09 E
Kuan Shan ∧	90	23.14 N	120.54 E
Kuantan	104	3.48 N	103.20 E
Kuantan ≃	104	3.50 N	103.17 E
Kuanyin	90	25.02 N	121.04 E
Kuanyün → Guanyun	88	34.20 N	119.17 E
Kuanza → Cuanza ≃	142	9.19 S	13.08 E
Kuba	74	41.22 N	48.31 E
Kuba → Cuba □[1]	230p	21.30 N	80.00 W
Kuban' ≃	62	45.20 N	37.30 E
Kubatly	74	39.22 N	46.34 E
Kubbī	130	11.08 N	25.14 E
Kubbum	130	11.47 N	23.47 E
Kubena ≃	66	59.36 N	39.39 E
Kubenskoje	66	59.26 N	39.40 E
Kubenskoje, Ozero ⊜	66	59.40 N	39.25 E
Kubiki	84	37.11 N	138.20 E
Kubinka	72	55.35 N	36.43 E
Kubitzer Bodden ⊂	50	54.24 N	13.12 E
Küblis	54	46.55 N	9.47 E
Kubn'a ≃	70	55.31 N	48.27 E
Kubokawa	86	33.12 N	133.08 E
Kubor, Mount ∧	154	6.05 S	144.45 E
Kubr' ≃	72	56.52 N	38.17 E
Kubrat	38	43.48 N	26.30 E
Kubu	105b	8.16 S	115.35 E
Kubuchaj	78	50.30 N	114.48 E
Kubu Gajah	104	5.10 N	100.41 E
Kubumesaai	102	1.31 N	115.06 E
Kubura	165d	24.27 N	122.57 E
Kubutambahan	105b	8.05 S	115.10 E
Kučema	24	65.37 N	42.28 E
Kučen'ajevo	70	54.44 N	46.24 E
Kučevo	38	44.27 N	21.44 E
Kuchaiburi	116	22.16 N	86.10 E
Kuchāman	110	27.09 N	74.52 E
Kuch'ang-ni	88	40.09 N	124.46 E
Kuche	80	41.43 N	82.54 E
Kuchelebai	144	1.29 N	35.01 E
Kuchen Spitze ∧	54	47.03 N	10.14 E
Kuchinarai	100	16.32 N	104.04 E
Kuching	102	1.33 N	110.20 E
Kuchinoerabu-jima I	83b	30.28 N	130.12 E
Kuchino-shima I	83b	29.57 N	129.57 E
Kuchiwa	86	34.53 N	132.55 E
Kuchl	58	47.37 N	13.09 E
Kūchnay Darvīshān	118	30.59 N	64.11 E
Kuchterin Lug	79	52.25 N	128.05 E
Kuchtinka	72	54.29 N	38.10 E
Kučino	255b	55.45 N	37.58 E
Kučkak	75	40.15 N	70.20 E
Kučki	70	53.01 N	44.29 E
Kuçovë → Stalin	38	40.48 N	19.54 E
Küçük Ağrı Dağı ∧	74	39.38 N	44.25 E
Küçükbahce	120	38.33 N	26.24 E
Küçükbakkal	257b	40.58 N	29.06 E
Küçükçekmece	257b	40.59 N	28.46 E
Küçükköy	257b	41.04 N	28.54 E
Küçükkuyu	120	39.32 N	26.36 E
Kučukskoje, Ozero ⊜	76	52.42 N	79.46 E
Kucur, Tanjung ≻	105a	8.39 S	114.34 E
Kučurgan ≃	68	46.43 N	29.53 E
Kūd	113	33.05 N	75.17 E
Kuda ≃	78	52.25 N	104.08 E
Kudaka-shima I	164m	26.09 N	127.54 E
Kudamatsu	86	34.00 N	131.52 E
Kudanggou	94	41.06 N	124.00 E
Kudap	104	1.17 N	102.26 E
Kudara, S.S.S.R.	75	38.25 N	72.41 E
Kudara, S.S.S.R.	78	52.13 N	106.39 E
Kudara ≃	75	38.19 N	72.28 E
Kudara-Somon	78	50.10 N	107.25 E
Kudat	102	6.53 N	116.50 E
Kudejevskij	76	54.52 N	56.46 E
Kudene	154	6.14 S	134.39 E
Kudever'	66	56.47 N	29.23 E
Kūdī, Qārat ∧∧[2]	136	23.30 N	23.52 E
Kudinovo	72	55.45 N	38.12 E
Kudirkos Naumiestis	66	54.46 N	22.53 E
Kudongho	88	35.31 N	126.29 E
Kudoyama	86	34.17 N	135.34 E
Kudremukh ∧	112	13.08 N	75.16 E
Kudrovo	255a	59.54 N	30.31 E
Kudus	105a	6.48 S	110.50 E
Kudyat al-Islām	132	27.32 N	30.45 E
Kudymkar	76	59.01 N	54.37 E
Kuee Ruins ⊥	219d	19.21 N	155.23 W
Kueishan Tao I	90	24.50 N	121.56 E
Kueisui → Huhehaote	92	40.51 N	111.40 E
Kueiyang → Guiyang	92	26.35 N	106.43 E
Kuekvun' ≃	170	69.14 N	179.25 E
Kuënlun → Kunlunshanmai ∧∧	110	36.30 N	88.00 E
Kuerbin	79	49.25 N	128.59 E
Kuerchahanbo ⊜	92	43.37 N	114.40 E
K'uerhlo → Kuerle	80	41.44 N	86.09 E
Kuerle	80	41.44 N	86.09 E
Kuerleikehu ⊜	92	37.20 N	96.54 E
Kufayr Yabūs	122	33.42 N	36.01 E
Küfre	120	38.02 N	42.00 E
Kufrinjah	122	32.18 N	35.42 E
Kufstein	58	47.35 N	12.10 E
Kufūr Bilshāy	132	30.51 N	30.48 E
Kufūr Najm	132	30.44 N	31.35 E
Kuga	86	34.05 N	132.05 E
Kugaluk ≃	170	69.10 N	131.00 W
Kugaly	76	44.29 N	78.40 E
Kugarčino	70	55.33 N	50.29 E
Kugart ≃	75	40.52 N	72.53 E
Kugas	75	38.21 N	70.48 E
Kugej	73	46.53 N	39.19 E
Kugesi	70	56.02 N	47.18 E
Kugmallit Bay ⊂	170	69.33 N	133.25 W
Kugo-Jeja ≃	68	46.34 N	39.38 E
Kuguno	84	36.03 N	137.16 E
Kuhaylī	130	19.25 N	32.50 E
Kūhdasht	118	33.32 N	47.36 E
Kūh-e-Geyshtasar ∧	74	38.51 N	47.14 E
Kuhlīyah, Wādī ∨	132	30.05 N	31.58 E
Kühlungsborn	50	54.09 N	11.43 E
Kuhmo	26	64.08 N	29.31 E
Kuhmoinen	26	61.34 N	25.11 E
Kühnhausen	50	51.02 N	10.58 E
Kūhpāyeh	118	32.43 N	52.26 E
Kūhrān, Kūh-e ∧	118	26.46 N	58.12 E
Kühren	50	51.20 N	12.50 E
Kuhstedt	48	53.23 N	8.58 E
Kui	154	7.30 S	147.15 E
Kuibyschew → Kujbyšev	70	53.12 N	50.09 E
Kuidesu	88	41.46 N	119.29 E
Kuidou	90	25.10 N	118.11 E
Kuikkol', Ozero ⊜	76	50.57 N	64.30 E
Kuikui, Cape ≻	219a	20.36 N	156.35 W
Kuikukang	79	53.07 N	124.46 E
Kuilāpāl	116	22.50 N	86.38 E
Kuinre	48	52.47 N	5.50 E
Kuiseb ≃	146	22.59 S	14.31 E
Kuishi-yama ∧, Nihon	86	33.51 N	133.35 E
Kuishi-yama ∧, Nihon	86	33.40 N	133.31 E
Kuitan	90	23.05 N	115.58 E
Kuitun	76	44.24 N	84.58 E
Kuiu Island I	170	57.45 N	134.10 W
Kuivaniemi	26	65.35 N	25.11 E
Kuivastu	66	58.35 N	23.22 E
Kuja, S.S.S.R.	24	67.46 N	53.10 E
Kuja, S.S.S.R.	24	65.05 N	40.06 E
Kujal'nickij Liman ⊜	68	46.40 N	30.42 E
Kujang	88	39.52 N	126.01 E
Kujani Game Reserve ◆[4]	140	7.10 N	0.50 W
Kujasovo	24	56.21 N	53.07 E
Kujawy ◆[1]	30	52.45 N	18.30 E
Kujbyšev, S.S.S.R.	70	53.12 N	50.09 E
Kujbyšev, S.S.S.R.	70	54.57 N	49.05 E
Kujbyšev, S.S.S.R.	76	55.27 N	78.19 E
Kujbyševka	68	47.37 N	31.42 E
Kujbyševo, S.S.S.R.	68	44.38 N	33.52 E
Kujbyševo, S.S.S.R.	68	47.22 N	36.39 E
Kujbyševo, S.S.S.R.	73	47.49 N	38.55 E
Kujbyševo, S.S.S.R.	75	40.22 N	71.17 E
Kujbyševskij	62	37.52 N	68.44 E
Kujbyševskij Zaton	70	55.09 N	49.12 E
Kujbyševskoje Vodochranilišče ⊜[1]	70	53.40 N	49.00 E
Kujbyshevskij	110	37.52 N	68.44 E
Kujeda	76	56.26 N	55.35 E
Kujgan	76	45.25 N	74.10 E
Kujgenkol'	70	49.17 N	47.59 E
Kuji	82	40.11 N	141.46 E
Kuji ≃	84	36.29 N	140.37 E
Kujirai	258	35.56 N	139.27 E
Kujl'uk	75	41.15 N	69.20 E
Kujman'	66	52.52 N	39.16 E
Kujŏng-ni	88	37.53 N	125.54 E
Kujtun	78	54.21 N	101.29 E
Kujū	86	33.01 N	131.18 E
Kujūkuri	84	35.35 N	140.30 E
Kujūkuri-hama •̲[2]	84	35.45 N	140.30 E
Kujū-san ∧	86	33.05 N	131.15 E
Kujvikej, Gora ∧	170	67.05 N	173.12 E
Kuk ∧	58	46.16 N	13.45 E
Kuk ≃	170	70.36 N	160.00 W
Kukaklek Lake ⊜	170	59.09 N	155.20 W

Symbols in the index entries represent the broad categories identified in the key at the right. Symbols with superior numbers (∧∧[2]) identify subcategories (see complete key on page *I* · *26*).

Kartensymbole in dem Registerverzeichnis stellen die rechts in Schlüssel erklärten Kategorien dar. Symbole mit hochgestellten Ziffern (∧∧[2]) bezeichnen Unterabteilungen einer Kategorie (vgl. vollständiger Schlüssel auf Seite *I* · *26*).

Los símbolos incluídos en el texto del índice representan las grandes categorias identificadas con la clave a la derecha. Los símbolos con numeros en su parte superior (∧∧[2]) identifican las subcategorías (véase la clave completa en la página *I* · *26*).

Les symboles de l'index représentent les catégories indiquées dans la légende à droite. Les symboles suivis d'un indice (∧∧[2]) représentent des sous-catégories (voir légende complète à la page *I* · *26*).

Os símbolos incluídos no texto do índice representam as grandes categorias identificadas com a chave à direita. Os símbolos com números em sua parte superior (∧∧[2]) identificam as subcategorias (veja-se a chave completa à página *I* · *26*).

Symbol	English	Deutsch	Español	Français	Português
∧	Mountain	Berg	Montaña	Montagne	Montanha
∧∧	Mountains	Berge	Montañas	Montagnes	Montanhas
)(	Pass	Pass	Paso	Col	Passo
∨	Valley, Canyon	Tal, Cañon	Valle, Cañón	Vallée, Canyon	Vale, Canhão
≚	Plain	Ebene	Llano	Plaine	Planície
≻	Cape	Kap	Cabo	Cap	Cabo
I	Island	Insel	Isla	Île	Ilha
II	Islands	Inseln	Islas	Îles	Ilhas
•̲	Other Topographic Features	Andere Topographische Objekte	Otros Elementos Topográficos	Autres données topographiques	Outros Elementos Topográficos

ESPAÑOL

Nombre	Página	Lat.°′	Long.°′ W=Oeste
Kukan	79	49.12 N	133.28 E
Kukarino	72	55.31 N	35.59 E
Kukawa	136	12.56 N	13.35 E
Kukerin	152	33.11 S	118.05 E
Kukës	38	42.05 N	20.24 E
Kukeshan ⛰	75	40.00 N	75.00 E
Kuki	84	36.04 N	139.40 E
Kukipi	154	8.10 S	146.05 E
Kukkola	26	65.59 N	24.04 E
Kukmor	70	56.13 N	50.54 E
Kukoboj	66	58.42 N	39.54 E
Kukol'	66	59.52 N	32.35 E
Kükong → Shaoguan	90	24.50 N	113.37 E
Kukpowruk ≃	170	69.35 N	163.00 W
Kukpuk ≃	170	68.23 N	166.20 W
Kukshi	110	22.12 N	74.45 E
Kukuj	66	59.21 N	32.33 E
Kuku-Nor → Qinghai ⊜	92	36.50 N	100.20 E
Kukunuoerling ⛰	92	37.06 N	99.05 E
Kukup	104	1.19 N	103.27 E
Kuku Point ≻	164a	19.18 N	166.34 E
Kukuri Mukuri Char I	116	21.56 N	90.39 E
Kukuštan	76	57.38 N	56.30 E
Kula, Blg.	38	43.53 N	22.31 E
Kula, Jugo.	38	45.36 N	19.32 E
Kula, Tür.	120	38.32 N	28.40 E
Kula, Haw., U.S.	219a	20.46 N	156.20 W
Kul'ab	110	37.55 N	69.46 E
Kulāchi	113	31.56 N	70.27 E
Kulagi	66	52.56 N	32.24 E
Kula Gulf ⋓	165e	8.05 S	157.18 E
Kulai	104	1.40 N	103.36 E
Kulaj	76	57.42 N	75.15 E
Kula Kangri ▲	114	28.03 N	90.27 E
Kulākh	134	21.18 N	40.41 E
Kulakovo, S.S.S.R.	72	55.06 N	37.28 E
Kulakovo, S.S.S.R.	76	58.06 N	93.57 E
Kulakši	76	47.12 N	55.24 E
Kulal, Mount ▲	144	2.43 N	36.56 E
Kulanak	75	41.22 N	75.31 E
Kulandy	76	46.08 N	59.31 E
Kulanutpes ≃	76	50.21 N	69.15 E
Kulasekharapatnam	112	8.24 N	78.03 E
Kulassein Island I	106	6.25 N	120.41 E
Kulautuva	66	54.58 N	23.38 E
Kulaykilī	130	11.21 N	25.36 E
Kul'či	79	53.33 N	139.36 E
Kuldīga	66	56.58 N	21.59 E
Kuldja → Yining	76	43.55 N	81.14 E
Kul'dur	79	49.13 N	131.38 E
Kule	146	23.05 S	20.05 E
Kulebaki	70	55.24 N	42.32 E
Kulejevo	76	59.40 N	80.59 E
Kulen Vakuf	36	44.34 N	16.06 E
Kulešovka	73	47.05 N	39.33 E
Kulevčinskij	76	53.12 N	61.26 E
Kulgam	113	33.39 N	75.01 E
Kulgera	152	25.50 S	133.18 E
Kulgunino	76	53.35 N	56.56 E
Kuligi	70	58.11 N	53.46 E
Kulik Lake ⊜	170	68.55 N	155.00 W
Kulikov	68	49.58 N	24.04 E
Kulikovka, S.S.S.R.	68	51.23 N	31.37 E
Kulikovka, S.S.S.R.	70	52.14 N	47.36 E
Kulikovo	66	52.14 N	39.35 E
Kulikovskij	70	50.51 N	42.34 E
Kulim	104	5.22 N	100.34 E
Kulin	152	32.40 S	118.10 E
Kuliushucun	95	40.07 N	116.34 E
Kulju	26	61.23 N	23.46 E
Kulkyne Creek ≃	156	30.16 S	144.12 E
Kullaberg ⛰[2]	41	56.18 N	12.30 E
Kullamaa	66	58.53 N	24.05 E
Küllenhahn ◆[8]	253	51.14 N	7.08 E
Küllstedt	52	51.16 N	10.17 E
Kulm	188	46.24 N	98.57 W
Kulmbach	50	50.06 N	11.27 E
Kulnura	160	33.14 S	151.13 E
Kuloj, S.S.S.R.	24	64.58 N	43.28 E
Kuloj, S.S.S.R.	24	61.02 N	42.29 E
Kuloj ≃	66	60.25 N	42.30 E
Kuloli	75	39.22 N	68.03 E
Kulongshan	88	41.43 N	116.54 E
Kulongshanpuzi	94	41.16 N	123.59 E
Kulotino	66	58.27 N	33.21 E
Kulpahār	114	25.19 N	79.39 E
Kulpara	158b	34.04 S	138.02 E
Kulpawn ≃	140	10.21 N	1.05 W
Kulpi	116	22.06 N	88.15 E
Kul'pino	72	56.18 N	37.09 E
Kulpmont	198	40.48 N	76.28 W
Kulpsville	275	40.15 N	75.20 W
Kul'sary	76	46.59 N	54.01 E
Kulsbjerge ⛰[2]	41	55.01 N	12.01 E
Külsheim	52	49.40 N	9.31 E
Kültepe ⊥	120	38.44 N	35.34 E
Kulti	116	23.44 N	86.51 E
Kultikri	116	22.10 N	87.09 E
Kultuk	78	51.44 N	103.42 E
Kulu, Bhārat	113	31.58 N	77.06 E
Kulu, Tür.	120	39.06 N	33.05 E
Kuluha, Jabal ▲	130	15.31 N	23.25 E
Kulumadau	154	9.03 S	152.43 E
Kulunda	76	52.35 N	78.57 E
Kulunda ≃	76	52.59 N	79.48 E
Kulundinskaja Step' ◆[1]	76	53.00 N	79.00 E
Kulundinskoje, Ozero ⊜	76	53.00 N	79.36 E
Kulunqi	88	42.44 N	121.40 E
Kuluqi	79	50.23 N	124.13 E
Kulwin	156	35.02 S	142.33 E
Kuma	86	33.39 N	132.54 E
Kuma ≃, Nihon	82	32.30 N	130.34 E
Kuma ≃, S.S.S.R.	62	44.56 N	47.00 E
Kumagaya	84	36.08 N	139.23 E
Kumai, Indon.	102	3.23 S	112.33 E
Kumai, Indon.	102	2.44 S	111.43 E
Kumai, Teluk C	102	3.00 S	111.43 E
Kumaishi	82a	42.08 N	139.59 E
Kumak	76	51.10 N	60.08 E
Kumakanda	78	52.44 N	116.55 E
Kumalarang	106	7.44 N	123.08 E
Kumamba, Kepulauan II	154	1.36 S	138.45 E
Kumamoto	82	32.48 N	130.43 E
Kumamoto □[5]	86	32.58 N	130.55 E
Kumani, Ostrov I	74	39.33 N	49.35 E
Kumano, Nihon	82	33.54 N	136.05 E
Kumano, Nihon	86	34.15 N	132.36 E
Kumano ≃	82	33.44 N	136.01 E
Kumano-nada ⊤[2]	82	33.47 N	136.20 E
Kumanovo	38	42.08 N	21.43 E
Kumār ≃[1], Bngl.	116	23.11 N	90.10 E
Kumār ≃[1], Bngl.	116	23.31 N	89.28 E
Kumara, N.Z.	162	42.38 S	171.11 E
Kumara, S.S.S.R.	79	51.37 N	126.47 E
Kumārapālaiyam	112	11.28 N	77.43 E
Kumarganj	116	22.59 N	87.44 E
Kumārgrām	114	26.37 N	89.50 E
Kumāri ≃	116	22.57 N	86.48 E
Kumārkhāli	114	23.51 N	89.15 E
Kumarl	152	32.47 S	121.33 E
Kumasi	140	6.41 N	1.35 W
Kumatori	260	34.24 N	135.22 E
Kumawa, Pegunungan ⛰	154	3.50 S	132.50 E
Kumba	142	4.38 N	9.25 E
Kumbakonam	112	10.58 N	79.23 E
Kumbar	130	12.03 N	30.16 E
Kumbarilla	156	27.19 S	150.53 E
Kumbe	154	8.21 S	140.13 E
Kumbel'	75	42.30 N	73.11 E
Kumbher	114	28.16 N	81.24 E
Kumbo	142	6.12 N	10.40 E
Kŭmch'ŏn	88	38.10 N	126.29 E
Kum-Dag	118	39.16 N	54.35 E
Kumdah ⊤[4]	134	20.23 N	45.05 E
Kumdan ▲	113	35.09 N	77.35 E

FRANÇAIS

Nom	Page	Lat.°′	Long.°′ W=Ouest
Kume	86	35.03 N	133.54 E
Kumenan	86	34.56 N	133.58 E
Kumeny	70	58.07 N	49.56 E
Kumertau	76	52.46 N	55.47 E
Kume-shima I	83b	26.20 N	126.47 E
Kŭmgang-san ▲	88	38.35 N	128.10 E
Kumha Pits	146	18.45 S	24.45 E
Kŭmhwa	88	38.17 N	127.28 E
Kumi	144	1.29 N	33.56 E
Kumihama	86	35.36 N	134.55 E
Kuminovskoje	76	57.48 N	64.07 E
Kuminskij	76	58.40 N	66.04 E
Kumiyama	260	34.53 N	135.45 E
Kumizawa ◆[8]	258	35.23 N	139.31 E
Kŭmje	88	35.48 N	126.52 E
Kumköy	257b	41.15 N	29.02 E
Kumla	40	59.08 N	15.08 E
Kumli	74	43.58 N	46.04 E
Kumlinge I	26	60.16 N	20.47 E
Kumluca, Tür.	120	41.27 N	32.28 E
Kumluca, Tür.	120	36.22 N	30.18 E
Kummelnäs	40	59.21 N	18.17 E
Kummerow	50	54.17 N	12.53 E
Kummerower See ⊜	50	53.49 N	12.52 E
Kumo	136	10.03 N	11.13 E
Kumon Range ⛰	92	26.30 N	97.15 E
Kumora	78	55.53 N	111.13 E
Kumosō-yama ▲	86	33.54 N	134.18 E
Kumotori-yama ▲	84	35.51 N	138.57 E
Kumphawapi	100	17.07 N	103.01 E
Kumrābād	116	24.10 N	87.16 E
Kŭmsan	88	36.07 N	127.30 E
Kŭmsan-ni	88	37.55 N	125.41 E
Kumsenga	144	3.47 S	30.25 E
Kumta	112	14.25 N	74.24 E
Kumu	144	3.04 N	25.09 E
Kumu ≃	104	1.24 N	100.43 E
Kumuch	74	42.11 N	47.07 E
Kumukahi, Cape ≻	219d	19.31 N	154.49 W
Kumukuli	110	37.33 N	88.50 E
Kumushi	76	42.14 N	88.11 E
Kumusi ≃	154	8.35 S	148.00 E
Kumylženskaja	70	49.53 N	42.36 E
Kumzār	118	26.20 N	56.25 E
Kuna	192	43.30 N	116.25 W
Kunar (Konar) ≃	113	34.26 N	70.32 E
Kunašak	76	55.43 N	61.36 E
Kunašir, Ostrov (Kunashiri-tō) I	82a	44.10 N	146.00 E
Kunayr, Wādī V	136	27.36 N	15.04 E
Kun'batar	74	44.17 N	45.34 E
Kunchenghu ⊜	96	31.35 N	120.45 E
Kunchha	114	28.08 N	84.20 E
Kunc'ovo ◆[8]	255b	55.44 N	37.26 E
Kunda, S.S.S.R.	66	59.29 N	26.32 E
Kunda, Zaïre	144	3.57 S	26.35 E
Kunda Hills ⛰[2]	112	11.10 N	76.30 E
Kundahit	116	23.58 N	87.10 E
Kundam	114	23.13 N	80.21 E
Kundar ≃, As.	110	31.56 N	69.19 E
Kundar ≃, Pāk.	113	34.18 N	73.28 E
Kundara	112	8.57 N	76.41 E
Kundat	76	55.14 N	87.51 E
Kunderu ≃	112	14.38 N	78.42 E
Kundi	144	1.08 S	40.41 E
Kundiān	113	32.27 N	71.28 E
Kundiawa	154	6.00 S	145.00 E
Kundima	154	4.14 S	143.52 E
Kundip	152	33.42 S	120.10 E
Kundl	58	47.28 N	11.59 E
Kundla	110	21.20 N	71.18 E
Kundr'učje ≃	73	47.52 N	40.15 E
Kundur, Pulau I	102	0.45 N	103.26 E
Kune ◆[7]	84	35.05 N	137.51 E
Kunene (Cunene) ≃	142	17.20 S	11.50 E
Kunersdorf, Forst ◆[3]	254a	52.17 N	12.59 E
Kunes	24	70.21 N	26.31 E
Kunga ≃[1]	114	21.45 N	89.30 E
Kungälv	26	57.52 N	11.58 E
Kungana	136	7.50 N	10.42 E
Kungchuling → Huaide	79	43.32 N	124.50 E
Kungej-Alatau, Chrebet ⛰	75	42.50 N	77.00 E
Kunghit Island I	172	52.06 N	131.04 W
Kunghsi	90	24.39 N	121.18 E
Kung Pei-tien	259d	25.05 N	121.39 E
Kungrad	76	43.06 N	58.54 E
Kungribingri)(	114	30.37 N	80.16 E
Kungsängen	40	59.29 N	17.45 E
Kungsbacka	26	57.29 N	12.04 E
Kungsgården	40	60.36 N	16.37 E
Kungshamn	26	58.22 N	11.15 E
Kungsör	40	59.25 N	16.05 E
Kungu	142	2.47 N	19.12 E
Kungur	76	57.25 N	56.57 E
Kungurri	156	21.05 S	148.44 E
Kungus ≃	78	55.39 N	95.44 E
Kungwe Mount ▲	128	6.07 S	29.48 E
Kunhegyes	30	47.22 N	20.38 E
Kunhing	100	21.18 N	98.26 E
Kuni	84	36.35 N	138.38 E
Kunia	219c	21.29 N	158.07 W
Kunimi	86	33.41 N	131.36 E
Kuningan	105a	6.59 S	108.29 E
Kunisaki	86	33.33 N	131.45 E
Kunisaki-hantō ≻[1]	86	33.30 N	131.40 E
Kuni Vyselki	72	54.18 N	38.41 E
Kunja	66	56.18 N	30.59 E
Kunja ≃, S.S.S.R.	66	57.09 N	31.10 E
Kunja ≃, S.S.S.R.	72	56.31 N	38.12 E
Kunjāh	113	32.32 N	73.59 E
Kunje	73	49.23 N	37.15 E
Kunkle	206	41.38 N	84.30 W
Kunkletown	200	40.51 N	75.27 W
Kunkuri	114	22.45 N	83.57 E
Kunlong	100	23.25 N	98.39 E
Kunlunshanmai ⛰	110	36.30 N	88.00 E
Kunming	92	25.05 N	102.40 E
Kunminghu ⊜	261a	39.59 N	116.15 E
Kunnamkulam	112	10.39 N	76.05 E
Kunost'	66	60.01 N	37.38 E
Kunovice	30	49.03 N	17.29 E
Kunow	50	53.00 N	12.07 E
Kunowice	50	52.20 N	14.50 E
Kunrau	50	52.35 N	11.01 E
Kunsan	88	35.58 N	126.41 E
Kunsangen Flygplats ⊠	40	58.36 N	16.15 E
Kunshan	96	31.23 N	120.57 E
Kunstmuseum ⍢	253	51.14 N	6.46 E
Kunszentmárton	30	46.51 N	20.18 E
Kuntair	140	13.32 N	16.13 W
Kuntaur	140	13.40 N	14.48 W
Kuntiki	76	58.29 N	76.24 E
Kunting	90	29.48 N	121.56 E
Kuntshankoie	142	3.20 S	23.34 E
Kuntuolun	92	45.13 N	115.21 E
Kununurra	154	15.47 S	128.44 E
Kunwi	88	36.15 N	128.34 E
Kunya	140	12.14 N	8.34 E
Künzelsau	52	49.16 N	9.41 E
Kunzulu	142	3.29 S	16.09 E
Kuocangshan ⛰	90	28.30 N	118.46 E
Kuohsing	90	24.02 N	120.51 E
Kuokegan	110	37.30 N	89.55 E
Kuolajarvi	24	66.58 N	29.12 E
Kuop Atoll I[1]	165c	7.03 N	151.56 E
Kuopio	26	62.54 N	27.41 E
Kuopion lääni □[4]	26	63.00 N	27.30 E
Kuortane	26	62.48 N	23.30 E
Kupa ≃	36	45.28 N	16.24 E
Kup'abal	261b	37.39 N	126.54 E
Kup'ačeje	73	48.10 N	39.37 E
Kupang	102	10.10 S	123.35 E
Kupang, Teluk C	102	10.04 S	123.40 E
Kup'ansk	73	49.42 N	37.38 E
Kupanskoje	72	56.51 N	38.43 E
Kup'ansk-Uzlovoj	73	49.39 N	37.39 E
Kuparuk ≃	170	70.25 N	148.55 W
Kupava	70	51.07 N	42.57 E

PORTUGUÊS

Nome	Página	Lat.°′	Long.°′ W=Oeste
Kupavna	255b	55.45 N	38.08 E
Kuper Island I	214	48.58 N	123.39 W
Kupferberg	253	51.09 N	7.27 E
Kupferdreh ◆[8]	253	51.23 N	7.05 E
Kupfermühle	41	54.50 N	9.24 E
Kupferzell	52	49.14 N	9.41 E
Kupičev	68	51.00 N	24.44 E
Kupino	76	54.22 N	77.18 E
Kupiškis	66	55.50 N	24.58 E
Küplü, Tür.	120	41.07 N	26.21 E
Küplu, Tür.	120	40.06 N	30.00 E
Kupol, Gora ▲	170	68.38 N	174.45 E
Kuppenheim	52	48.49 N	8.15 E
Kupper Airport ⊠	266	40.31 N	74.36 W
Kupreanof Island I	170	56.50 N	133.30 W
Kupreanof Point ≻	170	55.34 N	159.35 W
Kupres	36	44.00 N	17.17 E
Küps	50	50.11 N	11.16 E
Kupuri	79	54.44 N	130.30 E
Kur ≃	79	48.44 N	134.14 E
Kur, Pulau I	154	5.20 S	132.00 E
Kura (Kuruçay) ≃, As.	74	39.24 N	49.24 E
Kura ≃, S.S.S.R.	74	44.06 N	44.57 E
Kurabuchi	84	36.25 N	138.48 E
Kur'ačevka, S.S.S.R.	73	49.22 N	39.36 E
Kur'ačevka, S.S.S.R.	73	49.39 N	38.42 E
Kurach	74	41.36 N	47.46 E
Kurach ≃	74	41.40 N	48.11 E
Kurachovka	73	48.02 N	37.23 E
Kurachovo	73	47.59 N	37.16 E
Kuragaty	75	43.06 N	72.59 E
Kuragaty ≃	75	43.57 N	73.34 E
Kuragino	76	53.53 N	92.40 E
Kurahashi	86	34.06 N	132.30 E
Kurahashi-jima I	86	34.08 N	132.31 E
Kuraj	76	56.42 N	95.29 E
Kurajlysaj	70	50.07 N	51.51 E
Kurakake-tōge)(	84	35.12 N	136.25 E
Kurakaki	260	34.59 N	135.28 E
Kurakino, S.S.S.R.	70	52.33 N	44.03 E
Kurakino, S.S.S.R.	72	54.30 N	35.48 E
Kurakovo	72	54.05 N	37.14 E
Kūrāli	113	30.50 N	76.35 E
Kuram	75	43.33 N	78.08 E
Kuramā', Ḥarrat ◆[9]	118	24.30 N	40.15 E
Kurama-yama ▲	86	35.07 N	135.46 E
Kuraminskij Chrebet ⛰	75	40.45 N	70.10 E
Kuramo Waters C	263a	6.26 N	3.26 E
Kuranami	258	35.27 N	140.00 E
Kurāon	114	24.59 N	82.05 E
Kurar ◆[8]	262c	19.11 N	72.52 E
Kurašasaj	76	50.18 N	56.55 E
Kurashiki	86	34.35 N	133.46 E
Kurasiki → Kurashiki	86	34.35 N	133.46 E
Kurate	86	33.47 N	130.41 E
Kurauli	114	27.24 N	78.59 E
Kuraymah	130	18.33 N	31.51 E
Kurayoshi	86	35.26 N	133.49 E
Kurayyimah	122	32.16 N	35.36 E
Kurba	70	57.34 N	39.32 E
Kurba ≃	78	52.02 N	108.30 E
Kurbağa Gölü ⊜	120	38.21 N	35.17 E
Kurbalı Dere ≃	257b	40.59 N	29.02 E
Kurbatovo	76	55.34 N	91.10 E
Kurbulik	78	53.45 N	108.57 E
Kurčaloj	74	43.12 N	46.05 E
Kur-Čilik ≃	75	43.50 N	78.06 E
Kurčum	76	48.37 N	83.40 E
Kurdaj	75	43.21 N	74.59 E
K'urdamir	74	40.21 N	48.08 E
Kurdgelauri	74	41.58 N	45.32 E
Kurdistan □[9]	108	37.00 N	45.00 E
Kurdufān □[4]	130	13.00 N	30.00 E
Kurd'umovka	73	48.28 N	37.59 E
Kurduvādi	112	18.05 N	75.26 E
Kure, Nihon	86	34.14 N	132.34 E
Küre, Tür.	120	41.48 N	33.43 E
Kure Island I[1]	6	28.25 N	178.25 W
Kurejka ≃	64	66.30 N	87.12 E
Kurejskaja	78	58.56 N	111.20 E
Kuren'	68	51.09 N	32.44 E
Kurenalus	26	65.21 N	26.59 E
Kurenec	66	54.33 N	26.57 E
Kurgal'džino	76	50.36 N	70.01 E
Kurgan	76	55.26 N	65.18 E
Kurgan Mečetnyj, Gora ▲[2]	73	48.06 N	39.21 E
Kurgan-T'ube	110	37.50 N	68.48 E
Kurgasyn	76	49.15 N	66.43 E
Kurgatej	78	54.23 N	99.27 E
Kurgolovo	66	59.46 N	28.06 E
Kuria I	14	0.14 N	173.25 E
Kuria Muria Islands → Khūryān Mūryān II	108	17.30 N	56.00 E
Kuriasol	116	22.06 N	86.39 E
Kuridala	156	21.17 S	140.30 E
Kurīgrām	114	25.49 N	89.39 E
Kurihama	258	35.13 N	139.43 E
Kurihashi	84	36.08 N	139.42 E
Kurikka	26	62.37 N	22.25 E
Kurilen → Kuril'skije Ostrova II	64	46.10 N	152.00 E
Kurilen-Strasse → Pervyj Kuril'skij Proliv ⋓	64	50.50 N	156.36 E
Kuriles, Islas → Kuril'skije Ostrova II	64	46.10 N	152.00 E
Kuril Islands → Kuril'skije Ostrova II	64	46.10 N	152.00 E
Kurilovka	70	50.44 N	48.02 E
Kuril'sk	64	45.14 N	147.53 E
Kuril'skije Ostrova (Kuril Islands) II	64	46.10 N	152.00 E
Kuril Strait → Pervyj Kuril'skij Proliv ⋓	64	50.50 N	156.36 E
Kuril Trench ✢[1]	6	47.00 N	155.00 E
Kuřim	30	49.18 N	16.32 E
Kurimoto	84	35.49 N	140.30 E
Ku-ring-gai	160	33.45 S	151.08 E
Ku-ring-gai Chase National Park ♠	160	33.38 S	151.15 E
Kuring Kuru	142	17.38 S	18.35 E
Kurinjippadi	112	11.34 N	79.36 E
Kurinskaja Kosa ≻[2]	74	39.03 N	49.13 E
Kuripapango	162	39.23 S	176.21 E
Kuriyama, Nihon	82a	43.03 N	141.47 E
Kuriyama, Nihon	84	36.52 N	139.37 E
Kurja, S.S.S.R.	24	61.42 N	57.09 E
Kurja, S.S.S.R.	76	51.36 N	82.19 E
Kurjanovskaja	66	60.19 N	41.33 E
Kurkino, S.S.S.R.	66	53.26 N	38.40 E
Kurkino, S.S.S.R.	255b	55.53 N	37.23 E
Kurkliai	66	55.25 N	25.03 E
Kurl ◆[8]	253	51.35 N	7.35 E
Kurla ◆[8]	262c	19.05 N	72.53 E
Kurlackoje	73	47.21 N	39.03 E
Kurleja	78	52.11 N	119.11 E
Kurlin	70	51.48 N	51.00 E
Kurlovskij	70	55.27 N	40.36 E
Kurmanajevka	70	52.31 N	52.06 E
Kurmani	116	22.47 N	89.53 E
Kurmankol'	70	49.09 N	48.27 E
Kurmenty	75	42.48 N	78.15 E
Kurmitala Airport ⊠	116	23.46 N	90.23 E
Kurmuk	130	10.33 N	34.17 E
Kurnell	264a	34.01 S	151.13 E
Kurnool	112	15.50 N	78.03 E
Kurobane	84	36.51 N	140.07 E
Kurobe	84	36.51 N	137.26 E
Kurobe ≃	84	36.55 N	137.25 E
Kurobe-dam ◆[6]	84	36.36 N	137.38 E
Kurodashō	86	35.01 N	135.00 E
Kurogi	86	33.12 N	130.40 E
Kurohone	84	36.30 N	139.17 E
Kuroishi	82	40.38 N	140.36 E
Kuroiso	84	36.58 N	140.03 E
Kuroo-tōge)(	86	35.11 N	134.12 E
Kuropatkino, S.S.S.R.	70	46.32 N	45.20 E
Kuropatkino, S.S.S.R.	75	39.57 N	67.27 E
Kurort Darasun	78	51.12 N	113.44 E
Kurose	86	34.19 N	132.40 E
Kurose ≃	86	34.13 N	132.36 E
Kuro-shima I, Nihon	83b	30.50 N	129.57 E
Kuro-shima I, Nihon	165d	24.19 N	124.05 E
Kurosu	258	35.51 N	139.23 E
Kurovo	72	55.49 N	36.00 E
Kurovskoje	72	55.34 N	38.55 E
Kurow	162	44.44 S	170.28 E
Kuroya	258	35.55 N	139.44 E
Kurrajong	160	33.33 S	150.40 E
Kurram	110	30.06 N	66.31 E
Kurram □[5]	113	33.45 N	70.25 E
Kurram ≃	113	32.36 N	71.20 E
Kurri Kurri	160	32.49 S	151.29 E
Kursavka	74	44.28 N	42.31 E
Kursela	114	25.27 N	87.15 E
Kuršėnai	66	56.00 N	22.56 E
Kurseong	110	26.53 N	88.17 E
Kursk	68	51.42 N	36.12 E
Kursk □[4]	66	52.14 N	35.30 E
Kurskaja	74	44.03 N	44.27 E
Kurskaja Kosa ≻[2]	66	55.18 N	21.00 E
Kurskij Vokzal ◆[5]	255b	55.46 N	37.40 E
Kurskij Zaliv C	66	55.00 N	21.00 E
Kursole	134	2.16 N	45.28 E
Kuršumlija	38	43.08 N	21.17 E
Kurşunlu, Tür.	120	38.40 N	37.51 E
Kurşunlu, Tür.	120	40.51 N	33.16 E
Kurtalan, Tür.	118		
	120	37.57 N	41.42 E
Kurtamyš	76	54.55 N	64.27 E
Kurtatsch → Cortaccia	58	46.19 N	11.13 E
Kurten	212	30.47 N	96.16 W
Kürteşe	120	41.14 N	33.44 E
Kurthasanlı	120	38.20 N	32.11 E
Kurth Lake ⊜	212	31.26 N	94.42 W
Kūrtī	130	18.07 N	31.33 E
Kurtino	72	54.59 N	38.17 E
Kurtistown	219d	19.36 N	155.04 W
Kurtumo	134	7.28 N	49.00 E
Kurtušibinskij Chrebet ⛰	78	52.10 N	93.30 E
Kurty ≃	75	44.16 N	76.42 E
Kurtz	208	38.58 N	86.12 W
Kuru, Sūd.	130	7.43 N	26.31 E
Kuru, Suomi	26	61.52 N	23.44 E
Kuru ≃	130	9.08 N	26.57 E
Kuruca Geçidi)(	120	38.58 N	40.16 E
Kurucaşile	120	41.50 N	32.43 E
Kuruçay	120	39.39 N	38.29 E
Kuruçay (Kura) ≃	74	39.24 N	49.24 E
Kuruçeşme ◆[8]	257b	41.03 N	29.02 E
Kurudu, Pulau I	154	1.51 S	137.01 E
Kurukshetra	114	29.59 N	76.51 E
Kurum	154	4.45 S	145.55 E
Kuruman	148	27.28 S	23.28 E
Kuruman ≃	148	26.56 S	20.39 E
Kuruman Heuwels ⛰[2]	148	27.40 S	23.25 E
Kurumazaka-tōge)(	84	36.24 N	138.28 E
Kurumdy, Gora ▲	75	39.28 N	73.32 E
Kurume, Nihon	86	33.19 N	130.31 E
Kurume, Nihon	258	35.45 N	139.32 E
Kurumkan	78	54.18 N	110.18 E
Kurun ≃	134	5.30 N	34.17 E
Kurunegala	112	7.29 N	80.22 E
Kurungbaja, Tanjung ≻	105b	8.15 S	120.35 E
Kurung Tank ⊜[1]	114	22.19 N	82.14 E
Kurunzulaj	78	51.00 N	117.10 E
Kuruqi	79	48.58 N	123.50 E
Kurur, Jabal ▲	130	20.31 N	31.32 E
Kurusaj	75	40.35 N	69.24 E
Kurushima-kaikyo ⋓	86	34.07 N	133.00 E
Kuruson-zan ▲	86	34.21 N	130.51 E
Kurylys	76	48.38 N	60.47 E
Kuryŏng-gang ≃	88	39.43 N	125.47 E
Kuryongp'o	88	35.59 N	129.32 E
Kurzeme □[9]	66	56.50 N	22.30 E
Kusa	76	55.20 N	59.29 E
Kusabe	260	34.31 N	135.29 E
Kuşadası	120	37.51 N	27.15 E
Kuşadası Körfezi C	120	37.50 N	27.08 E
Kusaie I	14	5.19 N	162.59 E
Kušalino	66	57.07 N	36.05 E
Kusan	88	36.18 N	128.55 E
Kusan-ni	88	37.43 N	128.49 E
Kusary	74	41.27 N	48.25 E
Kusathu ⊜	110	35.43 N	92.45 E
Kusatsu, Nihon	84	35.00 N	135.57 E
Kusatsu, Nihon	84	36.37 N	138.36 E
Kusawa Lake ⊜	170	60.20 N	136.15 W
Kusaybah, Bi'r ⊤[4]	130	22.41 N	29.55 E
Kuščovskaja	68	46.33 N	39.37 E
Kuse	86	35.04 N	133.45 E
Kusel	52	49.32 N	7.24 E
Kušen'ki	68	48.53 N	34.07 E
Kusey	50	52.36 N	11.05 E
Kuş Gölü ⊜	120	40.10 N	27.57 E
Kushaka	140	10.32 N	6.48 E
Kushālgarh	110	23.10 N	74.27 E
Kusheriki	140	10.33 N	6.28 E
Kushi	164m	26.31 N	128.01 E
Kushida ≃	84	34.36 N	136.34 E
Kushigata	84	35.36 N	138.28 E
Kushihiki	258	35.55 N	139.36 E
Kushikino	82	31.44 N	130.16 E
Kushima	82	31.29 N	131.14 E
Kushimoto	82	33.28 N	135.47 E
Kushira	260	34.28 N	135.43 E
Kushiro	82a	42.58 N	144.23 E
Kushog Lake ⊜	202	45.05 N	78.48 W
Kushtia	114	23.55 N	89.07 E
Kushu	95	39.55 N	117.35 E
Kushui	92	42.11 N	94.25 E
Kusiro → Kushiro	82a	42.58 N	144.23 E
Kusiyāra ≃	110	24.36 N	91.44 E
Kuška	118	35.16 N	62.20 E
Kuška ≃	118	36.00 N	62.40 E
Kuskokwim ≃	170	60.17 N	162.27 W
Kuskokwim, North Fork ≃	170	63.06 N	154.37 W
Kuskokwim, South Fork ≃	170	63.06 N	154.37 W
Kuskokwim Bay C	170	59.45 N	162.25 W
Kuskokwim Mountains ⛰	170	62.30 N	156.00 W
Kuskovo ◆[8]	255b	55.44 N	37.49 E
Kuškušara	24	64.58 N	40.21 E
Kusma	114	28.14 N	83.41 E
Kušmurun	76	52.27 N	64.36 E
Kušmurun, Ozero ⊜	76	52.40 N	64.48 E
Küsnacht	54	47.19 N	8.35 E
Kušnarenkovo	76	55.06 N	55.22 E
Kušnica	68	48.27 N	23.14 E
Kusŏng	88	39.59 N	125.15 E
Kusria	262b	22.58 N	88.14 E
Kussharo-ko ⊜	82a	43.38 N	144.21 E
Küssnacht	54	47.05 N	8.27 E
Kustanaj	76	53.10 N	63.35 E
Kustar'ovka	70	54.16 N	42.16 E
Küsten-Gebirge → Coast Mountains ⛰	166	55.00 N	129.00 W
Küstenkanal ≍	48	52.57 N	7.18 E
Küsten-Ketten → Coast Ranges ⛰	168	41.00 N	123.30 W
Kusthalia	116	23.29 N	87.03 E
Kūstī	130	13.10 N	32.40 E
Küstrin → Kostrzyn	30	52.37 N	14.39 E
Kusu, Nihon	84	34.55 N	136.38 E
Kusu, Nihon	86	33.16 N	131.09 E
Kušugum	68	47.42 N	35.14 E
Kušum ≃	70	48.54 N	50.32 E
Kusumba	262b	22.27 N	88.24 E
Kusumbāni ▲	116	21.57 N	86.26 E
Kušumskij	70	51.38 N	48.21 E
Kusunoki	86	34.03 N	131.15 E
K'us'ur	64	70.39 N	127.15 E
Kušva	76	58.18 N	59.45 E
Kut, Ko I	100	11.40 N	102.35 E
Kuta	140	9.52 N	6.43 E
Kuta ≃	78	56.46 N	105.40 E
Kutabaru	102	0.44 S	102.56 E
Kutabuloh	104	3.28 N	97.04 E
Kutacane	104	3.30 N	97.48 E
Kütahya	120	39.25 N	29.59 E
Kütahya □[4]	120	39.20 N	29.30 E
Kutais	68	44.32 N	39.18 E
Kutaisi	74	42.15 N	42.40 E
Kutāmat al-Ghābah	132	30.55 N	30.54 E
Kutanibong	104	3.53 N	96.22 E
Kutaradja → Banda Aceh	104	5.34 N	95.20 E
Kutarere	162	38.03 S	177.09 E
Kutasawang	104	5.08 N	96.54 E
Kutch, Gulf of C	110	22.36 N	69.30 E
Kutchan	82a	42.54 N	140.45 E
Kutcharo-ko ⊜	82a	45.09 N	142.19 E
Kutejnikovo, S.S.S.R.	73	47.49 N	38.18 E
Kutejnikovo, S.S.S.R.	73	47.34 N	39.46 E
Kutenholz	48	53.29 N	9.19 E
Kutima	78	57.10 N	108.16 E
Kutima ≃	78	57.08 N	108.14 E
Kutina	36	45.29 N	16.46 E
Kutiyāna	110	21.38 N	69.59 E
Kutjino	72	55.26 N	37.27 E
Kutkai	100	23.27 N	97.56 E
Kutkašen	74	40.59 N	47.50 E
Kutluškino	70	55.14 N	50.24 E
Kutná Hora	30	49.57 N	15.16 E
Kutno	30	52.15 N	19.23 E
Kutoarjo	105a	7.43 S	109.54 E
Kutomara	78	51.06 N	118.49 E
Kutsuki	84	35.21 N	135.55 E
Küttigen	54	47.25 N	8.03 E
Kuttura	24	68.24 N	26.28 E
Kuttusoja	24	67.46 N	28.50 E
Kuttuzi	255a	59.45 N	30.04 E
Kutu	142	2.44 S	18.09 E
Kutubdia Island I	110	21.50 N	91.52 E
Kutubu, Lake ⊜	154	6.23 S	143.18 E
Kutukovo	70	54.26 N	40.31 E
Kutulik	78	53.21 N	102.48 E
Kutulo, Lagh ≃	144	2.08 N	40.56 E
Kutuluk ≃	70	53.19 N	51.09 E
Kutum	130	14.12 N	24.40 E
Kutu-Moke	142	3.12 S	17.21 E
Kúty, Česko.	30	48.40 N	17.03 E
Kuty, S.S.S.R.	68	48.16 N	25.10 E
Kutztown	200	40.31 N	75.47 W
Kuuli-Majak	118	40.14 N	52.42 E
Kuurne	46	50.51 N	3.17 E
Kuusamo	26	65.58 N	29.11 E
Kuusankoski	26	60.54 N	26.38 E
Kuva	75	40.32 N	72.05 E
Kuvak-Nikol'skoje	70	53.37 N	43.30 E
Kuvandyk	76	51.28 N	57.21 E
Kuvasaj	75	40.18 N	71.58 E
Kuvet ≃	170	69.14 N	175.00 E
Kuvšinovo	66	57.02 N	34.10 E
Kuwabara	260	34.53 N	135.15 E
Kuwait □[1]	108		
	118	29.30 N	47.45 E
Kuwait Bay → Kuwayt, Khalīj al- C	118	29.30 N	48.00 E
Kuwana	84	35.04 N	136.42 E
Kuwayt, Khalīj al- C	118	29.30 N	48.00 E
Kuyāli	116	22.31 N	86.11 E
Kuybyshev → Kujbyšev	70	53.12 N	50.09 E
Kūysanjaq	118	36.05 N	44.38 E
Kuyucak, Tür.	120	37.51 N	38.21 E
Kuyucak, Tür.	120	37.55 N	28.28 E
Kuyuwini ≃	236	2.16 N	58.16 W
Kuyuyukak, Cape ≻	170	56.54 N	156.50 W
Kuzaranda	24	62.22 N	35.37 E
Kuze	84	35.33 N	136.30 E
Kuze ◆[8]	260	34.57 N	135.49 E
Kuzedejevo	76	53.20 N	87.10 E
Kuzemino	68	50.09 N	34.39 E
Kuzemovka	73	49.31 N	37.59 E
Kužener	70	56.48 N	48.56 E
Kuženkino	66	57.44 N	33.59 E
Kuzitrin ≃	170	65.10 N	165.28 W
Kuzkejevo	70	55.46 N	52.48 E
Kuz'miniči	66	54.16 N	33.42 E
Kuz'minka ≃	255a	59.48 N	30.31 E
Kuz'minki ◆[8]	255b	55.42 N	37.48 E
Kuzmino, S.S.S.R.	72	55.09 N	37.53 E
Kuz'mino, S.S.S.R.	72	56.36 N	37.55 E
Kuzmiščevo	72	54.46 N	37.12 E
Kuz'movka	64	62.19 N	92.02 E
Kuznečicha	70	54.43 N	49.38 E
Kuznečikovo	72	56.13 N	36.35 E
Kuzneck, S.S.S.R.	70	53.07 N	46.36 E
Kuzneck → Novokuzneck, S.S.S.R.	76	53.45 N	87.06 E
Kuzneckij Alatau ⛰	76	54.45 N	88.00 E
Kuznecova	79	46.16 N	138.03 E
Kuznecovka	66	56.18 N	28.33 E
Kuznecovo, S.S.S.R.	72	55.27 N	36.57 E
Kuznecovo, S.S.S.R.	72	55.30 N	38.21 E
Kuznecovo, S.S.S.R.	76	59.15 N	63.28 E
Kuznecovo-Michajlovka	73	47.27 N	38.13 E
Kuznecovskij	70	47.25 N	40.57 E
Kuznecy	72	55.51 N	38.40 E
Kuznetsk → Kuzneck	70	53.07 N	46.36 E
Kuzomen', S.S.S.R.	24	64.17 N	42.53 E
Kuzomen', S.S.S.R.	24	66.17 N	36.54 E
Kuzovatovo	70	53.33 N	47.41 E
Kuztekke	120	41.48 N	33.16 E
Kuzucubelen	120	36.51 N	34.27 E
Kuzuha	260	34.52 N	135.41 E
Kuzuryū ≃	84	36.13 N	136.08 E
Kuzuu	84	36.24 N	139.37 E
Kvænangen C[2]	24	70.05 N	21.13 E
Kværndrup	41	55.10 N	10.32 E
Kvaisi	74	42.31 N	43.40 E
Kvaløya I, Nor.	24	69.40 N	18.30 E
Kvaløya I, Nor.	24	70.37 N	23.52 E
Kvam	26	61.40 N	9.42 E
Kvanløse	41	55.39 N	11.41 E
Kvanndal	26	60.29 N	6.36 E
Kvareli	74	41.56 N	45.54 E
Kvarner C	36	44.45 N	14.15 E
Kvarnerić ⋓	36	44.45 N	14.35 E
Kvarnsveden	40	60.31 N	15.24 E
Kvarntorp	40	59.08 N	15.15 E
Kvarsa	70	56.58 N	53.57 E
Kvarsebo	40	58.39 N	16.39 E
Kvašenki	72	56.48 N	37.33 E
Kvenna ≃	26	60.01 N	7.56 E
Kverkfjöll ▲	24a	64.43 N	16.38 W
Kvichak Bay C	170	58.48 N	157.30 W
Kvicksund	40	59.27 N	16.19 E
Kvidinge	41	56.08 N	13.04 E
Kvien ⊜	40	60.24 N	13.48 E
Kvikkjokk	24	66.55 N	17.50 E
Kvina ≃	26	58.17 N	6.56 E
Kvismare kanal ≍	40	59.12 N	15.11 E
Kvissleby	26	62.17 N	17.21 E
Kvistbro	40	59.09 N	14.49 E
Kvistgård	41	55.59 N	12.30 E
Kvitok	78	56.03 N	98.30 E
Kwa ≃	142	3.10 S	16.11 E
Kwachaga	144	5.38 S	38.08 E
Kwada	154	6.09 S	141.53 E
Kwahae-ri ◆[8]	261b	37.33 N	126.50 E
Kwahu Plateau ⛰[1]	140	6.30 N	0.30 W
Kwajalein I[1]	14	9.05 N	167.20 E
Kwajok	130	8.19 N	28.00 E
Kwakhanai	146	21.41 S	21.19 E
Kwakoegron	240	5.15 N	55.20 W
Kwale, Kenya	144	4.11 S	39.27 E
Kwale, Nig.	140	5.46 N	6.26 E
Kwali	140	8.56 N	7.00 E
Kwambilo ≃	263b	4.26 S	15.20 E
Kwa-Mbonambi	148	28.36 S	32.05 E
Kwamisa ▲	140	7.08 N	1.53 W
Kwamouth	142	3.10 S	16.12 E
Kwa Mtoro	144	5.14 S	35.26 E
Kwanak-san ▲	261b	37.27 N	126.58 E
Kwando (Cuando) ≃	142	18.27 S	23.32 E
Kwangchow → Guangzhou	90	23.06 N	113.16 E
Kwangju	88	35.09 N	126.54 E
Kwangnaru Bridge ◆[5]	261b	37.33 N	127.05 E
Kwango (Cuango) ≃	142	3.14 S	17.23 E
Kwangsi Chuang Autonomous Region → Guangxi Zhuang Zizhiqu □[4]	92	24.00 N	109.00 E
Kwangtung → Guangdong □[4]	80	23.00 N	113.00 E
Kwangwazi	144	7.47 S	38.15 E
Kwangyang	88	34.59 N	127.34 E
Kwanmo-bong ▲	88	41.42 N	129.13 E
Kwansan-ni	261b	37.43 N	126.51 E
Kwansei Gakuin University ⍢[2]	260	34.46 N	135.21 E
Kwanto Plain → Kantō-heiya ≚	84	36.00 N	139.30 E
Kwara □[3]	140	9.00 N	4.30 E
Kware	140	13.12 N	5.14 E
Kwa-Thema	263d	26.18 S	28.23 E
Kwatisore	154	3.15 S	134.57 E
Kweichow → Guizhou □[4]	92	27.00 N	107.00 E
Kweihwa → Huhehaote	92	40.51 N	111.40 E
Kweijang → Guiyang	92	26.35 N	106.43 E
Kweilin → Guilin	92	25.11 N	110.09 E
Kweisui → Huhehaote	92	40.51 N	111.40 E
Kweiyang → Guiyang	92	26.35 N	106.43 E
Kweneng □[5]	146	24.00 S	24.00 E
Kwenge (Caengo) ≃	142	4.50 S	18.42 E
Kwesimintim	140	4.54 N	1.47 W
Kwethluk	170	60.49 N	161.27 W
Kwethluk ≃	170	60.46 N	161.26 W
Kwidzyn	30	53.45 N	18.56 E
Kwiello	140	11.16 N	7.00 E
Kwigillingok	170	59.51 N	163.08 W
Kwiguk	170	62.45 N	164.28 W
Kwiha	134	13.31 N	39.32 E
Kwilu (Cuilo) ≃	142	3.22 S	17.22 E
Kwinana	158a	32.15 S	115.48 E
Kwisa ≃	30	51.35 N	15.25 E
Kwitaro ≃	236	3.19 N	58.47 W
Kwobrup	152	33.37 S	117.46 E
Kwoka, Gunung ▲	154	0.31 S	132.27 E
Kwolla	140	9.00 N	9.15 E
Kyabé	136	9.27 N	18.57 E
Kyabra	156	26.18 S	143.10 E
Kyabra Creek ≃	156	25.36 S	142.55 E
Kyabram	156	36.19 S	145.03 E
Kyaikkami	100	16.04 N	97.34 E
Kyaiklat	100	16.26 N	95.44 E
Kyaikto	100	17.18 N	97.01 E
Kya-in	100	16.02 N	98.08 E
Kyaka	144	1.16 S	31.25 E
Kyancutta	156	33.08 S	135.34 E
Ky-anh	100	18.05 N	106.18 E
Kyat-aw	100	12.29 N	98.19 E
Kyaukhnyat	100	18.15 N	97.31 E
Kyaukkyi	100	18.19 N	96.46 E
Kyaukme	100	22.32 N	97.02 E
Kyaukpa	100	13.05 N	98.59 E
Kyaukpyu, Mya.	100	19.26 N	93.33 E
Kyaukpyu, Mya.	100	19.05 N	93.52 E
Kyaukse	100	21.36 N	96.08 E
Kyauktaw	100	20.51 N	92.59 E
Kyaunggon	100	17.06 N	95.11 E
Kybartai	66	54.39 N	22.45 E
Kybean	161b	36.22 S	149.25 E
Kybeyan Range ⛰	161b	36.20 S	149.32 E
Kyburz	216	38.47 N	120.18 W
Kydra	161b	36.27 S	149.23 E
Kyeamba	161b	35.26 S	147.37 E
Kyeamba Creek ≃	161b	35.06 S	147.29 E
Kyebaiwa	144	0.33 N	34.48 E
Kyebang-san ▲	88	37.43 N	128.29 E
Kyegegwa	144	0.29 N	31.03 E
Kyeikdon	100	16.00 N	98.24 E
Kyeintali	100	18.00 N	94.29 E
Kyenjojo	144	0.37 N	30.38 E
Kyes Peak ▲	214	47.57 N	121.19 W
Kyffhäuser-Denkmal ⊥	50	51.23 N	11.06 E
Kyffhäuser Gebirge ⛰	50	51.23 N	11.05 E
Kyidaunggan	100	19.53 N	96.12 E
Kyindwe	100	20.58 N	93.51 E
Kyje ◆[8]	50	50.04 N	14.32 E
Kyjov	30	49.01 N	17.08 E
Kykladen → Kikládhes II	38	37.30 N	25.00 E
Kykva	70	57.22 N	53.50 E
Kylās ▲	114	25.18 N	90.45 E
Kyle, Sask., Can.	174	50.50 N	108.02 W
Kyle, S. Dak., U.S.	188	43.26 N	102.10 W
Kyle, Tex., U.S.	186	29.59 N	97.53 W
Kyle □[8]	42	55.32 N	4.25 W
Kyle, Lake ⊜[1]	144	20.14 S	31.00 E
Kyle National Park ♠	144	20.14 S	31.00 E
Kyle of Lochalsh	28	57.17 N	5.43 W
Kylertown	204	41.00 N	78.10 W
Kyll ≃	52	49.48 N	6.42 E
Kyllburg	52	50.02 N	6.35 E
Kym ≃	44	52.14 N	0.17 W
Kymen lääni □[4]	26	61.00 N	28.00 E
Kymijoki ≃	26	60.30 N	26.52 E
Kymynejvejem ≃	170	67.26 N	175.28 W
Kyn	76	57.52 N	58.38 E
Kyndby	41	55.48 N	11.56 E
Kyneton	159	37.15 S	144.27 E
Kynnefjäll ▲[2]	26	58.42 N	11.41 E
Kynšperk nad Ohří	50	50.04 N	12.32 E
Kynuna	156	21.35 S	141.55 E
Kyoga, Lake ⊜	144	1.30 N	33.00 E
Kyōga-saki ≻	86	35.46 N	135.13 E
Kyogle	156	28.37 S	153.00 E
Kyoha-ri	261b	37.46 N	126.46 E
Kyohyŏn-ni	261b	37.43 N	126.58 E
Kyom ≃	130	8.58 N	28.13 E
Kyŏmip'o → Songnim	88	38.44 N	125.38 E
Kyonan	84	35.07 N	139.50 E
Kyondo	100	16.35 N	98.03 E
Kyongbok Palace ⍢	261b	37.36 N	126.57 E
Kyŏnggi Do □[4]	88	37.30 N	127.15 E
Kyŏnggi-man C	88	37.25 N	126.00 E
Kyŏngju	88	35.51 N	129.14 E
Kyŏngsan	88	35.48 N	128.43 E
Kyŏngsang Namdo □[4]	88	35.15 N	128.30 E
Kyŏngsang Pukdo □[4]	88	36.15 N	128.45 E
Kyŏngsŏng, C.M.I.K.	88	41.35 N	129.36 E
Kyŏngsŏng → Sŏul, Taehan	88	37.33 N	126.58 E
Kyŏngwŏn	88	42.48 N	130.09 E
Kyŏnkadun	100	16.04 N	95.38 E

≃ River	Fluss	Río	Rivière	Rio
≍ Canal	Kanal	Canal	Canal	Canal
Waterfall, Rapids	Wasserfall, Stromschnellen	Cascada, Rápidos	Chute d'eau, Rapides	Cascata, Rápidos
⋓ Strait	Meeresstrasse	Estrecho	Détroit	Estreito
C Bay, Gulf	Bucht, Golf	Bahía, Golfo	Baie, Golfe	Baía, Golfo
⊜ Lake, Lakes	See, Seen	Lago, Lagos	Lac, Lacs	Lago, Lagos
Swamp	Sumpf	Pantano	Marais	Pântano
Ice Features, Glacier	Eis- und Gletscherformen	Accidentes Glaciales	Formes glaciaires	Acidentes Glaciares
Other Hydrographic Features	Andere Hydrographische Objekte	Otros Elementos Hidrográficos	Autres données hydrographiques	Outros Elementos Hidrográficos

✢ Submarine Features	Untermeerische Objekte	Accidentes Submarinos	Formes de relief sous-marin	Acidentes Submarinos
□ Political Unit	Politische Einheit	Unidad Politica	Entité politique	Unidade Política
⍢ Cultural Institution	Kulturelle Institution	Institución Cultural	Institution culturelle	Instituição Cultural
⊥ Historical Site	Historische Stätte	Sitio Histórico	Site historique	Sítio Histórico
♠ Recreational Site	Erholungs- und Ferienort	Sitio de Recreo	Centre de loisirs	Sítio de Lazer
⊠ Airport	Flughafen	Aeropuerto	Aéroport	Aeroporto
⊤ Military Installation	Militäranlage	Instalación Militar	Installation militaire	Instalação Militar
◆ Miscellaneous	Verschiedenes	Misceláneo	Divers	Miscelânea

Name	Page	Lat.	Long.
Kyonmange	100	16.30 N	95.50 E
Kyonpyaw	100	17.18 N	95.12 E
Kyotera	144	0.33 S	31.19 E
Kyōto	84		
	260	35.00 N	135.45 E
Kyōto □5	84	35.05 N	135.45 E
Kyōto-bonchi ⋀	260	35.03 N	135.45 E
Kyoto Race Club ▲	260	34.54 N	135.44 E
Kyoto University ʋ2	260	35.02 N	135.46 E
Kyōwa	84	36.19 N	140.03 E
Kyōyomi-dake ∧	86	33.31 N	131.02 E
Kypšak, Ozero ⊜	76	50.09 N	68.28 E
Kyra	78	49.36 N	111.58 E
Kyra ≃	78	49.27 N	112.13 E
Kyrčany	70	57.37 N	50.10 E
Kyren	78	51.41 N	102.08 E
Kyrenia → Kirínia	120	35.20 N	33.19 E
Kyritz	50	52.56 N	12.23 E
Kyrkheden	40	60.10 N	13.29 E
Kyrkkazyk	75	42.30 N	72.20 E
Kyrksæterøra	26	63.17 N	9.06 E
Kyrkslätt (Kirkkonumi)	26	60.07 N	24.26 E
Kyrö	26	60.42 N	22.45 E
Kyrönjoki ≃	26	63.14 N	21.45 E
Kyrösjärvi ⊜	26	61.45 N	23.10 E
Kyröskoski	26	61.40 N	23.11 E
Kyrta	24	64.04 N	57.42 E
Kyrykkuduk	70	49.51 N	51.54 E
Kyštovka	76	56.33 N	76.38 E
Kyštym	76	55.42 N	60.34 E
Kysykkamys	70	49.14 N	50.19 E
Kyte ≃	184	42.00 N	89.19 W
Kytlym	76	59.30 N	59.12 E
Kytmanovo	76	53.28 N	85.28 E
Kyūhōji	260	34.38 N	135.35 E
Kyūhōji ◆8	260	34.38 N	135.35 E
Kyunchaung	100	15.33 N	98.15 E
Kyundon	100	20.31 N	95.44 E
Kyungyi I	100	15.04 N	97.44 E
Kyunhla	100	23.21 N	95.18 E
Kyuquot	172	50.02 N	127.23 W
Kyuquot Sound Ш	172	50.05 N	127.15 W
Kyūroku-jima I	82	40.32 N	139.29 E
Kyū-shizudani-gakkō ⊥	86	34.45 N	134.13 E
Kyūshū I	82	33.00 N	131.00 E
Kyūshū-sanchi ⋀	82	32.35 N	131.17 E
Kywebwe	100	18.42 N	96.25 E
Kywong	156	34.59 S	146.44 E
Kyyjärvi	26	63.02 N	24.34 E
Kyzas	76	52.20 N	89.20 E
Kyzyl	78	51.42 N	94.27 E
Kyzylagačskij Zapovednik ◆4	74	39.10 N	49.00 E
Kyzylagaš	76	45.54 N	81.37 E
Kyzylaryk	75	43.57 N	70.42 E
Kyzylbejit	75	41.30 N	72.24 E
Kyzyl-Chaja	76	50.03 N	89.54 E
Kyzyl-Chem ≃	78	51.15 N	96.54 E
Kyzyl-Džar	75	41.17 N	72.02 E
Kyzylemgek	75	41.57 N	74.56 E
Kyzylespe	76	47.27 N	73.53 E
Kyzylkak, Ozero ⊜	76	53.25 N	73.48 E
Kyzyl-Kija	75	40.16 N	72.08 E
Kyzyl-Kommuna	76	48.44 N	67.32 E
Kyzylkum ◆2	62	42.00 N	64.00 E
Kyzylkup	118	40.38 N	53.58 E
Kyzyl-Mažalyk	76	51.10 N	90.32 E
Kyzyloba	70	49.37 N	50.38 E
Kyzylraj, Gora ∧	76	48.27 N	75.32 E
Kyzylsu ≃	75	39.17 N	71.23 E
Kyzyltas, Gory ⋀	76	48.30 N	74.50 E
Kyzyltau	76	47.53 N	72.05 E
Kyzylt'ob'o	75	42.13 N	75.16 E
Kyzyltu, S.S.S.R.	75	42.11 N	76.40 E
Kyzyltu, S.S.S.R.	76	47.46 N	59.08 E
Kyzyltu, S.S.S.R.	76	47.43 N	75.42 E
Kyzyluj	76	48.07 N	65.28 E
Kyzylžar	76	48.17 N	69.39 E
Kzyl-Kuga	70	48.28 N	53.01 E
Kzyl-Orda	76	44.48 N	65.28 E
Kzyl-Orda □4	75	45.00 N	65.00 E
Kzyltu	76	53.38 N	72.20 E

L

Name	Page	Lat.	Long.
La'a	92	29.44 N	101.26 E
Laa an der Thaya	30	48.43 N	16.23 E
Laab im Walde	254b	48.09 N	16.11 E
Laacher See ⊜	52	50.25 N	7.16 E
Laaerberg ∧2	254b	48.09 N	16.24 E
Laage	50	53.56 N	12.20 E
La Aguada, Zanjón de ≃	276e	33.30 S	70.47 W
La Aguja, Cabo de ≻	236	11.18 N	74.12 W
Laakajärvi ⊜	26	63.50 N	27.55 E
Laaken ◆8	253	51.15 N	7.15 E
Laakirchen	58	47.58 N	13.49 E
La Albuera	34	38.43 N	6.49 W
La Albufera ⊜	34	39.20 N	0.22 W
La Alcarria ◆1	34	40.30 N	2.45 W
La Aldea	224	20.54 N	101.29 W
La Aldehuela	256a	40.18 N	3.36 W
La Algaba	34	37.28 N	6.01 W
La Almarcha	34	39.41 N	2.22 W
La Almunia de Doña Godina	34	41.29 N	1.22 W
Laanecoorie Reservoir ⊜1	159	36.52 S	143.53 E
Laar ◆8	253	51.28 N	6.43 E
La Arena	226	7.58 N	80.28 W
Laas → Lasa	58	46.37 N	10.42 E
Laase	50	53.04 N	11.18 E
Laasphe	52	50.56 N	8.24 E
La Asunción	236	11.02 N	63.53 W
Laatzen	48	52.19 N	9.47 E
Laau Point ≻	219a	21.06 N	157.19 W
La Aurora	276e	33.36 S	70.38 W
La Azufrosa	186	28.14 N	100.50 W
Laba ≃	68	45.11 N	39.42 E
La Babia	222	28.34 N	102.04 W
L'Abacou, Pointe ≻	228	18.03 N	73.47 W
Labadie	209	38.32 N	90.51 W
Labadieville	184	29.50 N	90.57 W
La Balme-de-Sillingy	54	45.58 N	6.02 E
La Balme-les-Grottes	56	45.51 N	5.20 E
Laban	198	37.24 N	76.17 W
La Banda	242	27.44 S	64.15 W
La Bandera	276e	33.34 S	70.39 W
La Bañeza	34	42.18 N	5.54 W
La Barca	224	20.17 N	102.34 W
La Barge	190	42.16 N	110.12 W
LaBarge Creek ≃	190	42.14 N	110.10 W
La Barre-en-Ouche	46	48.57 N	0.40 E
La Barr Meadows	216	39.11 N	121.02 W
Labason	106	8.04 N	122.31 E
La Bassée	46	50.32 N	2.48 E
Labastide-Murat	32	44.39 N	1.34 E
La Bastide-Puylaurent	56	44.36 N	3.54 E
La Bâte	251	48.35 N	2.01 E
La Baule	32	47.17 N	2.24 W
La Bazoche-Gouet	46	48.08 N	0.59 E
L'Abbé	251	48.34 N	1.50 E
Labbezanga	140	14.57 N	0.42 E
Labé	140	11.19 N	12.17 W
Labé □4	140	11.23 N	12.07 W
Labe (Elbe) ≃	30	53.50 N	9.00 E
Labégude	56	44.39 N	4.22 E
La Bégude-Blanche	56	43.55 N	6.08 E
La Bégude-de-Mazenc	56	44.32 N	4.56 E
Labelle, Qué., Can.	196	46.16 N	74.44 W
La Belle, Fla., U.S.	210	26.46 N	81.26 W
La Belle, Mo., U.S.	209	40.07 N	91.55 W
Labelle □6	196	46.20 N	75.00 W
Labelle, Lac ⊜, Qué., Can.	196	46.13 N	74.52 W
La Belle, Lac ⊜, Wis., U.S.	206	43.08 N	88.31 W
Labengke, Pulau I	102	3.27 S	122.25 E
La Bérarde	56	44.56 N	6.18 E
Laberge, Lake ⊜	170	61.11 N	135.12 W
Laberinto de las Doce Leguas I	230p	20.35 N	78.30 W
La Berra ∧	54	46.41 N	7.11 E
Labes → Łobez	30	53.39 N	15.36 E
La Besace	52	49.34 N	4.58 E
Labette Creek ≃	184	37.03 N	95.05 W
Labi	102	4.25 N	114.22 E
La Biche ≃	172	55.01 N	112.44 W
Labico	60	41.47 N	12.53 E
Labin	36	45.05 N	14.07 E
Labinsk	74	44.38 N	40.44 E
Labis	104	2.23 N	103.02 E
La Bisbal	34	41.57 N	3.03 E
Łabiszyn	30	52.57 N	17.55 E
Lablābah, Wādī al- ∨	263c	30.02 N	31.19 E
La Blanca, Chile	276e	33.31 S	70.41 W
La Blanca, Méx.	224	22.40 N	102.06 W
La Blanquilla I	236	11.51 N	64.37 W
Labná ⊥	222	20.11 N	89.34 W
Labo	106	14.09 N	122.51 E
Labo ≃	106	14.11 N	122.56 E
Labo, Mount ∧	106	14.01 N	122.48 E
La Boca	224	23.56 N	99.17 W
Laboe	50	54.24 N	10.15 E
La Boissière	251	48.46 N	1.59 E
La Boissière-Ecole	251	48.41 N	1.39 E
La Bollène-Vésubie	56	43.59 N	7.20 E
La Bonneville-sur-Iton	46	49.00 N	1.02 E
Laboratory	204	40.09 N	80.13 W
Laborde, Arg.	242	33.09 S	62.51 W
La Borde, Fr.	251	48.32 N	2.50 E
Laborec ≃	30	48.31 N	21.54 E
Laborie	231f	13.45 N	61.00 W
Laborie Bay C	231f	13.45 N	61.01 W
Labouchere, Mount ∧	152	25.12 S	118.18 E
Labouheyre	32	44.13 N	0.55 W
Laboulaye	242	34.07 S	63.24 W
La Bouverie	46	50.24 N	3.52 E
La Boyera, Ven.	276c	10.25 N	66.50 W
La Boyera, Ven.	276c	10.23 N	66.57 W
Lābpur	116	23.50 N	87.49 E
Labrador ◆1	166	54.00 N	62.00 W
Labrador Basin ⊹1	16	54.00 N	47.00 W
Labrador City	166	52.57 N	66.55 W
Labrador Sea ⊤2	166	57.00 N	53.00 W
Lábrea, Bra.	238	7.16 S	64.47 W
La Brea, Trin.	231r	10.15 N	61.37 W
Labrède	32	44.41 N	0.31 W
La Bresse	54	48.00 N	6.53 E
La Brévine	54	46.59 N	6.36 E
Labrieville, Parc de ▲	176	49.20 N	69.40 W
La Brigue-de-Nice	56	44.04 N	7.37 E
La Brillanne	56	43.55 N	5.53 E
Labrit	32	44.07 N	0.33 W
La Broquerie	174	49.28 N	96.27 W
Labroye	46	50.17 N	1.59 E
Labry	52	49.10 N	5.52 E
Labuan, Pulau I	102	5.21 N	115.13 E
Labuchongshan ⋀	110	30.30 N	85.00 E
Labuha	154	0.37 S	127.29 E
Labuhan	105a	6.22 S	105.50 E
Labuhanbajo	105b	8.29 S	119.54 E
Labuhanbatu	104	2.12 N	100.12 E
Labuhanbilik	104	2.31 N	100.10 E
Labuhanhaji, Indon.	104	3.33 N	97.00 E
Labuhanhaji, Indon.	105b	8.42 S	116.34 E
Labuhanmarege	102	7.06 S	120.40 E
Labuhanmaringgai	105a	5.21 S	105.48 E
Labuhanpandan	105b	8.23 S	116.43 E
Labuhanruku	104	3.13 N	99.35 E
Labuhanwaiharu	102	5.44 S	104.26 E
Labuk ≃	102	5.54 N	117.30 E
Labuk, Teluk C	102	6.07 N	117.46 E
Labu Kananga	105b	8.08 S	117.47 E
Labutta	100	16.09 N	94.46 E
Labytnangi	62	66.39 N	66.21 E
Laç, Shq.	38	41.38 N	19.43 E
Lač, S.S.S.R.	24	63.18 N	54.28 E
Lac □5	136	13.30 N	14.15 E
Lača, Ozero ⊜	24	61.20 N	38.48 E
La Cadena	186	25.53 N	104.12 W
L'Acadie	265a	45.19 N	73.21 W
L'Acadie ≃	196	45.29 N	73.16 W
La Cadière-d'Azur	56	43.12 N	5.46 E
Lacadivas, Islas → Laccadive Islands II	112	10.00 N	73.00 E
La Cal ≃	238	17.27 S	58.15 W
Lac-à-la-Tortue	196	46.37 N	72.38 W
La Calera, Chile	242	32.47 S	71.12 W
La Calera, Perú	276d	12.12 S	76.54 W
Lac Allard	176	50.38 N	63.28 W
Lacamas Creek ≃	214	46.20 N	122.55 W
Lacamas Lake ⊜	214	45.37 N	122.26 W
La Campana, Esp.	34	37.34 N	5.26 W
La Campana, Méx.	224	22.45 N	105.35 W
La Cañada, Méx.	224	20.37 N	100.19 W
La Canada, Calif., U.S.	218	34.12 N	118.12 W
La Canada Verde Creek ≃	270	33.52 N	118.02 W
Lacanau	32	44.59 N	1.05 W
Lacanau, Étang de C	32	44.58 N	1.07 E
La Candelaria, Arg.	242	26.06 S	65.06 W
La Candelaria, Méx.	190	31.07 N	106.29 W
La Candelaria, Méx.	276a	19.20 N	99.09 W
La Cañiza	34	42.13 N	8.16 W
La Canourgue	32	44.26 N	3.13 E
Lacantum ≃	222	16.36 N	90.39 W
La Capelle-en-Thiérache	46	49.58 N	3.55 E
La Capelle-lès-Boulogne	46	50.44 N	1.42 E
Lacapelle-Marival	32	44.44 N	1.54 E
La Capilla, Méx.	224	18.30 N	96.40 W
La Capilla, Méx.	224	23.59 N	98.25 W
La Carlota, Arg.	242	33.26 S	63.18 W
La Carlota, Pil.	106	10.25 N	122.55 E
La Carlota, Aeropuerto ⊠	276c	10.29 N	66.50 W
Lacarne	204	41.31 N	83.03 W
La Carolina	34	38.15 N	3.37 W
La Casita	224	23.43 N	104.46 W
La Castellana	106	10.20 N	123.03 E
La Castrina, Aeropuerto ⊠	276e	33.31 S	70.38 W
Lacaune	32	43.43 N	2.42 E
La Cavalerie	32	44.00 N	3.10 E
Lac-Bellemare	196	46.34 N	72.55 W
Lac-Brome	196	45.13 N	72.31 W
Laccadive, Minicoy, and Amīndīvi → Lakshadweep □3	112	10.00 N	73.00 E
Laccadive Islands II	112	10.00 N	73.00 E
Laccadive Sea ⊤2	12	7.00 N	76.00 E
Lacchiarella	56	45.19 N	9.08 E
Lacco Ameno	60	40.45 N	13.54 E
Lac Courte Oreilles Indian Reservation ◆4	180	45.55 N	91.19 W
Lac du Flambeau	180	45.58 N	89.53 W
Lac du Flambeau Indian Reservation ◆4	180	45.59 N	89.53 W
Lacedonia	60	41.03 N	15.25 E
La Ceiba, Hond.	226	15.47 N	86.50 W
La Ceiba, Ven.	236	9.28 N	71.04 W
La Celle-les-Bordes	251	48.38 N	1.57 E
La Celle-Saint-Cyr	46	47.58 N	3.18 E
La Center, Ky., U.S.	184	37.04 N	88.58 W
La Center, Wash., U.S.	214	45.52 N	122.40 W
Lacepede Bay C	156	36.47 S	139.45 E
Lacerdónia	146	18.01 S	35.30 E
Laces (Latsch)	58	46.37 N	10.52 E
Lac-Etchemin	176	46.24 N	70.30 W
Lacey	214	47.07 N	122.49 W
Lacey Creek ≃	268	41.50 N	88.03 W
Laceyville	200	41.39 N	76.10 W
Lac-Frontière	176	46.42 N	70.00 W
Lac-giao	100	12.40 N	108.03 E
La Chaise-Dieu	56	45.19 N	3.42 E
La Chambre	56	45.22 N	6.18 E
La Chapelle-d'Angillon	46	47.22 N	2.26 E
La Chapelle-en-Vercors	56	44.58 N	5.25 E
La Chapelle-Gauthier	251	48.33 N	2.54 E
La Chapelle-la-Reine	46	48.19 N	2.35 E
La Chapelle-Saint-Mesmin	46	47.53 N	1.50 E
La Chapelle-Vendômoise	46	47.40 N	1.15 E
La Charité-sur-Loire	46	47.11 N	3.01 E
La Chartre-sur-le-Loir	46	47.44 N	0.35 E
La Châtaigneraie	32	46.39 N	0.44 W
La Châtre	32	46.35 N	1.59 E
Lachaussée, Étang de ⊜	52	49.02 N	5.48 E
La Chaux-de-Fonds	54	47.06 N	6.50 E
Lachay, Punta ≻	238	11.18 S	77.39 W
Lach Dennis	252	53.15 N	2.26 W
Lachdenpochja	24	61.31 N	30.08 E
Lachen	54	47.12 N	8.51 E
Lachendorf	48	52.37 N	10.14 E
Lachhmangarh Sīkar	110	27.49 N	75.02 E
L'achi	70	55.20 N	41.56 E
Lachine	196	45.26 N	73.40 W
Lachine, Canal de Ξ	265a	45.26 N	73.40 W
Lachine, Rapides de ↳	265a	45.25 N	73.36 W
La Chira, Punta ≻	276d	12.13 S	77.03 W
La Chivera	276c	10.37 N	66.54 W
Lachkaltsap Indian Reserve ◆4	172	55.03 N	129.34 W
Lachlan ≃	156	34.21 S	143.57 E
La Chorrera, Col.	236	0.44 S	73.01 W
La Chorrera, Pan.	226	8.53 N	79.47 W
L'achoviči, S.S.S.R.	66	52.23 N	27.55 E
L'achoviči, S.S.S.R.	66	53.02 N	26.16 E
L'achovskije Ostrova II	64	73.30 N	141.00 E
La Choza	248	34.47 S	59.07 W
La Choza, Arroyo ≃	248	34.40 S	58.58 W
Lachta ◆8	255a	60.00 N	30.09 E
Lachtinskij Razliv, Ozero ⊜	255a	60.00 N	30.11 E
Lachute	196	45.38 N	74.20 W
Lachva	68	52.13 N	27.04 E
La Ciénaga	242	27.30 S	66.57 W
La Ciénega	224	16.54 N	96.46 W
La Cinta Creek ≃	186	35.24 N	104.06 W
La Ciotat	56	43.10 N	5.36 E
La Cisterna	276e	33.33 S	70.41 W
La Citadelle ⊥	228	19.35 N	72.14 W
La Ciudad, Parque Nacional ▲	224	23.55 N	105.35 W
Lackawanna	200	42.49 N	78.50 W
Lackawanna □6	200	41.24 N	75.40 W
Lackawanna ≃	200	41.21 N	75.47 W
Lackawanna, Lake ⊜	266	40.57 N	74.42 W
Lackawanna State Park ▲	200	41.33 N	75.44 W
Lackawaxen	200	41.29 N	74.59 W
Lackawaxen ≃	200	41.29 N	74.59 W
Lackey	198	37.14 N	76.33 W
Lackland Air Force Base ■	186	29.27 N	98.37 W
Läckö	26	58.41 N	13.13 E
Lackoje	66	58.05 N	38.08 E
Lac La Belle	206	43.09 N	88.32 W
Lac la Biche	172	54.46 N	111.58 W
Lac la Hache	172	51.49 N	121.28 W
Lac la Ronge Provincial Park ▲	174	55.14 N	104.45 W
La Clayette	32	46.18 N	4.19 E
Laclede, Idaho, U.S.	172	49.58 N	116.45 W
La Clede, Ill., U.S.	209	38.53 N	88.43 W
Laclede, Mo., U.S.	184	39.47 N	93.10 W
La Clotilde	242	27.08 S	60.40 W
La Clusaz	56	45.54 N	6.25 E
La Cluse	54	46.10 N	5.34 E
La Cluse-et-Mijoux	54	46.53 N	6.23 E
Lacmalac	161b	35.19 S	148.19 E
Lac-Masson	196	46.02 N	74.04 W
Lac-Mégantic	178	45.36 N	70.53 W
Lacob ti-duyong, Mount ∧	106	17.35 N	121.09 E
La Cocha	242	27.47 S	65.34 W
La Cocha, Laguna de ⊜	236	1.05 N	77.09 W
Lacolle	196	45.05 N	73.22 W
Lacolle ≃	196	45.04 N	73.20 W
La Colle-sur-Loup	56	43.41 N	7.06 E
La Colmena	276a	19.36 N	99.18 W
La Colorada	222	28.41 N	110.25 W
La Columna → Bolívar, Pico ∧	236	8.30 N	71.02 W
Lacombe	172	52.28 N	113.44 W
Lacon	180	41.02 N	89.24 W
Lacona, Iowa, U.S.	180	41.12 N	93.23 W
Lacona, N.Y., U.S.	202	43.39 N	76.04 W
La Concepción, Méx.	224	18.15 N	102.27 W
La Concepción, Ven.	236	10.38 N	71.50 W
La Concordia	224	16.05 N	92.38 W
La Condamine-Châtelard	56	44.27 N	6.45 E
Laconia	178	43.31 N	71.29 W
La Conner	214	48.23 N	122.30 W
La Consulta	242	33.44 S	69.07 W
Lacoochee	210	28.28 N	82.10 W
La Coruña	34	43.22 N	8.23 W
Lacoste, Fr.	56	43.50 N	5.18 E
La Coste, Tex., U.S.	186	29.19 N	98.49 W
La Côte-Saint-André	56	45.23 N	5.15 E
La Courneuve	251	48.56 N	2.23 E
La Couronne	56	43.20 N	5.03 E
La Courtine	32	45.42 N	2.16 E
Lac qui Parle ≃	188	45.01 N	95.53 W
Lac qui Parle, West Branch ≃	188	44.55 N	96.02 W
La Crau	56	43.09 N	6.04 E
Lacre Punt ≻	231s	12.02 N	68.15 W
La Crescent	180	43.50 N	91.19 W
La Crescenta	218	34.12 N	118.12 W
La Creu	256d	41.32 N	2.07 E
La Croft	204	40.39 N	80.35 W
Lacroix-Saint-Ouen	46	49.21 N	2.47 E
La Crosse, Ind., U.S.	206	41.19 N	86.53 W
La Crosse, Kans., U.S.	188	38.32 N	99.18 W
La Crosse, Va., U.S.	182	36.42 N	78.06 W
Lacrosse, Wash., U.S.	192	46.49 N	117.53 W
La Crosse, Wis., U.S.	180	43.49 N	91.15 W
La Crosse ≃	180	43.49 N	91.16 W
La Cruz, Arg.	242	29.10 S	56.38 W
La Cruz, Col.	236	1.35 N	76.58 W
La Cruz, C.R.	226	11.04 N	85.39 W
La Cruz, Méx.	186	28.33 N	100.48 W
La Cruz, Ur.	248	33.56 S	56.15 W
La Cruz de Río Grande	226	13.06 N	84.10 W
Lac-Saguay	196	46.30 N	75.09 W
Lac Seul	174	50.20 N	92.16 W
Lac Seul Indian Reserve ◆4	174	50.15 N	92.10 W
La Cuchilla	224	18.54 N	103.19 W
La Cuesta, C.R.	226	8.30 N	82.50 W
La Cuesta, Méx.	224	20.10 N	104.51 W
La Cuesta, P.R.	230m	18.25 N	66.49 W
La Culebra, Cerro ∧	224	21.43 N	102.45 W
La Cumbre, Arg.	242	30.58 S	64.30 W
La Cumbre, Ven.	276c	10.32 N	66.57 W
La Cure	54	46.28 N	6.05 E
Lacy Fork ≃	212	32.24 N	96.08 W
La Cygne	188	38.21 N	94.46 W
Lacy-Lakeview	212	31.37 N	97.06 W
Lada, Teluk C	105a	6.29 S	105.44 E
Ladainha	245	17.39 S	41.44 W
Ladākh Range ⋀	110	34.00 N	78.00 E
Ladan	68	50.31 N	32.35 E
La Dang, Ko I	104	6.33 N	99.18 E
Ladang Jagor	104	4.42 N	101.35 E
Ladário	238	19.01 S	57.35 W
Ladbergen	48	52.08 N	7.44 E
Ladby	41	55.26 N	10.38 E
Ladd	180	41.23 N	89.13 W
Ladder Creek ≃	188	38.48 N	100.52 W
Laddingford	250	51.12 N	0.25 E
Laddonia	209	39.15 N	91.39 W
Ladeburg	254a	52.42 N	13.35 E
La Défense ʋ	251	48.53 N	2.15 E
La Dehesa	276e	33.22 S	70.33 W
La Dent d'Oche ∧	54	46.21 N	6.44 E
Ladera Heights	270	33.59 N	118.22 W
Ladesi	90	33.33 N	115.53 E
La Désirade I	231o	16.19 N	61.03 W
Ládhi	38	41.27 N	26.17 E
Ladhu I	165f	15.07 S	167.08 E
Ladhurka	116	23.22 N	86.32 E
La Digue I	128	4.21 S	55.50 E
Lâdik	120	40.55 N	35.55 E
L'adiny	24	61.33 N	38.20 E
Ladismith	148	33.30 S	21.16 E
Ladispoli	60	41.56 N	12.05 E
Lādīz	118	28.56 N	61.19 E
Ladner	172	49.05 N	123.05 W
Lādnun	110	27.39 N	74.23 E
Ladoga	184	39.55 N	86.48 W
Ladoga, Lake → Ladožskoje Ozero ⊜	24	61.00 N	31.30 E
La Dolorita	276c	10.29 N	66.47 W
Ladon	46	48.00 N	2.32 E
Ladonia	186	33.25 N	95.57 W
La Dorada	236	5.27 N	74.40 W
La Dormida	242	33.21 S	67.55 W
Lado Sarāi ◆8	262a	28.32 N	77.12 E
L'adova ≃	68	48.28 N	27.37 E
Ladovskaja Balka	70	45.38 N	41.25 E
Ladožskaja	68	45.19 N	39.54 E
Ladožskoje Ozero	66	60.08 N	30.01 E
Ladožskoje Ozero (Lake Ladoga) ⊜	24	61.00 N	31.30 E
Lādpur ◆8	262a	28.44 N	76.59 E
Ladrillero, Golfo C	244	49.20 S	75.37 W
Ladue ≃	170	63.09 N	140.25 W
Laduozong	92	31.27 N	97.19 E
Laduškin	66	54.36 N	20.11 E
Ladva	24	61.21 N	34.34 E
Ladva-Vetka	24	61.21 N	34.27 E
Ladvozero	24	65.00 N	29.50 E
Lādwa	114	29.59 N	77.03 E
Lady, Fr.	251	48.35 N	2.54 E
L'ady, S.S.S.R.	66	58.38 N	28.47 E
L'ady, S.S.S.R.	66	54.36 N	31.10 E
Lady Ann Strait Ш	166	75.40 N	79.50 W
Lady Barron	156	40.12 S	148.14 E
Ladybrand	148	29.19 S	27.25 E
Lady Elliot Island I	156	24.07 S	152.42 E
Lady Evelyn Lake ⊜	180	47.20 N	80.10 W
Lady Frere	148	31.44 S	27.16 E
Lady Grey	148	30.45 S	27.13 E
Lady Lake	210	28.55 N	81.55 W
Ladysmith, Austl.	161b	35.12 S	147.31 E
Ladysmith, B.C., Can.	172	48.58 N	123.49 W
Ladysmith, S. Afr.	148	28.34 S	29.45 E
Ladysmith, Wis., U.S.	180	45.28 N	91.12 W
Ladyženka	76	51.00 N	68.42 E
Ladyžin	68	48.41 N	29.15 E
Ladžanurges	74	42.37 N	42.50 E
Lae	154	6.45 S	147.00 E
Lae I1	14	8.56 N	166.14 E
Laem, Khao ∧	100	14.27 N	101.30 E
Laem Ngop	100	12.10 N	102.26 E
La Encantada	242	27.05 S	65.13 W
La Encantada, Cerro de ∧	222	31.00 N	115.24 W
La Encarnacion	224	23.23 N	98.01 W
Laer	48	52.03 N	7.21 E
Laer ◆8	253	51.28 N	7.16 E
Lærdalsøyri	26	61.06 N	7.29 E
La Escondida, Méx.	186	26.17 N	99.46 W
La Escondida, Méx.	222	25.40 N	98.18 W
La Esmeralda, Méx.	222	27.17 N	103.39 W
La Esmeralda, Para.	242	22.13 S	62.38 W
Læsø I	26	57.16 N	11.01 E
La Esperanza, Cuba	230p	22.27 N	80.06 W
La Esperanza, Cuba	230p	22.46 N	83.44 W
La Esperanza, Hond.	226	14.20 N	88.10 W
La Esperanza, Méx.	186	26.46 N	104.00 W
La Esperanza, Méx.	190	32.06 N	114.47 W
La Esperanza, P.R.	230m	18.22 N	66.07 W
La Esperanza ◆8	276b	23.03 N	82.22 W
La Estación	256d	41.34 N	2.14 E
La Estación ◆8	256a	40.27 N	3.48 W
La Estancia	224	18.05 N	101.25 W
La Estrada	34	42.41 N	8.29 W
La Estrella, Bol.	238	16.30 S	63.45 W
La Estrella, Chile	242	34.12 S	71.40 W
La Estrella, Col.	236	6.10 N	75.39 W
La Estrella, Ven.	276c	10.25 N	66.48 W
Lafa	79	43.50 N	127.19 E
La Falda	242	31.05 S	64.30 W
La Farge	180	43.35 N	90.38 W
LaFargeville	202	44.12 N	75.58 W
Lafayette, Fr.	56	45.35 N	5.04 E
Lafayette, Ala., U.S.	184	32.54 N	85.24 W
Lafayette, Calif., U.S.	216	37.54 N	122.07 W
Lafayette, Colo., U.S.	188	40.00 N	105.05 W
Lafayette, Ga., U.S.	182	34.42 N	85.17 W
Lafayette, Ind., U.S.	206	40.25 N	86.53 W
Lafayette, La., U.S.	184	30.14 N	92.01 W
Lafayette, Minn., U.S.	180	44.27 N	94.24 W
Lafayette, N.J., U.S.	200	41.06 N	74.41 W
La Fayette, N.Y., U.S.	200	42.54 N	76.06 W
La Fayette, Ohio, U.S.	206	40.46 N	83.57 W
Lafayette, Oreg., U.S.	214	45.15 N	123.07 W
La Fayette, R.I., U.S.	197	41.34 N	71.29 W
Lafayette, Tenn., U.S.	184	36.32 N	86.01 W
La Fayette, Tex., U.S.	212	32.54 N	94.51 W
Lafayette, Mount ∧	178	44.10 N	71.38 W
Lafayette Hill	275	40.05 N	75.15 W
Lafayette Reservoir ⊜1	272	37.53 N	122.08 W
Lafayette Water Tunnel ◆5	272	37.54 N	122.12 W
La Fère	46	49.40 N	3.22 E
La Feria	186	26.09 N	97.50 W
Laferrere	278	34.45 S	58.35 W
La Ferrière-sur-Risle	46	48.59 N	0.48 E
La Ferté-Alais	46	48.29 N	2.21 E
La Ferté-Bernard	46	48.11 N	0.40 E
La Ferté-Frênel	46	48.50 N	0.30 E
La Ferté-Gaucher	46	48.47 N	3.18 E
La Ferté-Macé	32	48.36 N	0.22 W
La Ferté-Milon	46	49.10 N	3.07 E
La Ferté-Saint-Aubin	46	47.43 N	1.56 E
La Ferté-sous-Jouarre	46	48.57 N	3.08 E
Laferté-sur-Amance	54	47.50 N	5.42 E
La Ferté-Vidame	46	48.37 N	0.55 E
La Ferté-Villeneuil	46	47.59 N	1.21 E
Lafferty	204	40.07 N	81.01 W
Laffrey	56	45.02 N	5.46 E
Lafia	140	8.30 N	8.30 E
Lafiagi	140	8.52 N	5.25 E
Laflamme ≃	180	48.56 N	77.18 W
Laflèche, Qué., Can.	265a	45.30 N	73.28 W
Laflèche, Sask., Can.	174	49.43 N	106.35 W
La Flèche, Fr.	32	47.42 N	0.05 W

ENGLISH

Name	Page	Lat.°′	Long.°′
La Flor	226	11.30 N	84.21 W
La Floresta	256d	41.27 N	2.04 E
La Florida, Chile	276e	33.33 S	70.34 W
La Florida, Esp.	256d	41.31 N	2.12 E
La Florida, Guat.	222	16.33 N	90.27 W
Lafnitz ≃	30	46.57 N	16.16 E
La Foa	165f	21.43 S	165.50 E
La Foce	56	44.08 N	9.47 E
La Follette	182	36.23 N	84.07 W
Lafon	144	5.02 N	32.27 E
Lafontaine, Qué., Can.	196	45.48 N	74.01 W
La Fontaine, Ind., U.S.	206	40.40 N	85.43 W
Lafontaine, Parc ▲	265a	45.32 N	73.34 W
La Forteleza, Río de ≃	238	10.40 S	77.52 W
La Fortuna	226	10.30 N	84.35 W
Lafourche, Bayou ≃	184	29.05 N	90.14 W
La Foux, Fr.	56	44.17 N	6.34 E
La Foux, Fr.	56	43.16 N	6.35 E
La Fragua	242	26.05 S	64.20 W
La Francia	242	31.24 S	62.38 W
La Fregeneda	34	40.59 N	6.52 W
La Frette-sur-Seine	251	48.58 N	2.11 E
La Fría	236	8.13 N	72.15 W
Lafrimbolle	54	48.36 N	7.01 E
La Fuente de San Esteban	34	40.48 N	6.15 W
Laga, Monti della ⋀	60	42.37 N	13.24 E
Lagaip ≃	154	5.05 S	142.40 E
La Galite I	138	37.32 N	8.56 E
La Gallareta	242	29.34 S	60.23 W
La Gallega	34	41.54 N	3.16 W
Lagan	26	56.55 N	13.59 E
Lagan ≃, Sve.	26	56.33 N	12.56 E
Lagan ≃, N. Ire., U.K.	42	54.37 N	5.53 W
Lagangzong	110	28.05 N	91.04 E
Lagantu	92	42.20 N	108.22 E
La Garde	56	43.07 N	6.01 E
La Garde-Freinet	56	43.19 N	6.28 E
La Garenne-Colombes	251	48.55 N	2.15 E
Lagarina, Val ∨	58	45.50 N	11.10 E
La Garita	224	19.43 N	103.10 W
Lagarto, Bra.	240	10.54 S	37.41 W
Lagarto, C.R.	226	10.07 N	84.56 W
Lagarto Creek ≃	186	28.08 N	97.56 W
Lagay	106	14.06 N	122.12 E
Lagayan	106	17.43 N	120.42 E
Lage, B.R.D.	48	51.59 N	8.48 E
Lage, Esp.	34	43.13 N	9.00 W
Lage, Zhg.	110	29.26 N	85.51 E
Lagechi ⊜	114	30.42 N	81.16 E
Lagedu	92	26.24 N	101.11 E
Lågen ≃, Nor.	26	61.08 N	10.25 E
Lågen ≃, Nor.	26	59.03 N	10.05 E
Lägerdorf	48	53.53 N	9.34 E
Lageuen	104	4.44 N	95.31 E
Lage Zwaluwe	48	51.43 N	4.41 E
Laggan Bay C	42	55.40 N	6.20 W
Lagginhorn ∧	54	46.11 N	8.01 E
Laghmān □4	110	35.00 N	70.15 E
Laghouat	138	33.50 N	2.59 E
Lagič	74	40.51 N	48.24 E
La Giettaz	56	45.52 N	6.30 E
La Giustiniana ◆8	257a	41.59 N	12.24 E
La Gleize	52	50.25 N	5.51 E
La Gloria	236	8.37 N	73.48 W
La Gloria, Bahía C	230p	21.50 N	77.40 W
Lagnieu	54	45.54 N	5.21 E
Lagny, Fr.	32	49.37 N	2.55 E
Lagny, Fr.	46	48.52 N	2.43 E
Lagny-le-Sec	251	49.05 N	2.45 E
Lago, Mount ∧	214	48.51 N	120.32 W
Lagoa	246	23.18 S	45.36 W
Lagoa Branca	246	21.54 S	47.02 W
Lagoa da Prata	245	20.01 S	45.33 W
Lagoa dos Gatos	240	8.39 S	35.54 W
Lagoa Dourada	245	20.55 S	44.05 W
Lagoa Formosa	245	18.47 S	46.24 W
Lago Argentino → Calafate	244	50.20 S	72.18 W
Lagoa Santa	245	19.38 S	43.53 W
Lagoa Vermelha	242	28.13 S	51.32 W
Lago Blanco	244	45.55 S	71.15 W
Lago da Pedra	240	4.20 S	45.10 W
Lago de Camécuaro, Parque Nacional ▲	224	19.51 N	102.18 W
Lagodechi	74	41.49 N	46.18 E
Lagodechskij Zapovednik ▲	74	41.53 N	46.22 E
Lago Futalaufquen	244	42.53 S	71.37 W
Lagoinha	246	23.06 S	45.11 W
Lagolândia	245	15.37 S	49.02 W
Lagolovo	255a	59.42 N	30.00 E
La Gomera	226	14.05 N	91.03 W
Lagonegro	36	40.07 N	15.46 E
Lagonglong	106	8.48 N	124.47 E
Lagonoy	106	13.44 N	123.31 E
Lagonoy Gulf C	106	13.35 N	123.45 E
Lago Posadas	244	47.32 S	71.45 W
Lagorai, Catena del ⋀	58	46.18 N	11.35 E
La Gorgue	46	50.38 N	2.42 E
Lagos, Ang.	142	16.04 S	17.03 E
Lagos, Nig.	140		
	263a	6.27 N	3.24 E
Lagos, Port.	34	37.06 N	8.40 W
Lagos □8	140	6.30 N	3.30 E
Lagos (Ikeja) Airport ⊠	263a	6.35 N	3.20 E
Lagos, University of ʋ2	263a	6.32 N	3.24 E
Lagosanto	60	44.46 N	12.08 E
Lagos de Moreno	224	21.21 N	101.55 W
Lagos Harbour C	263a	6.26 N	3.24 E
Lagos Island I	263a	6.27 N	3.26 E
Lagos Lagoon C	263a	6.30 N	3.26 E
Lagos Terminus ◆5	263a	6.28 N	3.23 E
La Goulette	138	36.49 N	10.18 E
Lago Viedma	244	49.48 S	72.07 W
La Grand Baie C	265a	45.29 N	74.00 W
La Grand'Combe	56	44.13 N	4.02 E
La Grande	192	45.20 N	118.05 W
La Grande ≃	166	53.50 N	79.00 W
La Grande Anse C	231o	16.19 N	61.48 W
La Grande Moucherolle ∧	56	45.00 N	5.34 E
La Grange, Austl.	152	18.41 S	121.45 E
LaGrange, Calif., U.S.	216	37.40 N	120.28 W
La Grange, Ga., U.S.	182	33.02 N	85.02 W
La Grange, Ill., U.S.	206	41.49 N	87.55 W
Lagrange, Ind., U.S.	206	41.39 N	85.25 W
La Grange, Ky., U.S.	208	38.24 N	85.23 W
La Grange, Maine, U.S.	178	45.10 N	68.51 W
La Grange, Mo., U.S.	209	40.03 N	91.35 W
La Grange, N.C., U.S.	182	35.19 N	77.47 W
Lagrange, Ohio, U.S.	204	41.14 N	82.07 W
La Grange, Tex., U.S.	212	29.54 N	96.52 W
Lagrange, Wyo., U.S.	188	41.38 N	104.10 W
Lagrange □6	206	41.39 N	85.25 W
Lagrange Bay C	152	18.38 S	121.42 E
La Grange Highlands	268	41.48 N	87.53 W
La Grange Lock and Dam ◆5	209	39.57 N	90.32 W
La Grange Park	268	41.50 N	87.52 W
Lagrangeville	200	41.39 N	73.46 W
La Granja	276e	33.32 S	70.39 W
La Gran Sabana ≚	236	5.30 N	61.30 W
La Grave	56	45.03 N	6.18 E
La Grita	236	8.08 N	71.59 W
Lagro	206	40.50 N	85.44 W
La Groise	46	50.05 N	3.41 E
La Grue Bayou ≃	184	34.05 N	91.10 W
Lagu	92	26.26 N	101.30 E
La Guadalupe	224	17.34 N	95.17 W
La Guadeloupe (Saint Evariste)	178	45.57 N	70.56 W

DEUTSCH

Name	Seite	Breite°′	Länge°′ E=Ost
La Guaira	236		
	276c	10.36 N	66.56 W
La Guajira □5	236	11.30 N	72.30 W
La Guajira, Península de ≻1	236	12.00 N	71.40 W
La Guardia, Arg.	242	29.33 S	65.27 W
La Guardia, Bol.	238	17.54 S	63.20 W
La Guardia, Esp.	34	41.54 N	8.53 W
Laguardia, Esp.	34	42.33 N	2.35 W
La Guardia Airport ⊠	200	40.46 N	73.53 W
Lagubu	114	29.08 N	87.14 E
La Gudiña	34	42.04 N	7.08 W
La Guêpière	251	48.35 N	1.50 E
La Guerche-de-Britagne	32	47.56 N	1.14 W
La Guerche-sur-l'Aubois	32	46.57 N	2.57 E
Laguiole	32	44.41 N	2.51 E
Laguna, Bra.	242	28.29 S	48.47 W
Laguna, N. Mex., U.S.	190	35.02 N	107.23 W
Laguna □4	106	14.10 N	121.20 E
Laguna ≃, Bra.	240	1.17 S	50.50 W
Laguna ≃, Calif., U.S.	216	38.16 N	121.23 W
Laguna, Ilha da I	240	1.40 S	51.00 W
Laguna Beach	218	33.33 N	117.51 W
Laguna Blanca	230p	20.27 N	76.07 W
Laguna Carapã	245	22.27 S	55.01 W
Laguna Creek ≃	190	36.54 N	109.45 W
Laguna Dam ◆6	190	32.50 N	114.31 W
Laguna de Jaco	222	27.50 N	104.00 W
Laguna Hills	218	33.37 N	117.43 W
Laguna Indian Reservation ◆4	190	35.00 N	107.20 W
Laguna Lake ⊜	216	35.16 S	120.42 W
Laguna Larga	242	31.46 S	63.48 W
Laguna Limpia	242	26.29 S	59.41 W
Laguna Park	212	31.52 N	97.23 W
Lagunas	238	5.14 S	75.38 W
Lagundo	58	46.41 N	11.08 E
Lagunillas, Bol.	238	19.38 S	63.43 W
Lagunillas, Méx.	224	21.34 N	99.35 W
Lagunillas → Ciudad Ojeda, Ven.	236	10.12 N	71.19 W
Lagunillas, Ven.	236	8.31 N	71.24 W
Lagunillás, Lago ⊜	238	15.44 S	70.43 W
Laguntara C	226	15.12 N	83.30 W
L'agušje	76	54.24 N	77.59 E
Laguyu	94	41.43 N	123.49 E
Laha	79	48.10 N	124.39 E
La Habana (Havana)	230p		
	276b	23.08 N	82.22 W
La Habana □4	230p	22.45 N	82.10 W
La Habana, Bahía de C	276b	23.08 N	82.20 W
La Habana, Universidad de ʋ2	276b	23.08 N	82.22 W
La Habra	218	33.56 N	117.57 W
La Habra Heights	270	33.57 N	117.57 W
Lahad Datu	102	5.02 N	118.19 E
Lahaina	219a	20.52 N	156.41 W
Laham	102	0.22 N	115.24 E
Lahār	114	26.12 N	78.57 E
La Harpe, Ill., U.S.	180	40.35 N	90.58 W
La Harpe, Kans., U.S.	188	37.55 N	95.18 W
Lāharpur	114	27.43 N	80.54 E
Lahaska	198	40.21 N	75.02 W
Lahat, Indon.	102	3.48 S	103.32 E
Lahat, Malay.	104	4.33 N	101.02 E
Lahaul and Spiti □5	113	32.40 N	77.15 E
La Hauteville	251	48.42 N	1.37 E
La Havane → La Habana	230p	23.08 N	82.22 W
La Have ≃	176	44.14 N	64.20 W
La Have Islands II	176	44.12 N	64.23 W
La Haye → 's-Gravenhage	48	52.06 N	4.18 E
La Haye-du-Puits	32	49.18 N	1.33 W
La Häy-les-Roses	251	48.47 N	2.21 E
Lähden	48	52.45 N	7.34 E
Lāhe	100	26.20 N	95.26 E
Laheria Sarai	114	26.07 N	85.54 E
Lahewa	104	1.24 N	97.11 E
Lahfān, Bi'r ⊤4	122	31.01 N	33.52 E
Lahi, Ava Ш	164w	21.02 S	175.11 W
La Higuera	242	29.30 S	71.17 W
Laḥij	134	13.02 N	44.54 E
Lāhījān	118	37.12 N	50.01 E
Lāhitah	122	32.59 N	36.35 E
Lähn → Wleń	30	51.01 N	15.40 E
Lahn ≃	52	50.18 N	7.37 E
Laholm	26	56.31 N	13.02 E
Laholmsbukten C	26	56.35 N	12.50 E
La Honda	216	37.19 N	122.16 W
La Honda Creek ≃	272	37.18 N	122.16 W
Lahontan Reservoir ⊜1	216	39.23 N	119.09 W
Lahontan State Recreation Area ▲	216	39.28 N	119.03 W
Lahor → Lahore, Pāk.	113	31.35 N	74.18 E
Lāhor, Pāk.	113	34.03 N	72.22 E
Lahore	113	31.35 N	74.18 E
La Horqueta	236	3.06 N	72.50 W
La Horqueta, Arroyo ≃	278	34.41 S	58.51 W
La Houssaye-en-Brie	251	48.45 N	2.53 E
Lahr	54	48.20 N	7.52 E
Lahri	110	29.11 N	68.13 E
Lahṭah, Wādī ∨	132	29.44 N	32.45 E
Lahti	26	60.58 N	25.40 E
La Huaca	238	4.54 S	80.57 W
La Huacana	224	18.58 N	101.49 W
La Huerta	224	19.28 N	104.39 W
La Hunière	251	48.36 N	1.52 E
Lahuy Island I	106	13.56 N	123.50 E
Laï	136	9.24 N	16.18 E
Laiagam	154	5.30 S	143.20 E
Laian	90	32.27 N	118.25 E
Laibach → Ljubljana	36	46.03 N	14.31 E
Laibin	92	23.42 N	109.22 E
Lai-chau	100	22.02 N	103.10 E
Laichingen	54	48.29 N	9.41 E
Laichow Bay → Laizhouwan C	88	37.36 N	119.30 E
Laidley	161a	27.38 S	152.24 E
Laidley Creek ≃	161a	27.31 S	152.24 E
Laie	219c	21.39 N	157.56 W
Laifang	90	25.56 N	116.54 E
Laifeng	92	29.31 N	109.15 E
Laifengchang	97	30.14 N	105.17 E
Laifengyi	97	29.26 N	106.13 E
L'Aigle	46	48.45 N	0.38 E
L'Aigle Creek ≃	184	33.12 N	92.08 W
Laignes	46	47.50 N	4.22 E
Laigou	90	33.56 N	117.06 E
Laigueglia	56	43.58 N	8.09 E
Laihia	26	62.58 N	22.01 E
Lai-hka	100	21.16 N	97.40 E
Laijiaqiao	97	29.38 N	106.23 E
Lailly-en-Val	46	47.46 N	1.41 E
Lainate	56	45.34 N	9.02 E
Laindon	44	51.34 N	0.26 E
Laingsburg, S. Afr.	148	33.11 S	20.51 E
Laingsburg, Mich., U.S.	206	42.54 N	84.21 W
Laingsnek ◆1	148	27.28 S	29.55 E
Lainioälven ≃	24	67.22 N	23.39 E
Lainville	251	49.04 N	1.49 E
Lainz ◆8	254b	48.11 N	16.17 E
Lainzer Tiergarten ▲	254b	48.10 N	16.14 E
Lair	208	38.20 N	84.20 W
Laird Hill	212	32.21 N	94.54 W
Lairdsville	200	41.14 N	76.37 W
Lairg	28	58.01 N	4.25 W
Laïri	136	10.49 N	17.06 E
Laïri, Batha de ≃	136	12.28 N	16.45 E

Symbols in the index entries represent the broad categories identified in the key at the right. Symbols with superior numbers (⋀²) identify subcategories (see complete key on page I · 26).

Kartensymbole in dem Registerverzeichnis stellen die rechts in Schlüssel erklärten Kategorien dar. Symbole mit hochgestellten Ziffern (⋀²) bezeichnen Unterabteilungen einer Kategorie (vgl. vollständiger Schlüssel auf Seite I · 26).

Los símbolos incluídos en el texto del índice representan las grandes categorias identificadas con la clave a la derecha. Los símbolos con numeros en su parte superior (⋀²) identifican las subcategorías (véase la clave completa en la página I · 26).

Les symboles de l'index représentent les catégories indiquées dans la légende à droite. Les symboles suivis d'un indice (⋀²) représentent des sous-catégories (voir légende complète à la page I · 26).

Os símbolos incluídos no texto do índice representam as grandes categorias identificadas com a chave à direita. Os símbolos com números em sua parte superior (⋀²) identificam as subcategorias (veja-se a chave completa à página I · 26).

∧ Mountain	Berg	Montaña	Montagne	Montanha
⋀ Mountains	Berge	Montañas	Montagnes	Montanhas
)(Pass	Pass	Paso	Col	Passo
∨ Valley, Canyon	Tal, Cañon	Valle, Cañón	Vallée, Canyon	Vale, Canhão
≚ Plain	Ebene	Llano	Plaine	Planície
≻ Cape	Kap	Cabo	Cap	Cabo
I Island	Insel	Isla	Île	Ilha
II Islands	Inseln	Islas	Îles	Ilhas
⊥ Other Topographic Features	Andere Topographische Objekte	Otros Elementos Topográficos	Autres données topographiques	Outros Elementos Topográficos

ESPAÑOL

Nombre	Página	Lat.°′	Long.°′ W=Oeste
Lais, Indon.	102	0.47 N	120.27 E
Lais, Indon.	102	3.32 S	102.03 E
Lais, Pil.	106	6.20 N	125.39 E
La Isabela	230p	22.57 N	80.01 W
Laisamis	144	1.36 N	37.48 E
Laiševo	70	55.24 N	49.32 E
Laishan	88	37.24 N	121.23 E
Laishui	95	39.23 N	115.42 E
Laissac	32	44.23 N	2.49 E
Laissey	54	47.18 N	6.14 E
Laisuchang	97	29.16 N	105.47 E
Laisvall	24	66.05 N	17.10 E
Laitan	97	29.06 N	106.10 E
Laitila	26	60.53 N	21.41 E
Laives (Leifers)	58	46.26 N	11.20 E
Laiwu	88	36.12 N	117.42 E
Laiwui	154	1.22 S	127.40 E
Laixi	88	36.51 N	120.29 E
Laiya	106	13.40 N	121.24 E
Laiyang	88	36.58 N	120.44 E
Laiyuan, Zhg.	88	39.18 N	114.44 E
Laiyuan, Zhg.	90	25.36 N	117.01 E
Laizhouwan C	88	37.36 N	119.30 E
Laja ≃	24	66.20 N	56.16 E
Laja, Laguna de la ⊜	242	37.21 S	71.19 W
Laja, Río de la ≃	224	20.30 N	100.46 W
Laja, Salto del ⌞	242	37.22 S	72.25 W
La Jalca	238	6.29 S	77.43 W
La Jara	190	37.16 N	105.58 W
La Jara ✦[1]	34	39.42 N	4.54 W
La Jara Canyon ∨	190	36.50 N	107.30 W
La Jara Creek ≃	190	37.22 N	105.46 W
La Jarita	222	28.03 N	103.20 W
La Jarrie	32	46.08 N	1.00 W
Lajas, Méx.	224	23.07 N	105.07 W
Lajas, P.R.	230m	18.03 N	67.04 W
La Javie	56	44.10 N	6.21 E
Laje	245	13.10 S	39.25 W
Laje, Ilha da I	277a	22.57 S	43.09 W
Laje, Ponta da >	256c	38.40 N	9.19 W
Laje, Ribeira de ≃	256c	38.41 N	9.19 W
Lajeado	242	29.27 S	51.58 W
Lajeado Velho ✦[8]	277b	23.32 S	46.23 W
Lajedo	240	8.40 S	36.19 W
Lajes, Bra.	240	5.41 S	36.14 W
Lajes, Bra.	242	27.48 S	50.19 W
Lajes, Ribeirão das ≃	246	22.38 S	43.42 W
Lajinha	245	20.09 S	41.37 W
Lajishan ⩕	92	36.13 N	102.15 E
Lajkovo	255b	55.42 N	37.13 E
La Jolla	218	32.51 N	117.16 W
La Jolla, Point >	218	32.51 N	117.17 W
Lajord	174	50.14 N	104.09 W
La Jose	204	40.50 N	78.41 W
Lajosmizse	30	47.02 N	19.34 E
La Joya, Méx.	186	26.26 N	101.08 W
La Joya, Méx.	222	32.08 N	114.01 W
La Joya, Perú	238	16.44 S	71.51 W
Lajtamak	76	58.25 N	67.25 E
Lajturi	74	41.55 N	41.55 E
La Junta, Méx.	222	28.28 N	107.20 W
La Junta, Colo., U.S.	188	37.59 N	103.33 W
Lakaband	110	31.00 N	69.30 E
Lakahia, Teluk C	154	4.00 S	134.38 E
Lakamané	140	14.31 N	9.55 W
Lakazangbuhe ≃	114	29.24 N	87.58 E
Lake	184	32.21 N	89.20 W
Lake □[6], Calif., U.S.	216	39.01 N	122.33 W
Lake □[6], Fla., U.S.	210	28.42 N	81.39 W
Lake □[6], Ill., U.S.	206	42.22 N	87.50 W
Lake □[6], Ind., U.S.	206	41.25 N	87.22 W
Lake □[6], Ohio, U.S.	204	41.43 N	81.15 W
Lake Accotink Park ♠	274c	38.48 N	77.14 W
Lake Albert	161b	35.10 S	147.23 E
Lake Alfred	210	28.05 N	81.44 W
Lake Alpine	216	38.28 N	120.00 W
Lake Andes	188	43.09 N	98.32 W
Lake Angelus	271	42.42 N	83.19 W
Lake Ariel	200	41.27 N	75.23 W
Lake Arrowhead	218	34.15 N	117.12 W
Lake Arthur, La., U.S.	184	30.05 N	92.41 W
Lake Arthur, N. Mex., U.S.	186	33.00 N	104.22 W
Lake Barcroft	274c	38.51 N	77.09 W
Lake Bathurst	160	35.01 S	149.36 E
Lake Benton	188	44.16 N	96.17 W
Lake Beseck	197	41.30 N	72.14 W
Lake Biddy	152	33.00 S	118.57 E
Lake Bluff	206	42.16 N	87.50 W
Lake Buena Vista	210	28.23 N	81.31 W
Lake Burragorang ⊜[1]	160	33.57 S	150.26 E
Lake Butler	182	30.01 N	82.20 W
Lake Cable	204	40.52 N	81.27 W
Lake Camm	152	32.59 S	119.35 E
Lake Cargelligo	156	33.18 S	146.23 E
Lake Carmel	200	41.27 N	73.40 W
Lake Charles	184	30.13 N	93.12 W
Lake Chelan National Recreation Area ♠	214	48.20 N	120.40 W
Lake City, Ark., U.S.	184	35.49 N	90.26 W
Lake City, Colo., U.S.	190	38.02 N	107.19 W
Lake City, Fla., U.S.	182	30.12 N	82.38 W
Lake City, Ill., U.S.	209	39.45 N	88.43 W
Lake City, Iowa, U.S.	188	42.16 N	94.44 W
Lake City, Mich., U.S.	180	44.20 N	85.13 W
Lake City, Minn., U.S.	180	44.27 N	92.16 W
Lake City, Pa., U.S.	204	42.01 N	80.21 W
Lake City, S.C., U.S.	182	33.52 N	79.45 W
Lake City, Tenn., U.S.	182	36.13 N	84.09 W
Lake Clarke Shores	210	26.39 N	80.04 W
Lake Coleridge	162	43.22 S	171.32 E
Lake Como, N.Y., U.S.	200	42.41 N	76.18 W
Lake Como, Pa., U.S.	200	41.51 N	75.20 W
Lake Cowichan	172	48.50 N	124.03 W
Lake Creek ≃, Oreg., U.S.	192	44.04 N	123.47 W
Lake Creek ≃, Tex., U.S.	212	30.16 N	95.29 W
Lake Crescent	214	48.06 N	123.50 W
Lake Crystal	180	44.06 N	94.13 W
Lake Dalecarlia	206	41.20 N	87.24 W
Lake Dallas	212	33.07 N	97.02 W
Lake Delta	200	43.17 N	75.28 W
Lake Delton	180	43.35 N	89.47 W
Lakedemonovka	73	47.12 N	38.33 E
Lake Denison State Park ♠	197	42.38 N	72.05 W
Lake District ✦[1]	42	54.30 N	3.10 W
Lake District National Park ♠	42	54.30 N	3.05 W
Lake Eliza	206	41.26 N	87.10 W
Lake Elsinore	218	33.40 N	117.20 W
Lake Elsinore State Recreation Area ♠	218	33.41 N	117.22 W
Lake Entrance Ц	160	33.05 S	151.39 E
Lake Errock	214	49.13 N	122.02 W
Lake Fenton	206	42.52 N	83.43 W
Lakefield, Ont., Can.	202	44.26 N	78.16 W
Lakefield, S. Afr.	263d	26.11 S	28.18 E
Lakefield, Minn., U.S.	188	43.41 N	95.10 W
Lake Forest, Fla., U.S.	182	30.24 N	81.41 W
Lake Forest, Ill., U.S.	206	42.15 N	87.50 W
Lake Forest, N.J., U.S.	266	40.58 N	74.36 W
Lake Forest Park	214	47.45 N	122.17 W
Lake Fork	209	39.58 N	89.21 W
Lake Fork ≃	190	40.13 N	110.07 W
Lake Fork Creek ≃	212	32.36 N	95.21 W
Lake Front Park ♠	268	42.03 N	87.40 W
Lake Garfield	210	27.54 N	81.47 W
Lake Geneva	206	42.36 N	88.26 W
Lake George	178	43.26 N	73.43 W
Lake Grace	152	33.06 S	118.28 E
Lake Grinnell	266	41.06 N	74.38 W
Lake Grove	266	40.51 N	73.07 W
Lake Hamilton	210	28.07 N	81.42 W

FRANÇAIS

Nom	Page	Lat.°′	Long.°′ W=Ouest
Lake Harbor	210	26.42 N	80.48 W
Lake Harbour	166	62.51 N	69.53 W
Lake Harmony	200	41.04 N	75.36 W
Lake Hattie Reservoir ⊜[1]	190	41.15 N	105.55 W
Lake Havasu City	190	34.27 N	114.22 W
Lake Helen	210	28.59 N	81.14 W
Lake Hiawatha	200	40.53 N	74.23 W
Lake Hill	200	42.04 N	74.11 W
Lake Hills, Ind., U.S.	206	41.28 N	87.27 W
Lake Hills, Wash., U.S.	214	47.36 N	122.08 W
Lake Hopatcong	200	40.55 N	74.39 W
Lake Hughes	218	34.40 N	118.26 W
Lake Huntington	200	41.41 N	75.00 W
Lakehurst	198	40.01 N	74.19 W
Lakehurst Naval Air Station ■	198	40.01 N	74.18 W
Lake Illawarra	160	34.33 S	150.52 E
Lake Intervale	266	40.53 N	74.25 W
Lake in the Hills	206	42.11 N	88.20 W
Lake Isabella	194	35.39 N	118.28 W
Lake Jackson	212	29.02 N	95.27 W
Lake Jem	210	28.45 N	81.40 W
Lakekamu ≃	154	8.10 S	146.15 E
Lake Katrine	200	41.59 N	73.59 W
Lake King	152	33.05 S	119.40 E
Lake Lackawanna	200	40.57 N	74.42 W
Lakeland, Fla., U.S.	210	28.03 N	81.57 W
Lakeland, Ga., U.S.	182	31.02 N	83.04 W
Lakeland, Mich., U.S.	206	42.28 N	83.51 W
Lakeland, N.Y., U.S.	200	43.06 N	76.15 W
Lakeland Park	206	42.21 N	88.17 W
Lakeland Village	218	33.39 N	117.22 W
Lake Lenape	200	41.01 N	74.44 W
Lake Linden	180	47.11 N	88.26 W
Lake Lookover	266	41.09 N	74.24 W
Lake Loramie State Park ♠	206	40.23 N	84.20 W
Lake Louise, Alta., Can.	172	51.26 N	116.11 W
Lake Louise, Wash., U.S.	214	47.05 N	122.36 W
Lake Lucerne	204	41.24 N	81.21 W
Lake Luzerne	200	43.19 N	73.50 W
Lake Magdalene	210	28.05 N	82.28 W
Lake Manyara National Park ♠	144	3.30 S	36.25 E
Lake Mary	210	28.46 N	81.19 W
Lakemba	264a	33.55 S	151.05 E
Lakemba I	165g	18.13 S	178.47 W
Lakemba Passage Ц	165g	17.53 S	178.32 W
Lake Mead National Recreation Area ♠	190	36.00 N	114.30 W
Lake Mills, Iowa, U.S.	180	43.25 N	93.32 W
Lake Milis, Wis., U.S.	206	43.05 N	88.55 W
Lake Milton	204	41.06 N	80.58 W
Lake Minchumina	170	63.53 N	152.19 W
Lake Monroe	210	28.50 N	81.19 W
Lakemont, N.Y., U.S.	200	42.31 N	76.56 W
Lakemont, Pa., U.S.	204	40.31 N	78.23 W
Lakemoor	206	42.20 N	88.12 W
Lakemore	204	41.01 N	81.25 W
Lake Murray State Park ♠	186	34.01 N	97.00 W
Lake Nakuru National Park ♠	144	0.20 S	36.05 E
Lake Nash	156	21.00 S	137.55 E
Lake Nepessing	206	43.02 N	83.22 W
Lakenheath	44	52.25 N	0.31 E
Lake Norden	188	44.35 N	97.13 W
Lake Normandy Estates	274c	39.03 N	77.11 W
Lake Odessa	206	42.47 N	85.08 W
Lake of the Ozarks State Park ♠	184	38.08 N	92.40 W
Lake of the Woods	206	41.26 N	86.14 W
Lake Orion	206	42.47 N	83.14 W
Lake Orion Heights	206	42.46 N	83.18 W
Lake Oroville State Recreational Area ♠	216	39.32 N	121.27 W
Lake Oswego	214	45.26 N	122.39 W
Lake Ozark	184	38.12 N	92.38 W
Lakepa	164v	18.59 S	169.48 W
Lake Panasoffkee	210	28.46 N	82.07 W
Lake Paringa	162	43.43 S	169.29 E
Lake Park, Fla., U.S.	210	26.49 N	80.04 W
Lake Park, Iowa, U.S.	188	43.27 N	95.19 W
Lake Park, Minn., U.S.	188	46.53 N	96.06 W
Lake Pine	198	39.52 N	74.51 W
Lake Placid, Fla., U.S.	210	27.18 N	81.22 W
Lake Placid, N.Y., U.S.	178	44.17 N	73.59 W
Lake Pleasant	178	43.28 N	74.25 W
Lakeport, Calif., U.S.	194	39.03 N	122.55 W
Lakeport, Mich., U.S.	180	43.07 N	82.30 W
Lakeport, N.Y., U.S.	200	43.09 N	75.52 W
Lake Preston	188	44.22 N	97.23 W
Lake Providence	184	32.48 N	91.11 W
Lake Pukaki	162	44.11 S	170.09 E
Lakeridge, Nev., U.S.	216	39.02 N	119.57 W
Lake Ridge, N.J., U.S.	266	40.24 N	74.15 W
Lake Riviera	198	40.03 N	74.10 W
Lake Saint Louis	209	38.48 N	90.45 W
Lake Sammamish State Park ♠	214	47.33 N	122.03 W
Lake San Marcos	218	33.09 N	117.12 W
Lake Sawyer	214	47.20 N	122.03 W
Lakes Bay C	198	39.22 N	74.30 W
Lakes Entrance	156	37.53 S	147.59 E
Lake Shawnee	266	40.59 N	74.36 W
Lakeshore, Calif., U.S.	216	37.15 N	119.12 W
Lake Shore, Fla., U.S.	182	30.17 N	81.43 W
Lake Shore, Mich., U.S.	206	42.38 N	86.14 W
Lake Shore, Wash., U.S.	214	45.42 N	122.42 W
Lakeside, N.S., Can.	176	44.38 N	63.41 W
Lakeside, S. Afr.	263d	26.06 S	28.09 E
Lakeside, Ariz., U.S.	190	34.09 N	109.58 W
Lakeside, Calif., U.S.	218	32.52 N	116.55 W
Lakeside, Conn., U.S.	197	41.41 N	73.15 W
Lakeside, Conn., U.S.	197	41.26 N	73.16 W
Lakeside, Mich., U.S.	206	41.51 N	86.40 W
Lakeside, Mont., U.S.	192	48.01 N	114.13 W
Lakeside, Ohio, U.S.	204	41.32 N	82.45 W
Lakeside, Oreg., U.S.	192	43.34 N	124.11 W
Lakeside, Va., U.S.	198	37.37 N	77.28 W
Lakeside Center ✦[9]	271	42.37 N	83.00 W
Lakeside Village	212	32.02 N	97.30 W
Lakes National Park ♠	156	38.05 S	147.40 E
Lake Station	206	41.34 N	87.15 W
Lake Stevens	214	48.01 N	122.04 W
Lake Stockholm	266	41.04 N	74.31 W
Lake Success	266	40.46 N	73.43 W
Lake Superior Provincial Park ♠	180	47.32 N	84.50 W
Lake Swannanoa	266	41.01 N	74.31 W
Lake Taghkanic State Park ♠	200	42.06 N	73.43 W
Lake Tahoe Airport ⊠	216	38.54 N	120.00 W
Lake Tahoe-Nevada State Park ♠	216	39.13 N	119.55 W
Lake Tamarack	200	41.06 N	74.32 W
Lake Tekapo	162	44.01 S	170.30 E
Lake Telemark	266	40.57 N	74.30 W
Lake Temescal Regional Park ♠	272	37.51 N	122.14 W
Laketon	206	40.58 N	85.50 W
Laketown	190	41.49 N	111.19 W
Lake Varley	152	32.46 S	119.27 E
Lakeview, Calif., U.S.	218	33.50 N	117.07 W
Lakeview, Ga., U.S.	182	34.59 N	85.16 W
Lake View, Iowa, U.S.	188	42.18 N	95.03 W
Lakeview, Mich., U.S.	206	42.18 N	85.11 W
Lake View, N.Y., U.S.	200	42.43 N	78.56 W

PORTUGUÊS

Nome	Página	Lat.°′	Long.°′ W=Oeste
Lakeview, Ohio, U.S.	206	40.29 N	83.56 W
Lakeview, Oreg., U.S.	192	42.11 N	120.21 W
Lake View, S.C., U.S.	182	34.21 N	79.10 W
Lakeview, Tex., U.S.	184	29.55 N	93.54 W
Lakeview, Tex., U.S.	186	34.40 N	100.42 W
Lakeview, Wash., U.S.	214	47.10 N	122.30 W
Lakeview ✦[8]	268	41.57 N	87.39 W
Lakeview Mountain ∧, B.C., Can.	172	49.03 N	120.09 W
Lakeview Mountain ∧, Wash., U.S.	214	46.22 N	121.24 W
Lake Village, Ark., U.S.	184	33.20 N	91.17 W
Lake Village, Ind., U.S.	206	41.08 N	87.27 W
Lakeville, Conn., U.S.	197	41.58 N	73.27 W
Lakeville, Ind., U.S.	206	41.31 N	86.16 W
Lakeville, Mich., U.S.	204	42.49 N	83.09 W
Lakeville, Minn., U.S.	180	44.39 N	93.14 W
Lakeville, N.Y., U.S.	200	42.50 N	77.42 W
Lakeville, Ohio, U.S.	204	40.40 N	82.07 W
Lakeville Lake ⊜	204	42.50 N	83.09 W
Lake Wales	210	27.54 N	81.35 W
Lake Whitney State Park ♠	212	31.55 N	97.22 W
Lake Wilson	188	43.59 N	95.57 W
Lake Winola	200	41.30 N	75.50 W
Lakewood, Calif., U.S.	218	33.50 N	118.08 W
Lakewood, Colo., U.S.	190	39.44 N	105.06 W
Lakewood, Ill., U.S.	206	39.19 N	88.54 W
Lakewood, Mich., U.S.	206	42.18 N	85.31 W
Lakewood, N.J., U.S.	198	40.06 N	74.13 W
Lakewood, N.Y., U.S.	204	42.06 N	79.20 W
Lakewood, Ohio, U.S.	204	41.29 N	81.48 W
Lakewood, Pa., U.S.	200	41.51 N	75.22 W
Lakewood, Wash., U.S.	214	48.09 N	122.12 W
Lakewood, Wis., U.S.	180	45.18 N	88.31 W
Lakewood Center	214	47.10 N	122.31 W
Lakewood Center ✦[9]	270	33.51 N	118.09 W
Lakewood Park	188	48.04 N	98.56 W
Lakewood Park ♠	269a	41.29 N	81.47 W
Lakewood Shores	206	41.17 N	88.10 W
Lake Worth, Fla., U.S.	210	26.37 N	80.03 W
Lake Worth, Tex., U.S.	212	32.49 N	97.27 W
Lake Zurich	206	42.12 N	88.06 W
Lakhdaria	34	36.34 N	3.35 E
Lākheri	114	25.40 N	76.10 E
Lakhīmpur	114	27.57 N	80.46 E
Lakhipur, Bhārat	110	24.48 N	93.01 E
Lakhipur, Bhārat	114	26.02 N	90.18 E
Lakhish	122	31.34 N	34.51 E
Lakhish ∨	122	31.48 N	34.38 E
Lakhnādon	114	22.36 N	79.36 E
Lakhpat	110	23.49 N	68.47 E
Lakhya ≃	116	23.35 N	90.31 E
L'aki	74	40.34 N	47.26 E
Laki ≃	105a	7.30 S	107.25 E
Lakin	188	37.56 N	101.15 W
Lakinskij	70	56.01 N	39.57 E
Lakkadiven → Laccadive Islands II	112	10.00 N	73.00 E
Lakki	113	32.36 N	70.55 E
Laknau → Lucknow	114	26.51 N	80.55 E
Lakonikós Kólpos C	38	36.25 N	22.37 E
Lakor, Pulau I	154	8.14 S	128.10 E
Lakota, C. Iv.	140	5.51 N	5.41 W
Lakota, Iowa, U.S.	180	43.23 N	94.06 W
Lakota, N. Dak., U.S.	188	48.02 N	98.21 W
Laksefjorden C[2]	24	70.58 N	27.00 E
Lakselv	24	70.04 N	24.56 E
Lakshadweep □[3]	112	10.00 N	73.00 E
Lakshamannāth	116	21.51 N	87.13 E
Lakshmanpur	262b	22.38 N	88.16 E
Lakshmeshwar	112	15.08 N	75.28 E
Lakshmi, Char I	116	21.57 N	90.33 E
Lakshmikantapur	116	22.07 N	88.20 E
Lakshmīpur	116	22.57 N	90.50 E
Lakshmisāgar	116	22.55 N	87.01 E
Lakulu	142	14.22 S	23.17 E
Lala	106	7.59 N	123.46 E
Lalafuta ≃	144	13.57 S	24.41 E
La Laguna → San Cristóbal de la Laguna	138	28.29 N	16.19 W
La Lajilla	222	26.47 N	99.37 W
Lāla Mūsa	113	32.42 N	73.58 E
Lalapanzi	144	19.16 S	30.15 E
Lâlapaşa	120	41.50 N	26.44 E
Lalatuncun	94	41.44 N	122.00 E
Lalbenque	32	44.20 N	1.33 E
Laleham	250	51.25 N	0.30 W
Lāleh Zār, Kūh-e ∧	118	29.24 N	56.46 E
Lâleli	120	41.03 N	37.37 E
La Leona	186	25.52 N	101.05 W
La Leonesa	242	27.03 S	58.43 W
Lalevade-d'Ardèche	56	44.39 N	4.19 E
Lālganj	114	25.52 N	85.11 E
Lālgarh	116	22.35 N	87.03 E
Lāliān	113	31.49 N	72.48 E
Lalibela	134	12.02 N	39.02 E
La Libertad, El Sal.	226	13.29 N	89.19 W
La Libertad, Guat.	222	16.47 N	90.07 W
La Libertad, Hond.	226	14.43 N	87.36 W
La Libertad, Méx.	222	29.55 N	112.43 W
La Libertad, Nic.	226	12.13 N	85.10 W
La Libertad □[5]	238	8.00 S	78.30 W
La Ligua	242	32.27 S	71.14 W
La Lima, Hond.	226	15.24 N	87.56 W
La Lima, It.	60	44.04 N	10.46 E
La Limpia, Laguna ⊜	248	35.37 S	57.49 W
Lalín	34	42.39 N	8.07 W
Lalinde	32	44.51 N	0.44 E
Lalindi	105b	10.12 S	120.10 E
Lalindu ≃	102	3.28 S	122.05 E
La Línea	34	36.10 N	5.19 W
Lalinhe ≃	79	45.29 N	125.26 E
L'alino	72	54.29 N	39.06 E
La Lisa	276b	23.04 N	82.26 W
Lalitpur, Bhārat	114	24.41 N	78.25 E
Lalitpur, Nepāl	114	27.41 N	85.20 E
La Llagosta	256d	41.31 N	2.12 E
Lalla Khedidja, Tamgout de ∧	34	36.27 N	4.15 E
Lālmai	114	23.19 N	91.07 E
Lālmanir Hāt	114	25.54 N	89.27 E
Laloa	102	4.50 S	121.54 E
La Loche	174	56.29 N	109.27 W
La Loche, Lac ⊜	174	56.25 N	109.30 W
Laloki	154	9.25 S	147.15 E
La Loma	224	22.53 N	105.51 W
La Londe	56	43.08 N	6.14 E
Lalo Point >	164n	14.55 N	145.38 E
La Lora ⩕[1]	34	42.45 N	4.00 W
Lalor Park	264a	33.45 S	150.56 E
La Loupe	46	48.28 N	1.01 E
Lalouvesc	56	45.07 N	4.32 E
La Louvière	46	50.28 N	4.11 E
L'Alpe-d'Huez	56	45.06 N	6.04 E
Lālpur, Bhārat	110	22.12 N	69.58 E
Lālpur, Bngl.	116	24.11 N	88.58 E
Lal'sk	24	60.44 N	47.34 E
Lālsot	114	26.34 N	76.20 E
La Luz	186	25.52 N	97.37 W
Lama ≃	72	56.29 N	36.10 E
Lama, Ozero ⊜	64	69.30 N	90.30 E
L'Amable Lake ⊜	202	45.01 N	77.49 W
La Macarena, Serranía de ⩕	236	2.45 N	73.55 W
La Maddalena	36	41.13 N	9.24 E
Lama dei Peligni	60	42.02 N	14.11 E
La Madeleine	46	50.39 N	3.04 E
Lamadong	88	40.39 N	119.39 E
La Madrague	56	43.14 N	5.22 E

Nome	Página	Lat.°′	Long.°′ W=Oeste
La Madrid, Arg.	242	27.38 S	65.15 W
Lamadrid, Méx.	186	27.05 N	101.50 W
Lamag	102	5.29 N	117.49 E
La Magdalena, Río de ≃	276a	19.21 N	99.11 W
La Magdalena Contreras □[7]	276a	19.16 N	99.16 W
Lamagoumen	95	40.52 N	116.39 E
Lamahuang	94	42.27 N	121.33 E
La Mailleraye-sur-Seine	46	49.29 N	0.46 E
La Majada	276c	10.27 N	67.01 W
Lama-Kara	140	9.33 N	1.12 E
La Malbaie	176	47.39 N	70.10 W
La Malinche, Parque Nacional ♠	224	19.15 N	98.05 W
Lamaline	176	46.52 N	55.49 W
La Malmaison ⊥	251	48.52 N	2.10 E
Lamaload Reservoir ⊜[1]	252	53.16 N	2.02 W
Lama Mocogno	58	44.18 N	10.45 E
La Mancha	222	24.52 N	102.47 W
La Mancha ✦[1]	34	39.05 N	3.00 W
La Mancha, Canal de → English Channel Ц	28	50.20 N	1.00 W
La Manche (English Channel) Ц	28	50.20 N	1.00 W
Lamandau ≃	102	2.42 S	111.34 E
La Mansión	226	10.06 N	85.22 W
Lamap	165f	16.26 S	167.43 E
Lamar, Colo., U.S.	188	38.05 N	102.37 W
Lamar, Mo., U.S.	184	37.29 N	94.17 W
Lamar, Pa., U.S.	200	41.01 N	77.32 W
Lamar, S.C., U.S.	182	34.10 N	80.04 W
Lamar ≃	192	44.56 N	110.24 W
La Mar, Parque ♠	276d	12.04 S	77.02 W
La Marañosa	256a	40.17 N	3.35 W
Lamarche	54	48.04 N	5.47 E
Lamarche-sur-Saône	54	47.16 N	5.23 E
La Mare, Pointe >	230e	14.47 N	61.13 W
La Mariposa, Embalse ⊜[1]	276c	10.24 N	66.56 W
La Mariscala	242	34.03 S	54.47 W
La Marolle-en-Sologne	46	47.35 N	1.47 E
La Maroma	186	28.34 N	100.45 W
Lamarque, Arg.	242	39.24 S	65.42 W
La Marque, Tex., U.S.	212	29.22 N	94.58 W
La Marsa	36	36.53 N	10.20 E
La Martre	56	43.46 N	6.36 E
Lamas	238	6.25 S	76.35 W
La Masica	226	15.37 N	87.07 W
Lamastre	56	44.59 N	4.35 E
La Matanza → San Justo	248	34.40 S	58.33 W
Lama Temple ⊕[1]	261a	39.56 N	116.25 E
La Mauricie, Parc National de (La Mauricie National Park) ♠	196	46.50 N	73.00 W
L'Amaury	46	48.47 N	1.49 E
La Maya, Cuba	230p	20.10 N	75.39 W
Lamaya, Zhg.	92	29.50 N	99.53 E
Lamayingzi	94	42.09 N	121.50 E
Lambach	58	48.05 N	13.53 E
Lamballe	32	48.28 N	2.31 W
Lambaréné	142	0.42 S	10.13 E
Lambari	246	21.58 S	45.21 W
Lambari ≃, Bra.	245	19.30 S	45.00 W
Lambari ≃, Bra.	246	21.47 S	45.13 W
Lambasa	165g	16.26 S	179.24 E
Lambayeque	238	6.42 S	79.55 W
Lambayeque □[5]	238	6.20 S	80.00 W
Lambayeque, Río de ≃	238	6.43 S	79.54 W
Lambay Island I	28	53.29 N	6.01 W
Lambe	263a	6.42 N	3.21 E
Lambersart	46	50.39 N	3.02 E
Lambert, Miss., U.S.	184	34.12 N	90.24 W
Lambert, Mont., U.S.	188	47.41 N	104.37 W
Lambert, Cape >, Austl.	152	20.35 S	117.10 E
Lambert, Cape >, Pap. N. Gui.	154	4.12 S	151.32 E
Lambert Glacier ⊼	9	71.00 S	70.00 E
Lamberton	188	44.14 N	95.16 W
Lambert-Saint Louis International Airport ⊠	209	38.45 N	90.22 W
Lambertsbaai → Lambert's Bay	148	32.05 S	18.17 E
Lambert's Bay	148	32.05 S	18.17 E
Lambertville, Mich., U.S.	206	41.46 N	83.35 W
Lambertville, N.J., U.S.	198	40.22 N	74.57 W
Lambesc	56	43.39 N	5.16 E
Lambeth	204	42.54 N	81.18 W
Lambeth ✦[8]	44	51.30 N	0.07 W
L'ambir'	70	54.17 N	45.07 E
Lambo Katenga	144	5.02 S	28.48 E
Lambomakondro	147b	22.41 S	44.44 E
Lambourn	44	51.31 N	1.31 W
Lambourne ≃	44	51.24 N	1.18 W
Lambourne End	250	51.38 N	0.08 E
Lambrama	238	13.52 S	72.46 W
Lambrate ✦[8]	256b	45.29 N	9.15 E
Lambrecht	52	50.08 N	8.56 E
Lambrechts Drift	148	28.31 S	21.43 E
Lambro ≃	56	45.08 N	9.32 E
Lambro, Parco ♠	256b	45.30 N	9.15 E
Lambs Creek	200	41.51 N	77.06 W
Lambs Terrace	275	39.46 N	75.02 W
Lambton	263d	26.15 S	28.10 E
Lambton □[6]	204	42.45 N	82.15 W
Lambton, Cape >	166	71.05 N	123.10 W
Lambu	154	3.09 S	151.41 E
Lambunao	106	11.03 N	122.29 E
Lambwe Valley Game Reserve ✦[4]	144	0.37 S	34.15 E
L'amca	24	64.27 N	37.04 E
Lamdessar-Timur	154	7.12 S	131.58 E
Lame, Nig.	140	10.23 N	9.13 E
Lamé, Tchad	136	9.15 N	14.32 E
La Meca → Makkah	134	21.27 N	39.49 E
La Mecque → Makkah	134	21.27 N	39.49 E
Lame Deer	192	45.37 N	106.40 W
La Méditerranée → Mediterranean Sea ⊤[2]	10	35.00 N	20.00 E
Lamego	34	41.06 N	7.49 W
La Meije ∧	56	45.00 N	6.18 E
La Membrolle-sur-Choisille	46	47.26 N	0.38 E
La Mendieta	242	24.19 S	64.58 W
L'amen'ga	66	59.51 N	44.31 E
Lamentin	231o	16.16 N	61.38 W
Lamentin, Cohé du C	230e	14.36 N	61.02 W
Lamenu	165f	16.34 S	168.11 E
Lamèque	176	47.47 N	64.38 W
La Merced, Arg.	242	28.10 S	65.41 W
La Merced, Arg.	242	24.58 S	65.29 W
La Merced, Perú	238	11.03 S	75.19 W
Lameroo	156	35.20 S	140.31 E
La Mesa, Pan.	226	8.09 N	81.11 W
La Mesa, Calif., U.S.	218	32.46 N	117.01 W
La Mesa, N. Mex., U.S.	190	32.07 N	106.42 W
Lamesa, Tex., U.S.	186	32.44 N	101.57 W
La Mesa, Cerro ∧	222	26.59 N	113.44 W
La Mesa Dam ✦[6]	259f	14.43 N	121.04 E
La Meta ∧	60	41.41 N	13.56 E
Lamía	38	38.54 N	22.26 E
L'amin ≃	64	61.18 N	71.48 E
Lamine ≃	184	38.59 N	92.51 W
La Minerve	196	46.15 N	74.56 W
Lamington ≃	200	40.38 N	74.41 W
Lamington National Park ♠	156	28.15 S	153.12 E

Nome	Página	Lat.°′	Long.°′ W=Oeste
Laminusa	106	5.33 N	120.55 E
La Mira	224	18.02 N	102.19 W
La Mirada	218	33.54 N	118.01 W
La Mirada Creek ≃	270	33.53 N	118.01 W
La Misión	194	32.05 N	116.50 W
Lamitan	106	6.39 N	122.08 E
Lamlam, Mount ∧	164p	13.20 N	144.40 E
Lamlash	42	55.32 N	5.08 W
Lammefjord C	41	55.48 N	11.43 E
Lammerlaw Top ∧	162	45.40 S	169.38 E
Lammermuir □[8]	42	55.50 N	2.25 W
Lammermuir Hills ⩕[2]	42	55.52 N	2.40 W
Lammeulo	104	5.15 N	95.56 E
Lammhulf	26	57.10 N	14.35 E
Lammi	26	61.05 N	25.01 E
Lamming Mills	172	53.22 N	120.18 W
Lamogai	154	5.50 S	149.20 E
La Moille, Ill., U.S.	180	41.32 N	89.17 W
Lamoille, Nev., U.S.	194	40.44 N	115.29 W
Lamoille ≃	178	44.35 N	73.10 W
La Moine ≃	184	39.59 N	90.31 W
La Moine, East Fork ≃	184	40.24 N	90.56 W
La Molina	276d	12.05 S	76.57 W
Lamon Bay C	106	14.25 N	122.00 E
La Moncada	224	20.16 N	100.48 W
Lamone ≃	60	44.31 N	12.15 E
Lamongan	105a	7.07 S	112.25 E
Lamongan, Gunung ∧	105a	7.58 S	113.20 E
Lamoni	180	40.37 N	93.56 W
Lamont, Alta., Can.	172	53.46 N	112.48 W
Lamont, Calif., U.S.	218	35.15 N	118.55 W
Lamont, Iowa, U.S.	180	42.36 N	91.39 W
Lamont, Mich., U.S.	206	43.01 N	86.09 W
Lamont, Okla., U.S.	186	36.41 N	97.33 W
La Monte	184	38.46 N	93.25 W
La Morita	222	28.30 N	104.28 W
La Mothe, Réservoir ⊜[1]	176	48.46 N	71.09 W
La Mothe-Achard	32	46.37 N	1.40 W
La Mothe-Saint-Héraye	32	46.22 N	0.07 W
Lamotrek I[1]	14	7.30 N	146.20 E
La Mott	275	40.04 N	75.08 W
La Motte, Lac ⊜	180	48.24 N	78.03 W
Lamotte-Beuvron	46	47.36 N	2.01 E
La Motte-Chalançon	56	44.29 N	5.23 E
La Motte-du-Caire	56	44.21 N	6.02 E
Lamoura	54	46.24 N	5.58 E
La Moure	188	46.21 N	98.18 W
La Moustique ≃	231o	16.11 N	61.35 W
Lampa	238	15.21 S	70.22 W
Lampang	100	18.18 N	99.31 E
Lampasas ≃	186	30.59 N	97.24 W
Lampedusa, Isola di I	36	35.31 N	12.35 E
Lampertheim	52	49.35 N	8.28 E
Lampeter, Wales, U.K.	44	52.07 N	4.05 W
Lampeter, Pa., U.S.	198	39.58 N	76.14 W
Lamphun	100	18.35 N	99.01 E
Lampinsaari	26	64.25 N	25.09 E
Lampione, Isolotto di I	36	35.33 N	12.19 E
Lampman	174	49.23 N	102.45 W
Lamprechtshausen	58	47.59 N	12.57 E
Lampung, Teluk C	105a	5.40 S	105.20 E
Lamskoje	66	52.57 N	38.02 E
Lamspringe	48	51.58 N	10.00 E
Lamstedt	48	53.38 N	9.05 E
Lāmta	114	22.08 N	80.07 E
Lamu, Kenya	144	2.16 S	40.54 E
Lāmu, Mya.	100	19.14 N	94.10 E
Lamud	238	6.09 S	77.55 W
Lamu Island I	144	2.17 S	40.52 E
Lam Uk Wei	261d	22.26 N	114.22 E
La Mure	56	44.54 N	5.47 E
Lamure-sur-Azergues	54	46.04 N	4.30 E
La Mutua	224	22.23 N	99.18 W
Lan' ≃	66	52.09 N	27.18 E
Lan, Loi ∧	100	19.40 N	97.55 E
Lana	58	46.37 N	11.09 E
Lana, Río de la ≃	224	17.49 N	95.09 W
Lanai I	219a	20.50 N	156.55 W
Lanai City	219a	20.50 N	156.55 W
Lanaihale ∧	219a	20.49 N	156.52 W
Lanaken	52	50.53 N	5.39 E
Lanalhue, Lago ⊜	242	37.55 S	73.18 W
La Nana, Bayou ≃	212	31.27 N	94.43 W
Lanao, Lake ⊜	106	7.53 N	124.15 E
Lanao del Norte □[4]	106	8.00 N	124.00 E
Lanao del Sur □[4]	106	7.50 N	124.25 E
La Napoule	56	43.31 N	6.56 E
Lanarce	56	44.44 N	4.00 E
Lanark, Ont., Can.	202	45.01 N	76.22 W
Lanark, Scot., U.K.	42	55.41 N	3.46 W
Lanark, Ill., U.S.	180	42.06 N	89.50 W
Lanark, Pa., U.S.	198	40.33 N	75.26 W
Lanark □[6]	202	45.05 N	76.20 W
La Nartelle	56	43.19 N	6.39 E
Lanas	102	5.20 N	116.30 E
La Nava de Ricomalillo	34	39.39 N	4.59 W
Lanbi Kyun I	100	10.50 N	98.15 E
Lanboyan Point >	106	8.18 N	122.56 E
Lancang	92	23.00 N	100.02 E
Lancangjiang → Mekong ≃	12	10.33 N	105.24 E
Lancashire □[6]	42	53.45 N	2.40 W
Lancashire Plain ⌣	42	53.40 N	2.45 W
Lancaster, Ont., Can.	196	45.08 N	74.30 W
Lancaster, Eng., U.K.	42	54.03 N	2.48 W
Lancaster, Calif., U.S.	218	34.42 N	118.08 W
Lancaster, Ky., U.S.	182	37.37 N	84.35 W
Lancaster, Mass., U.S.	197	42.28 N	71.41 W
Lancaster, Minn., U.S.	188	48.52 N	96.48 W
Lancaster, Mo., U.S.	184	40.31 N	92.32 W
Lancaster, N.H., U.S.	178	44.29 N	71.34 W
Lancaster, N.Y., U.S.	200	42.54 N	78.40 W
Lancaster, Ohio, U.S.	178	39.43 N	82.36 W
Lancaster, Pa., U.S.	198	40.02 N	76.19 W
Lancaster, S.C., U.S.	182	34.43 N	80.46 W
Lancaster, Tex., U.S.	212	32.36 N	96.46 W
Lancaster, Va., U.S.	198	37.46 N	76.28 W
Lancaster, Wis., U.S.	180	42.51 N	90.43 W
Lancaster □[6], Pa., U.S.	198	40.02 N	76.19 W
Lancaster □[6], Va., U.S.	198	37.45 N	76.30 W
Lancaster Canal ═	252	53.46 N	2.43 W
Lancaster Sound Ц	166	74.13 N	84.00 W
Lančchuti	74	42.06 N	42.01 E
Lance Creek	190	43.02 N	104.39 W
Lance Creek ≃	188	43.22 N	104.16 W
Lancefield	159	37.17 S	144.44 E
Lancelot, Mount ∧	152	26.13 S	123.12 E
Lancey	56	45.14 N	5.53 E
Lanchang	104	3.30 N	102.11 E
Lanchow → Lanzhou	92	36.03 N	103.41 E
Lanciano	60	42.14 N	14.23 E
Lancin, Fr.	56	45.43 N	5.24 E
Lančin, S.S.S.R.	68	48.34 N	24.45 E
Lancing	44	50.50 N	0.19 W
Lanco	244	39.24 S	72.46 W
Lancones	236	4.35 S	80.30 W
Łańcut	30	50.05 N	22.13 E
Lancy	54	46.11 N	6.07 E
Landang Gua	106	6.58 N	122.15 E
Landau	52	49.12 N	8.07 E
Landau an der Isar	30	48.40 N	12.43 E
Landay	118	30.31 N	63.47 E
Land Between the Lakes ♠	184	36.55 N	88.05 W
Landeck	54	47.08 N	10.34 E
Landeck in Westpreussen → Lędyczek	30	53.33 N	16.58 E
Landen	52	50.45 N	5.05 E

Nome	Página	Lat.°′	Long.°′ W=Oeste
Landenberg	198	39.47 N	75.46 W
Landenhausen	52	50.36 N	9.28 E
Lander	190	42.50 N	108.44 W
Lander ≃	152	20.25 S	132.00 E
Landerneau	32	48.27 N	4.15 W
Landes □[5]	32	44.20 N	1.00 W
Landesbergen	48	52.33 N	9.07 E
Landeskrone ∧[2]	50	51.08 N	14.56 E
Landess	206	40.37 N	85.34 W
Landete	34	39.54 N	1.22 W
Landham Brook ≃	273	42.22 N	71.25 W
Landhausen	253	51.24 N	7.45 E
Landi	88	36.35 N	119.59 E
Landi Kotal	113	34.06 N	71.09 E
Landina	76	59.12 N	67.02 E
Landing	200	40.54 N	74.40 W
Landing Lake ⊜	174	55.17 N	97.26 W
Landingville	198	40.38 N	76.07 W
Landis, Sask., Can.	174	52.12 N	108.28 W
Landis, N.C., U.S.	182	35.33 N	80.37 W
Landisburg	198	40.20 N	77.18 W
Landisville	198	40.06 N	76.25 W
Landivisiau	32	48.31 N	4.04 W
Landkirchen	50	54.27 N	11.08 E
Landl	58	47.35 N	12.02 E
Lando	182	34.43 N	81.01 W
Land O'Lakes, Fla., U.S.	210	28.11 N	82.34 W
Land O'lakes, Wis., U.S.	180	46.10 N	89.13 W
Landor	152	25.09 S	116.54 E
Landos	56	44.51 N	3.50 E
Landösjön ⊜	26	63.35 N	14.04 E
Landquart	54	46.58 N	9.33 E
Landquart ≃	54	46.58 N	9.32 E
Landrecies	46	50.08 N	3.42 E
Landres	52	49.19 N	5.48 E
Landreth Draw ∨	186	31.14 N	102.29 W
Landriano	56	45.19 N	9.15 E
Landri Sales	240	7.16 S	43.55 W
Landro (Höhlenstein)	58	46.39 N	12.14 E
Landrum	182	35.11 N	82.11 W
Landry	56	45.34 N	6.45 E
Landsberg	50	51.31 N	12.10 E
Landsberg am Lech	54	48.05 N	10.55 E
Landsberg an der Warthe → Gorzów Wielkopolski	30	52.44 N	15.15 E
Landsberg in Oberschlesien → Gorzów Śląski	30	51.02 N	18.24 E
Landsberg in Ostpreussen → Górowo Iławeckie	30	54.17 N	20.30 E
Landsborough	156	26.49 S	152.58 E
Landsborough Creek ≃	156	22.30 S	144.33 E
Landsbro	26	57.22 N	14.54 E
Land's End >, Eng., U.K.	28	50.03 N	5.44 W
Lands End >, R.I., U.S.	197	41.27 N	71.19 W
Landshut	30	48.33 N	12.09 E
Landskrona	41	55.52 N	12.50 E
Landsman Creek ≃	188	39.35 N	102.19 W
Landsmeer	48	52.26 N	4.52 E
Landstuhl	52	49.25 N	7.34 E
Landweg	253	51.29 N	7.37 E
Landwehrbach ≃	253	51.26 N	6.26 E
Land Wursten ✦[1]	48	53.40 N	8.35 E
Lane	209	40.07 N	88.51 W
Lane City	212	29.13 N	96.02 W
Lane Cove	264a	33.49 S	151.10 E
Lane Cove C	264a	33.48 S	151.09 E
Lane Cove National Park ♠	264a	33.47 S	151.09 E
La Negra	242	23.45 S	70.19 W
Lane Mountain ∧	218	35.05 N	116.56 W
Lanersbach	58	47.09 N	11.44 E
Lanesboro, Mass., U.S.	197	42.31 N	73.14 W
Lanesboro, Minn., U.S.	180	43.43 N	91.59 W
Lanesboro, Pa., U.S.	200	41.58 N	75.35 W
Lanesville, Ind., U.S.	208	38.14 N	85.59 W
Lanesville, N.Y., U.S.	200	42.08 N	74.16 W
Lanesville, Va., U.S.	198	37.37 N	76.59 W
Lanett	184	32.57 N	85.12 W
La Neuveville	54	47.04 N	7.06 E
Laneville	212	31.58 N	94.49 W
Lanexa	198	37.24 N	76.55 W
Lanezi Lake ⊜	172	53.03 N	120.56 W
Lang	174	49.56 N	104.23 W
La-nga ≃	100	11.12 N	107.16 E
Langadhás	38	40.45 N	23.04 E
Langádhia	38	37.41 N	22.02 E
Langa-Langa	142	3.54 S	15.56 E
Langan Creek ≃	206	40.57 N	87.49 W
Langano, Lake ⊜	134	7.35 N	38.48 E
Lan'gao	92	32.13 N	109.02 E
Langar, Afg.	110	37.02 N	73.47 E
L'angar, S.S.S.R.	75	40.25 N	73.07 E
L'angar, S.S.S.R.	113	37.02 N	72.42 E
Langara	102	4.02 S	123.00 E
Langara Island I	172	54.14 N	133.00 W
Langarūd	118	37.11 N	50.10 E
L'angasovo	70	58.32 N	49.30 E
Långban	40	59.51 N	14.15 E
Langbank	174	50.05 N	102.20 W
Lang Bay	172	49.47 N	124.21 W
Langburkersdorf	50	51.02 N	14.14 E
Langchuhe (Sutlej) ≃	110	29.23 N	71.02 E
Langda	92	31.12 N	96.59 E
Langdai	92	26.06 N	105.20 E
Langdale	184	32.44 N	85.11 W
Langdon	188	48.46 N	98.22 W
Langdondale	204	40.08 N	78.15 W
Langdonggangzi	94	41.40 N	122.20 E
Langdon Hills	250	51.34 N	0.25 E
Langeac	32	45.06 N	3.30 E
Langeais	46	47.20 N	0.24 E
Langebaan	148	33.06 S	18.02 E
Langeberg ⩕, S. Afr.	148	34.00 S	20.40 E
Langeberg ⩕, S. Afr.	148	28.20 S	22.35 E
Lange Berge ⩕[2]	52	50.20 N	10.55 E
Langebrück	50	51.07 N	13.50 E
Langeland I	41	55.00 N	10.50 E
Langelands Bælt Ц	41	54.50 N	10.55 E
Längelmävesi ⊜	26	61.32 N	24.22 E
Langeloth	204	40.23 N	80.24 W
Langelsheim	48	51.56 N	10.19 E
Langemark	46	50.55 N	2.55 E
Langen, B.R.D.	48	53.36 N	8.35 E
Langen, B.R.D.	52	49.59 N	8.41 E
Langenargen	54	47.35 N	9.32 E
Langenau, B.R.D.	54	48.30 N	10.07 E
Langenau, D.D.R.	50	50.50 N	13.18 E
Langenberg, B.R.D.	48	51.46 N	8.19 E
Langenberg, B.R.D.	52	51.21 N	7.09 E
Langenbernsdorf	50	50.45 N	12.19 E
Langenbielau → Bielawa	30	50.41 N	16.38 E
Langenbochum	253	51.37 N	7.07 E
Langenbruck	54	47.21 N	7.46 E
Langenbrücken	52	49.12 N	8.38 E
Langenburg, B.R.D.	52	49.15 N	9.50 E
Langenburg, Sask., Can.	174	50.50 N	101.43 W
Langendorf	50	51.11 N	11.58 E
Langendreer ✦[8]	253	51.28 N	7.19 E
Langeneichstädt	50	51.20 N	11.41 E
Langenfeld, B.R.D.	52	51.07 N	6.56 E
Längenfeld, Öst.	58	47.04 N	10.58 E
Langenhagen	48	52.27 N	9.44 E
Langenhagen, Flughafen ⊠	48	52.27 N	9.42 E
Langenhessen	50	50.45 N	12.22 E
Langenhorn	41	54.41 N	8.53 E
Langenhorst	253	51.22 N	7.02 E
Langennaundorf	50	51.36 N	13.20 E
Langenneufnach	54	48.16 N	10.36 E
Langenselbold	52	50.10 N	9.02 E

≃ River	Fluss	Río	Rivière	Rio
═ Canal	Kanal	Canal	Canal	Canal
⌞ Waterfall, Rapids	Wasserfall, Stromschnellen	Cascada, Rápidos	Chute d'eau, Rapides	Cascata, Rápidos
Ц Strait	Meeresstrasse	Estrecho	Détroit	Estreito
C Bay, Gulf	Bucht, Golf	Bahía, Golfo	Baie, Golfe	Baía, Golfo
⊜ Lake, Lakes	See, Seen	Lago, Lagos	Lac, Lacs	Lago, Lagos
≛ Swamp	Sumpf	Pantano	Marais	Pântano
⊼ Ice Features, Glacier	Eis- und Gletscherformen	Accidentes Glaciales	Formes glaciaires	Acidentes Glaciares
⊤ Other Hydrographic Features	Andere Hydrographische Objekte	Otros Elementos Hidrográficos	Autres données hydrographiques	Outros Elementos Hidrográficos

↞ Submarine Features	Untermeerische Objekte	Accidentes Submarinos	Formes de relief sous-marin	Acidentes Submarinos
□ Political Unit	Politische Einheit	Unidad Política	Entité politique	Unidade Política
⊕ Cultural Institution	Kulturelle Institution	Institución Cultural	Institution culturelle	Instituição Cultural
⊥ Historical Site	Historische Stätte	Sitio Histórico	Site historique	Sitio Histórico
♠ Recreational Site	Erholungs- und Ferienort	Sitio de Recreo	Centre de loisirs	Sítio de Lazer
⊠ Airport	Flughafen	Aeropuerto	Aéroport	Aeroporto
■ Military Installation	Militäranlage	Instalación Militar	Installation militaire	Instalação Militar
✦ Miscellaneous	Verschiedenes	Misceláneo	Divers	Miscelânea

ENGLISH

DEUTSCH

Symbols in the index entries represent the broad categories identified in the key at the right. Symbols with superior numbers (⛰[2]) identify subcategories (see complete key on page *I* · *26*).

Kartensymbole in dem Registerverzeichnis stellen die rechts in Schlüssel erklärten Kategorien dar. Symbole mit hochgestellten Ziffern (⛰[2]) bezeichnen Unterabteilungen einer Kategorie (vgl. vollständiger Schlüssel auf Seite *I* · *26*).

Los símbolos incluídos en el texto del índice representan las grandes categorias identificadas con la clave a la derecha. Los símbolos con numeros en su parte superior (⛰[2]) identifican las subcategorías (véase la clave completa en la página *I* · *26*).

Les symboles de l'index représentent les catégories indiquées dans la légende à droite. Les symboles suivis d'un indice (⛰[2]) représentent des sous-catégories (voir légende complète à la page *I* · *26*).

Os símbolos incluídos no texto do índice representam as grandes categorias identificadas com a chave à direita. Os símbolos com números em sua parte superior (⛰[2]) identificam as subcategorias (veja-se a chave completa à página *I* · *26*).

Symbol	English	Deutsch	Español	Français	Português
∧	Mountain	Berg	Montaña	Montagne	Montanha
⛰	Mountains	Berge	Montañas	Montagnes	Montanhas
)(	Pass	Pass	Paso	Col	Passo
∨	Valley, Canyon	Tal, Cañon	Valle, Cañón	Vallée, Canyon	Vale, Canhão
≃	Plain	Ebene	Llano	Plaine	Planície
≻	Cape	Kap	Cabo	Cap	Cabo
I	Island	Insel	Isla	Île	Ilha
II	Islands	Inseln	Islas	Îles	Ilhas
◆	Other Topographic Features	Andere Topographische Objekte	Otros Elementos Topográficos	Autres données topographiques	Outros Elementos Topográficos

ESPAÑOL: Nombre · Página · Lat.°′ · Long.°′ W=Oeste
FRANÇAIS: Nom · Page · Lat.°′ · Long.°′ W=Ouest
PORTUGUÊS: Nome · Página · Lat.°′ · Long.°′ W=Oeste

Nombre / Nom / Nome	Página / Page	Lat.°′	Long.°′ W=Oeste
Lauban → Lubań	30	51.08 N	15.18 E
Laubusch	50	51.28 N	14.10 E
Laubuseschbach	52	50.24 N	8.20 E
Lauca ≃	238	19.10 S	68.10 W
Laucha	50	51.13 N	11.41 E
Lauchhammer	50	51.30 N	13.47 E
Lauchheim	52	48.52 N	10.14 E
Lauda	52	49.34 N	9.41 E
Lauder	42	55.43 N	2.45 W
Lauderdale	184	32.31 N	88.31 W
Lauderdale ∨	42	55.43 N	2.42 W
Lauderdale-by-the-Sea	210	26.12 N	80.07 W
Lauderdale Lakes	210	26.11 N	80.12 W
Lauderhill	210	26.10 N	80.14 W
Laudun	56	44.06 N	4.40 E
Lauenbrück	48	53.12 N	9.33 E
Lauenburg, B.R.D.	48	53.22 N	10.33 E
Lauenburg → Lębork, Pol.	30	54.33 N	17.44 E
Lauenburgische Seen, Naturpark ♠	50	53.38 N	10.45 E
Lauenförde	48	51.39 N	9.23 E
Lauenstein, B.R.D.	48	52.04 N	9.33 E
Lauenstein, B.R.D.	50	50.31 N	11.20 E
Lauenstein, D.D.R.	50	50.47 N	13.49 E
Lauer ≃	52	50.18 N	10.10 E
Lauerzer See ⊜	54	47.02 N	8.36 E
Lauf an der Pegnitz	30	49.30 N	11.17 E
Läufelfingen	54	47.24 N	7.51 E
Laufen, B.R.D.	58	47.57 N	12.56 E
Laufen, Schw.	54	47.25 N	7.30 E
Laufenburg (Baden), B.R.D.	54	47.35 N	8.04 E
Laufenburg (Baden), Schw.	54	47.33 N	8.04 E
Laufersfort, Schloss ⊥	253	51.25 N	6.37 E
Lauffen	58	47.40 N	13.37 E
Lauffen am Neckar	52	49.05 N	9.10 E
Laugharne	44	51.47 N	4.28 W
Laughery Creek ≃	208	39.02 N	84.53 W
Laughlen, Mount ∧	152	23.23 S	134.23 E
Laughlin Air Force Base ■	186	29.22 N	100.47 W
Laughlin Peak ∧	186	36.38 N	104.12 W
Laughlintown	204	40.13 N	79.12 W
Lau Group II	165g	18.20 S	178.30 W
Lauingen	52	48.34 N	10.25 E
Lauis → Lugano	54	46.01 N	8.58 E
Laukaa	26	62.25 N	25.57 E
Laukuva	66	55.37 N	22.14 E
Laulii	164u	14.17 S	170.39 W
Laul'u	79	45.46 N	135.16 E
Laun	100	10.07 N	98.46 E
Launceston, Austl.	156	41.26 S	147.08 E
Launceston, Eng., U.K.	44	50.38 N	4.21 W
Laundi, Tanjung ≻	105b	9.28 S	120.12 E
Launglon	100	13.58 N	98.07 E
Laungowāl	113	30.13 N	75.41 E
La Unión, Chile	244	40.17 S	73.05 W
La Unión, Col.	236	1.36 N	77.09 W
La Unión, El Sal.	226	13.20 N	87.51 W
La Unión, Esp.	34	37.37 N	0.52 W
La Unión, Méx.	224	17.58 N	101.49 W
La Unión, Perú	238	5.24 S	80.45 W
La Unión, Perú	238	9.46 S	76.48 W
La Union, Pil.	106	6.42 N	126.05 E
La Union, N. Mex., U.S.	190	31.57 N	106.39 W
La Unión, Ven.	236	8.13 N	67.46 W
La Unión, Ven.	276c	10.25 N	66.48 W
La Union □[4]	106	16.35 N	120.25 E
La Unión de Coto	226	8.36 N	83.03 W
Launois-sur-Vence	52	49.39 N	4.32 E
Laupen	54	46.54 N	7.14 E
Laupendahl	253	51.21 N	6.56 E
Laupheim	54	48.14 N	9.52 E
Laur	106	15.35 N	121.11 E
Laura, Austl.	154	15.34 S	144.28 E
Laura, Ohio, U.S.	208	40.00 N	84.25 W
La Urbana	236	7.08 N	66.56 W
Laureana di Borrello	36	38.30 N	16.05 E
Laurel, Del., U.S.	198	38.33 N	75.34 W
Laurel, Fla., U.S.	210	27.08 N	82.27 W
Laurel, Ind., U.S.	208	39.30 N	85.11 W
Laurel, Md., U.S.	178	39.06 N	76.51 W
Laurel, Miss., U.S.	184	31.42 N	89.08 W
Laurel, Mont., U.S.	192	45.40 N	108.46 W
Laurel, Nebr., U.S.	188	42.26 N	97.06 W
Laurel, Va., U.S.	198	37.38 N	77.31 W
Laurel, Wash., U.S.	214	45.57 N	121.23 W
Laurel ≃	182	36.57 N	84.18 W
Laurel, Mount ∧[2]	275	39.56 N	74.53 W
Laurel Bay	182	32.27 N	80.48 W
Laureldale, N.J., U.S.	198	39.30 N	74.41 W
Laureldale, Pa., U.S.	198	40.23 N	75.55 W
Laureles	242	31.22 S	55.51 W
Laurel Gardens	269b	40.31 N	80.01 W
Laurel Hill	161b	35.37 S	148.05 E
Laurel Hill ∧	204	40.02 N	79.17 W
Laurel Hollow	266	40.52 N	73.28 W
Laurel Reservoir ⊜[1]	266	41.10 N	73.33 W
Laurel Ridge State Park ♠	178	39.58 N	79.23 W
Laurel Run	200	41.13 N	75.57 W
Laurel Run ≃	198	40.20 N	77.20 W
Laurel Springs	275	39.49 N	75.00 W
Laurelton	200	40.53 N	77.12 W
Laurelville, Ohio, U.S.	178	39.28 N	82.44 W
Laurelville, Pa., U.S.	204	40.09 N	79.29 W
Laurenburg	52	50.20 N	7.54 E
Laurence Harbor	266	40.27 N	74.15 W
Laurencekirk	28	56.50 N	2.29 W
Laurens, Iowa, U.S.	188	42.51 N	94.51 W
Laurens, N.Y., U.S.	200	42.32 N	75.06 W
Laurens, S.C., U.S.	182	34.30 N	82.01 W
Laurentides	196	45.51 N	73.46 W
Laurentides ∧∧[1]	16	50.00 N	70.00 W
Laurentides, Parc des ♠	176	47.40 N	71.30 W
Laurentum ⊥	60	41.43 N	12.20 E
Lauria	36	40.02 N	15.50 E
Laurie Island I	9	60.45 S	44.35 W
Laurie Lake ⊜	174	56.34 N	101.54 W
Laurier, Man., Can.	174	50.54 N	99.33 W
Laurier, Qué., Can.	196	46.32 N	71.38 W
Laurière	32	46.05 N	1.28 E
Laurierville	196	46.18 N	71.39 W
Laurinburg	182	34.47 N	79.27 W
Lauritsala	26	61.04 N	28.16 E
Lauritzen Bay C	9	69.05 S	156.50 E
Laurium	180	47.14 N	88.26 W
Lauriya Nandangarh	114	26.59 N	84.24 E
Lauro, Monte ∧	36	37.08 N	14.47 E
Lauro Müller	242	28.24 S	49.23 W
Laurys Station	198	40.43 N	75.32 W
Lausanne	54	46.31 N	6.38 E
Lauscha	50	50.28 N	11.10 E
Laut	76	59.18 N	66.02 E
Laut, Pulau I, Indon.	102	4.43 N	107.59 E
Laut, Pulau I, Indon.	102	3.40 S	116.10 E
Laut, Selat ⋓	102	3.25 S	116.03 E
Lauta	50	51.27 N	14.04 E
Lautaro	242	38.31 S	72.27 W
Lautenbach	54	47.57 N	7.09 E
Lautenthal	48	51.52 N	10.17 E
Lauter ≃, B.R.D.	52	49.39 N	7.35 E
Lauter ≃, Eur.	52	48.58 N	8.11 E
Lauterach	54	47.29 N	9.44 E
Lauterbach, B.R.D.	52	50.38 N	9.24 E
Lauterbach, B.R.D.	54	48.14 N	8.20 E
Lauterbourg	52	48.59 N	8.11 E
Lauterbrunnen	54	46.36 N	7.55 E
Lauterecken	52	49.39 N	7.35 E
Lauter [Sachsen]	50	50.33 N	12.44 E
Lauthala I	165g	16.45 S	179.41 W
Laut Kecil, Kepulauan II	102	4.50 S	115.45 E
Lautoka	165g	17.37 S	177.27 E
Lau Trough ✢[1]	14	20.00 S	177.00 W
Lauttakylä → Huittinen	26	61.11 N	22.42 E
Lauwe	46	50.48 N	3.11 E
Lauwerszee C	48	53.20 N	6.12 E
Lauzerte	32	44.15 N	1.08 E
Lauzon	196	46.50 N	71.10 W
Lauzun	32	44.38 N	0.28 E
Lava (Łyna) ≃	66	54.37 N	21.14 E
Lava, Nosy I	147b	14.33 S	47.36 E
Lava Beds National Monument ♠	194	41.42 N	121.30 W
Lavaca □[6]	212	29.22 N	96.55 W
Lavaca ≃	186	28.50 N	96.36 W
Lavaca Bay C	186	28.35 N	96.35 W
La Vacherie	56	44.53 N	5.11 E
Lavagh More ∧	28	54.45 N	8.05 W
Lavagna	56	44.18 N	9.20 E
Lavagna ≃	56	44.21 N	9.20 E
Lava Hot Springs	192	42.37 N	112.01 W
Lavaisse	242	33.49 S	65.25 W
Laval, Qué., Can.	196	45.35 N	73.45 W
Laval, Fr.	32	48.04 N	0.46 W
Laval-des-Rapides ⬥[8]	265a	45.33 N	73.42 W
La Valette → Valletta	36	35.54 N	14.31 E
La Valette-du-Var	56	43.08 N	5.59 E
Lavalle, Arg.	242	29.01 S	59.11 W
Lavalle, Arg.	242	28.12 S	65.08 W
Lavalleja → Minas	242	34.23 S	55.14 W
Lavallette	198	39.58 N	74.04 W
La Valley	190	37.06 N	105.22 W
Laval-Ouest ⬥[8]	265a	45.33 N	73.52 W
Lavaltrie	196	45.53 N	73.17 W
Lāvān, Jazīreh-ye I	118	26.48 N	53.15 E
Lavanono	147b	25.24 S	44.55 E
Lavapié, Punta ≻	242	37.09 S	73.35 W
Lávara	38	41.16 N	26.22 E
Lavaraty	147b	23.16 S	46.59 E
Lavardac	32	44.11 N	0.18 E
Lāvar Meydān ☷	118	30.20 N	54.30 E
Lavarone	58	45.56 N	11.15 E
Lavassaare	66	58.31 N	24.22 E
Lava Tudo ≃	242	28.26 S	50.25 W
Laveaga Peak ∧	216	36.53 N	121.11 W
La Vecilla de Curueño	34	42.51 N	5.24 W
La Vega	228	19.13 N	70.31 W
La Vega ⬥[8]	276c	10.28 N	66.57 W
Lavela, S.S.S.R.	24	63.38 N	45.31 E
La Vela, Ven.	236	11.27 N	69.34 W
La Vela, Cabo de ≻	236	12.15 N	72.11 W
Lavelanet	32	42.56 N	1.51 E
Lavelle	198	40.46 N	76.22 W
Lavello	36	41.03 N	15.48 E
Laven	41	56.07 N	9.43 E
La Venada	186	25.50 N	97.30 W
Lavendon	44	52.11 N	0.40 W
Lavenham	44	52.06 N	0.47 E
Laveno	54	45.55 N	8.37 E
Lavenone	58	45.44 N	10.26 E
La Venta ⊥	224	18.08 N	94.03 W
Laventie	46	50.38 N	2.46 E
La Ventura	222	24.38 N	100.54 W
Laver ≃	42	54.08 N	1.30 W
Lavéra	56	43.23 N	5.02 E
La Vera ⬥[1]	34	40.20 N	5.30 W
La Verde	248	34.44 S	59.16 W
La Verde, Arg.	242	27.08 S	59.23 W
La Verde, Arg.	248	34.44 S	59.16 W
Laverdière, Lac ⊜	196	46.50 N	74.28 W
L'Averdy, Cape ≻	165e	5.33 S	155.04 E
La Vérendrye, Parc de ♠	180	47.30 N	77.30 W
La Verna ⊍[1]	60	43.42 N	11.54 E
La Verne, Calif., U.S.	270	34.06 N	117.46 W
Laverne, Okla., U.S.	186	36.43 N	99.54 W
La Verne College ⊍[2]	270	34.07 N	117.47 W
La Vernia	186	29.21 N	98.07 W
Laverock	275	40.05 N	75.11 W
La Verpillière	56	45.38 N	5.09 E
La Verrière	251	48.45 N	1.57 E
Lavers Hill	159	38.40 S	143.24 E
Laverton, Austl.	152	28.38 S	122.25 E
Laverton, Austl.	159	37.52 S	144.45 E
Laverton Royal Australian Air Force Base ■	159	37.52 S	144.43 E
La Veta	190	37.31 N	105.00 W
Lavezares	106	12.32 N	124.20 E
Lavezzola	60	44.34 N	11.52 E
Lavia	26	61.36 N	22.36 E
Lavic Lake ⊜	194	34.40 N	116.21 W
La Victoria, Perú	276d	12.04 S	77.02 W
La Victoria, Ven.	236	10.14 N	67.20 W
Lavieille, Lake ⊜	180	45.51 N	78.14 W
La Vieja, Punta ≻	242	35.36 S	72.38 W
Lavik	26	61.06 N	5.30 E
La Villa	58	46.36 N	11.54 E
La Villa ≃	226	7.59 N	80.23 W
La Ville-du-Bois	251	48.40 N	2.16 E
La Villeneuve-Saint-Martin	251	49.04 N	1.58 E
Lavillette	176	47.16 N	65.18 W
Lavin	54	46.46 N	10.06 E
La Viña, Arg.	242	25.27 S	65.35 W
Lavina, Mont., U.S.	192	46.18 N	108.56 W
Lavinio Lido di Enea	60	41.30 N	12.05 E
Laviolette, Lac ⊜	196	46.51 N	73.58 W
La Virginia	236	4.54 N	75.53 W
Lavis	58	46.08 N	11.07 E
La Volla	194	32.51 N	117.16 W
Lavon	212	33.02 N	96.26 W
Lavonia	182	34.26 N	83.06 W
Lavon Lake ⊜[1]	212	33.05 N	96.28 W
La Voulte-sur-Rhône	56	44.48 N	4.47 E
Lavoûte-sur-Loire	56	45.07 N	3.54 E
Lavoutte Bay C	231f	14.06 N	60.56 W
Lavras	246	21.14 S	45.00 W
Lavras ≃	277a	23.00 S	43.33 W
Lavras da Mangabeira	240	6.45 S	38.57 W
Lavras do Sul	242	30.49 S	53.55 W
Lavrentija	170	65.35 N	171.00 W
Lavrentija, Zaliv C	170	65.40 N	171.15 W
Lavrinhas	246	22.35 S	44.54 W
Lávrion	38	37.44 N	24.04 E
Lavushi Manda Game Reserve ⬥[4]	144	12.20 S	30.50 E
Lawa	106	6.12 N	125.41 E
Lawai	219b	21.55 N	159.31 W
Lawang	105a	7.49 S	112.42 E
La Wantzenau	54	48.40 N	7.50 E
La Ward	212	28.51 N	96.28 W
Lawatu	102	2.53 S	120.18 E
Lawdar	134	13.53 N	45.52 E
Lawele	102	5.13 S	122.57 E
Lawrence □[6]	204	41.00 N	80.20 W
Lawers, Ben ∧	28	56.33 N	4.15 W
Laweueng	104	5.31 N	95.52 E
Lawford Lake ⊜	174	54.30 N	96.43 W
Lawgi	156	24.34 S	150.39 E
Lawin	104	5.18 N	101.04 E
Lawin, Pulau I	154	1.31 S	128.44 E
Lawksawk	100	21.15 N	96.52 E
Lawler	180	43.04 N	92.09 W
Lawlor, Mount ∧	270	34.16 N	118.06 W
Lawn, Newf., Can.	176	46.57 N	55.32 W
Lawn, Pa., U.S.	198	40.13 N	76.32 W
Lawn, Tex., U.S.	186	32.08 N	99.49 W
Lawn Bay C	176	46.53 N	55.35 W
Lawndale, Calif., U.S.	218	33.54 N	118.21 W
Lawndale, Ill., U.S.	209	40.13 N	89.17 W
Lawndale, N.C., U.S.	182	35.25 N	81.34 W
Lawndale ⬥[8], Ill., U.S.	268	41.51 N	87.43 W
Lawndale ⬥[8], Pa., U.S.	275	40.03 N	75.05 W
Lawnes Creek ≃	198	37.08 N	76.40 W
Lawn Hill	156	18.35 S	138.35 E
Lawn Hill Creek ≃	156	18.03 S	139.09 E
Lawnside	275	39.52 N	75.03 W
Lawowa	102	4.26 S	122.56 E
Lawqah	118	29.49 N	42.45 E
Lawra	140	10.39 N	2.52 W
Lawrence, N.Z.	162	45.55 S	169.41 E
Lawrence, Ind., U.S.	208	39.50 N	86.02 W
Lawrence, Kans., U.S.	188	38.58 N	95.14 W
Lawrence, Mass., U.S.	197		
	273	42.42 N	71.09 W
Lawrence, Mich., U.S.	206	42.13 N	86.03 W
Lawrence, Nebr., U.S.	188	40.17 N	98.16 W
Lawrence, N.Y., U.S.	266	40.38 N	73.42 W
Lawrence, Pa., U.S.	269b	40.18 N	80.09 W
Lawrence, Tex., U.S.	212	32.45 N	96.21 W
Lawrence □[6]	208	38.52 N	86.29 W
Lawrence, Lake ⊜	214	46.51 N	122.34 W
Lawrence Brook ≃	266	40.29 N	74.24 W
Lawrenceburg, Ind., U.S.	208	39.06 N	84.51 W
Lawrenceburg, Ky., U.S.	208	38.02 N	84.54 W
Lawrenceburg, Tenn., U.S.	184	35.15 N	87.20 W
Lawrence Institute of Technology ⊍[2]	271	42.28 N	83.15 W
Lawrence Marsh ☷	266	40.36 N	73.42 W
Lawrence Municipal Airport ⊠	273	42.43 N	71.07 W
Lawrence Park	204	42.09 N	80.01 W
Lawrencepur	113	33.50 N	72.30 E
Lawrenceville, Ill., U.S.	184	38.44 N	87.41 W
Lawrenceville, N.J., U.S.	198	40.18 N	74.44 W
Lawrenceville, Pa., U.S.	200	42.00 N	77.08 W
Lawrenceville, Va., U.S.	182	36.45 N	77.51 W
Lawrenceville ⬥[8]	269b	40.28 N	79.57 W
Lawson, Austl.	160	33.43 S	150.26 E
Lawson, Mo., U.S.	184	39.26 N	94.12 W
Lawson Heights	204	40.18 N	79.23 W
Lawsons Creek ≃	160	32.35 S	149.43 E
Lawtey	182	30.03 N	82.04 W
Lawton, Ky., U.S.	208	38.16 N	83.13 W
Lawton, Mich., U.S.	206	42.10 N	85.50 W
Lawton, N. Dak., U.S.	188	48.18 N	98.22 W
Lawton, Okla., U.S.	186	34.37 N	98.25 W
Lawton ⬥[8]	276b	23.06 N	82.21 W
Lawu, Gunung ∧	105a	7.38 S	111.11 E
Lawyer Creek ≃	192	46.14 N	116.01 W
Lawyersville	200	42.42 N	74.30 W
Lawz, Jabal al- ∧	118	28.40 N	35.18 E
Laxå	40	58.59 N	14.37 E
Laxenburg	254b	48.04 N	16.21 E
Laxenburger Park ♠	254b	48.04 N	16.22 E
Laxey	42	54.14 N	4.23 W
Laxou	54	48.41 N	6.09 E
Layang Layang	104	1.49 N	103.29 E
Laye ≃	56	43.54 N	5.48 E
La Yesca	224	21.19 N	104.02 W
Layhill	198	39.05 N	77.03 W
Laylā	134	22.17 N	46.45 E
Layou	231h	13.12 N	61.17 W
Layou ≃	230d	15.23 N	61.26 W
Lay-Saint-Christophe	52	48.45 N	6.12 E
Laysan Island I	14	25.50 N	171.50 W
Layton, N.J., U.S.	200	41.13 N	74.50 W
Layton, Utah, U.S.	190	41.04 N	111.58 W
Laytons Lake ⊜	275	39.42 N	75.26 W
Laytonville	194	39.41 N	123.29 W
Laz	70	57.11 N	49.14 E
La Zarca	222	25.50 N	104.44 W
Lazarev	79	52.13 N	141.32 E
Lazarevo	70	56.49 N	50.15 E
Lazarevskoje	74	43.55 N	39.20 E
Lazarivo	147b	23.54 S	44.59 E
Lazaro Cárdenas	186	25.23 N	103.10 W
Lazdijai	66	54.14 N	23.31 E
Lazha	92	26.26 N	101.50 E
Lazhulong	110	35.08 N	81.33 E
Lazi, Pil.	106	9.08 N	123.38 E
Lazi, Zhg.	110	29.10 N	87.42 E
Lazio □[4]	60	42.00 N	12.30 E
Lazise	58	45.30 N	10.44 E
Lazo	79	43.25 N	133.55 E
Lazorki	68	50.06 N	32.39 E
La Zorra, Quebrada ≃	276c	10.36 N	67.03 W
Lazzate	256b	45.40 N	9.05 E
Lea ≃	44	51.30 N	0.01 E
Léach	100	12.21 N	103.46 E
Leach ≃	44	51.41 N	1.39 W
Leach Pond ⊜	273	42.04 N	71.09 W
Leachville	184	35.56 N	90.15 W
Leacock	198	40.05 N	76.12 W
Lead	188	44.21 N	103.46 W
Leadbetter Point ≻	214	46.38 N	124.03 W
Leadburn	42	55.47 N	3.14 W
Leadenham	44	53.05 N	0.34 W
Leaden Roding	250	51.48 N	0.19 E
Leader	174	50.53 N	109.31 W
Leader Water ≃	42	55.36 N	2.41 W
Leadgate	42	54.52 N	1.48 W
Lead Hill ∧[2]	184	37.06 N	92.38 W
Leadhills	42	55.25 N	3.47 W
Leadon ≃	44	51.53 N	2.16 W
Leadore	192	44.41 N	113.21 W
Leadville	190	39.15 N	106.20 W
Leaf ≃, Minn., U.S.	188	46.29 N	94.53 W
Leaf ≃, Miss., U.S.	184	31.00 N	88.45 W
Leaf Lake ⊜	174	53.02 N	102.07 W
League City	212	29.31 N	95.05 W
Leakesville	184	31.09 N	88.33 W
Leakey	186	29.44 N	99.46 W
Leakin Park ♠	274b	39.18 N	76.42 W
Leak Run ≃	269b	40.27 N	79.47 W
Leaksville	182	36.29 N	79.53 W
Lealman	210	27.50 N	82.41 W
Lealui	142	15.10 S	23.02 E
Leam ≃	44	52.17 N	1.14 W
Leamington	204	42.03 N	82.36 W
Leamington Spa → Royal Leamington Spa	44	52.18 N	1.31 W
Lean	90	27.24 N	115.48 E
Leán ≃	226	15.47 N	87.20 W
Leander Point ≻	152	29.16 S	114.56 E
Leandro	240	5.59 S	44.55 W
Leandro, Serra do ∧∧	246	22.55 S	43.55 W
Leandro N. Alem	242	27.36 S	55.19 W
Leane, Lough ⊜	28	52.05 N	9.35 W
Leano, Monte ∧	60	41.20 N	13.13 E
Leary	182	31.29 N	84.31 W
Leaside □[8]	265b	43.42 N	79.22 W
Leask	174	53.00 N	106.45 W
Leatherhead	44	51.18 N	0.20 W
Leatherman Peak ∧	192	44.05 N	113.44 W
Leatherwood Creek ≃	208	38.49 N	86.30 W
Lea Town	252	53.46 N	2.48 W
Leavenworth, Kans., U.S.	188	39.19 N	94.55 W
Leavenworth, Wash., U.S.	214	47.36 N	120.40 W
Leavesden Aerodrome ⊠	250	51.42 N	0.27 W
Leavittsburg	204	41.14 N	80.53 W
Leawood	184	37.03 N	94.31 W
Łeba	30	54.47 N	17.33 E
Łeba ≃	30	54.47 N	17.33 E
Lebach	52	49.24 N	6.54 E
Lebak	106	6.32 N	124.03 E
Lebam	214	46.34 N	123.33 W
Lébamba	142	2.12 S	11.30 E
Lebango	142	0.22 N	14.49 E
Lebanon, Conn., U.S.	197	41.38 N	72.13 W
Lebanon, Ill., U.S.	209	38.36 N	89.49 W
Lebanon, Ind., U.S.	208	40.03 N	86.28 W
Lebanon, Kans., U.S.	188	39.49 N	98.33 W
Lebanon, Ky., U.S.	184	37.34 N	85.15 W
Lebanon, Mo., U.S.	184	37.41 N	92.40 W
Lebanon, N.H., U.S.	178	43.38 N	72.15 W
Lebanon, N.J., U.S.	200	40.39 N	74.50 W
Lebanon, N.Y., U.S.	200	42.47 N	75.39 W
Lebanon, Ohio, U.S.	208	39.26 N	84.13 W
Lebanon, Oreg., U.S.	192	44.32 N	122.54 W
Lebanon, Pa., U.S.	198	40.20 N	76.25 W
Lebanon, S. Dak., U.S.	188	45.04 N	99.46 W
Lebanon, Tenn., U.S.	184	36.12 N	86.18 W
Lebanon, Va., U.S.	182	36.54 N	82.05 W
Lebanon □[6]	198	40.20 N	76.25 W
Lebanon □[1]	108		
	118	33.50 N	35.50 E
Lebanon Junction	184	37.50 N	85.44 W
Lebanon Mountains → Lubnān, Jabal ∧∧	122	34.00 N	36.00 E
Lebanon Springs	200	42.29 N	73.23 W
Le Ban-Saint-Martin	52	49.07 N	6.09 E
Le Bar-sur-le-Loup	56	43.42 N	6.59 E
Leb'ažje, S.S.S.R.	70	57.25 N	49.32 E
Leb'ažje, S.S.S.R.	76	51.28 N	77.46 E
Leb'ažje, S.S.S.R.	76	55.16 N	66.29 E
Lebbeke	46	51.00 N	4.08 E
Le Béage	56	44.51 N	4.07 E
Le Beausset	56	43.12 N	5.48 E
Lebec	218	34.50 N	118.52 W
Lebed'an'	66	53.01 N	39.09 E
Lebedevka, S.S.S.R.	70	51.06 N	47.09 E
Lebedevka, S.S.S.R.	76	50.09 N	54.07 E
Lebedevka, S.S.S.R.	76	56.48 N	66.57 E
Lebedi	68	51.17 N	37.38 E
Lebedin, S.S.S.R.	68	50.36 N	34.30 E
Lebedin, S.S.S.R.	68	48.59 N	31.31 E
Lebedino	70	55.14 N	49.50 E
Leben, Oued el ∨	138	34.37 N	10.01 E
Lebesby	24	70.34 N	26.59 E
Le Bessat	56	45.22 N	4.31 E
Le Bihan Falls ⌊	148	29.51 S	28.03 E
Le Biot	54	46.16 N	6.38 E
Lebir ≃	104	5.33 N	102.12 E
Le Blanc	32	46.38 N	1.04 E
Le Blanc-Mesnil	251	48.56 N	2.28 E
Le Bleymard	56	44.29 N	3.44 E
Leblon ⬥[8]	277a	22.59 S	43.13 W
Lebo, Kans., U.S.	188	38.25 N	95.51 W
Lebo, Zaïre	142	4.29 N	23.57 E
Le Bois-de-Cise	46	50.05 N	1.26 E
Le Bois-Dieu	251	48.39 N	1.43 E
Le Bois-d'Oingt	54	45.55 N	4.35 E
Lebomboberge ∧∧	146	25.15 S	32.00 E
Lebombo Mountains ∧∧[2]	146	25.15 S	32.00 E
Lebongtandai	102	3.01 S	101.54 E
Lebon Régis	242	26.56 S	50.42 W
Le Boréon	56	44.07 N	7.17 E
Lębork	30	54.33 N	17.44 E
Le Boulay	251	48.47 N	1.40 E
Le Bourg-d'Oisans	56	45.03 N	6.02 E
Le Bourget	251	48.56 N	2.26 E
Le Bourget-du-Lac	56	45.39 N	5.52 E
Le Brassus	54	46.35 N	6.13 E
Lebrija	34	36.55 N	6.04 W
Lebrija ≃	236	8.08 N	73.47 W
Le Broc	56	43.49 N	7.10 E
Le Brugeron	56	45.43 N	3.43 E
Le Brusc	56	43.04 N	5.48 E
Łebsko, Jezioro C	30	54.44 N	17.24 E
Lebu	242	37.37 S	73.39 W
Le Bugue	32	44.55 N	0.56 E
Le Buisson de Massoury ♠	251	48.30 N	2.43 E
Lebus	50	52.25 N	14.32 E
Leça	102	8.45 S	126.34 E
Le Caire → Al-Qāhirah	132	30.03 N	31.15 E
Le Camp-du-Castellet	56	43.15 N	5.45 E
Le Cannet	56	43.34 N	7.01 E
Lecanto	210	28.51 N	82.29 W
Le Cap → Cap-Haïtien, Haï.	228	19.45 N	72.12 W
Le Cap → Cape Town, S. Afr.	148	33.55 S	18.22 E
Le Carbet	230e	14.43 N	61.11 W
Le Cateau	46	50.06 N	3.33 E
Le Catelet	46	50.00 N	3.15 E
Lecce	36	40.23 N	18.11 E
Lecce nei Marsi	60	41.56 N	13.41 E
Lečchumskij Chrebet ∧∧	74	42.45 N	43.05 E
Lecco	56	45.51 N	9.23 E
Lecco, Lago di ⊜	54	45.55 N	9.19 E
Le Center	180	44.24 N	93.44 W
Lech	54	47.12 N	10.09 E
Lech ≃	30	48.44 N	10.56 E
Le Châble, Fr.	54	46.06 N	6.06 E
Le Châble, Schw.	54	46.05 N	7.12 E
L'Échalp	56	44.45 N	7.00 E
Le Chambon-Feugerolles	56	45.24 N	4.19 E
Le Chambon-sur-Lignon	56	45.03 N	4.18 E
Le Champ-Renault	251	49.06 N	2.31 E
Lechang	90	25.09 N	113.21 E
Le Chasseral ∧	54	47.08 N	7.03 E
Le-Château-d'Oléron	32	45.53 N	1.11 W
Le Châtelard, Fr.	56	45.41 N	6.08 E
Le Châtelard, Schw.	54	46.04 N	6.58 E
Le Châtelet	32	46.39 N	2.17 E
Le Châtelet-en-Brie	46	48.30 N	2.48 E
Lechbruck	54	47.42 N	10.47 E
Leche, Laguna de C	230p	22.13 N	78.38 W
Le Chêne-Rogneux	251	48.46 N	1.46 E
Lecheng	100	19.14 N	110.34 E
Le Chesnay	251	48.50 N	2.07 E
Le Chesne	52	49.31 N	4.46 E
Le Cheylard	56	44.54 N	4.25 E
Lechfeld ☷	54	48.10 N	10.50 E
Lechiguanas, Islas de las II	242	33.26 S	59.42 W
Lechiguiri, Cerro ∧	224	16.43 N	95.30 W
Lechlade	44	51.43 N	1.41 W
Lechleiten	54	47.16 N	10.12 E
Lechta	24	60.49 N	48.28 E
Lechtaler Alpen ∧∧	58	47.15 N	10.30 E
Lechuga, Arroyo ≃	276b	23.01 N	82.16 W
Lecinone, Monte ∧	257a	41.59 N	12.48 E
Leck	41	54.46 N	8.58 E
Le Claire	180	41.36 N	90.21 W
l'Ecole	46	48.48 N	2.04 E
Lecompte	184	31.05 N	92.24 W
Léconi	142	1.35 S	14.14 E
Léconi ≃	142	1.11 S	13.16 E
Le Conquet	32	48.22 N	4.46 W
Lecontes Mills	204	41.05 N	78.17 W
Le Cornate ∧	60	43.10 N	10.57 E
Le Coudray-Montceaux	251	48.34 N	2.31 E
Le Coudray-Saint-Germer	46	49.25 N	1.50 E
Le Creusot	54	46.48 N	4.26 E
Le Croisic	32	47.18 N	2.31 W
Le Crotoy	46	50.13 N	1.37 E
Łęczna	30	51.19 N	22.52 E
Łęczyca	30	52.04 N	19.13 E
Leda ≃	48	53.12 N	7.26 E
Led'anaja, Gora ∧	64	61.53 N	171.09 W
Ledang, Gunong ∧	104	2.22 N	102.37 E
Ledbetter	212	30.09 N	96.48 W
Ledbury	44	52.02 N	2.25 W
Lede	46	50.58 N	3.58 E
Lederach	275	40.16 N	75.24 W
Le Deschaux	54	46.57 N	5.30 E
Ledesma	34	41.05 N	6.00 W
Ledgewood	266	40.53 N	74.39 W
Le Diamant	230e	14.29 N	61.02 W
Lediba	142	3.03 S	16.32 E
Lédignan	56	43.59 N	4.06 E
Ledkovo	24	67.14 N	50.30 E
Ledo, Bhārat	110	27.18 N	95.44 E
Ledo, Indon.	102	1.02 N	109.36 E
Lêdo, Cabo ≻	142	9.41 S	13.12 E
Ledong	100	18.45 N	109.12 E
Le Donjon	32	46.21 N	3.48 E
Le Dorat	32	46.13 N	1.05 E
Le Doré, Lac ⊜	176	51.17 N	61.23 W
Ledra ≃	58	46.13 N	13.02 E
Ledsham	252	53.16 N	2.58 W
Ledu	92	36.32 N	102.25 E
Leduc	172	53.16 N	113.33 W
Lędyczek	30	53.33 N	16.58 E
Lee, Ill., U.S.	206	41.48 N	88.56 W
Lee, Mass., U.S.	197	42.19 N	73.15 W
Lee □[6], Fla., U.S.	210	26.34 N	81.55 W
Lee □[6], Ill., U.S.	206	41.50 N	89.29 W
Lee □[6], Tex., U.S.	212	30.20 N	96.55 W
Lee Center	200	43.18 N	75.31 W
Leechburg	204	40.38 N	79.36 W
Leechburg Airport ⊠	269b	40.37 N	79.34 W
Leech Lake ⊜, Sask., Can.	174	51.04 N	102.30 W
Leech Lake ⊜, Minn., U.S.	180	47.09 N	94.23 W
Leech Lake Indian Reservation ⬥[4]	180	47.30 N	94.27 W
Leechtown	214	48.30 N	123.42 W
Leedey	186	35.52 N	99.21 W
Leeds, Eng., U.K.	42	53.50 N	1.35 W
Leeds, Ala., U.S.	184	33.33 N	86.33 W
Leeds, N. Dak., U.S.	188	48.17 N	99.27 W
Leeds, N.Y., U.S.	200	42.15 N	73.54 W
Leeds □[6]	202	44.35 N	76.00 W
Leeds and Bradford (Yeadon) Airport ⊠	42	53.52 N	1.38 W
Leeds and Liverpool Canal ☰	252	53.25 N	2.59 W
Leeds Point	198	39.30 N	74.26 W
Leeds Pond ⊜	266	40.49 N	73.42 W
Leegebruch	50	52.43 N	13.11 E
Leek, Ned.	48	53.09 N	6.24 E
Leek, Eng., U.K.	44	53.06 N	2.01 W
Leelanau, Lake ⊜	180	44.55 N	85.43 W
Leen ≃	44	52.57 N	1.11 W
Leende	48	51.21 N	5.33 E
Lee-on-the-Solent	44	50.47 N	1.12 W
Lee Park	200	41.14 N	75.55 W
Leeper	204	41.22 N	79.18 W
Leer	48	53.14 N	7.26 E
Leerdam	48	51.54 N	5.05 E
Leerhafe	48	53.32 N	7.47 E
Leersum	48	52.01 N	5.26 E
Lees	252	53.32 N	2.04 W
Leesburg, Fla., U.S.	210	28.49 N	81.53 W
Leesburg, Ga., U.S.	182	31.44 N	84.10 W
Leesburg, Ind., U.S.	206	41.20 N	85.51 W
Leesburg, N.J., U.S.	198	39.15 N	74.59 W
Leesburg, Ohio, U.S.	208	39.21 N	83.33 W
Leesburg, Tex., U.S.	212	32.59 N	95.05 W
Leesburg, Va., U.S.	198	39.07 N	77.34 W
Lees Creek ≃	208	39.21 N	83.29 W
Leese	48	52.30 N	9.06 E
Leesport	198	40.27 N	75.58 W
Lees Summit	184	38.55 N	94.23 W
Leeste	48	52.59 N	8.49 E
Leeston	162	43.46 S	172.18 E
Leesville, Ill., U.S.	206	41.01 N	87.33 W
Leesville, Ind., U.S.	208	38.51 N	86.18 W
Leesville, La., U.S.	184	31.08 N	93.16 W
Leesville, Ohio, U.S.	204	40.27 N	81.13 W
Leesville, Tex., U.S.	212	29.24 N	97.45 W
Leesville Lake ⊜[1], Ohio, U.S.	204	40.30 N	81.10 W
Leesville Lake ⊜[1], Va., U.S.	182	37.05 N	79.25 W
Leeton	156	34.33 S	146.24 E
Leetonia	204	40.53 N	80.45 W
Leetsdale	204	40.34 N	80.13 W
Leeudoringstad	148	27.15 S	26.10 E
Leeu-Gamka	148	32.47 S	21.59 E
Leeupan ⊜	148	26.34 S	28.59 E
Leeuwarden	48	53.12 N	5.46 E
Leeuwin, Cape ≻	152	34.22 S	115.08 E
Leeuwpan ☷	263d	26.14 S	28.19 E
Lee Vining	216	37.58 N	119.07 W
Leeward Islands II	228	17.00 N	63.00 W
Le Faouët	28	48.02 N	3.29 W
Le Fayet	54	45.55 N	6.42 E
Lefèvre, Cap ≻	165f	20.54 S	167.01 E
Leffe	56	45.48 N	9.53 E
Lefferts, Lake ⊜	266	40.25 N	74.14 W
Léfini ≃	142	2.57 S	16.10 E
Léfini, Réserve de Chasse de la ⬥[4]	142	2.58 S	15.25 E
Le Focette	58	43.55 N	10.13 E
Leforest	46	50.26 N	3.04 E
Lefors	186	35.26 N	100.48 W
Le François	230e	14.37 N	60.54 W
Le Freney-d'Oisans	56	45.02 N	6.07 E
Lefroy	202	44.16 N	79.34 W
Lefroy, Lake ⊜	152	31.15 S	121.40 E
Leftrook Lake ⊜	174	56.05 N	98.36 W
Lefu ≃	79	44.32 N	132.30 E
Legal	172	53.57 N	113.35 W
Leganés	256a	40.20 N	3.46 W
Legaspi → Legazpi	106	13.08 N	123.44 E
Legau	54	47.51 N	10.07 E
Legazpi	106	13.08 N	123.44 E
Legden	48	52.02 N	7.07 E
Légé	32	46.53 N	1.36 W
Lege Hida	134	7.55 N	41.00 E
Legendre ≃	196	45.44 N	71.08 W
Legendre Island I	152	20.23 S	116.54 E
Léger	46	48.43 N	1.46 E
Legges Tor ∧	156	41.32 S	147.40 E
Leggett, Calif., U.S.	194	39.52 N	123.43 W
Leggett, Tex., U.S.	212	30.49 N	94.52 W
Leghorn → Livorno	60	43.33 N	10.19 E
Legion Mine	144	21.23 S	28.33 E
Legion of Honor, Palace of the ⊍	272	37.47 N	122.30 W
Legionowo	30	52.25 N	20.56 E
L'Eglise	46	47.22 N	3.56 E
Legnago	58	45.11 N	11.18 E
Legnano	56	45.36 N	8.54 E
Legnica (Liegnitz)	30	51.13 N	16.09 E
Le Gosier	231o	16.12 N	61.30 W
Le Grand	216	37.14 N	120.15 W
LeGrand, Cape ≻	152	34.01 S	122.06 E
Le Grand-Lucé	46	47.52 N	0.28 E
Le Grand-Quevilly	46	49.25 N	1.02 E
Le Grand-Serre	56	45.16 N	5.06 E
Le Grand Wintersberg ∧[2]	52	48.59 N	7.37 E
Le Grau-du-Roi	56	43.32 N	4.08 E
Le Gua	56	45.01 N	5.37 E
Le Guelta	34	36.22 N	0.50 E
Leguga	144	3.23 N	25.02 E
Legume	156	28.25 S	152.19 E
Legundi, Pulau I	105a	5.50 S	105.16 E
Leh	113	34.10 N	77.35 E
Le Havre	46	49.30 N	0.08 E
Lehčevo	38	43.32 N	23.32 E
Le Hérie-la-Viéville	46	49.49 N	3.38 E
Lehesten	50	50.29 N	11.28 E
Lehi	190	40.24 N	111.51 W
Lehigh, Iowa, U.S.	180	42.22 N	94.03 W
Lehigh, Okla., U.S.	186	34.28 N	96.13 W
Lehigh □[6]	198	40.36 N	75.29 W
Lehigh ≃	200	40.41 N	75.12 W
Lehigh Acres	210	26.36 N	81.39 W
Lehighton	200	40.49 N	75.45 W
Lehman Caves National Monument ♠	194	39.01 N	114.14 W
Lehman College ⊍[2]	266	40.52 N	73.54 W
Lehnin	50	52.19 N	12.44 E
Lehnitz	50	52.44 N	13.15 E
Lehnitz See ⊜	254a	52.45 N	13.16 E
Leho	130	7.07 N	33.52 E
Le Hohwald	54	48.24 N	7.20 E
Le Houlme	46	49.31 N	1.02 E
Lehr	188	46.17 N	99.21 W
Lehra Gāga	113	29.55 N	75.49 E
Lehrbach	52	50.47 N	9.04 E
Lehrberg	52	49.21 N	10.30 E
Lehre	50	52.19 N	10.40 E
Lehrte	48	52.22 N	9.59 E
Lehtar	113	33.42 N	73.26 E
Lehtimäki	26	62.47 N	23.55 E
Lehtse	66	59.15 N	25.50 E
Lehua Island I	219b	22.01 N	160.06 W
Lehututu	146	23.58 S	21.51 E
Leiah	113	30.58 N	70.56 E
Leião	256c	38.44 N	9.18 W
Leibnitz	30	46.48 N	15.32 E
Leibo	92	28.19 N	103.21 E
Leicester, Eng., U.K.	44	52.38 N	1.05 W
Leicester, Mass., U.S.	197	42.15 N	71.55 W
Leicester, N.Y., U.S.	200	42.46 N	77.54 W
Leicestershire □[6]	44	52.40 N	1.10 W
Leichhardt	264a	33.53 S	151.07 E
Leichhardt ≃	156	17.35 S	139.48 E
Leichhardt Falls ⌊	156	18.14 S	139.53 E
Leichhardt Range ∧∧	156	20.40 S	147.25 E
Leichlingen	52	51.06 N	7.01 E
Leiden	48	52.09 N	4.30 E
Leiderdorp	48	52.09 N	4.32 E
Leidschendam	48	52.05 N	4.24 E
Leie (Lys) ≃	46	51.03 N	3.43 E
Leiferde	48	52.26 N	10.26 E
Leigh, N.Z.	162	36.17 S	174.49 E
Leigh, Eng., U.K.	42	53.30 N	2.33 W
Leigh, Eng., U.K.	250	51.12 N	0.13 E
Leigh Canal ☰	252	53.28 N	2.21 W
Leigh Creek	156	30.28 S	138.25 E
Leigh-on-Sea	44	51.33 N	0.38 E
Leighton	184	34.42 N	87.32 W
Leighton Buzzard	44	51.55 N	0.40 W
Leikanger	26	61.10 N	6.52 E
Leiktho	100	19.13 N	96.35 E
Leimbach	50	51.36 N	11.28 E
Leimstruth	52	50.59 N	8.19 E
Lein ≃	52	48.54 N	10.01 E
Leinan	174	50.30 N	107.46 W
Leinefelde	50	51.23 N	10.20 E
Leinfelden	52	48.41 N	9.08 E
Leinster □[9]	28	53.05 N	7.00 W
Leinster, Mount ∧	28	52.37 N	6.44 W
Leintwardine	44	52.23 N	2.51 W
Leipalingis	66	54.05 N	23.51 E
Leipheim	54	48.27 N	10.13 E
Leipoldtville	148	32.14 S	18.30 E
Leipsic, Del., U.S.	198	39.14 N	75.31 W
Leipsic, Ind., U.S.	208	38.40 N	86.22 W
Leipsic, Ohio, U.S.	206	41.06 N	83.59 W
Leipsic ≃	198	39.15 N	75.24 W
Leipzig	50	51.19 N	12.20 E
Leipzig □[5]	50	51.15 N	12.45 E
Leiria	34	39.45 N	8.48 W
Leirvik	26	59.45 N	5.30 E
Leisach	58	46.48 N	12.45 E
Leishendian	97	28.58 N	106.40 E
Leishui ≃	90	26.54 N	112.39 E
Leisi	66	58.34 N	22.39 E
Leisler, Mount ∧	152	23.28 S	129.17 E
Leisnig	50	51.09 N	12.56 E
Leisure City	210	25.30 N	80.26 W
Leitariegos, Puerto de)(	34	43.00 N	6.25 W
Leitchfield	184	37.29 N	86.18 W
Leiters Ford	206	41.07 N	86.23 W
Leith	42	55.59 N	3.10 W
Leith, Water of ≃	42	55.59 N	3.11 W
Leitha (Lajta) ≃, Eur.	30	47.54 N	17.17 E
Leitha ≃, Öst.	254b	48.00 N	16.35 E
Leithe ⬥[8]	253	51.29 N	7.06 E
Leith Hill ∧[2]	44	51.11 N	0.23 W
Leitre	154	2.50 S	141.40 E
Leitrim	28	54.00 N	8.04 W
Leitrim □[6]	28	54.20 N	8.20 W
Leitzkau	50	52.03 N	11.57 E
Lei U Mun ⋓	261d	22.16 N	114.14 E
Leiva	236	5.38 N	73.34 W
Leixi	90	27.10 N	112.52 E
Leiyang	90	26.24 N	112.51 E
Leizhoubandao ≻[1]	92	21.15 N	110.09 E
Leizhuang	88	39.47 N	118.34 E
Lejasciems	66	57.17 N	26.35 E
Lejía, Cerro ∧	242	23.33 S	67.46 W
Lek ≃	48	52.00 N	6.00 E
Lékana	142	2.19 S	14.36 E
Le Kef → El Kef	138	36.11 N	8.43 E
Lékéti ≃	142	1.36 S	14.57 E
Lékéti, Monts de la ∧∧	142	2.34 S	14.17 E
Lekhainá	38	37.56 N	21.17 E
Lekir	104	4.07 N	100.44 E
Lekitobi	102	1.58 S	124.33 E
Lekkeroog	148	30.43 S	20.00 E
Lekkerwater	146	23.38 S	17.14 E
Lekkous, Oued ≃	34	34.58 N	5.52 W
Lekma ≃	70	58.18 N	52.04 E
Łęknice	50	51.35 N	14.45 E
Lekotero	142	0.46 S	23.51 E
Lékoumou □[5]	142	3.00 S	13.00 E
Le Kreïder	138	34.06 N	0.02 E
Le Kremlin-Bicêtre	251	48.49 N	2.21 E
Leksand	26	60.44 N	14.59 E
Leksberg	40	59.41 N	13.49 E
Leksozero, Ozero ⊜	24	63.46 N	30.58 E
Leksvik	26	63.40 N	10.37 E
Lela	142	5.03 S	12.29 E
Le Lac-d'Issarlès	56	44.49 N	4.04 E
Le Lamentin	230e	14.37 N	61.01 W
Leland, Ill., U.S.	206	41.37 N	88.48 W
Leland, Mich., U.S.	180	45.01 N	85.45 W
Leland, Miss., U.S.	184	33.24 N	90.54 W
Leland Grove	209	39.47 N	89.41 W
Leland Lake ⊜	214	47.53 N	122.53 W
Lelång ⊜	26	59.08 N	12.10 E
Le Laus	56	44.31 N	6.09 E
Le Lauzet-Ubaye	56	44.26 N	6.26 E
Le Lavandou	56	43.08 N	6.22 E
Lel'čicy	68	51.47 N	28.19 E
Leleiwi Point ≻	219d	19.44 N	155.00 W
Lelepa I	165f	17.36 S	168.13 E
Leleque	244	42.23 S	71.03 W
Leles	105a	7.07 S	107.53 E
Lelewau	102	3.02 S	121.05 E
Lélex	54	46.18 N	5.57 E
Le Liège	46	47.13 N	1.06 E
Leling	88	37.45 N	117.12 E
Lelingluang	154	7.09 S	131.43 E
Lelintah	154	2.03 S	130.16 E
Le Lion-d'Angers	32	47.38 N	0.43 W
Lelishan ∧	110	33.26 N	81.42 E
Le Locle	54	47.03 N	6.45 E
Lelogama	102	9.44 S	123.57 E
Le Lorrain	230e	14.50 N	61.04 W
Le Luc	56	43.23 N	6.19 E
Le Lude	46	47.39 N	0.09 E
Lelystad	48	52.31 N	5.27 E
Lema	140	12.57 N	4.14 E
Le Madonie ∧∧	36	37.55 N	14.00 E
Lemahabang	105a	6.17 S	107.27 E
Le Maire, Estrecho de ⋓	244	54.50 S	65.00 W
Léman, Lac → Geneva, Lake ⊜	54	46.25 N	6.30 E
Lemanmanu Mission	165e	5.02 S	154.35 E
Le Mans	46	48.00 N	0.12 E
Le Marin	230e	14.28 N	60.53 W
Le Markstein	54	47.56 N	7.02 E
Le Mars	188	42.47 N	96.10 W

≃ River	Fluss	Río	Rivière	Rio
☰ Canal	Kanal	Canal	Canal	Canal
⌊ Waterfall, Rapids	Wasserfall, Stromschnellen	Cascada, Rápidos	Chute d'eau, Rapides	Cascata, Rápidos
⋓ Strait	Meeresstrasse	Estrecho	Détroit	Estreito
C Bay, Gulf	Bucht, Golf	Bahía, Golfo	Baie, Golfe	Baía, Golfo
⊜ Lake, Lakes	See, Seen	Lago, Lagos	Lac, Lacs	Lago, Lagos
☷ Swamp	Sumpf	Pantano	Marais	Pântano
Ice Features, Glacier	Eis- und Gletscherformen	Accidentes Glaciales	Formes glaciaires	Acidentes Glaciares
Other Hydrographic Features	Andere Hydrographische Objekte	Otros Elementos Hidrográficos	Autres données hydrographiques	Outros Elementos Hidrográficos

✢ Submarine Features	Untermeerische Objekte	Accidentes Submarinos	Formes de relief sous-marin	Acidentes Submarinos
□ Political Unit	Politische Einheit	Unidad Política	Entité politique	Unidade Política
⊍ Cultural Institution	Kulturelle Institution	Institución Cultural	Institution culturelle	Instituição Cultural
⊥ Historical Site	Historische Stätte	Sitio Histórico	Site historique	Sítio Histórico
♠ Recreational Site	Erholungs- und Ferienort	Sitio de Recreo	Centre de loisirs	Sítio de Lazer
⊠ Airport	Flughafen	Aeropuerto	Aéroport	Aeroporto
■ Military Installation	Militäranlage	Instalación Militar	Installation militaire	Instalação Militar
⬥ Miscellaneous	Verschiedenes	Misceláneo	Divers	Miscelânea

ENGLISH — Name, Page, Lat.°′, Long.°′
DEUTSCH — Name, Seite, Breite°′, Länge°′ E=Ost

Name	Page	Lat.	Long.
Lema Shilindi	134	4.55 N	42.02 E
Lemay	209	38.32 N	90.17 W
Lemay, Lac ◎	176	50.35 N	68.25 W
Le Mayet-de-Montagne	32	46.05 N	3.40 E
Lembach	52	49.00 N	7.48 E
Lembak	102	0.52 N	117.32 E
Lembang	105a	6.49 S	107.36 E
Lembeck	48	51.45 N	7.00 E
Lembeek	46	50.43 N	4.13 E
Lembeh, Pulau I	102	1.26 N	125.13 E
Lembeni	144	3.47 S	37.37 E
Lemberg, Sask., Can.	174	50.44 N	103.13 W
Lemberg, Fr.	52	49.00 N	7.23 E
Lemberg → L'vov, S.S.S.R.	68	49.50 N	24.00 E
Lemberg ∧	54	48.09 N	8.45 E
Lembruch	48	52.31 N	8.22 E
Lembu, Gunung ∧	104	4.12 N	97.24 E
Leme	245	22.12 S	47.24 W
Leme, Morro do ∧[2]	277a	22.58 S	43.10 W
Le Mée-sur-Seine	251	48.32 N	2.38 E
Lemei Rock ∧	214	46.01 N	121.46 W
Lemele	48	52.27 N	6.25 E
Le Mêle-sur-Sarthe	46	48.31 N	0.21 E
Lemene ≃	58	45.37 N	12.53 E
Lemeris, Cape ≻	154	3.15 S	152.03 E
Le Merlerault	46	48.42 N	0.18 E
Lemery	106	13.53 N	120.55 E
Lemeškino	70	51.01 N	44.27 E
Le Mesle	251	48.43 N	1.41 E
Le Mesnil-Amelot	251	49.01 N	2.36 E
Le Mesnil-Aubry	251	49.03 N	2.24 E
Le Mesnil-le-Roi	251	48.56 N	2.08 E
Le Mesnil-Saint-Denis	251	48.45 N	1.58 E
Le Mesnil-sur-Oger	46	48.57 N	4.01 E
Lemesós (Limassol)	120	34.40 N	33.02 E
Lemešovka	68	52.04 N	31.38 E
Lemeta	170	64.52 N	147.44 W
Lemförde	48	52.28 N	8.22 E
Lemfu	142	5.18 S	15.13 E
Lemgo	48	52.02 N	8.54 E
Lemhi ≃	192	45.12 N	113.53 W
Lemhi Pass)(	192	44.58 N	113.27 W
Lemhi Range ⛰	192	44.30 N	113.25 W
Lemie	56	45.14 N	7.17 E
Lemierzyce	50	52.35 N	14.56 E
Lemieux Islands II	166	64.30 N	64.40 W
Lemin	92	21.11 N	109.42 E
Leming	186	29.04 N	98.29 W
Lemitar	190	34.09 N	106.55 W
Lemke	48	52.39 N	9.09 E
Lemmatsi	66	58.20 N	26.37 E
Lemmenjoen Kansallispuisto ♠	24	68.40 N	26.00 E
Lemmer	48	52.50 N	5.42 E
Lemmon	188	45.56 N	102.10 W
Lemmon, Mount ∧	190	32.26 N	110.47 W
Lemnos → Límnos I	38	39.54 N	25.21 E
Lemoenshoek	148	33.51 S	20.51 E
Lemoine, Lac ◎	180	48.00 N	78.00 W
Lemon, Lake ◎	208	39.16 N	86.25 W
Le Monastier	56	44.56 N	4.00 E
Lemoncove	194	36.23 N	119.01 W
Lemon Creek ≃	266	40.31 N	74.12 W
Le Monêtier-les-Bains	56	44.59 N	6.31 E
Lemon Grove	218	32.44 N	117.02 W
Lemon Heights	270	33.46 N	117.48 W
Lemont, Ill., U.S.	206	41.40 N	88.00 W
Lemont, Pa., U.S.	204	40.49 N	77.49 W
Le Montet	32	46.25 N	3.03 E
Le Mont Saint-Michel ♥[1]	32	48.38 N	1.32 W
Lemoore	216	36.18 N	119.47 W
Lemoore Naval Air Station ■	216	36.15 N	119.57 W
Lemoro	102	1.25 S	121.05 E
Lemos	246	22.43 S	46.25 W
Lemotol Bay ⊂	165c	7.21 N	151.35 E
Le Moule	231o	16.20 N	61.21 W
Le Moutier	251	48.50 N	1.42 E
LeMoyne, Qué., Can.	265a	45.31 N	73.29 W
Lemoyne, Ohio, U.S.	204	41.30 N	83.28 W
Lemoyne, Pa., U.S.	198	40.15 N	76.54 W
Lempa ≃	226	13.14 N	88.49 W
Lempäälä	26	61.19 N	23.45 E
Lempe	102	1.40 S	120.14 E
Lempira □[5]	226	14.20 N	88.40 W
Lemro ≃	100	20.25 N	93.20 E
Lemsid ⏏[4]	138	26.32 N	13.49 W
Lemukutan, Pulau I	102	0.45 N	108.43 E
Le Murge ⛰[1]	36	40.52 N	16.42 E
Lemutan	102	3.03 N	115.49 E
Le Muy	56	43.28 N	6.33 E
Lemva ≃	24	66.30 N	61.48 E
Lemvig	26	56.32 N	8.18 E
Lemyethna	100	17.36 N	95.09 E
Len ≃	250	51.16 N	0.31 E
Lena, Ill., U.S.	180	42.23 N	89.50 W
Lena, Wis., U.S.	180	44.57 N	88.03 W
Lena ≃	64	72.25 N	126.40 E
Lenakel	165f	19.32 S	169.16 E
Lenangguar	105b	8.44 S	117.24 E
Lenape	275	39.55 N	75.38 W
Lenart	36	46.35 N	15.50 E
Lenawee □[6]	206	41.53 N	84.04 W
Lencloître	32	46.49 N	0.20 E
Lençóis	245	12.34 S	41.23 W
Lend	58	47.18 N	13.04 E
Lenda ≃	144	1.20 N	28.01 E
Lendelede	46	50.53 N	3.14 E
Lendery	24	63.26 N	31.03 E
Lendinara	58	45.05 N	11.36 E
Lendorf	58	46.50 N	13.26 E
Lendringsen	52	51.24 N	7.49 E
Le Neubourg	46	49.09 N	0.55 E
Lenga	104	2.17 N	102.49 E
Lengduqiao	96	30.27 N	119.15 E
Lengede	48	52.12 N	10.18 E
Lengefeld	50	50.43 N	13.11 E
Lengelscheid	253	51.08 N	7.40 E
Lengenfeld, D.D.R.	50	50.34 N	12.22 E
Lengenfeld, D.D.R.	52	51.13 N	10.13 E
Lenger	75	42.12 N	69.54 E
Lengerich, B.R.D.	48	52.11 N	7.50 E
Lengerich, B.R.D.	48	52.33 N	7.32 E
Lenggor ≃	104	2.25 N	103.37 E
Lenggries	58	47.41 N	11.34 E
Lenghu	80	38.30 N	93.15 E
Lengjiagou	94	41.40 N	121.37 E
Lengkong	105a	7.32 S	112.04 E
Lenglingen ◎	26	64.14 N	13.45 E
Lengnau	54	47.11 N	7.22 E
Lengoué	142	1.13 N	15.43 E
Lengshuichang	97	29.27 N	106.26 E
Lengshuikeng	90	27.55 N	117.08 E
Lengshuitan	92	26.14 N	111.29 E
Lengua de Vaca, Punta ≻	242	30.14 S	71.38 W
Lengulu	144	3.15 N	26.30 E
Lengzipu	94	41.42 N	122.47 E
Lenham	250	51.14 N	0.43 E
Lenhartsville	198	40.34 N	75.53 W
Lenhovda	26	57.00 N	15.17 E
Lenina, Gora ∧[2]	255b	55.42 N	37.31 E
Lenina, Ozero ◎	68	48.33 N	35.12 E
Lenina, Pik ∧	75	39.20 N	72.55 E
Leninabad	75	40.17 N	69.37 E
Leninakan	74	40.48 N	43.50 E
Lenindžol	75	41.03 N	72.38 E
Leningori	74	42.07 N	44.29 E
Leningrad	66		
	255a	59.55 N	30.15 E
Leningrad □[4]	255a	59.55 N	30.15 E
Leningrad, Aeroport ⊠	255a	59.48 N	30.16 E
Leningrad, Gorod □[7]	255a	59.55 N	30.15 E
Leningrado → Leningrad	66	59.55 N	30.15 E
Leningradskaja	68	46.19 N	39.24 E
Leningradskij Vokzal ⬥[5]	255b	55.47 N	37.39 E
Leningradskoje	76	53.33 N	71.35 E
Lenino	68	45.18 N	35.47 E
Lenino ⬥[8]	255b	55.37 N	37.41 E
Leninogorsk, S.S.S.R.	70	54.36 N	52.30 E
Leninogorsk, S.S.S.R.	76	50.27 N	83.32 E
Leninpol'	75	42.29 N	71.55 E
Leninsk, S.S.S.R.	68	45.16 N	35.54 E
Leninsk, S.S.S.R.	70	48.42 N	45.11 E
Leninsk, S.S.S.R.	70	46.08 N	43.46 E
Leninsk, S.S.S.R.	75	40.38 N	72.15 E
Leninsk, S.S.S.R.	76	54.55 N	59.54 E
Leninskaja Sloboda	70	56.05 N	44.28 E
Leninskij, S.S.S.R.	68	47.53 N	28.23 E
Leninskij, S.S.S.R.	70	56.34 N	45.58 E
Leninskij, S.S.S.R.	70	46.31 N	44.28 E
Leninskij, S.S.S.R.	72	54.18 N	37.28 E
Leninskij, S.S.S.R.	73	48.05 N	39.31 E
Leninskij, S.S.S.R.	76	52.13 N	76.47 E
Leninsk-Kuzneckij	76	54.38 N	86.10 E
Leninskoje, S.S.S.R.	68	51.27 N	33.18 E
Leninskoje, S.S.S.R.	70	58.19 N	47.06 E
Leninskoje, S.S.S.R.	70	49.03 N	49.56 E
Leninskoje, S.S.S.R.	75	40.42 N	73.11 E
Leninskoje, S.S.S.R.	75	41.45 N	69.23 E
Leninskoje, S.S.S.R.	76	50.44 N	57.53 E
Leninskoje, S.S.S.R.	79	47.56 N	132.38 E
Lenin-Stausee → Kujbyševskoje Vodochranilišče ◎[1]	70	53.40 N	49.00 E
Leninžol	70	49.20 N	47.05 E
Lenk	54	46.28 N	7.27 E
Lenkerville	198	40.32 N	76.58 W
Len'ki	76	52.57 N	80.26 E
Lenkoran'	74	38.45 N	48.50 E
Lenkoranskaja Nizmennost' ≍	74	38.50 N	48.50 E
Lenmalu	154	1.44 S	130.13 E
Lenne ≃	52	51.25 N	7.30 E
Lennegebirge ⛰	48	51.15 N	8.00 E
Lennep	52	51.11 N	7.15 E
Lennep ⬥[8]	48	51.12 N	7.15 E
Lenni	275	39.54 N	75.27 W
Lennon	206	42.59 N	83.56 W
Lennonville	152	27.58 S	117.50 E
Lennox, Calif., U.S.	218	33.56 N	118.21 W
Lennox, S. Dak., U.S.	188	43.21 N	96.53 W
Lennox □[9]	42	56.02 N	4.15 W
Lennox, Isla I	244	55.18 S	66.50 W
Lennox and Addington □[6]	202	44.30 N	77.00 W
Lennoxtown	42	55.59 N	4.12 W
Lennoxville	196	45.22 N	71.51 W
Leno	58	45.22 N	10.13 E
Lenoir	182	35.55 N	81.32 W
Lenoir City	182	35.48 N	84.16 W
Le Noirmont	54	47.13 N	6.58 E
Lenola	60	41.24 N	13.28 E
Lenora	30	48.56 N	13.48 E
Lenore Lake ◎	174	52.30 N	105.00 W
Le Nouvion-en-Thiérache	46	50.01 N	3.47 E
Lenox, Ga., U.S.	182	31.16 N	83.28 W
Lenox, Iowa, U.S.	188	40.53 N	94.34 W
Lenox, Mass., U.S.	197	42.22 N	73.17 W
Lenox, Tenn., U.S.	184	36.05 N	89.30 W
Lenox Dale	197	42.20 N	73.15 W
Lens	46	50.26 N	2.50 E
Lensahn	50	54.13 N	10.52 E
Lensk	64	61.00 N	114.50 E
Lenskoje	76	58.09 N	63.11 E
Lenswood	158b	34.55 S	138.49 E
Lentate sul Seveso	256b	45.41 N	9.07 E
Lentechi	74	42.48 N	42.44 E
Lenti	30	46.37 N	16.33 E
Lentini	36	37.17 N	15.00 E
Lentner	209	39.43 N	92.09 W
Lentua ◎	26	64.14 N	29.36 E
Lentvaris	66	54.39 N	25.03 E
Lenwood	218	34.53 N	117.07 W
Lenya	100	11.28 N	99.00 E
Lenya ≃	100	11.40 N	98.43 E
Lenz	263d	26.19 S	27.49 E
Lenzburg	54	47.23 N	8.11 E
Lenzen	50	53.05 N	11.28 E
Lenzerheide (Lai)	54	46.44 N	9.33 E
Lenzinghausen	48	52.07 N	8.28 E
Lenzkirch	54	47.52 N	8.12 E
Léo, H. Vol.	140	11.06 N	2.06 W
Leo, Ind., U.S.	206	41.13 N	85.01 W
Leoben	30	47.23 N	15.06 E
Leobschütz → Głubczyce	30	50.13 N	17.49 E
Leo Carrillo State Beach ♠	218	34.03 N	118.56 W
Léogâne	228	18.31 N	72.38 W
Leogang	58	47.26 N	12.45 E
Leola, Ark., U.S.	184	34.10 N	92.35 W
Leola, Pa., U.S.	198	40.05 N	76.11 W
Leola, S. Dak., U.S.	188	45.43 N	98.56 W
Leominster, Eng., U.K.	44	52.14 N	2.45 W
Leominster, Mass., U.S.	197	42.32 N	71.45 W
León, Esp.	34	42.36 N	5.34 W
Léon, Fr.	32	43.53 N	1.18 W
León, Nic.	226	12.26 N	86.53 W
Leon, Pil.	106	10.47 N	122.23 E
Leon, Iowa, U.S.	180	40.44 N	93.45 W
Leon, Kans., U.S.	188	37.42 N	96.46 W
Leon, N.Y., U.S.	200	42.18 N	79.01 W
León □[5]	226	12.35 N	86.35 W
Leon □[6]	212	31.18 N	95.55 W
León □[9]	34	42.00 N	6.00 W
Leon ≃	186	30.59 N	97.24 W
Leon, Arroyo ≃	272	37.28 N	122.25 W
León, Montes de ⛰	34	42.30 N	6.18 W
Leona	212	31.09 N	95.58 W
Leona ≃	186	28.45 N	99.11 W
Leona, Punta ≻	226	9.41 N	84.41 W
Leonard, Mich., U.S.	204	42.52 N	83.09 W
Leonard, Mo., U.S.	209	39.54 N	92.11 W
Leonard, N. Dak., U.S.	188	46.39 N	97.15 W
Leonard, Tex., U.S.	186	33.23 N	96.15 W
Leonardo	266	40.25 N	74.03 W
Leonardo da Vinci, Aeroporto Intercontinentale ⊠	60	41.48 N	12.13 E
Leonardsburg	204	40.21 N	82.59 W
Leonardsville	200	42.49 N	75.15 W
Leonardtown	178	38.17 N	76.38 W
Leonardville, Namibia	146	23.29 S	18.49 E
Leonardville, Kans., U.S.	188	39.22 N	96.51 W
Leonárison	120	35.28 N	34.08 E
Leona Vicario	190	32.10 N	115.10 W
Leonberg	52	48.48 N	9.01 E
Leonbronn	52	49.03 N	8.53 E
Leon Creek ≃	186	31.11 N	102.45 W
Leondárion	257c	37.59 N	23.51 E
León [de los Aldamas]	224	21.07 N	101.40 W
Leone	164u	14.20 S	170.47 W
Leone, Golfo del → Lion, Golfe du ⊂	32	43.00 N	4.00 E
Leone, Monte ∧	54	46.15 N	8.06 E
Leones	242	32.39 S	62.18 W
Leonessa	60	42.34 N	12.58 E
Leonforte	36	37.39 N	14.24 E
Leongatha	159	38.29 S	145.57 E
León Guzmán	186	25.31 N	103.34 W
Leonia	266	40.52 N	73.59 W
Leonicha	66	59.37 N	38.51 E
Leonidas	206	42.01 N	85.21 W
Leonídhion	38	37.10 N	22.52 E
Leonidovo	79	49.17 N	142.50 E
Leon Junction	212	31.20 N	97.36 W
Leonora	152	28.53 S	121.20 E
Leonovo	72	55.26 N	38.42 E
León Rougés	242	27.13 S	65.32 W
Leontjev Bajrak, Uročišče ♠	73	48.03 N	38.48 E
Leontjevka	75	43.03 N	69.50 E
Leontjevo	66	58.58 N	36.37 E
Leonville	184	30.29 N	91.59 W
Leopard	275	40.01 N	75.27 W
Leopold	159	38.11 S	144.28 E
Leopold, Camp ■	263b	4.18 S	15.17 E
Léopold, Mont ∧[2]	263b	4.19 S	15.15 E
Leopold and Astrid Coast ⏏[2]	9	67.10 S	84.10 E
Leopoldau ⬥[8]	254b	48.16 N	16.27 E
Leopold Downs	152	17.52 S	125.25 E
Léopold II, Lac → Mai-Ndombe, Lac ◎	142	2.00 S	18.20 E
Leopoldina	246	21.32 S	42.38 W
Leopoldkanaal ≌	46	51.14 N	3.46 E
Leopoldo de Bulhões	245	16.37 S	48.46 W
Leopoldo y Astrid, Costa → Leopold and Astrid Coast ⏏[2]	9	67.10 S	84.10 E
Leopoldsburg	52	51.07 N	5.15 E
Leopoldsdorf	254b	48.06 N	16.24 E
Leopoldshagen	50	53.46 N	13.53 E
Leopoldstadt ⬥[8]	254b	48.13 N	16.23 E
Léopoldville → Kinshasa	142	4.18 S	15.18 E
Leoti	188	38.29 N	101.21 W
Leoville	174	53.37 N	107.35 W
Leovo	68	46.29 N	28.15 E
Le Pailly	54	47.48 N	5.25 E
Le Palais	32	47.21 N	3.09 W
Lepanto, C.R.	226	9.57 N	85.02 W
Lepanto → Návpaktos, Ellás	38	38.23 N	21.50 E
Lepanto, Ark., U.S.	184	35.36 N	90.20 W
Lepar, Pulau I	102	2.57 S	106.50 E
Le Parcq	46	50.23 N	2.06 E
Le Pâté	251	48.32 N	2.18 E
Lepe	34	37.15 N	7.12 W
Le Péage-de-Roussillon	56	45.22 N	4.48 E
Le Pecq	251	48.54 N	2.07 E
Lepel'	66	54.53 N	28.42 E
Le Pellerin	32	47.12 N	1.45 W
Lepembusu, Keli ∧	105b	8.40 S	121.49 E
Le Perray-en-Yvelines	251	48.42 N	1.51 E
Le Perreux-sur-Marne	251	48.51 N	2.30 E
Leper Settlement ♥	219a	21.12 N	156.58 W
Lepeški	72	56.05 N	38.07 E
Le Petit-Clamart ♥	251	48.47 N	2.14 E
Le Petit-Couronne	46	49.23 N	1.01 E
Le Petit-Quevilly	46	49.26 N	1.02 E
Lephepe	146	23.20 S	25.50 E
Lépi	142	12.52 S	15.26 E
Le Piastre	60	44.00 N	10.50 E
Lepihué	244	41.37 S	73.36 W
Le Pin	251	48.55 N	2.38 E
Le Pin-au-Haras	46	48.44 N	0.09 E
L'Épine, Fr.	52	48.58 N	4.28 E
L'Épine, Fr.	251	48.32 N	2.21 E
Leping	90	28.57 N	117.05 E
Lepini, Monti ⛰	60	41.35 N	13.00 E
Lépin-le-Lac	56	45.32 N	5.47 E
L'Épiphanie	196	45.51 N	73.30 W
Lepl'avo	68	49.48 N	31.32 E
Le Plessis-aux-Bois	251	49.00 N	2.46 E
Le Plessis-Belleville	46	49.06 N	2.46 E
Le Plessis-Bouchard	251	49.00 N	2.14 E
Le Plessis-Pâté	251	48.37 N	2.20 E
Le Plessis-Trévise	251	48.49 N	2.34 E
Lépo, Lagoa de ◎	142	17.08 S	19.00 E
Le Poët	56	44.17 N	5.53 E
Le Pont	54	46.40 N	6.20 E
Le Pont-de-Beauvoisin	56	45.32 N	5.40 E
Le Pont-de-Montvert	56	44.22 N	3.45 E
Le Pontel	251	48.49 N	1.53 E
Lepontine, Alpi ⛰	54	46.25 N	8.40 E
Le Port	147c	20.55 S	55.18 E
Le Portel	46	50.42 N	1.34 E
Le Port-Marly	251	48.53 N	2.06 E
Le Pouzin	56	44.45 N	4.45 E
Leppävirta	26	62.29 N	27.47 E
Lepperton	162	39.04 S	174.13 E
Leppin	50	52.53 N	11.34 E
Leppington	264a	33.58 S	150.49 E
Le Pradet	56	43.06 N	6.01 E
Lepreau, Point ≻	176	45.04 N	66.27 W
Le Prêcheur	230e	14.48 N	61.14 W
Le Pré-Saint-Gervais	251	48.53 N	2.25 E
Le Prese	54	46.18 N	10.04 E
Lepsinsk	76	45.32 N	80.37 E
Lepsy, S.S.S.R.	76	46.18 N	78.20 E
Lepsy, S.S.S.R.	76	46.15 N	78.55 E
Leptis Magna ⊥	136	32.38 N	14.18 E
Le Puy	56	45.02 N	3.53 E
Leqing	90	28.08 N	120.58 E
Lequeitio	34	43.22 N	2.30 W
Le Quesnoy	46	50.15 N	3.38 E
Léraba ≃	140	9.42 N	4.35 W
Le Raincy	251	48.54 N	2.31 E
Le Rayol-Canadel-sur-Mer	56	43.10 N	6.28 E
Le Raysville	200	41.51 N	76.11 W
Lerberget	41	56.11 N	12.33 E
Lercara Friddi	36	37.45 N	13.36 E
Lerche	253	51.37 N	7.43 E
Lerderderg ≃	159	37.42 S	144.30 E
Lerdo → Ciudad Lerdo	186	25.32 N	103.32 W
Lerdo de Tejada	224	18.37 N	95.31 W
Léré, Fr.	46	47.28 N	2.52 E
Léré, Mali	140	15.43 N	4.55 W
Lere, Nig.	140	9.43 N	9.21 E
Léré, Tchad	136	9.39 N	14.13 E
Lereh	154	3.08 S	139.54 E
Lerek ∧	104	3.47 N	102.47 E
Le Renne, Rivière ≃	196	45.41 N	72.39 W
Le Reposoir	54	46.00 N	6.33 E
Leri ≃	44	52.32 N	4.02 W
Leribe	148	28.58 S	28.00 E
Lerici	58	44.04 N	9.55 E
Lérida, Col.	236	0.10 N	70.42 W
Lérida, Esp.	34	41.37 N	0.37 E
Lerik	74	38.46 N	48.25 E
Lérins, Îles de II	56	43.31 N	7.03 E
Lerma	34	42.02 N	3.45 W
Lerma ≃	224	20.13 N	102.46 W
Lermontovka	79	47.10 N	134.20 E
Lermoos	54	47.24 N	10.53 E
Le Robert	230e	14.41 N	60.57 W
Léros I, Ellás	38	37.08 N	26.52 E
Léros I, Ellás	257c	37.59 N	23.34 E
Lérouville	52	48.47 N	5.33 E
Leroux Wash ∨	190	34.54 N	110.12 W
Leroy, Ind., U.S.	206	41.22 N	87.16 W
Le Roy, Kans., U.S.	188	38.05 N	95.38 W
Le Roy, Minn., U.S.	180	43.31 N	92.30 W
Le Roy, N.Y., U.S.	200	42.59 N	77.59 W
Le Roy, Pa., U.S.	200	41.41 N	76.43 W
Leroy, Tex., U.S.	212	31.44 N	97.01 W
Lerum	26	57.46 N	12.16 E
Le Russey	54	47.10 N	6.44 E
Lerwick	28	60.09 N	1.09 W
Léry	196	45.21 N	73.48 W
Lesa	56	45.50 N	8.34 E
Les Abrets	56	45.32 N	5.35 E
Les Abymes	231o	16.16 N	61.31 W
Lesage, Lac ◎	196	46.19 N	75.03 W
Le Saint-Esprit	230e	14.34 N	60.57 W
Les Aix-d'Angillon	46	47.12 N	2.34 E
Les Allues	56	45.26 N	6.33 E
Les Alluets-le-Roi	251	48.55 N	1.55 E
Les Andelys	46	49.15 N	1.25 E
Les Anses-d'Arlets	230e	14.29 N	61.05 W
Le Sappey-en-Chartreuse	56	45.16 N	5.47 E
Les Arcs	56	43.27 N	6.29 E
Lesatima, Ol Doinyo ∧	144	0.19 S	36.37 E
Le Sauze	56	44.22 N	6.41 E
Les Baux-en-Provence	56	43.45 N	4.48 E
Les Bézards	46	47.48 N	2.44 E
Les Bordes	251	48.39 N	1.58 E
Lesbos → Lésvos I	38	39.10 N	26.20 E
Les Bouchoux	54	46.18 N	5.49 E
Les Bréviaires	251	48.42 N	1.49 E
Lesbury	42	55.24 N	1.36 W
L'Escarène	56	43.50 N	7.21 E
L'Escaut	46	50.27 N	3.35 E
Les Cayes	228	18.12 N	73.45 W
Les Chaises	251	48.39 N	1.42 E
Les Chapieux	56	45.42 N	6.44 E
Leschenault, Cape ≻	152	31.18 S	115.27 E
Leschenault Inlet ⊂	158a	33.15 S	115.42 E
Lesches	251	48.54 N	2.47 E
Leščinovka	68	49.16 N	34.14 E
Les Clayes-sous-Bois	251	48.49 N	1.59 E
Les Contamines-Montjoie	56	45.50 N	6.44 E
Les Diablerets	54	46.21 N	7.10 E
Les Diablerets ∧	54	46.19 N	7.12 E
Les Echarmeaux	54	46.10 N	4.27 E
Les Échelles	56	45.26 N	5.45 E
Les Écureuils	196	46.39 N	71.43 W
Le Semnoz ∧	56	45.48 N	6.07 E
Leseru	144	0.35 N	35.10 E
Les Essarts	32	46.46 N	1.14 W
Les Essarts-le-Roi	251	48.43 N	1.54 E
Les Estables	56	44.54 N	4.10 E
Les Étangs	52	49.09 N	6.23 E
Lesever, Mount ∧	152	30.10 S	115.11 E
Les Fonts	256d	41.32 N	2.02 E
Les Fourgs	54	46.50 N	6.25 E
Les Galleries d'Anjou ⬥[9]	265a	45.35 N	73.34 W
Les Gâtines	251	48.48 N	1.58 E
Les Gets	54	46.09 N	6.40 E
Les Granges-le-Roi	251	48.30 N	2.01 E
Les Halles	56	45.43 N	4.26 E
Leshan	97	29.34 N	103.45 E
Les Haudères	54	46.05 N	7.31 E
Les Hautes-Rivières	52	49.53 N	4.50 E
Les Herbiers	32	46.52 N	1.01 W
Les Houches	56	45.53 N	6.48 E
Leshui ≃	90	26.54 N	113.12 E
Lesignano de'Bagni	58	44.39 N	10.18 E
Lésigny	251	48.45 N	2.37 E
Lesima, Monte ∧	56	44.41 N	9.15 E
Lesina	60	41.52 N	15.21 E
Lesina, Lago di ⊂	60	41.53 N	15.26 E
Les Islettes	52	49.06 N	5.00 E
Lesjaskog	26	62.15 N	8.22 E
Lesjöfors	40	59.59 N	14.11 E
Lesken	74	43.16 N	43.48 E
Les'ki	68	49.19 N	32.13 E
Lesko	30	49.29 N	22.21 E
Leskovac	38	42.59 N	21.57 E
Leskov Island I	9	56.40 S	28.10 W
Les Laumes	54	47.32 N	4.27 E
Les Lecques	56	43.11 N	5.40 E
Leslie, S. Afr.	148	26.27 S	28.55 E
Leslie, Ark., U.S.	184	35.50 N	92.34 W
Leslie, Ga., U.S.	182	31.57 N	84.05 W
Leslie, Mich., U.S.	206	42.27 N	84.26 W
Leslie, W. Va., U.S.	178	38.03 N	80.43 W
Les Lilas	251	48.53 N	2.25 E
Les Loges	251	48.34 N	2.03 E
Les Loges-en-Josas	251	48.46 N	2.09 E
Lesmahagow	42	55.39 N	3.55 W
Les Marécottes	54	46.07 N	7.00 E
Les Mées	56	44.02 N	5.59 E
Les Mesnuls	46	48.45 N	1.50 E
Lesmo	256b	45.39 N	9.18 E
Les Molières	251	48.40 N	2.04 E
Les Monges ∧	56	44.16 N	6.12 E
Lesmont	46	48.26 N	4.25 E
Les Moroubas	142	6.11 N	20.13 E
Les Mosses	54	46.24 N	7.07 E
Les Mureaux	251	49.00 N	1.55 E
Leśna	30	51.02 N	15.16 E
Lesna ≃	66	52.10 N	23.33 E
Lesnaja	66	52.59 N	25.46 E
Les Neyrolles	54	46.08 N	5.38 E
Lešnica	38	44.39 N	19.19 E
Lesnoj, S.S.S.R.	70	54.11 N	40.27 E
Lesnoj, S.S.S.R.	76	56.57 N	67.15 E
Lesnoj ⬥[8]	255a	60.00 N	30.19 E
Lesnoje	66	58.17 N	35.32 E
Lesnoje Konobejevo	70	54.02 N	41.55 E
Lesnoje Mat'unino	70	53.27 N	47.26 E
Lesnoj Gorodok	255b	55.39 N	37.13 E
Lesnoj Park ♠	255a	59.59 N	30.21 E
Lesný ∧	30	50.02 N	12.37 E
Lesnyje Pol'any, S.S.S.R.	24	58.58 N	52.26 E
Lesnyje Pol'any, S.S.S.R.	255b	55.57 N	37.53 E
Lesogorsk, S.S.S.R.	70	55.06 N	43.56 E
Lesogorsk, S.S.S.R.	78	56.03 N	99.33 E
Lesogorsk, S.S.S.R.	79	49.27 N	142.08 E
Lesogorskij	24	61.02 N	28.53 E
Lesopil'noje	79	46.44 N	134.20 E
Lesotho □[1]	128		
	148	29.30 S	28.30 E
Lesovščina	68	50.47 N	28.35 E
Lesozavodsk	79	45.28 N	133.27 E
Lesozavodskij	24	66.44 N	32.49 E
Lesparre-Médoc	32	45.18 N	0.56 W
Les Pavillons-sous-Bois	251	48.55 N	2.30 E
Les Pieux	32	49.31 N	1.48 W
Les Planches-en-Montagne	54	46.40 N	6.01 E
Les Ponts-de-Martel	54	46.54 N	6.41 E
Les Praz-de-Chamonix	54	45.56 N	6.52 E
Lesquin	46	50.35 N	3.07 E
Les Riceys	46	47.59 N	4.22 E
Les Roches-l'Evêque	46	47.47 N	0.53 E
Les Rousses	54	46.29 N	6.04 E
Les Ruelles	251	48.40 N	1.37 E
Les Sables-d'Olonne	32	46.30 N	1.47 W
Lessach	58	47.11 N	13.49 E
Les Salles-sur-Verdon	56	43.46 N	6.12 E
Lessay	32	49.13 N	1.32 W
Les Scaffarels	56	43.57 N	6.41 E
Lesse ≃	52	50.14 N	4.54 E
Lessebo	26	56.45 N	15.16 E
Lessen → Lessines	46	50.43 N	3.50 E
Lesser Antilles II	228	15.00 N	61.00 W
Lesser Khingan Mountains → Xiaoxing'anling-shanmai ⛰	79	50.00 N	126.25 E
Lesser Slave ≃	172	55.10 N	114.03 W
Lesser Slave Lake ◎	172	55.25 N	115.30 W
Lessines (Lessen)	46	50.43 N	3.50 E
Lessini, Monti ⛰	58	45.41 N	11.13 E
L'Estaque	56	43.22 N	5.20 E
Lester, Pa., U.S.	275	39.52 N	75.17 W
Lester, Wash., U.S.	214	47.12 N	121.29 W
Les Thilliers-en-Vexin	46	49.14 N	1.36 E
Lestijärvi	26	63.32 N	24.39 E
Lestijoki ≃	26	64.04 N	23.38 E
Lestock	174	51.18 N	104.00 W
L'Estréchure	56	44.06 N	3.47 E
Les Trois Lacs ◎	196	45.48 N	71.54 W
Le Sueur	180	44.27 N	93.54 W
Le Sueur ≃	180	44.07 N	94.03 W
Lešukonskoje	24	64.54 N	45.40 E
Lesung, Tanjung ≻	105a	6.28 S	105.40 E
Lesunovo	70	55.40 N	43.07 E
Les Vans	56	44.24 N	4.08 E
Les Verrières	54	46.54 N	6.30 E
Lésvos I	38	39.10 N	26.20 E
Leszno	30	51.51 N	16.35 E
Letälven ≃	40	59.05 N	14.20 E
L'Étang-la-Ville	251	48.52 N	2.05 E
Letcher	188	43.54 N	98.08 W
Letchmore Heath	250	51.40 N	0.20 W
Letchworth	44	51.58 N	0.14 W
Letchworth State Park ♠	200	42.42 N	77.56 W
Letea, Ostrovul I	38	45.20 N	29.20 E
Le Teil	56	44.33 N	4.41 E
Le Temple	251	49.00 N	1.58 E
Letenye	30	46.26 N	16.43 E
Le Tertre-Saint-Denis	251	48.56 N	1.36 E
Lethbridge, Austl.	264a	33.44 S	150.48 E
Lethbridge, Alta., Can.	172	49.42 N	112.50 W
Lethbridge, Newf., Can.	176	48.21 N	53.52 W
Le Theil-sur-Huisne	46	48.16 N	0.42 E
Lethem	236	3.23 N	59.48 W
Le Thillot	54	47.53 N	6.46 E
Le Tholy	54	48.05 N	6.45 E
Le Thor	56	43.56 N	5.00 E
Le Thoronet	56	43.27 N	6.18 E
Leti, Kepulauan II	154	8.13 S	127.50 E
Leti, Pulau I	102	8.12 S	127.41 E
Letiahau ≃	146	21.16 S	24.00 E
Letičev	68	49.23 N	27.37 E
Leticia	236	4.09 S	69.57 W
Leting	88	39.27 N	118.53 E
Letino	60	41.26 N	14.17 E
Letjiesbos	148	32.34 S	22.16 E
Letka	24	59.36 N	49.22 E
Letlhakane	146	21.27 S	25.30 E
Letlhakeng	146	24.08 S	25.02 E
Letmathe	52	51.22 N	7.37 E
Letn'aja Zolotica	24	64.57 N	36.50 E
Letnerečenskij	24	64.17 N	34.23 E
Letong	102	2.58 N	105.42 E
Le Touquet-Paris-Plage	46	50.31 N	1.35 E
Le Touvet	56	45.21 N	5.57 E
Letovo	255b	55.34 N	37.24 E
Letpadan	100	17.47 N	95.45 E
Le Trait	46	49.28 N	0.49 E
Le Trayas	56	43.28 N	6.55 E
Le Tremblay-sur-Mauldre	251	48.47 N	1.53 E
Le Tréport	46	50.04 N	1.22 E
Letschin	50	52.39 N	14.21 E
Letsôk-aw Kyun I	100	11.37 N	98.15 E
Letter	48	52.24 N	9.38 E
Letterkenny	28	54.57 N	7.44 W
Letterston	44	51.56 N	5.00 W
Lettonie → Latvijskaja Sovetskaja Socialist českaja Respublika □[3]	66	57.00 N	25.00 E
Letts	208	39.14 N	85.35 W
Letzlingen	50	52.26 N	11.29 E
Leu	38	44.11 N	24.00 E
Léua	142	11.34 S	20.32 E
Leubnitz	50	50.43 N	12.21 E
Leubsdorf	50	50.48 N	13.08 E
Leucadia	218	33.04 N	117.18 W
Leucate, Étang de ⊂	32	42.51 N	3.00 E
Leudeville	251	48.34 N	2.20 E
Leuenberger Forst ⬥[3]	254a	52.40 N	13.53 E
Leuglay	54	47.49 N	4.48 E
Leuk	54	46.19 N	7.38 E
Leukerbad	54	46.23 N	7.38 E
Leulumoega	165a	13.49 S	171.55 W
Leumeah	264a	34.03 S	150.50 E
Leuna	50	51.19 N	12.01 E
Leupoldsgrün	50	50.17 N	11.47 E
Leura	160	33.43 S	150.20 E
Leura, Mount ∧[2]	159	38.15 S	143.09 E
Leuser, Gunung ∧	104	3.45 N	97.11 E
Leušinskij Tuman, Ozero ◎	76	59.42 N	65.35 E
Leutenberg	50	50.34 N	11.28 E
Leutersdorf	50	50.57 N	14.40 E
Leutershausen	52	49.18 N	10.24 E
Leutesdorf	52	50.27 N	7.23 E
Leutkirch	54	47.49 N	10.01 E
Leuven (Louvain)	52	50.53 N	4.42 E
Leuville-sur-Orge	251	48.37 N	2.16 E
Leuwiliang	105a	6.34 S	106.37 E
Leuze, Bel.	46	50.36 N	3.36 E
Leuze, Bel.	52	50.34 N	4.54 E
Levack	180	46.38 N	81.23 W
Levádhia	38	38.25 N	22.54 E
Levaja Mama ≃	78	57.10 N	111.54 E
Le Val-d'Ajol	54	47.55 N	6.29 E
Le Val-d'Albian	251	48.45 N	2.11 E
Levallois-Perret	251	48.54 N	2.18 E
Le Val-Saint-Germain	251	48.34 N	2.04 E
Levan	190	39.33 N	111.52 W
Levanger	26	63.45 N	11.18 E
Levanna, Monte ∧	56	45.24 N	7.12 E
Levant, Île du I	56	43.03 N	6.28 E
Levante, Riviera di ⏏[2]	56	44.15 N	9.30 E
Levanto	56	44.10 N	9.38 E
Levanzo, Isola di I	36	38.00 N	12.20 E
Levaši	74	42.27 N	47.20 E
Le Vauclin	230e	14.33 N	60.51 W
Levdym	76	60.29 N	66.19 E
Leveaux Mountain ∧[2]	180	47.37 N	90.47 W
Level, Isla I	244	44.29 S	74.23 W
Level Green	269b	40.24 N	79.43 W
Levelland	186	33.35 N	102.23 W
Levelock	170	59.07 N	156.52 W
Level Park	206	42.22 N	85.18 W
Leven ≃, Eng., U.K.	42	54.14 N	3.01 W
Leven ≃, Eng., U.K.	42	54.31 N	1.21 W
Leven Point ≻	148	27.55 S	32.35 E
Levens	56	43.52 N	7.13 E
Levenshulme ⬥[8]	252	53.27 N	2.10 W
Levent	120	38.27 N	37.52 E
Leventina, Valle ∨	54	46.25 N	9.52 E
L'Evêque	46	49.18 N	0.11 E
Leveque, Cape ≻	152	16.24 S	122.56 E
Leverett Glacier ⛉	9	85.30 S	150.00 W
Leveretts Chapel	212	32.19 N	94.55 W
Levering	180	45.38 N	84.47 W
Leverkusen	52	51.03 N	6.59 E
Levern	48	52.22 N	8.26 E
Lever Park ♠	252	53.37 N	2.34 W
Leverville	142	4.50 S	18.44 E
Le Vésinet	251	48.54 N	2.08 E
Le Vésuve → Vesuvio ∧[1]	60	40.49 N	14.26 E
Leviathan Peak ∧	216	38.41 N	119.37 W
Levice	30	48.13 N	18.37 E
Levicha	76	57.36 N	59.55 E
Levick, Mount ∧	9	74.08 S	163.12 E
Levico	58	46.01 N	11.18 E
Levie	36	41.42 N	9.07 E
Levier	54	46.57 N	6.08 E
Le Vigan	32	43.59 N	3.35 E
Levin	162	40.37 S	175.17 E
Levino	66	60.29 N	37.30 E
Lévis	196	46.48 N	71.11 W
Lévis □[6]	196	46.40 N	71.15 W
Lévis-Saint Nom	251	48.43 N	1.58 E
Levítha I	38	37.00 N	26.28 E
Levittown → Willingboro, N.J., U.S.	198	40.03 N	74.53 W
Levittown, N.Y., U.S.	200	40.41 N	73.31 W
Levittown, Pa., U.S.	198	40.09 N	74.50 W
Levittown Shop-A-Rama ⬥[9]	275	40.09 N	74.49 W
Lévka	120	35.07 N	32.51 E
Lévka Óri ⛰	38	35.18 N	24.01 E
Levkás	38	38.50 N	20.41 E
Levkás I	38	38.39 N	20.27 E
Levkímmi	38	39.25 N	20.04 E
Levkónoikon	120	35.15 N	33.45 E
Levkosía (Nicosia)	120	35.10 N	33.22 E
Levoča	30	49.02 N	20.36 E
Levokumskoje	74	44.48 N	44.39 E
Levroux	32	46.59 N	1.37 E
Levski	38	43.22 N	25.08 E
Lev Tolstoj	66	53.13 N	39.27 E
Levuka	165g	17.41 S	178.50 E
Lėvuo ≃	66	56.04 N	24.23 E
Levyj Tuzlov ≃	73	47.35 N	39.23 E
Lewapaku	105b	9.43 S	119.55 E
Lewbeach	200	42.00 N	74.47 W
Lewe	100	19.38 N	96.07 E
Lewedorp	48	51.30 N	3.45 E
Lewellen	188	41.20 N	102.09 W
Lewer ≃	146	25.30 S	17.45 E
Lewes, Eng., U.K.	44	50.52 N	0.01 E
Lewes, Del., U.S.	198	38.47 N	75.08 W
Lewin Brzeski	30	50.46 N	17.37 E
Lewis, Iowa, U.S.	188	41.18 N	95.05 W
Lewis, Kans., U.S.	188	37.56 N	99.15 W
Lewis □[6], Ky., U.S.	208	38.32 N	83.21 W
Lewis □[6], Mo., U.S.	209	40.08 N	91.45 W
Lewis □[6], N.Y., U.S.	202	43.47 N	75.29 W
Lewis □[6], Wash., U.S.	214	46.35 N	122.22 W
Lewis ≃	214	45.51 N	122.48 W
Lewis, Butt of ≻	28	58.31 N	6.15 W
Lewis, East Fork ≃	214	45.52 N	122.43 W
Lewis, Isle of I	28	58.10 N	6.40 W
Lewis, Mount ∧	194	40.24 N	116.51 W
Lewis and Clark ≃	214	46.10 N	123.52 W
Lewis and Clark Caverns State Park ♠	192	45.49 N	111.13 W
Lewis and Clark Lake ◎[1]	188	42.50 N	97.45 W
Lewisberry	198	40.08 N	76.52 W
Lewisburg, Ky., U.S.	184	36.59 N	86.57 W
Lewisburg, Ohio, U.S.	208	39.51 N	84.33 W
Lewisburg, Pa., U.S.	200	40.58 N	76.53 W
Lewisburg, Tenn., U.S.	184	35.27 N	86.48 W
Lewisburg, W. Va., U.S.	178	37.48 N	80.27 W
Lewis Center	204	40.12 N	83.01 W
Lewis Creek ≃, Calif., U.S.	216	35.17 N	120.58 W
Lewis Creek ≃, Ind., U.S.	208	39.22 N	85.51 W
Lewisdale	274c	38.58 N	76.58 W
Lewisetta	198	38.01 N	76.28 W
Lewis Gut ⊂	266	41.09 N	73.09 W
Lewisham	263d	26.07 S	27.49 E
Lewisham ⬥[8]	44	51.27 N	0.01 E
Lewis Hills ⛰[2]	176	48.48 N	58.30 W
Lewis Island I	210	27.44 N	82.38 W
Lewis-Lockport Airport ⊠	268	41.36 N	88.05 W
Lewis Pass)(	162	42.23 S	172.24 E
Lewisport	184	37.56 N	86.54 W
Lewisporte	176	49.15 N	55.03 W
Lewis Range ⛰, Austl.	152	20.20 S	128.40 E
Lewis Range ⛰, N.A.	192	48.30 N	113.15 W
Lewis Run	204	41.52 N	78.40 W
Lewis Run ≃	269b	40.17 N	79.55 W
Lewis Smith Lake ◎[1]	184	34.05 N	87.07 W
Lewiston, Calif., U.S.	194	40.43 N	122.48 W
Lewiston, Idaho, U.S.	192	46.25 N	117.01 W
Lewiston, Maine, U.S.	178	44.06 N	70.13 W
Lewiston, Mich., U.S.	180	44.53 N	84.18 W
Lewiston, Minn., U.S.	180	44.00 N	91.49 W
Lewiston, N.Y., U.S.	200	43.10 N	79.03 W
Lewiston, Utah, U.S.	190	41.58 N	111.51 W
Lewiston Orchards	192	46.23 N	116.59 W
Lewistown, Ill., U.S.	184	40.24 N	90.09 W
Lewistown, Md., U.S.	198	39.32 N	77.25 W
Lewistown, Mo., U.S.	209	40.05 N	91.49 W
Lewistown, Mont., U.S.	192	47.04 N	109.26 W
Lewistown, Ohio, U.S.	206	40.25 N	83.53 W
Lewistown, Pa., U.S.	198	40.36 N	77.31 W
Lewisville, N.B., Can.	176	45.06 N	64.46 W
Lewisville, Ark., U.S.	184	33.22 N	93.35 W
Lewisville, Ind., U.S.	208	39.48 N	85.21 W
Lewisville, Pa., U.S.	198	39.43 N	75.53 W
Lewisville, Tex., U.S.	212	33.03 N	97.00 W
Lewisville Dam ⬥[6]	212	33.05 N	96.55 W
Lewoleba	102	8.23 S	123.24 E
Lewotobi Lakilaki, Ili ∧	105b	8.32 S	122.46 E
Lewvan	174	50.00 N	104.06 W
Lexa	184	34.36 N	90.45 W
Lexington, Ga., U.S.	182	33.52 N	83.07 W
Lexington, Ill., U.S.	206	40.39 N	88.47 W
Lexington, Ind., U.S.	208	38.39 N	85.37 W
Lexington, Ky., U.S.	208	38.03 N	84.30 W
Lexington, Mass., U.S.	197	42.27 N	71.14 W
Lexington, Mich., U.S.	180	43.16 N	82.32 W
Lexington, Miss., U.S.	184	33.07 N	90.03 W
Lexington, Mo., U.S.	184	39.11 N	93.52 W
Lexington, Nebr., U.S.	188	40.47 N	99.45 W
Lexington, N.C., U.S.	182	35.49 N	80.15 W
Lexington, N.Y., U.S.	200	42.15 N	74.22 W
Lexington, Ohio, U.S.	204	40.41 N	82.35 W
Lexington, Okla., U.S.	186	35.01 N	97.20 W
Lexington, Oreg., U.S.	192	45.27 N	119.41 W
Lexington, S.C., U.S.	182	34.00 N	81.14 W
Lexington, Tenn., U.S.	184	35.39 N	88.24 W
Lexington, Tex., U.S.	212	30.25 N	97.01 W
Lexington, Va., U.S.	182	37.47 N	79.27 W
Lexington Park	178	38.16 N	76.27 W
Lexington Reservoir ◎[1]	216	37.12 N	121.59 W
Lexton	159	37.17 S	143.31 E
Leybourne	250	51.18 N	0.25 E
Leyburn	42	54.19 N	1.49 W
Leyden → Leiden	48	52.09 N	4.30 E
Leyland	42	53.42 N	2.42 W
Leyne	120	37.22 N	28.02 E
Leyond ≃	174	51.40 N	96.32 W
Leyou ≃	142	1.07 S	13.08 E
Leyre ≃	32	44.39 N	1.01 W
Leysdown-on-Sea	44	51.24 N	0.55 E
Leysin	54	46.21 N	7.01 E
Leyte	106	11.23 N	124.29 E
Leyte □[4]	106	10.50 N	124.55 E
Leyte I	106	10.50 N	124.50 E
Leyte Gulf ⊂	106	10.50 N	125.25 E
Leyu	96	31.55 N	120.43 E
Lèz ≃	56	44.13 N	4.43 E
Lèz ≌	56	43.31 N	3.55 E
Leža	66	58.56 N	40.45 E
Leža ≃	66	59.15 N	40.10 E
Leżajsk	30	50.16 N	22.24 E
Lezama	236	9.43 N	66.24 W
Lézard, Pointe à ≻	231o	16.08 N	61.47 W
Lézarde ≃	230e	14.36 N	61.01 W
Lézat	54	46.30 N	5.56 E
Lèze ≃	56	43.40 N	5.28 E
Lezhë	38	41.47 N	19.39 E
Lezhi	97	30.17 N	105.02 E
Ležn'ovo	70	56.46 N	40.53 E
Lezzeno	54	45.56 N	9.11 E
L'gov	68	51.43 N	35.17 E

Symbols in the index entries represent the broad categories identified in the key at the right. Symbols with superior numbers (⛰[2]) identify subcategories (see complete key on page I · 26).

Kartensymbole in dem Registerverzeichnis stellen die rechts in Schlüssel erklärten Kategorien dar. Symbole mit hochgestellten Ziffern (⛰[2]) bezeichnen Unterabteilungen einer Kategorie (vgl. vollständiger Schlüssel auf Seite I · 26).

Los símbolos incluídos en el texto del índice representan las grandes categorias identificadas con la clave a la derecha. Los símbolos con numeros en su parte superior (⛰[2]) identifican las subcategorías (véase la clave completa en la página I · 26).

Les symboles de l'index représentent les catégories indiquées dans la légende à droite. Les symboles suivis d'un indice (⛰[2]) représentent des sous-catégories (voir légende complète à la page I · 26).

Os símbolos incluídos no texto do índice representam as grandes categorias identificadas com a chave à direita. Os símbolos com números em sua parte superior (⛰[2]) identificam as subcategorias (veja-se a chave completa à página I · 26).

Symbol	English	Deutsch	Español	Français	Português
∧	Mountain	Berg	Montaña	Montagne	Montanha
⛰	Mountains	Berge	Montañas	Montagnes	Montanhas
)(	Pass	Pass	Paso	Col	Passo
∨	Valley, Canyon	Tal, Cañon	Valle, Cañón	Vallée, Canyon	Vale, Canhão
≍	Plain	Ebene	Llano	Plaine	Planície
≻	Cape	Kap	Cabo	Cap	Cabo
I	Island	Insel	Isla	Île	Ilha
II	Islands	Inseln	Islas	Îles	Ilhas
⏏	Other Topographic Features	Andere Topographische Objekte	Otros Elementos Topográficos	Autres données topographiques	Outros Elementos Topográficos

ESPAÑOL — Nombre | Página | Lat.°′ | Long.°′ W=Oeste
FRANÇAIS — Nom | Page | Lat.°′ | Long.°′ W=Ouest
PORTUGUÊS — Nome | Página | Lat.°′ | Long.°′ W=Oeste

Symbol	English	Deutsch	Español	Français	Português
≃	River	Fluss	Río	Rivière	Rio
≊	Canal	Kanal	Canal	Canal	Canal
⌊	Waterfall, Rapids	Wasserfall, Stromschnellen	Cascada, Rápidos	Chute d'eau, Rapides	Cascata, Rápidos
⊔	Strait	Meeresstrasse	Estrecho	Détroit	Estreito
C	Bay, Gulf	Bucht, Golf	Bahía, Golfo	Baie, Golfe	Baía, Golfo
◎	Lake, Lakes	See, Seen	Lago, Lagos	Lac, Lacs	Lago, Lagos
☷	Swamp	Sumpf	Pantano	Marais	Pântano
⊼	Ice Features, Glacier	Eis- und Gletscherformen	Accidentes Glaciales	Formes glaciaires	Acidentes Glaciares
≂	Other Hydrographic Features	Andere Hydrographische Objekte	Otros Elementos Hidrográficos	Autres données hydrographiques	Outros Elementos Hidrográficos
✢	Submarine Features	Untermeerische Objekte	Accidentes Submarinos	Formes de relief sous-marin	Acidentes Submarinos
□	Political Unit	Politische Einheit	Unidad Politica	Entité politique	Unidade Política
♉	Cultural Institution	Kulturelle Institution	Institución Cultural	Institution culturelle	Instituição Cultural
⊥	Historical Site	Historische Stätte	Sitio Histórico	Site historique	Sitio Histórico
♠	Recreational Site	Erholungs- und Ferienort	Sitio de Recreo	Centre de loisirs	Sítio de Lazer
⊠	Airport	Flughafen	Aeropuerto	Aéroport	Aeroporto
■	Military Installation	Militäranlage	Instalación Militar	Installation militaire	Instalação Militar
◆	Miscellaneous	Verschiedenes	Misceláneo	Divers	Miscelânea

Lingling 92 26.11 N 111.29 E
Linglongta 88 40.54 N 119.59 E
Lingma 92 23.22 N 107.53 E
Lingolsheim 54 48.34 N 7.41 E
Lingomo 142 0.38 N 21.59 E
Lingqiu, Zhg. 88 39.24 N 114.13 E
Lingqiu, Zhg. 92 39.28 N 113.40 E
Lingshan, Zhg. 88 36.33 N 120.27 E
Lingshan, Zhg. 92 22.28 N 109.17 E
Lingshanwei 88 35.58 N 120.13 E
Lingshi 92 36.54 N 111.43 E
Lingshou 88 38.18 N 114.24 E
Lingshui 100 18.31 N 110.01 E
Lingtangqiao 90 32.43 N 119.14 E
Lingu 110 29.26 N 87.36 E
Linguère 140 15.24 N 15.07 W
Lingwu 92 38.06 N 106.21 E
Lingxian, Zhg. 88 37.21 N 116.34 E
Lingxian, Zhg. 90 26.30 N 113.46 E
Lingxiazhu 90 29.03 N 119.46 E
Lingyuan 88 41.15 N 119.16 E
Lingzhuangzi 95 39.04 N 117.09 E
Lingzinan 95 39.29 N 115.15 E
Linh, Ngoc ∧ 100 15.04 N 107.59 E
Linhai 90 28.51 N 121.07 E
Linhares 245 19.25 S 40.04 W
Linh-cam 100 18.31 N 105.34 E
Linhe 92 40.51 N 107.30 E
Linhezhuang 95 40.04 N 117.39 E
Linhó 256c 38.46 N 9.23 W
Linhsia
→ Linxia 92 35.34 N 103.08 E
Linhuaiguan 90 32.55 N 117.40 E
Linhuanji 90 33.42 N 116.33 E
Lini
→ Linyi 88 35.04 N 118.22 E
Linjiang, Zhg. 88 41.49 N 126.54 E
Linjiang, Zhg. 90 27.50 N 118.26 E
Linjiang, Zhg. 92 28.04 N 115.21 E
Linjiang, Zhg. 92 33.01 N 105.01 E
Linjiangchang 97 29.14 N 105.58 E
Linjianghu 90 28.40 N 118.01 E
Linjiangsi, Zhg. 92 29.42 N 104.01 E
Linjiangsi, Zhg. 97 30.15 N 104.37 E
Linjiatai 94 40.43 N 123.58 E
Linkenheim 52 49.07 N 8.24 E
Linköping 26 58.25 N 15.37 E
Linkou 79 45.15 N 130.16 E
Linksfield ◆8 263d 26.10 S 28.06 E
Linksmakalnis 66 54.45 N 23.55 E
Linkuva 66 56.05 N 23.59 E
Linkwood 198 38.32 N 75.57 W
Linli 92 29.18 N 111.30 E
Linlithgow 42 55.59 N 3.37 W
Linmeyer 263d 26.16 S 28.04 E
Linmingguan 88 36.47 N 114.30 E
Linn, Kans., U.S. 188 39.41 N 97.05 W
Linn, Mo., U.S. 209 38.29 N 91.51 W
Linn ◆8 253 51.20 N 6.38 E
Linnancang 95 39.50 N 117.37 E
Linnansaaren Kansallispuisto ◆ 26 62.07 N 28.31 E
Linndale 269a 41.27 N 81.46 W
Linne 48 51.10 N 5.57 E
Linnell 216 36.21 N 119.11 W
Linnés Hammarby I 40 59.49 N 17.46 E
Linney Head ≻ 44 51.38 N 5.04 W
Linn Grove 206 40.39 N 85.02 W
Linnhe, Loch C 28 56.37 N 5.25 W
Linnich 52 50.59 N 6.16 E
Linntown 200 40.58 N 76.54 W
Linnville Bayou ≃ 212 28.57 N 95.42 W
Linosa, Isola di I 36 35.52 N 12.52 E
Linovica 68 50.28 N 32.22 E
Lin'ovo 70 50.53 N 44.51 E
Linow 50 53.06 N 12.49 E
Linpu 90 30.03 N 120.15 E
Linqi, Zhg. 88 35.48 N 113.53 E
Linqi, Zhg. 90 29.51 N 119.06 E
Linqing 88 36.53 N 115.41 E
Linqu 88 36.32 N 118.31 E
Linquan 90 33.06 N 115.13 E
Linru 90 34.11 N 112.49 E
Linruzhen 90 34.17 N 112.35 E
Lins 245 21.40 S 49.45 W
Linshanhe 90 30.44 N 114.52 E
Linshanwei 90 30.09 N 120.59 E
Linshui 92 30.21 N 106.59 E
Linshui ≃ 92 40.20 N 99.30 E
Linslade 44 51.55 N 0.41 W
Linstead 231q 18.08 N 77.02 W
Lintan 92 34.37 N 103.40 E
Lintao 92 35.27 N 103.46 E
Linté 142 5.24 N 11.42 E
Linth ≃ 54 47.07 N 9.07 E
Linthal, Fr. 54 47.56 N 7.08 E
Linthal, Schw. 54 46.55 N 9.00 E
Linthicum Heights 274b 39.12 N 76.39 W
Linthkanal ≃ 54 47.13 N 8.57 E
Linthwaite 252 53.37 N 1.51 W
Lintingkou 95 39.39 N 117.30 E
Linton, Austl. 159 37.41 S 143.34 E
Linton, N.Z. 162 40.26 S 175.33 E
Linton, Eng., U.K. 44 52.06 N 0.17 E
Linton, Eng., U.K. 250 51.13 N 0.31 E
Linton, Ind., U.S. 184 39.02 N 87.10 W
Linton, N. Dak., U.S. 188 46.16 N 100.14 W
Lintong 92 34.21 N 109.11 E
Lintorf 52 51.20 N 6.49 E
Linum 254a 52.46 N 12.53 E
Linville, Austl. 161a 26.51 S 152.16 E
Linville, N.C., U.S. 182 36.04 N 81.52 W
Linwood, Austl. 158b 34.21 S 138.46 E
Linwood, Ind., U.S. 208 40.12 N 85.41 W
Linwood, Mass., U.S. 197 42.06 N 71.39 W
Linwood, N.J., U.S. 198 39.21 N 74.34 W
Linwood, Pa., U.S. 275 39.49 N 75.24 W
Linwood, Wash., U.S. 192 47.42 N 117.23 W
Linworth 204 40.06 N 83.04 W
Linwu, Zhg. 88 36.14 N 119.17 E
Linwu, Zhg. 92 25.16 N 112.30 E
Linxi 80 43.30 N 118.00 E
Linxia 92 35.34 N 103.08 E
Linxian, Zhg. 88 36.04 N 113.50 E
Linxian, Zhg. 92 37.58 N 110.59 E
Linxiang 90 29.28 N 113.30 E
Linyanti 146 18.04 S 24.01 E
Linyanti (Chobe) ≃ 146 17.50 S 25.05 E
Linyi, Zhg. 88 35.04 N 118.22 E
Linyi, Zhg. 88 37.13 N 116.51 E
Linyi, Zhg. 92 35.15 N 110.59 E
Linying 90 33.50 N 113.57 E
Linyü
→ Shanhaiguan 88 40.01 N 119.44 E
Linyüan 90 22.30 N 120.25 E
Linz, B.R.D. 52 50.34 N 7.17 E
Linz, Öst. 30 48.18 N 14.18 E
Linze 92 39.19 N 100.17 E
Linzgau ◆1 54 47.45 N 9.16 E
Linzhai 90 24.18 N 115.03 E
Linzhang 88 36.21 N 114.36 E
Linzhi 110 29.25 N 94.22 E
Linzi, Zhg. 88 36.52 N 118.21 E
Linzi, Zhg. 90 33.03 N 119.38 E
Linzikou 90 28.42 N 112.46 E
Linzolo 142 4.25 S 15.07 E
Lioko, Zaïre 142 0.02 N 22.04 E
Lioko, Zaïre 142 1.25 N 23.07 E
Lio Matoh 102 3.10 N 115.14 E
Liomer 48 49.51 N 1.49 E
Lion, Golfe du C 32 43.00 N 4.00 E
Lionel Town 231q 17.48 N 77.14 W
Lion Rock Tunnel ◆5 261d 22.21 N 114.09 E
Lions Den 144 17.16 S 30.02 E
Lion's Head 202 44.59 N 81.15 W
Lionville 198 40.03 N 75.39 W
Lioppa 102 7.40 S 126.00 E
Liouesso 142 1.02 N 15.43 E
Liozno 66 55.02 N 30.48 E
Lipa 106 13.57 N 121.10 E
Lipan 186 32.31 N 98.03 W
Lipany 30 49.10 N 20.58 E
Lipari 36 38.28 N 14.57 E
Lipari, Isola I 36 38.30 N 14.57 E
Lipatkain 102 0.01 S 101.13 E
Lipayan 94 42.13 N 123.23 E
Lipcy 68 50.13 N 36.25 E
Lipeck 66 52.37 N 39.35 E
Lipeck □4 70 52.15 N 40.30 E
Lipeckoje Vtoroje 68 47.46 N 29.41 E
Liperi 26 62.32 N 29.22 E
Lipetsk
→ Lipeck 66 52.37 N 39.35 E
Lipez, Cordillera de ∧ 238 21.40 S 66.35 W
Liphook 44 51.05 N 0.49 W
Lipiany 30 53.00 N 14.59 E
Lipicy 66 53.22 N 37.17 E
Lipin Bor 66 60.16 N 37.57 E
Liping 92 26.17 N 109.00 E
Lipis ≃ 104 4.10 N 102.04 E
Lipiyu 94 41.09 N 123.36 E
Lipka ≃ 255b 55.45 N 37.11 E
Lipkany 68 48.16 N 26.48 E
Lipki 66 53.58 N 37.42 E
Lipník nad Bečvou 30 49.31 N 17.35 E
Lipniški 66 54.00 N 25.37 E
Lipno 30 52.51 N 19.10 E
Lipno, údolní nádrž @1 30 48.43 N 14.04 E
Lipoa Point ≻ 219a 21.02 N 156.38 W
Lipova 38 46.05 N 21.40 E
Lipovaja Dolina 68 50.35 N 33.48 E
Lipovcy 79 44.11 N 131.44 E
Lipovec 68 49.14 N 29.03 E
Lipovka, S.S.S.R. 68 50.52 N 40.02 E
Lipovka, S.S.S.R. 70 49.46 N 44.56 E
Lipovka, S.S.S.R. 70 52.26 N 46.11 E
Lippborg 48 51.40 N 8.02 E
Lippe ≃ 48 51.39 N 6.38 E
Lipperode 48 51.41 N 8.22 E
Lippoldsberg 48 51.37 N 9.33 E
Lippolthausen ◆8 253 51.37 N 7.29 E
Lippstadt 48 51.40 N 8.19 E
Lipscomb 186 36.14 N 100.16 W
Lipsko 30 51.09 N 21.39 E
Lipsoi I 38 37.20 N 26.45 E
Lipsós I 120 37.20 N 26.45 E
Lipton 174 50.54 N 103.50 W
Liptovská Teplička 30 48.59 N 20.06 E
Liptovský Mikuláš 30 49.06 N 19.37 E
Liptrap, Cape ≻ 156 38.54 S 145.55 E
Lipu 92 24.25 N 110.29 E
Lipu La)(114 30.21 N 81.05 E
Liqi 90 27.39 N 116.19 E
Liqiao 97 29.03 N 108.04 E
Lira, Ug. 144 2.15 N 32.54 E
Lira, Ven. 276c 10.26 N 66.46 W
Liranga 142 0.40 S 17.36 E
Lirangdian 95 39.14 N 116.14 E
Lircay 238 12.56 S 74.43 W
Liren 90 33.55 N 118.47 E
Lirentuncun 94 41.24 N 122.59 E
Liri ≃ 60 41.25 N 13.52 E
Liria 34 39.38 N 0.36 W
Liro ≃ 54 46.18 N 9.23 E
Lisa, Punta ≻ 226 8.00 N 80.22 W
Lisala 142 2.09 N 21.31 E
Lisavy 72 56.33 N 38.32 E
Lisboa (Lisbon) 34
256c 38.43 N 9.08 W
Lisboa □5 256c 38.48 N 9.16 W
Lisboa, Universidade de ◆2 256c 38.45 N 9.09 W
Lisbon
→ Lisboa, Port. 34 38.43 N 9.08 W
Lisbon, Ill., U.S. 206 41.29 N 88.29 W
Lisbon, Maine, U.S. 178 44.02 N 70.06 W
Lisbon, Md., U.S. 198 39.20 N 77.04 W
Lisbon, N.H., U.S. 178 44.13 N 71.55 W
Lisbon, N. Dak., U.S. 188 46.27 N 97.41 W
Lisbon, Ohio, U.S. 204 40.47 N 80.46 W
Lisbon Falls 178 44.03 N 70.03 W
Lisbonne
→ Lisboa 34 38.43 N 9.08 W
Lisburn 42 54.31 N 6.03 W
Lisburne, Cape ≻, N. Heb. 165f 15.40 S 166.43 E
Lisburne, Cape ≻, Alaska, U.S. 170 68.52 N 166.14 W
Liscannor Bay C 28 52.55 N 9.25 W
Liscia ≃ 36 41.11 N 9.19 E
Lisec 68 48.52 N 24.36 E
Liseleje 41 56.01 N 11.59 E
Lishan, Zhg. 90 31.50 N 113.16 E
Lishan, Zhg. 94 41.10 N 123.00 E
Lishangzhuang 95 39.35 N 118.11 E
Lishanke 88 40.41 N 119.53 E
Lishe 90 29.48 N 121.28 E
Lishehe ≃ 92 24.18 N 101.32 E
Lishi, Zhg. 92 37.32 N 111.09 E
Lishi, Zhg. 96 31.14 N 120.37 E
Lishi, Zhg. 97 29.20 N 105.24 E
Lishiba 97 29.04 N 106.15 E
Lishichang 97 29.10 N 105.42 E
Lishu 79 43.21 N 124.37 E
Lishui (Yunhe), Zhg. 90 28.06 N 119.34 E
Lishui, Zhg. 90 28.27 N 119.54 E
Lishui, Zhg. 95 40.03 N 115.51 E
Lishui, Zhg. 96 31.39 N 119.01 E
Lisi 79 45.05 N 130.41 E
Lisi 120 35.06 N 33.41 E
Lisianski Island I 14 26.02 N 174.00 W
Lisica ≃ 76 58.34 N 85.11 E
Lisičansk 73 48.55 N 38.26 E
Lisichansk
→ Lisičansk 73 48.55 N 38.26 E
Lisicy 72 56.47 N 36.21 E
Lisieux, Sask., Can. 174 49.17 N 105.59 W
Lisieux, Fr. 46 49.09 N 0.14 E
Lisij Nos 255a 60.01 N 30.00 E
Lisitu 144 9.39 S 34.39 E
Lisizhuang 95 38.55 N 115.07 E
Liska 70 45.50 N 44.50 E
Liska ≃ 70 48.32 N 43.08 E
Liskeard 44 50.28 N 4.28 W
Liski, S.S.S.R. 68 50.56 N 39.29 E
Liski
→ Georgiu-Dež, S.S.S.R. 68 50.59 N 39.30 E
L'Isle, Fr. 46 47.35 N 4.00 E
L'Isle, Schw. 54 46.37 N 6.25 E
Lisle, Ill., U.S. 206 41.48 N 88.05 W
Lisle, N.Y., U.S. 200 42.21 N 76.00 W
L'Isle Adam 46 49.07 N 2.14 E
L'Isle Jourdain, Fr. 32 46.14 N 0.41 E
L'Isle-Jourdain, Fr. 32 43.37 N 1.05 E
L'Isle-sur-la-Sorgue 56 43.55 N 5.03 E
L'Isle-sur-le-Doubs 54 47.27 N 6.35 E
Lisman 184 32.05 N 88.17 W
Lismore, Austl. 156 28.48 S 153.17 E
Lismore, Austl. 159 37.58 S 143.20 E
Lismore, N.S., Can. 176 45.42 N 62.16 W
Lismore Island I 28 56.30 N 5.30 W
Lišn'ovka 68 51.28 N 25.25 E
Lisö ≻1 40 58.55 N 17.45 E
Lišov 30 49.01 N 14.37 E
Liss 44 51.03 N 0.55 W
Lissabon
→ Lisboa 34 38.43 N 9.08 W
Lissberg 52 50.22 N 9.05 E
Lisse 48 52.15 N 4.33 E
Lisses 251 48.36 N 2.26 E
Lissewege 46 51.18 N 3.11 E
Lissie 212 29.33 N 96.13 W
Lissingen 52 50.14 N 6.38 E
Lissone 56 45.37 N 9.14 E
Lissy 251 48.38 N 2.42 E
Lista 70 47.44 N 45.54 E
Lista ≻1 26 58.07 N 6.40 E
Lister ≃ 253 51.05 N 7.45 E
Lištica 36 43.23 N 17.36 E
Listowel, Ont., Can. 202 43.44 N 80.57 W
Listowel, Eire 28 52.27 N 9.29 W
Listv'anka 78 51.52 N 104.51 E
Listv'anskij 76 54.27 N 83.29 E
Lisui 95 40.05 N 116.44 E
Lit 26 63.19 N 14.49 E
Lita 90 27.22 N 116.34 E
Litang, Malay. 102 5.20 N 118.31 E
Litang, Zhg. 92 23.11 N 109.05 E
Litang, Zhg. 92 29.59 N 100.19 E
Litanghe ≃ 92 28.04 N 101.30 E
Litani (Itany) ≃ 240 3.40 N 54.00 W
Līṭānī, Nahr al- ≃ 122 33.20 N 35.14 E
Litcham 44 52.44 N 0.47 E
Litchfield, Conn., U.S. 197 41.45 N 73.11 W
Litchfield, Ill., U.S. 209 39.11 N 89.39 W
Litchfield, Mich., U.S. 206 42.03 N 84.46 W
Litchfield, Minn., U.S. 180 45.08 N 94.31 W
Litchfield, Nebr., U.S. 188 41.09 N 99.09 W
Litchfield, Ohio, U.S. 204 41.10 N 82.02 W
Litchfield □6 197 41.45 N 73.11 W
Litchfield Park 190 33.30 N 112.22 W
Litchville 188 46.39 N 98.11 W
Literberry 209 39.51 N 90.12 W
Līth, Wādī al- ∨ 134 20.40 N 40.35 E
Lithgow 160 33.29 S 150.09 E
Lithia 210 27.51 N 82.10 W
Lithinon, Ákra ≻ 38 34.55 N 24.44 E
Lithonia 182 33.43 N 84.06 W
Lithuanian Soviet Socialist Republic → Litovskaja Sovetskaja Socialističeskaja Respublika □3 66 56.00 N 24.00 E
Litian 90 26.58 N 114.10 E
Litija 36 46.03 N 14.50 E
Litin 68 49.20 N 28.05 E
Litipāra 114 24.42 N 87.37 E
Lititz 198 40.09 N 76.18 W
Litke 79 53.57 N 140.15 E
Litókhoron 38 40.06 N 22.30 E
Litoko 144 1.13 S 24.47 E
Litoměřice 50 50.35 N 14.09 E
Litomyšl 30 49.52 N 16.19 E
Litoo 144 9.54 S 38.24 E
Litoral, Cordillera del ∧ 276c 10.33 N 66.52 W
Litouqiao 96 31.15 N 118.54 E
Litovel 30 49.42 N 17.05 E
Litovko 79 49.15 N 135.11 E
Litovskaja Sovetskaja Socialističeskaja Respublika □3 66 56.00 N 24.00 E
Littau 54 47.03 N 8.16 E
Little ≃, Austl. 159 38.01 S 144.35 E
Little ≃, Ont., Can. 271 42.20 N 82.56 W
Little ≃, U.S. 184 33.37 N 93.52 W
Little ≃, Ala., U.S. 184 34.16 N 85.40 W
Little ≃, Ala., U.S. 184 31.18 N 87.46 W
Little ≃, Conn., U.S. 197 41.36 N 72.03 W
Little ≃, Ga., U.S. 182 30.51 N 83.21 W
Little ≃, Ga., U.S. 182 33.39 N 82.32 W
Little ≃, Ind., U.S. 206 40.53 N 85.32 W
Little ≃, Ky., U.S. 184 36.51 N 87.58 W
Little ≃, Mass., U.S. 273 42.46 N 70.51 W
Little ≃, Mass., U.S. 273 42.37 N 70.42 W
Little ≃, N.C., U.S. 182 35.15 N 78.42 W
Little ≃, N.C., U.S. 182 35.21 N 78.02 W
Little ≃, N.Y., U.S. 200 43.18 N 75.43 W
Little ≃, Okla., U.S. 186 35.00 N 96.25 W
Little ≃, S.C., U.S. 182 34.10 N 81.11 W
Little ≃, S.C., U.S. 182 33.56 N 82.25 W
Little ≃, S.C., U.S. 182 34.11 N 81.45 W
Little ≃, Tenn., U.S. 182 35.51 N 83.57 W
Little ≃, Tex., U.S. 212 30.51 N 96.41 W
Little ≃, Va., U.S. 182 37.05 N 80.32 W
Little ≃, Va., U.S. 198 37.49 N 77.26 W
Little, Mountain Fork ≃ 184 33.57 N 94.34 W
Little Abaco Island I 228 26.53 N 77.43 W
Little Amwell 250 51.47 N 0.02 W
Little Andaman I 100 10.45 N 92.30 E
Little Arkansas ≃ 188 37.43 N 97.22 W
Little Auglaize ≃ 206 41.07 N 84.25 W
Little Averill Lake @ 196 44.57 N 71.44 W
Little Avon ≃ 44 51.42 N 2.28 W
Little Baddow 250 51.44 N 0.35 E
Littlebark Bay C 202 45.27 N 77.47 W
Little Barrier Island I 162 36.12 S 175.05 E
Little Bay Islands 176 49.39 N 55.47 W
Little Bear Creek ≃ 186 37.43 N 101.43 W
Little Beaver Creek ≃, U.S. 188 46.17 N 103.56 W
Little Beaver Creek ≃, U.S. 188 39.49 N 101.03 W
Little Beaver Creek ≃, U.S. 204 40.38 N 80.31 W
Little Beaver Creek ≃, Wash., U.S. 214 48.54 N 121.06 W
Little Beaver Creek, Middle Fork ≃ 204 40.43 N 80.37 W
Little Beaver Creek, West Fork ≃ 204 40.43 N 80.37 W
Little Belt Mountains ∧ 192 46.45 N 110.35 W
Little Berkhamsted 250 51.45 N 0.08 W
Little Bighorn ≃ 192 45.44 N 107.34 W
Little Billabong 161b 35.35 S 147.32 E
Little Bitterroot ≃ 192 47.30 N 114.19 W
Little Black ≃ 184 36.25 N 90.45 W
Little Black Bear Indian Reserve ◆4 174 51.00 N 103.12 W
Little Blackfoot ≃ 192 46.31 N 112.48 W
Little Blue ≃, U.S. 188 39.41 N 96.40 W
Little Blue ≃, Ind., U.S. 208 39.32 N 85.46 W
Littleborough 42 53.39 N 2.05 W
Little Bow ≃ 172 49.53 N 112.29 W
Little Bow Lake @ 172 50.12 N 112.41 W
Little Brazos ≃ 212 30.38 N 96.31 W
Little Brokenstraw Creek ≃ 204 41.50 N 79.23 W
Little Buffalo ≃ 166 61.00 N 113.46 W
Little Bullhead 174 51.40 N 96.51 W
Little Burstead 250 51.36 N 0.24 E
Little Calumet ≃ 278 41.39 N 87.34 W
Little Catalina 176 48.33 N 53.02 W
Little Cayman I 228 19.41 N 80.03 W
Little Cedar ≃ 180 42.57 N 92.31 W
Little Chalfont 250 51.40 N 0.34 W
Little Chariton, East Fork ≃ 184 39.20 N 92.50 W
Little Chartiers Creek ≃ 269b 40.17 N 80.08 W
Little Choptank River C 198 38.32 N 76.13 W
Little Churchill ≃ 174 57.15 N 95.21 W
Little Chute 180 44.17 N 88.16 W
Little Coco Island I 100 14.00 N 93.13 E
Little Colorado ≃ 190 36.11 N 111.48 W
Little Compton 196 41.31 N 71.10 W
Little Cooley 204 41.44 N 79.53 W
Little Cottonwood ≃ 188 44.15 N 94.20 W
Little Creek 198 39.10 N 75.27 W
Little Creek ≃, Ga., U.S. 182 33.13 N 83.24 W
Little Creek ≃, N.J., U.S. 275 39.56 N 74.48 W
Little Creek Naval Amphibious Base ■ 198 36.55 N 76.10 W
Little Cumbrae Island I 42 55.43 N 4.57 W
Little Current 180 45.58 N 81.56 W
Little Current ≃ 166 50.57 N 84.36 W
Little Cypress Bayou ≃ 184 32.41 N 94.15 W
Little Cypress Creek ≃ 212 32.39 N 94.42 W
Little Darby Creek ≃, Ohio, U.S. 208 39.53 N 83.13 W
Little Darby Creek ≃, Pa., U.S. 275 40.01 N 75.22 W
Little Dart ≃ 44 50.54 N 3.51 W
Little Deer Creek ≃, Ind., U.S. 206 40.36 N 86.28 W
Little Deer Creek ≃, Pa., U.S. 269b 40.33 N 79.50 W
Little Deschutes ≃ 192 43.51 N 121.27 W
Little Diomede Island I 170 65.45 N 168.57 W
Little Don ≃ 202 43.42 N 79.20 W
Little Dry Creek ≃, Calif., U.S. 216 39.22 N 121.52 W
Little Dry Creek ≃, Mont., U.S. 192 47.21 N 106.22 W
Little Ease Run ≃ 275 39.39 N 75.04 W
Little Eau Pleine ≃ 180 44.40 N 89.41 W
Little Egg Harbor C 198 39.35 N 74.18 W
Little Elkhart ≃ 206 41.43 N 85.49 W
Little End 250 51.41 N 0.14 E
Little Etobicoke Creek ≃ 265b 43.37 N 79.34 W
Little Fabius ≃ 209 39.59 N 91.59 W
Little Falls, Minn., U.S. 180 45.59 N 94.21 W
Little Falls, N.J., U.S. 266 40.53 N 74.14 W
Little Falls, N.Y., U.S. 200 43.03 N 74.52 W
Little Falls ≃ 198 39.36 N 76.38 W
Little Falls Dam ◆6 274c 38.57 N 77.08 W
Little Farms 208 39.57 N 83.10 W
Little Ferry 266 40.51 N 74.03 W
Littlefield 186 33.55 N 102.20 W
Little Flatrock ≃ 208 39.26 N 85.33 W
Littlefork 180 48.24 N 93.33 W
Little Fork ≃ 180 48.31 N 93.35 W
Little Fort 172 51.25 N 120.12 W
Little Genesee 200 42.02 N 78.13 W
Little Gold ≃ 152 18.01 S 126.29 E
Little Gunpowder Falls ≃ 198 39.23 N 76.22 W
Littlehampton 44 50.48 N 0.33 W
Little Harbour Deep 176 50.15 N 56.33 W
Little Haw Creek ≃ 182 29.23 N 81.24 W
Little Hawk Lake @ 202 45.10 N 78.42 W
Little Hoosic ≃ 200 42.49 N 73.20 W
Little Hope 204 42.06 N 79.49 W
Little Hulton 252 53.32 N 2.25 W
Little Humboldt ≃ 194 41.00 N 117.43 W
Little Humboldt, North Fork ≃ 194 41.24 N 117.10 W
Little Humboldt, South Fork ≃ 194 41.24 N 117.10 W
Little Hurricane Creek ≃ 182 31.23 N 82.19 W
Little Inagua I 228 21.30 N 73.00 W
Little Indian Creek ≃, Ill., U.S. 206 41.31 N 88.46 W
Little Indian Creek ≃, Ind., U.S. 208 38.12 N 86.08 W
Little Island Pond @ 273 42.43 N 71.17 W
Littlejohns Creek ≃ 216 37.52 N 121.14 W
Little Jost Van Dyke I 230m 18.27 N 64.43 W
Little Juniata ≃ 204 40.34 N 78.03 W
Little Juniata Creek ≃ 198 40.23 N 77.02 W
Little Kanawha ≃ 178 39.16 N 81.34 W
Little Kanawha, West Fork ≃ 178 38.57 N 81.16 W
Little Karroo (Klein Karroo) ∧1 148 33.45 S 21.30 E
Little Kentucky ≃ 208 38.41 N 85.12 W
Little Klickitat ≃ 214 45.51 N 121.04 W
Little Koniuji Island I 170 55.01 N 159.26 W
Little Lake 218 33.45 N 116.56 W
Little Lake @, Ont., Can. 202 44.26 N 79.40 W
Little Lake @, La., U.S. 184 29.30 N 90.10 W
Little Laramie ≃ 190 41.28 N 105.44 W
Little Laver 250 51.46 N 0.14 E
Little Leigh 252 53.17 N 2.35 W
Little Lever 252 53.34 N 2.22 W
Little Limestone Lake @ 174 53.46 N 99.18 W
Little London 231q 18.15 N 78.13 W
Little Lost ≃ 192 43.46 N 112.58 W
Little Lun ≃ 106 6.02 N 125.17 E
Little Mahoning Creek ≃ 204 40.49 N 79.00 W
Little Maitland ≃ 202 43.52 N 81.18 W
Little Malad ≃ 192 42.05 N 112.17 W
Little Manatee ≃ 210 27.42 N 82.28 W
Little Manatee, South Fork ≃ 210 27.39 N 82.18 W
Little Marco Pass C 210 26.01 N 81.46 W
Little Marsh 200 41.53 N 77.24 W
Little Meadows 200 41.59 N 76.08 W
Little Mecatina ≃ 166 50.28 N 59.35 W
Little Medicine Bow ≃ 190 41.58 N 106.18 W
Little Miami ≃ 208 39.05 N 84.26 W
Little Miami, North Fork ≃ 208 39.48 N 83.47 W
Little Miami, Todd Fork ≃ 208 39.21 N 84.08 W
Little Miami, Todd Fork, East Fork ≃ 208 39.09 N 84.18 W
Little Minch U 28 57.35 N 6.45 W
Little Mississippi ≃ 202 45.17 N 77.35 W
Little Missouri ≃, U.S. 188 47.30 N 102.25 W
Little Missouri ≃, Ark., U.S. 184 33.49 N 92.54 W
Little Mountain ∧ 198 40.47 N 76.40 W
Little Muddy ≃, Ill., U.S. 184 37.50 N 89.11 W
Little Muddy ≃, N. Dak., U.S. 188 48.12 N 103.36 W
Little Mulberry Creek ≃ 184 32.26 N 86.51 W
Little Muskegon ≃ 178 43.26 N 85.37 W
Little Nahant 273 42.25 N 70.56 W
Little Namaqualand □9 146 29.00 S 17.00 E
Little Neck ◆8 266 40.46 N 73.44 W
Little Neck Bay C 266 40.47 N 73.46 W
Little Nemaha ≃ 188 40.19 N 95.40 W
Little Neshaminy Creek ≃ 275 40.15 N 75.02 W
Little Niangua ≃ 184 38.04 N 92.54 W
Little Nicobar I 100 7.20 N 93.40 E
Little Ohoopee ≃ 182 32.27 N 82.24 W
Little Osage ≃ 184 38.02 N 94.14 W
Little Otter Creek ≃ 202 42.44 N 80.51 W
Little Ouse ≃ 44 52.30 N 0.22 E
Little Owyhee ≃ 192 42.28 N 117.15 W
Little Panoche Creek ≃ 216 36.50 N 120.42 W
Little Patuxent ≃ 274b 39.11 N 76.52 W
Little Peconic Bay C 197 40.59 N 72.24 W
Little Pee Dee ≃ 182 33.42 N 79.11 W
Little Pic ≃ 180 48.48 N 86.37 W
Little Pine and Lucky Man Indian Reserve ◆4 174 52.56 N 109.05 W
Little Pine Creek ≃, Pa., U.S. 200 41.18 N 77.22 W
Little Pine Creek ≃, Pa., U.S. 269b 40.31 N 79.57 W
Little Pine Island I 210 26.36 N 82.05 W
Little Pine Key I 210 24.44 N 81.19 W
Little Pine State Park ◆ 200 41.22 N 77.20 W
Little Pipe Creek ≃ 198 39.36 N 77.16 W
Little Platte ≃ 184 39.24 N 94.41 W
Little Plum Creek ≃ 269b 40.30 N 79.51 W
Little Popo Agie ≃ 192 42.54 N 108.35 W
Little Porcupine Creek ≃, Mont., U.S. 192 46.18 N 106.34 W
Little Porcupine Creek ≃, Mont., U.S. 192 48.02 N 106.04 W
Littleport 44 52.28 N 0.19 E
Little Portage Creek ≃ 206 42.00 N 85.27 W
Little Powder ≃ 188 45.28 N 105.20 W
Little Pucketa Creek ≃ 269b 40.33 N 79.45 W
Little Quill Lake @ 174 51.55 N 104.05 W
Little Rann of Kutch ≚ 110 23.25 N 71.15 E
Little Red ≃ 184 35.11 N 91.27 W
Little Red, Middle Fork ≃ 184 35.37 N 92.11 W
Little Red Deer ≃ 172 52.04 N 114.09 W
Little Red River Indian Reserve ◆4 174 53.30 N 105.58 W
Little Redstone Lake @ 202 45.13 N 78.34 W
Little River, Austl. 159 37.58 S 144.30 E
Little River, N.Z. 162 43.46 S 172.47 E
Little River, Kans., U.S. 188 38.24 N 98.01 W
Little River, Tex., U.S. 212 30.59 N 97.22 W
Little Rock, Ark., U.S. 184 34.44 N 92.15 W
Littlerock, Calif., U.S. 218 34.31 N 117.59 W
Little Rock, Ill., U.S. 206 41.43 N 88.34 W
Littlerock, Wash., U.S. 214 46.54 N 123.01 W
Little Rock ≃ 188 43.16 N 96.15 W
Little Rock Air Force Base ■ 184 34.55 N 92.10 W
Little Rock Creek ≃ 218 34.28 N 118.01 W
Little Rock Wash ∨ 218 34.42 N 118.02 W
Little Rocky Mountains ∧ 192 47.50 N 108.10 W
Little Rouge Creek ≃ 202 43.48 N 79.08 W
Little Sable Point ≻ 180 43.38 N 86.32 W
Little Sac ≃ 184 37.39 N 93.46 W
Little Sachigo Lake @ 174 54.09 N 92.11 W
Little Saint Bernard Pass → Petit-Saint-Bernard, Col du)(56 45.41 N 6.53 E
Little Salkehatchie ≃ 182 32.37 N 80.53 W
Little Salmon ≃, Idaho, U.S. 192 45.25 N 116.19 W
Little Salmon ≃, N.Y., U.S. 202 43.32 N 76.16 W
Little Salmon, North Branch ≃ 202 43.24 N 76.09 W
Little Salmon, South Branch ≃ 202 43.24 N 76.09 W
Little Salmon Lake @ 170 62.12 N 134.45 W
Little Salt Lake @ 190 37.55 N 112.53 W
Little Sandy ≃ 178 38.35 N 82.51 W
Little Sandy, East Fork ≃ 178 38.30 N 82.50 W
Little Sandy Creek ≃ 190 42.06 N 109.27 W
Little Scarcies ≃ 140 8.51 N 13.09 W
Little Scioto ≃, Ohio, U.S. 204 40.31 N 83.12 W
Little Scioto ≃, Ohio, U.S. 208 38.40 N 82.53 W
Little Sewickley Creek ≃, Pa., U.S. 269b 40.15 N 79.45 W
Little Sewickley Creek ≃, Pa., U.S. 269b 40.33 N 80.12 W
Little Silver 266 40.20 N 74.03 W
Little Sioux ≃ 188 41.49 N 96.04 W
Little Sioux, West Fork ≃ 188 42.04 N 96.00 W
Little Sitkin Island I 171a 51.55 N 178.30 E
Little Smoky ≃ 172 55.42 N 117.38 W
Little Snake ≃ 190 40.27 N 108.26 W
Little Sodus Bay C 200 43.20 N 76.43 W
Little Southwest Miramichi ≃ 176 46.57 N 65.50 W
Little Stanney 252 53.15 N 2.53 W
Little Stony Creek ≃ 216 39.20 N 122.31 W
Little Stour ≃ 44 51.19 N 1.15 E
Littlestown 198 39.45 N 77.05 W
Little Sugarloaf ∧2 264b 37.41 S 145.19 E
Little Sur ≃ 216 36.20 N 121.54 W
Little Sutton 252 53.17 N 2.57 W
Little Swatara Creek ≃ 198 40.24 N 76.29 W
Little Tallapoosa ≃ 182 33.18 N 85.34 W
Little Tanaga Island I 171a 51.48 N 176.10 W
Little Tennessee ≃ 182 35.47 N 84.15 W
Little Thurrock 250 51.28 N 0.21 E
Little Timber Creek ≃ 275 39.53 N 75.08 W
Little Tinicum Island I 275 39.51 N 75.17 W
Little Tobago I 231r 11.18 N 60.30 W
Little Tobago Island I 230m 18.26 N 64.51 W
Little Toby Creek ≃ 204 41.22 N 78.49 W
Littleton, Eng., U.K. 250 51.24 N 0.28 W
Littleton, Colo., U.S. 190 39.37 N 105.01 W
Littleton, Mass., U.S. 197 42.32 N 71.31 W
Littleton, N.H., U.S. 178 44.18 N 71.46 W
Littleton, N.C., U.S. 182 36.26 N 77.54 W
Littleton, W. Va., U.S. 178 39.42 N 80.31 W
Little Traverse Bay C 180 45.24 N 85.03 W
Little Truckee ≃ 216 39.25 N 120.05 W
Little Turtle ≃ 174 48.46 N 92.36 W
Little Turtle State Recreation Area ◆ 206 40.50 N 85.26 W
Little Valley 200 42.15 N 78.48 W
Little Valley Creek ≃ 275 40.04 N 75.28 W
Little Vermilion ≃ 206 41.20 N 89.05 W
Little Vermillion Lake @ 174 51.16 N 93.50 W
Little Wabash ≃ 184 37.54 N 88.05 W
Little Walsingham 44 52.54 N 0.51 E
Little Waltham 250 51.47 N 0.29 E
Little Warley 250 51.35 N 0.19 E
Little Washita ≃ 186 34.58 N 97.51 W
Little White ≃ 188 43.44 N 100.40 W
Little White Salmon ≃ 214 45.43 N 121.38 W
Little Wichita ≃ 186 33.54 N 97.59 W
Little Wichita, East Fork ≃ 186 33.52 N 98.07 W
Little Wind ≃ 192 42.57 N 108.29 W
Little Wind, North Fork ≃ 192 43.01 N 108.53 W
Little Wind, South Fork ≃ 192 43.01 N 108.53 W
Little Wolf ≃ 180 44.23 N 88.48 W
Little Wood ≃ 192 42.53 N 114.57 W
Little York, Ind., U.S. 208 38.42 N 85.54 W
Little York, N.Y., U.S. 200 42.42 N 76.10 W
Little Zab (Zāb-e Kūchek) (Az-Zāb as-Saghīr) ≃ 118 35.12 N 43.25 E
Litunga 142 13.17 S 16.43 E
Litvínov 50 50.37 N 13.36 E
Litvinovka, S.S.S.R. 70 48.24 N 40.53 E
Litvinovka, S.S.S.R. 73 49.18 N 39.27 E
Litvino 66 59.34 N 38.01 E
Litvinskoje 76 50.42 N 72.42 E
Litzmannstadt
→ Łódź 30 51.46 N 19.30 E
Liuan 90 31.44 N 116.31 E
Liuanzhuang 95 39.14 N 117.11 E
Liuba 92 33.32 N 107.07 E
Liubotong 90 31.26 N 116.00 E
Liucao 96 31.07 N 121.41 E
Liuchen 92 23.09 N 110.29 E
Liucheng, Zhg. 90 24.03 N 115.08 E
Liucheng, Zhg. 92 24.32 N 109.21 E
Liuchengba 92 27.27 N 102.53 E
Liuch'iu Hsü I 90 22.20 N 120.22 E
Liuch'iut'ai 90 23.12 N 120.48 E
Liuchonghe ≃ 92 29.40 N 107.25 E
Liuchow
→ Liuzhou 92 24.22 N 109.32 E
Liucun 96 30.44 N 119.23 E
Liucura 242 38.39 S 71.05 W
Liudaogou 88 41.34 N 127.12 E
Liudaohe 95 40.39 N 116.12 E
Liudiquan 88 34.25 N 116.06 E
Liudongqiao 96 31.03 N 119.32 E
Liudu 90 26.44 N 119.33 E
Liuduo 90 34.01 N 120.17 E
Liuduzhuang 95 39.27 N 117.50 E
Liuerbao 94 41.13 N 122.55 E
Liufang 90 27.56 N 116.22 E
Liufentzu 259d 24.57 N 121.35 E
Liugezhuang, Zhg. 88 38.33 N 116.30 E
Liugezhuang, Zhg. 95 40.03 N 118.16 E
Liugonghe 90 30.20 N 115.36 E
Liugou 95 40.57 N 118.14 E
Liuguan, Zhg. 90 29.56 N 113.08 E
Liuguan, Zhg. 95 39.22 N 116.18 E
Liuguantun 94 41.20 N 121.21 E
Liuhe, Zhg. 88 42.15 N 125.43 E
Liuhe, Zhg. 90 33.20 N 112.48 E
Liuhe, Zhg. 90 30.46 N 113.12 E
Liuhe, Zhg. 95 39.31 N 118.17 E
Liuhe, Zhg. 96 31.30 N 121.15 E
Liuhe ≃, Zhg. 88 40.38 N 118.09 E
Liuhe ≃, Zhg. 88 42.45 N 126.04 E
Liuhe ≃, Zhg. 96 31.31 N 121.18 E
Liuhegou, Zhg. 88 36.18 N 114.06 E
Liuhegou, Zhg. 94 41.56 N 122.44 E
Liuheita 94 42.09 N 123.56 E
Liuhejie 92 24.26 N 101.35 E
Liuhekou 95 40.39 N 118.09 E
Liuhekou C1 96 31.31 N 121.18 E
Liuhengdao I 90 29.43 N 122.08 E
Liuhuang 90 23.58 N 116.28 E
Liuhudang 94 42.31 N 122.22 E
Liujia, Zhg. 92 24.54 N 107.49 E
Liujia, Zhg. 96 32.04 N 121.30 E
Liujiachang 97 29.46 N 103.49 E
Liujiachuan 95 40.07 N 114.47 E
Liujiadai 96 31.57 N 120.23 E
Liujiadian 79 50.07 N 124.17 E
Liujiadu 96 32.15 N 120.33 E
Liujiafen 95 39.58 N 115.47 E
Liujiagangzi 94 41.28 N 122.33 E
Liujiagou 88 37.47 N 120.53 E
Liujiahang 96 31.21 N 121.22 E
Liujiahe, Zhg. 90 32.06 N 113.21 E
Liujiahe, Zhg. 94 40.40 N 123.58 E
Liujiang 88 40.04 N 119.34 E
Liujiashan 95 40.14 N 114.49 E
Liujiatun, Zhg. 94 42.08 N 122.44 E
Liujiatun, Zhg. 94 41.51 N 122.05 E
Liujiatun, Zhg. 94 41.52 N 122.44 E
Liujiawopeng 94 42.16 N 123.01 E
Liujiazi, Zhg. 88 41.00 N 120.13 E
Liujiazi, Zhg. 94 42.36 N 122.15 E
Liujiazi, Zhg. 94 41.48 N 123.47 E
Liujiazi, Zhg. 94 42.22 N 122.41 E
Liujingcun 95 39.27 N 115.26 E
Liujisu 95 40.01 N 117.13 E
Liukang Tenggaya, Kepulauan II 102 6.45 S 118.50 E
Liukedao I 90 22.34 N 114.52 E
Liukeshu 76 44.59 N 90.12 E
Liuku 92 25.48 N 98.52 E
Liuli 144 11.05 S 34.38 E
Liulicun 95 39.56 N 116.28 E
Liulidian 96 31.31 N 119.17 E
Liuligou 94 41.24 N 121.29 E
Liulihe 95 39.36 N 116.01 E
Liulin 88 36.41 N 115.42 E
Liulindian 90 31.34 N 113.14 E
Liuliwei 90 24.20 N 114.03 E
Liulongtai 94 41.32 N 120.56 E
Liumachang 97 29.51 N 104.54 E
Liumaogou 79 48.12 N 127.13 E
Liupangtun 94 41.36 N 123.28 E
Liupowu 88 37.38 N 117.25 E
Liuqianhutun 94 42.01 N 123.41 E
Liuquan 88 34.27 N 117.20 E
Liurenba 90 29.57 N 114.49 E
Liusheng 90 32.12 N 112.55 E
Liushi, Zhg. 88 38.33 N 115.44 E
Liushi, Zhg. 90 28.03 N 120.51 E
Liushilipu 90 32.45 N 115.58 E
Liushishan ∧ 110 36.15 N 82.05 E
Liushudian 88 35.54 N 119.30 E
Liushudixia 94 42.26 N 121.14 E
Liushuigou 90 31.34 N 112.27 E
Liushuituo 79 44.17 N 124.15 E
Liushuquan 95 39.21 N 118.06 E
Liusiqiao 90 29.47 N 116.21 E
Liusong 95 39.40 N 117.06 E
Liuta 88 35.52 N 115.18 E
Liutai 88 41.20 N 113.43 E
Liutaizi 94 41.46 N 122.39 E
Liutang 92 24.58 N 110.21 E
Liutiaozhaicun 94 41.29 N 123.12 E
Liutuan 88 36.56 N 119.22 E
Liutuhutun 94 40.44 N 120.32 E
Liuwanglou 88 34.48 N 116.28 E
Liuwa Plain ≚ 142 14.30 S 22.40 E
Liuwei 96 32.16 N 119.25 E
Liuwudian 90 24.36 N 118.13 E
Liuxia 96 30.15 N 120.03 E
Liuxiaoshuihang 96 31.45 N 121.48 E
Liuxihe ≃ 90 23.22 N 112.54 E
Liuyang 90 28.09 N 113.38 E
Liuyanghe ≃ 90 28.13 N 112.58 E
Liuyuan 88 36.10 N 114.34 E
Liuyuankou 88 34.54 N 114.20 E
Liuzhai 92 25.15 N 107.20 E
Liuzhou 92 24.22 N 109.32 E
Liuzhuang 90 33.10 N 120.19 E
Liuzong 96 32.12 N 121.19 E
Livada 38 47.52 N 23.07 E
Livadija 79 42.50 N 132.39 E
Livanátai 38 38.42 N 23.03 E
Līvāni 66 56.22 N 26.11 E
Livanjsko Polje ≚ 36 43.55 N 16.45 E
Livanovka 76 52.06 N 61.59 E
Livarot 46 49.01 N 0.09 E
Lively, Ont., Can. 180 46.26 N 81.09 W
Lively, Va., U.S. 198 37.47 N 76.31 W
Lively Island I 244 52.02 S 58.30 W
Livengood 170 65.32 N 148.33 W
Livenka, S.S.S.R. 68 50.26 N 38.18 E
Livenka, S.S.S.R. 68 50.44 N 40.14 E
Livenza ≃ 58 45.35 N 12.51 E
Live Oak, Calif., U.S. 216 39.17 N 121.40 W
Live Oak, Fla., U.S. 182 30.18 N 82.59 W
Live Oak Creek ≃ 186 30.39 N 101.42 W
Liverdun 52 48.45 N 6.03 E
Liverdy-en-Brie 251 48.42 N 2.47 E
Livergnano 60 44.19 N 11.21 E
Liveringa 152 18.03 S 124.10 E
Livermore, Calif., U.S. 216 37.41 N 121.46 W
Livermore, Iowa, U.S. 180 42.52 N 94.10 W
Livermore, Ky., U.S. 184 37.29 N 87.08 W
Livermore Falls 178 44.28 N 70.11 W
Liverpool, Austl. 160 33.54 S 150.56 E
Liverpool, N.S., Can. 176 44.02 N 64.43 W
Liverpool, Eng., U.K. 42
252 53.25 N 2.55 W
Liverpool, Ind., U.S. 206 41.34 N 87.18 W
Liverpool, N.Y., U.S. 200 43.06 N 76.13 W
Liverpool, Pa., U.S. 198 40.34 N 77.00 W
Liverpool, Tex., U.S. 212 29.18 N 95.17 W

Symbols in the index entries represent the broad categories identified in the key at the right. Symbols with superior numbers (∧²) identify subcategories (see complete key on page I · 26).

Kartensymbole in dem Registerverzeichnis stellen die rechts in Schlüssel erklärten Kategorien dar. Symbole mit hochgestellten Ziffern (∧²) bezeichnen Unterabteilungen einer Kategorie (vgl. vollständiger Schlüssel auf Seite I · 26).

Los símbolos incluidos en el texto del índice representan las grandes categorías identificadas con la clave a la derecha. Los símbolos con numeros en su parte superior (∧²) identifican las subcategorías (véase la clave completa en la página I · 26).

Les symboles de l'index représentent les catégories indiquées dans la légende à droite. Les symboles suivis d'un indice (∧²) représentent des sous-catégories (voir légende complète à la page I · 26).

Os símbolos incluídos no texto do índice representam as grandes categorias identificadas com a chave à direita. Os símbolos com números em sua parte superior (∧²) identificam as subcategorias (veja-se a chave completa à página I · 26).

Symbol	English	Deutsch	Español	Français	Português
∧	Mountain	Berg	Montaña	Montagne	Montanha
∧	Mountains	Berge	Montañas	Montagnes	Montanhas
)(	Pass	Pass	Paso	Col	Passo
∨	Valley, Canyon	Tal, Cañon	Valle, Cañón	Vallée, Canyon	Vale, Canhão
≚	Plain	Ebene	Llano	Plaine	Planície
≻	Cape	Kap	Cabo	Cap	Cabo
I	Island	Insel	Isla	Île	Ilha
II	Islands	Inseln	Islas	Îles	Ilhas
◆	Other Topographic Features	Andere Topographische Objekte	Otros Elementos Topográficos	Autres données topographiques	Outros Elementos Topográficos

ESPAÑOL
Nombre — Página — Lat.°′ — Long.°′ W=Oeste

Liverpool □[8] 252 53.25 N 2.55 W
Liverpool (Speke) Airport ⊠ 42 53.21 N 2.52 W
Liverpool, Cape ≻ 166 73.38 N 78.06 W
Liverpool, University of ♦[2] 252 53.24 N 2.58 W
Liverpool Bay ᑕ, N.W. Ter., Can. 170 69.45 N 130.00 W
Liverpool Bay ᑕ, N.S., Can. 176 44.02 N 64.41 W
Liverpool Bay ᑕ, Eng., U.K. 42 53.30 N 3.16 W
Liverpool Football Ground ♠ 252 53.26 N 2.57 W
Liverpool Heights 200 43.07 N 76.13 W
Liverpool Range ⋀ 156 31.40 S 150.30 E
Liverpool Street Station ⇀[5] 250 51.31 N 0.05 W
Livet-et-Gavet 56 45.06 N 5.56 E
Livigno 58 46.32 N 10.04 E
Livilliers 251 49.06 N 2.06 E
Lívingston, Guat. 226 15.50 N 88.45 W
Livingston, Ala., U.S. 184 32.35 N 88.11 W
Livingston, Calif., U.S. 216 37.23 N 120.43 W
Livingston, Ill., U.S. 184 38.58 N 89.46 W
Livingston, Ky., U.S. 182 37.18 N 84.13 W
Livingston, La., U.S. 184 30.30 N 90.45 W
Livingston, Mont., U.S. 192 45.40 N 110.34 W
Livingston, N.J., U.S. 200 40.48 N 74.19 W
Livingston, N.Y., U.S. 200 42.09 N 73.47 W
Livingston, Tenn., U.S. 184 36.23 N 85.19 W
Livingston, Tex., U.S. 212 30.43 N 94.56 W
Livingston, Wis., U.S. 180 42.54 N 90.26 W
Livingston □[6], Ill., U.S. 206 40.53 N 88.38 W
Livingston □[6], Mich., U.S. 206 42.38 N 83.50 W
Livingston □[6], N.Y., U.S. 200 42.48 N 77.49 W
Livingstone 144 17.50 S 25.53 E
Livingstone, Chutes de (Livingstone Falls) ↓ 142 4.50 S 14.30 E
Livingstone, Lake ⊜[1] 212 30.50 N 95.30 W
Livingstone Falls → Livingstone, Chutes de ↓ 142 4.50 S 14.30 E
Livingstone Lake ⊜ 202 45.22 N 78.43 W
Livingstone Mountains ⋀ 144 9.45 S 34.20 E
Livingstonia 144 10.36 S 34.07 E
Livingston Island ▌ 9 62.35 S 60.30 W
Livingston Mall ⇀[9] 266 40.47 N 74.21 W
Livingston Manor 200 41.54 N 74.50 W
Livno 36 43.50 N 17.01 E
Livny 66 52.25 N 37.37 E
Livojoki ≃ 26 65.24 N 26.48 E
Livonia, Ind., U.S. 208 38.34 N 86.17 W
Livonia, La., U.S. 184 30.33 N 91.33 W
Livonia, Mich., U.S. 206 42.25 N 83.23 W
Livonia, N.Y., U.S. 200 42.49 N 77.40 W
Livonia Center 200 42.49 N 77.38 W
Livonia Mall ⇀[9] 271 42.26 N 83.20 W
Livorno (Leghorn) 60 43.33 N 10.19 E
Livorno □[4] 60 43.14 N 10.35 E
Livorno Ferraris 56 45.17 N 8.05 E
Livourne → Livorno 60 43.33 N 10.19 E
Livramento → Santana do Livramento 242 30.53 S 55.31 W
Livramento do Brumado 245 13.39 S 41.50 W
Livron-sur-Drôme 56 44.46 N 4.51 E
Livry-Gargan 251 48.56 N 2.33 E
Livry-sur-Seine 251 48.31 N 2.41 E
Liwa 102 5.04 S 104.06 E
Liwale 144 9.46 S 37.56 E
Liwale Chini 144 9.41 S 38.01 E
Liwan 144 4.54 N 35.40 E
Liwonde 144 14.52 S 35.28 E
Liwung ≃ 105a 6.08 S 106.49 E
Lixi 90 29.15 N 114.46 E
Lixian, Zhg. 88 38.29 N 115.34 E
Lixian, Zhg. 95 39.33 N 116.26 E
Lixianjiang → Black ≃ 100 21.15 N 105.20 E
Lixin 90 26.52 N 116.42 E
Lixingji, Zhg. 88 34.38 N 115.54 E
Lixingji, Zhg. 90 33.28 N 115.28 E
Lixingzhuang 95 39.25 N 117.56 E
Lixoúrion 38 38.12 N 20.26 E
Lixus ⊥ 138 35.16 N 6.13 W
Liyang 96 31.26 N 119.29 E
Liyangzhen 92 29.30 N 111.37 E
Liyuanbao 90 25.16 N 112.55 E
Lizarda 240 9.36 S 46.41 W
Lizard Head Peak ∧ 190 42.47 N 109.11 W
Lizard Point ≻ 28 49.56 N 5.13 W
Lizard Point Indian Reserve ⇀[4] 174 50.40 N 100.57 W
Lizechang 97 30.10 N 106.10 E
Lizhai 96 31.34 N 121.45 E
Lizhou 92 28.08 N 102.10 E
Lizhu 90 29.56 N 120.30 E
Lizhuang 97 28.47 N 104.46 E
Lizhuangqiao 96 31.48 N 119.37 E
Lizino 73 49.33 N 38.51 E
Lizinovka 68 50.08 N 39.28 E
Liziwei 97 30.19 N 106.39 E
Lizy-sur-Ourcq 46 49.01 N 3.02 E
Lizzana 58 45.51 N 11.03 E
Lizzano in Belvedere 58 44.10 N 10.53 E
Ljalovo 72 56.03 N 37.14 E
Ljan 26 59.51 N 10.48 E
Ljubija 36 44.56 N 16.37 E
Ljubimec 38 41.50 N 26.05 E
Ljubinje 38 42.57 N 18.05 E
Ljubljana 36 46.03 N 14.31 E
Ljubovija 38 44.11 N 19.22 E
Ljubuški 36 43.12 N 17.33 E
Ljugarn 26 57.19 N 18.42 E
Ljunga 40 58.31 N 16.21 E
Ljungan ≃ 26 62.19 N 17.23 E
Ljungaverk 26 62.29 N 16.03 E
Ljungby 26 56.50 N 13.56 E
Ljungbyhed 41 56.04 N 13.12 E
Ljungbyholm 26 56.38 N 16.10 E
Ljungdalen 26 62.51 N 12.47 E
Ljungsbro 26 58.31 N 15.30 E
Ljungskile 26 58.14 N 11.55 E
Ljusdal 26 61.50 N 16.05 E
Ljusfallshammar 40 58.47 N 15.29 E
Ljusnan ≃ 26 61.12 N 17.08 E
Ljusnaren ⊜ 40 59.51 N 14.56 E
Ljusne 26 61.13 N 17.08 E
Ljusterö ▌ 40 59.31 N 18.37 E
Ljutomer 36 46.31 N 16.12 E
Llagas Creek ≃ 216 36.58 N 121.31 W
Llaima, Volcán ∧[1] 242 38.43 S 71.43 W
Llallagua 238 18.25 S 66.38 W
Llanaber 44 52.45 N 4.05 W
Llanaelhaiarn 44 52.59 N 4.24 W
Llanarth 44 52.12 N 4.18 W
Llanarthney 44 51.52 N 4.09 W
Llanbedrog 44 52.52 N 4.29 W
Llanberis, Pass of ∨ 44 53.06 N 4.04 W
Llanbister 44 52.21 N 3.27 W
Llanboidy 44 51.54 N 4.36 W
Llanbrynmair 44 52.37 N 3.57 W
Llanbyther 44 52.04 N 4.09 W
Llancañelo, Salina ☷ 242 35.40 S 69.08 W
Llandaff 44 51.30 N 3.14 W
Llandaff Cathedral ♦[1] 44 51.29 N 3.15 W
Llanddewi Brefi 44 52.10 N 3.57 W
Llandeilo 44 51.52 N 3.59 W

FRANÇAIS
Nom — Page — Lat.°′ — Long.°′ W=Ouest

L.L. Anderson Reservoir ⊜[1] 216 39.07 N 120.25 W
Llandilo 264a 33.43 S 150.45 E
Llandinam 44 52.29 N 3.26 W
Llandissilio 44 51.53 N 4.44 W
Llandovery 44 51.59 N 3.48 W
Llandrindod Wells 44 52.15 N 3.23 W
Llandudno 42 53.19 N 3.49 W
Llandybie 44 51.50 N 4.00 W
Llandyssul 44 52.02 N 4.19 W
Llanelli 44 51.42 N 4.10 W
Llanelltyd 44 52.45 N 3.54 W
Llanelly 159 36.44 S 143.51 E
Llanenddwyn 44 52.49 N 4.06 W
Llanerchymedd 42 53.20 N 4.22 W
Llanes 34 43.25 N 4.45 W
Llanfaethlu 42 53.21 N 4.32 W
Llanfair Caereinion 44 52.39 N 3.20 W
Llanfairfechan 42 53.15 N 3.58 W
Llanfrynach 44 51.56 N 3.21 W
Llanfyllin 44 52.46 N 3.17 W
Llanfynydd 44 51.56 N 4.06 W
Llanfyrnach 44 51.57 N 4.35 W
Llangadog 44 51.56 N 3.53 W
Llangefni 42 53.16 N 4.18 W
Llangennech 44 51.41 N 4.04 W
Llangollen 44 52.58 N 3.10 W
Llangollen Estates 198 39.39 N 75.37 W
Llangranog 44 52.09 N 4.29 W
Llangurig 44 52.25 N 3.36 W
Llangwryfon 44 52.19 N 4.03 W
Llangynog 44 52.50 N 3.25 W
Llanharan 44 51.33 N 3.25 W
Llanidloes 44 52.27 N 3.32 W
Llanilar 44 52.21 N 4.01 W
Llanllyfni 44 53.03 N 4.17 W
Llano 186 30.45 N 98.41 W
Llano ≃ 186 30.35 N 98.25 W
Llano Colorado 194 31.38 N 115.55 W
Llano Grande 224 20.28 N 105.37 W
Llanon 44 52.17 N 4.10 W
Llanos ☷ 236 5.00 N 70.00 W
Llanpumsaint 44 51.56 N 4.18 W
Llanquera 238 18.06 S 67.47 W
Llanquihue 244 41.15 S 73.01 W
Llanquihue □[4] 244 41.40 S 72.30 W
Llanquihue, Lago ⊜ 244 41.08 S 72.48 W
Llanrhaeadr-ym-Mochnant 44 52.51 N 3.17 W
Llanrhidian 44 51.37 N 4.11 W
Llanrhystyd 44 52.18 N 4.09 W
Llanrwst 44 53.08 N 3.48 W
Llansá 34 42.22 N 3.09 E
Llansantffraid-ym-Mechain 44 52.47 N 3.08 W
Llansawel 44 52.01 N 4.00 W
Llanta 242 26.20 S 69.49 W
Llantrisant 44 51.33 N 3.23 W
Llantwit Major 44 51.25 N 3.30 W
Llanuwchllyn 44 52.52 N 3.41 W
Llanwenog 44 52.06 N 4.12 W
Llanwrda 44 51.58 N 3.53 W
Llanwrtyd Wells 44 52.07 N 3.38 W
Llata 238 9.25 S 76.47 W
Llavallol ⇀[8] 278 34.48 S 58.28 W
Llay 44 53.06 N 2.59 W
Llentrisca, Cabo de ≻ 34 38.51 N 1.14 E
Llera 224 23.19 N 99.01 W
Llerena 34 38.14 N 6.01 W
Lleulleu, Lago ⊜ 242 38.09 S 73.20 W
Lleyn Peninsula ≻[1] 44 52.54 N 4.30 W
Llica 238 19.52 S 68.16 W
Llico 242 34.46 S 72.05 W
Llivia 32 42.28 N 1.59 E
Lljič 75 40.52 N 68.31 E
Llobregat ≃ 34 41.19 N 2.09 E
Llobregat, Delta del ☷[2] 256d 41.17 N 2.08 E
Llolleo 242 33.37 S 71.37 W
Llorente 106 11.25 N 125.33 E
Llorente ≃ 106 11.25 N 125.33 E
Lloyd 208 38.37 N 82.52 W
Lloyd Harbor 200 40.54 N 73.28 W
Lloyd Harbor ᑕ 266 40.55 N 73.27 W
Lloydminster 174 53.17 N 110.00 W
Lloyd Neck ≻[1] 266 40.56 N 73.28 W
Lloyd Point ≻ 200 40.57 N 73.29 W
Lloyds ≃ 176 48.33 N 57.13 W
Lluchmayor 34 39.29 N 2.54 E
Llullaillaco, Volcán ∧[1] 242 24.43 S 68.33 W
Llusco 238 14.21 S 72.07 W
Llyswen 44 52.02 N 3.17 W
I-n-Azaoua ⍑[4] 138 20.49 N 7.30 E
Lo ≃ 100 21.18 N 105.25 E
Loa 190 38.24 N 111.38 W
Loa ≃, Chile 238 21.26 S 70.04 W
Loa ≃, Congo 263b 4.30 S 15.10 E
Loami 184 39.40 N 89.51 W
Loanatit 165f 19.22 S 169.14 E
Loanda → Luanda, Ang. 142 8.48 S 13.14 E
Loanda, Bra. 245 22.54 S 53.10 W
Loanda, Gabon 142 0.55 S 9.00 E
Loande ≃ 142 8.41 S 17.56 E
Loange (Luangue) ≃ 142 4.17 S 20.02 E
Loango Buele 142 5.10 S 12.59 E
Loanhead 42 55.53 N 3.09 W
Loanja ≃ 144 17.22 S 24.48 E
Loano 56 44.08 N 8.15 E
Loantaka Brook ≃ 266 40.43 N 74.28 W
Lo Aranguiz 276e 33.23 S 70.40 W
Loay 106 9.36 N 124.01 E
Lob' ≃ 72 56.29 N 35.51 E
Lobamba 148 26.27 S 31.12 E
Loban 24 65.44 N 45.25 E
Loban' ≃ 70 56.58 N 51.12 E
Lobanovo 66 53.04 N 38.14 E
Lobanovskije Vyselki 72 54.18 N 38.58 E
Lobaski 70 54.38 N 45.09 E
Lobatos 224 22.49 N 103.24 W
Lobatse 146 25.11 S 25.40 E
Löbau 50 51.05 N 14.40 E
Lobau ☷ 254b 48.10 N 16.32 E
Lobaye □[5] 142 4.00 N 18.00 E
Lobaye ≃ 142 3.41 N 18.35 E
Lobbes 46 50.21 N 4.15 E
Lobbs Run ≃ 269b 40.15 N 79.55 W
Lobdell Lake ⊜ 206 42.48 N 83.48 W
Löbejün 50 51.38 N 11.53 E
Lo Benitez 276e 33.34 S 70.42 W
Lobenstein 50 50.26 N 11.38 E
Lobería 242 38.09 S 58.47 W
Lo Bernales 276e 33.34 S 70.34 W
Löberöd 41 55.47 N 13.30 E
Lobethal 158b 34.54 S 138.52 E
Łobez 30 53.39 N 15.36 E
Lobito 142 12.20 S 13.34 E
Lobitos 236 4.26 S 81.17 W
Lobitos Creek ≃ 272 37.22 N 122.24 W
Lobkoviči 66 53.50 N 31.45 E
Lobn'a 72 56.01 N 37.30 E
Löbnitz, D.D.R. 50 54.17 N 12.43 E
Löbnitz, D.D.R. 50 51.35 N 12.28 E
Lobo, Indon. 154 3.45 S 134.05 E
Lobo, Pil. 106 13.39 N 121.13 E
Lobo ≃ 140 6.02 N 6.47 W
Loboko 142 0.45 S 16.38 E
Lobos, Arg. 248 35.11 S 59.06 W
Lobos, Méx. 224 20.29 N 105.03 W
Lobos, Cabo ≻, Chile 238 18.47 S 70.21 W
Lobos, Cabo ≻, Méx. 222 29.55 N 112.46 W
Lobos, Estero de ᑕ 222 27.22 N 110.33 W
Lobos, Isla de ▌, Esp. 138 28.45 N 13.49 W
Lobos, Isla de ▌, Méx. 224 21.27 N 97.13 W
Lobos, Point ≻ 216 37.47 N 122.31 W
Lobos, Puerto de ᑕ 224 21.12 N 97.25 W
Lobos, Punta ≻, Chile 238 21.01 S 70.11 W
Lobos, Punta ≻, Ur. 248 34.54 S 56.15 W

PORTUGUÊS
Nome — Página — Lat.°′ — Long.°′ W=Oeste

Lobos de Afuera, Islas ▌▌ 238 6.57 S 80.42 W
Lobos de Tierra, Isla ▌ 238 6.27 S 80.52 W
Lo Boza 276e 33.23 S 70.46 W
Lobskoje 24 62.45 N 35.16 E
Lobstädt 50 51.08 N 12.29 E
Lobstick Lake ⊜ 166 54.00 N 64.50 W
Löbtau ⇀[8] 50 51.03 N 13.42 E
Loburg 50 52.07 N 12.05 E
Lobva 76 59.12 N 60.30 E
Łobżenica 30 53.16 N 17.15 E
Locana 56 45.25 N 7.27 E
Locana, Val di ∨ 56 45.25 N 7.27 E
Locarno 54 46.10 N 8.48 E
Lo Castillo, Aeropuerto ⊠ 276e 33.23 S 70.36 W
Locate Triulzi 56 45.21 N 9.13 E
Loccum 48 52.27 N 9.08 E
Loch 159 38.22 S 145.43 E
Lochaline 28 56.32 N 5.47 W
Lochar Water ≃ 42 54.59 N 3.27 W
Lo Chau ▌ 261d 22.11 N 114.15 E
Lochboisdale 28 57.09 N 7.19 W
Lochearn 274b 39.21 N 76.43 W
Lochem 48 52.09 N 6.25 E
Loches 46 47.08 N 1.00 E
Loch Garman → Wexford 28 52.20 N 6.27 W
Lochgelly 42 56.08 N 3.19 W
Lochgilphead 28 56.03 N 5.26 W
Lochiel 158b 33.56 S 138.10 E
Lochino 255b 55.42 N 37.19 E
Lochinver 28 58.09 N 5.15 W
Lochmaben 42 55.08 N 3.27 W
Lochranza 42 55.42 N 5.18 W
Loch Raven Dam ⇀[6] 274b 39.26 N 76.33 W
Loch Raven Reservoir ⊜[1] 198 39.27 N 76.34 W
Lochristi 46 51.06 N 3.50 E
Lochsa ≃ 192 46.08 N 115.36 W
Loch Sheldrake 200 41.46 N 74.39 W
Lochvica 68 50.22 N 33.16 E
Lochwinnoch 42 55.48 N 4.39 W
Lock 156 33.34 S 135.46 E
Locke, Calif., U.S. 216 38.15 N 121.31 W
Locke, Ind., U.S. 206 41.28 N 86.00 W
Locke, N.Y., U.S. 200 42.40 N 76.26 W
Lockeford 216 38.10 N 121.09 W
Lockeport 176 43.42 N 65.07 W
Lockerbie 42 55.07 N 3.22 W
Lockesburg 184 33.58 N 94.10 W
Lockhart, Austl. 156 35.14 S 146.43 E
Lockhart, Fla., U.S. 210 28.37 N 81.26 W
Lockhart, Tex., U.S. 212 29.53 N 97.41 W
Lock Haven 200 41.08 N 77.27 W
Lockheed Aircraft Corporation ♦[3], Calif., U.S. 270 34.12 N 118.22 W
Lockheed Aircraft Corporation ♦[3], Calif., U.S. 272 37.25 N 122.02 W
Lockington 206 40.12 N 84.13 W
Lockney 186 34.07 N 101.27 W
Löcknitz 50 53.27 N 14.12 E
Löcknitz ≃, D.D.R. 50 53.07 N 11.16 E
Löcknitz ≃, D.D.R. 254a 52.25 N 13.49 E
Lockport, Man., Can. 174 50.05 N 96.56 W
Lockport, Ill., U.S. 206 41.36 N 88.03 W
Lockport, La., U.S. 184 29.39 N 90.32 W
Lockport, N.Y., U.S. 200 43.10 N 78.42 W
Lockport Lock ⇀[5] 268 41.35 N 88.04 W
Locksley Park 200 42.45 N 78.52 W
Lockvattnet ⊜ 40 59.03 N 17.05 E
Lockview 269b 40.10 N 79.55 W
Lockwillow 263d 26.17 S 27.50 E
Lockwood, Calif., U.S. 216 35.56 N 121.05 W
Lockwood, Mo., U.S. 184 37.23 N 93.57 W
Lockwood Corners 204 41.00 N 81.34 W
Lockyer Creek ≃ 161a 27.25 S 152.36 E
Locminé 28 47.53 N 2.50 W
Loc-ninh 100 11.51 N 106.36 E
Loco, Bayou ≃ 212 31.28 N 94.44 W
Locon 46 50.34 N 2.40 E
Locri 36 38.14 N 16.16 E
Locroja 238 12.41 S 74.26 W
Locsin 106 13.09 N 123.43 E
Locumba 238 17.36 S 70.46 W
Locumba ≃ 238 17.54 S 70.57 W
Locust 198 40.24 N 74.01 W
Locust Creek ≃ 184 39.40 N 93.17 W
Locust Fork ≃ 184 33.33 N 87.11 W
Locust Grove, N.Y., U.S. 266 40.48 N 73.30 W
Locust Grove, Okla., U.S. 186 36.12 N 95.10 W
Locust Lake State Park ♠ 198 40.46 N 76.08 W
Locust Point ≻ 266 40.49 N 73.48 W
Locust Valley 200 40.53 N 73.36 W
Lod (Lydda) 122 31.58 N 34.54 E
Lod, Nemel-Te'ufa ⊠ 122 31.59 N 34.53 E
Loda 206 40.31 N 88.04 W
Lodal Creek ≃ 275 40.14 N 75.27 W
Löddeköpinge 41 55.46 N 13.01 E
Loddenhøj ∧[2] 41 56.13 N 9.48 E
Loddon 44 52.32 N 1.29 E
Loddon ≃, Austl. 159 36.41 S 143.55 E
Loddon ≃, Eng., U.K. 44 51.30 N 0.53 W
Lodejnoje Polje 66 60.44 N 33.30 E
Lodenau 50 51.24 N 14.57 E
Löderburg 50 51.52 N 11.32 E
Lodève 32 43.43 N 3.19 E
Lodge Creek ≃ 192 48.36 N 109.15 W
Lodge Grass 192 45.19 N 107.22 W
Lodgepole, Alta., Can. 172 53.06 N 115.19 W
Lodgepole, Nebr., U.S. 188 41.09 N 102.38 W
Lodgepole Creek ≃ 188 41.02 N 102.10 W
Lodhāsuli 116 22.19 N 87.03 E
Lodhrān 113 29.32 N 71.38 E
Lodi, It. 56 45.19 N 9.30 E
Lodi, Calif., U.S. 216 38.08 N 121.16 W
Lodi, N.J., U.S. 200 40.53 N 74.05 W
Lodi, N.Y., U.S. 200 42.37 N 76.50 W
Lodi, Ohio, U.S. 204 41.03 N 82.01 W
Lodi, Wis., U.S. 180 43.19 N 89.32 W
Lodi Park ♠ 262a 28.36 N 77.13 E
Lodi Vecchio 56 45.18 N 9.24 E
Lodja 142 3.29 S 23.26 E
Lodosa 34 42.25 N 2.05 W
Lodoyo 105a 8.10 S 112.13 E
Lodrone 58 45.50 N 10.32 E
Lods 54 47.03 N 6.15 E
Lodsch → Łódź 30 51.46 N 19.30 E
Lodwar 144 3.07 N 35.36 E
Łódź 30 51.46 N 19.30 E
Loe Āgra 113 34.35 N 71.43 E
Loei 100 17.29 N 101.35 E
Loei ≃ 100 17.51 N 101.37 E
Loen 26 61.52 N 6.52 E
Loenen 48 52.07 N 6.01 E
Loengo 144 4.45 S 26.27 E
Loeriesfontein 148 30.56 S 19.26 E
Lo Espejo 276e 33.32 S 70.43 W
Lofer 58 47.35 N 12.41 E
Loffa □[6] 140 7.40 N 10.00 W
Loffa ≃ 140 6.36 N 11.08 W
Löffingen 54 47.53 N 8.20 E
Lofoten ▌▌ 24 68.30 N 15.00 E
Lofthus 26 60.20 N 6.40 E
Loftus, Austl. 264a 34.03 S 151.03 E
Loftus, Eng., U.K. 42 54.33 N 0.53 W
Lofty, Mount ∧, Austl. 158b 34.59 S 138.42 E
Lofty, Mount ∧, Austl. 264b 37.43 S 145.17 E
Log 70 49.29 N 43.52 E
Loga, B.R.D. 48 53.14 N 7.29 E

Loga, Niger 140 13.37 N 3.14 E
Logačovka 70 52.23 N 52.21 E
Logan, Iowa, U.S. 188 41.39 N 95.47 W
Logan, Kans., U.S. 188 39.40 N 99.34 W
Logan, N. Mex., U.S. 186 35.22 N 103.25 W
Logan, Ohio, U.S. 178 39.32 N 82.25 W
Logan, Utah, U.S. 190 41.44 N 111.50 W
Logan, W. Va., U.S. 178 37.51 N 81.59 W
Logan □[6], Ill., U.S. 209 40.09 N 89.22 W
Logan □[6], Ohio, U.S. 206 40.22 N 83.46 W
Logan ⇀[8] 275 40.02 N 75.09 W
Logan ≃, Austl. 161a 27.43 S 153.18 E
Logan ≃, Alta., Can. 172 55.09 N 111.42 W
Logan ≃, Utah, U.S. 190 41.44 N 111.57 W
Logan, Mount ∧, Yukon, Can. 170 60.34 N 140.24 W
Logan, Mount ∧, Wash., U.S. 214 48.32 N 120.57 W
Logan Creek ≃, Calif., U.S. 216 39.22 N 122.06 W
Logan Creek ≃, Mo., U.S. 184 37.11 N 90.49 W
Logan Creek ≃, Nebr., U.S. 188 41.37 N 96.29 W
Logandale 194 36.36 N 114.29 W
Logan International Airport ⊠ 273 42.22 N 71.00 W
Logan Lake ⊜ 202 44.52 N 78.59 W
Logan Martin Lake ⊜[1] 184 33.40 N 86.15 W
Logan Mountains ⋀ 170 61.30 N 129.00 W
Logan Pass)(192 48.42 N 113.43 W
Logansport, Ind., U.S. 206 40.45 N 86.21 W
Logansport, La., U.S. 184 31.58 N 93.58 W
Logan Square ⇀[8] 268 41.56 N 87.42 W
Loganton 200 41.02 N 77.18 W
Loganville, Ga., U.S. 182 33.50 N 83.54 W
Loganville, Pa., U.S. 198 39.52 N 76.42 W
Logärden ⊜ 40 60.37 N 16.00 E
Lögdeälven ≃ 26 63.33 N 19.25 E
Logduz 66 60.00 N 44.41 E
Loge ≃, Ang. 142 10.12 S 17.00 E
Loge ≃, Ang. 142 7.49 S 13.06 E
Logia 154 2.55 S 151.27 E
Loginovo 72 55.42 N 38.44 E
Logirim 144 4.43 N 33.14 E
Logišin 66 52.20 N 25.59 E
Lognes 251 48.50 N 2.38 E
Lognes-Émerainville, Aérodrome de ⊠ 251 48.49 N 2.37 E
Logo 144 5.20 N 30.18 E
Logojsk 66 54.12 N 27.49 E
Logone ≃ 136 12.06 N 15.02 E
Logone Birni 136 11.47 N 15.06 E
Logone Gana 136 11.33 N 15.09 E
Logone Occidental □[5] 136 8.50 N 16.00 E
Logone Occidental ≃ 136 9.07 N 16.26 E
Logone Oriental □[5] 136 8.15 N 16.20 E
Logone Oriental ≃ 136 9.07 N 16.26 E
Logovskij 70 48.26 N 43.23 E
Log pod Mangartom 58 46.24 N 13.36 E
Logroño 34 42.28 N 2.27 W
Logrosán 34 39.20 N 5.29 W
Løgstør 26 56.58 N 9.15 E
Løgten 41 56.17 N 10.19 E
Logudoro ⇀[1] 36 40.38 N 8.38 E
Logue Brook Dam ⇀[6] 158a 33.00 S 115.57 E
Løgumgårde 41 55.05 N 8.57 E
Løgumkloster 41 55.03 N 8.57 E
Logumukum 144 0.27 N 36.05 E
Logy Creek ≃ 214 46.11 N 120.35 W
Loh ▌ 165f 13.21 S 166.38 E
Lohāgara 116 23.11 N 89.39 E
Lohals 41 55.08 N 10.55 E
Lohārdaga 114 23.26 N 84.41 E
Lohāru 110 28.27 N 75.49 E
Lohatlha 148 28.02 S 23.04 E
Lohausen ⇀[8] 253 51.16 N 6.44 E
Lohauserholz ⇀[8] 253 51.39 N 7.48 E
Lohberg 253 51.35 N 6.46 E
Löhdorf ⇀[8] 253 51.09 N 7.01 E
Lo Hermida 276e 33.29 S 70.33 W
Lohfelden 52 51.16 N 9.32 E
Lohheide 253 51.30 N 6.40 E
Lohiān 113 31.10 N 75.11 E
Lohiniva 24 67.10 N 24.58 E
Lohja 26 60.15 N 24.05 E
Lohjan harju ∧ 26 60.15 N 24.30 E
Lohjanjärvi ⊜ 26 60.15 N 23.55 E
Löhlbach 52 51.04 N 8.58 E
Lohmar 52 50.50 N 7.13 E
Lohme, D.D.R. 50 54.35 N 13.37 E
Löhme, D.D.R. 254a 52.37 N 13.40 E
Lohmen, D.D.R. 50 50.59 N 13.59 E
Lohmen, D.D.R. 50 53.41 N 12.05 E
Lohmühle 253 51.31 N 6.40 E
Lohne, B.R.D. 48 52.42 N 8.12 E
Löhne, B.R.D. 48 52.11 N 8.41 E
Löhnen 253 51.36 N 6.39 E
Lohnsburg 58 48.09 N 13.24 E
Loho → Luohe 90 33.35 N 114.01 E
Lohr am Main 52 50.00 N 9.34 E
Lohrville 188 42.17 N 94.33 W
Lohsa 50 51.23 N 14.24 E
Loi, Phou ∧ 100 20.16 N 103.12 E
Loiano 60 44.16 N 11.19 E
Loiborsoit 144 3.52 S 36.26 E
Loi-kaw 100 19.41 N 97.13 E
Loile ≃ 142 0.52 S 20.12 E
Loimaa 26 60.51 N 23.03 E
Loimijoki ≃ 26 61.13 N 22.38 E
Loi Mwe 100 21.11 N 99.46 E
Loing ≃ 46 48.23 N 2.48 E
Loing, Canal du ≋ 46 48.22 N 2.50 E
Loir ≃ 32 47.33 N 0.32 W
Loira → Loire ≃ 32 47.16 N 2.11 W
Loire 56 45.33 N 4.48 E
Loire □[5] 32 45.30 N 4.00 E
Loire ≃ 32 47.16 N 2.11 W
Loire, Canal latéral à la ≋ 46 47.37 N 2.44 E
Loire-Atlantique □[5] 32 47.20 N 1.35 W
Loiret □[5] 46 47.55 N 2.20 E
Loiret ≃ 46 47.52 N 1.48 E
Loir-et-Cher □[5] 46 47.30 N 1.30 E
Loïs, Lac ⊜ 180 48.34 N 78.44 W
Loisach ≃ 58 47.56 N 11.27 E
Loisia 54 46.29 N 5.27 E
Loison ≃ 52 49.30 N 5.17 E
Loitz 50 53.58 N 13.07 E
Loíza 230m 18.23 N 65.54 W
Loíza, Embalse de ⊜[1] 230m 18.17 N 66.00 W
Loíza Aldea 230m 18.26 N 65.53 W
Loja, Ec. 236 4.00 S 79.13 W
Loja, Esp. 34 37.10 N 4.09 W
Loja □[4] 236 4.10 S 79.30 W
Lojang → Luoyang 92 34.41 N 112.28 E
Lojas 246 22.47 S 42.53 W
Lojev 68 51.56 N 30.46 E
Lojga 24 61.05 N 44.37 E
Lojno 24 59.44 N 52.39 E
Løjt Kirkeby 41 55.05 N 9.28 E
Loka, Sūd. 144 4.16 N 31.01 E
Loka, Zaïre 142 0.20 N 17.57 E
Loka brunn 40 59.36 N 14.28 E
Lokači 68 50.44 N 24.39 E
Lokako 142 2.14 S 21.45 E
Lokalema 142 1.59 N 22.17 E
Lokan ≃ 106 5.25 N 117.44 E
Lokandu 144 2.31 S 25.47 E
Lokbatan 74 40.20 N 49.43 E
Løken 26 59.48 N 11.29 E
Loken tekojärvi ⊜[1] 24 67.55 N 27.40 E
Lokeren 46 51.06 N 4.00 E
Loket 50 50.09 N 12.43 E
Lokichar 144 2.23 N 35.39 E

Lokichokio 144 4.12 N 34.21 E
Lokitaung 144 4.16 N 35.45 E
Lokka 24 67.49 N 27.44 E
Løkken 26 57.22 N 9.43 E
Løkken verk 26 63.08 N 9.42 E
Lokn'a 66 56.50 N 30.09 E
Loknaš ≃ 72 56.11 N 36.04 E
Loko 140 8.02 N 7.49 E
Lokofa-Bokolongo 142 0.12 N 19.22 E
Lokoja 140 7.47 N 6.45 E
Lokolama 142 2.34 S 19.53 E
Lokolenge 142 1.11 N 22.40 E
Lokolo ≃ 142 0.43 S 19.40 E
Lokomo 142 2.41 N 15.19 E
Lokoro ≃ 142 1.43 S 18.23 E
Lokossa 140 6.38 N 1.43 E
Lokosso 140 10.19 N 3.40 W
Lokot', S.S.S.R. 66 52.34 N 34.34 E
Lokot', S.S.S.R. 76 51.11 N 81.11 E
Lokoua ≃ 263b 4.06 S 15.16 E
Loksa 66 59.35 N 25.45 E
Loks Land ▌ 166 62.26 N 64.38 W
Loktyši 66 52.50 N 26.43 E
Lokve 58 46.01 N 13.49 E
Loky 147b 12.47 S 49.39 E
Lokyang 261c 1.20 N 103.41 E
Lol 130 6.26 N 29.37 E
Lol ≃ 130 9.13 N 28.59 E
Lóla, Ang. 142 14.22 S 13.42 E
Lola, Guinée 140 7.48 N 8.32 W
Lola, Mount ∧ 216 39.26 N 120.22 W
Lolengi 142 0.07 N 20.59 E
Loleta 194 40.38 N 124.13 W
Lolingo 142 0.55 N 22.38 E
Loliondo 144 2.03 S 35.37 E
Lolita 212 28.50 N 96.32 W
Lolland ▌ 41 54.46 N 11.30 E
Lollar 52 50.39 N 8.42 E
Lolo, Mont., U.S. 192 46.45 N 114.05 W
Lolo, Zaïre 142 2.13 N 23.00 E
Lolo ≃ 142 1.07 S 12.28 E
Lolobau Island ▌ 154 4.55 S 151.10 E
Lolo Creek ≃, Idaho, U.S. 192 46.26 N 116.10 W
Lolo Creek ≃, Mont., U.S. 192 46.45 N 114.03 W
Lolodorf 142 3.14 N 10.44 E
Lolo Pass)(192 46.38 N 114.35 W
Lolotique 226 13.33 N 88.21 W
Lolowai 165f 15.18 S 168.00 E
Lolui Island ▌ 144 0.07 S 33.42 E
Lolwa 144 1.22 N 29.31 E
Lolworth Range ⋀ 156 20.20 S 145.15 E
Lom, Blg. 38 43.49 N 23.14 E
Lom, Česko. 50 50.37 N 13.40 E
Lom, Nor. 26 61.50 N 8.33 E
Lom, S.S.S.R. 70 57.54 N 39.12 E
Lom ≃, Afr. 142 5.20 N 13.24 E
Lom ≃, Blg. 38 43.50 N 23.15 E
Loma 134 6.55 N 37.34 E
Loma, Point ≻ 218 32.41 N 117.14 W
Loma Blanca, Chile 276e 33.30 S 70.47 W
Loma Blanca, Méx. 190 31.35 N 106.17 W
Loma Bonita 224 18.07 N 95.53 W
Lomakino 75 40.05 N 68.10 E
Lomako ≃ 142 0.50 N 20.50 E
Loma Linda, Méx. 276a 19.28 N 99.14 W
Loma Linda, Calif., U.S. 218 34.04 N 117.16 W
Lomaloma 165g 17.17 S 178.59 W
Loma Mansa ∧ 140 9.13 N 11.07 W
Lomami ≃ 128 0.46 N 24.16 E
Loma Mountains ⋀ 140 9.10 N 11.07 W
Loma Ridge ∧ 270 33.45 N 117.43 W
Lomas 238 15.34 S 74.50 W
Lomas, Bahía ᑕ 244 52.35 S 69.05 W
Lomas Alegres 224 17.38 N 92.36 W
Lomas Chapultepec ⇀[8] 276a 19.26 N 99.13 W
Lomas del Real 224 22.30 N 97.54 W
Lomas de Monreal 190 31.17 N 110.56 W
Lomas de Zamora 248 34.46 S 58.24 W
Lomas de Zamora □[5] 278 34.45 S 58.24 W
Loma Verde 248 35.16 S 58.24 W
Lomax, Ill., U.S. 180 40.41 N 91.04 W
Lomax, Tex., U.S. 212 29.41 N 95.04 W
Łomazy 30 51.55 N 23.10 E
Lomazzo 56 45.42 N 9.02 E
Lomba ≃ 142 15.36 S 21.32 E
Lombagin 102 0.55 N 124.04 E
Lombard 206 41.53 N 88.01 W
Lombarda, Serra ⋀[1] 240 2.50 N 51.50 W
Lombardia □[4] 36 45.40 N 9.30 E
Lombardy 263d 26.07 S 28.08 E
Lombe 142 9.27 S 16.13 E
Lomblen, Pulau ▌ 102 8.25 S 123.30 E
Lombo do Tejo, Mouchão do ▌ 256c 38.52 N 9.00 W
Lombok 105b 8.30 S 116.40 E
Lombok ▌ 105b 8.45 S 116.30 E
Lombok, Selat ⋃ 105b 8.30 S 115.50 E
Lombong 104 1.48 N 103.51 E
Lomé 140 6.08 N 1.13 E
Lomela 142 2.18 S 23.17 E
Lomela ≃ 142 0.14 S 20.42 E
Lomellina □[9] 56 45.15 N 8.45 E
Lomello 56 45.07 N 8.47 E
Lometa 186 31.13 N 98.24 W
Lomi 24 67.05 N 16.09 E
Lomié 142 3.10 N 13.37 E
Lomira 180 43.35 N 88.27 W
Lo Miranda 242 34.11 S 70.54 W
Lomita 218 33.48 N 118.19 W
Lom Kao 100 16.53 N 101.14 E
Lomma 41 55.41 N 13.05 E
Lommabukten ᑕ 41 55.40 N 12.58 E
Lommatzsch 50 51.12 N 13.18 E
Lomme 46 50.39 N 2.59 E
Lomme ≃ 52 50.08 N 5.10 E
Lommel 52 51.14 N 5.18 E
Lomnice nad Popelkou 30 50.32 N 15.22 E
Lomond 172 50.21 N 112.39 W
Lomond, Loch ⊜, N.S., Can. 176 45.46 N 60.35 W
Lomond, Loch ⊜, Ont., Can. 180 48.26 N 89.19 W
Lomond, Loch ⊜, Scot., U.K. 42 56.08 N 4.38 W
Lomond, Loch ⊜, Ill., U.S. 268 42.17 N 88.01 W
Lomonosov 255a 59.55 N 29.46 E
Lomonosovskij 76 52.50 N 66.28 E
Lomovatka 73 48.27 N 38.34 E
Lomovoje 24 64.01 N 40.40 E
Lompobatang, Gunung ∧ 102 5.20 S 119.55 E
Lompoc 194 34.38 N 120.27 W
Lom Sak 100 16.47 N 101.15 E
Lomy 78 52.17 N 117.59 E
Łomża 30 53.11 N 22.05 E
Lonaconing 178 39.34 N 78.59 W
Lonate Pozzolo 56 45.36 N 8.45 E
Lonato 58 45.27 N 10.29 E
Lonāvale 112 18.45 N 73.25 E
Lončakovo 79 47.05 N 134.10 E
Loncoche 244 39.22 S 72.38 W
Loncon ≃ 58 45.42 N 12.47 E
Loncopué 242 38.04 S 70.37 W
Londa 116 22.06 N 90.25 E
Londela-Kaye 142 4.51 S 13.24 E
Londerzeel 46 51.00 N 4.18 E
Londinières 46 49.50 N 1.24 E
Londo 144 2.03 N 25.43 E
Londoko 79 49.02 N 131.59 E
London, Ont., Can. 202 42.59 N 81.14 W
London, Gilb. Is. 164o 1.58 N 157.28 W
London, Eng., U.K. 44
250 51.30 N 0.10 W
London, Calif., U.S. 216 36.30 N 119.25 W
London, Ky., U.S. 182 37.08 N 84.05 W
London, Ohio, U.S. 208 39.53 N 83.27 W

London, Tex., U.S. 186 30.41 N 99.35 W
London, Wis., U.S. 206 43.03 N 89.01 W
London (Gatwick) Airport ⊠, Eng., U.K. 44 51.09 N 0.21 W
London (Heathrow) Airport ⊠, Eng., U.K. 250 51.27 N 0.28 W
London Bridge Station ⇀[5] 250 51.30 N 0.05 W
London Colney 250 51.43 N 0.18 W
Londonderry, N.S., Can. 176 45.29 N 63.36 W
Londonderry, N. Ire., U.K. 42 55.00 N 7.19 W
Londonderry, N.H., U.S. 197 42.51 N 71.22 W
Londonderry, Ohio, U.S. 204 39.16 N 82.47 W
Londonderry, Cape ≻ 154 13.45 S 126.55 E
Londonderry, Isla ▌ 244 55.03 S 70.35 W
Londontowne 198 38.55 N 76.33 W
London Zoo ♠ 250 51.32 N 0.09 W
Londres, Arg. 242 27.43 S 67.07 W
Londres → London, Eng., U.K. 44 51.30 N 0.10 W
Londrina 245 23.18 S 51.09 W
Lonedell 209 38.18 N 90.50 W
Lonely Lake ⊜ 174 51.09 N 99.05 W
Lonelyville 266 40.39 N 73.11 W
Lone Mountain ∧, Nev., U.S. 194 38.02 N 117.29 W
Lone Mountain ∧, S. Dak., U.S. 188 45.23 N 103.44 W
Lone Oak, Ky., U.S. 184 37.02 N 88.40 W
Lone Oak, Tex., U.S. 212 33.01 N 95.57 W
Lone Pine 194 36.36 N 118.04 W
Lone Rock 180 43.11 N 90.12 W
Lone Star 212 32.56 N 94.43 W
Lone Tree 180 41.29 N 91.26 W
Lone Tree Creek ≃, U.S. 190 40.25 N 104.35 W
Lone Tree Creek ≃, Calif., U.S. 216 37.53 N 121.14 W
Lone Wolf 186 34.59 N 99.15 W
Long 100 18.05 N 99.50 E
Long ≃ 46 47.41 N 0.28 E
Long, Loch ᑕ 42 56.04 N 4.50 W
Longa 142 14.42 S 18.32 E
Longa ≃, Ang. 142 16.25 N 19.04 E
Longa ≃, Ang. 142 10.15 S 13.30 E
Longá ≃, Bra. 240 3.09 S 41.56 W
Longa, Proliv ⋃ 64 70.20 N 178.00 E
Longairo 144 4.30 N 32.17 E
Long Akah 102 3.19 N 114.47 E
Long'an 92 25.03 N 109.00 E
Longanqiao 79 47.31 N 124.27 E
Longare 58 45.29 N 11.36 E
Longarone 58 46.16 N 12.18 E
Longasy 24 61.58 N 35.09 E
Longaví 242 35.58 S 71.41 W
Longbangun 102 0.36 N 115.11 E
Long Barn 216 38.05 N 120.08 W
Long Bay ᑕ, Austl. 264a 33.58 S 151.16 E
Long Bay ᑕ, Barb. 231g 13.04 N 59.29 W
Long Bay ᑕ, Jam. 231q 17.51 N 77.27 W
Long Bay ᑕ, U.S. 182 33.35 N 78.45 W
Long Beach, Calif., U.S. 218
270 33.46 N 118.11 W
Long Beach, Miss., U.S. 184 30.22 N 89.07 W
Long Beach, N.Y., U.S. 200 40.35 N 73.41 W
Long Beach, Wash., U.S. 214 46.21 N 124.03 W
Long Beach Breakwater ⇀[5] 270 33.43 N 118.09 W
Long Beach Middle Harbor ᑕ 270 33.45 N 118.13 W
Long Beach Municipal Airport ⊠ 270 33.49 N 118.09 W
Long Beach Naval Station ■ 270 33.45 N 118.14 W
Longbeleh 102 0.16 N 116.11 E
Long Belepai 102 2.45 N 114.04 E
Longbenton 42 55.02 N 1.35 W
Longboat Key 210 27.24 N 82.39 W
Longboat Key ▌ 210 27.23 N 82.39 W
Long Branch, N.J., U.S. 198 40.18 N 74.00 W
Longbranch, Wash., U.S. 214 47.13 N 122.46 W
Long Branch ≃ 209 39.23 N 91.49 W
Long Buckby 44 52.19 N 1.04 W
Longbuwei 90 25.32 N 115.24 E
Long Cane Creek ≃ 182 33.57 N 82.24 W
Long Canyon ∨ 216 38.59 N 120.41 W
Longchamp, Hippodrome de ♠ 251 48.51 N 2.14 E
Longchamps, Arg. 248 34.52 S 58.23 W
Longchamps, Bel. 52 50.03 N 5.42 E
Longchang, Zhg. 94 40.53 N 123.08 E
Longchang, Zhg. 97 29.21 N 105.17 E
Longchaumois 54 46.27 N 5.56 E
Longchêne 251 48.38 N 2.00 E
Longchuan, Zhg. 90 24.07 N 115.17 E
Longchuan, Zhg. 92 24.14 N 97.45 E
Long Creek, Ill., U.S. 209 39.48 N 88.50 W
Long Creek, Oreg., U.S. 192 44.43 N 119.06 W
Long Creek ≃ 174 49.07 N 103.00 W
Long Crendon 44 51.47 N 1.01 W
Longcun 90 23.34 N 115.33 E
Longde 92 35.28 N 106.22 E
Longdendale ∨ 252 53.29 N 1.56 W
Long Ditton 250 51.23 N 0.20 W
Longdongtuo 97 29.59 N 106.21 E
Longdou 90 27.25 N 117.24 E
Longdu 96 31.51 N 118.56 E
Long Eaton 44 52.54 N 1.15 W
Longeau 54 47.46 N 5.18 E
Long Eddy 200 41.51 N 75.08 W
Longeville-lès-Saint-Avold 52 49.07 N 6.38 E
Longfengchang 97 30.26 N 105.38 E
Longfengkan 94 41.51 N 124.01 E
Longfengyutun 94 40.39 N 122.57 E
Longfield 250 51.24 N 0.18 E
Longford, Austl. 156 38.10 S 147.05 E
Longford, Eire 28 53.44 N 7.47 W
Longford □[6] 28 53.40 N 7.40 W
Longford Park ♠ 252 53.27 N 2.17 W
Longframlington 42 55.18 N 1.47 W
Longgang, Zhg. 90 29.38 N 114.57 E
Longgang, Zhg. 90 33.22 N 120.04 E
Longgang, Zhg. 92 24.41 N 101.09 E
Longgangzi 94 42.09 N 123.26 E
Long Green 198 39.28 N 76.31 W
Long Grove 206 42.11 N 88.00 W
Longguan 95 40.47 N 115.34 E
Longgudu 90 27.45 N 116.14 E
Longguntur 102 0.13 N 112.12 E
Long Harbour 176 47.26 N 53.48 W
Long Harbour ᑕ, Newf., Can. 176 47.44 N 55.01 W
Long Harbour ᑕ, H.K. 261d 22.27 N 114.20 E
Longhe ≃ 95 39.23 N 116.49 E
Longhorn Cavern State Park ♠ 186 30.20 N 98.30 W
Longhorsley 42 55.15 N 1.46 W
Longhoughton 42 55.26 N 1.36 W
Longhua, Zhg. 88 41.17 N 117.37 E
Longhua, Zhg. 90 22.42 N 113.59 E
Longhua, Zhg. 90 23.37 N 114.14 E
Longhua, Zhg. 96 31.09 N 121.26 E
Longhua Airport ⊠ 96 31.09 N 121.26 E
Longhuasi 97 28.47 N 104.08 E

Symbol	English	Deutsch	Español	Français	Português
≃	River	Fluss	Río	Rivière	Rio
≋	Canal	Kanal	Canal	Canal	Canal
↓	Waterfall, Rapids	Wasserfall, Stromschnellen	Cascada, Rápidos	Chute d'eau, Rapides	Cascata, Rápidos
⋃	Strait	Meeresstrasse	Estrecho	Détroit	Estreito
ᑕ	Bay, Gulf	Bucht, Golf	Bahía, Golfo	Baie, Golfe	Baía, Golfo
⊜	Lake, Lakes	See, Seen	Lago, Lagos	Lac, Lacs	Lago, Lagos
☷	Swamp	Sumpf	Pantano	Marais	Pântano
⊓	Ice Features, Glacier	Eis- und Gletscherformen	Accidentes Glaciales	Formes glaciaires	Acidentes Glaciares
⍑	Other Hydrographic Features	Andere Hydrographische Objekte	Otros Elementos Hidrográficos	Autres données hydrographiques	Outros Elementos Hidrográficos

Symbol	English	Deutsch	Español	Français	Português
⟡	Submarine Features	Untermeerische Objekte	Accidentes Submarinos	Formes de relief sous-marin	Acidentes Submarinos
□	Political Unit	Politische Einheit	Unidad Politica	Entité politique	Unidade Política
♦	Cultural Institution	Kulturelle Institution	Institución Cultural	Institution culturelle	Instituição Cultural
⊥	Historical Site	Historische Stätte	Sitio Histórico	Site historique	Sitio Histórico
♠	Recreational Site	Erholungs- und Ferienort	Sitio de Recreo	Centre de loisirs	Sítio de Lazer
⊠	Airport	Flughafen	Aeropuerto	Aéroport	Aeroporto
■	Military Installation	Militäranlage	Instalación Militar	Installation militaire	Instalação Militar
⇀	Miscellaneous	Verschiedenes	Misceláneo	Divers	Miscelânea

ENGLISH | DEUTSCH

Name	Page	Lat. °′	Long. °′
Longhui (Taohuaping), Zhg.	92	27.00 N	110.59 E
Longhui, Zhg.	97	29.32 N	104.48 E
Longhuiwei	90	25.32 N	114.47 E
Longhutang	96	31.52 N	119.59 E
Longido	144	2.44 S	36.41 E
Longiram	102	0.02 S	115.38 E
Long Island I, Antig.	230c	17.08 N	61.45 W
Long Island I, Austl.	156	22.09 S	149.54 E
Long Island I, Ba.	228	23.15 N	75.07 W
Long Island I, Newf., Can.	176	47.35 N	54.05 W
Long Island I, N.W. Ter., Can.	166	54.50 N	79.20 W
Long Island I, N.S., Can.	176	44.20 N	66.15 W
Long Island I, Pap. N. Gui.	154	5.20 S	147.05 E
Long Island I, Alaska, U.S.	172	54.54 N	132.45 W
Long Island I, Mass., U.S.	273	42.19 N	70.58 W
Long Island I, N.Y., U.S.	178	40.50 N	73.00 W
Long Island I, Wash., U.S.	214	46.27 N	123.58 W
Long Island City ◆[8]	266	40.45 N	73.56 W
Long Island Sound ⊔	178	41.05 N	72.58 W
Long Island University ʊ[2], N.Y., U.S.	266	40.41 N	73.59 W
Long Island University (C.W. Post Center) ʊ[2], N.Y., U.S.	266	40.49 N	73.36 W
Longitudinal, Valle ∨	242	36.00 S	72.00 W
Long Jetty	160	33.22 S	151.29 E
Longji	97	29.23 N	106.04 E
Longjiadian	94	42.10 N	120.47 E
Longjiang, Zhg.	79	47.19 N	123.12 E
Longjiang, Zhg.	90	22.59 N	116.13 E
Longjiang, Zhg.	90	22.53 N	113.04 E
Longjiang ≃, Zhg.	90	23.26 N	114.38 E
Longjiang ≃, Zhg.	90	22.59 N	116.18 E
Longjie ∧	92	25.15 N	98.25 E
Longjiezhen	97	29.53 N	104.32 E
Longjin	90	28.37 N	116.37 E
Longjing	90	23.53 N	112.52 E
Longjingguan)(	95	40.23 N	118.08 E
Longjohn Slough ≃	268	41.43 N	87.53 W
Longjuchang	97	30.00 N	103.59 E
Longjumeau	46	48.42 N	2.18 E
Longka, Zhg.	110	31.10 N	84.00 E
Longka, Zhg.	110	33.12 N	79.47 E
Longkamp	52	59.53 N	7.07 E
Longkang	90	33.09 N	116.54 E
Long Ke	261d	22.23 N	114.22 E
Long Key I, Fla., U.S.	210	27.44 N	82.45 W
Long Key I, Fla., U.S.	210	24.49 N	80.49 W
Long King Creek ≃	212	30.34 N	94.58 W
Longkou, Zhg.	88	37.38 N	120.18 E
Longkou, Zhg.	90	32.55 N	114.59 E
Longkou, Zhg.	90	29.57 N	113.47 E
Longkou, Zhg.	90	26.11 N	115.15 E
Longkouqiao	75	39.40 N	77.09 E
Long Lake, Ill., U.S.	206	42.22 N	88.08 W
Long Lake, N.Y., U.S.	178	43.58 N	74.25 W
Long Lake, Tex., U.S.	212	31.39 N	95.47 W
Long Lake ⊜, Ont., Can.	202	45.00 N	79.36 W
Long Lake ⊜, Ont., Can.	202	44.41 N	76.45 W
Long Lake ⊜, Mich., U.S.	180	45.12 N	83.30 W
Long Lake ⊜, Mich., U.S.	271	42.36 N	83.28 W
Long Lake ⊜, Mich., U.S.	271	42.37 N	83.44 W
Long Lake ⊜, N. Dak., U.S.	188	46.43 N	100.07 W
Long Lake ⊜, N.Y., U.S.	178	44.04 N	74.20 W
Long Lake ⊜, Wash., U.S.	214	47.03 N	122.47 W
Long Lake Creek ≃	188	46.40 N	100.13 W
Long Lake Shores	271	42.35 N	83.19 W
Long Lama	102	3.46 N	114.24 E
Longlangshan ⋀	92	21.50 N	100.30 E
Longlaville	52	49.32 N	5.47 E
Longleaf	184	31.00 N	92.34 W
Long Leaf Park	182	34.12 N	77.56 W
Longleat ʊ	44	51.12 N	2.17 W
Long-legged Lake ⊜	174	50.46 N	94.08 W
Longli	92	26.26 N	106.58 E
Longlin	92	24.49 N	105.31 E
Longling	92	24.39 N	98.40 E
Longmeadow	197	42.03 N	72.34 W
Long Melford	44	52.05 N	0.43 E
Longmen, Zhg.	79	48.55 N	126.54 E
Longmen, Zhg.	90	29.53 N	119.57 E
Longmen, Zhg.	90	23.44 N	114.15 E
Longmen, Zhg.	90	24.56 N	118.04 E
Longmen, Zhg.	90	25.06 N	116.58 E
Longmen, Zhg.	97	29.27 N	104.59 E
Longmenchang	97	30.53 N	106.10 E
Longmensuo	88	40.56 N	115.54 E
Longmentan	97	29.12 N	106.13 E
Longmiaozhen	88	40.03 N	123.47 E
Longming	92	22.59 N	107.11 E
Longmire	214	46.45 N	121.49 W
Longmont	190	40.10 N	105.06 W
Long Mountain ∧	184	36.41 N	92.26 W
Long Mountain ∧[2]	44	52.39 N	3.09 W
Longmu	90	24.16 N	115.28 E
Longnan	90	24.54 N	114.48 E
Longnawan	102	1.54 N	114.53 E
Long Neck ≻[1]	266	41.03 N	73.29 W
Long Neck Point ≻	266	41.02 N	73.29 W
Longnüsi	97	30.23 N	106.11 E
Longny-au-Perche	46	48.32 N	0.45 E
Longperrier	251	49.03 N	2.40 E
Long Pine	188	42.32 N	99.42 W
Longping	90	29.53 N	115.41 E
Long Plains	158b	34.21 S	138.22 E
Long Point, Austl.	264a	34.01 S	150.54 E
Long Point, Ill., U.S.	206	41.00 N	88.54 W
Long Point ≻, Ba.	230b	25.01 N	77.20 W
Long Point ≻, Man., Can.	174	53.02 N	98.40 W
Long Point ≻, Newf., Can.	176	48.48 N	58.46 W
Long Point ≻, Ont., Can.	202	44.06 N	76.29 W
Long Point ≻, Pil.	106	9.39 N	118.20 E
Long Point ≻, Calif., U.S.	270	33.44 N	118.23 W
Long Point ≻, Vir. Is., U.S.	230m	18.18 N	64.53 W
Long Point ≻, Vir. Is., U.S.	231n	17.41 N	64.50 W
Long Point ≻[1]	204	42.34 N	80.15 W
Long Point ≻	202	44.32 N	80.18 W
Long Point Bay ⊂	202	42.40 N	80.14 W
Long Point Creek ≃	206	41.02 N	88.48 W
Long Point Provincial Park ♠	204	42.35 N	80.35 W
Long Pond ⊜, U.S.	273	42.41 N	71.21 W
Long Pond ⊜, Mass., U.S.	197	41.43 N	70.04 W
Long Pond ⊜, Mass., U.S.	197	41.48 N	70.57 W
Longpont	46	49.16 N	3.13 E
Longport	198	39.19 N	74.32 W
Long Prairie	188	45.59 N	94.52 W
Long Prairie ≃	188	46.20 N	94.36 W
Longpré-les-Corps-Saints	46	50.01 N	1.59 E
Long Preston	42	54.02 N	2.15 W
Longqiantai	94	41.23 N	120.52 E
Longqu, Zhg.	88	34.54 N	116.47 E
Longqu, Zhg.	88	34.16 N	114.49 E
Longquan	90	28.04 N	119.07 E
Longquanguan	88	38.55 N	113.51 E
Longquanshan ⋀	97	30.00 N	104.10 E
Longquansi	97	30.21 N	104.39 E
Longquanyi	97	30.34 N	104.16 E
Long Range Mountains ⋀	176	49.20 N	57.30 W
Longreach	156	23.26 S	144.15 E
Long Reach ⊂	176	45.26 N	66.09 W
Long Reach ⊔	202	44.07 N	77.04 W
Long Reef ÷[2]	154	11.11 S	151.40 E
Long Reef Point ≻	264a	33.45 S	151.19 E
Longridge	42	53.51 N	2.36 W
Long Run ≃, Ill., U.S.	268	41.37 N	88.03 W
Long Run ≃, Pa., U.S.	269b	40.20 N	79.48 W
Long Sault Dam ◆[6]	196	45.00 N	74.45 W
Long Sault Islands II	196	45.00 N	74.55 W
Longsegah	102	2.15 N	116.42 E
Longshan, Zhg.	90	33.36 N	116.18 E
Longshan, Zhg.	90	22.59 N	113.17 E
Longshan, Zhg.	92	29.28 N	109.20 E
Longshansuo	90	30.05 N	121.33 E
Longsheng	92	25.42 N	110.01 E
Longshengchang	97	30.36 N	105.21 E
Longshengzhuang	88	40.40 N	113.21 E
Longshizhen, Zhg.	97	29.23 N	105.10 E
Longshizhen, Zhg.	97	30.12 N	106.26 E
Longshuizhen	97	29.33 N	105.45 E
Longs Peak ∧	190	40.15 N	105.37 W
Long Sutton	44	52.47 N	0.08 E
Longtaichang	97	30.04 N	105.34 E
Longtan, Zhg.	90	23.40 N	113.24 E
Longtan, Zhg.	92	28.20 N	108.52 E
Longtan, Zhg.	96	32.11 N	119.04 E
Longtan, Zhg.	96	31.20 N	118.45 E
Longtan, Zhg.	97	29.19 N	104.35 E
Longtansi	97	30.42 N	104.10 E
Long Teru	102	3.52 N	114.15 E
Long-thanh	100	10.47 N	106.57 E
Longtian	90	25.38 N	119.28 E
Longtian'an	96	31.10 N	120.49 E
Long Tom ≃	192	44.23 N	123.15 W
Longton, Eng., U.K.	44	53.00 N	2.09 W
Longton, Eng., U.K.	252	53.44 N	2.48 W
Longton, Kans., U.S.	188	37.23 N	96.05 W
Longtou	88	38.51 N	121.18 E
Longtoupu	90	27.54 N	113.12 E
Longtouwei	90	25.14 N	115.24 E
Longtown	42	55.01 N	2.58 W
Long-truong	259c	10.49 N	106.49 E
Longué	32	47.23 N	0.06 W
Longueau	46	49.52 N	2.21 E
Longuesse	251	49.04 N	1.56 E
Longueuil	196	45.32 N	73.30 W
Longueville, Austl.	264a	33.50 S	151.10 E
Longueville, Fr.	46	48.31 N	3.15 E
Longueville-sur-Scie	46	49.48 N	1.06 E
Longuyon	52	49.26 N	5.36 E
Long Valley	200	40.47 N	74.47 W
Long Valley Creek ≃, Calif., U.S.	216	39.03 N	122.34 W
Long Valley Creek ≃, Nev., U.S.	216	39.31 N	119.39 W
Long Valley Wash ∨	194	39.56 N	116.39 W
Longvic	54	47.17 N	5.04 E
Longview, Alta., Can.	172	50.32 N	114.14 W
Longview, N.C., U.S.	182	35.44 N	81.23 W
Longview, Tex., U.S.	212	32.30 N	94.44 W
Longview, Wash., U.S.	214	46.08 N	122.57 W
Longview Heights	212	32.30 N	94.41 W
Longvilliers	251	48.35 N	2.00 E
Longvilly	52	50.01 N	5.50 E
Longwai	102	0.42 N	116.39 E
Longwan	95	38.57 N	116.10 E
Longwangmiao, Zhg.	88	36.12 N	115.13 E
Longwangmiao, Zhg.	92	40.36 N	95.52 E
Longwangmiao, Zhg.	94	42.35 N	123.42 E
Longwangmiao, Zhg.	94	41.38 N	121.04 E
Longwarry	159	38.07 S	145.46 E
Longwen	90	24.36 N	116.21 E
Longwo	90	23.28 N	115.17 E
Longwokou	96	32.18 N	119.52 E
Longwood	210	28.42 N	81.21 W
Longwood Gardens ♠	275	39.52 N	75.40 W
Longwood Lake	266	40.59 N	74.52 W
Longwood Park	182	34.55 N	79.42 W
Longworth	172	53.55 N	121.28 W
Longwy	52	49.31 N	5.46 E
Longxi → Zhangzhou, Zhg.	90	24.33 N	117.39 E
Longxi, Zhg.	92	34.56 N	104.47 E
Longxi, Zhg.	97	29.59 N	106.09 E
Longxi ≃, Zhg.	90	26.24 N	118.26 E
Longxi ≃, Zhg.	96	30.49 N	120.08 E
Longxian, Zhg.	92	34.51 N	106.59 E
Longxian, Zhg.	97	29.09 N	105.50 E
Longxumen	88	40.37 N	118.31 E
Long-xuyen	100	10.23 N	105.25 E
Longyan	90	25.08 N	117.02 E
Longyou	90	29.02 N	119.10 E
Longyouhe ≃	96	32.08 N	120.38 E
Longyuan	90	24.56 N	114.27 E
Longzhen	79	48.41 N	126.42 E
Longzhou	92	22.22 N	106.52 E
Longzi	110	28.25 N	92.31 E
Loni	262a	28.45 N	77.17 E
Lonigo	58	45.23 N	11.23 E
Löningen	48	52.44 N	7.46 E
Lonkala	142	4.37 S	23.14 E
Lönnewitz	50	51.34 N	13.11 E
Lonny	52	49.49 N	4.35 E
Lonoke	184	34.47 N	91.54 W
Lönsboda	26	56.24 N	14.19 E
Lønsdal	24	66.44 N	15.28 E
Lonsdale	180	44.29 N	93.25 W
Lonsdale, Point ≻	159	38.17 S	144.37 E
Lons-le-Saunier	54	46.40 N	5.33 E
Lonton	100	25.06 N	96.17 E
Lontra ≃	240	6.37 S	48.39 W
Lontra, Ribeirão ≃	245	21.28 S	53.37 W
Lonua ≃	142	1.16 N	22.38 E
Loo	74	43.43 N	39.36 E
Looc	106	12.16 N	121.59 E
Loogootee	184	38.41 N	86.55 W
Looking Glass ≃	206	42.52 N	84.54 W
Lookout	200	41.47 N	75.11 W
Lookout, Cape ≻, N.C., U.S.	182	34.35 N	76.32 W
Lookout, Cape ≻, Oreg., U.S.	214	45.20 N	124.00 W
Lookout, Point ≻, Austl.	161a	27.26 S	153.33 E
Lookout, Point ≻, Md., U.S.	198	38.02 N	76.19 W
Lookout Mountain ∧, U.S.	184	34.25 N	85.40 W
Lookout Mountain ∧, Oreg., U.S.	192	44.20 N	120.22 W
Lookout Mountain ∧, Oreg., U.S.	214	45.21 N	121.31 W
Lookout Mountain ∧, Wash., U.S.	214	48.40 N	122.22 W
Lookout Pass)(	192	47.27 N	115.42 W
Lookout Point Lake ⊜[1]	192	43.52 N	122.40 W
Lookout Ridge ⋀	170	69.07 N	158.36 W
Loolmalassin ∧[1]	144	3.03 S	35.49 E
Loomis, Calif., U.S.	216	38.49 N	121.12 W
Loomis, Nebr., U.S.	188	40.29 N	99.31 W
Loon	106	9.48 N	123.47 E
Loon ≃	174	55.50 N	101.59 W
Loon Creek ≃	192	44.49 N	114.49 W
Loongana	152	30.57 S	127.02 E
Loon Lake ⊜, Can.	174	55.51 N	102.00 W
Loon Lake ⊜, Mich., U.S.	271	42.41 N	83.22 W
Loon Lake ⊜[1]	216	39.00 N	120.18 W
Loon op Zand	48	51.38 N	5.04 E
Loop	186	32.55 N	102.25 W
Loop ◆[8]	268	41.53 N	87.38 W
Loop Head ≻	28	52.34 N	9.56 W
Lo Ortuzar	276e	33.28 S	70.45 W
Loos	46	50.37 N	3.01 E
Loosduinen ◆[8]	48	52.04 N	4.13 E
Loose, B.R.D.	41	54.31 N	9.53 E
Loose, Eng., U.K.	250	51.14 N	0.31 E
Loose Creek	209	38.30 N	91.57 W
Lop ≃	100	13.18 N	107.37 E
Lopandino	66	52.28 N	34.49 E
Lopanka	70	46.24 N	40.59 E
Lopar'ovo	70	58.20 N	42.41 E
Lopasn'a ≃	72	54.51 N	37.52 E
Lopatiči	66	53.34 N	30.53 E
Lopatin, S.S.S.R.	68	50.13 N	24.50 E
Lopatin, S.S.S.R.	74	43.53 N	47.41 E
Lopatina, Gora ∧	79	50.52 N	143.10 E
Lopatino, S.S.S.R.	70	52.37 N	45.47 E
Lopatino, S.S.S.R.	72	54.45 N	37.00 E
Lopatino, S.S.S.R.	79	48.24 N	142.15 E
Lopatinskij	72	55.21 N	38.34 E
Lopatka, Mys ≻	64	50.52 N	156.40 E
Lopatovo	66	56.08 N	29.12 E
Lop Buri	100	14.48 N	100.37 E
Lopes	246	22.02 S	44.33 W
Lopevi I	165f	16.30 S	168.21 E
Lopez, Pa., U.S.	200	41.27 N	76.20 W
Lopez, Wash., U.S.	214	48.31 N	122.54 W
López, Arroyo de ≃	248	35.26 S	57.35 W
Lopez, Cap ≻	142	0.37 S	8.43 E
Lopez Bay ⊂	106	13.56 N	122.12 E
López Collada	222	31.45 N	113.55 W
Lopez Dam ◆[6]	216	35.12 N	120.29 W
Lopez Island I	214	48.30 N	122.54 W
Lopik	48	51.58 N	4.56 E
Lop Nor → Luobubo ⊜	80	40.20 N	90.15 E
Lopori ≃	142	1.14 N	19.49 E
Lopotovo	72	56.04 N	36.49 E
Loppersum	48	53.19 N	6.45 E
Loppi	26	60.43 N	24.27 E
Lo Prado Arriba	276e	33.26 S	70.45 W
Lopšen'ga	24	64.58 N	37.41 E
L'Opton Ruisseau ≃	251	48.52 N	1.29 E
Lopt'uga	24	63.16 N	47.56 E
Lopuchovka, S.S.S.R.	70	50.37 N	44.29 E
Lopuchovka, S.S.S.R.	70	51.59 N	44.42 E
Łopuszno	30	50.57 N	20.15 E
Lora	113	33.53 N	73.17 E
Lora ≃	236	9.25 N	72.25 W
Lora, Hāmūn-i- ⊜	118	29.20 N	64.50 E
Lora Creek ≃	152	28.10 S	135.22 E
Lora del Río	34	37.39 N	5.32 W
Lorain	204		
	269a	41.28 N	82.10 W
Lorain □[6]	204	41.22 N	82.06 W
Lorain County Regional Airport ⊠	269a	41.20 N	82.11 W
Loraine, Calif., U.S.	218	35.19 N	118.25 W
Loraine, Ill., U.S.	209	40.09 N	91.13 W
Loraine, Tex., U.S.	186	32.25 N	100.43 W
Loralai	110	30.22 N	68.36 E
Loramie, Lake ⊜[1]	206	40.23 N	84.18 W
Loramie Creek ≃	206	40.11 N	84.14 W
Lorca	34	37.40 N	1.42 W
Lorch, B.R.D.	52	50.02 N	7.48 E
Lorch, B.R.D.	52	48.49 N	9.40 E
Lorchhausen	52	50.03 N	7.47 E
Lord Howe Island I	150	31.33 S	159.05 E
Lord Howe Rise ÷[3]	14	29.00 S	162.30 E
Lord Mayor Bay ⊂	166	69.44 N	92.00 W
Lordsburg	190	32.21 N	108.43 W
Lord's Cricket Ground ♠	250	51.32 N	0.10 W
Lordstown	204	41.09 N	80.53 W
Lords Valley	200	41.23 N	75.04 W
Loreauville	184	30.03 N	91.44 W
Loreley ♠	52	50.08 N	7.44 E
Lorena, Bra.	246	22.44 S	45.08 W
Lorena, Tex., U.S.	212	31.23 N	97.13 W
Lorengau	154	2.00 S	147.15 E
Lorentz ≃	154	5.23 S	138.04 E
Lorentzen	52	48.57 N	7.10 E
Lorenzago di Cadore	58	46.29 N	12.28 E
Lorenzo	186	33.40 N	101.32 W
Lorenzo Geyres (Queguay)	242	32.05 S	57.55 W
Loreo	58	45.04 N	12.11 E
Lorestān □[8]	118	33.30 N	48.30 E
Loreto, Arg.	242	27.46 S	57.17 W
Loreto, Bol.	238	15.13 S	64.40 W
Loreto, Bra.	240	7.05 S	45.09 W
Loreto, Col.	236	3.48 S	70.15 W
Loreto, It.	60	43.26 N	13.36 E
Loreto, Méx.	222	26.01 N	111.21 W
Loreto, Méx.	224	22.16 N	101.58 W
Loreto, Para.	242	23.16 S	57.11 W
Loreto, Pil.	106	10.21 N	125.34 E
Loreto, Pil.	106	8.12 N	125.45 E
Loreto □[5]	236	3.00 S	75.00 W
Loreto Aprutino	60	42.26 N	13.59 E
Lorette, Man., Can.	174	49.44 N	96.52 W
Lorette, Fr.	56	45.31 N	4.35 E
Loretteville	196	46.51 N	71.21 W
Loretto → Loreto, It.	60	43.26 N	13.36 E
Loretto, Pa., U.S.	204	40.31 N	78.38 W
Loretto, Tenn., U.S.	184	35.05 N	87.26 W
Lorgues	56	43.29 N	6.22 E
Lorian Swamp ≡	144	0.40 N	39.35 E
Lorica	236	9.14 N	75.49 W
Lorida	210	27.27 N	81.15 W
Lorient	32	47.45 N	3.22 W
L'Orignal	196	45.37 N	74.42 W
Lorimor	184	41.07 N	94.03 W
Loring, Aeródromo de ⊠	256a	40.22 N	3.47 W
Loring Air Force Base ■	176	46.57 N	67.54 W
Lorino	170	65.30 N	171.43 W
Loriol-sur-Drôme	56	44.45 N	4.49 E
Loris	182	34.04 N	78.53 W
Lorman	184	31.49 N	91.03 W
L'Orme	251	48.39 N	1.41 E
Lormes	46	47.17 N	3.49 E
Lorn, Firth of ⊂[2]	28	56.20 N	5.40 W
Lorna Glen	152	26.14 S	121.33 E
Lorne, Austl.	159	38.33 S	143.59 E
Lorne, N.B., Can.	176	47.53 N	66.08 W
Loro Ciuffenna	60	43.35 N	11.38 E
Loronyo	144	4.39 N	32.38 E
Lorquin	54	48.40 N	7.00 E
Lörrach	54	47.37 N	7.40 E
Lorrain, Rivière du ≃	230e	14.50 N	61.03 W
Lorraine □[9]	32	49.00 N	6.00 E
Lorrez-le-Bocage	46	48.14 N	2.54 E
Lorris	46	47.53 N	2.31 E
Lorsch	52	49.39 N	8.34 E
Lorsica	56	44.26 N	9.16 E
Lorup	48	52.55 N	7.38 E
Lorze ≃	54	47.15 N	8.25 E
Los	26	61.44 N	15.10 E
Los, Îles de II	140	9.30 N	13.48 W
Losada ≃	236	2.12 N	73.55 W
Los Aguacates	276c	10.35 N	66.48 W
Los Alamitos	270	33.48 N	118.04 W
Los Alamitos Naval Air Station ■	218	33.47 N	118.03 W
Los Alamitos Race Course ♠	270	33.48 N	118.03 W
Los Alamos, Méx.	222	28.40 N	103.30 W
Los Alamos, Calif., U.S.	194	34.44 N	120.17 W
Los Alamos, N. Mex., U.S.	190	35.53 N	106.19 W
Los Aldamas	222	26.03 N	99.11 W
Los Altos, Méx.	186	26.14 N	98.28 W
Los Altos, Calif., U.S.	216	37.23 N	122.06 W
Los Altos Hills	216	37.21 N	122.08 W
Los Amates, Guat.	226	15.16 N	89.06 W
Los Amates, Méx.	224	18.08 N	102.15 W
Los Andes	242	32.50 S	70.37 W
Los Ángeles, Chile	242	37.28 S	72.21 W
Los Ángeles, Nic.	226	13.14 N	85.47 W
Los Angeles	218		
	270	34.03 N	118.15 W
Los Angeles □[6]	218	34.20 N	118.10 W
Los Angeles ≃	218	33.46 N	118.12 W
Los Angeles Aqueduct ≡[1]	194	35.22 N	118.05 W
Los Angeles County Art Museum ʊ	270	34.05 N	118.22 W
Los Angeles County Fairgrounds ♠	270	34.05 N	117.46 W
Los Angeles Harbor ⊂	270	33.42 N	118.16 W
Los Angeles International Airport ⊠	218	33.56 N	118.24 W
Los Antiguos	244	46.33 S	71.37 W
Losantville	208	40.02 N	85.11 W
Losap I[1]	14	6.54 N	152.44 E
Los Arabos	230p	22.44 N	80.43 W
Losarang	105a	6.24 S	108.10 E
Los Arroyos, Lago de ⊜	238	12.38 S	65.00 W
Los Banos	216	37.04 N	120.51 W
Los Banos Creek ≃	216	37.20 N	120.57 W
Los Banos Creek, North Fork ≃	216	36.57 N	121.07 W
Los Banos Creek, South Fork ≃	216	36.57 N	121.07 W
Los Berros	242	31.57 S	68.39 W
Los Blancos	242	23.36 S	62.36 W
Los Burros	222	25.03 N	110.50 W
Los Cardales	248	34.20 S	58.59 W
Los Cerrillos, Arg.	242	31.57 S	65.28 W
Los Cerrillos, Ur.	248	34.37 S	56.22 W
Los Cerrillos, Aeropuerto ⊠	276e	33.30 S	70.43 W
Los Cerritos Center ◆[9]	270	33.52 N	118.05 W
Los Chacos	238	14.33 S	62.11 W
Löschenrod	52	50.30 N	9.41 E
Los Chiles	226	11.02 N	84.43 W
Los Conquistadores	242	30.36 S	58.28 W
Los Coronados, Islas II	194	32.25 N	117.15 W
Los Coyotes Indian Reservation ◆[4]	194	33.20 N	116.35 W
Los Cuatro Álamos	276e	33.32 S	70.44 W
Los Dos Caminos	276c	10.31 N	66.50 W
Los Ebanos, Méx.	222	24.40 N	97.45 W
Los Ebanos, Tex., U.S.	186	26.14 N	98.34 W
Loseley House ⊥	250	51.13 N	0.36 W
Los Encuentros	226	12.39 N	85.12 W
Los Esclavos ≃	226	13.50 N	90.20 W
Losevo	68	50.40 N	40.02 E
Los Flamencos, Laguna ⊜	248	35.36 S	58.42 W
Los Frentones	242	26.25 S	61.25 W
Los Fresnos	186	26.04 N	97.29 W
Los Garzas	186	26.23 N	99.46 W
Los Gatos	216	37.14 N	121.59 W
Los Gatos Creek ≃, Calif., U.S.	216	36.13 N	120.08 W
Los Gatos Creek ≃, Calif., U.S.	216	37.20 N	121.54 W
Los Glaciares, Parque Nacional ♠	244	49.52 S	73.05 W
Los Guerras	186	26.25 N	99.05 W
Loshan → Leshan	97	29.34 N	103.45 E
Los Haros	224	22.46 N	102.57 W
Losheim	52	49.30 N	6.44 E
Los Hermanos, Islas II	236	11.45 N	64.25 W
Los Herreras	186	25.55 N	99.24 W
Losi	263a	6.40 N	3.31 E
Łosice	30	52.14 N	22.43 E
Lošinj, Otok I	36	44.36 N	14.24 E
Losinoborskaja	76	58.27 N	89.28 E
Losino-Petrovskij	72	55.52 N	38.12 E
Losinovka	68	50.51 N	31.54 E
Los Jazmines, Presa ⊜[1]	276a	19.25 N	99.16 W
Los Juríes	242	28.28 S	62.06 W
Loškar'ovka	68	47.57 N	34.12 E
Loskopdam ◆[6]	146	25.23 S	29.20 E
Loskop Game Reserve ◆[4]	146	25.23 S	29.20 E
Los Lagos	244	39.51 S	72.50 W
Los Llanos	230m	18.03 N	66.24 W
Los Llanos [de Aridane]	138	28.39 N	17.54 W
Los López	186	26.15 N	99.05 W
Los Lunas	190	34.48 N	106.44 W
Los Mármoles, Parque Nacional ♠	224	20.55 N	99.12 W
Los Médanos, Istmo de ⊥[3]	231s	11.35 N	69.45 W
Los Menucos	244	40.50 S	68.08 W
Los Metates	224	23.46 N	106.02 W
Los'mino	66	55.04 N	34.24 E
Los Mochis	222	25.45 N	108.57 W
Los Molinos	194	40.03 N	122.06 W
Los Muemos	244	41.24 S	73.29 W
Los Naranjos	276c	10.27 N	66.48 W
Los Navalmorales	34	39.43 N	4.38 W
Lošnica	66	54.17 N	28.46 E
Los Nietos	270	33.58 N	118.04 W
Løsning	41	55.48 N	9.42 E
Los Nogales	186	26.16 N	99.43 W
Los Olmos Creek ≃, Tex., U.S.	186	26.21 N	98.48 W
Los Olmos Creek ≃, Tex., U.S.	186	27.20 N	97.40 W
Los Osos	216	35.19 N	120.50 W
Los Palacios, Arg.	242	29.22 S	68.11 W
Los Palacios, Cuba	230p	22.35 N	83.15 W
Los Palacios y Villafranca	34	37.10 N	5.56 W
Los Paraguas, Parque Nacional ♠	244	39.15 S	71.54 W
Los Perros, Arroyo ≃	278	34.37 S	58.46 W
Los Pinos ◆[8]	276b	23.04 N	82.23 W
Los Pinos ≃	190	36.56 N	107.36 W
Los Placeres	224	18.13 N	100.54 W
Los Polvorines	278	34.30 S	58.41 W
Los Quillayes	276e	33.34 S	70.37 W
Los Quirquinchos	242	33.22 S	61.43 W
Los Rábanos	230m	18.11 N	66.50 W
Los Ramones	186	25.42 N	99.37 W
Los Reyes	276a	19.21 N	99.07 W
Los Reyes de Salgado	224	19.35 N	102.29 W
Los Reyes la Paz	276a	19.21 N	98.58 W
Los Ríos □[4]	236	1.30 S	79.25 W
Los Roques, Islas II	236	11.50 N	66.45 W
Lossa	50	51.13 N	11.25 E
Lossa ≃	50	51.18 N	11.10 E
Los Santos	236	7.56 N	80.25 W
Los Santos □[4]	226	7.55 N	80.25 W
Los Santos de Maimona	34	38.27 N	6.23 W
Los Sauces, Chile	242	37.58 S	72.50 W
Los Sauces, Méx.	224	21.35 N	102.12 W
Lossburg	54	48.25 N	8.27 E
Lössel	253	51.21 N	7.39 E
Losser	48	52.15 N	7.00 E
Los Serranos	218	33.59 N	117.42 W
Lossiemouth	28	57.43 N	3.18 W
Lössnitz	50	50.37 N	12.43 E
Lost ≃, U.S.	192	41.56 N	121.30 W
Lost ≃, Ind., U.S.	184	38.33 N	86.49 W
Lost ≃, Minn., U.S.	188	47.51 N	96.02 W
Lost ≃, W. Va., U.S.	178	39.05 N	78.36 W
Lostant	206	41.09 N	89.04 W
Los Taques	236	11.50 N	70.16 W
Lost Bridge State Recreation Area ♠	206	40.45 N	85.37 W
Lost Creek ≃, Ala., U.S.	184	33.38 N	87.14 W
Lost Creek ≃, Ark., U.S.	184	34.10 N	92.31 W
Lost Creek ≃, Ohio, U.S.	208	39.58 N	84.09 W
Lost Creek ≃, Utah, U.S.	190	41.04 N	111.32 W
Lost Creek ≃, Wyo., U.S.	190	42.01 N	108.11 W
Lost Draw ∨	186	32.58 N	102.02 W
Los Telares	242	28.59 S	63.26 W
Los Teques	236	10.21 N	67.02 W
Los Testigos, Islas II	236	11.22 N	63.06 W
Lost Hills	194	35.37 N	119.41 W
Lostine ≃	192	45.33 N	117.29 W
Lost Lake ⊜, Oreg., U.S.	214	45.29 N	121.49 W
Lost Lake ⊜, Wash., U.S.	214	47.20 N	121.24 W
Lost Nation	180	41.58 N	90.49 W
Lostock ≃	252	53.40 N	2.48 W
Lostock Gralam	252	53.16 N	2.28 W
Los Torres	226	13.28 N	85.48 W
Los Trancos Creek ≃	272	37.25 N	122.12 W
Los Trancos Woods	272	37.21 N	122.12 W
Los Tres Palos	222	24.33 N	98.18 W
Lost River Range ⋀	192	44.10 N	113.35 W
Lost Trail Pass)(	192	45.41 N	113.57 W
Lostwithiel	44	50.25 N	4.40 W
Losuia	154	8.32 S	151.04 E
Los Vidrios	222	31.59 N	113.28 W
Los Vilos	242	31.55 S	71.31 W
Los Yébenes	34	39.34 N	3.53 W
Lot	164r	6.49 N	158.18 E
Lot □[5]	32	44.35 N	1.40 E
Lot ≃	32	44.18 N	0.20 E
Lota	242	37.05 S	73.10 W
Lotagipi Swamp (Lotikipi Plain) ⌣	134	4.36 N	34.55 E
Lotak	102	0.11 S	115.54 E
Lotbinière □[6]	196	46.30 N	71.40 W
Lotela, Lake ⊜	210	27.34 N	81.29 W
Løten	26	60.49 N	11.19 E
Lot-et-Garonne □[5]	32	44.20 N	0.20 E
Lotfābād	118	37.32 N	59.20 E
Lothair, S. Afr.	148	26.26 S	30.27 E
Lothair, Ky., U.S.	182	37.15 N	83.10 W
Lot Harbor ⊂	164r	6.48 N	158.19 E
Lothian □[8]	42	55.55 N	3.05 W
Lothian Region □[4]	42	55.50 N	3.15 W
Lothringen → Lorraine □[9]	32	49.00 N	6.00 E
Lotikipi Plain (Lotagipi Swamp) ⌣	134	4.36 N	34.55 E
Loto	142	2.49 S	22.29 E
Loto ≃	142	6.49 N	24.14 E
Lotofaga	165a	13.59 S	171.50 W
Lotoi ≃	142	1.35 S	18.30 E
Lotorp	40	58.44 N	15.50 E
Lotošino	66	56.14 N	35.38 E
Lotrului, Munții ⋀	38	45.30 N	23.52 E
Lotsane ≃	146	22.41 S	28.11 E
Lötschberg Tunnel ◆[5]	54	46.25 N	7.45 E
Lötschental ∨	54	46.25 N	7.50 E
Lotseninsel I	41	54.40 N	10.01 E
Lott	212	31.12 N	97.02 W
Lotta ≃	24	68.36 N	31.06 E
Lottaville	268	41.31 N	87.22 W
Lottivue	204	42.40 N	83.46 W
Löttringhausen ◆[8]	253	51.27 N	7.27 E
Lottsburg	198	37.57 N	76.31 W
Lotts Creek ≃	182	32.09 N	81.47 W
Lottsford Branch ≃	274c	38.55 N	76.49 W
Lottstetten	54	47.38 N	8.34 E
Lotuke, Jabal ∧	144	4.07 N	33.48 E
Lotung	90	24.41 N	121.46 E
Lötzen → Giżycko	30	54.03 N	21.47 E
Louame ≃	142	0.49 N	15.47 E
Louang Namtha	100	20.57 N	101.25 E
Louangphrabang	100	19.52 N	102.08 E
Louangphrabang □[4]	92	20.30 N	102.30 E
L'Ouarsenis, Massif de ⋀	34	35.40 N	1.50 E
Loubaresse	56	44.36 N	4.03 E
Loube, Montagne de la ∧	56	43.22 N	5.59 E
Loubetsi	142	3.12 S	12.10 E
Louchi	24	66.04 N	33.00 E
Loučná ∧	50	50.39 N	13.37 E
Loude	88	35.54 N	117.18 E
Loudéac	32	48.10 N	2.45 W
Louden Cove ⊂	266	41.05 N	73.43 W
Loudes	56	45.05 N	3.45 E
Loudi	92	27.47 N	111.37 E
Loudima Poste	142	4.07 S	13.04 E
Loudon	182	35.44 N	84.20 W
Loudonville, N.Y., U.S.	200	42.42 N	73.47 W
Loudonville, Ohio, U.S.	204	40.38 N	82.14 W
Loudoun □[6]	198	39.05 N	77.30 W
Loudun	32	47.01 N	0.05 E
Loué	32	48.00 N	0.09 W
Loue ≃	54	47.01 N	5.27 E
Louga	140	15.37 N	16.13 W
Louge	242	36.57 S	61.40 W
Louge ≃	32	43.27 N	1.20 E
Loughborough	44	52.47 N	1.11 W
Loughborough Lake ⊜	202	44.23 N	76.30 W
Loughermore ∧[2]	42	54.59 N	7.05 W
Loughman	210	28.14 N	81.34 W
Loughor	44	51.40 N	4.04 W
Loughor ≃	44	51.40 N	4.04 W
Loughrea	28	53.12 N	8.34 W
Loughros More Bay ⊂	28	54.47 N	8.35 W
Loughton	250	51.39 N	0.03 E
Louhans	54	46.38 N	5.13 E
Louin	184	31.59 N	89.16 W
Louisa, Ky., U.S.	182	38.07 N	82.36 W
Louisa, Va., U.S.	182	38.01 N	78.01 W
Louisa, Lac ⊜	196	45.46 N	74.25 W
Louisa, Lake ⊜, Ont., Can.	202	45.28 N	78.30 W
Louisa, Lake ⊜, Fla., U.S.	210	28.29 N	81.44 W
Louisbourg	176	45.55 N	59.58 W
Louis Bull Indian Reserve ◆[4]	172	52.53 N	113.31 W
Louisburg, Kans., U.S.	188	38.37 N	94.41 W
Louisburg, N.C., U.S.	182	36.06 N	78.18 W
Louisdale	176	45.36 N	61.04 W
Louise, Miss., U.S.	184	32.59 N	90.35 W
Louise, Tex., U.S.	212	29.06 N	96.25 W
Louise, Lake ⊜	170	62.20 N	146.30 W
Louise Island I	172	52.58 N	131.50 W
Louiseville	196	46.15 N	72.57 W
Louis Gentil → Youssoufia	138	32.16 N	8.33 W
Louisiade Archipelago II	150	11.00 S	153.00 E
Louisiade Rise ÷[3]	14	13.00 S	158.00 E
Louisiana	209	39.27 N	91.03 W
Louisiana □[3]	168		
	184	31.15 N	92.15 W
Louisiana ʊ	41	55.58 N	12.33 E
Lou Island I	154	2.25 S	147.20 E
Louis Trichardt	146	23.01 S	29.43 E
Louisvale	148	28.33 S	21.12 E
Louisville, Ont., Can.	204	42.28 N	82.07 W
Louisville, Ala., U.S.	184	31.47 N	85.33 W
Louisville, Ga., U.S.	182	33.00 N	82.24 W
Louisville, Ill., U.S.	184	38.46 N	88.30 W
Louisville, Ky., U.S.	208	38.16 N	85.45 W
Louisville, Miss., U.S.	184	33.07 N	89.03 W
Louisville, Nebr., U.S.	188	41.00 N	96.10 W
Louisville, Ohio, U.S.	204	40.50 N	81.16 W
Louisville Ridge ÷[3]	14	31.30 S	173.30 W
Louisville Seamount ÷[3]	14	31.15 S	172.20 W
Louis-XIV, Pointe ≻	166	54.37 N	79.45 W
Loujiaying	88	42.04 N	116.04 E
Loukanga	263b	4.20 S	15.09 E
Loukoua ≃	263b	4.07 S	15.10 E
Loulé	34	37.08 N	8.02 W
Loum	142	4.43 N	9.44 E
Loumou	263b	4.08 S	15.09 E
Lount Lake ⊜	174	50.10 N	94.20 W
Louny	50	50.19 N	13.46 E
Loup ≃, Fr.	56	43.38 N	7.09 E
Loup ≃, Nebr., U.S.	188	41.24 N	97.19 W
Loup, Gorge du ∨	52	49.47 N	6.23 E
Loup, Rivière du ≃	196	46.13 N	72.55 W
Loup City	188	41.17 N	98.58 W
Lourches	46	50.19 N	3.21 E
Lourdes, Newf., Can.	176	48.39 N	59.00 W
Lourdes, Fr.	32	43.06 N	0.03 W
Lourel de Baixo	256c	38.49 N	9.22 W
Lourenço	240	2.30 N	51.40 W
Lourenço Marques → Maputo	146	25.58 S	32.35 E
Lourenço Marques → Maputo □[5]	146	26.00 S	32.25 E
Lourenço Velho	246	22.22 S	45.19 W
Lourenço Velho ≃, Bra.	246	22.22 S	45.31 W
Lourenço Velho ≃, Bra.	246	23.26 S	45.35 W
Loures	34	38.50 N	9.10 W
Loures ≃	256c	38.50 N	9.08 W
Lourinhã	34	39.14 N	9.19 W
Lourmarin	56	43.46 N	5.22 E
Lourosa	34	40.19 N	7.56 W
Loury	46	48.00 N	2.05 E
Lousã, Port.	34	40.07 N	8.15 W
Lousa, Port.	256c	38.53 N	9.12 W
Louse Creek ≃	188	46.22 N	100.57 W
Loushan ∧	79	45.15 N	128.58 E
Louta	140	13.30 N	3.10 W
Loutang	96	31.26 N	121.12 E
Loutézou, Île de I	263b	4.22 S	15.10 E
Louth, Austl.	156	30.32 S	145.07 E
Louth, Eire	28	53.37 N	6.53 W
Louth, Eng., U.K.	42	53.22 N	0.01 W
Louth □[6]	28	53.55 N	6.30 W
Louth Bay ⊂	156	34.34 S	136.02 E
Louti, Mayo ≃	136	9.38 N	13.56 E
Loutit Bay ⊂	159	38.33 S	144.00 E
Loutrá Aidhipsoú	38	38.51 N	23.02 E
Loutre ≃	209	38.42 N	91.25 W
Loutre, Bayou de ≃	184	32.41 N	92.08 W
Loutrópirgos	257c	38.02 N	23.28 E
Louvain → Leuven	52	50.53 N	4.42 E
Louveciennes	251	48.52 N	2.07 E
Louveigné	52	50.32 N	5.42 E
Louveira	246	23.04 S	46.58 W
Louviers, Fr.	46	49.13 N	1.10 E
Louviers, Colo., U.S.	190	39.28 N	105.01 W
Louvigné-du-Désert	32	48.29 N	1.08 W
Louvre ʊ	251	48.52 N	2.20 E
Louvres	46	49.02 N	2.30 E
Louvroil	46	50.16 N	3.58 E
Louwsburg	148	27.37 S	31.07 E
Lou Yaeger, Lake ⊜[1]	209	39.10 N	89.37 W
Lóvago ≃	226	11.48 N	85.16 W
Lövånger	26	64.22 N	21.18 E
Lovat' ≃	66	58.14 N	31.28 E
Lovcy	72	55.00 N	39.15 E
Love	174	53.29 N	104.09 W
Loveč	38	43.08 N	24.43 E
Love Clough	252	53.44 N	2.17 W
Lovedale	269b	40.17 N	79.52 W
Lovejoy	209	38.39 N	90.10 W
Lovelady	212	31.08 N	95.27 W
Loveland, Colo., U.S.	190	40.24 N	105.05 W
Loveland, Ohio, U.S.	208	39.16 N	84.16 W
Lovell	192	44.50 N	108.24 W
Lovell Island I	273	42.20 N	70.56 W
Lovelock	194	40.11 N	118.28 W
Lovely	182	37.50 N	82.24 W
Love Point ≻	198	39.02 N	76.18 W
Lovere	58	45.49 N	10.04 E
Lovering Lake ⊜	196	45.10 N	72.09 W
Lovero	58	46.14 N	10.14 E
Loves Green	250	51.43 N	0.24 E
Loves Park	206	42.19 N	89.03 W
Loviisa → Lovisa	26	60.27 N	26.14 E
Lovilia	180	41.08 N	92.55 W
Loving, N. Mex., U.S.	186	32.17 N	104.06 W
Loving, Tex., U.S.	186	33.16 N	98.31 W
Lovingston	182	37.46 N	78.52 W
Lovington, Ill., U.S.	209	39.43 N	88.38 W
Lovington, N. Mex., U.S.	186	32.57 N	103.21 W
Lovisa (Loviisa)	26	60.27 N	26.14 E
Lovö I	40	59.20 N	17.50 E
Lovosice	50	50.31 N	14.03 E
Lovozero	24	68.00 N	35.00 E
Lovozero, Ozero ⊜	24	67.54 N	35.12 E
Lövstabruk	40	60.24 N	17.53 E
Lövstabukten ⊂	40	60.35 N	17.45 E
Lövstads slott ⊥	40	58.33 N	16.02 E
Lóvua, Ang.	142	7.20 S	20.16 E
Lóvua, Ang.	142	11.36 S	23.53 E
Lovua (Lóvua) ≃	142	6.07 S	20.35 E
Low	178	45.48 N	75.57 W
Low, Cape ≻	166	63.07 N	85.18 W
Lowa	144	1.24 S	25.51 E
Lowa ≃	144	1.24 S	25.51 E
Lowāda	116	22.27 N	87.37 E
Lowat → Lovat' ≃	66	58.14 N	31.28 E
Lowber	269b	40.15 N	79.46 W
Lowden	180	41.52 N	90.56 W
Lowder Brook ≃	273	43.14 N	71.11 W
Lowell, Ind., U.S.	206	41.18 N	87.25 W
Lowell, Mass., U.S.	197		
	273	42.39 N	71.18 W
Lowell, Mich., U.S.	206	42.56 N	85.20 W
Lowell, Oreg., U.S.	192	43.55 N	122.47 W
Lowell, Lake ⊜[1]	192	43.33 N	116.40 W
Lowell, University of ʊ[2]	273	42.39 N	71.20 W
Lowell-Dracut State Forest ♠	273	42.40 N	71.22 W
Lowelli	130	5.59 N	33.45 E
Lowellville	204	41.02 N	80.32 W
Löwen → Leuven, Bel.	52	50.53 N	4.42 E
Löwen → Lewin Brzeski, Pol.	30	50.46 N	17.37 E
Löwenberg, D.D.R.	50	52.54 N	13.08 E
Löwenberg → Lwówek Śląski, Pol.	30	51.07 N	15.35 E
Löwenbruch	254a	52.18 N	13.19 E
Löwenstein	52	49.06 N	9.22 E
Lowe Pine ♠	161a	27.32 S	152.57 E
Lowe Pond ⊜	273	42.41 N	70.59 W
Lower Arrow Lake ⊜	172	49.40 N	118.08 W
Lower Bear River Reservoir ⊜[1]	216	38.33 N	120.14 W
Lower Bershire Valley	266	40.54 N	74.37 W
Lower Beverly Lake ⊜	202	44.36 N	76.09 W
Lower Broughton ◆[8]	252	53.29 N	2.15 W

Symbols in the index entries represent the broad categories identified in the key at the right. Symbols with superior numbers (⋀[2]) identify subcategories (see complete key on page I · 26).

Kartensymbole in dem Registerverzeichnis stellen die rechts in Schlüssel erklärten Kategorien dar. Symbole mit hochgestellten Ziffern (⋀[2]) bezeichnen Unterabteilungen einer Kategorie (vgl. vollständiger Schlüssel auf Seite I · 26).

Los símbolos incluídos en el texto del índice representan las grandes categorias identificadas con la clave a la derecha. Los símbolos con numeros en su parte superior (⋀[2]) identifican las subcategorías (véase la clave completa en la página I · 26).

Les symboles de l'index représentent les catégories indiquées dans la légende à droite. Les symboles suivis d'un indice (⋀[2]) représentent des sous-catégories (voir légende complète à la page I · 26).

Os símbolos incluídos no texto do índice representam as grandes categorias identificadas com a chave à direita. Os símbolos com números em sua parte superior (⋀[2]) identificam as subcategorias (veja-se a chave completa à página I · 26).

∧ Mountain	Berg	Montaña	Montagne	Montanha
⋀ Mountains	Berge	Montañas	Montagnes	Montanhas
)(Pass	Pass	Paso	Col	Passo
∨ Valley, Canyon	Tal, Cañon	Valle, Cañón	Vallée, Canyon	Vale, Canhão
⌣ Plain	Ebene	Llano	Plaine	Planície
≻ Cape	Kap	Cabo	Cap	Cabo
I Island	Insel	Isla	Île	Ilha
II Islands	Inseln	Islas	Îles	Ilhas
⊥ Other Topographic Features	Andere Topographische Objekte	Otros Elementos Topográficos	Autres données topographiques	Outros Elementos Topográficos

ESPAÑOL

Nombre	Página	Lat. °′	Long. °′ W=Oeste
Lower Brule Indian Reservation ◆[4]	188	44.05 N	99.44 W
Lower Buckhorn Lake ⊜	202	44.33 N	78.17 W
Lower Burrell	204	40.35 N	79.44 W
Lower Chittering	158a	31.34 S	116.06 E
Lower Crystal Springs Reservoir ⊜[1]	216	37.32 N	122.22 W
Lower Darwen	252	53.43 N	2.28 W
Lower Eltham Park ♠	264b	37.45 S	145.09 E
Lower Elwha Indian Reservation ◆[4]	214	48.09 N	123.33 W
Lower Fort Garry National Historic Park ♠	174	50.07 N	96.55 W
Lower Ganga Canal ≊	114	26.27 N	80.17 E
Lower Gap C	202	44.10 N	76.35 W
Lower Halstow	250	51.22 N	0.40 E
Lower Hay Lake ⊜	202	45.25 N	78.13 W
Lower Higham	250	51.26 N	0.28 E
Lower Highland Creek Park ♠	265b	43.47 N	79.10 W
Lower Huron Metropolitan Park ♠	271	42.12 N	83.25 W
Lower Hutt	162	41.13 S	174.55 E
Lower Juba □[4]	134	0.15 S	42.10 E
Lower Kalskag	170	61.31 N	160.22 W
Lower Keechi Creek ≃	212	31.08 N	95.46 W
Lower Klamath Lake ⊜	194	41.55 N	121.42 W
Lower Lake	216	38.55 N	122.36 W
Lower Lake ⊜	194	41.15 N	120.02 W
Lower Loteni	148	29.32 S	29.36 E
Lower Manitou Lake ⊜	174	49.15 N	93.00 W
Lower Matecumbe Key I	210	24.51 N	80.43 W
Lower Montville	266	40.54 N	74.22 W
Lower Mystic Lake ⊜	273	42.26 N	71.09 W
Lower Nazeing	250	51.44 N	0.01 E
Lower New York Bay C	266	40.33 N	74.02 W
Lower Otay Reservoir ⊜[1]	218	32.37 N	116.55 W
Lower Paia	219a	20.55 N	156.23 W
Lower Paudash Lake ⊜	202	44.58 N	78.01 W
Lower Peover	252	53.16 N	2.23 W
Lower Place	252	53.36 N	2.09 W
Lower Plenty	264b	37.44 S	145.06 E
Lower Portland	160	33.27 S	150.53 E
Lower Post	166	59.55 N	128.30 W
Lower Red Lake ⊜	188	48.00 N	94.50 W
Lower River Rouge ≃	271	42.18 N	83.14 W
Lower Rouge Parkway ♠	271	42.18 N	83.20 W
Lower Stoke	250	51.27 N	0.38 E
Lower Ugashik Lake ⊜	170	57.30 N	156.56 W
Lower Van Norman Lake ⊜[1]	270	34.17 N	118.29 W
Lower West Pubnico	176	43.38 N	65.48 W
Lower Whitley	252	53.18 N	2.35 W
Lower Wood's Harbour	176	43.31 N	65.44 W
Lowery, Lake ⊜	210	28.07 N	81.41 W
Lowestoft	44	52.29 N	1.45 E
Lowgar □[4]	110	33.50 N	69.00 E
Lowick	42	55.38 N	2.00 W
Łowicz	30	52.07 N	19.56 E
Lowman	200	42.02 N	76.44 W
Lowmoor	182	37.47 N	79.53 W
Lowood	161a	27.28 S	152.35 E
Lowries Run ≃	269b	40.30 N	80.05 W
Low Rocky Point ≻	156	43.00 S	145.30 E
Lowry City	184	38.08 N	93.44 W
Lowther ≃	42	54.39 N	2.44 W
Lowther Hills ⋀[2]	42	55.19 N	3.38 W
Lowton	252	53.28 N	2.35 W
Lowton Common	252	53.29 N	2.33 W
Lowville, N.Y., U.S.	202	43.47 N	75.29 W
Lowville, Pa., U.S.	204	42.01 N	79.49 W
Loxahatchee	210	26.49 N	80.13 W
Loxley	184	30.37 N	87.45 W
Loxstedt	48	53.28 N	8.38 E
Loxten	48	52.03 N	8.08 E
Loxton, Austl.	156	34.27 S	140.35 E
Loxton, S. Afr.	148	31.30 S	22.22 E
Loyal	180	44.44 N	90.30 W
Loyalhanna	204	40.19 N	79.21 W
Loyalhanna Creek ≃	204	40.28 N	79.27 W
Loyalhanna Lake ⊜[1]	204	40.25 N	79.28 W
Loyalsock Creek ≃	200	41.14 N	76.56 W
Loyalton	194	39.41 N	120.14 W
Loyalty Islands → Loyauté, îles II	165f	21.00 S	167.00 E
Loyalty Ridge ✢[3]	14	21.30 S	168.00 E
Loyang → Luoyang	92	34.41 N	112.28 E
Loyauté, Îles (Loyality Islands) II	165f	21.00 S	167.00 E
Loyola Marymount University ⊍[2]	270	33.58 N	118.25 W
Loyola University ⊍[2]	268	42.00 N	87.39 W
Loyoro	144	3.21 N	34.16 E
Loysburg	204	40.10 N	78.23 W
Loysville	198	40.22 N	77.21 W
Lozano	248	34.51 S	59.03 W
Lozère □[5]	32	44.30 N	3.30 E
Lozère, Mont ⋀	56	44.25 N	3.46 E
Loznica	38	44.32 N	19.13 E
Ložnikovo, S.S.S.R.	76	56.54 N	73.56 E
Ložnikovo, S.S.S.R.	78	51.22 N	117.03 E
Lozno-Aleksandrovka	68	49.50 N	38.44 E
Loznoje	70	49.17 N	44.26 E
Lozovaja, S.S.S.R.	68	48.54 N	36.20 E
Lozovaja, S.S.S.R.	73	49.28 N	37.54 E
Lozovaja, S.S.S.R.	76	53.17 N	77.45 E
Lozovoje, S.S.S.R.	68	49.18 N	27.18 E
Lozovoje, S.S.S.R.	73	49.13 N	37.36 E
Lozovskij	73	48.33 N	38.54 E
Lozoyuela	34	40.55 N	3.37 W
Loz'va ≃	76	59.36 N	62.20 E
Lozzo di Cadore	58	46.29 N	12.27 E
Lterh, Oued V	138	21.39 N	2.30 E
Lu	56	45.00 N	8.29 E
Lua	142	5.18 S	16.06 E
Lua ≃	142	2.46 N	18.26 E
Luabo	146	18.30 S	36.10 E
Luabu ≃	142	2.46 S	18.19 E
Luachimo ≃	142	6.33 S	20.59 E
Luaha-sibuha	100	0.31 S	98.28 E
Luala ≃	144	17.57 S	36.30 E
Lualaba ≃	144	0.26 N	25.20 E
Luali	142	5.06 S	12.29 E
Lualoje ≃	142	12.18 S	21.38 E
Luama ≃	144	4.46 S	26.53 E
Lua Makika •[6]	219a	20.34 N	156.34 W
Luambe Game Reserve ◆[4]	144	12.25 S	32.15 E
Luambimba ≃	142	15.00 S	22.48 E
Luampa	144	15.03 S	24.28 E
Luampa ≃	144	14.33 S	24.10 E
Luana ≃	142	7.56 S	21.06 E
Luana Point ≻	231q	18.02 N	77.52 W
Luan Balu	104	2.38 N	96.13 E
Luancheng, Zhg.	88	37.53 N	114.39 E
Luancheng, Zhg.	92	22.45 N	108.51 E
Luanchuan	92	33.51 N	111.36 E
Luancundo ≃	142	16.25 S	21.27 E
Luanda	142	8.48 S	13.14 E
Luanda □[5]	142	8.30 S	13.20 E
Luanda ≃	142	7.16 S	16.00 E
Luando ≃	142	10.19 S	16.40 E

FRANÇAIS

Nom	Page	Lat. °′	Long. °′ W=Ouest
Luando, Reserva Natural Integral do ◆[4]	142	10.50 S	18.00 E
Luang ≃	100	18.01 N	103.04 E
Luang, Khao ⋀	100	8.31 N	99.47 E
Luang, Thale C	100	7.30 N	100.15 E
Luang Chiang Dao, Doi ⋀	100	19.23 N	98.54 E
Luanginga (Luanguinga) ≃	142	15.11 S	22.56 E
Luang Prabang → Louangphrabang	100	19.52 N	102.08 E
Luang Prabang Range ⋀	100	18.30 N	101.15 E
Luangue	142	7.19 S	19.38 E
Luangue (Loange) ≃	142	4.17 S	20.02 E
Luanguinga (Luanginga) ≃	142	15.11 S	22.56 E
Luangwa (Aruângua) ≃	144	15.36 S	30.25 E
Luangwa Valley Game Reserve (South) ◆[4], Zam.	144	12.50 S	31.45 E
Luangwa Valley Game Reserve (North) ◆[4], Zam.	144	11.50 S	32.15 E
Luanhe	95	40.57 N	117.44 E
Luanhe ≃	88	40.32 N	118.15 E
Luanping	88	40.57 N	117.20 E
Luanshishan	94	42.10 N	123.41 E
Luanshya	144	13.08 S	28.24 E
Luán Toro	242	36.12 S	65.06 W
Luanxian	88	39.45 N	118.44 E
Luanza	144	8.42 S	28.42 E
Luapula □[4]	144	10.55 S	29.00 E
Luapula ≃	144	9.26 S	28.33 E
Luar, Danau ⊜	102	0.55 N	111.59 E
Luarca	34	43.32 N	6.32 W
Luashi	142	10.56 S	23.37 E
Luashi ≃	142	10.41 S	22.55 E
Luassinga ≃	142	15.47 S	18.50 E
Luati	142	14.35 S	21.13 E
Luatira	142	12.52 S	17.14 E
Lua-Vindu ≃	142	3.38 N	19.16 E
Lubaantum ⊥	222	16.17 N	88.58 W
Lubaczów	30	50.10 N	23.07 E
Lubalo	142	9.12 S	19.16 E
Lubalo ≃	142	7.22 S	19.20 E
Lubamiti	142	2.29 S	17.47 E
Lubań, Pol.	30	51.08 N	15.18 E
L'uban', S.S.S.R.	66	59.21 N	31.13 E
L'uban', S.S.S.R.	66	52.37 N	29.08 E
L'uban', S.S.S.R.	66	52.48 N	27.59 E
Lubāna	66	56.54 N	26.43 E
Lubānas Ezers ⊜	66	56.46 N	26.53 E
Lubang	106	13.52 N	120.07 E
Lubang Islands II	106	13.46 N	120.15 E
Lubango	142	14.55 S	13.30 E
Lubanowo	50	53.09 N	14.36 E
Lubansenshi ≃	144	11.21 S	30.35 E
Lub'any	70	56.02 N	51.24 E
Lubao	90	23.22 N	112.55 E
L'ubar	68	49.55 N	27.44 E
Lübars, D.D.R.	50	52.10 N	12.09 E
Lübars, D.D.R.	50	52.39 N	12.02 E
Lübars ◆[8]	254a	52.37 N	13.22 E
Lubartów	30	51.28 N	22.38 E
L'ubašovka	68	47.51 N	30.15 E
Lubawa	30	53.30 N	19.45 E
Lubaynī, Baḥr al- ≊	263c	29.56 N	31.11 E
Lübbecke	48	52.18 N	8.36 E
Lübben	50	51.56 N	13.53 E
Lübbenau	50	51.52 N	13.57 E
Lubber Brook ≃	273	42.33 N	71.09 W
Lubbers Run ≃	266	40.56 N	74.43 W
Lübbesee ⊜	50	53.05 N	13.34 E
Lubbock	186	33.35 N	101.51 W
Lübbow	50	52.54 N	11.10 E
Lubbub Creek ≃	184	33.04 N	88.10 W
L'ubča	66	53.45 N	26.03 E
L'ubčany	72	55.15 N	37.33 E
L'ubeč, S.S.S.R.	68	51.42 N	30.39 E
Lubec, Maine, U.S.	178	44.52 N	66.59 W
Lübeck	48	53.52 N	10.40 E
Lubefu	142	4.43 S	24.25 E
Lubefu ≃	142	4.10 S	23.00 E
Lubelska, Wyżyna ⋀[2]	30	51.00 N	23.00 E
Lubembe (Luembe) ≃	142	6.37 S	21.05 E
Lüben → Lubin	30	51.24 N	16.13 E
Lubenec	50	50.06 N	13.20 E
L'ubercy	72	55.41 N	37.53 E
Lubéron, Montagne du ⋀	56	43.48 N	5.22 E
Lubersac	32	45.27 N	1.24 E
L'ubešov	68	51.46 N	25.31 E
Lübesse	50	53.29 N	11.28 E
Lubi ≃	142	4.58 S	23.26 E
Lubiana → Ljubljana	36	46.03 N	14.31 E
Lubic Island I	106	10.58 N	120.44 E
L'ubickoje	70	51.46 N	49.19 E
Lubień Kujawski	30	52.25 N	19.10 E
Lubilash ≃	142	6.02 S	23.45 E
Lubile	144	2.55 S	26.45 E
L'ubim	70	58.22 N	40.41 E
L'ubimovka, S.S.S.R.	68	51.31 N	35.37 E
L'ubimovka, S.S.S.R.	68	46.47 N	33.34 E
L'ubimovka, S.S.S.R.	76	52.15 N	66.45 E
L'ubimyj	73	47.53 N	39.28 E
Lubin, Pol.	30	51.24 N	16.13 E
Lubin, Pol.	50	53.50 N	14.25 E
L'ubino	76	56.32 N	88.46 E
L'ubinskij	76	55.09 N	72.42 E
Lubishi ≃	142	6.54 S	24.09 E
Lubja ≃	255a	59.58 N	30.30 E
Lublin	30	51.15 N	22.35 E
Lubliniec	30	50.40 N	18.41 E
L'ublino ◆[8]	255b	55.41 N	37.44 E
Lubmin	50	54.08 N	13.37 E
Lubnān, Jabal (Lebanon Mountains) ⋀	122	34.00 N	36.00 E
L'ubnica	66	57.58 N	32.42 E
Lubny	68	50.01 N	33.00 E
L'ubochna	66	53.31 N	34.23 E
Lubok China	104	2.27 N	102.04 E
Lubomierz	30	51.01 N	15.30 E
L'uboml'	68	51.14 N	24.01 E
Luboń	30	52.23 N	16.54 E
Lubondai	142	6.34 S	22.39 E
Lubondoi	144	8.02 S	26.31 E
L'ubostan'	68	51.19 N	35.44 E
L'ubotin	68	49.57 N	35.57 E
Lubraniec	30	52.33 N	18.50 E
Lubsko	30	51.46 N	14.59 E
Lübtheen	50	53.18 N	11.04 E
Lubu, Indon.	102	0.46 S	122.30 E
Lubu, Zhg.	92	23.09 N	112.13 E
Lubuagan	106	17.21 N	121.10 E
Lubudi, Zaïre	142	6.51 S	21.18 E
Lubudi, Zaïre	144	9.57 S	25.58 E
Lubudi ≃, Zaïre	142	4.03 S	21.23 E
Lubudi ≃, Zaïre	144	9.13 S	25.38 E
Lubue	142	4.09 S	19.52 E
Lubue ≃	142	4.10 S	19.53 E
Lubukambacang	102	0.37 S	101.25 E
Lubukbatang	102	4.03 S	104.12 E
Lubukbertubung	102	0.02 N	102.08 E
Lubuklinggau	102	3.18 S	102.52 E
Lubukpakam	104	3.33 N	98.52 E
Lubukraya, Dolok ⋀	104	1.29 N	99.13 E
Lubuksikaping	102	0.08 N	100.10 E
Lubumbaschi → Lubumbashi	144	11.40 S	27.28 E
Lubumbashi (Élisabethville)	144	11.40 S	27.28 E
Lubunda	144	5.10 S	26.40 E

PORTUGUÊS

Nome	Página	Lat. °′	Long. °′ W=Oeste
Lubutu	144	0.44 S	26.35 E
Luby	50	50.12 N	12.25 E
L'ubytino	66	58.49 N	33.23 E
Lübz	50	53.27 N	12.01 E
Lučak	75	38.23 N	67.25 E
Lucala	142	9.16 S	15.15 E
Lucala ≃	142	6.38 S	12.34 E
Lucan, Ont., Can.	180	43.11 N	81.24 W
Lucan, Eire	42	53.22 N	6.27 W
Lucanas	238	14.36 S	74.15 W
Lucania ◆[1]	36	40.30 N	16.00 E
Lucania, Mount ⋀	170	61.01 N	140.28 W
Lucano	142	11.16 S	21.38 E
Lucaogou	92	42.26 N	96.55 E
L'uca-Ongokton, Gora ⋀	64	67.52 N	106.24 E
Lucas, Iowa, U.S.	180	41.02 N	93.28 W
Lucas, Kans., U.S.	188	39.04 N	98.32 W
Lucas, Ohio, U.S.	204	40.42 N	82.25 W
Lucas, Tex., U.S.	212	33.05 N	96.35 W
Lucas □[6]	204	41.39 N	83.32 W
Lucas González	242	32.24 S	59.33 W
Lucas Valley	272	38.03 N	122.35 W
Lucasville	208	38.53 N	83.00 W
Lucban	106	14.06 N	121.33 E
Lucca	60	43.50 N	10.29 E
Lucca □[4]	58	44.02 N	10.27 E
Luce, Water of ≃	42	54.52 N	4.48 W
Lucea	231q	18.27 N	78.10 W
Luce Bay C	42	54.47 N	4.50 W
Luce Bayou ≃	212	30.03 N	95.07 W
Lucedale	184	30.55 N	88.35 W
Lucena, Esp.	34	37.24 N	4.29 W
Lucena, Pil.	106	13.56 N	121.37 E
Lucena del Cid	34	40.08 N	0.17 W
Lucenay-l'Évêque	32	47.05 N	4.15 E
Luc-en-Diois	56	44.37 N	5.27 E
Lučenec	30	48.20 N	19.40 E
Lucens	54	46.42 N	6.50 E
Luceque	142	14.41 S	15.04 E
Lucera	60	41.30 N	15.20 E
Lucéram	56	43.53 N	7.22 E
Lucerne → Luzern, Schw.	54	47.03 N	8.18 E
Lucerne, Calif., U.S.	194	39.06 N	122.48 W
Lucerne, Ind., U.S.	206	40.52 N	86.24 W
Lucerne, Lake → Vierwaldstätter See ⊜	54	47.00 N	8.28 E
Lucerne Lake ⊜	218	34.31 N	57.00 W
Lucernemines	204	40.34 N	79.09 W
Lucerne Valley	218	34.27 N	116.57 W
Lucero	190	30.49 N	106.30 W
Lucero, Lake ⊜	190	32.42 N	106.25 W
Lučesa ≃	66	55.10 N	30.11 E
Luch	70	57.01 N	42.15 E
Luch ≃	70	56.14 N	42.25 E
Luchena ≃	34	37.44 N	1.50 W
Lucheng, Zhg.	92	24.21 N	106.00 E
Lucheng, Zhg.	96	31.47 N	120.02 E
Lücheng, Zhg.	96	31.55 N	119.44 E
Luché-Pringé	46	47.42 N	0.05 E
Lucheringo ≃	144	11.43 S	36.17 E
Luchiang	90	24.04 N	120.26 E
Luchibe ≃	142	12.07 S	21.13 E
Luchico (Lushiko) ≃	142	6.13 S	19.40 E
Luchou	259d	25.05 N	121.28 E
Luchovicy	72	54.59 N	39.03 E
Lüchow, B.R.D.	50	52.58 N	11.10 E
Luchow → Luzhou, Zhg.	97	28.54 N	105.27 E
Lüchtringen	48	51.47 N	9.25 E
Luchuan	92	22.19 N	110.11 E
Luci	90	29.52 N	119.47 E
L'učicheza, Gora ⋀	79	45.10 N	135.48 E
Lucie ≃	240	3.35 N	57.38 W
Lucikou	90	28.56 N	116.04 E
Lučin	66	53.01 N	30.01 E
Lucinda	204	41.19 N	79.22 W
Lucindale	156	36.59 S	140.22 E
Lucipara, Kepulauan II	154	5.30 S	127.33 E
Lucira	142	13.51 S	12.31 E
Lucito	60	41.44 N	14.41 E
Luciyu I	90	25.07 N	119.22 E
Luck, S.S.S.R.	68	50.44 N	25.20 E
Luck, Wis., U.S.	180	45.34 N	92.28 W
Luck, Mount ⋀[2]	152	28.47 S	123.33 E
Lucka	50	51.06 N	12.20 E
Luckau	50	51.51 N	13.43 E
Luckeesarai	114	25.11 N	86.05 E
Luckenwalde	50	52.05 N	13.10 E
Luckey	204	41.27 N	83.29 W
Luckhoff	148	29.44 S	24.43 E
Luckiamute ≃	192	44.45 N	123.09 W
Luck Lake ⊜	174	51.05 N	107.07 W
Lucknow, Bhārat	114	26.51 N	80.55 E
Lucknow, Ont., Can.	180	43.57 N	81.31 W
Lucknow, Pa., U.S.	198	40.20 N	76.54 W
Lucky Lake	174	51.00 N	107.10 W
Lucky Peak Lake ⊜[1]	192	43.33 N	116.00 W
Luco dei Marsi	60	41.58 N	13.28 E
Lucomagno, Passo del)(, Schw.	54	46.33 N	8.49 E
Luçon, Fr.	32	46.27 N	1.10 W
Lucon, Pa., U.S.	275	40.14 N	75.25 W
Luconha ≃	142	12.54 S	21.15 E
Lucun, Zhg.	88	36.12 N	118.01 E
Lucun, Zhg.	96	30.49 N	119.26 E
Lucunga ≃	142	6.57 S	12.48 E
Lucungu ≃	142	6.41 S	14.26 E
Lucusse	142	12.32 S	20.48 E
Lucy Creek	156	22.25 S	136.20 E
Lüda (Dairen)	88	38.53 N	121.35 E
Luda Kamčija ≃	38	43.03 N	27.29 E
Ludanli	96	31.37 N	119.20 E
Ludao	79	43.51 N	129.19 E
Ludao I	88	39.44 N	123.45 E
Ludbreg	36	46.15 N	16.37 E
Luddan	113	29.54 N	72.34 E
Luddenden	252	53.44 N	1.56 W
Luddenham	264a	33.53 S	150.41 E
Luddesdown	250	51.22 N	0.24 E
Lüdenscheid	52	51.13 N	7.38 E
Lüdenscheid □[8]	253	51.09 N	7.33 E
Lüder ≃	52	50.31 N	9.27 E
Lüderitz, D.D.R.	50	52.30 N	11.44 E
Lüderitz, Namibia	146	26.38 S	15.10 E
Lüderitz □[5]	146	26.30 S	15.45 E
Lüdersdorf	50	53.47 N	10.46 E
Ludgershall	44	51.16 N	1.37 W
Ludgo	40	58.55 N	17.08 E
Ludhiāna	113	30.54 N	75.51 E
Ludian	92	27.11 N	103.33 E
Luding	92	29.55 N	102.15 E
Lüdinghausen	48	51.46 N	7.26 E
Lüdinghausen □[8]	253	51.41 N	7.30 E
Ludington	180	43.57 N	86.27 W
Ludingtonville	200	41.29 N	73.39 W
L'udinovo	66	53.52 N	34.27 E
L'udkovo	66	54.36 N	34.43 E
Ludlam Bay C	198	39.10 N	74.42 W
Ludlow, Eng., U.K.	44	52.22 N	2.43 W
Ludlow, Colo., U.S.	188	37.20 N	104.35 W
Ludlow, Ill., U.S.	206	40.23 N	88.08 W
Ludlow, Ky., U.S.	208	39.05 N	84.33 W
Ludlow, Mass., U.S.	197	42.10 N	72.29 W
Ludlow, Pa., U.S.	204	41.44 N	78.57 W
Ludlow, Vt., U.S.	178	43.24 N	72.42 W
Ludlow Falls	208	40.00 N	84.20 W
Ludlowville	200	42.33 N	76.32 W
Ludonghe	92	25.53 N	103.33 E
Ludoni	66	58.12 N	29.21 E
Ludowici	182	31.43 N	81.45 W
Luduqiao	96	31.28 N	121.11 E
Luduș	38	46.29 N	24.05 E
Ludvika	40	60.09 N	15.11 E
Ludwigsburg	52	48.53 N	9.11 E
Ludwigsfelde	50	52.17 N	13.16 E
Ludwigsfelder-Heide ◆[3]	254a	52.18 N	13.14 E
Ludwigshafen	52	49.29 N	8.26 E
Ludwigshafen am Bodensee	54	47.49 N	9.03 E
Ludwigslust	50	53.19 N	11.30 E
Ludwigsort → Laduškin	66	54.36 N	20.11 E
Ludwigsstadt	50	50.30 N	11.23 E
Ludwigstein, Burg ⊥	52	51.20 N	9.55 E
Ludza	66	56.33 N	27.43 E
Lue	160	32.39 S	149.51 E
Luebo	142	5.21 S	21.25 E
Lueders	186	32.48 N	99.37 W
Lueg, Pass)(	58	47.34 N	13.12 E
Lueki	144	3.22 S	25.51 E
Luele ≃	142	7.55 S	20.09 E
Luemba	144	3.42 S	28.40 E
Luembe (Lubembe) ≃	142	6.37 S	21.05 E
Luena	144	9.27 S	25.47 E
Luena ≃, Ang.	142	12.31 S	22.34 E
Luena ≃, Zam.	142	14.45 S	23.25 E
Luena Flats ☷	142	14.50 S	23.20 E
Luengué ≃	142	16.54 S	21.52 E
Luenha (Ruenya) ≃	144	16.24 S	33.48 E
Lueo ≃	142	9.06 S	23.51 E
Luepa	236	5.43 N	61.31 W
Lueta	142	7.19 S	22.06 E
Lueta ≃	142	7.04 S	21.40 E
Lueti ≃	142	16.14 S	23.13 E
Lueyang	92	33.19 N	106.19 E
Lüfangsicun	94	41.25 N	123.22 E
Lufeng, Zhg.	90	22.57 N	115.38 E
Lufeng, Zhg.	92	25.07 N	102.07 E
Lüfeng, Zhg.	97	29.51 N	105.58 E
Lufico	142	6.24 S	13.23 E
Lufira ≃	144	8.16 S	26.27 E
Lufkin	212	31.20 N	94.44 W
Lufubu ≃	144	8.36 S	30.47 E
Lufuidje ≃	142	12.52 S	22.47 E
Lufupa	144	10.37 S	24.56 E
Lufupa ≃	144	14.37 S	26.12 E
Luga	66	58.44 N	29.52 E
Luga ≃	66	59.40 N	28.18 E
Lugagnano Val d'Arda	56	44.49 N	9.50 E
Lugan' ≃	73	48.37 N	39.27 E
Lugančik ≃	73	48.35 N	39.32 E
Lugang, Zhg.	90	31.17 N	118.22 E
Lugang, Zhg.	90	27.23 N	115.36 E
Luganga	144	7.31 S	35.32 E
Lugano	54	46.01 N	8.58 E
Lugano, Lago di ⊜	54	46.00 N	9.00 E
Lugansk → Vorošilovgrad	73	48.34 N	39.20 E
Luganskoje	73	48.26 N	38.15 E
Luganville	165f	15.32 S	167.08 E
Lugards Falls ⌊	144	3.03 S	38.42 E
Lugareño	230p	21.33 N	77.28 W
Lugarno	264a	33.59 S	151.03 E
Lugau	50	50.44 N	12.44 E
Lügde	48	51.57 N	9.15 E
Lugela	144	16.25 S	36.43 E
Lugenda	144	12.30 S	37.43 E
Lugenda ≃	144	11.25 S	38.33 E
Lugg ≃	44	52.02 N	2.38 W
Luggarus → Locarno	54	46.10 N	8.48 E
Lugh Ganane	134	3.56 N	42.32 E
Luginino	66	57.43 N	35.17 E
Luginy	68	51.04 N	28.24 E
Lugnano in Teverina	60	42.34 N	12.20 E
Lugnaquillia Mountain ⋀	28	52.58 N	6.27 W
Lugnås	40	58.39 N	13.42 E
Lugny	54	46.28 N	4.49 E
Lugo, Esp.	34	43.00 N	7.34 W
Lugo, It.	60	44.25 N	11.54 E
Lugoj	38	45.41 N	21.54 E
Lugongshi	96	31.38 N	121.12 E
Lugos → Lugoj	38	45.41 N	21.54 E
Lugouqiao	95	39.51 N	116.13 E
Lugovaja Subbota	76	59.52 N	69.45 E
Lugovoj, S.S.S.R.	75	42.56 N	72.45 E
Lugovoj, S.S.S.R.	76	59.44 N	65.55 E
Lugovoje	75	42.55 N	72.43 E
Lugovskij	78	58.02 N	112.54 E
Lugovskoje	70	50.38 N	46.28 E
Lugu	92	28.21 N	102.09 E
Lugufu ≃	144	5.10 S	30.14 E
Lugunga ⋀	144	6.47 S	36.19 E
Luguru	144	2.55 S	33.58 E
Lugus Island I	106	5.41 N	120.50 E
Luhanka	26	61.47 N	25.42 E
Luhe ≃	48	53.18 N	10.11 E
Lühedian	90	32.33 N	114.28 E
Luhit ≃	110	27.48 N	95.28 E
Lühmannsdorf	50	54.00 N	13.38 E
Luhombero ≃	144	8.24 S	37.12 E
Luhsien → Luzhou	97	28.54 N	105.27 E
Luhuo	92	31.26 N	100.48 E
Lui ≃, Ang.	142	8.41 S	17.56 E
Lui ≃, Zam.	142	16.21 S	23.18 E
Luia	142	8.26 S	21.45 E
Luia (Ruya) ≃, Afr.	144	16.35 S	33.13 E
Luia ≃, Ang.	142	8.24 S	21.42 E
Lúia ≃, Moç.	144	15.34 S	32.58 E
Luiana	142	17.23 S	23.03 E
Luiana ≃	142	17.27 S	23.14 E
Luido	146	21.31 S	34.41 E
Luie ≃	142	4.33 S	17.41 E
Luik → Liège	52	50.38 N	5.34 E
Luilaka ≃	142	0.52 S	20.12 E
Luilu ≃	142	6.22 S	23.50 E
Luimbale	142	12.15 S	15.99 E
Luimneach → Limerick	28	52.40 N	8.38 W
Luing I	28	56.13 N	5.39 W
Luino	54	46.00 N	8.44 E
Luio ≃	142	13.15 S	21.39 E
Luipaardsvlei	263d	26.16 S	27.42 E
Luís Alves	242	26.44 S	48.57 W
Luisant	46	48.25 N	1.29 E
Luis Beltrán	242	39.19 S	65.46 W
Luís Correia	240	2.53 S	41.40 W
Luis D'Abreu (Calchaqui)	242	29.54 S	60.18 W
Luis de Saboya, Cerro ⋀	244	54.38 S	69.29 W
Luisen-Berg ⋀[2]	254a	52.27 N	13.07 E
Luisenthal	50	50.47 N	10.43 E
Luís Gomes	240	6.25 S	38.23 W
Luis Guillón	278	34.48 S	58.27 W
Luishia	144	11.10 S	27.02 E
Luisiânia	245	21.41 S	50.17 W
Luis Moya, Méx.	224	22.25 N	102.15 W
Luis Moya, Méx.	224	23.05 N	103.56 W
Luis Peña, Cayo de I	230m	18.18 N	65.20 W
Luis Pereira, Arroyo ≃	248	34.33 S	57.02 W
Luita	142	8.04 S	19.25 E
Luitpold Coast •[2]	9	78.30 S	32.00 W
Luiza	142	7.12 S	22.25 E
Luiza ≃	142	7.35 S	22.40 E
Luizavo ≃	142	11.42 S	23.12 E
Luizi	144	6.03 S	27.28 E
Luján, Arg.	242	32.22 S	65.57 W
Luján, Arg.	242	33.03 S	68.52 W
Luján, Arg.	248	34.34 S	59.07 W
Luján ≃	278	34.26 S	58.32 W
Lujia	96	31.15 N	121.37 E
Lujiabang	96	31.20 N	121.03 E
Lujiachang	97	30.14 N	105.34 E
Lujiagangzi	94	42.05 N	122.59 E
Lujiang	90	31.14 N	117.17 E
Lujiang ≃	90	27.02 N	115.03 E
Lujiao	90	29.10 N	112.52 E
Lujiaoxi	97	28.55 N	105.48 E
Lujiaqiao, Zhg.	96	31.47 N	120.27 E
Lujiaqiao, Zhg.	97	28.50 N	106.21 E
Lujiaqiao, Zhg.	97	30.16 N	104.25 E
Lujiatun, Zhg.	88	40.14 N	122.11 E
Lujiatun, Zhg.	94	41.58 N	122.38 E
Lujiatun, Zhg.	94	42.18 N	124.15 E
Lujiatun, Zhg.	94	41.10 N	121.56 E
Lujiazhou	90	28.16 N	114.35 E
L'uk	70	56.55 N	52.48 E
Lukachukai Wash V	190	36.39 N	109.36 W
Lukačok	79	53.03 N	132.16 E
Lukala	142	5.31 S	14.32 E
Lukanga, Zaïre	142	1.41 S	18.09 E
Lukanga, Zaïre	142	1.00 S	18.08 E
Lukanga Swamp ☷	144	14.25 S	27.45 E
Luk'anovo	72	54.52 N	37.25 E
Lukašin	74	40.12 N	44.01 E
Lukaškin Jar	76	60.20 N	78.24 E
Lukašovka	68	51.38 N	35.35 E
Luke, Mount ⋀	152	27.13 S	116.48 E
Lukenie ≃	142	2.44 S	18.09 E
Lukens, Mount ⋀	270	34.16 N	118.14 W
Lukeqin	76	42.44 N	89.42 E
Lukeville	190	31.53 N	112.49 W
Luki	66	53.29 N	26.15 E
Lukino, S.S.S.R.	72	55.26 N	37.04 E
Lukino, S.S.S.R.	72	55.50 N	36.49 E
Lukk	136	32.01 N	24.45 E
Lukka	130	14.33 N	23.42 E
Luk Kang	261d	22.27 N	114.02 E
Luknovo	70	56.12 N	42.03 E
Lukojanov	70	55.02 N	44.30 E
Lukolela, Zaïre	142	5.23 S	24.32 E
Lukolela, Zaïre	142	1.03 S	17.12 E
Lukong	97	29.31 N	105.39 E
Lukop	164r	6.54 N	158.19 E
Lukose ≃	144	7.28 S	36.31 E
Lukoshi ≃	142	10.05 S	22.59 E
Lukosi	144	18.30 S	26.30 E
Lukoškino	72	55.19 N	37.16 E
Lukou, Zhg.	90	27.42 N	113.08 E
Lukou, Zhg.	90	29.30 N	113.26 E
Lukou, Zhg.	90	27.14 N	114.04 E
Lukou, Zhg.	96	31.48 N	118.52 E
Lukouyu	90	28.24 N	113.18 E
Lukov	68	51.13 N	24.19 E
Lukovit	38	43.12 N	24.10 E
Lukovskaja	70	50.35 N	41.52 E
Łuków	30	51.56 N	22.23 E
Lukuga ≃	144	5.40 S	26.55 E
Lukula	142	5.23 S	12.57 E
Lukula ≃	142	5.08 S	12.28 E
Lukulu	142	14.25 S	23.12 E
Lukulu ≃	144	10.56 S	31.05 E
Lukumburu	144	9.45 S	35.09 E
Lukunga ≃	263b	4.25 S	15.14 E
Lukuni	142	5.52 S	17.11 E
Lukusashi ≃	144	14.38 S	30.00 E
Lukusuzi Game Reserve ◆[4]	144	12.50 S	32.35 E
Lula, Miss., U.S.	184	34.27 N	90.29 W
Lula, Zaïre	142	5.22 S	16.02 E
Luleå	26	65.34 N	22.10 E
Luleälven ≃	24	65.35 N	22.03 E
Lüleburgaz	120	41.24 N	27.21 E
Lules	242	26.56 S	65.21 W
Luliang	92	25.05 N	103.36 E
Lüliangshan ⋀	92	37.25 N	111.20 E
Luliāni	113	31.15 N	74.25 E
Luliao	259d	25.07 N	121.39 E
Luling	212	29.41 N	97.39 W
Lullingstone Castle ⊥	250	51.21 N	0.12 E
Lulo ≃	142	9.25 S	18.14 E
Lulong	88	39.54 N	118.50 E
Lulonga	142	0.37 N	18.23 E
Lulonga ≃	142	0.43 N	18.23 E
Lulu ≃	142	1.18 N	23.42 E
Lulua ≃	142	5.02 S	21.07 E
Luluabourg → Kananga	142	5.54 S	22.25 E
Lulu Island I, B.C., Can.	214	49.09 N	123.05 W
Lulu Island I, Alaska, U.S.	172	55.28 N	133.30 W
Luluozhen	88	37.06 N	113.58 E
Lulworth, Mount ⋀	152	26.53 S	117.42 E
Luma	164y	14.14 S	169.32 W
Lumai	142	13.31 S	21.21 E
Lumajang	105a	8.08 S	113.13 E
Lumaling	110	29.53 N	92.37 E
Lumb	252	53.42 N	1.58 W
Lumbala	142	12.39 S	22.34 E
Lumbala ≃	142	12.38 S	22.34 E
Lumban	106	14.18 N	121.27 E
Lumbanganjang	104	2.22 N	98.43 E
Lumbangaraga	104	1.53 N	99.04 E
Lumbanlobu	104	2.31 N	99.08 E
Lumbe ≃	142	16.42 S	23.42 E
Lumber ≃	182	34.12 N	79.10 W
Lumber City	182	31.56 N	82.41 W
Lumberport	178	39.23 N	80.21 W
Lumberton, Miss., U.S.	184	31.00 N	89.27 W
Lumberton, N.C., U.S.	182	34.37 N	79.00 W
Lumbis	102	4.18 N	116.15 E
Lumbo	144	15.00 S	40.44 E
Lumbovka	24	67.44 N	40.30 E
Lumbrales	34	40.56 N	6.43 W
Lumbrein	54	46.41 N	9.08 E
Lumbres	46	50.42 N	2.08 E
Lumbwa	144	0.12 S	35.28 E
Lumby	172	50.15 N	118.58 W
Lumding	110	25.45 N	93.10 E
Lumege ≃	142	11.55 S	20.58 E
Lumerau ≃	106	5.21 N	118.53 E
Lumiei ≃	58	46.24 N	12.51 E
Luminárias	246	21.30 S	44.54 W
Luminosa	246	22.35 S	45.38 W
Lumintao ≃	106	12.43 N	120.55 E
Lummen	52	50.59 N	5.12 E
Lummi Bay C	214	48.46 N	122.41 W
Lummi Indian Reservation ◆[4]	214	48.48 N	122.38 W
Lummi Island	214	48.42 N	122.40 W
Lummi Island I	214	48.42 N	122.40 W
Lumphăt	100	13.30 N	106.59 E
Lumpini Park ♠	259a	13.44 N	100.33 E
Lumpkin	182	32.03 N	84.48 W
Lumpun ≃	70	57.01 N	51.22 E
Lumsån ≃	40	59.59 N	15.26 E
Lumsås	41	55.57 N	11.31 E
Lumsden, N.B., Can.	176	49.19 N	53.37 W
Lumsden, Sask., Can.	174	50.34 N	104.53 W
Lumsden, N.Z.	162	45.44 S	168.27 E
Lumsheden	40	60.43 N	16.15 E
Lums Pond State Park ♠	198	39.34 N	75.43 W
Lumu, Indon.	102	2.11 S	119.09 E
Lumu, Zhg.	96	31.22 N	120.37 E
Lumuhu ⊜	110	33.45 N	79.30 E
Lumuna	144	3.46 S	26.24 E
Lumuna ≃	142	16.59 S	21.25 E
Lumut	104	4.14 N	100.38 E
Lumut, Tanjung ≻	102	3.50 S	105.57 E
Lumwana	144	11.50 S	25.10 E
Lün, Mong.	78	47.24 N	102.52 E
Lün, Mong.	78	47.52 N	105.15 E
Luna, Pil.	106	16.51 N	120.23 E
Luna, Pil.	106	18.18 N	121.21 E
Luna ≃	236	4.32 S	60.41 W
Lunada Bay C	270	33.46 N	118.25 W
Lunain ≃	46	48.20 N	2.47 E
Lunan	92	24.49 N	103.16 E
Lunano	60	43.44 N	12.26 E
Luna Pier	206	41.48 N	83.27 W
Lūnāvāda	110	23.08 N	73.37 E
Lund, B.C., Can.	172	49.58 N	124.44 W
Lund, Sve.	41	55.42 N	13.11 E
Lund, Nev., U.S.	194	38.52 N	115.00 W
Lunda □[5]	142	9.00 S	20.00 E
Lunda ≃, Ang.	142	6.07 S	13.52 E
L'unda ≃, S.S.S.R.	70	56.32 N	46.03 E
Lundåkrabukten C	41	55.48 N	12.53 E
Lundale	178	37.48 N	81.45 W
Lundar	174	50.42 N	98.02 W
Lundazi	144	12.19 S	33.13 E
Lundby	41	55.07 N	11.53 E
Lunde	41	55.29 N	10.21 E
Lundeborg	41	55.08 N	10.47 E
Lunden	41	54.20 N	9.01 E
Lunderskov	41	55.29 N	9.18 E
Lundevatn ⊜	26	58.22 N	6.36 E
Lundi ≃	144	21.43 S	32.34 E
Lundsberg	40	59.30 N	14.10 E
Lundsfjärden ⊜	40	59.38 N	14.41 E
Lundy I	44	51.10 N	4.40 W
Lundys Lane	204	41.53 N	80.21 W
Lune ≃	42	54.02 N	2.50 W
Lüneburg	48	53.15 N	10.23 E
Lüneburg □[6]	48	53.00 N	10.15 E
Lüneburger Heide ◆[1]	48	53.10 N	10.20 E
Lüneburger Heide, Naturpark ♠	48	53.10 N	9.55 E
Lunel	56	43.41 N	4.08 E
Lünen	48	51.36 N	7.32 E
Lunenburg, N.S., Can.	176	44.23 N	64.19 W
Lunenburg, Mass., U.S.	197	42.36 N	71.44 W
Lunenburg, Va., U.S.	182	36.58 N	78.16 W
Luneray	46	49.50 N	0.55 E
Lünern	253	51.33 N	7.46 E
Lunéville	52	48.36 N	6.30 E
Lunga ≃, Ang.	142	5.59 S	16.20 E
Lunga ≃, Zam.	144	14.34 S	26.25 E
Lunga Game Reserve ◆[4]	144	12.55 S	25.10 E
Lungälven ≃	40	59.34 N	14.10 E
Lunga Reservoir ⊜[1]	198	38.32 N	77.28 W
Lungau ◆[1]	58	47.07 N	13.39 E
Lungavilla	56	45.02 N	9.04 E
Lungch'i → Zhangzhou	90	24.33 N	117.39 E
Lunge	142	12.12 S	16.05 E
Lunge'nake	110	31.45 N	85.55 E
Lungern	54	46.47 N	8.10 E
Lunghezza ◆[8]	257a	41.55 N	12.35 E
Lunghua Pagoda ⊍[1]	259b	31.09 N	121.25 E
Lungi	140	8.38 N	13.13 W
Lungleh	110	22.53 N	92.44 E
Lung Shun Wan Chau I	261d	22.22 N	114.21 E
Lungt'an	90	24.52 N	121.12 E
Lungué-Bungo (Lungwebungu) ≃	142	14.19 S	23.14 E
Lunguya	144	3.23 S	32.24 E
Lungwebungu (Lungué-Bungo) ≃	142	14.19 S	23.14 E
Lūni	110	26.00 N	73.00 E
Lūni ≃	110	24.41 N	71.15 E
Luni ⊥	58	44.04 N	10.01 E
Lunia-Bubi	144	7.30 S	24.49 E
Lunigiana ◆[1]	58	44.15 N	9.50 E
Lunin	66	52.18 N	26.38 E
Luninec	66	52.15 N	26.48 E
Lunino, S.S.S.R.	70	53.35 N	45.14 E
Lunino, S.S.S.R.	72	54.09 N	38.29 E
Lunjiao	90	22.53 N	113.13 E
Lunnaja, Gora ⋀	170	68.14 N	174.20 E
Lunndörrsfjällen ⋀	26	63.00 N	13.00 E
Lunno	66	53.27 N	24.16 E
Lunongzha	96	31.59 N	120.55 E
Lunsar	140	8.41 N	12.32 W
Lunsemfwa ≃	144	14.54 S	30.12 E
Lunt	252	53.31 N	2.59 W
Lunteren	48	52.05 N	5.37 E
Lunyuk	105b	8.57 S	117.14 E
Lunzenau	50	50.58 N	12.45 E
Lunzhen	88	36.47 N	116.34 E
Luoba, Zhg.	90	24.51 N	114.13 E
Luoba, Zhg.	97	29.08 N	106.11 E
Luobei (Fengxiangzhen)	79	47.34 N	130.50 E
Luobo	92	28.22 N	101.38 E
Luobu	92	24.30 N	109.40 E
Luobubo (Lop Nor) ⊜	80	40.20 N	90.15 E
Luobumiao	92	40.19 N	107.30 E
Luobuqiongzi	114	29.02 N	89.15 E
Luochanghe	90	31.01 N	117.18 E
Luocheng	92	24.51 N	108.59 E
Luochengpu	97	29.23 N	104.01 E
Luochuan	92	35.55 N	109.26 E
Luoci	92	25.19 N	102.18 E
Luodian, Zhg.	92	22.47 N	111.31 E
Luodian, Zhg.	96	31.25 N	121.20 E
Luoding	100	22.47 N	111.31 E
Luoduoke	110	33.28 N	79.40 E
Luoduxi	97	30.22 N	106.35 E
Luofa	95	39.25 N	116.50 E
Luofang, Zhg.	90	28.40 N	115.04 E
Luofang, Zhg.	90	27.52 N	115.06 E
Luofu, Zaïre	144	0.10 S	29.14 E
Luofu, Zhg.	90	24.32 N	115.35 E
Luofushan ⋀	90	23.28 N	114.10 E
Luogang, Zhg.	90	24.25 N	115.38 E
Luogang, Zhg.	90	23.11 N	113.30 E
Luogosanto	36	41.02 N	9.12 E
Luoguhe	79	53.18 N	121.30 E
Luohanchang	97	28.55 N	105.29 E
Luohanshan ⋀	90	25.51 N	119.13 E
Luohe	90	33.35 N	114.01 E
Luohe ≃	92	34.42 N	110.15 E
Luohua	90	26.35 N	118.43 E
Luoji	90	32.06 N	117.16 E
Luojiachang	97	30.49 N	106.32 E
Luojiangzhen	92	31.21 N	104.28 E
Luojiatang	96	30.18 N	120.13 E
Luojiatun, Zhg.	88	40.11 N	118.34 E
Luojiatun, Zhg.	94	40.55 N	122.04 E
Luojiatun, Zhg.	94	42.06 N	122.44 E
Luojiawei	90	26.55 N	115.02 E
Luoke	90	24.07 N	114.28 E
Luokeng	90	24.32 N	113.23 E
Luokou, Zhg.	90	25.46 N	115.39 E
Luokou, Zhg.	90	25.39 N	112.46 E
Luokou, Zhg.	90	28.54 N	117.24 E
Luokou, Zhg.	90	26.46 N	115.59 E
Luolong	92	30.45 N	96.09 E
Luolongchang	97	28.49 N	104.57 E
Luomizhuang	88	35.46 N	118.54 E
Luonan	92	34.05 N	110.04 E
Luoning	92	34.25 N	111.42 E
Luoping	92	24.59 N	104.21 E
Luopu	110	37.02 N	80.15 E
Luoqi	92	29.48 N	106.56 E
Luoqiao	90	26.28 N	119.01 E
Luoquanjing	97	29.50 N	104.31 E
Luoshan, Zhg.	90	29.41 N	113.18 E
Luoshan, Zhg.	90	32.13 N	114.32 E
Luoshan, Zhg.	95	39.55 N	117.33 E
Luoshe, Zhg.	96	30.41 N	120.04 E
Luoshe, Zhg.	96	31.39 N	120.11 E
Luossa ≃	142	8.24 S	17.03 E
Luosuojiang ≃	92	21.51 N	101.13 E
Luotian	90	30.48 N	115.22 E
Luotuodian	90	32.13 N	113.49 E
Luotuoqiao	90	29.56 N	121.32 E
Luotuoshan	79	43.43 N	129.28 E
Luowenba	92	31.48 N	107.48 E
Luowenyu	95	40.16 N	117.57 E
Luoxi	90	29.05 N	114.58 E
Luoxiaoshan ⋀	90	26.00 N	114.00 E
Luoyang (Loyang)	92	34.41 N	112.28 E
Luoyangqiao	96	31.39 N	120.05 E
Luoyuan	90	26.31 N	119.32 E
Luozha	110	28.24 N	90.49 E
Luozhexi	97	29.02 N	103.54 E
Luozi	142	4.57 S	14.08 E
Lupala	146	17.50 S	19.06 E
Lupani	144	18.54 S	27.44 E
Lupao	106	15.53 N	120.54 E
Lupar ≃	102	1.30 N	111.00 E

	English	Deutsch	Español	Français	Português
≃	River	Fluss	Río	Rivière	Rio
≊	Canal	Kanal	Canal	Canal	Canal
⌊	Waterfall, Rapids	Wasserfall, Stromschnellen	Cascada, Rápidos	Chute d'eau, Rapides	Cascata, Rápidos
)(	Strait	Meeresstrasse	Estrecho	Détroit	Estreito
C	Bay, Gulf	Bucht, Golf	Bahía, Golfo	Baie, Golfe	Baía, Golfo
⊜	Lake, Lakes	See, Seen	Lago, Lagos	Lac, Lacs	Lago, Lagos
☷	Swamp	Sumpf	Pantano	Marais	Pântano
⍓	Ice Features, Glacier	Eis- und Gletscherformen	Accidentes Glaciales	Formes glaciaires	Acidentes Glaciares
•	Other Hydrographic Features	Andere Hydrographische Objekte	Otros Elementos Hidrográficos	Autres données hydrographiques	Outros Elementos Hidrográficos
✢	Submarine Features	Untermeerische Objekte	Accidentes Submarinos	Formes de relief sous-marin	Acidentes Submarinos
□	Political Unit	Politische Einheit	Unidad Politica	Entité politique	Unidade Política
⊍	Cultural Institution	Kulturelle Institution	Institución Cultural	Institution culturelle	Instituição Cultural
⊥	Historical Site	Historische Stätte	Sitio Histórico	Site historique	Sitio Histórico
♠	Recreational Site	Erholungs- und Ferienort	Sitio de Recreo	Centre de loisirs	Sítio de Lazer
⊠	Airport	Flughafen	Aeropuerto	Aéroport	Aeroporto
■	Military Installation	Militäranlage	Instalación Militar	Installation militaire	Instalação Militar
◆	Miscellaneous	Verschiedenes	Misceláneo	Divers	Miscelânea

Łupawa 30 54.26 N 17.24 E
Lupembe 144 9.15 S 35.15 E
Lupeni 38 45.22 N 23.13 E
Lupire 142 14.36 S 19.29 E
Lupiro 144 8.23 S 36.40 E
Lupon 106 6.54 N 126.00 E
Lupow → Łupawa 30 54.26 N 17.24 E
Luppa 50 51.20 N 12.57 E
Luputa 142 7.10 S 23.42 E
Luqiao, Zhg. 90 32.34 N 117.14 E
Luqiao, Zhg. 90 28.35 N 121.22 E
Luqu 92 34.41 N 102.22 E
Luque 34 37.33 N 4.16 W
Luquillo 230m 18.22 N 65.43 W
Luquillo, Sierra de ⛰ 230m 18.17 N 65.47 W
Lūrah ≃ 110 31.33 N 66.33 E
Luray 178 38.40 N 78.28 W
Lure 54 47.41 N 6.30 E
Lure, Montagne de ⛰ 56 44.07 N 5.47 E
Luremo 142 8.31 S 17.50 E
Lurgan 42 54.28 N 6.20 W
Luribay 238 17.06 S 67.39 W
Lurigancho 276d 12.02 S 77.01 W
Lurín 238 12.17 S 76.52 W
Lúrio 144 13.35 S 40.30 E
Lúrio ≃, Moç. 144 13.35 S 40.32 E
Lurio ≃, Suomi 24 67.08 N 27.29 E
Lurisia 56 44.18 N 7.42 E
Lurnea 264a 33.56 S 150.54 E
Lurö I 26 58.48 N 13.14 E
Lürrip ◆[8] 253 51.12 N 6.28 E
Lusahunga 144 2.52 S 31.15 E
Lusaka, Zaïre 144 7.10 S 29.27 E
Lusaka, Zam. 144 15.25 S 28.17 E
Lusakert 74 40.23 N 44.36 E
Lusambo 142 4.58 S 23.27 E
Lusancay Islands and Reefs II 154 8.25 S 150.20 E
Lusangaye 144 4.54 S 26.00 E
Lusangi 144 4.37 S 27.08 E
Luscar 172 53.04 N 117.24 W
Luseke 142 2.51 S 23.08 E
Luseland 174 52.05 N 109.30 W
Lusenga Plain Game Reserve ◆[4] 144 9.30 S 29.10 E
Lusengo 142 1.46 N 19.29 E
Luserna San Giovanni 56 44.48 N 7.15 E
Lush, Mount ∧ 154 17.02 S 127.30 E
Lushan, Zhg. 90 33.45 N 112.53 E
Lushan, Zhg. 92 30.15 N 102.58 E
Lushan ∧ 90 29.31 N 115.58 E
Lushanguanliju 90 29.33 N 115.58 E
Lushi 92 34.05 N 111.01 E
Lushiko (Luchico) ≃ 142 6.13 S 19.40 E
Lushnje 38 40.56 N 19.42 E
Lushoto 144 4.47 S 38.17 E
Lushui (Luzhang) 92 26.00 N 98.51 E
Lushui ≃ 90 27.04 N 115.00 E
Lüsi 96 32.03 N 121.36 E
Lusi ≃ 105a 7.05 S 110.55 E
Lusiana 58 45.47 N 11.34 E
Lusignan 32 46.26 N 0.07 E
Lusignan, Lac ⊜ 196 46.40 N 74.09 W
Lusigny-sur-Barse 46 48.15 N 4.16 E
Lusikisiki 148 31.25 S 29.30 E
L'usino 66 52.38 N 26.31 E
Lusk, Eire 42 53.32 N 6.10 W
Lusk, Wyo., U.S. 190 42.46 N 104.27 W
Lus-la-Croix-Haute 56 44.40 N 5.42 E
Luso 142 11.47 S 19.52 E
Lusongwa 142 12.58 S 24.16 E
Luspebryggan 24 67.01 N 19.51 E
Lussac-les-Châteaux 32 46.24 N 0.44 E
Lussan 56 44.09 N 4.22 E
Lustenau 54 47.26 N 9.39 E
Luster 26 61.26 N 7.24 E
Lustin 52 50.23 N 4.53 E
Lustrafjorden C[2] 26 61.20 N 7.22 E
Lüstringen 48 52.16 N 8.08 E
Luswishi ≃ 144 13.55 S 27.24 E
Lūt, Dasht-e ◆[2] 118 33.00 N 57.00 E
Lü-ta → Lüda 88 38.53 N 121.35 E
L'uta ≃ 66 58.37 N 28.40 E
Lutago (Luttach) 58 46.57 N 11.55 E
Lutaiji 90 33.32 N 115.03 E
Lütan, Zhg. 88 34.07 N 114.27 E
Lütan, Zhg. 90 28.57 N 119.46 E
Lutao 106 10.00 N 124.04 E
Lutcher 184 30.02 N 90.42 W
Lutembo 142 13.26 S 21.16 E
Lutembo ≃ 142 12.03 S 22.15 E
L'uten'ka 68 50.13 N 34.02 E
Lutesville 184 37.18 N 89.59 W
Lutéte ≃ 142 9.21 S 15.14 E
Lutexu ≃ 263b 4.24 S 15.12 E
Lütgendortmund ◆[8] 253 51.30 N 7.21 E
Luthe 48 52.26 N 9.28 E
Luther, Mich., U.S. 180 44.02 N 85.41 W
Luther, Okla., U.S. 186 35.40 N 97.12 W
Luther Lake ⊜ 202 43.55 N 80.26 W
Luthersburg 204 41.03 N 78.43 W
Lutherville-timonium 274b 39.25 N 76.37 W
Luti 165e 7.14 S 156.59 E
Lütian, Zhg. 90 23.48 N 113.56 E
Lütian, Zhg. 90 26.33 N 114.38 E
Lütjenburg 50 54.17 N 10.35 E
Lütjensee 48 53.39 N 10.22 E
Luton, Eng., U.K. 44 51.53 N 0.25 W
Luton, Eng., U.K. 250 51.22 N 0.32 E
Lutong 102 4.28 N 114.00 E
Lutosn'a ≃ 72 56.26 N 36.52 E
Lutouzhen 90 32.16 N 112.53 E
Lutry 54 46.30 N 6.41 E
Lutshi 144 4.09 S 26.30 E
Lutshima ≃ 142 5.22 S 18.59 E
Lutsk → Luck 68 50.44 N 25.20 E
Luttach → Lutago 58 46.57 N 11.55 E
Lutter am Barenberge 48 51.59 N 10.16 E
Lutterbach 54 47.46 N 7.17 E
Lutterworth 44 52.28 N 1.10 W
Lüttich → Liège 52 50.38 N 5.34 E
Luttrell 182 36.12 N 83.44 W
Lüttringhausen ◆[8] 253 51.13 N 7.14 E
Lutuai ≃ 142 12.33 S 20.16 E
Lutugino 73 48.24 N 39.13 E
Lutz 210 28.09 N 82.28 W
Lützel 52 50.58 N 8.10 E
Lutzelbourg 52 48.44 N 7.15 E
Lützelflüh 54 47.00 N 7.41 E
Lützen 50 51.15 N 12.08 E
Lutzerath 52 50.07 N 7.00 E
Lützow 50 53.40 N 11.11 E
Lützow-Holm Bay C 9 69.10 S 37.30 E
Lutzputs 148 28.03 S 20.40 E
Lützschena 50 51.23 N 12.16 E
Lutzville 148 31.33 S 18.22 E
Luus 92 45.12 N 105.42 E
Luverne, Ala., U.S. 184 31.43 N 86.16 W
Lu Verne, Iowa, U.S. 180 42.55 N 94.05 W
Luverne, Minn., U.S. 188 43.39 N 96.13 W
Luvo 142 5.51 S 14.05 E
Luvo ≃ 142 10.18 S 17.08 E
Luvua 144 8.48 S 25.19 E
Luvua ≃, Ang. 144 11.57 S 22.30 E
Luvua ≃, Zaïre 144 6.46 S 26.58 E
Luvuvhu ≃ 146 22.40 S 30.55 E
Luwegu ≃ 144 8.31 S 37.23 E
Luwei 96 31.02 N 120.49 E
Luwingu 144 10.15 S 29.55 E
Luwuk → Banggai, Indon. 102 1.34 S 123.30 E
Luwuk, Indon. 102 0.56 S 122.47 E
Luxana Bay C 172 52.03 N 131.00 W
Luxapallila Creek ≃ 184 33.28 N 88.26 W
Luxembourg 52 49.36 N 6.09 E
Luxembourg □[4] 52 50.00 N 5.30 E
Luxembourg □[1] 22; 52 49.45 N 6.05 E
Luxembourg, Jardin du ♠ 251 48.51 N 2.19 E
Luxemburg 180 44.32 N 87.42 W
Luxemburg → Luxembourg □[1] 52 49.45 N 6.05 E
Luxemburgo → Luxembourg □[1] 52 49.45 N 6.05 E
Luxeuil-les-Bains 54 47.49 N 6.23 E
Luxi, Zhg. 92 24.32 N 103.41 E
Luxi (Mangshi), Zhg. 92 24.20 N 98.25 E
Luxi ≃ 90 28.11 N 116.48 E
Lüxia 90 26.41 N 120.06 E
Luxiang, Zhg. 96 31.32 N 120.45 E
Lüxiang, Zhg. 96 30.50 N 121.10 E
Luxikou 90 29.54 N 113.42 E
Luxmanor 274c 39.02 N 77.07 W
Luxor → Al-Uqşur, Mişr 130 25.41 N 32.39 E
Luxor, Pa., U.S. 204 40.20 N 79.28 W
Luxora 184 35.45 N 89.56 W
Lu Xun Museum ♥ 259b 31.16 N 121.28 E
Lüxuqiao 96 31.50 N 119.31 E
Luy ≃ 32 43.39 N 1.08 W
Luyan 96 30.25 N 120.53 E
Lüyangyi 94 41.23 N 121.40 E
Luyanó ≃ 276b 23.07 N 82.21 W
Luyashan ⛰ 92 38.45 N 111.50 E
Luyeh 90 22.55 N 121.08 E
Luyi 90 33.53 N 115.28 E
Luyu 96 31.34 N 121.41 E
Luyuan, Zhg. 96 31.51 N 120.38 E
Luyuan, Zhg. 261a 39.54 N 116.27 E
Luz, Bra. 245 19.48 S 45.40 W
Luz, Bra. 277a 22.48 S 43.05 W
Luz ◆[8] 256c 38.46 N 9.10 W
Luz, Estação da ◆[5] 277b 23.32 S 46.38 W
Luz, Isla I 244 45.30 S 73.59 W
Luz, Ponta da ≻ 277a 22.47 S 43.05 W
Luza, S.S.S.R. 24 60.39 N 47.10 E
Luza, S.S.S.R. 24 62.42 N 37.06 E
Luža, S.S.S.R. 66 59.58 N 31.56 E
Luža ≃ 72 55.03 N 36.35 E
Luzarches 46 49.07 N 2.25 E
Luzern 54 47.03 N 8.18 E
Luzern □[3] 54 47.05 N 8.05 E
Luzerne 200 41.17 N 75.54 W
Luzerne □[6] 200 41.14 N 75.53 W
Luzhai, Zhg. 90 29.16 N 120.17 E
Luzhai, Zhg. 92 24.31 N 109.50 E
Luzhi 96 31.16 N 120.52 E
Luzhou 97 28.54 N 105.27 E
Luziânia 245 16.15 S 47.56 W
Lužické hory ⛰ 50 50.48 N 14.40 E
Luzilândia 240 3.28 S 42.22 W
Lužki, S.S.S.R. 66 55.21 N 27.52 E
Lužki, S.S.S.R. 72 54.51 N 37.36 E
Lužná 50 50.06 N 13.45 E
Lužniki ◆[8] 255b 55.43 N 37.33 E
Luzon 226 9.25 N 82.32 W
Luzon I 106 16.00 N 121.00 E
Luzon Strait ⊔ 98 20.30 N 121.00 E
Luzy 32 46.48 N 3.58 E
Luzzara 58 44.58 N 10.41 E
L'va ≃ 68 52.00 N 27.36 E
L'va Tolstogo 72 54.37 N 36.03 E
L'vov 68 49.50 N 24.00 E
L'vovskij 72 55.19 N 37.31 E
Lwów → L'vov 68 49.50 N 24.00 E
Lwówek 30 52.28 N 16.10 E
Lwówek Śląski 30 51.07 N 15.35 E
Lyall, Mount ∧ 162 45.17 S 167.34 E
Lyallpur 113 31.25 N 73.05 E
Lyantonde 144 0.24 S 31.09 E
Lybster 28 58.18 N 3.18 W
Lychen 50 53.12 N 13.19 E
Lyck → Ełk 30 53.50 N 22.22 E
Lyckeby 26 56.12 N 15.39 E
Lyčkovo, S.S.S.R. 66 57.55 N 32.24 E
Lyčkovo, S.S.S.R. 68 49.06 N 35.12 E
Lycksele 26 64.36 N 18.40 E
Lycoming □[6] 200 41.14 N 77.00 W
Lycoming Creek ≃ 200 41.13 N 77.02 W
Lydd 44 50.57 N 0.55 E
Lydda → Lod 122 31.58 N 34.54 E
Lydden ∨ 44 50.56 N 2.22 W
Lydenburg 146 25.10 S 30.29 E
Lydford 44 50.39 N 4.06 W
Lydgate 252 53.44 N 2.07 W
Lydham 44 52.31 N 2.58 W
Lydia Mills 182 34.28 N 81.55 W
Lydiate 252 53.32 N 2.57 W
Lydick 206 41.42 N 86.22 W
Lydney 44 51.44 N 2.32 W
Lye Green 250 51.43 N 0.35 W
Lyell, Mount ∧, Can. 172 51.57 N 117.06 W
Lyell, Mount ∧, Calif., U.S. 216 37.44 N 119.16 W
Lyell Brown, Mount ∧ 152 23.21 S 130.24 E
Lyell Island I 172 52.40 N 131.30 W
Lyford 186 26.24 N 97.48 W
Lygnern ⊜ 26 57.29 N 12.20 E
Lykens 198 40.34 N 76.43 W
Lykošino 66 58.07 N 33.43 E
Lyle, Minn., U.S. 180 43.30 N 92.57 W
Lyle, Wash., U.S. 214 45.42 N 121.17 W
Lyles 184 35.55 N 87.21 W
Lyman, Nebr., U.S. 188 41.55 N 104.02 W
Lyman, S.C., U.S. 182 34.56 N 82.09 W
Lyman, Wash., U.S. 214 48.31 N 122.04 W
Lyman, Wyo., U.S. 190 41.20 N 110.18 W
Lymbel'karamo 76 60.15 N 83.32 E
Lyme 197 41.19 N 72.10 W
Lyme Bay C 44 50.38 N 3.00 W
Lyme Hall ⊥ 252 53.20 N 2.03 W
Lyme Regis 44 50.44 N 2.57 W
Lyminge 44 51.08 N 1.05 E
Lymington 44 50.46 N 1.33 W
Lymkoj 76 59.31 N 70.22 E
Lymm 252 53.23 N 2.29 W
Lympne 44 51.05 N 1.02 E
Lyn 202 44.35 N 75.47 W
Łyna (Lava) ≃ 66 54.37 N 21.14 E
Lynæs 41 55.57 N 11.52 E
Lynbrook 266 40.39 N 73.41 W
Lynch, Ky., U.S. 182 36.58 N 82.55 W
Lynch, Nebr., U.S. 188 42.50 N 98.28 W
Lynch, Lac ⊜ 180 46.25 N 77.05 W
Lynchburg, Ohio, U.S. 208 39.14 N 83.48 W
Lynchburg, S.C., U.S. 182 34.04 N 80.04 W
Lynchburg, Tenn., U.S. 184 35.17 N 86.22 W
Lynchburg, Va., U.S. 182 37.24 N 79.10 W
Lynches ≃ 182 33.50 N 79.22 W
Lynchville 204 41.26 N 78.34 W
Lynd ≃ 154 16.28 S 143.18 E
Lynde Creek ≃ 202 43.51 N 78.57 W
Lynden, Ont., Can. 202 43.14 N 80.08 W
Lynden, Wash., U.S. 214 48.57 N 122.27 W
Lyndhurst, Austl. 156 30.17 S 138.21 E
Lyndhurst, Austl. 156 19.12 S 144.23 E
Lyndhurst, Austl. 264b 38.03 S 145.15 E
Lyndhurst, Eng., U.K. 44 50.52 N 1.34 W
Lyndhurst, N.J., U.S. 276 40.49 N 74.07 W
Lyndhurst, Ohio, U.S. 204 41.31 N 81.30 W
Lyndoch 158b 34.37 S 138.53 E
Lyndon, Austl. 152 23.37 S 115.15 E
Lyndon, Kans., U.S. 188 38.36 N 95.41 W
Lyndon, Ky., U.S. 208 38.16 N 85.36 W
Lyndon ≃ 152 23.29 S 114.06 E
Lyndon B. Johnson Space Center ♥[3] 212 29.34 N 95.05 W
Lyndonville, N.Y., U.S. 200 43.19 N 78.23 W
Lyndonville, Vt., U.S. 178 44.32 N 72.01 W
Lyndora 204 40.51 N 79.55 W
Lyne 250 51.23 N 0.33 W
Lyne ≃ 42 54.58 N 3.01 W
Lyneham 44 51.31 N 1.58 W
Lynemouth 42 55.12 N 1.31 W
Lyne Water ≃ 42 54.39 N 3.16 W
Lynga 70 57.17 N 53.04 E
Lyngdal 26 58.08 N 7.05 E
Lynge 41 55.51 N 12.17 E
Lyngen 24 69.34 N 20.10 E
Lyngen C[2] 24 69.58 N 20.30 E
Lyngør 26 58.38 N 9.10 E
Lynher ≃ 44 50.28 N 4.12 W
Lynmouth 44 51.15 N 3.50 W
Lynn, Ala., U.S. 184 34.03 N 87.33 W
Lynn, Ind., U.S. 208 40.03 N 84.56 W
Lynn, Mass., U.S. 197 42.28 N 70.57 W
Lynn ≃ 202 42.47 N 80.12 W
Lynn Canal C 170 58.50 N 135.15 W
Lynndyl 190 39.31 N 112.22 W
Lynne Acres 274b 39.21 N 76.45 W
Lynnfield 197 42.32 N 71.03 W
Lynn Garden 182 36.35 N 82.34 W
Lynn Harbor C 273 42.27 N 70.57 W
Lynn Haven 184 30.15 N 85.39 W
Lynn Lake 174 56.51 N 101.03 W
Lynnville 180 41.35 N 92.47 W
Lynnwood, Pa., U.S. 200 41.14 N 75.56 W
Lynnwood, Pa., U.S. 204 40.07 N 79.51 W
Lynnwood, Wash., U.S. 214 47.49 N 122.19 W
Lynton 44 51.15 N 3.50 W
Lyntupy 66 55.03 N 26.19 E
Lynwood, Calif., U.S. 218 33.55 N 118.12 W
Lynwood, Ill., U.S. 268 41.32 N 87.32 W
Lynx Lake ⊜ 166 62.25 N 106.15 W
Lyø I 41 55.02 N 10.10 E
Lyon 56 45.45 N 4.51 E
Lyon □[6] 216 39.00 N 119.15 W
Lyon ◆[5] 251 48.51 N 2.23 E
Lyon Inlet C 166 66.32 N 83.53 W
Lyon Mountain 178 44.43 N 73.55 W
Lyon Mountain ∧ 178 44.41 N 73.53 W
Lyonnais □[9] 56 45.45 N 4.30 E
Lyonnais, Monts du ⛰ 56 45.40 N 4.30 E
Lyons, Colo., U.S. 190 40.13 N 105.16 W
Lyons, Ga., U.S. 182 32.12 N 82.19 W
Lyons, Ill., U.S. 206 41.49 N 87.50 W
Lyons, Ind., U.S. 184 38.59 N 87.05 W
Lyons, Kans., U.S. 188 38.21 N 98.12 W
Lyons, Mich., U.S. 206 42.59 N 84.57 W
Lyons, Nebr., U.S. 188 41.56 N 96.28 W
Lyons, N.Y., U.S. 200 43.04 N 77.00 W
Lyons, Ohio, U.S. 206 41.42 N 84.04 W
Lyons, Tex., U.S. 212 30.23 N 96.34 W
Lyons, Wis., U.S. 206 42.39 N 88.21 W
Lyons ≃ 152 25.02 S 115.09 E
Lyon Satolas, Aérodrome de ⊠ 56 45.43 N 5.04 E
Lyons Creek ≃ 274a 43.03 N 79.04 W
Lyons Falls 202 43.37 N 75.22 W
Lyons-la-Forêt 46 49.24 N 1.28 E
Lyons Plains 197 41.13 N 73.21 W
Lyons Run ≃ 269b 40.25 N 79.43 W
Lyon Station 198 40.28 N 75.45 W
Lyonsville 266 40.57 N 74.25 W
Lyrestad 40 58.48 N 14.04 E
Lys (Leie) ≃, Eur. 46 51.03 N 3.43 E
Lys ≃, It. 56 45.36 N 7.47 E
Lysaja Gora 68 48.11 N 31.06 E
Lysaker 26 59.54 N 10.36 E
Lys'anka 68 49.16 N 30.50 E
Lysá pod Makytou 30 49.12 N 18.13 E
Lysefjorden C[2] 26 59.00 N 6.14 E
Lysekil 26 58.16 N 11.26 E
Łysica ∧ 30 50.54 N 20.55 E
Lysjön ⊜ 40 60.07 N 14.18 E
Lyskovo 70 56.04 N 45.02 E
Lysogorka 73 47.42 N 39.12 E
Lyss 54 47.04 N 7.18 E
Lysterfield 264b 37.56 S 145.18 E
Lysterfield Hills ⛰[2] 264b 37.56 S 145.16 E
Lysterfield Reservoir ⊜[1] 264b 37.58 S 145.18 E
Lyster Station 196 46.22 N 71.37 W
Lys'va 76 58.07 N 57.47 E
Lys'va ≃ 70 58.15 N 54.47 E
Lysyje Gory 70 51.32 N 44.46 E
Lytham Saint Anne's 42 53.45 N 2.57 W
Lytkarino 72 55.35 N 37.54 E
Lytle 186 29.14 N 98.48 W
Lytle Creek ≃ 218 34.09 N 117.23 W
Lyttelton, N.Z. 162 43.35 S 172.42 E
Lyttelton, S. Afr. 148 25.50 S 28.11 E
Lytton 172 50.14 N 121.34 W
Lytton Springs 212 30.00 N 97.37 W
Lyubertsy → L'ubercy 72 55.41 N 37.53 E

M

Ma ≃ 100 19.47 N 105.56 E
Ma, Oued el ∨, Alg. 138 27.45 N 7.45 W
Ma, Oued el- ∨, Maur. 138 24.03 N 9.10 W
Maad, Djebel bou ∧ 34 36.26 N 2.08 E
Maadid, Djebel ∧ 34 35.52 N 4.46 E
Maalaea Bay C 219a 20.47 N 156.29 W
Ma'alot-Tarshiḥa 122 33.01 N 35.17 E
Maan, Tür. 120 36.51 N 38.50 E
Ma'ān, Urd. 122 30.12 N 35.44 E
Ma'ān □[8] 122 30.20 N 36.30 E
Maaninka 26 63.09 N 27.18 E
Maanshan, Zhg. 90 31.42 N 118.30 E
Maanshan, Zhg. 97 29.52 N 104.59 E
Ma-ao 106 10.29 N 122.59 E
Maar 130 6.54 N 31.33 E
Maardu 66 59.28 N 25.02 E
Maarianhamina → Mariehamn 26 60.06 N 19.57 E
Ma'ārik, Qārat al- ∧[2] 132 29.59 N 30.52 E
Ma'arrat an-Nu'mān 120 35.38 N 36.40 E
Ma'arrat Mişrīn 120 36.01 N 36.40 E
Ma'arrat Şaydnāyā 122 33.41 N 36.23 E
Maarssen 48 52.08 N 5.08 E
Maas (Meuse) ≃ 30 51.49 N 5.01 E
Maasbracht 48 51.08 N 5.53 E
Maasdam 48 51.47 N 4.32 E
Maaseik 52 51.06 N 5.48 E
Maasholm 41 54.41 N 9.59 E
Maasin 106 10.08 N 124.50 E
Ma'āşir ash-Shūf 122 33.40 N 35.40 E
Maasniel 48 51.13 N 6.01 E
Maassluis 48 51.55 N 4.15 E
Maastricht 52 50.52 N 5.43 E
Maave 146 21.03 S 34.47 E
Ma-ayon ≃ 106 11.25 N 122.46 E
Maba, Zhg. 90 24.41 N 113.35 E
Maba, Zhg. 90 32.59 N 118.48 E
Maba, Ouadi ∨ 136 15.10 N 21.00 E
Mababe Depression ●[7] 146 18.50 S 24.15 E
Mabaduan 154 9.16 S 142.44 E
Mabaho, Mount ∧ 106 9.15 N 125.42 E
Mabaia 142 7.13 S 14.03 E
Mabalane 146 23.37 S 32.31 E
Mabana 142 [illegible]
Mabanga 142 1.30 N 19.06 E
Mabank 212 32.22 N 96.06 W
Mabaoquan 95 40.09 N 115.53 E
Ma'barot 122 32.22 N 34.54 E
Mabaruma 236 8.12 N 59.47 W
Mabashi 258 35.49 N 139.55 E
Mabau 102 2.14 S 111.54 E
Mabay 230p 20.16 N 76.40 W
Mabber, Ras ≻ 134 9.28 N 50.53 E
Mabel Creek 152 29.01 S 134.17 E
Mabeleapodi 146 20.58 S 22.36 E
Mabel Lake ⊜ 172 50.35 N 118.44 W
Maben 184 33.33 N 89.05 W
Mabenga-Cité 142 3.39 S 18.40 E
Mabenge 142 4.14 N 24.09 E
Maberry, Loch ⊜ 42 55.02 N 4.41 W
Mabeul 36 36.27 N 10.46 E
Mabi, Nihon 86 34.38 N 133.41 E
Mabi, Zhg. 90 26.21 N 119.36 E
Mabian 97 28.48 N 103.41 E
Mabian ≃ 97 29.04 N 103.43 E
Mabicun 92 35.59 N 112.15 E
Mablethorpe 42 53.21 N 0.15 E
Mableton 182 33.49 N 84.35 W
Mabole ≃ 140 9.01 N 12.44 W
Maboma 144 2.32 N 28.13 E
Mabonto 140 8.52 N 11.49 W
Mabote 146 22.03 S 34.09 E
Mabou 176 46.05 N 61.22 W
Mabrak, Jabal ∧ 122 30.13 N 35.29 E
Mabrous Tafidinga ●[4] 136 21.13 N 13.38 E
Mabrūk, Lībīya 136 29.50 N 17.10 E
Mabrūk, Sūd. 130 8.07 N 29.25 E
Mabton 192 46.13 N 120.00 W
Mabu 90 31.33 N 116.04 E
Mabuguai 90 29.49 N 112.42 E
Mabuki 144 2.59 S 33.11 E
Mabuni 164m 26.05 N 127.43 E
Mabwe 144 8.39 S 26.31 E
Mc → Mac 0.00 0.00
Mača, S.S.S.R. 64 59.54 N 117.35 E
Maca, Ven. 276c 10.28 N 66.48 W
Macá, Monte ∧ 244 45.06 S 73.12 W
Macabu ≃ 245 21.59 S 41.28 W
Macachín 242 37.09 S 63.39 W
Macaco, Morro do ∧[2] 277a 22.56 S 43.07 W
Macacos, Ilha dos I 240 1.20 S 50.35 W
Macacu ≃ 246 22.42 S 43.02 W
McAdam 176 45.36 N 67.20 W
McAdams Peak ∧[2] 209 38.58 N 90.32 W
McAdoo 200 40.55 N 76.00 W
McAdoo Heights 200 40.54 N 76.01 W
Macaé 245 22.23 S 41.47 W
McAfee 200 41.11 N 74.33 W
Macaíba 240 5.51 S 35.21 W
Macajalar Bay C 106 8.37 N 124.38 E
Macajuba 245 12.09 S 40.22 W
Macalaya 106 12.53 N 123.46 E
Macalelon 106 13.45 N 122.08 E
McAlester 186 34.56 N 95.46 W
Macalister 172 52.27 N 122.24 W
Macalister ≃ 156 38.02 S 146.59 E
Macalister, Mount ∧ 160 34.27 S 149.45 E
McAlisterville 198 40.38 N 77.16 W
McAllen 186 26.12 N 98.15 W
McAlpine 198 39.16 N 76.50 W
McAlpine Dam ◆[6] 208 38.16 N 85.47 W
MacAlpine Lake ⊜ 166 66.40 N 103.15 W
McAlveys Fort 204 40.39 N 77.50 W
Macambira 240 10.40 S 37.32 W
Macamic, Lac ⊜ 180 48.48 N 78.59 W
Macão 34 39.33 N 8.00 W
Macao → Macau □[2] 90 22.10 N 113.33 E
Macapá 240 0.02 N 51.03 W
Macaparana 240 7.34 S 35.27 W
Macar 120 37.06 N 30.56 E
Macará 236 4.23 S 79.57 W
Macarani 245 15.33 S 40.24 W
Macarao 276c 10.26 N 67.02 W
Macarao ≃ 276c 10.26 N 67.01 W
Macareo, Caño ≃[1] 236 9.47 N 61.37 W
Macari ≃ 240 1.52 N 50.31 W
MacArthur, Pil. 106 10.50 N 125.00 E
MacArthur, Ill., U.S. 268 41.39 N 87.44 W
McArthur 178 39.15 N 82.29 W
McArthur ≃ 154 15.54 S 136.40 E
McArthur River 154 16.27 S 136.07 E
Macaruma ≃ 236 7.37 N 61.48 W
Macas 236 2.19 S 78.07 W
Macatawa ≃ 206 42.48 N 86.05 W
Macatawa, Lake C 206 42.47 N 86.10 W
Macaterick, Loch ⊜ 42 55.12 N 4.26 W
Macau, Bra. 240 5.07 S 36.38 W
Macau (Aomen), Macau 90 22.14 N 113.35 E
Macau □[2] 80; 90 22.10 N 113.33 E
Macau, Ilha I 146 20.55 S 35.05 E
Macauã ≃ 238 9.13 S 68.44 W
Macaúbas 245 13.02 S 42.42 W
McAuley 174 50.16 N 101.23 W
Macaya ≃ 236 0.59 N 72.20 W
Macaya, Pic de ∧ 228 18.25 N 74.00 W
Macaza ≃ 196 46.21 N 74.47 W
McBain 180 44.12 N 85.13 W
McBee 182 34.28 N 80.15 W
McBeth 212 29.11 N 95.30 W
McBeth Fjord C[2] 166 69.38 N 68.30 W
McBride 172 53.18 N 120.10 W
McCall 192 44.55 N 116.06 W
McCall Creek 184 31.31 N 90.42 W
McCallum 176 47.38 N 56.15 W
McCallum Creek ≃ 159 37.03 S 143.49 E
McCamey 186 31.08 N 102.13 W
McCammon 192 42.39 N 112.12 W
Maccarese ◆[8] 257a 41.53 N 12.13 E
Maccarese, Bonifica di ◆[1] 257a 41.51 N 12.13 E
McCarteney Creek ≃ 192 47.13 N 120.05 W
Mccarthy 170 61.26 N 142.55 W
McCauley Island I 172 53.40 N 130.15 W
McCaysville 182 34.59 N 84.23 W
Macchiagodena 60 41.33 N 14.24 E
McChord Air Force Base ■ 214 47.08 N 122.29 W
McClarens Run ≃ 269b 40.27 N 80.12 W
McClarty Lake ⊜ 174 54.28 N 100.20 W
McCleary 214 47.03 N 123.16 W
McClees Creek ≃ 266 40.22 N 74.03 W
McClellan Air Force Base ■ 216 38.39 N 121.23 W
McClellan Creek ≃ 186 35.22 N 100.34 W
McClellanville 182 33.05 N 79.28 W
Macclenny 182 30.18 N 82.07 W
Macclesfield, Austl. 158b 35.10 S 138.50 E
Macclesfield, Eng., U.K. 42 53.16 N 2.07 W
Macclesfield □[8] 252 53.17 N 2.15 W
Macclesfield Canal ☰ 252 53.24 N 2.03 W
Macclesfield Forest ◆[3] 252 53.15 N 2.03 W
McClintock, Mount ∧ 9 80.13 S 157.26 E
McCloud 194 41.15 N 122.08 W
McCloud ≃ 194 40.46 N 122.18 W
McClure, Ill., U.S. 184 37.19 N 89.26 W
McClure, Ohio, U.S. 206 41.22 N 83.57 W
McClure, Pa., U.S. 200 40.42 N 77.19 W
McClure, Lake ⊜[1] 216 37.37 N 120.16 W
McClusky 188 47.29 N 100.27 W
McColl 182 34.40 N 79.33 W
McComas 182 37.23 N 81.17 W
McComb, Miss., U.S. 184 31.14 N 90.27 W
McComb, Ohio, U.S. 206 41.06 N 83.48 W
McConaughy, Lake ⊜[1] 188 41.15 N 101.50 W
McConnell Air Force Base ■ 188 37.38 N 97.15 W
McConnell Range ⛰ 170 64.00 N 123.00 W
McConnellsburg 178 39.56 N 77.59 W
McConnells Mill 269b 40.15 N 80.15 W
McConnells Mill State Park ♠ 204 40.57 N 80.11 W
McConnellstown 204 40.27 N 78.05 W

ENGLISH

Name	Page	Lat.°′	Long.°′
McConnellsville	200	43.16 N	75.42 W
McConnelsville	178	39.39 N	81.51 W
McCook, Ill., U.S.	268	41.48 N	87.50 W
McCook, Nebr., U.S.	188	40.12 N	100.38 W
McCordsville	208	39.54 N	85.55 W
McCormick	182	33.55 N	82.17 W
McCormick Place ♥	268	41.51 N	87.37 W
McCoy	214	45.03 N	123.13 W
McCoy Lake ⊜	174	52.35 N	92.19 W
McCrae Lake ⊜	202	44.55 N	79.48 W
McCraney Creek ≃	209	39.39 N	91.12 W
McCreary	174	50.46 N	99.30 W
McCrory	184	35.16 N	91.12 W
Mcculloch, Mount ∧	152	25.10 S	129.52 E
McCullom Lake	206	42.22 N	88.18 W
Mccullough	269b	40.22 N	79.38 W
McCullough Mountain ∧	194	35.36 N	115.11 W
McCune	188	37.21 N	95.01 W
McCurtain	186	35.09 N	94.58 W
McCusker ≃	174	55.32 N	108.40 W
McCutchenville	204	40.59 N	83.16 W
McDade	212	30.17 N	97.15 W
McDavid	184	30.52 N	87.19 W
McDermitt	194	41.59 N	117.36 W
McDermott	208	38.50 N	83.04 W
Macdhui, Ben ∧	148	30.39 S	27.58 E
MacDill Air Force Base ■	210	27.51 N	82.29 W
McDonald, Kans., U.S.	188	39.47 N	101.22 W
McDonald, Pa., U.S.	204; 269b	40.22 N	80.14 W
Macdonald ≃	160	33.23 S	150.59 E
McDonald, Lac ⊜	196	45.52 N	74.35 W
Macdonald, Lake ⊜	152	23.30 S	129.00 E
McDonald, Lake ⊜	192	48.35 N	113.55 W
Macdonald, Mount ∧	165f	17.36 S	168.23 E
McDonald Creek ≃	192	47.01 N	108.09 W
MacDonald Downs	152	22.27 S	135.13 E
McDonald Islands II	6	53.02 S	72.36 E
Macdonald Lake ⊜	202	45.14 N	78.34 W
McDonald Park ♠	272	37.18 N	122.17 W
MacDonald Pass)(	192	46.34 N	112.18 W
Macdonald Range ⛰	172	49.12 N	114.46 W
Macdonnell Ranges ⛰	152	23.45 S	133.20 E
McDonogh	274c	39.24 N	76.46 W
McDonough, Ga., U.S.	182	33.27 N	84.09 W
McDonough, N.Y., U.S.	200	42.30 N	75.46 W
McDouall Peak	152	29.51 S	134.55 E
McDougall, Mount ∧	190	42.54 N	110.36 W
MacDowell Lake ⊜	174	52.15 N	92.45 W
McDowell Peak ∧	190	33.40 N	111.50 W
Macduff	28	57.40 N	2.29 W
Macdui, Ben ∧	28	57.04 N	3.40 W
Mačecha	70	50.48 N	43.17 E
Mačechi	68	49.31 N	34.26 E
Maceday Lake ⊜	271	42.42 N	83.26 W
Macedo de Cavaleiros	34	41.32 N	6.58 W
Macedon	200	43.04 N	77.18 W
Macedon, Mount ∧	159	37.23 S	144.35 E
Macedonia, Conn., U.S.	197	41.47 N	73.30 W
Macedonia, Ohio, U.S.	204	41.19 N	81.31 W
Macedonia → Makedonija □[3]	38	41.50 N	22.00 E
Macedonia □[9]	38	41.00 N	23.00 E
Macedonia Brook State Park ♠	197	41.47 N	73.29 W
Macedonio Alcalá	224	17.52 N	96.02 W
Maceió	240	9.40 S	35.43 W
Maceira	256c	38.52 N	9.19 W
McElhattan	200	41.09 N	77.22 W
McElmo Creek ≃	190	37.13 N	109.12 W
Mc Ennen Airport ⊠	271	42.12 N	83.37 W
Mcensk	66	53.17 N	36.35 E
Macenta	140	8.33 N	9.28 W
Macenta □[4]	140	8.30 N	9.25 W
Maceo	236	6.33 N	74.47 W
Macerata	60	43.18 N	13.27 E
Macerata □[4]	60	43.12 N	13.10 E
Macerata Feltria	60	43.48 N	12.26 E
McEwen	184	36.06 N	87.38 W
McEwensville	200	41.05 N	76.49 W
McFadden	190	41.39 N	106.08 W
McFarland, Calif., U.S.	216	35.41 N	119.14 W
McFarland, Wis., U.S.	206	43.01 N	89.17 W
MacFarlane ≃	166	59.12 N	107.58 W
Macfarlane, Lake ⊜	156	31.55 S	136.42 E
Macfarlane, Mount ∧	162	43.56 S	169.23 E
McGavock Lake ⊜	174	56.32 N	101.25 W
McGehee	184	33.38 N	91.24 W
McGill	194	39.23 N	114.47 W
McGillivray, Lac ⊜	180	46.04 N	77.06 W
McGill University ♥[2]	265a	45.30 N	73.35 W
McGinnis Slough Wildlife Refuge ◆[4]	268	41.39 N	87.52 W
McGovern	204	40.14 N	80.13 W
Mcgrann	204	40.47 N	79.31 W
Mcgrath	170	62.58 N	155.38 W
McGraw	200	42.36 N	76.06 W
MacGregor	174	49.57 N	98.49 W
McGregor, Ont., Can.	204	42.09 N	82.58 W
McGregor, S. Afr.	148	33.57 S	19.50 E
McGregor, Iowa, U.S.	180	43.01 N	91.11 W
McGregor, Tex., U.S.	212	31.26 N	97.24 W
McGregor ≃	172	54.11 N	122.00 W
McGregor Creek ≃	204	42.24 N	82.11 W
McGregor Lake ⊜	172	50.31 N	112.53 W
McGregor Range ⛰	156	26.40 S	142.45 E
McGuffey	206	40.42 N	83.47 W
McGuire, Mount ∧	192	45.10 N	114.36 W
McGuire Air Force Base ■	198	40.02 N	74.35 W
Macha	238	18.49 S	66.05 W
Machacamarca	238	18.10 S	67.02 W
Machache ∧	148	29.21 S	27.55 E
Machachi	236	0.30 S	78.34 W
Machačkala	74	42.58 N	47.30 E
Machada, Mata Nacional da ♠	256c	38.36 N	9.02 W
Machadinho ≃	238	9.00 S	61.52 W
Machado	246	21.41 S	45.56 W
Machado ≃	246	21.38 S	45.52 W
Machadodorp	146	25.40 S	30.14 E
Machados	246	22.30 S	46.25 W
Machærus ⊥	122	31.34 N	35.38 E
Machagai	242	26.56 S	60.03 W
Machaila	146	22.15 S	32.55 E
Machakos	144	1.31 S	37.16 E
Machala	236	3.16 S	79.58 W
Machalí	242	34.11 S	70.40 W
Machalino	70	53.05 N	46.14 E
Māchalpur	114	24.08 N	76.18 E
Machaneng	146	23.10 S	27.26 E
Machang, Malay.	104	5.46 N	102.13 E
Machang, Zhg.	88	34.06 N	119.02 E
Machang, Zhg.	88	40.22 N	119.43 E
Machanga	146	20.58 S	34.59 E
Machangcun	95	38.54 N	115.26 E
Machangfu	95	25.14 N	103.45 E
Machangjianhe ≃	95	39.00 N	117.40 E
Macharadze	74	41.56 N	42.01 E
Machattie, Lake ⊜	156	24.50 S	139.48 E
Machault	46	49.21 N	4.30 E
Machava	146	25.54 S	32.29 E
Machaze	146	20.51 S	33.26 E
Machebu	90	29.25 N	119.32 E
Machece	146	19.17 S	35.33 E

DEUTSCH

Name	Seite	Breite°′	Länge°′ E=Os
Machecoul	32	47.00 N	1.50 W
Macheke	144	18.05 S	31.51 E
Machelen	46	50.55 N	4.26 E
Macheng	90	31.13 N	115.00 E
McHenry, Ill., U.S.	206	42.21 N	88.16 W
McHenry, Miss., U.S.	184	30.42 N	89.08 W
Mc Henry □[6]	206	42.19 N	88.27 W
McHenry Dam and Lake Defiance State Park ♠	206	42.18 N	88.15 W
Macherio	256b	45.38 N	9.16 E
Māchērla	112	16.29 N	79.26 E
Machern	50	51.21 N	12.37 E
Mcherrah ◆[1]	138	27.00 N	4.40 W
Machery	251	48.36 N	2.05 E
Machesna Mountain ∧	216	35.17 N	120.14 W
Machhīwara	113	30.55 N	76.12 E
Machhlīshahr	114	25.41 N	82.25 E
Machhuakhali	116	22.05 N	90.21 E
Machias, Maine, U.S.	178	44.43 N	67.28 W
Machias, N.Y., U.S.	200	42.25 N	78.30 W
Machias ≃	176	44.43 N	67.22 W
Machias Bay C	176	44.40 N	67.20 W
Machichaco, Cabo ≻	34	43.27 N	2.45 W
Machichi ≃	174	57.03 N	92.06 W
Machico	138	32.42 N	16.46 W
Machida	84	35.32 N	139.27 E
Machili ≃	144	17.26 S	25.02 E
Machilīpatnam (Bandar)	112	16.10 N	81.08 E
Machindžauri	74	41.40 N	41.43 E
Mchinga	144	9.44 S	39.42 E
Mchinji	144	13.41 S	32.55 E
Machiques	236	10.04 N	72.34 W
Machiya ≃	84	35.01 N	136.42 E
Machkund ⊜[1]	112	18.26 N	82.35 E
Machmud-Mekteb	74	44.26 N	45.13 E
Machn'ovo	76	58.27 N	61.42 E
Macho, Arroyo del ∨	186	33.36 N	104.28 W
Machočen, Porog ⌊	78	57.23 N	121.29 E
Machona, Laguna C	224	18.20 N	93.40 W
Machorovka	76	54.17 N	69.41 E
Machtaly	75	41.22 N	68.02 E
Mchungo	144	7.42 S	39.17 E
Machupicchu	238	13.07 S	72.34 W
Machu Picchu ⊥	238	13.07 S	72.34 W
Machupo ≃	238	12.34 S	64.25 W
Machynlleth	44	52.35 N	3.51 W
Maciá, Arg.	242	32.10 S	59.23 W
Macia, Moç.	146	25.03 S	33.10 E
Macias Nguema Biyogo I	142	3.30 N	8.42 E
Maciel, Arroyo ≃	248	33.42 S	57.59 W
Măcin	38	45.15 N	28.08 E
Macina ◆[1]	140	14.30 N	5.00 W
McInnes Lake ⊜	174	52.12 N	93.45 W
McIntosh, Ala., U.S.	184	31.16 N	88.02 W
McIntosh, Ill., U.S.	206	42.03 N	88.23 W
McIntosh, Minn., U.S.	188	47.38 N	95.53 W
McIntosh, S. Dak., U.S.	188	45.55 N	101.21 W
McIntosh Lake ⊜	174	55.45 N	105.08 W
McIntyre	204	40.34 N	79.18 W
Macintyre ≃, Austl.	156	29.25 S	148.45 E
Macintyre ≃, Austl.	156	28.38 S	150.47 E
McIntyre Bay C	172	54.05 N	131.55 W
Mačkassy	70	52.46 N	45.34 E
Mackay, Austl.	156	21.09 S	149.11 E
Mackay, Idaho, U.S.	192	43.55 N	113.37 W
MacKay ≃	174	57.03 N	111.55 W
Mackay, Lake ⊜	152	22.30 S	129.00 E
McKay, Mount ∧	152	22.26 S	120.01 E
McKay Creek ≃	192	45.40 N	118.50 W
MacKay Lake ⊜	166	63.55 N	110.25 W
McKean	204	41.59 N	80.09 W
McKean □[6]	204	41.49 N	78.27 W
McKeand ≃	166	65.26 N	68.10 W
McKee	182	37.25 N	84.01 W
McKee City	198	39.26 N	74.37 W
McKee Creek ≃	209	39.46 N	90.36 W
McKeesport	204	40.21 N	79.52 W
McKees Rocks	204	40.28 N	80.10 W
McKenna	214	46.56 N	122.33 W
Mackenrode	50	51.33 N	10.33 E
Mackenzie	236	6.00 N	58.17 W
McKenzie, Ala., U.S.	184	31.33 N	86.43 W
McKenzie, Tenn., U.S.	184	36.08 N	88.31 W
Mackenzie □[5]	166	65.00 N	115.00 W
Mackenzie ≃	166	69.15 N	134.08 W
McKenzie ≃	192	44.07 N	123.06 W
MacKenzie Bay C, Ant.	9	68.20 S	71.15 E
Mackenzie Bay C, Can.	170	69.00 N	136.30 W
McKenzie Bridge	192	44.05 N	123.04 W
McKenzie Creek ≃	202	43.02 N	79.53 W
McKenzie Island	174	51.05 N	93.48 W
McKenzie Lake ⊜, Ont., Can.	202	45.22 N	78.02 W
McKenzie Lake ⊜, Sask., Can.	174	54.12 N	102.30 W
Mackenzie Mountains ⛰	170	64.00 N	130.00 W
McKerrow, Lake ⊜	162	44.26 S	168.03 E
Mackeyville	200	41.03 N	77.28 W
McKillip Ditch ☰	206	40.50 N	86.51 W
Mackinac, Straits of ⊔	180	45.49 N	84.42 W
Mackinac Bridge ◆[5]	180	45.50 N	84.45 W
Mackinac Island	180	45.51 N	84.37 W
Mackinac Island I	180	45.51 N	84.38 W
Mackinac Island State Park ♠	180	45.52 N	84.40 W
Mackinaw	180	40.32 N	89.21 W
Mackinaw ≃	184	40.33 N	89.44 W
Mackinaw City	180	45.47 N	84.44 W
McKinlay	156	21.16 S	141.17 E
McKinlay ≃	156	20.50 S	141.28 E
McKinley, Mount ∧	170	63.30 N	151.00 W
McKinley Airport ⊠	271	42.33 N	82.58 W
Mc Kinley Park	170	63.44 N	148.54 W
McKinley Park ♠	269b	40.25 N	80.00 W
McKinleyville, Calif., U.S.	194	40.57 N	124.06 W
McKinleyville, W. Va., U.S.	204	40.15 N	80.36 W
McKinney	212	33.12 N	96.37 W
Mackinnon Road	144	3.44 S	39.03 E
McKittrick, Calif., U.S.	216	35.18 N	119.37 W
McKittrick, Mo., U.S.	209	38.44 N	91.27 W
McKittrick Summit ∧	216	35.18 N	119.46 W
Macklin	174	52.20 N	109.56 W
McKnight Lake ⊜	174	56.03 N	101.08 W
McKnightstown	198	39.52 N	77.20 W
McKnight Village	269b	40.31 N	80.00 W
M'ačkovo, S.S.S.R.	72	55.13 N	38.40 E
M'ačkovo, S.S.S.R.	72	56.21 N	39.03 E
McKownville	200	42.41 N	73.50 W
Macksville, Austl.	156	30.43 S	152.55 E
Macksville, Kans., U.S.	188	37.58 N	98.58 W
McLarty Hills ⛰[2]	152	19.29 S	123.33 E
McLaughlin	188	45.49 N	100.49 W
McLaughlin ≃	174	53.46 N	97.38 W
McLaughlin Run ≃	269b	40.22 N	80.07 W
McLaurin	184	31.10 N	89.13 W
Maclean	156	29.28 S	153.13 E
McLean, Sask., Can.	174	50.30 N	104.04 W
McLean, Ill., U.S.	184	40.19 N	89.10 W
McLean, N.Y., U.S.	200	42.33 N	76.17 W
McLean, Tex., U.S.	186	35.14 N	100.36 W
McLean, Va., U.S.	198	38.56 N	77.11 W
Mc Lean □[6]	206	40.20 N	88.45 W
McLean Lake ⊜	174	56.27 N	109.15 W

Symbols in the index entries represent the broad categories identified in the key at the right. Symbols with superior numbers (⛰[2]) identify subcategories (see complete key on page *I* · *26*).

Kartensymbole in dem Registerverzeichnis stellen die rechts in Schlüssel erklärten Kategorien dar. Symbole mit hochgestellten Ziffern (⛰[2]) bezeichnen Unterabteilungen einer Kategorie (vgl. vollständiger Schlüssel auf Seite *I* · *26*).

Los símbolos incluídos en el texto del índice representan las grandes categorías identificadas con la clave a la derecha. Los símbolos con numeros en su parte superior (⛰[2]) identifican las subcategorías (véase la clave completa en la página *I* · *26*).

Les symboles de l'index représentent les catégories indiquées dans la légende à droite. Les symboles suivis d'un indice (⛰[2]) représentent des sous-catégories (voir légende complète à la page *I* · *26*).

Os símbolos incluídos no texto do índice representam as grandes categorias identificadas com a chave à direita. Os símbolos com números em sua parte superior (⛰[2]) identificam as subcategorias (veja-se a chave completa à página *I* · *26*).

∧	Mountain	Berg	Montaña	Montagne	Montanha
⛰	Mountains	Berge	Montañas	Montagnes	Montanhas
)(	Pass	Pass	Paso	Col	Passo
∨	Valley, Canyon	Tal, Cañon	Valle, Cañón	Vallée, Canyon	Vale, Canhão
⌣	Plain	Ebene	Llano	Plaine	Planície
≻	Cape	Kap	Cabo	Cap	Cabo
I	Island	Insel	Isla	Île	Ilha
II	Islands	Inseln	Islas	Îles	Ilhas
◆	Other Topographic Features	Andere Topographische Objekte	Otros Elementos Topográficos	Autres données topographiques	Outros Elementos Topográficos

ESPAÑOL

Nombre	Página	Lat.°′	Long.°′ W=Oeste
McLean Mountain Λ	176	47.07 N	68.50 W
McLeansboro	184	38.06 N	88.32 W
Macleantown	148	32.47 S	27.45 E
Maclear	148	31.02 S	28.23 E
Macleay ≃	156	30.52 S	153.01 E
McLennan	172	55.42 N	116.54 W
McLennan □[6]	212	31.35 N	97.13 W
Macleod	264b	37.43 S	145.04 E
McLeod ≃	172	54.08 N	115.42 W
Macleod, Lake ◎	152	24.00 S	113.35 E
McLeod Bay C	166	62.53 N	110.00 W
McLeodganj	113	30.15 N	73.42 E
McLeodganj Road	113	30.09 N	73.44 E
McLeod Lake	172	54.59 N	123.02 W
McLoughlin, Mount Λ	192	42.27 N	122.19 W
McLoughlin Bay C	166	67.50 N	99.00 W
McLoughlin House National Historic Site ⊥	214	45.20 N	122.33 W
Maclovio Herrera	222	29.05 N	105.08 W
McLure	172	51.03 N	120.14 W
McMahan	212	29.51 N	97.31 W
McMahon	174	50.05 N	107.32 W
McMasterville	196	45.33 N	73.15 W
MacMillan ≃	170	62.52 N	135.55 W
McMillan, Lake ◎[1]	186	32.40 N	104.20 W
McMinnville, Oreg., U.S.	214	45.13 N	123.12 W
McMinnville, Tenn., U.S.	184	35.41 N	85.46 W
McMurdo ✿[3]	9	77.50 S	166.25 E
McMurdo Sound ⊔	9	77.30 S	165.00 E
McMurray	204	40.17 N	80.05 W
McNair	212	29.48 N	95.02 W
McNary	190	34.04 N	109.51 W
McNeil, Ark., U.S.	184	33.21 N	93.13 W
McNeil, Tex., U.S.	212	30.27 N	97.43 W
McNeil, Mount Λ	172	54.35 N	130.14 W
McNeil Island I	214	47.13 N	122.41 W
McNeill	184	30.40 N	89.38 W
McNulty	214	45.50 N	122.51 W
Macocha V	30	49.23 N	16.45 E
Macocolo	142	6.47 S	16.08 E
Macolin	54	47.09 N	7.14 E
Macolla, Punta >	231s	12.06 N	70.13 W
Macolo	142	7.05 S	16.48 E
Macomb	180	40.27 N	90.40 W
Macomb □[6]	204	42.40 N	82.54 W
Macomb Mall ◆[9]	271	42.32 N	82.55 W
Macomer	36	40.16 N	8.46 E
Macon, Bel.	46	50.03 N	4.13 E
Mâcon, Fr.	54	46.18 N	4.50 E
Macon, Ga., U.S.	182	32.50 N	83.38 W
Macon, Ill., U.S.	209	39.43 N	89.00 W
Macon, Miss., U.S.	184	33.07 N	88.34 W
Macon, Mo., U.S.	184	39.44 N	92.28 W
Macon □[6], Ill., U.S.	209	39.51 N	89.32 W
Macon □[6], Mo., U.S.	209	39.50 N	92.20 W
Macon, Bayou ≃	184	31.55 N	91.33 W
Macon Creek ≃	206	41.58 N	83.38 W
Macondo	142	12.35 S	23.44 E
Macondo ≃	142	13.23 S	23.03 E
Mâconnais, Monts du ⛰	54	46.18 N	4.45 E
Macorís, Cabo >	228	19.47 N	70.28 W
Macosquin	42	55.06 N	6.43 W
Macossa	146	17.52 S	33.56 E
Macouba, Pointe du >	230e	14.53 N	61.09 W
Macoun Lake ◎	174	56.32 N	103.50 W
Macoupin □[6]	209	39.17 N	89.53 W
Macoupin Creek ≃	209	39.11 N	90.36 W
Macouria	240	4.55 N	52.22 W
Macovane	146	21.28 S	35.04 E
McPhail ≃	174	52.44 N	96.31 W
McPhee Bay C	202	44.35 N	79.19 W
McPherson	188	38.22 N	97.40 W
Macpherson, Mount Λ[2]	152	21.49 S	121.35 E
McPherson Range ⛰	156	28.20 S	153.00 E
Macquarie ≃, Austl.	156	41.44 S	147.08 E
Macquarie ≃, Austl.	156	30.07 S	147.24 E
Macquarie, Lake ◎	160	33.05 S	151.35 E
Macquarie Fields	264a	33.59 S	150.53 E
Macquarie Harbour C	156	42.19 S	145.23 E
Macquarie Marshes ≡	156	30.50 S	147.32 E
Macquarie Ridge ⊹[3]	9	57.00 S	159.00 E
Macquarie Rise ⊹[3]	4	55.00 S	150.00 E
Macquarie University ✿[2]	264a	33.46 S	151.06 E
McQueeney	186	29.35 N	98.02 W
McRae, Ark., U.S.	184	35.07 N	91.49 W
McRae, Ga., U.S.	182	32.04 N	82.53 W
McRae, Mount Λ	152	22.17 S	117.35 E
Macritchie Reservoir ◎[1]	261c	1.21 N	103.50 E
McRoberts	182	37.12 N	82.40 W
Mac Robertson Coast •[2]	9	68.10 S	65.00 E
Macrohon	106	10.05 N	124.56 E
Macroom	28	51.54 N	8.57 W
McSherrystown	198	39.48 N	77.02 W
Mactan Airfield ■	106	10.18 N	123.58 E
Mactan Island I	106	10.18 N	123.58 E
MacTier	202	45.08 N	79.47 W
Macuapanim, Ilhas II	236	2.35 S	65.28 W
Macuelizo	226	15.18 N	88.31 W
Macugnaga	54	45.58 N	7.58 E
Macujer	236	0.24 N	73.07 W
Macul	276e	33.30 S	70.34 W
Macúl, Parque de ♣	276e	33.30 S	70.35 W
Maculabo Island I	106	14.24 N	122.49 E
Macuma ≃	236	2.44 S	77.24 W
Macumba ≃	152	27.45 S	136.50 E
Macun	120	36.58 N	30.50 E
Macungie	198	40.31 N	75.34 W
Macunqiao	90	33.50 N	116.13 E
Macuro	236	10.39 N	61.56 W
Maçururé ≃	240	8.47 S	38.59 W
Macusani	238	14.05 S	70.26 W
Macuspana	224	17.46 N	92.36 W
Macusse	142	17.51 S	20.21 E
Macuto	276c	10.37 N	66.53 W
Macuze	146	17.42 S	37.11 E
McVeigh	182	37.32 N	82.15 W
McVeytown	204	40.30 N	77.44 W
McVickers Brook ≃	266	40.45 N	74.38 W
McVille	188	47.46 N	98.11 W
McWilliams	184	31.50 N	87.06 W
Macy	206	40.58 N	86.08 W
Mad ≃, Ont., Can.	202	44.25 N	79.54 W
Mad ≃, Calif., U.S.	194	40.57 N	124.07 W
Mad ≃, N.Y., U.S.	202	43.20 N	75.44 W
Mad ≃, Ohio, U.S.	178	39.46 N	84.11 W
Mad ≃, Vt., U.S.	178	44.18 N	72.41 W
Mada ≃	140	7.59 N	7.55 E
Madaba, Tan.	144	8.40 S	37.47 E
Ma'dabā, Urd.	122	31.43 N	35.48 E
Madadi	136	18.28 N	20.45 E
Madagascar □[1]	128 147b	19.00 S	46.00 E
Madagascar Basin ⊹[1]	10	34.00 S	38.00 E
Madagascar Plateau ⊹[3]	10	31.00 S	45.00 E
Madagasikara → Madagascar □[1]	147b	19.00 S	46.00 E
Madagaskar → Madagascar □[1]	147b	19.00 S	46.00 E
Madagiz	74	40.19 N	46.44 E
Madā'in Ṣāliḥ	118	26.48 N	37.53 E
Madajevo	70	54.48 N	44.31 E
Madam	140	7.58 N	3.32 W
Madama	136	21.58 N	13.39 E
Madamarodi	134	2.37 N	44.37 E
Madame, Isle I	176	45.33 N	61.02 W
Madan	38	41.30 N	24.57 E

FRANÇAIS

Nom	Page	Lat.°′	Long.°′ W=Ouest
Madanapalle	112	13.33 N	78.30 E
Madang, Pap. N. Gui.	154	5.15 S	145.50 E
Madang, Zhg.	90	29.58 N	116.40 E
Madang □[5]	154	5.00 S	145.30 E
Madanpur	262b	22.40 N	88.32 E
Madanpur Dabās ◆[8]	262a	28.43 N	77.02 E
Madaoua	140	14.06 N	6.26 E
Mādār Gāng ≃[1]	116	22.12 N	89.04 E
Mādāri Hāt	114	26.42 N	89.17 E
Mādārīpur	114	23.10 N	90.12 E
Mādārpur	262b	22.54 N	88.27 E
Madawaska, Ont., Can.	202	45.30 N	77.59 W
Madawaska, Maine, U.S.	176	47.21 N	68.20 W
Madawaska ≃	202	45.27 N	76.21 W
Madawaska Highlands ⛰[1]	202	45.15 N	77.35 W
Madawaska Lake ◎	202	45.20 N	78.23 W
Madaya, Mya.	100	22.13 N	96.07 E
Maḍāyā, Sūrīy.	122	33.41 N	36.06 E
Madbar	130	6.19 N	30.40 E
Maddalena, Colle della (Col de Larche))(	56	44.25 N	6.53 E
Maddalena, Isola I	36	41.13 N	9.24 E
Maddaloni	60	41.02 N	14.23 E
Maddela	106	16.21 N	121.41 E
Madden, Mount Λ	152	33.12 S	119.51 E
Madden Lake ◎[1]	226	9.15 N	79.35 W
Maddington	158a	32.03 S	115.59 E
Maddock	188	47.58 N	99.32 W
Made	48	51.41 N	4.46 E
Madeir	130	7.50 N	29.12 E
Madeira	208	39.11 N	84.22 W
Madeira I	138	32.44 N	17.00 W
Madeira ≃	232	3.22 S	58.45 W
Madeira, Arquipélago da II	138	32.40 N	16.45 W
Madeira Beach	210	27.48 N	82.48 W
Madeirinha ≃	238	8.31 S	60.46 W
Madeirinha, Paraná ≃[1]	236	3.25 S	58.51 W
M'adel'	66	54.53 N	26.57 E
Mädelegabel Λ	54	47.18 N	10.18 E
Madeleine, Îles de la II	176	47.30 N	61.45 W
Madeleine, Pointe >	265a	45.27 N	73.57 W
Madeleine-Centre	176	49.15 N	65.21 W
Madeley, Eng., U.K.	44	52.39 N	2.28 W
Madeley, Eng., U.K.	44	52.59 N	2.20 W
Madelia	180	44.03 N	94.25 W
Madeline Island I	180	46.50 N	90.40 W
Maden	120	38.23 N	39.40 E
Maden ◆[8]	257b	40.52 N	29.08 E
Madenhanları	120	40.11 N	40.25 E
Madenijet	76	47.53 N	78.37 E
Madera, Méx.	222	29.12 N	108.07 W
Madera, Calif., U.S.	216	36.57 N	120.03 W
Madera, Pa., U.S.	204	40.50 N	78.26 W
Madera □[6]	216	37.15 N	119.45 W
Madera, Volcán Λ[1]	226	11.27 N	85.31 W
Madera Canal Ξ	216	37.05 N	119.59 W
Madera Lake ◎[1]	216	37.02 N	119.59 W
Madera Peak Λ	216	37.32 N	119.23 W
Maderas, Islas → Madeira, Arquipélago da II	138	32.40 N	16.45 W
Maderno	58	45.38 N	10.35 E
Madgaon (Margao)	112	15.18 N	73.57 E
Madh ◆[8]	262c	19.08 N	72.47 E
Madhipura	114	25.55 N	86.47 E
Madhkūr, Bi'r ⊤[4]	132	30.42 N	32.32 E
Mādhopur	113	32.22 N	75.36 E
Madhubani	114	26.22 N	86.05 E
Madhudaha	262b	22.31 N	88.25 E
Madhugiri	112	13.40 N	77.12 E
Madhukhāli	116	23.33 N	89.38 E
Madhumati ≃[1]	116	22.53 N	89.52 E
Madhupar	116	22.54 N	86.28 E
Madhupur	116	24.16 N	86.39 E
Madhya Bhārat Pathār ◆[1]	114	25.00 N	77.00 E
Madhyamgrām	262b	22.42 N	88.27 E
Madhya Pradesh □[4]	110	23.00 N	79.00 E
Madi □[5]	144	3.15 N	31.45 E
Mādi ≃	114	27.49 N	84.27 E
Madia	144	7.08 S	26.00 E
Madian	96	32.15 N	119.58 E
Madianzi	95	39.39 N	117.15 E
Madibi	142	4.18 S	18.24 E
Madibira	144	8.12 S	34.49 E
Madibogo	148	26.25 S	25.10 E
Madida	88	42.57 N	130.48 E
Madidi ≃	238	12.32 S	66.52 W
Madill	186	34.06 N	96.46 W
Madimba, Ang.	142	6.31 S	14.21 E
Madimba, Zaïre	142	4.58 S	15.08 E
Madina	140	13.24 N	8.51 W
Madina do Boé	140	11.45 N	14.13 W
Madinani	140	9.37 N	6.57 W
Madīnat ash-Sha'b	134	12.50 N	44.56 E
Madingo	142	4.07 S	11.22 E
Madingou	142	4.09 S	13.34 E
Madingzi	94	42.08 N	120.52 E
Madi Opei	144	3.37 N	33.05 E
Madirobe	147b	16.04 S	46.15 E
Madirovalo	147b	16.26 S	46.30 E
Madison, Ala., U.S.	184	34.42 N	86.45 W
Madison, Calif., U.S.	216	38.41 N	121.58 W
Madison, Conn., U.S.	197	41.17 N	72.36 W
Madison, Fla., U.S.	182	30.28 N	83.25 W
Madison, Ga., U.S.	182	33.36 N	83.28 W
Madison, Ill., U.S.	209	38.41 N	90.10 W
Madison, Ind., U.S.	208	38.44 N	85.23 W
Madison, Kans., U.S.	188	38.08 N	96.08 W
Madison, Maine, U.S.	178	44.48 N	69.53 W
Madison, Md., U.S.	198	38.31 N	76.13 W
Madison, Minn., U.S.	188	45.01 N	96.11 W
Madison, Mo., U.S.	209	39.28 N	92.13 W
Madison, Nebr., U.S.	188	41.50 N	97.27 W
Madison, N.J., U.S.	200	40.46 N	74.25 W
Madison, N.C., U.S.	182	36.23 N	79.58 W
Madison, N.Y., U.S.	200	42.54 N	75.31 W
Madison, Pa., U.S.	269b	40.15 N	79.41 W
Madison, S. Dak., U.S.	188	44.00 N	97.07 W
Madison, Va., U.S.	178	38.23 N	78.15 W
Madison, W. Va., U.S.	178	38.04 N	81.49 W
Madison, Wis., U.S.	206	43.05 N	89.22 W
Madison □[6], Ill., U.S.	209	38.49 N	89.58 W
Madison □[6], Ind., U.S.	208	40.10 N	85.41 W
Madison □[6], N.Y., U.S.	200	43.05 N	75.42 W
Madison □[6], Ohio, U.S.	208	39.53 N	83.27 W
Madison □[6], Tex., U.S.	212	30.58 N	95.55 W
Madison ≃	192	45.56 N	111.30 W
Madison, West Fork ≃	192	44.55 N	111.35 W
Madisonburg, Ohio, U.S.	204	40.51 N	81.55 W
Madisonburg, Pa., U.S.	200	40.55 N	77.31 W
Madison Heights, Mich., U.S.	206	42.30 N	83.06 W
Madison Heights, Va., U.S.	182	37.25 N	79.08 W
Madison Mills	208	39.40 N	83.20 W
Madison-on-the-lake	204	41.42 N	81.24 W
Madison Park	266	40.26 N	74.19 W
Madison Range ⛰	192	45.15 N	111.20 W
Madison Square Garden ♣	266	40.45 N	74.00 W
Madisonville, Ky., U.S.	184	37.20 N	87.30 W
Madisonville, La., U.S.	184	30.24 N	90.09 W
Madisonville, Tenn., U.S.	182	35.31 N	84.22 W

PORTUGUÊS

Nome	Página	Lat.°′	Long.°′ W=Oeste
Madisonville, Tex., U.S.	212	30.57 N	95.55 W
Madiun	105a	7.37 S	111.31 E
Madiun ≃	105a	7.23 S	111.27 E
Madiyi	92	28.14 N	110.30 E
Madjingo, Congo	142	1.23 N	14.06 E
Madjingo, Gabon	142	1.22 N	14.04 E
Madjori	140	11.26 N	1.15 E
Madlangampisiberg Λ	148	27.12 S	30.28 E
Madley, Mount Λ	152	24.31 S	123.58 E
Madoc	202	44.30 N	77.28 W
Mado Gashi	144	0.44 N	39.10 E
Madol	130	9.02 N	27.46 E
Madon ≃	54	48.36 N	6.06 E
Madona	66	56.51 N	26.13 E
Madonna (Unserfrau)	58	46.43 N	10.52 E
Madonna della Guardia ✿[1]	56	44.29 N	8.51 E
Madonna della Quercia ✿[1]	60	42.25 N	12.06 E
Madonna dell'Olmo	56	44.25 N	7.32 E
Madonna del Sasso ✿[1]	54	46.11 N	8.33 E
Madonna di Campiglio	58	46.14 N	10.49 E
Madonna di Tirano	58	46.13 N	10.09 E
Madora	66	53.09 N	30.11 E
Madougou	140	14.24 N	3.05 W
Madrakah	134	21.59 N	39.59 E
Madras, Bhārat	112	13.05 N	80.17 E
Madras, Oreg., U.S.	192	44.38 N	121.08 W
Madras □[3], Bhārat	112	11.00 N	78.15 E
Madras → Tamil Nadu □[3], Bhārat	112	11.00 N	78.15 E
Madre, Laguna C, Méx.	222	25.00 N	97.40 W
Madre, Laguna C, Tex., U.S.	186	27.00 N	97.35 W
Madre, Sierra ⛰	226	15.20 N	92.20 W
Madre, Sierra ⛰, Pil.	106	16.20 N	122.00 E
Madre de Deus	245	12.44 S	38.37 W
Madre de Deus de Minas	246	21.29 S	44.20 W
Madre de Dios □[5]	238	12.00 S	70.15 W
Madre de Dios ≃	238	10.59 S	66.08 W
Madre de Dios, Isla I	244	50.15 S	75.05 W
Madre del Sur, Sierra ⛰	224	17.00 N	100.00 W
Madre Occidental, Sierra ⛰	222	25.00 N	105.00 W
Madre Oriental, Sierra ⛰	222	22.00 N	99.30 W
Madre Vieja ≃	226	14.01 N	91.26 W
Madrid, Col.	236	4.44 N	74.16 W
Madrid, Esp.	34 256a	40.24 N	3.41 W
Madrid, Pil.	106	9.15 N	126.00 E
Madrid, Ala., U.S.	184	31.01 N	85.24 W
Madrid, Iowa, U.S.	180	41.53 N	93.49 W
Madrid, Nebr., U.S.	188	40.51 N	101.33 W
Madrid, Punta >	238	19.01 S	70.19 W
Madridejos, Esp.	34	39.28 N	3.32 W
Madridejos, Pil.	106	11.18 N	123.44 E
Madrigalejo	34	39.09 N	5.37 W
Madrillon	274c	38.55 N	77.14 W
Madriz □[5]	226	13.30 N	86.30 W
Madroñera	34	39.26 N	5.46 W
Madruga	230p	22.55 N	81.51 W
Madrūsah	136	24.48 N	14.32 E
Madsen	174	50.58 N	93.55 W
Madsūs, Bi'r ⊤[4]	132	29.15 N	32.19 E
Maducang Island I	106	10.42 N	120.15 E
Maduda	142	4.55 S	13.06 E
Maduo, Zaïre	142	1.24 S	20.44 E
Maduo (Huangheyan), Zhg.	92	34.53 N	98.24 E
Madura, Austl.	152	31.55 S	127.00 E
Madura → Madurai, Bhārat	112	9.56 N	78.08 E
Madura I, Indon.	102	7.00 S	113.20 E
Madura I, Indon.	105a	7.00 S	113.30 E
Madura, Selat ⊔	105a	7.25 S	113.25 E
Madurai	112	9.56 N	78.07 E
Madurāntakam	112	12.31 N	79.54 E
Madureira ◆[8]	277a	22.53 S	43.21 W
Madureira, Serra de ⛰	277a	22.49 S	43.31 W
Maduru ≃	112	7.52 N	81.31 E
Madwar al-Bighāl Λ[2]	132	29.09 N	29.54 E
Madyan ◆[1]	118	27.40 N	35.35 E
Madžalis	74	42.08 N	47.50 E
Mãe, Ilha da I	277a	22.59 S	43.04 W
Maeander Reef ⊹[2]	106	8.05 N	119.18 E
Maebaru	82	33.33 N	130.12 E
Maebashi	84	36.23 N	139.04 E
Maeda	260	34.55 N	135.08 E
Maegye-ri	88	34.45 N	126.18 E
Mae Hong Son	100	19.16 N	97.56 E
Mae Klong ≃	100	13.21 N	100.00 E
Mae Nam Khong → Mekong ≃	12	10.33 N	105.24 E
Maenclochog	44	51.54 N	4.48 W
Maengsan	88	39.40 N	126.30 E
Maeno ◆[8]	258	35.46 N	139.42 E
Maenza	60	41.31 N	13.11 E
Mae Ramat	100	16.58 N	98.31 E
Mae Rim	100	18.54 N	98.57 E
Maerkang	92	31.50 N	102.40 E
Maerkansu	75	39.19 N	73.53 E
Ma'erna	92	31.13 N	102.02 E
Maershan Λ	92	26.18 N	100.20 E
Mae Sariang	100	18.10 N	97.56 E
Maeser	190	40.28 N	109.32 W
Mae Sot	100	16.43 N	98.34 E
Maesteg	44	51.37 N	3.40 W
Maestra, Sierra ⛰	230p	20.00 N	76.45 W
Maestre de Campo Island I	106	12.56 N	121.42 E
Maestu	34	42.44 N	2.27 W
Mae Tha	100	18.28 N	99.08 E
Maevarano ≃	147b	14.35 S	47.58 E
Maevatanana	147b	16.56 S	46.49 E
Maewo I	165f	15.10 S	168.10 E
Ma'fan	136	25.55 N	14.29 E
Mafang	95	40.03 N	116.59 E
Mafangchang	97	29.24 N	106.06 E
Mafangcun	95	40.09 N	116.24 E
Ma Faro ⊹[2]	112	5.50 N	73.26 E
Mafeking, Man., Can.	174	52.41 N	101.06 W
Mafeking, S. Afr.	146	25.53 S	25.39 E
Mafembage	142	14.32 S	21.42 E
Mafengtun	94	40.49 N	122.54 E
Mafeteng	148	29.51 S	27.15 E
Maffliers	251	49.05 N	2.19 E
Maffra	156	37.58 S	146.59 E
Mafia Island I	144	7.50 S	39.50 E
Mafou ≃	140	10.32 N	10.08 W
Mafra, Bra.	242	26.07 S	49.49 W
Mafra, Port.	34	38.56 N	9.20 W
Magadan	64	59.34 N	150.48 E
Magadi	144	1.54 S	36.17 E
Magadi, Lake ◎	144	1.52 S	36.17 E
Magaguadavic Lake ◎	176	45.43 N	67.12 W
Magai-butsu ✿[1]	86	33.05 N	131.45 E
Magalhães Bastos ◆[8]	277a	22.53 S	43.23 W
Magalhães de Almeida	240	3.24 S	42.12 W
Magaliesberg Λ	148	25.50 S	27.30 E
Magallanes → Punta Arenas, Chile	244	53.09 S	70.55 W
Magallanes, Pil.	106	12.50 N	123.50 E
Magallanes □[4]	244	51.30 S	73.30 W
Magallanes, Estrecho de (Strait of Magellan) ⊔	244	54.00 S	71.00 W
Maganga	144	0.51 N	26.22 E
Magangué	236	9.14 N	74.45 W
Maganoy ≃	106	6.55 N	124.30 E
Magansk	78	55.52 N	93.15 E
Magara, Bhārat	116	22.34 N	87.34 E
Mağara, Tür.	120	36.43 N	33.52 E
Magaramkent	74	41.37 N	48.21 E
Magaria	140	13.00 N	8.54 E
Magat ≃	106	17.02 N	121.49 E
Magazine Mountain Λ	184	35.10 N	93.38 W
Magboro	263a	6.43 N	3.24 E
Magburaka	140	8.43 N	11.57 W
Magdagači	79	53.27 N	125.48 E
Magdalena, Arg.	248	35.04 S	57.32 W
Magdalena, Bol.	238	13.20 S	64.08 W
Magdalena, Méx.	222	30.38 N	110.57 W
Magdalena, Méx.	224	20.55 N	103.57 W
Magdalena, Perú	238	6.41 S	77.50 W
Magdalena, N. Mex., U.S.	190	34.07 N	107.14 W
Magdalena □[5]	236	10.00 N	74.00 W
Magdalena ≃, Col.	236	11.06 N	74.51 W
Magdalena ≃, Méx.	222	30.48 N	112.32 W
Magdalena, Bahía C	222	24.35 N	112.00 W
Magdalena, Isla I	244	44.40 S	73.10 W
Magdalena, Punta >	236	3.56 N	77.21 W
Magdalena Contreras	276a	19.18 N	99.17 W
Magdalena del Mar	276d	12.06 S	77.05 W
Magdalena Peñasco	224	17.14 N	97.34 W
Magdalena Tequisistlán	224	16.22 N	95.15 W
Magdalen Laver	250	51.45 N	0.11 E
Magdalinovka	68	48.55 N	34.54 E
Magdeborn	50	51.14 N	12.26 E
Magdeburg	50	52.07 N	11.38 E
Magdeburg □[5]	50	52.15 N	11.30 E
Magdeburger Börde ≡	50	52.00 N	11.30 E
Magdeburgo → Magdeburg	50	52.07 N	11.38 E
Magdiwang	106	12.30 N	122.31 E
Magdonskij, Porog ⌞	78	57.45 N	100.55 E
Magé, Bra.	246	22.39 S	43.02 W
Māge, Mya.	100	26.33 N	98.33 E
Magé □[7]	277a	22.41 S	43.07 W
Magé ≃	246	22.41 S	43.03 W
Magee	184	31.52 N	89.44 W
Magee, Island >[1]	42	54.48 N	5.43 W
Magelang	105a	7.28 S	110.13 E
Magellan, Strait of → Magallanes, Estrecho de ⊔	244	54.00 S	71.00 W
Magellan-Strasse → Magallanes, Estrecho de ⊔	244	54.00 S	71.00 W
Magé-Mirim	277a	22.40 S	43.01 W
Magen	122	31.18 N	34.26 E
Magenta	56	45.28 N	8.53 E
Magenta, Lake ◎	152	33.26 S	119.10 E
Magerov	68	50.08 N	23.43 E
Magerøya I	24	71.03 N	25.45 E
Magetan	105a	7.39 S	111.20 E
Magezhuang	95	40.08 N	117.59 E
Maggia	54	46.15 N	8.42 E
Maggia ≃	54	46.09 N	8.48 E
Maggia, Valle V	54	46.17 N	8.40 E
Maggie Creek ≃	194	40.43 N	116.05 W
Maggieville	156	17.27 S	141.10 E
Maggiorasca, Monte Λ	56	44.33 N	9.29 E
Maggiore ≃	257a	43.43 N	13.06 E
Maggiore, Fosso ≃	257a	41.54 N	12.16 E
Maggiore, Lago ◎	36	46.00 N	8.40 E
Maggiore, Monte Λ	60	41.14 N	14.12 E
Maghāghah	132	28.39 N	30.50 E
Maghama	140	15.31 N	12.51 W
Maghār	122	32.53 N	35.24 E
Maghdūshah	122	33.31 N	35.23 E
Maghera	42	54.51 N	6.40 W
Magherafelt	42	54.45 N	6.36 W
Maghnia	138	34.50 N	1.50 W
Magholpur ◆[8]	262a	28.42 N	77.06 E
Maghull	42	53.32 N	2.57 W
Magician Lake ◎	206	42.04 N	86.10 W
Magicienne Bay C	164n	15.08 N	145.46 E
Magic Mountain ♣	218	34.26 N	118.36 W
Magill Heights	269b	40.37 N	79.52 W
Magill Lake ◎, Man., Can.	174	54.45 N	94.58 W
Magill Lake ◎, Qué., Can.	196	45.35 N	71.17 W
Magina Λ	34	37.43 N	3.28 W
Maginu	258	35.35 N	139.36 E
Magiolobo Bay C	106	11.07 N	125.21 E
Magione	60	43.08 N	12.12 E
Magiscatzin	224	22.48 N	98.42 W
Magiss Lake ◎	174	52.59 N	91.40 W
Maglaj	38	44.33 N	18.06 E
Magliana ◆[8]	257a	41.50 N	12.25 E
Magliana, Fosso ≃	257a	41.49 N	12.25 E
Magliano dei Marsi	60	42.05 N	13.22 E
Magliano in Toscana	60	42.36 N	11.17 E
Magliano Sabina	60	42.22 N	12.29 E
Maglie	36	40.07 N	18.19 E
Maglód	254c	47.27 N	19.21 E
M'aglovo	255a	59.53 N	30.41 E
Magna	190	40.42 N	112.06 W
Magnago	256b	45.35 N	8.48 E
Magnanville	251	48.58 N	1.41 E
Magnet	174	51.19 N	99.30 W
Magnetawan ≃	180	45.46 N	80.37 W
Magnetic Island I	156	19.08 S	146.50 E
Magnetic Springs	204	40.21 N	83.16 W
Magnetischer Nordpol → North Magnetic Pole ◆	16	76.02 N	101.00 W
Magnetischer Südpol → South Magnetic Pole ◆	9	66.40 S	140.10 E
Magnières	54	48.27 N	6.34 E
Magnitka	76	55.21 N	59.43 E
Magnitogorsk	76	53.27 N	59.04 E
Magnitostroj	70	51.43 N	53.05 E
Magnolia, Ark., U.S.	184	33.16 N	93.14 W
Magnolia, Del., U.S.	198	39.04 N	75.29 W
Magnolia, Mass., U.S.	273	42.35 N	70.43 W
Magnolia, Minn., U.S.	188	43.39 N	96.05 W
Magnolia, Miss., U.S.	184	31.09 N	90.28 W
Magnolia, N.J., U.S.	275	39.51 N	75.02 W
Magnolia, N.C., U.S.	182	34.54 N	78.03 W
Magnolia, Ohio, U.S.	204	40.39 N	81.18 W
Magnolia, Tex., U.S.	212	30.13 N	95.45 W
Magnor	26	59.57 N	12.12 E
Magny-en-Vexin	46	49.09 N	1.47 E
Magny-le-Hongre	251	48.52 N	2.49 E
Magny-les-Hameaux	251	48.44 N	2.04 E
Mago	79	53.15 N	140.13 E
Màgoé	144	15.48 S	31.43 E
Magog	196	45.16 N	72.09 W
Magog ≃	196	45.24 N	71.54 W
Magog, Lake ◎	196	45.18 N	72.03 W
Magoito	256c	38.52 N	9.26 W
Magome ◆[8]	258	35.35 N	139.43 E
Magongdang ◎	96	31.27 N	119.43 E
Magoro	144	1.44 N	34.06 E
Magothy Bay C	198	37.10 N	75.55 W
Magothy River C	198	39.04 N	76.28 W
Magoúla	257c	38.04 N	23.32 E
Magoye	144	16.00 S	27.37 E
M'agozero	66	60.21 N	34.50 E
Magpie	176	50.19 N	64.30 W
Magpie ≃, Ont., Can.	180	47.56 N	84.50 W
Magpie ≃, Qué., Can.	176	50.19 N	64.27 W
Magpie, Lac ◎	176	51.00 N	64.41 W
Magpie-Ouest ≃	176	51.02 N	64.42 W
Magra	116	22.59 N	88.22 E
Magra ≃	58	44.03 N	9.58 E
Magra Hāt	116	22.14 N	88.23 E
Magrath	172	49.25 N	112.52 W
Magrè (Margreid)	58	46.17 N	11.12 E
Magro ≃	34	39.11 N	0.25 W
Magruder Mountain Λ	194	37.25 N	117.33 W
Magsaysay (Linugos)	106	9.01 N	125.11 E
Magsingal	106	17.41 N	120.25 E
Magu ≃	240	2.56 S	41.55 W
Maguan	92	22.59 N	104.19 E
Maguanying	261a	39.52 N	116.17 E
Magude	146	25.02 S	32.40 E
Magudu	148	27.31 S	31.40 E
Magumeri	136	12.08 N	12.50 E
Māgura	114	23.29 N	89.25 E
Maguru	140	12.28 N	6.35 E
Maguse Lake ◎	166	61.40 N	95.10 W
Maguzhan	110	31.15 N	88.00 E
Magwe, Mya.	100	20.09 N	94.55 E
Magwe, Sūd.	144	4.08 N	32.17 E
Magwe □[8]	100	23.00 N	95.00 E
Magwood Park ♣	265b	43.39 N	79.30 W
Magyarország → Hungary □[1]	30	47.00 N	20.00 E
Mahābād	118	36.45 N	45.43 E
Mahābaleshwar	112	17.55 N	73.40 E
Mahābalipuram	112	12.37 N	80.12 E
Mahabe	147b	17.05 S	45.20 E
Mahābhārat Range ⛰	114	27.40 N	84.30 E
Mahabo, Madag.	147b	20.23 S	44.40 E
Mahabo, Madag.	147b	23.40 S	46.08 E
Mahād	112	18.05 N	73.25 E
Mahadday Weyne	134	3.00 N	45.32 E
Mahādebpur	116	23.51 N	89.53 E
Mahādeo Hills ⛰[2]	112	22.22 N	78.34 E
Mahādeo Range ⛰	112	17.50 N	74.15 E
Mahaena, Passe de ⊔	164s	17.33 S	149.19 W
Mahaffey	204	40.53 N	78.44 W
Mahagi	144	2.18 N	30.59 E
Mahagi Port	144	2.09 N	31.14 E
Mahai	92	38.17 N	94.13 E
Mahaicony	236	6.36 N	57.48 W
Mahajamba ≃	147b	15.33 S	47.08 E
Mahajamba, Baie de la C	147b	15.24 S	47.05 E
Mahājan	113	28.47 N	73.50 E
Mahajilo ≃	147b	19.42 S	45.22 E
Maḥajjah	122	32.57 N	36.14 E
Mahakam ≃	102	0.35 S	117.17 E
Mahālandi	116	24.04 N	88.07 E
Mahalatswe	146	23.05 S	26.51 E
Mahali Mountains ⛰	144	6.12 S	29.50 E
Mahalla el-Kubra → Al-Maḥallah al-Kubrā	132	30.58 N	31.10 E
Maḥallāt	118	33.55 N	50.27 E
Maḥallat Kayl	132	31.01 N	30.17 E
Maḥallat Marḥūm	132	30.48 N	30.57 E
Maḥallat Minūf	132	30.53 N	30.58 E
Maḥallat Zayyād	132	31.02 N	31.14 E
Maham	114	28.59 N	76.18 E
Mahamba	148	27.07 S	31.10 E
Mahānadi ≃	108	20.19 N	86.45 E
Mahānadpati	116	23.00 N	88.16 E
Mahānanda ≃	114	24.29 N	88.18 E
Mahanay Island I	106	10.12 N	124.14 E
Mahanoro	147b	19.54 S	48.48 E
Mahanoy City	198	40.49 N	76.08 W
Mahanoy Creek ≃	198	40.42 N	76.51 W
Mahantango Creek ≃	198	40.47 N	76.56 W
Mahantango Mountain Λ	198	40.40 N	76.45 W
Mahao	79	43.09 N	127.55 E
Mahape	262c	19.07 N	73.01 E
Mahārājganj, Bhārat	114	26.07 N	84.29 E
Mahārājganj, Bhārat	114	27.09 N	83.34 E
Mahārājpur, Bhārat	114	25.01 N	79.44 E
Mahārājpur, Bhārat	262a	28.39 N	77.20 E
Mahārāshtra □[3]	112	19.00 N	76.00 E
Maḥārīq, Wādī V	132	27.48 N	31.47 E
Mahārlū, Daryācheh-ye ◎	118	29.25 N	52.50 E
Mahāsamund	110	21.06 N	82.06 E
Maha Sarakham	100	16.11 N	103.18 E
Maha Sawat, Khlong Ξ	259a	13.47 N	100.28 E
Mahasoa	147b	22.12 S	46.06 E
Mahasolo	147b	19.07 S	46.22 E
Mahāsu □[5]	113	31.10 N	77.10 E
Mahates	236	10.14 N	75.12 W
Mahatsinjo	147b	21.26 S	45.51 E
Maḥaṭṭat Abū al-Lasan	122	30.05 N	35.31 E
Maḥaṭṭat Abū Jirdhān	122	30.20 N	35.46 E
Maḥaṭṭat Abū Ṭarafah	122	30.00 N	35.56 E
Maḥaṭṭat al-Furayfirah	122	30.54 N	35.59 E
Maḥaṭṭat al-Ḥasā	122	30.49 N	35.59 E
Maḥaṭṭat al-Jīzah	122	31.43 N	35.58 E
Maḥaṭṭat al-Manzil	122	31.03 N	36.01 E
Maḥaṭṭat al-Qaṣr	122	31.54 N	35.56 E
Maḥaṭṭat al-Qaṭrānah	122	31.15 N	36.03 E
Maḥaṭṭat 'aqabat al-Ḥijāzīyah	122	29.44 N	35.52 E
Maḥaṭṭat ash-Shīdīyah	122	29.56 N	35.56 E
Maḥaṭṭat as-Suwāqah	122	31.22 N	36.07 E
Maḥaṭṭat Bḥamdūn	122	33.48 N	35.39 E
Maḥaṭṭat Ḍab'ah	122	31.36 N	36.04 E
Maḥaṭṭat Faṣṣū'ah	122	29.46 N	35.54 E
Maḥaṭṭat Jurf ad-Darāwīsh	122	30.42 N	35.52 E
Maḥaṭṭat Muṣawwal	122	30.05 N	35.52 E
Maḥaṭṭat Samnah	122	30.09 N	35.39 E
Maḥaṭṭat 'Unayzah	122	30.29 N	35.48 E
Mahaut	230d	15.21 N	61.25 W
Mahavavy ≃, Madag.	147b	15.57 S	45.54 E
Mahavavy ≃, Madag.	147b	13.00 S	48.55 E
Mahaweli ≃	112	8.27 N	81.13 E
Mahaxai	100	17.25 N	105.12 E
Maḥbas, Wādī al- V	130	15.50 N	29.45 E
Mahbés	138	27.13 N	9.44 W
Mahbūbābād	112	17.37 N	80.01 E
Mahbūbnagar	112	16.44 N	77.59 E
Mahd adh-Dhahab	118	23.30 N	40.52 E
Mahdāt, Bi'r al- ⊤[4]	132	30.44 N	32.32 E
Mahe	112	11.42 N	75.32 E
Mahébourg	147c	20.24 S	57.42 E
Mahé Island I	128	4.40 S	55.28 E
Mahendraganj	110	25.20 N	89.45 E
Mahendragarh	114	28.17 N	76.09 E
Mahendragarh □[5]	114	28.20 N	76.10 E
Mahendra Giri Λ	112	18.58 N	84.21 E
Mahenge, Tan.	144	7.38 S	36.16 E
Mahenge, Tan.	144	8.41 S	36.43 E
Maheno	162	45.10 S	170.50 E
Mahesgādi	262b	22.39 N	88.33 E
Maheshmunda	116	24.13 N	86.24 E
Maheshtala	262b	22.30 N	88.15 E
Maheshwar	110	22.11 N	75.35 E
Mahespur	114	23.21 N	88.55 E
Mahgawān	114	26.29 N	78.37 E
Mahi ≃	110	22.16 N	72.58 E
Mahia Peninsula >[1]	162	39.10 S	177.53 E
Mahiāri	262b	22.35 N	88.14 E
Māhikpur	262b	22.32 N	88.14 E
Mahilāra	116	22.56 N	90.16 E
Māhīm ◆[8]	262c	19.03 N	72.49 E
Māhīm ≃	262c	19.03 N	72.51 E
Māhīm Bay C	262c	19.02 N	72.50 E
Mahina	140	13.46 N	10.51 W
Mahinerangi, Lake ◎	162	45.51 S	170.03 E
Mahinog	106	9.09 N	124.47 E
Mahīshādal	116	22.11 N	87.59 E
Mahishdānga	262b	22.54 N	88.11 E
Mahlabatini, S. Afr.	148	28.14 S	31.30 E
Mahlabatini, S. Afr.	148	27.37 S	31.42 E
Mahlberg	54	48.17 N	7.48 E
Mahlow	50	52.22 N	13.24 E
Mahlsdorf	50	52.47 N	11.13 E
Mahlsdorf ◆[8]	254a	52.31 N	13.37 E
Mahlsdorf-Süd ◆[8]	254a	52.29 N	13.36 E
Mahmūdābād, Bhārat	114	27.18 N	81.07 E
Maḥmūdābād, Īrān	118	36.38 N	52.15 E
Mahmūd-e 'Erāqī	110	35.01 N	69.20 E
Maḥmūdīyah, Tur'at al- Ξ	132	31.11 N	29.53 E
Mahmudiye	120	39.30 N	31.00 E
Mahmūdpur, Bhārat	262a	28.46 N	77.22 E
Mahmudpur, Bhārat	262b	22.41 N	88.09 E
Mahmut Bendi ◆[6]	257b	41.10 N	28.57 E
Mahmutbey	257b	41.03 N	28.49 E
Mahmutşevketpaşa	257b	41.09 N	29.11 E
Mahnomen	188	47.19 N	96.01 W
Mahoba	114	25.17 N	79.52 E
Mahogany Mountain Λ	192	43.14 N	117.16 W
Mahomet	206	40.12 N	88.24 W
Mahón	34	39.53 N	4.15 E
Mahone Bay	176	44.27 N	64.23 W
Mahone Bay C	176	44.30 N	64.15 W
Mahoning □[6]	204	41.06 N	80.39 W
Mahoning ≃	204	40.58 N	80.23 W
Mahoning, West Branch ≃	204	41.12 N	80.57 W
Mahoning Creek ≃	204	40.55 N	79.27 W
Mahoning Creek Lake ◎[1]	204	40.50 N	79.10 W
Mahony Lake ◎	170	65.30 N	125.20 W
Mahood Falls	172	51.50 N	120.39 W
Mahood Lake ◎	172	51.55 N	120.24 W
Mahopac	200	41.22 N	73.45 W
Mahopac Falls	200	41.22 N	73.46 W
Mahora	34	39.13 N	1.44 W
Mahoras Brook ≃	266	40.25 N	74.08 W
Mahrāt, Jabal ⛰	134	17.05 N	51.30 E
Mahrauli ◆[8]	262a	28.31 N	77.11 E
Mähren → Morava □[9]	30	49.20 N	17.00 E
Mahroni	114	24.35 N	78.43 E
Mahtomedi	180	45.04 N	92.57 W
Mahuiling	90	29.24 N	115.48 E
Māhul ◆[8]	262c	19.01 N	72.53 E
Mahulia	116	22.39 N	86.24 E
Mahur Island I	154	2.50 S	152.40 E
Mahuta	144	10.52 S	39.27 E
Mahuva	110	21.05 N	71.48 E
Mahwah, Bhārat	114	27.03 N	76.56 E
Mahwah, N.J., U.S.	266	41.06 N	74.09 W
Mahwah ≃	266	41.06 N	74.10 W
Mai, Île de I	265a	45.36 N	73.50 W
Maia, Am. Sam.	164y	14.13 S	169.28 W
Maia, Port.	34	41.14 N	8.37 W
Mai Aché	136	12.00 N	15.44 E
Maianga	142	14.12 S	21.45 E
Maiano	58	46.11 N	13.04 E
Maiauatá	240	1.51 S	49.02 W
Maibara	84	35.19 N	136.17 E
Maicao	236	11.23 N	72.13 W
Maîche	54	47.15 N	6.48 E
Maichen	92	20.29 N	109.59 E
Maici ≃	238	6.30 S	61.43 W
Maicurú ≃	240	2.14 S	54.17 W
Maidan ♣	262b	22.33 N	88.21 E
Maiden	182	35.35 N	81.13 W
Maidenhead	44	51.32 N	0.44 W
Maiden Newton	44	50.46 N	2.35 W
Maidens Choice Run ≃	274b	39.17 N	76.40 W
Maidstone, Austl.	264b	37.47 S	144.52 E
Maidstone, Ont., Can.	204	42.13 N	82.53 W
Maidstone, Sask., Can.	174	53.06 N	109.18 W
Maidstone, Eng., U.K.	44	51.17 N	0.32 E
Maidstone □[8]	250	51.17 N	0.35 E
Maiduguri	136	11.51 N	13.10 E
Maie	144	2.46 N	30.34 E
Maiella, Montagna della ⛰	60	42.05 N	14.07 E
Maienfeld	54	47.00 N	9.32 E
Maifeld □[9]	52	50.20 N	7.20 E
Maigaiti	75	38.55 N	77.38 E
Maigatari	140	12.46 N	9.27 E
Maignelay	46	49.33 N	2.31 E
Maigudo, Mount Λ	134	7.33 N	37.15 E
Maihar	114	24.16 N	80.45 E
Maijdi	114	22.52 N	91.06 E
Maijoma	186	28.55 N	104.21 W
Maikala Plateau ⛰[1]	114	22.30 N	81.00 E
Maikala Range ⛰	112	22.30 N	81.30 E
Maikammer	52	49.18 N	9.07 E
Maiko ≃	144	0.14 N	25.33 E
Maikoor, Pulau I	154	6.15 S	134.15 E
Mailand → Milano	56	45.28 N	9.12 E
Mailāni	114	28.17 N	80.21 E
Maili	219c	21.25 N	158.11 W
Mailiao	90	23.45 N	120.15 E
Maillane	56	43.50 N	4.47 E
Mailley-et-Chazelot	54	47.32 N	6.03 E
Maillezais	32	46.22 N	0.44 W
Mailly-le-Camp	46	48.40 N	4.13 E
Mailly-le-Château	46	47.36 N	3.38 E
Mailly-Maillet	46	50.04 N	2.36 E
Mailsi	113	29.48 N	72.11 E
Maimbung	106	5.56 N	121.02 E
Mā'īn	122	31.41 N	35.44 E
Main ≃, B.R.D.	30	50.00 N	8.18 E
Main ≃, N. Ire., U.K.	42	54.43 N	6.18 W
Maināguri	114	26.34 N	88.49 E
Mainart ≃	245	20.27 S	43.17 W
Mainau	54	47.42 N	9.11 E
Mainburg	30	48.38 N	11.47 E
Main Canal Ξ, Calif., U.S.	216	37.25 N	121.05 W
Main Canal Ξ, Calif., U.S.	216	37.23 N	120.26 W
Main Canal Ξ, Wash., U.S.	214	47.07 N	120.44 W
Main Canal Extension Ξ	214	46.24 N	120.41 W
Main Channel ⊔	180	45.22 N	81.50 W
Maincourt-sur-Yvette	251	48.43 N	1.58 E
Main Creek ≃	266	40.34 N	74.11 W
Maincy	251	48.33 N	2.42 E
Mai-Ndome, Lac ◎	142	2.00 S	18.20 E
Main Duck Island I	202	43.56 N	76.37 W
Maine	200	42.12 N	76.04 W
Maine □[9]	32	48.15 N	0.05 W
Maine □[3]	168	45.15 N	69.15 W
Mainebene □[9]	52	50.00 N	8.45 E
Maine-et-Loire □[5]	32	47.25 N	0.30 W
Mainesburg	200	41.47 N	77.07 W
Maïné-Soroa	136	13.12 N	12.02 E
Maineville	208	39.18 N	84.13 W
Mainguerin	251	48.32 N	1.51 E
Mainhardt	52	49.04 N	9.33 E
Mainit	106	9.32 N	125.32 E
Mainit, Lake ◎	106	9.26 N	125.32 E
Mainland	275	40.15 N	75.22 W
Mainland I, Scot., U.K.	28	59.00 N	3.10 W
Mainland I, Scot., U.K.	28	60.20 N	1.22 W
Mainleus	50	50.06 N	11.22 E
Mainoru	154	14.02 S	134.05 E
Mainpuri	114	27.14 N	79.01 E
Mainpuri □[5]	114	27.10 N	79.00 E
Maintenon	46	48.35 N	1.35 E
Maintirano	147b	18.03 S	44.01 E
Main Topsail Λ	176	49.08 N	56.33 W
Mainvilliers	46	48.27 N	1.28 E
Mainz	52	50.01 N	8.16 E
Maio I	140a	15.15 N	23.10 W
Maiolati Spontini	60	43.28 N	13.06 E
Maiori	60	40.39 N	14.38 E
Maipa	154	8.21 S	146.33 E
Maipo ≃	242	33.37 S	71.39 W
Maipo, Volcán Λ[1]	242	34.10 S	69.50 W
Maipú, Arg.	242	36.52 S	57.52 W
Maipú, Arg.	242	32.58 S	68.47 W
Maipú, Chile	242	33.31 S	70.46 W
Maiqihamiao	79	43.22 N	120.46 E

≃	River	Fluss	Río	Rivière	Rio
Ξ	Canal	Kanal	Canal	Canal	Canal
⌞	Waterfall, Rapids	Wasserfall, Stromschnellen	Cascada, Rápidos	Chute d'eau, Rapides	Cascata, Rápidos
⊔	Strait	Meeresstrasse	Estrecho	Détroit	Estreito
C	Bay, Gulf	Bucht, Golf	Bahía, Golfo	Baie, Golfe	Baía, Golfo
◎	Lake, Lakes	See, Seen	Lago, Lagos	Lac, Lacs	Lago, Lagos
≡	Swamp	Sumpf	Pantano	Marais	Pântano
❄	Ice Features, Glacier	Eis- und Gletscherformen	Accidentes Glaciales	Formes glaciaires	Acidentes Glaciares
⇝	Other Hydrographic Features	Andere Hydrographische Objekte	Otros Elementos Hidrográficos	Autres données hydrographiques	Outros Elementos Hidrográficos

⊹	Submarine Features	Untermeerische Objekte	Accidentes Submarinos	Formes de relief sous-marin	Acidentes Submarinos
□	Political Unit	Politische Einheit	Unidad Politica	Entité politique	Unidade Política
✿	Cultural Institution	Kulturelle Institution	Institución Cultural	Institution culturelle	Instituição Cultural
⊥	Historical Site	Historische Stätte	Sitio Histórico	Site historique	Sitio Histórico
♣	Recreational Site	Erholungs- und Ferienort	Sitio de Recreo	Centre de loisirs	Sítio de Lazer
⊠	Airport	Flughafen	Aeropuerto	Aéroport	Aeroporto
■	Military Installation	Militäranlage	Instalación Militar	Installation militaire	Instalação Militar
◆	Miscellaneous	Verschiedenes	Misceláneo	Divers	Miscelânea

ENGLISH: Name / Page / Lat.°′ / Long.°′ — DEUTSCH: Name / Seite / Breite°′ / Länge°′ E=Ost

Maiquetía 236 10.36 N 66.57 W
Maiquetía, Aeropuerto ⊠ 276c 10.37 N 66.59 W
Maira ≃ 56 44.49 N 7.38 E
Maira, Valle ∨ 56 44.30 N 7.08 E
Mairabāri 110 26.28 N 92.26 E
Mairi 240 11.43 S 40.08 W
Mairinque 246 23.33 S 47.10 W
Mairiporã 246 23.19 S 46.35 W
Mairiporã □[7] 277b 23.24 S 46.37 W
Mairipotaba 245 17.18 S 49.28 W
Maisaka 84 34.41 N 137.37 E
Maishi 90 29.11 N 113.58 E
Maisí, Cabo ≻ 230p 20.15 N 74.09 W
Maišiagala 66 54.52 N 25.04 E
Maiskhāl Island I 110 21.36 N 91.56 E
Maison de Pierre, Lac de la ⊜ 196 46.53 N 74.42 W
Maisonneuve, Parc ♠ 265a 45.33 N 73.34 W
Maisons-Alfort 251 48.48 N 2.26 E
Maisons-Laffitte 46 48.57 N 2.09 E
Maisons-Laffitte, Château de ⊥ 251 48.57 N 2.09 E
Maisse 46 48.24 N 2.23 E
Maissin 52 49.58 N 5.11 E
Mait 134 10.57 N 47.06 E
Maitani 260 34.49 N 135.22 E
Maitengwe 146 20.06 S 27.13 E
Maitengwe ≃ 146 19.59 S 26.26 E
Maithon Reservoir ⊜[1] 116 23.50 N 86.43 E
Maitland, Austl. 158b 34.22 S 137.40 E
Maitland, Austl. 160 32.44 S 151.33 E
Maitland, N.S., Can. 176 45.19 N 63.30 W
Maitland, Ont., Can. 202 44.38 N 75.37 W
Maitland, Fla., U.S. 210 28.38 N 81.22 W
Maitland ≃ 180 43.45 N 81.43 W
Maitland, Lake ⊜ 152 27.11 S 121.03 E
Maixie 90 27.38 N 115.29 E
Maíz ≃ 226 11.17 N 83.52 W
Maizefield 148 26.28 S 29.31 E
Maizières-lès-Metz 52 49.13 N 6.09 E
Maizières-lès-Vic 54 48.43 N 6.46 E
Maizuru 86 35.27 N 135.20 E
Maja ≃ 79 54.31 N 134.41 E
Majābirah, Minqār al- •[4] 132 30.16 N 29.49 E
Majačka ≃ 73 48.44 N 37.33 E
Majačnyj 76 52.41 N 55.44 E
Majadahonda 256a 40.29 N 3.52 W
Majagua 230p 21.55 N 79.00 W
Majagual 236 8.33 N 74.38 W
Majaki, S.S.S.R. 68 46.25 N 30.16 E
Majaki, S.S.S.R. 73 48.57 N 37.37 E
Majakovskij 74 42.06 N 42.48 E
Majalengka 105a 6.50 S 108.13 E
Majana, Ensenada de C 230p 22.41 N 82.45 W
Majari ≃ 236 3.29 N 60.58 W
Majchura 75 39.02 N 68.35 E
Majdal 'Anjar 122 33.42 N 35.54 E
Majdantal 75 43.41 N 68.02 E
Majd el Kurūm 122 32.55 N 35.15 E
Majeigha 130 11.33 N 24.40 E
Majenang 105a 7.18 S 108.45 E
Majene 102 3.33 S 118.57 E
Majenica 206 40.46 N 85.27 W
Majes, Río de ≃ 238 16.39 S 72.46 W
Majevica ⋀⋀ 38 44.30 N 18.55 E
Maji 134 6.11 N 35.38 E
Majiacun 96 30.08 N 119.58 E
Majiahe 92 35.20 N 104.46 E
Majiahe ≃ 88 38.09 N 117.53 E
Majiahu 94 41.13 N 121.30 E
Majiaji 90 32.32 N 118.50 E
Majian, Zhg. 90 29.19 N 119.36 E
Majian, Zhg. 90 29.43 N 120.00 E
Majiang, Zhg. 92 23.48 N 111.09 E
Majiang, Zhg. 100 26.28 N 107.28 E
Majiangzong 110 30.27 N 90.03 E
Majiaoba 92 32.14 N 104.35 E
Majiaping 92 36.31 N 103.20 E
Majiasi 95 39.03 N 117.05 E
Majiawopu 94 41.46 N 121.06 E
Majiayan 90 27.26 N 112.56 E
Majiazhai 94 42.22 N 124.04 E
Majiazhou 90 26.46 N 114.47 E
Majidun Creek ≃ 263a 6.38 N 3.28 E
Majie, Zhg. 92 23.50 N 105.07 E
Majie, Zhg. 92 25.03 N 103.45 E
Majijo 164r 6.55 N 158.19 E
Majin 90 29.18 N 118.24 E
Majinxi ≃ 90 29.00 N 118.21 E
Majinzhuangzi 94 41.55 N 123.53 E
Majishan I 96 31.26 N 120.06 E
Majītha 113 31.46 N 74.57 E
Majja 64 61.44 N 130.18 E
Majkain 76 51.27 N 75.52 E
Majkop 74 44.35 N 40.07 E
Majkor 76 59.01 N 55.54 E
Majlibaš 76 45.49 N 62.39 E
Majli-Saj 75 41.17 N 72.29 E
Majlispur 116 24.13 N 90.53 E
Majma'ah 118 25.54 N 45.20 E
Majmak 75 42.40 N 71.15 E
Majna, S.S.S.R. 70 54.07 N 47.37 E
Majna, S.S.S.R. 76 53.00 N 91.28 E
Majnan 262b 22.59 N 88.09 E
Majnic, Ozero ⊜ 170 63.15 N 176.40 E
Majno-Gytkino 170 63.36 N 176.30 E
Majno-Pyl'gino 64 62.32 N 177.02 E
Majŏn-ni, C.M.I.K. 88 39.06 N 127.07 E
Majŏn-ni, Taehan 261b 37.36 N 126.41 E
Major, Puig ∧ 34 39.48 N 2.48 E
Majorca → Mallorca I 34 39.30 N 3.00 E
Major Isidoro 240 9.32 S 37.00 W
Majorque, Île → Mallorca I 34 39.30 N 3.00 E
Majrūr 130 14.01 N 30.27 E
Majrūr, Wādī ∨ 130 15.44 N 26.26 E
Majsk 76 57.49 N 77.16 E
Majskij, S.S.S.R. 73 47.43 N 40.03 E
Majskij, S.S.S.R. 74 43.38 N 44.04 E
Majskij, S.S.S.R. 79 52.18 N 129.38 E
Majskij, S.S.S.R. 79 49.00 N 140.10 E
Majskoje, S.S.S.R. 72 56.08 N 37.55 E
Majskoje, S.S.S.R. 76 50.55 N 78.15 E
Majtan 76 45.46 N 74.20 E
Majtobe 75 43.01 N 70.35 E
Māju 116 22.37 N 88.05 E
Majuba Hill •[1] 148 27.28 S 29.51 E
Majunga 147b 15.43 S 46.19 E
Majunga □[4] 147b 17.00 S 46.00 E
Majuqiao 95 39.46 N 116.32 E
Majuro I[1] 14 7.09 N 171.12 E
Majuzigou 94 41.49 N 121.38 E
Maka 140 13.40 N 14.17 W
Makabana 142 2.48 S 12.29 E
Makabe 84 36.16 N 140.06 E
Makadasa ≃ 106 7.22 N 124.36 E
Makaha, Rh. 144 17.17 S 32.37 E
Makaha, Haw., U.S. 219c 21.28 N 158.13 W
Makaha Point ≻ 219b 22.08 N 159.44 W
Makah Indian Reservation •[4] 214 48.20 N 124.41 W
Makahuena Point ≻ 219b 21.52 N 159.27 W
Makaising 114 27.53 N 84.41 E
Makak 142 3.33 N 11.02 E
Makalamabedi 146 20.19 S 23.51 E
Makale 102 3.06 S 119.51 E
Makallé 242 27.13 S 59.17 W
Makālu ≃ 114 27.54 N 87.06 E
Makamba 144 4.08 S 29.49 E
Makanapur 262a 28.38 N 77.21 E
Makanči 76 46.48 N 82.00 E
Makanya 144 4.20 S 37.51 E
Makaoo Indian Reserve •[4] 174 53.40 N 110.02 W
Makapu Point ≻ 164v 18.59 S 169.56 W
Makapuu Head ≻ 219c 21.19 N 157.39 W
Makarakskij 76 55.36 N 88.03 E
Makarewa 162 46.20 S 168.21 E
Makari 136 12.35 N 14.28 E
Makar-Ib 24 63.39 N 49.24 E
Makaricha 24 66.15 N 58.20 E
Makarje 70 58.35 N 48.11 E
Makarjev 70 57.52 N 43.48 E
Makarjevo 70 56.06 N 45.06 E
Makarov, S.S.S.R. 68 50.28 N 29.49 E
Makarov, S.S.S.R. 79 48.38 N 142.48 E
Makarovo, S.S.S.R. 70 52.18 N 43.20 E
Makarovo, S.S.S.R. 72 54.22 N 36.40 E
Makarovo, S.S.S.R. 78 57.29 N 107.52 E
Makarska 36 43.18 N 17.02 E
Makasar → Ujung Pandang 102 5.07 S 119.24 E
Makasar, Selat (Makassar Strait) ⊔ 102 2.00 S 117.30 E
Makaševka 70 51.30 N 42.36 E
Makassar Strait → Makasar, Selat ⊔ 102 2.00 S 117.30 E
Makasuko 144 6.00 S 34.56 E
Makat 70 47.39 N 53.19 E
Makatea I 14 15.50 S 148.15 W
Makati 259f 14.34 N 121.02 E
Makaw, Mya. 100 26.27 N 96.42 E
Makaw, Zaïre 142 3.29 S 18.19 E
Makawao 219a 20.52 N 156.19 W
Makaweli 219b 21.55 N 159.38 W
Makay, Massif du ⋀⋀ 147b 21.15 S 45.15 E
Makaya 142 3.22 S 18.02 E
Makaza)(38 41.16 N 25.26 E
Makedonija □[3] 38 41.50 N 22.00 E
Makefu 164v 18.59 S 169.55 W
Makehahu ⊜ 110 35.00 N 83.03 E
Makejevka, S.S.S.R. 68 50.40 N 31.50 E
Makejevka, S.S.S.R. 73 49.14 N 37.59 E
Makejevka, S.S.S.R. 73 48.02 N 37.58 E
Makemie Park 198 37.55 N 75.34 W
Makemo I[1] 14 16.35 S 143.40 W
Makena 219a 20.39 N 156.27 W
Makeni 140 8.53 N 12.03 W
Makere 144 4.17 S 30.25 E
Maketu 162 37.46 S 176.27 E
Makeyevka → Makejevka 73 48.02 N 37.58 E
Makgadikgadi Pans ⌣ 146 20.45 S 25.30 E
Makhachkala → Machačkala 74 42.58 N 47.30 E
Makhad 113 33.08 N 71.44 E
Makhaleng ≃ 148 30.20 S 27.23 E
Mākhālpur 262b 22.56 N 88.10 E
Makham 100 12.40 N 102.12 E
Makhdūmnagar 114 26.28 N 82.46 E
Makhfar al-Quwayrah 122 29.48 N 35.19 E
Makhrūq, Wādī al- ∨ 122 31.30 N 37.10 E
Makhyah, Wādī ∨ 134 16.55 N 48.41 E
Maki, Indon. 154 3.11 S 134.14 E
Maki, Nihon 82 37.45 N 138.53 E
Maki, Nihon 260 34.52 N 135.04 E
Makikihi 162 44.38 S 171.09 E
Makilala 106 6.55 N 125.05 E
Makin I[1] 14 3.07 N 172.48 E
Makindu 144 2.17 S 37.49 E
Makino, Nihon 84 35.28 N 136.05 E
M'akino, S.S.S.R. 255b 55.48 N 37.22 E
Makinsk 76 52.37 N 70.26 E
Makio-dam •[6] 84 35.50 N 137.36 E
Makioka 84 35.45 N 138.43 E
Makira Bay C 165e 10.25 S 161.29 E
M'akiševo 66 56.34 N 28.53 E
M'akit 64 61.24 N 152.09 E
Makkah (Mecca) 134 21.27 N 39.49 E
Makkavejevo 78 51.44 N 113.58 E
Makkum 48 53.04 N 5.24 E
Maklakovo 76 58.16 N 92.29 E
Makó, Magy. 30 46.13 N 20.29 E
Mako, Sén. 140 12.52 N 12.21 W
Makobe Lake ⊜ 180 47.27 N 80.25 W
Makoka 144 2.34 S 25.29 E
Makok-ni 261b 37.43 N 126.38 E
Makokou 142 0.34 N 12.52 E
Makoli 144 17.27 S 26.05 E
Makongai I 165g 17.27 S 178.58 E
Makongo 144 3.25 N 26.22 E
Makongolosi 144 8.24 S 33.09 E
Makopse 74 43.59 N 39.13 E
Makorako ∧ 162 39.09 S 176.02 E
Makoro 144 3.08 N 29.44 E
Makošino 68 51.27 N 32.18 E
Makotuku 162 40.07 S 176.14 E
Makoua 142 0.01 N 15.39 E
Makov 30 49.23 N 18.30 E
Makovskoje 76 58.12 N 90.52 E
Maków Mazowiecki 30 52.52 N 21.06 E
Maków Podhalański 30 49.44 N 19.41 E
Makrai 114 22.04 N 77.06 E
Makrampur 116 22.44 N 90.14 E
Makrāna 110 27.03 N 74.43 E
M'aksa 66 58.54 N 38.12 E
Maksaticha 66 57.48 N 35.53 E
Maksimicha 78 53.15 N 108.43 E
Maksimkin Jar 76 58.42 N 86.48 E
Maksimoviči 68 51.13 N 29.37 E
Maksimovka, S.S.S.R. 70 52.59 N 51.10 E
Maksimovka, S.S.S.R. 73 47.38 N 37.34 E
Maksimovo 72 56.20 N 35.58 E
Maksudangarh 114 24.03 N 77.15 E
Maktau 144 3.24 S 38.08 E
Makteïr ⊽[4] 138 22.10 N 10.50 W
Makthar 138 35.51 N 9.12 E
Mākū, Īrān 118 39.17 N 44.31 E
Maku, Zhg. 95 39.33 N 114.46 E
Makuhari 258 35.39 N 140.03 E
Makuliro 144 9.35 S 37.26 E
Mākum 92 27.30 N 95.27 E
Makumbako 144 8.51 S 34.50 E
Makumbi 142 5.51 S 20.41 E
Makunudu I 112 6.25 N 72.41 E
Makunudu Atoll I[1] 112 6.20 N 72.36 E
Makura I 165f 17.08 S 168.27 E
Makuragi-san ∧ 86 35.32 N 133.08 E
Makurazaki 82 31.16 N 130.19 E
Makurdi 140 7.45 N 8.32 E
Makushin Volcano ∧[1] 170 53.53 N 166.50 W
Makušino 76 55.13 N 67.13 E
Makuyuni 144 3.33 S 36.06 E
Makwa Lake ⊜ 174 54.04 N 109.15 W
Makwānpur Garhi 114 27.25 N 85.08 E
Makwassie 148 27.26 S 26.00 E
Makwende-Bayo 144 7.08 S 28.06 E
Makwiro 144 17.58 S 30.28 E
Māl, Bhārat 114 26.52 N 88.44 E
Mal, Maur. 140 16.58 N 13.23 W
Mala, Perú 238 12.39 S 76.38 W
Malå, Sve. 26 65.11 N 18.44 E
Mala, Punta ≻, C.R. 226 9.05 N 83.41 W
Mala, Punta ≻, Pan. 236 7.28 N 80.00 W
Mala, Río de ≃ 238 12.40 S 76.41 W
Malabadi 120 38.09 N 41.12 E
Malabang 106 7.38 N 124.03 E
Malabar, Austl. 264a 33.58 S 151.15 E
Malabar, Fla., U.S. 210 28.00 N 80.34 W
Malabar Coast •[2] 112 10.00 N 76.15 E
Malabar Farm ⊥ 204 40.38 N 82.25 W
Malabar Hill ∧[2] 262c 18.57 N 72.48 E
Malabar Point ≻ 262c 18.57 N 72.47 E
Malabo 142 3.45 N 8.47 E
Malabon 106 14.39 N 120.57 E
Mal Abrigo 248 34.09 S 56.57 W
Malabrigo Point ≻ 106 13.36 N 121.15 E
Malabuyoc 106 9.39 N 123.19 E
Malaca, Estrecho de → Malacca, Strait of ⊔ 100 2.30 N 101.20 E
Malacacheta 245 17.50 S 42.05 W
Malacca, Strait of ⊔ 100 2.30 N 101.20 E
Malachovka 72 55.39 N 38.00 E
Malachovo, S.S.S.R. 72 54.22 N 37.31 E
Malachovo, S.S.S.R. 72 54.45 N 37.27 E
Malachovskij 70 49.08 N 41.43 E
Malacky 30 48.27 N 17.00 E
Mālād •[8] 262c 19.11 N 72.51 E
Malad ≃ 190 41.35 N 112.07 W
Malad City 192 42.12 N 112.15 W
Malafede ≃ 257a 41.47 N 12.24 E
Málaga, Col. 236 6.42 N 72.44 W
Málaga, Esp. 34 36.43 N 4.25 W
Malaga, Calif., U.S. 216 36.42 N 119.46 W
Malaga, N.J., U.S. 198 39.34 N 75.02 W
Malaga, N. Mex., U.S. 186 32.14 N 104.04 W
Malagarasi 144 5.06 S 30.50 E
Malagarasi ≃ 144 5.12 S 29.47 E
Malagash 176 45.46 N 63.23 W
Malagasy Republic → Madagascar □[1] 147b 19.00 S 46.00 E
Malago ≃ 106 10.55 N 123.02 E
Malagón 34 39.10 N 3.51 W
Malagón ≃ 34 37.35 N 7.29 W
Malagrotta •[8] 60 41.53 N 12.20 E
Malahat 214 48.32 N 123.34 W
Malahide 42 53.27 N 6.09 W
Malaimbandy 147b 20.20 S 45.36 E
Malaisie → Malaysia □[1] 102 2.30 N 112.30 E
Malaita □[8] 165e 9.00 S 161.00 E
Malaita I 165e 9.00 S 161.00 E
Malaita Division □[5] 165e 9.00 S 161.00 E
Malaja Belaja ≃ 78 52.52 N 103.05 E
Malaja Beloz'orka 68 47.14 N 34.56 E
Malaja Bessergenovka 73 47.09 N 38.36 E
Malaja Bira ≃ 79 48.07 N 133.14 E
Malaja Borščovka 72 56.33 N 36.53 E
Malaja Bykovka 70 51.54 N 47.45 E
Malaja Čuja ≃ 78 58.56 N 112.13 E
Malaja Devica 68 50.41 N 32.10 E
Malaja Doroginka 72 54.06 N 38.56 E
Malaja Dubna 72 55.52 N 38.58 E
Malaja Istra ≃ 72 55.54 N 36.50 E
Malaja Ižmora 70 53.33 N 42.50 E
Malaja Janisol' 73 47.22 N 37.20 E
Malaja Jekaterinovka 70 51.26 N 44.17 E
Malaja Ket' ≃ 76 57.53 N 91.14 E
Malaja Kinel' ≃ 70 53.29 N 51.30 E
Malaja Kokšaga ≃ 70 56.09 N 47.53 E
Malaja Konkudera ≃ 78 57.26 N 112.37 E
Malaja Kuberle ≃ 70 47.22 N 42.17 E
Malaja Kuril'skaja Gr'ada (Habomai-shotō) II 82a 43.30 N 146.10 E
Malaja Laba ≃ 74 44.16 N 40.53 E
Malaja Neva ≃[1] 255a 59.57 N 30.15 E
Malaja Ochta •[8] 255a 59.56 N 30.24 E
Malaja Orlovka 70 47.18 N 41.24 E
Malaja Pera 24 64.11 N 54.47 E
Malaja Serdoba 70 52.28 N 44.56 E
Malaja Sestra ≃ 72 56.17 N 35.57 E
Malaja Tokmačevka 68 47.32 N 35.54 E
Malaja Višera 66 58.51 N 32.14 E
Malaja Viska 68 48.39 N 31.38 E
Malaka → Melaka 104 2.12 N 102.15 E
Malaka, Sempitan ⊔ 104 5.44 N 95.30 E
Malakāl 130 9.31 N 31.39 E
Malākand 113 34.34 N 71.56 E
Mala Kapela ⋀⋀ 36 44.50 N 15.30 E
Malakka, Strasse von → Malacca, Strait of ⊔ 100 2.30 N 101.20 E
Malakoff, Fr. 251 48.49 N 2.19 E
Malakoff, Tex., U.S. 212 32.10 N 96.01 W
Malakpur •[8] 262a 28.42 N 77.12 E
Malakwāl 113 32.34 N 73.13 E
Malala 154 5.15 S 147.10 E
Malalag 106 6.36 N 125.24 E
Malalbergo 58 44.43 N 11.32 E
Malam 136 11.27 N 20.59 E
Malamala 102 3.21 S 120.55 E
Malamaui Island I 106 6.44 N 121.58 E
Malambo, Arroyo ≃ 248 33.43 S 58.46 W
Malambunga 106 9.02 N 117.38 E
Malamocco 58 45.22 N 12.20 E
Malampaya Sound ⊔ 106 10.51 N 119.20 E
Malān 100 25.37 N 96.21 E
Malān, Rās ≻ 118 25.18 N 65.11 E
Malanao Island I 106 9.27 N 118.37 E
Malanas ≃ 106 17.41 N 120.43 E
Mālancha 262b 22.55 N 88.26 E
Mālancha ≃[1] 116 21.40 N 89.20 E
Mālandighi 116 23.33 N 87.24 E
Malandji 142 5.56 S 22.18 E
Malang 105a 7.59 S 112.37 E
Malang, Gunung ∧ 105a 7.02 S 107.01 E
Malangali 144 8.34 S 34.51 E
Malangas 106 7.37 N 123.01 E
Malanguan)(95 40.16 N 117.39 E
Malangwa 114 26.52 N 85.34 E
Malanipa Island I 106 6.53 N 122.16 E
Malanje 142 9.32 S 16.20 E
Malanje □[5] 142 9.30 S 16.30 E
Malanut Bay C 106 9.16 N 117.59 E
Malanville 140 11.52 N 3.23 E
Malanyu 95 40.14 N 117.39 E
Malanzán 242 30.48 S 66.37 W
Malapa I 165e 9.48 S 160.52 E
Malapane → Ozimek 30 50.41 N 18.13 E
Mała Panew ≃ 30 50.44 N 17.52 E
Malapantao, Mount ∧ 106 9.54 N 122.37 E
Malapardis Brook ≃ 266 40.49 N 74.25 W
Mala Pascua, Cabo ≻ 230m 17.59 N 65.55 W
Malapascua Island I 106 11.20 N 124.07 E
Mälaren ⊜ 40 59.30 N 17.12 E
Malargüe 242 35.28 S 69.35 W
Mälar-See → Mälaren ⊜ 40 59.30 N 17.12 E
Malartic 180 48.08 N 78.08 W
Malartic, Lac ⊜ 180 48.15 N 78.07 W
Malasia → Malaysia □[1] 102 2.30 N 112.30 E
Malasiqui 106 15.55 N 120.25 E
Malaspina 244 44.56 S 66.54 W
Malaspina Glacier ⊓ 170 59.50 N 140.30 W
Malaspina Strait ⊔ 172 49.44 N 124.20 W
Malassis 251 48.38 N 2.03 E
Malāṭīyah 132 28.42 N 30.51 E
Malatya 120 38.21 N 38.19 E
Malatya □[4] 120 38.30 N 38.10 E
Malaucène 56 44.10 N 5.08 E
Malaunay 46 49.32 N 1.02 E
Malaut 113 30.13 N 74.29 E
Malavalli 112 12.23 N 77.05 E
Malawali, Pulau I 102 7.03 N 117.18 E
Malawi □[1] 128; 144 13.30 S 34.00 E
Malawi, Lake → Nyasa, Lake ⊜ 144 12.00 S 34.30 E
Malawiya 130 15.16 N 36.12 E
Malaya □[9] 104 4.00 N 102.00 E
Malayal 106 7.12 N 121.57 E
Malaybalay 106 8.09 N 125.05 E
Malāyer 118 34.17 N 48.50 E
Malay Peninsula ≻[1] 100 6.00 N 101.00 E
Malay Reef ✦[2] 156 17.59 S 149.18 E
Malaysia □[1] 98; 102 2.30 N 112.30 E
Malazán, Sierra de ⋀⋀ 242 30.45 S 66.34 W
Malazgirt 120 39.09 N 42.31 E
Malbaie ≃ 176 47.39 N 70.09 W
Malbaie, Baie de C 176 48.35 N 64.14 W
Malbon 156 21.04 S 140.18 E
Malbooma 152 30.41 S 134.11 E
Malborghetto Valbruna 58 46.30 N 13.26 E
Malbork 30 54.02 N 19.01 E
Malbrán 242 29.21 S 62.27 W
Malbuisson 54 46.48 N 6.18 E
Malbun 54 47.35 N 9.33 E
Malcesine 58 45.46 N 10.48 E
Mal'cevo 72 55.56 N 37.57 E
Mal'čevskaja 68 49.04 N 40.21 E
Mal'čevsko-Polnenskaja 73 48.58 N 40.12 E
Malchanskij Chrebet ⋀⋀ 78 50.45 N 109.30 E
Malchin 50 53.44 N 12.46 E
Malchiner See ⊜ 50 53.43 N 12.38 E
Malchow 50 53.28 N 12.25 E
Malchow •[8] 254a 52.35 N 13.29 E
Malčin 78 49.44 N 93.18 E
Malcolm 152 28.56 S 121.30 E
Malcolm, Point ≻ 152 33.48 S 123.45 E
Malcom 180 41.43 N 92.33 W
Malcompeth → Mahābaleshwar 112 17.55 N 73.40 E
Malcontenta 58 45.25 N 12.13 E
Malczyce 30 51.14 N 16.29 E
Mālda 114 25.02 N 88.09 E
Mālda □[5] 114 25.00 N 88.10 E
Maldegem 46 51.13 N 3.27 E
Malden, Mass., U.S. 197 42.26 N 71.04 W
Malden, Mo., U.S. 184 36.34 N 89.57 W
Malden ≃ 273 42.24 N 71.05 W
Malden Bridge 200 42.28 N 73.35 W
Malden Island I 14 4.03 S 154.59 W
Malden on Hudson 200 42.06 N 73.56 W
Maldivas → Maldives □[1] 12 3.15 N 73.00 E
Maldive Islands → Maldives □[1] 12 3.15 N 73.00 E
Maldive Islands II 4 5.00 N 73.00 E
Maldives □[1] 12 3.15 N 73.00 E
Maldon, Austl. 159 37.00 S 144.04 E
Maldon, Eng., U.K. 44 51.45 N 0.40 E
Maldon □[8] 250 51.43 N 0.40 E
Maldonado 242 34.54 S 54.57 W
Maldonado, Punta ≻ 224 16.20 N 98.35 W
Male, It. 58 46.21 N 10.55 E
Male, Mald. 12 4.10 N 73.30 E
Male, Mya. 100 23.02 N 95.58 E
Maléa, Ákra ≻ 38 36.26 N 23.12 E
Malea, Dolok ∧ 104 0.56 N 99.38 E
Malediven → Maldives □[1] 12 3.15 N 73.00 E
Mālegaon 112 20.33 N 74.32 E
Malegno, It. 58 46.40 N 11.08 E
Malegno, It. 58 45.56 N 10.14 E
Malehra 114 24.34 N 79.19 E
Maleit, Lake ⊜ 130 7.55 N 28.35 E
Malejevka 68 47.29 N 32.43 E
Malek, S.S.S.R. 75 40.47 N 68.37 E
Malek, Sūd. 130 6.04 N 31.36 E
Malek Dīn 110 32.25 N 68.04 E
Malek Kandī 118 37.09 N 46.06 E
Malekula I 165f 16.15 S 167.30 E
Malela, Zaïre 144 4.22 S 26.08 E
Malela, Zaïre 144 2.28 S 26.09 E
Malen'ga 24 63.50 N 36.25 E
Malengoya 144 3.32 N 25.25 E
Malente 50 54.10 N 10.33 E
Maleo 56 45.10 N 9.46 E
Māler Kotla 114 30.31 N 75.53 E
Malesco 54 46.08 N 8.30 E
Malesherbes 46 48.18 N 2.25 E
Malestroit 32 47.49 N 2.23 W
Maleta 78 50.50 N 108.25 E
Malgas 148 34.18 S 20.35 E
Malgobek 74 43.32 N 44.34 E
Malgomaj ⊜ 26 64.47 N 16.12 E
Malha Wells 130 15.08 N 26.12 E
Malheur ≃ 192 44.03 N 116.59 W
Malheur, North Fork ≃ 192 43.45 N 118.04 W
Malheur, South Fork ≃ 192 43.33 N 118.10 W
Malheur Lake ⊜ 192 43.20 N 118.45 W
Mali, Cam. 136 8.28 N 12.35 E
Mali, Guinée 140 12.05 N 12.18 W
Mali, Zaïre 144 2.48 S 26.08 E
Mali □[4] 140 12.05 N 12.05 W
Mali □[1] 124 17.00 N 4.00 W
Mali I 165g 16.20 S 179.21 E
Mali ≃ 92 25.43 N 97.29 E
Maliangping 92 31.29 N 111.20 E
Malianjingzi 92 41.32 N 95.23 E
Malibamatso ≃ 148 29.20 S 29.28 E
Malibu 218 34.02 N 118.42 W
Malibu Lake ⊜[1] 218 34.07 N 118.45 W
Malienkang 259d 25.10 N 121.39 E
Maligay Bay C 106 7.30 N 123.14 E
Malighati 116 22.33 N 87.40 E
Maligne ≃ 172 52.56 N 118.02 W
Maligne Lake ⊜ 172 52.40 N 117.31 W
Malīhābād 114 26.55 N 80.43 E
Māliḥah, Wādī ∨ 132 29.21 N 32.35 E
Malik 102 0.34 S 123.14 E
Malik, Wādī al- ∨ 130 18.02 N 30.58 E
Malik Sīān, Kūh-i- ∧ 118 29.51 N 60.52 E
Mali Kyun I 100 13.06 N 98.16 E
Malili 102 2.38 S 121.06 E
Målilla 26 57.23 N 15.48 E
Malimba, Monts ⋀⋀ 144 7.32 S 29.30 E
Malim Nawar 104 4.21 N 101.07 E
Malimono 106 9.34 N 125.25 E
Malin, S.S.S.R. 68 50.46 N 29.15 E
Malin, Oreg., U.S. 192 42.01 N 121.24 W
Malinalco ⊥ 224 18.57 N 99.30 W
Malinaltepec 224 17.03 N 98.40 W
Malinau 102 3.35 N 116.38 E
Malindang, Mount ∧ 106 8.13 N 123.38 E
Malindi 144 3.13 S 40.07 E
Malindi Marinee National Park ♠ 144 3.15 S 40.10 E
Malines → Mechelen 46 51.02 N 4.28 E
Malinga 142 2.25 S 12.14 E
Malingguan)(88 37.20 N 114.00 E
Malingping 105a 6.46 S 106.01 E
Malingsbosjön ⊜ 40 59.55 N 15.27 E
Malin Head ≻ 28 55.23 N 7.24 W
Malinki 72 54.05 N 38.59 E
Malinniki 72 56.17 N 38.24 E
Malino, Indon. 102 5.15 S 119.51 E
Malino, S.S.S.R. 72 55.06 N 38.11 E
Malino, S.S.S.R. 255b 55.58 N 37.13 E
Malino, Bukit ∧ 102 0.45 N 120.47 E
Malinoa I 164w 21.02 S 175.08 W
Malinovka, S.S.S.R. 68 49.47 N 36.43 E
Malinovka, S.S.S.R. 70 51.47 N 43.26 E
Malinovka, S.S.S.R. 76 53.24 N 87.17 E
Malinta 206 41.19 N 84.02 W
Malinyi 144 8.56 S 36.08 E
Malipara 262b 22.57 N 88.14 E
Mali Rajinac ∧ 36 44.48 N 15.02 E
Malita 106 6.25 N 125.36 E
Malitbog 106 10.10 N 125.00 E
Maliuchang 97 29.05 N 104.07 E
Maliuping 97 29.55 N 106.23 E
Ma-Liu Shui 261d 22.25 N 114.12 E
Malivo 72 55.07 N 39.02 E
Maliwun 100 10.14 N 98.37 E
Māliya 110 23.05 N 70.46 E
Malizhen 92 23.10 N 104.35 E
Maljamar 186 32.51 N 103.46 W
Malka, S.S.S.R. 64 53.20 N 157.30 E
Malka, S.S.S.R. 74 43.47 N 43.21 E
Malka ≃ 74 43.44 N 44.15 E
Malkāpur 110 20.53 N 76.12 E
Malkapuram 112 17.42 N 83.16 E
Malkara 120 40.53 N 26.54 E
Malkerns 148 26.32 S 31.11 E
Malko Târnovo 38 41.59 N 27.32 E
Mallacoota National Park ♠ 156 37.30 S 149.50 E
Mallāḥ 122 32.30 N 36.51 E
Mallaig, Alta., Can. 172 54.13 N 111.22 W
Mallaig, Scot., U.K. 28 57.00 N 5.50 W
Mallala 158b 34.26 S 138.30 E
Mallamalla Range ⋀⋀ 112 15.30 N 78.50 E
Mallaoua 140 13.02 N 9.36 E
Mallapunyah 154 16.59 S 135.49 E
Mallard Reservoir ⊜[1] 272 38.01 N 122.03 W
Mallawī 132 27.44 N 30.50 E
Malleco □[4] 242 38.10 S 72.20 W
Mallémbé 142 3.32 S 10.53 E
Mallemort 56 43.44 N 5.11 E
Mallersdorf 30 48.47 N 12.16 E
Mallery Lake ⊜ 166 63.55 N 98.25 W
Malles Venosta (Mals) 58 46.41 N 10.32 E
Mallet 242 25.55 S 50.50 W
Mallig 106 17.08 N 121.41 E
Malligasta 242 29.11 S 67.26 W
Mallina 152 20.53 S 118.02 E
Malling 41 56.02 N 10.10 E
Mallnitz 58 46.59 N 13.10 E
Mallorca I 34 39.30 N 3.00 E
Mallorquinas 256d 41.28 N 2.16 E
Mallorytown 202 44.29 N 75.53 W
Mallow 28 52.08 N 8.39 W
Mallwitz → Małowice 30 51.34 N 15.27 E
Mallwood 206 42.51 N 89.02 W
Malm 26 64.04 N 11.13 E
Malmbäck 26 57.35 N 14.28 E
Malmberget 24 67.10 N 20.40 E
Malmédy 52 50.25 N 6.02 E
Malmesbury, S. Afr. 148 33.28 S 18.44 E
Malmesbury, Eng., U.K. 44 51.36 N 2.06 W
Malmesbury, Vale of ∨ 44 51.22 N 2.10 W
Malmköping 40 59.08 N 16.44 E
Malmö 41 55.36 N 13.00 E
Malmöhus Län □[6] 26 55.45 N 13.30 E
Malmsbury 159 37.12 S 144.23 E
Malmsbury Reservoir ⊜[1] 159 37.13 S 144.22 E
Malmslätt 26 58.25 N 15.30 E
Malmstrom Air Force Base ■ 192 47.30 N 111.10 W
Malmyž 70 56.31 N 50.41 E
Malna 106 8.08 N 124.27 E
Malnate 56 45.48 N 8.53 E
Malnoue 251 48.50 N 2.36 E
Malo 58 45.39 N 11.24 E
Malo I 165f 15.40 S 167.11 E
Malo, Arroyo ≃ 248 33.43 S 58.52 W
Maloarchangel'sk 66 52.24 N 36.30 E
Maloarchangel'skoje 78 50.24 N 108.50 E
Maloba 144 6.18 S 27.39 E
Maloca Velha, Igarapé da ≃ 240 6.17 S 54.32 W
Malodel'skaja 70 50.11 N 43.53 E
Maloduša 68 52.09 N 30.14 E
Maloelap I[1] 14 8.45 N 171.03 E
Malo-Iljinovka •[8] 73 48.38 N 37.59 E
Maloja 54 46.24 N 9.41 E
Malojapass)(54 46.24 N 9.41 E
Malojaroslavec 72 55.01 N 36.28 E
Malojaz 76 55.13 N 58.09 E
Maloje Goloustnoje 78 52.18 N 105.18 E
Maloje Jeravnoje, Ozero ⊜ 78 52.40 N 111.36 E
Malojekaterinovka 68 47.39 N 35.16 E
Maloje Kozino 70 56.26 N 43.41 E
Maloje More, Proliv ⊔ 78 53.20 N 107.25 E
Maloje Polesje •[1] 68 50.10 N 25.00 E
Maloje-Ščerbedino 70 51.59 N 42.50 E
Maloje Skuratovo 66 53.33 N 37.00 E
Malokirsanovka 73 47.28 N 38.31 E
Malokrasnojarka 76 56.28 N 76.01 E
Malo-les-Bains 46 51.03 N 2.24 E
Malolo 144 7.18 S 36.35 E
Malolos, Guam 164p 13.18 N 144.46 E
Malolos, Pil. 106 14.51 N 120.49 E
Malom 154 3.10 S 151.50 E
Maloma 148 27.00 S 31.40 E
Maloma ≃ 24 58.20 N 48.28 E
Malombe, Lake ⊜ 144 14.38 S 35.12 E
Malomichajlovka 68 48.06 N 36.23 E
Malonabatovskij 70 48.57 N 43.40 E
Malone, Fla., U.S. 182 30.57 N 85.10 W
Malone, N.Y., U.S. 178 44.51 N 74.17 W
Malone, Tex., U.S. 212 31.55 N 96.54 W
Malone, Wash., U.S. 214 46.58 N 123.20 W
Malonga 142 10.24 S 23.10 E
Malonno 58 46.07 N 10.18 E
Małopolska •[1] 30 50.10 N 21.30 E
Malor'azancevo 73 48.53 N 38.23 E
Malorita 68 51.47 N 24.05 E
Malorossijskij 76 53.12 N 62.30 E
Malo Strait ⊔ 165f 15.50 S 167.10 E
Malošujka 24 63.45 N 37.22 E
Maloti Mountains ⋀⋀ 148 29.05 S 28.20 E
Måløv 41 55.45 N 12.20 E
Małowice 30 51.34 N 15.27 E
Måløy 26 61.56 N 5.07 E
Malozemel'skaja Tundra •[1] 24 67.50 N 51.00 E
Malpaisillo 226 12.35 N 86.41 W
Malpartida de Plasencia 34 39.59 N 6.02 W
Malpas, Austl. 156 34.43 S 140.37 E
Malpas, Eng., U.K. 44 53.01 N 2.46 W
Malpaso 224 22.37 N 102.46 W
Malpaso, Presa de ⊜[1] 224 17.10 N 93.40 W
Malpe 112 13.21 N 74.43 E
Malpelo, Isla de I 232 3.59 N 81.35 W
Malpensa, Aeroporto di ⊠ 56 45.38 N 8.44 E
Malpeque Bay C 176 46.30 N 63.47 W
Malprabha ≃ 112 16.12 N 76.03 E
Mālpura 110 26.17 N 75.23 E
Mals → Malles Venosta 58 46.41 N 10.32 E
Mälsåkers slott ⊥ 40 59.23 N 17.18 E
Malsch 52 48.53 N 8.19 E
Målselva ≃ 24 69.14 N 18.30 E
Malta, Bra. 240 6.54 S 37.31 W
Malta, Öst. 58 46.57 N 13.30 E
Malta, S.S.S.R. 66 56.21 N 27.10 E
Malta, Ill., U.S. 206 41.56 N 88.52 W
Malta, Mont., U.S. 192 48.21 N 107.52 W
Malta, Ohio, U.S. 178 39.39 N 81.52 W
Malta □[1] 22; 36 35.50 N 14.35 E
Malta I 36 35.53 N 14.27 E
Malta ≃ 66 56.44 N 26.53 E
Maltahöhe 146 24.50 S 17.00 E
Maltahöhe □[5] 146 25.00 S 16.30 E
Malta-Tal ∨ 58 47.03 N 13.24 E
Maltby 42 53.26 N 1.11 W
Malte → Malta □[1] 36 35.50 N 14.35 E
Malte Brun, Mount ∧ 162 43.34 S 170.18 E
Maltepe, Tür. 120 40.02 N 27.58 E
Maltepe, Tür. 257b 40.55 N 29.08 E
Malton, Ont., Can. 265b 43.42 N 79.38 W
Malton, Eng., U.K. 42 54.08 N 0.48 W
Maltrata 224 18.48 N 97.16 W
Maltsch → Malczyce 30 51.14 N 16.29 E
Malugou 79 43.39 N 128.27 E
Maluku □[4] 154 5.00 S 130.00 E
Maluku (Moluccas) II 98 2.00 S 128.00 E
Maluku, Laut (Molucca Sea) ⊽[2] 98 0.00 S 125.00 E
Maluku-Maes 142 4.06 S 15.31 E
Ma'lūlā 120 33.50 N 36.33 E
Ma'lūlā, Jabal ∧ 122 33.54 N 36.36 E
Malu Mare 38 44.15 N 23.51 E
Malumfashi 140 11.47 N 7.37 E
Malunda 102 3.00 S 118.50 E
Malung 26 60.40 N 13.44 E
Maluso 106 6.33 N 121.53 E
Malūṭ 130 10.26 N 32.12 E
Maluti 116 24.09 N 87.41 E
Maluwe 140 8.40 N 2.17 W
Maluzhen 96 31.20 N 121.16 E
Malvaglia 54 46.25 N 8.59 E
Malvaglio 256b 45.31 N 8.47 E
Mālvan 112 16.04 N 73.28 E
Malveira 256c 38.45 N 9.27 W
Malvern, Austl. 264b 37.52 S 145.02 E
Malvern, Ark., U.S. 184 34.22 N 92.49 W
Malvern, Iowa, U.S. 188 41.00 N 95.35 W
Malvern, Ohio, U.S. 204 40.41 N 81.11 W
Malvern, Pa., U.S. 275 40.02 N 75.31 W
Malvern •[8] 263d 26.12 S 28.06 E
Malverne 266 40.40 N 73.40 W
Malvern East 263d 26.12 S 28.08 E
Malvern Hills 156 24.29 S 145.10 E
Malvern Hills ⋀⋀[2] 44 52.05 N 2.21 W
Malvern Link 44 52.08 N 2.18 W
Malvinas 242 29.37 S 58.59 W
Malwal 130 9.19 N 31.35 E
Mālwa Plateau ⋀⋀[1] 114 23.50 N 77.30 E
Malybaj 75 43.30 N 78.25 E
Malý Dunaj ≃ 30 48.08 N 17.09 E
Malyi Nesvetaj ≃ 73 47.32 N 39.49 E
Malyj, Ostrov I 66 60.02 N 28.02 E
Malyj An'uj ≃ 64 68.30 N 160.49 E
Malyj Barmamyt, Gora ∧ 74 43.41 N 42.27 E
Malyj Čeremšan ≃ 70 54.18 N 50.01 E
Malyj Chamar-Daban, Chrebet ⋀⋀ 78 51.00 N 105.00 E
Malyj Civil' ≃ 70 55.54 N 47.28 E
Malyje Alabuchi 70 51.33 N 42.10 E
Malyje Čany, Ozero ⊜ 76 54.33 N 78.02 E
Malyje Derbety 70 47.56 N 44.41 E
Malyje Gorod'atiči 66 52.33 N 28.20 E
Malyje Jagury 70 45.26 N 43.01 E
Malyje Kamkaly 76 44.44 N 71.31 E
Malyje Karmakuly 62 72.23 N 52.44 E
Malyje Porogi 255a 59.47 N 30.42 E
Malyj Irgiz ≃ 70 52.12 N 47.58 E
Malyj Jenisej (Ka-Chem) ≃ 78 51.43 N 94.26 E
Malyj Jugan ≃ 76 60.40 N 73.54 E
Malyj Kavkaz ⋀⋀ 74 41.00 N 44.35 E
Malyj Kemčug ≃ 76 56.55 N 91.49 E
Malyj Kundyš ≃ 70 56.22 N 47.53 E
Malyj L'achovskij, Ostrov I 64 74.07 N 140.36 E
Malyj Šantar, Ostrov I 79 54.30 N 137.36 E
Malyj Sarybulak 76 52.10 N 72.35 E
Malyj Tagul ≃ 78 54.50 N 97.23 E
Malyj Tajmyr, Ostrov I 64 78.08 N 107.12 E
Malyj T'uters, Ostrov I 66 59.49 N 26.56 E
Malyj Uran ≃ 70 52.30 N 53.01 E
Malyj Uzen' ≃ 70 48.50 N 49.39 E
Malyj Zelenčuk ≃ 74 44.24 N 41.56 E
Malyn' 72 54.36 N 38.40 E
Malyševo 66 57.50 N 35.36 E
Malzéville 54 48.43 N 6.12 E
Mama 78 58.18 N 112.54 E
Mama ≃ 78 58.18 N 112.55 E
Ma Ma Creek ≃ 161a 27.35 S 152.13 E
Mamadyš 70 55.44 N 51.25 E
Mamagota 165e 6.46 S 155.24 E
Mamahuolang 94 42.24 N 124.12 E
Mamaia 38 44.15 N 28.37 E
Mamajiecun 94 41.26 N 122.51 E
Mamakan 78 57.48 N 114.01 E
Mamaku 162 38.06 S 176.05 E
Mamakula 164v 18.57 S 169.54 W
Mamakwash Lake ⊜ 174 51.38 N 92.56 W
Mamala Bay C 219a 21.18 N 157.57 W
Mamalu Bay C 219a 20.37 N 156.09 W
Mamanguape 240 6.50 S 35.07 W
Mamanutha Group II 165g 17.34 S 177.04 E
Mamao, Hakau ✦[2] 164w 21.00 S 175.12 W
Mamara 238 14.14 S 72.35 W
Mamaregu 165e 6.32 S 155.12 E
Mamaroneck 200 40.57 N 73.44 W
Mamaroneck ≃ 266 40.57 N 73.44 W
Mamaroneck Harbor C 266 40.56 N 73.43 W
Mamasa 102 2.56 S 119.22 E
Mamasa ≃ 102 3.30 S 119.42 E
Mamba 84 36.07 N 138.55 E
Mambaí 245 14.28 S 46.07 W
Mambajao 106 9.15 N 124.43 E
Mambajao, Mount ∧ 106 9.10 N 124.44 E
Mambali 144 4.33 S 32.41 E
Mambalot 106 8.51 N 117.55 E
Mambare ≃ 154 8.20 S 147.55 E
Mambasa 144 1.21 N 29.03 E
Mambéllé 142 3.51 N 16.42 E
Mamberamo ≃ 154 1.26 S 137.53 E
Mambéré ≃ 142 3.31 N 16.03 E
Mambili ≃ 142 0.07 N 16.08 E
Mambrui 144 3.07 S 40.09 E
Mambucaba 246 23.01 S 44.31 W
Mambucaba ≃ 246 23.02 S 44.32 W
Mamburao 106 13.14 N 120.35 E
Mambusao ≃ 106 11.24 N 122.41 E
Mamdūḥ, Rujm ∧ 122 32.14 N 36.15 E
Mamedkala 74 42.10 N 48.06 E
Mamehaktebo 102 0.08 N 115.32 E
Ma-Me-O Beach 172 52.58 N 113.59 W
Mamera 276c 10.27 N 66.59 W
Mamera, Quebrada ≃ 276c 10.27 N 66.59 W
Mamers 46 48.21 N 0.23 E
Mamfe 142 5.46 N 9.17 E
Mamiá ≃ 240 1.55 S 55.07 W
Mamiá, Lago ⊜ 236 4.15 S 63.03 W
Mamie 182 36.08 N 75.50 W
Mamiña 238 20.05 S 69.14 W
Maminigui 140 7.24 N 5.50 W
Mamirolle 54 47.12 N 6.10 E
Mamisonskij, Pereval)(74 42.43 N 43.48 E
Maml'utka 76 54.57 N 68.35 E
Mammendorf 58 48.12 N 11.09 E
Mammola 36 38.22 N 16.15 E
Mammoth, Ariz., U.S. 190 32.43 N 110.38 W
Mammoth, W. Va., U.S. 178 38.16 N 81.22 W
Mammoth Cave National Park ♠ 184 37.08 N 86.13 W
Mammoth Lakes 194 37.38 N 118.58 W
Mammoth Pool Reservoir ⊜[1] 216 37.20 N 119.20 W
Mammoth Spring 184 36.30 N 91.33 W
Mamonovo, S.S.S.R. 66 54.28 N 19.57 E
Mamonovo, S.S.S.R. 255b 55.41 N 37.19 E
Mamont 269b 40.29 N 79.36 W
Mamontovo, S.S.S.R. 76 52.43 N 81.37 E
Mamontovo, S.S.S.R. 76 51.45 N 81.25 E
Mamoré ≃ 238 10.23 S 65.53 W
Mamori, Lago ⊜ 236 3.38 S 60.07 W
Mamoriá ≃ 238 7.30 S 66.21 W
Mamoriàzinho ≃ 238 7.27 S 65.18 W
Mamoritanas ≃ 236 1.39 S 67.22 W
Mamou, Guinée 140 10.23 N 12.05 W
Mamou, La., U.S. 184 30.38 N 92.25 W
Mamou □[4] 140 10.30 N 12.00 W
Mamoutzou 147a 12.47 S 45.14 E

Symbols in the index entries represent the broad categories identified in the key at the right. Symbols with superior numbers (⋀⋀[2]) identify subcategories (see complete key on page *I* · *26*).

Kartensymbole in dem Registerverzeichnis stellen die rechts in Schlüssel erklärten Kategorien dar. Symbole mit hochgestellten Ziffern (⋀⋀[2]) bezeichnen Unterabteilungen einer Kategorie (vgl. vollständiger Schlüssel auf Seite *I* · *26*).

Los símbolos incluídos en el texto del índice representan las grandes categorías identificadas con la clave a la derecha. Los símbolos con numeros en su parte superior (⋀⋀[2]) identifican las subcategorías (véase la clave completa en la página *I* · *26*).

Les symboles de l'index représentent les catégories indiquées dans la légende à droite. Les symboles suivis d'un indice (⋀⋀[2]) représentent des sous-catégories (voir légende complète à la page *I* · *26*).

Os símbolos incluídos no texto do índice representam as grandes categorias identificadas com a chave à direita. Os símbolos com números em sua parte superior (⋀⋀[2]) identificam as subcategorias (veja-se a chave completa à página *I* · *26*).

Symbol	English	Deutsch	Español	Français	Português
∧	Mountain	Berg	Montaña	Montagne	Montanha
⋀⋀	Mountains	Berge	Montañas	Montagnes	Montanhas
)(	Pass	Pass	Paso	Col	Passo
∨	Valley, Canyon	Tal, Cañon	Valle, Cañón	Vallée, Canyon	Vale, Canhão
⌣	Plain	Ebene	Llano	Plaine	Planície
≻	Cape	Kap	Cabo	Cap	Cabo
I	Island	Insel	Isla	Île	Ilha
II	Islands	Inseln	Islas	Îles	Ilhas
•	Other Topographic Features	Andere Topographische Objekte	Otros Elementos Topográficos	Autres données topographiques	Outros Elementos Topográficos

ESPAÑOL — Nombre | Página | Lat.°′ | Long.°′ W=Oeste
FRANÇAIS — Nom | Page | Lat.°′ | Long.°′ W=Ouest
PORTUGUÊS — Nome | Página | Lat.°′ | Long.°′ W=Oeste

Nombre	Página	Lat.°′	Long.°′ W=Oeste
Mampikony	147b	16.06 S	47.38 E
Mampong	140	7.04 N	1.24 W
Mamraš	74	41.44 N	48.19 E
Mamre	148	33.30 S	18.29 E
Mamry, Jezioro ⊜	30	54.08 N	21.42 E
Mamué	142	13.35 S	13.13 E
Mamuju	102	2.41 S	118.54 E
Mamulique	186	26.08 N	100.20 W
Ma'mūn	130	12.15 N	22.41 E
Mamuno	146	22.16 S	20.01 E
Mamure	120	40.08 N	35.18 E
Mamuru ≃	240	2.42 S	56.44 W
Mamykovo	70	54.38 N	50.37 E
Mamyl'	24	61.57 N	56.41 E
Man, Bhārat	110	33.51 N	78.32 E
Man, C. Iv.	140	7.24 N	7.33 W
Man, W. Va., U.S.	182	37.45 N	81.53 W
Man □[5]	140	7.15 N	7.30 W
Man (Île de) → Isle of Man □[2]	42	54.15 N	4.30 W
Man, Isle of → Isle of Man □[2]	42	54.15 N	4.30 W
Mana	219b	22.02 N	159.46 W
Mana ≃, Guy. fr.	240	5.44 N	53.54 W
Mana ≃, S.S.S.R.	76	55.57 N	92.28 E
Manabí □[4]	236	0.40 S	80.05 W
Manabique, Punta de ≻	226	15.56 N	88.37 W
Manacá ≃	236	2.52 S	61.50 W
Manacacías ≃	236	4.23 N	72.04 W
Manacapuru	236	3.18 S	60.37 W
Manacor	34	39.34 N	3.12 E
Manado	102	1.29 N	124.51 E
Managua, Cuba	276b	22.58 N	82.17 W
Managua, Nic.	226	12.09 N	86.17 W
Managua □[5]	226	12.00 N	86.25 W
Managua, Aeropuerto ⊠	276b	23.00 N	82.17 W
Managua, Lago de ⊜	226	12.20 N	86.20 W
Manahawkin	198	39.42 N	74.16 W
Manahawkin Bay C	198	39.40 N	74.12 W
Manaia	162	39.33 S	174.08 E
Manā'if, Bi'r al- ⍑[4]	132	30.31 N	32.12 E
Manajenki	66	53.42 N	36.27 E
Manakalampona ∧	147b	15.23 S	48.50 E
Manakara	147b	22.08 S	48.01 E
Manakau	162	40.43 S	175.13 E
Manakau ∧	162	42.14 S	173.37 E
Manākhah	134	15.07 N	43.44 E
Manalapan Brook ≃	266	40.24 N	74.23 W
Manāli	113	32.16 N	77.10 E
Manama → Al-Manāmah	118	26.13 N	50.35 E
Manambaroa ≃	147b	17.41 S	44.04 E
Manambato, Madag.	147b	13.14 S	49.54 E
Manambato, Madag.	147b	13.43 S	49.07 E
Manambolo ≃	147b	19.18 S	44.24 E
Manambolosy	147b	16.02 S	49.40 E
Manam Island I	154	4.05 S	145.05 E
Mánamo, Caño ≃[1]	236	9.55 N	62.16 W
Manamoc Island I	106	11.19 N	120.41 E
Manampatrana	147b	21.40 S	47.35 E
Manana I	219c	21.20 N	157.40 W
Mananantanana ≃	147b	21.25 S	45.33 E
Mananao	106	13.30 N	120.34 E
Mananara	147b	16.10 S	49.46 E
Mananara ≃	147b	23.21 S	47.42 E
Manandaza	147b	19.19 S	45.23 E
Mananjary	147b	21.13 S	48.20 E
Manankoro	140	10.28 N	7.27 W
Manantenina	147b	24.17 S	47.19 E
Manantiales Behr	244	45.41 S	67.31 W
Manantico Creek ≃	198	39.20 N	75.00 W
Mānānwala	113	31.38 N	74.18 E
Manaoag	106	16.03 N	120.29 E
Manaoba I	165e	8.18 S	160.47 E
Manáos → Manaus	236	3.08 S	60.01 W
Manapiare ≃	236	5.04 N	66.30 W
Manapire ≃	236	7.42 N	66.07 W
Manapla	106	10.58 N	123.07 E
Manapouri	162	45.34 S	167.36 E
Manapouri, Lake ⊜	162	45.30 S	167.30 E
Manappārai	112	10.36 N	78.25 E
Manaquiri, Lago ⊜	236	3.29 S	60.31 W
Manār ≃	112	18.39 N	77.44 E
Manaravolo	147b	23.59 S	45.39 E
Manas	134	2.52 N	43.26 E
Manās ≃	110	26.13 N	90.38 E
Manas, Gora ∧	75	42.18 N	71.01 E
Ma'nasaluowochi ⊜	110	30.42 N	81.27 E
Ma'nasi	76	44.18 N	86.13 E
Ma'nasihu ⊜	76	45.45 N	85.55 E
Manāslu ∧	114	28.33 N	84.33 E
Manasota Key I	210	26.58 N	82.23 W
Manasquan	198	40.07 N	74.03 W
Manasquan ≃	198	40.06 N	74.02 W
Manassa	190	37.11 N	105.56 W
Manassas	198	38.45 N	77.28 W
Manassas National Battlefield Park ♠	198	38.50 N	77.32 W
Manassas Park	198	38.47 N	77.28 W
Manastash Creek ≃	214	46.59 N	120.35 W
Manastash Creek, North Fork ≃	214	46.57 N	120.44 W
Manastash Creek, South Fork ≃	214	46.57 N	120.44 W
Manastash Ridge ∧	214	46.55 N	120.30 W
Manastırbükü	120	40.48 N	38.56 E
Manatang	102	8.26 S	124.28 E
Maná-Tará, Cerro ∧	236	10.06 N	72.52 W
Manatawny	198	40.17 N	75.41 W
Manatawny Creek ≃	198	40.14 N	75.39 W
Manatee □[6]	210	27.26 N	82.25 W
Manatee ≃	210	27.32 N	82.38 W
Manatee, Lake ⊜[1]	210	27.29 N	82.20 W
Manatí, Col.	236	10.27 N	74.58 W
Manatí, Cuba	230p	21.19 N	76.56 W
Manatí, P.R.	230m	18.26 N	66.29 W
Manatí ≃	230p	21.40 N	79.50 W
Manaul	106	12.27 N	121.25 E
Manaung	100	18.51 N	93.44 E
Manaus	236	3.08 S	60.01 W
Manavgat	120	36.47 N	31.26 E
Manawa	180	44.28 N	88.55 W
Manawai	165e	9.05 S	161.11 E
Manawan Lake ⊜	174	55.24 N	103.14 W
Manāwar	110	22.14 N	75.05 E
Manawatu ≃	162	40.28 S	175.13 E
Manawoka, Pulau I	154	4.05 S	131.20 E
Manay	106	7.13 N	126.32 E
Manayunk ⬥[8]	275	40.01 N	75.13 W
Manazuru	84	35.09 N	139.08 E
Manazuru-misaki ≻	84	35.08 N	139.10 E
Manban	92	23.04 N	103.11 E
Mānbāzār	116	23.04 N	86.39 E
Manbian	92	24.19 N	100.32 E
Manbij	120	36.31 N	37.57 E
Mancelona	180	44.54 N	85.04 W
Mancenillier, Anse du C	231o	16.15 N	61.15 W
Mancha Blanca	244	40.47 S	65.27 W
Mancha Real	34	37.47 N	3.37 W
Manchaug	197	42.06 N	71.45 W
Manche □[5]	32	49.00 N	1.10 W
Mancheng	95	38.56 N	115.20 E
Mancherāl	112	18.52 N	79.26 E
Manchester, Eng., U.K.	42, 252	53.30 N	2.15 W
Manchester, Conn., U.S.	197	41.47 N	72.31 W
Manchester, Ga., U.S.	182	32.51 N	84.37 W
Manchester, Ill., U.S.	209	39.33 N	90.20 W
Manchester, Iowa, U.S.	180	42.29 N	91.27 W
Manchester, Ky., U.S.	182	37.09 N	83.46 W
Manchester, Mass., U.S.	197	42.34 N	70.46 W
Manchester, Mich., U.S.	206	42.09 N	84.02 W
Manchester, N.H., U.S.	178	42.59 N	71.28 W
Manchester, N.Y., U.S.	200	42.58 N	77.14 W
Manchester, Ohio, U.S.	208	38.41 N	83.36 W
Manchester, Pa., U.S.	198	40.04 N	76.43 W
Manchester, Tenn., U.S.	184	35.29 N	86.05 W
Manchester, Vt., U.S.	178	43.10 N	73.05 W
Manchester, Wash., U.S.	214	47.33 N	122.33 W
Manchester □[8]	252	53.27 N	2.13 W
Manchester Airport ⊠	42	53.21 N	2.15 W
Manchester Bridge	200	41.41 N	73.52 W
Manchester City Football Ground ♠	252	53.27 N	2.14 W
Manchester Docks ⬥[5]	252	53.28 N	2.17 W
Manchester Race Course ♠	252	53.30 N	2.16 W
Manchester Ship Canal ☰	252	53.19 N	2.57 W
Manchester United Football Ground ♠	252	53.28 N	2.18 W
Manchioneal	231q	18.02 N	76.17 W
Manchouli → Manzhouli	78	49.35 N	117.22 E
Manchuria ⬥[1]	80	47.00 N	125.00 E
Manciano	60	42.35 N	11.31 E
Mancieulles	52	49.17 N	5.53 E
Máncora	236	4.06 S	81.05 W
Mancornado, Isla I	226	11.10 N	85.02 W
Mancos	190	37.21 N	108.18 W
Mancos ≃	190	36.59 N	108.59 W
Mand	118	26.07 N	62.03 E
Mānd ≃, Bhārat	110	21.42 N	83.15 E
Mand ≃, Bhārat	114	21.58 N	83.13 E
Mand ≃, Īrān	118	28.11 N	51.17 E
Manda, Bhārat	116	22.06 N	86.14 E
Manda, Tan.	144	7.58 S	32.26 E
Manda, Tan.	144	8.30 S	32.44 E
Manda, Tan.	144	10.28 S	34.35 E
Manda, Jabal ∧	130	8.39 N	24.27 E
Mandabe, Madag.	147b	21.03 S	44.55 E
Mandabe, Madag.	147b	20.55 S	45.49 E
Mandach	92	44.27 N	108.20 E
Mandaguaçu	245	23.20 S	52.05 W
Mandaguari, Bra.	245	23.32 S	51.42 W
Mandaguari, Bra.	246	21.31 S	45.43 W
Mandai	261c	1.25 N	103.45 E
Manda Island I	144	2.15 S	40.57 E
Mandal	26	58.02 N	7.27 E
Mandal, Jibāl ∧[2]	130	12.09 N	29.31 E
Mandala, Puncak ∧	154	4.44 S	140.20 E
Mandalay	100	22.00 N	96.05 E
Mandalay □[5]	100	22.00 N	96.00 E
Mandale	206	41.01 N	84.20 W
Mandale Station ⬥[5]	262c	19.03 N	72.56 E
Mandalgov'	92	45.45 N	106.20 E
Mandalī	118	33.45 N	45.32 E
Mandalkia	262b	22.43 N	88.08 E
Mandal-Ovoo	92	44.22 N	104.20 E
Mandalselva ≃	26	58.02 N	7.28 E
Mandaluyong	259f	14.35 N	121.02 E
Mandalya Körfezi C	120	37.12 N	27.20 E
Mandan	188	46.50 N	100.54 W
Mandāoli ⬥[8]	262a	28.38 N	77.18 E
Mandaon	106	12.14 N	123.17 E
Mandaoua Gadaoulé	136	14.14 N	11.01 E
Mandapeta	112	16.52 N	81.56 E
Mandapur	116	23.00 N	88.29 E
Mandar, Tanjung ≻	102	3.33 S	118.56 E
Mandar, Teluk C	102	3.40 S	119.15 E
Mandara Mountains (Monts Mandara) ∧∧	136	10.45 N	13.40 E
Mandas	36	39.39 N	9.08 E
Mandasor	110	24.04 N	75.04 E
Mandaue	106	10.20 N	123.56 E
Mandāwar	114	29.30 N	78.08 E
Mandeb, Bāb el- Ʉ	134	12.40 N	43.20 E
Mandehu	94	42.07 N	121.33 E
Mandel	118	33.17 N	61.52 E
Mandélia	136	11.43 N	15.15 E
Mandelieu	56	43.33 N	6.56 E
Mandello del Lario	54	45.54 N	9.19 E
Mandera	144	3.56 N	41.52 E
Manderfeld	52	50.20 N	6.20 E
Manderscheid	52	50.05 N	6.49 E
Manderson	192	44.16 N	107.58 W
Mandeure	54	47.27 N	6.48 E
Mandeville, Qué., Can.	196	46.22 N	73.22 W
Mandeville, Jam.	231q	18.02 N	77.30 W
Mandeville, N.Z.	162	46.00 S	168.49 E
Mandeville, La., U.S.	184	30.22 N	90.04 W
Mandi	113	31.43 N	76.55 E
Mandiana	140	10.38 N	8.41 W
Mandiangin	102	2.01 S	102.58 E
Mandi Angin, Gunong ∧	104	4.42 N	102.52 E
Mandi Bahāuddīn	113	32.35 N	73.30 E
Mandi Būrewāla	113	31.29 N	72.39 E
Mandi Dabwāli	113	29.58 N	74.42 E
Mandié	144	16.30 S	33.30 E
Mandimba	144	14.21 S	35.39 E
Mandinga	236	9.27 N	79.04 W
Mandioli, Pulau I	98	0.44 S	127.14 E
Mandioré, Lagoa ⊜	238	18.08 S	57.33 W
Mandira ⊜[1]	114	22.20 N	84.35 E
Mandiri ≃	105a	7.02 S	106.32 E
Mandi Sādiqganj	113	30.20 N	73.44 E
Mandjafa	136	11.11 N	15.25 E
Mandjé, Lac ⊜	142	1.01 S	9.31 E
Mandji-Kili	142	1.36 S	10.26 E
Mandla	114	22.36 N	80.23 E
Mandla □[5]	114	22.50 N	80.50 E
Mandling	58	47.24 N	13.34 E
Mandora	152	19.44 S	120.51 E
Mandoto	147b	19.34 S	46.17 E
Mandoul ≃	136	8.56 N	17.58 E
Mandouri	140	10.51 N	0.49 E
Māndrā, Bhārat	262b	22.55 N	88.07 E
Mándra, Ellás	257c	38.04 N	23.30 E
Mandra, Pāk.	113	33.22 N	73.14 E
Mandrare ≃	147b	25.10 S	46.27 E
Mandres-les-Roses	251	48.42 N	2.33 E
Mandriola ⬥[8]	257a	41.45 N	12.30 E
Mandriole	58	44.33 N	12.14 E
Mandrioli, Passo dei)(	58	43.48 N	11.55 E
Mandritsara	147b	15.50 S	48.49 E
Mandronarivo	147b	21.07 S	45.38 E
Māndu	112	22.22 N	75.23 E
Mandu ≃	246	22.14 S	45.55 W
Manduhu	94	41.36 N	122.38 E
Mandun	92	22.17 N	100.05 E
Mandurah	158a	32.32 S	115.43 E
Manduri	245	23.01 S	49.19 W
Manduria	36	40.24 N	17.38 E
Māndvi, Bhārat	110	21.15 N	73.18 E
Māndvi, Bhārat	110	22.50 N	69.22 E
Mandvi ⬥[8]	262c	18.57 N	72.50 E
Mandya	112	12.33 N	76.54 E
Mané	140	12.59 N	1.21 W
Måne ≃	26	59.00 N	9.40 E
Manea	44	52.30 N	0.11 E
Maneadero ≃	230p	21.42 N	78.47 W
Manebach	50	50.41 N	10.51 E
Mānebhanjyāng	114	27.12 N	86.26 E
Manek Urai	104	5.23 N	102.14 E
Manele Bay C	219a	20.45 N	156.53 W
Manendragarh	114	23.13 N	82.13 E
Manera	147b	22.55 S	44.20 E
Manerbio	58	45.21 N	10.08 E
Manevići	68	51.17 N	25.33 E
Manfalūṭ	132	27.19 N	30.58 E
Manfredonia	60	41.38 N	15.55 E
Manfredonia, Golfo di C	36	41.35 N	16.05 E
Manga, Bra.	245	14.46 S	43.56 W
Manga, H. Vol.	140	11.40 N	1.04 W
Manga, Ur.	248	34.49 S	56.06 W
Manga ⬥[1]	136	15.00 N	14.00 E
Mangabeiras, Chapada das ∧∧[2]	240	10.00 S	46.30 W
Mangagoy	106	8.11 N	126.21 E
Mangahao ≃	162	40.23 S	175.50 E
Mangai	154	2.45 S	151.05 E
Mangaia I	14	21.55 S	157.55 W
Mangakino	162	38.22 S	175.47 E
Mangala	142	1.02 N	23.50 E
Mangalagiri	112	16.26 N	80.33 E
Mangaldai	110	26.26 N	92.02 E
Mangalia	38	43.50 N	28.35 E
Mangalkot	116	23.33 N	87.54 E
Mangalmé	136	12.21 N	19.37 E
Mangalore	112	12.52 N	74.53 E
Mangalpaita	116	23.19 N	89.11 E
Mangalvedha	112	17.31 N	75.28 E
Mangamahu	162	39.49 S	175.22 E
Manganji	258	35.40 N	139.26 E
Mangaoka	147b	12.19 S	49.07 E
Mangapehi	162	38.31 S	175.18 E
Mangaratiba	246	22.57 S	44.02 W
Mangart, Monte (Mangrt) ∧	58	46.25 N	13.40 E
Mangarura dos Antigos ≃	245	13.36 S	51.30 W
Mangatarem	106	15.47 N	120.17 E
Mangawān	114	24.41 N	81.33 E
Mangaweka	162	39.48 S	175.47 E
Mangaweka ∧	162	39.49 S	176.05 E
Mangcao Point ≻	106	11.02 N	123.54 E
Mangchang	92	25.08 N	107.31 E
Mangde ≃	114	27.35 N	90.28 E
Mange, S.L.	140	8.55 N	12.51 W
Mange, Zaïre	142	0.54 N	20.30 E
Mange, Zhg.	110	32.25 N	83.35 E
Mangeigne	136	10.31 N	21.19 E
Mangela, Mount ∧	165e	8.16 S	157.43 E
Mangfall ≃	58	47.51 N	12.08 E
Manggar	102	2.53 S	108.16 E
Manggeng	104	3.36 N	96.55 E
Manggonggri	154	3.30 S	133.19 E
Mangguar, Tanjung ≻	154	2.53 S	134.51 E
Mangham	184	32.19 N	91.47 W
Mangichu ≃	116	23.24 N	90.48 E
Mangindrano	147b	14.17 S	48.58 E
Mangin Range ∧∧	100	24.20 N	95.42 E
Mangkalihat, Tanjung ≻	102	1.02 N	118.59 E
Mangkutana	102	2.24 S	120.48 E
Mangla	113	33.08 N	73.38 E
Mangla Dam ⬥[6]	113	33.09 N	73.44 E
Manglares, Cabo ≻	236	1.36 N	79.02 W
Manglaur	114	29.48 N	77.52 E
Manglisi	74	41.43 N	44.24 E
Mangnuiyingzi	94	41.37 N	120.43 E
Mango	210	28.00 N	82.19 W
Mango I	165g	17.27 S	179.09 W
Mangoche	144	14.28 S	35.16 E
Mangoky ≃, Madag.	147b	21.29 S	43.41 E
Mangoky ≃, Madag.	147b	23.27 S	45.13 E
Mangole, Pulau I	102	1.53 S	125.50 E
Mangombe	144	1.25 S	26.54 E
Mangonia Park	210	26.46 N	80.05 W
Mangonui	162	34.59 S	173.32 E
Mangoplah	161b	35.23 S	147.15 E
Mangoro ≃	147b	20.00 S	48.45 E
Mangotsfield	44	51.28 N	2.28 W
Mangoupa	130	5.53 N	24.40 E
Māngrol	110	21.07 N	70.07 E
Mangrove Cay I	228	24.10 N	77.45 W
Mangrove Creek ≃	160	33.28 S	151.10 E
Mangrove Mountain	160	33.19 S	151.14 E
Mangrove Point ≻	210	26.56 N	82.08 W
Mangrt (Monte Mangart) ∧	58	46.25 N	13.40 E
Mangrullo, Cuchilla ∧∧[2]	248	34.34 S	56.42 W
Mangrūl Pīr	112	20.19 N	77.21 E
Mångsälven ≃	40	59.59 N	14.36 E
Mangsang	102	2.10 S	104.00 E
Mangualde	34	40.36 N	7.46 W
Mangueira, Lagoa C	242	33.06 S	52.48 W
Mangueirinha	242	25.57 S	52.09 W
Mangueni, Plateau de ∧∧[1]	136	22.35 N	12.40 E
Mangues ≃	240	10.21 S	48.27 W
Manguinho, Aeroporto de ⊠	277a	22.52 S	43.15 W
Manguito	230p	22.35 N	80.55 W
Mangulile	226	15.03 N	86.49 W
Mangum	186	34.53 N	99.30 W
Mangungu	142	5.13 S	19.35 E
Mangut, S.S.S.R.	76	55.47 N	70.46 E
Mangut, S.S.S.R.	78	49.46 N	112.38 E
Mangya	80	37.40 N	90.50 E
Man'gyŏng	88	35.52 N	126.48 E
Manhã	245	12.43 S	46.24 W
Manhan ≃	197	42.17 N	72.38 W
Manhasset	266	40.48 N	73.42 W
Manhasset Bay C	266	40.50 N	73.43 W
Manhasset Hills	266	40.46 N	73.41 W
Manhasset Neck ≻[1]	266	40.50 N	73.42 W
Manhattan, Ill., U.S.	206	41.25 N	87.59 W
Manhattan, Kans., U.S.	188	39.11 N	96.35 W
Manhattan, Mont., U.S.	192	45.52 N	111.20 W
Manhattan □[8]	266	40.46 N	73.55 W
Manhattan Beach	218	33.54 N	118.24 W
Manhattan Bridge ⬥[5]	266	40.42 N	73.59 W
Manhattan College ᵾ[2]	266	40.53 N	73.54 W
Manhattan State Beach ♠	270	33.54 N	118.25 W
Manheim	198	40.10 N	76.24 W
Manhiça	146	25.24 S	32.48 E
Mān Hpāng	100	22.41 N	98.36 E
Manhuaçu	245	20.15 S	42.02 W
Manhuaçu ≃	245	19.30 S	41.06 W
Manhumirim	245	20.22 S	41.57 W
Maní, P.R.	230m	18.15 N	67.10 W
Mani, Zaïre	144	6.27 S	25.20 E
Māni', Jabal al- ∧	122	33.19 N	36.17 E
Mania ≃	147b	19.42 S	45.22 E
Maniago	58	46.10 N	12.43 E
Maniamba	144	12.43 S	35.00 E
Manianga	263b	4.08 S	15.17 E
Manica e Sofala □[5]	146	19.00 S	34.00 E
Manicahan	106	7.01 N	122.12 E
Manicaland □[4]	144	19.30 S	32.15 E
Manicani Island I	106	10.59 N	125.38 E
Manicaragua	230p	22.09 N	79.58 W
Manicoré	238	5.49 S	61.17 W
Manicoré ≃	238	5.51 S	61.19 W
Manicouagan ≃	176	49.11 N	68.13 W
Manicouagan, Réservoir ⊜[1]	176	51.30 N	68.19 W
Manifold ≃	44	53.03 N	1.47 W
Manigan'ge	92	32.01 N	99.11 E
Manigotagan	174	51.06 N	96.18 W
Manigotagan ≃	174	51.07 N	96.20 W
Maniguin Island I	106	11.36 N	121.45 E
Manihari	114	25.21 N	87.38 E
Manihiki I[1]	14	10.24 S	161.01 W
Manika, Plateau de la ∧∧[1]	144	10.00 S	26.00 E
Manikanāli	116	23.19 N	87.03 E
Mānikganj	114	23.52 N	90.00 E
Mānikpur	114	25.04 N	81.07 E
Manila, Pil.	106, 259f	14.35 N	121.00 E
Manila, Ark., U.S.	184	35.53 N	90.10 W
Manila, Utah, U.S.	190	40.59 N	109.43 W
Manila □[7]	259f	14.37 N	120.58 E
Manila Bay C, Pil.	106	14.30 N	120.45 E
Manila Bay C, Pil.	259f	14.35 N	120.55 E
Manila Cathedral ᵾ[1]	259f	14.35 N	120.59 E
Manilaid I	66	58.13 N	24.08 E
Manila International Airport ⊠	259f	14.31 N	121.01 E
Manilla, Austl.	156	30.45 S	150.43 E
Manilla, Ind., U.S.	208	39.35 N	85.37 W
Manilla, Iowa, U.S.	188	41.53 N	95.14 W
Manille → Manila	106	14.35 N	121.00 E
Manily	64	62.29 N	165.36 E
Mani Majra	113	30.43 N	76.50 E
Manimpé	140	14.09 N	5.31 W
Maningory ≃	147b	17.13 S	49.28 E
Maningrida	154	12.03 S	134.13 E
Maninian	140	10.00 N	7.50 W
Maninjau, Danau ⊜	102	0.20 S	100.11 E
Manino	66	53.58 N	34.20 E
Manipa, Pulau I	154	3.17 S	127.35 E
Manipa, Selat Ʉ	154	3.20 S	127.23 E
Manipur □[8]	110	25.00 N	94.00 E
Manique de Baixo	256c	38.44 N	9.22 W
Manirāmpur	116	23.01 N	89.14 E
Manisa	120	38.36 N	27.26 E
Manisa □[4]	120	38.50 N	28.10 E
Manistee	180	44.15 N	86.19 W
Manistee ≃	180	44.15 N	86.21 W
Manistique	180	45.57 N	86.15 W
Manistique ≃	180	45.57 N	86.15 W
Manistique, West Branch ≃	180	46.02 N	86.09 W
Manistique Lake ⊜	180	46.15 N	85.45 W
Manito	184	40.25 N	89.47 W
Manitoba □[4]	174, 166	54.00 N	97.00 W
Manitoba, Lake ⊜	174	51.00 N	98.45 W
Manito Lake ⊜	174	52.45 N	109.45 W
Manitou	174	49.15 N	98.31 W
Manitou ≃	174	48.58 N	93.20 W
Manitou, Lac ⊜, Qué., Can.	176	50.29 N	63.54 W
Manitou, Lac ⊜, Qué., Can.	176	50.54 N	65.18 W
Manitou, Lac ⊜, Qué., Can.	196	46.03 N	74.23 W
Manitou, Lake ⊜	206	41.03 N	86.11 W
Manitou Beach, Sask., Can.	174	51.43 N	105.26 W
Manitou Beach, Mich., U.S.	206	41.58 N	84.19 W
Manitou Lake ⊜	180	45.48 N	82.00 W
Manitoulin Island I	180	45.45 N	82.30 W
Manitou Springs	190	38.52 N	104.55 W
Manitouwabing Lake ⊜	202	45.29 N	79.54 W
Manitowaning	180	45.45 N	81.49 W
Manitowish Waters	180	46.09 N	89.53 W
Manitowoc	180	44.06 N	87.40 W
Manitowoc ≃	180	44.05 N	87.39 W
Manitsauá-Missu ≃	240	10.58 S	53.20 W
Maniwaki	178	46.23 N	75.58 W
Ma'nīyā	132	30.50 N	30.39 E
Manizales	236	5.05 N	75.32 W
Manja, Madag.	147b	21.26 S	44.20 E
Manjā, Urd.	122	31.45 N	35.51 E
Manjacaze	146	24.44 S	33.53 E
Manjakandriana	147b	18.55 S	47.47 E
Manjeri	112	11.07 N	76.07 E
Manjeshwara	112	12.42 N	74.53 E
Manjiang	88	41.57 N	127.36 E
Manjimup	152	34.14 S	116.09 E
Mānjra ≃	112	18.49 N	77.52 E
Manjuyod	106	9.41 N	123.09 E
Mankaiana	148	26.42 S	31.00 E
Mankanaj	76	48.58 N	60.58 E
Månkarbo	40	60.14 N	17.28 E
Mān Kāt	100	22.05 N	98.01 E
Mankato, Kans., U.S.	188	39.47 N	98.12 W
Mankato, Minn., U.S.	180	44.10 N	94.01 W
Mankent	75	42.25 N	69.50 E
Mankera	113	31.23 N	71.26 E
Mankim	142	5.01 N	12.00 E
Mankinholes	252	53.42 N	2.03 W
Mankono	140	8.04 N	6.12 W
Mankota	174	49.25 N	107.04 W
Man'kovka, S.S.S.R.	68	48.58 N	30.20 E
Man'kovka, S.S.S.R.	73	49.34 N	38.27 E
Man'kovo	73	49.24 N	40.17 E
Man'kovo-Ber'ozovskaja	70	48.47 N	41.33 E
Mankoya	144	14.47 S	24.48 E
Mānkundu	262b	22.50 N	88.22 E
Mānkur, Bhārat	116	23.20 N	87.33 E
Mānkur, Bhārat	116	22.30 N	87.54 E
Manlaj	92	44.06 N	107.01 E
Manley	252	53.14 N	2.45 W
Manley Hot Springs	170	65.00 N	150.37 W
Manleys Corner	273	42.03 N	71.04 W
Manlius	200	43.00 N	75.59 W
Manlléu	34	42.00 N	2.17 E
Manly, Austl.	160	33.48 S	151.17 E
Manly, Iowa, U.S.	180	43.17 N	93.12 W
Manly Warringah War Memorial Park ♠	264a	33.46 S	151.15 E
Manmād	112	20.15 N	74.27 E
Mann ≃	154	12.20 S	134.07 E
Mann, Mount ∧	152	25.59 S	129.42 E
Manna, Indon.	102	4.27 S	102.55 E
Mān Na, Mya.	100	23.27 N	97.14 E
Mannahill	156	32.26 S	139.59 E
Mannar	112	8.59 N	79.54 E
Mannar, Gulf of C	112	8.30 N	79.00 E
Mannārgudi	112	10.40 N	79.26 E
Mannar Island I	112	9.03 N	79.50 E
Mann Creek ≃	271	42.32 N	83.44 W
Männedorf	54	47.15 N	8.42 E
Mannheim	52	49.29 N	8.29 E
Manni	110	34.48 N	87.15 E
Manning, Iowa, U.S.	188	41.55 N	95.03 W
Manning, N. Dak., U.S.	188	47.14 N	102.47 W
Manning, S.C., U.S.	182	33.42 N	80.13 W
Manning, Cape ≻	164o	2.02 N	157.26 W
Manning Provincial Park ♠	172	49.07 N	120.54 W
Manning Strait Ʉ	165e	7.24 S	158.00 E
Mannington	178	39.32 N	80.20 W
Manningtree	44	51.57 N	1.04 E
Mannō	86	34.11 N	133.51 E
Mann Ranges ∧∧	152	26.00 S	129.30 E
Mannsville	202	43.43 N	76.04 W
Mannswörth ⬥[8]	254b	48.09 N	16.31 E
Mannu ≃	36	40.50 N	8.23 E
Mannus	161b	35.48 S	147.57 E
Mannus Creek ≃	161b	35.58 S	148.03 E
Mannville	172	53.20 N	111.10 W
Mano	140	8.02 N	12.06 W
Mano ≃	140	6.56 N	11.31 W
Manoa	238	9.40 S	65.27 W
Manohardi	116	24.08 N	90.43 E
Manoharpur, Bhārat	114	22.23 N	85.12 E
Manoharpur, Bhārat	116	21.59 N	87.18 E
Manokin ≃	198	38.05 N	75.55 W
Manokotak	170	58.40 N	159.09 W
Manokwari	154	0.52 S	134.05 E
Manolo Fortich (Maluko)	106	8.25 N	124.58 E
Manoma ≃	79	49.18 N	136.37 E
Manombo	147b	22.57 S	43.28 E
Manomet	197	41.55 N	70.34 W
Manomet Hill ∧[2]	197	41.55 N	70.36 W
Manong	104	4.36 N	100.53 E
Manonga ≃	144	4.08 S	34.12 E
Manono	144	7.18 S	27.25 E
Manono I	165a	13.50 S	172.05 W
Manoora	158b	34.00 S	138.49 E
Manoppello	60	42.15 N	14.03 E
Manor, Sask., Can.	174	49.36 N	102.05 W
Manor, Pa., U.S.	204	40.20 N	79.40 W
Manor, Tex., U.S.	212	30.20 N	97.33 W
Manorbier	44	51.39 N	4.48 W
Manorhamilton	28	54.18 N	8.10 W
Manorhaven	266	40.50 N	73.42 W
Manor Hill	204	40.38 N	77.55 W
Manori ⬥[8]	262c	19.12 N	72.47 E
Manori Creek C	262c	19.12 N	72.48 E
Manori Point ≻	262c	19.11 N	72.47 E
Manoron	100	11.38 N	99.04 E
Manorville	204	40.48 N	79.31 W
Manosque	56	43.50 N	5.47 E
Manotick	202	45.13 N	75.41 W
Manouane ≃	176	49.30 N	71.11 W
Manouane, Lac ⊜	176	50.41 N	70.45 W
Manouanis ≃	176	50.28 N	70.08 W
Manouanis, Lac ⊜	176	50.51 N	70.20 W
Manouba	36	36.50 N	10.06 E
Manovo ≃	136	9.12 N	20.29 E
Manown	269b	40.13 N	79.54 W
Manpaka	263b	4.18 S	15.12 E
Manpitou	90	22.17 N	112.52 E
Mānpur, Bhārat	112	20.22 N	80.43 E
Mānpur, Bhārat	114	23.46 N	81.08 E
Manqabād	132	27.12 N	31.07 E
Manqaṭīn	132	28.20 N	30.40 E
Manquehue, Cerro ∧	276e	33.21 S	70.36 W
Manresa	34	41.44 N	1.50 E
Manresa Island I	266	41.04 N	73.25 W
Mānsa, Bhārat	110	23.26 N	72.40 E
Mānsa, Bhārat	113	29.59 N	75.23 E
Mansa (Fort Rosebery), Zam.	144	11.12 S	28.53 E
Mansabá	140	12.18 N	15.15 W
Mansafīs	132	28.00 N	30.49 E
Mansalay	106	12.31 N	121.26 E
Mānsar	113	33.54 N	72.19 E
Mansara	140	13.20 N	4.39 W
Manse ≃	46	47.08 N	0.25 E
Manseau	196	46.22 N	72.00 W
Mānsehra	113	34.20 N	73.12 E
Mansein	100	25.12 N	95.58 E
Mansel Island I	166	62.00 N	79.50 W
Mansfeld	50	51.35 N	11.27 E
Mansfield, Austl.	159	37.03 S	146.05 E
Mansfield, Eng., U.K.	44	53.09 N	1.11 W
Mansfield, Ark., U.S.	184	35.04 N	94.13 W
Mansfield, Ga., U.S.	182	33.31 N	83.44 W
Mansfield, Ill., U.S.	206	40.13 N	88.31 W
Mansfield, La., U.S.	184	32.02 N	93.43 W
Mansfield, Mass., U.S.	197	42.02 N	71.13 W
Mansfield, Mo., U.S.	184	37.06 N	92.35 W
Mansfield, N.J., U.S.	275	40.05 N	74.43 W
Mansfield, Ohio, U.S.	204	40.46 N	82.31 W
Mansfield, Pa., U.S.	200	41.48 N	77.05 W
Mansfield, Tex., U.S.	212	32.34 N	97.09 W
Mansfield, Mount ∧	178	44.33 N	72.49 W
Mansfield Center	197	41.50 N	72.16 W
Mansfield Hollow Lake ⊜[1]	197	41.45 N	72.11 W
Mansfield Hollow State Park ♠	197	41.46 N	72.10 W
Mansfield Municipal Airport ⊠	273	42.00 N	71.12 W
Mansfield Woodhouse	44	53.11 N	1.12 W
Manshan I	96	31.14 N	120.17 E
Manshuijing	97	29.55 N	104.07 E
Mansieville Location	263d	26.05 S	27.45 E
Mānsinhapur	262b	22.39 N	88.09 E
Manskoje Belogorje ∧∧	78	54.35 N	94.00 E
Mansle	32	45.53 N	0.11 E
Manso ≃, Bra.	238	14.42 S	56.16 W
Manso ≃, Bra.	245	13.18 S	46.51 W
Mansôa	140	12.10 N	14.36 W
Manson	188	42.32 N	94.32 W
Manson ≃	172	55.42 N	123.47 W
Mansonville	196	45.03 N	72.23 W
Mansourah	34	36.04 N	4.28 E
Mansura → Al-Manṣūrah, Miṣr	132	31.03 N	31.23 E
Mansura, La., U.S.	184	31.04 N	92.03 W
Manṣūrah	122	33.08 N	35.48 E
Manṣūrīyah, Tur'at al- ☰	132	31.03 N	31.24 E
Mansurovo	72	55.52 N	36.36 E
Manta, Ec.	236	0.57 S	80.44 W
Manta, It.	56	44.37 N	7.29 E
Manta, Bahía de C	236	0.54 S	80.42 W
Mantabuan Island I	106	5.02 N	120.13 E
Mantagao ≃	174	51.50 N	97.48 W
Mantalingajan, Mount ∧	106	8.48 N	117.40 E
Mantalingajan Range ∧∧	106	8.46 N	117.40 E
Mantanani Besar, Pulau I	102	6.45 N	116.17 E
Mantangule Island I	106	8.10 N	117.10 E
Mantantale	142	2.10 S	20.06 E
Mantare	144	2.43 S	33.13 E
Mantaro ≃	238	12.15 S	73.58 W
Manteca	216	37.48 N	121.13 W
Mantecal	236	7.33 N	69.09 W
Mantekamuhu ⊜	110	34.30 N	89.15 E
Manteno	206	41.14 N	88.12 W
Manteo	182	35.55 N	75.40 W
Mantes-Chérence, Aérodrome de ⊠	251	49.05 N	1.41 E
Mantes-Gassicourt, Aérodrome de ⊠	251	49.00 N	1.41 E
Mantes-la-Jolie	46	48.59 N	1.43 E
Manteswar	116	23.26 N	88.06 E
Manthelan	46	47.08 N	0.47 E
Manti	190	39.16 N	111.38 W
Manticao	106	8.24 N	124.17 E
Mantilla ⬥[8]	276b	23.04 N	82.20 W
Mantin	104	2.49 N	101.54 E
Mantiqueira, Serra da ∧∧	246	22.45 S	45.45 W
Mant Islands II	164r	7.00 N	158.17 E
Mantok	102	1.09 S	123.14 E
Manton	180	44.24 N	85.24 W
Mantorville	180	44.05 N	92.45 W
Mantos Blancos	242	23.25 S	70.05 W
Mantou	94	42.27 N	122.26 E
Mantova	58	45.09 N	10.48 E
Mantova □[4]	58	45.10 N	10.47 E
Mant Passage Ʉ	164r	7.02 N	158.18 E
Māntri	116	21.39 N	86.49 E
Mänttä	26	62.02 N	24.38 E
Mantua, Cuba	230p	22.17 N	84.17 W
Mantua → Mantova, It.	58	45.09 N	10.48 E
Mantua, N.J., U.S.	198	39.48 N	75.10 W
Mantua, Ohio, U.S.	204	41.17 N	81.14 W
Mantua, Va., U.S.	274c	38.51 N	77.15 W
Mantua ≃	230p	22.12 N	84.25 W
Mantua Creek ≃	275	39.51 N	75.14 W
Mantua Creek, Bees Branch ≃	275	39.46 N	75.08 W
Mantua Creek, Chestnut Branch ≃	275	39.47 N	75.10 W
Mantua Creek, Porch Branch ≃	275	39.46 N	75.07 W
Mantua Terrace	275	39.48 N	75.10 W
Manturovo, S.S.S.R.	68	51.28 N	37.07 E
Manturovo, S.S.S.R.	70	58.20 N	44.46 E
Mäntyharju	26	61.25 N	26.53 E
Mäntyluoto	26	61.35 N	21.29 E
Manu	238	12.15 S	70.50 W
Manu ≃	238	12.16 S	70.51 W
Manuae I[1]	14	19.21 S	158.56 W
Manua Islands II	164y	14.13 S	169.35 W
Manu Chico ≃	238	11.41 S	71.48 W
Manuel	224	22.44 N	98.19 W
Manuel Alves da Natividade ≃	240	11.19 S	48.28 W
Manuel Alves Grande ≃	240	7.27 S	47.35 W
Manuel Benavides	222	29.05 N	103.55 W
Manuel Derqui	242	27.50 S	58.48 W
Manuel Duarte	246	22.06 S	43.34 W
Manuel M. Diéguez	224	19.34 N	102.55 W
Manuel Ribas	242	24.31 S	51.39 W
Manuel Rodríguez, Isla I	244	52.35 S	73.50 W
Manuel Urbano	238	8.53 S	69.18 W
Manuhangi I[1]	14	19.12 S	141.16 W
Manuherikia ≃	162	45.16 S	169.24 E
Manui, Pulau I	102	3.35 S	123.08 E
Manuilovskaja	66	60.29 N	40.40 E
Manu Island I	154	1.17 S	143.35 E
Manūjān	118	27.24 N	57.32 E
Manuk ≃	105a	6.14 S	108.13 E
Manuk, Pulau I	154	5.33 S	130.18 E
Manukan	106	8.31 N	123.06 E
Manukau	162	37.02 S	174.54 E
Manukau Harbour C	162	37.01 S	174.44 E
Manulu Lagoon C	164o	1.56 N	157.20 W
Manumuskin ≃	198	39.18 N	75.00 W
Manundi, Tanjung ≻	154	0.38 S	135.22 E
Manunui	162	38.53 S	175.20 E
Manupari ≃	238	11.50 S	67.16 W
Manurimi ≃	238	11.42 S	67.16 W
Manuripe (Manuripi) ≃	238	11.06 S	67.36 W
Manuro Point ≻	165f	17.41 S	168.36 E
Manursing Island I	266	40.58 N	73.40 W
Manursing Island Park ♠	266	40.58 N	73.40 W
Manus □[5]	154	2.00 S	147.00 E
Mānushmuria	116	22.22 N	86.47 E
Manus Island I	154	2.05 S	147.00 E
Manutahi	162	39.40 S	174.24 E
Manutuke	162	38.41 S	177.55 E
Manvel, N. Dak., U.S.	188	48.04 N	97.10 W
Manvel, Tex., U.S.	212	29.28 N	95.22 W
Manville, N.J., U.S.	200	40.32 N	74.36 W
Manville, R.I., U.S.	197	41.58 N	71.28 W
Manwakh	134	16.50 N	48.05 E
Mānwat	112	19.18 N	76.30 E
Many	184	31.34 N	93.29 W
Manyal Shīḥah	263c	29.57 N	31.14 E
Manyana	146	23.23 S	21.44 E
Manyani	144	3.05 S	38.30 E
Manyara, Lake ⊜	144	3.35 S	35.50 E
Manyberries	174	49.24 N	110.42 W
Manyč ≃	62	47.15 N	40.00 E
Manyč Gudilo, Ozero ⊜	70	46.24 N	42.38 E
Many Island Lake ⊜	174	50.08 N	110.03 W
Manyoni	144	5.45 S	34.50 E
Many Peaks	156	24.33 S	151.23 E
Manytsch → Manyč ≃	62	47.15 N	40.00 E
Manz'a	76	58.29 N	96.15 E
Mānzai	110	30.07 N	68.52 E
Manzanares	34	39.00 N	3.22 W
Manzanares ≃	34	40.19 N	3.32 W
Manzanares, Canal del ☰	256a	40.23 N	3.41 W
Manzanillo, Cuba	230p	20.21 N	77.07 W
Manzanillo, Méx.	224	19.03 N	104.20 W
Manzanillo, Punta ≻, Pan.	226	9.38 N	79.32 W
Manzanillo, Punta ≻, Ven.	231s	11.32 N	69.17 W
Manzanillo Bay ≃	228	19.45 N	71.46 W
Manzanita, Oreg., U.S.	214	45.43 N	123.56 W
Manzanita, Wash., U.S.	214	47.42 N	122.33 W
Manzano, It.	58	45.59 N	13.23 E
Manzano, N. Mex., U.S.	190	34.39 N	106.21 W
Manzanola	188	38.06 N	103.52 W
Manzano Peak ∧	190	34.35 N	106.26 W
Manželija	68	49.19 N	33.38 E
Manzhouli	78	49.35 N	117.22 E
Manziana	60	42.08 N	12.08 E
Manzil	110	29.15 N	63.05 E
Manzilah, Birkat al- ⊜	132	31.08 N	31.56 E
Manzilah, Buḥayrat al- ⊜	132	31.15 N	32.00 E
Manzini	148	26.30 S	31.25 E
Manzone	248	34.29 S	58.52 W
Manzovka	79	44.12 N	132.26 E
Manzurka	78	53.30 N	106.04 E
Mao	136	14.07 N	15.19 E
Maoba	92	30.02 N	108.59 E
Maocifan	90	31.40 N	112.53 E
Maocun	88	34.25 N	117.16 E
Maodianzi	97	30.42 N	104.25 E
Maodun'emuqi	79	48.50 N	118.51 E
Maoertuo	97	29.19 N	106.24 E
Mao Hsü I	90	23.19 N	119.19 E
Maojia	97	29.10 N	104.08 E
Maojiagou	94	40.58 N	120.51 E
Maojiaji	90	31.32 N	114.16 E
Maojiakou	90	29.53 N	112.58 E
Maojiaping	95	40.34 N	114.43 E
Maojiapuzi	94	41.10 N	123.32 E
Maojiashi	96	31.30 N	121.05 E
Maojiatun	94	41.05 N	121.58 E
Maojiazao	88	39.53 N	113.26 E
Maoke, Pegunungan ∧∧	154	4.00 S	138.00 E
Maolin, Zhg.	79	43.58 N	123.24 E
Maolin, Zhg.	90	30.32 N	118.14 E
Maoming	92	21.55 N	110.52 E
Maomu	92	40.18 N	99.28 E
Ma On Shan ∧	261d	22.25 N	114.15 E
Ma On Shan Tsuen	261d	22.25 N	114.14 E
Maoping	92	30.23 N	110.33 E
Maopora, Pulau I	102	7.35 S	127.35 E
Maoshi	90	26.57 N	113.05 E
Maospati	105a	7.36 S	111.26 E
Maouri, Dallol ∨	140	12.05 N	3.32 E
Maowen	92	31.30 N	103.39 E
Maoxing	79	45.32 N	124.33 E
Maozhou	95	38.51 N	116.06 E
Map I	164q	9.35 N	138.11 E
Mapaga	102	0.06 S	119.48 E
Mapai	148	25.51 S	31.58 E
Mapan	102	2.21 S	111.10 E
Mapanda	142	9.32 S	24.16 E
Mapane	102	1.24 S	120.40 E
Mapanza Mission	144	16.15 S	26.55 E
Mapaochang	97	29.38 N	105.50 E
Mapaoni ≃	240	1.55 N	54.13 W
Mapastepec	224	15.26 N	92.54 W
Mapaville	209	38.15 N	90.28 W
Mapfongui	142	1.15 S	12.59 E
Mapi	154	7.07 S	139.23 E
Mapi ≃	154	7.00 S	139.16 E
Mapia, Kepulauan II	98	0.50 N	134.20 E
Mapida	102	0.33 S	119.46 E
Mapimí	222	25.49 N	103.51 W
Mapimí, Bolsón de ⬥[2]	222	27.30 N	103.30 W
Mapimí, Bufa de ∧	186	25.47 N	103.48 W
Maping	90	24.16 N	117.54 E
Mapinga	144	6.36 S	39.04 E
Mapinggang	90	31.36 N	113.32 E
Mapinhane	146	22.19 S	35.03 E
Mapire	236	7.45 N	64.42 W
Mapiri	238	15.15 S	68.10 W
Mapiri ≃	238	9.52 S	66.21 W
Mapiripán, Laguna ⊜	236	2.58 N	71.45 W
Mapixari, Ilha I	236	2.10 S	65.08 W
Maple	265b	43.51 N	79.31 W
Maple Airfield ⊠	265b	43.51 N	79.31 W
Maple ≃, Iowa, U.S.	188	42.00 N	95.59 W

Symbol	English	Deutsch	Español	Français	Português
≃	River	Fluss	Río	Rivière	Rio
☰	Canal	Kanal	Canal	Canal	Canal
ᒪ	Waterfall, Rapids	Wasserfall, Stromschnellen	Cascada, Rápidos	Chute d'eau, Rapides	Cascata, Rápidos
Ʉ	Strait	Meeresstrasse	Estrecho	Détroit	Estreito
C	Bay, Gulf	Bucht, Golf	Bahía, Golfo	Baie, Golfe	Baía, Golfo
⊜	Lake, Lakes	See, Seen	Lago, Lagos	Lac, Lacs	Lago, Lagos
☷	Swamp	Sumpf	Pantano	Marais	Pântano
⩍	Ice Features, Glacier	Eis- und Gletscherformen	Accidentes Glaciales	Formes glaciaires	Acidentes Glaciares
⍑	Other Hydrographic Features	Andere Hydrographische Objekte	Otros Elementos Hidrográficos	Autres données hydrographiques	Outros Elementos Hidrográficos
✧	Submarine Features	Untermeerische Objekte	Accidentes Submarinos	Formes de relief sous-marin	Acidentes Submarinos
□	Political Unit	Politische Einheit	Unidad Política	Entité politique	Unidade Política
ᵾ	Cultural Institution	Kulturelle Institution	Institución Cultural	Institution culturelle	Instituição Cultural
⊥	Historical Site	Historische Stätte	Sitio Histórico	Site historique	Sítio Histórico
♠	Recreational Site	Erholungs- und Ferienort	Sitio de Recreo	Centre de loisirs	Sítio de Lazer
⊠	Airport	Flughafen	Aeropuerto	Aéroport	Aeroporto
▪	Military Installation	Militäranlage	Instalación Militar	Installation militaire	Instalação Militar
⬥	Miscellaneous	Verschiedenes	Misceláneo	Divers	Miscelânea

Name	Page	Lat.	Long.
Maple ≃, Mich., U.S.	180	42.59 N	84.57 W
Maple ≃, Minn., U.S.	180	44.05 N	94.00 W
Maple ≃, N. Dak., U.S.	188	46.56 N	96.55 W
Maple Airfield ⊠	265b	43.51 N	79.32 W
Maple Bay	214	48.49 N	123.36 W
Maple Bluff	206	43.07 N	89.22 W
Maple Creek	174	49.55 N	109.27 W
Maple Creek ≃	188	41.33 N	96.27 W
Maplecrest	200	42.17 N	74.11 W
Maple Cross	250	51.37 N	0.30 W
Mapledale	204	41.23 N	79.51 W
Maple Falls	214	48.56 N	122.05 W
Maple Glen	275	40.11 N	75.11 W
Maple Grove, Ont., Can.	202	43.55 N	78.44 W
Maple Grove, Qué., Can.	196	45.19 N	73.50 W
Maple Heights	204	41.25 N	81.34 W
Maple Lake	180	45.14 N	94.00 W
Maple Lake ⊜	202	45.06 N	78.40 W
Maple Lane	206	41.45 N	86.14 W
Maple Leaf Gardens ♦	265b	43.40 N	79.23 W
Maple Meadow Brook ≃	273	42.33 N	71.09 W
Maple Mount	184	37.42 N	87.26 W
Maple Park	206	41.55 N	88.36 W
Maples	206	41.01 N	84.58 W
Maple Springs	204	42.12 N	79.25 W
Maplesville	184	32.47 N	86.52 W
Mapleton, S. Afr.	148	26.20 S	28.14 E
Mapleton, Iowa, U.S.	188	42.10 N	95.47 W
Mapleton, Minn., U.S.	180	43.56 N	93.57 W
Mapleton, Oreg., U.S.	192	44.02 N	123.52 W
Mapleton, Utah, U.S.	190	40.08 N	111.36 W
Mapleton Depot	204	40.24 N	77.57 W
Maple Valley	214	47.25 N	122.03 W
Mapleville	197	41.57 N	71.39 W
Maplewood, Mo., U.S.	209	38.37 N	90.19 W
Maplewood, N.J., U.S.	266	40.44 N	74.17 W
Maplewood, Ohio, U.S.	206	40.23 N	84.02 W
Maplewood, Wash., U.S.	214	47.30 N	122.07 W
Maplewood Terrace	269b	40.17 N	79.32 W
Mapocho ≃	276e	33.25 S	70.47 W
Mapocho, Estación ⬥⁵	276e	33.26 S	70.40 W
Mapoi	144	5.28 N	27.40 E
Mappsville	198	37.51 N	75.34 W
Maprik	154	3.40 S	143.05 E
Mapuera ≃	240	1.05 S	57.02 W
Mapujiang	95	40.24 N	114.56 E
Mapulanguene	146	24.29 S	32.06 E
Mapulau ≃	236	1.23 N	63.24 W
Mapumulo	148	29.11 S	31.02 E
Maputa	148	26.59 S	32.46 E
Maputo (Lourenço Marques)	146	25.58 S	32.35 E
Maputo (Lourenço Marques) □⁵	146	26.00 S	32.25 E
Maputo (Great Usutu) ≃	148	26.11 S	32.42 E
Ma'qalā'	118	26.31 N	47.19 E
Maqiangou	95	39.30 N	115.02 E
Maqiao, Zhg.	90	29.48 N	114.22 E
Maqiao, Zhg.	96	30.28 N	120.42 E
Maquanhe ≃	114	29.35 N	84.10 E
Maqueda	34	40.04 N	4.22 W
Maqueda Bay C	106	11.44 N	124.58 E
Maqueda Channel ⊔	106	13.42 N	124.01 E
Maquela do Zombo	142	6.03 S	15.07 E
Maquereau, Pointe au ≻	176	48.12 N	64.47 W
Maquiling, Mount ∧	106	14.08 N	121.12 E
Maquinchao	244	41.15 S	68.44 W
Maquoketa	180	42.04 N	90.40 W
Maquoketa ≃	180	42.11 N	90.19 W
Maquoketa, North Fork ≃	180	42.05 N	90.40 W
Mar, Serra do •⁴	234	25.00 S	48.00 W
Mara, Bhārat	110	28.11 N	94.06 E
Mara, Perú	238	14.06 S	72.07 W
Mara, Zhg.	110	28.11 N	94.08 E
Mara □⁴	144	1.45 S	34.00 E
Mara ≃, Afr.	144	1.31 S	33.56 E
Mara ≃, S.S.S.R.	78	58.06 N	104.06 E
Maraã, Bra.	236	1.50 S	65.22 W
Maraa, Poly. fr.	164s	17.46 S	149.34 W
Maraa, Passe de ⊔	164s	17.44 S	149.34 W
Marabá	240	5.21 S	49.07 W
Marabahan	102	3.00 S	114.45 E
Marabut	106	11.07 N	125.13 E
Maracá ≃	240	0.26 S	51.26 W
Maracá, Ilha de I, Bra.	236	3.25 N	61.40 W
Maracá, Ilha de I, Bra.	240	2.05 N	50.25 W
Maracaçumé ≃	240	1.23 S	45.42 W
Maracaí	245	22.36 S	50.39 W
Maracaí, Lago de ⊜	236	1.28 S	65.44 W
Maracaibo	236	10.40 N	71.37 W
Maracaibo, Lago de ⊜	236	9.50 N	71.30 W
Maracajá ≃	245	12.21 S	51.00 W
Maracaju	245	21.38 S	55.09 W
Maracaju, Serra de ⋀²	245	23.57 S	55.01 W
Maracanã	240	0.46 S	47.27 W
Maracanã ⬥⁸	277a	22.54 S	43.14 W
Maracanã ≃	238	8.22 S	59.41 W
Maracanã, Estádio Municipal ♦	277a	22.55 S	43.14 W
Maracanaú	240	3.52 S	38.38 W
Maracás	245	13.26 S	40.27 W
Maracay	236	10.15 N	67.36 W
Maracossic Creek ≃	198	37.53 N	77.11 W
Marādah	136	29.14 N	19.13 E
Maradi	140	13.29 N	7.06 E
Maradi □⁵	140	14.00 N	7.00 E
Marae	164s	17.32 S	149.54 W
Marāghah, Sabkhat al- ⊜	120	35.39 N	37.39 E
Marāgheh	118	37.23 N	46.13 E
Maragini	154	3.33 S	141.34 E
Maragogi	240	9.01 S	35.13 W
Maragogipe	245	12.46 S	38.55 W
Mārahra	114	27.44 N	78.35 E
Marahuaca, Cerro ∧	236	3.34 N	65.27 W
Maraial	240	8.47 S	35.50 W
Maraiche Lake ⊜	174	54.28 N	102.01 W
Marainviller	54	48.35 N	6.36 E
Maraisburg	263d	26.11 S	27.56 E
Marais des Cygnes ≃	184	38.02 N	94.14 W
Marais Temps Clair ⊜	209	38.54 N	90.24 W
Marajó, Baía de C	240	1.00 S	48.30 W
Marajó, Ilha de I	240	1.00 S	49.30 W
Marakabei	148	29.32 S	28.09 E
Ma'rakah	122	33.16 N	35.18 E
Mārākand	74	38.52 N	45.14 E
Maralal	144	1.06 N	36.42 E
Maralaleng	146	25.47 S	22.45 E
Maraldy	76	52.26 N	77.45 E
Marali	142	6.01 N	18.24 E
Maralik	74	40.35 N	43.52 E
Maram	110	25.25 N	94.06 E
Maramag	106	7.46 N	125.00 E
Maramasike I	165e	9.32 S	161.27 E
Marambaia	246	22.26 S	44.48 W
Marambaia, Ilha da I	246	23.04 S	43.58 W
Marambaia, Pico da ∧	246	23.04 S	43.59 W
Marambaia, Ribeirão ≃	246	21.44 S	46.25 W
Marampa	140	8.41 N	12.28 W
Maramsilli Reservoir ⊜¹	112	20.32 N	81.41 E
Maramureș □⁴	38	47.40 N	24.00 E
Maramureșului, Munții ⋀	38	47.50 N	24.45 E
Maran	104	3.35 N	102.46 E
Mārān, Koh-i- ∧	110	29.26 N	66.49 E
Marana, Mali	140	14.38 N	11.55 W
Marana, Ariz., U.S.	190	32.27 N	111.13 W
Maranalgo	152	29.23 S	117.48 E
Maranboy	154	14.30 S	132.45 E
Maranchón	34	41.03 N	2.12 W
Marand	118	38.26 N	45.46 E
Marandellas	144	18.10 S	31.36 E
Maranello	58	44.32 N	10.52 E
Maranenuka	164t	1.29 N	173.02 E
Marang, Malay.	104	5.12 N	103.13 E
Marang, Mya.	100	10.27 N	98.47 E
Marangá ≃	277a	22.51 S	43.23 W
Marangani	238	14.22 S	71.10 W
Marangas	106	8.40 N	117.38 E
Marange-Zondrange	52	49.07 N	6.32 E
Maranguape	240	3.53 S	38.40 W
Maranhão □³	240	5.00 S	45.00 W
Maranhão ≃	245	14.34 S	49.02 W
Maranhão, Cachoeira ↳	240	4.49 S	56.18 W
Marano	256b	45.38 N	8.38 E
Marano, Laguna di C	58	45.44 N	13.10 E
Maranoa ≃	156	27.50 S	148.37 E
Marano di Napoli	60	40.54 N	14.11 E
Marano Lagunare	58	45.46 N	13.10 E
Marañón ≃	232	4.30 S	73.27 W
Marano sul Panaro	58	44.27 N	10.58 E
Marano Vicentino	58	45.41 N	11.25 E
Marans	32	46.19 N	1.00 W
Maraoli ⬥⁸	262c	19.03 N	72.54 E
Maraoné, Massif du ⋀	136	14.40 N	21.33 E
Marapanim	240	0.42 S	47.42 W
Marapendi, Lagoa de C	277a	23.01 S	43.24 W
Marapi ≃	240	0.37 N	55.58 W
Marapicu	246	22.48 S	43.35 W
Marapicu, Morro do ∧	277a	22.50 S	43.36 W
Marari ≃	236	0.53 N	64.25 W
Mararoa ≃	162	45.34 S	167.36 E
Mararui	144	1.56 S	41.18 E
Maras, Perú	238	13.20 S	72.09 W
Maraş, Tür.	120	37.36 N	36.55 E
Maraş □⁴	120	38.00 N	37.05 E
Marasany	70	57.27 N	54.25 E
Maraş Dağları ⋀	120	37.40 N	37.00 E
Marasende, Pulau I	102	5.08 S	118.09 E
Mărășești	38	45.52 N	27.14 E
Maratasã ≃	240	4.14 S	42.15 W
Maratea	36	39.59 N	15.45 E
Marathon, Austl.	156	20.49 S	143.34 E
Marathon, Ont., Can.	180	48.40 N	86.25 W
Marathón, Ellás	38	38.10 N	23.58 E
Marathon, Fla., U.S.	210	24.43 N	81.05 W
Marathon, N.Y., U.S.	200	42.26 N	76.02 W
Marathon, Tex., U.S.	186	30.12 N	103.15 W
Marathon, Wis., U.S.	180	44.56 N	89.50 W
Marathóvounon	120	35.13 N	33.37 E
Maratua, Pulau I	102	2.15 N	118.36 E
Marau, Bra.	242	28.27 S	52.12 W
Maraú, Bra.	245	14.06 S	39.00 W
Marauiá ≃	236	0.23 S	65.13 W
Maravari	165e	7.51 S	156.42 E
Maravatío de Ocampo	224	19.54 N	100.27 W
Marāveh Tappeh	118	37.55 N	55.57 E
Maravilha, Bra.	240	9.14 S	37.21 W
Maravilha, Bra.	242	26.47 S	53.09 W
Maravillas	222	27.22 N	104.29 W
Maravillas Creek ≃	186	29.34 N	102.47 W
Mara Vista	197	41.33 N	70.34 W
Marav Lake ⊜	110	29.04 N	69.18 E
Maravovo	165e	9.17 S	159.38 E
Marāwah	136	32.29 N	21.25 E
Marawi, Pil.	106	8.01 N	124.18 E
Marawī, Sūd.	130	18.29 N	31.49 E
Maraye-en-Othe	46	48.10 N	3.51 E
Marayes	242	31.29 S	67.20 W
Marayong	264a	33.45 S	150.54 E
Maraza	74	40.33 N	48.56 E
Marbach, B.R.D.	52	50.37 N	9.43 E
Marbach, D.D.R.	50	51.02 N	13.13 E
Marbach, Schw.	54	46.52 N	7.55 E
Marbach am Neckar	52	48.56 N	9.14 E
Marbache	52	48.48 N	6.05 E
Marbais	46	50.33 N	4.31 E
Marbeck	48	51.49 N	6.52 E
Marbella	34	36.31 N	4.53 W
Marble, Minn., U.S.	180	47.19 N	93.18 W
Marble, N.C., U.S.	182	35.10 N	83.55 W
Marble, Pa., U.S.	204	41.20 N	79.26 W
Marble Arch ⊥	136	30.29 N	18.35 E
Marble Bar	152	21.11 S	119.44 E
Marble Canyon ∨	190	36.30 N	111.50 W
Marble Falls	186	30.34 N	98.17 W
Marble Hall	146	24.57 S	29.13 E
Marblehead, Ill., U.S.	209	39.50 N	91.22 W
Marblehead, Mass., U.S.	197	42.30 N	70.51 W
Marblehead, Ohio, U.S.	204	41.32 N	82.44 W
Marblehead Neck ≻¹	273	42.29 N	70.51 W
Marble Hill	184	37.18 N	89.58 W
Marble Lake ⊜	206	41.54 N	84.54 W
Marblemount	214	48.32 N	121.26 W
Marble Rock	180	42.58 N	92.52 W
Marbleton	196	45.37 N	71.35 W
Marburg, Austl.	161a	27.34 S	152.35 E
Marburg, S. Afr.	148	30.44 S	30.26 E
Marburg, Lake ⊜¹	198	39.48 N	76.53 W
Marburg an der Drau → Maribor	36	46.33 N	15.39 E
Marburg an der Lahn	52	50.49 N	8.46 E
Marca, Ponta da ≻	142	16.31 S	11.42 E
Marcaconga	238	13.59 S	71.34 W
Marcal ≃	30	47.41 N	17.32 E
Marcala	226	14.07 N	88.00 W
Marcali	30	46.35 N	17.25 E
Marcallo con Casone	256b	45.29 N	8.52 E
Marcaria	58	45.07 N	10.32 E
Marceau, Lac ⊜	176	51.25 N	66.41 W
Marcelin	174	52.55 N	106.47 W
Marceline	184	39.43 N	92.57 W
Marcelino Ramos	242	27.28 S	51.54 W
Marcelino Vieira	240	6.18 S	38.10 W
Marcella	266	40.59 N	74.28 W
Marcellina	60	42.01 N	12.48 E
Marcellus, Mich., U.S.	206	42.03 N	85.49 W
Marcellus, N.Y., U.S.	200	42.59 N	76.20 W
Marcellus Falls	200	43.00 N	76.20 W
Marcevo	73	47.15 N	38.53 E
March	44	52.33 N	0.06 E
March (Morava) ≃	30	48.10 N	16.59 E
Marcha	64	61.49 N	122.20 E
March Air Force Base ■	218	33.54 N	117.15 W
Marchais	251	48.31 N	2.03 E
Marchal	142	5.16 S	14.58 E
Marchamat	75	40.30 N	72.19 E
Marchand	204	40.51 N	79.02 W
Marchaux	54	47.19 N	6.08 E
Marche □⁴	60	43.30 N	13.15 E
Marche □⁹	32	46.05 N	2.10 E
Marche-en-Famenne	52	50.12 N	5.20 E
Marchegg	30	48.17 N	16.55 E
Marche-les-Dames	52	50.29 N	4.58 E
Marchémoret	251	49.03 N	2.46 E
Marchena	34	37.20 N	5.24 W
Marchena, Isla I	236a	0.21 N	90.29 W
Marchenoir	46	47.49 N	1.24 E
Marchesa Bay C	106	6.35 N	117.40 E
Marchfeld ⬥¹	254b	48.17 N	16.31 E
Marchienne-au-Pont	46	50.24 N	4.23 E
Marchiennes	46	50.24 N	3.17 E
Mar Chiquita, Laguna C	242	37.37 S	57.24 W
Mar Chiquita, Laguna ⊜	242	30.42 S	62.36 W
Marciana	60	42.47 N	10.10 E
Marciana Marina	60	42.48 N	10.12 E
Marcianise	60	41.02 N	14.17 E
Marciano della Chiana	60	43.18 N	11.47 E
Marčichina Buda	68	51.58 N	34.03 E
Marcigny	32	46.17 N	4.02 E
Marcillac-Vallon	32	44.29 N	2.28 E
Marcilloles	56	45.20 N	5.11 E
Marcilly	251	49.02 N	2.53 E
Marcilly-la-Campagne	46	48.50 N	1.13 E
Marcilly-le-Hayer	46	48.21 N	3.38 E
Marcilly-sur-Eure	46	48.49 N	1.21 E
Marck	46	50.57 N	1.57 E
Marckolsheim	54	48.10 N	7.33 E
Marco, Bra.	240	3.08 S	40.09 W
Marco, It.	58	45.51 N	11.01 E
Marco, Fla., U.S.	210	25.58 N	81.44 W
Marcoing	46	50.07 N	3.11 E
Marco Island I	210	25.55 N	81.45 W
Marcola	192	44.10 N	122.52 W
Marcolino, Igarapé ≃	240	11.03 S	58.35 W
Marcona	238	15.03 S	75.01 W
Marco Polo Bridge ⬥⁵	261a	39.52 N	116.12 E
Marco Polo di Tessera, Aeroporto ⊠	58	45.30 N	12.21 E
Marcos Juárez	242	32.42 S	62.06 W
Marcos Paz	248	34.46 S	58.50 W
Marcos Paz □⁵	278	34.49 S	58.49 W
Marcotte, Lac ⊜	196	46.47 N	73.12 W
Marcounda	142	7.37 N	16.59 E
Marcoussis	251	48.39 N	2.14 E
Marcq	251	48.52 N	1.49 E
Marcq-en-Baroeul	46	50.40 N	3.05 E
Marčugi	72	55.21 N	38.33 E
Marcus	188	42.50 N	95.48 W
Marcus Baker, Mount ∧	170	61.26 N	147.45 W
Marcus Hook	198	39.49 N	75.25 W
Marcus Hook Creek ≃	275	39.49 N	75.25 W
Marcus Island → Minami-Tori-shima I	14	24.18 N	153.58 E
Marcus-Necker Ridge ⊹³	14	20.00 N	179.00 E
Marcy, Mount ∧	178	44.07 N	73.56 W
Marda	152	30.13 S	119.17 E
Mardakert	74	40.12 N	46.48 E
Mardalsfossen ↳	26	62.30 N	8.07 E
Mardān	113	34.12 N	72.02 E
Mardarovka	68	47.32 N	29.44 E
Mar de Cães, Vala de ≋	256c	38.51 N	8.59 W
Mar de Espanha	246	21.52 S	43.00 W
Mardela Springs	198	38.28 N	75.45 W
Mar del Plata	242	38.00 S	57.33 W
Mardi, Hadjer ∧	136	14.49 N	22.04 E
Mardie	152	21.11 S	115.57 E
Mardin	120	37.18 N	40.44 E
Mardin □⁴	120	37.25 N	41.00 E
Mare	154	9.10 S	141.40 E
Maré, Île I	165f	21.30 S	168.00 E
Mare, Muntele ∧	38	46.29 N	23.14 E
Marecchia ≃	60	44.04 N	12.34 E
Marechal Deodoro	240	9.43 S	35.54 W
Maree, Loch ⊜	28	57.40 N	5.30 W
Mareeba	156	17.00 S	145.26 E
Mareetsane	148	26.09 S	25.25 E
Mareg	134	3.47 N	47.18 E
Mareil-en-France	251	49.04 N	2.26 E
Mareil-le-Guyon	251	48.47 N	1.51 E
Mareil-Marly	251	48.53 N	2.05 E
Mare Island I	216	38.06 N	122.16 W
Mare Island Naval Shipyard ■	216	38.06 N	122.17 W
Mare Island Strait ⊔	272	38.06 N	122.17 W
Mareje, Gunung ∧	105b	8.46 S	116.08 E
Marek	102	4.48 S	120.21 E
Maremma ⬥¹	60	42.30 N	11.30 E
Marene	56	44.39 N	7.44 E
Marengo, Ill., U.S.	206	42.15 N	88.37 W
Marengo, Ind., U.S.	208	38.22 N	86.21 W
Marengo, Iowa, U.S.	180	41.48 N	92.04 W
Marengo, Mich., U.S.	206	42.17 N	84.51 W
Marengo, Ohio, U.S.	204	40.24 N	82.49 W
Marengo ⬥¹	56	44.55 N	8.40 E
Marengo ⊥	56	44.49 N	8.40 E
Marengo Cave •⁵	208	38.23 N	86.21 W
Marenisco	180	46.23 N	90.30 W
Marennes	32	45.50 N	1.06 W
Marerano	147b	21.23 S	44.52 E
Mareşalçakmak	120	39.22 N	39.13 E
Maresias	246	23.48 S	45.33 W
Marettimo, Isola I	36	37.58 N	12.04 E
Mareuil-en-Brie	46	48.57 N	3.45 E
Mareuil-lès-Meaux	251	48.56 N	2.52 E
Mareuil-sur-Aÿ	46	49.03 N	4.02 E
Mareuil-sur-Belle	32	45.28 N	0.28 E
Marevo	66	57.19 N	32.05 E
Marey-sur-Tille	54	47.35 N	5.03 E
Marfa	186	30.18 N	104.01 W
Marfinka	73	47.36 N	38.32 E
Marfino	70	46.25 N	48.44 E
Marfleet	42	53.45 N	0.17 W
Margam, Īrān	74	39.09 N	44.57 E
Margam, Wales, U.K.	44	51.34 N	3.44 W
Marganec	68	47.38 N	34.40 E
Margao → Madgaon	112	15.18 N	73.57 E
Margaree	176	46.24 N	61.05 W
Margaree Harbour	176	46.26 N	61.07 W
Margaret ≃	152	18.10 S	125.37 E
Margaret, Mount ∧	214	46.18 N	122.08 W
Margaret Bay	172	51.20 N	127.29 W
Margaret Creek ≃	156	29.26 S	137.07 E
Margarethenhöhe ⬥⁸	253	51.26 N	6.58 E
Margaret River, Austl.	152	18.38 S	126.52 E
Margaret River, Austl.	152	33.57 S	115.04 E
Margaret Roding	250	51.47 N	0.19 E
Margaretting	250	51.41 N	0.25 E
Margarettsville	198	36.32 N	77.21 W
Margaretville	200	42.09 N	74.39 W
Margarita, Bahía → Marguerite Bay C	9	68.30 S	68.30 W
Margarita, Isla I	236	9.05 N	74.30 W
Margarita, Isla de I	236	11.00 N	64.00 W
Margarita Belén	242	27.16 S	58.58 W
Margarita Peak ∧	218	33.26 N	117.23 W
Margaritovka	73	46.55 N	38.52 E
Margate, S. Afr.	148	30.55 S	30.15 E
Margate, Eng., U.K.	44	51.24 N	1.24 E
Margate, Fla., U.S.	210	26.18 N	80.12 W
Margate City	198	39.20 N	74.31 W
Margater ∧	113	35.14 N	72.35 E
Margecany	30	48.54 N	21.01 E
Margelan → Margilan	75	40.28 N	71.44 E
Margeride, Monts de la ⋀	32	44.50 N	3.30 E
Margès	56	45.09 N	5.03 E
Māgherita, Bhārat	110	27.17 N	95.41 E
Margherita → Jamame, Som.	134	0.04 N	42.46 E
Margherita di Savoia	36	41.23 N	16.09 E
Margherita Peak ∧	144	0.22 N	29.51 E
Marghī	110	34.58 N	66.31 E
Marghita	38	47.21 N	22.21 E
Marghūb, Kūh-e ∧	118	33.06 N	57.30 E
Margilan	75	40.28 N	71.44 E
Margit Híd ⬥⁵	254c	47.31 N	19.02 E
Margit-sziget I	254c	47.32 N	19.03 E
Margny-lès-Compiègne	46	49.26 N	2.49 E
Margone	56	45.13 N	7.11 E
Margonin	30	52.59 N	17.05 E
Margos	238	10.04 S	76.26 W
Margosatubig	106	7.34 N	123.10 E
Margot Lake ⊜	174	52.28 N	93.10 W
Māgow, Dasht-e ⬥²	118	30.45 N	63.10 E
Margreid → Magrè	58	46.17 N	11.12 E
Margua ≃	236	7.03 N	72.05 W
Margudol', Šivera ↳	78	56.55 N	102.02 E
Marguerite, Pic → Margherita Peak ∧	144	0.22 N	29.51 E
Marguerite Bay C	9	68.30 S	68.30 W
Marguerittes	56	43.51 N	4.27 E
Margut	52	49.35 N	5.16 E
Māri'	120	36.28 N	37.11 E
Mari ≃	238	7.05 S	64.34 W
Maria	106	9.12 N	123.39 E
Maria I¹	14	21.48 S	154.41 W
Maria Augustina Bank ⊹⁴	14	14.30 S	105.40 E
Mariabrunn ⬥⁸	254b	48.12 N	16.14 E
María Cleofas, Isla I	224	21.16 N	106.14 W
Maria da Fé	246	22.18 S	45.23 W
María Elena	242	22.21 S	69.40 W
Maria Enzersdorf	254b	48.06 N	16.17 E
Maria Gail	58	46.36 N	13.52 E
Mariager	26	56.39 N	10.00 E
María Grande	242	31.39 S	59.54 W
Mariāhu	114	25.37 N	82.37 E
María Ignacia (Vela)	242	37.24 S	59.30 W
Maria Island I, Austl.	154	14.52 S	135.40 E
Maria Island I, Austl.	156	42.39 S	148.04 E
Mariakani	144	3.52 S	39.28 E
Maria Laach ⋓¹	52	50.24 N	7.14 E
María la Baja	236	9.59 N	75.17 W
Maria Lanzendorf	254b	48.06 N	16.25 E
Maria Luggau	58	46.42 N	12.45 E
María Madre, Isla I	224	21.35 N	106.33 W
María Magdalena, Isla I	224	21.25 N	106.24 W
Marian, Lake ⊜	210	27.52 N	81.06 W
Mariana	245	20.23 S	43.25 W
Mariana Basin ⊹¹	14	12.00 N	154.00 E
Mariana Islands II	98	16.00 N	145.30 E
Marianao	230p	23.05 N	82.26 W
Marianao □⁷	276b	23.05 N	82.26 W
Mariana Ridge ⊹³	14	17.00 N	146.00 E
Mariana Trench ⊹¹	14	16.00 N	148.00 E
Marianhill	148	29.52 S	30.50 E
Mariāni	110	26.40 N	94.20 E
Marian Lake ⊜	166	63.00 N	116.10 W
Marianna, Ark., U.S.	184	34.46 N	90.46 W
Marianna, Fla., U.S.	182	30.47 N	85.14 W
Mariannelund	26	57.37 N	15.34 E
Mariano Acosta	248	34.43 S	58.48 W
Mariano Comense	56	45.42 N	9.11 E
Mariano del Friuli	58	45.55 N	13.27 E
Mariano J. Haedo	278	34.38 S	58.36 W
Mariano Machado	142	13.02 S	14.40 E
Mariano Moreno, Arg.	242	38.44 S	70.01 W
Mariano Moreno → Moreno, Arg.	248	34.39 S	58.48 W
Marianópolis	240	4.47 S	44.38 W
Mariánské Lázně	30	49.59 N	12.43 E
Maria Paula	277a	22.54 S	43.02 W
Mariar	154	2.48 S	132.50 E
Mariarano	147b	15.29 S	46.42 E
Marias ≃	192	47.56 N	110.30 W
Marias Pass)(	192	48.19 N	113.21 W
Maria Stein	206	40.24 N	84.28 W
María Teresa	242	34.01 S	61.54 W
Maria Theresa Reef ⊹²	14	37.00 S	151.15 W
Maria-Theresiopel → Subotica	38	46.06 N	19.39 E
Mariato, Punta ≻	236	7.13 N	80.53 W
Maria Van Diemen, Cape ≻	162	34.28 S	172.39 E
Mariaville	200	42.49 N	74.08 W
Mariazell	30	47.47 N	15.19 E
Ma'rib	134	15.30 N	45.20 E
Maribo	41	54.46 N	11.31 E
Maribojoc Bay C	106	9.42 N	123.50 E
Maribor	36	46.33 N	15.39 E
Maribyrnong	264b	37.46 S	144.54 E
Maribyrnong ≃	159	37.49 S	144.55 E
Marica, Blg.	38	42.02 N	25.50 E
Maricá, Bra.	246	22.55 S	42.49 W
Marica, S.S.S.R.	68	51.45 N	35.16 E
Maricá □⁷	277a	22.57 S	42.59 W
Marica (Évros) (Meriç) ≃	38	40.52 N	26.12 E
Maricá, Lagoa de C	246	22.56 S	42.50 W
Maricaban Island I	106	13.39 N	120.53 E
Maricao	230m	18.11 N	66.59 W
Maricás, Ilhas II	246	23.01 S	42.55 W
Maricha Bil ⊜	262b	22.55 N	88.31 E
Marico ≃	146	24.12 S	26.52 E
Maricopa, Ariz., U.S.	190	33.04 N	112.03 W
Maricopa, Calif., U.S.	194	35.03 N	119.24 W
Maricourt (Wakeham Bay)	166	61.36 N	71.58 W
Maricunga, Salar de ≚	242	26.55 S	69.05 W
Maridagao ≃	106	7.13 N	124.41 E
Marīdī	144	4.55 N	29.28 E
Marié ≃	236	0.27 S	66.26 W
Mariec	70	56.32 N	49.50 E
Marie Curtis Park ♦	265b	43.35 N	79.33 W
Mariedamm	40	58.51 N	15.09 E
Mariefred	40	59.16 N	17.13 E
Marie-Galante I	231o	15.56 N	61.16 W
Mariehamn	26	60.06 N	19.57 E
Marieholm	41	55.52 N	13.09 E
Mariel	230p	22.59 N	82.45 W
Marie Lake ⊜	174	54.37 N	110.18 W
Marie-Lefranc, Lac ⊜	196	46.08 N	75.00 W
Mariembourg	46	50.06 N	4.31 E
Marienbad → Mariánské Lázně	30	49.59 N	12.43 E
Marienbaum	48	51.41 N	6.22 E
Marienberg, B.R.D.	52	50.39 N	7.57 E
Marienberg, D.D.R.	50	50.39 N	13.10 E
Marienberg, Pap. N. Gui.	154	3.55 S	144.15 E
Marien-Berg ∧²	254a	52.22 N	13.32 E
Marienborn	50	52.12 N	11.08 E
Marienburg → Malbork	30	54.02 N	19.01 E
Mariendorf ⬥⁸	254a	52.26 N	13.23 E
Marienfelde ⬥⁸	254a	52.25 N	13.22 E
Marienhafe	48	53.31 N	7.16 E
Marienheide	52	51.05 N	7.32 E
Mariental, B.R.D.	50	52.16 N	10.59 E
Mariental, Namibia	146	24.36 S	17.59 E
Marienville	204	41.28 N	79.07 W
Maries □⁶	209	38.15 N	91.56 W
Maries ≃	184	38.30 N	92.01 W
Mariestad	40	58.43 N	13.51 E
Marieta ≃	236	5.02 N	66.38 W
Marietta, Fla., U.S.	182	30.19 N	81.47 W
Marietta, Ga., U.S.	182	33.57 N	84.33 W
Marietta, Ind., U.S.	208	39.27 N	85.53 W
Marietta, Minn., U.S.	188	45.01 N	96.25 W
Marietta, Ohio, U.S.	178	39.25 N	81.27 W
Marietta, Okla., U.S.	186	33.56 N	97.07 W
Marietta, Pa., U.S.	198	40.04 N	76.35 W
Marietta, Tex., U.S.	212	33.10 N	94.33 W
Marietta, Wash., U.S.	214	48.47 N	122.36 W
Marieville	196	45.26 N	73.10 W
Mariga ≃	140	9.40 N	5.55 E
Marigliano	60	40.56 N	14.27 E

ENGLISH

Name	Page	Lat.°′	Long.°′
Marignane	56	43.25 N	5.13 E
Marignier	54	46.06 N	6.31 E
Marigny-le-Châtel	46	48.24 N	3.44 E
Marigny-L'église	46	47.22 N	3.56 E
Marigot, Dom.	230d	15.32 N	61.18 W
Marigot, Guad.	228	18.04 N	63.06 W
Marihatag	106	8.48 N	126.18 E
Mariinsk	76	56.13 N	87.45 E
Mariinskoje	79	51.43 N	140.13 E
Marijskaja Avtonomnaja Sovetskaja Socialističeskaja Respublika □³	70	56.30 N	48.00 E
Marijskaja Nizina ≚	70	56.30 N	46.35 E
Marikana	148	25.42 S	27.30 E
Marikina	259f	14.38 N	121.06 E
Marikina ≃	259f	14.33 N	121.04 E
Marília	245	22.13 S	49.56 W
Marilla	200	42.50 N	78.33 W
Mari-Malmyž	70	56.30 N	50.52 E
Marimari ≃	236	3.58 S	58.49 W
Marimba	142	8.28 S	17.08 E
Marín, Esp.	34	42.23 N	8.42 W
Marín, Méx.	222	25.52 N	100.03 W
Marin □⁶	216	38.03 N	122.33 W
Marin, Cul-de-Sac du C	230e	14.27 N	60.53 W
Marina	216	36.41 N	121.48 W
Marina ⬥⁸	272	37.47 N	122.27 W
Marina del Rey	270	33.59 N	118.28 W
Marina del Rey C	270	33.58 N	118.27 W
Marina di Andora	56	43.57 N	8.08 E
Marina di Campo	60	42.44 N	10.14 E
Marina di Carrara	58	44.02 N	10.02 E
Marina di Cecina	60	43.18 N	10.29 E
Marina di Gioiosa Ionica	36	38.18 N	16.20 E
Marina di Grosseto	60	42.43 N	10.59 E
Marina di Massa	58	44.00 N	10.06 E
Marina di Minturno	60	41.16 N	13.45 E
Marina di Pietrasanta	58	43.56 N	10.12 E
Marina di Pisa	60	43.40 N	10.16 E
Marina di Ravenna	60	44.29 N	12.17 E
Marina Fall ↳	236	5.22 N	59.29 W
Marin City	272	37.52 N	122.21 W
Marinduque □⁴	106	13.25 N	121.55 E
Marinduque Island I	106	13.24 N	121.58 E
Marine	209	38.47 N	89.47 W
Marine City	204	42.43 N	82.30 W
Marine-Ehrenmal ⊥	50	54.23 N	10.15 E
Marineland of the Pacific ⋓³	218	33.44 N	118.24 W
Marine Museum ⋓	270	33.43 N	118.17 W
Marine Park ♦	273	42.20 N	71.01 W
Marine Parkway Bridge ⬥⁵	266	40.34 N	73.53 W
Mariners Museum ⋓	198	37.03 N	76.30 W
Marines	46	49.09 N	1.59 E
Marinette	180	45.06 N	87.38 W
Marine World / Africa USA ♦	272	37.32 N	122.16 W
Maringá	245	23.25 S	51.55 W
Maringa ≃	142	1.14 N	19.48 E
Maringe Lagoon C	165e	8.07 S	159.34 E
Maringouin	184	30.29 N	91.31 W
Marinha Grande	34	39.45 N	8.56 W
Marin Headlands State Park ♦	272	37.49 N	122.30 W
Marin Mall ⬥⁹	272	37.56 N	122.31 W
Marino	60	41.46 N	12.39 E
Marinovka, S.S.S.R.	68	47.46 N	30.53 E
Marinovka, S.S.S.R.	70	48.41 N	43.49 E
Marinovka, S.S.S.R.	73	47.54 N	38.51 E
Marin Peninsula ≻¹	272	37.51 N	122.31 W
Marins	246	22.27 S	45.08 W
Marinskij Posad	70	56.07 N	47.43 E
Marintu	102	0.34 N	110.00 E
Marinwood	216	38.02 N	122.32 W
Mario, Monte ∧²	257a	41.55 N	12.27 E
Marion, Austl.	158b	35.01 S	138.34 E
Marion, Ala., U.S.	184	32.32 N	87.26 W
Marion, Ark., U.S.	184	35.13 N	90.12 W
Marion, Conn., U.S.	197	41.34 N	72.56 W
Marion, Ill., U.S.	184	37.44 N	88.56 W
Marion, Ind., U.S.	206	40.33 N	85.40 W
Marion, Iowa, U.S.	180	42.02 N	91.36 W
Marion, Kans., U.S.	188	38.21 N	97.01 W
Marion, Ky., U.S.	184	37.20 N	88.05 W
Marion, La., U.S.	184	32.54 N	92.15 W
Marion, Mass., U.S.	197	41.42 N	70.46 W
Marion, Mich., U.S.	180	44.06 N	85.09 W
Marion, Miss., U.S.	184	32.25 N	88.39 W
Marion, N.C., U.S.	182	35.41 N	82.01 W
Marion, N. Dak., U.S.	188	46.37 N	98.20 W
Marion, N.Y., U.S.	200	43.08 N	77.11 W
Marion, Ohio, U.S.	204	40.35 N	83.08 W
Marion, S.C., U.S.	182	34.11 N	79.24 W
Marion, S. Dak., U.S.	188	43.25 N	97.16 W
Marion, Va., U.S.	182	36.50 N	81.31 W
Marion, Wis., U.S.	180	44.21 N	89.05 W
Marion □⁶, Fla., U.S.	210	29.00 N	82.03 W
Marion □⁶, Ill., U.S.	209	38.38 N	88.57 W
Marion □⁶, Ind., U.S.	208	39.46 N	86.09 W
Marion □⁶, Mo., U.S.	209	39.50 N	91.37 W
Marion □⁶, Ohio, U.S.	204	40.35 N	83.08 W
Marion □⁶, Oreg., U.S.	214	45.06 N	122.47 W
Marion □⁶, Tex., U.S.	212	32.48 N	94.33 W
Marion, Lake ⊜	210	28.05 N	81.32 W
Marion, Lake ⊜¹	182	33.30 N	80.25 W
Marion Bay C	156	42.48 S	147.55 E
Marion Center	204	40.46 N	79.03 W
Marion Downs	156	23.22 S	139.39 E
Marion Heights	200	40.48 N	76.28 W
Marion Hill	204	40.44 N	80.18 W
Marion Hills	268	41.45 N	87.57 W
Marion Junction	184	32.26 N	87.14 W
Marion Reef ⊹²	156	19.10 S	152.17 E
Marion Station	198	38.02 N	75.46 W
Marionville	184	37.00 N	93.38 W
Mariópolis	242	26.20 S	52.33 W
Maripá, Bra.	246	21.48 S	42.58 W
Maripa, Ven.	236	7.26 N	65.09 W
Maripipi Island I	106	11.47 N	124.19 E
Mariposa	216	37.29 N	119.58 W
Mariposa □⁶	216	37.29 N	119.58 W
Mariposa Creek ≃	216	37.14 N	120.26 W
Mariposa Slough ≃	216	37.12 N	120.46 W
Mariquita	236	5.12 N	74.54 W
Mariquita, Cerro ∧	224	23.13 N	98.22 W
Marisa	102	0.28 N	121.56 E
Marisa ≃	102	0.28 N	121.56 E
Mariscal Estigarribia	242	22.02 S	60.38 W
Marisco, Ponta do ≻	277a	23.01 S	43.17 W
Mariškino	72	55.21 N	38.37 E
Marissa	209	38.15 N	89.45 W
Maritime Alps (Alpes Maritimes) (Alpi Marittime) ⋀	56	44.15 N	7.10 E
Maritimes, Alpes → Maritime Alps ⋀	56	44.15 N	7.10 E
Marittime, Alpi → Maritime Alps ⋀	56	44.15 N	7.10 E
Mari-Turek	70	56.47 N	49.36 E
Maritzburg → Pietermaritzburg	148	29.37 S	30.16 E
Mariupol' → Ždanov	73	47.06 N	37.33 E
Mariusa, Caño ≃¹	236	9.43 N	61.26 W
Mariusa, Isla I	231r	9.39 N	61.19 W
Mariveles	106	14.26 N	120.29 E
Märjamaa	66	58.54 N	24.26 E
Marjanovka, S.S.S.R.	68	50.28 N	24.48 E
Marjanovka, S.S.S.R.	76	54.58 N	72.38 E
Marjanskaja	68	45.06 N	38.38 E

DEUTSCH

Name	Seite	Breite°′	Länge°′ E=Ost
Marjevka	76	53.46 N	67.24 E
Marjina Gorka	66	53.31 N	28.09 E
Marjinka	73	47.56 N	37.31 E
Marjino, S.S.S.R.	72	54.28 N	37.12 E
Marjino, S.S.S.R.	79	48.31 N	130.38 E
Marjino, S.S.S.R.	255a	59.50 N	29.56 E
Marjino, S.S.S.R.	255b	55.52 N	37.18 E
Marjinskaja	74	43.53 N	43.29 E
Marjinsko	66	58.49 N	28.32 E
Mārjirjis, Jūn C	122	33.54 N	35.33 E
Marj 'Uyūn	122	33.22 N	35.35 E
Mark ≃	46	50.43 N	3.50 E
Marka, Som.	134	1.47 N	44.52 E
Mārkā, Urd.	122	31.59 N	35.59 E
Mark Acres	269b	40.21 N	79.42 W
Markakol', Ozero ⊜	76	48.45 N	85.48 E
Markala	140	13.41 N	6.05 W
Markansu	75	39.18 N	73.20 E
Mārkāpur	112	15.44 N	79.17 E
Markaryd	26	56.26 N	13.36 E
Markdale	202	44.19 N	80.39 W
Markdorf	54	47.43 N	9.23 E
Marked Tree	184	35.32 N	90.25 W
Markelo	48	52.14 N	6.30 E
Markelovo	76	56.42 N	83.33 E
Marken I	48	52.28 N	5.03 E
Markendorf	50	51.59 N	13.10 E
Markerwaard ⬥¹	48	52.33 N	5.15 E
Markesan	180	43.42 N	88.59 W
Market Bosworth	44	52.37 N	1.24 W
Market Deeping	44	52.41 N	0.19 W
Market Drayton	44	52.54 N	2.29 W
Market Harborough	44	52.29 N	0.55 W
Markethill	42	54.18 N	6.31 W
Market Lavington	44	51.18 N	1.59 W
Market Rasen	42	53.24 N	0.21 W
Market Weighton	42	53.52 N	0.40 W
Markgröningen	52	48.54 N	9.05 E
Markham, Ont., Can.	202	43.52 N	79.16 W
Markham, Tex., U.S.	212	28.57 N	96.04 W
Markham ≃	154	6.35 S	146.25 E
Markham, Mount ∧	9	82.51 S	161.21 E
Markham Bay C	166	63.30 N	71.48 W
Märkisch Buchholz	50	52.07 N	13.46 E
Märkisch Friedland → Mirosławiec	30	53.21 N	16.05 E
Markkleeberg	50	51.17 N	12.23 E
Markland Dam ⬥⁶	208	38.47 N	84.58 W
Markle, Ind., U.S.	206	40.50 N	85.20 W
Markle, Pa., U.S.	269b	40.34 N	79.39 W
Markleeville	216	38.41 N	119.47 W
Markleville	208	39.59 N	85.37 W
Markley Canyon ∨	272	38.00 N	121.50 W
Marklissa → Leśna	30	51.02 N	15.16 E
Marknesse	48	52.43 N	5.52 E
Markneukirchen	50	50.18 N	12.19 E
Markoldendorf	48	51.48 N	9.46 E
Markópoulon	257c	37.54 N	23.54 E
Markovka	73	49.31 N	39.34 E
Markovo, S.S.S.R.	64	64.40 N	170.25 E
Markovo, S.S.S.R.	70	57.01 N	40.30 E
Markovo, S.S.S.R.	72	55.52 N	39.17 E
Markovo, S.S.S.R.	78	57.20 N	107.04 E
Markoye	140	14.39 N	0.02 E
Markranstädt	50	51.18 N	12.13 E
Marks, S.S.S.R.	70	51.42 N	46.46 E
Marks, Miss., U.S.	184	34.16 N	90.16 W
Marksuhl	52	50.55 N	10.11 E
Marksville	184	31.08 N	92.04 W
Markt Bibart	52	49.39 N	10.26 E
Marktbreit	52	49.40 N	10.08 E
Markt Erlbach	52	49.29 N	10.38 E
Marktheidenfeld	52	49.50 N	9.36 E
Marktleugast	50	50.10 N	11.38 E
Marktleuthen	50	50.08 N	12.00 E
Marktoberdorf	54	47.47 N	10.37 E
Marktredwitz	30	50.00 N	12.06 E
Markt Rettenbach	54	47.57 N	10.23 E
Marktschellenberg	58	47.42 N	13.02 E
Markt Schwaben	58	48.11 N	11.51 E
Mark Twain Cave •⁵	209	39.42 N	91.21 W
Mark Twain State Park ♦	209	39.29 N	91.48 W
Markulešty	68	47.52 N	28.14 E
Markundi	130	11.33 N	23.49 E
Markvue Manor	269b	40.20 N	79.46 W
Mark West Creek ≃	216	38.30 N	122.42 W
Marl	48	51.38 N	7.05 E
Marlasi	154	5.30 S	134.38 E
Marlboro, Alta., Can.	172	53.33 N	116.45 W
Marlboro, N.J., U.S.	198	40.19 N	74.15 W
Marlboro, N.Y., U.S.	200	41.36 N	73.58 W
Marlboro, Ohio, U.S.	204	40.53 N	81.12 W
Marlboro, Pa., U.S.	275	39.54 N	75.42 W
Marlborough, Austl.	156	22.49 S	149.53 E
Marlborough, Guy.	236	7.29 N	58.38 W
Marlborough, Eng., U.K.	44	51.26 N	1.43 W
Marlborough, Conn., U.S.	197	41.38 N	72.28 W
Marlborough, Mass., U.S.	197	42.21 N	71.33 W
Marlborough Downs ⋀¹	44	51.30 N	1.45 W
Marle	46	49.44 N	3.46 E
Marlenheim	54	48.37 N	7.30 E
Marles-en-Brie	251	48.44 N	2.53 E
Marles-les-Mines	46	50.30 N	2.31 E
Marlette	180	43.20 N	83.05 W
Marlette Lake ⊜	216	39.10 N	119.54 W
Marley	268	41.33 N	87.55 W
Marley Creek ≃	268	41.31 N	87.57 W
Marlieux	54	46.04 N	5.04 E
Marlin	212	31.18 N	96.53 W
Marlinton	178	38.13 N	80.06 W
Marl-Loemühle, Flughafen ⊠	253	51.39 N	7.10 E
Marlow, D.D.R.	50	54.09 N	12.34 E
Marlow, Eng., U.K.	44	51.35 N	0.48 W
Marlow, Okla., U.S.	186	34.39 N	97.57 W
Marlpit Hill	250	51.13 N	0.04 E
Marlton	198	39.54 N	74.55 W
Marlton Heights	275	39.40 N	75.21 W
Marly, Forêt de ♦	251	48.50 N	2.00 E
Marly-la-Ville	251	49.05 N	2.30 E
Marly-le-Roi	46	48.52 N	2.05 E
Marma, Sve.	26	61.16 N	16.52 E
Marma, Sve.	40	60.30 N	17.25 E
Marmaduke	184	36.11 N	90.23 W
Marmagne	54	46.50 N	4.21 E
Marmande	32	44.30 N	0.10 E
Marmara, Sea of → Marmara Denizi ⊤²	120	40.40 N	28.15 E
Marmara Adası I	120	40.38 N	27.37 E
Marmara Denizi (Sea of Marmara) ⊤²	120	40.40 N	28.15 E
Marmara Ereğlisi	120	40.58 N	27.57 E
Marmara Gölü ⊜	120	38.37 N	28.02 E
Marmaris	120	36.51 N	28.16 E
Marmarītā	120	34.47 N	36.15 E
Marmarth	188	46.18 N	103.54 W
Marmaton ≃	184	38.00 N	94.19 W
Marmelada ≃	245	19.01 S	45.08 W
Marmelos	238	6.08 S	61.50 W
Marmelos, Rio dos ≃	238	6.06 S	61.46 W
Marmet	178	38.15 N	81.04 W
Marmion Lake ⊜¹	180	48.54 N	91.30 W
Marmirolo	58	45.13 N	10.45 E
Marmolada ∧	58	46.26 N	11.51 E
Marmora, Ont., Can.	202	44.29 N	77.41 W
Marmora, N.J., U.S.	198	39.16 N	74.39 W
Marmora, Punta la ∧	36	39.59 N	9.19 E
Marmore	60	42.33 N	12.43 E
Marmore ≃	56	45.44 N	7.37 E
Marmore, Cascàta delle ↳	60	42.33 N	12.43 E
Marmot Bay C	170	58.00 N	152.20 W
Marmot Island I	170	58.13 N	151.51 W
Marmoutier	54	48.41 N	7.23 E

Symbols in the index entries represent the broad categories identified in the key at the right. Symbols with superior numbers (⋀²) identify subcategories (see complete key on page *I* · *26*).

Kartensymbole in dem Registerverzeichnis stellen die rechts in Schlüssel erklärten Kategorien dar. Symbole mit hochgestellten Ziffern (⋀²) bezeichnen Unterabteilungen einer Kategorie (vgl. vollständiger Schlüssel auf Seite *I* · *26*).

Los símbolos incluídos en el texto del índice representan las grandes categorias identificadas con la clave a la derecha. Los símbolos con numeros en su parte superior (⋀²) identifican las subcategorías (véase la clave completa en la página *I* · *26*).

Les symboles de l'index représentent les catégories indiquées dans la légende à droite. Les symboles suivis d'un indice (⋀²) représentent des sous-catégories (voir légende complète à la page *I* · *26*).

Os símbolos incluídos no texto do índice representam as grandes categorias identificadas com a chave à direita. Os símbolos com números em sua parte superior (⋀²) identificam as subcategorias (veja-se a chave completa à página *I* · *26*).

	English	Deutsch	Español	Français	Português
∧	Mountain	Berg	Montaña	Montagne	Montanha
⋀	Mountains	Berge	Montañas	Montagnes	Montanhas
)(	Pass	Pass	Paso	Col	Passo
∨	Valley, Canyon	Tal, Cañon	Valle, Cañón	Vallée, Canyon	Vale, Canhão
≚	Plain	Ebene	Llano	Plaine	Planície
≻	Cape	Kap	Cabo	Cap	Cabo
I	Island	Insel	Isla	Île	Ilha
II	Islands	Inseln	Islas	Îles	Ilhas
•	Other Topographic Features	Andere Topographische Objekte	Otros Elementos Topográficos	Autres données topographiques	Outros Elementos Topográficos

ESPAÑOL

Nombre	Página	Lat. °′	Long. °′ W=Oeste
Marnate	256b	45.38 N	8.54 E
Marnay	54	47.17 N	5.46 E
Marnaz	54	46.04 N	6.32 E
Marne, B.R.D.	48	53.57 N	9.00 E
Marne, Mich., U.S.	206	43.02 N	85.50 W
Marne □[5]	32	48.55 N	4.10 E
Marne ≃	32	48.49 N	2.24 E
Marneà la Saône, Canal de la ≍	54	48.44 N	4.36 E
Marne au Rhin, Canal de la ≍	52	48.35 N	7.47 E
Marneuli	74	41.28 N	44.50 E
Marnhull	44	50.58 N	2.18 W
Marnitz	50	53.19 N	11.56 E
Maroa, Ill., U.S.	209	40.02 N	88.57 W
Maroa, Ven.	236	2.43 N	67.33 W
Maroala	147b	15.23 S	47.59 E
Maroantsetra	147b	15.26 S	49.44 E
Maroc → Morocco □[1]	138	32.00 N	5.00 W
Maroelaboom	146	19.15 S	18.53 E
Marofandilia	147b	20.07 S	44.34 E
Marokko → Morocco □[1]	138	32.00 N	5.00 W
Marol ◆[8]	262c	19.07 N	72.53 E
Marolambo	147b	20.02 S	48.07 E
Maroldsweisach	52	50.12 N	10.39 E
Marolles-en-Brie	251	48.44 N	2.33 E
Marolles-en-Hurepoix	251	48.34 N	2.18 E
Marolles-les-Braults	46	48.15 N	0.19 E
Maromandia	147b	14.13 S	48.08 E
Maromme	46	49.28 N	1.02 E
Maromokotro ∧	147b	14.01 S	48.59 E
Marone	58	45.44 N	10.05 E
Marong	92	31.07 N	99.20 E
Maronghi Creek ≃	161a	26.58 S	152.22 E
Maroni (Marowijne) ≃	240	5.45 N	53.58 W
Maroon	161a	28.10 S	152.44 E
Maroondah Aqueduct ≍[1]	264b	37.42 S	145.01 E
Maros	102	5.00 S	119.34 E
Maros (Mureș) ≃	38	46.15 N	20.13 E
Maroseranana	147b	18.32 S	48.51 E
Marostica	58	45.45 N	11.39 E
Marosvásárhely → Tîrgu Mureș	38	46.33 N	24.33 E
Marotandrano	147b	16.10 S	48.50 E
Marotolana	147b	14.01 S	48.37 E
Marotta	60	43.46 N	13.08 E
Maroua	136	10.36 N	14.20 E
Maroubra	264a	33.57 S	151.16 E
Maroubra Bay C	264a	33.57 S	151.16 E
Marouini ≃	240	3.18 N	54.04 W
Marovato, Madag.	147b	16.28 S	48.25 E
Marovato, Madag.	147b	15.48 S	48.05 E
Marovoay	147b	16.06 S	46.39 E
Marovoay Nord	147b	16.57 S	44.34 E
Marovo Lagoon C	165e	8.29 S	158.04 E
Marowijne □[5]	240	4.15 N	54.35 W
Marowijne (Maroni) ≃	240	5.45 N	53.58 W
Marpent	46	50.18 N	4.05 E
Marpi Point ≻	164n	15.17 N	145.49 E
Marple	42	53.24 N	2.03 W
Marpo Point ≻	164n	14.57 N	145.40 E
Marqa I	134	18.13 N	41.19 E
Marquam	214	45.04 N	122.41 W
Marquand	184	37.26 N	90.10 W
Marquard	148	28.54 S	27.28 E
Marquardt	50	52.27 N	12.57 E
Marquartstein	58	47.45 N	12.28 E
Marquesas Islands → Marquises, Îles II	6	9.00 S	139.30 W
Marquesas Keys II	210	24.34 N	82.08 W
Marquette, Kans., U.S.	188	38.33 N	97.50 W
Marquette, Mich., U.S.	180	46.33 N	87.24 W
Marquette Park ♠	268	41.46 N	87.42 W
Márquez, Perú	276d	11.57 S	77.08 W
Marquez, Tex., U.S.	212	31.14 N	96.15 W
Marquina-Jemein	34	43.16 N	2.30 W
Marquion	46	50.13 N	3.05 E
Marquis	231k	12.06 N	61.37 W
Marquis, Cape ≻	231f	14.03 N	60.54 W
Marquise	46	50.49 N	1.42 E
Marquises, Îles (Marquesas Islands) II	6	9.00 S	139.30 W
Marrabel	158b	34.08 S	138.53 E
Marrabios, Cordillera de los ⩘	226	12.35 N	86.50 W
Marra Creek ≃	156	30.05 S	147.05 E
Marradi	60	44.04 N	11.37 E
Marradong	158a	32.52 S	116.27 E
Marrah, Jabal ∧	130	13.04 N	24.21 E
Marra Hills ⩘[2]	130	6.05 N	27.33 E
Marrakech	138	31.38 N	8.00 W
Marrawah	156	40.56 S	144.41 E
Marrecas, Serra das ⩘[1]	240	9.00 S	41.00 W
Marree	156	29.39 S	138.04 E
Marrero	184	29.54 N	90.07 W
Marrickville	264a	33.55 S	151.09 E
Marromeu	146	18.20 S	35.56 E
Marrowstone Island I	214	48.04 N	122.41 W
Marruecos → Morocco □[1]	138	32.00 N	5.00 W
Marrupa	144	13.08 S	37.30 E
Mars	204	40.42 N	80.06 W
Marsabit	144	2.20 N	37.59 E
Marsabit National Park ♠	144	2.20 N	38.00 E
Marsac-en-Livradois	56	45.29 N	3.44 E
Marṣafā wa Kafr Aḥmad Ḥashīsh	132	30.25 N	31.15 E
Marsal	52	48.48 N	6.36 E
Marsala	36	37.48 N	12.26 E
Marsangue, Ruisseau la ≃	251	48.43 N	2.45 E
Marsannay-la-Côte	54	47.16 N	4.59 E
Marsanne	56	44.39 N	4.52 E
Marsā Sūsah	136	32.54 N	21.58 E
Mars'aty	76	60.05 N	60.29 E
Marscheid ◆[8]	253	51.14 N	7.14 E
Marsciano	60	42.54 N	12.20 E
Marsden, Austl.	156	33.45 S	147.32 E
Marsden, Eng., U.K.	252	53.36 N	1.56 W
Marsden, Point ≻	158b	35.35 S	137.38 E
Marsden Park	264a	33.42 S	150.50 E
Marsdiep Ʉ	48	52.59 N	4.45 E
Marseille	56	43.18 N	5.24 E
Marseille-en-Beauvaisis	46	49.35 N	1.57 E
Marseille-Marignane, Aéroport de ⊠	56	43.27 N	5.13 E
Marseilles, Ill., U.S.	206	41.20 N	88.43 W
Marseilles, Ohio, U.S.	204	40.42 N	83.23 W
Marsella → Marseille	56	43.18 N	5.24 E
Marsfield	264a	33.47 S	151.07 E
Marsfjället ∧	24	65.05 N	15.28 E
Marshakala ∧	113	35.25 N	75.35 E
Marshall, Liber.	140	6.10 N	10.23 W
Marshall, Ark., U.S.	184	35.55 N	92.38 W
Marshall, Ill., U.S.	184	39.23 N	87.42 W
Marshall, Mich., U.S.	206	42.16 N	84.58 W
Marshall, Minn., U.S.	188	44.27 N	95.47 W
Marshall, Mo., U.S.	184	39.07 N	93.12 W
Marshall, N.C., U.S.	182	35.48 N	82.41 W
Marshall, Tex., U.S.	184	32.33 N	94.23 W
Marshall, Va., U.S.	178	38.52 N	77.52 W
Marshall, Wis., U.S.	206	43.10 N	89.04 W
Marshall □[6], Ill., U.S.	206	41.02 N	89.24 W
Marshall □[6], Ind., U.S.	206	41.21 N	86.19 W
Marshall ≃	152	22.59 S	136.59 E
Marshall Bennett Islands II	154	8.50 S	151.50 E

FRANÇAIS

Nom	Page	Lat. °′	Long. °′ W=Ouest
Marshallberg	182	34.44 N	76.31 W
Marshall Canyon Regional Park ♠	270	34.09 N	117.43 W
Marshall Gold Discovery State Historical Park ♠	216	38.48 N	120.53 W
Marshall Hall	198	38.41 N	77.06 W
Marshall Islands II	14	9.00 N	168.00 E
Marshalls Creek	200	41.03 N	75.08 W
Marshallton, Del., U.S.	198	39.45 N	75.39 W
Marshallton, Pa., U.S.	275	39.57 N	75.41 W
Marshalltown	180	42.03 N	92.55 W
Marshallville, Ga., U.S.	182	32.27 N	89.56 W
Marshallville, Ohio, U.S.	204	40.54 N	81.44 W
Marshbank Metropolitan Park ♠	271	42.36 N	83.23 W
Marshbrook	144	18.34 S	31.03 E
Marsh Creek ≃, Calif., U.S.	272	37.53 N	121.49 W
Marsh Creek ≃, Mich., U.S.	271	42.06 N	83.13 W
Marsh Creek ≃, Pa., U.S.	204	41.03 N	77.36 W
Marsh Creek ≃, Pa., U.S.	275	40.03 N	75.43 W
Marsh Creek ≃, Wis., U.S.	206	42.13 N	89.04 W
Marshes Creek ≃	266	40.36 N	74.13 W
Marshfield, Eng., U.K.	44	51.28 N	2.19 W
Marshfield, Mass., U.S.	197	42.07 N	70.43 W
Marshfield, Mo., U.S.	184	37.15 N	92.54 W
Marshfield, Wis., U.S.	180	44.40 N	90.10 W
Marshfield Airport ⊠	273	42.06 N	70.40 W
Marshfield Center	273	42.07 N	70.43 W
Marshfield Hills	197	42.09 N	70.44 W
Marsh Harbour	228	26.33 N	77.03 W
Marsh Hill	200	41.29 N	76.58 W
Mars Hill, Ind., U.S.	208	39.43 N	86.09 W
Mars Hill, Maine, U.S.	176	46.31 N	67.52 W
Mars Hill, N.C., U.S.	182	35.47 N	82.29 W
Marsh Island I	184	29.35 N	91.53 W
Marsh Lake ⊜	170	60.25 N	134.18 W
Marsh Peak ∧	190	40.43 N	109.50 W
Marshside	252	53.40 N	2.58 W
Marshville	182	34.59 N	80.26 W
Marshyhope Creek ≃	198	38.32 N	75.45 W
Marsica ◆[1]	60	41.50 N	13.45 E
Marsillargues	56	43.40 N	4.11 E
Marsing	192	43.33 N	116.48 W
Marske-by-the-Sea	42	54.36 N	1.01 W
Mars-la-Tour	52	49.06 N	5.54 E
Marson	52	48.55 N	4.32 E
Marssassoum	140	12.50 N	16.00 W
Marssum	48	53.12 N	5.42 E
Märsta	40	59.37 N	17.51 E
Marstal	41	54.51 N	10.31 E
Marsteller	204	40.39 N	78.47 W
Märstetten	54	47.36 N	9.04 E
Marston	252	53.16 N	2.30 W
Marston Moor ≚	42	53.57 N	1.17 W
Marstons Mills	197	41.39 N	70.25 W
Marstrand	26	57.53 N	11.35 E
Marsyandi ≃	114	28.05 N	84.28 E
Mart	212	31.33 N	96.50 W
Marta	60	42.32 N	11.55 E
Marta ≃	60	42.14 N	11.42 E
Martaban	100	16.32 N	97.37 E
Martaban, Gulf of C	100	16.30 N	97.00 E
Martap	142	6.54 N	13.03 E
Martapura, Indon.	102	4.19 S	104.22 E
Martapura, Indon.	102	3.25 S	114.51 E
Marte	136	12.22 N	13.51 E
Marteg ≃	44	52.20 N	3.33 W
Martel, Fr.	32	44.56 N	1.37 E
Martel, Ohio, U.S.	204	40.40 N	82.55 W
Martelange	52	49.50 N	5.44 E
Martell	216	38.22 N	120.48 W
Martello	58	46.34 N	10.47 E
Martello, Val V	58	46.31 N	10.45 E
Martemjanovskij	76	55.54 N	80.22 E
Marten ◆[8]	253	51.31 N	7.23 E
Marten Lake ⊜	180	46.42 N	79.41 W
Marten Mountain ∧	172	55.28 N	114.43 W
Martfeld	48	52.52 N	9.04 E
Marthaguy Creek ≃	156	30.16 S	147.35 E
Martha Lake	214	47.51 N	122.20 W
Marthall	252	53.17 N	2.18 W
Marthasville	209	38.38 N	91.04 W
Martha's Vineyard I	197	41.25 N	70.40 W
Martí, Cuba	230p	21.09 N	77.27 W
Martí, Cuba	230p	22.57 N	80.55 W
Martignacco	58	46.05 N	13.08 E
Martignat	54	46.13 N	5.36 E
Martigny	54	46.06 N	7.04 E
Martigny-les-Bains	54	48.06 N	5.49 E
Martigues	56	43.24 N	5.03 E
Martil	34	35.37 N	5.17 W
Martim Francisco	246	22.31 S	46.57 W
Martin, Česko.	30	49.05 N	18.55 E
Martin, Ky., U.S.	182	37.34 N	82.45 W
Martin, Mich., U.S.	206	42.37 N	85.39 W
Martin, N. Dak., U.S.	188	47.50 N	100.07 W
Martin, Ohio, U.S.	204	41.33 N	83.20 W
Martin, S. Dak., U.S.	188	43.10 N	101.44 W
Martin, Tenn., U.S.	184	36.21 N	88.51 W
Martin □[6]	210	27.07 N	80.31 W
Martín ≃	34	41.18 N	0.19 W
Martín, Arroyo ≃	278	34.51 S	58.04 W
Martina	54	46.53 N	10.30 E
Martina Franca	36	40.42 N	17.21 E
Martin Airport ⊠	274b	39.20 N	76.25 W
Martinborough	162	41.13 S	175.28 E
Martín Chico, Punta ≻	248	34.10 S	58.13 W
Martindale	186	29.50 N	97.51 W
Martindale Creek ≃	208	39.48 N	85.09 W
Martindale Pond ⊜	274a	43.11 N	79.16 W
Martin-Église	46	49.54 N	1.09 E
Martinengo	56	45.34 N	9.46 E
Mărtinești	38	45.30 N	27.18 E
Martinez	216	37.55 N	121.55 W
Martínez ◆[8]	248	34.29 S	58.30 W
Martínez de la Torre	224	20.04 N	97.03 W
Martín García, Isla I	248	34.13 S	58.15 W
Martinho Campos	245	19.20 S	45.13 W
Martinica → Martinique □[2]	230e	14.40 N	61.00 W
Martini Creek ≃	272	37.33 N	122.31 W
Martinique □[2]	220		
	230e	14.40 N	61.00 W
Martin Lake ⊜[1]	184	32.50 N	85.55 W
Martinniemi	26	65.13 N	25.18 E
Martinópole	240	3.15 S	40.41 W
Martin Peninsula ≻[1]	9	74.25 S	114.10 W
Martín Pérez ≃	276b	23.07 N	82.20 W
Martin Point ≻	170	70.08 N	143.16 W
Martin Run ≃	269a	41.27 N	82.12 W
Martins	240	6.05 S	37.55 W
Martinsberg	30	48.22 N	15.09 E
Martins Brook ≃	273	42.34 N	71.06 W
Martinsburg, Mo., U.S.	209	39.06 N	91.39 W
Martinsburg, N.Y., U.S.	202	43.44 N	75.28 W
Martinsburg, Ohio, U.S.	204	40.16 N	82.21 W
Martinsburg, Pa., U.S.	204	40.19 N	78.20 W
Martinsburg, W. Va., U.S.	178	39.27 N	77.58 W
Martins Creek	198	40.47 N	75.11 W
Martins Creek ≃	200	41.37 N	75.46 W
Martinscroft	252	53.24 N	2.31 W

PORTUGUÊS

Nome	Página	Lat. °′	Long. °′ W=Oeste
Martins Ferry	204	40.06 N	80.44 W
Martins Mills	212	32.25 N	95.47 W
Martins Pond ⊜	273	42.36 N	71.08 W
Martinstein	52	49.48 N	7.32 E
Martinsthal	52	50.03 N	8.07 E
Martinsville, Austl.	160	33.03 S	151.25 E
Martinsville, Ill., U.S.	184	39.20 N	87.53 W
Martinsville, Ind., U.S.	208	39.26 N	86.25 W
Martinsville, N.J., U.S.	266	40.36 N	74.34 W
Martinsville, Ohio, U.S.	208	39.19 N	83.49 W
Martinsville, Va., U.S.	182	36.41 N	79.52 W
Martinton	206	40.55 N	87.44 W
Martintown	196	45.09 N	74.42 W
Martin Van Buren National Historic Site ⊥	200	42.22 N	73.43 W
Martin Vaz, Ilhas II	234	20.30 S	28.51 W
Martisovo	66	56.34 N	31.55 E
Martock	44	50.59 N	2.46 W
Martofte	41	55.33 N	10.40 E
Marton, N.Z.	162	40.05 S	175.23 E
Marton, Eng., U.K.	252	53.12 N	2.13 W
Martorell	256d	41.29 N	1.56 E
Martorellas	256d	41.32 N	2.14 E
Martos	34	37.43 N	3.58 W
Martovaja	68	49.57 N	36.57 E
Martre, Lac la ⊜	166	63.15 N	116.55 W
Martti	24	67.28 N	28.28 E
Martūbah	136	32.35 N	22.46 E
Martuk	76	50.46 N	56.31 E
Martuni, S.S.S.R.	74	39.48 N	47.06 E
Martuni, S.S.S.R.	74	40.08 N	45.19 E
Martville	200	43.17 N	76.38 W
Martynoviči	68	51.17 N	29.37 E
Martynovka	68	49.38 N	31.18 E
Martynovo	70	50.43 N	50.23 E
Martynovskij	70	50.29 N	42.18 E
Maru	140	12.22 N	6.22 E
Marua	154	9.30 S	149.20 E
Marudi	102	4.11 N	114.19 E
Marudu, Teluk C	102	6.45 N	116.55 E
Marugame	86	34.17 N	133.47 E
Marui	154	4.05 S	143.00 E
Maruia	162	42.11 S	172.13 E
Maruia ≃	162	41.47 S	172.12 E
Maruim	240	10.45 S	37.05 W
Maruko	84	36.19 N	138.16 E
Marula	144	20.26 S	28.06 E
Marulan	160	34.43 S	150.00 E
Marulan South	160	34.46 S	150.02 E
Marum	48	53.08 N	6.16 E
Marum, Mount ∧	165f	16.15 S	168.07 E
Marunga	142	17.27 S	20.02 E
Marungu	144	3.44 S	30.48 E
Marungu ⩘	144	7.42 S	30.00 E
Maruoka	84	36.09 N	136.16 E
Mårup	41	55.57 N	10.35 E
Marusino	255b	55.42 N	37.59 E
Maruškino	72	55.36 N	37.12 E
Ma'rūt	110	31.34 N	67.03 E
Marutea I[1]	14	17.00 S	143.10 W
Maruyama	84	35.01 N	139.58 E
Maruyama ≃	86	35.39 N	134.50 E
Marv Dasht	118	29.50 N	52.40 E
Marve ◆[8]	262c	19.12 N	72.49 E
Marvejols	32	44.33 N	3.18 E
Marvell	184	34.33 N	90.55 W
Marvel Loch	152	31.28 S	119.28 E
Marviken	40	58.34 N	16.51 E
Marvila ◆[8]	256c	38.44 N	9.06 W
Marville	52	49.27 N	5.27 E
Marvin Creek ≃	204	41.48 N	78.26 W
Marvine, Mount ∧	190	38.40 N	111.39 W
Mar Vista ◆[8]	270	34.00 N	118.27 W
Mārwār	110	25.44 N	73.36 E
Marwayne	174	53.32 N	110.20 W
Marwitz	254a	52.41 N	13.09 E
Marwitzer Heide ◆[3]	254a	52.40 N	13.06 E
Marwood	204	40.48 N	79.47 W
Marxhagen	50	53.37 N	12.36 E
Marxloh ◆[8]	253	51.31 N	6.46 E
Mary	118	37.36 N	61.50 E
Mary □[4]	118	37.36 N	61.50 E
Mary ≃	154	12.53 S	131.38 E
Mary Anne Group II	152	21.13 S	115.32 E
Maryborough, Austl.	156	25.32 S	152.42 E
Maryborough, Austl.	159	37.03 S	143.45 E
Maryborough → Port Laoise, Eire	28	53.02 N	7.17 W
Mary D	198	40.45 N	76.04 W
Marydale	148	29.23 S	22.05 E
Marydel	198	39.07 N	75.45 W
Maryfield	174	49.48 N	101.32 W
Maryhill	214	45.41 N	120.49 W
Mary Jane, Lake ⊜	210	28.22 N	81.11 W
Mary Kathleen	156	20.49 S	139.58 E
Maryknoll	200	41.11 N	73.50 W
Mary Lake ⊜	202	45.15 N	79.15 W
Maryland, Rh.	144	17.39 S	30.29 E
Maryland, N.Y., U.S.	200	42.32 N	74.53 W
Maryland □[6]	140	4.40 N	8.00 W
Maryland □[3]	168		
	178	39.00 N	76.45 W
Maryland, University of (Baltimore County Campus) ɤ[2], Md., U.S.	274b	39.15 N	76.43 W
Maryland, University of ɤ[2], Md., U.S.	274c	38.59 N	76.57 W
Maryland City	198	39.06 N	76.50 W
Maryland Gardens Park ♠	265b	43.47 N	79.32 W
Maryland Heights	209	38.44 N	90.27 W
Maryland Line	198	39.43 N	76.40 W
Maryland Park	274c	38.53 N	76.54 W
Marylebone	252	53.34 N	2.38 W
Maryneal	186	32.14 N	100.27 W
Maryport	42	54.43 N	3.30 W
Marys ≃, Ill., U.S.	184	37.53 N	89.47 W
Marys ≃, Nev., U.S.	194	41.04 N	115.16 W
Marys Creek ≃	192	42.18 N	115.48 W
Mary's Igloo	170	65.09 N	165.04 W
Marys Peak ∧	192	44.30 N	123.33 W
Marystown	176	47.10 N	55.09 W
Marysvale	190	38.27 N	112.11 W
Marysville, Austl.	159	37.31 S	145.45 E
Marysville, B.C., Can.	172	49.38 N	115.57 W
Marysville, N.B., Can.	176	45.59 N	66.35 W
Marysville, Calif., U.S.	216	39.09 N	121.35 W
Marysville, Kans., U.S.	188	39.51 N	96.39 W
Marysville, Mich., U.S.	204	42.54 N	82.29 W
Marysville, Ohio, U.S.	204	40.14 N	83.22 W
Marysville, Pa., U.S.	198	40.20 N	76.56 W
Marysville, Wash., U.S.	214	48.03 N	122.11 W
Mār Yūsuf	122	33.53 N	35.33 E
Maryūt, Buḥayrat ⊜	132	31.08 N	29.54 E
Maryvale	161a	28.05 S	152.15 E
Maryvale ◆[8]	265b	43.46 N	79.18 W
Maryville, Mo., U.S.	184	40.21 N	94.52 W
Maryville, Tenn., U.S.	182	35.46 N	83.58 W
Marywood	206	41.48 N	88.18 W
Marzabotto	58	44.20 N	11.12 E
Marzagão	245	17.59 S	48.39 W
Marzahn ◆[8]	254a	52.33 N	13.33 E
Marzahna	50	52.00 N	12.46 E
Marzahne	50	52.31 N	12.31 E
Marzal, Aven de ●[5]	56	44.22 N	4.31 E
Marzo, Punta ≻	236	6.50 N	77.42 W
Marzolara	58	44.38 N	10.10 E
Marzūq	136	25.55 N	13.55 E
Marzūq, Ḥammādat ◆[2]	136	26.10 N	12.45 E
Marzūq, Idehan ●[8]	136	24.30 N	13.00 E
Masa	142	3.45 S	15.29 E
Masachapa	226	11.47 N	86.31 W
Mas'adah (Cæsarea Philippi)	122	33.14 N	35.45 E
Masada Landing Ground ⊠	122	31.19 N	35.21 E
Más Afuera, Isla → Alejandro Selkirk, Isla I	234	33.45 S	80.46 W
Masagua	226	14.12 N	90.51 W
Masaguisi	106	12.41 N	121.32 E
Masai	104	1.29 N	103.53 E
Masai-Amboseli Game Reserve ♠	144	2.30 S	37.00 E
Masai-Mara Game Reserve ♠	144	1.15 S	35.15 E
Masai Steppe ≚	144	4.45 S	37.00 E
Masak	75	43.37 N	78.18 E
Masaka	144	0.20 S	31.44 E
Masaka □[5]	144	0.30 S	31.35 E
Masaki, Nihon	86	33.47 N	132.42 E
Masaki, Nihon	258	35.13 N	140.02 E
Masalasef	136	11.43 N	17.08 E
Masalembo-besar I	102	5.34 S	114.26 E
Masally	74	39.03 N	48.40 E
Masalog Point ≻	164n	15.01 N	145.41 E
Masamba	102	2.32 S	120.20 E
Masan	88	35.11 N	128.32 E
Masangwe ∧	144	5.28 S	30.05 E
Masānjor	116	24.07 N	87.19 E
Masapelid Island I	106	9.42 N	125.39 E
Masapun	102	7.47 S	126.38 E
Masarah	132	27.29 N	30.50 E
Masaran	105a	7.28 S	110.55 E
Ma'ṣarat Samālūṭ	132	28.19 N	30.43 E
Masaryktown	210	28.27 N	82.28 W
Masasi	144	10.43 S	38.48 E
Masatepe	226	11.55 N	86.09 W
Más a Tierra, Isla → Róbinson Crusoe, Isla I	234	33.38 S	78.52 W
Masaya	226	11.58 N	86.06 W
Masaya □[5]	226	12.00 N	86.10 W
Masayama	140	8.15 N	10.49 W
Masba	136	11.30 N	13.00 E
Masbate	106	12.22 N	123.36 E
Masbate □[4]	106	12.20 N	123.30 E
Masbate Island I	106	12.15 N	123.30 E
Masbate Pass Ʉ	106	12.30 N	123.35 E
Mascara	138	35.45 N	0.01 E
Mascarene Basin ⊹[1]	12	27.00 S	55.00 E
Mascarene Islands II	147c	21.00 S	57.00 E
Mascasín	242	31.22 S	66.59 W
Maschen	48	53.24 N	10.02 E
Mascot, Austl.	264a	33.56 S	151.12 E
Mascot, Tenn., U.S.	182	36.04 N	83.44 W
Mascota	224	20.32 N	104.49 W
Mascotte	210	28.35 N	81.53 W
Mascouche	196	45.45 N	73.36 W
Mascouche ≃	196	45.41 N	73.40 W
Mascoutah	209	38.29 N	89.48 W
Mascuppic Lake ⊜	273	42.41 N	71.23 W
Mase	92	27.16 N	104.08 E
Mase ≃	84	35.40 N	137.10 E
Masefield	174	49.09 N	107.48 W
Masela, Pulau I	154	8.09 S	129.50 E
Maser	58	45.48 N	11.59 E
Maserada sul Piave	58	45.45 N	12.17 E
Maserti	120	37.24 N	40.58 E
Maseru	148	29.28 S	27.30 E
Masevaux	54	47.47 N	7.00 E
Maševka	68	49.26 N	34.52 E
Maševo	68	52.06 N	32.48 E
Masha	90	27.26 N	117.50 E
Mashaba	144	20.02 S	30.29 E
Mashaba Mountains ⩘	144	18.45 S	30.32 E
Mash'abbe Sade	122	31.00 N	34.47 E
Mashābih I	118	25.37 N	36.29 E
Mashai Pass)(	148	29.42 S	29.10 E
Mashalah	132	30.44 N	31.08 E
Masham	42	54.13 N	1.40 W
Mashan, Zhg.	79	45.13 N	130.35 E
Mashan, Zhg.	90	27.33 N	113.46 E
Mashan, Zhg.	92	23.50 N	108.16 E
Mashar	130	9.14 N	26.52 E
Mashbury	250	51.47 N	0.24 E
Mashel ≃	214	46.51 N	122.20 W
Mashenqiao	95	40.04 N	117.36 E
Masherbrum ∧	113	35.38 N	76.18 E
Mashgharah	122	33.32 N	35.39 E
Mashhad, Īrān	118	36.18 N	59.36 E
Mashhad, Yis.	122	32.44 N	35.19 E
Mashi, Nig.	140	13.00 N	7.54 E
Mashi, Zhg.	90	25.01 N	114.09 E
Mashi, Zhg.	90	29.05 N	114.22 E
Mashike	82a	43.51 N	141.31 E
Mashiko	84	36.28 N	140.06 E
Mashita ≃	84	35.40 N	137.10 E
Mashīz	118	29.56 N	56.37 E
Mashkai ≃	118	26.02 N	65.19 E
Māshkel (Māshkīd) ≃	118	28.02 N	63.25 E
Māshkel, Hāmūn-i- ⊜	118	28.15 N	63.00 E
Mashki Chāh	118	29.01 N	62.27 E
Māshkīd (Māshkel) ≃	118	28.02 N	63.25 E
Mashonaland North □[4]	144	16.30 S	30.00 E
Mashonaland South □[4]	144	18.15 S	30.45 E
Mashpee	197	41.39 N	70.29 W
Mashra'ar-Raqq	130	8.25 N	29.16 E
Mashtūl as-Sūq	132	30.22 N	31.22 E
Mashuikou	95	39.48 N	115.16 E
Mashū-ko ⊜	82a	43.35 N	144.32 E
Mashūray	110	32.12 N	68.21 E
Masibi	142	11.08 S	22.42 E
Masihi	104	2.47 N	99.40 E
Masīlah, Wādī V	134	15.10 N	51.05 E
Masi-Manimba	142	4.46 S	17.55 E
Masin	154	6.15 S	139.19 E
Masina	262b	22.55 N	88.32 E
Masindi	144	1.41 N	31.43 E
Masinloc	106	15.32 N	119.57 E
Masīr	132	31.03 N	31.00 E
Maṣīrah, Khalīj al- C	108	20.10 N	58.15 E
Masisea	238	8.36 S	74.19 W
Masisi	144	1.24 S	28.49 E
Masiwang, Tanjung ≻	154	3.27 S	130.49 E
Masjed Soleymān	118	31.58 N	49.18 E
Masjid Tanah	104	2.21 N	102.07 E
Mask, Lough ⊜	28	53.35 N	9.20 W
Maska	140	11.20 N	7.20 E
Maskanah	120	36.01 N	38.05 E
Maskelyne Islands II	165f	16.32 S	167.49 E
Maskharah, Jabal al- ∧	132	29.44 N	31.34 E
Maskin	118	23.35 N	56.39 E
Maškino	72	54.53 N	36.08 E
Maskinongé □[6]	196	46.35 N	73.30 W
Maskinongé ≃, Qué., Can.	196	46.10 N	73.01 W
Maskinongé ≃, Qué., Can.	196	45.49 N	74.40 W
Maskinongé, Lac ⊜	196	46.19 N	73.23 W
Maškoviči	72	54.11 N	36.17 E
Masku	26	60.34 N	22.06 E
Maskun, Ras ≻	134	11.12 N	43.35 E
Maskūtān	118	26.51 N	59.49 E
Maskwa ≃	174	50.33 N	96.08 W
Masl'anino	76	54.20 N	84.13 E
Masl'anskaja	76	55.56 N	70.08 E
Maslova	255a	59.47 N	30.48 E
Maslovka	68	51.33 N	39.14 E
Maslovo	76	60.13 N	60.10 E
Masnières	46	50.07 N	3.13 E
Masnou	256d	41.29 N	2.19 E
Maso	140	7.14 N	2.53 W
Masoala	147b	15.59 S	50.10 E
Masoala, Cap ≻	147b	15.59 S	50.13 E
Masoala, Presqu'île ≻[1]	147b	15.40 S	50.12 E
Masoarivo	147b	19.03 S	44.19 E
Masomeloka	147b	20.17 S	48.37 E
Mason, Mich., U.S.	206	42.35 N	84.26 W
Mason, Ohio, U.S.	208	39.17 N	84.19 W
Mason, Tenn., U.S.	184	35.25 N	89.33 W
Mason, Tex., U.S.	186	30.45 N	99.14 W
Mason, W. Va., U.S.	178	39.01 N	82.01 W
Mason □[6], Ill., U.S.	209	40.18 N	90.04 W
Mason □[6], Ky., U.S.	208	38.35 N	83.48 W
Mason □[6], Wash., U.S.	214	47.20 N	123.09 W
Mason, Lake ⊜	152	27.39 S	119.34 E
Mason Bay C	162	46.56 S	167.44 E
Mason City, Ill., U.S.	209	40.12 N	89.42 W
Mason City, Iowa, U.S.	180	43.09 N	93.12 W
Mason City, Nebr., U.S.	188	41.13 N	99.18 W
Mason Creek	172	55.40 N	124.29 W
Masone	56	44.30 N	8.42 E
Masonicus Brook ≃	266	41.06 N	74.09 W
Mason Lake ⊜	214	47.20 N	122.57 W
Masons Creek ≃	275	39.59 N	74.51 W
Masontown	178	39.51 N	79.54 W
Mason Valley V	216	39.07 N	119.10 W
Masonville, N.J., U.S.	275	39.59 N	74.52 W
Masonville, N.Y., U.S.	200	42.15 N	75.23 W
Maspalomas	138	27.45 N	15.34 W
Masparro, Punta ≻	236	10.40 N	66.15 W
Maspeth ◆[8]	266	40.43 N	73.55 W
Masqaṭ (Muscat)	118	23.37 N	58.35 E
Maṣra'	132	27.14 N	31.02 E
Massa	58	44.01 N	10.09 E
Massa-Carrara □[4]	58	44.15 N	10.03 E
Massachusetts □[3]	197		
	168	42.15 N	71.50 W
Massachusetts Bay C	197	42.20 N	70.50 W
Massachusetts Institute of Technology ɤ[2]	273	42.21 N	71.06 W
Massaciuccoli, Lago di ⊜	60	43.50 N	10.20 E
Massacre Lake ⊜	194	41.39 N	119.35 W
Massa Fermana	60	43.09 N	13.28 E
Massa Fiscaglia	60	44.48 N	12.01 E
Massafra	36	40.35 N	17.07 E
Massaguet	136	12.28 N	15.26 E
Massakory	136	13.00 N	15.44 E
Massa Lombarda	60	44.27 N	11.49 E
Massa Lubrense	60	40.36 N	14.20 E
Massa Marittima	60	43.03 N	10.53 E
Massa Martana	60	42.46 N	12.31 E
Massandra	68	44.32 N	34.12 E
Massangano	142	9.37 S	14.15 E
Massangena	146	21.32 S	32.57 E
Massapê	240	3.31 S	40.19 W
Massapequa	200	40.40 N	73.29 W
Massapequa Park	266	40.40 N	73.28 W
Massapequa State Park ♠	266	40.42 N	73.27 W
Massapoag Brook ≃	273	42.09 N	71.09 W
Massapoag Lake ⊜	273	42.06 N	71.11 W
Massara	146	18.20 S	34.09 E
Massarosa	60	43.52 N	10.20 E
Massasoit State Park ♠	197	41.53 N	71.01 W
Massaua → Mesewa	134	15.38 N	39.28 E
Massawa → Mesewa	134	15.38 N	39.28 E
Massawippi ≃	196	45.22 N	71.51 W
Massawippi, Lake ⊜	196	45.14 N	72.00 W
Massay	46	47.09 N	2.00 E
Massé, Ruisseau ≃	265a	45.28 N	73.17 W
Massello	56	44.57 N	7.04 E
Massen	48	51.32 N	7.38 E
Massena, Iowa, U.S.	188	41.15 N	94.46 W
Massena, N.Y., U.S.	196	44.56 N	74.54 W
Massenya	136	11.24 N	16.10 E
Masset	172	54.02 N	132.09 W
Masset Inlet C	172	53.42 N	132.20 W
Masseube	32	43.26 N	0.35 E
Massey	180	46.12 N	82.05 W
Massey Creek ≃	265b	43.42 N	79.20 W
Massiac	32	45.15 N	3.12 E
Massiaru	66	58.00 N	24.35 E
Massico, Monte ∧	60	41.10 N	13.55 E
Massieville	208	39.16 N	82.58 W
Massif Central → Central, Massif ⩘	32	45.00 N	3.10 E
Massillon	204	40.48 N	81.32 W
Massima	142	1.27 S	11.42 E
Massina	263b	4.08 S	15.19 E
Massinga	146	23.20 S	35.25 E
Massingir	146	23.51 S	32.04 E
Massive, Mount ∧	190	39.12 N	106.28 W
Masson, Lac ⊜	196	46.03 N	74.02 W
Masson Island I	9	66.08 S	96.34 E
Massy	251	48.44 N	2.17 E
Mastābah	134	20.49 N	39.20 E
Maṣṭabat ar-Ruwayān ∧[2]	132	29.06 N	30.08 E
Maštaga	74	40.32 N	50.00 E
Masterson	186	35.38 N	101.58 W
Masterton	162	40.57 S	175.40 E
Mas-Thibert	56	43.34 N	4.44 E
Mastic Point	182	25.03 N	77.57 W
Mastigouche ≃	196	46.20 N	73.24 W
Mastigouche-Nord ≃	196	46.24 N	73.25 W
Mastūj	113	36.17 N	72.31 E
Mastūj ≃	113	35.54 N	71.49 E
Mastung	110	29.48 N	66.51 E
Mastūrah	118	23.06 N	38.50 E
Masu	136	12.10 N	13.19 E
Masua	116	24.16 N	90.46 E
Masuda	86	34.40 N	131.51 E
Masuho	84	35.34 N	138.28 E
Masuie	144	18.05 S	25.45 E
Masuika	142	7.37 S	22.32 E
Masuku	144	17.12 S	27.07 E
Māsūleh	118	37.10 N	48.59 E
Masulipatam → Machilīpatnam	112	16.10 N	81.08 E
Masura	116	23.16 N	90.24 E
Masurai, Gunung ∧	102	2.30 S	101.51 E
Masury	204	41.13 N	80.33 W
Maṣyāf	120	35.03 N	36.21 E
Maszewo, Pol.	30	53.29 N	15.02 E
Maszewo, Pol.	50	52.06 N	14.55 E
Mat ≃	38	41.39 N	19.34 E
Mata, Indon.	105b	8.12 S	122.56 E
Mata, Zaïre	142	7.53 S	21.58 E
Mata Amarilla	244	49.36 S	71.13 W
Mataba, Mount ∧	259f	14.42 N	121.10 E
Matabeleland ◆[1]	146	19.30 S	28.00 E
Matabeleland North □[4]	144	19.00 S	27.15 E
Matabeleland South □[4]	144	21.00 S	29.15 E
Mātābhānga	114	26.20 N	89.13 E
Matabuena	34	41.10 N	3.40 W
Matachel ≃	34	38.50 N	6.17 W
Matachewan	180	47.56 N	80.39 W
Matad	78	47.12 N	115.35 E
Mata de Plátano, Quebrada ≃	276c	10.35 N	66.46 W
Matadero Creek ≃	272	37.26 N	122.08 W
Mata de São João	245	12.31 S	38.17 W
Matadi	142	5.49 S	13.27 E
Matador	186	34.01 N	100.49 W
Matagalpa	226	12.55 N	85.55 W
Matagalpa □[5]	226	13.00 N	85.30 W
Matag-ob	106	11.07 N	124.29 E
Matagorda	186	28.41 N	95.58 W
Matagorda □[6]	212	28.57 N	96.00 W
Matagorda Bay C	186	28.35 N	96.20 W
Matagorda Island I	186	28.15 N	96.30 W
Matagorda Peninsula ≻[1]	186	28.32 N	96.07 W
Mata Grande	240	9.07 S	37.44 W
Matahiae, Pointe ≻	164s	17.49 S	149.17 W
Mataiva I[1]	14	14.53 S	148.40 W
Mataj	76	45.53 N	78.43 E
Matajing	97	29.32 N	104.00 E
Matak, Pulau I	102	3.18 N	106.16 E
Matakana, Austl.	156	33.00 S	145.54 E
Matakana, N.Z.	162	36.21 S	174.43 E
Matakana Island I	162	37.35 S	176.05 E
Matakitaki ≃	162	41.48 S	172.19 E
Matala	142	14.46 S	15.04 E
Matale	112	7.28 N	80.37 E
Matam	140	15.40 N	13.15 W
Matama	86	33.36 N	131.28 E
Matama, Cerro ∧	226	9.47 N	83.15 W
Matamata	162	37.49 S	175.47 E
Matameye	140	13.26 N	8.28 E
Matamoras	200	41.22 N	74.42 W
Matamoros	222	25.53 N	97.30 W
Matamoros de la Laguna	222	25.32 N	103.15 W
Matan	102	1.52 S	110.00 E
Matana	144	3.46 S	29.41 E
Matana, Danau ⊜	102	2.28 S	121.20 E
Matanalem, Cape ≻	154	2.28 S	149.57 E
Matandu ≃	144	8.45 S	39.19 E
Matane	176	48.51 N	67.32 W
Matane, Parc de ♠	176	48.45 N	67.00 W
Matang, Malay.	104	4.49 N	100.41 E
Matang, Zhg.	90	29.17 N	113.05 E
Matang, Zhg.	90	32.20 N	121.04 E
Matangi	162	37.49 S	175.25 E
Matani	74	42.06 N	45.13 E
Matanni	113	33.48 N	71.34 E
Matanuska ≃	170	61.30 N	149.15 W
Matanza → San Justo	248	34.40 S	58.33 W
Matanza □[5]	278	34.46 S	58.37 W
Matanza ≃	248	34.42 S	58.28 W
Matanza, Aeródromo ⊠	278	34.44 S	58.30 W
Matanzas, Cuba	230p	23.03 N	81.35 W
Matanzas, Méx.	224	21.37 N	101.38 W
Matanzas □[4]	230p	22.40 N	81.10 W
Matanzas, Bahía de C	230p	23.04 N	81.30 W
Matão	245	16.13 S	49.12 W
Mata Ortiz	222	30.08 N	108.03 W
Matapa	146	23.11 S	24.39 E
Matapalo, Cabo ≻	226	8.23 N	83.19 W
Matape ≃	222	28.17 N	110.41 W
Matapédia	176	47.58 N	66.57 W
Matapédia, Lac ⊜	176	48.33 N	67.33 W
Matapi ≃	240	0.03 S	51.12 W
Matapu	162	39.29 S	174.14 E
Mataquito ≃	242	34.59 S	72.12 W
Matará, Perú	238	7.16 S	78.16 W
Matara, S. Lan.	112	5.56 N	80.33 E
Mataram	105b	8.35 S	116.07 E
Matarani	238	17.00 S	72.06 W
Mataranka	154	14.56 S	133.07 E
Matarca	236	0.30 S	72.38 W
Matārimah, Ra's ≻	132	29.27 N	32.42 E
Matarinao Bay C	106	11.14 N	125.34 E
Mataró	34	41.32 N	2.27 E
Matarraña ≃	34	41.14 N	0.22 E
Matas ∧	256d	41.30 N	2.16 E
Matasango	276d	12.05 S	76.58 W
Matasiri, Pulau I	102	4.48 S	115.48 E
Mataso I	165f	17.14 S	168.26 E
Mätäsvaara	26	63.26 N	29.36 E
Matata	162	37.53 S	176.45 E
Matatamane Point ≻	164v	19.07 S	169.51 W
Matatepai, Pointe ≻	164x	9.43 S	139.02 W
Matatiele	148	30.24 S	28.43 E
Matatindoc Point ≻	106	9.43 N	122.23 E
Matatula, Cape ≻	164u	14.15 S	170.34 W
Mataura	162	46.11 S	168.52 E
Mataurá ≃, Bra.	238	5.30 S	60.45 W
Mataura ≃, N.Z.	162	46.34 S	168.43 E
Matautu	165a	13.57 S	171.56 W
Matauvau, Passe Ʉ	164s	17.34 S	149.23 W
Matavai	165a	13.28 S	172.35 W
Matavai, Baie de C	164s	17.30 S	149.30 W
Matavera	164k	21.13 S	159.44 W
Matawai	162	38.21 S	177.32 E
Matawan	198	40.25 N	74.14 W
Matawin ≃	196	46.54 N	72.56 W
Matāy	132	28.25 N	30.46 E
Matbāri	116	22.18 N	89.57 E
Matbūl	132	31.05 N	31.02 E
Matča	75	39.27 N	69.39 E
Matchaponix Brook ≃	266	40.23 N	74.23 W
Matchi-Manitou, Lac ⊜	180	48.00 N	77.04 W
Matching	250	51.47 N	0.13 E
Matching Green	250	51.47 N	0.14 E
Matching Tye	250	51.47 N	0.12 E
Mateare	226	12.14 N	86.26 W
Mateba, Île de I	142	5.54 S	12.50 E
Matehuala	224	23.39 N	100.39 W
Mateira	245	18.54 S	50.30 W
Mateke Hills ⩘[2]	144	21.48 S	31.00 E
Mateko	142	4.03 S	18.55 E
Matelica	60	43.15 N	13.00 E
Matemo, Ilha I	144	12.13 S	40.36 E
Matera	36	40.40 N	16.37 E
Materborn	48	51.46 N	6.06 E
Matese, Lago del ⊜	60	41.25 N	14.25 E
Matese, Monti del ⩘	60	41.27 N	14.22 E
Mátészalka	30	47.57 N	22.19 E
Matete ≃	263b	4.24 S	15.20 E
Matetsi	144	18.16 S	25.56 E
Mateur	138	37.03 N	9.40 E
Matewan	182	37.37 N	82.10 W
Matfield	197	42.02 N	71.00 W
Matfors	26	62.21 N	17.02 E
Matha	32	45.52 N	0.19 W
Mathematicians Seamounts ⊹[3]	16	16.00 N	112.00 W
Mather, Man., Can.	174	49.06 N	99.07 W
Mather, Calif., U.S.	216	37.53 N	119.52 W
Mather, Pa., U.S.	178	39.56 N	80.05 W
Mather Air Force Base ■	216	38.34 N	121.18 W
Mather Gorge V	274c	38.59 N	77.15 W
Matheson	180	48.32 N	80.28 W
Matheson Island	174	51.44 N	96.56 W
Matheu	248	34.22 S	58.50 W
Mathews	198	37.26 N	76.19 W
Mathews □[6]	198	37.25 N	76.20 W
Mathews, Lake ⊜	218	33.51 N	117.26 W
Mathi	56	45.15 N	7.32 E
Mathis	186	28.06 N	97.50 W
Māthle	262b	22.35 N	88.14 E
Mathry	44	51.57 N	5.05 W
Mathura, Bhārat	112	10.57 N	78.27 E
Mathura, Bhārat	114	27.30 N	77.41 E
Mathura □[5]	114	27.35 N	77.35 E
Mathura Bil ⊜	262b	22.56 N	88.31 E
Mathurai → Madurai	112	9.56 N	78.07 E
Mathurāpur, Bngl.	116	23.17 N	89.15 E
Mathurāpur, Bngl.	116	24.02 N	88.47 E
Mati	106	6.57 N	126.13 E
Matiakhola	116	23.16 N	86.56 E
Matiakoali	140	12.22 N	1.02 E
Mātiāli	114	26.56 N	88.49 E
Matiāri	110	25.36 N	68.27 E
Matias Barbosa	246	21.53 S	43.20 W
Matías Romero	224	16.53 N	95.02 W
Mātibhānga	116	22.49 N	89.56 E
Maticora ≃	236	11.03 N	71.09 W
Matiere	162	38.45 S	175.06 E

Symbol	English	Deutsch	Español	Français	Português
≃	River	Fluss	Río	Rivière	Rio
≍	Canal	Kanal	Canal	Canal	Canal
∟	Waterfall, Rapids	Wasserfall, Stromschnellen	Cascada, Rápidos	Chute d'eau, Rapides	Cascata, Rápidos
Ʉ	Strait	Meeresstrasse	Estrecho	Détroit	Estreito
C	Bay, Gulf	Bucht, Golf	Bahía, Golfo	Baie, Golfe	Baía, Golfo
⊜	Lake, Lakes	See, Seen	Lago, Lagos	Lac, Lacs	Lago, Lagos
≚	Swamp	Sumpf	Pantano	Marais	Pântano
⊼	Ice Features, Glacier	Eis- und Gletscherformen	Accidentes Glaciales	Formes glaciaires	Acidentes Glaciares
↔	Other Hydrographic Features	Andere Hydrographische Objekte	Otros Elementos Hidrográficos	Autres données hydrographiques	Outros Elementos Hidrográficos

Symbol	English	Deutsch	Español	Français	Português
⊹	Submarine Features	Untermeerische Objekte	Accidentes Submarinos	Formes de relief sous-marin	Acidentes Submarinos
□	Political Unit	Politische Einheit	Unidad Política	Entité politique	Unidade Política
ɤ	Cultural Institution	Kulturelle Institution	Institución Cultural	Institution culturelle	Instituição Cultural
⊥	Historical Site	Historische Stätte	Sitio Histórico	Site historique	Sítio Histórico
♠	Recreational Site	Erholungs- und Ferienort	Sitio de Recreo	Centre de loisirs	Sitio de Lazer
⊠	Airport	Flughafen	Aeropuerto	Aéroport	Aeroporto
■	Military Installation	Militäranlage	Instalación Militar	Installation militaire	Instalação Militar
●	Miscellaneous	Verschiedenes	Misceláneo	Divers	Miscelânea

ENGLISH · DEUTSCH

Name	Page / Seite	Lat.°′ / Breite°′	Long.°′ / Länge°′ E=Ost
Matignon	32	48.36 N	2.18 W
Matiguás	226	12.50 N	85.28 W
Matillas, Laguna ⊜	224	18.02 N	92.42 W
Matinecock	266	40.53 N	73.38 W
Matinenda Lake ⊜	180	46.22 N	82.57 W
Matinha	240	3.06 S	45.02 W
Matinicock Point ≻	266	40.54 N	73.38 W
Matinicus Island I	178	43.54 N	68.55 W
Matipó	245	20.17 S	42.21 W
Matipó ≃	245	19.53 S	42.33 W
Maṭir Ṭāris	132	29.22 N	30.54 E
Matiyure ≃	236	7.36 N	67.39 W
Mātla ≃[1]	116	22.04 N	88.38 E
Matlab Bāzār	116	23.20 N	90.43 E
Matlacha	210	26.37 N	81.53 W
Matlacha Pass ɰ	210	26.37 N	82.04 W
Matlamanyane	146	19.33 S	25.57 E
Matlapa	224	21.15 N	98.50 W
M'atlevo	66	54.54 N	35.39 E
Mātli	110	25.02 N	68.39 E
Matlock, Eng., U.K.	44	53.08 N	1.32 W
Matlock, Wash., U.S.	214	47.14 N	123.25 W
Matmata	138	33.33 N	9.58 E
Matnog	106	12.35 N	124.05 E
Mato	144	8.01 S	24.55 E
Mato ≃	236	7.09 N	65.07 W
Mato, Cerro ∧	236	7.15 N	65.14 W
Matoaca	198	37.14 N	77.29 W
Matobe	102	2.42 S	100.11 E
Matočkin Šar	62	73.16 N	56.27 E
Matočkin Šar, Proliv ɰ	62	73.20 N	55.21 E
Mato do Gado	246	23.42 S	47.07 W
Mato Grosso	238	15.00 S	59.57 W
Mato Grosso □[3]	238	12.00 S	57.00 W
Mato Grosso, Planalto do ⩕[1]	232	15.30 S	56.00 W
Mato Grosso do Sul □[3]	238	20.00 S	56.00 W
Matola	146	25.59 S	32.29 E
Matola-Rio	146	25.58 S	32.26 E
Matombo	144	7.03 S	37.46 E
Mato Mole, Serra do ⩕[2]	246	23.00 S	46.12 W
Matong	154	5.35 S	151.45 E
Matonipi ≃	176	51.21 N	69.45 W
Matope	144	15.20 S	34.59 E
Matopo Hills ⩕[2]	144	20.36 S	28.28 E
Matopos	144	20.24 S	28.28 E
Matopos National Park ♠	144	20.33 S	28.20 E
Matos ≃	238	14.07 S	65.25 W
Matosinhos	34	41.11 N	8.42 W
Matoso, Ponta do ≻	277a	22.50 S	43.11 W
Matou, T'aiwan	90	23.11 N	120.16 E
Matou, Zhg.	88	36.29 N	114.26 E
Matou, Zhg.	90	25.14 N	118.22 E
Matou, Zhg.	90	29.49 N	115.35 E
Matou, Zhg.	95	39.46 N	116.49 E
Matou, Zhg.	95	39.18 N	116.45 E
Matouji	88	35.02 N	115.07 E
Matour	54	46.18 N	4.29 E
Matoury	240	4.51 N	52.20 W
Matouxi	97	30.15 N	106.31 E
Matouying	88	39.18 N	118.47 E
Matouzhen, Zhg.	88	34.39 N	118.18 E
Matouzhen, Zhg.	90	30.48 N	118.29 E
Matouzhen, Zhg.	90	33.32 N	118.56 E
Matouzhen, Zhg.	95	39.33 N	116.07 E
Mato Verde	245	15.23 S	42.52 W
Matozinhos	245	19.35 S	44.07 W
Mátra ⩕	30	47.55 N	20.00 E
Maṭraḥ	118	23.38 N	58.34 E
Matraville	264a	33.54 S	151.18 E
Matrei am Brenner	58	47.08 N	11.27 E
Matrei in Osttirol	58	47.00 N	12.32 E
Matru	140	7.36 N	12.11 W
Maṭrūḥ	130	31.21 N	27.14 E
Matsap	148	28.38 S	22.47 E
Matsapa	148	26.29 S	31.23 E
Matsari	142	5.21 N	12.14 E
Matsena	140	13.05 N	10.05 E
Matsiatra ≃	147b	21.25 S	45.33 E
Matsieng	148	29.36 S	27.32 E
Matsknutsgårdarna	40	60.28 N	15.22 E
Matsqui	214	49.12 N	122.25 W
Matsubara	86	34.34 N	135.33 E
Matsubushi	258	35.55 N	139.49 E
Matsuda	84	35.21 N	139.09 E
Matsudai	84	37.08 N	138.37 E
Matsudaira	84	35.03 N	137.13 E
Matsudo	84	35.47 N	139.54 E
Matsudo Race Track ♠	258	35.48 N	139.55 E
Matsue	86	35.28 N	133.04 E
Matsugasaki	258	35.53 N	139.58 E
Matsuida	84	36.19 N	138.48 E
Matsukawa, Nihon	84	35.36 N	137.55 E
Matsukawa, Nihon	84	36.25 N	137.51 E
Matsumae	82	41.26 N	140.07 E
Matsumoto	84	36.14 N	137.58 E
Matsuno	86	33.13 N	132.42 E
Matsunoyama	84	37.05 N	138.37 E
Matsuo	84	35.38 N	140.28 E
Matsuōji	258	35.08 N	140.01 E
Matsuoka	84	36.05 N	136.18 E
Matsuo-san ∧[2]	260	34.38 N	135.44 E
Matsusaka	82	34.34 N	136.32 E
Matsu Shan I	90	26.09 N	119.56 E
Matsushima	82	38.22 N	141.04 E
Matsutō	84	36.31 N	136.34 E
Matsuura	82	33.22 N	129.42 E
Matsuyama	86	33.50 N	132.45 E
Matsuzaka	84	34.34 N	136.32 E
Matsuzaki	84	34.45 N	138.47 E
Matta ≃	198	38.07 N	77.26 W
Mattagami ≃	166	50.43 N	81.29 W
Mattagami Heights	180	48.29 N	81.22 W
Mattagami Lake ⊜	180	47.54 N	81.35 W
Mattamuskeet, Lake ⊜	182	35.30 N	76.11 W
Mattāncheri	112	9.59 N	76.16 E
Mattapan ⬩[8]	273	42.16 N	71.06 W
Mattapoisett	197	41.40 N	70.49 W
Mattaponi	198	37.32 N	76.46 W
Mattaponi ≃	198	37.31 N	76.47 W
Mattarana	56	44.15 N	9.37 E
Mattarello	58	46.00 N	11.07 E
Mattawa, Ont., Can.	180	46.19 N	78.42 W
Mattawa, Wash., U.S.	192	46.44 N	119.54 W
Mattawa ≃	180	46.19 N	78.43 W
Mattawamkeag	178	45.31 N	68.21 W
Mattawamkeag ≃	178	45.30 N	68.24 W
Mattawan	206	42.12 N	85.47 W
Mattawana	204	40.30 N	77.44 W
Mattawoman Creek ≃	198	38.34 N	77.12 W
Matterhorn ∧, Eur.	54	45.59 N	7.43 E
Matterhorn ∧, Nev., U.S.	194	41.49 N	115.23 W
Mattersburg	30	47.44 N	16.25 E
Mattertal ∨	54	46.10 N	7.49 E
Matteson	206	41.30 N	87.40 W
Matteson Lake ⊜	206	41.56 N	85.12 W
Matthew Flinders Memorial ⊥	159	38.19 S	145.04 E
Matthews	206	40.23 N	85.30 W
Matthews Mountain ∧	184	37.29 N	90.21 W
Matthews Ridge	236	7.30 N	60.10 W
Matthew Town	228	20.57 N	73.40 W
Matthiessen State Park ♠	206	41.17 N	89.01 W
Maṭṭī, Sabkhat ⊜	118	23.51 N	52.00 E
Mattie, Lake ⊜	210	28.08 N	81.46 W
Mattig ≃	58	48.10 N	13.07 E
Mattighofen	58	48.06 N	13.09 E
Mattinata	60	41.42 N	16.03 E
Mattituck	197	40.59 N	72.32 W
Mattole ≃	194	40.18 N	124.21 W
Mattoon, Ill., U.S.	184	39.29 N	88.22 W
Mattoon, Wis., U.S.	180	45.01 N	89.02 W
Mattox Creek ≃	198	38.12 N	76.58 W
Mattox Draw ∨	188	38.03 N	101.11 W
Mattsee	58	47.58 N	13.06 E
Mattydale	200	43.06 N	76.09 W
Matu	102	2.41 N	111.32 E
Matua	102	2.59 S	110.45 E
Matuba	146	24.27 S	32.55 E
Matucana	238	11.51 S	76.24 W
Matudo → Matsudo	84	35.47 N	139.54 E
Matue → Matsue	86	35.28 N	133.04 E
Matuku I	165g	19.10 S	179.46 E
Matumoto → Matsumoto	84	36.14 N	137.58 E
Matungo ≃	142	16.25 S	21.27 E
Matunuck	197	41.23 N	71.32 W
Matuog	106	9.55 N	123.09 E
Matura Bay C	231r	10.38 N	61.01 W
Maturín	236	9.45 N	63.11 W
Maturino	66	59.06 N	37.55 E
Matusevich Glacier ⊏	9	69.11 S	157.20 E
Matusov	68	49.03 N	31.34 E
Matutina	245	19.13 S	45.58 W
Matuto	144	14.46 S	35.59 E
Matutum, Mount ∧	106	6.22 N	125.05 E
Matuzaka → Matsuzaka	84	34.34 N	136.32 E
Matvejevka	70	53.32 N	53.29 E
Matvejev-Kurgan	73	47.35 N	38.52 E
Matvejevo, S.S.S.R.	66	58.38 N	43.30 E
Matvejevo, S.S.S.R.	76	57.47 N	57.51 E
Mátyásföld ⬩[8]	254c	47.31 N	19.13 E
Mátyas-Templom ⬥[1]	254c	47.30 N	19.02 E
Matyra ≃	66	52.38 N	39.38 E
Matyševo	70	50.49 N	44.12 E
Mau	114	25.17 N	81.23 E
Maú (Ireng) ≃	236	3.33 N	59.51 W
Mauá, Bra.	246	23.40 S	46.27 W
Maúa, Moç.	144	13.51 S	37.10 E
Mauá □[7]	277b	23.40 S	46.27 W
Mau Aimma	114	25.42 N	81.55 E
Mauban	106	14.12 N	121.44 E
Maubara	102	8.37 S	125.12 E
Maubeuge	46	50.17 N	3.58 E
Ma-ubin	100	16.44 N	95.39 E
Mauchamps	251	48.32 N	2.12 E
Mauchline	42	55.31 N	4.24 W
Maud, Mo., U.S.	209	39.37 N	92.15 W
Maud, Ohio, U.S.	208	39.21 N	84.23 W
Maud, Okla., U.S.	186	35.08 N	96.46 W
Maud, Tex., U.S.	184	33.20 N	94.21 W
Maud, Point ≻	152	23.06 S	113.45 E
Maudaha	114	25.41 N	80.07 E
Maude	156	34.28 S	144.18 E
Maudétour-en-Vexin	251	49.06 N	1.47 E
Mau-é-ele	146	24.21 S	34.07 E
Mauensee	54	47.10 N	8.04 E
Mauer ⬩[8]	254b	48.09 N	16.16 E
Mauerbach	254b	48.15 N	16.10 E
Mauerbach ≃	254b	48.12 N	16.14 E
Mauerkirchen	58	48.11 N	13.08 E
Maués	240	3.24 S	57.42 W
Maués Açu ≃	240	3.22 S	57.44 W
Mau Escarpment ⏏[4]	144	0.40 S	36.02 E
Maug ≃	106	8.20 N	125.53 E
Mauganj	114	24.41 N	81.53 E
Mauga Silisili ∧	165a	13.35 S	172.27 W
Mauger, Île I	176	51.05 N	58.45 W
Maughold	42	54.18 N	4.17 W
Maug Islands II	98	20.01 N	145.13 E
Mauguio	56	43.37 N	4.01 E
Mauguio, Étang de C	56	43.35 N	4.02 E
Maui □[6]	219a	20.53 N	156.30 W
Maui I	219a	20.45 N	156.15 W
Mauk	105a	6.04 S	106.30 E
Mauke I	14	20.09 S	157.23 W
Maulbach	52	50.43 N	9.04 E
Maulbronn	52	49.00 N	8.49 E
Maulde	46	50.30 N	3.26 E
Mauldin	182	34.47 N	82.19 W
Mauldre ≃	251	48.58 N	1.49 E
Maule	46	48.55 N	1.51 E
Maule □[4]	242	35.45 S	72.15 W
Maule ≃	242	35.19 S	72.25 W
Maule, Laguna del ⊜	242	36.04 S	70.30 W
Mauléon	32	46.56 N	0.45 W
Maulette	251	48.48 N	1.37 E
Maullín	244	41.38 S	73.37 W
Maulvi Bāzār	110	24.29 N	91.47 E
Maumee	204	41.34 N	83.39 W
Maumee ≃	206	41.42 N	83.28 W
Maumee Bay C	206	41.43 N	83.26 W
Maumelle, Lake ⊜[1]	184	34.55 N	92.40 W
Maumere	105b	8.37 S	122.14 E
Maun	146	20.00 S	23.25 E
Maunabo	230m	18.01 N	65.54 W
Mauna Kea ∧[1]	219d	19.50 N	155.28 W
Maunaloa	219a	21.08 N	157.13 W
Mauna Loa ∧[1]	219d	19.29 N	155.36 W
Maunalua Bay C	219c	21.17 N	157.44 W
Maunath Bhanjan	114	25.57 N	83.33 E
Maunatlala	146	22.32 S	27.28 E
Maunesha ≃	206	43.13 N	88.57 W
Maunga Roa ∧	164k	21.13 S	159.48 W
Maungatapere	162	35.45 S	174.12 E
Maungaturoto	162	36.06 S	174.22 E
Maungdaw	100	20.50 N	92.21 E
Maungmagan	100	14.09 N	98.06 E
Maungu	144	3.33 S	38.45 E
Maunoir, Lac ⊜	170	67.30 N	125.00 W
Maupin	214	45.11 N	121.05 W
Maur	113	30.05 N	75.15 E
Mau Rānīpur	114	25.15 N	79.08 E
Maurecourt	251	49.00 N	2.04 E
Maure-de-Bretagne	32	47.54 N	1.59 W
Mauregard	251	49.02 N	2.35 E
Maurentanien → Mauritania □[1]	124	2.00 N	12.00 W
Maurepas, Lake ⊜	184	30.15 N	90.30 W
Maures ⩕, Fr.	34		
	56	43.16 N	6.23 E
Mauri ≃	238	17.18 S	68.41 W
Mauria, Passo della)(	58	46.27 N	12.31 E
Mauriac	32	45.13 N	2.20 E
Maurice (Île) → Mauritius □[2]	147c	20.17 S	57.33 E
Maurice ≃	198	39.13 N	75.02 W
Maurice, Lake ⊜	152	29.28 S	130.58 E
Maurice K. Goddard State Park ♠	204	41.23 N	81.10 W
Mauricetown	198	39.17 N	74.58 W
Mauriceville	162	40.47 S	175.42 E
Mauricio → Mauritius □[2]	147c	20.17 S	57.33 E
Maurienne ∨	56	45.13 N	6.30 E
Mauritania □[1]	124	20.00 N	12.00 W
Mauritanie → Mauritania □[1]	124	20.00 N	12.00 W
Mauriti	240	7.23 S	38.46 W
Mauritius □[1]	128		
	147c	20.17 S	57.33 E
Mauritius I	147c	20.17 S	57.33 E
Mauron	32	48.05 N	2.18 W
Maurs	32	44.43 N	2.11 E
Maurui	144	5.07 S	38.23 E
Maury ≃	178	37.50 N	79.25 W
Maury Channel ɰ	166	75.44 N	94.40 W
Maury Island ≻[1]	214	47.20 N	122.24 W
Maussane	56	43.43 N	4.48 E
Mauston	180	43.48 N	90.05 W
Mautala	116	22.25 N	89.05 E
Mautau, Pointe ≻	164x	9.42 S	138.58 W
Mauterndorf	58	47.08 N	13.40 E
Mauthausen	30	48.14 N	14.32 E
Mauthen	58	46.40 N	13.00 E
Mauvais Coulee ∨	188	48.21 N	99.06 W
Mauvaise Terre Creek ≃	209	39.43 N	90.38 W
Mauvaise Terre Lake ⊜[1]	209	39.42 N	90.12 W
Mauvezin	32	43.44 N	0.55 E
Mauzé-sur-le-Mignon	32	46.12 N	0.40 W
Mava	154	6.50 S	141.25 E
Mavá ≃	236	0.44 N	69.30 W
Mavaca ≃	236	2.31 N	65.11 W
Mavanza	146	22.43 S	35.08 E
Māvelikara	112	9.16 N	76.33 E
Mavinga	142	15.50 S	20.21 E
Mavita	146	19.33 S	33.10 E
Mavonde	146	18.32 S	33.02 E
Mavrovoúni ∧, Ellás	257c	37.55 N	23.30 E
Mavrovoúni ∧, Ellás	257c	37.54 N	23.48 E
Mavuradona Mountains ⩕	144	16.30 S	31.20 E
Mawa	144	2.43 N	26.42 E
Mawai	104	1.52 N	103.57 E
Mawan	88	37.24 N	118.14 E
Mawāna	114	29.06 N	77.55 E
Mawangkanlishan ∧	110	34.19 N	80.03 E
Mawangtang	96	30.43 N	120.41 E
Ma Wan Island I	261d	22.21 N	114.03 E
Mawasangka	102	5.17 S	122.18 E
Mawchi	100	18.49 N	97.09 E
Maw-daung Pass)(	100	11.47 N	99.39 E
Mawdesley	252	53.38 N	2.46 W
Mawdesley Lake ⊜	174	54.01 N	100.39 W
Maweigang	90	29.21 N	116.45 E
Mawi	262a	28.39 N	77.25 E
Mawiwi	144	3.06 N	27.40 E
Māwiyah	134	13.35 N	44.21 E
Mawjib, Wādī al- ∨	122	31.28 N	35.34 E
Mawkhi	100	16.17 N	98.53 E
Mawlaik	100	23.38 N	94.24 E
Mawlamyaing → Moulmein	100	16.30 N	97.38 E
Mawr, Wādī ∨	134	15.41 N	42.42 E
Mawshij	134	13.43 N	43.17 E
Mawson Escarpment ⏏[4]	9	73.05 S	68.10 E
Mawson Peninsula ≻[1]	9	68.35 S	154.11 E
Maw Taung ∧	100	11.39 N	99.35 E
Mawuba	92	29.50 N	108.11 E
Max	188	47.49 N	101.18 W
Maxaranguape	240	5.31 S	35.16 W
Maxatawny	198	40.33 N	75.41 W
Maxcanú	222	20.35 N	89.59 W
Maxéville	54	48.43 N	6.10 E
Maxglan, Flughafen ⊠	58	47.48 N	13.02 E
Maxiang	90	24.41 N	118.15 E
Maximo	204	40.53 N	81.11 W
Maximo Paz	248	34.56 S	58.37 W
Maxinkuckee, Lake ⊜	206	41.12 N	86.24 W
Maxixe	146	23.51 S	35.21 E
Maxon Creek ≃	186	29.53 N	102.24 W
Maxton	182	34.44 N	79.21 W
Maxville	196	45.17 N	74.51 W
Maxwell, Calif., U.S.	216	39.17 N	122.11 W
Maxwell, Ind., U.S.	208	39.51 N	85.46 W
Maxwell, Iowa, U.S.	180	41.53 N	93.24 W
Maxwell, Nebr., U.S.	188	41.05 N	100.31 W
Maxwell, N. Mex., U.S.	186	36.32 N	104.33 W
Maxwell, Tex., U.S.	212	29.53 N	97.48 W
Maxwell Air Force Base ■	184	32.23 N	86.21 W
Maxwell Bay C	166	74.35 N	89.00 W
Maxwelltown	42	55.04 N	3.38 W
May	186	31.59 N	98.55 W
May ≃, Alta., Can.	172	55.43 N	111.22 W
May ≃, Pap. N. Gui.	154	4.35 S	141.35 E
May, Cape ≻	198	38.58 N	74.55 W
May, Mount ∧	172	54.02 N	119.58 W
Maya, Pulau I	102	1.10 S	109.35 E
Mayaguana I	228	22.23 N	72.57 W
Mayaguana Passage ɰ	228	22.32 N	73.15 W
Mayagüez	230m	18.12 N	67.09 W
Mayagüez, Aeropuerto ⊠	230m	18.15 N	67.09 W
Mayagüez, Bahía de C	230m	18.12 N	67.10 W
Mayahi	140	13.58 N	7.40 E
Mayajigua	230p	22.14 N	79.04 W
Mayaka	142	5.17 S	16.52 E
Mayala	263b	4.21 S	15.09 E
Mayales, Punta ≻	226	11.52 N	85.26 W
Mayama	142	3.51 S	14.54 E
Mayamba	142	4.46 S	16.52 E
Mayāmey	118	36.24 N	55.42 E
Maya Mountains ⩕	222	16.40 N	88.50 W
Mayang (Gaocun)	92	27.41 N	109.35 E
Mayantoc	106	15.37 N	120.23 E
Mayao	96	30.50 N	120.23 E
Mayapan ⊥	222	20.38 N	89.27 W
Māyāpur	262b	22.27 N	88.08 E
Mayarí	230p	20.40 N	75.41 W
Mayarí Arriba	230p	20.25 N	75.32 W
Mayaro Bay C	231r	10.15 N	60.58 W
Maya-san ∧	86	34.44 N	135.12 E
May Ayini	134	14.46 N	39.10 E
Maybee	206	42.00 N	83.31 W
Maybeury	182	37.22 N	81.22 W
Maybole	42	55.21 N	4.41 W
Maybrook	200	41.29 N	74.13 W
Maychew	134	13.02 N	39.34 E
Maydelle	212	31.48 N	95.18 W
Maydena	156	42.55 S	146.30 E
Maydī	134	16.20 N	42.46 E
Maydolong	106	11.30 N	125.30 E
Maydūm	132	29.22 N	31.10 E
Mayen	52	50.19 N	7.13 E
Mayence → Mainz	52	50.01 N	8.16 E
Mayenne	32	48.18 N	0.37 W
Mayenne □[5]	32	48.05 N	0.40 W
Mayenne ≃	32	47.30 N	0.33 W
Mayer	190	34.24 N	112.14 W
Mayersville	184	32.54 N	91.03 W
Mayerthorpe	172	53.57 N	115.08 W
Mayet	46	47.46 N	0.17 E
Mayfair ⬩[8], S. Afr.	263d	26.12 S	28.01 E
Mayfair ⬩[8], Pa., U.S.	275	40.02 N	75.03 W
Mayfield, N.Z.	162	43.49 S	171.25 E
Mayfield, Eng., U.K.	44	53.01 N	1.45 W
Mayfield, Ind., U.S.	208	40.11 N	85.21 W
Mayfield, Ky., U.S.	184	36.44 N	88.38 W
Mayfield, N.Y., U.S.	200	43.06 N	74.16 W
Mayfield, Ohio, U.S.	269a	41.33 N	81.26 W
Mayfield, Utah, U.S.	190	39.07 N	111.42 W
Mayfield Creek ≃	184	36.57 N	89.05 W
Mayfield Dam ⬩[6]	214	46.30 N	122.35 W
Mayfield Heights	204	41.31 N	81.27 W
Mayfield Lake ⊜[1]	214	46.31 N	122.32 W
Mayford	250	51.18 N	0.34 W
May Inlet C	166	76.15 N	100.45 W
Māyir	120	36.23 N	37.02 E
May Jirgui	140	13.44 N	8.08 E
Maykop → Majkop	74	44.35 N	40.07 E
Maymont	174	52.33 N	107.40 W
Maymūn, Wādī ∨	136	30.10 N	10.27 E
Maymyo	100	22.02 N	96.28 E
Mayna	116	22.14 N	87.47 E
Maynāmati	114	23.29 N	91.07 E
Maynard, Iowa, U.S.	180	42.46 N	91.53 W
Maynard, Mass., U.S.	197	42.30 N	71.33 W
Maynard, Ohio, U.S.	204	40.07 N	80.53 W
Maynardville	182	36.15 N	83.48 W
Mayne	214	48.51 N	123.18 W
Mayne ≃	156	23.34 S	141.18 E
May Nefalis	134	14.57 N	38.23 E
Mayne Island I	214	48.51 N	123.17 W
Maynooth	28	53.23 N	6.35 W
Mayo, Yukon, Can.	170	63.35 N	135.54 W
Mayo, Tchad	136	9.07 N	18.11 E
Mayo, Fla., U.S.	182	30.03 N	83.10 W
Mayo, Md., U.S.	198	38.53 N	76.31 W
Mayo □[6]	28	53.50 N	9.30 W
Mayo ≃, Arg.	244	45.46 S	69.43 W
Mayo ≃, Col.	236	1.40 N	77.21 W
Mayo ≃, Méx.	222	26.45 N	109.47 W
Mayo ≃, Perú	238	6.37 S	76.16 W
Mayoba	144	17.13 S	26.16 E
Mayo Bay C	106	6.56 N	126.22 E
Mayodan	182	36.25 N	79.58 W
Mayo-Kebbi □[5]	136	10.00 N	15.30 E
Mayoko, Congo	142	2.18 S	12.49 E
Mayoko, Zaïre	142	1.05 S	23.49 E
Mayola ≃	42	54.45 N	6.31 W
Mayo Lake ⊜	170	63.46 N	135.10 W
Mayo Ndaga	136	6.54 N	11.25 E
Mayon Volcano ∧[1]	106	13.15 N	123.41 E
Mayor Buratovich	242	39.15 S	62.37 W
Mayor Island I	162	37.18 S	176.16 E
Mayotte □[8], Afr.	128		
	147a	12.50 S	45.10 E
Mayotte □[2]	128	12.50 S	45.10 E
Mayotte I	147a	12.50 S	45.10 E
Mayoyao	106	16.59 N	121.14 E
Maypearl	212	32.19 N	97.01 W
May Pen	231q	17.58 N	77.14 W
Mayraira Point ≻	106	18.39 N	120.51 E
Mayrán, Laguna de ☷	186	25.45 N	102.45 W
Mayres	56	44.40 N	4.07 E
Mayrhofen	58	47.10 N	11.52 E
Mays	208	39.45 N	85.26 W
Maysah, Tall al- ∧	122	31.08 N	35.40 E
Maysfield	212	30.54 N	96.51 W
Mays Landing	198	39.27 N	74.44 W
Mays Lick	208	38.31 N	83.50 W
Maysville, Ky., U.S.	208	38.39 N	83.46 W
Maysville, Mo., U.S.	184	39.48 N	94.35 W
Maysville, N.C., U.S.	182	34.59 N	77.14 W
Maysville, Okla., U.S.	186	34.49 N	97.24 W
Maythalūn	122	32.21 N	35.16 E
Maytiguid Island I	106	11.03 N	119.36 E
Maytown	198	40.04 N	76.35 W
Mayu	90	27.48 N	120.26 E
Mayumba	142	3.25 S	10.39 E
Mayūrākshi Dam ⬩[6]	116	24.03 N	86.29 E
Māyūram	112	11.06 N	79.40 E
Mayūrbhanj □[5]	116	21.50 N	86.30 E
Mayville, Mich., U.S.	180	43.20 N	83.21 W
Mayville, N. Dak., U.S.	188	47.30 N	97.19 W
Mayville, N.Y., U.S.	204	42.15 N	79.30 W
Mayville, Wis., U.S.	180	43.30 N	88.33 W
Maywood, Calif., U.S.	270	33.59 N	118.11 W
Maywood, Ill., U.S.	206	41.53 N	87.51 W
Maywood, Mo., U.S.	209	39.57 N	91.36 W
Maywood, Nebr., U.S.	188	40.39 N	100.37 W
Maywood, N.J., U.S.	266	40.56 N	74.04 W
Maywood, N.Y., U.S.	200	42.42 N	73.52 W
Maywood Race Track ♠	268	41.44 N	87.50 W
Maza, Arg.	242	36.50 S	63.19 W
Maza, S.S.S.R.	70	57.14 N	44.13 E
Mazabuka	144	15.51 S	27.46 E
Mazagan → El-Jadida	138	33.16 N	8.30 W
Mazagão	240	0.07 S	51.17 W
Mazagaon ⬩[8]	262c	18.57 N	72.50 E
Mazagão Velho	240	0.13 S	51.25 W
Ma'zah, Jabal ∧	120	35.51 N	40.38 E
Mazamet	32	43.30 N	2.24 E
Mazamitla	224	19.55 N	103.02 W
Mazamitote, Arroyo de ≃	222	24.51 N	103.12 W
Mazán ≃	236	3.28 S	73.11 W
Māzandarān □[4]	118	36.30 N	53.30 E
Mazanovo	79	51.40 N	128.52 E
Mazār, Jabal ∧	122	33.34 N	36.03 E
Mazar, Oued ∨	138	31.50 N	1.36 E
Mazara del Vallo	36	37.39 N	12.36 E
Mazār-e Sharīf	110	36.42 N	67.06 E
Mazargues	56	43.15 N	5.24 E
Mazarredo	244	47.05 S	66.42 W
Mazarrón	34	37.36 N	1.19 W
Mazarrón, Golfo de C	34	37.30 N	1.18 W
Mazarsu	75	41.56 N	72.40 E
Mazaruni ≃	236	6.25 N	58.38 W
Mazaruni-Potaro □[5]	236	6.00 N	60.00 W
Mazatenango	226	14.32 N	91.30 W
Mazatlán	224	23.13 N	106.25 W
Mazatlán de Flores	224	18.02 N	96.54 W
Mazatzal Mountains ⩕	190	34.00 N	111.55 W
Mazatzal Peak ∧	190	34.03 N	111.28 W
Maze	84	35.52 N	137.10 E
Mažeikiai	66	56.19 N	22.20 E
Mazenod	174	49.53 N	106.14 W
Mazeppa, Minn., U.S.	180	44.17 N	92.32 W
Mazeppa, Pa., U.S.	200	40.59 N	76.59 W
Mazha	90	23.27 N	114.00 E
Māzhān, Īrān	118	32.35 N	59.01 E
Mazhan, Zhg.	88	36.04 N	118.45 E
Mazhangfang	94	42.23 N	122.26 E
Mazhuang, Zhg.	88	37.47 N	115.17 E
Mazhuang, Zhg.	90	32.54 N	114.03 E
Mazhuang, Zhg.	95	39.11 N	116.15 E
Mazhūr, Khubb al- ⏏[8]	118	27.45 N	43.55 E
Mazigou	95	40.28 N	114.48 E
Mazilovo ⬩[8]	255b	55.44 N	37.26 E
Mazīnān	118	36.18 N	56.46 E
Mazinaw Lake ⊜	202	44.55 N	77.12 W
Mazirbe	66	57.41 N	22.21 E
Mazoco	144	11.40 S	35.48 E
Mazoe ≃	144	16.32 S	33.25 E
Mazomanie	180	43.11 N	89.48 W
Mazomba ≃	246	22.53 S	43.45 W
Mazon	206	41.14 N	88.25 W
Mazon ≃	206	41.21 N	88.25 W
Mazon, East Fork ≃	206	41.11 N	88.18 W
Mazon, West Fork ≃	206	41.15 N	88.21 W
Mazongshan ∧	92	41.27 N	97.00 E
Mazorra	276b	23.01 N	82.24 W
Mazou ≃	46	47.15 N	2.59 E
Mazoul ▿[4]	138	28.20 N	7.50 E
Mazoula	138	28.20 N	7.50 E
Mazowsze ⬩[1]	30	52.30 N	20.40 E
Mazra'at-Bayt Jinn	122	33.19 N	35.55 E
Mazsalaca	66	57.52 N	25.03 E
Mazul'skij	76	56.16 N	90.28 E
Mazunga	144	21.45 S	29.52 E
Mazury ⬩[1]	30	53.45 N	21.00 E
Mazzin	58	46.27 N	11.42 E
Mba	165g	17.33 S	177.41 E
Mba ≃	165g	17.29 S	177.40 E
Mbabala Island I	144	11.18 S	29.44 E
Mbabane	148	26.18 S	31.06 E
Mbabo, Tchabal ∧	142	7.16 N	12.09 E
Mbacké	140	14.48 N	15.55 W
Mbaéré ≃	142	3.47 N	17.31 E
Mbage	130	5.30 N	25.13 E
Mbahiakro	140	7.27 N	4.20 W
Mbaïki	142	3.53 N	18.00 E
Mbakana, Montagne de ∧	142	7.58 N	15.06 E
Mbakaou, Barrage de ⬩[5]	142	6.25 N	12.55 E
Mbala, Centraf.	142	7.48 N	20.51 E
Mbala (Abercorn), Zam.	144	8.50 S	31.22 E
Mbalam	142	2.13 N	13.49 E
Mbale	144	1.05 N	34.10 E
Mbali	142	2.50 S	16.12 E
Mbali, Kaga ⩕	142	7.14 N	21.30 E
Mbali Lim ≃	142	4.26 N	18.20 E
Mbalizi	144	8.56 S	33.22 E
Mbalmayo	142	3.31 N	11.30 E
Mbalouro	263b	4.09 S	15.21 E
Mbalouro ≃	263b	4.09 S	15.21 E
Mbam ≃	142	4.24 N	11.17 E
Mbamba Bay	144	11.17 S	34.46 E
Mbamou, Île I	263b	4.13 S	15.25 E
Mbamou, Pointe ≻	263b	4.16 S	15.19 E
Mbandaka (Coquilhatville)	142	0.04 N	18.16 E
Mbanga	142	3.52 N	10.49 E
Mbanio, Lagune C	142	3.35 S	11.00 E
Mbar	140	14.32 N	15.46 W
Mbarangandu ≃	144	8.57 S	37.24 E
Mbarara	144	0.37 S	30.39 E
Mbari ≃	142	4.34 N	22.43 E
Mbasay	136	7.39 N	15.40 E
Mbate	144	8.52 S	39.10 E
Mbatto	140	6.28 N	4.22 W
Mbé	142	3.18 N	15.54 E
Mbé ≃	142	0.27 N	9.41 E
Mbemba	144	10.03 S	38.36 E
Mbengga I	165g	18.23 S	178.08 E
Mbéré ≃	142	7.45 N	15.36 E
Mbereshi Mission	144	9.45 S	28.46 E
Mberubu	140	6.10 N	7.38 E
Mbeya	144	8.54 S	33.27 E
Mbeya □[4]	144	8.30 S	33.00 E
Mbia	130	6.15 N	29.19 E
Mbigou	142	1.53 S	11.56 E
Mbinda	142	2.00 S	12.55 E
Mbindawina	142	15.57 S	23.18 E
Mbinga	144	10.56 S	35.01 E
Mbingué	140	10.00 N	5.54 W
Mbirira	144	4.21 S	30.10 E
Mbirizi	144	0.23 S	31.27 E
Mbissa	142	0.41 N	10.59 E
Mbogo	144	7.26 S	33.26 E
Mboie	142	6.56 S	21.54 E
Mboli	142	4.08 N	23.09 E
Mbomou □[5]	142	5.00 N	23.30 E
Mbomou (Bomu) ≃	126	4.08 N	22.26 E
Mbonge	142	4.33 N	9.05 E
Mbor	142	6.24 N	11.19 E
Mboro, Sén.	140	15.09 N	16.54 W
Mboro, Sūd.	130	6.18 N	28.45 E
Mborong	105b	8.49 S	120.37 E
Mboté	142	3.56 S	12.43 E
Mbouda	142	5.38 N	10.15 E
Mboula	142	4.27 N	16.29 E
Mbour	140	14.24 N	16.58 W
Mbout	140	16.02 N	12.35 W
Mbrés	142	6.40 N	19.48 E
M'bridge ≃	142	7.14 S	12.52 E
Mbua	165g	16.48 S	178.37 E
Mbua Bay C	165g	16.49 S	178.35 E
Mbuji-Mayi (Bakwanga)	142	6.09 S	23.38 E
Mbulo I	165e	8.46 S	158.17 E
Mbulu	144	3.51 S	35.32 E
Mbulula	144	5.26 S	27.26 E
Mbuma	144	3.32 N	24.50 E
Mburucuyá	242	28.03 S	58.14 W
Mbutha	165g	16.39 S	179.50 E
Mbuyapey	242	26.12 S	56.50 W
Mbwemburu ≃	144	9.29 S	39.39 E
M'Chedallah	34	36.21 N	4.16 E
M'Clintock Channel ɰ	166	71.00 N	101.00 W
M'Clure, Cape ≻	166	74.35 N	121.08 W
M'Clure Strait ɰ	166	74.30 N	116.00 W
Mdandu	144	9.09 S	34.42 E
M'Daourouch	36	36.05 N	7.49 E
Meacham	174	52.08 N	105.45 W
Mead, Lake ⊜[1]	190	36.05 N	114.25 W
Meade, Kans., U.S.	188	37.17 N	100.20 W
Meade, Mich., U.S.	204	42.43 N	82.52 W
Meade ≃	170	70.50 N	156.25 W
Meaden Peak ∧	190	40.46 N	107.03 W
Meade Peak ∧	192	42.30 N	111.15 W
Meadow, Tex., U.S.	186	33.20 N	102.12 W
Meadow, Utah, U.S.	190	38.53 N	112.24 W
Meadowbank Park ♠	264a	33.49 S	151.06 E
Meadowbrook, Ill., U.S.	209	38.54 N	90.01 W
Meadowbrook, Ind., U.S.	206	41.03 N	85.03 W
Meadow Brook ≃, Mass., U.S.	273	42.03 N	70.58 W
Meadow Brook ≃, Pa., U.S.	275	40.07 N	75.04 W
Meadow Creek ≃	192	46.03 N	115.18 W
Meadowdale	268	41.32 N	87.21 W
Meadow Flat	160	33.26 S	149.56 E
Meadow Island I	266	40.36 N	73.33 W
Meadow Lake	174	54.08 N	108.26 W
Meadow Lake ⊜, Sask., Can.	174	54.07 N	108.20 W
Meadow Lake ⊜, N.Y., U.S.	266	40.44 N	73.50 W
Meadow Lake ⊜, Oreg., U.S.	214	45.19 N	123.26 W
Meadow Lake Provincial Park ♠	174	54.28 N	109.10 W
Meadowlands, S. Afr.	263d	26.13 S	27.54 E
Meadow Lands, Pa., U.S.	204	40.15 N	80.13 W
Meadowlark Airport ⊠	270	33.43 N	118.02 W
Meadowood, Del., U.S.	275	39.42 N	75.42 W
Meadowood, Md., U.S.	274c	39.04 N	77.00 W
Meadows	158b	35.11 S	138.46 E
Meadows, Island of I	266	40.34 N	74.12 W
Meadows Field ⊠	216	35.26 N	119.03 W
Meadowvale	265b	43.37 N	79.43 W
Meadow Valley Wash ∨	194	36.39 N	114.35 W
Meadowview	182	36.46 N	81.52 W
Meadow Vista	216	39.06 N	121.01 W
Meads Creek ≃	200	42.10 N	77.07 W
Meadville, Miss., U.S.	184	31.28 N	90.54 W
Meadville, Mo., U.S.	184	39.47 N	93.18 W
Meadville, Pa., U.S.	204	41.38 N	80.09 W
Meaford	202	44.36 N	80.35 W
Meaghers Grant	176	44.55 N	63.15 W
Me-akan-dake ∧	82a	43.23 N	144.01 E
Meakerville	170	60.32 N	145.00 W
Mealhada	34	40.22 N	8.27 W
Méan	52	50.22 N	5.20 E
Meana	118	36.55 N	60.30 E
Meandarra	156	27.20 S	149.53 E
Meander Creek Reservoir ⊜[1]	204	41.09 N	80.47 W
Meander River	166	59.02 N	117.42 W
Mearim ≃	240	3.04 S	44.35 W
Measham	44	52.43 N	1.29 W
Meath □[6]	28	53.35 N	6.40 W
Meath □[9]	28	53.40 N	7.00 W
Meaux	46	48.57 N	2.52 E
Meaux-Esbly, Aérodrome de ⊠	251	48.55 N	2.50 E
Mebane	182	36.06 N	79.16 W
Mebisere	263a	6.42 N	3.31 E
Mebtoûh, Oued el ≃	34	35.16 N	0.32 W
Meča ≃	72	54.50 N	39.10 E
Meca, La → Makkah	134	21.27 N	39.49 E
Mecanhelas	144	15.12 S	35.54 E
Mecatán	224	21.32 N	105.08 W
Mecatlán	224	20.13 N	97.41 W
Mecaya ≃	236	0.29 N	75.11 W
Mecca → Makkah	134	21.27 N	39.49 E
Mečebilovo	68	49.04 N	36.41 E
Mečetinskaja	68	46.46 N	40.27 E
Mečetka	68	50.54 N	40.05 E
Mechanic Falls	178	44.07 N	70.24 W
Mechanicsburg, Ill., U.S.	209	39.48 N	89.24 W
Mechanicsburg, Ind., U.S.	208	40.09 N	86.28 W
Mechanicsburg, Ohio, U.S.	208	40.04 N	83.34 W
Mechanicsburg, Pa., U.S.	178	40.13 N	77.01 W
Mechanicstown, N.Y., U.S.	200	41.27 N	74.24 W
Mechanicstown, Ohio, U.S.	204	40.37 N	80.57 W
Mechanicsville, Iowa, U.S.	180	41.54 N	91.15 W
Mechanicsville, Md., U.S.	198	38.26 N	76.44 W
Mechanicsville, Va., U.S.	182	37.36 N	77.22 W
Mechanicville	200	42.54 N	73.42 W
Mechara	134	8.32 N	40.22 E
Mechelen (Malines)	46	51.02 N	4.28 E
Mechel'ta	74	42.48 N	46.30 E
Méchéria	138	33.35 N	0.18 W
Mechernich	52	50.35 N	6.38 E
Mechita	242	35.04 S	60.24 W
Mechlin → Mechelen	46	51.02 N	4.28 E
Mechol	164q	9.37 N	138.10 E
Mechonskoje	76	56.09 N	64.34 E
Mechra Safsaf	34	34.52 N	2.36 W
Mechren'ga	24	61.46 N	40.57 E
Mechrenga ≃	24	63.15 N	41.20 E
Mechroha	36	36.21 N	7.51 E
Mecidiye, Tür.	120	38.53 N	27.42 E
Mecidiye, Tür.	120	40.38 N	26.32 E
Mečigmen	170	65.28 N	172.05 W
Mečigmeskij Zaliv C	170	65.25 N	172.00 W
Meçitözü	120	40.31 N	35.19 E
Meckelfeld	48	53.25 N	10.01 E
Meckenbeuren	54	47.42 N	9.34 E
Meckenheim	52	50.37 N	7.07 E
Meckering	152	31.38 S	117.01 E
Meckesheim	52	49.19 N	8.49 E
Meckinghoven	253	51.37 N	7.19 E
Mecklenburg, D.D.R.	50	53.47 N	11.28 E
Mecklenburg, N.Y., U.S.	200	42.27 N	76.43 W
Mecklenburg □[9]	50	53.30 N	13.00 E
Mecklenburger Bucht C	50	54.20 N	11.40 E
Mecklenburgische Seenplatte ⬩[1]	50	53.30 N	12.00 E
Meco	200	43.03 N	74.23 W
Mecoacán	224	18.23 N	93.07 W
Mecoacán, Laguna C	224	18.22 N	93.09 W
Meconta	144	14.49 S	39.50 E
Mecox Bay C	197	40.54 N	72.20 W
Mecque, La → Makkah	134	21.27 N	39.49 E
Mecrihan	120	37.08 N	39.03 E
Mecsek ⩕	30	46.15 N	18.05 E
Mecúfi	144	13.17 S	40.30 E
Mecula	144	12.04 S	37.40 E
Meda, It.	56	45.40 N	9.09 E
Meda, Port.	34	40.58 N	7.16 W
Medak	112	18.02 N	78.16 E
Medākul	116	23.03 N	90.11 E
Médan, Fr.	251	48.57 N	2.00 E
Medan, Indon.	104	3.35 N	98.40 E
Medang	104	2.06 N	101.38 E
Medang, Pulau I	105b	8.09 S	117.23 E
Medang, Tanjung ≻	104	2.08 N	101.39 E
Médanos	242	38.50 S	62.41 W
Medanosa, Punta ≻	244	48.06 S	65.55 W
Medaryville	206	41.05 N	86.55 W
Meddahia, 'Assâbet el ∧	138	22.08 N	11.58 W
Mede	56	45.06 N	8.44 E
Médéa	138	36.12 N	2.50 E
Medebach	52	51.12 N	8.42 E
Medeiros Neto	245	17.20 S	40.14 W
Medel, Val ∨	54	46.37 N	8.50 E
Medellín, Col.	236	6.15 N	75.35 W
Medellín, Pil.	106	11.08 N	123.58 E
Medelpad □[9]	26	62.40 N	16.15 E
Medemblik	48	52.46 N	5.06 E
Měděnec	50	50.25 N	13.05 E
Medenica	68	49.26 N	23.45 E
Médenine	138	33.21 N	10.30 E
Médenine □[5]	138	32.00 N	10.00 E
Mederdra	140	16.55 N	15.39 W
Medesano	58	44.45 N	10.08 E
Medevi	40	58.40 N	14.57 E
Medfield	197	42.11 N	71.18 W
Medford, Mass., U.S.	197	42.25 N	71.07 W
Medford, N.J., U.S.	198	39.54 N	74.49 W
Medford, N.Y., U.S.	200	40.49 N	73.00 W
Medford, Okla., U.S.	186	36.48 N	97.44 W
Medford, Oreg., U.S.	192	42.19 N	122.52 W
Medford, Wis., U.S.	180	45.09 N	90.20 W
Medford Farms	275	39.52 N	74.45 W
Medford Lakes	275	39.52 N	74.49 W
Medfra	170	63.06 N	154.44 W
Medgidia	38	44.15 N	28.16 E
Medgyes → Mediaș	38	46.10 N	24.21 E
Medi	144	5.04 N	30.44 E
Media	198	39.54 N	75.23 W
Media Agua	242	31.59 S	68.25 W
Media Luna, Arrecife de la ⊹[2]	226	15.13 N	82.36 W
Mediapolis	180	41.00 N	91.10 W
Mediaș	38	46.10 N	24.21 E
Medical Lake	192	47.34 N	117.41 W
Medicina	60	44.28 N	11.38 E
Medicine Bow	190	41.54 N	106.12 W
Medicine Bow ≃	190	42.00 N	106.40 W
Medicine Bow Mountains ⩕	190	41.10 N	106.10 W
Medicine Bow Peak ∧	190	41.21 N	106.19 W
Medicine Creek ≃, Mo., U.S.	184	39.43 N	93.24 W
Medicine Creek ≃, Nebr., U.S.	188	40.17 N	100.10 W
Medicine Creek ≃, S. Dak., U.S.	188	44.06 N	99.42 W
Medicine Hat	174	50.03 N	110.40 W
Medicine Knoll Creek ≃	188	44.19 N	100.05 W
Medicine Lake	188	48.30 N	104.30 W
Medicine Lake ⊜	188	48.28 N	104.24 W
Medicine Lodge	188	37.17 N	98.35 W
Medicine Lodge ≃	186	36.49 N	98.20 W
Medina → Al-Madīnah, Ar. Sa.	118	24.28 N	39.36 E
Medina, Bra.	245	16.15 S	41.29 W
Medina, Pil.	106	8.55 N	125.01 E
Medina, N. Dak., U.S.	188	46.54 N	99.18 W
Medina, N.Y., U.S.	200	43.13 N	78.23 W
Medina, Ohio, U.S.	204	41.08 N	81.52 W
Medina, Tex., U.S.	186	29.48 N	99.15 W
Medina □[6]	204	41.08 N	81.52 W
Medina ≃	186	29.12 N	98.20 W
Medinaceli	34	41.10 N	2.26 W
Medina del Campo	34	41.18 N	4.55 W
Medina de Ríoseco	34	41.53 N	5.02 W
Médina Gonassé	140	13.08 N	13.45 W
Medinah	268	41.59 N	88.01 W
Médina Saback	140	13.36 N	15.35 W
Medina-Sidonia	34	36.27 N	5.55 W
Medinat al-Faiyum → Al-Fayyūm	132	29.19 N	30.50 E
Medininkai	66	54.32 N	25.40 E
Medino	154	9.40 S	149.40 E
Medio, Arroyo del ≃	248	33.49 S	57.43 W
Medio Creek ≃	186	28.19 N	97.19 W
Mediterranean Sea ▿[2]	10	35.00 N	20.00 E
Mediterraneo, Mare → Mediterranean Sea ▿[2]	10	35.00 N	20.00 E
Mediterráneo, Mare → Mediterranean Sea ▿[2]	10	35.00 N	20.00 E
Medjana	34	36.08 N	4.41 E

Symbols in the index entries represent the broad categories identified in the key at the right. Symbols with superior numbers (⩕[2]) identify subcategories (see complete key on page *I* · 26).

Kartensymbole in dem Registerverzeichnis stellen die rechts in Schlüssel erklärten Kategorien dar. Symbole mit hochgestellten Ziffern (⩕[2]) bezeichnen Unterabteilungen einer Kategorie (vgl. vollständiger Schlüssel auf Seite *I* · 26).

Los símbolos incluídos en el texto del índice representan las grandes categorias identificadas con la clave a la derecha. Los símbolos con numeros en su parte superior (⩕[2]) identifican las subcategorías (véase la clave completa en la página *I* · 26).

Les symboles de l'index représentent les catégories indiquées dans la légende à droite. Les symboles suivis d'un indice (⩕[2]) représentent des sous-catégories (voir légende complète à la page *I* · 26).

Os símbolos incluídos no texto do índice representam as grandes categorias identificadas com a chave à direita. Os símbolos com números em sua parte superior (⩕[2]) identificam as subcategorias (veja-se a chave completa à página *I* · 26).

	English	Deutsch	Español	Français	Português
∧	Mountain	Berg	Montaña	Montagne	Montanha
⩕	Mountains	Berge	Montañas	Montagnes	Montanhas
)(	Pass	Pass	Paso	Col	Passo
∨	Valley, Canyon	Tal, Cañon	Valle, Cañón	Vallée, Canyon	Vale, Canhão
≃	Plain	Ebene	Llano	Plaine	Planície
≻	Cape	Kap	Cabo	Cap	Cabo
I	Island	Insel	Isla	Île	Ilha
II	Islands	Inseln	Islas	Îles	Ilhas
⏏	Other Topographic Features	Andere Topographische Objekte	Otros Elementos Topográficos	Autres données topographiques	Outros Elementos Topográficos

ESPAÑOL Nombre	Página	Lat.°′	Long.°′ W=Oeste
Medje	144	2.25 N	27.18 E
Medjerda, Monts de la ⛰	36	36.35 N	8.15 E
Medjerda, Oued ≃	138	37.07 N	10.13 E
Medjez el Bab	138	36.39 N	9.37 E
Medkovec	38	43.37 N	23.10 E
Mednogorsk	76	51.24 N	57.37 E
Mednoje	66	56.56 N	35.29 E
Mednyj, Ostrov I	64	54.45 N	167.35 E
Médoc ◆1	32	45.20 N	1.00 W
Medolla	58	44.51 N	11.04 E
Medora, Ill., U.S.	209	39.11 N	90.09 W
Medora, Ind., U.S.	208	38.49 N	86.10 W
Medora, N. Dak., U.S.	188	46.55 N	103.31 W
Médouneu	142	0.57 N	10.47 E
Medow	50	53.50 N	13.32 E
Medstead, Sask., Can.	174	53.19 N	108.02 W
Medstead, Eng., U.K.	44	51.08 N	1.04 W
Medua	116	22.38 N	90.44 E
Meductic	176	46.00 N	67.29 W
Medulla	210	27.58 N	81.58 W
Meduna ≃	58	45.49 N	12.34 E
Medveda	38	42.50 N	21.35 E
Medvedevo, S.S.S.R.	66	60.02 N	43.01 E
Medvedevo, S.S.S.R.	70	56.37 N	47.47 E
Medvedevo, S.S.S.R.	76	60.37 N	77.21 E
Medvedevskoje	66	58.58 N	35.58 E
Medvedica ≃, S.S.S.R.	66	57.05 N	37.32 E
Medvedica ≃, S.S.S.R.	70	49.35 N	42.41 E
Medvedickij	70	50.47 N	44.43 E
Medvedkovo ◆8	255b	55.53 N	37.38 E
Medvedok	70	57.23 N	50.05 E
Medvedovskaja	68	45.27 N	39.01 E
Medvėgalis ∧	66	55.38 N	22.45 E
Medvenka	72	54.15 N	37.42 E
Medvežij, Ostrov I	79	54.41 N	136.18 E
Medvežinka	73	48.10 N	39.31 E
Medvežje, Ozero ⊜	76	55.07 N	68.00 E
Medvežjegorsk	24	62.55 N	34.23 E
Medvežji Ostrova II, S.S.S.R.	64	70.52 N	161.26 E
Medvežji Ostrova II, S.S.S.R.	79	54.41 N	136.18 E
Medvežji Ozera ⊜	255b	55.52 N	38.00 E
Medvežji Oz'ora	255b	55.52 N	37.59 E
Medvežskaja	24	64.57 N	57.34 E
Medvin	68	49.23 N	30.47 E
Medv'onka	68	51.26 N	36.07 E
Medv'onka ≃	255b	55.44 N	37.12 E
Medway, Maine, U.S.	178	45.37 N	68.35 W
Medway, Mass., U.S.	197	42.08 N	71.24 W
Medway, Ohio, U.S.	208	39.53 N	83.59 W
Medway □8	250	51.24 N	0.31 E
Medway ≃, N.S., Can.	176	44.08 N	64.36 W
Medway ≃, Eng., U.K.	44	51.27 N	0.44 E
Medyn'	72	54.58 N	35.52 E
Medynka ≃	72	54.44 N	36.02 E
Medynskij Zavorot, Mys ➤	24	68.58 N	59.17 E
Medžibož	68	49.26 N	27.25 E
Medzilaborce	30	49.16 N	21.55 E
Meeberrie	152	26.58 S	115.58 E
Meekatharra	152	26.36 S	118.29 E
Meeker, Colo., U.S.	190	40.02 N	107.55 W
Meeker, Ohio, U.S.	204	40.39 N	83.18 W
Meeks Bay	216	39.02 N	120.08 W
Meelpaeg Lake ⊜1	176	48.16 N	56.35 W
Meenaar	158a	31.38 S	116.53 E
Meentheena	152	21.17 S	120.28 E
Meer	48	51.27 N	4.44 E
Meeralpen → Maritime Alps ⛰	56	44.15 N	7.10 E
Meerane	50	50.51 N	12.28 E
Meerbeck	253	51.28 N	6.39 E
Meerbeke	46	50.50 N	4.02 E
Meerhout	52	51.08 N	5.05 E
Meerhusener Moor ◆3	48	53.35 N	7.30 E
Meerkerk	48.	51.45 N	5.00 E
Meerle	48	51.28 N	4.48 E
Meersburg	54	47.41 N	9.16 E
Meerseen	52	50.53 N	5.45 E
Meerut	114	28.59 N	77.42 E
Meerut □5	114	29.00 N	77.35 E
Meese ≃	44	52.40 N	2.39 W
Meeteetse	192	44.09 N	108.52 W
Meetinghouse Branch ≃	274c	38.47 N	76.55 W
Mega, Indon.	154	0.41 S	131.53 E
Mega, Yai.	134	4.07 N	38.16 E
Mega, Pulau I	102	4.00 S	101.02 E
Megalo	134	6.55 N	41.48 E
Megálon Khoríon	38	36.27 N	27.21 E
Megalópolis	38	37.24 N	22.08 E
Meganom, Mys ➤	68	44.48 N	35.05 E
Mégantic □6	196	46.10 N	71.30 W
Mégantic, Lac ⊜	178	45.32 N	70.53 W
Mégantic, Mont ∧	196	45.28 N	71.09 W
Mégara	38	38.01 N	23.21 E
Megargel	186	33.27 N	98.56 W
Mégaron, Kólpos C	257c	37.56 N	23.20 E
Megasini ∧	110	21.38 N	86.21 E
Meget	78	52.24 N	104.03 E
Megève	56	45.52 N	6.37 E
Mégevette	54	46.12 N	6.30 E
Megezez, Mount ∧	134	9.13 N	37.37 E
Meghalaya □3	110	25.30 N	91.15 E
Meghna ≃	114	22.50 N	90.50 E
Mégiscane ≃	180	48.29 N	77.08 W
Mégiscane, Lac ⊜	180	48.35 N	75.55 W
Megi-shima I	86	34.24 N	134.03 E
Megorskaja Gr'ada ∧	66	60.30 N	36.00 E
Megra, S.S.S.R.	24	66.09 N	41.37 E
Megra, S.S.S.R.	66	60.10 N	37.13 E
Megrel'skij Chrebet ⛰	74	42.49 N	42.24 E
Megri	74	38.56 N	46.16 E
Meguro ◆8	258	35.38 N	139.42 E
Meguro ≃	258	35.37 N	139.45 E
Mehadia	38	44.55 N	22.22 E
Méhaigne ≃	52	50.32 N	5.13 E
Mehaïguène, Oued V	138	32.15 N	2.59 E
Mehakit	102	2.51 S	115.57 E
Mehar	110	27.11 N	67.49 E
Mehdia	138	35.26 N	1.40 E
Mehede	40	60.27 N	17.24 E
Mehedinţi □4	38	44.30 N	22.50 E
Meheisa	130	19.37 N	32.57 E
Mehekar	112	20.09 N	76.34 E
Mehendiganj	116	22.49 N	90.32 E
Meherpur	114	23.46 N	88.38 E
Meherrin ≃	182	36.26 N	76.57 W
Mehetia I	14	17.52 S	148.03 W
Mehidpur	110	23.49 N	75.40 E
Mehikoorma	66	58.14 N	27.28 E
Mehlem	52	50.39 N	7.11 E
Mehlsack → Pieniężno	30	54.15 N	20.08 E
Mehlteuer	50	50.32 N	12.02 E
Mehlville	209	38.31 N	90.19 W
Mehmetkân	120	38.26 N	41.17 E
Mehnagar	114	25.53 N	83.07 E
Mehndāwal	114	26.59 N	83.07 E
Mehoopany	200	41.34 N	76.04 W
Mehoopany Creek ≃	200	41.34 N	76.03 W
Mehpālpur ◆8	262a	28.33 N	77.08 E
Mehr	48	51.43 N	6.29 E
Mehrābād, Īrān	118	36.53 N	47.55 E
Mehrābād, Īrān	257d	35.40 N	51.20 E
Mehrābād Airport ⊠	257d	35.41 N	51.19 E
Mehram Nagar ◆8	262a	28.34 N	77.07 E
Mehrān	118	33.07 N	46.10 E
Mehring	52	49.48 N	6.49 E

FRANÇAIS Nom	Page	Lat.°′	Long.°′ W=Ouest
Mehrīz	118	31.35 N	54.28 E
Mehrow	254a	52.34 N	13.37 E
Mehrum	253	51.35 N	6.37 E
Mehsāna	110	23.36 N	72.24 E
Mè-hsa-tè	100	19.33 N	97.38 E
Mehtar Lām	110	34.39 N	70.10 E
Mehun-sur-Yèvre	46	47.09 N	2.13 E
Meia Meia	144	5.49 S	35.48 E
Meia Ponte ≃	245	18.32 S	49.36 W
Meichang	95	39.22 N	117.10 E
Meichuan	90	30.10 N	115.36 E
Meicun, Zhg.	90	25.30 N	116.56 E
Meicun, Zhg.	96	31.33 N	120.24 E
Meicun, Zhg.	96	30.22 N	119.01 E
Meicun, Zhg.	96	30.40 N	119.04 E
Meide	253	51.11 N	6.55 E
Meiderich ◆8	253	51.28 N	6.46 E
Meidling ◆8	254b	48.11 N	16.20 E
Méier ◆8	277a	22.54 S	43.16 W
Meierij ◆1	48	51.35 N	5.40 E
Meierkaisong	110	30.54 N	84.31 E
Meiersberg	253	51.17 N	6.57 E
Meiganga	142	6.31 N	14.11 E
Meigs	182	31.04 N	83.06 W
Meihe ≃	95	39.21 N	117.50 E
Meihekou	88	42.27 N	125.33 E
Meihsien → Meixian	90	24.21 N	116.08 E
Meihua	90	26.02 N	119.40 E
Meihuajie	90	25.14 N	113.05 E
Meijel	48	51.21 N	5.53 E
Meijiadang ⊜	96	30.56 N	120.43 E
Meijiang ≃, Zhg.	90	24.24 N	116.34 E
Meijiang ≃, Zhg.	90	26.00 N	115.23 E
Meijino-mori-minō-kokutei-kōen ♣	84	34.51 N	135.29 E
Meiji Shrine ♁1	258	35.41 N	139.42 E
Meiji University ♁2	258	35.41 N	139.45 E
Meikeng	90	23.59 N	114.05 E
Meikle Millyea ∧	42	55.07 N	4.19 W
Meikle Says Law ∧	42	55.55 N	2.40 W
Meiktila	100	20.52 N	95.52 E
Meila	50	51.09 N	13.13 E
Meilap	164r	6.54 N	158.09 E
Meilen	54	47.16 N	8.38 E
Meili	96	31.42 N	120.53 E
Meilie	90	26.18 N	117.38 E
Meilin, Zhg.	90	23.18 N	115.58 E
Meilin, Zhg.	96	30.35 N	119.04 E
Meillerie	54	46.24 N	6.43 E
Meilong	90	22.56 N	115.17 E
Meilunyingzi	94	42.18 N	122.10 E
Meina	56	45.47 N	8.32 E
Meine	48	52.23 N	10.32 E
Meiners Oaks	218	34.30 N	119.17 W
Meinerzhagen	52	51.06 N	7.38 E
Meiningen	50	50.34 N	10.25 E
Meinung	90	22.54 N	120.32 E
Meio ≃	240	7.42 S	36.35 W
Meio, Ilha do I	277a	23.02 S	43.17 W
Meio, Rio do ≃	245	17.47 S	39.47 W
Meiqi	96	30.48 N	119.45 E
Meiringen	54	46.43 N	8.12 E
Meisburg	52	50.06 N	6.41 E
Meisenheim	52	49.42 N	7.40 E
Meishan, Zhg.	90	28.52 N	113.38 E
Meishan, Zhg.	97	30.02 N	103.49 E
Meissen	50	51.10 N	13.28 E
Meissendorf	48	52.43 N	9.50 E
Meiss Lake ⊜	194	41.52 N	122.04 W
Meissner ∧	52	51.12 N	9.50 E
Meissner-Kaufunger Wald, Naturpark ♣	52	51.15 N	9.45 E
Meitan	92	27.46 N	107.35 E
Meitian	90	25.21 N	112.47 E
Meitik	164r	6.57 N	158.14 E
Meitingen	52	48.32 N	10.50 E
Meiwa	84	34.33 N	136.39 E
Meixian	90	24.21 N	116.08 E
Meiyao	79	49.37 N	124.30 E
Meiyino	130	6.12 N	34.40 E
Meizhai	92	25.30 N	108.50 E
Meizhou	90	23.50 N	117.20 E
Meizhoudao I	90	25.06 N	119.07 E
Meizhouwan C	90	25.06 N	119.00 E
Meizhu	96	31.16 N	119.13 E
Mejia	116	23.34 N	87.06 E
Mejillones	242	23.06 S	70.27 W
Mejillones del Sur, Bahía de C	242	23.03 S	70.27 W
Mejocote ≃	226	14.43 N	88.39 W
Mejorada del Campo	256a	40.24 N	3.29 W
Meka	152	27.26 S	116.48 E
Mekambo	142	1.01 N	13.56 E
Mekdela	134	11.28 N	39.23 E
Mekele	134	13.33 N	39.30 E
Mekerra, Oued ≃	34	35.00 N	0.45 W
Mekerrhane, Sebkha ☰	138	26.19 N	1.20 E
Mékhé	140	15.07 N	16.38 W
Mekhliganj	114	26.21 N	88.55 E
Mekhtar	110	30.29 N	69.22 E
Mékinac ≃	196	46.51 N	72.46 W
Mekka → Makkah	134	21.27 N	39.49 E
Meknès	138	33.53 N	5.37 W
Mekong ≃	12	10.33 N	105.24 E
Mekongga, Gunung ∧	102	3.38 S	121.15 E
Mekongga, Pegunungan ⛰	102	3.35 S	121.15 E
Mékôngk → Mekong ≃	12	10.33 N	105.24 E
Mekoryuk	170	60.23 N	166.12 W
Mékrou ≃	140	12.24 N	2.49 E
Mel	58	46.04 N	12.05 E
Melado ≃	242	35.43 S	71.05 W
Melah, Oued ≃	138	33.42 N	7.26 W
Melah, Oued el V, Alg.	138	28.21 N	6.00 E
Melah, Oued el V, Tun.	138	34.03 N	8.06 E
Melah, Sebkhet el ⊜	138	29.05 N	1.10 W
Melaka	104	2.12 N	102.15 E
Melaka □3	104	2.15 N	102.15 E
Melalap	102	5.14 N	116.00 E
Melanesia II	14	13.00 S	164.00 E
Melanesian Border Plateau ✧3	14	11.00 S	179.00 E
Melanesian Mission Station ♁1	164c	29.02 S	167.55 E
Melappālaiyam	112	8.42 N	77.43 E
Melara	58	45.03 N	11.11 E
Melaune	50	51.11 N	14.44 E
Melawi ≃	102	0.05 N	111.29 E
Melayu ≃	261c	1.27 N	103.42 E
Melbern	206	41.28 N	84.39 W
Melbourn	44	52.05 N	0.01 E
Melbourne, Austl.	159		
	264b	37.49 S	144.58 E
Melbourne, Ont., Can.	204	42.49 N	81.33 W
Melbourne, Eng., U.K.	44	52.49 N	1.25 W
Melbourne, Ark., U.S.	184	36.04 N	91.54 W
Melbourne, Fla., U.S.	210	28.05 N	80.37 W
Melbourne, Iowa, U.S.	180	41.57 N	93.06 W
Melbourne, University of ♁2	264b	37.48 S	144.58 E
Melbourne Beach	210	28.05 N	80.34 W
Melbourne Island I	166	68.30 N	104.45 W
Melbourne Regional Airport ⊠	210	28.06 N	80.38 W
Melby House	28	60.18 N	1.39 W
Mel'cany	70	54.28 N	44.43 E
Melcher	180	41.13 N	93.14 W
Melchor, Isla I	244	45.08 S	73.57 W
Melchor Ocampo	186	26.03 N	99.33 W
Melchor Romero ◆8	248	34.56 S	58.03 W

PORTUGUÊS Nome	Página	Lat.°′	Long.°′ W=Oeste
Melchtal	54	46.50 N	8.17 E
Melcombe Regis	44	50.38 N	2.28 W
Melcroft	204	40.03 N	79.24 W
Melderskin ∧	26	60.01 N	6.05 E
Meldola	60	44.07 N	12.05 E
Meldorf	30	54.05 N	9.05 E
Meldrum Bay	180	45.56 N	83.07 W
Meldrum Creek	172	52.07 N	122.20 W
Mele, Bhārat	262b	22.49 N	88.09 E
Mélé, Centraf.	136	9.46 N	21.33 E
Mele, It.	56	44.27 N	8.45 E
Mele, Capo ➤	56	43.57 N	8.10 E
Mele Bay C	165f	17.43 S	168.15 E
Melechovo	70	56.17 N	41.17 E
Meleck	76	57.25 N	90.12 E
Meledin	134	10.25 N	49.52 E
Melefan	120	38.11 N	41.34 E
Melegnano	56	45.21 N	9.19 E
Meleješt'	68	46.59 N	29.33 E
Melekeiok	165b	7.29 N	134.38 E
Melekess	70	54.14 N	49.39 E
Melena del Sur	230p	22.47 N	82.09 W
Melendiz Dağı ∧	120	38.07 N	34.25 E
Melenki	70	55.20 N	41.38 E
Meleškoviči	68	51.56 N	28.59 E
Meleuz	76	52.58 N	55.55 E
Mélèzes, Rivière aux ≃	166	57.40 N	69.29 W
Melfa	198	37.39 N	75.45 W
Melfa ≃	60	41.30 N	13.35 E
Melfi, It.	36	40.59 N	15.40 E
Melfi, Tchad	136	11.04 N	17.56 E
Melfort, Sask., Can.	174	52.52 N	104.36 W
Melfort, Rh.	144	17.59 S	31.19 E
Melgaço, Bra.	240	1.47 S	50.44 W
Melgaço, Port.	34	42.07 N	8.16 W
Melgar	236	4.12 N	74.39 W
Mel'guny	70	52.09 N	40.52 E
Melhus	26	63.17 N	10.16 E
Meli ≃	140	8.17 N	10.41 W
Meliau	102	0.08 S	110.18 E
Melibocus ∧	52	49.42 N	8.40 E
Melichovo, S.S.S.R.	68	50.42 N	36.48 E
Melichovo, S.S.S.R.	72	55.07 N	37.39 E
Melide	54	45.57 N	8.57 E
Meligalás	38	37.13 N	21.59 E
Melilla	34	35.19 N	2.58 W
Melimoyu, Monte ∧	244	44.05 S	72.52 W
Melincué	242	33.39 S	61.27 W
Melipilla	242	33.42 S	71.13 W
Mélisey	54	47.45 N	6.35 E
Melíssia	257c	38.03 N	23.50 E
Melita	174	49.16 N	101.00 W
Melito di Porto Salvo	36	37.56 N	15.47 E
Melitopol'	68	46.50 N	35.22 E
Melívoia	38	39.45 N	22.48 E
Melk	30	48.14 N	15.20 E
Melka Teka	134	6.05 N	43.08 E
Melkbosstrand	148	33.43 S	18.27 E
Melksham	44	51.23 N	2.09 W
Mella ≃	58	45.13 N	10.13 E
Mellansel	26	63.26 N	18.19 E
Mellau	54	47.21 N	9.53 E
Melle, B.R.D.	48	52.12 N	8.20 E
Melle, Fr.	32	46.13 N	0.09 W
Melleck	58	47.40 N	12.45 E
Mellègue, Oued ≃	36	36.32 N	8.51 E
Mellen	180	46.20 N	90.40 W
Mellendorf	48	52.33 N	9.43 E
Mellenville	200	42.15 N	73.40 W
Mellerud	26	58.42 N	12.28 E
Mellette	188	45.09 N	98.30 W
Mellid	34	42.55 N	8.00 W
Mellier ≃	52	49.43 N	5.32 E
Melling	252	53.30 N	2.56 W
Mellingen	50	50.56 N	11.23 E
Mellish Reef I1	150	17.25 S	155.50 E
Mellish Rise ✧3	14	17.00 S	156.00 E
Mellit	130	14.08 N	25.33 E
Mellone, Monte ∧	257a	41.50 N	12.43 E
Mellong Range ⛰	160	33.06 S	150.43 E
Mellor	252	53.46 N	2.32 W
Mellor Brook	252	53.47 N	2.33 W
Mellor Glacier ⊓	9	73.30 S	66.30 E
Mellösa	40	59.06 N	16.33 E
Melloulou, Oued ≃	138	34.13 N	3.21 W
Mellrichstadt	52	50.26 N	10.18 E
Mellum I	48	53.40 N	8.10 E
Melmerby	42	54.44 N	2.35 W
Melmore	204	41.02 N	83.07 W
Melmoth	148	28.38 S	31.24 E
Mel'nica-Podol'skaja	68	48.37 N	26.10 E
Mělník	50	50.20 N	14.29 E
Mel'nikovo, S.S.S.R.	75	40.19 N	70.19 E
Mel'nikovo, S.S.S.R.	76	56.34 N	84.05 E
Melo	242	32.22 S	54.11 W
Melo, Ilha de I	140	11.02 N	15.13 W
Melocheville	196	45.19 N	73.56 W
Meloco	144	13.25 S	39.08 E
Melolo	105b	9.53 S	120.40 E
Melolo ≃	105b	9.52 S	120.41 E
Melong	142	5.07 N	9.57 E
Melos → Mílos I	38	36.41 N	24.15 E
Melovaja ≃	73	49.23 N	40.16 E
Melovatka	73	49.21 N	38.11 E
Melovoje	73	49.22 N	40.06 E
Melovoj Syrt ∧	70	52.15 N	52.35 E
Melozitna ≃	170	64.46 N	155.29 W
Melrhir, Chott ⊜	138	34.20 N	6.20 E
Melrose, Austl.	152	27.56 S	121.19 E
Melrose, Austl.	156	32.42 S	146.58 E
Melrose, Scot., U.K.	42	55.36 N	2.44 W
Melrose, Mass., U.S.	197	42.27 N	71.04 W
Melrose, Minn., U.S.	188	45.40 N	94.49 W
Melrose, N. Mex., U.S.	186	34.26 N	103.38 W
Melrose, N.Y., U.S.	200	42.50 N	73.37 W
Melrose, Ohio, U.S.	206	41.05 N	84.25 W
Melrose, Wis., U.S.	180	44.08 N	91.01 W
Melrose ◆8	266	40.49 N	73.55 W
Melrose Abbey ♁1	42	55.37 N	2.45 W
Melrose Park, Fla., U.S.	210	26.06 N	80.12 W
Melrose Park, Ill., U.S.	206	41.54 N	87.51 W
Melrose Park, Pa., U.S.	275	40.04 N	75.08 W
Mels	54	47.03 N	9.25 E
Melsetter	144	19.48 S	32.50 E
Melstone	192	46.36 N	107.52 W
Melsungen	52	51.08 N	9.32 E
Melta, Mount ∧	106	5.41 N	117.20 E
Meltaus	24	66.54 N	25.22 E
Meltham	252	53.36 N	1.51 W
Melton, Austl.	158b	34.05 S	137.59 E
Melton, Austl.	159	37.41 S	144.35 E
Melton Constable	44	52.53 N	1.01 E
Melton Hill Lake ⊜1	182	36.00 N	84.15 W
Melton Mowbray	44	52.46 N	0.53 W
Melúa	236	3.55 N	72.50 W
Meluan	102	1.52 N	111.56 E
Meluco	144	12.36 S	39.38 E
Melúli ≃	144	16.28 S	39.44 E
Melun, Fr.	46	48.32 N	2.40 E
Melun, Mya.	100	20.14 N	93.24 E
Melunga	142	17.16 S	16.24 E
Melun-Villaroche, Aérodrome de ⊠	251	48.37 N	2.40 E
Melūr	112	10.03 N	78.20 E
Melvern	188	38.30 N	95.38 W
Melvich	28	58.33 N	3.55 W
Melville, Austl.	158a	32.03 S	115.49 E
Melville, Sask., Can.	174	50.55 N	102.48 W
Melville, La., U.S.	184	30.42 N	91.45 W
Melville, N.Y., U.S.	266	40.48 N	73.25 W
Melville ◆8	263d	26.11 S	28.00 E
Melville, Cape ➤, Austl.	154	14.11 S	144.30 E
Melville, Cape ➤, Pil.	106	7.49 N	117.01 E
Melville, Détroit de → Viscount Melville Sound ⊔	166	74.10 N	113.00 W
Melville, Lake ⊜	166	53.45 N	59.30 W
Melville Bugt C	16	75.30 N	63.00 W
Melville Hall Airport ⊠	230d	15.33 N	61.18 W
Melville Hills ⛰2	166	69.20 N	122.00 W
Melville Island I, Austl.	154	11.40 S	131.00 E
Melville Island I, N.W. Ter., Can.	16	75.15 N	110.00 W
Melville Peninsula ➤1	166	68.00 N	84.00 W
Melville Sound ⊔, N.W. Ter., Can.	166	68.05 N	107.30 W
Melville Sound ⊔, Ont., Can.	202	44.57 N	81.05 W
Melvin, Ill., U.S.	206	40.34 N	88.15 W
Melvin, Tex., U.S.	186	31.13 N	99.35 W
Melvin, Lough ⊜	28	54.26 N	8.10 W
Melvindale	204	42.17 N	83.11 W
Melvin Lake ⊜	174	57.08 N	100.15 W
Mélykút	30	46.13 N	19.24 E
Melzo	56	45.30 N	9.25 E
Memala	102	1.44 S	112.36 E
Memāri	116	23.12 N	88.07 E
Memba	144	14.11 S	40.30 E
Membalong	102	3.09 S	107.38 E
Memboro	105b	9.22 S	119.32 E
Membre	52	49.52 N	4.54 E
Même ≃	46	48.11 N	0.39 E
Memel, S. Afr.	148	27.43 S	29.30 E
Memel → Klaipėda, S.S.S.R.	66	55.43 N	21.07 E
Memel → Nemunas ≃	66	55.18 N	21.23 E
Mēmele ≃	66	56.24 N	24.10 E
Memewin, Lac ⊜	180	46.29 N	78.42 W
Memmert I	48	53.39 N	6.53 E
Memmingen	54	47.59 N	10.11 E
Memo ≃	236	9.16 N	66.40 W
Memori, Tanjung ➤	154	0.52 S	134.08 E
Memorial Bridge ◆5	259a	13.44 N	100.30 E
Memorial Coliseum and Sports Arena ♣	270	34.01 N	118.17 W
Mémót	100	11.49 N	106.11 E
Mempawah	102	0.22 N	108.58 E
Memphis, Fla., U.S.	210	27.32 N	82.34 W
Memphis, Ind., U.S.	208	38.29 N	85.46 W
Memphis, Mich., U.S.	204	42.54 N	82.46 W
Memphis, Mo., U.S.	184	40.28 N	92.10 W
Memphis, Tenn., U.S.	184	35.08 N	90.03 W
Memphis, Tex., U.S.	186	34.44 N	100.32 W
Memphis Naval Air Station ■	184	35.21 N	89.52 W
Memphremagog, Lake ⊜	196	45.05 N	72.15 W
Mena, S.S.S.R.	68	51.31 N	32.13 E
Mena, Ark., U.S.	184	34.35 N	94.15 W
Menado → Manado	102	1.29 N	124.51 E
Menaggio	54	46.01 N	9.14 E
Menahga	188	46.45 N	95.06 W
Menai	264a	34.01 S	151.01 E
Menai Bridge	42	53.14 N	4.10 W
Menai Strait ⊔	42	53.12 N	4.12 W
Ménaka	140	15.55 N	2.24 E
Menaldum	48	53.12 N	5.39 E
Mènam Khong → Mekong ≃	12	10.33 N	105.24 E
Menan	192	43.43 N	112.00 W
Menands	200	42.42 N	73.45 W
Menangina	152	29.50 S	121.54 E
Menarandra ≃	147b	25.17 S	44.30 E
Menard	186	30.55 N	99.47 W
Menard □6	209	40.01 N	89.51 W
Menard Creek ≃	212	30.29 N	94.50 W
Menars	46	47.38 N	1.24 E
Menasha	180	44.13 N	88.26 W
Menate	102	0.14 S	113.02 E
Menawashei	130	12.40 N	24.59 E
Menchang	95	38.54 N	117.01 E
Menčikury	68	47.04 N	34.48 E
Mencué	244	40.25 S	69.38 W
Menda	79	43.40 N	123.08 E
Mendanau, Pulau I	102	2.51 S	107.26 E
Mendarik, Pulau I	102	1.18 N	107.02 E
Mendatai	92	38.51 N	94.39 E
Mendatica	56	44.05 N	7.49 E
Mendawai	102	2.59 S	113.16 E
Mendawai ≃	102	3.17 S	113.21 E
Mendaya	105a	8.23 S	114.42 E
Mende	32	44.30 N	3.30 E
Mendebo Mountains ⛰	134	6.50 N	39.20 E
Mendel' ≃	76	58.13 N	90.08 E
Menden	52	51.26 N	7.47 E
Menden ◆8	253	51.24 N	6.54 E
Mendenhall, Miss., U.S.	184	31.58 N	89.52 W
Mendenhall, Pa., U.S.	275	39.51 N	75.38 W
Mendenhall, Cape ➤	170	59.51 N	166.15 W
Mendes	246	22.32 S	43.44 W
Méndez	236	2.43 S	78.19 W
Mendez-Nuñez	106	14.08 N	120.54 E
Mendham	200	40.46 N	74.36 W
Mendi, Pap. N. Gui.	154	6.10 S	143.40 E
Mendi, Yai.	134	9.50 N	35.06 E
Mendip Hills ⛰2	44	51.15 N	2.40 W
Mendlesham	44	52.16 N	1.05 E
Mendocino	194	39.19 N	123.48 W
Mendocino, Cape ➤	194	40.25 N	124.25 W
Mendocino Seascarp ✧4	16	41.00 N	140.00 W
Mendon, Ill., U.S.	209	40.05 N	91.17 W
Mendon, Mass., U.S.	197	42.06 N	71.33 W
Mendon, Mich., U.S.	206	42.00 N	85.27 W
Mendon, N.Y., U.S.	200	43.00 N	77.34 W
Mendon, Ohio, U.S.	206	40.40 N	84.31 W
Mendon, Pa., U.S.	269b	40.11 N	79.41 W
Mendota, Calif., U.S.	216	36.45 N	120.23 W
Mendota, Ill., U.S.	206	41.33 N	89.07 W
Mendota, Lake ⊜	206	43.05 N	89.25 W
Mendoza, Arg.	242	32.53 S	68.49 W
Mendoza, Perú	238	6.20 S	77.24 W
Mendoza, Perú	276d	12.06 S	76.59 W
Mendoza, Ur.	248	34.17 S	56.13 W
Mendoza □4	242	34.30 S	68.30 W
Mendoza, Arroyo de ≃	248	34.21 S	56.18 W
Mendrisio	54	45.52 N	8.59 E
Mend'ukino	72	54.47 N	38.51 E
Mendung	102	0.31 N	103.13 E
Ménéac	32	48.09 N	2.28 W
Mene de Mauroa	236	10.43 N	71.01 W
Mene Grande	236	9.49 N	70.56 W
Menemen	120	38.36 N	27.04 E
Menen	46	50.48 N	3.07 E
Meneng Point ➤	164b	0.32 S	166.57 E
Menes	105a	6.23 S	105.55 E
Menfi	36	37.36 N	12.58 E
Mengalum, Pulau I	102	6.16 N	115.12 E
Mengban	92	23.08 N	101.19 E
Mengbang	92	21.28 N	101.19 E
Mengcheng	90	33.17 N	116.33 E
Mengchihe ≃	97	29.47 N	104.56 E
Mengcun	88	38.06 N	117.05 E
Mengdapu	94	41.35 N	123.12 E
Mengede ◆8	253	51.34 N	7.23 E
Mengeh Jek	110	37.02 N	66.07 E
Mengen, B.R.D.	54	48.03 N	9.20 E
Mengen, Tür.	120	40.59 N	31.37 E
Mengeringhausen	52	51.22 N	8.59 E
Mengersgereuth-Hämmern	50	50.24 N	11.07 E
Menges Mills	198	39.52 N	76.54 W
Menggala	102	4.28 S	105.17 E
Menggu	92	26.34 N	102.57 E
Menggubao	94	42.27 N	122.23 E
Menggudai	92	38.10 N	108.15 E
Menghai	92	22.00 N	100.26 E
Menghe	96	32.03 N	119.47 E
Mengheyi	88	35.51 N	115.04 E
Mengisor, Ozero ⊜	76	54.33 N	67.57 E
Mengjiacun	96	31.33 N	118.46 E
Mengjiagang	79	46.22 N	130.40 E
Mengjiatai	94	42.06 N	123.21 E
Mengjiawan	92	38.35 N	109.25 E
Mengjiawopeng	94	41.22 N	121.51 E
Mengjiayuanjia	95	40.52 N	118.08 E
Mengka	92	25.10 N	98.01 E
Mengkibol	104	1.58 N	103.20 E
Mengkuang	104	3.11 N	102.24 E
Mengli	96	31.39 N	120.13 E
Menglian	92	22.20 N	99.38 E
Menglinghausen ◆8	253	51.28 N	7.25 E
Menglong	92	21.44 N	100.23 E
Mengluchang	97	29.19 N	103.35 E
Mengmucun	96	31.59 N	119.01 E
Mengo □5	144	0.30 N	32.15 E
Mengong	142	2.56 N	11.25 E
Mengqigou	94	42.00 N	121.08 E
Mengshan	92	24.07 N	110.33 E
Mengtong	97	30.44 N	105.53 E
Mengulek, Gora ∧	76	50.58 N	89.30 E
Mengwang	92	22.26 N	100.34 E
Mengyin	88	35.45 N	117.57 E
Mengyinzhai	88	36.04 N	117.47 E
Mengzhe	92	22.02 N	100.16 E
Mengzhi	92	24.10 N	99.46 E
Mengzi	92	23.22 N	103.20 E
Menihek Lakes ⊜	166	54.00 N	66.35 W
Ménil-la-Tour	52	48.46 N	5.52 E
Menindee	156	32.24 S	142.26 E
Menindee Lake ⊜	156	32.21 S	142.20 E
Meningie	156	35.42 S	139.20 E
Menjiaqiangzi	94	42.29 N	121.19 E
Menkoutang	96	31.01 N	119.27 E
Menlo	214	46.38 N	123.39 W
Menlo Park	216	37.28 N	122.13 W
Menlo Park Mall ◆9	266	40.32 N	74.20 W
Menlo Park Terrace	266	40.32 N	74.20 W
Mennecy	251	48.34 N	2.26 E
Mennetou-sur-Cher	46	47.16 N	1.53 E
Mennighüffen	48	52.13 N	8.43 E
Menno	188	43.14 N	97.34 W
Meno, Indon.	154	3.52 S	135.31 E
Meno, Okla., U.S.	186	36.24 N	98.11 W
Menominee	180	45.06 N	87.37 W
Menominee ≃	180	45.05 N	87.36 W
Menomonee ≃	206	43.02 N	87.54 W
Menomonee Falls	206	43.11 N	88.07 W
Menomonie	180	44.53 N	91.55 W
Menongue	142	14.36 S	17.48 E
Menor, Mar C	34	37.43 N	0.48 W
Menorca I	34	40.00 N	4.00 E
Mens	56	44.49 N	5.45 E
Menslage	48	52.41 N	7.49 E
Menstrup	41	55.13 N	11.36 E
Mentana	60	42.02 N	12.38 E
Mentasta Lake	170	62.55 N	143.45 W
Mentasta Mountains ⛰	170	62.40 N	143.07 W
Mentawai, Kepulauan II	98	2.00 S	99.30 E
Mentawai, Selat ⊔	102	1.56 S	100.12 E
Mentekab	104	3.29 N	102.21 E
Menteke, Peski ◆2	70	47.20 N	50.40 E
Menteng ◆8	259e	6.12 S	106.50 E
Menteroda	50	51.18 N	10.33 E
Menteşpiri	120	41.41 N	32.39 E
Menthon-Saint-Bernard	56	45.51 N	6.12 E
Menton	56	43.47 N	7.30 E
Mentone → Menton, Fr.	56	43.47 N	7.30 E
Mentone, Calif., U.S.	218	34.05 N	117.08 W
Mentone, Ind., U.S.	206	41.10 N	86.02 W
Mentone, Tex., U.S.	186	31.42 N	103.36 W
Mentor, Ky., U.S.	208	38.53 N	84.16 W
Mentor, Ohio, U.S.	204	41.40 N	81.20 W
Mentor-on-the-lake	204	41.43 N	81.21 W
Mentougou	95	39.56 N	116.03 E
Mentzdam ◆6	148	33.10 S	25.09 E
Menucourt	251	49.02 N	1.59 E
Menuma	84	36.13 N	139.23 E
Men'uša	66	58.23 N	30.42 E
Menyamya	154	7.10 S	146.00 E
Menyapa, Gunung ∧	102	1.05 N	116.05 E
Menyuan	92	37.27 N	101.48 E
Menza ≃	78	50.14 N	108.38 E
Menzel Bourguiba	138	37.10 N	9.48 E
Menzel Bou Zelfa	36	36.41 N	10.36 E
Menzel Djemil	36	37.14 N	9.55 E
Menzelen	48	51.37 N	6.32 E
Menzelerheide	253	51.37 N	6.31 E
Menzelinsk	70	55.43 N	53.08 E
Menzel Temime	138	36.47 N	10.59 E
Menzenschwand	54	47.49 N	8.04 E
Menzies	152	29.41 S	121.02 E
Menzies, Mount ∧	9	73.30 S	61.50 E
Menziken	54	47.14 N	8.12 E
Meob Bay C	146	24.25 S	14.34 E
Meola Āgri	262a	28.42 N	77.23 E
Meolo	58	45.37 N	12.27 E
Meon ≃	44	50.48 N	1.15 W
Meopham	250	51.22 N	0.22 E
Meopham Station	250	51.23 N	0.21 E
Meoqui	222	28.17 N	105.29 W
Meota	174	53.02 N	108.27 W
Méouge ≃	56	44.16 N	5.50 E
Méounes-lès-Montrieux	56	43.17 N	5.58 E
Mepal	44	52.24 N	0.07 E
Mepisckaro, Gora ∧	74	41.50 N	42.40 E
Meppel	48	52.42 N	6.11 E
Meppen	48	52.41 N	7.17 E
Mequon	206	43.13 N	87.58 W
Mer	46	47.42 N	1.30 E
Mera ≃	54	46.11 N	9.25 E
Merah	102	0.50 N	116.48 E
Merai	154	4.50 S	152.20 E
Meråker	26	63.26 N	11.45 E
Merakurak	105a	6.53 S	111.59 E
Mera Lava I	165f	14.25 S	168.03 E
Meram	120	37.50 N	32.27 E
Meramangye, Lake ⊜	152	28.25 S	132.13 E
Merambéllou, Kólpos C	38	35.14 N	25.47 E
Meramec ≃	184	38.23 N	90.21 W
Meramec Caverns ●5	209	38.15 N	91.06 W
Meramec State Park ♣	209	38.14 N	91.05 W
Meran → Merano, It.	58	46.40 N	11.09 E
Meran, Nig.	263a	6.38 N	3.16 E
Meranggau	102	0.12 S	110.17 E
Merangin ≃	102	2.09 S	102.47 E
Merano (Meran)	58	46.40 N	11.09 E
Merapi, Gunung ∧	105a	8.03 S	114.15 E
Merapoh	104	4.41 N	101.59 E
Merasheen	176	47.25 N	54.21 W
Merasheen Island I	176	47.30 N	54.15 W
Merate	56	45.42 N	9.25 E
Meratus, Pegunungan ⛰	102	2.45 S	115.40 E
Merauke	154	8.28 S	140.20 E
Merauke ≃	154	8.30 S	140.24 E
Merawang, Pulau I	261c	1.20 N	103.38 E
Merbabu, Gunung ∧	105a	7.33 S	110.26 E
Merbau	104	1.07 N	102.33 E
Merbein	156	34.11 S	142.04 E
Mer Bleue Peat Bog ☰	202	45.24 N	75.30 W
Merca → Marka	134	1.47 N	44.52 E
Mercaderes	236	1.47 N	77.10 W
Mercader y Millás	256d	41.21 N	2.05 E
Mercan Dağları ⛰	74	39.34 N	39.33 E
Mercāra	112	12.25 N	75.44 E
Mercatale	60	43.15 N	12.08 E
Mercato San Severino	60	40.47 N	14.46 E
Mercato Saraceno	60	43.57 N	12.12 E
Merced	216	37.18 N	120.29 W
Merced □6	216	37.15 N	120.40 W
Merced ≃	216	37.21 N	120.58 W
Merced, Lake ⊜	272	37.43 N	122.29 W
Merced, North Fork ≃	216	37.37 N	120.03 W
Merced, South Fork ≃	216	37.39 N	119.53 W
Merced Airport ⊠	216	37.17 N	120.31 W
Mercedario, Cerro ∧	242	31.59 S	70.07 W
Mercedes, Arg.	242	33.40 S	65.28 W
Mercedes, Arg.	242	29.12 S	58.05 W
Mercedes, Arg.	248	34.39 S	59.27 W
Mercedes, Pil.	106	14.07 N	123.01 E
Mercedes, Tex., U.S.	186	26.09 N	97.55 W
Mercedes, Ur.	242	33.16 S	58.01 W
Mercedita, Aeropuerto ⊠	230m	18.01 N	66.34 W
Mercer, N.Z.	162	37.16 S	175.03 E
Mercer, Mo., U.S.	184	40.31 N	93.32 W
Mercer, Ohio, U.S.	206	40.40 N	84.35 W
Mercer, Pa., U.S.	204	41.14 N	80.15 W
Mercer, Wis., U.S.	180	46.10 N	90.04 W
Mercer □6, N.J., U.S.	198	40.13 N	74.45 W
Mercer □6, Ohio, U.S.	206	40.33 N	84.34 W
Mercer □6, Pa., U.S.	204	41.14 N	80.15 W
Mercer Island	214	47.35 N	122.15 W
Mercersburg	178	39.50 N	77.54 W
Mercerville	198	40.14 N	74.41 W
Mercês, Bra.	246	21.12 S	43.21 W
Mercês, Port.	256c	38.47 N	9.19 W
Merchants Bay C	166	67.10 N	62.50 W
Merchants Millpond ⊜	198	36.26 N	76.41 W
Merchantville	275	39.57 N	75.03 W
Merchong ≃	104	3.03 N	103.27 E
Merchtem	46	50.58 N	4.14 E
Mercier (Saint-Philomène)	265a	45.19 N	73.45 W
Mercier, Pont ◆5	265a	45.25 N	73.39 W
Mercoal	172	53.10 N	117.05 W
Mercogliano	60	40.55 N	14.44 E
Mercümüt	120	38.25 N	39.04 E
Mercury	194	36.40 N	115.59 W
Mercury Islands II	162	36.35 S	175.55 E
Mercy Bay C	166	74.05 N	119.00 W
Mercy-le-Bas	52	49.23 N	5.45 E
Merdeka Bridge ◆5	261c	1.18 N	103.53 E
Merdeka Palace ♁	259e	6.10 S	106.49 E
Merdinik	120	40.48 N	42.36 E
Méré, Fr.	251	48.47 N	1.49 E
Mere, Eng., U.K.	44	51.06 N	2.16 W
Mere, Eng., U.K.	252	53.20 N	2.25 W
Mere Brow	252	53.40 N	2.53 W
Mereckij	75	43.48 N	74.42 E
Mereclough	252	53.46 N	2.11 W
Meredale	263d	26.17 S	27.59 E
Meredith, Austl.	159	37.51 S	144.04 E
Meredith, N.H., U.S.	178	43.39 N	71.30 W
Meredith, Cape ➤	244	52.15 S	60.39 W
Meredith, Lake ⊜1	186	35.36 N	101.42 W
Meredosia	209	39.50 N	90.34 W
Meredosia Lake ⊜	209	39.52 N	90.33 W
Merefa	68	49.49 N	36.03 E
Merelbeke	46	51.00 N	3.45 E
Merenkurkku (Norra Kvarken) ⊔	26	63.36 N	20.43 E
Merevari ≃	236	4.28 N	63.57 W
Méréville	46	48.19 N	2.05 E
Merewa	134	7.40 N	37.00 E
Merewether	160	32.57 S	151.46 E
Mereworth	250	51.15 N	0.23 E
Mergenevo	70	49.56 N	51.17 E
Mergozzo	54	45.58 N	8.26 E
Mergui (Myeik)	100	12.26 N	98.36 E
Mergui Archipelago II	100	12.00 N	98.00 E
Merḥavya	122	32.36 N	35.19 E
Meria	262b	22.59 N	88.20 E
Meribah	156	34.42 S	140.51 E
Méribel	56	45.25 N	6.34 E
Meriç (Marica) (Évros) ≃	38	40.52 N	26.12 E
Méricourt	46	50.24 N	2.52 E
Mérida, Esp.	34	38.55 N	6.20 W
Mérida, Méx.	190	32.39 N	114.58 W
Mérida, Méx.	222	20.58 N	89.37 W
Merida, Pil.	106	10.55 N	124.32 E
Mérida, Ven.	236	8.36 N	71.08 W
Mérida □3	236	8.30 N	71.10 W
Mérida, Cordillera de ⛰	236	8.40 N	71.00 W
Meridale	200	42.22 N	74.57 W
Meriden, Eng., U.K.	44	52.26 N	1.37 W
Meriden, Conn., U.S.	197	41.32 N	72.48 W
Meriden, N.J., U.S.	266	40.57 N	74.28 W
Meridian, Calif., U.S.	216	39.09 N	121.55 W
Meridian, Ga., U.S.	182	31.27 N	81.23 W
Meridian, Idaho, U.S.	192	43.37 N	116.24 W
Meridian, Miss., U.S.	184	32.22 N	88.42 W
Meridian, N.Y., U.S.	200	43.10 N	76.32 W
Meridian, Pa., U.S.	204	40.51 N	79.58 W
Meridian, Tex., U.S.	212	31.55 N	[illegible].39 W
Meridian Hills	208	39.53 N	86.09 W
Mériel	251	49.05 N	2.12 E
Mérignac	32	44.50 N	0.42 W
Merigold	184	33.50 N	90.50 W
Merikarvia	26	61.51 N	21.30 E
Merille ≃	134	1.25 N	38.26 E
Merimbula	156	36.53 S	149.54 E
Merín, Laguna (Lagoa Mirim) C	242	32.45 S	52.50 W
Merinda	156	20.01 S	148.10 E
Merin Gubai	134	1.27 N	44.23 E
Merino	188	40.29 N	103.21 W
Merinos	242	32.24 S	56.54 W
Merion Station	275	40.00 N	75.15 W
Merir I	98	4.19 N	132.19 E
Merishausen	54	47.45 N	8.37 E
Merit	212	33.13 N	96.17 W
Meriti ≃	277a	22.48 S	43.20 W
Merivale Gardens	202	45.19 N	75.44 W
Merizo	164p	13.16 N	144.40 E
Merke	75	42.52 N	73.11 E
Merkel	186	32.28 N	100.01 W
Merkem	46	50.57 N	2.51 E
Merkendorf	52	49.12 N	10.42 E
Merkinė	66	54.10 N	24.10 E
Merklingen	54	48.30 N	9.44 E
Merksem	46	51.15 N	4.27 E
Merksplas	52	51.22 N	4.52 E
Merkulovĭči	66	52.58 N	30.36 E
Merkys ≃	66	54.10 N	24.11 E
Merlara	58	45.10 N	11.26 E
Merlebach	52	49.09 N	6.48 E
Merlejevo	72	55.05 N	37.13 E
Merlimau, Pulau I	261c	1.17 N	103.42 E
Merlimont-Plage	46	50.28 N	1.35 E
Merlin, Ont., Can.	204	42.14 N	82.14 W
Merlin, Oreg., U.S.	192	42.31 N	123.25 W
Merlin Seamount ✧3	14	8.20 S	150.25 W
Merlo, Arg.	242	32.21 S	65.02 W
Merlo, Arg.	248	34.40 S	58.45 W
Merlo □5	278	34.40 S	58.45 W
Merlo, Aeródromo ⊠	278	34.41 S	58.45 W
Merlynston	264b	37.43 S	144.58 E
Mermaid Beach	161a	28.03 S	153.27 E
Mern	41	55.03 N	12.04 E
Merna	188	41.29 N	99.46 W
Mernye	30	46.30 N	17.50 E
Meron	122	32.59 N	35.26 E
Meron, Hare ∧	122	32.58 N	35.25 E

≃ River	Fluss	Río	Rivière	Rio
⩧ Canal	Kanal	Canal	Canal	Canal
Waterfall, Rapids	Wasserfall, Stromschnellen	Cascada, Rápidos	Chute d'eau, Rapides	Cascata, Rápidos
⊔ Strait	Meeresstrasse	Estrecho	Détroit	Estreito
C Bay, Gulf	Bucht, Golf	Bahía, Golfo	Baie, Golfe	Baía, Golfo
⊜ Lake, Lakes	See, Seen	Lago, Lagos	Lac, Lacs	Lago, Lagos
☰ Swamp	Sumpf	Pantano	Marais	Pântano
⊓ Ice Features, Glacier	Eis- und Gletscherformen	Accidentes Glaciales	Formes glaciaires	Acidentes Glaciares
Other Hydrographic Features	Andere Hydrographische Objekte	Otros Elementos Hidrográficos	Autres données hydrographiques	Outros Acidentes Hidrográficos

✧ Submarine Features	Untermeerische Objekte	Accidentes Submarinos	Formes de relief sous-marin	Acidentes Submarinos
□ Political Unit	Politische Einheit	Unidad Politica	Entité politique	Unidade Política
♁ Cultural Institution	Kulturelle Institution	Institución Cultural	Institution culturelle	Instituição Cultural
⊥ Historical Site	Historische Stätte	Sitio Histórico	Site historique	Sitio Histórico
♣ Recreational Site	Erholungs- und Ferienort	Sitio de Recreo	Centre de loisirs	Sítio de Lazer
⊠ Airport	Flughafen	Aeropuerto	Aéroport	Aeroporto
■ Military Installation	Militäranlage	Instalación Militar	Installation militaire	Instalação Militar
◆ Miscellaneous	Verschiedenes	Misceláneo	Divers	Miscelânea

Meros, Ponta dos ≻ 246 23.13 S 44.21 W
Merotai Besar 102 4.26 N 117.46 E
Merouana 34 35.38 N 5.55 E
Merouane, Chott ◎ 138 34.00 N 6.02 E
Mer'oža 66 59.02 N 36.23 E
Merredin 152 31.29 S 118.16 E
Merrick 266 40.40 N 73.33 W
Merrick ∧ 42 55.08 N 4.29 W
Merrick Bay C 266 40.38 N 73.33 W
Merrickville 202 44.55 N 75.50 W
Merri Creek ≃ 159 37.48 S 145.01 E
Merriewold Lake 200 41.22 N 74.12 W
Merrifield 274c 38.52 N 77.14 W
Merrill, Iowa, U.S. 188 42.43 N 96.15 W
Merrill, Mich., U.S. 180 43.25 N 84.20 W
Merrill, Oreg., U.S. 192 42.01 N 121.36 W
Merrill, Wis., U.S. 180 45.11 N 89.41 W
Merrillan 180 44.27 N 90.50 W
Merrill C. Meigs Field ⊠ 268 41.52 N 87.37 W
Merrill Lake ◎ 202 44.55 N 77.24 W
Merrillville 206 41.29 N 87.20 W
Merrimac 197 42.50 N 71.00 W
Merrimack ≃ 197 42.49 N 70.49 W
Merrimac Terrace 273 42.49 N 71.00 W
Merriman, S. Afr. 148 31.13 S 23.38 E
Merriman, Nebr., U.S. 188 42.55 N 101.42 W
Merrin, Mount ∧ 165f 19.35 S 169.22 E
Merrionette Park 268 41.41 N 87.42 W
Merriott 44 50.54 N 2.48 W
Merritt, B.C., Can. 172 50.07 N 120.47 W
Merritt, Wash., U.S. 214 47.47 N 120.51 W
Merritt, Lake ◎1 272 37.48 N 122.16 W
Merritt Island 210 28.21 N 80.42 W
Merritt Island I 210 28.33 N 80.40 W
Merritt Reservoir ◎1 188 42.35 N 100.55 W
Merriwa 156 32.08 S 150.21 E
Mer Rouge 184 32.47 N 91.48 W
Merrow 197 41.49 N 72.19 W
Merrygoen 156 31.50 S 149.14 E
Merrylands 264a 33.50 S 150.59 E
Merrymount Park ♠ 273 42.16 N 71.01 W
Merryville 184 30.45 N 93.33 W
Mersa Fatma 134 14.55 N 40.20 E
Mersa Matruh → Maṭrūḥ 130 31.21 N 27.14 E
Mersch 52 49.46 N 6.06 E
Merscheid ◆8 253 51.10 N 7.01 E
Merse ∨ 42 55.39 N 2.15 W
Merse ≃ 60 43.05 N 11.22 E
Mersea Island I 44 51.47 N 0.55 E
Merseburg 50 51.21 N 11.59 E
Mers el Kébir 138 35.45 N 0.43 W
Mersey ≃, Austl. 156 41.10 S 146.22 E
Mersey ≃, N.S., Can. 176 44.02 N 64.43 W
Mersey ≃, Eng., U.K. 252 53.26 N 3.01 W
Merseyside □6 252 53.29 N 2.59 W
Mersey Tunnel ◆5 252 53.24 N 3.00 W
Mersin 120 36.48 N 34.38 E
Mersing 104 2.26 N 103.50 E
Mers-les-Bains 46 50.04 N 1.23 E
Mērsrags 66 57.21 N 23.07 E
Merstham 250 51.16 N 0.09 W
Merta 110 26.39 N 74.02 E
Merta Road 110 26.43 N 73.55 E
Merthyr Tydfil 44 51.46 N 3.23 W
Merti 144 1.04 N 38.40 E
Mertingen 52 48.39 N 10.47 E
Mértola 34 37.38 N 7.40 W
Merton, Austl. 159 36.59 S 145.42 E
Merton, Wis., U.S. 206 43.09 N 88.18 W
Merton ◆8 44 51.25 N 0.12 W
Mertz Glacier Tongue ⊹ 9 67.40 S 144.45 E
Mertzon 186 31.16 N 100.49 W
Mertztown 198 40.30 N 75.40 W
Méru, Fr. 46 49.14 N 2.08 E
Meru, Kenya 144 0.03 N 37.39 E
Meru, Mount ∧ 144 3.14 S 36.40 E
Meru National Park ♠ 144 0.00 38.15 E
Meruoca 240 3.28 S 40.28 W
Merv → Mary 118 37.36 N 61.50 E
Mervans 54 46.48 N 5.11 E
Merville 46 50.38 N 2.38 E
Mervin 174 53.20 N 108.53 W
Merwede 148 31.38 S 23.48 E
Merweville 148 32.40 S 21.31 E
Merwin, Lake ◎1 214 45.59 N 122.26 W
Merxleben 50 51.07 N 10.40 E
Mery 72 55.49 N 36.36 E
Méry-la-Bataille 46 49.33 N 2.38 E
Méry-sur-Oise 251 49.04 N 2.11 E
Méry-sur-Seine 46 48.30 N 3.53 E
Merzdorf 50 51.23 N 14.32 E
Merzhausen 54 47.58 N 7.49 E
Merzifon 120 40.53 N 35.29 E
Merzig 52 49.27 N 6.36 E
Mesa, Moç. 144 13.00 S 39.33 E
Mesa, S. Afr. 148 26.29 S 26.59 E
Mesa, Ariz., U.S. 190 33.25 N 111.50 W
Mesa ≃ 34 41.15 N 1.48 W
Mesa, Cerro ∧ 244 48.46 S 71.29 W
Mesabi Range ⛰2 180 47.30 N 92.50 W
Mesachie Lake 214 48.49 N 124.07 W
Mesa del Nayar 224 22.16 N 104.35 W
Mesa de Santa Rita 224 23.04 N 105.31 W
Mesagne 36 40.33 N 17.49 E
Mes'agutovo 76 55.35 N 58.20 E
Mesaména 142 3.44 N 12.50 E
Mesa Mountain ∧ 190 37.55 N 106.38 W
Mesarás, Kólpos C 38 34.58 N 24.36 E
Mesa Verde National Park ♠ 190 37.13 N 108.30 W
Mescalero 190 33.09 N 105.46 W
Mescalero Indian Reservation ◆4 190 33.12 N 105.40 W
Meščerino, S.S.S.R. 66 53.37 N 37.23 E
Meščerino, S.S.S.R. 72 55.11 N 38.21 E
Meščerskij 255b 55.40 N 37.25 E
Meščerskoje 72 55.17 N 37.38 E
Meschede 52 51.20 N 8.17 E
Meschetskij Chrebet ⛰ 74 41.48 N 42.30 E
Mescit Dağı ∧ 120 40.22 N 41.11 E
Meščovsk 66 54.19 N 35.17 E
Meščura 24 63.20 N 50.52 E
Mese 54 46.17 N 9.21 E
Mèsè Atet 100 18.38 N 97.39 E
Mesen-Bucht → Mezenskaja Guba C 24 66.40 N 43.45 E
Meseritz → Międzyrzecz 30 52.28 N 15.35 E
Mesero 256b 45.30 N 8.51 E
Mesewa (Massaua) 134 15.38 N 39.28 E
Mesewa Channel ⋓ 134 15.30 N 40.00 E
Mesfinto 134 13.20 N 37.19 E
Mesgarābād 257d 35.37 N 51.31 E
Mesgouez, Lac ◎ 166 51.24 N 75.05 W
Meshed → Mashhad 118 36.18 N 59.36 E
Meshomasic Mountain ∧ 197 41.38 N 72.32 W
Meshoppen 200 41.34 N 76.03 W
Meshoppen Creek ≃ 200 41.37 N 76.03 W
Mesick 180 44.24 N 85.43 W
Mesilinka ≃ 172 56.09 N 124.28 W
Mesilla 190 32.16 N 106.48 W
Mesillas, Méx. 224 23.33 N 103.35 W
Mesillas, Méx. 224 23.14 N 106.03 W
Meskiana 138 35.39 N 7.41 E
Meskiana, Oued ≃ 36 35.49 N 7.53 E
Meşkinan 120 37.18 N 40.22 E
Meskine 136 11.25 N 15.21 E
Meškuičiai 66 56.05 N 23.28 E
Meskum 104 1.34 N 102.01 E
Meslay-du-Maine 32 47.57 N 0.33 W
Meslay-le-Grenet 46 48.22 N 1.23 E
Meslo 134 6.27 N 39.50 E
Mesnil-Val-Plage 46 50.03 N 1.20 E
Mesocco 54 46.23 N 9.14 E
Mesola 60 44.55 N 12.14 E
Mesolcina, Valle ∨ 54 46.20 N 9.10 E
Mesolóngion 38 38.21 N 21.17 E
Mésondo 142 3.43 N 10.28 E
Mesopotamia 204 41.27 N 80.57 W
Mesopotamia ◆1 118 34.00 N 44.00 E
Mesóyia □9 257c 37.56 N 23.53 E
Mespelbrunn ⊥ 52 49.54 N 9.19 E
Mesquita, Bra. 245 19.13 S 42.35 W
Mesquita, Bra. 246 22.48 S 43.26 W
Mesquite, Nev., U.S. 194 36.48 N 114.04 W
Mesquite, Tex., U.S. 212 32.46 N 96.36 W
Messaad, Oued ∨ 138 33.45 N 2.51 E
Messach Mellet ⛰2 136 24.30 N 11.35 E
Messalo ≃ 144 11.40 S 40.26 E
Messaoud, Oued ∨ 138 27.28 N 0.21 W
Messdorf 50 52.43 N 11.33 E
Messent National Park ♠ 156 36.05 S 139.50 E
Messina, It. 36 38.11 N 15.33 E
Messina, S. Afr. 146 22.23 S 30.00 E
Messina, Stretto di ⋓ 36 38.15 N 15.35 E
Messíni 38 37.04 N 22.00 E
Messíni ⊥ 38 37.11 N 21.57 E
Messiniakós Kólpos C 38 36.58 N 22.00 E
Messix Peak ∧ 192 41.29 N 112.31 W
Messkirch 54 47.59 N 9.07 E
Messojacha ≃ 64 67.52 N 77.27 E
Messtetten 54 48.11 N 8.58 E
Messy 251 48.58 N 2.42 E
Mestá 38 38.15 N 25.55 E
Mesta (Néstos) ≃ 38 40.41 N 24.44 E
Mestasa 138 35.07 N 4.25 W
Mestia 74 43.03 N 42.43 E
Mestlin 50 53.35 N 11.56 E
Mestre 58 45.29 N 12.15 E
Mestre, Espigão ⛰1 245 12.30 S 46.10 W
Mestrino 58 45.26 N 11.45 E
Mesudiye 120 40.28 N 37.46 E
Mesum 48 52.13 N 7.29 E
Meszah Peak ∧ 170 58.28 N 131.26 W
Meta, It. 60 40.39 N 14.24 E
Meta, Mo., U.S. 209 38.19 N 92.10 W
Meta □5 236 3.30 N 73.00 W
Meta ≃ 236 6.12 N 67.28 W
Métabief 54 46.47 N 6.21 E
Metagācha 262b 22.38 N 88.31 E
Metairie 184 29.59 N 90.09 W
Metalanim 164r 6.53 N 158.16 E
Metaline Falls 192 48.52 N 117.22 W
Metallifere, Colline ⛰ 60 43.15 N 11.00 E
Metallostroj 255a 59.47 N 30.33 E
Metamora, Ill., U.S. 180 40.47 N 89.22 W
Metamora, Ind., U.S. 208 39.27 N 85.08 W
Metamora, Mich., U.S. 206 42.57 N 83.17 W
Metamora, Ohio, U.S. 206 41.43 N 83.55 W
Metán 242 25.29 S 64.57 W
Metapán 226 14.20 N 89.27 W
Metapontum ⊥ 36 40.24 N 16.49 E
Metarica 144 14.20 S 36.48 E
Metaurilia 60 43.49 N 13.03 E
Metauro ≃ 60 43.50 N 13.03 E
Metcalfe 202 45.14 N 75.28 W
Metchosin 214 48.22 N 123.33 W
Metechi 74 41.55 N 44.21 E
Metedeconk, South Branch ≃ 198 40.04 N 74.09 W
Meteghan 176 44.11 N 66.10 W
Metehara 134 8.55 N 39.57 E
Metelen 48 52.08 N 7.12 E
Metema 134 12.57 N 36.12 E
Metéora ♉1 38 39.46 N 21.36 E
Meteor Seamount ⊹3 8 47.50 S 8.55 E
Metepec, Méx. 224 18.56 N 98.28 W
Metepec, Méx. 224 19.15 N 99.36 W
Metharaw 100 16.12 N 98.08 E
Methler 253 51.35 N 7.37 E
Methóni 38 36.50 N 21.43 E
Methow 172 48.08 N 120.00 W
Methow ≃ 214 48.40 N 120.32 W
Methuen 197 42.44 N 71.11 W
Methven 162 43.38 S 171.39 E
Methwold 44 52.31 N 0.33 E
Metiskow 174 52.24 N 110.38 W
Metković 36 43.03 N 17.39 E
Metlakatla, B.C., Can. 172 54.20 N 130.27 W
Metlakatla, Alaska, U.S. 170 55.08 N 131.35 W
Metlatonoc 224 17.11 N 98.20 W
Metlika 36 45.39 N 15.19 E
Metlili, Oued ∨ 138 31.54 N 4.53 E
Metlili Chaamba 138 32.18 N 3.40 E
Metmahu ◎ 110 34.15 N 82.20 E
Meto, Bayou ≃ 184 34.05 N 91.26 W
Metolius ≃ 192 44.36 N 121.17 W
Metomkin Bay C 198 37.43 N 75.35 W
Metomkin Inlet C 198 37.41 N 75.35 W
Metomkin Island I 198 37.43 N 75.33 W
Metro 105a 5.05 S 105.20 E
Metropolis 184 37.09 N 88.44 W
Metropolitan 180 46.00 N 87.53 W
Metropolitan Beach ♠ 271 42.35 N 82.48 W
Metropolitan Museum of Art ♉ 266 40.47 N 73.58 W
Metropolitan Oakland International Airport ⊠ 216 37.43 N 122.13 W
Metschow 50 53.49 N 12.58 E
Metsematluku 146 24.01 S 24.40 E
Metsera 144 2.35 S 26.07 E
Métsovon 38 39.46 N 21.11 E
Mettawa 268 42.14 N 87.56 W
Mettendorf 52 49.57 N 6.19 E
Metter 182 32.24 N 82.03 W
Mettet 52 50.19 N 4.40 E
Mettetal Airport ⊠ 271 42.21 N 83.27 W
Mettingen 48 52.18 N 7.46 E
Mettlach 52 49.30 N 6.36 E
Mettmach 58 48.10 N 13.21 E
Mettmann 52 51.15 N 6.58 E
Mettray 46 47.27 N 0.39 E
Mettuppālaiyam 112 11.18 N 76.57 E
Mettūr 112 11.48 N 77.48 E
Metu 134 8.20 N 35.36 E
Metuchen 200 40.33 N 74.22 W
Metuge 144 12.58 S 40.20 E
Metulla 122 33.16 N 35.35 E
Metundo, Ilha I 144 11.10 S 40.41 E
Metz 52 49.08 N 6.10 E
Metzervisse 52 49.19 N 6.17 E
Metzger 214 45.26 N 122.44 W
Metzingen 52 48.32 N 9.17 E
Metzkausen 253 51.16 N 6.57 E
Metztitlán, Laguna ◎ 224 20.40 N 98.50 W
Meu ≃ 32 48.02 N 1.47 W
Meuban 142 2.27 N 12.41 E
Meudon 251 48.48 N 2.14 E
Meudon, Bois de ♠ 251 48.47 N 2.12 E
Meulaboh 104 4.09 N 96.08 E
Meulan 46 49.01 N 1.54 E
Meulebeke 46 50.57 N 3.17 E
Meung-sur-Loire 46 47.50 N 1.42 E
Meureubo ≃ 104 4.09 N 96.09 E
Meureudu 104 5.16 N 96.16 E
Meursault 54 46.59 N 4.46 E
Meurthe ≃ 32 48.47 N 6.09 E
Meurthe-et-Moselle □5 32 48.35 N 6.10 E
Meuse 54 47.59 N 5.33 E
Meuse □5 52 49.00 N 5.30 E
Meuse (Maas) ≃ 30 51.49 N 5.01 E
Meuselwitz 50 51.02 N 12.17 E
Meux Creek ≃ 202 44.07 N 81.02 W
Mevagissey 44 50.16 N 4.48 W
Mewāt Plain ≚ 114 27.40 N 76.15 E
Mexborough 42 53.30 N 1.17 W
Mexia 212 31.41 N 96.29 W
Mexiana, Ilha I 240 0.02 S 49.35 W
Mexicali 222 32.40 N 115.29 W
Mexican Hat 190 37.09 N 109.52 W
Mexico, Ind., U.S. 206 40.49 N 86.07 W
Mexico, Maine, U.S. 178 44.34 N 70.33 W
Mexico, Mo., U.S. 209 39.10 N 91.53 W
Mexico, N.Y., U.S. 202 43.28 N 76.14 W
Mexico, Pa., U.S. 198 40.32 N 77.21 W
México □3 224 19.20 N 99.45 W
Mexico □1 220 / 222 23.00 N 102.00 W
México, Golfo de → Mexico, Gulf of C 220 25.00 N 90.00 W
Mexico, Gulf of C 220 25.00 N 90.00 W
Mexico Basin ⊹1 16 25.00 N 91.00 W
Mexico Bay C 202 43.31 N 76.17 W
Mexico City → Ciudad de México 224 19.24 N 99.09 W
Mexiko → Ciudad de México 224 19.24 N 99.09 W
Mexiko → Mexico □1 222 23.00 N 102.00 W
Mexiko, Golf von → Mexico, Gulf of C 220 25.00 N 90.00 W
Meximieux 54 45.54 N 5.12 E
Mexique → Mexico □1 220 23.00 N 102.00 W
Mexique, Golfe du → Mexico, Gulf of C 220 25.00 N 90.00 W
Mexticacán 224 21.13 N 102.43 W
Mey, Castle of ♠ 28 58.40 N 3.12 W
Meyanodas 154 7.38 S 131.38 E
Meycauayan 106 14.44 N 120.58 E
Meydan 120 38.21 N 41.47 E
Meydancik 120 41.25 N 42.14 E
Meydān-e Gel ≚ 118 29.04 N 54.50 E
Meydān Kalay 110 32.25 N 66.44 E
Meydān Khvolah 110 33.36 N 69.51 E
Meyenburg 50 53.18 N 12.14 E
Meyers Chuck 170 55.44 N 132.12 W
Meyersdale 178 39.45 N 79.05 W
Meyers Lake 204 40.52 N 81.24 W
Meyersville 212 28.55 N 97.21 W
Meyerton 148 26.33 S 28.01 E
Meyisti I 120 36.08 N 29.34 E
Meymac 32 45.32 N 2.09 E
Meymaneh 110 35.55 N 64.47 E
Meymeh 118 33.27 N 51.10 E
Meymeh ≃ 118 32.05 N 47.16 E
Meyo-Centre 142 2.33 N 11.02 E
Meyrargues 56 43.38 N 5.32 E
Meyrin 54 46.14 N 6.05 E
Meyronne 174 49.39 N 106.50 W
Meyrueis 32 44.10 N 3.26 E
Meẕada, Ḥorvot (Masada) ⊥ 122 31.19 N 35.21 E
Mezapa 226 15.33 N 87.23 W
Mezdra 38 43.09 N 23.42 E
Meždurečensk 76 53.42 N 88.03 E
Meždurečenskij 76 59.36 N 65.53 E
Mèze 32 43.25 N 3.36 E
Mézel 56 43.59 N 6.12 E
Mezen' 24 65.50 N 44.13 E
Mezen' ≃ 24 66.11 N 43.59 E
Mézenc, Mont ∧ 56 44.55 N 4.11 E
Mezenskaja Guba C 24 66.40 N 43.45 E
Meževaja 68 48.16 N 36.44 E
Mežgorje 68 48.32 N 23.30 E
Meziadin Lake ◎ 172 56.04 N 129.18 W
Mézières-en-Brenne 32 46.49 N 1.13 E
Mézières-sur-Seine 251 48.58 N 1.48 E
Mézilhac 56 44.48 N 4.21 E
Mézin 32 44.03 N 0.16 E
Mezinovskij 66 55.30 N 40.21 E
Mežirič 68 50.43 N 34.29 E
Mezőberény 30 46.50 N 21.02 E
Mezőcsát 30 47.49 N 20.55 E
Mezőkovácsháza 30 46.25 N 20.55 E
Mezőkövesd 30 47.50 N 20.34 E
Mezőtúr 30 47.00 N 20.38 E
Mezquital 224 23.29 N 104.23 W
Mezquital ≃ 222 22.54 N 104.54 W
Mezquital del Oro 224 21.10 N 103.23 W
Mezquitic 224 22.23 N 103.41 W
Mezraa 120 41.12 N 35.08 E
Mézy 251 49.00 N 1.53 E
Mezzana 58 46.19 N 10.48 E
Mezzano 58 46.09 N 11.48 E
Mezzenile 56 45.17 N 7.23 E
Mezzocorona 58 46.13 N 11.07 E
Mezzola, Lago di ◎ 54 46.12 N 9.26 E
Mezzoldo 54 46.01 N 9.40 E
Mezzolombardo 58 46.13 N 11.05 E
Mezzomerico 256b 45.37 N 8.36 E
Mfangano Island I 144 0.28 S 34.01 E
Mfou 142 3.43 N 11.38 E
Mgači 79 51.05 N 142.17 E
Mgeni ≃ 148 29.48 S 31.02 E
Mgeta 144 8.19 S 36.08 E
Mglin 66 53.04 N 32.51 E
M'goun, Irhil ∧ 138 31.31 N 6.25 W
M'hai, B'nom ∧ 100 11.21 N 107.50 E
Mhasvād 112 17.38 N 74.47 E
Mhlume 148 26.02 S 31.50 E
Mhow 110 22.33 N 75.46 E
Miacatlán 224 18.46 N 99.22 W
Mia-dong ◆8 261b 37.37 N 127.01 E
Miagao 106 10.39 N 122.14 E
Miahuatlán de Porfirio Díaz 224 16.20 N 96.36 W
Miajadas 34 39.09 N 5.54 W
Miājlar 110 26.15 N 70.23 E
Miaméré 136 8.52 N 19.50 E
Miami, Man., Can. 174 49.21 N 98.11 W
Miami, Rh. 144 16.40 S 29.46 E
Miami, Ariz., U.S. 190 33.24 N 110.52 W
Miami, Fla., U.S. 210 25.46 N 80.12 W
Miami, Ind., U.S. 206 40.37 N 86.06 W
Miami, Okla., U.S. 184 36.53 N 94.53 W
Miami, Tex., U.S. 186 35.42 N 100.38 W
Miami □6, Ind., U.S. 206 40.45 N 86.04 W
Miami □6, Ohio, U.S. 208 40.02 N 84.13 W
Miami ≃ 214 45.33 N 123.53 W
Miami Beach, Ont., Can. 202 44.13 N 79.29 W
Miami Beach, Fla., U.S. 210 25.47 N 80.08 W
Miami Canal ≍ 210 25.47 N 80.15 W
Miami Creek ≃ 216 37.21 N 119.44 W
Miami International Airport ⊠ 210 25.48 N 80.17 W
Miami Lakes 210 25.53 N 80.18 W
Miamisburg 208 39.38 N 84.17 W
Miamisburg Mound State Memorial ⊥ 208 39.38 N 84.17 W
Miami Shores 210 25.51 N 80.11 W
Miami Springs 210 25.49 N 80.17 W
Miami State Recreation Area ♠ 206 40.40 N 85.55 W
Miamiville 208 39.13 N 84.18 W
Mīānābād 118 37.02 N 57.27 E
Miān Channūn 113 30.27 N 72.22 E
Mianchi 92 34.48 N 111.49 E
Mīāndowāb 118 36.58 N 46.06 E
Miandrivazo 147b 19.31 S 45.28 E
Mianduhe 79 49.05 N 121.06 E
Miane 58 45.57 N 12.06 E
Mīāneh 118 37.26 N 47.42 E
Miang, Phu ∧ 100 17.42 N 101.01 E
Miangas, Pulau I 98 5.35 N 126.35 E
Mianhu 90 23.28 N 116.09 E
Mianhuadi 94 41.15 N 120.49 E
Miāni, Bhārat 110 21.51 N 69.23 E
Miāni, Pāk. 113 32.32 N 73.04 E
Miāni Hōr C 110 25.34 N 66.19 E
Mianning 92 28.39 N 102.09 E
Mianus ≃ 197 41.03 N 73.35 W
Mianus Reservoir ◎1 266 41.08 N 73.37 W
Miānwāli 113 32.35 N 71.33 E
Mianxian 92 33.09 N 106.48 E
Mianyang, Zhg. 90 30.23 N 113.25 E
Mianyang, Zhg. 92 31.30 N 104.49 E
Mianzhu, Zhg. 92 31.20 N 104.09 E
Mianzhu, Zhg. 92 32.17 N 110.02 E
Miaodaoqundao II 88 37.56 N 120.40 E
Miaoergou 76 45.32 N 83.52 E
Miaofengshan 95 40.04 N 116.13 E
Miaogou 94 41.12 N 120.40 E
Miaojiagou 94 42.16 N 123.22 E
Miaojiatun 94 40.54 N 120.55 E
Miaokou 88 35.48 N 114.09 E
Miaoli 90 24.34 N 120.48 E
Miaoling ⛰ 92 26.15 N 107.26 E
Miaopu 96 31.00 N 118.44 E
Miaoqian 90 30.33 N 117.44 E
Miaotou 96 30.58 N 120.33 E
Miaowan 90 33.07 N 114.41 E
Miaowan I 90 21.54 N 114.00 E
Miaoyang 88 40.49 N 124.24 E
Miaozhen 96 31.43 N 121.21 E
Miarayon 106 8.04 N 124.50 E
Miarinarivo, Madag. 147b 16.38 S 48.15 E
Miarinarivo, Madag. 147b 18.57 S 46.55 E
Miarinavaratra 147b 20.13 S 47.31 E
Miasa 84 36.34 N 137.53 E
Miass 76 54.59 N 60.06 E
Miass ≃ 76 56.06 N 64.30 E
Miasteczko Krajeńskie 30 53.06 N 17.01 E
Miastko 30 54.01 N 17.00 E
Miboro-dam ◆6 84 36.08 N 136.55 E
Mibu 84 36.25 N 139.48 E
Mibu ≃ 84 35.49 N 137.57 E
Mica 146 24.10 S 30.48 E
Mica Mountain ∧ 190 32.13 N 110.33 W
Micangshan ⛰ 92 32.32 N 107.49 E
Micanopy 182 29.30 N 82.17 W
Micaúne 146 18.18 S 36.35 E
Mičavičevnik 24 64.14 N 57.58 E
Micha-cchakaja 74 42.17 N 42.04 E
Michael, Mount ∧ 154 6.25 S 145.20 E
Michael J. Kirwan Reservoir ◎1 204 41.10 N 81.10 W
Michaga, Cerro ∧ 238 19.28 S 66.32 W
Michajlo-Koc'ubinskoje 68 51.27 N 31.04 E
Michajlov 72 54.14 N 39.02 E
Michajlovka, S.S.S.R. 68 47.16 N 35.14 E
Michajlovka, S.S.S.R. 68 49.19 N 36.28 E
Michajlovka, S.S.S.R. 68 49.53 N 39.38 E
Michajlovka, S.S.S.R. 70 50.05 N 43.15 E
Michajlovka, S.S.S.R. 70 47.38 N 46.54 E
Michajlovka, S.S.S.R. 73 48.30 N 38.54 E
Michajlovka, S.S.S.R. 73 48.09 N 37.22 E
Michajlovka, S.S.S.R. 73 48.44 N 37.16 E
Michajlovka, S.S.S.R. 75 42.50 N 75.42 E
Michajlovka, S.S.S.R. 75 42.37 N 78.20 E
Michajlovka, S.S.S.R. 75 43.06 N 71.36 E
Michajlovka, S.S.S.R. 76 51.49 N 79.45 E
Michajlovka, S.S.S.R. 76 56.26 N 78.53 E
Michajlovka, S.S.S.R. 76 53.51 N 76.32 E
Michajlovka, S.S.S.R. 78 52.57 N 103.18 E
Michajlovka, S.S.S.R. 78 50.26 N 104.10 E
Michajlovka, S.S.S.R. 78 55.30 N 114.09 E
Michajlovka, S.S.S.R. 78 51.07 N 119.20 E
Michajlovka, S.S.S.R. 78 51.53 N 110.28 E
Michajlovka, S.S.S.R. 79 49.13 N 129.56 E
Michajlovka, S.S.S.R. 79 43.56 N 132.00 E
Michajlovka, S.S.S.R. 255a 59.43 N 30.01 E
Michajlovka, S.S.S.R. 255a 60.04 N 30.14 E
Michajlovo 70 56.56 N 45.04 E
Michajlovo-Aleksandrovskij 73 49.13 N 40.15 E
Michajlovskaja 70 50.58 N 41.52 E
Michajlovskij, S.S.S.R. 66 60.05 N 43.29 E
Michajlovskij, S.S.S.R. 70 56.11 N 45.47 E
Michajlovskij, S.S.S.R. 76 51.41 N 79.47 E
Michajlovskij, S.S.S.R. 76 50.17 N 55.23 E
Michajlovskoje, S.S.S.R. 66 58.23 N 37.40 E
Michajlovskoje, S.S.S.R. 72 55.50 N 36.20 E
Michajlovskoje, S.S.S.R. 255b 55.35 N 37.35 E
Michalevo 72 55.27 N 38.26 E
Michali 72 55.17 N 39.05 E
Michalkovo 72 54.11 N 37.33 E
Michalovce 30 48.45 N 21.55 E
Michanoviči 66 53.45 N 27.40 E
Michaud Point ≻ 176 45.34 N 60.40 W
Michejevo 78 57.10 N 104.53 E
Michel 172 49.43 N 114.49 W
Michelago 161b 35.43 S 149.10 E
Michelau 52 50.10 N 11.06 E
Micheldever 44 51.09 N 1.15 W
Michel Peak ∧ 172 53.35 N 126.26 W
Michelson, Mount ∧ 170 69.19 N 144.17 W
Michel'sona 255b 55.42 N 37.54 E
Michelstadt 52 49.41 N 9.00 E
Michendorf 50 52.18 N 13.01 E
Miches 228 18.59 N 69.03 W
Micheta 74 41.52 N 44.44 E
Michiana 206 41.46 N 86.48 W
Michiana Regional Airport ⊠ 206 41.42 N 86.19 W
Michigamee ≃ 180 46.04 N 88.13 W
Michigan 188 48.07 N 98.07 W
Michigan □3 168 / 180 44.00 N 85.00 W
Michigan, Lake ◎ 180 44.00 N 87.00 W
Michigan, University of (North Campus) ♉2, Mich., U.S. 271 42.17 N 83.43 W
Michigan, University of ♉2, Mich., U.S. 271 42.17 N 83.44 W
Michigan Center 180 42.14 N 84.20 W
Michigan City 206 41.43 N 86.54 W
Michigan International Speedway ♠ 206 42.03 N 84.15 W
Michigan State Fair Grounds ♠ 271 42.27 N 83.07 W
Michigantown 206 40.20 N 86.23 W
Michika 136 10.38 N 13.24 E
Michikamau Lake ◎ 166 54.00 N 64.00 W
Michillinda 270 34.07 N 118.05 W
Michipicoten Bay C 180 47.55 N 84.56 W
Michipicoten Island I 180 47.45 N 85.45 W
Michnevo 72 55.07 N 37.58 E
Michninskaja 24 60.26 N 46.14 E
Michoacán 194 32.28 N 115.20 W
Michoacán □3 224 19.10 N 101.50 W
Michoacanejo 224 21.33 N 102.36 W
Michów 30 51.32 N 22.19 E
Michurinsk → Mičurinsk 70 52.54 N 40.30 E
Mickle Fell ∧ 42 54.37 N 2.18 W
Mickleham 250 51.16 N 0.19 W
Mickleover 44 52.24 N 1.34 W
Mickleton 275 39.47 N 75.14 W
Mickle Trafford 252 53.13 N 2.50 W
Mickleyville 208 39.45 N 86.16 W
Mico ≃ 226 12.11 N 84.16 W
Mico, Montañas del ⛰ 226 15.30 N 88.55 W
Mico, Punta ≻ 226 11.36 N 83.39 W
Miconge 142 4.26 S 12.51 E
Micos, Laguna de los C 226 15.45 N 87.36 W
Micoud 231f 13.50 N 60.54 W

ENGLISH Name	Page	Lat.°′	Long.°′

Micronesia II 14 11.00 N 159.00 E
Mičurin 38 42.10 N 27.51 E
Mičurinsk 70 52.54 N 40.30 E
Midai, Pulau I 102 3.00 N 107.47 E
Midale 174 49.22 N 103.27 W
Midar 138 34.58 N 3.30 W
Mid-Atlantic Ridge ⊹3 8 0.00 25.00 W
Midbar Yehuda → Wilderness of Judæa ◆2 122 31.30 N 35.18 E
Middalya 152 23.55 S 114.45 E
Middelburg, Ned. 48 51.30 N 3.37 E
Middelburg, S. Afr. 146 25.47 S 29.28 E
Middelburg, S. Afr. 148 31.30 S 25.00 E
Middelfart 41 55.30 N 9.45 E
Middelharnis 48 51.45 N 4.11 E
Middelkerke 46 51.11 N 2.49 E
Middelkerke, Vliegveld ⊠ 46 51.12 N 2.52 E
Middelpos 148 31.55 S 20.13 E
Middelstum 48 53.20 N 6.38 E
Middelvlei 263d 26.14 S 27.38 E
Middelwit 146 24.58 S 27.00 E
Middenbeemster 48 52.33 N 4.55 E
Middenin 148 27.43 S 28.02 E
Middenmeer 48 52.47 N 5.00 E
Middle ≃, B.C., Can. 172 54.50 N 125.08 W
Middle ≃, Calif., U.S. 216 38.03 N 121.31 W
Middle ≃, Iowa, U.S. 184 41.29 N 93.24 W
Middle ≃, Minn., U.S. 188 48.22 N 97.04 W
Middle ≃, Mo., U.S. 209 38.39 N 91.53 W
Middle Alkali Lake ◎ 194 41.28 N 120.04 W
Middle America Trench ⊹1 16 15.00 N 95.00 W
Middle Andaman I 100 12.30 N 92.50 E
Middle Bass 204 41.41 N 82.50 W
Middle Bass Island I 204 41.41 N 82.49 W
Middle Bay 176 51.28 N 57.30 W
Middle Bay C 266 40.37 N 73.36 W
Middleboro 197 41.49 N 70.55 W
Middle Bosque ≃ 212 31.31 N 97.16 W
Middlebourne 178 39.30 N 80.54 W
Middlebranch 204 40.54 N 81.20 W
Middle Breakwater ◆5 270 33.43 N 118.13 W
Middlebro 174 49.01 N 95.21 W
Middle Brook 176 48.45 N 54.13 W
Middle Brook ≃, N.J., U.S. 266 40.33 N 74.33 W
Middle Brook ≃, N.J., U.S. 266 40.39 N 74.41 W
Middle Brook, East Branch ≃ 266 40.35 N 74.33 W
Middle Brook, West Branch ≃ 266 40.35 N 74.33 W
Middleburg, Md., U.S. 198 39.36 N 77.16 W
Middleburg, N.Y., U.S. 200 42.36 N 74.20 W
Middleburg, Ohio, U.S. 206 40.18 N 83.35 W
Middleburg, Pa., U.S. 198 40.47 N 77.03 W
Middleburg, Va., U.S. 178 38.58 N 77.44 W
Middleburgh Heights 204 41.22 N 81.48 W
Middlebury, Conn., U.S. 197 41.32 N 73.07 W
Middlebury, Ind., U.S. 206 41.41 N 85.42 W
Middlebury, Vt., U.S. 178 44.01 N 73.10 W
Middlebush 266 40.29 N 74.32 W
Middle Cape ≻ 210 25.09 N 81.09 W
Middle Castor ≃ 202 45.16 N 75.24 W
Middle Channel ≃1, N.W. Ter., Can. 170 69.05 N 136.00 W
Middle Channel ≃1, Mich., U.S. 271 42.33 N 82.42 W
Middle Concho ≃ 186 31.27 N 100.25 W
Middle Creek ≃, U.S. 198 39.41 N 76.18 W
Middle Creek ≃, Pa., U.S. 200 41.28 N 75.11 W
Middle Creek ≃, Pa., U.S. 200 40.46 N 76.52 W
Middle Fabius ≃ 184 39.58 N 91.35 W
Middle Falls 200 43.07 N 73.32 W
Middlefield, Conn., U.S. 197 41.31 N 72.43 W
Middlefield, N.Y., U.S. 200 42.41 N 74.50 W
Middlefield, Ohio, U.S. 204 41.28 N 81.05 W
Middle Fork Reservoir ◎1 208 39.51 N 84.51 W
Middle Ground I 262c 18.55 N 72.51 E
Middle Ground ⊹2 164g 28.15 N 177.25 W
Middle Grove, Mo., U.S. 209 39.24 N 92.16 W
Middle Grove, N.Y., U.S. 200 43.05 N 73.55 W
Middle Haddam 197 41.33 N 72.33 W
Middleham 42 54.17 N 1.49 W
Middle Harbour C 264a 33.48 S 151.14 E
Middle Head ≻ 264a 33.50 S 151.16 E
Middle Hope 200 41.34 N 74.01 W
Middle Island 200 40.53 N 72.56 W
Middle Island I 152 34.07 S 123.12 E
Middle Level Main Drain ≍ 44 52.43 N 0.22 E
Middle Loup ≃ 188 41.17 N 98.23 W
Middle Maitland ≃ 202 43.53 N 81.19 W
Middlemarch 162 45.31 S 170.07 E
Middle Musquodoboit 176 45.03 N 63.09 W
Middle Oakville Creek ≃ 265b 43.32 N 79.47 W
Middle Pease ≃ 186 34.15 N 100.07 W
Middle Point 206 40.51 N 84.27 W
Middle Popo Aggie ≃ 192 42.51 N 108.42 W
Middleport, N.Y., U.S. 200 43.13 N 78.29 W
Middleport, Ohio, U.S. 178 39.00 N 82.03 W
Middleport, Pa., U.S. 198 40.44 N 76.05 W
Middle Raccoon ≃ 188 41.34 N 94.12 W
Middle Reef ⊹2 230c 17.01 N 61.52 W
Middle Reservoir ◎1 273 42.27 N 71.07 W
Middle River 198 39.19 N 76.27 W
Middle River C 198 39.19 N 76.25 W
Middle River Rouge ≃ 271 42.20 N 83.15 W
Middle Rouge Parkway ♠ 271 42.21 N 83.21 W
Middle Run ≃ 275 39.41 N 75.43 W
Middle Rush Creek ≃ 188 38.52 N 103.29 W
Middlesboro 182 36.36 N 83.43 W
Middlesbrough 42 54.35 N 1.14 W
Middlesex, Belize 222 17.02 N 88.31 W
Middlesex, N.C., U.S. 182 35.47 N 78.12 W
Middlesex, N.Y., U.S. 200 42.42 N 77.16 W
Middlesex □6, Ont., Can. 202 43.00 N 81.08 W
Middlesex □6, Conn., U.S. 197 41.33 N 72.39 W
Middlesex □6, Mass., U.S. 197 42.22 N 71.06 W
Middlesex □6, N.J., U.S. 198 40.29 N 74.27 W
Middlesex □6, Va., U.S. 198 37.40 N 76.35 W
Middlesex Fells Reservation ♠ 273 42.27 N 71.07 W
Middlesex Reservoir ◎1 266 40.37 N 74.19 W
Middle Stewiacke 176 45.13 N 63.08 W
Middle Swan 158a 31.52 S 116.00 E
Middle Thames ≃ 202 42.59 N 80.58 W
Middleton, Austl. 156 22.22 S 141.32 E
Middleton, N.S., Can. 176 44.57 N 65.04 W
Middleton, Eng., U.K. 42 53.33 N 2.13 W
Middleton, Eng., U.K. 42 53.45 N 1.32 W
Middleton, Eng., U.K. 44 52.43 N 0.28 E

DEUTSCH Name	Seite	Breite°′	Länge°′ E=Ost

Middleton, Mass., U.S. 197 42.36 N 71.01 W
Middleton, Mich., U.S. 180 43.11 N 84.43 W
Middleton, Tenn., U.S. 184 35.04 N 88.54 W
Middleton, Wis., U.S. 206 43.06 N 89.30 W
Middleton ≃ 156 22.35 S 141.51 E
Middleton in Teesdale 42 54.38 N 2.04 W
Middleton Island I 170 59.25 N 146.25 W
Middleton-on-the-Wolds 42 53.56 N 0.33 W
Middleton Pond ◎ 273 42.36 N 71.02 W
Middleton Reef I1 150 29.28 S 159.06 E
Middletown, N. Ire., U.K. 42 54.18 N 6.50 W
Middletown, Calif., U.S. 216 38.45 N 122.37 W
Middletown, Conn., U.S. 197 41.33 N 72.39 W
Middletown, Del., U.S. 198 39.25 N 75.47 W
Middletown, Ill., U.S. 209 40.11 N 89.35 W
Middletown, Ind., U.S. 208 40.03 N 85.32 W
Middletown, Ky., U.S. 208 38.15 N 85.32 W
Middletown, Md., U.S. 178 39.27 N 77.33 W
Middletown, Mo., U.S. 209 39.08 N 91.25 W
Middletown, N.J., U.S. 266 40.24 N 74.07 W
Middletown, N.Y., U.S. 200 41.27 N 74.25 W
Middletown, Ohio, U.S. 208 39.29 N 84.25 W
Middletown, Pa., U.S. 178 40.12 N 76.44 W
Middletown, Pa., U.S. 269b 40.16 N 79.37 W
Middletown, R.I., U.S. 197 41.32 N 71.17 W
Middletown, Va., U.S. 178 39.02 N 78.17 W
Middletown Park 208 40.09 N 85.26 W
Middle Tuolumne ≃ 216 37.50 N 120.01 W
Middleville, Mich., U.S. 206 42.43 N 85.28 W
Middleville, N.Y., U.S. 200 43.08 N 74.58 W
Middleville, N.Y., U.S. 266 41.54 N 73.17 W
Middlewich 44 53.11 N 2.27 W
Middle Yegua Creek ≃ 212 30.19 N 96.47 W
Middle Yuba ≃ 216 39.22 N 121.12 W
Midelt 138 32.41 N 4.43 W
Midfield 212 28.56 N 96.13 W
Midge Hall 252 53.42 N 2.45 W
Midgic 176 45.59 N 64.18 W
Mid Glamorgan □6 44 51.40 N 3.30 W
Midgley 252 53.44 N 1.58 W
Midhurst, Ont., Can. 202 44.27 N 79.44 W
Midhurst, Eng., U.K. 44 50.59 N 0.45 W
Midi, Aiguille du ∧ 56 45.52 N 6.53 E
Midi, Canal du ≍ 32 43.26 N 1.58 E
Midi de Bigorre, Pic du ∧ 32 42.56 N 0.08 E
Mid Illovo 148 29.59 S 30.25 E
Mid-Indian Basin ⊹1 12 10.00 S 80.00 E
Mid-Indian Ridge ⊹3 6 20.00 S 67.00 E
Mid-Island Plaza ◆9 266 40.46 N 73.32 W
Midland, Austl. 158a 31.53 S 116.00 E
Midland, Ont., Can. 202 44.45 N 79.53 W
Midland, Calif., U.S. 194 33.52 N 114.48 W
Midland, Mich., U.S. 180 43.37 N 84.14 W
Midland, N.C., U.S. 182 35.14 N 80.30 W
Midland, Ohio, U.S. 208 39.18 N 83.55 W
Midland, Pa., U.S. 204 40.38 N 80.27 W
Midland, Pa., U.S. 204 40.15 N 80.13 W
Midland, S. Dak., U.S. 188 44.04 N 101.10 W
Midland, Tex., U.S. 186 32.00 N 102.05 W
Midland, Wash., U.S. 214 47.10 N 122.24 W
Midland Bay C 202 44.47 N 79.52 W
Midland Beach ◆8 266 40.34 N 74.05 W
Midland City 209 40.09 N 89.08 W
Midland Park, Mich., U.S. 206 42.23 N 85.22 W
Midland Park, N.J., U.S. 266 41.00 N 74.09 W
Midland Park Lake ◎ 202 44.44 N 79.53 W
Midlands □4 144 19.00 S 29.45 E
Midleton 28 51.55 N 8.10 W
Midlothian, Ill., U.S. 206 41.38 N 87.42 W
Midlothian, Tex., U.S. 212 32.29 N 97.00 W
Midlothian Creek ≃ 268 41.39 N 87.40 W
Midlum 48 53.43 N 8.37 E
Midnapore, Bhārat 116 22.26 N 87.20 E
Midnapore, Alta., Can. 172 50.55 N 114.05 W
Midnapore □5 116 22.25 N 87.20 E
Midnapore Canal ≍ 116 22.25 N 87.53 E
Midnapore Plain ≚ 116 22.00 N 87.45 E
Mid-Ohio Race Course ♠ 204 40.40 N 82.38 W
Midongy Nord 147b 20.45 S 46.13 E
Midongy Sud 147b 23.35 S 47.01 E
Midori 86 34.43 N 132.37 E
Midou ≃ 32 43.54 N 0.30 W
Midpines 216 37.33 N 119.56 W
Midsayap 106 7.12 N 124.32 E
Midshipman Point ≻ 272 38.07 N 122.27 W
Midsland 48 53.22 N 5.16 E
Midsomer Norton 44 51.18 N 2.28 W
Miduzhen 92 25.22 N 100.31 E
Midvale, Del., U.S. 275 39.39 N 75.37 W
Midvale, Idaho, U.S. 192 44.28 N 116.44 W
Midvale, Ohio, U.S. 204 40.26 N 81.23 W
Midville 182 32.49 N 88.14 W
Midway, S. Afr. 263d 26.18 S 27.51 E
Midway, Ala., U.S. 184 32.05 N 85.31 W
Midway, Ind., U.S. 206 41.37 N 85.55 W
Midway, Ky., U.S. 208 38.09 N 84.41 W
Midway, Pa., U.S. 269b 40.16 N 79.34 W
Midway, Tex., U.S. 212 31.02 N 95.45 W
Midway, Utah, U.S. 190 40.31 N 111.28 W
Midway City 270 33.45 N 118.00 W
Midway Island □2 6 / 164g 28.13 N 177.22 W
Midway Mall ◆9 269a 41.24 N 82.07 W
Midway Naval Station ■ 164g 28.13 N 177.26 W
Midway Park 182 34.43 N 77.21 W
Midwest 190 43.25 N 106.16 W
Midwest City 186 35.27 N 97.24 W
Mid-Western □3 140 6.00 N 6.00 E
Midwolda 48 53.12 N 7.00 E
Midyat 120 37.25 N 41.23 E
Midžor (Midżur) ∧ 38 43.23 N 22.42 E
Mie 86 32.58 N 131.35 E
Mie □5 82 34.30 N 136.30 E
Miechów 30 50.23 N 20.01 E
Miedwie, Jezioro ◎ 50 53.17 N 14.52 E
Międzybórz 30 51.24 N 17.40 E
Międzychód 30 52.36 N 15.55 E
Międzylesie 30 50.10 N 16.40 E
Międzyrzec Podlaski 30 52.00 N 22.47 E
Międzyrzecz 30 52.28 N 15.35 E
Międzyzdroje 30 53.55 N 14.28 E
Miehuapu 95 39.11 N 117.44 E
Miejska Górka 30 51.40 N 16.58 E
Miélan 32 43.26 N 0.19 E
Mielec 30 50.18 N 21.25 E
Mielno 30 54.16 N 16.01 E
Mien ◎ 26 56.25 N 14.51 E
Mienga 142 17.17 S 19.48 E
Mienhua Hsü I 90 25.29 N 122.06 E
Mient'ienhuo Shan ∧ 259d 25.11 N 121.30 E
Miercurea-Ciuc 38 46.22 N 25.48 E
Mieres 34 43.15 N 5.46 W
Mierlo 48 51.27 N 5.37 E
Mieroszów 30 50.41 N 16.10 E
Miersdorf 254a 52.20 N 13.37 E

Symbols in the index entries represent the broad categories identified in the key at the right. Symbols with superior numbers (⛰2) identify subcategories (see complete key on page *I · 26*).

Kartensymbole in dem Registerverzeichnis stellen die rechts in Schlüssel erklärten Kategorien dar. Symbole mit hochgestellten Ziffern (⛰2) bezeichnen Unterabteilungen einer Kategorie (vgl. vollständiger Schlüssel auf Seite *I · 26*).

Los símbolos incluídos en el texto del índice representan las grandes categorias identificadas con la clave a la derecha. Los símbolos con numeros en su parte superior (⛰2) identifican las subcategorias (véase la clave completa en la página *I · 26*).

Les symboles de l'index représentent les catégories indiquées dans la légende à droite. Les symboles suivis d'un indice (⛰2) représentent des sous-catégories (voir légende complète à la page *I · 26*).

Os símbolos incluídos no texto do índice representam as grandes categorias identificadas com a chave à direita. Os símbolos com números em sua parte superior (⛰2) identificam as subcategorias (veja-se a chave completa à página *I · 26*).

∧ Mountain	Berg	Montaña	Montagne	Montanha
⛰ Mountains	Berge	Montañas	Montagnes	Montanhas
)(Pass	Pass	Paso	Col	Passo
∨ Valley, Canyon	Tal, Cañon	Valle, Cañón	Vallée, Canyon	Vale, Canhão
≚ Plain	Ebene	Llano	Plaine	Planície
≻ Cape	Kap	Cabo	Cap	Cabo
I Island	Insel	Isla	Île	Ilha
II Islands	Inseln	Islas	Îles	Ilhas
⊹ Other Topographic Features	Andere Topographische Objekte	Otros Elementos Topográficos	Autres données topographiques	Outros Elementos Topográficos

ESPAÑOL

Nombre	Página	Lat.°′	Long.°′ W=Oeste
Miersig	38	46.53 N	21.51 E
Mier y Noriega	224	23.25 N	100.07 W
Miesaituo	110	35.52 N	94.20 E
Miesau	52	49.24 N	7.26 E
Miesbach	58	47.47 N	11.50 E
Mieso	134	9.15 N	40.48 E
Mieste	50	52.28 N	11.11 E
Miesterhorst	50	52.27 N	11.09 E
Mieszkowice	30	52.46 N	14.30 E
Mifflin, Ohio, U.S.	204	40.47 N	82.22 W
Mifflin, Pa., U.S.	198	40.34 N	77.24 W
Mifflin □[6]	200	40.40 N	77.33 W
Mifflinburg	200	40.55 N	77.03 W
Mifflintown	198	40.34 N	77.24 W
Mifflinville	200	41.03 N	76.19 W
Miftāḥ, Wādī ∨	132	30.15 N	31.46 E
Migdal	122	32.50 N	35.30 E
Migdal Ha'Emeq	122	32.41 N	35.15 E
Migdol	148	26.54 S	25.27 E
Migennes	46	47.58 N	3.31 E
Mīghān	118	31.49 N	59.28 E
Migırtepe ∧	120	36.50 N	36.22 E
Migiurtinia □[4]	134	10.00 N	50.00 E
Migliarino	60	44.46 N	11.56 E
Migliaro	58	44.48 N	11.58 E
Mignano Monte Lungo	60	41.23 N	13.58 E
Mignone ≃	60	42.11 N	11.44 E
Mignoviči	66	54.16 N	31.34 E
Mignovillard	54	46.48 N	6.08 E
Migori ≃	144	0.59 S	34.15 E
Miguel Alemán, Presa ⊜[1]	224	18.13 N	96.32 W
Miguel Alves	240	4.10 S	42.54 W
Miguel Auza	222	24.18 N	103.25 W
Miguel Calmon	240	11.26 S	40.36 W
Miguel Couto	277a	22.43 S	43.27 W
Miguel de la Borda	226	9.09 N	80.19 W
Migueles, Arroyo de los ≃	256a	40.20 N	3.32 W
Miguelete	248	34.01 S	57.39 W
Miguelete, Arroyo ≃	248	34.14 S	57.54 W
Miguelópolis	245	20.12 S	48.03 W
Miguel Pereira	246	22.27 S	43.22 W
Miguel Riglos	242	36.51 S	63.42 W
Migulinskaja	70	49.42 N	41.16 E
Migyaunglaung	100	14.40 N	98.09 E
Mihăeşti	38	45.07 N	25.00 E
Mihai Viteazu	38	44.39 N	28.41 E
Mihajlovgrad	38	43.25 N	23.13 E
Mihalıççık	120	39.52 N	31.30 E
Mihama, Nihon	84	34.46 N	136.54 E
Mihama, Nihon	84	35.36 N	135.56 E
Mihama, Nihon	86	33.54 N	135.08 E
Mihara, Nihon	86	34.24 N	133.05 E
Mihara, Nihon	86	34.17 N	134.46 E
Mihara, Nihon	86	34.32 N	135.34 E
Mihara-yama ∧	84	34.43 N	139.23 E
Mihe ≃	88	37.12 N	119.10 E
Mihla	50	51.04 N	10.20 E
Mihmandar	120	36.52 N	35.18 E
Miho	84	36.00 N	140.18 E
Mihonoseki	86	35.34 N	133.19 E
Miho-wan C	86	35.30 N	133.23 E
Mihuangzhuang	95	39.07 N	116.12 E
Mijaly	76	48.57 N	53.42 E
Mijares ≃	34	39.55 N	0.01 W
Mijdaḥah	134	14.00 N	48.26 E
Mijdrecht	48	52.13 N	4.52 E
Mijiang	88	43.01 N	130.08 E
Mijoux	54	46.22 N	6.00 E
Mikabo-yama ∧	84	36.09 N	138.55 E
Mikame	86	33.25 N	132.27 E
Mikamo	86	35.09 N	133.37 E
Mikasa	82a	43.20 N	141.40 E
Mikaševiči	68	52.13 N	27.28 E
Mikata	84	35.33 N	135.55 E
Mikata-ko ⊜	84	35.34 N	135.53 E
Mikatou	263b	4.16 S	15.08 E
Mikawa, Nihon	84	36.29 N	136.29 E
Mikawa, Nihon	86	33.37 N	132.58 E
Mikawa-wan-kokutei-kōen ♠	84	34.42 N	137.10 E
Mikazuki	86	34.58 N	134.27 E
Mikese	144	6.46 S	37.54 E
Mikhaylov, Cape ≻	9	66.51 S	118.33 E
Miki, Nihon	86	34.48 N	134.59 E
Miki, Nihon	86	34.17 N	134.05 E
Mikínai ⊥	38	37.44 N	22.45 E
Mikindani	144	10.17 S	40.07 E
Mikinduri	144	0.07 N	37.50 E
Mikkabi	84	34.48 N	137.33 E
Mikkaichi	260	34.26 N	135.35 E
Mikkeli	26	61.41 N	27.15 E
Mikkelin lääni □[4]	26	62.00 N	27.30 E
Mikkwa ≃	166	58.25 N	114.45 W
Mikołajki	30	53.49 N	21.36 E
Mikołów	30	50.11 N	18.55 E
Mikomeseng	142	2.08 N	10.37 E
Mikomoto-jima I	84	34.34 N	138.56 E
Mikongo, Monts ∧∧	142	0.15 N	10.55 E
Mikonos	38	37.26 N	25.20 E
Mikonos I	38	37.29 N	25.25 E
Mikope	142	5.03 S	20.48 E
Mikre	38	43.02 N	24.31 E
Mikri Préspa, Límni ⊜	38	40.46 N	21.04 E
Miksimil	116	22.52 N	89.23 E
Mikšino	66	57.15 N	35.43 E
Mikstat	30	51.32 N	17.59 E
Mikulášovice	50	50.58 N	14.20 E
Mikulino	66	55.02 N	31.07 E
Mikulkin, Mys ≻	24	67.48 N	46.40 E
Mikulov	30	48.49 N	16.39 E
Mikumi	144	7.24 S	36.59 E
Mikumi National Park ♠	144	7.12 S	37.05 E
Mikun'	24	62.21 N	50.06 E
Mikuni	84	36.13 N	136.09 E
Mikuni-sammyaku ∧∧	84	36.50 N	138.40 E
Mikuni-tōge)(	84	36.46 N	138.50 E
Mikuni-yama ∧	84	35.59 N	138.43 E
Mikura-jima I	82	33.52 N	139.36 E
Mila	34	36.27 N	6.16 E
Milaca	180	45.45 N	93.39 W
Miladummadulu Atoll I[1]	112	6.15 N	73.15 E
Milagre	246	21.18 S	47.00 W
Milagres	240	7.17 S	38.57 W
Milagro, Arg.	242	31.01 S	65.59 W
Milagro, Ec.	236	2.07 S	79.36 W
Milagros	106	12.13 N	123.30 E
Milam □[6]	212	30.47 N	96.57 W
Milan → Milano, It.	56	45.28 N	9.12 E
Milan, Ga., U.S.	182	32.01 N	83.04 W
Milan, Ind., U.S.	208	39.07 N	85.08 W
Milan, Mich., U.S.	206	42.05 N	83.40 W
Milan, Minn., U.S.	188	45.07 N	95.55 W
Milan, Mo., U.S.	184	40.12 N	93.07 W
Milan, N. Mex., U.S.	190	35.09 N	107.54 W
Milan, Ohio, U.S.	204	41.18 N	82.36 W
Milan, Pa., U.S.	200	41.54 N	76.32 W
Milan, Tenn., U.S.	184	35.55 N	88.46 W
Milando	142	8.45 S	17.36 E
Milan Federal Correctional Institution ʋ	271	42.06 N	83.40 W
Milang	158b	35.25 S	138.58 E
Milano (Milan)	56		
	256b	45.28 N	9.12 E
Milano, Tex., U.S.	212	30.43 N	96.52 W
Milano □[4]	56	45.30 N	9.30 E
Milanoa	147b	13.35 S	49.47 E
Milano Marittima	60	44.16 N	12.21 E
Milanville	200	41.40 N	75.04 W
Milâs	120	37.19 N	27.47 E
Milaševiči	68	51.39 N	27.56 E
Mil'atino, S.S.S.R.	66	54.29 N	34.18 E
Mil'atino, S.S.S.R.	72	55.41 N	35.48 E
Milazzo	36	38.14 N	15.15 E

FRANÇAIS

Nom	Page	Lat.°′	Long.°′ W=Ouest
Milbank	188	45.13 N	96.38 W
Milbanke Sound Ц	172	52.18 N	128.33 W
Milborne Port	44	50.58 N	2.27 W
Milbridge	178	44.32 N	67.53 W
Milbuk	106	6.10 N	124.16 E
Milburn	186	34.14 N	96.33 W
Milburn Creek ≃	266	40.38 N	73.36 W
Milden	174	51.30 N	107.31 W
Mildenau	50	50.35 N	13.04 E
Mildenhall	44	52.21 N	0.30 E
Milders	58	47.06 N	11.16 E
Mildmay	202	44.03 N	81.07 W
Mildred, Ill., U.S.	209	39.46 N	89.38 W
Mildred, Pa., U.S.	200	41.29 N	76.23 W
Mildura	156	34.12 S	142.09 E
Mile	92	24.26 N	103.26 E
Miléai	38	39.20 N	23.09 E
Milepa	144	11.43 S	36.20 E
Mile Run ≃	266	40.31 N	74.28 W
Miles, Austl.	156	26.40 S	150.11 E
Miles, Tex., U.S.	186	31.36 N	100.11 W
Miles ≃	273	42.40 N	70.51 W
Milesburg	204	40.56 N	77.47 W
Miles City	192	46.25 N	105.51 W
Miles Creek C	198	38.46 N	76.12 W
Miles Creek ≃	216	37.12 N	120.21 W
Mile Seven Hundred Thirty Three	170	60.03 N	131.07 W
Milešovka ∧	50	50.33 N	13.56 E
Milestone	174	50.00 N	104.30 W
Milesville	269b	40.12 N	79.52 W
Miletto, Monte ∧	60	41.27 N	14.22 E
Miletus ⊥	120	37.28 N	27.15 E
Mileura	152	26.23 S	117.20 E
Milevsko	30	49.27 N	14.22 E
Milford, Eng., U.K.	44	51.11 N	1.38 W
Milford, Conn., U.S.	197	41.13 N	73.04 W
Milford, Del., U.S.	198	38.55 N	75.25 W
Milford, Ill., U.S.	206	40.38 N	87.42 W
Milford, Ind., U.S.	206	41.25 N	85.51 W
Milford, Iowa, U.S.	188	43.20 N	95.09 W
Milford, Ky., U.S.	208	38.35 N	84.10 W
Milford, Maine, U.S.	178	44.57 N	68.39 W
Milford, Md., U.S.	274b	39.21 N	76.44 W
Milford, Mass., U.S.	197	42.08 N	71.32 W
Milford, Mich., U.S.	206	42.35 N	83.36 W
Milford, N.H., U.S.	178	42.50 N	71.39 W
Milford, N.J., U.S.	200	40.34 N	75.06 W
Milford, N.Y., U.S.	200	42.35 N	74.57 W
Milford, Ohio, U.S.	208	39.11 N	84.18 W
Milford, Pa., U.S.	200	41.19 N	74.48 W
Milford, Tex., U.S.	212	32.07 N	96.57 W
Milford, Utah, U.S.	190	38.24 N	113.01 W
Milford, Va., U.S.	198	38.01 N	77.22 W
Milford Brook ≃	266	40.19 N	74.17 W
Milford Center	208	40.11 N	83.26 W
Milford Cross Roads	275	39.43 N	75.44 W
Milford Dam ◆[6]	188	39.02 N	96.54 W
Milford Haven	44	51.40 N	5.02 W
Milford Haven C	44	51.42 N	5.03 W
Milford Lake ⊜[1]	188	39.15 N	97.00 W
Milford-on-Sea	44	50.44 N	1.36 W
Milford Sound	162	44.40 S	167.54 E
Milford Sound Ц	162	44.35 S	167.47 E
Milford Station	176	45.03 N	63.26 W
Milgis ≃	144	1.48 N	38.06 E
Milgoo ∧	152	28.51 S	118.07 E
Mil'guvejem ≃	170	68.22 N	171.30 E
Milḥ, Baḥr al- ⊜	118	32.40 N	43.35 E
Milḥ, Ra's al- ≻	136	32.19 N	23.08 E
Milḥat Ashqar ⊜	118	35.18 N	41.55 E
Milhaud	56	43.47 N	4.18 E
Mili I[1]	14	6.08 N	171.55 E
Miliana	138	36.15 N	2.15 E
Miliane, Oued ≃	36	36.46 N	10.18 E
Milibangalala, Ponta ≻	148	26.26 S	32.56 E
Milicz	30	51.32 N	17.17 E
Milieu, Rivière du ≃	196	46.47 N	73.56 W
Milīj	132	30.36 N	31.03 E
Miling	152	30.30 S	116.21 E
Militsch → Milicz	30	51.32 N	17.17 E
Milk ≃	192	48.05 N	106.15 W
Milk Creek ≃, Colo., U.S.	190	40.24 N	107.45 W
Milk Creek ≃, Oreg., U.S.	214	45.15 N	122.41 W
Milk Hill ∧[2]	44	51.23 N	1.51 W
Mil'kovo	64	54.43 N	158.37 E
Milk River	172	49.09 N	112.05 W
Milk River Ridge ∧	172	49.15 N	112.30 W
Milk River Ridge Reservoir ⊜[1]	172	49.15 N	112.17 W
Mill	48	51.41 N	5.47 E
Mill ≃, Conn., U.S.	266	41.08 N	73.16 W
Mill ≃, Mass., U.S.	197	42.18 N	72.37 W
Mill ≃, Mass., U.S.	273	42.38 N	70.41 W
Mill ≃, Mass., U.S.	273	42.44 N	70.52 W
Mill ≃, Mass., U.S.	273	42.08 N	71.21 W
Mill ≃, Mass., U.S.	273	42.12 N	70.57 W
Mill ≃, N.Y., U.S.	266	40.38 N	73.39 W
Millard	188	41.13 N	96.07 W
Millau	32	44.06 N	3.05 E
Mill Bay	214	48.39 N	123.34 W
Millboro	182	37.59 N	79.36 W
Millbourne	275	39.58 N	75.15 W
Millbrae	216	37.36 N	122.24 W
Millbrook, Ont., Can.	202	44.09 N	78.27 W
Millbrook, Eng., U.K.	44	50.20 N	4.13 W
Millbrook, Mass., U.S.	273	42.03 N	70.41 W
Millbrook, N.J., U.S.	266	40.52 N	74.33 W
Millbrook, N.Y., U.S.	200	41.47 N	73.42 W
Mill Brook ≃, Mass., U.S.	273	42.31 N	71.18 W
Mill Brook ≃, N.J., U.S.	266	40.53 N	74.32 W
Mill Brook ≃, N.J., U.S.	266	40.29 N	74.23 W
Mill Brook ≃, N.J., U.S.	266	40.25 N	74.06 W
Millburn	266	40.44 N	74.20 W
Millbury, Mass., U.S.	197	42.11 N	71.46 W
Millbury, Ohio, U.S.	204	41.34 N	83.25 W
Mill City	192	44.45 N	122.29 W
Mill Creek, Pa., U.S.	204	40.26 N	77.56 W
Millcreek, Utah, U.S.	190	40.43 N	111.51 W
Mill Creek, W. Va., U.S.	178	38.44 N	79.58 W
Mill Creek ≃, U.S.	206	42.23 N	87.54 W
Mill Creek ≃, Calif., U.S.	216	36.49 N	119.21 W
Mill Creek ≃, Calif., U.S.	218	34.05 N	117.06 W
Mill Creek ≃, Del., U.S.	275	39.42 N	75.39 W
Mill Creek ≃, Ill., U.S.	209	39.50 N	91.24 W
Mill Creek ≃, Ind., U.S.	184	39.30 N	86.57 W
Mill Creek ≃, Ind., U.S.	206	41.01 N	86.36 W
Mill Creek ≃, Iowa, U.S.	188	42.47 N	95.31 W
Mill Creek ≃, Kans., U.S.	188	39.55 N	96.56 W
Mill Creek ≃, Ky., U.S.	208	38.28 N	84.20 W
Mill Creek ≃, N.J., U.S.	266	40.48 N	74.03 W
Mill Creek ≃, N.J., U.S.	275	40.02 N	74.55 W
Mill Creek ≃, N.Y., U.S.	202	43.57 N	76.08 W
Mill Creek ≃, N.Y., U.S.	266	40.31 N	74.14 W
Mill Creek ≃, Ohio, U.S.	204	41.06 N	80.40 W
Mill Creek ≃, Ohio, U.S.	204	40.14 N	83.09 W
Mill Creek ≃, Ohio, U.S.	208	39.06 N	84.32 W

PORTUGUÊS

Nome	Página	Lat.°′	Long.°′ W=Oeste
Mill Creek ≃, Ohio, U.S.	269a	41.25 N	81.38 W
Mill Creek ≃, Pa., U.S.	200	41.53 N	77.08 W
Mill Creek ≃, Pa., U.S.	204	41.09 N	79.03 W
Mill Creek ≃, Pa., U.S.	275	40.08 N	74.52 W
Mill Creek ≃, Pa., U.S.	275	40.03 N	75.16 W
Mill Creek ≃, Tex., U.S.	212	32.46 N	95.46 W
Mill Creek ≃, Tex., U.S.	212	29.50 N	96.07 W
Mill Creek ≃, Tex., U.S.	212	30.08 N	95.37 W
Mill Creek ≃, Va., U.S.	198	38.09 N	77.10 W
Mill Creek, East Fork ≃	212	29.55 N	96.17 W
Mill Creek, North Fork ≃	214	45.33 N	121.18 W
Mill Creek, South Fork ≃	214	45.36 N	121.12 W
Mill Creek, West Fork ≃	212	29.55 N	96.17 W
Millcreek Township	204	42.05 N	80.10 W
Milldale	197	41.34 N	72.53 W
Milledgeville, Ga., U.S.	182	33.04 N	83.14 W
Milledgeville, Ill., U.S.	180	41.58 N	89.46 W
Milledgeville, Ohio, U.S.	208	39.36 N	83.35 W
Mille Îles, Rivière des ≃	196	45.42 N	73.32 W
Mille Lacs, Lac des ⊜	180	48.50 N	90.30 W
Mille Lacs Kathio State Park ♠	180	46.08 N	93.43 W
Mille Lacs Lake ⊜	180	46.15 N	93.40 W
Millemont	251	48.49 N	1.45 E
Millen	182	32.48 N	81.57 W
Millendon	158a	31.48 S	116.02 E
Miller, Mo., U.S.	184	37.13 N	93.50 W
Miller, S. Dak., U.S.	188	44.31 N	98.59 W
Miller □[6]	209	38.15 N	92.15 W
Miller, Mount ∧	170	60.25 N	142.23 W
Miller City	206	41.06 N	84.08 W
Miller Creek ≃, Ont., Can.	274a	42.57 N	78.58 W
Miller Creek ≃, Calif., U.S.	272	38.02 N	122.30 W
Miller House	170	65.32 N	145.11 W
Miller Mountain ∧	194	38.03 N	118.12 W
Millerovo, S.S.S.R.	68	48.55 N	40.25 E
Millerovo, S.S.S.R.	73	47.49 N	39.15 E
Miller Peak ∧	190	31.23 N	110.17 W
Miller Place	200	40.58 N	73.00 W
Millers ≃	197	42.35 N	72.30 W
Millersburg, Ind., U.S.	206	41.32 N	85.42 W
Millersburg, Ind., U.S.	208	38.34 N	86.20 W
Millersburg, Ky., U.S.	208	38.18 N	84.10 W
Millersburg, Mich., U.S.	180	45.20 N	84.04 W
Millersburg, Ohio, U.S.	204	40.33 N	81.55 W
Millersburg, Pa., U.S.	198	40.33 N	76.58 W
Millers Creek ≃	186	33.27 N	99.14 W
Miller Seamount ⊹[3]	16	53.30 N	144.20 W
Millers Falls	197	42.35 N	72.30 W
Millers Ferry	184	32.06 N	87.22 W
Millers Flat	162	45.40 S	169.25 E
Millers Island	274b	39.14 N	76.24 W
Millers Pond ⊜	266	40.51 N	73.12 W
Millersport	178	39.54 N	82.32 W
Millers Run ≃	269b	40.22 N	80.07 W
Millerstown	200	40.33 N	77.09 W
Millersville, Ohio, U.S.	204	41.19 N	83.17 W
Millersville, Pa., U.S.	198	40.00 N	76.22 W
Millerton, N.Y., U.S.	200	41.57 N	73.31 W
Millerton, Pa., U.S.	200	41.59 N	76.56 W
Millerton Lake ⊜[1]	216	37.01 N	119.41 W
Millerton Lake State Recreation Area ♠	216	37.02 N	119.37 W
Millertown	176	48.49 N	56.33 W
Millertown Junction	176	49.01 N	56.21 W
Millesimo	56	44.22 N	8.12 E
Milles Sound Ц	230b	25.00 N	77.26 W
Millet	172	53.06 N	113.28 W
Millett, Mich., U.S.	206	42.42 N	84.38 W
Millett, Tex., U.S.	186	28.35 N	99.12 W
Milleur Point ≻	28	55.01 N	5.06 W
Millevaches, Plateau de ∧∧[1]	32	45.30 N	2.10 E
Mill Green	250	51.41 N	0.22 E
Mill Grove	206	40.25 N	85.17 W
Mill Hall	200	41.06 N	77.29 W
Mill Hill ◆[8]	250	51.37 N	0.13 W
Mill Hill ∧[2]	252	53.25 N	1.54 W
Millhousen	208	39.13 N	85.26 W
Millican	212	30.28 N	96.12 W
Millicent	156	37.36 S	140.22 E
Milligan, Fla., U.S.	184	30.45 N	86.38 W
Milligan, Nebr., U.S.	188	40.30 N	97.23 W
Milligantown	269b	40.33 N	79.41 W
Milliken	265b	43.49 N	79.18 W
Millingen aan de Rijn	48	51.52 N	6.02 E
Millington, Ill., U.S.	206	41.34 N	88.36 W
Millington, Md., U.S.	198	39.16 N	75.50 W
Millington, Mich., U.S.	180	43.17 N	83.32 W
Millington, N.J., U.S.	200	40.40 N	74.31 W
Millington, Tenn., U.S.	184	35.21 N	89.54 W
Millinocket	178	45.39 N	68.43 W
Millionnyj	79	54.30 N	126.19 E
Millis	197	42.10 N	71.22 W
Mill Island I, Ant.	9	65.30 S	100.40 E
Mill Island I, N.W. Ter., Can.	166	64.00 N	78.00 W
Mill Lake ⊜	202	45.22 N	80.00 W
Millmerran	156	27.52 S	151.16 E
Millmont	200	40.53 N	77.08 W
Mill Neck	266	40.52 N	73.34 W
Mill Neck ≻[1]	266	40.53 N	73.33 W
Mill Neck Creek C	266	40.54 N	73.33 W
Millom	42	54.13 N	3.18 W
Mill Pond ⊜	266	40.53 N	73.22 W
Millport, Scot., U.K.	28	55.46 N	4.55 W
Millport, Ala., U.S.	184	33.34 N	88.05 W
Millport, N.Y., U.S.	200	42.16 N	76.50 W
Millport, Pa., U.S.	204	41.55 N	78.07 W
Millrift	200	41.25 N	74.45 W
Mill River	197	42.07 N	73.16 W
Millry	184	31.33 N	88.19 W
Mills, Pa., U.S.	204	41.57 N	77.41 W
Mills, Wyo., U.S.	192	42.50 N	106.22 W
Mills, Lake ⊜[1]	214	47.59 N	123.36 W
Millsboro	198	38.36 N	75.17 W
Mills Creek ≃, Austl.	156	22.23 S	143.05 E
Mills Creek ≃, Calif., U.S.	272	37.27 N	122.25 W
Mills Lake ⊜	166	61.30 N	118.10 W
Mills/Norrie State Park ♠	200	41.52 N	73.57 W
Millstadt	209	38.28 N	90.06 W
Millstatt	58	46.48 N	13.35 E
Millstätter See ⊜	58	46.47 N	13.35 E
Millstone	266	40.30 N	74.35 W
Millstone ≃	266	40.33 N	74.34 W
Millstream, Austl.	152	21.35 S	117.04 E
Millstream, B.C., Can.	214	48.30 N	123.31 W
Milltown, Ind., U.S.	208	38.21 N	86.17 W
Milltown, Mont., U.S.	192	46.53 N	113.52 W
Milltown, N.J., U.S.	198	40.27 N	74.27 W
Milltown, Wis., U.S.	180	45.32 N	92.30 W
Milltown Malbay	28	52.52 N	9.23 W
Millvale	269b	40.29 N	79.58 W
Mill Valley	216	37.54 N	122.32 W
Mill Village	204	41.53 N	79.58 W
Millville, Mass., U.S.	197	42.02 N	71.35 W
Millville, N.J., U.S.	198	39.24 N	75.02 W
Millville, Ohio, U.S.	208	39.24 N	84.40 W
Millville, Pa., U.S.	200	41.07 N	76.32 W
Millville Lake	273	42.48 N	71.13 W
Millville Lake ⊜	273	42.48 N	71.13 W
Millwood, N.Y., U.S.	200	41.11 N	73.48 W
Millwood, Va., U.S.	178	39.04 N	78.02 W
Millwood Lake ⊜[1]	184	33.45 N	94.00 W
Milly-la-Forêt	46	48.24 N	2.28 E
Milly-Lamartine	54	46.21 N	4.42 E
Milmay	198	39.26 N	74.52 W
Milmersdorf	50	53.06 N	13.38 E
Milmine	209	39.54 N	88.39 W
Milmont Park	275	39.53 N	75.20 W
Milne Bay □[5]	154	10.00 S	152.30 E
Milne Bay C	154	10.22 S	150.30 E
Milner	214	49.20 N	122.42 W
Milnesville	200	40.59 N	75.59 W
Milngavie	42	55.57 N	4.20 W
Milnor	188	46.16 N	97.27 W
Milnrow	42	53.37 N	2.06 W
Milnthorpe	42	54.14 N	2.46 W
Milo, Alta., Can.	172	50.34 N	112.53 W
Milo, Iowa, U.S.	180	41.17 N	93.27 W
Milo, Maine, U.S.	178	45.15 N	68.59 W
Milo ≃	140	11.04 N	9.14 W
Milon-la-Chapelle	251	48.44 N	2.03 E
Mílos	38	36.45 N	24.27 E
Mílos I	38	36.41 N	24.15 E
Miloslaviči	66	53.41 N	32.15 E
Miloslavskoje	66	53.34 N	39.24 E
Miłosław	30	52.13 N	17.29 E
Milow, D.D.R.	50	52.31 N	12.18 E
Milow, D.D.R.	50	53.11 N	11.32 E
Milpa Alta	276a	19.11 N	99.01 W
Milpa Alta □[7]	276a	19.11 N	99.02 W
Milparinka	156	29.44 S	141.53 E
Milpitas	216	37.26 N	121.54 W
Milpitas Wash ∨	194	33.18 N	114.44 W
Milroy, Ind., U.S.	208	39.30 N	85.28 W
Milroy, Pa., U.S.	198	40.43 N	77.35 W
Milseburg ∧	52	50.32 N	9.53 E
Mil'skaja Step' ☷	74	40.00 N	48.00 E
Milspe	253	51.18 N	7.21 E
Miltenberg	52	49.42 N	9.15 E
Miltitz	50	51.19 N	12.16 E
Milton, Austl.	160	35.19 S	150.26 E
Milton, Ont., Can.	202	43.31 N	79.53 W
Milton, N.Z.	162	46.07 S	169.58 E
Milton, Del., U.S.	198	38.47 N	75.19 W
Milton, Fla., U.S.	184	30.38 N	87.03 W
Milton, Ill., U.S.	209	39.34 N	90.39 W
Milton, Ind., U.S.	208	39.47 N	85.09 W
Milton, Ind., U.S.	208	38.58 N	85.01 W
Milton, Iowa, U.S.	180	40.41 N	92.10 W
Milton, Ky., U.S.	208	38.43 N	85.22 W
Milton, Mass., U.S.	197	42.15 N	71.05 W
Milton, N.J., U.S.	266	41.02 N	74.32 W
Milton, N. Dak., U.S.	188	48.38 N	98.03 W
Milton, N.Y., U.S.	200	41.39 N	73.57 W
Milton, Pa., U.S.	200	41.01 N	76.51 W
Milton, Vt., U.S.	178	44.38 N	73.07 W
Milton, Wash., U.S.	214	47.15 N	122.19 W
Milton, W. Va., U.S.	178	38.26 N	82.08 W
Milton, Wis., U.S.	206	42.47 N	88.56 W
Milton, Lake ⊜	204	41.06 N	80.58 W
Milton Abbot	44	50.35 N	4.15 W
Milton-freewater	192	45.56 N	118.23 W
Milton Harbor C	266	40.57 N	73.42 W
Milton Point ≻	266	40.57 N	73.42 W
Miltonvale	188	39.21 N	97.27 W
Miltou	136	10.14 N	17.26 E
Miltzow	50	54.12 N	13.13 E
Milumba	144	7.06 S	31.04 E
Miluo	90	28.50 N	113.04 E
Mil'utinskaja	70	48.38 N	41.40 E
Mil'utke, Gora ∧	170	65.42 N	178.03 W
Milverton, Ont., Can.	202	43.34 N	80.55 W
Milverton, Eng., U.K.	44	51.02 N	3.16 W
Milwaukee	206	43.02 N	87.55 W
Milwaukee □[6]	206	43.02 N	87.58 W
Milwaukee ≃	180	43.02 N	87.54 W
Milwaukee Bay C	206	43.02 N	87.53 W
Milwaukie	214	45.27 N	122.38 W
Mim	140	6.54 N	2.34 W
Mima	86	33.17 N	132.36 E
Mimasaka	86	35.00 N	134.10 E
Mimbres ≃	190	32.13 N	107.28 W
Mimbres Mountains ∧∧	190	32.45 N	107.45 W
Mimi ≃	82	32.20 N	131.37 E
Mimico Creek ≃	265b	43.37 N	79.29 W
Mimizan	32	44.12 N	1.14 W
Mimmaya	82	41.12 N	140.26 E
Mimoň	50	50.40 N	14.44 E
Mimongo	142	1.11 S	11.36 E
Mimoso, Bra.	238	16.17 S	55.48 W
Mimoso, Bra.	245	15.10 S	48.05 W
Mimoso do Sul	245	21.04 S	41.22 W
Mims	210	28.40 N	80.51 W
Mimuro-yama ∧	86	35.14 N	134.28 E
Minā, Ar. Sa.	134	21.25 N	39.52 E
Mina, Méx.	186	26.01 N	100.32 W
Mina, Nev., U.S.	194	38.24 N	118.07 W
Mina ≃	102	10.09 S	124.12 E
Mîna, Oued ≃	34	35.47 N	0.30 E
Mīnā' al-Aḥmadī	118	29.04 N	48.08 E
Mīnāb	118	27.09 N	57.05 E
Mīnāb ≃	118	27.01 N	56.53 E
Minabe	86	33.46 N	135.19 E
Minabegawa	86	33.47 N	135.20 E
Minago ≃	174	54.34 N	98.08 W
Minahasa ≻[1]	102	1.00 N	124.35 E
Mināj ≃[1]	116	22.31 N	89.22 E
Minakami	84	36.46 N	138.58 E
Minakuchi	84	34.58 N	136.10 E
Minam ≃	192	45.37 N	117.43 W
Minamata	82	32.13 N	130.24 E
Minami	84	35.39 N	136.57 E
Minami ◆[8], Nihon	258	35.24 N	139.36 E
Minami ◆[8], Nihon	260	34.58 N	135.45 E
Minami ◆[8], Nihon	260	34.40 N	135.31 E
Minamiaiki	84	36.02 N	138.33 E
Minami-alps-kokuritsu-kōen ♠	84	35.40 N	138.13 E
Minamiashigara	84	35.19 N	139.07 E
Minami-bōsō-kokutei-kōen ♠	84	35.10 N	140.05 E
Minamichita	84	34.44 N	136.52 E
Minami-Daitō-jima I	80	25.50 N	131.15 E
Minami-iō-jima I	14	24.14 N	141.28 E
Minamiizu	84	34.39 N	138.50 E
Minamimaki	84	36.00 N	138.30 E
Minaminasu	84	36.39 N	140.06 E
Minamisenju ◆[8]	258	35.44 N	139.48 E
Minamishinano	84	35.19 N	137.56 E
Minami-Tori-shima (Marcus Island) I	14	24.18 N	153.58 E
Minano	84	36.04 N	139.06 E
Mina Pirquitas	242	22.41 S	66.31 W
Minard	148	31.17 S	27.35 E
Minas, Cuba	230p	21.29 N	77.37 W
Minas, Indon.	104	0.50 N	101.29 E
Minas, Ur.	242	34.23 S	55.14 W
Minas, Sierra de las ∧∧	226	15.10 N	89.40 W
Minas Basin C	176	45.20 N	64.00 W
Minas Channel Ц	176	45.15 N	64.45 W
Minas de Barroterán	222	27.40 N	101.20 W
Minas de Corrales	242	31.35 S	55.28 W
Minas de Matahambre	230p	22.35 N	83.57 W
Minas de Oro	226	14.46 N	87.20 W
Minas de Ríotinto	34	37.40 N	6.39 W
Minas Gerais □[3]	245	18.00 S	44.00 W
Minas Novas	245	17.15 S	42.36 W
Mînăstirea	38	44.13 N	26.54 E
Minatitlán	224	17.59 N	94.31 W
Minato ◆[8], Nihon	258	35.39 N	139.45 E
Minato ◆[8], Nihon	260	34.39 N	135.26 E
Minato ≃	258	35.13 N	139.52 E
Minbāl	132	28.24 N	30.41 E
Minbu	100	20.11 N	94.52 E
Minbulak	75	41.30 N	75.53 E
Minbya	100	20.22 N	93.15 E
Minbyin	100	19.17 N	93.32 E
Minchinābād	113	30.10 N	73.34 E
Minchinhampton	44	51.42 N	2.10 W
Minchinmávida, Volcán ∧[1]	244	42.49 S	72.28 W
Minchumina, Lake ⊜	170	63.52 N	152.15 W
Mincio ≃	58	45.04 N	10.59 E
Minco	186	35.19 N	97.57 W
Minčol ∧	30	49.15 N	20.59 E
Mind'ak	76	54.02 N	58.48 E
Mindanao I	106	8.00 N	125.00 E
Mindanao ≃	106	7.07 N	124.24 E
Mindanao Sea ⊤[2]	106	9.10 N	124.25 E
Mindanao Trench ⊹[1]	14	9.00 N	127.00 E
Mindego Creek ≃	272	37.18 N	122.15 W
Mindego Hill ∧[2]	272	37.18 N	122.13 W
Mindel ≃	54	48.31 N	10.23 E
Mindelheim	54	48.03 N	10.29 E
Mindelo	140a	16.53 N	25.00 W
Mindemoya	180	45.44 N	82.10 W
Minden, B.R.D.	48	52.17 N	8.55 E
Minden, Ont., Can.	202	44.55 N	78.43 W
Minden, La., U.S.	184	32.37 N	93.17 W
Minden, Nebr., U.S.	188	40.30 N	98.57 W
Minden, Nev., U.S.	216	38.57 N	119.45 W
Minden, W. Va., U.S.	178	37.59 N	81.07 W
Minden City	180	43.40 N	82.47 W
Mindenmines	184	37.28 N	94.35 W
Minderoo	152	22.00 S	115.02 E
Mindif	136	10.24 N	14.26 E
Mindiptana	154	5.45 S	140.42 E
Mindjik, Bahr ≃	136	10.01 N	20.41 E
Mindon	100	19.21 N	94.44 E
Mindoro I	106	12.50 N	121.05 E
Mindoro Occidental □[4]	106	13.00 N	121.00 E
Mindoro Oriental □[4]	106	13.00 N	121.20 E
Mindoro Strait Ц	106	12.20 N	120.40 E
Mindouli	142	4.17 S	14.21 E
Mindourou	142	4.06 N	14.34 E
Minduri	246	21.41 S	44.37 W
Mindživan	74	39.03 N	46.42 E
Mine, Nihon	86	33.17 N	130.26 E
Mine, Nihon	86	34.10 N	131.13 E
Mine, Yai.	134	8.20 N	40.09 E
Minear Lake ⊜	268	42.17 N	87.57 W
Minebank Run ≃	274b	39.25 N	76.32 W
Mine Brook ≃, Mass., U.S.	273	42.09 N	71.15 W
Mine Brook ≃, Mass., U.S.	273	42.08 N	71.26 W
Mine Brook ≃, N.J., U.S.	266	40.41 N	74.38 W
Mine Centre	180	48.45 N	92.37 W
Minehead	44	51.13 N	3.29 W
Mine Hill	200	40.53 N	74.36 W
Mineiros	245	17.34 S	52.34 W
Mineola, N.Y., U.S.	200	40.45 N	73.38 W
Mineola, Tex., U.S.	212	32.40 N	95.29 W
Mineral	214	46.43 N	122.11 W
Mineral City	204	40.36 N	81.25 W
Mineral Creek ≃	214	46.45 N	122.08 W
Mineral del Monte	224	20.08 N	98.40 W
Mineral del Oro	224	19.48 N	100.08 W
Mineral'nyje Vody	74	44.12 N	43.08 E
Mineral Point, Pa., U.S.	204	40.23 N	78.50 W
Mineral Point, Wis., U.S.	180	42.52 N	90.11 W
Mineral Ridge	204	41.08 N	80.46 W
Mineral Springs, Ark., U.S.	184	33.53 N	93.55 W
Mineral Springs, Pa., U.S.	204	41.00 N	78.22 W
Mineral Wells	186	32.48 N	98.07 W
Minerbe	58	45.14 N	11.20 E
Minerbio	58	44.37 N	11.29 E
Minersville, Pa., U.S.	198	40.41 N	76.16 W
Minersville, Utah, U.S.	190	38.13 N	112.55 W
Mine Run ≃	275	40.15 N	75.28 W
Minerva, Ky., U.S.	208	38.42 N	83.55 W
Minerva, Ohio, U.S.	204	40.44 N	81.06 W
Minerva, Tex., U.S.	212	30.46 N	96.59 W
Minerva Park	204	40.04 N	83.00 W
Minervino Murge	36	41.05 N	16.05 E
Minesing Swamp ☷	202	44.23 N	79.51 W
Minetto	200	43.24 N	76.29 W
Mineville	178	44.05 N	73.31 W
Mineyama	86	35.37 N	135.04 E
Minfeng	110	37.05 N	82.40 E
Minga	144	11.08 S	27.57 E
Mingala	142	5.06 N	21.49 E
Mingan	176	50.18 N	64.02 W
Mingan, Îles de II	176	50.12 N	63.35 W
Mingan Mountains ∧∧	106	15.29 N	121.24 E
Mingāora	113	34.47 N	72.22 E
Mingary	156	32.08 S	140.44 E
Mingcheng	79	43.11 N	125.59 E
Mingečaur	74	40.45 N	47.03 E
Mingečaurskoje Vodochranilišče ⊜[1]	74	40.50 N	46.50 E
Mingela	156	19.53 S	146.38 E
Mingenew	152	29.11 S	115.26 E
Mingera Creek ≃	156	20.38 S	138.10 E
Mingfankuangqu	90	27.21 N	120.24 E
Minggang	90	32.29 N	114.03 E
Minggao	90	34.20 N	112.15 E
Minggugong (Ming Palace) ʋ	96	32.01 N	118.46 E
Minghuang	96	31.41 N	119.56 E
Mingin	100	22.52 N	94.39 E
Mingjiaqiao	90	32.53 N	119.13 E
Mingjuesi	96	31.34 N	118.53 E
Minglanilla	34	39.32 N	1.36 W
Mingling (Ming Tombs) ⊥	95	40.22 N	116.12 E
Mingo, Congo	142	1.55 S	14.59 E
Mingo, Ohio, U.S.	206	40.13 N	83.38 W
Mingo Creek ≃, Pa., U.S.	269b	40.13 N	79.57 W
Mingo Creek ≃, Pa., U.S.	275	40.10 N	75.32 W
Mingo Junction	204	40.19 N	80.37 W
Mingo Lake ⊜	166	64.35 N	72.10 W
Mingorría	34	40.45 N	4.40 W
Mingoville	204	40.56 N	77.39 W
Mingoyo	144	10.06 S	39.38 E
Mingrel'skaja	68	45.01 N	38.20 E
Mingshantou	90	29.18 N	112.33 E
Mingshui, Zhg.	79	47.10 N	125.55 E
Mingshui, Zhg.	92	42.06 N	96.04 E
Mingulay I	28	56.50 N	7.40 W
Mingwan	96	31.04 N	120.17 E
Mingxi	90	26.24 N	117.13 E
Mingyuelu	75	39.34 N	75.26 E
Minhla, Mya.	100	19.58 N	95.03 E
Minhla, Mya.	100	17.59 N	95.43 E
Minho □[9]	34	41.40 N	8.30 W
Minho (Miño) ≃	34	41.52 N	8.51 W
Minhou	90	25.59 N	119.18 E
Minianko	140	9.58 N	8.22 W
Minićevo	38	43.41 N	22.18 E
Minicoy Island I	112	8.17 N	73.02 E
Minier	184	40.26 N	89.19 W
Minigwal, Lake ⊜	152	29.35 S	123.12 E
Minija ≃	66	55.21 N	21.17 E
Minilulan Point ≻	106	9.08 N	123.42 E
Minilya	152	23.51 S	113.58 E
Minilya ≃	152	23.56 S	113.51 E
Minimarg	113	34.47 N	75.05 E
Minīn	122	33.39 N	36.18 E
Miniota	174	50.08 N	101.00 W
Minirodo, Baie de C	147b	25.10 S	44.15 E
Minisinakwa Lake ⊜	180	47.40 N	81.43 W
Ministikwan Lake ⊜	174	54.01 N	109.39 W
Ministro Ramos Mexia	244	40.30 S	67.17 W
Ministro Rivadavia	278	34.51 S	58.22 W
Minitonas	174	52.07 N	101.00 W
Minj	154	5.54 S	144.39 E
Minjar	76	55.04 N	57.33 E
Minjary, Mount ∧	161b	35.14 S	148.08 E
Minjiadianzi	94	41.35 N	121.41 E
Minjiaji	90	31.08 N	115.01 E
Minjiang ≃, Zhg.	90	26.05 N	119.32 E
Minjiang ≃, Zhg.	92	28.54 N	105.28 E
Minjiangkou ≃[1]	90	26.06 N	119.40 E
Minkamman	130	6.03 N	31.32 E
Min'kovo	66	59.42 N	43.28 E
Minkulincy	68	49.24 N	25.38 E
Min-Kuš	75	41.41 N	74.28 E
Minlaton	158b	34.46 S	137.36 E
Minle, Zhg.	90	22.59 N	112.58 E
Minle, Zhg.	92	38.27 N	100.56 E
Minna	140	9.37 N	6.33 E
Minna Bluff ≻[1]	9	78.32 S	166.30 E
Minna-jima I	165d	24.45 N	124.42 E
Minna-shima I	164m	26.39 N	127.49 E
Minneapolis, Kans., U.S.	188	39.08 N	97.42 W
Minneapolis, Minn., U.S.	180	44.59 N	93.13 W
Minnechaduza Creek ≃	188	42.54 N	100.29 W
Minnedosa	174	50.14 N	99.51 W
Minnedosa ≃	174	49.53 N	100.08 W
Minnehaha	214	45.39 N	122.37 W
Minnehaha, Lake ⊜	210	28.31 N	81.46 W
Minneola, Fla., U.S.	210	28.35 N	81.45 W
Minneola, Kans., U.S.	188	37.26 N	100.01 W
Minneola, Lake ⊜	210	28.34 N	81.46 W
Minneota	188	44.58 N	93.12 W
Minnertsga	48	53.15 N	5.35 E
Minnesota □[3]	168	46.00 N	94.15 W
Minnesota ≃	180	44.54 N	93.10 W
Minnesota Lake	180	43.51 N	93.50 W
Minnewanka, Lake ⊜	172	51.15 N	115.20 W
Minnewaukan	188	48.04 N	99.15 W
Minnie Creek	152	24.02 S	115.42 E
Minnigaff	42	54.58 N	4.30 W
Minnipa	152	32.51 S	135.09 E
Minnitaki Lake ⊜	174	49.58 N	92.00 W
Minnoch, Water of ≃	42	55.02 N	4.33 W
Mino, Nihon	84	35.32 N	136.55 E
Minō	84		
	86	34.50 N	135.30 E
Miño (Minho) ≃, Eur.	34	41.52 N	8.51 W
Minō ≃, Nihon	260	34.47 N	134.57 E
Minoa	200	43.04 N	76.00 W
Minobu	84	35.22 N	138.26 E
Minobu-san ∧	84	35.24 N	138.25 E
Minobu-sanchi ∧∧	84	35.14 N	138.20 E
Minocqua	180	45.52 N	89.43 W
Mino-kamo	84	35.26 N	137.01 E
Mino-mikawa-kōgen ∧∧[1]	84	35.11 N	137.23 E
Minong	180	46.06 N	91.49 W
Minonk	180	40.54 N	89.02 W
Minōnoshō	260	34.39 N	135.59 E
Minooka	206	41.27 N	88.16 W
Minorca → Menorca I	34	40.00 N	4.00 E
Minori	84	36.14 N	140.21 E
Minorsville	208	38.20 N	84.42 W
Minot, Mass., U.S.	273	42.14 N	70.46 W
Minot, N. Dak., U.S.	188	48.14 N	101.18 W
Minot Air Force Base ■	188	48.26 N	101.21 W
Minowa	84	35.55 N	137.59 E
Minqin	92	39.03 N	103.38 E
Minqing	90	26.12 N	118.51 E
Minquadale	275	39.42 N	75.34 W
Minquan	88	34.41 N	115.11 E
Minsen	48	53.42 N	7.58 E
Minshan ∧∧	92	33.15 N	103.15 E
Minshāt Adh Dhahab	132	28.00 N	30.42 E
Minshat al-Amir Muhammad 'Ali	132	29.10 N	30.38 E
Minshāt al-Bakkārī	263c	30.01 N	31.08 E
Minshāt al-Ikhwah	132	30.56 N	31.21 E
Minshāt al-Mughālaqah	132	27.44 N	30.47 E
Minshāt Būlīn	132	31.11 N	30.10 E
Minshāt Sulṭān	132	30.32 N	30.55 E
Minsk	66	53.54 N	27.34 E
Minsk □[4]	24	54.30 N	28.00 E
Minskaja Vozvyšennost' ∧∧[1]	66	54.00 N	27.10 E
Mińsk Mazowiecki	30	52.11 N	21.34 E
Minster, Eng., U.K.	44	51.26 N	0.49 E
Minster, Eng., U.K.	44	51.20 N	1.19 E
Minster, Ohio, U.S.	206	40.24 N	84.23 W
Minsterley	44	52.39 N	2.55 W
Minta	142	4.35 N	12.48 E
Mintaka Pass)(	113	36.58 N	74.54 E
Mintard	253	51.22 N	6.54 E
Mintaro	158b	33.55 S	138.43 E
Mint Canyon	218	34.26 N	118.25 W
Minto, Austl.	264a	34.01 S	150.51 E
Minto, Man., Can.	174	49.25 N	100.01 W
Minto, N.B., Can.	176	46.05 N	66.05 W
Minto, Yukon, Can.	170	62.34 N	136.51 W
Minto, Alaska, U.S.	170	64.53 N	149.11 W
Minto, N. Dak., U.S.	188	48.17 N	97.15 W
Minto, Lac ⊜	166	51.00 N	73.37 W
Minto Inlet C	166	71.20 N	117.00 W
Mintom	142	2.42 N	13.17 E
Minton	174	49.05 N	105.35 W
Mintoum	142	0.27 N	12.16 E
Minturn	190	39.35 N	106.26 W
Minturnae ⊥	60	41.14 N	13.45 E
Minturno	60	41.15 N	13.45 E
Minūf	132	30.28 N	30.56 E
Minulovo	255a	60.03 N	30.45 E
Minumadai-yōsui Ξ	258	35.50 N	139.42 E
Minur'uk	75	40.56 N	73.22 E
Minusinsk	76	53.43 N	91.42 E
Minutang	110	28.13 N	96.32 E
Minute Man National Historical Park ♠	197	42.27 N	71.17 W
Minvoul	142	2.09 N	12.08 E
Minxian	92	34.22 N	104.08 E
Minya → Al-Minyā	132	28.06 N	30.45 E
Minyā al-Qamḥ	132	30.31 N	31.21 E
Minya Konka → Gonggashan ∧	92	29.35 N	101.51 E
Minyat an-Naṣr	132	31.07 N	31.39 E
Minyat as-Sīrij ◆[8]	263c	30.05 N	31.15 E
Minyat Sandūb	132	31.00 N	31.23 E
Minžir	68	46.40 N	28.19 E
Minzow	50	53.23 N	12.30 E
Mio	180	44.39 N	84.08 W
Mioglia	56	44.29 N	8.25 E
Mionica	38	44.15 N	20.05 E
Miory	66	55.37 N	27.38 E
Mipi	110	28.57 N	95.48 E
Miquan	76	44.06 N	87.35 E
Miquelon I	176	47.03 N	56.20 W
Miquihuana	224	23.34 N	99.47 W
Miquon	275	40.04 N	75.16 W
Mīr, Miṣr	132	27.27 N	30.44 E
Mir, Niger	136	14.05 N	11.59 E
Mir, S.S.S.R.	66	53.27 N	26.28 E
Mira, It.	58	45.26 N	12.08 E
Mira, Port.	34	40.26 N	8.44 W
Mira ≃, N.S., Can.	176	46.03 N	60.00 W
Mira ≃, Col.	236	1.36 N	79.01 W
Mira ≃, Port.	34	37.43 N	8.47 W
Mīrābād	118	30.25 N	61.50 E
Mira Bay C	176	46.02 N	59.56 W
Mirabeau	56	43.42 N	5.39 E

≃	River	Fluss	Río	Rivière	Rio
Ξ	Canal	Kanal	Canal	Canal	Canal
⌊	Waterfall, Rapids	Wasserfall, Stromschnellen	Cascada, Rápidos	Chute d'eau, Rapides	Cascata, Rápidos
Ц	Strait	Meeresstrasse	Estrecho	Détroit	Estreito
C	Bay, Gulf	Bucht, Golf	Bahía, Golfo	Baie, Golfe	Baía, Golfo
⊜	Lake, Lakes	See, Seen	Lago, Lagos	Lac, Lacs	Lago, Lagos
☷	Swamp	Sumpf	Pantano	Marais	Pântano
⍓	Ice Features, Glacier	Eis- und Gletscherformen	Accidentes Glaciales	Formes glaciaires	Acidentes Glaciares
⊤	Other Hydrographic Features	Andere Hydrographische Objekte	Otros Elementos Hidrográficos	Autres données hydrographiques	Outros Elementos Hidrográficos
⊹	Submarine Features	Untermeerische Objekte	Accidentes Submarinos	Formes de relief sous-marin	Acidentes Submarinos
□	Political Unit	Politische Einheit	Unidad Política	Entité politique	Unidade Política
ʋ	Cultural Institution	Kulturelle Institution	Institución Cultural	Institution culturelle	Instituição Cultural
⊥	Historical Site	Historische Stätte	Sitio Histórico	Site historique	Sítio Histórico
♠	Recreational Site	Erholungs- und Ferienort	Sitio de Recreo	Centre de loisirs	Sítio de Lazer
⊠	Airport	Flughafen	Aeropuerto	Aéroport	Aeroporto
■	Military Installation	Militäranlage	Instalación Militar	Installation militaire	Instalação Militar
◆	Miscellaneous	Verschiedenes	Misceláneo	Divers	Miscelânea

Mirabella Eclano 60 41.02 N 14.59 E
Mirabello, Ippodromo ♠ 256b 45.36 N 9.17 E
Mirabello Monferrato 56 45.02 N 8.31 E
Miracema do Norte 240 9.33 S 48.24 W
Mirada Hills → La Mirada 218 33.54 N 118.01 W
Mirador 240 6.22 S 44.22 W
Mirador, Cerro ∧ 276d 11.57 S 77.02 W
Miradouro 245 20.53 S 42.21 W
Miraflores, Arg. 242 28.36 S 65.55 W
Miraflores, Col. 236 1.25 N 72.13 W
Miraflores, Col. 236 5.12 N 73.12 W
Miraflores, Perú 276d 12.07 S 77.02 W
Miraflores, Palacio ʊ 276c 10.31 N 66.55 W
Miraflores Locks ◆[5] 226 9.00 N 79.36 W
Mīrah, Wādī al- ∨ 118 32.26 N 41.42 E
Miraí 246 21.12 S 42.37 W
Miraj 112 16.50 N 74.38 E
Miraki 75 39.02 N 67.10 E
Miraleste 218 33.46 N 118.19 W
Mira Loma 218 34.01 N 117.31 W
Miramar, Arg. 242 30.54 S 62.40 W
Miramar, Arg. 242 38.16 S 57.51 W
Miramar, C.R. 226 10.06 N 84.44 W
Miramar, Fr. 56 43.30 N 6.57 E
Miramar, Moç. 146 23.50 S 35.34 E
Miramar, Fla., U.S. 210 25.59 N 80.11 W
Miramar ◆[8] 276b 23.07 N 82.25 W
Miramar, Laguna @ 226 16.23 N 91.16 W
Miramare 60 44.02 N 12.38 E
Miramare, Aeroporto di ⊠ 60 44.02 N 12.35 E
Miramare, Castello di ⊥ 58 45.42 N 13.43 E
Miramar Naval Air Station ■ 218 32.52 N 117.07 W
Miramas 56 43.35 N 5.00 E
Mirambeau 32 45.23 N 0.34 W
Miramichi Bay C 176 47.08 N 65.08 W
Mira Monte 218 36.42 N 119.03 W
Mīram Shāh 110 33.00 N 70.04 E
Mīrān 113 31.24 N 70.43 E
Miranda, Austl. 264a 34.02 S 151.06 E
Miranda, Bra. 238 20.14 S 56.22 W
Miranda, Col. 236 3.15 N 76.14 W
Miranda, Moç. 144 12.30 S 35.28 E
Miranda, Calif., U.S. 194 40.14 N 123.49 W
Miranda □[3] 236 10.15 N 66.25 W
Miranda ≃ 238 19.25 S 57.20 W
Miranda de Ebro 34 42.41 N 2.57 W
Miranda do Douro 34 41.30 N 6.16 W
Mirande 32 43.31 N 0.25 E
Mirandela 34 41.29 N 7.11 W
Mirando City 186 27.26 N 99.00 W
Mirandola 58 44.53 N 11.04 E
Mirano 58 45.30 N 12.07 E
Mirantão 246 22.15 S 44.30 W
Mirante do Paranapanema 245 22.17 S 51.54 W
Mirapuxi ≃ 245 13.06 S 51.10 W
Mirasaka 86 34.46 N 132.58 E
Miravalles, Volcán ∧[1] 226 10.45 N 85.10 W
Miravete, Puerto de)(34 39.43 N 5.43 W
Mīr Bachcheh Kūt 110 34.45 N 69.08 E
Mir-Bašir 74 40.20 N 46.55 E
Mirbāṭ 108 17.00 N 54.45 E
Mirboo North 159 38.24 S 146.10 E
Mirebeau-sur-Bèze 54 47.24 N 5.19 E
Mirecourt 54 48.18 N 6.08 E
Miren 58 45.54 N 13.37 E
Mireny 68 46.58 N 29.04 E
Mirfield 42 53.40 N 1.41 W
Mirgorod 68 49.58 N 33.36 E
Mirgorodka 70 50.58 N 53.33 E
Miri 102 4.23 N 113.59 E
Miriam Vale 156 24.20 S 151.34 E
Miribel 56 45.49 N 4.57 E
Mirim, Lagoa (Laguna Merín) C 242 32.45 S 52.50 W
Mirimichi, Lake @ 273 42.02 N 71.18 W
Mirina 38 39.52 N 25.04 E
Miriñay ≃ 242 30.10 S 57.39 W
Mirinzal 240 2.01 S 44.43 W
Miriti 238 6.15 S 59.00 W
Miritiparaná ≃ 236 1.11 S 70.02 W
Miriyama 154 3.57 S 141.45 E
Mīrjāveh 118 29.01 N 61.28 E
Mirke ◆[8] 253 51.16 N 7.09 E
Mirna ≃ 58 45.19 N 13.36 E
Mirnock ∧ 58 46.46 N 13.43 E
Mirnoje Ozero 76 57.44 N 78.45 E
Mirnyj, S.S.S.R. 64 62.33 N 113.53 E
Mirnyj, S.S.S.R. 68 50.57 N 28.34 E
Mirnyj, S.S.S.R. 70 53.30 N 50.18 E
Mirnyy ʊ[3] 9 66.33 S 93.00 E
Mirond Lake @ 174 55.06 N 102.47 W
Mironeasa 38 46.58 N 27.25 E
Mironovka 68 49.39 N 30.59 E
Mironovo 78 58.19 N 109.38 E
Mironovskij 73 48.29 N 38.17 E
Miropol' 68 50.07 N 27.41 E
Miropolje 68 51.02 N 35.16 E
Miroslav 30 48.57 N 16.18 E
Mirosławiec 30 53.21 N 16.05 E
Mirovoje 68 47.45 N 34.45 E
Mirovskoje 68 48.05 N 33.23 E
Mirow 50 53.16 N 12.49 E
Mīrpur, Bngl. 116 23.56 N 88.59 E
Mīrpur, Bngl. 116 23.47 N 90.21 E
Mīrpur, Pāk. 113 33.11 N 73.46 E
Mīrpur Batoro 110 24.44 N 68.16 E
Mīrpur Bībīwāri 110 28.32 N 67.44 E
Mīrpur Khās 110 25.32 N 69.00 E
Mīrpur Sakro 110 24.33 N 67.37 E
Mirria 140 13.43 N 9.07 E
Mirror 172 52.28 N 113.07 W
Mirror Lake @, Mass., U.S. 273 42.05 N 71.20 W
Mirror Lake @, N.J., U.S. 266 40.29 N 74.22 W
Mirs Bay C 90 22.30 N 114.24 E
Mirskoj Chrebet ∧∧ 76 52.24 N 92.48 E
Mirtağ 120 38.23 N 41.56 E
Mirtóön Pélagos ▼[2] 38 36.51 N 23.18 E
Mirvan 120 38.33 N 39.48 E
Miryang 88 35.31 N 128.44 E
Miry Run ≃ 275 40.15 N 74.49 W
Mirza-Aki 75 40.45 N 73.25 E
Mirzaani 74 41.23 N 46.09 E
Mirzāganj 116 22.21 N 90.14 E
Mīrzakālu 116 22.29 N 90.48 E
Mirzāpur, Bhārat 114 25.09 N 82.35 E
Mirzāpur, Bhārat 262b 22.50 N 88.24 E
Mirzāpur, Bngl. 116 24.06 N 90.06 E
Mirzāpur □[5] 114 24.55 N 82.50 E
Mis 58 46.12 N 11.57 E
Misa ≃ 60 43.43 N 13.14 E
Misāḥah, Bi'r ▼[4] 130 22.12 N 27.57 E
Misailovo 255b 55.34 N 37.49 E
Misaka 84 35.38 N 138.40 E
Misaka-tōge)(86 33.42 N 132.52 E
Misaki, Nihon 84 35.18 N 140.22 E
Misaki → Miura, Nihon 84 35.08 N 139.37 E
Misaki, Nihon 86 33.23 N 132.07 E
Misaki, Nihon 86 34.19 N 135.09 E
Mi-saki ≻ 83b 30.50 N 131.04 E
Misakubo 84 35.09 N 137.52 E
Misallah, Ra's ≻ 132 29.50 N 32.36 E
Misamis Occidental □[4] 106 8.20 N 123.42 E
Misamis Oriental □[4] 106 8.45 N 125.00 E
Misano Adriatico 60 43.57 N 12.39 E
Misantla 224 19.56 N 96.50 W
Misasa 86 35.24 N 133.54 E
Misasagi → Fujiidera 86 34.34 N 135.36 E
Misato, Nihon 84 36.15 N 137.54 E
Misato, Nihon 84 34.43 N 136.24 E
Misato, Nihon 84 36.23 N 138.57 E
Misato, Nihon 86 34.09 N 135.22 E
Misato, Nihon 258 35.50 N 139.53 E
Misawa 82 40.41 N 141.24 E
Misawa Air Base (United States) ■ 82 40.45 N 141.23 E
Misbourne ≃ 250 51.34 N 0.29 W
Misburg 48 52.23 N 9.51 E
Miscou Centre 176 47.57 N 64.34 W
Miscou Island I 176 47.57 N 64.33 W
Miscou Point ≻ 176 48.03 N 64.32 W
Miševelka 78 52.51 N 103.09 E
Misema ≃ 180 47.54 N 79.53 W
Mi-sen ∧ 86 34.16 N 132.19 E
Misenheimer 182 35.29 N 80.17 W
Miseno 60 40.47 N 14.05 E
Misericórdia, Serra da ∧ 277a 22.51 S 43.17 W
Misgār 113 36.47 N 74.47 E
Mish'āb, Ra's al- ≻ 118 28.12 N 48.39 E
Mishan (Dongan) 79 45.33 N 131.52 E
Mishaua ≃ 238 11.13 S 72.59 W
Mishawaka 206 41.40 N 86.11 W
Mishawum Lake @ 273 42.30 N 71.08 W
Mishbiḥ, Jabal ∧ 130 22.38 N 34.44 E
Misheguk Mountain ∧ 170 68.15 N 161.03 W
Misheiti, Jabal al- ∧ 122 30.47 N 34.18 E
Mishe-Mokwa, Lake @ 275 39.52 N 74.48 W
Mishibishu Lake @ 180 48.05 N 85.25 W
Mishicot 180 44.14 N 87.38 W
Mishima, Nihon 84 35.07 N 138.55 E
Mishima → Settsu, Nihon 86 34.46 N 135.33 E
Mi-shima I 86 34.46 N 131.09 E
Mishmar HaNegev 122 31.21 N 34.43 E
Mishmar HaYarden 122 33.00 N 35.36 E
Mishmi Hills ∧∧[2] 110 29.00 N 96.00 E
Mishō 86 32.57 N 132.34 E
Mishqal, Jabal al- ∧ 122 31.53 N 36.08 E
Mishui ≃, Zhg. 90 27.09 N 112.51 E
Mishui ≃, Zhg. 90 28.50 N 113.06 E
Mišicha 78 51.38 N 105.35 E
Misikan 110 35.45 N 89.25 E
Misilmeri 36 38.01 N 13.27 E
Misima Island I 154 10.40 S 152.45 E
Misinto 256b 45.40 N 9.05 E
Misiones □[4] 242 27.00 S 55.00 W
Misiones □[5] 242 27.00 S 57.00 W
Misión San Francisco de Laishí 242 26.14 S 58.38 W
Misirevo 72 56.16 N 36.45 E
Misk 120 38.48 N 42.13 E
Miskī 130 14.51 N 24.13 E
Miski, Enneri ∨ 136 20.00 N 17.55 E
Miškino, S.S.S.R. 76 55.20 N 63.55 E
Miškino, S.S.S.R. 255a 59.42 N 30.45 E
Miskito Channel ∪ 226 14.20 N 83.08 W
Miskitos, Cayos II 226 14.23 N 82.46 W
Miskitos Reef ÷[2] 226 14.28 N 82.42 W
Miskolc 30 48.06 N 20.47 E
Misli 120 38.10 N 34.52 E
Mislippi 136 10.00 N 15.37 E
Mislivna ∧ 30 48.40 N 14.44 E
Mismār 130 18.13 N 35.38 E
Mismār, Jabal ∧ 130 18.06 N 35.42 E
Mišn'ovo 66 53.58 N 36.21 E
Misoke 144 1.06 S 28.38 E
Misool, Pulau I 154 1.52 S 130.10 E
Mispillion ≃ 198 38.57 N 75.20 W
Misquamaebin Lake @ 174 53.30 N 91.05 W
Misquamicut 197 41.20 N 71.49 W
Miṣr → Egypt □[1] 130 27.00 N 30.00 E
Miṣr al-Jadīdah (Heliopolis) ◆[8] 263c 30.06 N 31.20 E
Miṣr al-Qadīmah (Old Cairo) ◆[8] 263c 30.00 N 31.14 E
Misrātah 136 32.23 N 15.06 E
Misrātah □[4] 136 30.00 N 16.30 E
Misrikh 114 27.27 N 80.31 E
Missão Santa Cruz 142 16.14 S 21.57 E
Missão Velha 240 7.15 S 39.08 W
Misserghin 34 35.37 N 0.45 W
Missinaibi ≃ 166 50.44 N 81.29 W
Missinaibi Lake @ 180 48.23 N 83.40 W
Mission, S. Dak., U.S. 188 43.18 N 100.40 W
Mission, Tex., U.S. 186 26.13 N 98.20 W
Mission ◆[8] 272 37.45 N 122.25 W
Mission Bay C 218 32.47 N 117.15 W
Mission City 172 49.08 N 122.18 W
Mission Creek ≃ 272 37.32 N 121.55 W
Mission Hills ◆[8] 270 34.16 N 118.27 W
Mission Indian Reservation ◆[4] 218 33.22 N 116.58 W
Mission Mountain ∧ 184 34.15 N 94.33 W
Mission Peak ∧ 272 37.31 N 121.53 W
Mission Range ∧∧ 192 47.30 N 113.55 W
Mission Texas State Historic Park ♠ 212 31.33 N 95.15 W
Mission Valley 212 28.54 N 97.12 W
Mission Viejo 218 33.36 N 117.40 W
Missisquoi □[6] 196 45.10 N 72.55 W
Missisquoi ≃ 196 45.00 N 73.08 W
Missisquoi Bay C 196 45.05 N 73.10 W
Missisquoi-Nord ≃ 196 45.02 N 72.26 W
Mississagagon Lake @ 202 44.52 N 77.05 W
Mississagi ≃ 180 46.10 N 83.01 W
Mississagi Provincial Park ♠ 180 46.35 N 82.30 W
Mississagua ≃ 202 44.34 N 78.20 W
Mississagua Lake @ 202 44.42 N 78.19 W
Mississauga 202 43.35 N 79.37 W
Mississinewa ≃ 206 40.46 N 86.02 W
Mississinewa Lake @[1] 206 40.42 N 85.52 W
Mississippi □[3] 168
184 32.50 N 89.30 W
Mississippi ≃, Ont., Can. 202 45.26 N 76.16 W
Mississippi ≃, U.S. 168 29.00 N 89.15 W
Mississippi Bay C 152 34.00 S 122.17 E
Mississippi Delta ⌣[2] 184 29.10 N 89.15 W
Mississippi Lake @ 202 45.05 N 76.12 W
Mississippi Sound ∪ 184 30.15 N 88.40 W
Missolonghi → Mesolóngion 38 38.21 N 21.17 E
Missoula 192 46.52 N 114.01 W
Missouri □[3] 168
184 38.30 N 93.30 W
Missouri ≃ 168 38.50 N 90.08 W
Missouri, Coteau du ∧∧[2] 188 46.00 N 99.30 W
Missouri Buttes ∧ 188 44.37 N 104.47 W
Missouri City 212 29.37 N 95.32 W
Missouri Creek ≃ 209 40.07 N 90.43 W
Missouri Valley 188 41.33 N 95.53 W
Mistake, Mount ∧ 161a 27.52 S 152.20 E
Mistake Creek 154 17.06 S 129.04 E
Mistake Creek ≃ 156 21.38 S 146.50 E
Mistake Mountains ∧∧ 161a 27.52 S 152.22 E
Mistaken Point ≻ 176 46.38 N 53.10 W
Mistanipisipou ≃ 176 51.32 N 61.50 W
Mistassibi ≃ 166 48.53 N 72.13 W
Mistassibi-Nord-Est ≃ 176 49.50 N 71.56 W
Mistassini, Lac @ 166 51.00 N 73.37 W
Mistatim 174 52.52 N 103.22 W
Mistawasis Indian Reserve ◆[4] 174 53.06 N 106.48 W
Mistelbach an der Zaya 30 48.34 N 16.35 E
Misteln @ 40 59.07 N 16.57 E
Misterbianco 36 37.31 N 15.01 E
Misterei 130 13.07 N 22.09 E
Misterton, Eng., U.K. 42 53.27 N 0.51 W
Misterton, Eng., U.K. 44 50.52 N 2.47 W
Misti, Volcán ∧[1] 238 16.18 S 71.24 W
Mistikokan ≃ 174 57.00 N 91.27 W
Mistrás ⊥ 38 37.04 N 22.21 E
Mistretta 36 37.56 N 14.22 E
Misugi 84 34.33 N 136.16 E
Misumi, Nihon 82 32.37 N 130.27 E
Misumi, Nihon 86 34.46 N 131.58 E
Misumi, Nihon 86 34.22 N 131.15 E
Misumi ≃ 86 34.47 N 131.56 E
Misurina 58 46.35 N 12.15 E
Mišurin Rog 68 48.50 N 33.58 E
Mišutino, S.S.S.R. 66 59.31 N 36.01 E
Mišutino, S.S.S.R. 72 56.23 N 38.06 E
Mita, Punta de ≻ 224 20.47 N 105.33 W
Mīt Abū Ghālib 132 31.17 N 31.40 E
Mit'ajevo, S.S.S.R. 72 55.16 N 36.32 E
Mit'ajevo, S.S.S.R. 76 60.17 N 61.06 E
Mitaka 84 35.40 N 139.33 E
Mitake, Nihon 84 35.25 N 137.08 E
Mitake, Nihon 84 35.51 N 137.37 E
Mit'akinka ≃ 73 48.35 N 39.50 E
Mit'akino 72 54.24 N 38.50 E
Mit'akinskaja 73 48.36 N 39.47 E
Mīt al-'Āmil 132 30.54 N 31.21 E
Mitatib 130 16.03 N 36.11 E
Mitau → Jelgava 66 56.39 N 23.42 E
Mīt Badr Ḥalāwah 132 30.51 N 31.14 E
Mīt Bashshār 132 30.31 N 31.24 E
Mitcham, Austl. 158b 34.59 S 138.36 E
Mitcham, Austl. 264b 37.49 S 145.12 E
Mitcham ◆[8] 250 51.24 N 0.10 W
Mitcheldean 44 51.53 N 2.30 W
Mitchell, Austl. 156 26.29 S 147.58 E
Mitchell, Ont., Can. 202 43.28 N 81.12 W
Mitchell, Ill., U.S. 209 38.46 N 90.06 W
Mitchell, Ind., U.S. 208 38.44 N 86.28 W
Mitchell, Nebr., U.S. 188 41.57 N 103.48 W
Mitchell, Oreg., U.S. 192 44.34 N 120.09 W
Mitchell, S. Dak., U.S. 188 43.43 N 104.01 W
Mitchell ≃, Austl. 154 15.12 S 141.35 E
Mitchell ≃, Austl. 156 37.53 S 147.41 E
Mitchell, Lake @[1] 184 32.50 N 86.30 W
Mitchell, Mount ∧ 182 35.46 N 82.16 W
Mitchell Bay C 204 42.28 N 82.26 W
Mitchell Corners 202 43.57 N 78.48 W
Mitchell Field ⊠ 268 41.55 N 88.15 W
Mitchell Lake @, B.C., Can. 172 52.53 N 120.36 W
Mitchell Lake @, Ont., Can. 202 44.34 N 78.58 W
Mitchell Point ≻ 204 42.26 N 82.26 W
Mitchell River Mission 154 15.28 S 141.44 E
Mitchellville 180 41.40 N 93.22 W
Mitchelstown 28 52.16 N 8.16 W
Mīt Fāris 132 31.02 N 31.36 E
Mīt Ghamr 132 30.43 N 31.16 E
Mīt Ḥalfah 263c 30.10 N 31.14 E
Mīt Ḥamal 132 30.26 N 31.32 E
Mithapur 110 22.25 N 69.00 E
Mitha Tiwāna 113 32.14 N 72.07 E
Mithi 110 24.44 N 69.48 E
Míthimna 38 39.22 N 26.10 E
Mitiaro I 14 19.49 S 157.43 W
Mitidja, Plaine de la ⌣ 34 36.45 N 3.00 E
Mitilíni 38 39.06 N 26.32 E
Mitino 255b 55.51 N 37.21 E
Mitis, Lac @ 176 48.17 N 67.45 W
Mitishto ≃ 174 54.50 N 98.58 W
Mitiškovo 66 54.40 N 33.31 E
Mitiwanga 204 41.22 N 82.27 W
Mīt Kinānah 132 30.23 N 31.16 E
Mitkof Island I 170 56.45 N 132.50 W
Mitla ⊥ 224 16.55 N 96.17 W
Mitla, Laguna C 224 17.03 N 100.25 W
Mitla, Mamarr Mitla Pass)(132 30.00 N 32.53 E
Mito, Nihon 84 36.22 N 140.28 E
Mito, Nihon 84 34.49 N 137.19 E
Mitō, Nihon 86 34.13 N 131.21 E
Mito, Nihon 86 34.40 N 131.59 E
Mito, Nihon 258 35.10 N 139.37 E
Mito, Tchad 136 10.49 N 15.44 E
Mitomi 84 35.47 N 138.44 E
Mitoya 86 35.17 N 132.52 E
Mitra, Monte ∧ 142 1.23 N 9.57 E
Mitra do Bispo ∧ 246 22.10 S 44.34 W
Mitre ∧ 162 40.48 S 175.27 E
Mitre, Península ≻[1] 244 54.48 S 65.40 W
Mitre Peak ∧ 162 44.38 S 167.50 E
Mitrofania Island I 170 55.51 N 158.49 W
Mitrofanovka 68 49.58 N 39.42 E
Mitrofanovo 24 63.13 N 56.00 E
Mīt Ruhaynah 263c 29.51 N 31.15 E
Mīt Ruhaynah (Memphis) ⊥ 132 29.51 N 31.15 E
Mitry-le-Neuf 251 48.57 N 2.36 E
Mitry-Mory 251 48.59 N 2.37 E
Mitsamiouli 147a 11.23 S 43.18 E
Mitsinjo 147b 16.01 S 45.52 E
Mitsio, Nosy I 147b 12.54 S 48.36 E
Mitsu, Nihon 86 34.47 N 134.33 E
Mitsu, Nihon 86 34.48 N 133.56 E
Mitsubori 258 35.56 N 139.56 E
Mitsue 84 34.29 N 136.10 E
Mitsugi 86 34.30 N 133.09 E
Mitsuishi 86 34.48 N 134.16 E
Mitsukaidō, Nihon 84 36.01 N 139.59 E
Mitsuke 82 37.32 N 138.56 E
Mitsumarenge-dake ∧ 84 36.23 N 137.35 E
Mitsusawa Park Race Track ♠ 258 35.28 N 139.37 E
Mitsuzaku 258 35.25 N 140.00 E
Mitta, Oued el ∨ 138 34.20 N 6.44 E
Mittagong 160 34.27 S 150.27 E
Mittainville 251 48.40 N 1.39 E
Mitta Mitta ≃ 161b 36.12 S 147.11 E
Mitte ◆[8] 254a 52.31 N 13.24 E
Mittelberg, B.R.D. 54 47.38 N 10.25 E
Mittelberg, Öst. 54 47.20 N 10.10 E
Mitteldorf → Międzychód 30 52.36 N 15.55 E
Mittelfischach 52 49.02 N 9.52 E
Mittelfranken □[5] 52 49.20 N 10.40 E
Mittellandkanal ≚ 30 52.16 N 11.41 E
Mittelmeer → Mediterranean Sea ▼[2] 10 35.00 N 20.00 E
Mittelsaida 50 50.46 N 13.18 E
Mittenwald 58 47.27 N 11.15 E
Mittenwalde, D.D.R. 50 53.11 N 13.39 E
Mittenwalde, D.D.R. 50 52.16 N 13.32 E
Mitterndorf 58 47.33 N 13.55 E
Mittersill 58 47.16 N 12.29 E
Mittewald an der Drau 58 46.46 N 12.36 E
Mittwalde → Międzylesie 30 50.10 N 16.40 E
Mittweida 50 50.59 N 12.59 E
Mitú 236 1.08 N 70.03 W
Mitumba, Monts ∧∧ 144 6.00 S 29.00 E
Mituochang 97 28.53 N 105.37 E
Mitwaba 144 8.38 S 27.20 E
Mitwitz 52 50.15 N 11.12 E
Mityana 144 0.24 N 32.03 E
Mīt Yazīd 132 30.30 N 31.20 E
Mitzic 142 0.47 N 11.34 E
Miura 84 35.08 N 139.37 E
Miura-chosuichi @[1] 84 35.49 N 137.23 E
Miura-dam ◆[6] 84 35.49 N 137.24 E
Miura-hantō ≻[1] 84 35.15 N 139.39 E
Mius 70 51.26 N 47.56 E
Mius ≃ 73 47.18 N 38.49 E
Miusinsk 73 48.05 N 38.53 E
Miusskij Liman C[1] 73 47.15 N 38.40 E
Miwa, Nihon 84 36.39 N 140.18 E
Miwa, Nihon 84 35.11 N 136.47 E
Miwa, Nihon 84 36.12 N 139.49 E
Miwa, Nihon 86 35.12 N 135.14 E
Miwa, Nihon 86 34.13 N 132.06 E
Miwa, Nihon 260 34.31 N 135.51 E
Mi-Wuk Village 216 38.05 N 120.13 W
Mixcoac ◆[8] 276a 19.23 N 99.12 W
Mixcoac, Presa de @[1] 276a 19.22 N 99.14 W
Mixco Viejo ⊥ 226 14.52 N 90.40 W
Mixian 90 34.31 N 113.22 E
Mixin 97 30.23 N 105.46 E
Mixquiahuala 224 20.14 N 99.13 W
Mixquic 276a 19.13 N 98.58 W
Mixtán 224 17.55 N 95.51 W
Mixteco ≃ 224 18.11 N 98.30 W
Mixtlán 224 20.26 N 104.25 W
Miya 84 36.05 N 137.15 E
Miya ≃, Nihon 84 36.28 N 137.15 E
Miya ≃, Nihon 84 34.32 N 136.44 E
Miyagawa, Nihon 84 36.19 N 137.09 E
Miyagawa, Nihon 84 34.22 N 136.21 E
Miyagi □[5] 82 38.22 N 140.52 E
Miyāh, Wādī al- ∨ 130 25.00 N 33.23 E
Miyahara 258 35.56 N 139.37 E
Miyajima 86 34.18 N 132.19 E
Miyake 260 34.35 N 135.47 E
Miyake-jima I 82 34.05 N 139.32 E
Miyako 82 39.38 N 141.57 E
Miyakojima ◆[8] 260 34.43 N 135.33 E
Miyako-jima I 165d 24.47 N 125.20 E
Miyakonojō 82 31.44 N 131.04 E
Miyako-rettō II 165d 24.24 N 125.00 E
Miyama, Nihon 82 34.06 N 136.14 E
Miyama, Nihon 84 35.33 N 136.45 E
Miyama, Nihon 84 36.01 N 136.20 E
Miyama, Nihon 86 33.59 N 135.22 E
Miyama, Nihon 86 35.16 N 135.33 E
Miyamaki 260 34.49 N 135.47 E
Miyanojō 82 31.54 N 130.27 E
Miyanoura-dake ∧ 83b 30.20 N 130.31 E
Miyara 165d 24.20 N 124.14 E
Miyata 86 33.32 N 130.34 E
Miyazaki, Nihon 82 31.54 N 131.26 E
Miyazaki, Nihon 84 35.56 N 136.05 E
Miyazakino-hana ≻ 86 34.04 N 135.05 E
Miyazu 86 35.32 N 135.11 E
Miyi 92 27.00 N 102.08 E
Miyoshi, Nihon 86 34.02 N 133.52 E
Miyoshi, Nihon 86 33.57 N 133.03 E
Miyoshi, Nihon 86 34.48 N 132.51 E
Miyoshi, Nihon 258 35.50 N 139.31 E
Miyota 84 36.18 N 138.30 E
Miyun 95 40.22 N 116.50 E
Mizan Teferi 134 6.53 N 35.28 E
Mizar 120 37.26 N 39.26 E
Mizdah 136 31.26 N 12.59 E
Mize 184 31.52 N 89.34 W
Mizen Head ≻ 28 51.27 N 9.49 W
Miževiči 66 52.59 N 25.05 E
Mizhi 92 37.49 N 110.02 E
Mizil 38 45.00 N 26.26 E
Mizoč 68 50.24 N 26.09 E
Mizoguchi 86 35.21 N 133.26 E
Mizo Hills ∧∧[2] 110 22.50 N 93.00 E
Mizonokuchi 258 35.36 N 139.37 E
Mizonuma 258 35.48 N 139.36 E
Mizoram □[8] 110 23.30 N 93.00 E
Mizpah 198 39.29 N 74.50 W
Mizpah Creek ≃ 188 46.16 N 105.17 W
Mizpe Ramon 122 30.36 N 34.48 E
Mizque 238 17.56 S 65.19 W
Mizue ◆[8] 258 35.41 N 139.54 E
Mizuho, Nihon 84 35.46 N 139.21 E
Mizuho, Nihon 86 35.10 N 135.22 E
Mizuho, Nihon 86 34.51 N 132.31 E
Mizuko 258 35.50 N 139.34 E
Mizumaki 86 33.51 N 130.42 E
Mizunami 84 35.22 N 137.15 E
Mizunoko-jima I 86 33.02 N 132.11 E
Mizusawa 82 39.08 N 141.08 E
Mizushima-nada C 86 34.25 N 133.40 E
Mizutori 260 34.47 N 135.45 E
Mizuwake-tōge)(86 33.15 N 131.17 E
Mjälgen 40 60.33 N 15.07 E
Mjällom 26 62.59 N 18.26 E
Mjangad 76 48.15 N 91.57 E
Mjanji 144 0.15 N 33.59 E
Mjanyana 148 31.50 S 28.10 E
Mjölby 26 58.19 N 15.08 E
Mjøndalen 26 59.45 N 10.01 E
Mjörn @ 26 57.54 N 12.25 E
Mjøsa @ 26 60.40 N 11.00 E
Mkalama 144 4.07 S 34.38 E
Mkata 144 5.47 S 38.17 E
Mkhada, Garaet el ≡ 36 36.48 N 8.00 E
Mkokotoni 144 5.52 S 39.15 E
Mkomazi ≃ 148 30.12 S 30.50 E
Mkomazi Game Reserve ◆[4] 144 4.10 S 38.10 E
Mkondo ≃ 148 26.39 S 31.25 E
Mkulwe 144 8.35 S 32.19 E
Mkumvura ≃ 144 15.55 S 31.07 E
Mkunumbi 144 2.18 S 40.42 E
Mkushi 144 13.40 S 29.20 E
Mkushi ≃ 144 14.40 S 29.07 E
Mkushi River 144 13.32 S 29.45 E
Mkuze 148 27.10 S 32.00 E
Mkuze ≃ 148 27.53 S 32.29 E
Mkuze Game Reserve ◆[4] 148 27.40 S 32.15 E
Mkwaja 144 5.47 S 38.51 E
Mkwaya 144 10.06 S 39.40 E
Mladá Boleslav 50 50.23 N 14.59 E
Mladenovac 38 44.26 N 20.42 E
Mlala Hills ∧∧[2] 144 6.47 S 31.45 E
M'Lang 106 6.55 N 124.53 E
M'Lang ≃ 106 6.52 N 124.45 E
Mlanje Peak → Sapitwa ∧ 144 15.57 S 35.36 E
Mlava ≃ 38 44.45 N 21.13 E
Mława 30 53.06 N 20.23 E
Mlawula 148 26.11 S 32.01 E
Mliba 148 26.14 S 31.36 E
Mlinov 68 50.31 N 25.37 E
Mljet, Otok I 36 42.45 N 17.30 E
Mljetski Kanal ∪ 36 42.48 N 17.35 E
Mmadinare 146 21.57 S 27.52 E
Mmanford 44 51.48 N 3.59 W
Mnazi 144 8.54 S 39.06 E
Mncwasa Point ≻ 148 32.05 S 29.05 E
Mneni 144 20.38 S 30.03 E
Mnevniki ◆[8] 255b 55.45 N 37.28 E
Mníšek pod Brdy 30 49.52 N 14.16 E
Mo 24 66.15 N 14.08 E
Mo ≃ 140 8.45 N 11.36 W
Moa ≃, Afr. 140 6.59 N 11.36 W
Moa ≃, Bra. 238 7.39 S 72.41 W
Moa, Pulau I 154 8.10 S 127.56 E
Moab 190 38.35 N 109.33 W
Moabi 142 2.15 S 11.00 E
Moaco ≃ 238 7.41 S 68.18 W
Moa Island I 154 10.12 S 142.16 E
Moala I 165g 18.36 S 179.53 E
Moalboal 106 9.56 N 123.23 E
Moama 156 36.07 S 144.47 E
Moamba 146 25.35 S 32.13 E
Moana 158b 35.13 S 138.29 E
Moanda, Gabon 142 1.34 S 13.11 E
Moanda, Zaïre 142 5.56 S 12.21 E
Moanza 142 5.25 S 17.30 E
Moar Lake @ 174 52.00 N 95.09 W
Moate 28 53.24 N 7.58 W
Moatize 144 16.08 S 33.45 E
Moawhango 162 39.35 S 175.52 E
Moba, Nig. 263a 6.27 N 3.28 E
Moba, Zaïre 144 7.03 S 29.47 E
Mobara 84 35.25 N 140.18 E
Mobārakpur 116 22.58 N 89.10 E
Mobaye 142 4.19 N 21.11 E
Mobberley 252 53.19 N 2.20 W
Mobeetie 186 35.31 N 100.26 W
Mobeka 142 1.53 N 19.46 E

ENGLISH
Name Page Lat.°′ Long.°′

Mobenzélé 142 0.54 N 17.51 E
Moberly 184 39.25 N 92.26 W
Moberly ≃ 172 56.12 N 120.55 W
Moberly Lake 172 55.48 N 121.45 W
Mobile, Ala., U.S. 184 30.42 N 88.05 W
Mobile, Ariz., U.S. 190 33.03 N 112.16 W
Mobile Bay C 184 30.25 N 88.00 W
Mobjack 198 37.23 N 76.21 W
Mobjack Bay C 198 37.19 N 76.21 W
Mobridge 188 45.32 N 100.26 W
Mobu 90 26.50 N 117.42 E
Moca, P.R. 230m 18.24 N 67.07 W
Moca, Rep. Dom. 228 19.24 N 70.31 W
Moča ≃ 72 55.25 N 37.28 E
Mocajuba 240 2.35 S 49.30 W
Močalejevka 70 53.38 N 51.46 E
Močališče 70 56.21 N 48.23 E
Moçambique 144 15.03 S 40.42 E
Moçambique □[5] 144 15.00 S 39.00 E
Moçambique → Mozambique □[1] 128 18.15 S 35.00 E
Moçâmedes 142 15.10 S 12.09 E
Moçâmedes □[5] 142 15.20 S 12.30 E
Mocanaqua 200 41.08 N 76.08 W
Mocanguê Grande, Ilha I 277a 22.52 S 43.08 W
Mocassins, Lac des @ 196 46.35 N 74.25 W
Mo-cay 100 10.08 N 106.20 E
Moccasin, Calif., U.S. 216 37.49 N 120.18 W
Moccasin, Ill., U.S. 209 39.09 N 88.45 W
Moc-chau 100 20.51 N 104.37 E
Mocha → Al-Mukhā 134 13.19 N 43.15 E
Mocha, Isla I 242 38.22 S 73.56 W
Mocheng 96 31.35 N 120.43 E
Mochh 113 32.45 N 71.31 E
Mochigase 86 35.20 N 134.12 E
Mochitlán 224 17.30 N 99.18 W
Mochizuki 84 36.16 N 138.22 E
Mocho, Arroyo ≃ 216 37.41 N 121.55 W
Mochov 50 50.08 N 14.50 E
Mochovoje 66 52.57 N 36.34 E
Mochudi 146 24.28 S 26.05 E
Močily 72 54.20 N 38.41 E
Mocímboa da Praia 144 11.20 S 40.21 E
Mocímboa do Rovuma 144 11.20 S 39.18 E
Möckeln @, Sve. 26 56.40 N 14.10 E
Möckeln @, Sve. 40 59.18 N 14.30 E
Möckern 50 52.08 N 11.57 E
Mockfjärd 40 60.30 N 14.58 E
Mockhorn Island I 198 37.13 N 75.53 W
Möckmühl 52 49.19 N 9.22 E
Mockrehna 50 51.30 N 12.49 E
Mocksville 182 35.54 N 80.34 W
Moclips 214 47.14 N 124.13 W
Mocó ≃ 236 1.49 S 66.48 W
Môco, Serra ∧ 142 12.28 S 15.10 E
Mocoa 236 1.09 N 76.37 W
Mococa 246 21.28 S 47.01 W
Mocoduene 146 23.40 S 35.10 E
Mocomoco 238 15.22 S 68.59 W
Mocoretá 242 30.38 S 57.58 W
Mocorito 222 25.29 N 107.55 W
Moctezuma, Méx. 222 29.48 N 109.42 W
Moctezuma, Méx. 224 22.45 N 101.05 W
Moctezuma ≃, Méx. 222 29.09 N 109.40 W
Moctezuma ≃, Méx. 224 21.59 N 98.34 W
Mocuba 144 16.50 S 36.59 E
Mocubúri 144 14.39 S 38.54 E
Mocubúri ≃ 144 14.10 S 40.31 E
Močurica ≃ 38 42.31 N 26.32 E
Modane 56 45.12 N 6.40 E
Modaomen C 90 22.08 N 113.24 E
Modāsa 110 23.28 N 73.18 E
Modbury 44 50.21 N 3.53 W
Modder ≃ 148 29.02 S 24.37 E
Modderbee 263d 26.10 S 28.24 E
Modderfontein 148 26.05 S 28.10 E
Modderfontein ≃ 263d 26.13 S 28.10 E
Modderrivier 148 29.02 S 24.38 E
Model City 274a 43.11 N 78.59 W
Modena, It. 58 44.40 N 10.55 E
Modena, N.Y., U.S. 200 41.40 N 74.07 W
Modena □[4] 58 44.30 N 10.54 E
Moder ≃ 52 48.49 N 8.06 E
Möderath 52 50.53 N 6.43 E
Modern Art, Museum of ʊ 266 40.46 N 73.58 W
Modeste, Mount ∧ 214 48.37 N 124.06 W
Modesto, Calif., U.S. 216 37.39 N 121.00 W
Modesto, Ill., U.S. 209 39.29 N 89.59 W
Modesto City-County Airport ⊠ 216 37.39 N 120.57 W
Modesto Main Canal ≚ 216 37.39 N 120.27 W
Modesto Reservoir @[1] 216 37.26 N 121.58 W
Modica 36 36.51 N 14.47 E
Modigliana 60 44.09 N 11.47 E
Modjamboli 142 2.28 N 22.06 E
Modjeska 270 33.43 N 117.37 W
Mödling 254b 48.05 N 16.17 E
Mödling ≃ 254b 48.04 N 16.22 E
Modo 130 5.29 N 30.38 E
Modoc 208 40.03 N 85.08 W
Modon ≃ 46 47.16 N 1.27 E
Modowi 154 4.05 S 134.39 E
Modra, Česko. 30 48.21 N 17.17 E
Modra, Tchad 136 20.43 N 17.42 E
Modra Špilja •[5] 36 43.00 N 16.02 E
Modriča 38 44.57 N 18.18 E
Mo-duc 100 14.57 N 108.53 E
Moe 159 38.10 S 146.15 E
Moe ≃, Austl. 159 38.08 S 146.17 E
Moe ≃, Qué., Can. 196 45.19 N 71.49 W
Moecherville 206 41.44 N 88.17 W
Moeda 245 20.20 S 44.03 W
Moehau ∧ 162 36.35 S 175.24 E
Moel Fferna ∧ 44 52.57 N 3.18 W
Moelv 26 60.56 N 10.42 E
Moema 245 19.50 S 45.24 W
Moen 46 50.46 N 3.24 E
Moen I 165c 7.26 N 151.52 E
Moena 58 46.22 N 11.39 E
Moengo 240 5.37 N 54.24 W
Moenkopi 190 36.07 N 111.13 W
Moenkopi Wash ∨ 190 36.54 N 111.26 W
Moeraki Point ≻ 162 45.22 S 170.52 E
Moeranyah Lake @ 156 33.02 S 143.58 E
Moerbeke, Bel. 46 51.10 N 3.56 E
Moerbeke, Bel. 46 50.45 N 3.55 E
Moerdijk 48 51.43 N 4.38 E
Moerewa 162 35.23 S 174.02 E
Moergestel 48 51.33 N 5.11 E
Moero, Lago → Mweru, Lake @ 144 9.00 S 28.45 E
Moers 52 51.27 N 6.37 E
Moers □[8] 253 51.32 N 6.36 E
Moersbach ≃ 253 51.33 N 6.36 E
Moesa ≃ 54 46.13 N 9.03 E
Moffat 42 55.20 N 3.27 W
Moffat Peak ∧ 162 45.02 S 168.07 E
Moffatt 212 31.12 N 97.28 W
Moffatt Lake @ 196 45.34 N 71.19 W
Moffat Water ≃ 42 55.18 N 3.25 W
Moffet Point ≻ 170 55.26 N 162.32 W
Moffett Field Naval Air Station ■ 216 37.24 N 122.03 W
Moffit 188 46.41 N 100.18 W
Mofolo 263d 26.14 S 27.53 E
Mofoluku 263a 6.33 N 3.20 E
Moga 113 30.48 N 75.10 E
Mogadiscio → Mogadisho 134 2.01 N 45.20 E
Mogadisho 134 2.01 N 45.20 E
Mogador → Essaouira 138 31.30 N 9.47 W
Mogadore 204 41.03 N 81.24 W

DEUTSCH
Name Seite Breite°′ Länge°′ E=Ost

Mogadore Reservoir @[1] 204 41.04 N 81.21 W
Mogadouro 34 41.20 N 6.39 W
Mogalakwena ≃ 146 23.00 S 28.40 E
Mogalo 142 3.10 N 19.04 E
Mogami ≃ 82 38.55 N 139.48 E
Moganshan ∧ 96 30.36 N 119.52 E
Moganshan ∧∧ 96 30.34 N 119.50 E
Mogapinyana 146 22.19 S 27.27 E
Mogaung 100 25.18 N 96.56 E
Mogdy 79 50.35 N 133.51 E
Mogees 275 40.06 N 75.19 W
Møgeltønder 41 54.56 N 8.49 E
Mogenstrup 41 55.11 N 11.53 E
Mogent ≃ 256d 41.33 N 2.15 E
Moggio Udinese 58 46.25 N 13.12 E
Mogi, Serra do ∧∧ 277b 23.47 S 46.20 W
Mogi das Cruzes 246 23.31 S 46.11 W
Mogielnica 30 51.42 N 20.43 E
Mogi-Guaçu 246 22.22 S 46.57 W
Mogi-Guaçu ≃ 245 20.53 S 48.10 W
Mogila-Bel'mak, Gora ∧[2] 68 47.20 N 36.35 E
Mogila-Mečetnaja, Gora ∧[2] 73 48.16 N 38.53 E
Mogilev → Mogil'ov 66 53.54 N 30.21 E
Mogilno 30 52.40 N 17.58 E
Mogil'ov, S.S.S.R. 66 53.54 N 30.21 E
Mogil'ov, S.S.S.R. 68 48.52 N 34.29 E
Mogil'ov-Podol'skij 68 48.27 N 27.48 E
Mogi-Mirim 246 22.26 S 46.57 W
Mogincual 144 15.35 S 40.25 E
Moglal, Wādī ∨ 130 19.18 N 34.29 E
Moglia 58 44.56 N 10.55 E
Mogliano Veneto 58 45.33 N 12.14 E
Mogoča 78 53.44 N 119.44 E
Mogoča ≃ 66 58.00 N 36.26 E
Mogočin 76 57.43 N 83.34 E
Mogod 78 48.15 N 103.05 E
Mogogh 130 8.26 N 31.19 E
Mogojto 78 54.25 N 110.27 E
Mogojtuj 78 51.17 N 114.55 E
Mogok 100 22.55 N 96.30 E
Mogollon Mountains ∧∧ 190 33.25 N 108.40 W
Mogollon Rim •[4] 190 32.30 N 111.00 W
Mogor 110 32.52 N 67.47 E
Mogotes 236 6.30 N 72.58 W
Mogotes, Punta ≻ 242 38.06 S 57.33 W
Mogotón, Cerro ∧ 226 13.45 N 86.23 W
Mograt Island I 130 19.30 N 33.15 E
Mogroum 136 11.06 N 15.25 E
Moguer 34 37.16 N 6.50 W
Mogyoród 254c 47.36 N 19.15 E
Mogyoródi-patak ≃ 254c 47.36 N 19.05 E
Mogzon 78 51.45 N 111.58 E
Mohács 30 45.59 N 18.42 E
Mohaka 162 39.07 S 177.11 E
Mohaka ≃ 162 39.07 S 177.12 E
Mohale's Hoek 148 30.07 S 27.26 E
Mohall 188 48.46 N 101.31 W
Moḥammadābād 118 30.53 N 61.28 E
Mohammadia 138 35.33 N 0.03 E
Mohammedia (Fedala) 138 33.44 N 7.24 W
Mohana 114 25.54 N 77.45 E
Mohangi 144 0.03 N 29.05 E
Mohania 114 25.11 N 83.37 E
Mohanpur, Bhārat 116 21.51 N 87.26 E
Mohanpur, Bhārat 262a 28.44 N 77.10 E
Mohanpur, Bngl. 116 23.24 N 90.36 E
Mohave, Lake @[1] 194 35.25 N 114.38 W
Mohawk, Mich., U.S. 180 47.18 N 88.26 W
Mohawk, N.Y., U.S. 200 43.00 N 75.00 W
Mohawk ≃ 200 42.47 N 73.42 W
Mohawk, East Branch ≃ 202 43.22 N 75.28 W
Mohawk, Lake @ 200 41.02 N 74.41 W
Mohawk Mountain ∧ 197 41.49 N 73.17 W
Mohawk Point ≻ 202 42.51 N 79.29 W
Mohe 79 53.29 N 122.19 E
Moheda 26 57.00 N 14.34 E
Mohegan 197 41.28 N 72.06 W
Mohegan Lake 200 41.19 N 73.51 W
Moheli I 147a 12.15 S 43.45 E
Mohelnice 30 49.46 N 16.55 E
Mohican ≃ 204 40.22 N 82.09 W
Mohican, Black Fork ≃ 204 40.35 N 82.17 W
Mohican, Cape ≻ 170 60.12 N 167.28 W
Mohican, Clear Fork ≃ 204 40.35 N 82.12 W
Mohican, Jerome Fork ≃ 204 40.45 N 82.23 W
Mohican, Lake Fork ≃ 204 40.27 N 82.12 W
Mohican, Muddy Fork ≃ 204 40.45 N 82.08 W
Mohican State Park ♠ 204 40.37 N 82.16 W
Mohicanville Dam ◆[6] 204 40.44 N 82.09 W
Mohicanville Reservoir @[1] 204 40.45 N 82.00 W
Mohili ◆[8] 262c 19.06 N 72.53 E
Mohinora, Cerro ∧ 222 26.06 N 107.04 W
Möhlau 50 51.44 N 12.21 E
Mohlesi Pass)(148 29.29 S 29.21 E
Möhlin 54 47.34 N 7.51 E
Mohmand □[8] 113 34.30 N 71.20 E
Möhne ≃ 48 51.27 N 7.57 E
Möhnestausee @[1] 48 51.29 N 8.08 E
Mohns Ridge ÷[3] 10 73.00 N 5.00 E
Mohnton 198 40.17 N 75.59 W
Mohnyin 100 24.47 N 96.22 E
Moho ≃ 226 16.04 N 88.52 W
Moholm 40 58.37 N 14.02 E
Mohon 52 49.45 N 4.44 E
Mohorn 50 51.00 N 13.28 E
Mohoro 144 8.08 S 39.10 E
Mohoru 144 1.01 S 34.07 E
Möhringen 54 47.57 N 8.46 E
Mohrsville 198 40.28 N 75.59 W
Mohrungen → Morąg 30 53.56 N 19.56 E
Moi 26 58.28 N 6.32 E
Moiano 60 41.05 N 14.32 E
Moindou 165f 21.42 S 165.41 E
Moinești 38 46.28 N 26.29 E
Moingbi 130 5.46 N 28.49 E
Moinhos 246 22.43 S 46.20 W
Moinkum 75 43.48 N 73.41 E
Mointy 76 47.13 N 73.21 E
Moiporá 245 16.34 S 50.42 W
Moira ≃ 202 44.09 N 77.23 W
Moiraba 240 2.27 S 49.25 W
Moira Lake @ 202 44.29 N 77.27 W
Moirans 56 45.20 N 5.34 E
Moirans-en-Montagne 54 46.26 N 5.44 E
Mõisaküla 66 58.06 N 25.11 E
Moisdon 32 47.37 N 1.22 W
Moisejeviči 66 53.13 N 28.17 E
Moisejevka, S.S.S.R. 73 49.14 N 39.51 E
Moisejevka, S.S.S.R. 76 58.05 N 76.16 E
Moisejevo Alabuška 66 51.54 N 42.06 E
Moisenay 251 48.34 N 2.44 E
Moisés Ville 242 30.43 S 61.29 W
Moisie 176 50.11 N 66.05 W
Moisie, Baie C 176 50.16 N 65.56 W
Moisling ◆[8] 48 53.50 N 10.38 E
Moison Creek ≃ 271 42.18 N 82.40 W
Moissac 32 44.06 N 1.05 E
Moïssala 136 8.21 N 17.46 E
Moisselles 251 49.03 N 2.20 E
Moisson 251 49.05 N 1.40 E
Moisson, Forêt de ♠ 251 49.03 N 1.39 E
Moissy-Cramayel 251 48.38 N 2.36 E
Moita 34 38.39 N 8.59 W
Moitaco 236 8.01 N 64.21 W

Symbols in the index entries represent the broad categories identified in the key at the right. Symbols with superior numbers (∧∧[2]) identify subcategories (see complete key on page *I* · 26).

Kartensymbole in dem Registerverzeichnis stellen die rechts in Schlüssel erklärten Kategorien dar. …mbole mit hochgestellten Ziffern (∧∧[2]) bezeichnen …bteilungen einer Kategorie (vgl. vollständiger … auf Seite *I* · 26).

Los símbolos incluídos en el texto del índice representan las grandes categorias identificadas con la clave a la derecha. Los símbolos con numeros en su parte superior (∧∧[2]) identifican las subcategorías (véase la clave completa en la página *I* · 26).

Les symboles de l'index représentent les catégories indiquées dans la légende à droite. Les symboles suivis d'un indice (∧∧[2]) représentent des sous-catégories (voir légende complète à la page *I* · 26).

Os símbolos incluídos no texto do índice representam as grandes categorias identificadas com a chave à direita. Os símbolos com números em sua parte superior (∧∧[2]) identificam as subcategorias (veja-se a chave completa à página *I* · 26).

∧	Mountain	Berg	Montaña	Montagne	Montanha
∧∧	Mountains	Berge	Montañas	Montagnes	Montanhas
)(	Pass	Pass	Paso	Col	Passo
∨	Valley, Canyon	Tal, Cañon	Valle, Cañón	Vallée, Canyon	Vale, Canhão
⌣	Plain	Ebene	Llano	Plaine	Planície
≻	Cape	Kap	Cabo	Cap	Cabo
I	Island	Insel	Isla	Île	Ilha
II	Islands	Inseln	Islas	Îles	Ilhas
•	Other Topographic Features	Andere Topographische Objekte	Otros Elementos Topográficos	Autres données topographiques	Outros Elementos Topográficos

ESPAÑOL — Nombre / Página / Lat.° / Long.° W=Oeste
FRANÇAIS — Nom / Page / Lat.° / Long.° W=Ouest
PORTUGUÊS — Nome / Página / Lat.° / Long.° W=Oeste

Moivre ≃ 52 48.52 N 4.28 E
Mõja I 26 59.26 N 18.55 E
Mojácar 34 37.08 N 1.51 W
Mojana, Caño ≃[1] 236 9.02 N 74.46 W
Mojave 218 35.03 N 118.10 W
Mojave ≃ 194 35.06 N 116.04 W
Mojave Desert ◆[2] 194 35.00 N 117.00 W
Mojave River Forks Reservoir ⊜[1] 218 34.20 N 117.15 W
Moji 75 38.59 N 74.24 E
Mojiang 92 23.28 N 101.39 E
Mojjero ≃ 64 68.44 N 103.42 E
Mojnalyk 78 51.18 N 95.33 E
Mojo 134 8.38 N 39.07 E
Mojoagung 105a 7.34 S 112.21 E
Mojokerto 105a 7.28 S 112.26 E
Mojosari 105a 7.31 S 112.33 E
Mojstrana 58 46.27 N 13.56 E
Moju 240 1.53 S 48.46 W
Moju ≃ 240 1.40 S 48.25 W
Mōka 84 36.26 N 140.01 E
Mokai 162 38.32 S 175.54 E
Mokambo 144 12.25 S 28.21 E
Mokameh 114 25.24 N 85.55 E
Mokane 209 38.41 N 91.53 W
Mokapu Peninsula ≻[1] 219c 21.27 N 157.45 W
Mokaria 142 2.00 N 23.20 E
Mokau 162 38.41 S 174.37 E
Mokau ≃ 162 38.42 S 174.37 E
Moke 92 30.14 N 100.01 E
Mokelumne ≃ 216 38.13 N 121.28 W
Mokelumne, Middle Fork ≃ 216 38.22 N 120.37 W
Mokelumne, North Fork ≃ 216 38.22 N 120.37 W
Mokelumne, South Fork ≃ 216 38.23 N 120.35 W
Mokelumne Aqueduct ≍[1] 216 37.54 N 122.07 W
Mokelumne Hill 216 38.18 N 120.42 W
Mokena 206 41.32 N 87.53 W
Mokhotlong 148 29.22 S 29.02 E
Mokil I[1] 14 6.40 N 159.47 E
Mokimbo 144 6.20 S 28.42 E
Mokino 70 57.27 N 49.11 E
Mokkoidumis 134 1.40 N 44.32 E
Moklakan 78 54.56 N 118.56 E
Möklinta 40 60.05 N 16.32 E
Mokochu, Khao ∧ 100 15.56 N 99.06 E
Mokokchūng 110 26.20 N 94.32 E
Mokolo, Cam. 136 10.45 N 13.48 E
Mokolo, Zaïre 142 1.57 N 18.05 E
Mokombe 142 0.14 S 23.48 E
Mokoreta ≃ 162 46.21 S 168.51 E
Mokou 263b 4.13 S 15.13 E
Mokpalin 100 17.26 N 96.53 E
Mokp'o 88 34.48 N 126.22 E
Mokraja Jel'muta 70 46.51 N 41.41 E
Mokraja Ol'chovka 70 50.28 N 44.59 E
Mokraja Sura ≃ 68 48.19 N 35.09 E
Mokraja Volnovacha ≃ 73 47.30 N 37.15 E
Mokrany 68 51.50 N 24.14 E
Mokrisset 34 34.59 N 5.20 W
Mokro-Jelančik 73 47.42 N 38.31 E
Mokrous 70 51.14 N 47.37 E
Mokrousovo 76 55.48 N 66.45 E
Mokrušinskoje 76 57.31 N 93.11 E
Mokryje Jaly ≃ 68 48.05 N 36.44 E
Mokryj Gašun 70 46.53 N 42.45 E
Mokryj Jelančik ≃ 73 47.08 N 38.20 E
Mokryj Kor 72 54.34 N 37.58 E
Mokša ≃ 70 54.44 N 41.53 E
Moksan 70 53.26 N 44.37 E
Moku 144 2.57 N 29.22 E
Mokuleia 219c 21.35 N 158.09 W
Mokumbusu 142 1.44 N 21.04 E
Mokvin 68 50.57 N 26.48 E
Mokwa 140 9.20 N 5.02 E
Mol 52 51.11 N 5.06 E
Mola di Bari 36 41.04 N 17.05 E
Molale 134 10.08 N 39.42 E
Molalla 214 45.09 N 122.35 W
Molalla ≃ 214 45.18 N 122.43 W
Molalla, North Fork ≃ 214 45.05 N 122.29 W
Molanda 142 2.28 N 20.48 E
Molanosa 174 54.30 N 105.33 W
Moláoi 38 36.48 N 22.52 E
Molaretto 56 45.10 N 7.00 E
Molat, Otok I 36 44.15 N 14.49 E
Molbergen 48 52.51 N 7.55 E
Molčanovka 73 46.52 N 38.37 E
Molčanovo 76 57.35 N 83.48 E
Mold 44 53.10 N 3.08 W
Moldary 76 50.47 N 78.29 E
Moldau → Vltava ≃ 30 50.21 N 14.30 E
Moldavia □[9] 38 46.30 N 27.00 E
Moldavian Soviet Socialist Republic → Moldavskaja Sovetskaja Socialističeskaja Respublika □[3] 68 47.00 N 29.00 E
Moldavskaja Sovetskaja Socialističeskaja Respublika □[3] 68 47.00 N 29.00 E
Molde 26 62.44 N 7.11 E
Moldes 242 33.38 S 64.36 W
Moldotau, Chrebet ∧ 75 41.35 N 74.40 E
Moldova ≃ 38 46.54 N 26.58 E
Moldova-Nouă 38 44.44 N 21.40 E
Moldoveanu ∧ 38 45.36 N 24.44 E
Môle ≃, Fr. 56 43.15 N 6.32 E
Mole ≃, Eng., U.K. 44 51.24 N 0.21 W
Mole ≃, Eng., U.K. 44 50.57 N 3.54 W
Môle, Cap du ≻ 228 19.50 N 73.25 W
Mole Creek 156 41.33 S 146.24 E
Mole Game Reserve ◆ 140 9.30 N 2.00 W
Molegbe 142 4.14 N 20.53 E
Molenbeek-St.-Jean 50 50.51 N 4.19 E
Molepolole 146 24.25 S 25.30 E
Moléson ∧ 54 46.33 N 7.01 E
Molétai 66 55.14 N 25.25 E
Mole Valley □[8] 250 51.16 N 0.18 W
Molfetta 36 41.12 N 16.36 E
Molibagu 102 0.23 N 123.59 E
Molidawadawoerzu-zizhiqi (Buxi) 79 48.28 N 124.27 E
Molières-sur-Cèze 56 44.15 N 4.09 E
Molimiao 79 44.34 N 121.54 E
Molina 242 35.07 S 71.17 W
Molina de Aragón 34 40.51 N 1.53 W
Molina de Segura 34 38.03 N 1.12 W
Molina di Ledro 58 45.56 N 10.46 E
Molinara 60 41.18 N 14.54 E
Moline, Ill., U.S. 180 41.30 N 90.31 W
Moline, Kans., U.S. 198 37.22 N 96.18 W
Moline, Mich., U.S. 206 42.44 N 85.40 W
Molinella 58 44.37 N 11.40 E
Molinges 54 46.21 N 5.46 E
Molingguan 79 41.50 N 118.50 E
Molini di Tures (Mühlen) 58 46.54 N 11.56 E
Moliniere Point ≻ 231k 12.05 N 61.45 W
Molino 184 30.43 N 87.20 W
Molino de Rosas 276a 19.22 N 99.13 W
Molinos 242 25.25 S 66.19 W
Molins de Rey 34 41.25 N 2.01 E
Moliro 144 8.13 S 30.34 E
Molise □[4] 60 41.35 N 14.30 E
Molkābād 118 34.32 N 52.35 E
Mölkau 50 51.20 N 12.26 E
Mölln 40 59.36 N 13.43 E
Mölln 58 46.50 N 13.26 E
Mollahašan 120 39.22 N 47.37 E
Mollāhāt 116 22.56 N 89.48 E

Mollakendi 120 38.36 N 39.20 E
Mollaro 58 46.16 N 11.05 E
Möllbrücke 58 46.50 N 13.22 E
Mölle 41 56.17 N 12.29 E
Möllen 253 51.35 N 6.42 E
Möllenbeck, D.D.R. 50 53.17 N 11.44 E
Möllenbeck, D.D.R. 50 53.23 N 13.20 E
Mollendo 238 17.02 S 72.01 W
Möllensee ⊜ 254a 52.26 N 13.51 E
Mollepata 238 13.31 S 72.32 W
Moller, Port C 170 55.51 N 160.25 W
Möllersdorf 254b 48.02 N 16.18 E
Mollet 256d 41.33 N 2.13 E
Mollia 56 45.49 N 8.02 E
Molliens-Vidame 46 49.53 N 2.01 E
Mollington 252 53.13 N 2.55 W
Mollis 54 47.05 N 9.04 E
Mölln 50 53.37 N 10.41 E
Mollösund 26 58.04 N 11.28 E
Mollusk 198 37.44 N 76.32 W
Molly Ann Brook ≃ 266 40.55 N 74.11 W
Mölnbo 40 59.03 N 17.25 E
Mölndal 26 57.39 N 12.01 E
Mölnlycke 26 57.39 N 12.09 E
Mölntorp 40 59.33 N 16.15 E
Molocaboc Island I 106 10.58 N 123.34 E
Moločansk 68 47.12 N 35.36 E
Moločnaja ≃ 68 46.42 N 35.20 E
Moločnoje 66 59.17 N 39.41 E
Moločnoje, Ozero ⊜ 68 46.30 N 35.20 E
Molócuè ≃ 144 17.03 S 38.52 E
Molodečno 66 54.19 N 26.49 E
Molodežnaja ◆[3] 9 67.35 S 46.35 E
Molodi 72 55.17 N 37.31 E
Molodo 140 14.14 N 6.02 W
Molodogvardejsk 73 48.20 N 39.40 E
Molodoj Tud 66 56.26 N 33.36 E
Molod'ožnyj 79 50.23 N 136.48 E
Mologa ≃ 66 58.50 N 37.11 E
Molokai I 219a 21.07 N 157.00 W
Molokča ≃ 72 56.15 N 38.45 E
Molokini I 219a 20.38 N 156.30 W
Molokovo, S.S.S.R. 66 58.10 N 36.45 E
Molokovo, S.S.S.R. 72 55.34 N 37.52 E
Molong 156 33.06 S 148.52 E
Molonglo ≃ 161b 35.15 S 148.58 E
Molopo ≃ 146 28.30 S 20.13 E
Molotkoviči 68 52.07 N 25.56 E
Molotov → Perm' 76 58.00 N 56.15 E
Molotovsk → Severodvinsk 24 64.34 N 39.50 E
Molou 136 13.42 N 21.44 E
Moloundou 142 2.03 N 15.10 E
Molowaie 142 5.47 S 23.20 E
Moloy 54 47.32 N 4.55 E
Mols Bjerge ∧[2] 41 56.13 N 10.32 E
Molsheim 54 48.32 N 7.29 E
Molson Lake ⊜ 174 54.12 N 96.45 W
Molteno 148 31.22 S 26.22 E
Moltke, Cape ≻ 165e 6.03 S 154.52 E
Molu, Pulau I 154 6.45 S 131.33 E
Moluca, Mar de la → Maluku, Laut ≂[2] 98 0.00 125.00 E
Molucas, Islas → Maluku II 98 2.00 S 128.00 E
Moluccas → Maluku II 98 2.00 S 128.00 E
Molucca Sea → Maluku, Laut ≂[2] 98 0.00 125.00 E
Molukken → Maluku II 98 2.00 S 128.00 E
Molumbo 144 15.27 S 30.15 E
Molundo 106 7.56 N 124.23 E
Moluques → Maluku II 98 2.00 S 128.00 E
Molveno, Lago di ⊜ 58 46.08 N 10.57 E
Molvoticy 66 57.25 N 32.20 E
Molžaninovo 72 55.56 N 37.22 E
Moma, Moç. 144 16.44 S 39.14 E
Moma, Zaïre 142 1.36 S 23.57 E
Moma ≃ 64 66.26 N 143.06 E
Momanga 142 18.12 S 21.42 E
Momats ≃ 154 5.20 S 137.47 E
Momax 224 21.56 N 103.19 W
Momba 148 8.28 S 32.40 E
Mombaça 240 5.45 S 39.38 W
Mombachito, Cerro ∧ 226 12.24 N 85.34 W
Mombacho, Volcán ∧[1] 226 11.50 N 85.58 W
Mombango 142 1.45 N 24.26 E
Mombaruzzo 58 44.46 N 8.27 E
Mombasa 144 4.03 S 39.40 E
Mombetsu 82a 44.21 N 143.22 E
Mombo 144 4.53 S 38.17 E
Mombongo 142 1.39 N 23.09 E
Momboyo ≃ 142 0.16 S 19.00 E
Mombuey 34 42.02 N 6.20 W
Mombum 154 8.23 S 138.51 E
Momčilgrad 38 41.32 N 25.25 E
Momence 206 41.10 N 87.40 W
Momfafa, Tanjung ≻ 154 0.18 S 131.20 E
Momi 165g 17.55 S 177.17 E
Momignies 46 50.02 N 4.10 E
Mommark 41 54.55 N 10.03 E
Mommenheim 52 48.45 N 7.39 E
Momo 142 1.52 N 11.48 E
Momotombo, Volcán ∧[1] 226 12.26 N 86.33 W
Momozaka 260 34.51 N 135.02 E
Mompog Island I 106 13.31 N 122.11 E
Mompog Pass ≍ 106 13.34 N 122.13 E
Mompono 142 0.04 N 21.48 E
Mompós 236 9.14 N 74.26 W
Momskij Chrebet ≪ 64 66.00 N 146.00 E
Mon 41 54.57 N 12.18 E
Møn I 41 55.00 N 12.20 E
Mon □ 100 20.20 N 94.54 E
Mona 190 39.49 N 111.51 W
Mona, Canal de la ≍ 228 18.30 N 67.45 W
Mona, Isla I 228 18.05 N 67.54 W
Mona, Punta ≻ 226 9.38 N 82.37 W
Monaca 204 40.41 N 80.17 W
Monachovo 78 49.09 N 38.07 E
Monaco 56 43.42 N 7.23 E
Monaco □[1] 22 56 43.45 N 7.25 E
Monadhliath Mountains ≪ 28 57.15 N 4.10 W
Monadnock, Mount ∧ 197 42.52 N 72.07 W
Monagas □[3] 236 9.20 N 63.00 W
Monaghan 28 54.15 N 6.58 W
Monaghan □[6] 28 54.10 N 7.00 W
Monagrillo 226 7.59 N 80.26 W
Monahans 186 31.36 N 102.54 W
Monahans Draw ∨ 186 31.55 N 101.46 W
Monahans Sandhills State Park ◆ 186 31.38 N 102.50 W
Monakino 79 43.24 N 133.29 E
Mona Lake ⊜ 206 43.11 N 86.15 W
Monango 188 46.10 N 98.43 W
Monapo 144 14.55 S 40.17 E
Monapo ≃ 144 15.07 S 40.33 E
Mona Quimbundo 142 9.55 S 19.58 E
Monarch 182 34.43 N 81.35 W
Monarch Mountain ∧ 172 51.54 N 125.53 W
Monarch Pass ≍ 190 38.30 N 106.19 W
Monarto South 158b 35.08 S 139.08 E
Monaš 70 46.58 N 50.36 E
Monashee Mountains ≪ 172 50.30 N 118.30 W
Monashee Provincial Park ◆ 172 50.28 N 118.11 W

Monash University ◆[2] 264b 37.55 S 145.08 E
Monasterolo di Savigliano 56 44.40 N 7.37 E
Monastir → Bitola, Jugo. 38 41.01 N 21.20 E
Monastir, Tun. 138 35.47 N 10.50 E
Monastyrišče 68 49.00 N 29.49 E
Monastyriska 68 49.06 N 25.11 E
Monastyrščina 66 54.21 N 31.50 E
Monatélé 142 4.16 N 11.12 E
Mona Vale 160 33.41 S 151.18 E
Monbulk 264b 37.52 S 145.25 E
Monbulk Creek ≃ 264b 37.54 S 145.15 E
Moncada, Esp. 256d 41.29 N 2.11 E
Moncada, Pil. 106 15.44 N 120.34 E
Moncalieri 56 45.00 N 7.41 E
Moncalvo 56 45.03 N 8.16 E
Monção, Bra. 240 3.30 S 45.15 W
Monção, Port. 34 42.05 N 8.29 W
Monceau-sur-Sambre 46 50.25 N 4.22 E
Mončegorsk 24 67.54 N 32.58 E
Mönchengladbach 52 51.12 N 6.28 E
Mönchengladbach, Flughafen ⊠ 253 51.14 N 6.29 E
Monchique 34 37.19 N 8.33 W
Mönchröden 52 50.18 N 11.03 E
Mönchweiler 54 48.06 N 8.25 E
Moncks Corner 182 33.12 N 80.01 W
Monclova 222 26.54 N 101.25 W
Moncontour 32 48.21 N 2.39 W
Moncoutant 32 46.43 N 0.35 W
Moncton 176 46.06 N 64.47 W
Mondai 242 27.05 S 53.25 W
Mondaino 60 43.51 N 12.41 E
Mondavio 60 43.40 N 12.58 E
Monday ≃ 242 25.33 S 54.41 W
Mondego ≃ 34 40.09 N 8.52 W
Mondego, Cabo ≻ 34 40.11 N 8.55 W
Mondeodo 102 3.33 S 122.12 E
Mondeor 263d 26.17 S 28.00 E
Mondfeld 50 49.47 N 9.25 E
Mondimbi 142 1.43 N 22.58 E
Mondo, Tan. 144 4.59 S 35.54 E
Mondo, Tchad 136 13.47 N 15.32 E
Mondolé, Monte ∧ 56 44.13 N 7.46 E
Mondolfo 60 43.45 N 13.06 E
Mondombe 142 0.53 S 22.45 E
Mondoñedo 34 43.26 N 7.22 W
Mondorf-les-Bains 52 49.31 N 6.16 E
Mondoro 144 14.40 N 1.57 W
Mondoubleau 46 47.59 N 0.54 E
Mondovi, It. 56 44.23 N 7.49 E
Mondovi, Wis., U.S. 180 44.34 N 91.40 W
Mondragon, Fr. 56 44.14 N 4.43 E
Mondragon, Pil. 106 12.31 N 124.45 E
Mondragone 60 41.07 N 13.53 E
Mondrain Island I 152 34.08 S 122.15 E
Mondsee 58 47.52 N 13.21 E
Mondsee ⊜ 58 47.49 N 13.23 E
Monds Island I 275 39.50 N 75.19 W
Mondy 78 51.40 N 100.59 E
Monee 206 41.25 N 87.45 W
Moneglia 56 44.14 N 9.30 E
Monemvasia 38 36.41 N 23.03 E
Monero 190 36.54 N 106.52 W
Moneron, Ostrov I 79 46.17 N 141.15 E
Monesiglio 56 44.28 N 8.07 E
Monessen 204 40.09 N 79.53 W
Monesterio 34 38.05 N 6.16 W
Monestier-de-Clermont 56 44.54 N 5.38 E
Monetnyj 76 57.03 N 60.53 E
Monett 184 36.55 N 93.55 W
Monette 184 35.53 N 90.21 W
Money Creek ≃ 206 40.40 N 88.58 W
Moneymore 42 54.42 N 6.40 W
Monfalcone 58 45.49 N 13.32 E
Monferrato □[9] 56 44.55 N 8.05 E
Monflanquin 32 44.32 N 0.46 E
Monforte 34 39.03 N 7.26 W
Monforte de Lemos 34 42.31 N 7.30 W
Monfort Heights 208 39.12 N 84.37 W
Monga 142 4.12 N 22.49 E
Mongaguá 246 24.06 S 46.37 W
Monga-Musenge 142 4.04 S 19.34 E
Mongala ≃ 142 1.53 N 19.46 E
Mongalla 144 5.12 N 31.46 E
Mongandjo 142 1.21 N 24.20 E
Mongat 256d 41.28 N 2.17 E
Mongaup ≃ 200 41.25 N 74.45 W
Mongaup Valley 200 41.40 N 74.47 W
Mongbwalu 144 1.57 N 30.02 E
Mongbyŏn-ni 261b 37.40 N 126.44 E
Mong-cai 100 21.32 N 107.58 E
Monge ∧ 256c 38.46 N 9.26 W
Mongeri 140 8.19 N 11.44 W
Mongers Lake ⊜ 152 29.15 S 117.05 E
Mönggümp'o 88 38.09 N 124.47 E
Mong Hai 100 20.46 N 99.49 E
Mong Hawm 100 23.51 N 98.20 E
Monghidoro 58 44.13 N 11.19 E
Mong Hpāyak 100 20.53 N 99.54 E
Mong Hsat 100 20.32 N 99.15 E
Monghyr 114 25.23 N 86.28 E
Monghyr □[5] 114 25.10 N 86.10 E
Mongi 154 6.35 S 147.35 E
Mongibello → Etna, Monte ∧[1] 36 37.46 N 15.00 E
Mông Kung 100 21.36 N 97.32 E
Mong Ma 100 21.37 N 99.54 E
Mong Mit 100 23.07 N 96.41 E
Mong Nai 100 20.31 N 97.52 E
Mong Nawng 100 21.39 N 98.08 E
Mongo, Tchad 136 12.11 N 18.42 E
Mongo, Ind., U.S. 206 41.41 N 85.17 W
Mongo ≃ 140 9.34 N 12.11 W
Mongo ≃ 78 53.57 N 113.50 E
Mongol Altajn Nuruu ≪ 80 47.00 N 92.00 E
Mongol Ard Uls → Mongolia □[1] 80 46.00 N 105.00 E
Mongolei → Mongolia □[1] 80 46.00 N 105.00 E
Mongol Els ◆[2] 78 47.45 N 94.30 E
Mongolia □[1] 80 46.00 N 105.00 E
Mongolie → Mongolia □[1] 80 46.00 N 105.00 E
Mongomo 142 1.38 N 11.19 E
Mongönmor't 78 48.11 N 108.29 E
Mongororo 136 12.01 N 22.28 E
Mongoumba 142 3.38 N 18.36 E
Mông Pai 100 19.44 N 97.05 E
Mông Pan 100 20.19 N 98.22 E
Mông Pawn 100 20.49 N 97.28 E
Mông Ping 100 22.22 N 99.02 E
Mongpong ≃ 106 12.44 N 120.48 E
Mongrando 56 45.31 N 8.00 E
Mongrove, Punta ≻ 224 17.56 N 102.11 W
Mông Si 100 23.20 N 98.23 E
Mongu 142 15.15 S 23.09 E
Mongu ≃ 263b 4.25 S 15.24 E
Mongua 142 16.43 S 15.23 E
Mông Yai 144 22.25 N 98.02 E
Monguelfo (Welsberg) 58 46.45 N 12.06 E
Monguno 136 12.40 N 13.35 E
Mông Yai 100 22.25 N 98.02 E
Mông Yawng 100 21.11 N 100.22 E
Monheim, B.R.D. 52 51.05 N 6.52 E
Monheim, B.R.D. 58 48.50 N 10.51 E
Moniaive 42 55.12 N 5.53 W
Monico 180 45.35 N 89.09 W
Monida Pass ≍ 192 44.33 N 112.18 W
Mon Idée 46 49.53 N 4.23 E
Monie 144 4.00 S 17.22 E
Monie Bay C 198 38.13 N 75.51 W
Monie Creek ≃ 198 38.13 N 75.50 W
Moninger 204 40.11 N 80.32 W
Monino 72 55.50 N 38.11 E
Moniquirá 236 5.52 N 73.36 W

Mõniste 66 57.35 N 26.33 E
Monistrol-d'Allier 56 44.57 N 3.38 E
Monistrol-sur-Loire 56 45.17 N 4.10 E
Monitor Range ≪ 194 38.45 N 116.30 W
Monitor Valley ∨ 194 39.00 N 116.40 W
Monjolo 246 22.49 S 42.57 W
Monk, Pointe ≻ 265a 45.29 N 73.57 W
Monkayo 106 7.50 N 126.03 E
Mönkebude 50 53.46 N 13.57 E
Monken Hadley ◆[8] 250 51.40 N 0.11 W
Monkey Bay 144 14.05 S 34.55 E
Monkey River 226 16.22 N 88.29 W
Moñki 30 53.24 N 22.49 E
Monkira 156 24.49 S 140.34 E
Monkoto 142 1.38 S 20.39 E
Monks Heath 252 53.16 N 2.14 W
Monkton 202 43.35 N 81.05 W
Monmouth, Wales, U.K. 44 51.50 N 2.43 W
Monmouth, Ill., U.S. 180 40.55 N 90.39 W
Monmouth, Ind., U.S. 206 40.52 N 84.57 W
Monmouth, Oreg., U.S. 192 44.51 N 123.14 W
Monmouth □[6] 198 40.16 N 74.17 W
Monmouth Beach 266 40.20 N 73.59 W
Monmouth Hills 266 40.24 N 74.00 W
Monmouth Junction 198 40.20 N 74.36 W
Monmouth Mountain ∧ 172 51.00 N 123.47 W
Monmouth Peak ∧ 192 44.48 N 123.33 W
Monnickendam 48 52.27 N 5.02 E
Monnow ≃ 44 51.48 N 2.42 W
Mono □[5] 140 6.45 N 1.50 E
Mono □[6] 216 38.18 N 119.22 W
Mono I 165e 7.21 S 155.34 E
Mono ≃ 140 6.17 N 1.51 E
Monobe 86 33.42 N 133.53 E
Monobe ≃ 86 33.32 N 133.41 E
Monocacy ≃, Md., U.S. 198 39.13 N 77.27 W
Monocacy ≃, Pa., U.S. 198 39.13 N 77.27 W
Monocacy Station 198 40.16 N 75.46 W
Monogarovo 72 54.42 N 38.45 E
Mono Lake ⊜ 194 38.00 N 119.00 W
Monolith 218 35.07 N 118.22 W
Monomoy Island I 197 41.35 N 69.59 W
Monomoy Point ≻ 197 41.33 N 70.02 W
Monon 206 40.52 N 86.53 W
Monona, Iowa, U.S. 180 43.03 N 91.23 W
Monona, Wis., U.S. 206 43.04 N 89.20 W
Monona, Lake ⊜ 206 43.03 N 89.22 W
Monongah 204 40.11 N 79.56 W
Monongahela 204 40.27 N 80.00 W
Monongahela ≃ 204 40.27 N 80.00 W
Monongahela Brook ≃ 275 39.47 N 75.09 W
Monongahela Seamount ◆[3] 14 26.30 S 179.05 W
Monopoli 36 40.57 N 17.19 E
Monor 30 47.21 N 19.27 E
Mono Road Station 265b 43.51 N 79.51 W
Monos I 222 18.27 N 89.02 W
Monóvar 34 38.26 N 0.47 W
Monowai, Lake ⊜ 162 45.52 S 167.27 E
Monpazier 32 44.41 N 0.54 E
Monponsett 197 42.01 N 70.51 W
Monponsett Pond ⊜ 273 42.01 N 70.51 W
Monreal 34 42.42 N 1.30 W
Monreal del Campo 34 40.47 N 1.21 W
Monreale 36 38.05 N 13.17 E
Monroe, Conn., U.S. 197 41.18 N 73.16 W
Monroe, Fla., U.S. 210 30.28 N 84.17 W
Monroe, Ga., U.S. 182 33.47 N 83.43 W
Monroe, Ind., U.S. 206 40.45 N 84.56 W
Monroe, Iowa, U.S. 180 41.31 N 93.06 W
Monroe, La., U.S. 184 32.33 N 92.07 W
Monroe, Mich., U.S. 184 41.55 N 83.24 W
Monroe, Nebr., U.S. 188 41.28 N 97.36 W
Monroe, N.J., U.S. 266 41.07 N 74.38 W
Monroe, N.C., U.S. 182 34.59 N 80.33 W
Monroe, N.Y., U.S. 200 41.20 N 74.11 W
Monroe, Ohio, U.S. 208 39.27 N 84.22 W
Monroe, Oreg., U.S. 192 44.19 N 123.18 W
Monroe, Utah, U.S. 190 38.38 N 112.07 W
Monroe, Va., U.S. 182 37.30 N 79.08 W
Monroe, Wash., U.S. 214 47.51 N 121.58 W
Monroe, Wis., U.S. 180 42.36 N 89.38 W
Monroe □[6], Fla., U.S. 210 25.10 N 81.10 W
Monroe □[6], Ill., U.S. 209 38.20 N 90.09 W
Monroe □[6], Ind., U.S. 208 39.10 N 86.26 W
Monroe □[6], Mich., U.S. 206 41.55 N 83.26 W
Monroe □[6], Mo., U.S. 209 39.30 N 92.00 W
Monroe □[6], N.Y., U.S. 200 43.10 N 77.36 W
Monroe □[6], Pa., U.S. 200 40.59 N 75.12 W
Monroe, Lake ⊜ 210 28.52 N 81.16 W
Monroe Bridge 197 42.43 N 72.57 W
Monroe Center, Conn., U.S. 197 41.20 N 73.12 W
Monroe Center, Ill., U.S. 206 42.06 N 89.00 W
Monroe City, Ind., U.S. 184 38.37 N 87.21 W
Monroe City, Mo., U.S. 209 39.39 N 91.44 W
Monroe City, Tex., U.S. 212 29.47 N 94.35 W
Monroe Lake ⊜[1] 208 39.05 N 86.25 W
Monroe Manor 206 41.36 N 86.40 W
Monroeton 200 41.43 N 76.30 W
Monroeville, Ala., U.S. 184 31.31 N 87.20 W
Monroeville, Ind., U.S. 206 40.58 N 84.52 W
Monroeville, N.J., U.S. 198 39.38 N 75.10 W
Monroeville, Ohio, U.S. 204 41.15 N 82.42 W
Monroeville, Pa., U.S. 204 40.26 N 79.47 W
Monroeville Mall ◆[9] 269b 40.26 N 79.48 W
Monrovia, Liber. 140 6.18 N 10.47 W
Monrovia, Calif., U.S. 218 34.09 N 118.03 W
Monrovia, Ind., U.S. 208 39.35 N 86.29 W
Monrovia Mountain Park ◆ 270 34.10 N 118.10 W
Monrovia Peak ∧ 270 34.13 N 117.58 W
Mons (Bergen), Bel. 46 50.27 N 3.56 E
Mons, Fr. 56 43.41 N 6.43 E
Monsanto, Parque Florestal de ◆ 256c 38.43 N 9.11 W
Monsarás, Ponta do ≻ 245 19.35 S 39.45 W
Monschau 52 50.33 N 6.14 E
Monse 102 4.07 S 123.15 E
Monsefú 238 6.52 S 79.52 W
Monselice 58 45.14 N 11.45 E
Monsenhor Hipólito 240 6.59 S 41.07 W
Monsenhor Paulo 246 21.46 S 45.33 W
Monsenhor Tabosa 240 4.47 S 40.04 W
Monserrato 36 39.15 N 9.08 E
Monsey 200 41.07 N 74.04 W
Monsheim, B.R.D. 52 49.38 N 8.12 E
Monsheim, B.R.D. 52 48.52 N 8.52 E
Mons Klint ◆[4] 41 54.58 N 12.33 E
Monsols 54 46.13 N 4.31 E
Monson, Maine, U.S. 178 45.17 N 69.30 W
Monson, Mass., U.S. 197 42.06 N 72.19 W
Monster 48 52.02 N 4.10 E
Mönsterås 26 57.02 N 16.26 E
Monsummano Terme 60 43.52 N 10.49 E
Montà 56 44.49 N 7.57 E
Montabaur 52 50.26 N 7.50 E
Montacute 44 50.57 N 2.43 W
Montafon ∨ 58 47.02 N 9.57 E
Montagano 60 41.39 N 14.40 E
Montagnana 58 45.14 N 11.28 E
Montagnola ◆[8] 267a 41.51 N 12.29 E
Montagrier 32 45.16 N 0.29 E
Montagu 148 33.45 S 20.08 E
Montague, P.E.I., Can. 176 46.10 N 62.39 W
Montague, Calif., U.S. 194 41.44 N 122.32 W

Montague, Mass., U.S. 197 42.32 N 72.32 W
Montague, Mich., U.S. 180 43.25 N 86.22 W
Montague, Tex., U.S. 186 33.40 N 97.43 W
Montague, Isla I 222 31.45 N 114.48 W
Montague City 197 42.35 N 72.35 W
Montague Island I 170 60.00 N 147.30 W
Montague Peak ∧ 170 60.15 N 147.01 W
Montagu Island I 18 58.25 S 26.20 W
Montaigle, Château de ⊥ 52 50.18 N 4.49 E
Montaigu 32 46.59 N 1.19 W
Montaigut-en-Combraille 32 46.11 N 2.38 E
Montainville 251 48.53 N 1.56 E
Montaione 60 43.33 N 10.55 E
Montaj-Taš 75 42.06 N 68.58 E
Montalba 212 31.53 N 95.38 W
Montalbán 34 40.50 N 0.48 W
Montalbancito 276c 10.28 N 66.59 W
Montalbano Elicona 36 38.02 N 15.02 E
Montalbano Ionico 36 40.17 N 16.34 E
Montalcino 60 43.03 N 11.29 E
Montaldo di Cosola 56 44.40 N 9.11 E
Montale 60 43.56 N 11.01 E
Montalegre 34 41.49 N 7.48 W
Montalet-le-Bois 251 49.03 N 1.50 E
Montalieu-Vercieu 56 45.49 N 5.24 E
Mont Alto 198 39.50 N 77.34 W
Montalto ∧ 36 38.10 N 15.55 E
Montalto delle Marche 60 42.59 N 13.36 E
Montalto di Castro 60 42.21 N 11.37 E
Montalto Ligure 56 43.56 N 7.51 E
Montalto Uffugo 36 39.25 N 16.10 E
Montalvin Manor 216 37.59 N 122.21 W
Montalvo 218 34.15 N 119.12 W
Montana, Schw. 54 46.18 N 7.29 E
Montana, Alaska, U.S. 170 62.05 N 150.04 W
Montana □[3] 168
Montana 192 47.00 N 110.00 W
Montana de Oro State Park ◆ 216 35.15 N 120.50 W
Montana Indian Reserve ◆[4] 172 52.43 N 113.25 W
Montanaro 56 45.14 N 7.51 E
Montánchez 34 39.13 N 6.09 W
Montandon 200 40.58 N 76.51 W
Montara 216 37.33 N 122.31 W
Montara Beach ◆ 272 37.33 N 122.31 W
Montara Mountain ≪ 272 37.32 N 122.27 W
Montargil 34 39.05 N 8.10 W
Montargis 46 48.00 N 2.45 E
Montataire 46 49.16 N 2.26 E
Montauban 32 44.01 N 1.21 E
Montauban, Lac ⊜ 196 46.52 N 72.10 W
Montauban-les-Mines 196 46.50 N 72.20 W
Montauk 178 41.03 N 71.57 W
Montauk Harbor C 197 41.04 N 71.55 W
Montauk Point ≻ 197 41.04 N 71.52 W
Montauroux 56 43.37 N 6.46 E
Monta Vista 216 37.19 N 122.03 W
Montazzoli 60 41.57 N 14.26 E
Montbard 46 47.37 N 4.20 E
Montbarrey 54 47.01 N 5.39 E
Montbazon 46 47.17 N 0.43 E
Montbéliard 54 47.31 N 6.48 E
Mont Belvieu 212 29.51 N 94.54 W
Montbenoit 54 46.59 N 6.28 E
Mont Blanc Tunnel du ◆[5] 54 45.50 N 6.53 E
Montblanch 34 41.22 N 1.10 E
Mont-Bonvillers 52 49.20 N 5.51 E
Montbovon 54 46.29 N 7.03 E
Montbozon 54 47.28 N 6.16 E
Montbrison 56 45.36 N 4.03 E
Montbron 32 45.40 N 0.30 E
Montbronn 52 48.59 N 7.19 E
Montcalm □[6] 196 46.20 N 74.20 W
Montceau-les-Mines 54 46.40 N 4.22 E
Montcenis 54 46.47 N 4.23 E
Mont Cenis, Col du ≍ 56 45.15 N 6.54 E
Mont Cenis, Lac du ⊜ 56 45.14 N 6.55 E
Montcevelles, Lac ⊜ 176 51.07 N 60.38 W
Montchanin, Fr. 54 46.45 N 4.27 E
Montchanin, Del., U.S. 275 39.47 N 75.35 W
Montchauvet 251 48.54 N 1.38 E
Montclair, Calif., U.S. 218 34.06 N 117.41 W
Montclair, N.J., U.S. 200 40.49 N 74.13 W
Montclair State College ◆ 266 40.51 N 74.12 W
Montcornet 46 49.41 N 4.01 E
Montcresson 200 41.32 N 75.37 W
Mont-de-Marsan 32 43.53 N 0.30 W
Montdidier 46 49.39 N 2.34 E
Mont Dore 165f 22.16 S 166.34 E
Monte, Castel del ⊥ 36 41.05 N 16.15 E
Monte, Lago del ⊜ 242 37.00 S 62.28 W
Monte Adone, Galleria di ◆[5] 58 44.21 N 11.25 E
Monteagle 184 35.15 N 85.50 W
Monteagudo 238 19.49 S 63.59 W
Monte Albán ⊥ 224 17.02 N 96.45 W
Monte Alegre, Bra. 240 2.01 S 54.04 W
Monte Alegre, Bra. 240 6.04 S 35.20 W
Monte Alegre ≃ 245 17.16 S 50.41 W
Monte Alegre de Goiás 245 13.14 S 47.10 W
Monte Alegre de Minas 245 18.52 S 48.52 W
Monte Alegre de Sergipe 240 10.02 S 37.33 W
Monte Alegre do Piauí 240 9.46 S 45.18 W
Monte Alegre do Sul 246 22.40 S 46.41 W
Monte Azul 245 15.09 S 42.53 W
Monte Azul Paulista 245 20.55 S 48.38 W
Montebello, Qué., Can. 196 45.39 N 74.56 W
Montebello, It. 56 45.00 N 9.06 E
Montebello, P.R. 230m 18.22 N 66.31 W
Montebello, Calif., U.S. 218 34.01 N 118.06 W
Montebello Ionico 36 37.59 N 15.45 E
Montebello Islands II 152 20.25 S 115.32 E
Montebello Vicentino 58 45.27 N 11.23 E
Montebelluna 58 45.46 N 12.02 E
Monte Belo 246 21.20 S 46.23 W
Montebourg 32 49.29 N 1.23 W
Monte Buey 242 32.55 S 62.27 W
Montecalvo Irpino 60 41.11 N 15.02 E
Monte Campatri 257a 41.48 N 12.44 E
Montecarlo 242 26.34 S 54.47 W
Monte Carlo □[8] 56 43.44 N 7.25 E
Montecarotto 60 43.31 N 13.04 E
Monte Caseros 242 30.15 S 57.39 W
Montecassiano 60 43.21 N 13.26 E
Montecassino, Abbazia di ◆[1] 60 41.29 N 13.48 E
Montecastrilli 60 42.39 N 12.29 E
Montecatini Terme 60 43.53 N 10.46 E
Monte Cavallo 58 46.21 N 12.49 E
Montecchio 60 43.18 N 12.25 E
Montecchio Emilia 58 44.42 N 10.27 E
Montecchio Maggiore 58 45.30 N 11.24 E
Montecelio 60 42.01 N 12.44 E
Montechiaro d'Asti 56 45.01 N 8.07 E
Montechiarugolo 60 43.17 N 11.11 E
Monte Chingolo ◆[8] 278 34.45 S 58.20 W
Monteciccardo 60 43.49 N 12.48 E
Montecilfone 60 41.54 N 14.50 E
Montecillos, Cordillera de ≪ 226 14.25 N 87.51 W

Montecito 194 34.26 N 119.39 W
Monte Comán 242 34.36 S 67.54 W
Montecosaro 60 43.19 N 13.37 E
Monte Creek 172 50.39 N 119.57 W
Montecreto 58 44.14 N 10.41 E
Montecristi, Ec. 236 1.03 S 80.40 W
Montecristi, Rep. Dom. 228 19.52 N 71.39 W
Monte Cristo 238 14.43 S 61.14 W
Monte Cristo, Cerro ∧ 226 14.25 N 89.21 W
Montecristo, Isola di I 36 42.20 N 10.19 E
Montecuccolo ◆[1] 58 44.19 N 10.50 E
Montedinove 60 42.58 N 13.35 E
Monte di Procida 60 40.48 N 14.03 E
Monte do Carmo 240 10.45 S 48.07 W
Monte Escobedo 224 22.18 N 103.35 W
Monte Estoril 256c 38.42 N 9.24 W
Montefalcione 60 40.58 N 14.53 E
Montefalco 60 42.54 N 12.39 E
Montefalcone di Val Fortore 60 41.20 N 15.00 E
Montefano 60 43.25 N 13.26 E
Montefeltro ◆[1] 60 43.50 N 12.30 E
Montefiascone 60 42.32 N 12.02 E
Montefiorino 58 44.22 N 10.37 E
Monteforte d'Alpone 58 45.25 N 11.17 E
Monteforte Irpino 60 40.54 N 14.42 E
Montefrio 34 37.19 N 4.01 W
Montegallo 60 42.50 N 13.19 E
Montegiorgio 60 43.08 N 13.32 E
Monte Giovi, Passo di (Jaufen Pass) ≍ 58 46.50 N 11.19 E
Montego Bay 231q 18.28 N 77.55 W
Montegranaro 60 43.14 N 13.38 E
Monte Grande 242 30.06 S 70.31 W
Monte Grande, Aeródromo ⊠ 278 34.48 S 58.28 W
Monte Grimano 60 43.52 N 12.29 E
Montegrotto Terme 58 45.19 N 11.46 E
Montegut 184 29.29 N 90.33 W
Monteiro 240 7.53 S 37.07 W
Monteiro Lobato 246 22.58 S 45.50 W
Monteith, Mount ∧ 172 55.45 N 122.30 W
Montejicar 34 37.34 N 3.30 W
Montejinni 154 16.40 S 131.45 E
Montelavar 256c 38.51 N 9.20 W
Monteleone di Puglia 60 41.10 N 15.15 E
Monteleone di Spoleto 60 42.39 N 12.58 E
Monteleone Sabino 60 42.14 N 12.51 E
Montelíbano 236 8.05 N 75.29 W
Montélimar 56 44.34 N 4.45 E
Monte Lindo ≃ 242 23.56 S 57.12 W
Montella 60 40.51 N 15.01 E
Montellano 34 37.00 N 5.34 W
Montello, Nev., U.S. 194 41.16 N 114.12 W
Montello, Wis., U.S. 180 43.48 N 89.20 W
Montelluco ◆[1] 60 42.43 N 12.45 E
Montelungo 58 44.24 N 9.54 E
Montelupo Fiorentino 60 43.44 N 11.01 E
Montemagno 56 44.59 N 8.20 E
Monte Maíz 242 33.12 S 62.36 W
Montemarano 60 40.55 N 15.00 E
Montemarciano 60 43.38 N 13.19 E
Montemayor, Meseta de ◆[1] 244 44.20 S 66.10 W
Montemiletto 60 41.01 N 14.54 E
Montemor 256c 38.49 N 9.12 W
Montemor ∧ 256c 38.49 N 9.12 W
Montemorelos 222 25.12 N 99.49 W
Montemor-o-Novo 34 38.39 N 8.13 W
Montemor-o-Velho 34 40.10 N 8.41 W
Montemurro 32 45.17 N 0.24 W
Montenegro 242 29.42 S 51.28 W
Montenegro → Crna Gora □[3] 38 42.30 N 19.18 E
Montenero 60 43.30 N 10.21 E
Montenero di Bisaccia 60 41.57 N 14.47 E
Montenero di Bisaccia 60 42.05 N 14.39 E
Monte Oliveto Maggiore, Abbazia del ◆[1] 60 43.12 N 11.32 E
Monte Pascoal, Parque Nacional de ◆ 245 16.54 S 39.24 W
Monte Patria 242 30.42 S 70.58 W
Montepescali 60 42.53 N 11.05 E
Monte Porzio Catone 257a 41.49 N 12.43 E
Monteprandone 60 42.55 N 13.50 E
Montepuez 144 13.07 S 39.00 E
Montepuez ≃ 144 12.32 S 40.27 E
Montepulciano 60 43.05 N 11.47 E
Monte Quemado 242 25.48 S 62.52 W
Monterado 102 0.45 N 109.08 E
Monterchi 60 43.29 N 12.07 E
Montereale 60 42.31 N 13.15 E
Montereale Valcellina 58 46.10 N 12.39 E
Montereau 46 47.51 N 2.34 E
Montereau-faut-Yonne 46 48.23 N 2.57 E
Montereau-sur-le-Jard 251 48.35 N 2.40 E
Monterey, Calif., U.S. 216 36.37 N 121.55 W
Monterey, Ind., U.S. 206 41.09 N 86.29 W
Monterey, Ky., U.S. 208 38.25 N 84.52 W
Monterey, Mass., U.S. 197 42.11 N 73.13 W
Monterey, N.Y., U.S. 200 42.18 N 77.03 W
Monterey, Tenn., U.S. 184 36.09 N 85.16 W
Monterey, Va., U.S. 178 38.25 N 79.35 W
Monterey □[6] 216 36.40 N 121.38 W
Monterey Bay C 216 36.45 N 121.55 W
Monterey Park 218 34.04 N 118.07 W
Monterey Peninsula Airport ⊠ 216 36.35 N 121.51 W
Montería 236 8.46 N 75.53 W
Monteriggioni 60 43.23 N 11.13 E
Montero 238 17.20 S 63.15 W
Monte Romano 60 42.16 N 11.54 E
Monteroni d'Arbia 60 43.14 N 11.25 E
Monteros 242 27.10 S 65.30 W
Monterosso al Mare 56 44.09 N 9.39 E
Monterotondo 60 42.03 N 12.37 E
Monterotondo Marittimo 60 43.09 N 10.51 E
Monterrey, Méx. 222 25.40 N 100.19 W
Monterrey, Méx. 224 16.05 N 93.23 W
Monterrico, Hipódromo de ◆ 276d 12.06 S 76.59 W
Monterubbiano 60 43.05 N 13.43 E
Montes Altos 240 5.50 S 47.04 W
Monte San Biagio 60 41.21 N 13.21 E
Monte San Giovanni Campano 60 41.38 N 13.31 E
Monte San Savino 60 43.20 N 11.43 E
Montesano, It. 36 40.16 N 15.43 E
Montesano, Wash., U.S. 214 46.59 N 123.36 W
Monte Santa Maria Tiberina 60 43.26 N 12.09 E
Monte Sant'Angelo 60 41.42 N 15.57 E
Monte Santo, Bra. 240 9.54 S 49.03 W
Monte Santo, Bra. 240 10.26 S 39.20 W
Monte Santo de Minas 246 21.12 S 46.59 W
Monte Santu, Capo di ≻ 36 40.05 N 9.44 E
Montesarchio 60 41.04 N 14.38 E
Montes Claros 245 16.43 S 43.52 W
Montescudaio 60 43.18 N 10.40 E
Montese 58 44.16 N 10.56 E
Monte Sereno 216 37.15 N 122.01 W
Monte Sião 246 22.26 S 46.34 W
Montesilvano 60 42.29 N 14.08 E
Montespaccato ◆[8] 257a 41.54 N 12.23 E
Montespertoli 60 43.38 N 11.04 E
Montespluga 58 46.30 N 9.21 E
Montesson 251 48.55 N 2.09 E
Montets, Col des ≍ 54 46.00 N 6.55 E
Monteux 56 44.02 N 5.00 E
Montevallo 184 33.06 N 86.52 W

≃ River / Fluss / Río / Rivière / Rio
≂ Canal / Kanal / Canal / Canal / Canal
⌊ Waterfall, Rapids / Wasserfall, Stromschnellen / Cascada, Rápidos / Chute d'eau, Rapides / Cascata, Rápidos
≍ Strait / Meeresstrasse / Estrecho / Détroit / Estreito
C Bay, Gulf / Bucht, Golf / Bahía, Golfo / Baie, Golfe / Baía, Golfo
⊜ Lake, Lakes / See, Seen / Lago, Lagos / Lac, Lacs / Lago, Lagos
≛ Swamp / Sumpf / Pantano / Marais / Pântano
❄ Ice Features, Glacier / Eis- und Gletscherformen / Accidentes Glaciales / Formes glaciaires / Acidentes Glaciares
◆ Other Hydrographic Features / Andere Hydrographische Objekte / Otros Elementos Hidrográficos / Autres données hydrographiques / Outros Elementos Hidrográficos

◆ Submarine Features / Untermeerische Objekte / Accidentes Submarinos / Formes de relief sous-marin / Acidentes Submarinos
□ Political Unit / Politische Einheit / Unidad Política / Entité politique / Unidade Política
◆ Cultural Institution / Kulturelle Institution / Institución Cultural / Institution culturelle / Instituição Cultural
⊥ Historical Site / Historische Stätte / Sitio Histórico / Site historique / Sitio Histórico
◆ Recreational Site / Erholungs- und Ferienort / Sitio de Recreo / Centre de loisirs / Sítio de Lazer
⊠ Airport / Flughafen / Aeropuerto / Aéroport / Aeroporto
■ Military Installation / Militäranlage / Instalación Militar / Installation militaire / Instalação Militar
◆ Miscellaneous / Verschiedenes / Misceláneo / Divers / Miscelânea

ENGLISH: Name | Page | Lat.°′ | Long.°′
DEUTSCH: Name | Seite | Breite°′ | Länge°′ E=Ost

Name	Page	Lat.	Long.
Montevarchi	60	43.31 N	11.34 E
Monte Verde	142	8.43 S	16.51 E
Monte Verde ≃	246	21.55 S	43.33 W
Monteverde Nuovo ◆[8]	257a	41.51 N	12.27 E
Montevergine, Santuario di ✠[1]	60	40.55 N	14.45 E
Montevideo	188	44.57 N	95.43 W
Montevideo □[5]	248	34.50 S	56.12 W
Monte Vista	190	37.35 N	106.09 W
Montévrain	251	48.53 N	2.45 E
Montezemolo	56	44.22 N	8.08 E
Montezuma, Ga., U.S.	182	32.18 N	84.02 W
Montezuma, Ind., U.S.	184	39.48 N	87.22 W
Montezuma, Iowa, U.S.	180	41.35 N	92.32 W
Montezuma, Kans., U.S.	188	37.36 N	100.27 W
Montezuma, N.Y., U.S.	200	43.00 N	76.42 W
Montezuma, Ohio, U.S.	206	40.29 N	84.33 W
Montezuma Castle National Monument ♠	190	34.30 N	112.00 W
Montezuma Creek ≃	190	37.17 N	109.20 W
Montezuma Hills ⩓[2]	272	38.07 N	121.51 W
Montezuma Slough ≃	216	38.04 N	121.52 W
Montfaucon, Fr.	52	49.17 N	5.08 E
Montfaucon, Fr.	56	45.10 N	4.18 E
Montfaucon, Schw.	54	47.17 N	7.03 E
Montfermeil	251	48.54 N	2.34 E
Montfleur	54	46.19 N	5.26 E
Montflorit	256d	41.29 N	2.08 E
Montfoort	48	52.03 N	4.57 E
Montfort, Fr.	32	48.08 N	1.58 W
Montfort, Wis., U.S.	180	42.58 N	90.26 W
Montfort-l'Amaury	251	48.47 N	1.49 E
Montfort-le-Rotrou	46	48.03 N	0.25 E
Montfort-sur-Risle	46	49.18 N	0.40 E
Mont Fouari, Réserve du ◆[4]	142	2.45 S	11.35 E
Montfrin	56	43.53 N	4.36 E
Montgé	251	49.02 N	2.45 E
Montgenèvre	56	44.56 N	6.43 E
Montgenèvre, Col de)(	56	44.56 N	6.44 E
Montgeron	251	48.42 N	2.27 E
Montgeroult	251	49.05 N	2.00 E
Montgesoye	54	47.05 N	6.12 E
Montgomery → Sāhīwāl, Pāk.	113	30.40 N	73.06 E
Montgomery, Wales, U.K.	44	52.33 N	3.03 W
Montgomery, Ala., U.S.	184	32.23 N	86.18 W
Montgomery, Ill., U.S.	206	41.44 N	88.21 W
Montgomery, La., U.S.	184	31.40 N	92.53 W
Montgomery, Mich., U.S.	206	41.47 N	84.48 W
Montgomery, Minn., U.S.	180	44.26 N	93.35 W
Montgomery, N.Y., U.S.	200	41.32 N	74.14 W
Montgomery, Pa., U.S.	200	41.10 N	76.52 W
Montgomery, Tex., U.S.	212	30.23 N	95.42 W
Montgomery, W. Va., U.S.	178	38.11 N	81.19 W
Montgomery □[6], Ill., U.S.	209	39.09 N	89.29 W
Montgomery □[6], Md., U.S.	198	39.05 N	77.09 W
Montgomery □[6], Mo., U.S.	209	38.57 N	91.27 W
Montgomery □[6], N.Y., U.S.	200	42.57 N	74.22 W
Montgomery □[6], Ohio, U.S.	208	39.45 N	84.15 W
Montgomery □[6], Pa., U.S.	198	40.07 N	75.21 W
Montgomery □[6], Tex., U.S.	212	30.18 N	95.30 W
Montgomery City	209	38.59 N	91.30 W
Montgomery Dam ◆[6]	204	40.39 N	80.24 W
Montgomery Knolls	274b	39.14 N	76.48 W
Montgomery Mall ◆[9]	274c	39.01 N	77.09 W
Montgomeryville	275	40.15 N	75.15 W
Montgomeryville Airport ⊠	275	40.15 N	75.14 W
Montguyon	32	45.13 N	0.11 W
Monthermé	52	49.53 N	4.44 E
Monthey	54	46.15 N	6.57 E
Monthois	52	49.19 N	4.43 E
Monthureux-sur-Saône	54	48.02 N	5.58 E
Monthyon	251	49.00 N	2.50 E
Monticelli d'Ongina	58	45.05 N	9.56 E
Monticello, Ark., U.S.	184	33.38 N	91.47 W
Monticello, Fla., U.S.	182	30.33 N	83.52 W
Monticello, Ga., U.S.	182	33.18 N	83.40 W
Monticello, Ill., U.S.	184	40.01 N	88.34 W
Monticello, Ind., U.S.	206	40.45 N	86.46 W
Monticello, Iowa, U.S.	180	42.15 N	91.12 W
Monticello, Ky., U.S.	184	36.50 N	84.51 W
Monticello, Minn., U.S.	180	45.18 N	93.48 W
Monticello, Miss., U.S.	184	31.33 N	90.07 W
Monticello, Mo., U.S.	209	40.07 N	91.43 W
Monticello, N.Y., U.S.	200	41.39 N	74.42 W
Monticello, Utah, U.S.	190	37.52 N	109.21 W
Monticello, Wis., U.S.	180	42.45 N	89.35 W
Monticello ⊥	178	38.00 N	78.30 W
Monticello Conte Otto	58	45.35 N	11.35 E
Monticello Dam ◆[6]	216	38.30 N	122.07 W
Montichiari	58	45.25 N	10.23 E
Monticiano	60	43.08 N	11.11 E
Montiel, Campo de ≚	34	38.46 N	2.44 W
Montier-en-Der	54	48.29 N	4.46 E
Montieri	60	43.08 N	11.01 E
Montieri, Poggio di ∧	60	43.08 N	11.00 E
Montiers-sur-Saulx	54	48.32 N	5.16 E
Montignac	32	45.04 N	1.10 E
Montigny	54	48.31 N	6.48 E
Montigny-devant-Sassey	52	49.26 N	5.09 E
Montigny-le-Bretonneux	251	48.46 N	2.02 E
Montigny-le-Roi	54	48.00 N	5.30 E
Montigny-lès-Cormeilles	251	48.59 N	2.12 E
Montigny-sur-Aube	54	47.57 N	4.46 E
Montijo, Esp.	34	38.55 N	6.37 W
Montijo, Pan.	226	7.59 N	81.03 W
Montijo, Port.	34	38.42 N	8.58 W
Montijo, Aeroporto ⊠	256c	38.42 N	9.02 W
Montijo, Golfo de C	236	7.40 N	81.07 W
Montilla	34	37.35 N	4.38 W
Montividiu	245	17.24 S	51.14 W
Montividiu ≃	245	17.10 S	50.57 W
Montivilliers	46	49.33 N	0.12 E
Montjay-la-Tour	251	48.55 N	2.40 E
Montjoie, Lac ⊜, Qué., Can.	196	45.25 N	72.06 W
Montjoie, Lac ⊜, Qué., Can.	196	46.17 N	75.08 W
Mont-Joli	176	48.35 N	68.11 W
Montjovet	56	45.43 N	7.40 E
Montjuich, Castillo de ⊥	256d	41.22 N	2.10 E
Montjuich, Estadio de ♠	256d	41.22 N	2.09 E
Montjuich, Faro de ◆[5]	256d	41.21 N	2.11 E
Montjuich, Parque de ♠	256d	41.21 N	2.09 E
Mont-Laurier	166	46.33 N	75.30 W
Montlebon	54	47.02 N	6.37 E
Montlhéry	46	48.38 N	2.16 E
Montlhéry, Tour de ✠	251	48.38 N	2.16 E
Montlignon	251	49.01 N	2.17 E
Montlouet	251	48.31 N	1.43 E
Mont-Louis	32	42.31 N	2.07 E
Montlouis-sur-Loire	46	47.23 N	0.50 E
Montluçon	32	46.21 N	2.36 E
Montluel	56	45.51 N	5.03 E
Montmagny, Qué., Can.	176	46.59 N	70.33 W
Montmagny, Fr.	251	48.58 N	2.21 E
Montmajour, Abbaye de ✠[1]	56	43.43 N	4.40 E
Montmartre ◆[8]	251	48.53 N	2.21 E
Montmédy	52	49.31 N	5.22 E
Montmélian	56	45.30 N	6.04 E
Montmeló	256d	41.33 N	2.15 E
Montmerle-sur-Saône	54	46.05 N	4.46 E
Montmin	56	45.48 N	6.16 E
Montmirail, Fr.	46	48.52 N	3.32 E
Montmirail, Fr.	46	48.06 N	0.48 E
Montmirey-le-Château	54	47.13 N	5.32 E
Montmoreau-Saint-Cybard	32	45.24 N	0.08 E
Montmorenci	206	40.28 N	87.02 W
Montmorency, Austl.	264b	37.43 S	145.07 E
Montmorency, Qué., Can.	196	46.52 N	71.09 W
Montmorency ≃	176	46.53 N	71.07 W
Montmorency, Forêt de ♠	251	49.02 N	2.16 E
Montmorillon	32	46.26 N	0.52 E
Montmort	46	48.55 N	3.49 E
Monto	156	24.52 S	151.07 E
Montodine	56	45.17 N	9.42 E
Montoggio	56	44.31 N	9.03 E
Montoire-sur-le-Loir	46	47.45 N	0.52 E
Montone	60	43.22 N	12.20 E
Montone ≃, It.	58	44.24 N	12.14 E
Montone ≃, It.	60	43.22 N	12.20 E
Montopoli in Val d'Arno	60	43.40 N	10.45 E
Mont Orford, Parc du ♠	196	45.22 N	72.05 W
Montorio al Vomano	60	42.35 N	13.38 E
Montorio nei Frentani	60	41.46 N	14.55 E
Montorio Veronese	58	45.27 N	11.04 E
Montornés del Vallés	256d	41.33 N	2.16 E
Montoro	34	38.01 N	4.23 W
Mont'Orso, Galleria di ◆[5]	60	41.20 N	13.15 E
Montour □[6]	200	40.58 N	76.37 W
Montour Falls	200	42.21 N	76.51 W
Montour Run ≃, Pa., U.S.	269b	40.31 N	80.08 W
Montour Run ≃, Pa., U.S.	269b	40.36 N	79.57 W
Montoursville	200	41.15 N	76.55 W
Mont Park	264b	37.43 S	145.04 E
Montparnasse ◆[5]	251	48.51 N	2.19 E
Montpelier, Jam.	231q	18.22 N	77.56 W
Montpelier, Idaho, U.S.	192	42.19 N	111.18 W
Montpelier, Ind., U.S.	206	40.33 N	85.17 W
Montpelier, Miss., U.S.	184	33.43 N	88.57 W
Montpelier, Ohio, U.S.	206	41.35 N	84.36 W
Montpelier, Vt., U.S.	178	44.16 N	72.35 W
Montpellier	56	43.36 N	3.53 E
Montpezat-sous-Bauzon	56	44.43 N	4.12 E
Mont-Pichet	251	48.53 N	2.54 E
Montpon-Ménesterol	32	45.00 N	0.10 E
Montpont-en-Bresse	54	46.33 N	5.09 E
Montréal, Qué., Can.	196		
	265a	45.31 N	73.34 W
Montréal, Fr.	46	47.32 N	4.02 E
Montreal, Wis., U.S.	180	46.26 N	90.14 W
Montreal ≃, Ont., Can.	180	47.14 N	84.39 W
Montreal ≃, Ont., Can.	180	47.08 N	79.27 W
Montreal ≃, Sask., Can.	174	55.06 N	105.19 W
Montreal ≃, U.S.	180	46.44 N	90.25 W
Montréal, Île de I	196	45.30 N	73.40 W
Montréal, Université de ✠[2]	265a	45.30 N	73.37 W
Montréal-Est	196	45.38 N	73.31 W
Montreal International Airport ⊠	265a	45.28 N	73.45 W
Montreal Lake	174	54.03 N	105.46 W
Montreal Lake ⊜	174	54.20 N	105.40 W
Montreal Lake Indian Reserve ◆[4]	174	54.00 N	105.45 W
Montréal-Nord	196	45.36 N	73.38 W
Montreal Water Works Aqueduct ≖[1]	265a	45.26 N	73.36 W
Montrésor	46	47.09 N	1.12 E
Montret	54	46.41 N	5.07 E
Montreuil	251	48.52 N	2.27 E
Montreuil-Bellay	32	47.08 N	0.09 W
Montreuil-sous-Bois	46	48.52 N	2.26 E
Montreuil-sur-Mer	46	50.28 N	1.46 E
Montreux	54	46.26 N	6.55 E
Montrevel-en-Bresse	54	46.20 N	5.08 E
Montrichard	46	47.21 N	1.11 E
Montriond	54	46.12 N	6.41 E
Montrond-les-Bains	56	45.38 N	4.14 E
Montrose, Austl.	264b	37.49 S	145.21 E
Montrose, Scot., U.K.	28	56.43 N	2.29 W
Montrose, Calif., U.S.	218	34.12 N	118.13 W
Montrose, Colo., U.S.	190	38.29 N	107.53 W
Montrose, Iowa, U.S.	180	40.31 N	91.25 W
Montrose, Mich., U.S.	180	43.11 N	83.54 W
Montrose, N.Y., U.S.	200	41.15 N	73.56 W
Montrose, Ohio, U.S.	204	41.08 N	81.37 W
Montrose, Pa., U.S.	200	41.50 N	75.53 W
Montrose, S. Dak., U.S.	188	43.42 N	97.11 W
Montrose Harbor C	268	41.58 N	87.38 W
Montrose Hill	269b	40.30 N	79.51 W
Montross	198	38.06 N	76.50 W
Montrouge	251	48.49 N	2.19 E
Mont-Royal	196	45.31 N	73.39 W
Mont Royal, Parc ♠	265a	45.31 N	73.35 W
Mont Royal Tunnel ◆[5]	265a	45.31 N	73.38 W
Montry	251	48.53 N	2.50 E
Monts	46	47.17 N	0.37 E
Monts, Pointe des ≻	176	49.20 N	67.23 W
Mont-Saint-Aignan	46	47.16 N	1.23 E
Mont-Sainte-Anne, Parc du ♠	176	47.08 N	70.55 W
Mont-Saint-Hilaire	196	45.34 N	73.12 W
Mont-Saint-Martin	52	49.32 N	5.47 E
Mont-Saint-Michel → Le Mont Saint-Michel ✠[1]	32	48.38 N	1.32 W
Mont-Saint-Vincent	54	46.38 N	4.29 E
Montsauche	46	47.13 N	4.01 E
Montsec	52	48.53 N	5.43 E
Montserrado □[6]	140	6.40 N	10.40 W
Montserrat □[2]	220		
	228	16.45 N	62.12 W
Montserrat, Monasterio de ✠[1]	34	41.36 N	1.49 E
Montsoult	251	49.04 N	2.19 E
Mont-sur-Vaudrey	54	46.58 N	5.36 E
Mont Tremblant, Parc du ♠	196	46.42 N	74.20 W
Montuenga	34	41.03 N	4.37 W
Montvale, N.J., U.S.	266	41.03 N	74.02 W
Montvale, Va., U.S.	182	37.23 N	79.43 W
Montverde	210	28.36 N	81.41 W
Montville, Conn., U.S.	197	41.27 N	72.08 W
Montville, N.J., U.S.	266	40.52 N	74.22 W
Montville, Ohio, U.S.	204	41.36 N	81.03 W
Montville Airpark ⊠	266	40.56 N	74.20 W
Monument, S. Afr.	263d	26.06 S	27.43 E
Monument, Oreg., U.S.	192	44.49 N	119.25 W
Monument, Pa., U.S.	204	41.07 N	77.42 W
Monument Beach	197	41.43 N	70.37 W
Monument Draw V, U.S.	186	32.26 N	102.10 W
Monument Draw V, Tex., U.S.	186	30.51 N	102.33 W
Monument Hill State Historic Site ⊥	212	29.53 N	96.54 W
Monumento, Bra.	246	22.44 S	43.51 W
Monumento, Méx.	222	29.23 N	111.00 W
Monument Peak ∧, Colo., U.S.	190	39.43 N	107.55 W
Monument Peak ∧, Idaho, U.S.	192	42.07 N	114.14 W
Monument Valley V	190	37.05 N	110.20 W
Monveda	142	2.57 N	21.27 E
Monyo	100	17.59 N	95.30 E
Monywa	100	22.05 N	95.08 E
Monza	56	45.35 N	9.16 E
Monze	144	16.16 S	27.28 E
Monzen	82	37.17 N	136.46 E
Monzón, Esp.	34	41.55 N	0.12 E
Monzón, Perú	238	9.10 S	76.23 W
Moóca ◆[8]	277b	23.33 S	46.35 W
Moóca, Ribeirão da ≃	277b	23.36 S	46.35 W
Moodie Island I	166	64.37 N	65.30 W
Moodus	197	41.30 N	72.27 W
Moodus Reservoir ⊜[1]	197	41.30 N	72.24 W
Moody	212	31.19 N	97.21 W
Moody Air Force Base ■	182	30.59 N	83.11 W
Moody Wood Dale Airport ⊠	268	41.59 N	87.58 W
Mooers	196	44.58 N	73.35 W
Mooi ≃	148	28.45 S	30.34 E
Mooirivier	148	29.13 S	29.50 E
Mook	48	51.45 N	5.54 E
Mookane	146	24.59 S	24.33 E
Mooketsi	146	23.35 S	30.05 E
Moolalloo Point ≻	158a	31.48 S	115.44 E
Moolawatana	156	29.55 S	139.43 E
Moolman	148	27.10 S	30.53 E
Mooloogool	152	26.06 S	119.05 E
Moon	204	40.31 N	80.14 W
Moon ≃	202	45.07 N	79.55 W
Moonachie	266	40.50 N	74.03 W
Moonachie Creek ≃	266	40.48 N	74.03 W
Moonah Creek ≃	156	22.03 S	138.33 E
Moon Crest	269b	40.32 N	80.11 W
Moondarra Reservoir ⊜[1]	159	38.04 S	146.22 E
Moonee Valley Racecourse ♠	264b	37.46 S	144.56 E
Moonie ≃	156	29.19 S	148.43 E
Moon Island I, Ont., Can.	202	45.09 N	80.01 W
Moon Island I, Mass., U.S.	273	42.18 N	71.00 W
Moon Run	204	40.30 N	80.14 W
Moonta	158b	34.04 S	137.35 E
Moonyoonooka	152	28.47 S	114.43 E
Moor, Kepulauan II	154	2.57 S	135.45 E
Moora	152	30.39 S	116.00 E
Moorabbin	159	37.56 S	145.02 E
Moorabbin Airport ⊠	264b	37.59 S	145.09 E
Mooraberree	156	25.14 S	140.59 E
Moorabool ≃	159	38.09 S	144.19 E
Moorarie	152	25.56 S	117.35 E
Moorburg	48	53.17 N	7.53 E
Moorcroft	188	44.16 N	104.57 W
Moordorf	48	53.28 N	7.23 E
Moordrecht	48	51.59 N	4.40 E
Moore, Austl.	161a	26.53 S	152.18 E
Moore, Eng., U.K.	252	53.21 N	2.38 W
Moore, Idaho, U.S.	192	43.44 N	113.22 W
Moore, Mont., U.S.	192	46.59 N	109.42 W
Moore, Okla., U.S.	186	35.20 N	97.29 W
Moore, Tex., U.S.	186	29.03 N	99.01 W
Moore ≃	152	31.22 S	115.29 E
Moore, Lake ⊜	152	29.50 S	117.35 E
Moorea I	164s	17.32 S	149.50 W
Moorebank	264a	33.56 S	150.56 E
Moore Creek ≃	202	45.29 N	77.58 W
Moorefield, Ky., U.S.	208	38.16 N	83.56 W
Moorefield, Ohio, U.S.	204	40.12 N	81.10 W
Moorefield, W. Va., U.S.	178	39.04 N	78.58 W
Moore Haven	210	26.50 N	81.05 W
Moore Haven Lock ◆[5]	210	26.51 N	81.05 W
Moore Lake ⊜, Ont., Can.	202	45.26 N	78.01 W
Moore Lake ⊜, Ont., Can.	202	44.48 N	78.48 W
Moore Lake ⊜, Mich., U.S.	271	42.37 N	83.36 W
Mooreland, Ind., U.S.	208	39.60 N	85.15 W
Mooreland, Okla., U.S.	186	36.26 N	99.12 W
Moore Park ♠	264a	33.54 S	151.13 E
Moore Point ≻	265b	43.48 N	79.03 W
Moore Reservoir ⊜[1]	178	44.25 N	71.50 W
Mooresburg	200	40.59 N	76.43 W
Moores Creek National Military Park ♠	182	34.24 N	78.08 W
Moores Hill	208	39.07 N	85.05 W
Moore Station	212	32.11 N	95.35 W
Moorestown	198	39.58 N	74.57 W
Moorestown Airport ⊠	275	39.59 N	74.56 W
Moorestown Mall ◆[9]	275	39.56 N	74.58 W
Mooresville, Ind., U.S.	208	39.37 N	86.22 W
Mooresville, N.C., U.S.	182	35.35 N	80.48 W
Mooreville	271	42.06 N	83.44 W
Moorfoot Hills ⩓[2]	42	55.45 N	3.02 W
Moorhead, Minn., U.S.	188	46.53 N	96.45 W
Moorhead, Miss., U.S.	184	33.27 N	90.30 W
Mooring	212	30.41 N	96.33 W
Mooringsport	184	32.41 N	93.58 W
Moorooka	161a	27.32 S	153.02 E
Mooroolbark	264b	37.47 S	145.19 E
Moorpark	218	34.17 N	118.53 W
Moorreesburg	148	33.08 S	18.40 E
Moorrege	48	53.40 N	9.39 E
Moorriem	48	53.15 N	8.19 E
Moorsel	46	50.57 N	4.06 E
Moorside	252	53.34 N	2.04 W
Moors Island I	228	26.18 N	77.33 W
Moorslede	46	50.53 N	3.04 E
Moos → Moso, It.	58	46.41 N	12.23 E
Moos → Moso in Passiria, It.	58	46.50 N	11.10 E
Moosach ◆[8]	58	48.11 N	11.31 E
Moosbrunn	254b	48.01 N	16.28 E
Moosburg	30	48.29 N	11.57 E
Moose ≃	202	43.37 N	75.22 W
Moose Creek	196	45.15 N	74.58 W
Moose Creek ≃	196	45.23 N	75.04 W
Moosehead Lake ⊜	178	45.40 N	69.40 W
Mooseheart	206	41.49 N	88.20 W
Moose Heights	172	53.05 N	122.30 W
Moose Hill ∧[2]	273	42.07 N	71.13 W
Moose Island I	174	51.42 N	97.10 W
Moose Jaw	174	50.23 N	105.32 W
Moose Jaw ≃	174	50.34 N	105.17 W
Moose Lake, Man., Can.	174	53.43 N	100.20 W
Moose Lake, Minn., U.S.	180	46.26 N	92.45 W
Moose Lake ⊜, Alta., Can.	172	54.15 N	110.55 W
Moose Lake ⊜, Man., Can.	174	56.30 N	95.15 W
Moose Lake ⊜, Ont., Can.	202	45.09 N	78.28 W
Mooselookmeguntic Lake ⊜	178	44.53 N	70.48 W
Moose Mountain ∧	174	49.45 N	102.37 W
Moose Mountain Creek ≃	174	49.12 N	102.10 W
Moose Mountain Provincial Park ♠	174	49.48 N	102.25 W
Moose Pass	170	60.29 N	149.22 W
Moosomin	174	50.07 N	101.40 W
Moosomin Indian Reserve ◆[4]	174	53.06 N	108.14 W
Moosonee	166	51.17 N	80.39 W
Moosup	197	41.43 N	71.53 W
Mooti	134	0.40 N	41.58 E
Moots Creek ≃	206	40.32 N	86.47 W
Mopane	146	22.37 S	29.52 E
Mopanyang ⊔	90	29.32 N	122.16 E
Mopeia Velha	146	17.59 S	35.44 E
Mopelia I[1]	14	16.50 S	153.55 W
Mopipi	146	21.07 S	24.55 E
Mopo	90	33.07 N	113.02 E
Mopoï	144	5.08 N	26.55 E
Moppo → Mokp'o	88	34.48 N	126.22 E
Mopti	140	14.30 N	4.12 W
Mopti □[4]	140	14.40 N	4.15 W
Moqokorei	134	4.03 N	46.08 E
Moquegua	238	17.12 S	70.56 W
Moquegua □[5]	238	16.50 S	70.55 W
Mór	30	47.23 N	18.12 E
Mor ≃	116	24.01 N	88.03 E
Mora, Bhārat	262c	18.54 N	72.56 E
Mora, Cam.	136	11.03 N	14.09 E
Mora, Esp.	34	39.41 N	3.46 W
Mora, Port.	34	38.56 N	8.10 W
Mora, Sve.	26	61.00 N	14.33 E
Mora, Minn., U.S.	180	45.53 N	93.18 W
Mora, N. Mex., U.S.	190	35.58 N	105.20 W
Mora ≃	186	35.44 N	104.23 W
Moraby	40	60.23 N	15.35 E
Morača, Manastir ✠[1]	38	42.44 N	19.20 E
Morada	216	38.01 N	121.15 W
Morādābād	114	28.50 N	78.47 E
Morada Nova	240	5.07 S	38.23 W
Morada Nova de Minas	245	18.37 S	45.22 W
Mora de Rubielos	34	40.15 N	0.45 W
Morado, Cerro ∧	242	22.49 S	65.26 W
Moraduccio	60	44.10 N	11.29 E
Morafenobe	147b	17.49 S	44.55 E
Morag	30	53.56 N	19.56 E
Moraga	216	37.50 N	122.08 W
Mórahalom	30	46.13 N	19.54 E
Moraine	208	39.40 N	84.15 W
Moraine State Park ♠	204	40.56 N	80.07 W
Morainvilliers	251	48.56 N	1.56 E
Morākhi ≃	116	24.01 N	88.10 E
Mor'akovskij Zaton	76	56.45 N	84.41 E
Moral de Calatrava	34	38.50 N	3.35 W
Moraleda, Canal ⊔	244	44.30 S	73.30 W
Morales, Guat.	226	15.29 N	88.49 W
Morales, Méx.	224	22.10 N	101.02 W
Morales, Perú	238	6.28 S	76.28 W
Morales, Arroyo ≃	248	34.48 S	58.36 W
Morales, Laguna de C	224	23.35 N	97.47 W
Moramanga	147b	18.56 S	48.12 E
Moran, Kans., U.S.	188	37.55 N	95.10 W
Moran, Mich., U.S.	180	46.00 N	84.50 W
Moran, Tex., U.S.	186	32.33 N	99.10 W
Morangas, Ribeirão ≃	245	19.39 S	52.19 W
Morangis	251	48.42 N	2.20 E
Morangup Hill ∧[2]	158a	31.41 S	116.19 E
Morann	204	40.48 N	78.21 W
Morano sul Po	56	45.10 N	8.22 E
Moran State Park ♠	214	48.41 N	122.52 W
Morant Bay	231q	17.53 N	76.25 W
Morant Cays II	228	17.24 N	75.59 W
Morant Point ≻	231q	17.55 N	76.10 W
Mörarp	41	56.04 N	12.52 E
Morasverdes	34	40.36 N	6.16 W
Morat, Lac de (Murtensee) ⊜	54	46.55 N	7.05 E
Moratalla	34	38.12 N	1.53 W
Morattico	198	37.47 N	76.38 W
Moratuwa	112	6.46 N	79.53 E
Morava □[9]	30	49.20 N	17.00 E
Morava (March) ≃	30	48.10 N	16.59 E
Moravia, C.R.	226	9.51 N	83.26 W
Moravia, Iowa, U.S.	180	40.53 N	92.49 W
Moravia, N.Y., U.S.	200	42.43 N	76.25 W
Moravia → Morava □[9]	30	49.20 N	17.00 E
Moravian Indian Reserve ◆[4]	204	42.34 N	81.53 W
Moravská Ostrava → Ostrava	30	49.50 N	18.17 E
Moravská Třebová	30	49.45 N	16.40 E
Moravské Budějovice	30	49.03 N	15.49 E
Moravský Krumlov	30	49.03 N	16.19 E
Morawa	152	29.13 S	116.00 E
Morawhanna	236	8.16 N	59.45 W
Moraya	238	21.45 S	65.32 W
Morayfield	161a	27.07 S	152.57 E
Moray Firth C[1]	28	57.50 N	3.30 W
Morazán, Guat.	226	14.56 N	90.09 W
Morazán, Hond.	226	15.17 N	87.34 W
Morbach	52	49.48 N	7.07 E
Morbegno	36	46.08 N	9.34 E
Morbihan □[5]	32	47.55 N	2.50 W
Mörbylånga	26	56.31 N	16.23 E
Morcenx	32	44.02 N	0.55 W
Morciano di Romagna	60	43.55 N	12.38 E
Morcone	60	41.20 N	14.40 E
Morcote	54	45.56 N	8.55 E
Morcy	70	51.18 N	47.51 E
Morden	174	49.11 N	98.05 W
Morden ◆[8]	250	51.24 N	0.12 W
Mordialloc	159	38.00 S	145.05 E
Mordino	24	61.21 N	51.52 E
Mordoğan	120	38.30 N	26.37 E
Mordovo, S.S.S.R.	70	52.05 N	40.46 E
Mordovo, S.S.S.R.	70	51.07 N	45.48 E
Mordovo-Adel'akovo	70	53.47 N	51.36 E
Mordovskaja Avtonomnaja Sovetskaja Socialističeskaja Respublika □[3]	70	54.30 N	44.00 E
Mordovskij Buguruslan	70	53.48 N	52.31 E
Mordovskij Zapovednik ◆[4]	70	54.48 N	43.20 E
Mordves	72	54.34 N	38.13 E
Mordy	30	52.13 N	22.31 E
More, Ben ∧	28	56.23 N	4.31 W
More Assynt, Ben ∧	28	58.07 N	4.51 W
Moreau ≃, Mo., U.S.	209	38.33 N	92.06 W
Moreau ≃, S. Dak., U.S.	188	45.18 N	100.43 W
Moreau, North Fork ≃	188	45.09 N	102.50 W
Moreau, South Fork ≃	188	45.09 N	102.50 W
Morec	70	51.03 N	44.03 E
Morecambe	42	54.04 N	2.53 W
Morecambe Bay C	42	54.07 N	3.00 W
Moree, Austl.	156	29.28 S	149.51 E
Morée, Fr.	46	47.54 N	1.14 E
Morehead	208	38.11 N	83.25 W
Morehead ≃	154	9.00 S	141.25 E
Morehead City	182	34.43 N	76.43 W
Morehouse	184	36.51 N	89.41 W
Moreland, Ga., U.S.	182	33.17 N	84.46 W
Moreland, Ky., U.S.	184	37.30 N	84.49 W
Moreland Hills	269a	41.27 N	81.29 W
Morelia	224	19.42 N	101.07 W
Morell	176	46.25 N	62.42 W
Morella, Austl.	156	22.59 S	143.52 E
Morella, Esp.	34	40.37 N	0.06 W
Morelos, Méx.	186	28.25 N	100.53 W
Morelos, Méx.	222	26.42 N	107.40 W
Morelos, Méx.	224	22.53 N	102.37 W
Morelos □[3]	224	18.45 N	99.00 W
Morelos ◆[8]	276a	19.27 N	99.07 W
Morena	114	26.30 N	78.09 E
Morena □[5]	114	26.00 N	77.20 E
Morena, Serra ⩓	240	9.00 S	58.30 W
Morena, Sierra ∧	272	37.25 N	122.18 W
Morena, Sierra ⩓	34	38.00 N	5.00 W
Morenci, Ariz., U.S.	190	33.05 N	109.22 W
Morenci, Mich., U.S.	206	41.43 N	84.13 W
Moreni	38	45.00 N	25.39 E
Moreno, Arg.	248	34.39 S	58.48 W
Moreno, Calif., U.S.	218	33.55 N	117.09 W
Moreno □[5]	278	34.36 S	58.48 W
Moreno ≃	224	18.32 N	96.01 W
Moreno, Bahía C	242	23.35 S	70.30 W
Møre og Romsdal □[6]	26	62.40 N	7.50 E
Morere ≃	236	10.14 N	69.57 W
Moreru ≃	238	8.45 S	59.15 W
Moresby Island I, B.C., Can.	172	52.50 N	131.55 W
Moresby Island I, B.C., Can.	214	48.40 N	123.20 W
Moresnet	52	50.43 N	5.59 E
Morestel	56	45.40 N	5.28 E
Moreton, Austl.	154	12.28 S	142.38 E
Moreton, Eng., U.K.	250	51.44 N	0.14 E
Moreton, Eng., U.K.	252	53.24 N	3.07 W
Moreton, Cape ≻	161a	27.02 S	153.28 E
Moreton Bay C	161a	27.20 S	153.15 E
Moretonhampstead	44	50.40 N	3.45 W
Moreton-in-Marsh	44	51.59 N	1.42 W
Moreton Island I	161a	27.10 S	153.25 E
Moret-sur-Loing	46	48.22 N	2.49 E
Moretta	56	44.46 N	7.32 E
Moreuil	46	49.46 N	2.29 E
Morey Park	200	42.33 N	73.43 W
Morey Peak ∧	194	38.37 N	116.17 W
Morez	54	46.31 N	6.02 E
Morfa Nefyn	44	52.56 N	4.33 W
Mörfelden	52	49.58 N	8.34 E
Mórfou	120	35.12 N	32.59 E
Mórfou, Kólpos C	120	35.10 N	32.50 E
Morga	70	54.26 N	46.29 E
Morgan, Austl.	156	34.02 S	139.40 E
Morgan, Ga., U.S.	182	31.32 N	84.36 W
Morgan, Ky., U.S.	208	38.36 N	84.24 W
Morgan, Minn., U.S.	188	44.25 N	94.56 W
Morgan, Pa., U.S.	269b	40.22 N	80.08 W
Morgan, Tex., U.S.	212	32.01 N	97.37 W
Morgan, Utah, U.S.	190	41.02 N	111.41 W
Morgan □[6], Ill., U.S.	209	39.44 N	90.14 W
Morgan □[6], Ind., U.S.	208	39.30 N	86.25 W
Morgan, Mount ∧	161b	35.44 S	148.47 E
Morgan City, Ala., U.S.	184	34.28 N	86.34 W
Morgan City, La., U.S.	184	29.42 N	91.12 W
Morgan Creek ≃	186	32.19 N	100.55 W
Morganfield	184	37.41 N	87.55 W
Morgan Hill	216	37.08 N	121.39 W
Morganito	236	5.04 N	67.44 W
Morgan Park ◆[8]	268	41.42 N	87.40 W
Morgan's Bay	148	32.43 S	28.20 E
Morgan's Point	212	29.41 N	94.59 W
Morgans Point ≻	202	42.52 N	79.21 W
Morgan State College ✠[2]	274b	39.21 N	76.35 W
Morganton	182	35.45 N	81.41 W
Morgantown, Ind., U.S.	208	39.22 N	86.16 W
Morgantown, Ky., U.S.	184	37.14 N	86.41 W
Morgantown, Md., U.S.	198	38.21 N	76.58 W
Morgantown, Miss., U.S.	184	31.19 N	89.55 W
Morgantown, Ohio, U.S.	208	39.08 N	83.13 W
Morgantown, Pa., U.S.	198	40.09 N	75.54 W
Morgantown, W. Va., U.S.	178	39.38 N	79.57 W
Morganville	198	40.23 N	74.15 W
Morganza	184	30.44 N	91.36 W
Morgårdshammar	40	60.09 N	15.23 E
Morgauši	70	55.58 N	46.47 E
Morgenzon	148	26.45 S	29.36 E
Morges	54	46.31 N	6.30 E
Morgex	56	45.45 N	7.02 E
Morghāb (Murgab) ≃	118	38.18 N	61.12 E
Morghar	116	23.40 N	89.37 E
Morgongåva	40	59.56 N	16.57 E
Morguilla, Punta ≻	242	37.46 S	73.40 W
Morhange	52	48.55 N	6.38 E
Mori, It.	58	45.51 N	10.59 E
Mori, Nihon	82a	42.06 N	140.35 E
Mori, Nihon	84	34.50 N	137.56 E
Mori, Nihon	260	34.32 N	135.00 E
Mori ≃	154	10.00 S	148.30 E
Moriah	231r	11.15 N	60.43 W
Moriah, Mount ∧	194	39.17 N	114.12 W
Morialta Falls Reserve ♠	158b	34.55 S	138.40 E
Moriarty	190	34.59 N	106.03 W
Moriarty, Mount ∧	214	49.08 N	124.26 W
Morib	104	2.45 N	101.26 E
Moribaya	140	9.53 N	9.33 W
Morice ≃	172	54.24 N	126.45 W
Morice Lake ⊜	172	54.00 N	127.37 W
Morichal Largo ≃	236	9.27 N	62.25 W
Moricsala ♠	66	57.17 N	22.11 E
Morienval	46	49.18 N	2.56 E
Moriguchi	86	34.44 N	135.34 E
Morija	148	29.34 S	27.31 E
Moriki	140	12.52 N	6.30 E
Moringen	48	51.42 N	9.52 E
Morino, It.	60	41.53 N	13.25 E
Morino, S.S.S.R.	66	57.54 N	30.22 E
Morinville	172	53.48 N	113.39 W
Morioka	82	39.42 N	141.09 E
Morīri, Tso ⊜	110	32.54 N	78.20 E
Morisset	160	33.06 S	151.29 E
Moritzburg ⊥	50	51.09 N	13.40 E
Morivione ◆[8]	256b	45.26 N	9.12 E
Moriya	84	35.56 N	140.00 E
Moriyama	84	35.04 N	135.59 E
Moriyoshi-zan ∧	82	39.58 N	140.33 E
Morki	70	56.25 N	49.01 E
Morkill ≃	172	53.42 N	120.30 W
Morkiny Gory	66	57.33 N	36.18 E
Mörkö I	40	58.59 N	17.40 E
Morkoka ≃	64	65.10 N	115.52 E
Mørkøv	41	55.40 N	11.32 E
Morlaix	32	48.35 N	3.50 W
Morlanwelz	46	50.27 N	4.14 E
Morles	52	50.38 N	9.51 E
Morley, Eng., U.K.	42	53.46 N	1.36 W
Morley, Mich., U.S.	180	43.29 N	85.27 W
Morley, N.Y., U.S.	202	44.40 N	75.12 W
Morley Green	252	53.20 N	2.16 W
Mörlunda	26	57.19 N	15.51 E
Mormal'	66	52.45 N	29.53 E
Mormanno	36	39.53 N	16.00 E
Mormant	46	48.36 N	2.53 E
Mormoiron	56	44.04 N	5.11 E
Mormon Bar	216	37.28 N	119.57 W
Mormon Lake ⊜	190	34.57 N	111.27 W
Mormon Peak ∧	194	36.57 N	114.30 W
Mormon Reservoir ⊜[1]	192	43.16 N	114.49 W
Mormon Slough ≃	216	37.57 N	121.18 W
Mormon Station Historical State Monument ♠	216	39.00 N	119.50 W
Morna	262a	28.35 N	77.22 E
Mornant	56	45.37 N	4.40 E
Mornas	56	44.12 N	4.44 E
Morne, Pointe ≻	231o	16.20 N	61.18 W
Morne-à-l'Eau	231o	16.21 N	61.31 W
Morne-Rouge	230e	14.46 N	61.08 W
Morney	156	25.22 S	141.28 E
Morningdale	197	42.19 N	71.41 W
Morningside	274c	38.50 N	76.53 W
Morning Sun	180	41.05 N	91.15 W
Mornington	159	38.13 S	145.03 E
Mornington, Isla I	244	49.45 S	75.23 W
Mornington Island I	154	16.33 S	139.24 E
Mornington Peninsula ≻[1]	159	38.20 S	145.05 E
Morno	140	8.41 N	1.31 W
Mornou, Hadjer ∧	136	17.12 N	23.08 E
Moro, Pāk.	110	26.40 N	68.00 E
Moro, Oreg., U.S.	214	45.29 N	120.44 W
Moro ≃	140	7.25 N	11.03 W
Morobe	154	7.45 S	147.35 E
Morobe □[5]	154	7.00 S	146.30 E
Moroč'	66	52.34 N	27.36 E
Moroč' ≃	66	52.35 N	27.35 E
Morocco	206	40.57 N	87.27 W
Morocco □[1]	124		
	138	32.00 N	5.00 W
Morococala	238	18.10 S	66.44 W
Morococala, Cerro ∧	238	18.08 S	66.43 W
Morococha	238	11.37 S	76.09 W
Moro Creek ≃	184	33.18 N	92.22 W
Morogoro	144	6.49 S	37.40 E
Morogoro □[4]	144	8.00 S	37.00 E
Moro Gulf C	106	6.51 N	123.00 E
Moroka	263d	26.16 S	27.52 E
Morokweng	148	26.12 S	23.45 E
Moroleón	224	20.08 N	101.12 W
Morombe	147b	21.45 S	43.22 E
Morón, Arg.	248	34.39 S	58.37 W
Morón, Cuba	230p	22.06 N	78.38 W
Mörön, Mong.	78	47.27 N	110.14 E
Mörön, Mong.	78	49.38 N	100.10 E
Mörön, Mong.	78	48.15 N	100.23 E
Morón, Ven.	236	10.29 N	68.11 W
Morón □[5]	278	34.37 S	58.37 W
Mörön ≃	78	47.14 N	110.37 E
Morón, Aeródromo ⊠	278	34.41 S	58.38 W
Morón, Arroyo ≃	278	34.33 S	58.37 W
Morona ≃	236	4.45 S	77.04 W
Morona-Santiago □[4]	236	2.30 S	78.00 W
Morondava	147b	20.17 S	44.17 E
Morón de Almazán	34	41.25 N	2.25 W
Morón de la Frontera	34	37.08 N	5.27 W
Morones, Cerro ∧	224	21.45 N	103.05 W
Morong	106	14.41 N	120.16 E
Morongo Indian Reservation ◆[4]	194	33.59 N	116.50 W
Moroni, Comores	147a	11.41 S	43.16 E
Moroni, Utah, U.S.	190	39.32 N	111.35 W
Moros ≃	34	40.03 N	5.31 W
Morošečnoje	64	56.24 N	156.12 E
Morotai I	98	2.20 N	128.25 E
Moroto	144	2.32 N	34.39 E
Moroto ∧	144	2.32 N	34.46 E
Morovis	230m	18.20 N	66.24 W
Morovsk	68	51.06 N	30.50 E
Morowali	102	1.52 S	121.30 E
Moroyama	84	35.56 N	139.19 E
Morozkovo	76	59.29 N	61.01 E
Morozovka, S.S.S.R.	68	50.09 N	39.38 E
Morozovka, S.S.S.R.	73	49.28 N	39.54 E
Morozovsk	70	48.22 N	41.50 E
Morozovskaja	24	61.10 N	50.18 E
Morpeth, Ont., Can.	204	42.23 N	81.51 W
Morpeth, Eng., U.K.	42	55.10 N	1.41 W
Morphett Vale	158b	35.07 S	138.31 E
Morra, Monte ∧	257a	42.02 N	12.50 E
Morral	204	40.41 N	83.13 W
Morral, Arroyo del ≃	256d	41.29 N	2.03 E
Morrelganj	116	22.28 N	89.51 E
Morretes	242	25.28 S	48.49 W
Morrice	206	42.50 N	84.11 W
Morrill	188	41.58 N	103.56 W
Morrilton	184	35.09 N	92.45 W
Morrin	172	51.40 N	112.47 W
Morrinhos, Bra.	240	3.14 S	40.07 W
Morrinhos, Bra.	245	17.44 S	49.07 W
Morrinsville	162	37.39 S	175.32 E
Morris, Man., Can.	174	49.21 N	97.22 W
Morris, Conn., U.S.	197	41.43 N	73.15 W
Morris, Ill., U.S.	206	41.22 N	88.26 W
Morris, Ind., U.S.	208	39.17 N	85.11 W
Morris, Minn., U.S.	188	45.35 N	95.55 W
Morris, N.Y., U.S.	200	42.33 N	75.15 W
Morris, Okla., U.S.	186	35.36 N	95.51 W
Morris, Pa., U.S.	200	41.36 N	77.18 W
Morris □[6], N.J., U.S.	200	40.48 N	74.29 W
Morris □[6], Tex., U.S.	212	33.05 N	94.45 W
Morris ≃	174	49.21 N	97.22 W
Morris, Mount ∧	152	26.09 S	131.04 E
Morrisburg	202	44.54 N	75.11 W
Morrisdale	204	40.57 N	78.14 W
Morris Dam ◆[6]	270	34.11 N	117.53 W
Morris Jesup, Kap ≻	16	83.38 N	33.52 W
Morris Lake ⊜	266	41.03 N	74.37 W
Morrison, Arg.	242	32.36 S	62.50 W
Morrison, Ill., U.S.	180	41.49 N	89.58 W
Morrison, Mo., U.S.	209	38.40 N	91.38 W
Morrison Creek ≃	265b	43.28 N	79.39 W
Morrison Lake ⊜, Ont., Can.	202	44.52 N	79.28 W
Morrison Lake ⊜, Mich., U.S.	206	42.53 N	85.13 W
Morrisonville	209	39.25 N	89.27 W
Morris Park ♠	275	39.59 N	75.15 W
Morris Plains	200	40.49 N	74.29 W
Morris Reservoir ⊜[1]	218	34.12 N	117.52 W
Morris Run	200	41.41 N	77.01 W
Morristown, Ariz., U.S.	190	33.51 N	112.37 W
Morristown, Ill., U.S.	206	42.10 N	89.03 W
Morristown, Ind., U.S.	208	39.40 N	85.42 W
Morristown, Minn., U.S.	180	44.14 N	93.26 W
Morristown, N.J., U.S.	200	40.48 N	74.29 W
Morristown, N.Y., U.S.	202	44.35 N	75.39 W
Morristown, Ohio, U.S.	204	40.04 N	81.05 W
Morristown, S. Dak., U.S.	188	45.56 N	101.43 W
Morristown, Tenn., U.S.	182	36.13 N	83.18 W
Morristown Airport ⊠	266	40.48 N	74.25 W
Morristown National Historical Park ♠	200	40.46 N	74.32 W
Morrisville, N.Y., U.S.	200	42.54 N	75.39 W
Morrisville, Pa., U.S.	275	40.13 N	74.47 W
Morrisville, Vt., U.S.	178	44.34 N	72.44 W
Morrito	226	11.37 N	85.05 W
Morro	236	2.39 S	80.19 W
Morro, Castillo del (Morro Castle) ⊥	276b	23.09 N	82.21 W

Symbols in the index entries represent the broad categories identified in the key at the right. Symbols with superior numbers (⩓[2]) identify subcategories (see complete key on page *I · 26*).

Kartensymbole in dem Registerverzeichnis stellen die rechts in Schlüssel erklärten Kategorien dar. Symbole mit hochgestellten Ziffern (⩓[2]) bezeichnen Unterabteilungen einer Kategorie (vgl. vollständiger Schlüssel auf Seite *I · 26*).

Los símbolos incluídos en el texto del índice representan las grandes categorías identificadas con la clave a la derecha. Los símbolos con numeros en su parte superior (⩓[2]) identifican las subcategorías (véase la clave completa en la página *I · 26*).

Les symboles de l'index représentent les catégories indiquées dans la légende à droite. Les symboles suivis d'un indice (⩓[2]) représentent des sous-catégories (voir légende complète à la page *I · 26*).

Os símbolos incluídos no texto do índice representam as grandes categorias identificadas com a chave à direita. Os símbolos com números em sua parte superior (⩓[2]) identificam as subcategorias (veja-se a chave completa à página *I · 26*).

∧ Mountain	Berg	Montaña	Montagne	Montanha
⩓ Mountains	Berge	Montañas	Montagnes	Montanhas
)(Pass	Pass	Paso	Col	Passo
V Valley, Canyon	Tal, Cañon	Valle, Cañón	Vallée, Canyon	Vale, Canhão
≚ Plain	Ebene	Llano	Plaine	Planície
≻ Cape	Kap	Cabo	Cap	Cabo
I Island	Insel	Isla	Île	Ilha
II Islands	Inseln	Islas	Îles	Ilhas
⊥ Other Topographic Features	Andere Topographische Objekte	Otros Elementos Topográficos	Autres données topographiques	Outros Elementos Topográficos

ESPAÑOL — Nombre / Página / Lat.°′ / Long.°′ W=Oeste
FRANÇAIS — Nom / Page / Lat.°′ / Long.°′ W=Ouest
PORTUGUÊS — Nome / Página / Lat.°′ / Long.°′ W=Oeste

Morro, Punta ➤ 242 27.07 S 70.57 W
Morro, Punta del ➤ 224 19.51 N 96.27 W
Morro Agudo 277a 22.45 S 43.29 W
Morro Bay 216 35.22 N 120.51 W
Morro Bay C 216 35.20 N 120.51 W
Morro Bay State Park ♠ 216 35.20 N 120.52 W
Morro Creek ≃ 216 35.23 N 120.52 W
Morro de Mazatán 224 16.07 N 95.27 W
Morro do Chapéu, Bra. 240 11.33 S 41.09 W
Morro do Chapéu, Bra. 246 22.50 S 42.45 W
Morro do Pilar 245 19.12 S 43.23 W
Morro d'Oro 60 42.39 N 13.54 E
Morrone del Sannio 60 41.43 N 14.47 E
Morropón 238 5.15 S 80.00 W
Morros 240 2.52 S 44.03 W
Morrosquillo, Golfo de C 236 9.35 N 75.40 W
Morrow, La., U.S. 184 30.50 N 92.05 W
Morrow, Ohio, U.S. 208 39.21 N 84.08 W
Morrow □[6] 204 40.33 N 82.50 W
Morrow Island I 272 38.07 N 122.05 W
Morrow Point Reservoir @[1] 190 38.25 N 107.30 W
Mörrum 26 56.11 N 14.45 E
Morrumbala 144 17.22 S 35.36 E
Morrumbene 146 23.39 S 35.20 E
Mörrumsån ≃ 26 56.09 N 14.44 E
Mors I 26 56.50 N 8.45 E
Morsains 46 48.48 N 3.32 E
Morsang-sur-Orge 251 48.40 N 2.21 E
Moršansk 70 53.26 N 41.49 E
Morsbach 52 50.52 N 7.43 E
Mörsch 52 48.58 N 8.17 E
Morschwiller-le-Bas 54 47.45 N 7.16 E
Morščichino 255b 55.56 N 37.20 E
Morse, Sask., Can. 174 50.25 N 107.03 W
Morse, La., U.S. 184 30.08 N 92.30 W
Morse, Tex., U.S. 186 36.04 N 101.29 W
Morse Mill 209 38.17 N 90.40 W
Mörsenbroich ◆[8] 253 51.15 N 6.48 E
Morse Reservoir @[1] 208 40.06 N 86.02 W
Morses Pond @ 273 42.18 N 71.19 W
Morsi 110 21.21 N 78.00 E
Morskaja Masel'ga 24 63.06 N 34.54 E
Morskaja Pristan' ◆[5] 255a 59.53 N 30.11 E
Morskoj Bir'uček, Ostrov I 74 44.42 N 47.02 E
Morskoj Passažirskij Port ◆[5] 255a 59.55 N 30.14 E
Morskoj Vokzal ◆[5] 255a 59.57 N 30.17 E
Morson 174 49.03 N 94.18 W
Morsott 36 35.40 N 8.01 E
Morstein 275 40.01 N 75.35 W
Mort 262a 28.43 N 77.25 E
Morta 262a 28.44 N 77.27 E
Mortagne 32 48.31 N 0.33 E
Mortagne ≃ 54 48.33 N 6.27 E
Mortagne-au-Perche 46 48.31 N 0.33 E
Mortagne-sur-Sèvre 32 47.00 N 0.57 W
Mortain 32 48.39 N 0.56 W
Mortana 152 33.02 S 134.07 E
Mortara 56 45.15 N 8.44 E
Mortcho ◆[1] 136 16.00 N 21.10 E
Morteau 54 47.04 N 6.37 E
Mortefontaine 46 49.07 N 2.36 E
Mortegliano 58 45.57 N 13.10 E
Morte Point ➤ 44 51.11 N 4.13 W
Morteratsch, Piz ʌ 54 46.22 N 9.51 E
Morteros 242 30.42 S 62.00 W
Mortes, Rio das ≃ 246 21.18 S 43.58 W
Mortesoro 130 10.12 N 34.09 E
Mort-Homme, Forêt du ◆[3] 52 49.15 N 5.15 E
Mortlach 174 50.28 N 106.03 W
Mortlake, Austl. 156 38.05 S 142.48 E
Mortlake, Austl. 264a 33.51 S 151.07 E
Mortlake ◆[8] 250 51.28 N 0.16 W
Mortola Inferiore 56 43.47 N 7.33 E
Morton, Ill., U.S. 180 40.37 N 89.28 W
Morton, Minn., U.S. 188 44.33 N 94.59 W
Morton, Miss., U.S. 184 32.21 N 89.40 W
Morton, N.Y., U.S. 200 43.20 N 78.00 W
Morton, Pa., U.S. 275 39.55 N 75.20 W
Morton, Tex., U.S. 186 33.44 N 102.46 W
Morton, Wash., U.S. 214 46.33 N 122.17 W
Morton, Mount ʌ[2] 264b 37.56 S 145.20 E
Morton Arboretum ◆[4] 268 41.49 N 88.04 W
Morton Craig Range ʌʌ 152 28.12 S 124.41 E
Morton Grove 206 42.02 N 87.47 W
Mortons Gap 184 37.14 N 87.28 W
Mortrée 46 48.38 N 0.05 E
Mörtschach 58 46.55 N 12.55 E
Mortsel 46 51.10 N 4.28 E
M'ortvyj Donec ≃ 73 47.15 N 39.14 E
Morty 70 55.49 N 51.44 E
Morumbi, Estádio do ♠ 277b 23.37 S 46.43 W
Morungaba 246 22.52 S 46.48 W
Morungole ʌ 144 3.49 N 34.02 E
Moruya 156 35.55 S 150.05 E
Morvan ʌʌ 32 47.05 N 4.00 E
Morven, Austl. 156 26.25 S 147.07 E
Morven, N.Z. 162 44.50 S 171.07 E
Morven, Ga., U.S. 182 30.56 N 83.30 W
Morven, N.C., U.S. 182 34.52 N 80.01 W
Morven ʌ 28 58.13 N 3.42 W
Morvi 110 22.49 N 70.50 E
Morwell 159 38.14 S 146.24 E
Morwell ≃ 159 38.10 S 146.23 E
Morwenstow 44 50.54 N 4.33 W
Moryń 30 52.49 N 14.13 E
Morzalândia 245 14.47 S 50.35 W
Morženga 66 59.37 N 40.12 E
Morzhovoi 170 54.55 N 163.18 W
Morzine 54 46.11 N 6.43 E
Moržovec, Ostrov I 24 66.44 N 42.35 E
Moša ≃, S.S.S.R. 24 62.25 N 39.46 E
M'oša ≃, S.S.S.R. 70 55.25 N 49.22 E
Mosal'sk 66 54.29 N 34.59 E
Mosambik → Mozambique □[1] 128 18.15 S 35.00 E
Mošanicy 72 54.56 N 38.23 E
Mosås 40 59.12 N 15.08 E
Mosbach 52 49.21 N 9.08 E
Mosby 26 58.14 N 7.54 E
Moscavide 256c 38.47 N 9.06 W
Mosciano Sant'Angelo 60 42.45 N 13.53 E
Moščnyj, Ostrov I 66 60.01 N 27.50 E
Moscos Islands II 100 14.00 N 97.45 E
Moscou → Moskva 72 55.45 N 37.35 E
Moscow → Moskva, S.S.S.R. 72 55.45 N 37.35 E
Moscow, Idaho, U.S. 192 46.44 N 117.00 W
Moscow, Ind., U.S. 208 39.29 N 85.34 W
Moscow, Ohio, U.S. 208 38.52 N 84.14 W
Moscow, Pa., U.S. 200 41.20 N 75.31 W
Moscow, Tex., U.S. 212 30.55 N 94.50 W
Moscow → Moskva ≃ 66 55.05 N 38.50 E
Moscow Mills 209 38.57 N 90.55 W
Moscú → Moskva 72 55.45 N 37.35 E
Moscufo 60 42.25 N 14.03 E
Mosel 50 50.47 N 12.28 E
Mosel (Moselle) ≃ 32 50.22 N 7.36 E
Moselebe ≃ 146 25.03 S 23.13 E
Moselle, Miss., U.S. 184 31.30 N 89.17 W
Moselle, Mo., U.S. 209 38.23 N 90.54 W
Moselle □[5] 52 49.00 N 6.30 E
Moselle (Mosel) ≃ 32 50.22 N 7.36 E
Moselotte ≃ 54 48.01 N 6.38 E
Mošenskoje 66 58.31 N 34.35 E
Mosermandl ʌ 58 47.12 N 13.24 E

Mosers River 176 44.59 N 62.15 W
Moses Lake 192 47.08 N 119.17 W
Moses Point 170 64.42 N 162.03 W
Moses Power Plant ◆[6] 274a 43.09 N 79.02 W
Mosetse 146 20.37 S 26.32 E
Mosgiel 162 45.53 S 170.21 E
Moshannon 204 41.02 N 78.00 W
Moshannon Creek ≃ 204 41.04 N 78.06 W
Moshanpu 90 29.34 N 112.41 E
Mosheim, Tenn., U.S. 182 36.11 N 82.57 W
Mosheim, Tex., U.S. 212 31.38 N 97.36 W
Moshi 144 3.21 S 37.20 E
Moshiyu 94 41.15 N 124.05 E
Moshupa 146 24.50 S 25.31 E
Mosier 214 45.41 N 121.24 W
Mosina 30 52.16 N 16.51 E
Mosinee 180 44.47 N 89.43 W
Mosjøen 24 65.50 N 13.10 E
Moskal'vo 79 53.35 N 142.30 E
Moskau → Moskva 72 55.45 N 37.35 E
Moskenesøya I 24 67.59 N 13.00 E
Moskháton 257c 37.57 N 23.41 E
Moškino 70 57.45 N 45.20 E
Moskito-Golf → Mosquitos, Golfo de los C 226 9.00 N 81.15 W
Moškovo 76 55.18 N 83.37 E
Moskovskaja Slav'anka 255a 59.45 N 30.30 E
Moskovskij 75 40.44 N 72.03 E
Moskovskij Aerovokzal ʋ 255b 55.48 N 37.32 E
Moskovskij Park Pobedy ♠ 255a 59.52 N 30.20 E
Moskovskij Vokzal ◆[5] 255a 59.56 N 30.22 E
Moskva (Moscow) 72; 255b 55.45 N 37.35 E
Moskva □[4] 72 55.45 N 37.30 E
Moskva ≃ 66 55.05 N 38.50 E
Moskva, Gorod □[7] 255b 55.45 N 37.35 E
Moskva, Pik ʌ 75 38.57 N 71.49 E
Mosman 160 33.49 S 151.14 E
Mosman Park 158a 32.01 S 115.46 E
Mošny 68 49.32 N 31.44 E
Moso (Moos) 58 46.41 N 12.23 E
Moso in Passiria (Moos) 58 46.50 N 11.10 E
Mošok 70 55.48 N 41.17 E
Mosolovo 70 54.17 N 40.32 E
Mosomane 146 24.04 S 26.15 E
Mosonmagyaróvár 30 47.51 N 17.17 E
Mospino 73 47.53 N 38.03 E
Mosqueiro 240 1.10 S 48.28 W
Mosquera 236 2.30 N 78.29 W
Mosquero 186 35.47 N 103.58 W
Mosquic, Lac @ 196 46.39 N 74.28 W
Mosquito, Punta ➤ 236 9.07 N 77.53 W
Mosquito Brook ≃ 273 42.40 N 71.02 W
Mosquito Creek ≃, Iowa, U.S. 188 41.11 N 95.50 W
Mosquito Creek ≃, Ohio, U.S. 204 41.10 N 80.45 W
Mosquito Creek ≃, Pa., U.S. 204 41.07 N 78.07 W
Mosquito Creek Lake @[1] 204 41.22 N 80.45 W
Mosquito Indian Reserve ◆[4] 174 52.30 N 108.15 W
Mosquito Island I 230m 18.31 N 64.24 W
Mosquito Lagoon C 210 28.45 N 80.45 W
Mosquitos, Costa de •[2] 226 13.00 N 83.45 W
Mosquitos, Golfo de los C 226 9.00 N 81.15 W
Mosquitos, Riacho ≃ 242 22.02 S 57.57 W
Mosquitos, Serra dos ʌʌ[2] 246 22.36 S 46.39 W
Mosquito State Park ♠ 204 41.09 N 80.46 W
Moss 26 59.26 N 10.42 E
Mossaka 142 1.13 S 16.48 E
Mossâmedes 245 16.07 S 50.11 W
Mossbank, Sask., Can. 174 49.55 N 105.59 W
Moss Bank, Eng., U.K. 252 53.29 N 2.44 W
Moss Bank Park ♠ 252 53.36 N 2.28 W
Moss Beach 272 37.32 N 122.31 W
Mossburn 162 45.40 S 168.15 E
Mosselbaai (Mossel Bay) 148 34.11 S 22.08 E
Mosselbaai C 148 34.06 S 22.20 E
Mossendjo 142 2.57 S 12.44 E
Mosses, Col des)(54 46.24 N 7.06 E
Mossgiel 156 33.15 S 144.34 E
Moss Hill 212 30.15 N 94.45 W
Mössingen 54 48.24 N 9.03 E
Moss Landing 216 36.48 N 121.47 W
Mossleigh 172 50.43 N 113.20 W
Mossley 42 53.32 N 2.02 W
Mossley Hill ◆[8] 252 53.23 N 2.55 W
Mossman 154 16.28 S 145.22 E
Mossmans Brook ≃ 266 41.03 N 74.27 W
Moss Moor ◆[3] 252 53.37 N 2.00 W
Moss Mountain ʌ 184 34.50 N 92.40 W
Mossø @ 41 56.02 N 9.48 E
Mosson ≃ 56 43.33 N 3.54 E
Mossoró 240 5.11 S 37.20 W
Mosso Santa Maria 56 45.38 N 8.08 E
Moss Point 184 30.25 N 88.29 W
Moss Point ➤ 269a 41.37 N 81.32 W
Moss Side 252 53.46 N 2.57 W
Mossuril 144 14.58 S 40.42 E
Moss Vale 160 34.33 S 150.22 E
Mossy ≃ 174 54.05 N 103.00 W
Mossyrock 214 46.32 N 122.29 W
Mossyrock Dam ◆[6] 214 46.32 N 122.25 W
Most 50 50.32 N 13.39 E
Mosta 70 56.32 N 42.10 E
Mostaganem 138 35.51 N 0.07 E
Mostar 36 43.20 N 17.49 E
Mostardas 242 31.06 S 50.57 W
Møsting, Kap ➤ 166 64.00 N 41.00 W
Mostiska 68 49.48 N 23.09 E
Mostiștea ≃ 38 44.15 N 27.10 E
Mostizzolo 58 46.24 N 11.01 E
Mostki 73 49.19 N 38.30 E
Most na Soči 58 46.09 N 13.44 E
Mostok 66 53.59 N 30.28 E
Móstoles 256a 40.19 N 3.52 W
Mostoos Hills ʌʌ[2] 174 54.50 N 108.45 W
Mostovaja 66 56.13 N 33.08 E
Mostovoje 68 47.24 N 30.59 E
Mostovskoj 74 44.25 N 40.48 E
Mostovskoje 76 55.46 N 66.22 E
Mosty 66 53.25 N 24.32 E
Mostyn, Malay. 102 4.40 N 118.11 E
Mostyn, Wales, U.K. 42 53.19 N 3.16 W
Mosul → Al-Mawṣil 118 36.20 N 43.08 E
Møsvatnet @ 26 59.52 N 8.05 E
Mota 134 11.02 N 37.52 E
Mota I 165f 13.49 S 167.42 E
Motaba ≃ 142 2.03 N 18.03 E
Mota del Cuervo 34 39.30 N 2.52 W
Mota del Marqués 34 41.38 N 5.10 W
Motagua ≃ 226 15.44 N 88.14 W
Motala 26 58.33 N 15.03 E
Motala ström ≃ 40 58.38 N 16.10 E
Motane I 164x 9.59 S 138.49 W
Motatán 236 9.24 N 70.36 W
Motaze 146 24.48 S 32.52 E
Motegi 84 36.32 N 140.11 E
Mote Park ♠ 250 51.17 N 0.34 E
Moteve, Cap ➤ 164x 9.58 S 139.02 W
Moth 114 25.43 N 78.57 E
Mothe I 165g 18.40 S 178.30 W

Mother Brook ⌶ 273 42.15 N 71.10 W
Motherwell 42 55.48 N 4.00 W
Motīhāri 114 26.39 N 84.55 E
Motilla del Palancar 34 39.34 N 1.53 W
Motiong 106 11.47 N 125.00 E
Motiti Island I 162 37.38 S 176.26 E
Motjärnshyttan 40 59.56 N 13.58 E
Motloutse 146 21.28 S 27.24 E
Motloutse ≃ 146 22.15 S 29.00 E
Moto-ara ≃ 84 35.53 N 139.50 E
Motol' 66 52.19 N 25.36 E
Motomachi 82 34.45 N 139.21 E
Motomura 84 34.45 N 139.22 E
Motopu 164x 9.55 S 139.03 W
Motor Island I 274a 42.58 N 78.56 W
Motorki 70 56.53 N 51.29 E
Motorovo 76 56.31 N 71.10 E
Motosu 84 35.29 N 136.40 E
Motosu-ko @ 84 35.28 N 138.35 E
Motou 96 32.18 N 120.34 E
Motovilovo 70 55.36 N 43.51 E
Motovun 58 45.20 N 13.50 E
Motoyama 86 33.45 N 133.35 E
Moto-yama ʌ[2] 164f 24.48 N 141.20 E
Motozintla de Mendoza 222 15.22 N 92.14 W
Motril 34 36.45 N 3.31 W
Motrone 58 43.54 N 10.12 E
Motru 38 44.50 N 23.00 E
Mott 188 46.22 N 102.20 W
Motta 58 45.36 N 11.29 E
Motta di Livenza 58 45.47 N 12.36 E
Motta Montecorvino 60 41.30 N 15.07 E
Motta Visconti 56 45.17 N 8.59 E
Möttingen 52 48.48 N 10.35 E
Mottingham ◆[8] 250 51.26 N 0.03 E
Mottisfont 44 51.02 N 1.32 W
Mottola 36 40.38 N 17.03 E
Mottram in Longdendale 252 53.27 N 2.01 W
Motts Creek ≃ 266 40.38 N 73.45 W
Mottville, Mich., U.S. 206 41.48 N 85.45 W
Mottville, N.Y., U.S. 200 42.59 N 76.27 W
Motu ≃ 162 37.51 S 177.35 E
Motueka 162 41.07 S 173.00 E
Motueka ≃ 162 41.05 S 173.01 E
Motuo 110 29.20 N 95.15 E
Motupe 238 6.09 S 79.44 W
Motupena Point ➤ 165e 6.32 S 155.09 E
Moturiki I 165g 17.46 S 178.45 E
Motutapu 164v 19.02 S 169.52 W
Motutapu I 164k 21.14 S 159.43 W
Motygino 76 58.11 N 94.40 E
Motyklejka 64 59.26 N 148.38 E
Motyžin 68 50.23 N 29.55 E
Motyzlej 70 54.54 N 42.54 E
Mou 165f 21.05 S 165.26 E
Mouangko 142 3.39 N 9.49 E
Mouans-Sartoux 56 43.37 N 6.58 E
Mouchard 54 46.58 N 5.48 E
Mouchoir Bank ✢[4] 228 20.55 N 70.45 W
Mouchoir Passage ʮ 228 21.10 N 71.00 W
Moúdhros 38 39.52 N 25.16 E
Mouding 92 25.24 N 101.35 E
Moudjéria 140 17.53 N 12.20 W
Moudon 54 46.40 N 6.48 E
Moudongouma ≃ 142 1.36 N 17.24 E
Mougdi 136 11.30 N 17.34 E
Mouila 142 1.52 S 11.01 E
Mouit 140 16.35 N 13.05 W
Mouka 142 7.16 N 21.52 E
Moukden → Shenyang 94 41.48 N 123.27 E
Moulamein 156 35.05 S 144.02 E
Moulay-bou-Selham 34 34.53 N 6.15 W
Moulay-Idriss 138 34.02 N 5.27 W
Mouldsworth 252 53.14 N 2.44 W
Moule à Chique, Cap ➤ 231f 13.43 N 60.57 W
Moulhoulé 134 12.36 N 43.12 E
Moulin, Île du I 265a 45.41 N 73.32 W
Moulin-des-Ponts 54 46.20 N 5.19 E
Moulineaux 46 49.21 N 0.58 E
Moulinet 56 43.57 N 7.25 E
Moulins 32 46.34 N 3.20 E
Moulins-la-Marche 46 48.39 N 0.29 E
Moulmein 100 16.30 N 97.38 E
Moulmeingyun 100 16.23 N 95.16 E
Moulouya, Oued ≃ 138 35.05 N 2.25 W
Moulton, Eng., U.K. 252 53.13 N 2.31 W
Moulton, Ala., U.S. 184 34.29 N 87.18 W
Moulton, Iowa, U.S. 180 40.41 N 92.41 W
Moulton, Tex., U.S. 212 29.34 N 97.09 W
Moultrie 182 31.11 N 83.47 W
Moultrie □[6] 209 39.36 N 88.37 W
Moultrie, Lake @[1] 182 33.20 N 80.05 W
Mound 212 31.21 N 97.38 W
Mound City, Ill., U.S. 184 37.05 N 89.10 W
Mound City, Kans., U.S. 188 38.08 N 94.49 W
Mound City, Mo., U.S. 184 40.07 N 95.14 W
Mound City, S. Dak., U.S. 188 45.44 N 100.04 W
Mound City Group National Monument ♠ 208 39.23 N 83.00 W
Mound Lake @ 209 40.05 N 90.17 W
Moundou 136 8.34 N 16.05 E
Moundridge 188 38.12 N 97.31 W
Mounds, Ill., U.S. 184 37.07 N 89.12 W
Mounds, Okla., U.S. 186 35.53 N 96.04 W
Mounds State Park ♠ 208 40.07 N 85.37 W
Mounds State Recreation Area ♠ 208 39.30 N 84.59 W
Moundsville 178 39.55 N 80.44 W
Moundville 184 32.59 N 87.38 W
Moungahaumi ʌ 162 38.18 S 177.40 E
◆[8]Gali 263b 4.15 S 15.17
Moung Roessei 100 12.46 N 103.27 E
Mounianghi ≃ 142 0.32 N 12.52 E
Mounier, Mont ʌ 56 44.09 N 6.58 E
Mounimangqishan ʌʌ 92 32.35 N 100.35 E
Mounlapamôk 100 14.20 N 105.52 E
Mount, Cape ➤ 140 6.47 N 11.20 W
Mount Aetna 198 40.25 N 76.18 W
Mountain 180 45.11 N 88.28 W
Mountain □[4] 106 17.20 N 121.10 E
Mountain ≃ 170 65.41 N 128.50 W
Mountainair 190 34.31 N 106.15 W
Mountain Ash 44 51.42 N 3.24 W
Mountain Brook 184 33.29 N 86.46 W
Mountain Chute Dam ◆[6] 202 45.11 N 76.54 W
Mountain City, Ga., U.S. 182 34.55 N 83.23 W
Mountain City, Nev., U.S. 194 41.50 N 115.58 W
Mountain City, Tenn., U.S. 182 36.28 N 81.48 W
Mountain Creek 184 32.43 N 86.29 W
Mountain Creek ≃, Pa., U.S. 198 40.09 N 77.11 W
Mountain Creek ≃, Tex., U.S. 212 32.42 N 96.58 W
Mountain Creek Lake @[1] 212 32.43 N 96.58 W
Mountain Dale 200 41.41 N 74.32 W
Mountain Grove 184 37.08 N 92.16 W
Mountain Home, Ark., U.S. 184 36.20 N 92.23 W
Mountain Home, Idaho, U.S. 192 43.08 N 115.41 W
Mountainhome, Pa., U.S. 200 41.11 N 75.17 W
Mountain Home Air Force Base ■ 192 43.03 N 115.52 W
Mountain Iron 180 47.32 N 92.37 W
Mountain Lake, Fla., U.S. 210 27.57 N 81.36 W

Mountain Lake, Minn., U.S. 188 43.57 N 94.56 W
Mountain Lake @, Ont., Can. 202 44.59 N 78.43 W
Mountain Lake @, Ont., Can. 202 44.42 N 81.03 W
Mountain Lake @, N.J., U.S. 266 40.53 N 74.27 W
Mountain Lakes 200 40.54 N 74.27 W
Mountain Lodge 200 41.23 N 74.09 W
Mountain Nile (Baḥr al-Jabal) ≃ 126 9.30 N 30.30 E
Mountain Park 172 52.55 N 117.14 W
Mountain Pine 184 34.34 N 93.10 W
Mountain Point 170 55.18 N 131.32 W
Mountain Ranch 216 38.14 N 120.33 W
Mountainside 198 40.40 N 74.21 W
Mountain Spring Lakes 266 41.02 N 74.23 W
Mountain Valley Lake @ 269b 40.18 N 79.35 W
Mountain View, Ark., U.S. 184 35.52 N 92.07 W
Mountain View, Calif., U.S. 216 37.23 N 122.04 W
Mountain View, Mo., U.S. 184 36.59 N 91.42 W
Mountain View, Okla., U.S. 186 35.06 N 98.45 W
Mountain View, Wyo., U.S. 190 41.16 N 110.20 W
Mountain View, Wyo., U.S. 190 42.52 N 106.55 W
Mountain View Acres 218 34.31 N 117.24 W
Mountain Village 170 62.05 N 163.44 W
Mountain Zebra National Park ♠ 148 32.16 S 25.29 E
Mount Airy, Md., U.S. 178 39.23 N 77.09 W
Mount Airy, N.C., U.S. 182 36.31 N 80.37 W
Mount Airy ◆[8] 275 40.04 N 75.12 W
Mount Albert 202 44.08 N 79.19 W
Mount Alford 161a 28.04 S 152.36 E
Mount Alida 148 29.09 S 30.18 E
Mount Alverno 275 39.53 N 75.25 W
Mount Angel 214 45.04 N 122.48 W
Mount Ann Park ♠ 273 42.37 N 70.44 W
Mount Apo National Park ♠ 106 6.57 N 125.16 E
Mount Arayat National Park ♠ 106 15.13 N 120.46 E
Mount Arlington 200 40.56 N 74.38 W
Mount Assiniboine Provincial Park ♠ 172 50.54 N 115.40 W
Mount Auburn 209 39.46 N 89.16 W
Mount Augustus 152 24.19 S 116.54 E
Mount Ayliff 148 30.54 S 29.20 E
Mount Ayr, Ind., U.S. 206 40.57 N 87.18 W
Mount Ayr, Iowa, U.S. 188 40.43 N 94.14 W
Mount Baldy 270 34.14 N 117.40 W
Mount Barker, Austl. 152 34.38 S 117.40 E
Mount Barker, Austl. 158b 35.04 S 138.52 E
Mount Bethel 200 40.54 N 75.07 W
Mount Blanchard 206 40.54 N 83.33 W
Mount Bold Reservoir @[1] 158b 35.07 S 138.42 E
Mount Brydges 204 42.54 N 81.29 W
Mount Buller 159 37.10 S 146.27 E
Mount Calm 212 31.45 N 96.53 W
Mount Carmel, Newf., Can. 176 47.09 N 53.29 W
Mount Carmel, Ill., U.S. 184 38.25 N 87.46 W
Mount Carmel, Ky., U.S. 208 38.29 N 83.38 W
Mount Carmel, Ohio, U.S. 208 39.06 N 84.21 W
Mount Carmel, Pa., U.S. 198 40.48 N 76.25 W
Mount Carmel Heights 208 39.07 N 84.18 W
Mount Carroll 180 42.06 N 89.58 W
Mount Cavenagh 152 25.58 S 133.15 E
Mount Charles 265b 43.41 N 79.40 W
Mount Clare 178 39.13 N 80.21 W
Mount Clemens 204 42.36 N 82.53 W
Mount Colah 264a 33.41 S 151.07 E
Mount Compass 158b 35.22 S 138.37 E
Mount Cook National Park ♠ 162 43.35 S 170.15 E
Mount Cory 206 40.56 N 83.50 W
Mount Crawford 158b 34.40 S 138.57 E
Mount Crosby 161a 27.32 S 152.48 E
Mount Dandenong 264b 37.50 S 145.22 E
Mount Dennis ◆[8] 265b 43.42 N 79.30 W
Mount Desert Island I 178 44.20 N 68.20 W
Mount Diablo Creek ≃ 272 38.02 N 122.02 W
Mount Diablo State Park ♠ 216 37.51 N 121.55 W
Mount Dora 210 28.48 N 81.38 W
Mount Doreen 152 22.03 S 131.18 E
Mount Druitt 264a 33.46 S 150.49 E
Mount Dutton 152 27.50 S 135.43 E
Mount Eaton 204 40.42 N 81.42 W
Mount Eba 156 30.12 S 135.40 E
Mount Eden 216 37.38 N 122.06 W
Mount Eden Creek ≃ 272 37.36 N 122.09 W
Mount Edgecumbe 170 57.03 N 135.21 W
Mount Edwards 161a 28.01 S 152.31 E
Mount Elgon National Park ♠ 144 1.07 N 34.44 E
Mount Emu Creek ≃ 159 38.18 S 142.55 E
Mount Enterprise 212 31.55 N 94.41 W
Mount Ephraim 275 39.53 N 75.06 W
Mount Evelyn 264b 37.47 S 145.23 E
Mount Fern 266 40.52 N 74.34 W
Mount Field National Park ♠ 156 43.10 S 146.45 E
Mount Fletcher 148 30.40 S 28.30 E
Mount Forest 202 43.59 N 80.44 W
Mount Freedom 200 40.50 N 74.34 W
Mount Frere 148 31.00 S 28.58 E
Mount Gambier 156 37.50 S 140.46 E
Mount Garnet 156 17.41 S 145.07 E
Mount Gay 178 37.51 N 82.00 W
Mount Gilead, N.C., U.S. 182 35.10 N 79.56 W
Mount Gilead, Ohio, U.S. 204 40.33 N 82.50 W
Mount Glorious National Park ♠ 161a 27.19 S 152.47 E
Mount Gravatt 161a 27.33 S 153.06 E
Mount Greenwood ◆[8] 268 41.42 N 87.43 W
Mount Hagen 154 5.50 S 144.15 E
Mount Hawthorn 158a 31.55 S 115.50 E
Mount Healthy 208 39.14 N 84.33 W
Mount Hebron 274b 39.18 N 76.50 W
Mount Helena 158a 31.53 S 116.13 E
Mount Hermon, Calif., U.S. 216 37.03 N 122.04 W
Mount Hermon, Mass., U.S. 197 42.40 N 72.29 W
Mount Holly, N.J., U.S. 198 39.59 N 74.47 W
Mount Holly, N.C., U.S. 182 35.18 N 81.01 W
Mount Holly Springs 198 40.07 N 77.11 W
Mount Hope, Austl. 156 34.07 S 135.23 E
Mount Hope, Ont., Can. 202 43.09 N 79.55 W
Mount Hope, Kans., U.S. 188 37.52 N 97.40 W
Mount Hope, N.J., U.S. 266 40.56 N 74.33 W
Mount Hope, Ohio, U.S. 204 40.38 N 81.47 W
Mount Hope, W. Va., U.S. 178 37.54 N 81.10 W

Mount Hope Lake @ 266 40.56 N 74.32 W
Mount Horeb 180 43.00 N 89.44 W
Mount Houston 212 29.54 N 95.18 W
Mount Howitt 156 26.31 S 142.16 E
Mount Hunter Rivulet ≃ 264a 34.02 S 150.40 E
Mount Ida 184 34.34 N 93.38 W
Mount Isa 156 20.44 S 139.30 E
Mount Jackson, Pa., U.S. 204 40.58 N 80.26 W
Mount Jackson, Va., U.S. 178 38.45 N 78.39 W
Mount Jewett 204 41.44 N 78.38 W
Mount Juliet 184 36.12 N 86.31 W
Mount Kenya National Park ♠ 144 0.09 S 37.19 E
Mount Kisco 200 41.12 N 73.44 W
Mount Kokeby 158a 32.13 S 116.58 E
Mountlake Terrace 214 47.47 N 122.18 W
Mount Laurel 275 39.56 N 74.54 W
Mount Lebanon 204 40.23 N 80.03 W
Mount Liberty 204 40.21 N 82.38 W
Mount Lofty Ranges ʌʌ, Austl. 158b 35.15 S 138.50 E
Mount Lofty Ranges ʌʌ, Austl. 158b 34.45 S 139.00 E
Mount Magnet 152 28.04 S 117.49 E
Mount Manara 156 32.29 S 143.56 E
Mount Margaret 156 26.54 S 143.21 E
Mount Marion 200 42.02 N 73.59 W
Mount Martha 159 38.17 S 145.01 E
Mount Maunganui 162 37.37 S 176.11 E
Mount Mayon National Park ♠ 106 13.16 N 123.39 E
Mount McKinley National Park ♠ 170 63.30 N 150.00 W
Mount Mee 161a 27.04 S 152.46 E
Mountmellick 28 53.07 N 7.20 W
Mount Misery Point ➤ 266 40.58 N 73.05 W
Mount Molloy 154 16.41 S 145.20 E
Mount Monger 152 30.59 S 121.53 E
Mount Morgan 156 23.39 S 150.23 E
Mount Morris, Ill., U.S. 180 42.03 N 89.26 W
Mount Morris, Mich., U.S. 180 43.07 N 83.42 W
Mount Morris, N.Y., U.S. 200 42.44 N 77.53 W
Mount Mulligan 156 16.51 S 144.52 E
Mount Nebo 269b 40.33 N 80.06 W
Mount Nebo National Park ♠ 161a 27.22 S 152.43 E
Mountnessing 250 51.39 N 0.21 E
Mount Nimba National Park ♠ 140 7.40 N 8.27 W
Mount Olive, Ill., U.S. 209 39.04 N 89.43 W
Mount Olive, Miss., U.S. 184 31.46 N 89.39 W
Mount Olive, N.C., U.S. 182 35.12 N 78.04 W
Mount Oliver 269b 40.28 N 79.59 W
Mount Olivet 208 38.32 N 84.02 W
Mount Orab 208 39.02 N 83.56 W
Mount Penn 198 40.20 N 75.54 W
Mount Perry 156 25.11 S 151.39 E
Mount Pilchuck State Park ♠ 214 48.04 N 121.48 W
Mount Pleasant, Austl. 158b 34.47 S 139.02 E
Mount Pleasant, Ont., Can. 202 43.05 N 80.19 W
Mount Pleasant, Ind., U.S. 208 38.07 N 86.31 W
Mount Pleasant, Iowa, U.S. 180 40.58 N 91.33 W
Mount Pleasant, Mich., U.S. 180 43.35 N 84.47 W
Mount Pleasant, N.C., U.S. 182 35.24 N 80.26 W
Mount Pleasant, Ohio, U.S. 204 40.11 N 80.48 W
Mount Pleasant, Pa., U.S. 204 40.09 N 79.33 W
Mount Pleasant, S.C., U.S. 182 32.47 N 79.52 W
Mount Pleasant, Tenn., U.S. 184 35.32 N 87.13 W
Mount Pleasant, Tex., U.S. 212 33.09 N 94.58 W
Mount Pleasant, Utah, U.S. 190 39.33 N 111.27 W
Mount Pleasant Mills 198 40.43 N 77.01 W
Mount Pleasant Park ♠ 274b 39.22 N 76.35 W
Mount Pocono 200 41.08 N 75.22 W
Mount Pritchard 264a 33.54 S 150.54 E
Mount Prospect, S. Afr. 148 27.29 S 29.53 E
Mount Prospect, Ill., U.S. 206 42.04 N 87.56 W
Mount Pulaski 209 40.01 N 89.17 W
Mount Rainier 274c 38.56 N 76.58 W
Mount Rainier National Park ♠ 214 46.52 N 121.43 W
Mount Rebecca 152 26.48 S 135.10 E
Mount Repose 208 39.10 N 84.14 W
Mount Revelstoke National Park ♠ 172 51.06 N 118.00 W
Mount Riddock 152 23.03 S 134.40 E
Mount Robson Provincial Park ♠ 172 52.58 N 118.50 W
Mount Roskill 162 36.55 S 174.45 E
Mount Royal 275 39.49 N 75.13 W
Mount Rushmore National Memorial ⊥ 188 43.50 N 103.24 W
Mount Sandiman 152 24.24 S 115.23 E
Mount Sarah 152 26.57 S 135.22 E
Mount Savage 178 39.42 N 78.53 W
Mount's Bay C 28 50.03 N 5.25 W
Mount Selinda 144 20.25 S 32.43 E
Mount Selman 212 32.04 N 95.17 W
Mount Seymour Provincial Park ◆[4] 172 49.23 N 122.57 W
Mount Shasta 194 41.19 N 122.19 W
Mount Sinai 266 40.57 N 73.02 W
Mount Sinai Harbor C 266 40.57 N 73.02 W
Mount Sinai Ridge ʌ 208 39.04 N 84.58 W
Mount Somers 162 43.43 S 171.24 E
Mountsorrel 44 52.44 N 1.07 W
Mount Spokane State Park ♠ 192 47.58 N 117.13 W
Mount Sterling, Ill., U.S. 209 39.59 N 90.45 W
Mount Sterling, Ky., U.S. 182 38.04 N 83.56 W
Mount Sterling, Mo., U.S. 209 38.28 N 91.38 W
Mount Sterling, Ohio, U.S. 208 39.43 N 83.16 W
Mount Stewart, P.E.I., Can. 176 46.22 N 62.52 W
Mount Stewart, S. Afr. 148 33.10 S 24.26 E
Mount Stromlo Observatory ʋ[3] 161b 35.20 S 149.00 E
Mount Summit 208 40.00 N 85.23 W
Mount Surprise 156 18.09 S 144.19 E
Mount Sylvia 161a 27.44 S 152.14 E
Mount Tamalpais State Park ♠ 216 37.54 N 122.34 W
Mount Torrens 158b 34.52 S 138.57 E
Mount Tremper 200 42.03 N 74.17 W
Mount Uniacke 176 44.54 N 63.50 W
Mount Union 204 40.23 N 77.53 W
Mount Upton 200 42.26 N 75.23 W
Mount Vernon, Austl. 152 24.13 S 118.14 E
Mount Vernon, Ala., U.S. 184 31.05 N 88.01 W

Mount Vernon, Ga., U.S. 182 32.11 N 82.36 W
Mount Vernon, Ill., U.S. 209 38.19 N 88.55 W
Mount Vernon, Ind., U.S. 184 37.56 N 87.54 W
Mount Vernon, Iowa, U.S. 180 41.55 N 91.23 W
Mount Vernon, Ky., U.S. 182 37.21 N 84.20 W
Mount Vernon, Mo., U.S. 184 37.06 N 93.49 W
Mount Vernon, N.Y., U.S. 200 42.45 N 78.53 W
Mount Vernon, N.Y., U.S. 200 40.54 N 73.50 W
Mount Vernon, Ohio, U.S. 204 40.23 N 82.29 W
Mount Vernon, Oreg., U.S. 192 44.25 N 119.07 W
Mount Vernon, Pa., U.S. 269b 40.17 N 79.48 W
Mount Vernon, S. Dak., U.S. 188 43.43 N 104.16 W
Mount Vernon, Tex., U.S. 212 33.11 N 95.13 W
Mount Vernon, Wash., U.S. 214 48.25 N 122.20 W
Mount Vernon ⊥ 198 38.47 N 77.06 W
Mount Victoria 160 33.35 S 150.15 E
Mount Victory 206 40.32 N 83.31 W
Mount View 197 41.39 N 71.25 W
Mountville 198 40.02 N 76.26 W
Mount Vision 200 42.35 N 75.04 W
Mount Washington ◆[8] 274b 39.22 N 76.40 W
Mount Waverley 264b 37.53 S 145.08 E
Mount Wedge, Austl. 152 22.45 S 132.09 E
Mount Wedge, Austl. 152 33.29 S 135.10 E
Mount Wellington 162 36.54 S 174.51 E
Mount Willoughby 152 27.58 S 134.08 E
Mount Wilson Observatory ʋ[3] 218 34.14 N 118.03 W
Mount Wolf 198 40.04 N 76.43 W
Mount Zion 209 39.46 N 88.53 W
Mounyaz 136 10.41 N 21.18 E
Mouping 88 37.24 N 121.35 E
Moura, Bra. 236 1.27 S 61.38 W
Moura, Port. 34 38.08 N 7.27 W
Moura, Tchad 136 13.47 N 21.13 E
Mourdi, Dépression du •[7] 136 18.10 N 23.00 E
Mourdiah 140 14.28 N 7.28 W
Mouriès 56 43.41 N 4.52 E
Mourmelon-le-Grand 46 49.08 N 4.22 E
Mourne Mountains ʌʌ 42 54.10 N 6.04 W
Mouscron 46 50.44 N 3.13 E
Mousgougou 136 10.47 N 16.09 E
Moussa Ali ʌ 134 12.28 N 42.24 E
Mousseaux-sur-Seine 251 49.03 N 1.39 E
Moussey 54 48.40 N 6.47 E
Moussoro 136 13.39 N 16.29 E
Moussy-le-Neuf 251 49.04 N 2.36 E
Moussy-le-Vieux 251 49.03 N 2.38 E
Moustiers-Sainte-Marie 56 43.51 N 6.13 E
Mouthe 54 46.43 N 6.12 E
Mouthier-Haute-Pierre 54 47.02 N 6.16 E
Moutier 54 47.17 N 7.23 E
Moûtiers 56 45.29 N 6.32 E
Moutiers-au-Perche 46 48.29 N 0.51 E
Moutohora 162 38.17 S 177.32 E
Moutomoukadi 142 4.41 S 13.15 E
Moutong 102 0.28 N 121.13 E
Mouton Island I 176 43.54 N 64.46 W
Moux 46 47.10 N 4.09 E
Mouy 46 49.19 N 2.19 E
Mouydir, Monts du ʌʌ 138 24.45 N 4.05 E
Mouyombi-Tali 142 2.32 S 10.48 E
Mouyondzi 142 3.58 S 13.57 E
Mouzákion 38 39.26 N 21.40 E
Mouzon 52 49.36 N 5.05 E
Mouzon ≃ 54 48.21 N 5.41 E
Móvano 222 26.42 N 103.39 W
Moville, Eire 28 55.11 N 7.03 W
Moville, Iowa, U.S. 188 42.29 N 96.04 W
Mowangzui 90 30.31 N 113.34 E
Moweaqua 209 39.38 N 89.01 W
Mowein 130 7.36 N 28.11 E
Mowry Slough ≃ 272 37.29 N 122.03 W
Mowrystown 208 39.02 N 83.45 W
Mowshera 113 34.01 N 71.59 E
Moxhe 52 50.38 N 5.05 E
Moxi 97 30.18 N 105.41 E
Moxico □[5] 142 13.00 S 20.30 E
Moxos, Llanos de ⌣ 238 15.00 S 65.00 W
Moxotó ≃ 240 9.19 S 38.14 W
Moy 42 54.27 N 6.42 W
Moy ≃ 28 54.12 N 9.08 W
Moya, Comores 147a 12.18 S 44.27 E
Moya, Perú 238 12.24 S 75.10 W
Moyagee 152 27.45 S 117.54 E
Moyahua 224 21.16 N 103.10 W
Moyale, Kenya 144 3.32 N 39.03 E
Moyale, Yai. 134 3.30 N 39.07 E
Moyamba 140 8.10 N 12.26 W
Moydans 56 44.24 N 5.30 E
Moÿ-de-l'aisne 46 49.45 N 3.22 E
Moyedao I 88 36.55 N 122.32 E
Moyen Atlas ʌʌ 138 33.30 N 5.00 W
Moyen-Chari □[5] 136 9.00 N 18.00 E
Moyenmoutier 54 48.23 N 6.55 E
Moyenneville 46 50.04 N 1.45 E
Moyen-Ogooué □[4] 142 0.30 S 10.30 E
Moyenvic 52 48.47 N 6.33 E
Moyeuvre-Grande 52 49.15 N 6.02 E
Moyie 172 49.17 N 115.50 W
Moyie ≃ 172 48.42 N 116.11 W
Moyie Springs 192 48.43 N 116.11 W
Moylan 275 39.54 N 75.23 W
Moyo 144 3.39 N 31.43 E
Moyo ≃ 105b 8.26 S 117.28 E
Moyo, Pulau I 105b 8.15 S 117.34 E
Moyobamba 238 6.03 S 76.58 W
Moyock 198 36.32 N 76.11 W
Moyogalpa 226 11.32 N 85.42 W
Moyu 110 37.17 N 79.44 E
Moyuta, Volcán ʌ[1] 226 14.02 N 90.06 W
Moẕa 122 31.47 N 35.09 E
M'oža ≃, S.S.S.R. 66 55.27 N 30.43 E
M'oža ≃, S.S.S.R. 70 58.23 N 44.54 E
Možajevka 73 48.44 N 39.45 E
Možajsk 72 55.30 N 36.01 E
Možajskij 255a 59.43 N 30.07 E
Možajskoje Vodochranilišče @[1] 72 55.35 N 35.50 E
Mozambique → Moçambique 144 15.03 S 40.42 E
Mozambique □[1] 128 18.15 S 35.00 E
Mozambique Channel ʮ 128 19.00 S 41.00 E
Mozambique Plateau ✢[3] 10 34.00 S 35.00 E
Možarovka 76 51.09 N 59.05 E
Možarov Majdan 70 55.37 N 45.53 E
Možary 70 53.53 N 41.02 E
Mozdok 74 43.44 N 44.38 E
Možga 70 56.23 N 52.17 E
Mozhabong Lake @ 180 46.57 N 82.05 W
Mozhugongka 110 29.50 N 91.45 E
Mozichang 97 29.20 N 103.53 E
Mozolevo 66 59.19 N 33.51 E
Mozu 260 34.34 N 134.29 E
Mozuli 66 56.36 N 28.11 E
Mozyr' 68 52.03 N 29.14 E
Mozzanica 56 45.29 N 9.41 E
Mozzano 60 42.50 N 13.31 E

Symbol / English	Deutsch	Español	Français	Português
≃ River	Fluss	Río	Rivière	Rio
⌶ Canal	Kanal	Canal	Canal	Canal
Waterfall, Rapids	Wasserfall, Stromschnellen	Cascada, Rápidos	Chute d'eau, Rapides	Cascata, Rápidos
ʮ Strait	Meeresstrasse	Estrecho	Détroit	Estreito
C Bay, Gulf	Bucht, Golf	Bahía, Golfo	Baie, Golfe	Baía, Golfo
@ Lake, Lakes	See, Seen	Lago, Lagos	Lac, Lacs	Lago, Lagos
Swamp	Sumpf	Pantano	Marais	Pântano
Ice Features, Glacier	Eis- und Gletscherformen	Accidentes Glaciales	Formes glaciaires	Acidentes Glaciares
Other Hydrographic Features	Andere Hydrographische Objekte	Otros Elementos Hidrográficos	Autres données hydrographiques	Outros Elementos Hidrográficos
✢ Submarine Features	Untermeerische Objekte	Accidentes Submarinos	Formes de relief sous-marin	Acidentes Submarinos
□ Political Unit	Politische Einheit	Unidad Politica	Entité politique	Unidade Política
ʋ Cultural Institution	Kulturelle Institution	Institución Cultural	Institution culturelle	Instituição Cultural
⊥ Historical Site	Historische Stätte	Sitio Histórico	Site historique	Sitio Histórico
♠ Recreational Site	Erholungs- und Ferienort	Sitio de Recreo	Centre de loisirs	Sítio de Lazer
⊠ Airport	Flughafen	Aeropuerto	Aéroport	Aeroporto
■ Military Installation	Militäranlage	Instalación Militar	Installation militaire	Instalação Militar
◆ Miscellaneous	Verschiedenes	Misceláneo	Divers	Miscelânea

Mozzate 256b 45.41 N 8.57 E
Mpaka 148 26.26 S 31.47 E
Mpala 144 6.45 S 29.31 E
Mpama ≐ 142 0.57 S 15.39 E
Mpanda 144 6.22 S 31.02 E
Mpé 142 2.54 S 14.43 E
Mpelé, Mont ∧ 142 3.15 S 11.14 E
Mpese 142 5.14 S 15.33 E
Mpessoba 140 12.40 N 5.43 W
Mphoengs 144 21.10 S 27.51 E
Mpigi 144 0.13 N 32.42 E
Mpika 144 11.54 S 31.26 E
Mpila 263b 4.14 S 15.18 E
Mpimbe 144 15.18 S 35.04 E
Mpoka 142 1.26 S 17.02 E
Mponela 144 13.21 S 33.43 E
Mporokoso 144 9.23 S 30.05 E
Mpouya 142 2.37 S 16.13 E
Mpraeso 140 6.35 N 0.44 W
Mpui 144 8.21 S 31.50 E
Mpulungu 144 8.46 S 31.07 E
Mpwapwa 144 6.21 S 36.29 E
Mqanduli 148 31.48 S 28.46 E
Mragowo 30 53.52 N 21.19 E
Mrakovo 76 52.43 N 56.38 E
Mranggen 105a 7.01 S 110.31 E
Mras-su ≐ 76 53.45 N 87.49 E
Mrewa 144 17.39 S 31.47 E
Mrhila, Djebel ∧ 138 35.25 N 9.14 E
Mrijo 144 5.10 S 36.15 E
Mrkonjić Grad 36 44.25 N 17.05 E
Mrkopalj 36 45.19 N 14.51 E
Mrocza 30 53.14 N 17.36 E
Msagali 144 6.21 S 36.18 E
Msaken 138 35.44 N 10.35 E
Msata 144 6.20 S 38.23 E
Msec 50 50.10 N 13.54 E
Mšeno 50 50.27 N 14.38 E
M'Sila 138 35.46 N 4.31 E
Mšinskaja 66 59.01 N 29.57 E
Msoro Mission 144 13.36 S 31.55 E
Msta 66 57.55 N 34.29 E
Msta ≐ 66 58.25 N 31.20 E
Mstera 70 56.23 N 41.56 E
Mstislavl' 66 54.02 N 31.42 E
Mstiž 66 54.34 N 28.10 E
Mszana Dolna 30 49.42 N 20.05 E
Mszczonów 30 51.58 N 20.31 E
Mtakataka 144 14.12 S 34.32 E
Mtakuja 144 7.22 S 30.37 E
Mtama 144 10.18 S 39.22 E
Mtamvuna ≐ 148 31.06 S 30.12 E
Mtelo ∧ 144 1.39 N 35.23 E
Mtilikwe ≐ 144 21.09 S 31.30 E
Mtito Andei 144 2.41 S 38.10 E
Mtoko 144 17.24 S 32.13 E
Mtowabaga 144 2.30 S 35.53 E
Mtubatuba 148 28.30 S 32.08 E
Mtunzini 148 28.57 S 31.46 E
Mtwara 144 10.16 S 40.11 E
Mtwara □4 144 10.00 S 39.00 E
Mtyangimbori 144 10.16 S 35.31 E
Mu ≐, Mya. 100 21.56 N 95.38 E
Mu ≐, Nihon 82a 42.33 N 141.56 E
Mu, Cerro ∧ 236 9.29 N 73.07 W
Mua 164w 21.11 S 175.07 W
Muacandala 142 10.02 S 19.40 E
Mualama 144 16.53 S 38.17 E
Mualang 102 0.42 N 111.18 E
Mu'allaqah 130 13.28 N 23.57 E
Muan 88 34.58 N 126.26 E
Muaná 240 1.32 S 49.13 W
Muangai 142 12.32 S 19.51 E
Muang Bèng 100 20.22 N 101.44 E
Muang Hay 100 21.03 N 101.49 E
Muang Hinboun 100 17.35 N 104.36 E
Muang Hôngsa 100 19.43 N 101.20 E
Muang Houn 100 20.09 N 101.27 E
Muang Hounxianghoung 100 21.37 N 102.18 E
Muang Huang 100 18.45 N 103.42 E
Muang Khammouan 100 17.24 N 104.48 E
Muang Khao 100 19.47 N 103.29 E
Muang Khi 100 18.27 N 101.46 E
Muang Không 100 14.07 N 105.51 E
Muang Khôngxédôn 100 15.34 N 105.49 E
Muang Khoua 100 21.05 N 102.31 E
Muang La 100 20.52 N 102.07 E
Muang Liap 100 18.29 N 101.40 E
Muang Long 100 20.57 N 100.48 E
Muang Meung 100 20.43 N 100.28 E
Muang Ngoy 100 20.43 N 102.41 E
Muang Nong 100 16.22 N 106.30 E
Muang Ou Nua 100 22.18 N 101.48 E
Muang Ou Tai 100 22.07 N 101.48 E
Muang Pakbèng 100 19.54 N 101.08 E
Muang Pak-Lay 100 18.12 N 101.25 E
Muang Paktha 100 20.06 N 100.36 E
Muang Pakxan 100 18.22 N 103.39 E
Muang Peun 100 20.13 N 103.52 E
Muang Phalan 100 16.39 N 105.34 E
Muang Phiang 100 19.06 N 101.32 E
Muang Phônthong 100 15.05 N 105.39 E
Muang Phoun 100 19.07 N 102.43 E
Muang Sam Sip 100 15.31 N 104.44 E
Muang Sing 100 21.11 N 101.09 E
Muang Soum 100 18.45 N 102.36 E
Muang Souvannakhili 100 15.23 N 105.49 E
Muang Souy 100 19.33 N 102.52 E
Muang Sung 100 20.19 N 102.27 E
Muang Thadua 100 19.26 N 101.50 E
Muang Thatèng 100 15.26 N 106.23 E
Muang Thathôm 100 19.00 N 103.36 E
Muang Va 100 21.53 N 102.19 E
Muang Vangviang 100 18.56 N 102.27 E
Muang Vapi 100 15.40 N 105.55 E
Muang Xaignabouri 100 19.15 N 101.45 E
Muang Xamtong 100 19.51 N 103.51 E
Muang Xay 100 20.42 N 101.59 E
Muang Xépôn 100 16.41 N 106.14 E
Muang Xon 100 20.27 N 103.19 E
Muang Yo 100 21.31 N 101.51 E
Muang You 100 19.49 N 102.50 E
Muanza 146 18.59 S 34.48 E
Muar (Bandar Maharani) 104 2.02 N 102.34 E
Muar ≐ 104 2.03 N 102.35 E
Muara 102 5.02 N 115.02 E
Muaraaman 102 3.07 S 102.12 E
Muaraancalung 102 0.27 N 116.41 E
Muarabeliti 102 3.15 S 103.02 E
Muarabenangin 102 0.58 S 115.19 E
Muarabinuangeun 105a 6.50 S 105.53 E
Muarabulian 102 1.42 S 103.15 E
Muarabungo 102 1.28 S 102.07 E
Muaradua 102 4.32 S 104.05 E
Muaraenim 102 3.39 S 103.48 E
Muaragusung 102 1.35 N 117.17 E
Muarajuloi 102 0.12 S 114.03 E
Muarakaman 102 0.09 S 116.43 E
Muarakelingi 102 3.05 S 103.14 E
Muarakumpe 102 1.24 S 104.00 E
Muaralabuh 102 1.29 S 101.03 E
Muaralakitan 102 2.51 S 103.19 E
Muaralasan 102 1.48 N 117.12 E
Muaralembu 102 0.24 S 101.21 E
Muaramawai 102 0.37 N 116.49 E
Muarapangean 102 2.36 N 116.41 E
Muarapantai 102 0.45 S 101.43 E
Muarapayang 102 1.32 S 115.48 E
Muararupit 102 2.44 S 102.54 E
Muarasabak 102 1.08 S 103.51 E
Muarasiberut 98 1.36 S 99.11 E
Muarasipongi 102 0.37 N 99.51 E
Muaratebo 102 1.30 S 102.26 E
Muarateladang 102 2.50 S 103.58 E
Muaratembesi 102 1.42 S 103.07 E
Muaratewe 102 0.57 S 114.53 E
Muaratuhup 102 0.37 S 114.50 E
Muaratunan 102 1.24 S 116.39 E
Muarawahau 102 1.02 N 116.52 E
Muāri, Rās ⋟ 110 24.49 N 66.40 E
Muasdale 42 55.36 N 5.41 W
Muá Ximica 142 9.50 S 18.41 E
Mubārakpur 114 26.05 N 83.18 E
Mubārakpur Dabās ✲8 262a 28.43 N 77.03 E
Mubayyad ⊸4 132 30.55 N 32.48 E
Mubende 144 0.35 N 31.23 E
Mubende □5 144 0.45 N 31.10 E
Mubi 136 10.18 N 13.20 E
Mubian 102 3.07 S 116.38 E
Mubur, Pulau I 102 3.20 N 106.12 E
Mucacata 144 13.20 S 39.59 E
Mucaitá ≐ 240 6.59 S 42.40 W
Mucajaí ≐ 236 2.25 N 60.52 W
Mucambo 240 3.54 S 40.44 W
Mucari 142 9.30 S 16.54 E
Muccan 152 20.38 S 120.04 E
Muccia 60 43.05 N 13.02 E
Much 52 50.54 N 7.25 E
Mucha 259d 24.59 N 121.34 E
Muchangfu 90 31.55 N 116.35 E
Muchanovo 72 56.31 N 38.20 E
Muchavec ≐ 66 52.05 N 23.39 E
Much Dewchurch 44 51.59 N 2.46 W
Muchea 158a 31.35 S 115.59 E
Mücheln 50 51.18 N 11.48 E
Muchen 79 48.10 N 136.13 E
Muchengjie 97 29.47 N 103.29 E
Much Hoole 252 53.42 N 2.48 W
Muchinga Escarpment ⊸4 144 13.40 S 31.00 E
Muchinga Mountains ⋏
Muchino, S.S.S.R. 144 12.00 S 31.45 E
Muchino, S.S.S.R. 70 58.11 N 51.02 E
Muchino, S.S.S.R. 79 52.16 N 127.14 E
Muchino-Konduj 78 52.25 N 113.16 E
Muchoršibir' 78 51.03 N 107.50 E
Muchrani 74 41.56 N 44.35 E
Muchtadir 74 41.41 N 48.46 E
Muchtolovo 70 55.27 N 43.13 E
Muchuan 97 28.55 N 103.58 E
Much Wenlock 44 52.36 N 2.34 W
Mucifal 256c 38.48 N 9.26 W
Mučikan 78 53.02 N 120.27 E
Muck I 28 56.50 N 6.14 W
Mücka 50 51.18 N 14.40 E
Muckadilla 156 26.35 S 148.23 E
Muckalee Creek ≐ 182 31.38 N 84.09 W
Mučkapskij 70 51.52 N 42.28 E
Muckas 24 64.02 N 48.27 E
Mücke 52 50.38 N 9.03 E
Muckendorf an der Donau 254b 48.20 N 16.09 E
Mucking 250 51.30 N 0.26 E
Muckleshoot Indian Reservation ⊸4 214 47.16 N 122.09 W
Mucoma 142 15.18 S 13.39 E
Mucope, Ang. 142 8.42 S 21.43 E
Mucope, Ang. 142 16.24 S 14.53 E
Mucrone, Monte ∧ 56 45.36 N 7.56 E
Mucubela 144 16.55 S 37.52 E
Mucuchies 236 8.45 N 70.55 W
M'uc'ucl'u 74 40.28 N 47.55 E
Mucugê 240 13.00 S 41.23 W
Mucuim ≐ 238 6.33 S 64.18 W
Muculo 142 16.47 S 14.51 E
Muçum 242 29.10 S 51.53 W
Mucumbura 144 16.09 S 31.31 E
Mucun 90 26.44 N 114.00 E
Mucupia 146 18.01 S 36.48 E
Mucupina, Monte ∧ 226 15.08 N 86.38 W
Mucur 120 39.04 N 34.23 E
Mucuri 245 18.05 S 39.34 W
Mucuri ≐ 245 18.05 S 39.34 W
Mucusso 142 17.51 S 20.21 E
Mud ≐, Ky., U.S. 184 37.13 N 86.54 W
Mud ≐, W. Va., U.S. 178 38.25 N 82.17 W
Muda ≐ 104 5.33 N 100.22 E
Mudanjiang 79 44.35 N 129.36 E
Mudanjiang ≐ 79 46.22 N 129.33 E
Mudanya 120 40.22 N 28.52 E
Mudar 52 49.32 N 9.11 E
Mudaysīsāt, Jabal ∧ 122 31.39 N 36.14 E
Mud Creek ≐, U.S. 188 43.17 N 96.15 W
Mud Creek ≐, Ill., U.S. 209 38.21 N 89.48 W
Mud Creek ≐, Ind., U.S. 206 41.06 N 86.21 W
Mud Creek ≐, Ind., U.S. 206 40.26 N 85.55 W
Mud Creek ≐, Nebr., U.S. 188 41.01 N 98.54 W
Mud Creek ≐, N.Y., U.S. 200 43.05 N 78.43 W
Mud Creek ≐, N.Y., U.S. 200 42.17 N 77.13 W
Mud Creek ≐, N.Y., U.S. 200 42.59 N 77.23 W
Mud Creek ≐, Okla., U.S. 186 33.55 N 97.28 W
Mud Creek ≐, S. Dak., U.S. 188 45.11 N 98.24 W
Mud Creek ≐, Tex., U.S. 212 31.48 N 94.58 W
Mud Creek ≐, Vt., U.S. 196 45.02 N 72.12 W
Muddus Nationalpark ⊸ 24 67.00 N 20.16 E
Muddy ≐, Nev., U.S. 194 36.27 N 114.22 W
Muddy ≐, Wash., U.S. 214 46.04 N 122.01 W
Muddy Boggy Creek ≐ 186 34.03 N 95.47 W
Muddy Branch ≐ 274c 39.03 N 77.18 W
Muddy Brook ≐ 266 41.07 N 73.20 W
Muddy Creek ≐, U.S. 266 41.03 N 74.02 W
Muddy Creek ≐, Mo., U.S. 184 38.51 N 93.03 W
Muddy Creek ≐, Mont., U.S. 192 47.56 N 111.46 W
Muddy Creek ≐, Ohio, U.S. 204 41.27 N 83.03 W
Muddy Creek ≐, Pa., U.S. 198 39.47 N 76.18 W
Muddy Creek ≐, Utah, U.S. 190 38.24 N 110.42 W
Muddy Creek ≐, Wyo., U.S. 188 42.35 N 104.57 W
Muddy Creek ≐, Wyo., U.S. 190 41.01 N 107.42 W
Muddy Creek ≐, Wyo., U.S. 190 41.59 N 106.08 W
Muddy Creek ≐, Wyo., U.S. 190 41.32 N 110.13 W
Muddy Fork ≐ 192 43.17 N 108.14 W
Muddy Gut C 274b 39.17 N 76.26 W
Muddy Peak ∧ 194 36.18 N 114.42 W
Müden, B.R.D. 48 52.52 N 10.07 E
Müden, B.R.D. 50 52.31 N 10.22 E
Müdersbach 52 50.49 N 7.56 E
Mudgee 156 32.36 S 149.35 E
Mudgeeraba 161a 28.04 S 153.22 E
Mudhol 112 16.21 N 75.17 E
Mud Island I 161a 27.20 S 153.15 E
Mud Islands II 159 38.17 S 144.45 E
Mudjatik ≐ 174 56.02 N 107.36 W
Mudjuga 24 63.46 N 39.15 E
Mud Lake ◎, Idaho, U.S. 192 43.53 N 112.24 W
Mud Lake ◎, Minn., U.S. 188 48.20 N 95.58 W
Mud Lake ◎, Nev., U.S. 194 37.52 N 117.04 W
Mud Lake ◎, N.Y., U.S. 202 44.30 N 75.28 W
Mud Lake Reservoir ◎1 188 45.50 N 98.10 W
Mudon 100 16.15 N 97.44 E
Mudongzhen 92 29.35 N 106.51 E
Mudu 96 31.15 N 120.30 E
Mudugh □4 134 5.50 N 47.10 E
Mudurnu 120 40.28 N 31.13 E
Mudurnu ≐ 120 40.49 N 30.33 E
M'ud'ur'um ≐ 75 40.53 N 76.36 E
Mueda 144 11.39 S 39.33 E
Muelle de los Bueyes 226 12.04 N 84.32 W
Mueller, Mount ∧ 152 19.54 S 127.51 E
Muenster 186 33.39 N 97.23 W
Muerchang 97 29.48 N 106.37 E
Muerte, Valle de la → Death Valley ∨ 194 36.30 N 117.00 W
Muerto, Mar C 224 16.10 N 94.10 W
Muerto, Mar → Dead Sea ◎ 122 31.30 N 35.30 E
Mufulira 144 12.33 S 28.14 E
Mufuma 142 9.04 S 17.06 E
Mufushan ∧ 90 29.02 N 113.54 E
Mufushan ⋏ 90 29.00 N 114.00 E
Muganskaja Step' ⊸ 74 39.40 N 48.15 E
Mugazine 148 26.07 S 32.30 E
Mugegawa 84 35.31 N 136.51 E
Mugello ∨ 60 43.55 N 11.30 E
Mügeln 50 51.14 N 13.02 E
Muger ≐ 134 9.54 N 37.57 E
Müggelberge ⋏2 254a 52.25 N 13.39 E
Müggelheim ✲8 254a 52.25 N 13.40 E
Muggia 58 45.36 N 13.46 E
Muggio 256b 45.36 N 9.14 E
Mughalsarai 114 25.18 N 83.07 E
Mughr 122 33.05 N 35.43 E
Mugi, Nihon 84 35.33 N 136.59 E
Mugi, Nihon 86 33.40 N 134.25 E
Mu Gia, Deo ⋊ 100 17.40 N 105.47 E
Muginga 142 8.20 S 17.37 E
Mugla 120 37.12 N 28.22 E
Mugla □4 120 37.10 N 28.30 E
Mugodžarskaja 76 48.36 N 58.27 E
Mugodžary ⋏2 76 49.00 N 58.40 E
Mugombazi 144 5.50 S 30.14 E
Mugo-ri 88 38.58 N 126.31 E
Mugrejevskij 70 56.36 N 42.21 E
Mugron 32 43.45 N 0.45 W
Mūgu Karnāli ≐ 114 29.38 N 81.52 E
Mugur-Aksy 76 50.21 N 90.30 E
Mūh, Sabkhat ◎ 120 34.30 N 38.20 E
Muhala 144 5.40 S 28.43 E
Muhamdi 114 27.57 N 80.13 E
Muhammad, Ra's ⋟ 130 27.44 N 34.15 E
Muhammadābād 114 26.02 N 83.23 E
Muhammadpur 116 23.24 N 89.36 E
Muhammad Qawl 130 20.54 N 37.05 E
Muhayshir, Birkat ◎ 132 30.43 N 31.56 E
Muheza 144 5.10 S 38.47 E
Muhīt, Maṣrif al- ≐ 263c 30.07 N 31.06 E
Mühlacker 52 48.57 N 8.50 E
Mühlau 50 50.54 N 12.45 E
Mühlbach am Hochkönig 58 47.22 N 13.08 E
Mühlbach-sur-Munster 54 48.02 N 7.05 E
Mühlberg 50 51.26 N 13.13 E
Mühldorf 30 48.15 N 12.32 E
Mühlen → Molini de Tures 58 46.54 N 11.56 E
Mühlenbeck 254a 52.40 N 13.22 E
Mühlenbecker See ◎ 254a 52.41 N 13.24 E
Mühlenberg 200 41.14 N 76.09 W
Mühlen-Berg ⋏2 254a 52.23 N 13.15 E
Mühlen Eichsen 50 53.45 N 11.15 E
Mühlenfliess ≐ 254a 52.26 N 13.41 E
Mühlenrahmede 253 51.16 N 7.40 E
Mühlhausen, B.R.D. 253 51.33 N 7.44 E
Mühlhausen, D.D.R. 50 51.12 N 10.27 E
Mühlhausen im Täle 52 48.34 N 9.39 E
Mühlheim, B.R.D. 52 49.54 N 7.01 E
Mühlheim, B.R.D. 52 50.07 N 8.50 E
Mühlheim an der Donau 54 48.01 N 8.53 E
Mühlig-Hofmann Mountains ⋏ 9 72.00 S 5.20 E
Mühltroff 254b 48.10 N 16.34 E
Mühlviertel ⊸1 50 50.32 N 11.55 E
Muhola 30 48.25 N 14.10 E
Muhos 26 63.20 N 25.05 E
Muḥradah 26 64.48 N 25.59 E
Mühringen 120 35.15 N 36.35 E
Muhu I 54 48.25 N 8.46 E
Muhula 66 58.38 N 23.15 E
Muhulu 144 13.53 S 39.30 E
Muhushan 144 1.03 S 27.17 E
Muhu Väin ⋃ 94 40.42 N 120.36 E
Muhuwesi ≐ 144 1.33 S 31.42 E
Mui ≐ 66 58.45 N 23.20 E
Muiden 144 11.16 S 37.58 E
Muiderslot ⊥ 142 17.51 S 15.41 E
Muides-sur-Loire 48 52.19 N 5.04 E
Muié 48 52.20 N 5.12 E
Muikaichi 46 47.40 N 1.31 E
Muikamachi 142 14.25 S 20.36 E
Muir, Mich., U.S. 86 34.21 N 131.56 E
Muir, Pa., U.S. 84 37.04 N 138.53 E
Muir, Mount ∧ 206 43.00 N 84.56 W
Muir Beach 198 40.36 N 76.31 W
Muir Gorge ∨ 170 61.06 N 148.24 W
Muirkirk, Scot., U.K. 272 37.52 N 122.35 W
Muirkirk, Md., U.S. 216 37.57 N 119.32 W
Muiron Islands II 42 55.31 N 4.04 W
Muir Seamount ⊹3 274c 39.04 N 76.53 W
Muir Woods 152 21.35 S 114.20 E
Muir Woods National Monument ♠ 16 33.30 N 62.30 W
Muiskraal 272 37.53 N 122.34 W
Muisne 216 37.54 N 122.33 W
Muite 148 33.56 S 21.13 E
Mui Wo 236 0.36 N 80.02 W
Muizen 144 14.02 S 39.00 E
Muja, S.S.S.R. 261d 22.16 N 113.59 E
Muja, Yai. 46 51.01 N 4.31 E
Muja ≐ 78 56.24 N 115.39 E
Mujāhidpur ✲8 78 56.24 N 115.39 E
Mujang-ni 12 12.02 N 39.29 E
Mujeres, Isla I 78 56.24 N 115.39 E
Mujezerskij 262a 28.34 N 77.13 E
Mujiapucun 88 35.26 N 126.34 E
Mujiayu 222 21.13 N 86.43 W
Mujimbeji Mission 24 63.57 N 31.55 E
Mujnak 94 41.06 N 122.48 E
Muju 95 40.24 N 116.55 E
Mujunkum, Peski ⊸2, S.S.S.R. 144 12.11 S 24.57 E
Mujunkum, Peski ⊸2, S.S.S.R. 76 43.48 N 59.02 E
Muka 88 36.02 N 127.40 E
Mukačevo 75 44.00 N 71.40 E
Mukah 76 44.20 N 71.00 E
Mukaishima 78 56.42 N 104.41 E
Mukalla → Al-Mukallā 68 48.27 N 22.45 E
Mukandpur ✲8 102 2.54 N 112.06 E
Mukandwara 86 34.20 N 133.10 E
Mukawa
Mukāwir 134 14.32 N 49.08 E
Mukawwar I 262a 28.44 N 77.11 E
Mukdahan 110 24.49 N 75.59 E
Mukden → Shenyang 84 35.47 N 138.23 E
Mukebo 122 31.34 N 35.38 E
Mukeriān 130 20.48 N 37.13 E
Mukeru 100 16.32 N 104.43 E
Mukharram al-Fawqānī
Mukhmās 94 41.48 N 123.27 E
Mukho 144 6.49 S 28.03 E
Mukilteo 114 31.57 N 75.37 E
Mukinbudin 165b 7.25 N 134.30 E
Mukinge Hill
Mukō 120 34.49 N 37.04 E
Muko ≐ 122 31.52 N 35.17 E
88 37.33 N 129.06 E
214 47.57 N 122.18 W
158 30.54 S 118.13 E
144 13.29 S 25.12 E
84 34.56 N 135.42 E
86 34.41 N 135.23 E
Mukomuko 102 2.35 S 101.07 E
Mukomwenze 144 6.52 S 27.16 E
Mukoshima-rettō II 14 27.37 N 142.10 E
Mukry 118 37.36 N 65.44 E
Muksi-ri 88 39.52 N 125.54 E
Muksu ≐ 75 39.15 N 71.23 E
Muksüdpur 116 23.18 N 89.51 E
Muktāgācha 116 24.46 N 90.14 E
Muktsar 112 30.29 N 74.31 E
Mukuleshi ≐ 144 12.09 S 29.49 E
Mukumbura 142 10.21 S 24.30 E
Mukur 76 48.03 N 54.30 E
Mukusaki 105b 8.33 S 121.37 E
Mukutan 144 0.38 N 36.16 E
Mukutawa ≐ 174 53.10 N 97.28 W
Mukwela 144 17.02 S 26.39 E
Mukwonago 206 42.52 N 88.20 W
Mūl 112 20.04 N 79.40 E
Mula 34 38.03 N 1.30 W
Mula ≐, Bhārat 112 18.34 N 74.20 E
Mula ≐, Pāk. 110 27.57 N 67.36 E
Mulādi 116 22.54 N 90.25 E
Muladu I 112 7.01 N 72.59 E
Mulaly 76 45.27 N 78.19 E
Mulan 79 45.57 N 128.03 E
Muland ✲8 262c 19.10 N 72.57 E
Mulanda 144 14.41 S 21.48 E
Mulanje, Malawi 144 16.03 S 35.31 E
Mulanje, Moç. 144 16.03 S 35.45 E
Mulanje Mountains ⋏ 144 15.58 S 35.38 E
Mulas, Punta ⋟ 230m 18.09 N 65.27 W
Mulashi 92 29.40 N 100.39 E
Mulatos 222 28.39 N 108.51 W
Mulatupo 236 8.57 N 77.45 W
Mulayt Taung ∧ 100 16.11 N 98.32 E
Mulazzo 58 44.19 N 9.53 E
Mulbāgal 112 13.10 N 78.24 E
Mulberry, Ark., U.S. 184 35.30 N 94.03 W
Mulberry, Fla., U.S. 210 27.54 N 81.59 W
Mulberry, Ind., U.S. 206 40.21 N 86.40 W
Mulberry, Ohio, U.S. 208 39.11 N 84.15 W
Mulberry ≐ 184 35.28 N 94.03 W
Mulberry Creek ≐, Ala., U.S. 182 32.27 N 86.52 W
Mulberry Creek ≐, Tex., U.S. 186 34.37 N 100.55 W
Mulberry Fork ≐ 184 33.33 N 87.11 W
Mulberry Grove 184 38.56 N 89.16 W
Mulberry Mountain ∧ 209
Mulchatna ≐ 184 35.42 N 92.56 W
Mulchén 170 59.39 N 157.08 W
Mulda, D.D.R. 242 37.43 S 72.14 W
Mul'da, S.S.S.R. 50 50.48 N 13.25 E
Mulde ≐ 24 67.28 N 63.34 E
Muldenstein 50 51.10 N 12.48 E
Muldersdrifseloop ≐ 50 51.40 N 12.19 E
Muldersvlei 263d 26.06 S 27.51 E
Muldoon 148 30.41 S 22.13 E
Muldraugh 212 29.49 N 97.04 W
Muldrow 184 37.56 N 85.59 W
Muleba 184 35.24 N 94.36 W
Mule Creek 144 1.49 S 31.40 E
Mulegé 188 37.05 N 99.00 W
Mulegns 222 26.53 N 112.01 W
Mulei 56 46.33 N 9.37 E
Muleng 76 43.49 N 90.11 E
Mulengzhen 79 44.56 N 130.31 E
Mules (Mauls) 79 44.31 N 130.13 E
Mules, Pulau I 58 46.51 N 11.31 E
Muleshoe 105b 8.54 S 120.17 E
Mulevala 186 34.13 N 102.43 W
Mulga Downs 144 16.30 S 37.36 E
Mulgathing 152 22.08 S 118.26 E
Mulgathing Rocks ⋏ 152 30.15 S 134.00 E
Mulghar 152 30.14 S 133.58 E
Mulgoa 116 22.46 N 89.45 E
Mulgoa Creek ≐ 160 33.50 S 150.40 E
Mulgowie 264a 33.46 S 150.39 E
Mulgrave, Austl. 161a 27.43 S 152.22 E
Mulgrave, N.S., Can. 264b 37.56 S 145.12 E
Mulgrave Hills ⋏2 176 45.37 N 61.23 W
Mulgul 170 67.42 N 163.24 W
Mulhacén ∧ 152 24.49 S 118.26 E
Mulhall 34 37.03 N 3.19 W
Mülhausen → Mulhouse 186 36.04 N 97.24 W
Mülheim an der Ruhr 54 47.45 N 7.20 E
Mülheimer Ruhrtalbrüke ⊸5 52 51.24 N 6.54 E
Mulhouse (Mülhausen) 253 51.23 N 6.54 E
Muli, N. Cal. 54 47.45 N 7.20 E
Muli, Zhg. 165f 20.42 S 166.25 E
Mulinhe ≐ 92 28.10 N 100.47 E
Mulino 92 42.20 N 100.20 E
Mulino 214 45.13 N 122.35 W
Mülki 106 7.18 N 124.52 E
Mull, Island of I 112 13.06 N 74.48 E
Mullaghcleevaun ∧ 42 56.27 N 6.00 W
Mullaghmore ∧ 42 53.06 N 6.24 W
Mullan 42 54.52 N 6.51 W
Mullen 192 47.28 N 115.48 W
Mullenbach 188 42.03 N 101.01 W
Mullengudgery 52 50.19 N 6.55 E
Mullens 156 31.41 S 147.26 E
Muller, Pegunungan ⋏ 188 37.35 N 81.23 W
Muller Creek ≐
Muller Range ⋏ 102 0.40 N 113.50 E
Mullet Key I 152 22.29 S 134.30 E
Mullett Lake ◎ 154 5.35 S 142.15 E
Mullewa 41 55.30 N 11.13 E
Müllheim 210 27.37 N 82.44 W
Müllhyttan 190 45.30 N 84.30 W
Mullica ≐ 152 28.33 S 115.31 E
Mullica, Alquatka Branch ≐ 54 47.48 N 7.38 E
Mullica Hill 40 59.09 N 14.41 E
Mulligan ≐ 198 39.33 N 74.25 W
Mullikon
Mullin 275 39.47 N 74.48 W
Mullinavat 198 39.44 N 75.13 W
Mullingar 156 25.00 S 138.30 E
Mullins 206 42.46 N 84.54 W
Mullinville 186 31.33 N 98.40 W
Mullovka 28 53.32 N 7.20 W
Mullrose 182 34.12 N 79.15 W
Mullsjö 188 37.35 N 99.28 W
Mullumbimby 70 54.13 N 49.25 E
Mulobezi 50 52.14 N 14.25 E
Mulonda Funda 40 57.55 N 13.53 E
Mulondo 156 28.33 S 153.30 E
Mulondo Funda 144 16.48 S 25.09 E
Mulongoie 144 11.06 S 25.28 E
Mulshi 142 15.39 S 15.14 E
Mulshi Lake ◎ 144 7.50 S 27.00 E
Multai 112 18.30 N 73.30 E
Multān 112 21.46 N 78.15 E
Multé 110 30.11 N 71.29 E
Multia 222 17.41 N 91.24 W
Multien ◎ 26 62.25 N 24.47 E
Multnomah □6 26 62.25 N 24.47 E
Multnomah Channel ≐ 214 45.30 N 122.00 W
Multnomah Falls ∟ 214 45.51 N 122.52 W
Mulu, Gunong ∧ 214 45.35 N 122.07 W
Mulumba, Monts ⋏ 102 4.04 N 114.56 E
Mulungu 240 8.16 S 28.16 E
Mulungushi 240 7.02 S 35.28 W
Mulungushi Dam ⊸6 144 14.40 S 28.45 E
Mulunguzi 144 14.48 S 28.52 E
Mulwusuhe ≐ 104 14.48 S 28.52 E
Mulvane 110 34.40 N 95.30 E
Mulwad 188 37.29 N 97.14 W
Mulyah Mountain ∧ 112 16.53 N 75.45 E
Muma 156 30.37 S 144.31 E
Mumbles Head ⋟ 142 3.14 S 23.23 E
Mumbwa 44 51.35 N 3.59 W
Mumcular 144 14.59 S 27.04 E
Mume 120 37.05 N 27.40 E
Mumen 144 9.40 S 27.26 E
Mumeng 92 32.09 N 106.28 E
154 7.00 S 146.35 E
Mumford, N.Y., U.S. 200 42.59 N 77.52 W
Mumford, Tex., U.S. 212 30.44 N 96.34 W
Mumias 144 0.20 N 34.29 E
Muminabad 75 38.06 N 70.01 E
Mümling ≐ 52 49.50 N 9.09 E
Mumoni ∧ 144 0.31 S 38.01 E
Mumra 70 45.47 N 47.41 E
Mumser Knob ⋏2 204 40.40 N 81.54 W
Mumu 130 12.06 N 23.42 E
Mumungwe 146 21.59 S 26.24 E
Mun ≐ 100 15.19 N 105.30 E
Mun, Jabal ∧ 130 14.08 N 22.42 E
Muna 222 20.29 N 89.43 W
Muna ≐ 64 67.52 N 123.06 E
Muna, Pulau I 102 5.00 S 122.30 E
Muna, Selat ⋃ 102 5.15 S 122.10 E
Munā al-Amīr 132 29.54 N 31.15 E
Munābāo 110 25.45 N 70.17 E
Munajly 76 46.47 N 54.31 E
Munakata 86 33.50 N 130.35 E
Munamägi ⋏2 66 57.43 N 27.04 E
Munam-ni 88 38.41 N 126.54 E
Munbong-ni 261b 37.43 N 126.49 E
Muncar 105a 8.26 S 114.20 E
Münchberg 50 50.11 N 11.47 E
Müncheberg 50 52.30 N 14.08 E
Münchehofe 254a 52.30 N 13.40 E
München (Munich) 58 48.08 N 11.34 E
Münchenbernsdorf 50 50.49 N 11.56 E
Münchenbuchsee 54 47.01 N 7.27 E
Münchendorf 254b 48.02 N 16.23 E
München-Gladbach → Mönchengladbach 52 51.12 N 6.28 E
München-Riem, Flughafen ⊠ 58 48.08 N 11.41 E
Münchenstein 54 47.31 N 7.37 E
Münchhausen 52 50.57 N 8.43 E
Munchique, Cerro ∧ 236 2.32 N 76.57 W
Munch'ŏn 88 39.16 N 127.15 E
Muncie 206 40.11 N 85.23 W
Muncunsun 120 38.54 N 35.38 E
Muncy 200 41.12 N 76.47 W
Muncy Creek ≐ 200 41.13 N 76.48 W
Muncy Valley 200 41.21 N 76.35 W
Mundare 172 53.36 N 112.20 W
Mundaring 158a 31.54 S 116.10 E
Munday 186 33.27 N 99.38 W
Mundelein 206 42.16 N 88.00 W
Mündelheim ✲8 253 51.21 N 6.41 E
Münden 52 51.25 N 9.39 E
Münden, Naturpark ⊸
Munderfing 52 51.20 N 9.40 E
Munderkingen 58 48.05 N 13.11 E
Munderoo ∧ 54 48.14 N 9.38 E
Mundesley 161b 35.48 S 147.47 E
Mundijong 44 52.53 N 1.26 E
Mundiwindi 158a 32.18 S 115.59 E
Mundka ✲8 152 23.52 S 120.09 E
Mundo ≐ 262a 28.41 N 77.02 E
Mundolsheim 34 38.19 N 1.40 W
Mundon Hill 54 48.39 N 7.42 E
Mundo Novo 250 51.41 N 0.42 E
Mundra 245 11.52 S 40.28 W
Mundrabilla 110 22.51 N 69.44 E
Munduba, Ponta ⋟ 152 31.52 S 127.51 E
Mundubbera 246 24.05 S 46.18 W
Munducurus 156 25.36 S 151.18 E
Mundybaš 236 4.47 S 58.16 W
Mundytau, Gora ∧ 76 53.14 N 87.19 E
Munenga 75 38.00 N 68.27 E
Munera 142 10.02 S 14.41 E
Munford 34 39.02 N 2.28 W
Munfordville 184 35.27 N 89.47 W
Mungallala 184 37.16 N 85.54 W
Mungallala Creek ≐ 156 26.27 S 147.33 E
Mungana 156 28.05 S 147.15 E
Mungaoli 156 17.07 S 144.24 E
Mungari 114 24.25 N 78.06 E
Mungar Junction 144 17.12 S 33.31 E
Mungbere 156 25.36 S 152.36 E
Mungeli 142 13.56 S 21.55 E
Mungeranie 144 2.38 N 28.30 E
Mungindi 114 22.04 N 81.41 E
Mungla 156 28.00 S 138.36 E
Mungra Badshāhpur 156 28.58 S 148.59 E
Mungun-Tajga, Gora ∧ 116 22.19 N 89.36 E
114 25.40 N 82.11 E
Mun'gyŏng 76 50.16 N 90.05 E
Munhall 88 36.44 N 128.07 E
Munhamade 204 40.24 N 79.53 W
Munhango 144 16.37 S 36.58 E
Munhango ≐ 142 12.12 S 18.42 E
Munhoz 142 11.54 S 18.44 E
Munhye-ri 246 22.37 S 46.22 W
Munich → München 88 38.10 N 127.19 E
Muniesa 58 48.08 N 11.34 E
Munim ≐ 34 41.02 N 0.48 W
Munirka ✲8 240 2.45 S 44.04 W
Munising 262a 28.34 N 77.10 E
Munith 180 46.25 N 86.40 W
Muñiz 206 42.23 N 84.12 W
Muniz Freire 248 34.33 S 58.42 W
Munkács → Mukačevo 245 20.28 S 41.25 W
Munka-Ljungby 68 48.27 N 22.45 E
Munkebjerg ⋏2 41 56.15 N 12.58 E
Munkebo 41 55.41 N 9.37 E
Munkedal 41 55.27 N 10.34 E
Munkerud 26 58.29 N 11.41 E
Munkfors 40 59.50 N 13.31 E
Munksund 40 59.50 N 13.32 E
Munktorp 26 65.17 N 21.29 E
Munku-Sardyk, Gora ∧ 40 59.32 N 16.08 E
Münnerstadt 78 51.45 N 100.32 E
Munnsville 52 50.15 N 10.11 E
Munntown 200 42.59 N 75.35 W
Muñoz 269b 40.14 N 80.05 W
Muñoz ≐ 230p 21.22 N 78.32 W
Munozero 24 67.05 N 34.12 E
Muñoz Gamero, Peninsula ⋟1 244 52.30 S 73.10 W
Munpal-li 261b 37.45 N 126.43 E
Munro ✲8 278 34.32 S 58.31 W
Munroe Falls 204 41.08 N 81.26 W
Munro Lake ◎ 174 54.38 N 95.16 W
Munsan 88 37.51 N 126.48 E
Munsarpur 114 24.18 N 88.26 E
Munsey Park 266 40.48 N 73.41 W
Munshiganj 116 23.33 N 90.32 E
Münsing 58 47.54 N 11.22 E
Münsingen, B.R.D. 58 48.25 N 9.29 E
Münsingen, Schw. 54 46.53 N 7.34 E
Munsö I 40 59.23 N 17.35 E
Munson, Alta., Can. 172 51.34 N 112.45 W
Munson, Pa., U.S. 204 40.57 N 78.10 W
Munsons Corners 200 42.35 N 76.13 W
Munster, B.R.D. 48 51.57 N 7.37 E
Munster, B.R.D. 48 52.59 N 10.05 E
Munster, Fr. 52 48.45 N 8.44 E
Munster, Fr. 54 48.03 N 7.08 E
Munster, Schw. 54 46.29 N 8.16 E
Munster, Ind., U.S. 206 41.34 N 87.30 W
Munster □6 28 52.30 N 9.00 W
Münster □9 28 52.25 N 8.20 W
Münsterberg → Ziębice 30 50.37 N 17.00 E
Münsterkirche ⊍1 253 51.27 N 7.01 E
Münsterland ⊸1 48 52.00 N 7.30 E
Münsterlingen 54 47.38 N 9.14 E
Münstermaifeld 52 50.15 N 7.21 E
Muntadgin 152 31.45 S 118.34 E
Muntahak ∧ 104 1.52 N 103.47 E
Munte 106 2.03 N 121.08 E
Muntendam 48 53.07 N 6.53 E
Muntok 102 2.04 S 105.11 E
Mununzi 144 0.36 N 29.15 E
Munuscong Lake ◎ 180 46.10 N 84.08 W
Münzenberg 52 50.27 N 8.46 E
Munzur Silsilesi ⋏ 120 39.30 N 39.10 E
Muojärvi ◎ 26 65.56 N 29.36 E
Muolea Point ⋟ 219a 20.41 N 156.01 W
Muong Het 100 20.49 N 104.01 E
Muong-hinh 100 19.49 N 105.03 E
Muong Luong Nam Tha 92 20.57 N 101.25 E
Muong Saiapoun 100 18.24 N 101.31 E
Muong-sen 100 19.24 N 104.08 E
Muong-te 100 22.28 N 102.37 E
Muonio 24 67.57 N 23.42 E
Muoro 36 40.20 N 9.20 E
Muotathal 54 46.59 N 8.46 E
Mupa 142 16.10 S 15.44 E
Mupa, Parque Nacional da ⊸4 142 16.00 S 15.35 E
Mupa Game Reserve ⊸4 142 15.35 S 14.40 E
Mupini 146 17.50 S 19.40 E
Mup'ungjang 88 35.58 N 127.49 E
Muqaddam, Wādī ∨ 130 18.04 N 31.30 E
Muqatta' 130 14.40 N 35.51 E
Muqaybirah, Bi'r al- ⊸4
Muqayshiț I 132 30.53 N 32.50 E
Muqi 118 24.12 N 53.42 E
Muqsam, Jabal ∧ 88 41.46 N 124.39 E
Muquequete 130 13.38 N 27.40 E
Muqui 142 14.50 S 14.16 E
Mura (Mur) ≐ 245 20.57 S 41.20 W
Mura (Mur) ≐, Eur. 30 46.18 N 16.53 E
Mura ≐, S.S.S.R. 30 46.18 N 16.53 E
Muradiye, Tür. 78 58.27 N 98.34 E
Muradiye, Tür. 118 38.59 N 43.46 E
Murādnagar 120 38.39 N 27.21 E
Murafa ≐ 114 28.47 N 77.30 E
Murāgācha 68 48.13 N 28.14 E
Muraglione, Passo del ⋊ 116 23.32 N 88.24 E
Murajá 60 43.56 N 11.39 E
Murakami 240 0.47 S 47.57 W
Murallón, Cerro ∧ 82 38.14 N 139.29 E
Muramvya 244 49.48 S 73.25 W
Murañ 144 3.16 S 29.37 E
Murana 30 48.46 N 20.02 E
Murano, Isola di I 154 3.33 S 133.49 E
Muranskij Porog ∟ 58 45.28 N 12.21 E
Muraoka 78 58.02 N 112.16 E
Murarai 86 35.28 N 134.35 E
Murași 114 24.27 N 87.52 E
Muraški 24 59.24 N 48.55 E
Murat 255b 55.59 N 37.45 E
Murat ≐ 32 45.07 N 2.52 E
Muratbaşı ∧ 120 38.39 N 39.50 E
Muratdağı ∧ 74 39.24 N 43.21 E
Muratkovo 120 38.55 N 29.43 E
Muratlı 76 58.26 N 62.23 E
Muratovo 120 41.10 N 27.30 E
Muratsu 73 48.48 N 38.45 E
Murau 262b 22.59 N 88.27 E
Murauaú ≐ 30 47.07 N 14.10 E
Muravera 236 0.09 N 60.40 W
Muravjevka 36 39.25 N 9.35 E
Muravjovo 79 49.50 N 127.44 E
Murayama, Nihon 66 56.14 N 34.14 E
Murayama, Nihon 82 38.28 N 140.22 E
Murayama-chosuichi ◎1 258 35.45 N 139.23 E
Murayr, Jabal ⋏2 258 35.45 N 139.25 E
Murča 132 30.31 N 30.36 E
Mürcheh Khvort 34 41.24 N 7.27 W
Murchin 118 33.06 N 51.30 E
Murchison, Austl. 50 53.54 N 13.44 E
Murchison, N.Z. 156 36.37 S 145.14 E
Murchison, Tex., U.S. 162 41.48 S 172.20 E
Murchison ≐ 212 32.17 N 95.45 W
Murchison, Mount ∧, Austl. 152 27.42 S 114.09 E
Murchison, Mount ∧, N.Z. 152 26.46 S 116.25 E
Murchison Falls ∟, Malawi 162 43.01 S 171.22 E
Murchison Falls ∟, Ug. 144 15.54 S 34.44 E
Murchison Falls National Park ♠ 144 2.17 N 31.41 E
Murchison Range ⋏ 144 2.15 N 31.50 E
Murcia, Esp. 152 20.11 S 134.26 E
Murcia, Pil. 34 37.59 N 1.07 W
Murcia □9 106 10.36 N 123.02 E
Murciélago 34 38.30 N 1.45 W
Murciélagos, Islas II 226 10.55 N 85.44 W
Murcielagos Bay C 226 10.51 N 85.57 W
Mur-de-Barrez 106 8.39 N 123.33 E
Murdeduke, Lake ◎ 32 44.51 N 2.39 E
Murder Creek ≐, Ala., U.S. 159 38.11 S 143.53 E
Murder Creek ≐, N.Y., U.S. 184 31.04 N 87.06 W
Murderkill ≐ 200 43.05 N 78.31 W
Murdo 198 39.03 N 75.24 W
Murdock 188 43.53 N 100.43 W
Mure 210 27.01 N 82.09 W
Mureaux, Aérodrome des ⊠ 36 46.35 N 138.14 E
Mureck 251 49.00 N 1.57 E
Mürefte 30 46.42 N 15.46 E
Mureș □4 120 40.40 N 27.14 E
Mureș (Maros) ≐ 38 46.35 N 24.40 E
Muret 38 46.15 N 20.13 E
Murfreesboro, Ark., U.S. 32 43.28 N 1.21 E
Murfreesboro, N.C., U.S. 184 34.04 N 93.41 W
Murfreesboro, Tenn., U.S. 182 36.27 N 77.06 W
Murg 184 35.51 N 86.23 W
Murg ≐ 54 47.33 N 8.01 E
Murgab 52 48.55 N 8.10 E
Murgab (Morghāb) ≐ 75 38.10 N 73.59 E
Murgab ≐, S.S.S.R. 118 38.18 N 61.12 E
Murgeni 75 38.20 N 72.30 E
Murgenthal 38 46.12 N 28.01 E
Murgha Faqīrzai 54 47.16 N 7.50 E
Murgha Kibzai 110 31.03 N 67.46 E
Murgon 110 30.44 N 69.25 E
Murguia 156 26.15 S 151.57 E
Muri 34 42.57 N 2.49 W
Muri, Cook Is. 54 47.17 N 8.21 E
Muri, Schw. 164k 21.15 S 159.43 W
Muri, Schw. 54 46.56 N 7.29 E
Muria, Gunung ∧ 54 47.16 N 8.21 E
Muriaé 102 6.36 S 110.53 E
Muriaé ≐ 245 21.08 S 42.22 W
Muriás de Paredes 34 42.51 N 6.11 W
Muribeca dos Guararapes 240 10.26 S 36.59 W
Murici 240 8.10 S 35.01 W
Muricizal ≐ 240 9.19 S 35.56 W
Muridke 240 6.40 S 48.40 W
Muriége 142 31.48 N 74.16 E
Muriel Lake ◎ 142 9.58 S 21.11 E
Murih, Pulau I 172 54.10 N 110.40 W
Murila 102 0.42 N 109.03 E
Murilo I[1] 144 10.44 S 20.20 E
Murinda 14 8.40 N 152.11 E
Murinéli 113 30.47 N 76.29 E
Murinja 240 22.05 S 42.39 W
Murino, S.S.S.R. 78 54.47 N 107.21 E
Murino, S.S.S.R. 78 51.30 N 104.23 E
Murinskij ≐ 255a 60.03 N 30.27 E
Murisengo 255a 60.01 N 30.28 E
Muritiba 277a 22.52 S 43.02 W
Müritz ◎ 56 45.05 N 8.08 E
Murivai 245 12.39 S 38.59 W
Murkong Selek 50 53.25 N 12.43 E
Murliganj 162 38.46 S 177.55 E
110 27.49 N 95.16 E
114 25.54 N 86.59 E

Symbols in the index entries represent the broad categories identified in the key at the right. Symbols with superior numbers (⋏²) identify subcategories (see complete key on page I · 26).

Kartensymbole in dem Registerverzeichnis stellen die rechts in Schlüssel erklärten Kategorien dar. Symbole mit hochgestellten Ziffern (⋏²) bezeichnen Unterabteilungen einer Kategorie (vgl. vollständiger Schlüssel auf Seite I · 26).

Los símbolos incluidos en el texto del índice representan las grandes categorías identificadas con la clave a la derecha. Los símbolos con números en su parte superior (⋏²) identifican las subcategorías (véase la clave completa en la página I · 26).

Les symboles de l'index représentent les catégories indiquées dans la légende à droite. Les symboles suivis d'un indice (⋏²) représentent des sous-catégories (voir légende complète à la page I · 26).

Os símbolos incluídos no texto do índice representam as grandes categorias identificadas com a chave à direita. Os símbolos com números em sua parte superior (⋏²) identificam as subcategorias (veja-se a chave completa à página I · 26).

ENGLISH	DEUTSCH	ESPAÑOL	FRANÇAIS	PORTUGUÊS
∧ Mountain	Berg	Montaña	Montagne	Montanha
⋏ Mountains	Berge	Montañas	Montagnes	Montanhas
⋊ Pass	Pass	Paso	Col	Passo
∨ Valley, Canyon	Tal, Cañon	Valle, Cañón	Vallée, Canyon	Vale, Canhão
⊸ Plain	Ebene	Llano	Plaine	Planície
⋟ Cape	Kap	Cabo	Cap	Cabo
I Island	Insel	Isla	Île	Ilha
II Islands	Inseln	Islas	Îles	Ilhas
⊻ Other Topographic Features	Andere Topographische Objekte	Otros Elementos Topográficos	Autres données topographiques	Outros Elementos Topográficos

ESPAÑOL / FRANÇAIS / PORTUGUÊS

Nombre / Nom / Nome	Página / Page / Página	Lat.°′	Long.°′ W=Oeste / W=Ouest / W=Oeste
Murlo	60	43.09 N	11.23 E
Murmansk	24	68.58 N	33.05 E
Murmansk Rise ✣[3]	10	74.00 N	37.00 E
Murmaši	24	68.47 N	32.42 E
Murmerwoude	48	53.16 N	6.00 E
Murmino	70	54.36 N	40.03 E
Murnau	58	47.40 N	11.12 E
Murnei	130	12.57 N	22.52 E
Murō	84	34.34 N	136.02 E
Muro, Capo di ≻	36	41.44 N	8.40 E
Muro Lucano	36	40.45 N	15.30 E
Murom	70	55.34 N	42.02 E
Muromcevo	76	56.23 N	75.14 E
Muroran	82a	42.18 N	140.59 E
Muros	34	42.47 N	9.02 W
Muros y Noya, Ría de C[1]	34	42.45 N	9.00 W
Muroto	86	33.18 N	134.09 E
Muroto-anan-kaigan-kokutei-kōen ♠	86	33.41 N	134.32 E
Muroto-zaki ≻	86	33.15 N	134.11 E
Murovanyje Kurilovcy	68	48.43 N	27.31 E
Murowana Goślina	30	52.35 N	17.01 E
Murphy, Idaho, U.S.	192	43.13 N	116.33 W
Murphy, Mo., U.S.	209	38.27 N	90.28 W
Murphy, N.C., U.S.	182	35.05 N	84.01 W
Murphy Lake ⊜	172	52.00 N	121.00 W
Murphys	216	38.08 N	120.28 W
Murphysboro	184	37.46 N	89.20 W
Murphy Slough ≃	216	36.28 N	120.00 W
Murr ≃	52	48.57 N	9.16 E
Murr, Wādī ∨	132	28.27 N	32.18 E
Murrah, Qārat al- ∧[2]	132	30.00 N	32.41 E
Murra Murra	156	28.16 S	146.48 E
Murrāt, Ābār ⍑[4]	130	21.03 N	32.55 E
Murray, Iowa, U.S.	180	41.03 N	93.57 W
Murray, Ky., U.S.	184	36.37 N	88.19 W
Murray, Utah, U.S.	190	40.40 N	111.53 W
Murray ≃, Austl.	156	35.22 S	139.22 E
Murray ≃, Austl.	158a	32.35 S	115.46 E
Murray ≃, B.C., Can.	172	55.40 N	121.10 W
Murray, Lake ⊜	154	7.00 S	141.30 E
Murray, Lake ⊜[1]	182	34.04 N	81.23 W
Murray, Mount ∧	170	60.54 N	128.49 W
Murray Bay → La Malbaie	176	47.39 N	70.10 W
Murray Bridge	158b	35.07 S	139.17 E
Murray Canal ≍	202	44.04 N	77.35 W
Murray City	178	39.31 N	82.10 W
Murray Downs	152	21.04 S	134.40 E
Murray Fracture Zone ✣	16	34.00 N	133.00 W
Murray Harbour	176	46.00 N	62.31 W
Murray Head ≻	176	46.00 N	62.28 W
Murray Maxwell Bay C	166	70.00 N	80.00 W
Murray Mouth ≃[1]	158b	35.34 S	138.54 E
Murray Ridge ✣[3]	12	20.00 N	61.00 E
Murraysburg	148	31.58 S	23.47 E
Murrayville, B.C., Can.	214	49.10 N	122.36 W
Murrayville, Ill., U.S.	184	39.35 N	90.15 W
Murrébuè	144	13.02 S	40.30 E
Murree	113	33.54 N	73.24 E
Mürren	54	46.34 N	7.54 E
Murrhardt	52	48.59 N	9.34 E
Murri ≃	236	6.33 N	76.52 W
Murrieta	218	33.33 N	117.13 W
Murrin Murrin	152	28.55 S	121.49 E
Murrumbidgee ≃	156	34.43 S	143.12 E
Murrumburrah	156	34.33 S	148.21 E
Murrupula	144	15.27 S	38.47 E
Murrurundi	156	31.46 S	150.50 E
Murry Hill	269b	40.17 N	80.09 W
Murrysville	269b	40.26 N	79.42 W
Mursala, Pulau I	104	1.38 N	98.32 E
Mürsel	120	39.11 N	37.59 E
Murshidābād	116	24.11 N	88.16 E
Murshidābād □[5]	116	24.05 N	88.10 E
Mürşitpınar	120	36.54 N	38.19 E
Murska Sobota	36	46.40 N	16.10 E
Murskij, Porog ⌞	78	58.27 N	98.30 E
Murtajāpur	112	20.44 N	77.23 E
Murtal	256c	38.42 N	9.22 W
Murtee	156	31.35 S	143.30 E
Murten	54	46.56 N	7.07 E
Murtensee → Morat, Lac de ⊜	54	46.55 N	7.05 E
Murter, Otok I	36	43.48 N	15.37 E
Murtle Lake ⊜	172	52.08 N	119.38 W
Murtoa	156	36.37 S	142.28 E
Murton	42	54.49 N	1.24 W
Murtosa	34	40.44 N	8.38 W
Muru	130	6.36 N	29.15 E
Muru ≃	238	8.09 S	70.45 W
Muruasigar ∧	144	3.08 N	35.02 E
Murud	112	18.19 N	72.58 E
Murud, Gunong ∧	102	3.52 N	115.30 E
Murukta	64	67.46 N	102.01 E
Murung ≃	102	0.12 S	114.03 E
Murupara	162	38.28 S	176.42 E
Murutinga	236	3.26 S	59.12 W
Murvaul, Lake ⊜[1]	212	32.03 N	94.28 W
Murvaul Creek ≃	184	32.05 N	94.12 W
Murwāra	114	23.51 N	80.24 E
Murwillumbah	156	28.19 S	153.24 E
Mürzzuschlag	30	47.36 N	15.41 E
Muş	120	38.44 N	41.30 E
Muş □[4]	120	39.00 N	42.00 E
Musa	142	2.40 N	19.18 E
Musa ≃, Pap. N. Gui.	154	9.25 S	148.50 E
Mūsa (Mūša) ≃, S.S.S.R.	66	56.24 N	24.10 E
Mūsā, Jabal (Mount Sinai) ∧	130	28.32 N	33.59 E
Mūsā, 'Uyūn (Springs of Moses) ⍑[4]	132	29.52 N	32.39 E
Musabeyli	120	39.51 N	34.37 E
Musadi	142	2.34 S	22.47 E
Mūsa Khel	113	32.38 N	71.44 E
Mūsa Khel Bāzār	110	30.52 N	69.49 E
Musala ∧	38	42.11 N	23.34 E
Musan	88	42.14 N	129.13 E
Musao	144	7.43 S	26.17 E
Mūsā Qal'eh	110	32.22 N	64.46 E
Mūsā Qal'eh ≃	118	32.05 N	64.51 E
Musar	262b	22.54 N	88.14 E
Musara	154	10.00 S	149.50 E
Musasa	144	3.21 S	31.33 E
Musashi → Iruma, Nihon	84	35.50 N	139.28 E
Musashi, Nihon	86	33.30 N	131.43 E
Musashino	84	35.42 N	139.34 E
Musashino-daichi ⋀[1]	258	35.44 N	139.28 E
Musau	54	47.32 N	10.40 E
Musay'īd	118	24.59 N	51.32 E
Musaymīr	134	13.27 N	44.37 E
Musazade	120	41.22 N	41.16 E
Mūsāzai	110	30.23 N	66.32 E
Muscat → Masqaṭ	118	23.37 N	58.35 E
Muscat and Oman → Oman □[1]	108	22.00 N	58.00 E
Muscatatuck ≃	208	38.46 N	86.10 W
Muscatatuck, Grassy Fork ≃	208	39.45 N	85.07 W
Muscatatuck, Vernon Fork ≃	208	38.46 N	85.54 W
Muscatine	180	41.25 N	91.03 W
Müsch	52	50.23 N	6.49 E
Mus-Chaja, Gora ∧	64	62.35 N	140.50 E
Muschwitz	50	51.11 N	12.07 E
Muscle Shoals	184	34.45 N	87.40 W
Musclow, Mount ∧	172	53.17 N	127.09 W
Musclow Lake ⊜	174	51.25 N	94.56 W
Muscoda	180	43.11 N	90.27 W
Musconetcong ≃	200	40.36 N	75.11 W
Musconetcong, Lake ⊜	266	40.54 N	74.42 W
Muscongus Bay C	176	43.55 N	69.20 W
Muscooten Bay ⊜	209	40.05 N	90.25 W
Muscote Bay C	202	44.06 N	77.18 W
Muscoy	218	34.09 N	117.19 W
Muse	204	40.18 N	80.12 W
Musengezi ≃	144	15.43 S	31.14 E
Museo Nacional de Antropologia ⊌	276a	19.25 N	99.11 W
Müsgebi	120	37.02 N	27.21 E
Musgrave, Austl.	154	14.47 S	143.30 E
Musgrave, B.C., Can.	214	48.45 N	123.32 W
Musgrave, Mount ∧	162	43.48 S	170.43 E
Musgrave Ranges ⋀	152	26.10 S	131.50 E
Musgravetown	176	48.24 N	53.53 W
Mūshā	132	27.08 N	31.18 E
Mushābani	116	22.31 N	86.27 E
Mushandike National Park ♠	144	20.10 S	30.38 E
Mushāsh, Jabal al- ∧[2]	132	28.54 N	31.11 E
Mushenge	142	4.32 S	21.21 E
Mushie	142	3.01 S	16.54 E
Mushigang	90	29.44 N	115.14 E
Mushilin	90	23.36 N	117.06 E
Mushima	144	14.13 S	25.05 E
Mushin	140	6.32 N	3.22 E
Mushitageshan ∧	110	38.17 N	75.11 E
Mushui ≃	90	27.00 N	119.41 E
Mushu Island I	154	3.25 S	143.35 E
Mūsi ≃, Bhārat	112	16.41 N	79.40 E
Musi ≃, Indon.	102	2.20 S	104.56 E
Musishan ∧	110	36.03 N	80.07 E
Muskauer Heide •[3]	50	51.25 N	14.40 E
Muskeg ≃	172	54.01 N	119.03 W
Muskeget Channel ⊔	197	41.25 N	70.20 W
Muskeget Island I	197	41.20 N	70.18 W
Muskeg Lake Indian Reserve •[4]	174	52.58 N	106.57 W
Muskego	206	42.54 N	88.08 W
Muskego Lake ⊜	206	42.53 N	88.07 W
Muskegon	206	43.14 N	86.16 W
Muskegon ≃	180	43.14 N	86.20 W
Muskegon County Airport ⊠	206	43.10 N	86.14 W
Muskegon Heights	206	43.12 N	86.12 W
Muskegon Lake ⊜	206	43.14 N	86.17 W
Muskegon State Park ♠	206	43.14 N	86.20 W
Mušketova, Gora ∧	78	53.35 N	113.32 E
Muskingum □[6]	204	40.06 N	81.51 W
Muskingum ≃	204	40.03 N	81.59 W
Muskingum Brook ≃	275	39.48 N	74.44 W
Muskira	114	25.40 N	79.48 E
Muskö I	40	59.00 N	18.06 E
Muskoday Indian Reserve •[4]	174	53.06 N	105.30 W
Muskogee	186	35.45 N	95.22 W
Muskoka □[6]	202	45.05 N	79.03 W
Muskoka, Lake ⊜	202	45.00 N	79.25 W
Muskoka, North Branch ≃	202	45.02 N	79.19 W
Muskoka, South Branch ≃	202	45.02 N	79.19 W
Muskosh Channel ⊔	202	44.55 N	79.53 W
Muskowekwan Indian Reserve •[4]	174	51.19 N	104.06 W
Muskrat Creek ≃	192	43.09 N	108.11 W
Muskratdam Lake ⊜	174	53.25 N	91.40 W
Muskrat Lake ⊜	180	45.40 N	76.55 W
Muskwa ≃	166	58.45 N	122.35 W
Muskwa Lake ⊜	172	56.09 N	114.38 W
Musl'umovo	70	55.18 N	53.12 E
Muşmuş	122	32.32 N	35.09 E
Musocco •[8]	256b	45.30 N	9.08 E
Musofu Mission	144	13.31 S	29.02 E
Musoma	144	1.30 S	33.48 E
Musone ≃, It.	58	45.50 N	11.55 E
Musone ≃, It.	60	43.28 N	13.38 E
Musoshi	144	11.54 S	27.46 E
Musquanousse, Lac ⊜	176	50.22 N	61.05 W
Musquapsink Brook ≃	266	40.59 N	74.01 W
Musquaro, Lac ⊜	176	50.38 N	61.05 W
Musquash ≃	202	44.57 N	79.52 W
Musquash Brook ≃	273	42.42 N	71.26 W
Musquashcut Pond ⊜	273	42.13 N	70.46 W
Musquodoboit Harbour	176	44.47 N	63.09 W
Mussau Island I	154	1.30 S	149.40 E
Musselburgh	42	55.57 N	3.04 W
Musselkanaal	48	52.56 N	7.00 E
Musselshell ≃	192	47.21 N	107.58 W
Mussel Slough ≃	216	36.11 N	119.47 W
Mussende	142	10.32 S	16.05 E
Mussidan	32	45.02 N	0.22 E
Mussolo	142	9.59 S	17.19 E
Mussomeli	36	37.35 N	13.46 E
Mussoorie	114	30.27 N	78.05 E
Mussuco	142	17.08 S	19.05 E
Mussum	48	51.48 N	6.34 E
Mussuma	142	14.14 S	21.59 E
Mussy-sur-Seine	54	47.58 N	4.30 E
Mustafakemalpaşa	120	40.02 N	28.24 E
Mustafino	70	55.01 N	53.38 E
Mustahil	134	5.12 N	44.17 E
Müstair	54	46.37 N	10.27 E
Mustajevo	70	51.48 N	53.25 E
Mustajõe	66	57.59 N	26.58 E
Mustāng	114	29.11 N	83.58 E
Mustang Draw ∨	186	32.12 N	101.36 W
Mustang Island I	186	28.00 N	96.55 W
Mustāy	132	30.37 N	31.09 E
Musters, Lago ⊜	244	45.27 S	69.13 W
Mustinka ≃	188	45.45 N	96.38 W
Mustjala	66	58.28 N	22.14 E
Mustla	66	58.14 N	25.52 E
Musṭurud	263c	30.08 N	31.17 E
Mustvee	66	58.51 N	26.56 E
Musu-dan ≻	88	40.50 N	129.43 E
Musun	74	39.42 N	43.49 E
Muswellbrook	156	32.16 S	150.53 E
Muszyna	30	49.21 N	20.54 E
Mūt, Miṣr	130	25.29 N	28.59 E
Mut, Tür.	120	36.39 N	33.27 E
Mutá, Ponta do ≻	245	13.52 S	38.56 W
Mu'tah	122	31.06 N	35.42 E
Mutalau	164v	18.56 S	169.50 W
Mutambara	144	19.36 S	32.33 E
Mutanchiang → Mudanjiang	79	44.35 N	129.36 E
Mutanda, Moç.	146	21.02 S	33.31 E
Mutanda, Zaïre	142	5.17 S	16.34 E
Mutanda Mission	144	12.24 S	26.16 E
Mutankiang → Mudanjiang	79	44.35 N	129.36 E
Mutarammil, Jabal al- ∧	122	31.04 N	36.06 E
Mutayyin	134	15.59 N	43.04 E
Mutbīn	122	33.09 N	36.15 E
Mutějovice	50	50.09 N	13.41 E
Mutha	144	1.48 S	38.26 E
Mutiko	144	1.39 S	28.12 E
Muting	154	7.23 S	140.20 E
Mutis, Gunung ∧	102	9.34 S	124.14 E
Mutmur	120	38.51 N	38.31 E
Mutok Harbor C	164r	6.48 N	158.16 E
Mutombo-Mukulu	142	7.58 S	24.00 E
Mutoraj	64	61.20 N	100.30 E
Mutoto	142	5.42 S	22.42 E
Mutouchengzi	88	41.20 N	119.59 E
Mutouhao	97	28.49 N	105.04 E
Mutquín	242	28.19 S	66.10 W
Mutsamudu	147a	12.09 S	44.25 E
Mutshatsha	142	10.39 S	24.27 E
Mutsu	82	41.17 N	141.10 E
Mutsuai	258	35.08 N	139.38 E
Mutsumi	86	34.26 N	131.34 E
Mutsuura •[8]	258	35.19 N	139.37 E
Mutsu-wan C	82	41.05 N	140.55 E
Muttaburra	156	22.36 S	144.33 E
Mutte Kopf ∧	54	47.16 N	10.39 E
Muttenz	54	47.32 N	7.39 E
Mutters	58	47.14 N	11.23 E
Mutterstadt	52	49.26 N	8.21 E
Mutton Bay	176	50.47 N	59.02 W
Muttontown	266	40.49 N	73.33 W
Muttra → Mathura	114	27.30 N	77.41 E
Muttyāluppettai	112	11.57 N	79.50 E
Mutual, Ohio, U.S.	208	40.05 N	83.38 W
Mutual, Pa., U.S.	269b	40.14 N	79.30 W
Muṭūbis	132	31.18 N	30.31 E
Mutuca, Ribeirão da ≃	246	21.36 S	45.39 W
Mutucu, Lago ⊜	240	1.21 N	50.24 W
Mutuípe	245	13.15 S	39.31 W
Mutum, Bra.	245	19.49 S	41.26 W
Mutum, Bra.	245	15.48 S	54.53 W
Mutum ≃, Bra.	236	4.25 S	68.03 W
Mutum ≃, Bra.	245	20.25 S	52.56 W
Mutumbo	142	13.14 S	17.17 E
Mutunópolis	245	13.40 S	49.15 W
Mutu-Nui, Islote I	164z	27.12 S	109.28 W
Muturi	154	2.06 S	133.43 E
Muturi ≃	154	2.13 S	133.40 E
Mututi, Ilha I	240	0.45 S	51.00 W
Mutzig	54	48.32 N	7.28 E
Mutzschen	50	51.16 N	12.53 E
Mūvattupula	112	9.58 N	76.35 E
Muvukoni	144	0.24 S	38.14 E
Muwan	96	30.44 N	118.43 E
Muwopu	94	41.03 N	121.12 E
Muxaluando	142	8.07 S	14.17 E
Muxihe	90	31.06 N	115.22 E
Muxima	142	9.31 S	13.56 E
Muyaga	144	3.14 S	30.33 E
Muyang	90	27.06 N	119.34 E
Muyinga	144	2.51 S	30.20 E
Muymanu ≃	238	11.27 S	69.03 W
Muy Muy	226	12.46 N	85.38 W
Muyuka	142	4.17 N	9.25 E
Muyumba	144	7.15 S	26.59 E
Mužač'	72	54.22 N	36.21 E
Muzaffarābād	113	34.22 N	73.28 E
Muzaffargarh	113	30.04 N	71.12 E
Muzaffarnagar	114	29.28 N	77.41 E
Muzaffarnagar □[5]	114	29.30 N	77.30 E
Muzaffarpur	114	26.07 N	85.24 E
Muzaffarpur □[5]	114	26.00 N	85.20 E
Muzambinho	246	21.22 S	46.32 W
Muzambinho ≃	246	21.15 S	46.26 W
Muzambo ≃	246	21.27 S	46.05 W
Muzayrīb	122	32.42 N	36.01 E
Muzbek, Gora ∧	75	40.23 N	69.39 E
Muzbel' •[1]	76	50.15 N	70.50 E
Muzeze	142	15.03 S	17.43 E
Muzhen	90	30.43 N	117.56 E
Muži	64	65.22 N	64.40 E
Mužiči	74	43.03 N	44.59 E
Mužiksu	76	47.42 N	84.58 E
Muzillac	32	47.33 N	2.29 W
Muzkol, Chrebet ⋀	75	38.25 N	73.30 E
Muzoka	144	16.41 S	27.19 E
Muzon, Cape ≻	170	54.41 N	132.44 W
Muz Tau ∧	76	43.50 N	85.40 E
Muzūrah	132	28.53 N	30.48 E
Muzzana del Turgnano	58	45.49 N	13.08 E
Mvadhi-Ousyé	142	1.13 N	13.12 E
Mvam	142	0.13 S	9.39 E
Mvangane	142	2.38 N	11.44 E
Mvela	144	14.46 S	35.16 E
Mvengué	142	3.17 N	11.01 E
Mvolo	130	6.03 N	29.56 E
Mvomero	144	6.20 S	37.25 E
Mvoung ≃	142	0.04 N	12.18 E
Mvouti	142	4.15 S	12.29 E
Mvuha	144	7.12 S	37.51 E
Mwadi-Kalumba	142	7.53 S	18.46 E
Mwadui	144	3.33 S	33.36 E
Mwanangumune	142	15.31 S	23.30 E
Mwango	142	6.51 S	24.13 E
Mwanza, Malawi	144	15.37 S	34.31 E
Mwanza, Tan.	144	2.31 S	32.54 E
Mwanza, Zaïre	144	7.54 S	26.45 E
Mwanza, Zam.	142	17.02 S	24.27 E
Mwanza □[4]	144	2.45 S	32.45 E
Mwaya, Tan.	144	9.33 S	33.57 E
Mwaya, Tan.	144	8.55 S	36.50 E
Mweelrea ∧	28	53.38 N	9.50 W
Mwehu	144	5.44 S	26.40 E
Mweka	142	4.51 S	21.34 E
Mwemena	144	10.19 S	27.28 E
Mwenda	144	12.01 S	28.44 E
Mwendjila	142	7.12 S	18.51 E
Mwene-Ditu	142	7.03 S	23.27 E
Mwenga	144	3.02 S	28.26 E
Mwepo	144	11.56 S	26.11 E
Mwerasandu	144	0.59 S	30.23 E
Mwereni	144	4.20 S	39.08 E
Mweru, Lake ⊜	144	9.00 S	28.45 E
Mweru Marsh Game Reserve •[4]	144	8.45 S	29.30 E
Mweru Wantipa, Lake ⊜	144	8.45 S	29.40 E
Mwetshi	142	4.42 S	22.39 E
Mwilambwe	144	8.07 S	25.00 E
Mwimbi	144	8.39 S	31.40 E
Mwingi	144	0.56 S	38.04 E
Mwinilunga	142	11.44 S	24.26 E
Mwitikira	144	6.31 S	35.39 E
Mwombezhi ≃	144	12.52 S	25.00 E
Mya, Oued ∨	138	30.47 N	4.54 E
Myaing	100	21.37 N	94.51 E
Myakka ≃	210	26.56 N	82.11 W
Myakka, Lake ⊜	210	27.16 N	82.17 W
Myakka City	210	27.21 N	82.10 W
Myakka River State Park ♠	210	27.15 N	82.17 W
Myall Range ⋀	160	32.58 S	151.22 E
Myanaung	100	18.17 N	95.19 E
Myanma → Burma □[1]	100	22.00 N	98.00 E
Myaungmya	100	16.36 N	94.56 E
Myawadi	100	16.41 N	98.31 E
Myckelgensjö	26	63.34 N	17.37 E
Myebon	100	20.03 N	93.22 E
Myeik → Mergui	100	12.26 N	98.36 E
Myers, Ky., U.S.	208	38.21 N	83.57 W
Myers, N.Y., U.S.	200	42.32 N	76.32 W
Myerstown	198	40.22 N	76.19 W
Myingyan	100	21.28 N	95.23 E
Myinmoletkat Taung ∧	100	13.28 N	98.48 E
Myitkyinā	100	25.23 N	97.24 E
Myitta	100	14.10 N	98.31 E
Myittha	100	21.25 N	96.08 E
Myittha ≃	100	23.12 N	94.17 E
Myjava	30	48.45 N	17.34 E
Myjeldino	24	61.46 N	54.48 E
Myjlybulak	76	48.57 N	75.13 E
Myk	75	39.39 N	68.25 E
Myla	24	65.25 N	50.48 E
Mylau	50	50.37 N	12.16 E
Myl'džino	76	59.03 N	78.29 E
Myllendonk, Schloss ⊥	253	51.13 N	6.29 E
Myllykoski	26	60.47 N	26.48 E
Myllymäki	26	62.32 N	24.17 E
Mylor	158b	35.03 S	138.45 E
Mymensingh	114	24.45 N	90.24 E
Mynämäki	26	60.40 N	22.00 E
Mynaral	76	45.25 N	73.41 E
Mynbulak, Gora ∧	75	41.43 N	69.49 E
Mynfontein	148	30.55 S	23.57 E
Mynydd Bach ∧[2]	44	52.15 N	4.05 W
Mynydd Eppynt ∧	44	52.05 N	3.30 W
Mynydd Hiraethog ∧	44	53.05 N	3.33 W
Mynydd Pencarreg ∧[2]	44	52.04 N	4.04 W
Mynydd Prescelly ∧	44	51.58 N	4.42 W
Mynžilgi, Gora ∧	75	43.49 N	68.40 E
Myōgi	84	36.17 N	138.49 E
Myōgi-san ∧	84	36.17 N	138.44 E
Myo-gyi	100	21.27 N	96.22 E
Myohaung	100	20.36 N	93.10 E
Myohyang-san ⋀	88	40.02 N	126.17 E
Myohyang-sanmaek ⋀	88	40.30 N	127.00 E
Myojin-dake ∧	260	34.57 N	135.36 E
Myōjin-ga-take ∧	84	35.17 N	139.03 E
Myōjin-san ∧	86	33.34 N	133.04 E
Myōken-san ∧	86	35.24 N	134.39 E
Myōken-zan ∧[2]	260	34.30 N	134.57 E
Myōkō	84	36.56 N	138.13 E
Myōkō-kōgen	84	36.52 N	138.12 E
Myōkō-zan ∧	84	36.52 N	138.07 E
Myŏnmong-ni •[8]	261b	37.35 N	127.05 E
Myponga	158b	35.24 S	138.28 E
Myra ⊥	120	36.15 N	29.54 E
Mýrdalsjökull ▽	24a	63.40 N	19.05 W
Myrnam	172	53.40 N	111.14 W
Myroodah	152	18.08 S	124.16 E
Myrskylä (Mörskom)	26	60.40 N	25.51 E
Myrtle Beach	182	33.42 N	78.52 W
Myrtle Beach Air Force Base ■	182	33.41 N	78.56 W
Myrtle Creek	192	43.01 N	123.17 W
Myrtle Grove	184	30.25 N	87.18 W
Myrtle Point	192	43.04 N	124.08 W
Myrtle Springs	212	32.37 N	95.56 W
Myrtletowne	194	40.47 N	124.04 W
Myrtleville	160	34.29 S	149.49 E
Myšega	72	54.31 N	37.02 E
Mysen	26	59.33 N	11.20 E
Mysingen ⊔	40	59.00 N	18.15 E
Myski	76	53.42 N	87.48 E
Myškino	66	57.47 N	38.27 E
Myśla ≃	50	52.40 N	14.29 E
Myślenice	30	49.51 N	19.56 E
Myślibórz	30	52.55 N	14.52 E
Mysłowice	30	50.15 N	19.07 E
Mysore	112	12.18 N	76.39 E
Mysore □[3]	112	14.00 N	76.00 E
Mys Šmidta	170	68.56 N	179.26 W
Mystic, Conn., U.S.	197	41.21 N	71.58 W
Mystic, Iowa, U.S.	180	40.47 N	92.57 W
Mystic ≃	273	42.23 N	71.03 W
Mystic Seaport ⊌	197	41.22 N	71.58 W
Mys Vchodnoj	64	73.53 N	86.43 E
Mysy	24	60.34 N	53.57 E
Mys Želanija	62	76.56 N	68.35 E
Myszków	30	50.36 N	19.20 E
Myszyniec	30	53.24 N	21.21 E
Myt	70	56.48 N	42.21 E
My-tho	100	10.21 N	106.21 E
Mytholm	252	53.44 N	2.01 W
Mytholmroyd	252	53.44 N	1.59 W
Mytilene → Mitilíni	38	39.06 N	26.32 E
Mytišči	72	55.55 N	37.46 E
Mytishchi → Mytišči	72	55.55 N	37.46 E
Myton	190	40.12 N	110.04 W
Mývatn ⊜	24a	65.37 N	16.58 W
Myzovo	68	51.22 N	24.31 E
Mzab, Oued ∨	138	32.19 N	5.24 E
Mže ≃	30	49.46 N	13.24 E
Mzenga	144	6.56 S	38.43 E
Mziha	144	5.54 S	37.47 E
Mzimba	144	11.52 S	33.34 E
Mzimkulu ≃	148	30.44 S	30.28 E
Mzimvubu ≃	148	31.38 S	29.32 E
Mzuzu	144	11.27 S	33.55 E
Mzymta ≃	74	43.27 N	39.56 E
N			
Na I	164r	6.52 N	158.22 E
Naab ≃	30	49.01 N	12.02 E
Naach, Jbel ∧	34	34.53 N	3.22 W
Naachtpunkt Brook ≃	266	40.54 N	74.15 W
Naaldwijk	48	52.00 N	4.12 E
Naalehu	219d	19.04 N	155.35 W
Na'ām	130	9.42 N	28.27 E
Naama, Sebkret en ☷	138	33.20 N	0.16 W
Naaman Creek ≃	275	39.48 N	75.27 W
Naantali	26	60.27 N	22.02 E
Naarden	48	52.17 N	5.09 E
Naas	28	53.13 N	6.39 W
Naas ≃	161b	35.36 S	149.04 E
Naast	46	50.33 N	4.05 E
Na'azuz, Har ∧	122	30.01 N	35.00 E
Nabā, Jabal an- (Mount Nebo) ∧	122	31.46 N	35.45 E
Nababiep	146	29.36 S	17.46 E
Nabābpur	262b	22.42 N	88.12 E
Nabadid	134	9.39 N	43.28 E
Nabadwīp	116	23.25 N	88.22 E
Nabaganga ≃[1]	116	22.59 N	89.34 E
Nabagram	116	24.12 N	88.06 E
Nabalat al-Ḥajanah	130	13.13 N	29.02 E
Nabari	84	34.37 N	136.05 E
Nabari ≃	84	34.45 N	136.01 E
Nabarūh	132	31.06 N	31.18 E
Nabas	106	11.50 N	122.05 E
Nabasta	116	23.15 N	88.01 E
Nabb	208	38.36 N	85.38 W
Nabberu, Lake ⊜	152	25.36 S	120.30 E
Nabburg	30	49.28 N	12.11 E
Nabeina	164t	1.26 N	173.05 E
Naberera	144	4.12 S	36.56 E
Nabereżnoje	255b	55.57 N	37.58 E
Nabereżnyje Čelny	70	55.42 N	52.19 E
Nabesna	170	62.22 N	143.00 W
Nabesna ≃	170	63.03 N	141.52 W
Nabeul	138	36.27 N	10.44 E
Nabeul □[8]	36	36.35 N	10.45 E
Nābha	113	30.22 N	76.09 E
Nab Hill ∧[2]	252	53.47 N	1.57 W
Nabī Hārūn, Jabal an- ∧	122	30.19 N	35.24 E
Nabileque ≃	238	20.55 S	57.49 W
Nabire	154	3.22 S	135.29 E
Nabisipi ≃	176	50.14 N	62.13 W
Nabiswera	144	1.28 N	32.16 E
Nabī Yūnus, Ra's an- ≻	122	33.39 N	35.24 E
Nabnasset	197	42.37 N	71.25 W
Nabnasset Pond ⊜	273	42.37 N	71.26 W
Nabogame	222	26.14 N	106.57 W
Naboomspruit	146	24.32 S	28.36 E
Nabordo	140	10.10 N	9.20 E
Nabou	140	11.27 N	2.43 W
Nabq	130	28.04 N	34.25 E
Nabua	106	13.24 N	123.22 E
Nabudalin	79	50.14 N	120.10 E
Nabula	110	31.55 N	80.10 E
Nābulus	122	32.13 N	35.16 E
Nābulus □[8]	122	32.18 N	35.17 E
Nabunturan	106	7.35 N	125.58 E
Nacajuca	224	18.08 N	93.01 W
Nacala	144	14.34 S	40.41 E
Nacala-Velha	144	14.32 S	40.37 E
Načalovo	70	46.20 N	48.11 E
Nacaome	226	13.31 N	87.30 W
Nacastillo	224	19.35 N	104.55 W
Nacereddine	34	36.08 N	3.26 E
Nachabinka ≃	255b	55.51 N	37.12 E
Nachabino	72	55.51 N	37.11 E
Naches	214	46.44 N	120.42 W
Naches ≃	192	46.38 N	120.31 W
Nachičevan'	74	39.13 N	45.24 E
Nachičevanskaja Avtonomnaja Sovetskaja Socialističeskaja Respublika □[3]	74	39.20 N	45.30 E
Nachi-katsuura	82	33.30 N	135.55 E
Nāchinda	116	21.53 N	87.46 E
Nachingwea	144	10.23 S	38.46 E
Nāchna	110	27.30 N	71.43 E
Náchod	30	50.25 N	16.10 E
Nachodka	79	42.48 N	132.52 E
Nachrodt-Wiblingwerde	52	51.19 N	7.37 E
Nächstebreck •[8]	253	51.18 N	7.14 E
Nachterstedt	50	51.49 N	11.20 E
Nachuge	100	10.45 N	92.22 E
Nachvak Fiord C[2]	166	59.03 N	63.45 W
Naci	106	6.19 N	124.46 E
Nacimiento	242	37.30 S	72.40 W
Nacimiento ≃	216	35.49 N	120.45 W
Nacimiento Reservoir ⊜[1]	216	35.45 N	121.00 W
Nacka	40	59.18 N	18.10 E
Naco, Méx.	222	31.20 N	109.56 W
Naco, Ariz., U.S.	190	31.20 N	109.57 W
Nacogdoches	212	31.36 N	94.39 W
Nacogdoches □[6]	212	31.40 N	94.45 W
Nácori Chico	222	29.39 N	109.01 W
Nacozari [de García]	222	30.24 N	109.39 W
Ñacunday	242	26.01 S	54.46 W
Nada	212	29.24 N	96.23 W
Nada •[8]	260	34.44 N	135.14 E
Nadābhānga	262b	22.24 N	88.14 E
Nadachi	84	37.09 N	138.06 E
Nadasaki	86	34.32 N	133.52 E
Nadbai	114	27.14 N	77.12 E
Nadder ≃	44	51.03 N	1.48 W
Nadedinskoje	79	48.21 N	133.08 E
Nadela	34	42.58 N	7.30 W
Nadelkap → Agulhas, Cape ≻	148	34.52 S	20.00 E
Naden Harbour C	172	54.00 N	132.35 W
Nadi	130	18.40 N	33.42 E
Nadia □[5]	116	23.30 N	88.30 E
Nadiād	110	22.42 N	72.52 E
Nādir, Miṣr	132	30.33 N	30.51 E
Nadir, Vir. Is., U.S.	230m	18.19 N	64.53 W
Nădlac	38	46.10 N	20.45 E
Nador	138	35.12 N	2.55 W
Nadporožje	66	60.28 N	34.17 E
Nadrin	52	50.10 N	5.41 E
Nadterečnaja	74	43.37 N	45.22 E
Nadvoicy	24	63.52 N	34.15 E
Nadvornaja	68	48.38 N	24.34 E
Nadym	62	65.35 N	72.42 E
Nadym ≃	64	66.12 N	72.00 E
Nadyrovo	70	54.53 N	52.28 E
Naeba-san ∧	84	36.51 N	138.41 E
Nae-dong	88	37.16 N	126.27 E
Naenwa	110	25.46 N	75.51 E
Nærbø	26	58.40 N	5.39 E
Næsby	41	55.25 N	10.22 E
Næstved	41	55.14 N	11.46 E
Nafada	136	11.08 N	11.20 E
Nafadji	140	12.37 N	11.37 W
Nafarros	256c	38.49 N	9.25 W
Nafāzah, 'Alam ∧[2]	132	30.30 N	29.42 E
Näfels	54	47.06 N	9.04 E
Nafīshah	132	30.34 N	32.15 E
Nafoora	136	29.20 N	21.20 E
Naftalan	74	40.31 N	46.50 E
Nafūsah, Jabal ⋀[2]	136	31.50 N	12.00 E
Nafutan Point ≻	164n	15.05 N	145.45 E
Nāg	110	27.24 N	65.08 E
Naga, Nihon	86	34.16 N	135.26 E
Naga, Pil.	106	13.37 N	123.11 E
Naga, Pil.	106	10.13 N	123.45 E
Nâga, Kreb en ⍑[4]	138	24.00 N	6.00 W
Naga, Oued en ∨	138	27.53 N	7.10 W
Nagaga	144	10.54 S	39.07 E
Nagahama, Nihon	84	35.23 N	136.16 E
Nagahama, Nihon	86	33.36 N	132.29 E
Nagai, Nihon	82	38.06 N	140.02 E
Nagai, Nihon	258	35.12 N	139.37 E
Nagai Island I	170	55.11 N	159.55 W
Nāgāland □[3]	110	26.00 N	95.00 E
Nagambie	159	36.47 S	145.10 E
Nagannu-shima I	164m	26.16 N	127.33 E
Nagano	84	36.39 N	138.11 E
Nagano □[5]	84	36.00 N	138.00 E
Nagano-dam •[6]	84	35.50 N	136.33 E
Naganohara	84	36.33 N	138.38 E
Nagao, Nihon	86	34.16 N	134.10 E
Nagao, Nihon	260	34.50 N	135.43 E
Nagao-hana ≻	86	35.32 N	134.01 E
Nagaoka, Nihon	82	37.27 N	138.51 E
Nagaoka, Nihon	84	34.55 N	135.42 E
Nāgappattinam	112	10.46 N	79.50 E
Nagar, Bhārat	113	32.07 N	77.10 E
Nagar, Bhārat	114	27.26 N	77.06 E
Nagara	260	34.26 N	135.44 E
Nagara ≃	84	35.01 N	136.43 E
Nagareyama	84	35.51 N	139.54 E
Nāgārjuna Sāgar ⊜[1]	112	16.35 N	79.21 E
Nagarote	226	12.16 N	86.34 W
Nagar Pārkar	110	24.22 N	70.45 E
Nāgarpur	114	24.03 N	89.53 E
Nagar Untāri	114	24.17 N	83.30 E
Nagas	106	13.06 N	123.18 E
Nagasa	84	35.08 N	140.02 E
Nagasaka	84	35.49 N	138.22 E
Nagasaki	82	32.48 N	129.55 E
Nagasawa	258	35.12 N	139.41 E
Nagashima, Nihon	82	34.12 N	136.20 E
Nagashima, Nihon	84	35.05 N	136.42 E
Naga-shima I, Nihon	86	33.49 N	132.05 E
Naga-shima I, Nihon	86	34.41 N	134.15 E
Nagashino ⊥	84	34.56 N	137.32 E
Nagasin Lake ⊜	180	47.44 N	83.37 W
Nagasu → Usa, Nihon	86	33.31 N	131.22 E
Nagasu, Nihon	86	32.56 N	130.27 E
Nagata •[8]	260	34.40 N	135.09 E
Nagataki	260	34.23 N	135.20 E
Nagatino •[8]	255b	55.41 N	37.41 E
Nagato, Nihon	84	36.15 N	138.16 E
Nagato, Nihon	86	34.21 N	131.10 E
Nagatsuta •[8]	258	35.32 N	139.30 E
Nāgaur	110	27.12 N	73.44 E
Nāgāvali ≃	112	18.13 N	83.56 E
Nagavskaja	70	47.47 N	42.50 E
Nagawa	84	36.05 N	137.41 E
Nagawicka Lake ⊜	206	43.05 N	88.23 W
Nagcarlan	106	14.08 N	121.25 E
Nāgda	110	23.27 N	75.25 E
Nagele	48	52.37 N	5.44 E
Nāgercoil	112	8.10 N	77.26 E
Nagi	86	35.07 N	134.11 E
Nagiba	106	13.41 N	120.53 E
Nagibino	76	55.46 N	72.43 E
Nagichot	144	4.16 N	33.34 E
Nagīna	114	29.27 N	78.27 E
Nāgirāt	116	23.38 N	89.18 E
Nagi-san ∧	86	35.10 N	134.11 E
Nagiso	84	35.36 N	137.37 E
Nagla	262a	28.31 N	77.22 E
Naglarby	40	60.25 N	15.34 E
Nagłowice	30	50.41 N	20.06 E
Nago, It.	58	45.53 N	10.53 E
Nago, Nihon	164m	26.35 N	127.59 E
Nāgod	114	24.34 N	80.36 E
Nagog Pond ⊜	273	42.31 N	71.26 W
Nagoja → Nagoya	84	35.10 N	136.55 E
Nagold	52	48.33 N	8.43 E
Nagold ≃	52	48.52 N	8.42 E
Nagol'naja ≃	73	47.57 N	38.58 E
Nagol'no-Tarasovka	73	48.00 N	39.29 E
Nagorje	66	56.55 N	38.16 E
Nagornoje	68	45.26 N	28.27 E
Nagorno-Karabachskaja Avtonomnaja Oblast' □[4]	74	40.00 N	46.40 E
Nagornyj, S.S.S.R.	64	55.58 N	124.57 E
Nagornyj, S.S.S.R.	255a	59.43 N	30.16 E
Nagorsk	24	59.18 N	50.48 E
Nagorskoje	72	56.54 N	38.06 E
Nago-wan C	164m	26.34 N	127.57 E
Nagoya	84	35.10 N	136.55 E
Nagoya-kūkō ⊠	84	35.15 N	136.55 E
Nāgpur	110	21.09 N	79.06 E
Nagrai	113	34.23 N	72.41 E
Nāgrākata	114	26.54 N	88.55 E
Nagrota	113	32.03 N	76.05 E
Nagu I	26	60.10 N	21.48 E
Nagua	228	19.23 N	69.50 W
Naguabo	230m	18.13 N	65.44 W
Naguilian	106	17.01 N	121.50 E
Nagumbuaya Point ≻	106	13.34 N	124.21 E
Naguri	84	35.53 N	139.11 E
Naguri I	112	6.39 N	72.55 E
Nagyatád	30	46.14 N	17.22 E
Nagybajom	30	46.23 N	17.31 E
Nagybánya → Baia-Mare	38	47.40 N	23.35 E
Nagyecsed	30	47.52 N	22.24 E
Nagykálló	68	47.53 N	21.51 E
Nagykanizsa	30	46.27 N	17.00 E
Nagykáta	30	47.25 N	19.45 E
Nagy-Kevély ∧	254c	47.37 N	18.59 E
Nagykőrös	30	47.02 N	19.43 E
Nagy-Milic ∧	30	48.35 N	21.28 E
Nagytarcsa	254c	47.32 N	19.17 E
Nagytétény •[8]	254c	47.24 N	18.58 E
Nagyvarad → Oradea	38	47.03 N	21.57 E
Naha	164m	26.13 N	127.40 E
Naha Airfield ⊠	164m	26.13 N	127.40 E
Nahabuan	102	0.49 N	114.05 E
Nahakki	113	34.25 N	71.20 E
Nahalal	122	32.41 N	35.12 E
Naḥal 'Oz	122	31.28 N	34.30 E
Nāhan	114	30.33 N	77.18 E
Nahang (Nihing) ≃	118	26.00 N	62.44 E
Nahant	197	42.25 N	70.55 W
Nahant Bay C	197	42.27 N	70.55 W
Nahari	86	33.25 N	134.01 E
Nahari ≃	86	33.25 N	134.01 E
Nahariyya	122	33.00 N	35.05 E
Nahar Ouassel, Oued ≃	138	35.42 N	2.33 E
Naharpur •[8]	262a	28.42 N	77.07 E
Nahāta	116	23.20 N	89.31 E
Nahāvand	118	34.12 N	48.22 E
Nahcotta	214	46.30 N	124.02 W
Nahe	79	48.28 N	124.52 E
Nahe ≃	52	49.58 N	7.57 E
Naḥf	122	32.56 N	35.19 E
Nahma	180	45.50 N	86.40 W
Nahmer	253	51.20 N	7.35 E
Nahmer ≃	253	51.21 N	7.35 E
Nahoe	164x	9.45 S	138.55 W
Nahon ≃	46	47.14 N	1.39 E
Nahuala, Laguna C	224	16.46 N	99.44 W
Nahualate ≃	226	14.03 N	91.32 W
Nahuatzén	224	19.42 N	101.50 W
Nahuel Huapi	244	41.03 S	71.09 W
Nahuel Huapi, Lago ⊜	244	40.58 S	71.30 W
Nahuel Huapi, Parque Nacional ♠	244	41.00 S	71.48 W
Nahuel Niyeu	244	40.30 S	66.33 W
Nahuizalco	226	13.46 N	89.45 W
Nahunta	182	31.12 N	81.59 W
Nāhyā	132	30.03 N	31.07 E
Naia ≃	60	42.46 N	12.22 E
Naic	106	14.19 N	120.46 E
Naicá	222	27.53 N	105.31 W
Naicam	174	52.25 N	104.30 W
Naidong	110	29.14 N	31.46 E
Naiguatá, Pico ∧	276c	10.33 N	66.46 W
Naihāti, Bhārat	116	22.54 N	88.25 E
Naihāti, Bngl.	116	22.49 N	89.37 E
Naikliu	102	9.30 S	123.50 E
Naila	50	50.19 N	11.42 E
Nailin	88	41.53 N	119.15 E
Nails Creek ≃	212	30.16 N	96.44 W
Nailsea	44	51.26 N	2.43 W
Nailsworth	44	51.42 N	2.14 W
Nā'im, Jabal an- ∧	122	31.04 N	35.55 E
Naimanqi	79	42.55 N	120.43 E
Nain, Newf., Can.	166	56.32 N	61.41 W
Nā'īn, Īrān	118	32.52 N	53.05 E
Nain ⊜	40	60.14 N	13.50 E
Naini Tāl	114	29.23 N	79.27 E
Naini Tāl □[5]	114	29.20 N	79.30 E
Nainpur	114	22.26 N	80.07 E
Naipli, Tür.	120	39.48 N	27.13 E
Naipli, Tür.	120	40.19 N	38.07 E
Naiqiguolehe ≃	110	35.58 N	95.00 E
Nairai I	165g	17.49 S	179.24 E
Nairn	28	57.35 N	3.53 W
Nairne	158b	35.02 S	138.54 E
Nairobi	144	1.17 S	36.49 E
Nairobi Airport ⊠	266	41.08 N	74.21 W
Nairobi National Park ♠	144	1.24 S	36.50 E
Naissaar I	66	59.33 N	24.32 E
Naita, Mount ∧	144	5.32 N	35.19 E
Naitaumba I	165g	17.31 S	179.17 W
Naivasha	144	0.43 S	36.26 E
Naivasha, Lake ⊜	144	0.46 S	36.21 E
Naivos	104	2.30 N	96.10 E
Naizifang	95	39.36 N	116.47 E
Najac	32	44.17 N	2.00 E
Najafābād	118	32.37 N	51.21 E
Najafgarh •[8]	262a	28.37 N	76.59 E
Najafgarh Drain ≍	262a	28.43 N	77.14 E
Najasa ≃	230p	20.42 N	77.55 W
Najd □[8]	134	21.00 N	46.00 E
Nájera	34	42.25 N	2.44 W
Najhā	122	33.23 N	36.22 E
Naj' Hammādī	130	26.03 N	32.15 E
Najiajie	94	41.37 N	123.47 E
Najībābād	114	29.38 N	78.20 E
Najin	88	42.15 N	130.18 E
Najinkouzi	79	50.23 N	126.57 E
Najio	260	34.50 N	135.18 E
Najramdal Uul ∧	76	49.10 N	87.52 E
Najstenjarvi	24	62.16 N	32.38 E
Naju	88	35.03 N	126.43 E
Najza, Gora ∧	76	49.24 N	70.42 E
Naka, Nihon	84	36.25 N	140.28 E
Naka, Nihon	86	35.02 N	134.55 E
Naka, Nihon	258	35.49 N	140.03 E
Naka, Nihon	260	34.50 N	135.48 E
Naka, Nihon	260	34.42 N	135.45 E
Naka •[8]	258	35.27 N	139.39 E
Naka ≃, Nihon	84	35.39 N	139.51 E
Naka ≃, Nihon	84	36.20 N	140.36 E
Naka ≃, Nihon	86	33.56 N	134.42 E
Nakadōri-shima I	82	32.57 N	129.04 E
Nakagami	258	35.49 N	139.21 E
Nakagawa	84	35.38 N	137.56 E
Nakagawa •[8]	258	35.33 N	139.35 E
Nakagō	84	36.58 N	138.14 E
Nakagusuku-wan C	164m	26.14 N	127.53 E
Nakagyō •[8]	260	35.01 N	135.45 E
Nakaheji	86	33.47 N	135.31 E
Nakai	84	35.20 N	139.14 E
Nakaizu	84	34.57 N	139.00 E
Nakajima, Nihon	84	37.07 N	136.51 E
Nakajima, Nihon	86	33.58 N	132.07 E
Nakajima, Nihon	258	35.26 N	139.56 E
Nakajima, Nihon	258	35.18 N	139.58 E
Naka-jima I	86	33.58 N	132.37 E
Nakajō, Nihon	82	38.03 N	139.24 E
Nakajō, Nihon	84	36.36 N	138.02 E
Nakakawane	84	35.03 N	138.05 E
Nāka Khārari	110	25.15 N	66.44 E
Nakalele Point ≻	219a	21.02 N	156.35 W
Nākālia	116	24.02 N	89.40 E
Nakama	86	33.50 N	130.43 E
Nakaminato	84	36.21 N	140.36 E
Nakamura	86	32.59 N	132.56 E
Nakanai Mountains ⋀	154	5.35 S	151.10 E
Nakano, Nihon	84	36.45 N	138.22 E

	English	Deutsch	Español	Français	Português
≃	River	Fluss	Río	Rivière	Rio
≍	Canal	Kanal	Canal	Canal	Canal
⌞	Waterfall, Rapids	Wasserfall, Stromschnellen	Cascada, Rápidos	Chute d'eau, Rapides	Cascata, Rápidos
⊔	Strait	Meeresstrasse	Estrecho	Détroit	Estreito
C	Bay, Gulf	Bucht, Golf	Bahía, Golfo	Baie, Golfe	Baía, Golfo
⊜	Lake, Lakes	See, Seen	Lago, Lagos	Lac, Lacs	Lago, Lagos
☷	Swamp	Sumpf	Pantano	Marais	Pântano
▽	Ice Features, Glacier	Eis- und Gletscherformen	Accidentes Glaciales	Formes glaciaires	Acidentes Glaciares
⍑	Other Hydrographic Features	Andere Hydrographische Objekte	Otros Elementos Hidrográficos	Autres données hydrographiques	Outros Elementos Hidrográficos
✣	Submarine Features	Untermeerische Objekte	Accidentes Submarinos	Formes de relief sous-marin	Acidentes Submarinos
□	Political Unit	Politische Einheit	Unidad Política	Entité politique	Unidade Política
⊌	Cultural Institution	Kulturelle Institution	Institución Cultural	Institution culturelle	Instituição Cultural
⊥	Historical Site	Historische Stätte	Sitio Histórico	Site historique	Sítio Histórico
♠	Recreational Site	Erholungs- und Ferienort	Sitio de Recreo	Centre de loisirs	Sítio de Lazer
⊠	Airport	Flughafen	Aeropuerto	Aéroport	Aeroporto
■	Military Installation	Militäranlage	Instalación Militar	Installation militaire	Instalação Militar
•	Miscellaneous	Verschiedenes	Misceláneo	Divers	Miscelânea

ENGLISH

DEUTSCH

Symbols in the index entries represent the broad categories identified in the key at the right. Symbols with superior numbers (⛰[2]) identify subcategories (see complete key on page I · 26).

Kartensymbole in dem Registerverzeichnis stellen die rechts im Schlüssel erklärten Kategorien dar. Symbole mit hochgestellten Ziffern (⛰[2]) bezeichnen Unterabteilungen einer Kategorie (vgl. vollständiger Schlüssel auf Seite I · 26).

Los símbolos incluidos en el texto del índice representan las grandes categorías identificadas con la clave a la derecha. Los símbolos con numeros en su parte superior (⛰[2]) identifican las subcategorías (véase la clave completa en la página I · 26).

Les symboles de l'index représentent les catégories indiquées dans la légende à droite. Les symboles suivis d'un indice (⛰[2]) représentent des sous-catégories (voir légende complète à la page I · 26).

Os símbolos incluídos no texto do índice representam as grandes categorias identificadas com a chave à direita. Os símbolos com numeros em sua parte superior (⛰[2]) identificam as subcategorias (veja-se a chave completa à página I · 26).

∧ Mountain	Berg	Montaña	Montagne	Montanha
⛰ Mountains	Berge	Montañas	Montagnes	Montanhas
)(Pass	Pass	Paso	Col	Passo
V Valley, Canyon	Tal, Cañon	Valle, Cañón	Vallée, Canyon	Vale, Canhão
= Plain	Ebene	Llano	Plaine	Planície
> Cape	Kap	Cabo	Cap	Cabo
I Island	Insel	Isla	Île	Ilha
II Islands	Inseln	Islas	Îles	Ilhas
◆ Other Topographic Features	Andere Topographische Objekte	Otros Elementos Topográficos	Autres données topographiques	Outros Elementos Topográficos

ESPAÑOL

Nombre	Página	Lat.°′	Long.°′ W=Oeste
Natagaima	236	3.37 N	75.06 W
Nātāgarh	262b	22.42 N	88.25 E
Natal, Bra.	240	5.47 S	35.13 W
Natal, B.C., Can.	172	49.44 N	114.50 W
Natal, Indon.	100	0.33 N	99.07 E
Natal □[3]	148	28.40 S	30.40 E
Natalia	186	29.11 N	98.52 W
Natal'jevka	73	47.10 N	38.29 E
Nataljin Jar	70	51.46 N	50.35 E
Nataljino	70	52.56 N	49.02 E
Natalkuz Lake ⊜	172	53.26 N	125.20 W
Natalspruit	263d	26.19 S	28.09 E
Natalspruit ≃	263d	26.19 S	28.10 E
Natan, Cabo ≻	226	11.07 N	85.48 W
Natanes Plateau ⋏⋏[1]	190	33.35 N	110.15 W
Natash, Wādī V	130	24.25 N	33.26 E
Natashō	86	35.24 N	135.38 E
Natashquan	176	50.12 N	61.49 W
Natashquan ≃	166	50.06 N	61.49 W
Natashquan, Pointe de ≻	176	50.06 N	61.44 W
Natashquan-Est ≃	176	51.20 N	61.40 W
Natchez	184	31.34 N	91.23 W
Natchez Trace National Parkway ♠	184	36.08 N	86.49 W
Natchitoches	184	31.46 N	93.05 W
Natco Lake ⊜	266	40.26 N	74.09 W
Natércia	246	22.07 S	45.30 W
Naters	54	46.20 N	7.59 E
Natewa Bay C	165g	16.35 S	179.40 E
Na Thawi	100	6.45 N	100.42 E
Nāthdwāra	110	24.56 N	73.49 E
Nathia Gali	113	34.04 N	73.24 E
Nathula I	165g	16.53 S	177.25 E
Natick	197	42.17 N	71.21 W
Natick Laboratories ■	273	42.17 N	71.22 W
Natimuk	156	36.45 S	141.57 E
Nation ≃	172	55.28 N	125.35 W
National Accelerator Laboratory ♉[3]	206	41.50 N	88.15 W
National Agricultural Research Center ♉[3]	274c	39.02 N	76.52 W
National Airport ⊠	271	42.19 N	83.25 W
National Arboretum ♠	274c	38.54 N	76.58 W
National Art Gallery ♉	259d	25.02 N	121.30 E
National Assembly ♉	259a	13.46 N	100.31 E
National Baseball Hall of Fame and Museum ♉	200	42.42 N	74.57 W
National City	218	32.40 N	117.06 W
National Gallery ♉	250	51.31 N	0.08 W
National Institute of Health ♉	274c	39.00 N	77.06 W
National Maritime Museum ♉	250	51.29 N	0.00
National Park	275	39.51 N	75.12 W
National Taiwan Normal University ♉[2]	259d	25.02 N	121.31 E
National Taiwan University ♉[2]	259d	25.01 N	121.32 E
National Zoological Park ♠	274c	38.56 N	77.03 W
Nation Lakes ⊜	172	55.10 N	125.00 W
Natipi, Lac ⊜	176	51.27 N	71.23 W
Natisone ≃	58	45.57 N	13.22 E
Natitingou	140	10.19 N	1.22 E
Native Bay C	166	63.52 N	82.30 W
Natividade	240	11.43 S	47.47 W
Natividade da Serra	246	23.24 S	45.26 W
Nativitas	276a	19.14 N	99.05 W
Nativity, Church of the ♉[1]	122	31.43 N	35.12 E
Natkyizin	100	14.55 N	97.57 E
Natl	122	31.39 N	35.52 E
Natoma	188	39.11 N	99.01 W
Natong	92	23.01 N	107.50 E
Nator	114	24.25 N	88.59 E
Natori	82	38.08 N	140.55 E
Natorp	253	51.30 N	7.38 E
Natron, Lake ⊜	144	2.25 S	36.00 E
Natrona Heights	204	40.38 N	79.44 W
Naṭrūn, Wādī an- ●[7]	132	30.25 N	30.13 E
Natsui ≃	84	37.03 N	140.59 E
Nattai ≃	160	34.05 S	150.25 E
Nattai River	160	34.04 S	150.27 E
Nattam	112	10.14 N	78.14 E
Nåttarö I	40	58.52 N	18.07 E
Nattastunturit ⋏	24	68.12 N	27.20 E
Nattaung ⋏	100	18.48 N	97.02 E
Natters	58	47.14 N	11.22 E
Nattwerder	254a	52.26 N	12.56 E
Natuchajevskaja	68	44.54 N	37.34 E
Nātudaha	116	23.39 N	88.41 E
Natukanaoka Pan ☷	146	18.40 S	15.45 E
Natu La)(	114	27.23 N	88.51 E
Natuna Besar I	102	4.00 N	108.15 E
Natural Arch And Cave ♠	161a	28.10 S	153.14 E
Natural Bridge	202	44.04 N	75.30 W
Natural Bridges National Monument ♠	190	37.30 N	110.08 W
Natural Bridge State Park ♠	182	37.47 N	83.42 W
Naturaliste, Cape ≻	152	33.32 S	115.01 E
Naturaliste Channel Ц	152	25.25 S	113.00 E
Naturita	190	38.14 N	108.34 W
Naturita Creek ≃	190	38.13 N	108.32 W
Naturno (Naturns)	58	46.39 N	11.00 E
Natzungen	48	51.36 N	9.14 E
Nau	75	40.09 N	69.22 E
Naucalpan → Ciudad de Naucalpan de Juárez	276a	19.28 N	99.14 W
Naucalpan □[7]	276a	19.26 N	99.17 W
Naucelle	32	44.12 N	2.20 E
Naučnyj	68	44.44 N	34.01 E
Naude	262c	19.03 N	73.06 E
Nauders	54	46.53 N	10.30 E
Nauen	50	52.36 N	12.52 E
Nauener Luch ☰	254a	52.37 N	12.55 E
Nauener Stadtforst ♠	254a	52.38 N	12.58 E
Naugachhia	114	25.24 N	87.06 E
Naugatuck	197	41.30 N	73.04 W
Naugatuck ≃	197	41.19 N	73.05 W
Naughton	180	46.24 N	81.12 W
Naugol'noje	72	56.22 N	38.11 E
Naui	130	18.28 N	30.43 E
Naujamiestis	66	55.44 N	23.10 E
Naujan	106	13.20 N	121.18 E
Naujan, Lake ⊜	106	13.10 N	121.21 E
Naujoji Akmenė	66	56.19 N	22.55 E
Naukan	170	66.01 N	169.43 W
Naulavaara ⋏[2]	26	63.53 N	28.13 E
Naulila	142	17.12 S	14.42 E
Naumburg, B.R.D.	52	51.15 N	9.10 E
Naumburg, D.D.R.	50	51.09 N	11.48 E
Naumburg am Queiss → Nowogrodziec	30	51.12 N	15.25 E
Naumovščina	66	58.23 N	28.20 E
Naunak	76	59.00 N	80.13 E
Naundorf	50	50.56 N	13.25 E
Naunglon	100	16.48 N	97.45 E
Naungpale	100	19.33 N	97.08 E
Naunhof	50	51.16 N	12.35 E
Naupada ◂[8]	262c	19.04 N	72.50 E
Ñaupe	238	5.36 S	79.54 W
Nā'ūr	122	31.53 N	35.50 E
Nauraushaun Brook ≃	266	41.03 N	73.59 W
Nauroth	52	50.42 N	7.52 E
Nauroz Kalāt	118	28.47 N	65.38 E

FRANÇAIS

Nom	Page	Lat.°′	Long.°′ W=Ouest
Naurskaja	74	43.38 N	45.19 E
Nauru □[1]	14		
	164b	0.32 S	166.55 E
Naushahra	113	33.09 N	74.14 E
Naushahro Fīroz	110	26.50 N	68.07 E
Naushon Island I	197	41.29 N	70.45 W
Nauški	78	50.28 N	106.07 E
Nausori	165g	18.02 S	175.32 E
Naustdal	26	61.31 N	5.43 E
Nauta	236	4.32 S	73.33 W
Nautanwa	114	27.26 N	83.25 E
Nautilus Park	197	41.22 N	72.05 W
Nautla	224	20.13 N	96.47 W
Nautla ≃	224	20.15 N	96.47 W
Nauvoo	180	40.33 N	91.23 W
Nava	222	28.25 N	100.46 W
Nava, Arroyo de la ≃	256a	40.31 N	3.46 W
Nava, Colle di)(	56	44.05 N	7.53 E
Nava del Rey	34	41.20 N	5.05 W
Navahermosa	34	39.38 N	4.28 W
Navajo ≃	190	37.01 N	107.10 W
Navajo Creek ≃	190	36.59 N	111.24 W
Navajo Indian Reservation ◂[4]	190	36.25 N	110.00 W
Navajo Mountain ⋏	190	37.02 N	110.52 W
Navajo National Monument ♠	190	36.40 N	110.33 W
Navajo Reservoir ⊜[1]	190	36.55 N	107.30 W
Naval	106	11.34 N	124.23 E
Navalcarnero	34	40.18 N	4.00 W
Navalmoral de la Mata	34	39.54 N	5.32 W
Naval Ordnance Test Station ■	218	35.32 N	117.05 W
Navalvillar de Pela	34	39.06 N	5.28 W
Navan	28	53.39 N	6.41 W
≃Vāpur	110	21.10 N	73.48
Navarin, Mys ≻	170	62.16 N	179.10 E
Navarino → Pílos	38	36.55 N	21.43 E
Navarino, Isla I	244	55.05 S	67.40 W
Navarra □[4]	34	42.40 N	1.30 W
Navarre, Austl.	159	36.54 S	143.07 E
Navarre, Ohio, U.S.	204	40.43 N	81.32 W
Navarro	248	35.01 S	59.16 W
Navarro □[6]	212	32.05 N	96.30 W
Navarro ≃	194	39.11 N	123.45 W
Navarro, Cañada ≃	248	35.00 S	59.18 W
Navarro Mills Lake ⊜[1]	212	31.56 N	96.45 W
Navašino	70	55.32 N	42.12 E
Navasota	212	30.23 N	96.05 W
Navasota ≃	212	30.20 N	96.09 W
Navassa	182	34.16 N	77.58 W
Navassa Island I	228	18.24 N	75.01 W
Nave	58	45.35 N	10.17 E
Nävekvarn	40	58.38 N	16.49 E
Navenne	54	47.36 N	6.10 E
Navesink	266	40.24 N	74.02 W
Navesink River C	266	40.23 N	73.58 W
Navesnoje	66	52.17 N	37.57 E
Nâves-Parmelan	54	45.56 N	6.11 E
Navesti ≃	66	58.30 N	24.54 E
Navestock	250	51.39 N	0.13 E
Navestock Side	250	51.39 N	0.16 E
Navia, Arg.	242	34.47 S	66.35 W
Navia, Esp.	34	43.32 N	6.43 W
Navia ≃	34	43.33 N	6.44 W
Navibandar	110	21.26 N	69.48 E
Navidad, Chile	242	33.57 S	71.50 W
Navidad, Méx.	224	20.35 N	104.42 W
Navidad ≃	186	28.41 N	96.35 W
Navidad, Bahía C	224	19.12 N	104.43 W
Navio, Riacho do ≃	240	8.39 S	38.36 W
Naviraí	245	23.08 S	54.13 W
Navis	58	47.07 N	11.32 E
Naviti I	165g	17.07 S	177.15 E
Navl'a	66	52.51 N	34.30 E
Navl'a ≃	66	52.42 N	34.01 E
Navoi	62	40.15 N	65.15 E
Navojoa	222	27.06 N	109.26 W
Navolato	222	24.47 N	107.42 W
Navoloki	70	57.28 N	41.59 E
Navotas	259f	14.40 N	120.57 E
Návpaktos	38	38.23 N	21.50 E
Návplion	38	37.34 N	22.48 E
Navrongo	140	10.54 N	1.06 W
Navşar	118	37.18 N	44.35 E
Navsāri	110	20.51 N	72.55 E
Navua	165g	18.14 S	178.10 E
Navua ≃	165g	18.15 S	178.09 E
Navy Island I	274a	43.04 N	79.01 W
Navy Pier ◂[5]	268	41.53 N	87.36 W
Navy Yard City	214	47.32 N	122.41 W
Nawa, Nihon	86	35.26 N	133.30 E
Nawa → Naha, Nihon	164m	26.13 N	127.40 E
Nawá, Sūrīy.	122	32.53 N	36.03 E
Nawābganj, Bhārat	114	26.52 N	82.08 E
Nawābganj, Bhārat	114	28.33 N	79.38 E
Nawābganj, Bhārat	114	26.56 N	81.13 E
Nawābganj, Bngl.	114	24.36 N	88.17 E
Nawābganj, Bngl.	116	23.40 N	90.10 E
Nawābshāh	110	26.15 N	68.25 E
Nawāda	114	24.53 N	85.32 E
Nāwah	110	32.19 N	67.53 E
Nawākot, Nepāl	114	27.55 N	85.10 E
Nawa Kot, Pāk.	110	28.20 N	71.22 E
Nawalapitiya	112	7.03 N	80.32 E
Nawalgarh	110	27.51 N	75.16 E
Nawān Kot	113	31.06 N	71.32 E
Nawāpāra, Bhārat	112	20.58 N	81.51 E
Nawapārā, Bhārat	116	23.29 N	88.15 E
Nawāpāra, Bngl.	116	23.02 N	89.23 E
Nawasā al-Ghayṭ	132	30.58 N	31.19 E
Nawāshahr, Bhārat	113	31.07 N	76.08 E
Nawāshahr, Pāk.	113	34.10 N	73.16 E
Nawāṣif, Ḥarrat ●[9]	134	21.20 N	42.10 E
Nawāy	132	27.47 N	30.46 E
Nawiliwili Bay C	219b	21.57 N	159.21 W
Nawinda Kuta	142	16.25 S	24.28 E
Nawŏn-ni	88	36.25 N	126.40 E
Naxera	198	37.20 N	76.27 W
Naxi	97	28.47 N	105.22 E
Náxos	38	37.06 N	25.23 E
Náxos I	38	37.02 N	25.35 E
Naxuebiruzong	110	31.30 N	93.51 E
Nayābās	262a	28.35 N	77.19 E
Nayāgaon	116	23.32 N	90.46 E
Nayāgarh	110	20.08 N	85.06 E
Nayāgrām	116	22.02 N	87.11 E
Nayak	110	34.44 N	66.57 E
Nayāpāra	116	21.35 N	87.01 E
Nayarit	194	32.20 N	115.19 W
Nayarit □[3]	224	22.00 N	105.00 W
Nayau I	165g	17.58 S	179.03 W
Nāy Band, Īrān	118	32.20 N	57.34 E
Nāy Band, Īrān	118	27.23 N	52.38 E
Nāy Band, Kūh-e ⋏	118	32.27 N	57.23 E
Nayé	140	14.25 N	12.12 W
Nayland	44	51.59 N	0.52 E
Naylor	184	36.34 N	90.36 W
Nayong	92	26.50 N	105.13 E
Nayoro	82a	44.21 N	142.28 E
Nayyāl, Wādī V	118	28.40 N	39.26 E
Nazālī Ṭāhā'	132	28.11 N	30.42 E
Nazaré, Bra.	240	6.23 S	47.40 W
Nazaré, Bra.	245	13.02 S	39.00 W
Nazaré, Port.	34	39.36 N	9.04 W
Nazaré da Mata	240	7.44 S	35.14 W
Nazaré do Piauí	240	6.59 S	42.40 W
Nazareno	246	21.13 S	44.37 W
Nazaré Paulista	246	23.11 S	46.24 W
Nazareth, Bel.	46	50.58 N	3.36 E
Nazareth, Pa., U.S.	198	40.44 N	75.19 W
Nazareth → Nazerat, Yis.	122	32.42 N	35.18 E
Nazareth Bank ✧[4]	12	14.30 S	60.45 E
Nazário	245	16.36 S	49.54 W
Nazarjevo, S.S.S.R.	72	55.22 N	36.24 E
Nazarjevo, S.S.S.R.	255b	55.59 N	37.16 E
Nazarovo	76	56.01 N	90.26 E

PORTUGUÊS

Nome	Página	Lat.°′	Long.°′ W=Oeste
Nazarovskij	68	49.33 N	40.56 E
Nazas	222	25.14 N	104.08 W
Nazas ≃	222	25.35 N	105.00 W
Nazca	238	14.50 S	74.57 W
Naze	83b	28.23 N	129.30 E
Nazeing	250	51.44 N	0.03 E
N'azepetrovsk	76	56.03 N	59.36 E
Naẕerat (Nazareth)	122	32.42 N	35.18 E
Naẕerat 'Illit	122	32.42 N	35.19 E
Nazeret	134	8.32 N	39.22 E
Nazija	66	59.50 N	31.35 E
Nazik Gölü ⊜	120	38.53 N	42.16 E
Nazilli	120	37.55 N	28.21 E
Nazimicha	255b	55.59 N	38.08 E
Nazımiye	120	39.11 N	39.50 E
Nazimovo	76	59.30 N	90.58 E
Nazina	76	60.07 N	78.52 E
Nāzira	110	26.55 N	94.44 E
Nāzir Hāt	110	22.38 N	91.47 E
Nāzirpur	116	22.43 N	89.58 E
Nazko ≃	172	53.07 N	123.34 W
Nazlat al-'Amūdayn	132	28.14 N	30.42 E
Nazlat al-Badramān	132	27.40 N	30.44 E
Nazlat as-Sammān	263c	29.59 N	31.08 E
Nazlat Khalīfah	263c	30.01 N	31.10 E
Nazlat Quftan Bāshā	132	28.57 N	30.49 E
Nazlat Thābit	132	28.25 N	30.47 E
Nazran'	74	43.13 N	44.46 E
Nazwā	118	22.56 N	57.32 E
Nazyvajevsk	76	55.34 N	71.21 E
N. B. C. Studios ♉[3]	270	34.09 N	118.20 W
Nchanga	144	12.30 S	27.53 E
Nchelenge	144	9.20 S	28.50 E
Ncheu	144	14.49 S	34.38 E
Ncue	142	2.01 N	10.28 E
Ndabala	144	13.28 S	29.50 E
Ndai I	165e	7.57 S	160.37 E
Ndala	144	4.46 S	33.16 E
Ndali	140	9.51 N	2.43 E
Ndande	140	15.16 N	16.30 W
Ndélé	136	8.24 N	20.39 E
Ndélélé	142	4.02 N	14.56 E
Ndemba	142	0.11 N	14.19 E
Ndendé	142	2.23 S	11.23 E
Ndikiniméki	142	4.46 N	10.50 E
Ndjamena	136	12.07 N	15.03 E
Ndjili ◂[8]	263b	4.20 S	15.22 E
Ndjili ≃	263b	4.19 S	15.24 E
Ndjim ≃	142	4.38 N	11.24 E
Ndjo	142	1.15 S	14.30 E
Ndjolé	142	0.11 S	10.45 E
Ndogo, Lagune C	142	2.35 S	10.00 E
Ndola	144	12.58 S	28.38 E
Ndolo ◂[8]	263b	4.19 S	15.19 E
Ndomayop	142	1.21 N	10.18 E
Ndona	105b	8.46 S	121.45 E
Ndongo	142	2.19 S	13.38 E
Ndoro Hills ⋏⋏[2]	136	7.15 N	11.00 E
Ndoto Mountains ⋏⋏	144	1.45 N	37.07 E
Ndouba	142	0.11 S	14.09 E
Ndouci	140	5.52 N	4.46 W
Ndougou	142	1.39 S	9.40 E
Ndreketi ≃	165g	16.34 S	178.53 E
Ndrhamcha, Sebkha de ⊜	140	18.45 N	15.48 W
Ndu	142	4.41 N	22.49 E
Nduguti	144	4.18 S	34.42 E
Ndumbwe	144	10.14 S	39.58 E
Ndumo Game Reserve ◂[4]	148	26.53 S	32.15 E
Ndundure, Île I	165f	21.20 S	167.44 E
Nduye	144	1.50 N	29.01 E
Ne	258	35.47 N	140.03 E
Nea ≃	26	63.13 N	11.02 E
Neabul Creek ≃	156	27.45 S	147.32 E
Néa Erithraía	257c	38.05 N	23.49 E
Néa Filadhélfia	257c	38.02 N	23.44 E
Neagari	84	36.27 N	136.27 E
Neagh, Lough ⊜	42	54.38 N	6.24 W
Neah Bay	214	48.22 N	124.37 W
Néa Ionía	257c	38.02 N	23.45 E
Neajlov ≃	38	44.11 N	26.12 E
Néa Khalkidhón	257c	38.02 N	23.43 E
Neale, Lake ⊜	152	24.22 S	130.00 E
Neales ≃	152	28.08 S	136.47 E
Neales Flat	158b	34.15 S	139.10 E
Néa Liósia	257c	38.02 N	23.42 E
Neamt □[4]	38	47.00 N	26.30 E
Neandertal, Naturschutzgebiet ♠	253	51.15 N	7.00 E
Néa Páfos (Paphos)	120	34.45 N	32.25 E
Neapel → Napoli	60	40.51 N	14.17 E
Néa Pendéli	257c	38.04 N	23.52 E
Néa Péramos	257c	38.00 N	23.26 E
Neápolis, Ellás	38	35.15 N	25.37 E
Neápolis, Ellás	38	36.30 N	23.04 E
Neapolis, Ohio, U.S.	206	41.29 N	83.52 W
Néa Psará	38	38.23 N	23.48 E
Near Islands II	171a	52.40 N	173.30 E
Near North Side ◂[8]	268	41.54 N	87.38 W
Néa Smírni	257c	37.57 N	23.43 E
Neasons Hill	204	41.37 N	80.08 W
Neatahwanta, Lake ⊜	200	43.18 N	76.27 W
Neath	44	51.40 N	3.48 W
Neath ≃	44	51.37 N	3.50 W
Neauphle-le-Château	46	48.49 N	1.54 E
Neauphle-le-Vieux	251	48.49 N	1.52 E
Neavitt	198	38.44 N	76.17 W
Neba	84	35.15 N	137.35 E
Néba, Île I	165f	20.09 S	163.56 E
Nebaj	226	15.24 N	91.08 W
Nebbou	140	11.18 N	1.53 W
Nebelhorn ⋏	54	47.25 N	10.20 E
Nebeur	36	36.17 N	8.47 E
Nebine Creek ≃	156	29.07 S	146.56 E
Nebit-Dag	118	39.30 N	54.22 E
Nebo	184	39.27 N	90.47 W
Nebo, Mount ⋏, Utah, U.S.	190	39.49 N	111.46 W
Nebo, Mount → Nabā, Jabal an- ⋏, Urd.	122	31.46 N	35.45 E
Nebolči	66	59.08 N	33.18 E
Nebra	50	51.17 N	11.34 E
Nebraska	208	39.04 N	85.28 W
Nebraska □[3]	168		
	188	41.30 N	100.00 W
Nebraska City	188	40.41 N	95.52 W
Nebrodi ⋏⋏	36	37.55 N	14.35 E
Nebyloje	70	56.22 N	39.59 E
Nečajannoje	68	46.57 N	31.33 E
Nečajevka	70	53.17 N	44.27 E
Nečajevo	72	54.42 N	37.23 E
Nečatka, Ozero ⊜	78	57.45 N	117.30 E
Necaxa ≃	224	20.16 N	97.27 W
Necedah	180	44.02 N	90.05 W
Nechajevskaja	70	50.25 N	41.44 E
Nechako ≃	172	53.56 N	122.42 W
Nechako Plateau ⋏⋏[1]	172	54.00 N	124.30 W
Nechako Range ⋏⋏	172	53.20 N	124.30 W
Nechako Reservoir ⊜[1]	172	53.25 N	125.10 W
Neche	188	48.59 N	97.33 W
Neches	212	31.52 N	95.30 W
Neches ≃	184	29.55 N	93.52 W
Nechí	236	8.07 N	74.46 W
Nechí ≃	236	8.08 N	74.46 W
Nechmeya	36	36.36 N	7.31 E
Nechranická Přehradová Nádrž ⊜[1]	50	50.20 N	13.20 E
Nechvorošča	68	49.09 N	34.44 E
Neckar ≃	30	49.31 N	8.26 E
Neckarailfingen	52	48.36 N	9.16 E
Neckarbischofsheim	52	49.17 N	8.57 E
Neckarelz	52	49.20 N	9.06 E
Neckargemünd	52	49.23 N	8.47 E
Neckarsteinach	52	49.25 N	8.53 E
Neckarsulm	52	49.12 N	9.13 E
Neckartenzlingen	52	48.35 N	9.14 E
Neck Creek ≃	266	40.36 N	74.12 W
Necker	274b	39.23 N	76.29 W
Necker Island I	14	23.35 N	164.42 W
Necochea	242	38.33 S	58.45 W
Necropoli di Spina ⊥	60	44.43 N	12.08 E
Necrópolis ◂	256a	40.25 N	3.38 W
Nedančiči	68	51.30 N	30.37 E
Ned Brown Preserve ♠	268	42.02 N	88.01 W
Nedel'noje	72	54.50 N	36.39 E
Nederbrakel	46	50.48 N	3.46 E
Nederland	184	29.58 N	93.60 W
Nederland → Netherlands □[1]	30	52.15 N	5.30 E
Nederlandse Antillen → Netherlands Antilles □[2]	231s	12.15 N	69.00 W
Neder-Rijn ≃[1]	48	51.59 N	6.20 E
Nederweert	48	51.17 N	5.45 E
Nederzwalm-Hermelgem	46	50.53 N	3.41 E
Nedlands	158a	31.59 S	115.49 E
Nedlitz	50	52.04 N	12.14 E
Nedlitz ◂[8]	254a	52.26 N	13.03 E
Nedre Soppero	24	68.01 N	21.44 E
Nedre Vättern ⊜	40	59.49 N	15.40 E
Nedrigajlov	68	50.50 N	33.53 E
Nédroma	138	35.01 N	1.45 W
Nedrow	200	42.59 N	76.09 W
Nedstrand	26	59.21 N	5.51 E
Neebish Island I	180	46.16 N	84.09 W
Neede	48	52.08 N	6.36 E
Needham, Ind., U.S.	208	39.32 N	85.58 W
Needham, Mass., U.S.	197	42.17 N	71.14 W
Needham Market	44	52.09 N	1.03 E
Needhams Point ≻	231g	13.05 N	59.36 W
Needle Mountain ⋏	192	44.05 N	109.37 W
Needles	194	34.51 N	114.37 W
Needville	212	29.24 N	95.51 W
Neelyton	204	40.10 N	77.50 W
Ñeembucú □[5]	242	27.00 S	58.00 W
Neenah	180	44.11 N	88.28 W
Neepawa	174	50.13 N	99.29 W
Neerim South	159	38.01 S	145.58 E
Neermoor	48	53.18 N	7.26 E
Neeroeteren	52	51.05 N	5.42 E
Neerpelt	52	51.13 N	5.25 E
Neersen	253	51.15 N	6.29 E
Nee Soon	261c	1.24 N	103.49 E
Neetze	48	53.15 N	10.39 E
Neetze ≃	50	53.20 N	10.28 E
Nefedjevo	72	54.39 N	37.56 E
Nefern ≃	44	52.02 N	4.50 W
Neffs	198	40.42 N	75.37 W
Neffsville	198	40.06 N	76.18 W
Nef'odovo	76	58.48 N	72.34 E
Nefta	138	33.52 N	7.33 E
Nefteabad	75	40.12 N	70.34 E
Neftečala	74	39.23 N	49.16 E
Neftegorsk	74	44.22 N	39.42 E
Neftekamsk	70	56.06 N	54.17 E
Neftekumsk	74	44.45 N	44.48 E
Nefyn	44	52.57 N	4.31 W
Negage	142	7.45 S	15.16 E
Négala	140	12.52 N	8.27 W
Negapatam → Nāgappattinam	112	10.46 N	79.50 E
Negara, Indon.	102	2.37 S	115.06 E
Negara, Indon.	105a	8.22 S	114.37 E
Negara ≃	102	3.00 S	114.45 E
Negast	50	54.15 N	13.01 E
Negaunee	180	46.30 N	87.36 W
Negba	122	31.40 N	34.41 E
Negele	134	5.20 N	39.36 E
Negenborn	48	51.53 N	9.34 E
Negeribatin	102	4.35 S	104.32 E
Negeri Sembilan □[3]	104	2.45 N	102.10 E
Negev → HaNegev ◂[1]	122	30.30 N	34.55 E
Negishi	258	35.51 N	139.23 E
Negley	204	40.48 N	80.32 W
Negola	142	14.10 S	14.30 E
Negomano	144	11.27 S	38.31 E
Negombo	112	7.13 N	79.50 E
Negoreloje	66	53.36 N	27.04 E
Negotin	38	44.14 N	22.32 E
Negra, Cordillera ⋏⋏	238	9.25 S	77.40 W
Negra, Laguna ⊜	242	34.03 S	53.40 W
Negra, Ponta ≻	246	22.58 S	42.42 W
Negra, Punta ≻, Belize	222	16.17 N	88.34 W
Negra, Punta ≻, Perú	238	6.06 S	81.09 W
Negra, Puntilla ≻	138	22.54 N	16.18 W
Negra, Serra ⋏, Bra.	240	6.30 S	46.15 W
Negra, Serra ⋏, Bra.	246	21.58 S	43.54 W
Negra, Serranía ⋏⋏	238	13.45 S	60.58 W
Negra, Sierra ⋏⋏	244	42.49 S	69.52 W
Negrais	256c	38.53 N	9.17 W
Negras, Lomas ⋏[2]	276d	11.55 S	77.06 W
Negreira	34	42.54 N	8.44 W
Nègres, Pointe des ≻	230e	14.36 N	61.06 W
Negrești	38	46.50 N	27.27 E
Negrești-Oaș	38	47.52 N	23.25 E
Negrine	138	34.30 N	7.30 E
Negritos	236	4.38 S	81.19 W
Negro ≃, Arg.	244	41.02 S	62.47 W
Negro ≃, Bol.	238	9.49 S	65.42 W
Negro ≃, Bol.	238	14.11 S	63.07 W
Negro ≃, Bra.	238	19.13 S	57.17 W
Negro ≃, Bra.	238	5.15 S	70.53 W
Negro ≃, Bra.	240	9.15 S	47.34 W
Negro ≃, Bra.	242	26.01 S	50.30 W
Negro ≃, Col.	236	5.44 N	74.39 W
Negro ≃, N.A.	226	13.02 N	87.17 W
Negro ≃, Para.	242	24.23 S	57.11 W
Negro ≃, S.A.	236	3.08 S	59.55 W
Negro ≃, S.A.	242	33.24 S	58.22 W
Negro ≃, Ven.	236	9.36 N	72.15 W
Negro, Cerro ⋏, Arg.	244	46.55 S	70.12 W
Negro, Cerro ⋏, Arg.	244	44.09 S	69.30 W
Negro, Mar → Black Sea ⊤[2]	22	43.00 N	35.00 E
Negro Bay C	134	7.52 N	49.50 E
Negros I	106	10.00 N	123.00 E
Negros Occidental □[4]	106	10.20 N	123.00 E
Negros Oriental □[4]	106	9.40 N	123.00 E
Negru-Vodă	38	43.50 N	28.12 E
Neguac	176	47.15 N	65.05 W
Nehalem	214	45.43 N	123.54 W
Nehalem ≃	214	45.40 N	123.56 W
Nehawka	188	40.50 N	95.59 W
Nehbandān	118	31.32 N	60.02 E
Neheim-Hüsten	52	51.27 N	7.57 E
Nehonsey Brook ≃	275	39.49 N	75.18 W
Néhoué, Baie de C	165f	20.21 S	164.09 E
Neiba	228	18.28 N	71.25 W
Neiba, Bahía de C	228	18.15 N	71.02 W
Neichiang → Neijiang	97	29.35 N	105.03 E
Neidenburg → Nidzica	30	53.22 N	20.26 E
Neidpath	174	50.08 N	107.15 W
Neige, Crêt de la ⋏	54	46.16 N	5.56 E
Neiges, Piton des ⋏	147c	21.05 S	55.29 E
Neihart	192	46.56 N	110.44 W
Neiheshui ≃	90	22.54 N	115.38 E
Neihu	259d	25.05 N	121.35 E
Neihuang	88	35.59 N	114.55 E
Neijiang	97	29.35 N	105.03 E
Neikiang → Neijiang	97	29.35 N	105.03 E
Neilburg	174	52.50 N	109.38 W
Neillsville	180	44.34 N	90.36 W
Neilston	42	55.47 N	4.27 W
Neimen	253	51.29 N	7.48 E
Neimenggu Zizhiqu (Inner Mongolia) □[4]	80	43.00 N	115.00 E
Nein	122	32.38 N	35.21 E
Neindorf	50	52.20 N	10.50 E
Neinstedt	50	51.45 N	11.05 E
Neiqiu	88	37.17 N	114.31 E
Neira	236	5.10 N	75.32 W
Neirone	56	44.27 N	9.11 E
Neishuishan	259d	25.09 N	121.43 E
Neisse → Nysa	30	50.29 N	17.20 E
Neisse (Nysa Łużycka) (Nisa) ≃	30	52.04 N	14.46 E
Neiva	236	2.56 N	75.18 W
Neiva ≃	236	4.35 S	77.53 W
Neiwufuquan	95	40.11 N	117.39 E
Neixiang	92	33.12 N	111.57 E
Neizengshan ⋏	90	24.02 N	117.32 E
Neja	70	58.18 N	43.54 E
Neja ≃	70	57.48 N	43.42 E
Nejapa de Madero	224	16.37 N	95.59 W
Nejdek	50	50.17 N	12.42 E
Nejo	134	9.30 N	35.30 E
Nejva ≃	76	57.54 N	62.18 E
Nekalagba	144	2.50 N	28.01 E
Nekemte	134	9.02 N	36.31 E
Nekhab ⊥	130	25.10 N	32.48 E
Nekoosa	180	44.19 N	89.54 W
Neko-zaki ≻	86	35.40 N	134.46 E
Nekrasino	72	56.18 N	36.33 E
Nekrasovka	255b	55.41 N	37.56 E
Nekrasovo, S.S.S.R.	70	51.10 N	45.18 E
Nekrasovo, S.S.S.R.	72	54.30 N	38.57 E
Nekrasovskoje	70	57.41 N	40.22 E
Nekselø I	41	55.47 N	11.18 E
Neksø	26	55.04 N	15.09 E
Nela Park ♠	269a	41.33 N	81.33 W
Nel'aty	78	56.29 N	115.41 E
Nelichu ⋏	130	6.08 N	34.25 E
Nelidovo	66	56.13 N	32.46 E
Neligh	188	42.08 N	98.02 W
Nel'kan	64	57.40 N	136.13 E
Nellie	204	40.20 N	82.04 W
Nellikuppam	112	11.46 N	79.41 E
Nellingen, B.R.D.	52	48.44 N	9.18 E
Nellingen, B.R.D.	52	48.33 N	9.47 E
Nellis Air Force Base ■	194	36.14 N	115.02 W
Nelliston	200	42.56 N	74.37 W
Nellore	112	14.26 N	79.58 E
Nel'ma	79	47.39 N	139.09 E
Nelson, B.C., Can.	172	49.29 N	117.17 W
Nelson, N.Z.	162	41.17 S	173.17 E
Nelson, Eng., U.K.	42	53.51 N	2.13 W
Nelson, Nebr., U.S.	188	40.12 N	98.04 W
Nelson, Pa., U.S.	200	41.59 N	77.14 W
Nelson ≃	174	57.04 N	92.30 W
Nelson, Cape ≻, Austl.	156	38.26 S	141.33 E
Nelson, Cape ≻, Pap. N. Gui.	154	9.00 S	149.15 E
Nelson, Estrecho Ц	244	51.37 S	75.00 W
Nelson Creek ≃, Nev., U.S.	194	40.36 N	114.28 W
Nelson Creek ≃, Tex., U.S.	212	30.56 N	95.31 W
Nelson House	174	55.47 N	98.51 W
Nelson Island I	170	60.35 N	164.45 W
Nelson-Kennedy Ledges State Park ♠	204	41.18 N	81.04 W
Nelson Lake ⊜	174	55.44 N	100.00 W
Nelson Lakes National Park ♠	162	41.50 S	172.40 E
Nelson Reservoir ⊜[1]	192	48.30 N	107.34 W
Nelsons Dockyard ⊥	230c	17.00 N	61.46 W
Nelsonville, N.Y., U.S.	200	41.25 N	73.57 W
Nelsonville, Ohio, U.S.	178	39.27 N	82.14 W
Nelspoort	148	32.07 S	23.00 E
Nelspoortjie	148	29.58 S	22.25 E
Nelspruit	146	25.30 S	30.58 E
Néma, Maur.	140	16.37 N	7.15 W
Nema, S.S.S.R.	70	57.31 N	50.31 E
Néma, Dhar ●[4]	140	16.40 N	7.13 W
Nemacolin	178	39.52 N	79.56 W
Nemadji ≃	180	46.41 N	92.02 W
Nemaha	188	40.20 N	95.40 W
Nemam	112	8.27 N	77.01 E
Neman (Ragnit)	66	55.02 N	22.02 E
Neman (Nemunas) ≃	66	55.18 N	21.23 E
Nematābād	257d	35.38 N	51.21 E
Nembe	140	4.35 N	6.26 E
Nembrala	102	10.53 S	122.50 E
Nembro	56	45.45 N	9.45 E
Nemčinovka	255b	55.43 N	37.23 E
Nemda ≃, S.S.S.R.	70	57.35 N	48.56 E
Nemda ≃, S.S.S.R.	70	57.21 N	43.08 E
Nemegosenda ≃	180	48.31 N	82.53 W
Nemegt Uul ⋏⋏	92	43.40 N	101.10 E
Nemeiben Lake ⊜	174	55.20 N	105.20 W
Nemenčinė	66	54.51 N	25.29 E
Nemeriči	66	53.51 N	33.59 E
Nemi	60	41.43 N	12.43 E
Nemi, Lago di ⊜	257a	41.43 N	12.42 E
Nemira ⋏	38	46.15 N	26.19 E
Nemirov, S.S.S.R.	68	48.58 N	28.50 E
Nemirov, S.S.S.R.	68	50.07 N	23.25 E
Nemirovo	72	55.54 N	36.12 E
Nemo	212	32.16 N	97.39 W
Nemours	46	48.16 N	2.42 E
Nemoviči	68	51.16 N	26.38 E
Nemrut Gölü ⊜	120	38.37 N	42.12 E
Nemuna, Bjeshkët e ⋏⋏	38	42.27 N	19.47 E
Nemunas (Neman) ≃	66	55.18 N	21.23 E
Nemuro	82a	43.20 N	145.35 E
Nemuro-hantō ≻[1]	82a	43.21 N	145.42 E
Nemuro Strait Ц	82a	44.00 N	145.20 E
Nemzeti Múzeum ♉	254c	47.29 N	19.05 E
Nena Creek ≃	214	45.07 N	121.07 W
Nenagh	28	52.52 N	8.12 W
Nenana	170	64.34 N	149.07 W
Nenana ≃	170	64.30 N	149.00 W
Nenaševo	72	54.34 N	37.28 E
Nenasi	104	3.08 N	103.27 E
Nendö I	14	10.45 S	165.54 E
Nendaz	54	46.11 N	7.18 E
Nendeln	54	47.12 N	9.32 E
Nene ≃	44	52.48 N	0.13 E
Neneckij Nacionalnyj Okrug □[8]	24	67.30 N	54.00 E
Nenggiri ≃	104	4.53 N	101.48 E
Nengjia	94	41.38 N	120.46 E
Nengo ≃	142	14.27 S	22.09 E
Nengonengo I[1]	14	18.47 S	141.48 W
Nenndorf	48	53.23 N	9.53 E
Nenneper ≃	253	51.32 N	6.26 E
Neno	144	15.24 S	34.39 E
Nentón ≃	226	15.48 N	91.52 W
Nenzing	54	47.11 N	9.42 E
Neo	84	35.38 N	136.37 E
Neo ≃	84	35.24 N	136.34 E
Neodesha	188	37.25 N	95.41 W
Neoga	184	39.19 N	88.27 W
Neola, Iowa, U.S.	188	41.27 N	95.37 W
Neola, Utah, U.S.	190	40.26 N	110.02 W
Neon	182	37.12 N	82.43 W
Néon Fáliron	257c	37.57 N	23.40 E
Néon Karlovásion	38	37.48 N	26.44 E
Néon Psikhikón	257c	38.00 N	23.47 E
Neopit	180	44.59 N	88.50 W
Neópolis	240	10.18 S	36.35 W
Neosho	184	36.52 N	94.22 W
Neosho ≃	184	35.48 N	95.18 W
Neotsu	214	45.00 N	123.59 W
Nepa	78	59.14 N	108.14 E
Nepa ≃	78	59.16 N	108.16 E
Nepal (Nepāl) □[1]	108		
	114	28.00 N	84.00 E
Nepālganj	114	28.03 N	81.37 E
Nepa Nagar	110	21.28 N	76.23 E
Nepaug Reservoir ⊜[1]	197	41.48 N	72.57 W
Nepean ≃	160	33.27 S	150.53 E
Nepean, Point ≻	159	38.18 S	144.39 E
Nepean Bay C	158b	35.42 S	137.44 E
Nepean Island I	164c	29.04 S	167.58 E
Nepean Reservoir ⊜[1]	160	34.22 S	150.35 E
Nepecino	72	55.12 N	38.37 E
Nepeña	238	9.10 S	78.23 W
Nepewassi Lake ⊜	180	46.20 N	80.40 W
Nephi	190	39.43 N	111.50 W
Nephin ⋏	28	54.01 N	9.22 W
Nepi	60	42.14 N	12.21 E
Nepisiguit ≃	176	47.37 N	65.38 W
Nepisiguit Bay C	176	47.46 N	65.32 W
Népliget ♠	254c	47.29 N	19.07 E
Nepoko ≃	144	1.40 N	27.01 E
Nepomuceno	246	21.14 S	45.15 W
Nepomuk	30	49.29 N	13.36 E
Neponset ≃	273	42.17 N	71.02 W
Neponset Reservoir ⊜[1]	273	42.05 N	71.15 W
Neponset River Reservation ♠	273	42.13 N	71.08 W
Neppermin	50	53.56 N	14.02 E
Nepr'adva ≃	66	53.40 N	38.39 E
Népstadion ♠	254c	47.30 N	19.06 E
Nép-sziget I	254c	47.34 N	19.05 E
Neptune, N.J., U.S.	198	40.12 N	74.02 W
Neptune, Ohio, U.S.	206	40.36 N	84.30 W
Neptune Beach	182	30.19 N	81.24 W
Neptune City	198	40.12 N	74.03 W
Neqarot, Naḥal V	122	30.40 N	35.15 E
Nera ≃, Eur.	38	44.49 N	21.22 E
Nera ≃, It.	60	42.26 N	12.24 E
Nérac	32	44.08 N	0.20 E
Nerákion	257c	38.01 N	23.27 E
Nerang	161a	28.00 S	153.20 E
Nerang ≃	161a	28.03 S	153.17 E
Nerastro, Sarīr ◂[2]	136	24.20 N	20.37 E
Neratovice	50	50.14 N	14.31 E
Nerča ≃	78	51.56 N	116.40 E
Nerchau	50	51.16 N	12.47 E
Nerčinsk	78	51.58 N	116.35 E
Nerčinskij Chrebet ⋏⋏	78	50.50 N	117.50 E
Nerčinskij Zavod	78	51.19 N	119.36 E
Nerčugan ≃	78	53.26 N	116.38 E
Nère ≃	46	47.34 N	2.18 E
Nerechta	70	57.28 N	40.34 E
Nerenstetten	52	48.31 N	10.06 E
Neresheim	52	48.45 N	10.15 E
Nereta	66	56.13 N	25.18 E
Nereto	60	42.49 N	13.49 E
Neretva ≃	36	43.01 N	17.27 E
Nerevoznoje	70	56.53 N	53.54 E
Nerima ◂[8]	258	35.44 N	139.42 E
Nerima, Camp ■	258	35.45 N	139.39 E
Neringa	66	55.18 N	21.01 E
Neriquinha	142	15.45 S	21.42 E
Neris ≃	66	54.54 N	23.53 E
Nerito	60	42.32 N	13.28 E
Nerja	34	36.44 N	3.52 W
Nerka, Lake ⊜	170	59.30 N	158.45 W
Nerl', S.S.S.R.	66	57.03 N	37.59 E
Nerl', S.S.S.R.	70	56.40 N	40.24 E
Nerl' ≃, S.S.S.R.	66	57.07 N	37.39 E
Nerl' ≃, S.S.S.R.	70	56.11 N	40.34 E
Nero, Ozero ⊜	70	57.07 N	39.27 E
Neroj	78	54.28 N	97.49 E
Néronde	56	45.50 N	4.14 E
Nérondes	32	47.00 N	2.49 E
Nerópolis	245	16.25 S	49.14 W
Nerriga	160	35.07 S	150.05 E
Nerrima	152	18.24 S	124.29 E
Nerrimunga Creek ≃	160	34.57 S	150.04 E
Nersingen	54	48.25 N	10.07 E
Nerskaja ≃	72	55.23 N	38.35 E
Nerul	262c	19.02 N	73.01 E
Nerus ≃	104	5.20 N	103.05 E
Nerussa ≃	66	52.33 N	33.47 E
Nerva	34	37.42 N	6.32 W
Nervi	56	44.23 N	9.02 E
Nervia ≃	56	43.47 N	7.38 E
Nerviano	56	45.33 N	8.58 E
Nerville-la-Forêt	251	49.05 N	2.17 E
Nes, Ned.	48	53.26 N	5.45 E
Nes, Ned.	48	53.04 N	5.51 E
Nes, Nor.	26	60.34 N	9.59 E
Nes', S.S.S.R.	24	66.37 N	44.36 E
Nes, Har ⋏	122	30.22 N	34.37 E
Nesbyen	26	60.34 N	9.09 E
Neščerdo, Ozero ⊜	66	55.54 N	29.04 E
Neščeretovo	73	49.24 N	38.48 E
Nesco	198	39.38 N	74.42 W
Nescochague Creek ≃	275	39.39 N	74.41 W
Nescochague Creek, Great Swamp Branch ≃	275	39.41 N	74.43 W
Nesconset	266	40.50 N	73.09 W
Nescopeck	200	41.03 N	76.13 W
Nescopeck Creek ≃	200	41.03 N	76.14 W
Nescopeck Mountain ⋏	200	41.03 N	76.05 W
Nesebâr	38	42.39 N	27.44 E
Neshaminy Creek ≃	198	40.04 N	74.55 W
Neshaminy Hills	275	40.10 N	74.57 W
Neshannock Creek ≃	204	40.59 N	80.21 W
Nesher	122	32.46 N	35.03 E
Neškan	170	67.03 N	173.01 W
Neškanpil'gun, Laguna C	170	66.57 N	172.45 W
Neskaupstaður	24a	65.10 N	13.43 W
Neskowin	214	45.05 N	123.59 W
Nesle	46	49.46 N	2.55 E
Nesna	24	66.12 N	13.02 E
Nesque ≃	56	43.59 N	4.59 E
Nesquehoning	200	40.52 N	75.49 W
Ness	252	53.17 N	3.03 W
Ness, Loch ⊜	28	57.15 N	4.30 W
Ness City	188	38.27 N	99.54 W
Nesse ≃	50	50.59 N	10.32 E
Nesselrode, Mount ⋏	170	58.58 N	134.18 W
Nesselwang	54	47.37 N	10.30 E
Nesselwängle	54	47.29 N	10.37 E
Nesslau	54	47.13 N	9.13 E
Nessmersiel	48	53.40 N	7.21 E
Nesso	54	45.55 N	9.08 E
Neštěmice	50	50.40 N	14.07 E
Nesterkovo	66	59.10 N	30.33 E
Nesterov, S.S.S.R.	66	54.38 N	22.34 E
Nesterov, S.S.S.R.	68	50.04 N	23.58 E
Nesterovka	70	52.26 N	53.42 E
Nesterovo, S.S.S.R.	70	54.31 N	41.49 E
Nesterovo, S.S.S.R.	72	56.45 N	36.30 E
Nesterovo, S.S.S.R.	78	52.22 N	107.53 E
Nestiary	70	56.34 N	45.21 E
Nestoita	68	47.47 N	29.21 E
Neston	42	53.18 N	3.04 W
Nestore ≃	60	43.21 N	12.15 E
Néstos (Mesta) ≃	38	40.41 N	24.44 E
Nesttun	26	60.19 N	5.20 E
Nestucca ≃	214	45.12 N	123.57 W
Nesvetaj	73	47.27 N	39.40 E
Nesviž	66	53.13 N	26.40 E
Nes Ẕiyyona	122	31.55 N	34.48 E
Netanya	122	32.20 N	34.51 E
Netarhāt	114	23.29 N	84.16 E
Netarts	214	45.26 N	123.57 W
Netarts Bay C	214	45.24 N	123.56 W
Netcong	200	40.54 N	74.42 W
Nethan ≃	42	55.42 N	3.52 W
Nether Alderley	252	53.17 N	2.14 W
Netherdale	156	21.08 S	148.32 E
Netherlands □[1]	22		
	30	52.15 N	5.30 E

≃ River	Fluss	Río	Rivière	Rio
☰ Canal	Kanal	Canal	Canal	Canal
Waterfall, Rapids	Wasserfall, Stromschnellen	Cascada, Rápidos	Chute d'eau, Rapides	Cascata, Rápidos
Ц Strait	Meeresstrasse	Estrecho	Détroit	Estreito
C Bay, Gulf	Bucht, Golf	Bahía, Golfo	Baie, Golfe	Baía, Golfo
⊜ Lake, Lakes	See, Seen	Lago, Lagos	Lac, Lacs	Lago, Lagos
☷ Swamp	Sumpf	Pantano	Marais	Pântano
Ice Features, Glacier	Eis- und Gletscherformen	Accidentes Glaciales	Formes glaciaires	Acidentes Glaciares
⊤ Other Hydrographic Features	Andere Hydrographische Objekte	Otros Elementos Hidrográficos	Autres données hydrographiques	Outros Elementos Hidrográficos
✧ Submarine Features	Untermeerische Objekte	Accidentes Submarinos	Formes de relief sous-marin	Acidentes Submarinos
□ Political Unit	Politische Einheit	Unidad Politica	Entité politique	Unidade Política
♉ Cultural Institution	Kulturelle Institution	Institución Cultural	Institution culturelle	Instituição Cultural
⊥ Historical Site	Historische Stätte	Sitio Histórico	Site historique	Sítio Histórico
♠ Recreational Site	Erholungs- und Ferienort	Sitio de Recreo	Centre de loisirs	Sítio de Lazer
⊠ Airport	Flughafen	Aeropuerto	Aéroport	Aeroporto
■ Military Installation	Militäranlage	Instalación Militar	Installation militaire	Instalação Militar
◂ Miscellaneous	Verschiedenes	Misceláneo	Divers	Miscelânea

ENGLISH: Name — Page — Lat.°′ — Long.°′
DEUTSCH: Name — Seite — Breite°′ — Länge°′ E=Ost

Netherland Antilles □2 220
231s 12.15 N 69.00 W
Netherton 252 53.30 N 2.58 W
Netia 144 14.48 S 39.59 E
Netley Marsh 44 50.53 N 1.21 W
Neto ≏ 36 39.13 N 17.08 E
Netolice 30 49.03 N 14.12 E
Netra 52 51.06 N 10.05 E
Netrakona 114 24.53 N 90.43 E
Netstal 54 47.03 N 9.03 E
Nettancourt 52 48.52 N 4.57 E
Nette 48 52.02 N 10.05 E
Nette ≏8 253 51.33 N 7.25 E
Nettelstedt 48 52.18 N 8.41 E
Nettetal 52 51.18 N 6.16 E
Nettilling Fiord C2 166 66.02 N 68.12 W
Nettilling Lake ⊜ 166 66.30 N 70.40 W
Nett Lake ⊜ 180 48.10 N 93.10 W
Nett Lake Indian Reservation ◆4 180 48.06 N 93.10 W
Nettlebed 44 51.35 N 1.00 W
Nettle Creek ≏ 208 40.03 N 83.48 W
Nettleden 250 51.47 N 0.32 W
Nettlestead 250 51.14 N 0.25 E
Nettlestead Green 250 51.14 N 0.25 E
Nettleton 184 34.05 N 88.44 W
Nettuno 60 41.27 N 12.39 E
Netze → Noteć ≏ 30 52.44 N 15.26 E
Netzschkau 50 50.36 N 12.14 E
Neuastenberg 52 51.10 N 8.29 E
Neubeckum 48 51.48 N 8.01 E
Neu Bentschen → Zbąszynek 30 52.15 N 15.50 E
Neubrandenburg 50 53.33 N 13.15 E
Neubrandenburg □5 50 53.30 N 13.15 E
Neubraunschweig → New Brunswick □4 176 46.30 N 66.15 W
Neubritannien → New Britain I 154 6.00 S 150.00 E
Neu Büddenstedt 50 52.10 N 10.31 E
Neubukow 50 54.02 N 11.40 E
Neuburg an der Donau 30 48.44 N 11.11 E
Neuchâtel 54 46.59 N 6.56 E
Neuchâtel □3 54 47.00 N 6.55 E
Neuchâtel, Lac de ⊜ 54 46.52 N 6.50 E
Neudamm → Dębno 30 52.45 N 14.40 E
Neu-Delhi → New Delhi 114 28.36 N 77.12 E
Neudenau 52 49.17 N 9.16 E
Neudietendorf 50 50.55 N 10.55 E
Neudorf, B.R.D. 52 49.10 N 8.29 E
Neudorf, Sask., Can. 174 50.44 N 102.59 W
Neudorf, D.D.R. 50 50.29 N 12.58 E
Neudorf ◆8 253 51.25 N 6.47 E
Neue Hebriden → New Hebrides □2 165f 16.00 S 167.00 E
Neuemühle 254a 52.18 N 13.39 E
Neuenbürg, B.R.D. 48 53.23 N 7.57 E
Neuenbürg, B.R.D. 52 48.50 N 8.35 E
Neuenbürg, B.R.D. 54 47.49 N 7.35 E
Neuenburg → Neuchâtel, Schw. 54 46.59 N 6.56 E
Neuendettelsau 52 49.17 N 10.47 E
Neuendorf 50 54.31 N 13.05 E
Neuendorfer See ⊜ 50 52.07 N 13.55 E
Neuenegg 54 46.54 N 7.18 E
Neuenhagen bei Berlin 50 52.32 N 13.41 E
Neuenhaus 48 52.30 N 6.59 E
Neuenhof ◆8 253 51.10 N 7.13 E
Neuenhoven 253 51.08 N 6.31 E
Neue Niers ≏ 253 51.16 N 6.26 E
Neuenkamp ◆8 253 51.26 N 6.44 E
Neuenkirchen, B.R.D. 48 53.14 N 8.31 E
Neuenkirchen, B.R.D. 48 52.30 N 8.04 E
Neuenkirchen, B.R.D. 48 53.02 N 9.42 E
Neuenkirchen, B.R.D. 48 52.14 N 7.22 E
Neuenkirchen, B.R.D. 48 51.50 N 8.26 E
Neuenkirchen, B.R.D. 48 53.46 N 8.53 E
Neuenkirchen, D.D.R. 50 54.32 N 13.20 E
Neuenland, Flughafen ⊠ 48 53.03 N 8.46 E
Neuenrade 52 51.17 N 7.47 E
Neuensalz 50 50.30 N 12.13 E
Neuenstadt am Kocher 52 49.14 N 9.20 E
Neuenwalde 48 53.40 N 8.40 E
Neuerburg 52 50.00 N 6.17 E
Neu-Erlaa ◆8 254b 48.08 N 16.19 E
Neues Palais ⊥ 254a 52.24 N 13.01 E
Neu Fahrland 254a 52.26 N 13.03 E
Neuf-Brisach 54 48.01 N 7.32 E
Neufchâteau, Bel. 52 49.50 N 5.26 E
Neufchâteau, Fr. 54 48.21 N 5.42 E
Neufchâtel-en-Bray 46 49.44 N 1.27 E
Neufchâtel-sur-Aisne 46 49.26 N 4.02 E
Neuffen 52 48.33 N 9.22 E
Neuffossé, Canal de ≅ 46 50.45 N 2.15 E
Neufmanil 52 49.49 N 4.48 E
Neuf-Marché 46 49.25 N 1.43 E
Neufmontiers-lès-Meaux 251 48.58 N 2.50 E
Neufundland → Newfoundland □4 166 52.00 N 56.00 W
Neufvilles 46 50.34 N 4.00 E
Neugersdorf 50 50.59 N 14.36 E
Neuglobsow 50 53.09 N 13.02 E
Neugraben-Fischbek ◆8 48 53.28 N 9.52 E
Neuguinea → New Guinea I 154 5.00 S 140.00 E
Neuharlingersiel 48 53.42 N 7.42 E
Neu-Hartmannsdorf 254a 52.22 N 13.51 E
Neuhaus, B.R.D. 54 47.46 N 8.34 E
Neuhaus, D.D.R. 50 50.30 N 11.08 E
Neuhaus, D.D.R. 50 53.17 N 10.55 E
Neuhaus an der Oste 48 53.48 N 9.02 E
Neuhausen, B.R.D. 54 47.58 N 8.55 E
Neuhausen, D.D.R. 50 50.41 N 13.28 E
Neuhausen, Schw. 54 47.41 N 8.37 E
Neuhausen → Gurjevsk, S.S.S.R. 66 54.47 N 20.38 E
Neuhausen auf den Fildern 52 48.41 N 9.16 E
Neuhaus im Solling 48 51.45 N 9.31 E
Neuhaus-Schierschnitz 50 50.19 N 11.14 E
Neuheum 104 5.34 N 95.32 E
Neuhof 52 50.27 N 9.40 E
Neuhof an der Zenn 52 49.27 N 10.38 E
Neuillé-Pont-Pierre 46 47.33 N 0.33 E
Neuilly-en-Thelle 46 49.13 N 2.17 E
Neuilly-l'Évêque 54 47.55 N 5.26 E
Neuilly-Saint-Front 46 49.10 N 3.16 E
Neuilly-sur-Marne 251 48.51 N 2.32 E
Neuilly-sur-Seine 46 48.53 N 2.16 E
Neuirland → New Ireland I 154 3.20 S 152.00 E
Neu-Isenburg 52 50.03 N 8.41 E
Neukagran ◆8 254b 48.14 N 16.27 E
Neukaledonien → New Caledonia □2 165f 21.30 S 165.30 E
Neukalen 50 53.49 N 12.47 E
Neu Kaliss 50 53.10 N 11.17 E
Neukieritzsch 50 51.10 N 12.25 E
Neukirch, B.R.D. 54 47.39 N 9.41 E
Neukirch, D.D.R. 50 51.05 N 14.20 E
Neukirch, D.D.R. 50 51.17 N 13.58 E
Neukirchen, B.R.D. 41 54.52 N 8.44 E
Neukirchen, B.R.D. 50 54.19 N 11.01 E
Neukirchen, B.R.D. 52 49.29 N 6.50 E
Neukirchen, B.R.D. 52 50.46 N 9.41 E
Neukirchen, B.R.D. 253 51.07 N 6.41 E
Neukirchen, D.D.R. 50 50.47 N 12.22 E
Neukirchen, D.D.R. 50 51.05 N 12.32 E
Neukirchen, D.D.R. 50 50.46 N 12.52 E
Neukirchen, Öst. 58 47.15 N 12.17 E
Neukirchen, Öst. 58 47.52 N 13.42 E
Neukirchen-Vluyn 52 51.27 N 6.33 E
Neukloster 50 53.52 N 11.41 E
Neukölln ◆8 254a 52.29 N 13.27 E
Neukuhren → Pionerskij 66 54.57 N 20.20 E
Neulangerwisch 254a 52.19 N 13.04 E
Neulienen 50 53.27 N 14.22 E
Neu Lübbenau 50 52.04 N 13.53 E
Neulussheim 52 49.17 N 8.31 E
Neumagen 52 49.51 N 6.53 E
Neuman Creek ≏ 274a 42.42 N 78.48 W
Neumark 50 50.39 N 12.21 E
Neumarkt → Środa Śląska, Pol. 30 51.10 N 16.36 E
Neumarkt → Tîrgu Mureș 38 46.33 N 24.33 E
Neumarkt → Tîgu-Secuiesc 38 46.00 N 26.08 E
Neumarkt am Wallersee 58 47.57 N 13.14 E
Neumarkt [im Hausruckkreis] 30 48.16 N 13.45 E
Neumarkt in der Oberpfalz 30 49.16 N 11.28 E
Neumarkt in Steiermark 30 47.05 N 14.26 E
Neumarkt-Sankt Veit 30 48.22 N 12.30 E
Neumittelwalde → Międzybórz 30 51.24 N 17.40 E
Neumünster 30 54.04 N 9.59 E
Neun ≏ 100 19.42 N 104.03 E
Neunburg vorm Wald 30 49.21 N 12.24 E
Neundorf 50 51.49 N 11.34 E
Neung-sur-Beuvron 46 47.32 N 1.48 E
Neunkirchen, B.R.D. 52 50.32 N 8.06 E
Neunkirchen, Öst. 30 47.43 N 16.05 E
Neunkirchen am Brand 52 49.37 N 11.07 E
Neunkirchen am Potzberg 52 49.30 N 7.29 E
Neunkirchen / saar 52 49.20 N 7.10 E
Neupetershain 50 51.36 N 14.09 E
Neuquén 242 38.57 S 68.04 W
Neuquén □4 244 39.00 S 70.00 W
Neuquén ≏ 242 38.59 S 68.00 W
Neurara 242 24.10 S 68.29 W
Neuravensburg 54 47.38 N 9.46 E
Neureisenberg 254b 48.01 N 16.30 E
Neurode → Nowa Ruda 30 50.35 N 16.31 E
Neuruppin 50 52.55 N 12.48 E
Neusalz → Nowa Sól 30 51.48 N 15.44 E
Neusalza-Spremberg 50 51.02 N 14.32 E
Neu Sankt Johann 54 47.14 N 9.12 E
Neusatz → Novi Sad 38 45.15 N 19.50 E
Neuschottland → Nova Scotia □4 176 45.00 N 63.00 W
Neuschwanstein, Schloss ♥ 54 47.35 N 10.44 E
Neuse ≏ 182 35.06 N 76.30 W
Neuseddin 254a 52.18 N 12.59 E
Neuseeland → New Zealand □1 162 41.00 S 174.00 E
Neusibirische Inseln → Novosibirskije Ostrova II 64 75.00 N 142.00 E
Neusiedler See ⊜ 30 47.50 N 16.46 E
Neusohl → Banská Bystrica 30 48.44 N 19.07 E
Neuss 52 51.12 N 6.41 E
Neusserweyhe ◆8 253 51.13 N 6.39 E
Neustadt, B.R.D. 52 50.51 N 9.07 E
Neustadt, Ont., Can. 202 44.05 N 81.00 W
Neustadt, D.D.R. 50 51.01 N 14.13 E
Neustadt, D.D.R. 50 50.44 N 11.44 E
Neustadt, D.D.R. 50 52.52 N 12.25 E
Neustadt ◆8 48 53.04 N 8.47 E
Neustadt am Rübenberge 48 52.30 N 9.28 E
Neustadt an der Aisch 52 49.34 N 10.37 E
Neustadt an der Waldnaab 30 49.44 N 12.11 E
Neustadt an der Weinstrasse 52 49.21 N 8.08 E
Neustadt bei Coburg 52 50.19 N 11.07 E
Neustädtel → Nowe Miasteczko 30 51.42 N 15.45 E
Neustädter Bucht C 50 54.02 N 10.50 E
Neustadt-Glewe 50 53.25 N 11.36 E
Neustadt in Holstein 50 54.06 N 10.48 E
Neustadt in Oberschlesien → Prudnik 30 50.19 N 17.34 E
Neustettin → Szczecinek 30 53.43 N 16.42 E
Neustift am Walde ◆8 254b 48.15 N 16.18 E
Neustift im Stubaital 58 47.07 N 11.19 E
Neustrelitz 50 53.21 N 13.04 E
Neuteich → Nowy Staw 30 54.09 N 19.00 E
Neu Töplitz 254a 52.27 N 12.54 E
Neutral Hills ◆2 174 52.10 N 110.50 W
Neutral Zone □2 118 29.10 N 45.30 E
Neutrebbin 50 52.40 N 14.13 E
Neu-Ulm 54 48.23 N 10.01 E
Neuve-Chapelle 46 50.35 N 2.47 E
Neuves-Maisons 54 48.37 N 6.06 E
Neuvic 46 45.23 N 2.16 E
Neuville-aux-Bois 46 48.04 N 2.03 E
Neuville-de-Poitou 32 46.41 N 0.15 E
Neuville-en-Condroz 52 50.32 N 5.27 E
Neuville-lès-Dieppe 46 49.55 N 1.06 E
Neuville-sur-Oise 251 49.01 N 2.04 E
Neuville-sur-Saône 56 45.52 N 4.51 E
Neuvy-le-Roi 46 47.36 N 0.36 E
Neuvy-sur-Barangeon 46 47.19 N 2.15 E
Neuvy-sur-Loire 46 47.31 N 2.53 E
Neuwaldegg ◆8 254b 48.14 N 16.17 E
Neuwarp → Nowe Warpno 30 53.44 N 14.16 E
Neuwedell → Drawno 30 53.13 N 15.45 E
Neuwerk ◆8 253 51.13 N 6.28 E
Neuwerk I 48 53.55 N 8.30 E
Neuwied 52 50.25 N 7.27 E
Neuwiller-lès-Saverne 52 48.49 N 7.24 E
Neuwirtshaus 52 50.11 N 9.50 E
Neu Wulmstorf 48 53.28 N 9.48 E
Neuzelle 50 52.05 N 14.38 E
Neu Zittau 50 52.23 N 13.44 E
Neva ≏ 255a 59.55 N 30.15 E
Nevache 56 45.01 N 6.37 E
Nevada, Iowa, U.S. 180 42.01 N 93.27 W
Nevada, Mo., U.S. 184 37.51 N 94.22 W
Nevada, Ohio, U.S. 204 40.49 N 83.08 W
Nevada, Tex., U.S. 212 33.02 N 96.22 W
Nevada □6 216 39.16 N 121.01 W
Nevada □3 168
194 39.00 N 117.00 W
Nevada, Sierra ◆, Esp. 34 37.05 N 3.10 W
Nevada, Sierra ◆, Calif., U.S. 194 38.00 N 119.15 W
Nevada City 216 39.16 N 121.01 W
Nevada Creek ≏ 192 46.54 N 113.02 W
Nevada de Santa Marta, Sierra ◆ 236 10.50 N 73.40 W
Nevado, Cerro ◆ 242 35.35 S 68.30 W
Nevado, Sierra del ◆ 242 35.40 S 68.30 W
Nevado de Toluca, Parque Nacional ◆ 224 19.10 N 99.50 W
Neval'cevo 76 58.38 N 81.53 E
Nevali 262c 19.01 N 73.07 E
Nevanka 78 56.30 N 98.54 E
Neve, Serra da ◆ 142 13.52 S 13.26 E
Nevel' 66 56.02 N 29.55 E
Nevel'sk 79 46.40 N 141.53 E
Nevel'skogo, Proliv U 79 52.05 N 141.35 E
Nevendon 250 51.36 N 0.30 E
Never 79 53.58 N 124.05 E
Neverkino 70 52.47 N 46.44 E
Neverovo 70 55.07 N 44.24 E
Nevers 32 47.00 N 3.09 E
Neversink ≏ 200 41.21 N 74.42 W
Neversink Reservoir ⊜1 200 41.48 N 74.42 W
Nevertire 156 31.52 S 147.39 E
Neves 246 22.51 S 43.06 W
Nevesinje 38 43.15 N 18.07 E
Nevežis ≏ 66 54.56 N 23.46 E
Nevežkino 70 53.07 N 43.19 E
Neviano degli Arduini 58 44.35 N 10.19 E
Neviges 52 51.19 N 7.05 E
Neville Island 269b 40.31 N 80.08 W
Neville Island I 269b 40.31 N 80.08 W
Nevinnomyssk 74 44.38 N 41.56 E
Nevis I 228 17.10 N 62.34 W
Nevis, Ben ◆ 28 56.48 N 5.01 W
Nevjansk 76 57.32 N 60.13 E
Nevlunghamn 26 58.58 N 9.52 E
Nevon 78 58.07 N 102.49 E
Nevşehir 120 38.38 N 34.43 E
Nevşehir □4 120 38.50 N 34.40 E
Nevskoje 66 58.08 N 30.26 E
New ≏, Belize 222 18.22 N 88.24 W
New ≏, Guy. 236 3.23 N 57.36 W
New ≏, N.A. 194 33.08 N 115.44 W
New ≏, U.S. 182 38.10 N 81.12 W
New ≏, Ariz., U.S. 190 33.31 N 112.18 W
New ≏, Fla., U.S. 182 29.50 N 84.40 W
New ≏, Fla., U.S. 182 29.55 N 82.25 W
New ≏, N.C., U.S. 182 34.32 N 77.20 W
New ≏, S.C., U.S. 182 32.09 N 80.50 W
New ≏, Tenn., U.S. 182 36.25 N 84.38 W
Newabāgam 262b 22.48 N 88.24 E
New Abbey 42 54.59 N 3.38 W
New Addington ◆8 250 51.21 N 0.01 W
Newala 144 10.56 S 39.18 E
New Albany, Ind., U.S. 208 38.18 N 85.49 W
New Albany, Miss., U.S. 184 34.29 N 89.00 W
New Albany, Ohio, U.S. 204 40.05 N 82.49 W
New Albany, Pa., U.S. 200 41.36 N 76.27 W
New Albin 180 43.30 N 91.17 W
New Alexandria, Ohio, U.S. 204 40.17 N 80.40 W
New Alexandria, Pa., U.S. 204 40.24 N 79.25 W
New Alexandria, Va., U.S. 274c 38.47 N 77.03 W
New Alfa 130 15.10 N 35.40 E
New Almaden 216 37.11 N 121.49 W
New Alresford 44 51.06 N 1.10 W
New Amsterdam 236 6.15 N 57.31 W
New Angledool 156 29.07 S 147.57 E
Newark, Ark., U.S. 184 35.42 N 91.27 W
Newark, Calif., U.S. 216 37.32 N 122.02 W
Newark, Del., U.S. 198 39.41 N 75.45 W
Newark, Ill., U.S. 206 41.32 N 88.35 W
Newark, Md., U.S. 198 38.15 N 75.17 W
Newark, Mo., U.S. 209 39.60 N 91.59 W
Newark, N.J., U.S. 200
266 40.44 N 74.10 W
Newark, N.Y., U.S. 200 43.03 N 77.06 W
Newark, Ohio, U.S. 204 40.04 N 82.24 W
Newark, Tex., U.S. 212 33.00 N 97.29 W
Newark, Port C 266 40.42 N 74.08 W
Newark Airport ⊠ 200 40.42 N 74.10 W
Newark Bay C 266 40.39 N 74.09 W
Newark Bay Bridge ◆5 266 40.42 N 74.07 W
Newark Lake ⊜ 194 39.41 N 115.44 W
Newark Slough ≏ 272 37.31 N 122.05 W
Newark-upon-Trent 44 53.05 N 0.49 W
Newark Valley 200 42.14 N 76.11 W
New Athens, Ill., U.S. 209 38.19 N 89.53 W
New Athens, Ohio, U.S. 204 40.11 N 81.00 W
New Augusta 184 31.12 N 89.02 W
Newaukum, North Fork ≏ 214 46.36 N 122.51 W
Newaukum, South Fork ≏ 214 46.36 N 122.51 W
Newaygo 180 43.25 N 85.48 W
New Baden, Ill., U.S. 209 38.32 N 89.42 W
New Baden, Tex., U.S. 212 31.03 N 96.26 W
New Baltimore, Mich., U.S. 204 42.41 N 82.44 W
New Baltimore, N.Y., U.S. 200 42.27 N 73.47 W
New Bavaria 204 41.12 N 84.10 W
New Bedford, Mass., U.S. 197 41.38 N 70.56 W
New Bedford, Pa., U.S. 204 41.06 N 80.30 W
New Bedford ◆ 44 52.35 N 0.20 E
Newberg 214 45.18 N 122.58 W
New Berlin, Ill., U.S. 209 39.44 N 89.55 W
New Berlin, N.Y., U.S. 200 42.38 N 75.20 W
New Berlin, Pa., U.S. 200 40.53 N 76.59 W
New Berlin, Wis., U.S. 206 42.58 N 88.07 W
New Berlinville 198 40.20 N 75.38 W
Newbern, Ala., U.S. 184 32.36 N 87.38 W
Newbern, Ill., U.S. 209 39.01 N 90.20 W
New Bern, N.C., U.S. 182 35.07 N 77.03 W
Newberry, Fla., U.S. 182 29.39 N 82.37 W
Newberry, Mich., U.S. 180 46.21 N 85.30 W
Newberry, S.C., U.S. 182 34.17 N 81.37 W
New Bethlehem 204 41.00 N 79.20 W
Newbiggin-by-the-Sea 42 55.11 N 1.30 W
New Bloomfield, Mo., U.S. 209 38.43 N 92.05 W
New Bloomfield, Pa., U.S. 198 40.25 N 77.11 W
New Bloomington 204 40.35 N 83.19 W
Newbold Island I 275 40.08 N 74.45 W
Newboro 202 44.39 N 76.19 W
Newboro Lake ⊜ 202 44.38 N 76.20 W
Newborough, Austl. 159 38.11 S 146.17 E
Newborough, Wales, U.K. 42 53.09 N 4.22 W
New Boston, Ill., U.S. 180 41.10 N 91.00 W
New Boston, Mich., U.S. 206 42.10 N 83.24 W
New Boston, Ohio, U.S. 208 38.45 N 82.56 W
New Boston, Tex., U.S. 184 33.28 N 94.25 W
New Braintree 197 42.19 N 72.07 W
New Braunfels 186 29.42 N 98.08 W
New Bremen 206 40.26 N 84.23 W
Newbridge → Droichead Nua 28 53.11 N 6.48 W
Newbridge on Wye 42 52.13 N 3.27 W
New Brighton, N.Z. 162 43.31 S 172.44 E
New Brighton, Eng., U.K. 252 53.26 N 3.03 W
New Brighton, Pa., U.S. 204 40.44 N 80.19 W
New Brighton ◆8 266 40.38 N 74.06 W
New Britain, Conn., U.S. 197 41.40 N 72.47 W
New Britain, Pa., U.S. 198 40.18 N 75.11 W
New Britain I 154 6.00 S 150.00 E
New Britain Trench ◆1 14 6.00 S 152.30 E
New Brockton 184 31.23 N 85.57 W
Newbrook 172 54.19 N 112.57 W
New Brunswick, Ind., U.S. 208 39.57 N 86.31 W
New Brunswick, N.J., U.S. 198 40.29 N 74.27 W
New Brunswick □4 166
176 46.30 N 66.15 W
New Buffalo, Mich., U.S. 206 41.47 N 86.45 W
New Buffalo, Pa., U.S. 198 40.27 N 76.58 W
New Bullards Bar Reservoir ⊜1 216 39.25 N 121.08 W
Newburg, Mo., U.S. 184 37.55 N 91.54 W
Newburg, Pa., U.S. 198 40.08 N 77.32 W
Newburg, Pa., U.S. 204 40.31 N 78.25 W
Newburgh, Ont., Can. 202 44.19 N 76.52 W
Newburgh, Eng., U.K. 252 53.35 N 2.47 W
Newburgh, Ind., U.S. 184 37.57 N 87.24 W
Newburgh, N.Y., U.S. 200 41.30 N 74.01 W
Newburgh Heights 269a 41.27 N 81.40 W
Newburn 42 54.59 N 1.43 W
Newbury, Ont., Can. 204 42.41 N 81.48 W
Newbury, Eng., U.K. 44 51.25 N 1.20 W
Newbury, Mass., U.S. 197 42.48 N 70.52 W
Newbury Old Town 197 42.46 N 70.51 W
Newbury Park 218 34.11 N 118.53 W
Newburyport 197 42.49 N 70.53 W
Newby 42 54.20 N 0.28 W
Newby Bridge 42 54.16 N 2.58 W
New Caledonia □2 14
165f 21.30 S 165.30 E
New Canaan 197 41.09 N 73.30 W
New Caney 222 30.09 N 95.13 W
New Canton 209 39.38 N 91.06 W
New Carlisle, Qué., Can. 176 48.01 N 65.20 W
New Carlisle, Ind., U.S. 206 41.42 N 86.31 W
New Carlisle, Ohio, U.S. 208 39.56 N 84.02 W
New Carrollton 274c 38.58 N 76.53 W
New Cassel 266 40.44 N 73.36 W
Newcastle, Austl. 160 32.56 S 151.46 E
Newcastle, N.B., Can. 176 47.00 N 65.34 W
Newcastle, Ont., Can. 202 43.55 N 78.35 W
Newcastle, S. Afr. 148 27.49 S 29.55 E
Newcastle, Eng., U.K. 44 52.26 N 3.06 W
Newcastle, N. Ire., U.K. 42 54.12 N 5.54 W
Newcastle, Calif., U.S. 216 38.53 N 121.08 W
New Castle, Colo., U.S. 190 39.34 N 107.32 W
New Castle, Del., U.S. 198 39.40 N 75.34 W
New Castle, Ind., U.S. 208 39.55 N 85.22 W
New Castle, Ky., U.S. 208 38.26 N 85.10 W
Newcastle, Maine, U.S. 178 44.02 N 69.33 W
Newcastle, Nebr., U.S. 188 42.39 N 96.53 W
Newcastle, Ohio, U.S. 204 40.20 N 82.10 W
New Castle, Pa., U.S. 204 41.00 N 80.20 W
Newcastle, Tex., U.S. 186 33.12 N 98.44 W
New Castle, Va., U.S. 192 37.30 N 80.07 W
Newcastle, Wyo., U.S. 188 43.50 N 104.11 W
New Castle □6 198 39.44 N 75.33 W
Newcastle (Ouston) Airport ⊠ 42 55.01 N 1.53 W
Newcastle Bay C 154 10.50 S 142.37 E
Newcastle Bight C3 160 32.51 S 151.54 E
Newcastle Creek ≏ 154 17.20 S 133.23 E
Newcastle Emlyn 44 52.02 N 4.28 W
Newcastle Mine 172 51.28 N 112.46 W
Newcastleton 42 55.11 N 2.49 W
Newcastle-under-Lyme 44 53.00 N 2.14 W
Newcastle upon Tyne 42 54.59 N 1.35 W
Newcastle Waters 152 17.24 S 133.24 E
Newcastle West 28 52.27 N 9.03 W
New Centerville 275 40.04 N 75.26 W
New Chicago 206 41.34 N 87.16 W
Newchurch, Wales, U.K. 44 52.09 N 3.08 W
New Church, Va., U.S. 198 37.59 N 75.32 W
New City 200 41.09 N 73.59 W
Newclare ◆8 263d 26.11 S 27.58 E
New Columbia 200 41.02 N 76.52 W
New Columbus 200 41.10 N 76.18 W
Newcomerstown 204 40.16 N 81.36 W
New Concord 178 40.00 N 81.44 W
New Corydon 206 40.34 N 84.51 W
New Croton Aqueduct ≅1 266 41.11 N 73.49 W
New Croton Reservoir ⊜1 200 41.14 N 73.46 W
New Cumberland, Pa., U.S. 198 40.14 N 76.53 W
New Cumberland, W. Va., U.S. 204 40.30 N 80.36 W
New Cumberland Dam ◆6 204 40.32 N 80.37 W
New Cumnock 42 55.24 N 4.12 W
New Dayton 172 49.25 N 112.23 W
Newdegate 152 33.06 S 119.01 E
New Delhi 114
262a 28.36 N 77.12 E•
New Delhi Railroad Station ◆5 262a 28.39 N 77.13 E
New Denver 172 49.59 N 117.22 W
New Derry 204 40.21 N 79.19 W
New Don Pedro Reservoir ⊜1 216 37.43 N 120.23 W
New Dundee 202 43.21 N 80.31 W
New Dungeness Bay C 214 48.10 N 123.07 W
New Eagle 204 40.12 N 79.56 W
New Edinburg 184 33.46 N 92.14 W
New Effington 188 45.51 N 96.55 W
New Egypt 198 40.04 N 74.32 W
Newell, Iowa, U.S. 188 42.36 N 95.00 W
Newell, S. Dak., U.S. 186 44.43 N 103.25 W
Newell, W. Va., U.S. 204 40.36 N 80.36 W
Newell, Lake ⊜, Austl. 152 24.50 S 126.10 E
Newell, Lake ⊜, Alta., Can. 172 50.25 N 111.56 W
New Ellenton 182 33.24 N 81.42 W
Newellton 184 32.10 N 91.14 W
New Eltham ◆8 250 51.26 N 0.04 E
New Empire 218 35.15 N 119.21 W
New England 188 46.32 N 102.52 W
New England National Park ◆ 156 30.30 S 152.15 E
New England Range ◆ 156 30.00 S 151.50 E
Newenham, Cape ≻ 170 58.37 N 162.12 W
Newent 44 51.56 N 2.24 W
New Enterprise 204 40.10 N 78.25 W
New Ermelo 148 26.32 S 30.02 E
Newfane, N.Y., U.S. 200 43.17 N 78.43 W
Newfane, Vt., U.S. 178 42.59 N 72.39 W
New Ferry 252 53.22 N 2.59 W
Newfield, N.J., U.S. 198 39.33 N 75.01 W
Newfield, N.Y., U.S. 200 42.22 N 76.35 W
Newfield Pond ⊜ 273 42.38 N 71.22 W
New Field Workshops ♥3 164b 0.31 S 166.56 E
New Florence, Mo., U.S. 209 38.54 N 91.27 W
New Florence, Pa., U.S. 204 40.23 N 79.05 W
New Forest ◆3 44 50.53 N 1.35 W
New Fork ≏ 190 42.33 N 109.58 W
Newfound Gap)(182 35.37 N 83.25 W
Newfoundland, N.J., U.S. 266 41.03 N 74.26 W
Newfoundland, Pa., U.S. 200 41.19 N 75.19 W
Newfoundland □4 166 52.00 N 56.00 W
Newfoundland I 176 48.30 N 56.00 W
Newfoundland Basin ◆1 16 43.00 N 43.00 W
New Franklin 184 39.01 N 92.44 W
New Freedom 198 39.44 N 76.42 W
New Galilee 204 40.50 N 80.24 W
New Galloway 42 55.05 N 4.10 W
New Garden 275 39.49 N 75.45 W
Newgate 172 49.00 N 115.10 W
Newgate Street 250 51.44 N 0.07 W
New Georgia I 165e 8.15 S 157.30 E
New Georgia Group II 165e 8.30 S 157.20 E
New Germantown 198 40.18 N 77.34 W
New Germany 176 44.33 N 64.43 W
New Glarus 180 42.49 N 89.38 W
New Glasgow 176 45.35 N 62.39 W
New Gretna 198 39.35 N 74.28 W
New Guinea I 154 5.00 S 140.00 E
New Guinea, Territory of → Papua New Guinea □1 154 6.00 S 150.00 E
Newgulf 212 29.16 N 95.54 W
Newhalem 214 48.41 N 121.16 W
Newhalen 170 59.43 N 154.54 W
Newhall, Eng., U.K. 44 52.48 N 1.34 W
Newhall, Calif., U.S. 218 34.23 N 118.31 W
Newham ◆8 44 51.32 N 0.03 E
New Hamburg, Ont., Can. 202 43.23 N 80.42 W
New Hamburg, N.Y., U.S. 200 41.35 N 73.57 W
New Hampshire 206 40.33 N 83.57 W
New Hampshire □3 168
178 43.35 N 71.40 W
New Hampton, Iowa, U.S. 180 43.03 N 92.19 W
New Hampton, N.Y., U.S. 200 41.25 N 74.24 W
New Hanover, S. Afr. 148 29.23 S 30.28 E
New Hanover, Ill., U.S. 209 38.23 N 90.13 W
New Hanover I 154 2.30 S 150.15 E
New Harmony 184 38.08 N 87.56 W
New Hartford, Conn., U.S. 197 41.53 N 72.59 W
New Hartford, Iowa, U.S. 180 42.34 N 92.37 W
New Hartford, Mo., U.S. 209 39.12 N 91.16 W
New Hartford, N.Y., U.S. 200 43.04 N 75.18 W
Newhaven, Eng., U.K. 44 50.47 N 0.03 E
New Haven, Conn., U.S. 197 41.18 N 72.56 W
New Haven, Ill., U.S. 184 37.55 N 88.08 W
New Haven, Ind., U.S. 206 41.04 N 85.01 W
New Haven, Ky., U.S. 184 37.39 N 85.36 W
New Haven, Mich., U.S. 204 42.44 N 82.48 W
New Haven, Mo., U.S. 209 38.37 N 91.13 W
New Haven, N.Y., U.S. 202 43.29 N 76.19 W
New Haven, Ohio, U.S. 204 41.02 N 82.41 W
New Haven, W. Va., U.S. 178 38.59 N 81.58 W
New Haven □6 197 41.18 N 72.56 W
New Hazelton 172 55.15 N 127.35 W
New Hebrides □2 14
165f 16.00 S 167.00 E
New Hebrides (Nouvelles-Hébrides) II 165f 16.00 S 167.00 E
New Hebrides Basin ◆1 14 16.00 S 162.00 E
New Hebrides Trench ◆1 14 19.00 S 168.00 E
Newhebron 184 31.44 N 83.58 W
New Hempstead 266 41.08 N 74.03 W
New Hey 252 53.36 N 2.06 W
New Hogan Lake ⊜1 216 38.09 N 120.48 W
New Holland, Eng., U.K. 42 53.42 N 0.22 W
New Holland, Ill., U.S. 209 40.11 N 89.36 W
New Holland, Ohio, U.S. 208 39.33 N 83.15 W
New Holland, Pa., U.S. 198 40.06 N 76.05 W
New Holstein 180 43.57 N 88.05 W
New Hope, Ala., U.S. 184 34.32 N 86.24 W
New Hope, Pa., U.S. 198 40.22 N 74.57 W
New Hudson 271 42.31 N 83.37 W
New Hudson Airport ⊠ 271 42.30 N 83.37 W
New Hyde Park 266 40.44 N 73.41 W
New Hythe 250 51.19 N 0.27 E
New Iberia 184 30.00 N 91.49 W
Newington, Eng., U.K. 44 51.05 N 1.08 E
Newington, Eng., U.K. 250 51.21 N 0.40 E
Newington, Conn., U.S. 197 41.43 N 72.45 W
New Ipswich 197 42.46 N 71.51 W
New Ireland □5 154 3.00 S 151.30 E
New Ireland I 154 3.20 S 152.00 E
New Island I 116 21.31 N 88.12 E
New Jersey □3 168
178 40.15 N 74.30 W
New Jersey Institute of Technology ♥2 266 40.45 N 74.11 W
New Jersey Sports Center ◆ 266 40.49 N 74.05 W
New Kensington 204 40.34 N 79.46 W
New Kent 198 37.31 N 76.59 W
New Kent □6 198 37.30 N 77.00 W
New Kingstown 198 40.13 N 77.07 W
Newkirk 186 36.53 N 97.03 W
Newkirk Estates 275 39.42 N 75.42 W
New Knoxville 206 40.30 N 84.19 W
New Kowloon (Xinjiulong) 261d 22.20 N 114.10 E
New Lagos ◆8 263a 6.30 N 3.22 E
New Lake ⊜ 182 35.38 N 76.20 W
Newland 182 36.05 N 81.56 W
Newland Head ≻ 158b 35.39 S 138.31 E
Newland Range ◆ 152 27.53 S 123.58 E
Newlands ◆8 263d 26.11 S 27.58 E
New Lane 252 53.37 N 2.52 W
New Lebanon, N.Y., U.S. 200 42.28 N 73.24 W
New Lebanon, Ohio, U.S. 208 39.45 N 84.23 W
New Lebanon, Pa., U.S. 204 41.25 N 80.04 W
New Lebanon Center 200 42.28 N 73.25 W
New Leipzig 188 46.22 N 101.57 W
New Lenox 206 41.31 N 87.58 W
New Lexington 178 39.43 N 82.13 W
New Liberty 208 38.37 N 84.54 W
New Lisbon 180 43.53 N 90.10 W
New Liskeard 178 47.30 N 79.40 W
New London, Conn., U.S. 197 41.21 N 72.07 W
New London, Iowa, U.S. 180 40.55 N 91.24 W
New London, Minn., U.S. 188 45.18 N 94.56 W
New London, Mo., U.S. 209 39.35 N 91.24 W
New London, N.H., U.S. 178 43.25 N 71.59 W
New London, Ohio, U.S. 204 41.05 N 82.24 W
New London, Pa., U.S. 198 39.47 N 75.52 W
New London, Tex., U.S. 212 32.15 N 94.56 W
New London, Wis., U.S. 180 44.23 N 88.45 W
New London □6 197 41.21 N 72.07 W
New London Submarine Base ■ 197 41.24 N 72.05 W
New Longton 252 53.44 N 2.45 W
Newlonsburg 269b 40.25 N 79.40 W
New Lyme 204 41.36 N 80.47 W
Newlyn 159 37.25 S 143.59 E
Newlyn East 44 50.22 N 5.03 W
New Machavie 148 26.48 S 26.57 E
New Madison 208 39.58 N 84.43 W
New Madrid 184 36.36 N 89.32 W
Newmains 42 55.47 N 3.53 W
Newman, Calif., U.S. 216 37.19 N 121.01 W
Newman, Ill., U.S. 184 39.48 N 87.59 W
Newman, Mount ◆ 152 23.16 S 119.33 E
New Manchester 204 40.31 N 80.35 W
Newman Grove 188 41.45 N 97.47 W
Newmanstown 198 40.21 N 76.13 W
New Mansville 209 40.00 N 90.01 W
New Marion 208 39.00 N 85.22 W
Newmarket, Austl. 161a 27.25 S 153.01 E
Newmarket, Ont., Can. 202 44.03 N 79.28 W
Newmarket, Eire 28 52.13 N 9.00 W
Newmarket, S. Afr. 263d 26.17 S 28.08 E
Newmarket, Eng., U.K. 44 52.15 N 0.25 E
New Market, Ala., U.S. 184 34.55 N 86.24 W
New Market, Iowa, U.S. 188 40.44 N 94.54 W
New Market, Md., U.S. 198 39.23 N 77.16 W
Newmarket, N.H., U.S. 178 43.05 N 70.56 W
New Market, N.J., U.S. 266 40.34 N 74.27 W
New Market, Va., U.S. 178 38.39 N 78.40 W
Newmarket Race Course ◆ 263d 26.17 S 28.08 E
New Martinsville 178 39.39 N 80.52 W
New Meadows 192 44.58 N 116.32 W
New Melle 209 38.43 N 90.53 W
New Melones Lake ⊜1 216 38.00 N 120.32 W
New Memphis 209 38.29 N 89.41 W
New Mexico □3 168 34.30 N 106.00 W
New Miami 208 39.26 N 84.32 W
New Middletown 204 40.58 N 80.34 W
New Milford, Conn., U.S. 197 41.35 N 73.25 W
New Milford, Ill., U.S. 206 42.11 N 89.04 W
New Milford, N.J., U.S. 266 40.56 N 74.01 W
New Milford, Pa., U.S. 200 41.52 N 75.44 W
New Millpond ⊜ 266 40.50 N 73.13 W
New Millport 204 40.54 N 78.32 W
New Mills 42 53.23 N 2.00 W
Newmilns 42 55.37 N 4.20 W
New Milton 44 50.44 N 1.40 W
New Minden 209 38.26 N 89.22 W
New Munster 206 42.35 N 88.14 W
Newnan 182 33.23 N 84.48 W
Newnans Lake ⊜ 182 29.39 N 82.13 W
Newnham 44 51.49 N 2.27 W
New Norcia 152 30.58 S 116.13 E
New Norfolk 156 42.47 S 147.03 E
New Norway 172 52.53 N 112.58 W
New Orleans 184 29.58 N 90.07 W
New Oxford 198 39.52 N 77.04 W
New Palestine 208 39.43 N 85.53 W
New Paltz 200 41.45 N 74.05 W
New Paris, Ind., U.S. 206 41.30 N 85.50 W
New Paris, Ohio, U.S. 208 39.51 N 84.48 W
New Paris, Pa., U.S. 204 40.06 N 78.39 W
New Philadelphia, Ohio, U.S. 204 40.30 N 81.27 W
New Philadelphia, Pa., U.S. 198 40.43 N 76.07 W
New Pine Creek 192 42.01 N 120.18 W
New Pittsburg 204 40.50 N 82.06 W
New Plymouth, N.Z. 162 39.04 S 174.05 E
New Plymouth, Idaho, U.S. 192 43.58 N 116.49 W
New Point 208 39.19 N 85.20 W
New Point Comfort ≻ 198 37.18 N 76.17 W
Newport, Austl. 264a 33.40 S 151.19 E
Newport, Austl. 264b 37.51 S 144.53 E
Newport, Qué., Can. 176 48.16 N 64.45 W
New Port, Ned. Ant. 231s 12.03 N 68.49 W
Newport, Eng., U.K. 44 50.42 N 1.18 W
Newport, Eng., U.K. 44 52.47 N 2.22 W
Newport, Scot., U.K. 28 56.27 N 2.56 W
Newport, Wales, U.K. 44 52.01 N 4.51 W
Newport, Wales, U.K. 44 51.35 N 3.00 W
Newport, Ark., U.S. 184 35.37 N 91.17 W
Newport, Del., U.S. 198 39.43 N 75.36 W
Newport, Ind., U.S. 184 39.53 N 87.24 W
Newport, Ky., U.S. 208 39.06 N 84.29 W
Newport, Maine, U.S. 178 44.50 N 69.17 W
Newport, Md., U.S. 198 38.25 N 76.54 W
Newport, Mich., U.S. 206 42.00 N 83.18 W
Newport, N.H., U.S. 178 43.21 N 72.09 W
Newport, N.J., U.S. 198 39.18 N 75.11 W
Newport, N.Y., U.S. 200 43.11 N 75.01 W
Newport, Ohio, U.S. 206 39.23 N 81.14 W
Newport, Oreg., U.S. 192 44.38 N 124.03 W
Newport, Pa., U.S. 178 40.29 N 77.08 W
Newport, R.I., U.S. 197 41.13 N 71.18 W
Newport, Tenn., U.S. 182 35.58 N 83.11 W
Newport, Vt., U.S. 178 44.57 N 72.12 W
Newport, Wash., U.S. 192 48.11 N 117.03 W
Newport □6 197 41.35 N 71.15 W
Newport Bay C 198 38.14 N 75.13 W
Newport Beach 218 33.37 N 117.56 W
Newport Center 196 44.57 N 72.19 W
Newport Hills 214 47.33 N 122.10 W
Newport News 198 37.04 N 76.28 W
Newport Pagnell 44 52.05 N 0.44 W
New Port Richey 210 28.16 N 82.43 W
Newportville 275 40.09 N 74.53 W
Newportville Terrace 275 40.07 N 74.54 W
New Prague 180 44.32 N 93.34 W
New Preston 197 41.40 N 73.21 W
New Providence, N.J., U.S. 200 40.42 N 74.24 W
New Providence, Pa., U.S. 198 39.56 N 76.12 W
New Providence, Tenn., U.S. 184 36.32 N 87.23 W
New Providence I 230b 25.02 N 77.24 W
Newquay, Eng., U.K. 44 50.25 N 5.05 W
New Quay, Wales, U.K. 44 52.13 N 4.22 W
New Redruth 263d 26.16 S 28.07 E
New Richland 180 43.54 N 93.30 W
New Richmond, Qué., Can. 176 48.10 N 65.52 W
New Richmond, Ohio, U.S. 208 38.57 N 84.17 W
New Richmond, Wis., U.S. 180 45.07 N 92.32 W
New Riegel 204 41.03 N 83.19 W
New Rim Ditch ≅ 218 35.08 N 118.58 W
New Ringgold 198 40.41 N 76.00 W
New Road 176 44.45 N 63.28 W
New Roads 184 30.42 N 91.26 W
New Rochelle 178 40.55 N 73.47 W
New Rockford 188 47.41 N 99.08 W
New Romney 44 50.59 N 0.57 E
New Ross, N.S., Can. 176 44.44 N 64.27 W
New Ross, Eire 28 52.24 N 6.56 W
New Rossington 42 53.29 N 1.04 W
Newry, N. Ire., U.K. 42 54.11 N 6.20 W
Newry, Pa., U.S. 204 40.24 N 78.26 W
Newry, S.C., U.S. 182 34.43 N 82.55 W
New Salem, Ind., U.S. 208 39.32 N 85.22 W
New Salem, N. Dak., U.S. 188 46.51 N 101.25 W
New Salisbury 208 38.19 N 86.06 W
New Sarum → Salisbury 44 51.05 N 1.48 W

Symbols in the index entries represent the broad categories identified in the key at the right. Symbols with superior numbers (◆2) identify subcategories (see complete key on page I · 26).

Kartensymbole in dem Registerverzeichnis stellen die rechts in Schlüssel erklärten Kategorien dar. Symbole mit hochgestellten Ziffern (◆2) bezeichnen Unterabteilungen einer Kategorie (vgl. vollständiger Schlüssel auf Seite I · 26).

Los símbolos incluidos en el texto del índice representan las grandes categorías identificadas con la clave a la derecha. Los símbolos con números en su parte superior (◆2) identifican las subcategorías (véase la clave completa en la página I · 26).

Les symboles de l'index représentent les catégories indiquées dans la légende à droite. Les symboles suivis d'un indice (◆2) représentent des sous-catégories (voir légende complète à la page I · 26).

Os símbolos incluídos no texto do índice representam as grandes categorias identificadas com a chave à direita. Os símbolos com números em sua parte superior (◆2) identificam as subcategorias (veja-se a chave completa à página I · 26).

English	Deutsch	Español	Français	Português
Mountain	Berg	Montaña	Montagne	Montanha
Mountains	Berge	Montañas	Montagnes	Montanhas
Pass	Pass	Paso	Col	Passo
Valley, Canyon	Tal, Cañon	Valle, Cañón	Vallée, Canyon	Vale, Canhão
Plain	Ebene	Llano	Plaine	Planície
Cape	Kap	Cabo	Cap	Cabo
Island	Insel	Isla	Île	Ilha
Islands	Inseln	Islas	Îles	Ilhas
Other Topographic Features	Andere Topographische Objekte	Otros Elementos Topográficos	Autres données topographiques	Outros Elementos Topográficos

ESPAÑOL — Nombre | Página | Lat.°′ | Long.°′ W=Oeste
FRANÇAIS — Nom | Page | Lat.°′ | Long.°′ W=Ouest
PORTUGUÊS — Nome | Página | Lat.°′ | Long.°′ W=Oeste

New Schwabenland ⊹[1] 9 72.30 S 1.00 E
Newsham Park ♠ 252 53.25 N 2.56 W
New Sharon 180 41.28 N 92.39 W
New Sheffield 204 40.36 N 80.17 W
New Shrewsbury 266 40.19 N 74.04 W
Newsiedl am See 30 47.57 N 16.51 E
New Smyrna Beach 210 29.02 N 80.56 W
Newsome 212 32.59 N 95.08 W
Newsoms 198 36.37 N 77.14 W
New South Wales □[3] 156 33.00 S 146.00 E
New South Wales, University of ⊍[2] 264a 33.55 S 151.14 E
New South Wales Lawn Tennis Association Courts ♠ 264a 33.53 S 151.14 E
New Springfield 204 40.55 N 80.36 W
New Square 266 41.08 N 74.02 W
New Stanton 204 40.13 N 79.37 W
Newstead 159 37.07 S 144.04 E
New Stuyahok 170 59.29 N 157.20 W
New Suffolk 197 41.00 N 72.28 W
New Summerfield 212 31.59 N 95.06 W
New Terrell City Lake @[1] 212 32.44 N 96.14 W
New Territories □[8] 261d 22.24 N 114.10 E
New Thunderchild Indian Reserve ◆[4] 174 53.30 N 108.50 W
Newtok 170 60.56 N 164.38 W
Newton, Eng., U.K. 42 53.57 N 2.27 W
Newton, Eng., U.K. 42 53.16 N 2.43 W
Newton, Ga., U.S. 182 31.19 N 84.20 W
Newton, Ill., U.S. 184 38.59 N 88.10 W
Newton, Iowa, U.S. 180 41.42 N 93.03 W
Newton, Kans., U.S. 188 38.03 N 97.21 W
Newton, Mass., U.S. 197 42.21 N 71.11 W
Newton, Miss., U.S. 184 32.19 N 89.10 W
Newton, N.J., U.S. 200 41.03 N 74.45 W
Newton, N.C., U.S. 182 35.40 N 81.13 W
Newton, Tex., U.S. 184 30.51 N 93.46 W
Newton □[6] 266 40.46 N 87.27 W
Newton Abbot 44 50.32 N 3.36 W
Newton Arlosh 42 54.53 N 3.15 W
Newton Aycliffe 42 54.36 N 1.32 W
Newton Brook ◆[8] 265b 43.48 N 79.24 W
Newton Center 273 42.20 N 71.12 W
Newton Falls, N.Y., U.S. 178 44.13 N 74.59 W
Newton Falls, Ohio, U.S. 204 41.11 N 80.59 W
Newton Ferrers 44 50.18 N 4.02 W
Newton Flotman 44 52.32 N 1.16 E
Newtongrange 42 55.52 N 3.04 W
Newton Hamilton 204 40.24 N 77.51 W
Newton Highlands 273 42.19 N 71.13 W
Newton-le-Willows 42 53.28 N 2.37 W
Newton Lower Falls 273 42.19 N 71.23 W
Newton Stewart 42 54.57 N 4.29 W
Newtonsville 208 39.11 N 84.05 W
Newton Upper Falls 273 42.19 N 71.13 W
Newtonville, Ont., Can. 202 43.56 N 78.30 W
Newtonville, Mass., U.S. 273 42.21 N 71.13 W
Newtonville, N.J., U.S. 198 39.34 N 74.52 W
Newtown, Austl. 159 38.09 S 144.20 E
Newtown, Newf., Can. 176 49.12 N 53.31 W
Newtown, Eng., U.K. 252 53.21 N 2.00 W
Newtown, Wales, U.K. 44 52.32 N 3.19 W
Newtown, Conn., U.S. 197 41.25 N 73.19 W
Newtown, Ind., U.S. 206 40.12 N 87.09 W
Newtown, Ky., U.S. 208 38.13 N 84.57 W
New Town, N. Dak., U.S. 188 47.59 N 102.30 W
Newtown, Pa., U.S. 198 40.14 N 74.56 W
Newtown ◆[8] 264a 33.54 S 151.11 E
Newtownabbey 28 54.42 N 5.54 W
Newtownards 42 54.36 N 5.41 W
Newtown Creek ≃, N.Y., U.S. 266 40.44 N 73.58 W
Newtown Creek ≃, Pa., U.S. 275 40.13 N 74.56 W
Newtown Crommelin 42 55.00 N 6.13 W
Newtownhamilton 42 54.12 N 6.35 W
Newtown Saint Boswells 42 55.34 N 2.40 W
Newtown Square 198 39.59 N 75.24 W
New Tredegar 44 51.43 N 3.14 W
New Tripoli 198 40.41 N 75.45 W
New Troy 206 41.53 N 86.33 W
New Truxton 209 38.58 N 91.15 W
New Ulm, Minn., U.S. 180 44.19 N 94.28 W
New Ulm, Tex., U.S. 212 29.53 N 96.29 W
New Usenow 50 53.47 N 13.46 E
New Utrecht ◆[8] 266 40.36 N 73.59 W
New Vernon 266 40.45 N 74.30 W
New Vienna 208 39.19 N 83.42 W
Newville, Ind., U.S. 206 41.21 N 84.51 W
Newville, Pa., U.S. 198 40.10 N 77.24 W
New Vineyard 178 44.48 N 70.07 W
New Washington, Pil. 106 11.39 N 122.26 E
New Washington, Ind., U.S. 208 38.34 N 85.33 W
New Washington, Ohio, U.S. 204 40.58 N 82.51 W
New Waterford, N.S., Can. 176 46.15 N 60.05 W
New Waterford, Ohio, U.S. 204 40.51 N 80.37 W
New Waverly, Ind., U.S. 206 40.46 N 86.12 W
New Waverly, Tex., U.S. 212 30.32 N 95.29 W
New Westminster 172 49.12 N 122.55 W
New Whiteland 208 39.33 N 86.05 W
New Wilmington 204 41.07 N 80.20 W
New Windsor → Windsor, Eng., U.K. 44 51.29 N 0.38 W
New Windsor, N.Y., U.S. 200 41.29 N 74.02 W
New Woodbine Racetrack ♠ 265b 43.43 N 79.36 W
New Woodstock 200 42.51 N 75.51 W
New World Island I 176 49.35 N 54.40 W
New Year Creek ≃ 212 30.08 N 96.12 W
New York 200 / 266 40.43 N 74.01 W
New York □[6] 266 40.43 N 74.01 W
New York □[3], U.S. 168 / 178 43.00 N 75.00 W
New York, City College of ⊍[2] 266 40.49 N 73.57 W
New York, Polytechnic Institute of ⊍[2] 266 40.42 N 73.59 W
New York, State University of (Stony Brook) ⊍[2], N.Y., U.S. 266 40.55 N 73.08 W
New York, State University of (Buffalo) ⊍[2], N.Y., U.S. 274a 42.57 N 78.49 W
New York, State University of, College at Buffalo ⊍[2] 274a 42.56 N 78.53 W
New York Mills, Minn., U.S. 188 46.31 N 95.22 W
New York Mills, N.Y., U.S. 200 43.06 N 75.18 W
New York State Barge Canal ☰ 200 43.05 N 78.43 W
New York Stock Exchange ⊍ 266 40.42 N 74.01 W
New York University ⊍[2] 266 40.51 N 73.55 W
New Zealand □[1], Oc. 14 / 162 41.00 S 174.00 E
New Zealand Plateau ⊹[3] 9 51.00 S 170.00 E
Nexapa ≃ 224 18.07 N 98.46 W
Nexon 32 45.41 N 1.11 E
Nexpa ≃ 224 18.05 N 102.46 W
Ney 206 41.23 N 84.32 W
Neyagawa 86 34.46 N 135.38 E
Neye 253 51.07 N 7.22 E
Neyestausee @[1] 253 51.08 N 7.24 E
Ney Lake @ 174 54.38 N 92.25 W
Neyland 44 51.43 N 4.57 W
Neylandville 212 33.12 N 96.00 W
Neyrīz 118 29.12 N 54.19 E
Neyshābūr 118 36.12 N 58.50 E
Neyyāttinkara 112 8.24 N 77.05 E
Nezamajevskaja 68 46.09 N 40.16 E
Nezameno-toko ♠ 84 35.46 N 137.42 E
Nezavertajlovka 68 46.37 N 29.56 E
Nežin 68 51.03 N 31.54 E
Nezlobnaja 74 44.08 N 43.23 E
Neznanka ≃ 255b 55.34 N 37.21 E
Neznanovo 70 54.02 N 40.06 E
Nezperce 192 46.14 N 116.14 W
Nez Perce Indian Reservation ◆[4] 192 46.20 N 116.30 W
Nez Perce National Historical Park ♠ 192 45.50 N 116.15 W
Ngabang 102 0.23 N 109.57 E
Ngabé 142 3.12 S 16.11 E
Ngabordamlu, Tanjung ⟩ 154 6.56 S 134.11 E
Ngadirojo 105a 8.13 S 111.19 E
Ngadza 142 5.10 N 20.12 E
Ngahere 162 42.24 S 171.27 E
Ngala 136 12.20 N 14.10 E
Ngale 142 2.56 N 21.20 E
Ngali 142 2.27 S 19.20 E
Ngalipaeng 102 3.24 N 125.37 E
Ngaloa Harbour C 165g 19.06 S 178.11 E
Ngamakoussou ≃ 263b 4.10 S 15.19 E
Ngamba 263b 4.15 S 15.18 E
Ngambé 142 4.14 N 10.37 E
Ngamdu 136 11.48 N 12.18 E
Ngamegei Passage ⋓ 165b 7.44 N 134.34 E
Ngami, Lake @ 146 20.37 S 22.40 E
Ngamiland □[5] 146 19.09 S 22.47 E
Ngamo 144 19.08 S 27.32 E
Ngamouéri 263b 4.14 S 15.14 E
Ngangala 144 4.42 N 31.55 E
Ngangerabeli Plain 144 1.30 S 40.15 E
Ngang Kong C 261d 22.16 N 114.00 E
Nganjuk 105a 7.36 S 111.55 E
Ngao 100 18.46 N 99.59 E
Ngaoundéré 142 7.19 N 13.35 E
Ngapara 162 44.57 S 170.45 E
Ngape 100 20.04 N 94.38 E
Ngaputaw 100 16.32 N 94.42 E
Ngara 144 2.28 S 30.39 E
Ngardmau 165b 7.37 N 134.35 E
Ngardmau Bay C 165b 7.39 N 134.35 E
Ngarimbi 144 8.28 S 38.36 E
Ngaruawahia 162 37.40 S 175.09 E
Ngaruroro ≃ 162 39.34 S 176.56 E
Ngasamo 144 2.33 S 33.53 E
Ngat ≃ 100 19.09 N 99.01 E
Ngatangiia 164k 21.14 S 159.43 W
Ngatangiia Harbour C 164k 21.14 S 159.45 W
Ngatea 162 37.17 S 175.30 E
Ngathainggyaung 100 17.24 N 95.05 E
Ngatik I[1] 14 5.51 N 157.16 E
Ngau I 165g 18.02 S 179.18 E
Ngauruhoe, Mount ∧ 162 39.09 S 175.38 E
Ngau Tau Kok → Tai Wan Tsun 261d 22.19 N 114.12 E
Ngawen 105a 7.00 S 111.18 E
Ngawi 105a 7.24 S 111.26 E
Ngaya ∧ 130 9.18 N 23.28 E
Ngay Nua 100 21.50 N 101.54 E
Ngebel 105a 7.46 S 111.37 E
Ngele 142 0.29 S 20.25 E
Ngele ≃ 148 30.35 S 29.35 E
Ngemelis Islands II 165b 7.07 N 134.15 E
Ngerengere 144 6.45 S 38.07 E
Ngetera 136 12.31 N 12.38 E
Ngezi National Park ♠ 144 18.40 S 30.28 E
Nggamea I 165g 16.46 S 179.46 W
Nggele Group II 165e 9.00 S 160.10 E
Nggele Levu I 165g 16.05 S 179.09 W
Nghabe ≃ 146 20.22 S 22.58 E
Nghia-hanh 100 15.03 N 108.47 E
Nghia-hung 100 19.18 N 105.26 E
Nghia-lo 100 21.36 N 104.31 E
Ngiap ≃ 100 18.24 N 103.36 E
Ngidinga 142 5.37 S 15.17 E
Ngila 142 4.43 N 11.41 E
Ngimbang 105a 7.17 S 112.12 E
Ng'iro, Ewaso ≃, Kenya 144 2.04 S 36.07 E
Ng'iro, Ewaso ≃, Kenya 144 0.28 N 39.55 E
Ngo 142 2.29 S 15.45 E
Ngoap 142 4.09 N 12.51 E
Ngobé, Lagune C 142 1.55 S 9.25 E
Ngoboli 144 4.57 N 32.37 E
Ngo Ki 261d 22.18 N 113.58 E
Ngoko ≃ 142 1.40 N 16.03 E
Ngol-Kedju Hill ∧[2] 142 6.20 N 9.45 E
Ngolo 136 9.56 N 22.16 E
Ngoma 144 2.11 S 29.18 E
Ngomahuru 144 20.26 S 30.43 E
Ngomba 144 8.23 S 32.53 E
Ngomba ∧ 144 5.43 S 35.52 E
Ngombe, Zaïre 142 6.35 S 20.42 E
Ngombe, Zaïre 263b 4.24 S 15.11 E
Ngome 148 27.46 S 31.28 E
Ngomedzap 142 3.15 N 11.12 E
Ngomeni, Ras ⟩ 144 2.59 S 40.14 E
Ngong 144 1.22 S 36.39 E
Ngongotaha 162 38.05 S 176.12 E
Ngono ≃ 144 1.08 S 31.35 E
Ngon Shun Chau I 261d 22.19 N 114.08 E
Ngonye Falls ⌊ 142 16.40 S 23.35 E
Ngop 130 6.16 N 30.12 E
Ngora 144 1.27 N 33.46 E
Ngorengore 144 1.02 S 35.30 E
Ngoro 105a 7.41 S 112.16 E
Ngorongoro Crater ●[6] 144 3.10 S 35.35 E
Ngosa Farm 144 12.18 S 27.28 E
Ngote 144 2.14 N 30.48 E
Ngotto 142 4.00 N 17.21 E
Ngoui 140 16.09 N 13.55 W
Ngoulémakong 142 3.07 N 11.25 E
Ngouma 140 15.38 N 3.22 W
Ngounié □[4] 142 2.00 S 11.00 E
Ngounié ≃ 142 0.37 S 10.18 E
Ngouo, Mont ∧ 130 7.55 N 24.38 E
Ngouri 136 13.38 N 15.22 E
Ngoywa 144 5.56 S 32.48 E
Ngozi 144 2.54 S 29.50 E
Ngqeleni 148 31.40 S 29.02 E
Ngudiabaka ≃ 263b 4.25 S 15.11 E
Nguélémendouka 142 4.23 N 12.55 E
Nguigmi 136 14.15 N 13.07 E
Nguiroungou 142 6.27 N 22.37 E
Ngulu I[1] 98 8.27 N 137.29 E
Ngum ≃ 100 18.09 N 103.06 E
Nguna I 165f 17.26 S 168.21 E
Ngunga 144 3.41 S 33.34 E
Ngunju, Tanjung ⟩ 105b 10.19 S 120.28 E
Ngunut 105a 8.06 S 112.01 E
Ngurore 136 9.18 N 12.14 E
Nguru 136 12.52 N 10.27 E
Nguru Mountains ∧∧ 144 6.00 S 37.30 E
Ngwakets □[5] 146 24.45 S 24.00 E
Ngweni 148 27.56 S 32.15 E
Ngwenya ∧ 148 26.11 S 31.02 E
Ngwerere 144 15.18 S 28.20 E
Ngwezi ≃ 144 17.40 S 25.07 E
Nha-be 259c 10.42 N 106.44 E
Nha-be ≃ 259c 10.39 N 106.44 E
Nhacoongo 146 24.18 S 35.14 E
Nhamacolomo 146 18.05 S 34.26 E
Nhamundá 240 2.14 S 56.43 W
Nhamundá ≃ 236 2.12 S 56.41 W
Nha-nam 100 21.27 N 106.06 E
Nhandeara 245 20.40 S 50.02 W
Nhareia 142 11.25 S 17.03 E
Nha-trang 100 12.15 N 109.11 E
Nhecolândia 238 19.16 S 57.04 W
Nhia ≃ 142 10.15 S 14.12 E
Nhill 156 36.20 S 141.39 E
Nhlazatshe 148 28.10 S 31.14 E
Nhon-trach 259c 10.43 N 106.51 E
Nhundo 142 14.25 S 21.23 E
Nhunguaçu 246 22.21 S 42.53 W
Niabembe 144 2.14 S 27.44 E
Niafounké 140 15.56 N 4.00 W
Niagara 180 45.46 N 88.02 W
Niagara □[6], Ont., Can. 202 43.05 N 79.20 W
Niagara □[6], N.Y., U.S. 200 43.10 N 78.42 W
Niagara ≃ 202 43.15 N 79.04 W
Niagara County Historical Center ⊍ 274a 43.10 N 78.43 W
Niagara Falls, Ont., Can. 202 / 274a 43.06 N 79.04 W
Niagara Falls, N.Y., U.S. 200 / 274a 43.06 N 79.02 W
Niagara Falls ⌊ 202 43.05 N 79.04 W
Niagara Falls Airport ⊠ 274a 43.02 N 79.08 W
Niagara Falls International Airport ⊠ 274a 43.06 N 78.56 W
Niagara-on-the-Lake 202 43.15 N 79.04 W
Niagara University ⊍[2] 274a 43.08 N 79.02 W
Niagassola 140 12.19 N 9.07 W
Niah 102 3.52 N 113.44 E
Niakaramandougou 140 8.40 N 5.17 W
Niamey 140 13.31 N 2.07 E
Niamey □[5] 140 14.00 N 2.00 E
Niamtougou 140 9.46 N 1.06 E
Nianbadu 90 28.17 N 118.28 E
Niandan Koro 140 11.05 N 9.15 W
Nianforando 140 9.32 N 10.31 W
Niangara 144 3.42 N 27.52 E
Niangay, Lac @ 140 15.50 N 3.00 W
Niangmake 92 30.14 N 99.40 E
Niangnianggong 94 41.00 N 121.13 E
Niangniangmiao 88 42.34 N 118.05 E
Niangniangwa 95 40.33 N 117.30 E
Niangoloko 140 10.17 N 4.55 W
Niangua ≃ 184 37.58 N 92.48 W
Niangzizhuang 95 40.02 N 118.05 E
Nia-Nia 144 1.24 N 27.36 E
Nianpan 94 41.48 N 124.02 E
Nianqingtanggula-shanmai ∧∧ 110 30.00 N 90.00 E
Niantan ≃ 140 10.30 N 10.26 W
Niantic, Conn., U.S. 197 41.19 N 72.12 W
Niantic, Ill., U.S. 209 39.51 N 89.10 W
Nianyuogou 94 42.00 N 123.59 E
Nianyushan 90 29.11 N 117.04 E
Nianzhuang 88 34.19 N 117.47 E
Nianzigang 90 31.03 N 114.18 E
Nianzishan 89 47.32 N 122.52 E
Niapu 144 2.25 N 26.28 E
Niari □[5] 142 3.15 S 12.30 E
Niari ≃ 142 3.56 S 12.12 E
Niaro 130 10.38 N 31.31 E
Nias, Pulau I 104 1.05 N 97.35 E
Niassa □[5] 144 13.30 S 36.00 E
Nibbiano 56 44.54 N 9.19 E
Nibe 36 56.59 N 9.38 E
Nibong Tebal 104 5.10 N 100.29 E
Nibria 262b 22.36 N 88.16 E
Nīca 66 56.19 N 21.04 E
Nica ≃ 76 57.29 N 64.33 E
Nicaragua □[1], N.A. 220 / 226 13.00 N 85.00 W
Nicaragua, Lago de @ 226 11.30 N 85.30 W
Nicaro 230p 20.42 N 75.33 W
Nicastro (Lamezia Terme) 36 38.59 N 16.20 E
Nice 56 43.42 N 7.15 E
Nice-Côte d'Azur, Aéroport de ⊠ 56 43.40 N 7.14 E
Niceville 184 30.31 N 86.29 W
Nichelino 56 44.59 N 7.38 E
Nichengjiao 96 30.55 N 121.49 E
Nichihara 86 34.30 N 131.50 E
Nichinan, Nihon 82 31.36 N 131.23 E
Nichinan, Nihon 86 35.09 N 133.16 E
Nicholas □[6] 208 38.20 N 84.02 W
Nicholas Channel ⋓ 228 23.25 N 80.05 W
Nicholas Research Institute ⊍[3] 264b 37.53 S 145.21 E
Nicholasville 182 37.53 N 84.34 W
Nicholls 182 31.31 N 82.38 W
Nichols, Calif., U.S. 272 38.02 N 121.59 W
Nichols, Fla., U.S. 210 27.54 N 82.02 W
Nichols, N.Y., U.S. 200 42.01 N 76.22 W
Nichols Brook ≃ 273 42.37 N 70.59 W
Nicholson, Austl. 152 18.02 S 128.54 E
Nicholson, Ky., U.S. 208 38.54 N 84.33 W
Nicholson, Miss., U.S. 184 30.29 N 89.42 W
Nicholson, Pa., U.S. 200 41.38 N 75.47 W
Nicholson ≃, Austl. 152 17.34 S 128.38 E
Nicholson ≃, Austl. 154 17.31 S 139.36 E
Nicholson Island I 202 43.56 N 77.32 W
Nicholson Range ∧∧ 152 27.15 S 116.45 E
Nichols Run ≃ 274b 39.03 N 77.18 W
Nickerie □[5] 240 4.00 N 57.30 W
Nickerie ≃ 240 5.59 N 57.00 W
Nickerson 188 38.08 N 98.05 W
Nickol Bay C 152 20.39 S 116.52 E
Nicktown 204 40.37 N 78.48 W
Nicobar Basin ⊹[1] 12 5.00 N 92.00 E
Nicobar Islands II 100 8.00 N 93.30 E
Nicola 172 50.10 N 120.40 W
Nicola ≃ 172 50.25 N 121.18 W
Nicolae Bălcescu 38 47.34 N 26.52 E
Nicolai Mountain ∧ 214 46.05 N 123.28 W
Nicola Lake @ 172 50.10 N 120.25 W
Nicola Mameet Indian Reserve ◆[4] 172 50.11 N 120.49 W
Nicolás Bravo 224 18.21 N 93.10 W
Nicolás Pérez, Sierra de ∧∧ 224 22.27 N 99.08 W
Nicolás Romero □[7] 276a 19.37 N 99.17 W
Nicolaus 216 38.54 N 121.35 W
Nicolet 196 46.13 N 72.37 W
Nicolet □[6] 196 46.15 N 72.20 W
Nicolet ≃ 196 46.14 N 72.39 W
Nicolet, Lac @ 196 45.50 N 71.33 W
Nicolet-Centre ≃ 196 45.46 N 71.50 W
Nicolet-Sud-Ouest ≃ 196 46.13 N 72.36 W
Nicoll Bay C 266 40.43 N 73.07 W
Nicollet 180 44.17 N 94.11 W
Nicoll Point ⟩ 266 40.42 N 73.09 W
Nicolls Town 228 25.08 N 78.00 W
Nicosia, It. 36 37.45 N 14.24 E
Nicosia → Levkosía, Kípros 120 35.10 N 33.22 E
Nicotera 36 38.34 N 15.57 E
Nicoya 226 10.09 N 85.27 W
Nicoya, Golfo de C 226 9.47 N 84.48 W
Nicoya, Península de ⟩[1] 226 10.00 N 85.25 W
Nictheroy → Niterói 246 22.53 S 43.07 W
Nida ≃ 30 50.18 N 20.52 E
Nidadavole 112 16.55 N 81.40 E
Nidau 54 47.07 N 7.14 E
Nidd ≃ 42 54.01 N 1.12 W
Nidda 52 50.24 N 9.00 E
Nidda ≃ 52 50.06 N 8.34 E
Nidder ≃ 52 50.12 N 8.47 E
Nide 92 31.51 N 96.19 E
Nideck, Château et Cascade du ⊥ 54 48.34 N 7.16 E
Nideggen 52 50.47 N 6.29 E
Nidelva ≃ 26 58.24 N 8.48 E
Nidwalden □[3] 54 46.55 N 8.28 E
Nidže (Nítse Óros) ≃ 38 40.58 N 21.49 E
Nidzica 30 53.22 N 20.26 E
Niebüll 41 54.48 N 8.50 E
Nied ≃ 52 49.23 N 6.40 E
Niederaden ◆[8] 253 51.36 N 7.34 E
Niederanven 52 49.39 N 6.16 E
Niederaschau 58 47.47 N 12.19 E
Niederau 50 51.10 N 13.32 E
Niederaula 52 50.48 N 9.36 E
Niederbipp 54 47.16 N 7.39 E
Niederbobritzsch 50 50.54 N 13.26 E
Niederbonsfeld 253 51.23 N 7.08 E
Niederbronn-les-Bains 52 48.57 N 7.38 E
Niederdonk 253 51.14 N 6.41 E
Niederelfringhausen 253 51.21 N 7.10 E
Niedere Tauern ∧∧ 30 47.18 N 14.00 E
Niederfinow 50 52.50 N 13.55 E
Niederfrohna 50 50.53 N 12.43 E
Niederhaverbeck 48 53.09 N 9.54 E
Niederheimbach 52 50.02 N 7.48 E
Niederhohne 52 51.13 N 10.06 E
Nieder-Kassel ◆[8] 253 51.14 N 6.45 E
Niederkrüchten 52 51.12 N 6.13 E
Nieder-Lahnstein 52 50.19 N 7.36 E
Niederlande → Netherlands □[1] 30 52.15 N 5.30 E
Niederländische Antillen → Netherlands Antilles □[2] 231s 12.15 N 69.00 W
Niederlausitz □[9] 50 51.40 N 14.15 E
Niederlehme 50 52.19 N 13.39 E
Niedermarsberg 52 51.28 N 8.50 E
Niedermarschacht 48 53.25 N 10.21 E
Nieder-Mörlen 52 50.23 N 8.43 E
Niederndodeleben 50 52.08 N 11.30 E
Nieder-Neuendorf 254a 52.37 N 13.12 E
Niedernhall 52 49.17 N 9.36 E
Niedernwöhren 48 52.21 N 9.08 E
Niederoderwitz 50 50.57 N 14.44 E
Nieder-Ohmen 52 50.38 N 9.02 E
Nieder-Olm 52 49.55 N 8.11 E
Niederorschel 50 51.22 N 10.25 E
Niederösterreich □[3] 30 48.20 N 15.50 E
Niedersachsen □[3] 30 52.00 N 10.00 E
Niedersachswerfen 50 51.33 N 10.46 E
Niederschöneweide ◆[8] 254a 52.27 N 13.31 E
Niederschönhausen ◆[8] 50 52.35 N 13.23 E
Niedersee → Ruciane-Nida 30 53.39 N 21.35 E
Niederselters 52 50.20 N 8.14 E
Niedersonthofen 54 47.38 N 10.13 E
Niederstetten 52 49.24 N 9.55 E
Niederstotzingen 52 48.32 N 10.14 E
Niederurnen 54 47.07 N 9.03 E
Niederwald 54 46.26 N 8.12 E
Niederwalgern 52 50.44 N 8.41 E
Niederweningen 54 47.30 N 8.23 E
Niederwiesa 50 50.51 N 13.01 E
Nieder-Wöllstadt 52 50.16 N 8.46 E
Niederwürschnitz 50 50.43 N 12.45 E
Niedu 90 25.28 N 114.08 E
Niefang 142 1.50 N 10.14 E
Nieheim 48 51.48 N 9.06 E
Niekerkshoop 148 29.19 S 22.51 E
Niel 46 51.07 N 4.20 E
Niélé 140 10.12 N 5.38 W
Niellim 136 9.42 N 17.49 E
Nielson Airport ⊠ 259f 14.34 N 121.01 E
Niem 142 6.12 N 15.14 E
Niemba 144 5.57 S 28.26 E
Niemegk 50 52.04 N 12.41 E
Niemeyer ◆[8] 277a 23.00 S 43.15 W
Niemodlin 30 50.39 N 17.37 E
Niéna 140 11.26 N 6.21 W
Nienberge 48 52.00 N 7.34 E
Nienborg-Wigbold 48 52.08 N 7.06 E
Nienburg, B.R.D. 48 52.38 N 9.13 E
Nienburg, D.D.R. 50 51.50 N 11.46 E
Niendorf 50 53.59 N 10.50 E
Nienhagen, B.R.D. 48 52.33 N 10.05 E
Nienhagen, D.D.R. 50 51.57 N 11.09 E
Niénokoué, Mont ∧ 140 5.26 N 7.10 W
Niepkuhlen ≃ 253 51.29 N 6.31 E
Niepołomice 30 50.03 N 20.13 E
Nieppe 46 50.42 N 2.50 E
Niéré 136 14.30 N 21.09 E
Niéri Ko ≃ 140 13.21 N 13.23 W
Nierong 110 32.09 N 92.11 E
Niers ≃, B.R.D. 253 51.10 N 6.28 E
Niers ≃, Eur. 48 51.43 N 5.57 E
Nierst 253 51.19 N 6.43 E
Nierstein 52 49.52 N 8.20 E
Niesen ∧ 54 46.39 N 7.39 E
Niesky 50 51.17 N 14.49 E
Nieszawa 30 52.50 N 18.55 E
Nieto, Cañada de ≃ 248 34.00 S 58.15 W
Nieu Bethesda 148 31.51 S 24.34 E
Nieuw-Amsterdam, Ned. 48 52.44 N 6.51 E
Nieuw Amsterdam, Sur. 240 5.53 N 55.05 W
Nieuw-Buinen 48 52.57 N 6.55 E
Nieuwefontein 148 28.01 S 19.06 E
Nieuwe-Niedorp 48 52.45 N 4.54 E
Nieuwe-Pekela 48 53.04 N 6.58 E
Nieuweschans 48 53.11 N 7.12 E
Nieuwkoop 48 52.08 N 4.47 E
Nieuw Nickerie 240 5.57 N 56.59 W
Nieuwolda 48 53.14 N 6.59 E
Nieuwoudtville 148 31.23 S 19.07 E
Nieuwpoort 46 51.08 N 2.45 E
Nieuwpoort-Bad 46 51.09 N 2.42 E
Nieuw-Schoonebeek 48 52.38 N 6.59 E
Nieuw-Vennep 48 52.16 N 4.38 E
Nieuw-Weerdinge 48 52.52 N 6.59 E
Nievenheim 52 51.07 N 6.46 E
Nievería 276d 11.59 S 76.55 W
Nieves 224 24.00 N 103.01 W
Nièvre □[5] 32 47.05 N 3.30 E
Nièvre ≃ 46 47.10 N 3.13 E
Nif 164q 9.28 N 138.04 E
Nīfī Ya'qūb 122 31.50 N 35.14 E
Niga 140 13.38 N 5.27 W
Nigan 116 23.30 N 87.59 E
Niğde 120 37.59 N 34.42 E
Niğde □[4] 120 38.15 N 34.15 E
Nigel 148 26.30 S 28.28 E
Niger □[1] 124 16.00 N 8.00 E
Niger ≃ 140 5.33 N 6.33 E
Niger Delta ☷[2] 140 4.50 N 6.00 E
Nigeria □[1] 124 10.00 N 8.00 E
Nigerian Museum ⊍ 263a 6.20 N 3.24 E
Nighāsan 114 28.14 N 80.52 E
Nightcaps 162 45.58 S 168.02 E
Night Hawk Lake @ 180 48.28 N 81.00 W
Nightingale Island I 10 37.24 S 12.28 W
Nightmute 170 60.29 N 164.00 W
Nigou 88 34.43 N 117.41 E
Nigríta 38 40.55 N 23.30 E
Nigwar 134 13.54 N 36.33 E
Nihe 94 41.27 N 121.13 E
Nihing (Nahang) ≃ 118 26.00 N 62.44 E
Nihoa I 14 23.06 N 161.58 W
Nihommatsu 82 37.35 N 140.26 E
Nihon → Japan □[1] 82 36.00 N 138.00 E
Nihonbashi ◆[8] 258 35.41 N 139.47 E
Nihon-kai → Japan, Sea ⟩ ⫪[2] 80 40.00 N 135.00 E
Nihon University ⊍[2] 258 35.42 N 139.45 E
Nihtaur 114 29.20 N 78.23 E
Nihuil, Embalse de @[1] 242 35.05 S 68.45 W
Niida ≃ 86 33.11 N 132.58 E
Niigata 82 37.55 N 139.03 E
Niigata □[5] 84 37.08 N 138.30 E
Niigata-heiya ☷ 82 37.45 N 139.00 E
Niihama 86 33.58 N 133.16 E
Niihari 84 36.07 N 140.09 E
Niiharu 84 36.41 N 138.55 E
Niihau I 219b 21.55 N 160.10 W
Nii-jima I 84 34.22 N 139.16 E
Niimi 86 34.59 N 133.28 E
Niinisalo 26 61.50 N 22.29 E
Nii-shima I 82 34.22 N 139.16 E
Niitsu 82 37.48 N 139.07 E
Niiza 84 35.48 N 139.34 E
Níjar 34 36.58 N 2.12 W
Nijil 122 30.31 N 35.33 E
Nijkerk 48 52.13 N 5.30 E
Nijlen 52 51.10 N 4.39 E
Nijmegen 48 51.50 N 5.50 E
Nijo Castle ⊥ 260 35.01 N 135.45 E
Nijvel → Nivelles 46 50.36 N 4.20 E
Nijverdal 48 52.22 N 6.27 E
Níkaia 257c 37.58 N 23.39 E
Nike 140 6.26 N 7.29 E
Nikel' 24 69.24 N 30.12 E
Nikel'tau 76 50.23 N 58.13 E
Nikiforovo 255b 55.50 N 38.05 E
Nikiniki 102 9.49 S 124.28 E
Nikip Lake @ 174 52.53 N 91.53 W
Nikishka 170 60.44 N 151.19 W
Nikitovka, S.S.S.R. 68 50.23 N 38.25 E
Nikitovka, S.S.S.R. 73 48.21 N 38.02 E
Nikitskoje, S.S.S.R. 72 55.13 N 35.46 E
Nikitskoje, S.S.S.R. 72 55.18 N 38.28 E
Nikki 140 9.56 N 3.12 E
Nikkō 84 36.45 N 139.37 E
Nikkō-kokuritsu-kōen ♠ 84 36.49 N 139.33 E
Niklā al-'Inab 132 30.55 N 30.46 E
Nikobaren → Nicobar Islands II 100 8.00 N 93.30 E
Nikolai 170 62.58 N 154.09 W
Nikolaiken → Mikołajki 30 53.49 N 21.36 E
Nikolajev, S.S.S.R. 68 49.32 N 23.58 E
Nikolajev, S.S.S.R. 68 46.58 N 32.00 E
Nikolajevka, S.S.S.R. 68 51.04 N 34.02 E
Nikolajevka, S.S.S.R. 68 44.58 N 33.37 E
Nikolajevka, S.S.S.R. 68 46.23 N 29.24 E
Nikolajevka, S.S.S.R. 68 47.06 N 34.14 E
Nikolajevka, S.S.S.R. 68 47.33 N 40.44 E
Nikolajevka, S.S.S.R. 68 47.38 N 33.12 E
Nikolajevka, S.S.S.R. 70 53.08 N 47.12 E
Nikolajevka, S.S.S.R. 70 52.28 N 49.14 E
Nikolajevka, S.S.S.R. 70 52.11 N 48.04 E
Nikolajevka, S.S.S.R. 70 46.21 N 47.44 E
Nikolajevka, S.S.S.R. 73 47.18 N 38.50 E
Nikolajevka, S.S.S.R. 73 48.46 N 38.20 E
Nikolajevka, S.S.S.R. 73 47.39 N 37.41 E
Nikolajevka, S.S.S.R. 73 48.51 N 37.46 E
Nikolajevka, S.S.S.R. 76 54.57 N 75.44 E
Nikolajevka, S.S.S.R. 76 49.10 N 81.59 E
Nikolajevka, S.S.S.R. 76 56.29 N 95.06 E
Nikolajevka, S.S.S.R. 78 55.46 N 98.10 E
Nikolajevka, S.S.S.R. 79 48.34 N 134.47 E
Nikolajevo 66 58.16 N 29.29 E
Nikolajevo-Kozlovskij 73 47.13 N 38.21 E
Nikolajevskaja 70 47.37 N 41.29 E
Nikolajevskij 70 50.01 N 45.28 E
Nikolajevsk-na-Amure 79 53.08 N 140.44 E
Nikolajevskoje, S.S.S.R. 68 45.08 N 39.36 E
Nikolajevskoje, S.S.S.R. 78 51.04 N 111.48 E
Nikolajevskoje, S.S.S.R. 78 52.21 N 117.00 E
Nikolassee ◆[8] 254a 52.26 N 13.12 E
Nikolayev → Nikolajev 68 46.58 N 32.00 E
Nikolo-Berezovec 66 58.38 N 42.17 E
Nikolo-Ber'ozovka 70 56.08 N 54.09 E
Nikolo-Chovanskoje 255b 55.36 N 37.27 E
Nikologory 70 56.09 N 41.59 E
Nikolo-Kropotki 72 56.44 N 37.55 E
Nikolo-L'vovsk 79 43.54 N 131.23 E
Nikolo-Makarovo 70 57.38 N 43.34 E
Nikolsdorf 58 46.47 N 12.55 E
Nikol'sk, S.S.S.R. 24 59.30 N 45.27 E
Nikol'sk, S.S.S.R. 70 53.45 N 46.05 E
Nikolski 170 53.15 N 168.22 W
Nikol'skij, S.S.S.R. 24 60.55 N 34.00 E
Nikol'skij, S.S.S.R. 76 56.18 N 68.58 E
Nikol'skij, S.S.S.R. 76 47.55 N 67.28 E
Nikol'skij Toržok 66 59.53 N 38.46 E
Nikol'skoje, S.S.S.R. 64 55.12 N 166.00 E
Nikol'skoje, S.S.S.R. 66 59.23 N 44.36 E
Nikol'skoje, S.S.S.R. 66 55.26 N 35.04 E
Nikol'skoje, S.S.S.R. 66 52.39 N 36.04 E
Nikol'skoje, S.S.S.R. 66 59.30 N 42.32 E
Nikol'skoje, S.S.S.R. 68 50.35 N 41.10 E
Nikol'skoje, S.S.S.R. 70 52.37 N 43.49 E
Nikol'skoje, S.S.S.R. 70 47.46 N 46.24 E
Nikol'skoje, S.S.S.R. 72 54.03 N 37.10 E
Nikol'skoje, S.S.S.R. 72 54.30 N 36.50 E
Nikol'skoje, S.S.S.R. 72 55.37 N 36.41 E
Nikol'skoje, S.S.S.R. 72 54.18 N 35.53 E
Nikol'skoje, S.S.S.R. 72 56.09 N 36.43 E
Nikol'skoje, S.S.S.R. 72 55.53 N 36.26 E
Nikol'skoje, S.S.S.R. 72 55.15 N 36.04 E
Nikol'skoje, S.S.S.R. 72 54.27 N 36.24 E
Nikol'skoje, S.S.S.R. 72 54.51 N 35.53 E
Nikol'skoje, S.S.S.R. 73 47.46 N 37.18 E
Nikol'skoje, S.S.S.R. 76 52.02 N 55.43 E
Nikol'skoje, S.S.S.R. 76 57.12 N 84.21 E
Nikol'skoje, S.S.S.R. 255a 59.41 N 30.47 E
Nikol'skoje, S.S.S.R. 255b 55.46 N 37.54 E
Nikol'skoje-na-Čeremšane 70 54.03 N 49.14 E
Nikol'skoje-na-Dnepre 68 48.12 N 35.12 E
Nikol'skoje-Ur'upino 255b 55.48 N 37.13 E
Nikonorovka 73 49.07 N 39.59 E
Nikonova Gora 66 60.22 N 36.07 E
Nikonovskoje 72 55.17 N 38.10 E
Nikopol, Blg. 38 43.42 N 24.54 E
Nikopol', S.S.S.R. 68 47.35 N 34.25 E
Niksar 120 40.36 N 36.58 E
Nīkshahr 118 26.13 N 60.12 E
Nikšić 38 42.46 N 18.56 E
Nikulino, S.S.S.R. 66 55.16 N 33.46 E
Nikulino, S.S.S.R. 70 58.05 N 44.14 E
Nikulino, S.S.S.R. 72 56.48 N 35.50 E
Nikulino ◆[8] 255b 55.40 N 37.28 E
Nikulkino 72 56.07 N 38.38 E
Nikul'skoje 72 55.10 N 38.41 E
Nikunau I 14 1.23 S 176.26 E
Nil → Nile ≃ 130 30.10 N 31.06 E
Nīl, Nahr an- → Nile ≃ 130 30.10 N 31.06 E
Nila, Pulau I 154 6.44 S 129.31 E
Nilakka @ 26 63.07 N 26.33 E
Niland 194 33.14 N 115.31 W
Nil Blanc → White Nile ≃ 130 15.38 N 32.31 E
Nile (Nahr an-Nīl) ≃ 130 30.10 N 31.06 E
Nīleh, Kūh-e ∧ 118 32.59 N 50.32 E
Nileke 76 43.47 N 82.20 E
Niles, Ill., U.S. 268 42.01 N 87.49 W
Niles, Mich., U.S. 206 41.50 N 86.15 W
Niles, Ohio, U.S. 204 41.11 N 80.45 W
Nileshwar 112 12.15 N 75.06 E
Niles Pond @ 273 42.35 N 70.40 W
Nilgani 262b 22.46 N 88.26 E
Nilgaut, Lac @ 180 46.36 N 77.15 W
Nīlgiri 116 21.28 N 86.46 E
Nilo → Nile ≃ 130 30.10 N 31.06 E
Nilo Azul → Blue Nile ≃ 130 15.38 N 32.31 E
Nilo Blanco → White Nile ≃ 130 15.38 N 32.31 E
Nilópolis 246 22.49 S 43.25 W
Nilópolis □[7] 277a 22.49 S 43.26 W
Nilphāmāri 114 25.56 N 88.51 E
Nilsiä 26 63.12 N 28.05 E
Niltepec 224 16.34 N 94.37 W
Nīlwāl ◆[8] 262a 28.40 N 76.59 E
Nilwood 209 39.24 N 89.49 W
Nima 86 35.09 N 132.24 E
Nīmach 110 24.28 N 74.52 E
Niman ≃ 79 51.24 N 132.45 E
Nimančik 79 52.09 N 133.47 E
Nimba □[6] 140 7.40 N 8.50 W
Nīmbahera 110 24.37 N 74.41 E
Nimba Mountains ∧∧ 140 7.30 N 8.30 W
Nimelen ≃ 79 52.27 N 136.32 E
Nîmes 56 43.50 N 4.21 E
Nimis 58 46.12 N 13.16 E
Nimishillen Creek ≃ 204 40.38 N 81.22 W
Nimisila 204 40.56 N 81.34 W
Nimisila Reservoir @[1] 204 40.57 N 81.31 W
Nīm Ka Thāna 110 27.44 N 75.48 E
Nimmitabel 156 36.31 S 149.16 E
Nimmonsburg 200 42.09 N 75.55 W
Nimpkish Lake @ 172 50.25 N 126.59 W
Nimrod Glacier ⩗ 9 82.27 S 161.00 E
Nimrod Lake @[1] 184 34.55 N 93.20 W
Nīmrūz □[4] 118 30.30 N 62.00 E
Nims ≃ 52 49.51 N 6.28 E
Nimta 262b 22.40 N 88.25 E
Nimule 144 3.36 N 32.03 E
Nimy 46 50.28 N 3.57 E
Nina Bang Lake @ 166 70.51 N 79.07 W
Nin Bay C 106 12.13 N 123.15 E
Ninda 142 14.47 S 21.24 E
Nindigully 156 28.21 S 148.49 E
Nindirí 226 12.00 N 86.08 W
Nine Ashes 250 51.42 N 0.18 E
Nine Degree Channel ⋓, As. 112 9.00 N 73.00 E
Nine Degree Channel ⋓, Bhārat 112 9.00 N 73.00 E
Ninemile Creek ≃, N.Y., U.S. 200 43.11 N 75.20 W
Ninemile Creek ≃, N.Y., U.S. 200 43.24 N 76.38 W
Ninemile Creek ≃, N.Y., U.S. 200 43.06 N 76.14 W
Nine Mile Creek ≃, Utah, U.S. 190 39.50 N 109.53 W
Ninemile Island I 269b 40.29 N 79.52 W
Nine Mile Lake @ 202 44.57 N 79.34 W
Nine Mile Point ⟩ 202 44.09 N 76.34 W
Ninepin Group II 261d 22.16 N 114.21 E
Ninette 174 49.22 N 99.43 W
Ninetyeast Ridge ⊹[3] 12 15.00 S 88.00 E
Ninety Mile Beach ●[2], Austl. 156 38.13 S 147.23 E
Ninety Mile Beach ●[2], N.Z. 162 34.48 S 173.00 E
Ninety Six 182 34.11 N 82.01 W
Nineveh, Ind., U.S. 208 39.22 N 86.05 W
Nineveh, N.Y., U.S. 200 42.12 N 75.36 W
Nineveh ⊥ 118 36.25 N 43.10 E
Ninfa ⊥ 60 41.36 N 12.58 E
Ninfas, Punta ⟩ 244 42.56 S 64.20 W
Ninfield 44 50.53 N 0.25 E
Ninga 174 49.13 N 99.51 W
Ningan 79 44.22 N 129.25 E
Ningari 140 14.40 N 3.16 W
Ningbo 90 29.52 N 121.31 E
Ningcheng (Tianyi) 88 41.33 N 119.20 E
Ningde 90 26.43 N 119.33 E
Ningdu 90 26.31 N 115.58 E
Ninggang 90 26.50 N 114.02 E
Ningguo 96 30.38 N 118.58 E
Ninghai 90 29.17 N 121.25 E
Ninghe (Lutai) 95 39.20 N 117.48 E
Ninghepu 95 40.43 N 116.07 E
Ninghua 90 26.15 N 116.38 E
Ningi 140 11.04 N 9.32 E
Ningjin, Zhg. 88 37.37 N 114.55 E
Ningjin, Zhg. 88 37.39 N 116.48 E
Ningjing 92 29.40 N 98.30 E
Ningjingshan ∧∧ 92 30.41 N 98.12 E
Ningling 88 34.27 N 115.21 E
Ningming 92 22.07 N 107.09 E
Ningnan 92 27.11 N 102.36 E
Ningpo → Ningbo 90 29.52 N 121.31 E
Ningqiang 92 32.44 N 106.19 E
Ningshan (Guankou) 92 33.04 N 108.39 E
Ningshuo (Xiaobabao) 92 37.58 N 106.02 E
Ningsia → Yinchuan 92 38.30 N 106.18 E
Ningsia Hut Autonomous Region → Ningxia Huizu Zizhiqu □[4] 92 37.00 N 106.00 E
Ningwu 92 39.01 N 112.21 E
Ningxi 90 28.35 N 121.00 E
Ningxia Huizu Zizhiqu □[4] 92 37.00 N 106.00 E
Ningxian 92 35.31 N 108.01 E
Ningxiang 90 28.15 N 112.33 E
Ningyang 88 35.47 N 115.49 E
Ningyō-tōge)(86 35.19 N 133.56 E
Ningyuan 92 25.37 N 111.46 E
Ningyuanbao 92 38.38 N 102.30 E
Ningyuanpu 95 40.44 N 114.54 E
Ninh-binh 100 20.15 N 105.59 E
Ninh-hoa 100 12.29 N 109.08 E
Ninhue 242 36.24 S 72.24 W
Ninigo Group II 154 1.15 S 144.15 E
Ninilchik 170 60.03 N 151.41 W
Ninnescah ≃ 188 37.20 N 97.10 W
Ninnescah, North Fork ≃ 188 37.34 N 97.42 W
Ninnescah, South Fork ≃ 188 37.34 N 97.42 W
Ninnis Glacier Tongue ⩗ 9 68.12 S 147.12 E
Ninomiya, Nihon 84 35.18 N 139.16 E
Ninomiya, Nihon 84 36.22 N 139.58 E
Ninove 46 50.50 N 4.01 E
Niny 74 44.29 N 43.57 E
Nio 86 34.12 N 133.39 E
Nioaque 238 21.08 S 55.48 W
Nioaque ≃ 238 20.46 S 56.04 W
Niobe 204 42.01 N 79.27 W
Niobrara 188 42.45 N 98.02 W
Niobrara ≃ 188 42.45 N 98.00 W
Nioka 144 2.10 N 30.39 E
Nioki 142 2.43 S 17.41 E
Niokolo Koba 140 13.04 N 12.43 W
Niokolo Koba, Parc National du ♠ 140 13.00 N 13.00 W
Niono 140 14.15 N 6.00 W
Nionsamoridougou 140 8.43 N 8.50 W
Niordenskiold ≃ 170 62.05 N 136.18 W
Nioro du Rip 140 13.45 N 15.48 W
Nioro du Sahel 140 15.15 N 9.35 W
Niort 32 46.19 N 0.27 W
Niota 182 35.31 N 84.33 W
Niout ⫪[4] 140 16.03 N 6.52 W

Symbol	English	Deutsch	Español	Français	Português
≃	River	Fluss	Río	Rivière	Rio
☰	Canal	Kanal	Canal	Canal	Canal
⌊	Waterfall, Rapids	Wasserfall, Stromschnellen	Cascada, Rápidos	Chute d'eau, Rapides	Cascata, Rápidos
⋓	Strait	Meeresstrasse	Estrecho	Détroit	Estreito
C	Bay, Gulf	Bucht, Golf	Bahía, Golfo	Baie, Golfe	Baía, Golfo
@	Lake, Lakes	See, Seen	Lago, Lagos	Lac, Lacs	Lago, Lagos
☷	Swamp	Sumpf	Pantano	Marais	Pântano
⩗	Ice Features, Glacier	Eis- und Gletscherformen	Accidentes Glaciales	Formes glaciaires	Acidentes Glaciares
⫪	Other Hydrographic Features	Andere Hydrographische Objekte	Otros Elementos Hidrográficos	Autres données hydrographiques	Outros Elementos Hidrográficos
⊹	Submarine Features	Untermeerische Objekte	Accidentes Submarinos	Formes de relief sous-marin	Acidentes Submarinos
□	Political Unit	Politische Einheit	Unidad Politica	Entité politique	Unidade Política
⊍	Cultural Institution	Kulturelle Institution	Institución Cultural	Institution culturelle	Instituição Cultural
⊥	Historical Site	Historische Stätte	Sitio Histórico	Site historique	Sitio Histórico
♠	Recreational Site	Erholungs- und Ferienort	Sitio de Recreo	Centre de loisirs	Sítio de Lazer
⊠	Airport	Flughafen	Aeropuerto	Aéroport	Aeroporto
■	Military Installation	Militäranlage	Instalación Militar	Installation militaire	Instalação Militar
◆	Miscellaneous	Verschiedenes	Misceláneo	Divers	Miscelânea

ENGLISH — Name | Page | Lat.°′ | Long.°′
DEUTSCH — Name | Seite | Breite°′ | Länge°′ E=Ost

Nipan 156 24.47 S 150.01 E
Nipāni 112 16.24 N 74.23 E
Nipawin 174 53.22 N 104.00 W
Nipawin Provincial Park ▲ 174 54.00 N 104.40 W
Nipe, Bahía de C 230p 20.47 N 75.42 W
Nipe, Sierra de ⛰ 230p 20.28 N 75.49 W
Nipekamew Lake ⊜ 174 54.24 N 104.58 W
Nipepe 144 14.01 S 37.55 E
Nipigon 180 49.01 N 88.16 W
Nipigon, Lake ⊜ 166 49.50 N 88.30 W
Nipigon Bay C 180 48.53 N 87.50 W
Nipin ≃ 174 55.45 N 109.02 W
Nipisi Lake ⊜ 172 55.47 N 114.57 W
Nipissing □6 202 45.30 N 78.50 W
Nipissing, Lake ⊜ 180 46.17 N 80.00 W
Nipissis, Lac ⊜ 176 51.02 N 66.10 W
Nipisso, Lac ⊜ 176 50.52 N 65.50 W
Nipomo 194 35.03 N 120.29 W
Nippenicket, Lake ⊜ 273 41.58 N 71.03 W
Nippers Harbour 176 49.48 N 55.52 W
Nippersink Creek ≃ 206 42.23 N 88.22 W
Niqichang 97 29.02 N 104.16 E
Niqiuji 90 33.25 N 115.38 E
Niquelândia 245 14.27 S 48.27 W
Niquero 230p 20.03 N 77.35 W
Niquivil 242 30.25 S 68.42 W
Nīr 118 38.02 N 47.59 E
Nīr, Jabal an- ⛰2 118 24.10 N 43.20 E
Nīra ≃ 112 17.59 N 75.07 E
Nir'am 122 31.31 N 34.35 E
Nirasaki 84 35.42 N 138.27 E
Nirayama 84 35.03 N 138.57 E
Nirgua 236 10.09 N 68.34 W
Nirim 122 31.20 N 34.24 E
Nirmal 112 19.06 N 78.21 E
Nirmali 114 26.19 N 86.35 E
Nirsa 116 23.47 N 86.43 E
Nirwāno 118 26.22 N 62.43 E
Niš 38 43.19 N 21.54 E
Nisa 34 39.31 N 7.39 W
Nisa (Neisse) (Nysa Łużycka) ≃ 30 52.04 N 14.46 E
Nišava ≃ 38 43.22 N 21.46 E
Nisbet 200 41.13 N 77.07 W
Niscemi 36 37.08 N 14.24 E
Nischintāpur 262b 22.26 N 88.22 E
Nişf Thānī Bashbīsh 132 31.07 N 31.11 E
Nish → Niš 38 43.19 N 21.54 E
Nishan 110 32.17 N 83.30 E
Nishi ◆8, Nihon 258 35.27 N 139.38 E
Nishi ◆8, Nihon 260 34.41 N 135.30 E
Nishiarai ◆8 258 35.47 N 139.47 E
Nishiazai 84 35.31 N 136.10 E
Nishibetsuin 260 34.58 N 135.31 E
Nishigō 84 37.09 N 140.10 E
Nishiiyayama 86 33.53 N 133.49 E
Nishiizu 84 34.46 N 138.47 E
Nishi-jima I 86 34.39 N 134.29 E
Nishikata 84 36.28 N 139.45 E
Nishikatsura 84 35.31 N 138.51 E
Nishiki 86 34.16 N 131.57 E
Nishiki ≃ 86 34.09 N 132.15 E
Nishikiori 260 34.29 N 135.34 E
Nishimori ◆8 260 34.45 N 135.01 E
Nishinari ◆8 260 34.38 N 135.28 E
Nishinasuno 84 36.53 N 139.59 E
Nishinomiya 86 34.43 N 135.20 E
Nishinoomote 83b 30.44 N 131.00 E
Nishio 84 34.52 N 137.03 E
Nishitani 84 35.52 N 136.30 E
Nishitoda ◆8 260 34.43 N 135.00 E
Nishitosa 86 33.09 N 132.47 E
Nishiwaki 86 34.59 N 134.58 E
Nishiyodogawa ◆8 260 34.42 N 135.27 E
Nisi 92 28.06 N 99.33 E
Nisinomiya → Nishinomiya 86 34.43 N 135.20 E
Nisiros I 38 36.35 N 27.10 E
Niska Lake ⊜ 174 55.35 N 108.38 W
Niskayuna 200 42.46 N 73.50 W
Nisling ≃ 170 62.27 N 139.30 W
Nismes 52 50.05 N 4.33 E
Nispen 48 51.29 N 4.28 E
Nisporeny 68 47.06 N 28.11 E
Nisqually ≃ 214 47.06 N 122.42 W
Nisqually Indian Reservation ◆4 214 47.02 N 122.42 W
Nisqually Reach C 214 47.07 N 122.45 W
Nissan ≃ 26 56.40 N 12.51 E
Nissequogue 266 40.54 N 73.12 W
Nissequogue ≃ 266 40.54 N 73.13 W
Nissequogue, Northeast Branch ≃ 266 40.50 N 73.13 W
Nissequogue River State Park ▲ 266 40.51 N 73.13 W
Nisser ⊜ 26 59.10 N 8.30 E
Nisshin 84 35.08 N 137.02 E
Nissum Bredning C 26 56.38 N 8.22 E
Nissum Fjord C2 26 56.21 N 8.14 E
Nisswa 180 46.31 N 94.17 W
Nistelrode 48 51.43 N 5.33 E
Nisutlin ≃ 170 60.10 N 132.30 W
Nita, Indon. 105b 8.40 S 122.11 E
Nita, Nihon 86 35.12 N 133.01 E
Nitalas 262c 19.06 N 73.08 E
Nītaure 66 57.10 N 25.10 E
Niterói 246
 277a 22.53 S 43.07 W
Niterói □7 277a 22.56 S 43.04 W
Nith ≃, Ont., Can. 202 43.12 N 80.22 W
Nith ≃, Scot., U.K. 42 55.00 N 3.35 W
Nithāri 262a 28.35 N 77.21 E
Nithāri ◆8 262a 28.42 N 77.03 E
Nithi River 172 54.01 N 125.01 W
Nithsdale ∨ 42 55.14 N 3.46 W
Nitibe 102 9.19 S 124.12 E
Nitinat 214 48.55 N 124.29 W
Nitinat ≃ 214 48.49 N 124.37 W
Nitinat Lake ⊜ 172 48.45 N 124.45 W
Niton 44 50.35 N 1.16 W
Nitra 30 48.20 N 18.05 E
Nitra ≃ 30 47.46 N 18.10 E
Nitro 178 38.25 N 81.50 W
Nitry 46 47.40 N 3.53 E
Nítse Óros (Nidže) ∧ 38 40.58 N 21.49 E
Nitta 84 36.17 N 139.18 E
Nittälven ≃ 40 59.51 N 14.50 E
Nittany Mountain ∧ 200 41.00 N 77.25 W
Nittedal 26 60.04 N 10.53 E
Niuaunofo ≻ 164w 21.04 S 175.20 W
Niubaotun 95 39.46 N 116.41 E
Niubu 90 31.02 N 117.39 E
Niuchutuncun 94 41.28 N 122.58 E
Niudouguang 90 24.51 N 115.44 E
Niue □2 14
 164v 19.02 S 169.52 W
Niuerhe ≃ 79 52.04 N 120.48 E
Niufentai 79 47.05 N 120.02 E
Niufodu 97 29.23 N 105.02 E
Niuhang 90 28.44 N 115.51 E
Niujiazhuang 88 37.21 N 118.29 E
Niujingjie 100 25.46 N 100.33 E
Niujouch'i 90 23.17 N 120.24 E
Niuke 110 30.41 N 82.01 E
Niulake 92 28.10 N 94.49 E
Niulanjiang ≃ 92 27.28 N 103.10 E
Niulanshan 95 40.13 N 116.39 E
Niulongxi 97 29.29 N 103.48 E
Niumaowu 88 40.58 N 124.59 E
Niupeng 96 31.32 N 121.50 E
Niupichang 97 30.35 N 103.40 E
Niuquanzi 88 41.39 N 116.26 E
Niushan 88 34.30 N 118.47 E
Niushandao I 90 25.26 N 119.56 E
Niushitun 88 35.18 N 114.24 E
Niut, Gunung ∧ 102 1.00 N 109.55 E
Niutanchang 97 29.05 N 105.21 E
Niutao I 14 6.06 S 177.17 E
Niuti 90 32.58 N 113.35 E
Niutianwei 90 27.17 N 115.44 E
Niutoushan 79 45.09 N 126.45 E
Niutuozhen 95 39.15 N 116.20 E
Niuxichang 97 28.47 N 104.31 E
Niuxintai 94 41.21 N 123.53 E
Niuxintun 94 41.56 N 121.21 E
Niuyuanzi 95 40.20 N 117.47 E
Niuzhuang 94 40.58 N 122.32 E
Nivå 41 55.56 N 12.31 E
Nivala 26 63.55 N 24.58 E
Nive ≃, Austl. 156 26.02 S 146.25 E
Nive ≃, Fr. 32 43.30 N 1.29 W
Nive Downs 156 25.30 S 146.32 E
Nivelles (Nijvel) 46 50.36 N 4.20 E
Nivernais □9 32 47.00 N 3.30 E
Nivernais, Canal du ≋ 46 47.40 N 3.40 E
Niverville, Man., Can. 174 49.37 N 97.01 W
Niverville, N.Y., U.S. 200 42.26 N 73.40 W
Nivillers 46 49.28 N 2.10 E
Nivnoje 66 53.11 N 32.35 E
Nivskij 24 67.16 N 32.23 E
Nixa 184 37.03 N 93.18 W
Nixichang 92 29.09 N 104.08 E
Nixon, Nev., U.S. 194 39.50 N 119.21 W
Nixon, Pa., U.S. 204 40.45 N 79.56 W
Nixon, Tex., U.S. 212 29.16 N 97.46 W
Niyodo 86 33.32 N 133.08 E
Niyodo ≃ 86 33.27 N 133.29 E
Niyor 104 2.05 N 103.17 E
Niża 24 66.20 N 43.16 E
Nizam ◆8 257b 40.52 N 29.07 E
Nizāmābād 112 18.40 N 78.07 E
Nizamghāt 110 28.16 N 95.42 E
Nizām Sāgar ⊜1 112 18.10 N 77.55 E
Nižankoviči 68 49.40 N 22.47 E
Nīzgān ≃ 118 33.13 N 63.40 E
Nizhniy Tagil → Nižnij Tagil 76 57.55 N 59.57 E
Nizhny Novgorod → Gor'kij 70 56.20 N 44.00 E
Nižin 66 52.38 N 28.10 E
Nizino 255a 59.50 N 29.53 E
Nizip 120 37.01 N 37.46 E
Nízke Beskydy ⛰ 30 49.20 N 21.30 E
Nízke Tatry ⛰ 30 48.54 N 19.40 E
Nižn'aja 70 56.34 N 49.07 E
Nižn'aja Čvorovaja 76 59.11 N 77.31 E
Nižnaja Dobrinka 70 50.18 N 45.42 E
Nižn'aja Duvanka 68 49.35 N 38.10 E
Nižn'aja-Gerasimovka 73 48.46 N 39.44 E
Nižn'aja Grajvoronka 68 51.47 N 37.45 E
Nižn'aja Irga 76 56.51 N 57.26 E
Nižn'aja Ivanovka ◆8 73 48.09 N 38.46 E
Nižn'aja Karelina 78 57.55 N 107.44 E
Nižn'aja Keul'skaja, Šivera ⌊ 78 58.25 N 102.46 E
Nižn'aja Krynka 73 48.07 N 38.11 E
Nižnaja Matrenka 70 52.16 N 40.06 E
Nižn'aja-Ol'chovaja 73 48.44 N 39.35 E
Nižn'aja Omka 76 55.26 N 74.55 E
Nizn'aja Omra 24 62.46 N 55.46 E
Nižn'aja Ošma 70 55.44 N 51.18 E
Nižn'aja Ouvanka 73 49.35 N 38.10 E
Nižn'aja Peša 24 66.43 N 47.36 E
Nižn'aja Pojma 78 56.11 N 97.13 E
Nižn'aja Pokrovka 70 51.40 N 50.07 E
Nižn'aja Šachtama 78 51.24 N 117.40 E
Nižn'aja Salda 76 58.05 N 60.43 E
Nižn'aja Syzran' 70 53.04 N 48.34 E
Nižn'aja Tavda 76 57.40 N 66.12 E
Nižn'aja Tojma 24 62.24 N 44.10 E
Nižn'aja Tunguska ≃ 64 65.48 N 88.04 E
Nižn'aja Tura 76 58.37 N 59.49 E
Nižn'aja Vol'dža 76 58.19 N 79.20 E
Nižn'aja Zaimka 78 56.09 N 98.14 E
Nižneangarsk 78 55.47 N 109.33 E
Nižnebakanskij 68 44.52 N 37.52 E
Nižne-Baranikovka 73 49.05 N 39.51 E
Nižnečujskij 75 43.12 N 74.21 E
Nižnedevick 68 51.33 N 38.20 E
Nižne-Gnilovskoj ◆8 73 47.11 N 39.36 E
Nižnegnutov 70 48.02 N 42.22 E
Nižnegorskij 68 45.27 N 34.44 E
Nižneilimsk 78 57.11 N 103.16 E
Nižneje 73 48.46 N 38.37 E
Nižneje Al'kejevo 70 54.46 N 50.03 E
Nižn'eje Gir'unino 78 51.12 N 116.58 E
Nižneje Kučukovo 70 56.13 N 52.57 E
Nižneje Kujto, Ozero ⊜ 24 64.58 N 31.38 E
Nižneje M'ačkovo 72 55.33 N 37.59 E
Nižneje Platino 73 48.48 N 39.30 E
Nižnejepravalje ≃ 73 48.17 N 39.57 E
Nižneje Romanovo 76 59.47 N 69.35 E
Nižneje Sančelejevo 70 53.40 N 49.27 E
Nižnekamskij 70 55.32 N 51.58 E
Nižnekundr'učenskaja 70 47.45 N 40.57 E
Nižnelemskij 24 64.01 N 56.16 E
Nižne Mit'akin Pervyj 73 48.41 N 40.02 E
Nižnenagol'naja 73 49.00 N 39.59 E
Nižneoz'ornoje 70 51.37 N 53.56 E
Nižne-Podpol'nyj 73 47.12 N 40.01 E
Nižne-Pokrovka 73 49.13 N 38.38 E
Nižnetambovskoje 79 50.54 N 138.13 E
Nižne-T'oploje 73 48.48 N 39.23 E
Nižnetroickij 70 54.20 N 53.41 E
Nižneudinsk 78 54.54 N 99.03 E
Nižnij Baskunčak 70 48.13 N 46.50 E
Nižnij Časučej 78 50.31 N 115.08 E
Nižnij Čir 70 48.22 N 43.03 E
Nižnij Čulym 76 54.37 N 78.56 E
Nižnije Černi 70 47.41 N 43.26 E
Nižnije Čeršely 70 54.40 N 52.08 E
Nižnije Sergi 76 56.40 N 59.18 E
Nižnije Serogozy 68 46.49 N 33.24 E
Nižnije Timers'any 70 54.34 N 47.45 E
Nižnije V'azovyje 70 55.49 N 48.32 E
Nižnij Ingaš 78 56.12 N 96.31 E
Nižnij Kisl'aj 68 50.50 N 40.11 E
Nižnij Kuranach 64 58.49 N 125.32 E
Nižnij Lomov 70 53.32 N 43.41 E
Nižnij Mamon 68 50.11 N 40.30 E
Nižnij Odec 24 63.40 N 54.52 E
Nižnij Ol'šan 68 50.45 N 38.55 E
Nižnij Oseredok, Ostrov I 70 45.45 N 48.35 E
Nižnij P'andž 110 37.08 N 68.32 E
Nižnij Paramonov 70 47.57 N 41.55 E
Nižnij Rogačik 68 47.21 N 34.02 E
Nižnij Serebr'akov 70 47.58 N 41.02 E
Nižnij Škaft 70 53.36 N 45.40 E
Nižnij Stan 78 52.18 N 115.44 E
Nižnij Tagil 76 57.55 N 59.57 E
Nižnij Takanyš 70 55.57 N 51.04 E
Nižnij Trojanov Val ⊥ 68 45.40 N 28.30 E
Nižnij Ufalej 76 55.55 N 59.59 E
Nižnij V'aloz'orskij 24 66.44 N 35.10 E
Nižnyj Nagol'čik 73 48.01 N 39.04 E
Nizy 68 50.47 N 34.46 E
Nizy-le-Comte 46 49.34 N 4.03 E
Nizza Monferrato 56 44.46 N 8.21 E
Niẕẕana, Naḥal ∨ 122 30.57 N 34.23 E
Niẕẕanim 122 31.43 N 34.38 E
Njassa-See → Nyasa, Lake ⊜ 144 12.00 S 34.30 E
Njinjo 144 8.48 S 38.54 E
Njoko ≃ 142 17.10 S 24.05 E
Njombe 144 9.20 S 34.46 E
Njombe ≃ 144 6.56 S 35.06 E
Njupeskär ⌊ 26 61.38 N 12.41 E
Njurunda 26 62.16 N 17.22 E
Nkai 144 19.00 S 28.54 E
Nkala Mission 144 15.55 S 26.00 E
Nkambe 142 6.38 N 10.40 E
Nkandla 148 28.37 S 31.05 E
Nkawkaw 140 6.33 N 0.47 W
Nkhata Bay 144 11.33 S 34.18 E
Nkhota Kota 144 12.57 S 34.17 E
Nkolabona 142 1.14 N 11.43 E
Nkomi, Lagune C 142 1.35 S 9.17 E
Nkongsamba 142 4.57 N 9.56 E
Nkonko 144 6.20 S 34.58 E
Nkoso 142 2.42 S 22.39 E
Nkoto 142 1.56 S 19.41 E
Nkunga 142 4.41 S 18.34 E
Nkwalini 148 28.45 S 31.33 E
Nmai ≃ 92 25.42 N 97.30 E
Nnewi 140 6.00 N 6.59 E
Nō 84 37.06 N 137.59 E
Noābād 262b 22.34 N 88.31 E
Noailles 46 49.20 N 2.12 E
Noākhāli 114 22.49 N 91.06 E
Noak Hill ◆8 250 51.37 N 0.14 E
Noale 58 45.32 N 12.04 E
Noamundi 114 22.09 N 85.32 E
Noank 197 41.19 N 72.01 W
Noarlunga 158b 35.11 S 138.30 E
Noasca 56 45.27 N 7.19 E
Noatak 170 67.34 N 162.59 W
Noatak ≃ 170 67.00 N 162.30 W
Nobby 161a 27.51 S 151.54 E
Nobel 202 45.25 N 80.06 W
Nobeoka 82 32.35 N 131.40 E
Nobéré 140 11.33 N 1.12 W
Nobidome 258 35.48 N 139.34 E
Nobidome-yōsui ≋1 258 35.44 N 139.27 E
Nōbi-heiya ≚ 84 35.15 N 136.45 E
Nobitz 50 50.58 N 12.29 E
Noble, Ill., U.S. 184 38.42 N 88.13 W
Noble, Okla., U.S. 186 35.08 N 97.24 W
Noble □6 206 41.24 N 85.25 W
Noble Park 264b 37.58 S 145.10 E
Noblestown 269b 40.24 N 80.12 W
Noblesville 208 40.03 N 86.01 W
Nobleton, Ont., Can. 202 43.54 N 79.40 W
Nobleton, Fla., U.S. 210 28.39 N 82.16 W
Noboribetsu 82a 42.27 N 141.11 E
Noborito 258 35.37 N 139.34 E
Nobres 238 14.44 S 56.20 W
Nobsa 236 5.46 N 72.57 W
Nocatee 210 27.09 N 81.53 W
Noccundra 156 27.50 S 142.36 E
Nocé 46 48.22 N 0.42 E
Noce ≃ 58 46.09 N 11.04 E
Nocera Inferiore 60 40.44 N 14.38 E
Nocera Superiore 60 40.44 N 14.40 E
Nocera Umbra 60 43.05 N 12.47 E
Noceto 58 44.48 N 10.11 E
Nochistlán 224 21.22 N 102.51 W
Nochixtlán 224 17.28 N 97.14 W
Nochten 50 51.26 N 14.36 E
Noci 36 40.48 N 17.08 E
Nockamixon Lake ⊜1 198 40.28 N 75.14 W
Nockamixon State Park ▲ 198 40.27 N 75.16 W
Nockatunga 156 27.43 S 142.43 E
Nocona 186 33.47 N 97.44 W
Nocupétaro 224 18.48 N 101.04 W
Noda 84 35.56 N 139.52 E
Nodagawa 86 35.31 N 135.06 E
Noda-sogo Baseball Ground ▲ 258 35.57 N 139.52 E
Nodaway ≃ 184 39.54 N 94.58 W
Nodera 260 34.45 N 134.56 E
Nodier, Lac ⊜ 180 47.38 N 78.26 W
Nodol' ≃ 72 56.07 N 36.42 E
Nods 54 47.06 N 6.20 E
Noé, Ouadi ∨ 136 15.39 N 21.19 E
Noel 184 36.33 N 94.29 W
Noenieput 148 27.29 S 20.06 E
Noer 41 54.27 N 10.00 E
Noetinger 242 32.22 S 62.19 W
Nœux-les-Mines 46 50.29 N 2.40 E
Nofels 54 47.15 N 9.34 E
Nogajsk 68 46.44 N 36.20 E
Nogajskaja Step' ≚ 74 44.17 N 46.05 E
Nogal ≃ 134 7.58 N 49.52 E
Nogales, Chile 242 32.44 S 71.15 W
Nogales, Méx. 222 31.20 N 110.56 W
Nogales, Méx. 224 18.49 N 97.10 W
Nogales, Ariz., U.S. 190 31.20 N 110.56 W
Nogal Valley ∨ 134 8.35 N 48.35 E
Nogami 84 36.07 N 139.07 E
Nogangjin 88 39.30 N 125.23 E
Nogara 58 45.11 N 11.04 E
Nogaro 32 43.46 N 0.02 W
Nōgata 86 33.44 N 130.44 E
Nogent-en-Bassigny 54 48.02 N 5.21 E
Nogent-le-Roi 46 48.39 N 1.32 E
Nogent-le-Rotrou 46 48.19 N 0.50 E
Nogent-sur-Marne 46 48.50 N 2.29 E
Nogent-sur-Oise 46 49.16 N 2.28 E
Nogent-sur-Seine 46 48.29 N 3.30 E
Nogent-sur-Vernisson 46 47.51 N 2.45 E
Nogi 84 36.14 N 139.44 E
Noginsk 72 55.51 N 38.27 E
Nogisaki 258 35.57 N 139.58 E
Nogles Creek ≃ 202 44.35 N 78.31 W
Nogliki 79 51.48 N 143.10 E
Nogoa ≃ 156 23.33 S 148.32 E
Nōgohaku-san ∧ 84 35.46 N 136.31 E
Nogoonnuur 76 49.33 N 90.17 E
Nogoyá 242 32.24 S 59.48 W
Nógrád □6 30 48.00 N 19.35 E
Noguera Pallarese ≃ 34 42.15 N 0.54 E
Noguera Ribagorzana ≃ 34 41.40 N 0.43 E
Nohain ≃ 46 47.24 N 2.55 E
Nohar 113 29.11 N 74.46 E
Noheji 82 40.52 N 141.08 E
Nohili Point ≻ 219b 22.04 N 159.47 W
Nohjhīl 114 27.51 N 77.39 E
Nohta 114 23.40 N 79.34 E
Noichi 86 33.33 N 133.42 E
Noir, Causse ⛰1 32 44.10 N 3.15 E
Noir, Isla I 244 54.29 S 73.02 W
Noir, Montagne ⛰ 32 43.28 N 2.18 E
Noire ≃, Qué., Can. 180 45.54 N 76.57 W
Noire ≃, Qué., Can. 196 46.39 N 72.08 W
Noire ≃, Qué., Can. 196 45.33 N 72.58 W
Noire, Mer du → Black Sea ▾2 22 43.00 N 35.00 E
Noire, Montagne ∧ 196 46.14 N 74.18 W
Noirétable 56 45.49 N 3.46 E
Noirmoutier 32 47.00 N 2.14 W
Noirmoutier, Île de I 32 47.00 N 2.15 W
Noiseau 251 48.47 N 2.33 E
Noisiel 251 48.51 N 2.37 E
Noisy ≃ 202 44.19 N 80.08 W
Noisy-le-Grand 251 48.51 N 2.33 E
Noisy-le-Roi 251 48.51 N 2.04 E
Nojember'an 74 41.12 N 45.01 E
Nojima-zaki ≻ 84 34.56 N 139.53 E
Nojiri-ko ⊜ 84 36.49 N 138.13 E
Nojon 92 43.10 N 102.12 E
Nojon Uul ⛰ 92 43.10 N 101.30 E
Nokami 86 34.15 N 135.20 E
Nokaneng 146 19.40 S 22.16 E
Nōke 260 34.26 N 135.29 E
Nokha 110 27.35 N 73.29 E
Nokia 26 61.28 N 23.30 E
Nokilalaki, Bulu ∧ 102 1.13 S 120.08 E
Nok Kundi 110 28.48 N 62.46 E
Nokogiri-yama ∧ 258 35.09 N 139.51 E
Nokomis, Sask., Can. 174 51.30 N 105.00 W
Nokomis, Fla., U.S. 210 27.07 N 82.27 W
Nokomis, Ill., U.S. 209 39.18 N 89.18 W
Nokomis Lake ⊜ 174 56.58 N 103.02 W
Nokou 136 14.35 N 14.47 E
Nokrek ∧ 114 25.27 N 90.20 E
Nola, Centraf. 142 3.32 N 16.04 E
Nola, It. 60 40.55 N 14.33 E
Nolan ≃ 212 32.07 N 97.26 W
Nolan Creek ≃ 212 31.02 N 97.26 W
Nolanville 212 31.05 N 97.36 W
Nolay 54 46.57 N 4.38 E
Nole 56 45.15 N 7.35 E
Noli 56 44.12 N 8.26 E
Noli, Capo di ≻ 56 44.12 N 8.25 E
Nolichucky ≃ 182 36.07 N 83.14 W
Nolin ≃ 184 37.13 N 86.15 W
Nolin Lake ⊜1 184 37.20 N 86.10 W
Nolinsk 70 57.33 N 49.57 E
Nomahegan Brook ≃ 266 40.41 N 74.18 W
Nomans Land I 197 41.15 N 70.49 W
Noma Omuramba ≃ 146 18.52 S 20.53 E
Nombre de Dios, Méx. 222 28.41 N 106.05 W
Nombre de Dios, Méx. 224 23.51 N 104.14 W
Nombre de Dios, Pan. 226 9.35 N 79.28 W
Nome 170 64.30 N 165.24 W
Nomény 52 48.54 N 6.14 E
Nomexy 54 48.18 N 6.23 E
Nomgon, Mong. 92 45.27 N 105.05 E
Nomgon, Mong. 92 42.57 N 104.55 E
Nomgon Uul ⛰ 92 43.00 N 104.50 E
Nomini Bay C 198 38.09 N 76.43 W
Nominingue 196 46.24 N 75.02 W
Nominingue, Lac ⊜ 196 46.26 N 74.59 W
Nomozaki 82 32.35 N 129.45 E
Nomtsas 146 24.22 S 16.47 E
Nomura 86 33.22 N 132.38 E
Nonacho Lake ⊜ 166 61.42 N 109.40 W
Nonancourt 46 48.46 N 1.12 E
Nonant-le-Pin 46 48.42 N 0.13 E
Nonantola 58 44.41 N 11.02 E
Nonburg 24 65.34 N 50.32 E
Nonceveux 52 50.28 N 5.44 E
Nondalton 170 60.00 N 154.49 W
Nondwa 144 6.26 S 35.20 E
Nondweni 148 28.11 S 30.49 E
None 56 44.56 N 7.32 E
Nonette ≃ 46 49.12 N 2.24 E
None-yama ∧ 86 33.29 N 134.10 E
Nong'an, Zhg. 79 44.22 N 124.36 E
Nong'an, Zhg. 79 44.25 N 125.10 E
Nong Bua Lamphu 100 17.11 N 102.25 E
Nong Han 100 17.21 N 103.07 E
Nong Hèt 100 19.29 N 103.59 E
Nong Khai 100 17.52 N 102.44 E
Nongoma 148 27.58 S 31.35 E
Nongpoh 110 25.54 N 91.53 E
Nongstoin 110 25.31 N 91.16 E
Nonnenhorn 54 47.34 N 9.36 E
Nonnevitz 50 54.39 N 13.17 E
Nonning 156 32.30 S 136.30 E
Nonnweiler 52 49.36 N 6.58 E
Nonoai 242 27.21 S 52.47 W
Nonoava 222 27.28 N 106.44 W
Nonoc Island I 106 9.51 N 125.37 E
9 de Julho, Túnel ◆5 277b 23.34 S 46.39 W
Nonogasta 242 29.18 S 67.30 W
Nonoichi 84 36.32 N 136.37 E
Nonouti I1 14 0.40 S 174.21 E
Nonsan 88 36.12 N 127.05 E
Nonsuch Bay C 230c 17.03 N 61.42 W
Nonthaburi 100 13.50 N 100.29 E
Nonthaburi □4 259a 13.52 N 100.27 E
Non Thai 100 15.12 N 102.19 E
Nontron 32 45.32 N 0.40 E
Nonvianuk Lake ⊜ 170 59.00 N 155.15 W
Noojee 159 37.55 S 146.00 E
Nookawarra 152 26.19 S 116.52 E
Nooksack 214 48.55 N 122.19 W
Nooksack ≃ 214 48.46 N 122.35 W
Nooksack, Middle Fork ≃ 214 48.50 N 122.08 W
Nooksack, North Fork ≃ 214 48.50 N 122.11 W
Nooksack, South Fork ≃ 214 48.50 N 122.11 W
Noonamah 154 12.38 S 131.04 E
Noonan 188 48.54 N 103.01 W
Noon Hill ∧2 273 42.09 N 71.19 W
Noonkanbah 152 18.30 S 124.50 E
Noorat 159 38.12 S 142.56 E
Noord-Beveland I 48 51.35 N 3.45 E
Noord-Brabant □4 48 51.30 N 5.00 E
Noord-Holland □4 48 52.40 N 4.50 E
Noordhorn 48 53.16 N 6.24 E
Noordoewer 146 28.45 S 17.37 E
Noordoost Polder ◆1 48 52.42 N 5.45 E
Noordpunt ≻ 231s 12.23 N 69.10 W
Noord-Scharwoude 48 52.43 N 4.47 E
Noordwijk aan Zee 48 52.14 N 4.26 E
Noordwijk-Binnen 48 52.13 N 4.27 E
Noordwijkerhout 48 52.15 N 4.30 E
Noordwolde 48 52.54 N 6.09 E
Noormarkku 26 61.35 N 21.52 E
Noorvik 170 66.50 N 161.12 W
Noosaville 156 26.24 S 153.04 E
Nootka Island I 172 49.32 N 126.42 W
Nootka Sound ⊔ 172 49.33 N 126.38 W
Nopaltepec 224 18.17 N 95.59 W
No Point, Point ≻ 266 41.09 N 73.08 W
Nóqui 142 5.51 S 13.25 E
Nora, Sve. 40 59.31 N 15.02 E
Nora, Ind., U.S. 208 39.55 N 86.08 W
Nora ≃ 79 52.26 N 129.58 E
Nor Ačin 74 40.19 N 44.35 E
Norah Head ≻ 160 33.17 S 151.35 E
Nora Islands II 134 16.02 N 39.58 E
Norala 106 6.28 N 124.38 E
Noralee 172 53.59 N 126.26 W
Noranda 180 48.15 N 79.02 W
Noraskög ⛰ 40 59.39 N 14.50 E
Nora Springs 180 43.09 N 93.01 W
Norberg 40 60.04 N 15.56 E
Norberto de la Riestra 242 35.16 S 59.46 W
Norborne 184 39.18 N 93.40 W
Norbottens Län □6 24 66.00 N 20.00 E
Norcan Lake ⊜ 202 45.10 N 76.53 W
Norcatur 188 39.50 N 100.11 W
Norchia ⊥ 60 42.20 N 11.57 E
Norcia 60 42.48 N 13.05 E
Norco 218 33.56 N 117.33 W
Norcott, Mount ∧ 152 32.07 S 121.59 E
Norcross 182 33.57 N 84.13 W
Nord □4 136 9.00 N 13.30 E
Nord □5 46 50.20 N 3.40 E
Nord ◆5 251 48.53 N 2.21 E
Nord, Canal du ≋ 46 47.14 N 2.27 E
Nord, Cap → Nordkapp ≻ 24 71.11 N 25.48 E
Nord, Rivière du ≃ 196 45.31 N 74.20 W
Nordamerika → North America •1 16 45.00 N 100.00 W
Nordanholen 40 60.30 N 14.57 E
Nordausques 46 50.49 N 2.05 E
Nordaustlandet I 12 79.48 N 22.24 E
Nordbögge 253 51.37 N 7.44 E
Nordborg 41 55.03 N 9.45 E
Nordby 41 55.58 N 10.34 E
Nord Dakota → North Dakota □3 188 47.30 N 100.15 W
Norddeich 48 53.37 N 7.09 E
Nordegg 172 52.28 N 116.04 W
Nordegg ≃ 172 52.53 N 115.18 W
Nordeifel, Naturpark ▲ 52 50.40 N 6.20 E
Norden, B.R.D. 48 53.36 N 7.12 E
Norden, Eng., U.K. 252 53.38 N 2.13 W
Norden, Calif., U.S. 216 39.20 N 120.22 W
Nordendorf 52 48.36 N 10.50 E
Nordenham 48 53.29 N 8.28 E
Nordenšel'da, Archipelag II 64 76.45 N 96.00 E
Norderney 48 53.42 N 7.08 E
Norderney I 48 53.42 N 7.10 E
Norderstapel 41 54.21 N 9.14 E
Norderstedt 48 53.43 N 10.00 E
Nordfjord C2 26 61.54 N 5.12 E
Nordfjordeid 26 61.54 N 6.00 E
Nordfold 24 67.46 N 15.12 E
Nordfriesische Inseln → North Frisian Islands II 24 54.50 N 8.12 E
Nordgermersleben 50 52.13 N 11.20 E
Nordhalben 50 50.22 N 11.30 E
Nordhausen 50 51.30 N 10.47 E
Nordheim 212 28.55 N 97.36 W
Nordheim von der Rhön 52 50.28 N 10.11 E
Nordhelle ∧2 253 51.09 N 7.46 E
Nordhorn 48 52.27 N 7.05 E
Nordic Park 268 41.57 N 88.02 W
Nordingrå 26 62.56 N 18.16 E
Nordirland → Northern Ireland □8 28 54.40 N 6.45 W
Nordiyya 122 32.19 N 34.54 E
Nordkanal ≋ 253 51.10 N 6.42 E
Nordkapp ≻ 24 71.11 N 25.48 E
Nordkinnhalvøya ≻1 24 70.55 N 27.45 E
Nordkirchen 48 51.44 N 7.31 E
Nordkjosbotn 24 69.13 N 19.30 E
Nord-Korea → Korea, North □1 88 40.00 N 127.00 E
Nordland 214 48.03 N 122.41 W
Nordland □6 24 67.00 N 14.40 E
Nördliche Dwina → Severnaja Dvina ≃ 24 64.32 N 40.30 E
Nördlicher Teutoburger Wald-Wiehengebirge, Naturpark ▲ 48 52.20 N 8.05 E
Nördliches Eismeer → Arctic Ocean ▾1 16 85.00 N 170.00 E
Nördlingen 52 48.51 N 10.30 E
Nordmaling 26 63.34 N 19.30 E
Nordmark 40 59.50 N 14.06 E
Nordmarka ◆1 26 60.00 N 10.25 E
Nordostrundingen ≻ 16 81.36 N 12.09 W
Nord-Ostsee-Kanal ≋ 30 53.53 N 9.08 E
Nordpfälzer Bergland ⛰ 52 49.40 N 7.40 E
Nordradde ≃ 48 52.43 N 7.17 E
Nordreisa 24 69.46 N 21.03 E
Nordre Strømfjord C2 166 67.50 N 52.00 W
Nordrhein-Westfalen □3 30 51.30 N 7.30 E
Nordsee → North Sea ▾2 22 55.20 N 3.00 E
Nordstemmen 48 52.09 N 9.46 E
Nordstrand I 41 54.30 N 8.53 E
Nordstrandischmoor I 41 54.33 N 8.48 E
Nord-Trøndelag □6 24 64.25 N 12.00 E
Nordvik 64 74.02 N 111.32 E
Nordwalde 48 52.05 N 7.28 E
Nordwest-Kap → North West Cape ≻ 152 21.45 S 114.10 E
Nore 26 60.10 N 9.01 E
Nore ≃ 28 52.25 N 6.58 W
Noremberg → Nürnberg 52 49.27 N 11.04 E
Nörenberg → Ińsko 30 53.27 N 15.33 E
Norf 253 51.09 N 6.43 E
Norfbach ≃ 253 51.11 N 6.44 E
Norfolk, Conn., U.S. 197 41.59 N 73.12 W
Norfolk, Mass., U.S. 273 42.07 N 71.19 W
Norfolk, Nebr., U.S. 188 42.02 N 97.25 W
Norfolk, Va., U.S. 198 36.40 N 76.14 W
Norfolk □6, Ont., Can. 204 42.48 N 80.25 W
Norfolk □6, Eng., U.K. 44 52.35 N 1.00 E
Norfolk □6, Mass., U.S. 197 42.15 N 71.10 W
Norfolk Broads ◆1 44 52.40 N 1.30 E
Norfolk-Insel → Norfolk Island □2 164c 29.02 S 167.57 E
Norfolk Island □2 14
 164c 29.02 S 167.57 E
Norfolk Island Aerodome ⊠ 164c 29.03 S 167.56 E
Norfolk Island Ridge ✧3 4 29.00 S 167.00 E
Norfolk Island Trough ✧1 14 30.00 S 165.00 E
Norfolk Naval Base ■ 198 36.57 N 76.18 W
Norfolk Naval Shipyard ■ 198 36.49 N 76.18 W
Norfolk Regional Airport ⊠ 198 36.54 N 76.12 W
Norfolk Ridge ✧3 14 29.00 S 167.00 E
Norfork Lake ⊜1 184 36.25 N 92.10 W
Norg 48 53.04 N 6.27 E
Norge 198 37.22 N 76.46 W
Norge → Norway □1 24 62.00 N 10.00 E
Norham 42 55.43 N 2.10 W
Norheimsund 26 60.22 N 6.08 E
Norikura-dake ∧ 84 36.06 N 137.33 E
Noril'sk 64 69.20 N 88.06 E
Noring, Gunong ∧ 104 5.24 N 101.44 E
Norland, Ont., Can. 202 44.43 N 78.49 W
Norland, Fla., U.S. 210 25.57 N 80.12 W
Norlane 159 38.06 S 144.21 E
Norley 252 53.15 N 2.39 W
Norlina 182 36.27 N 78.12 W
Norma, It. 60 41.35 N 12.58 E
Norma, N.J., U.S. 198 39.29 N 75.05 W
Normal, Ala., U.S. 184 34.47 N 86.34 W
Normal, Ill., U.S. 206 40.31 N 88.59 W
Norman, Ark., U.S. 184 34.27 N 93.41 W
Norman, Ind., U.S. 208 38.57 N 86.16 W
Norman, Okla., U.S. 186 35.13 N 97.26 W
Norman ≃ 156 17.28 S 140.49 E
Norman, Lake ⊜1 182 35.35 N 80.55 W
Normanby, Austl. 161a 27.28 S 153.01 E
Normanby, N.Z. 162 39.32 S 174.17 E
Normanby ≃ 154 14.25 S 144.08 E
Normanby Island I 154 10.05 S 151.05 E
Norman Creek C 274b 39.18 N 76.25 W
Normandie □9 32 49.00 N 0.05 W
Normandien 148 27.57 S 29.47 E
Normandy → Normandie □9 32 49.00 N 0.05 W
Normandy Heights 274b 39.17 N 76.48 W
Normandy Park 214 47.27 N 122.21 W
Normangee 212 31.02 N 96.07 W
Normanhurst 264a 33.43 S 151.06 E
Normanhurst, Mount ∧ 152 25.04 S 122.32 E
Norman Island I 230m 18.20 N 64.37 W
Normannische Inseln → Channel Islands II 28 49.20 N 2.20 W
Norman Park 182 31.16 N 83.38 W
Normans Kill ≃ 200 42.36 N 73.44 W
Normanton, Austl. 156 17.40 S 141.05 E
Normanton, Eng., U.K. 42 53.41 N 1.27 W
Normanville 158b 35.27 S 138.19 E
Norman Wells 170 65.17 N 126.51 W
Nor Marsh ≡ 250 51.24 N 0.38 E
Nornalup 152 35.00 S 116.49 E
Norogachic 222 27.15 N 107.07 W
Noroton ≃ 266 41.03 N 73.31 W
Noroton Point ≻ 266 41.03 N 73.26 W
Norovlin 78 48.44 N 112.59 E
Noroy-le-Bourg 54 47.37 N 6.18 E
Norphlet 184 33.19 N 92.40 W
Norquay 174 51.53 N 102.05 W
Ñorquincó 244 41.51 S 70.54 W
Norra Björkfjärden C 40 59.27 N 17.28 E
Norrahammar 26 57.42 N 14.06 E
Norra Hörken ⊜ 40 60.04 N 14.53 E
Norra Kvarken (Merenkurkku) ⊔ 26 63.36 N 20.43 E
Norra Kvills Nationalpark ▲ 26 57.44 N 15.37 E
Norrälgen ⊜ 40 59.50 N 14.34 E
Norra Rörum 41 56.01 N 13.30 E
Norra Storfjället ∧ 24 65.52 N 15.18 E
Norrboda 40 60.28 N 18.25 E
Norrbotten □9 26 66.45 N 23.00 E
Nørre Åby 41 55.27 N 9.54 E
Nørre Alslev 41 54.54 N 11.54 E
Nørre Broby 41 55.15 N 10.14 E
Nørre Nærå 41 55.34 N 10.17 E
Norrent-Fontes 46 50.35 N 2.24 E
Nørre Snede 41 55.58 N 9.25 E
Nørresundby 26 57.04 N 9.55 E
Nørre Vejrup 41 55.31 N 8.47 E
Norrfjärden 26 65.25 N 21.27 E
Norridge 206 41.57 N 87.49 W
Norridgewock 178 44.43 N 69.48 W
Norris 182 36.12 N 84.04 W
Norris, Lake ⊜ 210 28.57 N 81.32 W
Norris Arm 176 49.05 N 55.15 W
Norris Bridge ◆5 198 37.37 N 76.26 W
Norris City 184 37.59 N 88.20 W
Norrish Creek ≃ 214 49.10 N 122.08 W
Norris Lake ⊜1 182 36.20 N 83.55 W
Norris Point 176 49.31 N 57.53 W
Norristown 198 40.07 N 75.21 W
Norrköping 40 58.36 N 16.11 E
Norroway Brook ≃ 273 42.11 N 71.03 W
Norrskedika 40 60.17 N 18.17 E
Norrsundet 26 60.56 N 17.08 E
Norrtälje 40 59.46 N 18.42 E
Norrtäljeviken C 40 59.47 N 18.53 E
Norseman 152 32.12 S 121.46 E
Norsewood 162 40.04 S 176.13 E
Norsjå ⊜ 26 59.18 N 9.20 E
Norsjö 26 64.55 N 19.29 E
Norsk 79 52.20 N 129.55 E
Norsminde 41 56.01 N 10.16 E
Norte □4 138 26.50 N 11.15 W
Norte, Cabo ≻, Bra. 240 1.40 N 49.55 W
Norte, Cabo ≻, Chile 164z 27.03 S 109.24 W
Norte, Canal do ⊔ 240 0.30 N 50.30 W
Norte, Cayo I 230m 18.20 N 65.15 W
Norte, Estación del ◆5, Esp. 256a 40.25 N 3.43 W
Norte, Estación del ◆5, Esp. 256d 41.24 N 2.02 E
Norte, Mar del → North Sea ▾2 22 55.20 N 3.00 E
Norte, Punta ≻, Arg. 242 36.17 S 56.47 W
Norte, Punta ≻, Arg. 244 42.04 S 63.45 W
Norte, Serra do ⛰1 238 11.20 S 59.00 W
Norte Cabo → Nordkapp •2 24 71.11 N 25.48 E
Norte de Santander □5 236 8.00 N 73.00 W
Nortelândia 238 14.25 S 56.48 W
Nörten-Hardenberg 48 51.38 N 9.56 E
North, S.C., U.S. 182 33.37 N 81.06 W
North, Va., U.S. 198 37.27 N 76.25 W
North ≃, Newf., Can. 166 57.30 N 62.05 W
North ≃, Ont., Can. 202 44.44 N 79.39 W
North ≃, Ala., U.S. 184 33.15 N 87.30 W
North ≃, Iowa, U.S. 184 41.31 N 93.27 W
North ≃, Mass., U.S. 273 42.10 N 70.43 W
North ≃, Mo., U.S. 209 39.52 N 91.27 W
North ≃, Wash., U.S. 214 46.45 N 123.53 W
North, Cape ≻ 18 53.58 S 37.44 W
North, Cape •2 176 47.02 N 60.25 W
North Abington 197 42.08 N 70.57 W
North Adams, Mass., U.S. 197 42.42 N 73.07 W
North Adams, Mich., U.S. 206 41.58 N 84.32 W
North Albany 192 44.39 N 123.06 W
Northallerton 42 54.20 N 1.26 W
Northam, Austl. 158a 31.39 S 116.40 E
Northam, S. Afr. 146 25.03 S 27.11 E
Northam, Eng., U.K. 44 51.02 N 4.12 W
North America •1 4
 16 45.00 N 100.00 W
North American Basin ✧1 8 31.00 N 62.00 W
North Amherst 197 42.25 N 72.32 W
North Amityville 266 40.42 N 73.26 W
Northampton, Austl. 152 28.21 S 114.37 E
Northampton, Eng., U.K. 44 52.14 N 0.54 W
Northampton, Mass., U.S. 197 42.19 N 72.38 W
Northampton, N.Y., U.S. 197 40.54 N 72.40 W
Northampton, Pa., U.S. 198 40.41 N 75.30 W
Northampton □6, N.C., U.S. 198 36.28 N 77.21 W
Northampton □6, Pa., U.S. 200 40.45 N 75.18 W
Northampton □6, Va., U.S. 198 37.20 N 75.50 W
Northamptonshire □6 44 52.20 N 0.50 W
North Andaman I 100 13.15 N 92.55 E
North Andover 197 42.42 N 71.08 W
North Andrews Gardens 210 26.12 N 80.07 W
North Anna ≃ 182 37.48 N 77.25 W
North Anson 178 44.52 N 69.54 W
North Apollo 204 40.35 N 79.34 W
North Arlington 266 40.47 N 74.08 W
North Arm ≃1 214 49.12 N 123.10 W
North Atlanta 182 33.51 N 84.21 W
North Attleboro 197 41.59 N 71.20 W
North Attleboro National Fish Hatchery ▲ 273 42.00 N 71.17 W
North Auburn 264a 33.50 S 151.02 E
North Augusta 182 33.30 N 81.58 W
North Aulatsivik Island I 166 59.50 N 64.00 W
North Aurora 206 41.48 N 88.20 W
Northaw 250 51.42 N 0.09 W
North Babylon 266 40.44 N 73.19 W
North Balabac Strait ⊔ 106 8.10 N 117.04 E
North Baltimore 206 41.11 N 83.41 W
North Balwyn 264b 37.48 S 145.05 E
North Bannister 158a 32.35 S 116.26 E
North Barrackpore 116 22.46 N 88.22 E
North Bass Island I 204 41.43 N 82.49 W
North Battleford 174 52.47 N 108.17 W
North Bay, Ont., Can. 180 46.19 N 79.28 W
North Bay, N.Y., U.S. 200 43.14 N 75.45 W
North Bay, Wis., U.S. 206 42.46 N 87.47 W
North Bay C, Ont., Can. 202 44.53 N 79.48 W
North Bay C, Wash., U.S. 214 46.59 N 124.04 W
North Bay Village 210 25.51 N 80.08 W
North Beach 158a 31.52 S 115.45 E
North Beach ◆8 272 37.48 N 122.25 W
North Belle Vernon 204 40.08 N 79.52 W
North Bellmore 266 40.41 N 73.32 W
North Bend, B.C., Can. 172 49.53 N 121.27 W
North Bend, Nebr., U.S. 188 41.28 N 96.47 W
North Bend, Ohio, U.S. 208 39.09 N 84.45 W
North Bend, Oreg., U.S. 192 43.24 N 124.14 W
North Bend, Pa., U.S. 204 41.21 N 77.42 W
North Bend, Wash., U.S. 214 47.30 N 121.47 W

Symbols in the index entries represent the broad categories identified in the key at the right. Symbols with superior numbers (⛰²) identify subcategories (see complete key on page *I* · 26).

Kartensymbole in dem Registerverzeichnis stellen die rechts in Schlüssel erklärten Kategorien dar. Symbole mit hochgestellten Ziffern (⛰²) bezeichnen Unterabteilungen einer Kategorie (vgl. vollständiger Schlüssel auf Seite *I* · 26).

Los símbolos incluídos en el texto del índice representan las grandes categorías identificadas con la clave a la derecha. Los símbolos con numeros en su parte superior (⛰²) identifican las subcategorías (véase la clave completa en la página *I* · 26).

Les symboles de l'index représentent les catégories indiquées dans la légende à droite. Les symboles suivis d'un indice (⛰²) représentent des sous-catégories (voir légende complète à la page *I* · 26).

Os símbolos incluídos no texto do índice representam as grandes categorias identificadas com a chave à direita. Os símbolos com números em sua parte superior (⛰²) identificam as subcategorias (veja-se a chave completa à página *I* · 26).

Symbol	English	Deutsch	Español	Français	Português
∧	Mountain	Berg	Montaña	Montagne	Montanha
⛰	Mountains	Berge	Montañas	Montagnes	Montanhas
)(	Pass	Pass	Paso	Col	Passo
∨	Valley, Canyon	Tal, Cañon	Valle, Cañón	Vallée, Canyon	Vale, Canhão
≚	Plain	Ebene	Llano	Plaine	Planície
≻	Cape	Kap	Cabo	Cap	Cabo
I	Island	Insel	Isla	Île	Ilha
II	Islands	Inseln	Islas	Îles	Ilhas
•	Other Topographic Features	Andere Topographische Objekte	Otros Elementos Topográficos	Autres données topographiques	Outros Elementos Topográficos

ESPAÑOL

Nombre	Página	Lat.°′	Long.°′ W=Oeste
North Benfleet	250	51.35 N	0.32 E
North Bengal Plains ⌣	114	26.20 N	88.30 E
North Bennington	178	42.56 N	73.15 W
North Bergen	266	40.48 N	74.01 W
North Berwick, Scot., U.K.	42	56.04 N	2.44 W
North Berwick, Maine, U.S.	178	43.17 N	70.45 W
North Bethlehem	200	42.40 N	73.50 W
North Bihar Plains ⌣	114	26.20 N	86.00 E
North Billerica	197	42.35 N	71.17 W
North Bloomfield	204	41.28 N	80.52 W
North Boggy Creek ≃	186	34.23 N	96.04 W
North Bonneville	214	45.39 N	121.57 W
Northborough	197	42.19 N	71.39 W
North Bosque ≃	186	31.40 N	97.24 W
North Boston	200	42.41 N	78.47 W
North Bourke	156	30.03 S	145.57 E
North Box Hill	264b	37.48 S	145.07 E
North Braddock	269b	40.24 N	79.52 W
North Branch, Mich., U.S.	180	43.14 N	83.12 W
North Branch, Minn., U.S.	180	45.31 N	92.58 W
North Branch, N.J., U.S.	200	40.36 N	74.41 W
North Branch, N.J., U.S.	266	40.35 N	74.41 W
North Branch Canal ≍	214	47.12 N	120.40 W
North Branford	197	41.20 N	72.46 W
North Breakers ⊹[2]	164g	28.14 N	177.25 W
Northbridge, Austl.	264a	33.49 S	151.13 E
Northbridge, Mass., U.S.	197	42.09 N	71.39 W
North Bristol	204	41.24 N	80.52 W
Northbrook, Ont., Can.	202	44.44 N	77.10 W
Northbrook, Ill., U.S.	206	42.08 N	87.50 W
Northbrook, Pa., U.S.	275	39.55 N	75.41 W
North Brookfield, Mass., U.S.	197	42.16 N	72.05 W
North Brookfield, N.Y., U.S.	200	42.51 N	75.24 W
North Brunswick	198	40.28 N	74.28 W
North Caicos I	228	21.56 N	71.59 W
North Caldwell	266	40.52 N	74.16 W
North Canton, Conn., U.S.	197	41.54 N	72.54 W
North Canton, Ga., U.S.	182	34.15 N	84.29 W
North Canton, Ohio, U.S.	204	40.53 N	81.24 W
North Cape	206	42.47 N	88.05 W
North Cape ≻, N.Z.	162	34.25 S	173.02 E
North Cape → Nordkapp ≻, Nor.	24	71.11 N	25.48 E
North Cape ≻, Pap. N. Gui.	154	2.32 S	150.49 E
North Cape May	198	38.59 N	74.57 W
North Cape Rise ⊹[3]	14	32.00 S	173.00 E
North Captiva Island I	210	26.35 N	82.13 W
North Caribou Lake ⊜	166	52.50 N	90.40 W
North Carlsbad	218	33.11 N	117.21 W
North Carolina □[3]	168		
	182	35.30 N	80.00 W
North Carver	197	41.55 N	70.48 W
North Cascades National Park ♠, Wash., U.S.	172	48.45 N	121.14 W
North Cascades National Park ♠, Wash., U.S.	214	48.30 N	121.00 W
North Castor ≃	202	45.16 N	75.24 W
North Catasauqua	198	40.40 N	75.29 W
North Cemetery ◆	259f	14.38 N	120.59 E
North-Central □[3]	140	11.00 N	7.45 E
North Chagrin Reservation ♠	269a	41.34 N	81.26 W
North Channel Ɯ, Ont., Can.	180	46.02 N	82.50 W
North Channel Ɯ, Ont., Can.	202	44.10 N	76.45 W
North Channel Ɯ, U.K.	42	55.10 N	5.40 W
North Channel ≃[1]	271	42.38 N	82.40 W
North Charleroi	204	40.09 N	79.54 W
North Charleston	182	32.53 N	80.00 W
North Chatham	200	42.29 N	73.38 W
North Chelmsford	197	42.38 N	71.23 W
North Chicago	206	42.20 N	87.51 W
North Chili	200	43.06 N	77.45 W
Northchurch	250	51.46 N	0.36 W
North City	214	47.30 N	121.47 W
North Cleveland	212	30.21 N	95.06 W
Northcliff ◆[8]	263d	26.09 S	27.58 E
Northcliffe	152	34.36 S	116.07 E
North Clymer	204	42.04 N	79.34 W
North Cohasset	273	42.16 N	70.51 W
North Cohocton	200	42.34 N	77.28 W
North College Hill	208	39.12 N	84.32 W
North Collins	200	42.36 N	78.56 W
North Concho ≃	186	31.27 N	100.25 W
North Conway	178	44.03 N	71.08 W
Northcote	264b	37.46 S	145.00 E
North Cray ◆[8]	250	51.26 N	0.08 E
North Creek	178	43.42 N	73.59 W
North Creek ≃	268	41.33 N	87.37 W
Northcrest	212	31.38 N	97.06 W
North Crosswicks	275	40.10 N	74.39 W
North Dakota □[3]	168		
	188	47.30 N	100.15 W
North Dandalup	158a	32.31 S	115.58 E
North Dartmouth	197	41.38 N	70.59 W
North Dighton	197	41.52 N	71.08 W
North Dorset Downs ΛΛ[1]	44	50.47 N	2.30 W
North Downs ΛΛ[1]	44	51.20 N	0.10 E
North Dum-Dum	116	22.38 N	88.23 E
North East, Md., U.S.	178	39.36 N	75.56 W
North East, Pa., U.S.	204	42.13 N	79.50 W
North East □[5]	146	21.00 S	27.30 E
Northeast Cape	170	63.18 N	168.42 W
Northeast Cape ≻	170	63.17 N	168.45 W
Northeast Cape Fear ≃	182	34.11 N	77.57 W
Northeast Creek ≃	274b	39.18 N	76.29 W
North-Eastern □[3]	136	11.00 N	12.00 E
North Eastern □[4]	144	1.00 N	40.15 E
Northeastern University ɤ[2]	273	42.20 N	71.05 W
North Eastham	197	41.52 N	69.59 W
Northeast Harbor	178	44.18 N	68.17 W
Northeast Henrietta	200	43.04 N	77.36 W
Northeast Islands II	165c	7.36 N	151.57 E
North Easton	197	42.04 N	71.06 W
Northeast Pass Ɯ	165c	7.30 N	151.59 E
Northeast Point ≻, Ba.	228	22.43 N	73.50 W
Northeast Point ≻, Ba.	228	21.20 N	73.01 W
North East Point ≻, Gilb. Is.	164o	1.57 N	157.16 W
Northeast Point ≻, St. Vin.	231h	13.03 N	61.13 W
Northeast Providence Channel Ɯ	228	25.40 N	77.09 W
North Edwards	218	35.01 N	117.44 W
North Egremont	197	42.12 N	73.26 W
Northeim	48	51.42 N	10.00 E
North Elkhorn Creek ≃	208	38.13 N	84.48 W
North Elm Creek ≃	212	30.53 N	97.00 W
North English	180	41.31 N	92.05 W
Northern □[4], Ghana	140	9.30 N	1.00 W
Northern □[4], Malawi	144	11.00 S	34.00 E
Northern □[4], S.L.	140	9.15 N	11.45 W

FRANÇAIS

Nom	Page	Lat.°′	Long.°′ W=Ouest
Northern □[4], Zam.	144	11.00 S	31.00 E
Northern □[5]	154	9.00 S	148.30 E
Northern Aire Estates	268	42.08 N	88.02 W
Northern Arm	176	49.10 N	55.23 W
Northern Cheyenne Indian Reservation ◆[4]	192	45.31 N	106.45 W
Northern Circārs ΛΛ[2]	112	18.00 N	83.15 E
Northern Division □[5], Fiji	165g	16.30 S	179.30 E
Northern Division □[5], N. Heb.	165f	14.30 S	167.00 E
Northern Dvina → Severnaja Dvina ≃	24	64.32 N	40.30 E
Northern Indian Lake ⊜	166	57.20 N	97.20 W
Northern Ireland □[8]	28	54.40 N	6.45 W
Northern Light Lake ⊜	180	48.15 N	90.38 W
Northern Territory □[8]	150	20.00 S	134.00 E
North Esk ≃	42	55.54 N	3.04 W
North Essendon	264b	37.45 S	144.54 E
North Evans	200	42.42 N	78.56 W
Northey Island I	250	51.44 N	0.43 E
North Fabius ≃	184	39.54 N	91.30 W
North Fairfield	204	41.06 N	82.37 W
North Fair Oaks	272	37.28 N	122.12 W
North Falmouth	197	41.39 N	70.37 W
Northfield, B.C., Can.	214	49.11 N	123.59 W
Northfield, Conn., U.S.	197	41.42 N	73.07 W
Northfield, Ill., U.S.	268	42.06 N	87.46 W
Northfield, Mass., U.S.	197	42.42 N	72.27 W
Northfield, Minn., U.S.	180	44.27 N	93.09 W
Northfield, N.J., U.S.	198	39.22 N	74.33 W
Northfield, Ohio, U.S.	204	41.20 N	81.32 W
Northfield, Vt., U.S.	178	44.09 N	72.40 W
Northfield Airport ⊠	269a	41.17 N	81.31 W
Northfield Center	269a	41.19 N	81.32 W
Northfield Park Race Track ♠	269a	41.21 N	81.31 W
Northfield Village	269a	41.21 N	81.31 W
Northfield Woods	268	42.05 N	87.52 W
North Fiji Basin ⊹[1]	14	17.00 S	173.00 E
North Fillmore	218	34.24 N	118.56 W
North Fitzroy	264b	37.47 S	144.59 E
Northfleet	44	51.27 N	0.21 E
North Flinders Range ΛΛ	156	31.00 S	139.00 E
North Fond du Lac	180	43.38 N	88.28 W
Northford	197	41.24 N	72.48 W
North Foreland ≻	44	51.23 N	1.27 E
North Fork	216	37.14 N	119.31 W
North Fork ≃	184	36.13 N	92.17 W
North Fork Lake ⊜[1]	216	38.56 N	121.00 W
North Fork Reservoir ⊜[1]	214	45.13 N	122.15 W
North Fork Village	208	39.21 N	83.02 W
North Fort Myers	210	26.40 N	81.54 W
North Freedom	180	43.27 N	89.52 W
North Frisian Islands II	24	54.50 N	8.12 E
Northgate	206	43.01 N	85.36 W
Northgate ◆[9]	272	38.00 N	122.33 W
North Georgetown	204	40.51 N	80.59 W
North Germiston	263d	26.14 S	28.09 E
North Glanford	202	43.11 N	79.54 W
North Glen Ellyn	268	41.54 N	88.04 W
North Gower	202	45.08 N	75.43 W
North Grafton	197	42.14 N	71.42 W
North Granby	197	41.59 N	72.50 W
North Grand Island Bridge ◆[5]	274a	43.04 N	78.59 W
North Great River	266	40.45 N	73.11 W
North Grosvenordale	197	41.59 N	71.54 W
North Grove	206	40.37 N	85.58 W
North Hadley	197	42.23 N	72.36 W
North Haledon	266	40.58 N	74.11 W
North Hampton	208	39.59 N	83.56 W
North Hanover	273	42.09 N	70.52 W
North Haven	197	41.23 N	72.52 W
North Havre	192	48.36 N	109.41 W
North Hawaiian Seamount Range ⊹[3]	6	29.00 N	163.00 W
North Head ≻	264a	33.49 S	151.18 E
North Henik Lake ⊜	166	61.45 N	97.40 W
North Hero	178	44.49 N	73.18 W
North Highlands	216	38.40 N	121.23 W
North Hill	44	50.34 N	4.25 W
North Hills, Del., U.S.	275	39.46 N	75.30 W
North Hills, Ill., U.S.	268	42.18 N	88.01 W
North Hills, N.Y., U.S.	266	40.47 N	73.41 W
North Hinksey	44	51.45 N	1.16 W
North Hogan Creek ≃	208	39.03 N	84.54 W
North Hollywood ◆[8]	270	34.10 N	118.23 W
North Holmwood	250	51.13 N	0.20 W
North Honcut Creek ≃	216	39.19 N	121.36 W
North Hoosick	200	42.56 N	73.21 W
North Hornell	200	42.21 N	77.40 W
North Horr	144	3.19 N	37.04 E
North Houston	212	29.54 N	95.31 W
North Hudson	180	44.59 N	92.46 W
North Industry	204	40.45 N	81.22 W
North Irwin	269b	40.20 N	79.43 W
North Island I, Bhārat	112	10.08 N	72.20 E
North Island I, Kenya	144	4.04 N	36.03 E
North Island I, N.Z.	162	39.00 S	176.00 E
North Islet I	106	8.56 N	120.02 E
North Jackson	204	41.06 N	80.52 W
North Java	200	42.41 N	78.20 W
North Judson	206	41.13 N	86.46 W
North Kingstown	197	41.34 N	71.27 W
North Kingsville	204	41.54 N	80.42 W
North Knife Lake ⊜	166	58.05 N	97.05 W
North Knob Λ	200	41.43 N	75.33 W
North Korea → Korea, North □[1]	88	40.00 N	127.00 E
Northlake, Ill., U.S.	268	41.55 N	87.54 W
North Lake, Wis., U.S.	206	43.10 N	88.22 W
North Lake ⊜, N.Y., U.S.	266	41.09 N	73.41 W
North Lake ⊜, Tex., U.S.	212	32.57 N	96.58 W
North Lakhimpur	110	27.14 N	94.07 E
Northland ◆[9]	271	42.27 N	83.13 W
North Landing ≃	198	36.31 N	76.01 W
North Laramie ≃	188	42.08 N	104.56 W
North Las Vegas	194	36.12 N	115.07 W
North La Veta Pass)(	190	37.37 N	105.11 W
North Lawrence	204	40.51 N	81.38 W
Northleach	44	51.51 N	1.50 W
North Lewisburg	206	40.13 N	83.33 W
North Liberty	206	41.32 N	86.26 W
North Lima	204	40.57 N	80.40 W
North Lindenhurst	266	40.43 N	73.23 W
North Line Island I	266	40.38 N	73.29 W
Northline Terrace	212	29.55 N	95.25 W
North Little Rock	184	34.46 N	92.14 W
North Llano ≃	186	30.30 N	99.46 W
North Logan	192	41.45 N	111.49 W
North Loma Linda	218	34.02 N	117.05 W
North Loon Mountain Λ	192	45.07 N	115.52 W
North Loup	188	41.30 N	98.46 W
North Loup ≃	188	41.17 N	98.23 W
North MacMillan ≃	170	63.03 N	133.18 W
North Madagascar Basin ⊹[1]	10	14.00 S	44.00 E
North Madison	204	41.48 N	81.03 W
North Magnetic Pole ◆	16	76.02 N	101.00 W
North Malosmadulu Atoll I[1]	112	5.35 N	72.55 E

PORTUGUÊS

Nome	Página	Lat.°′	Long.°′ W=Oeste
North Mamm Peak Λ	190	39.23 N	107.52 W
North Manchester	206	41.00 N	85.46 W
North Manitou Island I	180	45.06 N	86.01 W
North Mankato	180	44.10 N	94.00 W
North Manly	264a	33.46 S	151.16 E
North Maroota	160	33.29 S	150.56 E
North Marshfield	273	42.09 N	70.47 W
North Massapequa	266	40.43 N	73.28 W
Northmead, Austl.	264a	33.47 S	151.00 E
Northmead, S. Afr.	263d	26.10 S	28.20 E
North Merrick	266	40.41 N	73.34 W
North Miami	210	25.54 N	80.11 W
North Miami Beach	210	25.56 N	80.09 W
North Middleboro	197	41.53 N	70.55 W
North Milk ≃	192	49.08 N	112.23 W
North Mokelumne ≃	216	38.08 N	121.35 W
North Moose Lake ⊜	174	54.08 N	100.13 W
North Moreau Creek ≃	184	38.30 N	92.18 W
North Muskegon	206	43.15 N	86.17 W
North Myrtle Beach	182	33.48 N	78.42 W
North Nahanni ≃	170	62.05 N	124.30 W
North Naples	210	26.12 N	81.48 W
North Narrabeen	264a	33.42 S	151.18 E
North Nemah ≃	214	46.30 N	123.53 W
North New Hyde Park	266	40.45 N	73.41 W
North New River Canal ≍	210	26.05 N	80.12 W
North Niles	206	41.52 N	86.15 W
North Ninepin Island I	261d	22.16 N	114.20 E
North Norwich	200	42.37 N	75.32 W
North Oaks	212	30.22 N	97.41 W
North Ockendon ◆[8]	250	51.32 N	0.18 E
North Ogden	190	41.18 N	112.00 W
North Olmsted	204	41.25 N	81.56 W
Northolt Aerodrome ⊠	250	51.33 N	0.23 W
Northome	180	47.52 N	94.17 W
Northop	252	53.12 N	3.08 W
North Ore Creek ≃	271	42.43 N	83.47 W
North Orwell	200	41.55 N	76.19 W
Northowram	252	53.44 N	1.50 W
North Oxford	197	42.10 N	71.53 W
North Palisade Λ	194	37.06 N	118.31 W
North Palm Beach	210	26.49 N	80.04 W
North Para ≃	158b	34.36 S	138.45 E
North Park	206	42.20 N	89.02 W
North Park ◆[8]	268	41.59 N	87.43 W
North Park ♠	269b	40.36 N	80.00 W
North Park Lake ⊜	269b	40.36 N	80.00 W
North Parramatta	264a	33.48 S	151.00 E
North Pass Ɯ	165c	7.41 N	151.48 E
North Patchogue	266	40.47 N	73.01 W
North Peak Λ, Alaska, U.S.	170	62.34 N	162.23 W
North Peak Λ, Calif., U.S.	272	37.33 N	122.28 W
North Pease ≃	186	34.15 N	100.07 W
North Pelham, N.H., U.S.	273	42.47 N	71.21 W
North Pelham, N.Y., U.S.	266	40.55 N	73.48 W
North Pembroke	197	42.05 N	70.47 W
North Pender Island I	214	48.49 N	123.17 W
North Perry	204	41.47 N	81.07 W
North Petherton	44	51.06 N	3.01 W
North Philadelphia ◆[8]	275	39.58 N	75.09 W
North Philadelphia Airport ⊠	275	40.05 N	75.01 W
North Pine Grove	204	41.24 N	79.13 W
North Piney Creek ≃	190	42.31 N	110.05 W
North Pitcher	200	42.37 N	75.49 W
North Plainfield	200	40.37 N	74.25 W
North Plains	214	45.36 N	123.00 W
North Platte	188	41.08 N	100.46 W
North Platte ≃	168	41.15 N	100.45 W
North Pleasureville	208	38.22 N	85.07 W
North Plympton	273	41.59 N	70.48 W
North Point, H.K.	261d	22.17 N	114.12 E
Northpoint, Pa., U.S.	204	40.54 N	79.08 W
North Point ◆[8]	261d	22.17 N	114.11 E
North Point ≻, Barb.	231g	13.20 N	59.36 W
North Point ≻, P.E.I., Can.	176	47.05 N	64.00 W
North Point ≻, Mich., U.S.	180	45.02 N	83.16 W
North Pole	170	64.40 N	147.07 W
North Pole ◆	16	90.00 N	0.00
North Popo Aggie ≃	192	42.51 N	108.42 W
Northport, Ala., U.S.	184	33.14 N	87.35 W
North Port, Fla., U.S.	210	27.01 N	82.10 W
Northport, Mich., U.S.	180	45.08 N	85.37 W
Northport, N.Y., U.S.	200	40.53 N	73.20 W
Northport, Wash., U.S.	192	48.55 N	117.48 W
North Portal	174	49.00 N	102.33 W
Northport Harbor C	266	40.53 N	73.22 W
North Powder	192	45.13 N	117.55 W
North Pownal	197	42.48 N	73.16 W
North Prairie	206	42.56 N	88.24 W
North Providence	197	41.50 N	71.25 W
North Puyallup	214	47.12 N	122.17 W
North Queensferry	42	56.01 N	3.25 W
North Quincy	209	39.58 N	91.24 W
North Raisin ≃	196	45.09 N	74.43 W
North Ram ≃	172	52.16 N	115.38 W
North Randall	269a	41.27 N	81.32 W
North Rat Island Ridge ⊹[3]	12	54.00 N	177.00 E
North Reading	197	42.34 N	71.05 W
North Reservoir ⊜[1]	273	42.28 N	71.07 W
North Richland Hills	212	32.51 N	97.12 W
North Richmond	272	37.57 N	122.22 W
Northridge, Ohio, U.S.	208	39.59 N	83.47 W
Northridge, Ohio, U.S.	208	39.49 N	84.12 W
Northridge ◆[8]	270	34.14 N	118.33 W
Northridge Fashion Center ◆[9]	270	34.13 N	118.33 W
North Ridge Village	208	39.57 N	86.09 W
North Ridgeville	204	41.23 N	82.01 W
North Rim	190	36.12 N	112.03 W
North River C	198	37.25 N	76.25 W
North Riverside	268	41.51 N	87.49 W
North Robinson	204	40.48 N	82.51 W
North Rocks	264a	33.46 S	151.02 E
North Ronaldsay I	28	59.25 N	2.30 W
North Rose	200	43.11 N	76.54 W
North Royalton	204	41.19 N	81.44 W
North Rustico	176	46.27 N	63.19 W
North Ryde	264a	33.48 S	151.07 E
North Salem	204	40.09 N	81.33 W
North Salt Lake	190	40.50 N	111.55 W
North San Juan	216	39.22 N	121.06 W
North Santiam ≃	192	44.41 N	123.00 W
North Saskatchewan ≃	166	53.15 N	105.06 W
North Saugeen ≃	202	44.19 N	81.17 W
North Scituate, Mass., U.S.	197	42.14 N	70.47 W
North Scituate, R.I., U.S.	197	41.50 N	71.35 W
North Sea ⍑[2]	22	55.20 N	3.00 E
North Seaton Colliery	42	55.11 N	1.32 W
North Seven ≃	186	32.35 N	104.23 W
North Shafter	216	35.31 N	119.18 W
Norths Highland ΛΛ[1]	9	66.40 S	126.00 E
North Shoal Lake ⊜	174	50.29 N	97.40 W
North Shore	206	42.16 N	88.23 W
Northshore Center ◆[9]	273	42.32 N	70.57 W
North Shore Channel ≍	268	42.05 N	87.41 W
North Shores	206	41.50 N	83.25 W
North Shoshone Peak Λ	194	39.09 N	117.29 W
North Siberian Lowland → Severo-Sibirskaja Nizmennost' ⌣	64	73.00 N	100.00 E
Northside	164h	2.47 S	171.43 W
North Side ◆[8]	269b	40.28 N	80.01 W
North Skunk ≃	184	41.15 N	92.02 W
North Somercotes	42	53.28 N	0.08 E
North Sound Ɯ	28	59.18 N	2.45 W
North Spicer Island I	166	68.30 N	78.55 W
North Spirit Lake ⊜	174	52.30 N	92.53 W
North Spot I	226	16.15 N	88.11 W
North Springfield, Pa., U.S.	204	41.59 N	80.26 W
North Springfield, Va., U.S.	274c	38.48 N	77.13 W
North Stamford Reservoir ⊜[1]	266	41.08 N	73.32 W
North Star	206	40.19 N	84.34 W
North Stradbroke Island I	161a	27.35 S	153.28 E
North Sudbury	273	42.23 N	71.24 W
North Sulphur ≃	186	33.23 N	95.18 W
North Sunday Creek ≃	192	46.27 N	105.54 W
North Sunderland	42	55.34 N	1.39 W
North Swansea	197	41.47 N	71.16 W
North Sydenham ≃	204	42.35 N	82.23 W
North Sydney, Austl.	264a	33.50 S	151.13 E
North Sydney, N.S., Can.	176	46.13 N	60.15 W
North Syracuse	200	43.08 N	76.08 W
North Tamborine	161a	27.56 S	153.11 E
North Taranaki Bight C[3]	162	38.42 S	174.15 E
North Tarrytown	266	41.05 N	73.52 W
North Tawton	44	50.48 N	3.53 W
North Terre Haute	184	39.31 N	87.22 W
North Tewksbury	273	42.38 N	71.15 W
North Thames ≃	202	42.59 N	81.16 W
North Thompson ≃	172	50.41 N	120.21 W
North Tidworth	44	51.16 N	1.40 W
North Toe ≃	182	36.00 N	82.16 W
North Tokelau Trough ⊹[1]	14	4.00 S	168.00 W
North Tonawanda	200	43.02 N	78.53 W
North Towanda	200	41.47 N	76.28 W
North Troy	178	45.00 N	72.24 W
North Truro	197	42.02 N	70.06 W
North Tule Draw V	186	34.30 N	101.36 W
North Turlock	216	37.31 N	120.51 W
North Turramurra	264a	33.43 S	150.09 E
North Twin Lake ⊜	176	49.16 N	55.56 W
North Tyne ≃	42	54.59 N	2.08 W
North Ubian Island I	106	6.09 N	120.27 E
North Uist I	28	57.37 N	7.22 W
Northumberland	200	40.54 N	76.48 W
Northumberland □[6], Ont., Can.	202	44.10 N	78.00 W
Northumberland □[6], Eng., U.K.	42	55.15 N	2.05 W
Northumberland □[6], Pa., U.S.	200	40.49 N	76.39 W
Northumberland □[6], Va., U.S.	198	37.50 N	76.25 W
Northumberland Isles II	156	21.40 S	150.00 E
Northumberland National Park ♠	42	55.15 N	2.20 W
Northumberland Strait Ɯ	176	46.00 N	63.30 W
North Umpqua ≃	192	43.16 N	123.27 W
North Uxbridge	197	42.06 N	71.39 W
Northvale	266	41.00 N	73.57 W
North Valley Stream	266	40.41 N	73.41 W
North Vancouver	172	49.19 N	123.04 W
North Vassalboro	178	44.29 N	69.37 W
North Vernon	208	39.00 N	85.38 W
North Versailles	269b	40.22 N	79.48 W
North Vietnam → Vietnam □[1]	100	16.00 N	108.00 E
North Vijayapuri	112	16.52 N	79.35 E
Northville, Mich., U.S.	206	42.26 N	83.29 W
Northville, N.Y., U.S.	200	43.13 N	74.11 W
Northville Downs ♠	271	42.26 N	83.29 W
Northvue	204	40.54 N	79.56 W
North Wabasca Lake ≃	172	56.00 N	113.55 W
North Wales	198	40.13 N	75.17 W
North Walsham	44	52.50 N	1.24 E
North Wantagh	266	40.41 N	73.30 W
North Warren	204	41.38 N	79.09 W
North Washington, Pa., U.S.	204	41.03 N	79.49 W
North Washington, Pa., U.S.	269b	40.32 N	79.36 W
Northway	170	62.59 N	141.43 W
North Wazīristān □[5]	113	33.05 N	70.40 E
North Weald Bassett	44	51.43 N	0.10 E
North Webster	206	41.19 N	85.42 W
North Weissport	200	40.50 N	75.41 W
North West □[5]	236	7.45 N	59.30 W
Northwest ≃	198	36.31 N	76.05 W
North West Cape ≻, Austl.	152	21.45 S	114.10 E
Northwest Cape ≻, Alaska, U.S.	170	63.46 N	171.45 W
Northwest Cape ≻, Fla., U.S.	210	25.13 N	81.11 W
North Westchester	197	41.35 N	72.24 W
Northwest Christmas Island Ridge ⊹[3]	14	6.30 N	159.00 W
North Western	200	43.20 N	75.22 W
North-Western □[3]	140	11.00 N	5.30 E
North-Western □[4]	144	13.00 S	25.00 E
Northwestern University (Chicago Campus) ɤ[2], Ill., U.S.	268	41.54 N	87.37 W
Northwestern University ɤ[2], Ill., U.S.	268	42.04 N	87.40 W
Northwest Frontier □[4]	110	33.30 N	71.30 E
Northwest Gander ≃	176	48.50 N	55.00 W
Northwest Harbor C	274b	39.16 N	76.35 W
Northwest Head ≻	106	10.08 N	118.45 E
Northwest Miramichi ≃	176	46.58 N	65.35 W
North West Point ≻	164o	2.02 N	157.29 W
Northwest Providence Channel Ɯ	228	26.10 N	78.20 W
North West River	166	53.32 N	60.08 W
Northwest Territories □[4]	166	70.00 N	100.00 W
North Weymouth	273	42.15 N	70.57 W
Northwich	42	53.16 N	2.32 W
North Wichita ≃	186	33.43 N	99.29 W
North Wilbraham	197	42.09 N	72.25 W
North Wildwood	198	39.00 N	74.48 W
North Wilkesboro	182	36.10 N	81.09 W
North Willow Creek ≃	192	46.51 N	107.54 W
North Wilmington	273	42.34 N	71.10 W
North Windham, Conn., U.S.	197	41.45 N	72.09 W
North Windham, Maine, U.S.	178	43.50 N	70.26 W
Northwold	44	52.33 N	0.35 E
Northwood, Iowa, U.S.	180	43.27 N	93.13 W
Northwood, Mich., U.S.	206	42.19 N	85.38 W
Northwood, N. Dak., U.S.	188	47.44 N	97.34 W
Northwood, Ohio, U.S.	204	41.37 N	83.30 W
Northwood ◆[8]	250	51.37 N	0.25 W
North Woodslee	271	42.13 N	82.43 W
North Yamhill ≃	214	45.13 N	123.08 W
North Yelta	158b	34.03 S	137.37 E
North York	202	43.46 N	79.25 W
North York Moors ΛΛ[2]	42	54.24 N	0.53 W
North York Moors National Park ♠	42	54.23 N	0.50 W
North Yorkshire □[6]	42	54.15 N	1.30 W
North Yuba ≃	216	39.22 N	121.08 W
North Zulch	212	30.55 N	96.07 W
Norton, N.B., Can.	176	45.38 N	65.42 W
Norton, Eng., U.K.	42	54.09 N	0.47 W
Norton, Eng., U.K.	252	53.20 N	2.40 W
Norton, Kans., U.S.	188	39.50 N	99.53 W
Norton, Mass., U.S.	197	41.58 N	71.11 W
Norton, Ohio, U.S.	204	41.01 N	81.39 W
Norton, Vt., U.S.	196	45.00 N	71.48 W
Norton, Va., U.S.	182	36.56 N	82.38 W
Norton Air Force Base ■	218	34.06 N	117.14 W
Norton Basin C	266	40.36 N	73.47 W
Norton Bay C	170	64.45 N	161.15 W
Norton Canes	44	52.41 N	1.59 W
Norton Creek ≃	271	42.34 N	83.34 W
Norton de Matos	142	12.21 S	14.46 E
Norton Fitzwarren	44	51.02 N	3.09 W
Norton Grove	197	42.00 N	71.12 W
Norton Heath	250	51.43 N	0.19 E
Norton Hill	200	42.25 N	74.04 W
Norton Pond ⊜	196	44.56 N	71.51 W
Norton Reservoir ⊜[1]	273	41.59 N	71.12 W
Norton Shores	206	43.10 N	86.14 W
Norton Sound Ɯ	170	63.50 N	164.00 W
Nortonville, Ont., Can.	265b	43.43 N	79.44 W
Nortonville, Kans., U.S.	188	39.25 N	95.20 W
Nortorf	48	53.55 N	9.16 E
Nort-sur-Erdre	32	47.26 N	1.30 W
Noruega → Norway □[1]	24	62.00 N	10.00 E
Noruega, Mar de → Norwegian Sea ⍑[2]	10	70.00 N	2.00 E
Norumbega Reservoir ⊜[1]	273	42.20 N	71.18 W
Nørup	41	55.43 N	9.19 E
Norval	202	43.39 N	79.51 W
Norvalspont	148	30.38 S	25.27 E
Norvège → Norway □[1]	24	62.00 N	10.00 E
Norvegia, Cape ≻	9	71.25 S	12.18 W
Norvell	206	42.10 N	84.11 W
Norvelt	204	40.12 N	79.32 W
Norvin Green State Forest ♠	266	41.03 N	74.20 W
Norwalk, Calif., U.S.	218	33.54 N	118.05 W
Norwalk, Conn., U.S.	197	41.07 N	73.27 W
Norwalk, Iowa, U.S.	180	41.29 N	93.41 W
Norwalk, Ohio, U.S.	204	41.15 N	82.37 W
Norwalk ≃	197	41.06 N	73.25 W
Norwalk Harbor C	266	41.06 N	73.24 W
Norwalk Islands II	266	41.03 N	73.23 W
Norway, Ind., U.S.	206	40.47 N	86.46 W
Norway, Iowa, U.S.	180	41.54 N	91.55 W
Norway, Maine, U.S.	178	44.13 N	70.32 W
Norway, Mich., U.S.	180	45.47 N	87.55 W
Norway □[1]	22		
	24	62.00 N	10.00 E
Norway Bay C	166	71.08 N	104.35 W
Norway House	174	53.59 N	97.50 W
Norway Lake ⊜	202	45.20 N	76.43 W
Norwegen → Norway □[1]	24	62.00 N	10.00 E
Norwegian Basin ⊹[1]	10	70.00 N	5.00 E
Norwegian Sea ⍑[2]	10	70.00 N	2.00 E
Norwell	273	42.10 N	70.48 W
Norwich, Ont., Can.	202	42.59 N	80.36 W
Norwich, Eng., U.K.	44	52.38 N	1.18 E
Norwich, Conn., U.S.	197	41.32 N	72.05 W
Norwich, Kans., U.S.	188	37.27 N	97.51 W
Norwich, N.Y., U.S.	200	42.32 N	75.31 W
Norwich Airport ⊠	44	52.31 N	1.15 E
Norwin Heights	269b	40.20 N	79.44 W
Norwood, Ont., Can.	202	44.23 N	77.59 W
Norwood, Colo., U.S.	190	38.08 N	108.20 W
Norwood, Mass., U.S.	197	42.11 N	71.12 W
Norwood, Minn., U.S.	180	44.46 N	93.55 W
Norwood, N.J., U.S.	266	40.60 N	73.57 W
Norwood, N.C., U.S.	182	35.14 N	80.07 W
Norwood, N.Y., U.S.	178	44.45 N	75.00 W
Norwood, Ohio, U.S.	208	39.10 N	84.28 W
Norwood, Pa., U.S.	275	39.53 N	75.18 W
Norwood ◆[8]	263d	26.10 S	28.04 E
Norwood Memorial Airport ⊠	273	42.11 N	71.10 W
Norwood Park ◆[8]	268	41.59 N	87.48 W
Norwood Pond ⊜	273	42.35 N	70.52 W
Norwoodville	180	41.39 N	93.33 W
Noryang	88	34.56 N	127.52 E
Norzagaray	106	14.54 N	121.02 E
Nosaka	84	35.39 N	140.34 E
Nosate	256b	45.33 N	8.43 E
Nosbonsing, Lake ⊜	180	46.12 N	79.13 W
Nose	86	34.58 N	135.24 E
Nose ◆[8]	260	34.49 N	135.09 E
Nose Creek ≃	172	54.53 N	119.28 W
Noshiro	82	40.12 N	140.02 E
Noska ≃	76	58.53 N	68.40 E
Nosova	76	59.30 N	63.13 E
Nosovaja, S.S.S.R.	24	68.15 N	54.35 E
Nosovaja, S.S.S.R.	70	57.15 N	45.35 E
Nosovka	68	50.55 N	31.35 E
Nosovo, S.S.S.R.	66	57.07 N	27.50 E
Nosovo, S.S.S.R.	73	47.16 N	38.40 E
Nosovščina	24	62.56 N	37.03 E
Noṣratābād	118	29.54 N	59.59 E
Nossa Senhora da Aparecida	246	22.02 S	42.48 W
Nossa Senhora das Dores	240	10.29 S	37.13 W
Nossa Senhora do Amparo	246	22.22 S	44.05 W
Nossa Senhora do Livramento	238	15.48 S	56.22 W
Nossa Senhora do Ó ◆[8]	277b	23.30 S	46.41 W
Nossa Senhora Mãe dos Homens	246	22.52 S	46.37 W
Nossebro	26	58.11 N	12.43 E
Nossen	50	51.03 N	13.17 E
Nossentiner Heide ◆[3]	50	53.35 N	12.25 E
Nossi-Bé I	147b	13.20 S	48.15 E
Nossob	146	22.18 S	17.10 E
Nossob (Nossop) ≃	146	26.55 S	20.37 E
Nossombougou	140	13.06 N	7.56 W
Nošul'	24	60.09 N	49.28 E
Nosy Varika	147b	20.35 S	48.32 E
Notasulga	184	32.34 N	85.40 W
Notch Cliff	274b	39.27 N	76.31 W
Notch Peak Λ	190	39.08 N	113.24 W
Noteć ≃	30	52.44 N	15.26 E
Notengo, Laguna de C	224	16.12 N	98.07 W
Notigi Lake ⊜	174	55.57 N	99.18 W
Notikewin ≃	166	57.15 N	117.05 W
Noto, It.	36	36.53 N	15.05 E
Noto, Nihon	82	37.18 N	137.09 E
Noto ≃	79	44.41 N	134.04 E
Noto, Golfo di C	36	36.50 N	15.15 E
Notodden	26	59.34 N	9.17 E
Notogawa	84	35.10 N	136.10 E
Noto-hantō ≻[1]	82	37.20 N	137.00 E
Noto-hantō-kokutei-kōen ♠	84	37.10 N	136.50 E
Notojima	84	37.08 N	137.00 E
Nōtori-dake Λ	84	35.37 N	138.15 E
Notoro-ko ⊜	82a	44.05 N	144.10 E
Notozero, Ozero ⊜	24	66.28 N	32.05 E
Notre-Dame, N.B., Can.	176	46.19 N	64.43 W
Notre Dame, Ind., U.S.	206	41.42 N	86.14 W
Notre-Dame ɤ[1]	251	48.51 N	2.21 E
Notre-Dame, Bois ♠	251	48.45 N	2.35 E
Notre Dame, Monts ΛΛ	176	48.10 N	68.00 W
Notre-Dame, Ruisseau ≃	265a	45.41 N	73.26 W
Notre Dame Bay C	176	49.45 N	55.15 W
Notre-Dame-de-Bellecombe	56	45.48 N	6.31 E
Notre-Dame-de-Lorette ɤ[1]	46	50.25 N	2.42 E
Notre-Dame-de-Lourdes	174	49.32 N	98.33 W
Notre-Dame-de-Pierreville	196	46.06 N	72.53 W
Notre-Dame-des-Victoires ◆[8]	265a	45.35 N	73.34 W
Notre-Dame-du-Haut ɤ[1]	32	47.43 N	6.37 E
Notre-Dame-du-Laus	178	46.05 N	75.37 W
Notre-Dame-du-Nord	180	47.36 N	79.30 W
Notrees	186	31.55 N	102.45 W
Notreure ≃	46	47.41 N	2.36 E
Notsu	86	33.02 N	131.42 E
Notsuharu	86	33.09 N	131.32 E
Nottawa	206	41.55 N	85.27 W
Nottawa Creek ≃	206	42.01 N	85.24 W
Nottawasaga ≃	202	44.32 N	80.01 W
Nottawasaga Bay C	202	44.40 N	80.30 W
Nottaway ≃	166	51.22 N	79.55 W
Nottingham, Eng., U.K.	44	52.58 N	1.10 W
Nottingham, Pa., U.S.	198	39.45 N	76.01 W
Nottingham, Pa., U.S.	275	40.07 N	74.58 W
Nottingham Island I	166	63.20 N	77.55 W
Nottingham Park	268	41.46 N	87.48 W
Nottingham Road	148	29.22 S	30.00 E
Nottinghamshire □[6]	44	53.00 N	1.00 W
Notting Hill	264b	37.54 S	145.08 E
Nottleben	50	50.58 N	10.50 E
Nottoway	182	37.08 N	78.05 W
Nottoway ≃	182	36.33 N	76.55 W
Nottuln	48	51.55 N	7.22 E
Notukeu Creek ≃	174	49.55 N	106.30 W
Notwani ≃	146	23.35 S	26.58 E
Nouadhibou	138	20.54 N	17.04 W
Nouakchott	140	18.06 N	15.57 W
Nouamrhar	140	19.22 N	16.31 W
Nouan-le-Fuzelier	46	47.32 N	2.02 E
Nouans-les-Fontaines	46	47.08 N	1.18 E
Nouméa	165f	22.16 S	166.27 E
Noun ≃	142	4.55 N	11.06 E
Nouna	140	12.44 N	3.52 W
Nounsley	250	51.46 N	0.36 E
Noupoort	148	31.10 S	24.57 E
Nous	148	28.44 S	19.52 E
Nouveau Brunswick → New Brunswick □[4]	176	46.30 N	66.15 W
Nouveau Mexique → New Mexico □[3]	168	34.30 N	106.00 W
Nouveau-Québec, Cratère du •[6]	166	61.17 N	73.40 W
Nouvelle	176	48.08 N	66.19 W
Nouvelle ≃	176	48.07 N	66.18 W
Nouvelle-Anvers	142	1.36 N	19.07 E
Nouvelle-Calédonie → New Caledonia □[2]	165f	21.30 S	165.30 E
Nouvelle-Calédonie I	165f	21.30 S	165.30 E
Nouvelle Écosse → Nova Scotia □[4]	176	45.00 N	63.00 W
Nouvelle-France, Cap de ≻	166	62.27 N	73.42 W
Nouvelle Galles du Sud → New South Wales □[3]	156	33.00 S	146.00 E
Nouvelle-Orléans → New Orleans	184	29.58 N	90.07 W
Nouvelles-Hébrides → New Hebrides □[2]	165f	16.00 S	167.00 E
Nouvelle Zélande → New Zealand □[1]	162	41.00 S	174.00 E
Nouvelle Zemble → Novaja Zeml'a II	62	74.00 N	57.00 E
Nouvion-en-Ponthieu	46	50.12 N	1.47 E
Nouvion-sur-Meuse	52	49.42 N	4.48 E
Nouzonville	52	49.49 N	4.45 E
Nova	204	41.02 N	82.18 W
Nova, Ilha I	240	0.20 N	49.40 W
Nova, Serra ΛΛ[1]	238	9.30 S	62.48 W
Nova América	245	15.01 S	49.56 W
Nova Anadia	102	8.56 S	125.52 E
Nova Andradina	245	22.10 S	53.15 W
Nova Aurora	245	18.04 S	48.16 W
Novabad, S.S.S.R.	75	38.37 N	68.45 E
Novabad, S.S.S.R.	75	39.01 N	70.09 E
Nová Baňa	30	48.26 N	18.39 E
Nová Bystřice	30	49.01 N	15.06 E
Nova Cachoeirinha ◆[8]	277b	23.28 S	46.40 W
Nova Caipemba	142	7.26 S	14.38 E
Novacella ɤ[1]	58	46.44 N	11.39 E
Nova Chaves	142	10.34 S	21.17 E
Nova Cintra	246	22.13 S	46.46 W
Nova Era	245	19.45 S	43.03 W
Nova Esperança	245	23.08 S	52.13 W
Nova Fátima	245	23.29 S	50.33 W
Novafeltria	60	43.53 N	12.17 E
Nova Freixo	144	14.49 S	36.33 E
Nova Friburgo	246	22.16 S	42.32 W
Nova Gaia	142	10.09 S	17.31 E
Nova Goa → Panaji	112	15.29 N	73.50 E
Nova Gorica	58	45.57 N	13.39 E
Nova Gradiška	36	45.16 N	17.23 E
Nova Granada	245	20.29 S	49.19 W
Nova Iguaçu	246	22.45 S	43.27 W
Nova Iguaçu □[7]	277a	22.45 S	43.29 W
Nova Iorque	240	6.45 S	44.03 W
Novaja, S.S.S.R.	72	55.13 N	38.54 E
Novaja, S.S.S.R.	255b	55.48 N	38.03 E
Novaja ◆[8]	255a	60.02 N	30.28 E
Novaja Astrachan'	73	49.07 N	38.36 E
Novaja Belaja	68	49.46 N	39.11 E
Novaja Binaradka	70	53.48 N	49.56 E
Novaja Borovaja	68	50.42 N	28.39 E
Novaja Čigla	68	51.13 N	40.28 E
Novaja Derevn'a, S.S.S.R.	72	54.01 N	38.53 E
Novaja Derevn'a, S.S.S.R.	78	57.15 N	103.08 E
Novaja Ivanovka	68	45.55 N	29.05 E
Novaja Janisol'	73	47.17 N	37.16 E
Novaja Kachovka	68	46.45 N	33.23 E
Novaja Kalitva	68	50.06 N	40.01 E
Novaja Kazanka	70	48.57 N	49.36 E
Novaja Kazmaska	70	56.49 N	53.31 E
Novaja Kriuša	68	50.16 N	41.16 E
Novaja Ladoga	66	60.05 N	32.16 E
Novaja L'al'a	76	59.03 N	60.36 E
Novaja Majačka	68	46.36 N	33.14 E
Novaja Maluksa	66	59.39 N	31.21 E
Novaja Malykla	70	54.13 N	49.57 E
Novaja Mojgora	72	54.27 N	33.32 E
Novaja Odessa	68	47.19 N	31.47 E
Novaja Porubežka	70	51.45 N	49.40 E
Novaja Praga	68	48.33 N	32.54 E
Novaja Ropša	255a	59.45 N	29.53 E

Symbol	English	Deutsch	Español	Français	Português
≃	River	Fluss	Río	Rivière	Rio
≍	Canal	Kanal	Canal	Canal	Canal
↳	Waterfall, Rapids	Wasserfall, Stromschnellen	Cascada, Rápidos	Chute d'eau, Rapides	Cascata, Rápidos
Ɯ	Strait	Meeresstrasse	Estrecho	Détroit	Estreito
C	Bay, Gulf	Bucht, Golf	Bahía, Golfo	Baie, Golfe	Baía, Golfo
⊜	Lake, Lakes	See, Seen	Lago, Lagos	Lac, Lacs	Lago, Lagos
☷	Swamp	Sumpf	Pantano	Marais	Pântano
⍓	Ice Features, Glacier	Eis- und Gletscherformen	Accidentes Glaciales	Formes glaciaires	Acidentes Glaciares
⍑	Other Hydrographic Features	Andere Hydrographische Objekte	Otros Elementos Hidrográficos	Autres données hydrographiques	Outros Elementos Hidrográficos
⊹	Submarine Features	Untermeerische Objekte	Accidentes Submarinos	Formes de relief sous-marin	Acidentes Submarinos
□	Political Unit	Politische Einheit	Unidad Politica	Entité politique	Unidade Política
ɤ	Cultural Institution	Kulturelle Institution	Institución Cultural	Institution culturelle	Instituição Cultural
⊥	Historical Site	Historische Stätte	Sitio Histórico	Site historique	Sitio Histórico
♠	Recreational Site	Erholungs- und Ferienort	Sitio de Recreo	Centre de loisirs	Sítio de Lazer
⊠	Airport	Flughafen	Aeropuerto	Aéroport	Aeroporto
■	Military Installation	Militäranlage	Instalación Militar	Installation militaire	Instalação Militar
◆	Miscellaneous	Verschiedenes	Misceláneo	Divers	Miscelânea

Novaja Sibir', Ostrov I 64 75.00 N 149.00 E
Novaja Sloboda 68 51.23 N 34.08 E
Novaja Slobodka 72 54.56 N 36.47 E
Novaja Šul'ba 76 50.33 N 81.20 E
Novaja Uda 78 54.07 N 103.33 E
Novaja Ušica 68 48.49 N 27.16 E
Novaja Usman' 68 51.37 N 39.24 E
Novaja Vodolaga 68 49.43 N 35.52 E
Novaja Zburjevka 68 46.28 N 32.24 E
Novaja Zeml'a II 62 74.00 N 57.00 E
Nováky 30 48.43 N 18.34 E
Nova Lamego 140 12.19 N 14.11 W
Novalesa 56 45.11 N 7.01 E
Novaliches Watershed Reservation ⊜[1] 259f 14.43 N 121.05 E
Nova Lima 245 19.59 S 43.51 W
Nova Lisboa → Huambo 142 12.44 S 15.47 E
Nova Lusitânia 146 19.54 S 34.35 E
Nova Mambone 146 20.59 S 35.01 E
Nova Milanese 256b 45.35 N 9.12 E
Nova Nabúri 144 16.46 S 38.57 E
Nova Olinda 240 7.06 S 39.40 W
Nova Olinda, Riacho ≃ 240 8.05 S 42.34 W
Nova Olinda do Norte 236 3.45 S 59.03 W
Nová Paka 30 50.29 N 15.31 E
Nova Ponente (Deutschnofen) 58 46.25 N 11.25 E
Nova Ponte 245 19.08 S 47.41 W
Nova Prata 242 28.47 S 51.36 W
Novar 202 45.27 N 79.15 W
Novara 56
256b 45.28 N 8.38 E
Novara □[4] 54 46.00 N 8.25 E
Nova Resende 245 21.08 S 46.25 W
Nová Role 50 50.15 N 12.47 E
Nova Roma 245 13.51 S 46.57 W
Nova Russas 240 4.42 S 40.34 W
Nova Sagres 102 8.24 S 127.15 E
Nova Scotia □[4] 166
176 45.00 N 63.00 W
Nova Sintra 142 12.09 S 17.16 E
Nova Sofala 146 20.09 S 34.42 E
Nova Soure 240 11.14 S 38.29 W
Novate Mezzola 54 46.15 N 9.27 E
Novate Milanese 256b 45.32 N 9.08 E
Nova Timboteua 240 1.12 S 47.24 W
Novato 216 38.06 N 122.34 W
Novato Creek ≃ 272 38.06 N 122.29 W
Nova Varoš 38 43.28 N 19.48 E
Nova Venécia 245 18.43 S 40.24 W
Nova Veneza 242 28.39 S 49.30 W
Nova Vida 238 10.11 S 62.47 W
Nova Vida, Cachoeira ⌊ 238 9.25 S 63.36 W
Novaya Zemlya Ridge ✦[3] 10 73.00 N 51.00 E
Nova Zagora 38 42.29 N 26.01 E
Nova Zembla Island I 166 72.10 N 74.50 W
Nove 58 45.43 N 11.40 E
Nové Hrady 30 48.47 N 14.37 E
Novelda 34 38.23 N 0.46 W
Novellara 58 44.51 N 10.44 E
Novelty 209 40.01 N 92.12 W
Nové Město 30 50.21 N 16.09 E
Nové Město nad Váhom 30 48.46 N 17.49 E
Nové Město na Moravě 30 49.34 N 16.04 E
Noventa di Piave 58 45.39 N 12.31 E
Noventa Padovana 58 45.24 N 11.58 E
Noventa Vicentina 58 45.17 N 11.32 E
Noves 56 43.52 N 4.54 E
Nové Sedlo 50 50.10 N 12.42 E
Nové Strašecí 50 50.07 N 13.53 E
Nové Zámky 30 47.59 N 18.11 E
Novgorod 66 58.31 N 31.17 E
Novgorodka 68 48.21 N 32.39 E
Novgorod-Severskij 68 51.59 N 33.16 E
Novgorodskoje 73 48.20 N 37.50 E
Novi 206 42.29 N 83.28 W
Novi Bečej 38 45.36 N 20.08 E
Novice 186 31.59 N 99.37 W
Novičicha 76 52.13 N 81.24 E
Novi di Modena 58 44.54 N 10.54 E
Novigrad, Jugo. 36 44.11 N 15.33 E
Novigrad, Jugo. 36 45.19 N 13.34 E
Novikovo, S.S.S.R. 76 58.15 N 80.39 E
Novikovo, S.S.S.R. 79 46.23 N 143.20 E
Novi Ligure 56 44.46 N 8.47 E
Noville 52 50.40 N 5.23 E
Novi Lyon Drain ≍ 271 42.30 N 83.38 W
Novinger 184 40.19 N 92.42 W
Novinka 66 59.49 N 33.20 E
Novion-Porcien 46 49.36 N 4.25 E
Novi Pazar, Blg. 38 43.21 N 27.12 E
Novi Pazar, Jugo. 38 43.08 N 20.31 E
Novi Sad 38 45.15 N 19.50 E
Novi Vinodolski 36 45.08 N 14.48 E
Novka 66 55.27 N 30.24 E
Novki 70 56.22 N 41.06 E
Novl'anka 70 55.48 N 41.44 E
Novlenskoje 66 59.37 N 39.20 E
Novo ≃, Bra. 238 4.55 S 70.33 W
Novo ≃, Bra. 240 4.30 S 53.50 W
Novo ≃, Bra. 246 21.23 S 42.44 W
Novo, Lago ⊜ 240 1.30 N 50.40 W
Novoachtyrka 73 48.55 N 38.49 E
Nôvo Acôrdo 245 13.10 S 46.48 W
Novoajdar 73 48.57 N 39.00 E
Novoaleksandrovka, S.S.S.R. 70 51.56 N 52.26 E
Novoaleksandrovka, S.S.S.R. 73 49.08 N 39.17 E
Novoaleksandrovka, S.S.S.R. 73 48.17 N 39.37 E
Novoaleksandrovka, S.S.S.R. 76 51.47 N 68.49 E
Novoaleksandrovo 255b 55.59 N 37.33 E
Novoaleksandrovskaja 70 45.29 N 41.16 E
Novoaleksejevka, S.S.S.R. 68 46.13 N 34.39 E
Novoaleksejevka, S.S.S.R. 68 46.06 N 32.30 E
Novoaleksejevka, S.S.S.R. 76 52.47 N 74.54 E
Novoaleksejevka, S.S.S.R. 76 52.56 N 64.41 E
Novoaleksejevka, S.S.S.R. 76 50.08 N 55.39 E
Novoaltajsk 76 53.24 N 83.58 E
Novoamvrosijevskoje 73 47.49 N 38.29 E
Novoanninskij 70 50.32 N 42.41 E
Novoarchangel'sk 68 48.39 N 30.48 E
Novoarchangel'skoje 255b 55.55 N 37.33 E
Novo Aripuanã 236 5.08 S 60.22 W
Novoasbest 76 57.44 N 60.45 E
Novoazorskoje 73 47.08 N 38.05 E
Novobachmutovka 73 48.15 N 37.48 E
Novobatajsk 73 46.54 N 39.47 E
Novobelaja 68 49.49 N 39.18 E
Novobessergenovka 73 47.11 N 38.51 E
Novobogatinskoje 70 47.22 N 51.11 E
Novobogdanovka 68 47.06 N 35.29 E
Novobogorodskoje 70 53.11 N 53.56 E
Novoborovaja 73 49.15 N 38.33 E
Nôvo Brasil 245 16.11 S 50.38 W
Novobratcevskij 72 55.51 N 37.23 E
Novoburejskij 79 49.49 N 129.54 E
Novo Čeremšansk 70 54.21 N 50.10 E
Novočerkassk 73 47.25 N 40.06 E
Novočernorečenskij 76 56.16 N 91.06 E
Novocharitonovo 72 55.35 N 38.30 E
Novocherkassk → Novočerkassk 73 47.25 N 40.06 E
Novochop'orsk 70 51.07 N 41.37 E
Novochop'orskij 70 51.06 N 41.33 E
Novochovrino ✦[8] 255b 55.52 N 37.30 E
Novociml'anskaja 70 47.59 N 42.17 E
Nôvo Cruzeiro 245 17.29 S 41.53 W
Novodanilovka 68 46.38 N 35.00 E
Novoderev'ankovskaja 68 46.19 N 38.45 E
Novoderkul 73 49.08 N 39.38 E
Novodevičje 70 53.37 N 48.52 E
Novodolinka 76 51.12 N 72.33 E
Novodolinskij 76 49.44 N 72.45 E
Novodoroninskoje 78 51.08 N 112.08 E
Novodružesk 73 48.58 N 38.21 E
Novodubovoje 66 52.19 N 39.13 E
Novodugino 66 55.38 N 34.18 E
Novodžerelijevskaja 68 45.46 N 38.41 E
Novoekonomičeskoje 73 48.18 N 37.15 E
Novofetinino 72 56.14 N 39.17 E
Novogaritovo 70 52.47 N 40.07 E
Novogirejevo ✦[8] 255b 55.45 N 37.49 E
Novogorbovo 72 55.43 N 36.29 E
Novogornyj 76 55.37 N 60.47 E
Novograd-Volynskij 68 50.36 N 27.36 E
Novogrigorjevka 68 46.24 N 34.59 E
Novogrigorjevskaja 70 49.26 N 43.37 E
Novogrigorjevskoje 74 44.25 N 43.51 E
Novogrodovka 73 48.13 N 37.20 E
Novogroznenskij 74 43.15 N 46.15 E
Novogrudok 66 53.36 N 25.50 E
Novogupalovka 68 48.02 N 35.26 E
Nôvo Hamburgo 242 29.41 S 51.08 W
Novo Horizonte 245 21.28 S 49.13 W
Novoignatjevka 73 47.38 N 37.41 E
Novoiljinsk 78 51.42 N 108.41 E
Novoiljinskij 76 57.54 N 55.30 E
Novoivanovka, S.S.S.R. 68 49.44 N 33.28 E
Novoivanovka, S.S.S.R. 73 47.41 N 38.23 E
Novoivanovka, S.S.S.R. 75 43.08 N 71.26 E
Novoivanovskoje 255b 55.43 N 37.22 E
Novoizborsk 66 57.50 N 27.59 E
Novojampol' 79 52.55 N 127.38 E
Novojamskoje 66 52.14 N 34.28 E
Novoje, S.S.S.R. 72 55.38 N 38.55 E
Novoje, S.S.S.R. 76 58.53 N 68.40 E
Novoje Alechnovo 72 56.02 N 36.49 E
Novojegorjevskoje 76 51.46 N 80.53 E
Novojekaterinovka 73 47.43 N 38.07 E
Novoje Koval'ovo 255a 59.59 N 30.34 E
Novoje Leušino 70 56.48 N 40.32 E
Novojel'n'a 66 53.28 N 25.35 E
Novojenisejsk 76 58.16 N 92.24 E
Novoje Pavšino 72 54.15 N 37.07 E
Novoje Zarečje 66 57.43 N 34.22 E
Novokadinsk 78 54.46 N 101.24 E
Novokamala 78 55.58 N 94.58 E
Novokarasuk 76 56.16 N 71.46 E
Novokaširovo 70 54.58 N 52.32 E
Novokaširsk 72 54.51 N 38.15 E
Novokazalinsk 76 45.50 N 62.10 E
Novokijevskij 70 50.27 N 43.08 E
Novokorsunskaja 68 45.38 N 39.09 E
Novokrasn'anka 73 49.08 N 38.18 E
Novokrasnoje 68 48.01 N 31.21 E
Novokručininskij 78 51.46 N 113.48 E
Novokubanka 76 51.40 N 70.44 E
Novokujbyševsk 70 53.07 N 49.58 E
Novokurovka 79 48.51 N 134.20 E
Novokuzneck 76 53.45 N 87.06 E
Novokuznetsk → Novokuzneck 76 53.45 N 87.06 E
Novoladožskij Kanal ≍ 255a 60.26 N 32.48 E
Novolakskoje 74 43.07 N 46.29 E
Novolazarevskaja ⊍[3] 9 70.45 S 11.50 E
Novoleuškovskaja 68 45.59 N 39.58 E
Novolimarevka 73 49.17 N 39.36 E
Novolukoml' 66 54.40 N 29.08 E
Novol'vovsk 66 53.55 N 38.47 E
Novomalorossijskaja 68 45.38 N 39.53 E
Novomansurkino 70 53.52 N 51.52 E
Novomargaritovka 73 46.54 N 38.50 E
Novomariinka 78 55.27 N 96.01 E
Novomarkovka 76 51.44 N 72.17 E
Novomel'nikov 74 43.56 N 45.09 E
Novomelovatka 68 50.27 N 40.46 E
Novomelovoje 68 51.23 N 38.13 E
Novo Mesto 36 45.48 N 15.10 E
Novomichajlovka, S.S.S.R. 73 47.51 N 37.29 E
Novomichajlovka, S.S.S.R. 76 55.13 N 81.57 E
Novomichajlovskij 76 53.55 N 54.36 E
Novomichajlovskoje, S.S.S.R. 68 44.15 N 38.51 E
Novomichajlovskoje, S.S.S.R. 72 55.25 N 37.10 E
Novominskaja 68 46.19 N 38.57 E
Novomirgorod 68 48.47 N 31.39 E
Novomoskovsk, S.S.S.R. 68 48.37 N 35.12 E
Novomoskovsk, S.S.S.R. 72 54.05 N 38.13 E
Novomyšastovskaja 68 45.12 N 38.35 E
Novonagajevo 70 55.56 N 54.15 E
Novonikolajevka, S.S.S.R. 68 46.13 N 32.45 E
Novonikolajevka, S.S.S.R. 68 47.59 N 35.55 E
Novonikolajevka, S.S.S.R. 73 46.59 N 39.36 E
Novonikolajevka, S.S.S.R. 75 42.26 N 70.28 E
Novonikolajevskij 70 50.58 N 42.22 E
Novonikolayevsk → Novosibirsk 76 55.02 N 82.55 E
Novonikol'skoje, S.S.S.R. 66 59.25 N 33.13 E
Novonikol'skoje, S.S.S.R. 70 49.09 N 45.00 E
Novonikol'skoje, S.S.S.R. 73 49.21 N 39.51 E
Novonikol'skoje, S.S.S.R. 76 59.46 N 79.12 E
Novonikol'skoje, S.S.S.R. 255b 55.50 N 37.15 E
Novoomel'kovo 73 49.08 N 39.05 E
Novo Oriente 240 5.32 S 40.42 W
Novoorsk 76 51.23 N 58.58 E
Novopavlovka, S.S.S.R. 78 51.13 N 109.14 E
Novopavlovka, S.S.S.R. 78 50.49 N 106.30 E
Novopavlovskaja 74 43.58 N 43.38 E
Novopavlovskoje 78 50.56 N 111.35 E
Novopetrovo 76 57.11 N 69.10 E
Novopetrovskoje 72 55.59 N 36.28 E
Novopiscovo 66 57.19 N 41.54 E
Novopodrezkovo 72 55.57 N 37.21 E
Novopokrovka, S.S.S.R. 68 48.03 N 34.37 E
Novopokrovka, S.S.S.R. 75 42.52 N 74.45 E
Novopokrovka, S.S.S.R. 76 50.41 N 80.28 E
Novopokrovka, S.S.S.R. 76 53.43 N 67.45 E
Novopokrovka, S.S.S.R. 79 45.52 N 134.28 E
Novopokrovskoje 70 51.35 N 43.36 E
Novopolevodino 70 51.46 N 47.29 E
Novopolock 66 55.31 N 28.38 E
Novopskov 73 49.33 N 39.05 E
Novorajčichinsk 79 49.47 N 129.38 E
Novor'ažsk 70 53.44 N 40.07 E
Novo Redondo 142 11.13 S 13.50 E
Novorepnoje 70 51.06 N 48.24 E
Novorossijka 75 42.44 N 76.07 E
Novorossijsk 68 44.45 N 37.45 E
Novorossijskoje 76 50.13 N 58.00 E
Novorossiysk → Novorossijsk 68 44.45 N 37.45 E
Novorossoš' 73 49.32 N 39.15 E
Novorudnyj 76 51.30 N 58.10 E
Novorybinka 76 51.51 N 71.14 E
Novorybnoje 64 72.50 N 105.50 E
Novoržev 66 57.02 N 29.20 E
Novošachtinsk 73 47.47 N 39.56 E
Novosaratovka 255a 59.50 N 30.32 E
Novoščerbinovskaja 68 46.28 N 38.38 E
Novosel'e 76 54.10 N 76.53 E
Novoselenginsk 78 51.06 N 106.37 E
Novoselica 68 48.14 N 26.17 E
Novoselickoje 74 44.45 N 43.26 E
Novoselišče 68 49.48 N 25.03 E
Novoselje 255a 59.48 N 30.05 E
Novoselki, S.S.S.R. 72 55.08 N 37.33 E
Novoselki, S.S.S.R. 72 54.49 N 38.55 E
Novosel'nyj 76 50.00 N 54.38 E
Novoselovka Pervaja 73 48.12 N 37.31 E
Novoselovo, S.S.S.R. 72 56.04 N 39.04 E
Novoselovo, S.S.S.R. 76 55.04 N 91.07 E
Novoselovo, S.S.S.R. 78 56.04 N 107.42 E
Novosel'skoje 68 45.20 N 28.33 E
Novosemejkino 70 53.23 N 50.22 E
Novosergijevka, S.S.S.R. 70 52.06 N 53.39 E
Novosergijevka, S.S.S.R. 255a 59.54 N 30.34 E
Novoseslavino 70 53.21 N 40.26 E
Novošešminsk 70 55.04 N 51.15 E
Novoshakhtinsk → Novošachtinsk 73 47.47 N 39.56 E
Novosibirsk 76 55.02 N 82.55 E
Novosibirskije Ostrova II 64 75.00 N 142.00 E
Novosibirskoje Vodochranilišče ⊜[1] 64 54.35 N 82.35 E
Novosil' 66 52.58 N 37.03 E
Novosil'skoje 68 51.56 N 38.31 E
Novosokol'niki 66 56.21 N 30.10 E
Novos'olki, S.S.S.R. 66 56.01 N 33.37 E
Novos'olki, S.S.S.R. 66 52.24 N 28.33 E
Novos'olki, S.S.S.R. 68 52.02 N 24.21 E
Novos'olki, S.S.S.R. 70 54.50 N 39.46 E
Novos'olki, S.S.S.R. 70 55.48 N 42.41 E
Novos'olki, S.S.S.R. 255a 59.42 N 30.17 E
Novos'olovka 73 49.04 N 37.42 E
Novos'olovskoje 68 45.26 N 33.34 E
Novospasovka 73 47.42 N 39.04 E
Novospasskoje 70 53.08 N 47.45 E
Novostrel'covka 73 49.20 N 39.55 E
Novostrojevo 66 54.27 N 21.50 E
Novosvetlovka 73 48.30 N 39.30 E
Novotavolžanka 68 50.22 N 36.50 E
Novotitarovskaja 68 45.14 N 39.00 E
Novotroick 76 51.12 N 58.20 E
Novotroickoje, S.S.S.R. 68 46.22 N 34.20 E
Novotroickoje, S.S.S.R. 70 58.28 N 47.06 E
Novotroickoje, S.S.S.R. 73 47.43 N 37.35 E
Novotroickoje, S.S.S.R. 75 43.42 N 73.46 E
Novotroickoje, S.S.S.R. 76 56.11 N 78.41 E
Novo-Troitsk → Novotroick 76 51.12 N 58.20 E
Novotulka, S.S.S.R. 70 50.50 N 47.34 E
Novotulka, S.S.S.R. 70 52.38 N 48.45 E
Novotul'skij 72 54.10 N 37.43 E
Novoukolovo 68 51.02 N 38.25 E
Novoukrainka 68 48.19 N 31.32 E
Novouljanovsk 70 54.08 N 48.24 E
Novoural'sk 76 51.15 N 57.16 E
Novouzensk 70 50.28 N 48.08 E
Novovaršavka 76 54.11 N 74.42 E
Novovasiljevka, S.S.S.R. 68 46.48 N 35.44 E
Novovasiljevka, S.S.S.R. 68 46.51 N 36.46 E
Novov'atsk 70 58.29 N 49.44 E
Novov'azniki 70 56.12 N 42.10 E
Novovolynsk 68 50.50 N 24.05 E
Novovoroncovka 68 47.29 N 33.54 E
Novovoronežskij 68 51.16 N 39.11 E
Novovoskresenovka 75 42.50 N 73.32 E
Novovoskresenskoje 68 47.21 N 33.37 E
Novozacharkino 70 52.11 N 48.29 E
Novozagorje 72 55.39 N 38.38 E
Novozavidovskij 72 56.33 N 36.26 E
Novožilovskaja 24 64.50 N 51.20 E
Novozizevka 70 50.48 N 49.08 E
Novozybkov 66 52.32 N 31.56 E
Novska 36 45.21 N 16.59 E
Nový Bohumín 30 49.56 N 18.20 E
Nový Bor 50 50.45 N 14.33 E
Novyj 76 55.39 N 86.39 E
Novyj Afon 74 43.06 N 40.48 E
Novyj Bor 24 66.43 N 52.16 E
Novyj Bug 68 47.41 N 32.30 E
Novyj Bujan 70 53.41 N 50.04 E
Novyj Bykov 68 50.36 N 31.39 E
Novyj Donbass ✦[8] 73 48.05 N 38.46 E
Novyj Dvor 66 52.50 N 24.21 E
Novyje Ajbesi 70 54.49 N 47.02 E
Novyje Aneny 68 46.52 N 29.14 E
Novyje Basy 68 50.53 N 34.51 E
Novyje Burasy 70 52.08 N 46.06 E
Novyje Denisoviči 66 54.12 N 29.13 E
Novyje Gorki 70 56.42 N 41.06 E
Novyje Maty 70 55.15 N 54.04 E
Novyje Salty 70 54.06 N 53.26 E
Novyje Senžary 68 49.21 N 34.19 E
Novyje Z'atcy 70 57.27 N 52.36 E
Nový Jičín 30 49.36 N 18.00 E
Novyj Jaryčev 68 49.55 N 24.18 E
Novyj Jegorlyk 70 46.24 N 41.54 E
Novyj Karačaj 74 43.49 N 41.56 E
Novyj Karamass 70 56.11 N 48.58 E
Novyj Kiner 70 56.24 N 49.44 E
Novyj Multan 70 57.09 N 52.19 E
Novyj Nekouz 66 57.54 N 38.04 E
Novyj Oskol 68 50.46 N 37.53 E
Novyj Pogost 66 55.30 N 27.29 E
Novyj Port 64 67.40 N 72.52 E
Novyj Put' 75 43.29 N 73.52 E
Novyj Ropsk 66 52.18 N 32.19 E
Novyj Stan 72 56.18 N 37.00 E
Novyj Svet 73 47.48 N 38.00 E
Novyj Tap 76 57.04 N 67.49 E
Novyj Terek ≃ 74 43.37 N 47.25 E
Novyj Tevriz 76 59.04 N 78.08 E
Novyj Torjal 70 57.00 N 48.44 E
Novyj Vas'ugan 76 58.34 N 76.29 E
Nowa Dęba 30 50.26 N 21.46 E
Nowaja Semlja → Novaja Zeml'a II 62 74.00 N 57.00 E
Nowa Ruda 30 50.35 N 16.31 E
Nowa Sól (Neusalz) 30 51.48 N 15.44 E
Nowata 186 36.42 N 95.38 W
Nowater Creek ≃ 192 43.57 N 108.00 W
Nowbarān 118 35.08 N 48.42 E
Nowe 30 53.40 N 18.43 E
Nowe Miasteczko 30 51.42 N 15.45 E
Nowe Miasto Lubawskie 30 53.27 N 19.35 E
Nowe Miasto nad Pilicą 30 51.38 N 20.35 E
Nowendoc 156 31.32 S 151.43 E
Nowe Warpno 30 53.44 N 14.16 E
Nowgong, Bhārat 110 26.21 N 92.40 E
Nowgong, Bhārat 114 25.04 N 79.27 E
Nowingi 156 34.36 S 142.14 E
Nowitna ≃ 170 65.55 N 154.17 W
Nowogard 30 53.40 N 15.08 E
Nowogród 30 53.15 N 21.53 E
Nowogrodziec 30 51.12 N 15.25 E
Nowokusnezk → Novokuzneck 76 53.45 N 87.06 E
Nowood ≃ 192 44.17 N 107.58 W
Nowosibirsk → Novosibirsk 76 55.02 N 82.55 E
Nowra 160 34.53 S 150.36 E
Nowrangapur 112 19.14 N 82.33 E
Nowshāk ∧ 113 36.26 N 71.50 E
Nowshera 110 34.01 N 71.59 E
Nowy Dwór Gdański 30 54.13 N 19.06 E
Nowy Dwór Mazowiecki 30 52.26 N 20.43 E
Nowy Sącz 30 49.38 N 20.42 E
Nowy Staw 30 54.09 N 19.00 E
Nowy Targ 30 49.29 N 20.02 E
Nowy Tomyśl 30 52.20 N 16.07 E
Now Zād 110 32.24 N 64.28 E
Noxapater 184 33.00 N 89.04 W
Noxe ≃ 46 48.33 N 3.35 E
Noxen 200 41.25 N 76.03 W
Noxon 192 48.01 N 115.47 W
Noxon Reservoir ⊜[1] 192 47.54 N 115.40 W
Noy ≃ 100 17.05 N 105.02 E
Noya 34 42.47 N 8.53 W
Noya ≃, Esp. 34 41.28 N 1.56 E
Noya ≃, Gabon 142 0.58 N 9.48 E
Noyant 46 47.31 N 0.08 E
Noye ≃ 46 49.51 N 2.20 E
Noyelles-sur Mer 46 50.11 N 1.43 E
Noyers 46 47.42 N 4.00 E
Noyers, Ruisseau des ≃ 265a 45.21 N 73.22 W
Noyes Island I 170 55.30 N 133.40 W
Noyon 46 49.35 N 3.00 E
Nožaj-Jurt 74 43.05 N 46.24 E
Nozawa-onsen 84 36.55 N 138.27 E
Nozay, Fr. 32 47.34 N 1.38 W
Nozay, Fr. 251 48.40 N 2.14 E
Nozeroy 54 46.47 N 6.02 E
Nozori-dam ✦[6] 84 36.43 N 138.39 E
Nozori-ko ⊜ 84 36.42 N 138.39 E
Nozuta 258 35.35 N 139.27 E
Nozza 58 45.42 N 10.23 E
Nqamakwe 148 32.12 S 27.56 E
Nqutu 148 28.13 S 30.32 E
N'Rougas 148 29.07 S 21.09 E
Nsa, Oued en ∨ 138 32.28 N 5.24 E
Nsaba 140 5.39 N 0.45 W
Nsah 142 2.22 S 15.19 E
Nsang 142 2.02 N 10.56 E
Nsanje 144 16.55 S 35.12 E
Nsawam 140 5.50 N 0.20 W
Nsefu Game Reserve ✦[4] 144 13.07 S 32.10 E
Nsele ≃ 142 4.14 S 15.33 E
Nseleni 148 28.33 S 31.39 E
Nsok 142 1.08 N 11.16 E
Nsoko 148 27.02 S 31.57 E
Nsontin 142 3.09 S 18.00 E
Nsouélé 263b 4.12 S 15.11 E
Nsukka 140 6.52 N 7.24 E
Nsuta 140 5.17 N 1.58 W
Ntakat ✦[4] 140 16.49 N 11.43 W
Ntambanana 148 28.36 S 31.45 E
Ntandembele 142 2.11 S 17.08 E
Ntchisi 144 13.19 S 33.58 E
Ntem ≃ 142 2.15 N 9.45 E
Ntoum 142 0.23 N 9.47 E
Ntsama 142 0.32 S 14.38 E
Ntui 142 4.27 N 11.38 E
Ntumba 144 8.20 S 32.05 E
Ntusi 144 0.03 N 31.13 E
Ntwetwe Pan ⊻ 146 20.30 S 25.20 E
Nuala 144 13.27 S 28.16 E
Nuanchitang 94 41.02 N 120.41 E
Nuanetsi 144 21.22 S 30.45 E
Nuanetsi ≃ 146 22.40 S 31.50 E
Nuangola 200 41.09 N 75.58 W
Nuanli 92 23.26 N 100.51 E
Nuannuan 259d 25.06 N 121.44 E
Nuanshui 90 28.53 N 117.51 E
Nuanzhouying 90 25.22 N 117.22 E
Nuasjärvi ⊜ 26 64.10 N 28.05 E
Nuatabu 164t 1.33 N 172.59 E
Nuatja 140 6.57 N 1.10 E
Nu'aymah 122 32.38 N 36.10 E
Nūbah 132 30.29 N 31.33 E
Nūbah, Jibāl an- ∧∧ 130 12.00 N 30.45 E
Nūbārīyah, Tur'at an- ≍ 132 30.43 N 30.46 E
Nubian Desert ✦[2] 130 20.30 N 33.00 E
Ñuble □[4] 242 36.35 S 71.50 W
Ñuble ≃ 242 36.39 S 72.27 W
Nubra ≃ 113 34.39 N 77.36 E
Nucet 38 46.28 N 22.35 E
Nucetto 56 44.20 N 8.04 E
Nucha → Šeki 74 41.12 N 47.12 E
Nuchatlitz Inlet ⊂ 172 49.45 N 126.55 W
N'uchča 24 63.27 N 46.28 E
Nuch'ŏn-ni 88 38.14 N 126.16 E
Nucla 190 38.16 N 108.33 W
Núcleo Colonial São Bento 277a 22.44 S 43.18 W
N'učpas 24 60.51 N 51.18 E
Nucuray ≃ 236 5.02 S 75.34 W
Nuda, Monte la ∧ 58 44.17 N 10.15 E
Nudaybah 132 30.59 N 30.22 E
Nudlung Fiord ⊂[2] 166 68.21 N 67.22 W
Nudol'-Šarino 72 56.06 N 36.31 E
Nudow 254a 52.20 N 13.10 E
Nudž 74 40.56 N 47.41 E
Nueces ≃ 186 27.50 N 97.30 W
Nueces Plains ⊻ 186 28.30 N 99.15 W
Nueltin Lake ⊜ 166 60.20 N 99.50 W
Nuenen 48 51.29 N 5.33 E
Nüerhe 94 41.04 N 121.00 E
Nüerhe ≃ 88 40.57 N 121.19 E
Nuestra Señora de las Lajas ⊍[1] 236 0.49 N 77.36 W
Nuestra Señora de Talavera 242 25.26 S 63.48 W
Nueva, Isla I 244 55.13 S 66.30 W
Nueva Antioquia 236 6.05 N 69.26 W
Nueva Atzacoalco 276a 19.29 N 99.05 W
Nueva Brunswick → New Brunswick □[4] 176 46.30 N 66.15 W
Nueva Caledonia → New Caledonia □[2] 165f 21.30 S 165.30 E
Nueva California 242 32.45 S 68.20 W
Nueva Casas Grandes 222 30.25 N 107.55 W
Nueva Chicago ✦[8] 278 34.40 S 58.30 W
Nueva Ciudad Guerrero 222 26.35 N 99.15 W
Nueva Concepción 226 14.08 N 89.18 W
Nueva Coronela 276b 23.04 N 82.28 W
Nueva Cuadrilla 224 18.04 N 101.33 W
Nueva Ecija □[4] 106 15.35 N 121.00 E
Nueva Escocia → Nova Scotia □[4] 176 45.00 N 63.00 W
Nueva Esparta □[3] 236 11.00 N 64.00 W
Nueva Francia 242 28.11 S 64.12 W
Nueva Galia 242 35.07 S 65.15 W
Nueva Germania 242 23.54 S 56.45 W
Nueva Gerona 230p 21.53 N 82.48 W
Nueva Guinea, Isla → New Guinea I 154 5.00 S 140.00 E
Nueva Hébridas → New Hebrides □[2] 165f 16.00 S 167.00 E
Nueva Helvecia 248 34.19 S 57.13 W
Nueva Imperial 242 38.44 S 72.57 W
Nueva Italia de Ruiz 224 19.01 N 102.06 W
Nueva Lubecka 244 44.32 S 70.24 W
Nueva Palmira 248 33.53 S 58.25 W
Nueva Paz 230p 22.46 N 81.45 W
Nueva Pompeya ✦[8] 278 34.39 S 58.25 W
Nueva Rosita 222 27.57 N 101.13 W
Nueva San Salvador 226 13.41 N 89.17 W
Nueva Segovia □[5] 226 13.40 N 86.10 W
Nueva Siberia, Islas → Novosibirskije Ostrova II 64 75.00 N 142.00 E
Nueva Venecia 226 14.03 N 91.33 W
Nueva Vizcaya □[4] 106 16.20 N 121.20 E
Nueva Zelandia → New Zealand □[1] 162 41.00 S 174.00 E
Nueva Zembla, Isla de → Novaja Zeml'a II 62 74.00 N 57.00 E
Nueve de Julio 242 35.27 S 60.52 W
Nuevitas 230p 21.33 N 77.16 W
Nuevitas, Bahía de ⊂ 230p 21.30 N 77.12 W
Nuevo 218 33.48 N 117.09 W
Nuevo, Golfo ⊂ 244 42.42 S 64.36 W
Nuevo Berlín 242 32.59 S 58.03 W
Nuevo Camarón 186 27.05 N 99.55 W
Nuevo Chagres 226 9.14 N 80.05 W
Nuevo Laredo 222 27.30 N 99.31 W
Nuevo Léon 194 32.20 N 115.12 W
Nuevo León □[3] 222 25.40 N 100.00 W
Nuevo Morelos 224 17.31 N 95.02 W
Nuevo Mundo, Cerro ∧ 238 21.55 S 66.53 W
Nuevo Necaxa 224 20.13 N 98.00 W
Nuevo Poblado el Oro 186 26.50 N 101.19 W
Nuevo Primero de Mayo 186 26.01 N 98.02 W
Nuevo Progreso 222 18.38 N 92.18 W
Nuevo Rocafuerte 236 0.56 S 75.24 W
Nuevo Saucillo 186 27.20 N 104.54 W
Nugget Point ≻ 162 46.27 S 169.49 E
Nûgssuaq ≻[1] 166 71.45 N 53.00 W
Nugu ⊜[1] 112 11.58 N 76.28 E
Nuguria Islands II 14 3.20 S 154.45 E
Nūh 114 28.07 N 77.01 E
Nūh, Rās ≻ 118 25.05 N 62.24 E
Nuhaka 162 39.03 S 177.45 E
Nuhaydāt as-Sūd, Jabal an- ∧ 132 28.01 N 32.21 E
Nuhūd, Jabal an- ∧ 130 14.50 N 29.53 E
Nui I[1] 14 7.15 S 177.10 E
Nuia 66 58.04 N 25.33 E
Nuits-Saint-Georges 54 47.08 N 4.57 E
Nuits-sur-Armançon 46 47.44 N 4.12 E
N'uja 64 60.32 N 116.14 E
N'uja ≃ 64 60.32 N 116.20 E
Nujiang 92 29.58 N 97.25 E
N'uk, Ozero ⊜ 24 64.27 N 31.45 E
Nuka Island I 170 59.21 N 150.42 W
Nukata 84 34.55 N 137.17 E
Nukey Bluff ✦[4] 156 32.33 S 135.40 E
Nukhayb 118 32.02 N 42.15 E
Nukhaylah ✦[4] 130 19.03 N 26.19 E
Nukiki 165e 6.46 S 156.28 E
N'uksenica 24 60.25 N 44.13 E
Nuktal', Chrebet ∧∧ 74 42.15 N 46.35 E
Nukualofa 164w 21.08 S 175.12 W
Nukufetau I[1] 14 8.00 S 178.22 E
Nukuhu 154 5.35 S 149.25 E
Nukulailai I[1] 14 9.23 S 179.52 E
Nukumanu Islands II 14 4.30 S 159.30 E
Nukunonu I 14 9.12 S 171.54 W
Nukunuku 164w 21.08 S 175.18 W
Nukuoro I[1] 14 3.51 N 154.58 E
Nukus 62 42.50 N 59.29 E
Nulato 170 64.43 N 158.06 W
Nules 34 39.51 N 0.09 W
Nullagine 152 21.53 S 120.06 E
Nullagine ≃ 152 20.43 S 120.33 E
Nullarbor 152 31.26 S 130.55 E
Nullarbor Plain ⊻ 152 31.00 S 129.00 E
Nulltown 208 39.35 N 85.10 W
Nuluerhushan ∧∧ 94 42.20 N 120.35 E
Nul'vand 75 38.16 N 70.32 E
Num, Pulau I 154 1.30 S 135.13 E
Numabin Bay ⊂ 174 56.30 N 103.08 W
Numakuma 86 34.20 N 133.20 E
Numana 60 43.31 N 13.37 E
Numancia 106 9.52 N 125.58 E
Numancia ⊥ 34 41.48 N 2.25 W
Numansdorp 48 51.44 N 4.26 E
Numara I 112 6.26 N 73.03 E
Numarán 224 20.15 N 101.56 W
Numata, Nihon 82a 43.48 N 141.57 E
Numata, Nihon 84 36.38 N 139.03 E
Numata, Nihon 86 34.27 N 132.24 E
Numatinna ≃ 130 7.14 N 27.37 E
Numazu 84 35.06 N 138.52 E
Numbargulme, Mount ∧ 154 14.56 S 145.03 E
Number 5 Mine 204 41.08 N 80.11 W
Numedal ∨ 26 60.06 N 9.06 E
Numeralla 161b 36.11 S 149.20 E
Numfoor, Pulau I 154 1.03 S 134.54 E
Numidia 200 40.53 N 76.24 W
Numila 219b 21.54 N 159.34 W
Nu Mine 204 40.48 N 79.18 W
Numto 64 63.40 N 71.20 E
Numurkah 156 36.06 S 145.26 E
Nun ≃[1] 140 4.20 N 6.00 E
Nun'amo 170 65.37 N 170.40 W
Nunapitchuk 170 60.54 N 162.29 W
Nunawading 159 37.49 S 145.10 E
Nünchritz 50 51.18 N 13.23 E
Nunda 200 42.35 N 77.57 W
Nundah 161a 27.24 S 153.04 E
Nundu 144 3.49 S 29.05 E
Nuneaton 44 52.32 N 1.28 W
Núñez ✦[8] 278 34.33 S 58.27 W
Nunez ≃ 140 10.36 N 14.40 W
Núñez, Isla I 244 53.31 S 73.48 W
Nungarin 152 31.11 S 118.06 E
Nungesser Lake ⊜ 174 51.28 N 93.35 W
Nungwe 144 2.46 S 32.01 E
Nunica 206 43.10 N 86.04 W
Nunivak Island I 170 60.00 N 166.30 W
Nunjiang 79 49.10 N 125.11 E
Nunjiang ≃ 79 45.25 N 124.40 E
Nunjikompita 152 32.16 S 134.19 E
Nunkiní 222 20.20 N 90.11 W
Nunkun ∧ 113 33.59 N 76.01 E
Nunligran 170 64.48 N 175.24 W
Nunnelly 184 35.52 N 87.28 W
Ñuñoa 276e 33.28 S 70.36 W
Nunshan 79 48.59 N 125.14 E
Nunspeet 48 52.23 N 5.46 E
Nuomindashan ∧ 79 50.15 N 122.46 E
Nuominhe ≃ 79 48.06 N 124.26 E
Nuorang 110 27.36 N 92.59 E
Nuoro 36 40.19 N 9.20 E
Nuqruș, Jabal ∧ 130 24.49 N 34.36 E
Nuquí 236 5.42 N 77.17 W
Nura 76 48.53 N 62.20 E
Nura ≃ 76 50.30 N 69.59 E
Nuraghe San Antine ⊥ 36 40.30 N 8.46 E
Nurakita I 14 10.45 S 179.30 E
Nurallao 36 39.46 N 9.05 E
Nuratau, Chrebet ∧∧ 75 40.20 N 67.15 E
N'urba 64 63.17 N 118.20 E
Nürburg 52 50.21 N 6.57 E
Nürburgring ✦ 52 50.21 N 6.58 E
Nur Dağları ∧∧ 120 36.45 N 36.20 E
Nure ≃ 56 45.03 N 9.49 E
Nurek 75 38.23 N 69.19 E
Nuremberg → Nürnberg, B.R.D. 52 49.27 N 11.04 E
Nuremberg, Pa., U.S. 200 40.56 N 76.10 W
Nürenbei 97 30.11 N 106.04 E
Nurettin 120 39.14 N 42.25 E
Nurhak 120 37.58 N 37.25 E
Nuri 222 28.02 N 109.22 W
Nuria, Monte ∧ 60 42.21 N 13.05 E
Nuriootpa 158b 34.29 S 139.00 E
Nurlat 70 54.26 N 50.46 E
Nurlaty 70 55.37 N 48.18 E
Nūrmahal 113 31.06 N 75.36 E
Nurmes 26 63.33 N 29.07 E
Nurmijärvi 26 60.28 N 24.48 E
Nurnagar 116 22.20 N 89.03 E
Nürnberg 52 49.27 N 11.04 E
Nürnberg, Flughafen ⊠ 52 49.30 N 11.06 E
Nūrpur, Bhārat 113 32.18 N 75.54 E
Nūrpur, Bhārat 113 31.10 N 76.29 E
Nurpur, Bhārat 116 22.13 N 88.05 E
Nūrpur, Pāk. 113 31.53 N 71.54 E
Nurra ✦[1] 36 40.45 N 8.15 E
Nurrari Lakes ⊜ 152 29.01 S 130.05 E
Nurri 36 39.42 N 9.14 E
Nurri, Mount ∧ 156 31.42 S 146.02 E
Nursery 212 28.56 N 97.06 W
Nürtingen 52 48.38 N 9.20 E
Nuruhak Dağı ∧ 120 38.04 N 37.29 E
Nus 56 45.45 N 7.28 E
Nūsa 134 14.00 N 46.43 E
Nusa Barung, Pulau I 105a 8.28 S 113.20 E
Nusa Tenggara Barat (Lesser Sunda Islands) □[4] 105b 8.50 S 117.30 E
Nusa Tenggara Timur □[4] 102 9.30 S 122.00 E
Nusaybin 120 37.03 N 41.13 E
Nusco 60 40.53 N 15.05 E
Nushagak ≃ 170 59.00 N 158.30 W
Nushagak Bay ⊂ 170 58.40 N 158.40 W
Nushagak Peninsula ≻[1] 170 58.30 N 159.00 W
Nushan ∧∧ 92 28.41 N 98.24 E
Nu-shima I 86 34.10 N 134.50 E
Nushki 110 29.33 N 66.01 E
Nusplingen 54 48.08 N 8.53 E
Nuśpoly 72 56.39 N 37.44 E
Nussdorf ✦[8] 254b 48.15 N 16.22 E
Nussdorf am Attersee 58 47.53 N 13.31 E
Nuta ≃ 86 34.23 N 133.04 E
Nutae 164s 17.44 S 149.15 W
Nutauge, Laguna ⊂ 170 67.55 N 176.45 W
Nutepel'men, S.S.S.R. 170 67.26 N 174.56 W
Nutepelmen, S.S.S.R. 170 65.31 N 178.30 W
Nutfield 250 51.14 N 0.07 W
Nuth 52 50.55 N 5.54 E
Nuthe ≃, D.D.R. 50 52.23 N 13.04 E
Nuthe ≃, D.D.R. 50 51.58 N 11.53 E
Nut Lake Indian Reserve ✦[4] 174 52.20 N 103.30 W
Nutley 200 40.49 N 74.10 W
Nutrioso 190 33.57 N 109.13 W
Nut Swamp Brook ≃ 266 40.21 N 74.06 W
Nuttby Mountain ∧[2] 176 45.33 N 63.13 W
Nutter Fort 178 39.20 N 80.19 W
Nutting Lake 197 42.32 N 71.16 W
Nutting Lake ⊜ 273 42.32 N 71.16 W
Nutwood 209 39.05 N 90.39 W
Nutwood Downs 154 15.49 S 134.10 E
Nutzotin Mountains ∧∧ 170 62.10 N 141.40 W
Nu'ūmīyah, Wādī an- ∨ 132 29.31 N 31.17 E
Nuupere, Pointe ≻ 164s 17.36 S 149.47 W
Nuuuli 164u 14.18 S 170.42 W
N'uvčim 24 61.22 N 50.42 E
Nuwa-jima I 86 33.58 N 132.38 E
Nuwākot 114 28.08 N 83.53 E
Nuwara-Eliya 112 6.58 N 80.46 E
Nuwaybi' al-Muzayyinah 130 28.58 N 34.39 E
Nuwerus 148 31.08 S 18.24 E
Nuweveldberge ∧∧ 148 32.13 S 21.40 E
Nuyakuk Lake ⊜ 170 60.00 N 158.40 W
Nuyts, Point ≻ 152 35.04 S 116.37 E
Nuyts Archipelago II 152 32.35 S 133.17 E
Nūzvīd 112 16.47 N 80.51 E
N'Vinda 142 13.04 S 18.57 E
Nwa 142 6.30 N 11.00 E
Nxainxai 146 19.50 S 21.13 E
Nxaunxau 146 18.19 S 21.04 E
Nyaake 140 4.52 N 7.37 W
Nyabéssan 142 2.24 N 10.24 E
Nyabing 152 33.32 S 118.09 E
Nyac 170 61.01 N 159.57 W
Nyack 200 41.05 N 73.55 W
Nyack Beach State Park ✦ 266 41.07 N 73.55 W
Nyadiri ≃ 144 16.44 S 32.33 E
Nyahanga 144 2.23 S 33.33 E
Nyahua 144 5.24 S 33.19 E
Nyah West 156 35.11 S 143.22 E
Nyakabindi 144 2.38 S 33.59 E
Nyakakiri 144 2.15 S 31.28 E
Nyakanazi 144 3.00 S 31.15 E
Nyakrom 140 5.37 N 0.48 W
Nyakulenga 142 13.03 S 23.29 E
Nyala 130 12.03 N 24.53 E
Nyalas 104 2.26 N 102.28 E
Nyamandhlovu 144 19.50 S 28.16 E
Nyamina 140 13.19 N 6.59 W
Nyamlell 130 9.07 N 26.58 E
Nyamtumbo 144 10.29 S 36.02 E
Nyamwage 144 8.08 S 39.00 E
Nyandekwa 144 3.55 S 32.30 E
Nyanding, Khawr ∨ 130 8.40 N 32.41 E
Nyanga □[4] 142 3.00 S 11.00 E
Nyanga ≃ 142 2.58 S 10.15 E
Nyanga, Lake ⊜ 152 29.57 S 126.10 E
Nyanga, Réserve de la ✦[4] 142 3.00 S 11.45 E
Nyangana 142 18.00 S 20.41 E
Nyangui ∧ 144 17.53 S 32.44 E
Nyanji Mission 144 14.23 S 31.48 E
Nyanza 144 2.21 S 29.45 E
Nyanza □[4] 144 0.30 S 34.30 E
Nyanza-Lac 144 4.21 S 29.36 E
Nyasa, Lake (Lake Malawi) ⊜ 144 12.00 S 34.30 E
Nyaunglebin 100 17.57 N 96.44 E
Nyavikungu 144 11.26 S 25.54 E
Nyazvidzi ≃ 144 20.00 S 32.17 E
Nybergsund 26 61.15 N 12.19 E
Nyborg 41 55.19 N 10.48 E
Nybro 26 56.45 N 15.54 E
Nyda 64 66.36 N 72.54 E
Nyenchentangiha ∧ 114 30.22 N 90.35 E
Nyengo Swamp ≋ 142 14.51 S 22.07 E
Nyenyam 110 28.11 N 85.58 E
Nyeri 144 0.25 S 36.57 E
Nyerol 130 8.41 N 32.02 E
Nyfer ≃ 44 52.02 N 4.50 W
Nygligan, Mys ≻ 170 65.05 N 172.06 W
Nyhammar 40 60.17 N 14.58 E
Nyhyttan 40 59.40 N 14.48 E
Nyiel 130 6.06 N 31.13 E
Nyika Plateau ∧∧[1] 144 10.40 S 33.50 E
Nyilumba 144 10.29 S 40.20 E
Nyimba 144 14.35 S 30.52 E
Nyíradony 30 47.41 N 21.55 E
Nyírbátor 30 47.50 N 22.08 E
Nyíregyháza 30 47.59 N 21.43 E
Nyiri Desert ✦[2] 144 2.25 S 37.20 E
Nyiru, Mount ∧ 144 2.08 N 36.51 E
Nykøbing, Dan. 26 56.48 N 8.52 E
Nykøbing, Dan. 41 54.46 N 11.53 E
Nykøbing, Dan. 41 55.55 N 11.41 E
Nyköping 40 58.45 N 17.00 E
Nykroppa 40 59.38 N 14.18 E
Nykvarn 40 59.11 N 17.26 E
Nyland 26 63.00 N 17.46 E
Nyland Acres 218 34.14 N 119.09 W
Nylga, S.S.S.R. 70 56.46 N 52.22 E
Nylga, S.S.S.R. 79 51.38 N 127.35 E
Nylstroom 146 24.42 S 28.20 E
Nymagee 156 32.04 S 146.20 E
Nymboida ≃ 156 29.39 S 152.30 E
Nymburk 30 50.11 N 15.03 E
Nymphenburg ✦[8] 58 48.09 N 11.30 E
Nynäshamn 40 58.54 N 17.57 E
Nyngan 156 31.34 S 147.11 E
Nyoma 110 33.11 N 78.38 E
Nyon 54 46.23 N 6.14 E
Nyong ≃ 142 3.17 N 9.54 E

Symbols in the index entries represent the broad categories identified in the key at the right. Symbols with superior numbers (∧∧[2]) identify subcategories (see complete key on page *I · 26*).

Kartensymbole in dem Registerverzeichnis stellen die rechts in Schlüssel erklärten Kategorien dar. Symbole mit hochgestellten Ziffern (∧∧[2]) bezeichnen Unterabteilungen einer Kategorie (vgl. vollständiger Schlüssel auf Seite *I · 26*).

Los símbolos incluídos en el texto del índice representan las grandes categorias identificadas con la clave a la derecha. Los símbolos con numeros en su parte superior (∧∧[2]) identifican las subcategorías (véase la clave completa en la página *I · 26*).

Les symboles de l'index représentent les catégories indiquées dans la légende à droite. Les symboles suivis d'un indice (∧∧[2]) représentent des sous-catégories (voir légende complète à la page *I · 26*).

Os símbolos incluídos no texto do índice representam as grandes categorias identificadas com a chave à direita. Os símbolos com números em sua parte superior (∧∧[2]) identificam as subcategorias (veja-se a chave completa à página *I · 26*).

∧	Mountain	Berg	Montaña	Montagne	Montanha
∧∧	Mountains	Berge	Montañas	Montagnes	Montanhas
)(	Pass	Pass	Paso	Col	Passo
∨	Valley, Canyon	Tal, Cañon	Valle, Cañón	Vallée, Canyon	Vale, Canhão
⊻	Plain	Ebene	Llano	Plaine	Planície
≻	Cape	Kap	Cabo	Cap	Cabo
I	Island	Insel	Isla	Île	Ilha
II	Islands	Inseln	Islas	Îles	Ilhas
✦	Other Topographic Features	Andere Topographische Objekte	Otros Elementos Topográficos	Autres données topographiques	Outros Elementos Topográficos

≃ River	Fluss	Río	Rivière	Rio
☲ Canal	Kanal	Canal	Canal	Canal
ɭ Waterfall, Rapids	Wasserfall, Stromschnellen	Cascada, Rápidos	Chute d'eau, Rapides	Cascata, Rápidos
⊔ Strait	Meeresstrasse	Estrecho	Détroit	Estreito
C Bay, Gulf	Bucht, Golf	Bahía, Golfo	Baie, Golfe	Baía, Golfo
⊜ Lake, Lakes	See, Seen	Lago, Lagos	Lac, Lacs	Lago, Lagos
☷ Swamp	Sumpf	Pantano	Marais	Pântano
• Ice Features, Glacier	Eis- und Gletscherformen	Accidentes Glaciales	Formes glaciaires	Acidentes Glaciares
▾ Other Hydrographic Features	Andere Hydrographische Objekte	Otros Elementos Hidrográficos	Autres données hydrographiques	Outros Acidentes Hidrográficos

✢ Submarine Features	Untermeerische Objekte	Accidentes Submarinos	Formes de relief sous-marin	Acidentes Submarinos
□ Political Unit	Politische Einheit	Unidad Politica	Entité politique	Unidade Política
ʊ Cultural Institution	Kulturelle Institution	Institución Cultural	Institution culturelle	Instituição Cultural
⊥ Historical Site	Historische Stätte	Sitio Histórico	Site historique	Sítio Histórico
♠ Recreational Site	Erholungs- und Ferienort	Sitio de Recreo	Centre de loisirs	Sítio de Lazer
⊠ Airport	Flughafen	Aeropuerto	Aéroport	Aeroporto
■ Military Installation	Militäranlage	Instalación Militar	Installation militaire	Instalação Militar
◆ Miscellaneous	Verschiedenes	Misceláneo	Divers	Miscelânea

Ohey 52 50.26 N 5.08 E
O'Higgins □[4] 242 34.15 S 70.45 W
O'Higgins, Cabo ≻ 164z 27.05 S 109.15 W
O'Higgins, Cerro ▲ 244 48.48 S 73.11 W
O'Higgins, Lago (Lago San Martín) ⊜ 244 49.00 S 72.40 W
Ohingaiti 162 39.52 S 175.43 E
Ohio 180 41.34 N 89.28 W
Ohio □[6], Ind., U.S. 208 38.57 N 84.51 W
Ohio □[6], W. Va., U.S. 204 40.09 N 80.35 W
Ohio □[3] 168
178 40.15 N 82.45 W
Ohio ≃ 168 36.59 N 89.08 W
Ohio Brush Creek ≃ 208 38.41 N 83.27 W
Ohio Brush Creek, Baker Fork ≃ 208 39.02 N 83.26 W
Ohio Brush Creek, Little West Fork ≃ 208 38.58 N 83.34 W
Ohio Brush Creek, West Fork ≃ 208 38.56 N 83.28 W
Ohio Caverns •[5] 206 40.14 N 83.43 W
Ohio City 206 40.46 N 84.37 W
Ohio Peak ▲ 190 38.49 N 107.07 W
Ohiopyle State Park ♠ 178 39.50 N 79.31 W
Ohioville, N.Y., U.S. 200 41.45 N 74.03 W
Ohioville, Pa., U.S. 204 40.41 N 80.30 W
Ōhira 84 36.20 N 139.42 E
Ōhira-yama ▲ 86 34.20 N 133.57 E
Ōhito 84 34.59 N 138.56 E
Ohlau → Oława 30 50.57 N 17.17 E
Ohligs ◆[8] 253 51.09 N 7.00 E
Ohlman 209 39.21 N 89.13 W
Ohlsdorf 58 47.57 N 13.47 E
Ohm ≃ 52 50.51 N 8.48 E
Ōho 84 36.08 N 140.06 E
Ohoitom 154 5.56 S 132.41 E
Ohonua 164w 21.20 S 174.57 W
Ohoopee ≃ 182 31.54 N 82.07 W
Ohopoho 142 18.03 S 13.45 E
Ōhori 258 35.20 N 139.52 E
Ohorn 50 51.10 N 14.02 E
Ohra Stausee ⊜[1] 50 50.46 N 10.42 E
Ohrdruf 50 50.50 N 10.44 E
Ohre ≃, Eur. 50 52.18 N 11.47 E
Ohře (Eger) ≃, Eur. 50 50.32 N 14.08 E
Ohrid 38 41.07 N 20.47 E
Ohrid, Lake ⊜ 38 41.02 N 20.43 E
Ohrigstad 146 24.49 S 30.33 E
Öhringen 52 49.12 N 9.29 E
Ohrnberg 52 49.15 N 9.27 E
Ohuira, Bahía de ⊂ 222 25.38 N 108.58 W
Ohura 162 38.50 S 174.59 E
Ōi, Nihon 86 35.28 N 135.37 E
Ōi, Nihon 258 35.51 N 139.30 E
Ōi ≃, Nihon 84 34.46 N 138.18 E
Ōi ≃, Nihon 86 35.01 N 135.39 E
Oiapoque 240 3.50 N 51.50 W
Oiapoque (Oyapock) ≃ 240 4.08 N 51.40 W
Oies, Île aux I 176 47.07 N 70.30 W
Ōigawa 84 34.48 N 138.17 E
Oignies 46 50.28 N 2.59 E
Oik 75 43.46 N 70.58 E
Oil Center 186 32.30 N 103.16 W
Oil City, La., U.S. 184 32.45 N 93.58 W
Oil City, Pa., U.S. 204 41.26 N 79.42 W
Oil Creek ≃ 204 41.26 N 79.42 W
Oil Creek State Park ♠ 204 41.33 N 79.40 W
Oildale 216 35.25 N 119.01 W
Oil Springs 204 42.47 N 82.07 W
Oilton, Okla., U.S. 186 36.05 N 96.35 W
Oilton, Tex., U.S. 186 27.33 N 98.59 W
Oinville-sur-Montcient 251 49.02 N 1.51 E
Oir, Beinn an ▲ 42 55.54 N 6.00 W
Oirschot 48 51.30 N 5.18 E
Oise □[5] 46 49.30 N 2.30 E
Oise ≃ 46 49.00 N 2.04 E
Oise à l'Aisne, Canal de l' ≅ 46 49.36 N 3.11 E
Oisemont 46 49.57 N 1.46 E
Ōiso, Nihon 84 35.18 N 139.19 E
Ōiso, Nihon 260 34.33 N 135.01 E
Oissel 46 49.20 N 1.06 E
Oissery 251 49.04 N 2.49 E
Oisterwijk 48 51.35 N 5.12 E
Oistins 231g 13.04 N 59.32 W
Oistins Bay ⊂ 231g 13.03 N 59.33 W
Ōita 86 33.14 N 131.36 E
Ōita □[5] 86 33.15 N 131.30 E
Ōita ≃ 86 33.15 N 131.37 E
Oiticica 240 5.03 S 41.05 W
Oituz, Pasul)(38 46.03 N 26.23 E
Ōiwa 260 34.53 N 135.33 E
Ōizumi, Nihon 84 36.15 N 139.25 E
Ōizumi, Nihon 84 35.52 N 138.23 E
Oizuruga-take ▲ 84 36.18 N 136.47 E
Öja I 40 58.45 N 17.52 E
Oja ≃ 76 53.26 N 91.55 E
Ojai 218 34.27 N 119.15 W
Öjaren ⊜ 40 60.43 N 16.50 E
Ojat' ≃ 66 60.31 N 33.00 E
Ojcowski Park Narodowy ♠ 30 50.15 N 19.50 E
Öje 26 60.49 N 13.51 E
Ojek 78 52.35 N 104.27 E
Ojgon Nuur ⊜ 78 49.10 N 96.36 E
Ojgor 76 49.10 N 89.17 E
Ōji 86 34.35 N 135.42 E
Ojika-hantō ≻[1] 82 38.20 N 141.30 E
Ōjima 84 36.15 N 139.20 E
Ojinaga 222 29.34 N 104.25 W
Ojitlán 224 18.04 N 96.23 W
Ojiya 82 37.18 N 138.48 E
Ojm'akon 64 63.28 N 142.49 E
Ojocaliente 224 22.34 N 102.15 W
Ojo de Agua de Alférez 224 22.51 N 99.42 W
Ojo de la Casa 190 31.23 N 106.32 W
Ojo de Liebre, Laguna ⊂ 222 27.45 N 114.15 W
Ojos del Salado, Cerro ▲ 242 27.06 S 68.32 W
Ojota 263a 6.35 N 3.23 E
Ojtal, S.S.S.R. 75 42.55 N 73.17 E
Ojtal, S.S.S.R. 75 40.24 N 74.06 E
Oju 140 6.53 N 8.26 E
Ojuelos de Jalisco 224 21.52 N 101.35 W
Ojus 210 25.57 N 80.09 W
Oka 140 7.29 N 5.49 E
Oka ≃, S.S.S.R. 70 56.20 N 43.59 E
Oka ≃, S.S.S.R. 78 55.15 N 102.10 E
Okaba 154 8.06 S 139.42 E
Okabe, Nihon 84 36.12 N 139.15 E
Okabe, Nihon 84 34.55 N 138.17 E
Okagaki 86 33.50 N 130.38 E
Okahandja 146 21.59 S 16.58 E
Okahandja □[5] 146 21.30 S 17.00 E
Okahukura 162 38.47 S 175.13 E
Okahumpka 210 28.45 N 81.54 W
Okaihau 162 35.19 S 173.47 E
Okalataka 142 0.20 S 14.59 E
Okaloacoochee Slough ≃ 210 26.16 N 81.17 W
Okam 120 40.53 N 42.36 E
Okamoto 260 34.59 N 135.58 E
Okamoto ◆[8] 260 34.44 N 135.16 E
Okanagan (Okanogan) ≃ 172 48.06 N 119.43 W
Okanagan Centre 172 50.03 N 119.27 W
Okanagan Falls 172 49.21 N 119.34 W
Okanagan Indian Reserve ◆[4] 172 50.21 N 119.17 W
Okanagan Lake ⊜ 172 50.00 N 119.28 W
Okanagan Landing 172 50.14 N 119.22 W
Okanagan Range ⛰ 192 48.40 N 119.45 W
Okanda, Parc National de l' ♠ 142 0.30 S 11.40 E
Okanogan 192 48.22 N 119.35 W
Okanogan □[6] 214 48.39 N 120.41 W
Okanogan Range (Okanagan Range) ⛰ 172 49.00 N 120.00 W
Okapilco Creek ≃ 182 30.45 N 83.30 W
Okaputa 146 20.09 S 16.56 E
Okāra 113 30.49 N 73.27 E
Okarche 186 35.44 N 97.58 W
Okarito 162 43.14 S 170.11 E
Okasaki 260 34.46 N 135.52 E
Okato 162 39.12 S 173.53 E
Okau 164q 9.32 N 138.06 E
Okauchee 206 43.07 N 88.26 W
Okauchee Lake ⊜ 206 43.07 N 88.26 W
Okaukuejo 146 19.10 S 15.54 E
Okavango (Cubango) ≃ 128 18.50 S 22.25 E
Okavango Swamp ≡ 146 18.45 S 22.45 E
Ōkawa, Nihon 82 33.12 N 130.23 E
Ōkawa, Nihon 84 35.05 N 138.15 E
Ōkawa, Nihon 86 33.47 N 133.26 E
Ōkawachi 86 35.04 N 134.45 E
Ōkawado 258 35.56 N 139.49 E
Okawville 209 38.26 N 89.33 W
Okaya 84 36.03 N 138.03 E
Okayama 86 34.39 N 133.55 E
Okayama □[5] 86 35.00 N 134.00 E
Okayama-heiya ≚ 82 34.35 N 133.51 E
Okazaki 84 34.57 N 137.10 E
Okch'ŏn 88 36.20 N 127.34 E
Oke-Aro 263a 6.41 N 3.19 E
Okeechobee 210 27.15 N 80.50 W
Okeechobee □[6] 210 27.25 N 80.52 W
Okeechobee, Lake ⊜ 210 26.55 N 80.45 W
O'Keefe Centre ⌂ 265b 43.37 N 79.22 W
Okeene 186 36.07 N 98.19 W
Okefenokee Swamp ≡ 182 30.42 N 82.20 W
Okegawa 84 36.00 N 139.35 E
Okehampton 44 50.44 N 4.00 W
Oke-Igbo 140 7.09 N 4.43 E
Okemah 186 35.26 N 96.19 W
Okemasis and Beardy Indian Reserve ◆[4] 174 52.48 N 106.20 W
Okement ≃ 44 50.50 N 4.01 W
Okemos 206 42.43 N 84.26 W
Okene 140 7.33 N 6.15 E
Oke-Ode 140 8.33 N 5.02 E
Oke Ogbe 263a 6.24 N 3.23 E
Oker 48 51.54 N 10.29 E
Oker ≃ 50 52.30 N 10.22 E
Okere ≃ 144 2.07 N 33.55 E
Oker Talsperre ◆[6] 48 51.48 N 10.27 E
Okhaldhunga 114 27.19 N 86.30 E
Okhla ◆[8] 262a 28.34 N 77.18 E
Okhotsk, Sea of (Ochotskoje More) ⊤[2] 64 53.00 N 150.00 E
Okhotsk Basin ✦[1] 12 53.00 N 148.00 E
Okiep 146 29.39 S 17.53 E
Oki-guntō II 82 36.15 N 133.15 E
Okinawa □[5] 83b 26.31 N 127.59 E
Okinawa-jima I 164m 26.30 N 128.00 E
Okino-Daitō-jima I 80 24.28 N 131.11 E
Okino-Erabu-shima I 83b 27.22 N 128.35 E
Okinokami-shima I 165d 24.11 N 123.33 E
Okino-Kl'uči 78 50.36 N 107.06 E
Okino-shima I, Nihon 84 35.12 N 136.04 E
Okino-shima I, Nihon 86 34.07 N 135.06 E
Okino-Tori-Shima I 80 20.25 N 136.00 E
Okinskij Chrebet ⛰ 78 53.10 N 99.50 E
Okitipupa 140 6.29 N 4.46 E
Okitsu-zaki ≻ 86 33.09 N 133.14 E
Okkang-ni 88 40.18 N 124.42 E
Okkerbil' ≃ 255a 59.56 N 30.26 E
Okladnevo 66 58.36 N 33.39 E
Oklahoma, Pa., U.S. 204 41.07 N 78.44 W
Oklahoma, Pa., U.S. 269b 40.35 N 79.35 W
Oklahoma □[3] 168
186 35.30 N 98.00 W
Oklahoma City 186 35.28 N 97.32 W
Oklawaha 210 29.03 N 81.56 W
Oklawaha ≃ 182 29.28 N 81.41 W
Oklee 188 47.50 N 95.51 W
Okmulgee 186 35.37 N 95.58 W
Oknica 68 48.24 N 27.29 E
Okno 68 48.34 N 25.58 E
Oko, Wādī ∨ 130 21.15 N 35.56 E
Okobojo Creek ≃ 188 44.38 N 100.28 W
Ōkōchi 84 35.09 N 138.22 E
Okok ≃ 144 2.06 N 33.53 E
Okoka 142 2.57 S 23.27 E
Okola 142 4.01 N 11.23 E
Okollo 144 2.40 N 31.08 E
Okolo 142 3.46 S 23.55 E
Okolona, Ark., U.S. 184 34.00 N 93.20 W
Okolona, Ky., U.S. 184 38.08 N 85.41 W
Okolona, Miss., U.S. 184 34.00 N 88.45 W
Okombahe 146 21.23 S 15.22 E
Okondja 142 0.41 S 13.47 E
Okonek 30 53.33 N 16.50 E
Okonešnikovo 76 54.50 N 75.05 E
Okorokovo 72 54.02 N 36.40 E
Okotoks 172 50.44 N 113.59 W
Okoyo 142 1.28 S 15.04 E
Okpara ≃ 140 7.40 N 2.35 E
Okrika 140 4.47 N 7.04 E
Oksbøl 26 55.38 N 8.17 E
Okskij Zapovednik ◆[4] 70 54.45 N 40.45 E
Oksko-Donskaja Ravnina ≚ 70 53.00 N 40.30 E
Oksovskij 24 62.37 N 39.55 E
Oksskolten ▲ 24 65.59 N 14.15 E
Oksu ≃, S.S.S.R. 75 40.12 N 69.16 E
Oksu ≃, S.S.S.R. 75 38.09 N 73.57 E
Okt'abr', S.S.S.R. 66 57.50 N 37.26 E
Okt'abr', S.S.S.R. 75 43.41 N 77.12 E
Okt'abr', S.S.S.R. 76 45.45 N 61.34 E
Okt'abr'sk 70 53.11 N 48.40 E
Okt'abr'skij, S.S.S.R. 24 61.04 N 43.08 E
Okt'abr'skij, S.S.S.R. 24 59.29 N 48.50 E
Okt'abr'skij, S.S.S.R. 66 53.47 N 39.29 E
Okt'abr'skij, S.S.S.R. 66 52.38 N 28.53 E
Okt'abr'skij, S.S.S.R. 68 44.56 N 39.00 E
Okt'abr'skij, S.S.S.R. 68 50.26 N 36.22 E
Okt'abr'skij, S.S.S.R. 70 54.28 N 53.28 E
Okt'abr'skij, S.S.S.R. 70 57.08 N 40.20 E
Okt'abr'skij, S.S.S.R. 70 47.58 N 43.38 E
Okt'abr'skij, S.S.S.R. 70 56.17 N 44.12 E
Okt'abr'skij, S.S.S.R. 70 58.19 N 44.19 E
Okt'abr'skij, S.S.S.R. 70 56.35 N 53.58 E
Okt'abr'skij, S.S.S.R. 72 54.14 N 38.54 E
Okt'abr'skij, S.S.S.R. 72 55.37 N 37.58 E
Okt'abr'skij, S.S.S.R. 73 47.28 N 40.04 E
Okt'abr'skij, S.S.S.R. 75 38.33 N 68.22 E
Okt'abr'skij, S.S.S.R. 76 56.31 N 57.12 E
Okt'abr'skij, S.S.S.R. 76 49.38 N 83.35 E
Okt'abr'skij, S.S.S.R. 76 52.35 N 62.40 E
Okt'abr'skij, S.S.S.R. 78 56.05 N 99.26 E
Okt'abr'skij, S.S.S.R. 78 50.04 N 118.04 E
Okt'abr'skij, S.S.S.R. 79 49.02 N 140.11 E
Okt'abr'skij, S.S.S.R. 79 53.01 N 128.37 E
Okt'abr'skoje, S.S.S.R. 64 62.28 N 66.03 E
Okt'abr'skoje, S.S.S.R. 66 52.18 N 39.44 E
Okt'abr'skoje, S.S.S.R. 68 48.38 N 33.04 E
Okt'abr'skoje, S.S.S.R. 68 45.18 N 34.09 E
Okt'abr'skoje, S.S.S.R. 70 45.37 N 42.49 E
Okt'abr'skoje, S.S.S.R. 70 52.54 N 46.30 E
Okt'abr'skoje, S.S.S.R. 73 48.28 N 37.22 E
Okt'abr'skoje, S.S.S.R. 76 54.26 N 62.44 E
Okt'abr'skoje, S.S.S.R. 76 52.20 N 55.30 E
Okt'abr'skoje, S.S.S.R. 76 52.07 N 65.40 E
Okt'abr'skoj Revol'ucii, Ostrov I 64 79.30 N 97.00 E
Oktember'an 74 40.09 N 44.02 E
Oktong-ni 88 38.27 N 127.07 E
Oktwin 100 18.49 N 96.26 E
Oktyabr'skiy → Okt'abr'skij 70 54.28 N 53.28 E
Oku 86 34.40 N 134.05 E
Ōkubo, Nihon 258 35.21 N 139.56 E
Ōkubo, Nihon 260 34.41 N 134.47 E
Ōkubo ◆[8] 258 35.24 N 139.35 E
Okučani 36 45.16 N 17.12 E
Ōkuchi, Nihon 82 32.04 N 130.37 E
Okuchi, Nihon 84 36.17 N 136.39 E
Okuku ≃ 162 43.16 S 172.28 E
Okulovka 66 58.26 N 33.18 E
Okuma Bay ⊂ 9 77.48 S 158.35 W
Okumi 74 42.43 N 41.45 E
Okumyōgata 84 35.51 N 137.02 E
Okundi 140 6.22 N 8.44 E
Okun'ov Nos 24 66.15 N 52.28 E
Ōkura-yama ▲ 86 35.08 N 133.22 E
Okusawa ◆[8] 258 35.36 N 139.40 E
Okushiri 82a 42.10 N 139.31 E
Okushiri-tō I 82a 42.10 N 139.27 E
Ōkusu-yama ▲ 258 35.15 N 139.38 E
Okuta 140 9.14 N 3.15 E
Okutadami Dam ◆[6] 84 37.09 N 139.15 E
Okutama-ko ⊜ 84 35.47 N 139.02 E
Okutango-hantō ≻[1] 86 35.40 N 135.10 E
Okutsu 86 35.14 N 133.56 E
Ōkuwa 84 35.41 N 137.40 E
Okwa ≃ 146 22.30 S 23.00 E
Okwoga 140 7.01 N 7.50 E
Olá, Pan. 226 8.25 N 80.39 W
Ola, S.S.S.R. 64 59.35 N 151.17 E
Ola, Ark., U.S. 184 35.02 N 93.13 W
Ola ≃ 66 52.41 N 29.39 E
Ólafsfjördur 24a 66.06 N 18.38 W
Olancha 194 36.17 N 118.01 W
Olancha Peak ▲ 194 36.16 N 118.07 W
Olanchito 226 15.30 N 86.35 W
Olancho □[5] 226 14.45 N 86.00 W
Öland I 26 56.45 N 16.38 E
Olandsån ≃ 40 60.20 N 18.14 E
Olango Island I 106 10.16 N 124.03 E
Olanta 182 33.58 N 79.56 W
Olar 182 33.11 N 81.11 W
Olarevo 66 59.22 N 40.04 E
Olaria, Bra. 246 21.52 S 43.56 W
Olaria, Bra. 277a 22.41 S 43.08 W
Olaria ◆[8] 277a 22.52 S 43.15 W
Olary 156 32.17 S 140.19 E
Olascoaga 242 35.12 S 60.36 W
Olasore 263a 6.40 N 3.17 E
Olathe, Colo., U.S. 190 38.36 N 107.59 W
Olathe, Kans., U.S. 188 38.53 N 94.49 W
Olavarría 242 36.54 S 60.17 W
Olavinlinna ⊥ 26 61.52 N 29.00 E
Oława 30 50.57 N 17.17 E
Olbernhau 50 50.39 N 13.20 E
Olbersdorf 50 50.52 N 14.46 E
Olbersleben 50 51.09 N 11.20 E
Olbia 36 40.55 N 9.29 E
Ølby Lyng 41 55.29 N 12.09 E
Olca, Volcán ▲[1] 238 20.57 S 68.30 W
Ol'chi 70 53.53 N 41.28 E
Ol'chon, Ostrov I 78 53.09 N 107.24 E
Ol'chovaja ≃, S.S.S.R. 70 48.47 N 40.51 E
Ol'chovaja ≃, S.S.S.R. 73 48.35 N 39.17 E
Ol'chovatka, S.S.S.R. 68 50.18 N 39.17 E
Ol'chovatka, S.S.S.R. 73 48.15 N 38.25 E
Ol'chovčik ◆[8] 73 48.04 N 38.31 E
Ol'chovka, S.S.S.R. 70 49.52 N 44.34 E
Ol'chovka, S.S.S.R. 76 56.22 N 63.46 E
Ol'chovka ◆[8] 73 48.24 N 39.07 E
Ol'chovoje 73 48.40 N 39.34 E
Olcott 200 43.20 N 78.43 W
Old ≃, Calif., U.S. 216 38.04 N 121.35 W
Old ≃, Tex., U.S. 212 30.25 N 96.19 W
Old Bahama Channel ⋓ 228 22.30 N 78.50 W
Old Bedford ≃ 44 52.35 N 0.20 E
Old Bennington 200 42.52 N 73.13 W
Old Bethpage 266 40.45 N 73.28 W
Old Bethpage Village ⊥ 266 40.47 N 73.28 W
Old Bight 228 24.15 N 75.21 W
Old Brazoria 212 29.04 N 95.34 W
Old Bridge 266 40.25 N 74.22 W
Old Brookville 266 40.49 N 73.36 W
Oldbury 44 52.30 N 2.00 W
Old Cairo → Mişr al-Qadīmah ◆[8] 263c 30.00 N 31.14 E
Oldcastle 28 53.46 N 7.10 W
Old Colwyn 42 53.18 N 3.43 W
Old Cork 156 22.56 S 141.52 E
Old Crow 170 67.35 N 139.50 W
Old Crow ≃ 170 67.35 N 139.50 W
Oldeani 144 3.21 S 35.33 E
Oldebroek 48 52.26 N 5.54 E
Old Economy ⊥ 269b 40.36 N 80.14 W
Olden, Nor. 26 61.50 N 6.49 E
Olden, Tex., U.S. 186 32.25 N 98.45 W
Oldenbrok 48 53.17 N 8.23 E
Oldenburg, B.R.D. 48 53.08 N 8.13 E
Oldenburg, Ind., U.S. 208 39.20 N 85.12 W
Oldenburg □[6] 48 53.10 N 8.10 E
Oldenburg in Holstein 50 54.17 N 10.52 E
Oldendorf 48 53.35 N 9.14 E
Oldenstadt 48 52.58 N 10.35 E
Oldenswort 41 54.22 N 8.56 E
Oldenzaal 48 52.19 N 6.56 E
Oldersum 48 53.20 N 7.20 E
Old Faithful Geyser ⊤ 192 44.30 N 110.45 W
Old Farm 274c 39.03 N 77.09 W
Old Field 266 40.57 N 73.08 W
Old Field Point ≻ 266 40.58 N 73.07 W
Old Fletton 44 52.33 N 0.15 W
Old Ford Mountain ▲ 172 55.05 N 126.30 W
Old Forge, N.Y., U.S. 178 43.43 N 74.58 W
Old Forge, Pa., U.S. 200 41.22 N 75.44 W
Old Forge Village 266 40.49 N 74.29 W
Old Fort 204 41.15 N 83.09 W
Old Fort Bay 176 51.26 N 57.49 W
Old Fort Erie ⊥ 274a 42.53 N 78.56 W
Old Fort Henry ⊥ 202 44.14 N 76.28 W
Old Fort Niagara ⊥ 200 43.16 N 79.03 W
Old Fort Parker State Historic Site ⊥ 212 31.34 N 96.34 W
Old Fort Point ≻, Antig. 230c 17.02 N 61.53 W
Old Fort Point ≻, Ba. 230b 25.03 N 77.29 W
Old Greenwich 266 41.02 N 73.34 W
Oldham, Eng., U.K. 42 53.33 N 2.07 W
Oldham, S. Dak., U.S. 188 44.14 N 97.19 W
Oldham □[6] 208 38.23 N 85.27 W
Oldham □[8] 252 53.34 N 2.03 W
Oldham Pines 273 42.05 N 70.50 W
Oldham Pond ⊜ 273 42.03 N 70.51 W
Oldham Village 197 42.04 N 70.50 W
Old Harbor 170 57.12 N 153.19 W
Old Harbour 231q 17.56 N 77.07 W
Old Hickory Lake ⊜[1] 184 36.18 N 86.30 W
Old Howe ≃ 42 53.57 N 0.21 W
Oldisleben 50 51.18 N 11.10 E
Old Lyme 197 41.19 N 72.20 W
Old Malden ◆[8] 250 51.23 N 0.15 W
Oldman ≃ 172 49.56 N 111.42 W
Old Man House ⊥ 214 47.43 N 122.34 W
Old Man Mountain ▲ 176 49.08 N 57.43 W
Old Manor 266 40.24 N 74.11 W
Oldmans Creek ≃ 198 39.47 N 75.27 W
Oldmeldrum 28 57.20 N 2.20 W
Old Mkushi 144 14.22 S 29.22 E
Old Monroe 209 38.56 N 90.45 W
Old Mystic 197 41.23 N 71.58 W
Old Nene ≃ 44 52.40 N 0.10 E
Old Noranside 156 22.13 S 140.04 E
Old North Church ⌂[1] 273 42.22 N 71.03 W
Old Ocean 212 29.05 N 95.45 W
Ol Doinyo National Park ♠ 144 1.09 S 37.12 E
Ol'doj ≃ 79 53.33 N 123.21 E
Old Orchard ◆[9] 268 42.04 N 87.45 W
Old Orchard Beach 178 43.31 N 70.23 W
Old Perlican 176 48.05 N 53.01 W
Old Place Creek ≃ 266 40.38 N 74.12 W
Old Point Comfort ≻ 198 37.00 N 76.19 W
Old Rhodes Key I 210 25.22 N 80.14 W
Old Ripley 209 38.54 N 89.34 W
Old Road 230c 17.01 N 61.50 W
Old Road Bay ⊂ 274b 39.12 N 76.27 W
Old Road Bluff ≻ 230c 16.59 N 61.50 W
Old Round Rock 212 30.31 N 97.42 W
Olds 172 51.47 N 114.06 W
Old Saybrook 197 41.18 N 72.23 W
Oldsmar 210 28.02 N 82.40 W
Old Speck Mountain ▲ 178 44.34 N 70.57 W
Old Sturbridge Village ⊥ 197 42.07 N 72.07 W
Old Swamp ≃ 273 42.11 N 70.57 W
Old Swedes Church ⌂[1] 275 39.44 N 75.32 W
Old Tampa Bay ⊂ 210 27.56 N 82.35 W
Old Tappan 266 41.01 N 73.59 W
Old Tate 146 21.22 S 27.46 E
Old Town 178 44.56 N 68.39 W
Old Trafford Cricket Ground ♠ 252 53.28 N 2.17 W
Old Trap 182 36.15 N 76.02 W
Olduvai Gorge ∨ 144 2.58 S 35.22 E
Old Westbury 266 40.47 N 73.37 W
Old Westbury Gardens ♠ 266 40.46 N 73.36 W
Oldwick 200 40.40 N 74.45 W
Old Windsor 250 51.28 N 0.35 W
Old Wives Lake ⊜ 174 50.06 N 106.00 W
Old Woman Creek ≃ 188 43.19 N 104.21 W
Öldzijt, Mong. 78 48.10 N 102.34 E
Öldzijt, Mong. 92 45.20 N 106.20 E
Old Zoinsville 198 40.29 N 75.31 W
Olean 200 42.05 N 78.26 W
Olean Creek ≃ 200 42.04 N 78.25 W
O'Leary 176 46.42 N 64.13 W
Olecko 30 54.03 N 22.30 E
Olegário Maciel 246 22.19 S 45.35 W
Oleggio 56 45.36 N 8.38 E
Olekma → Ol'okma ≃ 64 60.22 N 120.42 E
Olema 24 64.30 N 46.08 E
Olen, Bel. 52 51.09 N 4.51 E
Ølen, Nor. 26 59.36 N 5.48 E
Ölen ⊜ 40 59.13 N 14.31 E
Olenegorsk 24 68.09 N 33.15 E
Olenevka 68 45.23 N 32.32 E
Olenguj ≃ 78 51.46 N 113.46 E
Olenica 24 66.29 N 35.20 E
Olenij, Ostrov I 64 72.25 N 77.45 E
Olenino 66 56.12 N 33.29 E
Olenja Rečka 76 52.48 N 93.14 E
Olen'kovo 72 54.34 N 38.06 E
Olen'ok 64 68.33 N 112.18 E
Olen'ok ≃ 64 73.00 N 119.55 E
Olen'okskij Zaliv ⊂ 64 73.20 N 121.00 E
Olentangy ≃ 204 39.58 N 83.06 W
Olenty 70 50.02 N 52.07 E
Olenty ≃ 70 49.50 N 52.03 E
Oleopolis 204 41.27 N 79.37 W
Oléron, Île d' I 32 45.56 N 1.15 W
Olesko 68 49.58 N 24.53 E
Oleśnica 30 51.13 N 17.23 E
Olesno 30 50.53 N 18.25 E
Olevano Romano 60 41.52 N 13.02 E
Olevsk 68 51.13 N 27.39 E
Olevuga I 165e 8.58 S 160.05 E
Oley 198 40.23 N 75.47 W
Olfen 48 51.42 N 7.23 E
Ol'ga, S.S.S.R. 79 43.45 N 135.18 E
Olga, Wash., U.S. 214 48.37 N 122.50 W
Olga, Mount ▲, Austl. 152 25.19 S 130.46 E
Olga, Mount ▲, Vt., U.S. 197 42.51 N 72.48 W
Olgiata 257a 42.02 N 12.22 E
Olgiate Comasco 56 45.48 N 8.58 E
Olgiate Olona 56 45.38 N 8.53 E
Ölgij, Mong. 76 48.59 N 92.01 E
Ölgij, Mong. 76 48.56 N 89.57 E
Olginate 56 45.48 N 9.24 E
Ol'ginka, S.S.S.R. 68 44.14 N 38.53 E
Ol'ginka, S.S.S.R. 73 47.42 N 37.31 E
Ol'gino, S.S.S.R. 76 54.59 N 71.54 E
Ol'gino, S.S.S.R. 79 52.53 N 125.47 E
Ol'gino ◆[8] 255a 60.00 N 30.09 E
Ol'ginskaja, S.S.S.R. 68 45.57 N 38.34 E
Ol'ginskaja, S.S.S.R. 73 47.11 N 39.56 E
Ølgod 26 55.49 N 8.37 E
Ol'gopol' 68 48.12 N 29.29 E
Ol'govo 72 56.16 N 37.21 E
Olhão 34 37.02 N 8.50 W
Ôlho d'Água 245 16.02 S 48.36 W
Ôlho-d'Água das Flores 240 9.33 S 37.17 W
Ôlho-d'Água Grande 240 4.43 S 44.34 W
Oli ≃ 140 9.45 N 4.38 E
Olib, Otok I 36 44.22 N 14.48 E
Oliden 248 35.11 S 57.57 W
Oliena 36 40.16 N 9.24 E
Olifants (Rio dos Elefantes) ≃, Afr. 146 24.10 S 32.40 E
Olifants ≃, Namibia 146 25.30 S 19.30 E
Olifants ≃, S. Afr. 148 33.41 S 21.42 E
Olifants ≃, S. Afr. 148 31.42 S 18.12 E
Olifantshoek 148 27.57 S 22.42 E
Olifantsrivierberge ⛰ 148 32.40 S 19.00 E
Oliki 255a 59.46 N 29.55 E
Olimarao I[1] 98 7.41 N 145.52 E
Olimbía ⊥ 38 37.38 N 21.41 E
Ólimbos 38 35.44 N 27.11 E
Ólimbos ▲, Ellás 38 40.05 N 22.21 E
Ólimbos ▲, Kípros 120 34.56 N 32.52 E
Olímpia 245 20.44 S 48.54 W
Olímpico, Estadio ♠ 276a 19.20 N 99.12 W
Olimpio Noronha 246 22.04 S 45.16 W
Olimpo □[5] 238 20.30 S 58.45 W
Olimpo → Ólimbos ▲ 38 40.05 N 22.21 E
Olin 180 42.00 N 91.09 W
Olinalá 224 17.50 N 98.51 W
Olinda, Austl. 160 32.50 S 150.08 E
Olinda, Austl. 264b 37.51 S 145.22 E
Olinda, Bra. 240 8.01 S 34.51 W
Olinda, Bra. 246 22.49 S 43.25 W
Olinda, Mount ▲ 264b 37.52 S 145.21 E
Olinda Creek ≃ 264b 37.41 S 145.21 E
Olindina 240 11.22 S 38.21 W
Olinsk 78 52.24 N 116.13 E
Olio 156 21.54 S 143.13 E
Olišovka 68 51.13 N 31.18 E
Olite 34 42.29 N 1.39 W
Oliva, Arg. 242 32.03 S 63.34 W
Oliva, Esp. 34 38.55 N 0.07 W
Oliva de la Frontera 34 38.16 N 6.55 W

ENGLISH

Name | Page | Lat.°′ | Long.°′

Olivais ◆[8] 256c 38.46 N 9.06 E
Olival Basto 256c 38.47 N 9.10 W
Olivar de los Padres 276a 19.21 N 99.13 W
Olive Branch 184 34.58 N 89.50 W
Olivebridge 200 41.55 N 74.13 W
Olive Hill 208 38.16 N 83.10 W
Olivehurst 216 39.06 N 121.34 W
Oliveira 245 20.41 S 44.49 W
Oliveira dos Brejinhos 245 12.19 S 42.54 W
Oliveira Fortes 246 21.20 S 43.27 W
Oliveira Salazar, Barragem ◆[6] 146 19.08 S 33.00 E
Olivelifuri I 112 5.17 N 73.35 E
Olive Mount ◆[8] 252 53.24 N 2.55 W
Olivença 144 11.47 S 35.13 E
Olivenza 34 38.41 N 7.06 W
Oliver 172 49.11 N 119.33 W
Olivera 248 34.38 S 59.15 W
Oliver Creek ≃ 212 33.06 N 97.17 W
Oliver Ditch ≅ 206 41.00 N 87.10 W
Oliverea 200 42.04 N 74.28 W
Oliver Lake ⊜ 174 56.56 N 103.22 W
Oliver Springs 182 36.03 N 84.20 W
Olivet, Fr. 46 47.52 N 1.54 E
Olivet, Mich., U.S. 206 42.27 N 84.56 W
Olivet, S. Dak., U.S. 188 43.14 N 97.40 W
Olivette 209 38.40 N 90.24 W
Olivia 188 44.46 N 94.59 W
Olivine Range ⛰ 162 44.18 S 168.30 E
Olivo 106 10.52 N 123.53 E
Olivone 54 46.32 N 8.57 E
Olivos ◆[8] 248 34.32 S 58.29 W
Öljaren ⊜ 40 59.08 N 16.02 E
Olla 184 31.54 N 92.14 W
Ollagüe 238 21.14 S 68.16 W
Ollagüe, Volcán (Volcán Oyahue) ▲[1] 238 21.18 S 68.12 W
Ollainville 251 48.35 N 2.13 E
Ollantaitambo 238 13.16 S 72.16 W
Ollerton, Eng., U.K. 42 53.12 N 1.00 W
Ollerton, Eng., U.K. 252 53.17 N 2.20 W
Ollerup 41 55.04 N 10.30 E
Olliergues 56 45.40 N 3.38 E
Ollioules 56 43.08 N 5.51 E
Ollomont 56 45.50 N 7.22 E
Ollon 54 46.18 N 7.00 E
Olloua 142 0.56 S 14.34 E
Olmedillo de Roa 34 41.47 N 3.56 W
Olmedo 34 41.23 N 4.41 W
Olmo al Brembo 54 45.58 N 9.39 E
Olmos 238 5.59 S 79.46 W
Olmsted 204 41.24 N 81.44 W
Olmsted Falls 269a 41.22 N 81.55 W
Olmütz → Olomouc 30 49.36 N 17.16 E
Olney, Eng., U.K. 44 52.81 N 0.43 W
Olney, Ill., U.S. 184 38.44 N 88.05 W
Olney, Mo., U.S. 209 39.05 N 91.15 W
Olney, Tex., U.S. 186 33.22 N 98.45 W
Olney ◆[8] 275 40.02 N 75.08 W
Olofström 26 56.16 N 14.30 E
Oloj ≃ 64 66.29 N 159.29 E
Ol'okma ≃ 64 60.22 N 120.42 E
Ol'okminsk 64 60.24 N 120.24 E
Ol'okminskij Stanovik ⛰ 78 54.30 N 120.00 E
Olokui ▲ 219a 21.08 N 156.51 W
Olomane ≃ 176 50.14 N 60.37 W
Olombo 142 1.18 S 15.53 E
Olomega, Laguna ⊜ 226 13.19 N 88.04 W
Olomouc 30 49.36 N 17.16 E
Olona ≃ 56 45.06 N 9.21 E
Olonec 24 61.00 N 32.57 E
Olongapo 106 14.50 N 120.16 E
Olonki 78 52.54 N 103.45 E
Olorgasailie National Monument ♠ 144 1.40 S 36.22 E
Oloron, Gave d' ≃ 32 43.33 N 1.05 W
Oloron-Sainte-Marie 32 43.12 N 0.36 W
Olosega 164y 14.11 S 169.39 W
Olosega I 164y 14.11 S 169.39 W
Olot 34 42.11 N 2.29 E
Olov'annaja, S.S.S.R. 78 50.56 N 115.35 E
Olov'annaja, S.S.S.R. 170 66.10 N 178.59 W
Oloví 50 50.11 N 12.33 E
Olpe, B.R.D. 52 51.02 N 7.52 E
Olpe, Kans., U.S. 188 38.16 N 96.10 W
Olperer ▲ 58 47.03 N 11.39 E
Ol'ša 66 54.51 N 31.52 E
Ol'šana, S.S.S.R. 68 49.47 N 37.46 E
Ol'šana, S.S.S.R. 68 49.13 N 31.13 E
Ol'šana, S.S.S.R. 68 50.48 N 34.02 E
Ol'šanka, S.S.S.R. 68 51.46 N 35.25 E
Ol'šanka, S.S.S.R. 68 48.14 N 30.52 E
Ol'šany, S.S.S.R. 68 52.05 N 27.20 E
Ol'šany, S.S.S.R. 68 50.03 N 35.53 E
Olsberg 52 51.21 N 8.29 E
Ølsemagle 41 55.30 N 12.10 E
Olshammar 40 58.45 N 14.48 E
Olst 48 52.20 N 6.06 E
Ølstykke 41 55.47 N 12.11 E
Olsufjevo 66 53.36 N 33.40 E
Olsztyn (Allenstein) 30 53.48 N 20.29 E
Olsztynek 30 53.36 N 20.17 E
Olt □[4] 38 44.20 N 24.30 E
Olt ≃ 38 43.43 N 24.51 E
Olta 242 30.37 S 66.16 W
Olten 54 47.21 N 7.54 E
Olteni 38 44.10 N 25.18 E
Oltenița 38 44.05 N 26.39 E
Olteț ≃ 38 44.14 N 24.27 E
Olton 186 34.11 N 102.08 W
Oltre il Colle 58 45.54 N 9.46 E
Oltu 120 40.33 N 41.59 E
Oltu ≃ 120 40.50 N 41.40 E
Oluan Pi ≻ 90 21.54 N 120.51 E
Olukonda 146 18.03 S 16.00 E
Olu Malau Islands II 165e 10.10 S 161.57 E
Olur 120 40.50 N 42.08 E
Olustee, Fla., U.S. 182 30.12 N 82.26 W
Olustee, Okla., U.S. 186 34.33 N 99.25 W
Olustee Creek ≃ 182 29.57 N 82.32 W
Oluta 224 17.55 N 94.54 W
Olutanga (Suba Nipa) 106 7.26 N 122.54 E
Olutanga Island I 106 7.22 N 122.52 E
Olutaya Island I 106 11.39 N 122.50 E
Olute 263a 6.28 N 3.16 E
Ol'utorskij, Mys ≻ 64 59.55 N 170.27 E
Ol'utorskij Zaliv ⊂ 64 59.55 N 170.27 E
Oluwo 263a 6.42 N 3.18 E
Olvenstedt 50 52.09 N 11.34 E
Olvera 34 36.56 N 5.16 W
Olychovatka 68 50.12 N 37.31 E
Olyka 68 50.42 N 25.51 E
Olym 68 51.42 N 38.10 E
Olymp → Ólimbos ▲ 38 40.05 N 22.21 E
Olympe, Mont → Ólimbos ▲ 38 40.05 N 22.21 E
Olympia 214 47.03 N 122.53 W
Olympia → Olimbía ⊥ 38 37.38 N 21.41 E
Olympia Fields 206 41.32 N 87.42 W
Olympia Heights 210 25.43 N 80.17 W
Olympia-Stadion ♠ 254a 52.31 N 13.14 E
Olympia Stadium ♠ 271 42.21 N 83.06 W
Olympic Mountains ⛰ 214 47.50 N 123.45 W
Olympic National Park ♠ 214 47.48 N 123.30 W
Olympic Park ♠ 264b 37.49 S 144.59 E
Olympic Valley 216 39.13 N 120.14 W
Olympic View 214 47.43 N 122.45 W
Olympieion ⊥ 257c 37.58 N 23.44 E
Olympus, Mount → Ólimbos ▲, Ellás 38 40.05 N 22.21 E
Olympus, Mount ▲, Ky., U.S. 182 38.03 N 83.39 W

DEUTSCH

Name | Seite | Breite°′ | Länge°′ E=Ost

Olympus, Mount ▲, Wash., U.S. 214 47.48 N 123.43 W
Olyphant 200 41.28 N 75.37 W
Ol'zony 78 52.57 N 105.15 E
Om' ≃ 76 54.59 N 73.22 E
Ōmachi, Nihon 84 36.30 N 137.52 E
Ōmachi, Nihon 260 34.28 N 135.25 E
Omaezaki 84 34.35 N 138.13 E
Omae-zaki ≻ 84 34.36 N 138.14 E
Ōmagari 82 39.27 N 140.29 E
Omagh, Ont., Can. 265b 43.30 N 79.49 W
Omagh, N. Ire., U.K. 28 54.36 N 7.18 W
Ōmagi 258 35.52 N 139.42 E
Omaguas 236 4.08 S 73.15 W
Omaha, Nebr., U.S. 188 41.16 N 95.57 W
Omaha, Tex., U.S. 212 33.11 N 94.45 W
Omaha Indian Reservation ◆[4] 188 42.08 N 96.22 W
Omak 192 48.24 N 119.31 W
Omakau 162 45.05 S 169.36 E
Omak Lake ⊜ 192 48.16 N 119.23 W
Omalo 74 42.23 N 45.38 E
Omal'skij Chrebet ⛰ 79 52.47 N 137.30 E
Ōmama 84 36.26 N 139.17 E
Oman □[1] 108 22.00 N 58.00 E
Oman, Gulf of ⊂ 108 24.30 N 58.30 E
Omar 182 37.46 N 82.00 W
Omarama 162 44.29 S 169.58 E
'Omar Gambon 134 3.12 N 45.50 E
Omaruru 146 21.28 S 15.56 E
Omaruru □[5] 146 21.00 S 15.45 E
Omaruru ≃ 146 22.07 S 14.15 E
Omas 238 12.31 S 76.17 W
Omatako ▲ 146 21.07 S 16.43 E
Omate 238 16.41 S 70.59 W
Omatena 105b 9.53 S 119.47 E
Ōma-zaki ≻ 82a 41.32 N 140.55 E
Ombella-Mpoko □[5] 142 5.00 N 18.00 E
Omberg ▲[2] 26 58.20 N 14.39 E
Ombersley 44 52.17 N 2.13 W
Ombombo 146 18.43 S 13.53 E
Omboué 142 1.34 S 9.15 E
Ombrone ≃ 60 42.39 N 11.00 E
Ombúes de Lavalle 248 33.55 S 57.47 W
Ombutosu ▲ 146 21.22 S 16.50 E
Ombwe 144 4.22 S 25.35 E
Omčak 64 61.38 N 147.55 E
Omčaly 118 40.47 N 53.43 E
Omdraaisvlei 148 30.08 S 23.08 E
Omdurman → Umm Durmān 130 15.38 N 32.30 E
Ōme 84 35.47 N 139.15 E
Omega, Ga., U.S. 182 31.21 N 83.36 W
Omega, Ohio, U.S. 208 39.09 N 82.55 W
Omegna 56 45.53 N 8.24 E
Omel'nik 68 49.12 N 33.32 E
Omemee 202 44.18 N 78.33 W
Omeo 156 37.06 S 147.36 E
Ömerin 120 37.18 N 42.04 E
Ömerköy 120 39.48 N 28.03 E
Ömerli 120 41.05 N 29.19 E
Omerville 196 45.17 N 72.07 W
Ometepe, Isla de I 226 11.30 N 85.35 W
Ometepec 224 16.41 N 98.25 W
Ometepec ≃ 224 16.30 N 98.45 W
Om Hajer 134 14.24 N 36.46 E
Ōmi, Nihon 84 36.27 N 138.03 E
Ōmi, Nihon 84 35.20 N 136.24 E
Ōmi, Nihon 84 37.01 N 137.48 E
Omigawa 84 35.51 N 140.37 E
Ōmi-hachiman 84 35.08 N 136.06 E
Omin 164q 9.36 N 138.10 E
Ōminato → Mutsu 82 41.17 N 141.10 E
Omineca ≃ 172 56.05 N 124.30 W
Omineca Mountains ⛰ 172 56.00 N 125.00 W
Omin-ni ◆[8] 261b 37.27 N 127.01 E
Ōmino 260 34.32 N 135.33 E
Omišalj 36 45.13 N 14.34 E
Ōmi-shima I 86 34.25 N 131.13 E
Omitara 146 22.18 S 18.01 E
Omitlán ≃ 224 17.06 N 99.34 W
Ōmiya, Nihon 84 35.54 N 139.38 E
Ōmiya, Nihon 84 36.33 N 140.25 E
Ōmiya, Nihon 86 35.35 N 135.06 E
Ōmiya-daichi ⛰[1] 258 35.56 N 139.38 E
Omiya Park Race Track ♠ 258 35.55 N 139.38 E
Øm Kloster ⊥ 41 56.03 N 9.45 E
Ommaney, Cape ≻ 170 56.10 N 134.39 W
Ommanney Bay ⊂ 166 73.07 N 100.11 W
Omme Å ≃ 41 55.53 N 8.40 E
Ommen 48 52.32 N 6.25 E
Ömnödelger 78 47.58 N 109.53 E
Ömnögov' 76 49.08 N 91.43 E
Ömnögov' □[4] 92 43.00 N 104.00 E
Omø I 41 55.09 N 11.10 E
Omo ≃ 134 4.51 N 36.55 E
Omoa, Bahía de ⊂ 226 15.45 N 88.10 W
Omodeo, Lago ⊜ 36 40.08 N 8.55 E
Omogo 86 33.41 N 133.02 E
Omoi ≃ 84 36.09 N 139.41 E
Omoko 140 5.20 N 6.39 E
Omole 263a 6.38 N 3.22 E
Omoloj ≃ 64 71.10 N 132.08 E
Omolon ≃ 64 68.42 N 158.36 E
Omono ≃ 82 39.46 N 140.03 E
Omont 52 49.36 N 4.44 E
Omo Ranch 216 38.35 N 120.35 W
Ōmori ◆[8] 258 35.34 N 139.44 E
Omotegō 84 37.03 N 140.18 E
Omrel'kaj ≃ 170 68.34 N 170.30 E
Omro 180 44.02 N 88.44 W
Omsino 70 58.36 N 50.28 E
Omsk 76 55.00 N 73.24 E
Omsukčan 64 62.32 N 155.48 E
O-mu, Mya. 100 22.58 N 99.18 E
Ōmu, Nihon 82a 44.34 N 142.58 E
Omu-Aran 140 8.09 N 5.07 E
Ōmuda → Ōmuta 86 33.02 N 130.27 E
Omul ▲ 38 45.26 N 25.26 E
Omulew ≃ 30 53.05 N 21.32 E
Ōmura 82 32.54 N 129.57 E
Omuramba Omatako ≃ 146 17.59 S 20.30 E
Ōmuro 258 35.54 N 139.58 E
Omurtag 38 43.06 N 26.25 E
Ōmuta 86 33.02 N 130.27 E
Omutinskij 76 56.31 N 67.41 E
Omutninsk 76 58.40 N 52.12 E
Ŏmyŏnbo 88 41.16 N 127.36 E
On 100 21.40 N 106.35 E
Ona, Nor. 26 62.52 N 6.34 E
Ona, Fla., U.S. 210 27.29 N 81.55 W
Ona ≃, S.S.S.R. 76 52.34 N 89.50 E
Ona → Bir'usa ≃, S.S.S.R. 78 57.43 N 95.24 E
Onadikondo 142 3.52 S 24.10 E
Onaga 188 39.29 N 96.10 W
Onagawa 82 38.26 N 141.27 E
Onalaska, Tex., U.S. 212 30.48 N 95.07 W
Onalaska, Wash., U.S. 214 46.35 N 122.42 W
Onalaska, Wis., U.S. 180 43.53 N 91.14 W
Onamia 180 46.04 N 93.40 W
Onancock 198 37.43 N 75.45 W
Onangué, Lac ⊜ 142 0.57 S 10.04 E
Onaping ≃ 180 46.37 N 81.18 W
Onaping Lake ⊜ 180 46.57 N 81.30 W
Onarga 206 40.43 N 88.01 W
Ōnari 258 35.55 N 139.37 E
Onatchiway, Lac ⊜ 176 49.00 N 71.03 W
Onawa 188 42.02 N 96.06 W
Onaway 180 45.21 N 84.14 W
Oncativo 242 31.55 S 63.40 W
Once ◆[8] 278 34.36 S 58.24 W
Onchāi 262b 22.57 N 88.19 E
Onchan 42 54.11 N 4.27 W
Onchi 260 34.37 N 135.38 E
Onch'ŏn-dong 88 40.51 N 129.07 E

Symbols in the index entries represent the broad categories identified in the key at the right. Symbols with superior numbers (⛰[2]) identify subcategories (see complete key on page I · 26).

Kartensymbole in dem Registerverzeichnis stellen die rechts in Schlüssel erklärten Kategorien dar. Symbole mit hochgestellten Ziffern (⛰[2]) bezeichnen Unterabteilungen einer Kategorie (vgl. vollständiger Schlüssel auf Seite I · 26).

Los símbolos incluídos en el texto del índice representan las grandes categorias identificadas con la clave a la derecha. Los símbolos con numeros en su parte superior (⛰[2]) identifican las subcategorias (véase la clave completa en la página I · 26).

Les symboles de l'index représentent les catégories indiquées dans la légende à droite. Les symboles suivis d'un indice (⛰[2]) représentent des sous-catégories (voir légende complète à la page I · 26).

Os símbolos incluídos no texto do índice representam as grandes categorias identificadas com a chave à direita. Os símbolos com números em sua parte superior (⛰[2]) identificam as subcategorias (veja-se a chave completa à página I · 26).

▲	Mountain	Berg	Montaña	Montagne	Montanha
⛰	Mountains	Berge	Montañas	Montagnes	Montanhas
)(	Pass	Pass	Paso	Col	Passo
∨	Valley, Canyon	Tal, Cañon	Valle, Cañón	Vallée, Canyon	Vale, Canhão
≚	Plain	Ebene	Llano	Plaine	Planície
≻	Cape	Kap	Cabo	Cap	Cabo
I	Island	Insel	Isla	Île	Ilha
II	Islands	Inseln	Islas	Îles	Ilhas
•	Other Topographic Features	Andere Topographische Objekte	Otros Elementos Topográficos	Autres données topographiques	Outros Elementos Topográficos

ESPAÑOL

Nombre	Página	Lat.°′	Long.°′ W=Oeste
Oncócua	142	16.34 S	13.28 E
Onda, Bhārat	116	23.08 N	87.12 E
Onda, Esp.	34	39.58 N	0.15 W
Ondangua	146	17.55 S	16.00 E
Ondas, Rio das ≃	245	12.08 S	45.00 W
Ondava ≃	30	48.27 N	21.48 E
Onderdijk	48	52.45 N	5.07 E
Onder-Sneeuberg ⋀	148	32.10 S	23.47 E
Onderstedorings	148	30.13 S	20.37 E
Ondo, Nig.	140	7.04 N	4.47 E
Ondo, Nihon	86	34.11 N	132.32 E
Ondo-ōhashi ◆[5]	86	34.12 N	132.33 E
Öndörchaan (Cecer Chaan)	78	47.19 N	110.39 E
Öndörchangaj	78	49.20 N	94.50 E
Öndör-Önc	92	45.51 N	103.11 E
Öndöršireet	78	47.27 N	104.50 E
Öndör-Ulaan	78	48.06 N	100.27 E
O'Neals	216	37.08 N	119.42 W
One Arrow Indian Reserve ◆[4]	174	52.48 N	106.03 W
Oneata I	165g	18.27 S	178.29 W
Oneco, Conn., U.S.	197	41.42 N	71.48 W
Oneco, Fla., U.S.	210	27.27 N	82.33 W
Onega	24	63.55 N	38.05 E
Onega ≃	24	63.58 N	37.55 E
Onega, Lake → Onežskoje Ozero ⊜	24	61.30 N	35.45 E
Oneglia	56	43.53 N	8.02 E
One Hundred and Two ≃	184	39.44 N	94.43 W
One Hundred and Two, West Fork ≃	184	40.26 N	94.49 W
One Hundred Fifty Mile House	172	52.07 N	121.56 W
One Hundred Mile House	172	51.39 N	121.18 W
Oneida, Ill., U.S.	180	41.04 N	90.13 W
Oneida, Ky., U.S.	182	37.16 N	83.39 W
Oneida, N.Y., U.S.	200	43.06 N	75.39 W
Oneida, Ohio, U.S.	208	40.42 N	81.09 W
Oneida, Pa., U.S.	200	40.54 N	76.08 W
Oneida, Tenn., U.S.	182	36.30 N	84.31 W
Oneida □[6]	200	43.10 N	75.20 W
Oneida ≃	200	43.12 N	76.17 W
Oneida Castle	200	43.05 N	75.40 W
Oneida County Airport ⊠	200	43.09 N	75.23 W
Oneida Creek ≃	200	43.10 N	75.44 W
Oneida Indian Reservation ◆[4]	180	44.30 N	88.10 W
Oneida Indian Reserve ◆[4]	204	42.49 N	81.24 W
Oneida Lake ⊜	200	43.13 N	76.00 W
O'Neil Forebay ⊜[1]	216	37.05 N	121.03 W
O'Neill	188	42.27 N	98.39 W
Onekama	180	44.22 N	86.12 W
Onekotan, Ostrov I	64	49.25 N	154.45 E
Onema	142	4.33 S	24.31 E
Oneman Lake ⊜	174	50.20 N	94.45 W
Onemen, Zaliv C	170	64.45 N	176.35 E
Oneonta, Ala., U.S.	184	33.57 N	86.29 W
Oneonta, N.Y., U.S.	200	42.27 N	75.04 W
Oneroa I	164k	21.15 S	159.43 W
One Tree Hill	158b	34.43 S	138.46 E
One Tree Hill ∧[2]	264b	37.52 S	145.19 E
One Tree Hill Lookout ♠	159	36.48 S	144.18 E
Onevai I	164w	21.05 S	175.07 W
Onežskaja Guba C	24	64.20 N	36.30 E
Onežskij Poluostrov >[1]	24	64.35 N	38.00 E
Onežskoje Ozero (Lake Onega) ⊜	24	61.30 N	35.45 E
Onga ≃	86	33.54 N	130.39 E
Ongaonga	162	39.55 S	176.25 E
Ongarue	162	38.43 S	175.17 E
Ong-con, Cu-lao I	259c	10.45 N	106.50 E
Ongea Levu I	165g	19.08 S	178.24 W
Ongers ≃	148	31.04 S	23.13 E
Ongerup	152	33.58 S	118.29 E
Ongijn Gol ≃	92	44.30 N	103.40 E
Ongjin	88	37.57 N	125.21 E
Ongoka	144	1.23 S	26.02 E
Ongole	112	15.31 N	80.04 E
Ongon	92	45.41 N	113.05 E
Ongudaj	76	50.45 N	86.09 E
Oni	74	42.34 N	43.27 E
Onida	188	44.42 N	100.04 W
Onigajō-yama ∧	86	33.07 N	132.41 E
Onilahy ≃	147b	23.34 S	43.45 E
Onin, Jazirah >[1]	154	2.50 S	132.05 E
Onion Creek ≃	212	30.12 N	97.35 W
Onion Peak ∧	214	45.49 N	123.53 W
Onishi	84	36.09 N	139.04 E
Onistagane, Lac ⊜	176	50.42 N	71.19 W
Onitsha	140	6.09 N	6.47 E
Onjuku	84	35.11 N	140.22 E
Onkaparinga ≃	158b	35.10 S	138.28 E
Onkivesi ⊜	26	63.18 N	27.18 E
Onko	142	4.07 S	19.59 E
Onley	198	37.41 N	75.43 W
Onna	164m	26.30 N	127.51 E
Onnaing	46	50.23 N	3.36 E
Onno	54	45.55 N	9.17 E
Onny ≃	44	52.23 N	2.45 W
Ōno, Nihon	84	35.28 N	136.38 E
Ōno, Nihon	84	35.59 N	136.29 E
Ōno, Nihon	86	33.02 N	131.30 E
Ōno, Nihon	86	34.51 N	134.56 E
Ōno, Nihon	86	34.18 N	132.17 E
Ono, Nihon	260	34.57 N	135.14 E
Ono, Pa., U.S.	198	40.24 N	76.32 W
Ono I	165g	18.55 S	178.29 E
Ōno ≃	86	33.15 N	131.43 E
Onochoj	78	51.58 N	108.01 E
Onoda	86	33.59 N	131.11 E
Ōno-dam ◆[6]	86	35.15 N	135.27 E
Onogami	84	36.33 N	138.56 E
Onohara	86	34.05 N	133.40 E
Ono-i-lau I	14	20.39 S	178.42 W
Ōnomi	86	33.21 N	133.09 E
Onomichi	86	34.25 N	133.12 E
Onon	78	49.09 N	112.35 E
Onon ≃	78	51.42 N	115.50 E
Onondaga, Mich., U.S.	206	42.27 N	84.34 W
Onondaga, N.Y., U.S.	200	43.00 N	76.11 W
Onondaga □[6]	200	43.03 N	76.09 W
Onondaga Creek ≃	200	43.04 N	76.11 W
Onondaga Indian Reservation ◆[4]	200	42.55 N	76.09 W
Onor	79	50.11 N	142.40 E
Onota Lake ⊜	197	42.28 N	73.17 W
Onoto	236	9.36 N	65.12 W
Onotoa I[1]	14	1.52 S	175.34 E
Onoway	172	53.42 N	114.12 W
Ons, Isla de I	34	42.23 N	8.56 W
Onsbjerg	41	55.51 N	10.35 E
Onseepkans	148	28.46 S	19.14 E
Onsen	86	35.33 N	134.29 E
Onset	197	41.45 N	70.39 W
Onslow	152	21.39 S	115.06 E
Onslow Bay C	182	34.20 N	77.20 W
Onslow Village	250	51.14 N	0.36 W
Onsted	206	42.00 N	84.11 W
Onstmettingen	54	48.17 N	9.00 E
Onstwedde	48	53.02 N	7.02 E
Ontake-san ∧	84	35.53 N	137.29 E
Ontario, Calif., U.S.	218	34.04 N	117.39 W
Ontario, Ind., U.S.	206	41.43 N	85.23 W
Ontario, N.Y., U.S.	200	43.13 N	77.17 W
Ontario, Ohio, U.S.	204	40.46 N	82.39 W
Ontario, Oreg., U.S.	192	44.02 N	116.58 W
Ontario □[6], Ont., Can.	202	44.15 N	79.05 W
Ontario □[6], N.Y., U.S.	200	42.54 N	77.17 W
Ontario □[4]	166	51.00 N	85.00 W
Ontario, Lake ⊜	180	43.45 N	78.00 W

FRANÇAIS

Nom	Page	Lat.°′	Long.°′ W=Ouest
Ontario Center	200	43.14 N	77.19 W
Ontario International Airport ⊠	218	34.04 N	117.36 W
Ontario Place ♠	265b	43.38 N	79.25 W
Ontario Science Centre ⊍	265b	43.43 N	79.21 W
Ontelaunee, Lake ⊜	198	40.27 N	75.55 W
Onteniente	34	38.49 N	0.37 W
Ontojärvi ⊜	26	64.08 N	29.09 E
Ontonagon	180	46.52 N	89.19 W
Ontonagon ≃	180	46.52 N	89.20 W
Ontonagon, East Branch ≃	180	46.42 N	89.11 W
Ontonagon, Middle Branch ≃	180	46.42 N	89.10 W
Ontonagon, West Branch ≃	180	46.42 N	89.11 W
Ontong Java Atoll I[1]	165e	5.20 S	159.30 E
Ontong Java Rise ✣[3]	14	7.00 S	160.00 E
Onufrijevka	68	48.54 N	33.26 E
Onufrijevo	72	55.51 N	36.31 E
Ōnuma	258	35.32 N	139.25 E
Onverwacht	240	5.36 N	55.12 W
Onward	206	40.42 N	86.12 W
Ŏnyang	88	35.34 N	129.07 E
Onzain	46	47.30 N	1.11 E
Onzo ≃	142	8.12 S	13.16 E
Oodnadatta	152	27.33 S	135.28 E
Oog van Wonderfontein ≃	263d	26.16 S	27.42 E
Ōoka	84	36.30 N	137.59 E
Ooldea	152	30.27 S	131.50 E
Oolitic	208	38.54 N	86.31 W
Oologah Lake ⊜[1]	186	36.33 N	95.36 W
Ooma	164d	0.53 S	169.36 E
Oombergen	46	50.54 N	3.50 E
Oona River	172	53.57 N	130.18 W
Ooratippra	152	22.00 S	136.00 E
Ooratippra Creek ≃	152	21.55 S	136.05 E
Oos	52	48.47 N	8.11 E
Oos-Londen → East London	148	33.00 S	27.55 E
Oostakker	46	51.06 N	3.46 E
Oostburg, Ned.	48	51.20 N	3.30 E
Oostburg, Wis., U.S.	180	43.37 N	87.48 W
Oost-Cappel	46	50.55 N	2.36 E
Oostduinkerke	46	51.07 N	2.41 E
Oostelijk Flevoland ◆[1]	48	52.30 N	5.45 E
Oostende (Ostende)	46	51.13 N	2.55 E
Oosterbeek	48	52.00 N	5.50 E
Oosterend	48	53.05 N	4.52 E
Oosterhout	48	51.38 N	4.51 E
Ooster Schelde C	48	51.30 N	4.00 E
Oosterwolde	48	52.59 N	6.17 E
Oosterzele	46	50.57 N	3.48 E
Oosthuizen	48	52.35 N	5.00 E
Oostkamp	46	51.09 N	3.14 E
Oostmahorn	48	53.24 N	6.09 E
Oostmalle	52	51.18 N	4.44 E
Oostrozebeke	46	50.55 N	3.20 E
Oost-Souburg	48	51.27 N	3.35 E
Oost-Vlaanderen □[4]	46	51.00 N	3.45 E
Oostvleteren	46	50.56 N	2.44 E
Oost-Vlieland	48	53.17 N	5.04 E
Oostvoorne	48	51.55 N	4.06 E
Ootacamund	112	11.24 N	76.42 E
Ootmarsum	48	52.25 N	6.54 E
Ootsa Lake	172	53.47 N	126.03 W
Ootsa Lake ⊜	172	53.49 N	126.18 W
Ootse	146	25.02 S	25.45 E
Ootua, Mont ∧	164x	9.47 S	138.58 W
Opaka	38	43.27 N	26.10 E
Opala	142	0.37 S	24.21 E
Opalaca, Sierra de ⋀	226	14.30 N	88.20 W
Opal Cliffs	216	36.58 N	121.58 W
Opale, Côte d' •[2]	46	50.40 N	1.35 E
Opalenica	30	52.19 N	16.23 E
Opalicha	255b	55.49 N	37.15 E
Opa Locka	210	25.54 N	80.15 W
Opari	144	3.56 N	32.03 E
Oparino	24	59.52 N	48.17 E
Opasatica, Lac ⊜	180	48.05 N	79.18 W
Opasatika Lake ⊜	180	49.04 N	83.08 W
Opasquia	174	53.16 N	93.35 W
Opasquia Lake ⊜	174	53.18 N	93.34 W
Opatija	36	45.21 N	14.19 E
Opatów	30	50.49 N	21.26 E
Opava	30	49.56 N	17.54 E
Opečenskij Posad	66	58.16 N	34.07 E
Opeepeesway Lake ⊜	180	47.38 N	82.14 W
Opeilu	263a	6.42 N	3.18 E
Opelika	184	32.39 N	85.23 W
Opelousas	184	30.32 N	92.05 W
Open Bay C	154	4.50 S	151.20 E
Open Door	248	34.30 S	59.05 W
Opeongo Lake ⊜	180	45.42 N	78.23 W
Opequon Creek ≃	178	39.35 N	77.52 W
Operaház ⊍	254c	47.30 N	19.04 E
Ophain-Bois-Seigneur-Isaac	46	50.40 N	4.21 E
Ophasselt	46	50.49 N	3.53 E
Opheim	192	48.51 N	106.24 W
Opherdicke	253	51.29 N	7.38 E
Opheusden	48	51.56 N	5.38 E
Ophir, Alaska, U.S.	170	63.10 N	156.31 W
Ophir, Oreg., U.S.	192	42.34 N	124.23 W
Ophirton ◆[8]	263d	26.14 S	28.01 E
Ophthalmia Range ⋀	152	23.17 S	119.30 E
Opi	60	41.47 N	13.50 E
Opienge	144	0.12 N	27.30 E
Opihikao	219d	19.26 N	154.53 W
Opinaca ≃	166	52.15 N	78.02 W
Opinicon Lake ⊜	202	44.33 N	76.20 W
Opiscotéo, Lac ⊜	166	53.10 N	68.10 W
Opladen	52	51.04 N	7.00 E
Opmeer	48	52.43 N	4.56 E
Opobo	140	4.34 N	7.27 E
Opobo Town	140	4.30 N	7.30 E
Opočka	66	56.43 N	28.38 E
Opoczno	30	51.23 N	20.17 E
Opol	106	8.31 N	124.34 E
Opole (Oppeln)	30	50.41 N	17.55 E
Opole Lubelskie	30	51.09 N	21.58 E
Opon → Lapu-lapu	106	10.19 N	123.57 E
Oponono Lake ⊜	146	18.08 S	15.45 E
Opopeo	224	19.24 N	101.36 W
Oporto → Porto	34	41.11 N	8.36 W
Opošn'a	68	49.58 N	34.37 E
Opotiki	162	38.00 S	177.17 E
Opp	184	31.17 N	86.22 W
Oppach	50	51.03 N	14.30 E
Oppdal	26	62.36 N	9.40 E
Oppelhain	50	51.33 N	13.35 E
Oppeln → Opole	30	50.41 N	17.55 E
Oppenau	54	48.28 N	8.10 E
Oppenheim, B.R.D.	52	49.51 N	8.21 E
Oppenheim, N.Y., U.S.	200	43.04 N	74.42 W
Oppenhuizen	48	53.00 N	5.42 E
Oppido Mamertina	36	38.16 N	16.00 E
Oppio	60	44.03 N	10.50 E
Oppland □[6]	26	61.10 N	9.40 E
Opportunity, Mont., U.S.	192	46.07 N	112.49 W
Opportunity, Wash., U.S.	192	47.39 N	117.15 W
Oppum ◆[8]	253	51.19 N	6.37 E
Opsa	66	55.32 N	26.47 E
Opsaheden	40	60.28 N	13.59 E
Optic Lake	174	54.46 N	101.13 W
Opua	162	35.19 S	174.07 E
Opunake	162	39.27 S	173.51 E
Opwijk	46	50.58 N	4.11 E
Oquawka	180	40.56 N	90.57 W

PORTUGUÊS

Nome	Página	Lat.°′	Long.°′ W=Oeste
Oquendo, Perú	276d	11.58 S	77.08 W
Oquendo, Pil.	106	12.08 N	124.32 E
O'Quinn	212	29.50 N	96.58 W
Or' ≃	76	51.12 N	58.30 E
Or, Côte d' ∧	54	47.10 N	4.50 E
Or, Étang d' ⊜	251	48.38 N	1.51 E
Ora (Auer), It.	58	46.21 N	11.18 E
Ora, Lībīya	136	28.33 N	19.24 E
Ōra, Nihon	164m	26.33 N	128.02 E
Ora Banda	152	30.22 S	121.04 E
Oracle	190	32.37 N	110.46 W
Oradea	38	47.03 N	21.57 E
Oradell	266	40.57 N	74.02 W
Oradell Reservoir ⊜[1]	266	40.58 N	74.01 W
Öræfajökull ⊼	24a	64.03 N	16.38 W
Orahovica	38	45.31 N	17.53 E
Orai	114	25.59 N	79.28 E
Oraibi	190	35.53 N	110.37 W
Oraibi Wash ∨	190	35.26 N	110.49 W
Oraison	56	43.55 N	5.55 E
Oran (Ouahran), Alg.	138	35.43 N	0.43 W
Oran, Mo., U.S.	184	37.05 N	89.39 W
Oran, Sebkra d' ⊜	138	35.30 N	1.00 W
Orange, Austl.	156	33.17 S	149.06 E
Orange, Fr.	56	44.08 N	4.48 E
Orange, Calif., U.S.	218	33.47 N	117.51 W
Orange, Conn., U.S.	197	41.17 N	73.02 W
Orange, Mass., U.S.	197	42.35 N	72.19 W
Orange, Ohio, U.S.	269a	41.26 N	81.29 W
Orange, Tex., U.S.	184	30.01 N	93.44 W
Orange, Va., U.S.	178	38.15 N	78.07 W
Orange □[6], Calif., U.S.	218	33.43 N	117.54 W
Orange □[6], Fla., U.S.	210	28.32 N	81.16 W
Orange □[6], Ind., U.S.	208	38.33 N	86.28 W
Orange □[6], N.Y., U.S.	200	41.24 N	74.20 W
Orange (Oranje) ≃	146	28.41 S	16.28 E
Orange, Cabo >	240	4.24 N	51.33 W
Orange Bowl ♠	210	25.46 N	80.14 W
Orangeburg, Ky., U.S.	208	38.35 N	83.39 W
Orangeburg, N.Y., U.S.	200	41.03 N	73.57 W
Orangeburg, S.C., U.S.	182	33.30 N	80.52 W
Orange City, Fla., U.S.	210	28.57 N	81.17 W
Orange City, Iowa, U.S.	188	43.00 N	96.03 W
Orange County Airport ⊠	218	33.40 N	117.51 W
Orange Cove	216	36.37 N	119.19 W
Orange Free State (Oranje-Vrystaat) □[3]	148	28.30 S	27.00 E
Orange Grove	186	27.58 N	97.56 W
Orange Grove ◆[8]	263d	26.10 S	28.05 E
Orange Lake, Fla., U.S.	182	29.25 N	82.13 W
Orange Lake, N.Y., U.S.	200	41.33 N	74.06 W
Orange Lake ⊜	182	29.29 N	82.10 W
Orangemouth → Oranjemund	146	28.38 S	16.24 E
Orange Park	182	30.10 N	81.42 W
Orange Park Acres	270	33.48 N	117.47 W
Orangevale	216	38.41 N	121.13 W
Orangeville, Ont., Can.	202	43.55 N	80.06 W
Orangeville, S. Afr.	148	27.00 S	28.15 E
Orangeville, Ohio, U.S.	204	41.20 N	80.31 W
Orangeville, Pa., U.S.	200	41.05 N	76.25 W
Orangeville, Utah, U.S.	190	39.13 N	111.03 W
Orange Walk	222	18.06 N	88.33 W
Orango, Ilha de I	140	11.10 N	16.08 W
Orani	106	14.49 N	120.32 E
Oranienbaum	50	51.48 N	12.24 E
Oranienburg	50	52.45 N	13.14 E
Oraniye ◆[8]	257b	41.03 N	29.01 E
Oranje	48	52.55 N	6.28 E
Oranje → Orange ≃	146	28.41 S	16.28 E
Oranjefontein	146	23.25 S	27.41 E
Oranje Gebergte ⋀	240	3.00 N	55.05 W
Oranjemund	146	28.38 S	16.24 E
Oranjerivier	148	29.40 S	24.12 E
Oranjestad	231s	12.33 N	70.06 W
Oranki	70	55.53 N	43.44 E
Ŏran-ni	88	34.22 N	126.29 E
Oranžerei	70	45.50 N	47.36 E
Oraparinna	156	31.22 S	138.43 E
Or 'Aqiva	122	32.30 N	34.55 E
Orarak	130	6.15 N	32.23 E
Orari ≃	162	44.15 S	171.25 E
Oras	106	12.09 N	125.26 E
Oras ≃	106	12.08 N	125.26 E
Oras Bay C	106	12.07 N	125.28 E
Orăștie	38	45.50 N	23.12 E
Orașul Stalin → Brașov	38	45.39 N	25.37 E
Oratório, Ribeirão do ≃	277b	23.37 S	46.32 W
Oratov	68	49.12 N	29.32 E
Oravais (Oravainen)	26	63.18 N	22.23 E
Oravița	38	45.02 N	21.41 E
Orawia	162	46.03 S	167.49 E
Orb ≃	32	43.15 N	3.18 E
Orba ≃	56	44.53 N	8.37 E
Orbassano	56	45.01 N	7.32 E
Orbe	54	46.43 N	6.32 E
Orbe ≃	54	46.47 N	6.39 E
Orbec-en-Auge	46	49.01 N	0.25 E
Orbetello	60	42.27 N	11.13 E
Orbetello, Laguna di C	60	42.27 N	11.14 E
Orbey	54	48.08 N	7.10 E
Orbieu ≃	32	43.14 N	2.54 E
Orbigny	46	47.12 N	1.14 E
Orbigo ≃	34	41.58 N	5.40 W
Orbiquet ≃	46	49.09 N	0.14 E
Orbisonia	204	40.15 N	77.54 W
Orbost	156	37.42 S	148.27 E
Örbyhus	40	60.14 N	17.42 E
Orcadas, Islas → Orkney Islands II	28	59.00 N	3.00 W
Orcadas del Sur, Islas → South Orkney Islands II	9	60.35 S	45.30 W
Orcades du Sud, Îles → South Orkney Islands II	9	60.35 S	45.30 W
Orcas	214	48.36 N	122.57 W
Orcas Island I	214	48.39 N	122.55 W
Orce ≃	34	37.44 N	2.28 W
Orcemont	251	48.35 N	1.49 E
Orcera	34	38.19 N	2.39 W
Orchamps	54	47.09 N	5.40 E
Orchard, Nebr., U.S.	188	42.20 N	98.14 W
Orchard, Tex., U.S.	212	29.36 N	95.58 W
Orchard City	190	38.51 N	107.58 W
Orchard Hills, Austl.	264a	33.47 S	150.43 E
Orchard Hills, Pa., U.S.	269b	40.35 N	79.32 W
Orchard Homes	192	46.55 N	114.04 W
Orchard Island	206	40.28 N	83.53 W
Orchard Lake ⊜	271	42.35 N	83.22 W
Orchard Park	200	42.43 N	78.45 W
Orchard Park Airport ⊠	274a	42.48 N	78.45 W
Orchard Peak ∧	216	35.44 N	120.08 W
Orchards	214	45.40 N	122.34 W
Orchard Valley	190	41.06 N	104.19 W
Orchard View	275	40.04 N	74.53 W
Orchha	114	25.21 N	78.39 E
Orchies	46	50.28 N	3.14 E
Orchon	78	49.09 N	105.21 E
Orchon ≃	78	50.21 N	106.05 E
Orchontuul	78	48.58 N	104.59 E
Orcia ≃	60	42.58 N	11.21 E
Orcières	56	44.41 N	6.20 E
Orčik ≃	68	49.10 N	35.04 E

Orco ≃	56	45.10 N	7.52 E
Orcotuna	238	11.58 S	75.20 W
Ord	188	41.36 N	98.56 W
Ord ≃	154	15.30 S	128.21 E
Ord, Mount ∧	150	17.20 S	125.34 E
Orda	76	57.12 N	56.54 E
Ordenes	34	43.04 N	8.24 W
Orderville	190	37.16 N	112.38 W
Ordesa, Parque Nacional de ♠	34	42.39 N	0.02 E
Ordine di Malta, Sovrano Internazionale Militare (S.M.O.M.) ⊍	257a	41.55 N	12.29 E
Ord Mountain ∧	194	34.40 N	116.49 W
Ord Mountains ⋀	218	34.42 N	117.10 W
Ordoqui	242	35.54 S	61.10 W
Ord River	152	17.23 S	128.51 E
Ordu, Tür.	120	35.56 N	36.01 E
Ordu, Tür.	120	41.00 N	37.53 E
Ordu □[4]	120	37.45 N	37.30 E
Ordubad	74	38.56 N	46.02 E
Ordway	188	38.13 N	103.46 W
Ordynskoje	76	54.22 N	81.56 E
Ordzhonikidze → Jenakijevo, S.S.S.R.	73	48.14 N	38.13 E
Ordzhonikidze → Ordžonikidze, S.S.S.R.	74	43.03 N	44.40 E
Ordžonikidze, S.S.S.R.	68	44.57 N	35.22 E
Ordžonikidze, S.S.S.R.	68	47.40 N	34.04 E
Ordžonikidze, S.S.S.R.	74	43.03 N	44.40 E
Ordžonikidze, S.S.S.R.	74	40.53 N	47.23 E
Ordžonikidze, S.S.S.R.	74	42.01 N	43.12 E
Ordžonikidze, S.S.S.R.	75	41.21 N	69.22 E
Ordžonikidzeabad	75	38.34 N	69.01 E
Ordžonikidzevskaja	74	43.18 N	45.03 E
Ordžonikidzevskij, S.S.S.R.	74	43.51 N	41.54 E
Ordžonikidzevskij, S.S.S.R.	76	54.46 N	88.59 E
Ore	140	6.44 N	4.52 E
Ore ≃	42	56.10 N	3.15 W
Oreälven ≃	26	63.32 N	19.44 E
Oreana	209	39.56 N	88.52 W
Örebro	40	59.17 N	15.13 E
Örebro Län □[6]	40	59.30 N	15.00 E
Orechov	68	47.34 N	35.47 E
Orechovka, S.S.S.R.	70	52.56 N	48.14 E
Orechovka, S.S.S.R.	73	48.17 N	39.13 E
Orechovo	70	58.28 N	41.58 E
Orechovo-Zujevo	72	55.49 N	38.59 E
Orechovsk	66	54.41 N	30.30 E
Orechov'skij ◆[8]	73	48.01 N	38.42 E
Ore City	212	32.48 N	94.43 W
Oredež	66	58.49 N	30.20 E
Oredež ≃	66	58.49 N	30.00 E
Orefield	198	40.38 N	75.35 W
Oregon, Ill., U.S.	180	42.01 N	89.20 W
Oregon, Mo., U.S.	184	39.59 N	95.09 W
Oregon, Ohio, U.S.	204	41.38 N	83.28 W
Oregon, Wis., U.S.	206	42.56 N	89.23 W
Oregon □[3]	168 192	44.00 N	121.00 W
Oregon Caves National Monument ♠	192	42.06 N	123.24 W
Oregon City	214	45.21 N	122.36 W
Oregon Creek ≃	216	39.23 N	121.05 W
Oregon Dunes National Recreation Area ♠	192	43.45 N	124.12 W
Oregon House	216	39.21 N	121.17 W
Öregrund	40	60.20 N	18.26 E
Öregrundsgrepen C	40	60.27 N	18.18 E
Orehoved	41	54.57 N	11.52 E
Orekhovo-Zuyevo → Orechovo-Zujevo	72	55.49 N	38.59 E
Orel → Or'ol	66	52.59 N	36.05 E
Orel', Ozero ⊜	79	53.30 N	139.42 E
Oreland	275	40.07 N	75.11 W
Orellana	238	6.54 S	75.04 W
Orellana, Embalse de ⊜[1]	34	39.00 N	5.25 W
Orem	190	40.19 N	111.42 W
Orenburg	76	51.54 N	55.06 E
Orenburg □[4]	70	52.38 N	53.00 E
Örencik	120	39.16 N	29.33 E
Oreng	104	4.03 N	97.28 E
Orense, Arg.	242	38.40 S	59.47 W
Orense, Esp.	34	42.20 N	7.51 W
Orepuki	162	46.17 S	167.44 E
Oreški	72	55.43 N	36.21 E
Oressa ≃	66	52.33 N	28.45 E
Orestes	206	40.16 N	85.44 W
Orestiás	38	41.30 N	26.31 E
Orestimba Creek ≃	216	37.25 N	121.00 W
Øresund → The Sound Џ	41	55.50 N	12.40 E
Oreti ≃	162	46.28 S	168.17 E
Orewa	162	36.34 S	174.42 E
Oreye	52	50.44 N	5.22 E
Orfanoú, Kólpos C	38	40.40 N	23.50 E
Orford, Eng., U.K.	44	52.06 N	1.31 E
Orford, Eng., U.K.	252	53.25 N	2.35 W
Orford Ness >	44	52.05 N	1.34 E
Orfordville	180	42.38 N	89.16 W
Organ Needle ∧	190	32.21 N	106.33 W
Órganos, Sierra de los ⋀	230p	22.25 N	84.00 W
Organ Pipe Cactus National Monument ♠	190	32.00 N	112.55 W
Órgãos, Serra dos ⋀	246	22.22 S	42.45 W
Orgaz	34	39.39 N	3.54 W
Orge ≃	46	48.42 N	2.24 E
Orgejev	68	47.23 N	28.48 E
Orgelet	54	46.31 N	5.37 E
Orgères-en-Beauce	46	48.09 N	1.42 E
Orgerus	251	48.50 N	1.42 E
Orgeval	46	48.55 N	1.59 E
Orgiano	58	45.21 N	11.28 E
Orgnac, Aven d' •[5]	56	44.19 N	4.27 E
Orgnac-l'Aven	56	44.19 N	4.27 E
Orgof	134	3.03 N	43.44 E
Orgon	56	43.47 N	5.02 E
Orgtrud	70	56.12 N	40.37 E
Orgūn	110	32.51 N	69.07 E
Orhangazi	120	40.30 N	29.18 E
Orhanlar	120	39.54 N	27.37 E
Oria	144	3.17 N	30.41 E
Orica	226	14.41 N	86.56 W
Oriçanga ≃	246	22.18 S	47.03 W
Oriči	70	58.24 N	49.05 E
Orick	194	41.17 N	124.04 W
Oricola	60	42.02 N	13.02 E
Orient, Iowa, U.S.	188	41.12 N	94.25 W
Orient, N.Y., U.S.	197	41.08 N	72.18 W
Orient, Ohio, U.S.	208	39.48 N	83.09 W
Oriental, Méx.	224	19.22 N	97.37 W
Oriental, N.C., U.S.	182	35.02 N	76.42 W
Oriental, Cordillera ⋀, Bol.	238	17.30 S	64.30 W
Oriental, Cordillera ⋀, Col.	236	6.00 N	73.00 W
Oriental, Cordillera ⋀, Perú	238	13.00 S	72.00 W
Oriental, Pico ∧	276c	10.32 N	66.50 W
Oriental de Zapata, Ciénaga ☷	230p	22.15 N	80.50 W
Orientaliă, Poarta)(	38	45.06 N	22.18 E
Oriental Park	204	42.09 N	79.22 W
Oriente	242	38.44 S	60.37 W
Oriente □[4]	230p	20.35 N	76.00 W
Orientos	156	28.05 S	141.14 E
Origgio	256b	45.36 N	9.01 E
Origny-en-Thiérache	46	49.54 N	4.01 E
Origny-Sainte-Benoite	46	49.50 N	3.30 E
Orihuela	34	38.05 N	0.57 W
Orillia	202	44.37 N	79.25 W
Orimattila	26	60.48 N	25.45 E
Orinda	216	37.53 N	122.11 W
Orinduik	236	4.42 N	60.01 W
Orini	162	37.34 S	175.18 E
Orinin	68	48.46 N	26.24 E
Orinoco ≃	236	8.37 N	62.15 W
Orinoco, Delta del ≚[2]	236	9.15 N	61.30 W
Oriole, Md., U.S.	198	38.10 N	75.49 W
Oriole, Pa., U.S.	200	41.08 N	77.13 W
Oriomo	154	8.50 S	143.15 E
Orion, Pil.	106	14.37 N	120.34 E
Orion, Ill., U.S.	180	41.21 N	90.23 W
Oripää	26	60.51 N	22.41 E
Oriskany	200	43.09 N	75.20 W
Oriskany Battle Monument ⊥	200	43.11 N	75.23 W
Oriskany Creek ≃	200	43.10 N	75.20 W
Oriskany Falls	200	42.56 N	75.28 W
Orissa □[3]	112	20.00 N	84.00 E
Orissaare	66	58.34 N	23.05 E
Orissa Coast Canal ☰	116	21.51 N	87.41 E
Oristano	36	40.00 N	8.40 E
Orituco ≃	236	8.45 N	67.27 W
Orivesi	26	61.41 N	24.21 E
Orivesi ⊜	26	62.16 N	29.24 E
Oriximiná	240	1.45 S	55.52 W
Orizaba	224	18.51 N	97.06 W
Orizaba, Pico de → Citlaltépetl, Volcán ∧[1]	224	19.01 N	97.16 W
Orizona	245	17.03 S	48.18 W
Orjahovo	38	43.45 N	23.57 E
Ørje	26	59.29 N	11.39 E
Orjen ∧	38	42.30 N	18.38 E
Orjiva	34	36.54 N	3.25 W
Orkanger	26	63.19 N	9.52 E
Örkelljunga	41	56.17 N	13.17 E
Orken	253	51.06 N	6.34 E
Örkenez	120	38.12 N	31.17 E
Orkla ≃	26	63.18 N	9.50 E
Orkney, Sask., Can.	174	49.08 N	107.55 W
Orkney, S. Afr.	148	27.00 S	26.39 E
Orkney Islands □[4]	28	59.00 N	3.00 W
Orkney Islands II	28	59.00 N	3.00 W
Orl'a	66	53.30 N	24.59 E
Orla ≃	50	50.46 N	11.31 E
Orlamünde	50	50.47 N	11.31 E
Orland, Calif., U.S.	194	39.45 N	122.11 W
Orland, Ind., U.S.	206	41.44 N	85.10 W
Orlândia	245	20.43 S	47.53 W
Orland Lake ⊜	268	41.38 N	87.52 W
Orlando, S. Afr.	263d	26.14 S	27.55 E
Orlando, Fla., U.S.	210	28.32 N	81.23 W
Orlando Jetport ⊠	210	28.26 N	81.19 W
Orlando Naval Training Center ■	210	28.34 N	81.20 W
Orlando West Extension	263d	26.15 S	27.54 E
Orland Park	206	41.38 N	87.52 W
Orleães	242	28.21 S	49.18 W
Orléanais □[9]	46	47.50 N	2.00 E
Orléans, Ont., Can.	202	45.28 N	75.31 W
Orléans, Fr.	46	47.55 N	1.54 E
Orleans, Calif., U.S.	194	41.18 N	123.32 W
Orleans, Ind., U.S.	208	38.40 N	86.27 W
Orleans, Mass., U.S.	197	41.47 N	70.00 W
Orleans, Nebr., U.S.	188	40.08 N	99.27 W
Orleans, Vt., U.S.	178	44.49 N	72.12 W
Orleans □[6], N.Y., U.S.	200	43.15 N	78.12 W
Orleans □[6], Vt., U.S.	196	44.57 N	72.12 W
Orléans, Canal d' ☰	46	47.54 N	1.55 E
Orleans, Île d' I	176	46.55 N	70.58 W
Orléansville → El Asnam	138	36.10 N	1.20 E
Orlenga ≃	78	56.03 N	105.53 E
Orlik, S.S.S.R.	70	48.17 N	51.32 E
Orlik, S.S.S.R.	78	52.30 N	99.55 E
Orlinga	78	56.03 N	105.53 E
Orlinnaja, Gora ∧	170	62.35 N	178.30 E
Orlová	30	49.50 N	18.24 E
Orlov Gaj	70	50.57 N	48.12 E
Orlovista	210	28.32 N	81.28 W
Orlovka, S.S.S.R.	68	51.02 N	40.32 E
Orlovka, S.S.S.R.	68	51.54 N	32.47 E
Orlovka, S.S.S.R.	68	45.40 N	33.21 E
Orlovka, S.S.S.R.	73	48.10 N	37.39 E
Orlovka, S.S.S.R.	76	59.03 N	85.59 E
Orlovka ≃	76	58.40 N	86.08 E
Orlovo, S.S.S.R.	68	51.45 N	39.35 E
Orlovo, S.S.S.R.	255b	55.38 N	37.23 E
Orlovskij	70	46.52 N	42.03 E
Orlu	140	5.47 N	7.02 E
Orly	251	48.45 N	2.24 E
Ormanlı	120	41.10 N	31.39 E
Ormāra	118	25.12 N	64.38 E
Ormāra, Rās >	110	25.09 N	64.35 E
Orme, Rivière à l' ≃	265a	45.27 N	73.56 W
Ormea	56	44.09 N	7.54 E
Ormesby	42	54.33 N	1.11 W
Ormesby Saint Margaret	44	52.40 N	1.42 E
Ormiston	174	49.45 N	105.22 W
Ormoc	106	11.00 N	124.37 E
Ormoc Bay C	106	10.58 N	124.35 E
Ormond	264b	37.54 S	145.03 E
Ormond Beach	182	29.17 N	81.02 W
Ormož	36	46.25 N	16.09 E
Ormsby	204	41.48 N	78.33 W
Ormsby □[6]	216	39.11 N	119.46 W
Ormsjön ⊜	26	64.23 N	16.03 E
Ormskirk	42	53.35 N	2.54 W
Ormstown	196	45.08 N	74.00 W
Ormtjernkampen Nasjonalpark ♠	26	61.12 N	9.48 E
Ornain ≃	54	48.46 N	4.47 E
Ornans	54	47.06 N	6.09 E
Ornäs	40	60.31 N	15.32 E
Ornavasso	54	45.58 N	8.24 E
Orne □[5]	32	48.40 N	0.05 E
Orne ≃, Fr.	46	48.08 N	0.11 E
Orne ≃, Fr.	46	48.39 N	0.14 E
Orne ≃, Fr.	52	49.17 N	6.11 E
Ornes	26	61.18 N	7.22 E
Orneta	30	54.08 N	20.08 E
Ornö I	40	59.04 N	18.24 E
Örnsköldsvik	26	63.18 N	18.43 E
Oro	88	40.02 N	127.26 E
Orø I	41	55.46 N	11.49 E
Oro, Río de ≃	236	9.06 N	72.45 W
Oro, Río del ≃, Méx.	222	25.35 N	105.03 W
Oro, Río del ≃, Méx.	224	18.27 N	100.57 W
Orobie, Alpi ⋀	58	46.00 N	10.00 E
Oročanskij Golec, Gora ∧	78	53.29 N	114.18 E
Oročen	64	58.28 N	125.26 E
Orocovis	230m	18.14 N	66.23 W
Orocué	236	4.48 N	71.20 W
Orocuina	226	13.26 N	87.06 W
Orodara	140	10.59 N	4.55 W
Orofino	192	46.29 N	116.15 W
Örög Nuur ⊜, Mong.	76	50.10 N	91.00 E
Orog Nuur ⊜, Mong.	92	45.03 N	100.42 E
Oro Grande	218	34.36 N	117.20 W
Orohena, Mont ∧	164s	17.37 S	149.28 W
Orok, Ol Doinyo ∧	144	2.29 S	36.46 E
Oroku	164m	26.12 N	127.39 E
Or'ol, S.S.S.R.	66	52.59 N	36.05 E
Or'ol, S.S.S.R.	76	59.21 N	56.35 E
Or'ol □[4]	68	52.00 N	38.00 E
Or'ol' ≃	68	48.30 N	34.54 E
Oroluk I[1]	14	7.32 N	155.18 E
Oromocto	176	45.51 N	66.29 W
Oromocto Lake ⊜	176	45.36 N	67.00 W
Oron, Nig.	140	4.48 N	8.14 E
Oron, S.S.S.R.	78	57.11 N	116.28 E
Oron, Ozero ⊜	78	57.06 N	116.30 E
Oronato ≃	236	7.23 N	62.01 W
Oron-la-Ville	54	46.34 N	6.50 E
Orono, Ont., Can.	202	43.59 N	78.37 W
Orono, Maine, U.S.	178	44.53 N	68.40 W
Oronogue ≃	236	2.45 N	57.25 W
Orono Lake ⊜	174	52.13 N	94.55 W
Oronsay I	28	56.01 N	6.14 W
Orontes → Asi ≃	120	36.02 N	35.58 E
Oropeo	224	18.50 N	101.48 W
Oroquieta	106	8.29 N	123.48 E
Oroquieta ≃	106	8.29 N	123.48 E
Orós	240	6.15 S	38.55 W
Orós, Açude ⊜[1]	240	6.15 S	39.05 W
Orosei, Golfo di C	36	40.10 N	9.50 E
Orosháza	30	46.34 N	20.40 E
Orosi	216	36.33 N	119.17 W
Orosi, Volcán ∧[1]	226	10.59 N	85.29 W
Oroszlány	30	47.30 N	18.19 E
Orote Peninsula >[1]	164p	13.26 N	144.38 E
Orotina	226	9.54 N	84.31 W
Oroville, Calif., U.S.	216	39.31 N	121.33 W
Oroville, Wash., U.S.	192	48.56 N	119.26 W
Oroville, Lake ⊜[1]	194	39.32 N	121.25 W
Orowoc Creek ≃	266	40.43 N	73.13 W
Orphin	251	48.35 N	1.47 E
Orpierre	56	44.19 N	5.41 E
Orpington ◆[8]	250	51.23 N	0.06 E
Orrefors	26	56.50 N	15.45 E
Orrell	252	53.32 N	2.43 W
Orrick	184	39.13 N	94.07 W
Orrin	188	48.05 N	100.10 W
Orrius	256d	41.33 N	2.21 E
Orr Lake ⊜, Man., Can.	174	56.07 N	97.11 W
Orr Lake ⊜, Ont., Can.	202	44.37 N	79.47 W
Orroroo	156	32.44 S	138.37 E
Orrs Island	178	43.46 N	69.59 W
Orrtanna	198	39.51 N	77.22 W
Orrville, Ala., U.S.	184	32.18 N	87.15 W
Orrville, Ohio, U.S.	204	40.50 N	81.46 W
Orrville, Pa., U.S.	269b	40.33 N	79.47 W
Orša, S.S.S.R.	66	54.30 N	30.24 E
Orsa, Sve.	26	61.07 N	14.37 E
Orša ≃	72	56.48 N	36.11 E
Orsago	58	45.56 N	12.25 E
Orsainville	196	46.51 N	71.14 W
Orsan	56	44.08 N	4.40 E
Oršanka	70	56.55 N	47.53 E
Orsara di Puglia	60	41.17 N	15.16 E
Orsasjön ⊜	26	61.07 N	14.34 E
Orsay	46	48.48 N	2.11 E
Orsett	250	51.31 N	0.22 E
Orsières	54	46.02 N	7.09 E
Orsjön ⊜	26	61.35 N	16.20 E
Orsk	76	51.12 N	58.34 E
Örskär I	40	60.31 N	18.23 E
Ørslev	41	55.02 N	11.59 E
Orsogna	60	42.13 N	14.17 E
Orson	200	41.49 N	75.27 W
Orșova	38	44.42 N	22.24 E
Orsoy	48	51.31 N	6.41 E
Ørsta	26	62.12 N	6.09 E
Ørsted	41	55.20 N	10.04 E
Örsundaån ≃	40	59.44 N	17.21 E
Örsundsbro	40	59.44 N	17.18 E
Országház ⊍	254c	47.31 N	19.03 E
Orta	120	40.38 N	33.06 E
Orta, Lago d' ⊜	56	45.49 N	8.24 E
Ortaca	120	36.49 N	28.47 E
Ortaklar	120	37.53 N	27.30 E
Ortaköy, Tür.	120	38.44 N	34.03 E
Ortaköy, Tür.	120	38.00 N	34.23 E
Ortaköy, Tür.	120	40.27 N	38.02 E
Ortaköy, Tür.	120	40.17 N	35.16 E
Ortaköy ◆[8]	257b	41.03 N	29.01 E
Orta Nova	60	41.19 N	15.42 E
Orta San Giulio	56	45.48 N	8.25 E
Orte	60	42.27 N	12.23 E
Ortega	236	3.56 N	75.13 W
Ortega Channel Џ	165e	8.22 S	159.37 E
Ortegal, Cabo >	34	43.45 N	7.53 W
Orteguaza ≃	236	0.43 N	75.16 W
Ortelsburg → Szczytno	30	53.34 N	21.00 E
Ortenberg, B.R.D.	52	50.21 N	9.02 E
Ortenberg, B.R.D.	54	48.27 N	7.58 E
Orth	50	54.27 N	11.03 E
Orthez	32	43.29 N	0.46 W
Ortigalita Creek ≃	216	36.57 N	120.52 W
Ortigalita Peak ∧	216	36.48 N	120.55 W
Ortigara, Monte ∧	58	46.00 N	11.29 E
Ortigueira, Bra.	242	24.12 S	50.55 W
Ortigueira, Esp.	34	43.41 N	7.51 W
Ortigueira, Ría de C[1]	34	43.42 N	7.51 W
Orting	214	47.06 N	122.12 W
Ortisei (Sankt Ulrich)	58	46.34 N	11.40 E
Ortiz, Méx.	222	28.17 N	110.43 W
Ortiz, Ven.	236	9.37 N	67.17 W
Ortles (Otler) ∧	58	46.31 N	10.33 E
Örtofta	41	55.47 N	13.14 E
Ortón ≃	238	10.50 S	66.04 W
Ortona	60	42.21 N	14.24 E
Ortona Lock ◆[5]	210	26.47 N	81.18 W
Orton Park ♠	265b	43.46 N	79.12 W
Ortonura	75	41.29 N	76.12 E
Ortonville, Mich., U.S.	206	42.51 N	83.27 W
Ortonville, Minn., U.S.	188	45.19 N	96.27 W
Ortonville State Recreation Area ♠	206	42.52 N	83.26 W
Ortoterek	75	41.56 N	71.21 E
Orto-Tokoj	75	42.21 N	76.01 E
Ortovero	56	44.03 N	8.07 E
Ortrand	50	51.22 N	13.45 E
Örträsk	26	64.08 N	18.59 E
Ortúzar, Canal de ☰	276e	33.33 S	70.47 W
Örtze ≃	48	52.40 N	9.57 E
Oruanui	162	38.35 S	176.02 E
Oruba	263a	6.35 N	3.25 E
Orubskoje Gorodišče ⊥	72	55.12 N	36.45 E
Orudjevo	72	56.26 N	37.32 E
Oruro	238	17.59 S	67.09 W
Oruro □[5]	238	18.40 S	67.30 W
Or'us-Mijele ≃	78	58.35 N	121.30 E
Orust I	26	58.10 N	11.38 E
Orūzgān (Qala-i-Hazār Qadam)	110	32.56 N	66.38 E
Orūzgān □[4]	110	33.15 N	66.00 E
Orval, Abbaye d' ⊍[1]	52	49.38 N	5.22 E
Orvanne ≃	46	48.22 N	2.50 E
Orvieto	60	42.43 N	12.07 E
Orvilla	198	40.16 N	75.17 W
Orvilliers	251	48.52 N	1.39 E
Orvin ≃	46	48.28 N	3.23 E
Orvinio	60	42.08 N	12.56 E
Orviston	204	41.06 N	77.45 W
Orvyn, Gora ∧	170	65.14 N	175.20 W
Orwell, Ont., Can.	204	42.46 N	81.02 W
Orwell, N.Y., U.S.	202	43.35 N	76.00 W
Orwell, Ohio, U.S.	204	41.32 N	80.52 W
Orwell ≃	44	51.57 N	1.17 E
Orwigsburg	198	40.39 N	76.06 W
Orwin	198	40.35 N	76.31 W
Or Yehuda	122	32.01 N	34.51 E
Oryu-dong ◆[8]	261b	37.29 N	126.51 E
Oržev	68	50.45 N	26.07 E
Orževka	70	52.43 N	42.55 E
Oržica	68	49.48 N	32.42 E

≃ River	Fluss	Río	Rivière	Rio
☰ Canal	Kanal	Canal	Canal	Canal
⌊ Waterfall, Rapids	Wasserfall, Stromschnellen	Cascada, Rápidos	Chute d'eau, Rapides	Cascata, Rápidos
Џ Strait	Meeresstrasse	Estrecho	Détroit	Estreito
C Bay, Gulf	Bucht, Golf	Bahía, Golfo	Baie, Golfe	Baía, Golfo
⊜ Lake, Lakes	See, Seen	Lago, Lagos	Lac, Lacs	Lago, Lagos
☷ Swamp	Sumpf	Pantano	Marais	Pântano
⊼ Ice Features, Glacier	Eis- und Gletscherformen	Accidentes Glaciales	Formes glaciaires	Acidentes Glaciares
⊤ Other Hydrographic Features	Andere Hydrographische Objekte	Otros Elementos Hidrográficos	Autres données hydrographiques	Outros Elementos Hidrográficos

✣ Submarine Features	Untermeerische Objekte	Accidentes Submarinos	Formes de relief sous-marin	Acidentes Submarinos
□ Political Unit	Politische Einheit	Unidad Politica	Entité politique	Unidade Política
⊍ Cultural Institution	Kulturelle Institution	Institución Cultural	Institution culturelle	Instituição Cultural
⊥ Historical Site	Historische Stätte	Sitio Histórico	Site historique	Sitio Histórico
♠ Recreational Site	Erholungs- und Ferienort	Sitio de Recreo	Centre de loisirs	Sítio de Lazer
⊠ Airport	Flughafen	Aeropuerto	Aéroport	Aeroporto
■ Military Installation	Militäranlage	Instalación Militar	Installation militaire	Instalação Militar
◆ Miscellaneous	Verschiedenes	Misceláneo	Divers	Miscelânea

ENGLISH

Name	Page	Lat.°′	Long.°′
Orzinuovi	56	45.24 N	9.55 E
Orzyc ≃	30	52.47 N	21.13 E
Orzysz	30	53.49 N	21.56 E
Os, Nor.	26	62.30 N	11.12 E
Oš, S.S.S.R.	75	40.33 N	72.48 E
Ōsa, Nihon	86	35.05 N	133.34 E
Osa, S.S.S.R.	76	57.17 N	55.26 E
Osa, S.S.S.R.	78	53.24 N	103.53 E
Osa, Península de ≻[1]	226	8.34 N	83.31 W
Osage, Iowa, U.S.	180	43.17 N	92.49 W
Osage, Mo., U.S.	209	38.25 N	92.02 W
Osage, N.J., U.S.	275	39.51 N	75.01 W
Osage, Wyo., U.S.	188	43.59 N	104.25 W
Osage □[6]	209	38.27 N	91.50 W
Osage ≃	184	38.35 N	91.57 W
Osage Beach	184	38.09 N	92.37 W
Osage City	188	38.38 N	95.50 W
Osaka, Nihon	84	35.57 N	137.16 E
Ōsaka, Nihon	86		
	260	34.40 N	135.30 E
Ōsaka □[5]	86	34.30 N	135.30 E
Osaka Castle ⊥	260	34.41 N	135.32 E
Ōsaka-hana ≻	86	35.11 N	132.25 E
Ōsaka-heiya ≚	84	34.42 N	135.35 E
Osaka International Airport ⊠	260	34.47 N	135.26 E
Ōsaka-kō C	260	34.38 N	135.26 E
Ōsaka-kokusai-kūkō ⊠	86	34.47 N	135.26 E
Osakarovka	76	50.32 N	72.39 E
Ōsaka-tōge)(, Nihon	86	33.49 N	135.36 E
Ōsaka-tōge)(, Nihon	260	34.56 N	135.18 E
Osaka University ♁[2]	260	34.42 N	135.30 E
Ōsaka-wan C	86	34.30 N	135.18 E
Ōsaki-bana ≻	86	33.19 N	132.23 E
Ōsaki-ga-hana ≻	86	35.11 N	132.25 E
Ōsaki-kami-shima I	86	34.14 N	132.54 E
Osakis	188	45.52 N	95.09 W
Ōsaki-shimo-jima I	86	34.10 N	132.50 E
Osâm ≃	38	43.42 N	24.51 E
Osan	88	37.11 N	127.04 E
Osanovo	72	54.12 N	38.41 E
Osasco	246	23.32 S	46.46 W
Osasco □[7]	277b	23.32 S	46.46 W
Ōsawa	84	35.15 N	139.51 E
Ōsawano	84	36.34 N	137.12 E
Osawatomie	188	38.31 N	94.57 W
Ōsa-yama ∧	86	34.45 N	132.12 E
Osbaldeston	252	53.47 N	2.32 W
Osborne, Kans., U.S.	188	39.26 N	98.42 W
Osborne, Pa., U.S.	269b	40.32 N	80.10 W
Osburger Hochwald •[3]	52	49.40 N	6.50 E
Osburn	192	47.30 N	116.00 W
Osby	26	56.22 N	13.59 E
Osbyholm	41	55.51 N	13.36 E
Oscar Peak ∧	172	54.51 N	129.07 W
Oscarville	170	60.43 N	161.46 W
Oscawana Lake	200	41.23 N	73.52 W
Osceola, Ark., U.S.	184	35.42 N	89.58 W
Osceola, Ind., U.S.	206	41.40 N	86.04 W
Osceola, Iowa, U.S.	180	41.02 N	93.46 W
Osceola, Mo., U.S.	184	38.03 N	93.42 W
Osceola, Nebr., U.S.	188	41.11 N	97.33 W
Osceola, Pa., U.S.	200	41.59 N	77.21 W
Osceola, Tex., U.S.	212	32.08 N	97.14 W
Osceola, Wis., U.S.	180	45.19 N	92.42 W
Osceola □[6]	210	28.00 N	81.15 W
Osceola Mills	204	40.51 N	78.16 W
Oščepkovo	76	56.29 N	70.42 E
Os Césares	246	22.47 S	46.49 W
Oschatz	50	51.17 N	13.07 E
Oschersleben	50	52.01 N	11.13 E
Oscoda	180	44.26 N	83.20 W
Öse ≃	253	51.26 N	7.49 E
Osečenka	66	57.33 N	34.48 E
Osečina	38	44.23 N	19.36 E
Osejevskaja	72	55.53 N	38.10 E
Ošejkino	72	56.15 N	35.54 E
Osek	50	50.37 N	13.40 E
Ösel → Saaremaa I	66	58.25 N	22.30 E
Osen	24	64.17 N	10.30 E
Osetrovo	78	56.47 N	105.47 E
Ōse-zaki ≻	84	35.02 N	138.47 E
Osgood, Ind., U.S.	208	39.08 N	85.17 W
Osgood, Ohio, U.S.	206	40.20 N	84.30 W
Osgoode	202	45.08 N	75.36 W
Osh → Oš	75	40.33 N	72.48 E
Oshamambe	82a	42.30 N	140.22 E
O'Shanassy ≃	156	18.59 S	138.46 E
O'Shaughnessy Dam •[6]	216	37.57 N	119.47 W
O'Shaughnessy Reservoir ⊜[1]	204	40.12 N	83.09 W
Oshawa	202	43.54 N	78.51 W
Oshawa Creek ≃	202	43.52 N	78.49 W
Oshibe •[8]	260	34.45 N	135.04 E
Oshigambo	146	17.47 S	16.05 E
Oshika, Nihon	82	38.16 N	141.32 E
Ōshika, Nihon	84	35.34 N	138.02 E
Oshikango	146	17.25 S	15.56 E
Ōshima, Nihon	82	33.03 N	129.33 E
Ōshima, Nihon	84	37.07 N	138.30 E
Ōshima, Nihon	86	33.55 N	132.15 E
Ō-shima I, Nihon	82	33.28 N	135.50 E
Ō-shima I, Nihon	82a	41.30 N	139.22 E
Ō-shima I, Nihon	84	34.43 N	139.24 E
Ō-shima I, Nihon	84	36.15 N	136.07 E
Ō-shima I, Nihon	86	33.38 N	134.30 E
Ō-shima I, Nihon	86	33.54 N	130.26 E
Ō-shima I, Nihon	86	34.09 N	133.04 E
Ō-shima I, Nihon	86	34.30 N	131.25 E
Ō-shima I, Nihon	86	34.00 N	133.22 E
Oshima-hantō ≻[1]	82a	42.00 N	140.30 E
Oshimizu	84	36.49 N	136.46 E
Oshino	84	35.28 N	138.51 E
Oshivre •[8]	262c	19.09 N	72.51 E
Oshkosh, Nebr., U.S.	188	41.24 N	102.21 W
Oshkosh, Wis., U.S.	180	44.01 N	88.33 W
Oshnovīyeh	118	37.02 N	45.06 E
Oshodi	263a	6.34 N	3.21 E
Oshoek	148	26.13 S	30.59 E
Oshogbo	140	7.47 N	4.34 E
Oshtemo	206	42.15 N	85.41 W
Oshtorān Kūh ∧	118	33.20 N	49.16 E
Oshtorīnān	118	34.01 N	48.38 E
Oshwe	142	3.24 S	19.30 E
Osi	140	8.08 N	5.14 E
Osiān	110	26.43 N	72.55 E
Osica de Jos	38	44.15 N	24.17 E
Osich'ŏn-ni	88	41.25 N	128.16 E
Osiek	30	50.31 N	21.28 E
Osiglia	56	44.17 N	8.12 E
Osijek	38	45.33 N	18.41 E
Osilinka ≃	172	56.05 N	124.29 W
Osilo	36	40.44 N	8.39 E
Osimo	60	43.29 N	13.29 E
Osinki	70	52.51 N	49.30 E
Osinniki, S.S.S.R.	70	58.03 N	47.02 E
Osinniki, S.S.S.R.	76	53.37 N	87.21 E
Osinovka, S.S.S.R.	73	49.34 N	39.05 E
Osinovka, S.S.S.R.	78	50.34 N	109.27 E
Osinovka, S.S.S.R.	78	56.19 N	101.56 E
Osinovskij Chrebet ⛰	170	67.10 N	175.00 E
Osinów Dolny	50	52.48 N	14.10 E
Osintorf	66	54.42 N	30.39 E
Osio Sotto	56	45.36 N	9.35 E
Osipaonica	38	44.33 N	21.04 E
Osipenko → Berd'ansk	68	46.45 N	36.49 E
Osipoviči	66	53.18 N	28.38 E
Osipovo Selo	66	56.51 N	30.30 E
Osire	146	20.59 S	17.19 E
Oskaloosa, Iowa, U.S.	180	41.18 N	92.39 W
Oskaloosa, Kans., U.S.	188	39.13 N	95.19 W
Oskar-Fredriksborg	40	59.24 N	18.26 E
Oskarshamn	26	57.16 N	16.26 E
Oskarström	26	56.48 N	12.58 E
Os'kino	68	51.14 N	39.02 E
Oskol ≃	68	49.06 N	37.25 E
Oskolkovo	24	67.58 N	53.42 E
Oskū	118	37.55 N	46.06 E
Oskuj	66	59.17 N	32.05 E
Oskuja ≃	66	59.14 N	31.54 E
Oslava ≃	30	49.05 N	16.22 E
Ösling □[9]	52	49.55 N	6.00 E
Oslo	26	59.55 N	10.45 E
Oslob	106	9.31 N	123.26 E
Oslofjorden C[2]	26	59.20 N	10.35 E
Os'ma ≃	66	54.55 N	33.24 E
Osmānābād	112	18.10 N	76.02 E
Osmancık	120	40.59 N	34.49 E
Osmaneli	120	40.22 N	30.01 E
Osmaniye	120	37.05 N	36.14 E
Osmanlı	120	41.52 N	34.37 E
Osmanpaşa	120	39.38 N	34.58 E
Ošm'anskaja Vozvyšennost' ⛰[1]	66	54.20 N	26.00 E
Ošm'any	66	54.25 N	25.56 E
Osmeña	106	10.11 N	125.31 E
Osmington	44	50.38 N	2.22 W
Os'mino	66	59.01 N	29.06 E
Osminog, Gora ∧	170	67.54 N	176.50 E
Ösmo	40	58.59 N	17.54 E
Osmond	188	42.22 N	97.36 W
Osmore, Río de ≃	238	17.33 S	71.12 W
Osmoy	251	48.52 N	1.43 E
Osmussaar I	66	59.18 N	23.22 E
Osnabrück	48	52.16 N	8.02 E
Osnabrück □[6]	48	52.30 N	7.40 E
Ośno	30	52.28 N	14.50 E
Osny	251	49.04 N	2.04 E
Oso	214	48.16 N	121.56 W
Oso ≃	144	1.09 S	27.22 E
Oso, Gran Lago del → Great Bear Lake ⊜	166	66.00 N	120.00 W
Ośoba	75	40.44 N	70.26 E
Osogna	54	46.18 N	9.00 E
Osoppo	58	46.15 N	13.05 E
Osorakan-zan ∧	86	34.36 N	132.08 E
Osore-san ∧	82	41.18 N	144.05 E
Osório	242	29.54 S	50.16 W
Osorio, Quebrada ≃	276c	10.36 N	66.56 W
Osório Fonseca	240	3.40 S	58.13 W
Osorno, Chile	244	40.34 S	73.09 W
Osorno, Esp.	34	42.24 N	4.22 W
Osorno □[4]	244	40.45 S	73.00 W
Osorun	263a	6.33 N	3.29 E
Os'otr ≃	72	54.58 N	38.46 E
Osoyoos	172	49.02 N	119.28 W
Osoyoos Indian Reserve •[4]	172	49.08 N	119.30 W
Osoyoos Lake ⊜	172	49.00 N	119.26 W
Osøyra	26	60.11 N	5.28 E
Ospedaletti	56	43.48 N	7.43 E
Ospedaletto, It.	58	46.03 N	11.33 E
Ospedaletto, It.	58	46.17 N	13.07 E
Ospino	236	9.18 N	69.27 W
Ospitale di Cadore	58	46.20 N	12.19 E
Ospitaletto	58	45.33 N	10.04 E
Osprey	210	27.12 N	82.29 W
Osprey Reef ✣[2]	154	13.55 S	146.38 E
Ospwagan Lake ⊜	174	55.35 N	98.03 W
Os Ribeiros	246	22.06 S	46.49 W
Oss	48	51.46 N	5.31 E
Ossa, Mount ∧	156	41.54 S	146.01 E
Ossabaw Island I	182	31.47 N	81.06 W
Osse ≃, Fr.	32	44.07 N	0.17 E
Osse ≃, Nig.	140	6.10 N	5.20 E
Ossenberg	253	51.34 N	6.35 E
Ossendrecht	48	51.24 N	4.19 E
Osseo, Mich., U.S.	206	41.53 N	84.33 W
Osseo, Wis., U.S.	180	44.35 N	91.12 W
Ossett	42	53.41 N	1.35 W
Ossiacher See ⊜	58	46.40 N	13.55 E
Ossian, Ind., U.S.	206	40.53 N	85.10 W
Ossian, Iowa, U.S.	180	43.09 N	91.46 W
Ossining	200	41.10 N	73.52 W
Ossipee	178	43.41 N	71.07 W
Ossjøen ⊜	26	61.13 N	11.53 E
Ossling	50	51.21 N	14.09 E
Ossokmanuan Lake ⊜	166	53.25 N	65.00 W
Ossona	256b	45.30 N	8.54 E
Ossora	64	59.20 N	163.13 E
Ossum-Bösinghoven	253	51.18 N	6.39 E
Ošta	24	60.49 N	35.32 E
Ostaboningue, Lac ⊜	180	47.09 N	78.53 W
Östanå, Sve.	40	60.38 N	16.48 E
Östanå, Sve.	40	59.33 N	18.35 E
Östanbyn	40	60.39 N	16.48 E
Ostankino •[8]	255b	55.49 N	37.37 E
Östansjö	40	59.03 N	14.59 E
Ostapje	68	49.33 N	33.46 E
Ostaškov	66	57.09 N	33.06 E
Ostašovo	72	55.52 N	35.52 E
Ost-Berlin → Berlin (Ost)	254a	52.30 N	13.25 E
Ostbevern	48	52.02 N	7.50 E
Østbirk	41	55.58 N	9.46 E
Ostbüren	253	51.31 N	7.46 E
Østby	26	61.15 N	12.32 E
Ostchinesisches Meer → East China Sea ▾[2]	80	30.00 N	126.00 E
Oste ≃	48	53.33 N	9.10 E
Osted	41	55.34 N	11.58 E
Osteen	210	28.51 N	81.10 W
Ostellato	60	44.45 N	11.56 E
Ostende → Oostende	46	51.13 N	2.55 E
Ostenfelde	48	51.52 N	8.04 E
Oster, S.S.S.R.	66	54.01 N	32.48 E
Oster, S.S.S.R.	68	50.57 N	30.53 E
Oster ≃	66	53.47 N	31.46 E
Osterath	52	51.16 N	6.37 E
Osterbönen	253	51.37 N	7.48 E
Osterburg, D.D.R.	50	52.47 N	11.44 E
Osterburg, Pa., U.S.	204	40.16 N	78.31 W
Osterburken	52	49.26 N	9.26 E
Österbybruk	40	60.12 N	17.54 E
Österbymo	26	57.50 N	15.16 E
Ostercappeln	48	52.20 N	8.13 E
Österdalälven ≃	26	60.33 N	15.08 E
Østerdalen ∨	26	61.15 N	11.10 E
Österfärnebo	40	60.18 N	16.48 E
Osterfeld	50	51.05 N	11.56 E
Osterfeld •[8]	253	51.30 N	6.53 E
Östergötland □[9]	26	58.24 N	15.34 E
Östergötlands Län □[6]	26	58.25 N	15.45 E
Österhaninge	40	59.08 N	18.12 E
Øster Højst	41	55.00 N	9.03 E
Osterholz-Scharmbeck	48	53.14 N	8.47 E
Osterley Park ♠	250	51.30 N	0.21 W
Österlövsta	40	60.26 N	17.47 E
Ostermundigen	54	46.58 N	7.29 E
Osternienburg	50	51.48 N	12.01 E
Osterode, B.R.D.	48	51.44 N	10.11 E
Osterode → Ostróda, Pol.	30	53.43 N	19.59 E
Osterøya I	26	60.33 N	5.35 E
Österreich → Austria □[1]	30	47.20 N	13.20 E
Österreichische Alpen ⛰	30	47.40 N	15.10 E
Osterrönfeld	41	54.17 N	9.41 E
Östersjön → Baltic Sea ▾[2]	24	57.00 N	19.00 E
Österskär	40	59.28 N	18.18 E
Östersund	26	63.11 N	14.39 E
Östervåla	40	60.11 N	17.11 E
Osterville	197	41.38 N	70.22 W
Osterwick	48	52.01 N	7.13 E
Osterwieck	50	51.58 N	10.42 E
Ostfeld	253	51.40 N	7.45 E
Østfold □[6]	26	59.20 N	11.30 E
Ostfriesische Inseln II	48	53.44 N	7.25 E
Ostfriesland □[9]	48	53.20 N	7.40 E
Ost-Ghats → Eastern Ghāts ⛰	112	14.00 N	78.50 E
Ostgrossefehn	48	53.24 N	7.36 E
Östhammar	40	60.16 N	18.22 E
Ostheim vor der Rhön	52	50.27 N	10.14 E
Osthofen	52	49.42 N	8.19 E
Ostia, Bonifica di •[1]	257a	41.46 N	12.18 E
Ostia Antica ⊥	60	41.45 N	12.16 E
Ostiano	58	45.13 N	10.15 E
Ostiglia	58	45.04 N	11.08 E
Ostki	68	51.16 N	27.22 E
Östliche Sierra Madre → Madre Oriental, Sierra ⛰	222	22.00 N	99.30 W
Östmark	26	60.17 N	12.45 E
Ost'or ≃	68	50.56 N	30.52 E
Ostpeene ≃	50	53.43 N	12.46 E
Ostra	60	43.37 N	13.09 E
Östraby	41	55.46 N	13.41 E
Ostrach	54	47.57 N	9.23 E
Ostrach ≃	54	48.04 N	9.24 E
Östra Grevie	41	55.28 N	13.08 E
Östra Husby	40	58.35 N	16.33 E
Östra Laxsjön ⊜	40	58.54 N	14.42 E
Östra Ljungby	41	56.11 N	13.04 E
Ostrander	204	40.16 N	83.13 W
Ostrau → Ostrava, Česko.	30	49.50 N	18.17 E
Ostrau, D.D.R.	50	51.12 N	13.09 E
Ostrava	30	49.50 N	18.17 E
Ostra Vetere	60	43.36 N	13.03 E
Ostredok ∧	30	48.55 N	19.04 E
Ostrhauderfehn	48	53.08 N	7.37 E
Östrich	253	51.40 N	6.55 E
Ostricourt	46	50.27 N	3.02 E
Östringen	52	49.13 N	8.43 E
Ostritz	50	51.01 N	14.56 E
Ostróda	30	53.43 N	19.59 E
Ostrog	68	50.20 N	26.31 E
Ostrog, Manastir ♁[1]	38	42.39 N	19.00 E
Ostrogožsk	68	50.52 N	39.05 E
Ostrokonje	66	59.52 N	42.02 E
Ostrołęka	30	53.06 N	21.34 E
Ostroróg	30	52.39 N	16.27 E
Ostrošickij Gorodok	66	54.04 N	27.42 E
Ostrov, Česko.	50	50.17 N	12.57 E
Ostrov, Rom.	38	44.06 N	27.22 E
Ostrov, S.S.S.R.	66	52.53 N	25.59 E
Ostrov, S.S.S.R.	66	57.20 N	28.22 E
Ostrov, S.S.S.R.	66	60.34 N	37.55 E
Ostrov, S.S.S.R.	255b	55.35 N	37.51 E
Ostrov •[1]	30	47.55 N	17.35 E
Ostrov'anskij	70	46.45 N	42.13 E
Ostrovcy	72	55.35 N	38.01 E
Ostrovec	66	54.37 N	25.57 E
Ostrovki	255a	59.48 N	30.50 E
Ostrovno	66	55.08 N	29.53 E
Ostrovskaja	70	50.26 N	44.27 E
Ostrovskoje	70	57.48 N	42.15 E
Ostrov-Zalit	66	58.01 N	28.04 E
Ostrowiec Świętokrzyski	30	50.57 N	21.23 E
Ostrów Lubelski	30	51.30 N	22.52 E
Ostrów Mazowiecka	30	52.49 N	21.54 E
Ostrów Wielkopolski	30	51.39 N	17.49 E
Ostryna	66	53.44 N	24.32 E
Ostrzeszów	30	51.25 N	17.57 E
Ostsee → Baltic Sea ▾[2]	24	57.00 N	19.00 E
Ostseebad Ahrenshoop	50	54.23 N	12.25 E
Ostseebad Boltenhagen	50	54.00 N	11.12 E
Ostseebad Dierhagen	41	54.17 N	12.22 E
Ostseebad Graal-Müritz	50	54.15 N	12.12 E
Ostseebad Nienhagen	50	54.09 N	11.58 E
Ostseebad Rerik	50	54.06 N	11.37 E
Ostseebad Wustrow	50	54.21 N	12.23 E
Ost-Sümmern	253	51.26 N	7.44 E
Osttirol •[1]	58	46.55 N	12.30 E
Ostuacán	224	17.25 N	93.18 W
Ostula	224	18.30 N	103.28 W
Ostuni	36	40.44 N	17.35 E
Ostwald	54	48.33 N	7.43 E
Osuga	66	56.02 N	34.18 E
Osuga ≃	66	57.16 N	34.49 E
Osuka	84	34.41 N	137.59 E
Osum ≃	38	40.48 N	19.52 E
Ōsumi	260	34.50 N	135.45 E
Ōsumi-hantō ≻[1]	82	31.20 N	130.55 E
Ōsumi-kaikyō ⋃	82	31.00 N	131.00 E
Ōsumi-shotō II	83b	30.30 N	130.00 E
Osuna	34	37.14 N	5.07 W
Osu-ri	88	35.31 N	127.18 E
Osvaldo Cruz	245	21.47 S	50.50 W
Osveja	66	56.01 N	28.06 E
Osvejskoje, Ozero ⊜	66	56.03 N	28.08 E
Ošvor	24	66.58 N	62.53 E
Oswaldtwistle	42	53.43 N	2.26 W
Oswaldtwistle Moor •[3]	252	53.43 N	2.23 W
Oswald West State Park ♠	214	45.45 N	123.58 W
Oswayo	204	41.55 N	78.01 W
Oswayo Creek ≃	200	42.02 N	78.21 W
Oswegatchie ≃	202	44.42 N	75.30 W
Oswego, Ill., U.S.	206	41.41 N	88.21 W
Oswego, Ind., U.S.	206	41.19 N	85.47 W
Oswego, Kans., U.S.	188	37.10 N	95.06 W
Oswego, N.Y., U.S.	202	43.27 N	76.31 W
Oswego □[6]	202	43.22 N	76.15 W
Oswego ≃, N.J., U.S.	198	39.40 N	74.32 W
Oswego ≃, N.Y., U.S.	202	43.28 N	76.31 W
Oswestry	44	52.52 N	3.04 W
Oświęcim	30	50.03 N	19.12 E
Osyka	184	31.00 N	90.28 W
Ōta, Nihon	84	36.18 N	139.22 E
Ōta, Nihon	86	33.31 N	131.33 E
Ōta •[8]	258	35.35 N	139.44 E
Ōta ≃, Nihon	84	34.40 N	137.54 E
Ōta ≃, Nihon	86	34.22 N	132.25 E
Otago Peninsula ≻[1]	162	45.52 S	170.40 E
Otahuhu	162	36.57 S	174.51 E
Ōtake	86	34.12 N	132.13 E
Otaki, N.Z.	162	40.45 S	175.09 E
Ōtaki, Nihon	84	35.48 N	137.33 E
Ōtaki, Nihon	84	35.57 N	138.56 E
Ōtaki, Nihon	84	35.17 N	140.15 E
Ōtaki ≃	84	35.49 N	137.40 E
Ōtaki-yama ∧	86	34.07 N	134.08 E
Otane	162	39.53 S	176.38 E
Otanmäki	26	64.07 N	27.06 E
Otar	75	43.33 N	75.13 E
Otari	84	36.46 N	137.54 E
Otaru	82a	43.13 N	141.00 E
Otatara	162	46.26 S	168.18 E
Otatitlán	224	18.12 N	96.02 W
Otautau	162	46.09 S	168.00 E
Otava	26	61.39 N	27.04 E
Otava ≃	30	49.26 N	14.12 E
Otavalo	236	0.14 N	78.16 W
Otavi	146	19.39 S	17.20 E
Ōtawara	84	36.52 N	140.02 E
Otawa-yama ∧	260	34.28 N	135.53 E
Otay	218	32.36 N	117.04 W
Otchinjau	142	16.30 S	13.57 E
Oteapan	224	18.00 N	94.39 W
Otego	200	42.24 N	75.11 W
Otego Creek ≃	200	42.25 N	75.07 W
Otélé	142	3.35 N	11.15 E
Otematata	162	44.37 S	170.16 E
Otepää	66	58.03 N	26.30 E
Oteros ≃	222	26.55 N	108.22 W
Otford, Austl.	160	34.12 S	151.01 E
Otford, Eng., U.K.	44	51.19 N	0.12 E
Otgon	78	47.16 N	97.33 E
Otgon Tenger Uul ∧	78	47.35 N	97.35 E
Otham	250	51.15 N	0.35 E
Othello	192	46.50 N	119.10 W
Othery	44	51.05 N	2.53 W
Othfresen	48	52.00 N	10.23 E
Othis	251	49.04 N	2.41 E
Othonoí I	38	39.50 N	19.26 E
Oti ≃	140	8.40 N	0.13 E
Otibanda	154	7.15 S	146.30 E
Otinapa	222	24.11 N	105.02 W
Otira	162	42.50 S	171.33 E
Otis, Colo., U.S.	188	40.09 N	102.58 W
Otis, Ind., U.S.	206	41.36 N	86.54 W
Otis, Kans., U.S.	188	38.32 N	99.03 W
Otis, Mass., U.S.	197	42.12 N	73.06 W
Otisco	208	38.33 N	85.40 W
Otisco Lake ⊜	200	42.52 N	76.18 W
Otish, Monts ⛰	166	52.22 N	70.30 W
Otis Reservoir ⊜[1]	197	42.09 N	73.02 W
Otisville	200	41.28 N	74.32 W
Otjassy	70	53.14 N	41.39 E
Otjikondo	146	19.50 S	15.23 E
Otjimbingue	146	22.19 S	16.10 E
Otjimbingwe Game Reserve •[4]	146	22.20 S	16.05 E
Otjinene	146	21.13 S	18.42 E
Otjituuo	146	19.40 S	18.32 E
Otjiwarongo	146	20.29 S	16.36 E
Otjiwarongo □[5]	146	21.45 S	17.00 E
Otjiwero	146	17.59 S	13.22 E
Otjosondjou ≃	146	19.30 S	20.04 E
Otju	146	18.15 S	13.18 E
Otju □[5]	146	20.00 S	15.00 E
Otley	42	53.54 N	1.41 W
Otm'ok, Pereval)(	75	42.20 N	73.10 E
Otmuchów	30	50.28 N	17.10 E
Otnes	26	61.45 N	11.14 E
Ōtō	86	33.41 N	135.35 E
Otočac	36	44.52 N	15.14 E
Oton	106	10.42 N	122.29 E
Otonabee ≃	202	44.08 N	78.14 W
Otoque, Isla I	226	8.36 N	79.36 W
Ōtori-kita	260	34.33 N	135.27 E
Otorma	70	53.32 N	42.32 E
Otorohanga	162	38.11 S	175.12 E
Otoskwin ≃	166	52.13 N	88.06 W
Otowa	84	34.51 N	137.18 E
Otowa-yama ∧	260	34.58 N	135.51 E
Otowa-yama-tunnel •[5]	84	34.58 N	135.51 E
Ōtoyo	86	33.46 N	133.40 E
Otra ≃	26	58.09 N	8.00 E
Otradnaja	74	44.23 N	41.31 E
Otradnoje	255a	59.47 N	30.49 E
Otradnyj	70	53.22 N	51.21 E
Otranto	36	40.09 N	18.30 E
Otranto, Strait of ≃[1]	38	40.00 N	19.00 E
Otricoli	60	42.25 N	12.29 E
Otrokovice	30	49.13 N	17.31 E
Ötscher ∧	30	47.52 N	15.12 E
Otsego	206	42.27 N	85.42 W
Otsego □[6]	200	42.42 N	74.56 W
Otsego Lake ⊜	200	42.45 N	74.52 W
Otselic ≃	200	42.20 N	75.58 W
Ōtsu, Nihon	86	35.00 N	135.52 E
Ōtsu, Nihon	258	35.16 N	139.42 E
Ōtsu ≃	260	34.30 N	135.24 E
Ōtsuchi	82	39.21 N	141.54 E
Ōtsuki	84	35.36 N	138.57 E
Ōtsu-shima I	86	34.00 N	131.42 E
Otta, Nig.	140	6.42 N	3.10 E
Otta, Nor.	26	61.46 N	9.32 E
Otta ≃	26	61.46 N	9.31 E
Ottakring •[8]	254b	48.12 N	16.19 E
Otta Pass ⋃	165c	7.09 N	151.53 E
Ottarnic Pond ⊜	273	42.46 N	71.25 W
Ottavia •[8]	257a	41.58 N	12.24 E
Ottaviano	60	40.51 N	14.28 E
Ottawa, Ont., Can.	202	45.25 N	75.42 W
Ottawa, Ill., U.S.	206	41.21 N	88.51 W
Ottawa, Kans., U.S.	188	38.37 N	95.16 W
Ottawa, Ohio, U.S.	206	41.01 N	84.03 W
Ottawa □[6], Mich., U.S.	206	42.57 N	86.02 W
Ottawa □[6], Ohio, U.S.	204	41.31 N	82.56 W
Ottawa ≃, Can.	166	45.20 N	73.58 W
Ottawa ≃, Ohio, U.S.	204	41.44 N	83.28 W
Ottawa ≃, Ohio, U.S.	206	41.00 N	84.15 W
Ottawa-Carleton □[6]	202	45.15 N	75.45 W
Ottawa Hills	204	41.40 N	83.39 W
Ottawa International Airport ⊠	202	45.19 N	75.40 W
Ottawa Islands II	166	59.30 N	80.10 W
Ottbergen	48	51.42 N	9.18 E
Ottenby	26	56.14 N	16.25 E
Ottendorf-Okrilla	50	51.11 N	13.50 E
Ottenhöfen	54	48.34 N	8.09 E
Otter ≃	44	50.46 N	3.17 W
Otterbach ≃	52	49.07 N	8.21 E
Otterbäcken	40	58.57 N	14.02 E
Otterbein	206	40.29 N	87.06 W
Otterberg	52	49.30 N	7.46 E
Otterburn	42	55.14 N	2.10 W
Otterburne	174	49.30 N	97.03 W
Otterburn Park	196	45.33 N	73.13 W
Otter Creek	182	29.19 N	82.48 W
Otter Creek ≃, Ont., Can.	202	44.06 N	81.07 W
Otter Creek ≃, Ont., Can.	202	42.44 N	80.51 W
Otter Creek ≃, Ind., U.S.	208	38.58 N	85.37 W
Otter Creek ≃, Iowa, U.S.	184	41.20 N	93.30 W
Otter Creek ≃, Mo., U.S.	209	39.31 N	91.51 W
Otter Creek ≃, Mont., U.S.	192	45.36 N	106.17 W
Otter Creek ≃, N.Y., U.S.	202	43.43 N	75.23 W
Otter Creek ≃, Utah, U.S.	190	38.10 N	112.02 W
Otter Creek ≃, Vt., U.S.	178	44.13 N	73.17 W
Otter Creek Reservoir ⊜[1]	190	38.12 N	111.59 W
Otterhöfen	52	48.33 N	8.12 E
Otter Lake, Qué., Can.	178	45.51 N	76.26 W
Otter Lake, Mich., U.S.	180	43.13 N	83.28 W
Otter Lake ⊜, Ont., Can.	202	44.47 N	76.07 W
Otter Lake ⊜, Ont., Can.	202	45.17 N	79.56 W
Otter Lake ⊜, Sask., Can.	174	55.35 N	104.39 W
Otterlo	48	52.06 N	5.45 E
Otterndorf	48	53.48 N	8.53 E
Otterøya I	26	62.42 N	6.48 E
Otter River	197	42.36 N	72.03 W
Ottersberg	48	53.06 N	9.08 E
Ottershaw	250	51.22 N	0.32 W
Ottersleben •[8]	50	52.05 N	11.34 E
Otter Tail Lake ≃	188	46.16 N	96.36 W
Otterup	41	55.31 N	10.24 E
Otterville, Ont., Can.	202	42.55 N	80.36 W
Otterville, Ill., U.S.	209	39.03 N	90.24 W
Otterville, Mo., U.S.	184	38.42 N	93.00 W
Ottery ≃	44	50.39 N	4.20 W
Ottery Saint Mary	44	50.45 N	3.17 W
Ottignies	52	50.40 N	4.34 E
Ottine	212	29.36 N	97.35 W
Ottleben	50	52.05 N	11.07 E
Ottmachau → Otmuchów	30	50.28 N	17.10 E
Ottmarsbocholt	48	51.49 N	7.32 E
Ottnang	58	48.06 N	13.40 E
Ottnaren ⊜	40	60.29 N	16.37 E
Otto, N.Y., U.S.	200	42.21 N	78.50 W
Otto, Tex., U.S.	212	31.27 N	96.49 W
Ottobeuren	54	47.56 N	10.18 E
Ottobeuren, Klosterkirche ♁[1]	54	48.01 N	10.28 E
Ottobiano	56	45.09 N	8.50 E
Ottobrunn	58	48.04 N	11.40 E
Ottone	56	44.37 N	9.20 E
Ottoschwanden	54	48.12 N	7.52 E
Ottosdal	148	26.58 S	26.00 E
Ottoshoop	146	25.45 S	25.59 E
Ottoville	206	40.54 N	84.18 W
Ottuk, S.S.S.R.	75	41.38 N	75.51 E
Ottuk, S.S.S.R.	75	42.18 N	76.18 E
Ottumwa	180	41.01 N	92.25 W
Ottweiler	52	49.24 N	7.09 E
Otty Lake ⊜	202	44.50 N	76.13 W
Otu, Nig.	140	8.14 N	3.24 E
Otu → Ōtsu, Nihon	86	35.00 N	135.52 E
Otukpa	140	7.09 N	7.41 E
Otumpa	242	27.19 S	62.13 W
Otun	263a	6.42 N	3.22 E
Oturkpo	140	7.14 N	8.08 E
Otuzco	238	7.54 S	78.35 W
Otway, Bahía ⋃	244	53.20 S	74.00 W
Otway, Cape ≻	156	38.52 S	143.31 E
Otway, Seno de C	244	53.05 S	71.30 W
Otway Range ⛰	159	38.30 S	143.50 E
Otwock	30	52.07 N	21.16 E
Otyn'a	68	48.44 N	24.51 E
Ötztal ∨	58	47.05 N	10.55 E
Ötztaler Ache ≃	58	47.14 N	10.50 E
Ötztaler Alpen (Alpi Venoste) ⛰	58	46.45 N	10.55 E
Ou ≃	100	20.04 N	102.13 E
Ouachita ≃	184	31.38 N	91.49 W
Ouachita, Lake ⊜[1]	184	34.40 N	93.25 W
Ouachita Mountains ⛰	184	34.40 N	94.25 W
Ouaco	165f	20.50 S	164.29 E
Ouada, Djebel ∧	136	8.56 N	23.26 E
Ouadane	138	20.56 N	11.37 W
Ouadda	142	8.04 N	22.24 E
Ouaddai □[5]	136	13.00 N	21.00 E
Ouadey, Ouadi el ∨	136	13.34 N	18.03 E
Ouadou ∨	140	15.40 N	9.53 W
Ouagadougou	140	12.22 N	1.31 W
Ouah ≃	142	0.43 N	12.55 E
Ouahigouya	140	13.35 N	2.25 W
Ouahran → Oran	138	35.43 N	0.43 W
Ouak	142	7.43 N	13.30 E
Ouaka □[5]	142	6.00 N	21.00 E
Ouaka ≃	142	4.59 N	19.56 E
Oualâta	140	17.18 N	7.02 W
Oualâta, Dhar •[4]	140	17.48 N	7.24 W
Oualidia	138	32.44 N	9.08 W
Ouallam	140	14.19 N	2.05 E
Ouallene	138	24.37 N	1.14 E
Oualto	140	9.01 N	10.06 W
Ouamiri	142	6.12 N	20.45 E
Ouanary	240	4.13 N	51.40 W
Ouanda Djallé	136	8.54 N	22.48 E
Ouandjia ≃	136	9.35 N	21.43 E
Ouango	142	4.19 N	22.33 E
Ouani	140	16.46 N	0.17 W
Ouanne ≃	46	47.57 N	2.47 E
Ouan Taredert	138	27.33 N	9.32 E
Ouaquaga	200	42.08 N	75.39 W
Ouarane •[1]	124	21.00 N	10.30 W
Ouararda, Passe de)(	138	21.01 N	13.03 W
Ouareau ≃	196	45.56 N	73.25 W
Ouareau, Lac ⊜[1]	196	46.17 N	74.09 W
Ouargaye	140	11.32 N	0.01 E
Ouargla	138	31.59 N	5.25 E
Ouarkoye	140	12.05 N	3.40 W
Ouarkziz, Jbel ⛰	138	28.50 N	9.00 W
Ouarra ≃	144	5.05 N	24.26 E
Ouarsenis, Djebel ∧	34	35.53 N	1.38 E
Ouarville	46	48.21 N	1.46 E
Ouarzazate	138	30.57 N	6.50 W
Ouassoulou ≃	140	11.35 N	8.11 W
Ouatcha	140	13.22 N	9.18 E
Oubangui (Ubangi) ≃	142	0.30 S	17.42 E
Ouche ≃	54	47.06 N	5.16 E
Ōuchi	86	34.16 N	134.18 E
Oucques	46	47.49 N	1.18 E
Ōuda	84	34.28 N	135.56 E
Oudaze Lake ⊜	202	45.27 N	79.11 W
Oud-Beijerland	48	51.49 N	4.25 E
Ouddorp	48	51.18 N	3.56 E
Oude IJssel (Issel) ≃	48	52.00 N	6.10 E
Oudenaarde	46	50.51 N	3.36 E
Oudenbosch	48	51.35 N	4.31 E
Oudenburg	46	50.46 N	3.53 E
Oude-Pekela	48	53.04 N	6.58 E
Oude Rijn ≃	48	52.05 N	4.20 E
Oudeschild	48	53.02 N	4.50 E
Oude-Tonge	48	51.41 N	4.12 E
Oudewater	48	52.02 N	4.52 E
Oud-Gastel	48	51.35 N	4.27 E
Oudjda → Oujda	138	34.41 N	1.45 W
Oud-Loosdrecht	48	52.13 N	5.04 E
Oudtshoorn	148	33.35 S	22.14 E
Oudyoumoudi	140	14.04 N	0.28 W
Oued Athmenia	34	36.15 N	6.17 E
Oued Cheham	36	36.23 N	7.46 E
Oued Fodda	34	36.11 N	1.32 E
Oued Meliz	36	36.27 N	8.34 E
Oued Rhiou	34	35.58 N	0.55 E
Oued Tlelat	34	35.34 N	0.27 W
Oued Zarga	36	36.40 N	9.25 E
Oued-Zem	138	32.55 N	6.33 W
Ouellé	140	7.18 N	4.01 W
Ouémé □[5]	140	7.00 N	2.35 E
Ouémé ≃	140	6.29 N	2.32 E
Ouen, Île I	165f	22.26 S	166.49 E
Ouenkoro	140	13.23 N	3.50 W
Ouenza	138	35.57 N	8.04 E
Ouenza, Djebel ∧	36	35.57 N	8.05 E
Ouenzé	263b	4.14 S	15.17
Ouergayo	140	6.19 N	5.56 W
Ouessa	140	11.03 N	2.47 W
Ouessant, Île d' I	32	48.28 N	5.05 W
Ouesso	142	1.37 N	16.04 E
Ouest, Pointe de l' ≻	176	49.52 N	64.31 W
Ouest, Rivière de l' ≃	196	45.39 N	74.21 W
Ouezzane	138	34.52 N	5.35 W
Ouffet	52	50.26 N	5.28 E
Ouganda → Uganda □[1]	144	1.00 N	32.00 E
Ougarou	140	12.09 N	0.56 E
Oughter, Lough ⊜	42	54.07 N	6.42 W
Ouham □[5]	142	7.00 N	18.00 E
Ouham-Pendé □[5]	142	7.00 N	16.00 E
Ouidah	140	6.22 N	2.05 E
Ouistreham	32	49.17 N	0.15 W
Oujda	138	34.41 N	1.45 W
Oujiamiao	92	31.55 N	112.09 E
Oujiang ≃	90	28.04 N	120.35 E
Oulainen	26	64.16 N	24.48 E
Oulangan Kansallispuisto ♠	24	66.12 N	29.30 E
Oulchy-le-Château	46	49.12 N	3.21 E
Oule ≃	56	44.25 N	5.21 E
Ouled Agla	34	35.58 N	4.45 E
Ouled Djellal	138	34.28 N	5.02 E
Ouled-Naïl, Monts des ⛰	138	34.33 N	3.28 E
Ouleout Creek ≃	200	42.20 N	75.18 W
Oulins	46	48.52 N	1.28 E
Oullins	56	45.43 N	4.48 E
Oulou, Bahr ≃	136	9.48 N	21.32 E
Oulton Broad	44	52.31 N	1.42 E
Oulu	26	65.01 N	25.28 E

DEUTSCH

Name	Seite	Breite°′	Länge°′ E=Ost
Oulujärvi ⊜	26	64.20 N	27.15 E
Oulujoki ≃	26	65.01 N	25.25 E
Oulun lääni □[4]	24	65.00 N	27.00 E
Oulx	56	45.02 N	6.50 E
Oum Chalouba	136	15.48 N	20.46 E
Oumé	140	6.23 N	5.25 W
Oum er Rbia, Oued ≃	138	33.19 N	8.21 W
Oum Hadjer	136	13.18 N	19.41 E
Oum Hadjer, Ouadi ∨	136	16.38 N	20.14 E
Oumm ed Droûs Guebli, Sebkhet ⊜	138	24.03 N	11.45 W
Oumm ed Drous Telli, Sebkhet ⊜	138	24.20 N	11.30 W
Ounara	138	31.33 N	9.28 W
Ounasjoki ≃	24	66.30 N	25.45 E
Oundle	44	52.29 N	0.29 W
Ounianga Kébir	136	19.04 N	20.29 E
Ouolossébougou	140	12.00 N	7.55 W
Our ≃	52	49.53 N	6.18 E
Oural, Monts → Ural'skije Gory ⛰	62	60.00 N	60.00 E
Ōura-wan C	164m	26.32 N	128.04 E
Ouray	190	38.01 N	107.40 W
Ouray, Mount ∧	190	38.25 N	106.14 W
Ource ≃	54	48.06 N	4.23 E
Ourcq ≃	46	49.01 N	3.01 E
Ourcq, Canal de l' ≅	46	48.51 N	2.22 E
Ourém	240	1.33 S	47.06 W
Ouri	136	21.34 N	19.13 E
Ouri, Tarso ∧	136	21.25 N	18.56 E
Ouricuri	240	7.53 S	40.05 W
Ourimbah	160	33.22 S	151.23 E
Ourinhos	245	22.59 S	49.52 W
Ourique	34	37.39 N	8.13 W
Ournie	161b	35.56 S	147.51 E
Ouro, Paraná do ≃	238	8.29 S	70.30 W
Ouro, Ponta do ≻	148	26.51 S	32.54 E
Ouro, Rio d' ≃	277a	22.42 S	43.35 E
Ouro Branco	240	6.42 S	36.57 W
Ouro Fino	246	22.17 S	46.22 W
Ouro Prêto	245	20.23 S	43.30 W
Ouro Prêto ≃	238	11.02 S	65.13 W
Ouroufa, Vallée d' ∨	140	14.42 N	7.00 E
Ouroux	46	47.11 N	3.57 E
Ours, Grand Lac de l' → Great Bear Lake ⊜	166	66.00 N	120.00 W
Oursi	140	14.41 N	0.27 W
Ourthe ≃	52	50.38 N	5.35 E
Ourville-en-Caux	46	49.44 N	0.36 E
Ōu-sammyaku ⛰	82	38.45 N	140.50 E
Ouse	156	42.29 S	146.42 E
Ouse ≃, Ont., Can.	202	44.17 N	78.03 W
Ouse ≃, Eng., U.K.	42	53.42 N	0.41 W
Ouse ≃, Eng., U.K.	44	50.47 N	0.03 E
Oust ≃	32	47.39 N	2.06 W
Outardes, Baie aux C	176	49.02 N	68.30 W
Outardes, Rivière aux ≃	166	49.04 N	68.28 W
Outardes Est, Rivière aux ≃	196	45.06 N	74.04 W
Outarville	46	48.13 N	2.01 E
Outcalt	266	40.23 N	74.24 W
Outeiro	246	22.46 S	42.51 W
Outeniekwaberge ⛰	148	33.53 S	22.35 E
Outerbridge Crossing •[5]	266	40.31 N	74.15 W
Outer Harbour	158b	34.47 S	138.30 E
Outer Hebrides II	28	57.50 N	7.32 W
Outer Island I	180	47.03 N	90.30 W
Outer Santa Barbara Passage ⋃	218	33.10 N	118.30 W
Outjo	146	20.08 S	16.08 E
Outlane	252	53.39 N	1.53 W
Outlet Bay C	198	37.22 N	75.49 W
Outlook, Sask., Can.	174	51.30 N	107.03 W
Outlook, Mont., U.S.	188	48.53 N	104.47 W
Outokumpu	26	62.44 N	29.01 E
Outpost Mountain ∧	170	69.08 N	151.12 W
Outreau	46	50.42 N	1.35 E
Outremont	196	45.31 N	73.38 W
Outside Canal ≅	216	37.13 N	121.02 W
Outwell	44	52.37 N	0.14 E
Outwood	42	53.42 N	1.30 W
Ouvèze ≃	56	43.59 N	4.51 E
Ouvidor	245	18.14 S	47.50 W
Ouvidor, Ribeirão do ≃	246	21.40 S	45.43 W
Ouye, Forêt de l' ♠	251	48.32 N	2.00 E
Ouyen	156	35.04 S	142.20 E
Ouzinkie	170	57.55 N	152.30 W
Ouzouer-le-Marché	46	47.55 N	1.32 E
Ouzouer-sur-Loire	46	47.46 N	2.29 E
Ovacık	120	41.05 N	32.55 E
Ovada	56	44.38 N	8.38 E
Oval	200	41.09 N	77.11 W
Ovalau I	165g	17.40 S	178.48 E
Ovalle	242	30.36 S	71.12 W
Ovamboland □[5]	146	18.00 S	16.00 E
Ovamboland □[9]	146	17.45 S	16.30 E
Ovando, Bahía de C	230p	20.08 N	74.13 W
Ovar	34	40.52 N	8.38 W
Ovaro	58	46.29 N	12.52 E
Ovau I	165e	6.47 S	156.01 E
Ovčinino	72	56.02 N	39.03 E
Ovcyno	255a	59.48 N	30.37 E
Övedskloster	41	55.41 N	13.38 E
Ovejas	236	9.32 N	75.14 W
Ovelgönne	48	53.20 N	8.25 E
Ovenden	252	53.44 N	1.53 W
Oveng	142	2.25 N	12.16 E
Overath	52	50.55 N	7.14 E
Overberge	253	51.37 N	7.41 E
Overbrook	188	38.47 N	95.33 W
Overbrook •[8], Pa., U.S.	269b	40.24 N	79.59 W
Overbrook •[8], Pa., U.S.	275	39.58 N	75.16 W
Overdinkel	48	52.14 N	7.01 E
Overflakkee I	48	51.45 N	4.10 E
Overflowing ≃	174	53.10 N	101.05 W
Overhalla	24	64.30 N	11.57 E
Overijse	52	50.46 N	4.32 E
Overijssel □[4]	48	52.25 N	6.30 E
Over Jerstal	41	55.12 N	9.18 E
Överkalix	24	66.21 N	22.56 E
Overland	209	38.42 N	90.21 W
Overland Park	188	38.59 N	94.40 W
Overlea	198	39.22 N	76.31 W
Overloon	48	51.35 N	5.57 E
Övermark (Ylimarkku)	26	62.38 N	21.30 E
Overpeck Creek ≃	266	40.51 N	74.02 W
Overpelt	52	51.13 N	5.25 E
Overseal	44	52.44 N	1.34 W
Overstrand	44	52.56 N	1.20 E
Overton, Eng., U.K.	44	51.15 N	1.15 W
Overton, Nebr., U.S.	188	40.44 N	99.32 W
Overton, Nev., U.S.	194	36.33 N	114.27 W
Overton, Tex., U.S.	212	32.16 N	94.59 W
Overton Arm C	194	36.20 N	114.25 W
Övertorneå	24	66.23 N	23.40 E
Överum	26	57.59 N	16.19 E
Over Wallop	44	51.09 N	1.35 W
Ovett	184	31.29 N	89.02 W
Ovid, Mich., U.S.	206	43.01 N	84.22 W
Ovid, N.Y., U.S.	200	42.41 N	76.49 W
Ovidiopol'	68	46.17 N	30.27 E
Oviedo, Esp.	34	43.22 N	5.50 W
Oviedo, Fla., U.S.	210	28.40 N	81.13 W
Oviglio	56	44.52 N	8.29 E
Oviken	26	62.59 N	14.24 E
Oviksfjällen ⛰	26	63.02 N	13.51 E

Symbols in the index entries represent the broad categories identified in the key at the right. Symbols with superior numbers (⛰[2]) identify subcategories (see complete key on page *I* · *26*).

Kartensymbole in dem Registerverzeichnis stellen die rechts in Schlüssel erklärten Kategorien dar. Symbole mit hochgestellten Ziffern (⛰[2]) bezeichnen Unterabteilungen einer Kategorie (vgl. vollständiger Schlüssel auf Seite *I* · *26*).

Los símbolos incluídos en el texto del índice representan las grandes categorias identificadas con la clave a la derecha. Los símbolos con numeros en su parte superior (⛰[2]) identifican las subcategorías (véase la clave completa en la página *I* · *26*).

Les symboles de l'index représentent les catégories indiquées dans la légende à droite. Les symboles suivis d'un indice (⛰[2]) représentent des sous-catégories (voir légende complète à la page *I* · *26*).

Os símbolos incluídos no texto do índice representam as grandes categorias identificadas com a chave à direita. Os símbolos com números em sua parte superior (⛰[2]) identificam as subcategorias (veja-se a chave completa à página *I* · *26*).

∧	Mountain	Berg	Montaña	Montagne	Montanha
⛰	Mountains	Berge	Montañas	Montagnes	Montanhas
)(	Pass	Pass	Paso	Col	Passo
∨	Valley, Canyon	Tal, Cañon	Valle, Cañón	Vallée, Canyon	Vale, Canhão
≚	Plain	Ebene	Llano	Plaine	Planície
≻	Cape	Kap	Cabo	Cap	Cabo
I	Island	Insel	Isla	Île	Ilha
II	Islands	Inseln	Islas	Îles	Ilhas
•	Other Topographic Features	Andere Topographische Objekte	Otros Elementos Topográficos	Autres données topographiques	Outros Elementos Topográficos

ESPAÑOL / FRANÇAIS / PORTUGUÊS

Nombre / Nom / Nome	Página / Page	Lat.°′	Long.°′ W=Oeste / W=Ouest
Ovilla	212	32.32 N	96.53 W
Ovindoli	60	42.08 N	13.31 E
Ovinišče	66	58.22 N	37.02 E
Ovino	66	59.41 N	33.11 E
Oviši	66	57.34 N	21.45 E
Övörchangaj □[4]	92	46.00 N	102.30 E
Øvre Anarjokka Nasjonalpark ♠	24	69.00 N	25.00 E
Øvre Årdal	26	61.19 N	7.48 E
Øvre Dividalen Nasjonalpark ♠	24	68.39 N	19.45 E
Øvre Pasvik Nasjonalpark ♠	24	69.06 N	28.55 E
Øvre Rendal	26	61.53 N	11.05 E
Övre Vättern ⊜	40	59.52 N	15.40 E
Ovruč	68	51.21 N	28.49 E
Ovs'anikovo	66	60.09 N	45.16 E
Ovs'anka, S.S.S.R.	76	55.57 N	92.33 E
Ovs'anka, S.S.S.R.	79	53.35 N	126.57 E
Ovs'annikovo	72	56.54 N	37.33 E
Ovstug	66	53.24 N	33.52 E
Ōwada	258	35.49 N	139.33 E
Owaka	162	46.27 S	169.40 E
Owaneco	209	39.29 N	89.12 W
Owasco	200	42.51 N	76.28 W
Owasco Inlet ≃	200	42.45 N	76.28 W
Owasco Lake ⊜	200	42.52 N	76.32 W
Owasco Outlet ≃	200	43.04 N	76.39 W
Owase	82	34.04 N	136.12 E
Owasso	186	36.16 N	95.51 W
Owatonna	180	44.05 N	93.14 W
Owbeh	118	34.22 N	63.10 E
Owe	262c	19.04 N	73.04 E
Owego	200	42.06 N	76.16 W
Owego Creek, East Branch ≃	200	42.10 N	76.15 W
Owen, Austl.	158b	34.16 S	138.33 E
Owen, B.R.D.	52	48.35 N	9.27 E
Owen, Ind., U.S.	208	38.27 N	85.34 W
Owen, Wis., U.S.	180	44.57 N	90.33 W
Owen □[6]	208	38.33 N	84.49 W
Owen, Mount ∧	162	41.33 S	172.32 E
Owen Falls Dam ◆[6]	144	0.27 N	33.11 E
Owen River	162	41.39 S	172.27 E
Owens ≃	194	36.31 N	117.57 W
Owensboro	184	37.46 N	87.07 W
Owens Creek ≃	216	37.13 N	120.42 W
Owens Lake ⊜	194	36.25 N	117.56 W
Owen Sound	202	44.34 N	80.56 W
Owen Sound C	202	44.40 N	80.55 W
Owen Stanley Range ⋀	154	9.20 S	147.55 E
Owensville, Ind., U.S.	184	38.16 N	87.41 W
Owensville, Mo., U.S.	209	38.21 N	91.29 W
Owensville, Ohio, U.S.	208	39.07 N	84.08 W
Owenton, Ky., U.S.	208	38.32 N	84.50 W
Owenton, Va., U.S.	198	37.53 N	77.06 W
Owentown	212	32.26 N	95.12 W
Owerri	140	5.29 N	7.02 E
Owhango	162	39.00 S	175.23 E
Owia Bay C	231h	13.22 N	61.09 W
Owikeno Lake ⊜	172	51.41 N	127.00 W
Owings	198	38.43 N	76.36 W
Owings Mills	274b	39.25 N	76.47 W
Owingsville	178	38.09 N	83.46 W
Owl ≃, Alta., Can.	172	54.54 N	111.57 W
Owl ≃, Man., Can.	166	57.51 N	92.44 W
Owl Creek ≃, U.S.	188	44.41 N	103.29 W
Owl Creek ≃, Mont., U.S.	192	45.18 N	107.21 W
Owl Creek ≃, Wyo., U.S.	192	43.41 N	108.11 W
Owl Creek, South Fork ≃	192	43.43 N	108.32 W
Owl Creek Mountains ⋀	192	43.30 N	108.35 W
Owo	140	7.15 N	5.37 E
Oworonsoki	263a	6.33 N	3.24 E
Owosso	206	43.00 N	84.10 W
Owyhee	194	41.57 N	116.06 W
Owyhee ≃	192	43.46 N	117.02 W
Owyhee, Lake ⊜[1]	192	43.28 N	117.20 W
Owyhee, South Fork ≃	192	42.26 N	116.53 W
Oxapampa	238	10.34 S	75.24 W
Oxbow, Sask., Can.	174	49.14 N	102.11 W
Oxbow, Mich., U.S.	271	42.38 N	83.28 W
Oxbow, N.Y., U.S.	202	44.17 N	75.37 W
Oxbow Lake ⊜	271	42.38 N	83.28 W
Ox Creek ≃	188	48.37 N	100.17 W
Oxelösund	40	58.40 N	17.06 E
Oxford, N.S., Can.	176	45.44 N	63.52 W
Oxford, N.Z.	162	43.18 S	172.11 E
Oxford, Eng., U.K.	44	51.46 N	1.15 W
Oxford, Ala., U.S.	184	33.37 N	85.50 W
Oxford, Conn., U.S.	197	41.20 N	73.07 W
Oxford, Fla., U.S.	210	28.56 N	82.02 W
Oxford, Ind., U.S.	206	40.31 N	87.15 W
Oxford, Iowa, U.S.	180	41.43 N	91.47 W
Oxford, Kans., U.S.	188	37.16 N	97.10 W
Oxford, Ky., U.S.	208	38.16 N	84.30 W
Oxford, Maine, U.S.	178	44.08 N	70.30 W
Oxford, Md., U.S.	198	38.42 N	76.10 W
Oxford, Mass., U.S.	197	42.07 N	71.52 W
Oxford, Mich., U.S.	206	42.49 N	83.16 W
Oxford, Miss., U.S.	184	34.22 N	89.32 W
Oxford, Nebr., U.S.	188	40.15 N	99.38 W
Oxford, N.J., U.S.	200	40.48 N	75.00 W
Oxford, N.C., U.S.	182	36.19 N	78.35 W
Oxford, N.Y., U.S.	200	42.27 N	75.36 W
Oxford, Ohio, U.S.	208	39.30 N	84.44 W
Oxford, Pa., U.S.	198	39.47 N	75.59 W
Oxford, Wis., U.S.	180	43.47 N	89.34 W
Oxford □[6]	202	43.08 N	80.50 W
Oxford Falls	264a	33.44 S	151.15 E
Oxford House	174	54.56 N	95.16 W
Oxford House Indian Reserve ◆[4]	174	54.54 N	95.15 W
Oxford Junction	180	41.59 N	90.57 W
Oxford Lake ⊜	174	54.51 N	95.37 W
Oxford Peak ∧	192	42.16 N	112.06 W
Oxfordshire □[6]	44	51.50 N	1.15 W
Oxhey	250	51.39 N	0.23 W
Oxie	41	55.33 N	13.04 E
Oxley	156	34.12 S	144.06 E
Oxley Creek ≃	161a	27.32 S	153.00 E
Oxnard	218	34.12 N	119.11 W
Oxnard Beach	218	34.09 N	119.13 W
Oxon Hill	274c	38.48 N	76.59 W
Oxon Run ≃	274b	38.49 N	77.00 W
Ox Pasture Brook ≃	273	42.45 N	70.54 W
Oxshott	250	51.20 N	0.21 W
Oxted	44	51.16 N	0.01 W
Oxtongue ≃	202	45.19 N	79.01 W
Oxtongue Lake ⊜	202	45.22 N	78.55 W
Oxus → Amu Darya ≃	62	43.40 N	59.01 E
Oy	54	47.38 N	10.28 E
Oya, Malay.	102	2.52 N	111.53 E
Ōya, Nihon	86	35.20 N	134.40 E
Oya ≃	102	2.52 N	111.52 E
Oyabe	84	36.40 N	136.52 E
Oyabe ≃	84	36.48 N	137.04 E
Oyahue, Volcán (Volcán Ollagüe) ∧[1]	238	21.18 S	68.12 W
Ōyake-yama ∧[2]	260	34.48 N	135.51 E
Oyama, B.C., Can.	172	50.07 N	119.22 W
Ōyama, Nihon	84	36.36 N	137.18 E
Ōyama, Nihon	84	35.21 N	139.00 E
Oyama, Nihon	84	36.18 N	139.48 E
Ōyama, Nihon	258	35.36 N	139.22 E
Ōyamada	84	34.46 N	136.13 E
Ōya-magaibutsu ♥[1]	84	36.38 N	139.48 E
Ōyamazaki	260	34.54 N	135.42 E
Oyameles	224	19.43 N	97.32 W
Oyano	82	32.35 N	130.30 E
Oyapock (Oiapoque) ≃	240	4.08 N	51.40 W
Oyashirazu ♠	84	36.59 N	137.40 E
Oybin	50	50.50 N	14.44 E
Oye-et-Pallet	54	46.51 N	6.20 E
Oyem	142	1.37 N	11.35 E
Oyen	174	51.22 N	110.28 W
Øyeren ⊜	26	59.48 N	11.14 E
Oymyakon → Ojm'akon	64	63.28 N	142.49 E
Oyo, Congo	142	0.01 N	15.54 E
Oyo, Nig.	140	7.51 N	3.56 E
Oyo ≃	105a	7.57 S	110.22 E
Ōyodo	86	34.23 N	135.48 E
Ōyodo ◆[8]	260	34.43 N	135.30 E
Ōyodo ≃	82	31.53 N	131.28 E
Oyón	238	10.39 S	76.47 W
Oyonnax	54	46.15 N	5.40 E
Ōyorogi-san ∧	86	35.05 N	132.51 E
Oyotún	238	6.51 S	79.19 W
Oyster	198	37.17 N	75.55 W
Oyster Bay	200	40.52 N	73.32 W
Oyster Bay C, Austl.	158b	34.54 S	137.48 E
Oyster Bay C, Austl.	264a	34.00 S	151.06 E
Oyster Bay Cove	266	40.52 N	73.31 W
Oyster Bay Harbor C	266	40.53 N	73.32 W
Oyster Creek	212	29.00 N	95.20 W
Oyster Creek ≃	212	29.59 N	95.18 W
Oyster Point ∧	272	37.50 N	121.52 W
Oyster Point ≻	158b	34.55 S	137.48 E
Oyster Rock I[2]	262c	18.54 N	72.50 E
Oysterville	214	46.33 N	124.02 W
Øystese	26	60.23 N	6.13 E
Oyten	48	53.04 N	9.01 E
Ozaki	258	35.59 N	139.51 E
Ozala, Parc National d' ♠	142	1.00 S	15.00 E
Ozamiz	106	8.08 N	123.50 E
Ozanne ≃	46	48.11 N	1.22 E
Ozariči	66	52.28 N	29.16 E
Ozark, Ala., U.S.	184	31.28 N	85.38 W
Ozark, Ark., U.S.	184	35.29 N	93.50 W
Ozark, Mo., U.S.	184	37.01 N	93.12 W
Ozark Escarpment •[4]	184	36.15 N	91.15 W
Ozark Plateau ⋀[1]	184	37.00 N	93.00 W
Ozarks, Lake of the ⊜[1]	184	38.10 N	92.50 W
Ozaukee □[6]	206	44.14 N	88.00 W
Ozbourn Seamount ✢[3]	14	25.55 S	174.50 W
Ózd	30	48.14 N	20.18 E
Ozd'atiči	66	54.06 N	28.50 E
Oze ≃	86	34.12 N	132.14 E
Ozeblin ∧	36	44.35 N	15.53 E
Ozek	76	46.35 N	60.41 E
Ozereckoje	72	56.04 N	37.23 E
Ožerelje	72	54.48 N	38.17 E
Ožerelki	72	55.51 N	38.52 E
Ozerišče	66	54.48 N	33.13 E
Ozerki, S.S.S.R.	70	51.32 N	45.16 E
Ozerki, S.S.S.R.	70	52.01 N	45.29 E
Ozerki, S.S.S.R.	70	51.13 N	53.56 E
Ozerki, S.S.S.R.	76	53.38 N	83.44 E
Ozerki, S.S.S.R.	255a	59.54 N	30.44 E
Ozerna ≃	72	55.44 N	36.08 E
Ozernoje	68	50.11 N	28.42 E
Ozernovskij	64	51.30 N	156.31 E
Ozernyj	170	66.24 N	179.06 W
Ozero	70	56.58 N	44.43 E
Ozero Stambovskoje ♠	72	56.42 N	35.53 E
Ozery	72	54.51 N	38.34 E
Ozette Lake ⊜	214	48.06 N	124.38 W
Ozgol	257d	35.47 N	51.30 E
Ozgoryš	75	41.15 N	74.45 E
Ozieri	36	40.35 N	9.00 E
Ozimek	30	50.41 N	18.13 E
Ozinki	70	51.12 N	49.45 E
Ožogino, Ozero ⊜	64	69.16 N	146.36 E
Ozoir-la-Ferrière	251	48.46 N	2.40 E
Ozona, Fla., U.S.	210	28.04 N	82.47 W
Ozona, Tex., U.S.	186	30.43 N	101.12 W
Ozone Park ◆[8]	266	40.40 N	73.51 W
Ozorków	30	51.58 N	19.19 E
Oz'ornaja	76	53.25 N	63.15 E
Oz'ornoje, S.S.S.R.	70	51.46 N	51.28 E
Oz'ornoje, S.S.S.R.	76	56.48 N	71.15 E
Oz'ornyj, S.S.S.R.	70	57.10 N	40.59 E
Oz'ornyj, S.S.S.R.	76	51.08 N	60.50 E
Oz'orsk, S.S.S.R.	66	54.25 N	22.01 E
Oz'orsk, S.S.S.R.	68	51.43 N	26.24 E
Oz'orskij	79	46.36 N	143.08 E
Oz'ory	66	53.43 N	24.11 E
Ozouer-le-Voulgis	251	48.40 N	2.47 E
Ōzu, Nihon	82	32.52 N	130.52 E
Ōzu, Nihon	86	33.30 N	132.33 E
Ozubulu	140	5.57 N	6.51 E
Ozuluama	224	21.40 N	97.51 W
Ozumba de Alzate	224	19.03 N	98.48 W
P			
Pâ	140	11.33 N	3.15 W
Paadekraal Monument ⊥	263d	26.06 S	27.47 E
Paagoumène	165f	20.29 S	164.11 E
Paal	52	51.02 N	5.11 E
Paama I	165f	16.28 S	168.14 E
Pa-an	100	16.53 N	97.38 E
Paar ≃	58	48.13 N	10.59 E
Paaren	254a	52.39 N	12.59 E
Paarl	148	33.45 S	18.56 E
Paarlshoop ◆[8]	263d	26.13 S	27.59 E
Paasbach ≃	253	51.25 N	7.11 E
Paauilo	219d	20.02 N	155.22 W
Pabarabuk	154	6.05 S	144.05 E
Pabbay I	28	57.47 N	7.20 W
Pabbi	113	34.01 N	71.47 E
Pabbiring, Kepulauan II	102	4.55 S	119.25 E
Pabean	102	6.50 S	115.19 E
Pabellón, Ensenada del C	222	24.27 N	107.36 W
Pabianice	30	51.40 N	19.22 E
Pablo	192	47.36 N	114.07 W
Pābna	114	24.00 N	89.15 E
Pabo	144	3.00 N	32.09 E
Pabradė	66	54.59 N	25.44 E
Paca	105b	8.29 S	120.11 E
Pacaás Novos ≃	238	10.51 S	65.20 W
Pacaás Novos, Serra dos ⋀	238	10.45 S	64.15 W
Pacaembu	245	21.34 S	51.17 W
Pacaembú, Estádio do ♠	277b	23.33 S	46.39 W
Pacahuaras ≃	238	10.04 S	65.46 W
Pacajá ≃	240	1.56 S	50.50 W
Pacajus	240	4.10 S	38.28 W
Pacaltsdorp	148	34.00 S	22.28 E
Pacaraima, Sierra de → Pakaraima Mountains ⋀	236	5.30 N	60.40 W
Pacarán	238	12.52 S	76.03 W
Pacaraos	238	11.11 S	76.44 W
Pacasmayo	238	7.24 S	79.34 W
Pacatu	245	11.57 S	38.58 W
Pacatuba	240	3.58 S	38.37 W
Paccha ≃	238	9.05 S	76.54 W
Pace	184	33.42 N	90.52 W
Pačelma, S.S.S.R.	70	53.15 N	43.21 E
Pačelma, S.S.S.R.	70	53.20 N	43.20 E
Pacet	105a	6.45 S	107.03 E
Pachača	64	60.34 N	169.03 E
Pachacamac	238	12.14 S	76.53 W
Pachacamac ⊥	238	12.14 S	76.52 W
Pachāgarh	114	26.20 N	88.34 E
Pachamba	116	24.12 N	86.16 E
Pachaug Pond ⊜	197	41.34 N	71.54 W
Pacheco	216	37.59 N	122.04 W
Pacheco Creek ≃	216	36.58 N	121.28 W
Pacheco Pass)(	216	37.03 N	121.13 W
Pachecos	246	22.48 S	42.50 W
Pāchh Elāsin	116	24.08 N	89.54 E
Pāchi I	257c	37.58 N	23.22 E
Pachino	36	36.42 N	15.06 E
Pachitea ≃	238	8.46 S	74.32 W
Pachiza	238	7.16 S	76.46 W
Pachkoli ◆[8]	262c	19.08 N	72.54 E
Pachmarhi	114	22.28 N	78.26 E
Pacho	236	5.08 N	74.10 W
Pachomovo	72	54.38 N	37.33 E
Pachor	114	23.42 N	76.44 E
Pāchora	112	20.40 N	75.21 E
Pachotnyj Ugol	70	52.58 N	41.56 E
Pachra ≃	72	55.32 N	37.59 E
Pachtaabad	75	38.28 N	68.10 E
Pachuca [de Soto]	224	20.07 N	98.44 W
Paciência ◆[8]	246	22.55 S	43.38 W
Pacific, B.C., Can.	172	54.46 N	128.17 W
Pacific, Mo., U.S.	209	38.29 N	90.45 W
Pacific, Wash., U.S.	214	47.16 N	122.15 W
Pacific □[6]	214	46.30 N	123.39 W
Pacifica	216	37.38 N	122.29 W
Pacific Beach	214	47.13 N	124.12 W
Pacific City	214	45.12 N	123.57 W
Pacific Creek ≃	190	42.08 N	109.24 W
Pacific Gardens	216	37.58 N	121.20 W
Pacific Grove	216	36.38 N	121.56 W
Pacific Islands Trust Territory □[2]	14	10.00 N	155.00 E
Pacífico, Océano → Pacific Ocean ⊤[1]	6	10.00 S	150.00 W
Pacific Ocean ⊤[1]	4, 6	10.00 S	150.00 W
Pacifico Mountain ∧	218	34.23 N	118.02 W
Pacific Palisades ◆[8]	270	34.03 N	118.32 W
Pacific Ranges ⋀	172	50.45 N	125.30 W
Pacific Rim National Park ♠	214	48.35 N	124.40 W
Pacifique, Océan → Pacific Ocean ⊤[1]	6	10.00 S	150.00 W
Pacijan Island I	106	10.39 N	124.20 E
Paciran	105a	6.52 S	112.20 E
Pacitan	105a	8.12 S	111.07 E
Packanack Brook ≃	266	40.55 N	74.17 W
Packanack Lake ⊜	266	40.56 N	74.15 W
Packard Mountain ∧[2]	197	42.28 N	72.21 W
Pack Monadnock Mountain ∧	197	42.52 N	71.52 W
Packwood	214	46.36 N	121.40 W
Packwood Lake ⊜	214	46.35 N	121.34 W
Pacllón	238	10.18 S	77.07 W
Pacock Brook ≃	266	41.05 N	74.31 W
Paço de Arcos	256c	38.42 N	9.17 W
Paço do Lumiar	240	2.31 S	44.07 W
Pacoima ◆[8]	270	34.16 N	118.26 W
Pacolet ≃	182	34.50 N	81.27 W
Pacolet Mills	182	34.55 N	81.45 W
Pácora, Col.	236	5.31 N	75.27 W
Pacora, Pan.	236	9.05 N	79.17 W
Pacoti	240	4.13 S	38.56 W
Pacov	30	49.28 N	15.00 E
Pacquet	176	49.59 N	55.53 W
Pacuare ≃	226	10.14 N	83.17 W
Pacuí ≃	245	16.46 S	45.01 W
Pacuneiro ≃	245	13.02 S	53.25 W
Pacy-sur-Eure	46	49.01 N	1.23 E
Paczkow	30	50.27 N	17.00 E
Padada	106	6.42 N	125.22 E
Padada ≃	106	6.42 N	125.23 E
Padaido, Kepulauan II	154	1.15 S	136.30 E
Padam	113	33.28 N	76.53 E
Padamarang, Pulau I	102	4.07 S	121.24 E
Padamo ≃	236	2.54 N	65.17 W
Padampur	110	20.59 N	83.04 E
Padang, Indon.	102	1.39 S	108.55 E
Padang, Indon.	102	6.11 S	120.26 E
Padang, Indon.	102	2.59 N	105.40 E
Padang, Indon.	102	0.57 S	100.21 E
Padang, Pulau I	104	1.10 N	102.20 E
Padang Besar	104	6.40 N	100.19 E
Padangbetuah	102	3.39 S	102.13 E
Padang Endau	104	2.40 N	103.37 E
Padangpanjang	102	0.27 S	100.25 E
Padangsidempuan	104	1.22 N	99.16 E
Padangtiji	104	5.22 N	95.50 E
Padangtikar, Pulau I	102	0.50 S	109.30 E
Padang Tungku	104	4.14 N	101.59 E
Padany	24	63.17 N	33.22 E
Padas	105a	7.25 S	111.32 E
Padas ≃	102	5.14 N	115.34 E
Padasjoki	26	61.21 N	25.17 E
Padauari ≃	236	0.15 S	64.05 W
Padborg	41	54.49 N	9.22 E
Padcaya	238	21.52 S	64.48 W
Paddington ◆[8]	250	51.31 N	0.10 W
Paddington Station ◆[5]	250	51.31 N	0.11 W
Paddle ≃	172	54.05 N	114.15 W
Paddle Prairie	166	57.57 N	117.29 W
Paddock Lake	206	42.34 N	88.07 W
Paddock Wood	44	51.11 N	0.23 E
Padea	38	44.01 N	23.52 E
Padea-besar I	102	3.30 S	123.05 E
Padeghar	262c	18.58 N	73.03 E
Paden City	178	39.36 N	80.56 W
Paderborn	48	51.43 N	8.45 E
Paderno Dugnano	256b	45.34 N	9.10 E
Paderno Ponchielli	58	45.14 N	9.55 E
Padghe	262c	19.03 N	73.07 E
Padibe	144	3.28 N	32.50 E
Padiham	42	53.49 N	2.19 W
Padilla, Bol.	238	19.19 S	64.20 W
Padilla, Méx.	224	24.01 N	98.47 W
Padilla Bay C	214	48.35 N	122.32 W
Padingge	110	32.52 N	88.39 E
Padirac, Gouffre de •[5]	32	44.44 N	1.27 E
Padjelanta Nationalpark ♠	24	67.28 N	16.41 E
Padle	262c	19.09 N	73.03 E
Padloping Island I	166	67.07 N	62.35 W
Padma → Ganges ≃	114	23.22 N	90.32 E
Padmanābhapuram	112	8.14 N	77.20 E
Padola	58	46.36 N	12.28 E
Padoue → Padova	58	45.25 N	11.53 E
Padova	58	45.25 N	11.53 E
Padova □[4]	58	45.21 N	11.49 E
Padovka	70	52.28 N	49.31 E
Pādra	110	22.14 N	73.05 E
Padrão, Ponta do ≻	142	6.03 S	12.18 E
Padrauna	114	26.55 N	83.59 E
Padre Bernardo	245	15.21 S	48.30 W
Padre Brito	246	21.18 S	43.59 W
Padre Burgos	106	10.02 N	125.01 E
Padre Island I	186	27.00 N	97.15 W
Padre Island National Seashore ♠	186	26.26 N	27.43 W
Padre Miguel ◆[8]	277a	22.53 S	43.26 W
Padre Paraíso	245	17.06 S	41.31 W
Padrón	34	42.44 N	8.40 W
Padrone, Cape ≻	148	33.46 S	26.30 E
Padstow, Austl.	264a	33.57 S	151.02 E
Padstow, Eng., U.K.	44	50.33 N	4.56 W
Padua → Padova	58	45.25 N	11.53 E
Paduari ≃	236	2.08 S	61.15 W
Paducah, Ky., U.S.	184	37.05 N	88.36 W
Paducah, Tex., U.S.	186	34.01 N	100.18 W
Paduli	60	41.10 N	14.53 E
Padunskaja	76	55.02 N	85.02 E
Pădurea Craiului, Munții ⋀	38	46.55 N	22.20 E
Paea	164s	17.41 S	149.35 W
Paedun	88	35.03 N	128.21 E
Paekakariki	162	40.59 S	174.57 E
Paektu-san ∧	88	42.00 N	128.03 E
Paengaroa	162	37.49 S	176.25 E
Paerdegat Basin C	266	40.37 N	73.54 W
Paeroa	162	37.23 S	175.40 E
Paesana	56	44.41 N	7.16 E
Paese	58	45.40 N	12.10 E
Paestum ⊥	36	40.25 N	15.00 E
Paete	106	14.23 N	121.29 E
Páez ≃	236	2.28 N	75.34 W
Pafúri	146	22.27 S	31.21 E
Pag	36	44.27 N	15.04 E
Pag, Otok I	36	44.30 N	15.00 E
Paga	140	10.58 N	1.06 W
Pagadenbaru	105a	6.28 S	107.48 E
Pagadian	106	7.49 N	123.25 E
Pagadian Bay C	106	7.48 N	123.31 E
Pagai Selatan, Pulau I	102	3.00 S	100.20 E
Pagai Utara, Pulau I	102	2.42 S	100.07 E
Pagalu I	128	1.25 S	5.36 E
Pagalungan	106	7.04 N	124.41 E
Pagan	100	21.10 N	94.51 E
Pagan I	98	18.07 N	145.46 E
Pagancillo	242	29.34 S	68.03 W
Paganella ∧	58	46.08 N	11.02 E
Pagani	60	40.45 N	14.37 E
Paganica	60	42.21 N	13.28 E
Paganico	60	42.56 N	11.16 E
Pagaralam	102	4.01 S	103.16 E
Pagaran Tonga	104	1.14 N	99.46 E
Pagasitikós Kólpos C	38	39.15 N	22.51 E
Pagatan	102	3.36 S	115.56 E
Pagato ≃	174	55.49 N	102.05 W
Pagato Lake ⊜	174	56.08 N	102.30 W
Pagbilao	106	13.58 N	121.41 E
Pagbilao Grande Island I	106	13.55 N	121.46 E
Pagdanan Bay C	106	10.31 N	119.15 E
Page, Ariz., U.S.	190	36.57 N	111.27 W
Page, N. Dak., U.S.	188	47.09 N	97.34 W
Page Field ⊠	210	26.35 N	81.52 W
Pagėgiai	66	55.09 N	21.54 E
Pageland	182	34.46 N	80.24 W
Page Manor	208	39.45 N	84.07 W
Pagerdewa	102	3.46 S	105.18 E
Paget, Mount ∧	234	54.26 S	36.33 W
Paghmān	110	34.36 N	68.57 E
Paglia ≃	60	42.42 N	12.11 E
Paglieta	60	42.10 N	14.30 E
Pagliete, Bonifica delle ◆[1]	257a	41.53 N	12.12 E
Pagny-sur-Moselle	52	48.59 N	6.01 E
Pago Bay C	164p	13.25 N	144.48 E
Pagoda Peak ∧	190	40.10 N	107.20 W
Pagoda Point ≻	100	15.57 N	94.15 E
Pago Pago	164u	14.16 S	170.42 W
Pago Pago Harbor C	164u	14.17 S	170.40 W
Pagosa Springs	190	37.16 N	107.01 W
Pagote	262c	18.54 N	72.59 E
Pagouda	140	9.45 N	1.19 E
Pagsangahan	106	13.13 N	122.33 E
Pagsanjan	106	14.15 N	121.25 E
Pagua Bay C	230d	15.32 N	61.17 W
Paguate	190	35.08 N	107.23 W
Pagudpud	106	18.34 N	120.47 E
Pagueras, Torrente de ≃	256d	41.28 N	1.58 E
Paguilou	142	1.12 S	9.31 E
Paguyaman ≃	102	0.31 N	122.38 E
Pah, Tür.	74	39.08 N	39.40 E
Pah, Tür.	120	39.08 N	30.10 E
Pahādi ◆[8]	262c	19.10 N	72.51 E
Pahala	219d	19.12 N	155.29 W
Pahang □[3]	104	3.30 N	102.45 E
Pahang ≃	104	3.32 N	103.28 E
Pahāsu	114	28.11 N	78.03 E
Pahau Point ≻	219b	21.49 N	160.15 W
Pahi	104	5.28 N	102.13 E
Pahia Point ≻	162	46.19 S	167.41 E
Pahiatua	162	40.27 S	175.50 E
Pahlād Garhi	262a	28.40 N	77.21 E
Pahlavī → Bandar-e Pahlavī	118	37.28 N	49.27 E
Pahlavī Dezh, Īrān	118	37.01 N	54.30 E
Pahlavī Dezh, Īrān	118	35.51 N	46.02 E
Pahlevi → Bandar-e Pahlavī	118	37.28 N	49.27 E
Pahlgām	113	34.02 N	75.20 E
Pahoa	219d	19.28 N	154.51 W
Pahokee	210	26.49 N	80.40 W
Pahrump	194	36.12 N	115.59 W
Pahsimeroi ≃	192	44.41 N	114.03 W
Pahuatlán de Valle	224	20.17 N	98.09 W
Pai	100	19.19 N	98.27 E
Pai ≃	100	19.09 N	97.33 E
Pai, Ilha do I	277a	22.59 S	43.05 W
Paia	219a	20.54 N	156.22 W
Paianía	257c	37.57 N	23.51 E
Paicines	216	36.44 N	121.17 W
Paico	238	14.02 S	73.39 W
Paide	66	58.54 N	25.33 E
Paifangchang	97	30.31 N	106.38 E
Paige	212	30.13 N	97.07 W
Paignton	44	50.26 N	3.34 W
Paiguano	242	30.01 S	70.32 W
Paiho	90	23.21 N	120.25 E
Paiján	238	7.44 S	79.19 W
Päijänne ⊜	26	61.35 N	25.30 E
Pāikgācha	116	22.35 N	89.20 E
Pail, Bhārat	113	30.43 N	76.03 E
Pail, Pāk.	113	32.38 N	72.27 E
Paila ≃	238	16.02 S	64.12 W
Pailin	100	12.51 N	102.36 E
Pailitas	236	8.58 N	73.38 W
Pailolo Channel ⋃	219a	21.05 N	156.42 W
Pailoutou	96	30.56 N	121.16 E
Pailoutun	94	40.44 N	122.49 E
Paimboeuf	32	47.17 N	2.02 W
Paimio	26	60.27 N	22.42 E
Paimpol	32	48.46 N	3.03 W
Painan	102	1.21 S	100.34 E
Paincourt	204	42.23 N	82.17 W
Paine Medio, Cerro ∧	244	50.59 S	72.58 W
Painesdale	180	47.02 N	88.41 W
Painesville	204	41.43 N	81.15 W
Pains	245	20.22 S	45.40 W
Painscastle	44	52.07 N	3.12 W
Painswick	44	51.48 N	2.11 W
Paint ≃	180	45.58 N	88.15 W
Paint Creek ≃, Mich., U.S.	271	42.06 N	83.36 W
Paint Creek ≃, Ohio, U.S.	208	39.18 N	82.56 W
Paint Creek ≃, Pa., U.S.	204	41.10 N	79.28 W
Paint Creek ≃, Tex., U.S.	186	30.18 N	99.54 W
Paint Creek, East Fork ≃	208	39.32 N	83.25 W
Paint Creek, North Fork ≃	208	39.18 N	83.02 W
Paint Creek Lake ⊜[1]	208	39.15 N	83.22 W
Painted Desert ◆[2]	190	36.00 N	111.20 W
Painted Post	200	42.07 N	77.08 W
Painter	198	37.34 N	75.44 W
Painter Creek ≃	208	40.05 N	84.21 W
Paintertown	269b	40.21 N	79.42 W
Paint Lake ⊜	174	55.28 N	97.57 W
Paint Rock	186	31.30 N	99.55 W
Paint Rock ≃	184	34.28 N	86.28 W
Paintsville	182	37.49 N	82.48 W
Paiol da Vargem	246	22.41 S	46.26 W
Paiolinho	246	21.52 S	45.54 W
Paisco	58	46.04 N	10.17 E
Paisha	90	23.37 N	119.35 E
Paisley, Austl.	264b	37.51 S	144.51 E
Paisley, Ont., Can.	202	44.18 N	81.16 W
Paisley, Scot., U.K.	42	55.50 N	4.26 W
Paisley, Fla., U.S.	210	28.60 N	81.32 W
Paisley, Oreg., U.S.	192	42.42 N	120.32 W
Païta, N. Cal.	165f	22.08 S	166.22 E
Paita, Perú	238	5.06 S	81.07 W
Paita, Bahía de C	238	5.04 S	81.05 W
Paitan	90	23.31 N	113.46 E
Paitan ≃	106	6.30 N	117.30 E
Paitan Bay C	106	6.45 N	117.20 E
Paiton	105a	7.43 S	113.30 E
Paiva	246	21.18 S	43.25 W
Paiva ≃	34	41.04 N	8.16 W
Paiva Couceiro	142	14.51 S	14.30 E
Paizhou	90	30.13 N	113.56 E
Paj	24	61.13 N	34.24 E
Pajacuarán	224	20.07 N	102.34 W
Pajala	24	67.11 N	23.22 E
Paján	236	1.34 S	80.25 W
Pajapan	224	18.15 N	94.42 W
Pajares, Puerto de)(	34	43.00 N	5.46 W
Pajaro	216	36.54 N	121.39 W
Pajaro ≃	216	36.51 N	121.48 W
Pajaros Point ≻	230m	18.31 N	64.18 W
Paj-Choj ⋀[2]	62	69.00 N	63.00 E
Pajdugina ≃	76	58.50 N	81.47 E
Pajęczno	30	51.09 N	19.00 E
Pajeú ≃	240	8.55 S	38.42 W
Pajiangkou	90	23.46 N	113.14 E
Pajjer, Gora ∧	62	66.42 N	64.25 E
Pajtok	75	40.53 N	72.15 E
Pak ≃	100	21.05 N	102.31 E
Paka	104	4.39 N	103.26 E
Paka ≃	104	4.40 N	103.27 E
Pākāla	112	13.28 N	79.07 E
Pakanbaru	102	0.32 N	101.27 E
Pakaraima Mountains ⋀	236	5.30 N	60.40 W
Pakaur	114	24.38 N	87.51 E
Pak Ban	100	21.14 N	102.28 E
Pakch'ŏn	88	39.45 N	125.35 E
Pakeng	130	6.55 N	30.40 E
Pakenham, Austl.	159	38.04 S	145.29 E
Pakenham, Ont., Can.	202	45.20 N	76.17 W
Pākhāl ⊜[1]	112	17.57 N	79.59 E
Pákhi	257c	37.59 N	23.22 E
Pákhna	120	34.46 N	32.48 E
Pakhoi → Beihai	92	21.29 N	109.05 E
Pakin I[1]	14	7.04 N	157.48 E
Pakipaki	162	39.41 S	176.48 E
Pakistan (Pākistān) □[1]	108	30.00 N	70.00 E
Pakistan, East → Bangladesh □[1]	110	24.00 N	90.00 E
Pak Kong Tsun	261d	22.23 N	114.15 E
Pak Kret	259a	13.55 N	100.30 E
Pakokku	100	21.20 N	95.05 E
Pakość	30	52.49 N	18.05 E
Pakouabo	140	7.10 N	5.48 W
Pakowki Lake ⊜	174	49.22 N	110.57 W
Pākpattan	113	30.21 N	73.24 E
Pak Phanang	100	8.21 N	100.12 E
Pak Phayun	100	7.21 N	100.19 E
Pakrac	36	45.26 N	17.12 E
Pākrāganj	116	24.00 N	90.41 E
Pakruojis	66	55.58 N	23.52 E
Paks	30	46.39 N	18.53 E
Pak Sane → Muang Pakxan	100	18.22 N	103.39 E
Pāksey	116	24.05 N	89.03 E
Pak Thong Chai	100	14.43 N	102.01 E
Paktīā □[4]	110	33.30 N	69.30 E
Pākundia	116	24.20 N	90.42 E
P'akupur ≃	64	65.00 N	77.48 E
Pakwach	144	2.28 N	31.30 E
Pakwash Lake ⊜	174	50.45 N	93.30 W
Pakxé	100	15.07 N	105.47 E
Pala, Mya.	100	12.51 N	98.40 E
Pala, Tchad	136	9.22 N	14.54 E
Pala, Calif., U.S.	218	33.22 N	117.05 W
Palaau State Park ♠	219a	21.11 N	157.00 W
Palabek	144	3.26 N	32.34 E
Palacios	186	28.42 N	96.13 W
Paladru	56	45.28 N	5.33 E
Palagano	58	44.20 N	10.39 E
Palagonia	36	37.19 N	14.45 E
Palagruža, Otoci II	36	42.24 N	16.15 E
Palai	112	9.44 N	76.41 E
Palaia	60	43.36 N	10.46 E
Palaiá Epídhavros	38	37.38 N	23.09 E
Palaiá Kórinthos ⊥	38	37.54 N	22.56 E
Palaiá Psará	38	38.46 N	25.36 E
Palaikhóri	120	34.55 N	33.05 E
Pala Indian Reservation ◆[4]	218	33.21 N	117.04 W
Palaiokhóra	38	35.14 N	23.41 E
Palaión Fáliron	257c	37.55 N	23.41 E
Palaiseau	46	48.43 N	2.15 E
Pālakollu	112	16.32 N	81.44 E
Pālam ◆[8]	262a	28.35 N	77.05 E
Palam Airport ⊠	113	28.35 N	77.07 E
Palamás	38	39.28 N	22.05 E
Palāmau □[5]	114	24.00 N	84.00 E
Pālam International Airport ⊠	262a	28.35 N	77.07 E
Palamós	34	41.51 N	3.08 E
Pālampur	113	32.07 N	76.32 E
Palamuse	66	58.41 N	26.35 E
Palamut	120	38.59 N	27.41 E
Palana	64	59.07 N	159.58 E
Palanan, Mount ∧	106	17.03 N	122.15 E
Palanan Bay C	106	17.09 N	122.27 E
Palanan Point ≻	106	17.09 N	122.30 E
Palanas	106	12.09 N	123.55 E
Palandöken Dağları ⋀	120	39.47 N	41.15 E
Pālang	116	23.13 N	90.21 E
Pālang ≃[1]	116	23.15 N	90.21 E
Palanga	66	55.55 N	21.03 E
Palanganene	142	6.26 S	18.50 E
Palangkaraya	102	2.16 S	113.56 E
Pālanpur	110	24.10 N	72.26 E
Palanquinos	34	42.27 N	5.31 W
Palanzano	58	44.26 N	10.11 E
Palaoa Point ≻	219a	20.44 N	156.58 W
Palapag	106	12.33 N	125.07 E
Palapye	146	22.37 S	27.06 E
Pālār ≃	112	12.28 N	80.10 E
Palasan Island I	106	14.52 N	122.03 E
Palas del Rey	34	42.52 N	7.52 W
Palāshdānga	116	23.24 N	87.22 E
Palāspol	116	22.43 N	89.05 E
Palāstha	116	23.51 N	87.03 E
Palata	60	41.53 N	14.47 E
Palatcy	76	49.09 N	83.43 E
Palatine	206	42.07 N	88.03 W
Palatine Bridge	200	42.55 N	74.35 W
Palatka, S.S.S.R.	64	60.06 N	150.54 E
Palatka, Fla., U.S.	182	29.39 N	81.38 W
Palau	186	27.54 N	101.26 W
Palau □[5]	165b	7.30 N	134.30 E
Palauig	106	15.26 N	119.54 E
Palaui Island I	106	18.33 N	122.08 E
Palau Islands II	165b	7.30 N	134.30 E
Palauk	100	13.16 N	98.38 E
Palau-Kyushu Ridge ✢[3]	14	13.00 N	135.00 E
Pal'avaam ≃	170	68.50 N	170.45 E
Pal'avaamskij Chrebet ⋀	170	68.20 N	177.00 E
Palavas-les-Flots	56	43.32 N	3.56 E
Palaw	100	12.58 N	98.39 E
Palawai Basin ≌[1]	219a	20.47 N	156.55 W
Palawan I	106	9.30 N	118.30 E
Palawan Passage ⋃	106	10.00 N	118.00 E
Palayan	106	15.33 N	121.06 E
Pālayankottai	112	8.43 N	77.44 E
Palazzolo Acreide	36	37.03 N	14.54 E
Palazzolo dello Stella	58	45.48 N	13.05 E
Palazzolo sull'Oglio	56	45.36 N	9.53 E
Palazzolo Vercellese	56	45.11 N	8.14 E
Palazzo San Gervasio	36	40.56 N	16.00 E
Palazzuolo sul Senio	60	44.07 N	11.33 E
P'albong-san ∧	88	40.16 N	127.57 E
Palca, Bol.	238	16.34 S	67.59 W
Palca, Perú	238	11.21 S	75.31 W
Palcamayo	238	11.18 S	75.46 W
Pal'co	66	53.17 N	34.56 E
Paldi	214	48.48 N	123.51 W
Paldiski	66	59.20 N	24.06 E
Pāldor ∧	114	28.16 N	85.11 E
Palech	70	56.48 N	41.51 E
Palel	110	24.27 N	94.02 E
Paleleh	102	1.04 N	121.57 E
Palembang	102	2.55 S	104.45 E
Palena	60	41.59 N	14.08 E
Palena ≃	244	43.50 S	72.59 W
Palena, Lago (Lago General Vintter) ⊜	244	43.55 S	71.40 W
Palencia	34	42.01 N	4.32 W
Palen Dry Lake ⊜	194	33.46 N	115.12 W
Palenque	222	17.31 N	91.58 W
Palenque ≃	236	1.02 S	79.28 W
Palenque ⊥	222	17.30 N	92.00 W
Palenque, Punta ≻	228	18.14 N	70.09 W
Palenville	200	42.10 N	74.01 W
Palermo, Col.	236	2.54 N	75.26 W
Palermo, It.	36	38.07 N	13.21 E
Palermo, Calif., U.S.	216	39.26 N	121.33 W
Palermo, Ur.	242	33.48 S	55.59 W
Palermo ◆[8]	278	34.35 S	58.25 W
Palermo, Golfo di C	36	38.10 N	13.30 E
Palestina, Bra.	245	20.23 S	49.25 W
Palestina, Méx.	186	29.10 N	100.55 W
Palestine, Ill., U.S.	184	39.00 N	87.37 W
Palestine, Ohio, U.S.	208	40.03 N	84.45 W
Palestine, Tex., U.S.	212	31.46 N	95.38 W
Palestine □[1]	122	31.25 N	34.20 E
Palestine, Lake ⊜[1]	212	32.06 N	95.27 W
Palestrina	60	41.50 N	12.53 E
Paletwa	100	21.18 N	92.51 E
Palézieux	54	46.33 N	6.50 E
Pālghāt	112	10.47 N	76.39 E
Palgrave, Mount ∧	152	23.22 S	115.58 E
Palgrave Point ≻	146	20.45 S	13.20 E
Palhais	256c	38.37 N	9.03 W
Palhano	240	4.44 S	37.57 W
Palhano ≃	240	4.33 S	37.42 W
Pāli, Bhārat	110	25.46 N	73.20 E
Pali, Bhārat	114	25.51 N	76.33 E
Paliano	60	41.48 N	13.03 E
Palikea ∧	219c	21.26 N	158.06 W
Palikir Passage ⋃	164r	6.59 N	158.08 E
Palima	102	4.20 S	120.22 E
Palimanan	105a	6.42 S	108.26 E
Palimbang	106	6.12 N	124.12 E
Palimé	140	6.54 N	0.38 E
Palín	226	14.24 N	90.42 W
Palin, Mount ∧	106	6.21 N	117.08 E
Palinges	32	46.33 N	4.13 E
Palisade, Colo., U.S.	190	39.07 N	108.21 W
Palisade, Nebr., U.S.	188	40.21 N	101.07 W
Palisades, Idaho, U.S.	192	43.21 N	111.13 W
Palisades, N.Y., U.S.	266	41.01 N	73.55 W
Palisades Amusement Park ♠	266	40.50 N	73.59 W
Palisades Interstate Park ♠	200	40.56 N	73.55 W
Palisades Park, Mich., U.S.	206	42.18 N	86.19 W
Palisades Park, N.J., U.S.	266	40.51 N	74.00 W
Palisades Reservoir ⊜[1]	192	43.15 N	111.05 W
Paliseul	52	49.54 N	5.08 E
Palit, Kep i ≻	38	41.24 N	19.24 E
Pālitāna	110	21.31 N	71.50 E
Palivere	66	58.59 N	23.52 E
Palizada	222	18.15 N	92.05 W
Paljakka ∧[2]	26	64.41 N	28.08 E
Pälkäne	26	61.20 N	24.16 E
Palk Bay C	112	9.30 N	79.15 E
Palkino, S.S.S.R.	66	57.32 N	28.01 E
Palkino, S.S.S.R.	70	58.15 N	42.56 E
Pālkonda	112	18.36 N	83.45 E
Pālkonda Hills ⋀[2]	112	14.05 N	79.05 E
Palk Strait ⋃	112	10.00 N	79.45 E
Palla Bianca (Weisskugel) ∧	58	46.48 N	10.44 E
Pallamana	158b	35.02 S	139.12 E
Pallasca	238	8.15 S	78.01 W
Pallas-Ounastunturin Kansallispuisto ♠	24	68.06 N	24.00 E
Pallasovka	70	50.03 N	46.53 E
Pallastunturi ∧	24	68.06 N	24.00 E
Pallejá	256d	41.25 N	2.00 E
Pallier	165f	14.53 S	166.35 E
Palling	172	54.21 N	125.55 W
Pallíni	257c	38.00 N	23.53 E
Pallinup ≃	152	34.29 S	118.54 E
Pallisa	144	1.10 N	33.42 E
Palliser, Cape ≻	162	41.37 S	175.17 E
Palliser Bay C	162	41.25 S	175.05 E
Pallu	113	28.56 N	74.13 E
Palluau	32	46.48 N	1.37 W
Palma, Bra.	245	21.22 S	42.19 W
Palma, Moç.	144	10.46 S	40.29 E
P'al'ma, S.S.S.R.	24	62.26 N	35.53 E
Palma ≃	245	12.33 S	47.52 W
Palma, Bahía de C	34	39.27 N	2.35 E
Palma, Río de la ≃	230p	23.03 N	80.54 W
Palma, Sierra de la ⋀	186	25.50 N	101.30 W
Palma Campania	60	40.52 N	14.33 E
Palmácia	240	4.08 S	38.50 W
Palma del Río	34	37.42 N	5.17 W
Palma [de Mallorca]	34	39.34 N	2.39 E
Palma di Montechiaro	36	37.11 N	13.46 E
Palmahim	122	31.56 N	34.42 E
Palmanova	58	45.54 N	13.19 E
Palma Pegada	224	22.42 N	101.48 W
Palmar ≃	236	10.10 N	71.50 W
Palmar Camp	222	16.26 N	88.53 W
Palmar de Cariaco	276c	10.34 N	66.55 W
Palmar de Sepúlveda	222	25.43 N	107.55 W
Palmar de Varela	236	10.45 N	74.45 W
Palmarejo	230m	18.03 N	67.05 W
Palmares, Bra.	240	8.41 S	35.36 W
Palmares, C.R.	226	10.03 N	84.26 W
Palmares, C.R.	226	9.21 N	83.40 W
Palmares do Sul	242	30.16 S	50.31 W
Palmaria, Isola I	56	44.02 N	9.51 E
Palmarito	236	7.37 N	70.10 W
Palmarito [Tochapan]	224	18.54 N	97.37 W
Palmarola, Isola I	60	40.56 N	12.51 E
Palmar Sur	226	8.58 N	83.29 W
Palmas	242	26.30 S	52.00 W
Palmas, Canal de las ≍	278	34.36 S	58.18 W
Palmas, Cape ≻	140	4.22 N	7.44 W
Palmas, Golfo di C	36	39.00 N	8.30 E
Palmas, Ilha das I	277a	23.02 S	43.12 W
Palmas Bellas	226	9.14 N	80.05 W
Palmas de Monte Alto	245	14.16 S	43.10 W
Palma Sola	210	27.31 N	82.38 W
Palma Soriano	230p	20.13 N	76.00 W
Palm Bay	210	28.02 N	80.35 W
Palm Beach, Austl.	160	33.36 S	151.19 E
Palm Beach, Austl.	161a	28.08 S	153.28 E
Palm Beach, Fla., U.S.	210	26.42 N	80.02 W
Palm Beach □[6]	210	26.38 N	80.27 W
Palm Beach Gardens	210	26.49 N	80.06 W
Palm Beach International Airport ⊠	210	26.41 N	80.05 W
Palm City	210	27.09 N	80.16 W
Palmdale, Calif., U.S.	218	34.35 N	118.07 W
Palmdale, Fla., U.S.	210	26.57 N	81.19 W
Palmdale, Pa., U.S.	198	40.18 N	76.37 W
Palmdale, Lake ⊜[1]	218	34.33 N	118.07 W
Palm Desert	194	33.43 N	116.22 W
Palmeira, Bra.	242	25.25 S	50.00 W

Symbol	English	Deutsch	Español	Français	Português
≃	River	Fluss	Río	Rivière	Rio
≍	Canal	Kanal	Canal	Canal	Canal
⌊	Waterfall, Rapids	Wasserfall, Stromschnellen	Cascada, Rápidos	Chute d'eau, Rapides	Cascata, Rápidos
⋃	Strait	Meeresstrasse	Estrecho	Détroit	Estreito
C	Bay, Gulf	Bucht, Golf	Bahía, Golfo	Baie, Golfe	Baía, Golfo
⊜	Lake, Lakes	See, Seen	Lago, Lagos	Lac, Lacs	Lago, Lagos
≌	Swamp	Sumpf	Pantano	Marais	Pântano
⊼	Ice Features, Glacier	Eis- und Gletscherformen	Accidentes Glaciales	Formes glaciaires	Acidentes Glaciares
⊤	Other Hydrographic Features	Andere Hydrographische Objekte	Otros Elementos Hidrográficos	Autres données hydrographiques	Outros Elementos Hidrográficos
✢	Submarine Features	Untermeerische Objekte	Accidentes Submarinos	Formes de relief sous-marin	Acidentes Submarinos
□	Political Unit	Politische Einheit	Unidad Política	Entité politique	Unidade Política
♥	Cultural Institution	Kulturelle Institution	Institución Cultural	Institution culturelle	Instituição Cultural
⊥	Historical Site	Historische Stätte	Sitio Histórico	Site historique	Sítio Histórico
♠	Recreational Site	Erholungs- und Ferienort	Sitio de Recreo	Centre de loisirs	Sítio de Lazer
⊠	Airport	Flughafen	Aeropuerto	Aéroport	Aeroporto
▪	Military Installation	Militäranlage	Instalación Militar	Installation militaire	Instalação Militar
◆	Miscellaneous	Verschiedenes	Misceláneo	Divers	Miscelânea

Name	Page	Lat.°′	Long.°′
Palmeira, C.V.	140a	16.46 N	22.59 W
Palmeira das Missões	242	27.55 S	53.17 W
Palmeira d'Oeste	245	20.23 S	50.47 W
Palmeira dos Índios	240	9.25 S	36.37 W
Palmeirais	240	5.58 S	43.04 W
Palmeiral	246	21.38 S	46.31 W
Palmeirante	240	7.49 S	48.09 W
Palmeiras, Bra.	245	12.31 S	41.34 W
Palmeiras, Bra.	246	22.33 S	43.28 W
Palmeiras ≃, Bra.	240	12.22 S	47.08 W
Palmeiras ≃, Bra.	245	15.25 S	51.10 W
Palmeirina	240	8.56 S	36.17 W
Palmeirinhas, Ponta das ≻	142	9.05 S	13.00 E
Palmelo	245	17.20 S	48.27 W
Palmer, Austl.	158b	34.51 S	139.10 E
Palmer, P.R.	230m	18.22 N	65.46 W
Palmer, Alaska, U.S.	170	61.36 N	149.07 W
Palmer, Ill., U.S.	209	39.27 N	89.24 W
Palmer, Mass., U.S.	197	42.09 N	72.20 W
Palmer, Mich., U.S.	180	46.27 N	87.35 W
Palmer, Nebr., U.S.	188	41.13 N	98.15 W
Palmer, Tenn., U.S.	184	35.21 N	85.34 W
Palmer, Tex., U.S.	212	32.26 N	96.40 W
Palmer ≃, Austl.	152	24.46 S	133.25 E
Palmer ≃, Austl.	154	15.34 S	142.26 E
Palmer ≃, Qué., Can.	196	46.19 N	71.27 W
Palmerah ◆[8]	259e	6.12 S	106.47 E
Palmer Heights	198	40.42 N	75.16 W
Palmer Lake	190	39.07 N	104.55 W
Palmer Land ◆[1]	9	71.30 S	65.00 W
Palmer Mill Brook ≃	273	41.58 N	70.52 W
Palmer Park	274c	38.55 N	76.52 W
Palmer Park ♠	271	42.26 N	83.07 W
Palmers Crossing	184	31.16 N	89.15 W
Palmerston, Ont., Can.	202	43.50 N	80.51 W
Palmerston, N.Z.	162	45.29 S	170.43 E
Palmerston I[1]	14	18.04 S	163.10 W
Palmerston, Cape ≻	156	21.32 S	149.29 E
Palmerston Lake ⊜	202	45.01 N	76.50 W
Palmerston North	162	40.21 S	175.37 E
Palmerton	200	40.48 N	75.37 W
Palmerville	154	15.59 S	144.05 E
Palmetto, Fla., U.S.	210	27.31 N	82.35 W
Palmetto, Ga., U.S.	182	33.31 N	84.40 W
Palmetto, La., U.S.	184	30.43 N	91.55 W
Palmford	148	27.11 S	29.42 E
Palm Harbor	210	28.05 N	82.46 W
Palmi	36	38.21 N	15.51 E
Palminópolis	245	16.47 S	50.08 W
Palmira, Arg.	242	33.03 S	68.34 W
Palmira, Col.	236	3.32 N	76.16 W
Palmira, Cuba	230p	22.14 N	80.23 W
Palmira, Ec.	236	2.05 S	78.43 W
Palmira, Méx.	186	28.58 N	100.47 W
Palmital	246	23.14 S	45.33 W
Palmital, Serra do ∧∧	246	23.00 S	45.47 W
Palmitas	242	33.31 S	57.49 W
Palmito, Presa ⊜[1]	222	25.35 N	105.02 W
Palmitos	242	27.05 S	53.08 W
Palmnicken → Jantarnyj	66	54.52 N	19.57 E
Palmoli	60	41.56 N	14.32 E
Palm River	210	27.56 N	82.23 W
Palms ◆[8]	270	34.02 N	118.25 W
Palm Shores	210	28.11 N	80.35 W
Palm Springs, Calif., U.S.	194	33.50 N	116.33 W
Palm Springs, Fla., U.S.	210	26.39 N	80.06 W
Palmyra → Tudmur, Sūrīy.	120	34.33 N	38.17 E
Palmyra, Ill., U.S.	209	39.26 N	89.60 W
Palmyra, Ind., U.S.	208	38.24 N	86.07 W
Palmyra, Mich., U.S.	206	41.52 N	83.56 W
Palmyra, Mo., U.S.	209	39.48 N	91.31 W
Palmyra, N.J., U.S.	198	40.00 N	75.01 W
Palmyra, N.Y., U.S.	200	43.04 N	77.14 W
Palmyra, Ohio, U.S.	204	41.07 N	81.02 W
Palmyra, Pa., U.S.	198	40.18 N	76.36 W
Palmyra, Va., U.S.	182	37.51 N	78.16 W
Palmyra, Wis., U.S.	206	42.53 N	88.35 W
Palmyra ⊥	120	34.33 N	38.17 E
Palmyra Atoll I[1]	14	5.52 N	162.06 W
Palni	112	10.28 N	77.32 E
Palo, It.	60	41.56 N	12.06 E
Palo, Pil.	106	11.10 N	124.59 E
Palo Alto, Méx.	186	26.32 N	99.45 W
Palo Alto, Calif., U.S.	216	37.27 N	122.09 W
Palo Alto, Pa., U.S.	198	40.41 N	76.11 W
Palo Alto Airport ⊠	272	37.28 N	122.07 W
Palo Blanco, Méx.	186	26.45 N	101.32 W
Palo Blanco, P.R.	230m	18.26 N	66.39 W
Palo Blanco Creek ≃	186	27.10 N	97.52 W
Paločka	76	58.25 N	84.32 E
Palo Duro Canyon State Park ♠	186	34.55 N	101.42 W
Palo Duro Creek ≃, U.S.	186	36.39 N	100.58 W
Palo Duro Creek ≃, Tex., U.S.	186	35.00 N	101.55 W
Paloemeu ≃	240	3.21 N	55.26 W
Palo Flechado Pass)(	190	36.30 N	105.30 W
Paloh, Indon.	102	1.43 N	109.18 E
Paloh, Malay.	102	2.25 N	111.15 E
Paloh, Malay.	104	2.11 N	103.12 E
Paloich, Sūd.	130	10.28 N	32.32 E
Paloich, Sūd.	130	6.45 N	30.08 E
Palojoensuu	24	68.17 N	23.05 E
Paloma Creek ≃	216	36.15 N	121.26 W
Palomares	276d	12.00 S	77.01 W
Palomares Creek ≃	272	37.42 N	122.02 W
Palomar Mountain ∧	194	33.22 N	116.50 W
Palomar Mountain State Park ♠	218	33.19 N	116.53 W
Palomar Park	272	37.29 N	122.16 W
Palomas	186	28.43 N	103.45 W
Palomas, Mesa de ∧	222	28.46 N	103.41 W
Palomas Creek ≃	190	33.03 N	107.16 W
Palombara Sabina	60	42.04 N	12.46 E
Palometillas ≃	238	16.36 S	64.18 W
Palominos, Isla I	230m	18.21 N	65.34 W
Palompon	106	11.03 N	124.23 E
Palo Negro	236	10.11 N	67.33 W
Palo Pinto	186	32.46 N	98.18 W
Palo Pinto Reservoir ⊜[1]	186	32.38 N	98.18 W
Palopo	102	3.00 S	120.12 E
Palora ≃	236	1.51 S	77.49 W
Palos	230p	22.48 N	81.44 W
Palos, Cabo de ≻	34	37.38 N	0.41 W
Palo Santo	242	25.34 S	59.21 W
Palo Seco	230m	18.28 N	66.09 W
Palos Gardens	268	41.40 N	87.48 W
Palos Heights	206	41.40 N	87.48 W
Palos Hills	268	41.41 N	87.49 W
Palos Hills ♠	268	41.42 N	87.53 W
Palos Park	268	41.40 N	87.50 W
Palos Verdes Estates	218	33.48 N	118.24 W
Palos Verdes Hills ∧∧[2]	270	33.46 N	118.21 W
Palos Verdes Point ≻	218	33.47 N	118.26 W
Palotai-sziget I	254c	47.35 N	19.05 E
Paloúkia	257c	37.58 N	23.31 E
Palouse	192	46.55 N	117.04 W
Palouse ≃	192	46.35 N	118.13 W
Palo Verde	194	33.26 N	114.44 W
P'alovskoje Vodochranilišče ⊜[1]	72	56.03 N	37.40 E
Palpa	238	14.32 S	75.11 W
Palpalá	242	24.15 S	65.12 W
Pålsboda	40	59.04 N	15.20 E
Pālsit	116	23.12 N	88.03 E
Paltamo	26	64.25 N	27.50 E
Palu, Indon.	102	0.53 S	119.53 E
Palu, Tür.	120	38.42 N	39.57 E
Palu ≃	102	0.52 S	119.51 E
Palu, Pulau I	105b	8.20 S	121.43 E
Palu, Teluk C	102	0.40 S	119.45 E
Paluan	106	13.25 N	120.28 E
Paluan Bay C	106	13.23 N	120.25 E
Palù del Fersina	58	46.08 N	11.21 E
Paluga	24	65.16 N	45.11 E
Paluke	140	5.02 N	8.06 W
Paluxy ≃	186	32.15 N	97.43 W
Paluzza	58	46.32 N	13.01 E
Palvantaš	75	40.34 N	72.12 E
Palvart	118	38.11 N	64.34 E
Palwal	114	28.09 N	77.20 E
Pal-Waukee Airport ⊠	268	42.07 N	87.54 W
Pam	165f	20.16 S	164.19 E
Pama	140	11.15 N	0.42 E
Pama ≃	142	4.23 N	18.27 E
Pama, Réserve de ◆[4]	140	11.30 N	1.00 E
Pamaluan	102	1.04 S	116.39 E
Pamangkat	102	1.10 N	108.58 E
Pamanukan	105a	6.16 S	107.49 E
Pamarayan	105a	6.16 S	106.17 E
Pam'ati 13 Borcov	76	56.13 N	92.20 E
Pam'atnaja	76	56.01 N	65.42 E
Pam'at' Parižskoj Kommuny	70	56.06 N	44.31 E
Pāmban Channel ⊔	112	9.17 N	79.10 E
Pāmban Island I	112	9.15 N	79.20 E
Pambegua	140	10.40 N	8.19 E
Pambuhan	106	13.59 N	123.05 E
Pambujan	106	12.34 N	124.56 E
Pambunan ≃	106	12.34 N	124.55 E
Pamekasan	105a	7.10 S	113.28 E
Pamel	46	50.50 N	4.04 E
Pamenang	102	2.07 S	102.31 E
Pameungpeuk	105a	7.38 S	107.43 E
Pamiers	32	43.07 N	1.36 E
Pamir ∧∧, As.	62	38.00 N	73.00 E
Pamir ∧∧, S.S.S.R.	75	38.00 N	73.00 E
Pamlico ≃	182	35.20 N	76.30 W
Pamlico Sound ⊔	182	35.20 N	75.55 W
Pamotan	105a	6.46 S	111.29 E
Pampa	186	35.32 N	100.58 W
Pampã ≃	245	17.43 S	40.36 W
Pampa Almirón	242	26.42 S	59.08 W
Pampacolca	238	15.43 S	72.33 W
Pampa del Castillo	244	45.48 S	68.05 W
Pampa del Chañar	242	30.11 S	68.43 W
Pampa del Indio	242	26.02 S	59.55 W
Pampa del Infierno	242	26.31 S	61.10 W
Pampa de los Guanacos	242	26.14 S	61.51 W
Pampa Grande	238	18.05 S	64.06 W
Pampana ≃	140	8.24 N	12.00 W
Pampanga □[4]	106	15.05 N	120.40 E
Pampanga ≃	106	14.47 N	120.39 E
Pampanua	102	4.14 S	120.08 E
Pamparato	56	44.17 N	7.55 E
Pampas	238	12.24 S	74.54 W
Pampas ≃	238	13.23 S	73.15 W
Pampas ◆[1]	242	35.00 S	63.00 W
Pampeluna → Pamplona	34	42.49 N	1.38 W
Pamplico	182	34.00 N	79.34 W
Pamplona, Col.	236	7.23 N	72.39 W
Pamplona, Esp.	34	42.49 N	1.38 W
Pampoenpoort	148	31.03 S	22.40 E
Pampow	50	53.32 N	14.15 E
Pāmpur	113	34.01 N	74.56 E
Pamukova	120	40.31 N	30.09 E
Pamunkey ≃	198	37.32 N	76.48 W
Pana	209	39.23 N	89.05 W
Panabá	222	21.17 N	88.16 W
Panabo	106	7.19 N	125.42 E
Panaca	194	37.47 N	114.23 W
Panacachi	238	18.23 S	66.21 W
Panacan	106	9.16 N	118.25 E
Panacea	182	30.02 N	84.23 W
Panache, Lake ⊜	180	46.15 N	81.20 W
Panadura	112	6.43 N	79.54 E
Panaete Island I	154	10.40 S	152.20 E
Panāgar	114	23.18 N	79.59 E
Panagjurište	38	42.30 N	24.11 E
Panagtaran Point ≻	106	9.41 N	118.45 E
Panahan	102	1.44 S	111.49 E
Panaitan, Pulau I	105a	6.36 S	105.12 E
Panaitan, Selat ⊔	105a	6.40 S	105.16 E
Panaji (Panjim)	112	15.29 N	73.50 E
Pānākua	262b	22.23 N	88.21 E
Panakudi	112	8.19 N	77.36 E
Panamá, Bra.	245	18.11 S	49.21 W
Panamá, Pan.	226	8.58 N	79.32 W
Panama, Ill., U.S.	209	39.02 N	89.32 W
Panama, N.Y., U.S.	204	42.05 N	79.29 W
Panama, Okla., U.S.	184	35.10 N	94.40 W
Panamá □[4]	226	8.48 N	79.55 W
Panama □[1]	220		
	236	9.00 N	80.00 W
Panama, Bay of C	236	8.50 N	79.20 W
Panama, Gulf of C	236	8.00 N	79.30 W
Panama, Isthmus of •[3]	228	9.00 N	79.00 W
Panama Canal ≌	226	9.20 N	79.55 W
Panama City	184	30.10 N	85.41 W
Panamá Viejo ⊥	226	9.00 N	79.29 W
Panambi	242	28.18 S	53.30 W
Panamint Range ∧∧	194	36.30 N	117.20 W
Panamint Valley ∨	194	36.15 N	117.20 W
Pan'an	90	29.06 N	120.27 E
Panao, Perú	238	9.49 S	76.00 W
Pan'ao, Zhg.	97	30.09 N	103.37 E
Panaon Island I	106	10.03 N	125.13 E
Panarea, Isola I	36	38.38 N	15.05 E
Panaro ≃	58	44.55 N	11.25 E
Panarukan	105a	7.42 S	113.56 E
Panasoffkee, Lake ⊜	210	28.47 N	82.08 W
Pana Tinai Island I	154	11.15 S	153.10 E
Panay I	106	11.15 N	122.30 E
Panay ≃	106	11.35 N	122.43 E
Panay Gulf C	106	10.15 N	122.15 E
Panayía	38	39.56 N	25.20 E
Panay Island I	106	13.58 N	124.20 E
Pancalieri	56	44.50 N	7.35 E
Pancas	256c	38.48 N	8.55 W
Pancas ≃	245	19.30 S	40.36 W
Pančevo, Jugo.	38	44.52 N	20.39 E
Pančevo, S.S.S.R.	68	48.44 N	31.51 E
Pānchāl	116	23.15 N	87.18 E
Pānchet Hill ∧[2]	116	23.37 N	86.47 E
Pānchet Hill Reservoir ⊜[1]	116	23.42 N	86.35 E
Pānchghara	262b	22.44 N	88.16 E
Panchgram	116	24.12 N	88.01 E
Panch'iao	259d	25.01 N	121.27 E
Panchla	116	22.32 N	88.09 E
Panchor	104	2.10 N	102.43 E
Pancho Simón, Arroyo ≃	276b	23.03 N	82.21 W
Pānchur	262b	22.32 N	88.16 E
Pānchuria	262b	22.33 N	88.29 E
Panciu	38	45.55 N	27.05 E
Panda	146	24.02 S	34.45 E
Panda Gongoue	147a	11.50 S	43.24 E
Pandakan	105a	7.39 S	112.41 E
Pandalāyini	112	11.28 N	75.43 E
Pandamatenga	146	18.35 S	25.42 E
Pandan, Malay.	102	3.09 N	113.22 E
Pandan, Pil.	106	11.43 N	122.06 E
Pandan, Pil.	106	14.03 N	124.10 E
Pandan, Selat ⊔	261c	1.15 N	103.44 E
Pandanan Island I	106	8.17 N	117.13 E
Pandan Bay C	106	11.43 N	122.04 E
Pandaria	114	22.14 N	81.25 E
Pandarochan Bay C	106	12.12 N	121.10 E
Pandasan	102	6.28 N	116.32 E
Pandaveswar	116	23.43 N	87.17 E
Pan de Azúcar	242	34.48 S	55.14 W
Pan de Azucar Island I	106	11.17 N	123.10 E
Pandeglang	105a	6.18 S	106.06 E
Pandeiros, Riacho ≃	245	15.42 S	44.36 W
Pandėlys	66	56.01 N	25.13 E
Pāndharkawada	112	20.01 N	78.32 E
Pandharpur	112	17.40 N	75.20 E
Pāndhurna	112	21.36 N	78.31 E
Pandino	56	45.24 N	9.33 E
Pando	242	34.43 S	55.57 W
Pando □[5]	238	11.20 S	67.40 W
Pando, Cerro ∧	226	8.55 N	82.43 W
Pandora	206	40.57 N	83.58 W
Pandua, Bhārat	114	25.08 N	88.10 E
Pandua, Bhārat	116	23.05 N	88.17 E
P'andž (Āb-i-Panja) ≃, As.	62	37.06 N	68.20 E
P'andž (Panj) ≃, As.	110	37.06 N	68.20 E
Panela ≃	246	21.38 S	45.23 W
Panelas	240	8.40 S	36.01 W
Panerzhuang	95	39.20 N	117.28 E
Paneveggio	58	46.18 N	11.44 E
Panevėžys	66	55.44 N	24.21 E
Panfang	90	27.54 N	115.57 E
Panfilov	76	44.10 N	80.01 E
Panfilovo	70	50.26 N	42.55 E
Pang	58	47.49 N	12.05 E
Panga	144	1.51 N	26.25 E
Pangaduni Island I	116	21.35 N	88.52 E
Pangala	142	3.19 S	14.34 E
Pangalanes, Canal des ≌	147b	22.40 S	47.50 E
Pangandaran	105a	7.41 S	108.39 E
Pangani	144	5.26 S	38.58 E
Pangani ≃	144	5.26 S	38.58 E
Panganiran	106	13.02 N	123.26 E
Pangantocan	106	7.50 N	124.49 E
Panganuran	106	7.24 N	122.03 E
Pangasinan □[4]	106	16.00 N	120.20 E
Pangbourne	44	51.29 N	1.05 W
Pangburn	184	35.15 N	91.51 W
Pange	52	49.05 N	6.22 E
Pangfou → Bangbu	90	32.58 N	117.24 E
Pangga, Tanjung ≻	105b	8.55 S	116.02 E
Panggezhuang, Zhg.	95	39.38 N	116.19 E
Panggezhuang, Zhg.	95	39.16 N	115.49 E
Panghkam	100	23.53 N	97.37 E
Pangi	144	3.11 S	26.38 E
Pangian	102	1.06 S	119.24 E
Pangjiabao	95	40.42 N	115.23 E
Pangkah	105a	6.58 S	109.10 E
Pangkajene	102	4.50 S	119.32 E
Pangkalanberandan	104	4.01 N	98.17 E
Pangkalanbuun	102	2.41 S	111.37 E
Pangkalansusu	104	4.06 N	98.14 E
Pangkalaseang, Tanjung ≻	102	0.42 S	123.26 E
Pangkalpinang	102	2.08 S	106.08 E
Pangkatan	104	2.09 N	100.00 E
Pangkor, Pulau I	104	4.13 N	100.33 E
Panglao	106	9.35 N	123.45 E
Panglao Island I	106	9.35 N	123.48 E
Pangman	174	49.39 N	104.38 W
Pangnirtung	166	66.08 N	65.44 W
Pangnirtung Fiord C[2]	166	66.06 N	65.58 W
Pango Aluquém	142	8.43 S	14.27 E
Pangong Tso ⊜	110	33.45 N	78.43 W
Pangŏ-ri	88	35.29 N	129.26 E
Pangp'u → Bangbu	90	32.58 N	117.24 E
Pangsa	116	23.47 N	89.25 E
Pangtara	100	20.57 N	96.40 E
Pangubatan	106	6.57 N	125.47 E
Panguil Bay C	106	8.01 N	123.43 E
Panguipulli, Lago ⊜	244	39.43 S	72.13 W
Panguiranan	106	12.04 N	123.19 E
Panguitch	190	37.49 N	112.26 W
Pangururan	104	2.37 N	98.42 E
Pangushan	90	25.46 N	115.30 E
Pangutaran	106	6.18 N	120.35 E
Pangutaran Group II	106	6.15 N	120.30 E
Pangutaran Island I	106	6.18 N	120.34 E
Pangutaran Passage ⊔	106	6.13 N	120.30 E
Pangyan	106	5.42 N	125.17 E
Pangzidian	97	30.38 N	105.04 E
Panhame (Hunyani) ≃	144	15.37 S	30.39 E
Panhandle	186	35.21 N	101.23 W
Panhe ≃	90	33.11 N	115.07 E
Paniai, Danau ⊜	154	3.50 S	136.15 E
Pania-Mutombo	142	5.11 S	23.51 E
Panian I	164r	6.47 N	158.16 E
Paniau ∧	219b	21.57 N	160.05 W
Panié, Mont ∧	165f	20.36 S	164.46 E
Pānihāti	116	22.42 N	88.22 E
Panika	70	50.59 N	50.11 E
Panikoviči	66	57.41 N	27.34 E
Panindícuaro	224	19.59 N	101.46 W
Panino, S.S.S.R.	66	56.25 N	34.34 E
Panino, S.S.S.R.	68	51.38 N	40.08 E
Panino-Nesterovo	72	55.23 N	38.11 E
Panīpāt	114	29.23 N	76.58 E
Paniqui	106	15.40 N	120.35 E
Panissières	56	45.47 N	4.20 E
Panitian	106	9.05 N	118.05 E
Panj (P'andž) ≃	110	37.06 N	68.20 E
Panjāb	110	34.22 N	67.01 E
Panjang	105a	5.28 S	105.18 E
Pānjāng ≃	114	29.28 N	82.50 E
Panjang, Pulau I	102	2.44 N	108.55 E
Panje	262c	18.54 N	72.57 E
Panjgūr	118	26.58 N	64.06 E
Panji	104	2.34 N	97.50 E
Panjiadian	88	36.38 N	116.27 E
Panjiapie	90	32.54 N	120.42 E
Panjiasha I	96	31.25 N	121.38 E
Panjiatun	94	41.04 N	121.38 E
Panjim → Panaji	112	15.29 N	73.50 E
Pānjkora ≃	113	34.39 N	71.44 E
Panjnad ≃	113	28.57 N	70.30 E
Panjpāi	110	29.55 N	66.30 E
Pankakoski	26	63.19 N	30.09 E
Panke ≃	254a	52.32 N	13.22 E
Panker	50	54.20 N	10.34 E
Pānkhāli	116	22.37 N	89.31 E
Pankof, Cape ≻	170	54.40 N	163.04 W
Pankow ◆[8]	50	52.34 N	13.25 E
Pankratovo	66	59.10 N	43.30 E
Pankshin	140	9.20 N	9.24 E
Panlı	120	38.52 N	33.56 E
Panlong, Zhg.	90	25.52 N	114.52 E
Panlong, Zhg.	96	31.11 N	121.16 E
Panlong, Zhg.	96	31.58 N	121.35 E
Panlong, Zhg.	97	29.31 N	105.17 E
P'anmunjŏm	88	37.57 N	126.40 E
Panna	114	24.43 N	80.12 E
Panna □[5]	114	24.30 N	80.10 E
Panni	60	41.13 N	15.16 E
Panningen	48	51.20 N	5.59 E
Pannonhalma ⛪[1]	30	47.28 N	17.50 E
Panoche Creek ≃	216	36.44 N	120.31 W
Panola	184	32.57 N	88.16 W
Panola □[6]	212	32.07 N	94.30 W
Panopah	102	1.56 S	111.11 E
Páno Panayiá	120	34.55 N	32.38 E
Páno Plátres	120	34.53 N	32.52 E
Panora	188	41.42 N	94.22 W
Panorama	245	21.21 S	51.51 W
Pánormos	38	37.38 N	25.02 E
Panovo, S.S.S.R.	24	59.48 N	46.27 E
Panovo, S.S.S.R.	78	58.58 N	101.58 E
P'anp'yŏng-ni	88	40.28 N	125.49 E
Panruti	112	11.46 N	79.33 E
Pansfelde	50	51.39 N	11.16 E
Panshan	94	41.12 N	122.04 E
Panshanger Aerodrome ⊠	250	51.48 N	0.08 W
Pansic ∟	226	14.30 N	85.15 W
Pansionat	255b	55.59 N	37.41 E
Pānskura	116	22.25 N	87.42 E
Pantabañgan	106	15.50 N	121.09 E
Pantajevka	68	48.41 N	32.53 E
Pantanaw	100	16.59 N	95.28 E
Pântano	246	22.23 S	46.01 W
Pântano, Ribeirão do ≃	246	22.15 S	45.59 W
Pantar, Pulau I	102	8.25 S	124.07 E
Pantelejmonovka	73	48.12 N	37.59 E
Pantelleria	36	36.49 N	11.57 E
Pantelleria, Isola di I	36	36.47 N	12.00 E
Panteón Nacional ⊥	276c	10.31 N	66.55 W
Pantepec ≃	224	20.56 N	97.44 W
Pantha	100	23.49 N	94.33 E
Pantheon ⊥	257a	41.55 N	12.29 E
Panther Creek ≃, Idaho, U.S.	192	45.19 N	114.24 W
Panther Creek ≃, Ky., U.S.	184	37.45 N	87.19 W
Panther Creek, South Fork ≃	184	37.42 N	87.05 W
Panther Lake	200	43.19 N	75.54 W
Pantin	46	48.54 N	2.24 E
Pantitlán	276a	19.25 N	99.05 W
Panto, Tanjung ≻	105a	6.51 S	105.54 E
Panton, Mount ∧	152	17.21 S	129.13 E
Pantonlabu	104	5.08 N	97.28 E
Pantry Brook ≃	273	42.24 N	71.22 W
Panu	142	3.48 S	19.07 E
Pánuco	224	22.03 N	98.10 W
Pánuco ≃	224	22.16 N	97.47 W
Panukulan	106	14.56 N	121.49 E
Panulcillo	242	30.27 S	71.14 W
Pānuria	116	23.49 N	86.58 E
Pan'utino	68	48.56 N	36.17 E
Panvel	112	18.59 N	73.06 E
Panvel ≃	262c	19.01 N	73.04 W
Panvel Creek ≃	262c	18.59 N	73.00 E
Panwāri	114	25.27 N	79.29 E
Panxi	96	30.35 N	119.20 E
Panxian	92	25.50 N	104.36 E
Panxidu	88	35.39 N	115.52 E
Panyabungan	104	0.51 N	99.33 E
Panyam	140	9.25 N	9.13 E
Panyang	130	10.04 N	29.58 E
Panyčevo	76	57.05 N	81.49 E
Panyu	90	22.57 N	113.20 E
Panzerstausee ⊜[1]	253	51.11 N	7.16 E
Panzi	142	7.13 S	17.58 E
Panzós	226	15.24 N	89.40 W
Pao ≃, Thai	100	16.13 N	103.43 E
Pao ≃, Ven.	236	8.06 N	64.17 W
Pao ≃, Ven.	236	8.33 N	68.01 W
Paochi → Baoji	92	34.22 N	107.14 E
Pão de Açúcar	240	9.45 S	37.26 W
Pão de Açúcar (Sugar Loaf) ∧	277a	22.57 S	43.09 W
Paoki → Baoji	92	34.22 N	107.14 E
Paola, It.	36	39.22 N	16.03 E
Paola, Kans., U.S.	188	38.35 N	94.53 W
Paoli, Ind., U.S.	208	38.33 N	86.28 W
Paoli, Pa., U.S.	198	40.02 N	75.29 W
Paoli, Wis., U.S.	206	42.56 N	89.32 W
Paonia	190	38.52 N	107.36 W
Paonta	114	30.27 N	77.37 E
Paoshenmiao	88	41.12 N	118.17 E
Paotaiyingzi	88	41.48 N	115.12 E
Paoting → Baoding	95	38.52 N	115.29 E
Paotow → Baotou	92	40.40 N	109.59 E
Paoua	142	7.15 N	16.26 E
Paoying → Baoying	90	33.16 N	119.20 E
Paôy Pêt	100	13.39 N	102.33 E
P'aozero, Ozero ⊜	24	66.05 N	30.58 E
Paozi	94	42.17 N	122.20 E
Pap	75	40.53 N	71.07 E
Pápa	30	47.19 N	17.28 E
Papagaio	240	6.01 S	45.21 W
Papagaio ≃	236	1.53 S	62.35 W
Papagayo ≃	224	16.46 N	99.43 W
Papagayo, Golfo del C	226	10.42 N	85.50 W
Papago Indian Reservation ◆[4]	190	32.20 N	112.00 W
Papai I	261d	22.15 N	114.02 E
Papaikou	219d	19.47 N	155.06 W
Papakating Creek ≃	266	41.11 N	74.38 W
Papakura	162	37.04 S	174.57 E
Papale, Palazzo ⛪	257a	41.45 N	12.39 E
Papalia	102	5.58 S	124.01 E
Papaloapan ≃	224	18.42 N	95.38 W
Papanoa	224	17.21 N	101.02 W
Papantla [de Olarte]	224	20.27 N	97.19 W
Papar, Indon.	105a	7.41 S	112.04 E
Papar, Malay.	102	5.44 N	115.56 E
Paparoa	162	36.06 S	174.14 E
Paparoa Range ∧∧	162	42.00 S	171.35 E
Papatoetoe	162	36.58 S	174.52 E
Papawai Point ≻	219a	20.47 N	156.33 W
Papa Westray I	28	59.22 N	2.54 W
Papa Yacu, Lago ⊜	238	5.03 S	76.25 W
Papeete	164s	17.32 S	149.34 W
Papelón	276c	10.27 N	66.47 W
Papenburg	48	53.05 N	7.23 E
Papendrecht	48	51.50 N	4.40 E
Papenoo	164s	17.30 S	149.25 W
Papenoo ≃	164s	17.30 S	149.25 W
Papetoai	164s	17.29 S	149.52 W
Papetoai, Baie de C	164s	17.30 S	149.51 W
Papey I	24a	64.37 N	14.11 W
Paphos → Néa Páfos	120	34.45 N	32.25 E
Papigochic ≃	222	29.09 N	109.40 W
Papilė	66	56.09 N	22.48 E
Papillion	188	41.09 N	96.03 W
Papineau	206	40.58 N	87.43 W
Papineau □[6]	196	45.50 N	75.00 W
Papineau, Lac ⊜	196	45.48 N	74.46 W
Papineau, Parc de ♠	178	45.55 N	75.20 W
Papineau Creek ≃	202	45.13 N	77.43 W
Papineau Lake ⊜	202	45.20 N	77.50 W
Papineauville	196	45.37 N	75.01 W
Papiol	256d	41.26 N	2.01 E
Paposo	242	25.01 S	70.28 W
Papouasie Nouvelle-Guinée → Papua New Guinea □[1]	154	6.00 S	150.00 E
Papozze	58	44.59 N	12.02 E
Pappenheim, B.R.D.	52	48.56 N	10.58 E
Pappenheim, D.D.R.	50	50.47 N	10.27 E
Paps of Jura ∧	42	55.55 N	6.00 W
Papua, Gulf of C	154	8.30 S	145.00 E
Papua Neuguinea → Papua New Guinea □[1]	154	6.00 S	150.00 E
Papua New Guinea □[1]	14	6.00 S	150.00 E
Papua New Ginea □[1]	154	6.00 S	150.00 E
Papua Passage ⊔	164k	21.15 S	159.47 W
Papuasia Nueva Guinea → Papua New Guinea □[1]	154	6.00 S	150.00 E
Papudo	242	32.31 S	71.27 W
Papulovo	24	60.34 N	48.00 E
Papun	100	18.04 N	97.27 E
Papunaua ≃	236	2.09 N	70.32 W
Papunya	152	23.16 S	131.54 E
Papurí ≃	236	0.36 N	69.11 W
Paquemar, Cul-de-Sac du C	230e	14.31 N	60.50 W
Paquequer ≃	246	22.12 S	42.54 W
Paquequer, Serra do ∧∧	246	22.12 S	42.48 W
Paquequer Pequeno	246	22.20 S	43.02 W
Paquera	226	9.50 N	84.56 W
Paquetá, Ilha de I	277a	22.46 S	43.06 W
Paquica, Cabo ≻	242	21.54 S	70.12 W
Par	44	50.21 N	4.43 W
Pará → Belém	240	1.27 S	48.29 W
Pará □[3]	240	4.00 S	53.00 W
Pará ≃, Bra.	240	1.30 S	48.55 W
Pará ≃, Bra.	245	19.13 S	45.07 W
Para ≃, S.S.S.R.	70	54.23 N	40.52 E
Pará, Ilha do I	240	0.18 S	51.15 W
Para, Pulau I	102	3.05 N	125.30 E
Parabel'	76	58.43 N	81.31 E
Parabel' ≃	76	58.44 N	81.35 E
Parabiago	56	45.33 N	8.57 E
Paracale	106	14.17 N	122.48 E
Paracambi	246	22.37 S	43.43 W
Paracari ≃	240	4.36 S	57.47 W
Paracas, Península ≻[1]	238	13.48 S	76.24 W
Paracatu	245	17.13 S	46.52 W
Paracatu ≃, Bra.	245	16.30 S	45.04 W
Paracatu ≃, Bra.	245	16.35 S	45.06 W
Paracel Islands II	98	16.30 N	112.15 E
Parachilna	156	31.08 S	138.23 E
Pārachinār	110	33.54 N	70.06 E
Paracho [de Verduzco]	224	19.39 N	102.04 W
Paraćin	38	43.52 N	21.24 E
Paraconi	236	3.58 S	58.48 W
Parácuaro	224	20.09 N	100.46 W
Paracuellos de Jarama	256a	40.30 N	3.32 W
Paracuru	240	3.24 S	39.04 W
Parád	30	47.55 N	20.02 E
Parada, Punta ≻	238	15.22 S	75.12 W
Parada Pucheta	242	29.54 S	57.34 W
Paradas	34	37.18 N	5.30 W
Paradino	66	53.59 N	31.51 E
Paradise, Calif., U.S.	194	39.46 N	121.37 W
Paradise, Mont., U.S.	192	47.23 N	114.48 W
Paradise, Nev., U.S.	194	36.09 N	115.10 W
Paradise, Pa., U.S.	198	40.01 N	76.08 W
Paradise, Tex., U.S.	212	33.09 N	97.41 W
Paradise Hill, Sask., Can.	174	53.32 N	109.28 W
Paradise Hill, S. Afr.	263d	26.18 S	28.00 E
Paradise Hill, Alaska, U.S.	170	62.25 N	160.03 W
Paradise Island I	230b	25.05 N	77.19 W
Paradise Mountain ∧	161a	27.45 S	152.02 E
Paradise Valley, Ariz., U.S.	190	33.32 N	111.57 W
Paradise Valley, Nev., U.S.	194	41.30 N	117.32 W
Parado	105b	8.45 S	118.36 E
Parado ≃	240	10.17 S	55.39 W
Parafield	158b	34.47 S	138.38 E
Parafijevka	68	50.53 N	32.38 E
Paragačaj	74	39.07 N	45.56 E
Paragon	208	39.24 N	86.34 W
Paragonah	190	37.53 N	112.46 W
Paragould	184	36.03 N	90.29 W
Paraguá ≃, Bol.	238	13.34 S	61.53 W
Paragua ≃, Ven.	236	6.55 N	62.55 W
Paraguaçu	246	21.33 S	45.44 W
Paraguaçu ≃	245	12.45 S	38.54 W
Paraguaçu Paulista	245	22.25 S	50.34 W
Paraguaipoa	236	11.21 N	71.57 W
Paraguaná, Península de ≻[1]	236	11.55 N	70.00 W
Paraguarí	242	25.38 S	57.09 W
Paraguarí □[5]	242	26.00 S	57.10 W
Paraguay □[1]	18	23.00 S	58,00 W
Paraguay (Paraguai) ≃, S.A.	18	27.18 S	58.38 W
Paraguay ≃, S.A.	234	27.18 S	58.38 W
Parahi	140	11.09 N	13.07 W
Parahyba → João Pessoa	240	7.07 S	34.52 W
Paraíba □[3]	240	7.15 S	36.30 W
Paraíba ≃	240	6.58 S	34.51 W
Paraíba do Sul	246	22.09 S	43.17 W
Paraíba do Sul ≃	245	21.37 S	41.03 W
Paraibano	240	6.30 S	44.01 W
Paraibuna	246	23.23 S	45.39 W
Paraibuna ≃, Bra.	246	22.06 S	43.08 W
Paraibuna ≃, Bra.	246	23.22 S	45.40 W
Paraíso, Bra.	245	19.03 S	52.59 W
Paraíso, Bra.	246	22.19 S	45.42 W
Paraíso, C.R.	226	9.50 N	83.51 W
Paraíso, Méx.	224	18.24 N	93.14 W
Paraiso, Pan.	**226**	**9.02 N**	**79.38 W**
Paraíso, Serra do ∧∧[1]	245	15.53 S	53.47 W
Paraíso do Norte	245	23.13 S	52.38 W
Paraíso Garcia	246	21.32 S	43.53 W
Paraíso Novillero	224	18.16 N	95.59 W
Paraisópolis	246	22.33 S	45.47 W
Paraitinga ≃, Bra.	246	23.34 S	46.02 W
Paraitinga ≃, Bra.	246	23.22 S	45.40 W
Paraitinguinho	246	23.31 S	45.50 W
Parakan	105a	7.17 S	110.06 E
Parakou	140	9.21 N	2.37 E
Paralía Aspropírgos	257c	38.02 N	23.35 E
Paralímni	120	35.02 N	33.59 E
Param I	164r	7.01 N	158.15 E
Paramagudi	112	9.33 N	78.36 E
Parama Island I	154	9.00 S	143.25 E
Paramaribo	240	5.50 N	55.10 W
Parambu	240	6.13 S	40.43 W
Paramillo ∧	236	7.04 N	75.55 W
Paramirim	245	13.26 S	42.15 W
Paramirim ≃	240	11.34 S	43.18 W
Paramithiá	38	39.28 N	20.30 E
Paramonga	238	10.40 S	77.50 W
Paramoti	240	4.06 S	39.15 W
Paramount	218	33.53 N	118.09 W
Paramus	200	40.57 N	74.04 W
Paramušir, Ostrov I	64	50.25 N	155.50 E
Paramus Park ◆[9]	266	40.57 N	74.04 W
Paran, Naḥal (Wādī al-Jirāfī) ∨	122	30.24 N	35.10 E
Paraná, Arg.	242	31.44 S	60.32 W
Paranã, Bra.	245	12.33 S	47.52 W
Paraná □[3]	242	24.00 S	51.00 W
Paranã ≃, Bra.	245	12.30 S	48.14 W
Paraná ≃, S.A.	18	33.43 S	59.15 W
Paranabi	246	23.54 S	45.14 W
Paraná Bravo ≃[1]	248	33.53 S	58.27 W
Paraná de las Palmas ≃[1]	248	34.18 S	58.33 W
Paranaguá	242	25.31 S	48.30 W
Paranaguá, Baía de C	242	25.29 S	48.33 W
Paraná Guazú ≃[1]	248	34.00 S	58.25 W
Paranaiba	245	19.40 S	51.11 W
Paranaíba ≃	245	20.07 S	51.05 W
Paraná Ibicuy ≃[1]	248	33.48 S	59.10 W
Paranaidji	240	6.33 S	47.27 W
Paranaíta ≃	240	9.28 S	56.43 W
Paranam	240	5.37 N	55.06 W
Paraná Miní ≃[1]	248	34.13 S	58.25 W
Paranapanema ≃	245	22.40 S	53.09 W
Paranapiacaba	246	23.47 S	46.19 W
Paranapiacaba, Serra do ∧∧	242	24.20 S	49.00 W
Parañaque	259f	14.30 N	120.59 E
Paranavaí	245	23.04 S	52.28 W
Parang, Pil.	106	5.55 N	120.54 E
Parang, Pil.	106	7.23 N	124.16 E
Parang, Pulau I	105a	5.45 S	110.14 E
Paran'ga	70	56.43 N	49.24 E
Parangaba	240	3.45 S	38.33 W
Paranhos	245	23.55 S	55.25 W

Name	Seite	Breite°′	Länge°′ E=Ost
Paranjang	88	37.08 N	126.55 E
Paraopeba	245	19.18 S	44.25 W
Parapara	236	9.44 N	67.18 W
Paraparaumu	162	40.55 S	175.01 E
Paraparaumu Beach	162	40.54 S	174.59 E
Parapayè	54	45.55 N	7.32 E
Parapetí ≃	238	18.58 S	62.21 W
Parara	102	2.37 S	120.07 E
Parás, Méx.	186	26.30 N	99.31 W
Paras, Perú	238	13.30 S	74.35 W
Parasan	106	8.05 N	123.33 E
Parāsi	114	27.32 N	83.40 E
Parāsia	114	22.12 N	78.46 E
Parasida	116	23.46 N	87.20 E
Parasnāth	114	23.59 N	86.02 E
Parasnath Jain Temple ⛪[1]	262b	22.36 N	88.23 E
Paratei	246	23.14 S	46.00 W
Paratei ≃	246	23.12 S	46.00 W
Parati	246	23.13 S	44.43 W
Paratico	58	45.39 N	9.57 E
Parati-Mirim	246	23.14 S	44.38 W
Paratinga	245	12.42 S	43.10 W
Paratoo	156	32.42 S	139.22 E
Parauapebas ≃	240	5.35 S	49.41 W
Parauari ≃	240	4.36 S	57.47 W
Paraúna	245	17.02 S	50.26 W
Paravani, Ozero ⊜	74	41.26 N	43.48 E
Paray-le-Monial	32	46.27 N	4.07 E
Parbakalan	104	2.38 N	98.27 E
Pārbati ≃	114	25.51 N	76.36 E
Pārbatipur	114	25.39 N	88.55 E
Parbhani	112	19.16 N	76.47 E
Parbig	76	57.14 N	81.24 E
Parbig ≃	76	57.37 N	82.18 E
Parbold	252	53.36 N	2.46 W
Parburuan	104	1.52 N	99.55 E
Parchen	50	52.21 N	12.05 E
Parchim	50	53.25 N	11.51 E
Parchment	206	42.19 N	85.33 W
Parchomenko	73	48.34 N	39.43 E
Parchomovka	68	50.08 N	35.01 E
Parchwitz → Prochowice	30	51.17 N	16.22 E
Parcines (Partschins)	58	46.41 N	11.04 E
Parczew	30	51.39 N	22.54 E
Pardee Reservoir ⊜[1]	216	38.16 N	120.51 W
Pardeeville	180	43.32 N	89.18 W
Pardes Ḥanna	122	32.28 N	34.58 E
Pārdi	112	20.31 N	72.57 E
Pardo ≃, Bra.	240	5.21 S	52.53 W
Pardo ≃, Bra.	242	29.59 S	52.23 W
Pardo ≃, Bra.	245	20.10 S	48.38 W
Pardo ≃, Bra.	245	15.39 S	38.57 W
Pardo ≃, Bra.	245	22.55 S	49.58 W
Pardo ≃, Bra.	245	15.48 S	44.48 W
Pardo ≃, Bra.	245	21.46 S	52.09 W
Pardo ≃, Bra.	246	21.25 S	42.39 W
Pardo ≃, Bra.	246	23.32 S	45.30 W
Pardomuan	104	2.06 N	98.20 E
Pardubice	30	50.02 N	15.47 E
Pare	105a	7.46 S	112.11 E
Parece Vela → Okino-Tori-Shima I	80	20.25 N	136.00 E
Parecis	238	14.09 S	56.56 W
Parecis ≃	238	12.56 S	56.43 W
Parecis, Serra dos ∧∧	238	13.00 S	60.00 W
Parede	256c	38.41 N	9.21 W
Paredes de Nava	34	42.09 N	4.41 W
Paredes do Sapucaí	246	21.48 S	45.43 W
Paredón	222	25.56 N	100.58 W
Parelhas	240	6.41 S	36.39 W
Parelheiros ◆[5]	246	23.51 S	46.44 W
Pareloup, Lac de ⊜	32	44.15 N	2.45 E
Paremata	162	41.07 S	174.52 E
Paren'	64	62.28 N	163.05 E
Paren' ≃	64	62.25 N	163.10 E
Parengarenga Harbour C	162	34.31 S	172.57 E
Parent	166	47.55 N	74.37 W
Parent, Lac ⊜	180	48.38 N	77.03 W
Parentis-en-Born	32	44.21 N	1.05 W
Pareora	162	44.30 S	171.12 E
Parepare	102	4.01 S	119.38 E
Parera	242	35.08 S	64.32 W
Parey	50	52.22 N	11.59 E
Parfenjevo, S.S.S.R.	24	61.21 N	42.43 E
Parfenjevo, S.S.S.R.	70	58.29 N	43.25 E
Parfentevo	72	55.06 N	38.49 E
Parfino	66	57.58 N	31.41 E
Parforce-Heide ◆[3]	254a	52.22 N	13.10 E
Párga	38	39.17 N	20.23 E
Pārgaon	262c	18.59 N	73.05 E
Pargarutan	104	1.28 N	99.20 E
Pargas (Parainen)	26	60.18 N	22.18 E
Pargey Creek ≃	275	39.49 N	75.18 W
Pargny-sur-Saulx	52	48.46 N	4.50 E
Pargolovo	66	60.04 N	30.18 E
Parham	230c	17.05 N	61.46 W
Parham Harbour C	230c	17.07 N	61.46 W
Parhebangan	104	2.15 N	98.45 E
Pari	114	27.44 N	89.09 E
Pari ◆[8]	277b	23.32 S	46.37 W
Paria ≃	190	36.52 N	111.36 W
Paria, Gulf of C	236	10.20 N	62.00 W
Paria, Península de ≻[1]	231r	10.40 N	62.10 W
Pariaguán	236	8.51 N	64.43 W
Pariaman	102	0.38 S	100.08 E
Pariamanu ≃	238	12.26 S	69.16 W
Paricá, Lago ⊜	236	1.53 S	65.45 W
Pariči	66	52.48 N	29.25 E
Parícutin ∧[1]	224	19.28 N	102.15 W
Parida, Isla I	226	8.07 N	82.20 W
Pariette Draw ∨	190	40.02 N	109.45 W
Parigi, Indon.	102	0.48 S	120.10 E
Parigi, Indon.	105a	6.12 S	106.22 E
Parigné-l'Évêque	46	47.56 N	0.22 E
Parika	236	6.52 N	58.25 W
Parikkala	26	61.33 N	29.30 E
Parima ≃	236	3.34 N	63.47 W
Parima, Sierra ∧∧	236	2.30 N	64.00 W
Pariñas, Punta ≻	236	4.40 S	81.20 W
Parîngul ∧	38	45.22 N	23.33 E
Parintins	240	2.36 S	56.44 W
Paripiranga	240	10.41 S	37.52 W
Pariquera-Açu	242	24.43 S	47.53 W
Paris, Ont., Can.	202	43.12 N	80.23 W
Paris, Fr.	46		
	251	48.52 N	2.20 E
Paris, Gilb. Is.	164o	1.56 N	157.29 W
Paris, Ark., U.S.	184	35.18 N	93.44 W
Paris, Idaho, U.S.	192	42.14 N	111.24 W
Paris, Ill., U.S.	184	39.36 N	87.42 W
Paris, Ky., U.S.	208	38.13 N	84.14 W
Paris, Maine, U.S.	178	44.16 N	70.30 W
Paris, Mo., U.S.	209	39.29 N	92.00 W
Paris, Ohio, U.S.	204	40.48 N	81.10 W
Paris, Pa., U.S.	204	40.24 N	80.31 W
Paris, Tenn., U.S.	184	36.19 N	88.20 W
Paris, Tex., U.S.	186	33.40 N	95.33 W
Paris □[5]	251	48.52 N	2.20 E
Paris, Port de C	251	48.57 N	2.17 E
Parish	200	43.24 N	76.08 W
Parisien de Pantin, Cimetière ◆	251	48.54 N	2.23 E
Paris-le-Bourget, Aéroport de ⊠	251	49.00 N	2.25 E
Parismina	226	10.12 N	83.38 W
Parismina ≃	226	10.19 N	83.21 W
Paris-Orly, Aeroport de ⊠	46	48.43 N	2.22 E
Paris-Plage, Aéroport ⊠	46	50.31 N	1.38 E
Parit	102	3.10 S	104.38 E
Parita, Bahía de C	226	8.08 N	80.24 W
Parit Bunga	104	2.04 N	102.33 E
Parit Buntar	104	5.07 N	100.30 E
Pariti	102	10.01 S	123.43 E
Parit Jawa	104	1.57 N	102.39 E

Symbols in the index entries represent the broad categories identified in the key at the right. Symbols with superior numbers (∧∧[2]) identify subcategories (see complete key on page *I · 26*).

Kartensymbole in dem Registerverzeichnis stellen die rechts in Schlüssel erklärten Kategorien dar. Symbole mit hochgestellten Ziffern (∧∧[2]) bezeichnen Unterabteilungen einer Kategorie (vgl. vollständiger Schlüssel auf Seite *I · 26*).

Los símbolos incluidos en el texto del índice representan las grandes categorías identificadas con la clave a la derecha. Los símbolos con numeros en su parte superior (∧∧[2]) identifican las subcategorías (véase la clave completa en la página *I · 26*).

Les symboles de l'index représentent les catégories indiquées dans la légende à droite. Les symboles suivis d'un indice (∧∧[2]) représentent des sous-catégories (voir légende complète à la page *I · 26*).

Os símbolos incluídos no texto do índice representam as grandes categorias identificadas com a chave à direita. Os símbolos com números em sua parte superior (∧∧[2]) identificam as subcategorias (veja-se a chave completa à página *I · 26*).

	English	Deutsch	Español	Français	Português
∧	Mountain	Berg	Montaña	Montagne	Montanha
∧∧	Mountains	Berge	Montañas	Montagnes	Montanhas
)(	Pass	Pass	Paso	Col	Passo
∨	Valley, Canyon	Tal, Cañon	Valle, Cañón	Vallée, Canyon	Vale, Canhão
∟	Plain	Ebene	Llano	Plaine	Planície
≻	Cape	Kap	Cabo	Cap	Cabo
I	Island	Insel	Isla	Île	Ilha
II	Islands	Inseln	Islas	Îles	Ilhas
⊥	Other Topographic Features	Andere Topographische Objekte	Otros Elementos Topográficos	Autres données topographiques	Outros Elementos Topográficos

ESPAÑOL Nombre / FRANÇAIS Nom / PORTUGUÊS Nome	Página / Page / Página	Lat.°′	Long.°′ W=Oeste / W=Ouest
Parižskaja Kommuna ◄[8]	73	48.26 N	38.49 E
Park ≃	188	48.28 N	97.09 W
Park, North Branch ≃	188	48.26 N	97.27 W
Park, South Branch ≃	188	48.26 N	97.27 W
Parka	144	4.31 N	27.20 E
Parkano	26	62.01 N	23.01 E
Parkany	68	46.49 N	29.31 E
Parkchester	275	40.00 N	75.35 W
Park City, Ill., U.S.	206	42.21 N	87.53 W
Park City, Kans., U.S.	188	37.46 N	97.19 W
Park City, Mont., U.S.	192	45.38 N	108.55 W
Park City, Utah, U.S.	190	40.39 N	111.30 W
Park Creek ≃	275	40.13 N	75.08 W
Parkdale, P.E.I., Can.	176	46.15 N	63.07 W
Parkdale, Mo., U.S.	209	38.29 N	90.32 W
Parkdale, Oreg., U.S.	214	45.31 N	121.36 W
Parkdene	263d	26.14 S	28.16 E
Parkent	75	41.18 N	69.40 E
Parker, Ariz., U.S.	190	34.09 N	114.17 W
Parker, Fla., U.S.	184	30.08 N	85.36 W
Parker, Pa., U.S.	204	41.06 N	79.41 W
Parker, S. Dak., U.S.	188	43.24 N	97.08 W
Parker □[6]	212	32.48 N	97.42 W
Parker ≃	197	42.45 N	70.49 W
Parker, Cape ≻	166	75.04 N	79.40 W
Parker, Lake ⊜	210	28.04 N	81.56 W
Parker City	208	40.11 N	85.12 W
Parker Dam	194	34.17 N	114.09 W
Parker Dam ◄[6]	190	34.18 N	114.10 W
Parker Ford	275	40.12 N	75.35 W
Parker Peak Λ	188	43.24 N	103.41 W
Parker Range	152	31.38 S	119.35 E
Parker River National Wildlife Refuge ◄[4]	273	42.45 N	70.48 W
Parkersburg, Ill., U.S.	184	38.36 N	88.03 W
Parkersburg, Iowa, U.S.	180	42.35 N	92.47 W
Parkersburg, W. Va., U.S.	178	39.17 N	81.32 W
Parkers Creek ≃	275	40.00 N	74.53 W
Parkers Prairie	188	46.09 N	95.20 W
Parkerville	158a	31.53 S	116.09 E
Parker Volcano Λ[1]	106	6.07 N	124.54 E
Parkes	156	33.08 S	148.11 E
Parkesburg	198	39.58 N	75.55 W
Park Falls	180	45.56 N	90.32 W
Park Forest	206	41.28 N	87.38 W
Park Forest South	206	41.36 N	87.39 W
Parkgate, Eng., U.K.	252	53.18 N	3.05 W
Parkgate, Eng., U.K.	252	53.16 N	2.20 W
Park Hall	198	38.13 N	76.26 W
Parkhill, Ont., Can.	180	43.09 N	81.41 W
Parkhill, Pa., U.S.	204	40.22 N	78.52 W
Parkhill Gardens	263d	26.14 S	28.11 E
Parkin	184	35.16 N	90.34 W
Parkitapo	144	1.29 S	35.34 E
Park Lake	206	42.48 N	84.27 W
Parkland, Pa., U.S.	275	40.09 N	74.56 W
Parkland, Wash., U.S.	214	47.09 N	122.26 W
Parklawn	274c	38.50 N	77.09 W
Park Layne	208	39.53 N	84.03 W
Parklea	264a	33.44 S	150.57 E
Parkman	204	41.22 N	81.04 W
Park Meadows	269b	40.18 N	79.44 W
Parkmore	42	55.02 N	6.06 W
Park Orchards	264b	37.46 S	145.13 E
Park Plateau ΛΛ[1]	188	37.15 N	104.45 W
Park Range ΛΛ	190	40.00 N	106.30 W
Park Rapids	188	46.55 N	95.04 W
Park Ridge, Ill., U.S.	206	42.01 N	87.50 W
Park Ridge, N.J., U.S.	266	41.02 N	74.02 W
Park Ridge Farms	275	40.10 N	74.42 W
Park Ridge Manor	268	42.02 N	87.50 W
Park River	188	48.24 N	97.45 W
Parkrose	214	45.34 N	122.33 W
Park Rynie	148	30.25 S	30.35 E
Parks Creek ≃	202	44.17 N	77.21 W
Park Shore Resort	206	41.55 N	85.59 W
Parkside, Md., U.S.	274c	39.02 N	77.06 W
Parkside, Pa., U.S.	275	39.52 N	75.23 W
Parksley	198	37.47 N	75.39 W
Park Station ◄[5]	263d	26.12 S	28.03 E
Parkston	188	43.24 N	97.59 W
Parksville, B.C., Can.	172	49.19 N	124.19 W
Parksville, N.Y., U.S.	200	41.52 N	74.46 W
Parkview	269b	40.30 N	79.56 W
Parkville, Md., U.S.	198	39.23 N	76.32 W
Parkville, Mo., U.S.	188	39.11 N	94.41 W
Parkwater	192	47.40 N	117.18 W
Parkway, Calif., U.S.	216	38.30 N	121.27 W
Parkway, Mo., U.S.	209	38.20 N	90.57 W
Parkwood	274c	39.01 N	77.05 W
Parlākimidi	112	18.46 N	84.05 E
Parlament ⊍	254b	48.12 N	16.22 E
Parliament, Houses of ⊍	250	51.30 N	0.07 W
Parlier	216	36.37 N	119.32 W
Parma, It.	58	44.48 N	10.20 E
Parma, Idaho, U.S.	192	43.47 N	116.57 W
Parma, Mich., U.S.	206	42.15 N	84.36 W
Parma, Mo., U.S.	184	36.37 N	89.48 W
Parma, Ohio, U.S.	204	41.22 N	81.43 W
Parma □[4]	58	44.40 N	10.10 E
Parma ≃	58	44.56 N	10.26 E
Parma Heights	204	41.23 N	81.45 W
Parmain	251	49.07 N	2.12 E
Parmatown Center ◄[9]	269a	41.23 N	81.44 W
Parnaguá	240	10.13 S	44.38 W
Parnaguá, Lagoa de ⊜	240	10.15 S	44.40 W
Parnahyba → Parnaíba	240	2.54 S	41.47 W
Parnaíba	240	2.54 S	41.47 W
Parnaíba ≃	240	3.00 S	41.50 W
Parnaibinha ≃	240	9.17 S	45.55 W
Parnamirim, Bra.	240	5.55 S	35.15 W
Parnamirim, Bra.	240	8.05 S	39.34 W
Parnarama	240	5.41 S	43.06 W
Parnassós Λ	38	38.32 N	22.35 E
Parnassus	162	42.43 S	173.18 E
Parnell	206	40.14 N	88.42 W
Párnis Λ	38	38.11 N	23.42 E
Párnis Óros ΛΛ	257c	38.07 N	23.41 E
Parnon ΛΛ	38	37.18 N	22.35 E
Pärnu	66	58.24 N	24.32 E
Pärnu ≃	66	58.23 N	24.29 E
Pärnu-Jaagupi	66	58.37 N	24.30 E
Pärnu Laht C	66	58.15 N	24.25 E
Paro	114	27.26 N	89.25 E
Pārola	110	20.53 N	75.07 E
Paromaj	79	52.50 N	143.02 E
Parona	120	37.31 N	41.58 E
Paroo	152	26.16 S	119.46 E
Paroo ≃	156	31.28 S	143.32 E
Parorā	262b	22.48 N	88.09 E
Páros	38	37.04 N	25.08 E
Páros ▮	38	37.08 N	25.12 E
Parow	148	33.53 S	18.37 E
Parowan	190	37.51 N	112.57 W
Parpaillon ΛΛ	56	44.30 N	6.40 E
Parpan	54	46.46 N	9.33 E
Parpik Pass)(	113	36.58 N	75.25 E
Parques Nacionales depuertode los Ángeles y Barranca de	224	23.40 N	105.18 W
Parr	206	41.02 N	87.13 W
Parral, Chile	242	36.09 S	71.50 W
Parral → Hidalgo del Parral, Méx.	222	26.56 N	105.40 W
Parral, Ohio, U.S.	204	40.33 N	81.30 W
Parramatta	160	33.49 S	151.00 E
Parramatta ≃	264a	33.51 S	151.14 E
Parramatta Park ♠	264a	33.49 S	151.00 E
Parramore Island ▮	198	37.32 N	75.38 W
Parras de la Fuente	222	25.25 N	102.11 W
Parrett ≃	44	51.13 N	3.01 W
Parrish, Ala., U.S.	184	33.44 N	87.17 W
Parrish, Fla., U.S.	210	27.35 N	82.25 W
Parris Island Marine Corps Recruit Depot ■	132	32.21 N	80.41 W
Parrita	226	9.30 N	84.19 W
Parrsboro	176	45.24 N	64.20 W
Parrudo ≃	246	21.53 S	46.17 W
Parry, Cape ≻	166	70.08 N	124.24 W
Parry, Mount Λ	172	52.53 N	128.45 W
Parry Bay C	166	68.07 N	82.00 W
Parry Island ▮	202	45.18 N	80.10 W
Parry Island Indian Reserve ◄[4]	202	45.18 N	80.10 W
Parry Peninsula ≻[1]	170	69.45 N	124.30 W
Parry Sound	202	45.21 N	80.02 W
Parry Sound □[6]	202	45.25 N	79.55 W
Parry Sound ⊔	202	45.21 N	80.06 W
Parryville	198	40.49 N	75.40 W
Parsad	110	24.11 N	73.42 E
Parsberg	30	49.09 N	11.43 E
Parsdorf	58	48.09 N	11.47 E
Parseier Spitze Λ	54	47.10 N	10.28 E
Parsęta ≃	30	54.12 N	15.33 E
Parshall	188	47.57 N	102.08 W
Parshallville	271	42.41 N	83.46 W
Paršino	78	59.10 N	111.48 E
Parsippany	200	40.52 N	74.26 W
Parsippany, Lake ⊜	266	40.51 N	74.26 W
Parsnāth Λ	114	23.53 N	86.08 E
Parsnip ≃	172	55.10 N	123.00 W
Parsoburan	104	2.19 N	99.20 E
Parsonage Island ▮	266	40.37 N	73.37 W
Parsonne, Morne Λ[2]	231o	15.58 N	61.13 W
Parsons, Kans., U.S.	188	37.20 N	95.16 W
Parsons, Tenn., U.S.	184	35.39 N	88.07 W
Parsons, W. Va., U.S.	178	39.06 N	79.41 W
Parson's Pond	176	50.02 N	57.43 W
Parsons Pond ⊜	176	50.00 N	57.35 W
Parsons Range ΛΛ	154	13.30 S	135.15 E
Parsteiner See ⊜	50	52.55 N	13.59 E
Pärsti	66	58.25 N	25.32 E
Partābpur	114	23.29 N	83.13 E
Partanna	36	37.43 N	12.53 E
Partāppur	116	21.48 N	86.44 E
Partenen	54	46.58 N	10.03 E
Parthala	262a	28.36 N	77.24 E
Parthe ≃	50	51.22 N	12.21 E
Parthenay	32	46.39 N	0.15 W
Partille	26	57.44 N	12.07 E
Partington	252	53.25 N	2.26 W
Partinico	36	38.03 N	13.07 E
Partizánske	30	48.39 N	18.23 E
Partizanskoje	76	55.30 N	94.24 E
Parton	42	54.34 N	3.35 W
Partridge, Point ≻	214	48.13 N	122.46 W
Partridge Creek ≃	202	44.44 N	77.13 W
Partridge Crop Lake ⊜	174	55.38 N	97.27 W
Partridge Point ≻	176	50.09 N	56.10 W
Partschins → Parcines	58	46.41 N	11.04 E
Paru ≃, Bra.	240	1.33 S	52.38 W
Parú ≃, Ven.	236	4.20 N	66.27 W
Parubcan	106	13.43 N	123.45 E
Parucito, Caño ≃	236	5.18 N	65.59 W
Paru de Este ≃	240	1.10 N	54.40 W
Paru de Oeste (Cuminá) ≃	240	1.30 S	56.00 W
Parung	105a	6.25 S	106.42 E
Pårup, Dan.	41	55.24 N	10.20 E
Pårup, Dan.	41	56.08 N	9.21 E
Parūr	112	10.09 N	76.14 E
Paruro	238	13.46 S	71.51 W
Parutino	68	46.43 N	31.53 E
Parvān □[4]	110	35.15 N	69.30 E
Pārvatīpuram	112	18.47 N	83.26 E
Parvin State Park ♠	198	39.30 N	75.09 W
Pârvomaj	38	42.06 N	25.13 E
Påryd	26	56.34 N	15.55 E
Parys	148	27.04 S	27.16 E
Paša ≃	66	60.29 N	32.55 E
Paşabahçe ◄[8]	257b	41.06 N	29.05 E
Pasacao	106	13.31 N	123.03 E
Pasaco	226	13.59 N	90.12 W
Pasadena, Newf., Can.	176	49.01 N	57.36 W
Pasadena, Calif., U.S.	218	34.09 N	118.09 W
Pasadena, Tex., U.S.	212	29.42 N	95.13 W
Pasado, Cabo ≻	236	0.22 S	80.30 W
Pasaje	236	3.20 S	79.49 W
Pasaje ≃	242	25.35 S	63.57 W
Pasaje Talavera ≃[1]	248	33.53 S	58.55 W
Pa Sak ≃	100	14.21 N	100.35 E
Pasaleng Bay C	106	18.36 N	120.56 E
Paşalimanı Adası ▮	120	40.28 N	27.37 E
Pasān	114	22.51 N	82.12 E
Pasanauri	74	42.21 N	44.41 E
Pasangkayu	102	1.10 S	119.20 E
Pasarbantal	102	2.45 S	101.20 E
Pasarseluma	102	4.09 S	102.32 E
Pasar Senen Station ◄[5]	259e	6.10 S	106.50 E
Pasarwajo	102	5.29 S	122.50 E
Pasatiempo	216	37.02 N	122.02 W
Pasaunda	262a	28.42 N	77.21 E
Paşavenk	120	38.53 N	39.29 E
Pasawng	100	18.52 N	97.18 E
Pasay	259f	14.33 N	121.00 E
Pasayten, Middle Fork ≃	214	48.53 N	120.37 W
Pasayten, West Fork ≃	214	48.53 N	120.37 W
Pascack Brook ≃	266	40.59 N	73.59 W
Pascagama, Lac ⊜	180	48.34 N	75.36 W
Pascagoula	184	30.23 N	88.31 W
Pascagoula ≃	184	30.21 N	88.34 W
Pascalis, Lac ⊜	180	48.16 N	77.24 W
Paşcani	38	47.15 N	26.44 E
Pasco, Fla., U.S.	210	28.20 N	82.22 W
Pasco, Wash., U.S.	192	46.14 N	119.06 W
Pasco □[5]	238	10.30 S	75.15 W
Pasco □[6]	210	28.20 N	82.27 W
Pascoag	197	41.57 N	71.42 W
Pascoe Vale	264b	37.44 S	144.56 E
Pasco Seamount ✢[3]	14	13.00 S	174.30 W
Pascua, Isla de (Easter Island) ▮	164z	27.07 S	109.22 W
Pascuales, Boca ≃[1]	224	18.52 N	103.58 W
Pas-de-Calais □[5]	46	50.30 N	2.20 E
Pas-en-Artois	46	50.09 N	2.30 E
Pasewalk	50	53.30 N	14.00 E
Pasian di Prato	58	46.03 N	13.11 E
Pasiano di Pordenone	58	45.51 N	12.37 E
Pasig	106	14.35 N	121.05 E
Pasig ≃	259f	14.36 N	120.58 E
Pāsighāt	110	28.04 N	95.20 E
Pašija	76	58.26 N	58.16 E
P'asina ≃	64	73.50 N	87.10 E
Pasing ◄[8]	58	48.08 N	11.27 E
Pasinler (Hasankale)	120	39.59 N	41.41 E
Pašino	76	55.11 N	83.00 E
P'asino, Ozero ⊜	64	69.45 N	87.45 E
P'asinskij Zaliv C	64	74.00 N	86.00 E
Pasión, Rió de la ≃	222	16.28 N	90.33 W
Pasirganting	102	2.02 S	100.53 E
Pasir Gudang	261c	1.27 N	103.53 E
Pasirian	105a	8.13 S	113.06 E
Pasir Mas	104	6.02 N	102.08 E
Pasir Panjang	261c	1.17 N	103.47 E
Pasirpengarayan	104	0.51 N	100.16 E
Pasir Puteh, Malay.	104	5.50 N	102.24 E
Pasir Puteh, Malay.	261c	1.26 N	103.56 E
Påskallavik	26	57.10 N	16.27 E
Paskeville	158b	34.02 S	137.54 E
Paškovo, S.S.S.R.	70	53.39 N	42.25 E
Paškovo, S.S.S.R.	79	48.54 N	130.42 E
Paškovskij	68	45.02 N	39.06 E
Pasłęk	30	54.05 N	19.39 E
Pasłęka ≃	30	54.26 N	19.45 E
Pasley, Cape ≻	152	33.57 S	123.31 E
Pasley Bay C	166	70.40 N	96.27 W
Pašman, Otok ▮	36	43.58 N	15.21 E
Pasmore ≃	156	31.07 S	139.48 E
Pašn'a	24	63.21 N	56.28 E
Pasni	118	25.16 N	63.28 E
Paso de Indios	244	43.52 S	69.06 W
Paso del Cerro	242	31.29 S	55.50 W
Paso del Limay	244	40.33 S	70.26 W
Paso del Macho	224	18.58 N	96.43 W
Paso de los Libres	242	29.43 S	57.05 W
Paso de los Toros	242	32.49 S	56.31 W
Paso del Rey	278	34.39 S	58.46 W
Paso del Toro	224	19.02 N	96.07 W
Paso de Ovejas	224	19.17 N	96.26 W
Paso de Patria	242	27.13 S	58.35 W
Paso de San Antonio	186	29.05 N	103.55 W
Paso Hondo	222	15.49 N	92.02 W
Pasorapa	238	18.16 S	64.37 W
Paso Real de Sarabia	224	17.03 N	95.01 W
Paso Robles	216	35.38 N	120.41 W
Paso Seco	230m	17.59 N	66.23 W
Pašozero	66	60.02 N	34.37 E
Pasqua Indian Reserve ◄[4]	174	50.45 N	104.02 W
Pasque Island ▮	197	41.27 N	70.50 W
Pasquia Hills ΛΛ[2]	174	53.13 N	102.37 W
Pasquia Lake ⊜	174	53.37 N	101.20 W
Pasquotank □[6]	198	36.26 N	76.26 W
Pasquotank ≃	182	36.10 N	76.03 W
Pasrūr	113	32.16 N	74.40 E
Passa Cinco, Corredeira ∟	246	21.19 S	43.08 W
Passadumkeag	178	45.11 N	68.37 W
Passadumkeag Mountain Λ	178	45.10 N	68.20 W
Passagem	245	12.11 S	43.14 W
Passagem Franca	240	6.10 S	43.47 W
Passage West	28	51.52 N	8.20 W
Passaic	200	40.51 N	74.08 W
Passaic □[6]	200	40.55 N	74.10 W
Passaic ≃	266	40.43 N	74.07 W
Passamaquoddy Bay C	176	45.06 N	66.59 W
Passa Quatro	246	22.23 S	44.58 W
Passa Três	246	22.42 S	44.00 W
Passau	30	48.35 N	13.28 E
Passa Vinte	246	22.13 S	44.15 W
Pass Creek ≃	188	43.45 N	101.28 W
Passero, Capo ≻	36	36.40 N	15.09 E
Passignano sul Trasimeno	60	43.11 N	12.08 E
Passirio (Passer) ≃	58	46.41 N	11.10 E
Pass Island	176	47.29 N	56.11 W
Pašskij Perevoz	66	60.24 N	32.59 E
Passo Corese	60	42.09 N	12.39 E
Passo de Camaragibe	240	9.14 S	35.29 W
Passo Fundo	242	28.15 S	52.24 W
Passo Fundo ≃	242	27.16 S	52.42 W
Passos	245	20.43 S	46.37 W
Passow	50	53.08 N	14.06 E
Passy	54	45.55 N	6.41 E
Passy ◄[8]	32	48.52 N	2.17 E
Pastaza □[4]	236	1.45 S	76.50 W
Pastaza ≃	236	4.50 S	76.25 W
Pastecho ≃	172	56.07 N	114.15 W
Pasteur, Lac ⊜	176	50.13 N	66.58 W
Pastillo	230m	17.59 N	66.29 W
Pasto	236	1.13 N	77.17 W
Pastol Bay C	170	63.07 N	163.15 W
Pastora Peak Λ	190	36.47 N	109.10 W
Pastoría, Laguna de C	224	15.59 N	97.40 W
Pastoria Creek ≃	218	35.01 N	118.51 W
Pastos Bons	240	6.36 S	44.05 W
Pastrana	34	40.25 N	2.55 W
Pastrengo	58	45.29 N	10.48 E
Pašukovo	72	55.55 N	38.16 E
Pasuquin	106	18.20 N	120.37 E
Pasur	120	38.30 N	41.02 E
Pasuruan	105a	7.38 S	112.54 E
Pasvalys	66	56.04 N	24.24 E
Pásztó	30	47.55 N	19.42 E
Pata	106	5.51 N	121.10 E
Patacamaya	238	17.14 S	67.55 W
Pātāchārkuchi	110	26.31 N	91.16 E
Patache, Punta ≻	238	20.49 S	70.13 W
Patagonia	190	31.33 N	110.45 W
Patagonia ◄[1]	244	44.00 S	68.00 W
Pataha Creek ≃	192	46.31 N	117.59 W
Pata Island ▮	106	5.49 N	121.10 E
Patamban	224	19.48 N	102.18 W
Pātan, Bhārat	110	23.50 N	72.07 E
Pātan, Bhārat	114	23.18 N	79.42 E
Patan → Lalitpur, Nepāl	114	27.41 N	85.20 E
Patapsco	198	39.32 N	76.54 W
Patapsco ≃	198	39.09 N	76.27 W
Patapsco, Cooks Branch ≃	274b	39.27 N	76.53 W
Patapsco, Davis Branch ≃	274b	39.19 N	76.51 W
Patapsco, North Branch ≃	198	39.21 N	76.53 W
Patapsco, Rockburn Branch ≃	274b	39.14 N	76.43 W
Patapsco, Soapstone Branch ≃	274b	39.13 N	76.43 W
Patapsco River Neck ≻[1]	274b	39.14 N	76.27 W
Patapsco State Park ♠	198	39.20 N	76.55 W
Patargān, Daqq-e ☷	118	33.30 N	60.40 E
Pataudi	114	28.19 N	76.47 E
Pataula Creek ≃	182	31.46 N	85.02 W
Patay	46	48.03 N	1.42 E
Pataz	238	7.44 S	77.37 W
Patcham	44	50.52 N	0.08 W
Patchewollock	156	35.23 S	142.11 E
Patchogue	200	40.46 N	73.00 W
Patchogue Bay C	266	40.44 N	73.01 W
Patchway	44	51.32 N	2.34 W
Pat Cleburne, Lake ⊜[1]	212	32.25 N	97.30 W
Pate	144	2.08 S	41.00 E
Patea	162	39.45 S	174.28 E
Patea ≃	162	39.46 S	174.29 E
Patearoa	162	45.16 S	170.03 E
Pategi	140	8.44 N	5.44 E
Pate Island ▮	144	2.07 S	41.03 E
Pateley Bridge	42	54.05 N	1.45 W
Patel Nagar ◄[8]	262a	28.39 N	77.10 E
Patensie	148	33.46 S	24.49 E
Patéras Óros Λ	257c	38.07 N	23.25 E
Patergassen	58	46.49 N	13.52 E
Paterna	34	39.30 N	0.26 W
Paternion	58	46.43 N	13.38 E
Paternò	36	37.34 N	14.54 E
Pateros, Pil.	259f	14.33 N	121.04 E
Pateros, Wash., U.S.	192	48.03 N	119.54 W
Paterson, Austl.	160	32.36 S	151.37 E
Paterson, S. Afr.	148	33.26 S	25.58 E
Paterson, N.J., U.S.	200 / 266	40.55 N	74.10 W
Paterson, Cape ≻	159	38.40 S	145.36 E
Paterswolde	48	53.08 N	6.35 E
Pātghāti	116	22.53 N	89.55 E
Pathalgaon	114	22.34 N	83.28 E
Pathānkot	113	32.17 N	75.39 E
Pathānkot Airport ⊠	113	32.15 N	75.37 E
Pātharghāra	262b	22.34 N	88.35 E
Pātharghāta	116	22.02 N	89.58 E
Patharia	114	23.54 N	79.12 E
Pathfinder Reservoir ⊜[1]	190	42.30 N	106.50 W
Pathfinder Seamount ✢[3]	16	50.55 N	143.20 W
Pathiong	130	6.46 N	30.54 E
Pathiu	100	10.42 N	99.19 E
Pāthrāil	116	24.12 N	89.56 E
Pathro ≃	116	24.12 N	86.48 E
Pathum Thani	100	14.01 N	100.32 E
Pati, Indon.	102	0.33 S	111.19 E
Pati, Indon.	105a	6.45 S	111.01 E
Pati ≃	236	3.41 S	67.37 W
Patía	236	2.04 N	77.04 W
Patía ≃	236	2.13 N	78.40 W
Patiāla	113	30.19 N	76.24 E
Patiāla □[5]	114	30.20 N	76.20 E
Patiāla Λ	113	32.32 N	72.11 E
P'atichatki	68	48.24 N	33.42 E
Pati do Alferes	246	22.25 S	43.25 W
P'atigorsk	74	44.03 N	43.04 E
Pātihāl	262b	22.39 N	88.08 E
Patikul	106	6.04 N	121.06 E
Patillas	230m	18.00 N	66.01 W
P'atimar	70	49.31 N	50.32 E
Patinti, Selat ⊔	154	0.30 S	127.45 E
Patipāda	262c	19.04 N	73.05 E
Pati Point ≻	164p	13.36 N	144.57 E
Pātiram	114	25.19 N	88.45 E
Pătîrlagele	38	45.19 N	26.22 E
Pativilca	238	10.42 S	77.47 W
Pativilca ≃	238	10.44 S	77.48 W
Pātkai Range ΛΛ	110	27.00 N	96.00 E
Patman	212	32.57 N	94.34 W
Pátmos ▮	120	37.20 N	26.33 E
Patna, Bhārat	114	25.36 N	85.07 E
Patna, Bhārat	116	21.56 N	87.52 E
Pātna, Bhārat	262b	22.59 N	88.18 E
Patna □[5]	114	25.20 N	85.30 E
Patnāgarh	112	20.43 N	83.09 E
Patnanongan Island ▮	106	14.48 N	122.11 E
P'atnica, S.S.S.R.	72	54.46 N	38.09 E
P'atnica, S.S.S.R.	72	56.05 N	36.48 E
P'atnickoje, S.S.S.R.	68	50.25 N	37.51 E
P'atnickoje, S.S.S.R.	72	54.20 N	35.53 E
Pātnoli	262c	18.57 N	73.05 E
Patnoñgon	106	10.55 N	122.00 E
Patnos	74	39.14 N	42.52 E
Pato Branco	242	26.13 S	52.40 W
Patoka	209	38.45 N	89.06 W
Patoka ≃	184	38.25 N	87.44 W
Patokino	72	56.27 N	39.06 E
Patomskoje Nagorje ΛΛ[1]	78	59.00 N	114.00 E
Patonga	144	2.46 N	33.18 E
Patos	240	7.01 S	37.16 W
Patos, Cachoeira dos ∟	238	9.20 S	60.15 W
Patos, Lagoa dos C	242	31.06 S	51.15 W
Patos, Río de los ≃	242	31.18 S	69.25 W
Patos, Rio dos ≃, Bra.	238	13.33 S	56.29 W
Patos, Rio dos ≃, Bra.	245	14.59 S	48.46 W
Patos de Minas	245	18.35 S	46.32 W
Patos Island ▮	214	48.47 N	122.56 W
P'atovskij	72	54.41 N	36.04 E
Patquía	242	30.03 S	66.53 W
Pátrai	38	38.15 N	21.44 E
Patraïkós Kólpos C	38	38.14 N	21.15 E
Patras → Pátrai	38	38.15 N	21.44 E
Pātrasāer	114	23.13 N	87.31 E
Patricio Lynch, Isla ▮	244	48.37 S	75.26 W
Patrick Air Force Base ■	210	28.15 N	80.36 W
Patrick Henry International Airport ⊠	198	37.08 N	76.30 W
Patrick Point ≻	204	42.35 N	81.28 W
Patrington	42	53.41 N	0.02 W
Patriot	208	38.50 N	84.49 W
Patrocínio	245	18.57 S	46.59 W
Patrocínio Paulista	245	20.38 S	47.17 W
Patsaliga Creek ≃	184	31.22 N	86.31 W
Patscherkofel Λ	58	47.13 N	11.28 E
Pattada	36	40.35 N	9.07 E
Pattani	100	6.52 N	101.16 E
Pattani ≃, Thai	100	6.53 N	101.16 E
Pattani ≃, Thai	104	6.45 N	101.18 E
Patten	178	46.01 N	68.27 W
Pattenburg	200	40.38 N	75.01 W
Pattensen	48	52.15 N	9.46 E
Pattenville	273	42.35 N	71.14 W
Patterdale	42	54.32 N	2.56 W
Patterson, Calif., U.S.	216	37.28 N	121.07 W
Patterson, Ga., U.S.	182	31.23 N	82.08 W
Patterson, Ill., U.S.	209	39.29 N	90.29 W
Patterson, La., U.S.	184	29.42 N	91.18 W
Patterson, N.Y., U.S.	200	41.31 N	73.36 W
Patterson, Ohio, U.S.	206	40.47 N	83.32 W
Patterson, Mount Λ	170	64.04 N	134.39 W
Patterson Creek ≃	178	39.34 N	78.23 W
Patterson Gardens	206	41.56 N	83.25 W
Patterson Heights	204	40.45 N	80.19 W
Patterson Island ▮	180	48.39 N	87.00 W
Patterson Park ♠	274b	39.17 N	76.35 W
Pattersonville	200	42.53 N	74.05 W
Patteson, Port C	165f	13.49 S	167.34 E
Patteson Passage ⊔	165f	15.26 S	168.12 E
Patti, Bhārat	113	31.17 N	74.51 E
Patti, Bhārat	114	25.55 N	82.12 E
Patti, It.	36	38.09 N	14.58 E
Patti, Golfo di C	36	38.12 N	15.05 E
Pattison, Miss., U.S.	184	31.53 N	90.53 W
Pattison, Tex., U.S.	212	29.49 N	95.60 W
Pattoki	113	31.01 N	73.51 E
Patton	204	40.38 N	78.39 W
Patton, Cape ≻	159	38.42 S	143.50 E
Patton Park ♠	271	42.19 N	83.10 W
Pattonsburg	184	40.03 N	94.08 W
Patton Seamount Group ✢[3]	16	55.30 N	149.30 W
Pattscheid	253	51.05 N	7.03 E
Pattukkottai	112	10.26 N	79.19 E
Pattullo, Mount Λ	170	56.14 N	129.39 W
Patu	240	6.06 S	37.38 W
Pātua	116	22.06 N	90.23 E
Patuākhāli	114	22.21 N	90.21 E
Patuca ≃	226	15.50 N	84.17 W
Patuca, Punta ≻	226	15.51 N	84.18 W
Patuha, Gunung Λ	105a	7.10 S	107.23 E
Pātul	262b	22.45 N	88.10 E
Pātuli, Bhārat	116	23.33 N	88.15 E
Pātuli, Bngl.	116	24.13 N	89.54 E
Patulul	226	14.25 N	91.10 W
Patumahoe	162	37.11 S	174.50 E
Pat'ung Kuan)(	90	23.30 N	121.01 E
Pātūr	112	20.27 N	76.56 E
Patusi	154	2.10 S	147.10 E
Patutu Λ	162	39.15 S	175.51 E
Patuxent ≃	198	38.18 N	76.25 W
Patuxent, Western Branch ≃	198	38.47 N	76.43 W
Patuxent River Naval Air Test Center ■	198	38.17 N	76.25 W
Patwāri	262a	28.35 N	77.27 E
Pátzcuaro	224	19.31 N	101.36 W
Pátzcuaro, Lago de ⊜	224	19.35 N	101.35 W
Patzicía	226	14.38 N	90.56 W
Patzig	50	54.28 N	13.24 E
Patzún	226	14.41 N	91.01 W
Pau	32	43.18 N	0.22 W
Pau, Gave de ≃	32	43.33 N	1.12 W
Pau Brasil	245	15.27 S	39.39 W
Paucarbamba	238	12.25 S	74.36 W
Paucarpata	238	16.26 S	71.30 W
Paucartambo	238	13.18 S	71.40 W
Paudalho	240	7.54 S	35.10 W
Pau d'Arco	240	7.30 S	49.22 W
Paudash Lake ⊜	202	44.58 N	78.04 W
Pau dos Ferros	240	6.07 S	38.10 W
Pauh	102	2.08 S	102.48 E
Pauhunri Λ	114	27.58 N	88.50 E
Pauini	238	7.40 S	66.58 W
Pauini ≃, Bra.	236	1.42 S	62.50 W
Pauini ≃, Bra.	238	7.47 S	67.05 W
Pauk	100	21.27 N	94.27 E
Pauksa Taung Λ	100	19.55 N	94.18 E
Paul	192	42.40 N	113.36 W
Paul, Lac à ⊜	176	49.52 N	70.46 W
Paula Lima	246	21.35 S	43.29 W
Paularo	58	46.32 N	13.07 E
Paulaya ≃	226	15.51 N	85.06 W
Paulding, Miss., U.S.	184	32.02 N	89.02 W
Paulding, Ohio, U.S.	206	41.08 N	84.35 W
Paulding □[6]	206	41.08 N	84.35 W
Paulding Bay C	9	66.35 S	123.00 E
Paulhan	32	43.32 N	3.27 E
Paulicéia	245	21.17 S	51.51 W
Paulina Peak Λ	192	43.41 N	121.15 W
Pauline, Mount Λ	172	53.33 N	119.54 W
Paulinenaue	50	52.40 N	12.43 E
Paulínia	246	22.45 S	47.10 W
Paulino Neves	240	2.43 S	42.33 W
Paulins Kill	200	41.03 N	74.49 W
Paulins Kill ≃	200	40.55 N	75.05 W
Paulinzella ⊥	50	50.42 N	11.06 E
Paulis → Isiro	144	2.47 N	27.37 E
Paulista	240	7.57 S	34.53 W
Paulistana	240	8.09 S	41.09 W
Paulistas	245	18.25 S	42.52 W
Paullina	188	42.59 N	95.41 W
Paull Lake ⊜	174	56.08 N	104.50 W
Paullo	56	45.25 N	9.24 E
Paulo Afonso	240	9.21 S	38.14 W
Paulo Afonso, Parque Nacional de ♠	240	9.20 S	38.12 W
Paulo de Faria	245	20.02 S	49.24 W
Paulo e Virginia, Gruta •[5]	277a	22.57 S	43.18 W
Pauloff Harbor (Pavlof Harbor)	170	54.27 N	162.42 W
Paulpietersburg	148	27.30 S	30.51 E
Paul Roux	148	28.18 S	27.59 E
Paulsboro	198	39.50 N	75.15 W
Pauls Cross Roads	198	37.52 N	76.53 W
Paul Seamount ✢[3]	14	18.30 N	172.30 W
Pauls Valley	186	34.44 N	97.13 W
Paulton	269b	40.34 N	79.34 W
Pāunān	262b	22.57 N	88.17 E
Paung	100	16.37 N	97.28 E
Paungbyin	100	24.16 N	94.49 E
Paungde	100	18.29 N	95.30 E
Paunggyi	100	17.19 N	96.11 E
Pauni	112	20.47 N	79.38 E
Paup	154	3.15 S	142.35 E
Paupack	200	41.24 N	75.14 W
Pauri, Bhārat	114	25.32 N	77.21 E
Pauri, Bhārat	114	30.09 N	78.47 E
Pausa, D.D.R.	50	50.35 N	12.00 E
Pausa, Perú	238	15.16 S	73.20 W
Pausania	36	40.55 N	9.06 E
Pausin	254a	52.38 N	13.03 E
Paute	236	2.47 S	78.50 W
Paute ≃	236	2.46 S	78.16 W
Pauto ≃	236	5.09 N	70.55 W
Pautou → Baotou	92	40.40 N	109.59 E
Pauwalu Point ≻	219a	20.52 N	156.08 W
Pauwela	219a	20.56 N	156.19 W
Pauwela Point ≻	219a	20.57 N	156.19 W
Pavai ◄[8]	262c	19.07 N	72.55 E
Pavai Lake ⊜	262c	19.07 N	72.55 E
Pavant Range ΛΛ	190	38.45 N	112.15 W
Pavda	76	59.15 N	59.30 E
Pāveh	118	35.03 N	46.22 E
Pavel'cevo	72	56.15 N	36.26 E
Pavelec	66	53.50 N	39.16 E
Paveleckij Vokzal ◄[5]	255b	55.44 N	37.38 E
Pavia	56	45.10 N	9.10 E
Pavia □[4]	56	45.07 N	9.08 E
Pavia, Naviglio di ≅	256b	45.27 N	9.11 E
Pavia di Udine	58	45.59 N	13.17 E
Pavilion, B.C., Can.	172	50.52 N	121.50 W
Pavilion, N.Y., U.S.	200	42.53 N	78.01 W
Pavilion Key ▮	210	25.42 N	81.22 W
Pavillion	190	43.15 N	108.42 W
Pavilly	46	49.34 N	0.58 E
Pāvilosta	66	56.53 N	21.14 E
Pavino	24	59.07 N	46.07 E
Pavione, Monte Λ	58	46.07 N	11.50 E
Pavlikeni	38	43.14 N	25.18 E
Pavliščevo, S.S.S.R.	72	55.34 N	35.59 E
Pavliščevo, S.S.S.R.	72	55.11 N	35.59 E
Pavlodar	76	52.18 N	76.57 E
Pavlof Bay C	170	55.30 N	161.32 W
Pavlof Volcano Λ[1]	170	55.24 N	161.52 W
Pavlograd	68	48.32 N	35.53 E
Pavlogradka	76	54.12 N	73.33 E
Pavlopol'	73	47.16 N	37.47 E
Pavlovka, S.S.S.R.	68	47.45 N	37.14 E
Pavlovka, S.S.S.R.	70	52.41 N	47.09 E
Pavlovka, S.S.S.R.	73	49.36 N	38.42 E
Pavlovka, S.S.S.R.	73	48.08 N	39.33 E
Pavlovka, S.S.S.R.	76	51.55 N	54.47 E
Pavlovka, S.S.S.R.	76	55.25 N	56.33 E
Pavlovo, S.S.S.R.	66	60.05 N	45.17 E
Pavlovo, S.S.S.R.	70	55.58 N	43.04 E
Pavlovo, S.S.S.R.	255a	59.56 N	30.40 E
Pavlovo, S.S.S.R.	255a	59.49 N	30.54 E
Pavlovsk, S.S.S.R.	66	59.41 N	30.27 E
Pavlovsk, S.S.S.R.	68	50.27 N	40.08 E
Pavlovsk, S.S.S.R.	76	53.20 N	82.59 E
Pavlovskaja	68	46.08 N	39.48 E
Pavlovskaja Sloboda	72	55.49 N	37.05 E
Pavlovskij, S.S.S.R.	70	57.50 N	54.51 E
Pavlovskij, S.S.S.R.	76	52.32 N	63.06 E
Pavlovskij Posad	72	55.47 N	38.40 E
Pavlyš	68	48.55 N	33.21 E
Pavne	262c	19.05 N	73.01 E
Pavo	182	30.57 N	83.45 W
Pavón	248	34.23 S	59.03 W
Pavón, Col.	236	3.37 N	72.15 W
Pavón, Arroyo ≃	248	34.30 S	57.05 W
Pavona	257a	41.43 N	12.37 E
Pavonia	204	40.49 N	82.26 W
Pavšino	255b	55.49 N	37.21 E
Pavšozero	66	60.38 N	35.34 E
Pavullo nel Frignano	58	44.20 N	10.50 E
Pavuna, Arroio ≃	277a	22.58 S	43.23 W
Pavuvu ▮	165e	9.03 S	159.06 E
Pavy	66	58.03 N	29.30 E
Pawai, Pulau ▮	261c	1.12 N	103.43 E
Pawan ≃	102	1.51 S	109.57 E
Pawāyan	114	28.04 N	80.06 E
Pawcatuck	197	41.22 N	71.52 W
Paw Creek	182	35.17 N	80.56 W
Päwesin	50	52.31 N	12.42 E
Pawhuska	186	36.40 N	96.20 W
Pawling	200	41.34 N	73.36 W
Pawnee, Ill., U.S.	209	39.35 N	89.35 W
Pawnee, Okla., U.S.	186	36.20 N	96.48 W
Pawnee ≃	188	38.10 N	99.06 W
Pawnee City	188	40.07 N	96.09 W
Pawnee Creek ≃	188	40.34 N	103.14 W
Pawnee Rock	188	38.16 N	99.01 W
Pawota	100	17.46 N	97.17 E
Pawpaw, Ill., U.S.	206	41.41 N	88.59 W
Paw Paw, Mich., U.S.	206	42.13 N	85.53 W
Paw Paw, W. Va., U.S.	178	39.32 N	78.27 W
Paw Paw ≃	206	42.07 N	86.29 W
Paw Paw Creek ≃	206	40.52 N	85.58 W
Paw Paw Lake	206	42.12 N	86.15 W
Paw Paw Lake ⊜	206	42.12 N	86.16 W
Pawtucket	197	41.53 N	71.23 W
Pawtucket Falls ∟	197	42.39 N	71.20 W
Paxoí ▮	38	39.12 N	20.12 E
Paxson	170	63.02 N	145.30 W
Paxton, Austl.	160	32.54 S	151.16 E
Paxton, Ill., U.S.	206	40.27 N	88.06 W
Paxton, Mass., U.S.	197	42.19 N	71.56 W
Paxton, Nebr., U.S.	188	41.07 N	101.21 W
Paxtonia	198	40.19 N	76.48 W
Paxtonville	198	40.46 N	77.05 W
Paya	226	15.37 N	85.17 W
Paya Besar	104	3.47 N	103.16 E
Payadapu	104	3.05 N	97.23 E
Payāgpur	114	27.25 N	81.48 E
Payagyi	100	17.29 N	96.32 E
Payakumbuh	102	0.14 S	100.38 E
Paya Lebar	261c	1.22 N	103.53 E
Paya Lebar Airport ⊠	261c	1.21 N	103.54 E
Payamlı	120	37.01 N	38.35 E
Payangan	105b	8.26 S	115.15 E
Payas	120	36.47 N	36.10 E
Payas, Cerro Λ	226	15.50 N	85.00 W
Payerne	54	46.49 N	6.56 E
Payeti	105b	9.41 S	120.20 E
Payette	192	44.05 N	116.56 W
Payette ≃	192	44.05 N	116.57 W
Payette, Middle Fork ≃	192	44.05 N	116.07 W
Payette, North Fork ≃	192	44.05 N	116.07 W
Payette, South Fork ≃	192	44.06 N	116.00 W
Payette Lake ⊜[1]	192	44.57 N	116.05 W
Paylampur	262b	22.47 N	88.16 E
Payne	206	41.05 N	84.44 W
Payne ≃	196	45.14 N	75.08 W
Payne, Bassin C	166	60.00 N	70.00 W
Payne, Lac ⊜	166	59.25 N	74.00 W
Payneham	158b	34.53 S	138.38 E
Paynes Creek ≃	194	40.16 N	122.11 W
Paynes Find	152	29.15 S	117.41 E
Paynesville, S. Afr.	263d	26.14 S	28.28 E
Paynesville, Minn., U.S.	188	45.23 N	94.43 W
Paynesville, Mo., U.S.	209	39.16 N	90.54 W
Paynetown State Recreation Area ♠	208	39.05 N	86.27 W
Paynton	174	53.01 N	108.56 W
Paysandú	242	32.19 S	58.05 W
Pays-Bas → Netherlands □[1]	30	52.15 N	5.30 W
Payson, Ariz., U.S.	190	34.14 N	111.20 W
Payson, Ill., U.S.	209	39.49 N	73.14 W
Payson, Utah, U.S.	190	40.03 N	111.44 W
Payún, Cerro Λ	242	36.30 S	69.18 W
Paz ≃	226	13.45 N	90.08 W
Paz, Cañada de la ≃	278	34.53 S	58.38 W
Paz, Ribeirão da ≃	240	9.14 S	52.01 W
Pazanji	112	10.41 N	76.04 E
Pazar, Tür.	120	41.11 N	40.53 E
Pazar, Tür.	120	40.17 N	36.18 E
Pazarcık, Tür.	120	37.31 N	37.19 E
Pazarcık, Tür.	120	40.00 N	29.54 E
Pazardžik	38	42.12 N	24.20 E
Pazarköy, Tür.	120	39.51 N	27.24 E
Pazarköy, Tür.	120	40.55 N	32.11 E
Pazarviran	120	38.41 N	36.11 E
Pazaryeri, Tür.	120	41.57 N	34.01 E
Pazaryeri, Tür.	120	38.05 N	28.14 E
Paz de Ariporo	236	5.53 N	71.54 W
Paz de Rio	236	5.59 N	72.47 W
Pazifischer Ozean → Pacific Ocean ⊤[1]	6	10.00 S	150.00 W
P'ažijeva Sel'ga	24	61.29 N	34.29 E
Pazin	36	45.14 N	13.56 E
Pazña	238	18.36 S	66.55 W
Paznaun ∨	54	47.03 N	10.20 E
Pčevža	66	59.23 N	32.20 E
Pčevža ≃	66	59.21 N	31.54 E
Pchery	50	50.10 N	14.08 E
Pe	100	13.28 N	98.31 E
Pea	164w	21.10 S	175.14 W
Pea ≃	184	31.01 N	85.51 W
Peabody, Kans., U.S.	188	38.10 N	97.07 W
Peabody, Mass., U.S.	197	42.32 N	70.55 W
Peace ≃, Can.	166	59.00 N	111.25 W
Peace ≃, Fla., U.S.	210	26.55 N	82.05 W
Peace Arch ⊥	214	49.00 N	122.45 W
Peace Bridge ◄[5]	274a	42.54 N	78.55 W
Peace Dale	197	41.27 N	71.30 W
Peacehaven	44	50.47 N	0.01 E
Peace River	172	56.14 N	117.17 W
Peach Creek	178	37.53 N	81.59 W
Peach Creek ≃, Tex., U.S.	212	30.07 N	95.10 W
Peach Creek ≃, Tex., U.S.	212	29.24 N	97.19 W
Peach Creek, Sandy Fork ≃	212	29.34 N	97.19 W
Peachdale	148	26.30 S	24.42 E
Peachland	172	49.46 N	119.44 W
Peach Springs	190	35.32 N	113.25 W
Peacock Hills ΛΛ[2]	166	66.05 N	110.45 W
Peacock Point ≻, Ont., Can.	202	42.47 N	79.59 W
Peacock Point ≻, Wake I.	164a	19.16 N	166.37 E
Peacock Sound ⊔	9	72.55 S	100.00 W
Pea Hill Branch ≃	274c	38.45 N	76.57 W
Peak Crossing	161a	27.47 S	152.44 E
Peak Dale	252	53.17 N	1.52 W
Peak District National Park ♠	28	53.17 N	1.45 W
Peake Creek ≃	152	28.05 S	136.07 E
Peaked Mountain Λ	176	46.34 N	68.49 W
Peak Forest	252	53.19 N	1.50 W
Peak Forest Canal ≅	252	53.29 N	2.06 W
Peak Hill, Austl.	152	25.38 S	118.43 E
Peak Hill, Austl.	156	32.44 S	148.12 E
Peakhurst	264a	33.58 S	151.04 E
Peakview	161b	36.04 S	149.24 E
Peäldoaivi Λ	24	69.11 N	26.36 E
Peale, Mount Λ	190	38.26 N	109.14 W
Peale Island ▮	164a	19.19 N	166.35 E
Peapack Brook ≃	266	40.41 N	74.39 W
Pearblossom	218	34.30 N	117.55 W
Pearce	190	31.54 N	109.49 W
Peard Bay C	170	70.[illegible] N	159.10 W
Pea Ridge Λ	208	38.25 N	83.36 W
Pea Ridge National Military Park ♠	184	36.29 N	94.06 W
Pearisburg	182	37.20 N	80.44 W
Pearl, Ill., U.S.	184	39.28 N	90.38 W
Pearl, Miss., U.S.	184	32.18 N	90.12 W
Pearl ≃	184	30.11 N	89.32 W
Pearl, Lake ⊜	273	42.04 N	71.21 W
Pearland	212	29.34 N	95.17 W
Pearl and Hermes Reef ✢[2]	14	27.55 N	175.45 W
Pearl Bank ✢[4]	106	5.49 N	119.42 E
Pearl Beach	204	42.37 N	82.35 W
Pearl City	219c	21.24 N	157.59 W
Pearl Creek ≃	188	44.15 N	98.08 W
Pearl Harbor C	219c	21.22 N	157.58 W
Pearl Harbor Naval Base ■	219c	21.21 N	157.57 W
Pearl Peak Λ	194	40.14 N	115.32 W
Pearl River, La., U.S.	184	30.23 N	89.45 W
Pearl River, N.Y., U.S.	200	41.04 N	74.02 W
Pearls Airport ⊠	231k	12.09 N	61.37 W
Pearns Point ≻	230c	17.05 N	61.54 W
Pearsall	186	28.53 N	99.06 W
Pearse Island ▮	172	54.51 N	130.21 W
Pearsoll Peak Λ	192	42.18 N	123.50 W
Pearson	182	31.18 N	82.51 W
Pearson Lake ⊜	174	56.15 N	97.15 W
Pearston	148	32.35 S	25.08 E
Peary Land ◄[1]	16	83.00 N	35.00 W
Pease ≃	186	34.12 N	99.07 W
Pease Air Force Base ■	178	43.06 N	70.49 W
Peaster	212	32.52 N	97.52 W
Pebane	144	17.10 S	38.08 E
Pebas	236	3.20 S	71.49 W
Pebble Beach	216	36.34 N	121.57 W
Pebble Island ▮	244	51.18 S	59.35 W
Peć	38	42.40 N	20.19 E
Pecan Bayou ≃	186	31.28 N	98.43 W
Pecangakan	105a	6.41 S	110.42 E
Pecan Gap	186	33.26 N	95.51 W
Peçanha	245	18.33 S	42.34 W
Peças, Ilha das ▮	242	25.26 S	48.19 W
Pecatonica	180	42.19 N	89.22 W
Pecatonica ≃	180	42.27 N	89.05 W

Symbol	English	Deutsch	Español	Français	Português
≃	River	Fluss	Río	Rivière	Rio
≅	Canal	Kanal	Canal	Canal	Canal
∟	Waterfall, Rapids	Wasserfall, Stromschnellen	Cascada, Rápidos	Chute d'eau, Rapides	Cascata, Rápidos
⊔	Strait	Meeresstrasse	Estrecho	Détroit	Estreito
C	Bay, Gulf	Bucht, Golf	Bahía, Golfo	Baie, Golfe	Baía, Golfo
⊜	Lake, Lakes	See, Seen	Lago, Lagos	Lac, Lacs	Lago, Lagos
☷	Swamp	Sumpf	Pantano	Marais	Pântano
⊼	Ice Features, Glacier	Eis- und Gletscherformen	Accidentes Glaciales	Formes glaciaires	Acidentes Glaciares
⊤	Other Hydrographic Features	Andere Hydrographische Objekte	Otros Elementos Hidrográficos	Autres données hydrographiques	Outros Elementos Hidrográficos

Symbol	English	Deutsch	Español	Français	Português
✢	Submarine Features	Untermeerische Objekte	Accidentes Submarinos	Formes de relief sous-marin	Acidentes Submarinos
□	Political Unit	Politische Einheit	Unidad Política	Entité politique	Unidade Política
⊍	Cultural Institution	Kulturelle Institution	Institución Cultural	Institution culturelle	Instituição Cultural
⊥	Historical Site	Historische Stätte	Sitio Histórico	Site historique	Sitio Histórico
♠	Recreational Site	Erholungs- und Ferienort	Sitio de Recreo	Centre de loisirs	Sítio de Lazer
⊠	Airport	Flughafen	Aeropuerto	Aéroport	Aeroporto
■	Military Installation	Militäranlage	Instalación Militar	Installation militaire	Instalação Militar
◄	Miscellaneous	Verschiedenes	Misceláneo	Divers	Miscelânea

ENGLISH: Name | Page | Lat.°′ | Long.°′
DEUTSCH: Name | Seite | Breite°′ | Länge°′ E=Ost

Symbols in the index entries represent the broad categories identified in the key at the right. Symbols with superior numbers (⛰[2]) identify subcategories (see complete key on page *I · 26*).

Kartensymbole in dem Registerverzeichnis stellen die rechts in Schlüssel erklärten Kategorien dar. Symbole mit hochgestellten Ziffern (⛰[2]) bezeichnen Unterabteilungen einer Kategorie (vgl. vollständiger Schlüssel auf Seite *I · 26*).

Los símbolos incluídos en el texto del índice representan las grandes categorias identificadas con la clave a la derecha. Los símbolos con numeros en su parte superior (⛰[2]) identifican las subcategorías (véase la clave completa en la página *I · 26*).

Les symboles de l'index représentent les catégories indiquées dans la légende à droite. Les symboles suivis d'un indice (⛰[2]) représentent des sous-catégories (voir légende complète à la page *I · 26*).

Os símbolos incluídos no texto do índice representam as grandes categorias identificadas com a chave à direita. Os símbolos com números em sua parte superior (⛰[2]) identificam as subcategorias (veja-se a chave completa à página *I · 26*).

	English	Deutsch	Español	Français	Português
Λ	Mountain	Berg	Montaña	Montagne	Montanha
⛰	Mountains	Berge	Montañas	Montagnes	Montanhas
)(	Pass	Pass	Paso	Col	Passo
∨	Valley, Canyon	Tal, Cañon	Valle, Cañón	Vallée, Canyon	Vale, Canhão
≚	Plain	Ebene	Llano	Plaine	Planície
≻	Cape	Kap	Cabo	Cap	Cabo
I	Island	Insel	Isla	Île	Ilha
II	Islands	Inseln	Islas	Îles	Ilhas
•	Other Topographic Features	Andere Topographische Objekte	Otros Elementos Topográficos	Autres données topographiques	Outros Elementos Topográficos

ESPAÑOL

Nombre	Página	Lat.°′	Long.°′ W=Oeste
Perijá, Sierra de ⋀	236	10.00 N	73.00 W
Perim → Barīm I	134	12.40 N	43.25 E
Peri-Mirim	240	2.38 S	44.54 W
Perinaldo	56	43.52 N	7.40 E
Peringat	104	6.02 N	102.17 E
Periperi de Poções	245	14.39 S	40.29 W
Periprava	38	45.24 N	29.32 E
Peristérion	257c	38.01 N	23.42 E
Perito Moreno	244	46.36 S	70.56 W
Peritoró	240	4.20 S	44.18 W
Perivale ◆[8]	250	51.32 N	0.19 W
Periyakulam	112	10.07 N	77.33 E
Periyār ≃	112	10.11 N	76.13 E
Periyār Lake ⊜	112	9.32 N	77.12 E
Perkam, Tanjung ≻	154	1.28 S	137.54 E
Perkasie	198	40.22 N	75.18 W
Perkins	186	35.58 N	97.02 W
Perkinsfield	202	44.42 N	79.57 W
Perkins Observatory ⊍[3]	204	40.14 N	83.02 W
Perkinston	184	30.47 N	89.08 W
Perkinsville, Ind., U.S.	208	40.09 N	85.52 W
Perkinsville, N.Y., U.S.	200	42.32 N	77.38 W
Perkiomen Creek ≃	198	40.07 N	75.28 W
Perkiomen Creek, East Branch ≃	198	40.15 N	75.27 W
Perkiomen Junction Pawling	275	40.21 N	75.28 W
Perkiomen Valley Airport ⊠	275	40.12 N	75.25 W
Perl	52	49.28 N	6.36 E
Perlas, Archipiélago de las II	236	8.25 N	79.00 W
Perlas, Laguna de C	226	12.30 N	83.40 W
Perlas, Punta de ≻	226	12.23 N	83.30 W
Perleberg	50	53.04 N	11.51 E
Perlez	38	45.12 N	20.24 E
Perlis □[3]	104	6.30 N	100.15 E
Perl'ovka	68	51.51 N	38.51 E
Perm'	76	58.00 N	56.15 E
Perm' □[4]	70	59.00 N	56.00 E
Permanente Creek ≃	272	37.25 N	122.05 W
Permas	24	59.20 N	45.34 E
Përmet	38	40.14 N	20.21 E
Permisi	70	54.06 N	45.48 E
Permskaja Oblast' □[4]	24	59.00 N	56.00 E
Pernambuco → Recife	240	8.03 S	34.54 W
Pernambuco □[3]	240	8.00 S	37.00 W
Pernate	256b	45.27 N	8.41 E
Pernatty Lagoon ⊜	156	31.31 S	137.14 E
Pernay	46	47.27 N	0.30 E
Pernes-les-Fontaines	56	44.00 N	5.03 E
Pernik	38	42.36 N	23.02 E
Pernink	50	50.20 N	12.45 E
Perniö	26	60.12 N	23.08 E
Pernovo	72	55.58 N	39.10 E
Pero	256b	45.31 N	9.05 E
Peroba, Ribeirão do ≃	277b	23.27 S	46.22 W
Perobas	246	22.46 S	42.47 W
Pérols, Étang de C	56	43.33 N	3.56 E
Peron, Cape ≻	158a	32.17 S	115.41 E
Péronne	46	49.56 N	2.56 E
Péronnes	46	50.26 N	4.08 E
Peron Peninsula ≻[1]	152	24.50 S	113.30 E
Pero Pinheiro	256c	38.51 N	9.20 W
Perosa Argentina	56	44.58 N	7.10 E
Perote	224	19.34 N	97.14 W
Perotó	238	14.50 S	64.31 W
Pérou → Peru □[1]	232	10.00 S	76.00 W
Pérouges	54	45.54 N	5.11 E
Peroulaz	56	45.42 N	7.19 E
Perovo ◆[8]	255b	55.44 N	37.46 E
Perow	172	54.31 N	126.26 W
Perpendicular, Point ≻	160	35.06 S	150.48 E
Perpignan	32	42.41 N	2.53 E
Perranporth	44	50.20 N	5.09 W
Perrault Falls	174	50.19 N	93.11 W
Perray ≃	251	48.31 N	1.42 E
Perrero	56	44.56 N	7.05 E
Perriers-sur-Andelle	46	49.25 N	1.22 E
Perrignier	54	46.18 N	6.27 E
Perrigny	54	46.40 N	5.35 E
Perrin	186	33.02 N	98.04 W
Perrine	210	25.36 N	80.21 W
Perrineville	198	40.14 N	74.27 W
Perris	218	33.47 N	117.14 W
Perris, Lake ⊜[1]	218	33.50 N	117.10 W
Perro, Laguna del ⊜	190	34.40 N	105.57 W
Perro, Punta del ≻	34	36.45 N	6.25 W
Perros ≃	224	16.20 N	94.59 W
Perros, Bahía de C	230p	22.25 N	78.30 W
Perros-Guirec	32	48.49 N	3.27 W
Perrot, Île I	196	45.22 N	73.57 W
Perry, Fla., U.S.	182	30.07 N	83.35 W
Perry, Ga., U.S.	182	32.27 N	83.44 W
Perry, Ill., U.S.	209	39.47 N	90.45 W
Perry, Iowa, U.S.	180	41.50 N	94.06 W
Perry, Kans., U.S.	188	39.05 N	95.24 W
Perry, Mich., U.S.	206	42.50 N	84.13 W
Perry, Mo., U.S.	209	39.26 N	91.40 W
Perry, N.Y., U.S.	200	42.43 N	78.00 W
Perry, Ohio, U.S.	204	41.46 N	81.09 W
Perry, Okla., U.S.	186	36.17 N	97.17 W
Perry, Tex., U.S.	212	31.25 N	96.55 W
Perry, Utah, U.S.	190	35.18 N	105.22 W
Perry □[6]	198	40.25 N	77.11 W
Perrydale	214	45.03 N	123.16 W
Perry Hall	198	39.25 N	76.28 W
Perry Heights	204	40.48 N	81.24 W
Perry-jōriku-kinenhi ⊥	84	35.14 N	139.43 E
Perry Lake ⊜[1]	188	39.20 N	95.30 W
Perrymont	269b	40.33 N	80.02 W
Perryopolis	204	40.05 N	79.45 W
Perry Park	208	38.33 N	85.00 W
Perrysburg, N.Y., U.S.	200	42.27 N	79.00 W
Perrysburg, Ohio, U.S.	204	41.33 N	83.38 W
Perry's Landing Monument ⊥	258	35.14 N	139.43 E
Perry's Victory and International Peace Memorial ⊥	204	41.33 N	82.50 W
Perrysville, Ohio, U.S.	204	40.40 N	82.19 W
Perrysville, Pa., U.S.	204	40.32 N	80.02 W
Perrysville, Pa., U.S.	269b	40.31 N	79.32 W
Perryton	186	36.24 N	100.48 W
Perryville, Alaska, U.S.	170	55.54 N	159.10 W
Perryville, Ark., U.S.	184	35.00 N	92.48 W
Perryville, Mo., U.S.	184	37.43 N	89.52 W
Perryville, N.Y., U.S.	200	43.01 N	75.48 W
Peršaj	66	54.02 N	26.41 E
Persan	46	49.09 N	2.16 E
Perșani, Munții ⋀	38	45.40 N	25.15 E
Persberg	40	59.45 N	14.15 E
Perşembe	120	41.04 N	37.46 E
Perseverance, Mount ∧	161a	27.25 S	152.10 E
Perseverancia	238	14.44 S	62.48 W
Pershagen	40	59.10 N	17.39 E
Pershing	208	39.49 N	85.08 W
Pershore	44	52.07 N	2.05 W
Pershyttan	40	59.30 N	15.00 E
Persia	188	41.34 N	95.35 W
Persia → Iran □[1]	118	32.00 N	53.00 E
Persian Gulf C	118	27.00 N	51.00 E
Pérsico, Golfo → Persian Gulf C	118	27.00 N	51.00 E
Persimmon Creek ≃	184	31.31 N	86.50 W

FRANÇAIS

Nom	Page	Lat.°′	Long.°′ W=Ouest
Persique, Golfe → Persian Gulf C	118	27.00 N	51.00 E
Persischer Golf → Persian Gulf C	118	27.00 N	51.00 E
Peršotravensk	68	50.12 N	27.39 E
Peršotravnevoje, S.S.S.R.	68	48.22 N	36.24 E
Peršotravnevoje, S.S.S.R.	68	51.24 N	28.53 E
Peršotravnevoje, S.S.S.R.	73	47.03 N	37.18 E
Perštejn	50	50.23 N	13.08 E
Perstorp	41	56.08 N	13.23 E
Pertandangan, Tanjung ≻	104	2.41 N	100.14 E
Pertang ≃	104	3.14 N	102.19 E
Pertek	120	38.50 N	39.22 E
Perth, Austl.	158a	31.56 S	115.50 E
Perth, Ont., Can.	202	44.54 N	76.15 W
Perth, Scot., U.K.	28	56.24 N	3.28 W
Perth, N.Y., U.S.	200	43.03 N	74.12 W
Perth □[6]	202	43.30 N	81.05 W
Perth Amboy	200	40.31 N	74.16 W
Perth-Andover	176	46.45 N	67.42 W
Perthes	54	48.39 N	4.49 E
Perth International Airport ⊠	158a	31.57 S	115.58 E
Perthois ◆[1]	54	48.40 N	4.45 E
Pertisau	58	47.26 N	11.42 E
Pertovo	70	54.22 N	41.31 E
Pertuis	56	43.41 N	5.30 E
Peru, Ill., U.S.	206	41.20 N	89.08 W
Peru, Ind., U.S.	206	40.45 N	86.04 W
Peru, Nebr., U.S.	188	40.29 N	95.44 W
Peru, N.Y., U.S.	178	44.35 N	73.32 W
Peru □[1]	232	10.00 S	76.00 W
Peruacu ≃	245	15.11 S	44.07 W
Peruc	50	50.19 N	13.59 E
Perugia	60	43.08 N	12.22 E
Perugia □[4]	60	43.03 N	12.33 E
Perugorria	242	29.20 S	58.37 W
Peruíbe	242	24.19 S	47.00 W
Peruípe ≃	245	17.43 S	39.16 W
Peruque Creek ≃	209	38.53 N	90.39 W
Perus ◆[8]	246	23.25 S	46.45 W
Perus ≃	277b	23.23 S	46.46 W
Perušić	36	44.39 N	15.23 E
Péruwelz	46	50.31 N	3.35 E
Pervaja Maja	76	48.55 N	67.25 E
Pervenchères	46	48.26 N	0.26 E
Pervesinka	70	52.13 N	43.15 E
Pervijze	46	51.05 N	2.47 E
Pervoavgustovskij	66	52.14 N	35.03 E
Pervoje Pole	170	63.05 N	179.19 W
Pervomajka, S.S.S.R.	73	49.09 N	37.58 E
Pervomajka, S.S.S.R.	76	51.17 N	70.08 E
Pervomajka ◆[8]	73	48.17 N	39.50 E
Pervomajsk, S.S.S.R.	68	48.04 N	30.52 E
Pervomajsk, S.S.S.R.	70	54.53 N	43.49 E
Pervomajsk, S.S.S.R.	73	49.05 N	39.37 E
Pervomajsk, S.S.S.R.	73	48.37 N	38.35 E
Pervomajsk, S.S.S.R.	76	57.59 N	94.12 E
Pervomajsk, S.S.S.R.	78	58.01 N	94.10 E
Pervomajskij, S.S.S.R.	24	64.26 N	40.47 E
Pervomajskij, S.S.S.R.	66	54.04 N	32.29 E
Pervomajskij, S.S.S.R.	66	53.54 N	25.23 E
Pervomajskij, S.S.S.R.	68	49.24 N	36.12 E
Pervomajskij, S.S.S.R.	70	53.15 N	40.18 E
Pervomajskij, S.S.S.R.	70	53.22 N	51.38 E
Pervomajskij, S.S.S.R.	70	51.22 N	48.54 E
Pervomajskij, S.S.S.R.	72	55.32 N	37.09 E
Pervomajskij, S.S.S.R.	72	54.03 N	37.32 E
Pervomajskij, S.S.S.R.	72	55.57 N	37.52 E
Pervomajskij, S.S.S.R.	73	47.58 N	38.47 E
Pervomajskij, S.S.S.R.	75	42.51 N	74.04 E
Pervomajskij, S.S.S.R.	76	54.52 N	61.08 E
Pervomajskij, S.S.S.R.	76	53.43 N	55.43 E
Pervomajskij, S.S.S.R.	76	59.29 N	61.24 E
Pervomajskij, S.S.S.R.	78	51.44 N	115.39 E
Pervomajskoje, S.S.S.R.	66	52.56 N	33.36 E
Pervomajskoje, S.S.S.R.	68	45.43 N	33.51 E
Pervomajskoje, S.S.S.R.	70	55.05 N	47.22 E
Pervomajskoje, S.S.S.R.	70	46.03 N	42.13 E
Pervomajskoje, S.S.S.R.	70	50.56 N	46.46 E
Pervomajskoje, S.S.S.R.	70	46.21 N	43.37 E
Pervomajskoje, S.S.S.R.	70	51.28 N	47.37 E
Pervomajskoje, S.S.S.R.	70	48.50 N	41.14 E
Pervomajskoje, S.S.S.R.	75	42.05 N	69.53 E
Pervomajskoje, S.S.S.R.	76	53.45 N	84.08 E
Pervomajskoje, S.S.S.R.	76	57.06 N	86.12 E
Pervoural'sk	76	56.54 N	59.58 E
Pervušino	70	58.02 N	41.56 E
Pervyj Kuril'skij Proliv)(	64	50.50 N	156.36 E
Perwenitz	254a	52.40 N	13.01 E
Pes'	66	58.55 N	34.19 E
Pes' ≃	66	59.08 N	35.18 E
Pesa ≃	60	43.44 N	11.01 E
Pes'akov, Ostrov I	24	68.47 N	57.35 E
Pesangrohan ≃	259e	6.11 S	106.45 E
Pesaro	60	43.54 N	12.55 E
Pesaro e Urbino □[4]	60	43.40 N	12.38 E
Pesca	236	5.33 N	73.03 W
Pescadero	216	37.15 N	122.23 W
Pescadero, Laguna C	224	22.12 N	105.20 W
Pescadero Creek ≃, Calif., U.S.	216	37.16 N	122.25 W
Pescadero Creek ≃, Calif., U.S.	216	36.42 N	121.17 W
Pescadores → P'enghu Liehtao II	90	23.30 N	119.30 E
Pescadores, Punta ≻, Méx.	222	23.46 N	109.43 W
Pescadores, Punta ≻, Perú	238	16.21 S	73.15 W
Pescaglia	60	43.58 N	10.25 E
Pesčanaja	68	48.08 N	29.44 E
Pesčanka, S.S.S.R.	68	48.12 N	28.53 E
Pesčanka, S.S.S.R.	70	51.18 N	43.40 E
Pesčanoje, S.S.S.R.	24	62.12 N	35.45 E
Pesčanoje, S.S.S.R.	68	49.44 N	31.50 E
Pesčanoje, S.S.S.R.	73	49.34 N	37.51 E
Pesčanoje, S.S.S.R.	76	53.01 N	76.19 E
Pesčanokopskoje	70	46.12 N	41.04 E
Pescantina	58	45.29 N	10.51 E
Pesčanyj	73	47.02 N	37.28 E
Pesčanyje, Ostrova II	73	46.52 N	38.17 E
Pescara	60	42.28 N	14.13 E
Pescara □[4]	60	42.20 N	13.57 E
Pescara ≃	60	42.28 N	14.13 E
Pescasseroli	60	41.48 N	13.47 E
Pesch	253	51.11 N	6.32 E
Pesch, Schloss ⊥	253	51.18 N	6.39 E

PORTUGUÊS

Nome	Página	Lat.°′	Long.°′ W=Oeste
Peschici	60	41.57 N	16.01 E
Peschiera del Garda	58	45.26 N	10.42 E
Peschio, Monte ∧	257a	41.43 N	12.46 E
Pescia	60	43.54 N	10.41 E
Pescina	60	42.02 N	13.39 E
Pescocostanzo	60	41.53 N	14.04 E
Pescolanciano	60	41.41 N	14.20 E
Pescorocchiano	60	42.12 N	13.09 E
Pesco Sannita	60	41.14 N	14.49 E
Pesé	226	7.54 N	80.37 W
Pesek, Pulau I	261c	1.17 N	103.41 E
Peseux	54	46.59 N	6.53 E
Peshastin	214	47.34 N	120.36 W
Peshastin Creek ≃	214	47.33 N	120.35 W
Peshāwar	113	34.01 N	71.33 E
Peshīn Jān	118	33.25 N	61.28 E
Peshkopi	38	41.41 N	20.26 E
Peshmāl	113	35.26 N	72.36 E
Peshtigo	180	45.03 N	87.45 W
Peshtigo ≃	180	44.58 N	87.40 W
Pesio ≃	56	44.28 N	7.53 E
Pesjane	72	56.01 N	38.48 E
Peski, S.S.S.R.	66	53.21 N	24.38 E
Peski, S.S.S.R.	68	50.23 N	33.27 E
Peski, S.S.S.R.	70	51.16 N	42.27 E
Peski, S.S.S.R.	72	55.13 N	38.46 E
Peški, S.S.S.R.	72	56.08 N	37.04 E
Peski, S.S.S.R.	73	49.26 N	38.59 E
Peski-Rad'kovskije	73	49.17 N	37.36 E
Peskovatskoje	72	54.03 N	36.16 E
Peskovka, S.S.S.R.	68	50.42 N	29.38 E
Peskovka, S.S.S.R.	76	59.04 N	52.22 E
Peškovo	73	47.02 N	39.24 E
Peškovo Grecovo	72	54.26 N	37.36 E
Peškovskoje	76	53.45 N	62.23 E
Pesmes	54	47.17 N	5.34 E
Pesočenskij	72	54.10 N	36.06 E
Pesočin	68	49.57 N	36.06 E
Pesočn'a	70	54.07 N	40.50 E
Pesočnoje, S.S.S.R.	66	53.20 N	27.06 E
Pesočnoje, S.S.S.R.	70	58.01 N	39.10 E
Pesočnyj	66	60.07 N	30.08 E
Peso da Régua	34	41.10 N	7.47 W
Pespire	226	13.35 N	87.22 W
Pesqueira	240	8.22 S	36.42 W
Pesquería	186	25.47 N	100.03 W
Pesquesía, Arroyo ≃	248	34.07 S	58.58 W
Pessac	32	44.48 N	0.38 W
Pessáni	120	41.05 N	26.06 E
Pessegueiros	246	22.18 S	42.58 W
Pessin	50	52.38 N	12.40 E
Pessinetto	56	45.17 N	7.24 E
Pest □[6]	30	47.25 N	19.20 E
Pest'aki	70	56.43 N	42.40 E
Peštera	38	42.02 N	24.18 E
Pesterzsébet ◆[8]	254c	47.26 N	19.07 E
Pesthidegkút ◆[8]	254c	47.34 N	18.58 E
Pestimre ◆[8]	254c	47.24 N	19.12 E
Pestlőrinc ◆[8]	254c	47.26 N	19.12 E
Pestovo, S.S.S.R.	66	58.36 N	35.48 E
Pestovo, S.S.S.R.	70	57.12 N	46.44 E
Pestovskoje Vodochranilišče ⊜[1]	72	56.06 N	37.40 E
Pestravka	70	52.24 N	49.58 E
Pestrecy	70	55.46 N	49.39 E
Pestrikovo	72	55.05 N	38.53 E
Pestújhely ◆[8]	254c	47.32 N	19.07 E
Petacalco, Bahía de C	224	17.57 N	102.05 W
Petah Tiqwa	122	32.05 N	34.53 E
Petäjävesi	26	62.15 N	25.12 E
Petal	184	31.21 N	89.17 W
Petalcingo	222	17.17 N	92.27 W
Petaling Jaya	104	3.05 N	101.39 E
Petalión, Kólpos C	38	37.59 N	24.02 E
Petaluma	216	38.14 N	122.39 W
Petaluma ≃	216	38.06 N	122.30 W
Pétange	52	49.34 N	5.52 E
Petare	236	10.29 N	66.49 W
Petatlán	224	17.31 N	101.16 W
Petatlán, Bahía de C	224	17.34 N	101.30 W
Petauke	144	14.15 S	31.20 E
Petawawa	180	45.54 N	77.17 W
Petawawa ≃	180	45.55 N	77.15 W
Pété	136	10.58 N	14.30 E
Petegem	46	50.58 N	3.32 E
Petén Itzá, Lago ⊜	222	16.59 N	89.50 W
Petenwell Dam ◆[6]	180	44.01 N	90.02 W
Petenwell Lake ⊜[1]	180	44.10 N	89.57 W
Peterboro	200	42.58 N	75.41 W
Peterborough, Austl.	156	32.58 S	138.50 E
Peterborough, Ont., Can.	202	44.18 N	78.19 W
Peterborough, Eng., U.K.	44	52.35 N	0.15 W
Peterborough, N.H., U.S.	178	42.53 N	71.57 W
Peterborough □[6]	202	44.33 N	78.15 W
Peterculter	28	57.05 N	2.16 W
Peterhead	28	57.30 N	1.49 W
Peter I Island I	9	68.47 S	90.35 W
Peter Island I	230m	18.22 N	64.35 W
Peter Lake ⊜, N.W. Ter., Can.	166	63.08 N	92.48 W
Peter Lake ⊜, Sask., Can.	174	57.15 N	103.53 W
Peterlee	42	54.46 N	1.19 W
Petermann Ranges ⋀	152	25.00 S	129.46 E
Peter Pond Lake ⊜	174	55.55 N	108.44 W
Peter Pond Lake Indian Reserve ◆[4]	174	55.55 N	109.00 W
Petersberg	52	50.33 N	9.43 E
Peters Brook ≃	266	40.33 N	74.37 W
Petersburg, Alaska, U.S.	170	56.50 N	132.59 W
Petersburg, Ill., U.S.	209	40.01 N	89.51 W
Petersburg, Mich., U.S.	206	41.54 N	83.43 W
Petersburg, Nebr., U.S.	188	41.51 N	98.05 W
Petersburg, N.J., U.S.	198	39.15 N	74.43 W
Petersburg, N.Y., U.S.	200	42.45 N	73.21 W
Petersburg, Ohio, U.S.	204	40.55 N	80.32 W
Petersburg, Pa., U.S.	204	40.34 N	78.03 W
Petersburg, Tenn., U.S.	184	35.19 N	86.38 W
Petersburg, Tex., U.S.	186	33.52 N	101.36 W
Petersburg, Va., U.S.	198	37.13 N	77.24 W
Petersburg, W. Va., U.S.	178	39.00 N	79.07 W
Petersburg National Battlefield ♠	198	37.14 N	77.22 W
Peters Canyon Reservoir ⊜[1]	270	33.47 N	117.45 W
Peters Creek ≃, Calif., U.S.	272	37.15 N	122.13 W
Peters Creek ≃, Pa., U.S.	269b	40.18 N	79.52 W
Peters Creek, Piney Fork ≃	269b	40.16 N	79.58 W
Petersdorf	50	54.29 N	11.04 E
Petersfield	44	51.00 N	0.56 W
Petershagen, B.R.D.	48	52.23 N	8.58 E
Petershagen, D.D.R.	50	52.24 N	14.20 E
Petershagen bei Berlin	50	52.31 N	13.46 E
Petersham, Austl.	264a	33.54 S	151.09 E
Petersham, Mass., U.S.	197	42.29 N	72.11 W
Peterskirchen	58	48.05 N	12.29 E
Peterson	188	42.55 N	95.21 W
Peters Pond ⊜	273	42.43 N	71.16 W
Peterswald Hill ∧[2]	152	26.43 S	123.39 E
Pétervására	30	48.01 N	20.06 E
Petilia Policastro	36	39.07 N	16.47 E
Pétionville	228	18.31 N	72.17 W
Petit	263d	26.06 S	28.22 E

Name	Page	Lat.°′	Long.°′
Petit Bois Island I	184	30.12 N	88.26 W
Petit-Bourg	231o	16.12 N	61.36 W
Petit-Canal	231o	16.23 N	61.29 W
Petitcodiac	176	45.56 N	65.10 W
Petitcodiac ≃	176	45.50 N	64.33 W
Petit Cul-de-Sac Marin C	231o	16.12 N	61.33 W
Petite-Cascapedia, Parc de la ♠	176	48.30 N	65.50 W
Petite-Nation, Rivière de la ≃	196	45.35 N	75.06 W
Petite Rivière de La Baleine ≃	166	56.00 N	76.45 W
Petite Rivière du Chêne ≃	196	46.34 N	72.02 W
Petite Rivière Noire, Piton de la ∧	147c	20.24 S	57.24 E
Petite Rivière Rouge ≃	196	45.45 N	75.00 W
Petite Sauldre ≃	46	47.27 N	2.05 E
Petite-Synthe	46	51.01 N	2.19 E
Petite Terre, Îles de la II	231o	16.10 N	61.07 W
Petit-Fort-Philippe	46	51.00 N	2.07 E
Petit-Goâve	228	18.26 N	72.52 W
Petit Havre C	231o	16.12 N	61.27 W
Petit Jean ≃	184	35.10 N	92.56 W
Petit Jean State Park ♠	184	35.06 N	92.57 W
Petit Lac du Nord ⊜	176	50.50 N	67.10 W
Petit Lac Nominingue ⊜	196	46.21 N	75.00 W
Petit Loango	142	2.16 S	9.35 E
Petit Loango, Parc National du ♠	142	2.15 S	9.36 E
Petit Mécatina, Île du I	176	50.33 N	59.20 W
Petit-Mecatina, Rivière du ≃	166	50.28 N	59.35 W
Petit Morin ≃	46	48.56 N	3.07 E
Petitot ≃	166	60.14 N	123.29 W
Petit Rhône ≃	56	43.27 N	4.24 E
Petit-Saint-Bernard, Col du)(	56	45.41 N	6.53 E
Petitsikapau Lake ⊜	166	54.45 N	66.25 W
Petit Trou, Point du ≻	231k	12.02 N	61.39 W
Petkeljärven Kansallispuisto ♠	24	62.35 N	31.12 E
Petkus	50	51.59 N	13.21 E
Petlād	110	22.28 N	72.48 E
Petlalcingo	224	18.05 N	97.54 W
Petnahor	257b	41.11 N	28.53 E
Petnjička Pećina •[5]	38	44.15 N	19.54 E
Peto	222	20.08 N	88.55 W
Petoh	104	2.53 N	103.15 E
Petone	162	41.13 S	174.52 E
Petorca	242	32.15 S	70.56 W
Petoskey	180	45.22 N	84.57 W
Petownikip Lake ⊜	174	52.56 N	92.02 W
Petra ⊥	122	30.20 N	35.26 E
Petralia Soprana	36	37.47 N	14.06 E
Petras, Mount ∧	9	75.52 S	128.38 W
Petre, Point ≻	202	43.50 N	77.09 W
Petrecovo	24	61.18 N	57.07 E
Petrella, Monte ∧	60	41.18 N	13.40 E
Petrella Salto	60	42.18 N	13.04 E
Petrella Tifernina	60	41.41 N	14.42 E
Petrič	38	41.24 N	23.13 E
Petrie	161a	27.16 S	152.59 E
Petrified Forest National Park ♠	190	34.55 N	109.49 W
Petrikov	68	52.08 N	28.30 E
Petrikovka	68	48.43 N	34.37 E
Petrila	38	45.27 N	23.25 E
Petrinja	36	45.26 N	16.17 E
Petriščevo, S.S.S.R.	72	55.30 N	36.18 E
Petriščevo, S.S.S.R.	72	54.37 N	36.57 E
Petrodvorec	66	59.53 N	29.54 E
Petrograd → Leningrad	66	59.55 N	30.15 E
Petrogrado-Doneckoje ◆[8]	73	48.42 N	38.41 E
Petrohanski prohod)(	38	43.08 N	23.08 E
Petrohué	244	41.08 S	72.25 W
Petrokrepost'	66	59.57 N	31.02 E
Petrolândia	240	9.05 S	38.18 W
Petrólea	236	8.30 N	72.35 W
Petroleum	206	40.37 N	85.09 W
Petrolia, Ont., Can.	204	42.52 N	82.09 W
Petrolia, Pa., U.S.	204	41.01 N	79.43 W
Petrolia, Tex., U.S.	186	34.01 N	98.14 W
Petrolina	240	9.24 S	40.30 W
Petrolina de Goiás	245	16.06 S	49.20 W
Petrominsk	24	64.47 N	38.25 E
Petrona, Punta ≻	230m	17.56 N	66.23 W
Petronila Creek ≃	186	27.32 N	97.32 W
Petropavlovka, S.S.S.R.	68	50.06 N	40.54 E
Petropavlovka, S.S.S.R.	68	48.27 N	36.26 E
Petropavlovka, S.S.S.R.	73	49.43 N	37.42 E
Petropavlovka, S.S.S.R.	78	50.38 N	105.19 E
Petropavlovsk, S.S.S.R.	76	56.20 N	57.09 E
Petropavlovsk, S.S.S.R.	76	54.54 N	69.06 E
Petropavlovskaja Krepost' ⊥	255a	59.57 N	30.19 E
Petropavlovsk-Kamčatskij	64	53.01 N	158.39 E
Petropavlovskoje, S.S.S.R.	76	52.06 N	85.06 E
Petropavlovskoje, S.S.S.R.	78	58.13 N	108.59 E
Petrópolis	246	22.31 S	43.10 W
Petros	182	36.06 N	84.26 W
Petroșani	38	45.25 N	23.22 E
Petro-Slav'anka	255a	59.48 N	30.31 E
Petroso, Monte ∧	60	41.44 N	13.55 E
Petroúpolis	257c	38.03 N	23.41 E
Petrovac	38	44.22 N	21.27 E
Petrovgrad → Zrenjanin	38	45.23 N	20.24 E
Petrovka, S.S.S.R.	68	46.54 N	30.44 E
Petrovka, S.S.S.R.	70	53.13 N	51.58 E
Petrovka, S.S.S.R.	73	48.53 N	39.52 E
Petrovka, S.S.S.R.	73	48.48 N	39.16 E
Petrovo, S.S.S.R.	66	58.22 N	35.09 E
Petrovo, S.S.S.R.	68	48.20 N	33.16 E
Petrovo, S.S.S.R.	72	55.00 N	38.08 E
Petrovo, S.S.S.R.	78	54.30 N	105.15 E
Petrovo-Dal'neje	255b	55.45 N	37.11 E
Petrovo-Krasnoselje ◆[8]	73	48.18 N	38.52 E
Petrovsk	70	52.19 N	45.23 E
Petrovskaja	68	45.25 N	37.57 E
Petrovskij, S.S.S.R.	70	50.45 N	41.59 E
Petrovskij, S.S.S.R.	70	56.39 N	40.19 E
Petrovskij, S.S.S.R.	72	54.29 N	36.59 E
Petrovskoje, S.S.S.R.	68	49.10 N	36.54 E
Petrovskoje, S.S.S.R.	70	52.39 N	40.15 E
Petrovskoje, S.S.S.R.	70	57.01 N	39.16 E
Petrovskoje, S.S.S.R.	72	55.32 N	36.59 E
Petrovskoje, S.S.S.R.	72	55.27 N	38.21 E
Petrovskoje, S.S.S.R.	73	48.18 N	38.52 E
Petrovskoje, S.S.S.R.	255b	55.36 N	37.53 E
Petrovsko-Razumovskoje ◆[8]	255b	55.50 N	37.34 E
Petrovsk-Zabajkal'skij	78	51.17 N	108.50 E
Petrov Val	70	50.09 N	45.12 E
Petrozavodsk	24	61.47 N	34.20 E
Petrozsény → Petroșani	38	45.25 N	23.22 E
Petru I, Pam'atnik ⊥	255a	59.56 N	30.18 E
Petrun'	24	66.28 N	60.43 E
Petrusburg	148	29.08 S	25.27 E

Name	Page	Lat.°′	Long.°′
Petrušino	255a	59.48 N	30.50 E
Petrus Steyn	148	27.38 S	28.08 E
Petrusville	148	30.05 S	24.41 E
Petschora → Pečora ≃	24	68.13 N	54.15 E
Petten	48	52.45 N	4.39 E
Petteril ≃	42	54.54 N	2.55 W
Petticoat Creek ≃	265b	43.48 N	79.06 W
Pettisville	206	41.32 N	84.14 W
Pettneu am Arlberg	54	47.09 N	10.20 E
Pettus	186	28.37 N	97.48 W
Petty Harbour	176	47.28 N	52.43 W
Petty Island I	275	39.58 N	75.07 W
Petua	262b	22.25 N	88.27 E
Petuchovo	76	55.06 N	67.58 E
Petuški	70	55.55 N	39.28 E
Petworth	44	50.59 N	0.38 W
Petzow	254a	52.21 N	12.56 E
Peudada	104	5.12 N	96.35 E
Peuerbach	30	48.21 N	13.56 E
Peuetsagoe, Gunung ∧	104	4.55 N	96.20 E
Peumo	242	34.24 S	71.10 W
Peureulak	104	4.48 N	97.53 E
Peureulak ≃	104	4.54 N	97.53 E
Peureulak, Ujung ≻	104	4.54 N	97.54 E
Peusangan ≃	104	5.16 N	96.51 E
Peusangan, Ujung ≻	104	5.18 N	96.50 E
Pevek	64	69.42 N	170.17 E
Pevely	209	38.17 N	90.24 W
Pevensey	44	50.49 N	0.20 E
Pevensey Levels ☷	44	50.50 N	0.20 E
Peveragno	56	44.20 N	7.37 E
Pewamo	206	43.00 N	84.51 W
Pewaukee	206	43.05 N	88.16 W
Pewaukee Lake ⊜	206	43.04 N	88.19 W
Pewee Valley	208	38.19 N	85.29 W
Pews Creek ≃	266	40.27 N	74.06 W
Pewsey	44	51.21 N	1.46 W
Pewsey, Vale of ∨	44	51.20 N	1.48 W
Pewsum	48	53.26 N	7.05 E
Péyia	120	34.53 N	32.23 E
Peykjahlid	24a	65.40 N	16.50 W
Peyrolles-en-Provence	56	43.39 N	5.35 E
Peyruis	56	44.02 N	5.56 E
Peza ≃	24	65.36 N	44.35 E
Pezas	76	54.39 N	87.46 E
Pezawa Taung ∧	100	19.33 N	94.31 E
Pézenas	32	43.27 N	3.25 E
Pežemga	66	59.10 N	44.16 E
Pezinok	30	48.18 N	17.17 E
Pezu	113	32.19 N	70.44 E
Pezzana	56	45.16 N	8.29 E
Pfäfers	54	46.59 N	9.30 E
Pfaffenhausen	54	48.07 N	10.27 E
Pfaffenhofen an der Ilm	30	48.31 N	11.30 E
Pfaffenhoffen	52	48.51 N	7.37 E
Pfaffenöden ∧[2]	254b	48.04 N	16.33 E
Pfäffikersee ⊜	54	47.21 N	8.48 E
Pfäffikon, Schw.	54	47.12 N	8.46 E
Pfäffikon, Schw.	54	47.22 N	8.47 E
Pfaffnau	54	47.14 N	7.54 E
Pfaffstätten	254b	48.01 N	16.16 E
Pfalz □[5]	52	49.20 N	8.00 E
Pfalzdorf	48	51.42 N	6.11 E
Pfalzel	52	49.47 N	6.41 E
Pfälzer Wald, Naturpark ♠	52	49.15 N	7.50 E
Pfänder ∧	54	47.30 N	9.47 E
Pfarrkirchen	30	48.27 N	12.56 E
Pfarrweisach	52	50.09 N	10.44 E
Pfastatt	54	47.47 N	7.18 E
Pfaueninsel, Schloss ⊥	254a	52.26 N	13.07 E
Pfeddersheim	52	49.38 N	8.16 E
Pfeiffer-Big Sur State Park ♠	216	36.15 N	121.47 W
Pferderennbahn ♠	253	51.31 N	7.32 E
Pflugerville	212	30.26 N	97.37 W
Pförten → Brody	30	51.45 N	14.45 E
Pforzen	54	47.55 N	10.37 E
Pforzheim	52	48.54 N	8.42 E
Pfrimm ≃	52	49.39 N	8.22 E
Pfronten	54	47.34 N	10.33 E
Pfuhl	54	48.24 N	10.02 E
Pfullendorf	54	47.55 N	9.15 E
Pfullingen	54	48.28 N	9.13 E
Pfunds	54	46.58 N	10.33 E
Pfungstadt	52	49.48 N	8.36 E
Pfyn	54	47.36 N	8.57 E
Phachi ≃	100	13.56 N	99.24 E
Phaéton, Port C	164s	17.44 S	149.21 W
Phagwāra	113	31.14 N	75.46 E
Phala	146	23.45 S	26.57 E
Phalaborwa	146	23.55 S	31.13 E
Phalanx	204	41.15 N	80.58 W
Phalempin	46	50.31 N	3.01 E
Phālia	113	32.26 N	73.35 E
Phalodi	110	27.08 N	72.22 E
Phalsbourg	52	48.46 N	7.16 E
Phaltan	112	17.59 N	74.26 E
Phalti	262b	22.46 N	88.34 E
Phan	100	19.28 N	99.43 E
Phanat Nikhom	100	13.27 N	101.11 E
Phangan, Ko I	100	9.45 N	100.04 E
Phang Hoei, Khao ∧	100	15.15 N	101.23 E
Phangnga	100	8.28 N	98.32 E
Phaniang ≃	100	16.49 N	102.24 E
Phanom Dongrak, Thiu Khao ⋀	100	14.25 N	103.30 E
Phanom Thuan	100	14.07 N	99.42 E
Phan-rang	100	11.34 N	108.59 E
Phan-thiet	100	10.56 N	108.06 E
Phan Thong	100	13.28 N	101.06 E
Phantom Lake	206	42.52 N	88.21 W
Pharenda	114	27.06 N	83.17 E
Phariāro	110	27.12 N	68.59 E
Pharr	186	26.12 N	98.11 W
Phasi Charoen	259a	13.43 N	100.26 E
Phasi Charoen, Khlong ⩳	259a	13.44 N	100.30 E
Phat-diem	100	20.06 N	106.06 E
Phato	100	9.48 N	98.48 E
Phatthalung	100	7.37 N	100.05 E
Phayao	100	19.10 N	99.55 E
Pheasant Creek ≃	174	50.35 N	103.28 W
Pheba	184	33.35 N	88.57 W
Phelan	218	34.25 N	117.34 W
Phelps, N.Y., U.S.	200	42.57 N	77.03 W
Phelps, Tex., U.S.	212	30.42 N	95.27 W
Phelps, Wis., U.S.	180	46.04 N	89.05 W
Phelps Lake ⊜	182	35.46 N	76.27 W
Phenix City	182	32.29 N	85.01 W
Phet Buri	100	13.06 N	99.57 E
Phet Buri ≃	100	13.13 N	99.59 E
Phetchabun	100	16.25 N	101.08 E
Phetchabun, Thiu Khao ⋀	100	16.20 N	100.55 E
Phibun Mangsahan	100	15.14 N	105.14 E
Phichai	100	17.17 N	100.05 E
Phichit	100	16.26 N	100.22 E
Philadelphia, S. Afr.	148	33.40 S	18.36 E
Philadelphia, Ill., U.S.	209	39.58 N	90.07 W
Philadelphia, Miss., U.S.	184	32.46 N	89.07 W
Philadelphia, Mo., U.S.	209	39.50 N	91.44 W
Philadelphia, N.Y., U.S.	202	44.09 N	75.43 W
Philadelphia, Pa., U.S.	198, 275	39.57 N	75.07 W
Philadelphia, Tenn., U.S.	182	35.41 N	84.24 W
Philadelphia □[6]	275	39.57 N	75.07 W
Philadelphia International Airport ⊠	198	39.53 N	75.14 W

Name	Page	Lat.°′	Long.°′
Philadelphia Naval Shipyard ▪	275	39.53 N	75.11 W
Philae ⊥	130	24.01 N	32.53 E
Phil Campbell	184	34.21 N	87.42 W
Philip	188	44.02 N	101.40 W
Philipp	184	33.45 N	90.12 W
Philippeville → Skikda, Alg.	138	36.50 N	6.58 E
Philippeville, Bel.	46	50.12 N	4.32 E
Philippi	178	39.09 N	80.02 W
Philippi, Lake ⊜	156	24.22 S	139.00 E
Philippi Glacier ⍓	9	66.45 S	88.20 E
Philippine Basin ✢[1]	14	18.00 N	133.00 E
Philippinen → Philippines □[1]	106	13.00 N	122.00 E
Philippines □[1]	98, 106	13.00 N	122.00 E
Philippines, University of the ⊍[2]	259f	14.39 N	121.04 E
Philippine Sea ⊤[2]	14	20.00 N	135.00 E
Philippolis	148	30.19 S	25.13 E
Philippopolis → Plovdiv	38	42.09 N	24.45 E
Philippsthal	254a	52.20 N	13.09 E
Philipsburg, Qué., Can.	196	45.02 N	73.05 W
Philipsburg, Ned. Ant.	228	17.59 N	63.10 W
Philipsburg, Mont., U.S.	192	46.20 N	113.18 W
Philipsburg, Pa., U.S.	204	40.53 N	78.05 W
Philipsburg Manor ⊥	266	41.05 N	73.52 W
Philipse Manor ⊥	266	40.56 N	73.54 W
Philip Smith Mountains ⋀	170	68.30 N	148.00 W
Philipstown	148	30.26 S	24.29 E
Phillaur	113	31.01 N	75.47 E
Phillip Island I	159	38.29 S	145.14 E
Phillips, Maine, U.S.	178	44.49 N	70.21 W
Phillips, Tex., U.S.	186	35.42 N	101.22 W
Phillips, Wis., U.S.	180	45.41 N	90.24 W
Phillipsburg, Kans., U.S.	188	39.45 N	99.19 W
Phillipsburg, N.J., U.S.	200	40.42 N	75.12 W
Philmont	200	42.15 N	73.39 W
Philo, Ill., U.S.	184	40.01 N	88.09 W
Philo, Ohio, U.S.	178	39.52 N	81.55 W
Philomath	192	44.32 N	123.22 W
Philpots Island I	166	74.48 N	80.00 W
Phimai	100	15.13 N	102.30 E
Phinga	262b	22.41 N	88.25 E
Phitsanulok	100	16.50 N	100.15 E
Phnom Penh → Phnum Pénh	100	11.33 N	104.55 E
Phnum Pénh	100	11.33 N	104.55 E
Phnum Tbêng Méanchey	100	13.49 N	104.58 E
Pho ≃	114	27.41 N	89.53 E
Phoenicia	200	42.05 N	74.19 W
Phoenix, Ariz., U.S.	190	33.27 N	112.05 W
Phoenix, Ill., U.S.	268	41.37 N	87.38 W
Phoenix, Md., U.S.	198	39.31 N	76.37 W
Phoenix, N.Y., U.S.	200	43.14 N	76.18 W
Phoenix I[1]	14	3.43 S	170.43 W
Phoenix Islands II	14	4.00 S	172.00 W
Phoenix Lake ⊜[1]	272	37.57 N	122.35 W
Phoenix Trough ✢[1]	14	6.00 S	172.30 W
Phoenixville	198	40.08 N	75.31 W
Phon	100	15.49 N	102.36 E
Phong ≃	100	16.23 N	102.56 E
Phôngsali	100	21.41 N	102.06 E
Phong Saly □[4]	92	21.40 N	102.05 E
Phong-tho	100	22.32 N	103.21 E
Phon Phisai	100	18.01 N	103.05 E
Phrae	100	18.09 N	100.08 E
Phra Khanong ◆[8]	259a	13.42 N	100.35 E
Phra Nakhon → Krung Thep	100	13.45 N	100.31 E
Phra Nakhon Si Ayutthaya	100	14.21 N	100.33 E
Phran Kratai	100	16.40 N	99.36 E
Phrao	100	19.22 N	99.13 E
Phra Phutthabat	100	14.43 N	100.48 E
Phra Pradaeng	259a	13.40 N	100.32 E
Phra Rop, Khao ∧	100	13.11 N	99.31 E
Phrom Phiram	100	17.02 N	100.12 E
Phsar Réam	100	10.30 N	103.37 E
Phu-cat	100	14.01 N	109.03 E
Phu-cuong	100	10.58 N	106.39 E
Phu-huu, Viet.	100	18.58 N	105.31 E
Phu-huu, Viet.	259c	10.43 N	106.47 E
Phuket	100	7.53 N	98.24 E
Phuket, Ko I	100	8.00 N	98.22 E
Phularwān	113	32.22 N	73.00 E
Phulbari	116	21.52 N	88.08 E
Phulbāria	116	23.22 N	89.50 E
Phuljhuri	116	22.12 N	90.04 E
Phulkusma	116	22.43 N	86.52 E
Phu-loc	100	16.16 N	107.53 E
Phūlpur	114	25.33 N	82.06 E
Phulra	113	34.20 N	73.03 E
Phultala	116	22.59 N	89.28 E
Phu-ly	100	20.32 N	105.56 E
Phum Duang ≃	100	9.10 N	99.20 E
Phumĭ Bâ Khăm	100	13.51 N	107.22 E
Phumĭ Banam	100	11.19 N	105.18 E
Phumĭ Béng	100	13.05 N	104.18 E
Phumĭ Châmbák	100	11.14 N	104.49 E
Phumĭ Chângho Ândêng	100	12.39 N	104.35 E
Phumĭ Chhuk	100	10.50 N	104.28 E
Phumĭ Chruŏy Slêng	100	13.14 N	105.57 E
Phumĭ Dăk Dăm	100	12.20 N	107.21 E
Phumĭ Kâmpóng Srâlau	100	14.05 N	105.46 E
Phumĭ Kâmpóng Trâbâk	100	13.06 N	105.14 E
Phumĭ Kântuŏt Sâmraông	100	14.12 N	104.37 E
Phumĭ Kaôh Kért	100	13.47 N	104.32 E
Phumĭ Kaôh Kŏng	100	11.26 N	103.11 E
Phumĭ Khpôb	100	11.02 N	105.12 E
Phumĭ Krĕk	100	11.46 N	105.56 E
Phumĭ Lvéa Kraôm	100	13.21 N	102.54 E
Phumĭ Moŭng	100	13.45 N	103.33 E
Phumĭ Narŭng	100	13.53 N	105.34 E
Phumĭ Phnum Srâlau	100	11.03 N	103.42 E
Phumĭ Prêk Kák	100	12.15 N	105.32 E
Phumĭ Prêk Sândêk	100	11.51 N	105.22 E
Phumĭ Prey Toch	100	12.54 N	103.23 E
Phumĭ Puŏk Chăs	100	13.26 N	103.44 E
Phumĭ Rôluŏs Chăs	100	13.19 N	104.00 E
Phumĭ Sâmraông	100	14.11 N	103.31 E
Phumĭ Spœ Tbong	100	12.20 N	105.19 E
Phumĭ Srê Kôkir	100	13.08 N	106.04 E
Phumĭ Srê Rônéam	100	12.16 N	106.25 E
Phumĭ Tbêng	100	13.35 N	104.55 E
Phumĭ Thalabârĭvăt	100	13.33 N	105.57 E
Phumĭ Thmâ Pôk	100	13.57 N	103.04 E
Phumĭ Tnaôt	100	12.56 N	104.34 E
Phumĭ Tœk Choŭ	100	13.36 N	103.24 E
Phu-my	100	14.10 N	109.03 E
Phung-hiep	100	9.49 N	105.50 E
Phuntsholing	114	26.53 N	89.23 E
Phuoc-binh	100	11.50 N	106.58 E
Phuoc Khanh	259c	10.40 N	106.48 E
Phuoc-le	98	10.30 N	107.10 E
Phuoc-long	100	9.26 N	105.28 E
Phuoc-long-xa	259c	10.49 N	106.46 E
Phuoc-luong	259c	10.45 N	106.48 E
Phu-quoc, Dao I	100	10.12 N	104.00 E
Phurphura	262b	22.44 N	88.08 E
Phu-tho	100	21.24 N	105.13 E
Phu-tho-hoa	259c	10.46 N	106.38 E
Phu Tho Race Track ♠	259c	10.46 N	106.40 E
Phutthaisong	100	15.32 N	103.01 E
Phu-vang	100	16.31 N	107.37 E
Phu-vinh	100	9.56 N	106.20 E
Phu-yen	100	21.16 N	104.39 E

≃ River	Fluss	Río	Rivière	Rio
⩳ Canal	Kanal	Canal	Canal	Canal
⌊ Waterfall, Rapids	Wasserfall, Stromschnellen	Cascada, Rápidos	Chute d'eau, Rapides	Cascata, Rápidos
)(Strait	Meeresstrasse	Estrecho	Détroit	Estreito
C Bay, Gulf	Bucht, Golf	Bahía, Golfo	Baie, Golfe	Baía, Golfo
⊜ Lake, Lakes	See, Seen	Lago, Lagos	Lac, Lacs	Lago, Lagos
☷ Swamp	Sumpf	Pantano	Marais	Pântano
⍓ Ice Features, Glacier	Eis- und Gletscherformen	Accidentes Glaciales	Formes glaciaires	Acidentes Glaciares
⊤ Other Hydrographic Features	Andere Hydrographische Objekte	Otros Elementos Hidrográficos	Autres données hydrographiques	Outros Elementos Hidrográficos

✢ Submarine Features	Untermeerische Objekte	Accidentes Submarinos	Formes de relief sous-marin	Acidentes Submarinos
□ Political Unit	Politische Einheit	Unidad Política	Entité politique	Unidade Política
⊍ Cultural Institution	Kulturelle Institution	Institución Cultural	Institution culturelle	Instituição Cultural
⊥ Historical Site	Historische Stätte	Sitio Histórico	Site historique	Sitio Histórico
♠ Recreational Site	Erholungs- und Ferienort	Sitio de Recreo	Centre de loisirs	Sítio de Lazer
⊠ Airport	Flughafen	Aeropuerto	Aéroport	Aeroporto
▪ Military Installation	Militäranlage	Instalación Militar	Installation militaire	Instalação Militar
◆ Miscellaneous	Verschiedenes	Misceláneo	Divers	Miscelânea

Symbols in the index entries represent the broad categories identified in the key at the right. Symbols with superior numbers (∧2) identify subcategories (see complete key on page I · 26).

Kartensymbole in dem Registerverzeichnis stellen die rechts in Schlüssel erklärten Kategorien dar. Symbole mit hochgestellten Ziffern (∧2) bezeichnen Unterabteilungen einer Kategorie (vgl. vollständiger Schlüssel auf Seite I · 26).

Los símbolos incluidos en el texto del índice representan las grandes categorías identificadas con la clave a la derecha. Los símbolos con números en su parte superior (∧2) identifican las subcategorías (véase la clave completa en la página I · 26).

Les symboles de l'index représentent les catégories indiquées dans la légende à droite. Les symboles suivis d'un indice (∧2) représentent des sous-catégories (voir légende complète à la page I · 26).

Os símbolos incluídos no texto do índice representam as grandes categorias identificadas com a chave à direita. Os símbolos com números em sua parte superior (∧2) identificam as subcategorias (veja-se a chave completa à página I · 26).

∧ Mountain	Berg	Montaña	Montagne	Montanha
∧ Mountains	Berge	Montañas	Montagnes	Montanhas
)(Pass	Pass	Paso	Col	Passo
∨ Valley, Canyon	Tal, Cañon	Valle, Cañón	Vallée, Canyon	Vale, Canhão
≃ Plain	Ebene	Llano	Plaine	Planície
≻ Cape	Kap	Cabo	Cap	Cabo
I Island	Insel	Isla	Île	Ilha
II Islands	Inseln	Islas	Îles	Ilhas
◆ Other Topographic Features	Andere Topographische Objekte	Otros Elementos Topográficos	Autres données topographiques	Outros Elementos Topográficos

ESPAÑOL
Nombre | Página | Lat.°' | Long.°' W=Oeste

Pintos, Arroyo de ≃ 248 33.55 S 56.51 W
Pintos Negreiros 246 22.18 S 45.13 W
Pintoyacu ≃ 236 3.35 S 73.55 W
Pinturas ≃ 244 46.35 S 70.18 W
Pintuyan 106 9.57 N 125.15 E
Pin'ug 24 60.15 N 47.48 E
Pinukpuk 106 17.35 N 121.22 E
Pinwherry 42 55.09 N 4.50 W
Pinxton 44 53.06 N 1.19 W
Pinzano al Tagliamento 58 46.11 N 12.57 E
Pinzgau ∨ 58 47.15 N 12.40 E
Pinzón, Isla I 236a 0.36 S 90.40 W
Piobbico 60 43.35 N 12.31 E
Pioche 194 37.56 N 114.27 W
Pio IX 240 6.50 S 40.37 W
Piolenc 56 44.11 N 4.46 E
Piombino 60 42.55 N 10.32 E
Piombino, Canale di Ʊ 60 42.53 N 10.30 E
Pioneer, Austl. 152 31.48 S 121.43 E
Pioneer, Calif., U.S. 216 38.25 N 120.33 W
Pioneer, Ohio, U.S. 206 41.41 N 84.33 W
Pioneer Mine 172 50.46 N 122.46 W
Pioneer Mountains ∧∧ 192 45.40 N 113.00 W
Pioneer Park ♠ 263d 26.10 S 28.04 E
Pioner, Ostrov I 64 79.50 N 92.30 E
Pionerskij [Neukuhren] 66 54.57 N 20.20 E
Pionierbivak 154 2.16 S 138.02 E
Pionki 30 51.30 N 21.27 E
Pio Pico State Historical Park ♠ 270 33.59 N 118.04 W
Piopio 162 38.28 S 175.01 E
Piora, Mount ∧ 154 6.45 S 146.00 E
Pioraco 60 43.11 N 12.59 E
Piorini ≃ 236 3.23 S 63.30 W
Piorini, Lago ⊜ 236 3.34 S 63.15 W
Piotrków Trybunalski 30 51.25 N 19.42 E
Piotta 54 46.31 N 8.40 E
Pio V. Corpus (Limbujan) 106 11.53 N 124.03 E
Piove di Sacco 58 45.18 N 12.02 E
Piovene-Rocchette 58 45.45 N 11.25 E
Pio XII 240 3.53 S 45.17 W
Pipa 97 29.07 N 105.05 E
Pipalkoti 114 30.26 N 79.27 E
Pīpār 110 26.23 N 73.32 E
Piparia 114 22.45 N 78.21 E
Pīpar Road 110 26.27 N 73.27 E
Pipas 142 14.56 S 12.12 E
Pipe Creek ≃, Ind., U.S. 184 40.08 N 85.52 W
Pipe Creek ≃, Ind., U.S. 206 40.45 N 86.13 W
Pipe Creek ≃, Ind., U.S. 208 39.26 N 85.06 W
Piper City 206 40.45 N 88.11 W
Pipe Spring National Monument ♠ 190 36.43 N 112.33 W
Pipestem Creek ≃ 188 46.54 N 98.43 W
Pipestone 188 43.58 N 96.19 W
Pipestone ≃ 166 52.53 N 89.23 W
Pipestone Creek ≃, Can. 174 49.42 N 100.45 W
Pipestone Creek ≃, Mich., U.S. 206 42.04 N 86.24 W
Pipestone National Monument ♠ 188 44.00 N 96.18 W
Pipi ≃ 136 7.27 N 22.48 E
Pipinas 248 35.32 S 57.20 W
Piping Brook ≃ 266 41.08 N 73.37 W
Pipiriki 162 39.29 S 175.03 E
Piplān 113 32.17 N 71.21 E
Piplūn 116 23.21 N 88.07 E
Pipmouacane, Réservoir ⊜[1] 176 49.35 N 70.30 W
Pipri 114 23.58 N 82.40 E
Pipriac 28 47.49 N 1.57 W
Piqiang 75 40.20 N 77.38 E
Piqiao 96 31.34 N 119.27 E
Piqua 208 40.09 N 84.15 W
Piquet Carneiro 240 5.48 S 39.25 W
Piquete 246 22.36 S 45.11 W
Piquete, Ribeirão ≃ 246 22.36 S 45.01 W
Piquiri ≃, Bra. 238 17.23 S 55.38 W
Piquiri ≃, Bra. 242 24.03 S 54.14 W
Pira 140 8.30 N 1.44 E
Piracaia 246 23.03 S 46.21 W
Piracanjuba 245 17.18 S 49.01 W
Piracanjuba ≃, Bra. 245 18.14 S 48.48 W
Piracanjuba ≃, Bra. 245 17.18 S 48.13 W
Piracão ≃ 277a 23.02 S 43.36 W
Piracicaba 245 22.43 S 47.38 W
Piracicaba ≃ 245 22.36 S 48.19 W
Piracuruca 240 3.56 S 41.42 W
Piraeus → Piraiévs 38 37.57 N 23.38 E
Pirahmet 120 38.11 N 39.51 E
Piraí 246 22.38 S 43.54 W
Piraí ≃ 246 22.28 S 43.50 W
Piraí do Sul 242 24.31 S 49.56 W
Piraiévs (Piraeus) 38 / 257c 37.57 N 23.38 E
Piraju 245 23.12 S 49.23 W
Pirajuba 245 19.54 S 48.42 W
Pirajucara, Ribeirão ≃ 277b 23.34 S 46.43 W
Pirajuí 245 21.59 S 49.29 W
Pirakata 116 22.34 N 87.11 E
Piramida, Gora ∧ 78 54.15 N 95.45 E
Piramidal'nyj, Pik ∧ 75 39.34 N 69.57 E
Pirámide de Cuicuilco ⊥ 276a 19.18 N 99.11 W
Pirámide de Santa Cecilia ⊥ 276a 19.35 N 99.11 W
Pirámide de Tenayuca ⊥ 276a 19.32 N 99.11 W
Pirámide Xochicalco ⊥ 224 18.48 N 99.19 W
Piram Island I 110 21.36 N 72.41 E
Piran, Jugo. 36 45.32 N 13.34 E
Piran, Tür. 120 38.22 N 40.04 E
Piraña, Arroyo ≃ 278 34.24 S 58.30 W
Piranê 242 25.43 S 59.06 W
Piranga 245 20.41 S 43.18 W
Pirangaí 246 22.34 S 44.37 W
Pirangi ≃ 240 4.23 S 37.48 W
Piranguinho 246 22.24 S 45.32 W
Piranhas, Bra. 240 9.27 S 37.46 W
Piranhas, Bra. 245 16.31 S 51.51 W
Piranhas ≃, Bra. 240 8.40 S 49.28 W
Piranhas ≃, Bra. 240 5.15 S 36.45 W
Piranhas ≃, Bra. 240 5.56 S 48.15 W
Pīrān Shahr 118 36.41 N 45.08 E
Pirapemas 240 3.43 S 44.14 W
Pirapetinga, Bra. 245 21.39 S 42.21 W
Pirapetinga, Bra. 246 21.54 S 43.40 W
Pirapetinga ≃ 246 21.37 S 42.32 W
Pirapetinga, Ribeirão ≃ 246 21.49 S 43.36 W
Pirapó ≃ 245 22.30 S 52.01 W
Pirapora 245 17.21 S 44.56 W
Pirapora do Bom Jesus □[7] 277b 23.24 S 46.56 W
Piraputanga 245 20.26 S 55.32 W
Piraquara 242 25.26 S 49.04 W
Piraquê ≃ 277a 23.01 S 43.37 W
Pirarajá 242 33.44 S 54.45 W
Piraras, Cachoeira de ⅃ 245 14.02 S 53.25 W
Pirassununga 245 21.59 S 47.25 W
Pirata, Monte ∧[2] 230m 18.06 N 65.33 W
Pirate Creek ≃ 272 37.33 N 121.52 W
Pir'atin 68 50.15 N 32.30 E
Piratinga ≃ 245 15.41 S 46.07 W
Piratini 242 31.27 S 53.06 W
Piratini ≃ 242 28.06 S 55.27 W
Piratininga 277a 22.57 S 43.04 W
Piratininga, Lagoa de C 246 22.57 S 43.05 W
Piratuba 242 27.27 S 51.48 W

FRANÇAIS
Nom | Page | Lat.°' | Long.°' W=Ouest

Piratuba, Lago C 240 1.37 N 50.10 W
Piratucu ≃ 240 1.59 S 56.58 W
Piraúba 246 21.17 S 43.02 W
Piraube, Lac ⊜ 176 50.33 N 71.42 W
Piray ≃ 238 16.32 S 63.45 W
Pirbright 250 51.18 N 0.39 W
Pirdop 38 42.42 N 24.11 E
Pirenópolis 245 15.51 S 48.57 W
Pires, Ribeirão ≃ 277b 23.43 S 46.25 W
Pires do Rio 245 17.18 S 48.17 W
Pírgos 38 37.41 N 21.28 E
Piriá 240 1.40 S 50.02 W
Piriápolis 242 34.54 S 55.17 W
Piribebuy 242 25.29 S 57.03 W
Pirin ∧∧ 38 41.40 N 23.30 E
Pirinçşiköy 257b 41.10 N 28.50 E
Pirineos → Pyrenees ∧∧ 34 42.40 N 1.00 E
Piripiri 240 4.16 S 41.47 W
Piritiba 240 11.44 S 40.34 W
Píritu, Ven. 236 9.23 N 69.12 W
Píritu, Ven. 236 11.22 N 69.08 W
Pirituba ◆[8] 277b 23.29 S 46.43 W
Pīr Jo Goth 110 27.36 N 68.37 E
Pirk 50 50.25 N 12.04 E
Pirlerkondu 120 36.55 N 32.31 E
Pīr Mahal 113 30.46 N 72.26 E
Pirmasens 52 49.12 N 7.36 E
Pirna 50 50.58 N 13.56 E
Piroči 72 55.04 N 38.57 E
Pirogovka 68 51.54 N 33.18 E
Pirogovskij 255b 55.59 N 37.44 E
Pirogovskoje Vodochranilišče ⊜[1] 72 55.58 N 37.40 E
Pirojpur 116 22.34 N 89.59 E
Pirón ≃ 34 41.23 N 4.31 W
Pirongia 162 38.00 S 175.12 E
Pirot 38 43.09 N 22.35 E
Pirovano 242 36.30 S 61.34 W
Pirovskoje 76 57.37 N 92.16 E
Pirpirituba 240 6.46 S 35.30 W
Pirrașit Dağı ∧ 74 38.56 N 43.51 E
Pirrís ≃ 226 9.29 N 84.19 W
Pirsagat 74 39.54 N 49.24 E
Pirsagat ≃ 74 39.53 N 49.19 E
Pirtleville 190 31.22 N 109.34 W
Piru, Indon. 154 3.04 S 128.12 E
Piru, Calif., U.S. 218 34.25 N 118.48 W
Piru, Lake ⊜[1] 218 34.30 N 118.45 W
Piru Creek ≃ 218 34.23 N 118.47 W
Pisa 60 43.43 N 10.23 E
Pisa □[4] 60 43.25 N 10.43 E
Pisa ∧[2] 26 63.13 N 28.18 E
Pisa ≃ 30 53.15 N 21.52 E
Pisa, Certosa di ɤ[1] 60 43.45 N 10.31 E
Pisa, Mount ∧ 162 44.52 S 169.11 E
Pisac ⊥ 238 13.25 S 71.53 W
Pisagua 238 19.36 S 70.13 W
Pisam-bong ∧ 88 40.41 N 126.34 E
Pisang, Pulau I 154 1.23 S 128.55 E
Pisarevka 68 49.53 N 40.12 E
Pisarve 262c 19.06 N 73.05 E
Pisau, Tanjong › 102 6.04 N 118.03 E
Piščalje 70 58.14 N 48.42 E
Piscasaw Creek ≃ 206 42.16 N 88.49 W
Piscataway 200 40.34 N 74.27 W
Piscataway Creek ≃, Md., U.S. 198 38.42 N 77.02 W
Piscataway Creek ≃, Va., U.S. 198 37.54 N 76.50 W
Pișchia 38 45.55 N 21.20 E
Pisco 238 13.42 S 76.13 W
Pisco ≃ 238 13.42 S 76.15 W
Pisco, Bahía de C 238 13.45 S 76.18 W
Pișcolt 38 47.35 N 22.18 E
Piscovo 70 57.11 N 40.32 E
Piseco Lake ⊜ 200 43.23 N 74.36 W
Písek 30 49.19 N 14.10 E
Pisgah 208 39.19 N 84.22 W
Pishan 110 37.37 N 78.18 E
Pishan I 90 28.06 N 121.30 E
Pishīn 110 30.35 N 67.00 E
Pishīn Lora (Lowrah) ≃ 110 29.09 N 64.55 E
Pisinemo 190 32.02 N 112.19 W
Pising 102 5.05 S 121.54 E
Pis'mennoje 68 48.13 N 35.48 E
Pismo Beach, Calif., U.S. 194 / 216 35.09 N 120.38 W
Pišnur 70 57.47 N 47.58 E
Piso, Lake ⊜ 140 6.48 N 11.17 W
Pisogne 58 45.48 N 10.06 E
Pisqui ≃ 238 7.45 S 75.01 W
Pissila 140 13.10 N 0.49 W
Pissos 32 44.19 N 0.47 W
Pistakee 206 42.25 N 88.11 W
Pistakee Lake ⊜ 206 42.23 N 88.12 W
Pisticci 36 40.23 N 16.34 E
Pistoia 60 43.55 N 10.54 E
Pistoia □[4] 58 43.58 N 10.50 E
Pistolet Bay C 176 51.32 N 55.50 W
Pistuk Peak ∧ 170 59.43 N 159.42 W
Pisuerga ≃ 34 41.33 N 4.52 W
Pisz 30 53.38 N 21.49 E
Pit ≃ 194 40.45 N 122.22 W
Pit, North Fork ≃ 194 41.28 N 120.33 W
Pit, South Fork ≃ 194 41.28 N 120.33 W
Pita 140 11.05 N 12.24 W
Pita □[4] 140 11.00 N 12.45 W
Pital 236 2.16 N 75.49 W
Pitalito 236 1.51 N 76.02 W
Pitampura Kālan ◆[8] 262a 28.42 N 77.08 E
Pitanga 242 24.46 S 51.44 W
Pitangueiras 245 21.02 S 48.13 W
Pitangueiras, Ribeirão das ≃ 246 21.27 S 44.27 W
Pitangui 245 19.40 S 44.54 W
Pitcairn 269b 40.24 N 79.47 W
Pitcairn □[2] 6 / 164e 25.04 S 130.05 W
Pitcairn Island I 6 25.04 S 130.06 W
Pitcher 200 42.35 N 75.52 W
Pitch Place 250 51.16 N 0.36 W
Piteå 26 65.20 N 21.30 E
Piteälven ≃ 24 65.14 N 21.32 E
Piteglio 60 44.01 N 10.46 E
Pitelino 70 54.34 N 41.49 E
Piterka 70 50.42 N 47.27 E
Pitești 38 44.52 N 24.52 E
Pithāpuram 112 17.07 N 82.16 E
Pithara 152 30.24 S 116.40 E
Pithiviers 46 48.10 N 2.15 E
Pithoragarh 114 29.35 N 80.13 E
Pithoragarh □[5] 114 30.10 N 80.30 E
Piti 164p 13.28 N 144.41 E
Piti, Lagoa ⊜ 148 26.34 S 32.53 E
Pitigliano 60 42.38 N 11.40 E
Pitillal del Norte 224 20.40 N 105.01 W
Pitim 70 53.12 N 42.21 E
Pitiquito 222 30.42 N 112.02 W
Pitk'aranta 24 61.34 N 31.27 E
Pitkas Point 170 62.02 N 163.17 W
Pitlochry 28 56.43 N 3.45 W
Pitman 198 39.44 N 75.08 W
Pitman Airport ⊠ 275 39.45 N 75.08 W
Pitner Ditch ≍ 206 41.14 N 86.53 W
Pitogo 106 10.08 N 124.33 E
Pitomača 36 45.57 N 17.14 E
Pitou, Zhg. 90 25.01 N 114.35 E
Pitou, Zhg. 90 23.34 N 116.05 E
Pitou, Zhg. 90 24.26 N 114.22 E
Pitrufquén 244 38.59 S 72.39 W
Pitsani 146 25.30 S 25.35 E
Pitschen → Byczyna 30 51.07 N 18.11 E
Pitsea 250 51.34 N 0.31 E
Pitseng 148 28.58 S 28.16 E
Pitsford Reservoir ⊜[1] 44 52.20 N 0.52 W
Pitt ≃ 214 49.12 N 122.47 W
Pitt, Mount ∧ 164c 29.01 S 167.56 E

PORTUGUÊS
Nome | Página | Lat.°' | Long.°' W=Oeste

Pittem 46 51.00 N 3.16 E
Pitti Island I 112 10.50 N 72.38 E
Pitt Island I 172 53.35 N 129.45 W
Pitt Lake ⊜ 172 49.25 N 122.32 W
Pittsboro, Ind., U.S. 208 39.52 N 86.28 W
Pittsboro, Miss., U.S. 184 33.56 N 89.20 W
Pittsboro, N.C., U.S. 182 35.43 N 79.11 W
Pittsburg, Calif., U.S. 216 38.02 N 121.53 W
Pittsburg, Kans., U.S. 188 37.25 N 94.42 W
Pittsburg, N.H., U.S. 196 45.03 N 71.21 W
Pittsburg, Tex., U.S. 212 32.60 N 94.58 W
Pittsburgh, Pa., U.S. 204 / 269b 40.26 N 80.00 W
Pittsburgh, University of ɤ[2] 269b 40.27 N 79.58 W
Pittsburgh-Monroeville Airport ⊠ 269b 40.27 N 79.46 W
Pittsfield, Ill., U.S. 209 39.36 N 90.48 W
Pittsfield, Maine, U.S. 178 44.47 N 69.23 W
Pittsfield, Mass., U.S. 197 42.27 N 73.15 W
Pittsfield, N.H., U.S. 178 43.18 N 71.19 W
Pittsfield, Pa., U.S. 204 41.50 N 79.23 W
Pittsford, Mich., U.S. 206 41.52 N 84.28 W
Pittsford, N.Y., U.S. 200 43.05 N 77.31 W
Pitt Stadium ♠ 269b 40.27 N 79.58 W
Pittston 200 41.19 N 75.47 W
Pittsview 184 32.11 N 85.10 W
Pittsville 198 38.24 N 75.52 W
Pittsworth 156 27.43 S 151.38 E
Pituil 242 28.34 S 67.27 W
Pitumarca 238 13.59 S 71.25 W
Pituri Creek ≃ 156 22.58 S 138.50 E
Pitz Bach ≃ 58 47.13 N 10.46 E
Pitztal ∨ 54 47.07 N 10.47 E
Piu, Cerro ∧ 226 13.38 N 84.52 W
Piũí 245 20.28 S 45.58 W
Pium 240 10.27 S 49.11 W
Pium ≃ 240 10.12 S 49.57 W
Piumafua ∧ 164y 14.10 S 169.39 W
Piura 238 5.12 S 80.38 W
Piura □[5] 238 5.10 S 80.00 W
Piura ≃ 238 5.32 S 80.53 W
Piute Peak ∧ 194 35.27 N 118.24 W
Piute Reservoir ⊜[1] 190 38.17 N 112.12 W
Piuthān 114 28.06 N 82.54 E
Piva ≃ 38 43.21 N 18.51 E
Pivan' 79 50.29 N 137.06 E
Piverone 56 45.27 N 8.00 E
Pivijay 236 10.28 N 74.37 W
Piwniczna 30 49.27 N 20.42 E
Pixian 92 30.49 N 103.49 E
Pixley 216 35.58 N 119.17 W
Piyadin 120 37.01 N 29.58 E
Pižanka 70 57.28 N 48.33 E
Pizarro 236 4.58 N 77.22 W
Pižma 70 57.52 N 47.06 E
Pižma ≃ 70 57.37 N 48.58 E
Pizzighettone 56 45.11 N 9.47 E
Pizzo 36 38.44 N 16.10 E
Pizzoferrato 60 41.55 N 14.14 E
Pizzoli 60 42.26 N 13.18 E
Pizzone 60 41.40 N 14.02 E
Pjalka 24 66.43 N 40.59 E
Pjana ≃ 70 55.40 N 45.57 E
Pjöngjang → P'yŏngyang 88 39.01 N 125.45 E
Place Bonaventure ◆[9] 265a 45.30 N 73.34 W
Placentia, Newf., Can. 176 47.14 N 53.58 W
Placentia, Calif., U.S. 218 33.52 N 117.46 W
Placentia Bay C 176 47.15 N 54.30 W
Placer, Pil. 106 11.52 N 123.55 E
Placer, Pil. 106 9.39 N 125.36 E
Placer □[6] 216 38.54 N 121.04 W
Placeres de Picacho 224 23.11 N 105.42 W
Placerville 216 38.43 N 120.48 W
Placetas 230p 22.19 N 79.40 W
Place Versailles ◆[9] 265a 45.35 N 73.32 W
Plachino 66 54.28 N 39.20 E
Plachtejevka 68 46.07 N 29.43 E
Placid, Lake ⊜ 210 27.14 N 81.22 W
Placida 210 26.50 N 82.16 W
Plácido de Castro 238 10.20 S 67.11 W
Plácido Rosas 242 32.45 S 53.44 W
Plačkovica ∧∧ 38 41.45 N 22.35 E
Plaffeien 54 46.44 N 7.17 E
Plages, Lac des ⊜ 196 45.59 N 74.54 W
Plage-Sainte-Cécile 46 50.34 N 1.35 E
Plailly 251 49.06 N 2.35 E
Plai Mat ≃ 100 15.22 N 102.45 E
Plain 214 47.46 N 120.39 W
Plain City, Ohio, U.S. 204 40.06 N 83.16 W
Plain City, Utah, U.S. 190 41.18 N 112.06 W
Plain Dealing 184 32.54 N 93.42 W
Plaines, Île aux I 265a 45.21 N 73.50 W
Plainfield, Conn., U.S. 197 41.41 N 71.55 W
Plainfield, Ill., U.S. 206 41.37 N 88.12 W
Plainfield, Ind., U.S. 208 39.42 N 86.24 W
Plainfield, Mass., U.S. 197 42.31 N 72.55 W
Plainfield, N.J., U.S. 200 40.37 N 74.26 W
Plainfield, Ohio, U.S. 204 40.13 N 81.43 W
Plainfield, Pa., U.S. 198 40.12 N 77.17 W
Plainfield, Wis., U.S. 180 44.13 N 89.30 W
Plainfield Heights 206 43.01 N 85.37 W
Plains, Ga., U.S. 182 32.02 N 84.24 W
Plains, Kans., U.S. 188 37.16 N 100.35 W
Plains, Mont., U.S. 192 47.27 N 114.53 W
Plains, Tex., U.S. 186 33.11 N 102.50 W
Plainsboro 198 40.20 N 74.36 W
Plainview, Ark., U.S. 184 34.60 N 93.18 W
Plainview, Calif., U.S. 216 36.08 N 119.08 W
Plainview, Ill., U.S. 209 39.10 N 89.59 W
Plainview, Minn., U.S. 180 44.10 N 92.10 W
Plainview, Nebr., U.S. 188 42.21 N 97.47 W
Plainview, N.Y., U.S. 200 40.46 N 73.28 W
Plainview, Tex., U.S. 186 34.11 N 101.43 W
Plainville, Conn., U.S. 197 41.41 N 72.51 W
Plainville, Ill., U.S. 209 39.47 N 91.11 W
Plainville, Ind., U.S. 184 38.48 N 87.09 W
Plainville, Kans., U.S. 188 39.14 N 99.18 W
Plainville, Mass., U.S. 197 42.00 N 71.20 W
Plainville, N.Y., U.S. 200 43.10 N 76.27 W
Plainwell 206 42.27 N 85.38 W
Plaisance, Baie de C 176 47.18 N 61.53 W
Plaisir 251 48.49 N 1.57 E
Plaistow 178 42.50 N 71.06 W
Plaksino 66 56.11 N 30.42 E
Plamondon 172 54.51 N 112.19 W
Plampang 105b 8.48 S 117.48 E
Planá 30 49.52 N 12.44 E
Plana, Isla I 34 38.10 N 0.28 W
Planada 216 37.18 N 120.19 W
Planaltina 245 15.37 S 47.40 W
Planalto 242 27.20 S 53.03 W
Planches 46 48.42 N 0.22 E
Plandome 266 40.48 N 73.42 W
Plandome Heights 266 40.48 N 73.42 W
Plandome Manor 266 40.49 N 73.42 W
Plan-d'Orgon 56 43.48 N 5.00 E
Plane ≃ 50 52.23 N 12.30 E
Planegg 58 48.06 N 11.25 E
Planerskoje 68 44.57 N 35.14 E
Planeta Rica 236 8.25 N 75.36 W
Plangeross 54 46.59 N 10.52 E
Plankinton 188 43.43 N 98.29 W
Plano, Ill., U.S. 206 41.40 N 88.32 W
Plano, Tex., U.S. 212 33.01 N 96.42 W
Plansee ⊜ 58 47.28 N 10.48 E
Planta de Evaporación ɤ[3] 276a 19.35 N 99.00 W
Plantagenet 196 45.32 N 75.00 W
Plantation, Fla., U.S. 210 24.59 N 80.33 W
Plantation, Fla., U.S. 210 26.05 N 80.14 W
Plantation, Ky., U.S. 208 38.17 N 85.36 W
Plantation Key I 210 24.58 N 80.33 W
Plant City 210 28.01 N 82.08 W
Plantersville, Ala., U.S. 184 32.40 N 86.55 W

Plantersville, Miss., U.S. 184 34.12 N 88.40 W
Plantersville, Tex., U.S. 212 30.20 N 95.52 W
Planting Fields Arboretum ♠ 266 40.52 N 73.33 W
Plantsite 190 33.02 N 109.21 W
Plantsville 197 41.35 N 72.54 W
Plaquemine 184 30.17 N 91.14 W
Plaridel, Pil. 106 8.37 N 123.43 E
Plaridel, Pil. 106 10.32 N 124.46 E
Plasencia 34 40.02 N 6.05 W
Plaški 36 45.05 N 15.22 E
Plassey 116 23.47 N 88.15 E
Plast 76 54.22 N 60.50 E
Plaster City 222 32.47 N 115.51 W
Plaster Rock 176 46.54 N 67.24 W
Plastovo 72 54.17 N 37.03 E
Plastun 79 44.45 N 136.19 E
Plastunovskaja 68 45.18 N 39.16 E
Plasy 30 49.56 N 13.24 E
Plata, Río de la C[1] 248 35.00 S 57.00 W
Plata, Río de la ≃ 230m 18.29 N 66.15 W
Platani ≃ 36 37.23 N 13.16 E
Plátanos 278 34.47 S 58.11 W
Plátanos, Arroyo ≃ 278 34.45 S 58.08 W
Plate, Île I 265a 45.22 N 73.48 W
Platea 204 41.57 N 80.20 W
Plateau Creek ≃ 190 39.11 N 108.18 W
Plateaux □[5] 142 2.15 S 15.30 E
Plathe → Płoty 30 53.49 N 15.16 E
Platinum 170 59.01 N 161.49 W
Platnirovskaja 68 45.23 N 39.23 E
Plato 236 9.47 N 74.47 W
Platono-Petrovka 73 46.59 N 39.28 E
Platonovka 70 52.43 N 41.57 E
Platón Sánchez 224 21.17 N 98.22 W
Platovo 73 48.05 N 39.53 E
Platrand 148 27.08 S 29.29 E
Platt 250 51.17 N 0.20 E
Platta 54 46.40 N 8.51 E
Platte 188 43.23 N 98.51 W
Platte ≃, U.S. 184 39.16 N 94.50 W
Platte ≃, Minn., U.S. 180 45.47 N 94.17 W
Platte ≃, Nebr., U.S. 188 41.04 N 95.53 W
Platte ≃, Wis., U.S. 180 42.37 N 90.40 W
Platte Center 188 41.32 N 97.29 W
Platte City 184 39.22 N 94.47 W
Platte Creek ≃ 188 43.19 N 99.00 W
Platte Island I 128 5.52 S 55.23 E
Plattekill 200 41.37 N 74.05 W
Platteville, Colo., U.S. 190 40.13 N 104.49 W
Platteville, Wis., U.S. 180 42.44 N 90.29 W
Platt Hall ⊥ 252 53.27 N 2.13 W
Plattling 30 48.47 N 12.53 E
Plattsburg 184 39.34 N 94.27 W
Plattsburgh 178 44.42 N 73.28 W
Plattsburgh Air Force Base ■ 178 44.40 N 73.28 W
Plattsmouth 188 41.01 N 95.53 W
Plattsville 202 43.18 N 80.37 W
Platveld 146 19.58 S 17.07 E
Plau 50 53.27 N 12.16 E
Plaue, D.D.R. 50 52.24 N 12.25 E
Plaue, D.D.R. 50 50.47 N 10.54 E
Plauen 50 50.30 N 12.08 E
Plauer See ⊜ 50 53.30 N 12.20 E
Plav 38 42.36 N 19.56 E
Plave 58 46.02 N 13.36 E
Pļaviņas 66 56.37 N 25.43 E
Plavsk 66 53.43 N 37.18 E
Plaxtol 250 51.15 N 0.18 E
Playa Azul 224 17.59 N 102.24 W
Playa Baracoa 276b 23.03 N 82.34 W
Playa Bonita 226 9.39 N 84.27 W
Playa de Fajardo 230m 18.20 N 65.38 W
Playa de Guayanés 230m 18.04 N 65.49 W
Playa de Guayanilla 230m 18.01 N 66.46 W
Playa del Rey ◆[8] 270 33.58 N 118.26 W
Playa de Naguabo 230m 18.12 N 65.43 W
Playa de Ponce 230m 17.59 N 66.37 W
Playa Noriega, Laguna ⊜ 222 29.10 N 111.50 W
Playas Lake ⊜ 190 31.50 N 108.34 W
Playa Vicente 224 17.50 N 95.49 W
Playa Vicente ≃ 224 18.31 N 95.42 W
Playford ≃ 152 19.03 S 135.35 E
Playgreen Lake ⊜ 174 54.00 N 98.10 W
Playland ♠ 266 40.58 N 73.41 W
Playon Grande 236 9.21 N 78.20 W
Plaza 188 48.01 N 101.58 W
Plaza de Caisan 226 8.46 N 82.45 W
Plaza de Mayo ♠ 278 34.36 S 58.23 W
Plaza de Toros ♠ 256a 40.26 N 3.39 W
Plaza de Toros Las Arenas ♠ 256d 41.23 N 2.09 W
Plaza de Toros Monumental ♠ 256d 41.24 N 2.11 E
Plaza Huincul 242 38.55 S 69.09 W
Plaza Park 275 40.04 N 74.53 W
Plazas de Soberanía en el Norte de África → Spanish North Africa □[2] 34 35.53 N 5.19 W
Pleasant 265b 43.41 N 79.49 W
Pleasant, Lake ⊜[1] 190 33.53 N 112.16 W
Pleasant, Mount ∧ 182 37.44 N 79.10 W
Pleasant, Mount ∧[2] 230c 17.09 N 61.49 W
Pleasant Bay 176 46.49 N 60.48 W
Pleasantdale, Sask., Can. 174 52.35 N 104.30 W
Pleasantdale, N.Y., U.S. 200 42.47 N 73.40 W
Pleasant Gap 204 40.52 N 77.45 W
Pleasant Garden 182 35.58 N 79.46 W
Pleasant Grove, Calif., U.S. 216 38.49 N 121.29 W
Pleasant Grove, Utah, U.S. 190 40.22 N 111.44 W
Pleasant Grove Creek ≃ 216 38.48 N 121.32 W
Pleasant Hill, Calif., U.S. 216 37.56 N 122.04 W
Pleasant Hill, Ill., U.S. 209 39.27 N 90.52 W
Pleasant Hill, La., U.S. 184 31.49 N 93.31 W
Pleasant Hill, Mo., U.S. 184 38.47 N 94.16 W
Pleasant Hill, N.C., U.S. 198 36.32 N 77.32 W
Pleasant Hill, Ohio, U.S. 208 40.03 N 84.20 W
Pleasant Hill Lake ⊜[1] 204 40.38 N 82.21 W
Pleasant Hills 204 40.20 N 79.58 W
Pleasant Home 214 45.28 N 122.20 W
Pleasant Lake, Ind., U.S. 206 41.35 N 85.01 W
Pleasant Lake, Mich., U.S. 206 42.23 N 84.22 W
Pleasant Lake ⊜ 206 42.13 N 83.56 W
Pleasant Mills 206 40.47 N 84.51 W
Pleasant Mount 200 41.44 N 75.26 W
Pleasant Mountain ∧[2] 176 45.26 N 66.49 W
Pleasanton, Calif., U.S. 216 37.40 N 121.53 W
Pleasanton, Kans., U.S. 188 38.11 N 94.43 W
Pleasanton, Tex., U.S. 186 28.58 N 98.29 W
Pleasanton Ridge ∧ 272 37.40 N 121.55 W
Pleasant Plains, Ill., U.S. 209 39.52 N 89.55 W
Pleasant Plains, N.J., U.S. 198 40.00 N 74.13 W
Pleasant Point 162 44.16 S 171.08 E
Pleasant Prairie 206 42.33 N 87.57 W
Pleasant Ridge 271 42.31 N 83.10 W
Pleasant Unity 204 40.15 N 79.28 W

Pleasant Valley, N.Y., U.S. 200 41.45 N 73.50 W
Pleasant Valley, Ohio, U.S. 208 39.22 N 83.03 W
Pleasant Valley, Pa., U.S. 269b 40.31 N 75.18 W
Pleasantville, Iowa, U.S. 180 41.23 N 93.18 W
Pleasantville, Md., U.S. 274b 39.11 N 76.38 W
Pleasantville, N.J., U.S. 198 39.23 N 74.32 W
Pleasantville, N.Y., U.S. 200 41.08 N 73.48 W
Pleasantville, Pa., U.S. 204 41.36 N 79.35 W
Pleasington 252 53.44 N 2.34 W
Pleasure Beach 197 41.18 N 72.08 W
Pleasure Ridge Park 208 38.10 N 85.50 W
Pleasureville 208 38.21 N 85.07 W
Pléaux 32 45.08 N 2.14 E
Plechanovo 72 54.14 N 37.33 E
Plechanovskoje 66 52.39 N 39.50 E
Plechovo 68 51.07 N 35.18 E
Pledger 212 29.11 N 95.55 W
Pleebo 140 4.35 N 7.40 W
Pleiku 100 13.59 N 108.00 E
Pleine d'Aleria ◆[1] 36 42.05 N 9.25 E
Pleinfeld 52 49.06 N 10.59 E
Pleissa 50 50.50 N 12.46 E
Pleisse ≃ 50 51.20 N 12.22 E
Pléneuf 32 48.36 N 2.33 W
Plenty 174 51.47 N 108.36 W
Plenty ≃, Austl. 152 23.25 S 136.31 E
Plenty ≃, Austl. 264b 37.45 S 145.07 E
Plenty, Bay of C 162 37.40 S 177.00 E
Plentywood 188 48.47 N 104.34 W
Plered 105a 6.38 S 107.23 E
Pleščejevo, Ozero ⊜ 72 56.46 N 38.47 E
Pleščenicy 66 54.25 N 27.50 E
Pleseck 24 62.43 N 40.20 E
Plešivka 72 54.23 N 37.09 E
Plesna ≃ 50 50.07 N 12.28 E
Pless, B.R.D. 54 48.05 N 10.08 E
Pless → Pszczyna, Pol. 30 49.59 N 18.57 E
Plessa 50 51.28 N 13.37 E
Plessisville 196 46.14 N 71.47 W
Pleszew 30 51.54 N 17.48 E
Pletenevka 72 54.31 N 36.06 E
Pleternica 38 45.17 N 17.48 E
Plétipi, Lac ⊜ 166 51.44 N 70.06 W
Plet'onyj Tašlyk 68 48.29 N 31.40 E
Plettenberg 52 51.13 N 7.52 E
Plettenbergbaai 148 34.04 S 23.22 E
Pleurs 46 48.41 N 3.52 E
Pleven 38 43.25 N 24.37 E
Plevna, Mo., U.S. 209 39.58 N 92.05 W
Plevna, Mont., U.S. 188 46.25 N 104.31 W
Pleyben 28 48.14 N 3.58 W
Pliening 58 48.12 N 11.48 E
Pliezhausen 52 48.33 N 9.12 E
Plimmerton 162 41.05 S 174.52 E
Plimoth Plantation ⊥ 197 41.57 N 70.38 W
Plintovka 255a 60.01 N 30.46 E
Pliski 68 51.07 N 32.24 E
Pliskov 68 49.23 N 29.18 E
Plitvička Jezera ⊜ 36 44.53 N 15.38 E
Plješevica ∧∧ 36 44.40 N 15.45 E
Pljevlja 38 43.21 N 19.21 E
Ploaghe 36 40.40 N 8.44 E
Ploče 36 43.04 N 17.26 E
Plochingen 52 48.42 N 9.25 E
Płock 30 52.33 N 19.43 E
Plöckenpass)(58 46.36 N 12.58 E
Pločno ∧ 36 43.23 N 17.57 E
Plodorodnoje 70 46.44 N 41.06 E
Ploegsteert 46 50.43 N 2.53 E
Ploërmel 32 47.56 N 2.24 W
Ploești → Ploiești 38 44.56 N 26.02 E
Ploiești 38 44.56 N 26.02 E
Plomárion 38 38.59 N 26.22 E
Plomb du Cantal ∧ 32 45.03 N 2.46 E
Plombières-les-Bains 54 47.58 N 6.29 E
Plombières-lès-Dijon 54 47.20 N 4.58 E
Plomer 248 34.48 S 59.02 W
Plomer, Point › 156 31.19 S 152.58 E
Plön 50 54.09 N 10.25 E
Plonge, Lac la ⊜ 174 55.08 N 107.25 W
Płońsk 30 52.38 N 20.23 E
Pl'os 70 57.27 N 41.31 E
Plose, Cima delle ∧ 58 46.42 N 11.44 E
Ploskij 68 46.17 N 40.15 E
Ploskoje 66 52.45 N 38.21 E
Ploskoš' 66 56.46 N 31.16 E
Pl'oso 66 59.47 N 35.43 E
Plotbišče 70 56.50 N 50.35 E
Plotina 73 48.33 N 40.05 E
Plotnica 68 52.03 N 26.39 E
Plottier 242 38.58 S 68.14 W
Płoty 30 53.49 N 15.16 E
Plötz 50 51.38 N 11.56 E
Plouay 32 47.55 N 3.20 W
Ploučnice ≃ 50 50.47 N 14.13 E
Ploudalmézeau 32 48.32 N 4.39 W
Plouescat 32 48.40 N 4.10 W
Plouguenast 32 48.17 N 2.43 W
Plouha 32 48.41 N 2.56 W
Plovdiv 38 42.09 N 24.45 E
Plover ≃ 180 44.29 N 89.35 W
Plover Islands II 170 71.15 N 155.30 W
Pluckemin 266 40.39 N 74.39 W
Plum, Pa., U.S. 204 40.28 N 79.44 W
Plum, Pa., U.S. 204 41.35 N 79.51 W
Plum, Tex., U.S. 212 29.56 N 96.58 W
Pluma Hidalgo 224 15.55 N 96.25 W
Plumas 174 50.25 N 99.02 W
Plumbon 105a 6.42 S 108.28 E
Plum Brook ≃ 271 42.34 N 82.58 W
Plum Creek ≃, Ill., U.S. 268 41.33 N 87.29 W
Plum Creek ≃, Nebr., U.S. 188 40.41 N 99.40 W
Plum Creek ≃, S. Dak., U.S. 188 44.13 N 100.43 W
Plum Creek ≃, Tex., U.S. 186 29.38 N 97.36 W
Plum Creek, Clear Fork ≃ 212 29.45 N 97.37 W
Plumerville 184 35.10 N 92.38 W
Plum Grove 212 30.15 N 95.05 W
Plum Grove Estates 268 42.04 N 88.02 W
Plum Island 273 42.49 N 70.59 W
Plum Island I, Mass., U.S. 197 42.45 N 70.48 W
Plum Island I, N.Y., U.S. 197 41.11 N 72.12 W
Plum Island Airport ⊠ 273 42.48 N 70.50 W
Plum Island Sound Ʊ 273 42.45 N 70.48 W
Plumley 252 53.17 N 2.25 W
Plummer 192 47.20 N 116.53 W
Plummers Landing 208 38.19 N 83.33 W
Plumper Sound Ʊ 214 48.47 N 123.13 W
Plum Point › 266 40.50 N 40.43 W
Plumpton 264a 33.45 S 150.50 E
Plumridge Lakes ⊜ 152 29.30 S 125.25 E
Plum Run ≃ 269b 40.15 N 80.13 W
Plumsteadville 198 40.23 N 75.09 W
Plumtree 144 20.30 S 27.50 E
Plumville 204 40.48 N 79.11 W
Plumwood 208 40.01 N 83.23 W
Plungė 66 55.55 N 21.51 E
Pl'usa 66 58.26 N 29.21 E
Pl'uskovo 66 52.46 N 33.49 E
Pl'ussa ≃ 66 59.19 N 28.11 E
Plym ≃ 44 50.12 N 4.07 W
Plymouth, Monts. 228 16.42 N 62.13 W
Plymouth, Trin. 231r 11.13 N 60.47 W

Plymouth, Eng., U.K. 44 50.23 N 4.10 W
Plymouth, Calif., U.S. 216 38.29 N 120.51 W
Plymouth, Conn., U.S. 197 41.40 N 73.03 W
Plymouth, Ill., U.S. 184 40.29 N 90.58 W
Plymouth, Ind., U.S. 206 41.21 N 86.19 W
Plymouth, Mass., U.S. 197 41.58 N 70.41 W
Plymouth, Mich., U.S. 206 42.22 N 83.28 W
Plymouth, Nebr., U.S. 188 40.18 N 97.00 W
Plymouth, N.H., U.S. 178 43.45 N 71.41 W
Plymouth, N.C., U.S. 182 35.52 N 76.43 W
Plymouth, N.Y., U.S. 200 42.37 N 75.36 W
Plymouth, Ohio, U.S. 204 40.59 N 82.40 W
Plymouth, Pa., U.S. 200 41.14 N 75.58 W
Plymouth, Wis., U.S. 180 43.45 N 87.58 W
Plymouth □[6] 197 41.58 N 70.41 W
Plymouth ≃ 273 42.12 N 70.54 W
Plymouth Bay C 197 41.57 N 70.37 W
Plymouth Harbor C 273 41.58 N 70.39 W
Plymouth Meeting 275 40.06 N 75.15 W
Plymouth Rock ⊥ 197 41.57 N 70.39 W
Plympton, Eng., U.K. 44 50.23 N 4.03 W
Plympton, Mass., U.S. 197 41.57 N 70.49 W
Plymptonville 204 41.03 N 78.28 W
Plymstock 44 50.22 N 4.04 W
Plynlimon ∧ 44 52.28 N 3.47 W
Plzeň 30 49.45 N 13.23 E
Pniewy 30 52.31 N 16.15 E
Pô 140 11.10 N 1.09 W
Po ≃ 36 44.57 N 12.04 E
Po, Foci del ≃[1] 58 44.52 N 12.30 E
Poá 246 23.32 S 46.20 W
Poá □[7] 277b 23.33 S 46.21 W
Poá ≃ 277b 23.37 S 46.45 W
Poana ≃ 240 0.56 N 57.03 W
Poané, Baie de C 165f 21.24 S 168.02 E
Poás, Volcán ∧[1] 226 10.11 N 84.13 W
Pobé, Benin 140 6.58 N 2.41 E
Pobé, H. Vol. 140 13.53 N 1.45 W
Pobeda, Gora ∧ 64 65.12 N 146.12 E
Pobeda Ice Island I 9 64.30 S 97.00 E
Pobedino 79 49.51 N 142.49 E
Pobedy, Pik ∧ 62 42.02 N 80.05 E
Pobershau 50 50.38 N 13.13 E
Poblado Cerro Gordo 230m 18.29 N 66.20 W
Poblado Jacaguas 230m 18.03 N 66.32 W
Poblado Medianía Alta 230m 18.26 N 65.50 W
Poblado Sábalos 230m 18.11 N 67.09 W
Poblado Santana 230m 18.27 N 66.40 W
Poblet 248 35.04 S 57.57 W
Pocahontas, Ark., U.S. 184 36.16 N 90.58 W
Pocahontas, Ill., U.S. 209 38.50 N 89.33 W
Pocahontas, Iowa, U.S. 188 42.44 N 94.40 W
Pocahontas State Park ♠ 198 37.23 N 77.34 W
Počajev 68 50.01 N 25.31 E
Pocantico Hills 266 41.06 N 73.50 W
Pocantico Lake ⊜ 266 41.07 N 73.50 W
Poção 240 8.11 S 36.42 W
Poção, Lago do ⊜ 240 2.09 S 55.40 W
Pocasset 197 41.41 N 70.37 W
Pocatalico ≃ 178 38.29 N 81.49 W
Pocatello 192 42.52 N 112.27 W
Počegda 24 62.42 N 43.23 E
Počep 66 52.56 N 33.27 E
Počepy 66 53.17 N 31.20 E
Pocé-sur-Cisse 46 47.26 N 0.59 E
Počet 78 57.10 N 96.30 E
Pöchlarn 30 48.12 N 15.13 E
Pochutla 224 15.44 N 96.28 W
Pochvistnevo 70 53.38 N 52.08 E
Pocinhos 240 7.04 S 36.03 W
Pocinhos do Rio Verde 246 21.56 S 46.25 W
Počinki 70 54.42 N 44.51 E
Počinnaja Sopka 66 58.25 N 34.22 E
Počinok 66 54.25 N 32.27 E
Pocitos 242 22.04 S 63.43 W
Pockau 50 50.40 N 13.27 E
Pöcking 58 47.58 N 11.17 E
Pocklington 42 53.56 N 0.46 W
Pocoata 238 18.41 S 66.11 W
Poço Do Bispo ◆[8] 256c 38.44 N 9.06 W
Poções 245 14.31 S 40.21 W
Poço Fundo 246 21.48 S 45.58 W
Poço Fundo, Cachoeira do ⅃ 246 22.10 S 44.13 W
Pocol 58 46.31 N 12.07 E
Pocomoke ≃ 198 37.58 N 75.39 W
Pocomoke City 178 38.05 N 75.34 W
Pocomoke Sound Ʊ 198 37.52 N 75.49 W
Pocona 238 17.39 S 65.24 W
Poconé 238 16.15 S 56.37 W
Pocono International Raceway ♠ 200 41.03 N 75.31 W
Pocono Lake 200 41.06 N 75.31 W
Pocono Manor 200 41.06 N 75.22 W
Pocono Mountains ∧∧[2] 200 41.10 N 75.20 W
Pocono Pines 200 41.05 N 75.29 W
Pocono Summit 200 41.07 N 75.25 W
Pocopson 275 39.54 N 75.37 W
Pocopson Creek ≃ 275 39.54 N 75.37 W
Poço Redondo 240 9.49 S 37.41 W
Poços de Caldas 246 21.48 S 46.34 W
Poço Verde 240 10.42 S 38.11 W
Pocrane 245 19.37 S 41.37 W
Pocrí 226 8.16 N 80.33 W
Podbel'skaja 70 53.37 N 51.50 E
Podberezje, S.S.S.R. 66 56.57 N 30.38 E
Podberezje, S.S.S.R. 72 56.46 N 37.10 E
Podbořany 50 50.11 N 13.25 E
Podborki 72 54.11 N 35.56 E
Podborovje 66 59.28 N 34.43 E
Podbuž 68 49.22 N 23.15 E
Podbužje 66 53.30 N 34.56 E
Podčerje 24 63.53 N 57.57 E
Podchožeje 72 54.19 N 38.34 E
Podčinnyj 70 50.52 N 45.13 E
Poddębice 30 51.53 N 18.58 E
Poddemjur 24 64.05 N 53.26 E
Poddolgoje 66 53.12 N 38.04 E
Poddorje 66 57.28 N 31.07 E
Poděbrady 30 50.08 N 15.07 E
Po della Donzella ≃ 58 44.48 N 12.25 E
Po delle Tolle ≃ 58 44.50 N 12.28 E
Podensac 32 44.39 N 0.22 W
Podenzano 56 44.57 N 9.41 E
Podgajcy 68 49.16 N 25.08 E
Podgorenskij 68 50.24 N 39.39 E
Podgorica → Titograd 38 42.26 N 19.14 E
Podgornaja 68 50.28 N 41.10 E
Podgornoje, S.S.S.R. 68 50.27 N 39.37 E
Podgornoje, S.S.S.R. 68 51.43 N 39.07 E
Podgornoje, S.S.S.R. 70 46.33 N 43.07 E
Podgornoje, S.S.S.R. 75 42.55 N 72.25 E
Podgornoje, S.S.S.R. 76 57.47 N 82.36 E
Podgorodnaja 68 48.07 N 30.51 E
Podgorodnoje 68 48.34 N 35.08 E
Podhale ∧∧[2] 30 49.25 N 20.00 E
Podi 102 1.08 S 121.16 E
Po di Goro ≃ 58 44.48 N 12.27 E
Po di Volano ≃ 58 44.49 N 12.15 E
Podjom-Michajlovka 70 52.49 N 50.32 E
Podjuchy ◆[8] 50 53.20 N 14.36 E
Podkamen' 68 49.57 N 25.19 E
Podkamennaja Tunguska 64 61.36 N 90.09 E
Podkamennaja Tunguska ≃ 64 61.36 N 90.18 E
Podkoren 58 46.30 N 13.45 E
Podkumok ≃ 74 44.14 N 43.36 E
Podlasie ◆[1] 30 52.30 N 23.00 E
Podlesnoje, S.S.S.R. 68 48.47 N 32.15 E
Podlesnoje, S.S.S.R. 70 51.50 N 47.03 E
Podlopatki 78 50.55 N 107.05 E
Podmošje 72 56.23 N 37.24 E

≃ River	Fluss	Río	Rivière	Rio
≍ Canal	Kanal	Canal	Canal	Canal
⅃ Waterfall, Rapids	Wasserfall, Stromschnellen	Cascada, Rápidos	Chute d'eau, Rapides	Cascata, Rápidos
Ʊ Strait	Meeresstrasse	Estrecho	Détroit	Estreito
C Bay, Gulf	Bucht, Golf	Bahía, Golfo	Baie, Golfe	Baía, Golfo
⊜ Lake, Lakes	See, Seen	Lago, Lagos	Lac, Lacs	Lago, Lagos
Swamp	Sumpf	Pantano	Marais	Pântano
Ice Features, Glacier	Eis- und Gletscherformen	Accidentes Glaciales	Formes glaciaires	Acidentes Glaciares
Other Hydrographic Features	Andere Hydrographische Objekte	Otros Elementos Hidrográficos	Autres données hydrographiques	Outros Elementos Hidrográficos

Submarine Features	Untermeerische Objekte	Accidentes Submarinos	Formes de relief sous-marin	Acidentes Submarinos
□ Political Unit	Politische Einheit	Unidad Politica	Entité politique	Unidade Política
ɤ Cultural Institution	Kulturelle Institution	Institución Cultural	Institution culturelle	Instituição Cultural
⊥ Historical Site	Historische Stätte	Sitio Histórico	Site historique	Sitio Histórico
♠ Recreational Site	Erholungs- und Ferienort	Sitio de Recreo	Centre de loisirs	Sítio de Lazer
⊠ Airport	Flughafen	Aeropuerto	Aéroport	Aeroporto
■ Military Installation	Militäranlage	Instalación Militar	Installation militaire	Instalação Militar
◆ Miscellaneous	Verschiedenes	Misceláneo	Divers	Miscelânea

ENGLISH — Name | Page | Lat.°′ | Long.°′
DEUTSCH — Name | Seite | Breite°′ | Länge°′ E=Ost

Podol'sk 72 55.26 N 37.33 E
Podol'skaja Vozvyšennost' ⋀[1] 68 49.00 N 27.00 E
Podor, Maur. 140 16.40 N 15.00 W
Podor, Sén. 140 16.40 N 14.57 W
Podora 24 62.22 N 54.19 E
Podosinovec 24 60.17 N 47.04 E
Podoz'orskij 70 57.14 N 40.20 E
Podporožje 24 60.53 N 34.07 E
Podravina ◂[1] 38 45.40 N 17.40 E
Podravska Slatina 38 45.42 N 17.42 E
Podrezčicha 24 59.22 N 51.28 E
Podstepnyj 70 51.08 N 51.28 E
Podsvilje 66 55.09 N 27.58 E
Podt'osovo 78 58.36 N 92.06 E
Pod'uga 24 61.06 N 40.53 E
Podujevo 38 42.55 N 21.11 E
Poduškino 255b 55.43 N 37.17 E
Podu Turcului 38 46.12 N 27.23 E
Podvoločisk 68 49.33 N 26.09 E
Podymachino 78 56.59 N 106.11 E
Podyvotje 68 52.03 N 34.08 E
Poe 206 40.56 N 85.05 W
Poel I 50 54.00 N 11.26 E
Poeldijk 48 52.01 N 4.12 E
Poelela, Lagoa ⊜ 146 24.38 S 35.00 E
Poelkapelle 46 50.55 N 2.57 E
Poestenkill 200 42.41 N 73.34 W
Poesten Kill ≃ 200 42.43 N 73.42 W
Pofadder 148 29.10 S 19.22 E
Pogamasing Lake ⊜ 180 46.57 N 81.50 W
Pogan, Zhg. 90 28.18 N 116.46 E
Pogan, Zhg. 90 27.40 N 116.46 E
Pogăniș ≃ 38 45.41 N 21.22 E
Pogar 66 52.33 N 33.16 E
Poge, Cape ≻ 197 41.25 N 70.27 W
Poggendorf 50 54.03 N 13.07 E
Poggibonsi 60 43.28 N 11.09 E
Poggio 58 44.30 N 10.00 E
Poggio Berni 60 44.02 N 12.24 E
Poggio Bustone 60 42.30 N 12.53 E
Poggio Imperiale 60 41.49 N 15.22 E
Poggiomarino 60 40.48 N 14.32 E
Poggio Mirteto 60 42.16 N 12.41 E
Poggio Moiano 60 42.12 N 12.53 E
Poggio Renatico 58 44.46 N 11.29 E
Poggio Rusco 58 44.59 N 11.07 E
Poggio Sannita 60 41.47 N 14.25 E
Pogibi 79 52.12 N 141.42 E
Pogliano 256b 45.32 N 8.59 E
Pogny 52 48.52 N 4.29 E
Pogoanele 38 44.54 N 27.00 E
Pogodajev 70 51.37 N 51.04 E
Pogoniani 38 40.00 N 20.25 E
Pogoreloje Gorodišče 66 56.08 N 34.56 E
Pogoso 142 6.46 S 17.12 E
Pogost, S.S.S.R. 66 52.51 N 27.39 E
Pogost, S.S.S.R. 66 53.51 N 29.09 E
Pogost, S.S.S.R. 70 57.39 N 42.33 E
Pogost, S.S.S.R. 72 56.52 N 39.04 E
Pogožeje 68 51.36 N 37.16 E
Pogradec 38 40.54 N 20.39 E
Po Grande ≃ 58 44.57 N 12.26 E
Pograničnoje 70 50.32 N 48.38 E
Pograničnyj, S.S.S.R. 70 46.57 N 45.46 E
Pograničnyj, S.S.S.R. 79 44.25 N 131.24 E
Pogrebišče 68 49.29 N 29.16 E
Pogromni Volcano ∧[1] 170 54.33 N 164.45 W
Pogromnoje 70 52.35 N 52.32 E
Pogruznaja 70 54.14 N 50.29 E
Poh 102 0.46 S 122.49 E
P'ohang 88 36.03 N 129.20 E
Pohatcong Creek ≃ 200 40.37 N 75.11 W
Pohick Creek ≃ 274c 38.46 N 77.14 W
Pohick Creek, Rabbit Branch ≃ 274c 38.48 N 77.17 W
Pohick Creek, Sideburn Branch ≃ 274c 38.48 N 77.17 W
Pohjanmaa ◂[1] 26 64.00 N 25.00 E
Pohjois-Karjalan lääni □[4] 24 63.00 N 30.00 E
Pöhl, Talsperre ◂[6] 50 50.33 N 12.12 E
Pöhla 50 50.31 N 12.49 E
Pöhlde 48 51.37 N 10.18 E
Pohl-Göns 52 50.28 N 8.39 E
Pohopoco Creek ≃ 200 40.49 N 75.40 W
Pohořelice 30 48.59 N 16.32 E
Pohorje ⋀ 36 46.30 N 15.20 E
Pohsien → Boxian 90 33.53 N 115.45 E
Pohue Bay C 219d 19.00 N 155.48 W
Poiana Mare 38 43.55 N 23.04 E
Poiana Ruscăi, Munții ⋀ 38 45.41 N 22.30 E
Pöide 66 58.31 N 23.03 E
Poigny-la-Forêt 251 48.41 N 1.45 E
Poim 70 53.01 N 43.11 E
Poinsett, Cape ≻ 9 65.42 S 113.18 E
Poinsett, Lake ⊜, Fla., U.S. 210 28.20 N 80.50 W
Poinsett, Lake ⊜, S. Dak., U.S. 188 44.34 N 97.05 W
Point 212 32.56 N 95.52 W
Point Arena 194 38.55 N 123.41 W
Point Au Fer Island I 184 29.15 N 91.15 W
Point Baker 170 56.21 N 133.37 W
Pointblank 212 30.45 N 95.13 W
Point Chautauqua 204 42.14 N 79.28 W
Point Cloates 152 22.35 S 113.41 E
Point Comfort 186 28.41 N 96.33 W
Point Cook 264b 37.56 S 144.45 E
Point Cook Royal Australian Air Force Station ■ 159 37.56 S 144.45 E
Point du Jour, Ruisseau du ≃ 196 45.50 N 73.25 W
Pointe-à-la-Frégate 176 49.12 N 64.55 W
Pointe-à-la-Garde 176 48.05 N 66.32 W
Pointe a la Hache 184 29.35 N 89.48 W
Pointe-à-Maurier 176 50.20 N 59.48 W
Pointe-à-Pitre 231o 16.14 N 61.32 W
Pointe-à-Pitre-le Raizet, Aérodrome de ⊠ 231o 16.17 N 61.32 W
Pointe-au-Chêne 196 45.38 N 74.45 W
Pointe Aux Peaux Farms 206 41.57 N 83.16 W
Pointe-aux-Trembles 196 45.39 N 73.30 W
Pointe-Calumet 265a 45.30 N 73.58 W
Pointe-Claire 196 45.26 N 73.50 W
Pointe-des-Cascades 265a 45.20 N 73.58 W
Pointe-des-galets → Le Port 147c 20.55 S 55.18 E
Pointe-du-Moulin 265a 45.22 N 73.52 W
Point Edward 204 43.00 N 82.24 W
Pointe-Gatineau 202 45.28 N 75.42 W
Pointe-Noire, Congo 142 4.48 S 11.51 E
Pointe-Noire, Guad. 231o 16.14 N 61.47 W
Point Enterprise 212 31.40 N 96.26 W
Pointers 198 39.36 N 75.28 W
Point Fortin 231r 10.11 N 61.41 W
Point Hope 170 68.21 N 166.41 W
Point Imperial ∧ 190 36.16 N 111.58 W
Point Independence 197 41.44 N 70.39 W
Point Lake ⊜ 166 65.15 N 113.04 W
Point Leamington 176 49.20 N 55.24 W
Point Lookout 266 40.35 N 73.35 W
Point Marion 178 39.44 N 79.53 W
Point McLeay 158b 35.32 S 139.06 E
Point Mugu Naval Air Station ■ 218 34.07 N 119.07 W
Point of Rocks 198 39.17 N 77.32 W
Point O'Woods 266 40.39 N 73.08 W
Point Pass 158b 34.05 S 139.03 E
Point Pelee National Park ♠ 204 41.57 N 82.30 W
Point Peninsula ≻[1] 202 44.01 N 76.15 W
Point Pleasant, Md., U.S. 274b 39.11 N 76.35 W
Point Pleasant, N.J., U.S. 198 40.05 N 74.04 W
Point Pleasant, Ohio, U.S. 208 38.54 N 84.14 W
Point Pleasant, Pa., U.S. 198 40.25 N 75.04 W
Point Pleasant, W. Va., U.S. 178 38.52 N 82.08 W
Point Pleasant Beach 198 40.05 N 74.03 W
Point Reyes National Seashore ♠ 194 38.00 N 122.58 W
Point Roberts 214 48.59 N 123.13 W
Point Samson 152 20.36 S 117.12 E
Point Sapin 176 46.58 N 64.50 W
Point View Reservoir ⊜[1] 266 40.58 N 74.15 W
Point Whiteshed 170 60.28 N 145.57 W
Poirino 56 44.55 N 7.51 E
Poiseevo 70 55.32 N 53.30 E
Poison Creek ≃ 192 43.15 N 108.09 W
Poison Spider Creek ≃ 190 42.46 N 106.31 W
Poisson Blanc, Réservoir du ⊜[1] 178 46.00 N 75.45 W
Poissonnier Point ≻ 152 19.57 S 119.11 E
Poissons 54 48.25 N 5.13 E
Poissy 46 48.56 N 2.03 E
Poitiers 32 46.35 N 0.20 E
Poitou □[9] 32 46.20 N 0.30 W
Poix 46 49.47 N 1.59 E
Poix-Terron 52 49.39 N 4.39 E
Pojarkovo 79 49.38 N 128.38 E
Pojiang ≃ 90 28.57 N 116.39 E
Pojma ≃ 78 56.54 N 97.48 E
Pojo 238 17.45 S 64.49 W
Pojoaque Valley 190 35.53 N 105.59 W
Pojuca 245 12.21 S 38.20 W
Pojuca ≃ 245 12.34 S 38.03 W
Pok 164r 6.49 N 158.12 E
Pokagon State Park ♠ 206 41.43 N 85.01 W
Pokaran 110 26.55 N 71.55 E
Pokataroo 156 29.35 S 148.42 E
Pokatejeva 78 56.59 N 97.25 E
Pokatilovka, S.S.S.R. 70 51.06 N 51.53 E
Pokatilovka, S.S.S.R. 76 45.23 N 80.10 E
Poke Run ≃ 269b 40.30 N 79.33 W
Pokhara 114 28.14 N 83.59 E
Pokharia 116 23.55 N 86.37 E
Pok Liu Chau I 261d 22.12 N 114.07 E
Poko, Sūd. 130 5.38 N 31.50 E
Poko, Zaïre 144 3.09 N 26.53 E
Pokojnoje 74 44.48 N 44.16 E
Pokok Sena 104 6.10 N 100.32 E
Pokol'ubiči 66 52.30 N 31.02 E
Pokrov 72 55.55 N 39.10 E
Pokrovka, S.S.S.R. 68 47.59 N 36.14 E
Pokrovka, S.S.S.R. 70 53.47 N 53.19 E
Pokrovka, S.S.S.R. 70 48.22 N 46.04 E
Pokrovka, S.S.S.R. 75 42.20 N 78.01 E
Pokrovka, S.S.S.R. 75 42.45 N 71.36 E
Pokrovka, S.S.S.R. 76 54.17 N 68.15 E
Pokrovka, S.S.S.R. 76 49.28 N 81.28 E
Pokrovka, S.S.S.R. 79 43.57 N 131.39 E
Pokrov-Konopl'anskaja Gr'ada ∧ 66 58.25 N 36.30 E
Pokrovo-Kirejevo 73 47.38 N 38.16 E
Pokrovsk 64 61.29 N 129.06 E
Pokrovskaja Arčada 70 52.56 N 44.13 E
Pokrovskij 68 46.32 N 31.38 E
Pokrovskoje, S.S.S.R. 66 52.38 N 36.51 E
Pokrovskoje, S.S.S.R. 68 49.44 N 38.13 E
Pokrovskoje, S.S.S.R. 70 53.54 N 40.26 E
Pokrovskoje, S.S.S.R. 70 54.04 N 43.37 E
Pokrovskoje, S.S.S.R. 72 56.25 N 37.03 E
Pokrovskoje, S.S.S.R. 72 55.53 N 36.19 E
Pokrovskoje, S.S.S.R. 73 48.37 N 38.09 E
Pokrovskoje, S.S.S.R. 73 47.25 N 38.54 E
Pokrovskoje, S.S.S.R. 76 57.14 N 66.48 E
Pokrovskoje, S.S.S.R. 255a 59.44 N 30.46 E
Pokrovskoje ◂[8] 255b 55.37 N 37.37 E
Pokrovsko-Strešnevo ◂[8] 255b 55.49 N 37.29 E
Pokrovsk-Ural'skij 76 60.10 N 59.49 E
Pokur 64 61.02 N 75.26 E
Pola → Pula, Jugo. 58 44.52 N 13.50 E
Pola, Pil. 106 13.09 N 121.26 E
Pola, S.S.S.R. 66 57.56 N 31.50 E
Pola ≃ 66 58.04 N 31.37 E
Pola Bay C 106 13.10 N 121.28 E
Polacca 190 35.50 N 110.23 W
Polacca Wash ∨ 190 35.22 N 110.50 W
Pola de Laviana 34 43.15 N 5.34 W
Pola de Lena 34 43.10 N 5.49 W
Pola de Siero 34 43.23 N 5.40 W
Polān 118 25.35 N 61.12 E
Polanco 242 33.54 S 55.09 W
Poland, Gilb. Is. 164o 1.59 N 157.32 W
Poland, Ohio, U.S. 204 41.01 N 80.37 W
Poland □[1] 22 / 30 52.00 N 19.00 E
Polangui 106 13.17 N 123.29 E
Polanów 30 54.08 N 16.39 E
Polapare ≃ 105b 9.43 S 119.06 E
Pol'arnik 170 67.00 N 179.15 W
Pol'arnyj 24 69.12 N 33.22 E
Pol'arnyj Ural ⋀ 24 66.55 N 64.30 E
Polar Record Glacier ⊓ 9 69.49 S 75.30 E
Polatlı 120 39.36 N 32.09 E
Polba 262b 22.57 N 88.18 E
Polch 52 50.18 N 7.18 E
Polcirkeln 24 66.34 N 21.05 E
Polcura 242 37.17 S 71.43 W
Połczyn Zdrój 30 53.46 N 16.06 E
Polden Hills ⋀[2] 44 51.08 N 2.50 W
Poldnevica 70 58.37 N 46.38 E
Pol'dorak 75 39.25 N 69.56 E
Poleang 102 4.42 S 121.46 E
Polecat Creek ≃ 186 36.00 N 95.57 W
Polee, Pulau I 154 2.12 S 130.15 E
Polegate 44 50.49 N 0.15 E
Pol-e Khomrī 110 35.56 N 68.43 E
Pole Moor 252 53.39 N 1.54 W
Pole Mountain ∧ 190 41.14 N 105.23 W
Polen → Poland □[1] 30 52.00 N 19.00 E
Polenezköy 257b 41.07 N 29.12 E
Polenia Bay C 165f 18.43 S 169.11 E
Pol-e Safīd 118 36.06 N 53.01 E
Polesella 58 44.58 N 11.45 E
Polesine □[9] 58 45.00 N 11.45 E
Polesine Parmense 58 45.01 N 10.04 E
Polesje 66 53.05 N 31.17 E
Polesje ◂[1] 62 52.30 N 27.30 E
Polessk [Labiau] 66 54.52 N 21.05 E
Polesskoje 68 51.14 N 29.22 E
Polesworth 44 52.37 N 1.36 W
Polevaja 68 51.37 N 36.30 E
Polevskoj 76 56.26 N 60.11 E
Polewali 102 3.25 S 119.20 E
Polgár 30 47.52 N 21.08 E
Pŏlgyo 88 34.52 N 127.21 E
Poli 136 8.29 N 13.15 E
Políaigos I 38 36.46 N 24.38 E
Policastro, Golfo di C 36 40.00 N 15.30 E
Police 30 53.35 N 14.33 E
Polička 30 49.43 N 16.16 E
Polignac 56 45.04 N 3.52 E
Poligny 54 46.50 N 5.43 E
Políkastron 38 41.00 N 22.34 E
Polikhnítos 38 39.05 N 26.11 E
Polillo 106 14.43 N 121.56 E
Polillo Island I 106 14.50 N 121.57 E
Polillo Islands II 106 14.50 N 122.05 E
Polillo Strait ⊔ 106 14.44 N 121.51 E
Polinesia Francesa → French Polynesia □[2] 14 15.00 S 140.00 W
Polinik ∧ 58 46.54 N 13.09 E
Polinyá 256d 41.33 N 2.10 E
Pólis 120 35.02 N 32.25 E
Polist' ≃ 66 58.06 N 31.31 E
Polistena 36 38.25 N 16.05 E
Politécnico Nacional, Instituto ♦[2] 276a 19.30 N 99.08 W
Politotdel'skoje 73 47.33 N 39.05 E
Pölitz → Police 30 53.35 N 14.33 E
Polivanovo 70 53.36 N 47.23 E
Políyiros 38 40.23 N 23.27 E
Polk, Nebr., U.S. 188 41.05 N 97.46 W
Polk, Ohio, U.S. 204 40.57 N 82.13 W
Polk, Pa., U.S. 204 41.22 N 79.56 W
Polk □[6], Fla., U.S. 210 28.01 N 81.37 W
Polk □[6], Oreg., U.S. 214 45.00 N 123.23 W
Polk □[6], Tex., U.S. 212 30.45 N 94.48 W
Polk City 210 28.11 N 81.50 W
Pol'kino 64 71.10 N 99.13 E
Polkton 182 35.00 N 80.12 W
Polla 36 40.30 N 15.30 E
Pollāchi 112 10.40 N 77.01 E
Pollaphuca Reservoir ⊜[1] 28 53.08 N 6.31 W
Pöllau 30 47.18 N 15.51 E
Polleben 50 51.34 N 11.36 E
Pollenza 60 43.16 N 13.21 E
Polling 58 47.48 N 11.09 E
Pollino, Monte ∧ 36 39.55 N 16.11 E
Pollnow → Polanów 30 54.08 N 16.39 E
Polloc Harbor C 106 7.23 N 124.12 E
Pollock, La., U.S. 184 31.31 N 92.24 W
Pollock, S. Dak., U.S. 188 45.55 N 100.17 W
Pollock Pines 216 38.46 N 120.34 W
Pollock Run ≃ 269b 40.14 N 79.47 W
Pollok 212 31.27 N 94.52 W
Pollutri 60 42.08 N 14.35 E
Pollux ∧ 162 44.14 S 168.53 E
Polmak 24 70.04 N 28.00 E
Polná 30 49.29 N 15.43 E
Polnaja ≃ 73 48.54 N 39.50 E
Pol'noje-Jaltunovo 70 53.59 N 41.52 E
Polnovo-Seliger 66 57.32 N 32.55 E
Polo, Pil. 259f 14.42 N 120.57 E
Polo, Ill., U.S. 180 41.59 N 89.35 W
Polo, Mo., U.S. 184 39.33 N 94.03 W
Polochic ≃ 226 15.28 N 89.22 W
Polock, S.S.S.R. 66 55.31 N 28.46 E
Polock, S.S.S.R. 76 52.46 N 59.42 E
Pologi 68 47.29 N 36.15 E
Pologne → Poland □[1] 30 52.00 N 19.00 E
Pologoje Zajmišče 70 48.29 N 45.57 E
Pologrudovo 76 57.07 N 74.13 E
Polom, S.S.S.R. 24 59.13 N 50.50 E
Polom, S.S.S.R. 70 57.47 N 53.29 E
Polo Magnético del Sur → South Magnetic Pole ◂ 9 66.40 S 140.10 E
Pölömäki ∧[2] 26 63.21 N 27.03 E
Polomet' ≃ 66 57.41 N 32.12 E
Polonia → Poland □[1] 30 52.00 N 19.00 E
Polonia, Arroyo ≃ 248 34.10 S 57.15 W
Poloninskij Chrebet ⋀ 68 48.40 N 23.20 E
Polonio, Cabo ≻ 242 34.24 S 53.46 W
Polonio Pass)(216 35.37 N 120.11 W
Polonnaruwa 112 7.56 N 81.00 E
Polonnaruwa ⊥ 112 7.56 N 81.00 E
Polonnoje 68 50.07 N 27.30 E
Polos 120 41.50 N 27.04 E
Pološkovo 72 54.08 N 35.53 E
Polo Sur → South Pole ◂ 9 90.00 S 0.00
Polotn'anyj 72 55.44 N 36.00 E
Polotsk → Polock 66 55.31 N 28.46 E
Polovinkino 73 49.14 N 38.55 E
Polovinnoje, S.S.S.R. 76 54.43 N 63.50 E
Polovinnoje, S.S.S.R. 76 53.46 N 79.15 E
Polovo 66 57.03 N 32.27 E
Polperro 44 50.19 N 4.31 W
Polruan 44 50.19 N 4.36 W
Polska → Poland □[1] 30 52.00 N 19.00 E
Polski Trâmbeš 38 43.22 N 25.38 E
Polson 192 47.41 N 114.09 W
Polsum 48 51.37 N 7.03 E
Poltava 68 49.35 N 34.34 E
Poltavka 76 54.22 N 71.45 E
Poltevy Pen'ki 70 54.35 N 42.06 E
Poltimore 178 45.47 N 75.43 W
Põltsamaa 66 58.38 N 25.58 E
Põltsamaa ≃ 66 58.27 N 26.09 E
Poludino 76 54.51 N 69.55 E
Poluj ≃ 64 66.31 N 66.33 E
Polunočnoje 62 60.52 N 60.25 E
Poluokenushan ⋀ 76 44.06 N 83.10 E
Polūr 112 12.30 N 79.08 E
Polur'adinki 72 54.51 N 38.41 E
Poluškino 255b 55.41 N 38.05 E
Pol'ustrovo ◂[8] 255a 59.58 N 30.25 E
Põlva 66 58.03 N 27.03 E
Polvaredas 248 35.35 S 59.30 W
Polverigi 60 43.31 N 13.23 E
Polvijärvi 26 62.51 N 29.22 E
Polvoranca 256a 40.19 N 3.48 W
Polynesia II 14 4.00 S 156.00 W
Polynésie française → French Polynesia □[2] 14 15.00 S 140.00 W
Polynnoje 70 46.51 N 46.56 E
Polysajevo 76 54.35 N 86.14 E
Pölzig 50 50.57 N 12.11 E
Pomabamba 238 8.50 S 77.28 W
Pomacanchi 238 14.02 S 71.34 W
Pomacocha 238 5.50 S 77.55 W
Pomahaka ≃ 162 46.09 S 169.34 E
Pomán 242 28.24 S 66.13 W
Pomarance 60 43.18 N 10.52 E
Pomarkku 26 61.42 N 22.00 E
Pomaro 224 18.20 N 103.18 W
Pomata 238 16.16 S 69.18 W
Pomáz 254c 47.39 N 19.02 E
Pomba ≃ 246 21.24 S 42.32 W
Pombais, Ribeira de ≃ 256c 38.48 N 9.07 W
Pombal, Bra. 240 6.46 S 37.47 W
Pombal, Port. 34 39.55 N 8.38 W
Pombas, Rio das ≃ 238 6.27 S 60.18 W
Pombia 256b 45.39 N 8.38 E
Pomellen 50 53.20 N 14.23 E
Pomene 146 22.53 S 35.33 E
Pomerania □[3] 50 53.40 N 14.35 E
Pomeranian Bay C 50 54.00 N 14.15 E
Pomerene 190 32.01 N 110.17 W
Pomerode 242 26.45 S 49.11 W
Pomeroon ≃ 236 7.37 N 58.45 W
Pomeroy, S. Afr. 148 28.33 S 30.26 E
Pomeroy, N. Ire., U.K. 42 54.36 N 6.55 W
Pomeroy, Iowa, U.S. 188 42.33 N 94.41 W
Pomeroy, Ohio, U.S. 178 39.02 N 82.02 W
Pomeroy, Pa., U.S. 198 39.58 N 75.53 W
Pomeroy, Wash., U.S. 192 46.28 N 117.36 W
Pomezia 60 41.40 N 12.30 E
Pomfret, S. Afr. 146 25.50 S 23.32 E
Pomfret, Conn., U.S. 197 41.54 N 71.58 W
Pomfret, Md., U.S. 198 38.35 N 77.02 W
Pomi 38 47.42 N 23.19 E
Pomigliano d'Arco 60 40.54 N 14.23 E
Pominovo 72 55.26 N 39.11 E
Pomio 154 5.30 S 151.30 E
Pommard 54 47.01 N 4.47 E
Pomme de Terre ≃, Minn., U.S. 188 45.10 N 96.05 W
Pomme de Terre ≃, Mo., U.S. 184 38.11 N 93.24 W
Pomme de Terre Reservoir ⊜[1] 184 37.51 N 93.19 W
Pommera 46 50.10 N 2.26 E
Pommern → Pomerania □[9] 30 53.40 N 14.35 E
Pommersche Bucht → Pomeranian Bay C 50 54.00 N 14.15 E
Pommersfelden 52 49.46 N 10.49 E
Pomona, Arg. 244 39.28 S 65.30 W
Pomona, Namibia 146 27.09 S 15.18 E
Pomona, Calif., U.S. 218 34.04 N 117.45 W
Pomona, Kans., U.S. 188 38.36 N 95.27 W
Pomona, N.J., U.S. 198 39.29 N 74.35 W
Pomona, N.Y., U.S. 266 41.10 N 74.02 W
Pomona Estates 263d 26.06 S 28.15 E
Pomona Lake ⊜[1] 188 38.40 N 95.35 W
Pomona Park 182 29.30 N 81.36 W
Pomongo 142 5.00 S 19.08 E
Pomor'any 68 49.38 N 24.56 E
Pomorie 38 42.33 N 27.39 E
Pomorze → Pomerania □[9] 30 53.40 N 14.35 E
Pomošnaja 68 48.14 N 31.26 E
Pomozdino 24 62.12 N 54.06 E
Pompano Beach 210 26.15 N 80.07 W
Pompano Beach Highlands 210 26.18 N 80.11 W
Pompei 60 40.45 N 14.30 E
Pompei ⊥ 60 40.45 N 14.30 E
Pompéia 245 22.08 S 50.10 W
Pompejevka 79 48.23 N 130.46 E
Pompeston Creek ≃ 275 40.01 N 75.01 W
Pompéu 245 19.12 S 44.59 W
Pompey, Fr. 52 48.46 N 6.07 E
Pompey, N.Y., U.S. 200 42.54 N 76.01 W
Pomponio Beach ♠ 272 37.17 N 122.24 W
Pomponio Creek ≃ 272 37.18 N 122.25 W
Pomponne 251 48.53 N 2.41 E
Pompon-yama ∧ 260 34.56 N 135.37 E
Pomposa 60 44.49 N 12.11 E
Pompton ≃ 266 40.54 N 74.16 W
Pompton Lakes 200 41.00 N 74.17 W
Pompton Lakes ⊜ 266 41.00 N 74.17 W
Pompton Plains 266 40.58 N 74.18 W
Pomquet 176 45.38 N 61.51 W
Pomssen 50 51.14 N 12.37 E
Ponape 164r 6.58 N 158.13 E
Ponape □[5] 164r 6.52 N 158.15 E
Ponape I 164r 6.55 N 158.15 E
Ponape Harbor C 164r 7.00 N 158.13 E
Ponask Lake ⊜ 174 54.00 N 92.41 W
Ponass Lake ⊜ 174 52.18 N 103.58 W
Ponazyrevo 70 58.21 N 46.19 E
Ponca 188 42.34 N 96.43 W
Ponca City 186 36.42 N 97.05 W
Ponca Creek ≃ 188 42.48 N 98.05 W
Ponce 230m 18.01 N 66.37 W
Ponce de Leon 184 30.44 N 85.56 W
Ponce de Leon Bay C 210 25.21 N 81.07 W
Ponce de Leon Inlet C 182 29.04 N 80.55 W
Poncé-sur-le-Loir 46 47.46 N 0.40 E
Poncha Pass)(190 38.25 N 106.05 W
Ponchatoula 184 30.26 N 90.26 W
Poncin 54 46.05 N 5.24 E
Poncitlán 224 20.22 N 102.55 W
Pond Brook ≃, N.J., U.S. 266 41.02 N 74.15 W
Pond Brook ≃, Ohio, U.S. 269a 41.17 N 81.24 W
Pondcreek 186 36.40 N 97.48 W
Pond Creek ≃, Colo., U.S. 188 38.17 N 103.40 W
Pond Creek ≃, Tex., U.S. 212 31.02 N 96.46 W
Pond Eddy 200 41.27 N 74.49 W
Ponder 212 33.11 N 97.17 W
Pondera Coulee ∨ 192 48.16 N 111.03 W
Ponders End ◂[8] 250 51.39 N 0.03 W
Pondicherry 112 11.56 N 79.53 E
Pondicherry □[8] 112 11.56 N 79.50 E
Pond Inlet 166 72.41 N 78.00 W
Pond Inlet C 166 72.46 N 77.00 W
Pondok Tanjong 104 5.00 N 100.44 E
Pondoland ◂[1] 148 31.10 S 29.30 E
Pondosa 194 41.12 N 121.41 W
Pond Run ≃ 275 40.13 N 74.44 W
Poneas Island I 106 9.55 N 125.57 E
Ponente, Riviera di ⊥[2] 56 44.10 N 8.20 E
Ponérihouen 165f 21.05 S 165.24 E
Poneto 206 40.39 N 85.13 W
Ponežukaj 68 44.53 N 39.22 E
Ponferrada 34 42.33 N 6.35 W
Pong 100 19.10 N 100.17 E
Pongani 154 9.05 S 148.35 E
Pongara, Pointe ≻ 142 0.21 N 9.21 E
Pongaroa 162 40.33 S 176.11 E
Pongau ∨ 58 47.21 N 13.14 E
Ponghyŏn 88 37.49 N 125.36 E
Pongo ≃ 130 8.42 N 27.40 E
Pongola ≃ 148 26.57 S 32.17 E
Pon'goma 24 65.21 N 34.25 E
Pong Tamale 140 9.41 N 0.49 W
Ponhook Lake ⊜ 176 44.18 N 64.54 W
Poni ≃ 198 38.07 N 77.26 W
Poniatowa 30 51.11 N 22.05 E
Poniec 30 51.47 N 16.50 E
Ponil Creek ≃ 186 36.29 N 104.48 W
Poninka 68 50.12 N 27.32 E
Ponino 70 58.16 N 52.49 E
Pönitz, B.R.D. 50 54.03 N 10.40 E
Ponitz, D.D.R. 50 50.51 N 12.25 E
Ponizovje 66 55.17 N 31.04 E
Ponkapog Pond ⊜ 273 42.12 N 71.06 W
Pônley 100 12.26 N 104.27 E
Ponnaiyār ≃ 112 11.46 N 79.47 E
Ponnāni 112 10.46 N 75.54 E
Ponnūru Nidubrolu 112 16.04 N 80.34 E
Pono 154 6.22 S 134.36 E
Ponoj 24 67.05 N 41.07 E
Ponoj ≃ 24 66.59 N 41.17 E
Ponoka 172 52.42 N 113.35 W
Ponomar'ovka, S.S.S.R. 70 53.19 N 54.08 E
Ponomar'ovka, S.S.S.R. 76 56.08 N 82.23 E
Ponornica 68 51.43 N 32.49 E
Ponorogo 105a 7.52 S 111.27 E
Ponpāj 262b 22.56 N 88.15 E
Pons, Esp. 34 41.55 N 1.12 E
Pons, Fr. 32 45.35 N 0.33 W
Ponsacco 60 43.37 N 10.38 E
Ponson Island I 106 10.46 N 124.32 E
Ponsul ≃ 34 39.40 N 7.31 W
Pont 56 45.34 N 7.07 E
Ponta ≃ 240 7.46 S 51.09 W
Pont-à-Celles 46 50.30 N 4.21 E
Ponta da Areia 245 17.44 S 39.14 W
Ponta Delgada 138a 37.44 N 25.40 W
Ponta de Pedras 240 1.23 S 48.52 W
Ponta Grossa 242 25.05 S 50.09 W
Pontal ≃ 240 9.08 S 40.12 W
Pontalete 246 21.27 S 45.40 W
Pontalina 245 17.31 S 49.27 W
Pontallier-sur-Saône 54 47.18 N 5.25 E
Pont-à-Marcq 46 50.31 N 3.07 E
Pont-à-Mousson 52 48.54 N 6.04 E
Pontão 34 39.55 N 8.22 W
Ponta Porã 245 22.32 S 55.43 W
Pontardawe 44 51.44 N 3.51 W
Pontardulais 44 51.43 N 4.03 W
Pontarlier 54 46.54 N 6.22 E
Pontas de Pedras 240 7.38 S 34.48 W
Pontassieve 60 43.46 N 11.26 E
Pontaubert 46 47.29 N 3.52 E
Pont-Audemer 46 49.21 N 0.31 E
Pontault-Combault 251 48.47 N 2.36 E
Pontaumur 32 45.52 N 2.40 E
Pont-Aven 32 47.51 N 3.45 W
Pontbriand 196 46.09 N 71.15 W
Pont Canavese 56 45.25 N 7.36 E
Pontcarré 251 48.48 N 2.42 E
Pontcharra 56 45.26 N 6.01 E
Pontchartrain 251 48.48 N 1.54 E
Pontchartrain, Lake ⊜ 184 30.10 N 90.10 W
Pontchâteau 32 47.26 N 2.05 W
Pont-Croix 32 48.02 N 4.29 W
Pont-d'Ain 54 46.03 N 5.20 E
Pont-de-Bonne 52 50.27 N 5.17 E
Pont-de-Chéruy 56 45.45 N 5.11 E
Pont-de-l'Arche 46 49.18 N 1.10 E
Pont-de-Pany 54 47.18 N 4.49 E
Pont-de-Poitte 54 46.35 N 5.41 E
Pont-de-Roide 54 47.23 N 6.46 E
Pont-de-Ruan 46 47.15 N 0.35 E
Pont-de-Salars 32 44.17 N 2.44 E
Pont de Suert 34 42.24 N 0.45 E
Pont-de-Vaux 54 46.26 N 4.56 E
Pont-de-Veyle 54 46.16 N 4.53 E
Ponte a Elsa 60 43.41 N 10.54 E
Ponte Alta 246 22.26 S 47.06 W
Ponte Alta, Ribeirão da ≃ 246 21.32 S 44.03 W
Ponte Alta do Bom Jesus 245 12.06 S 46.29 W
Ponte Alta do Norte 240 10.45 S 47.34 W
Ponte a Moriano 60 43.54 N 10.31 E
Pontebba 58 46.30 N 13.18 E
Ponte Branca 245 16.27 S 52.40 W
Ponte Caffaro 58 45.50 N 10.32 E
Pontecchio Marconi 58 44.25 N 11.15 E
Pontecchio Polesine 58 45.01 N 11.49 E
Pontecorvo 60 41.27 N 13.40 E
Pontecurone 56 44.57 N 8.56 E
Ponte da Barca 34 41.48 N 8.25 W
Ponte d'Arbia 60 43.10 N 11.28 E
Ponte delle Arche 58 46.02 N 10.52 E
Ponte dell'Olio 56 44.52 N 9.39 E
Pontedera 60 43.40 N 10.38 E
Ponte de Sor 34 39.15 N 8.01 W
Ponte di Barbarano 58 45.23 N 11.34 E
Ponte di Legno 58 46.16 N 10.31 E
Ponte di Nava 56 44.08 N 7.53 E
Ponte di Piave 58 45.43 N 12.28 E
Ponte do Lima 34 41.46 N 8.35 W
Ponte do Púngoè 146 19.30 S 34.32 E
Pontefract 42 53.42 N 1.18 W
Ponte Galeria ◂[8] 257a 41.49 N 12.21 E
Ponte Gardena (Waidbruck) 58 46.36 N 11.32 E
Ponte Ghiereto 60 43.59 N 11.15 E
Pontegrande 54 45.59 N 8.09 E
Ponte in Valtellina 58 46.12 N 9.59 E
Ponteix 174 49.49 N 107.30 W
Pontelagoscuro 58 44.53 N 11.36 E
Ponteland 42 55.03 N 1.44 W
Pontelandolfo 60 41.17 N 14.41 E
Pontelongo 58 45.15 N 12.02 E
Ponte nell'Alpi 58 46.11 N 12.16 E
Ponte Nova 245 20.24 S 42.54 W
Pont-en-Royans 56 45.04 N 5.21 E
Ponte Nuovo 60 43.01 N 12.28 E
Pontenure 56 44.59 N 9.47 E
Pontepetri 60 44.02 N 10.53 E
Pontericcioli 60 43.26 N 12.38 E
Ponte Rocchetta 58 46.14 N 11.04 E
Ponterwyd 44 52.25 N 3.50 W
Pontes 246 22.26 S 46.28 W
Ponte San Giovanni 60 43.05 N 12.26 E
Ponte San Pietro 56 45.42 N 9.35 E
Pontesbury 44 52.39 N 2.54 W
Ponte Selva 58 45.52 N 9.54 E
Ponte Serrada 242 26.52 S 51.58 W
Pontestura 56 45.08 N 8.20 E
Ponte Tresa 54 45.58 N 8.52 E
Pontevedra, Arg. 248 34.45 S 58.42 W
Pontevedra, Esp. 34 42.26 N 8.38 W
Pontevedra, Pil. 106 10.22 N 122.52 E
Pontevedra, Ría de C[1] 34 42.22 N 8.45 W
Pont-Évêque 56 45.32 N 4.55 E
Pontevico 58 45.16 N 10.05 E
Pontfaverger-Moronvilliers 46 49.18 N 4.19 E
Pontgibaud 32 46.50 N 2.51 E
Ponthévrard 251 48.33 N 1.55 E
Ponthierry 251 48.32 N 2.33 E
Ponthierville → Ubundi 144 0.21 S 25.29 E
Pontiac, Ill., U.S. 180 40.53 N 88.38 W
Pontiac, Mich., U.S. 206 42.37 N 83.18 W
Pontiac □[6] 202 46.30 N 77.00 W
Pontiac, Parc de ♠ 180 46.25 N 76.35 W
Pontiac Lake 271 42.40 N 83.28 W
Pontiac Lake ⊜ 271 42.40 N 83.28 W
Pontiac Lake State Recreation Area ♠ 206 42.41 N 83.28 W
Pontiac Mall ◂[9] 271 42.39 N 83.20 W
Pontiac Metropolitan Stadium ♠ 271 42.39 N 83.15 W
Pontianak 102 0.02 S 109.20 E
Pontian Kechil 104 1.29 N 103.23 E
Pontida 56 45.43 N 9.30 E
Pontigny 46 47.55 N 3.43 E
Pontinha ◂[8] 256c 38.46 N 9.11 W
Pontinia 60 41.24 N 13.02 E
Pontivy 32 48.04 N 2.59 W
Pont-l'Abbé 32 47.52 N 4.13 W
Pont-lès-Moulins 54 47.19 N 6.22 E
Pont-l'évêque 46 49.18 N 0.11 E
Pontlevoy 46 47.23 N 1.15 E
Pontoise 46 49.03 N 2.06 E
Pontoise-Cormeilles-en-Vexin, Aérodrome ⊠ 251 49.06 N 2.02 E
Ponton Creek ≃ 152 31.10 S 124.25 E
Pontonnyj 255a 59.47 N 30.38 E
Pontoon Beach 209 38.43 N 90.04 W
Pontorson 32 48.33 N 1.31 W
Pontotoc, Miss., U.S. 184 34.15 N 89.00 W
Pontotoc, Tex., U.S. 186 30.54 N 98.59 W
Pontremoli 56 44.22 N 9.53 E
Pont-Remy 46 50.03 N 1.55 E
Pontresina 54 46.28 N 9.53 E
Pontrhydfendigaid 44 52.17 N 3.51 W
Pont-Rouge 196 46.45 N 71.42 W
Pont-Royal 56 43.43 N 5.11 E
Pont-Sainte-Marie 46 48.19 N 4.06 E
Pont-Sainte-Maxence 46 49.18 N 2.36 E
Pont-Saint-Esprit 56 44.15 N 4.39 E
Pont-Saint-Martin 56 45.36 N 7.48 E
Pont-Saint-Vincent 54 48.36 N 6.06 E
Pont-Scorff 28 47.50 N 3.24 W
Ponts Quentin, Ruisseau des ≃ 251 48.44 N 1.48 E
Pont-sur-Yonne 46 48.17 N 3.12 E
Pontuda, Ilha I 277a 23.02 S 43.18 W
Pontvallain 46 47.45 N 0.12 E
Pont-Viau ◂[8] 265a 45.34 N 73.41 W
Pontyberem 44 51.17 N 4.09 W
Pontycymmer 44 51.37 N 3.34 W
Pontypool 44 51.43 N 3.02 W
Pontypridd 44 51.37 N 3.22 W
Pony 192 45.40 N 111.54 W
Ponyri 66 52.19 N 36.20 E
Ponza 60 40.54 N 12.58 E
Ponziane, Isole I 60 40.55 N 12.57 E
Ponziane, Isole II 60 40.55 N 12.57 E
Ponzone 56 44.35 N 8.27 E
Poochera 152 32.43 S 134.51 E
Pool □[5] 142 3.30 S 15.00 E
Poole 44 50.43 N 1.59 W
Poole, Mount ∧ 156 29.37 S 141.46 E
Poole Bay C 44 50.42 N 1.52 W
Pooler 182 32.07 N 81.15 W
Pooles Island I 198 39.17 N 76.16 W
Poolesville 198 39.09 N 77.25 W
Pooley Island I 172 52.44 N 128.16 W
Poolville 212 32.58 N 97.52 W
Poona → Pune 112 18.32 N 73.52 E
Poona-Bayabo (Gata) 106 7.51 N 124.22 E
Pooncarie 156 33.23 S 142.34 E
Poondinna, Mount ∧ 152 27.20 S 129.59 E
Poopó 238 18.23 S 66.59 W
Poopó, Lago de ⊜ 238 18.45 S 67.07 W
Pooraka 158b 34.50 S 138.37 E
Poor Knights Islands II 162 35.30 S 174.45 E
Poor Man Indian Reserve ◂[4] 174 51.30 N 104.23 W
Poor Meadow Brook ≃ 273 42.01 N 70.55 W
Poortjie 148 30.13 S 22.44 E
Poowong 159 38.21 S 145.46 E
Popa, Isla I 226 9.11 N 82.07 W
Popasnaja 73 48.37 N 38.20 E
Popasnoje 68 48.48 N 35.31 E
Popayán 236 2.27 N 76.36 W
Pope 184 34.13 N 89.57 W
Pope Creek ≃ 216 38.37 N 122.17 W
Popel'n'a 68 49.57 N 29.27 E
Popel'nastoje 68 48.39 N 33.43 E
Poperečnoje 78 52.23 N 110.42 E
Poperinge 46 50.51 N 2.43 E
Popești-Leordeni 38 44.23 N 26.10 E
Pope Valley 216 38.37 N 122.26 W
Popham Bay C 166 64.10 N 65.10 W
Popigaj 64 71.55 N 110.47 E
Popigaj ≃ 64 72.54 N 106.36 E
Popilta Lake ⊜ 156 33.10 S 141.43 E
Popinci 38 42.25 N 24.17 E
Popki 70 50.11 N 44.30 E
Popkum 214 49.12 N 121.44 W
Poplar, Calif., U.S. 216 36.03 N 119.08 W
Poplar, Mont., U.S. 188 48.07 N 105.12 W
Poplar, Wis., U.S. 180 46.35 N 91.48 W
Poplar ◂[8] 250 51.31 N 0.01 W
Poplar ≃, Can. 174 53.00 N 97.24 W
Poplar ≃, N.A. 188 48.05 N 105.11 W
Poplar ≃, Minn., U.S. 188 47.51 N 96.04 W
Poplar, West Fork ≃ 188 48.31 N 105.22 W
Poplar Bluff 184 36.45 N 90.24 W
Poplar Grove 206 42.22 N 88.49 W
Poplar Heights 274c 38.53 N 77.12 W
Poplar Hill 174 52.05 N 94.18 W
Poplar Mountain ∧ 184 36.43 N 85.03 W
Poplar Point 174 50.04 N 97.57 W
Poplar Ridge 200 42.44 N 76.37 W
Poplar Springs 198 39.21 N 77.06 W
Poplarville 184 30.51 N 89.32 W
Poplevinskij 66 53.41 N 39.33 E
Popo Aggie ≃ 192 43.01 N 108.21 W
Popocatépetl, Volcán ∧[1] 224 19.02 N 98.38 W
Popof Island I 170 55.17 N 160.25 W
Popoh 105a 8.15 S 111.48 E
Popokabaka 142 5.42 S 16.35 E
Popoli 60 42.10 N 13.50 E
Popomanasiu, Mount ∧ 165e 9.42 S 160.04 E
Popondetta 154 8.46 S 148.14 E
Popova 79 42.58 N 131.42 E
Popovka, S.S.S.R. 66 60.08 N 39.21 E
Popovka, S.S.S.R. 70 49.14 N 41.12 E
Popovkino 72 56.07 N 36.01 E
Popovo 38 43.21 N 26.13 E
Poppel 52 51.27 N 5.02 E
Poppenbüttel ◂[8] 48 53.39 N 10.04 E
Poppenhausen 52 50.06 N 10.08 E
Poppi 60 43.43 N 11.46 E
Popple ≃ 180 45.50 N 88.21 W
Poprad 30 49.03 N 20.18 E
Poprad ≃ 30 49.38 N 20.42 E
Popricani 38 47.18 N 27.31 E
Pŏpsŏng 88 35.22 N 126.27 E
Pŏptong 88 38.59 N 127.05 E
Poptún 226 16.21 N 89.26 W
Populonia 60 42.59 N 10.29 E
Poputnaja 74 44.31 N 41.27 E
Poqinshumu 94 42.24 N 121.36 E
Poquessing Creek ≃ 275 40.03 N 74.58 W
Poquetanuck 197 41.29 N 72.03 W
Poquonock 197 41.54 N 72.41 W
Poquonock Bridge 197 41.19 N 72.11 W
Poquoson 198 37.07 N 76.21 W
Poquoson ≃ 198 37.10 N 76.24 W
Poquott 266 40.57 N 73.05 W
Porādaha 116 23.51 N 89.01 E
Porādiha 116 21.33 N 86.26 E
Porāli Nai ≃ 110 25.58 N 66.26 E
Poranga 240 4.44 S 40.55 W
Porangahau 162 40.18 S 176.37 E
Porangatu 245 13.26 S 49.10 W
Porbandar 110 21.38 N 69.36 E
Porce ≃ 236 7.28 N 74.53 W
Porcelette 52 49.09 N 6.36 E
Por Chaman 118 33.08 N 63.51 E
Porcher Island I 172 53.57 N 130.30 W
Porcheville 251 48.58 N 1.47 E
Porchov 66 57.46 N 29.34 E
Porcia 58 45.57 N 12.36 E
Porciúncula 245 20.58 S 42.02 W
Porco 238 19.50 S 65.59 W
Porcos, Ilha dos I, Bra. 240 0.25 S 51.05 W
Porcos, Ilha dos I, Bra. 246 23.33 S 45.04 W
Porcos, Rio dos ≃ 245 12.42 S 45.07 W
Porcuna 34 37.52 N 4.11 W
Porcupine ≃ 170 66.35 N 145.15 W
Porcupine Brook ≃ 273 42.46 N 71.13 W
Porcupine Dome ∧ 170 65.31 N 145.31 W
Porcupine Hills ⋀[2] 174 52.30 N 101.45 W
Porcupine Mountains ⋀ 180 46.40 N 89.40 W
Porcupine Mountains State Park ♠ 180 46.47 N 89.50 W
Porcupine Point ≻ 170 60.45 N 146.44 W
Pordenone 58 45.57 N 12.39 E
Pordenone □[4] 58 46.00 N 12.45 E
Pordim 38 43.23 N 24.51 E
Poreč 36 45.13 N 13.37 E
Porecatu 245 22.43 S 51.24 W
Porečje, S.S.S.R. 66 56.06 N 30.29 E
Porečje, S.S.S.R. 66 55.43 N 35.33 E
Porečje, S.S.S.R. 66 53.55 N 24.07 E
Porečje Rybnoje 70 57.06 N 39.23 E
Poreckoje 70 55.12 N 46.20 E
Porez 70 57.40 N 51.10 E
Pori 26 61.29 N 21.47 E
Poricy Brook ≃ 266 40.21 N 74.05 W
Porirua 162 41.08 S 174.51 E
Porjaguba 24 66.47 N 33.45 E
Porkkala 26 59.59 N 24.26 E
Porlamar 236 10.57 N 63.51 W
Porlezza 54 46.03 N 9.07 E
Porlock 44 51.14 N 3.36 W
Porma ≃ 34 42.29 N 5.28 W
Pornassio 56 44.04 N 7.52 E
Pornic 32 47.07 N 2.06 W
Porog, S.S.S.R. 24 63.50 N 38.29 E
Porog, S.S.S.R. 66 59.16 N 33.24 E
Porogi 255a 59.46 N 30.47 E
Poro Island I 106 10.40 N 124.27 E
Porokylä 26 63.33 N 29.06 E
Poroma 238 18.29 S 65.30 W
Poronaj ≃ 79 49.14 N 143.06 E
Poronajsk 79 49.14 N 143.04 E
Porong 105a 7.32 S 112.41 E
Porong ≃ 105a 7.32 S 112.51 E
Poropotank ≃ 198 37.27 N 76.42 W
Poror ∧ 144 1.14 N 36.37 E
Poroškovo 68 48.41 N 22.45 E
Porosozero 24 62.43 N 32.42 E
Poroto Mountains ⋀ 144 9.00 S 33.45 E
Porozovo 66 52.56 N 24.22 E
Porožskij 78 56.04 N 101.46 E
Porpoise Bay C 9 66.30 S 128.30 E
Porpoise Channel ⊔ 266 40.55 N 73.09 W
Porquerolles 56 43.00 N 6.12 E

Symbols in the index entries represent the broad categories identified in the key at the right. Symbols with superior numbers (⋀[2]) identify subcategories (see complete key on page I · 26).

Kartensymbole in dem Registerverzeichnis stellen die rechts in Schlüssel erklärten Kategorien dar. Symbole mit hochgestellten Ziffern (⋀[2]) bezeichnen Unterabteilungen einer Kategorie (vgl. vollständiger Schlüssel auf Seite I · 26).

Los símbolos incluídos en el texto del índice representan las grandes categorias identificadas con la clave a la derecha. Los símbolos con numeros en su parte superior (⋀[2]) identifican las subcategorías (véase la clave completa en la página I · 26).

Les symboles de l'index représentent les catégories indiquées dans la légende à droite. Les symboles suivis d'un indice (⋀[2]) représentent des sous-catégories (voir légende complète à la page I · 26).

Os símbolos incluídos no texto do índice representam as grandes categorias identificadas com a chave à direita. Os símbolos com números em sua parte superior (⋀[2]) identificam as subcategorias (veja-se a chave completa à página I · 26).

	English	Deutsch	Español	Français	Português
∧	Mountain	Berg	Montaña	Montagne	Montanha
⋀	Mountains	Berge	Montañas	Montagnes	Montanhas
)(	Pass	Pass	Paso	Col	Passo
∨	Valley, Canyon	Tal, Cañon	Valle, Cañón	Vallée, Canyon	Vale, Canhão
≃	Plain	Ebene	Llano	Plaine	Planície
≻	Cape	Kap	Cabo	Cap	Cabo
I	Island	Insel	Isla	Île	Ilha
II	Islands	Inseln	Islas	Îles	Ilhas
⊥	Other Topographic Features	Andere Topographische Objekte	Otros Elementos Topográficos	Autres données topographiques	Outros Elementos Topográficos

ESPAÑOL Nombre	Página	Lat.°′	Long.°′ W=Oeste

FRANÇAIS Nom	Page	Lat.°′	Long.°′ W=Ouest

PORTUGUÊS Nome	Página	Lat.°′	Long.°′ W=Oeste

Porquerolles, Île de I 56 43.00 N 6.13 E
Porrentruy 54 47.25 N 7.05 E
Porretta Terme 58 44.09 N 10.59 E
Porsangen C[2] 24 70.58 N 27.00 E
Porsangerhalvøya ≻[1] 24 70.50 N 25.00 E
Porsea 104 2.27 N 99.09 E
Porsgrunn 26 59.09 N 9.40 E
Porsuk ≃ 120 39.42 N 31.59 E
Port → Le Port 147c 20.55 S 55.18 E
Portachuelo 238 17.21 S 63.24 W
Port Adelaide 158b 34.51 S 138.30 E
Porta di Roma, Necropoli del ⊥ 257a 41.46 N 12.16 E
Portadown 42 54.26 N 6.27 W
Portaferry 42 54.23 N 5.33 W
Portage, Alaska, U.S. 170 60.50 N 148.58 W
Portage, Ind., U.S. 206 41.34 N 87.14 W
Portage, Mich., U.S. 206 42.12 N 85.41 W
Portage, Ohio, U.S. 206 41.20 N 83.39 W
Portage, Pa., U.S. 204 40.23 N 78.41 W
Portage, Utah, U.S. 190 41.59 N 112.14 W
Portage, Wis., U.S. 180 43.33 N 89.28 W
Portage □[6] 204 41.09 N 81.15 W
Portage ≃, Mich., U.S. 206 41.57 N 85.38 W
Portage ≃, Ohio, U.S. 204 41.31 N 83.05 W
Portage, East Branch ≃ 206 41.17 N 83.31 W
Portage, Middle Branch ≃ 206 41.22 N 83.28 W
Portage, North Branch ≃ 206 41.25 N 83.27 W
Portage, South Branch ≃ 206 41.22 N 83.30 W
Portage Bay C 174 51.33 N 98.50 W
Portage Des Sioux 209 38.55 N 90.21 W
Portage Lake ⊜, Mich., U.S. 206 42.03 N 85.31 W
Portage Lake ⊜, Mich., U.S. 206 42.25 N 83.54 W
Portage Lakes 204 40.59 N 81.32 W
Portage Lakes ⊜ 204 40.59 N 81.32 W
Portage Lakes State Park ♠ 204 40.57 N 81.32 W
Portage-la-Prairie 174 49.59 N 98.18 W
Portage Park •[8] 268 41.57 N 87.46 W
Portageville, Mo., U.S. 184 36.26 N 89.42 W
Portageville, N.Y., U.S. 200 42.34 N 78.02 W
Portal, Ga., U.S. 182 32.33 N 81.56 W
Portal, N. Dak., U.S. 188 48.59 N 102.33 W
Port Alberni 172 49.14 N 124.48 W
Portal del Infierno ⌊ 226 14.22 N 85.38 W
Portalegre, Bra. 240 6.02 S 38.00 W
Portalegre, Port. 34 39.17 N 7.26 W
Portales 186 34.11 N 103.20 W
Port Alexander 170 56.15 N 134.39 W
Port-Alfred, Qué., Can. 176 48.19 N 70.53 W
Port Alfred (Kowie), S. Afr. 148 33.36 S 26.55 E
Port Alice 172 50.23 N 127.27 W
Port Allegany 204 41.49 N 78.17 W
Port Allen 184 30.27 N 91.12 W
Port Alma, Austl. 156 23.35 S 150.51 E
Port Alma, Ont., Can. 204 42.11 N 82.15 W
Port Alsworth 170 60.12 N 154.20 W
Port Angeles 214 48.07 N 123.27 W
Port Angeles Harbor C 214 48.07 N 123.24 W
Port Anson 176 49.32 N 55.50 W
Port Antonio 231q 18.11 N 76.28 W
Port Aransas 186 27.50 N 97.04 W
Portarlington, Austl. 159 38.07 S 144.39 E
Portarlington, Eire 28 53.10 N 7.11 W
Port Arthur, Austl. 156 43.09 S 147.51 E
Port Arthur → Thunder Bay, Ont., Can. 180 48.23 N 89.15 W
Port Arthur, Tex., U.S. 184 29.55 N 93.55 W
Port Ashton 170 60.04 N 148.01 W
Port Askaig 42 55.51 N 6.07 W
Port Augusta 156 32.30 S 137.46 E
Port au Port 176 48.33 N 58.44 W
Port au Port Bay C 176 48.40 N 58.45 W
Port au Port Peninsula ≻[1] 176 48.35 N 59.00 W
Port-au-Prince 228 18.32 N 72.20 W
Port-au-Prince, Baie de C 228 18.40 N 72.30 W
Port Austin 180 44.03 N 83.01 W
Port aux Basques → Channel-Port-aux-Basques 176 47.34 N 59.09 W
Porta Westfalica 48 52.14 N 8.55 E
Porta Westfalica ♠ 48 52.14 N 8.55 E
Port Bannatyne 42 55.52 N 5.05 W
Port Barre 184 30.34 N 91.57 W
Port Bell 144 0.17 N 32.39 E
Port-Bergé 147b 15.33 S 47.40 E
Port Blair 100 11.40 N 92.45 E
Port Blakely 214 47.37 N 122.28 W
Port Blandford 176 48.21 N 54.10 W
Port Bolivar 212 29.23 N 94.46 W
Port Borden 176 46.15 N 63.42 W
Port-Bouët 140 5.15 N 3.58 W
Port Broughton 156 33.36 S 137.56 E
Port Burwell 172 42.39 N 80.49 W
Port Byron, Ill., U.S. 180 41.36 N 90.20 W
Port Byron, N.Y., U.S. 200 43.02 N 76.38 W
Port Campbell 159 38.37 S 143.00 E
Port Campbell National Park ♠ 159 38.38 S 142.55 E
Port Canning 116 22.18 N 88.40 E
Port Carbon 198 40.42 N 76.10 W
Port Carling 202 45.07 N 79.35 W
Port-Cartier-Quest 176 50.01 N 66.52 W
Port-Cartier-Sept-Îles, Parc de ♠ 176 50.35 N 67.10 W
Port Chalmers 162 45.49 S 170.37 E
Port Charlotte 210 26.59 N 82.06 W
Port Chester 210 41.00 N 73.40 W
Port Chester Harbor C 266 40.59 N 73.40 W
Port Chicago 216 38.03 N 122.01 W
Port Clements 172 53.42 N 132.11 W
Port Clinton, Austl. 158b 34.14 S 138.01 E
Port Clinton, Ohio, U.S. 204 41.31 N 82.56 W
Port Clinton, Pa., U.S. 198 40.35 N 76.02 W
Port Clyde 178 43.56 N 69.15 W
Port Colborne 202 42.53 N 79.14 W
Port Colden 202 40.46 N 74.57 W
Port Columbus International Airport ⊠ 208 40.00 N 82.53 W
Port Coquitlam 172 49.16 N 122.46 W
Port Costa 216 38.03 N 122.11 W
Port Crane 200 42.10 N 75.50 W
Port Credit 202 43.33 N 79.35 W
Port-Cros 56 43.00 N 6.24 E
Port-Cros, Île de I 56 43.00 N 6.24 E
Port-Daniel, Parc de ♠ 176 48.18 N 64.55 W
Port-Daniel, Réserve (Port Daniel Reserve) ♠ 176 48.18 N 64.55 W
Port-de-Bouc 56 43.24 N 4.59 E
Port-de-Paix 228 19.57 N 72.50 W
Port Dickinson 200 42.08 N 75.53 W
Port Dickson 120 2.31 N 101.48 E
Port Dover 202 42.47 N 80.12 W
Porte Crayon, Mount ∧ 178 38.56 N 79.27 W
Port Edward, B.C., Can. 172 54.14 N 130.18 W
Port Edward, S. Afr. 148 31.02 S 30.13 E
Port Edward → Weihai, Zhg. 88 37.28 N 122.07 E
Port Edwards 180 44.21 N 90.05 W
Portegolpe 226 10.20 N 85.46 W
Porteiras 240 7.31 S 39.07 W
Porteirinha 245 15.44 S 43.02 W
Portel, Bra. 240 1.57 S 50.49 W
Portel, Port. 34 38.18 N 7.42 W
Portel, Baía do C 240 1.55 S 50.47 W
Portela ≃ 277a 23.00 S 43.27 W
Portela, Aeroporto da ⊠ 256c 38.46 N 9.08 W
Port Elgin, N.B., Can. 176 46.03 N 64.05 W
Port Elgin, Ont., Can. 180 44.26 N 81.24 W
Port Elizabeth, St. Vin. 231h 13.03 N 61.13 W
Port Elizabeth, S. Afr. 148 33.58 S 25.40 E
Port Elizabeth, N.J., U.S. 198 39.19 N 74.59 W
Port Ellen 42 55.39 N 6.12 W
Port Elliot 158b 35.32 S 138.41 E
Porteña 242 31.01 S 62.04 W
Port-en-Bessin 32 49.21 N 0.45 W
Porter, Ind., U.S. 206 41.37 N 87.04 W
Porter, Okla., U.S. 196 35.52 N 95.31 W
Porter, Tex., U.S. 212 30.06 N 95.14 W
Porter, Wash., U.S. 214 46.56 N 123.18 W
Porter □[6] 206 41.28 N 87.04 W
Port'Ercole 60 42.23 N 11.12 E
Porter Corners 200 43.09 N 73.53 W
Porter Creek ≃ 269a 41.41 N 81.56 W
Port Erin 42 54.06 N 4.44 W
Porter Lake ⊜ 174 56.21 N 107.20 W
Porter Springs 212 31.16 N 95.36 W
Porters Retreat 160 34.00 S 149.48 E
Porters River ≃ 269b 40.27 N 79.33 W
Portersville 204 40.56 N 80.09 W
Porterville, S. Afr. 148 33.00 S 19.00 E
Porterville, Calif., U.S. 194 36.04 N 119.01 W
Porterville, Miss., U.S. 184 32.41 N 88.28 W
Portes-lès-Valence 56 44.52 N 4.53 E
Port Essington 172 54.09 N 129.57 W
Portete, Bahía de C 226 12.13 N 71.55 W
Port-Étienne → Nouadhibou 138 20.54 N 17.04 W
Port Ewen 200 41.54 N 73.59 W
Porteynon 44 51.33 N 4.13 W
Porteynon Point ≻ 44 51.32 N 4.12 W
Portezuelo 224 20.25 N 102.31 W
Port Fairy 158 38.23 S 142.14 E
Port Fitzroy 162 36.10 S 175.21 E
Port Gamble 214 47.51 N 122.35 W
Port Gamble Indian Reservation ✦[4] 214 47.53 N 122.34 W
Port-Gentil 142 0.43 S 8.47 E
Port Germein 156 33.01 S 138.00 E
Port Gibson, Miss., U.S. 184 31.58 N 90.58 W
Port Gibson, N.Y., U.S. 200 43.02 N 77.09 W
Port Glasgow 42 55.56 N 4.41 W
Portglenone 42 54.52 N 6.29 W
Port Graham 170 59.21 N 151.50 W
Port Greville 176 45.24 N 64.33 W
Porth 44 51.38 N 3.25 W
Port Hacking 264a 34.04 S 151.08 E
Port Hacking Point ≻ 264a 34.05 S 151.10 E
Port Hammond 214 49.13 N 122.39 W
Port Harcourt 140 4.43 N 7.05 E
Port Hardy 172 50.43 N 127.29 W
Port Hawkesbury 176 45.37 N 61.21 W
Porthcawl 44 51.29 N 3.43 W
Port Hedland 152 20.19 S 118.34 E
Port Heiden 170 56.55 N 158.41 W
Port Henry 178 44.03 N 73.28 W
Port Hill 176 46.35 N 63.53 W
Porth Neigwl C 44 52.48 N 4.34 W
Port Hood 176 46.01 N 61.32 W
Port Hope, Ont., Can. 202 43.57 N 78.18 W
Port Hope, Mich., U.S. 180 43.57 N 82.43 W
Port Hueneme 218 34.09 N 119.12 W
Port Hughes 158b 34.04 S 137.32 E
Port Huron 204 42.58 N 82.27 W
Portici 60 40.49 N 14.20 E
Porticino di Romagna 60 44.01 N 11.47 E
Port-Il'ič 74 38.53 N 48.48 E
Portillo 230p 19.55 N 77.11 W
Portimão 34 37.08 N 8.32 W
Portinho, Rio do ≃ 277a 23.03 S 43.35 W
Port Isaac 44 50.35 N 4.49 W
Port Isabel 186 26.04 N 97.13 W
Portishead 44 51.30 N 2.46 W
Port Jefferson, N.Y., U.S. 200 40.57 N 73.04 W
Port Jefferson, Ohio, U.S. 206 40.20 N 84.06 W
Port Jefferson Harbor C 266 40.58 N 73.05 W
Port Jefferson Station 200 40.56 N 73.03 W
Port Jervis 200 41.22 N 74.41 W
Port-Katon 73 46.52 N 38.46 E
Port Keats Mission 154 14.13 S 129.32 E
Port Kembla 160 34.29 S 150.54 E
Port Kennedy 275 40.06 N 75.25 W
Port Kenny 152 33.10 S 134.42 E
Port Lairge → Waterford 28 52.15 N 7.06 W
Port Lambton 204 42.39 N 82.30 W
Portland, Austl. 158 38.21 S 141.36 E
Portland, Austl. 160 33.22 S 150.00 E
Portland, N.Z. 162 35.48 S 174.19 E
Portland, Ark., U.S. 184 33.14 N 91.30 W
Portland, Conn., U.S. 197 41.34 N 72.38 W
Portland, Ind., U.S. 206 40.26 N 84.59 W
Portland, Maine, U.S. 178 43.39 N 70.17 W
Portland, Mich., U.S. 206 42.52 N 84.54 W
Portland, Mo., U.S. 209 38.43 N 91.43 W
Portland, N. Dak., U.S. 188 47.30 N 97.22 W
Portland, N.Y., U.S. 204 42.23 N 79.28 W
Portland, Oreg., U.S. 214 45.33 N 122.36 W
Portland, Pa., U.S. 200 40.55 N 75.06 W
Portland, Tenn., U.S. 184 36.35 N 86.31 W
Portland, Tex., U.S. 186 27.53 N 97.20 W
Portland, Wis., U.S. 206 43.12 N 88.58 W
Portland, Bill of ≻ 44 50.31 N 2.27 W
Portland, Cape ≻ 156 40.45 S 147.57 E
Portland, Isle of I 44 50.33 N 2.26 W
Portland Bay C 158 38.19 S 141.47 E
Portland Bight C[3] 231q 17.53 N 77.08 W
Portland Canal C 170 55.10 N 130.08 W
Portland Creek Pond ⊜ 176 50.12 N 57.34 W
Portland Inlet C 172 54.50 N 130.15 W
Portland International Airport ⊠ 214 45.35 N 122.36 W
Portland Island I 162 39.17 S 177.52 E
Portland Mills 204 41.23 N 78.50 W
Portland Point ≻ 231q 17.42 N 77.11 W
Portlandville 200 42.32 N 74.58 W
Port Laoise 28 53.02 N 7.17 W
Port Lavaca 212 28.37 N 96.38 W
Port-Lesney 54 47.00 N 5.49 E
Port Leyden 202 43.35 N 75.20 W
Port Lincoln 156 34.44 S 135.52 E
Port Lions 170 57.52 N 152.53 W
Portlock Reefs ✦[2] 154 9.30 S 144.45 E
Port Lockroy ↓[3] 9 64.48 S 63.30 W
Port Logan 42 54.43 N 4.57 W
Port Loko 140 8.46 N 12.47 W
Port-Louis, Fr. 32 47.43 N 3.21 W
Port-Louis, Guad. 231o 16.25 N 61.32 W
Port Louis, Maus. 147c 20.10 S 57.30 E
Port Ludlow 214 47.56 N 122.41 W
Port-Lyautey → Kenitra 136 34.16 N 6.40 W
Port MacDonnell 156 38.03 S 140.42 E
Port Macquarie 156 31.26 S 152.55 E
Port Madison Indian Reservation ✦[4] 214 47.45 N 122.35 W
Portmadoc 44 52.55 N 4.08 W
Portmahomack 28 57.49 N 3.50 W
Port Maitland, N.S., Can. 176 43.59 N 66.09 W
Port Maitland, Ont., Can. 204 42.52 N 79.34 W
Port Maria 231q 18.22 N 76.54 W
Port Matilda 204 40.48 N 78.03 W
Port Mayaca 210 26.59 N 80.36 W
Port McNeill 172 50.35 N 127.06 W
Port McNicoll 202 44.45 N 79.49 W
Port Melbourne 264b 37.51 S 144.56 E
Port Mellon 172 49.32 N 123.29 W
Port-Menier 176 49.48 N 64.20 W
Port Moller 170 55.59 N 160.34 W
Port Monmouth 266 40.26 N 74.07 W
Port Moody 172 49.17 N 122.51 W
Port Morant 231q 17.54 N 76.19 W
Port Moresby 154 9.30 S 147.10 E
Port Morien 176 46.08 N 59.52 W
Port Morris 266 40.54 N 74.41 W
Port Mouton 176 43.56 N 64.51 W
Port Murray 200 40.47 N 74.55 W
Portnahaven 42 55.41 N 6.31 W
Port Neches 184 29.59 N 93.58 W
Port Neill 156 34.07 S 136.20 E
Port Nelson 174 57.03 N 92.36 W
Portneuf 196 46.42 N 71.53 W
Portneuf □[6] 196 46.45 N 72.00 W
Portneuf ≃, Qué., Can. 176 48.38 N 69.05 W
Portneuf ≃, Qué., Can. 196 46.42 N 71.53 W
Portneuf ≃, Idaho, U.S. 192 42.58 N 112.35 W
Portneuf, Lac ⊜ 176 49.08 N 70.18 W
Portneuf-Station 196 46.43 N 71.54 W
Portneuf-sur-Mer 176 48.37 N 69.06 W
Port Neville 172 50.29 N 126.05 W
Port Noarlunga 158b 35.09 S 138.28 E
Port Nolloth 146 29.17 S 16.51 E
Port Norris 198 39.15 N 75.02 W
Port-Nouveau-Québec 166 58.32 N 65.54 W
Pôrto, Bra. 240 3.54 S 42.42 W
Pôrto, Port. 34 41.11 N 8.36 W
Pôrto, Bonifica di ⊥ 257a 41.48 N 12.16 E
Pôrto Acre 238 9.34 S 67.31 W
Pôrto Alegre, Bra. 242 30.04 S 51.11 W
Pôrto Alegre, S. Tom./P. 142 0.02 N 6.32 E
Pôrto Alexandre 142 15.49 S 11.53 E
Pôrto Amazonas 242 25.33 S 49.53 W
Pôrto Amboim 142 10.44 S 13.44 E
Pôrto Amélia 144 12.58 S 40.30 E
Porto Azzurro 60 42.46 N 10.24 E
Portobello 42 55.58 N 3.07 W
Pôrto Belo, Bra. 242 27.10 S 48.33 W
Portobelo, Pan. 226 9.33 N 79.39 W
Pôrto Calvo 240 9.04 S 35.24 W
Porto Ceresio 54 45.54 N 8.55 E
Pôrto das Caixas 246 22.42 S 42.53 W
Pôrto d'Ascoli 60 42.55 N 13.53 E
Pôrto das Flores 246 22.05 S 43.34 W
Pôrto das Gabarras 240 3.07 S 44.34 W
Pôrto de Mós 240 1.33 S 52.14 W
Pôrto de Moz 240 1.45 S 52.14 W
Pôrto de Pedras 240 9.10 S 35.17 W
Porto di Potenza Picena 60 43.21 N 13.42 E
Porto Empedocle 36 37.17 N 13.32 E
Pôrto Esperança 238 19.37 S 57.27 W
Pôrto Esperidião 238 15.51 S 58.28 W
Pôrto Farina 36 37.10 N 10.12 E
Pôrto Feliz 245 23.13 S 47.32 W
Portoferraio 60 42.49 N 10.19 E
Pôrto Ferreira 245 21.51 S 47.28 W
Portofino 56 44.18 N 9.12 E
Pôrto Franco 240 6.20 S 47.24 W
Port of Spain 231r 10.39 N 61.31 W
Porto Garibaldi 60 44.41 N 12.14 E
Pôrto Grande 240 0.42 N 51.24 W
Portogruaro 58 45.47 N 12.50 E
Pôrto Inglês 140a 15.08 N 23.13 W
Portola 194 39.48 N 120.28 W
Portola State Park ♠ 216 37.15 N 122.13 W
Portola Valley 216 37.23 N 122.13 W
Pôrto Lucena 242 27.51 S 55.01 W
Pörtom (Pirttikylä) 26 62.42 N 21.37 E
Portomaggiore 58 44.42 N 11.48 E
Pôrto Maurizio 56 43.52 N 8.01 E
Pôrto Mendes 242 24.30 S 54.20 W
Pôrto Murtinho 238 21.42 S 57.52 W
Pôrto Nacional 240 10.42 S 48.25 W
Porto-Novo, Benin 140 6.29 N 2.37 E
Porto Novo, Bhārat 112 11.29 N 79.46 E
Porto Novo Creek C 263a 6.26 N 3.20 E
Port Orange 182 29.09 N 80.59 W
Port Orchard 214 47.32 N 122.38 W
Pôrto Real 246 22.25 S 44.20 W
Pôrto Real do Colégio 240 10.11 S 36.49 W
Porto Recanati 60 43.26 N 13.40 E
Port Orford 192 42.45 N 124.30 W
Porto Rico 142 6.08 S 12.30 E
Porto Rico → Puerto Rico □[2] 230m 18.15 N 66.30 W
Portorož 58 45.31 N 13.36 E
Porto Salvo 256c 38.43 N 9.18 W
Porto San Giorgio 60 43.11 N 13.48 E
Porto Sant'Elpidio 60 43.15 N 13.45 E
Porto Santo I 138 33.04 N 16.20 W
Porto Santo Stefano 60 42.26 N 11.07 E
Pôrto São José 245 22.43 S 53.10 W
Pôrto Seguro, Bra. 245 16.26 S 39.05 W
Porto-Séguro, Togo 140 6.12 N 1.29 E
Porto Tolle 60 44.56 N 12.22 E
Porto Torres 36 40.50 N 8.23 E
Pôrto União 242 26.15 S 51.05 W
Pôrto Valter 238 8.15 S 72.45 W
Porto Valtravaglia 54 45.58 N 8.41 E
Porto-Vecchio 36 41.35 N 9.16 E
Pôrto Velho 238 8.46 S 63.54 W
Pôrto Velho da Cunha 246 21.50 S 42.32 W
Portovenere 56 44.03 N 9.51 E
Portoviejo 236 1.03 S 80.27 W
Portpatrick 42 54.51 N 5.07 W
Port Penn 198 39.31 N 75.35 W
Port Perry 202 44.06 N 78.57 W
Port Phillip Bay C 159 38.07 S 144.48 E
Port Pirie 156 33.11 S 138.01 E
Port Providence 275 40.08 N 75.30 W
Port Radium 166 66.05 N 118.02 W
Port Reading 266 40.34 N 74.16 W
Portree 28 57.24 N 6.12 W
Port Renfrew 172 48.33 N 124.25 W
Port Republic 198 39.31 N 74.29 W
Port Rexton 176 48.23 N 53.20 W
Port Richey 210 28.16 N 82.44 W
Port Richmond 198 37.33 N 76.49 W
Port Rowan 204 42.37 N 80.28 W
Port Royal, Jam. 231q 17.56 N 76.51 W
Port Royal, Ky., U.S. 208 38.33 N 85.05 W
Port Royal, Pa., U.S. 198 40.32 N 77.23 W
Port Royal, Va., U.S. 198 38.10 N 77.12 W
Port-Royal-des-Champs, Abbaye de ⊥ 251 48.45 N 2.01 E
Port Royal National Historic Park ♠ 176 44.44 N 65.40 W
Portrush 42 55.12 N 6.40 W
Port Said → Būr Sa'īd 132 31.16 N 32.18 E
Port-Sainte-Marie 32 44.15 N 0.24 E
Port Saint Joe 182 29.49 N 85.18 W
Port Saint Johns 148 31.38 S 29.33 E
Port-Saint-Louis 56 43.23 N 4.48 E
Port Saint Lucie 210 27.20 N 80.20 W
Port Saint Mary 42 54.05 N 4.43 W
Port-Saint-Servan 176 51.19 N 58.02 W
Port Salerno 210 27.09 N 80.12 W
Port Sanilac 180 43.26 N 82.33 W
Port Saunders 176 50.39 N 57.18 W
Portsea 159 38.19 S 144.43 E
Port Seton 42 55.58 N 2.57 W
Port Shepstone 148 30.46 S 30.22 E
Port Simpson 172 54.33 N 130.25 W
Portslade 44 50.50 N 0.11 W
Portsmouth, Dom. 230d 15.35 N 61.28 W
Portsmouth, Eng., U.K. 44 50.48 N 1.05 W
Portsmouth, N.H., U.S. 178 43.04 N 70.46 W
Portsmouth, Ohio, U.S. 208 38.45 N 82.59 W
Portsmouth, R.I., U.S. 197 41.36 N 71.15 W
Portsmouth, Va., U.S. 198 36.52 N 76.24 W
Portsmouth Naval Shipyard ■ 178 43.05 N 70.45 W
Portsoy 28 57.41 N 2.41 W
Port Stanley, Ont., Can. 204 42.40 N 81.13 W
Port Stanley → Stanley, Falk. Is. 244 51.42 S 57.51 W
Portstewart 42 55.11 N 6.43 W
Port Sudan → Būr Sūdān 130 19.37 N 37.14 E
Port Sulphur 184 29.29 N 89.42 W
Port Sunlight 252 53.21 N 2.59 W
Port-sur-Saône 54 47.41 N 6.03 E
Port Talbot 44 51.36 N 3.47 W
Porttipahdan tekojärvi ⊜[1] 24 68.08 N 26.40 E
Port Tobacco River C 198 38.27 N 77.02 W
Port Townsend 214 48.07 N 122.46 W
Port Trevorton 198 40.42 N 76.52 W
Portugal □[1] 22, 34 39.30 N 8.00 W
Portugal, Cachoeira ⌊ 238 9.55 S 64.16 W
Portugal Cove South 176 46.42 N 53.15 W
Portugalete 34 43.19 N 3.01 W
Portugália 142 7.20 S 20.47 E
Portuguesa □[3] 236 9.10 N 69.15 W
Portuguesa ≃ 236 7.57 N 67.32 W
Portuguese Guinea → Guinea-Bissau □[1] 140 12.00 N 15.00 W
Portumna 28 53.06 N 8.13 W
Port Union, Newf., Can. 176 48.30 N 53.05 W
Port Union, Ont., Can. 265b 43.47 N 79.08 W
Port-Vendres 32 42.31 N 3.07 E
Port Victoria → Victoria 128 4.38 S 55.27 E
Portville 200 42.02 N 78.20 W
Port Vincent 158b 34.47 S 137.51 E
Port-Vladimir 24 69.25 N 33.06 E
Port Vue 269b 40.20 N 79.52 W
Port Wakefield, Austl. 158b 34.11 S 138.09 E
Port Wakefield, Alaska, U.S. 170 57.52 N 152.51 W
Port Washington, B.C., Can. 214 48.49 N 123.19 W
Port Washington, N.Y., U.S. 200 40.49 N 73.41 W
Port Washington, Ohio, U.S. 204 40.20 N 81.31 W
Port Washington, Wis., U.S. 180 43.23 N 87.53 W
Port Weld 104 4.50 N 100.38 E
Port Wentworth 182 32.09 N 81.10 W
Port William, Scot., U.K. 42 54.46 N 4.35 W
Port William, Ohio, U.S. 208 39.33 N 83.47 W
Port Wing 180 46.47 N 91.23 W
Porum 186 35.22 N 95.16 W
Porus 231q 18.02 N 77.25 W
Porvenir 244 53.18 S 70.22 W
Porvoo → Borgå 26 60.24 N 25.40 E
Porvoonjoki ≃ 26 60.23 N 25.40 E
Porz 52 50.53 N 7.03 E
Porzdni 70 57.00 N 42.33 E
Porzuna 34 39.09 N 4.09 W
Posada 36 40.38 N 9.43 E
Posada ≃ 36 40.39 N 9.45 E
Posadas, Arg. 242 27.23 S 55.53 W
Posadas, Esp. 34 37.48 N 5.06 W
Posavina ∨ 36 45.10 N 17.20 E
Poščharv 75 38.24 N 71.10 E
Poschiavino ≃ 54 46.12 N 10.10 E
Poschiavo 54 46.18 N 10.04 E
Pošechonje-Volodarsk 66 58.30 N 39.07 E
Posen → Poznań, Pol. 30 52.25 N 16.55 E
Posen, Ill., U.S. 268 41.38 N 87.41 W
Posen, Mich., U.S. 180 45.16 N 83.42 W
Poseritz 50 54.18 N 13.16 E
Posesión, Bahía C 244 52.17 S 69.14 W
Posets, Pico de ∧ 34 42.39 N 0.25 E
Posevnaja 76 54.18 N 83.20 E
Poshan → Boshan 88 36.29 N 117.50 E
Poshiwu 96 30.22 N 119.36 E
Posieux 58 46.46 N 7.06 E
Posina 58 45.47 N 11.15 E
Posio 26 66.06 N 28.09 E
Positano 60 40.38 N 14.29 E
Posjet 79 42.39 N 130.50 E
Poso 102 1.23 S 120.44 E
Poso, Danau ⊜ 102 1.52 S 120.35 E
Poso, Teluk C 102 1.15 S 120.55 E
Poso Creek ≃ 194 35.36 N 119.23 W
Pos'olki 70 53.08 N 46.29 E
Pos'olok 255a 59.43 N 30.23 E
Posŏng 88 34.47 N 127.04 E
Posooy, Mount ∧ 106 17.21 N 120.48 E
Pospelicha 76 51.57 N 81.46 E
Possagno 58 45.51 N 11.51 E
Posse 245 14.05 S 46.22 W
Posse dos Coutinhos 246 22.49 S 42.45 W
Possendorf 50 50.57 N 13.42 E
Posses 246 21.43 S 46.08 W
Possession Sound ⋈ 214 48.00 N 122.20 W
Possidhonia ⊥ 38 37.40 N 24.00 E
Pössneck 50 50.42 N 11.37 E
Possum Kingdom Lake ⊜[1] 186 32.55 N 98.28 W
Post 186 33.12 N 101.23 W
Posta 60 42.31 N 13.06 E
Postal (Burgstall) 58 46.36 N 11.11 E
Postavy 66 55.07 N 26.50 E
Post Creek ≃ 200 42.09 N 77.02 W
Poste-de-la-Baleine 166 55.17 N 77.45 W
Poste-Mistassini 166 50.25 N 73.52 W
Poste Ramartina 147b 19.38 S 45.58 E
Posterholt 48 51.07 N 6.03 E
Poste Weygand 138 24.28 N 0.39 E
Post Falls 192 47.43 N 116.57 W
Postmasburg 148 28.18 S 23.05 E
Post Maurice Cortier (Bidon Cinq) 138 22.18 N 1.05 E
Pôsto do Registro 246 22.23 S 42.35 W
Postojna 36 45.47 N 14.13 E
Postojnska Jama •[7] 36 45.47 N 14.12 E
Postoloprty 50 50.20 N 13.40 E
P'ostraja Dresva 64 61.34 N 156.41 E
Postre Valle 238 18.29 S 63.51 W
Postsee ⊜ 50 54.13 N 10.13 E
Poststadion ♠ 254a 52.32 N 13.21 E
Postville 180 43.05 N 91.34 W
Pota 105b 8.20 S 120.46 E
Potaizi 94 41.34 N 121.08 E
Potake Pond ⊜ 266 41.08 N 74.13 W
Pótam 222 27.36 N 110.23 W
Potanino 66 60.16 N 32.47 E
Potapovo Vtoroje 255b 55.56 N 37.58 E
Potaro ≃ 236 5.22 N 58.54 W
Potaro Landing 236 5.23 N 59.08 W
Potato Creek ≃, Ga., U.S. 182 32.47 N 84.21 W
Potato Creek ≃, Pa., U.S. 204 41.53 N 78.23 W
Potawatomie Woods ♠ 268 42.08 N 87.53 W
Potawatomi Indian Reservation ✦[4] 188 39.20 N 95.50 W
Potchefstroom 148 26.46 S 27.01 E
Potè 245 17.49 S 41.49 W
Poteau 184 35.03 N 94.37 W
Poteau ≃ 184 35.23 N 94.26 W
Potechino 79 54.33 N 127.46 E
Poteet 186 29.02 N 98.34 W
Potengi 240 7.06 S 40.00 W
Potengi ≃ 240 5.47 S 35.16 W
Potenitz 50 53.57 N 10.58 E
Pötenitzer Wiek C 50 53.55 N 10.55 E
Potenza 36 40.38 N 15.49 E
Potenza ≃ 60 43.25 N 13.40 E
Potenza Picena 60 43.22 N 13.37 E
Poteriteri, Lake ⊜ 162 46.06 S 167.08 E
Potes 34 43.09 N 4.37 W
Potfontein 148 30.12 S 24.08 E
Potgietersrus 146 24.15 S 28.55 E
Poth 186 29.04 N 98.05 W
Potholes Reservoir ⊜[1] 192 47.01 N 119.19 W
Poti 74 42.09 N 41.40 E
Poti ≃ 240 5.02 S 42.50 W
Potic Creek ≃ 200 42.16 N 73.55 W
Potijevka 68 50.37 N 28.58 E
Potiraguá 245 15.36 S 39.53 W
Potirendaba 245 21.08 S 49.08 W
Potiská nížina ⌣ 30 48.40 N 22.00 E
Potiskum 136 11.43 N 11.05 E
Potlatch 192 46.55 N 116.54 W
Potlatch ≃ 192 46.28 N 116.46 W
Poto 238 14.42 S 69.33 W
Po Toi Group II 261d 22.11 N 114.16 E
Po Toi Island I 261d 22.10 N 114.15 E
Potol Point ≻ 106 11.56 N 121.57 E
Potomac, Ill., U.S. 206 40.18 N 87.48 W
Potomac, Md., U.S. 274c 39.01 N 77.12 W
Potomac ≃ 178 38.00 N 76.18 W
Potomac, South Branch ≃ 178 39.04 N 78.59 W
Potomac Creek ≃ 198 38.21 N 77.18 W
Potomac Creek, Long Branch ≃ 198 38.23 N 77.29 W
Potomac Heights 178 38.36 N 77.08 W
Poto Poto •[8] 263b 4.15 S 15.18 E
Potosi, Bol. 238 19.35 S 65.45 W
Potosi, Mo., U.S. 184 37.56 N 90.47 W
Potosí □[5] 238 20.40 S 67.00 W
Potosi, Cerro ∧ 222 24.52 N 100.13 W
Pototan 106 10.55 N 122.40 E
Potrerillos, Chile 242 26.26 S 69.29 W
Potrerillos, Hond. 226 15.11 N 87.58 W
Potrerillos Arriba 226 8.41 N 82.30 W
Potrero •[8] 272 37.48 N 122.24 W
Potrero de Gallegos 224 22.38 N 103.41 W
Potrero del Llano 186 29.12 N 104.28 W
Potrero Grande, C.R. 226 9.00 N 83.11 W
Potrero Grande, Méx. 222 24.59 N 106.26 W
Potsdam, D.D.R. 50 52.24 N 13.04 E
Potsdam, S. Afr. 148 32.56 S 27.42 E
Potsdam, N.Y., U.S. 178 44.40 N 74.59 W
Potsdam, Ohio, U.S. 208 39.58 N 84.25 W
Potsdam □[5] 50 52.30 N 12.45 E
Potsdam, Staatsforst ♠ 254a 52.26 N 13.04 E
Potshausen 48 53.11 N 7.37 E
Pott, Île I 165f 19.35 S 163.36 E
Pottawatomie Creek ≃ 184 38.29 N 94.55 W
Potten End 250 51.46 N 0.31 W
Potter 188 41.13 N 103.19 W
Potter □[6] 204 41.47 N 78.01 W
Potter Heigham 44 52.44 N 1.33 E
Potter Hollow 200 42.25 N 74.13 W
Potter Lake 206 44.07 N 88.06 W
Potter Point ≻ 264a 34.03 S 151.13 E
Potters Bar 44 51.42 N 0.11 W
Potters Mills 198 40.48 N 77.32 W
Potter Street 44 51.46 N 0.08 E
Pottersville 266 40.43 N 74.44 W
Potterville 206 42.38 N 84.45 W
Potton 44 52.08 N 0.14 W
Potts Camp 184 34.39 N 89.18 W
Potts Creek ≃ 182 37.45 N 80.00 W
Potts Grove 200 40.60 N 76.48 W
Potts Hill Reservoirs •[5] ⊜[1] 264a 33.54 S 151.02 E
Pott Shrigley 252 53.19 N 2.05 W
Pottstown 198 40.15 N 75.38 W
Pottstown Limerick Airport ⊠ 275 40.14 N 75.34 W
Pottsville 198 40.41 N 76.12 W
Potwin 188 37.56 N 97.01 W
Pötzleinsdorf •[8] 254b 48.15 N 16.19 E
Pötzleinsdorfer Park ♠ 254b 48.14 N 16.18 E
P'otzu 90 23.29 N 120.16 E
Pouancé 32 47.44 N 1.11 W
Pouce Coupe 172 55.43 N 120.08 W
Pouce Coupé ≃ 172 56.08 N 119.52 W
Pouch 50 51.37 N 12.24 E
Pouch Cove 176 47.46 N 52.46 W
Pouebo 165f 20.24 S 164.04 E
Pouembout 165f 21.08 S 164.53 E
Poughkeepsie 200 41.42 N 73.56 W
Poughquag 200 41.37 N 73.41 W
Pouilly-en-Auxois 54 47.16 N 4.33 E
Pouilly-sur-Loire 46 47.17 N 2.57 E
Pouilly-sur-Meuse 52 49.32 N 5.07 E
Poulain, Étang ⊜ 251 48.43 N 1.44 E
Poulan 182 31.31 N 83.47 W
Poulin-de-Courval, Lac ⊜ 176 48.52 N 70.27 W
Poulsbo 214 47.44 N 122.39 W
Poulter, Lac ⊜ 180 47.07 N 76.45 W
Poultney 178 43.31 N 73.14 W
Poulton-le-Fylde 42 53.51 N 2.59 W
Poume 165f 20.14 S 164.02 E
Poŭn 88 36.29 N 127.43 E
Pound 182 37.07 N 82.36 W
Poundmaker Indian Reserve ✦[4] 174 52.51 N 109.00 W
Poundstock 44 50.46 N 4.33 W
Pouoanuu, Mont ∧ 164x 9.49 S 139.07 W
Pourri, Mont ∧ 56 45.32 N 6.52 E
Pouru-Saint-Rémy 52 49.41 N 5.05 E
Pourville-sur-Mer 46 49.55 N 1.02 E
Pouso Alegre 246 22.13 S 45.56 W
Pouso Alto 246 22.11 S 44.58 W
Pouso Frio, Serra do ∧ 246 22.18 S 45.18 W
Pouso Redondo 242 27.15 S 49.57 W
Pouso Sêco 246 22.41 S 44.10 W
Pouss 136 10.51 N 15.03 E
Poutasi 165a 14.01 S 171.41 W
Poŭthĭsăt 100 12.32 N 103.55 E
Poŭthĭsăt ≃ 100 12.41 N 104.09 E
Pouxeux 54 48.06 N 6.34 E
Pouzauges 32 46.47 N 0.50 W
Považská Bystrica 30 49.08 N 18.27 E
Povenec 24 62.51 N 34.45 E
Poverennyj 62 45.40 N 43.12 E
Poverty Bay C 162 38.42 S 177.58 E
Povetkino 72 54.20 N 38.23 E
Poviglio 58 44.50 N 10.32 E
Povljen ∧ 38 43.55 N 19.30 E
Póvoa, Mouchão da I 256c 38.51 N 9.03 W
Povoação 138 37.45 N 25.15 W
Póvoa de Santa Iria 256c 38.52 N 9.04 W
Póvoa de Santo Adrião 256c 38.48 N 9.10 W
Póvoa de Varzim 34 41.23 N 8.46 W
Povorino 70 51.12 N 42.14 E
Povorotnyj, Mys ≻ 79 42.42 N 133.04 E
Povorsk 68 51.16 N 25.07 E
Povrly 50 50.40 N 14.10 E
Povungnituk 166 60.02 N 77.10 W
Povungnituk, Rivière de ≃ 166 60.03 N 77.15 W
Powassan 180 46.05 N 79.22 W
Poway 218 32.58 N 117.02 W
Poway Creek ≃ 218 32.56 N 117.15 W
Powder ≃, Mont., U.S. 168 46.44 N 105.26 W
Powder ≃, Oreg., U.S. 192 44.45 N 117.03 W
Powder, Dry Fork ≃ 190 43.47 N 106.15 W
Powder, Middle Fork ≃ 190 43.42 N 106.33 W
Powder, North Fork ≃ 192 43.42 N 106.33 W
Powder, Red Fork ≃ 192 43.39 N 106.47 W
Powder, South Fork ≃ 192 43.40 N 106.30 W
Powder Horn Lake ⊜ 268 41.38 N 87.32 W
Powderly 186 33.49 N 95.31 W
Powdermaker Ditch ≡ 269a 41.30 N 82.02 W
Powder River Pass)(192 44.09 N 107.04 W
Powell, Ohio, U.S. 204 40.09 N 83.05 W
Powell, Pa., U.S. 200 41.42 N 76.31 W
Powell, Tex., U.S. 212 32.07 N 96.20 W
Powell, Wyo., U.S. 192 44.45 N 108.46 W
Powell ≃ 182 36.29 N 83.42 W
Powell, Lake ⊜[1] 190 37.25 N 110.45 W
Powell, Mount ∧ 190 39.46 N 106.20 W
Powell Creek ≃, Austl. 156 25.02 S 143.40 E
Powell Creek ≃, Ohio, U.S. 206 41.17 N 84.21 W
Powellhurst 214 45.31 N 122.31 W
Powell Lake ⊜ 172 50.11 N 124.24 W
Powell River 172 49.52 N 124.33 W
Powells Valley 198 40.26 N 76.56 W
Powellton 178 38.05 N 81.19 W
Powers, Mich., U.S. 180 45.39 N 87.32 W
Powers, Oreg., U.S. 192 42.53 N 124.04 W
Powers Lake, N. Dak., U.S. 188 48.34 N 102.39 W
Powers Lake, Wis., U.S. 206 42.33 N 88.17 W
Powers Lookout ♠ 159 36.50 S 146.22 E
Powhatan, La., U.S. 184 31.52 N 93.12 W
Powhatan, Va., U.S. 182 37.29 N 77.55 W
Powhatan Point 178 39.52 N 80.49 W
Powis, Vale of ∨ 44 52.38 N 3.08 W
Powissett Brook ≃ 273 42.16 N 71.14 W
Powlett ≃ 159 38.35 S 145.32 E
Pownal 200 42.46 N 73.14 W
Powys □[6] 44 52.17 N 3.20 W
Poxoreu 245 15.50 S 54.23 W
Poya 165f 21.19 S 165.07 E
Poyang 90 28.59 N 116.40 E
Poyanghu ⊜ 90 29.00 N 116.25 E
Poyen 184 34.19 N 92.38 W
Poygan, Lake ⊜ 180 44.19 N 88.50 W
Poyle 250 51.28 N 0.31 W
Poynette 180 43.24 N 89.24 W
Poynor 212 32.04 N 95.36 W
Poynton 252 53.21 N 2.07 W
Poyntzpass 42 54.18 N 6.23 W
Poyraz 257b 41.12 N 29.07 E
Poyraz Burnu ≻ 257b 41.12 N 29.09 E
Poza Grande 222 25.50 N 112.05 W
Pozantı 120 37.25 N 34.52 E
Požarevac 38 44.37 N 21.11 E
Poza Rica de Hidalgo 224 20.33 N 97.27 W
Požarskoje 79 46.16 N 134.04 E
Pozdejevka 79 50.36 N 128.56 E
Požega 38 43.50 N 20.02 E
Poznań 30 52.25 N 16.55 E
Pozo Alcón 34 37.42 N 2.56 W
Pozo Almonte 238 20.16 S 69.48 W
Pozoblanco 34 38.22 N 4.51 W
Pozo-Cañada 34 38.48 N 1.45 W
Pozo del Molle 242 32.02 S 62.55 W
Pozo del Tigre 242 24.54 S 60.19 W
Pozo Hondo 242 27.10 S 64.30 W
Pozos 224 21.14 N 100.29 W
Pozos, Arroyo de los ≃ 278 34.57 S 58.45 W
Pozos, Punta ≻ 244 47.57 S 65.47 W
Pozsony → Bratislava 30 48.09 N 17.07 E
Pozuelo de Alarcón 34 40.26 N 3.49 W
Pozuelo de Alarcón •[8] 256a 40.26 N 3.49 W
Pozuelos 236 10.11 N 64.39 W
Pozuelos, Laguna de ⊜ 242 22.22 S 66.01 W
Pozuzo 238 10.04 S 75.32 W
Pozuzo ≃ 238 9.43 S 75.29 W
Požva 76 59.05 N 56.05 E
Pozzallo 36 36.43 N 14.52 E
Pozzolo Formigaro 56 44.48 N 8.47 E
Pozzuoli 60 40.49 N 14.07 E
Pozzuolo del Friuli 58 45.59 N 13.12 E
Pra ≃, Ghana 140 5.01 N 1.37 W
Pra ≃, S.S.S.R. 70 54.45 N 41.01 E
Prabuty 30 53.46 N 19.10 E
Praça Sêca •[8] 277a 22.53 S 43.21 W
Prachantakham 100 14.04 N 101.31 E
Prachatice 30 49.01 N 14.00 E
Prachin Buri 100 14.03 N 101.22 E
Prachuap Khiri Khan 100 11.49 N 99.48 E
Pracuí ≃ 240 2.26 S 51.09 W
Pracupí ≃ 240 2.06 S 51.30 W
Pradelles 56 44.46 N 3.53 E
Pradera 236 3.25 N 76.15 W
Pradleves 56 44.25 N 7.17 E
Prado 245 17.21 S 39.13 W
Prado, Museo del ⊥ 256a 40.25 N 3.41 W
Prado Churubusco 276a 19.21 N 99.07 W
Prado Dam ♠[6] 270 33.54 N 117.39 W
Prado Flood Control Basin ⊜[1] 270 33.54 N 117.38 W
Prados 245 21.03 S 44.05 W
Pr'adovka 68 48.55 N 34.41 E
Prads 56 44.13 N 6.27 E
Præstø 41 55.07 N 12.03 E
Prag → Praha 50 50.05 N 14.26 E
Praga → Praha 50 50.05 N 14.26 E
Pragelato 56 45.01 N 6.57 E
Praglia, Monastero di ♥[1] 58 45.23 N 11.45 E
Prägraten 58 47.01 N 12.23 E
Prague → Praha, Česko. 50 50.05 N 14.26 E
Prague, Nebr., U.S. 188 41.19 N 96.48 W
Prague, Okla., U.S. 186 35.29 N 96.41 W
Praha (Prague) 50 50.05 N 14.26 E
Praha ∧ 30 49.40 N 13.49 E
Prahova □[4] 38 45.00 N 26.00 E
Prahova ≃ 38 44.43 N 26.27 E
Prahran 264b 37.51 S 144.59 E
Praia 140a 14.55 N 23.31 W
Praia da Cruz Quebrada 256c 38.42 N 9.14 W
Praia das Maçãs 256c 38.50 N 9.28 W
Praia da Vitória 138a 38.44 N 27.04 W
Praia de Araçatiba 246 23.06 S 44.15 W
Praia Funda, Ponta da ≻ 277a 23.05 S 43.33 W
Praia Grande 242 29.12 S 49.57 W
Praiano 60 40.37 N 14.32 E
Praikalogu 105b 9.45 S 119.25 E
Prainha, Bra. 238 7.16 S 60.23 W
Prainha, Bra. 240 1.48 S 53.29 W

≃ River	Fluss	Río	Rivière	Rio
Canal	Kanal	Canal	Canal	Canal
⌊ Waterfall, Rapids	Wasserfall, Stromschnellen	Cascada, Rápidos	Chute d'eau, Rapides	Cascata, Rápidos
⋈ Strait	Meeresstrasse	Estrecho	Détroit	Estreito
C Bay, Gulf	Bucht, Golf	Bahía, Golfo	Baie, Golfe	Baía, Golfo
⊜ Lake, Lakes	See, Seen	Lago, Lagos	Lac, Lacs	Lago, Lagos
Swamp	Sumpf	Pantano	Marais	Pântano
Ice Features, Glacier	Eis- und Gletscherformen	Accidentes Glaciales	Formes glaciaires	Acidentes Glaciares
Other Hydrographic Features	Andere Hydrographische Objekte	Otros Elementos Hidrográficos	Autres données hydrographiques	Outros Elementos Hidrográficos

✦ Submarine Features	Untermeerische Objekte	Accidentes Submarinos	Formes de relief sous-marin	Acidentes Submarinos
□ Political Unit	Politische Einheit	Unidad Política	Entité politique	Unidade Política
♥ Cultural Institution	Kulturelle Institution	Institución Cultural	Institution culturelle	Instituição Cultural
⊥ Historical Site	Historische Stätte	Sitio Histórico	Site historique	Sítio Histórico
♠ Recreational Site	Erholungs- und Ferienort	Sitio de Recreo	Centre de loisirs	Sítio de Lazer
⊠ Airport	Flughafen	Aeropuerto	Aéroport	Aeroporto
■ Military Installation	Militäranlage	Instalación Militar	Installation militaire	Instalação Militar
• Miscellaneous	Verschiedenes	Misceláneo	Divers	Miscelânea

ENGLISH — Name / Page / Lat.°′ / Long.°′

DEUTSCH — Name / Seite / Breite°′ / Länge°′ E=Ost

Prairie 156 20.52 S 144.36 E
Prairie ≃, Mich., U.S. 206 41.55 N 85.38 W
Prairie ≃, Minn., U.S. 180 47.18 N 93.29 W
Prairie ≃, Wis., U.S. 180 45.10 N 89.42 W
Prairie City, Ill., U.S. 180 40.37 N 90.28 W
Prairie City, Iowa, U.S. 180 41.36 N 93.14 W
Prairie City, Oreg., U.S. 192 44.28 N 118.43 W
Prairie Creek ≃, Fla., U.S. 210 26.59 N 81.56 W
Prairie Creek ≃, Ill., U.S. 206 40.24 N 88.01 W
Prairie Creek ≃, Ill., U.S. 206 41.21 N 88.12 W
Prairie Creek ≃, Ill., U.S. 206 40.55 N 87.49 W
Prairie Creek ≃, Mich., U.S. 206 42.59 N 85.01 W
Prairie Creek ≃, Nebr., U.S. 188 41.22 N 97.32 W
Prairie Creek Reservoir ⊜[1] 208 40.08 N 85.17 W
Prairie Dog Creek ≃ 188 40.00 N 99.23 W
Prairie du Chien 180 43.03 N 91.09 W
Prairie du Sac 180 43.17 N 89.43 W
Prairie Elk Creek ≃ 188 48.00 N 105.51 W
Prairie Grove 184 35.59 N 94.19 W
Prairie Hill 212 31.39 N 96.47 W
Prairie Lea 212 29.44 N 97.45 W
Prairie River 174 52.52 N 103.00 W
Prairies, Coteau des ⋀[2] 188 44.30 N 96.45 W
Prairies, Rivière des ≃ 265a 45.42 N 73.29 W
Prairie View, Ill., U.S. 268 42.12 N 87.57 W
Prairie View, Tex., U.S. 212 30.04 N 96.00 W
Prairie Village 188 39.01 N 94.38 W
Prajekan 105a 7.47 S 113.59 E
Prakhon Chai 100 14.37 N 103.05 E
Pralboino 58 45.16 N 10.13 E
Prali 56 44.54 N 7.03 E
Pralls Island I 266 40.37 N 74.12 W
Pralognan-la-Vanoise 56 45.23 N 6.43 E
Pramaggiore, Monte ∧ 58 46.22 N 12.33 E
Prambanan 105a 7.45 S 110.30 E
Pr'amicyno 68 51.39 N 35.56 E
Pramort 50 54.26 N 12.55 E
Prampram 140 5.42 N 0.07 E
Pran Buri 100 12.23 N 99.55 E
Pran Buri ≃ 100 12.24 N 100.00 E
Prang 140 7.59 N 0.53 W
Prangli I 66 59.38 N 25.02 E
Pranzo 58 45.55 N 10.48 E
Prapa, Khlong ≋ 259a 13.46 N 100.32 E
Prapat 104 2.40 N 98.56 E
Praraye 54 45.55 N 7.32 E
Praskovejevka 73 48.40 N 38.00 E
Praslin, Lac ⊜ 176 50.03 N 69.48 W
Praslin, Port C 231f 13.53 N 60.54 W
Praslin Island I 128 4.19 S 55.44 E
Prasónisi, Ákra ≻ 38 35.42 N 27.46 E
Praszka 30 51.04 N 18.26 E
Prat, Isla I 244 48.15 S 75.00 W
Prata, Bra. 240 7.41 S 37.06 W
Prata, Bra. 245 19.18 S 48.55 W
Prata, Bra. 246 22.23 S 42.58 W
Prata, Bra. 277a 22.45 S 43.25 W
Prata, Rio da ≃, Bra. 245 18.49 S 49.54 W
Prata, Rio da ≃, Bra. 245 18.50 S 52.11 W
Prata, Rio da ≃, Bra. 245 17.28 S 46.35 W
Prata, Rio da ≃, Bra. 277a 22.56 S 43.34 W
Pratāpgarh 110 24.02 N 74.47 E
Pratapgarh □[5] 114 25.55 N 82.00 E
Pratāpnagar 116 22.23 N 89.13 E
Pratápolis 245 20.45 S 46.52 W
Pratas Islands → Dongshaqundao II 80 20.42 N 116.43 E
Pratau 50 51.50 N 12.38 E
Prat de Llobregat 34 41.20 N 2.06 E
Pratella 60 41.24 N 14.11 E
Prater ♠ 254b 48.12 N 16.25 E
Prathet Thai → Thailand □[1] 100 15.00 N 100.00 E
Pratinha 245 19.46 S 46.24 W
Prato 60 43.53 N 11.06 E
Prato allo Stelvio 58 46.37 N 10.35 E
Pratola Peligna 60 42.06 N 13.52 E
Pratola Serra 60 40.59 N 14.51 E
Pratolino 60 43.52 N 11.18 E
Pratomagno ⋀ 60 43.39 N 11.39 E
Pratt 188 37.39 N 98.44 W
Pratteln 54 47.31 N 7.42 E
Prättigau ∨ 54 46.55 N 9.45 E
Pratt's Bottom ◆[8] 250 51.20 N 0.07 E
Prattsburg 200 42.32 N 77.17 W
Prattsville 200 42.19 N 74.26 W
Prattville 184 32.28 N 86.29 W
Pratudão ≃ 245 13.56 S 44.55 W
Prauthoy 54 47.40 N 5.17 E
Pravaja Mama ≃ 78 57.10 N 111.54 E
Pravda 79 47.00 N 142.01 E
Pravdinsk, S.S.S.R. 66 54.27 N 21.01 E
Pravdinsk, S.S.S.R. 70 56.32 N 43.34 E
Pravdinskij 72 56.04 N 37.51 E
Pravia 34 43.29 N 6.07 W
Prawet Buri Rom, Khlong ≋ 259a 13.42 N 100.35 E
Prawle Point ≻ 44 50.13 N 3.42 W
Praya 105b 8.42 S 116.17 E
Pr'aža 24 61.42 N 33.35 E
Praz-sur-Arly 56 45.50 N 6.34 E
Prazzo 56 44.29 N 7.03 E
Preakness Brook ≃ 266 40.54 N 74.15 W
Preakness Mountain ∧ 266 40.58 N 74.13 W
Preakness Valley Park ♠ 266 40.55 N 74.14 W
Preble, Ind., U.S. 206 40.50 N 85.01 W
Preble, N.Y., U.S. 200 42.44 N 76.09 W
Preble □[6] 208 39.45 N 84.38 W
Preci 60 42.53 N 13.02 E
Prečistoje, S.S.S.R. 66 55.41 N 34.56 E
Prečistoje, S.S.S.R. 66 55.31 N 32.22 E
Prečistoje, S.S.S.R. 70 58.27 N 40.19 E
Précy-sous-Thil 46 47.23 N 4.19 E
Précy-sur-Marne 251 48.56 N 2.47 E
Précy-sur-Oise 46 49.12 N 2.22 E
Preda 54 46.36 N 9.46 E
Predappio 60 44.06 N 11.58 E
Predazzo 58 46.19 N 11.36 E
Predeal 38 45.30 N 25.35 E
Prédecelle ≃ 251 48.35 N 2.07 E
Predești 38 44.21 N 23.36 E
Predgornoje 76 47.10 N 81.02 E
Predivinsk 76 57.04 N 93.27 E
Predkarpatje ⋀[1] 68 49.00 N 24.30 E
Predlitz 58 47.04 N 13.55 E
Predmostnoje 68 45.57 N 34.37 E
Predoi (Prettau) 58 47.02 N 12.06 E
Predore 58 45.40 N 10.01 E
Preeceville 174 51.58 N 102.40 W
Pré-en-Pail 32 48.27 N 0.12 W
Preetz 50 54.14 N 10.16 E
Pregarten 30 48.21 N 14.32 E
Pregel → Pregol'a ≃ 66 54.41 N 20.22 E
Pregnana 256b 45.31 N 9.00 E
Pregol'a ≃ 66 54.41 N 20.22 E
Pregonero 236 8.01 N 71.46 W
Pregos 246 21.46 S 42.54 W
Pregradnaja 74 43.58 N 41.12 E
Pregradnoje 70 45.49 N 41.45 E
Preguiças ≃ 240 2.34 S 42.44 W
Preila 66 55.22 N 21.04 E
Preiļi 66 56.18 N 26.43 E
Preissac, Lac ⊜ 180 48.20 N 78.20 W
Prekestolen ♠ 26 59.00 N 6.01 E
Preko 36 44.05 N 15.11 E
Prěk Poŭthĭ 100 11.51 N 105.07 E
Prelate 174 50.51 N 109.23 W
Přelouč 30 50.02 N 15.34 E
Premana 54 46.03 N 9.25 E
Prembun 105a 7.43 S 109.48 E
Prémery 46 47.10 N 3.20 E
Premiá de Mar 256d 41.29 N 2.21 E
Premier Grand Ruisseau ≃ 265a 45.39 N 73.12 W
Premnitz 50 52.32 N 12.19 E
Prémont, Qué., Can. 196 46.22 N 73.03 W
Premont, Tex., U.S. 186 27.22 N 98.08 W
Prémontré 46 49.33 N 3.24 E
Premosello 54 46.00 N 8.20 E
Premuda, Otok I 36 44.20 N 14.37 E
Prenestini, Monti ⋀ 60 41.50 N 12.55 E
Prenjas 38 41.04 N 20.32 E
Prentice 180 45.33 N 90.17 W
Prentiss 184 31.36 N 89.52 W
Prenton 252 53.22 N 3.03 W
Prenzlau 50 53.19 N 13.52 E
Prenzlauer Berg ◆[8] 254a 52.32 N 13.26 E
Preobražennoje 73 49.32 N 38.10 E
Preobraženovka 79 48.04 N 131.55 E
Preparis Island I 100 14.52 N 93.41 E
Preparis North Channel ⊔ 100 15.27 N 94.05 E
Preparis South Channel ⊔ 100 14.40 N 94.00 E
Přerov 30 49.27 N 17.27 E
Prerow 50 54.26 N 12.35 E
Pré-Saint-Didier 56 45.46 N 6.59 E
Presanella, Cima ∧ 58 46.13 N 10.40 E
Prescot 42 53.26 N 2.48 W
Prescott, Ont., Can. 202 44.43 N 75.31 W
Prescott, Ariz., U.S. 190 34.33 N 112.28 W
Prescott, Ark., U.S. 184 33.48 N 93.23 W
Prescott, Oreg., U.S. 214 46.03 N 122.54 W
Prescott, Wis., U.S. 180 44.45 N 92.48 W
Prescott □[6] 196 45.30 N 74.45 W
Prescott Island I 166 73.01 N 96.50 W
Preseglie 58 45.40 N 10.24 E
Preševo 38 42.18 N 21.39 E
Presho 188 43.54 N 100.04 W
Presidencia de la Plaza 242 27.01 S 59.51 W
Presidencia Roca 242 26.08 S 59.36 W
Presidencia Roque Sáenz Peña 242 26.47 S 60.27 W
Presidente Costa e Silva, Ponte ◆[5] 277a 22.53 S 43.10 W
Presidente Derqui 248 34.29 S 58.51 W
Presidente Dutra 240 5.15 S 44.30 W
Presidente Epitácio 245 21.46 S 52.06 W
Presidente Getúlio 242 27.03 S 49.37 W
Presidente Hayes □[5] 242 24.00 S 59.00 W
Presidente Nicolás Avellaneda, Parque ♠ 278 34.39 S 58.29 W
Presidente Olegário 245 18.25 S 46.25 W
Presidente Prudente 245 22.07 S 51.22 W
Presidente Ríos, Lago ⊜ 244 46.28 S 74.25 W
Presidente Roosevelt, Estação ◆[5] 277b 23.33 S 46.36 W
Presidente Venceslau 245 21.52 S 51.50 W
Presidential Heights 269b 40.34 N 80.03 W
President Roxas 106 11.26 N 122.56 E
Presidio 186 29.33 N 104.23 W
Presidio, Río del ≃ 224 23.06 N 106.17 W
Presidio of San Francisco ■ 216 37.48 N 122.28 W
Presles 52 50.23 N 4.35 E
Presles-en-Brie 251 48.43 N 2.45 E
Presnogor'kovka 76 54.30 N 65.45 E
Presnovka 76 54.40 N 67.09 E
Presolana, Passo della)(58 45.55 N 10.06 E
Prešov 30 49.00 N 21.15 E
Prespa, Lake ⊜ 38 40.55 N 21.00 E
Prespansko Jezero → Prespa, Lake ⊜ 38 40.55 N 21.00 E
Prespuntal ≃ 236 10.08 N 64.39 W
Presque Isle 176 46.41 N 68.01 W
Presque Isle ≻[1] 204 42.09 N 80.06 W
Presque Isle ≃ 180 46.43 N 89.59 W
Presque Isle State Park ♠ 204 42.09 N 80.06 W
Presqu'ile Bay C 202 44.01 N 77.43 W
Presqu'ile Point ≻, Ont., Can. 202 44.42 N 80.54 W
Presqu'ile Point ≻, Ont., Can. 202 44.00 N 77.41 W
Presqu'ile Provincial Park ♠ 202 44.00 N 77.42 W
Pressana 58 45.17 N 11.24 E
Pressburg → Bratislava 30 48.09 N 17.07 E
Pressel 50 51.34 N 12.41 E
Prestatyn 42 53.20 N 3.24 W
Prestbury 252 53.17 N 2.09 W
Prestea 140 5.27 N 2.08 W
Presteigne 44 52.17 N 3.00 W
Přeštice 30 49.34 N 13.20 E
Presto, Bol. 238 18.55 S 64.56 W
Presto, Pa., U.S. 269b 40.23 N 80.07 W
Preston, Austl. 159 37.45 S 145.01 E
Preston, Cuba 230p 20.46 N 75.39 W
Preston, Eng., U.K. 42 53.46 N 0.12 W
Preston, Eng., U.K. 42 / 252 53.46 N 2.42 W
Preston, Ga., U.S. 182 31.59 N 84.37 W
Preston, Idaho, U.S. 192 42.06 N 111.53 W
Preston, Iowa, U.S. 180 42.03 N 90.24 W
Preston, Kans., U.S. 188 37.46 N 98.33 W
Preston, Md., U.S. 198 38.43 N 75.54 W
Preston, Minn., U.S. 180 43.40 N 92.05 W
Preston, Wash., U.S. 214 47.31 N 121.56 W
Preston □[8] 252 53.48 N 2.42 W
Preston ≃, Austl. 158a 33.20 S 115.40 E
Preston ≃, Qué., Can. 196 46.05 N 75.04 W
Preston, Cape ≻ 152 20.51 S 116.12 E
Preston, Lac ⊜ 196 46.05 N 75.04 W
Preston, Lake ⊜, Austl. 158a 32.59 S 115.42 E
Preston, Lake ⊜, Fla., U.S. 210 28.18 N 81.08 W
Preston Airport ⊠ 266 40.22 N 74.15 W
Preston Brook 252 53.19 N 2.39 W
Preston Brook Canal Tunnel ◆[5] 252 53.19 N 2.38 W
Preston Heights 206 41.28 N 88.08 W
Preston Hollow 200 42.27 N 74.13 W
Preston North End Football Ground ♠ 252 53.47 N 2.42 W
Prestonpans 42 55.57 N 3.00 W
Preston Peak ∧ 194 41.50 N 123.37 W
Prestonsburg 182 37.40 N 82.46 W
Prestrud Inlet C 9 78.18 S 156.00 W
Preststranda 26 59.06 N 9.04 E
Prestville 172 55.45 N 118.06 W
Prestwich 42 53.32 N 2.17 W
Prestwick 42 55.30 N 4.37 W
Prestwick Airport ⊠ 42 55.30 N 4.36 W
Prêto ≃, Bra. 236 1.41 S 63.48 W
Prêto ≃, Bra. 238 8.03 S 62.54 W
Prêto ≃, Bra. 240 11.21 S 43.52 W
Prêto ≃, Bra. 240 3.32 S 43.46 W
Prêto ≃, Bra. 245 20.08 S 49.38 W
Prêto ≃, Bra. 245 18.44 S 50.23 W
Prêto ≃, Bra. 245 18.25 S 39.47 W
Prêto ≃, Bra. 245 13.37 S 48.06 W
Prêto ≃, Bra. 245 19.22 S 41.56 W
Prêto ≃, Bra. 245 17.00 S 46.12 W
Prêto ≃, Bra. 246 22.14 S 43.07 W
Prêto ≃, Bra. 246 22.01 S 43.20 W
Prêto, Igarapé ≃ 236 4.10 S 68.57 W
Prêto do Igapó-Açu ≃ 236 4.26 S 59.48 W
Pretoria 148 25.45 S 28.10 E
Pretoriusvlei 148 28.30 S 22.59 E
Prettau → Predoi 58 47.02 N 12.06 E
Prettin 50 51.39 N 12.55 E
Prettyboy Reservoir ⊜[1] 198 39.38 N 76.45 W
Pretty Prairie 188 37.47 N 98.01 W
Pretzier 50 52.49 N 11.15 E
Pretzsch 50 51.42 N 12.48 E
Preussisch Eylau → Bagrationovsk 66 54.23 N 20.39 E
Preussisch Friedland → Debrzno 30 53.33 N 17.14 E
Preussisch Holland → Pasłęk 30 54.05 N 19.39 E
Preussisch Königsdorf → Olesno 30 50.53 N 18.25 E
Preussisch-Oldendorf 48 52.18 N 8.30 E
Preussisch-Ströhen 48 52.29 N 8.40 E
Préveza 38 38.57 N 20.44 E
Prevost Island I 214 48.50 N 123.22 W
Prey Lvéa 100 11.10 N 104.57 E
Prey Nób 100 10.38 N 103.47 E
Prey Vêng 100 11.29 N 105.19 E
Prezza, Monte ∧ 60 42.02 N 13.49 E
Priaral'skije Karakumy ◆[2] 76 47.00 N 63.30 E
Priargunsk 78 50.27 N 119.00 E
Priay 54 46.00 N 5.17 E
Priazovskaja Vozvyšennost' ⋀[1] 73 47.30 N 37.30 E
Priazovskoje 68 46.43 N 35.38 E
Pribel'skij, Zapovednik ♠ 76 53.01 N 56.53 E
Pribilof Islands II 170 57.00 N 170.00 W
Priboj 38 43.35 N 19.31 E
Příbor 30 49.39 N 18.10 E
Příbram 30 49.42 N 14.01 E
Pribylovo 66 60.26 N 28.40 E
Price, Austl. 158b 34.17 S 138.00 E
Price, Tex., U.S. 212 32.08 N 94.57 W
Price, Utah, U.S. 190 39.36 N 110.48 W
Price ≃ 190 39.10 N 110.06 W
Price, Cape ≻ 100 13.34 N 93.03 E
Price Bend C 266 40.55 N 73.24 W
Price Island I 172 52.23 N 128.36 W
Prichard 184 30.44 N 88.07 W
Prickly Point ≻ 231k 11.59 N 61.45 W
Pričornomorskaja Nizmennost' ≚ 68 47.00 N 33.00 E
Priddy 186 31.40 N 98.31 W
Pridneprovsk 68 48.24 N 35.09 E
Pridneprovskaja Nizmennost' ≚ 68 50.00 N 32.00 E
Pridneprovskaja Vozvyšennost' ⋀[1] 68 49.00 N 32.00 E
Priego 34 40.27 N 2.18 W
Priego de Córdoba 34 37.26 N 4.11 W
Priekule, S.S.S.R. 66 56.26 N 21.35 E
Priekulė, S.S.S.R. 66 55.33 N 21.19 E
Prienai 66 54.38 N 23.57 E
Prien am Chiemsee 58 47.51 N 12.20 E
Prieros 50 52.13 N 13.46 E
Prieska 148 29.40 S 22.42 E
Priest ≃ 192 48.11 N 116.53 W
Priestewitz 50 51.15 N 13.30 E
Priest Lake ⊜ 192 48.34 N 116.52 W
Priestley, Mount ∧ 172 55.13 N 128.53 W
Priest River 192 48.11 N 116.55 W
Prieta, Loma ∧ 216 37.07 N 121.51 W
Prieta, Peña ∧ 34 43.01 N 4.44 W
Prieto ≃ 230m 18.15 N 66.54 W
Prieto Diaz 106 13.02 N 124.12 E
Prievidza 30 48.47 N 18.37 E
Prignitz ◆[1] 50 53.05 N 12.15 E
Priirtyšskaja Ravnina ≚ 76 52.30 N 76.15 E
Priiskovyj, S.S.S.R. 76 54.39 N 88.42 E
Priiskovyj, S.S.S.R. 78 51.57 N 116.39 E
Prijedor 36 44.59 N 16.43 E
Prijepolje 38 43.23 N 19.39 E
Prijutnoje 70 46.06 N 43.31 E
Prijutovo 70 53.54 N 53.56 E
Prikaspijskaja Nizmennost' ≚ 70 48.00 N 52.00 E
Prikolotnoje 68 50.09 N 37.21 E
Prikubanskaja Nizmennost' ≚ 68 46.00 N 39.30 E
Prikumsk 74 44.46 N 44.09 E
Prilep 38 41.20 N 21.33 E
Prilepy 72 54.03 N 37.42 E
Prilly 54 46.32 N 6.36 E
Priluki, S.S.S.R. 66 59.16 N 39.53 E
Priluki, S.S.S.R. 68 50.36 N 32.24 E
Priluki, S.S.S.R. 72 54.51 N 37.53 E
Prima Porta ◆[8] 257a 42.00 N 12.29 E
Primavera 240 0.56 S 47.06 W
Primeira Cruz 240 2.30 S 43.26 W
Primeiro de Maio 245 22.48 S 51.01 W
Primera 186 26.14 N 97.43 W
Primero de Mayo 186 27.12 N 101.15 W
Primghar 188 43.05 N 95.38 W
Primkenau → Przemków 30 51.32 N 15.48 E
Primolano 58 45.58 N 11.42 E
Primorje [Warnicken] 66 54.57 N 20.02 E
Primorka 73 47.16 N 39.03 E
Primorsk, S.S.S.R. 66 60.22 N 28.36 E
Primorsk, S.S.S.R. 66 54.44 N 20.01 E
Primorsk, S.S.S.R. 70 49.16 N 45.03 E
Primorsk, S.S.S.R. 74 40.13 N 49.33 E
Primorskij, S.S.S.R. 68 45.07 N 35.29 E
Primorskij, S.S.S.R. 79 43.07 N 131.38 E
Primorskij Chrebet ⋀ 78 52.30 N 106.00 E
Primorskij Kraj □[4] 79 45.25 N 135.25 E
Primorsko 38 42.16 N 27.46 E
Primorsko-Achtarsk 68 46.03 N 38.11 E
Primorskoje 73 47.11 N 37.42 E
Primos 275 39.55 N 75.18 W
Primrose, S. Afr. 263d 26.12 S 28.10 E
Primrose, Pa., U.S. 200 40.42 N 76.17 W
Primrose, Pa., U.S. 269b 40.21 N 80.16 W
Primrose Brook ≃ 266 40.43 N 74.31 W
Primrose Lake ⊜ 174 54.55 N 109.45 W
Prims ≃ 52 49.20 N 6.44 E
Primstal 52 49.32 N 6.58 E
Prince, Lake ⊜[1] 198 36.48 N 76.38 W
Prince Albert, Ont., Can. 202 44.05 N 78.58 W
Prince Albert, Sask., Can. 174 53.12 N 105.46 W
Prince Albert, S. Afr. 148 33.13 S 22.02 E
Prince Albert Mountains ⋀ 9 76.00 S 161.30 E
Prince Albert National Park ♠ 174 54.00 N 106.25 W
Prince Albert Road 148 33.01 S 21.40 E
Prince Albert Sound ⊔ 166 70.25 N 115.00 W
Prince Alexander Mountains ⋀ 154 3.30 S 142.50 E
Prince Alfred Hamlet 148 33.18 S 19.20 E
Prince Charles Island I 166 67.50 N 76.00 W
Prince Charles Mountains ⋀ 9 72.00 S 67.00 E
Prince-de-Galles, Cap du ≻ 166 61.36 N 71.30 W
Prince-de-Galles, Île du → Prince of Wales Island I, Austl. 154 10.40 S 142.10 E
Prince-de-Galles, Île du → Prince of Wales Island I, N.W. Ter., Can. 166 72.40 N 99.00 W
Prince Edward □[6] 202 44.00 N 77.15 W
Prince Edward Bay C 202 43.57 N 76.57 W
Prince Edward Island □[4], Can. 166 46.20 N 63.20 W
Prince Edward Island □[4] 176 46.20 N 63.20 W
Prince Edward Island □[4] 176 46.31 N 63.26 W
Prince Edward Islands II 6 46.35 S 37.56 E
Prince Edward Park ♠ 264a 34.02 S 151.03 E
Prince Edward Point ≻ 202 44.56 N 76.52 W
Prince Frederick 178 38.33 N 76.35 W
Prince Gallitzin State Park ♠ 204 40.40 N 78.32 W
Prince George, B.C., Can. 172 53.55 N 122.45 W
Prince George, Va., U.S. 198 37.13 N 77.17 W
Prince George □[6] 198 37.13 N 77.10 W
Prince Georges □[6] 198 38.49 N 76.45 W
Prince Kemal el Din's Monument ⊥ 130 22.51 N 25.48 E
Prince Leopold Island I 166 74.02 N 89.55 W
Prince of Wales, Cape ≻ 170 65.40 N 168.05 W
Prince of Wales Island I, Austl. 154 10.40 S 142.10 E
Prince of Wales Island I, N.W. Ter., Can. 166 72.40 N 99.00 W
Prince of Wales Island I, Alaska, U.S. 170 55.47 N 132.50 W
Prince of Wales Strait ⊔ 166 73.00 N 117.00 W
Prince Olav Coast •[2] 9 68.30 S 42.30 E
Prince Patrick Island I 16 76.45 N 119.30 W
Prince Regent Inlet C 166 73.00 N 90.30 W
Prince Rupert 172 54.19 N 130.19 W
Prince Rupert Bay C 230d 15.34 N 61.29 W
Prince Rupert Bluff Point ≻ 230d 15.35 N 61.29 W
Princesa, Puerto C 106 9.45 N 118.43 E
Princesa Astrid, Costa → Princess Astrid Coast •[2] 9 70.45 S 12.30 E
Princesa Carlota, Bahía → Princess Charlotte Bay C 154 14.25 S 144.00 E
Princesa Isabel 240 7.44 S 38.00 W
Princesa Marta, Costa → Princess Martha Coast •[2] 9 72.00 S 7.30 W
Princesa Ragnhild, Costa → Princess Ragnhild Coast •[2] 9 70.15 S 27.30 E
Princes Bay C 266 40.31 N 74.12 W
Princes Risborough 44 51.44 N 0.51 W
Princess Anne 178 38.12 N 75.41 W
Princess Astrid Coast •[2] 9 70.45 S 12.30 E
Princess Charlotte Bay C 154 14.25 S 144.00 E
Princess Martha Coast •[2] 9 72.00 S 7.30 W
Princess Ragnhild Coast •[2] 9 70.15 S 27.30 E
Princess Ranges ⋀ 152 26.08 S 121.55 E
Princess Royal Channel ⊔ 172 53.10 N 128.37 W
Princess Royal Island I 172 52.57 N 128.49 W
Princes Town 231r 10.16 N 61.23 W
Princeton, B.C., Can. 172 49.27 N 120.31 W
Princeton, Newf., Can. 176 48.25 N 53.36 W
Princeton, Ont., Can. 202 43.10 N 80.32 W
Princeton, Calif., U.S. 216 39.24 N 122.01 W
Princeton, Fla., U.S. 210 25.32 N 80.25 W
Princeton, Ill., U.S. 180 41.23 N 89.28 W
Princeton, Ind., U.S. 184 38.21 N 87.34 W
Princeton, Ky., U.S. 184 37.07 N 87.53 W
Princeton, Maine, U.S. 178 45.13 N 67.34 W
Princeton, Mich., U.S. 180 46.17 N 87.29 W
Princeton, Minn., U.S. 180 45.34 N 93.35 W
Princeton, Mo., U.S. 184 40.24 N 93.35 W
Princeton, N.J., U.S. 198 40.21 N 74.40 W
Princeton, N.C., U.S. 182 35.28 N 78.10 W
Princeton, Tex., U.S. 212 33.11 N 96.30 W
Princeton, W. Va., U.S. 182 37.22 N 81.06 W
Princeton, Wis., U.S. 180 43.51 N 89.08 W
Princeton Airfield ⊠ 266 40.24 N 74.39 W
Princeton Battlefield Park ⊥ 266 40.20 N 74.41 W
Princeton Junction 198 40.19 N 74.37 W
Princeton Township 266 40.22 N 74.40 W
Princeton University ⊻[2] 266 40.21 N 74.39 W
Princetown 44 50.33 N 4.00 W
Princeville, Qué., Can. 196 46.10 N 71.53 W
Princeville, Ill., U.S. 180 40.45 N 89.45 W
Princeville, N.C., U.S. 182 35.53 N 77.82 W
Prince William □[6] 198 38.42 N 77.27 W
Prince William Forest Park ♠ 198 38.36 N 77.23 W
Prince William Sound ⊔ 170 60.40 N 147.00 W
Príncipe I 142 1.37 N 7.25 E
Príncipe Alberto, Montes → Prince Albert Mountains ⋀ 9 76.00 S 161.30 E
Príncipe Carlos, Montes → Prince Charles Mountains ⋀ 9 72.00 S 67.00 E
Principe Channel ⊔ 172 53.28 N 130.00 W
Príncipe da Beira 238 12.25 S 64.25 W
Príncipe de Gales, Isla → Prince of Wales Island I, Austl. 154 10.40 S 142.10 E
Príncipe de Gales, Isla → Prince of Wales Island I, N.W. Ter., Can. 166 72.40 N 99.00 W
Príncipe Eduardo, Isla → Prince Edward Island I 176 46.20 N 63.20 W
Príncipe Olav, Costa → Prince Olav Coast •[2] 9 68.30 S 42.30 E
Príncipe Patricio, Isla → Prince Patrick Island I 16 76.45 N 119.30 W
Prineville 192 44.18 N 120.51 W
Prineville Reservoir ⊜[1] 192 44.08 N 120.42 W
Prineville Southeast 192 44.17 N 120.53 W
Pringgabaja 105b 8.34 S 116.37 E
Pringy 251 48.31 N 2.34 E
Prinsenbeek 48 51.36 N 4.42 E
Prinses Margrietkanaal ≋ 48 53.10 N 5.55 E
Prinskof 148 32.06 S 20.53 E
Prinzapolca 226 13.24 N 83.34 W
Prinzapolca ≃ 226 13.24 N 83.34 W
Prinzessin Astrid-Küste → Princess Astrid Coast •[2] 9 70.45 S 12.30 E
Prinzessin Charlotte Bucht → Princess Charlotte Bay C 154 14.25 S 144.00 E
Prinzessin Martha-Küste → Princess Martha Coast •[2] 9 72.00 S 7.30 W
Prinzessin Ragnhild-Küste → Princess Ragnhild Coast •[2] 9 70.15 S 27.30 E
Priobskoje Plato ⋀[1] 76 52.40 N 83.00 E
Prioksko-Terrasnyj Zapovednik ◆[4] 72 54.51 N 37.36 E
Prior, Cabo ≻ 34 43.34 N 8.19 W
Priort 254a 52.31 N 12.58 E
Priozernyj 70 47.23 N 45.14 E
Prioz'ornyj 76 47.50 N 84.13 E
Prioz'orsk 24 61.02 N 30.04 E
Prip'at' ≃ 68 51.21 N 30.09 E
Pripet → Prip'at' ≃ 68 51.21 N 30.09 E
Pripet Marshes → Polesje ◆[1] 62 52.30 N 27.30 E
Pripjat → Prip'at' ≃ 68 51.21 N 30.09 E
Pripjet → Prip'at' ≃ 68 51.21 N 30.09 E
Pripol'arnyj Ural ⋀ 24 65.00 N 60.00 E
Priputni 68 50.57 N 32.14 E
Prirečje 78 55.07 N 101.03 E
Prirečnyj 70 51.03 N 52.26 E
Přísečnice 50 50.27 N 13.06 E
Priselje 66 55.09 N 32.49 E
Prišib, S.S.S.R. 68 47.16 N 35.21 E
Prišib, S.S.S.R. 74 39.08 N 48.36 E
Prislon 72 56.48 N 37.16 E
Pristan'-Prževal'sk 75 42.34 N 78.18 E
Pristen', S.S.S.R. 68 51.15 N 36.41 E
Pristen', S.S.S.R. 73 49.36 N 37.38 E
Priština 38 42.39 N 21.10 E
Pritchett 188 37.22 N 102.52 W
Pritzerbe 50 52.30 N 12.27 E
Pritzier 50 53.22 N 11.04 E
Pritzwalk 50 53.09 N 12.10 E
Priural'nyj 70 51.29 N 53.06 E
Privas 56 44.44 N 4.36 E
Priverno 60 41.28 N 13.11 E
Privetnoje 68 44.50 N 34.41 E
Privodino 24 61.05 N 46.28 E
Privokzal'nyj, S.S.S.R. 72 55.59 N 35.56 E
Privokzal'nyj, S.S.S.R. 76 58.53 N 60.43 E
Privolje, S.S.S.R. 73 48.52 N 37.16 E
Privolje, S.S.S.R. 73 49.01 N 38.18 E
Privol'naja 68 46.09 N 38.42 E
Privol'n'anskij ◆[8] 73 48.41 N 38.28 E
Privol'noje, S.S.S.R. 68 47.29 N 32.17 E
Privol'noje, S.S.S.R. 70 50.57 N 46.06 E
Privolžje 70 52.52 N 48.37 E
Privolžsk 70 57.23 N 41.17 E
Privolžskaja Vozvyšennost' ⋀[1] 70 52.00 N 46.00 E
Privolžskij, S.S.S.R. 70 51.24 N 46.02 E
Privolžskij, S.S.S.R. 70 46.24 N 48.00 E
Privolžskoje 70 51.06 N 45.57 E
Prizren 38 42.12 N 20.44 E
Prizzi 36 37.43 N 13.26 E
Prnjavor 36 44.52 N 17.40 E
Pró 276d 11.57 S 77.05 W
Probolinggo 105a 7.45 S 113.13 E
Proboštov 50 50.39 N 13.50 E
Probstzella 50 50.32 N 11.22 E
Probus 44 50.17 N 4.57 W
Procchio 60 42.47 N 10.15 E
Prochladnoje 76 48.30 N 82.41 E
Prochladnyj 74 43.46 N 44.00 E
Prochorkino 76 59.34 N 79.26 E
Prochorovka 72 54.07 N 38.11 E
Prochowice 30 51.17 N 16.22 E
Procida 60 40.46 N 14.02 E
Procida, Isola di I 60 40.45 N 14.01 E
Procter 172 49.37 N 116.57 W
Proctor, Minn., U.S. 180 46.45 N 92.13 W
Proctor, Vt., U.S. 178 43.40 N 73.02 W
Proctor Brook ≃ 273 42.32 N 70.54 W
Proctor Lake ⊜ 218 35.07 N 118.21 W
Proctor Lake ⊜[1] 186 32.02 N 98.32 W
Proddatūr 112 14.44 N 78.33 E
Proença-a-Nova 34 39.45 N 7.55 W
Profen 50 51.07 N 12.13 E
Professor Dr. Ir. W. J. van Blommestein Meer ⊜[1] 240 4.45 N 55.00 W
Pro Football Hall of Fame ⊻ 204 40.49 N 81.25 W
Prognoj 73 48.45 N 39.51 E
Progreso, Méx. 186 27.28 N 100.59 W
Progreso, Méx. 222 21.17 N 89.40 W
Progreso, Ur. 248 34.40 S 56.13 W
Progreso Industrial 224 19.38 N 99.21 W
Progress, S.S.S.R. 79 49.42 N 129.39 E
Progress, Oreg., U.S. 214 45.28 N 122.47 W
Progress, Pa., U.S. 198 40.08 N 76.34 W
Project City 194 40.41 N 122.21 W
Prokopjeva 78 58.03 N 100.39 E
Prokopjevsk 76 53.53 N 86.45 E
Prokopyevsk → Prokopjevsk 76 53.53 N 86.45 E
Prokuplje 38 43.14 N 21.36 E
Prokuševo 66 59.55 N 34.56 E
Prokutskoje 76 56.19 N 69.46 E
Proletarij 66 58.26 N 31.44 E
Proletarsk, S.S.S.R. 68 48.56 N 38.23 E
Proletarsk, S.S.S.R. 75 40.10 N 69.30 E
Proletarsk ◆[8] 73 48.56 N 38.23 E
Proletarskaja 70 46.42 N 41.44 E
Proletarskij, S.S.S.R. 68 50.47 N 35.47 E
Proletarskij, S.S.S.R. 72 55.01 N 37.23 E
Proletarskij ◆[8] 73 48.08 N 39.18 E
Prolysovo 66 52.54 N 34.09 E
Prome (Pyè) 100 18.49 N 95.13 E
Promised Land State Park ♠ 200 41.18 N 75.11 W
Promissão 245 21.32 S 49.52 W
Promitorio 257a 42.03 N 12.39 E
Promontogno 54 46.21 N 9.34 E
Prompton 200 41.35 N 75.19 W
Prompton Lake ⊜[1] 200 41.36 N 75.20 W
Prompton State Park ♠ 200 41.37 N 75.22 W
Promyšlennaja 76 54.55 N 85.40 E
Promyšlennovskij 76 55.29 N 86.12 E
Promyšlennyj 24 67.35 N 63.55 E
Promyslovka, S.S.S.R. 70 45.44 N 47.10 E
Promyslovka, S.S.S.R. 79 43.00 N 132.24 E
Pron'a ≃, S.S.S.R. 66 53.25 N 31.01 E
Pron'a ≃, S.S.S.R. 70 54.21 N 40.24 E
Pron'a Gorodišče 72 54.15 N 38.43 E
Pronin 70 49.12 N 42.11 E
Pronsfeld 52 50.10 N 6.20 E
Pronsk 66 54.07 N 39.37 E
Prony, Baie du C 165f 22.22 S 166.53 E
Prophet ≃ 166 58.45 N 122.45 W
Prophetstown 184 41.40 N 89.56 W
Propriá 240 10.13 S 36.51 W
Propriano 36 41.40 N 8.55 E
Prorer Wiek C 50 54.27 N 13.38 E
Prorva 76 46.03 N 53.15 E
Proryvnoje 76 54.23 N 64.26 E
Pros'anaja 68 48.07 N 36.23 E
Pros'anov 68 49.42 N 35.47 E
Prösen 50 51.25 N 13.30 E
Proserpine 156 20.24 S 148.34 E
Prosigk 50 51.42 N 12.03 E
Proskoveja 74 44.43 N 44.12 E
Proskurov → Chmel'nickij 68 49.25 N 27.00 E
Prosna ≃ 30 52.10 N 17.39 E
Prosnica 70 58.26 N 50.15 E
Prosotsáni 38 41.10 N 23.59 E
Prospect, Austl. 158b 34.54 S 138.35 E
Prospect, Austl. 264a 33.48 S 150.56 E
Prospect, Conn., U.S. 197 41.30 N 72.59 W
Prospect, N.Y., U.S. 200 43.18 N 75.09 W
Prospect, Ohio, U.S. 204 40.27 N 83.11 W
Prospect, Pa., U.S. 204 40.54 N 80.03 W
Prospect Bay C 198 38.56 N 76.14 W
Prospect Heights 268 42.06 N 87.56 W
Prospect Hill 158b 35.13 S 138.44 E
Prospect Hill ∧[2], Mass., U.S. 197 41.21 N 70.45 W
Prospect Hill ∧[2], Mass., U.S. 273 42.23 N 71.15 W
Prospect Hill Park ♠ 273 42.23 N 71.15 W
Prospect Meadows 268 42.05 N 87.57 W
Prospect Park, N.J., U.S. 266 40.56 N 74.10 W
Prospect Park, Pa., U.S. 204 41.31 N 78.13 W
Prospect Park, Pa., U.S. 275 39.53 N 75.19 W
Prospect Park ♠ 266 40.40 N 73.58 W
Prospect Park Lake ⊜ 266 40.39 N 73.57 W
Prospect Plains 266 40.19 N 74.28 W
Prospect Point 266 40.58 N 74.38 W
Prospect Point ≻ 266 40.52 N 73.43 W
Prospect Reservoir ⊜[1] 264a 33.49 S 150.54 E
Prospectville 275 40.13 N 75.11 W
Prosper 212 33.14 N 96.48 W
Prosperi Airport ⊠ 268 41.33 N 87.47 W
Prosperidad 106 8.34 N 125.52 E
Prosser 192 46.12 N 119.46 W
Prosser Creek ≃ 216 39.22 N 120.07 W
Prosser Creek Reservoir ⊜[1] 216 39.22 N 120.08 W
Prostějov 30 49.29 N 17.07 E
Prostken → Prostki 30 53.43 N 22.26 E
Prostki 30 53.43 N 22.26 E
Proston 156 26.10 S 151.36 E
Proszowice 30 50.12 N 20.18 E
Protasovo, S.S.S.R. 72 54.48 N 38.35 E
Protasovo, S.S.S.R. 72 54.11 N 37.00 E
Protasovo, S.S.S.R. 72 56.08 N 37.36 E
Protasy 66 52.47 N 29.05 E
Protea 263d 26.17 S 27.51 E
Protection 188 37.12 N 99.29 W
Protection Island I 214 48.07 N 122.55 W
Protem 148 34.16 S 20.05 E
Protestantes 246 22.44 S 46.18 W
Protoka ≃ 68 45.43 N 37.46 E
Protva 72 55.01 N 36.41 E
Protva ≃ 72 54.51 N 37.16 E
Protville 36 36.54 N 10.01 E
Prötzel 50 52.38 N 13.59 E
Proud Lake State Recreational Area ♠ 271 42.35 N 83.29 W
Proud Lake State Recreation Area ♠ 271 42.34 N 83.33 W
Proulxville 196 46.40 N 72.30 W
Provadija 38 43.11 N 27.26 E
Proval, Zaliv C 78 52.21 N 106.45 E
Provence □[9] 56 44.00 N 6.00 E
Provence, Alpes de ⋀ 56 43.40 N 6.00 E
Provenchères-sur-Fave 54 48.19 N 7.05 E
Providence, Ky., U.S. 184 37.24 N 87.39 W
Providence, R.I., U.S. 197 41.50 N 71.25 W
Providence, Utah, U.S. 190 41.43 N 111.49 W
Providence □[6] 197 41.52 N 71.36 W
Providence ≃ 197 41.43 N 71.21 W
Providence Forge 198 37.27 N 77.02 W
Providence Island I 128 9.14 S 51.02 E
Providência, Bra. 246 21.40 S 42.35 W
Providencia, Chile 276e 33.26 S 70.37 W
Providencia, Méx. 186 27.06 N 103.32 W
Providencia, Isla de I 226 13.21 N 81.22 W
Providência, Serra da ⋀[1] 238 10.30 S 61.25 W
Providenciales I 228 21.47 N 72.17 W
Providenija 64 64.23 N 173.18 W
Providenija, Buchta C 170 64.30 N 173.20 W
Provincetown 197 42.03 N 70.11 W
Provincia, Cerro de la ∧ 276e 33.25 S 70.26 W
Provincial Capital ⊻ 259f 14.35 N 121.04 E
Provins 46 48.33 N 3.18 E
Provo 190 40.14 N 111.39 W
Provo ≃ 190 40.14 N 111.44 W
Provost 174 52.21 N 110.16 W
Prozor 36 43.49 N 17.37 E
Prud'anka 68 50.14 N 36.09 E
Prudence Island I 197 41.37 N 71.19 W
Prudentópolis 242 25.12 S 50.57 W
Prudentov 70 49.39 N 46.19 E
Prudhoe 42 54.58 N 1.51 W
Prudhoe Bay C 170 70.20 N 148.20 W
Prudhoe Island I 156 21.19 S 149.40 E
Prudišči 72 54.24 N 38.26 E
Prudki 72 54.46 N 36.29 E
Prudnik 30 50.19 N 17.34 E
Prudy 66 53.47 N 26.32 E
Pruggern 58 47.25 N 13.52 E
Prüm 52 50.12 N 6.25 E
Prüm ≃ 52 49.49 N 6.28 E
Prunay-le-Temple 251 48.52 N 1.40 E
Prunay-sous-Ablis 251 48.32 N 1.48 E
Prunedale 216 36.47 N 121.40 W
Pruněřov 50 50.25 N 13.16 E
Prunières 56 44.33 N 6.20 E
Pruszków 30 52.11 N 20.48 E
Prut (Prutul) ≃ 68 45.28 N 28.12 E
Pruth → Prut ≃ 68 45.28 N 28.12 E
Prutting 58 47.53 N 12.11 E
Prutul (Prut) ≃ 68 45.28 N 28.12 E
Prutz 54 47.05 N 10.40 E
Pružany 66 52.33 N 24.28 E
Prydz Bay C 9 69.00 S 76.00 E
Pryor 186 36.19 N 95.19 W
Pryor Creek ≃ 192 45.54 N 108.19 W
Pryor Mountain ∧[2] 212 31.43 N 95.12 W
Prysor ≃ 44 52.56 N 4.00 W
Przasnysz 30 53.01 N 20.55 E
Przedbórz 30 51.06 N 19.53 E
Przemków 30 51.32 N 15.48 E
Przemocze 50 53.27 N 14.55 E
Przemyśl 30 49.47 N 22.47 E
Prževal'sk 75 42.29 N 78.24 E
Przeworsk 30 50.05 N 22.29 E
Przewóz 50 51.29 N 14.59 E
Przybiernów 50 53.46 N 14.46 E
Przysucha 30 51.22 N 20.38 E
Pšagar 75 39.58 N 68.08 E
Psakhná 38 38.35 N 23.38 E
Psará I 38 38.35 N 25.37 E
Psárion 38 37.20 N 21.51 E
Psebaj 74 44.07 N 40.47 E
Pšecha ≃ 68 44.47 N 39.48 E
Psekups ≃ 68 45.00 N 39.09 E
Pselec 68 51.17 N 36.32 E
Psikhikón 257c 38.01 N 23.46 E
Pšiš ≃ 68 45.01 N 39.18 E
Pšiš, Gora ∧ 74 43.24 N 41.12 E
Psittália I 257c 37.56 N 23.35 E
Pskem 75 41.56 N 70.22 E
Pskem ≃ 75 41.38 N 70.01 E
Pskent 75 40.54 N 69.20 E
Pskov 66 57.50 N 28.20 E
Pskovskoje Ozero ⊜ 66 58.00 N 28.00 E

Symbols in the index entries represent the broad categories identified in the key at the right. Symbols with superior numbers (⋀[2]) identify subcategories (see complete key on page I · 26).

Kartensymbole in dem Registerverzeichnis stellen die rechts in Schlüssel erklärten Kategorien dar. Symbole mit hochgestellten Ziffern (⋀[2]) bezeichnen Unterabteilungen einer Kategorie (vgl. vollständiger Schlüssel auf Seite I · 26).

Los símbolos incluídos en el texto del índice representan las grandes categorias identificadas con la clave a la derecha. Los símbolos con numeros en su parte superior (⋀[2]) identifican las subcategorías (véase la clave completa en la página I · 26).

Les symboles de l'index représentent les catégories indiquées dans la légende à droite. Les symboles suivis d'un indice (⋀[2]) représentent des sous-catégories (voir légende complète à la page I · 26).

Os símbolos incluídos no texto do índice representam as grandes categorias identificadas com a chave à direita. Os símbolos com números em sua parte superior (⋀[2]) identificam as subcategorias (veja-se a chave completa à página I · 26).

	English	Deutsch	Español	Français	Português
∧	Mountain	Berg	Montaña	Montagne	Montanha
⋀	Mountains	Berge	Montañas	Montagnes	Montanhas
)(	Pass	Pass	Paso	Col	Passo
∨	Valley, Canyon	Tal, Cañon	Valle, Cañón	Vallée, Canyon	Vale, Canhão
≚	Plain	Ebene	Llano	Plaine	Planície
≻	Cape	Kap	Cabo	Cap	Cabo
I	Island	Insel	Isla	Île	Ilha
II	Islands	Inseln	Islas	Îles	Ilhas
•	Other Topographic Features	Andere Topographische Objekte	Otros Elementos Topográficos	Autres données topographiques	Outros Elementos Topográficos

ESPAÑOL — Nombre | Página | Lat.°′ | Long.°′ W=Oeste
FRANÇAIS — Nom | Page | Lat.°′ | Long.°′ W=Ouest
PORTUGUÊS — Nome | Página | Lat.°′ | Long.°′ W=Oeste

Symbol	English	Deutsch	Español	Français	Português
≃	River	Fluss	Río	Rivière	Rio
≍	Canal	Kanal	Canal	Canal	Canal
⌊	Waterfall, Rapids	Wasserfall, Stromschnellen	Cascada, Rápidos	Chute d'eau, Rapides	Cascata, Rápidos
Ʉ	Strait	Meeresstrasse	Estrecho	Détroit	Estreito
C	Bay, Gulf	Bucht, Golf	Bahía, Golfo	Baie, Golfe	Baía, Golfo
⊜	Lake, Lakes	See, Seen	Lago, Lagos	Lac, Lacs	Lago, Lagos
≋	Swamp	Sumpf	Pantano	Marais	Pântano
☰	Ice Features, Glacier	Eis- und Gletscherformen	Accidentes Glaciales	Formes glaciaires	Acidentes Glaciares
◆	Other Hydrographic Features	Andere Hydrographische Objekte	Otros Elementos Hidrográficos	Autres données hydrographiques	Outros Elementos Hidrográficos
✢	Submarine Features	Untermeerische Objekte	Accidentes Submarinos	Formes de relief sous-marin	Acidentes Submarinos
□	Political Unit	Politische Einheit	Unidad Politica	Entité politique	Unidade Política
ʊ	Cultural Institution	Kulturelle Institution	Institución Cultural	Institution culturelle	Instituição Cultural
⊥	Historical Site	Historische Stätte	Sitio Histórico	Site historique	Sítio Histórico
♠	Recreational Site	Erholungs- und Ferienort	Sitio de Recreo	Centre de loisirs	Sítio de Lazer
⊠	Airport	Flughafen	Aeropuerto	Aéroport	Aeroporto
■	Military Installation	Militäranlage	Instalación Militar	Installation militaire	Instalação Militar
◆	Miscellaneous	Verschiedenes	Misceláneo	Divers	Miscelânea

ENGLISH — DEUTSCH

Name	Page	Lat.°′	Long.°′
Qianertaizi	94	42.04 N	122.42 E
Qianfang	90	28.32 N	116.13 E
Qianguoerluosi	79	45.08 N	124.47 E
Qiangzilu	95	40.26 N	117.13 E
Qianhonghepu	94	41.23 N	123.07 E
Qianhuang	96	31.36 N	119.58 E
Qianji	90	33.55 N	118.56 E
Qianjiadian	79	43.42 N	122.35 E
Qianjiang, Zhg.	90	30.25 N	112.51 E
Qianjiang, Zhg.	92	23.37 N	109.00 E
Qianjian'gangzi	94	41.34 N	122.26 E
Qianjiangtai	94	41.46 N	122.03 E
Qianjiaqiao	96	30.53 N	121.31 E
Qianjiaying	95	39.35 N	118.21 E
Qianjiazhai	94	41.28 N	122.02 E
Qianjiazhuang	96	32.16 N	120.17 E
Qianjing	96	31.33 N	121.15 E
Qianjinmiao	90	25.09 N	118.20 E
Qiankeng	96	30.43 N	119.47 E
Qiankoutou	95	39.42 N	117.01 E
Qianlijiazhuang	95	39.25 N	118.17 E
Qianluanshanzi	94	42.17 N	122.27 E
Qianmajiagushanzi	94	42.23 N	123.33 E
Qianmen Station ⇠[5]	261a	39.54 N	116.23 E
Qianmintun	94	41.49 N	123.15 E
Qianning	92	30.30 N	101.31 E
Qianpai	92	22.22 N	111.11 E
Qianqi	90	27.20 N	120.20 E
Qianqianjianglugou	94	41.59 N	120.58 E
Qiansandaoliangzi	94	42.06 N	120.44 E
Qianshahezi	94	41.46 N	123.01 E
Qianshan (Hekou), Zhg.	90	28.18 N	117.41 E
Qianshan, Zhg.	90	22.16 N	113.33 E
Qianshan, Zhg.	90	30.38 N	116.33 E
Qianshan, Zhg.	96	31.06 N	120.24 E
Qianshanyang ⊜	96	30.50 N	120.08 E
Qianshuangshanzi	94	41.22 N	121.13 E
Qiansongshu-lianggou	94	41.47 N	120.59 E
Qiansuo	90	28.44 N	121.27 E
Qiantangjiang ≃	96	30.23 N	120.33 E
Qiantangzhen	97	30.12 N	106.18 E
Qianwei	88	40.12 N	120.06 E
Qianxi, Zhg.	92	26.57 N	106.00 E
Qianxi (Xingcheng), Zhg.	95	40.09 N	118.19 E
Qianxiatazi	94	42.23 N	123.53 E
Qianyamen	94	42.04 N	121.26 E
Qianyao	96	30.54 N	120.54 E
Qianyaopu	94	42.02 N	123.37 E
Qianzhou	96	31.44 N	120.13 E
Qiaodunmen	90	27.29 N	120.18 E
Qiaoershan ⩕	92	31.48 N	99.10 E
Qiaogou	90	32.26 N	115.45 E
Qiaohengjin	92	29.30 N	99.50 E
Qiaojia	92	26.57 N	102.52 E
Qiaokou	90	25.55 N	113.10 E
Qiaolima	110	34.35 N	81.00 E
Qiaolin	90	31.57 N	118.32 E
Qiaomu	88	39.34 N	114.27 E
Qiaopurikebazha	75	38.48 N	76.19 E
Qiaoqi	96	31.49 N	120.18 E
Qiaoshe	90	28.48 N	115.58 E
Qiaosi	96	30.21 N	120.18 E
Qiaotou, Zhg.	90	33.05 N	112.46 E
Qiaotou, Zhg.	92	28.17 N	99.22 E
Qiaotou, Zhg.	94	41.13 N	123.44 E
Qiaotou, Zhg.	96	32.11 N	119.14 E
Qiaotou, Zhg.	97	29.18 N	104.39 E
Qiaotoucun	96	30.36 N	119.08 E
Qiaotouji	90	31.45 N	117.34 E
Qiaotouyi	90	28.24 N	112.58 E
Qiaotouzhen, Zhg.	96	30.49 N	119.13 E
Qiaotouzhen, Zhg.	96	30.33 N	118.50 E
Qiaowei	92	22.51 N	109.50 E
Qiaoxia	96	31.09 N	119.35 E
Qiaoxiajie	90	28.10 N	120.34 E
Qiaozhen	96	31.39 N	121.24 E
Qibao	96	31.09 N	121.20 E
Qibyā	122	31.59 N	35.01 E
Qichun (Caohe)	90	30.17 N	115.26 E
Qidong, Zhg.	88	37.04 N	117.29 E
Qidong, Zhg.	92	26.44 N	112.04 E
Qidong, Zhg.	96	31.49 N	121.40 E
Qidu	90	30.16 N	117.46 E
Qiemo	110	38.08 N	85.32 E
Qiesanglinzi	94	41.42 N	123.30 E
Qieshikou	261a	39.59 N	116.24 E
Qiezixi	97	29.25 N	106.30 E
Qifṭ (Coptos)	130	26.00 N	32.49 E
Qiganka	79	53.02 N	120.33 E
Qigong	92	28.38 N	100.38 E
Qigongtai	94	41.50 N	123.08 E
Qihe	88	36.42 N	116.47 E
Qiji	88	37.16 N	115.21 E
Qijiadian	79	46.48 N	125.36 E
Qijiang	97	29.02 N	106.39 E
Qijiang ≃, Zhg.	97	29.01 N	106.36 E
Qijiang ≃, Zhg.	97	30.38 N	105.26 E
Qijiapuzi	94	40.54 N	122.31 E
Qijiawan	90	30.53 N	114.13 E
Qijiawopeng	94	41.02 N	121.26 E
Qijiazi	94	41.54 N	122.58 E
Qijizhen	88	36.17 N	116.03 E
Qika	79	50.35 N	119.16 E
Qikou	88	38.35 N	117.31 E
Qila Abdullāh	110	30.43 N	66.38 E
Qila Dīdār Singh	113	32.08 N	74.01 E
Qilagugannishan ∧	110	28.46 N	87.38 E
Qila Lādgasht	118	27.54 N	62.57 E
Qila Saifullāh	110	30.43 N	68.21 E
Qila Sobha Singh	113	32.14 N	74.46 E
Qili	90	30.13 N	117.27 E
Qilianshanmai (Nanshan) ⩕	92	39.06 N	98.40 E
Qilihai ⊜	95	39.19 N	117.33 E
Qilihe, Zhg.	94	41.21 N	121.16 E
Qilihe, Zhg.	94	41.30 N	121.15 E
Qilihezi	94	40.56 N	121.02 E
Qilin	96	31.56 N	121.21 E
Qiling	90	24.05 N	115.27 E
Qilingzicun	94	41.05 N	123.06 E
Qilinhu ⊜	110	31.50 N	89.00 E
Qilinmen	96	32.04 N	118.55 E
Qiliping	90	31.27 N	114.39 E
Qiliqiao	96	31.35 N	120.48 E
Qilizhen, Zhg.	92	35.43 N	108.59 E
Qilizhen, Zhg.	96	32.19 N	121.05 E
Qilṭ, 'Ayn al- ⊤[4]	122	31.50 N	35.23 E
Qimafang	88	40.48 N	114.31 E
Qiman al-'Arūs	132	29.18 N	31.10 E
Qimen, Zhg.	90	25.18 N	113.15 E
Qimen, Zhg.	90	29.52 N	117.42 E
Qimoudi	95	39.35 N	115.32 E
Qinā	130	26.10 N	32.43 E
Qinā, Wādī ∨, Miṣr	130	26.12 N	32.44 E
Qinā, Wādī ∨, Miṣr	132	29.39 N	31.53 E
Qincaigou	94	40.38 N	120.37 E
Qing'an	79	46.52 N	128.30 E
Qingbaikou	95	40.01 N	115.50 E
Qingcao'ai)(	90	27.40 N	119.34 E
Qingcaoge	90	30.50 N	116.46 E
Qingcaohu ⊜	96	31.06 N	118.48 E
Qingchengzi	94	40.44 N	123.36 E
Qingcungang	96	30.56 N	121.34 E
Qingdao (Tsingtao)	88	36.06 N	120.19 E
Qingdian	95	39.51 N	117.22 E
Qingduizi, Zhg.	88	39.50 N	123.18 E
Qingduizi, Zhg.	94	41.28 N	121.53 E
Qingfengtuo	88	40.59 N	116.04 E
Qingfu	92	28.29 N	104.35 E
Qinggang	79	46.43 N	126.07 E
Qingguang	95	39.11 N	117.02 E
Qingguji	88	34.45 N	115.47 E
Qinghai □[4]	80	36.00 N	96.00 E
Qinghai ⊜	92	36.50 N	100.20 E
Qinghe, Zhg.	76	46.36 N	90.39 E
Qinghe, Zhg.	88	40.02 N	122.35 E
Qinghe, Zhg.	95	40.01 N	116.20 E
Qinghecheng	94	41.28 N	124.15 E
Qinghechengzi	94	41.44 N	121.25 E
Qinghemen	94	41.45 N	121.25 E
Qinghetou	88	35.51 N	115.41 E
Qinghezhen	88	37.16 N	117.39 E
Qinghu	90	28.40 N	118.34 E
Qinghua	90	29.24 N	117.46 E
Qinghuashui ≃	90	25.00 N	114.00 E
Qinghuayuan	95	40.00 N	116.19 E
Qinghuazhen	90	32.55 N	112.19 E
Qingjian	92	37.10 N	110.00 E
Qingjiang, Zhg.	90	28.05 N	115.29 E
Qingjiang, Zhg.	97	29.17 N	105.34 E
Qingjiang ≃	92	30.22 N	111.20 E
Qingjiangdu	90	28.16 N	121.06 E
Qingjujie	97	30.42 N	106.07 E
Qinglian	90	24.27 N	112.45 E
Qingliu	90	26.12 N	116.52 E
Qingliuzhen	97	29.56 N	105.19 E
Qinglong, Zhg.	88	40.24 N	118.54 E
Qinglong, Zhg.	92	25.50 N	105.10 E
Qinglongchang, Zhg.	97	29.51 N	105.40 E
Qinglongchang, Zhg.	97	29.28 N	103.27 E
Qinglongchang, Zhg.	97	30.20 N	103.51 E
Qinglongchang, Zhg.	97	28.50 N	106.31 E
Qinglonggang	96	31.51 N	121.15 E
Qinglongguan	97	30.25 N	104.48 E
Qinglonghe ≃	95	39.35 N	117.46 E
Qinglongji	88	34.05 N	116.37 E
Qinglongwanhe ≃	95	38.51 N	117.19 E
Qinglongwei	90	25.28 N	114.28 E
Qingmuguan	97	29.41 N	106.18 E
Qingningsi	96	31.16 N	121.33 E
Qingong	90	33.38 N	119.12 E
Qingping, Zhg.	88	36.47 N	116.06 E
Qingping, Zhg.	97	29.00 N	106.21 E
Qingpu	96	31.09 N	121.06 E
Qingshan, Zhg.	90	31.33 N	116.22 E
Qingshan, Zhg.	90	30.38 N	114.23 E
Qingshan, Zhg.	96	30.16 N	119.48 E
Qingshan, Zhg.	96	30.36 N	119.41 E
Qingshan ⩕	92	35.20 N	97.50 E
Qingshanpu	90	29.27 N	114.01 E
Qingshanshi	90	28.31 N	113.08 E
Qingshen	97	29.50 N	103.50 E
Qingshui	92	34.42 N	106.21 E
Qingshuibao	92	39.23 N	99.09 E
Qingshuihe ≃, Zhg.	92	37.30 N	105.30 E
Qingshuihe ≃, Zhg.	97	29.09 N	104.00 E
Qingshuijian	95	39.59 N	115.58 E
Qingshuilangshan ⩕	92	26.15 N	99.35 E
Qingshuipu	97	30.11 N	103.57 E
Qingshuixi	97	29.09 N	103.55 E
Qingtan	90	31.48 N	112.48 E
Qingtang, Zhg.	90	24.14 N	113.51 E
Qingtang, Zhg.	90	26.28 N	115.48 E
Qingtian	90	28.10 N	120.17 E
Qingtuosi	88	35.29 N	118.20 E
Qingtuozi, Zhg.	94	41.05 N	121.28 E
Qingtuozi, Zhg.	95	39.08 N	117.45 E
Qingxi, Zhg.	79	49.19 N	127.10 E
Qingxi, Zhg.	90	31.40 N	118.00 E
Qingxi, Zhg.	97	30.40 N	106.14 E
Qingxian	88	38.34 N	116.46 E
Qingyang, Zhg.	79	45.20 N	128.47 E
Qingyang, Zhg.	90	30.38 N	117.48 E
Qingyang, Zhg.	92	36.06 N	107.47 E
Qingyang, Zhg.	96	31.46 N	120.15 E
Qingyihu ⊜	88	34.22 N	118.54 E
Qingyijiang	90	30.55 N	118.28 E
Qingyijiang ≃	97	29.34 N	103.42 E
Qingyuan, Zhg.	88	42.13 N	124.56 E
Qingyuan, Zhg.	90	23.43 N	113.01 E
Qingyuan, Zhg.	90	27.38 N	119.04 E
Qingyuan, Zhg.	92	24.35 N	108.45 E
Qingyuan → Baoding, Zhg.	95	38.52 N	115.29 E
Qingyun	88	37.52 N	117.21 E
Qingyunbao	94	42.34 N	123.50 E
Qingzhen, Zhg.	92	26.29 N	106.22 E
Qingzhen, Zhg.	96	30.45 N	120.30 E
Qingzhou	90	23.39 N	116.57 E
Qinhuaihe ≃	96	32.01 N	118.50 E
Qinhuangdao (Chinwangtao)	88	39.56 N	119.36 E
Qinjia	79	46.47 N	127.00 E
Qinjiang ≃, Zhg.	90	23.58 N	115.47 E
Qinjiang ≃, Zhg.	90	26.16 N	115.52 E
Qinlanzhen	90	32.37 N	119.08 E
Qinlingshanmai ⩕	92	34.00 N	108.00 E
Qinnancang	90	33.16 N	119.55 E
Qinshui	92	35.41 N	112.11 E
Qinshui ≃	92	27.08 N	109.36 E
Qinxian, Zhg.	92	36.48 N	112.41 E
Qinxian (Qinzhou), Zhg.	92	21.59 N	108.36 E
Qinyang	92	35.06 N	112.57 E
Qinyuan	92	36.30 N	112.15 E
Qionghai (Jiaji)	100	19.20 N	110.30 E
Qionglai	97	30.25 N	103.27 E
Qionglaishan ⩕	92	31.21 N	102.50 E
Qionglongshan ∧	96	31.15 N	120.25 E
Qiongzhouhaixia ⊔	92	20.10 N	110.15 E
Qipandi	95	39.46 N	115.12 E
Qipanshan	88	42.05 N	117.30 E
Qiqihaer (Tsitsihar)	79	47.19 N	123.55 E
Qiryat	122	32.49 N	35.06 E
Qiryat 'Anavim	122	31.48 N	35.07 E
Qiryat Bialik	122	32.50 N	35.05 E
Qiryat Binyamin	122	32.48 N	35.05 E
Qiryat Gat	122	31.36 N	34.46 E
Qiryat Ḥayyim	122	32.49 N	35.04 E
Qiryat Mal'akhi	122	31.44 N	34.44 E
Qiryat Motzkin	122	32.50 N	35.04 E
Qiryat Ono	122	32.04 N	34.51 E
Qiryat Shemona	122	33.13 N	35.34 E
Qiryat Tiv'on	122	32.43 N	35.08 E
Qiryat Yam	122	32.51 N	35.04 E
Qirzah, Wādī ∨	136	30.56 N	14.31 E
Qiseqishan ∧	79	48.37 N	122.32 E
Qishn	134	15.26 N	51.40 E
Qishon ≃	122	32.49 N	35.02 E
Qishrān I	134	20.14 N	40.05 E
Qishudang	97	29.13 N	104.39 E
Qishui ≃	90	30.09 N	115.20 E
Qishuyan	96	31.44 N	120.04 E
Qiṣrāyā	120	34.53 N	36.26 E
Qitaizi	94	41.33 N	122.11 E
Qitamu	79	44.22 N	126.20 E
Qitangzhen	97	29.47 N	106.16 E
Qitao	88	34.12 N	119.52 E
Qiting	90	31.02 N	114.44 E
Qitingqiao	96	31.26 N	119.52 E
Qitou	90	24.54 N	117.29 E
Qiubei	92	24.07 N	104.12 E
Qiuchang	97	28.59 N	104.42 E
Qiuji	90	33.51 N	118.01 E
Qiujia	96	31.49 N	121.51 E
Qiujiatun	94	41.20 N	121.00 E
Qiujin	90	29.10 N	115.42 E
Qiuxian	88	36.49 N	115.10 E
Qiuxihe	92	29.59 N	104.33 E
Qiuxihe ≃	97	29.58 N	104.40 E
Qiweigang	96	32.01 N	119.59 E
Qixia	88	37.17 N	120.48 E
Qixian, Zhg.	90	33.28 N	117.01 E
Qixian, Zhg.	90	34.33 N	114.47 E
Qixiashan	96	32.10 N	118.57 E
Qixiasi Temple ᵿ[1]	96	32.12 N	118.58 E
Qixinglizi ∧	79	46.35 N	130.52 E
Qixingqiao	96	30.49 N	120.51 E
Qiyang	92	26.29 N	111.43 E
Qiyi	90	32.30 N	112.54 E
Qiying	92	36.38 N	106.25 E
Qīzān	134	16.54 N	42.29 E
Qizhou	90	30.04 N	115.20 E
Qizil Jilga	110	35.21 N	78.52 E
Qizil Langar	110	35.13 N	77.59 E
Qizimei I	96	30.17 N	121.36 E
Qolhak	257d	35.47 N	51.26 E
Qom	118	34.39 N	50.54 E
Qom ≃	118	34.48 N	51.02 E
Qondūz	110	37.45 N	68.51 E
Qondūz □[4]	110	36.45 N	68.30 E
Qondūz ≃	110	37.00 N	68.16 E
Qorveh	118	35.10 N	47.48 E
Qoṭbābād	118	28.42 N	53.34 E
Qoṭūr	118	38.28 N	44.25 E
Quabbin Reservoir ⊜[1]	197	42.22 N	72.18 W
Quaddick Reservoir ⊜[1]	197	41.57 N	71.49 W
Quadra Island I	172	50.08 N	125.16 W
Quadraro ⇠[8]	257a	41.51 N	12.33 E
Quadrath-Ichendorf	52	50.56 N	6.41 E
Quadros, Lagoa dos C	242	29.42 S	50.05 W
Quail Valley	218	33.43 N	117.15 W
Quairading	152	32.01 S	117.25 E
Quakake	200	40.51 N	76.02 W
Quakenbrück	48	52.40 N	7.57 E
Quaker Hill, Conn., U.S.	197	41.24 N	72.07 W
Quaker Hill, N.Y., U.S.	200	41.35 N	73.33 W
Quakers Hill	160	33.43 S	150.53 E
Quakers Knob ∧[2]	204	40.21 N	80.24 W
Quaker Street	200	42.44 N	74.11 W
Quakertown, N.J., U.S.	200	40.34 N	74.57 W
Quakertown, Pa., U.S.	198	40.26 N	75.21 W
Qualicum Beach	172	49.21 N	124.27 W
Quambatook	156	35.51 S	143.31 E
Quanah	186	34.18 N	99.44 W
Quangang	90	28.10 N	115.34 E
Quang-ngai	100	15.07 N	108.48 E
Quanjiangyan	90	27.43 N	113.59 E
Quanjiao	90	32.06 N	118.16 E
Quan-long (Ca-mau)	100	9.11 N	105.08 E
Quanmian	94	42.02 N	122.13 E
Quannan	90	24.44 N	114.31 E
Quannapowitt, Lake ⊜	273	42.31 N	71.05 W
Quanshang	90	26.25 N	116.55 E
Quanshengpu	94	41.59 N	123.22 E
Quanshui	94	41.18 N	124.11 E
Quanshuitou	95	40.24 N	116.39 E
Quantico, Md., U.S.	198	38.23 N	75.44 W
Quantico, Va., U.S.	198	38.31 N	77.17 W
Quantico Marine Corps Air Station ■	198	38.31 N	77.19 W
Quantock Hills ⩕[2]	44	51.07 N	3.10 W
Quantou	79	42.52 N	124.07 E
Quanxishi	90	26.51 N	112.45 E
Quanyanhezi	94	40.52 N	123.26 E
Quanzhou	90	24.54 N	118.35 E
Quanzhougang C	90	24.52 N	118.37 E
Qu'Appelle	174	50.33 N	103.52 W
Qu'Appelle ≃	174	50.25 N	101.20 W
Qu'Appelle Dam ⇠[6]	174	51.00 N	106.25 W
Quaraí	242	30.23 S	56.27 W
Quaraí (Guareim) ≃	242	30.12 S	57.36 W
Quaregnon	46	50.26 N	3.51 E
Quarles, Pegunungan ⩕	102	2.55 S	119.30 E
Quarrata	60	43.51 N	10.58 E
Quarré-les-Tombes	46	47.22 N	3.59 E
Quarry	212	30.18 N	96.30 W
Quarry Heights	266	41.04 N	73.45 W
Quarryville, Conn., U.S.	197	41.32 N	72.42 W
Quarryville, Pa., U.S.	198	39.54 N	76.10 W
Quartu Sant'Elena	36	39.14 N	9.11 E
Quartz Hill	218	34.39 N	118.13 W
Quartz Lake ⊜	166	70.55 N	80.33 W
Quartz Mountain ∧	192	43.10 N	122.40 W
Quartzsite	190	33.40 N	114.13 W
Quatá	245	22.16 S	50.42 W
Quatis	246	22.25 S	44.16 W
Quatre Isle I	231h	12.57 N	61.15 W
Quatre Piliers, Forêt des ⇠[3]	251	48.49 N	1.42 E
Quatsino Sound ⊔	172	50.25 N	127.55 W
Qubei	114	28.18 N	86.53 E
Qūchān	118	37.06 N	58.30 E
Quchijie	92	28.03 N	111.53 E
Qudaym	120	35.03 N	38.25 E
Qudi	88	37.06 N	117.15 E
Qudsia Gardens ♠	262a	28.40 N	77.13 E
Quê ≃	142	14.45 S	14.45 E
Queanbeyan	161b	35.21 S	149.14 E
Queanbeyan ≃	161b	35.20 S	149.14 E
Québec	196	46.49 N	71.14 W
Québec □[6]	196	46.50 N	71.20 W
Quebec (Québec) □[4]	166	52.00 N	72.00 W
Quebec Airport ⊠	196	46.47 N	71.23 W
Quebec House ⊥	250	51.14 N	0.05 E
Quebeck	184	35.49 N	85.34 W
Quebra-Anzol ≃	245	19.09 S	47.38 W
Quebra-cangalha, Serra ⩕	246	22.55 S	45.10 W
Quebracho	242	31.57 S	57.53 W
Quebrada Seca	230m	18.14 N	65.40 W
Quebradillas	230m	18.29 N	66.56 W
Quebrangulo	240	9.20 S	36.29 W
Quecholac	224	18.57 N	97.40 W
Quechultenango	224	17.25 N	99.13 W
Quecreek	204	40.06 N	79.05 W
Quedal, Cabo ≻	244	40.59 S	73.59 W
Quedas	146	19.30 S	33.29 E
Quedlinburg	50	51.48 N	11.09 E
Queen	204	40.16 N	78.31 W
Queen Alexandra Range ⩕	9	84.00 S	168.00 E
Queen Anne	198	38.55 N	75.57 W
Queen Anne Creek ≃	275	40.08 N	74.53 W
Queen Annes □[6]	198	39.03 N	76.04 W
Queen Bess, Mount ∧	172	51.16 N	124.34 W
Queenborough	44	51.26 N	0.45 E
Queen Charlotte	172	53.16 N	132.05 W
Queen Charlotte Bay C	244	51.50 S	60.40 W
Queen Charlotte Islands II	172	53.00 N	132.00 W
Queen Charlotte Mountains ⩕	172	53.00 N	132.00 W
Queen Charlotte Sound ⊔	172	51.30 N	129.30 W
Queen Charlotte Strait ⊔	172	50.50 N	127.25 W
Queen City, Mo., U.S.	184	40.25 N	92.34 W
Queen City, Tex., U.S.	184	33.09 N	94.09 W
Queen Elizabeth II Reservoir ⊜[1]	250	51.23 N	0.24 W
Queen Elizabeth Islands II	16	78.00 N	95.00 W
Queen Elizabeth National Park ♠	144	0.15 S	30.00 E
Queen Fabiola Mountains ⩕	9	71.30 S	35.40 E
Queen Mary ⇠	270	33.45 N	118.12 W
Queen Mary Coast •[2]	9	67.00 S	96.00 E
Queen Mary Reservoir ⊜[1]	250	51.25 N	0.28 W
Queen Maud Gulf C	166	68.25 N	102.30 W
Queen Maud Land ⇠[1]	9	72.30 S	12.00 E
Queen Maud Mountains ⩕	9	86.00 S	160.00 W
Queens □[6]	200	40.34 N	73.52 W
Queensbury	42	53.46 N	1.50 W
Queens Channel II	166	76.11 N	96.00 W
Queens Channel ⊔	154	14.46 S	129.24 E
Queenscliff	159	38.16 S	144.40 E
Queens College ᵿ[2]	266	40.44 N	73.49 W
Queensferry, Scot., U.K.	42	55.59 N	3.25 W
Queensferry, Wales, U.K.	42	53.12 N	3.01 W
Queensland □[3]	150	22.00 S	145.00 E
Queens Park ♠, Austl.	264a	33.54 S	151.16 E
Queens Park ♠, Ont., Can.	265b	43.40 N	79.24 W
Queens Park ♠, Eng., U.K.	252	53.30 N	2.13 W
Queen's Park ♠, Eng., U.K.	252	53.44 N	2.28 W
Queens Park ♠, Eng., U.K.	252	53.35 N	2.27 W
Queensport	176	45.20 N	61.16 W
Queens Sound ⊔	172	51.55 N	128.11 W
Queenston Chippawa Power Canal ≍	274a	43.08 N	79.03 W
Queenstown, Austl.	156	42.05 S	145.33 E
Queenstown → Cobh, Eire	28	51.51 N	8.17 W
Queenstown, Guy.	236	7.12 N	58.29 W
Queenstown, N.Z.	162	45.02 S	168.40 E
Queenstown, S. Afr.	148	31.52 S	26.52 E
Queenstown, Md., U.S.	198	38.59 N	76.09 W
Queensville	202	44.08 N	79.28 W
Queen Victoria Park ♠	274a	43.05 N	79.05 W
Queerhe	94	40.57 N	121.35 E
Queets	214	47.32 N	124.20 W
Queets ≃	214	47.33 N	124.21 W
Queguay Grande ≃	242	32.09 S	58.09 W
Queige	56	45.43 N	6.28 E
Queimada	246	22.27 S	45.09 W
Queimada, Ilha I	240	0.10 S	50.50 W
Queimada Nova	240	8.35 S	41.25 W
Queimadas	240	10.58 S	39.38 W
Queimadinhas	245	13.03 S	40.45 W
Queimados	246	22.42 S	43.34 W
Quela	142	9.16 S	17.02 E
Quelimane	146	17.53 S	36.51 E
Quelizhen	96	30.54 N	121.26 E
Quelle	48	52.00 N	8.29 E
Quellendorf	50	51.45 N	12.07 E
Quelo	142	6.27 S	12.48 E
Quelpart Island → Cheju-do I	80	33.20 N	126.30 E
Queluz → Conselheiro Lafaiete, Bra.	245	20.40 S	43.48 W
Queluz, Bra.	246	22.32 S	44.46 W
Queluz, Port.	256c	38.45 N	9.15 W
Quemado, N. Mex., U.S.	190	34.20 N	108.30 W
Quemado, Tex., U.S.	186	28.56 N	100.38 W
Quemado de Güines	230p	22.48 N	80.15 W
Quemahoning Reservoir ⊜[1]	204	40.09 N	78.57 W
Quembo ≃	142	14.57 S	20.22 E
Quemchi	244	42.09 S	73.29 W
Quemoy → Chinmen Tao I	90	24.27 N	118.23 E
Quemú Quemú	242	36.03 S	63.33 W
Quend	46	50.19 N	1.38 E
Quend Plage	46	50.19 N	1.33 E
Queñi, Nevado de ∧	244	40.14 S	71.49 W
Quenouilles, Lac aux ⊜	196	46.10 N	74.23 W
Quentin	198	40.17 N	76.26 W
Quepe ≃	244	38.46 S	72.55 W
Quepos	226	9.27 N	84.09 W
Que Que	144	18.55 S	29.49 E
Quequén	242	38.32 S	58.42 W
Quequén Salado ≃	244	38.56 S	60.31 W
Quercianella	60	43.27 N	10.22 E
Quercy □[9]	32	44.30 N	1.25 E
Querecotillo	238	4.50 S	80.40 W
Querenburg ⇠[8]	253	51.27 N	7.16 E
Querência do Norte	245	23.00 S	53.28 W
Querenhorst	50	52.20 N	10.57 E
Querétaro	224	20.36 N	100.23 W
Querétaro □[3]	224	21.00 N	99.55 W
Querfurt	50	51.23 N	11.36 E
Quero	58	45.55 N	11.56 E
Querobabi	222	30.03 N	111.01 W
Querobamba	238	13.52 S	73.50 W
Quesada, C.R.	226	10.19 N	84.26 W
Quesada, Esp.	34	37.51 N	3.04 W
Queset Brook ≃	273	42.02 N	71.04 W
Queshan	90	32.48 N	114.01 E
Quesnel	172	52.59 N	122.30 W
Quesnel ≃	172	53.00 N	122.30 W
Quesnel Lake ⊜	172	52.32 N	121.05 W
Quesnoy	46	50.43 N	3.00 E
Que-son	100	15.40 N	108.14 E
Questa	190	36.42 N	105.36 W
Questembert	32	47.40 N	2.27 W
Quetena	238	22.10 S	67.25 W
Quetico Lake ⊜	180	48.34 N	91.52 W
Quetico Provincial Park ♠	180	48.30 N	91.30 W
Quetta	110	30.12 N	67.00 E
Quettehou	32	49.36 N	1.18 W
Quetzala ≃	224	16.35 N	98.30 W
Quevedo	236	1.02 S	79.29 W
Quezaltenango	226	14.50 N	91.31 W
Quezaltenango □[5]	226	14.45 N	91.40 W
Quezaltepeque, El Sal.	226	13.50 N	89.17 W
Quezaltepeque, Guat.	226	14.38 N	89.27 W
Quezon	106	14.01 N	122.11 E
Quezon	106	15.34 N	120.49 E
Quezon □[4]	106	13.58 N	122.02 E
Quezon □[7]	259f	14.38 N	121.03 E
Quezon City, Pil.	106 / 259f	14.38 N	121.00 E
Quezon Memorial ⊥	259f	14.39 N	121.03 E
Quezon National Park ♠	106	14.01 N	121.51 E
Qufu	88	35.36 N	117.02 E
Qugou, Zhg.	92	36.10 N	100.56 E
Qugou, Zhg.	95	39.17 N	116.15 E
Quiabaya	238	15.37 S	68.46 W
Quibala	142	10.46 S	14.59 E
Quibaxi	142	8.29 S	14.36 E
Quibdó	236	5.42 N	76.40 W
Quiberon	32	47.29 N	3.07 W
Quiberville	46	49.54 N	0.55 E
Quíbor	236	9.56 N	69.37 W
Quibray Bay C	264a	34.01 S	151.11 E
Quibú ≃	276b	23.05 N	82.27 W
Quiçama, Parque Nacional de ♠	142	9.45 S	13.30 E
Qui-chau	100	19.33 N	105.06 E
Quiches	238	8.25 S	77.27 W
Quickborn	48	53.44 N	9.53 E
Quicksand Creek ≃	182	37.32 N	83.21 W
Quiculungo	142	8.31 S	15.19 E
Quidapil Point ≻	106	6.49 N	123.57 E
Quidnessett	197	41.39 N	71.26 W
Quidnick	197	41.42 N	71.33 W
Quien Sabe Creek ≃	216	36.43 N	121.09 W
Quiévrain	46	50.24 N	3.41 E
Quiévy	46	50.10 N	3.25 E
Quiindy	242	25.58 S	57.16 W
Quijiang ≃	97	29.59 N	106.16 E
Quijos ≃	236	0.14 S	77.43 W
Quilá	222	24.23 N	107.13 W
Quilalí	226	13.34 N	86.02 W
Quilán, Cabo ≻	244	43.16 S	74.23 W
Quilates, Cap ≻	34	35.20 N	3.45 W
Quilcene	214	47.49 N	122.53 W
Quilenda	142	10.33 S	14.22 E
Quilengues	142	14.05 S	14.04 E
Quileute Indian Reservation ⇠[4]	214	47.55 N	124.38 W
Quilicura	276e	33.22 S	70.45 W
Quilicura, Canal de ≍	276e	33.22 S	70.47 W
Quilimarí	242	32.07 S	71.30 W
Quilino	242	30.12 S	64.29 W
Quillabamba	238	12.49 S	72.43 W
Quillacas	238	19.14 S	66.58 W
Quillacollo	238	17.26 S	66.17 W
Quillagua	238	21.39 S	69.33 W
Quillan	32	42.52 N	2.11 E
Quillebeuf-sur-Seine	46	49.29 N	0.31 E
Quill Lake	174	52.05 N	104.15 W
Quillota	242	32.53 S	71.16 W
Quilmes	248	34.44 S	58.16 W
Quilmes □[5]	278	34.44 S	58.16 W
Quilmes, Aeródromo ⊠	278	34.42 S	58.15 W
Quilombo ≃	246	23.52 S	46.21 W
Quilon	112	8.53 N	76.36 E
Quilotosa Wash ∨	190	32.56 N	112.46 W
Quilpie	156	26.37 S	144.15 E
Quilpué	242	33.03 S	71.27 W
Quimarí, Alto de ∧	236	8.07 N	76.23 W
Quimbango	142	11.01 S	17.26 E
Quimbaya	236	4.38 N	75.47 W
Quimbele	142	6.28 S	16.13 E
Quimbo	142	13.59 S	16.05 E
Quimbonge	142	8.36 S	18.30 E
Quimbumbe	142	7.50 S	14.03 E
Quimby	188	42.38 N	95.38 W
Quime	238	17.02 S	67.15 W
Quimichis	224	22.21 N	105.32 W
Quimilí	242	27.38 S	62.25 W
Quimper	32	48.00 N	4.06 W
Quimperlé	32	47.52 N	3.33 W
Quimpitirique	238	12.15 S	73.52 W
Quinalasag Island I	106	13.56 N	123.38 E
Quinault	214	47.28 N	123.50 W
Quinault ≃	214	47.23 N	124.18 W
Quinault, North Fork ≃	214	47.32 N	123.40 W
Quinault Indian Reservation ⇠[4]	214	47.24 N	124.10 W
Quinault Lake ⊜	214	47.28 N	123.52 W
Quinby Inlet C	198	37.28 N	75.40 W
Quincampoix	46	49.32 N	1.11 E
Quincemil	238	13.16 S	70.38 W
Quinches	238	12.13 S	76.05 W
Quincy, Calif., U.S.	194	39.56 N	120.57 W
Quincy, Ill., U.S.	209	39.56 N	91.23 W
Quincy, Ky., U.S.	208	38.37 N	83.07 W
Quincy, Mass., U.S.	197	42.15 N	71.01 W
Quincy, Mich., U.S.	206	41.57 N	84.53 W
Quincy, Ohio, U.S.	206	40.18 N	83.58 W
Quincy, Oreg., U.S.	214	46.04 N	123.05 W
Quincy, Pa., U.S.	198	39.48 N	77.35 W
Quincy, Wash., U.S.	192	47.14 N	119.51 W
Quincy Bay C	273	42.17 N	70.58 W
Quincy Hills ⩕[2]	184	39.55 N	91.15 W
Quincy-sous-Sénart	251	48.40 N	2.33 E
Quincy-Voisins	251	48.54 N	2.53 E
Quindanning	158a	33.03 S	116.34 E
Quindío □[5]	236	4.30 N	75.40 W
Quinebaug	197	42.01 N	71.57 W
Quinebaug ≃	197	41.33 N	72.03 W
Quines	242	32.13 S	65.48 W
Quinga	144	15.49 S	40.15 E
Quingey	54	47.06 N	5.53 E
Quinhagak	170	59.45 N	161.43 W
Quinh-luu	100	19.10 N	105.42 E
Qui-nhon	100	13.46 N	109.14 E
Quiniluban Group II	106	11.27 N	120.48 E
Quinjenje	142	12.49 S	14.55 E
Quinlan	212	32.55 N	96.08 W
Quinn ≃	194	40.58 N	119.05 W
Quiñones, Arroyo de los ≃	256a	40.33 N	3.34 W
Quinson	56	43.42 N	6.02 E
Quinta da Boa Vista ♠	277a	22.54 S	43.15 W
Quintanar de la Orden	34	39.34 N	3.03 W
Quintana Roo □[3]	222	19.40 N	88.30 W
Quinta Normal	276e	33.27 S	70.42 W
Quinta Normal de Agricultura ᵿ[2]	276e	33.27 S	70.42 W
Quinte, Bay of C	202	44.07 N	77.15 W
Quinter	188	39.04 N	100.14 W
Quintero	242	32.47 S	71.32 W
Quintin	32	48.24 N	2.55 W
Quintino Sella, Canale ≍	256b	45.29 N	8.38 E
Quinto	34	41.25 N	0.29 W
Quinto Creek ≃	216	37.11 N	121.02 W
5 de Noviembre, Presa ⇠[6]	226	13.59 N	88.44 W
Quinton, Sask., Can.	174	51.23 N	104.24 W
Quinton, N.J., U.S.	198	39.33 N	75.25 E
Quinton, Okla., U.S.	186	35.07 N	95.22 W
Quinto Romano ⇠[8]	256b	45.29 N	9.05 E
Quinzano d'Oglio	58	45.19 N	10.00 E
Quinzáu	142	6.51 S	12.46 E
Quinze, Lac des ⊜	180	47.35 N	79.05 W
Quionga	144	10.37 S	40.30 E
Quiotepec ≃	224	17.35 N	97.00 W
Quiotepec ⊥	224	17.54 N	96.58 W
Quipapá	240	8.50 S	36.02 W
Quipar ≃	34	38.14 N	1.36 W
Quipeio	142	12.26 S	15.30 E
Quipemba	142	7.12 S	15.06 E
Quipit ≃	106	8.04 N	122.29 E
Quirauk Mountain ∧	198	39.42 N	77.31 W
Quiriguá ⊥	226	15.17 N	89.04 W
Quirihue	242	36.17 S	72.32 W
Quirima	142	10.48 S	18.09 E
Quirimbo	142	10.36 S	14.12 E
Quirindi	156	31.31 S	150.41 E
Quirinópolis	245	18.32 S	50.30 W
Quiriquire	236	9.59 N	63.13 W
Quiriri ≃	142	15.13 S	18.47 E
Quiririm	246	23.02 S	45.38 W
Quirke Lake ⊜	180	46.28 N	82.33 W
Quiroga, Esp.	34	42.29 N	7.16 W
Quiroga, Méx.	224	19.40 N	101.32 W
Quirós	242	28.47 S	65.07 W
Quiros, Cape ≻	165f	14.55 S	167.01 E
Quirpon Island I	176	51.35 N	55.25 W
Quiruvilca	238	8.00 S	78.19 W
Quissac	56	43.55 N	4.00 E
Quissanga	144	12.25 S	40.29 E
Quissico	146	24.42 S	34.44 E
Quissongo	142	10.01 S	15.07 E
Quistello	58	45.00 N	10.59 E
Quitapa	142	10.23 S	18.14 E
Quitaque	186	34.22 N	101.04 W
Quita Sueño Bank ✢[4]	226	14.20 N	81.15 W
Quitaúna	277b	23.31 S	46.47 W
Quiterajo	144	11.48 S	40.25 E
Quitéria ≃	245	20.16 S	51.08 W
Quitexe	142	7.56 S	15.02 E
Quitilipi	242	26.52 S	60.13 W
Quitman, Ga., U.S.	182	30.47 N	83.33 W
Quitman, Miss., U.S.	184	32.03 N	88.43 W
Quitman, Tex., U.S.	212	32.48 N	95.27 W
Quito	236	0.13 S	78.30 W
Quivilla	238	9.32 S	76.41 W
Quixadá	240	4.58 S	39.01 W
Quixeramobim	240	5.12 S	39.17 W
Quixeré	240	5.05 S	37.59 W
Quixico	142	7.59 S	14.25 E
Quixinge	142	9.52 S	14.23 E
Quixito ≃	236	4.29 S	70.18 W
Quizenga	142	9.21 S	15.28 E
Qujiadian	79	43.13 N	123.53 E
Qujiang, Zhg.	90	28.15 N	115.45 E
Qujiang, Zhg.	90	24.48 N	113.17 E
Qujing	92	25.32 N	103.41 E
Qujiu	92	22.28 N	107.40 E
Quke	110	28.16 N	87.24 E
Qukou	95	39.46 N	117.07 E
Qulay'ah, Ra's al- ≻	118	28.53 N	48.18 E
Qulbān al-'Īsāwīyah	118	30.38 N	37.53 E
Qulin	184	36.36 N	90.15 W
Qulubbā	132	27.45 N	30.50 E
Qulūd, Jabal ∧[2]	130	11.41 N	29.31 E
Qulūṣanā	132	28.21 N	30.44 E
Qulzum, Baḥr al- C	132	29.55 N	32.31 E
Qumalai (Sewugou)	92	34.35 N	95.27 E
Qumbu	148	31.10 S	28.48 E
Qumo	88	36.54 N	114.43 E
Qumrān, Khirbat ⊥	122	31.44 N	35.27 E
Qunayfidhah, Nafūd •[8]	118	24.45 N	45.30 E
Qunbush al-Ḥamrā'	132	29.00 N	30.59 E
Qunshen'guan	95	39.49 N	117.59 E
Quobba, Point ≻	152	24.23 S	113.24 E
Quoich ≃	166	64.00 N	93.30 W
Quoile ≃	42	54.21 N	5.42 W
Quoin Point ≻	148	34.46 S	19.37 E
Quonochontaug	197	41.21 N	71.43 W
Quorn	156	32.21 S	138.03 E
Quorndon	44	52.45 N	1.09 W
Qurayn, Kawlat al- ∧	132	29.25 N	31.55 E
Qurayyah, Wādī ∨	122	30.26 N	34.01 E
Qurayyāt, Al- □[4]	122	31.28 N	37.05 E
Qurdūd	130	10.17 N	29.56 E
Qurrāṣah	130	14.38 N	32.12 E
Qurūn Ḥarḥash ∧[2]	132	28.09 N	31.42 E
Qūṣ	130	25.55 N	32.45 E
Quṣayr ad-Daffah ⊥	136	30.20 N	23.57 E
Qushan I	90	30.27 N	122.20 E
Qūshchī	118	37.59 N	45.03 E
Qushui	110	29.22 N	90.43 E
Qushuichang	97	30.41 N	106.02 E
Qutang	90	32.30 N	120.21 E
Qutbapur ⇠[8]	262a	28.35 N	77.01 E
Qutb Minar ᵿ[1]	262a	28.32 N	77.11 E
Qutdligssat	166	70.04 N	53.01 W
Quthing	148	30.30 S	27.36 E
Quṭūr	132	30.59 N	30.57 E
Quwaysinā	132	30.34 N	31.09 E
Quxi, Zhg.	90	28.00 N	120.31 E
Quxi, Zhg.	90	23.36 N	116.26 E
Quxia	96	32.06 N	120.09 E
Quxian, Zhg.	90	28.58 N	118.52 E
Quxian, Zhg.	92	30.51 N	106.59 E
Quxingji	88	34.52 N	114.39 E
Quxiong	92	31.09 N	96.00 E
Quyang	88	38.34 N	114.42 E
Qūyjāq-e-Bālā	74	39.16 N	47.07 E
Quyon	178	45.31 N	76.14 W
Quyquyhó	242	26.14 S	57.01 W
Quzaymah, Jabal ∧	122	30.34 N	36.21 E
Quzhou	88	36.46 N	114.57 E
Quzong	92	30.08 N	96.00 E

R

Name	Seite	Breite°′	Länge°′ E=Ost
Råå	41	56.00 N	12.44 E
Raab → Győr	30	47.42 N	17.38 E
Raab (Rába) ≃	30	47.42 N	17.38 E
Raadt ⇠[8]	253	51.24 N	6.56 E
Raahe	26	64.41 N	24.29 E
Rääkkylä	26	62.19 N	29.37 E
Raalte	48	52.24 N	6.16 E
Raamsdonksveer	48	51.42 N	4.56 E
Ra'anana	122	32.11 N	34.53 E
Raas, Pulau I	105a	7.09 S	114.32 E
Raasay I	28	57.25 N	6.04 W
Raasdorf	254b	48.15 N	16.34 E
Raasiku	66	59.22 N	25.11 E
Rab	36	44.46 N	14.46 E
Rab, Otok I	36	44.47 N	14.45 E
Raba	105b	8.27 S	118.46 E
Rába (Raab) ≃, Eur.	30	47.42 N	17.38 E
Raba ≃, Pol.	30	50.09 N	20.30 E
Rabableh	134	8.14 N	48.18 E
Rabaçal ≃	34	41.30 N	7.12 W
Rábade	34	43.07 N	7.37 W
Rabai	144	3.58 S	39.37 E
Rabak	130	13.09 N	32.44 E
Rabal	154	6.22 S	134.52 E
Rabat, Magreb	138	34.02 N	6.51 W
Rabat, Malta	36	35.52 N	14.25 E
Rabat (Victoria), Malta	36	36.02 N	14.14 E
Rabaul	154	4.12 S	152.12 E
Rabbit ≃	206	42.38 N	86.06 W
Rabbit, Lac ⊜	180	47.30 N	78.22 W
Rabbit Creek ≃, S. Dak., U.S.	188	45.13 N	102.10 W
Rabbit Creek ≃, Tex., U.S.	212	32.26 N	94.47 W
Rabbit Ears Pass)(	190	40.23 N	106.37 W
Rabbit Lake ⊜, Ont., Can.	180	47.00 N	79.37 W
Rabbit Lake ⊜, Calif., U.S.	218	34.27 N	117.01 W
Rabbs Creek ≃	212	29.59 N	96.55 W
R'abcevo	66	54.39 N	32.19 E
Rabeira, Ponta da ≻	277a	22.49 S	43.10 W
Rabenau	50	50.57 N	13.38 E
Rabette, Ruisseau la ≃	251	48.35 N	2.00 E
Rābigh	118	22.48 N	39.01 E
Rabinal	226	15.06 N	90.27 W
Rabiusa ≃	54	46.48 N	9.20 E
Rabka	30	49.36 N	19.56 E
Rabkavi Banhatti	112	16.28 N	75.06 E
Rabnābād Channel ⊔	116	21.50 N	90.19 E
Rabočeostrovsk	24	64.02 N	34.46 E
Rabočij	76	59.07 N	79.00 E
Rabong, Gunong ∧	104	4.48 N	102.07 E
Rabotki	70	56.03 N	44.38 E
R'abovskij	70	50.01 N	41.53 E
Rabun Bald ∧	182	34.58 N	83.18 W
Raby	252	53.19 N	3.02 W
Răcari	38	44.38 N	25.45 E
Racconigi	56	44.46 N	7.46 E
Raccoon ≃	184	41.35 N	93.37 W
Raccoon Creek ≃, N.J., U.S.	198	39.48 N	75.23 W
Raccoon Creek ≃, Ohio, U.S.	204	40.02 N	82.24 W
Raccoon Creek ≃, Pa., U.S.	204	40.38 N	80.22 W
Raccoon Creek ≃, Pa., U.S.	275	39.48 N	75.23 W
Raccoon Creek ≃, Va., U.S.	198	36.48 N	77.10 W
Raccoon Creek State Park ♠	204	40.30 N	80.27 W
Raccoon Island I	275	39.49 N	75.22 W
Raccoon Lake ⊜[1]	209	38.32 N	89.08 W
Race, Cape ≻	176	46.40 N	53.10 W
Raceland	184	29.48 N	90.40 W
Race Point ≻	197	42.04 N	70.14 W
Racette, Lac ⊜	196	46.34 N	74.03 W
Racette, Ruisseau ≃	196	46.36 N	74.04 W
Raceview	263d	26.17 S	28.08 E
Rach'a	66	60.05 N	30.49 E
Rach-gia	100	10.01 N	105.05 E
Rach-gia, Vinh C	100	10.00 N	105.00 E
Rachmanovka, S.S.S.R.	68	47.48 N	33.13 E
Rachmanovka, S.S.S.R.	70	51.57 N	49.29 E
Rachmanovo	72	55.44 N	38.37 E
Rachny Lesovyje	68	48.47 N	28.29 E
Rachov	68	48.03 N	24.12 E
Raciąż	30	52.47 N	20.06 E
Racibórz (Ratibor)	30	50.06 N	18.13 E
Racine, Pa., U.S.	204	40.49 N	80.20 W
Racine, Wis., U.S.	206	42.43 N	87.48 W
Racine □[6]	206	42.45 N	88.05 W
Racines	58	46.52 N	11.18 E
Račinskij Chrebet ⩕	74	42.30 N	43.30 E
Rackerby	216	39.26 N	121.20 W
Ráckeve	30	47.10 N	18.56 E
R'ad	66	57.56 N	35.04 E
Råda	40	60.00 N	13.36 E
Radama, Îles II	147b	14.00 S	47.47 E
Radama, Presqu'île ≻[1]	147b	14.16 S	47.53 E
Rådasjön ⊜	40	59.58 N	13.38 E
Radaur	114	30.02 N	77.09 E

Symbols in the index entries represent the broad categories identified in the key at the right. Symbols with superior numbers (⩕[2]) identify subcategories (see complete key on page *I · 26*).

Kartensymbole in dem Registerverzeichnis stellen die rechts in Schlüssel erklärten Kategorien dar. Symbole mit hochgestellten Ziffern (⩕[2]) bezeichnen Unterabteilungen einer Kategorie (vgl. vollständiger Schlüssel auf Seite *I · 26*).

Los símbolos incluídos en el texto del índice representan las grandes categorias identificadas con la clave a la derecha. Los símbolos con numeros en su parte superior (⩕[2]) identifican las subcategorias (véase la clave completa en la página *I · 26*).

Les symboles de l'index représentent les catégories indiquées dans la légende à droite. Les symboles suivis d'un indice (⩕[2]) représentent des sous-catégories (voir légende complète à la page *I · 26*).

Os símbolos incluídos no texto do índice representam as grandes categorias identificadas com a chave à direita. Os símbolos com números em sua parte superior (⩕[2]) identificam as subcategorias (veja-se a chave completa à página *I · 26*).

	English	Deutsch	Español	Français	Português
∧	Mountain	Berg	Montaña	Montagne	Montanha
⩕	Mountains	Berge	Montañas	Montagnes	Montanhas
)(	Pass	Pass	Paso	Col	Passo
∨	Valley, Canyon	Tal, Cañon	Valle, Cañón	Vallée, Canyon	Vale, Canhão
≚	Plain	Ebene	Llano	Plaine	Planície
≻	Cape	Kap	Cabo	Cap	Cabo
I	Island	Insel	Isla	Île	Ilha
II	Islands	Inseln	Islas	Îles	Ilhas
•	Other Topographic Features	Andere Topographische Objekte	Otros Elementos Topográficos	Autres données topographiques	Outros Elementos Topográficos

ESPAÑOL · FRANÇAIS · PORTUGUÊS

Nombre / Nom / Nome	Página / Page	Lat.°′	Long.°′ W=Oeste / W=Ouest
Rădăuţi	38	47.51 N	25.55 E
Radbuza ≃	30	49.46 N	13.24 E
Radčenskoje	68	49.48 N	40.32 E
Radcliff	184	37.51 N	85.57 W
Radcliffe	42	53.34 N	2.20 W
Radcliffe-on-Trent	44	52.57 N	1.03 W
Radda in Chianti	60	43.29 N	11.22 E
Råde	26	59.21 N	10.51 E
Radebaugh	269b	40.19 N	79.35 W
Radeberg	50	51.07 N	13.55 E
Radebeul	50	51.06 N	13.40 E
Radeburg	50	51.13 N	13.43 E
Radeče	36	46.04 N	15.11 E
Radechov	68	50.18 N	24.37 E
Radegast	50	51.39 N	12.05 E
Radenthein	58	46.48 N	13.43 E
Radevormwald	52	51.12 N	7.21 E
Radford	182	37.08 N	80.34 W
Rādhānagar, Bhārat	116	23.09 N	87.19 E
Rādhānagar, Bhārat	262b	22.27 N	88.28 E
Rādhanpur	110	23.50 N	71.36 E
Radici, Foce delle)(	58	44.12 N	10.31 E
Radicofani	60	42.54 N	11.46 E
Radicondoli	60	43.16 N	11.02 E
Rădinești	38	44.48 N	23.46 E
Radiščevo	70	52.51 N	47.53 E
Radisson	174	52.27 N	107.23 W
Radiumbad Brambach	50	50.13 N	12.19 E
Radium Hot Springs	172	50.38 N	116.03 W
Radix, Point ≻	231r	10.20 N	60.59 W
Radkersburg	30	46.41 N	15.59 E
Rad'kovka	68	51.06 N	36.58 E
Radlett	44	51.42 N	0.20 W
Radlett Aerodrome ⊠	250	51.43 N	0.19 W
Radley Run ≃	275	39.54 N	75.37 W
Rådmansö ≻[1]	40	59.45 N	18.55 E
Radnevo	38	42.18 N	25.56 E
Radnice	30	49.51 N	13.37 E
Radnor, Ohio, U.S.	204	40.23 N	83.09 W
Radnor, Pa., U.S.	275	40.02 N	75.21 W
Radnor Forest ∧	44	52.18 N	3.10 W
Radnor Mere @	252	53.17 N	2.14 W
Radofinnikovo	66	59.09 N	30.55 E
Radogošča	66	59.47 N	34.51 E
Radoj'a	68	47.44 N	28.09 E
Radolfzell	54	47.44 N	8.58 E
Radom, Pol.	30	51.25 N	21.10 E
Radom, Ill., U.S.	209	38.17 N	89.12 W
Radomicko	50	52.10 N	14.58 E
Radomir	38	42.33 N	22.58 E
Radomka	68	51.56 N	32.32 E
Radomka ≃	30	51.43 N	21.26 E
Radomsko	30	51.05 N	19.25 E
Radomyšl'	68	50.30 N	29.14 E
Radomyśl Wielki	30	50.12 N	21.16 E
Radoškoviči	66	54.09 N	27.14 E
Radotín	30	50.00 N	14.22 E
Radovicy	70	55.06 N	39.32 E
Radoviš	38	41.38 N	22.28 E
Radovljica	36	46.21 N	14.11 E
Radstadt	58	47.23 N	13.27 E
Radstädter Tauern)(	58	47.15 N	13.24 E
Radstock	44	51.18 N	2.28 W
Radul'	68	51.49 N	30.42 E
Radun'	66	54.03 N	25.00 E
Radušnoje	68	47.49 N	33.29 E
Radutino	66	52.39 N	33.57 E
Radvaniči	68	52.02 N	24.02 E
Radviliškis	66	55.50 N	23.31 E
Radville	174	49.27 N	104.17 W
Radwā, Jabal ∧	118	24.34 N	38.18 E
Radway	172	54.04 N	112.57 W
Radykovskoje	70	45.56 N	41.57 E
Radymno	30	49.57 N	22.48 E
Radziejów	30	52.38 N	18.32 E
Radzyń Chełmiński	30	53.24 N	18.56 E
Radzyń Podlaski	30	51.48 N	22.38 E
Rae	166	62.50 N	116.03 W
Rae ≃	166	67.55 N	115.30 W
Rāe Bareli	114	26.13 N	81.14 E
Rāe Bareli □[5]	114	26.20 N	81.20 E
Raeford	182	34.59 N	79.14 W
Rae Isthmus •[3]	166	66.55 N	86.10 W
Rāenda	116	22.18 N	89.51 E
Raeren	52	50.41 N	6.07 E
Raesfeld	48	51.46 N	6.50 E
Raeside, Lake @	152	29.30 S	122.00 E
Rae Strait ⊔	166	68.45 N	95.00 W
Raetihi	162	39.26 S	175.17 E
Raevavae I	14	23.52 S	147.40 W
Rafael, Cachoeira do ⌞	238	10.25 S	63.15 W
Rafaela	242	31.16 S	61.29 W
Rafael Calzada	248	34.48 S	58.22 W
Rafael Castillo	278	34.43 S	58.37 W
Rafael Perazza	248	34.32 S	56.47 W
Rafah	122	31.18 N	34.15 E
Rafaï	142	4.58 N	23.56 E
Rafalovka	68	51.22 N	25.52 E
Raffadali	36	37.24 N	13.33 E
Raffelberg, Rennbahn ♠	253	51.26 N	6.50 E
Raffili Mission	130	6.53 N	27.58 E
Rafḥā'	118	29.42 N	43.30 E
Rafinesque, Mount ∧	200	42.47 N	73.37 W
Rafsanjān	118	30.24 N	56.01 E
Raft ≃	192	42.37 N	113.15 W
Raft River Mountains ⩕	190	41.55 N	113.25 W
Rafz	54	47.37 N	8.32 E
Raga	130	8.28 N	25.41 E
Ragada	58	46.10 N	10.38 E
Ragang, Mount ∧	106	7.43 N	124.32 E
Ragay	106	13.49 N	122.47 E
Ragay Gulf C	106	13.30 N	122.45 E
Rågeleje	41	56.06 N	12.10 E
Rägelin	50	53.01 N	12.38 E
Ragewitz	50	51.14 N	12.51 E
Ragged, Mount ∧	152	33.27 S	123.25 E
Ragged Island I	228	22.12 N	75.44 W
Ragged Lake @	202	45.28 N	78.38 W
Ragged Point ≻	231g	13.10 N	59.25 W
Ragged Top Mountain ∧	190	41.27 N	105.20 W
Raghabpur	262b	22.25 N	88.21 E
Rāghogarh	114	24.27 N	77.12 E
Raghumāthbāri	116	22.22 N	87.47 E
Raghunāthpur, Bhārat	116	23.33 N	86.40 E
Raghunāthpur, Bngl.	116	23.12 N	89.31 E
Raglan, Austl.	160	33.26 S	149.36 E
Raglan, N.Z.	162	37.48 S	174.53 E
Raglan, Wales, U.K.	44	51.47 N	2.51 W
Ragland	184	33.45 N	86.09 W
Ragnit → Neman	66	55.02 N	22.02 E
Ragow	254a	52.17 N	13.33 E
Ragozino	76	59.15 N	77.52 E
Rågsveden	40	60.29 N	14.05 E
Raguhn	50	51.42 N	12.17 E
Raguli	70	45.38 N	43.42 E
Ragusa, It.	36	36.55 N	14.44 E
Ragusa → Dubrovnik, Jugo.	38	42.38 N	18.07 E
Raguva	66	55.34 N	24.36 E
Raha	102	4.51 S	122.43 E
Raḥā, Ḥarrat ar- •[9]	130	27.40 N	36.35 E
Rahad, Nahr ar- (Rahad) ≃	130	14.28 N	33.31 E
Rahad al-Baraī	130	11.18 N	23.53 E
Rahaṭ, Ḥarrat •[9]	134	22.20 N	40.05 E
Rahatgaon	114	22.15 N	77.14 E
Rāhatgarh	114	23.47 N	78.22 E
Raḥbah	120	34.30 N	36.09 E
Rahden	48	52.26 N	8.36 E
Rahimatpur	112	17.36 N	74.12 E
Rahīm ki Bāzār	110	24.19 N	69.10 E
Rahīmyār Khān	110	28.25 N	70.18 E
Rahīmyār Khān □[5]	113	28.50 N	70.50 E
Rahlstedt ◆[8]	48	53.36 N	10.09 E
Rahm	253	51.26 N	6.26 E
Rahm ◆[8], B.R.D.	253	51.32 N	7.23 E
Rahm ◆[8], B.R.D.	253	51.21 N	6.47 E
Rahmer See @	254a	52.45 N	13.25 E
Rahns	275	40.12 N	75.27 W
Rahnsdorf ◆[8]	254a	52.26 N	13.42 E
Rāhon	113	31.03 N	76.07 E
Rahotu	162	39.20 S	173.48 E
Rahouia	34	35.32 N	1.01 E
Rāhwāli	113	32.15 N	74.10 E
Rahway	200	40.37 N	74.17 W
Rahway ≃	266	40.35 N	74.12 W
Rahway, East Branch ≃	266	40.42 N	74.18 W
Rahway, Robinsons Branch ≃	266	40.37 N	74.17 W
Rahway, South Branch ≃	266	40.36 N	74.17 W
Rahway, West Branch ≃	266	40.42 N	74.18 W
Rahway River Parkway ♠	266	40.41 N	74.19 W
Raiano	60	42.06 N	13.49 E
Raiatea I	14	16.50 S	151.25 W
Rāichūr	112	16.12 N	77.22 E
Raidak ≃	114	26.22 N	89.45 E
Rāidighi	116	22.00 N	88.26 E
Raiford	182	30.04 N	82.14 W
Raiganj	114	25.37 N	88.07 E
Raigarh	112	21.54 N	83.24 E
Raigarh □[5]	114	22.20 N	83.30 E
Raijua, Pulau I	102	10.37 S	121.36 E
Rāikot	113	30.39 N	75.36 E
Railroad	198	39.46 N	76.42 W
Railroad Canyon Reservoir @[1]	218	33.42 N	117.16 W
Railroad Creek ≃	214	48.12 N	120.36 W
Rail Road Flat	216	38.20 N	120.30 W
Railroad Valley ∨	194	38.25 N	115.40 W
Railton	156	41.21 S	146.25 E
Raimangal ≃[1]	116	21.47 N	89.08 E
Rain	52	48.41 N	10.55 E
Rainbow	218	33.24 N	117.10 W
Rainbow Bridge ◆[5]	274a	43.05 N	79.04 W
Rainbow Bridge National Monument ♠	190	36.58 N	110.56 W
Rainbow City	226	9.21 N	79.53 W
Rainbow Falls ⌞	172	52.23 N	119.59 W
Rainbow Lakes	266	40.52 N	74.28 W
Rainbow Park ♠	268	41.46 N	87.33 W
Rainbow Shores	202	43.37 N	76.12 W
Rainelle	178	37.58 N	80.47 W
Rainford	42	53.30 N	2.48 W
Rainham	44	51.23 N	0.36 E
Rainham ◆[8]	44	51.31 N	0.11 E
Rainhill	42	53.26 N	2.46 W
Rainhill Stoops	252	53.24 N	2.45 W
Rainier, Oreg., U.S.	214	46.06 N	122.56 W
Rainier, Wash., U.S.	214	46.53 N	122.41 W
Rainier, Mount ∧	214	46.52 N	121.46 W
Rainow	252	53.17 N	2.04 W
Rains → Riva di Tures	58	46.57 N	12.04 E
Rains □[6]	212	32.50 N	95.47 W
Rainsboro	208	39.13 N	83.25 W
Rainsford Island I	273	42.18 N	70.57 W
Rainworth	44	53.07 N	1.08 W
Rainy ≃, N.A.	174	48.50 N	94.41 W
Rainy ≃, Mich., U.S.	180	45.27 N	84.13 W
Rainy Lake @, Ont., Can.	202	45.32 N	79.30 W
Rainy Lake @, N.A.	174	48.42 N	93.10 W
Rainy River	180	48.43 N	94.29 W
Raipur, Bhārat	112	21.14 N	81.38 E
Raipur, Bhārat	114	30.19 N	78.06 E
Raipur, Bhārat	116	22.48 N	86.57 E
Raipur, Bhārat	262a	28.32 N	77.20 E
Raipur, Bhārat	262b	22.24 N	88.09 E
Rāipur, Bngl.	116	23.03 N	90.46 E
Rāipura	116	23.59 N	90.53 E
Raipur Uplands ⩕[1]	112	21.00 N	82.20 E
Rairākhol	110	21.04 N	84.21 E
Ra'īs	118	23.34 N	38.36 E
Raisdorf	50	54.17 N	10.16 E
Raisen	114	23.20 N	77.48 E
Raisen □[5]	114	23.10 N	78.10 E
Raisin	216	36.36 N	119.54 W
Raisin ≃, Ont., Can.	196	45.08 N	74.29 W
Raisin ≃, Mich., U.S.	206	41.53 N	83.20 W
Raisinghnagar	113	29.32 N	73.27 E
Raismes	46	50.23 N	3.29 E
Raita	116	24.07 N	88.57 E
Raiti	226	14.35 N	85.02 W
Rāiwind	113	31.15 N	74.13 E
Raizeux	251	48.37 N	1.41 E
Raja, Gili I	105a	7.14 S	113.47 E
Raja, Ujung ≻	104	3.45 N	96.33 E
Rājābari	116	23.23 N	90.28 E
Rajabasa	102	5.25 S	104.24 E
Rājābhāt Khāwa	114	26.37 N	89.32 E
Rājābhita	116	23.52 N	86.20 E
Rājahmundry	112	16.59 N	81.47 E
Rajāj	130	10.55 N	24.43 E
Rāja Jang	113	31.13 N	74.16 E
Raja-Jooseppi	24	68.28 N	28.21 E
Rājākhera	114	26.55 N	78.11 E
Rājaldesar	110	28.02 N	74.28 E
Raj-Aleksandrovka	73	48.48 N	37.51 E
Rājāluka	116	22.09 N	86.38 E
Rajamäki	26	60.32 N	24.45 E
Rājampet	112	14.11 N	79.10 E
Rajang ≃	102	2.04 N	111.12 E
Rājanpur	110	29.06 N	70.19 E
Rājapālaiyam	112	9.27 N	77.34 E
Rājāpur, Bhārat	112	16.40 N	73.31 E
Rājāpur, Bhārat	114	25.23 N	81.09 E
Rājāpur, Bhārat	262b	22.39 N	88.11 E
Rājāpur, Bngl.	116	22.34 N	90.09 E
Rājasthān □[4]	110	27.00 N	74.00 E
Rājasthān Canal ≅	110	31.10 N	75.00 E
Rājauri	113	33.23 N	74.18 E
Rājbāri, Bhārat	116	22.25 N	88.48 E
Rājbāri, Bngl.	114	23.46 N	89.39 E
Raj Bhawan ⛉	262b	22.34 N	88.21 E
Rajčichinsk	79	49.46 N	129.25 E
Rājendrapur	116	24.06 N	90.27 E
Rajevskij	76	54.04 N	54.56 E
Rāj Gāngpur	114	22.11 N	84.36 E
Rājganj ≃[1]	116	22.21 N	90.16 E
Rājgarh, Bhārat	113	28.38 N	75.23 E
Rājgarh, Bhārat	114	23.56 N	76.58 E
Rājgarh, Bhārat	114	27.14 N	76.38 E
Rājgarh □[5]	114	23.45 N	76.50 E
Rajghat ⛉[1]	262a	28.39 N	77.15 E
Rājgīr	114	25.02 N	85.25 E
Rajgorod	70	48.26 N	44.55 E
Rajgorodka, S.S.S.R.	73	48.50 N	39.04 E
Rajgorodka, S.S.S.R.	73	49.22 N	37.57 E
Rajgorodok, S.S.S.R.	70	48.48 N	52.53 E
Rajgorodok, S.S.S.R.	73	48.54 N	37.43 E
Rajgród	30	53.44 N	22.42 E
Rājhāt	262b	22.56 N	88.21 E
Rājibpur	262b	22.49 N	88.34 E
Rajik	102	2.36 S	105.56 E
Rajka	30	48.02 N	17.11 E
Rājkot	110	22.18 N	70.47 E
Rajkuzi	255a	59.47 N	29.57 E
Rājmahāl	114	25.03 N	87.50 E
Rājmahāl Hills ⩕[2]	114	24.40 N	87.25 E
Rājnagar	116	23.57 N	87.19 E
Rāj-Nāndgaon	110	21.06 N	81.02 E
Rajokri ◆[8]	262a	28.31 N	77.07 E
Rājpīpla	110	21.47 N	73.34 E
Rājpur, Bhārat	110	21.56 N	75.08 E
Rājpur, Bhārat	116	22.25 N	88.25 E
Rājpur, Bhārat	262a	28.44 N	77.22 E
Rājpur ◆[8]	262a	28.41 N	77.12 E
Rājpura	114	30.29 N	76.36 E
Rājshāhi	114	24.22 N	88.36 E
Rajskoje	73	48.34 N	37.25 E
Rajula	112	21.03 N	71.26 E
Rakaia	162	43.45 S	172.01 E
Rakaia ≃	162	43.56 S	172.13 E
Rakamaz	30	48.08 N	21.30 E
Rakaposhi ∧	113	36.10 N	74.30 E
Rakata, Pulau I	105a	6.10 S	105.26 E
Rakha La)(	114	27.53 N	87.34 E
Rakhawt, Wādī ∨	134	17.40 N	51.40 E
Rakhneh	118	31.39 N	59.13 E
Rakhni	110	30.03 N	69.55 E
Rakhshān ≃	118	27.00 N	64.08 E
Rākīn	122	31.14 N	35.42 E
Rakitnoje, S.S.S.R.	68	49.42 N	30.27 E
Rakitnoje, S.S.S.R.	68	51.17 N	27.14 E
Rakitnoje, S.S.S.R.	68	50.51 N	35.50 E
Rakitnoje, S.S.S.R.	79	45.36 N	134.17 E
Rakke	66	58.59 N	26.15 E
Rakkestad	26	59.26 N	11.21 E
Rakoniewice	30	52.10 N	16.16 E
Rakops	146	21.00 S	24.32 E
Rákoscsaba ◆[8]	254c	47.29 N	19.17 E
Rákoshegy ◆[8]	254c	47.28 N	19.14 E
Rákoskeresztúr ◆[8]	254c	47.29 N	19.15 E
Rákoskert ◆[8]	254c	47.28 N	19.19 E
Rákosliget ◆[8]	254c	47.30 N	19.16 E
Rákospalota ◆[8]	254c	47.34 N	19.08 E
Rákos-patak ≃	254c	47.33 N	19.04 E
Rákosszentmihály ◆[8]	254c	47.32 N	19.11 E
Rakovnická plošina ⩕[1]	50	50.08 N	13.47 E
Rakovník	50	50.05 N	13.43 E
Rakovski	38	42.18 N	24.58 E
Rakša	70	53.33 N	41.37 E
Raksakiny	76	60.37 N	73.52 E
Rakuša	70	47.03 N	52.47 E
Råkvåg	26	63.46 N	10.05 E
Rakvere	66	59.22 N	26.20 E
Rakwa	154	2.42 S	134.30 E
Raleigh, Newf., Can.	176	51.34 N	55.44 W
Raleigh, Miss., U.S.	184	32.02 N	89.30 W
Raleigh, N.C., U.S.	182	35.47 N	78.39 W
Raleigh Hills	214	45.29 N	122.46 W
Ralls	186	33.41 N	101.23 W
Ralls □[6]	209	39.34 N	91.30 W
Ralsko ∧	50	50.42 N	14.47 E
Ralston, Nebr., U.S.	188	41.12 N	96.03 W
Ralston, Pa., U.S.	200	41.31 N	76.57 W
Ram ≃	172	52.23 N	115.25 W
Rama, Nic.	226	12.09 N	84.15 W
Rama, Yis.	122	32.56 N	35.22 E
Rama ≃	226	12.08 N	84.13 W
Ramacca	36	37.23 N	14.42 E
Ramachandrapuram	112	16.51 N	82.01 E
Ramādah	134	13.38 N	43.56 E
Ramah	190	35.08 N	108.30 W
Rama Indian Reserve ◆[4]	202	44.41 N	79.15 W
Ramales de la Victoria	34	43.15 N	3.27 W
Ramalho, Serra do ⩕	245	13.45 S	44.00 W
Rām Allāh	122	31.54 N	35.12 E
Ramallo	242	33.29 S	60.00 W
Raman	113	29.58 N	74.58 E
Rāmanagaram	112	12.43 N	77.18 E
Rāmanāthapuram	112	9.23 N	78.50 E
Ramanāthpur	262b	22.41 N	88.14 E
Ramanbāti	262b	22.47 N	88.08 E
Ramanetaka, Baie C	147b	14.13 S	47.52 E
Rāmānuj Ganj	114	23.48 N	83.42 E
Ramapo	266	41.08 N	74.10 W
Ramapo ≃	266	40.58 N	74.17 W
Ramapo Lake @	266	41.02 N	74.16 W
Ramapo Mountains ⩕	266	41.08 N	74.12 W
Ramapo Valley Airport ⊠	266	41.06 N	74.02 W
Ramas, Cape ≻	112	15.07 N	73.55 E
Ramasucha	66	52.46 N	33.33 E
Ramat Gan	122	32.05 N	34.49 E
Ramat HaSharon	122	32.09 N	34.50 E
Ramat HaShofet	122	32.37 N	35.06 E
Ramathlabama	146	25.40 S	25.35 E
Ramatuelle	56	43.13 N	6.37 E
Ramat Yoḥanan	122	32.47 N	35.07 E
Rama VI Bridge ◆[5]	259a	13.48 N	100.31 E
Rāmban	113	33.15 N	75.15 E
Rambervillers	54	48.21 N	6.38 E
Rambi I	165g	16.30 S	179.59 E
Rambipuji	105a	8.13 S	113.36 E
Rambleton Acres	198	39.39 N	75.38 W
Rambouillet	46	48.39 N	1.50 E
Rambouillet, Château de ⊥	251	48.39 N	1.49 E
Rambouillet, Forêt de ♠	251	48.40 N	1.50 E
Rambutyo Island I	154	2.20 S	147.50 E
Rām Dās	113	31.58 N	74.54 E
Rāmdia	116	23.42 N	89.32 E
Rāmdurg	112	15.57 N	75.18 E
Ramea	176	47.31 N	57.23 W
Ramea Islands II	176	47.31 N	57.21 W
Rāmechhāp	114	27.20 N	86.05 E
Rame Head ≻, S. Afr.	148	31.48 S	29.22 E
Rame Head ≻, Eng., U.K.	44	50.19 N	4.13 W
Rämen @	40	60.18 N	15.10 E
Ramenje, S.S.S.R.	66	60.17 N	43.46 E
Ramenje, S.S.S.R.	72	56.34 N	37.13 E
Ramenka ◆[8]	255b	55.41 N	37.30 E
Ramenskoje	72	55.34 N	38.14 E
Ramer	184	32.03 N	86.13 W
Ramerupt	46	48.31 N	4.18 E
Rameški	66	57.21 N	36.03 E
Rāmeswaram	112	9.17 N	79.18 E
Ramey	204	40.48 N	78.24 W
Ramey Air Force Base ■	230m	18.30 N	67.08 W
Rāmganj	116	23.06 N	90.51 E
Rāmgarh, Bhārat	110	27.22 N	70.30 E
Rāmgarh, Bhārat	110	27.15 N	75.11 E
Rāmgarh, Bhārat	114	24.34 N	87.15 E
Rāmgarh, Bhārat	114	23.38 N	85.31 E
Rāmgarh, Bhārat	116	22.42 N	87.04 E
Rāmgarh, Bngl.	110	22.59 N	91.44 E
Rāmgarh Hills ⩕[2]	114	22.50 N	83.10 E
Ram Head ≻	230m	18.18 N	64.42 W
Rāmhormoz	118	31.16 N	49.36 E
Ramingstein	58	47.04 N	13.50 E
Ramírez, Méx.	186	25.57 N	97.46 W
Ramírez, Méx.	186	27.20 N	100.58 W
Ramiriquí	236	5.24 N	73.20 W
Ramis ≃	134	7.59 N	41.34 E
Ramit	75	38.44 N	69.17 E
Ramit Zapovednik ♠	75	38.52 N	69.20 E
Rāmjībanpur	116	22.50 N	87.37 E
Rāmkānāli	116	23.35 N	86.45 E
Raml, Qārat ar- ∧[2]	132	30.02 N	30.39 E
Ramla	122	31.55 N	34.52 E
Ramlo ∧	134	13.20 N	41.45 E
Ramm, Jabal ∧	122	29.35 N	35.24 E
Rämmen	40	60.07 N	14.08 E
Rāmnagar, Bhārat	113	32.49 N	75.19 E
Rāmnagar, Bhārat	114	25.17 N	83.02 E
Rāmnagar, Bhārat	114	29.24 N	79.07 E
Rāmnagar, Bhārat	116	21.41 N	87.33 E
Rāmnagar, Bhārat	262b	22.23 N	88.19 E
Ramnäs	40	59.46 N	16.12 E
Ramon'	68	51.54 N	39.20 E
Ramon, Har ∧	122	30.30 N	34.38 E
Ramon, Makhtesh •[7]	122	30.36 N	34.49 E
Ramon, Naḥal ∨	122	30.36 N	34.55 E
Ramona, Calif., U.S.	218	33.08 N	116.52 W
Ramona, Okla., U.S.	186	36.32 N	95.55 W
Ramona, S. Dak., U.S.	188	44.07 N	97.13 W
Ramos	224	22.50 N	101.55 W
Ramos ◆[8]	277a	22.51 S	43.15 W
Ramos ≃[1]	140	5.08 N	5.22 E
Ramos Arizpe	222	25.33 N	100.58 W
Ramosch	54	46.50 N	10.22 E
Ramos Island I, Pil.	106	8.06 N	117.02 E
Ramos Island I, Sol.Is.	165e	8.15 S	160.11 E
Ramos Mejía	248	34.38 S	58.34 W
Ramotswa	146	24.56 S	25.50 E
Rāmpāl	116	22.34 N	89.39 E
Rampart	170	65.30 N	150.10 W
Ramparts ≃	170	66.11 N	129.03 W
Rampillon	46	48.33 N	3.04 E
Rampside	42	54.05 N	3.10 W
Rāmpur, Bhārat	110	31.27 N	77.38 E
Rāmpur, Bhārat	113	29.49 N	77.27 E
Rāmpur, Bhārat	114	28.49 N	79.02 E
Rāmpur □[5]	114	28.50 N	79.05 E
Rāmpura	110	24.28 N	75.26 E
Rāmpura Phūl	113	30.17 N	75.14 E
Rampur Boalia → Rājshāhi	114	24.22 N	88.36 E
Rāmpur Hāt	116	24.10 N	87.47 E
Ramrath	253	51.06 N	6.41 E
Ramree Island I	100	19.06 N	93.48 E
Rāmsāgar	116	23.05 N	87.17 E
Rāmsar	118	36.53 N	50.41 E
Ramsau	58	47.36 N	12.54 E
Ramsay Range ⩕	152	18.31 S	127.03 E
Ramsbeck	52	51.18 N	8.24 E
Ramsberg	40	59.46 N	15.17 E
Ramsbottom	42	53.40 N	2.19 W
Ramsden Bellhouse	250	51.37 N	0.29 E
Ramsden Heath	250	51.38 N	0.28 E
Ramsdorf	48	51.54 N	6.55 E
Ramsele	26	63.33 N	16.29 E
Ramseur	182	35.44 N	79.39 W
Ramsey, I. of Man	42	54.20 N	4.21 W
Ramsey, Eng., U.K.	44	51.56 N	1.14 E
Ramsey, Eng., U.K.	44	52.27 N	0.07 W
Ramsey, Ill., U.S.	209	39.08 N	89.06 W
Ramsey, N.J., U.S.	200	41.03 N	74.09 W
Ramsey Bay C	42	54.20 N	4.20 W
Ramsey Brook ≃	266	41.02 N	74.08 W
Ramsey Creek ≃	209	39.03 N	89.04 W
Ramsey Island I	44	51.52 N	5.10 W
Ramsey Lake @	180	47.15 N	82.16 W
Ramsey Lake State Park ♠	209	39.10 N	89.08 W
Ramsgate, Austl.	264a	33.59 S	151.08 E
Ramsgate, Eng., U.K.	44	51.20 N	1.25 E
Rāmshai	114	26.44 N	88.51 E
Rāmshīr	118	30.54 N	49.24 E
Ramshorn Peak ∧	192	45.09 N	111.06 W
Ramshyttan	40	60.18 N	15.13 E
Ramsjö	26	62.11 N	15.39 E
Ramsloh	48	53.06 N	7.40 E
Ramstein	52	49.27 N	7.33 E
Rāmtek	110	21.24 N	79.20 E
Rāmu, Bngl.	110	21.25 N	92.07 E
Ramu, Kenya	144	3.56 N	41.13 E
Ramu ≃	154	5.00 S	144.40 E
Ramuševo	66	57.50 N	31.37 E
Ramvik	26	62.49 N	17.51 E
Ramville, Îlet I	230e	14.42 N	60.53 W
Ramygala	66	55.31 N	24.18 E
Ramzaj	70	53.18 N	44.44 E
Rānāghāt	116	23.11 N	88.35 E
Rana Kao, Volcán ∧[1]	164z	27.11 S	109.27 W
Ranalt	58	47.02 N	11.13 E
Rana Roi, Volcán ∧[1]	164z	27.05 S	109.23 W
Rana Roraka, Volcán ∧[1]	164z	27.07 S	109.18 W
Rånäs	40	59.48 N	18.17 E
Ranau	102	5.58 N	116.41 E
Ranau, Danau @	102	4.50 S	103.55 E
Ranbīrsinghpura	113	32.38 N	74.44 E
Ranburne	184	33.31 N	85.21 W
Ranburn Woods	268	41.33 N	87.22 W
Rancabali	105a	7.08 S	107.21 E
Rancagua	242	34.10 S	70.45 W
Rancah	105a	7.12 S	108.30 E
Rance ≃	32	48.31 N	1.59 W
Rancevo, S.S.S.R.	66	56.56 N	34.03 E
Rancevo, S.S.S.R.	66	56.40 N	33.02 E
Rancharia	245	22.15 S	50.55 W
Rancheria	170	60.05 N	130.40 W
Ranchería ≃	236	11.34 N	72.54 W
Rancheria Rock ∧	192	44.53 N	120.08 W
Ranches of Taos	190	36.22 N	105.37 W
Ranchester	192	44.54 N	107.16 W
Rānchī	114	23.21 N	85.20 E
Rānchi □[5]	114	23.00 N	85.00 E
Ranchillos	242	26.57 S	65.03 W
Rānchi Plateau ⩕[1]	114	23.20 N	84.50 E
Rancho Boyeros	276b	23.00 N	82.23 W
Rancho Colorado, Presa de @[1]	276a	19.29 N	99.17 W
Rancho Cordova	216	38.36 N	121.17 W
Rancho Del Mar	216	38.10 N	122.15 W
Rancho Nuevo, Méx.	186	26.22 N	99.54 W
Rancho Nuevo, Méx.	224	23.12 N	97.48 W
Rancho Palos Verdes, Calif., U.S.	218		
	270	33.45 N	118.24 W
Rancho Rinconado	216	37.18 N	122.01 W
Rancho Santa Fe	218	33.01 N	117.12 W
Rancho Veloz	230p	22.53 N	80.23 W
Ranchuelo	230p	22.23 N	80.09 W
Ranco, Lago @	244	40.14 S	72.24 W
Rancocas	198	40.01 N	74.52 W
Rancocas Creek, North Branch ≃	198	40.00 N	74.52 W
Rancocas Creek, South Branch ≃, N.J., U.S.	198	40.00 N	74.52 W
Rancocas Creek, South Branch ≃, N.J., U.S.	275	39.57 N	74.48 W
Rancocas Creek, Southwest Branch ≃	275	39.57 N	74.48 W
Rancocas Heights	275	39.59 N	74.51 W
Rancocas Woods	275	39.59 N	74.52 W
Rancul	242	35.03 S	64.42 W
Rand	156	35.36 S	146.35 E
Rand (Germiston) Airport ⊠	263d	26.15 S	28.09 E
Randa	54	46.07 N	7.47 E
Randall Lake @	206	41.57 N	85.02 W
Randall Park ◆[9]	269a	41.26 N	81.32 W
Randalls Island I	266	40.48 N	73.55 W
Randallstown	274b	39.22 N	76.48 W
Randalstown	42	54.45 N	6.19 W
Randan	32	46.01 N	3.21 E
Randazzo	36	37.53 N	14.57 E
Randbøl	41	55.42 N	9.16 E
Randburg	263d	26.06 S	27.59 E
Rānder	110	21.14 N	72.47 E
Randers	26	56.28 N	10.03 E
Randfontein	148	26.11 S	27.42 E
Randgate	263d	26.11 S	27.41 E
Randhurst ◆[9]	268	42.05 N	87.56 W
Randle	214	46.32 N	121.57 W
Randleman	182	35.49 N	79.48 W
Randlett	186	34.11 N	98.28 W
Randolph, Ariz., U.S.	190	32.55 N	111.31 W
Randolph, Maine, U.S.	178	44.19 N	69.46 W
Randolph, Mass., U.S.	197	42.10 N	71.03 W
Randolph, Nebr., U.S.	188	42.23 N	97.21 W
Randolph, N.Y., U.S.	200	42.10 N	78.59 W
Randolph, Ohio, U.S.	204	41.02 N	81.15 W
Randolph, Utah, U.S.	190	41.40 N	111.11 W
Randolph, Vt., U.S.	178	43.55 N	72.40 W
Randolph, Wis., U.S.	180	43.35 N	89.00 W
Randolph □[6], Ind., U.S.	208	40.10 N	85.00 W
Randolph □[6], Mo., U.S.	209	39.22 N	92.20 W
Randolph Air Force Base ■	186	29.32 N	98.16 W
Randolph Hills	274c	39.03 N	77.06 W
Randolph Village	274c	38.53 N	76.52 W
Random Island I	176	48.08 N	53.45 W
Random Lake	180	43.33 N	87.57 W
Randow ≃	50	53.41 N	14.04 E
Randowaya	154	1.52 S	136.31 E
Randowbruch ≡	50	53.15 N	14.10 E
Randsburg	218	35.22 N	117.39 W
Randsfjorden @	26	60.25 N	10.24 E
Rand Stadium ♠	263d	26.14 S	28.03 E
Randublatung	105a	7.12 S	111.23 E
Randudongkal	105a	7.06 S	109.19 E
Randwick	160	33.55 S	151.15 E
Randwick Racecourse ♠	264a	33.54 S	151.14 E
Råneå	26	65.52 N	22.18 E
Ranelagh	248	34.48 S	58.12 W
Rāner	113	28.53 N	73.17 E
Ranérou	140	15.18 N	13.58 W
Rāneswar	116	24.02 N	87.25 E
Raneue	104	5.03 N	95.20 E
Ranford	158a	32.48 S	116.31 E
Ranfurly, N.Z.	162	45.08 S	170.06 E
Ranfurly, Scot., U.K.	42	55.52 N	4.33 W
Rangae	104	6.17 N	101.44 E
Rāngāmāti	110	22.38 N	92.12 E
Rangantemiang	102	0.35 S	113.19 E
Rangasa, Tanjung ≻	102	2.38 S	118.49 E
Rangaunu Bay C	162	34.50 S	173.15 E
Range Creek ≃	190	39.18 N	110.04 W
Range Indian Reserve ◆[4]	172	49.09 N	119.50 W
Rangeley	178	44.58 N	70.39 W
Rangely	190	40.05 N	108.48 W
Ranger	186	32.28 N	98.41 W
Ranger Lake @	180	46.54 N	83.35 W
Rangersdorf	58	46.51 N	12.58 E
Ranghezhen	90	33.43 N	112.51 E
Rangia	110	26.28 N	91.38 E
Rangiora	162	43.18 S	172.36 E
Rangitaiki ≃	162	37.54 S	176.53 E
Rangitata ≃	162	44.12 S	171.30 E
Rangitikei ≃	162	40.18 S	175.14 E
Rangitukia	162	37.46 S	178.27 E
Rangkasbitung	105a	6.21 S	106.15 E
Rangkul'	75	38.29 N	74.22 E
Rangoon	100	16.47 N	96.10 E
Rangoon ≃	100	16.29 N	96.21 E
Rangpo	114	27.11 N	88.32 E
Rangpur, Bngl.	114	25.45 N	89.15 E
Rangpur, Pāk.	113	30.31 N	71.34 E
Rangpuri ⊥	262a	28.33 N	77.08 E
Rangsang, Pulau I	104	1.00 N	102.55 E
Rangsdorf	50	52.17 N	13.25 E
Rangsdorfer See @	254a	52.17 N	13.24 E
Ranguana Cay I	226	16.20 N	88.09 W
Ranguana Entrance ⊔	226	16.19 N	88.09 W
Rangun → Rangoon	100	16.47 N	96.10 E
Ranholas	256c	38.47 N	9.22 W
Rānībāndh	116	22.52 N	86.47 E
Rānībennur	112	14.37 N	75.37 E
Rānīganj	116	23.37 N	87.08 E
Rānīkhet	114	29.39 N	79.25 E
Ranino	70	52.58 N	40.15 E
Rānipet	112	12.56 N	79.20 E
Ranis	50	50.39 N	11.34 E
Rāniwāra	110	24.45 N	72.13 E
Rāniyah	118	36.15 N	44.53 E
Ranken ≃	156	20.31 S	137.36 E
Ranken Store	156	19.35 S	136.55 E
Rankin, Ill., U.S.	206	40.28 N	87.54 W
Rankin, Mich., U.S.	206	42.55 N	83.46 W
Rankin, Pa., U.S.	269b	40.25 N	79.53 W
Rankin, Tex., U.S.	186	31.13 N	101.56 W
Rankin Inlet	166	62.45 N	92.10 W
Rankins Springs	156	33.50 S	146.16 E
Rānkūs	122	33.45 N	36.23 E
Rankweil	54	47.17 N	9.39 E
Ranlo	182	35.17 N	81.07 W
Rannersdorf	254b	48.08 N	16.28 E
Rannij	70	51.29 N	52.37 E
Rannoch, Loch @	28	56.41 N	4.20 W
Rann of Kutch ≡	110	24.00 N	70.00 E
Ranobe ≃	147b	17.10 S	44.08 E
Ranohira	147b	22.29 S	45.24 E
Ranomafana, Madag.	147b	18.57 S	48.50 E
Ranomafana, Madag.	147b	24.36 S	46.58 E
Ranomena	147b	23.25 S	47.17 E
Ranong	100	9.58 N	98.38 E
Ranopiso	147b	25.03 S	46.40 E
Ranot	100	7.46 N	100.19 E
Ranotsara Nord	147b	22.48 S	46.36 E
Rānsai	262c	18.53 N	73.05 E
Ransäter	40	59.46 N	13.26 E
Ranshaw	198	40.47 N	76.31 W
Ransiki	154	1.30 S	134.10 E
Ransom, Ill., U.S.	206	41.09 N	88.39 W
Ransom, Kans., U.S.	188	38.38 N	99.56 W
Ransom, Pa., U.S.	200	41.24 N	75.50 W
Ransom Creek ≃	274a	43.04 N	78.45 W
Ransomville	200	43.14 N	78.55 W
Ranson	178	39.18 N	77.52 W
Ransta	40	59.48 N	16.38 E
Ranstadt	52	50.21 N	8.59 E
Rantabe	147b	15.42 S	49.39 E
Rantasalmi	26	62.04 N	28.18 E
Rantau, Indon.	102	2.56 S	115.09 E
Rantau, Malay.	104	2.35 N	101.58 E
Rantaukampar	104	1.24 N	100.59 E
Rantaupanjang, Indon.	102	1.51 S	102.19 E
Rantaupanjang, Indon.	102	1.16 S	101.49 E
Rantaupanjang, Indon.	104	0.58 N	99.13 E
Rantauprapat	104	2.06 N	99.50 E
Rantekombola, Bulu ∧	102	3.21 S	120.01 E
Rantepao	102	2.59 S	119.54 E
Rantigny	46	49.20 N	2.26 E
Rantoul	206	40.19 N	88.09 W
Rantsila	26	64.31 N	25.39 E
Rantzau	50	54.15 N	10.30 E
Ranua	26	65.55 N	26.32 E
Rānvād	262c	18.53 N	72.55 E
Ranwanlenau	146	19.35 S	22.47 E
Råö	26	57.24 N	11.56 E
Raoerdun	90	28.48 N	117.40 E
Raohe	79	46.47 N	134.00 E
Raon-l'Étape	54	48.24 N	6.51 E
Raon-sur-Plaine	54	48.31 N	7.06 E
Raoping	90	23.43 N	117.01 E
Raoui, Erg er ◆[2]	138	29.17 N	2.20 W
Raoul Island I	14	29.16 S	177.54 W
Raowu	92	29.30 N	96.46 E
Raoyang	88	38.16 N	115.44 E
Raoyanghe	94	41.46 N	122.26 E
Raoyanghe ≃	94	41.11 N	122.02 E
Rapa I	14	27.36 S	144.20 W
Rapa, Ponta do ≻	242	27.22 S	48.26 W
Rapallo	56	44.21 N	9.14 E
Rapang	102	3.50 S	119.48 E
Rāpar	110	23.34 N	70.38 E
Rapatovo	70	55.04 N	54.37 E
Rāpch ≃	118	25.28 N	59.21 E
Rapel ≃	242	33.55 S	71.51 W
Rapelli	242	26.24 S	64.29 W
Rapid ≃, Mich., U.S.	180	45.55 N	86.58 W
Rapid ≃, Minn., U.S.	188	48.42 N	94.26 W
Rapid ≃, Wash., U.S.	214	47.48 N	121.18 W
Rapidan ≃	178	38.22 N	77.37 W
Rapid Bay	158b	35.32 S	138.12 E
Rapid City, Man., Can.	174	50.08 N	100.02 W
Rapid City, Mich., U.S.	180	44.50 N	85.17 W
Rapid City, S. Dak., U.S.	188	44.05 N	103.14 W
Rapid Creek ≃	188	43.54 N	102.37 W
Rapide Taureau, Barrage du ◆[6]	196	46.52 N	73.39 W
Rapid River	180	45.56 N	86.58 W
Räpina	66	58.06 N	27.27 E
Rapkan	75	40.22 N	70.40 E
Rapla	66	59.01 N	24.47 E
Rapolano Terme	60	43.17 N	11.36 E
Raposo ∧[2]	256c	38.40 N	9.11 W
Rappahannock ≃	198	37.34 N	76.18 W
Rappbodestausee @[1]	50	51.09 N	10.58 E
Rappenlochschlucht ∨	54	47.23 N	9.47 E
Rapperswil	54	47.14 N	8.50 E
Rāpti ≃, As.	114	26.17 N	83.41 E
Rāpti ≃, Nepāl	114	27.33 N	84.07 E
Rápulo ≃	238	13.43 S	65.32 W
Rapu-Rapu	106	13.11 N	124.08 E
Rapu-Rapu Island I	106	13.12 N	124.09 E
Raqabah, Khashm ar- ∧[2]	132	28.18 N	31.43 E
Rāqūbah	136	29.04 N	19.08 E
Raquette ≃	196	45.00 N	74.42 W
Raraka I[1]	14	16.10 S	144.54 W
Rāribahāl	116	24.05 N	87.21 E
Raritan	200	40.34 N	74.38 W
Raritan ≃	198	40.29 N	74.17 W
Raritan, North Branch ≃	200	40.33 N	74.41 W
Raritan, South Branch ≃	200	40.33 N	74.41 W
Raritan Bay C	198	40.28 N	74.12 W
Raroia I	14	16.01 S	142.27 W
Raron	54	46.19 N	7.48 E
Rarotonga I	164k	21.14 S	159.46 W
Rarz	75	39.23 N	68.44 E
Rasa, Ilha I	277a	23.04 S	43.09 W
Rasa, Punta ≻, Arg.	244	40.51 S	62.19 W
Rasa, Punta ≻, Méx.	224	21.02 N	105.20 W
Rašaant	78	49.13 N	101.26 E
Rasa da Guaratiba, Ilha I	246	23.05 S	43.34 W
Rasa Island I	106	9.14 N	118.27 E
Ra's al-'Ayn	120	36.51 N	40.04 E
Ra's al-Barr	132	31.31 N	31.50 E
Ra's al-Khalīj	132	31.15 N	31.39 E
Ra's al-Khaymah	118	25.47 N	55.57 E
Ra's al-Ushsh ◆[8]	132	31.08 N	32.18 E
Ra's an-Naqb, Miṣr	122	29.36 N	34.51 E
Ra's an-Naqb, Urd.	122	30.00 N	35.29 E
Rasawi	154	2.04 S	134.01 E
Ra's Ba'labakk	120	34.15 N	36.25 E
Rasbo	40	59.57 N	17.53 E
Raschau	50	50.32 N	12.50 E
Ras Dashen ∧	134	13.10 N	38.26 E
Ras Djebel	36	37.13 N	10.09 E
Rasdorf	52	50.43 N	9.53 E
Raseborg	26	59.59 N	23.39 E
Raseiniai	66	55.24 N	23.07 E
Râs el Aïoun	36	35.30 N	8.18 E
Ras el Ma, Alg.	138	34.31 N	0.46 W
Râs el Mâ, Mali	140	16.37 N	4.28 W
Ras el Oued	138	35.57 N	5.03 E
Rasen-Antholz → Anterselva di Sopra	58	46.52 N	12.08 E
Raševka	68	50.14 N	33.54 E
Rashād	130	11.51 N	31.04 E
Rāshayyā	122	33.30 N	35.51 E
Rashīd (Rosetta)	132	31.24 N	30.25 E
Rashīd, Far' ≃	132	31.30 N	30.21 E
Rashīd, Maṣabb (Rosetta Mouth) ≃[1]	132	31.30 N	30.21 E
Rashīd Qal'eh	110	31.31 N	67.31 E
Rashin → Najin	88	42.15 N	130.18 E
Rasht	118	37.16 N	49.36 E
Rashtrapati Bhawan ⛉	262a	28.37 N	77.12 E
Rasiga 'Alula ≻	134	11.59 N	50.50 E
Rasina ≃	38	43.37 N	21.22 E
Rāsipuram	112	11.28 N	78.10 E
Rasi Salai	100	15.20 N	104.09 E
Rāsk	118	26.13 N	61.25 E
Raška	38	43.17 N	20.37 E
Rask Mølle	41	55.52 N	9.37 E
Rās Koh ∧	118	28.50 N	65.12 E
Raškov	68	47.57 N	28.50 E
Raskunda	116	22.48 N	87.26 E
Rasm al-Arwām, Sabkhat @	120	35.53 N	37.40 E
R'asna	66	54.01 N	31.12 E
R'asnopol'	68	47.04 N	31.12 E
Raso, Cabo ≻, Arg.	244	44.20 S	65.14 W
Raso, Cabo ≻, Port.	256c	38.43 N	9.29 W
Raso, Ilhéu I	140a	16.37 N	24.36 W
Rason Lake @	152	28.46 S	124.20 E
Raspberry Peak ∧	184	34.23 N	94.01 W
Raspopinskaja	70	49.24 N	42.52 E
Rasra	114	25.51 N	83.51 E
Rasskazovka	255b	55.38 N	37.20 E
Rasskazovo	70	52.40 N	41.53 E
Rassua, Ostrov I	64	47.45 N	153.01 E
Rassudovo	72	55.29 N	36.54 E
Rassvet	74	43.58 N	46.44 E
Rassypnaja	70	51.35 N	53.37 E
Rassypnoje	73	48.08 N	38.34 E
Rast	38	43.53 N	23.17 E
Rastälven ≃	40	59.37 N	14.56 E
Rastatt	52	48.51 N	8.12 E
Rastavica ≃	68	49.44 N	30.01 E
Rastede	48	53.15 N	8.11 E
Rastegai'sa ∧	24	70.00 N	26.18 E
Rastenberg	50	51.10 N	11.25 E
Rastenburg → Kętrzyn	30	54.06 N	21.23 E
Rastorf	50	54.16 N	10.19 E
Rastorgujevo	72	55.33 N	37.41 E
Rastovcy	72	56.39 N	37.35 E
Rastunovo	72	55.16 N	37.50 E
Rasu, Monte ∧	36	40.25 N	9.00 E
Rasūl	113	32.42 N	73.34 E
Rasūlnagar	113	32.20 N	73.47 E
Rasulpur	262a	28.37 N	77.22 E
Rasulpur ◆[8]	262a	28.42 N	77.01 E
Rasun di sopra	58	46.48 N	12.03 E
Rasun di sotto	58	46.47 N	12.02 E
Rasura	54	46.06 N	9.33 E
Råsvalen @	40	59.40 N	15.10 E
Răsvani	38	44.25 N	26.53 E
Rat ≃, Man., Can.	174	49.35 N	97.08 W
Rat ≃, Man., Can.	174	55.41 N	99.04 W
Ratahan	102	1.04 N	124.48 E
Ratangarh	110	28.05 N	74.36 E
Ratanpur, Bhārat	116	23.07 N	87.04 E
Ratanpur, Bhārat	262b	22.50 N	88.14 E
Rätansbyn	26	62.29 N	14.32 E
Rat Burana	259a	13.41 N	100.30 E
Ratčino, S.S.S.R.	70	53.02 N	39.55 E
Ratčino, S.S.S.R.	72	55.16 N	38.39 E
Ratcliff	212	31.24 N	95.08 W
Rateče	58	46.30 N	13.43 E
Ratekau	50	53.57 N	10.44 E
Rāth	114	25.35 N	79.34 E
Rath ◆[8]	253	51.17 N	6.49 E
Rathbone	200	42.08 N	77.19 W
Rathbun Lake @	202	44.47 N	78.12 W
Rathbun Lake @[1]	180	40.54 N	93.05 W
Rathdowney	161a	28.12 S	152.52 E
Rathdrum, Éire	28	52.56 N	6.13 W
Rathdrum, Idaho, U.S.	192	47.49 N	116.54 W
Rathebur	50	53.44 N	13.46 E
Ratheim	48	51.04 N	6.10 E
Rathenow	50	52.36 N	12.20 E
Rathfriland	42	54.14 N	6.10 W
Rathkeale	28	52.32 N	8.56 W
Rathlin Island I	42	55.18 N	6.13 W
Rathlin Sound ⊔	42	55.15 N	6.15 W
Rath Luirc (Charleville)	28	52.21 N	8.41 W
Rathmecke	253	51.15 N	7.38 E
Rathstock	50	52.31 N	14.32 E

Symbol	English	Deutsch	Español	Français	Português
≃	River	Fluss	Río	Rivière	Rio
≅	Canal	Kanal	Canal	Canal	Canal
⌞	Waterfall, Rapids	Wasserfall, Stromschnellen	Cascada, Rápidos	Chute d'eau, Rapides	Cascata, Rápidos
⊔	Strait	Meeresstrasse	Estrecho	Détroit	Estreito
C	Bay, Gulf	Bucht, Golf	Bahía, Golfo	Baie, Golfe	Baía, Golfo
@	Lake, Lakes	See, Seen	Lago, Lagos	Lac, Lacs	Lago, Lagos
≡	Swamp	Sumpf	Pantano	Marais	Pântano
⊓	Ice Features, Glacier	Eis- und Gletscherformen	Accidentes Glaciales	Formes glaciaires	Acidentes Glaciares
•	Other Hydrographic Features	Andere Hydrographische Objekte	Otros Elementos Hidrográficos	Autres données hydrographiques	Outros Elementos Hidrográficos
✧	Submarine Features	Untermeerische Objekte	Accidentes Submarinos	Formes de relief sous-marin	Acidentes Submarinos
□	Political Unit	Politische Einheit	Unidad Política	Entité politique	Unidade Política
⛉	Cultural Institution	Kulturelle Institution	Institución Cultural	Institution culturelle	Instituição Cultural
⊥	Historical Site	Historische Stätte	Sitio Histórico	Site historique	Sítio Histórico
♠	Recreational Site	Erholungs- und Ferienort	Sitio de Recreo	Centre de loisirs	Sítio de Lazer
⊠	Airport	Flughafen	Aeropuerto	Aéroport	Aeroporto
■	Military Installation	Militäranlage	Instalación Militar	Installation militaire	Instalação Militar
◆	Miscellaneous	Verschiedenes	Misceláneo	Divers	Miscelânea

ENGLISH

Name	Page	Lat. °′	Long. °′
Rathwell	174	49.40 N	98.32 W
Ratibor → Racibórz	30	50.06 N	18.13 E
Raticosa, Passo della)(	60	44.10 N	11.20 E
Rätikon ∧∧	54	47.03 N	9.40 E
Ratingen	52	51.18 N	6.51 E
Ratisbon → Regensburg	30	49.01 N	12.06 E
Rätische Alpen → Rhaetian Alps ∧∧	54	46.30 N	10.00 E
Rat Island I	171a	51.55 N	178.20 E
Rat Islands II	171a	52.00 N	178.00 E
Rat'kovo	72	56.01 N	38.38 E
Rat Lake ⊜	174	56.10 N	99.40 W
Ratlām	110	23.19 N	75.04 E
Ratmanova, Ostrov I	170	65.46 N	169.02 W
Ratnāgiri	112	16.59 N	73.18 E
Ratnapura	112	6.41 N	80.24 E
Ratno	68	51.40 N	24.31 E
Ratodero	110	27.48 N	68.18 E
Ratomka	66	53.56 N	27.21 E
Raton	186	36.54 N	104.24 W
Ratt ≃	214	47.27 N	124.21 W
Rattanaburi	100	15.19 N	103.51 E
Rattaphum	100	7.08 N	100.16 E
Rattenberg	58	47.26 N	11.54 E
Rattlesnake	192	46.56 N	113.59 W
Rattlesnake Creek ≃, Kans., U.S.	188	38.13 N	98.22 W
Rattlesnake Creek ≃, Ohio, U.S.	208	39.16 N	83.23 W
Rattlesnake Creek ≃, Oreg., U.S.	192	42.44 N	117.47 W
Rattlesnake Creek ≃, Wash., U.S.	214	46.45 N	120.55 W
Rattlesnake Creek ≃, Wash., U.S.	214	45.48 N	121.29 W
Rattlesnake Hills ∧∧[2]	190	42.45 N	107.10 W
Rattlesnake Mountain ∧	197	41.42 N	72.50 W
Rattlesnake Peak ∧	270	34.16 N	117.47 W
Rattling Brook	176	49.38 N	56.10 W
Rattling Run ≃	269b	40.33 N	79.32 W
Rattu	113	35.08 N	74.48 E
Rättvik	26	60.53 N	15.06 E
Ratz, Mount ∧	170	57.23 N	132.19 W
Ratzebuhr → Okonek	30	53.33 N	16.50 E
Ratzeburg	50	53.42 N	10.46 E
Ratzeburger See ⊜	50	53.45 N	10.47 E
Rätzlingen	50	52.23 N	11.08 E
Rau	102	0.34 N	100.01 E
Raub, Malay.	104	3.48 N	101.52 E
Raub, Ind., U.S.	206	40.44 N	87.29 W
Raubsville	198	40.38 N	75.12 W
Rauch	242	36.46 S	59.06 W
Rauchenwarth	254b	48.05 N	16.32 E
Rauchtown	200	41.07 N	77.14 W
Raucourt-et-Flaba	52	49.36 N	4.57 E
Rauen	50	52.20 N	14.01 E
Rauenstein	50	50.24 N	11.03 E
Raufarhöfn	24a	66.30 N	15.57 W
Raufoss	26	60.43 N	10.37 E
Rauhe Ebrach ≃	52	49.50 N	10.56 E
Raukumara Range ∧∧	162	37.47 S	178.02 E
Raul Soares	245	20.05 S	42.22 W
Rauma	26	61.08 N	21.30 E
Rauma ≃	26	62.33 N	7.43 E
Raumünzach	52	48.38 N	8.21 E
Rauna	66	57.20 N	25.43 E
Raunds	44	52.21 N	0.33 W
Raung, Gunung ∧	105a	8.08 S	114.03 E
Raunheim	52	50.01 N	8.28 E
Raupal'an	170	65.28 N	171.59 W
Raurimu	162	39.07 S	175.24 E
Rauris	58	47.13 N	13.00 E
Raurkela	114	22.13 N	84.53 E
Rauschenberg	52	50.53 N	8.55 E
Rausu	82a	44.01 N	145.12 E
Rautalampi	26	62.38 N	26.50 E
Rāutara	262b	22.51 N	88.28 E
Rautavaara	26	63.29 N	28.18 E
Ravahere I[1]	14	18.14 S	142.09 W
Ravalgaon	112	20.38 N	74.25 E
Ravanica, Manastir ♁[1]	38	43.58 N	21.26 E
Ravānsar	118	34.43 N	46.40 E
Ravanusa	36	37.16 N	13.58 E
Rāvar	118	31.15 N	56.53 E
Ravarano	58	44.35 N	10.04 E
Ravarino	58	44.44 N	11.06 E
Rava-Russkaja	68	50.14 N	23.37 E
Ravascletto	58	46.32 N	12.57 E
Ravat	75	39.54 N	70.10 E
Ravello	60	40.39 N	14.37 E
Ravelo	238	18.48 S	65.32 W
Ravena	200	42.29 N	73.49 W
Ravenglass	42	54.21 N	3.24 W
Raven Lake ⊜	202	45.13 N	78.51 W
Ravenna, It.	60	44.25 N	12.12 E
Ravenna, Ky., U.S.	182	37.41 N	83.57 W
Ravenna, Mich., U.S.	206	43.11 N	85.56 W
Ravenna, Nebr., U.S.	188	41.02 N	98.55 W
Ravenna, Ohio, U.S.	204	41.09 N	81.15 W
Ravenna □[4]	60	44.25 N	11.59 E
Ravensbourne	161a	27.22 S	152.10 E
Ravensbourne National Park ♠	161a	27.21 S	152.15 E
Ravensburg	54	47.47 N	9.37 E
Ravenscrag	174	49.30 N	109.05 W
Ravensdale	214	47.21 N	121.59 W
Ravenshoe	156	17.37 S	145.29 E
Ravensthorpe, Austl.	152	33.35 S	120.02 E
Ravensthorpe, Eng., U.K.	42	53.42 N	1.35 W
Ravenswood, S. Afr.	263d	26.11 S	28.15 E
Ravenswood, Mich., U.S.	206	42.45 N	84.36 W
Ravenswood, W. Va., U.S.	178	38.57 N	81.46 W
Ravenswood Park ♠	273	42.36 N	70.42 W
Ravenswood Point ›	272	37.30 N	122.08 W
Ravensworth	274c	38.48 N	77.13 W
Rāver	110	21.15 N	76.02 E
Ravernet ≃	42	54.30 N	6.04 W
Rāvi ≃	113	30.35 N	71.48 E
Ravières	46	47.45 N	4.17 E
Ravine	198	40.34 N	76.24 W
Ravine Lake ⊜[1]	266	40.43 N	74.38 W
Ravinia Park ♠	268	42.09 N	87.46 W
Ravlı	120	40.08 N	33.06 E
Ravna Gora	36	45.23 N	14.57 E
Ravnina	118	37.57 N	62.40 E
Ravsted	41	55.01 N	9.08 E
Rāwah	118	34.28 N	41.55 E
Rāwala Kot	113	33.52 N	73.46 E
Rāwalpindi	113	33.36 N	73.04 E
Rawa Mazowiecka	30	51.46 N	20.16 E
Rāwāndūz	118	36.37 N	44.31 E
Rawang	104	3.19 N	101.35 E
Rawas ≃	102	2.42 S	103.24 E
Rawḍah ⊜	120	35.15 N	41.05 E
Rawḍah, Wādī ar- ∨	120	34.22 N	37.21 E
Rawd al-Faraj ♦[8]	263c	30.05 N	31.14 E
Rawdon	196	46.03 N	73.44 W
Rawene	162	35.24 S	173.30 E
Rawḥah	134	19.28 N	41.48 E
Rawhide Creek ≃	188	42.06 N	104.20 W
Rawhide Lake ⊜	180	46.39 N	82.37 W
Rawhide Mountain ∧	194	38.17 N	116.25 W
Rawi, Ko I	104	6.33 N	99.14 E
Rawicz	30	51.37 N	16.52 E
Rawlinna	152	31.01 S	125.20 E
Rawlins	190	41.47 N	107.14 W
Rawlinson, Mount ∧	152	25.58 S	127.28 E
Rawlinson Range ∧∧	152	24.51 S	128.00 E
Rawmarsh	42	53.27 N	1.21 W
Rawreth	250	51.37 N	0.35 E
Rawson, Arg.	242	34.36 S	60.04 W
Rawson, Arg.	244	43.18 S	65.06 W
Rawson, Ohio, U.S.	206	40.57 N	83.47 W
Rawsonville, S. Afr.	148	33.41 S	19.20 E
Rawsonville, Mich., U.S.	271	42.13 N	83.32 W
Rawtenstall	42	53.42 N	2.18 W
Raxaul	114	26.59 N	84.51 E
Ray, Ill., U.S.	209	40.12 N	90.29 W
Ray, Ind., U.S.	206	41.45 N	84.53 W
Ray, N. Dak., U.S.	188	48.21 N	103.10 W
Ray ≃, Eng., U.K.	44	51.48 N	1.15 W
Ray ≃, Eng., U.K.	44	51.38 N	1.49 W
Ray, Cape ›	176	47.40 N	59.18 W
Raya	102	1.05 N	118.32 E
Raya, Bukit ∧	102	0.40 S	112.41 E
Raya, Pulau I	104	4.52 N	95.22 E
Rāyachoti	112	14.03 N	78.45 E
Rāyadrug	112	14.42 N	76.52 E
Rāyagada	112	19.10 N	83.25 E
Rayburn	212	30.25 N	94.56 W
Rayen, B.R.D.	253	51.28 N	6.32 E
Rāyen, Īrān	118	29.34 N	57.26 E
Ray Hubbard, Lake ⊜[1]	212	32.53 N	96.35 W
Rayland	204	40.11 N	80.41 W
Rayleigh	44	51.36 N	0.36 E
Raymond, Alta., Can.	172	49.27 N	112.39 W
Raymond, Calif., U.S.	216	37.13 N	119.54 W
Raymond, Ill., U.S.	209	39.19 N	89.34 W
Raymond, Minn., U.S.	188	45.01 N	95.14 W
Raymond, Miss., U.S.	184	32.15 N	90.25 W
Raymond, Ohio, U.S.	206	40.20 N	83.28 W
Raymond, Wash., U.S.	214	46.41 N	123.44 W
Raymond Terrace	160	32.46 S	151.44 E
Raymondville	186	26.29 N	97.47 W
Raymore	174	50.25 N	104.31 W
Ray Mountains ∧∧	170	65.45 N	151.30 W
Rāyna	116	23.05 N	87.54 E
Rayne	184	30.14 N	92.16 W
Rayner Glacier ⊓	9	67.40 S	48.30 E
Raynham	197	41.57 N	71.04 W
Raynham Dog Track ♠	273	41.59 N	71.04 W
Rayón, Méx.	222	29.43 N	110.35 W
Rayón, Méx.	224	17.12 N	93.00 W
Rayón, Méx.	224	21.51 N	99.40 W
Rayón, Parque Nacional ♠	224	19.54 N	100.10 W
Rayones	222	25.01 N	100.05 W
Rayong	100	12.40 N	101.17 E
Rāypur	262b	22.25 N	88.31 E
Rayrah ⊤[4]	130	15.21 N	34.41 E
Rayse Creek ≃	209	38.13 N	89.00 W
Rayton	148	25.45 S	28.32 E
Raytown	184	39.00 N	94.28 W
Rayville	184	32.28 N	91.45 W
Raywood	212	30.02 N	94.40 W
Rayyikhah I	118	26.12 N	36.21 E
Raz, Pointe du ›	32	48.02 N	4.44 W
Razan, Īrān	118	35.23 N	49.02 E
R'azan', S.S.S.R.	70	54.38 N	39.44 E
R'azan □[4]	72	54.15 N	39.00 E
R'azancevo	72	56.42 N	39.12 E
Ražanj	38	43.40 N	21.33 E
R'azanovo	72	55.29 N	37.31 E
Razāq, Kūh-e ∧∧	257d	35.42 N	51.35 E
Razbegaj	255a	59.47 N	29.56 E
Războeni	38	47.05 N	26.32 E
Razdan	74	40.30 N	44.46 E
Razdan ≃	74	39.58 N	44.27 E
Razdel'naja	68	46.51 N	30.05 E
Razdolinsk	76	58.25 N	94.38 E
Razdolje	78	52.27 N	103.13 E
Razdol'noje, S.S.S.R.	68	45.47 N	33.29 E
Razdol'noje, S.S.S.R.	73	47.37 N	38.01 E
Razdol'noje, S.S.S.R.	79	43.30 N	131.52 E
Razdol'nyj	70	46.38 N	42.57 E
Razdorskaja	68	47.33 N	40.38 E
Razdory, S.S.S.R.	68	48.21 N	35.42 E
Razdory, S.S.S.R.	255b	55.45 N	37.18 E
Razelm, Lacul ⊜	38	44.54 N	28.57 E
R'aženoje	73	47.31 N	38.52 E
Raževo	76	56.09 N	68.25 E
Razgrad	38	43.32 N	26.31 E
Razlog	38	41.53 N	23.28 E
Razmachnino	78	51.47 N	115.28 E
Razmitelevo	255a	59.54 N	30.41 E
Raznočinovka	70	46.37 N	47.57 E
Raznomojka	76	52.29 N	55.52 E
Razorback Mountain ∧	172	51.35 N	124.42 W
R'ažsk	70	53.43 N	40.04 E
Razvil'noje	70	46.14 N	41.18 E
Ré, Île de I	32	46.12 N	1.25 W
Rea ≃, Eng., U.K.	44	52.30 N	1.51 W
Rea ≃, Eng., U.K.	44	52.18 N	2.32 W
Read	252	53.49 N	2.21 W
Reading, Eng., U.K.	44	51.28 N	0.59 W
Reading, Ill., U.S.	206	41.05 N	88.51 W
Reading, Kans., U.S.	188	38.31 N	95.58 W
Reading, Mass., U.S.	197	42.31 N	71.07 W
Reading, Mich., U.S.	206	41.50 N	84.45 W
Reading, Ohio, U.S.	208	39.14 N	84.27 W
Reading, Pa., U.S.	198	40.20 N	75.56 W
Reading Center	200	42.26 N	76.56 W
Reading Station ♦[5]	275	39.57 N	75.10 W
Readington	200	40.34 N	74.44 W
Readlyn	180	42.42 N	92.13 W
Readsboro	197	42.46 N	72.57 W
Readstown	180	43.27 N	90.45 W
Reagan	212	31.13 N	96.47 W
Real	106	14.40 N	121.36 E
Real ≃	240	11.27 S	37.22 W
Real, Cordillera ∧∧	238	17.00 S	67.10 W
Real, Estero ≃	226	12.55 N	87.23 W
Real Corona ≃	236	7.33 N	64.06 W
Real del Castillo	222	31.58 N	116.19 W
Real del Padre	242	34.50 S	67.46 W
Real de San Carlos	248	34.26 S	57.53 W
Realengo ♦[8]	246	22.53 S	43.25 W
Real Felipe, Castillo ⊥	276d	12.04 S	77.09 W
Realicó	242	35.02 S	64.15 W
Realitos	186	27.27 N	98.32 W
Réalmont	32	43.47 N	2.12 E
Reamstown	198	40.13 N	76.08 W
Reana del Roiale	58	46.12 N	13.13 E
Reardan	192	47.40 N	117.53 W
Reata	222	26.08 N	101.05 W
Reatini, Monti ∧∧	60	42.28 N	13.00 E
Réau	251	48.37 N	2.38 E
Reay	28	58.33 N	3.47 W
Rebais	46	48.51 N	3.14 E
Rebecca, Lake ⊜	152	29.53 S	122.10 E
Rebecq-Rognon	46	50.40 N	4.08 E
Rebeida, Wādī ∨	130	20.45 N	34.06 E
Rebel Hill	275	40.04 N	75.20 W
Rebersburg	200	40.57 N	77.27 W
Rebi	154	6.23 S	134.06 E
Rebiana ⊤[4]	136	24.15 N	22.00 E
Rebiana Sand Sea → Nerastro, Sarīr ♦[2]	136	24.20 N	20.37 E
Rebild ♁	26	56.50 N	9.51 E
Rebojo, Cachoeira do L	240	9.13 S	58.38 W
Reboly	24	63.50 N	30.47 E
Rebouças	242	25.36 S	50.42 W
Rebricha	76	53.05 N	82.20 E
Rebun-jima I	82a	45.23 N	141.02 E
Recalde	242	36.39 S	61.05 W
Recanati	60	43.24 N	13.32 E
Rečane	66	56.25 N	31.39 E
Recco	56	44.22 N	9.09 E
Recey-sur-Ource	54	47.47 N	4.52 E
Rechāh Lām	110	34.58 N	70.51 E
Rechberghausen	52	48.44 N	9.38 E
Recherche, Archipelago of the II	152	34.05 S	122.45 E
Recherche, Cape ›	165e	10.11 S	161.19 E
Réchicourt-le-Château	54	48.40 N	6.51 E
Rechlin	50	53.21 N	12.43 E
Rechna Doāb ∧∧[1]	113	31.35 N	73.30 E
Rečica, S.S.S.R.	66	52.22 N	30.25 E
Rečica, S.S.S.R.	68	51.52 N	26.48 E
Recife	240	8.03 S	34.54 W
Recife, Kaap ›	148	34.02 S	25.44 E
Recinto	242	36.48 S	71.44 W
Recke	48	52.22 N	7.43 E
Rečki	68	51.07 N	34.30 E
Recklinghausen	48	51.36 N	7.13 E
Recklinghausen □[8]	253	51.38 N	7.02 E
Recklinghausen-Süd ♦[8]	253	51.34 N	7.13 E
Recknitz ≃	50	54.14 N	12.28 E
Recoaro Terme	58	45.42 N	11.13 E
Recogne	52	49.55 N	5.22 E
Recologne	54	47.16 N	5.50 E
Reconquista	242	29.09 S	59.39 W
Reconquista ≃	278	34.25 S	58.35 W
Recovery Glacier ⊓	9	81.10 S	28.00 W
Recreio, Bra.	238	8.11 S	58.14 W
Recreio, Bra.	245	21.32 S	42.28 W
Recreo	242	29.16 S	65.04 W
Rector	184	36.16 N	90.17 W
Rectorville	208	38.34 N	83.39 W
Recuay	238	9.43 S	77.28 W
Recz	30	53.16 N	15.33 E
Red (Hong-ha) (Yuanjiang) ≃, As.	100	20.17 N	106.34 E
Red ≃, Qué., Can.	196	45.38 N	71.22 W
Red ≃, N.A.	168	50.24 N	96.48 W
Red ≃, U.S.	168	31.00 N	91.40 W
Red ≃, U.S.	184	36.32 N	87.22 W
Red ≃, Idaho, U.S.	192	45.48 N	115.28 W
Red ≃, Ky., U.S.	182	37.51 N	84.05 W
Red ≃, N. Mex., U.S.	190	36.39 N	105.42 W
Red ≃, Wis., U.S.	180	44.49 N	88.38 W
Red, Elm Fork ≃	186	34.53 N	99.19 W
Red, North Fork ≃	186	34.24 N	99.14 W
Red, Salt Fork ≃	186	34.27 N	99.22 W
Red, South Fork ≃	184	36.41 N	86.56 W
Reda	30	54.37 N	18.21 E
Redang, Pulau I	104	5.47 N	103.00 E
Redange	52	49.46 N	5.54 E
Redang Panjang	104	5.07 N	100.47 E
Red Bank, N.J., U.S.	266	40.21 N	74.03 W
Red Bank, Tenn., U.S.	184	35.07 N	85.17 W
Red Bank Battle Monument ⊥	275	39.52 N	75.11 W
Redbank Creek ≃	204	40.58 N	79.33 W
Red Banks	184	34.50 N	89.34 W
Red Bay, Newf., Can.	176	51.44 N	56.25 W
Red Bay, Ala., U.S.	184	34.27 N	88.09 W
Redbay, Fla., U.S.	184	30.35 N	85.57 W
Red Bay C	42	55.04 N	6.02 W
Redberry Lake ⊜	174	52.40 N	107.10 W
Redbird	204	41.48 N	81.06 W
Red Bird ≃	182	37.16 N	83.38 W
Red Bluff	194	40.11 N	122.15 W
Red Bluff Reservoir ⊜[1]	186	31.57 N	103.56 W
Red Boiling Springs	184	36.32 N	85.51 W
Redbourn	44	51.48 N	0.24 W
Redbridge ♦[8]	44	51.34 N	0.05 E
Red Bud	209	38.13 N	89.59 W
Red Canyon ∨	188	43.18 N	103.49 W
Redcar	42	54.37 N	1.04 W
Red Cedar ≃, Mich., U.S.	206	42.43 N	84.33 W
Red Cedar ≃, Wis., U.S.	180	44.42 N	91.53 W
Red Cedar Lake ⊜	180	46.45 N	79.54 W
Red Clay Creek ≃	275	39.43 N	75.39 W
Red Clay Creek, East Branch ≃	275	39.49 N	75.42 W
Red Clay Creek, West Branch ≃	275	39.49 N	75.42 W
Redcliff, Alta., Can.	174	50.05 N	110.47 W
Redcliff, Rh.	144	19.02 S	29.50 E
Redcliff, Colo., U.S.	190	39.31 N	106.22 W
Redcliffe	161a	27.14 S	153.07 E
Redcliffe, Mount ∧	152	28.25 S	121.32 E
Red Cliff Indian Reservation ♦[4]	180	46.50 N	90.47 W
Red Cliffs	156	34.19 S	142.11 E
Red Cloud	188	40.05 N	98.32 W
Red Creek	200	43.15 N	76.43 W
Red Creek ≃	184	30.41 N	88.40 W
Red Cross Lake ⊜	174	55.05 N	92.55 W
Red Deer	172	52.16 N	113.48 W
Red Deer ≃, Can.	166	50.56 N	109.54 W
Red Deer ≃, Can.	174	52.53 N	101.01 W
Red Deer Lake ⊜, Alta., Can.	172	52.43 N	113.02 W
Red Deer Lake ⊜, Man., Can.	174	52.56 N	101.20 W
Reddersburg	148	29.38 S	26.07 E
Red Devil	170	61.46 N	157.18 W
Red Dial	42	54.48 N	3.10 W
Reddick	206	41.06 N	88.15 W
Redding, Calif., U.S.	194	40.35 N	122.24 W
Redding, Conn., U.S.	197	41.18 N	73.23 W
Redding Ridge	197	41.19 N	73.21 W
Reddish	252	53.26 N	2.09 W
Redditch	44	52.19 N	1.56 W
Rede ≃	42	55.08 N	2.13 W
Redefin	50	53.21 N	11.11 E
Redelinghuys	148	32.30 S	18.33 E
Redenção	240	4.13 S	38.43 W
Redenção da Serra	246	23.16 S	45.33 W
Redesdale ∨	42	55.17 N	2.16 W
Redes Mere ⊜	252	53.15 N	2.14 W
Redeye ≃	188	46.26 N	94.49 W
Redfield, Iowa, U.S.	188	41.35 N	94.12 W
Redfield, N.Y., U.S.	202	43.32 N	75.49 W
Redfield, S. Dak., U.S.	188	44.53 N	98.31 W
Redfish Lake ⊜	192	44.07 N	114.56 W
Redford	186	29.47 N	104.10 W
Redford ♦[8]	271	42.25 N	83.16 W
Redford Township	206	42.25 N	83.16 W
Red Fort ⊥	262a	28.40 N	77.14 E
Redhead	231r	10.47 N	60.57 W
Red Hill, Austl.	152	21.59 S	116.03 E
Redhill, Eng., U.K.	44	51.14 N	0.11 W
Red Hill, Calif., U.S.	270	33.45 N	117.48 W
Red Hill, Pa., U.S.	198	40.22 N	75.29 W
Red Hill ∧	162	41.38 S	173.04 E
Redhill Aerodrome ⊠	250	51.12 N	0.07 W
Red Hill Branch ≃	274b	39.14 N	76.51 W
Red Hook	200	41.55 N	73.53 W
Redhouse Creek ≃	274b	39.18 N	76.31 W
Red Indian Lake ⊜	176	48.40 N	56.50 W
Redington Beach	210	27.49 N	82.49 W
Redington Shores	210	27.50 N	82.50 W
Red Island I	176	47.23 N	54.11 W
Redja ≃	66	58.05 N	31.33 E
Redkey	206	40.21 N	85.09 W
Redkino	72	56.38 N	36.17 E
Red Lake	174	51.03 N	93.49 W
Red Lake ⊜, Ont., Can.	174	51.01 N	94.05 W
Red Lake ⊜, Ariz., U.S.	190	35.40 N	114.04 W
Red Lake ⊜, Fla., U.S.	210	28.24 N	81.15 W
Red Lake ⊜, S. Dak., U.S.	188	43.44 N	99.13 W
Red Lake ⊜[1]	212	31.40 N	95.58 W
Red Lake ≃	188	47.55 N	97.01 W
Red Lake Falls	188	47.53 N	96.16 W
Red Lake Indian Reservation ♦[4]	180	48.05 N	95.05 W
Red Lake Road	174	49.58 N	93.22 W
Redland	212	31.25 N	94.43 W
Redland Bay	161a	27.37 S	153.18 E
Redlands	218	34.03 N	117.11 W
Red Level	184	31.24 N	86.36 W
Red Lick	184	31.48 N	90.59 W
Redlin	50	53.22 N	12.01 E
Red Lion, Pa., U.S.	178	39.54 N	76.36 W
Red Lion, Pa., U.S.	275	39.53 N	75.41 W
Red Lodge	192	45.11 N	109.15 W
Red Mill	196	46.25 N	72.28 W
Redmond, Oreg., U.S.	192	44.17 N	121.11 W
Redmond, Utah, U.S.	190	39.00 N	111.52 W
Redmond, Wash., U.S.	214	47.40 N	122.07 W
Red Mountain	218	35.21 N	117.37 W
Red Mountain ∧, Calif., U.S.	194	41.35 N	123.06 W
Red Mountain ∧, Calif., U.S.	218	35.21 N	117.36 W
Red Mountain ∧, Mont., U.S.	192	47.07 N	112.44 W
Red Mountain Pass)(	190	37.54 N	107.43 W
Rednitz ≃	52	49.28 N	10.59 E
Red Oak, Iowa, U.S.	188	41.01 N	95.14 W
Red Oak, Okla., U.S.	186	34.57 N	95.05 W
Red Oak, Tex., U.S.	212	32.31 N	96.48 W
Red Oak Creek ≃	212	32.28 N	96.30 W
Red Oaks Mill	200	41.40 N	73.53 W
Redon	32	47.39 N	2.05 W
Redonda I	228	16.55 N	62.19 W
Redonda, Ilha I	246	23.04 S	43.12 W
Redonda, Isla I	231r	9.52 N	61.35 W
Redonda Islands II	172	50.13 N	124.48 W
Redondela	34	42.17 N	8.36 W
Redondo, Port.	34	38.39 N	7.33 W
Redondo, Wash., U.S.	214	47.21 N	122.19 W
Redondo, Mount ∧	106	10.21 N	125.38 E
Redondo Beach	218	33.51 N	118.23 W
Redondo State Beach ♠	270	33.50 N	118.24 W
Redoubt, Mount ∧	214	48.57 N	121.18 W
Redoubt Volcano ∧[1]	170	60.29 N	152.45 W
Red Pass	172	52.59 N	118.59 W
Red Pheasant Indian Reserve ♦[4]	174	52.30 N	108.07 W
Red Pine Lake ⊜	202	45.12 N	78.42 W
Red Point ›	160	34.29 S	150.55 E
Red Rock, B.C., Can.	172	53.39 N	122.41 W
Red Rock, Ont., Can.	180	48.58 N	88.15 W
Red Rock, Tex., U.S.	212	29.58 N	97.27 W
Red Rock I	272	37.56 N	122.26 W
Red Rock ≃	192	44.59 N	112.52 W
Red Rock, Lake ⊜[1]	180	41.30 N	93.20 W
Red Rock Canyon Park ♠	218	35.23 N	118.00 W
Red Rock Creek ≃	186	36.36 N	97.03 W
Red Rocks Point ›	152	32.13 S	127.32 E
Red Root Creek ≃	266	40.30 N	74.19 W
Red Run ≃, Md., U.S.	274b	39.24 N	76.47 W
Red Run ≃, Mich., U.S.	271	42.34 N	82.58 W
Redruth	28	50.13 N	5.14 W
Red Sea ⊤[2]	126	20.00 N	38.00 E
Red Springs	182	34.49 N	79.11 W
Redstone	172	52.08 N	123.42 W
Redstone ≃, N.W. Ter., Can.	170	64.17 N	124.33 W
Redstone ≃, Ont., Can.	180	48.27 N	81.03 W
Redstone Creek ≃	188	44.04 N	98.05 W
Redstone Lake ⊜	202	45.11 N	78.32 W
Red Sucker ≃	174	55.19 N	92.31 W
Red Sucker Lake ⊜	174	54.09 N	93.40 W
Reduction	269b	40.11 N	79.46 W
Redut	70	47.22 N	51.53 E
Redvers	174	49.33 N	101.39 W
Redwater	172	53.57 N	113.06 W
Redwater ≃, U.S.	188	44.40 N	103.51 W
Redwater ≃, Mont., U.S.	188	48.03 N	105.13 W
Red Wharf Bay C	42	53.18 N	4.10 W
Redwillow ≃	172	55.04 N	119.21 W
Red Willow Creek ≃	188	40.13 N	100.29 W
Red Wing	180	44.34 N	92.31 W
Redwood	202	44.18 N	75.48 W
Redwood ≃	188	44.34 N	95.05 W
Redwood City	216	37.29 N	122.13 W
Redwood Creek ≃, Calif., U.S.	194	41.18 N	124.05 W
Redwood Creek ≃, Calif., U.S.	216	38.18 N	122.18 W
Redwood Creek ≃, Calif., U.S.	272	37.31 N	122.12 W
Redwood Creek ≃, Calif., U.S.	272	37.52 N	122.35 W
Redwood Estates	216	37.10 N	121.59 W
Redwood Falls	188	44.32 N	95.07 W
Redwood National Park ♠	194	41.30 N	124.05 W
Redwood Point ›	272	37.32 N	122.12 W
Redwood Regional Park ♠	272	37.38 N	122.10 W
Redwood Terrace	272	37.19 N	122.18 W
Redwood Valley	194	39.16 N	123.12 W
Ree, Lough ⊜	28	53.35 N	8.00 W
Reed City	180	43.53 N	85.31 W
Reeder	188	46.06 N	102.57 W
Reeders	200	41.01 N	75.20 W
Reeders Point ›	161a	27.22 S	153.55 E
Reed Lake ⊜, Man., Can.	174	54.37 N	100.30 W
Reed Lake ⊜, Sask., Can.	174	50.24 N	107.05 W
Reedley	216	36.36 N	119.27 W
Reedsburg, Ohio, U.S.	204	40.49 N	82.07 W
Reedsburg, Wis., U.S.	180	43.32 N	90.00 W
Reeds Peak ∧	190	33.09 N	107.51 W
Reedsport	192	43.42 N	124.06 W
Reedsville, Pa., U.S.	198	40.40 N	77.36 W
Reedsville, Wis., U.S.	180	44.09 N	87.57 W
Reedurban	204	40.47 N	81.22 W
Reedville	198	37.51 N	76.17 W
Reedy Creek ≃	210	28.04 N	81.21 W
Reedy Creek Swamp Ξ	210	28.17 N	81.31 W
Reedy Lake ⊜	210	27.44 N	81.22 W
Reef Islets II	165f	13.36 S	167.32 E
Reef Point ›	148	34.11 S	24.36 E
Reefton	162	42.07 S	171.52 E
Reelfoot Lake ⊜	184	36.25 N	89.22 W
Reepham	44	52.46 N	1.07 E
Reersø ›[1]	41	55.31 N	11.06 E
Rees	48	51.45 N	6.23 E
Rees □[8]	253	51.41 N	6.45 E
Reese	180	43.27 N	83.42 W
Reese ≃	194	40.39 N	116.54 W
Reese Air Force Base ■	186	33.36 N	102.02 W
Reese Village	186	33.36 N	102.01 W
Reeseville	180	43.18 N	88.51 W
Reesville	208	39.29 N	83.41 W
Reetz	50	53.11 N	11.52 E
Reetz in der Neumark → Recz	30	53.16 N	15.33 E
Refaa, Djebel ∧	34	35.34 N	5.52 E
Refahiye	120	39.54 N	38.46 E
Reform	184	33.23 N	88.01 W
Reforma de Pineda	224	16.24 N	94.28 W
Refton	198	39.57 N	76.14 W
Refuge Cove	172	50.07 N	124.50 W
Refugio	186	28.18 N	97.17 W
Refugio, Cerro del ∧	224	22.19 N	104.15 W
Refugio, Isla I	244	43.58 S	73.12 W
Refugio Creek ≃	272	38.01 N	122.17 W
Refugio Island I	106	10.28 N	123.21 E
Rega ≃	30	54.10 N	15.18 E
Regaïa	34	35.38 N	5.46 W
Regar	75	38.32 N	68.13 E
Regau	58	47.59 N	13.41 E
Regen	30	48.59 N	13.07 E
Regen ≃	30	49.01 N	12.06 E
Regency Estates	274c	39.03 N	77.10 W
Regeneração	240	6.15 S	42.41 W
Regensburg	30	49.01 N	12.06 E
Regensdorf	54	47.26 N	8.28 E
Regent, Austl.	264b	37.44 S	145.00 E
Regent, N. Dak., U.S.	188	46.25 N	102.33 W
Regents Park	264a	33.53 S	151.02 E
Regents Park ♦[8]	263d	26.15 S	28.04 E
Regentville	264a	33.47 S	150.40 E
Reggane	138	26.42 N	0.10 E
Regge ≃	48	52.31 N	6.22 E
Reggello	60	43.41 N	11.32 E
Reggio di Calabria	36	38.07 N	15.39 E
Reggiolo	58	44.55 N	10.48 E
Reggio nell'Emilia	58	44.43 N	10.36 E
Reggio nell'Emilia □[4]	58	44.37 N	10.37 E
Regharen ⊜	40	58.54 N	15.46 E
Reghin	38	46.47 N	24.42 E
Regina, Sask., Can.	174	50.25 N	104.39 W
Régina, Guy. fr.	240	4.19 N	52.08 W
Regina, S. Afr.	148	27.02 S	26.30 E
Regina Beach	174	50.47 N	105.00 W
Regina Elena, Canale Ξ	256b	45.41 N	8.39 E
Regis-Breitingen	50	51.05 N	12.26 E
Registro	242	24.30 S	47.50 W
Registro do Araguaia	245	15.44 S	51.50 W
Regiwar	110	25.57 N	65.44 E
Regla	230p	23.08 N	82.20 W
Regla □[7]	276b	23.07 N	82.20 W
Regnéville	32	49.01 N	1.33 W
Regnitz ≃	52	49.54 N	10.49 E
Rego Park ♦[8]	266	40.44 N	73.52 W
Regozero	24	65.28 N	31.10 E
Regresso, Cachoeira do L	240	0.58 S	54.51 W
Regstrup	41	55.40 N	11.37 E
Reguengos de Monsaraz	34	38.25 N	7.32 W
Reh	253	51.22 N	7.33 E
Rehau	50	50.15 N	12.02 E
Rehberg	50	52.43 N	12.10 E
Reh-Berge ∧∧[2]	254a	52.35 N	13.11 E
Rehberge, Volkspark ♠	254a	52.33 N	13.20 E
Rehburg	48	52.28 N	9.13 E
Rehden	48	52.37 N	8.29 E
Rehe	52	50.38 N	8.07 E
Rehe ≃	95	40.54 N	117.55 E
Rehefeld-Zaunhaus	50	50.43 N	13.42 E
Rehfelde	50	52.30 N	13.54 E
Rehli	114	23.38 N	79.05 E
Rehme	48	52.12 N	8.49 E
Rehna	50	53.47 N	11.03 E
Rehoboth	146	23.18 S	17.03 E
Rehoboth □[5]	146	23.30 S	17.30 E
Rehoboth Bay C	198	38.40 N	75.06 W
Rehoboth Beach	198	38.43 N	75.05 W
Rehoboth Seamount ✧[3]	16	37.35 N	59.55 W
Réhon	52	49.30 N	5.45 E
Reḥovot	122	31.54 N	34.49 E
Rehti	114	22.44 N	77.26 E
Reiche Ebrach ≃	52	49.49 N	10.58 E
Reiche Liesing ≃	254b	48.08 N	16.16 E
Reichelsheim	52	49.43 N	8.50 E
Reichenau, B.R.D.	54	47.41 N	9.03 E
Reichenau → Bogatynia, Pol.	50	50.53 N	15.00 E
Reichenau, Schw.	54	46.49 N	9.24 E
Reichenbach, D.D.R.	50	50.37 N	12.18 E
Reichenbach, D.D.R.	50	51.08 N	14.48 E
Reichenbach → Dzierżoniów, Pol.	30	50.44 N	16.39 E
Reichenbach, Schw.	54	46.38 N	7.42 E
Reichenberg → Liberec	30	50.46 N	15.03 E
Reichenhofen	54	47.50 N	9.58 E
Reichensachsen	52	51.09 N	9.59 E
Reichen Spitze ∧	58	47.09 N	12.07 E
Reichertsheim	58	48.12 N	12.17 E
Reichsbrücke ♦[5]	254b	48.14 N	16.25 E
Reichshoffen	52	48.56 N	7.40 E
Reid	152	30.49 S	128.26 E
Reid, Mount ∧, Austl.	152	17.58 S	130.38 E
Reid, Mount ∧, Alaska, U.S.	170	55.42 N	131.15 W
Reid Lake ⊜[1]	174	50.02 N	108.05 W
Reidsville, Ga., U.S.	182	32.06 N	82.07 W
Reidsville, N.C., U.S.	182	36.21 N	79.40 W
Reiffton	198	40.19 N	75.53 W
Reigate	44	51.14 N	0.13 W
Reigate and Banstead □[8]	250	51.17 N	0.12 W
Reignac-sur-Indre	46	47.13 N	0.55 E
Reignier	54	46.08 N	6.16 E
Reigoldswil	54	47.24 N	7.41 E
Reihoku	82	32.31 N	130.02 E
Reillanne	56	43.53 N	5.40 E
Reims	46	49.15 N	4.02 E
Reims, Montagne de ∧∧[2]	46	49.08 N	4.00 E
Reina Adelaida, Archipiélago II	244	52.10 S	74.25 W
Reina Alejandra → Queen Alexandra Range ∧∧	9	84.00 S	168.00 E
Reina Carlota, Estrecho de la → Queen Charlotte Sound U	172	51.30 N	129.30 W
Reinach, Schw.	54	47.15 N	8.11 E
Reinach, Schw.	54	47.30 N	7.35 E
Reina Fabiola → Queen Fabiola Mountains ∧∧	9	71.30 S	35.40 E
Reina Maria, Costa de la → Queen Mary Coast ⊻[2]	9	67.00 S	96.00 E
Reina Maud, Tierras de la → Queen Maud Land ♦[1]	9	72.30 S	12.00 E
Reinbeck	180	42.19 N	92.36 W
Reinbek	48	53.31 N	10.14 E
Reinberg	50	54.12 N	13.15 E
Reindeer ≃	174	55.36 N	103.11 W
Reindeer Island I	174	52.25 N	98.00 W
Reindeer Lake ⊜	166	57.15 N	102.40 W
Reindeer Station	170	68.42 N	134.06 W
Reine Charlotte, Détroit de la → Queen Charlotte Sound U	172	51.30 N	129.30 W
Reineck	54	47.28 N	9.34 E
Reinerton	198	40.36 N	76.34 W
Reinfeld	48	53.49 N	10.28 E
Reinga, Cape ›	162	34.25 S	172.41 E
Reinhardswald ♦[3]	48	51.30 N	9.30 E
Reinhardtsdorf	50	50.53 N	14.11 E
Reinheim	52	49.49 N	8.50 E
Reinickendorf ♦[8]	254a	52.35 N	13.21 E
Reinosa	34	43.00 N	4.08 W
Reino Unido → United Kingdom □[1]	28	54.00 N	2.00 W
Reinsdorf, D.D.R.	50	50.42 N	12.33 E
Reinsdorf, D.D.R.	50	51.54 N	12.37 E
Reinshagen ♦[8]	253	51.10 N	7.09 E
Reinstorf	50	53.50 N	11.38 E
Reis	120	38.16 N	31.35 E
Reisach	58	46.39 N	13.09 E
Reisaelva ≃	24	69.48 N	21.00 E
Reisdorf	52	49.53 N	6.15 E
Reisholz ♦[8]	253	51.11 N	6.52 E
Reisjärvi	26	63.37 N	24.54 E
Reisterstown	178	39.28 N	76.50 W
DEUTSCH Name	Seite	Breite °′	Länge °′ E=Ost
Reisterstown Plaza ♦[9]	274b	39.02 N	76.42 W
Reitdiep Ξ	48	53.20 N	6.18 E
Reiteralpe ∧∧	58	47.37 N	12.47 E
Reith bei Seefeld	58	47.18 N	11.12 E
Reit im Winkl	58	47.40 N	12.28 E
Reitz	148	27.53 S	28.31 E
Reitzenhain	50	50.33 N	13.13 E
Reivilo	148	27.36 S	24.08 E
Reixach	256d	41.30 N	2.12 E
Rejinagar	116	23.53 N	88.15 E
Rejmyra	40	58.50 N	15.55 E
Rejowiec Fabryczny	30	51.08 N	23.13 E
Rekarne	40	59.26 N	16.20 E
Rekarne □[9]	40	59.17 N	16.25 E
Reken	48	51.50 N	7.02 E
Rekjoāti	262b	22.37 N	88.28 E
Rela	110	29.27 N	89.45 E
Reliance	190	41.40 N	109.12 W
Relief Reservoir ⊜[1]	216	38.16 N	119.44 W
Reliz Creek ≃	216	36.19 N	121.18 W
Rellingen	48	53.39 N	9.49 E
Rellinghausen ♦[8]	253	51.25 N	7.04 E
Reloncaví, Seno C	244	41.40 S	72.35 W
Remada	138	32.19 N	10.24 E
Remagen	52	50.34 N	7.13 E
Rémalard	46	48.26 N	0.47 E
Remansão	240	4.25 S	49.34 W
Remanso	240	9.41 S	42.04 W
Remarde ≃	251	48.35 N	2.15 E
Remarkable, Mount ∧	152	32.48 S	138.10 E
Rembang	105a	6.42 S	111.20 E
Rembau	104	2.35 N	102.06 E
Rembia	104	2.20 N	102.13 E
Remchi	34	35.04 N	1.26 W
Remecó	242	37.38 S	63.39 W
Remedios, Col.	236	7.02 N	74.41 W
Remedios, Cuba	230p	22.30 N	79.33 W
Remedios, Pan.	226	8.14 N	81.51 W
Remedios, Punta ›	226	13.31 N	89.49 W
Remedios, Santuario de los ♁[1]	276a	19.28 N	99.15 W
Remedios de Escalada ♦[8]	248	34.43 S	58.23 W
Remels	48	53.18 N	7.44 E
Remennicy	72	56.43 N	36.36 E
Remer	180	47.03 N	93.55 W
Remeshk	118	26.50 N	58.49 E
Remhoogte	148	29.33 S	23.01 E
Remich	52	49.33 N	6.22 E
Remich Airport ⊠	269b	40.36 N	79.49 W
Rémigny, Lac ⊜	180	47.51 N	79.12 W
Rémilly	52	49.01 N	6.24 E
Reminderville	204	41.20 N	81.23 W
Remington, Ind., U.S.	206	40.46 N	87.09 W
Remington, Va., U.S.	178	38.32 N	77.49 W
Rémire	240	4.53 N	52.17 W
Remiremont	54	48.01 N	6.35 E
Remo	134	6.50 N	41.15 E
Remo □[8]	263a	6.42 N	3.29 E
Remolá, Laguna del C	256d	41.17 N	2.04 E
Remollon	56	44.28 N	6.10 E
Remontnoje	70	46.33 N	43.39 E
Remoray	54	46.46 N	6.14 E
Remoulins	56	43.56 N	4.34 E
Removka ♦[8]	73	47.59 N	38.43 E
Rempang, Pulau I	104	0.51 N	104.10 E
Remptendorf	50	50.31 N	11.39 E
Rems ≃	52	48.52 N	9.16 E
Remscheid	52		
	253	51.11 N	7.11 E
Remscheider-Stausee ⊜[1]	253	51.10 N	7.14 E
Remsen, Iowa, U.S.	188	42.49 N	95.58 W
Remsen, N.Y., U.S.	200	43.19 N	75.11 W
Remsfeld	52	51.00 N	9.29 E
Remuna	116	21.33 N	86.54 E
Remus	180	43.36 N	85.09 W
Rémuzat	56	44.24 N	5.21 E
Rena	26	61.08 N	11.22 E
Renaix → Ronse	46	50.45 N	3.36 E
Renāla Khurd	113	30.53 N	73.36 E
Rena Point ›	106	16.10 N	119.45 E
Renard Islands II	154	10.50 S	153.05 E
Renascença	236	3.50 S	66.21 W
Renata	172	49.26 N	118.06 W
Renaud Island I	9	65.40 S	66.00 W
Renbu	114	29.10 N	89.59 E
Renca	276e	33.24 S	70.44 W
Renca, Cerro ∧	276e	33.23 S	70.43 W
Rencēni	66	57.44 N	25.26 E
Renchen	52	48.35 N	8.01 E
Rencontre East	176	47.38 N	55.12 W
Rencun	88	36.19 N	113.50 E
Renda, S.S.S.R.	66	57.09 N	22.22 E
Renda, Yai.	134	14.30 N	39.53 E
Rende	36	39.19 N	16.11 E
Rendena, Valle ∨	54	46.08 N	10.42 E
Rend Lake ⊜[1]	184	38.05 N	88.58 W
Rendova I	165e	8.32 S	157.20 E
Rendsburg	41	54.18 N	9.40 E
Renens	54	46.32 N	6.35 E
Rene Reef ✧[2]	14	16.20 N	178.50 E
Renesse	48	51.44 N	3.46 E
Renews	176	46.56 N	52.56 W
Renfrew, Ont., Can.	202	45.28 N	76.41 W
Renfrew, Scot., U.K.	42	55.53 N	4.24 W
Renfrew, Pa., U.S.	204	40.46 N	79.58 W
Renfrew □[6]	202	45.25 N	77.05 W
Rengam	104	1.53 N	103.24 E
Ren'gang	96	32.01 N	120.50 E
Rengasdengklok	105a	6.09 S	107.17 E
Rengat	102	0.24 S	102.33 E
Rengel	105a	7.04 S	112.00 E
Rengen ⊜	26	64.05 N	14.03 E
Ren'gezhuang	95	39.45 N	118.10 E
Rengit	104	1.41 N	103.09 E
Rengkang	102	1.07 N	112.10 E
Rengo	242	34.25 S	70.52 W
Rengsdorf	52	50.30 N	7.29 E
Reng Tlāng ∧	110	21.59 N	92.36 E
Renhe, Zhg.	90	27.41 N	115.15 E
Renhe, Zhg.	90	33.32 N	114.02 E
Renhechang	97	30.30 N	105.56 E
Renheji	90	31.56 N	115.07 E
Renhua	90	25.06 N	113.44 E
Renhuai	92	27.48 N	106.18 E
Reni, Bhārat	113	28.41 N	75.02 E
Reni, S.S.S.R.	68	45.27 N	28.17 E
Renick	178	38.00 N	80.22 W
Renjiawopeng	94	41.27 N	122.18 E
Renjiaxu	96	30.49 N	121.00 E
Renju	90	24.51 N	115.54 E
Renko	26	60.54 N	24.17 E
Renkum	48	51.58 N	5.45 E
Renliuchang	97	29.13 N	106.39 E
Renlongchang	97	30.32 N	105.47 E
Renmark	156	34.11 S	140.45 E
Renmei	90	25.50 N	117.56 E
Renmin	79	46.37 N	125.32 E
Renminshenliqu Ξ	88	35.10 N	113.55 E
Rennau	50	52.17 N	10.55 E
Renne, Lac du → Reindeer Lake ⊜	166	57.15 N	102.40 W
Rennell I	150	11.40 S	160.10 E
Rennell, Islas II	244	52.00 S	74.00 W
Rennell Ridge ✧[3]	14	11.30 S	158.00 E
Renner	212	32.59 N	96.47 W
Rennerdale	269b	40.24 N	80.08 W
Rennerod	52	50.36 N	8.04 E
Renner Springs	152	18.20 S	133.48 E
Rennertshofen	52	48.45 N	11.02 E
Rennes	32	48.05 N	1.41 W
Rennick Bay C	9	70.18 S	161.45 E
Rennick Glacier ⊓	9	70.30 S	161.45 E
Rennie	174	49.51 N	95.33 W
Renningen	52	48.46 N	8.56 E

Symbols in the index entries represent the broad categories identified in the key at the right. Symbols with superior numbers (∧∧[2]) identify subcategories (see complete key on page *I* · 26).

Kartensymbole in dem Registerverzeichnis stellen die rechts in Schlüssel erklärten Kategorien dar. Symbole mit hochgestellten Ziffern (∧∧[2]) bezeichnen Unterabteilungen einer Kategorie (vgl. vollständiger Schlüssel auf Seite *I* · 26).

Los símbolos incluídos en el texto del índice representan las grandes categorias identificadas con la clave a la derecha. Los símbolos con numeros en su parte superior (∧∧[2]) identifican las subcategorías (véase la clave completa en la página *I* · 26).

Les symboles de l'index représentent les catégories indiquées dans la légende à droite. Les symboles suivis d'un indice (∧∧[2]) représentent des sous-catégories (voir légende complète à la page *I* · 26).

Os símbolos incluídos no texto do índice representam as grandes categorias identificadas com a chave à direita. Os símbolos com números em sua parte superior (∧∧[2]) identificam as subcategorias (veja-se a chave completa à página *I* · 26).

∧ Mountain	Berg	Montaña	Montagne	Montanha
∧∧ Mountains	Berge	Montañas	Montagnes	Montanhas
)(Pass	Pass	Paso	Col	Passo
∨ Valley, Canyon	Tal, Cañon	Valle, Cañón	Vallée, Canyon	Vale, Canhão
Plain	Ebene	Llano	Plaine	Planície
› Cape	Kap	Cabo	Cap	Cabo
I Island	Insel	Isla	Île	Ilha
II Islands	Inseln	Islas	Îles	Ilhas
Other Topographic Features	Andere Topographische Objekte	Otros Elementos Topográficos	Autres données topographiques	Outros Elementos Topográficos

ESPAÑOL

Nombre	Página	Lat.°′	Long.°′ W=Oeste
Renntier-See → Reindeer Lake ⊜	166	57.15 N	102.40 W
Rennweg	58	47.01 N	13.37 E
Reno, Nev., U.S.	216	39.31 N	119.48 W
Reno, Pa., U.S.	204	41.25 N	79.45 W
Reno, Tex., U.S.	212	32.56 N	97.05 W
Reno ≃	58	44.37 N	12.17 E
Reno Beach	204	41.40 N	83.15 W
Reno Hill ∧	190	42.35 N	106.03 W
Reno International Airport ⊠	216	39.30 N	119.46 W
Renous	176	46.49 N	65.48 W
Renous ≃	176	46.50 N	65.50 W
Renovo	204	41.20 N	77.38 W
Renqiao	90	33.27 N	117.16 E
Renqiu	88	38.43 N	116.05 E
Rens	41	54.54 N	9.06 E
Renshan	90	22.50 N	114.48 E
Renshou	90	27.08 N	117.51 E
Rensjön	24	68.05 N	19.49 E
Rensselaer, Ind., U.S.	206	40.57 N	87.09 W
Rensselaer, Mo., U.S.	209	39.40 N	91.33 W
Rensselaer, N.Y., U.S.	200	42.39 N	73.44 W
Rensselaer □[6]	200	42.43 N	73.40 W
Rensselaer Falls	202	44.35 N	75.19 W
Rensselaerville	200	42.31 N	74.08 W
Rentería	34	43.19 N	1.54 W
Rentfort ◂[8]	253	51.35 N	6.57 E
Renton	214	47.30 N	122.11 W
Rentuo	97	29.14 N	106.23 E
Rentweinsdorf	52	50.04 N	10.47 E
Renun ≃	104	3.05 N	97.55 E
Renville	188	44.48 N	95.13 W
Renwez	52	49.50 N	4.36 E
Renwick, N.Z.	162	41.30 S	173.50 E
Renwick, Iowa, U.S.	180	42.50 N	93.59 W
Renyizhen	97	29.29 N	105.28 E
Renziehalusen Park ♠	269b	40.21 N	79.50 W
Réo, H. Vol.	140	12.19 N	2.28 W
Reo, Indon.	105b	8.19 S	120.30 E
Reola ◂[8]	262a	28.34 N	76.59 E
Repartición	276d	12.00 S	77.04 W
Repartimento ≃	240	6.06 S	50.40 W
Repaupo	275	39.48 N	75.18 W
Repbäcken	40	60.31 N	15.20 E
Répce ≃	30	47.41 N	17.03 E
Repentigny	196	45.44 N	73.28 W
Repetek	118	38.34 N	63.11 E
Repetekskij Zapovednik ◂[4]	118	38.28 N	63.18 E
Repino	66	60.10 N	29.52 E
Repjovka, S.S.S.R.	68	51.05 N	38.39 E
Repjovka, S.S.S.R.	70	53.09 N	48.06 E
Repki	68	51.48 N	31.05 E
Repolka	66	59.16 N	29.34 E
Repolovo	76	60.40 N	69.50 E
Reporoa	162	38.26 S	176.21 E
Reposaari	26	61.37 N	21.27 E
Reppen → Rzepin	50	52.22 N	14.50 E
Repton	184	31.25 N	87.14 W
Republic, Kans., U.S.	188	39.55 N	97.49 W
Republic, Mich., U.S.	180	46.22 N	87.59 W
Republic, Mo., U.S.	184	37.07 N	93.29 W
Republic, Ohio, U.S.	204	41.08 N	83.01 W
Republic, Wash., U.S.	192	48.39 N	118.44 W
Republic Airport ⊠	266	40.44 N	73.25 W
Republican ≃	188	39.03 N	96.48 W
Republican, South Fork ≃	188	40.03 N	101.31 W
Republic Observatory Ʊ[3]	263d	26.11 S	28.05 E
Republic Steel Corporation Ʊ[3]	269a	41.28 N	81.40 W
Republik Kongo → Zaïre □[1]	10	0.00	25.00 E
République démocratique du Congo → Zaïre □[1]	10	0.00	25.00 E
Repueblo de Oriente	186	25.51 N	99.39 W
Repulse Bay	166	66.32 N	86.15 W
Repulse Bay ⊂	156	20.36 S	148.43 E
Repvåg	24	70.45 N	25.41 E
Requena, Esp.	34	39.29 N	1.06 W
Requena, Perú	238	4.58 S	73.50 W
Réquista	32	44.02 N	2.32 E
Rère ≃	46	47.22 N	1.50 E
Reriutaba	240	4.10 S	40.35 W
Reşadiye, Tür.	120	40.24 N	37.21 E
Reşadiye, Tür.	257b	41.05 N	29.15 E
Reşadiye Yarımadası ≻[1]	120	36.40 N	27.45 E
Resang, Tanjong ≻	104	2.35 N	103.51 E
Resarö	40	59.26 N	18.20 E
Rescalda	256b	45.38 N	8.56 E
Rescaldina	256b	45.37 N	8.57 E
Reschenpass (Passo di Resia))(	58	46.50 N	10.30 E
Reschenscheideck)(	58	46.51 N	10.31 E
Rescue	198	36.59 N	76.34 W
Research	264b	37.42 S	145.11 E
Reseda ◂[8]	270	34.12 N	118.31 W
Resen	38	41.05 N	21.00 E
Resende	246	22.28 S	44.27 W
Reserva	242	24.38 S	50.52 W
Reserve, La., U.S.	184	30.04 N	90.34 W
Reserve, N. Mex., U.S.	190	33.43 N	108.45 W
Reserve Township	269b	40.29 N	79.59 W
Reservoir	264b	37.43 S	145.00 E
Reservoir Pond ⊜	273	42.10 N	71.07 W
Rešetilovka	68	49.34 N	34.04 E
Rešetnikovo	72	56.27 N	36.34 E
Reshou	97	30.00 N	104.08 E
Reshui	88	42.09 N	119.18 E
Reshuitang	92	24.10 N	103.09 E
Resistencia	242	27.27 S	58.59 W
Reşiţa	38	45.17 N	21.53 E
Resiutta	58	46.23 N	13.13 E
Resko	30	53.47 N	15.25 E
Rešma	70	57.24 N	42.34 E
Rešn'ovka	68	49.47 N	27.25 E
Resolute	166	74.41 N	94.54 W
Resolution Island I, N.W. Ter., Can.	166	61.30 N	65.00 W
Resolution Island I, N.Z.	162	45.40 S	166.40 E
Resolven	44	51.42 N	3.42 W
Rešoty	66	57.09 N	28.30 E
Resplandes	240	6.17 S	45.13 W
Resplendor	245	19.20 S	41.15 W
Ressa ≃	66	54.45 N	35.10 E
Ressaca	246	21.57 S	45.30 W
Ressaca, Ribeirão ≃	277b	23.38 S	46.51 W
Resse ◂[8]	253	51.34 N	7.07 E
Resseta ≃	66	53.49 N	35.15 E
Ressons-sur-Matz	46	49.33 N	2.45 E
Resta ≃	66	53.36 N	30.56 E
Resthaven	206	41.16 N	88.09 W
Restigouche ≃	176	48.04 N	66.20 W
Restinga	34	35.42 N	5.23 W
Restinga Sêca	242	29.49 S	53.23 W
Reston, Man., Can.	174	49.35 N	101.02 W
Reston, Scot., U.K.	42	55.51 N	2.11 W
Reston, Va., U.S.	198	38.58 N	77.21 W
Restoule Lake ⊜	180	46.03 N	79.47 W
Restrepo, Col.	236	3.48 N	76.31 W
Restrepo, Col.	236	4.15 N	73.33 W
Resülhınzır ≻	120	36.22 N	35.45 E
Resurrección	224	19.06 N	98.07 W
Retalhuleu	226	14.32 N	91.41 W
Retalhuleu □[5]	226	14.20 N	91.50 W
Retamosa	242	33.35 S	54.44 W
Retelimba	165f	16.06 S	167.25 E
Retem, Oued er ∨	138	33.30 N	5.45 E
Řetenice	50	50.38 N	13.46 E
Retezat, Munţii Ѧ	38	45.25 N	23.00 E
Rethel	46	49.31 N	4.22 E
Rethem	48	52.45 N	9.23 E
Réthimnon	38	35.22 N	24.29 E

FRANÇAIS

Nom	Page	Lat.°′	Long.°′ W=Ouest
Retiche, Alpi → Rhaetian Alps Ѧ	54	46.30 N	10.00 E
Retie	52	51.16 N	5.04 E
Retiers	28	47.55 N	1.23 W
Retiro	246	21.53 S	45.47 W
Retiro, Estacion ◂[5]	278	34.36 S	58.22 W
Retiro, Parque del ♠	256a	40.25 N	3.41 W
Retournac	56	45.12 N	4.02 E
Retreat	212	32.03 N	96.29 W
Retsof	200	42.50 N	77.53 W
Rettenberg	54	47.35 N	10.17 E
Rettendon	250	51.39 N	0.33 E
Rettendon Place	250	51.38 N	0.34 E
Rettichovka	79	44.10 N	132.47 E
Rettin	50	54.06 N	10.53 E
Return Creek ≃	216	37.56 N	119.28 W
Retzow	50	52.37 N	12.41 E
Reu	164r	6.49 N	158.16 E
Reuden	50	52.04 N	12.18 E
Reungeut	104	4.34 N	96.22 E
Reunion □[2]	128		
	147c	21.06 S	55.36 E
Reus	34	41.09 N	1.07 E
Reuschenberg ◂[8]	253	51.10 N	6.42 E
Reusel	48	51.21 N	5.22 E
Reusrath	253	51.06 N	6.57 E
Reuss ≃	54	47.28 N	8.14 E
Reut ≃	68	47.15 N	29.09 E
Reuterstadt Stavenhagen	50	53.42 N	12.53 E
Reutlingen	54	48.29 N	9.11 E
Reutov	72	55.46 N	37.52 E
Reutte	54	47.29 N	10.43 E
Reuver	48	51.17 N	6.05 E
Rev'akino	72	54.22 N	37.40 E
Reval → Tallinn	66	59.25 N	24.45 E
Revda, S.S.S.R.	24	67.55 N	34.30 E
Revda, S.S.S.R.	76	56.48 N	59.57 E
Réveillon, Ruisseau le ≃	251	48.42 N	2.30 E
Revel	56	45.11 N	5.52 E
Revelganj	114	25.47 N	84.40 E
Revelstoke	172	50.59 N	118.12 W
Reventazón	238	6.10 S	80.58 W
Reventazón ≃	226	10.17 N	83.24 W
Revere, It.	58	45.03 N	11.08 E
Revere, Mass., U.S.	197	42.24 N	71.01 W
Revere, Pa., U.S.	198	40.31 N	75.10 W
Revermont Ѧ[2]	54	46.27 N	5.25 E
Revesby	264a	33.57 S	151.01 E
Revest-du-Bion	56	44.05 N	5.33 E
Révia	144	13.23 S	36.31 E
Reviga	38	44.42 N	27.06 E
Revigny-sur-Ornain	52	48.50 N	4.59 E
Revilla del Campo	34	42.13 N	3.32 W
Revillagigedo, Islas de II	222	19.00 N	111.30 W
Revillagigedo Channel ⋓	172	55.10 N	131.13 W
Revillagigedo Island I	172	55.35 N	131.23 W
Revillo	188	45.01 N	96.34 W
Revin	52	49.56 N	4.38 E
Revloc	204	40.29 N	78.46 W
Řevničov	50	50.08 N	13.45 E
Revò	58	46.23 N	11.03 E
Revol'ucii, Muzej Ʊ	255b	55.46 N	37.36 E
Revol'ucii, Pik ∧	75	38.31 N	72.21 E
Revsundssjön ⊜	26	62.49 N	15.17 E
Revúboè ≃	144	16.13 S	33.37 E
Revuè ≃	146	19.49 S	34.00 E
Revuelto Creek ≃	186	35.22 N	103.23 W
Rew	204	41.54 N	78.32 W
Rewa	114	24.32 N	81.18 E
Rewa □[5]	114	24.45 N	81.30 E
Rewa ≃	165g	18.08 S	178.33 E
Rewāri	114	28.11 N	76.37 E
Rewataya, Taka ✢[2]	102	6.05 S	118.55 E
Rex, Mount ∧	9	74.57 S	76.00 W
Rexburg	192	43.49 N	111.47 W
Rexdale ◂[8]	265b	43.43 N	79.35 W
Rexford, Kans., U.S.	188	39.28 N	100.45 W
Rexford, Mont., U.S.	192	48.53 N	115.13 W
Rexhame	273	42.07 N	70.41 W
Rexton	176	46.39 N	64.52 W
Rexville, Ind., U.S.	268	41.31 N	87.21 W
Rexville, N.Y., U.S.	200	42.05 N	77.40 W
Rey	118	35.35 N	51.25 E
Rey, Arroyo del ≃	278	34.46 S	58.27 W
Rey, Estrecho del → King Sound ⋓	152	17.00 S	123.30 E
Rey, Isla del I	236	8.22 N	78.55 W
Rey, Laguna del ⊜	186	27.01 N	103.26 W
Rey Bouba	136	8.40 N	14.11 E
Reyes	238	14.19 S	67.23 W
Reyes, Point ≻	194	38.00 N	123.01 W
Reyes Peak ∧	218	34.38 N	119.17 W
Reyhanlı	120	36.18 N	36.32 E
Rey Jorge, Estrecho → King George Sound ⋓	152	35.03 S	117.57 E
Rey Jorge, Isla → King George Island I	9	62.00 S	58.15 W
Reykjanes ≻[1]	24a	63.49 N	22.43 W
Reykjanes Ridge ✢[3]	10	60.00 N	28.00 W
Reykjavík	24a	64.09 N	21.51 W
Reynaldo Cullen	242	31.19 S	60.39 W
Reynella	158b	35.06 S	138.32 E
Reynolds, Ga., U.S.	182	32.34 N	84.06 W
Reynolds, Ind., U.S.	206	40.45 N	86.52 W
Reynolds, N. Dak., U.S.	188	47.40 N	97.07 W
Reynolds Channel ⋓	266	40.36 N	73.40 W
Reynolds Creek ≃, Austl.	161a	27.56 S	152.36 E
Reynolds Creek ≃, Ont., Can.	202	42.59 N	80.58 W
Reynoldsville	204	41.06 N	78.53 W
Reynosa	222	26.07 N	98.18 W
Reyssouze ≃	54	46.27 N	4.54 E
Rež	76	57.23 N	61.24 E
Rež ≃	76	57.54 N	62.18 E
Reza, Gora Kūh-e Rīzeh) ∧	118	37.47 N	58.05 E
Rezā'īyeh	118	37.33 N	45.04 E
Rezā'īyeh, Daryācheh-ye ⊜	118	37.40 N	45.30 E
Rezé	32	47.12 N	1.34 W
Rēzekne	66	56.30 N	27.19 E
Rēzekne ≃	66	56.46 N	26.58 E
Rezeny	68	46.46 N	28.54 E
Rezina	68	47.44 N	28.58 E
Rezino	76	55.51 N	75.18 E
Rēznas Ezers ⊜	66	56.20 N	27.27 E
Rezonville	52	49.06 N	6.00 E
Rezovo	38	41.59 N	28.02 E
Rezovska (Rezve) ≃	120	41.59 N	28.01 E
Rezvāndeh	118	37.33 N	49.09 E
Rezve (Rezovska) ≃	120	41.59 N	28.01 E
Rezzato	58	45.31 N	10.19 E
Rezzoaglio	56	44.32 N	9.23 E
Rezzonico	54	46.04 N	9.16 E
Rhade	48	53.19 N	9.07 E
Rhadeswood Reservoir ⊜[1]	252	53.29 N	1.56 W
Rhaetian Alps (Rätische Alpen) (Alpi Retiche) Ѧ	54	46.30 N	10.00 E
Rhallamane, Sebkha de ≡	138	23.41 N	9.50 W
Rhame	188	46.14 N	103.39 W
Rharbi, Chott ⊜	138	33.50 N	1.30 W
Rharbi, Oued el ∨	138	31.50 N	0.51 E
Rharbi, Zahrez ⊜	138	34.50 N	2.50 E
Rharsa, Chott el ⊜	138	34.06 N	7.50 E
Rhaunen	52	49.52 N	7.20 E

PORTUGUÊS

Nome	Página	Lat.°′	Long.°′ W=Oeste
Rhayader	44	52.18 N	3.30 W
Rhea Creek ≃	192	45.30 N	119.46 W
Rheda-Wiedenbrück	48	51.50 N	8.18 E
Rhede, B.R.D.	48	51.50 N	6.11 E
Rhede, B.R.D.	48	53.03 N	7.16 E
Rheden	48	52.01 N	6.02 E
Rheems	198	40.08 N	76.34 W
Rheem Valley	216	37.52 N	122.07 W
Rheidol ≃	44	52.25 N	4.05 W
Rheims → Reims	46	49.15 N	4.02 E
Rhein, Sask., Can.	174	51.22 N	102.10 W
Rhein → Ryn, Pol.	30	53.56 N	21.33 E
Rhein → Rhine ≃	30	51.52 N	6.02 E
Rheinbach	52	50.37 N	6.57 E
Rheinberg	48	51.33 N	6.35 E
Rheinbischofsheim	52	48.39 N	7.55 E
Rheinböllen	52	50.00 N	7.40 E
Rheinbrohl	52	50.30 N	7.19 E
Rheinbrücke ◂[5]	253	51.12 N	6.44 E
Rheindürkheim	52	49.42 N	8.21 E
Rheine	48	52.17 N	7.26 E
Rheinen	253	51.27 N	7.38 E
Rheinfall ⌊	54	47.41 N	8.38 E
Rheinfelden, B.R.D.	54	47.33 N	7.47 E
Rheinfelden, Schw.	54	47.33 N	7.48 E
Rheinhausen	52	51.24 N	6.44 E
Rhein-Herne-Kanal ≊	253	51.27 N	6.47 E
Rheinhessen □[5]	52	49.40 N	8.40 E
Rheinisch-Bergischer Kreis □[8]	253	51.06 N	7.25 E
Rheinkamp	48	51.30 N	6.37 E
Rheinland-Pfalz □[3]	52	50.00 N	7.00 E
Rhein-Main-Donau-Kanal ≊	52	49.45 N	11.00 E
Rheinpark ♠	253	51.15 N	6.46 E
Rheinsberg	50	53.06 N	12.53 E
Rheinstadion ♠	253	51.16 N	6.44 E
Rheinstein, Burg ⊥	52	50.00 N	7.50 E
Rheinwald ∨	54	46.32 N	9.17 E
Rheinwaldhorn ∧	54	46.30 N	9.02 E
Rhein-Westerwald, Naturpark ♠	52	50.35 N	7.20 E
Rhein-Wupper-Kreis □[8]	253	51.07 N	7.06 E
Rheinzabern	52	49.07 N	8.16 E
Rhêmes-Notre-Dame	56	45.34 N	7.07 E
Rhenen	48	51.57 N	5.34 E
Rhens	52	50.17 N	7.37 E
Rheurdt	253	51.28 N	6.28 E
Rheydt	52		
	253	51.10 N	6.25 E
Rheydt, Schloss ⊥	253	51.11 N	6.29 E
Rhin ≃, D.D.R.	50	52.59 N	12.55 E
Rhin → Rhine ≃, Eur.	30	51.52 N	6.02 E
Rhinau	54	48.19 N	7.42 E
Rhine	182	31.59 N	83.12 W
Rhine (Rhein) (Rhin) ≃	30	51.52 N	6.02 E
Rhinebeck	200	41.56 N	73.55 W
Rhinecliff	200	41.55 N	73.57 W
Rhineland	209	38.43 N	91.31 W
Rhinelander	180	45.38 N	89.25 W
Rhin Kanal ≊	50	52.47 N	12.24 E
Rhinluch ≡	50	52.50 N	12.50 E
Rhinns of Kells Ѧ	42	55.07 N	4.22 W
Rhino Camp	144	2.58 N	31.24 E
Rhinow	50	52.45 N	12.20 E
Rhiou, Oued ≃	34	36.00 N	0.55 E
Rhir, Cap ≻	138	30.38 N	9.55 W
Rhis, Oued ≃	34	35.14 N	3.57 W
Rhiw ≃	44	52.36 N	3.11 W
Rho, It.	56	45.32 N	9.02 E
Rho, N. Cal.	165f	21.22 S	167.50 E
Rhode Island □[3]	197		
	168	41.40 N	71.30 W
Rhode Island I	197	41.33 N	71.15 W
Rhode Island Sound ⋓	197	41.25 N	71.15 W
Rhoden	48	51.28 N	9.00 E
Rhodes, Austl.	264a	33.50 S	151.05 E
Rhodes → Ródhos, Ellás	38	36.26 N	28.13 E
Rhodes, S. Afr.	148	30.47 S	27.59 E
Rhodes, Eng., U.K.	252	53.33 N	2.14 W
Rhodes → Ródhos I	38	36.10 N	28.00 E
Rhodesia □[2]	128		
	144	20.00 S	30.00 E
Rhodésie → Rhodesia □[2]	144	20.00 S	30.00 E
Rhodesien → Rhodesia □[2]	144	20.00 S	30.00 E
Rhodes Inyanga National Park ♠	144	18.12 S	32.45 E
Rhodes Park ♠	263d	26.12 S	28.06 E
Rhodes Peak ∧	192	46.41 N	114.47 W
Rhodes Salt Marsh ≡	194	38.17 N	118.06 W
Rhodes' Tomb ♠	144	20.30 S	28.30 E
Rhododendron	214	45.20 N	121.55 W
Rhododendron State Park ♠	197	42.47 N	72.12 W
Rhodon	251	48.43 N	2.04 E
Rhodon, Ruisseau le ≃	251	48.42 N	2.04 E
Rhodope Mountains Ѧ	38	41.30 N	24.30 E
Rhodt	52	49.16 N	8.07 E
Rhome	212	33.03 N	97.28 W
Rhondda	44	51.40 N	3.27 W
Rhône ≃	32	43.20 N	4.50 E
Rhône à Sète, Canal du ≊	56	43.25 N	3.42 E
Rhône au Rhin, Canal du ≊	54	47.06 N	5.19 E
Rhosesmor	252	53.12 N	3.10 W
Rhosllanerchrugog	44	53.00 N	3.03 W
Rhosneigr	42	53.14 N	4.31 W
Rhos-on-Sea	42	53.19 N	3.45 W
Rhossilli	44	51.34 N	4.17 W
Rhuddlan	42	53.18 N	3.27 W
Rhue ≃	32	45.23 N	2.29 E
Rhum I	28	57.00 N	6.20 W
Rhyl	42	53.19 N	3.29 W
Rhymney	44	51.46 N	3.18 W
Rhymney ≃	44	51.28 N	3.10 W
Riachão	240	7.22 S	46.37 W
Riachão ≃	240	11.05 S	45.30 W
Riachão do Dantas	240	11.04 S	37.44 W
Riachão do Jacuípe	240	11.48 S	39.21 W
Riacho de Santana	245	13.37 S	42.57 W
Riacho Grande	246	23.48 S	46.35 W
Riachos, Isla de los I	244	40.10 S	62.08 W
Riachuelo, Bra.	240	10.44 S	37.11 W
Riachuelo, Chile	244	40.49 S	73.21 W
Riachuelo, Ur.	248	34.28 S	57.43 W
Riachuelo, Arroyo ≃	248	34.27 S	57.44 W
Rialma	245	15.18 S	49.34 W
Rialto, Bra.	246	22.35 S	44.16 W
Rialto, Calif., U.S.	218	34.06 N	117.22 W
Rianápolis	245	15.29 S	49.28 W
Riāng	110	27.32 N	92.56 E
Riangnom	130	9.55 N	30.01 E
Riaño	34	42.58 N	5.01 W
Rians	56	43.37 N	5.45 E
Riánsares ≃	34	39.32 N	3.18 W
Riāsi	113	33.05 N	74.50 E
Riau □[4]	102	1.00 N	102.00 E
Riau, Kepulauan II	102	1.00 N	104.30 E
Riaz	54	46.38 N	7.04 E
Riaza	34	41.17 N	3.28 W
Riaza ≃	34	41.42 N	3.55 W
Rib ≃	44	51.48 N	0.04 W
Ribadavia	34	42.17 N	8.08 W
Ribadeo	34	43.32 N	7.02 W
Ribadesella	34	43.28 N	5.04 W
Ribagorza ◂[1]	34	42.15 N	0.30 E
Ribamar	240	2.33 S	44.03 W
Ribarroja, Embalse de ⊜[1]	34	41.12 N	0.20 E
Ribas de Jarama	256a	40.23 N	3.31 W
Ribas do Rio Pardo	245	20.27 S	53.46 W
Ribauè	144	14.57 S	38.17 E
Ribble ≃	42	53.44 N	2.50 W
Ribbleton	252	53.46 N	2.40 W
Ribble Valley □[8]	252	53.48 N	2.31 W
Ribbon Fall ⌊	216	37.44 N	119.39 W
Ribchester	252	53.49 N	2.32 W
Ribe	41	55.21 N	8.46 E
Ribe □[6]	41	55.35 N	8.50 E
Ribe Å ≃	41	55.21 N	8.40 E
Ribeauvillé	54	48.12 N	7.19 E
Ribécourt	46	49.31 N	2.55 E
Ribeira	242	24.40 S	49.01 W
Ribeira de Iguape ≃	242	24.40 S	47.24 W
Ribeira do Amparo	240	11.03 S	38.26 W
Ribeira do Pombal	240	10.50 S	38.32 W
Ribeira Grande, C.V.	140a	17.11 N	25.04 W
Ribeira Grande, Port.	138a	37.49 N	25.31 W
Ribeirão, Bra.	240	8.31 S	35.23 W
Ribeirão, Bra.	246	23.17 S	45.36 W
Ribeirão, Bra.	277b	23.35 S	46.55 W
Ribeirão das Lajes, Reprêsa do ⊜[1]	246	22.45 S	43.55 W
Ribeirão de São Joaquim	246	22.17 S	44.11 W
Ribeirão do Pinhal	245	23.24 S	50.18 W
Ribeirão do Pote	246	23.36 S	45.50 W
Ribeirão Fundo	246	22.40 S	46.15 W
Ribeirão Grande	246	22.48 S	45.27 W
Ribeirão Pires	246	23.43 S	46.25 W
Ribeirão Prêto	245	21.10 S	47.48 W
Ribeirão Vermelho	245	21.11 S	45.03 W
Ribeirãozinho	245	16.27 S	52.35 W
Ribeiro Gonçalves	240	7.32 S	45.14 W
Ribeiro Junqueira	246	21.28 S	42.31 W
Ribeirópolis	240	10.32 S	37.26 W
Ribemont	46	49.48 N	3.28 E
Ribera	36	37.30 N	13.16 E
Ribérac	32	45.15 N	0.20 E
Riberalta	238	10.59 S	66.06 W
Riberão Pires □[7]	277b	23.43 S	46.21 W
Ribiers	56	44.14 N	5.52 E
Rib Lake	180	45.20 N	90.12 W
Ribnica	36	45.44 N	14.44 E
Ribnitz-Damgarten	50	54.15 N	12.28 E
Ribstone Creek ≃	174	52.51 N	110.05 W
Ricarda, Laguna de la ⊂	256d	41.18 N	2.07 E
Ricardo Flores Magón	222	29.58 N	106.58 W
Ricaurte	236	1.13 N	77.59 W
Riccall	42	53.50 N	1.04 W
Riccarton	162	43.32 S	172.36 E
Riccia	60	41.29 N	14.50 E
Riccione	60	43.59 N	12.39 E
Rice	212	32.15 N	96.30 W
Rice Creek ≃	206	42.16 N	84.57 W
Rice Lake	180	45.30 N	91.44 W
Rice Lake ⊜, Ont., Can.	180	47.42 N	82.08 W
Rice Lake ⊜, Ont., Can.	202	44.08 N	78.13 W
Rice Lake Indian Reserve ◂[4]	202	44.10 N	78.12 W
Riceville, Iowa, U.S.	180	43.22 N	92.33 W
Riceville, Pa., U.S.	204	41.47 N	79.48 W
Riceville, Tenn., U.S.	182	35.23 N	84.42 W
Rich, Cape ≻	202	44.43 N	80.38 W
Richan	174	49.59 N	92.49 W
Richard Collinson Inlet ⊂	166	72.45 N	113.45 W
Richards	212	30.32 N	95.51 W
Richard's Bay	148	28.47 S	32.06 E
Richard's Bay ⊂	148	28.50 S	32.02 E
Richard's Bay Game Reserve ◂[4]	148	28.48 S	32.05 E
Richards-Gebaur Air Force Base ■	184	38.51 N	94.33 W
Richard's Harbour	176	47.37 N	56.24 W
Richards Island I	170	69.20 N	134.30 W
Richardson, Tex., U.S.	212	32.57 N	96.44 W
Richardson, Wash., U.S.	214	48.27 N	122.54 W
Richardson ≃	166	58.30 N	111.30 W
Richardson, Mount ∧	152	28.49 S	119.59 E
Richardson Bay ⊂	272	37.52 N	122.29 W
Richardson Lakes ⊜	178	44.50 N	70.52 W
Richardson Mountains Ѧ, Can.	170	67.15 N	136.30 W
Richardson Mountains Ѧ, N.Z.	162	44.45 S	168.31 E
Richardsville	204	41.14 N	79.01 W
Richard-Toll	140	16.28 N	15.41 W
Richardton	188	46.53 N	102.19 W
Rîchât, Guelb er ∧	138	21.07 N	11.24 W
Richboro	198	40.13 N	75.01 W
Richburg	200	42.05 N	78.09 W
Riche, Pointe ≻	176	50.42 N	57.25 W
Richebourg	251	48.49 N	1.38 E
Richelieu, Qué., Can.	196	45.27 N	73.15 W
Richelieu, Fr.	32	47.01 N	0.19 E
Richelieu □[6]	196	45.55 N	73.00 W
Richelieu ≃	196	46.03 N	73.07 W
Richer	174	49.39 N	96.28 W
Richey	188	47.39 N	105.04 W
Richfield, Idaho, U.S.	192	43.03 N	114.09 W
Richfield, Minn., U.S.	180	44.53 N	93.17 W
Richfield, Ohio, U.S.	204	41.14 N	81.39 W
Richfield, Pa., U.S.	198	40.41 N	77.07 W
Richfield, Utah, U.S.	190	38.46 N	112.05 W
Richfield Springs	200	42.51 N	74.59 W
Richford, N.Y., U.S.	200	42.21 N	76.12 W
Richford, Vt., U.S.	178	45.00 N	72.40 W
Rich Fountain	209	38.24 N	91.53 W
Richgrove	216	35.48 N	119.07 W
Rich Hill	184	38.06 N	94.22 W
Richibucto	176	46.41 N	64.52 W
Richisau	54	47.02 N	8.54 E
Richland, Ga., U.S.	182	32.06 N	84.39 W
Richland, Mich., U.S.	206	42.22 N	85.31 W
Richland, Mo., U.S.	184	37.51 N	92.26 W
Richland, N.J., U.S.	198	39.30 N	74.52 W
Richland, N.Y., U.S.	202	43.34 N	76.03 W
Richland, Pa., U.S.	198	40.21 N	76.16 W
Richland, Tex., U.S.	212	32.57 N	95.49 W
Richland, Tex., U.S.	212	31.56 N	96.26 W
Richland, Wash., U.S.	192	46.17 N	119.18 W
Richland □[6]	204	40.46 N	82.31 W
Richland Center	180	43.20 N	90.23 W
Richland Creek ≃, Ill., U.S.	209	38.14 N	89.54 W
Richland Creek ≃, Mo., U.S.	209	38.53 N	91.53 W
Richland Creek ≃, Tenn., U.S.	184	35.02 N	86.55 W
Richland Creek ≃, Tex., U.S.	212	31.58 N	96.03 W
Richland Hills	212	32.49 N	97.14 W
Richlands, N.C., U.S.	182	34.54 N	77.34 W
Richlands, Va., U.S.	182	37.06 N	81.48 W
Richland Springs	186	31.16 N	98.57 W
Richmond, Austl.	156	20.44 S	143.08 E
Richmond, Austl.	160	33.36 S	150.46 E
Richmond, Austl.	264b	37.49 S	145.00 E
Richmond, B.C., Can.	172	49.10 N	123.10 W
Richmond, Ont., Can.	202	45.11 N	75.50 W
Richmond, Qué., Can.	196	45.40 N	72.09 W
Richmond, N.Z.	162	41.20 S	173.11 E
Richmond, S. Afr.	148	29.54 S	30.08 E
Richmond, S. Afr.	148	31.23 S	23.56 E
Richmond, S. Afr.	263d	26.19 S	28.13 E
Richmond, Eng., U.K.	42	54.24 N	1.44 W
Richmond, Calif., U.S.	216	37.57 N	122.22 W
Richmond, Ill., U.S.	206	42.28 N	88.18 W
Richmond, Ind., U.S.	208	39.50 N	84.54 W
Richmond, Kans., U.S.	188	38.24 N	95.15 W
Richmond, Ky., U.S.	182	37.45 N	84.18 W
Richmond, Maine, U.S.	178	44.05 N	69.48 W
Richmond, Mass., U.S.	197	42.23 N	73.22 W
Richmond, Mich., U.S.	204	42.49 N	82.45 W
Richmond, Minn., U.S.	180	45.27 N	94.31 W
Richmond, Mo., U.S.	184	39.17 N	93.58 W
Richmond, Ohio, U.S.	204	40.26 N	80.46 W
Richmond, Tex., U.S.	212	29.35 N	95.46 W
Richmond, Utah, U.S.	190	41.55 N	111.48 W
Richmond, Vt., U.S.	178	44.24 N	72.59 W
Richmond, Va., U.S.	198	37.30 N	77.28 W
Richmond □[6], Qué., Can.	196	45.40 N	72.00 W
Richmond □[6], N.Y., U.S.	200	40.38 N	74.05 W
Richmond □[6], Va., U.S.	198	37.32 N	77.28 W
Richmond ◂[8], Eng., U.K.	44	51.28 N	0.18 W
Richmond ◂[8], Calif., U.S.	272	37.46 N	122.29 W
Richmond ◂[8], Pa., U.S.	275	39.59 N	75.06 W
Richmond, Mount ∧	162	41.29 S	173.24 E
Richmond, Point ≻	272	37.55 N	122.23 W
Richmond Beach	214	47.46 N	122.23 W
Richmond College Ʊ[2]	266	40.38 N	74.05 W
Richmond Creek ≃	266	40.34 N	74.11 W
Richmond Heights, Fla., U.S.	210	25.58 N	80.22 W
Richmond Heights, Mo., U.S.	209	38.38 N	90.19 W
Richmond Heights, Ohio, U.S.	204	41.33 N	81.29 W
Richmond Highlands	214	47.46 N	122.22 W
Richmond Hill, Ont., Can.	202	43.52 N	79.27 W
Richmond Hill, Ga., U.S.	182	31.56 N	81.18 W
Richmond Hill ◂[8]	266	40.42 N	73.49 W
Richmond Mall ◂[9]	269a	41.32 N	81.30 W
Richmond National Battlefield Park ♠	198	37.25 N	77.23 W
Richmond Park ♠	250	51.26 N	0.16 W
Richmond Peak ∧	231h	13.17 N	61.13 W
Richmond Range Ѧ	162	41.27 S	173.30 E
Richmond Royal Australian Air Force Base ■	160	33.37 S	150.48 E
Richmond-San Rafael Bridge ◂[5]	272	37.56 N	122.27 W
Richmondtown Restoration ⊥	266	40.34 N	74.09 W
Richmond Valley ◂[8]	266	40.31 N	74.13 W
Richmondville	200	42.38 N	74.34 W
Richrath	253	51.08 N	6.56 E
Rich Square	182	36.16 N	77.17 W
Richtenberg	50	54.12 N	12.53 E
Richterswil	54	47.13 N	8.42 E
Richton	184	31.16 N	88.56 W
Richton Park	206	41.29 N	87.43 W
Richvale, Ont., Can.	202	43.51 N	79.26 W
Richvale, Calif., U.S.	216	39.30 N	121.45 W
Richview	209	38.23 N	89.11 W
Richville, N.Y., U.S.	202	44.25 N	75.23 E
Richville, Ohio, U.S.	204	40.45 N	81.27 W
Richwood, N.J., U.S.	275	39.43 N	75.10 W
Richwood, Ohio, U.S.	204	40.26 N	83.18 W
Richwood, W. Va., U.S.	178	38.14 N	80.32 W
Richwood Village	212	29.04 N	95.25 W
Rickenbacker Air Force Base ■	208	39.48 N	82.56 W
Rickenpass)(	54	47.14 N	9.02 E
Ricken Tunnel ◂[5]	54	47.12 N	9.05 E
Ricketts Glen State Park ♠	200	41.20 N	76.18 W
Ricketts Point ≻	264b	38.00 S	145.02 E
Rickleån ≃	26	64.05 N	20.56 E
Rickling	50	54.01 N	10.13 E
Rickmansworth	44	51.39 N	0.29 W
Rico	190	37.41 N	108.02 W
Ricoa ≃	231s	11.30 N	69.12 W
Ricobayo, Embalse de ⊜[1]	34	41.30 N	5.55 W
Ricupe	142	14.37 S	21.25 E
Ridā'	134	14.38 N	44.54 E
Ridanna (Ridnaun)	58	46.55 N	11.15 E
Riddarhyttan	40	59.48 N	15.33 E
Ridderkerk	48	51.52 N	4.36 E
Riddes	54	46.10 N	7.13 E
Riddle	192	42.57 N	123.22 W
Riddle Mountain ∧	192	43.07 N	118.30 W
Riddlesburg	204	40.10 N	78.15 W
Riddlewood	275	39.54 N	75.26 W
Riddon, Loch ⊂	42	55.58 N	5.12 W
Rideau ≃	202	45.27 N	75.42 W
Ridge, Eng., U.K.	250	51.41 N	0.15 W
Ridge, N.Y., U.S.	197	40.54 N	72.53 W
Ridge, Tex., U.S.	212	31.09 N	96.19 W
Ridge Acres	266	40.41 N	74.32 W
Ridgecrest, Calif., U.S.	194	35.38 N	117.36 W
Ridgecrest, Wash., U.S.	214	47.45 N	122.21 W
Ridgedale	174	53.04 N	104.09 W
Ridge Farm	184	39.54 N	87.39 W
Ridgefield, Conn., U.S.	197	41.17 N	73.30 W
Ridgefield, Ill., U.S.	206	42.16 N	88.22 W
Ridgefield, N.J., U.S.	200	40.50 N	74.00 W
Ridgefield, Wash., U.S.	214	45.49 N	122.45 W
Ridgefield Park	266	40.51 N	74.01 W
Ridgeland	182	32.29 N	80.59 W
Ridgely	184	36.16 N	89.29 W
Ridge Manor	210	28.31 N	82.10 W
Ridgemont	200	43.13 N	77.43 W
Ridgetown	204	42.26 N	81.54 W
Ridgeville, Man., Can.	174	49.04 N	97.01 W
Ridgeville, Ind., U.S.	206	40.18 N	85.02 W
Ridgeville, Md., U.S.	198	39.22 N	77.10 W
Ridgeville, S.C., U.S.	182	33.06 N	80.19 W
Ridgeville Corners	206	41.26 N	84.16 W
Ridgeway, Mich., U.S.	206	41.59 N	83.52 W
Ridgeway, Mo., U.S.	184	40.23 N	93.56 W
Ridgeway, N.J., U.S.	198	40.02 N	74.17 W
Ridgeway, Ohio, U.S.	206	40.31 N	83.34 W
Ridgeway, Tex., U.S.	212	33.11 N	95.46 W
Ridgeway, Wis., U.S.	180	43.01 N	90.01 W
Ridgeway Ditch ≊	269a	41.25 N	82.05 W
Ridgewood, Ill., U.S.	268	41.48 N	87.54 W
Ridgewood, N.J., U.S.	200	40.59 N	74.07 W
Ridgewood ◂[8]	266	40.42 N	73.53 W
Ridgewood Reservoir ⊜[1]	266	40.41 N	73.53 W
Ridgway, Colo., U.S.	190	38.09 N	107.46 W
Ridgway, Ill., U.S.	184	37.48 N	88.16 W
Ridgway, Pa., U.S.	204	41.26 N	78.44 W
Riding Mountain ∧	174	50.37 N	99.37 W
Riding Mountain National Park ♠	174	50.55 N	100.25 W
Ridley Creek ≃	275	39.51 N	75.21 W
Ridley Park	275	39.53 N	75.19 W
Ridnaun → Ridanna	58	46.55 N	11.15 E
Ridotta Capuzzo	136	31.35 N	25.03 E
Riebeek-Kasteel	148	33.23 S	18.53 E
Riebeek-Oos	148	33.10 S	26.10 E
Riebeek-Wes	148	33.21 S	18.52 E
Riecawr, Loch ⊜	42	55.13 N	4.27 W
Riedelbach	52	50.18 N	8.23 E
Rieder	50	51.44 N	11.10 E
Riederalp	54	46.23 N	8.01 E
Riedern	52	49.40 N	9.23 E
Ried im Innkreis	58	48.13 N	13.30 E
Ried im Oberinntal	54	47.03 N	10.39 E
Riedisheim	54	47.45 N	7.22 E
Riedlingen	54	48.09 N	9.28 E
Riegel	54	48.09 N	7.45 E
Riegelsville, N.J., U.S.	200	40.36 N	75.11 W
Riegelsville, Pa., U.S.	198	40.36 N	75.12 W
Riegersdorf	58	46.33 N	13.47 E
Riehen	54	47.35 N	7.39 E
Rieka → Rijeka	36	45.20 N	14.27 E
Rielasingen	54	47.44 N	8.50 E
Riemke ◂[8]	253	51.30 N	7.13 E
Riemst	52	50.48 N	5.36 E
Rieneck	52	50.05 N	9.38 E
Rienza (Rienz) ≃	58	46.43 N	11.39 E
Rienzi	184	34.46 N	88.38 W
Riesa	50	51.18 N	13.17 E
Riesco, Isla I	244	53.00 S	72.30 W
Rieseby	41	54.32 N	9.48 E
Riesel	212	31.28 N	96.56 W
Riesenbeck	48	52.16 N	7.37 E
Riesenburg → Prabuty	30	53.46 N	19.10 E
Riese Pio X	58	45.44 N	11.55 E
Riesi	36	37.17 N	14.05 E
Riestedt	50	51.29 N	11.21 E
Riet ≃	148	29.00 S	23.54 E
Rietavas	66	55.44 N	21.56 E
Rietberg	48	51.47 N	8.25 E
Rietbron	148	32.54 S	23.10 E
Rietfontein, Namibia	146	21.58 S	20.58 E
Rietfontein, S. Afr.	148	26.44 S	20.01 E
Riethuiskraal	148	34.20 S	21.22 E
Rieti	60	42.24 N	12.51 E
Rieti □[4]	60	42.18 N	12.52 E
Rietschen	50	51.23 N	14.47 E
Rietspruit ≃	263d	26.06 S	27.39 E
Rietvlei	148	30.29 S	29.51 E
Rietzer See ⊜	50	52.22 N	12.39 E
Riez	56	43.49 N	6.06 E
Riezlern	54	47.21 N	10.11 E
Rif Ѧ	138	35.00 N	4.00 W
Rifflart	263b	4.25 S	15.21 E
Rifiano (Riffian)	58	46.42 N	11.11 E
Rifle	190	39.32 N	107.47 W
Rifle ≃	180	44.00 N	83.45 W
Rifstangi ≻	24a	66.35 N	16.10 W
Rifton	200	41.50 N	74.03 W
Rift Valley □[4]	144	0.30 N	36.00 E
Rift Valley ∨	10	3.00 S	29.00 E
Rīga, S.S.S.R.	66	56.57 N	24.06 E
Riga, S.S.S.R.	78	56.36 N	106.17 E
Riga, Mich., U.S.	206	41.49 N	83.50 W
Riga, Gulf of → Rižskij Zaliv ⊂	66	57.30 N	23.35 E
Riga, Mount ∧	152	21.59 S	116.25 E
Rigacikun	140	10.40 N	7.28 E
Rigaih	104	4.40 N	95.34 E
Rīgān	118	28.37 N	58.58 E
Rīgas Jūras Līcis → Rižskij Zaliv ⊂	66	57.30 N	23.35 E
Rigaud	196	45.29 N	74.18 W
Rigaud ≃	196	45.29 N	74.18 W
Rigby	192	43.40 N	111.55 W
Rīgestān ◂[1]	118	31.00 N	65.00 E
Riggins	192	45.25 N	116.19 W
Riggisberg	54	46.48 N	7.29 E
Riggston	209	39.42 N	90.25 W
Righedo, Passo del)(	58	44.27 N	9.55 E
Rigi ∧	54	47.05 N	8.30 E
Rignano Flaminio	60	42.12 N	12.29 E
Rignano Garganico	60	41.40 N	15.35 E
Rignano sull'Arno	60	43.43 N	11.27 E
Rigney	54	47.23 N	6.11 E
Rigney Bluff	200	43.19 N	77.38 W
Rigny-Ussé	46	47.15 N	0.18 E
Rigo	154	9.47 S	147.34 E
Rigolet	166	54.20 N	58.35 W
Rig-Rig	136	14.16 N	14.21 E
Riguldi	66	59.08 N	23.33 E
Rīḥ, Jazīrat ar- I	130	18.10 N	38.27 E
Riḥāb	122	32.19 N	36.06 E
Rihand ≃	114	24.33 N	82.59 E
Rihand Dam ◂[6]	114	24.05 N	82.45 E
Rihand Reservoir ◂[6]	110	24.05 N	82.45 E
Riihimäki	26	60.45 N	24.46 E
Riiser-Larsen Peninsula ≻[1]	9	68.55 S	34.00 E
Rijau	140	11.07 N	5.14 E
Riječki Zaljev ⊂	36	45.15 N	14.25 E
Rijeka	36	45.20 N	14.27 E
Rijen	48	51.35 N	4.55 E
Rijkevorsel	52	51.21 N	4.46 E
Rijksdorp	48	52.09 N	4.25 E
Rijn → Rhine ≃	30	51.52 N	6.02 E
Rijnsburg	48	52.12 N	4.27 E
Rijssel → Lille	46	50.38 N	3.04 E
Rijssen	48	52.18 N	6.30 E
Rijswijk	48	52.04 N	4.20 E
Rikaze	110	29.17 N	88.53 E
Rike	134	10.42 N	39.55 E
Rikers Island I	266	40.47 N	73.53 W
Rikers Island Channel ⋓	266	40.47 N	73.52 W
Rikkavesi ⊜	26	62.50 N	28.44 E
Riksgränsen	24	68.24 N	18.12 E
Rikuchūkaigan-kokuritsu-kōen ♠	82	39.25 N	141.57 E
Rikujō-jieitai-asahikawa-chūtonchi ■	82a	43.49 N	142.25 E
Rikujō-jieitai-chitose-chūtonchi ■	82a	42.46 N	141.40 E
Rikujō-jieitai-fukuoka-chūtonchi ■	86	33.32 N	130.28 E
Rikujō-jieitai-kaitaichi-chūtonchi ■	86	34.21 N	132.32 E
Rikujō-jieitai-kengun-chūtonchi ■	82	32.46 N	130.45 E
Rikujō-jieitai-sōmahara-chūtonchi ■	84	36.23 N	139.58 E
Rikuzen-takata	82	39.01 N	141.38 E
Rila Ѧ	38	42.08 N	23.33 E
Riley	188	39.18 N	96.50 W
Riley Creek ≃	206	41.02 N	84.00 W
Riley Lake ⊜	202	44.50 N	79.11 W
Rileys Range Ѧ	160	34.21 S	150.10 E
Rillieux	56	45.49 N	4.54 E
Rillington	42	54.09 N	0.42 W
Rillito	190	32.25 N	111.09 W
Rillton	204	40.17 N	79.44 W
Rilly-la-Montagne	46	49.10 N	4.03 E
Rilski manastir Ʊ[1]	38	42.08 N	23.20 E
Rima ≃	140	13.04 N	5.10 E
Rímac	276d	12.03 S	77.03 W
Rímac ≃	238	12.02 S	77.09 W
Rimachi, Lago ⊜	236	4.25 S	76.43 W
Rimāḥ, Jabal ar- ∧	122	32.19 N	36.52 E
Rima San Giuseppe	56	45.52 N	8.00 E
Rimatara I	14	22.38 S	152.51 W
Rimavská Sobota	30	48.23 N	20.02 E
Rimbey	172	52.38 N	114.14 W
Rimbo	40	59.45 N	18.22 E
Rimé, Ouadi ∨	136	14.02 N	18.03 E
Rimersburg	204	41.02 N	79.30 W
Rimforsa	26	58.08 N	15.40 E
Rimi	140	12.58 N	7.43 E
Rimini	60	44.04 N	12.34 E
Rîmna ≃	38	45.39 N	27.19 E

≃ River	Fluss	Río	Rivière	Rio
≊ Canal	Kanal	Canal	Canal	Canal
⌊ Waterfall, Rapids	Wasserfall, Stromschnellen	Cascada, Rápidos	Chute d'eau, Rapides	Cascata, Rápidos
⋓ Strait	Meeresstrasse	Estrecho	Détroit	Estreito
⊂ Bay, Gulf	Bucht, Golf	Bahía, Golfo	Baie, Golfe	Baía, Golfo
⊜ Lake, Lakes	See, Seen	Lago, Lagos	Lac, Lacs	Lago, Lagos
≡ Swamp	Sumpf	Pantano	Marais	Pântano
⩍ Ice Features, Glacier	Eis- und Gletscherformen	Accidentes Glaciales	Formes glaciaires	Acidentes Glaciares
⍑ Other Hydrographic Features	Andere Hydrographische Objekte	Otros Elementos Hidrográficos	Autres données hydrographiques	Outros Elementos Hidrográficos

✢ Submarine Features	Untermeerische Objekte	Accidentes Submarinos	Formes de relief sous-marin	Acidentes Submarinos
□ Political Unit	Politische Einheit	Unidad Politica	Entité politique	Unidade Política
Ʊ Cultural Institution	Kulturelle Institution	Institución Cultural	Institution culturelle	Instituição Cultural
⊥ Historical Site	Historische Stätte	Sitio Histórico	Site historique	Sitio Histórico
♠ Recreational Site	Erholungs- und Ferienort	Sitio de Recreo	Centre de loisirs	Sítio de Lazer
⊠ Airport	Flughafen	Aeropuerto	Aéroport	Aeroporto
■ Military Installation	Militäranlage	Instalación Militar	Installation militaire	Instalação Militar
◂ Miscellaneous	Verschiedenes	Misceláneo	Divers	Miscelânea

ENGLISH / DEUTSCH — Name · Page · Lat.°′ · Long.°′ / Name · Seite · Breite°′ · Länge°′ E=Ost

Rîmnicu-Sărat 38 45.23 N 27.03 E
Rîmnicu-Vîlcea 38 45.06 N 24.22 E
Rimo Glacier ⊓ 113 35.25 N 77.30 E
Rimogne 52 49.50 N 4.33 E
Rimouski 176 48.26 N 68.33 W
Rimouski ≃ 176 48.27 N 68.32 W
Rimouski, Parc de ♦ 176 48.07 N 68.10 W
Rimpar 52 49.51 N 9.57 E
Rimrock Lake ⊜[1] 214 46.38 N 121.12 W
Rimsko-Korsakovka 70 51.34 N 48.31 E
Rin → Rhine ≃ 30 51.52 N 6.02 E
Rinca 105b 8.37 S 119.48 E
Rinca, Pulau I 105b 8.41 S 119.42 E
Rinčinlchümbe 78 51.07 N 99.40 E
Rincón, C.R. 226 8.42 N 83.29 W
Rincón, Cuba 276b 22.57 N 82.25 W
Rincon, Ned. Ant. 231s 12.15 N 68.20 W
Rincón, P.R. 230m 18.20 N 67.15 W
Rincon, Ga., U.S. 182 32.18 N 81.14 W
Rincon, N. Mex., U.S. 190 32.40 N 107.04 W
Rincón, Bahía de C 230m 17.58 N 66.20 W
Rinconada, Arg. 242 22.26 S 66.10 W
Rinconada, Méx. 186 25.42 N 100.43 W
Rinconada, Hipódromo de la ♦ 276c 10.26 N 66.56 W
Rincón del Ocote, Cerro ∧ 226 13.36 N 87.10 W
Rincón de Romos 224 22.14 N 102.18 W
Rincón de Tamayo 224 20.25 N 100.45 W
Rincon Indian Reservation ◆[4] 218 33.15 N 116.57 W
Rincon Valley 216 38.28 N 122.39 W
Rindal 26 63.03 N 9.13 E
Ringe 41 55.14 N 10.29 E
Ringebu 26 61.31 N 10.10 E
Ringenwalde 50 53.03 N 13.42 E
Ringertown 269b 40.25 N 79.36 W
Ringford 42 54.54 N 4.03 W
Ringgau ◆[1] 52 51.04 N 10.04 E
Ringgit, Gunung ∧ 105a 7.43 S 113.50 E
Ringgold, Ga., U.S. 182 34.55 N 85.07 W
Ringgold, La., U.S. 184 32.20 N 93.17 W
Ringgold, Pa., U.S. 204 41.00 N 79.10 W
Ringgold Isles II 165g 16.15 S 179.25 W
Ringim 140 12.08 N 9.10 E
Ringkøbing 26 56.05 N 8.15 E
Ringkøbing □[6] 41 56.10 N 8.50 E
Ringkøbing Fjord C[2] 26 56.00 N 8.15 E
Ringlet 104 4.25 N 101.23 E
Ringling 186 34.10 N 97.36 W
Ringling Museums ♥ 210 27.23 N 82.34 W
Ringmer 44 50.53 N 0.04 E
Ringoes 198 40.26 N 74.52 W
Rings Island 273 42.49 N 70.52 W
Ringsjön ⊜ 41 55.52 N 13.32 E
Ringsted, Dan. 41 55.27 N 11.49 E
Ringsted, Iowa, U.S. 188 43.18 N 94.31 W
Ringtown 200 40.51 N 76.14 W
Rīngus 110 27.21 N 75.34 E
Ringvassøya I 24 69.55 N 19.15 E
Ringwood, Austl. 159 37.49 S 145.14 E
Ringwood, Eng., U.K. 44 50.51 N 1.47 W
Ringwood, N.J., U.S. 200 41.08 N 74.16 W
Ringwood Manor ⊥ 266 41.08 N 74.15 W
Ringwood North 264b 37.48 S 145.14 E
Ringwood State Park ♦ 200 41.08 N 74.16 W
Riñihue 244 39.49 S 72.27 W
Riñihue, Lago ⊜ 244 39.50 S 72.18 W
Rinjani, Gunung ∧ 105b 8.24 S 116.28 E
Rinkenæs 41 54.54 N 9.34 E
Rinkerode 48 51.50 N 7.41 E
Rinns of Islay ⋀ 42 55.45 N 6.25 W
Rinns Point ≻ 28 55.40 N 6.30 W
Rinnthal 52 49.13 N 7.55 E
Rinsumageest 48 53.18 N 5.57 E
Rinteln 48 52.11 N 9.04 E
Rinxent 46 50.48 N 1.44 E
Rio, Fla., U.S. 210 27.15 N 80.14 W
Rio, Wis., U.S. 180 43.27 N 89.14 W
Rio Acima 246 23.17 S 46.32 W
Río Ariguaisa 236 9.35 N 72.40 W
Rio Azul 242 25.43 S 50.47 W
Río Balsas 224 17.59 N 99.47 W
Riobamba 236 1.40 S 78.38 W
Río Benito 142 1.35 N 9.37 E
Río Blanco, Chile 242 32.55 S 70.19 W
Río Blanco (Tenango de Río Blanco), Méx. 224 18.50 N 97.09 W
Rio Bonito 246 22.43 S 42.37 W
Rio Bonito ◆[8] 277b 23.43 S 46.41 W
Rio Branco, Bra. 238 9.58 S 67.48 W
Río Branco, Ur. 242 32.34 S 53.25 W
Río Bravo, Méx. 186 28.17 N 100.55 W
Río Bravo, Méx. 222 25.59 N 98.06 W
Rio Brilhante 245 21.48 S 54.33 W
Río Bueno 244 40.19 S 72.58 W
Río Caribe 236 10.42 N 63.07 W
Rio Casca 245 20.13 S 42.39 W
Río Cauto 230p 20.33 N 76.55 W
Río Ceballos 242 31.10 S 64.20 W
Río Chico 244 41.43 S 70.30 W
Rio Claro, Bra. 245 22.24 S 47.33 W
Rio Claro, Bra. 246 22.43 S 44.09 W
Rio Claro, Trin. 231r 10.18 N 61.11 W
Rio Claro, Represa do ⊜[1] 246 23.39 S 45.54 W
Río Colorado 242 39.01 S 64.05 W
Rio Comprido ◆[8] 277a 22.55 S 43.12 W
Río Cuarto 242 33.08 S 64.21 W
Rio da Conceição 240 11.24 S 46.54 W
Rio das Antas 242 26.55 S 51.04 W
Rio das Flores 246 22.10 S 43.35 W
Rio das Pedras 146 23.12 S 35.23 E
Rio de Contas 245 13.36 S 41.48 W
Rio de Janeiro 246; 277a 22.54 S 43.14 W
Rio de Janeiro □[3] 245 22.00 S 42.30 W
Rio de Janeiro □[7] 277a 22.55 S 43.30 W
Río de Jesús 226 7.59 N 81.10 W
Río de las Playas 224 17.51 N 94.02 W
Rio Dell 194 40.30 N 124.07 W
Rio-del-Rey C[1] 142 4.31 N 8.45 E
Rio de Mouro 256c 38.46 N 9.20 W
Río de Oro 236 8.17 N 73.23 W
Río de Oro, Bahía de C 138 23.45 N 15.47 W
Río Deseado, Valle del ∨ 244 46.42 S 69.00 W
Rio d'Oeste 242 27.12 S 49.48 W
Rio do Prado 245 16.35 S 40.34 W
Rio do Sul 242 27.13 S 49.39 W
Rio d'Ouro, Bra. 246 22.51 S 42.59 W
Rio d'Ouro, Bra. 277a 22.39 S 43.32 W
Rio Espera 245 20.51 S 43.29 W
Rio Fortuna 242 28.06 S 49.07 W
Río Gallegos 244 51.38 S 69.13 W
Río Grande, Arg. 244 53.47 S 67.42 W
Rio Grande, Bra. 242 32.02 S 52.05 W
Río Grande, Méx. 224 15.59 N 97.27 W
Río Grande, Méx. 224 23.50 N 103.02 W
Río Grande, Nic. 226 12.54 N 83.32 W
Río Grande, Pan. 226 8.37 N 81.17 W
Río Grande, P.R. 230m 18.23 N 65.50 W
Rio Grande, N.J., U.S. 198 39.01 N 74.53 W
Río Grande, Ven. 276c 10.35 N 66.57 W
Rio Grande, Barragem do ◆[6] 277b 23.42 S 46.40 W
Rio Grande, Ponte do ◆[5] 277b 23.46 S 46.31 W
Rio Grande, Reservatório do ⊜[1] 246 23.47 S 46.37 W
Rio Grande City 186 26.23 N 98.49 W
Rio Grande do Norte □[3] 240 5.45 S 36.00 W
Rio Grande do Sul → Rio Grande 242 32.02 S 52.05 W
Rio Grande do Sul □[3] 242 30.00 S 54.00 W
Rio Grande Ridge ⟡[3] 18 31.00 S 35.00 W
Riograndina 246 22.11 S 42.30 W
Ríohacha 236 11.33 N 72.55 W
Río Hato 226 8.23 N 80.10 W
Río Hondo, Méx. 276a 19.25 N 99.16 W
Rio Hondo, Tex., U.S. 186 26.14 N 97.35 W
Rioja 238 6.05 S 77.09 W
Río Jueyes 230m 18.01 N 66.20 W
Riola 58 44.16 N 11.04 E
Río Lagartos 222 21.36 N 88.10 W
Riolândia 245 19.59 S 49.40 W
Rio Largo 240 9.29 S 35.51 W
Rio Linda 216 38.41 N 121.27 W
Riolo Terme 60 44.16 N 11.43 E
Río Luján 248 34.17 S 58.54 W
Riom 32 45.54 N 3.07 E
Riomaggiore 56 44.06 N 9.44 E
Rio Marina 60 42.49 N 10.25 E
Río Mayo 244 45.41 S 70.16 W
Río Mulato 238 19.42 S 66.47 W
Río Muni □[4] 142 1.30 N 10.30 E
Rional Reef ⟡[2] 14 17.00 N 177.50 E
Riondel 172 49.46 N 116.52 W
Rio Negrinho 242 26.15 S 49.31 W
Rio Negro, Bra. 242 26.06 S 49.48 W
Rio Negro, Bra. 245 19.27 S 54.58 W
Río Negro, Chile 244 40.47 S 73.14 W
Ríonegro, Col. 236 6.09 N 75.22 W
Ríonegro, Col. 236 7.16 N 73.09 W
Río Negro □[4] 244 40.00 S 67.00 W
Río Negro, Embalse del ⊜[1] 242 32.45 S 56.00 W
Rio Negro, Pantanal do ☷ 238 19.00 S 56.00 W
Rionero in Vulture 36 40.56 N 15.41 E
Rionero Sannitico 60 41.42 N 14.08 E
Rioni ≃ 74 42.08 N 41.39 E
Rio Novo 246 21.29 S 43.08 W
Rio Novo do Sul 245 20.52 S 40.56 W
Riópar 34 38.30 N 2.27 W
Rio Pardo 242 29.59 S 52.22 W
Rio Pardo de Minas 245 15.37 S 42.33 W
Rio Pequeno, Reservatório do ⊜[1] 277b 23.46 S 46.30 W
Río Pico 244 44.13 S 71.21 W
Río Piedras, Arg. 242 25.18 S 64.54 W
Río Piedras, P.R. 230m 18.24 N 66.03 W
Río Pilcomayo, Parque Nacional ♦ 242 25.10 S 58.00 W
Rio Piracicaba 245 19.55 S 43.11 W
Rio Pomba 246 21.17 S 43.11 W
Rio Prêto, Bra. 246 22.06 S 43.50 W
Rio Prêto, Bra. 246 22.48 S 45.46 W
Rio Prêto → São José do Rio Prêto, Bra.
Rio Real 246 22.10 S 42.57 W
Rio Real 240 11.28 S 37.56 W
Rio Saliceto 58 44.49 N 10.49 E
Río San Juan □[5] 226 11.10 N 84.30 W
Rio Sêco, Bra. 246 22.46 S 42.40 W
Río Seco, Chile 238 21.02 S 70.10 W
Río Segundo 242 31.40 S 63.55 W
Rio Sorocaba, Represa do ⊜[1] 246 23.37 S 47.16 W
Ríosucio, Col. 236 7.27 N 77.07 W
Ríosucio, Col. 236 5.25 N 75.42 W
Río Tercero 242 32.11 S 64.06 W
Rio Tinto 240 6.48 S 35.05 W
Riotord 56 45.14 N 4.24 E
Rio Tuba 106 8.30 N 117.25 E
Riou, Île de I 56 43.11 N 5.24 E
Rioveggio 58 44.17 N 11.14 E
Rio Verde, Bra. 245 17.43 S 50.56 W
Ríoverde, Méx. 224 21.56 N 99.59 W
Rio Verde de Mato Grosso 245 18.56 S 54.52 W
Rio Vermelho 245 18.18 S 43.00 W
Rio Vista, Calif., U.S. 216 38.10 N 121.42 W
Rio Vista, Tex., U.S. 212 32.14 N 97.23 W
Rioz 54 47.25 N 6.04 E
Riozinho ≃, Bra. 236 2.55 S 67.07 W
Riozinho ≃, Bra. 240 10.22 S 49.50 W
Riozinho ≃, Bra. 240 8.25 S 45.43 W
Říp ∧ 50 50.24 N 14.18 E
Ripalti, Punta dei ≻ 60 42.42 N 10.25 E
Ripatransone 60 43.00 N 13.46 E
Ripley, Eng., U.K. 44 53.03 N 1.24 W
Ripley, Eng., U.K. 250 51.18 N 0.29 W
Ripley, Ill., U.S. 209 40.01 N 90.38 W
Ripley, Ind., U.S. 206 41.06 N 86.39 W
Ripley, Miss., U.S. 184 34.44 N 88.57 W
Ripley, N.Y., U.S. 204 42.16 N 79.43 W
Ripley, Ohio, U.S. 208 38.45 N 83.51 W
Ripley, Tenn., U.S. 184 35.45 N 89.32 W
Ripley, W. Va., U.S. 178 38.49 N 81.43 W
Ripley □[6] 208 39.04 N 85.15 W
Ripoll 34 42.12 N 2.12 E
Ripoll ≃ 256d 41.29 N 2.12 E
Ripollet 256d 41.30 N 2.10 E
Ripon, Qué., Can. 196 45.47 N 75.06 W
Ripon, Eng., U.K. 42 54.08 N 1.31 W
Ripon, Calif., U.S. 216 37.44 N 121.07 W
Ripon, Wis., U.S. 180 43.51 N 88.50 W
Riposto 36 37.45 N 15.12 E
Rippling Ridge 274b 39.11 N 76.37 W
Ripponden 42 53.41 N 1.57 W
Rippowam ≃ 266 41.03 N 73.33 W
Riquewihr 54 48.10 N 7.18 E
Ririba, Laga ≃ 144 3.34 N 37.15 E
Riri Bāzār 114 27.57 N 83.26 E
Ririe 192 43.38 N 111.46 W
Risālpur Cantonment 113 34.04 N 72.00 E
Risaralda □[5] 236 5.00 N 76.00 W
Risasi 144 0.25 S 25.44 E
Risbäck 26 64.42 N 15.32 E
Risca 44 51.37 N 3.07 W
Rischenau 48 51.53 N 9.17 E
Risción, Punta de la ≻ 222 25.10 N 108.22 W
Riscle 32 43.40 N 0.05 W
Rī Shahr 118 28.55 N 50.50 E
Rishīkesh 114 30.07 N 78.42 E
Rishiri-suidō)(82a 45.10 N 141.25 E
Rishiri-tō I 82a 45.11 N 141.15 E
Rishiri-zan ∧ 82a 45.11 N 141.15 E
Rishmayyā 122 33.44 N 35.36 E
Rishon leẒiyyon 122 31.58 N 34.48 E
Rishpon 122 32.12 N 34.49 E
Rishra 262b 22.43 N 88.21 E
Rishrāsh, Wādī ∨ 132 29.29 N 31.16 E
Rishton 252 53.46 N 2.25 W
Rishworth 252 53.40 N 1.57 W
Rishworth Moor ◆[3] 252 53.39 N 2.01 W
Risinge 40 58.42 N 15.51 E
Rising Star 186 32.06 N 98.58 W
Rising Sun, Ind., U.S. 208 38.57 N 84.51 W
Rising Sun, Md., U.S. 178 39.42 N 76.04 W
Risingsun, Ohio, U.S. 204 41.16 N 83.25 W
Risle ≃ 46 49.26 N 0.23 E
Risnjak ∧ 36 45.26 N 14.37 E
Rîşnov 38 45.36 N 25.28 E
Risø 41 55.42 N 12.06 E
Rison, Ark., U.S. 184 33.58 N 92.11 W
Rison, Md., U.S. 198 38.33 N 77.11 W
Risør 26 58.43 N 9.14 E
Ris-Orangis 46 48.39 N 2.25 E
Riss ≃ 54 48.17 N 9.49 E
Rissani 138 31.23 N 4.09 W
Risskov ◆[8] 41 56.11 N 10.14 E
Risstissen 54 48.16 N 9.49 E
Rişşū, Jabal ∧[2] 132 29.53 N 30.25 E
Risti 66 58.59 N 24.03 E
Ristiina 26 61.30 N 27.16 E
Ristijärvi 26 64.44 N 28.24 E
Ristinge 41 54.50 N 10.38 E
Ristna 66 58.56 N 22.05 E
Risum-lindholm 41 54.45 N 8.53 E
Rita Blanca Creek ≃ 186 35.40 N 102.29 W
Ritchie, S. Afr. 148 29.02 S 24.38 E
Ritchie, Md., U.S. 274c 38.52 N 76.52 W
Ritchie Branch ≃ 274c 38.53 N 76.52 W
Rithāla ◆[8] 262a 28.43 N 77.06 E
Ritidian Point ≻ 164p 13.39 N 144.51 E
Ritscher Upland ⋀[1] 9 73.20 S 9.30 W
Ritsumeikan University ♥[2] 260 35.01 N 135.46 E
Ritsurin-kōen ♦ 86 34.21 N 134.02 E
Ritta Island I 210 26.44 N 80.48 W
Ritter, Mount ∧ 216 37.42 N 119.12 W
Ritterhude 48 53.11 N 8.45 E
Rittersgrün 50 50.29 N 12.47 E
Rittman 204 40.58 N 81.47 W
Rittō 84 35.01 N 136.00 E
Ritzleben 50 52.50 N 11.21 E
Ritzville 192 47.08 N 118.23 W
Riu 110 28.19 N 95.03 E
Riva, It. 58 45.53 N 10.50 E
Riva, Md., U.S. 198 38.57 N 76.35 W
Rivadavia, Arg. 242 35.28 S 62.57 W
Rivadavia, Arg. 242 33.11 S 68.28 W
Rivadavia, Arg. 242 24.11 S 62.53 W
Rivadavia, Arg. 242 31.33 S 68.37 W
Rivadavia, Chile 242 29.58 S 70.34 W
Riva del Sole 60 42.46 N 10.52 E
Riva Deresi ≃ 257b 41.14 N 29.12 E
Riva di Tures (Rain) 58 46.57 N 12.04 E
Rivaköy 257b 41.13 N 29.12 E
Rivanazzano 56 44.56 N 9.01 E
Rivanna ≃ 182 37.45 N 78.10 W
Rivare 206 40.49 N 84.50 W
Rivarolo Canavese 56 45.19 N 7.43 E
Rivarolo Mantovano 58 45.04 N 10.26 E
Rivas 226 11.26 N 85.50 W
Rivas □[5] 226 11.25 N 85.50 W
Rivasdale 263d 26.17 S 27.56 E
Rīvash 118 35.26 N 58.26 E
Rivas-Vaciamadrid 256a 40.20 N 3.31 W
Riva Trigoso 56 44.16 N 9.26 E
Rive, Île de la I 263b 4.21 S 15.26 E
Rive d'Arcano 58 46.08 N 13.02 E
Rive-de-Gier 56 45.32 N 4.37 E
Rivera, Arg. 242 37.12 S 63.14 W
Rivera, Col. 236 2.47 N 75.15 W
Rivera, Ur. 242 30.54 S 55.31 W
Riverbank 216 37.44 N 120.56 W
River Cess 140 5.28 N 9.32 W
Riverdale, Calif., U.S. 216 36.26 N 119.52 W
Riverdale, Ill., U.S. 268 41.38 N 87.38 W
Riverdale, Md., U.S. 274c 38.58 N 76.55 W
Riverdale, N.J., U.S. 266 40.59 N 74.32 W
Riverdale, N. Dak., U.S. 188 47.30 N 101.22 W
Riverdale, Oreg., U.S. 214 45.27 N 122.41 W
Riverdale ◆[8] 266 40.54 N 73.54 W
Riverdale Park ♦ 265b 43.40 N 79.21 W
River Drive Park 202 44.08 N 79.31 W
River Edge, N.J., U.S. 266 40.56 N 74.02 W
River Edge, Ohio, U.S. 269a 41.25 N 81.51 W
River Falls, Ala., U.S. 184 31.21 N 86.33 W
River Falls, Wis., U.S. 180 44.52 N 92.38 W
River Forest 268 41.53 N 87.49 W
Rivergaro 56 44.55 N 9.36 E
River Grove 268 41.56 N 87.50 W
River Haven 206 41.05 N 85.02 W
Riverhead, Eng., U.K. 250 51.17 N 0.10 E
Riverhead, N.Y., U.S. 197 40.55 N 72.40 W
River Hébert 176 45.42 N 64.23 W
River Hill 269b 40.12 N 79.54 W
River Hills 206 43.12 N 87.57 W
Riverhurst 174 50.53 N 106.52 W
Riverina ◆[1] 156 35.30 S 145.30 E
River John 176 45.45 N 63.03 W
River Jordan 172 48.25 N 124.03 W
Riverlea 204 40.05 N 83.02 W
River Lea Navigation ≍ 250 51.32 N 0.02 W
River Meadow Brook ≃ 273 42.38 N 71.17 W
Rivero, Isla I 244 45.37 S 74.20 W
River of Ponds 176 50.32 N 57.24 W
River Pines, Calif., U.S. 216 38.33 N 120.45 W
River Pines, Mass., U.S. 197 42.34 N 71.17 W
River Plaza 198 40.21 N 74.05 W
River Road 192 44.03 N 123.05 W
River Rouge 206 42.16 N 83.08 W
River Rouge Park ♦ 271 42.22 N 83.15 W
Rivers 174 50.02 N 100.12 W
Rivers □[3] 140 4.30 N 6.30 E
Rivers, Lake of the ⊜ 174 49.45 N 105.45 W
Riversdale, N.Z. 162 45.54 S 168.45 E
Riversdale, S. Afr. 148 34.07 S 21.15 E
Riverside, Calif., U.S. 218 33.59 N 117.22 W
Riverside, Conn., U.S. 266 41.02 N 73.35 W
Riverside, Ill., U.S. 268 41.50 N 87.49 W
Riverside, Iowa, U.S. 180 41.29 N 91.35 W
Riverside, Mich., U.S. 206 42.11 N 86.23 W
Riverside, Mich., U.S. 206 42.17 N 84.29 W
Riverside, N.J., U.S. 198 40.02 N 74.58 W
Riverside, N.Y., U.S. 200 42.08 N 77.01 W
Riverside, N.Y., U.S. 200 42.55 N 73.40 W
Riverside, Pa., U.S. 200 40.57 N 76.38 W
Riverside, Tex., U.S. 212 30.57 N 95.24 W
Riverside □[6] 218 33.45 N 117.10 W
Riverside ◆[8] 271 42.20 N 82.57 W
Riverside International Raceway ♦ 218 33.57 N 117.17 W
Riverside Park ♦, Mich., U.S. 271 42.22 N 83.26 W
Riverside Park ♦, N.Y., U.S. 274a 42.57 N 78.54 W
Rivers Inlet 172 51.41 N 127.15 W
Rivers Inlet C 172 51.39 N 127.30 W
Riversleigh 156 19.02 S 138.44 E
Riverstone 160 33.40 S 150.52 E
Riverton, Austl. 158b 34.09 S 138.45 E
Riverton, Man., Can. 174 50.59 N 96.59 W
Riverton, N.Z. 162 46.21 S 168.01 E
Riverton, Ill., U.S. 209 39.51 N 89.33 W
Riverton, Nebr., U.S. 188 40.05 N 98.46 W
Riverton, N.J., U.S. 198 40.01 N 75.01 W
Riverton, Utah, U.S. 190 40.31 N 111.56 W
Riverton, Va., U.S. 178 38.57 N 78.12 W
Riverton, Wyo., U.S. 190 43.02 N 108.23 W
Riverton Heights, Wash., U.S. 192; 214 47.28 N 122.17 W
River Vale 266 40.59 N 74.01 W
River View, S. Afr. 148 28.27 S 32.10 E
River View, Ala., U.S. 184 32.47 N 85.09 W
Riverview, Fla., U.S. 210 27.52 N 82.20 W
Riverview, Mich., U.S. 206 42.11 N 83.10 W
Riverview Park ♦ 269b 40.29 N 80.01 W
Riverwood, Austl. 264a 33.57 S 151.03 E
Riverwood, Ind., U.S. 208 40.06 N 85.58 W
Riverwoods 268 42.10 N 87.54 W
Rives, Fr. 56 45.21 N 5.30 E
Rives, Tenn., U.S. 184 36.21 N 89.04 W
Rivesaltes 32 42.46 N 2.52 E
Rives Junction 206 42.23 N 84.28 W
Rive Sud, Canal de la ≍ 265a 45.25 N 73.41 W
Rivesville 178 39.32 N 80.07 W
Riviera, Ariz., U.S. 194 35.04 N 114.35 W
Riviera, Tex., U.S. 186 27.18 N 97.49 W
Riviera ∨ 54 46.15 N 8.58 E
Riviera Beach 210 26.47 N 80.04 W
Rivière-à-Claude 176 49.13 N 65.54 W
Rivière à Goyaves, Pointe de la ≻ 231o 16.11 N 61.35 W
Rivière-au-Tonnerre 176 50.16 N 64.47 W
Rivière-Bleue 176 47.26 N 69.03 W
Rivière-Bois-Clair 196 46.34 N 71.50 W
Rivière-de-la-Chaloupe 176 49.08 N 62.32 W
Rivière-du-Loup 176 47.50 N 69.32 W
Rivière-du-Moulin 176 48.26 N 71.02 W
Rivière du Rempart 147c 20.06 S 57.41 E
Rivière-Matane 176 48.39 N 67.20 W
Rivière-Mékinac 196 46.47 N 72.48 W
Rivière-Pentecôte 176 49.47 N 67.10 W
Rivière-Pilote 230e 14.29 N 60.54 W
Rivière-Salée 230e 14.32 N 60.59 W
Rivière-Trois-Pistoles 176 48.07 N 69.10 W
Riviersonderend 148 34.09 S 19.55 E
Rivignano 58 45.52 N 13.03 E
Rivington 252 53.37 N 2.34 W
Rivington Reservoirs ⊜[1] 252 53.37 N 2.34 W
Rivisondoli 60 41.52 N 14.04 E
Rivoli 56 45.04 N 7.31 E
Rivoli Bay C 156 37.32 S 140.04 E
Rivolta d'Adda 56 45.28 N 9.31 E
Rivoltella 58 45.27 N 10.33 E
Riwaka 162 41.05 S 173.00 E
Rixford 204 41.55 N 78.30 W
Rixheim 54 47.46 N 7.24 E
Riyadh → Ar-Riyāḍ 118 24.38 N 46.43 E
Rīyāq 122 33.51 N 36.00 E
Rīz 118 32.23 N 51.20 E
Rizal, Pil. 106 15.43 N 121.06 E
Rizal → Pasay, Pil. 259f 14.33 N 121.00 E
Rizal □[4], Pil. 106 14.35 N 121.50 E
Rizal □[4], Pil. 259f 14.35 N 121.03 E
Rizal Memorial Stadium ♦ 259f 14.34 N 120.59 E
Rize 120 41.02 N 40.31 E
Rize □[4] 120 40.55 N 40.55 E
Rīzeh, Kūh-e (Gora Reza) ∧ 118 37.47 N 58.05 E
Rizhao 88 35.27 N 119.29 E
Rizokárpason 120 35.36 N 34.23 E
Rižskij Vokzal ◆[5] 255b 55.48 N 37.38 E
Rižskij Zaliv C 66 57.30 N 23.35 E
Rizzuto, Capo ≻ 36 38.54 N 17.06 E
Rjukan 26 59.52 N 8.34 E
Roa, Esp. 34 41.42 N 3.55 W
Roa, N.Z. 162 42.21 S 171.23 E
Roa, Nor. 26 60.17 N 10.37 E
Roa, Zaïre 144 3.49 N 24.56 E
Roachdale 184 39.51 N 86.48 W
Roadhead 42 55.04 N 2.46 W
Roadknight, Point ≻ 159 38.26 S 144.11 E
Roadside 148 27.31 S 28.52 E
Road Town 230m 18.27 N 64.37 W
Roana 58 45.52 N 11.28 E
Roan Cliffs ⊥[4] 190 39.20 N 109.40 W
Roan Creek ≃ 190 39.20 N 108.13 W
Roan Fell ∧ 42 55.13 N 2.52 W
Roan Mountain 182 36.12 N 82.05 W
Roann 206 40.55 N 85.55 W
Roanne 32 46.02 N 4.04 E
Roanoke, Ala., U.S. 184 33.09 N 85.22 W
Roanoke, Ill., U.S. 180 40.48 N 89.12 W
Roanoke, Ind., U.S. 206 40.58 N 85.22 W
Roanoke, Tex., U.S. 212 32.60 N 97.14 W
Roanoke, Va., U.S. 182 37.16 N 79.57 W
Roanoke (Staunton) ≃ 182 35.56 N 76.43 W
Roanoke Island I 182 35.53 N 75.39 W
Roanoke Rapids 182 36.28 N 77.40 W
Roanoke Rapids Dam ◆[6] 182 36.24 N 77.40 W
Roanoke Rapids Lake ⊜[1] 182 36.30 N 77.45 W
Roans Prairie 212 30.35 N 95.57 W
Roaring ≃ 214 45.13 N 122.12 W
Roaring Branch 200 41.34 N 76.57 W
Roaring Brook ≃ 202 43.44 N 75.24 W
Roaring Fork ≃ 190 39.33 N 107.20 W
Roaring River Slough ≃ 272 38.05 N 121.55 W
Roaring Run ≃ 269b 40.33 N 79.32 W
Roaring Spring 204 40.20 N 78.24 W
Roaring Springs 186 33.54 N 100.52 W
Roatán 226 16.18 N 86.35 W
Roatán, Isla de I 226 16.23 N 86.30 W
Robâa Oued Yahia 36 36.05 N 9.35 E
Robāṭ 118 30.04 N 54.49 E
Robāṭ Karīm 118 35.28 N 51.05 E
Robbeneiland I 148 33.49 S 18.22 E
Robbers Cave State Park ♦ 186 35.01 N 95.27 W
Robbins, Calif., U.S. 216 38.53 N 121.42 W
Robbins, Ill., U.S. 206 41.39 N 87.42 W
Robbins, N.C., U.S. 182 35.26 N 79.35 W
Robbins, Tenn., U.S. 182 36.21 N 84.35 W
Robbins Airport ⊠ 273 42.34 N 70.58 W
Robbins Ditch ≍ 206 41.21 N 86.43 W
Robbins Island I 156 40.41 S 144.57 E
Robbins Pond ⊜ 273 42.00 N 70.55 W
Robbins Rest 266 40.39 N 73.10 W
Robbinston 178 45.05 N 67.07 W
Robbinsville, N.J., U.S. 198 40.13 N 74.37 W
Robbinsville, N.C., U.S. 182 35.19 N 83.48 W
Robbio 56 45.17 N 8.35 E
Robe 156 37.11 S 139.45 E
Robe ≃, Austl. 152 21.19 S 115.40 E
Robe ≃, Eire 28 53.37 N 9.16 W
Robe, Mount ∧ 156 31.40 S 141.20 E
Robecchetto con Induno 256b 45.32 N 8.46 E
Robecco d'Oglio 58 45.15 N 10.04 E
Robecco sul Naviglio 256b 45.26 N 8.53 E
Röbel 50 53.23 N 12.35 E
Robeline 184 31.41 N 93.18 W
Röberget ∧[2] 40 59.45 N 14.54 E
Robersonville 182 35.50 N 77.15 W
Robert, Havre du C 230e 14.40 N 60.55 W
Roberta 182 32.43 N 84.01 W
Roberta Mills 182 35.22 N 80.38 W
Robert College ♥[2] 257b 41.04 N 29.02 E
Robert E. Lee Memorial Park ♦ 274b 39.23 N 76.39 W
Robert-Espagne 52 48.45 N 5.02 E
Robert F. Kennedy Memorial Stadium ♦ 274c 38.53 N 76.58 W
Robert H. Treman State Park ♦ 200 42.24 N 76.35 W
Robert Lee 186 31.54 N 100.29 W
Robert Louis Stevenson Memorial State Park ♦ 216 38.40 N 122.36 W
Robert Louis Stevenson's Tomb ⊥ 165a 13.50 S 171.44 W
Robert McIlwaine National Park ♦ 144 17.55 S 30.50 E
Robert Morse College ♥[2] 269b 40.31 N 80.12 W
Robert Moses State Park ♦ 200 40.37 N 73.16 W
Robert Mueller Municipal Airport ⊠ 212 30.18 N 97.42 W
Roberto Payró 248 35.10 S 57.39 W
Robert Point ≻ 158a 32.31 S 115.42 E
Roberts, Idaho, U.S. 192 43.43 N 112.08 W
Roberts, Ill., U.S. 206 40.37 N 88.11 W
Roberts, Mont., U.S. 192 45.22 N 109.10 W
Roberts, Mount ∧ 161a 28.13 S 152.28 E
Roberts, Point ≻ 214 49.00 N 123.06 W
Robert's Arm 176 49.29 N 55.49 W
Robertsbridge 44 50.59 N 0.29 E
Roberts Canyon ∨ 270 34.11 N 117.54 W
Roberts Creek Mountain ∧ 194 39.52 N 116.18 W
Robertsdale, Ala., U.S. 184 30.33 N 87.43 W
Robertsdale, Pa., U.S. 204 40.11 N 78.07 W
Robertsfield 140 6.15 N 10.24 W
Robertsfors 26 64.11 N 20.51 E
Robertsganj 114 24.42 N 83.04 E
Robertsham ◆[8] 263d 26.15 S 28.00 E
Robertsholm 40 60.35 N 76.16 E
Robert S. Kerr Lake ⊜[1] 184 35.25 N 95.00 W
Roberts Mountain ∧ 170 60.03 N 166.16 W
Robertson, Austl. 160 34.35 S 150.35 E
Robertson, S. Afr. 148 33.46 S 19.50 E
Robertson □[6], Ky., U.S. 208 38.32 N 84.04 W
Robertson □[6], Tex., U.S. 212 31.00 N 96.30 W
Robertson, Lac ⊜ 176 51.00 N 59.10 W
Robertson Bay C 9 71.25 S 170.00 E
Robertson Range ⋀ 152 23.10 S 121.00 E
Robertsonville 196 46.09 N 71.13 W
Roberts Park 268 41.44 N 87.49 W
Roberts Peak ∧ 172 52.57 N 120.32 W
Robertsport 140 6.45 N 11.22 W
Robertstown 158b 34.00 S 139.05 E
Robertsville 204 40.46 N 81.11 W
Robertville 52 50.27 N 6.07 E
Robert Williams 142 12.51 S 15.33 E
Roberval 166 48.31 N 72.13 W
Robi 134 7.51 N 39.46 E
Robin Hood's Bay 42 54.25 N 0.33 W
Robins Air Force Base ■ 182 32.38 N 83.35 W
Robins Island I 197 40.58 N 72.28 W
Robinson, S. Afr. 263d 26.09 S 27.43 E
Robinson, Ill., U.S. 184 39.00 N 87.44 W
Robinson, Tex., U.S. 212 31.31 N 97.06 W
Robinson ≃ 154 16.03 S 137.16 E
Robinson Brook ≃ 273 43.02 N 71.13 W
Robinson Creek ≃ 216 38.16 N 119.15 W
Róbinson Crusoe, Isla (Isla Más A Tierra) I 234 33.38 S 78.52 W
Robinson Gorge National Park ♦ 156 25.15 S 149.10 E
Robinson Lake ⊜ 212 29.35 N 94.36 W
Robinson Pond ⊜ 273 42.48 N 71.23 W
Robinson Range ⋀ 152 25.45 S 119.00 E
Robinson Run ≃ 269b 40.23 N 80.06 W
Robinson Run, North Branch ≃ 269b 40.23 N 80.11 W
Robinsons 176 48.15 N 58.48 W
Robinvale 156 34.36 S 142.46 E
Robleda 34 40.23 N 6.36 W
Robledo 34 38.46 N 2.26 W
Roblin 174 51.14 N 101.21 W
Röblingen 50 51.28 N 11.40 E
Roboré 238 18.20 S 59.45 W
Röbrinken 40 58.36 N 15.53 E
Rob Roy Island I 165e 7.25 S 157.35 E
Robson, Mount ∧ 172 53.07 N 119.09 W
Robstown 186 27.47 N 97.40 W
Roby, Eng., U.K. 252 53.25 N 2.51 W
Roby, Ill., U.S. 209 39.44 N 89.24 W
Roby, Tex., U.S. 186 32.45 N 100.23 W
Roby Mill 252 53.34 N 2.44 W
Roca, Cabo da ≻ 34 38.47 N 9.30 W
Roçadas 142 16.43 S 15.01 E
Roca del Toro, Punta ≻ 190 31.19 N 113.43 W
Roçado 240 6.40 S 44.19 W
Rocafuerte 236 0.55 S 80.28 W
Roça Grande 246 21.36 S 42.58 W
Rocanville 174 50.24 N 101.43 W
Roca Partida, Isla I 222 19.01 N 112.02 W
Roca Partida, Punta ≻ 224 18.42 N 95.10 W
Rocas, Atol das I[1] 240 3.52 S 33.59 W
Roccacasale 60 42.07 N 13.53 E
Roccadaspide 36 40.26 N 15.12 E
Rocca di Cambio 60 42.14 N 13.29 E
Rocca di Mezzo 60 42.12 N 13.31 E
Rocca di Papa 60 41.46 N 12.42 E
Roccafluvione 60 42.51 N 13.29 E
Roccalbegna 60 42.47 N 11.30 E
Rocca Massima 60 41.41 N 12.55 E
Roccamonfina 60 41.17 N 13.59 E
Rocca Pia 60 41.56 N 13.59 E
Rocca Pietore 58 46.26 N 11.59 E
Roccaprebalza 58 44.31 N 9.57 E
Rocca Priora 257a 41.48 N 12.45 E
Roccaraso 60 41.51 N 14.05 E
Rocca San Casciano 60 44.03 N 11.50 E
Rocca Santa Maria 60 42.41 N 13.30 E
Roccasecca 60 41.33 N 13.40 E
Roccasecca dei Volsci 60 41.29 N 13.13 E
Roccastrada 60 43.00 N 11.10 E
Roccavione 56 44.19 N 7.29 E
Roccavivara 60 41.50 N 14.36 E
Rocchetta Sant'Antonio 60 41.06 N 15.27 E
Rocciamelone ∧ 56 45.12 N 7.05 E
Roch ≃ 42 53.34 N 2.18 W
Rocha, Bra. 246 21.28 S 45.49 W
Rocha, Ur. 242 34.29 S 54.20 W
Rocha da Gale, Barragem ◆[6] 34 37.42 N 7.35 W
Rocha Miranda ◆[8] 277a 22.52 S 43.22 W
Rocha Sobrinho 277a 22.47 S 43.25 W
Rochdale, Eng., U.K. 42 53.38 N 2.09 W
Rochdale, Mass., U.S. 197 42.12 N 71.54 W
Rochdale, N.Y., U.S. 200 41.43 N 73.50 W
Rochdale □[8] 252 53.37 N 2.08 W
Rochdale Canal (disused) ≍ 252 53.43 N 1.54 W
Roche 44 50.24 N 4.48 W
Rochebrune, Pic de ∧ 56 44.49 N 6.51 E
Rochechouart 32 45.50 N 0.50 E
Rochedinho, Bra. 238; 245 20.14 S 54.33 W
Rochedo 245 19.57 S 54.52 W
Rochedo de Minas 246 21.38 S 43.01 W
Rochefort, Bel. 52 50.10 N 5.13 E
Rochefort, Fr. 32 45.57 N 0.58 W
Rochefort-en-Yvelines 46 48.35 N 1.59 E
Rochefort-Montagne 32 45.41 N 2.48 E
Rochefort-sur-Nenon 54 47.07 N 5.34 E
Roche Harbor 214 48.36 N 123.09 W
Rochehaut 52 49.51 N 5.00 E
Roche-la-Molière 56 45.26 N 4.19 E
Roche-lez-Beaupré 54 47.17 N 6.07 E
Rochelle, Ga., U.S. 182 31.57 N 83.27 W
Rochelle, Ill., U.S. 206 41.56 N 89.04 W
Rochelle, Tex., U.S. 186 31.13 N 99.13 W
Rochelle Park 266 40.55 N 74.04 W
Rochemaure 56 44.35 N 4.42 E
Roche-Percée 174 49.03 N 102.45 W
Rochepot, Château de la ⊥ 54 46.57 N 4.40 E
Rochester, Austl. 156 36.22 S 144.42 E
Rochester, Eng., U.K. 42 55.16 N 2.16 W
Rochester, Eng., U.K. 44 51.24 N 0.30 E
Rochester, Ill., U.S. 209 39.45 N 89.32 W
Rochester, Ind., U.S. 206 41.04 N 86.13 W
Rochester, Mass., U.S. 197 41.44 N 70.49 W
Rochester, Mich., U.S. 204 42.41 N 83.08 W
Rochester, Minn., U.S. 180 44.02 N 92.29 W
Rochester, N.H., U.S. 178 43.18 N 70.59 W
Rochester, N.Y., U.S. 200 43.10 N 77.36 W
Rochester, Ohio, U.S. 204 41.07 N 82.18 W
Rochester, Pa., U.S. 204 40.43 N 80.17 W
Rochester, Tex., U.S. 186 33.19 N 99.51 W
Rochester, Wash., U.S. 214 46.49 N 123.06 W
Rochester, Wis., U.S. 206 42.45 N 88.14 W
Rochester City Airport ⊠ 250 51.21 N 0.30 E
Rochester Mills 204 40.49 N 78.59 W
Rochester-Monroe County Airport ⊠ 200 43.07 N 77.40 W
Rochester-Utica State Recreation Area ♦ 204 42.39 N 83.04 W
Rochetaillée 56 45.25 N 4.27 E
Rocheuses → Rocky Mountains ⋀ 16 48.00 N 116.00 W
Rochford 44 51.36 N 0.43 E
Rochford □[8] 250 51.36 N 0.39 E
Rochlitz 50 51.03 N 12.47 E
Rochon, Lacs ⊜ 196 46.43 N 75.14 W
Rock 180 46.04 N 87.10 W
Rock □[6] 206 42.41 N 89.05 W
Rock ≃, U.S. 180 41.29 N 90.37 W
Rock ≃, U.S. 188 43.05 N 96.27 W
Rockall I 22 57.35 N 13.48 W
Rockall Rise ⟡[3] 10 59.00 N 14.00 W
Rockanje 48 51.53 N 4.05 E
Rockaway, N.J., U.S. 200 40.54 N 74.31 W
Rockaway, Oreg., U.S. 214 45.37 N 123.57 W
Rockaway ≃ 200 40.51 N 74.21 W
Rockaway Inlet C 266 40.34 N 73.55 W
Rockaway Neck 266 40.51 N 74.21 W
Rockaway Park ◆[8] 266 40.35 N 73.50 W
Rockaway Point ◆[8] 266 40.33 N 73.55 W
Rockaway Point ≻ 266 40.33 N 73.56 W
Rockaways' Playland ♦ 266 40.35 N 73.49 W
Rockbank 264b 37.43 S 144.39 E
Rock Bay 172 50.20 N 125.29 W
Rockbridge 209 39.16 N 90.12 W
Rock Bridge State Park ♦ 209 38.53 N 92.19 W
Rock Brook ≃ 266 40.25 N 74.40 W
Rock Candy Mountain ∧ 214 47.01 N 123.07 W
Rockcastle ≃ 182 36.58 N 84.21 W
Rock City Falls 200 43.04 N 73.55 W
Rockcliffe Park 202 45.27 N 75.41 W
Rock Creek, B.C., Can. 172 49.06 N 118.58 W
Rock Creek, Ohio, U.S. 204 41.40 N 80.52 W
Rock Creek ≃, N.A. 192 48.25 N 107.05 W
Rock Creek ≃, U.S. 198 38.54 N 77.04 W
Rock Creek ≃, Calif., U.S. 216 37.55 N 120.58 W
Rock Creek ≃, Idaho, U.S. 192 42.39 N 113.01 W
Rock Creek ≃, Ill., U.S. 206 41.12 N 87.59 W
Rock Creek ≃, Ind., U.S. 206 40.42 N 86.35 W
Rock Creek ≃, Ind., U.S. 206 40.49 N 85.23 W
Rock Creek ≃, Mont., U.S. 192 45.31 N 108.49 W
Rock Creek ≃, Mont., U.S. 192 46.43 N 113.40 W
Rock Creek ≃, Nev., U.S. 194 40.39 N 116.54 W
Rock Creek ≃, Oreg., U.S. 192 45.34 N 120.25 W
Rock Creek ≃, Oreg., U.S. 192 42.39 N 119.08 W
Rock Creek ≃, Oreg., U.S. 214 45.51 N 123.12 W
Rock Creek ≃, S. Dak., U.S. 188 43.44 N 97.58 W
Rock Creek ≃, Utah, U.S. 190 40.17 N 110.30 W
Rock Creek ≃, Wash., U.S. 192 46.55 N 117.56 W
Rock Creek ≃, Wash., U.S. 192 45.42 N 120.29 W
Rock Creek ≃, Wyo., U.S. 190 41.54 N 106.08 W
Rock Creek Butte ∧ 192 44.49 N 118.07 W
Rock Creek Park ♦ 274c 38.58 N 77.03 W
Rock Cut State Park ♦ 206 42.20 N 89.00 W
Rockdale, Austl. 160 33.57 S 151.08 E
Rockdale, Ill., U.S. 206 41.30 N 88.06 W
Rockdale, Md., U.S. 274b 39.21 N 76.46 W
Rockdale, Pa., U.S. 275 39.53 N 75.26 W
Rockdale, Tex., U.S. 212 30.39 N 97.00 W
Rockdale, W. Va., U.S. 204 40.18 N 80.35 W
Rockefeller Center ♥ 266 40.45 N 74.00 W
Rockefeller Park ♦ 269a 41.32 N 81.38 W
Rockefeller Plateau ⋀[1] 9 80.00 S 135.00 W
Rockenhausen 52 49.38 N 7.49 E
Rockensüss 52 51.03 N 9.50 E
Rockfall 197 41.28 N 72.44 W
Rock Falls 180 41.47 N 89.41 W
Rock Ferry 252 53.22 N 3.00 W
Rockfield 206 40.39 N 86.34 W
Rock Flat 161b 36.21 S 149.12 E
Rockford, Ala., U.S. 184 32.53 N 86.13 W
Rockford, Ill., U.S. 206 42.17 N 89.06 W
Rockford, Ind., U.S. 208 38.59 N 85.54 W
Rockford, Iowa, U.S. 180 43.03 N 92.57 W
Rockford, Mich., U.S. 180 43.07 N 85.33 W
Rockford, Ohio, U.S. 206 40.42 N 84.39 W
Rockford, Tenn., U.S. 182 35.49 N 83.56 W
Rock Forest 196 45.20 N 71.59 W
Rockglen, Sask., Can. 174 49.10 N 105.57 W
Rock Glen, N.Y., U.S. 200 42.41 N 78.07 W
Rock Hall 178 39.08 N 76.14 W
Rockhammar 40 59.32 N 15.26 E
Rockhampton 156 23.23 S 150.31 E
Rockhampton Downs 152 18.57 S 135.01 E
Rock Hill, N.Y., U.S. 200 41.38 N 74.36 W
Rock Hill, S.C., U.S. 182 34.56 N 81.01 W
Rockhill Furnace 204 40.15 N 77.54 W
Rockingham, Austl. 158a 32.17 S 115.44 E
Rockingham, N.C., U.S. 182 34.56 N 79.46 W
Rockingham □[6] 197 42.50 N 71.15 W
Rockingham ⊥ 266 40.24 N 74.37 W
Rockingham Bay C 156 18.10 S 146.05 E
Rockingham Forest ◆[3] 44 52.30 N 0.37 W
Rockingham Park ♦ 273 42.45 N 71.14 W
Rock Island, Qué., Can. 196 45.01 N 72.06 W
Rock Island, Ill., U.S. 180 41.30 N 90.34 W
Rock Island, Tex., U.S. 212 29.32 N 96.35 W
Rocklake 188 48.47 N 99.15 W
Rock Lake ⊜, Man., Can. 174 49.11 N 99.12 W
Rock Lake ⊜, Ont., Can. 202 45.30 N 78.23 W
Rock Lake ⊜, Ill., U.S. 268 41.40 N 88.03 W
Rock Lake ⊜, Wis., U.S. 206 43.04 N 88.56 W
Rockland, Del., U.S. 275 39.48 N 75.34 W
Rockland, Idaho, U.S. 192 42.34 N 112.53 W
Rockland, Maine, U.S. 178 44.06 N 69.06 W
Rockland, Mass., U.S. 197 42.08 N 70.55 W
Rockland, Mich., U.S. 180 46.41 N 89.11 W
Rockland, N.Y., U.S. 200 41.58 N 74.54 W
Rockland □[6] 200 41.09 N 73.59 W
Rockland Lake 266 41.09 N 73.55 W
Rockland Lake ⊜ 266 41.08 N 73.55 W
Rockland Lake State Park ♦ 266 41.08 N 73.55 W
Rocklands Reservoir ⊜[1] 156 37.15 S 142.00 E
Rockledge, Fla., U.S. 210 28.20 N 80.43 W
Rockledge, Pa., U.S. 275 40.03 N 75.05 W

Symbols in the index entries represent the broad categories identified in the key at the right. Symbols with superior numbers (⋀[2]) identify subcategories (see complete key on page *I* · 26).

Kartensymbole in dem Registerverzeichnis stellen die rechts in Schlüssel erklärten Kategorien dar. Symbole mit hochgestellten Ziffern (⋀[2]) bezeichnen Unterabteilungen einer Kategorie (vgl. vollständiger Schlüssel auf Seite *I* · 26).

Los símbolos incluídos en el texto del índice representan las grandes categorías identificadas con la clave a la derecha. Los símbolos con numeros en su parte superior (⋀[2]) identifican las subcategorías (véase la clave completa en la página *I* · 26).

Les symboles de l'index représentent les catégories indiquées dans la légende à droite. Les symboles suivis d'un indice (⋀[2]) représentent des sous-catégories (voir légende complète à la page *I* · 26).

Os símbolos incluídos no texto do índice representam as grandes categorias identificadas com a chave à direita. Os símbolos com números em sua parte superior (⋀[2]) identificam as subcategorias (veja-se a chave completa à página *I* · 26).

	English	Deutsch	Español	Français	Português
∧	Mountain	Berg	Montaña	Montagne	Montanha
⋀	Mountains	Berge	Montañas	Montagnes	Montanhas
)(	Pass	Pass	Paso	Col	Passo
∨	Valley, Canyon	Tal, Cañon	Valle, Cañón	Vallée, Canyon	Vale, Canhão
⊻	Plain	Ebene	Llano	Plaine	Planície
≻	Cape	Kap	Cabo	Cap	Cabo
I	Island	Insel	Isla	Île	Ilha
II	Islands	Inseln	Islas	Îles	Ilhas
⊥	Other Topographic Features	Andere Topographische Objekte	Otros Elementos Topográficos	Autres données topographiques	Outros Elementos Topográficos

ESPAÑOL

Nombre	Página	Lat.°′	Long.°′ W=Oeste
Rockleigh	266	41.00 N	73.56 W
Rocklin	216	38.48 N	121.14 W
Rockmart	182	34.00 N	85.02 W
Rock Meadow Brook ≃	273	42.16 N	71.13 W
Rock Point	198	38.16 N	76.50 W
Rock Point ≻	165f	15.55 S	168.17 E
Rock Pond ⊜	273	42.44 N	71.00 W
Rockport, Ill., U.S.	209	39.32 N	91.00 W
Rockport, Ky., U.S.	184	37.20 N	86.59 W
Rockport, Maine, U.S.	178	44.11 N	69.06 W
Rockport, Mass., U.S.	197	42.39 N	70.36 W
Rock Port, Mo., U.S.	184	40.25 N	95.31 W
Rockport, Tex., U.S.	186	28.01 N	97.04 W
Rock Rapids	188	43.26 N	96.10 W
Rock River	190	41.44 N	105.58 W
Rock Run	198	39.59 N	75.50 W
Rock Run ≃	274c	38.58 N	77.11 W
Rock Sound	228	24.54 N	76.12 W
Rocksprings, Tex., U.S.	186	30.01 N	100.13 W
Rock Springs, Wyo., U.S.	190	41.35 N	109.13 W
Rockstone	236	5.59 N	58.33 W
Rock Stream	200	42.28 N	76.56 W
Rockton, Ill., U.S.	206	42.27 N	89.04 W
Rockton, Pa., U.S.	204	41.05 N	78.39 W
Rock Valley	188	43.12 N	96.18 W
Rockville, N.Z.	162	40.44 S	172.38 E
Rockville, Conn., U.S.	197	41.52 N	72.27 W
Rockville, Ind., U.S.	184	39.46 N	87.14 W
Rockville, Md., U.S.	274c	39.05 N	77.09 W
Rockville, Mass., U.S.	273	42.08 N	71.22 W
Rockville, Pa., U.S.	198	40.20 N	76.54 W
Rockville, R.I., U.S.	197	41.31 N	71.46 W
Rockville Centre	200	40.40 N	73.37 W
Rockwall	212	32.56 N	96.28 W
Rockwall □6	212	32.55 N	96.23 W
Rockwell, Iowa, U.S.	180	42.59 N	93.11 W
Rockwell, N.C., U.S.	182	35.33 N	80.25 W
Rockwell, Lake ⊜	204	41.12 N	81.19 W
Rockwell City	188	42.24 N	94.38 W
Rockwell International Corporation ♁3	270	33.52 N	117.51 W
Rockwood, Ont., Can.	202	43.37 N	80.08 W
Rockwood, Maine, U.S.	178	45.41 N	69.44 W
Rockwood, Mich., U.S.	206	42.10 N	83.15 W
Rockwood, Oreg., U.S.	214	45.31 N	122.28 W
Rockwood, Pa., U.S.	178	39.54 N	79.09 W
Rockwood, Tenn., U.S.	182	35.52 N	84.41 W
Rockwood Lake ⊜	266	41.06 N	73.38 W
Rockwood Lake Brook ≃	266	41.03 N	73.36 W
Rocky	186	35.09 N	99.04 W
Rocky ≃, Alta., Can.	172	53.08 N	117.59 W
Rocky ≃, Mich., U.S.	206	41.57 N	85.39 W
Rocky ≃, N.C., U.S.	182	35.37 N	79.09 W
Rocky ≃, Ohio, U.S.	204	41.30 N	81.49 W
Rocky, East Branch ≃	269a	41.24 N	81.53 W
Rocky, West Branch ≃	204	41.24 N	81.53 W
Rocky Arroyo V	186	32.32 N	104.21 W
Rocky Boys Indian Reservation ✦4	192	48.18 N	109.45 W
Rocky Branch ≃	274c	38.53 N	77.19 W
Rocky Comfort Creek ≃	182	32.59 N	82.25 W
Rocky Coulee V	192	47.10 N	119.16 W
Rocky Creek ≃	182	35.53 N	80.47 W
Rockyford, Alta., Can.	172	51.13 N	113.08 W
Rocky Ford, Colo., U.S.	188	38.03 N	103.43 W
Rocky Ford Creek ≃	206	41.19 N	83.37 W
Rocky Fork Lake ⊜	208	39.11 N	83.28 W
Rocky Fork State Park ♠	208	39.11 N	83.30 W
Rocky Gorge Reservoir ⊜1	198	39.07 N	77.54 W
Rocky Grove	204	41.25 N	79.49 W
Rocky Gully	152	34.30 S	116.48 E
Rocky Harbour	176	49.36 N	57.55 W
Rocky Harbour C	261d	22.20 N	114.19 E
Rocky Hill, Conn., U.S.	197	41.40 N	72.39 W
Rocky Hill, N.J., U.S.	266	40.24 N	74.38 W
Rocky Island Lake ⊜1	180	46.56 N	83.04 W
Rocky Lake ⊜	174	54.08 N	101.30 W
Rocky Mount, N.C., U.S.	182	35.56 N	77.48 W
Rocky Mount, Va., U.S.	182	37.00 N	79.54 W
Rocky Mountain ∧	192	47.49 N	112.49 W
Rocky Mountain House	172	52.22 N	114.55 W
Rocky Mountain National Park ♠	190	40.19 N	105.42 W
Rocky Mountains ∧∧	16	48.00 N	116.00 W
Rocky Point, N.Y., U.S.	197	40.57 N	72.56 W
Rocky Point, Wash., U.S.	214	47.35 N	122.41 W
Rocky Point ≻, Ba.	182	26.00 N	77.25 W
Rocky Point ≻, Namibia	146	19.03 S	12.30 E
Rocky Point ≻, Norf. I.	164c	29.03 S	167.55 E
Rocky Point ≻, Alaska, U.S.	170	64.25 N	163.10 W
Rocky Point ≻, Mass., U.S.	197	41.57 N	70.35 W
Rocky Point ≻, N.Y., U.S.	266	40.55 N	73.32 W
Rocky Ridge	204	41.32 N	83.13 W
Rocky Ridge ∧	272	37.48 N	122.03 W
Rocky River	204	41.30 N	81.40 W
Rocky River Reservation ♠	269a	41.27 N	81.50 W
Rocky Run ≃, N. Dak., U.S.	188	47.38 N	99.02 W
Rocky Run ≃, Pa., U.S.	275	39.54 N	75.28 W
Rocky Run ≃, Va., U.S.	274c	38.58 N	77.15 W
Rocky Saugeen ≃	202	44.13 N	80.53 W
Rocky Top ∧	192	44.47 N	122.17 W
Roclenge-sur-Geer	52	50.45 N	5.36 E
Rocosas, Montañas → Rocky Mountains ∧∧	16	48.00 N	116.00 W
Rocquencourt	251	48.50 N	2.07 E
Rocroi	46	49.55 N	4.31 E
Roda	182	36.58 N	82.50 W
Roda ≃	50	50.52 N	11.44 E
Rodach	52	50.20 N	10.46 E
Rodach ≃	52	50.08 N	10.52 E
Rodakovo	73	48.33 N	39.02 E
Rodalben	52	49.14 N	7.38 E
Rodalquilar	34	37.40 N	2.08 W
Rodas	230p	22.20 N	80.33 W
Rodas,, Isla de → Ródhos I	38	36.10 N	28.00 E
Rodaun ✦8	254b	48.08 N	16.16 E
Rødberg	26	60.16 N	8.58 E
Rødby	41	54.42 N	11.24 E
Rødbyhavn	41	54.39 N	11.21 E
Roddickton	176	50.52 N	56.08 W
Rødding	41	55.23 N	9.06 E
Rodeio	242	26.57 S	49.23 W
Rodeiro	246	21.12 S	42.52 W
Rødekro	41	55.04 N	9.21 E
Roden	48	53.07 N	6.26 E
Roden ≃	44	52.43 N	2.36 W
Rodenberg	48	52.18 N	9.21 E

FRANÇAIS

Nom	Page	Lat.°′	Long.°′ W=Ouest
Rodenkirchen, B.R.D.	48	53.24 N	8.26 E
Rodenkirchen, B.R.D.	52	50.54 N	6.59 E
Rodeo, Arg.	242	30.12 S	69.06 W
Rodeo, Méx.	222	25.11 N	104.34 W
Rodeo, Calif., U.S.	216	38.02 N	122.09 W
Rodeo, N. Mex., U.S.	190	31.50 N	109.02 W
Röderau	50	51.19 N	13.19 E
Roderick ≃	152	26.57 S	116.13 E
Roderick Island I	172	52.40 N	128.22 W
Rodewisch	50	50.32 N	12.24 E
Rodez	32	44.21 N	2.35 E
Rodheim-Bieber	52	50.37 N	8.35 E
Rodhópis, Orosirá → Rhodope Mountains ∧∧	38	41.30 N	24.30 E
Ródhos (Rhodes)	38	36.26 N	28.13 E
Ródhos I	38	36.10 N	28.00 E
Rodi Garganico	60	41.55 N	15.53 E
Rodina	78	57.44 N	95.14 E
Roding	30	49.12 N	12.32 E
Roding ≃	44	51.31 N	0.06 E
Rodinga	152	24.34 S	134.05 E
Rodinka	70	57.24 N	43.34 E
Rodino, S.S.S.R.	66	58.57 N	44.59 E
Rodino, S.S.S.R.	76	52.30 N	80.15 E
Rodionovo-Nesvetajskoje	73	47.36 N	39.42 E
Rodman	170	57.28 N	135.21 W
Rodman Naval Station ■	226	8.58 N	79.36 W
Rodn'a	66	56.22 N	34.55 E
Rodnei, Munții ∧∧	38	47.35 N	24.40 E
Rodney, Ont., Can.	204	42.34 N	81.41 W
Rodney, Miss., U.S.	184	31.52 N	91.12 W
Rodney, Cape ≻, N.Z.	162	36.17 S	174.49 E
Rodney, Cape ≻, Alaska, U.S.	170	64.39 N	166.24 W
Rodney Village	198	39.08 N	75.31 W
Rodničok	70	51.26 N	42.54 E
Rodniki, S.S.S.R.	70	57.06 N	41.44 E
Rodniki, S.S.S.R.	255b	55.39 N	38.04 E
Rodnikovskij	76	50.39 N	57.12 E
Rodolfo, Lago → Rudolf, Lake ⊜	134	3.30 N	36.05 E
Rodolfo Iselín	242	34.39 S	68.01 W
Rodonit, Kep i ≻	38	41.35 N	19.27 E
Rodostov	68	51.58 N	24.57 E
Rødovre	41	55.41 N	12.29 E
Rodrigo de Freitas, Lagoa C	277a	22.58 S	43.13 W
Rodrigues I	12	19.42 S	63.25 E
Rodríguez, Méx.	186	27.10 N	100.01 W
Rodríguez, Méx.	222	27.11 N	101.21 W
Rodríguez, Ur.	248	34.23 S	56.33 W
Rodríguez, Arroyo ≃	278	34.52 S	58.02 W
Rodstock, Cape ≻	152	33.12 S	134.20 E
Roduco	198	36.28 N	76.49 W
Rødven	26	62.38 N	7.33 E
Rødvig	41	55.15 N	12.23 E
Roe ≃	42	55.07 N	6.59 W
Roebling	198	40.07 N	74.47 W
Roebourne	152	20.47 S	117.09 E
Roebuck Bay C	152	19.04 S	122.17 E
Roehampton ✦8	250	51.27 N	0.14 W
Roe Island I	272	38.04 N	122.02 W
Roeland Park	188	39.02 N	94.37 W
Roelands	158a	33.18 S	115.50 E
Roeliff Jansen Kill ≃	200	42.11 N	73.52 W
Roelofarendsveen	48	52.12 N	4.38 E
Roelofskamp	148	26.10 S	24.24 E
Roen, Monte ∧	58	46.22 N	11.11 E
Roer (Rur) ≃	52	51.12 N	5.59 E
Roermond	48	51.12 N	6.00 E
Roesbrugge-Haringe	46	50.55 N	2.37 E
Roeselare (Roulers)	46	50.57 N	3.08 E
Roesinger, Lake ⊜	214	47.58 N	121.55 W
Roessleville	200	42.42 N	73.49 W
Roes Welcome Sound Ψ	166	64.00 N	88.00 W
Roetgen	52	50.39 N	6.12 E
Rœulx	46	50.30 N	4.06 E
Rofan Spitze ∧	58	47.27 N	11.46 E
Roff	186	34.38 N	96.50 W
Röfors	40	58.57 N	14.37 E
Rogačevo	72	56.26 N	37.10 E
Rogačov	66	53.05 N	30.03 E
Rogačovka	68	51.30 N	39.34 E
Rogagua, Lago ⊜	238	13.43 S	66.54 W
Rogaland □6	26	59.00 N	6.15 E
Rogalik	73	48.56 N	40.03 E
Rogan'	68	49.54 N	36.29 E
Rogans Hill	264a	33.44 S	151.01 E
Rogan's Seat ∧	42	54.25 N	2.07 W
Rogäsen	50	52.19 N	12.20 E
Rogaška Slatina	36	46.14 N	15.38 E
Rogatica	38	43.48 N	19.00 E
Rogatin	68	49.25 N	24.37 E
Rogätz	50	52.19 N	11.46 E
Rogen ⊜	26	62.19 N	12.23 E
Roger, Lac ⊜	180	47.50 N	78.51 W
Roger Island I	273	42.43 N	70.50 W
Rogers, Ark., U.S.	184	36.20 N	94.07 W
Rogers, Conn., U.S.	197	41.50 N	71.54 W
Rogers, Ohio, U.S.	204	40.48 N	80.38 W
Rogers, Tex., U.S.	212	30.56 N	97.14 W
Rogers, Mount ∧	182	36.39 N	81.33 W
Rogers City	180	45.25 N	83.49 W
Rogers Lake ⊜	218	34.52 N	117.51 W
Rogers Park ✦8	268	42.01 N	87.40 W
Rogersville, N.B., Can.	176	46.44 N	65.26 W
Rogersville, Ala., U.S.	184	34.50 N	87.17 W
Rogersville, Tenn., U.S.	182	36.25 N	83.02 W
Roggeveldberge ∧∧	148	32.17 S	20.08 E
Roggewein, Cabo ≻	164z	27.07 S	109.15 W
Roggiano Gravina	36	39.37 N	16.09 E
Rogliano, Fr.	56	42.57 N	9.25 E
Rogliano, It.	36	39.11 N	16.20 E
Rognac	56	43.29 N	5.14 E
Rognedino	66	53.48 N	33.33 E
Rögnitz ≃	50	53.19 N	10.57 E
Rognon ≃	54	48.23 N	5.10 E
Rogny	46	47.45 N	2.53 E
Rogoaguado, Lago ⊜	238	12.52 S	65.43 W
Rogojampi	105a	8.19 S	114.17 E
Rogovatoje	68	51.14 N	38.22 E
Rogovo	72	55.13 N	37.05 E
Rogovskaja	68	45.44 N	38.44 E
Rogovskoje	70	58.33 N	50.43 E
Rogožkino	73	47.10 N	39.21 E
Rogoźno	30	52.46 N	17.00 E
Rogozov	68	50.14 N	31.03 E
Rogue ≃, Mich., U.S.	180	43.04 N	85.35 W
Rogue ≃, Oreg., U.S.	192	42.26 N	124.25 W
Rogue River	192	42.26 N	123.10 W
Rohdenhaus	253	51.18 N	7.01 E
Rohilkhand Plains ≚	114	28.20 N	79.30 E
Rohinjan	262c	19.06 N	73.04 E
Rohitpur	116	23.42 N	90.19 E
Rohl ≃	130	6.22 N	29.46 E
Röhlinghausen ✦8	253	51.36 N	7.14 E
Rohnert Park	216	38.21 N	122.42 W
Rohrbach-lès-Bitche	52	49.03 N	7.16 E
Rohrbeck	254a	52.32 N	13.02 E
Rohrberg	50	52.42 N	11.02 E
Rohrbrunn	52	49.54 N	9.23 E
Röhrenfurth	52	51.09 N	9.32 E
Rohri	110	27.41 N	68.54 E
Röhrsdorf	50	50.51 N	12.50 E
Rohtak	113	28.54 N	76.34 E
Roi	164r	6.56 N	158.17 E
Roi, Île du → King Island I	156	39.50 S	144.00 E
Roia (Roya) ≃	56	43.48 N	7.35 E
Roi Baudouin ♁3	9	70.25 S	24.20 E
Roi Et	100	16.03 N	103.40 E

PORTUGUÊS

Nome	Página	Lat.°′	Long.°′ W=Oeste
Roi Georges, Îles du II	14	14.32 S	145.08 W
Roi Léopold, Monts du → King Leopold Ranges ∧∧	150	17.30 S	125.45 E
Roine ⊜	26	61.24 N	24.06 E
Roinville	251	48.32 N	2.03 E
Roisel	46	49.57 N	3.06 E
Roissy	251	48.47 N	2.39 E
Roissy-en-France	251	49.00 N	2.31 E
Roitzsch	50	51.34 N	12.16 E
Roja, S.S.S.R.	66	57.30 N	22.49 E
Roja, S.S.S.R.	73	47.59 N	37.20 E
Rojas	242	34.12 S	60.44 W
Rojl'anka	68	46.17 N	29.46 E
Rojo → Red ≃	168	31.00 N	91.40 W
Rojo, Cabo ≻, Méx.	224	21.33 N	97.20 W
Rojo, Cabo ≻, P.R.	230m	17.56 N	67.11 W
Rojo, Mar → Red Sea ✢2	126	20.00 N	38.00 E
Rokan	102	0.34 N	100.25 E
Rokan ≃	104	2.00 N	100.52 E
Rokan-kanan ≃	104	1.23 N	100.56 E
Rokan-kiri ≃	104	1.23 N	100.56 E
Röke	41	56.14 N	13.30 E
Rokel ≃	140	8.33 N	12.48 W
Rokewood	159	37.54 S	143.43 E
Rokewood Junction	159	37.51 S	143.41 E
Rokheh	110	35.16 N	69.28 E
Rokiškis	66	55.58 N	25.35 E
Rokkō-sanchi ∧∧	260	34.45 N	135.13 E
Rokkō-zan ∧	86	34.46 N	135.16 E
Roklum	50	52.04 N	10.44 E
Roksana	263d	26.07 S	28.04 E
Rokuan Kansallispuisto ♠	26	64.32 N	26.33 E
Rokugō	84	35.29 N	138.27 E
Rokugō ✦8	258	35.33 N	139.43 E
Rokusei	84	36.58 N	136.52 E
Rokycany	30	49.45 N	13.36 E
Rolampont	54	47.57 N	5.16 E
Roland, Man., Can.	174	49.25 N	97.55 W
Roland, Ark., U.S.	184	34.54 N	92.30 W
Roland, Iowa, U.S.	180	42.10 N	93.30 W
Roland, Lake ⊜1	274b	39.23 N	76.38 W
Roland C. Nickerson State Park ♠	197	41.46 N	70.03 W
Rolândia	245	23.18 S	51.22 W
Roland Park ✦8	274b	39.22 N	76.39 W
Roland Run ≃	274b	39.23 N	76.39 W
Rolava ≃	50	50.15 N	12.51 E
Røldal	26	59.49 N	6.48 E
Roldán	242	32.54 S	60.54 W
Roldanillo	236	4.24 N	76.09 W
Rolde	48	52.58 N	6.38 E
Roldskov ✦3	26	56.48 N	9.50 E
Rolette	188	48.40 N	99.51 W
Roleystone	158a	32.08 S	116.04 E
Rolfe	188	42.49 N	94.31 W
Roll, Ariz., U.S.	190	32.45 N	113.59 W
Roll, Ind., U.S.	206	40.33 N	85.23 W
Roll, Cape ≻	231h	13.22 N	61.11 W
Rolla, B.C., Can.	172	55.54 N	120.09 W
Rolla, Kans., U.S.	188	37.07 N	101.38 W
Rolla, Mo., U.S.	184	37.57 N	91.46 W
Rolla, N. Dak., U.S.	188	48.52 N	99.37 W
Rolle	54	46.28 N	6.20 E
Rolle, Passo di)(	58	46.18 N	11.47 E
Rolleboise	251	49.01 N	1.36 E
Rolleston, Austl.	156	24.28 S	148.37 E
Rolleston, N.Z.	162	43.35 S	172.23 E
Rolling Acres	274b	39.17 N	76.52 W
Rollingbay	214	47.40 N	122.30 W
Rolling Fork	184	32.55 N	90.52 W
Rolling Fork ≃	184	37.55 N	85.50 W
Röllinghausen ✦8	253	51.31 N	7.08 E
Rolling Hills	270	33.46 N	118.21 W
Rolling Hills Estates	270	33.47 N	118.22 W
Rolling Meadows	206	42.04 N	88.01 W
Rolling Prairie	206	41.40 N	86.37 W
Rolling River Indian Reserve ✦4	174	50.27 N	100.00 W
Rollingstone	156	19.03 S	146.24 E
Rollingwood	216	37.57 N	122.20 W
Rolvsøya I	24	71.00 N	24.00 E
Rom → Roma	60	41.54 N	12.29 E
Roma, Austl.	156	26.35 S	148.47 E
Roma (Rome), It.	60		
	257a	41.54 N	12.29 E
Roma, Leso.	148	29.27 S	27.45 E
Roma □4	60	41.58 N	12.40 E
Romagna ✦1	58	44.30 N	12.15 E
Romagnano Sesia	56	45.38 N	8.23 E
Romagne-sous-Montfaucon	52	49.20 N	5.05 E
Romain, Cape ≻	182	33.00 N	79.22 W
Romaine ≃	166	50.18 N	63.47 W
Romainmôtier	54	46.42 N	6.29 E
Romainville	251	48.53 N	2.26 E
Romakloster	26	57.31 N	18.27 E
Roman, Blg.	38	43.09 N	23.55 E
Roman, Rom.	38	46.55 N	26.56 E
Roman ≃	44	51.51 N	0.57 E
Romanche ≃	56	45.05 N	5.43 E
Romanche Gap ✢1	10	0.10 S	18.15 W
Romang, Pulau I	154	7.35 S	127.26 E
Romang, Selat Ψ	154	7.30 S	127.00 E
Romania □1	22		
	38	46.00 N	25.30 E
Roman-Koš, Gora ∧	68	44.37 N	34.15 E
Romankovcy	68	48.29 N	27.13 E
Roman Nose Mountain ∧	192	43.55 N	123.44 W
Romano, Cape ≻	210	25.50 N	81.41 W
Romano, Cayo I	230p	22.04 N	77.50 W
Romano di Lombardia	56	45.31 N	9.45 E
Romanova	78	57.04 N	103.24 E
Romanovka, S.S.S.R.	70	51.24 N	47.23 E
Romanovka, S.S.S.R.	70	51.45 N	42.45 E
Romanovka, S.S.S.R.	70	49.47 N	45.05 E
Romanovka, S.S.S.R.	76	54.38 N	76.03 E
Romanovka, S.S.S.R.	78	53.14 N	112.46 E
Romanovka, S.S.S.R.	255a	60.03 N	30.42 E
Romanovo, S.S.S.R.	72	56.39 N	39.14 E
Romanovo, S.S.S.R.	76	52.37 N	81.14 E
Romanovo, S.S.S.R.	76	59.09 N	61.30 E
Romanovo, S.S.S.R.	76	53.58 N	80.30 E
Romans d'Isonzo	58	45.53 N	13.26 E
Romanshorn	54	47.34 N	9.22 E
Romans-sur-Isère	56	45.03 N	5.03 E
Romanzof Mountains ∧∧	170	69.00 N	144.00 W
Romaški	70	50.13 N	46.41 E
Romaškino	70	52.29 N	51.48 E
Romaškovo	255b	55.44 N	37.20 E
Romayor	212	30.27 N	94.50 W
Rombari	144	4.33 N	31.02 E
Romblon	106	12.35 N	122.15 E
Romblon □4	106	12.30 N	122.10 E
Romblon Island I	106	12.33 N	122.17 E
Romblon Passage Ψ	106	12.27 N	122.12 E
Rombo, Ilhéus do II	140a	14.58 N	24.40 W
Rome → Roma, It.	60	41.54 N	12.29 E
Rome, Ga., U.S.	182	34.16 N	85.11 W
Rome, Ill., U.S.	180	40.53 N	89.30 W
Rome, Miss., U.S.	184	33.52 N	90.29 W
Rome, N.Y., U.S.	200	43.13 N	75.27 W
Rome, Ohio, U.S.	204	41.36 N	80.52 W
Rome, Pa., U.S.	200	41.51 N	76.21 W
Rome, Wis., U.S.	206	42.58 N	88.38 W
Rome City	206	41.30 N	85.23 W
Romeleåsen ∧∧2	41	55.34 N	13.33 E
Romenay	54	46.30 N	5.04 E
Romeno	58	46.24 N	11.07 E
Romentino	56	45.28 N	8.42 E
Romeo	180	42.48 N	83.01 W
Romeoville	206	41.39 N	88.05 W
Rometan	118	39.56 N	64.23 E
Romfartuna	40	59.44 N	16.35 E
Romford ✦8	250	51.35 N	0.11 E
Römhild	50	50.24 N	10.32 E
Romiley	252	53.25 N	2.05 W
Romilly, Mount ∧	152	20.27 S	126.34 E
Romilly-sur-Seine	46	48.31 N	3.43 E
Romita	224	20.52 N	101.31 W
Romitorio	257a	42.01 N	12.39 E
Rommani	138	34.34 N	6.37 W
Romme	40	60.26 N	15.30 E
Rommerskirchen	52	51.02 N	6.40 E
Romney, Ind., U.S.	206	40.15 N	86.54 W
Romney, W. Va., U.S.	178	39.21 N	78.45 W
Romney Marsh ☰	44	51.03 N	0.55 E
Romny, S.S.S.R.	68	50.45 N	33.30 E
Romny, S.S.S.R.	79	50.44 N	129.15 E
Rømø I	26	55.08 N	8.31 E
Romodan	68	49.59 N	33.19 E
Romodanovo	70	54.26 N	45.20 E
Romoland	218	33.45 N	117.10 W
Romont	54	46.42 N	6.55 E
Romorantin-Lanthenay	46	47.22 N	1.45 E
Rompin, Malay.	104	2.42 N	102.31 E
Rompin, Malay.	104	2.48 N	103.29 E
Rompin ≃	104	2.49 N	103.29 E
Romrod	52	50.43 N	9.13 E
Romsdalen V	26	62.15 N	8.05 E
Romsdalsfjorden C2	26	62.39 N	7.15 E
Romsey, Austl.	159	37.21 S	144.45 E
Romsey, Eng., U.K.	44	50.59 N	1.30 W
Romsø I	41	55.31 N	10.48 E
Romulus, Mich., U.S.	206	42.13 N	83.24 W
Romulus, N.Y., U.S.	200	42.45 N	76.50 W
Røn, Nor.	26	61.03 N	9.03 E
Ron, Viet.	100	17.53 N	106.27 E
Rona, Schw.	54	46.34 N	9.38 E
Rona, Zaïre	144	2.14 N	30.52 E
Rona I	28	59.07 N	5.49 W
Ronald	214	47.14 N	121.01 W
Ronan	192	47.32 N	114.06 W
Ronas Hill ∧2	28	60.31 N	1.28 W
Ronay I	28	57.28 N	7.07 W
Roncade	58	45.38 N	12.22 E
Roncador, Serra do ∧∧1	232	12.00 S	52.00 W
Roncador Bank ✢4	226	13.32 N	80.03 W
Roncador Reef ✢2	165e	6.13 S	159.22 E
Roncegno	58	46.03 N	11.25 E
Roncesvalles	34	43.01 N	1.19 W
Ronceverte	182	37.45 N	80.28 W
Ronchamp	54	47.42 N	6.39 E
Ronchi dei Legionari	58	45.50 N	13.30 E
Ronchin	46	50.36 N	3.06 E
Ronchis	58	45.49 N	13.00 E
Ronciglione	60	42.17 N	12.13 E
Ronco	54	46.08 N	8.44 E
Ronco Canavese	56	45.30 N	7.32 E
Roncofreddo	60	44.02 N	12.20 E
Roncone	58	45.59 N	10.40 E
Ronco Scrivia	56	44.37 N	8.59 E
Roncq	46	50.45 N	3.07 E
Ronda	34	36.44 N	5.10 W
Ronda, Serranía de ∧∧	34	36.44 N	5.03 W
Rondane ∧	26	61.55 N	9.45 E
Rondane nasjonalpark ♠	26	61.50 N	9.50 E
Rønde	41	56.18 N	10.29 E
Ronde, Point ≻	230d	15.33 N	61.29 W
Rondeau Harbour C	204	42.18 N	81.53 W
Rondeau Provincial Park ♠	204	42.16 N	81.51 W
Rondebult	263d	26.18 S	28.14 E
Ronde Island I	231k	12.18 N	61.35 W
Rondissone	56	45.15 N	7.58 E
Rondon	245	23.23 S	52.48 W
Rondônia	238	10.52 S	61.57 W
Rondônia □8	238	11.00 S	63.00 W
Rondonópolis	245	16.28 S	54.38 W
Rondout	268	42.17 N	87.53 W
Rondout Creek ≃	200	41.55 N	73.53 W
Rondout Reservoir ⊜1	200	41.50 N	74.29 W
Rone ≃	46	50.46 N	3.27 E
Ronehamn	26	57.10 N	18.29 E
Ronga	70	56.43 N	48.32 E
Rongai	144	0.10 S	35.51 E
Rongan	92	25.10 N	109.20 E
Rongbacha	92	31.48 N	99.40 E
Rongchang	97	29.24 N	105.36 E
Rongcheng, Zhg.	88	37.08 N	122.23 E
Rongcheng, Zhg.	95	39.03 N	115.52 E
Rongding	97	28.57 N	103.40 E
Ronge, Lac la ⊜	174	55.10 N	105.00 W
Rongelap I1	14	11.20 N	166.50 E
Rongjiang	92	25.52 N	108.37 E
Rongjiatun	94	42.12 N	123.37 E
Rongkop	105a	8.10 S	110.45 E
Rongola	148	27.22 S	31.37 E
Rongotea	162	40.18 S	175.25 E
Rõngu	66	58.09 N	26.15 E
Rongui, Ilha I	144	10.50 S	40.40 E
Rongwanshi	90	28.10 N	112.57 E
Rongxian, Zhg.	92	22.50 N	110.38 E
Rongxian, Zhg.	97	29.28 N	104.25 E
Roniu ∧	164s	17.49 S	149.12 W
Ronkiti	164r	6.49 N	158.10 E
Ronkiti Harbor C	164r	6.48 N	158.10 E
Ronkonkoma	266	40.49 N	73.07 W
Ronkonkoma, Lake ⊜	266	40.50 N	73.07 W
Ron-ma, Mui ≻	100	18.07 N	106.22 E
Rønne	26	55.06 N	14.42 E
Rönne å ≃	41	56.16 N	12.50 E
Ronneburg	50	50.51 N	12.10 E
Ronneby	26	56.12 N	15.18 E
Ronne Entrance C	9	72.30 S	74.00 W
Ronne Ice Shelf ⊓	9	78.30 S	61.00 W
Ronnenberg	48	52.20 N	9.40 E
Rönneshytta	40	58.56 N	15.02 E
Rönninge	40	59.12 N	17.44 E
Ronroni	165e	9.37 S	159.58 E
Rönsahl	253	51.07 N	7.30 E
Ronsdorf ✦8	253	51.14 N	7.12 E
Ronse (Renaix-gleiche)	46	50.45 N	3.36 E
Röntgenmuseum ♁	253	51.12 N	7.16 E
Ronuro ≃	245	11.56 S	53.33 W
Roodepoort-Maraisburg	148	26.11 S	27.54 E
Roodeschool	48	53.25 N	6.45 E
Roodhouse	209	39.29 N	90.22 W
Roof Butte ∧	190	36.28 N	109.05 W
Rooiberge ∧	148	28.27 S	28.26 E
Rooiboklaagte ≃	146	20.50 S	21.00 E
Rooidam	148	28.07 S	21.15 E
Rooiduinepunt ≻	148	31.57 S	18.17 E
Rooilyf	148	28.49 S	21.57 E
Rooks Creek ≃	206	40.57 N	88.44 W
Rookwood Cemetery ✦	264a	33.53 S	151.04 E
Roon, Pulau I	154	2.23 S	134.33 E
Roordahuizum	48	53.06 N	5.46 E
Roorkee	114	29.52 N	77.53 E
Roosendaal	48	51.32 N	4.28 E
Roosevelt, Ariz., U.S.	190	33.40 N	111.09 W
Roosevelt, Minn., U.S.	188	48.48 N	95.06 W
Roosevelt, N.J., U.S.	198	40.13 N	74.29 W
Roosevelt, N.Y., U.S.	266	40.41 N	73.36 W
Roosevelt, Okla., U.S.	186	34.51 N	99.01 W
Roosevelt, Utah, U.S.	190	40.18 N	109.59 W
Roosevelt ≃	238	7.35 S	60.20 W
Roosevelt Beach	200	43.19 N	78.52 W
Roosevelt-Campobello International Park ♠	176	44.52 N	66.58 W
Roosevelt Field ✦9	266	40.45 N	73.37 W
Roosevelt Island I	9	79.30 S	162.00 W
Roosevelt Park	206	43.11 N	86.16 W
Roosevelt Park ♠	266	40.33 N	74.21 W
Roosevelt Raceway ♠	266	40.44 N	73.36 W
Roosevelt Roads Naval Station ■	230m	18.15 N	65.38 W
Roosevelt Terrace	216	38.08 N	122.16 W
Root	54	47.07 N	8.23 E
Root ≃, N.W. Ter., Can.	170	62.50 N	123.40 W
Root ≃, Minn., U.S.	180	43.46 N	91.15 W
Root ≃, Wis., U.S.	206	42.44 N	87.47 W
Root, North Branch ≃	180	43.49 N	92.10 W
Root, South Branch ≃	180	43.44 N	91.58 W
Root Lake ⊜	174	54.04 N	101.24 W
Rootstown	204	41.06 N	81.15 W
Rooty Hill	160	33.46 S	150.50 E
Ropang	105b	8.52 S	117.29 E
Ropaži	66	57.08 N	24.30 E
Ropča	24	63.02 N	52.16 E
Ropczyce	30	50.03 N	21.37 E
Roper	182	35.53 N	76.37 W
Roper ≃	154	14.43 S	135.27 E
Roper River Mission	154	14.44 S	134.44 E
Roper Valley	154	14.56 S	134.00 E
Ropesville	186	33.26 N	102.09 W
Roppe	54	47.40 N	6.55 E
Ropša	255a	59.44 N	29.52 E
Roque	240	3.01 S	45.23 W
Roquebillière	56	44.01 N	7.18 E
Roquebrune-Cap-Martin	56	43.46 N	7.28 E
Roquebrune-sur-Argens	56	43.26 N	6.38 E
Roquefavour, Aqueduc de Ξ1	56	43.31 N	5.19 E
Roquefort	32	44.02 N	0.19 W
Roquemaure	56	44.03 N	4.47 E
Roque Pérez	248	35.25 S	59.20 W
Roquestéron	56	43.52 N	7.00 E
Roquevaire	56	43.21 N	5.36 E
Roraima □8	236	1.00 N	61.00 W
Roraima, Mount ∧	236	5.12 N	60.44 W
Rörbäcksnäs	26	61.08 N	12.49 E
Roreto Chisone	56	44.59 N	7.06 E
Rorey Lake ⊜	170	66.55 N	128.25 W
Rørholtfjorden ⊜	26	59.01 N	9.15 E
Rorke Lake ⊜	174	54.33 N	92.30 W
Rorke's Drift ⊥	148	28.20 S	30.32 E
Rorketon	174	51.26 N	99.32 W
Røros	26	62.35 N	11.20 E
Rorschach	54	47.29 N	9.30 E
Rørvig	41	55.57 N	11.46 E
Ros' ≃	68	49.39 N	31.35 E
Rosà, It.	58	45.43 N	11.45 E
Rosa, Zam.	144	9.38 S	31.21 E
Rosa, Cap ≻	138	36.57 N	8.14 E
Rosa, Monte ∧	54	45.55 N	7.53 E
Rosairinho	256c	38.40 N	9.01 W
Rošal'	70	55.40 N	39.51 E
Rosales, Méx.	222	28.12 N	105.33 W
Rosales, Pil.	106	15.54 N	120.38 E
Rosalia	192	47.14 N	117.22 W
Rosalie, Lake ⊜	210	27.58 N	81.28 W
Rosamond, Calif., U.S.	218	34.52 N	118.10 W
Rosamond, Ill., U.S.	209	39.23 N	89.10 W
Rosamond Lake ⊜	218	34.50 N	118.04 W
Rosamorada	224	22.08 N	105.12 W
Rosander, Mount ∧	214	48.46 N	124.42 W
Rosanky	212	29.56 N	97.18 W
Rosanna	264b	37.45 S	145.04 E
Rosans	56	44.23 N	5.28 E
Rosario, Arg.	242	32.57 S	60.40 W
Rosário, Bra.	240	2.57 S	44.14 W
Rosario, Méx.	222	26.31 N	105.40 W
Rosario, Méx.	222	30.01 N	115.40 W
Rosario, Méx.	224	23.00 N	105.52 W
Rosario, Para.	242	24.27 S	57.03 W
Rosario, Pil.	106	13.51 N	121.12 E
Rosario, Pil.	106	16.14 N	120.29 E
Rosario, Ur.	248	34.19 S	57.21 W
Rosario ≃	242	24.50 S	65.43 W
Rosario, Bahía del C	222	29.52 N	115.45 W
Rosario, Cayo del I	230p	21.38 N	81.53 W
Rosario, Islas de II	236	10.10 N	75.46 W
Rosario, Laguna ⊜	224	17.52 N	93.48 W
Rosario, Sierra del ∧∧	230p	22.48 N	83.15 W
Rosario Bank ✢4	228	18.30 N	84.00 W
Rosario de la Frontera	242	25.48 S	64.58 W
Rosario de Lerma	242	24.59 S	65.35 W
Rosario del Tala	242	32.18 S	59.09 W
Rosário de Minas	246	21.43 S	43.38 W
Rosário do Sul	242	30.15 S	54.55 W
Rosário Oeste	238	14.50 S	56.25 W
Rosarito, Méx.	194	32.20 N	117.02 W
Rosarito, Méx.	222	26.27 N	111.38 W
Rosarito, Méx.	222	28.38 N	114.04 W
Rosarito, Embalse de ⊜1	34	40.05 N	5.15 W
Rosarno	36	38.29 N	15.59 E
Rosas	186	26.09 N	103.27 W
Rosas, Golfo de C	34	42.10 N	3.15 E
Rosazza	56	45.41 N	7.58 E
Rosbach	52	50.48 N	7.37 E
Rosboom	148	28.36 S	29.44 E
Rošča	72	54.47 N	36.51 E
Roščino	66	60.15 N	29.37 E
Rosciolo	60	42.07 N	13.20 E
Roscoe, Ill., U.S.	206	42.25 N	89.01 W
Roscoe, N.Y., U.S.	200	41.56 N	74.55 W
Roscoe, Pa., U.S.	204	40.05 N	79.52 W
Roscoe, S. Dak., U.S.	188	45.27 N	99.20 W
Roscoe, Tex., U.S.	186	32.27 N	100.32 W
Roscoe Glacier ⊓	9	66.30 S	95.20 E
Roscoe Village ⊥	204	40.18 N	81.54 W
Roscommon, Eire	28	53.38 N	8.11 W
Roscommon, Mich., U.S.	180	44.30 N	84.35 W
Roscommon □6	28	53.40 N	8.30 W
Roscrea	28	52.57 N	7.47 W
Rosdorf	48	51.30 N	9.53 E
Rose	200	43.09 N	76.53 W
Rose, Mount ∧	216	39.21 N	119.55 W
Rose, Pointe de la ≻	230e	14.40 N	60.53 W
Roseau, Dom.	230d	15.18 N	61.24 W
Roseau, Minn., U.S.	188	48.51 N	95.46 W
Roseau ≃, Dom.	230d	15.18 N	61.24 W
Roseau ≃, N.A.	188	49.08 N	97.15 W
Roseau ≃, St. Luc.	231f	13.58 N	61.02 W
Rosebank ✦8	263d	26.09 S	28.02 E
Rosebank Station	265b	43.47 N	79.07 W
Roseberry Lakes ⊜	174	52.40 N	92.30 W
Roseberth	156	25.47 S	139.37 E
Rosebery	156	41.46 S	145.32 E
Rosebery ✦8	264a	33.55 S	151.12 E
Rose-Blanche	176	47.37 N	58.41 W
Roseboom	200	42.45 N	74.47 W
Roseboro	182	34.58 N	78.31 W
Rose Bowl ♠	270	34.10 N	118.09 W
Rosebud, Austl.	159	38.21 S	144.54 E
Rosebud, Mo., U.S.	209	38.23 N	91.25 W
Rosebud, Mont., U.S.	192	46.16 N	106.27 W
Rose Bud, Pa., U.S.	204	40.45 N	78.33 W
Rosebud, S. Dak., U.S.	188	43.14 N	100.51 W
Rosebud, Tex., U.S.	212	31.04 N	96.59 W
Rosebud ≃	172	51.25 N	112.37 W
Rosebud Creek ≃	192	46.16 N	106.28 W
Rosebud Indian Reservation ✦4	188	43.25 N	100.28 W
Roseburg	192	43.13 N	123.20 W
Rosebush	180	43.42 N	84.46 W
Rose City	180	44.25 N	84.07 W
Rose Creek ≃, U.S.	188	40.04 N	97.07 W
Rose Creek ≃, Calif., U.S.	216	38.07 N	120.24 W
Rosecroft Raceway ♠	274c	38.48 N	76.58 W
Rosedal	276a	19.20 N	99.09 W
Rosedale, Austl.	156	24.38 S	151.55 E
Rosedale, Alta., Can.	172	51.25 N	112.38 W
Rosedale, B.C., Can.	214	49.11 N	121.48 W
Rosedale, Ind., U.S.	184	39.37 N	87.17 W
Rosedale, La., U.S.	184	30.27 N	91.27 W
Rosedale, Md., U.S.	274b	39.19 N	76.31 W
Rosedale, Miss., U.S.	184	33.51 N	91.02 W
Rosedale ✦8, Ont., Can.	265b	43.41 N	79.22 W
Rosedale ✦8, N.Y., U.S.	266	40.39 N	73.45 W
Rosedale Hills	208	39.42 N	86.07 W
Rosedene	148	32.01 S	22.07 E
Rose Hall	236	6.16 N	57.21 W
Rosehearty	28	57.42 N	2.07 W
Rose Hill, Maus.	147c	20.14 S	57.27 E
Rose Hill, N.C., U.S.	182	34.50 N	78.02 W
Rose Hill, Va., U.S.	182	36.40 N	83.22 W
Rose Hill, Wash., U.S.	214	47.42 N	122.10 W
Rosehill Cemetery ✦	268	41.59 N	87.41 W
Rosehill Racecourse ♠	264a	33.49 S	151.02 E
Rose Hills Memorial Park ✦	270	34.01 N	118.02 W
Roseira	246	22.54 S	45.18 W
Roseiras	246	22.49 S	46.17 W
Rose Island I	182	25.06 N	77.14 W
Rose Lake	172	54.24 N	126.02 W
Roseland, Calif., U.S.	216	38.25 N	122.44 W
Roseland, Ind., U.S.	206	41.42 N	86.15 W
Roseland, La., U.S.	184	30.46 N	90.31 W
Roseland, N.J., U.S.	266	40.49 N	74.18 W
Roseland, Ohio, U.S.	204	40.47 N	82.32 W
Roseland ✦8	268	41.42 N	87.38 W
Roselawn	206	41.09 N	87.19 W
Roselle, Ill., U.S.	206	41.59 N	88.05 W
Roselle, N.J., U.S.	266	40.40 N	74.16 W
Roselle Field ⊠	268	41.59 N	88.06 W
Rosellen	253	51.08 N	6.43 E
Roselle Park	266	40.40 N	74.16 W
Rosellerheide	253	51.07 N	6.44 E
Rose Lodge	214	45.01 N	123.52 W
Rosemary	172	50.46 N	112.05 W
Rosemary Brook ≃	273	42.19 N	71.15 W
Rosemead	270	34.04 N	118.03 W
Rosemère	196	45.38 N	73.48 W
Rosemont, Calif., U.S.	216	38.34 N	121.20 W
Rosemont, Ill., U.S.	268	41.59 N	87.52 W
Rosemont, Ky., U.S.	208	38.01 N	84.32 W
Rosemont, Ohio, U.S.	204	41.03 N	80.53 W
Rosemont, Pa., U.S.	275	40.01 N	75.19 W
Rosenberg → Susz, Pol.	30	53.44 N	19.20 E
Rosenberg, Tex., U.S.	212	29.33 N	95.48 W
Rosendaël	46	51.02 N	2.24 E
Rosendal, Nor.	26	59.59 N	6.01 E
Rosendal, S. Afr.	148	28.30 S	27.55 E
Rosendale	200	41.51 N	74.05 W
Roseneath	263d	26.17 S	28.11 E
Rosenfeld	54	48.17 N	8.43 E
Rosenhayn	198	39.29 N	75.08 W
Rosenheim	58	47.51 N	12.07 E
Rosenhügel ✦8	253	51.10 N	7.12 E
Rosenthal, B.R.D.	52	50.58 N	8.52 E
Rosenthal, D.D.R.	50	50.51 N	14.04 E
Rosenthal ✦8	254a	52.36 N	13.23 E
Rose Peak ∧	190	33.26 N	109.22 W
Rosepine	184	30.55 N	93.17 W
Rose Point ≻	172	54.13 N	131.35 W
Rosersberg	40	59.35 N	17.53 E
Rosersberg ⊥	40	59.34 N	17.50 E
Roseto	200	40.53 N	75.15 W
Roseto degli Abruzzi	60	42.41 N	14.01 E
Roseto Valfortore	60	41.22 N	15.06 E
Rosetown	174	51.33 N	108.00 W
Rose Tree	275	39.56 N	75.23 W
Rosetta → Rashīd	132	31.24 N	30.25 E
Rosetta Mouth → Rashīd, Maṣabb ≃1	132	31.30 N	30.21 E
Rosettenville ✦8	263d	26.15 S	28.03 E
Rosevale	161a	27.51 S	152.29 E
Rose Valley, Sask., Can.	174	52.18 N	103.50 W
Rose Valley, Pa., U.S.	275	40.10 N	75.13 W
Rose Valley, Pa., U.S.	275	39.53 N	75.23 W
Rose Valley, Wash., U.S.	214	46.06 N	122.50 W
Roseville, Austl.	264a	33.47 S	151.11 E
Roseville, Calif., U.S.	216	38.45 N	121.17 W
Roseville, Ill., U.S.	180	40.44 N	90.40 W
Roseville, Mich., U.S.	204	42.30 N	82.56 W
Roseville, Minn., U.S.	180	45.01 N	93.09 W
Roseville, Ohio, U.S.	178	39.49 N	82.05 W
Roseville, Pa., U.S.	200	41.11 N	79.09 W
Roseville Park	275	39.42 N	75.43 W
Rosewood, Austl.	161a	27.39 S	152.35 E
Rosewood, Austl.	161b	35.41 S	147.52 E
Rosewood, Ohio, U.S.	206	40.13 N	83.58 W
Rosewood Heights	209	38.52 N	90.06 W
Roseworthy	158b	34.32 S	138.44 E
Roshanara Gardens ♠	262a	28.40 N	77.12 E
Rosharon	212	29.21 N	95.28 W
Rosheim	54	48.30 N	7.28 E
Rosherville Dam ✦6	263d	26.14 S	28.07 E
Rosh Ha'Ayin	122	32.06 N	34.57 E
Rosholt, S. Dak., U.S.	188	45.52 N	96.44 W
Rosholt, Wis., U.S.	180	44.38 N	89.18 W
Rosh Pinna	122	32.58 N	35.32 E
Rosh Pinna, Sede-Te'ufa ⊠	122	32.59 N	35.34 E
Rosica ≃	38	43.15 N	25.42 E
Rosice	30	49.11 N	16.23 E
Rosiclare	184	37.25 N	88.20 W
Rosières-aux-Salines	54	48.36 N	6.20 E
Rosières-en-Santerre	46	49.49 N	2.43 E
Rosiers, Rivière des ≃	196	45.59 N	72.07 W
Rosignano Marittimo	60	43.24 N	10.28 E
Rosignano Solvay	60	43.23 N	10.26 E
Rosignol	236	6.17 N	57.32 W
Roșiori-de-Vede	38	44.07 N	25.00 E
Rosita	226	13.53 N	84.24 W
Rositz	50	51.01 N	12.22 E
Ros'ka ≃	68	49.27 N	29.45 E
Roskilde	41	55.39 N	12.05 E
Roskilde □6	41	55.30 N	12.05 E
Roskilde Fjord C	41	55.56 N	12.00 E
Roskow	50	52.28 N	12.42 E
Roslagen □9	40	59.30 N	18.40 E
Roslags-Bro	40	59.50 N	18.44 E
Roslags-Näsby	40	59.26 N	18.04 E
Rosl'akovo	24	69.03 N	33.09 E
Rosl'atino	66	59.46 N	44.15 E
Roslavl'	66	53.57 N	32.52 E
Roslev	26	56.42 N	8.59 E
Roslindale ✦8	273	42.18 N	71.07 W
Roslyn, N.Y., U.S.	266	40.48 N	73.39 W
Roslyn, Pa., U.S.	275	39.57 N	75.36 W
Roslyn, Pa., U.S.	275	40.07 N	75.08 W
Roslyn, Wash., U.S.	214	47.13 N	120.59 W
Roslyn Estates	266	40.47 N	73.40 W
Roslyn Harbor	266	40.49 N	73.38 W
Roslyn Heights	266	40.47 N	73.39 W
Rosmalen	48	51.43 N	5.22 E
Rosman	182	35.03 N	82.49 W
Rosmead	148	31.29 S	25.08 E
Ros Mhic Treoin → New Ross	28	52.24 N	6.56 W
Røsnæs ≻1	41	55.44 N	10.59 E
Rosne, Ruisseau le ≃	251	48.58 N	2.25 E
Rosny-sous-Bois	251	48.53 N	2.29 E
Rosny-sur-Seine	46	49.00 N	1.38 E

≃ River	Fluss	Río	Rivière	Rio
Ξ Canal	Kanal	Canal	Canal	Canal
ᒪ Waterfall, Rapids	Wasserfall, Stromschnellen	Cascada, Rápidos	Chute d'eau, Rapides	Cascata, Rápidos
Ψ Strait	Meeresstrasse	Estrecho	Détroit	Estreito
C Bay, Gulf	Bucht, Golf	Bahía, Golfo	Baie, Golfe	Baía, Golfo
⊜ Lake, Lakes	See, Seen	Lago, Lagos	Lac, Lacs	Lago, Lagos
☰ Swamp	Sumpf	Pantano	Marais	Pântano
⊓ Ice Features, Glacier	Eis- und Gletscherformen	Accidentes Glaciales	Formes glaciaires	Acidentes Glaciares
≃1 Other Hydrographic Features	Andere Hydrographische Objekte	Otros Elementos Hidrográficos	Autres données hydrographiques	Outros Elementos Hidrográficos

✢ Submarine Features	Untermeerische Objekte	Accidentes Submarinos	Formes de relief sous-marin	Acidentes Submarinos
□ Political Unit	Politische Einheit	Unidad Politica	Entité politique	Unidade Política
♁ Cultural Institution	Kulturelle Institution	Institución Cultural	Institution culturelle	Instituição Cultural
⊥ Historical Site	Historische Stätte	Sitio Histórico	Site historique	Sitio Histórico
♠ Recreational Site	Erholungs- und Ferienort	Sitio de Recreo	Centre de loisirs	Sítio de Lazer
⊠ Airport	Flughafen	Aeropuerto	Aéroport	Aeroporto
■ Military Installation	Militäranlage	Instalación Militar	Installation militaire	Instalação Militar
✦ Miscellaneous	Verschiedenes	Misceláneo	Divers	Miscelânea

Rosolina 58 45.05 N 12.15 E
Rošore 75 38.20 N 72.19 E
Rosporden 32 47.58 N 3.50 W
Rösrath 52 50.54 N 7.11 E
Ross, Austl. 156 42.02 S 147.29 E
Ross, N.Z. 162 42.54 S 170.49 E
Ross', S.S.S.R. 66 53.17 N 24.24 E
Ross, Calif., U.S. 216 37.55 N 122.32 W
Ross, Ind., U.S. 268 41.32 N 87.23 W
Ross, Ohio, U.S. 208 39.19 N 84.39 W
Ross □6 208 39.20 N 83.06 W
Ross ≃ 170 61.59 N 132.26 W
Ross, Cape ≻ 106 10.56 N 119.13 E
Ross, Mount ∧ 162 41.28 S 175.21 E
Ross, Point ≻ 164c 29.04 S 167.56 E
Ross, Pointe ≻ 265a 45.21 N 73.48 W
Rossa 54 46.22 N 9.08 E
Rossach 52 50.09 N 10.56 E
Rossano 36 39.35 N 16.39 E
Rossan Point ≻ 28 54.42 N 8.48 W
Rossasna 66 54.39 N 30.53 E
Rossau 50 52.47 N 11.38 E
Rossbach 50 51.15 N 11.53 E
Ross Barnett Reservoir ⊜1 184 32.30 N 90.00 W
Ross-Béthio 140 16.16 N 16.08 W
Rossburg 206 40.17 N 84.38 W
Rossburn 174 50.40 N 100.52 W
Ross Dam ⬩6 214 48.44 N 121.04 W
Rossdorf 52 49.51 N 8.45 E
Rosseau 202 45.16 N 79.39 W
Rosseau, Lake ⊜ 202 45.10 N 79.35 W
Rossel, Cap ≻ 165f 20.23 S 166.36 E
Rossel Island I 150 11.21 S 154.09 E
Rossell y Rius 242 33.11 S 55.42 W
Rossen ⊜ 40 60.19 N 16.26 E
Rossendale □8 252 53.43 N 2.14 W
Rossendale ∨ 42 53.45 N 2.47 W
Rosser 212 32.28 N 96.27 W
Rossford 204 41.37 N 83.33 W
Ross Fork Creek ≃ 192 47.05 N 109.43 W
Rosshaupten 54 47.39 N 10.43 E
Rosshyttan 40 60.04 N 16.21 E
Ross Ice Shelf ⊠ 9 81.30 S 175.00 W
Rossiglione 56 44.34 N 8.40 E
Rossignol, Lake ⊜ 176 44.10 N 65.10 W
Rössing 146 22.31 S 14.52 E
Rossio, Estação do ⬩5 256c 38.43 N 9.09 W
Ross Island I, Ant. 9 77.30 S 168.00 E
Ross Island I, Man., Can. 174 54.14 N 97.45 W
Rossiter 204 40.53 N 78.56 W
Rossitten → Rybačij 66 55.09 N 20.51 E
Rossla 50 51.28 N 11.04 E
Ross Lake ⊜1 214 48.53 N 121.04 W
Ross Lake National Recreation Area ♠ 214 48.45 N 121.00 W
Rossland 172 49.05 N 117.48 W
Rosslare 28 52.17 N 6.23 W
Rosslau 50 51.53 N 12.14 E
Rossleben 50 51.17 N 11.25 E
Rosslyn Farms 269b 40.26 N 80.05 W
Rossmoor 270 33.47 N 118.04 W
Rossmore 264a 33.57 S 150.46 E
Rossmoyne 198 40.13 N 76.57 W
Rosso 140 16.30 N 15.49 W
Rosso, Cap ≻ 36 42.14 N 8.33 E
Rossön 26 63.55 N 16.21 E
Ross-on-Wye 44 51.55 N 2.35 W
Rossony 66 55.53 N 28.49 E
Rossoš', S.S.S.R. 68 50.12 N 39.34 E
Rossoš', S.S.S.R. 68 51.08 N 38.29 E
Rossouw 148 31.09 S 27.18 E
Ross River 170 61.59 N 132.27 W
Ross-Schelfeis → Ross Ice Shelf ⊠ 9 81.30 S 175.00 W
Ross Sea ▾2 9 76.00 S 175.00 W
Rosstal 52 49.25 N 10.52 E
Rosston 208 40.03 N 86.17 W
Røssvatnet ⊜ 24 65.45 N 14.00 E
Rossville, Ga., U.S. 182 34.59 N 85.16 W
Rossville, Ill., U.S. 206 40.23 N 87.40 W
Rossville, Ind., U.S. 206 40.25 N 86.36 W
Rossville, Kans., U.S. 188 39.08 N 95.57 W
Rossville, Md., U.S. 274b 39.20 N 76.29 W
Rosswein 50 51.03 N 13.10 E
Røst II 24 67.28 N 11.59 E
Rostāg 110 37.07 N 69.49 E
Röstånga 41 56.00 N 13.17 E
Rostavatn ⊜ 24 68.45 N 20.30 E
Rosthern 174 52.40 N 106.17 W
Rostherne 252 53.21 N 2.23 W
Rostherne Mere ⊜ 252 53.21 N 2.23 W
Roštkala 110 37.16 N 71.49 E
Rostock 50 54.05 N 12.07 E
Rostock □5 50 54.15 N 12.30 E
Rostov 70 57.11 N 39.25 E
Rostov □4 73 47.30 N 39.30 E
Rostov-na-Donu 73 47.14 N 39.42 E
Rostov-na-Donu, Aeroport ⊠ 73 47.17 N 39.39 E
Rostraver Airport ⊠ 269b 40.13 N 79.50 W
Rostraville 148 26.49 S 25.39 E
Rostrevor 42 54.06 N 6.12 W
Rosvinskoje 24 66.32 N 52.26 E
Roswell, Ga., U.S. 182 34.01 N 84.22 W
Roswell, N. Mex., U.S. 186 33.24 N 104.32 W
Roswell, Ohio, U.S. 204 40.28 N 81.21 W
Rosyth 42 56.03 N 3.26 W
Rot ≃ 54 48.19 N 9.54 E
Rota 34 36.37 N 6.21 W
Rota I 98 14.10 N 145.12 E
Rot am See 52 49.15 N 10.01 E
Rotan 186 32.51 N 100.28 W
Rotanda 146 19.33 S 32.50 E
Rotary Island I 275 40.14 N 74.49 W
Rotbach ≃ 253 51.34 N 6.41 E
Rotberg 254a 52.21 N 13.31 E
Rote-Erde, Stadion ♠ 253 51.30 N 7.27 E
Rotem 52 51.03 N 5.44 E
Rotenburg 48 53.06 N 9.24 E
Rotenburg an der Fulda 52 51.00 N 9.45 E
Roter Main ≃ 50 50.03 N 11.27 E
Rotes Meer → Red Sea ▾2 126 20.00 N 38.00 E
Roth 52 50.46 N 7.42 E
Rötha 50 51.12 N 12.25 E
Rothaargebirge ⛰ 52 51.05 N 8.15 E
Rothaargebirge, Naturpark ♠ 52 51.05 N 8.15 E
Roth bei Nürnburg 52 49.14 N 11.04 E
Rothbury 42 55.19 N 1.55 W
Rothbury Forest ⬩3 42 55.18 N 1.54 W
Rothemühl 50 53.36 N 13.49 E
Rothemühle 52 50.57 N 7.49 E
Röthenbach, B.R.D. 54 47.37 N 9.59 E
Röthenbach, Schw. 54 46.51 N 7.45 E
Rothenburg 50 51.20 N 14.58 E
Rothenburg an der Oder → Czerwieńsk 30 52.01 N 15.25 E
Rothenburg ob der Tauber 52 49.23 N 10.10 E
Rothenkirchen 50 50.33 N 12.30 E
Rothenschirmbach 50 51.27 N 11.33 E
Rothenstein ∧2 253 51.07 N 7.41 E
Rother ≃ 44 50.57 N 0.32 W
Rotherham, N.Z. 162 42.42 S 172.57 E
Rotherham, Eng., U.K. 42 53.26 N 1.20 W
Rothes 28 57.31 N 3.13 W
Rothesay, N.B., Can. 176 45.23 N 66.00 W
Rothesay, Scot., U.K. 42 55.51 N 5.03 W
Roth-neusiedl ⬩8 254b 48.08 N 16.23 E
Rothrist 54 47.19 N 7.53 E
Rothsay, Austl. 152 29.17 S 116.53 E
Rothsay, Minn., U.S. 188 46.28 N 96.17 W
Rothschild 180 44.54 N 89.50 W
Rothsville 198 40.09 N 76.15 W
Rothwell, N.B., Can. 176 46.04 N 66.04 W
Rothwell, Eng., U.K. 42 53.46 N 1.29 W
Rothwell, Eng., U.K. 44 52.25 N 0.48 W
Roti, Pulau I 102 10.45 S 123.10 E
Roti, Selat ⊔ 102 10.25 S 123.25 E
Roto 156 33.03 S 145.28 E
Rotoiti, Lake ⊜ 162 38.02 S 176.25 E
Rotomanu 162 42.39 S 171.32 E
Rotondella 36 40.10 N 16.32 E
Rotondo, Monte ∧ 36 42.13 N 9.03 E
Rotoroa, Lake ⊜ 162 41.52 S 172.38 E
Rotorua 162 38.09 S 176.15 E
Rotorua, Lake ⊜ 162 38.05 S 176.16 E
Rotours, Canal des ≅ 231o 16.20 N 61.28 W
Rotowaro 162 37.36 S 175.05 E
Rott 58 47.54 N 10.59 E
Rottach-Egern 58 47.41 N 11.46 E
Rott am Inn 58 47.59 N 12.07 E
Rotten ≃ 54 46.17 N 7.33 E
Röttenbach 52 49.09 N 11.02 E
Rottenbach-Tremersdorf 52 50.21 N 10.56 E
Rottenbuch 58 47.44 N 10.58 E
Rottenburg am Neckar 54 48.28 N 8.56 E
Rottenburg an der Laaber 30 48.42 N 12.02 E
Rottenmann 30 47.31 N 14.22 E
Rotterdam, Ned. 48 51.55 N 4.28 E
Rotterdam, N.Y., U.S. 200 42.48 N 74.01 W
Rotterdam Junction 200 42.52 N 74.03 W
Rotthausen ⬩8 253 51.30 N 7.05 E
Rottingdean 44 50.48 N 0.04 W
Röttingen 52 49.30 N 9.58 E
Rottleberode 50 51.31 N 10.57 E
Rottnest Island I 158a 32.00 S 115.30 E
Rottofreno 56 45.03 N 9.34 E
Rottum 253 51.36 N 7.42 E
Rottumeroog I 48 53.30 N 6.30 E
Rottumerplaat I 48 53.32 N 6.30 E
Rottweil 54 48.10 N 8.37 E
Rotuma I 14 12.30 S 177.05 E
Rotwand ⬩4 58 47.39 N 11.56 E
Roubaix 46 50.42 N 3.10 E
Roubideau Creek ≃ 190 38.44 N 108.10 W
Roubidoux Creek ≃ 184 37.51 N 92.13 W
Roubion ≃ 56 44.31 N 4.42 E
Rouceux 54 48.22 N 5.41 E
Roudnice [nad Labem] 50 50.22 N 14.16 E
Rouen 46 49.26 N 1.05 E
Rougé 32 47.47 N 1.27 W
Rouge ≃, Ont., Can. 202 43.47 N 79.01 W
Rouge ≃, Qué., Can. 196 45.39 N 74.42 W
Rouge → Red ≃, U.S. 168 31.00 N 91.40 W
Rouge, Bell Branch ≃ 271 42.23 N 83.16 W
Rouge, Lac ⊜ 196 46.56 N 74.38 W
Rouge, Mer → Red Sea ▾2 126 20.00 N 38.00 E
Rouge, River ≃ 271 42.17 N 83.06 W
Rougeau, Forêt de ♠ 251 48.35 N 2.30 E
Rougemont, Fr. 54 47.29 N 6.21 E
Rougemont, Schw. 54 46.29 N 7.12 E
Rougemont-le-Château 54 47.44 N 6.58 E
Rough ≃ 184 37.29 N 87.08 W
Rough And Ready 216 39.14 N 121.08 W
Rough River Lake ⊜1 184 37.40 N 86.25 W
Rouiba 34 36.44 N 3.17 E
Rouillac 32 45.47 N 0.04 W
Rouillon 251 48.33 N 2.00 E
Roujol, Pointe de ≻ 231o 16.12 N 61.35 W
Rouku 154 8.40 S 141.35 E
Roulans 54 47.19 N 6.14 E
Rouleau 174 50.11 N 104.55 W
Roulers → Roeselare 46 50.57 N 3.08 E
Roulette 204 41.47 N 78.09 W
Roulo 271 42.12 N 83.29 W
Roumanie → Romania □1 38 46.00 N 25.30 E
Round Harbour 176 47.37 N 56.00 W
Roundhead 206 40.34 N 83.50 W
Round Hill Head ≻ 156 24.10 S 151.53 E
Round Hill Regional Park ♠ 269b 40.15 N 79.51 W
Round Island I 147c 19.51 S 57.48 E
Round Lake, Ill., U.S. 268 42.21 N 88.05 W
Round Lake, Minn., U.S. 188 43.32 N 95.28 W
Round Lake, N.Y., U.S. 200 42.56 N 73.48 W
Round Lake ⊜, Newf., Can. 176 51.08 N 56.33 W
Round Lake ⊜, Ont., Can. 180 45.38 N 77.32 W
Round Lake ⊜, Ont., Can. 202 44.30 N 77.52 W
Round Lake ⊜, Ont., Can. 202 45.28 N 79.24 W
Round Lake ⊜, Sask., Can. 174 50.33 N 102.23 W
Round Lake ⊜, Mich., U.S. 206 41.58 N 84.17 W
Round Lake Beach 206 42.23 N 88.05 W
Round Lake Park 206 42.21 N 88.04 W
Round Mound ∧2 188 38.55 N 99.39 W
Round Mountain 194 38.43 N 117.04 W
Round Mountain ∧ 161b 36.15 S 148.34 E
Round Mountain ∧2 156 30.27 S 152.14 E
Round Pond ⊜, Newf., Can. 176 48.10 N 56.00 W
Round Pond ⊜, Mass., U.S. 273 42.36 N 70.49 W
Round Rock 212 30.31 N 97.41 W
Round Top 200 42.16 N 74.02 W
Round Top ∧2 198 40.30 N 76.42 W
Roundtop Mountain ∧ 196 45.05 N 72.33 W
Round Top Regional Park ♠ 272 37.51 N 122.12 W
Roundup 192 46.27 N 108.33 W
Round Valley Indian Reservation ⬩4 194 39.50 N 123.20 W
Round Valley Reservoir ⊜1 200 40.36 N 74.50 W
Roura 240 4.44 N 52.20 W
Rourkela → Raurkela 114 22.13 N 84.53 E
Rousay I 28 59.01 N 3.02 W
Rouse Hill 264a 33.41 S 150.56 E
Rouses Point 196 44.59 N 73.22 W
Rouseville 204 41.28 N 79.42 W
Rousies 46 50.16 N 4.00 E
Rousset, Col de)(56 44.50 N 5.24 E
Roussigny 251 48.39 N 2.06 E
Roussillon, Fr. 56 45.22 N 4.49 E
Roussillon, Fr. 56 43.54 N 5.17 E
Roussillon □9 32 42.30 N 2.30 E
Roussy-le-Village 52 49.27 N 6.10 E
Routhierville 176 48.11 N 67.09 W
Routot 46 49.23 N 0.44 E
Rouveen 48 52.36 N 6.11 E
Rouvignies 46 50.20 N 3.26 E
Rouville □6 196 45.23 N 73.04 W
Rouvray 46 47.25 N 4.06 E
Rouvray, Lac ⊜ 176 49.18 N 70.49 W
Rouxville 148 30.29 S 26.46 E
Rouyn 180 48.15 N 79.01 W
Rouzerville 198 39.44 N 77.32 W
Rovaniemi 24 66.34 N 25.48 E
Rovasenda 56 45.32 N 8.19 E
Rovato 58 45.34 N 10.00 E
Rovbick 66 52.40 N 24.05 E
Rove, Tunnel du ⬩5 56 43.22 N 5.17 E
Rovegno 56 44.35 N 9.17 E
Rovellasca 56 45.40 N 9.03 E
Rovello Porro 56 45.39 N 9.02 E
Roven'ki, S.S.S.R. 68 49.56 N 38.54 E
Roven'ki, S.S.S.R. 73 48.05 N 39.21 E
Rovenskaja Sloboda 68 52.13 N 30.19 E
Roverbella 58 45.16 N 10.46 E
Rovere 60 42.10 N 13.31 E
Roverè della Luna 58 46.15 N 11.10 E
Roveredo 54 46.14 N 9.08 E
Rovereto 58 45.53 N 11.02 E
Roverè Veronese 58 45.36 N 11.03 E
Rövershagen 50 54.10 N 12.15 E
Roversi 242 27.35 S 61.57 W
Roverud 26 60.15 N 12.03 E
Roviano 60 42.01 N 13.00 E
Rovigo 58 45.04 N 11.47 E
Rovigo □4 58 45.02 N 11.50 E
Rovinj 36 45.05 N 13.38 E
Rovira 236 4.14 N 75.14 W
Rovno 68 50.37 N 26.15 E
Rovnoje, S.S.S.R. 68 48.15 N 31.45 E
Rovnoje, S.S.S.R. 70 50.47 N 46.05 E
Rovnoje, S.S.S.R. 75 42.53 N 73.32 E
Rovuma (Ruvuma) ≃ 144 10.29 S 40.28 E
Rów 50 52.58 N 14.45 E
Rowan □6 208 38.17 N 83.26 W
Rowan Lake ⊜ 174 49.18 N 93.32 W
Rowanty Creek ≃ 198 36.58 N 77.21 W
Rowena, Austl. 156 29.49 S 148.54 E
Rowena, Tex., U.S. 186 31.39 N 100.03 W
Rowe Park ♠ 263a 6.30 N 3.23 E
Rowhill 263d 26.14 S 28.26 E
Rowland, N.C., U.S. 182 34.32 N 79.18 W
Rowland, Pa., U.S. 200 41.28 N 75.03 W
Rowland Flat 158b 34.35 S 138.56 E
Rowland Heights 270 33.59 N 117.54 W
Rowlands Gill 42 54.54 N 1.45 W
Rowlesburg 178 39.21 N 79.40 W
Rowlett 212 32.54 N 96.34 W
Rowlett, Isla I 244 44.48 S 74.25 W
Rowlett Creek ≃ 212 32.49 N 96.31 W
Rowley 197 42.43 N 70.53 W
Rowley ≃, N.W. Ter., Can. 166 70.16 N 77.45 W
Rowley ≃, Mass., U.S. 273 42.43 N 70.49 W
Rowley Island I 166 69.08 N 78.50 W
Rowley Regis 44 52.29 N 2.03 W
Rowley Shoals ⬩2 152 17.30 S 119.00 E
Rowntree Mill Park ♠ 265b 43.45 N 79.35 W
Rowsburg 204 40.52 N 82.10 W
Rowville 264b 37.56 S 145.14 E
Roxa, Ilha I 140 11.15 N 15.40 W
Roxana 209 38.50 N 90.04 W
Roxas (Capiz), Pil. 98 11.35 N 122.45 E
Roxas, Pil. 106 10.20 N 119.21 E
Roxas, Pil. 106 17.08 N 121.36 E
Roxas, Pil. 106 12.35 N 121.31 E
Roxas (Capiz), Pil. 106 11.35 N 122.45 E
Roxboro, Qué., Can. 265a 45.31 N 73.48 W
Roxboro, N.C., U.S. 182 36.24 N 78.59 W
Roxborough 231r 11.15 N 60.35 W
Roxborough ⬩8 275 40.02 N 75.13 W
Roxborough Downs 156 22.30 S 138.50 E
Roxburgh, N.Z. 162 45.32 S 169.19 E
Roxburgh, Scot., U.K. 42 55.34 N 2.30 W
Roxbury, Conn., U.S. 197 41.45 N 73.11 W
Roxbury, N.Y., U.S. 200 42.17 N 74.34 W
Roxbury, Pa., U.S. 204 40.07 N 77.40 W
Roxbury, Va., U.S. 198 37.28 N 77.09 W
Roxbury ⬩8, Mass., U.S. 273 42.20 N 71.06 W
Roxbury ⬩8, N.Y., U.S. 266 40.34 N 73.54 W
Roxel 48 51.57 N 7.32 E
Roxen ⊜ 26 58.30 N 15.41 E
Roxie 184 31.30 N 91.04 W
Roxo, Cap ≻ 140 12.20 N 16.43 W
Roxton 186 33.33 N 95.44 W
Roxton Pond (Sainte-Pudentienne) 196 45.29 N 72.40 W
Roxwell 250 51.45 N 0.23 E
Roy, N. Mex., U.S. 186 35.57 N 104.12 W
Roy, Utah, U.S. 190 41.10 N 112.02 W
Roy, Wash., U.S. 214 47.00 N 122.33 W
Roya (Roia) ≃ 56 43.48 N 7.35 E
Royal 188 43.04 N 95.17 W
Royal Albert Hall ⊥ 250 51.30 N 0.11 W
Royal Bangkok Sports Club ♠ 259a 13.44 N 100.33 E
Royal Botanic Gardens ♠, Austl. 264a 33.52 S 151.13 E
Royal Botanic Gardens ♠, Austl. 264b 37.50 S 144.59 E
Royal Canal ≅ 28 53.21 N 6.15 W
Royal Center 206 40.52 N 86.30 W
Royal City 192 46.54 N 119.38 W
Royale, Isle I 180 48.00 N 89.00 W
Royal Festival Hall ⊥ 250 51.30 N 0.07 W
Royal Island I 182 25.31 N 76.51 W
Royalla 161b 35.31 S 149.09 E
Royal Leamington Spa 44 52.18 N 1.31 W
Royal Natal National Park ♠ 148 28.45 S 28.57 E
Royal Naval College ⊥2 160 35.07 S 150.42 E
Royal Oak, B.C., Can. 214 48.30 N 123.23 W
Royal Oak, Md., U.S. 198 38.44 N 76.11 W
Royal Oak, Mich., U.S. 206 42.30 N 83.08 W
Royal Oak Township 271 42.27 N 83.10 W
Royal Observatory ⊥3 261d 22.18 N 114.10 E
Royal Ontario Museum ⊥ 265b 43.40 N 79.24 W
Royal Opera House ⊥ 250 51.30 N 0.08 W
Royal Palms State Beach ♠ 270 33.44 N 118.19 W
Royal Park ♠ 264b 37.47 S 144.57 E
Royal Roads ⊂ 214 48.26 N 123.26 W
Royalton, Ind., U.S. 208 39.56 N 86.21 W
Royalton, Minn., U.S. 180 45.50 N 94.18 W
Royalton, Pa., U.S. 198 40.11 N 76.44 W
Royal Tunbridge Wells → Tunbridge Wells 44 51.08 N 0.16 E
Royal Turf Club ♠ 259a 13.46 N 100.32 E
Royan 32 45.37 N 1.01 W
Royaume-Uni → United Kingdom □1 28 54.00 N 2.00 W
Roybon 56 45.15 N 5.15 E
Royce Brook ≃ 266 40.32 N 70.35 W
Roydon 44 51.46 N 0.03 E
Roye 46 49.42 N 2.48 E
Royersford 198 40.11 N 75.32 W
Royerton 206 40.16 N 85.22 W
Roy Hill 152 22.38 S 119.57 E
Royse City 212 32.59 N 96.20 W
Royston, Eng., U.K. 42 53.37 N 1.27 W
Royston, Eng., U.K. 44 52.03 N 0.01 W
Royston, Ga., U.S. 182 34.17 N 83.06 W
Royton 42 53.34 N 2.08 W
Rožaj 38 42.50 N 20.10 E
Różan 30 52.53 N 21.25 E
Rozay-en-Brie 46 48.41 N 2.58 E
Roždestvenka, S.S.S.R. 76 55.42 N 70.00 E
Roždestvenka, S.S.S.R. 76 50.52 N 71.22 E
Roždestvenka, S.S.S.R. 76 55.21 N 77.29 E
Roždestveno, S.S.S.R. 66 57.44 N 37.57 E
Roždestveno, S.S.S.R. 70 53.15 N 50.04 E
Roždestveno, S.S.S.R. 72 55.57 N 36.23 E
Roždestveno, S.S.S.R. 72 56.51 N 36.33 E
Roždestvenskaja Chava 68 51.38 N 39.40 E
Roždestvenskoje, S.S.S.R. 70 58.09 N 45.35 E
Roždestvenskoje, S.S.S.R. 70 52.47 N 42.10 E
Roždestvenskoje, S.S.S.R. 70 51.14 N 42.10 E
Roždestvo 66 57.36 N 33.48 E
Rozelle 264a 33.52 S 151.10 E
Rozewie, Przylądek ≻ 30 54.51 N 18.21 E
Rozhnof, Cape ≻ 170 55.58 N 160.58 W
Rožišče 68 50.54 N 25.15 E
Rožki 70 56.41 N 50.31 E
Rožkov 70 51.39 N 52.19 E
Rožn'atov 68 48.56 N 24.09 E
Rožňava 30 48.40 N 20.32 E
Roznov 38 46.50 N 26.31 E
Rožnov pod Radhoštěm 30 49.28 N 18.10 E
Rożnów 30 49.46 N 20.42 E
Rozovka 68 47.23 N 37.04 E
Rozoy-sur-Serre 46 49.43 N 4.08 E
Roztocze ∧ 30 50.30 N 23.20 E
Roztoky 50 50.09 N 14.22 E
Rrëshen 38 41.47 N 19.54 E
Rrogozhinë 38 41.05 N 19.40 E
Rtiščevo 70 52.16 N 43.47 E
Ru, Tanjong ≻ 104 2.50 N 101.17 E
Ruabon 44 52.59 N 3.02 W
Ruacaná 142 17.25 S 14.12 E
Ruacana Falls ⤷ 142 17.22 S 14.12 E
Ruaha National Park ♠ 144 7.30 S 34.40 E
Ruahine Range ⛰ 162 40.00 S 176.06 E
Ruahmi, Ra's ≻ 132 28.44 N 32.50 E
Ruanda 144 10.33 S 34.57 E
Ruanda → Rwanda □1 144 2.30 S 30.00 E
Ruango 154 5.35 S 150.10 E
Ruapehu, Mount ∧ 162 39.17 S 175.34 E
Ruapuke Island I 162 46.47 S 168.30 E
Rua Sura I 165e 9.30 S 160.37 E
Ruatahuna 162 38.33 S 176.57 E
Ruatapu 162 42.48 S 170.53 E
Ruatoria 162 37.53 S 178.20 E
Ruaus, Wādī ∨ 136 30.26 N 15.24 E
Ruawai 162 36.08 S 174.02 E
Ruba 66 26.08 N 30.19 E
Rub'al Khali → Ar-Rab'al-Khālī ⬩2 126 20.00 N 51.00 E
Rubanovka 68 47.00 N 34.10 E
Rubbestadneset 26 59.49 N 5.17 E
Rubcovsk 76 51.33 N 81.10 E
Rubcy 73 49.12 N 37.33 E
Rubeho Mountains ⛰ 144 6.55 S 36.30 E
Rubel' 68 51.58 N 27.04 E
Rübeland 50 51.45 N 10.50 E
Rubelles 251 48.34 N 2.41 E
Rubery 44 52.24 N 2.00 W
Rubeshibe 82a 43.47 N 143.38 E
Rubežka 70 51.26 N 51.59 E
Rubežnoje 73 49.01 N 38.23 E
Rubí, Esp. 256d 41.29 N 2.02 E
Rubi, Zaïre 144 2.49 N 25.14 E
Rubi ≃ 142 2.48 N 23.54 E
Rubiana 56 45.08 N 7.23 E
Rubiataba 245 15.08 S 49.48 W
Rubicon ≃ 216 39.00 N 120.44 W
Rubicone ≃ 60 44.08 N 12.28 E
Rubidoux 218 34.00 N 117.25 W
Rubiera 58 44.39 N 10.45 E
Rubim 245 16.23 S 40.32 W
Rubio, Méx. 222 28.45 N 106.53 W
Rubio, Ven. 236 7.43 N 72.22 W
Rubio Woods ♠ 268 41.38 N 87.46 W
Rubl'ovka 68 49.15 N 33.19 E
Rubl'ovo 72 55.47 N 37.21 E
Ruboani 130 8.06 N 30.45 E
Rubona 144 0.33 N 30.10 E
Rubondo Island I 144 2.20 S 31.52 E
Rubtsovsk → Rubcovsk 76 51.33 N 81.10 E
Ruby, Alaska, U.S. 170 64.44 N 155.30 W
Ruby, N.Y., U.S. 200 42.01 N 74.01 W
Ruby ≃ 192 45.34 N 112.21 W
Ruby Creek ≃ 214 48.43 N 120.59 W
Ruby Dome ∧ 194 40.37 N 115.28 W
Ruby Lake ≋ 194 40.10 N 115.30 W
Ruby Mountains ⛰ 194 40.25 N 115.35 W
Ruby Range ⛰ 192 45.15 N 112.15 W
Ruby Valley ∨ 194 40.30 N 115.15 W
Rucava 66 56.09 N 21.10 E
Ruchan' 66 53.33 N 32.48 E
Rucheng 90 25.34 N 113.41 E
Ruciane-Nida 30 53.39 N 21.35 E
Ručji ⬩8 255a 60.01 N 30.24 E
Ručjuvom 24 66.42 N 61.08 E
Rucphen 48 51.32 N 4.34 E
Ruda 58 45.50 N 13.24 E
Rudall 156 33.41 S 136.16 E
Rudall ≃ 152 22.16 S 122.47 E
Ruda Śląska 30 50.18 N 18.51 E
Rudauli 114 26.45 N 81.45 E
Ruḍaymah Lioûa 122 33.01 N 36.35 E
Rūdbār, Afg. 118 30.09 N 62.36 E
Rūdbār, Īrān 118 36.48 N 49.24 E
Rūdbar, Īrān 118 33.35 N 47.00 E
Rudbøl 41 54.54 N 8.45 E
Ruddervoorde 46 51.06 N 3.12 E
Ruddiman Terrace 206 43.12 N 86.17 W
Rudelsburg ⊥ 50 51.07 N 11.43 E
Ruden I 50 54.12 N 13.46 E
Rudensk 66 53.36 N 27.52 E
Rüdersdorf 50 52.29 N 13.47 E
Rüdersdorf, Forst ⬩3 254a 52.26 N 13.50 E
Rüdesheim am Rheim 52 49.59 N 7.56 E
Rudeville 266 41.09 N 74.33 W
Rudewa 144 10.06 S 34.39 E
Rudge Ramos 277b 23.41 S 46.34 W
Rüdinghausen ⬩8 253 51.27 N 7.25 E
Rūdiškės 66 54.31 N 24.50 E
Rudki 68 49.39 N 23.29 E
Rudkino 68 51.27 N 39.01 E
Rudkøbing 41 54.56 N 10.43 E
Rudn'a, S.S.S.R. 66 54.57 N 31.06 E
Rudn'a, S.S.S.R. 70 50.48 N 44.33 E
Rudnevka ≃ 255b 55.43 N 37.56 E
Rudnevo 72 54.44 N 38.09 E
Rudnica 68 48.15 N 28.55 E
Rudničnyj, S.S.S.R. 24 59.38 N 52.27 E
Rudničnyj, S.S.S.R. 76 44.40 N 78.55 E
Rudničnyj, S.S.S.R. 76 59.42 N 60.18 E
Rudničnyj, S.S.S.R. 76 56.08 N 86.12 E
Rudnik 30 50.28 N 22.15 E
Rüdnitz 50 52.43 N 13.37 E
Rudnyj 76 52.57 N 63.07 E
Rudo 38 43.37 N 19.22 E
Rudolf, Lake ⊜ 134 3.30 N 36.05 E
Rudolph 206 41.18 N 83.40 W
Rudolstadt 50 50.43 N 11.20 E
Rudong, Zhg. 92 21.39 N 111.23 E
Rudong, Zhg. 96 32.19 N 121.12 E
Rudovka, S.S.S.R. 70 53.07 N 42.23 E
Rudovka, S.S.S.R. 73 49.24 N 38.27 E
Rudow ⬩8 254a 52.25 N 13.30 E
Rudrón ≃ 34 42.47 N 3.45 W
Rūd Sar 118 37.08 N 50.18 E
Ruds Vedby 41 55.33 N 11.23 E
Rudyard, Mich., U.S. 180 46.14 N 84.36 W
Rudyard, Mont., U.S. 192 48.34 N 110.33 W
Rudyerd Bay ⊂ 172 55.35 N 130.44 W
Rue, Fr. 46 50.16 N 1.40 E
Rue, Schw. 54 46.37 N 6.50 E

ENGLISH

Name | Page | Lat.°′ | Long.°′

Ruecas ≃ 34 39.00 N 5.55 W
Rueil-Malmaison 251 48.53 N 2.11 E
Ruen ∧ 38 42.10 N 22.31 E
Ruenya (Luenha) ≃ 144 16.24 S 33.48 E
Rufā'ah 130 14.46 N 33.22 E
Ruffec 32 46.02 N 0.42 E
Ruffieu 54 46.00 N 5.40 E
Ruffieux 56 45.51 N 5.50 E
Ruffin 182 33.00 N 80.49 W
Ruffle Bar I 266 40.36 N 46.51 W
Rufford 252 53.38 N 2.49 W
Rufford Old Hall ⊥ 252 53.38 N 2.49 W
Ruffs Dale 269b 40.10 N 79.37 W
Rufidschi → Rufiji ≃ 144 8.00 S 39.20 E
Rufiji ≃ 144 8.00 S 39.20 E
Rufina 60 43.49 N 11.29 E
Rufino 242 34.16 S 62.42 W
Rufisque 140 14.43 N 17.17 W
Rufunsa 144 15.05 S 29.40 E
Rufus 214 45.42 N 120.44 W
Rufus, Mount ∧ 158b 34.20 S 139.07 E
Rugāji 66 57.00 N 27.08 E
Rugao 90 32.25 N 120.36 E
Rugby, Eng., U.K. 44 52.23 N 1.15 W
Rugby, N. Dak., U.S. 188 48.22 N 100.00 W
Rugeley 44 52.46 N 1.55 W
Rügen I 50 54.25 N 13.24 E
Rügenwalde → Darłowo 30 54.26 N 16.23 E
Rüggeberg 253 51.16 N 7.22 E
Rugged Mountain ∧ 172 50.02 N 126.41 W
Ruggles Beach 204 41.22 N 82.29 W
Rugles 46 48.49 N 0.42 E
Ruguj 66 59.28 N 32.50 E
Ruḥama 122 31.30 N 34.42 E
Ruhea 114 26.10 N 88.25 E
Ruhengeri 144 1.30 S 29.38 E
Ruhla 50 50.53 N 10.22 E
Ruhland 50 51.27 N 13.52 E
Ruhlsdorf 254a 52.23 N 13.16 E
Ruhner Berge ⛰2 50 53.17 N 11.55 E
Ruhnu Saar I 66 57.48 N 23.15 E
Ruhpolding 58 47.45 N 12.38 E
Ruhr ≃ 48 51.27 N 6.44 E
Ruhr, Universität ⊥2 253 51.27 N 7.16 E
Ruhrort ⬩8 253 51.26 N 6.45 E
Ruhudji ≃ 144 8.52 S 36.01 E
Ruhuhu ≃ 144 10.31 S 34.34 E
Ruian 90 27.49 N 120.38 E
Rui Barbosa 245 12.18 S 40.27 W
Ruichang 90 29.41 N 115.40 E
Ruicheng 92 34.45 N 110.45 E
Ruidoso 190 33.20 N 105.40 W
Ruidoso, Rio ≃ 190 33.23 N 105.16 W
Ruifengsha I 96 31.25 N 121.36 E
Ruijin 90 25.50 N 116.00 E
Ruinen 48 52.46 N 6.22 E
Ruinforme de l'Isalo, Massif ⛰ 147b 22.45 S 45.15 E
Ruiselede 46 51.03 N 3.24 E
Ruislip ⬩8 250 51.34 N 0.25 W
Ruit 52 48.43 N 9.14 E
Ruivos, Angra de los ⊂ 138 24.45 N 15.05 W
Ruiz 224 21.57 N 105.09 W
Ruiz, Nevado del ∧ 236 4.54 N 75.18 W
Ruiz de Montoya 242 26.59 S 55.03 W
Rūjiena 66 57.54 N 25.21 E
Rujm ar-Rashīd, Jabal ∧ 122 31.53 N 36.18 E
Rujm aṣ-Ṣakhrī 122 31.02 N 35.43 E
Rukan-shō ⬩2 164m 26.06 N 127.32 E
Rukatunturi ∧2 26 66.09 N 29.10 E
Ruki ≃ 142 0.05 N 18.17 E
Rukni 116 23.33 N 86.33 E
Rukungiri 144 0.48 S 29.55 E
Rukuruku Bay ⊂ 165g 16.42 S 178.33 E
Rukwa, Lake ⊜ 144 8.00 S 32.25 E
Rule 186 33.11 N 99.54 W
Rule Creek ≃ 188 38.02 N 103.02 W
Ruleville 184 33.44 N 90.33 W
Rulle 48 52.20 N 8.04 E
Rully 54 46.52 N 4.45 E
Rulo 188 40.03 N 95.26 W
Rum ≃ 180 45.11 N 93.23 W
Ruma 38 45.00 N 19.49 E
Rumaat 154 5.49 S 132.48 E
Rumahtinggih 154 6.23 S 140.17 E
Rum'ancevo, S.S.S.R. 72 55.58 N 36.32 E
Rum'ancevo, S.S.S.R. 72 55.38 N 37.26 E
Rum'ancevo ⬩8 73 48.21 N 38.06 E
Rumänien → Romania □1 38 46.00 N 25.30 E
Rumaysh 122 33.05 N 35.22 E
Rumbalara 152 25.20 S 134.29 E
Rumbek 130 6.48 N 29.41 E
Rumbeke 46 50.56 N 3.10 E
Rumberpon, Pulau I 154 1.50 S 134.15 E
Rumburk 50 50.57 N 14.32 E
Rum Cay I 228 23.40 N 74.53 W
Rumelange 52 49.28 N 6.02 E
Rumelifeneri 257b 41.14 N 29.06 E
Rumelihisarı ⬩8 257b 41.05 N 29.03 E
Rumelihisarı ⊥ 257b 41.05 N 29.02 E
Rumelikavağı ⬩8 257b 41.11 N 29.04 E
Rumeln-Kaldenhausen 52 51.23 N 6.40 E
Rumford 178 44.33 N 70.33 W
Rumford ≃ 273 41.58 N 71.11 W
Rumia 30 54.35 N 18.25 E
Rumigny 46 49.48 N 4.16 E
Rumilly 56 45.52 N 5.57 E
R'uminskoje 72 56.31 N 38.47 E
Rum Jungle 154 13.01 S 131.00 E
R'umki 255a 59.47 N 30.02 E
Rumkiğ 120 39.00 N 39.18 E
Rümlang 54 47.27 N 8.32 E
Rummah, Wādī ar- ∨ 118 26.12 N 44.04 E
Rummān, Wādī ∨ 122 29.43 N 35.23 E
Rummānah 132 31.01 N 32.40 E
Rummānah, Bi'r ar- ▾4 132 31.00 N 32.40 E
Rummel 204 40.13 N 78.48 W
Rummelsburg → Miastko 30 54.01 N 17.00 E
Rummelsburg ⬩8 254a 52.30 N 13.29 E
Rummenohl 253 51.17 N 7.32 E
Rumney 44 51.31 N 3.07 W
Rumoi 82a 43.56 N 141.39 E
Rumont 52 48.50 N 5.17 E
Rumphi 144 11.01 S 33.52 E
Rump Mountain ∧ 178 45.12 N 71.04 W
Rumson 198 40.22 N 74.00 W
Rumst 46 51.05 N 4.25 E
Rumula 154 16.35 S 145.20 E
Rumung I 164q 9.37 N 138.10 E
Rumuruti 144 0.16 N 36.32 E
Runan 90 33.01 N 114.22 E
Runanga 162 42.24 S 171.16 E
Runaway, Cape ≻ 162 37.32 S 177.59 E
Runazi 144 2.47 S 31.28 E
Runcorn 42 53.20 N 2.44 W
Rundeng 104 2.39 N 97.52 E
Rundēni 66 56.16 N 27.50 E
Ründeroth 52 50.59 N 7.28 E
Rundvik 26 63.32 N 19.26 E
Runere 144 3.06 S 33.16 E
Rŭng, Kaôh I 100 10.44 N 103.14 E
Rungāni 110 26.38 N 65.43 E
Runge 212 28.54 N 97.43 W
Rungis 251 48.45 N 2.21 E
Rungis-Halles, Marché de ⊥ 251 48.46 N 2.21 E
Rungsted 41 55.53 N 12.33 E
Rungus Point ≻ 106 13.43 N 123.58 E
Rungwa, Tan. 144 7.21 S 31.40 E
Rungwa, Tan. 144 6.57 S 33.31 E

DEUTSCH

Name | Seite | Breite°′ | Länge°′ E=Ost

Rungwa ≃ 144 7.36 S 31.50 E
Rungwa River Game Reserve ⬩4 144 7.00 S 34.10 E
Rungwe 144 9.10 S 33.36 E
Runhällen 40 60.02 N 16.49 E
Runheji 90 32.30 N 116.05 E
Runkel 52 50.24 N 8.10 E
Runmarö I 40 59.17 N 18.46 E
Runn ⊜ 40 60.33 N 15.40 E
Runnemede 275 39.51 N 75.04 W
Running Springs 218 34.12 N 117.07 W
Running Water Draw ∨ 186 33.58 N 101.30 W
Runnymede □8 250 51.24 N 0.32 W
Runnymede ⊥ 250 51.26 N 0.34 W
Rünthe 253 51.39 N 7.39 E
Runtu 146 17.52 S 19.43 E
Runu 164q 9.35 N 138.09 E
Runwell 250 51.37 N 0.32 E
Ruo'ergai 92 33.16 N 102.55 E
Ruoheng 90 28.24 N 121.31 E
Ruokolahti 26 61.17 N 28.50 E
Ruoms 56 44.27 N 4.21 E
Ruoqiang 80 38.30 N 88.05 E
Ruoshui ≃ 92 41.00 N 100.10 E
Ruovesi 26 61.59 N 24.05 E
Ruoxi 90 29.18 N 115.20 E
Rupanco 244 40.46 S 72.42 W
Rupanco, Lago ⊜ 244 40.49 S 72.28 W
Rūpar 113 30.59 N 76.31 E
Rupari 158b 35.37 S 139.09 E
Rupat, Pulau I 104 1.50 N 101.35 E
Rupat, Selat ⊔ 104 1.50 N 101.25 E
Rupdia 116 23.08 N 89.18 E
Rupea 38 46.02 N 25.13 E
Rupert, Idaho, U.S. 192 42.37 N 113.41 W
Rupert, Vt., U.S. 200 43.16 N 73.13 W
Rupert, W. Va., U.S. 178 37.58 N 80.41 W
Rupert, Rivière de ≃ 166 51.29 N 78.45 W
Rupert Creek ≃ 156 20.53 S 142.23 E
Rupert House 166 51.30 N 78.45 W
Rupganj 116 23.48 N 90.31 E
Rūpnārāyan ≃ 116 22.13 N 88.03 E
Ruponda 144 10.15 S 38.42 E
Ruppertenrod 52 50.37 N 9.05 E
Ruppiner See ⊜ 50 52.48 N 12.50 E
Rupt de Mad ≃ 52 49.01 N 6.02 E
Rupt-sur-Moselle 54 47.56 N 6.40 E
Rupununi □5 236 3.00 N 59.00 W
Rupununi ≃ 236 4.03 N 58.34 W
Rur (Roer) ≃ 52 51.12 N 5.59 E
Rural Hall 182 36.15 N 80.18 W
Rural Ridge 269b 40.35 N 79.50 W
Rural Valley 204 40.48 N 79.18 W
Rurberg 52 50.37 N 6.22 E
Ruri-kei ♠ 86 35.04 N 135.28 E
Rurrenabaque 238 14.28 S 67.34 W
Rurstausee ⊜1 52 50.36 N 6.22 E
Rurutu I 14 22.26 S 151.20 W
Rusambo 144 16.35 S 32.12 E
Rušan 110 37.58 N 71.30 E
Rusanov 68 50.29 N 31.09 E
Rusanovka 68 50.32 N 33.44 E
Rusape 144 18.32 S 32.07 E
Rusavkina-Popovščina 255b 55.42 N 38.04 E
Ruṣayriṣ, Khazzān ar- ⊜1 130 11.40 N 34.20 E
Ruschuk → Ruse 38 43.50 N 25.57 E
Ruscom ≃ 204 42.18 N 82.38 W
Ruscom Station 204 42.13 N 82.39 W
Ruse 38 43.50 N 25.57 E
Rusera 114 25.45 N 86.02 E
Rusfontein 148 30.28 S 29.17 E
Rush, Eire 42 53.32 N 6.06 W
Rush, N.Y., U.S. 200 42.59 N 77.39 W
Rush, Pa., U.S. 200 41.47 N 76.03 W
Rush □6 208 39.37 N 85.27 W
Rush ≃, N. Dak., U.S. 188 47.00 N 96.54 W
Rush ≃, Wis., U.S. 180 44.34 N 92.19 W
Rushan (Xiacun) 88 36.54 N 121.29 E
Rush Center 188 38.28 N 99.19 W
Rush City 180 45.41 N 92.58 W
Rush Creek ≃, Colo., U.S. 188 38.22 N 102.32 W
Rush Creek ≃, Nebr., U.S. 188 41.27 N 102.32 W
Rush Creek ≃, N.Y., U.S. 274a 42.00 N 78.52 W
Rush Creek ≃, Ohio, U.S. 178 39.38 N 82.33 W
Rush Creek ≃, Ohio, U.S. 204 40.34 N 83.20 W
Rush Creek ≃, Okla., U.S. 186 34.42 N 97.10 W
Rushden 44 52.17 N 0.36 W
Rushford, Minn., U.S. 180 43.49 N 91.46 W
Rushford, N.Y., U.S. 200 42.24 N 78.15 W
Rush Hill 209 39.13 N 91.43 W
Rush Lake ⊜, Ont., Can. 180 47.48 N 82.12 W
Rush Lake ⊜, Wis., U.S. 180 43.49 N 89.00 W
Rushland 275 40.15 N 75.02 W
Rushmore 188 43.37 N 95.48 W
Rusholme ⬩8 252 53.27 N 2.12 W
Rush Springs 186 34.47 N 97.58 W
Rushsylvania 206 40.28 N 83.41 W
Rushville, Ill., U.S. 209 40.07 N 90.34 W
Rushville, Ind., U.S. 208 39.37 N 85.27 W
Rushville, Nebr., U.S. 188 42.43 N 102.28 W
Rushville, N.Y., U.S. 200 42.46 N 77.14 W
Rusinga Island I 144 0.24 S 34.10 E
Rusizi (Ruzizi) ≃ 144 3.16 S 29.14 E
Rusk 212 31.48 N 95.09 W
Rusk □6 212 32.10 N 94.50 W
Rusken ⊜ 26 57.17 N 14.20 E
Ruskin, B.C., Can. 214 49.12 N 122.28 W
Ruskin, Fla., U.S. 210 27.43 N 82.26 W
Rusnė 66 55.18 N 21.22 E
Rušonu Ezers ⊜ 66 56.11 N 27.02 E
Russa 262b 22.29 N 88.21 E
Russas 240 4.56 S 37.58 W
Russbach ≃ 254b 48.17 N 16.35 E
Russee 41 54.18 N 10.04 E
Russel 140 8.15 N 13.05 W
Russell, Man., Can. 174 50.47 N 101.15 W
Russell, Ont., Can. 202 45.17 N 75.17 W
Russell, N.Z. 162 35.16 S 174.07 E
Russell, Calif., U.S. 216 37.39 N 122.08 W
Russell, Iowa, U.S. 180 40.59 N 93.12 W
Russell, Kans., U.S. 188 38.54 N 98.52 W
Russell, Ky., U.S. 178 38.32 N 82.42 W
Russell, Mass., U.S. 197 42.11 N 72.51 W
Russell, Minn., U.S. 188 44.19 N 95.57 W
Russell, Pa., U.S. 204 41.56 N 79.08 W
Russell □6 202 45.25 N 75.15 W
Russell, Cape ≻ 166 75.15 N 117.35 W
Russell, Mount ∧ 170 62.48 N 151.52 W
Russell Cave National Monument ♠ 184 34.54 N 85.48 W
Russell Creek ≃ 184 37.14 N 85.30 W
Russell Gardens 266 40.47 N 73.43 W
Russell Island I 166 73.55 N 98.25 W
Russell Islands II 165e 9.04 S 159.12 E
Russellkonda 110 19.56 N 84.35 E
Russell Lake ⊜ 174 56.15 N 101.30 W
Russell Point ≻ 166 73.30 N 115.00 W
Russell Range ⛰ 152 33.24 S 123.28 E
Russells Point 206 40.28 N 83.54 W
Russell Springs 184 37.03 N 85.05 W
Russellton 204 40.37 N 79.50 W
Russellville, Ala., U.S. 184 34.30 N 87.44 W
Russellville, Ark., U.S. 184 35.17 N 93.08 W
Russellville, Ky., U.S. 184 36.51 N 86.53 W
Russellville, Mo., U.S. 184 38.31 N 92.26 W
Russellville, Ohio, U.S. 208 38.52 N 83.47 W

Symbols in the index entries represent the broad categories identified in the key at the right. Symbols with superior numbers (⛰2) identify subcategories (see complete key on page *I* · 26).

Kartensymbole in dem Registerverzeichnis stellen die rechts in Schlüssel erklärten Kategorien dar. Symbole mit hochgestellten Ziffern (⛰2) bezeichnen Unterabteilungen einer Kategorie (vgl. vollständiger Schlüssel auf Seite *I* · 26).

Los símbolos incluídos en el texto del índice representan las grandes categorias identificadas con la clave a la derecha. Los símbolos con numeros en su parte superior (⛰2) identifican las subcategorías (véase la clave completa en la página *I* · 26).

Les symboles de l'index représentent les catégories indiquées dans la légende à droite. Les symboles suivis d'un indice (⛰2) représentent des sous-catégories (voir légende complète à la page *I* · 26).

Os símbolos incluídos no texto do índice representam as grandes categorias identificadas com a chave à direita. Os símbolos com números em sua parte superior (⛰2) identificam as subcategorias (veja-se a chave completa à página *I* · 26).

	English	Deutsch	Español	Français	Português
∧	Mountain	Berg	Montaña	Montagne	Montanha
⛰	Mountains	Berge	Montañas	Montagnes	Montanhas
)(	Pass	Pass	Paso	Col	Passo
∨	Valley, Canyon	Tal, Cañon	Valle, Cañón	Vallée, Canyon	Vale, Canhão
≚	Plain	Ebene	Llano	Plaine	Planície
≻	Cape	Kap	Cabo	Cap	Cabo
I	Island	Insel	Isla	Île	Ilha
II	Islands	Inseln	Islas	Îles	Ilhas
⬩	Other Topographic Features	Andere Topographische Objekte	Otros Elementos Topográficos	Autres données topographiques	Outros Elementos Topográficos

ESPAÑOL

Nombre	Página	Lat.	Long. W=Oeste
Russellville, Oreg., U.S.	214	45.31 N	122.32 W
Rüsselsheim	52	50.00 N	8.25 E
Russi	60	44.22 N	12.02 E
Russia	206	40.14 N	84.24 W
Russian ≃	194	38.27 N	123.08 W
Russian Mission	170	61.34 N	159.34 W
Russian Soviet Federated Socialist Republic → Rossijskaja Sovetskaja Federativnaja Socialističeskaja Respublika □[3]	64	60.00 N	100.00 E
Russiaville	206	40.25 N	86.16 W
Russka	66	58.59 N	28.30 E
Russkaja Bujlovka	68	50.22 N	40.03 E
Russkaja Gavan'	64	76.10 N	62.35 E
Russkaja Pol'ana	76	53.47 N	73.53 E
Russkaja Ţalovka	70	49.59 N	49.05 E
Russkaja Žuravka	70	50.21 N	40.33 E
Russkij	79	43.03 N	131.50 E
Russkij, Ostrov I	64	77.00 N	96.00 E
Russkij Aktaš	70	55.02 N	52.07 E
Russkij Brod	66	52.36 N	37.22 E
Russkij Kameškir	70	52.52 N	46.06 E
Russkij Pervyj	74	43.50 N	44.37 E
Russkij Turek	70	57.03 N	50.13 E
Russkij Vožoj	70	56.57 N	53.22 E
Russkij Zavorot, Mys ≻	24	68.58 N	54.34 E
Russkoje	73	47.45 N	38.56 E
Russkoje-Dobrino	70	54.22 N	52.28 E
Russko-Vysockoje	255a	59.42 N	29.56 E
Rust, B.R.D.	54	48.16 N	7.43 E
Rust, Öst.	30	47.48 N	16.41 E
Rustajskij	70	56.31 N	44.49 E
Rustam	113	34.21 N	72.17 E
Rustavi	74	41.33 N	45.02 E
Rustburg	182	37.17 N	79.06 W
Rustenburg	148	25.37 S	27.08 E
Rustic Canyon ∨	270	34.04 N	118.31 W
Rustington	44	50.48 N	0.31 W
Ruston, La., U.S.	184	32.32 N	92.38 W
Ruston, Wash., U.S.	214	47.19 N	122.32 W
Rusville	263d	26.10 S	28.18 E
Rutaki Passage ⩌	164k	21.15 S	159.48 W
Rutana	144	3.55 S	30.00 E
Rutčenkovo	73	47.57 N	37.44 E
Rute	34	37.19 N	4.22 W
Rütenbrock	48	52.50 N	7.10 E
Ruteng	105b	8.36 S	120.27 E
Rutenga	144	21.08 S	30.45 E
Rutersville	212	29.57 N	96.48 W
Rutgers University (Newark) ʊ[2], N.J., U.S.	266	40.44 N	74.10 W
Rutgers University ʊ[2], N.J., U.S.	266	40.30 N	74.27 W
Rutgers University (Camden) ʊ[2], N.J., U.S.	275	39.56 N	75.07 W
Ruth, Miss., U.S.	184	31.23 N	90.19 W
Ruth, Nev., U.S.	194	39.17 N	114.59 W
Rüthen	48	51.29 N	8.25 E
Rutherford, Calif., U.S.	216	38.28 N	122.25 W
Rutherford, N.J., U.S.	200	40.49 N	74.07 W
Rutherford, Tenn., U.S.	184	36.08 N	88.59 W
Rutherfordton	182	35.22 N	81.57 W
Rutherglen, Scot., U.K.	42	55.50 N	4.12 W
Ruther Glen, Va., U.S.	198	37.56 N	77.27 W
Ruthin	44	53.07 N	3.18 W
Ruthton	188	44.11 N	96.06 W
Ruthven, Ont., Can.	204	42.03 N	82.40 W
Ruthven, Iowa, U.S.	188	43.08 N	94.54 W
Rüti	54	47.16 N	8.51 E
Rutig	148	27.22 S	27.09 E
Rutka ≃	70	56.22 N	46.38 E
Rutland, B.C., Can.	172	49.53 N	119.24 W
Rutland, Fla., U.S.	210	28.51 N	82.13 W
Rutland, Ill., U.S.	206	40.59 N	89.03 W
Rutland, Mass., U.S.	197	42.23 N	71.57 W
Rutland, N. Dak., U.S.	188	46.03 N	97.30 W
Rutland, Vt., U.S.	178	43.36 N	72.59 W
Rutland □[6]	200	43.21 N	73.15 W
Rutland Island I	100	11.25 N	92.40 E
Rutland State Park ♠	197	42.23 N	72.01 W
Rutledge, Ga., U.S.	182	33.38 N	83.37 W
Rutledge, Pa., U.S.	275	39.54 N	75.20 W
Rutledge, Tenn., U.S.	182	36.17 N	83.31 W
Rütli ⊥	54	46.58 N	8.36 E
Rutshuru	144	1.11 S	29.27 E
Rüttenscheid ◆[8]	253	51.26 N	7.00 E
Rutter	180	46.06 N	80.40 W
Rutul	74	41.33 N	47.25 E
Ruukki	26	64.40 N	25.06 E
Ruurlo	48	52.05 N	6.26 E
Ruvu	144	6.48 S	38.39 E
Ruvu ≃	144	6.23 S	38.52 E
Ruvubu ≃	144	2.23 S	30.47 E
Ruvuma □[4]	144	11.00 S	36.00 E
Ruvuma (Rovuma) ≃	144	10.29 S	40.28 E
Ruwayān, Wādī ar- •[7]	132	29.07 N	30.10 E
Ruwaybah ⊤[4]	130	15.39 N	28.45 E
Ruwayfī, Jabal ar- ∧	122	31.12 N	36.00 E
Ruwenzori ⩕	144	0.23 N	29.54 E
Ruwer	52	49.47 N	6.43 E
Ruwer ≃	52	49.47 N	6.42 E
Ruya (Luia) ≃	144	16.34 S	33.12 E
Ruyang	90	34.10 N	112.26 E
Ruyigi	144	3.29 S	30.15 E
Ruyton-Eleven-Towns	44	52.48 N	2.54 W
Ruza	72	55.42 N	36.12 E
Ruza ≃	72	55.38 N	36.17 E
Ruzajevka, S.S.S.R.	70	54.04 N	44.57 E
Ruzajevka, S.S.S.R.	76	52.49 N	66.57 E
Ružany	66	52.52 N	24.53 E
Ružičnaja	68	49.24 N	26.58 E
Ružin	68	49.43 N	29.14 E
Ruzizi (Rusizi) ≃	144	3.16 S	29.14 E
Ružomberok	30	49.06 N	19.18 E
Ruzyně ⊠	50	50.06 N	14.17 E
Ruzzah, Jabal ∧[2]	132	30.01 N	30.26 E
Rwanda □[1]	128		
	144	2.30 S	30.00 E
Rwashamaire	144	0.49 S	30.08 E
Ry	41	56.05 N	9.46 E
Ryal Fold	252	53.41 N	2.30 W
Ryan	186	34.01 N	97.57 W
Ryan ≃	172	50.25 N	122.43 W
Ryan, Loch C	42	54.58 N	5.02 W
Ryan Peak ∧	192	43.54 N	114.25 W
Ryarsh	250	51.19 N	0.24 E
Ryazan' → R'azan'	70	54.38 N	39.44 E
Ryazovo	120	41.59 N	28.02 E
Rybačij (Rossitten)	66	55.09 N	20.51 E
Rybačij, Poluostrov ≻[1]	24	69.42 N	32.36 E
Rybačje, S.S.S.R.	75	42.28 N	76.10 E
Rybačje, S.S.S.R.	76	46.27 N	81.32 E
Rybackaja ◆[8]	255a	60.00 N	30.30 E
Rybackoje ◆[8]	255a	59.50 N	30.30 E
Rybakovka	68	46.37 N	31.20 E
Rybinsk	66	58.03 N	38.52 E
Rybinsker Stausee → Rybinskoje Vodochranilišče ⊜[1]	66	58.30 N	38.25 E
Rybinskije Budy	68	51.13 N	35.57 E
Rybinskoje	76	55.47 N	94.47 E
Rybinskoje Vodochranilišče ⊜[1]	66	58.30 N	38.25 E

FRANÇAIS

Nom	Page	Lat.	Long. W=Ouest
Rybkino	70	54.15 N	43.46 E
Rybnaja Sloboda	70	55.28 N	50.09 E
Rybnica	68	47.45 N	29.01 E
Rybnik	30	50.06 N	18.32 E
Rybnoje, S.S.S.R.	66	54.44 N	39.30 E
Rybnoje, S.S.S.R.	76	58.08 N	94.30 E
Rybnovsk	79	53.12 N	141.50 E
Ryburn ≃	252	53.43 N	1.54 W
Rybuška	70	51.17 N	45.26 E
Rychnov nad Kněžnou	30	50.10 N	16.17 E
Rychwał	30	52.05 N	18.09 E
Ryčkovo	76	58.09 N	61.43 E
Rycroft	172	55.45 N	118.43 W
Ryd	26	56.28 N	14.41 E
Rydaholm	26	56.59 N	14.16 E
Rydal, Austl.	160	33.29 S	150.02 E
Rydal, Pa., U.S.	275	40.06 N	75.06 W
Rydalmere	264a	33.49 S	151.02 E
Rydbo	40	59.28 N	18.11 E
Ryde, Austl.	160	33.49 S	151.06 E
Ryde, Eng., U.K.	44	50.44 N	1.10 W
Ryder	188	47.55 N	101.40 W
Ryder's Hill ∧[2]	44	50.31 N	3.53 W
Ryderwood	214	46.23 N	123.03 W
Rydsgård	41	55.28 N	13.35 E
Rydzyna	30	51.48 N	16.40 E
Rye, Austl.	159	38.23 S	144.49 E
Rye, Eng., U.K.	44	50.57 N	0.44 E
Rye, N.Y., U.S.	200	40.59 N	73.41 W
Rye, Tex., U.S.	212	30.27 N	94.46 W
Rye ≃	42	54.10 N	0.45 W
Ryegate	192	46.18 N	109.15 W
Rye Hills-Rye Brook	266	41.00 N	73.41 W
Rye Lake ⊜	266	41.04 N	73.43 W
Ryeosu → Yŏsu	88	34.46 N	127.44 E
Rye Patch Reservoir ⊜[1]	194	40.38 N	118.18 W
Ryer Island I	272	38.05 N	122.01 W
Ryes	32	49.19 N	0.37 W
Ryfoss	26	61.09 N	8.49 E
Ryfylke ◆[1]	26	59.30 N	5.30 E
Rygge	26	59.23 N	10.43 E
Rygnestad	26	59.16 N	7.29 E
Ryhope	42	54.52 N	1.21 W
Rykaartspos	148	26.32 S	26.39 E
Ryker Lake ⊜	266	41.03 N	74.33 W
Rykerts	172	49.00 N	116.35 W
Ryki	30	51.39 N	21.56 E
Rykonec	66	59.33 N	36.34 E
Ryley	172	53.17 N	112.26 W
Rylovići	66	52.31 N	32.04 E
Ryl'sk	68	51.36 N	34.43 E
Rylstone	160	32.48 S	149.58 E
Rymanów	30	49.34 N	21.53 E
Rýmařov	30	49.56 N	17.16 E
Ryn	30	53.56 N	21.33 E
Rynfield	263d	26.09 S	28.20 E
Rynok	70	45.39 N	47.34 E
Ryn-Peski ◆[2]	70	48.24 N	49.00 E
Ryō	260	34.44 N	135.55 E
Ryōhaku-sanchi ⩕	84	36.09 N	136.45 E
Ryōkami	84	36.00 N	138.58 E
Ryōke	258	35.58 N	139.33 E
Ryōnan	86	33.15 N	133.55 E
Ryōtsu	82	38.05 N	138.26 E
Rypin	30	53.05 N	19.25 E
Ryškany	68	47.58 N	27.32 E
Ryslinge	41	55.15 N	10.33 E
Rysy ∧	30	49.12 N	20.04 E
Ryton	42	54.59 N	1.46 W
Ryton ≃	42	53.25 N	1.00 W
Ryton-on-Dunsmore	44	52.22 N	1.26 W
Ryūga-do •[5]	86	33.39 N	133.45 E
Ryūgasaki	84	35.54 N	140.11 E
Ryūjin	86	33.53 N	135.29 E
Ryukyu Islands → Nansei-shotō II	80	26.30 N	128.00 E
Ryūmon-dake ∧	260	34.26 N	135.53 E
Ryūō, Nihon	84	35.04 N	136.07 E
Ryūō, Nihon	84	35.39 N	138.30 E
Ryūsen	260	34.28 N	135.37 E
Ryūyō	84	34.40 N	137.48 E
Ržaksa-Vyselki	70	52.09 N	42.02 E
Ržanica	66	53.26 N	33.55 E
Ržava	68	51.14 N	36.43 E
Rzepin	30	52.22 N	14.50 E
Rzeszów	30	50.03 N	22.00 E
Ržev	66	56.16 N	34.20 E
Ržiščov	68	49.58 N	31.03 E
Ržovka ◆[8]	255a	59.58 N	30.30 E

S

Nom	Page	Lat.	Long. W=Ouest
Sa	100	18.34 N	100.45 E
Saa	142	4.22 N	11.27 E
Sa'ad	122	31.28 N	34.32 E
Sa'ādatābād	118	30.06 N	53.08 E
Sääksjärvi ⊜	26	61.24 N	22.24 E
Saal	50	54.19 N	12.29 E
Saalach ≃	58	47.51 N	13.00 E
Saal an der Saale	52	50.19 N	10.21 E
Saalbach	58	47.23 N	12.38 E
Saalburg	50	50.30 N	11.43 E
Saaldorf	50	50.27 N	11.41 E
Saale ≃	50	51.57 N	11.55 E
Saaler Bodden C	50	54.20 N	12.28 E
Saales	54	48.21 N	7.07 E
Saaletalsperre ◆[6]	50	50.30 N	11.35 E
Saalfeld	50	50.39 N	11.22 E
Saalfelden	58	47.25 N	12.51 E
Şā al-Ḩajar	132	30.58 N	30.46 E
Saamar	78	50.08 N	106.10 E
Saâne ≃, Fr.	46	49.54 N	0.56 E
Saane ≃, Schw.	54	46.59 N	7.16 E
Saanen	54	46.29 N	7.16 E
Saanenmöser	54	47.32 N	7.18 E
Saanich Inlet C	214	48.38 N	123.30 W
Saar → Saarland □[3]	30	49.20 N	7.00 E
Saar (Sarre) ≃	52	49.42 N	6.34 E
Saarbrücken	52	49.14 N	6.59 E
Saarburg	52	49.36 N	6.33 E
Sääre	66	57.56 N	22.02 E
Saarelouis → Saarlouis	52	49.21 N	6.45 E
Saaremaa I	66	58.25 N	22.30 E
Saarijärvi	26	62.43 N	25.16 E
Saarland □[3]	52	49.20 N	7.00 E
Saarlautern → Saarlouis	52	49.21 N	6.45 E
Saarlouis	52	49.21 N	6.45 E
Saarmund	254a	52.19 N	13.07 E
Saarn ◆[8]	253	51.24 N	6.53 E
Saarnberg ◆[8]	253	51.25 N	6.53 E
Saas Almagell	54	46.07 N	7.58 E
Saas Fee	54	46.07 N	7.55 E
Saas Grund	54	46.08 N	7.56 E
Saastal ∨	54	46.10 N	7.56 E
Saatly	74	39.56 N	48.23 E
Saavedra	242	37.45 S	62.22 W
Saavedra ◆[8]	278	34.33 S	58.28 W
Sab, Tônlé ⊜	100	13.00 N	104.00 E
Saba	142	7.50 N	17.49 E
Saba I	228	17.38 N	63.10 W
Saba ≃, Nihon	86	34.02 N	131.30 E
Saba ≃, S.S.S.R.	66	59.08 N	29.00 E
Saba Bank ✦[4]	228	17.25 N	63.30 W
Šabac	38	44.45 N	19.42 E
Sabadell	34		
	256d	41.33 N	2.06 E
Sabae	84	35.57 N	136.11 E
Sabah □[3]	102	5.20 N	117.10 E
Sa'Bah, Qārat as- ∧[2]	136	27.20 N	17.10 E
Saba Island I	230m	18.18 N	65.00 W
Sabajevo	70	53.59 N	45.43 E
Sabak, Cape ≻	171a	52.20 N	173.45 E
Sabak Bernam	104	3.46 N	100.59 E
Sabal	102	0.59 S	123.14 E
Sabalān, Kūhhā-ye ∧	118	38.15 N	47.49 E

PORTUGUÊS

Nome	Página	Lat.	Long. W=Oeste
Sabalgarh	114	26.15 N	77.24 E
Sabaloyacú, Quebrada ≃	236	2.23 S	72.39 W
Sabana	230m	18.20 N	65.44 W
Sabana ≃	186	32.03 N	98.34 W
Sabana, Archipiélago de II	230p	23.00 N	80.00 W
Sabana-Camagüey, Archipiélago de II	230p	22.30 N	79.00 W
Sabana de la Mar	228	19.04 N	69.23 W
Sabana de Mendoza	236	9.26 N	70.46 W
Sabanagrande, Hond.	226	13.50 N	87.15 W
Sabana Grande, P.R.	230m	18.05 N	66.58 W
Sabanalamar, Bahía de C	230p	21.20 N	76.52 W
Sabanalamar, Ensenada C	230p	21.36 N	78.44 W
Sabanalarga	236	10.38 N	74.55 W
Sabana Llana	230m	18.02 N	66.15 W
Sabancuy	222	18.58 N	91.11 W
Sabaneta	236	8.46 N	69.56 W
Sābang, Bhārat	116	22.11 N	87.36 E
Sabang (Dampelas), Indon.	102	0.11 N	119.51 E
Sabang, Indon.	104	5.55 N	95.19 E
Şabanilla	222	25.08 N	101.44 W
Šabanovo	72	55.38 N	38.43 E
Şabanözü	120	40.29 N	33.18 E
Sabará	245	19.54 S	43.48 W
Sabarei	144	4.20 N	36.55 E
Sābari ≃	112	17.34 N	81.15 E
Sābarmati ≃	110	22.18 N	72.22 E
Sabasţīyah (Samaria)	122	32.17 N	35.12 E
Sab'atayn, Ramlat as- •[8]	134	15.30 N	46.20 E
Sabathu	113	30.59 N	76.59 E
Sabatini, Monti ⩕	60	42.10 N	12.15 E
Sabato ≃	60	41.08 N	14.45 E
Sabaudia	60	41.18 N	13.01 E
Sabaudia, Lago di C	60	41.16 N	13.02 E
Sabaúna	246	23.29 S	46.05 W
Saba Wanak	134	10.33 N	44.09 E
Sabaya	238	19.01 S	68.23 W
Sabažo	74	42.14 N	41.48 E
Sabbioneta	58	45.00 N	10.39 E
Şabe	262c	19.11 N	73.02 E
Šabel'kovka	73	48.45 N	37.29 E
Šabel'sk	73	46.51 N	38.29 E
Şāberī, Hāmūn-e ⊜	118	31.30 N	61.20 E
Sabetha	188	39.54 N	95.48 W
Şabḩā	122	32.20 N	36.30 E
Sabhah	136	27.03 N	14.26 E
Sabhah □[4]	136	28.00 N	14.00 E
Sābhār	116	23.51 N	90.15 E
Sabi (Save) ≃, Afr.	146	21.00 S	35.02 E
Sabi ≃, Nihon	84	36.48 N	140.04 E
Sabicy	66	58.50 N	29.18 E
Sabidana, Jabal ∧	130	18.04 N	36.50 E
Sabie	146	25.10 S	30.48 E
Sabie (Sábiè) ≃	146	25.19 S	32.18 E
Sabile	66	57.03 N	22.35 E
Sabillasville	198	39.42 N	77.27 W
Sabina	208	39.29 N	83.38 W
Sabina ◆[1]	36	42.15 N	12.42 E
Sabinal	186	29.19 N	99.28 W
Sabinal ≃	186	29.06 N	99.27 W
Sabinal, Cayo I	230p	21.40 N	77.18 W
Sabiñánigo	34	42.31 N	0.22 W
Sabinas	222	27.51 N	101.07 W
Sabinas ≃, Méx.	222	27.37 N	100.42 W
Sabinas ≃, Méx.	222	26.51 N	99.34 W
Sabinas ≃, Méx.	224	22.59 N	98.58 W
Sabinas Hidalgo	222	26.30 N	100.10 W
Sabine ≃	168	30.00 N	93.45 W
Sabine, Mount ∧, Ant.	9	71.55 S	169.33 E
Sabine, Mount ∧, Austl.	159	38.38 S	143.44 E
Sabine, South Fork ≃	212	32.52 N	96.10 W
Sabine Bay C	166	75.35 N	109.30 W
Sabine Lake ⊜	184	29.50 N	93.50 W
Sabine Pass C	184	29.44 N	93.52 W
Sabine Peninsula ≻[1]	166	76.20 N	109.30 W
Sabini, Monti ⩕	60	42.13 N	12.50 E
Sabinópolis	245	18.40 S	43.06 W
Sabinov	30	49.06 N	21.06 E
Sabinsville	200	41.52 N	77.31 W
Şabirabad	74	40.01 N	48.29 E
Šabla	38	43.32 N	28.32 E
Sabl'a, Gora ∧	24	64.48 N	58.50 E
Sablayan	106	12.50 N	120.46 E
Sable, Anse au C	265a	45.21 N	73.56 W
Sable, Anse de C	231o	16.07 N	61.34 W
Sable, Cape ≻, N.S., Can.	176	43.25 N	65.35 W
Sable, Cape ≻, Fla., U.S.	210	25.12 N	81.05 W
Sable, Île de I, N. Cal.	150	19.15 S	159.56 E
Sable, Île de I, N. Cal.	165f	19.15 S	163.48 E
Sable, Rivière du ≃	166	55.30 N	68.21 W
Sable Island I	176	43.55 N	59.50 W
Sables, Lac aux ⊜	196	46.53 N	72.22 W
Sables, River aux ≃	180	46.13 N	82.04 W
Sablé-sur-Sarthe	32	47.50 N	0.20 W
Şablinskoje	74	44.31 N	43.14 E
Şablykino	66	52.51 N	35.12 E
Šabo	68	46.08 N	30.23 E
Saboeiro	240	6.32 S	39.54 W
Saboga, Isla I	236	8.37 N	79.04 W
Sabogal ≃	226	10.55 N	84.43 W
Sāboli ◆[8]	262a	28.43 N	77.18 E
Sabonkafi	140	14.38 N	8.45 E
Sabor ≃	34	41.10 N	7.07 W
Sabou	140	12.04 N	2.14 W
Sabourin, Lac ⊜	180	47.58 N	77.41 W
Sabra, Tanjung ≻	154	2.17 S	132.19 E
Sabrata ⊥	136	32.47 N	12.29 E
Sabres	32	44.09 N	0.44 W
Sabrevois	196	45.12 N	73.14 W
Sabrina Coast •[2]	9	67.00 S	119.30 E
Sabuda, Pulau I	154	2.38 S	131.36 E
Sabugal	34	40.21 N	7.05 W
Sabugo	256c	38.49 N	9.18 W
Sabuka	263b	4.27 S	15.10 E
Sabula	180	42.04 N	90.10 W
Sabunči	74	40.26 N	49.56 E
Sabuncu	120	39.33 N	30.12 E
Saburovo	255b	55.53 N	37.16 E
Saburovo ◆[8]	255b	55.38 N	37.42 E
Sabyin	100	19.06 N	94.11 E
Sabyndy	76	50.53 N	70.33 E
Sabzevār	118	36.13 N	57.42 E
Sac ≃	184	38.01 N	93.43 W
Sacaba	238	17.23 S	66.02 W
Sacaca	238	18.05 S	66.26 W
Sacacomie, Lac ⊜	196	46.31 N	73.14 W
Sacajawea Peak ∧	192	45.15 N	117.17 W
Sacanche	238	7.05 S	76.44 W
Sacandaga ≃	200	43.19 N	73.50 W
Sacandaga, West Branch ≃	200	43.22 N	74.17 W
Sacandica	142	5.58 S	15.56 E
Sacaola	142	12.57 S	22.25 E
Sacaton	190	33.05 N	111.44 W
Sacavém	256c	38.47 N	9.06 W
Sačchere	74	42.21 N	43.23 E
Sac City	188	42.25 N	95.00 W
Sacco ≃	60	41.31 N	13.32 E
Sacedón	34	40.29 N	2.43 W
Săcele	38	45.37 N	25.42 E
Šacha ≃	72	56.45 N	39.10 E
Sachalin □[4]	79	50.00 N	143.00 E
Sachalin, Ostrov I	79	51.00 N	143.00 E
Şachalinskij Zaliv C	79	53.45 N	141.30 E
Šachand	75	40.54 N	71.28 E
Şachayoj	242	26.41 S	61.50 W
Šachbuz	74	39.25 N	45.34 E
Šachdagskij Chrebet ⩕	74	40.24 N	45.35 E
Saché	46	47.14 N	0.33 E
Šache ≃	74	43.47 N	39.27 E
Sachicapa	142	10.21 S	19.59 E
Sachigo ≃	166	55.06 N	88.58 W
Sachigo Lake ⊜	174	53.49 N	92.08 W
Sachimbo	142	9.14 S	20.16 E
Şachnovščina	68	49.08 N	35.53 E
Šachovskaja	66	56.02 N	35.29 E
Şachrang	58	47.41 N	12.15 E
Šachrinau	75	38.34 N	68.20 E
Šachrisabz	62	39.03 N	66.50 E
Šachristan	75	39.47 N	68.49 E
Šachristan, Pereval)(	75	39.33 N	68.33 E
Šachrovka	70	58.34 N	52.12 E
Sachse	212	32.59 N	96.36 W
Sachseln	54	46.52 N	8.15 E
Sachsen □[9]	50	51.00 N	13.30 E
Sachsen-Anhalt □[9]	50	52.20 N	11.40 E
Sachsenbrunn	50	50.27 N	10.56 E
Sachsenburg	58	46.50 N	13.21 E
Sachsenhagen	48	52.24 N	9.16 E
Sachsenhausen, B.R.D.	52	51.15 N	9.00 E
Sachsenhausen, D.D.R.	50	52.47 N	13.14 E
Sachs Harbour	166	72.00 N	125.00 W
Sächsische Schweiz ◆[1]	50	50.55 N	14.10 E
Şachterskij	170	64.42 N	177.40 E
Šachtinsk	76	49.40 N	72.37 E
Šachtnoje	73	47.57 N	38.17 E
Šacht'orsk, S.S.S.R.	73	48.03 N	38.28 E
Šacht'orsk, S.S.S.R.	79	49.11 N	142.07 E
Šacht'orskij ◆[8]	73	48.09 N	39.08 E
Šachty	73	47.42 N	40.13 E
Šachunja	70	57.40 N	46.37 E
Sachy	52	49.40 N	5.08 E
Sacile	58	45.57 N	12.30 E
Şacır (Sājūr) ≃	120	36.40 N	38.05 E
Šack, S.S.S.R.	66	53.25 N	27.41 E
Šack, S.S.S.R.	68	51.31 N	23.57 E
Šack, S.S.S.R.	70	54.01 N	41.43 E
Sackets Harbor	202	43.57 N	76.07 W
Säckingen	54	47.33 N	7.56 E
Sackville	176	45.54 N	64.22 W
Saclay	251	48.44 N	2.10 E
Saclay, Étang de ⊜	251	48.45 N	2.10 E
Saco, Maine, U.S.	178	43.29 N	70.28 W
Saco, Mont., U.S.	192	48.28 N	107.21 W
Saco ≃	176	43.27 N	70.22 W
Saco Bay C	178	43.30 N	70.15 W
Sacol Island I	106	6.58 N	122.13 E
Sacotes	256c	38.48 N	9.20 W
Sacra, Isola I	257a	41.45 N	12.15 E
Sacra Família do Tinguá	246	22.29 S	43.36 W
Sacramento, Bra.	245	19.53 S	47.27 W
Sacramento, Calif., U.S.	216	38.35 N	121.30 W
Sacramento □[6]	216	38.35 N	121.30 W
Sacramento ≃	194	38.03 N	121.56 W
Sacramento, Pampa del ≃	238	8.00 S	75.50 W
Sacramento Deep Water Channel ≊	216	38.15 N	121.40 W
Sacramento Metropolitan Airport ⊠	216	38.42 N	121.37 W
Sacramento Mountains ⩕	190	33.10 N	105.50 W
Sacramento South	216	38.32 N	121.26 W
Sacramento Valley ∨	194	39.15 N	122.00 W
Sacramento Wash ∨	190	34.43 N	114.28 W
Sacre ≃	238	12.56 S	58.18 W
Sacré-Cœur ʊ[1]	251	48.53 N	2.21 E
Sacred Heart	188	44.47 N	95.21 W
Sacro Monte ʊ[1]	56	45.49 N	8.15 E
Sacrow ◆[8]	254a	52.26 N	13.06 E
Sacrower See ⊜	254a	52.27 N	13.06 E
Săcueni	38	47.21 N	22.06 E
Sacul	212	31.50 N	94.56 W
Sacupana	236	8.35 N	61.39 W
Sacuriuiná ≃	238	12.52 S	57.22 W
Sada, Esp.	34	43.21 N	8.15 W
Sada, Nihon	86	35.15 N	132.43 E
Sádaba	34	42.17 N	1.16 W
Sadābād, Bhārat	114	27.27 N	78.03 E
Sa'dābād, Īrān	118	29.23 N	51.07 E
Şadad	120	34.18 N	36.56 E
Şa'dah	134	16.52 N	43.37 E
Şadaik Taung ∧	100	15.09 N	98.12 E
Sada-misaki ≻	86	33.20 N	132.01 E
Sada-misaki-hantō ≻[1]	86	33.26 N	132.13 E
Sadamitsu	86	34.02 N	134.04 E
Sadane ≃	105a	6.01 S	106.37 E
Sadang ≃	102	3.43 S	119.27 E
Sadanga	106	17.09 N	121.02 E
Sadani	144	6.03 S	38.47 E
Sadao	100	6.38 N	100.26 E
Sādarpur, Bhārat	262a	28.33 N	77.21 E
Sādarpur, Bngl.	116	23.28 N	90.02 E
Sadčikovka	76	53.01 N	63.27 E
Sadda	110	33.42 N	70.20 E
Saddle ≃	266	40.52 N	74.07 W
Saddleback ∧	42	54.38 N	3.03 W
Saddle Brook	266	40.54 N	74.06 W
Saddlebunch Keys II	210	24.37 N	81.37 W
Saddle Island I	165f	13.40 S	167.40 E
Saddle Lake Indian Reserve ◆[4]	172	54.00 N	111.40 W
Saddle Mountain ∧, Colo., U.S.	190	38.50 N	105.28 W
Saddle Mountain ∧, Oreg., U.S.	214	45.58 N	123.41 W
Saddle Mountains ⩕	192	46.50 N	119.55 W
Saddle Mountain State Park ♠	214	45.58 N	123.41 W
Saddle Peak ∧	100	13.09 N	93.01 E
Saddle River	266	41.02 N	74.06 W
Saddle Rock	266	40.48 N	73.45 W
Saddleworth, Austl.	158b	34.05 S	138.47 E
Saddleworth, Eng., U.K.	42	53.33 N	1.59 W
Saddleworth Moor ◆[3]	252	53.33 N	1.57 W
Sa-dec	100	10.18 N	105.46 E
Sadelkow	50	53.36 N	13.26 E
Sādhaura	114	30.23 N	77.13 E
Sādhuhāti	116	23.34 N	89.01 E
Sadieville	208	38.23 N	84.32 W
Sadiola	140	13.53 N	11.42 W
Şādiqābad	110	28.18 N	70.08 E
Sadiya	110	27.50 N	95.40 E
Sa'dīyah, Wādī ∨	134	20.35 N	39.38 E
Sa'dīyāt, Ra's as- ≻	122	33.41 N	35.25 E
Sadler Lake ⊜	174	55.17 N	103.45 W
Sado I	82	38.00 N	138.25 E
Sado ≃	34	38.29 N	8.55 W
Sado-kaikyō ⩌	82	37.50 N	138.40 E
Sadon	74	42.51 N	44.00 E
Sadovoje, S.S.S.R.	70	47.46 N	44.30 E
Sadovoje, S.S.S.R.	70	46.56 N	44.23 E
Sadovoje Pervoje	68	51.33 N	40.29 E
Sadowara	82	32.02 N	131.26 E
Şādri	110	25.11 N	73.26 E
Šadrina	79	51.33 N	130.22 E
Şadrino	76	55.52 N	91.06 E
Šadrinsk	76	56.05 N	63.38 E
Sadsburyville	198	39.59 N	75.53 W
Sadulgarh	113	29.35 N	74.19 E
Sadulpur	113	28.38 N	75.24 E
Sädvaluspen	24	66.24 N	16.51 E
Sæby, Dan.	26	57.20 N	10.32 E
Sæby, Dan.	41	55.33 N	11.19 E
Saegertown	204	41.43 N	80.09 W
Sae Islands II	154	0.45 S	145.15 E
Saeki, Nihon	86	34.22 N	132.11 E
Saeki, Nihon	86	34.51 N	134.06 E
Saeki → Saiki, Nihon	86	32.57 N	131.54 E
Saerbeck	48	52.10 N	7.38 E
Saerluojiahu ⊜	110	33.55 N	86.55 E
Særslev, Dan.	41	55.31 N	10.11 E
Særslev, Dan.	41	55.43 N	11.23 E
Saeul	52	49.44 N	5.59 E
Şafā, Tulul aş- ∧[1]	122	33.02 N	37.12 E
Safad → Ẓefat	122	32.58 N	35.30 E
Safājah, Jazīrat I	130	26.45 N	33.59 E
Safakulevo	76	54.59 N	62.33 E
Şafānīyah	132	28.49 N	30.48 E
Şafarābād	118	38.59 N	47.27 E
Šafárikovo	30	48.27 N	20.20 E
Safata Bay C	165a	14.00 S	171.50 W
Safdar Jang Airport ⊠	262a	28.37 N	77.13 E
Safdar Jang's Tomb ⊥	262a	28.36 N	77.13 E
Safed Koh Range ⩕	113	33.58 N	70.25 E
Safe Harbor Dam ◆[6]	198	39.59 N	76.28 W
Safety Bay	158a	32.18 S	115.43 E
Safety Harbor	210	27.59 N	82.42 W
Säffle	26	59.08 N	12.56 E
Safford	190	32.50 N	109.43 W
Saffron Walden	44	52.01 N	0.15 E
Safi	138	32.20 N	9.17 W
Safia	154	9.35 S	148.40 E
Safia, Hamada ◆[2]	138	23.10 N	4.15 W
Şafīābād	118	36.45 N	57.58 E
Safīd ≃, Afg.	110	36.44 N	65.38 E
Safīd ≃, Īrān	118	37.26 N	49.55 E
Safīdābeh	118	30.56 N	60.35 E
Safīd Kūh, Selseleh-ye ⩕	118	34.30 N	63.30 E
Safidon	114	29.25 N	76.40 E
Safiental ∨	54	46.40 N	9.18 E
Safioune, Sebkret ☷	138	32.16 N	5.27 E
Safipur	116	23.01 N	90.22 E
Safonovo, S.S.S.R.	24	65.42 N	47.39 E
Safonovo, S.S.S.R.	66	55.06 N	33.15 E
Safonovo, S.S.S.R.	72	55.33 N	38.17 E
Safraköy	257b	41.00 N	28.47 E
Safranbolu	120	41.15 N	32.45 E
Şaft al-'Inab	132	30.49 N	30.41 E
Şaft al-Khammār	132	28.02 N	30.42 E
Şaft al-Laban	263c	30.02 N	31.10 E
Şaft al-Mulūk	132	30.49 N	30.41 E
Şaft Rāshīn	132	28.58 N	30.55 E
Şaft Turāb	132	30.54 N	31.07 E
Şafwān	118	30.07 N	47.43 E
Saga, Nihon	82	33.15 N	130.18 E
Saga, Nihon	86	33.05 N	133.06 E
Saga, S.S.S.R.	76	49.25 N	55.17 E
Saga, S.S.S.R.	76	50.23 N	64.15 E
Saga, Zhg.	110	29.30 N	85.22 E
Saga □[5]	86	33.21 N	130.28 E
Sagaba	142	11.17 S	23.07 E
Sagae	82	38.22 N	140.17 E
Sagaing	100	21.52 N	95.59 E
Sagaing □[8]	100	24.00 N	95.00 E
Sagak, Cape ≻	170	52.48 N	169.08 W
Şagalaherang	105a	6.40 S	107.39 E
Šagalakasa	70	46.54 N	50.43 E
Sagami ≃	84	35.14 N	139.23 E
Sagamihara	84	35.32 N	139.23 E
Sagamihara-daichi ⩕[1]	258	35.25 N	139.27 E
Sagamiko	84	35.37 N	139.12 E
Sagami-ko ⊜	84	35.35 N	139.16 E
Sagami-nada C	84	35.00 N	139.30 E
Sagami-wan C	84	35.14 N	139.24 E
Sagamore, Mass., U.S.	197	41.45 N	70.33 W
Sagamore, Pa., U.S.	204	40.47 N	79.14 W
Sagamore Beach	197	41.48 N	70.32 W
Sagamore Hill National Historic Site ⊥	266	40.53 N	73.30 W
Sagamore Hills	204	41.19 N	81.34 W
Sagan → Żagań	30	51.37 N	15.19 E
Šagan ≃, S.S.S.R.	76	50.37 N	79.15 E
Sagån ≃, Sve.	40	59.35 N	16.54 E
Sagan ≃, Yai.	134	4.28 N	36.04 E
Saganaga Lake ⊜	180	48.14 N	90.52 W
Saganashkee Slough ≃	268	41.41 N	87.53 W
Saganash Lake ⊜	180	49.04 N	82.35 W
Saganoseki	86	33.15 N	131.53 E
Şaganthit Kyun I	100	11.56 N	98.29 E
Šagany, Ozero ⊜	68	45.43 N	29.53 E
Sagaon	262c	19.12 N	73.06 E
Sāgar, Bhārat	112	14.10 N	75.02 E
Sāgar, Bhārat	114	23.50 N	78.43 E
Sagara	84	34.41 N	138.12 E
Sagaranten	105a	7.13 S	106.52 E
Sagard	50	54.31 N	13.33 E
Sāgardīghi	116	24.17 N	88.06 E
Sagaredžo	74	41.44 N	45.20 E
Sāgar Island I	116	21.43 N	88.06 E
Sāgar Plateau ⩕[1]	114	23.30 N	78.30 E
Sagavanirktok ≃	170	70.20 N	148.00 W
Sage, Mount ∧	230m	18.25 N	64.39 W
Sage Creek ≃, N.A.	192	48.58 N	110.06 W
Sage Creek ≃, U.S.	192	44.50 N	108.26 W
Sage Creek ≃, Mont., U.S.	192	48.20 N	110.03 W
Sage Creek ≃, Mont., U.S.	192	47.16 N	109.43 W
Sagerton	186	33.05 N	99.58 W
Sag Harbor	197	41.00 N	72.18 W
Şaghbīn	122	33.37 N	35.42 E
Šagil	76	50.20 N	91.40 E
Saginaw, Mich., U.S.	180	43.25 N	83.58 W
Saginaw, Tex., U.S.	212	32.52 N	97.22 W
Saginaw ≃	180	43.39 N	83.51 W
Saginaw Bay C	180	43.50 N	83.40 W
Sagiz, S.S.S.R.	70	47.31 N	53.16 E
Sagiz, S.S.S.R.	76	48.12 N	54.56 E
Sagiz ≃	76	47.32 N	53.20 E
Sagleipie	140	7.00 N	8.52 W
Saglek Bay C	166	58.35 N	63.00 W
Şaglouc	166	62.14 N	75.38 W
Šaglyteniz, Ozero ⊜	76	54.08 N	69.52 E
Šagonar	76	51.32 N	92.48 E
Sagra di San Michele ʊ[1]	56	45.11 N	7.21 E
Sagrado	58	45.52 N	13.29 E
Sagres	34	37.00 N	8.56 W
Sag Sag	154	5.35 S	148.20 E
Sagsaj	76	48.54 N	89.37 E
Sagu, Indon.	102	8.15 S	123.13 E
Şagu, Rom.	38	46.03 N	21.17 E
Şaguache	190	38.05 N	106.08 W
Saguache Creek ≃	190	37.52 N	105.51 W
Sagua de Tánamo	230p	20.35 N	75.14 W
Sagua la Chica ≃	230p	22.45 N	79.39 W
Sagua la Grande	230p	22.49 N	80.05 W
Sagua la Grande ≃	230p	22.56 N	80.01 W
Saguaro National Monument ♠	190	32.12 N	110.38 W
Saguenay ≃	166	48.08 N	69.44 W
Saguna	262b	22.59 N	88.29 E
Sagunay Lake	206	41.43 N	86.34 W
Sagunovka	68	49.17 N	32.23 E
Sagunto	34	39.41 N	0.16 W
Saguny	68	50.36 N	39.43 E
Sagutjevo	66	52.28 N	33.28 E
Sāgwāra	110	23.41 N	74.01 E
Sagy	251	49.03 N	1.57 E
Sagyndyk, Mys ≻	74	44.02 N	50.52 E
Sah	140	15.38 N	4.03 W
Saḩāb	122	31.53 N	36.00 E
Sahaba	130	18.55 N	30.28 E
Sahagún, Col.	236	8.57 N	75.27 W
Sahagún, Esp.	34	42.22 N	5.02 W
Saḩam	122	32.42 N	35.47 E
Saḩam al-Jawlān	122	32.46 N	35.56 E
Sahana Ambodipont	147b	14.37 S	50.11 E
Sahand, Kūh-e ∧	118	37.44 N	46.27 E
Sahara ◆[2]	126	26.00 N	13.00 E
Sahāranpur	114	29.58 N	77.33 E
Sahārānpur □[5]	114	30.00 N	77.35 E
Sahara Occidental → Western Sahara □[2]	138	24.30 N	13.00 W
Sahara Occidentale → Western Sahara □[2]	138	24.30 N	13.00 W
Saharsa	114	25.53 N	86.36 E
Sahasinaka	147b	21.49 S	47.49 E
Sahasrail	116	23.19 N	89.43 E
Sahaswān	114	28.05 N	78.45 E
Sahe ≃	95	40.22 N	117.58 E
Sahel, Canal du ≊	140	13.44 N	6.05 W
Sahel, Oued ≃	34	36.45 N	5.04 E
Saheqiao	95	40.20 N	118.14 E
Sāhibabad	262a	28.40 N	77.22 E
Sahibābad ◆[8]	262a	28.45 N	77.05 E
Sāhibganj	114	25.15 N	87.39 E
Şahin	120	41.01 N	26.50 E
Sāhiwāl (Montgomery), Pāk.	113	30.40 N	73.06 E
Sāhiwāl, Pāk.	113	31.58 N	72.20 E
Sahlenburg	48	53.52 N	8.38 E
Şaḩneh	118	34.29 N	47.41 E
Şaḩrā', Bi'r ⊤[4]	130	22.52 N	28.37 E
Şaḩrā', Jabal ∧	130	28.00 N	34.08 E
Şahrajat al-Kubrā wa Kafr Jirjis Yūsuf	132	30.38 N	31.17 E
Sahtlam	214	48.48 N	123.54 W
Sahuaripa	222	29.03 N	109.14 W
Sahuarita	190	31.57 N	110.58 W
Sahuayo	224	20.04 N	102.43 W
Sahul Shelf ✦[4]	14	12.00 S	127.00 E
Şahwat al-Qamḩ	122	32.36 N	36.23 E
Šahy	30	48.05 N	18.57 E
Saï	140	13.50 N	5.00 W
Sai ≃, Bhārat	114	25.39 N	82.47 E
Sai ≃, Nihon	84	36.36 N	136.35 E
Sai ≃, Nihon	84	36.37 N	138.14 E
Saibai Island I	154	9.24 S	142.40 E
Sai Buri	100	6.42 N	101.37 E
Sai Buri ≃	100	6.43 N	101.39 E
Saïda	138	34.50 N	0.09 E
Saidābād, Bngl.	116	24.18 N	89.43 E
Sa'īdābād, Īrān	257d	35.40 N	51.11 E
Saidaiji	86	34.39 N	134.02 E
Saïdia	138	35.04 N	2.15 W
Saido	258	35.52 N	139.41 E
Saidor	154	5.35 S	146.30 E
Saidpur, Bhārat	114	25.33 N	83.11 E
Saidpur, Bngl.	114	25.47 N	88.54 E
Saidu	113	34.45 N	72.21 E
Saigawa	86	33.39 N	130.57 E
Saignelégier	54	47.15 N	7.00 E
Saignon	56	43.52 N	5.26 E
Saigō	82	36.12 N	133.20 E
Sai-gon → Thanh-pho Ho Chi Minh, Viet.	100		
	259c	10.45 N	106.40 E
Sai-gon ≃	259c	10.45 N	106.45 E
Saihaku	86	35.20 N	133.20 E
Saihantaolai	92	41.41 N	100.26 E
Saijō, Nihon	86	34.25 N	132.45 E
Saijō, Nihon	86	33.55 N	133.11 E
Saijō ≃	86	34.48 N	132.51 E
Sai-kai-kokuritsu-kōen ♠	82	32.12 N	129.22 E
Sai Kang	261d	22.26 N	114.16 E
Saiki	86	32.57 N	131.54 E
Saiki-wan C	86	33.00 N	131.58 E
Saileati	75	38.57 N	74.45 E
Sailimuhu ⊜	76	44.36 N	81.13 E
Sailkupa	116	23.41 N	89.15 E
Saillans	56	44.42 N	5.11 E
Sailly	251	49.02 N	1.48 E
Sailmouille, Ruisseau ≃	251	48.37 N	2.17 E
Sailor Creek ≃	192	42.56 N	115.29 W
Şail-sous-Couzan	56	45.44 N	3.57 E
Šaim	76	60.21 N	64.14 E
Saima	88	41.00 N	124.14 E
Saimaa ⊜	26	61.15 N	28.15 E
Saimaan kanava (Saimaa Canal) ≊	26	61.05 N	28.18 E
Saimbeyli	120	38.00 N	36.06 E
Saín Alto	224	23.35 N	103.15 W
Sain-Bel	54	45.49 N	4.36 E
Saindak	118	29.17 N	61.34 E
Sainghin-en-Weppes	46	50.33 N	2.54 E
Sainjang	88	39.15 N	125.51 E
Sainō-ha'iji ⊥	86	35.29 N	133.39 E
Sains-du-Nord	46	50.06 N	4.00 E
Sains-en-Gohelle	46	50.27 N	2.41 E
Sains-Richaumont	46	49.49 N	3.42 E
Saint Abb's Head ≻	42	55.54 N	2.09 W
Sainte-Adèle	196	45.57 N	74.07 W
Sainte-Adresse	46	49.30 N	0.05 E
Saint-Adrien	196	45.49 N	71.43 W
Saint-Affrique	32	43.57 N	2.53 E
Saint-Agapit	196	46.34 N	71.27 W
Saint Agatha	202	43.26 N	80.36 W
Sainte-Agathe, Man., Can.	174	49.34 N	97.10 W
Sainte-Agathe, Fr.	56	45.49 N	3.37 E
Sainte-Agathe [-de-Lotbinière]	196	46.23 N	71.24 W
Sainte-Agathe-des-Monts	196	46.03 N	74.17 W
Sainte-Agnès, Fr.	56	43.48 N	7.28 E
Saint Agnes, Eng., U.K.	44	50.18 N	5.13 W
Saint-Agrève	56	45.01 N	4.24 E
Saint-Aimé (Massueville)	196	45.55 N	72.56 W
Saint Albans, Austl.	159	37.44 S	144.48 E
Saint Albans, Austl.	160	33.17 S	150.59 E
Saint Alban's, Newf., Can.	176	47.52 N	55.51 W
Saint Albans, Eng., U.K.	44	51.46 N	0.21 W
Saint Albans, Mo., U.S.	209	38.35 N	90.46 W
Saint Albans, Vt., U.S.	178	44.49 N	73.05 W
Saint Albans, W. Va., U.S.	178	38.23 N	81.49 W
Saint Albans □[8]	250	51.45 N	0.20 W
Saint Albans ◆[8]	266	40.42 N	73.46 W
Saint Albans, Cape ≻	158b	35.49 S	138.07 E
Saint Albans Cathedral ʊ[1]	250	51.45 N	0.20 W
Saint Albert, Alta., Can.	172	53.38 N	113.38 W
Saint-Albert, Qué., Can.	196	46.00 N	72.05 W
Saint Aldhelm's Head ≻	44	50.34 N	2.04 W
Saint-Alexandre-de-Kamouraska	176	47.41 N	69.38 W
Saint-Alexis-des-Monts	196	46.28 N	73.08 W
Saint-Amand	52	48.49 N	4.36 E
Saint-Amand-en-Puisaye	46	47.31 N	3.04 E
Saint-Amand-les-Eaux	46	50.26 N	3.26 E
Saint-Amand-Longpré	46	47.41 N	1.01 E
Saint-Amand-Mont-Rond	32	46.44 N	2.30 E
Saint-Amant-Roche-Savine	56	45.34 N	3.38 E
Saint-Amarin	54	47.53 N	7.01 E
Saint-Ambroix	56	44.15 N	4.11 E
Sainte-Amélie	174	50.59 N	99.21 W
Saint-Amour	54	46.26 N	5.21 E
Saint-André	147c	20.57 S	55.39 E
Saint-André ≃	196	45.33 N	74.20 W
Saint-André, Cap ≻	147b	16.11 S	44.27 E

≃ River	Fluss	Río	Rivière	Rio	
≊ Canal	Kanal	Canal	Canal	Canal	
⌊ Waterfall, Rapids	Wasserfall, Stromschnellen	Cascada, Rápidos	Chute d'eau, Rapides	Cascata, Rápidos	
⩌ Strait	Meeresstrasse	Estrecho	Détroit	Estreito	
C Bay, Gulf	Bucht, Golf	Bahía, Golfo	Baie, Golfe	Baía, Golfo	
⊜ Lake, Lakes	See, Seen	Lago, Lagos	Lac, Lacs	Lago, Lagos	
☷ Swamp	Sumpf	Pantano	Marais	Pântano	
◸ Ice Features, Glacier	Eis- und Gletscherformen	Accidentes Glaciales	Formes glaciaires	Acidentes Glaciares	
⊤ Other Hydrographic Features	Andere Hydrographische Objekte	Otros Elementos Hidrográficos	Autres données hydrographiques	Outros Elementos Hidrográficos	

✦ Submarine Features	Untermeerische Objekte	Accidentes Submarinos	Formes de relief sous-marin	Acidentes Submarinos
□ Political Unit	Politische Einheit	Unidad Politica	Entité politique	Unidade Política
ʊ Cultural Institution	Kulturelle Institution	Institución Cultural	Institution culturelle	Instituição Cultural
⊥ Historical Site	Historische Stätte	Sitio Histórico	Site historique	Sitio Histórico
♠ Recreational Site	Erholungs- und Ferienort	Sitio de Recreo	Centre de loisirs	Sítio de Lazer
⊠ Airport	Flughafen	Aeropuerto	Aéroport	Aeroporto
▪ Military Installation	Militäranlage	Instalación Militar	Installation militaire	Instalação Militar
◆ Miscellaneous	Verschiedenes	Misceláneo	Divers	Miscelânea

Saint-André, Ruisseau ≃ 265a 45.22 N 73.29 W
Saint-André-Avellin 196 45.43 N 75.03 W
Saint-André-de-Cubzac 32 45.00 N 0.27 W
Saint-André-de-l'Eure 46 48.54 N 1.17 E
Saint-André-de-Valborgne 56 44.09 N 3.41 E
St.-André-Est 196 45.34 N 74.20 W
Saint-André-les-Alpes 56 43.58 N 6.30 E
Saint-André-les-Vergers 46 48.17 N 4.03 E
Saint Andrew 231g 13.15 N 59.33 W
Saint Andrew, Mount ▲ 231h 13.11 N 61.13 W
Saint Andrew Lakes ⊜ 202 44.36 N 76.40 W
Saint Andrews, Scot., U.K. 28 56.20 N 2.48 W
Saint Andrews, S.C., U.S. 182 32.47 N 80.00 W
Saint Andrew's Cathedral ✝1 261c 1.18 N 103.51 E
Saint Andrew's Channel ⋓ 176 46.03 N 60.38 W
Saint Ann 209 38.43 N 90.23 W
Sainte-Anne, Guad. 231o 16.14 N 61.23 W
Sainte-Anne, Mart. 230e 14.26 N 60.53 W
Saint Anne, Ill., U.S. 206 41.01 N 87.43 W
Sainte-Anne ≃ 196 46.33 N 72.12 W
Saint Anne, Cathedral of ✝1 263b 4.18 S 15.19 E
Sainte-Anne, Lac ⊜, Alta., Can. 172 53.43 N 114.27 W
Sainte-Anne, Lac ⊜, Qué., Can. 176 50.05 N 67.50 W
Sainte-Anne-de-Beaupré 176 47.02 N 70.56 W
Sainte-Anne-de-Bellevue 265a 45.24 N 73.57 W
Sainte-Anne-de-la-Pérade 196 46.35 N 72.12 W
Sainte-Anne-de-Madawaska 176 47.15 N 68.02 W
Sainte-Anne-des-Chênes 174 49.40 N 96.40 W
Sainte-Anne-des-Monts 176 49.08 N 66.30 W
Sainte-Anne-des-Plaines 196 46.46 N 73.48 W
Saint Anne of the Congo ✝1 263b 4.16 S 15.17 E
Saint Anne's 42 53.45 N 3.02 W
Saint Ann's Bay 231g 18.26 N 77.08 W
Saint Ann's Bay C 176 46.20 N 60.30 W
Saint Ann's Head ≻ 44 51.41 N 5.10 W
Saint-Anselme 176 46.37 N 70.58 W
Saint Ansgar 180 43.23 N 92.55 W
Saint-Anthème 56 45.31 N 3.55 E
Saint Anthony, Newf., Can. 176 51.22 N 55.35 W
Saint Anthony, Idaho, U.S. 192 43.58 N 111.41 W
St.-Antoine, N.B., Can. 176 46.22 N 64.45 W
Saint-Antoine, Qué., Can. 196 45.46 N 73.59 W
Saint-Antoine, Fr. 56 45.10 N 5.13 E
Saint-Antonin 32 44.09 N 1.45 E
Saint-Apollinaire (Francoeur) 196 46.37 N 71.31 W
Saint Arnaud 156 36.37 S 143.15 E
Saint-Arnoult, Forêt de ♠ 251 48.35 N 1.55 E
Saint-Arnoult-en-Yvelines 46 48.34 N 1.56 E
Saint Arvans 44 51.40 N 2.41 W
Saint Asaph 42 53.16 N 3.26 W
Saint-Astier 32 45.09 N 0.32 E
Saint Athan 44 51.24 N 3.25 W
Saint-Auban 56 43.51 N 6.44 E
Saint-Aubert, Mont ▲2 46 59.30 N 3.24 E
Saint Aubert Island I 209 38.40 N 91.52 W
Saint-Aubin, Fr. 46 49.53 N 0.53 E
Saint-Aubin, Fr. 54 47.02 N 5.20 E
Saint-Aubin, Schw. 54 46.54 N 6.47 E
Saint-Aubin-d'Aubigné 32 48.15 N 1.36 W
Saint-Aubin-lès-Elbeuf 46 49.18 N 1.01 E
Saint-Aubin-sur-Aire 54 48.42 N 5.27 E
St.-Augustin 147b 23.33 S 43.46 E
Saint-Augustin ≃ 166 51.14 N 58.41 W
Saint-Augustin-Deux-Montagnes 265a 45.38 N 73.59 W
Saint Augustine 182 29.54 N 81.19 W
Saint-Augustin-Nord-Ouest ≃ 176 51.16 N 58.42 W
Saint-Augustin-Saguenay 176 51.14 N 58.39 W
Saint-Aulaye 32 45.12 N 0.08 E
Saint Austell 44 50.20 N 4.48 W
Saint-Avertin 46 47.22 N 0.44 E
Saint-Avold 52 49.06 N 6.42 E
Saint-Ay 46 47.51 N 1.45 E
Saint-Aygulf 56 43.23 N 6.44 E
Saint-Barthélemy I 228 17.54 N 62.50 W
Saint-Basile 176 47.21 N 68.14 W
Saint-Basile-de-Portneuf 196 46.45 N 71.49 W
Saint-Basile-le-Grand 196 45.32 N 73.17 W
Saint Bathans, Mount ▲ 162 44.44 S 169.46 E
Sainte-Baume, Chaîne de la ⩚ 56 43.20 N 5.45 E
Saint-Béat 32 42.55 N 0.42 E
Saint Bees Head ≻ 42 54.32 N 3.38 W
Saint Benedict 204 40.38 N 78.44 W
Saint-Benoît, Fr. 251 48.40 N 1.55 E
Saint-Benoît, Réu. 147c 21.02 S 55.43 E
Saint-Benoît-du-Sault 32 46.27 N 1.23 E
Saint-Benoît-en-Woëvre 52 48.59 N 5.47 E
Saint Bernard 208 39.10 N 84.30 W
Saint-Bernard, Île I 265a 45.23 N 73.45 W
Saint-Bernard-de-Dorchester 196 46.30 N 71.08 W
Saint-Béron 56 45.30 N 5.43 E
Saint-Blaise, Qué., Can. 196 45.13 N 73.17 W
Saint-Blaise, Schw. 54 47.01 N 6.59 E
Saint-Blaise-la-Roche 54 48.24 N 7.10 E
Saint Blaize, Cape ≻ 148 34.11 S 22.10 E
Saint Blazey 44 50.22 N 4.43 W
Saint-Blin 54 48.16 N 5.25 E
Saint-Bonaventure, Qué., Can. 196 45.58 N 72.41 W
Saint Bonaventure, N.Y., U.S. 200 42.05 N 78.28 W
Saint Boniface 174 49.55 N 97.06 W
Saint-Boniface-de-Shawinigan 196 46.30 N 72.49 W
Saint-Bonnet 56 44.41 N 6.05 E
Saint-Bonnet-de-Joux 56 46.29 N 4.27 E
Saint-Bonnet-le-Château 56 45.25 N 4.04 E
Saint-Bonnet-le-Froid 56 45.09 N 4.27 E
Saint Brendan's 176 48.52 N 53.40 W
Saint-Brice-sous-Forêt 251 49.00 N 2.21 E
Saint Bride, Mount ▲ 172 51.30 N 115.57 W
Saint Bride's 176 46.55 N 54.10 W
Saint Brides Bay C 44 51.48 N 5.15 W
Saint Bride's Major 44 51.28 N 3.38 W
Saint-Brieuc 32 48.31 N 2.47 W
Saint Brieux 174 52.38 N 104.52 W
Saint-Broing-les-Moines 54 47.41 N 4.50 E
Saint-Bruno 196 45.32 N 73.21 W
Saint-Bruno, Mont ▲2 265a 45.33 N 73.19 W
Saint-Calais 46 47.55 N 0.45 E
Saint-Calixte-de-Kilkenny 196 45.57 N 73.51 W
Saint-Cannat 56 43.37 N 5.18 E
Saint-Casimir 196 46.40 N 72.08 W
Saint Catharines 202
274a 43.10 N 79.15 W
Saint Catharines Airport ⊠ 274a 43.11 N 79.10 W
Saint Catherine 210 28.37 N 82.08 W
Saint Catherine, Monastery of ✝1 130 28.29 N 34.01 E
Saint Catherine, Mount ▲ 231k 12.10 N 61.40 W
Sainte-Catherine-de-Fierbois 46 47.09 N 0.39 E
Saint Catherines Island I 182 31.38 N 81.10 W
Saint Catherine's Point ≻ 44 50.34 N 1.15 W
Saint-Célestin (Annaville) 196 46.13 N 72.26 W
Saint-Céré 32 44.52 N 1.53 E
Saint-Cergue 54 46.27 N 6.09 E
Saint-Césaire 196 45.25 N 73.00 W
Saint-Cézaire-sur-Siagne 56 43.39 N 6.48 E
Saint-Chamas 56 43.33 N 5.02 E
Saint-Chamond 56 45.28 N 4.30 E
Saint-Chaptes 56 43.58 N 4.17 E
Saint Charles, Ark., U.S. 184 34.22 N 91.08 W
Saint Charles, Idaho, U.S. 192 42.07 N 111.23 W
Saint Charles, Ill., U.S. 206 41.54 N 88.19 W
Saint Charles, Mich., U.S. 180 43.18 N 84.09 W
Saint Charles, Minn., U.S. 180 43.58 N 92.04 W
Saint Charles, Mo., U.S. 209 38.47 N 90.29 W
Saint Charles □6 209 38.47 N 90.43 W
Saint-Charles ≃ 265a 45.40 N 73.27 W
Saint-Charles, Lac ⊜ 196 46.55 N 71.23 W
Saint-Charles-de-Drummond 196 45.54 N 72.28 W
Saint-Charles-Richelieu 196 45.41 N 73.11 W
Saint-Chef 56 45.38 N 5.22 E
Saint-Chély-d'Apcher 32 44.48 N 3.17 E
Saint-Chéron 251 48.33 N 2.07 E
Saint-Christophe-en-Bazelle 46 47.11 N 1.43 E
Saint-Christophe-Nevis → Saint Kitts-Nevis □2 228 17.20 N 62.45 W
Saint Christopher (Saint Kitts) I 228 17.20 N 62.45 W
Saint-Chrysostome 196 45.06 N 73.46 W
Saint-Ciers-sur-Gironde 32 45.18 N 0.37 W
Saint Clair, Mich., U.S. 180 42.49 N 82.30 W
Saint Clair, Mo., U.S. 209 38.20 N 90.59 W
Saint Clair, Pa., U.S. 198 40.43 N 76.11 W
Saint Clair, Pa., U.S. 269b 40.16 N 79.33 W
Saint Clair □6, Ill., U.S. 209 38.31 N 90.00 W
Saint Clair □6, Mich., U.S. 204 42.50 N 82.42 W
Saint Clair ≃ 204 42.37 N 82.31 W
Saint Clair, Lake ⊜ 204 42.25 N 82.41 W
Saint Clair Beach 271 42.19 N 82.51 W
Saint Clair Flats 204 42.32 N 82.37 W
Saint Clair Flats ≃ 271 42.35 N 82.36 W
Saint Clair Flats Canal ≅ 204 42.20 N 82.58 W
Saint Clair Flats State Wildlife Area ♠4 271 42.36 N 82.40 W
Saint Clair Haven 204 42.34 N 82.47 W
Saint Clair Shores 204 42.30 N 82.54 W
Saint-Clair-sur-Epte 46 49.12 N 1.41 E
Saint Clairsville, Ohio, U.S. 204 40.05 N 80.54 W
Saint Clairsville, Pa., U.S. 204 40.09 N 78.31 W
Saint Clair Tunnel ♠5 204 42.57 N 82.25 W
Saint-Claud 32 45.53 N 0.23 E
Saint-Claude, Man., Can. 174 49.40 N 98.22 W
Saint-Claude, Fr. 54 46.23 N 5.52 E
Saint-Claude, Guad. 231o 16.02 N 61.42 W
Saint Clears 44 51.50 N 4.30 W
Saint-Clément 54 48.32 N 6.36 E
Saint Clements 204 43.31 N 80.39 W
Saint Clements Bay C 198 38.17 N 76.42 W
Sainte-Clothilde 196 45.59 N 72.14 W
Saint Cloud, Fr. 46 48.50 N 2.11 E
Saint Cloud, Fla., U.S. 210 28.15 N 81.17 W
Saint Cloud, Minn., U.S. 180 45.33 N 94.10 W
Saint-Cloud, Parc de ♠ 251 48.50 N 2.13 E
Saint-Cloud, Ruisseau ≃ 265a 45.25 N 73.28 W
Saint-Colomban-des-Villards 56 45.18 N 6.14 E
Sainte-Colombe 54 47.52 N 4.32 E
Saint Columb Major 44 50.26 N 5.03 W
Saint-Constant 196 45.22 N 73.37 W
Saint-Cosme-en-Vairais 46 48.16 N 0.28 E
Sainte-Croix, Qué., Can. 196 46.38 N 71.44 W
Sainte-Croix, Schw. 54 46.49 N 6.31 E
Saint Croix I 231n 17.45 N 64.45 W
Saint Croix ≃, N.A. 176 45.10 N 67.10 W
Saint Croix ≃, U.S. 180 44.45 N 92.49 W
Sainte-Croix-aux-Mines 54 48.16 N 7.13 E
Saint Croix Falls 180 45.24 N 92.38 W
Saint Croix Island I 148 33.48 S 25.45 E
Saint Croix Island National Monument ♠ 176 45.08 N 67.08 W
Saint Croix National Scenic Riverway ♠ 198 46.00 N 92.25 W
Saint Croix State Park ♠ 180 46.00 N 92.40 W
Sainte-Croix-Vallée-Française 56 44.11 N 3.44 E
Saint-Cuthbert 196 46.09 N 73.14 W
Saint-Cyprien 32 44.52 N 1.02 E
Saint-Cyrille-de-Wendover 196 45.56 N 72.26 W
Saint-Cyr-l'École 46 48.48 N 2.04 E
Saint-Cyr-l'École, Aérodrome de ⊠ 251 48.49 N 2.04 E
Saint Cyr Range ⩚ 170 61.10 N 131.10 W
Saint-Cyr-sous-Dourdan 251 48.34 N 2.02 E
Saint-Cyr-sur-Loire 46 47.24 N 0.40 E
Saint-Cyr-sur-Mer 56 43.11 N 5.43 E
Saint-Dalmas-de-Tende 56 44.03 N 7.35 E
Saint-Damien-de-Brandon 196 46.20 N 73.29 W
Saint David, Ariz., U.S. 190 31.54 N 110.13 W
Saint David, Ill., U.S. 180 40.30 N 90.03 W
Saint David Bay C 230d 15.26 N 61.15 W
Saint David's, Newf., Can. 176 48.12 N 58.52 W
Saint Davids, Ont., Can. 274a 43.10 N 79.06 W
Saint David's, Wales, U.K. 44 51.54 N 5.16 W
Saint Davids, Pa., U.S. 275 40.02 N 75.22 W
Saint David's Cathedral ✝1 44 51.54 N 5.16 W
Saint David's Head ≻ 44 51.55 N 5.19 W
Saint Davids Island I 230a 32.22 N 64.39 W
Saint-Denis, Fr. 46 48.56 N 2.22 E
Saint-Denis, Réu. 147c 20.52 S 55.28 E
Saint-Denis, Basilique ✝1 251 48.56 N 2.22 E
Saint-Denis-de-l'Hôtel 46 47.52 N 2.07 E
Saint-Denis-en-Bugey 54 45.57 N 5.20 E
Saint-Denis-Rivière-Richelieu 196 45.47 N 73.09 W
Saint Dennis 44 50.23 N 4.53 W
Saint-Didier-en-Velay 56 45.18 N 4.17 E
Saint-Didier-les-Bains 56 44.00 N 5.07 E
Saint-Dié 54 48.17 N 6.57 E
Saint-Disdier 56 44.44 N 5.54 E
Saint-Dizier 54 48.38 N 4.57 E
Saint Dogmaels 44 52.05 N 4.40 W
Saint-Donat-de-Montcalm 196 46.19 N 74.13 W
Saint-Donat-sur-l'Herbasse 56 45.07 N 5.00 E
Sainte-Dorothée ♠8 265a 45.32 N 73.49 W
Saint-Dyé-sur-Loire 46 47.39 N 1.29 E
Sainte → Saint
Saint-Édouard-de-Maskinongé 196 46.20 N 73.09 W
Saint Edward 188 41.34 N 97.52 W
Saint-Égrève 56 45.14 N 5.41 E
Saint Eleanor's 176 46.25 N 63.49 W
Sainte-Éleuthère 176 47.29 N 69.17 W
Saint Elias, Cape ≻ 170 59.52 N 144.30 W
Saint Elias, Mount ▲ 170 60.18 N 140.55 W
Saint Elias Mountains ⩚ 170 60.30 N 139.30 W
Saint-Elie 240 4.50 N 53.17 W
Saint Elmo 209 39.02 N 88.51 W
Saint-Éloi 176 48.02 N 69.14 W
Saint-Émile-de-Montcalm 196 46.06 N 74.00 W
Saint-Émile-de-Québec 196 46.52 N 71.20 W
Saint-Émile-de-Suffolk 196 45.56 N 74.55 W
Sainte-Énimie 56 44.22 N 3.26 E
Saint-Épain 46 47.08 N 0.32 E
Saint-Esprit ≃ 196 45.52 N 73.27 W
Saint-Étienne 56 45.26 N 4.24 E
Saint-Étienne-de-Lugdarès 56 44.39 N 3.57 E
Saint-Étienne-de-Saint-Geoirs 56 45.20 N 5.21 E
Saint-Étienne-des-Grès 196 46.26 N 72.46 W
Saint-Étienne-du-Rouvray 46 49.23 N 1.06 E
Saint-Étienne-en-Dévoluy 56 44.42 N 5.56 E
Saint-Étienne-le-Laus 56 44.30 N 6.10 E
Saint-Étienne-les-Orgues 56 44.03 N 5.47 E
Saint-Étienne-lès-Remiremont 54 48.02 N 6.37 E
Saint-Eugène 196 45.30 N 74.28 W
Saint-Eustache 196 45.33 N 73.54 W
Saint-Evroult-Notre-Dame-du-Bois 46 48.48 N 0.28 E
Saint-Fabien 176 48.18 N 68.52 W
Saint Faith's 148 30.30 S 30.12 E
Saint-Fargeau 46 47.38 N 3.04 E
Saint-Fargeau-Ponthierry 251 48.33 N 2.32 E
Saint-Félicien, Qué., Can. 166 48.39 N 72.26 W
Saint-Félicien, Fr. 56 45.05 N 4.38 E
Sainte-Félicité 176 48.54 N 67.20 W
Saint-Félix 56 45.48 N 5.58 E
Saint-Félix-de-Kingsey 196 45.48 N 72.12 W
Saint-Félix-de-Valois 196 46.10 N 73.26 W
Saint-Ferdinand (Bernierville) 196 46.06 N 71.34 W
Saintfield 42 54.28 N 5.50 W
Saint-Firmin 56 44.47 N 6.02 E
Saint-Firmin-sur-Loire 46 47.37 N 2.44 E
Saint-Flavien 196 46.31 N 71.36 W
Saint-Florentin 46 48.00 N 3.44 E
Saint-Florent-sur-Cher 32 46.59 N 2.15 E
Saint-Floris, Parc National de ♠ 136 9.40 N 21.35 E
Saint-Flour 32 45.02 N 3.05 E
Saint-Fons 56 45.42 N 4.52 E
Saint-Fortunat 196 45.58 N 71.36 W
Sainte-Foy 196 46.47 N 71.17 W
Sainte-Foy-la-Grande 32 44.50 N 0.13 E
Sainte-Foy-l'Argentière 56 45.42 N 4.28 E
Sainte-Foy-lès-Lyon 56 45.44 N 4.48 E
Sainte-Foy-Tarentaise 56 45.35 N 6.53 E
Saint Francis, Kans., U.S. 188 39.46 N 101.48 W
Saint Francis, S. Dak., U.S. 188 43.09 N 100.54 W
Saint Francis, Wis., U.S. 206 42.58 N 87.52 W
Saint Francis ≃, N.A. 176 47.10 N 68.57 W
Saint Francis ≃, U.S. 184 34.38 N 90.35 W
Saint Francis, Cape ≻, Newf., Can. 176 47.50 N 52.47 W
Saint Francis, Cape ≻, S. Afr. 148 34.14 S 24.49 E
Saint Francis, Lake ⊜ 196 45.08 N 74.25 W
Saint Francis Bay C 148 34.35 S 25.10 E
Saint Francisville 184 30.47 N 91.23 W
Saint-François 231o 16.15 N 61.17 W
Saint-François ≃ 196 46.07 N 72.55 W
Saint-François, Lac ⊜ 196 45.55 N 71.10 W
Saint-François de Boundji 142 1.03 S 15.22 E
Saint-François-de-Laval ♠8 265a 45.40 N 73.34 W
Saint-François-du-Lac 196 46.04 N 72.50 W
Saint Francois Mountains ⩚2 184 37.30 N 90.35 W
Saint-François-sur-Bugeon 56 45.24 N 6.21 E
Saint-Front 56 44.59 N 4.08 E
Saint-Gabriel 196 46.17 N 73.23 W
Saint-Gabriel-deGaspé 176 48.31 N 64.32 W
Saint-Gabriel-de-Rimouski 176 48.25 N 68.10 W
Saint-Gall → Sankt Gallen 54 47.25 N 9.23 E
Saint-Galmier 56 45.35 N 4.19 E
Sainte-Gauburge-Sainte-Colombe 46 48.42 N 0.26 E
Saint-Gaudens 32 43.07 N 0.44 E
Saint-Gaudens National Historic Site ⊥ 178 43.29 N 72.19 W
Saint-Gaultier 32 46.38 N 1.25 E
Saint-Gély-du-Fesc 56 43.42 N 3.48 E
Saint-Genest-Lerpt 56 45.27 N 4.20 E
Saint-Genest-Malifaux 56 45.20 N 4.25 E
Sainte-Geneviève, Qué., Can. 265a 45.29 N 73.52 W
Sainte Genevieve, Mo., U.S. 184 37.59 N 90.03 W
Sainte-Geneviève-de-Batiscan 196 46.32 N 72.20 W
Sainte-Geneviève-des-Bois 46 48.38 N 2.20 E
Saint-Gengoux-le-National 54 46.37 N 4.39 E
Saint-Genis-de-Saintonge 32 45.29 N 0.34 W
Saint-Genis-Laval 56 45.41 N 4.48 E
Saint-Genis-Pouilly 54 46.15 N 6.01 E
Saint-Genix-sur-Guiers 56 45.36 N 5.38 E
Saint-Geoire-en-Valdaine 56 45.27 N 5.38 E
Saint George, Austl. 156 28.02 S 148.35 E
Saint George, Ber. 230a 32.22 N 64.40 W
Saint George, N.B., Can. 176 45.08 N 66.49 W
Saint George, Ont., Can. 202 43.15 N 80.15 W
Saint George, Alaska, U.S. 170 56.36 N 169.32 W
Saint George, Pa., U.S. 204 41.15 N 79.47 W
Saint George, S.C., U.S. 182 33.11 N 80.35 W
Saint George, Utah, U.S. 190 37.06 N 113.35 W
Saint George ♠8 266 40.39 N 74.05 W
Saint George, Cape ≻, Newf., Can. 176 48.27 N 59.15 W
Saint George, Cape ≻, Pap. N. Gui. 154 4.52 S 152.52 E
Saint George, Cape ≻, Fla., U.S. 182 29.35 N 85.04 W
Saint George, Point ≻ 194 41.47 N 124.15 W
Saint George Island 198 38.07 N 76.29 W
Saint George Island I, Alaska, U.S. 170 56.35 N 169.35 W
Saint George Island I, Fla., U.S. 182 29.39 N 84.55 W
Saint George's, Newf., Can. 176 48.26 N 58.29 W
Saint-Georges, Qué., Can. 196 46.37 N 72.40 W
Saint-Georges, Fr. 54 48.40 N 6.56 E
Saint George's, Gren. 231k 12.03 N 61.45 W
Saint-Georges, Guy. fr. 240 3.54 N 51.48 W
Saint Georges, Del., U.S. 198 39.33 N 75.39 W
Saint Georges Basin C 160 35.07 S 150.36 E
Saint George's Bay C, Newf., Can. 176 48.20 N 59.00 W
Saint Georges Bay C, N.S., Can. 176 45.50 N 61.45 W
Saint George's Channel ⋓, Eur. 28 52.00 N 6.00 W
Saint George's Channel ⋓, Pap. N. Gui. 154 4.30 S 152.30 E
Saint-Georges-de-Reneins 54 46.04 N 4.43 E
Saint-Georges-de-Windsor 196 45.42 N 71.50 W
Saint-Georges-en-Couzan 56 45.42 N 3.56 E
Saint Georges Harbour C 230a 32.22 N 64.40 W
Saint Georges Head ≻ 160 35.12 S 150.42 E
Saint Georges Island I 230a 32.22 N 64.40 W
Saint George Sound ⋓ 182 29.47 N 84.42 W
Saint Georges Ranges ⩚ 152 18.40 S 125.00 E
Saint-Gérard, Bel. 52 50.21 N 4.45 E
Saint-Gérard, Qué., Can. 196 45.46 N 71.25 W
Saint-Germain 32 48.54 N 2.05 E
Saint-Germain ≃ 196 45.55 N 72.30 W
Saint-Germain, Forêt de ♠ 251 48.55 N 2.05 E
Saint-Germain-de-Calberte 56 44.13 N 3.48 E
Saint-Germain-de-Grantham 196 45.50 N 72.34 W
Saint-Germain-des-Joux 54 46.11 N 5.44 E
Saint-Germain-des-Champs 46 47.25 N 3.55 E
Saint-Germain-du-Bois 54 46.45 N 5.15 E
Saint-Germain-du-Plain 54 46.42 N 4.58 E
Saint-Germain-en-Laye 46 48.54 N 2.05 E
Saint-Germain-en-Laye, Château de ⊥ 251 48.54 N 2.06 E
Saint-Germain-Laval 56 45.50 N 4.01 E
Saint-Germain-Laxis 251 48.35 N 2.43 E
Saint-Germain-Lembron 32 45.28 N 3.14 E
Saint-Germain-lès-Arlay 54 46.46 N 5.34 E
Saint-Germain-lès-Corbeil 251 48.37 N 2.29 E
Saint-Germain-l'Herm 32 45.28 N 3.33 E
Saint-Germain-sur-Morin 251 48.53 N 2.51 E
Saint Germans 44 50.24 N 4.18 W
Saint-Germer-de-Fly 46 49.27 N 1.47 E
Saint-Gervais-d'Auvergne 32 46.02 N 2.49 E
Saint-Gervais-les-Bains 56 45.54 N 6.43 E
Saint-Gervasy 56 43.53 N 4.29 E
Saint-Géry 32 44.29 N 1.35 E
Saint-Gilles, Bel. 46 50.49 N 4.20 E
Saint-Gilles, Qué., Can. 196 46.31 N 71.22 W
Saint-Gilles, Fr. 56 43.41 N 4.26 E
Saint-Gilles-croix-de-Vie 32 46.42 N 1.57 W
Saint-Gingolph 54 46.24 N 6.52 E
Saint-Girons 32 42.59 N 1.09 E
Saint-Gobain 46 49.36 N 3.23 E
Saint Gotthard Pass → San Gottardo, Passo del ⩘ 54 46.33 N 8.34 E
Saint Govan's Head ≻ 44 51.36 N 4.55 W
Saint-Gratien 251 48.58 N 2.17 E
Saint-Grégoire (Larochelle) 196 46.16 N 72.30 W
Saint Gregory, Mount ▲ 176 49.19 N 58.13 W
Saint-Guénolé 32 47.49 N 4.20 W
Saint-Guillaume-d'Upton 196 45.53 N 72.46 W
Saint-Héand 56 45.31 N 4.22 E
Saint Helena 216 38.30 N 122.28 W

ENGLISH — Name, Page, Lat.°′, Long.°′
DEUTSCH — Name, Seite, Breite°′, Länge°′ E = Ost

Saint Helena □2 8 15.57 S 5.42 W
Saint Helena I 8 15.57 S 5.42 W
Saint Helena, Mount ▲ 216 38.40 N 122.38 W
Saint Helenabaai C 148 32.43 S 18.05 E
Saint Helena Sound ⋓ 182 32.27 N 80.25 W
Sainte-Hélène, Île I 265a 45.31 N 73.32 W
Sainte-Hélène-de-Bagot 196 45.44 N 72.44 W
Saint Helens, Austl. 156 41.20 S 148.15 E
Saint Helens, Eng., U.K. 42 53.28 N 2.44 W
Saint Helens, Eng., U.K. 44 50.42 N 1.06 W
Saint Helens, Eng., U.K. 252 53.28 N 2.44 W
Saint Helens, Oreg., U.S. 214 45.52 N 122.48 W
Saint Helens □8 252 53.28 N 2.45 W
Saint Helens, Mount ▲ 214 46.12 N 122.11 W
Saint Helens Canal ≅ 252 53.27 N 2.42 W
Saint Helier 28 49.12 N 2.37 W
Saint Henry 206 40.25 N 84.38 W
Sainte-Hermine 32 46.33 N 1.04 W
Sainthia 116 23.57 N 87.40 E
Saint-Hilaire-du-Harcouët 32 48.35 N 1.06 W
Saint-Hilaire-Est 196 45.34 N 73.11 W
Saint-Hilarion 251 48.37 N 1.44 E
Saint-Hippolyte, Fr. 54 47.19 N 6.49 E
Saint-Hippolyte, Fr. 56 43.38 N 4.45 E
Saint-Hippolyte-de-Kilkenny 196 45.56 N 74.01 W
Saint-Hippolyte-du-Fort 56 43.58 N 3.51 E
Saint-Honorat, Mont ▲ 56 44.05 N 6.46 E
Saint-Hubert, Bel. 52 50.01 N 5.23 E
Saint-Hubert, Qué., Can. 196 45.30 N 73.25 W
Saint-Hubert, Étang de ⊜ 251 48.43 N 1.51 E
Saint-Hubert-le-Roi 251 48.43 N 1.52 E
Saint-Hugues 196 45.48 N 72.52 W
Saint-Hyacinthe 196 45.37 N 72.57 W
Saint-Hyacinthe □6 196 45.40 N 73.05 W
Saint-Ignace, N.B., Can. 176 46.42 N 65.05 W
Saint Ignace, Mich., U.S. 180 45.52 N 84.43 W
Saint Ignace Island I 180 48.48 N 87.55 W
Saint Ignatius 192 47.19 N 114.06 W
Saint Ignatius Mission 236 3.20 N 59.47 W
Saint-Imier 54 47.09 N 7.00 E
Saint-Imier, Vallon de V 54 47.10 N 7.00 E
Saint-Isidore 176 47.33 N 65.03 W
Saint-Isidore-d'Auckland 196 45.16 N 71.31 W
Saint-Isidore-de-Laprairie 265a 45.18 N 73.41 W
Saint Ives, Austl. 264a 33.44 S 151.10 E
Saint Ives, Eng., U.K. 28 50.12 N 5.29 W
Saint Ives, Eng., U.K. 44 52.20 N 0.05 W
Saint Jacob 209 38.43 N 89.46 W
Saint Jacobs 202 43.32 N 80.33 W
Saint-Jacques 196 45.57 N 73.34 W
Saint-Jacques ≃ 265a 45.26 N 73.29 W
Saint James, Ill., U.S. 209 38.57 N 88.51 W
Saint James, Mich., U.S. 180 45.45 N 85.31 W
Saint James, Minn., U.S. 188 43.59 N 94.38 W
Saint James, Mo., U.S. 184 38.00 N 91.37 W
Saint James, N.Y., U.S. 200 40.53 N 73.09 W
Saint James, Cape ≻ 172 51.56 N 131.01 W
Saint James City 210 26.30 N 82.04 W
Saint James Islands II 230m 18.19 N 64.50 W
Saint James Palace ✝ 250 51.30 N 0.08 W
Saint-Jean 196 45.19 N 73.16 W
Saint-Jean □6 196 45.15 N 73.20 W
Saint-Jean ≃, Qué., Can. 176 50.17 N 64.20 W
Saint-Jean ≃, Qué., Can. 176 48.46 N 64.26 W
Saint-Jean, Île I 265a 45.41 N 73.39 W
Saint-Jean, Lac ⊜ 166 48.35 N 72.05 W
Saint-Jean, Rapides de ⊔ 265a 45.19 N 73.15 W
Saint-Jean Airport ⊠ 265a 45.18 N 73.17 W
Saint-Jean-aux-Bois 46 49.21 N 2.55 E
Saint-Jean-Baptiste 174 49.16 N 97.21 W
Saint-Jean-Baptiste-de-Rouville 196 45.31 N 73.07 W
Saint-Jean-Cap-Ferrat 56 43.41 N 7.20 E
Saint-Jean-d'Angély 32 45.57 N 0.31 W
Saint-Jean-d'Assé 46 48.09 N 0.07 E
Saint-Jean-de-Bournay 56 45.29 N 5.08 E
Saint-Jean-de-Braye 46 47.54 N 1.58 E
Saint-Jean-de-Losne 54 47.06 N 5.15 E
Saint-Jean-de-Luz 32 43.23 N 1.40 W
Saint-Jean-de-Maurienne 56 45.17 N 6.21 E
Saint-Jean-de-Monts 32 46.48 N 2.03 W
Saint-Jean-des-Piles 196 46.41 N 72.45 W
Saint-Jean-du-Gard 56 44.06 N 3.53 E
Saint-Jean-en-Royans 56 45.01 N 5.18 E
Saint-Jean-Pied-de-Port 32 43.10 N 1.14 W
Saint-Jean-Port-Joli 176 47.13 N 70.16 W
Saint-Jean-Soleymieux 56 45.30 N 4.02 E
Saint-Jeoire 56 46.09 N 6.28 E
Saint-Jérôme 196 45.47 N 74.00 W
Saint Jo 186 33.42 N 97.31 W
Saint Joachim 204 42.16 N 82.38 W
Saint Joe 206 41.19 N 84.54 W
Saint Joe ≃ 192 47.21 N 116.42 W
Saint John, N.B., Can. 176 45.16 N 66.03 W
Saint John, Ind., U.S. 206 41.27 N 87.28 W
Saint John, Kans., U.S. 188 38.00 N 98.46 W
Saint John, N. Dak., U.S. 188 48.57 N 99.43 W
Saint John, Wash., U.S. 192 47.05 N 117.35 W
Saint John I 230m 18.20 N 64.45 W
Saint John ≃, Liber. 140 6.40 N 9.10 W
Saint John ≃, N.A. 176 45.15 N 66.04 W
Saint John, Cape ≻ 176 50.00 N 55.32 W
Saint John, Lake ⊜, Newf., Can. 176 48.23 N 54.40 W
Saint John, Lake ⊜, Ont., Can. 202 44.41 N 79.20 W
Saint John Bay C 176 50.54 N 57.08 W
Saint John Island I 176 50.49 N 57.14 W
Saint Johns, Antig. 230c 17.06 N 61.51 W
Saint John's, Newf., Can. 176 47.34 N 52.43 W
Saint Johns → Saint-Jean, Qué., Can. 196 45.19 N 73.16 W
Saint John's, I. of Man 42 54.13 N 4.38 W
Saint Johns, Ariz., U.S. 190 34.30 N 109.22 W
Saint Johns, Mich., U.S. 206 43.00 N 84.33 W
Saint Johns, Mo., U.S. 209 38.43 N 90.22 W
Saint Johns, Ohio, U.S. 206 40.33 N 84.05 W
Saint Johns ≃, Calif., U.S. 216 36.25 N 119.25 W
Saint Johns ≃, Fla., U.S. 182 30.24 N 81.24 W
Saint Johnsburg 200 43.05 N 78.53 W
Saint Johnsbury 178 44.25 N 72.01 W
Saint Johns Creek ≃ 209 38.34 N 91.01 W
Saint John's Jerusalem ⊥ 250 51.25 N 0.14 E
Saint Johns Marsh ⩸ 210 27.40 N 80.35 W
Saint John's University ✝2 266 40.43 N 73.48 W
Saint Johnsville 200 43.00 N 74.41 W
Saint Joseph, N.B., Can. 176 45.59 N 64.34 W
Saint-Joseph, Qué., Can. 196 45.38 N 72.56 W
Saint-Joseph, Dom. 230d 15.26 N 61.26 W
Saint-Joseph, Mart. 230e 14.40 N 61.03 W
Saint-Joseph, Réu. 147c 21.22 S 55.36 E
Saint Joseph, Ill., U.S. 184 40.07 N 88.02 W
Saint Joseph, La., U.S. 184 31.55 N 91.14 W
Saint Joseph, Mich., U.S. 206 42.06 N 86.29 W
Saint Joseph, Minn., U.S. 180 45.34 N 94.19 W
Saint Joseph, Mo., U.S. 184 39.46 N 94.51 W
Saint Joseph □6, Ind., U.S. 206 41.41 N 86.15 W
Saint Joseph □6, Mich., U.S. 206 41.55 N 85.31 W
Saint Joseph ≃, U.S. 206 42.07 N 86.29 W
Saint Joseph ≃, U.S. 206 41.05 N 85.08 W
Saint-Joseph, Île I 265a 45.41 N 73.42 W
Saint-Joseph, Lac ⊜ 196 46.54 N 71.38 W
Saint Joseph, Lake ⊜ 166 51.05 N 90.35 W
Saint Joseph, West Branch ≃ 206 41.39 N 84.34 W
Saint Joseph Bay C 182 29.47 N 85.21 W
Saint Joseph Channel ⋓ 180 46.16 N 83.51 W
Saint Joseph d'Alma → Alma 176 48.33 N 71.39 W
Saint-Joseph-de-Beauce 176 46.18 N 70.53 W
Saint-Joseph-de-Mékinac 196 46.55 N 72.42 W
Saint-Joseph-de-Sorel 196 46.02 N 73.07 W
Saint-Joseph-du-Lac 265a 45.32 N 74.00 W
Saint Joseph Island I 180 46.13 N 83.57 W
Saint Joseph's College ✝2 275 40.00 N 75.14 W
Saint-Jouin-Bruneval 46 49.39 N 0.10 E
Saint-Jovite 196 46.07 N 74.36 W
Sainte-Julie 196 45.35 N 73.19 W
Saint-Julien 54 46.23 N 5.27 E
Saint-Julien-Chapteuil 56 45.02 N 4.04 E
Saint-Julien-du-Sault 46 48.02 N 3.18 E
Saint-Julien-du-Verdon 56 43.55 N 6.32 E
Saint-Julien-en-Beauchêne 56 44.37 N 5.42 E
Saint-Julien-en-Born 32 44.04 N 1.14 W
Saint-Julien-en-Genevois 54 46.08 N 6.05 E
Saint-Julien-en-Jarez 56 45.28 N 4.31 E
Saint-Julien-les-Villas 46 48.16 N 4.06 E
Saint-Julien-Molin-Molette 56 45.19 N 4.37 E
Sainte-Julienne 196 45.58 N 73.43 W
Saint-Junien 32 45.53 N 0.54 E
Saint Just 230m 18.23 N 66.00 W
Saint-Just-en-Chaussée 46 49.30 N 2.26 E
Saint-Just-en-Chevalet 32 45.55 N 3.50 E
Saint-Justin 196 46.15 N 73.05 W
Saint-Just-Malmont 56 45.20 N 4.19 E
Saint-Just-sur-Loire 56 45.29 N 4.16 E
Saint Kilda, Austl. 158b 34.44 S 138.32 E
Saint Kilda, Austl. 159 37.52 S 144.59 E
Saint Kilda, N.Z. 162 45.54 S 170.30 E
Saint Kilda I 28 57.49 N 8.36 W
Saint Kitts → Saint Christopher I 228 17.20 N 62.45 W
Saint Kitts-Nevis □2 228 17.20 N 62.45 W
Saint-Lambert, Qué., Can. 178 45.30 N 73.30 W
Saint-Lambert, Fr. 251 48.44 N 2.01 E
Saint Landry 184 30.51 N 92.15 W
Saint-Laurent, Man., Can. 174 50.24 N 97.56 W
Saint-Laurent, Qué., Can. 196 45.30 N 73.40 W
Saint-Laurent, Fr. 54 48.09 N 6.27 E
Saint-Laurent → Saint Lawrence ≃ 166 49.30 N 67.00 W
Saint-Laurent-Blangy 46 50.18 N 2.48 E
Saint-Laurent-de-Chamousset 56 45.44 N 4.28 E
Saint-Laurent-du-Maroni 240 5.30 N 54.02 W
Saint-Laurent-du-Var, Fr. 56 43.40 N 7.11 E
Saint-Laurent-du-Var, Fr. 56 45.23 N 5.44 E
Saint-Laurent-en-Caux 46 49.45 N 0.53 E
Saint-Laurent-en-Grandvaux 54 46.35 N 5.57 E
Saint-Laurent-et-Benon 32 45.09 N 0.49 W
Saint-Laurent-les-Bains 56 44.37 N 3.58 E
Saint-Laurent-sur-Saône 54 46.18 N 4.50 E
Saint Lawrence, Austl. 156 22.21 S 149.31 E
Saint Lawrence, Newf., Can. 176 46.55 N 55.24 W
Saint Lawrence □6 202 44.30 N 75.27 W
Saint Lawrence ≃ 166 49.30 N 67.00 W
Saint Lawrence, Cape ≻ 176 47.03 N 60.37 W
Saint Lawrence, Gulf of C 176 48.00 N 62.00 W
Saint Lawrence Island I 170 63.30 N 170.30 W
Saint Lawrence Islands National Park ♠ 202 44.18 N 76.08 W
Saint-Lazare 174 50.26 N 101.12 W
Saint-Lazare ♠5 251 48.53 N 2.20 E
Saint-Léandre 176 48.44 N 67.36 W
Saint-Léger-en-Yvelines 251 48.43 N 1.46 E
Saint-Léger-sur-Dheune 54 46.51 N 4.38 E
Saint Leo 210 28.21 N 82.14 W
Saint Leon 208 39.17 N 84.57 W
Saint-Léonard, N.B., Can. 176 47.10 N 67.56 W
Saint-Léonard, Qué., Can. 196 45.35 N 73.35 W
Saint Leonard, Md., U.S. 198 38.28 N 76.30 W

Symbols in the index entries represent the broad categories identified in the key at the right. Symbols with superior numbers (⩚²) identify subcategories (see complete key on page I · 26).

Kartensymbole in dem Registerverzeichnis stellen die rechts in Schlüssel erklärten Kategorien dar. Symbole mit hochgestellten Ziffern (⩚²) bezeichnen Unterabteilungen einer Kategorie (vgl. vollständiger Schlüssel auf Seite I · 26).

Los símbolos incluidos en el texto del índice representan las grandes categorías identificadas con la clave a la derecha. Los símbolos con numeros en su parte superior (⩚²) identifican las subcategorías (véase la clave completa en la página I · 26).

Les symboles de l'index représentent les catégories indiquées dans la légende à droite. Les symboles suivis d'un indice (⩚²) représentent des sous-catégories (voir légende complète à la page I · 26).

Os símbolos incluídos no texto do índice representam as grandes categorias identificadas com a chave à direita. Os símbolos com números em sua parte superior (⩚²) identificam as subcategorias (veja-se a chave completa à página I · 26).

English	Deutsch	Español	Français	Português
▲ Mountain	Berg	Montaña	Montagne	Montanha
⩚ Mountains	Berge	Montañas	Montagnes	Montanhas
⩘ Pass	Pass	Paso	Col	Passo
V Valley, Canyon	Tal, Cañon	Valle, Cañón	Vallée, Canyon	Vale, Canhão
⊟ Plain	Ebene	Llano	Plaine	Planície
≻ Cape	Kap	Cabo	Cap	Cabo
I Island	Insel	Isla	Île	Ilha
II Islands	Inseln	Islas	Îles	Ilhas
⊥ Other Topographic Features	Andere Topographische Objekte	Otros Elementos Topográficos	Autres données topographiques	Outros Elementos Topográficos

ESPAÑOL

Nombre	Página	Lat.°′	Long.°′ W=Oeste
Saint-Léonard-d'Aston	196	46.06 N	72.22 W
Saint-Léonard-de-Noblat	32	45.50 N	1.29 E
Saint Leonards	44	50.51 N	0.34 E
Saint-Leu-d'Esserent	46	49.13 N	2.25 E
Saint-Leu-la-Forêt	46	49.01 N	2.15 E
Saint-Liboire	196	45.39 N	72.46 W
Saint-Lô	32	49.07 N	1.05 W
Saint-Louis, Sask., Can.	174	52.56 N	105.49 W
Saint-Louis, Fr.	54	47.35 N	7.34 E
Saint-Louis, Guad.	231o	15.57 N	61.19 W
Saint-Louis, Réu.	147c	21.16 S	55.25 E
Saint-Louis, Sén.	140	16.02 N	16.30 W
Saint Louis, Mich., U.S.	180	43.25 N	84.36 W
Saint Louis, Mo., U.S.	209	38.38 N	90.11 W
Saint Louis, Tex., U.S.	212	32.18 N	95.20 W
Saint Louis □[6]	209	38.39 N	90.25 W
Saint-Louis ≃	265a	45.19 N	73.53 W
Saint-Louis, Baie de C	231o	15.57 N	61.20 W
Saint-Louis, Lac @	196	45.24 N	73.48 W
Saint-Louis, Pointe ≻	265a	45.19 N	73.53 W
Saint-Louis, Rivière de ≃	231o	15.57 N	61.20 W
Saint Louis Crossing	208	39.19 N	85.51 W
Saint-Louis-de-Champlain	196	46.25 N	72.36 W
Saint-Louis-de-Kent	176	46.44 N	64.58 W
Saint Louis Park	180	44.56 N	93.22 W
Saint Louisville	204	40.10 N	82.25 W
Saint-Loup-sur-Aujon	54	47.53 N	5.05 E
Saint-Loup-sur-Semouse	54	47.53 N	6.16 E
Saint-Luc, Qué., Can.	196	45.22 N	73.18 W
Saint-Luc, Schw.	54	46.13 N	7.36 E
Sainte-Luce	230e	14.28 N	60.56 W
Saint Lucia □[1]	**220**		
	231f	**13.53 N**	**60.58 W**
Saint Lucia, Cape ≻	148	28.25 S	32.25 E
Saint Lucia, Lake @	148	28.05 S	32.26 E
Saint Lucia Bay C	148	28.25 S	32.25 E
Saint Lucia Channel Ʊ	228	14.09 N	60.57 W
Saint Lucia Estuary	148	28.22 S	32.25 E
Saint Lucia Game Reserve ◆[4]	148	28.10 S	32.28 E
Sainte-Lucie, Fr.	36	41.42 N	9.22 E
Saint Lucie, Fla., U.S.	210	27.30 N	80.20 W
Saint Lucie □[6]	210	27.23 N	80.26 W
Saint Lucie ≃	210	27.10 N	80.11 W
Saint Lucie Canal ≋	210	27.10 N	80.15 W
Saint Lucie Inlet C	210	27.10 N	80.10 W
Saint Lucie Lock ◆[5]	210	27.07 N	80.17 W
Saint-Lucien	251	48.39 N	1.38 E
Saint-Lupicin	54	46.24 N	5.47 E
Sainte-Magnance	46	47.27 N	4.04 E
Saint Magnus Bay C	28	60.25 N	1.35 W
Saint-Malo, Qué., Can.	196	45.12 N	71.30 W
Saint-Malo, Fr.	32	48.39 N	2.01 W
Saint-Malo, Golfe de C	32	48.45 N	2.00 W
Saint-Mamert-du-Gard	56	43.53 N	4.12 E
Saint-Mammès	46	48.23 N	2.49 E
Saint-Mandé	251	48.50 N	2.25 E
Saint-Mandrier-sur-Mer	56	43.04 N	5.56 E
Saint-Marc, Qué., Can.	265a	45.41 N	73.12 W
Saint-Marc, Haï.	228	19.07 N	72.42 W
Saint-Marc, Canal de Ʊ	228	18.50 N	72.45 W
Saint-Marc-des-Carrières	196	46.41 N	72.03 W
Saint-Marcel	54	46.47 N	4.54 E
Saint-Marcellin	56	45.09 N	5.19 E
Saint-Marcelline-de-Kildare	196	46.07 N	73.36 W
Saint-Mard	251	49.02 N	2.42 E
Saint Margaret Bay C	176	51.01 N	56.58 W
Saint Margaret's at Cliffe	44	51.09 N	1.24 E
Saint Margaret's Bay C	176	44.35 N	64.00 W
Sainte-Marguerite ≃	166	50.09 N	66.36 W
Sainte-Marguerite, Baie C	176	50.06 N	66.36 W
Sainte-Marguerite-sur-Mer	46	49.55 N	0.57 E
Sainte-Marie	230e	14.47 N	61.00 W
Sainte-Marie, Cap ≻	147b	25.36 S	45.08 E
Sainte-Marie, Île I	147b	16.50 S	49.55 E
Sainte-Marie-aux-Mines (Markirch)	54	48.15 N	7.11 E
Saint Maries	192	47.19 N	116.35 W
Saint Maries ≃	192	47.19 N	116.33 W
Saint-Marin → San Marino □[1]	60	43.56 N	12.25 E
Saint Marks, S. Afr.	148	32.01 S	27.22 E
Saint Marks, Fla., U.S.	182	30.09 N	84.12 W
Saint Marks ≃	182	30.08 N	84.12 W
Sainte-Marthe-de-Gaspé	176	49.12 N	66.10 W
Saint-Martin (Sint Maarten) I	228	18.04 N	63.04 W
Saint-Martin, Cap ≻	230e	14.52 N	61.13 W
Saint Martin, Lake @	174	51.37 N	98.29 W
Saint-Martin-Boulogne	46	50.43 N	1.38 E
Saint-Martin-d'Ardèche	56	44.18 N	4.35 E
Saint-Martin-d'Auxigny	46	47.12 N	2.25 E
Saint-Martin-de-Belleville	56	45.23 N	6.30 E
Saint-Martin-de-Bossenay	46	48.26 N	3.41 E
Saint-Martin-de-Bréthencourt	251	48.31 N	1.56 E
Saint-Martin-de-Crau	56	43.38 N	4.49 E
Saint-Martin-de-Londres	56	43.47 N	3.44 E
Saint-Martin-de-Nigelles	251	48.37 N	1.37 E
Saint-Martin-d'Entraunes	56	44.08 N	6.46 E
Saint-Martin-des-Champs	251	48.53 N	1.43 E
Saint-Martin-de-Valamas	56	44.56 N	4.22 E
Saint-Martin-d'Hères	56	45.10 N	5.46 E
Saint-Martin-du-Puy	46	47.20 N	3.52 E
Saint-Martin-du-Tertre	251	49.06 N	2.21 E
Saint-Martin-du-Var	56	43.49 N	7.12 E
Sainte-Martine	196	45.15 N	73.48 W
Saint-Martin-en-Bresse	54	46.49 N	5.04 E
Saint-Martin-la-Garenne	251	49.02 N	1.41 E
Saint-Martin-la-Plaine	56	45.32 N	4.36 E
Saint Martins	176	45.21 N	65.32 W
Saint Martins Keys II	210	28.47 N	82.44 W
Saint-Martin-Vésubie	56	44.04 N	7.15 E
Saint Martinville	184	30.07 N	91.50 W
Saint Mary ≃, B.C., Can.	172	49.37 N	115.38 W

FRANÇAIS

Nom	Page	Lat.°′	Long.°′ W=Ouest
Saint Mary ≃, N.A.	172	49.37 N	112.52 W
Saint Mary, Cape ≻, N.S., Can.	176	44.05 N	66.13 W
Saint Mary, Cape ≻, Gam.	140	13.28 N	16.40 W
Saint Mary, Mount ∧	154	8.10 S	147.00 E
Saint Mary Bourne	44	51.16 N	1.24 W
Saint Mary Cray ◆[8]	250	51.23 N	0.07 E
Saint Mary Lake @	192	48.40 N	113.30 W
Saint Marylebone ◆[8]	250	51.31 N	0.10 W
Saint Mary of the Lake Seminary ʊ[2]	268	42.17 N	88.00 W
Saint Mary Peak ∧	156	31.30 S	138.33 E
Saint Mary Reservoir @[1]	172	49.19 N	113.12 W
Saint Marys, Austl.	156	41.35 S	148.10 E
Saint Marys, Austl.	160	33.47 S	150.47 E
Saint Mary's, Newf., Can.	176	46.55 N	53.34 W
Saint Mary's, Ont., Can.	202	43.16 N	81.08 W
Saint Marys, Alaska, U.S.	170	62.04 N	163.10 W
Saint Marys, Ga., U.S.	182	30.44 N	81.33 W
Saint Marys, Kans., U.S.	188	39.12 N	96.04 W
Saint Marys, Ohio, U.S.	206	40.33 N	84.23 W
Saint Marys, Pa., U.S.	204	41.26 N	78.34 W
Saint Marys, W. Va., U.S.	178	39.23 N	81.12 W
Saint Marys □[6]	198	38.17 N	76.38 W
Saint Mary's ≃, N.S., Can.	176	45.02 N	61.54 W
Saint Marys ≃, U.S.	182	30.43 N	81.27 W
Saint Marys ≃, U.S.	206	41.05 N	85.08 W
Saint Marys ≃, Md., U.S.	198	38.06 N	76.26 W
Saint Mary's, Cape ≻	176	46.49 N	54.12 W
Saint Marys, North Prong ≃	182	30.22 N	82.06 W
Saint Marys, South Prong ≃	182	30.22 N	82.06 W
Saint Mary's Bay	44	51.00 N	0.58 E
Saint Mary's Bay C, Newf., Can.	176	46.50 N	53.47 W
Saint Mary's Bay C, N.S., Can.	176	44.25 N	66.10 W
Saint Marys City	198	38.11 N	76.26 W
Saint Mary's Hoo	250	51.28 N	0.26 E
Saint Marys Lake @	268	42.17 N	87.59 W
Saint Mary's Marshes ☷	250	51.28 N	0.35 E
Saint-Mathieu	32	45.42 N	0.46 E
Saint-Mathieu, Pointe de ≻	32	48.20 N	4.46 W
Saint-Mathieu-de-Laprairie	265a	45.19 N	73.31 W
Saint Matthew Island I	170	60.30 N	172.45 W
Saint Matthews, Ky., U.S.	208	38.15 N	85.39 W
Saint Matthews, S.C., U.S.	182	33.40 N	80.46 W
Saint Matthias Group II	154	1.30 S	149.40 E
Saint-Maur-des-Fossés	46	48.48 N	2.30 E
Sainte-Maure-du-Touraine	32	47.07 N	0.37 E
Saint-Maurice, Fr.	251	48.49 N	2.25 E
Saint-Maurice, Schw.	54	46.13 N	7.00 E
Saint-Maurice □[6]	196	46.35 N	73.00 W
Saint-Maurice ≃	166	46.21 N	72.31 W
Saint-Maurice, Parc de ♠	196	46.52 N	73.10 W
Saint-Maurice-de-Beynost	56	45.50 N	5.00 E
Saint-Maurice-en-Montagne	54	46.34 N	5.50 E
Saint-Maurice-Montcouronne	251	48.35 N	2.07 E
Saint Mawes	44	50.09 N	5.01 W
Saint Mawgan	44	50.28 N	4.58 W
Saint-Max	54	48.42 N	6.13 E
Sainte-Maxime	56	43.18 N	6.38 E
Saint-Maximin-la-Sainte-Baume	56	43.27 N	5.52 E
Saint-Méen-le-Grand	32	48.11 N	2.12 W
Saint Meinrad	184	38.10 N	86.49 W
Sainte-Menehould	52	49.05 N	4.54 E
Saint-Menges	52	49.44 N	4.56 E
Sainte-Mère-Église	32	49.25 N	1.19 W
Saint Merryn	44	50.31 N	4.58 W
Saint-Méry	251	48.35 N	2.50 E
Sainte-Mesme	251	48.32 N	1.58 E
Saint-Mesmes	251	48.59 N	2.42 E
Saint Michael, Alaska, U.S.	170	63.29 N	162.02 W
Saint Michael, Pa., U.S.	204	40.20 N	78.46 W
Saint Michaels	178	38.47 N	76.14 W
Saint-Michel, Fr.	46	49.55 N	4.08 E
Saint-Michel, Fr.	56	45.13 N	6.28 E
Saint-Michel-de-Napierville	196	45.14 N	73.34 W
Saint-Michel-des-Saints	196	46.41 N	73.55 W
Saint-Michel-sur-Meurthe	54	48.19 N	6.54 E
Saint-Michel-sur-Orge	251	48.38 N	2.18 E
Saint-Mihiel	52	48.54 N	5.33 E
Sainte-Montaine	46	47.29 N	2.19 E
Saint-Moritz → Sankt Moritz	54	46.30 N	9.50 E
Saint-Narcisse	196	46.34 N	72.28 W
Saint-Nazaire	32	47.17 N	2.12 W
Saint-Nazaire-en-Royans	56	45.04 N	5.15 E
Saint-Nazaire-le-Désert	56	44.34 N	5.17 E
Saint Nazianz	180	44.00 N	87.55 W
Saint Neots	44	52.14 N	0.17 W
Saint-Nicéphore	196	45.50 N	72.25 W
Saint-Nicolas → Sint-Niklaas, Bel.	46	51.10 N	4.08 E
Saint-Nicolas, Qué., Can.	196	46.42 N	71.24 W
Saint-Nicolas-aux-Bois	46	49.36 N	3.25 E
Saint-Nicolas-d'Aliermont	46	49.53 N	1.13 E
Saint-Nicolas-de-Port	54	48.38 N	6.18 E
Saint-Nizier-du-Moucherotte	56	45.10 N	5.38 E
Saint-Nom-la-Bretèche	251	48.51 N	2.01 E
Saint Nora Lake @	202	45.08 N	78.49 W
Saint-Norbert-d'Arthabaska	196	46.07 N	71.50 W
Sainte Odile ʊ[1]	54	48.26 N	7.24 E
Saint-Omer	46	50.45 N	2.15 E
Saintonge □[9]	32	45.30 N	0.30 W
Saint-Ouen, Fr.	46	50.02 N	2.03 E
Saint-Ouen, Fr.	251	48.54 N	2.20 E
Saint-Ouen-l'Aumône	46	49.03 N	2.06 E
Saint-Pacôme	176	47.24 N	69.57 W
Saint-Pamphile	176	46.58 N	69.47 W
Saint Pancras ◆[8]	250	51.32 N	0.07 W
Saint Pancras Station ◆[5]	250	51.32 N	0.08 W
Saint Paris	208	40.07 N	83.58 W
Saint-Pascal	176	47.32 N	69.49 W
Saint-Paterne	46	48.24 N	0.07 E
Saint-Pathus	251	49.04 N	2.48 E
Saint-Patrick, Lac @	178	46.22 N	77.21 W
Saint Paul, Alta., Can.	172	53.59 N	111.17 W

PORTUGUÊS

Nome	Página	Lat.°′	Long.°′ W=Oeste
Saint-Paul, Fr.	56	43.42 N	7.07 E
Saint-Paul, Fr.	56	44.31 N	6.45 E
Saint-Paul, Réu.	147c	21.00 S	55.16 E
Saint Paul, Ind., U.S.	208	39.26 N	85.38 W
Saint Paul, Minn., U.S.	180	44.58 N	93.07 W
Saint Paul, Nebr., U.S.	188	41.13 N	98.27 W
Saint Paul, Oreg., U.S.	214	45.12 N	122.58 W
Saint Paul, Va., U.S.	182	36.54 N	82.19 W
Saint-Paul ≃, Can.	166	51.26 N	57.40 W
Saint Paul ≃, Liber.	140	7.10 N	10.00 W
Saint Paul, Cape ≻	140	5.49 N	0.57 E
Saint-Paul, Lac @	196	46.18 N	72.29 W
Saint Paul Bay C	106	10.14 N	118.54 E
Saint-Paul-de-Chester (Chesterville)	196	45.57 N	71.49 W
Saint-Paul-en-Jarez	56	45.29 N	4.35 E
Saint-Paul-et-Valmalle	56	43.38 N	3.40 E
Saint-Paulien	56	45.08 N	3.49 E
Saint-paulin	196	46.25 N	73.01 W
Saint Paul Island	170	57.07 N	170.17 W
Saint Paul Island I, N.S., Can.	176	47.15 N	60.10 W
Saint Paul Island I, Alaska, U.S.	170	57.10 N	170.15 W
Saint-Paul-l'Ermite	196	45.45 N	73.28 W
Saint Pauls	182	34.48 N	78.58 W
Saint Paul's Cathedral ʊ[1]	250	51.31 N	0.06 W
Saint Paul's Cray ◆[8]	250	51.24 N	0.07 E
Saint Pauls Inlet C	176	49.50 N	57.45 W
Saint Paul's Point ≻	164e	25.04 S	130.05 W
Saint-Paul-Trois-Châteaux	56	44.21 N	4.46 E
Saint-péravy-la-Colombe	46	48.00 N	1.42 E
Saint-Péray	56	44.57 N	4.50 E
Saint-Père	46	47.28 N	3.46 E
Saint Peter, Ill., U.S.	209	38.52 N	88.51 W
Saint Peter, Minn., U.S.	180	44.17 N	93.57 W
Saint Peter, Lake @	202	45.18 N	78.02 W
Saint Peter Island I	152	32.17 S	133.35 E
Saint Peter Port	32	49.27 N	2.32 W
Saint Peters, N.S., Can.	176	45.40 N	60.52 W
Saint Peters, Mo., U.S.	209	38.48 N	90.38 W
Saint Peters, Pa., U.S.	275	40.11 N	75.44 W
Saint Peters Bay	176	46.25 N	62.35 W
Saint Petersburg → Leningrad, S.S.S.R.	66	59.55 N	30.15 E
Saint Petersburg, Fla., U.S.	210	27.46 N	82.38 W
Saint Petersburg, Pa., U.S.	204	41.10 N	79.37 W
Saint Petersburg Beach	210	27.45 N	82.45 W
Saint Peter's College ʊ[2]	266	40.44 N	74.05 W
Saint Philip and Saint James Bay C	165f	15.06 S	166.54 E
Saint-Philippe-d'Argenteuil	196	45.37 N	74.25 W
Saint-Philippe-de-Laprairie	265a	45.21 N	73.28 W
Saint-Pie	196	45.30 N	72.54 W
Saint-Pierre, It.	56	45.42 N	7.14 E
Saint-Pierre, Mart.	230e	14.45 N	61.11 W
Saint-Pierre, Réu.	147c	21.19 S	55.29 E
Saint-Pierre, St. P./M.	176	46.40 N	56.00 W
Saint-Pierre I	176	46.47 N	56.11 W
Saint-Pierre ≃	265a	45.23 N	73.34 W
Saint-Pierre, Lac @	196	46.12 N	72.52 W
Saint-Pierre, Rade de ⊤[3]	230e	14.44 N	61.11 W
Saint Pierre and Miquelon □[2]	166		
	176	46.55 N	56.10 W
Saint-Pierre-d'Albigny	56	45.34 N	6.09 E
Saint-Pierre-de-Bœuf	56	45.22 N	4.45 E
Saint-Pierre-de-Broughton	196	46.15 N	71.12 W
Saint-Pierre-de-Chartreuse	56	45.20 N	5.49 E
Saint-Pierre-des-Corps	46	47.23 N	0.44 E
Saint-Pierre-de-Vacquière	56	43.52 N	4.13 E
Saint-Pierre-du-Vauvray	46	49.14 N	1.13 E
Saint-Pierre-Église	32	49.40 N	1.24 W
Saint-Pierre-en-Port	46	49.48 N	0.29 E
Saint-Pierre-et-Miquelon → Saint Pierre and Miquelon □[2]	176	46.55 N	56.10 W
Saint Pierre Island I	128	9.19 S	50.43 E
Saint-Pierre-Jolys	174	49.26 N	96.59 W
Saint-Pierre-la-Bourlhonne	56	45.40 N	3.45 E
Saint Pierre-le-Moûtier	32	46.48 N	3.07 E
Saint-Pierre-lès-Elbeuf	46	49.16 N	1.03 E
Saint-Pierreville	56	44.49 N	4.29 E
Saint-Point, Lac de @	54	46.49 N	6.19 E
Saint-Pol-de-Léon	32	48.41 N	3.59 W
Saint-Pol-sur-Mer	46	51.02 N	2.21 E
Saint-Pol-sur-Ternoise	46	50.23 N	2.20 E
Saint-Polycarpe	196	45.18 N	74.18 W
Saint-Pons	32	43.29 N	2.46 E
Saint-Pourçain-sur-Sioule	32	46.19 N	3.17 E
Saint-Prex	54	46.29 N	6.28 E
Saint-Priest	56	45.42 N	4.57 E
Saint-Priest-en-Jarez	56	45.28 N	4.22 E
Saint-Prix	251	49.01 N	2.16 E
Saint-Prosper-de-Dorchester	178	46.13 N	70.29 W
Saint-Quentin, N.B., Can.	176	47.30 N	67.23 W
Saint-Quentin, Fr.	46	49.51 N	3.17 E
Saint-Quentin, Canal de ≋	46	49.36 N	3.11 E
Saint-Quentin, Étang de @	251	48.47 N	2.01 E
Saint-Rambert-d'Albon	56	45.17 N	4.49 E
Saint-Rambert-en-Bugey	54	45.57 N	5.26 E
Saint-Rambert-sur-Loire	56	45.30 N	4.15 E
Saint-Raphaël	56	43.25 N	6.46 E
Saint-Raymond	196	46.54 N	71.50 W
Saint-Rédempter-de-Lévis	196	46.42 N	71.17 W
Saint Regis	192	47.18 N	115.06 W
Saint-Régis ≃, Qué., Can.	265a	45.24 N	73.34 W
Saint Regis ≃, Mont., U.S.	192	47.18 N	115.05 W
Saint Regis Falls	178	44.40 N	74.33 W
Saint Regis Indian Reservation ◆[4]	196	44.58 N	74.39 W
Saint-Rémi	196	45.16 N	73.37 W
Saint-Rémi-d'Amherst	196	46.01 N	74.46 W
Saint-Rémy (lès-Chevreuse), Fr.	46	48.42 N	2.05 E
Saint-Rémy, Fr.	54	46.46 N	4.50 E
Saint Remy, N.Y., U.S.	200	41.54 N	74.01 W
Saint-Rémy-de-Provence	56	43.47 N	4.50 E
Saint-Rémy-en-Bouzemont	54	48.38 N	4.39 E
Saint-Rémy-l'Honoré	251	48.45 N	1.53 E
Saint-Rémy-sur-Avre	46	48.46 N	1.15 E
Saint-Renan	32	48.26 N	4.37 W
Saint-Révérien	46	47.13 N	3.30 E
Saint-Rhémy	56	45.50 N	7.11 E
Saint-Riquier	46	50.08 N	1.57 E
Saint-Roch-de-l'Achigan	196	45.51 N	73.36 W
Saint-Romain-de-Colbosc	46	49.32 N	0.22 E
Saint-Romain-le-Puy	56	45.33 N	4.07 E
Saint-Romans	56	45.07 N	5.19 E
Saint-Romuald-d'Etchemin	196	46.45 N	71.14 W
Sainte-Rosalie	196	45.38 N	72.54 W
Sainte-Rose	231o	16.20 N	61.42 W
Sainte-Rose ◆[8]	265a	45.36 N	73.47 W
Sainte-Rose-du-Lac	174	51.03 N	99.32 W
Saintry-sur-Seine	251	48.36 N	2.30 E
Saintes, Bel.	46	50.42 N	4.10 E
Saintes, Fr.	32	45.45 N	0.52 W
Saintes, Îles des II	231o	15.52 N	61.37 W
Saint-Saëns	46	49.40 N	1.17 E
Saint-Saturnin-d'Apt	56	43.56 N	5.23 E
Saint-Sauveur, Fr.	46	47.37 N	3.12 E
Saint-Sauveur, Fr.	54	47.48 N	6.23 E
Saint-Sauveur-des-Monts	196	45.52 N	74.10 W
Saint-Sauveur-sur-Tinée	56	44.05 N	7.06 E
Saint-Savin	32	46.34 N	0.52 E
Sainte-Savine	46	48.18 N	4.03 E
Sainte-Scholastique	196	45.39 N	74.05 W
Saint Sebastian Bay C	148	34.25 S	21.00 E
Saint-Sébastien	196	45.07 N	73.09 W
Saint-Sébastien, Cap ≻	147b	12.26 S	48.44 E
Saint-Seine-l'Abbaye	54	47.26 N	4.47 E
Saint Servan	32	48.38 N	2.01 W
Saint Séverin	52	50.32 N	5.25 E
Saint Shotts	176	46.38 N	53.35 W
Sainte-Sigolène	56	45.14 N	4.15 E
Saint-Simon	46	49.45 N	3.10 E
Saint Simons Island	182	31.08 N	81.24 W
Saint Simons Island I	182	31.14 N	81.21 W
Saint-Sixte ≃	196	45.39 N	75.08 W
Saintes-Maries, Golfe des C	56	43.25 N	4.31 E
Saintes-Maries-de-la-Mer	56	43.27 N	4.26 E
Sainte-Sophie-de-Mégantic	196	46.09 N	71.42 W
Saint-Soupplets	251	49.02 N	2.48 E
Saint Stanislas Bay C	164o	1.53 N	157.30 W
Saint-Stanislas-de-Kosta	196	45.11 N	74.08 W
Saint Stephen, N.B., Can.	176	45.12 N	67.17 W
Saint Stephen, S.C., U.S.	182	33.24 N	79.55 W
Saint-Sulpice-de-Favières	251	48.33 N	2.11 E
Saint-Sulpice-les-Feuilles	32	46.19 N	1.22 E
Sainte-Suzanne	54	47.30 N	6.46 E
Saint-Sylvestre	196	46.22 N	71.14 W
Saint-Symphorien, Fr.	32	44.26 N	0.30 W
Saint-Symphorien, Fr.	251	48.31 N	1.46 E
Saint-Symphorien-d'Ozon	56	45.38 N	4.52 E
Saint-Symphorien-sur-Coise	56	45.38 N	4.27 E
Sainte-Thècle	196	46.49 N	72.31 W
Saint-Théodore-d'Acton	196	45.41 N	72.35 W
Sainte-Thérèse, Île I, Qué., Can.	265a	45.41 N	73.28 W
Sainte-Thérèse, Île I, Qué., Can.	265a	45.22 N	73.15 W
Sainte-Thérèse-de-Blainville	196	45.38 N	73.51 W
Saint-Thibault-des-Vignes	251	48.52 N	2.41 E
Saint Thomas, Ont., Can.	202	42.47 N	81.12 W
Saint Thomas, Mo., U.S.	209	38.23 N	92.13 W
Saint Thomas, N. Dak., U.S.	188	48.37 N	97.27 W
Saint Thomas → Charlotte Amalie, Vir. Is., U.S.	230m	18.21 N	64.56 W
Saint Thomas I	230m	18.21 N	64.55 W
Saint Timothée	196	45.18 N	74.02 W
Saint-Tite	196	46.44 N	72.34 W
Saint-Tite-des-Caps	176	47.08 N	70.47 W
Saint Tome et Principauté → Sao Tome and Principe □[1]	142	1.00 N	7.00 E
Saint-Trivier-de-Courtes	54	46.28 N	5.05 E
Saint-Trivier-sur-Moignans	54	46.04 N	4.54 E
Saint-Tropez	56	43.16 N	6.38 E
Saint Tudy	44	50.33 N	4.43 W
Sainte-Tulle	56	43.47 N	5.46 E
Saint-Ubald	196	46.45 N	72.16 W
Saint-Urbain-de-Charlevoix	176	47.33 N	70.32 W
Saint-Ursanne	54	47.22 N	7.10 E
Saint-Uze	56	45.11 N	4.52 E
Saint-Valérien	46	48.11 N	3.06 E
Saint-Valéry-en-Caux	46	49.52 N	0.44 E
Saint-Valéry-sur-Somme	46	50.11 N	1.38 E
Saint-Vallier, Fr.	54	46.38 N	4.22 E
Saint-Vallier, Fr.	56	45.10 N	4.49 E
Saint-Vallier-de-Thiey	56	43.42 N	6.51 E
Saint-Varent	32	46.53 N	0.14 W
Saint-Venant	46	50.37 N	2.33 E
Saint-Véran	56	44.42 N	6.52 E
Sainte-Victoire, Montagne ∧	56	43.32 N	5.39 E
Saint-Victoret	56	43.25 N	5.14 E
Saint Vincent	188	48.58 N	97.14 W
Saint Vincent □[2]	220		
	231h	13.15 N	61.12 W
Saint-Vincent, Baie de C	165f	22.00 S	166.05 E
Saint-Vincent, Cap ≻	147b	21.57 S	43.16 E
Saint Vincent, Cape ≻	156	43.18 S	145.50 E
Saint Vincent, Gulf C	158b	35.00 S	138.05 E
Saint Vincent Cape → São Vicente, Cabo de ≻	34	37.01 N	9.00 W
Saint-Vincent-de-Paul ◆[8]	265a	45.37 N	73.39 W
Saint-Vincent-de-Tyrosse	32	43.40 N	1.18 W
Saint Vincent Passage Ʊ	228	13.30 N	61.00 W
Saint Vincent's	176	46.48 N	53.38 W
Saint-Vit	54	47.11 N	5.49 E
Saint-Vith	52	50.17 N	6.08 E
Saint-Vivien-de-Médoc	32	45.26 N	1.02 W
Saint-Vrain	251	48.33 N	2.20 E
Saint Walburg	174	53.39 N	109.12 W
Saint-Wandrille-Rançon	46	49.32 N	0.46 E
Saint-Wenceslas ≃	196	46.18 N	72.23 W
Saint Williams	202	42.40 N	80.25 W
Saint-Witz	251	49.05 N	2.34 E
Saint-Yrieix-la-Perche	32	45.31 N	1.12 E
Saint-Yvon	176	49.10 N	64.48 W
Saint-Zacharie	56	43.23 N	5.43 E
Saint-Zénon	196	46.33 N	73.49 W
Saipan	165b	6.54 N	134.08 E
Saipan I	164n	15.12 N	145.45 E
Saipan Channel Ʊ	164n	15.05 N	145.41 E
Saiqi	90	27.00 N	119.43 E
Sa'īr	122	31.35 N	35.09 E
Sairecábur, Cerro ∧	238	22.43 S	67.54 W
Saishu-to → Cheju-do I	80	33.20 N	126.30 E
Saita	86	34.08 N	133.49 E
Saita ≃	86	34.08 N	133.38 E
Saitama □[5]	84	36.00 N	139.30 E
Saitama University ʊ[2]	258	35.52 N	139.38 E
Saito	82	32.06 N	131.24 E
Saitula	110	36.21 N	78.02 E
Saiyidān ◆[8]	262a	28.40 N	77.05 E
Sai Yok	100	14.07 N	99.08 E
Sajak	76	47.02 N	77.22 E
Sajam	154	0.53 S	132.41 E
Sajama	238	18.07 S	69.00 W
Sajama, Nevado ∧	238	18.06 S	68.54 W
Sajan → Sayan Mountains ∧∧	78	52.45 N	96.00 E
Sajantuj	78	51.44 N	107.30 E
Sajasan	74	43.03 N	46.17 E
Sajat	118	38.47 N	63.53 E
Sajchan	78	48.40 N	102.39 E
Sajchandulaan	92	44.42 N	109.01 E
Sajchin	70	48.50 N	46.47 E
Şajen	105a	7.40 S	112.31 E
Šajgino	70	57.46 N	46.51 E
Sajhan-Ovoo	92	45.27 N	103.52 E
Sajia	110	28.55 N	88.05 E
Şajīd I	134	16.52 N	41.50 E
Šajmak'	110	37.27 N	74.44 E
Sajnšand	92	44.55 N	110.11 E
Sajó ≃	30	47.56 N	21.08 E
Sajószentpéter	30	48.13 N	20.44 E
Sajram	75	42.18 N	69.45 E
Sajukino	70	52.47 N	41.59 E
Sājūr (Sacır) ≃	120	36.40 N	38.05 E
Sak ≃	148	30.52 S	20.25 E
Saka	144	0.09 S	39.20 E
Sakado	84	35.57 N	139.24 E
Sakae, Nihon	84	35.50 N	140.15 E
Sakae, Nihon	84	36.58 N	138.35 E
Sa Kaeo	100	13.49 N	102.04 E
Sakahogi	84	35.26 N	136.59 E
Sakai, Nihon	84	36.16 N	139.15 E
Sakai, Nihon	84	36.06 N	139.48 E
Sakai, Nihon	84	36.10 N	136.14 E
Sakai, Nihon	86	34.35 N	135.28 E
Sakai, Nihon	258	35.25 N	139.22 E
Sakai ≃	84	35.18 N	139.29 E
Sakaide	86	34.19 N	133.52 E
Sakaigawa	84	35.35 N	138.37 E
Sakai-minato	86	35.33 N	133.15 E
Sakākah	118	29.59 N	40.06 E
Sakakawea, Lake @[1]	188	47.50 N	102.20 W
Sakaki	84	36.28 N	138.11 E
Sakakita	84	36.25 N	138.01 E
Sakala, Pulau I	102	6.54 S	116.15 E
Sakami ≃	166	53.40 N	76.40 W
Sakami, Lac @	166	53.15 N	76.45 W
Sakania	144	12.45 S	28.34 E
Sakar	118	38.56 N	63.45 E
Sakar ∧∧	38	41.59 N	26.16 E
Sakaraha	147b	22.55 S	44.32 E
Sakar-Čaga	118	37.38 N	61.40 E
Sakar Island I	154	5.25 S	148.05 E
Sakarya □[4]	120	40.45 N	30.35 E
Sakashita	84	35.34 N	137.32 E
Sakasso	140	7.27 N	5.18 W
Sakata	82	38.55 N	139.50 E
Sakau	165f	16.49 S	168.24 E
Sakau I	165f	14.57 S	167.08 E
Sakauchi	84	35.36 N	136.25 E
Sakawa	86	33.30 N	133.17 E
Sakawa ≃	84	35.15 N	139.11 E
Sakchu	88	40.23 N	125.01 E
Sakesar	113	32.33 N	71.56 E
Sakété	140	6.43 N	2.40 E
Sakhā	132	31.05 N	30.57 E
Sakhalin → Sachalin, Ostrov I	79	51.00 N	143.00 E
Sākhar	110	32.57 N	65.32 E
Sakhi Sarwar	110	29.59 N	70.18 E
Sakhnīn	122	32.52 N	35.17 E
Şakhrīyāt, Jabal aş- ∧	122	31.01 N	36.21 E
Saki	68	45.09 N	33.35 E
Şāki ◆[8]	262c	19.06 N	72.53 E
Šakiai	66	54.57 N	23.03 E
Sākib	122	32.17 N	35.49 E
Sakiet Sidi Youssef	36	36.13 N	8.22 E
Sakijang Bendera, Pulau I	261c	1.13 N	103.51 E
Sakijang Pelepah, Pulau I	261c	1.13 N	103.52 E
Sakishima-guntō I	165d	24.46 N	124.00 E
Sakito	82	33.02 N	129.32 E
Sakkara → Şaqqārah	132	29.51 N	31.13 E
Sakleshpur	112	12.58 N	75.47 E
Sakmara ≃	76	51.46 N	55.01 E
Sako	260	34.53 N	135.47 E
Sākoli	110	21.05 N	79.59 E
Sakon Nakhon	100	17.10 N	104.09 E
Sakonnet	197	41.28 N	71.12 W
Sakoyra	140	14.17 N	1.24 E
Sakra, Pulau I	261c	1.16 N	103.42 E
Sakrān, Wādī ∨	132	30.22 N	31.53 E
Sakrand	110	26.08 N	68.16 E
Sakri	110	20.59 N	74.19 E
Sakrivier	148	30.54 S	20.28 E
Sakrow-Paretzer Kanal ≋	254a	52.28 N	12.55 E
Saksagan' ≃	68	47.53 N	33.18 E
Saksauldala ◆[2]	76	44.30 N	73.00 E
Sakskøbing	41	54.48 N	11.39 E
Sakti	114	22.02 N	82.58 E
Saku	84	36.09 N	138.26 E
Sakubva	144	19.00 S	32.10 E
Sakugi	86	34.52 N	132.43 E
Sakuma	84	35.05 N	137.48 E
Sakuma-dam ◆[6]	84	35.05 N	137.47 E
Sakuma-ko @[1]	84	35.08 N	137.47 E
Sakura	84	35.43 N	140.14 E
Sakura ≃	84	36.05 N	140.14 E
Sakurae	86	34.57 N	132.20 E
Sakurai	86	34.30 N	135.51 E
Sakura-tōge)(	260	34.36 N	135.53 E
Saku-shima I	84	34.43 N	137.03 E
Sakutō	86	35.01 N	134.14 E
Sakwaso Lake @	174	53.01 N	91.55 W
Säkylä	26	61.02 N	22.20 E
Sakyō ◆[8]	260	35.02 N	135.48 E
Sal I	140a	16.45 N	22.55 W
Sal ≃	70	47.31 N	40.45 E
Sal, Cay I	228	23.42 N	80.24 W
Sal, Ponta do ≻	256c	38.41 N	9.22 W
Şal, Punta ≻	226	15.53 N	87.37 W
Šal'a, Česko.	30	48.09 N	17.52 E
Šal'a, S.S.S.R.	76	57.15 N	58.43 E
Sala, Sve.	40	59.55 N	16.36 E
Sala, Yai.	134	16.58 N	37.27 E
Sala, Ouadi ∨	136	17.00 N	20.53 E
Sala Baganza	58	44.43 N	10.14 E
Salabangka, Kepulauan II	102	3.02 S	122.25 E
Salaberry, Île de I	196	45.17 N	74.07 W
Salaca ≃	66	57.45 N	24.21 E
Salacgrīva	66	57.45 N	24.21 E
Sala Consilina	36	40.24 N	15.36 E
Salada, Gran Pampa ☷	238	20.35 S	67.15 W
Salada, Laguna @	222	32.20 N	115.40 W
Saladas	242	28.15 S	58.38 W
Saladillo	242	35.38 S	59.46 W
Saladillo ≃	242	29.05 S	63.25 W
Saladillo, Arroyo ≃	248	35.33 S	59.04 W
Saladillo Dulce ≃	242	31.25 S	60.33 W
Salado, Arg.	242	28.18 S	67.15 W
Salado, Chile	242	26.25 S	70.19 W
Salado, Tex., U.S.	212	30.57 N	97.32 W
Salado ≃, Arg.	242	35.44 S	57.21 W
Salado ≃, Arg.	242	38.49 S	64.57 W
Salado ≃, Arg.	242	31.42 S	60.44 W
Salado ≃, Cuba	230p	20.36 N	76.56 W
Salado ≃, Méx.	222	26.52 N	99.19 W
Salado ≃, Méx.	224	18.44 N	103.36 W
Salado, Arroyo ≃, Arg.	244	41.37 S	65.02 W
Salado, Arroyo ≃, Arg.	244	40.35 S	66.33 W
Salado, Arroyo ≃, Méx.	222	24.25 N	111.34 W
Salado, Rio ≃	190	34.16 N	106.52 W
Salado Creek ≃, N. Mex., U.S.	186	34.35 N	104.25 W
Salado Creek ≃, Tex., U.S.	186	29.14 N	98.25 W
Salado Creek ≃, Tex., U.S.	212	30.59 N	97.25 W
Salaga	140	8.33 N	0.31 W
Salagle	134	1.50 N	42.18 E
Sālah	122	32.38 N	36.46 E
Salahin	134	2.58 N	46.45 E
Salailua	165a	13.41 S	172.34 W
Salair	76	54.13 N	85.47 E
Salairskij Kr'až ∧	76	54.15 N	85.30 E
Sălaj □[4]	38	47.15 N	23.00 E
Salak, Gunung ∧	105a	6.42 S	106.44 E
Şalakas	66	55.35 N	26.08 E
Šalakuša	24	62.15 N	40.17 E
Salal	136	14.51 N	17.13 E
Salala, Chile	242	30.41 S	71.32 W
Salala, Liber.	140	6.40 N	10.05 W
Salālah, Sūd.	130	21.19 N	36.13 E
Şalālah, 'Umān	108	17.00 N	54.06 E
Salamá, Guat.	226	15.06 N	90.16 W
Salamá, Hond.	226	14.50 N	86.36 W
Salaman	105a	7.35 S	110.08 E
Salamanca, Chile	242	31.47 S	70.58 W
Salamanca, Esp.	34	40.58 N	5.39 W
Salamanca, Méx.	224	20.34 N	101.12 W
Salamanca, Perú	238	15.31 S	72.50 W
Salamanca, Perú	276d	12.05 S	77.00 W
Salamanca, N.Y., U.S.	200	42.09 N	78.43 W
Salamanga	148	26.28 S	32.39 E
Salamat □[5]	136	11.00 N	20.30 E
Salamat, Bahr ≃	136	9.27 N	18.06 E
Salāmbek	110	28.16 N	65.08 E
Salamina	236	5.25 N	75.29 W
Salamínos, Órmos C	257c	37.56 N	23.27 E
Salamís	38	37.59 N	23.28 E
Salamís I	38	37.54 N	23.26 E
Salamis ⊥	120	35.10 N	33.54 E
Salām Khān	110	31.47 N	66.45 E
Salamonia	206	40.23 N	84.52 W
Salamonie ≃	206	40.50 N	85.43 W
Salamonie Lake @[1]	206	40.46 N	85.37 W
Salāmūn	132	31.04 N	31.28 E
Salanda	120	38.50 N	34.32 E
Salani	165a	14.00 S	171.33 W
Salantai	66	56.04 N	21.32 E
Salapaly, Baie de C	147b	24.40 S	43.55 E
Salaqi	92	40.38 N	110.29 E
Salaquí	236	7.18 N	77.33 W
Salaquí ≃	236	7.27 N	77.07 W
Salāqūs	132	28.44 N	30.50 E
Salara	58	44.59 N	11.25 E
Salard	38	47.13 N	22.03 E
Salarjovo	255b	55.37 N	37.26 E
Salas	238	6.16 S	79.37 W
Salas de los Infantes	34	42.01 N	3.17 W
Salat ≃	32	43.10 N	0.58 E
Salatiga	105a	7.19 S	110.30 E
Salauš	70	55.59 N	52.53 E
Salavat, S.S.S.R.	76	53.21 N	55.55 E
Salavat, Tür.	120	41.53 N	34.55 E
Salavaux	54	46.55 N	7.02 E
Salaverry	238	8.14 S	78.58 W
Salavina	242	28.48 S	63.25 W
Salawati I	154	1.07 S	130.52 E
Salawe	144	3.19 S	32.52 E
Salay	106	8.52 N	124.47 E
Salāya	110	22.19 N	69.35 E
Sala y Gómez, Isla I	18	26.28 S	105.28 W
Salazgor'	70	54.07 N	43.09 E
Salba	78	53.14 N	92.36 E
Sālbani	116	22.38 N	87.20 E
Salbohed	40	59.55 N	16.19 E
Salbosjön @	40	59.50 N	14.54 E
Salbris	46	47.26 N	2.03 E
Šalbuzdag, Gora ∧	74	41.19 N	47.48 E
Salcajá	226	14.53 N	91.27 W
Salcantay, Nevado ∧	238	13.20 S	72.33 W
Salcedo, Ec.	236	1.02 S	78.34 W
Salcedo, Pil.	106	11.09 N	125.40 E
Salcedo, Rep. Dom.	228	19.23 N	70.25 W
Salcha ≃	170	64.29 N	147.00 W
Şalcia	38	43.57 N	24.56 E
Šalčininkai	66	54.18 N	25.23 E
Salcombe	44	50.13 N	3.47 W
Salda ≃	76	58.48 N	61.20 E
Şalda Gölü @	120	37.33 N	29.42 E
Šaldaj	76	51.56 N	78.48 E
Saldaña	34	42.31 N	4.44 W
Saldaña ≃	236	4.01 N	74.52 W
Saldanha	148	33.00 S	17.56 E
Saldanhabaai C	148	33.04 S	18.00 E
Šaldež	70	56.52 N	44.46 E
Saldungaray	242	38.12 S	61.47 W
Saldus	66	56.40 N	22.30 E
Sale, Austl.	156	38.06 S	147.04 E
Sale, It.	56	44.59 N	8.48 E
Salé, Magreb	138	34.04 N	6.50 W
Sale, Eng., U.K.	42	53.26 N	2.19 W
Sale ≃	174	49.45 N	97.08 W
Salebabu, Pulau I	98	3.55 N	126.40 E
Salechard	64	66.33 N	66.40 E
Sale Creek	184	35.23 N	85.07 W
Salée, Rivière Ʊ	231o	16.17 N	61.33 W
Saleh, Teluk C	105b	8.34 S	117.57 E
Salelologa	165a	13.44 S	172.10 W
Salem, Bhārat	112	11.39 N	78.10 E
Salem, B.R.D.	54	47.46 N	9.16 E
Salem, Ont., Can.	202	43.42 N	80.27 W
Salem, S. Afr.	148	33.28 S	26.29 E
Salem, Sve.	40	59.13 N	17.44 E
Salem, Ark., U.S.	184	36.22 N	91.49 W
Salem, Ill., U.S.	209	38.38 N	88.57 W
Salem, Ind., U.S.	208	38.36 N	86.06 W
Salem, Iowa, U.S.	180	40.51 N	91.38 W
Salem, Mass., U.S.	197		
	273	42.31 N	70.55 W
Salem, Mich., U.S.	271	42.24 N	83.35 W
Salem, Mo., U.S.	184	37.39 N	91.32 W
Salem, N.H., U.S.	178	42.47 N	71.12 W
Salem, N.J., U.S.	198	39.34 N	75.28 W
Salem, N.Y., U.S.	200	43.10 N	73.20 W
Salem, Ohio, U.S.	204	40.54 N	80.52 W
Salem, Oreg., U.S.	214	44.57 N	123.01 W
Salem, S. Dak., U.S.	188	43.44 N	97.23 W
Salem, Utah, U.S.	190	40.03 N	111.40 W
Salem, Va., U.S.	182	37.17 N	80.03 W
Salem, W. Va., U.S.	178	39.17 N	80.34 W

Symbol	English	Deutsch	Español	Français	Português
≃	River	Fluss	Río	Rivière	Rio
≋	Canal	Kanal	Canal	Canal	Canal
⊾	Waterfall, Rapids	Wasserfall, Stromschnellen	Cascada, Rápidos	Chute d'eau, Rapides	Cascata, Rápidos
Ʊ	Strait	Meeresstrasse	Estrecho	Détroit	Estreito
C	Bay, Gulf	Bucht, Golf	Bahía, Golfo	Baie, Golfe	Baía, Golfo
@	Lake, Lakes	See, Seen	Lago, Lagos	Lac, Lacs	Lago, Lagos
☷	Swamp	Sumpf	Pantano	Marais	Pântano
⊼	Ice Features, Glacier	Eis- und Gletscherformen	Accidentes Glaciales	Formes glaciaires	Acidentes Glaciares
⊤	Other Hydrographic Features	Andere Hydrographische Objekte	Otros Elementos Hidrográficos	Autres données hydrographiques	Outros Elementos Hidrográficos
✣	Submarine Features	Untermeerische Objekte	Accidentes Submarinos	Formes de relief sous-marin	Acidentes Submarinos
□	Political Unit	Politische Einheit	Unidad Politica	Entité politique	Unidade Política
ʊ	Cultural Institution	Kulturelle Institution	Institución Cultural	Institution culturelle	Instituição Cultural
⊥	Historical Site	Historische Stätte	Sitio Histórico	Site historique	Sitio Histórico
♠	Recreational Site	Erholungs- und Ferienort	Sitio de Recreo	Centre de loisirs	Sítio de Lazer
⊠	Airport	Flughafen	Aeropuerto	Aéroport	Aeroporto
■	Military Installation	Militäranlage	Instalación Militar	Installation militaire	Instalação Militar
◆	Miscellaneous	Verschiedenes	Misceláneo	Divers	Miscelânea

Symbols in the index entries represent the broad categories identified in the key at the right. Symbols with superior numbers (⋀²) identify subcategories (see complete key on page *I* · *26*).

Kartensymbole in dem Registerverzeichnis stellen die rechts in Schlüssel erklärten Kategorien dar. Symbole mit hochgestellten Ziffern (⋀²) bezeichnen Unterabteilungen einer Kategorie (vgl. vollständiger Schlüssel auf Seite *I* · *26*).

Los símbolos incluidos en el texto del índice representan las grandes categorías identificadas con la clave a la derecha. Los símbolos con números en su parte superior (⋀²) identifican las subcategorías (véase la clave completa en la página *I* · *26*).

Les symboles de l'index représentent les catégories indiquées dans la légende à droite. Les symboles suivis d'un indice (⋀²) représentent des sous-catégories (voir légende complète à la page *I* · *26*).

Os símbolos incluídos no texto do índice representam as grandes categorias identificadas com a chave à direita. Os símbolos com números em sua parte superior (⋀²) identificam as subcategorias (veja-se a chave completa à página *I* · *26*).

∧ Mountain	Berg	Montaña	Montagne	Montanha
⋀ Mountains	Berge	Montañas	Montagnes	Montanhas
)(Pass	Pass	Paso	Col	Passo
∨ Valley, Canyon	Tal, Cañon	Valle, Cañón	Vallée, Canyon	Vale, Canhão
⌣ Plain	Ebene	Llano	Plaine	Planície
≻ Cape	Kap	Cabo	Cap	Cabo
I Island	Insel	Isla	Île	Ilha
II Islands	Inseln	Islas	Îles	Ilhas
⊥ Other Topographic Features	Andere Topographische Objekte	Otros Elementos Topográficos	Autres données topographiques	Outros Elementos Topográficos

ESPAÑOL | FRANÇAIS | PORTUGUÊS

Nombre / Nom / Nome	Página / Page	Lat.°′	Long.°′ W=Oeste / W=Ouest
San Benito Mountain ∧	216	36.22 N	120.38 W
San Bernard ≃	212	28.52 N	95.27 W
San Bernardino, Schw.	54	46.28 N	9.12 E
San Bernardino, Calif., U.S.	218	34.06 N	117.17 W
San Bernardino □6	218	34.40 N	117.17 W
San Bernardino, Passo del)(	54	46.30 N	9.11 E
San Bernardino, Río de ≃	190	30.48 N	109.11 W
San Bernardino Mountains ⛰	194	34.10 N	117.00 W
San Bernardino National Forest ♠	270	34.12 N	117.38 W
San Bernardino Strait ⊔	106	12.32 N	124.10 E
San Bernardo, Arg.	242	27.17 S	60.42 W
San Bernardo, Chile	242	33.36 S	70.43 W
San Bernardo, Méx.	222	25.59 N	105.33 W
San Bernardo □5	276e	33.35 S	70.44 W
San Bernardo, Canal ☰	276e	33.36 S	70.41 W
San Bernardo, Isla I	226	11.32 N	85.06 W
San Bernardo, Islas de II	236	9.45 N	75.50 W
San Bernardo del Viento	236	9.21 N	75.57 W
San Biagio	60	44.35 N	11.52 E
San Biagio di Callalta	58	45.41 N	12.22 E
San Biagio Saracinisco	60	41.37 N	13.55 E
San Blas, Méx.	222	26.05 N	108.46 W
San Blas, Méx.	224	21.31 N	105.16 W
San Blas, Cape >	182	29.40 N	85.22 W
San Blas, Cordillera de ⛰	236	9.18 N	79.00 W
San Blas, Golfo de C	236	9.30 N	79.00 W
San Blas Atempa	224	16.16 N	95.10 W
San Blas de los Sauces	242	28.24 S	67.05 W
San Bonifacio	58	45.24 N	11.16 E
San Borja	238	14.49 S	66.51 W
Sanborn, Iowa, U.S.	188	43.11 N	95.39 W
Sanborn, Minn., U.S.	188	44.13 N	95.08 W
Sanborn, N. Dak., U.S.	188	46.57 N	98.13 W
Sanborn, N.Y., U.S.	200	43.08 N	78.53 W
San Bovio	256b	45.28 N	9.19 E
San Bruno	216	37.37 N	122.25 W
San Bruno, Point >	272	37.39 N	122.22 W
San Bruno Mountain ∧	272	37.42 N	122.25 W
Sanbu	84	35.39 N	140.23 E
San Buena Ventura, Bol.	238	14.28 S	67.35 W
San Buenaventura, Méx.	222	27.05 N	101.32 W
San Buenaventura → Ventura, Calif., U.S.	218	34.17 N	119.18 W
San Buono	60	41.59 N	14.34 E
Sanbuzhen	92	22.23 N	112.35 E
San Candido (Innichen)	58	46.44 N	12.17 E
Sancanghe	90	32.45 N	120.43 E
San Carlo	54	46.25 N	8.32 E
San Carlos, Arg.	242	25.56 S	65.56 W
San Carlos, Arg.	242	33.46 S	69.02 W
San Carlos, Arg.	242	27.45 S	55.54 W
San Carlos, Chile	242	36.25 S	71.58 W
San Carlos, Chile	276e	33.36 S	70.35 W
San Carlos, Gui. Ecu.	142	3.27 N	8.33 E
San Carlos, Méx.	222	24.35 N	98.56 W
San Carlos, Méx.	222	29.01 N	100.51 W
San Carlos, Nic.	226	11.07 N	84.47 W
San Carlos, Pan.	226	8.29 N	79.57 W
San Carlos, Para.	242	22.16 S	57.18 W
San Carlos, Pil.	106	10.30 N	123.25 E
San Carlos, Pil.	106	15.55 N	120.20 E
San Carlos, Ariz., U.S.	190	33.21 N	110.27 W
San Carlos, Calif., U.S.	216	37.31 N	122.16 W
San Carlos, Ur.	242	34.48 S	54.55 W
San Carlos, Ven.	236	9.40 N	68.36 W
San Carlos ≃, C.R.	226	10.47 N	84.12 W
San Carlos ≃, Para.	242	22.51 S	57.51 W
San Carlos ≃, Ariz., U.S.	190	33.16 N	110.27 W
San Carlos ≃, Ven.	236	9.07 N	68.25 W
San Carlos, Canal ☰	276e	33.25 S	70.38 W
San Carlos, Isla I	236	11.01 N	71.43 W
San Carlos Airport ⊠	272	37.31 N	122.15 W
San Carlos Bay C	210	26.28 N	82.03 W
San Carlos Borromeo, Mission ʊ1	216	36.34 N	121.55 W
San Carlos Centro	242	31.44 S	61.06 W
San Carlos de Bariloche	244	41.09 S	71.18 W
San Carlos de Chena	276e	33.35 S	70.44 W
San Carlos de Guaroa	236	3.44 N	73.14 W
San Carlos de la Rápita	34	40.37 N	0.36 E
San Carlos del Zulia	236	9.01 N	71.55 W
San Carlos de Río Negro	236	1.55 N	67.04 W
San Carlos Indian Reservation ◆4	190	33.23 N	110.09 W
San Carlos Reservoir @1	190	33.13 N	110.24 W
San Carpoforo Creek ≃	216	35.47 N	121.19 W
San Casciano dei Bagni	60	42.52 N	11.53 E
San Casciano in Val di Pesa	60	43.39 N	11.11 E
San Cataldo	36	37.29 N	14.04 E
San Cayetano	242	38.20 S	59.37 W
Sancergues	46	47.09 N	2.55 E
Sancerre	46	47.20 N	2.51 E
Sancerrois, Collines du ⛰2	46	47.25 N	2.45 E
San Cesario sul Panaro	58	44.34 N	11.02 E
Sancey-le-Grand	54	47.18 N	6.35 E
Sanch'a, T'aiwan	90	24.25 N	120.46 E
Sancha, Zhg.	95	40.27 N	116.26 E
Sancha, Zhg.	96	31.52 N	119.06 E
Sanchaba	97	30.19 N	104.14 E
Sanchakou, Zhg.	95	39.47 N	117.19 E
Sanchakou, Zhg.	95	39.11 N	114.50 E
Sanchang	96	31.54 N	121.15 E
Sanchazi	94	41.07 N	124.15 E
Sanchazicun	94	42.03 N	123.59 E
Sanchenglong	79	44.02 N	120.58 E
Sánchez, Méx.	222	27.27 N	99.40 W
Sánchez, Rep. Dom.	228	19.14 N	69.36 W
Sanchez Creek ≃	212	32.36 N	97.50 W
Sánchez Magallanes	224	18.14 N	93.52 W
Sānchi	114	23.29 N	77.44 E
Sanchih	90	25.14 N	121.37 E
Sanch'ŏng	88	35.26 N	127.54 E
Sanchung	259d	25.04 N	121.29 E
Sanch'ungch'iao	259d	25.11 N	121.35 E
San Clemente, Esp.	34	39.24 N	2.26 W
San Clemente, Calif., U.S.	218	33.26 N	117.37 W
San Clemente, Arroyo de ≃	256d	41.20 N	2.00 E
San Clemente a Casauria ʊ1	60	42.14 N	13.55 E
San Clemente de Llobregat	256d	41.20 N	2.00 E
San Clemente Island I	218	32.54 N	118.29 W
Sancoins	32	46.50 N	2.55 E
San Colombano al Lambro	56	45.11 N	9.29 E
Sanco Point >	106	8.15 N	126.27 E
San Cosme	242	27.22 S	58.31 W
San Cosme Xalostoc	224	19.24 N	98.03 W
San Cristóbal, Arg.	242	30.19 S	61.14 W
San Cristóbal, Cuba	230p	22.43 N	83.03 W
San Cristóbal, Rep. Dom.	228	18.25 N	70.06 W
San Cristóbal, Ven.	236	7.46 N	72.14 W
San Cristóbal I	165e	10.36 S	161.45 E
San Cristóbal ≃	224	18.02 N	96.12 W
San Cristóbal, Bahía de C	222	27.23 N	114.38 W
San Cristóbal, Cerro ∧, Chile	276e	33.25 S	70.39 W
San Cristóbal, Cerro ∧, Perú	276d	12.02 S	77.01 W
San Cristóbal, Isla I	236a	0.50 S	89.26 W
San Cristóbal, Nevis → Saint Kitts-Nevis □2	228	17.20 N	62.45 W
San Cristóbal, Volcán ∧1	226	12.42 N	87.01 W
San Cristóbal de la Barranca	224	21.03 N	103.26 W
San Cristóbal de la Laguna	138	28.29 N	16.19 W
San Cristóbal las Casas	224	16.45 N	92.38 W
San Cristóbal Totonicapán	226	14.55 N	91.26 W
San Cristobal Trench ✢1	14	11.00 S	161.00 E
San Cristóbal Verapaz	226	15.23 N	90.24 W
San Cristobal Wash V	190	32.47 N	113.44 W
Sancti-Spíritus	230p	21.56 N	79.27 W
San Cugat, Riera de ≃	256d	41.29 N	2.11 E
San Cugat del Vallés	256d	41.28 N	2.05 E
Sančursk	70	56.57 N	47.15 E
Sand, B.R.D.	52	48.32 N	7.55 E
Sand, Nor.	26	59.29 N	6.15 E
Sand ≃, Alta., Can.	174	54.22 N	111.05 W
Sand ≃, S. Afr.	146	22.25 S	30.05 E
Sand ≃, S. Afr.	148	28.05 S	26.25 E
Sanda, Nihon	86	34.53 N	135.14 E
Sanda, Nihon	258	35.28 N	139.21 E
Sandafā al-Fa'r	132	28.32 N	30.40 E
Sandagou	79	43.43 N	134.52 E
Sandai	102	1.15 S	110.31 E
Sanda Island I	42	55.18 N	5.34 W
Sandakan	102	5.50 N	118.07 E
Sandakan Harbour C	106	5.45 N	118.05 E
Sandal, Baie du C	165f	20.50 S	167.05 E
San Damián	238	12.02 S	76.24 W
San Damiano d'Asti	56	44.50 N	8.04 E
San Damiano Macra	56	44.29 N	7.16 E
Sândăn	100	12.42 N	106.01 E
Sandan, Chāh ⊤4	118	28.59 N	63.27 E
Sandane	26	61.46 N	6.13 E
San Daniele del Friuli	58	46.09 N	13.00 E
Sandan-kyō ♠	86	34.38 N	132.13 E
Sandanski	38	41.34 N	23.17 E
Sandaogang	79	46.08 N	130.05 E
Sandaogou, Zhg.	94	41.39 N	121.45 E
Sandaogou, Zhg.	95	39.33 N	115.27 E
Sandaohe	76	44.21 N	85.37 E
Sandaoliangzi	94	41.20 N	122.07 E
Sandaolingzi	94	40.58 N	124.08 E
Sandaozhen	79	47.25 N	126.25 E
Sandaré	140	14.42 N	10.18 W
Sandared	26	57.43 N	12.47 E
Sandarne	26	61.16 N	17.10 E
Sand Arroyo Creek ≃	186	37.29 N	101.29 W
Sandata	70	46.16 N	41.46 E
Sandau	50	52.47 N	12.02 E
Sanday I	28	59.15 N	2.30 W
Sandbach	44	53.09 N	2.22 W
Sandbank	42	55.59 N	4.58 W
Sandbanks Provincial Park ♠	202	43.55 N	77.17 W
Sandbochum	253	51.40 N	7.41 E
Sand City	216	36.37 N	121.51 W
Sand Coulee	192	47.24 N	111.10 W
Sand Coulee Creek ≃	192	47.27 N	111.18 W
Sand Creek ≃, U.S.	190	41.13 N	105.43 W
Sand Creek ≃, Ariz., U.S.	190	35.46 N	112.27 W
Sand Creek ≃, Ind., U.S.	208	39.03 N	85.51 W
Sand Creek ≃, Minn., U.S.	180	45.56 N	92.39 W
Sand Creek ≃, Mont., U.S.	192	47.18 N	106.45 W
Sand Creek ≃, S. Dak., U.S.	188	44.02 N	98.05 W
Sand Creek ≃, Wyo., U.S.	190	41.02 N	107.52 W
Sand Creek ≃, Wyo., U.S.	192	44.16 N	107.55 W
Sand Cut	210	26.56 N	80.35 W
Sande, B.R.D.	48	51.45 N	8.39 E
Sande, B.R.D.	48	53.30 N	8.01 E
Sandefjord	26	59.08 N	10.14 E
San Demetrio ne'Vestini	60	42.17 N	13.34 E
Sanders, Ariz., U.S.	190	35.13 N	109.20 W
Sanders, Ky., U.S.	208	38.39 N	84.57 W
Sandersdorf	50	51.37 N	12.15 E
Sandersleben	50	51.40 N	11.34 E
Sanderson	186	30.09 N	102.24 W
Sanderstead ◆8	250	51.20 N	0.05 W
Sanderston	158b	34.46 S	139.13 E
Sandersville, Ga., U.S.	182	32.59 N	82.48 W
Sandersville, Miss., U.S.	184	31.47 N	89.02 W
Sandeshkhali	116	22.22 N	88.53 E
Sandesneben	48	53.41 N	10.30 E
Sandfly Lake @	174	55.45 N	106.05 W
Sand Fork	178	38.55 N	80.45 W
Sandgate, Austl.	161a	27.20 S	153.05 E
Sandgate, Eng., U.K.	44	51.05 N	1.08 E
Sandhammaren >	26	55.23 N	14.12 E
Sandhamn	40	59.17 N	18.55 E
Sandhead	42	54.48 N	4.58 W
Sandheuwel	148	31.46 S	20.48 E
Sandhill, Ont., Can.	265b	43.50 N	79.49 W
Sand Hill, Mass., U.S.	197	42.13 N	70.44 W
Sand Hill ∧2	200	42.31 N	77.37 W
Sand Hill ≃	188	47.36 N	96.52 W
Sand Hills ⛰2	188	42.00 N	101.00 W
Sandhorst	48	53.29 N	7.29 E
Sandhurst	44	51.19 N	0.48 W
Sāndi	114	27.18 N	79.57 E
Sandia	238	14.17 S	69.26 W
Sandia Crest ∧	190	35.13 N	106.27 W
Sandian	90	30.56 N	114.48 E
San Diego, Calif., U.S.	218	32.43 N	117.09 W
San Diego, Tex., U.S.	186	27.46 N	98.14 W
San Diego □6	218	33.00 N	117.05 W
San Diego ≃, Cuba	230p	22.20 N	83.16 W
San Diego ≃, Calif., U.S.	194	32.46 N	117.13 W
San Diego, Cabo >	244	54.38 S	65.07 W
San Diego Aqueduct ☰1	218	32.55 N	116.55 W
San Diego Bay C	218	32.37 N	117.07 W
San Diego Creek ≃	186	27.47 N	98.03 W
San Diego de Alcala, Mission ʊ1	218	32.48 N	117.06 W
San Diego de la Unión	224	21.28 N	100.52 W
San Diego Naval Air Station ■	218	32.42 N	117.12 W
San Diego Naval Training Center ■	218	32.44 N	117.13 W
San Dieguito ≃	218	32.58 N	117.16 W
Sandies Creek ≃	212	29.06 N	97.20 W
Sandıklı	120	38.28 N	30.17 E
Sandīla	114	27.05 N	80.31 E
Sandilands	158b	34.31 S	137.46 E
Sandilands Village	230b	25.02 N	77.18 W
San Dimas	218	34.06 N	117.49 W
San Dimas Canyon V	270	34.10 N	117.46 W
San Dimas Reservoir @1	270	34.09 N	117.43 W
San Dionisio, Nic.	226	12.45 N	85.51 W
San Dionisio, Pil.	106	11.16 N	123.06 E
Sand Island I	164g	28.12 N	177.23 W
Sand Islet I	164g	28.16 N	177.23 W
Sandiway	252	53.14 N	2.36 W
Sand Key I	210	27.53 N	82.51 W
Sandkrug	50	52.53 N	13.52 E
Sand Lake	200	42.38 N	73.32 W
Sand Lake @, Ont., Can.	174	50.05 N	94.39 W
Sand Lake @, Ont., Can.	202	44.34 N	76.15 W
Sand Lake @, Ont., Can.	202	44.56 N	77.02 W
Sandling ∧	58	47.39 N	13.43 E
Sandnes	26	58.51 N	5.44 E
Sandoa	142	9.41 S	22.52 E
Sandogora	70	58.12 N	40.59 E
Sandomierz	30	50.41 N	21.45 E
San Domingo Creek ≃	216	38.07 N	120.40 W
San Dominio, Isola I	60	42.07 N	15.29 E
Sandon	250	51.43 N	0.32 E
Sandoná	236	1.17 N	77.28 W
San Donà di Piave	58	45.38 N	12.34 E
San Donato Milanese	56	45.24 N	9.16 E
San Donato Val di Comino	60	41.42 N	13.49 E
Sandongo	142	15.30 S	21.28 E
San Dorligo della Valle	58	45.36 N	13.51 E
Sandouping	92	30.48 N	110.49 E
Sandoval	209	38.37 N	89.07 W
Sandovalina	245	22.27 S	51.44 W
Sandover ≃	152	21.43 S	136.32 E
Sandovo	66	58.28 N	36.25 E
Sandoway	100	18.28 N	94.22 E
Sandown	44	50.39 N	1.09 W
Sandown Park Racecourse ♠, Austl.	264b	37.57 S	145.10 E
Sandown Park Race Course ♠, Eng., U.K.	250	51.22 N	0.22 W
Sand Point, Alaska, U.S.	170	55.20 N	160.30 W
Sandpoint, Idaho, U.S.	192	48.16 N	116.33 W
Sand Point >	204	41.30 N	82.43 W
Sandrancourt	251	49.02 N	1.39 E
Sandray I	28	56.54 N	7.25 W
Sandridge, Eng., U.K.	250	51.47 N	0.18 W
Sand Ridge, N.Y., U.S.	200	43.15 N	76.14 W
Sandrigo	58	45.39 N	11.36 E
Sandringham, Austl.	156	24.05 S	139.04 E
Sandringham, Austl.	159	37.57 S	145.00 E
Sandringham, Eng., U.K.	44	52.50 N	0.30 E
Sandringham ◆8	263d	26.09 S	28.07 E
Sandringham House ⊥	44	52.50 N	0.30 E
Sand River Valley	148	28.28 S	29.33 E
Šandrovka	68	48.57 N	35.46 E
Sands Key I	210	25.30 N	80.11 W
Sandslån	26	63.01 N	17.47 E
Sandspit	172	53.14 N	131.50 W
Sands Point	266	40.51 N	73.43 W
Sands Point >	266	40.52 N	73.44 W
Sand Springs	186	36.09 N	96.07 W
Sandspruit	148	27.18 S	29.48 E
Sandspruit ≃	263d	26.07 S	28.04 E
Sandstedt	48	53.21 N	8.31 E
Sandston	198	37.31 N	77.19 W
Sandstone, Austl.	152	27.59 S	119.17 E
Sandstone, Minn., U.S.	180	46.08 N	92.52 W
Sandstone Creek ≃	206	42.23 N	84.33 W
Sandu, Zhg.	90	29.46 N	120.12 E
Sandu, Zhg.	90	26.02 N	113.16 E
Sandu, Zhg.	90	29.12 N	114.40 E
Sandu, Zhg.	92	25.57 N	107.58 E
Sanduan	94	41.10 N	121.27 E
Sandūb	132	31.01 N	31.23 E
Sandugan Point >	106	9.18 N	123.36 E
Sandumba	142	13.45 S	17.29 E
Sandun, Zhg.	96	31.52 N	121.50 E
Sandun, Zhg.	96	30.19 N	120.05 E
Sanduo	90	32.49 N	119.42 E
Sanduozhu	90	23.02 N	114.56 E
Sandusky, Ind., U.S.	208	39.25 N	85.29 W
Sandusky, Mich., U.S.	180	43.25 N	82.50 W
Sandusky, N.Y., U.S.	200	42.30 N	78.23 W
Sandusky, Ohio, U.S.	204	41.27 N	82.42 W
Sandusky □6	204	41.21 N	83.07 W
Sandusky ≃	204	41.27 N	83.00 W
Sandusky Bay C	204	41.27 N	82.52 W
Sandvig	26	55.17 N	14.47 E
Sandvika	26	59.54 N	10.31 E
Sandviken	40	60.37 N	16.46 E
Sandweiler	52	49.37 N	6.13 E
Sandwich, Eng., U.K.	44	51.17 N	1.20 E
Sandwich, Ill., U.S.	206	41.39 N	88.37 W
Sandwich, Mass., U.S.	197	41.46 N	70.30 W
Sandwich, Port C	165f	16.27 S	167.46 E
Sandwich Bay C, Newf., Can.	166	53.35 N	57.15 W
Sandwich Bay C, Namibia	146	23.22 S	14.30 E
Sandwich del Sur, Islas → South Sandwich Islands II	18	57.45 S	26.30 W
Sandwick	172	49.42 N	124.59 W
Sandwīp	114	22.29 N	91.26 E
Sandwīp Channel ⊔	114	22.30 N	91.35 E
Sandwīp Island I	114	22.30 N	91.25 E
Sandy, Eng., U.K.	44	52.08 N	0.18 W
Sandy, Oreg., U.S.	214	45.24 N	122.16 W
Sandy, Pa., U.S.	204	41.07 N	78.47 W
Sandy ≃, Maine, U.S.	178	44.45 N	69.52 W
Sandy ≃, Oreg., U.S.	214	45.34 N	122.24 W
Sandy ≃, Va., U.S.	182	36.35 N	79.25 W
Sandy Bay C, Nic.	226	14.28 N	83.16 W
Sandy Bay C, Mass., U.S.	273	42.40 N	70.37 W
Sandy Bay Indian Reserve ◆4	174	50.33 N	98.40 W
Sandy Bay Mountain ∧	178	45.47 N	70.25 W
Sandy Beach	200	43.04 N	78.55 W
Sandy Branch ≃	274c	39.03 N	77.16 W
Sandy Cape >, Austl.	156	24.42 S	153.17 E
Sandy Cape >, Austl.	156	41.25 S	144.45 E
Sandy Creek	202	43.39 N	76.05 W
Sandy Creek ≃, U.S.	186	34.25 N	99.35 W
Sandy Creek ≃, U.S.	186	36.50 N	98.10 W
Sandy Creek ≃, Ill., U.S.	209	39.34 N	90.35 W
Sandy Creek ≃, N.C., U.S.	182	36.08 N	78.02 W
Sandy Creek ≃, N.Y., U.S.	202	43.20 N	77.55 W
Sandy Creek ≃, N.Y., U.S.	202	43.44 N	76.15 W
Sandy Creek ≃, Ohio, U.S.	204	40.38 N	81.26 W
Sandy Creek ≃, Pa., U.S.	204	41.18 N	79.51 W
Sandy Creek ≃, Tex., U.S.	186	30.34 N	98.26 W
Sandy Creek ≃, Tex., U.S.	212	29.02 N	96.33 W
Sandy Creek, East Branch ≃	200	43.17 N	78.03 W
Sandy Creek, West Branch ≃	200	43.17 N	78.03 W
Sandy Desert ◆2, Pāk.	110	28.40 N	62.30 E
Sandy Desert ◆2, Pāk.	118	28.15 N	64.30 E
Sandy Hook, Conn., U.S.	197	41.25 N	73.17 W
Sandy Hook, Ky., U.S.	182	38.05 N	83.08 W
Sandy Hook, Miss., U.S.	184	31.02 N	89.48 W
Sandy Hook >2	198	40.27 N	74.00 W
Sandy Hook Bay C	266	40.26 N	74.03 W
Sandykači	118	36.33 N	62.34 E
Sandy Key I	210	25.02 N	81.01 W
Sandy Lake	204	41.22 N	80.05 W
Sandy Lake @, Newf., Can.	176	49.16 N	57.00 W
Sandy Lake @, Ont., Can.	174	53.00 N	93.07 W
Sandy Lake @, Ont., Can.	202	44.33 N	78.24 W
Sandy Lick Creek ≃	204	41.09 N	79.05 W
Sandy Point	228	17.22 N	62.50 W
Sandy Point >, Austl.	158b	34.16 S	138.09 E
Sandy Point >, R.I., U.S.	197	41.14 N	71.35 W
Sandy Pond @	273	42.26 N	71.19 W
Sandy Ridge	204	40.49 N	78.14 W
Sandy Springs	182	33.55 N	84.23 W
Sandyville, Md., U.S.	198	39.31 N	76.55 W
Sandyville, Ohio, U.S.	204	40.38 N	81.23 W
Sandžak ◆1	38	43.10 N	19.30 E
San Eladio	248	34.46 S	59.11 W
San Elizario	190	31.35 N	106.16 W
San Emigdio Creek ≃	218	35.02 N	119.11 W
San Emilio	106	17.14 N	120.37 E
Sanen ≃	105a	8.23 S	113.37 E
San Enrique	242	35.47 S	60.22 W
San Estanislao, Col.	236	10.24 N	75.09 W
San Estanislao, Para.	242	24.39 S	56.26 W
San Esteban	226	15.17 N	85.52 W
San Esteban, Bahía C	222	25.38 N	109.14 W
San Esteban, Isla I	222	28.42 N	112.36 W
San Esteban de Gormaz	34	41.35 N	3.12 W
San Fabian	106	16.05 N	120.25 E
San Fausto de Campcentellas	256d	41.31 N	2.14 E
San Felice (Sankt Felix)	58	46.30 N	11.08 E
San Felice Circeo	60	41.14 N	13.05 E
San Felice sul Panaro	58	44.50 N	11.08 E
San Felipe, Chile	242	32.45 S	70.44 W
San Felipe, Col.	236	1.55 N	67.06 W
San Felipe, Méx.	222	31.00 N	114.52 W
San Felipe, Méx.	224	21.29 N	101.13 W
San Felipe, Pil.	106	15.04 N	120.04 E
San Felipe, Tex., U.S.	212	29.48 N	96.06 W
San Felipe, Ven.	236	10.20 N	68.44 W
San Felipe, Castillo de ⊥	226	15.39 N	89.01 W
San Felipe, Cayos de II	230p	21.58 N	83.30 W
San Felipe, Punta >	190	31.03 N	114.51 W
San Felipe Aztatán	224	22.23 N	105.24 W
San Felipe Creek ≃	194	33.09 N	115.46 W
San Felipe de Puerto Plata → Puerto Plata	228	19.48 N	70.41 W
San Felipe Nuevo Mercurio	222	24.22 N	102.06 W
San Felipe Pueblo	190	35.27 N	106.28 W
San Felipe Terremotos	276a	19.22 N	99.04 W
San Felíu de Guixols	34	41.47 N	3.02 E
San Felíu de Llobregat	256d	41.23 N	2.03 E
San Félix ≃	226	8.10 N	81.51 W
San Félix, Isla I	234	26.17 S	80.05 W
San Fermín	186	26.20 N	104.49 W
San Fermín, Punta >	222	30.25 N	114.40 W
San Fernando, Arg.	248	34.26 S	58.34 W
San Fernando, Chile	242	34.35 S	71.00 W
San Fernando, Esp.	34	36.28 N	6.12 W
San Fernando, Méx.	186	28.32 N	100.54 W
San Fernando, Méx.	190	31.16 N	110.36 W
San Fernando, Méx.	222	24.50 N	98.10 W
San Fernando, Méx.	224	16.52 N	93.13 W
San Fernando, Pil.	106	16.37 N	120.19 E
San Fernando, Pil.	106	12.30 N	123.46 E
San Fernando, Pil.	106	15.01 N	120.41 E
San Fernando, Trin.	231r	10.17 N	61.28 W
San Fernando, Calif., U.S.	218	34.17 N	118.26 W
San Fernando □5	278	34.28 S	58.34 W
San Fernando ≃	222	24.55 N	97.40 W
San Fernando, Aeródromo ⊠	278	34.27 S	58.35 W
San Fernando Airport ⊠	270	34.17 N	118.25 W
San Fernando Creek ≃	186	27.28 N	97.46 W
San Fernando de Apure	236	7.54 N	67.28 W
San Fernando de Atabapo	236	4.03 N	67.42 W
San Fernando de Henares	256a	40.25 N	3.32 W
San Fernando Mission ʊ1	270	34.16 N	118.28 W
San Fernando Point >	106	16.38 N	120.17 E
San Fernando Valley V	270	34.13 N	118.27 W
Sånfjället ∧	26	62.17 N	13.32 E
Sånfjallets Nationalpark ♠	26	62.20 N	13.40 E
San Floriano	58	46.02 N	12.18 E
Sanford, Colo., U.S.	190	37.16 N	105.54 W
Sanford, Fla., U.S.	210	28.48 N	81.16 W
Sanford, Maine, U.S.	178	43.26 N	70.46 W
Sanford, Mich., U.S.	180	43.40 N	84.23 W
Sanford, N.C., U.S.	182	35.29 N	79.10 W
Sanford, Tex., U.S.	186	35.42 N	101.32 W
Sanford ≃	152	27.22 S	115.53 E
Sanford, Mount ∧	170	62.13 N	144.09 W
San Francesco, Convento ʊ1	257a	42.03 N	12.46 E
San Francisco, Arg.	242	31.26 S	62.05 W
San Francisco, Col.	236	1.11 N	76.53 W
San Francisco, C.R.	226	9.49 N	85.15 W
San Francisco, Pan.	226	8.15 N	80.58 W
San Francisco, Perú	276d	12.12 S	76.55 W
San Francisco, Pil.	106	8.30 N	125.56 E
San Francisco, Pil.	106	10.04 N	125.09 E
San Francisco, Calif., U.S.	216 / 272	37.48 N	122.24 W
San Francisco □6	216	37.45 N	122.22 W
San Francisco ≃, Arg.	242	23.16 S	64.03 W
San Francisco → São Francisco ≃, Bra.	232	10.30 S	36.24 W
San Francisco ≃, U.S.	190	32.59 N	109.22 W
San Francisco, Arroyo ≃	278	34.43 S	58.19 W
San Francisco, Cabo de >	236	0.40 N	80.05 W
San Francisco, La Cadena ⛰	230m	18.19 N	67.10 W
San Francisco, Paso de)(	242	26.53 S	68.19 W
San Francisco, Sierra de ⛰	224	22.40 N	105.25 W
San Francisco, University of ʊ2	272	37.46 N	122.26 W
San Francisco Bay C	216	37.43 N	122.17 W
San Francisco Creek ≃	186	29.53 N	102.19 W
San Francisco Culhuacán	276a	19.20 N	99.06 W
San Francisco de Arriba	222	26.15 N	102.50 W
San Francisco de Borja	222	27.53 N	106.41 W
San Francisco de Horizonte	186	25.56 N	103.26 W
San Francisco de la Paz	226	14.55 N	86.14 W
San Franciscó del Carnicero	226	12.30 N	86.18 W
San Francisco del Chañar	242	29.47 S	63.56 W
San Francisco del Mar	224	16.14 N	94.39 W
San Francisco del Monte de Oro	242	32.36 S	66.08 W
San Francisco del Oro	222	26.52 N	105.51 W
San Francisco del Rincón	224	21.01 N	101.51 W
San Francisco de Macorís	228	19.18 N	70.15 W
San Francisco de Mostazal	242	33.59 S	70.43 W
San Francisco de Paula	276b	23.04 N	82.18 W
San Francisco el Grande, Iglesia de ʊ1	256a	40.25 N	3.43 W
San Francisco Gotera	226	13.42 N	88.06 W
San Francisco International Airport ⊠	216	37.37 N	122.23 W
San Francisco Ixhuatán	224	16.22 N	94.29 W
San Francisco Maritime State Historical Park ♠	272	37.48 N	122.27 W
San Francisco Mountains ⛰	190	33.45 N	109.00 W
San Francisco-Oakland Bay Bridge ◆5	272	37.48 N	122.22 W
San Francisco State Beach ♠	272	37.47 N	122.29 W
San Francisco State Fish and Game Refuge ◆4	272	37.35 N	122.25 W
San Francisco State University ʊ2	272	37.43 N	122.28 W
San Francisco Tlalcilalcalpa	224	19.18 N	99.46 W
San Francisquito Creek ≃	272	37.28 N	122.07 W
San Fratello	36	38.01 N	14.36 E
Sanga, Ang.	142	11.07 S	15.22 E
Sanga, H. Vol.	140	11.10 N	0.10 E
Sanga, Mali	140	14.28 N	3.19 W
Sanga, Zaïre	144	7.02 S	28.21 E
Sang'a, Zhg.	88	36.26 N	115.37 E
San Gabriel, Ec.	236	0.36 N	77.49 W
San Gabriel, Calif., U.S.	218	34.07 N	118.06 W
San Gabriel ≃, Calif., U.S.	270	33.45 N	118.07 W
San Gabriel ≃, Tex., U.S.	212	30.46 N	97.01 W
San Gabriel, Isla I	248	34.28 S	57.54 W
San Gabriel, North Fork ≃, Calif., U.S.	270	34.15 N	117.52 W
San Gabriel, North Fork ≃, Tex., U.S.	212	30.38 N	97.40 W
San Gabriel, South Fork ≃	186	30.38 N	97.41 W
San Gabriel Arcangel, Mission ʊ1	270	34.06 N	118.06 W
San Gabriel Chilac	224	18.19 N	97.21 W
San Gabriel Dam ◆6	270	34.13 N	117.52 W
San Gabriel Mountains ⛰	218	34.20 N	118.00 W
San Gabriel Peak ∧	270	34.15 N	118.06 W
San Gabriel Reservoir @1	218	34.13 N	117.51 W
Sangačal, Mys >	74	40.07 N	49.30 E
San Galgano, Abbazia di ʊ1	60	43.10 N	11.10 E
Šangaly	24	61.08 N	43.19 E
Sangamankanda Point >	112	7.01 N	81.52 E
Sangamner	112	19.34 N	74.13 E
Sangamon □6	209	39.47 N	89.40 W
Sangamon ≃	184	40.07 N	90.20 W
Sangamon, South Fork ≃	209	39.48 N	89.32 W
Sangamon, South Fork, Flat Branch ≃	209	39.33 N	89.16 W
Sang'angqu	92	29.15 N	96.59 E
Sanga Puitã	245	22.40 S	55.36 W
Sangar	64	63.55 N	127.31 E
Sangāreddi	112	17.38 N	78.07 E
Sangar Sarāy	110	34.24 N	70.38 E
Sangasanga-dalam	102	0.40 S	117.14 E
Sanga Sanga Island I	106	5.04 N	119.47 E
Sangat	113	30.05 N	74.50 E
Sangatte	46	50.56 N	1.45 E
San Gavino Monreale	36	39.33 N	8.48 E
Sangay, Volcán ∧1	236	2.00 S	78.20 W
Sangayán, Isla de I	238	13.51 S	76.28 W
Sang Bast	118	35.59 N	59.46 E
Sangbé	142	6.03 N	12.28 E
Sangchris Lake State Park ♠	209	39.38 N	89.28 W
Sangchungshih	90	25.04 N	121.29 E
Sangeang, Pulau I	105b	8.12 S	119.04 E
Sang-e Māsheh	110	33.08 N	67.27 E
San Gemini	60	42.37 N	12.33 E
San Genesio Atesino	58	46.32 N	11.20 E
Sangenjaya ◆8	258	35.38 N	139.40 E
Sanger, Calif., U.S.	216	36.42 N	119.27 W
Sanger, Tex., U.S.	186	33.22 N	97.10 W
Sangerhausen	50	51.28 N	11.17 E
San Germán, Cuba	230p	20.36 N	76.08 W
San Germán, P.R.	230m	18.05 N	67.03 W
San Germano Vercellese	56	45.21 N	8.15 E
San Geronimo	216	38.01 N	122.39 W
Sangerville	178	45.10 N	69.21 W
Sangezhan	79	52.34 N	126.02 E
Sangganhe ≃	95	40.21 N	115.21 E
Sanggar, Teluk C	105b	8.20 S	118.18 E
Sanggau	102	0.08 N	110.36 E
Sangge-ri ◆8	261b	37.41 N	127.05 E
Sanggi	102	5.27 S	104.30 E
Sanggona	102	3.52 S	121.46 E
Sangha □5	142	2.00 N	15.00 E
Sangha ≃	142	1.13 S	16.49 E
Sanghar	110	26.02 N	68.57 E
San Giacomo (Sankt Jakob in Pfitsch)	58	46.57 N	11.36 E
San Giacomo Filippo	54	46.20 N	9.21 E
Sangihe, Kepulauan II	102	3.00 N	125.30 E
Sangihe, Pulau I	102	3.35 N	125.32 E
Sangijn Dalaj Nuur @	78	49.17 N	99.00 E
San Gil	236	6.33 N	73.08 W
Sangilen, Chrebet ⛰	78	50.18 N	96.30 E
San Gimignano	60	43.28 N	11.02 E
San Ginês de Vilasar	256d	41.31 N	2.22 E
San Ginesio	60	43.06 N	13.19 E
San Gion	54	46.38 N	8.50 E
San Giorgio Canavese	56	45.20 N	7.48 E
San Giorgio della Richinvelda	58	46.03 N	12.52 E
San Giorgio del Sannio	60	41.04 N	14.51 E
San Giorgio di Lomellina	56	45.10 N	8.47 E
San Giorgio di Nogaro	58	45.50 N	13.13 E
San Giorgio di Piano	58	44.39 N	11.22 E
San Giorgio la Molara	60	41.16 N	14.55 E
San Giorgio Monferrato	56	45.07 N	8.23 E
San Giorgio Piacentino	56	44.57 N	9.44 E
San Giorgio su Legnano	256b	45.34 N	8.55 E
San Giovanni (Sankt Johann)	58	46.38 N	11.44 E
San Giovanni al Timavo (Sankt Johann in Ahrn)	58	46.58 N	11.57 E
San Giovanni-Bianco	54	45.52 N	9.39 E
San Giovanni d'Asso	60	43.09 N	11.35 E
San Giovanni Ilarione	58	45.30 N	11.15 E
San Giovanni in Croce	58	45.05 N	10.22 E
San Giovanni in Fiore	36	39.16 N	16.42 E
San Giovanni in Laterano ʊ1	257a	41.53 N	12.30 E
San Giovanni in Persiceto	58	44.38 N	11.11 E
San Giovanni Lupatoto	58	45.23 N	11.03 E
San Giovanni Rotondo	60	41.42 N	15.44 E
San Giovanni Valdarno	60	43.34 N	11.32 E
San Giuliano Milanese	256b	45.24 N	9.17 E
San Giuliano Terme	60	43.46 N	10.26 E
San Giuseppe	56	44.22 N	8.18 E
San Giuseppe Vesuviano	60	40.50 N	14.30 E
San Giustino	60	43.33 N	12.10 E
San Giusto, Aeroporto di ⊠	60	43.11 N	10.21 E
San Giusto Canavese	56	45.19 N	7.49 E
Sangjiatun	94	42.24 N	122.42 E
Sangju	88	36.26 N	128.09 E
Sangkapura	105a	5.52 S	112.40 E
Sângkê ≃	100	13.13 N	103.41 E
Sangkhai	100	14.39 N	103.52 E
Sangkhla	100	15.07 N	98.28 E
Sangkulirang	102	0.59 N	117.58 E
Sāngla	113	31.43 N	73.23 E
Sangley Point Naval Station (United States) ■	106	14.30 N	120.54 E
Sāngli	112	16.52 N	74.34 E
Sanglin	90	27.54 N	114.46 E
Sangluoshu	88	37.31 N	117.43 E
Sangmélima	142	2.56 N	11.59 E
Sangnyŏng-ni	88	38.14 N	126.54 E
Sango	260	34.36 N	135.42 E
San Godenzo	60	43.55 N	11.37 E
Sāngola	112	17.26 N	75.12 E
Sangolquí	236	0.19 S	78.27 W
San Gorgonio Mountain ∧	194	34.06 N	116.50 W
San Gottardo, Passo del)(	54	46.33 N	8.34 E
San'gou	88	41.02 N	118.11 E
Sangre de Cristo Mountains ⛰	190	37.30 N	105.15 W
San Gregorio, Arg.	242	34.19 S	62.02 W
San Gregorio, It.	60	42.19 N	13.29 E
San Gregorio, Calif., U.S.	216	37.20 N	122.23 W
San Gregorio, Ur.	242	32.37 S	55.40 W
San Gregorio, Ur.	248	33.57 S	56.45 W
San Gregorio, Arroyo ≃	248	33.59 S	56.50 W
San Gregorio Atlapulco	276a	19.15 N	99.03 W
San Gregorio Beach ♠	272	37.19 N	122.24 W
San Gregorio Creek ≃	272	37.19 N	122.25 W
Sangre Grande	231r	10.35 N	61.07 W
Sangro ≃	60	42.14 N	14.32 E
Sangrūr	113	30.14 N	75.50 E
Sangrūr ◆1	113	30.16 N	75.52 E
Sangshuyuan	76	42.23 N	88.30 E
Sangsues, Lac aux @	180	46.29 N	77.57 W
Sangtuda	75	38.04 N	69.04 E
Sanguandian	90	31.19 N	118.05 E
Sanguang	96	31.47 N	121.16 E
Sanguanmiao	90	32.25 N	114.04 E
Sanguanyingzi	94	41.39 N	120.44 E
Sangudo	172	53.53 N	114.54 W
Sangue, Rio do ≃	238	11.01 S	58.39 W
Sangüesa	34	42.35 N	1.17 W
Sanguinetto	58	45.11 N	11.09 E
Sanguliu	94	40.45 N	124.14 E
Sāngurli	262c	18.56 N	73.07 E
Sangvor, S.S.S.R.	75	38.47 N	71.12 E
Sangvor, S.S.S.R.	75	38.53 N	71.06 E
Sangwa	144	5.30 S	26.00 E
Sangwei	88	34.18 N	118.51 E
Sangya	110	30.52 N	91.40 E
Sangyuanbao	95	40.15 N	115.32 E
Sangyuanbu	96	31.37 N	118.53 E
Sangyuanzhen	97	30.30 N	103.26 E
Sangzhi	92	29.18 N	110.02 E
Sangzidian	88	36.46 N	116.55 E
Sanhala	140	10.03 N	6.51 W
Sanharó	240	8.21 S	36.34 W
Sanhe, Zhg.	88	42.28 N	129.39 E
Sanhe, Zhg.	90	31.30 N	117.14 E
Sanhe, Zhg.	95	39.59 N	117.04 E
Sanheba	90	24.24 N	116.34 E
Sanhecha	79	44.59 N	126.04 E
Sanhechang, Zhg.	92	31.22 N	106.48 E
Sanhechang, Zhg.	97	30.04 N	105.01 E
Sanheji	90	32.42 N	117.55 E
Sanhekou	96	31.50 N	120.08 E
Sanhetun	94	42.38 N	123.38 E
Sanhezhuang	95	40.04 N	116.18 E
San Hipólito, Punta >	222	26.59 N	113.59 W
Sanhsient'ai I	90	23.08 N	121.26 E
Sanhsing	90	24.40 N	121.39 E
Sanhu	90	27.55 N	115.24 E
Sanhuiba	97	30.07 N	106.39 E
Sanhuichang	97	29.57 N	105.53 E
Sanhūr	132	29.25 N	30.46 E
Sanhūr al-Madīnah	132	31.07 N	30.44 E
Sanibel	210	26.27 N	82.01 W
Sanibel Island I	210	26.27 N	82.06 W
San Ignacio, Arg.	242	27.16 S	55.32 W
San Ignacio, Bol.	238	16.23 S	60.59 W
San Ignacio, Bol.	238	14.53 S	65.36 W
San Ignacio, C.R.	226	9.48 N	84.09 W
San Ignacio, Hond.	226	14.38 N	87.02 W
San Ignacio, Méx.	222	27.27 N	112.51 W
San Ignacio, Méx.	224	23.55 N	106.25 W
San Ignacio, Méx.	224	23.12 N	100.12 W
San Ignacio, Para.	242	26.52 S	57.03 W
San Ignacio, Isla de I	222	25.25 N	108.54 W

Symbol	English	Deutsch	Español	Français	Português
≃	River	Fluss	Río	Rivière	Rio
☰	Canal	Kanal	Canal	Canal	Canal
⌊	Waterfall, Rapids	Wasserfall, Stromschnellen	Cascada, Rápidos	Chute d'eau, Rapides	Cascata, Rápidos
⊔	Strait	Meeresstrasse	Estrecho	Détroit	Estreito
C	Bay, Gulf	Bucht, Golf	Bahía, Golfo	Baie, Golfe	Baía, Golfo
@	Lake, Lakes	See, Seen	Lago, Lagos	Lac, Lacs	Lago, Lagos
☷	Swamp	Sumpf	Pantano	Marais	Pântano
❄	Ice Features, Glacier	Eis- und Gletscherformen	Accidentes Glaciales	Formes glaciaires	Acidentes Glaciares
≈	Other Hydrographic Features	Andere Hydrographische Objekte	Otros Elementos Hidrográficos	Autres données hydrographiques	Outros Elementos Hidrográficos
✢	Submarine Features	Untermeerische Objekte	Accidentes Submarinos	Formes de relief sous-marin	Acidentes Submarinos
□	Political Unit	Politische Einheit	Unidad Politica	Entité politique	Unidade Política
ʊ	Cultural Institution	Kulturelle Institution	Institución Cultural	Institution culturelle	Instituição Cultural
⊥	Historical Site	Historische Stätte	Sitio Histórico	Site historique	Sítio Histórico
♠	Recreational Site	Erholungs- und Ferienort	Sitio de Recreo	Centre de loisirs	Sítio de Lazer
⊠	Airport	Flughafen	Aeropuerto	Aéroport	Aeroporto
■	Military Installation	Militäranlage	Instalación Militar	Installation militaire	Instalação Militar
◆	Miscellaneous	Verschiedenes	Misceláneo	Divers	Miscelânea

Name	Page	Lat.	Long.
San Ignacio, Laguna ⊜	222	26.54 N	113.13 W
San Ildefonso, Cape ≻	106	16.02 N	121.59 E
San Ildefonso, Cerro ∧	226	15.31 N	88.17 W
San Ildefonso o La Granja	34	40.54 N	4.00 W
San Ildefonso Peninsula ≻[1]	106	16.10 N	122.05 E
San'in-kaigan-kokuritsu-kōen ♠	86	35.38 N	134.38 E
Sanino	255a	59.50 N	29.54 E
Sani Pass)(	148	29.34 S	29.19 E
San Isabel Creek ≃	186	27.39 N	99.38 W
San Isidro, Arg.	242	28.27 S	65.44 W
San Isidro, Arg.	248	34.27 S	58.30 W
San Isidro, Méx.	190	31.31 N	106.18 W
San Isidro, Méx.	224	21.55 N	100.15 W
San Isidro, Nic.	226	12.56 N	86.12 W
San Isidro, Perú	276d	12.07 S	77.03 W
San Isidro, Pil.	106	11.24 N	124.21 E
San Isidro, Tex., U.S.	186	26.43 N	98.27 W
San Isidro □[5]	278	34.29 S	58.33 W
San Isidro del General	226	9.22 N	83.42 W
San Isidro el Real, Catedral de ✠[1]	256a	40.25 N	3.42 W
Sanitaria Springs	200	42.09 N	75.46 W
Sanitz	50	54.04 N	12.22 E
San Jacinto, Col.	236	9.50 N	75.08 W
San Jacinto, Méx.	186	25.29 N	103.44 W
San Jacinto, Pil.	106	12.34 N	123.44 E
San Jacinto, Calif., U.S.	218	33.47 N	116.57 W
San Jacinto □[6]	212	30.35 N	95.10 W
San Jacinto ≃, Calif., U.S.	218	33.43 N	117.16 W
San Jacinto ≃, Tex., U.S.	212	29.46 N	95.05 W
San Jacinto, East Fork ≃	212	30.05 N	95.09 W
San Jacinto, West Fork ≃	212	30.02 N	95.15 W
San Jacinto Monument ⊥	212	29.45 N	95.01 W
San Jacinto Peak ∧	194	33.49 N	116.41 W
San Jacinto Valley ∨	218	33.50 N	117.05 W
Sanjahā	132	30.50 N	31.38 E
San Javier, Arg.	242	27.53 S	55.08 W
San Javier, Arg.	242	30.35 S	59.57 W
San Javier, Bol.	238	14.34 S	64.42 W
San Javier, Bol.	238	16.20 S	62.38 W
San Javier, Chile	242	35.35 S	71.45 W
San Javier, Méx.	186	26.16 N	99.27 W
San Javier, Ur.	242	32.41 S	58.08 W
San Javier ≃	242	31.30 S	60.20 W
Sanjāwi	110	30.17 N	68.21 E
Sanje	144	0.46 S	31.30 E
San Jerónimo	226	15.03 N	90.12 W
San Jerónimo, Arroyo ≃	248	33.57 S	56.05 W
San Jerónimo de Juárez	224	17.08 N	100.28 W
San Jerónimo Lídice	276a	19.20 N	99.13 W
San Jerónimo Norte	242	31.33 S	61.05 W
Sanjiachang	97	30.17 N	105.32 E
Sanjiadian, Zhg.	95	39.22 N	115.58 E
Sanjiadian, Zhg.	95	39.58 N	116.06 E
Sanjiadian, Zhg.	95	40.09 N	116.36 E
Sanjiang	92	25.42 N	109.23 E
Sanjiangkou	97	29.59 N	104.54 E
Sanjiangying	90	32.18 N	119.42 E
Sanjiangzhen, Zhg.	97	29.33 N	104.03 E
Sanjiangzhen, Zhg.	97	30.31 N	103.48 E
Sanjiaocheng	92	36.47 N	104.40 E
Sanjiaopao	94	41.22 N	122.17 E
Sanjiaoshancun	94	40.42 N	122.49 E
Sanjiazi, Zhg.	94	41.53 N	121.42 E
Sanjiazi, Zhg.	94	40.42 N	123.16 E
Sanjiazi, Zhg.	94	42.33 N	121.38 E
Sanjiazi, Zhg.	94	40.54 N	121.59 E
Sanjiaziyingzi	94	41.52 N	120.49 E
Sanjie, Zhg.	90	32.35 N	118.08 E
Sanjie, Zhg.	92	25.01 N	101.02 E
Sanjō	82	37.37 N	138.57 E
San Joaquín, Bol.	238	13.04 S	64.49 W
San Joaquín, Para.	242	24.57 S	56.07 W
San Joaquin, Pil.	106	10.35 N	122.08 E
San Joaquin, Calif., U.S.	216	36.36 N	120.11 W
San Joaquin □[6]	216	37.57 N	121.17 W
San Joaquín ≃, Bol.	238	13.08 S	63.41 W
San Joaquin ≃, Calif., U.S.	216	38.03 N	121.50 W
San Joaquin, Middle Fork ≃	216	37.32 N	119.11 W
San Joaquin, North Fork ≃	216	37.32 N	119.11 W
San Joaquin, South Fork ≃	216	37.26 N	119.14 W
San Joaquin Valley ∨	194	36.50 N	120.10 W
San Jon	186	35.06 N	103.20 W
San Jorge, Arg.	242	31.54 S	61.52 W
San Jorge, El Sal.	226	13.25 N	88.21 W
San Jorge, Nic.	226	11.27 N	85.48 W
San Jorge ≃	236	9.07 N	74.44 W
San Jorge, Bahía de C	222	31.12 N	113.15 W
San Jorge, Cabo ≻	244	45.47 S	67.21 W
San Jorge, Canal de → Saint George's Channel ⊔	28	52.00 N	6.00 W
San Jorge, Golfo C	244	46.00 S	67.00 W
San Jorge, Golfo de C	34	40.53 N	1.00 E
San Jorge Island I	165e	8.27 S	159.35 E
San José, Arg.	242	27.46 S	55.47 W
San José, Arg.	242	28.23 S	65.42 W
San José, C.R.	226	9.56 N	84.05 W
San José, Ec.	236	1.42 S	79.01 W
San José, Hond.	226	14.54 N	88.44 W
San José, Méx.	186	28.16 N	100.15 W
San José, Méx.	222	27.32 N	110.09 W
San José, Para.	242	25.33 S	56.45 W
San Jose, Pil.	106	15.48 N	121.00 E
San Jose, Pil.	106	10.45 N	121.56 E
San Jose, Pil.	106	12.27 N	121.03 E
San Jose, Calif., U.S.	216 / 272	37.20 N	121.53 W
San Jose, Fla., U.S.	182	30.15 N	81.36 W
San Jose, Ill., U.S.	184	40.18 N	89.36 W
San Jose, N. Mex., U.S.	190	35.24 N	105.29 W
San José, Ven.	276c	10.34 N	66.57 W
San José □[4]	226	9.40 N	84.00 W
San José □[5]	248	34.15 S	56.45 W
San Jose ≃, B.C., Can.	172	52.14 N	122.15 W
San José ≃, Ur.	248	34.38 S	56.29 W
San Jose, Arroyo ≃	272	38.03 N	122.30 W
San José, Golfo C	244	42.20 S	64.18 W
San José, Isla I, Méx.	222	25.00 N	110.38 W
San José, Isla I, Pan.	236	8.15 N	79.07 W
San José, Laguna C	230m	18.25 N	66.01 W
San Jose, Mission ✠[1]	272	37.32 N	121.55 W
San José, Serranía de ⋏[2]	238	17.52 S	60.49 W
San José Ayuquila	224	17.58 N	97.57 W
San Jose Creek ≃	270	34.01 N	118.03 W
San José de Aura	186	27.34 N	101.23 W
San Jose de Buan	106	12.02 N	125.01 E
San José de Chiquitos	238	17.51 S	60.47 W
San José de Chupiamonas	238	14.13 S	68.05 W
San José de Feliciano	242	30.23 S	58.45 W
San José de Galipán	276c	10.35 N	66.54 W
San José de Galipán, Quebrada ≃	276c	10.37 N	66.54 W
San José de Gauribe	236	9.52 N	65.48 W
San José de Gracia	224	20.40 N	102.35 W
San José de Guanipa	236	8.54 N	64.09 W
San José de la Esquina	242	33.06 S	61.42 W
San José de la Popa	186	26.10 N	100.47 W
San José de las Flores	224	17.20 N	95.24 W
San José de las Lajas	230p	22.58 N	82.09 W
San José del Cabo	222	23.03 N	109.41 W
San José del Guaviare	236	2.35 N	72.38 W
San José de Llanetes	224	22.55 N	103.16 W
San José de los Molinos	238	13.57 S	75.41 W
San José de Lourdes	224	23.18 N	103.01 W
San José de Mayo	248	34.20 S	56.42 W
San José de Ocoa	228	18.33 N	70.30 W
San José de Ocuné	236	4.15 N	70.20 W
San José de Raíces	222	24.35 N	100.14 W
San José de Río Chico	236	10.18 N	65.59 W
San José de Sisa	238	6.37 S	76.39 W
San José de Tiznados	236	9.23 N	67.33 W
San Jose Hills ⋏[2]	270	34.04 N	117.49 W
San Jose Island I	186	28.10 N	96.45 W
San José Iturbide	224	21.00 N	100.23 W
San Jose Municipal Airport ⊠	216	37.22 N	121.56 W
San Jose State University ✠[2]	272	37.20 N	121.53 W
San Juan, Arg.	242	31.32 S	68.31 W
San Juan, Guat.	226	15.52 N	88.53 W
San Juan, Méx.	186	29.34 N	104.36 W
San Juan, Méx.	222	27.47 N	103.57 W
San Juan, Pil.	106	16.40 N	120.20 E
San Juan, Pil.	106	8.25 N	126.20 E
San Juan, Pil.	106	13.50 N	121.24 E
San Juan, P.R.	230m	18.28 N	66.07 W
San Juan □[4]	242	31.00 S	69.00 W
San Juan □[6]	214	48.34 N	122.59 W
San Juan ≃, Arg.	242	32.17 S	67.22 W
San Juan ≃, Bol.	238	21.02 S	65.19 W
San Juan ≃, B.C., Can.	214	48.34 N	124.24 W
San Juan ≃, Col.	236	4.03 N	77.27 W
San Juan ≃, Méx.	222	26.22 N	98.51 W
San Juan ≃, N.A.	226	10.56 N	83.42 W
San Juan ≃, Perú	238	13.27 S	76.11 W
San Juan ≃, Pil.	259f	14.35 N	121.01 E
San Juan ≃, Rep. Dom.	228	18.40 N	71.04 W
San Juan ≃, S.A.	236	1.11 N	78.33 W
San Juan ≃, U.S.	190	37.18 N	110.28 W
San Juan ≃, Ven.	236	10.14 N	62.38 W
San Juan, Bahía de C	230m	18.27 N	66.07 W
San Juan, Cabezas de ≻	230m	18.23 N	65.37 W
San Juan, Cabo ≻, Arg.	244	54.44 S	63.44 W
San Juan, Cabo ≻, Gui. Ecu.	142	1.08 N	9.23 E
San Juan, Embalse de ⊜[1]	34	40.30 N	4.15 W
San Juan, Pasaje de ⊔	230m	18.24 N	65.37 W
San Juan, Pico ∧	230p	21.59 N	80.09 W
San Juan, Port C	214	48.34 N	124.27 W
San Juan, Punta ≻	164z	27.03 S	109.22 W
San Juan Basin ═[1]	190	36.15 N	108.20 W
San Juan Bautista, Esp.	34	39.05 N	1.30 E
San Juan Bautista, Méx.	186	26.58 N	101.24 W
San Juan Bautista, Para.	242	26.38 S	57.10 W
San Juan Bautista, Calif., U.S.	216	36.51 N	121.32 W
San Juan Bautista State Historical Park ♠	216	36.51 N	121.31 W
San Juan Capistrano	218	33.30 N	117.40 W
San Juan Capistrano Mission ✠[1]	218	33.31 N	117.40 W
San Juan Colorado	224	16.32 N	97.55 W
San Juan Cotzal	226	15.26 N	91.01 W
San Juan Creek ≃, Calif., U.S.	216	35.40 N	120.22 W
San Juan Creek ≃, Calif., U.S.	218	33.28 N	117.41 W
San Juan de Abajo	224	20.48 N	105.13 W
San Juan de Aragón	276a	19.28 N	99.05 W
San Juan de Aragón, Bosque ♠	276a	19.28 N	99.04 W
San Juan de Aragón, Zoológico de ♠	276a	19.28 N	99.05 W
San Juan de Colón	236	8.02 N	72.16 W
San Juan de Dios	276c	10.35 N	66.55 W
San Juan de Guadalupe	222	24.38 N	102.44 W
San Juan [de la Maguana]	228	18.48 N	71.14 W
San Juan de la Vega	224	20.38 N	100.46 W
San Juan del César	236	10.46 N	73.01 W
San Juan de Lima, Punta ≻	224	18.36 N	103.42 W
San Juan de Limay	226	13.10 N	86.37 W
San Juan del Monte	259f	14.36 N	121.02 E
San Juan del Norte	226	10.55 N	83.42 W
San Juan del Norte, Bahía de C	226	11.15 N	83.45 W
San Juan de los Cayos	236	11.10 N	68.25 W
San Juan de los Lagos	224	21.15 N	102.18 W
San Juan de los Lagos ≃	224	21.18 N	102.33 W
San Juan de los Morros	236	9.55 N	67.21 W
San Juan del Piray	238	20.27 S	64.09 W
San Juan del Río, Méx.	222	24.47 N	104.27 W
San Juan del Río, Méx.	224	20.23 N	100.00 W
San Juan del Río ≃	224	20.40 N	99.30 W
San Juan del Salado	224	23.18 N	101.56 W
San Juan del Sur	226	11.15 N	85.52 W
San Juan de Micay ≃	236	3.05 N	77.32 W
San Juan de Payara	236	7.39 N	67.36 W
San Juan de Pirque	276e	33.38 S	70.30 W
San Juan de Sabinas	186	27.55 N	101.18 W
San Juan Despí	256d	41.22 N	2.04 E
San Juan de Vilasar	256d	41.30 N	2.24 E
San Juan Evangelista	224	17.54 N	95.08 W
San Juanico, Isla I	224	21.43 N	106.38 W
San Juanillo	226	10.02 N	85.44 W
San Juan Island I	214	48.32 N	123.05 W
San Juan Islands II	214	48.36 N	122.50 W
San Juan Islands National Historical Park ♠	214	48.28 N	123.00 W
San Juan Ixcaquixtla	224	18.27 N	97.49 W
San Juan Ixtayopan	276a	19.14 N	99.00 W
San Juan Lachao	224	16.14 N	97.09 W
San Juan Mazatlán	224	17.02 N	95.25 W
San Juan Mountains ⋏	190	37.35 N	107.10 W
San Juan Naval Station ▪	230m	18.28 N	66.06 W
San Juan Nepomuceno, Col.	236	9.57 N	75.05 W
San Juan Nepomuceno, Para.	242	26.06 S	55.58 W
San Juan Peyotán	224	22.24 N	104.21 W
San Juan Quiahije	224	16.17 N	97.20 W
San Juan Sacatepéquez	226	14.43 N	90.39 W
San Juan Sayultepec	224	17.27 N	97.17 W
San Juan y Martínez	230p	22.16 N	83.50 W
San Judas	224	23.15 N	100.52 W
San Julián, Arg.	244	49.18 S	67.43 W
San Julián, Méx.	224	21.01 N	102.10 W
San Julian, Pil.	106	11.45 N	125.27 E
San Julian, Quebrada ≃	276c	10.37 N	66.51 W
San Justo, Arg.	242	30.47 S	60.35 W
San Justo, Arg.	248	34.40 S	58.33 W
San Justo, Aeródromo ⊠	278	34.44 S	58.36 W
San Justo Desvern	256d	41.23 N	2.05 E
Sankanbiriwa ∧	140	8.56 N	10.48 W
Sankaranayinārkovil	112	9.10 N	77.33 E
Sankarani ≃	140	12.01 N	8.19 W
Sankarpur	262b	22.51 N	88.27 E
Sānkdaha	116	22.46 N	89.10 E
Sankeng	90	23.40 N	112.58 E
Sankertown	204	40.28 N	78.35 W
Sankeshu	94	42.38 N	122.25 E
Sankeshwar	112	16.16 N	74.29 E
Sankh ≃	114	22.15 N	84.48 E
Sankheda	110	22.10 N	73.35 E
Sankosh ≃	114	26.24 N	89.47 E
Sānkrāil	262b	22.34 N	88.14 E
Sankt Aegyd am Neuwalde	30	47.52 N	15.35 E
Sankt Andrä vor dem Hagenthale	254b	48.19 N	16.13 E
Sankt Andreasberg	50	51.43 N	10.31 E
Sankt Anton am Arlberg	54	47.08 N	10.16 E
Sankt Antönien	54	46.58 N	9.49 E
Sankt Bartholomä ✠[1]	58	47.32 N	12.58 E
Sankt Blasien	54	47.46 N	8.07 E
Sankt Christopher-Nevis → Saint Kitts-Nevis □[2]	228	17.20 N	62.45 W
Sankt Egidien	50	50.47 N	12.36 E
Sankt Gallen, Öst.	30	47.41 N	14.37 E
Sankt Gallen, Schw.	54	47.25 N	9.23 E
Sankt Gallen □[3]	54	47.10 N	9.08 E
Sankt Gallenkirch	54	47.01 N	9.59 E
Sankt Georgen, B.R.D.	54	47.59 N	7.47 E
Sankt Georgen, B.R.D.	54	48.07 N	8.20 E
Sankt Georgen im Attergau	58	47.56 N	13.29 E
Sankt Gertraud → Santa Gertrude	58	46.29 N	10.53 E
Sankt Gertrud ◆[8]	50	53.52 N	10.47 E
Sankt Gilgen	58	47.46 N	13.22 E
Sankt Goar	52	50.09 N	7.43 E
Sankt Goarshausen	52	50.09 N	7.44 E
Sankt Helena → Saint Helena □[2]	8	15.57 S	5.42 W
Sankt Hubert	52	51.23 N	6.26 E
Sankt Ingbert	52	49.17 N	7.06 E
Sankt Jakob → San Giacomo	58	46.57 N	11.36 E
Sankt Jakob im Lesachtal	58	46.41 N	12.56 E
Sankt Jakob in Defereggen	58	46.55 N	12.20 E
Sankt Johann → San Giovanni	58	46.38 N	11.44 E
Sankt Johann am Tauern	30	47.22 N	14.29 E
Sankt Johann im Pongau	58	47.21 N	13.12 E
Sankt Johann im Walde	58	46.54 N	12.37 E
Sankt Johann in Tirol	58	47.31 N	12.26 E
Sankt Leonhard → San Leonardo	58	46.49 N	11.15 E
Sankt Leonhard im Pitztal	54	47.04 N	10.51 E
Sankt Lorenz ◆[8]	48	53.51 N	10.40 E
Sankt Lorenz → Saint Lawrence ≃	166	49.30 N	67.00 W
Sankt Lorenzen → San Lorenzo de Sebato	58	46.47 N	11.54 E
Sankt Lorenzen im Lesachtal	58	46.42 N	12.47 E
Sankt Lorenz-Golf → Saint Lawrence, Gulf of C	176	48.00 N	62.00 W
Sankt Lorenz-Insel → Saint Lawrence Island I	170	63.30 N	170.30 W
Sankt Mang	54	47.44 N	10.21 E
Sankt Märgen	54	48.00 N	8.05 E
Sankt Margrethen	54	47.27 N	9.36 E
Sankt Martin	58	47.28 N	13.23 E
Sankt Martin in Gsies → San Martino in Casies	58	46.49 N	12.14 E
Sankt Mauritz	48	51.57 N	7.39 E
Sankt Michael im Lungau	58	47.06 N	13.38 E
Sankt Michel → Mikkeli	26	61.41 N	27.15 E
Sankt Moritz	54	46.30 N	9.50 E
Sankt Niklaus → San Nicolò d'Ultimo, It.	58	46.30 N	10.55 E
Sankt Niklaus, Schw.	54	46.11 N	7.48 E
Sankt Paul [im Lavanttal]	30	46.42 N	14.52 E
Sankt Peter, B.R.D.	30	54.18 N	8.38 E
Sankt Peter, B.R.D.	54	48.01 N	8.01 E
Sankt Peter ✠[1]	253	51.37 N	7.12 E
Sankt Peterzell	54	47.19 N	9.11 E
Sankt Pölten	30	48.12 N	15.37 E
Sankt-Quirinus-Dom ✠[1]	253	51.12 N	6.42 E
Sankt Stefan an der Gail	58	46.37 N	13.31 E
Sankt Ulrich → Ortisei	58	46.34 N	11.40 E
Sankt Valentin	30	48.10 N	14.32 E
Sankt Veit an der Glan	30	46.46 N	14.21 E
Sankt Veit im Pongau	58	47.20 N	13.09 E
Sankt-Viktors-Dom ✠[1]	253	51.40 N	6.27 E
Sankt Vincent → Saint Vincent □[2]	231h	13.15 N	61.12 W
Sankt Wallburg → Santa Valburga	58	46.33 N	11.00 E
Sankt Wendel	52	49.28 N	7.10 E
Sankt-Willibrodi-Dom ✠[1]	253	51.40 N	6.37 E
Sankt Wolfgang im Salzkammergut	58	47.44 N	13.27 E
Sankuru ≃	142	4.17 S	20.25 E
San Lázaro	242	22.10 S	57.55 W
San Lázaro, Cabo ≻	222	24.48 N	112.19 W
San Lazzaro di Savena	58	44.28 N	11.25 E
San Leandro	216	37.43 N	122.09 W
San Leandro Creek ≃	272	37.45 N	122.12 W
San Leo	60	43.54 N	12.21 E
San Leon	212	29.29 N	94.55 W
San Leonardo (Sankt Leonhard), It.	58	46.49 N	11.15 E
San Leonardo, Méx.	186	27.28 N	104.55 W
Sanlicheng	90	31.48 N	114.12 E
Sanlidian	90	30.48 N	118.15 E
Sanlifan	90	30.51 N	115.15 E
Sanlintang	96	31.08 N	121.29 E
Sanlipu	96	31.46 N	119.03 E
Sanliuji	90	32.08 N	116.19 E
San Lope	236	6.12 N	71.56 W
San Lorenzo, Arg.	242	28.08 S	58.46 W
San Lorenzo, Arg.	242	32.45 S	60.44 W
San Lorenzo, Bol.	238	21.26 S	64.47 W
San Lorenzo, Ec.	236	1.17 N	78.50 W
San Lorenzo, Hond.	226	13.25 N	87.27 W
San Lorenzo, Méx.	186	25.37 N	97.35 W
San Lorenzo, Méx.	222	25.32 N	102.11 W
San Lorenzo, Nic.	226	12.23 N	85.40 W
San Lorenzo, Nic.	226	12.07 N	86.34 W
San Lorenzo, P.R.	230m	18.11 N	65.58 W
San Lorenzo, Calif., U.S.	216	37.41 N	122.08 W
San Lorenzo, Ven.	236	9.47 N	71.04 W
San Lorenzo ≃, Méx.	222	24.15 N	107.24 W
San Lorenzo ≃, Méx.	276a	19.28 N	99.16 W
San Lorenzo → Saint Lawrence ≃, N.A.	166	49.30 N	67.00 W
San Lorenzo ≃, Calif., U.S.	216	36.58 N	122.01 W
San Lorenzo, Bahía C	226	13.19 N	87.30 W
San Lorenzo, Cabo ≻	236	1.04 S	80.56 W
San Lorenzo, Cerro ∧	244	47.37 S	72.19 W
San Lorenzo, Golfo del → Saint Lawrence, Gulf of C	176	48.00 N	62.00 W
San Lorenzo, Isla I, Méx.	222	28.38 N	112.51 W
San Lorenzo, Isla I, Perú	238	12.05 S	77.15 W
San Lorenzo Creek ≃, Calif., U.S.	216	36.12 N	120.38 W
San Lorenzo Creek ≃, Calif., U.S.	272	37.39 N	122.09 W
San Lorenzo de El Escorial	34	40.35 N	4.09 W
San Lorenzo de la Parrilla	34	39.51 N	2.22 W
San Lorenzo di Sebato (Sankt Lorenzen)	58	46.47 N	11.54 E
San Lorenzo in Campo	60	43.36 N	12.56 E
San Lorenzo Nuovo	60	42.41 N	11.54 E
San Lorenzo Tenoxtitlan ⊥	224	17.44 N	94.45 W
San Lorenzo Tezonco	276a	19.18 N	99.04 W
Sanlúcar de Barrameda	34	36.47 N	6.21 W
Sanlúcar la Mayor	34	37.23 N	6.12 W
San Lucas, Bol.	238	20.06 S	65.07 W
San Lucas, Ec.	236	3.45 S	79.15 W
San Lucas, Méx.	222	22.53 N	109.54 W
San Lucas, Méx.	222	24.13 N	103.04 W
San Lucas, Calif., U.S.	216	36.08 N	121.01 W
San Lucas, Cabo ≻	222	22.52 N	109.53 W
San Lucas, Isla I	226	9.56 N	84.54 W
San Lucas, Serranía de ⋏	236	8.00 N	74.20 W
San Lucas Ocampo	222	24.44 N	104.39 W
San Luis, Arg.	242	33.18 S	66.21 W
San Luis, Cuba	230p	20.12 N	75.51 W
San Luis, Cuba	230p	22.17 N	83.46 W
San Luis, Guat.	226	16.14 N	89.27 W
San Luis, Ariz., U.S.	190	32.29 N	114.47 W
San Luis, Colo., U.S.	190	37.12 N	105.25 W
San Luis, Ven.	236	11.07 N	69.42 W
San Luis □[4]	242	34.00 S	66.00 W
San Luis ◆[8]	276b	23.05 N	82.20 W
San Luis, Arroyo ≃	248	34.10 S	57.44 W
San Luis, Lago de ⊜	238	13.45 S	64.00 W
San Luis, Sierra de ⋏	242	32.40 S	65.50 W
San Luis Acatlán	224	16.48 N	98.45 W
San Luis Creek ≃	190	37.42 N	105.44 W
San Luis de la Loma	224	17.18 N	100.55 W
San Luis de la Paz	224	21.18 N	100.31 W
San Luis del Cordero	222	25.26 N	104.18 W
San Luis del Palmar	242	27.31 S	58.34 W
San Luis Gonzaga	222	24.55 N	111.16 W
San Luis Gonzaga, Bahía C	222	29.48 N	114.22 W
San Luis Jilotepeque	226	14.39 N	89.44 W
San Luis Obispo	216	35.17 N	120.40 W
San Luis Obispo □[6]	216	35.30 N	120.30 W
San Luis Pass C	212	29.05 N	95.08 W
San Luis Peak ∧	190	37.59 N	106.56 W
San Luis Potosí	224	22.09 N	100.59 W
San Luis Potosí □[3]	224	22.30 N	100.30 W
San Luis Reservoir ⊜[1]	216	37.07 N	121.05 W
San Luis Rey	218	33.14 N	117.20 W
San Luis Rey ≃	194	33.12 N	117.24 W
San Luis Rey, Mission ✠[1]	218	33.14 N	117.20 W
San Luis Río Colorado	222	32.29 N	114.48 W
San Luis Soyatlán	224	20.12 N	103.18 W
San Luis State Recreation Area ♠	216	37.04 N	121.05 W
San Luis Tlaxialtemalco	276a	19.15 N	99.03 W
San Luis Valley ∨	190	37.25 N	106.00 W
Sanluri	36	39.33 N	8.54 E
San Macario	256b	45.36 N	8.47 E
Sanmaiden	260	34.39 N	135.51 E
San Mamete	54	46.02 N	9.04 E
San Manuel, Arg.	242	37.47 S	58.50 W
San Manuel, Méx.	224	17.37 N	93.24 W
San Manuel, Pil.	106	16.04 N	120.40 E
San Manuel, Ariz., U.S.	190	32.36 N	110.38 W
San Marcelino, El Sal.	226	13.22 N	89.03 W
San Marcelino, Pil.	106	14.58 N	120.09 E
San Marcello Pistoiese	60	44.03 N	10.47 E
San Marcial, Punta ≻	222	25.30 N	111.01 W
San Marco, Chile	276e	33.37 S	70.38 W
San Marco, Esp.	34	43.13 N	8.17 W
San Marco dei Cavoti	60	41.18 N	14.53 E
San Marco in Lamis	60	41.43 N	15.38 E
San Marco la Catola	60	41.31 N	15.00 E
San Marcos, Chile	242	30.56 S	71.03 W
San Marcos, Col.	236	8.39 N	75.08 W
San Marcos, C.R.	226	9.40 N	84.01 W
San Marcos, El Sal.	226	13.39 N	89.11 W
San Marcos, Guat.	226	14.58 N	91.48 W
San Marcos, Hond.	226	14.24 N	88.56 W
San Marcos, Hond.	226	15.17 N	88.23 W
San Marcos, Méx.	222	26.41 N	102.07 W
San Marcos, Méx.	224	20.47 N	104.11 W
San Marcos, Méx.	224	16.48 N	99.21 W
San Marcos, Méx.	224	20.02 N	99.20 W
San Marcos, Calif., U.S.	218	33.09 N	117.10 W
San Marcos, Tex., U.S.	186	29.53 N	97.57 W
San Marcos □[5]	226	15.00 N	91.55 W
San Marcos ≃	186	29.29 N	97.28 W
San Marcos, Estadio de ♠	276d	12.04 S	77.05 W
San Marcos, Isla I	222	27.13 N	112.06 W
San Marcos, Laguna de ⊜	224	20.17 N	103.33 W
San Marcos, Universidad de ✠[2]	276d	12.03 S	77.05 W
San Marcos Arteaga	224	17.45 N	97.58 W
San Marcos de Colón	226	13.26 N	86.48 W
San Marino, S. Mar.	60	43.55 N	12.28 E
San Marino, Calif., U.S.	270	34.07 N	118.07 W
San Marino □[1]	22 / 60	43.56 N	12.25 E
San Martín, Arg.	242	29.14 S	65.46 W
San Martín, Arg.	242	33.04 S	68.28 W
San Martín → General San Martín, Arg.	248	34.34 S	58.32 W
San Martín, Col.	236	3.42 N	73.42 W
San Martin, Calif., U.S.	216	37.05 N	121.37 W
San Martín, Ur.	248	33.45 S	57.37 W
San Martín □[5]	238	7.00 S	76.50 W
San Martín ≃	238	13.08 S	63.43 W
San Martín, Arroyo ≃	248	33.49 S	57.44 W
San Martín, Cerro ∧[1]	224	18.19 N	94.48 W
San Martín, Cuchilla ⋏[2]	248	33.45 S	57.54 W
San Martín, Lago (Lago O'Higgins) ⊜	244	49.00 S	72.40 W
San Martín, Volcán ∧[1]	224	18.33 N	95.12 W
San Martín de Bolaños	224	21.29 N	103.58 W
San Martín [de las Pirámides]	224	19.42 N	98.50 W
San Martín de las Vacas	186	25.30 N	101.20 W
San Martín del Boracho, Sierra ⋏	190	30.45 N	105.42 W
San Martín de los Andes	244	40.10 S	71.21 W
San Martín de Valdeiglesias	34	40.21 N	4.24 W
San Martín Hidalgo	224	20.27 N	103.57 W
San Martino, It.	56	45.27 N	8.47 E
San Martino (Sankt Martin), It.	58	46.47 N	11.13 E
San Martino Buon Albergo	58	45.25 N	11.05 E
San Martino di Castrozza	58	46.16 N	11.48 E
San Martino di Lupari	58	45.39 N	11.51 E
San Martino in Badia (Saint Martin)	58	46.41 N	11.52 E
San Martino in Casies (Sankt Martin in Gsies)	58	46.49 N	12.14 E
San Martino in Rio	58	44.44 N	10.48 E
San Martino Valle Caudina	60	41.01 N	14.39 E
San Martín Peras	224	17.19 N	98.15 W
San Martín Texmelucan	224	19.17 N	98.26 W
San Marzano sul Sarno	60	40.46 N	14.35 E
San Mateo, Esp.	34	40.28 N	0.11 E
San Mateo, Méx.	224	22.59 N	103.30 W
San Mateo, Pil.	259f	14.42 N	121.07 E
San Mateo, Calif., U.S.	216	37.35 N	122.19 W
San Mateo, Fla., U.S.	182	29.36 N	81.35 W
San Mateo, N. Mex., U.S.	190	35.20 N	107.39 W
San Mateo, Ven.	236	9.45 N	64.33 W
San Mateo □[6]	216	37.25 N	122.20 W
San Mateo ≃	276a	19.30 N	99.17 W
San Mateo Atenco	224	19.16 N	99.32 W
San Mateo Bridge ◆[5]	272	37.36 N	122.13 W
San Mateo Canyon ∨	218	33.23 N	117.36 W
San Mateo Creek ≃	272	37.34 N	122.18 W
San Mateo del Mar	224	16.12 N	95.00 W
San Mateo Ixtatán	226	15.50 N	91.29 W
San Mateo Memorial Park ♠	272	37.17 N	122.18 W
San Mateo Point ≻	218	33.23 N	117.36 W
San Mateo Tlaltenango	276a	19.21 N	99.17 W
San Mateo Xalpa	276a	19.14 N	99.07 W
San Matías	238	16.22 S	58.24 W
San Matías, Golfo C	244	41.30 S	64.15 W
San Mauro Torinese	56	45.06 N	7.46 E
San Medi, Arroyo de ≃	256d	41.28 N	2.06 E
Sanmen	90	29.06 N	121.24 E
Sanmen I	90	22.26 N	114.38 E
San Menaio	60	41.56 N	15.58 E
Sanmendao I	90	29.55 N	121.52 E
Sanmenwan C	90	29.08 N	121.44 E
Sanmenxia (Shanxian)	92	34.45 N	111.05 E
Sanmiaochang	97	30.14 N	106.06 E
San Michele all'Adige	58	46.12 N	11.08 E
San Michele al Tagliamento	58	45.46 N	12.59 E
San Michele Mondovì	56	44.23 N	7.54 E
San Miguel, Arg.	242	28.00 S	57.36 W
San Miguel → General Sarmiento, Arg.	248	34.33 S	58.43 W
San Miguel, Bol.	238	16.42 S	61.01 W
San Miguel, Chile	276e	33.30 S	70.40 W
San Miguel, Ec.	236	1.44 S	79.01 W
San Miguel, El Sal.	226	13.29 N	88.11 W
San Miguel, Esp.	138	28.05 N	16.37 W
San Miguel, Méx.	224	23.23 N	98.10 W
San Miguel, Pan.	236	8.27 N	78.56 W
San Miguel, Perú	238	13.01 S	73.58 W
San Miguel, Perú	238	7.00 S	78.51 W
San Miguel, Perú	276d	12.06 S	77.07 W
San Miguel, Pil.	106	15.09 N	120.59 E
San Miguel, Calif., U.S.	216	35.45 N	120.42 W
San Miguel ≃, Bol.	238	13.52 S	63.56 W
San Miguel ≃, Méx.	190	30.51 N	110.45 W
San Miguel ≃, Méx.	222	29.16 N	110.53 W
San Miguel ≃, Méx.	224	18.16 N	100.40 W
San Miguel ≃, S.A.	238	19.15 S	59.20 W
San Miguel ≃, Colo., U.S.	190	38.23 N	108.48 W
San Miguel, Cerro ∧[2]	238	19.19 S	60.36 W
San Miguel, Golfo de C	236	8.22 N	78.17 W
San Miguel, Volcán de ∧[1]	226	13.26 N	88.16 W
San Miguel Arcángel, Mission ✠[1]	216	35.44 N	120.42 W
San Miguel Bay C	106	13.50 N	123.10 E
San Miguel Canoa	224	19.09 N	98.05 W
San Miguel Chimalapa	224	16.43 N	94.41 W
San Miguel Creek ≃	186	28.30 N	98.25 W
San Miguel de Allende	224	20.55 N	100.45 W
San Miguel de Cruces	222	24.25 N	105.51 W
San Miguel del Monte	248	35.27 S	58.48 W
San Miguel del Padrón	230p	23.05 N	82.19 W
San Miguel de Tucumán	242	26.49 S	65.13 W
San Miguel el Alto	224	21.01 N	102.21 W
San Miguel Island I, Pil.	106	13.23 N	123.48 E
San Miguel Island I, Calif., U.S.	194	34.02 N	120.22 W
San Miguel Islands II	106	7.45 N	118.28 E
San Miguelito	226	11.24 N	84.54 W
San Miguel Ixtahuacán	226	15.15 N	91.45 W
San Miguel Mountain ∧	218	32.42 N	116.56 W
San Miguel Octopan	224	20.34 N	100.44 W
San Miguel [o San Graciano]	222	29.10 N	101.28 W
San Miguel Talea de Castro	224	17.22 N	96.15 W
San Miguel Tenango	224	16.16 N	95.36 W
San Miguel Totolapan	224	18.08 N	100.23 W
Sanming, Zhg.	90	26.14 N	117.36 E
Sanming, Zhg.	90	26.25 N	117.13 E
San Miniato	60	43.41 N	10.51 E
San Murezzan → Sankt Moritz	54	46.30 N	9.50 E
Sannahed	40	59.06 N	15.09 E
Sannan	86	35.04 N	135.02 E
Sannār	130	13.33 N	33.38 E
San Narciso, Pil.	106	15.01 N	120.05 E
San Narciso, Pil.	106	13.34 N	122.34 E
Sannazzaro de'Burgondi	56	45.06 N	8.54 E
Sannicandro Garganico	60	41.50 N	15.34 E
San Nicola, Isola I	60	42.07 N	15.30 E
San Nicolás, Esp.	138	27.59 N	15.46 W
San Nicolás, Hond.	226	15.00 N	88.45 W
San Nicolás, Méx.	224	16.26 N	98.32 W
San Nicolas, Méx.	224	19.05 N	101.07 W
San Nicolás, Perú	238	15.13 S	75.12 W
San Nicolas, Pil.	106	16.04 N	120.46 E
San Nicolas, Pil.	106	18.09 N	120.38 E
San Nicolás ≃	224	19.40 N	105.14 W
San Nicolás, Bahía C	238	15.13 S	75.15 W
San Nicolás, Punta ≻	238	15.15 S	75.14 W
San Nicolás de Bari	230p	22.47 N	81.55 W
San Nicolás de los Arroyos	242	33.20 S	60.13 W
San Nicolás de los Garzas	186	25.45 N	100.18 W
San Nicolas Island I	194	33.15 N	119.31 W
San Nicolás Totolapan	276a	19.17 N	99.16 W
San Nicolò di Comelico	58	46.35 N	12.31 E
San Nicolò d'Ultimo (Sankt Nikolaus)	58	46.30 N	10.55 E
San Nicolò Ferrarese	58	44.42 N	11.42 E
Sannieshof	148	26.30 S	25.47 E
Sannikova, Proliv ⊔	64	74.30 N	140.00 E
Şannīn, Jabal ∧	122	33.57 N	35.52 E
Sannio, Monti del ⋏	60	41.30 N	14.45 E
Sanniquellie	140	7.22 N	8.43 W
Sannohe	82	40.22 N	141.15 E
Sannois	251	48.58 N	2.15 E
Sannō-tōge)(	84	37.04 N	139.45 E
Sannūr, Wādī ∨	132	28.58 N	31.03 E
Sano	84	36.19 N	139.35 E
Sañogasta	242	29.18 S	67.36 W
Sanok	30	49.34 N	22.13 E
Sânon ≃	54	48.38 N	6.20 E
San Onofre	236	9.44 N	75.32 W
San Onofre Mountain ∧	218	33.22 N	117.30 W
San Pablo, Chile	244	40.24 S	73.01 W
San Pablo, Col.	236	1.40 N	77.00 W
San Pablo, Pil.	106	14.04 N	121.19 E
San Pablo, Pil.	106	7.40 N	123.27 E
San Pablo, Calif., U.S.	216	37.57 N	122.21 W
San Pablo ≃	226	7.51 N	81.10 W
San Pablo, Point ≻	272	37.58 N	122.26 W
San Pablo, Punta ≻	222	27.14 N	114.29 W
San Pablo Autopan	224	19.21 N	99.40 W
San Pablo Balleza	222	26.57 N	106.21 W
San Pablo Bay C	216	38.06 N	122.22 W
San Pablo Creek ≃	272	37.58 N	122.30 W
San Pablo Huitzo	224	17.15 N	96.52 W
San Pablo Huixtepec	224	16.50 N	96.46 W
San Pablo Ostotepec	276a	19.11 N	99.04 W
San Pablo Reservoir ⊜[1]	272	37.56 N	122.15 W
San Pablo Ridge ∧	272	37.55 N	122.15 W
San Pablo Strait ⊔	272	37.58 N	122.26 W
San Pablo Villa de Mitla	224	16.55 N	96.24 W
Sanpāda	262c	19.04 N	73.01 E
San Pancrazio Salentino	36	40.25 N	17.50 E
San Paolo	58	46.29 N	11.15 E
San Paolo di Civitate	60	41.44 N	15.15 E
San Pascual	106	13.08 N	122.59 E
San Pasqual Indian Reservation ◆[4]	218	33.12 N	116.58 W
San Pedro, Arg.	242	27.57 S	65.10 W
San Pedro, Arg.	242	24.14 S	64.52 W
San Pedro, Arg.	242	33.40 S	59.40 W
San Pedro, Bol.	238	14.20 S	64.50 W
San Pedro, Chile	242	21.57 S	68.34 W
San Pedro, Chile	242	33.54 S	71.28 W
San Pedro, Col.	236	9.24 N	75.04 W
San Pedro, C.R.	226	9.56 N	84.03 W
San Pedro, Cuba	276b	23.03 N	82.27 W
San Pedro, Para.	242	24.07 S	56.59 W
San Pedro, Tex., U.S.	186	27.48 N	97.41 W
San Pedro, Ur.	248	34.21 S	57.51 W
San Pedro, Ven.	236	8.50 N	71.58 W
San Pedro □[5]	242	24.15 S	56.30 W
San Pedro ◆[8]	218	33.44 N	118.18 W
San Pedro ≃, Cuba	230p	21.09 N	78.30 W
San Pedro ≃, Méx.	224	21.45 N	105.30 W
San Pedro ≃, N.A.	190	32.59 N	110.47 W
San Pedro ≃, N.A.	222	17.45 N	91.25 W
San Pedro ≃, Ven.	276c	10.35 N	66.48 W
San Pedro, Arroyo ≃	248	34.21 S	57.56 W
San Pedro, Point ≻, Calif., U.S.	272	37.35 N	122.31 W
San Pedro, Point ≻, Calif., U.S.	272	37.59 N	122.27 W
San Pedro, Punta ≻, Chile	242	25.30 S	70.38 W
San Pedro, Punta ≻, C.R.	226	8.39 N	83.45 W
San Pedro, Río de ≃	224	19.23 N	103.51 W
San Pedro, Volcán ∧[1]	242	21.53 S	68.25 W
San Pedro Apóstol	224	16.44 N	96.44 W
San Pedro Atocpan	276a	19.12 N	99.03 W
San Pedro Ayampuc	226	14.47 N	90.27 W
San Pedro Bay C, Pil.	106	11.11 N	125.05 E
San Pedro Bay C, Calif., U.S.	218	33.45 N	118.11 W
San Pedro Breakwater ◆[5]	270	33.42 N	118.16 W
San Pedro Carchá	226	15.29 N	90.16 W
San Pedro Channel ⊔	218	33.35 N	118.25 W
San Pedro Creek ≃, Calif., U.S.	272	37.36 N	122.30 W
San Pedro Creek ≃, Tex., U.S.	212	31.34 N	95.14 W
San Pedro de Arriba	248	34.18 S	57.47 W
San Pedro de Atacama	242	22.55 S	68.13 W
San Pedro de Buena Vista	238	18.13 S	65.59 W
San Pedro de la Cueva	222	29.18 N	109.44 W
San Pedro de las Colonias	222	25.45 N	102.59 W
San Pedro del Gallo	222	25.33 N	104.18 W
San Pedro de Lloc	238	7.26 S	79.31 W
San Pedro del Norte	226	13.04 N	84.33 W
San Pedro del Paraná	242	26.46 S	56.15 W
San Pedro de Macorís	228	18.27 N	69.18 W
San Pedro de Premiá	256d	41.31 N	2.21 E
San Pedro El Alto	224	16.01 N	96.28 W
San Pedro Huamelula	224	16.02 N	95.40 W
San Pedro Jicayán	224	16.25 N	97.59 W
San Pedro Juchatengo	224	16.21 N	97.06 W
San Pedro Mártir	276a	19.16 N	99.10 W

Symbols in the index entries represent the broad categories identified in the key at the right. Symbols with superior numbers (⋏[2]) identify subcategories (see complete key on page I · 26).

Kartensymbole in dem Registerverzeichnis stellen die rechts in Schlüssel erklärten Kategorien dar. Symbole mit hochgestellten Ziffern (⋏[2]) bezeichnen Unterabteilungen einer Kategorie (vgl. vollständiger Schlüssel auf Seite I · 26).

Los símbolos incluidos en el texto del índice representan las grandes categorías identificadas con la clave a la derecha. Los símbolos con numeros en su parte superior (⋏[2]) identifican las subcategorías (véase la clave completa en la página I · 26).

Les symboles de l'index représentent les catégories indiquées dans la légende à droite. Les symboles suivis d'un indice (⋏[2]) représentent des sous-catégories (voir légende complète à la page I · 26).

Os símbolos incluídos no texto do índice representam as grandes categorias identificadas com a chave à direita. Os símbolos com números em sua parte superior (⋏[2]) identificam as subcategorias (veja-se a chave completa à página I · 26).

∧ Mountain	Berg	Montaña	Montagne	Montanha
⋏ Mountains	Berge	Montañas	Montagnes	Montanhas
)(Pass	Pass	Paso	Col	Passo
∨ Valley, Canyon	Tal, Cañon	Valle, Cañón	Vallée, Canyon	Vale, Canhão
═ Plain	Ebene	Llano	Plaine	Planície
≻ Cape	Kap	Cabo	Cap	Cabo
I Island	Insel	Isla	Île	Ilha
II Islands	Inseln	Islas	Îles	Ilhas
◆ Other Topographic Features	Andere Topographische Objekte	Otros Elementos Topográficos	Autres données topographiques	Outros Elementos Topográficos

ESPAÑOL — FRANÇAIS — PORTUGUÊS

Nombre / Nom / Nome	Página / Page	Lat.°′	Long.°′ W=Oeste / W=Ouest
San Pedro Mártir, Sierra ⋀	222	30.45 N	115.13 W
San Pedro Mixtepec	224	16.00 N	97.07 W
San Pedro Peaks ⋀	190	36.07 N	106.49 W
San Pedro Piedra Gorda	224	22.27 N	102.21 W
San Pedro Pinula	226	14.40 N	89.51 W
San Pedro Sacatepéquez	226	14.58 N	91.46 W
San Pedro Sula	226	15.27 N	88.02 W
San Pedro Tapanatepec	224	16.21 N	94.12 W
San Pedro Xalostoc	276a	19.32 N	99.05 W
San Pedro y Miquelon → Saint Pierre and Miquelon □2	176	46.55 N	56.10 W
San Pedro Zacatenco	276a	19.31 N	99.08 W
San Pelayo	236	8.58 N	75.51 W
San Pellegrino Terme	56	45.50 N	9.40 E
San Piero a Grado	60	43.41 N	10.21 E
San Piero in Bagno	60	43.51 N	11.58 E
San Pierre	206	41.12 N	86.53 W
San Pietro (Sankt Peter)	58	47.01 N	12.03 E
San Pietro, Isola di I	36	39.08 N	8.18 E
San Pietro di Cadore	58	46.34 N	12.35 E
San Pietro in Casale	58	44.42 N	11.24 E
San Pietro in Gu	58	45.37 N	11.40 E
San Pietro in Palazzi	60	43.20 N	10.30 E
San Pietro in Vaticano ♅1	257a	41.54 N	12.28 E
San Pietro Vara	56	44.20 N	9.35 E
San Pitch ≃	190	39.03 N	111.51 W
Sanpoil ≃	192	47.53 N	118.41 W
San Policarpio	106	12.11 N	125.30 E
San Polo d'Enza	58	44.38 N	10.26 E
Sanpu, Zhg.	88	34.09 N	117.10 E
Sanpu, Zhg.	90	33.38 N	117.09 E
Sanqiaobu	96	30.35 N	119.58 E
San Quentin	272	37.56 N	122.29 W
San Quentin State Prison ♅	272	37.56 N	122.28 W
Sanquhar	42	55.22 N	3.56 W
San Quintin	106	16.00 N	120.50 E
San Quintín, Bahía de C	222	30.22 N	115.55 W
San Quintín, Cabo >	222	30.21 N	116.00 W
San Quintin, Ventisquero ⛋	244	46.52 S	74.05 W
San Quirico de Tarrasa	256d	41.32 N	2.05 E
San Quirico d'Orcia	60	43.03 N	11.36 E
Sanquntan	90	27.17 N	115.04 E
San Rafael, Arg.	242	34.36 S	68.20 W
San Rafael, Chile	242	35.19 S	71.32 W
San Rafael, Méx.	222	28.34 N	111.42 W
San Rafael, Méx.	222	25.01 N	100.33 W
San Rafael, Méx.	224	20.12 N	96.51 W
San Rafael, Calif., U.S.	216	37.59 N	122.31 W
San Rafael, N. Mex., U.S.	190	35.06 N	107.53 W
San Rafael, Ven.	238	10.58 N	71.44 W
San Rafael ≃	190	38.47 N	110.07 W
San Rafael Bay C	272	37.58 N	122.28 W
San Rafael de Arriba	222	31.05 N	116.05 W
San Rafael de las Tortillas	186	26.49 N	99.32 W
San Rafael del Norte	226	13.12 N	86.06 W
San Rafael del Sur	226	11.51 N	86.27 W
San Rafael Hills ⋀2	270	34.10 N	118.12 W
San Rafael Mountains ⋀	194	34.45 N	119.50 W
San Rafael Oriente	226	13.23 N	88.21 W
San Rafael Swell ⋀1	190	38.40 N	110.45 W
San Ramón, Arg.	242	27.42 S	64.17 W
San Ramón, Bol.	238	13.17 S	64.43 W
San Ramón, C.R.	226	10.06 N	84.28 W
San Ramón, Nic.	226	14.45 N	84.50 W
San Ramón, Perú	238	11.08 S	75.20 W
San Ramon, Pil.	106	13.16 N	124.05 E
San Ramon, Calif., U.S.	272	37.47 N	121.59 W
San Ramón, Ur.	242	34.18 S	55.58 W
San Ramón, Bahía C	222	30.45 N	116.03 W
San Ramon Creek ≃	272	37.54 N	122.03 W
San Ramón de la Nueva Orán	242	23.08 S	64.20 W
San Ramon Valley V	272	37.46 N	121.58 W
Sanrao	90	23.59 N	116.50 E
San-rei ⋀	86	33.50 N	133.59 E
San Remigio	106	11.05 N	123.56 E
San Remo, Austl.	159	38.31 S	145.22 E
San Remo, It.	56	43.49 N	7.46 E
San Remo, N.Y., U.S.	200	40.54 N	73.13 W
San Rodrigo ≃	186	28.54 N	100.37 W
San Román ≃	226	16.21 N	90.22 W
San Román, Cabo >	236	12.12 N	70.00 W
San Roque, Arg.	242	28.34 S	58.43 W
San Roque, Arg.	242	30.17 S	68.41 W
San Roque, Esp.	34	36.13 N	5.24 W
San Roque, Pil.	259f	14.29 N	120.54 E
San Roque, Cabo → São Roque, Cabo de >	240	5.29 S	35.16 W
San Rosendo	242	37.16 S	72.43 W
San Saba	186	31.12 N	98.43 W
San Saba ≃	186	31.15 N	98.35 W
San Saep, Khlong ≃	259a	13.45 N	100.36 E
San Salvador, Arg.	242	31.37 S	58.30 W
San Salvador, Arg.	242	29.16 S	57.31 W
San Salvador, El Sal.	226	13.42 N	89.12 W
San Salvador (Watling Island) I	228	24.02 N	74.28 W
San Salvador ≃	248	33.37 S	58.06 W
San Salvador, Cuchilla de ⋀2	248	33.56 S	57.45 W
San Salvador, Isla I	236a	0.14 S	90.45 W
San Salvador, Volcán de ⋀1	226	13.44 N	89.17 W
San Salvador de Jujuy	242	24.11 S	65.18 W
San Salvador el Seco	224	19.08 N	97.39 W
San Salvatore Monferrato	56	44.59 N	8.34 E
San Salvatore Telesino	60	41.14 N	14.30 E
San Salvo	60	42.03 N	14.44 E
Sansanding Dam ⋅6	140	13.44 N	6.00 W
Sansanné-Mango	140	10.21 N	0.28 E
Sans Bois Creek ≃	186	35.20 N	94.50 W
San Sebastián, El Sal.	226	13.44 N	88.50 W
San Sebastián, Esp.	34	43.19 N	1.59 W
San Sebastián, Guat.	226	14.34 N	91.39 W
San Sebastián, Hond.	226	14.34 N	88.42 W
San Sebastián, Méx.	224	22.10 N	104.19 W
San Sebastián, Méx.	224	21.26 N	102.21 W
San Sebastián, Méx.	224	20.47 N	104.51 W
San Sebastián, P.R.	230m	18.20 N	66.59 W
San Sebastián, Bahía C	244	53.12 S	68.20 W
San Sebastián de la Gomera	138	28.06 N	17.06 W
San Sebastián de los Reyes	256a	40.33 N	3.38 W
San Sebastián de Yali	226	13.18 N	86.11 W
San Sebastiano Curone	56	44.47 N	9.04 E
San Secondo Parmense	58	44.55 N	10.14 E
Sansepolcro	60	43.34 N	12.08 E
Sanserre	46	47.22 N	2.50 E
San Severino Marche	60	43.13 N	13.10 E
San Severo	60	41.41 N	15.23 E
Sansha	90	26.58 N	120.12 E
Sanshanzhen	88	39.29 N	114.20 E
Sanshawan C	90	26.35 N	119.50 E
Sanshengchang	79	44.51 N	120.21 E
Sanshierzhan	79	53.16 N	121.49 E
Sanshijia	88	41.44 N	119.15 E
Sanshijiazi	88	41.05 N	119.03 E
Sanshilibao	88	39.15 N	121.48 E
Sanshiling	96	30.51 N	119.29 E
Sanshilitun	90	32.54 N	112.30 E
Sanshisanzhan	79	53.10 N	121.27 E
Sanshui	90	23.11 N	112.53 E
San Sigismondo (Sankt Sigmund)	58	46.49 N	11.46 E
San Simeon	216	35.39 N	121.11 W
San Simon, Méx.	194	30.30 N	115.58 W
San Simon, Ariz., U.S.	190	32.16 N	109.14 W
San Simón ≃, Bol.	238	13.13 S	63.31 W
San Simon ≃, Ariz., U.S.	190	32.50 N	109.39 W
San Simon Wash V	190	31.45 N	112.25 W
San Siro ⋅8	256b	45.29 N	9.07 E
Sanski Most	36	44.46 N	16.40 E
Sanso	140	11.43 N	6.51 W
San Solano	242	31.29 S	65.55 W
Sansom Park Village	212	32.48 N	97.24 W
Sanson	162	40.13 S	175.25 E
Sans Souci	264a	33.59 S	151.08 E
Sans-Souci ⊥	228	19.37 N	72.12 W
Sanssouci, Schloss ♅	50	52.24 N	13.02 E
San Stefano Ticino	256b	45.29 N	8.55 E
Santa, Perú	238	8.59 S	78.36 W
Santa, Pil.	106	17.29 N	120.26 E
Santa ≃	238	8.58 S	78.39 W
Santa, Isla de I	238	9.02 S	78.40 W
Santa Adélia	245	21.16 S	48.48 W
Santa Albertina	245	20.02 S	50.44 W
Santa Amalia	34	39.01 N	6.01 W
Santa Amelia ≃	226	16.13 N	90.01 W
Santa Ana, Arg.	242	27.22 S	55.34 W
Santa Ana, Bol.	238	15.31 S	67.30 W
Santa Ana, Bol.	238	13.45 S	65.35 W
Santa Ana, Bol.	238	18.43 S	58.44 W
Santa Ana, Col.	236	9.19 N	74.35 W
Santa Ana, Ec.	236	1.13 S	80.23 W
Santa Ana, El Sal.	226	13.59 N	89.34 W
Santa Ana, Méx.	222	24.04 N	100.30 W
Santa Ana, Méx.	222	30.33 N	111.07 W
Santa Ana, Méx.	224	19.19 N	98.11 W
Santa Ana, Méx.	224	18.15 N	93.28 W
Santa Ana, Calif., U.S.	218, 270	33.43 N	117.54 W
Santa Ana ≃	218	33.38 N	117.57 W
Santa Ana, Cuchilla de (Coxilha de Santana) ⋀2	242	31.15 S	55.15 W
Santa Ana, Volcán de ⋀1	226	13.50 N	89.38 W
Santa Ana Canyon V	270	33.53 N	117.43 W
Santa Ana de Barcelona	236	9.19 N	64.39 W
Santa Ana de Chena	276e	33.34 S	70.47 W
Santa Ana Heights	218	33.39 N	117.54 W
Santa Ana Island I	165e	10.50 S	162.28 E
Santa Ana Marine Corps Air Station ⊠	270	33.43 N	117.50 W
Santa Ana Mountains ⋀	218	33.45 N	117.35 W
Santa Ana Pacueco	224	20.22 N	102.00 W
Santa Anita	224	20.33 N	103.27 W
Santa Anita Canyon V	270	34.12 N	118.01 W
Santa Anita Park ♠	270	34.08 N	118.03 W
Santa Anna	186	31.45 N	99.19 W
Santa Apolonia	186	25.38 N	97.59 W
Santa Bárbara, Chile	242	37.40 S	72.01 W
Santa Bárbara, Col.	236	5.53 N	75.35 W
Santa Bárbara, Hond.	226	14.53 N	88.14 W
Santa Bárbara, Méx.	222	26.48 N	105.49 W
Santa Bárbara, Méx.	224	18.52 N	101.07 W
Santa Barbara, Calif., U.S.	194	34.25 N	119.42 W
Santa Bárbara, Ven.	236	3.57 N	67.06 W
Santa Bárbara, Ven.	236	7.47 N	71.10 W
Santa Barbara □5	226	15.10 N	88.20 W
Santa Barbara □6	218	33.28 N	119.02 W
Santa Bárbara ≃	238	16.58 S	61.39 W
Santa Bárbara, Morro de ⋀	277a	22.57 S	43.28 W
Santa Bárbara, Ribeirão ≃	246	22.00 S	45.43 W
Santa Bárbara, Serra de ⋀1	238	15.30 S	59.20 W
Santa Bárbara, Sierra ⋀	242	24.07 S	64.29 W
Santa Bárbara, Túnel ⋅5	277a	22.56 S	43.12 W
Santa Barbara Channel U	194	34.15 N	119.55 W
Santa Bárbara do Monte Verde	246	21.58 S	43.42 W
Santa Bárbara do Sul	242	28.22 S	53.15 W
Santa Barbara Island I	218	33.28 N	119.02 W
Santa Branca	246	23.24 S	45.53 W
Santaca	148	26.36 S	32.32 E
Santa Catalina, Arg.	242	21.57 S	66.04 W
Santa Catalina, Pan.	226	8.47 N	81.20 W
Santa Catalina, Pil.	106	9.20 N	122.51 E
Santa Catalina, Ur.	248	33.49 S	57.29 W
Santa Catalina, Arroyo ≃	278	34.46 S	58.27 W
Santa Catalina, Gulf of C	218	33.20 N	117.45 W
Santa Catalina, Isla I	222	25.40 N	110.47 W
Santa Catalina, Laguna ⓔ	278	34.46 S	58.27 W
Santa Catalina de Armara	34	43.02 N	8.49 W
Santa Catalina Island I	218	33.23 N	118.24 W
Santa Catarina, Méx.	194	31.37 N	115.48 W
Santa Catarina, Méx.	222	25.41 N	100.28 W
Santa Catarina, Méx.	224	21.19 N	101.10 W
Santa Catarina □3	242	27.00 S	50.00 W
Santa Catarina ≃	245	17.46 S	46.34 W
Santa Catarina, Ilha de I	242	27.36 S	48.30 W
Santa Catarina Yecahuizotl	276a	19.19 N	98.58 W
Santa Catarina Yosonotú	224	16.59 N	97.39 W
Santa Caterina Valfurva	58	46.25 N	10.29 E
Santa Cecilio	242	26.56 S	50.27 W
Santa Cesarea Terme	36	40.02 N	18.29 E
Santa Clara, Arg.	242	29.33 S	68.31 W
Santa Clara, Col.	236	2.43 S	69.43 W
Santa Clara, Cuba	230p	22.24 N	79.58 W
Santa Clara, Méx.	222	29.17 N	107.01 W
Santa Clara, Méx.	224	19.41 N	102.30 W
Santa Clara, Calif., U.S.	216	37.21 N	121.57 W
Santa Clara, Utah, U.S.	190	37.08 N	113.39 W
Santa Clara □6	216	37.20 N	121.53 W
Santa Clara ≃, Calif., U.S.	218	34.14 N	119.16 W
Santa Clara ≃, Utah, U.S.	190	37.05 N	113.36 W
Santa Clara, Bahía de C	230p	23.05 N	80.30 W
Santa Clara, Isla I	234	33.42 S	79.00 W
Santa Clara, University of ♅2	272	37.21 N	121.56 W
Santa Clara Coatitla	276a	19.34 N	99.04 W
Santa Clara de Olimar	242	32.55 S	54.58 W
Santa Clara Valley V	216	37.10 N	121.40 W
Santa Clarita	276d	12.00 S	77.01 W
Santa Clotilde	236	2.34 S	73.44 W
Santa Coloma de Cervelló	256d	41.22 N	2.01 E
Santa Coloma de Farnés	34	41.52 N	2.40 E
Santa Coloma de Gramanet	256d	41.27 N	2.13 E
Santa Comba Dão	34	40.24 N	8.08 W
Santa Cristina	58	46.34 N	11.43 E
Santa Croce	58	46.05 N	12.18 E
Santa Croce, Lago di ⓔ	58	46.10 N	12.20 E
Santa Croce del Sannio	60	41.23 N	14.43 E
Santa Croce di Magliano	60	41.42 N	14.59 E
Santa Cruz, Arg.	244	50.01 S	68.31 W
Santa Cruz, Bol.	238	17.48 S	63.10 W
Santa Cruz, Bra.	240	6.13 S	36.01 W
Santa Cruz, Bra.	245	19.56 S	40.09 W
Santa Cruz, Chile	242	34.38 S	71.22 W
Santa Cruz, C.R.	226	10.16 N	85.36 W
Santa Cruz, Méx.	190	31.14 N	110.35 W
Santa Cruz, Méx.	224	23.05 N	97.50 W
Santa Cruz, Perú	238	6.37 S	78.57 W
Santa Cruz, Pil.	106	6.50 N	125.25 E
Santa Cruz, Pil.	106	15.46 N	119.55 E
Santa Cruz, Pil.	106	14.17 N	121.25 E
Santa Cruz (Tubajon), Pil.	106	10.19 N	125.33 E
Santa Cruz, Pil.	106	13.04 N	120.43 E
Santa Cruz, Pil.	106	13.29 N	122.02 E
Santa Cruz, Calif., U.S.	216	36.58 N	122.01 W
Santa Cruz, Ven.	236	8.25 N	71.39 W
Santa Cruz, Ven.	276c	10.26 N	67.01 W
Santa Cruz □4	244	49.00 S	70.00 W
Santa Cruz □5	238	17.30 S	61.30 W
Santa Cruz □6	216	36.58 N	122.01 W
Santa Cruz ⋅8, Bhārat	262c	19.05 N	72.50 E
Santa Cruz ⋅8, Bra.	246	22.56 S	43.41 W
Santa Cruz ≃, Arg.	244	50.08 S	68.20 W
Santa Cruz ≃, Cuba	276b	23.04 N	82.29 W
Santa Cruz, Ilha I	277a	22.52 S	43.07 W
Santa Cruz, Isla I	236a	0.38 S	90.23 W
Santa Cruz, Sierra de ⋀	226	15.40 N	89.15 W
Santa Cruz Basin ⋅1	14	13.00 S	163.00 E
Santa Cruz Cabrália	245	16.17 S	39.02 W
Santa Cruz da Boa Vista	246	22.39 S	46.52 W
Santa Cruz da Graciosa	138a	39.05 N	28.01 W
Santa Cruz das Flores	138a	39.27 N	31.07 W
Santa Cruz da Vitória	245	14.57 S	39.48 W
Santa Cruz de Goiás	245	17.19 S	48.30 W
Santa Cruz de Juventino Rosas	224	20.39 N	101.00 W
Santa Cruz de la Palma	138	28.41 N	17.45 W
Santa Cruz de la Zarza	34	39.58 N	3.10 W
Santa Cruz del Norte	230p	23.09 N	81.55 W
Santa Cruz del Quiché	226	15.02 N	91.08 W
Santa Cruz del Sur	230p	20.43 N	78.00 W
Santa Cruz de Mudela	34	38.38 N	3.28 W
Santa Cruz de Tenerife	138	28.27 N	16.14 W
Santa Cruz do Capibaribe	240	7.57 S	36.12 W
Santa Cruz do Piauí	240	7.09 S	41.48 W
Santa Cruz do Prata	246	21.12 S	46.45 W
Santa Cruz do Rio Abaixo	246	23.18 S	45.24 W
Santa Cruz do Rio Pardo	245	22.55 S	49.37 W
Santa Cruz do Sul	242	29.43 S	52.26 W
Santa Cruz International Airport ⊠	262c	19.05 N	72.52 E
Santa Cruz Island I	194	34.01 N	119.45 W
Santa Cruz Islands II	14	11.00 S	166.15 E
Santa Cruz Meyehualco	276a	19.20 N	99.03 W
Santa Cruz Mountains ⋀	216	37.15 N	122.00 W
Santa Cruz Point >	106	15.44 N	119.52 E
Santa Cruz Tacache de Mina	224	17.51 N	98.07 W
Santadang ☰	96	31.23 N	119.15 E
Santa Eduviges	276e	33.33 S	70.39 W
Santa Elena, Arg.	242	30.57 S	59.48 W
Santa Elena, Ec.	236	2.14 S	80.51 W
Santa Elena, El Sal.	226	13.22 N	88.25 W
Santa Elena, Méx.	186	27.59 N	103.56 W
Santa Elena, Méx.	222	27.28 N	102.33 W
Santa Elena, Méx.	224	18.39 N	101.34 W
Santa Elena, Bahía C	226	10.59 N	85.50 W
Santa Elena, Bahía de C	236	2.06 S	80.53 W
Santa Elena, Cabo >	226	10.54 N	85.57 W
Santa Elena del Gomero	276e	33.29 S	70.46 W
Santa Elena de Uairén	236	4.37 N	61.08 W
Santa Emilia	276e	33.23 S	70.39 W
Santa Eugenia	34	42.33 N	9.00 W
Santa Eulalia, Esp.	34	40.34 N	1.19 W
Santa Eulalia, Guat.	226	15.45 N	91.29 W
Santa Eulalia del Río	34	38.59 N	1.31 E
Santa Fe, Arg.	242	31.38 S	60.42 W
Santa Fé, Bra.	245	15.40 S	51.16 W
Santa Fé, Bra.	245	23.01 S	51.48 W
Santa Fé, Cuba	230p	21.45 N	82.45 W
Santa Fé, Cuba	276b	23.05 N	82.31 W
Santa Fé, Esp.	34	37.11 N	3.43 W
Santa Fé, Hond.	226	15.55 N	86.05 W
Santa Fe, Méx.	276a	19.23 N	99.14 W
Santa Fe, Pan.	226	8.31 N	81.05 W
Santa Fe, Pil.	106	16.10 N	120.57 E
Santa Fe, Pil.	106	11.09 N	123.47 E
Santa Fe, Pil.	106	12.10 N	122.00 E
Santa Fe, Mo., U.S.	209	39.22 N	91.49 W
Santa Fe, N. Mex., U.S.	190	35.42 N	106.57 W
Santa Fe □4	242	31.00 S	61.00 W
Santa Fe ≃, Fla., U.S.	182	29.53 N	82.53 W
Santa Fe ≃, N. Mex., U.S.	190	35.36 N	106.20 W
Santa Fé, Aeropuerto ⊠	276b	23.04 N	82.28 W
Santa Fe, Cerro ⋀	224	20.30 N	103.02 W
Santa Fe, Isla I	236a	0.49 S	90.04 W
Santa Fé, Ribeirão ≃	277b	23.24 S	46.48 W
Santa Fe Baldy ⋀	190	35.50 N	105.46 W
Santa Fe Dam ⋅6	270	34.07 N	117.58 W
Santa Fé do Sul	245	20.13 S	50.56 W
Santa Fe Flood Control Basin ⋅1	270	34.07 N	117.58 W
Santa Fe Springs	270	33.56 N	118.04 W
Santa Filomena	240	9.07 S	45.56 W
Santa Fiora	60	42.50 N	11.35 E
Sant'Agata Bolognese	58	44.40 N	11.08 E
Sant'Agata de'Goti	60	41.05 N	14.30 E
Sant'Agata di Militello	36	38.04 N	14.38 E
Sant'Agata di Puglia	60	41.09 N	15.23 E
Sant'Agata Feltria	60	43.52 N	12.12 E
Sant'Agata sul Santerno	60	44.26 N	11.51 E
Santa Gertrude (Sankt Gertraud)	58	46.29 N	10.53 E
Santa Gertrudis	186	26.09 N	98.44 W
Sant'Agostino	58	44.48 N	11.23 E
Sāntāhār	114	24.48 N	88.59 E
Santa Helena	240	2.14 S	45.18 W
Santa Helena de Goiás	245	17.43 S	50.35 W
Santai, Zhg.	75	39.14 N	77.42 E
Santai, Zhg.	76	44.35 N	81.18 E
Santai, Zhg.	88	42.37 N	123.22 E
Santai, Zhg.	92	31.10 N	105.02 E
Santai, Zhg.	94	41.48 N	121.53 E
Santai, Zhg.	95	38.58 N	115.49 E
Santa Inês	245	13.17 S	39.48 W
Santa Inés, Bahía C	222	26.59 N	111.59 W
Santa Inés, Isla I	244	53.45 S	72.45 W
Santa Inés Ahuatempan	224	18.25 N	98.01 W
Santa Inés Zacatelco	224	19.13 N	98.14 W
Santa Iria de Azóia	256c	38.51 N	9.05 W
Santa Isabel, Arg.	242	36.15 S	66.56 W
Santa Isabel, Arg.	242	33.54 S	61.42 W
Santa Isabel, Bra.	246	23.19 S	46.14 W
Santa Isabel, Ec.	236	3.21 S	79.19 W
Santa Isabel → Malabo, Gui. Ecu.	142	3.45 N	8.47 E
Santa Isabel, P.R.	230m	17.58 N	66.24 W
Santa Isabel I	165e	8.00 S	159.00 E
Santa Isabel, Pico de ⋀	142	3.35 N	8.46 E
Santa Isabel de las Lajas	230p	22.25 N	80.18 W
Santa Isabel de Sihuas	238	16.20 S	72.06 W
Santa Isabel do Araguaia	240	6.07 S	48.19 W
Santa Isabel do Pará	240	1.16 S	48.11 W
Santa Isabel do Rio Prêto	246	22.14 S	44.05 W
Santaizi, Zhg.	94	41.56 N	123.11 E
Santaizi, Zhg.	94	41.21 N	121.36 E
Santa Josefa	106	8.02 N	125.57 E
Santa Julia	276e	33.30 S	70.38 W
Santa Juliana	245	19.19 S	47.32 W
Sant'Alberto	60	44.32 N	12.09 E
Santa Leopoldina	245	20.06 S	40.32 W
Santāl Parganas □5	114	24.30 N	87.20 E
Sāntālpur	110	23.45 N	71.10 E
Santa Luce	60	43.28 N	10.34 E
Santa Lucía, Arg.	242	28.59 S	59.06 W
Santa Lucía, Arg.	242	31.32 S	68.29 W
Santa Lucía, Cuba	230p	22.40 N	83.58 W
Santa Lucía, Cuba	230p	20.59 N	77.25 W
Santa Lucía, Cuba	230p	21.02 N	76.00 W
Santa Lucia, It.	58	46.28 N	10.21 E
Santa Lucía, Ur.	248	34.27 S	56.24 W
Santa Lucía, Ven.	236	8.07 N	69.46 W
Santa Lucia → Saint Lucia □2	231f	13.53 N	60.58 W
Santa Lucía ≃	248	34.48 S	56.22 W
Santa Lucía, Cabo → Saint Lucia, Cape >	148	28.25 S	32.25 E
Santa Lucía, Cuchilla de ⋀2	248	34.09 S	56.11 W
Santa Lucía Chico ≃	248	34.21 S	56.20 W
Santa Lucía Cotzumalguapa	226	14.20 N	91.01 W
Santa Lucia Creek ≃	216	36.13 N	121.30 W
Santa Lucia di Piave	58	45.51 N	12.17 E
Santa Lucia Range ⋀	216	36.00 N	121.20 W
Santa Lugarda, Punta >	222	26.44 N	109.48 W
Santa Luisa de Baixo	246	22.46 S	45.49 W
Santaluz	240	11.15 S	39.22 W
Santa Luzia, Bra.	240	6.53 S	36.56 W
Santa Luzia, Port.	34	37.44 N	8.24 W
Santa Luzia I	140a	16.46 N	24.45 W
Santa Magdalena, Isla I	222	24.55 N	112.15 W
Santa Margarita	216	35.23 N	120.37 W
Santa Margarita ≃	218	33.14 N	117.25 W
Santa Margarita, Isla de I	222	24.27 N	111.50 W
Santa Margarita Lake ⓔ1	216	35.20 N	120.28 W
Santa Margarita Mountains ⋀	218	33.30 N	117.25 W
Santa Margherita Ligure	56	44.20 N	9.12 E
Santa María, Arg.	242	26.41 S	66.02 W
Santa Maria, Bra.	242	29.41 S	53.48 W
Santa María, C.R.	226	9.39 N	83.57 W
Santa Maria, C.V.	140a	16.36 N	22.54 W
Santa María, Méx.	186	28.02 N	101.38 W
Santa María, Pan.	226	8.07 N	80.40 W
Santa María, Perú	276d	11.59 S	77.00 W
Santa Maria, Pil.	106	14.49 N	120.58 E
Santa Maria, Pil.	106	17.22 N	120.29 E
Santa María, P.R.	230m	18.09 N	65.26 W
Santa Maria, Schw.	54	46.36 N	10.24 E
Santa Maria, Schw.	54	46.16 N	9.09 E
Santa Maria, Calif., U.S.	194	34.57 N	120.26 W
Santa Maria I	138a	36.58 N	25.06 W
Santa María ≃, Arg.	242	26.03 S	65.50 W
Santa Maria ≃, Bra.	242	29.48 S	54.53 W
Santa María ≃, Méx.	222	31.00 N	107.14 W
Santa María ≃, Méx.	224	21.48 N	99.10 W
Santa María ≃, Pan.	226	8.06 N	80.29 W
Santa Maria ≃, Ariz., U.S.	190	34.19 N	114.31 W
Santa María ≃, Ven.	236	7.54 N	60.37 W
Santa María, Bahía de C	222	25.04 N	108.06 W
Santa Maria, Cabo → Sainte-Marie, Cap >, Madag.	147b	25.36 S	45.08 E
Santa María, Cabo >, Ur.	248	34.40 S	54.10 W
Santa Maria, Cabo de >, Ang.	142	13.25 S	12.32 E
Santa Maria, Cabo de >, Moç.	148	26.05 S	32.58 E
Santa Maria, Cabo de >, Port.	34	36.58 N	7.54 W
Santa Maria, Cape >	228	23.41 N	75.19 W
Santa María, Cayo I	230p	22.40 N	79.00 W
Santa María, Cerro ⋀	276d	11.56 S	76.57 W
Santa Maria, Giogo di (Pass Umbrail))(	58	46.34 N	10.25 E
Santa María, Isla I, Chile	242	37.02 S	73.33 W
Santa María, Isla I, Ec.	236a	1.17 S	90.26 W
Santa María, Laguna de ⓔ	222	31.07 N	107.16 W
Santa María, Riacho ≃	240	8.08 S	43.02 W
Santa María, Ribeirão ≃	240	7.10 S	49.13 W
Santa María, Volcán ⋀1	226	14.45 N	91.33 W
Santa María Ajoloapan	224	19.58 N	99.03 W
Santa Maria a Monte	60	43.42 N	10.42 E
Santa Maria a Vico	60	41.02 N	14.29 E
Santa Maria Capua Vetere	60	41.05 N	14.15 E
Santa María Chimalapa	224	16.55 N	94.41 W
Santa María Colotepec	224	15.53 N	96.55 W
Santa Maria da Boa Vista	240	8.49 S	39.49 W
Santa Maria das Barreiras	240	8.52 S	49.43 W
Santa Maria da Vitória	245	13.24 S	44.12 W
Santa María de Barbará	256d	41.31 N	2.08 E
Santa Maria degli Angeli	60	43.03 N	12.34 E
Santa María de Ipire	236	8.49 N	65.19 W
Santa Maria de Itabira	245	19.27 S	43.08 W
Santa Maria della Versa	56	44.59 N	9.18 E
Santa Maria delle Grazie ♅1	256b	45.27 N	9.10 E
Santa María del Oro	222	25.56 N	105.22 W
Santa María de los Ángeles	224	22.11 N	103.14 W
Santa María del Refugio	224	23.44 N	101.14 W
Santa María del Río	224	21.48 N	100.45 W
Santa María del Rosario	276b	23.04 N	82.15 W
Santa María del Rosario □7	276b	23.03 N	82.15 W
Santa María del Valle	224	20.54 N	102.22 W
Santa Maria di Galeria ⋅8	257a	42.01 N	12.19 E
Santa Maria di Leuca, Capo >	36	39.47 N	18.22 E
Santa Maria do Suaçuí	245	18.12 S	42.25 W
Santa Maria Island I	165f	14.15 S	167.30 E
Santa María Jalapa [del Marqués]	224	16.30 N	95.28 W
Santa María la Real de Nieva	34	41.04 N	4.24 W
Santa Maria Madalena	245	21.57 S	42.01 W
Santa Maria Magdalena [Cahuacán]	224	19.38 N	99.25 W
Santa Maria Maggiore	54	46.08 N	8.28 E
Santa Maria Maggiore ♅1	257a	41.53 N	12.30 E
Santa Maria Nuova	60	43.29 N	13.18 E
Santa-Maria-Siché	36	41.52 N	8.59 E
Santa María Tulpetlac	276a	19.34 N	99.03 W
Santa María Zoquitlán	224	16.33 N	96.23 W
Santa Marinella	60	42.02 N	11.51 E
Santa Marta, Col.	236	11.15 N	74.13 W
Santa Marta, Guat.	226	13.58 N	91.18 W
Santa Marta, Perú	276d	12.02 S	76.56 W
Santa Marta ≃	238	8.47 S	76.13 W
Santa Marta, Cabo de >	142	13.52 S	12.25 E
Santa Marta Grande, Cabo de >	242	28.38 S	48.45 W
Santa Martha Acatitla	276a	19.22 N	99.01 W
Sant'Ambrogio	58	45.31 N	10.50 E
Santa Mónica, Méx.	186	28.12 N	100.37 W
Santa Monica, Calif., U.S.	218	34.01 N	118.30 W
Santa Mónica ⋅8	276c	10.29 N	66.53 W
Santa Monica Bay C	218	33.54 N	118.25 W
Santa Monica Mountains ⋀	218	34.05 N	118.40 W
Santa Monica Municipal Airport ⊠	270	34.01 N	118.27 W
Santa Monica State Beach ♠	270	34.01 N	118.30 W
Santan	102	0.03 S	117.28 E
Santana	245	12.59 S	44.03 W
Santana ⋅8	277b	23.29 S	46.38 W
Santana ≃, Bra.	240	8.35 S	44.01 W
Santana ≃, Bra.	245	19.43 S	51.02 W
Santana, Cachoeira ∟	245	14.45 S	49.10 W
Santana, Coxilha de (Cuchilla De Santa Ana) ⋀2	242	31.15 S	55.15 W
Santana, Ribeirão ≃	240	9.47 S	50.13 W
Santana, Serra de ⋀	246	22.30 S	42.35 W
Santana da Boa Vista	242	30.52 S	53.07 W
Santana da Vargem	246	21.15 S	45.30 W
Santana de Caldas	246	21.50 S	46.24 W
Santana de Cataguases	246	21.17 S	42.33 W
Santana de Parnaíba	246	23.27 S	46.55 W
Santana de Parnaíba □7	277b	23.27 S	46.54 W
Santana do Acaraú	240	3.27 S	40.12 W
Santana do Capivari	246	22.14 S	44.56 W
Santana do Cariri	240	7.11 S	39.44 W
Santana do Deserto	246	21.57 S	43.11 W
Santana do Garambéu	246	21.36 S	44.06 W
Santana do Ipanema	240	9.22 S	37.14 W
Santana do Livramento	242	30.53 S	55.31 W
Santana do Matos	240	5.57 S	36.39 W
Sant'Anastasia	60	40.52 N	14.24 E
Santander, Col.	236	3.01 N	76.28 W
Santander, Esp.	34	43.28 N	3.48 W
Santander, Pil.	106	9.25 N	123.20 E
Santander □5	236	7.00 N	73.15 W
Santander, Norte de □3	228	9.15 N	73.00 W
Santander Jiménez	222	24.13 N	98.28 W
Santa Nella	216	37.03 N	121.02 W
Santanésia	246	22.30 S	43.42 W
Santang	90	28.44 N	116.32 E
Sant'angelo, Castel ♅	257a	41.55 N	12.28 E
Sant'Angelo, Monte ⋀	257a	41.56 N	12.49 E
Sant'Angelo dei Lombardi	60	40.56 N	15.11 E
Sant'Angelo in Vado	60	43.40 N	12.25 E
Sant'Angelo Lodigiano	56	45.14 N	9.24 E
Sant'Angelo Romano	257a	42.02 N	12.42 E
Santanghu	92	44.13 N	93.22 E
Sant'Antimo	60	40.56 N	14.14 E
Sant' Antioco	36	39.04 N	8.27 E
Sant'Antioco, Isola di I	36	39.00 N	8.25 E
Sant'Antonio Abate	60	40.43 N	14.32 E
Sant'Antonio Morignone	58	46.24 N	10.21 E
Santaný	34	39.22 N	3.07 E
Santa Paula	218	34.21 N	119.04 W
Santa Paula Creek ≃	218	34.21 N	119.03 W
Santa Perpetua de Moguda	256d	41.32 N	2.11 E
Santapogue Creek ≃	266	40.40 N	73.21 W
Santa Pola, Cabo de >	34	38.12 N	0.31 W
Sant'Apollinare in Classe ♅1	60	44.22 N	12.15 E
Santaquin	190	39.59 N	111.47 W
Santa Quitéria, Bra.	240	4.20 S	40.10 W
Santa Quitéria, Esp.	34	41.34 N	2.19 E
Santa Quitéria do Maranhão	240	3.31 S	42.32 W
Sant'Arcangelo	36	40.15 N	16.17 E
Santarcangelo di Romagna	60	44.04 N	12.27 E
Sant'Arcangelo Trimonte	60	41.10 N	14.56 E
Santarém, Bra.	240	2.26 S	54.42 W
Santarém, Port.	34	39.14 N	8.41 W
Santarém □5	256c	38.50 N	8.56 W
Santarém Novo	240	0.56 S	47.23 W
Santa Rita, Bra.	240	7.08 S	34.58 W
Santa Rita, Bra.	277a	22.41 S	43.28 W
Santa Rita, Col.	236	1.04 N	73.58 W
Santa Rita, Hond.	226	15.09 N	87.53 W
Santa Rita, Méx.	186	27.29 N	100.33 W
Santa Rita, Pil.	106	11.27 N	124.56 E
Santa Rita, Ven.	236	10.32 N	71.32 W
Santa Rita, Riacho ≃	245	12.49 S	43.21 W
Santa Rita, Serra de ⋀2	240	5.22 S	39.48 W
Santa Rita de Caldas	246	22.02 S	46.20 W
Santa Rita de Catuna	242	30.57 S	66.13 W
Santa Rita de Jacutinga	246	22.09 S	44.06 W
Santa Rita del Rucio	224	23.04 N	100.19 W
Santa Rita do Araguaia	245	17.20 S	53.12 W
Santa Rita do Sapucaí	246	22.15 S	45.42 W
Santa Rita do Weil	236	3.29 S	69.19 W
Santa Rita Park	216	37.03 N	120.36 W
Santa Rosa, Arg.	242	28.02 S	67.37 W
Santa Rosa, Arg.	242	32.20 S	65.12 W
Santa Rosa, Arg.	242	23.22 S	64.30 W
Santa Rosa, Arg.	242	36.37 S	64.17 W
Santa Rosa, Bol.	238	10.36 S	67.25 W
Santa Rosa, Bol.	238	14.10 S	66.53 W
Santa Rosa, Bol.	238	17.07 S	63.35 W
Santa Rosa, Bra.	242	27.52 S	54.29 W
Santa Rosa, Bra.	245	15.01 S	47.13 W
Santa Rosa, Col.	236	2.31 N	68.13 W
Santa Rosa, C.R.	226	10.51 N	85.38 W
Santa Rosa, Ec.	236	3.27 S	79.58 W
Santa Rosa, Méx.	194	31.59 N	116.45 W
Santa Rosa, Méx.	224	22.18 N	104.24 W
Santa Rosa, Méx.	224	19.41 N	100.02 W
Santa Rosa, Para.	238	21.46 S	61.43 W
Santa Rosa, Para.	242	26.52 S	56.49 W
Santa Rosa, Perú	276d	12.00 S	77.06 W
Santa Rosa, Calif., U.S.	216	38.26 N	122.43 W
Santa Rosa, N. Mex., U.S.	186	34.57 N	104.41 W
Santa Rosa, Tex., U.S.	186	26.15 N	97.50 W
Santa Rosa, Ur.	248	34.30 S	56.03 W
Santa Rosa, Ven.	236	8.26 N	69.24 W
Santa Rosa, Ven.	276c	10.30 N	66.46 W
Santa Rosa □5	226	14.10 N	90.18 W
Santa Rosa, Mount ⋀2	164p	13.32 N	144.55 E
Santa Rosa Beach	184	30.23 N	86.14 W
Santa Rosa Creek ≃	216	35.34 N	121.06 W
Santa Rosa de Aguán	226	15.57 N	85.43 W
Santa Rosa de Amanadona	236	1.29 N	66.55 W
Santa Rosa de Cabal	236	4.52 N	75.38 W
Santa Rosa [de Copán]	226	14.47 N	88.46 W
Santa Rosa de Huechuraba	276e	33.21 S	70.41 W
Santa Rosa de la Roca	238	16.04 S	61.32 W
Santa Rosa de Leales	242	27.09 S	65.15 W
Santa Rosa de Lima	226	13.37 N	87.53 W
Santa Rosa de Locobe	276e	33.26 S	70.33 W
Santa Rosa del Palmar	238	16.54 S	62.24 W
Santa Rosa de Osos	236	6.39 N	75.28 W
Santa Rosa de Río Primero	242	31.09 S	63.23 W
Santa Rosa de Sucumbíos	236	0.22 N	77.10 W
Santa Rosa de Viterbo	236	5.53 N	72.59 W
Santa Rosa Indian Reservation ⋅4	194	33.35 N	116.35 W
Santa Rosa Island I, Calif., U.S.	194	33.58 N	120.06 W
Santa Rosa Island I, Fla., U.S.	184	30.22 N	86.55 W
Santa Rosa Jáuregui	224	20.44 N	100.27 W
Santa Rosalía, Méx.	186	26.08 N	98.59 W
Santa Rosalía, Méx.	222	27.19 N	112.17 W
Santa Rosalía, Ven.	236	9.02 N	69.01 W
Santa Rosalía, Bahía C	222	28.37 N	114.13 W
Santa Rosa Range ⋀	194	41.00 N	117.40 W
Santa Rosa Wash V	190	33.00 N	112.00 W
Santa Rosita	276d	12.03 S	76.59 W
Santarskije Ostrova II	79	55.00 N	137.36 E
Santa Santissima Trinità di Saccargia ♅1	36	40.42 N	8.37 E
Santa Severa	60	42.02 N	11.57 E
Santa Sofia	60	43.57 N	11.54 E
Santa Susana	218	34.16 N	118.43 W
Santa Susana Mountains ⋀	218	34.20 N	118.42 W
Santa Sylvina	242	27.49 S	61.09 W
Santa Tecla → Nueva San Salvador	226	13.41 N	89.17 W
Santa Teresa, Arg.	242	33.26 S	60.47 W
Santa Teresa, Bra.	245	19.55 S	40.36 W
Santa Teresa, Bra.	245	13.38 S	49.01 W
Santa Teresa, Méx.	186	29.34 N	104.39 W
Santa Teresa, Méx.	190	30.52 N	111.33 W
Santa Teresa, Méx.	224	22.28 N	104.44 W
Santa Teresa ≃	245	11.47 S	48.37 W
Santa Teresa, Embalse de ⓔ1	34	40.40 N	5.30 W
Santa Teresa de lo Ovalle	276e	33.23 S	70.47 W
Santa Teresa del Tuy	236	10.14 N	66.40 W
Santa Teresa Gallura	36	41.15 N	9.12 E
Santa Teresinha	245	12.45 S	39.32 W
Santa Úrsula Coapa	276a	19.17 N	99.11 W
Santa Valburga (Sankt Wallburg)	58	46.33 N	11.00 E
Santa Venetia	216	38.01 N	122.31 W
Santa Vitória	245	18.50 S	50.08 W
Santa Vitória do Palmar	242	33.31 S	53.21 W
Santa Vittoria in Matenano	60	43.01 N	13.29 E
Santa Ynez ≃	194	35.41 N	120.36 W
Santa Ynez Canyon V	270	34.04 N	118.34 W
Santa Ysabel Indian Reservation ⋅4	194	33.11 N	116.41 W
Santee	218	32.50 N	116.58 W
Santee ≃	182	33.14 N	79.28 W
Santee Dam ⋅6	182	33.24 N	80.12 W
Santee Indian Reservation ⋅4	188	42.45 N	97.50 W
Sant'Egidio alla Vibrata	60	42.49 N	13.42 E
Sant'Elena	58	45.12 N	11.43 E
Sant'Elia a Pianisi	60	41.38 N	14.52 E
Sant'Elia Fiumerapido	60	41.32 N	13.52 E
San Telmo, Bahía de C	224	18.38 N	103.42 W
San Telmo, Cerro ⋀	224	18.37 N	103.37 W
Sant'Elpidio a Mare	60	43.14 N	13.41 E
Santena	54	44.57 N	7.45 E
Santenay	54	46.55 N	4.41 E
Santeny	251	48.43 N	2.34 E
Santerno ≃	60	44.34 N	11.58 E
Santerre □9	46	49.40 N	2.40 E
Sant'Eufemia, Golfo di C	36	38.50 N	16.00 E
Sant'Eufemia a Maiella	60	42.07 N	14.02 E
Sānthia, Bngl.	116	24.03 N	89.33 E

English	Deutsch	Español	Français	Português
≃ River	Fluss	Río	Rivière	Rio
Canal	Kanal	Canal	Canal	Canal
∟ Waterfall, Rapids	Wasserfall, Stromschnellen	Cascada, Rápidos	Chute d'eau, Rapides	Cascata, Rápidos
U Strait	Meeresstrasse	Estrecho	Détroit	Estreito
C Bay, Gulf	Bucht, Golf	Bahía, Golfo	Baie, Golfe	Baía, Golfo
ⓔ Lake, Lakes	See, Seen	Lago, Lagos	Lac, Lacs	Lago, Lagos
Swamp	Sumpf	Pantano	Marais	Pântano
⛋ Ice Features, Glacier	Eis- und Gletscherformen	Accidentes Glaciales	Formes glaciaires	Acidentes Glaciares
Other Hydrographic Features	Andere Hydrographische Objekte	Otros Elementos Hidrográficos	Autres données hydrographiques	Outros Elementos Hidrográficos
Submarine Features	Untermeerische Objekte	Accidentes Submarinos	Formes de relief sous-marin	Acidentes Submarinos
□ Political Unit	Politische Einheit	Unidad Política	Entité politique	Unidade Política
♅ Cultural Institution	Kulturelle Institution	Institución Cultural	Institution culturelle	Instituição Cultural
⊥ Historical Site	Historische Stätte	Sitio Histórico	Site historique	Sítio Histórico
♠ Recreational Site	Erholungs- und Ferienort	Sitio de Recreo	Centre de loisirs	Sítio de Lazer
⊠ Airport	Flughafen	Aeropuerto	Aéroport	Aeroporto
Military Installation	Militäranlage	Instalación Militar	Installation militaire	Instalação Militar
Miscellaneous	Verschiedenes	Misceláneo	Divers	Miscelânea

Santhià, It. 56 45.22 N 8.10 E
Santiago, Bol. 238 18.19 S 59.34 W
Santiago, Bra. 242 29.11 S 54.53 W
Santiago, Chile 242 / 276e 33.27 S 70.40 W
Santiago, C.R. 226 9.51 N 84.18 W
Santiago → Santiago de Compostela, Esp. 34 42.53 N 8.33 W
Santiago, Méx. 222 25.25 N 100.09 W
Santiago, Méx. 222 23.28 N 109.43 W
Santiago, Pan. 226 8.06 N 80.59 W
Santiago, Para. 242 27.09 S 56.47 W
Santiago, Perú 238 14.11 S 75.44 W
Santiago, Pil. 106 16.41 N 121.33 E
Santiago □[4] 242 33.30 S 70.50 W
Santiago □[5] 276e 33.25 S 70.40 W
Santiago ≃, Méx. 224 20.40 N 103.13 W
Santiago ≃, S.A. 236 4.27 S 77.38 W
Santiago, Cape ≻ 106 13.46 N 120.39 E
Santiago, Cerro ∧ 226 8.33 N 81.44 W
Santiago, Isla I 278 34.50 S 57.53 W
Santiago, Río de ≃ 222 25.11 N 105.26 W
Santiago, Serranía de ∧∧ 238 18.25 S 59.25 W
Santiago Acahualtepec 276a 19.21 N 99.01 W
Santiago Apóstol 224 16.49 N 96.42 W
Santiago Atitlán 226 14.38 N 91.14 W
Santiago Creek ≃, Calif., U.S. 218 35.06 N 119.17 W
Santiago Creek ≃, Calif., U.S. 218 33.46 N 117.54 W
Santiago Dam ◆[6] 270 33.47 N 117.43 W
Santiago de Cao 238 7.58 S 79.15 W
Santiago de Chocorvos 238 13.50 S 75.16 W
Santiago de Chuco 238 8.09 S 78.11 W
Santiago de Compostela 34 42.53 N 8.33 W
Santiago de Cuba 230p 20.01 N 75.49 W
Santiago de Huata 238 16.06 S 68.53 W
Santiago de la Peña 224 20.57 N 97.24 W
Santiago de las Vegas 276b 22.58 N 82.23 W
Santiago de las Vegas □[7] 276b 22.58 N 82.23 W
Santiago del Estero 242 27.47 S 64.16 W
Santiago del Estero □[4] 242 28.00 S 63.30 W
Santiago [de los Caballeros] 228 19.27 N 70.42 W
Santiago de Machaca 238 17.05 S 69.16 W
Santiago do Cacém 34 38.01 N 8.42 W
Santiago Island I 106 16.24 N 119.56 E
Santiago Ixcuintla 224 21.49 N 105.13 W
Santiago Ixtayutla 224 16.33 N 97.39 W
Santiago Lachiguirí 224 16.41 N 95.32 W
Santiago Larre 248 35.34 S 59.10 W
Santiago Maravatío 224 20.10 N 101.00 W
Santiago Papasquiaro 222 25.03 N 105.25 W
Santiago Peak ∧, Calif., U.S. 218 33.42 N 117.32 W
Santiago Peak ∧, Tex., U.S. 186 29.47 N 103.25 W
Santiago Reservoir ⊜[1] 218 33.47 N 117.43 W
Santiago Rodríguez 228 19.30 N 71.21 W
Santiago Tepalcatlalpan 276a 19.15 N 99.08 W
Santiago Tulantepec 224 20.02 N 98.22 W
Santiago Tutla 224 17.10 N 95.26 W
Santiago Tuxtla 224 18.28 N 95.18 W
Santiago Vázquez 248 34.48 S 56.21 W
Santiago Yaveo 224 17.19 N 95.42 W
Santiago Zacatepec 224 17.11 N 95.51 W
Santiaguillo, Laguna de ⊜ 222 24.48 N 104.48 W
Santiam Pass)(192 44.25 N 121.51 W
Santianzhu (Three Indian Temples) ♁[1] 96 30.15 N 120.08 E
Santiao Chiao ≻ 90 25.02 N 121.59 E
Santiaoqiao 96 31.36 N 121.22 E
Santigi 102 1.20 N 120.54 E
Santiguila 140 12.42 N 7.26 W
Sant'Ilario d'Enza 58 44.46 N 10.27 E
San Timoteo 236 9.48 N 71.04 W
San Timoteo Canyon ∨ 218 34.04 N 117.17 W
Sāntipur 116 23.15 N 88.26 E
Säntis ∧ 54 47.15 N 9.21 E
Santissimo ◆[8] 277a 22.53 S 43.31 W
Santisteban del Puerto 34 38.15 N 3.12 W
Santō, Nihon 84 35.21 N 136.22 E
Santō, Nihon 86 35.19 N 134.53 E
Santo, Tex., U.S. 186 32.36 N 98.13 W
Santo Aleixo 246 22.34 S 43.04 W
Santo Amaro, Bra. 240 2.33 S 43.14 W
Santo Amaro, Bra. 245 12.32 S 38.43 W
Santo Amaro ◆[8] 277b 23.39 S 46.42 W
Santo Amaro, Ilha de I 246 23.57 S 46.14 W
Santo Amaro das Brotas 240 10.47 S 37.04 W
Santo Anastácio 245 21.58 S 51.39 W
Santo Anastácio ≃ 245 21.49 S 52.11 W
Santo André 246 23.40 S 46.31 W
Santo André □[7] 277b 23.44 S 46.29 W
Santo Ângelo 242 28.18 S 54.16 W
Santo Antão I 140a 17.05 N 25.10 W
Santo Antônio, Bra. 240 6.18 S 35.27 W
Santo Antônio, Bra. 242 29.50 S 50.32 W
Santo Antônio, Bra. 242 26.02 S 53.44 W
Santo António, S. Tom./P. 142 1.39 N 7.26 E
Santo Antônio ≃, Bra. 240 11.31 S 48.37 W
Santo Antônio ≃, Bra. 245 17.30 S 45.37 W
Santo Antônio ≃, Bra. 277a 22.42 S 43.37 W
Santo Antônio, Cachoeira ⌊ 238 9.46 S 60.35 W
Santo Antônio, Igarapé ≃ 236 1.32 S 59.48 W
Santo Antônio da Boa Vista 245 15.52 S 44.09 W
Santo António da Charneca 256c 38.37 N 9.02 W
Santo Antônio de Jesus 245 12.58 S 39.16 W
Santo Antonio de Posse 246 22.36 S 46.55 W
Santo Antônio do Amparo 245 20.57 S 44.55 W
Santo Antônio do Içá 236 3.05 S 67.57 W
Santo Antônio do Jardim 246 22.07 S 46.41 W
Santo Antônio do Leverger 238 15.52 S 56.05 W
Santo Antônio do Pinhal 246 22.47 S 45.41 W
Santo Antônio do Rio Verde 245 17.57 S 47.27 W
Santo António do Zaire 142 6.07 S 12.18 E
Santo Augusto 242 27.51 S 53.47 W
Santo Corazón 238 17.59 S 58.51 W
Santo Cristo 242 27.50 S 54.40 W
Santo Domingo, Arg. 242 29.16 S 63.56 W
Santo Domingo, Cuba 230p 22.35 N 80.15 W
Santo Domingo, Méx. 186 25.38 N 101.05 W
Santo Domingo, Méx. 186 25.48 N 104.28 W
Santo Domingo, Méx. 222 25.32 N 112.02 W
Santo Domingo, Méx. 224 23.20 N 101.44 W
Santo Domingo, Nic. 226 12.16 N 85.05 W
Santo Domingo, Rep. Dom. 228 18.28 N 69.54 W
Santo Domingo ≃, Méx. 224 18.10 N 96.08 W
Santo Domingo ≃, Méx. 224 16.41 N 93.00 W
Santo Domingo ≃, Méx. 224 17.40 N 98.07 W
Santo Domingo ≃, Méx. 226 16.15 N 91.17 W
Santo Domingo ≃, Ven. 236 8.01 N 69.33 W
Santo Domingo, Arroyo ≃, Méx. 194 30.43 N 116.03 W
Santo Domingo, Arroyo ≃, Méx. 222 25.29 N 112.05 W
Santo Domingo, Isla → Hispaniola I 228 19.00 N 71.00 W
Santo Domingo de la Calzada 34 42.26 N 2.57 W
Santo Domingo de los Colorados 236 0.15 S 79.09 W
Santo Domingo Nuxaá 224 17.08 N 97.02 W
Santo Domingo Pueblo 190 35.31 N 106.22 W
Santo Domingo Teojomulco 224 16.36 N 97.14 W
Santo Estevão 245 12.26 S 39.13 W
Sant'Olcese 56 44.30 N 8.58 E
Santolea, Embalse de ⊜[1] 34 40.47 N 0.19 W
San Tomé 236 8.58 N 64.08 W
San Tommaso 60 42.11 N 13.58 E
Sant'Omobono Imagna 56 45.48 N 9.32 E
Santoña 34 43.27 N 3.27 W
Santonghe ≃ 88 42.39 N 126.03 E
Santo Nino Island I 106 11.55 N 124.27 E
Sant' Onofrio ◆[8] 257a 41.56 N 12.25 E
Santo Onofre ≃ 245 12.34 S 43.12 W
Santo Peak ∧ 165f 15.27 S 166.48 E
Sant'Oreste 60 42.14 N 12.32 E
Santorini → Thíra I 38 36.24 N 25.29 E
Santorso 58 45.44 N 11.23 E
Santos 246 23.57 S 46.20 W
Santos, Baía de C 246 24.00 S 46.21 W
Santos Dumont 246 21.28 S 43.34 W
Santos Dumont, Aeroporto ⊠ 246 22.55 S 43.10 W
Santoshpur 262b 22.40 N 88.10 E
Santo Stefano, Isola I 60 40.47 N 13.27 E
Santo Stefano Belbo 56 44.43 N 8.14 E
Santo Stefano d'Aveto 56 44.35 N 9.27 E
Santo Stefano di Cadore 58 46.33 N 12.32 E
Santo Stefano di Magra 58 44.10 N 9.55 E
Santo Stino di Livenza 58 45.44 N 12.41 E
Santo Tirso 34 41.21 N 8.28 W
Santo Tomás, Col. 236 10.46 N 74.45 W
Santo Tomás, Méx. 222 31.33 N 116.24 W
Santo Tomás, Nic. 226 12.04 N 85.05 W
Santo Tomás, Nic. 226 13.11 N 86.56 W
Santo Tomás, Perú 238 14.29 S 72.06 W
Santo Tomás, Perú 238 6.36 S 77.48 W
Santo Tomas, Pil. 106 7.29 N 125.38 E
Santo Tomás, Ven. 236 8.53 N 64.33 W
Santo Tomás ≃, Méx. 194 31.32 N 116.40 W
Santo Tomás ≃, Perú 238 13.47 S 72.09 W
Santo Tomás, Punta ≻ 222 31.34 N 116.42 W
Santo Tomas, University of ♁[2] 259f 14.37 N 120.59 E
Santo Tomás, Volcán ∧[1] 236a 0.48 S 91.07 W
Santo Tomás Ocotepec 224 17.08 N 97.46 W
Santo Tomás y Principe → Sao Tome and Principe □[1] 142 1.00 N 7.00 E
Santo Tomé, Arg. 242 28.33 S 56.03 W
Santo Tomé, Arg. 242 31.40 S 60.46 W
Santo Tomé de Guayana → Ciudad Guayana 236 8.22 N 62.40 W
Santouwan 92 38.06 N 100.33 E
Santpoort 48 52.25 N 4.38 E
Santuanjiang 96 30.54 N 121.43 E
Santuario di Oropa ♁[1] 56 45.38 N 7.58 E
Santunying 95 40.14 N 118.12 E
San Ubaldo 226 11.51 N 85.20 W
Sanuki 258 35.55 N 139.53 E
Sanuki-sammyaku ∧∧ 86 34.09 N 134.11 E
Şānūr 122 32.21 N 35.15 E
San Valentín, Monte ∧ 244 46.36 S 73.20 W
San Valentino in Abruzzo Citeriore 60 42.14 N 13.59 E
San Valentino Torio 60 40.48 N 14.36 E
San Venanzo 60 42.52 N 12.16 E
San Vendemiano 58 45.54 N 12.20 E
San Vicente, Arg. 242 28.30 S 64.09 W
San Vicente, Arg. 248 34.58 S 58.22 W
San Vicente, Chile 242 34.26 S 71.05 W
San Vicente, El Sal. 226 13.38 N 88.48 W
San Vicente, Méx. 222 31.20 N 116.15 W
San Vicente □[5] 278 34.56 S 58.24 W
San Vicente → Saint Vincent □[2] 231h 13.15 N 61.12 W
San Vicente, Cabo → São Vicente, Cabo de ≻ 34 37.01 N 9.00 W
San Vicente, Volcán de ∧[1] 226 13.36 N 88.51 W
San Vicente Creek ≃ 272 37.32 N 122.31 W
San Vicente de Alcántara 34 39.21 N 7.08 W
San Vicente de Baracaldo 34 43.18 N 2.59 W
San Vicente de Chucurí 236 6.54 N 73.25 W
San Vicente de la Barquera 34 43.26 N 4.24 W
San Vicente del Caguán 236 2.07 N 74.46 W
San Vicente dels Horts 256d 41.24 N 2.01 E
San Vicente Mountain ∧ 270 34.08 N 118.31 W
San Vicente Reservoir ⊜[1] 218 32.55 N 116.55 W
San Vicente Tancuayalab 224 21.44 N 98.34 W
San Vigilio 58 45.34 N 10.41 E
San Vigilio ♁[1] 58 46.37 N 11.07 E
San Vincenzo 60 43.06 N 10.32 E
San Vito, C.R. 226 8.50 N 82.58 W
San Vito, It. 36 39.27 N 9.32 E
San Vito, Capo ≻ 36 38.11 N 12.43 E
San Vito al Tagliamento 58 45.54 N 12.52 E
San Vito Chietino 60 42.18 N 14.27 E
San Vito dei Normanni 36 40.39 N 17.42 E
San Vito Romano 60 41.53 N 12.59 E
Sanwa, Nihon 84 37.07 N 138.21 E
Sanwa, Nihon 86 34.42 N 133.15 E
Sanwa, Nihon 86 34.39 N 132.51 E
San Xavier Indian Reservation ◆[4] 190 32.05 N 111.08 W
Sanxi, Zhg. 90 30.22 N 118.25 E
Sanxi, Zhg. 90 27.42 N 120.04 E
Sanxing, Zhg. 96 31.47 N 121.35 E
Sanxing, Zhg. 96 31.58 N 121.07 E
Sanxingchang, Zhg. 97 30.32 N 104.38 E
Sanxingchang, Zhg. 97 30.19 N 104.09 E
Sanxingjie 96 32.06 N 121.01 E
Sanxizhen 97 29.32 N 105.40 E
Sanyang, Zhg. 90 28.37 N 116.15 E
Sanyang, Zhg. 96 31.55 N 121.29 E
Sanyangdian 90 31.20 N 113.10 E
Sanyangqiao 90 27.57 N 114.22 E
Sanyanjing, Zhg. 88 42.11 N 119.00 E
Sanyanjing, Zhg. 94 41.28 N 122.27 E
Sanyanqiao 90 28.39 N 113.43 E
San Ygnacio 186 27.03 N 99.27 W
Sanyindalai 92 38.11 N 105.17 E
Sanyō, Nihon 86 34.02 N 131.10 E
Sanyō, Nihon 86 34.45 N 134.01 E
Sanyu 96 32.08 N 121.19 E
Sanyuan 92 34.35 N 108.54 E
Sanyuanpu 88 42.02 N 125.44 E
Sanyuhao 88 42.30 N 117.34 E
Sanzaodao I 90 22.03 N 113.21 E
Sanza Pombo 142 7.19 S 15.59 E
Sanzar ≃ 75 40.00 N 67.40 E
San Zeno di Montagna 58 45.37 N 10.43 E
Sanzha 88 41.44 N 114.39 E
Sanzhan, Zhg. 79 49.36 N 126.38 E
Sanzhan, Zhg. 79 49.37 N 125.23 E
Sanzuodian 88 41.36 N 118.49 E
São Benedito 240 4.03 S 40.53 W
São Benedito ≃ 240 9.11 S 57.02 W
São Benedito das Areias 246 21.19 S 47.02 W
São Benedito do Rio Prêto 240 3.20 S 43.35 W
São Bento, Bra. 236 3.02 N 60.30 W
São Bento, Bra. 240 2.42 S 44.50 W
São Bento, Mosteiro e Igreja de ♁[1] 277a 22.54 S 43.11 W
São Bento, Ribeirão ≃ 246 21.42 S 45.18 W
São Bento de Caldas 246 22.08 S 46.18 W
São Bento do Norte 240 5.04 S 36.02 W
São Bento do Sapucaí 246 22.42 S 45.43 W
São Bento do Sul 242 26.15 S 49.23 W
São Bento do Una 240 8.32 S 36.22 W
São Bernardino 246 22.39 S 43.26 W
São Bernardo 240 3.22 S 42.24 W
São Bernardo do Campo 246 23.42 S 46.33 W
São Bernardo do Campo □[7] 277b 23.44 S 46.33 W
São Borja 242 28.39 S 56.00 W
São Brás 240 10.05 S 36.55 W
São Brás de Alportel 34 37.09 N 7.53 W
São Braz, Cabo de ≻ 142 9.59 S 13.19 E
São Caetano de Odivelas 240 0.45 S 48.02 W
São Caetano do Sul 246 23.36 S 46.34 W
São Caetano do Sul □[7] 277b 23.37 S 46.33 W
São Caitano 240 8.21 S 36.06 W
São Carlos, Bra. 242 27.04 S 52.59 W
São Carlos, Bra. 245 22.01 S 47.54 W
São Cristóvão 240 11.01 S 37.12 W
São Cristóvão ◆[8] 277a 22.54 S 43.14 W
Saodatun 94 42.02 N 123.31 E
São Domingos, Bra. 242 26.34 S 52.32 W
São Domingos, Bra. 245 13.24 S 46.19 W
São Domingos, Bra. 246 21.41 S 42.47 W
São Domingos, Gui.-B. 140 12.22 N 16.08 W
São Domingos ≃, Bra. 238 12.28 S 64.13 W
São Domingos ≃, Bra. 245 19.13 S 50.44 W
São Domingos ≃, Bra. 245 13.24 S 47.12 W
São Domingos ≃, Bra. 245 20.03 S 53.13 W
São Domingos, Ribeirão ≃ 246 21.39 S 45.40 W
São Domingos da Bocaina 246 21.50 S 44.01 W
São Domingos do Maranhão 240 5.42 S 44.22 W
São Félix 240 11.36 S 50.39 W
São Félix de Balsas 240 7.08 S 44.52 W
São Félix do Piauí 240 5.56 S 42.07 W
São Filipe, Bra. 245 14.49 S 41.23 W
São Filipe, C.V. 140a 14.54 N 24.31 W
São Francisco, Bra. 245 15.57 S 44.52 W
São Francisco, Bra. 246 22.36 S 45.18 W
São Francisco ≃, Bra. 232 10.30 S 36.24 W
São Francisco ≃, Bra. 242 24.40 S 54.20 W
São Francisco ≃, Bra. 245 11.45 S 43.20 W
São Francisco ≃, Bra. 245 16.09 S 40.39 W
São Francisco ≃, Bra. 246 21.50 S 42.42 W
São Francisco ≃, Bra. 277a 22.57 S 43.20 W
São Francisco, Baía de C 242 26.10 S 48.34 W
São Francisco, Ilha de I 242 26.18 S 48.37 W
São Francisco de Assis 242 29.33 S 55.08 W
São Francisco de Goiás 245 15.55 S 49.16 W
São Francisco de Paula 242 29.27 S 50.35 W
São Francisco do Croará 277a 22.42 S 43.08 W
São Francisco do Maranhão 240 6.15 S 42.52 W
São Francisco do Piauí 240 7.15 S 42.32 W
São Francisco do Sul 242 26.14 S 48.39 W
São Francisco Xavier 246 22.54 S 45.58 W
São Gabriel, Bra. 242 30.20 S 54.19 W
São Gabriel, Bra. 245 19.01 S 40.32 W
São Gabriel de Goiás 245 15.12 S 47.34 W
São Gonçalo, Bra. 246 22.51 S 43.04 W
São Gonçalo, Bra. 246 21.36 S 46.19 W
São Gonçalo □[7] 277a 22.48 S 43.01 W
São Gonçalo do Abaeté 245 18.20 S 45.49 W
São Gonçalo do Amarante 240 3.36 S 38.58 W
São Gonçalo do Pará 245 19.59 S 44.51 W
São Gonçalo do Sapucaí 246 21.54 S 45.36 W
São Gonçalo dos Campos 245 12.25 S 38.58 W
Sao Hill 144 8.20 S 35.12 E
São Jerônimo 242 29.58 S 51.43 W
São Jerônimo, Serra de ∧∧[1] 245 17.00 S 54.50 W
São Jerônimo da Serra 245 23.43 S 50.44 W
São Joana ≃ 245 19.31 S 40.43 W
São João 140 11.32 N 15.26 W
São João ≃, Bra. 245 20.41 S 46.45 W
São João ≃, Bra. 245 12.27 S 51.07 W
São João ≃, Bra. 246 22.33 S 42.29 W
São João ≃, Bra. 277b 23.31 S 46.51 W
São João, Ribeirão ≃ 246 21.28 S 42.49 W
São João da Aliança 245 14.42 S 47.32 W
São João da Barra 245 21.38 S 41.03 W
São João da Boa Vista 246 21.58 S 46.47 W
São João da Madeira 34 40.54 N 8.30 W
São João da Mata 246 21.56 S 45.56 W
São João da Ponte 245 15.56 S 44.01 W
São João da Serra 246 21.28 S 43.27 W
São João das Lampas 256c 38.52 N 9.24 W
São João de Côrtes 240 2.12 S 44.32 W
São João del Rei 245 21.09 S 44.16 W
São João de Meriti 246 22.48 S 43.22 W
São João de Meriti □[7] 277a 22.48 S 43.21 W
São João de Meriti ≃ 277a 22.48 S 43.18 W
São João de Pirabas 240 0.46 S 47.10 W
São João do Araguaia 240 5.23 S 48.46 W
São João do Caiuá 245 22.48 S 52.22 W
São João do Cariri 240 7.23 S 36.31 W
São João do Jaguaribe 240 5.16 S 38.16 W
São João do Paraíso 245 15.19 S 42.01 W
São João do Piauí 240 8.21 S 42.15 W
São João do Sabugi 240 6.43 S 37.12 W
São João dos Patos 240 6.30 S 43.42 W
São João do Triunfo 242 25.40 S 50.20 W
São João Evangelista 245 18.32 S 42.45 W
São João Nepomuceno 246 21.33 S 43.01 W
São João Nôvo 246 23.33 S 47.01 W
São Joaquim 242 28.18 S 49.56 W
São Joaquim, Parque Nacional de ♠ 242 28.15 S 49.57 W
São Joaquim da Barra 245 20.35 S 47.53 W
São Joaquim dos Melos 240 5.48 S 44.44 W
São Jorge 245 23.24 S 52.17 W
São Jorge I 138a 38.38 N 28.03 W
São Jorge, Castelo de ⊥ 256c 38.43 N 9.08 W
São José 242 27.38 S 48.39 W
São José ≃, Bra. 245 19.10 S 40.12 W
São José ≃, Bra. 277a 22.39 S 43.27 W
São José, Ponta de ≻ 142 12.36 S 13.12 E
São José da Lagoa Tapada 240 6.57 S 38.10 W
São José da Laje 240 9.01 S 36.03 W
São José das Palmeiras 246 22.33 S 47.12 W
São José de Anauá 236 1.00 N 61.23 W
São José de Encoge 142 7.38 S 14.41 E
São José de Mipibu 240 6.05 S 35.15 W
São José de Piranhas 240 7.07 S 38.30 W
São José do Alegre 246 22.19 S 45.32 W
São José do Barreiro 246 22.38 S 44.35 W
São José do Belmonte 240 7.52 S 38.46 W
São José do Calçado 245 21.02 S 41.40 W
São José do Campestre 240 6.18 S 35.42 W
São José do Cedro 242 26.30 S 53.30 W
São José do Egito 240 7.28 S 37.16 W
São José do Goiabal 245 19.56 S 42.42 W
São José do Gurupi 240 1.36 S 46.13 W
São José do Jacuri 245 18.16 S 42.40 W
São José do Norte 242 32.01 S 52.03 W
São José do Peixe 240 7.24 S 42.34 W
São José do Piriá 240 1.17 S 46.18 W
São José do Rio Pardo 246 21.36 S 46.54 W
São José do Rio Prêto, Bra. 245 20.48 S 49.23 W
São José do Rio Prêto, Bra. 246 22.10 S 42.57 W
São José dos Campos, Bra. 246 23.11 S 45.53 W
São José dos Campos, Bra. 246 22.10 S 45.06 W
São José dos Lopes 246 21.48 S 43.53 W
São José dos Pinhais 242 25.31 S 49.13 W
São José do Turvo 246 22.21 S 43.59 W
São Julião da Barra 256c 38.40 N 9.21 W
São Julião do Tojal 256c 38.51 N 9.08 W
São Leopoldo 242 29.46 S 51.09 W
São Lourenço 246 22.07 S 45.03 W
São Lourenço ≃ 238 17.53 S 57.27 W
São Lourenço, Pantanal de ≡ 238 17.30 S 56.30 W
São Lourenço da Serra 246 23.52 S 46.57 W
São Lourenço d'Oeste 242 26.24 S 52.46 W
São Lourenço do Ipixuna 240 4.28 S 44.54 W
São Lourenço do Sul 242 31.22 S 51.58 W
São Luís 240 2.31 S 44.16 W
São Luís de Montes Belos 245 16.32 S 50.20 W
São Luís do Curu 240 3.40 S 39.14 W
São Luís Do Paraitinga 246 23.14 S 45.20 W
São Luís do Quitunde 240 9.20 S 35.33 W
São Luís do Tocantins 245 14.17 S 47.59 W
São Luís Gonzaga 242 28.24 S 54.58 W
São Mamede 240 6.56 S 37.06 W
São Manuel 245 22.44 S 48.34 W
São Mateus, Bra. 245 18.44 S 39.51 W
São Mateus, Bra. 246 22.49 S 43.23 W
São Mateus, Port. 138a 38.26 N 28.27 W
São Mateus ≃, Bra. 245 13.48 S 46.54 W
São Mateus ≃, Bra. 245 18.35 S 39.44 W
São Mateus do Sul 242 25.52 S 50.23 W
São Miguel, Bra. 240 6.13 S 38.30 W
São Miguel, Bra. 246 21.44 S 46.25 W
São Miguel I 138a 37.47 N 25.30 W
São Miguel ≃, Bra. 245 16.03 S 46.07 W
São Miguel ≃, Bra. 245 16.26 S 41.00 W
São Miguel do Anta 245 20.42 S 42.43 W
São Miguel do Araguaia 245 13.19 S 50.13 W
São Miguel d'Oeste 242 26.45 S 53.34 W
São Miguel dos Campos 240 9.47 S 36.05 W
São Miguel dos Macacos 240 1.11 S 50.28 W
São Miguel do Tapuio 240 5.30 S 41.20 W
São Miguel Paulista (Baquiriru) ◆[8] 246 23.30 S 46.26 W
Saona, Isla I 228 18.09 N 68.40 W
Saonara 58 45.22 N 11.59 E
Saône ≃ 56 45.44 N 4.50 E
Saône-et-Loire □[5] 32 46.42 N 4.45 E
Saonek 154 0.28 S 130.47 E
Saoner 110 21.23 N 78.54 E
São Nicolau 142 14.15 S 12.21 E
São Nicolau I 140a 16.35 N 24.15 W
São Nicolau ≃ 240 5.45 S 42.02 W
São Paulo 246 / 277b 23.32 S 46.37 W
São Paulo □[3] 245 22.00 S 49.00 W
São Paulo □[7] 277b 23.33 S 46.38 W
São Paulo ≃ 246 22.16 S 46.37 W
São Paulo de Olivença 236 3.27 S 68.48 W
São Paulo do Potengi 240 5.55 S 35.45 W
São Pedro, Bra. 245 19.53 S 51.55 W
São Pedro, Bra. 246 22.12 S 46.46 W
São Pedro ≃ 245 16.30 S 41.17 W
São Pedro de Viseu 240 2.33 S 49.33 W
São Pedro do Estoril 256c 38.42 N 9.22 W
São Pedro do Ivaí 245 23.51 S 51.51 W
São Pedro do Piauí 240 5.56 S 42.43 W
São Pedro do Sul, Bra. 242 29.37 S 54.10 W
São Pedro do Sul, Port. 34 40.45 N 8.04 W
São Rafael 240 5.47 S 36.55 W
São Raimundo das Mangabeiras 240 7.01 S 45.29 W
São Raimundo de Codó 240 4.21 S 43.37 W
São Raimundo Nonato 240 9.01 S 42.42 W
Saorge 56 43.59 N 7.33 E
Saori 84 35.11 N 136.44 E
São Romão 245 16.22 S 45.04 W

ENGLISH

Name | Page | Lat.°′ | Long.°′

São Roque 246 23.32 S 47.08 W
São Roque, Cabo de ≻ 240 5.29 S 35.16 W
São Roque da Fartura 246 21.51 S 46.45 W
São Roque do Paraguaçu 245 12.51 S 38.51 W
Saorre, Mount ∧ 166 64.27 N 84.30 W
São Salvador → Salvador 245 12.59 S 38.31 W
São Salvador do Congo 142 6.16 S 14.15 E
São Sebastião 246 23.48 S 45.25 W
São Sebastião, Canal de ⋃ 246 23.48 S 45.23 W
São Sebastião, Ilha de I 246 23.50 S 45.18 W
São Sebastião, Pico de ∧ 246 23.52 S 45.23 W
São Sebastião, Ponta ≻ 146 22.07 S 35.30 E
São Sebastião da Bela Vista 246 22.10 S 45.45 W
São Sebastião da Boa Vista 240 1.42 S 49.31 W
São Sebastião da Grama 246 21.43 S 46.49 W
São Sebastião da Vitória 246 21.14 S 44.25 W
São Sebastião do Barreado 246 22.04 S 43.38 W
São Sebastião do Maranhão 245 18.05 S 42.35 W
São Sebastião do Paraíso 245 20.55 S 47.00 W
São Sebastião do Rio Claro 245 15.45 S 51.30 W
São Sebastião do Rio Verde 246 22.13 S 44.58 W
São Sebastião dos Peitudos 246 22.19 S 46.29 W
São Sebastião dos Robertos 246 22.13 S 46.32 W
São Sebastião do Umbuzeiro 240 8.09 S 37.01 W
São Sepé 242 30.10 S 53.34 W
São Simão, Bra. 245 18.56 S 50.30 W
São Simão, Bra. 245 21.30 S 47.33 W
São Simão ≃ 238 12.40 S 63.04 W
São Tiago 245 20.55 S 44.30 W
São Tiago I 140a 15.05 N 23.40 W
São Timóteo 245 13.51 S 42.11 W
São Tomé, Bra. 240 5.58 S 36.04 W
São Tomé, S. Tom./P. 142 0.20 N 6.44 E
São Tomé I 142 0.12 N 6.39 E
São Tomé ≃ 240 8.10 S 58.13 W
São Tomé, Cabo de ≻ 245 21.59 S 40.59 W
São Tomé, Pico de ∧ 142 0.16 N 6.33 E
São Tomé, Ribeirão ≃ 246 21.26 S 46.02 W
Sao Tome and Principe □[1] 128 / 142 1.00 N 7.00 E
São Tomé das Letras 246 21.43 S 44.59 W
Saou 56 44.39 N 5.04 E
Saoura □[5] 138 28.00 N 3.00 W
Saoura, Oued ∨ 138 29.00 N 0.55 W
São Valério ≃ 240 11.20 S 48.28 W
São Vicente, Bra. 240 6.13 S 36.41 W
São Vicente, Bra. 246 22.22 S 47.12 W
São Vicente, Bra. 246 23.58 S 46.23 W
São Vicente I 140a 16.50 N 25.00 W
São Vicente, Cabo de ≻ 34 37.01 N 9.00 W
São Vicente, Ribeirão ≃ 246 21.59 S 45.40 W
São Vicente de Minas 246 21.42 S 44.27 W
São Vicente Ferrer, Bra. 240 7.35 S 35.30 W
São Vicente Ferrer, Bra. 240 2.53 S 44.52 W
Sápai 38 41.02 N 25.41 E
Sapallanga 238 12.09 S 75.11 W
Sapanca 120 40.41 N 30.16 E
Sapang Baho ≃ 259f 14.33 N 121.06 E
Sapao 106 10.01 N 126.02 E
Sapão ≃ 240 11.01 S 45.32 W
Saparua, Pulau I 154 3.34 S 128.40 E
Sapatgrām 114 26.20 N 90.08 E
Sapayán, Ciénaga ⊜ 236 10.08 N 74.45 W
Sapé, Bra. 240 7.06 S 35.13 W
Sapé, Bra. 246 22.16 S 46.34 W
Sape, Indon. 105b 8.34 S 118.59 E
Sapé ≃ 277a 22.52 S 43.02 W
Sape, Selat ⋃ 105b 8.39 S 119.18 E
Sapeaçu 245 12.44 S 39.13 W
Sapele 140 5.54 N 5.41 E
Sapello ≃ 190 35.47 N 104.59 W
Sapelo Island I 182 31.28 N 81.15 W
Saperkino 70 54.05 N 51.38 E
Şaphane 120 39.01 N 29.14 E
Sapian Bay C 106 11.33 N 122.37 E
Sapindji 142 9.39 S 23.12 E
Sapitwa ∧ 144 15.57 S 35.36 E
Šapki 66 59.36 N 31.14 E
Šapkina ≃ 24 66.44 N 52.25 E
Šapkino 70 51.42 N 42.24 E
Šapkovo, S.S.S.R. 66 55.47 N 33.20 E
Sapkovo, S.S.S.R. 72 54.34 N 39.10 E
Sapo, Serranía del ∧∧ 236 7.50 N 78.17 W
Saponé 140 12.03 N 1.36 W
Sap'o-ri 88 40.49 N 129.31 E
Sap'ornyj 255a 59.46 N 30.41 E
Saporoschje → Zaporožje 68 47.50 N 35.10 E
Saposoa 238 6.56 S 76.48 W
Sapožok 70 53.56 N 40.41 E
Sappa Creek ≃ 188 40.07 N 99.38 W
Sappa Creek, South Fork ≃ 188 39.47 N 100.35 W
Sappada 58 46.34 N 12.41 E
Sappemeer 48 53.09 N 6.50 E
Sapphire Mountains ∧∧ 192 46.20 N 113.45 W
Sappho 172 48.04 N 124.16 W
Sappington 209 38.32 N 90.23 W
Sapporo 82a 43.03 N 141.21 E
Şapri 36 40.04 N 15.38 E
Šapša 66 60.34 N 34.01 E
Sap Songkhla, Thale C 100 7.13 N 100.30 E
Šapsugskaja 68 44.45 N 38.05 E
Sapta-ri 261b 37.43 N 126.44 E
Sapt Kosi ≃, As. 114 26.30 N 86.55 E
Sapt Kosi ≃, Nepāl 114 26.31 N 86.58 E
Sapu 142 12.29 S 19.26 E
Sapucaí 246 22.19 S 46.42 W
Sapucaí ≃, Bra. 245 20.08 S 48.27 W
Sapucaí ≃, Bra. 246 21.33 S 45.40 W
Sapucaia 246 22.00 S 42.54 W
Sapucaí-Mirim 246 22.44 S 45.45 W
Sapucaí-Mirim ≃ 246 22.12 S 45.53 W
Sapudi, Pulau I 105a 7.06 S 114.20 E
Sapulpa 186 36.00 N 96.06 W
Sapulu 105a 6.54 S 112.57 E
Sapuran 105a 7.28 S 109.58 E
Sapwe 144 10.57 S 28.10 E
Sāq, Jabal ∧[2] 118 26.17 N 43.16 E
Sāqiat al-'Abd 130 20.48 N 30.19 E
Saqiqiao 90 27.19 N 117.35 E
Saqishanling ∧∧ 79 48.55 N 122.45 E
Sāqiyat Makkī 132 30.00 N 31.13 E
Şaqqārah 132 29.51 N 31.13 E
Saqqez 118 36.14 N 46.16 E
Saquarema 246 22.56 S 42.30 W
Saquarema, Lagoa de C 246 22.55 S 42.33 W
Saquena 238 4.40 S 73.31 W
Saquish Neck ≻[1] 273 42.00 N 70.37 W

DEUTSCH

Name | Seite | Breite°′ | Länge°′ E=Ost

Saquisilí 236 0.51 S 78.40 W
Sāra, Bngl. 116 24.07 N 89.02 E
Sara, H. Vol. 140 11.43 N 3.50 W
Sara, Niger 136 20.46 N 12.28 E
Sara, Pil. 106 11.16 N 123.01 E
Şara, S.S.S.R. 70 54.38 N 46.46 E
Šaraargun ≃ 74 43.02 N 45.44 E
Sarāb 118 37.56 N 47.32 E
Sarabia 224 20.31 N 101.05 W
Sarabia ≃ 224 17.11 N 94.56 W
Sarābiyūm 132 30.23 N 32.17 E
Sara Buri 100 14.32 N 100.55 E
Saracen 148 27.16 S 24.02 E
Saraceno, Monte ∧ 60 41.27 N 14.44 E
Saracura ≃ 245 12.18 S 40.07 W
Saracuruna ≃ 277a 22.41 S 43.13 W
Saraféré 140 15.50 N 3.42 W
Saragosa 186 31.01 N 103.39 W
Saragossa → Zaragoza 34 41.38 N 0.53 W
Saraguay ◆[8] 265a 45.31 N 73.45 W
Saraguro 236 3.36 S 79.13 W
Sarai 70 53.44 N 41.00 E
Saraikela 114 22.43 N 85.57 E
Sarāi Naurang 113 32.50 N 70.47 E
Saraipali 110 21.20 N 83.00 E
Säräisniemi 26 64.27 N 26.47 E
Sarajas de Madrid ◆[8] 256a 40.28 N 3.35 W
Sarajčik 70 47.30 N 51.43 E
Sarajevo 38 43.52 N 18.25 E
Saraj-Gir 70 53.36 N 53.24 E
Sarajskij 70 47.19 N 40.45 E
Sarakhs 118 36.32 N 61.11 E
Saraktaš 76 51.47 N 56.22 E
Sarala 76 54.52 N 89.14 E
Saraland 184 30.49 N 88.04 W
Šaraldaj 78 51.01 N 107.38 E
Saralžinskaja 70 49.12 N 48.55 E
Saramacca □[5] 240 4.45 N 56.00 W
Saramacca ≃ 240 5.51 N 55.53 W
Saramaguacán ≃ 230p 21.30 N 77.17 W
Šaran, S.S.S.R. 70 54.49 N 54.00 E
Saran', S.S.S.R. 76 49.46 N 72.52 E
Saran □[5] 114 26.00 N 84.30 E
Saran, Gunung ∧ 102 0.25 S 111.18 E
Saranac 206 42.56 N 85.13 W
Saranac ≃ 178 44.42 N 73.27 W
Saranac Lake 178 44.20 N 74.08 W
Saranakan, Gora ∧ 78 52.35 N 113.50 E
Saranap 216 37.53 N 122.06 W
Šaranbaš-Kn'azevo 70 54.58 N 54.09 E
Saranda 144 5.43 S 34.59 E
Sarandapótamos ≃ 257c 38.26 N 23.54 E
Sarandë 38 39.52 N 20.00 E
Sarandi 242 27.56 S 52.55 W
◆[8]Ndí 248 34.40 S 58.21
Sarandí del Yi 242 33.21 S 55.38 W
Sarandí Grande 248 33.44 S 56.20 W
Sarandira 246 21.50 S 43.11 W
Šaranga 70 57.11 N 46.34 E
Sarangani Bay C 106 5.57 N 125.11 E
Sarangani Island I 106 5.27 N 125.28 E
Sarangani Islands II 106 5.25 N 125.26 E
Sarangani Strait ⋃ 106 5.31 N 125.23 E
Sārangarh 110 21.36 N 83.05 E
Sārangpur 114 23.34 N 76.28 E
Sārankhola 116 22.18 N 89.47 E
Saranpaul' 24 64.14 N 60.53 E
Saransk 70 54.11 N 45.11 E
Sarantina, Valle ∨ 58 46.35 N 11.25 E
Saraphi 100 18.43 N 99.03 E
Sarapiquí ≃ 226 10.43 N 83.56 W
Şarapó ≃ 277a 22.46 S 43.37 W
Šarapovo, S.S.S.R. 70 55.17 N 44.42 E
Šarapovo, S.S.S.R. 72 55.11 N 37.16 E
Sarapuí ≃ 277a 22.46 S 43.24 W
Sarapuí, Canal ≋ 277a 22.44 S 43.16 W
Sarapul 70 56.28 N 53.48 E
Sarapul'skaja Vozvyšennost' ∧∧[1] 70 56.15 N 53.30 E
Sarapul'skoje 79 48.52 N 135.59 E
Sarāqib 120 35.52 N 36.48 E
Sarare 236 9.47 N 69.10 W
Sarar Plain ⌣ 134 9.35 N 46.15 E
Sará-Sará 246 23.40 S 47.05 W
Sarasara, Nevado ∧ 238 15.19 S 73.27 W
Sarasota 210 27.20 N 82.34 W
Sarasota □[6] 210 27.10 N 82.21 W
Sarasota Bay C 210 27.23 N 82.39 W
Sarasota-Bradenton Airport ⊠ 210 27.24 N 82.33 W
Sarasota Springs 210 27.17 N 82.28 W
Saraswati ≃ 262b 22.59 N 88.22 E
Sarata 68 46.02 N 29.38 E
Sarath 116 24.14 N 86.50 E
Saratoga, Austl. 160 33.28 S 151.21 E
Saratoga, Calif., U.S. 216 37.16 N 122.02 W
Saratoga, Ind., U.S. 206 40.14 N 84.55 W
Saratoga, Tex., U.S. 212 30.17 N 94.31 W
Saratoga, Wyo., U.S. 190 41.27 N 106.48 W
Saratoga □[6] 200 43.00 N 73.51 W
Saratoga Battle Monument ⊥ 200 43.05 N 75.36 W
Saratoga Creek ≃ 272 37.25 N 121.58 W
Saratoga Lake ⊜ 200 43.01 N 73.39 W
Saratoga National Historical Park ♠ 200 43.00 N 73.38 W
Saratoga Passage ⋃ 214 48.10 N 122.30 W
Saratoga Spa State Park ♠ 200 43.03 N 73.50 W
Saratoga Springs 200 43.05 N 73.47 W
Šara Togot 78 53.01 N 106.43 E
Saratok 102 1.44 N 111.20 E
Saratov 70 51.34 N 46.02 E
Saratov □[4] 66 52.00 N 42.40 E
Saratovka 76 51.12 N 54.54 E
Saraurcu, Cerro ∧ 236 0.06 S 77.55 W
Sarāvān, Īrān 118 27.15 N 62.40 E
Saravan, Lao 100 15.43 N 106.25 E
Sarawak □[3] 102 2.30 N 113.30 E
Saray 120 41.26 N 27.55 E
Saraya, Guinée 140 10.46 N 10.24 W
Saraya, Sén. 140 12.50 N 11.45 W
Sarayakpınar 120 41.46 N 26.29 E
Sarāyān 118 33.51 N 58.31 E
Saraycık 120 40.57 N 35.08 E
Sarayevo → Sarajevo 38 43.52 N 18.25 E
Sarayköy 120 37.55 N 28.58 E
Sarayönü 120 38.17 N 32.25 E
Sarbaj 70 53.39 N 51.34 E
Sarbāz 118 26.39 N 61.15 E
Sarbinowo 50 52.40 N 14.40 E
Sárbogárd 30 46.53 N 18.38 E
Sarca ≃ 58 45.52 N 10.52 E
Sarce ≃ 46 48.09 N 4.18 E
Sarcee Indian Reserve ◆[4] 172 50.58 N 114.06 W
Sarcelle, Passe de la ⋃ 165f 22.29 S 167.12 E
Sarcelles 46 49.00 N 2.23 E
Sarche di Calavino 58 46.03 N 10.57 E
Şarcidano ◆[1] 36 39.55 N 9.05 E
Šarčino 76 53.09 N 81.45 E
Sarcoxie 184 37.03 N 94.07 W
Sārda (Kāli) ≃ 114 27.22 N 81.23 E
Sard Āb)(113 36.40 N 71.32 E
Sārda Canal ≋ 114 28.59 N 80.07 E
Sardagna 58 46.03 N 11.06 E
Sardah 114 24.18 N 88.44 E
Sardalas 136 25.46 N 10.34 E
Sardanyola 256d 41.30 N 2.09 E
Sardaq 118 34.48 N 58.07 E
Sardār Chāh 118 27.58 N 64.50 E
Sardārpur 110 22.39 N 74.59 E
Sardārshahr 110 28.26 N 74.29 E
Sar Dasht, Īrān 118 32.32 N 48.52 E
Sar Dasht, Īrān 118 36.09 N 45.28 E
Sardegna □[4] 36 40.00 N 9.00 E

Symbols in the index entries represent the broad categories identified in the key at the right. Symbols with superior numbers (∧∧[2]) identify subcategories (see complete key on page I · 26).

Kartensymbole in dem Registerverzeichnis stellen die rechts in Schlüssel erklärten Kategorien dar. Symbole mit hochgestellten Ziffern (∧∧[2]) bezeichnen Unterabteilungen einer Kategorie (vgl. vollständiger Schlüssel auf Seite I · 26).

Los símbolos incluídos en el texto del índice representan las grandes categorias identificadas con la clave a la derecha. Los símbolos con numeros en su parte superior (∧∧[2]) identifican las subcategorías (véase la clave completa en la página I · 26).

Les symboles de l'index représentent les catégories indiquées dans la légende à droite. Les symboles suivis d'un indice (∧∧[2]) représentent des sous-catégories (voir légende complète à la page I · 26).

Os símbolos incluídos no texto do índice representam as grandes categorias identificadas com a chave à direita. Os símbolos com números em sua parte superior (∧∧[2]) identificam as subcategorias (veja-se a chave completa à página I · 26).

Symbol	English	Deutsch	Español	Français	Português
∧	Mountain	Berg	Montaña	Montagne	Montanha
∧∧	Mountains	Berge	Montañas	Montagnes	Montanhas
)(	Pass	Pass	Paso	Col	Passo
∨	Valley, Canyon	Tal, Cañon	Valle, Cañón	Vallée, Canyon	Vale, Canhão
⌣	Plain	Ebene	Llano	Plaine	Planície
≻	Cape	Kap	Cabo	Cap	Cabo
I	Island	Insel	Isla	Île	Ilha
II	Islands	Inseln	Islas	Îles	Ilhas
⊥	Other Topographic Features	Andere Topographische Objekte	Otros Elementos Topográficos	Autres données topographiques	Outros Elementos Topográficos

ESPAÑOL — Nombre | Página | Lat.°′ | Long.°′ W=Oeste
FRANÇAIS — Nom | Page | Lat.°′ | Long.°′ W=Ouest
PORTUGUÊS — Nome | Página | Lat.°′ | Long.°′ W=Oeste

Sardegna (Sardinia) I 36 40.00 N 9.00 E
Sardhana 114 29.09 N 77.37 E
Sardiha 116 22.22 N 87.09 E
Sardina 236 2.02 N 67.07 W
Sardinal 226 10.31 N 85.39 W
Sardinata 236 8.05 N 72.48 W
Sardinia, N.Y., U.S. 200 42.32 N 78.31 W
Sardinia, Ohio, U.S. 208 39.05 N 83.49 W
Sardinia → Sardegna I 36 40.00 N 9.00 E
Sardinien → Sardegna I 36 40.00 N 9.00 E
Sardis, B.C., Can. 214 49.08 N 121.57 W
Sardis, Ala., U.S. 184 32.17 N 86.59 W
Sardis, Ga., U.S. 182 32.58 N 81.46 W
Sardis, Ky., U.S. 208 38.32 N 83.57 W
Sardis, Miss., U.S. 184 34.26 N 89.55 W
Sardis, Pa., U.S. 269b 40.29 N 79.42 W
Sardis, Tenn., U.S. 184 35.27 N 88.18 W
Şardona, Piz ∧ 54 46.55 N 9.15 E
Šardonem' 24 63.56 N 44.37 E
Sareks Nationalpark ♠ 24 67.15 N 17.30 E
Sarektjåkkå ∧ 24 67.25 N 17.46 E
Sārenga, Bhārat 116 22.46 N 87.02 E
Sārenga, Bhārat 262b 22.31 N 88.13 E
Sarentino (Sarnthein) 58 46.38 N 11.21 E
Sar-e Pol-e Żahāb 118 34.28 N 45.52 E
Sarepta 184 32.54 N 93.27 W
Sarezskoje, Ozero ⊜ 75 38.13 N 72.45 E
Sarezzo 58 45.39 N 10.12 E
Sargans 54 47.03 N 9.26 E
Sargatskoje 76 55.37 N 73.30 E
Sargé-lès-le-Mans 46 48.02 N 0.14 E
Sargent 188 41.38 N 99.22 W
Sargent Creek ≃ 216 35.57 N 120.52 W
Sargento Paixão, Serra do ∧∧[1] 238 11.13 S 60.30 W
Şargodha 113 32.05 N 72.40 E
Šargol'džin 78 52.21 N 114.42 E
Šargorod 68 48.44 N 28.05 E
Šargou ≃ 75 43.25 N 73.50 E
Šargul', Ozero ⊜ 76 54.35 N 78.51 E
Šargun 75 38.37 N 67.53 E
Sarh 136 9.09 N 18.23 E
Sarhli, Djebel ∧ 34 36.06 N 0.40 E
Sarhro, Jbel ∧∧ 138 31.00 N 5.55 W
Sārī 118 36.34 N 53.04 E
Saría I 38 35.50 N 27.15 E
Saribi, Tanjung ≻ 154 1.36 S 135.25 E
Sáric 222 31.08 N 111.23 W
Saricumbe 142 12.12 S 19.46 E
Sarigan I 98 16.42 N 145.47 E
Sarıgazi 257b 41.01 N 29.12 E
Sarıgöl 120 38.14 N 28.43 E
Sarıkamış 120 40.20 N 42.35 E
Sarıkaya 120 38.47 N 32.15 E
Sarikei 102 2.07 N 111.31 E
Sarıköy 120 40.12 N 27.36 E
Sarilhos Grandes 256c 38.41 N 8.58 W
Sarilhos Pequenos 256c 38.41 N 8.59 W
Sarim 144 0.23 S 40.58 E
Sarimbun, Pulau I 261c 1.26 N 103.41 E
Sarina 156 21.26 S 149.13 E
Sarine ≃ 54 46.54 N 7.14 E
Sariñena 34 41.48 N 0.10 W
Sarıoğlan, Tür. 120 39.05 N 35.59 E
Sarıoğlan, Tür. 120 37.12 N 32.33 E
Saripul' 75 38.26 N 70.08 E
Sarīr 136 27.36 N 22.32 E
Sarısu 74 39.01 N 42.55 E
Sarita 186 37.13 N 97.47 W
Sariwŏn 88 38.31 N 125.44 E
Sarıyar Gölü ⊜[1] 120 40.02 N 31.40 E
Şarıyer 120 41.10 N 29.03 E
Šarja 70 58.24 N 45.30 E
Sarju (Babai) ≃ 114 27.42 N 81.16 E
Sark I 28 49.26 N 2.21 W
Sark ≃ 42 54.58 N 3.04 W
Şarkad 30 46.44 N 21.23 E
Šarkan 70 57.18 N 53.53 E
Sarkand 76 45.26 N 79.54 E
Şarkîkaraağaç 120 38.04 N 31.23 E
Şarkışla 120 39.21 N 36.26 E
Šarkovščina 66 55.22 N 27.28 E
Şarköy 120 40.37 N 27.06 E
Şarlat-la-Canéda 32 44.53 N 1.13 E
Šarlauk 118 38.13 N 55.38 E
Şarles 188 48.57 N 99.00 W
Šarlyk 76 52.55 N 54.45 E
Sarmakovo 74 43.43 N 43.12 E
Sarmanovo 70 55.15 N 52.36 E
Sărmașu 38 46.46 N 24.11 E
Sarmatskaja ≃ 73 47.20 N 38.48 E
Sármellék 30 46.44 N 17.10 E
Sarmi 154 1.51 S 138.44 E
Sarmiento 244 45.36 S 69.05 W
Sarmiento ≃ 278 34.25 S 58.35 W
Sarmiento, Lago ⊜ 244 51.04 S 72.45 W
Sarmiento, Monte ∧ 244 54.27 S 70.50 W
Särna 26 61.41 N 13.08 E
Sarna, Ozero ⊜ 70 48.24 N 44.38 E
Sarnano 60 43.02 N 13.18 E
Sārnāth ⊥ 114 25.24 N 83.01 E
Sarnen 54 46.54 N 8.15 E
Sârnena ∧∧ 38 42.35 N 25.10 E
Sarner See ⊜ 54 46.52 N 8.13 E
Sarnia 204 42.58 N 82.23 W
Sarnico 58 45.40 N 9.57 E
Sarno 60 40.49 N 14.37 E
Sarnow 50 53.45 N 13.37 E
Sarnowa 30 51.38 N 16.54 E
Sarnthein → Sarentino 58 46.38 N 11.21 E
Šarnutovskij 70 47.40 N 43.46 E
Sarny 68 51.21 N 26.36 E
Saroako 102 2.31 S 121.22 E
Sarolangun 102 2.18 S 102.42 E
Saroma-ko ⊜ 82a 44.08 N 143.50 E
Saron 148 33.11 S 19.01 E
Saronikós Kólpos C 38 37.54 N 23.12 E
Saronno 56 45.38 N 9.02 E
Saros Körfezi C 120 40.30 N 26.20 E
Sárospatak 30 48.19 N 21.34 E
Šarovka 68 50.01 N 35.27 E
Şarpa 70 47.07 N 45.29 E
Šarpajevka 68 48.34 N 40.59 E
Sar Passage U 165b 7.12 N 134.23 E
Sarpinskaja Nizmennost' ☷ 70 47.30 N 45.30 E
Sarpinskije Ozera ⊜ 70 47.30 N 45.00 E
Šar Planina ∧∧ 38 42.05 N 20.50 E
Sarpsborg 26 59.17 N 11.07 E
Sarpy Creek ≃ 192 46.15 N 107.09 W
Sarralbe 52 49.00 N 7.01 E
Sarras 56 45.11 N 4.48 E
Sarrath, Oued V 36 35.59 N 8.23 E
Sarratt 250 51.41 N 0.29 W
Sarre 56 45.43 N 7.15 E
Sarre (Saar) ≃ 52 49.42 N 6.34 E
Sarre Blanche ≃ 52 48.41 N 7.01 E
Sarrebourg 54 48.44 N 7.03 E
Sarrebruck → Saarbrücken 52 49.14 N 6.59 E
Sarreguemines 52 49.06 N 7.03 E
Sarre Rouge ≃ 52 48.41 N 7.01 E
Sarre-Union 52 48.56 N 7.05 E
Sarria 34 42.47 N 7.24 W
Sarriá ◂[8] 256d 41.24 N 2.08 E
Sarro 140 13.43 N 5.15 W
Sars 76 56.33 N 57.07 E
Sarsfield 202 45.27 N 75.21 W
Sarsina 60 43.55 N 12.08 E
Sarsol 262c 19.02 N 73.01 E
Sarstedt 48 52.14 N 9.51 E
Sarstein ∧ 58 47.36 N 13.41 E
Sarstoon ≃ 226 15.53 N 88.55 W
Sarsuna 262b 22.28 N 88.18 E
Sart 52 50.31 N 5.56 E
Sartang ≃ 64 67.44 N 133.12 E
Sarteano 60 42.59 N 11.52 E
Sartell 180 45.37 N 94.12 W
Sartène 36 41.36 N 8.59 E
Sarthe □[5] 32 48.00 N 0.05 E
Sarthe ≃ 32 47.30 N 0.32 W
Sartičala 74 41.43 N 45.10 E
Sartilly 32 48.45 N 1.27 W
Sartirana Lomellina 56 45.07 N 8.39 E
Sartlan, Ozero ⊜ 76 55.00 N 78.35 E
Sartol'gen 70 48.57 N 47.03 E
Sartrouville 251 48.57 N 2.10 E
Saru 75 42.20 N 77.55 E
Saru ≃ 82a 42.30 N 142.00 E
Sarufutsu 82a 45.16 N 142.12 E
Saruhanlı 120 38.44 N 27.34 E
Şarūr 118 23.22 N 58.07 E
Šar Us ≃ 78 47.08 N 97.38 E
Saru-shima I 258 35.17 N 139.42 E
Sarvadyk 70 46.07 N 44.07 E
Sárvár 30 47.15 N 16.57 E
Sarver 204 40.44 N 79.45 W
Sarvestān 118 29.16 N 53.13 E
Sárvíz ≃ 30 46.24 N 18.41 E
Saryagač 75 41.27 N 69.10 E
Saryassija 75 38.25 N 67.57 E
Sarybarak 75 43.24 N 71.30 E
Sarybasat 76 46.38 N 60.27 E
Sarybulak, S.S.S.R. 75 40.54 N 73.49 E
Sarybulak, S.S.S.R. 76 49.27 N 76.27 E
Saryč, Mys ≻ 68 44.23 N 33.45 E
Sarychosor 75 38.32 N 69.49 E
Sarydala 75 41.11 N 70.27 E
Saryg-Sep 78 51.30 N 95.36 E
Sary-Išikotrau ◂[2] 76 45.30 N 76.00 E
Sarykoby 75 43.44 N 72.35 E
Sarykol'skij Chrebet ∧∧ 110 38.00 N 74.30 E
Sarykomej 76 45.12 N 74.11 E
Sarykopa, Ozero ⊜ 76 50.22 N 64.08 E
Sarymogol 75 39.55 N 72.47 E
Sarymoin, Ozero ⊜ 76 51.36 N 64.30 E
Şaryozek 76 44.22 N 77.59 E
Šarypovo 76 55.33 N 89.12 E
Saryšagan 76 46.07 N 73.38 E
Sarysu 76 48.23 N 69.59 E
Sarysu ≃ 76 45.12 N 66.36 E
Sary-Taš 75 39.44 N 73.15 E
Sarytau 76 49.54 N 76.41 E
Saryżaz 62 42.55 N 79.38 E
Sarzana 58 44.07 N 9.58 E
Sarzanello, Fortezza di ⊥ 58 44.08 N 9.58 E
Sarzeau 32 47.32 N 2.46 W
S'as' ≃ 66 60.09 N 32.30 E
Sasa, Nihon 82 33.14 N 129.39 E
Sa'sa', Sūrīy. 122 33.17 N 36.02 E
Sasa, Yis. 122 33.02 N 35.24 E
Sasabe 190 31.27 N 111.31 W
Sasabeneh 134 7.55 N 43.39 E
Sasaga-mine ∧ 86 33.49 N 133.17 E
Sasaginnigak Lake ⊜ 174 51.36 N 95.40 W
Sasago-tunnel ◂[5] 84 35.38 N 138.47 E
Sasaguri 86 33.37 N 130.32 E
Sasak 100 0.01 S 99.42 E
Sasakwa 186 34.57 N 96.31 W
Sasamungga 165e 7.02 S 156.47 E
Sasao 260 34.57 N 135.20 E
Sasar, Tanjung ≻ 105b 9.17 S 119.56 E
Sasarām 114 24.57 N 84.02 E
Sasayama 86 35.04 N 135.13 E
Sasa-yama ∧ 86 33.03 N 132.40 E
Sasbach 54 48.08 N 7.37 E
Sasco Brook ≃ 266 41.07 N 73.18 W
Sásd 30 46.15 N 18.06 E
Sasebo 82 33.10 N 129.43 E
Sasebo Naval Base (United States) ▪ 82 33.09 N 129.45 E
Saseenos 214 48.24 N 123.40 W
Saseginaga, Lac ⊜ 180 47.06 N 78.35 W
Sashalom ◂[8] 254c 47.31 N 19.11 E
Sas-hegy ∧[2] 254c 47.23 N 19.18 E
Sashima 84 36.08 N 139.58 E
Sasiki 164m 26.10 N 127.47 E
Saskatchewan □[4] 174 / 166 54.00 N 105.00 W
Saskatchewan ≃ 174 53.12 N 99.16 W
Saskatoon 174 52.07 N 106.38 W
Saskylach 64 71.55 N 114.01 E
Sasmik, Cape ≻ 170 51.36 N 177.55 W
Sāsni 114 27.43 N 78.05 E
Sasolburg 148 26.48 S 27.45 E
Sason Dağları ∧∧ 120 38.15 N 41.32 E
Sasovo 70 54.21 N 41.54 E
Saspamco 186 29.14 N 98.18 W
Saspul Gompa 113 34.15 N 77.09 E
Sassafras 264b 37.52 S 145.21 E
Sassafras ≃ 198 39.23 N 76.02 W
Sassafras Mountain ∧ 182 35.03 N 82.48 W
Sassandra 140 4.58 N 6.05 W
Sassandra □[5] 140 5.20 N 6.40 W
Sassandra ≃ 140 4.58 N 6.05 W
Sassari 36 40.44 N 8.33 E
Sasse ≃ 56 44.15 N 5.55 E
Sassello 56 44.29 N 8.30 E
Sassenage 56 45.12 N 5.40 E
Sassenberg 48 51.59 N 8.02 E
Sassenheim 48 52.13 N 4.31 E
Sassnitz 50 54.31 N 13.38 E
Sassocorvaro 60 43.47 N 12.30 E
Sassoferrato 60 43.26 N 12.51 E
Sasso Marconi 58 44.24 N 11.15 E
S'as'stroj 66 60.08 N 32.34 E
Sassuolo 58 44.33 N 10.47 E
Sas-Tobe 75 42.34 N 70.00 E
Sastown 140 4.40 N 8.26 W
Sastre 242 31.45 S 61.50 W
Sasumua Dam ⊜ 144 0.45 S 36.40 E
Sas van Gent 48 51.14 N 3.47 E
Sasyk, Ozero ⊜ 68 45.12 N 33.31 E
Sasykkol', Ozero ⊜ 76 46.35 N 81.00 E
Şasykoli 70 47.33 N 47.00 E
Šat ≃ 72 54.08 N 37.47 E
Satadougou 140 12.21 N 10.07 W
Satah Mountain ∧ 172 52.29 N 124.41 W
Şatakunta ◂[1] 26 61.30 N 23.00 E
Šatalovka 68 51.09 N 38.16 E
Šatalovo 66 54.20 N 32.27 E
Sata-misaki ≻ 82 30.59 N 130.40 E
Satāna 112 20.35 N 74.12 E
Satanov 68 49.15 N 26.16 E
Satanta 188 37.26 N 100.59 W
Sátão 34 40.44 N 7.44 W
Sātāra, Bhārat 112 17.41 N 73.59 E
Satara, S. Afr. 146 24.29 S 31.47 E
Sataua 165a 13.28 S 172.40 W
Sātbāria, Bhārat 262b 22.25 N 88.33 E
Sātbāria, Bngl. 116 23.52 N 89.26 E
Satellite Beach 210 28.11 N 80.35 W
Satellite Channel U 214 48.43 N 123.30 W
Satema 142 4.18 N 21.42 E
Säter 40 60.21 N 15.45 E
Sātgāchia 116 23.16 N 88.08 E
Sātghara 262b 22.44 N 88.21 E
Saticoy 218 34.17 N 119.09 W
Satilla ≃ 182 30.59 N 81.28 W
Satilpa Creek ≃ 184 31.39 N 88.05 W
Satin 212 31.21 N 97.02 W
Satipo 238 11.16 S 74.37 W
Satırlar 120 37.30 N 29.46 E
Sátiro Dias 240 11.36 S 38.36 W
Satis 70 55.02 N 43.48 E
Satīt (Tekeze) ≃ 130 14.20 N 35.50 E
Satka 76 55.03 N 59.01 E
Satkānia 110 22.04 N 92.03 E
Şātkhira 114 22.43 N 89.06 E
Šatki 70 55.11 N 44.08 E
Satla Bīl ☷ 116 22.54 N 90.04 E
Satluj → Sutlej ≃ 110 29.23 N 71.02 E
Satna 114 24.35 N 80.50 E
Satna □[5] 114 24.30 N 80.50 E
Sato, Cañada de ≃ 278 34.35 S 58.38 W
Satomi 84 36.43 N 140.30 E
Satoou 140 13.38 N 6.58 E
Şátoraljaújhely 30 48.24 N 21.39 E
Šatovo 72 54.56 N 37.14 E
Satow 50 53.59 N 11.51 E
Sātpura Range ∧∧ 112 22.00 N 78.00 E
Şätrabrunn 40 59.51 N 16.27 E
Šatrovo 76 56.31 N 64.38 E
Satrup 41 54.41 N 9.35 E
Satsop ≃ 214 47.03 N 123.30 W
Satsop, Middle Fork ≃ 214 47.05 N 123.30 W
Satsop, West Fork ≃ 214 47.02 N 123.32 W
Satsuma 184 30.51 N 88.03 W
Satsuma-hantō ≻[1] 82 31.25 N 130.25 E
Satsunan-shotō II 83b 29.00 N 130.00 E
Sattahip 100 12.40 N 100.54 E
Sattānkulam 112 8.27 N 77.56 E
Satte 84 36.04 N 139.43 E
Sattel 54 47.05 N 8.42 E
Sattenapalle 112 16.24 N 80.11 E
Satthwa 100 17.46 N 94.30 E
Satui 102 3.47 S 115.27 E
Sātuli 262b 22.33 N 88.34 E
Satu Mare 38 47.48 N 22.53 E
Satu Mare □[5] 38 47.40 N 23.00 E
Şatun 100 6.37 N 100.04 E
Šatura 70 55.34 N 39.32 E
Saturna 214 48.43 N 123.11 W
Saturna Island I 214 48.47 N 123.08 W
Şaturnino M. Laspiur 242 31.42 S 62.29 W
Šaturtorf 66 55.34 N 39.26 E
Satus Creek ≃ 192 46.16 N 120.07 W
Satus Peak ∧ 214 46.15 N 120.45 W
Satyamangalam 112 11.31 N 77.15 E
Satzkorn 254a 52.29 N 12.59 E
Sau ≃ 259c 10.46 N 106.48 E
Sauble ≃ 202 44.40 N 81.17 W
Sauce, Arg. 242 30.05 S 58.46 W
Sauce, Perú 238 6.44 S 76.10 W
Sauce, Ur. 248 34.39 S 56.04 W
Sauce, Arroyo ≃ 248 33.53 S 56.49 W
Sauce, Arroyo del ≃, Arg. 278 34.41 S 58.50 W
Sauce, Arroyo del ≃, Ur. 248 34.26 S 57.28 W
Sauce, Arroyo del ≃, Ur. 248 33.56 S 56.45 W
Sauce Chico ≃ 242 38.47 S 62.18 W
Sauce Corto, Arroyo ≃ 242 36.55 S 61.48 W
Sauce Grande ≃ 242 38.59 S 61.07 W
Saucier 184 30.38 N 89.08 W
Saucillo 222 28.01 N 105.17 W
Sauda 26 59.39 N 6.20 E
Saudade 246 21.56 S 43.03 W
Sauđárkrókur 24a 65.46 N 19.41 W
Saúde 240 10.56 S 40.24 W
Saúde ◂[8] 277b 23.37 S 46.37 W
Saudi Arabia □[1] 108 25.00 N 45.00 E
Saudi-Arabien → Saudi Arabia □[1] 108 25.00 N 45.00 E
Saudron 54 48.30 N 5.20 E
Saueniná ≃ 238 12.24 S 58.40 W
Sauer (Sûre) ≃ 52 49.44 N 6.31 E
Sauerkohl-Berge ∧∧[2] 254a 52.20 N 13.45 E
Sauerlach 58 47.58 N 11.38 E
Sauerland ◂[1] 48 51.10 N 8.00 E
Saueruiná ≃ 238 12.00 S 58.43 W
Saug ≃ 106 7.27 N 125.44 E
Saugatuck 206 42.40 N 86.12 W
Saugatuck ≃ 266 41.07 N 73.22 W
Saugatuck Reservoir ⊜[1] 197 41.16 N 73.22 W
Saugeen ≃ 180 44.30 N 81.22 W
Saugerties 200 42.05 N 73.57 W
Saughall 252 53.13 N 2.58 W
Saugor → Sāgar 114 23.50 N 78.43 E
Saugor □[5] 114 24.00 N 78.50 E
Saugstad, Mount ∧ 172 52.15 N 126.31 W
Saugus, Calif., U.S. 218 34.25 N 118.32 W
Saugus, Mass., U.S. 197 42.27 N 71.01 W
Saugus ≃ 273 42.28 N 70.58 W
Sauh, Tanjong ≻ 104 3.46 N 100.49 E
Saujil 242 28.11 S 66.14 W
Saujon 32 45.40 N 0.56 W
Sauk ≃, Minn., U.S. 188 45.36 N 94.10 W
Sauk ≃, Wash., U.S. 214 48.30 N 121.37 W
Sauk Centre 188 45.44 N 94.57 W
Sauk City 180 43.17 N 89.43 W
Sauk Rapids 180 45.34 N 94.09 W
Sauksaj ≃ 75 39.11 N 72.15 E
Sauk Village 206 41.30 N 87.34 W
Saukville 180 43.23 N 87.55 W
Şaül 240 3.37 N 53.12 W
Šaul'der 75 42.47 N 68.24 E
Sauldre ≃ 46 47.16 N 1.30 E
Sauldre, Canal de la ⩸ 46 47.36 N 2.06 E
Saulgau 54 48.01 N 9.30 E
Saulgrub 58 47.40 N 11.01 E
Saulieu 46 47.16 N 4.14 E
Saulkrasti 66 57.17 N 24.25 E
Saulnot 54 47.34 N 6.38 E
Sault-au-Mouton 176 48.33 N 69.15 W
Sault au Récollet ◂[8] 265a 45.34 N 73.39 W
Sault aux Cochons, Rivière du ≃ 176 48.44 N 69.04 W
Sault-de-Vaucluse 56 44.05 N 5.25 E
Saulteaux ≃ 172 55.16 N 114.25 W
Saulteaux Indian Reserve ◂[4] 174 53.08 N 108.18 W
Sault-lès-Rethel 46 49.30 N 4.22 E
Sault Sainte Marie, Ont., Can. 180 46.31 N 84.20 W
Sault Sainte Marie, Mich., U.S. 180 46.30 N 84.21 W
Saulx ≃, Fr. 52 48.45 N 4.35 E
Saulx ≃, Fr. 251 48.41 N 2.19 E
Saulx-de-Vesoul 54 47.42 N 6.17 E
Saulx-les-Chartreux 251 48.42 N 2.16 E
Saulxures-sur-Moselotte 54 47.57 N 6.46 E
Šaum'ani 74 41.23 N 44.45 E
Šaum'anovsk 74 40.26 N 46.34 E
Saumarez Reef ✣[2] 156 21.50 S 153.40 E
Saumâtre, Étang ⊜ 228 18.35 N 72.00 W
Saumlaki 154 7.57 S 131.19 E
Saumon, Rivière au ≃ 196 45.41 N 71.27 W
Saumons, Rivíere aux ≃ 176 49.25 N 62.15 W
Saumur 32 47.16 N 0.05 W
Saundatti 112 15.47 N 75.07 E
Saundersfoot 44 51.43 N 4.43 W
Saunders Island I 18 57.47 S 26.27 W
Saunders Point ∧[2] 152 27.52 S 125.38 E
Saunderstown 197 41.30 N 71.25 W
Saunemin 206 40.54 N 88.24 W
Saupite 142 13.54 S 17.43 E
Sauquoit 200 43.00 N 75.16 W
Sauquoit Creek ≃ 200 43.08 N 75.16 W
Saura 74 44.14 N 50.50 E
Sauran 75 43.29 N 67.50 E
Saurimo 142 9.39 S 20.24 E
Saur-Mogila ⊥ 73 47.56 N 38.46 E
Sausalito 216 37.51 N 122.29 W
Sausar 110 21.39 N 78.47 E
Sauškin 70 49.30 N 43.32 E
Sausset-les-Pins 56 43.20 N 5.07 E
Saussy 54 47.28 N 4.57 E
Sausu 102 1.00 S 120.30 E
Saútar 142 11.06 S 18.27 E
Sauteurs 231k 12.14 N 61.38 W
Sauteurs Bay C 231k 12.14 N 61.38 W
Sauvas 56 44.19 N 4.09 E
Sauve 56 43.56 N 3.57 E
Sauveterre 56 44.02 N 4.48 E
Sauveterre, Causse ∧∧[1] 32 44.20 N 3.10 E
Sauveterre-de-Béarn 34 43.29 N 0.06 W
Sauveterre-de-Guyenne 32 44.42 N 0.05 W
Sauvie Island I 214 45.41 N 122.49 W
Sauvo 26 60.21 N 22.42 E
Sauwald ◂[3] 30 48.28 N 13.40 E
Sauzal 190 31.37 N 106.18 W
Sauze di Cesana 56 44.56 N 6.51 E
Sauze d'Oulx 56 45.02 N 6.52 E
Sava, It. 36 40.24 N 17.34 E
S'ava, S.S.S.R. 70 58.01 N 46.22 E
Sava ≃ 38 44.50 N 20.26 E
Sävaån ≃ 40 59.45 N 17.24 E
Savage, Md., U.S. 198 39.08 N 76.49 W
Savage, Mont., U.S. 192 47.27 N 104.21 W
Savai'i I 165a 13.35 S 172.25 W
Savala ≃ 70 51.03 N 41.30 E
Savalen ⊜ 26 62.15 N 10.29 E
Savalou 140 7.56 N 1.58 E
Savana Island I 230m 18.20 N 65.05 W
Savana Passage U 230m 18.21 N 65.04 W
Savane ≃ 176 51.08 N 71.26 W
Savanna, Ill., U.S. 180 42.05 N 90.08 W
Savanna, Okla., U.S. 186 34.50 N 95.51 W
Savannah, Ga., U.S. 182 32.04 N 81.05 W
Savannah, Mo., U.S. 184 39.56 N 94.50 W
Savannah, N.Y., U.S. 200 43.04 N 76.46 W
Savannah, Ohio, U.S. 204 40.58 N 82.22 W
Savannah, Tenn., U.S. 184 35.14 N 88.14 W
Savannah ≃ 182 32.02 N 80.53 W
Savannah Beach 182 32.01 N 80.51 W
Savannah Sound 182 25.06 N 76.09 W
Savannakhét 100 16.33 N 104.45 E
Savanna-la-Mar 231q 18.13 N 78.08 W
Savanna Portage State Park ♠ 180 46.51 N 93.10 W
Sāvantvādi 112 15.54 N 73.49 E
Savanūr 112 14.58 N 75.21 E
Sävar 26 63.54 N 20.34 E
Savara ≃ 56 45.42 N 7.12 E
Savasse ≃ 56 45.03 N 5.02 E
Savaştepe 120 39.22 N 27.40 E
Savcılıbüyükoba 120 39.14 N 33.41 E
Savé 140 8.02 N 2.29 E
Save (Sabi) ≃, Afr. 146 21.00 S 35.02 E
Save ≃, Fr. 32 43.47 N 1.17 E
Sāveh 118 35.01 N 50.20 E
Savelli 36 39.19 N 16.47 E
Savelovskij Vokzal ◂[5] 255b 55.48 N 37.35 E
Savelugu 140 9.37 N 0.49 W
Savenay 32 47.22 N 1.57 W
Săveni 38 47.57 N 26.52 E
Saverdun 32 43.14 N 1.35 E
Savernake Forest ◂[3] 44 51.24 N 1.38 W
Saverne 52 48.44 N 7.22 E
Savery Creek ≃ 190 41.01 N 107.27 W
Saviano 60 40.54 N 14.30 E
Saviči, S.S.S.R. 66 52.25 N 29.03 E
Saviči, S.S.S.R. 68 51.37 N 30.17 E
Savick Brook ≃ 252 53.49 N 2.37 W
Savièse 54 46.16 N 7.20 E
Savigliano 56 44.38 N 7.40 E
Savignano Irpino 60 41.14 N 15.11 E
Savignano sul Panaro 58 44.29 N 11.02 E
Savignano sul Rubicone 60 44.05 N 12.24 E
Savignone 56 44.34 N 8.58 E
Savigny-lès-Beaune 54 47.04 N 4.49 E
Savigny-le-Temple 251 48.35 N 2.35 E
Savigny-sur-Braye 46 47.53 N 0.49 E
Savigny-sur-Orge 46 48.40 N 2.21 E
Savincy 68 49.24 N 37.04 E
Savines 56 44.32 N 6.24 E
Savinka, S.S.S.R. 70 50.06 N 47.06 E
Savinka, S.S.S.R. 72 54.27 N 38.52 E
Savino 70 56.35 N 41.13 E
Savino-Borisovskaja 24 62.38 N 44.34 E
Savinsk 79 52.10 N 140.23 E
Savinskij 24 62.58 N 40.08 E
Savio 60 44.18 N 12.18 E
Savio ≃ 60 44.19 N 12.20 E
Saviore dell'Adamello 58 46.05 N 10.24 E
Săvîrşin 38 46.01 N 22.14 E
Şavitaipale 26 61.12 N 27.42 E
Šavnik 38 42.57 N 19.05 E
Savo I 165e 9.08 S 159.49 E
Savognin 54 40.36 N 9.36 E
Savoie □[5] 32 45.30 N 6.25 E
Savolaks ◂[1] 26 62.00 N 28.00 E
Sav'olovo 72 56.52 N 37.22 E
Savona, B.C., Can. 172 50.45 N 120.50 W
Savona, It. 56 44.17 N 8.30 E
Savona, N.Y., U.S. 200 42.17 N 77.13 W
Savona □[4] 56 44.18 N 8.16 E
Savonlinna 26 61.52 N 28.53 E
Savonnières 46 47.21 N 0.33 E
Savonranta 26 62.11 N 29.12 E
Savoonga 170 63.42 N 170.27 W
Savory Creek ≃ 152 23.22 S 122.37 E
Savoureuse ≃ 54 47.31 N 6.51 E
Savran' 68 48.09 N 30.04 E
Savruši 70 55.02 N 50.40 E
Sävsjö 26 57.25 N 14.40 E
S'avta 24 67.08 N 61.45 E
Savu Basin ✣[1] 14 9.30 S 122.00 E
Savudrija 58 45.30 N 13.30 E
Savur 120 37.33 N 40.53 E
Savusavu 165g 16.16 S 179.21 E
Savusavu Bay C 165g 16.45 S 179.15 E
Savu Sea → Sawu, Laut ▼[2] 105b 9.40 S 122.00 E
Savvatejevka 78 52.20 N 103.39 E
Savvino, S.S.S.R. 72 55.43 N 36.48 E
Savvino, S.S.S.R. 72 56.33 N 37.47 E
Savvo-Borz'a 78 50.46 N 118.18 E
Şawāb, Wādī aş- V 120 34.36 N 40.25 E
Sawada 165d 24.50 N 125.09 E
Sawah 102 2.23 N 115.14 E
Sawahlunto 102 0.40 S 100.47 E
Sawai 154 2.58 S 129.09 E
Sawai, Teluk C 154 2.52 S 129.12 E
Sawai Mādhopur 114 25.59 N 76.22 E
Sawai Madhopur □[5] 114 26.15 N 74.45 E
Sawākin 130 19.07 N 37.20 E
Sawal, Gunung ∧ 105a 7.12 S 108.16 E
Sawan, Indon. 105b 8.08 S 115.11 E
Sawan, Mya. 100 24.30 N 96.19 E
Sawang 104 0.45 N 103.21 E
Sawankhalok 100 17.19 N 99.50 E
Sawara 84 35.53 N 140.30 E
Sawata 82 38.00 N 138.16 E
Sawatch Range ∧∧ 190 39.10 N 106.25 W
Sawbridgeworth 44 51.50 N 0.09 E
Sawdā', Jabal as- ∧∧[2] 136 28.40 N 15.30 E
Sawdā', Qurnat as- ∧ 120 34.18 N 36.07 E
Sawdirī 130 14.25 N 29.05 E
Sawel Mountain ∧ 42 54.49 N 7.02 W
Sawhāj 130 26.33 N 31.42 E
Sawi 100 10.14 N 99.07 E
Sawin, Lac ⊜ 196 46.32 N 73.54 W
Sawknah 136 29.04 N 15.47 E
Şawl 132 29.21 N 31.14 E
Sawla 140 9.17 N 2.25 W
Saw Log Creek ≃ 188 38.07 N 99.42 W
Saw Mill ≃ 266 40.56 N 73.53 W
Sawmill Brook ≃, Mass., U.S. 273 42.34 N 70.46 W
Sawmill Brook ≃, N.J., U.S. 266 40.28 N 74.26 W
Sawmill Creek ≃, N.J., U.S. 266 40.46 N 74.05 W
Sawmill Creek ≃, Pa., U.S. 269b 40.10 N 79.58 W
Sawmill Pond Brook ≃ 266 41.10 N 74.23 W
Sawmill Run ≃ 275 40.07 N 75.21 W
Sawmills 144 19.31 S 28.02 E
Sawqarah, Dawḥat C 108 18.35 N 57.15 E
Sawston 44 52.07 N 0.10 E
Sawtayr ▼[4] 130 17.03 N 30.24 E
Sawtooth National Recreation Area ♠ 192 44.00 N 114.55 W
Sawtry 44 52.27 N 0.17 W
Sawu, Laut (Savu Sea) ▼[2] 105b 9.40 S 122.00 E
Sawu, Pulau I 102 10.30 S 121.54 E
Şawwān, Arḍ aş- ☷ 118 30.45 N 37.15 E
Sawyer, Mich., U.S. 206 41.53 N 86.35 W
Sawyer, N. Dak., U.S. 188 48.05 N 101.03 W
Sawyers Hill ∧[2] 176 47.11 N 53.52 W
Sawyers Valley 158a 31.54 S 116.13 E
Sawyerville, Qué., Can. 196 45.20 N 71.34 W
Sawyerville, Ill., U.S. 209 39.05 N 89.48 W
Sawyerwood 204 41.02 N 81.27 W
Saxby ≃ 156 18.25 S 140.53 E
Saxdalen 40 60.09 N 14.57 E
Saxen ⊜ 40 59.46 N 14.25 E
Saxike 110 30.44 N 86.22 E
Saxilby 42 53.17 N 0.40 W
Saxis 198 37.55 N 75.43 W
Saxmundham 44 52.13 N 1.29 E
Saxon, Schw. 54 46.09 N 7.11 E
Saxon, Wis., U.S. 180 46.29 N 90.25 W
Saxonburg 204 40.45 N 79.49 W
Saxon Woods Park ♠ 266 40.59 N 73.45 W
Saxony → Sachsen □[9] 50 51.00 N 13.30 E
Saxton 204 40.13 N 78.15 W
Say 140 13.07 N 2.21 E
Sāy, Jazīrat I 130 20.42 N 30.20 E
Saya 140 9.28 N 3.11 E
Saya de Malha Bank ✣[4] 12 10.30 S 61.00 E
Sayama, Nihon 84 35.51 N 139.24 E
Sayama, Nihon 260 34.31 N 135.34 E
Sayán 238 11.08 S 77.12 W
Sayan Mountains ∧∧ 78 52.45 N 96.00 E
Sayaxché 222 16.31 N 90.10 W
Saybrook, Ill., U.S. 206 40.26 N 88.32 W
Saybrook, Ohio, U.S. 204 41.50 N 80.51 W
Saybrook Manor 197 41.17 N 72.24 W
Sayda, D.D.R. 50 50.43 N 13.25 E
Şaydā (Sidon), Lubnān 122 33.33 N 35.22 E
Şaydnāyā 122 33.42 N 36.22 E
Sayghān 110 35.11 N 67.42 E
Sayḥūt 134 15.12 N 51.14 E
Sayil ⊥ 222 20.16 N 89.42 W
Saylah 132 29.21 N 30.58 E
Saylorsburg 200 40.54 N 75.19 W
Saylorville Lake ⊜[1] 180 41.48 N 93.46 W
Säynätsalo 26 62.08 N 25.46 E
Sayō 86 35.00 N 134.22 E
Şayq, Wādī V 134 14.36 N 47.47 E
Şayqal, Baḥr ⊜ 122 33.40 N 37.06 E
Sayre, Okla., U.S. 186 35.18 N 99.38 W
Sayre, Pa., U.S. 200 41.59 N 76.32 W
Sayreville 198 40.28 N 74.21 W
Sayula, Méx. 222 29.22 N 111.33 W
Sayula, Méx. 224 19.52 N 103.37 W
Sayula, Laguna de ⊜ 224 20.03 N 103.31 W
Sayula de Alemán 224 17.52 N 94.57 W
Say'ūn 134 15.56 N 48.47 E
Sayville 200 40.44 N 73.05 W
Sayward 172 50.22 N 125.55 W
Sazanit I 38 40.30 N 19.16 E
Sázava ≃ 30 49.53 N 14.24 E
Sazdy, S.S.S.R. 70 46.57 N 49.19 E
Sazdy, S.S.S.R. 76 47.22 N 61.48 E
Saze 56 43.56 N 4.41 E
Sažino 76 56.20 N 58.11 E
Sazlijka ≃ 38 42.02 N 25.52 E
Şazonovo 66 59.04 N 35.14 E
Šazud 110 37.43 N 72.11 E
Sazykul', Ozero ⊜ 76 55.22 N 67.34 E
Sba 138 28.13 N 0.08 W
Sbeïtla 138 35.14 N 9.08 E
Sbiba 36 35.33 N 9.05 E
Scaddan 152 33.27 S 121.43 E
Scaër 32 48.02 N 3.42 E
Scafati 60 40.45 N 14.31 E
Scafell Pikes ∧ 42 54.27 N 3.12 W
Scaggsville 198 39.09 N 76.54 W
Scajaquada Creek ≃ 274a 42.56 N 78.53 W
Scala, Teatro alla ⊻ 256b 45.28 N 9.11 E
Scalby 42 54.18 N 0.27 W
Scalea 36 39.49 N 15.48 E
Scalpay I 28 57.18 N 6.00 W
Scalp Level 204 40.15 N 78.51 W
Scammon 188 37.17 N 94.49 W
Scammon Bay 170 61.53 N 165.38 W
Scammon Bay C 170 61.53 N 165.54 W
Scandia 188 39.48 N 97.47 W
Scandiano 58 44.36 N 10.43 E
Scandicci 60 43.45 N 11.11 E
Scandinavian Peninsula ≻[1] 4 65.00 N 16.00 E
Scanlon 180 46.42 N 92.23 W
Scanno 60 41.54 N 13.53 E
Scansano 60 42.41 N 11.20 E
Scantic ≃ 197 41.52 N 72.38 W
Scapa 172 51.52 N 111.59 W
Scapa Flow U 28 58.54 N 3.05 W
Scapegoat Mountain ∧ 192 47.19 N 112.50 W
Ščapino 64 55.19 N 159.25 E
Ščapov 70 51.01 N 51.11 E
Ščapovo 72 55.09 N 38.11 E
Şcappoose 214 45.45 N 122.53 W
Ščara ≃ 66 53.27 N 24.45 E
Scarba I 28 56.11 N 5.42 W
Scarborough, Austl. 158a 31.54 S 115.45 E
Scarborough, Ont., Can. 202 43.44 N 79.16 W
Scarborough, Trin. 231r 11.11 N 60.44 W
Scarborough, Eng., U.K. 42 54.17 N 0.24 W
Scarborough Bluffs ◂[8] 265b 43.42 N 79.14 W
Scarborough Centre ◂[9] 265b 43.47 N 79.16 W
Scarborough Point ≻ 161a 27.12 S 153.07 E
Scarborough Shoal I[1] 106 15.08 N 117.46 E
Scargill 162 42.56 S 172.57 E
Scarisbrick 252 53.37 N 2.56 W
Scărișoara 38 44.00 N 24.35 E
Scarlino 60 42.54 N 10.51 E
Scarp I 28 58.02 N 7.15 W
Scarpe ≃ 46 50.30 N 3.27 E
Scarperia 60 44.00 N 11.21 E
Scarper Peak ∧ 272 37.32 N 122.26 W
Scarsdale, Austl. 159 37.40 S 143.40 E
Scarsdale, N.Y., U.S. 200 40.59 N 73.49 W
Scarth Hill 252 53.33 N 2.52 W
Ščastje 73 48.44 N 39.14 E
Scatarie Island I 176 46.00 N 59.44 W
Scatter Creek ≃ 214 46.48 N 123.06 W
Scauri 60 41.15 N 13.42 E
Scawfell Island I 156 20.52 S 149.36 E
Sceale Bay 152 33.01 S 134.12 E
Sceaux 46 48.47 N 2.17 E
Sceaux, Château de ⊥ 251 48.46 N 2.18 E
Ščedrin 66 52.53 N 29.33 E
Ščedro, Otok I 36 43.05 N 16.42 E
Ščedrovka 73 49.30 N 40.17 E
Ščeglovo 255a 60.02 N 30.46 E
Ščeljajur 24 65.21 N 53.21 E
Ščelkovo 66 55.55 N 38.00 E
Ščemilovo 255b 55.48 N 38.05 E
Scena 58 46.41 N 11.12 E
Scenery Hill 204 40.05 N 80.04 W
Scenic 214 47.43 N 121.09 W
Şceptre 174 50.51 N 109.15 W
Ščerbakovo, S.S.S.R. 64 65.15 N 160.30 E
Ščerbakovo, S.S.S.R. 76 57.04 N 73.47 E
Ščerbakty 76 52.29 N 78.09 E
Ščerbinka 72 55.31 N 37.35 E
Ščerbinovka 73 48.26 N 37.50 E
Scerni 60 42.07 N 14.34 E
Scey-sur-Saône-et-Saint-Albin 54 47.40 N 5.58 E
Schaale ≃ 50 53.21 N 10.49 E
Schaalsee ⊜ 50 53.35 N 10.57 E
Schaan 54 47.10 N 9.31 E
Schabs → Sciaves 58 46.46 N 11.40 E
Schaefferstown 198 40.18 N 76.18 W
Schaephuysen 253 51.26 N 6.29 E
Schaerbeek 46 50.51 N 4.23 E
Schaf-Berg ∧ 58 47.47 N 13.27 E
Schäferberg ∧[2] 254a 52.25 N 13.08 E
Schaffhausen 54 47.42 N 8.38 E
Schaffhausen □[3] 54 47.40 N 8.35 E
Schafstädt 50 51.23 N 11.46 E
Schäftlarn 58 47.59 N 11.28 E
Schagen 48 52.46 N 4.47 E
Schaghticoke 200 42.54 N 73.35 W
Schalchen 58 48.07 N 13.10 E
Schale 48 52.26 N 7.37 E
Schalkau 50 50.24 N 11.00 E
Schalke ◂[8] 253 51.31 N 7.05 E
Schälker Heide ◂[3] 253 51.24 N 7.36 E
Schalksmühle 52 51.14 N 7.31 E
Schaller 188 42.30 N 95.18 W
Schanck, Cape ≻ 159 38.30 S 144.53 E
Schandelah 50 52.16 N 10.41 E
S-Chane 54 46.36 N 9.59 E
Schanfigg V 54 46.51 N 9.38 E
Schanghai → Shanghai 96 31.14 N 121.28 E
Schangnau 54 46.50 N 7.52 E
Schapbach 54 48.22 N 8.17 E
Schapen 48 52.24 N 7.33 E
Schapenrust 263d 26.16 S 28.22 E
Schaprode 50 54.31 N 13.10 E
Schardenberg ∧[2] 253 51.27 N 6.28 E
Schärding 30 48.27 N 13.26 E
Scharfling 58 47.48 N 13.25 E
Schari → Chari ≃ 136 12.58 N 14.31 E
Scharl 253 51.06 N 7.40 E
Scharmützelsee ⊜ 50 52.15 N 14.03 E
Scharnhörn I 48 53.57 N 8.25 E
Scharnhorst ◂[8] 253 51.32 N 7.32 E
Scharnitz 58 47.23 N 11.17 E
Scharrel 48 53.04 N 7.42 E
Scharzfeld 48 51.37 N 10.22 E
Schässburg → Sighișoara 38 46.13 N 24.48 E
Schauinsland ∧ 54 47.55 N 7.54 E
Schaumburg 206 42.02 N 88.05 W
Schaut 74 43.43 N 42.32 E
Schebeli → Shebele ≃ 134 0.01 S 42.45 E
Scheessel 48 53.10 N 9.29 E
Scheffau an der Lammer 58 47.35 N 13.12 E
Schefferville 166 54.48 N 66.50 W
Scheggia 60 43.24 N 12.40 E
Scheggino 60 42.43 N 12.50 E
Scheibbs 30 48.00 N 15.10 E
Scheibenberg 50 50.32 N 12.55 E
Scheiblingstein 254b 48.16 N 16.13 E
Scheidegg 54 47.35 N 9.51 E
Scheinfeld 52 49.40 N 10.27 E
Schelde (Escaut) ≃ 46 51.22 N 4.15 E
Schelklingen 54 48.22 N 9.44 E
Schell Creek Range ∧∧ 194 39.10 N 114.40 W
Schellsburg 204 40.03 N 78.39 W
Schelsen ◂[8] 253 51.09 N 6.31 E
Schenectady 200 42.47 N 73.53 W
Schenectady □[6] 200 42.47 N 73.53 W
Schenefeld 48 53.36 N 9.49 E
Schenevus 200 42.33 N 74.50 W
Schenevus Creek ≃ 200 42.29 N 74.59 W
Schenkendorf 254a 52.16 N 13.35 E
Schenkenhorst 254a 52.20 N 13.12 E
Schenklengsfeld 52 50.49 N 9.50 E
Schenley 204 40.41 N 79.40 W
Schenley Park ♠ 269b 40.26 N 79.56 W
Schepsdorf-Lohne 48 52.30 N 7.16 E
Schererville 206 41.30 N 87.27 W
Scherfede 48 51.32 N 9.02 E
Scherlebeck 253 51.37 N 7.08 E
Schermbeck 48 51.41 N 6.52 E
Schermerhorn 48 52.36 N 4.52 E
Schermützelsee ⊜ 50 52.34 N 14.04 E
Scherpenheuve 52 50.59 N 4.59 E
Scherpenzeel 48 52.05 N 5.30 E
Schertz 186 29.33 N 98.16 W
Schesch, Erg → Chech, Erg ◂[2] 138 25.00 N 2.15 W
Schesslitz 52 49.59 N 11.01 E
Schevelinge-Stausee ⊜[1] 253 51.08 N 7.26 E
Scheveningen ◂[8] 48 52.06 N 4.18 E
Schiedam 48 51.55 N 4.24 E
Schieder 48 51.55 N 9.09 E
Schiefbahn 52 51.14 N 6.31 E
Schierke 50 51.46 N 10.40 E
Schiermonnikoog 48 53.24 N 6.10 E
Schiermonnikoog I 48 53.28 N 6.15 E
Schiers 54 46.59 N 9.41 E
Schiessen 54 48.18 N 10.14 E
Schiffdorf 48 53.32 N 8.39 E
Schiffenensee ⊜ 54 46.50 N 7.10 E
Schifferstadt 52 49.23 N 8.22 E
Schiffshebewerk ◂[5] 253 51.37 N 7.19 E
Schihkiatschwang → Shijiazhuang 88 38.03 N 114.28 E
Schijndel 48 51.37 N 5.25 E
Schikoku → Shikoku I 82 33.45 N 133.30 E
Schildau 50 51.27 N 12.56 E
Schilde 52 51.14 N 4.34 E
Schilde ≃ 50 53.26 N 10.53 E
Schildow 50 52.38 N 13.23 E
Schildwolde 48 53.14 N 6.49 E
Schiller Park 206 41.58 N 87.52 W
Schillingsfürst 52 49.17 N 10.15 E
Schillingstedt 50 51.14 N 11.11 E
Schilpario 58 46.01 N 10.09 E
Schiltach 54 48.17 N 8.20 E
Schiltigheim 54 48.36 N 7.45 E
Schimborn 52 50.03 N 9.11 E
Schimmert 52 50.55 N 5.50 E
Schinveld 52 50.57 N 5.59 E
Schinznach Bad 54 47.27 N 8.10 E
Schio 58 45.43 N 11.21 E
Schiphol, Luchthaven ⊠ 48 52.17 N 4.40 E
Schipkau 50 51.31 N 13.53 E
Schippenbeil → Sępopol 30 54.15 N 21.00 E
Schirgiswalde 50 51.05 N 14.27 E
Schirmeck 54 48.29 N 7.13 E
Schirnding 50 50.05 N 12.13 E
Schisuoka → Shizuoka 84 34.58 N 138.23 E
Schivelbein → Świdwin 30 53.47 N 15.47 E
Schjetman Reef ✣[2] 14 15.10 N 178.40 W
Schkeuditz 50 51.24 N 12.13 E
Schkoder-See → Scutari, Lake ⊜ 38 42.12 N 19.18 E
Schkölen 50 51.02 N 11.49 E
Schkopau 50 51.23 N 11.59 E
Schladen 50 52.01 N 10.32 E
Schladming 58 47.23 N 13.41 E
Schlanders → Silandro 58 46.38 N 10.46 E

Symbol	English	Deutsch	Español	Français	Português
≃	River	Fluss	Río	Rivière	Rio
⩸	Canal	Kanal	Canal	Canal	Canal
⌊	Waterfall, Rapids	Wasserfall, Stromschnellen	Cascada, Rápidos	Chute d'eau, Rapides	Cascata, Rápidos
U	Strait	Meeresstrasse	Estrecho	Détroit	Estreito
C	Bay, Gulf	Bucht, Golf	Bahía, Golfo	Baie, Golfe	Baía, Golfo
⊜	Lake, Lakes	See, Seen	Lago, Lagos	Lac, Lacs	Lago, Lagos
☷	Swamp	Sumpf	Pantano	Marais	Pântano
⩢	Ice Features, Glacier	Eis- und Gletscherformen	Accidentes Glaciales	Formes glaciaires	Acidentes Glaciares
▼	Other Hydrographic Features	Andere Hydrographische Objekte	Otros Elementos Hidrográficos	Autres données hydrographiques	Outros Elementos Hidrográficos
✣	Submarine Features	Untermeerische Objekte	Accidentes Submarinos	Formes de relief sous-marin	Acidentes Submarinos
□	Political Unit	Politische Einheit	Unidad Política	Entité politique	Unidade Política
⊻	Cultural Institution	Kulturelle Institution	Institución Cultural	Institution culturelle	Instituição Cultural
⊥	Historical Site	Historische Stätte	Sitio Histórico	Site historique	Sitio Histórico
♠	Recreational Site	Erholungs- und Ferienort	Sitio de Recreo	Centre de loisirs	Sítio de Lazer
⊠	Airport	Flughafen	Aeropuerto	Aéroport	Aeroporto
▪	Military Installation	Militäranlage	Instalación Militar	Installation militaire	Instalação Militar
◂	Miscellaneous	Verschiedenes	Misceláneo	Divers	Miscelânea

Schlangen 48 51.49 N 8.50 E
Schlangenbad 52 50.05 N 8.05 E
Schlänitz-See 254a 52.27 N 12.57 E
Schlanstedt 50 52.00 N 11.02 E
Schlater 184 33.38 N 90.21 W
Schlegel Lake 266 40.59 N 74.03 W
Schlei 41 54.36 N 9.51 E
Schleiden 52 50.31 N 6.28 E
Schleife 50 51.32 N 14.32 E
Schleinitz Range 154 3.10 S 151.40 E
Schleithal 52 48.59 N 8.02 E
Schleitheim 54 47.45 N 8.29 E
Schleiz 50 50.34 N 11.49 E
Schlema 50 50.40 N 12.40 E
Schlepzig 50 52.01 N 13.53 E
Schlesischer (Ost) Bahnhof 254a 52.30 N 13.26 E
Schleswig, B.R.D. 41 54.31 N 9.33 E
Schleswig, Iowa, U.S. 188 42.10 N 95.26 W
Schleswig-Holstein □3 30 54.00 N 10.30 E
Schlettau 50 50.33 N 12.56 E
Schlettstadt → Sélestat 54 48.16 N 7.27 E
Schleusingen 50 50.31 N 10.45 E
Schlichtingsheim → Szlichtyngowa 30 51.43 N 16.15 E
Schlicke 54 47.31 N 10.37 E
Schlieben 50 51.43 N 13.23 E
Schliengen 54 47.46 N 7.35 E
Schlieren 54 47.24 N 8.27 E
Schliersee 58 47.44 N 11.51 E
Schlitz 52 50.40 N 9.33 E
Schlochau → Człuchów 30 53.41 N 17.21 E
Schloppe → Człopa 30 53.06 N 16.08 E
Schloss Holte 48 51.52 N 8.35 E
Schloss Neuhaus 48 51.44 N 8.43 E
Schlossvippach 50 51.06 N 11.08 E
Schloss Zeil 58 47.52 N 10.00 E
Schlotheim 50 51.14 N 10.39 E
Schluchsee 54 47.49 N 8.10 E
Schluchsee 54 47.49 N 8.10 E
Schlucht, Col de la 54 48.04 N 7.02 E
Schlüchtern 52 50.20 N 9.31 E
Schluderns → Sluderno 58 46.40 N 10.35 E
Schlüsselburg 48 52.29 N 9.04 E
Schlüsselfeld 52 49.45 N 10.37 E
Schlutup 50 53.53 N 10.48 E
Schmachtendorf 253 51.32 N 6.49 E
Schmalfeld 48 53.52 N 9.58 E
Schmalkalden 50 50.43 N 10.26 E
Schmallenberg 52 51.09 N 8.17 E
Schmalnau 52 50.27 N 9.47 E
Schmannewitz 50 51.24 N 12.58 E
Schmarsau 50 52.54 N 11.21 E
Schmelz 52 49.27 N 6.51 E
Schmidmühlen 30 49.16 N 11.56 E
Schmidt 52 50.39 N 6.25 E
Schmidtsdrif 148 28.41 S 24.02 E
Schmiedeberg, D.D.R. 50 50.50 N 13.40 E
Schmiedefeld 50 50.37 N 10.49 E
Schmilka 50 50.53 N 14.14 E
Schmöckwitz 254a 52.23 N 13.39 E
Schmölln 50 50.53 N 12.20 E
Schmutter 54 48.42 N 10.46 E
Schnackenburg 50 53.02 N 11.32 E
Schnait 52 48.47 N 9.23 E
Schnaitsee 58 48.04 N 12.22 E
Schnakenbek 48 53.23 N 10.30 E
Schnecksville 198 40.41 N 75.36 W
Schneeberg 50 50.36 N 12.38 E
Schneeberg 50 50.03 N 11.51 E
Schneegattern 58 48.01 N 13.18 E
Schneidemühl → Piła 30 53.10 N 16.44 E
Schneider 206 41.11 N 87.27 W
Schneifel 52 50.15 N 6.25 E
Schneverdingen 48 53.07 N 9.47 E
Schney 52 50.09 N 11.13 E
Schober Gruppe 58 46.55 N 12.42 E
Schobüll 41 54.30 N 9.00 E
Schodn'a 72 55.57 N 37.18 E
Schodn'a 255b 55.50 N 37.25 E
Schoenbrunn Village State Memorial 204 40.27 N 81.24 W
Schofield 180 44.54 N 89.36 W
Schofield Barracks 219c 21.30 N 158.04 W
Schofields 264a 33.42 S 150.52 E
Schöftland 54 47.18 N 8.03 E
Schoharie 200 42.40 N 74.19 W
Schoharie □6 200 42.40 N 74.19 W
Schoharie Creek 200 42.57 N 74.18 W
Schoharie Reservoir 200 42.22 N 74.26 W
Scholen 48 52.44 N 8.46 E
Schollene 50 52.41 N 12.13 E
Schöllenen 54 46.40 N 8.35 E
Schöller 253 51.14 N 7.01 E
Schöllkrippen 52 50.05 N 9.14 E
Scholls 214 45.24 N 122.56 W
Scholven 253 51.36 N 7.01 E
Schömberg, B.R.D. 52 48.47 N 8.38 E
Schömberg, B.R.D. 54 48.13 N 8.46 E
Schomberg, Ont., Can. 202 44.00 N 79.41 W
Schönach 54 48.08 N 8.11 E
Schönaich 52 48.39 N 9.03 E
Schönau, B.R.D. 52 49.26 N 8.49 E
Schönau, B.R.D. 54 47.47 N 7.53 E
Schönau, B.R.D. 58 47.37 N 12.59 E
Schönau → Świerzawa, Pol. 30 51.01 N 15.54 E
Schönbeck 50 53.34 N 13.34 E
Schönberg, B.R.D. 50 54.23 N 10.22 E
Schönberg, D.D.R. 50 50.11 N 12.19 E
Schönberg, D.D.R. 50 53.50 N 11.38 E
Schönberg, D.D.R. 50 50.31 N 11.57 E
Schönberger Strand 50 54.25 N 10.24 E
Schönberg im Stubaital 58 47.11 N 11.25 E
Schönbrunn 50 50.32 N 10.53 E
Schönbrunn, Schloss 254b 48.11 N 16.19 E
Schönbrunner Schlosspark 254b 48.11 N 16.19 E
Schondra 52 50.07 N 9.44 E
Schönebeck, D.D.R. 50 53.03 N 12.13 E
Schönebeck, D.D.R. 50 52.01 N 11.44 E
Schönebeck 253 51.28 N 6.56 E
Schöneberg 254a 52.29 N 13.21 E
Schöneck 50 50.23 N 12.20 E
Schönecken 52 50.09 N 6.27 E
Schönefeld 254a 52.23 N 13.30 E
Schönefeld, Zentralflughafen 50 52.23 N 13.31 E
Schöneiche 50 52.28 N 13.41 E
Schönenwerd 54 47.22 N 8.00 E
Schönerlinde 254a 52.39 N 13.27 E
Schönewalde 50 51.49 N 13.13 E
Schönfeld 254a 52.41 N 13.44 E
Schönfliess 254a 52.39 N 13.20 E
Schongau 54 47.49 N 10.54 E
Schönhagen, B.R.D. 50 54.38 N 10.01 E
Schönhagen, B.R.D. 48 51.41 N 9.33 E
Schönhausen, B.R.D. 50 51.37 N 7.38 E
Schönhausen, D.D.R. 50 52.35 N 12.02 E
Schönheide 50 50.30 N 12.31 E
Schönholthausen 52 51.11 N 8.00 E
Schöningen 50 52.08 N 10.58 E
Schönkirchen 50 54.20 N 10.15 E
Schönlanke → Trzcianka 30 53.03 N 16.28 E
Schönmünzach 52 48.36 N 8.22 E
Schönnebeck 253 51.29 N 7.04 E
Schönningstedt 48 53.32 N 10.15 E
Schönow 50 52.40 N 13.32 E
Schonungen 52 50.03 N 10.18 E
Schönwald 54 48.06 N 8.11 E
Schönwalde, B.R.D. 50 54.11 N 10.45 E
Schönwalde, D.D.R. 50 52.37 N 13.07 E
Schönwalde, D.D.R. 50 52.40 N 13.26 E
Schönwalde, Forst 254a 52.42 N 13.28 E
Schönwies 54 47.11 N 10.39 E
Schoodic Lake 176 45.21 N 68.54 W
Schoolcraft 206 42.07 N 85.38 W
Schoolhouse Run 275 40.13 N 75.27 W
Schoombee 148 31.28 S 25.30 E
Schoondijke 48 51.21 N 3.32 E
Schoonebeek 48 52.39 N 6.52 E
Schoonhoven 48 51.56 N 4.51 E
Schoorl 48 52.42 N 4.41 E
Schopfheim 54 47.39 N 7.49 E
Schopfloch 52 49.07 N 10.18 E
Schopp 52 49.21 N 7.41 E
Schöppenstedt 50 52.08 N 10.46 E
Schöppingen 48 52.05 N 7.14 E
Schorfheide 50 52.56 N 13.43 E
Schorfheide 50 52.55 N 13.35 E
Schörfling 58 47.56 N 13.36 E
Schorndorf 52 48.48 N 9.31 E
Schortens 48 53.31 N 7.56 E
Schoten 46 51.15 N 4.30 E
Schötmar 48 52.04 N 8.45 E
Schotten 52 50.30 N 9.07 E
Schottland → Scotland □8 28 57.00 N 4.00 W
Schouten, Kepulauan II 154 0.55 S 135.55 E
Schouten Island I 156 42.19 S 148.17 E
Schouten Islands II 154 3.30 S 144.40 E
Schouwen I 48 51.43 N 3.50 E
Schrader Creek 200 41.43 N 76.30 W
Schrader Range 154 5.05 S 144.15 E
Schramberg 54 48.13 N 8.23 E
Schram City 209 39.10 N 89.27 W
Schrankogel 58 47.03 N 11.06 E
Schraplau 50 51.26 N 11.40 E
Schreiber 180 48.48 N 87.15 W
Schriever 184 29.45 N 90.49 W
Schrobenhausen 30 48.33 N 11.17 E
Schröcken 54 47.15 N 10.05 E
Schroon 178 43.29 N 73.49 W
Schroon Lake 178 43.47 N 73.46 W
Schrozberg 52 49.20 N 9.59 E
Schruns 54 47.04 N 9.55 E
Schulenburg, B.R.D. 48 52.12 N 9.47 E
Schulenburg, Tex., U.S. 212 29.41 N 96.54 W
Schull 28 51.32 N 9.33 W
Schuls → Scuol 54 46.48 N 10.18 E
Schultz Lake 166 64.45 N 97.30 W
Schulzendorf 52 52.22 N 13.35 E
Schulzenhöhe 254a 52.29 N 13.47 E
Schumacher 180 48.28 N 81.18 W
Schüpfheim 54 46.57 N 8.01 E
Schüren 253 51.30 N 7.32 E
Schussen 54 47.37 N 9.32 E
Schussenried 54 48.00 N 9.40 E
Schutter 54 48.34 N 7.50 E
Schüttorf 48 52.19 N 7.13 E
Schützenbruch → Kalety 30 50.34 N 18.54 E
Schuyler, Nebr., U.S. 188 41.27 N 97.04 W
Schuyler, Va., U.S. 192 37.47 N 78.42 W
Schuyler □6, Ill., U.S. 209 40.07 N 90.34 W
Schuyler □6, N.Y., U.S. 200 42.23 N 76.52 W
Schuyler Lake 200 42.47 N 75.02 W
Schuylerville 200 43.06 N 73.35 W
Schuylkill □6 200 40.41 N 76.12 W
Schuylkill 198 39.53 N 75.12 W
Schuylkill Canal 275 40.14 N 75.42 W
Schuylkill Haven 198 40.38 N 76.10 W
Schwaan 50 53.56 N 12.06 E
Schwabach 52 49.20 N 11.01 E
Schwaben □5 54 48.15 N 10.30 E
Schwaben □9 54 48.15 N 10.30 E
Schwabing 58 48.10 N 11.34 E
Schwäbische Alb 54 48.25 N 9.30 E
Schwäbisch Gmünd 52 48.48 N 9.47 E
Schwäbisch Hall 52 49.07 N 9.44 E
Schwabmünchen 58 48.11 N 10.45 E
Schwabstedt 41 54.23 N 9.11 E
Schwadorf 254b 48.04 N 16.35 E
Schwafheim 253 51.25 N 6.39 E
Schwagstorf 48 52.31 N 7.45 E
Schwaigern 52 49.08 N 9.03 E
Schwalenberg 48 51.52 N 9.11 E
Schwalm 52 51.10 N 9.25 E
Schwalm-Nette, Naturpark 52 51.15 N 6.15 E
Schwalmtal 52 51.13 N 6.16 E
Schwanden 54 47.00 N 9.04 E
Schwandorf in Bayern 30 49.20 N 12.08 E
Schwanebeck, D.D.R. 50 52.37 N 13.32 E
Schwanebeck, D.D.R. 50 51.58 N 11.07 E
Schwanenstadt 58 48.03 N 13.46 E
Schwanenwerder 254a 52.27 N 13.10 E
Schwaner, Pegunungan 102 0.40 S 112.40 E
Schwanewede 48 53.14 N 8.35 E
Schwangau 54 47.35 N 10.44 E
Schwansen 41 54.35 N 9.50 E
Schwante 254a 52.43 N 13.07 E
Schwarme 48 52.54 N 9.01 E
Schwarmstedt 48 52.40 N 9.37 E
Schwartau 50 53.56 N 10.41 E
Schwarza, D.D.R. 50 50.41 N 11.19 E
Schwarza, D.D.R. 50 50.38 N 10.32 E
Schwarza, D.D.R. 50 50.41 N 11.19 E
Schwarza, Öst. 30 47.43 N 16.13 E
Schwarzach 54 47.27 N 9.45 E
Schwarzach im Pongau 58 47.19 N 13.09 E
Schwarzbach 58 47.46 N 12.55 E
Schwarzbach, B.R.D. 52 49.16 N 7.18 E
Schwarzbach, B.R.D. 253 51.19 N 6.44 E
Schwarzburg 50 50.38 N 11.12 E
Schwarze Elster 50 51.49 N 12.51 E
Schwarzenbach am Wald 50 50.17 N 11.37 E
Schwarzenbach an der Saale 50 50.13 N 11.56 E
Schwarzenbek 48 53.30 N 10.29 E
Schwarzenberg, B.R.D. 253 51.24 N 6.42 E
Schwarzenberg, D.D.R. 50 50.32 N 12.47 E
Schwarzenberg Park 254b 48.14 N 16.15 E
Schwarzenborn 52 50.37 N 9.58 E
Schwarzenburg 54 46.49 N 7.21 E
Schwarze Pumpe 50 51.32 N 14.20 E
Schwarzer Berg 253 51.41 N 7.12 E
Schwarzer Mann 52 50.15 N 6.21 E
Schwarzes Meer → Black Sea 22 43.00 N 35.00 E
Schwarzheide 50 51.29 N 13.51 E
Schwarzrand 146 25.37 S 16.50 E
Schwarzsee 54 46.40 N 7.20 E
Schwarzwald (Black Forest) 54 48.00 N 8.15 E
Schwarzwälder Hochwald 52 49.39 N 6.55 E
Schwatka Mountains 170 67.25 N 157.00 W
Schwaz 58 47.20 N 11.42 E
Schwechat 254b 48.08 N 16.29 E
Schwechat 254b 48.08 N 16.29 E
Schweden → Sweden □1 24 62.00 N 15.00 E
Schwedeneck 41 54.27 N 10.05 E
Schwedt 50 53.03 N 14.17 E
Schweez 50 53.53 N 12.24 E
Schweflinghausen 253 51.16 N 7.25 E
Schwegenheim 52 49.16 N 8.20 E
Schwei 48 53.24 N 8.21 E
Schweich 52 49.49 N 6.45 E
Schweidnitz → Świdnica 30 50.51 N 16.29 E
Schweighausen 54 48.13 N 7.57 E
Schweighausen-sur-Moder 52 48.49 N 7.44 E
Schweinfurt 52 50.03 N 10.14 E
Schweinitz 50 51.48 N 13.01 E
Schweinrich 50 53.10 N 12.37 E
Schweiz → Switzerland □1 54 47.00 N 8.00 E
Schweizer-Reneke 148 27.11 S 25.18 E
Schwelm 52 51.17 N 7.17 E
Schwendi 54 48.10 N 9.58 E
Schwenke 253 51.11 N 7.26 E
Schwenksville 275 40.16 N 75.28 W
Schwepnitz 50 51.20 N 13.57 E
Schwerin 50 53.38 N 11.25 E
Schwerin □5 50 53.30 N 11.30 E
Schwerin 253 51.33 N 7.20 E
Schweriner See 50 53.45 N 11.28 E
Schwerte 52 51.26 N 7.34 E
Schwetzingen 52 49.23 N 8.34 E
Schweyen 52 49.10 N 7.24 E
Schwieberdingen 52 48.52 N 9.04 E
Schwiebus → Świebodzin 30 52.15 N 15.32 E
Schwielochsee 50 52.03 N 14.12 E
Schwielowsee, D.D.R. 50 52.20 N 12.57 E
Schwielow-See, D.D.R. 254a 52.20 N 12.57 E
Schwitten 253 51.27 N 7.48 E
Schwyz 54 47.02 N 8.40 E
Schwyz □3 54 47.05 N 8.40 E
Sciacca 36 37.30 N 13.06 E
Sciaves (Schabs) 58 46.48 N 11.40 E
Scicli 36 36.47 N 14.43 E
Scie 46 49.55 N 1.02 E
Science and Industry, Museum of 268 41.47 N 87.35 W
Sciez 54 46.20 N 6.23 E
Ščigry 68 51.53 N 36.55 E
Scilla 36 38.15 N 15.44 E
Scilly I 14 16.30 S 154.40 W
Scilly, Isles of II 28 49.55 N 6.20 W
Ścinawa 30 51.25 N 16.27 E
Scio, N.Y., U.S. 200 42.10 N 77.59 W
Scio, Ohio, U.S. 204 40.24 N 81.05 W
Scio, Oreg., U.S. 192 44.42 N 122.51 W
Scionzier 54 46.03 N 6.34 E
Sciota 200 40.56 N 75.19 W
Scioto 204 38.48 N 83.01 W
Scioto □6 208 38.48 N 83.01 W
Scioto 178 38.44 N 83.01 W
Scioto Brush Creek 208 38.50 N 83.01 W
Scipio, Ind., U.S. 208 39.05 N 85.43 W
Scipio, Utah, U.S. 190 39.15 N 112.06 W
Scipio Center 200 42.47 N 76.34 W
Scippo Creek 208 39.31 N 82.59 W
Ščit 36 44.02 N 17.47 E
Ščitkoviči 66 53.13 N 27.59 E
Scituate 197 42.12 N 70.44 W
Scituate Reservoir 197 41.47 N 71.36 W
Sciuĕref 135 29.53 N 14.08 E
Scobey 192 48.47 N 105.29 W
Scoffera, Passo della 56 44.29 N 9.07 E
Scofield Reservoir 190 39.47 N 111.09 W
Ščokino 66 54.01 N 37.31 E
Scole 44 52.22 N 1.10 E
Ščolkovo 72 55.55 N 38.00 E
Scoltenna 58 44.15 N 10.50 E
Scolt Head 44 52.58 N 0.42 E
Scone 156 32.03 S 150.52 E
Scooba 184 32.50 N 88.29 W
Scopello 56 45.46 N 8.06 E
Scordia 36 37.18 N 14.51 E
Scoresby 264b 37.54 S 145.14 E
Scorno, Punta di 36 41.07 N 8.19 E
Scorrano 60 42.35 N 13.49 E
Ščors 68 51.49 N 31.59 E
Ščorsk 68 48.22 N 34.06 E
Scorzè 58 45.34 N 12.06 E
Scotch 196 45.27 N 74.59 W
Scotch Plains 200 40.37 N 74.24 W
Scotchtown 200 41.29 N 74.21 W
Scotia, Nebr., U.S. 188 41.28 N 98.42 W
Scotia, N.Y., U.S. 200 44.54 N 73.33 W
Scotia Lake 180 47.05 N 81.23 W
Scotia Ridge 9 57.00 S 27.00 W
Scotia Sea 9 56.00 S 40.00 W
Scotland, Ont., Can. 202 43.01 N 80.22 W
Scotland, Pa., U.S. 198 39.58 N 77.35 W
Scotland, S. Dak., U.S. 188 43.09 N 97.43 W
Scotland, Tex., U.S. 186 33.40 N 98.28 W
Scotland □8 28 57.00 N 4.00 W
Scotland Neck 182 36.02 N 77.32 W
Scotland Run 275 39.39 N 75.03 W
Scotlandville 184 30.31 N 91.11 W
Ščot'ovo 73 48.09 N 39.04 E
Scotrun 200 41.04 N 75.19 W
Scotsburn 176 45.39 N 62.51 W
Scotstown 196 45.32 N 71.17 W
Scott, Sask., Can. 174 52.21 N 108.50 W
Scott, Miss., U.S. 184 33.36 N 91.04 W
Scott, Ohio, U.S. 206 40.59 N 84.35 W
Scott □6, Ill., U.S. 209 39.38 N 90.27 W
Scott □6, Ind., U.S. 208 38.41 N 85.46 W
Scott □6, Ky., U.S. 208 38.18 N 84.35 W
Scott 194 41.48 N 123.02 W
Scott, Cape 172 50.47 N 128.26 W
Scott, Mount, Okla., U.S. 186 34.44 N 98.32 W
Scott, Mount, Oreg., U.S. 192 42.56 N 122.01 W
Scott Air Force Base 209 38.32 N 89.52 W
Scott Base 9 77.50 S 166.25 E
Scottburgh 148 30.19 S 30.40 E
Scott City 188 38.29 N 100.54 W
Scott Cove 266 41.03 N 73.28 W
Scott Creek 216 37.02 N 122.13 W
Scottdale, Mich., U.S. 206 42.03 N 86.27 W
Scottdale, Pa., U.S. 204 40.06 N 79.35 W
Scott Glacier, Ant. 9 85.45 S 153.00 W
Scott Glacier, Ant. 9 66.15 S 100.05 E
Scott Haven 269b 40.15 N 79.47 W
Scott Island I 202 44.36 N 76.20 W
Scott Islands II 172 50.48 N 128.40 W
Scott Mountain 192 44.11 N 115.47 W
Scott Peak 190 44.21 N 112.50 W
Scott Reef 150 14.00 S 121.50 E
Scott Run 274c 38.51 N 77.13 W
Scotts 206 42.11 N 85.25 W
Scottsbluff 188 41.52 N 103.40 W
Scotts Bluff National Monument 188 41.49 N 103.41 W
Scottsboro 184 34.40 N 86.02 W
Scottsburg, Ind., U.S. 208 38.41 N 85.46 W
Scottsburg, N.Y., U.S. 200 42.40 N 77.43 W
Scottsdale, Austl. 156 41.10 S 147.31 E
Scottsdale, Ariz., U.S. 190 33.30 N 111.56 W
Scotts Flat Reservoir 216 39.17 N 120.55 W
Scotts Head 230d 15.13 N 61.23 W
Scotts Level Branch 274b 39.22 N 76.45 W
Scottsmoor 210 28.46 N 80.53 W
Scott State Park 188 38.40 N 100.54 W
Scotts Valley 216 37.03 N 122.02 W
Scottsville, Ky., U.S. 184 36.45 N 86.11 W
Scottsville, N.Y., U.S. 200 43.01 N 77.45 W
Scott Township 269b 40.24 N 80.06 W
Scottville, Ill., U.S. 209 39.29 N 90.06 W
Scottville, Mich., U.S. 180 43.57 N 86.17 W
Scour 42 55.13 N 3.46 W
Scourie 28 58.20 N 5.08 W
Scout Lake 174 49.22 N 106.00 W
Scranton, Iowa, U.S. 188 42.01 N 94.33 W
Scranton, N. Dak., U.S. 188 46.09 N 103.09 W
Scranton, N.Y., U.S. 200 42.44 N 78.50 W
Scranton, Pa., U.S. 200 41.24 N 75.40 W
Scremerston 42 55.44 N 1.59 W
Screven 182 31.29 N 82.01 W
Screw 154 3.55 S 142.50 E
Scribner 188 41.40 N 96.40 W
Scripps Institution of Oceanography 218 32.52 N 117.15 W
Scrivia 56 45.03 N 8.54 E
Scroggins 212 32.58 N 95.11 W
Scrooby 42 53.25 N 1.01 W
Scrub Island I 230m 18.28 N 64.31 W
Ščučin 66 53.36 N 24.45 E
Ščučinsk 76 52.56 N 70.12 E
Ščučje, S.S.S.R. 70 51.46 N 40.29 E
Ščučje, S.S.S.R. 76 55.17 N 63.59 E
Ščučje Ozero 76 56.28 N 56.38 E
Scugog 202 44.24 N 78.45 W
Scugog, Lake 202 44.10 N 78.51 W
Scugog Indian Reserve 202 44.11 N 78.54 W
Scugog Island I 202 44.10 N 78.53 W
Ščukino 72 54.28 N 37.01 E
Scunthorpe 42 53.36 N 0.38 W
Scuol (Schuls) 54 46.48 N 10.18 E
Scuppernong 206 42.54 N 88.42 W
Scurcola Marsicana 60 42.03 N 13.20 E
Ščurovo 72 55.03 N 38.49 E
Scurry 212 32.31 N 96.23 W
Scutari → Shkodër, Shq. 38 42.05 N 19.30 E
Scutari → Üsküdar, Tür. 120 41.01 N 29.01 E
Scutari, Lake 38 42.12 N 19.18 E
Sé 277b 23.33 S 46.37 W
Seabeck 214 47.38 N 122.51 W
Sea Bird Island Indian Reserve 172 49.17 N 121.42 W
Seaboard 182 36.24 N 77.26 W
Sea Bright 200 40.22 N 73.59 W
Seabrook, Md., U.S. 274c 38.58 N 76.51 W
Seabrook, N.J., U.S. 198 39.30 N 74.14 W
Seabrook, Tex., U.S. 212 29.34 N 95.02 W
Seabrook, Lake 152 30.56 S 119.40 E
Sea Cliff 200 40.51 N 73.38 W
Seacock Swamp 198 36.48 N 76.51 W
Seacombe 252 53.25 N 3.01 W
Sea Dog Island I 266 40.36 N 73.35 W
Seadrift 186 28.30 N 96.47 W
Seaford, Eng., U.K. 44 50.46 N 0.06 E
Seaford, Del., U.S. 198 38.39 N 75.37 W
Seaford, N.Y., U.S. 266 40.40 N 73.30 W
Seaford, Va., U.S. 198 37.12 N 76.26 W
Seaford Creek 266 40.38 N 73.29 W
Seaforth, Austl. 264a 33.48 S 151.15 E
Seaforth, Ont., Can. 180 43.33 N 81.24 W
Seaforth, Eng., U.K. 252 53.28 N 3.01 W
Seafox Seamount 14 30.30 S 172.40 W
Seager Wheeler Lake 174 54.27 N 103.30 W
Seagoville 212 32.38 N 96.32 W
Seagraves 186 32.57 N 102.34 W
Seaham 42 54.52 N 1.21 W
Seaholme 264b 37.52 S 144.50 E
Seahorse Point 166 63.47 N 80.09 W
Seahorse Shoal 102 5.30 N 112.37 E
Seahouses 42 55.35 N 1.38 W
Seahurst 214 47.28 N 122.22 W
Sea Island I 214 49.12 N 123.10 W
Sea Islands II 182 31.20 N 81.20 W
Sea Isle City 198 39.09 N 74.42 W
Seal 250 51.17 N 0.14 E
Seal 166 59.04 N 94.48 W
Seal, Cape 148 34.07 S 23.25 E
Sea Lake 156 35.30 S 142.51 E
Sealand 252 53.12 N 2.58 W
Sealark Channel 165e 9.18 S 160.20 E
Seal Bay 9 71.40 S 12.25 W
Seal Beach 218 33.44 N 118.06 W
Seal Beach Naval Weapons Station ■ 270 33.45 N 118.03 W
Seal Cove, N.B., Can. 176 44.39 N 66.51 W
Seal Cove, Newf., Can. 176 47.28 N 53.05 W
Sealdah Railroad Station 262b 22.34 N 88.23 E
Seale 184 32.18 N 85.10 W
Sealevel 182 34.52 N 76.23 W
Seal Harbor 176 44.18 N 68.14 W
Seal Islands II 272 38.03 N 122.03 W
Seal Lake 166 54.18 N 61.40 W
Seal Rocks II 272 37.47 N 122.31 W
Sealston 198 38.16 N 77.20 W
Sealy 212 29.47 N 96.09 W
Seaman 208 38.56 N 83.34 W
Seanor 204 40.13 N 78.54 W
Sear 242 27.07 S 52.17 W
Searchlight 190 35.28 N 114.55 W
Searcy 184 35.15 N 91.44 W
Searles Lake 194 35.43 N 117.20 W
Sears Lake 271 42.35 N 83.39 W
Searsport 178 44.28 N 68.56 W
Searsville Lake 272 37.24 N 122.14 W
Seascale 42 54.24 N 3.29 W
Seashore State Park 198 36.54 N 76.02 W
Seaside, Calif., U.S. 216 36.37 N 121.50 W
Seaside, Oreg., U.S. 214 46.02 N 123.55 W
Seaside Park 198 39.55 N 74.05 W
Seaside Park 266 41.10 N 73.12 W
Seaton, Eng., U.K. 42 53.54 N 0.14 W
Seaton, Eng., U.K. 42 54.41 N 3.33 W
Seaton, Eng., U.K. 44 50.43 N 3.05 W
Seaton 44 50.22 N 4.22 W
Seaton Delaval 42 55.04 N 1.31 W
Seat Pleasant 274c 38.53 N 76.54 W
Seattle 214 47.36 N 122.20 W
Seattle, Mount 170 60.06 N 139.11 W
Seattle Heights 214 47.48 N 122.20 W
Seattle-tacoma International Airport 214 47.27 N 122.18 W
Seatuck National Wildlife Refuge 266 40.43 N 73.13 W
Sea View, Mass., U.S. 273 42.08 N 70.43 W
Seaview, N.Y., U.S. 266 40.39 N 73.09 W
Seaview, Wash., U.S. 214 46.20 N 124.03 W
Seaward Kaikoura Range 162 42.14 S 173.39 E
Seaward Roads 164g 28.13 N 177.25 W
Seawell Airport 231g 13.04 N 59.29 W
Sea World, Fla., U.S. 210 28.25 N 81.28 W
Sea World, Ohio, U.S. 204 41.21 N 81.23 W
Seba 102 10.29 S 121.50 E
Sebaco 236 12.51 N 86.06 W
Sebago Lake 178 43.50 N 70.35 W
Se Bai 100 15.13 N 105.48 E
Sebakor, Teluk 154 3.35 S 132.50 E
Sebakung 102 1.37 S 116.26 E
Sebakwe National Park 144 19.00 S 30.14 E
Šebalino, S.S.S.R. 70 47.22 N 43.36 E
Šebalino, S.S.S.R. 86 51.17 N 85.40 E
Sebanga 104 1.24 N 101.10 E
Sebangan, Teluk 102 3.18 S 114.35 E
Sebaou, Oued 34 36.55 N 3.55 E
Sebarok, Pulau I 261c 1.13 N 103.48 E
Sebastian, Fla., U.S. 210 27.49 N 80.28 W
Sebastian, Tex., U.S. 186 26.20 N 97.47 W
Sebastian, Cape 192 42.19 N 124.26 W
Sebastian Inlet 210 27.51 N 80.26 W
Sebastián Vizcaíno, Bahía 222 28.00 N 114.30 W
Sebastião de Lacerda 246 22.17 S 43.35 W
Sebastopol, Austl. 159 37.36 S 143.51 E
Sebastopol, Calif., U.S. 194 38.24 N 122.49 W
Sebastopol, Miss., U.S. 184 32.34 N 89.27 W
Sebatik, Pulau I 102 4.08 N 117.47 E
Sebba 140 13.26 N 0.32 E
Sebderat 134 15.26 N 36.40 E
Sébé 142 1.02 S 13.06 E
Sebec Lake 176 45.18 N 69.18 W
Sebei □5 144 1.25 N 34.25 E
Sebeka 188 46.38 N 95.05 W
Šebekino 68 50.25 N 36.56 E
Sébékoro 140 12.57 N 8.59 W
Šebelinka 68 49.27 N 36.30 E
Seben 120 40.24 N 31.34 E
Sebenico → Šibenik 36 43.44 N 15.54 E
Seberi 242 27.29 S 53.24 W
Seberida 102 0.43 S 102.31 E
Seberta 78 54.40 N 99.54 E
Sebeş 38 45.58 N 23.34 E
Sebesi, Pulau I 105a 5.57 S 105.30 E
Sebes Körös (Crişu Repede) 38 46.55 N 20.59 E
Sebeşului, Munţii 38 45.38 N 23.27 E
Sebewaing 180 43.44 N 83.27 W
Sebež 66 56.17 N 28.29 E
Sebidiro 154 9.00 S 142.15 E
Sebille Manor 271 42.39 N 82.49 W
Sebinkarahisar 120 40.18 N 38.26 E
Sebiş 38 46.23 N 22.08 E
Sebnitz 50 50.58 N 14.16 E
Sebou, Oued 138 34.15 N 6.40 W
Sebree 184 37.36 N 87.32 W
Sebrell 198 36.47 N 77.07 W
Sebring, Fla., U.S. 210 27.30 N 81.26 W
Sebring, Ohio, U.S. 204 40.55 N 81.01 W
Sebringville 202 43.24 N 81.04 W
Sebseb, Oued 138 32.04 N 4.19 E
Sebuku 102 4.03 N 116.56 E
Sebuku, Pulau I, Indon. 102 3.30 S 116.22 E
Sebuku, Pulau I, Indon. 105a 5.53 S 105.31 E
Šebunino 79 46.27 N 141.51 E
Sêca, Ilha I 277a 22.50 S 43.11 W
Secane 198 39.55 N 75.18 W
Secang 105a 7.23 S 110.15 E
Secas, Islas II 226 7.58 N 82.02 W
Secaucus 266 40.47 N 74.04 W
Secchia 58 45.04 N 11.00 E
Šečenovo 70 55.13 N 45.54 E
Secesh 192 45.02 N 115.43 W
Séchault 52 49.16 N 4.44 E
Sechelt 172 49.28 N 123.45 W
Sechman' 66 52.32 N 40.29 E
Sechura 238 5.33 S 80.51 W
Sechura, Bahía de 238 5.42 S 81.00 W
Sechura, Desierto de 238 5.50 S 80.40 W
Seckach 52 49.26 N 9.20 E
Seclantas 242 25.18 S 66.15 W
Seclin 46 50.33 N 3.02 E
Seco, Esp. 256d 41.30 N 2.09 E
Seco, Méx. 190 30.41 N 111.56 W
Seco, Arroyo, Calif., U.S. 216 36.25 N 121.20 W
Seco, Arroyo, Calif., U.S. 270 34.05 N 118.13 W
Seco Creek, N. Mex., U.S. 190 32.59 N 107.18 W
Seco Creek, Tex., U.S. 186 29.02 N 99.08 W
Seco Island I 106 11.19 N 121.40 E
Second 266 40.47 N 74.09 W
Second Cliff 273 42.12 N 70.43 W
Second Herring Brook 273 42.09 N 70.47 W
Second Lake 196 45.09 N 71.10 W
Second Mountain 198 40.33 N 76.30 W
Second Swamp 198 37.08 N 77.12 W
Second Valley 158b 35.33 S 138.14 E
Second Watchung Mountain 266 40.55 N 74.13 W
Sečovce 30 48.43 N 21.40 E
Sečovská Polianka 30 48.47 N 21.42 E
Secretário, Ribeirão do 246 22.11 S 43.25 W
Secretary 198 38.37 N 75.57 W
Secretary Island I 162 45.15 S 166.55 E
Section 184 34.35 N 85.59 W
Secubun Island I 106 5.06 N 120.18 E
Sécure 238 15.10 S 64.52 W
Security 188 38.45 N 104.44 W
Séd 30 47.00 N 18.31 E
Seda, S.S.S.R. 66 57.40 N 25.46 E
Seda, S.S.S.R. 66 56.10 N 22.04 E
Seda, Zhg. 92 32.20 N 100.41 E
Seda 66 57.41 N 25.15 E
Sedah 102 10.46 S 123.12 E
Sedalia, Alta., Can. 174 51.41 N 110.40 W
Sedalia, Ind., U.S. 206 40.25 N 86.31 W
Sedalia, Mo., U.S. 188 38.42 N 93.14 W
Sedalia, Ohio, U.S. 208 39.44 N 83.29 W
Sedan, Austl. 158b 34.35 S 139.18 E
Sedan, Fr. 52 49.42 N 4.57 E
Sedan, Kans., U.S. 188 37.08 N 96.11 W
Sedanka, Cape 170 53.49 N 166.06 W
Sedanka Island I 170 53.50 N 166.10 W
Sedano 34 42.43 N 3.45 W
Sedano, Tanjung 105a 7.49 S 114.27 E
Sedanovo 78 56.58 N 101.22 E
Sedanovskaja, Šivera 78 56.24 N 101.21 E
Sedari, Tanjung 105a 5.57 S 107.18 E
Sedayu 105a 6.59 S 112.33 E
Sedbergh 42 54.20 N 2.31 W
Sedco Hills 218 33.39 N 117.24 W
Seddin-Berg 254a 52.24 N 13.40 E
Seddinsee 254a 52.23 N 13.41 E
Seddon 162 41.40 S 174.05 E
Seddonville 162 41.33 S 171.59 E
Sede Boqer 122 30.52 N 34.47 E
Sede Dov, Sede-Te'ufa 122 32.06 N 34.47 E
Sedel'nikovo 76 56.57 N 75.18 E
Sederberge 148 32.23 S 19.20 E
Sederon 56 44.12 N 5.32 E
Sederot 122 31.31 N 34.35 E
Sedgefield, Eng., U.K. 42 54.39 N 1.26 W
Sedgefield, N.J., U.S. 266 40.51 N 74.28 W
Sedgefield, N.C., U.S. 182 36.01 N 79.51 W
Sedge Island I 266 40.21 N 73.59 W
Sedgewick 174 52.46 N 111.41 W
Sedgewick, Mount 190 35.11 N 108.06 W
Sedgley 44 52.33 N 2.08 W
Sedgwick, Colo., U.S. 188 40.56 N 102.31 W
Sedgwick, Kans., U.S. 188 37.55 N 97.25 W
Sedgwick, Maine, U.S. 178 44.18 N 68.37 W
Sédhiou 140 12.44 N 15.33 W
Sedico 58 46.06 N 12.06 E
Sedini 36 40.50 N 8.49 E
Sedlčany 30 49.40 N 14.26 E
Sedley 198 36.46 N 76.59 W
Sedlitz 50 51.33 N 14.03 E
Sedlo 50 50.36 N 14.17 E
Šedn'ov 68 51.39 N 31.34 E
Sedok 74 44.13 N 40.52 E
Sedom 122 31.04 N 35.24 E
Sedom (Sodom) 122 31.04 N 35.23 E
Sedona 190 34.52 N 111.46 W
Sedot Yam 122 32.29 N 34.53 E
Sedova, Pik 62 73.29 N 54.58 E
Sedovo 73 47.03 N 38.10 E
Sedovo-Vasiljevka 73 47.14 N 38.08 E
Sedrata 36 36.08 N 7.32 E
Sedriano 56 45.29 N 8.58 E
Sedrina 56 45.47 N 9.38 E
Sedro Woolley 214 48.30 N 122.14 W
Sedrun 54 46.41 N 8.46 E
Šedtim 24 66.25 N 56.20 E
Šeduva 66 55.46 N 23.46 E
Sędziszów 30 50.04 N 21.41 E
See, Öst. 54 47.05 N 10.28 E
See, Öst. 58 47.48 N 13.27 E
Seebad Ahlbeck 50 53.56 N 14.11 E
Seebad Bansin 50 53.57 N 14.07 E
Seebad Heringsdorf 50 53.56 N 14.08 E
Seeberg, D.D.R. 254a 52.33 N 13.41 E
Seeberg, Schw. 54 47.09 N 7.40 E
Seeber Lake 174 53.52 N 93.03 W
Seeboden 58 46.49 N 13.30 E
Seebruck 58 47.56 N 12.28 E
Seebrugg 54 47.49 N 8.13 E
Seeburg, D.D.R. 254a 52.31 N 13.07 E
Seeburg → Jeziorany, Pol. 30 53.58 N 20.46 E
Seefeld, B.R.D. 48 53.27 N 8.21 E
Seefeld, D.D.R. 50 52.37 N 13.40 E
Seefeld in Tirol 58 47.20 N 11.11 E
Seeg 54 47.38 N 10.36 E
Seegatterl 58 47.39 N 12.32 E
Seehaus 58 47.45 N 13.17 E
Seehausen, D.D.R. 50 52.53 N 11.45 E
Seehausen, D.D.R. 50 52.06 N 11.17 E
Seeheim 146 26.50 S 17.45 E
Seehof 254a 52.24 N 13.17 E
Seeis 146 22.29 S 17.39 E
Seekaskootch Indian Reserve 174 53.43 N 109.55 W
Seekirchen Markt 58 47.54 N 13.08 E
Seekoegat 148 33.03 S 22.31 E
Seekoei 148 30.18 S 25.01 E
Seekonk 197 41.49 N 71.20 W
Seelbach 54 48.18 N 7.56 E
Seeley Lake 192 47.11 N 113.29 W
Seeleys Bay 202 44.29 N 76.14 W
Seelingstädt 50 50.46 N 12.14 E
Seelow 50 52.32 N 14.23 E
Seelyville, Ind., U.S. 184 39.30 N 87.16 W
Seelyville, Pa., U.S. 200 41.35 N 75.17 W
Seelze 48 52.24 N 9.35 E
Seemalik Butte 170 60.09 N 167.08 W
Seemenbach 52 50.17 N 8.59 E
Seemore Downs 152 30.42 S 125.15 E
Seen 54 47.29 N 8.46 E
Seengen 54 47.19 N 8.13 E
Seeon 58 47.58 N 12.26 E
Seer Green 250 51.37 N 0.36 W
Seergu 92 30.20 N 103.33 E
Seerhausen 50 51.16 N 13.15 E
Sées 46 48.36 N 0.10 E
Seesen 48 51.53 N 10.10 E
Seeshaupt 58 47.49 N 11.18 E
Seest 41 55.29 N 9.27 E
Seevetal 48 53.23 N 9.59 E
Seewalchen am Attersee 58 47.57 N 13.35 E
Seewis 54 47.00 N 9.32 E
Séez 56 45.37 N 6.48 E
Seez 54 47.07 N 9.18 E
Şefaatli 120 39.31 N 34.46 E
Sefadu 140 8.39 N 10.59 W
Seferihisar 120 38.11 N 26.51 E
Sefeto 140 14.08 N 9.49 W
Seffner 210 27.59 N 82.17 W
Sefhare 146 23.02 S 27.28 E
Sefrou 138 33.50 N 4.50 W
Sefton, N.Z. 162 43.15 S 172.40 E
Sefton, Eng., U.K. 252 53.30 N 2.58 W
Sefton □8 252 53.34 N 3.14 W
Sefton, Mount 162 43.41 S 170.03 E
Sefton Park 252 53.23 N 2.56 W
Segaliud 106 5.43 N 117.55 E
Segama 106 5.27 N 118.48 E
Segamat 104 2.30 N 102.49 E
Segang 90 31.58 N 114.18 E
Segangane 34 35.09 N 3.00 W
Şegarcea 38 44.06 N 23.45 E
Šegarka 76 57.16 N 84.05 E
Segbana 140 10.56 N 3.42 E
Segbwema 140 8.00 N 10.57 W
Segeg 134 7.42 N 42.50 E
Ségélo-Koro 140 9.25 N 7.09 W
Segera 154 8.15 S 143.30 E
Segeri 102 4.39 S 119.32 E
Segesta 36 37.56 N 12.50 E
Segesvár → Sighişoara 38 46.13 N 24.48 E
Segeža 24 63.44 N 34.19 E
Seggeuer, Oued es 138 31.39 N 2.26 E
Seggiano 60 42.56 N 11.33 E
Segmas 24 64.43 N 49.14 E
Segni 60 41.41 N 13.01 E
Segno 212 30.35 N 94.41 W
Segorbe 34 39.51 N 0.29 W
Ségou 140 13.27 N 6.16 W
Ségou □4 140 14.00 N 6.20 W
Segovary 24 62.23 N 42.57 E
Segovia, Col. 236 7.07 N 74.42 W
Segovia, Esp. 34 40.57 N 4.07 W
Segozero, Ozero 24 63.18 N 33.45 E
Segrate 256b 45.29 N 9.17 E
Segré 32 47.41 N 0.53 W
Seguam Island I 170 52.17 N 172.30 W
Seguam Pass 170 52.08 N 172.45 W
Séguédine 136 20.12 N 12.59 E
Séguéla, C. Iv. 140 7.57 N 6.40 W
Séguéla, Mali 140 14.07 N 6.44 W
Séguéla □5 140 8.30 N 6.30 W
Séguénéga 140 13.27 N 1.58 W
Seguí 242 31.57 S 60.08 W
Seguin 186 29.34 N 97.58 W
Seguin 202 45.21 N 80.01 W
Seguine Point 266 40.31 N 74.12 W
Segula Island I 171a 52.01 N 178.07 E
Segundo 188 37.07 N 104.45 W
Segundo 242 31.21 S 62.59 W
Seguntur 102 1.54 N 117.47 E
Segura 34 39.50 N 6.59 W
Segura 34 38.06 N 0.38 W
Segura, Sierra de 34 38.00 N 2.43 W
Sehāni Kalān 262a 28.41 N 77.25 E
Sehāni Khurd 262a 28.42 N 77.25 E
Sehāra Bāzār 116 23.06 N 87.49 E
Sehithwa 146 20.23 S 22.45 E
Sehlaba-Thebe 148 29.53 S 29.05 E
Sehma 50 50.32 N 13.00 E
Sehnde 48 52.18 N 9.57 E
Sehnkwehn 140 5.13 N 9.12 W
Sehnkwehn 140 5.12 N 9.21 W
Sehore 114 23.12 N 77.05 E
Sehore □5 114 23.00 N 77.00 E
Sehwān 110 26.26 N 67.52 E
Sehyŏn-ni 88 38.20 N 127.41 E
Seia 34 40.25 N 7.42 W
Seibeeshiden 258 35.34 N 139.22 E
Seibert 188 39.18 N 102.52 W
Seiches-sur-le-Loir 32 47.35 N 0.22 W
Seidan 86 34.19 N 134.45 E
Seidersville 200 40.35 N 75.23 W
Seiffen 50 50.39 N 13.26 E
Seifhennersdorf 50 50.56 N 14.36 E
Seignelay 46 47.54 N 3.36 E
Seigneurial, Lac 265a 45.33 N 73.50 W
Seika 260 34.46 N 135.48 E
Seikpyu 100 20.55 N 94.47 E
Seiland I 24 70.25 N 23.15 E
Seilhac 32 45.22 N 1.42 E
Seiling 186 36.09 N 98.56 W
Seillans 56 43.36 N 6.38 E
Seille, Fr. 52 49.07 N 6.11 E
Seille, Fr. 54 46.31 N 4.56 E
Seilo 130 12.20 N 23.50 E

Symbols in the index entries represent the broad categories identified in the key at the right. Symbols with superior numbers (⋆2) identify subcategories (see complete key on page I · 26).

Kartensymbole in dem Registerverzeichnis stellen die rechts in Schlüssel erklärten Kategorien dar. Symbole mit hochgestellten Ziffern (⋆2) bezeichnen Unterabteilungen einer Kategorie (vgl. vollständiger Schlüssel auf Seite I · 26).

Los símbolos incluidos en el texto del índice representan las grandes categorías identificadas con la clave a la derecha. Los símbolos con numeros en su parte superior (⋆2) identifican las subcategorías (véase la clave completa en la página I · 26).

Les symboles de l'index représentent les catégories indiquées dans la légende à droite. Les symboles suivis d'un indice (⋆2) représentent des sous-catégories (voir légende complète à la page I · 26).

Os símbolos incluídos no texto do índice representam as grandes categorias identificadas com a chave à direita. Os símbolos com números em sua parte superior (⋆2) identificam as subcategorias (veja-se a chave completa à página I · 26).

Mountain	Berg	Montaña	Montagne	Montanha
Mountains	Berge	Montañas	Montagnes	Montanhas
Pass	Pass	Paso	Col	Passo
Valley, Canyon	Tal, Cañon	Valle, Cañón	Vallée, Canyon	Vale, Canhão
Plain	Ebene	Llano	Plaine	Planície
Cape	Kap	Cabo	Cap	Cabo
Island	Insel	Isla	Île	Ilha
Islands	Inseln	Islas	Îles	Ilhas
Other Topographic Features	Andere Topographische Objekte	Otros Elementos Topográficos	Autres données topographiques	Outros Elementos Topográficos

ESPAÑOL Nombre	Página	Lat.°′	Long.°′ W=Oeste
Seim → Sejm ≃	68	51.27 N	32.34 E
Sein, Île de I	32	48.02 N	4.51 W
Seinaiji	84	35.30 N	137.42 E
Seinäjoki	26	62.47 N	22.50 E
Seine □[5]	46	48.50 N	2.10 E
Seine ≃, Man., Can.	174	49.54 N	97.07 W
Seine ≃, Ont., Can.	180	48.40 N	92.49 W
Seine ≃, Fr.	32	49.26 N	0.26 E
Seine, Baie de la C[1]	46	49.25 N	0.15 E
Seine, Baie de la ≃	32	49.30 N	0.30 W
Seine-et-Marne □[5]	46	48.30 N	3.00 E
Seine-et-Oise □[5]	46	48.45 N	2.00 E
Seine-Maritime □[5]	46	49.45 N	1.00 E
Seine-Port	46	48.33 N	2.33 E
Seine-Saint-Denis □[5]	251	48.55 N	2.30 E
Seip Mound State Memorial ⊥	208	39.15 N	83.13 W
Seipstown	198	40.35 N	75.40 W
Seis de Septiembre → Morón	248	34.39 S	58.37 W
Seishin → Ch'ŏngjin	88	41.47 N	129.50 E
Seitovka	70	46.43 N	48.03 E
Seiwa, Nihon	84	34.29 N	136.30 E
Seiwa, Nihon	84	35.15 N	140.00 E
Seixal	34	38.38 N	9.06 W
Seize-Îles, Lac des ⊜	196	45.54 N	74.28 W
Sejaka	102	3.34 S	116.12 E
Sejerø I	41	55.53 N	11.09 E
Sejerø Bugt C	41	55.50 N	11.15 E
Sejm ≃	68	51.27 N	32.34 E
Sejmčan	64	62.53 N	152.26 E
Šejno	70	53.22 N	43.12 E
Sejny	30	54.07 N	23.20 E
Sejorong	105b	9.02 S	116.48 E
Sejs	41	56.09 N	9.36 E
Seka	134	8.12 N	36.55 E
Sekači	70	50.30 N	43.37 E
Sekadau	102	0.01 S	110.54 E
Sekake's	148	29.58 S	28.27 E
Sekampung ≃	105a	5.36 S	105.50 E
Sekayam ≃	102	0.07 N	110.38 E
Sekayu	102	2.51 S	103.51 E
Seke	144	3.20 S	33.31 E
Seke-Banza	142	5.20 S	13.16 E
Sekeladi	102	2.38 S	102.14 E
Sekenke	144	4.16 S	34.10 E
Seki, Nihon	84	34.51 N	136.24 E
Seki, Nihon	84	35.29 N	136.55 E
Šeki (Nucha), S.S.S.R.	74	41.12 N	47.12 E
Seki, Tür.	120	36.24 N	29.13 E
Sekidō-san ∧	84	36.58 N	136.59 E
Sekigahara	84	35.22 N	136.28 E
Sekigane	86	35.22 N	133.46 E
Sekijō	84	36.14 N	139.55 E
Sekima	102	1.41 S	111.31 E
Sekinomiya	86	35.22 N	134.38 E
Sekiu	172	48.16 N	124.18 W
Sekiya	260	34.27 N	135.42 E
Sekiyado	84	36.06 N	139.47 E
Sek Kong	261d	22.26 N	114.06 E
Sek Kong Airfield ⊠	261d	22.27 N	114.05 E
Sekoma	146	24.41 S	23.50 E
Sekondi-Takoradi	140	4.59 N	1.43 W
Sekong Bay C	106	5.45 N	118.00 E
Sekota	134	12.38 N	39.03 E
Sekpiegu	140	9.33 N	0.02 W
Sekretaris ≃	259e	6.10 S	106.47 E
Sekretarka	70	52.36 N	44.11 E
Šekšema	70	58.22 N	45.11 E
Šeksna	66	59.13 N	38.30 E
Sekudai	104	1.32 N	103.40 E
Sela ≃[1]	116	21.54 N	89.39 E
Sela, Ponta da ≻	246	23.54 S	45.27 W
Šelabolicha	76	53.25 N	82.37 E
Sela Dingay	134	9.59 N	39.33 E
Šelagskij, Mys ≻	64	70.06 N	170.26 E
Selah	192	46.39 N	120.32 W
Selai ≃	104	2.13 N	103.26 E
Šelajevo	78	56.56 N	97.42 E
Selama	104	5.13 N	100.42 E
Šelanger	70	56.13 N	48.16 E
Selangor □[3]	104	3.20 N	101.30 E
Selangor ≃	104	3.20 N	101.15 E
Selaön I	40	59.24 N	17.12 E
Selaphum	100	16.02 N	103.57 E
Selaru, Pulau I	154	8.09 S	131.00 E
Selatan, Tanjung ≻	102	4.10 S	114.38 E
Sel'atin	68	47.53 N	25.12 E
Selatpanjang	104	1.00 N	102.43 E
Selawik	170	66.37 N	160.03 W
Selawik ≃	170	66.36 N	160.20 W
Selawik Lake ⊜	170	66.30 N	160.40 W
Selayar, Pulau I	102	6.05 S	120.30 E
Selayar, Selat ⋃	102	5.42 S	120.28 E
Selb	50	50.10 N	12.08 E
Selbach	52	49.32 N	7.02 E
Selbeck ⊸[8]	253	51.22 N	6.52 E
Selbecke ⊸[8]	253	51.20 N	7.28 E
Selbitz	50	50.19 N	11.44 E
Selborne	44	51.06 N	0.56 W
Selbu	26	63.13 N	11.02 E
Selbusjøen ⊜	26	63.14 N	10.54 E
Selby, Austl.	264b	37.55 S	145.22 E
Selby, Eng., U.K.	42	53.48 N	1.04 W
Selby, S. Dak., U.S.	188	45.31 N	100.02 W
Selby ⊸[8]	263d	26.13 S	28.02 E
Selby Creek ≃	202	44.09 N	77.08 W
Selbyville	198	38.28 N	75.13 W
Selchow	254a	52.21 N	13.28 E
Sel'co, S.S.S.R.	24	63.18 N	41.22 E
Sel'co, S.S.S.R.	66	53.22 N	34.06 E
Selcourt	263d	26.18 S	28.27 E
Selčuga ≃	79	49.42 N	133.20 E
Selçuk	120	37.56 N	27.22 E
Sel'cy, S.S.S.R.	66	57.57 N	35.59 E
Sel'cy, S.S.S.R.	255a	59.57 N	30.43 E
Selden, Kans., U.S.	188	39.33 N	100.34 W
Selden, N.Y., U.S.	200	40.51 N	73.02 W
Seldovia	170	59.27 N	151.43 W
Sele, Selat ⋃	154	1.10 S	131.05 E
Sele, Tanjung ≻	154	1.26 S	130.55 E
Selec	66	52.33 N	33.35 E
Selec-Cholopejev	66	53.23 N	30.24 E
Selečn'a	66	52.23 N	34.23 E
Selection Park	263d	26.18 S	28.27 E
Selemadeg	105b	8.29 S	115.02 E
Selembao	263b	4.22 S	15.17 E
Selemdža ≃	79	51.42 N	128.53 E
Selemdžinsk	79	52.36 N	131.08 E
Šelemeti	70	57.27 N	48.07 E
Selendi	120	38.46 N	27.53 E
Selenduma	78	50.55 N	106.10 E
Selenga (Selenge Mörön) ≃	78	52.16 N	106.16 E
Selenge, Mong.	78	49.25 N	103.59 E
Selenge, Zaïre	142	1.58 S	18.11 E
Selenge □[4]	78	50.15 N	106.12 E
Selenge Mörön (Selenga) ≃	78	52.16 N	106.16 E
Selenginsk	78	52.06 N	107.01 E
Selenicë	38	40.32 N	19.38 E
Selenn'ach ≃	64	67.48 N	144.54 E
Selent	50	54.17 N	10.26 E
Selenter See ⊜	50	54.17 N	10.28 E
Selepür	74	39.36 N	39.54 E
Sélestat (Schlettstadt)	54	48.16 N	7.27 E
Seletar	261c	1.25 N	103.53 E
Seletar ≃	261c	1.25 N	103.52 E
Seletar, Pulau I	261c	1.27 N	103.52 E
Seletar Airfield ⊠	261c	1.16 N	103.53 E
Seletar Reservoir ⊜[1]	261c	1.24 N	103.48 E
Selety ≃	76	53.06 N	73.22 E
Seletyteniz, Ozero ⊜	76	53.15 N	73.15 E
Selezen'ovo	66	59.12 N	42.18 E
Selezni, S.S.S.R.	66	55.39 N	31.29 E
Selezni, S.S.S.R.	70	52.48 N	41.15 E

FRANÇAIS Nom	Page	Lat.°′	Long.°′ W=Ouest
Selezn'ovo	66	60.45 N	28.39 E
Self Defense Fleet Headquarters ■	258	35.18 N	139.38 E
Selfoss	24a	63.56 N	20.57 W
Selfridge	188	46.02 N	100.56 W
Selghar	262c	18.57 N	73.02 E
Sel'gon	79	49.36 N	135.26 E
Sélibaby	140	15.10 N	12.11 W
Šelichino	79	50.22 N	137.38 E
Šelichov	78	52.13 N	104.08 E
Šelichova, Zaliv C	64	60.00 N	158.00 E
Šelichovo	78	55.42 N	97.41 E
Selidovo	73	48.08 N	37.18 E
Seligenstadt	52	50.02 N	8.58 E
Seligenthal	50	50.45 N	10.28 E
Seliger, Ozero ⊜	66	57.13 N	33.05 E
Seligman, Ariz., U.S.	190	35.20 N	112.53 W
Seligman, Mo., U.S.	184	36.31 N	93.56 W
Seliksa	70	53.13 N	45.18 E
Selim	104	3.51 N	101.29 E
Selimbau	102	0.37 N	112.08 E
Selimiye	120	37.24 N	27.40 E
Selim River	104	3.50 N	101.24 E
Selínia	257c	37.56 N	23.32 E
Selinsgrove	198	40.48 N	76.52 W
Selinus ⊥	36	37.35 N	12.49 E
Selišče, S.S.S.R.	24	64.58 N	46.18 E
Selišče, S.S.S.R.	66	56.53 N	33.16 E
Selitrennoje	70	47.11 N	47.27 E
Selivanovskaja	70	48.52 N	41.42 E
Seližarovo	66	56.51 N	33.27 E
Selje	26	62.03 N	5.22 E
Seljord	26	59.29 N	8.37 E
Selkämeri (Bottenhavet) C	26	62.00 N	20.00 E
Šelkan ≃	70	50.47 N	43.33 E
Selke ≃	50	51.52 N	11.14 E
Selkirk, Man., Can.	174	50.09 N	96.52 W
Selkirk, Ont., Can.	202	42.49 N	79.56 W
Selkirk, Scot., U.K.	42	55.33 N	2.50 W
Selkirk, N.Y., U.S.	200	42.32 N	73.48 W
Selkirk Mountains Λ	172	51.00 N	117.40 W
Selkirk Shores State Park ♠	202	43.33 N	76.12 W
Šelkovka	72	55.32 N	36.22 E
Šelkovskaja	74	43.30 N	46.22 E
Sella	58	46.00 N	11.25 E
Sella, Monte ∧	58	46.40 N	12.02 E
Sella, Paso di)(	58	46.30 N	11.45 E
Sella di Corno	60	42.21 N	13.14 E
Sellam, Oued Bou ≃	34	36.12 N	5.00 E
Sellano	60	42.54 N	12.55 E
Selle ≃	46	49.54 N	2.17 E
Seller Lake ⊜	174	55.00 N	94.32 W
Sellero	58	46.03 N	10.20 E
Sellers	182	34.17 N	79.28 W
Sellersburg	208	38.24 N	85.45 W
Sellersville	198	40.22 N	75.19 W
Selles-sur-Cher	46	47.16 N	1.33 E
Sellières	54	46.50 N	5.34 E
Sellin	50	54.22 N	13.41 E
Sells	190	31.55 N	111.53 W
Selly Oak ⊸[8]	44	52.25 N	1.52 W
Selm	48	51.42 N	7.28 E
Selma, Ala., U.S.	184	32.25 N	87.01 W
Selma, Calif., U.S.	216	36.34 N	119.37 W
Selma, Ind., U.S.	208	40.12 N	85.16 W
Selma, N.C., U.S.	182	35.32 N	78.17 W
Selman City	212	32.11 N	94.58 W
Selmer	184	35.11 N	88.36 W
Selmigerheide	253	51.38 N	7.47 E
Selmsdorf	50	53.48 N	10.50 E
Selommes	46	47.45 N	1.12 E
Šelon' ≃	66	58.14 N	30.50 E
Seloncourt	54	47.28 N	6.52 E
Selong	105b	8.39 S	116.32 E
Selongey	54	47.35 N	5.10 E
Šelopugino	78	51.39 N	117.33 E
Selouane	34	35.04 N	2.58 W
Selous, Mount ∧	170	62.57 N	132.31 W
Selous Game Reserve ⊸[4]	144	9.10 S	37.10 E
Selsdon ⊸[8]	250	51.21 N	0.04 W
Selsey	44	50.44 N	0.48 W
Selsey Bill ≻	44	50.43 N	0.48 W
Selsingen	48	53.22 N	9.13 E
Selston	44	53.04 N	1.20 W
Selters	52	50.32 N	7.44 E
Selty	70	57.19 N	52.10 E
Seltz	52	48.53 N	8.06 E
Seltzer	198	40.42 N	76.14 W
Selu, Pulau I	154	7.32 S	130.54 E
Selukwe	144	19.40 S	30.00 E
Selva, Arg.	242	29.46 S	62.03 W
Selva, It.	58	46.33 N	11.46 E
Sel'vačevo	72	55.25 N	37.57 E
Selva di Cadore	58	46.27 N	12.02 E
Selvagens, Ilhas II	138	30.05 N	15.55 W
Selvānā	118	37.25 N	44.51 E
Selvas ⊸[3]	232	5.00 S	68.00 W
Selvino	56	45.48 N	9.45 E
Selway ≃	192	46.08 N	115.36 W
Selwyn	156	21.32 S	140.30 E
Selwyn, Mount ∧	172	55.59 N	123.36 W
Selwyn Lake ⊜	166	59.55 N	104.35 W
Selwyn Mountains Λ	170	63.10 N	130.20 W
Selwyn Range Λ	156	21.35 S	140.35 E
Selwyn Strait ⋃	165f	16.03 S	168.12 E
Šelz ≃	52	49.59 N	8.02 E
Šemacha, S.S.S.R.	74	40.38 N	48.39 E
Šemacha, S.S.S.R.	76	56.15 N	59.16 E
Semai, Pulau I	154	3.08 S	132.30 E
Semakau, Pulau I	261c	1.12 N	103.46 E
Seman ≃	38	40.56 N	19.24 E
Semanggol	104	4.57 N	100.38 E
Semangka, Teluk C	102	5.36 S	104.42 E
Šemanicha	70	57.18 N	45.24 E
Semans	174	51.25 N	104.44 W
Semanu	105a	8.00 S	110.39 E
Semara	138	26.44 N	11.41 W
Semarang	105a	6.58 S	110.25 E
Semaria	114	24.16 N	79.54 E
Sematan	102	1.48 N	109.46 E
Semau, Pulau I	102	10.13 S	123.22 E
Semayang, Danau ⊜	102	0.14 S	116.28 E
Sembabule	144	0.05 S	31.27 E
Sembadel	56	45.16 N	3.41 E
Sembakung ≃	102	3.47 N	117.30 E
Sembawang	261c	1.27 N	103.50 E
Sembawang Airfield ⊠	261c	1.25 N	103.49 E
Sembé	142	1.39 N	14.36 E
Semberong ≃	104	2.27 N	103.37 E
Sembilan, Selat ⋃	261c	1.18 N	103.42 E
Semblançay	46	47.30 N	0.35 E
Sembo ≃	142	7.42 S	13.01 E
Semcy	66	52.51 N	33.28 E
Semejkino	73	48.19 N	39.32 E
Semeliškės	66	54.40 N	24.40 E
Semena ≃	148	29.33 S	28.42 E
Semendua	142	3.11 S	18.05 E
Semène ≃	56	45.23 N	4.13 E
Semenic, Munții Λ	38	45.05 N	22.05 E
Semenovka	68	49.36 N	33.10 E
Semenyih	104	2.57 N	101.51 E
Semertak	79	52.57 N	132.34 E
Šemeru, Gunung ∧	105a	8.06 S	112.55 E
Šemetovo	72	54.28 N	38.30 E
Semeževo	66	52.58 N	27.00 E
Semiahmoo Bay C	214	48.58 N	122.48 W
Semibalki	73	47.00 N	39.03 E
Semibratovo	70	57.18 N	39.32 E
Semibugry	70	46.11 N	48.16 E
Semichi Islands II	171a	52.42 N	174.00 E
Semides'atnoje	68	51.21 N	38.44 E
Semidi Islands II	170	56.07 N	156.44 W
Semien National Park ♠	134	13.08 N	38.15 E
Semijarka	76	50.54 N	78.20 E

PORTUGUÊS Nome	Página	Lat.°′	Long.°′ W=Oeste
Semikarakorskij	70	47.31 N	40.48 E
Semilej	70	53.57 N	45.21 E
Semilovo	70	55.04 N	42.10 E
Semiluki	68	51.41 N	39.02 E
Semily	30	50.36 N	15.20 E
Seminary	184	31.34 N	89.30 W
Seminoe Reservoir ⊜[1]	190	42.00 N	106.50 W
Seminoe State Park ♠	192	42.05 N	106.55 W
Seminole, Fla., U.S.	210	27.50 N	82.47 W
Seminole, Okla., U.S.	186	35.14 N	96.41 W
Seminole, Tex., U.S.	186	32.43 N	102.39 W
Seminole □[6]	210	28.45 N	81.13 W
Seminole, Lake ⊜[1]	182	30.46 N	84.50 W
Seminole Draw ∨	186	32.26 N	102.10 W
Seminole Park	210	27.52 N	82.45 W
Seminskij Chrebet Λ	76	51.05 N	85.50 E
Semiozerje	78	49.52 N	110.23 E
Semioz'ornoje	76	52.22 N	64.08 E
Semioz'ornyj	78	53.44 N	120.25 E
Semipalatinsk	76	50.28 N	80.13 E
Semipolka	76	54.07 N	67.16 E
Semipolki	68	50.43 N	30.56 E
Semirara Island I	106	12.04 N	121.23 E
Semisopochnoi Island I	171a	52.00 N	179.35 E
Semitau	102	0.33 N	111.58 E
Semizbugy	76	50.12 N	74.48 E
Semjany	70	56.02 N	45.59 E
Semli Kalān	114	24.10 N	76.39 E
Semliki ≃	144	1.14 N	30.28 E
Seml'ovo	66	55.03 N	33.58 E
Semmade	134	7.10 N	48.39 E
Semmens Lake ⊜	174	55.03 N	94.11 W
Semnān	118	35.33 N	53.24 E
Semnān □[8]	118	35.30 N	54.00 E
Semois ≃	52	49.53 N	4.45 E
Šemonaicha	76	50.39 N	81.54 E
Sem'ono-Aleksandrovka	68	51.03 N	40.12 E
Sem'onov	24	56.48 N	44.30 E
Sem'onovka, S.S.S.R.	68	52.10 N	32.35 E
Sem'onovka, S.S.S.R.	75	42.43 N	77.32 E
Sem'onovka, S.S.S.R.	76	51.20 N	70.46 E
Sem'onovskoje, S.S.S.R.	72	55.18 N	38.21 E
Sem'onovskoje, S.S.S.R.	72	55.03 N	37.46 E
Šemordan	70	56.11 N	50.26 E
Semouse ≃	54	47.49 N	6.12 E
Sempach	54	47.08 N	8.11 E
Sempacher See ⊜	54	47.09 N	8.09 E
Sempang Mengayau, Tanjong ≻	102	7.02 N	116.45 E
Semple Lake ⊜	174	55.02 N	95.38 W
Sempol	105a	8.01 S	114.08 E
Semporna	102	4.28 N	118.36 E
Sempu, Pulau I	105a	8.26 S	112.42 E
Semuda	102	2.51 S	112.58 E
Semur-en-Auxois	46	47.29 N	4.20 E
Šemurša	70	54.53 N	47.32 E
Šemyšejka	70	52.54 N	45.24 E
Semža	24	66.09 N	44.08 E
Sên ≃	100	12.32 N	104.28 E
Sena, Bol.	238	11.32 S	67.11 W
Seňa, Česko.	30	48.34 N	21.15 E
Sena, Moç.	144	17.27 S	35.00 E
Sena → Seine ≃	32	49.26 N	0.26 E
Senador Amaral	246	22.35 S	46.11 W
Senador Canedo	245	16.43 S	49.05 W
Senador Côrtes	246	21.48 S	42.56 W
Senador Firmino	245	20.55 S	43.06 W
Senador José Bento	246	22.10 S	46.10 W
Senador Pompeu	240	5.35 S	39.22 W
Senago	256b	45.35 N	9.07 E
Senahú	226	15.24 N	89.50 W
Senai	104	1.36 N	103.39 E
Senainville	251	48.30 N	1.37 E
Senaja	102	6.45 N	117.03 E
Senale	58	46.31 N	11.06 E
Senales, Val di ∨	58	46.45 N	10.50 E
Sena Madureira	238	9.04 S	68.40 W
Senamaninik	104	0.45 N	100.47 E
Senanayake Samudra ⊜[1]	112	7.11 N	81.29 E
Senang, Pulau I	261c	1.11 N	103.44 E
Senanga	142	16.06 S	23.16 E
Sénart, Forêt de ♠	251	48.40 N	2.30 E
Sénas	56	43.45 N	5.05 E
Senate	174	49.18 N	109.41 W
Senath	184	36.08 N	90.10 W
Senatobia	184	34.39 N	89.58 W
Šenber	76	49.46 N	66.09 E
Šenbertal	76	48.43 N	60.20 E
Senča	68	50.16 N	33.20 E
Send	250	51.17 N	0.31 W
Sendafa	134	9.07 N	39.00 E
Sendai, Nihon	82	38.15 N	140.53 E
Sendai, Nihon	82	31.49 N	130.18 E
Sendai ≃, Nihon	82	31.51 N	130.12 E
Sendai ≃, Nihon	86	35.02 N	134.11 E
Sendai-heiya =	82	38.15 N	141.00 E
Sendai-wan C	82	38.18 N	141.18 E
Sendamangalam	112	11.18 N	78.14 E
Senden, B.R.D.	48	51.51 N	7.29 E
Senden, B.R.D.	54	48.19 N	10.03 E
Sendenhorst	48	51.50 N	7.49 E
Sendhwa	110	21.41 N	75.06 E
Sendlingsdrift	146	28.12 S	16.53 E
Sendurjana	110	21.32 N	78.17 E
Senduruhan	102	1.00 S	110.46 E
Sene ≃	140	7.30 N	0.33 W
Senec	30	48.14 N	17.24 E
Seneca, Ill., U.S.	206	41.19 N	88.36 W
Seneca, Kans., U.S.	188	39.50 N	96.04 W
Seneca, Md., U.S.	274c	39.04 N	77.17 W
Seneca, Mo., U.S.	184	36.51 N	94.37 W
Seneca, Oreg., U.S.	192	44.08 N	118.58 W
Seneca, Pa., U.S.	204	41.23 N	79.42 W
Seneca, S.C., U.S.	182	34.41 N	82.57 W
Seneca □[6], N.Y., U.S.	200	42.54 N	76.52 W
Seneca □[6], Ohio, U.S.	204	41.07 N	83.11 W
Seneca ≃	200	43.12 N	76.17 W
Seneca, Mount ∧	200	42.01 N	78.49 W
Seneca Castle	200	42.53 N	77.06 W
Seneca Caverns ⊸[5]	204	41.11 N	82.53 W
Seneca Creek C	274b	39.19 N	76.22 W
Seneca Creek ≃	186	36.36 N	102.52 W
Seneca Falls	200	42.55 N	76.48 W
Seneca Lake ⊜	200	42.40 N	76.57 W
Seneca State Park ♠	198	39.08 N	77.15 W
Senecaville Lake ⊜[1]	178	39.55 N	81.25 W
Senecú	222	31.43 N	106.23 W
Seneffe	46	50.31 N	4.15 E
Senegal □[1]	124, 140	14.00 N	14.00 W
Sénégal ≃	140	15.48 N	16.32 W
Sénégal Oriental □[4]	140	14.00 N	13.00 W
Senekal	148	28.30 S	27.32 E
Senetosa, Punta di ≻	36	41.33 N	8.47 E
Sénez	56	43.55 N	6.24 E
Seneżskoje, Ozero ⊜	72	56.12 N	37.00 E
Senftenberg	50	51.31 N	14.00 E
Senga Hill	144	9.22 S	31.12 E
Sengbachstausee ⊜[1]	253	51.08 N	7.09 E
Sengejskij, Ostrov I	24	68.27 N	51.05 E
Šengel'šij	76	48.33 N	57.28 E
Sengés	245	24.06 S	49.29 W
Senggarang	104	1.45 N	103.03 E
Senghenydd	44	51.36 N	3.16 W
Sengilej	70	53.58 N	48.46 E
Sengkamang	104	0.42 N	101.55 E
Senguerr ≃	244	45.32 S	68.54 W
Sengwa ≃	144	17.07 S	28.05 E
Sengwarden	48	53.35 N	8.02 E
Senhāti	116	22.53 N	89.33 E
Senhora do Pôrto	245	18.53 S	43.06 W
Senhor do Bonfim	240	10.27 S	40.11 W
Senica	30	48.41 N	17.22 E
Senigallia	60	43.43 N	13.13 E
Senirkent	120	38.07 N	30.33 E
Senise	36	40.09 N	16.18 E
Senj	36	44.59 N	14.54 E
Senja I	24	69.20 N	17.30 E
Senjō-san ∧	86	35.26 N	133.36 E
Senkevičevka	68	50.32 N	25.02 E
Senkobo	144	17.38 S	25.58 E
Sen'kovo	73	49.31 N	37.43 E
Şenköy	120	36.05 N	36.05 E
Šenkursk	24	62.08 N	42.53 E
Senlac	174	52.29 N	109.41 W
Şenlikköy ⊸[8]	257b	40.59 N	28.47 E
Senlis	46	49.12 N	2.35 E
Senlisse	251	48.41 N	1.59 E
Senmonorom	100	12.27 N	107.12 E
Sennaja	68	45.15 N	37.01 E
Sennan	86	34.22 N	135.17 E
Senne ≃	46	51.04 N	4.26 E
Sennecey-le-Grand	54	46.39 N	4.52 E
Senne I	48	51.57 N	8.31 E
Senne II → Sennestadt	48	51.59 N	8.37 E
Sennestadt (Senne II)	48	51.59 N	8.37 E
Senneterre	180	48.23 N	77.15 W
Senneville	265a	45.27 N	73.57 W
Sennevoy-le-Bas	46	47.48 N	4.17 E
Senno	66	54.49 N	29.43 E
Sennoj, S.S.S.R.	70	52.11 N	46.57 E
Sennoj, S.S.S.R.	70	50.16 N	43.37 E
Sennokura-yama ∧	84	36.49 N	138.50 E
Sennori	36	40.48 N	8.34 E
Sennwald	54	47.16 N	9.30 E
Sennybridge	44	51.57 N	3.34 W
Senogawa	86	34.25 N	132.35 E
Senoia	182	33.18 N	84.33 W
Senonches	46	48.33 N	1.02 E
Senones	54	48.24 N	6.59 E
Senoo	86	34.36 N	133.52 E
Sénou	140	12.31 N	6.56 W
Sénouire ≃	56	45.16 N	3.25 E
Senqu → Orange ≃	146	28.41 S	16.28 E
Senriyama	260	34.47 N	135.30 E
Sens	46	48.12 N	3.17 E
Sensburg → Mrągowo	30	53.52 N	21.19 E
Sense ≃	54	46.54 N	7.14 E
Sensée ≃	46	50.16 N	3.06 E
Sensée, Canal de la Ξ	46	50.14 N	3.17 E
Sensuntepeque	226	13.52 N	88.38 W
Šenta	38	45.56 N	20.04 E
Šentala	70	54.27 N	51.29 E
Sentani, Danau ⊜	154	2.36 S	140.34 E
Sentarum, Danau ⊜	102	0.51 N	112.06 E
Sentas	76	49.19 N	82.28 E
Sentelek	76	51.13 N	83.44 E
Sentery	144	5.22 S	25.45 E
Sentinel	186	35.09 N	99.10 W
Sentinel Butte ∧	188	46.53 N	103.50 W
Sentinel Peak ∧	172	54.54 N	121.57 W
Sentinel Plain =	190	32.45 N	113.15 W
Sentinel Range Λ	9	78.10 S	85.30 W
Šentino ≃	60	43.24 N	12.59 E
Šentjur	36	46.13 N	15.24 E
Sentolo	105a	7.50 S	110.13 E
Sentosa I	261c	1.15 N	103.50 E
Sento Sé	240	9.40 S	41.18 W
Sentsū-zan ∧	86	35.09 N	133.11 E
Senyavin Islands II	14	6.55 N	158.00 E
Senye	142	1.34 N	9.50 E
Senza	144	3.02 N	26.19 E
Senzaki-wan C	86	34.24 N	131.15 E
Sen-zan ∧	86	34.21 N	134.51 E
Senzig	50	52.17 N	13.39 E
Senzō, Camp ■	260	34.47 N	135.24 E
Senzu-dake ∧	260	34.57 N	135.52 E
Seo de Urgel	34	42.21 N	1.28 E
Seohāra	114	29.13 N	78.35 E
Seon	54	47.21 N	8.10 E
Seonāth ≃	112	21.44 N	82.28 E
Seoni	114	22.05 N	79.32 E
Seoni Mālwa	114	22.27 N	77.28 E
Seorīnārāyan	110	21.44 N	82.35 E
Seoul → Sŏul	88	37.33 N	126.58 E
Seoul Airport ⊠	261b	37.32 N	126.56 E
Seoul National University ♥[2]	261b	37.28 N	126.57 E
Seoul Stadium ♠	261b	37.35 N	127.02 E
Seoul Station ⊸[5]	261b	37.34 N	126.58 E
Sepahat	104	1.34 N	101.53 E
Sepang	104	2.42 N	101.45 E
Sepanjang, Pulau I	102	7.10 S	115.50 E
Separation Creek ≃	190	41.59 N	107.28 W
Separation Point ≻	162	40.47 S	173.00 E
Sepasu	102	0.43 N	117.35 E
Sepatini ≃	238	7.36 S	65.24 W
Sépeaux	46	47.57 N	3.14 E
Sepetiba ⊸[8]	246	22.58 S	43.42 W
Sepetiba, Baía de C	246	23.00 S	43.48 W
Šepetovka	68	50.11 N	27.04 E
Sepi	165e	8.33 S	159.50 E
Sepino	60	41.24 N	14.37 E
Sep'o	88	38.39 N	127.22 E
Sępólno Krajeńskie	30	53.28 N	17.32 E
Sépone → Muang Xépôn	100	16.41 N	106.14 E
Sepopa	146	18.13 S	22.13 E
Sępopol	30	54.15 N	21.00 E
Sepoti ≃	238	6.43 S	61.38 W
Sepotuba ≃	238	15.56 S	57.39 W
Seppenrade	48	51.46 N	7.23 E
Sepphoris → Zippori	122	32.45 N	35.17 E
Seppois-le-Bas	54	47.33 N	7.10 E
Septeuil	251	48.54 N	1.41 E
Sept-Frères, Lac des ⊜	196	46.20 N	75.10 W
Sept-Îles (Seven Islands)	176	50.12 N	66.23 W
Septvaux	46	49.34 N	3.23 E
Sepulga ≃	184	31.11 N	86.46 W
Sepúlveda	34	41.18 N	3.45 W
Sepulveda ⊸[8]	270	34.13 N	118.28 W
Sepulveda Dam ⊸[6]	270	34.10 N	118.29 W
Sepulveda Flood Control Basin =[1]	218	34.11 N	118.29 W
Seputih ≃	102	4.40 S	105.51 E
Sepyč	70	58.11 N	54.08 E
Sequals	58	46.10 N	12.50 E
Sequatchie ≃	182	35.02 N	85.38 W
Sequeros	34	40.31 N	6.01 W
Sequillo ≃	34	41.45 N	5.30 W
Sequim	214	48.05 N	123.06 W
Sequim Bay C	214	48.03 N	123.02 W
Sequoia National Park ♠	194	36.30 N	118.30 W
Sera	86	34.36 N	133.03 E
Şera, Pulau I	154	7.40 S	131.05 E
Šerabad	118	37.40 N	67.01 E
Serafeddin Dağları Λ	120	39.05 N	41.10 E
Šerafimovič	70	49.36 N	42.43 E
Šeragul	78	54.29 N	100.56 E
Seraidi	36	36.55 N	7.41 E
Seraing	52	50.36 N	5.29 E
Seraja ≃	72	56.15 N	38.45 E
Seram (Ceram) I	154	3.00 S	129.00 E
Seram, Laut (Ceram Sea) ⍑[2]	154	2.30 S	128.00 E
Serampore	116	22.45 N	88.21 E
Serang	105a	6.07 S	106.09 E
Serang ≃	105a	6.43 S	110.35 E
Serangoon	261c	1.22 N	103.54 E
Serangoon ≃	261c	1.24 N	103.56 E
Serangoon, Pulau I	261c	1.25 N	103.56 E
Serangoon Harbour C	261c	1.23 N	103.57 E
Serapo	60	41.13 N	13.34 E
Serasan, Pulau I	102	2.30 N	109.03 E
Serasan, Selat ⋃	102	2.20 N	109.00 E
Seravalle Sesia	56	45.41 N	8.19 E
Seravezza	58	43.59 N	10.13 E
Seraya, Pulau I	261c	1.16 N	103.43 E
Serayevo → Sarajevo	38	43.52 N	18.25 E
Şerayu ≃	105a	7.41 S	109.06 E
Šerbakul'	76	54.38 N	72.24 E
Serbeulangit, Pegunungan Λ	104	3.45 N	97.50 E
Serbia → Srbija □[3]	38	44.00 N	21.00 E
Serchio ≃	58	43.47 N	10.16 E
Serdar	120	37.08 N	36.27 E
Serdce-Kamen', Mys ≻	170	66.57 N	171.40 W
Serdež	70	57.17 N	48.17 E
Serditoje	73	48.02 N	38.24 E
Serdoba ≃	70	52.34 N	44.01 E
Serdobsk	70	52.28 N	44.13 E
Serebr'anka, S.S.S.R.	73	48.55 N	38.08 E
Serebr'anka, S.S.S.R.	76	57.13 N	70.42 E
Serebr'anka, S.S.S.R.	255b	55.45 N	37.55 E
Serebr'anka ≃	255b	55.47 N	37.42 E
Serebr'ansk	76	49.43 N	83.20 E
Serebr'anyj Bor ⊸[8]	255b	55.48 N	37.30 E
Serebr'anyje Prudy	72	54.28 N	38.44 E
Serebrovo	78	55.24 N	97.52 E
Serechoviči	68	51.25 N	24.40 E
Sered'	30	48.17 N	17.44 E
Sereda, S.S.S.R.	66	55.54 N	35.31 E
Şereda, S.S.S.R.	70	58.00 N	40.27 E
Šeredar' ≃	72	55.56 N	39.04 E
Seredejskij	66	54.03 N	35.14 E
Seredići	66	53.35 N	35.51 E
Seredina-Buda	68	52.11 N	34.01 E
Serednikovo, S.S.S.R.	70	55.15 N	39.40 E
Serednikovo, S.S.S.R.	255b	55.56 N	37.14 E
Seredn'ovo	255b	55.35 N	37.18 E
Seredžius	66	55.05 N	23.25 E
Şereflikoçhisar	120	38.56 N	33.33 E
Šereges	76	52.57 N	88.02 E
Seregno	56	45.39 N	9.12 E
Serein ≃	46	47.55 N	3.31 E
Şeremban	104	2.43 N	101.56 E
Šeremetjevka	70	55.23 N	51.32 E
Šeremetjevo, Aeroport ⊠	72	55.59 N	37.24 E
Šeremetjevskij	72	55.59 N	37.30 E
Serena	206	41.29 N	88.44 W
Seren del Grappa	58	45.59 N	11.51 E
Serengeti National Park ♠	144	2.20 S	34.50 E
Serengeti Plain =	144	2.50 S	35.00 E
Serengka	102	1.40 S	110.40 E
Serenje	144	13.15 S	30.14 E
Serenli	134	2.22 N	42.20 E
Şereno	246	21.19 S	42.39 W
Šereševo	66	52.33 N	24.13 E
Seret ≃	68	48.38 N	25.52 E
Serfaus	54	47.02 N	10.36 E
Ser'ga	76	57.46 N	56.52 E
Sergač	70	55.32 N	45.28 E
Sergeant	204	41.38 N	78.45 W
Sergeant Bluff	188	42.24 N	96.22 W
Sergeja Kirova, Ostrova II	64	77.12 N	89.30 E
Sergejeviči	66	53.30 N	27.45 E
Sergejevka, S.S.S.R.	73	48.40 N	37.22 E
Sergejevka, S.S.S.R.	76	53.51 N	67.25 E
Sergejevka, S.S.S.R.	76	51.39 N	68.13 E
Sergejevka, S.S.S.R.	79	44.22 N	131.39 E
Sergejevka, S.S.S.R.	79	43.23 N	133.22 E
Sergejevo	76	57.18 N	86.02 E
Sergen	38	41.42 N	27.42 E
Sergijevka	68	51.46 N	41.05 E
Sergijevskaja, S.S.S.R.	66	60.16 N	43.54 E
Sergijevskaja, S.S.S.R.	70	50.16 N	43.47 E
Sergijevskij	70	51.56 N	51.54 E
Sergili	75	41.13 N	69.14 E
Sergines	46	48.20 N	3.15 E
Sergipe □[3]	240	10.30 S	37.30 W
Sergokala	74	42.27 N	47.40 E
Sergozero, Ozero ⊜	24	66.47 N	36.42 E
Seria	102	4.39 N	114.23 E
Serian	102	1.10 N	110.34 E
Seriana, Valle ∨	58	45.55 N	9.55 E
Seriate	56	45.41 N	9.43 E
Seribu, Kepulauan II	105a	5.36 S	106.33 E
Seribudolok, Indon.	104	2.56 N	98.37 E
Seribudolok, Indon.	104	2.51 N	99.04 E
Sericho	144	2.30 N	40.10 E
Seridó ≃	240	6.12 S	37.10 W
Sérifontaine	46	49.21 N	1.46 E
Sérifos	38	37.09 N	24.31 E
Sérifos I	38	37.11 N	24.31 E
Sérignan-du-Comtat	56	44.11 N	4.51 E
Sérigny ≃	166	56.47 N	66.00 W
Seringa, Serra da Λ[1]	240	7.00 S	50.40 W
Seringapatam	112	12.25 N	76.42 E
Serino	60	40.51 N	14.51 E
Serio ≃	56	45.16 N	9.45 E
Serir Dağı ∧	120	39.39 N	42.41 E
Seritinga	246	21.54 S	44.30 W
Serjol	24	60.02 N	48.58 E
Serkout, Djebel ∧	138	23.30 N	6.48 E
Serkovo	72	54.28 N	38.46 E
Şerles ∧	58	47.08 N	11.23 E
Šerlovaja Gora	78	50.34 N	116.15 E
Serm ⊸[8]	253	51.21 N	6.42 E
Sermaise	251	48.32 N	2.05 E
Sermaises	46	48.18 N	2.12 E
Sermaize-les-Bains	52	48.47 N	4.55 E
Serman	70	53.34 N	46.22 E
Sermata, Kepulauan II	154	8.10 S	128.40 E
Sermide	58	45.00 N	11.18 E
Sermizelles	46	47.32 N	3.48 E
Şermoneta	60	41.33 N	12.59 E
Šerna ≃	72	55.51 N	38.34 E
Sernambitiba	277a	22.41 S	42.59 W
Sernambitiba, Pontal de ≻	277a	23.02 S	43.27 W
Serniki	68	51.49 N	26.14 E
Sernovodsk	70	53.56 N	51.17 E
Sernur	70	56.56 N	49.09 E
Sernyy Zavod	118	39.59 N	58.50 E
Séro	140	14.48 N	11.04 W
Serock	30	52.31 N	21.03 E
Serodino	242	32.37 S	60.57 W
Ser'odka	66	58.10 N	28.12 E
Seroglazka	70	47.01 N	47.29 E
Ser'ogovo	24	62.20 N	50.36 E
Serooskerke	48	51.42 N	3.50 E
Seropédica	246	22.44 S	43.43 W
Serov	76	59.29 N	60.31 E
Serovo	75	40.27 N	71.12 E
Serowe	146	22.25 S	26.44 E
Ser'oža ≃	70	55.34 N	42.29 E
Serpa	34	37.56 N	7.36 W
Serpa, Ilha de I	240	3.07 S	58.19 W
Serpeddi, Punta ∧	36	39.22 N	9.18 E
Serpejsk	66	54.20 N	34.59 W
Serpent, Lac du ⊜	176	49.50 N	71.37 W
Serpent, Rivière au ≃	176	49.33 N	71.14 W
Serpentine	158a	32.22 S	115.59 E
Serpentine ≃, Austl.	158a	32.33 S	115.46 E
Serpentine ≃, B.C., Can.	214	49.05 N	122.50 W
Serpentine Dam ⊸[6]	158a	32.25 S	116.08 E
Serpentine Lakes ⊜	152	28.32 S	129.09 E
Serpent Mound State Memorial ⊥	208	39.02 N	83.26 W
Serpents Mouth ⋃	231r	10.00 N	62.00 W
Serpis ≃	34	38.59 N	0.09 W
Serpnevoje	68	46.18 N	29.02 E
Serpuchov	72	54.55 N	37.25 E
Serpukhov → Serpuchov	72	54.55 N	37.25 E
Serqo → Sark I	28	49.26 N	2.21 W
Serra	245	20.07 S	40.18 W
Serra, Monte ∧	60	43.46 N	10.33 E
Serra Branca	240	7.29 S	36.40 W
Serra Caiada	240	6.06 S	35.42 W
Serracapriola	60	41.48 N	15.09 E
Serrada	58	45.53 N	11.09 E
Serra de'Conti	60	43.33 N	13.02 E
Serra do Navio	240	0.59 N	52.03 W
Serra do Salitre	245	19.06 S	46.41 W
Serra dos Órgãos, Parque Nacional da ♠	246	22.26 S	43.02 W
Serra Grande	240	7.15 S	38.19 W
Sérrai	38	41.05 N	23.32 E
Serramanna	36	39.25 N	8.54 E
Serramazzoni	58	44.25 N	10.47 E
Serramonte Center ⊸[9]	272	37.40 N	122.28 W
Serrana	245	21.14 S	47.36 W
Serrana Bank ⊹[4]	226	14.23 N	80.12 W
Serra Negra	246	22.36 S	46.42 W
Serra Negra do Norte	240	6.40 S	37.24 W
Serrania	245	21.33 S	46.03 W
Serranilla Bank ⊹[4]	226	15.50 N	79.50 W
Serrano, Isla I	244	48.30 S	74.45 W
Serranópolis	245	18.16 S	52.00 W
Serranos, Bra.	246	22.42 S	45.44 W
Serranos, Bra.	246	21.51 S	44.30 W
Serra Preta	245	12.09 S	39.20 W
Serrara	60	40.42 N	13.54 E
Serraria, Bra.	240	6.49 S	35.38 W
Serraria, Bra.	246	22.01 S	43.12 W
Serra San Bruno	36	38.35 N	16.20 E
Serra San Quirico	60	43.27 N	13.01 E
Serrat, Cap ≻	36	37.14 N	9.13 E
Serra Talhada	240	7.59 S	38.18 W
Serravalle, It.	60	43.57 N	12.30 E
Serravalle, It.	60	42.47 N	13.01 E
Serravalle all'Adige	58	45.49 N	11.01 E
Serravalle Pistoiese	60	43.54 N	10.49 E
Serravalle Scrivia	56	44.43 N	8.51 E
Serre ≃	46	49.41 N	3.23 E
Serre Ponçon, Barrage de ⊸[6]	56	44.33 N	6.30 E
Serre-Ponçon, Lac de ⊜[1]	56	44.30 N	6.17 E
Serres	56	44.26 N	5.43 E
Serrezuela	242	30.38 S	65.23 W
Serri	36	39.41 N	9.09 E
Serrières	56	45.19 N	4.45 E
Serrinha	240	11.39 S	39.00 W
Serriola, Bocca)(	60	43.31 N	12.21 E
Serris	251	48.51 N	2.47 E
Serrita	240	7.56 S	39.19 W
Sêrro	245	18.37 S	43.23 W
Serrote ≃	245	21.27 S	54.40 W
Şersale	36	39.01 N	16.44 E
Šerstin	66	52.39 N	31.03 E
Šerstobitovo	76	57.16 N	78.52 E
Sertã	34	39.48 N	8.06 W
Sertaneja	245	23.03 S	50.50 W
Sertânia	240	8.05 S	37.16 W
Sertãozinho	246	22.19 S	46.03 W
Sertig-Dörfli	54	46.44 N	9.51 E
Sertung, Pulau I	105a	6.06 S	105.24 E
Seru	134	7.50 N	40.28 E
Şerua, Pulau I	154	6.18 S	130.01 E
Šerubaj-Nura ≃	76	49.54 N	72.31 E
Serui	154	1.53 S	136.14 E
Seruini ≃	238	7.42 S	66.42 W
Serule	146	21.58 S	27.20 E
Serutu, Pulau I	102	1.42 S	108.45 E
Seruwai	104	4.21 N	98.10 E
Sérvia	38	40.11 N	22.00 E
Servi Burnu ≻	120	41.40 N	28.06 E
Service Creek Reservoir ⊜[1]	204	40.34 N	80.21 W
Servigliano	60	43.05 N	13.29 E
Servon	251	48.43 N	2.35 E
Servoz	54	45.56 N	6.46 E
Serwaru	102	8.10 S	127.42 E
Seryševo	79	51.08 N	128.20 E
Şes, Munții Λ	38	47.05 N	22.30 E
Šešan	170	66.46 N	171.26 W
Sesayap ≃	102	3.36 N	117.15 E
Sesayap-lama	102	3.36 N	117.03 E
Seščinskij	66	53.45 N	33.23 E
Sese Islands II	144	0.20 S	32.20 E
Seseke ≃	253	51.37 N	7.32 E
Sesfontein	146	19.07 S	13.39 E
Sesheke	142	17.29 S	24.18 E
Seshu	95	39.33 N	115.37 E
Sesia ≃	56	45.05 N	8.37 E
Sesia, Val ∨	56	45.47 N	8.05 E
Sesibu	102	4.02 N	116.33 E
Seskar, Ostrov I	66	60.02 N	28.23 E
Şeskarön	26	65.44 N	23.44 E
Šešma ≃	70	55.27 N	51.05 E
Sesmarias ≃	246	22.28 S	44.27 W
Sesoko-jima I	164m	26.38 N	127.52 E
Sespe	218	34.23 N	118.58 W
Sespe Creek ≃	194	34.23 N	118.57 W
Sessa	142	13.56 S	20.38 E
Sessa Aurunca	60	41.14 N	13.56 E
Sessenheim	52	48.48 N	7.59 E
Şesta Godano	56	44.17 N	9.40 E
Şestakovka	68	48.32 N	31.58 E
Şestakovo, S.S.S.R.	72	56.21 N	35.49 E
Şestakovo, S.S.S.R.	78	56.29 N	103.59 E
Şestao	34	43.18 N	3.00 W
Šestern'a	68	47.33 N	33.16 E
Sestino	60	43.42 N	12.18 E
Sesto (Sexten)	58	46.42 N	12.21 E
Sesto Calende	56	45.44 N	8.38 E
Sesto Fiorentino	60	43.50 N	11.12 E
Sestola	58	44.14 N	10.46 E
Sesto San Giovanni	56	45.32 N	9.14 E
Sestra ≃, S.S.S.R.	70	52.11 N	49.36 E
Sestra ≃, S.S.S.R.	72	56.43 N	37.14 E
Sestriere	56	44.57 N	6.53 E
Sestri Levante	56	44.16 N	9.24 E
Sestri Ponente	56	44.25 N	8.51 E
Sestroreck	66	60.06 N	29.58 E
Sestroreckij Razliv, Ozero ⊜	255a	60.04 N	30.00 E
Šešupe ≃	66	55.30 N	22.12 E
Şešurga	70	57.29 N	47.35 E
Šešuvis ≃	66	55.13 N	22.15 E
Şeta, Nihon	260	34.58 N	135.55 E
Šeta, S.S.S.R.	66	55.17 N	24.15 E
Seta ≃	260	34.56 N	135.54 E
Setagaya ⊸[8]	258	35.39 N	139.40 E
Setail ≃	105a	8.30 S	114.21 E
Setaka	86	33.09 N	130.28 E
Setana	82a	42.26 N	139.51 E
Setapak	104	3.11 N	101.42 E
Setauket	200	40.57 N	73.07 W
Sète	56	43.24 N	3.41 E
Sete Barras	242	24.23 S	47.55 W
Sete Cachoeiras, Ribeirão das ≃	246	21.27 S	45.33 W
Sete Cidades, Parque Nacional de ♠	240	3.50 S	41.40 W
Sete de Setembro ≃	245	12.56 S	52.51 W
Sete Lagoas	245	19.27 S	44.14 W
Setentrional, Cordillera Λ	228	19.35 N	70.45 W
Sete Pontes	246	22.51 S	43.05 W
Sete Quedas, Cachoeira das ⌊	240	9.27 S	56.41 W

Symbol	English	Deutsch	Español	Français	Português
≃	River	Fluss	Río	Rivière	Rio
Ξ	Canal	Kanal	Canal	Canal	Canal
⌊	Waterfall, Rapids	Wasserfall, Stromschnellen	Cascada, Rápidos	Chute d'eau, Rapides	Cascata, Rápidos
⋃	Strait	Meeresstrasse	Estrecho	Détroit	Estreito
C	Bay, Gulf	Bucht, Golf	Bahía, Golfo	Baie, Golfe	Baía, Golfo
⊜	Lake, Lakes	See, Seen	Lago, Lagos	Lac, Lacs	Lago, Lagos
☷	Swamp	Sumpf	Pantano	Marais	Pântano
⍗	Ice Features, Glacier	Eis- und Gletscherformen	Accidentes Glaciales	Formes glaciaires	Acidentes Glaciares
⍑	Other Hydrographic Features	Andere Hydrographische Objekte	Otros Elementos Hidrográficos	Autres données hydrographiques	Outros Elementos Hidrográficos
⊹	Submarine Features	Untermeerische Objekte	Accidentes Submarinos	Formes de relief sous-marin	Acidentes Submarinos
□	Political Unit	Politische Einheit	Unidad Politica	Entité politique	Unidade Política
♥	Cultural Institution	Kulturelle Institution	Institución Cultural	Institution culturelle	Instituição Cultural
⊥	Historical Site	Historische Stätte	Sitio Histórico	Site historique	Sitio Histórico
♠	Recreational Site	Erholungs- und Ferienort	Sitio de Recreo	Centre de loisirs	Sítio de Lazer
⊠	Airport	Flughafen	Aeropuerto	Aéroport	Aeroporto
■	Military Installation	Militäranlage	Instalación Militar	Installation militaire	Instalação Militar
⊸	Miscellaneous	Verschiedenes	Misceláneo	Divers	Miscelânea

ENGLISH — Name | Page | Lat.°′ | Long.°′
DEUTSCH — Name | Seite | Breite°′ | Länge°′ E=Ost

Name	Page	Lat.°′	Long.°′
Sete Quedas, Parque Nacional de ♠	242	24.02 S	54.12 W
Sete Quedas, Salto das (Salto del Guairá) L	242	24.02 S	54.16 W
Sete Rios •[8]	256c	38.45 N	9.10 W
Setesdal ∨	26	59.25 N	7.25 E
Seth Ward	186	34.13 N	101.42 W
Seti ≃	114	28.58 N	81.06 E
Sétif	138	36.09 N	5.26 E
Setlagodi	148	26.16 S	25.06 E
Seto, Nihon	84	35.14 N	137.06 E
Seto, Nihon	86	33.27 N	132.15 E
Seto, Nihon	86	34.44 N	134.02 E
Setoda	86	34.18 N	133.05 E
Seto-naikai ⊤[2]	82	34.20 N	133.30 E
Seto-naikai-kokuritsu-kōen ♠	86	34.15 N	133.28 E
Seton Hall University ʋ[2]	266	40.45 N	74.15 W
Seton Lake ≃	172	50.45 N	122.05 W
Seton Portage	172	50.43 N	122.18 W
Seto-saki ≻	164m	26.51 N	128.18 E
Setouchi	83b	28.10 N	129.15 E
Seto-zaki ≻	86	33.40 N	135.20 E
Setraki	68	49.23 N	40.49 E
Setta ≃	58	44.22 N	11.14 E
Settat	138	33.04 N	7.37 W
Sette Bagni ≃	257a	42.00 N	12.31 E
Sette Cama	142	2.32 S	9.45 E
Settecamini •[8]	257a	41.56 N	12.37 E
Sette-Daban, Chrebet ⩕	64	62.00 N	138.00 E
Settee Lake @	174	57.03 N	96.55 W
Settepani, Monte ∧	56	44.15 N	8.12 E
Settimo Milanese	256b	45.29 N	9.03 E
Settimo Torinese	56	45.09 N	7.46 E
Settimo Vittone	56	45.33 N	7.50 E
Setting Lake @	174	55.00 N	98.38 W
Settle	42	54.04 N	2.16 W
Settlement Point ≻	159	38.25 S	145.25 E
Settlers	146	25.02 S	28.30 E
Settlers Cabin Regional Park ♠	269b	40.26 N	80.10 W
Settons, Lac des @	46	41.11 N	4.04 E
Settsu	86	34.46 N	135.33 E
Setúbal	34	38.32 N	8.54 W
Setúbal □[5]	256c	38.37 N	9.00 W
Setúbal, Baía de C	34	38.27 N	8.53 W
Setun' ≃	255b	55.44 N	37.33 E
Seui	36	39.50 N	9.20 E
Seúl → Sŏul	88	37.33 N	126.58 E
Seul, Lac @	174	50.20 N	92.30 W
Seul Choix Point ≻	180	45.56 N	85.52 W
Seulimeum	104	5.22 N	95.35 E
Seurre	54	47.00 N	5.09 E
Seutakan ≃	170	65.38 N	176.58 W
Seuzach	54	47.32 N	8.44 E
Sev ≃	66	52.24 N	34.10 E
Sevagram	112	20.45 N	78.30 E
Sevan	74	40.34 N	44.57 E
Sevan, Ozero @	74	40.20 N	45.20 E
Sévaré	140	14.32 N	4.06 W
Sevastopol'	68	44.36 N	33.32 E
Sevastopol'skij	76	53.08 N	65.44 E
Ševčenko	62	43.35 N	51.05 E
Ševčenkovo, S.S.S.R.	68	51.40 N	33.39 E
Ševčenkovo, S.S.S.R.	68	49.41 N	37.10 E
Ševčenkovo, S.S.S.R.	68	45.33 N	29.20 E
Ševčenkovo Vtoroje	68	47.29 N	36.08 E
Sevelen, B.R.D.	48	51.29 N	6.25 E
Sevelen, Schw.	54	47.07 N	9.29 E
Ševelevskaja	24	60.52 N	44.12 E
Ševelevskij Majdan	70	54.25 N	42.15 E
Seven ≃	42	54.11 N	0.52 W
Seven Caves •[5]	208	39.13 N	83.23 W
Seven Harbors	206	42.40 N	83.34 W
Sevenhill	158b	33.53 S	138.38 E
Seven Hills, Austl.	264a	33.46 S	150.57 E
Seven Hills, Ohio, U.S.	204	41.22 N	81.41 W
Seven Islands → Sept-Îles	176	50.12 N	66.23 W
Seven Kings •[8]	250	51.34 N	0.05 E
Seven Mile	208	39.29 N	84.33 W
Sevenmile Bridge •[5]	210	24.41 N	81.11 W
Sevenmile Creek ≃	208	39.28 N	84.33 W
Sevenoaks, Eng., U.K.	44	51.16 N	0.12 E
Seven Oaks, Tex., U.S.	212	30.51 N	94.51 W
Sevenoaks □[8]	250	51.18 N	0.10 E
Sevenoaks Weald	250	51.14 N	0.12 E
Seven Palm Lake @	210	25.12 N	80.44 W
Seven Persons	174	49.52 N	110.54 W
Seven Sisters	44	51.46 N	3.43 W
Seven Sisters Peaks ⩕	172	54.58 N	128.10 W
Seventy Mile House	172	51.18 N	121.24 W
Seven Valleys	198	39.51 N	76.46 W
Sévérac-le-château	32	44.19 N	3.04 E
Severance Center •[9]	269a	41.31 N	81.33 W
Sever'anskij Les ♠	73	48.55 N	38.00 E
Severka ≃	72	55.10 N	38.45 E
Severn, S. Afr.	148	26.36 S	22.52 E
Severn, N.C., U.S.	198	36.31 N	77.11 W
Severn, Va., U.S.	198	37.18 N	76.25 W
Severn ≃, Ont., Can.	166	56.02 N	87.36 W
Severn ≃, Ont., Can.	202	44.52 N	79.41 W
Severn ≃, Eng., U.K.	44	51.35 N	2.40 W
Severn ≃, Md., U.S.	198	38.58 N	76.28 W
Severn, Mouth of the ≃	44	51.25 N	3.00 W
Severnaja Dvina ≃	24	64.32 N	40.30 E
Severnaja Sos'va ≃, S.S.S.R.	62		
	64	64.10 N	65.28 E
Severnaja Zeml'a II	64	79.30 N	98.00 E
Severna Park	198	39.04 N	76.33 W
Severn Bridge •[5]	44	51.39 N	2.42 W
Severnoje, S.S.S.R.	70	58.02 N	41.26 E
Severnoje, S.S.S.R.	70	54.06 N	52.32 E
Severnoje, S.S.S.R.	73	48.04 N	38.44 E
Severnoje, S.S.S.R.	74	44.49 N	42.51 E
Severnoje, S.S.S.R.	76	56.21 N	78.23 E
Severn River C	198	37.19 N	76.25 W
Severn Tunnel •[5]	44	51.35 N	2.44 W
Severnyj, S.S.S.R.	24	67.38 N	64.06 E
Severnyj, S.S.S.R.	255b	55.56 N	37.33 E
Severnyje Uvaly ⩕[2]	24	59.30 N	49.00 E
Severnyj Kommunar	70	58.23 N	54.02 E
Severnyj Prijut	74	43.16 N	41.51 E
Severnyj Sučan	79	43.13 N	133.11 E
Severnyj Ural ⩕	24	63.00 N	59.00 E
Severo-Bajkal'skoje Nagorje ⩕[1]	78	57.00 N	111.00 E
Severočeský Kraj □[4]	32	50.35 N	14.15 E
Severodoneck	73	48.58 N	38.27 E
Severodvinsk	24	64.34 N	39.50 E
Severo-Dvinskij Kanal Ξ	66	59.45 N	38.22 E
Severo-Jenisejskij	64	60.22 N	93.01 E
Severo-Kazachstanskaja Oblast' □[4]	76	54.30 N	69.00 E
Severo-Kuril'sk	64	50.40 N	156.08 E
Severomoravský Kraj □[4]	30	49.45 N	17.50 E
Severomorsk	24	69.05 N	33.24 E
Severo-Mujskij Chrebet ⩕	78	56.30 N	114.00 E
Severo-Osetinskaja Avtonomnaja Sovetskaja Socialističeskaja Respublika □[3]	74	43.00 N	44.15 E
Severo-Sibirskaja Nizmennost' ⌣	64	73.00 N	100.00 E
Severoural'sk	76	60.09 N	59.57 E
Severo-Zadonsk	72	54.00 N	38.23 E
Severskaja	68	44.51 N	38.42 E
Severskij Donec ≃	62	48.20 N	40.15 E
Severskij Donec-Donbass, Kanal Ξ	73	48.55 N	37.45 E
Severucha	76	58.28 N	63.25 E
Severy	188	37.37 N	96.14 W
Seveso	56	45.39 N	9.09 E
Seveso ≃	256b	45.30 N	9.12 E
Sevettijärvi	24	69.26 N	28.38 E
Sevier ≃	190	39.04 N	113.06 W
Sevier, East Fork ≃	190	38.14 N	112.12 W
Sevier Bridge Reservoir @[1]	190	39.21 N	111.57 W
Sevier Desert •[2]	190	39.25 N	112.50 W
Sevier Lake @	190	38.55 N	113.09 W
Sevierville	182	35.52 N	83.34 W
Sevilla, Col.	236	4.16 N	75.57 W
Sevilla, Esp.	34	37.23 N	5.59 W
Sevilla, Isla I	226	8.14 N	82.24 W
Seville → Sevilla, Esp.	34	37.23 N	5.59 W
Seville, Fla., U.S.	182	29.19 N	81.30 W
Seville, Ohio, U.S.	204	41.01 N	81.52 W
Sevir	120	39.12 N	38.13 E
Şevketiye	120	40.05 N	27.51 E
Ševli ≃	79	54.08 N	133.04 E
Sevlievo	38	43.01 N	25.06 E
Sevran	46	48.56 N	2.32 E
Sevrej	92	43.31 N	102.35 E
Sèvres	46	48.49 N	2.12 E
Sévrier	54	45.52 N	6.08 E
Şevsk	68	52.09 N	34.30 E
Ševykan	78	54.20 N	106.49 E
Sewa ≃	140	7.18 N	12.08 W
Sewanee	184	35.12 N	85.55 W
Seward, Alaska, U.S.	170	60.06 N	149.26 W
Seward, Nebr., U.S.	188	40.55 N	97.06 W
Seward, N.Y., U.S.	200	42.43 N	74.37 W
Seward, Pa., U.S.	204	40.25 N	79.01 W
Seward Glacier ⊓	170	60.22 N	140.15 W
Seward Peninsula ≻[1]	170	65.00 N	164.00 W
Sewaren	266	40.33 N	74.16 W
Sewekow	50	53.15 N	12.39 E
Sewell, Chile	242	34.05 S	70.23 W
Sewell, N.J., U.S.	198	39.46 N	75.09 W
Sewen	54	47.48 N	5.54 E
Sewernaja-Semlja → Severnaja Zeml'a II	64	79.30 N	98.00 E
Seweweekspoort	148	33.22 S	21.25 E
Sewickley	204	40.33 N	80.11 W
Sewickley Creek ≃	269b	40.14 N	79.47 W
Sewickley Heights	269b	40.33 N	80.09 W
Sewickley Hills	269b	40.34 N	80.08 W
Sewri •[8]	262c	19.00 N	72.51 E
Sewu, Pegunungan ⩕	105a	8.05 S	110.35 E
Sexcello	142	3.58 S	11.38 E
Sexsmith	172	55.21 N	118.47 W
Sexten → Sesto	58	46.42 N	12.21 E
Sexton	208	39.42 N	85.27 W
Sexton Island I	266	40.39 N	73.14 W
Seya	258	35.29 N	139.29 E
Seybaplaya	222	19.39 N	90.40 W
Seybaplaya, Punta ≻	222	19.39 N	90.42 W
Seybouse, Oued ≃	138	36.54 N	7.47 E
Seychellen → Seychelles □[2]	128	4.35 S	55.40 E
Seychelles □[1]	128	4.35 S	55.40 E
Seychelles-Mauritius Ridge ÷[3]	12	14.00 S	61.00 E
Seyches	32	44.33 N	0.18 E
Seyda	50	51.53 N	12.53 E
Şeydābād	118	34.51 N	50.36 E
Şeydim	120	40.33 N	34.45 E
Seydişehir	120	37.25 N	31.51 E
Seyđisfjörđur	24a	65.16 N	14.00 W
Seyfe Gölü @	120	39.13 N	34.23 E
Seyhan ≃	120	36.43 N	34.53 E
Seyhan Gölü @[1]	120	37.05 N	35.13 E
Seyitgazi	120	39.27 N	30.43 E
Seymour, Austl.	159	37.02 S	145.08 E
Seymour, S. Afr.	148	32.33 S	26.46 E
Seymour, Conn., U.S.	197	41.24 N	73.04 W
Seymour, Ind., U.S.	208	38.58 N	85.53 W
Seymour, Iowa, U.S.	180	40.44 N	93.07 W
Seymour, Mo., U.S.	184	37.09 N	92.46 W
Seymour, Tex., U.S.	186	33.35 N	99.16 W
Seymour, Wis., U.S.	180	44.31 N	88.20 W
Seymour ≃	172	51.05 N	126.50 W
Seymour Inlet C	172	51.03 N	127.10 W
Seymour Range ⩕	214	48.40 N	124.00 W
Seyne-les-Alpes	56	44.21 N	6.21 E
Seyring	254b	48.20 N	16.29 E
Seyringer Graben Ξ	254b	48.18 N	16.33 E
Seyssel	54	45.57 N	5.49 E
Şeytan ≃	257b	41.06 N	28.59 E
Sežana	36	45.42 N	13.52 E
Sézanne	46	48.43 N	3.43 E
Sezela	148	30.24 S	30.42 E
Şezha	92	31.40 N	95.12 E
Sežim	24	62.07 N	58.21 E
Sezimbra	34	38.26 N	9.06 W
Sezimovo Ústí	30	49.23 N	14.42 E
Sezze	60	41.30 N	13.03 E
Sfax	138	34.44 N	10.46 E
Sfîntu-Gheorghe	38	45.52 N	25.47 E
Sfîntu Gheorghe, Braţul ≃[1]	38	44.53 N	29.36 E
Sfîntu Gheorghe, Ostrovul I	38	45.07 N	29.22 E
Sfizef	138	35.14 N	0.15 W
Sforzesco, Castello ⊥	256b	45.28 N	9.11 E
's-Gravendeel	48	51.46 N	4.37 E
's-Gravenhage (The Hague)	48	52.06 N	4.18 E
's-Gravenzande	48	52.00 N	4.10 E
Sgué ⊤[4]	140	17.45 N	7.43 W
Sgurgola	60	41.40 N	13.09 E
Sha'alav, Har ∧	122	30.04 N	35.06 E
Sha'alvim	122	31.52 N	34.59 E
Sha'ar HaGolan	122	32.41 N	35.36 E
Sha'ar Menashe	122	32.27 N	35.01 E
Shab'ā	122	33.21 N	35.45 E
Shaba □[4]	144	8.00 S	27.00 E
Shābah	132	31.11 N	30.46 E
Shabakunk Creek ≃	275	40.15 N	74.43 W
Shabani	144	20.20 S	30.02 E
Shabās al-Milḩ	132	31.12 N	30.39 E
Shabās ash-Shuhadā'	132	31.05 N	30.45 E
Shabās 'Umayr	132	31.06 N	30.48 E
Shabbona	206	41.46 N	88.52 W
Shabestar	118	38.11 N	45.42 E
Shabomeka Lake @	202	44.54 N	77.09 W
Shabotik ≃	180	48.50 N	85.34 W
Shabqadar	113	34.13 N	71.34 E
Shabrāmant	132	29.56 N	31.12 E
Shabshīr al-Ḩişşah	132	30.52 N	31.04 E
Shabunda	144	2.42 S	27.20 E
Shabwah	134	15.22 N	47.01 E
Shacheng	95	40.25 N	115.31 E
Shackan Indian Reserve •[4]	172	50.17 N	112.10 W
Shackleton Glacier ⊓	9	84.35 S	176.15 W
Shackleton Ice Shelf ⊓	9	66.00 S	100.00 E
Shackleton Range ⩕	9	80.40 S	26.00 W
Shaddādī	120	36.02 N	40.45 E
Shādegān	118	30.40 N	48.38 E
Shade Gap	204	40.11 N	77.52 W
Shadehill Reservoir @[1]	188	45.45 N	102.15 W
Shade Mountain ∧	198	40.34 N	77.30 W
Shades Creek ≃	184	33.11 N	87.02 W
Shades Glen	200	41.11 N	75.42 W
Shadi	90	26.08 N	114.49 E
Shadian	88	35.30 N	114.26 E
Shading	92	31.20 N	94.40 E
Shadow Lake @, Ont., Can.	202	44.43 N	78.48 W
Shadow Lake @, Mass., U.S.	273	42.50 N	71.14 W
Shadow Lake @, N.J., U.S.	266	40.21 N	74.06 W
Shadow Mountain National Recreation Area ♠	190	40.07 N	105.48 W
Shado-Wood Village	204	40.35 N	79.12 W
Shadrinsk → Šadrinsk	76	56.05 N	63.38 E
Shadui	92	31.30 N	100.10 E
Shadwān, Jazīrat I	130	27.30 N	33.59 E
Shady Cove	192	42.37 N	122.49 W
Shady Grove, Fla., U.S.	182	30.17 N	83.38 W
Shady Grove, Tex., U.S.	212	32.48 N	97.01 W
Shady Hills	206	40.36 N	85.41 W
Shady Shores	212	33.10 N	97.02 W
Shadyside	178	39.58 N	80.45 W
Sha'f	122	32.38 N	36.51 E
Shafer, Lake @	206	40.47 N	86.46 W
Shafer Butte ∧	192	43.47 N	116.05 W
Shafir	122	31.42 N	34.44 E
Shaft	118	37.12 N	49.24 E
Shaftesbury	44	51.01 N	2.12 W
Shafton	269b	40.20 N	79.42 W
Shaftsburg	206	42.48 N	84.18 W
Shaftsbury	200	42.57 N	73.13 W
Shafu	90	22.25 N	113.01 E
Shagamu	140	6.51 N	3.39 E
Shageluk	170	62.36 N	159.32 W
Shagou, Zhg.	90	33.09 N	119.45 E
Shagou, Zhg.	97	29.10 N	104.22 E
Shag Rocks II[1]	234	53.33 S	42.02 W
Shaguotun	94	41.10 N	120.38 E
Shāhābād, Bhārat	112	17.08 N	76.56 E
Shāhābād, Bhārat	113	30.10 N	76.53 E
Shāhābād, Bhārat	114	27.39 N	79.57 E
Shāhābād, Bhārat	262c	19.01 N	73.02 E
Shāhābād, Īrān	118	37.32 N	56.54 E
Shāhābād, Īrān	118	34.06 N	46.31 E
Shāhābād, Īrān	257d	35.49 N	51.29 E
Shāhābād □[5]	114	25.10 N	84.00 E
Shāhāda	110	21.28 N	74.18 E
Shahba	122	32.51 N	36.37 E
Shāhbandar	110	24.10 N	67.54 E
Shāhbāz Kalāt	118	26.42 N	63.58 E
Shāhbāzpur ⊻	114	22.05 N	90.50 E
Shāhdādkot	110	27.51 N	67.54 E
Shāhdādpur	110	25.56 N	68.37 E
Shāhdara	113	31.38 N	74.18 E
Shāhdara •[8]	262a	28.30 N	77.25 E
Shahdol	114	23.17 N	81.21 E
Shahdol □[5]	114	23.30 N	81.10 E
Shahe, Zhg.	88	34.44 N	118.58 E
Shahe, Zhg.	88	35.49 N	116.23 E
Shahe, Zhg.	88	37.01 N	119.43 E
Shahe, Zhg.	88	36.56 N	114.30 E
Shahe, Zhg.	90	29.36 N	115.52 E
Shahe, Zhg.	92	22.06 N	109.43 E
Shahe, Zhg.	95	40.08 N	116.15 E
Shahe ≃, Zhg.	88	37.31 N	117.50 E
Shahe ≃, Zhg.	88	38.20 N	115.22 E
Shahe ≃, Zhg.	90	33.38 N	114.36 E
Shahedian	90	33.01 N	113.44 E
Shaheji	90	32.26 N	118.14 E
Shahepu	94	41.08 N	121.01 E
Shaheyi	88	39.53 N	118.31 E
Shaheying	94	40.50 N	120.46 E
Shahezi	79	46.05 N	129.20 E
Shāhganj	114	26.03 N	82.41 E
Shāhgarh, Bhārat	110	27.07 N	69.54 E
Shāhgarh, Bhārat	114	24.19 N	79.08 E
Shaḩḩāt	136	32.49 N	21.52 E
Shāhī	118	36.28 N	52.53 E
Shāhī Kowt	113	34.16 N	70.34 E
Shāh-i-Mashhad	118	35.03 N	63.58 E
Shāhīn Dezh	118	36.40 N	46.33 E
Shāhjahānpur	114	27.53 N	79.55 E
Shāhjahānpur □[5]	114	28.00 N	79.55 E
Shāh Jūy	110	32.31 N	67.25 E
Shāh Kot	113	31.34 N	73.29 E
Shah Mosque ʋ[1]	257d	35.40 N	51.25 E
Shāh Pasand	118	37.07 N	55.16 E
Shāhpur, Bhārat	112	16.42 N	76.50 E
Shāhpūr, Īrān	118	38.11 N	44.47 E
Shāhpur, Pāk.	110	28.43 N	68.25 E
Shāhpur, Pāk.	113	32.16 N	72.28 E
Shāhpura, Bhārat	110	27.23 N	75.58 E
Shāhpura, Bhārat	110	25.38 N	74.56 E
Shāhpura, Bhārat	114	23.11 N	80.42 E
Shāhpur Chākar	110	26.09 N	68.39 E
Shahrak	110	34.06 N	64.18 E
Shahr-e Bābak	118	30.07 N	55.09 E
Shahr-e Monjān	110	36.02 N	70.46 E
Shahr-e Şafā	118	31.50 N	66.22 E
Shahrestān	110	34.22 N	66.47 E
Shahreẕā	118	32.01 N	51.52 E
Shahr Kord	118	32.19 N	50.50 E
Shāhrūd	118	36.25 N	55.01 E
Shāhrūd ≃	118	37.17 N	48.43 E
Shahsavār	118	36.49 N	50.53 E
Shahu	90	30.11 N	113.39 E
Shāhzādpur	116	24.10 N	89.36 E
Shā'ib al-Banāt, Jabal ∧	130	26.59 N	33.29 E
Shaighālu	110	31.11 N	68.49 E
Shaikhpura	114	25.09 N	85.51 E
Sha'īrah, Jabal ∧[2]	122	30.06 N	34.17 E
Sha'īrah, Jabal ash- ⩕	122	29.31 N	34.29 E
Shājāpur	114	23.26 N	76.16 E
Shājāpur □[5]	114	23.45 N	76.15 E
Shajian	90	24.46 N	117.38 E
Shajianzi	88	41.01 N	125.26 E
Shajiazhuang	96	32.13 N	120.53 E
Shajing	90	23.36 N	114.06 E
Shajingzi	92	37.42 N	105.09 E
Shakaga-hana ≻	86	34.25 N	134.14 E
Shakaga-take ∧	86	33.11 N	130.53 E
Shakaga-take-tunnel •[5]	86	33.27 N	130.52 E
Shakardarra	113	33.14 N	71.30 E
Shakargarh	113	32.16 N	75.10 E
Shakarpura	262a	28.46 N	77.21 E
Shakarpur Khās •[8]	262a	28.38 N	77.17 E
Shakaskraal	148	29.26 S	31.14 E
Shakawe	146	18.23 S	21.50 E
Shakeng	88	42.13 N	116.35 E
Shaker Heights	204	41.29 N	81.36 W
Shaker Heights Park ♠	269a	41.29 N	81.33 W
Shakespeare	202	43.22 N	80.49 W
Shākhen	118	33.22 N	59.32 E
Shakhty → Šachty	73	47.42 N	40.13 E
Shaki	140	8.39 N	3.25 E
Shakopee	180	44.48 N	93.32 W
Shakotan-hantō ≻[1]	82a	43.20 N	140.30 E
Shakou	90	24.25 N	113.32 E
Shakshūk	132	29.28 N	30.42 E
Shaktoolik	170	64.20 N	161.09 W
Shakūrpur •[8]	262a	28.41 N	77.09 E
Shala, Lake @	134	7.25 N	38.30 E
Shalalth	172	50.44 N	122.13 W
Shalamulunhe ≃	92	43.02 N	111.20 E
Shalatayn, Bi'r ⊤[4]	130	23.08 N	35.36 E
Shaleitiandao I	88	39.03 N	118.44 E
Shaler Mountains ⩕	166	72.35 N	110.45 W
Shaleshanto	146	19.09 S	23.58 E
Shalford	250	51.13 N	0.34 W
Shālimah	132	31.14 N	30.52 E
Shalimar Railroad Station •[5]	262b	22.33 N	88.19 E
Shaling	94	41.09 N	122.22 E
Shalingpu	94	41.47 N	123.11 E
Shalingzi	95	40.42 N	114.55 E
Shaliuhe, Zhg.	92	36.28 N	98.57 E
Shaliuhe, Zhg.	95	39.53 N	117.56 E
Shallotte	182	33.58 N	78.23 W
Shallowater	186	33.41 N	101.59 W
Shallow Brook ≃	266	40.21 N	74.35 W
Shallow Lake	202	44.36 N	81.05 W
Shaluhe	79	51.08 N	126.00 E
Shām, Bādiyat ash- •[2]	118	32.00 N	40.00 E
Shām, Jabal ash- ∧	118	23.13 N	57.16 E
Shaman	75	38.50 N	75.36 E
Shamattawa	174	55.52 N	92.05 W
Shambat	130	15.40 N	32.32 E
Shambe	130	7.07 N	30.46 E
Shambi	142	1.49 S	22.39 E
Shambu	134	9.40 N	37.03 E
Shambuanda	142	6.38 S	20.13 E
Shām Churasi	113	31.30 N	75.45 E
Shamei	90	24.32 N	118.25 E
Shamepūr •[8]	262a	28.45 N	77.09 E
Shamīl	118	27.30 N	56.53 E
Shāmli	114	29.27 N	77.19 E
Shammākh	122	30.30 N	35.30 E
Shammar, Jabal ⩕	118	27.20 N	41.45 E
Shamo, Lake @	134	5.49 N	37.35 E
Shamokin	198	40.47 N	76.34 W
Shamokin Dam	200	40.51 N	76.49 W
Shamona Creek ≃	275	40.02 N	75.43 W
Shamrock, Fla., U.S.	182	29.39 N	83.08 W
Shamrock, Tex., U.S.	186	35.13 N	100.15 W
Shamsābād	114	27.01 N	78.08 E
Shamsher	262a	28.44 N	77.24 E
Shamsol Emareh Palace ʋ	257d	35.41 N	51.25 E
Shamva	144	17.18 S	31.34 E
Shan □[3]	100	22.00 N	98.00 E
Shanbiao	88	35.28 N	113.57 E
Shanchengbao	92	37.01 N	107.00 E
Shanchengzhen	88	42.23 N	125.26 E
Shanchengzi	94	42.02 N	123.47 E
Shandaken	200	42.07 N	74.24 W
Shandan	92	38.48 N	101.20 E
Shandatgyi	100	19.37 N	94.43 E
Shandī	130	16.42 N	33.26 E
Shandianhe	88	42.22 N	116.15 E
Shandianhe ≃	88	42.23 N	116.21 E
Shandīd	132	30.55 N	30.40 E
Shandon	216	35.39 N	120.22 W
Shandong	97	29.31 N	106.25 E
Shandong □[4]	88	36.00 N	118.00 E
Shandongbandao ≻[1]	88	37.00 N	121.00 E
Shaner	269b	40.17 N	79.47 W
Shanesville	204	40.31 N	81.39 W
Shangani	144	19.47 S	29.22 E
Shangani ≃	144	18.41 S	27.10 E
Shang'ao	96	30.41 N	119.25 E
Shangbahe	90	30.40 N	115.05 E
Shangbai	96	30.29 N	119.58 E
Shangbancheng	95	40.50 N	118.03 E
Shangbatang	92	32.46 N	96.20 E
Shangcai	90	33.16 N	114.15 E
Shangcang	95	39.54 N	117.23 E
Shangchen	96	30.07 N	119.53 E
Shangcheng	90	31.48 N	115.24 E
Shangchewan	90	29.48 N	113.01 E
Shangch'iu → Shangqiu	88	34.27 N	115.42 E
Shangchuandao I	92	21.40 N	112.48 E
Shangdang	96	32.06 N	119.24 E
Shangdayangqi	79	51.09 N	124.02 E
Shangdian	90	34.07 N	112.23 E
Shangdianmiao	96	30.56 N	120.51 E
Shangdouying	95	40.36 N	115.33 E
Shangdu	88	41.29 N	113.34 E
Shangduichunshi	94	41.00 N	123.02 E
Shangdundu	90	27.56 N	116.15 E
Shangduxianghuangqi	88	42.27 N	113.55 E
Shangfu	90	28.40 N	114.59 E
Shanggaixin	92	23.25 N	100.02 E
Shanggan	90	25.56 N	119.22 E
Shanggang	90	33.30 N	120.04 E
Shanggangzi	94	42.26 N	123.03 E
Shanggao	90	28.18 N	114.54 E
Shanggecun	96	31.49 N	119.07 E
Shanggu	88	40.47 N	118.28 E
Shangguan	96	31.39 N	119.15 E
Shangguanying	88	41.18 N	117.07 E
Shanghai, Va., U.S.	198	37.37 N	76.47 W
Shanghai, Zhg.	96	31.14 N	121.28 E
Shanghai, Zhg.	96	31.01 N	121.25 E
Shanghai, Zhg.	259b	31.14 N	121.28 E
Shanghailingao	94	41.57 N	120.55 E
Shanghai Museum ʋ	259b	31.13 N	121.28 E
Shanghai Shih □[7]	96	31.10 N	121.30 E
Shanghai Station •[5]	259b	31.15 N	121.28 E
Shanghang	90	25.06 N	116.25 E
Shanghe	88	37.19 N	117.07 E
Shanghekou	88	40.26 N	124.47 E
Shanghetou	95	39.12 N	116.59 E
Shanghewantun	94	41.42 N	123.23 E
Shanghu @	96	31.39 N	120.41 E
Shanghuang	96	31.33 N	119.34 E
Shanghuangqi	88	41.29 N	116.31 E
Shanghucun	95	40.45 N	115.45 E
Shangjao → Shangrao	90	28.26 N	117.58 E
Shangjiafen	94	41.18 N	121.10 E
Shangjiahe	88	41.51 N	124.28 E
Shangjialin	88	38.19 N	116.05 E
Shangjiaodao	90	29.00 N	119.54 E
Shangjiatai	94	40.53 N	123.35 E
Shangjie	90	27.06 N	116.06 E
Shangjiuwu	90	33.59 N	113.01 E
Shangkasa	110	33.45 N	80.12 E
Shangkou	88	37.03 N	118.45 E
Shanglanjiagou	94	40.52 N	120.37 E
Shanglin, Zhg.	92	23.28 N	108.33 E
Shanglin, Zhg.	94	41.31 N	122.14 E
Shanglishi	90	27.52 N	113.46 E
Shangliuhezicun	94	41.28 N	123.32 E
Shangliulinzi	94	41.02 N	123.13 E
Shangmagushan	94	41.41 N	124.10 E
Shangmatai	95	39.22 N	117.15 E
Shangmatun	94	40.57 N	123.22 E
Shangmengyun	92	23.01 N	99.50 E
Shangmingdian	96	31.12 N	120.57 E
Shangmingju	95	39.41 N	115.12 E
Shangnan	92	33.31 N	110.45 E
Shangpan I	96	30.31 N	121.18 E
Shangpandaoling	94	41.42 N	121.14 E
Shangping, Zhg.	90	24.29 N	114.38 E
Shangping, Zhg.	90	25.57 N	117.33 E
Shangping, Zhg.	90	24.43 N	115.27 E
Shangpufou	96	31.28 N	119.13 E
Shangpuzi	94	41.37 N	121.35 E
Shangqianbu	96	30.27 N	120.04 E
Shangqiao	90	31.02 N	117.42 E
Shangqikou	90	29.44 N	118.02 E
Shangqing, Zhg.	90	25.53 N	118.36 E
Shangqing, Zhg.	90	28.02 N	117.00 E
Shangqingshuicun	95	39.56 N	115.38 E
Shangqitai	94	41.14 N	121.14 E
Shangqiu, Zhg.	88	34.27 N	115.42 E
Shangqiu, Zhg.	88	34.23 N	115.37 E
Shangrao	90	28.26 N	117.58 E
Shangshe	92	38.15 N	113.20 E
Shangshibatai	94	42.02 N	120.51 E
Shangshui	90	33.39 N	114.39 E
Shangsi	92	22.09 N	107.57 E
Shangtai	90	28.34 N	118.37 E
Shangtan	96	30.27 N	118.42 E
Shangtang	90	33.23 N	118.02 E
Shanguan)(	90	27.30 N	117.06 E
Shangweiniuchang	94	40.54 N	120.44 E
Shangxian	92	33.51 N	109.54 E
Shangxingbu	96	31.32 N	119.15 E
Shangxinhe	96	32.02 N	118.43 E
Shangxinqiu	94	42.27 N	121.37 E
Shangyangbao	88	42.30 N	124.14 E
Shangyangcun	96	30.48 N	118.40 E
Shangye	88	35.26 N	117.59 E
Shangyi	88	41.04 N	114.03 E
Shangying	79	44.10 N	127.17 E
Shangyinkou	92	32.52 N	103.04 E
Shangyou	90	25.51 N	114.30 E
Shangyoushui ≃	90	25.55 N	113.56 E
Shangyu	90	30.02 N	120.54 E
Shangyuan	94	41.39 N	120.55 E
Shangzhai	88	39.13 N	114.17 E
Shangzhaoshugou	94	42.12 N	121.58 E
Shangzhazi	95	40.52 N	117.42 E
Shangzhenzhuang	95	40.20 N	117.06 E
Shangzhi	79	45.13 N	127.59 E
Shangzhuang	88	37.01 N	122.15 E
Shangzhuangtai	95	39.41 N	115.25 E
Shanhaiguan	88	40.01 N	119.44 E
Shanhaikwan → Shanhaiguan	88	40.01 N	119.44 E
Shanhe	110	33.38 N	79.50 E
Shanhecun	79	45.38 N	128.27 E
Shanhetun	79	44.44 N	127.12 E
Shanjiang	90	27.32 N	115.08 E
Shanjiazhuang	95	38.52 N	115.45 E
Shanklin	44	50.38 N	1.10 W
Shankou, Zhg.	90	28.58 N	115.12 E
Shankou, Zhg.	90	26.40 N	117.46 E
Shankou, Zhg.	90	28.48 N	114.29 E
Shankou, Zhg.	92	21.38 N	109.43 E
Shanlenggang	92	28.33 N	103.23 E
Shanli	90	29.52 N	117.21 E
Shanlian	96	30.42 N	120.19 E
Shanmenjie	96	30.40 N	118.52 E
Shanmulong	92	24.39 N	98.05 E
Shannanguan	90	31.36 N	116.52 E
Shannock	197	41.27 N	71.38 W
Shannon, N.Z.	162	40.33 S	175.25 E
Shannon, S. Afr.	148	29.08 S	26.18 E
Shannon, Ga., U.S.	182	34.20 N	85.04 W
Shannon, Ill., U.S.	180	42.09 N	89.44 W
Shannon, Miss., U.S.	184	34.07 N	88.43 W
Shannon ≃	28	52.36 N	9.41 W
Shannon, Lake @	214	48.37 N	121.42 W
Shannons Flat	161b	35.54 S	148.58 E
Shannontown	182	33.53 N	80.21 W
Shannonville	202	44.12 N	77.13 W
Shanpo	90	30.06 N	114.20 E
Shanrendong	79	46.50 N	123.08 E
Shanrenqiao	96	31.16 N	120.27 E
Shanshan	76	42.52 N	90.10 E
Shanshenmiao	95	40.45 N	117.11 E
Shanshūr	132	30.21 N	31.00 E
Shansi → Shānxī □[4]	92	37.00 N	112.00 E
Shanting	88	35.09 N	117.29 E
Shantou (Swatow)	90	23.23 N	116.41 E
Shantouguan)(	90	27.54 N	117.26 E
Shantung → Shandong □[4]	88	36.00 N	118.00 E
Shantung Peninsula → Shandongbandao ≻[1]	88	37.00 N	121.00 E
Shanty Bay	202	44.25 N	79.36 W
Shanwa	144	3.10 S	33.46 E
Shanwangchang	97	29.38 N	104.38 E
Shanwei, Zhg.	90	22.47 N	115.21 E
Shanwei, Zhg.	92	22.21 N	107.58 E
Shānxī □[4], Zhg.	92	37.00 N	112.00 E
Shǎnxī □[4], Zhg.	92	35.00 N	109.00 E
Shanxian → Sanmenxia	92	34.45 N	111.05 E
Shanxiawu	90	28.52 N	113.52 E
Shanyang, Zhg.	90	26.43 N	119.13 E
Shanyang, Zhg.	92	33.35 N	109.49 E
Shanyang, Zhg.	96	31.19 N	120.16 E
Shanyao	90	25.08 N	118.53 E
Shanyaqiao	96	31.15 N	119.25 E
Shanyin	92	39.35 N	112.58 E
Shanzhangjiafen	95	40.37 N	116.44 E
Shanzui	95	40.48 N	118.13 E
Shanzuizi	94	41.55 N	120.30 E
Shaobo	90	32.30 N	119.32 E
Shaodenggao	94	42.13 N	121.47 E
Shaodian, Zhg.	88	34.05 N	118.30 E
Shaodian, Zhg.	90	33.10 N	114.18 E
Shaoguan	90	24.50 N	113.37 E
Shaogudian	88	36.57 N	115.32 E
Shaoguyingzi	94	41.33 N	120.27 E
Shaohing → Shaoxing	90	30.00 N	120.35 E
Shaohsing → Shaoxing	90	30.00 N	120.35 E
Shaohuyingzi	94	41.46 N	121.35 E
Shaojiaolou	96	31.05 N	121.32 E
Shaokuan → Shaoguan	90	24.50 N	113.37 E
Shaowu	90	27.20 N	117.28 E
Shaoxing	90	30.00 N	120.35 E
Shaoyang, Zhg.	92	26.53 N	111.13 E
Shaoyang, Zhg.	92	27.06 N	111.25 E
Shaozihe	88	40.13 N	123.33 E
Shap	42	54.32 N	2.41 W
Shapinsay I	28	59.03 N	2.51 W
Shāpūr ≃	118	29.39 N	51.03 E
Shaq'ah, Ra's ash- ≻	120	34.19 N	35.41 E
Shaqqā	122	32.53 N	36.42 E
Shaqq al-Ju'ayfir, Wādī ∨	130	15.16 N	26.00 E
Shaqrā, Lubnān	122	33.12 N	35.28 E
Shaqrā', Sūrīy.	122	32.54 N	36.14 E
Shaquan	76	44.33 N	83.25 E
Shaquzhen	97	30.33 N	103.45 E
Shār ≃	118	34.50 N	58.32 E
Sharafābād	262a	28.36 N	77.23 E
Sharafkhāneh	118	38.11 N	45.29 E
Sha'rah, Khabrat @	122	33.52 N	37.02 E
Sharan Jogīzai	110	31.02 N	68.33 E
Sharatin Mountain ∧	170	57.49 N	152.41 W
Sharbatāt, Ra's ash- ≻	108	17.52 N	56.22 E
Sharbīn, Jabal ∧	122	33.43 N	36.21 E
Sharbot Lake	202	44.46 N	76.41 W
Sharbot Lake @	202	44.46 N	76.41 W
Share	140	8.50 N	4.56 E
Shari	82a	43.55 N	144.50 E
Shari-dake ∧	82a	43.46 N	144.43 E
Shark ≃	210	25.21 N	81.05 W
Shark Bay C	152	25.30 S	113.30 E
Shark Point ≻, Austl.	264a	33.55 S	151.17 E
Shark Point ≻, Fla., U.S.	210	25.23 N	81.09 W
Shark River Hills	198	40.12 N	74.03 W
Sharnūb	132	31.01 N	30.35 E
Sharon, Ont., Can.	202	44.06 N	79.26 W
Sharon, Ont., Can.	204	42.53 N	81.22 W
Sharon, Conn., U.S.	197	41.53 N	73.29 W
Sharon, Mass., U.S.	197	42.05 N	71.11 W
Sharon, N. Dak., U.S.	188	47.36 N	97.54 W
Sharon, Pa., U.S.	204	41.14 N	80.31 W
Sharon, Wis., U.S.	206	42.30 N	88.44 W
Sharon Center	204	41.06 N	81.44 W
Sharon Hill	275	39.55 N	75.16 W
Sharon Park	208	39.23 N	84.35 W
Sharon Springs, Kans., U.S.	188	38.54 N	101.45 W
Sharon Springs, N.Y., U.S.	200	42.48 N	74.37 W
Sharon Valley	197	41.54 N	73.30 W
Sharonville	208	39.16 N	84.25 W
Sharpe Lake @	174	54.24 N	93.30 W
Sharpes	210	28.26 N	80.46 W
Sharp Park ♠	272	37.37 N	122.29 W
Sharp Peak ∧	106	5.58 N	125.31 E
Sharpsburg, Ill., U.S.	209	39.37 N	89.21 W
Sharpsburg, Ky., U.S.	208	38.12 N	83.56 W
Sharps Hill	269b	40.30 N	79.56 W
Sharps Run ≃	275	39.54 N	74.49 W
Sharpsville, Ind., U.S.	206	40.23 N	86.05 W
Sharpsville, Pa., U.S.	204	41.15 N	80.29 W
Sharptown	275	39.39 N	74.22 W
Sharqpur	113	31.28 N	74.06 E
Sharshar, Jabal ∧[2]	130	23.52 N	30.20 E
Shartlesville	198	40.31 N	76.06 W
Shārūnah	132	28.36 N	30.51 E
Shārūnah, Wādī ∨	132	28.36 N	30.52 E
Shasha	134	6.20 N	35.57 E
Shashi	92	30.19 N	112.14 E
Shashi ≃	146	22.14 S	29.20 E
Shashibu	90	25.48 N	114.54 E
Shasi → Shashi	92	30.19 N	112.14 E
Shasta	194	40.36 N	122.29 W
Shasta ≃	194	41.50 N	122.35 W
Shasta, Mount ∧[1]	194	41.20 N	122.20 W
Shasta Lake @[1]	194	40.50 N	122.25 W
Shatangjiang	96	31.25 N	120.01 E
Shaţānūf	132	30.14 N	31.04 E
Shatawī	130	14.39 N	32.06 E
Shāti', Wādī ash- ∨	136	27.30 N	13.15 E
Shatian, Zhg.	90	23.59 N	113.56 E
Shatian, Zhg.	90	25.53 N	113.44 E
Sha Tin Hoi C	261d	22.24 N	114.12 E
Sha Tin New Town	261d	22.23 N	114.11 E
Shattuck	186	36.16 N	99.53 W
Shatuji	88	35.18 N	115.45 E
Shatuosi	92	31.20 N	108.51 E
Shauck	204	40.37 N	82.40 W
Shaunavon	174	49.40 N	108.25 W
Shaver Lake	216	37.09 N	119.18 W
Shaver Lake @[1]	216	37.08 N	119.17 W
Shavertown	200	41.19 N	75.55 W
Shave Ziyyon	122	32.59 N	35.05 E
Shaw, Eng., U.K.	252	53.35 N	2.06 W
Shaw, Miss., U.S.	184	33.36 N	90.46 W
Shaw ≃	152	20.20 S	119.17 E
Shaw Air Force Base ■	182	33.58 N	80.29 W
Shawan, Zhg.	76	44.34 N	85.48 E
Shawan, Zhg.	90	27.52 N	119.28 E
Shawan, Zhg.	97	29.25 N	103.33 E
Shawanaga Inlet C	180	45.32 N	80.24 W
Shawangunk Kill ≃	200	41.41 N	74.10 W
Shawangunk Mountains ⩕	200	41.35 N	74.30 W
Shawano	180	44.47 N	88.36 W
Shawbridge	196	45.52 N	74.05 W
Shawbury	44	52.47 N	2.39 W
Shaw Creek ≃	182	33.34 N	81.30 W
Shawhan	208	38.18 N	84.16 W
Shawinigan	196	46.33 N	72.45 W
Shawinigan ≃	196	46.32 N	72.46 W
Shawinigan, Lac @	196	46.41 N	73.10 W
Shawinigan Falls → Shawinigan	196	46.33 N	72.45 W
Shawinigan-Sud	196	46.31 N	72.45 W
Shaw Island I	214	48.34 N	122.57 W
Shawmere ≃	180	48.40 N	82.29 W
Shawnee, Kans., U.S.	188	39.01 N	94.43 W
Shawnee, Ohio, U.S.	178	39.36 N	82.13 W
Shawnee, Okla., U.S.	186	35.20 N	96.55 W
Shawnee, Lake @	266	40.58 N	74.35 W
Shawnee Hills	204	40.07 N	83.09 W
Shawnee On Delaware	200	41.01 N	75.07 W
Shawnee State Park ♠	208	38.43 N	83.10 W
Shawneetown	184	37.42 N	88.08 W
Shawnī	132	30.45 N	30.55 E
Shawnigan Lake	214	48.38 N	123.35 W
Shawnigan Lake @	214	48.37 N	123.37 W
Shawo, Som.	134	3.26 N	45.22 E
Shawo, Zhg.	88	34.28 N	114.37 E
Shawo, Zhg.	90	31.44 N	115.08 E
Shawo, Zhg.	90	28.52 N	114.47 E
Shaw River	152	20.43 S	119.20 E
Shawsheen ≃	273	42.42 N	71.08 W
Shawtown	269b	40.20 N	79.42 W
Shawville	178	45.36 N	76.30 W
Shaxi, Zhg.	90	24.38 N	113.42 E
Shaxi, Zhg.	90	28.34 N	118.06 E
Shaxi, Zhg.	90	26.53 N	115.34 E
Shaxi, Zhg.	96	31.34 N	121.04 E
Shaxi ≃	90	26.34 N	118.02 E
Shaxian	90	26.24 N	117.47 E
Shaxikou	90	26.33 N	118.02 E
Shaximiao	97	29.57 N	106.19 E
Shayangzhen	90	30.42 N	112.33 E
Shaybārā I	118	25.27 N	36.48 E
Shaykh, Jabal ash- (Mount Hermon) ∧	122	33.26 N	35.51 E
Shaykh, Wādī ash- ∨	132	28.48 N	30.55 E
Shaykh al-Ḩadīd	120	36.30 N	36.35 E
Shaykh Sa'd	118	32.34 N	46.17 E
Shaykh 'Uthmān	134	12.52 N	44.59 E
Shayuan	90	27.45 N	120.38 E
Shazhen	88	36.23 N	115.47 E
Shazihe	92	32.12 N	106.42 E
Shchekino → Ščokino	66	54.01 N	37.31 E
Shchelkovo → Ščelkovo	66	55.55 N	38.00 E
Shcherbakov → Rybinsk	66	58.03 N	38.52 E
Sheaf ≃	42	53.23 N	1.26 W
Shea Island I	266	41.03 N	73.24 W
Sheakhala	116	22.46 N	88.10 E
Sheakleyville	204	41.27 N	80.13 W
Shea Stadium ♠	266	40.45 N	73.51 W
Shebele	134	9.43 N	42.43 E
Shebele (Shebelle) ≃	134	0.01 S	42.45 E
Sheberghān	110	36.41 N	65.45 E
Shebeshekong ≃	202	45.26 N	80.19 W
Sheboygan	180	43.46 N	87.36 W
Sheboygan ≃	180	43.45 N	87.42 W
Sheboygan Falls	180	43.44 N	87.49 W
Shebu	90	27.40 N	112.48 E
Shechem → Nābulus	122	32.13 N	35.16 E
Shechem ⊥	122	32.13 N	35.15 E
Shecheng	92	37.14 N	113.05 E
Shedden	204	42.44 N	81.21 W
Shedfield	44	50.55 N	1.12 W
Shediac	176	46.13 N	64.32 W
Shedin Peak ∧	172	55.55 N	127.32 W
Sheenjek ≃	170	66.45 N	144.33 W
Sheep ≃	172	50.44 N	113.51 W
Sheep Creek ≃, Alta., Can.	172	54.04 N	119.00 W
Sheep Creek ≃, U.S.	192	42.27 N	115.36 W
Sheep Creek ≃, Wyo., U.S.	190	42.03 N	106.04 W
Sheep Haven C	28	55.10 N	7.52 W
Sheepmoor	148	26.42 S	30.13 E
Sheep Mountain ∧, Ariz., U.S.	190	32.32 N	114.14 W
Sheep Mountain ∧, Wyo., U.S.	190	43.33 N	110.32 W
Sheep Peak ∧	186	31.14 N	104.59 W
Sheepranch	216	38.13 N	120.28 W
Sheep Range ⩕	194	36.45 N	115.05 W
Sheepscot ≃	178	44.00 N	69.50 W
Sheepshead Bay •[8]	266	40.35 N	73.56 W
's-Heerenberg	48	51.53 N	6.15 E
's-Heerenhoek	48	51.27 N	3.46 E
Sheerness	44	51.27 N	0.45 E
Sheet Harbour	176	44.55 N	62.32 W
Shefar'am	122	32.48 N	35.10 E
Sheffield, N.Z.	162	43.23 S	172.01 E
Sheffield, Eng., U.K.	42	53.23 N	1.30 W
Sheffield, Ala., U.S.	184	34.46 N	87.40 W
Sheffield, Ill., U.S.	180	41.21 N	89.44 W
Sheffield, Iowa, U.S.	180	42.54 N	93.13 W
Sheffield, Mass., U.S.	197	42.05 N	73.21 W
Sheffield, Ohio, U.S.	204	41.28 N	82.03 W
Sheffield, Pa., U.S.	204	41.42 N	79.02 W
Sheffield, Tex., U.S.	186	30.41 N	101.49 W
Sheffield Island I	266	41.03 N	73.25 W
Sheffield Island Harbor C	266	41.03 N	73.25 W
Sheffield Lake	204	41.29 N	82.07 W

Symbols in the index entries represent the broad categories identified in the key at the right. Symbols with superior numbers (⩕[2]) identify subcategories (see complete key on page *I* · 26).

Kartensymbole in dem Registerverzeichnis stellen die rechts in Schlüssel erklärten Kategorien dar. Symbole mit hochgestellten Ziffern (⩕[2]) bezeichnen Unterabteilungen einer Kategorie (vgl. vollständiger Schlüssel auf Seite *I* · 26).

Los símbolos incluídos en el texto del índice representan las grandes categorias identificadas con la clave a la derecha. Los símbolos con numeros en su parte superior (⩕[2]) identifican las subcategorías (véase la clave completa en la página *I* · 26).

Les symboles de l'index représentent les catégories indiquées dans la légende à droite. Les symboles suivis d'un indice (⩕[2]) représentent des sous-catégories (voir légende complète à la page *I* · 26).

Os símbolos incluídos no texto do índice representam as grandes categorias identificadas com a chave à direita. Os símbolos com números em sua parte superior (⩕[2]) identificam as subcategorias (veja-se a chave completa à página *I* · 26).

∧	Mountain	Berg	Montaña	Montagne	Montanha
⩕	Mountains	Berge	Montañas	Montagnes	Montanhas
)(	Pass	Pass	Paso	Col	Passo
∨	Valley, Canyon	Tal, Cañon	Valle, Cañón	Vallée, Canyon	Vale, Canhão
⌣	Plain	Ebene	Llano	Plaine	Planície
≻	Cape	Kap	Cabo	Cap	Cabo
I	Island	Insel	Isla	Île	Ilha
II	Islands	Inseln	Islas	Îles	Ilhas
•	Other Topographic Features	Andere Topographische Objekte	Otros Elementos Topográficos	Autres données topographiques	Outros Elementos Topográficos

ESPAÑOL

Nombre	Página	Lat.°′	Long.°′ W=Oeste
Sheffield Lake ⊜	176	49.20 N	56.35 W
Shefford	44	52.02 N	0.20 W
Shefford □[6]	196	45.25 N	72.30 W
Shefuwei	90	26.11 N	115.22 E
Shegangshi	90	28.32 N	113.36 E
Shegaon	112	20.47 N	76.41 E
Sheho	174	51.38 N	103.12 W
Shehojele	134	10.40 N	35.09 E
Shehong (Taihezhon)	92	30.56 N	105.22 E
Shehongmiao	97	30.44 N	106.03 E
Shekatika Bay	176	51.17 N	58.20 W
Shēkhābād	110	34.05 N	68.45 E
Shek Hasan	134	12.09 N	35.54 E
Shekhūpura	113	31.42 N	73.59 E
Sheki → Šeki	74	41.12 N	47.12 E
Shekki → Zhongshan	90	22.31 N	113.22 E
Shek Ku Chau I	261d	22.12 N	113.59 E
Shekou	90	30.44 N	114.20 E
Shelagyote Peak ʌ	172	55.58 N	127.12 W
Shelbina	209	39.47 N	92.02 W
Shelbourne	159	36.52 S	144.01 E
Shelburn	184	39.11 N	87.24 W
Shelburne, N.S., Can.	176	43.46 N	65.19 W
Shelburne, Ont., Can.	202	44.04 N	80.12 W
Shelburne Bay C	154	11.49 S	143.00 E
Shelburne Falls	197	42.36 N	72.44 W
Shelby, Ind., U.S.	206	41.12 N	87.21 W
Shelby, Iowa, U.S.	188	41.31 N	95.27 W
Shelby, Mich., U.S.	180	43.37 N	86.22 W
Shelby, Miss., U.S.	184	33.57 N	90.46 W
Shelby, Mont., U.S.	192	48.30 N	111.51 W
Shelby, Nebr., U.S.	188	41.12 N	97.26 W
Shelby, N.C., U.S.	182	35.17 N	81.32 W
Shelby, Ohio, U.S.	204	40.53 N	82.40 W
Shelby □[6], Ill., U.S.	209	39.24 N	88.48 W
Shelby □[6], Ind., U.S.	208	39.31 N	85.47 W
Shelby □[6], Ky., U.S.	208	38.15 N	85.13 W
Shelby □[6], Mo., U.S.	209	39.49 N	92.03 W
Shelby □[6], Ohio, U.S.	206	40.17 N	84.09 W
Shelby Village	204	42.38 N	83.04 W
Shelbyville, Ill., U.S.	209	39.24 N	88.48 W
Shelbyville, Ind., U.S.	208	39.31 N	85.47 W
Shelbyville, Ky., U.S.	208	38.13 N	85.14 W
Shelbyville, Mo., U.S.	209	39.48 N	92.02 W
Shelbyville, Tenn., U.S.	184	35.29 N	86.27 W
Shelbyville, Lake ⊜[1]	209	39.30 N	88.40 W
Sheldon, Ill., U.S.	206	40.46 N	87.34 W
Sheldon, Iowa, U.S.	188	43.11 N	95.51 W
Sheldon, Mich., U.S.	206	42.17 N	83.28 W
Sheldon, Mo., U.S.	184	37.40 N	94.18 W
Sheldon, Tex., U.S.	212	29.52 N	95.08 W
Sheldon Brook ≃	266	41.03 N	73.52 W
Sheldon Creek ≃	202	44.07 N	79.53 W
Sheldon Point	170	62.32 N	164.52 W
Sheldon Reservoir ⊜[1]	212	29.52 N	95.10 W
Sheldonville	273	42.02 N	71.23 W
Sheldrake ≃	266	40.57 N	73.44 W
Sheldrake Lake ⊜, Ont., Can.	202	44.49 N	77.16 W
Sheldrake Lake ⊜, N.Y., U.S.	266	40.57 N	73.46 W
Shelikof Strait ⋃	170	57.30 N	155.00 W
Shell ≃	174	50.58 N	101.24 W
Shellbrook	174	53.13 N	106.24 W
Shell Creek ≃, U.S.	190	40.56 N	108.37 W
Shell Creek ≃, Nebr., U.S.	188	41.27 N	96.58 W
Shell Creek ≃, N. Dak., U.S.	188	47.59 N	102.17 W
Shell Creek ≃, Wyo., U.S.	192	44.31 N	108.03 W
Shelley, B.C., Can.	172	54.00 N	122.37 W
Shelley, Idaho, U.S.	192	43.23 N	112.07 W
Shellharbour	160	34.35 S	150.52 E
Shell Lake, Sask., Can.	174	53.18 N	107.07 W
Shell Lake, Wis., U.S.	180	45.45 N	91.55 W
Shell Lakes ⊜	152	29.21 S	127.25 E
Shellman	182	31.46 N	84.37 W
Shellow Bowells	250	51.45 N	0.20 E
Shell Rock	180	42.43 N	92.35 W
Shell Rock ≃	180	42.38 N	92.30 W
Shellrock Peak ʌ	214	46.43 N	121.14 W
Shellsburg	180	42.06 N	91.52 W
Shelocta	204	40.39 N	79.18 W
Shelter, Port C	261d	22.21 N	114.17 E
Shelter Island	197	41.05 N	72.21 W
Shelter Island I	261d	22.20 N	114.17 E
Shelter Island Heights	197	41.05 N	72.21 W
Shelter Island Sound ⋃	197	41.03 N	72.22 W
Shelton, Conn., U.S.	197	41.19 N	73.05 W
Shelton, Nebr., U.S.	188	40.47 N	98.44 W
Shelton, Wash., U.S.	214	47.13 N	123.06 W
Shemanker ≃	140	8.12 N	9.45 E
Shemogue	176	46.09 N	64.11 W
Shemya Station	170	52.43 N	174.05 E
Shenandoah, Iowa, U.S.	188	40.46 N	95.22 W
Shenandoah, Pa., U.S.	198	40.49 N	76.12 W
Shenandoah, Va., U.S.	178	38.29 N	78.37 W
Shenandoah ≃	178	39.19 N	92.03 W
Shenandoah, North Fork ≃	178	38.57 N	78.12 W
Shenandoah, South Fork ≃	178	38.57 N	78.12 W
Shenandoah Heights	200	40.49 N	76.12 W
Shenandoah National Park ♠	178	38.48 N	78.12 W
Shenango	204	41.23 N	80.24 W
Shenango ≃	204	40.57 N	80.23 W
Shenango River Lake ⊜[1]	204	41.22 N	80.28 W
Shenchi	92	39.09 N	112.19 E
Shencottah	112	8.58 N	77.16 E
Shencun	96	31.04 N	118.51 E
Shendam	140	8.53 N	9.32 E
Shendang	96	30.34 N	120.49 E
Shenduncun	96	30.48 N	120.25 E
Shenfield	250	51.38 N	0.19 E
Shengang, Zhg.	90	27.20 N	116.18 E
Shen'gang, Zhg.	96	31.54 N	120.08 E
Shengcitang	96	32.03 N	120.10 E
Shenge	140	7.55 N	12.57 W
Shengfang	95	39.04 N	116.42 E
Shengfo	97	30.12 N	104.29 E
Shenggongjing	96	31.07 N	119.48 E
Shenghongxiang	90	30.12 N	114.56 E
Shengjiachi	97	30.28 N	105.03 E
Shengjiaqiao	96	31.27 N	121.24 E
Shengjiatun	94	41.14 N	121.22 E
Shengjin'gao	94	42.04 N	120.43 E
Shengqing	94	41.34 N	121.36 E
Shengshanshi	96	30.50 N	120.15 E
Shengshui	88	35.45 N	119.39 E
Shengshuihezi	88	42.27 N	125.59 E
Shengsi I	90	30.41 N	122.28 E
Shengsiqundao II	90	30.42 N	122.20 E
Shengtian	90	27.14 N	113.06 E
Shengxian	90	29.36 N	120.48 E
Shengze	96	30.55 N	120.39 E
Shengzigou	94	41.35 N	124.04 E
Shenhou	90	34.08 N	113.13 E
Shenhu	90	24.38 N	118.39 E
Shenhuwan C	90	24.40 N	118.42 E
Shenipsit Lake ⊜	197	41.53 N	72.26 W
Shenji	88	34.47 N	115.09 E
Shenjia	79	46.06 N	126.46 E
Shenjiadian	79	46.35 N	130.38 E
Shenjiamen	90	29.58 N	122.17 E
Shenjiatai	94	41.22 N	120.50 E
Shenjiawan	96	31.43 N	121.19 E
Shenjiazhuang	96	32.18 N	120.26 E
Shenjing, Zhg.	92	21.59 N	112.28 E
Shenjing, Zhg.	95	40.24 N	114.49 E
Shenjingzi	94	41.47 N	123.41 E

FRANÇAIS

Nom	Page	Lat.°′	Long.°′ W=Ouest
Shenk'eng	259d	25.00 N	121.36 E
Shenkou	90	28.42 N	116.02 E
Shenley	250	51.41 N	0.17 W
Shenmu	92	38.56 N	110.19 E
Shennanling	95	39.01 N	114.50 E
Shenorock	200	41.20 N	73.44 W
Shenqiu	90	33.24 N	115.02 E
Shenquan	90	22.59 N	116.20 E
Shenquangang C	90	22.54 N	116.18 E
Shensi → Shănxī □[4]	92	35.00 N	109.00 E
Shenton, Mount ʌ	152	28.00 S	123.22 E
Shentuan	88	35.30 N	119.17 E
Shenxian	88	38.01 N	115.33 E
Shenxian'gou ≃	88	37.53 N	118.47 E
Shenyang (Mukden)	94	41.48 N	123.27 E
Shenze	88	38.11 N	115.11 E
Shenzha	110	30.57 N	88.38 E
Sheo	110	26.11 N	71.15 E
Sheoganj	110	25.09 N	73.04 E
Sheopur	114	25.40 N	76.42 E
Shepard	172	50.57 N	113.55 W
Shepard Island I	9	74.25 S	132.30 W
Shepards Brook ≃	273	42.08 N	71.25 W
Shepaug ≃	197	41.28 N	73.19 W
Shepherd, Mich., U.S.	180	43.32 N	84.41 W
Shepherd, Tex., U.S.	212	30.30 N	95.00 W
Shepherd Bay C	166	68.56 N	93.40 W
Shepherd Islands II	165f	16.55 S	168.36 E
Shepherdstown	178	39.26 N	77.48 W
Shepherdsville	184	37.59 N	85.43 W
Sheppard Air Force Base ■	186	33.58 N	98.30 W
Sheppard Peak ʌ	170	57.41 N	132.37 W
Sheppard Pond ⊜	266	41.08 N	74.13 W
Shepparton	156	36.23 S	145.25 E
Shepperd, Lake ⊜	152	29.55 S	123.09 E
Shepperton	250	51.24 N	0.27 W
Sheppey, Isle of I	44	51.24 N	0.50 E
Sheppler Hill ʌ[2]	269b	40.09 N	79.49 W
Sheppton	200	40.54 N	76.07 W
Shepshed	44	52.47 N	1.18 W
Shepton Mallet	44	51.12 N	2.33 W
Shepway	250	51.15 N	0.33 E
Sheqizhen	90	33.03 N	112.57 E
Sherab	130	10.43 N	24.47 E
Sherada	134	7.21 N	36.32 E
Sheraden ⬥[8]	269b	40.28 N	80.05 W
Sherard, Cape ≻	166	74.36 N	80.25 W
Sherborn	273	42.14 N	71.22 W
Sherborne	44	50.57 N	2.31 W
Sherborne Lake ⊜	202	45.11 N	78.47 W
Sherborne Saint John	44	51.18 N	1.07 W
Sherbro ≃	140	7.45 N	12.55 W
Sherbro Island I	140	7.45 N	12.55 W
Sherbrooke, N.S., Can.	176	45.08 N	61.59 W
Sherbrooke, Qué., Can.	196	45.24 N	71.54 W
Sherbrooke □[6]	196	45.25 N	71.55 W
Sherbrooke Forest Park ♠	159	37.53 S	145.22 E
Sherbrooke Lake ⊜	176	44.40 N	64.35 W
Sherburn	188	43.39 N	94.43 W
Sherburne	200	42.41 N	75.30 W
Sherburne Reef ⟡[2]	154	3.20 S	148.00 E
Shercock	42	54.00 N	6.54 W
Shere	250	51.13 N	0.28 W
Sheridan, Ark., U.S.	184	34.19 N	92.24 W
Sheridan, Calif., U.S.	216	38.59 N	121.22 W
Sheridan, Ill., U.S.	206	41.32 N	88.41 W
Sheridan, Ind., U.S.	208	40.08 N	86.13 W
Sheridan, Mont., U.S.	192	45.27 N	112.12 W
Sheridan, Oreg., U.S.	192	45.06 N	123.24 W
Sheridan, Pa., U.S.	198	40.21 N	76.14 W
Sheridan, Tex., U.S.	212	29.29 N	96.40 W
Sheridan, Wyo., U.S.	192	44.48 N	106.58 W
Sheridan, Mount ʌ	192	44.16 N	110.32 W
Sheridan Park ♠	274a	42.59 N	78.54 W
Sheringa	152	33.51 S	135.15 E
Sheringham	44	52.57 N	1.12 E
Sherkston	274a	42.53 N	79.08 W
Sherlock ≃	152	20.44 S	117.35 E
Sherman, Conn., U.S.	197	41.35 N	73.30 W
Sherman, Ill., U.S.	209	39.54 N	89.36 W
Sherman, Ky., U.S.	208	38.44 N	84.36 W
Sherman, Miss., U.S.	184	34.22 N	88.57 W
Sherman, N.Y., U.S.	204	42.10 N	79.36 W
Sherman, Tex., U.S.	186	33.38 N	96.36 W
Sherman □[6]	214	45.25 N	120.49 W
Sherman Creek ≃	198	40.23 N	77.02 W
Sherman Mills	178	45.52 N	68.23 W
Sherman Mountain ʌ	184	36.01 N	93.17 W
Sherman Oaks ⬥[8]	270	34.09 N	118.26 W
Sherman Reservoir ⊜[1]	188	41.20 N	98.55 W
Sherman Station	178	45.54 N	68.26 W
Sherpur, Bngl.	114	25.01 N	90.01 E
Sherpur, Bngl.	114	24.41 N	89.25 E
Sher Qila	113	36.06 N	74.03 E
Sherrard	180	41.19 N	90.31 W
Sherridon	174	55.07 N	101.05 W
Sherrill	200	43.04 N	75.35 W
Sherri Park	268	42.02 N	87.51 W
Sherrodsville	204	40.30 N	81.15 W
Sher Shāh	113	30.06 N	71.21 E
Shertallai	112	9.42 N	76.20 E
's-Hertogenbosch	48	51.41 N	5.19 E
Sherwood, Ont., Can.	265b	43.50 N	79.31 W
Sherwood, P.E.I., Can.	176	46.17 N	63.08 W
Sherwood, Md., U.S.	198	38.36 N	76.19 W
Sherwood, Mich., U.S.	206	42.00 N	85.14 W
Sherwood, N. Dak., U.S.	188	48.58 N	101.38 W
Sherwood, Ohio, U.S.	206	41.17 N	84.33 W
Sherwood, Oreg., U.S.	214	45.21 N	122.50 W
Sherwood, Tenn., U.S.	184	35.05 N	85.56 W
Sherwood, Lake ⊜	271	42.36 N	83.33 W
Sherwood Forest, Calif., U.S.	216	37.57 N	122.17 W
Sherwood Forest, Md., U.S.	274c	39.05 N	77.01 W
Sherwood Forest ⬥[3]	44	53.08 N	1.08 W
Sherwood Island State Park ♠	266	41.07 N	73.20 W
Sherwood Manor	197	42.01 N	72.38 W
Sherwood Park, Alta., Can.	172	53.31 N	113.19 W
Sherwood Park, N.Y., U.S.	200	42.36 N	73.43 W
Sherwood Park ♠	265b	43.43 N	79.24 W
Sherwood Point ≻	266	41.07 N	73.20 W
Sheshan ʌ[2]	96	31.06 N	121.11 E
Sheshan I	90	28.26 N	121.53 E
Sheshea ≃	238	9.36 S	74.10 W
Shesh Gāv	110	33.45 N	68.33 E
Shet Bandar	262c	18.58 N	72.56 E
Shetland del Sur, Islas → South Shetland Islands II	9	62.00 S	58.00 W
Shetland Islands □[4]	28	60.30 N	0.15 W
Shetland Islands II	28	60.30 N	1.30 W
Shetou	96	31.39 N	119.27 E
Shetrunji ≃	110	21.19 N	72.07 E
Shetucket ≃	197	41.31 N	72.05 W
Sheva	262c	18.56 N	72.57 E
Sheva Nhava	262c	18.58 N	72.58 E
Shevaroy Hills ⛰[2]	112	11.50 N	78.16 E
Shevington	252	53.34 N	2.42 W
Shevington Moor	252	53.35 N	2.41 W
Shevut 'Am	122	32.19 N	34.55 E
Shewa □[4]	134	9.00 N	39.00 E
Shewa Gimira	134	7.00 N	35.50 E
Shexian	90	29.53 N	118.26 E
Sheyang (Hede), Zhg.	90	33.46 N	120.18 E
Sheyang, Zhg.	90	33.20 N	119.38 E
Sheyanghu ⊜	90	33.19 N	119.46 E

PORTUGUÊS

Nome	Página	Lat.°′	Long.°′ W=Oeste
Sheyenne	188	47.39 N	99.07 W
Sheyenne ≃	188	47.05 N	96.50 W
Shezhu	96	31.19 N	119.16 E
Shḥīm	122	33.37 N	35.29 E
Shiant Islands II	28	57.54 N	6.30 W
Shiawassee □[6]	206	42.56 N	84.09 W
Shiawassee ≃	206	43.06 N	84.10 W
Shiawassee, South Branch ≃	206	42.49 N	83.56 W
Shiba	90	32.45 N	118.07 E
Shiba ≃	258	35.37 N	139.44 E
Shibadu	92	28.01 N	110.51 E
Shibakawa	84	35.13 N	138.33 E
Shibām	134	15.56 N	48.38 E
Shibandeng	97	30.18 N	104.28 E
Shibanxi	97	29.17 N	103.51 E
Shibaocheng	92	39.48 N	96.10 E
Shibarni	130	14.50 N	24.25 E
Shibasaki	258	35.39 N	139.34 E
Shibata	82	37.57 N	139.20 E
Shibayama	84	35.41 N	140.25 E
Shibayama-gata ⊜	84	36.21 N	136.23 E
Shibecha	82a	43.17 N	144.36 E
Shibetsu, Nihon	82a	43.40 N	145.08 E
Shibetsu, Nihon	82a	44.10 N	142.23 E
Shibi	90	26.43 N	120.02 E
Shibīn al-Kawm	132	30.33 N	31.01 E
Shibīn al-Qanāṭir	132	30.19 N	31.19 E
Shibing	92	26.50 N	108.04 E
Shiblanjah	132	30.28 N	31.16 E
Shibotsu-tō I	82a	43.30 N	146.09 E
Shibu, Zhg.	88	36.09 N	119.06 E
Shibu, Zhg.	88	36.25 N	119.44 E
Shibukawa	84	36.29 N	139.00 E
Shibure-yama ʌ[2]	260	34.45 N	135.05 E
Shibushi	82	31.28 N	131.07 E
Shibutsu-san ʌ	84	36.54 N	139.11 E
Shibuya ⬥[8]	258	35.40 N	139.42 E
Shicha	90	28.24 N	115.50 E
Shichangyu	94	41.12 N	123.14 E
Shicheng, Zhg.	88	40.39 N	124.17 E
Shicheng, Zhg.	90	26.22 N	116.22 E
Shicheng, Zhg.	90	25.18 N	119.21 E
Shichengdao I	88	39.31 N	123.02 E
Shichisō	84	35.33 N	137.07 E
Shichiyo I	165c	7.23 N	151.40 E
Shichuan	92	36.10 N	103.57 E
Shickley	188	40.25 N	97.43 W
Shickshinny	200	41.09 N	76.09 W
Shicun	96	31.09 N	119.20 E
Shidai	90	30.20 N	117.56 E
Shidao	88	36.53 N	122.23 E
Shideng	92	26.44 N	99.11 E
Shidler	186	36.47 N	96.40 W
Shido	86	34.19 N	134.10 E
Shidong, Zhg.	97	28.59 N	105.27 E
Shidong, Zhg.	97	30.25 N	105.20 E
Shidongzigou	95	40.41 N	118.23 E
Shiducun	88	39.37 N	115.36 E
Shields ≃	192	45.43 N	110.28 W
Shiercun	96	30.31 N	119.34 E
Shiershan ʌ	90	29.18 N	118.08 E
Shierwei, Zhg.	96	31.59 N	120.43 E
Shierwei, Zhg.	96	32.15 N	119.14 E
Shierzhan	79	51.13 N	125.52 E
Shifang	90	25.01 N	116.14 E
Shifengxi ≃	90	28.52 N	121.04 E
Shifnal	44	52.40 N	2.21 W
Shifo	97	29.58 N	103.50 E
Shifobao	94	41.28 N	121.27 E
Shifochang	97	30.19 N	105.07 E
Shifodian	90	32.06 N	115.46 E
Shifosi	94	42.08 N	123.20 E
Shifoya	88	40.12 N	123.10 E
Shifuhu ⊜	110	31.20 N	83.25 E
Shiga, Nihon	84	35.09 N	135.55 E
Shiga, Nihon	84	36.20 N	137.59 E
Shiga □[5]	86	35.15 N	136.00 E
Shigaib	130	15.01 N	23.36 E
Shigaise → Rikaze	110	29.17 N	88.53 E
Shigang	90	32.16 N	121.00 E
Shigaopu	97	30.16 N	104.01 E
Shigar ≃	113	34.39 N	75.51 E
Shigaraki	84	34.52 N	136.03 E
Shigaraki-gū ❦[1]	84	34.54 N	136.04 E
Shiga University ❦[2]	260	35.00 N	135.53 E
Shigenobu	86	33.48 N	132.50 E
Shigenobu ≃	86	33.48 N	132.41 E
Shigezhuang, Zhg.	95	38.59 N	115.36 E
Shigezhuang, Zhg.	95	39.18 N	116.53 E
Shigezhuang, Zhg.	95	38.57 N	116.19 E
Shiggar ≃	113	34.35 N	75.59 E
Shigoubao	92	37.44 N	106.26 E
Shigu, Zhg.	90	34.10 N	113.39 E
Shigu, Zhg.	90	29.27 N	117.14 E
Shigu, Zhg.	92	26.50 N	99.55 E
Shiguantun	94	41.38 N	123.39 E
Shigulingyu	95	40.38 N	116.54 E
Shīḥān ʌ	122	31.23 N	35.44 E
Shihch'i → Zhongshan	90	22.31 N	113.22 E
Shihchiachuang → Shijiazhuang	88	38.03 N	114.28 E
Shihe	88	39.19 N	121.52 E
Shihe ≃	90	32.18 N	114.31 E
Shihengyuanyu	96	31.50 N	121.45 E
Shihkiachwang → Shijiazhuang	88	38.03 N	114.28 E
Shihlin	259d	25.05 N	121.31 E
Shihti	259d	25.02 N	121.44 E
Shihting	259d	24.59 N	121.39 E
Shihu, Zhg.	88	41.29 N	126.18 E
Shihu, Zhg.	95	40.04 N	117.17 E
Shihuajie	92	32.20 N	111.25 E
Shihudang	96	30.58 N	121.07 E
Shihuiqiao	90	26.58 N	114.23 E
Shihuixi	97	29.02 N	105.04 E
Shihuiyaozi	94	42.08 N	123.47 E
Shihuxia	95	40.48 N	117.22 E
Shiida	86	33.39 N	131.04 E
Shijiaba	97	30.18 N	104.46 E
Shijiagang	90	30.41 N	114.32 E
Shijiagangzi	94	42.19 N	123.34 E
Shijiagou	94	42.27 N	123.28 E
Shijiao	90	23.36 N	112.59 E
Shijiaqiao	96	32.18 N	119.26 E
Shijiawu	95	39.21 N	116.15 E
Shijiaxiang	97	29.38 N	104.59 E
Shijiayaozhuang	96	32.13 N	120.29 E
Shijiazhai	88	38.56 N	114.18 E
Shijiazhen	96	31.51 N	121.10 E
Shijiazhuang	88	38.03 N	114.28 E
Shijiazi, Zhg.	94	42.12 N	122.14 E
Shijiazi, Zhg.	94	42.39 N	122.06 E
Shijiedu	96	30.57 N	119.13 E
Shijing, Zhg.	90	24.40 N	118.24 E
Shijing, Zhg.	95	39.54 N	114.58 E
Shijingshan	95	39.56 N	116.07 E
Shijiuhu ⊜	96	31.28 N	118.53 E
Shijiusuo	88	35.24 N	119.29 E
Shijiutuo I	88	39.11 N	118.56 E
Shijōnawate	260	34.45 N	135.39 E
Shijūmagari-tōge)(	86	35.11 N	133.32 E
Shijushan	92	39.20 N	106.50 E
Shika	84	37.01 N	136.47 E
Shikami-yama ʌ	260	34.47 N	135.10 E
Shikano	86	35.28 N	134.04 E
Shikārpur, Bhārat	112	14.16 N	75.21 E
Shikārpur, Bhārat	114	28.17 N	78.01 E
Shikārpur, Pāk.	110	27.57 N	68.38 E
Shikata	86	34.49 N	134.49 E
Shikatsu	84	35.14 N	136.53 E
Shikewusumiao	92	40.13 N	108.52 E
Shiki	258	35.50 N	139.35 E
Shiki I	165c	7.24 N	151.53 E
Shikishima	84	35.41 N	138.32 E
Shikohābād	114	27.06 N	78.36 E
Shikoku I	82	33.45 N	133.30 E
Shikoku-sanchi ⛰	86	33.47 N	133.30 E
Shikoma	258	35.11 N	139.56 E
Shikongling ʌ	90	24.56 N	113.00 E
Shikotsu-ko ⊜	82a	42.45 N	141.20 E

Shikotsu-tōya-kokuritsu-kōen ♠	82a	42.47 N	141.00 E
Shikuang	96	31.54 N	121.24 E
Shil	262c	19.09 N	73.03 E
Shilabo	134	6.05 N	44.48 E
Shilbottle	42	55.23 N	1.42 W
Shildon	42	54.38 N	1.39 W
Shiliangji	90	33.54 N	115.14 E
Shilibao	95	39.55 N	116.29 E
Shilihe	94	41.31 N	123.22 E
Shiling	96	30.26 N	119.35 E
Shilipeng	96	31.14 N	119.35 E
Shilipu, Zhg.	95	39.29 N	116.18 E
Shilipu, Zhg.	95	39.11 N	115.59 E
Shilipu, Zhg.	95	40.15 N	117.58 E
Shiliuban	90	24.11 N	117.31 E
Shiliugu	88	34.14 N	115.52 E
Shillelagh	28	52.45 N	6.32 W
Shillingstone	44	50.54 N	2.14 W
Shillington	198	40.18 N	75.58 W
Shillong	110	25.34 N	91.53 E
Shiloh, Ill., U.S.	209	38.34 N	89.54 W
Shiloh, N.J., U.S.	198	39.27 N	75.18 W
Shiloh, Ohio, U.S.	204	40.58 N	82.36 W
Shiloh, Pa., U.S.	198	39.59 N	76.49 W
Shiloh National Military Park ♠	184	35.06 N	88.21 W
Shilong	90	23.07 N	113.48 E
Shilongchang	97	30.15 N	106.34 E
Shilou	90	22.58 N	113.29 E
Shima, Nihon	82	34.13 N	136.51 E
Shima, Nihon	260	34.59 N	135.20 E
Shima, Zhg.	90	24.27 N	117.49 E
Shimabara	82	32.47 N	130.22 E
Shimachang, Zhg.	97	28.59 N	105.55 E
Shimachang, Zhg.	97	29.03 N	105.36 E
Shimada, Nihon	84	34.49 N	138.11 E
Shimada, Nihon	258	35.59 N	139.25 E
Shimagahara	84	34.46 N	136.03 E
Shima-hantō ≻[1]	84	34.26 N	136.33 E
Shimamiao	96	32.08 N	119.20 E
Shimamoto	86	34.53 N	135.40 E
Shimane □[5]	86	35.00 N	132.30 E
Shimane-hantō ≻[1]	86	35.30 N	133.00 E
Shimantan	90	33.17 N	113.28 E
Shimanto ≃	86	32.56 N	133.00 E
Shimata ≃	86	33.57 N	131.55 E
Shimba Hills National Reserve ⬥[4]	144	4.15 S	39.25 E
Shimei	96	32.14 N	120.10 E
Shimen, Zhg.	88	39.44 N	118.52 E
Shimen, Zhg.	92	29.28 N	111.17 E
Shimen, Zhg.	95	40.06 N	117.42 E
Shimen, Zhg.	97	29.36 N	106.27 E
Shimencun, Zhg.	96	31.21 N	119.34 E
Shimencun, Zhg.	96	30.23 N	119.41 E
Shimendong	90	28.16 N	120.07 E
Shimengou	94	40.40 N	123.43 E
Shimenjie	90	29.34 N	116.44 E
Shimenlou	90	28.58 N	114.51 E
Shimenwan	96	30.37 N	120.26 E
Shimenzi	79	48.30 N	121.31 E
Shimian (Nongchang)	92	29.18 N	102.22 E
Shimiaozi	94	40.39 N	123.31 E
Shimizu, Nihon	82	35.01 N	138.29 E
Shimizu → Tosa-shimizu, Nihon	82	32.46 N	132.57 E
Shimizu, Nihon	82a	43.01 N	142.53 E
Shimizu, Nihon	84	36.02 N	136.09 E
Shimizu, Nihon	84	35.01 N	138.29 E
Shimizu, Nihon	86	34.05 N	135.26 E
Shimizu-tunnel ⬥[5]	84	36.52 N	138.55 E
Shimminato	84	36.47 N	137.04 E
Shimobe	84	35.27 N	138.29 E
Shimoda	84	34.40 N	138.57 E
Shimodate	84	36.18 N	139.59 E
Shimofusa	84	35.52 N	140.21 E
Shimofusa-daichi ⛰[1]	258	35.45 N	139.58 E
Shimoga	112	13.55 N	75.34 E
Shimogawara	258	35.56 N	139.21 E
Shimogōri	258	35.21 N	140.03 E
Shimogyō ⬥[8]	260	34.59 N	135.45 E
Shimohōya	258	35.45 N	139.34 E
Shimoichi	86	34.22 N	135.47 E
Shimoigusa ⬥[8]	258	35.43 N	139.37 E
Shimoji-shima I	165d	24.49 N	125.09 E
Shimojō	84	35.24 N	137.47 E
Shimokawa	82a	44.18 N	142.39 E
Shimokita-hantō ≻[1]	82	41.15 N	141.00 E
Shimomatsu	260	34.27 N	135.23 E
Shimomizo	258	35.31 N	139.23 E
Shimoni	144	4.39 S	39.23 E
Shimoniikura	258	35.47 N	139.38 E
Shimonita	84	36.13 N	138.47 E
Shimonoseki	86	33.57 N	130.57 E
Shimookudomi	258	35.53 N	139.26 E
Shimosakamoto	260	35.03 N	135.53 E
Shimoshakujii ⬥[8]	258	35.45 N	139.37 E
Shimosuwa	84	36.04 N	138.05 E
Shimotajiri	260	34.57 N	135.28 E
Shimotomi	258	35.50 N	139.29 E
Shimotsu	86	34.10 N	135.08 E
Shimotsuchidana	258	35.24 N	139.27 E
Shimotsuma	84	36.11 N	139.58 E
Shimotsuruma	258	35.29 N	139.28 E
Shimoya	258	35.23 N	139.21 E
Shimoyama	84	35.02 N	137.19 E
Shimoyugi	258	35.38 N	139.23 E
Shimpuru Rapids ᒪ	146	17.50 S	19.56 E
Shimura ⬥[8]	258	35.46 N	139.41 E
Shin, Loch ⊜	28	58.07 N	4.32 W
Shinagawa ⬥[8]	258	35.37 N	139.45 E
Shinan	92	22.43 N	109.54 E
Shinano	84	36.48 N	138.13 E
Shinano ≃	82	37.56 N	139.03 E
Shinarā	132	28.47 N	30.46 E
Shināṣ	118	24.46 N	56.28 E
Shināwari	113	33.32 N	70.48 E
Shinbārī	263c	30.07 N	31.09 E
Shīndand	118	33.18 N	62.08 E
Shindo	258	35.21 N	139.21 E
Shiner	212	29.26 N	97.10 W
Shingbwiyang	100	26.41 N	96.13 E
Shingishū → Sinŭiju	88	40.05 N	124.24 E
Shinglehouse	204	41.58 N	78.12 W
Shingle Springs	216	38.40 N	120.56 W
Shingō	86	34.54 N	133.29 E
Shingū, Nihon	82	33.44 N	135.59 E
Shingū, Nihon	86	34.55 N	134.33 E
Shingwidzi	146	23.05 S	31.25 E
Shinichi	86	34.33 N	133.16 E
Shining Tor ʌ	252	53.16 N	2.01 W
Shinīrah	122	32.22 N	36.45 E
Shiniujie	90	28.26 N	119.48 E
Shinji	86	35.24 N	132.54 E
Shinji-ko ⊜	86	35.27 N	132.58 E
Shinjō, Nihon	82	38.46 N	140.18 E
Shinjō, Nihon	260	34.30 N	135.44 E
Shinjuku ⬥[8]	258	35.41 N	139.42 E
Shinkawa	84	35.09 N	136.50 E
Shīnkay	110	31.57 N	67.26 E
Shinkolobwe	144	11.02 S	26.35 E
Shinmachi	84	36.16 N	139.07 E
Shinminato ≃	260	34.38 N	135.09 E
Shinnārah, Minqār ⏚[4]	132	28.52 N	30.38 E
Shīn Naray	110	31.19 N	66.43 E
Shinnecock Bay C	197	40.52 N	72.28 W
Shinnel Water ≃	42	55.13 N	3.49 W
Shinnston	178	39.24 N	80.18 W
Shino-jima I	84	34.39 N	137.00 E
Shinshār	120	34.36 N	36.44 E
Shinshiro	84	34.54 N	137.30 E
Shinshū-shinmachi	84	36.34 N	138.01 E
Shintone	84	35.50 N	140.20 E
Shinyanga	144	3.40 S	33.26 E
Shinyanga □[4]	144	3.45 S	33.00 E
Shin-yōdo ≃[1]	260	34.41 N	135.26 E
Shio	84	36.52 N	136.48 E
Shiobara	84	36.58 N	139.49 E

Shiocton	180	44.27 N	88.35 W
Shioda	84	36.21 N	138.12 E
Shiogama	82	38.19 N	141.01 E
Shiojiri	84	36.06 N	137.58 E
Shiojiri-tōge)(	84	36.05 N	138.02 E
Shiokawa	165d	24.40 N	124.41 E
Shiomi-dake ʌ	84	35.34 N	138.12 E
Shionoe	86	34.10 N	134.05 E
Shiono-misaki ≻	80	33.26 N	135.45 E
Shiono-zaki ≻	82	33.26 N	135.45 E
Shioya	84	36.46 N	139.51 E
Shioya ⬥[8]	260	34.38 N	135.06 E
Shioya-zaki ≻, Nihon	82	33.26 N	135.45 E
Shioya-zaki ≻, Nihon	84	37.00 N	140.59 E
Shiozawa	84	37.02 N	138.51 E
Shipai, Zhg.	90	23.08 N	113.21 E
Shipai, Zhg.	96	31.30 N	120.55 E
Shipanpu	97	30.28 N	104.23 E
Shipantuo	97	30.25 N	106.13 E
Ship Bottom	198	39.39 N	74.11 W
Shipbourne	250	51.15 N	0.17 E
Ship Cove	176	47.06 N	54.05 W
Shipdham	44	52.37 N	0.53 E
Shiping, Zhg.	92	23.47 N	102.30 E
Shiping, Zhg.	92	28.20 N	107.42 E
Ship Island I	184	30.13 N	88.55 W
Shipley	42	53.50 N	1.47 W
Shipman, Ill., U.S.	209	39.07 N	90.03 W
Shipman, Va., U.S.	182	37.43 N	78.51 W
Shippan Point ≻	266	41.01 N	73.32 W
Shippegan	176	47.45 N	64.42 W
Shippegan Island I	176	47.48 N	64.36 W
Shippensburg	198	40.03 N	77.31 W
Shippenville	204	41.15 N	79.28 W
Shippingport	204	40.38 N	80.25 W
Shippō	84	35.40 N	136.47 E
Shiprock	190	36.47 N	108.41 W
Ship Rock ʌ	190	36.42 N	108.50 W
Shipshewana	206	41.41 N	85.35 W
Shipston-on-Stour	44	52.04 N	1.37 W
Shipu, Zhg.	90	29.13 N	121.55 E
Shipu, Zhg.	96	31.15 N	121.03 E
Shiqi → Zhongshan	90	22.31 N	113.22 E
Shiqian	92	27.31 N	108.20 E
Shiqiao, Zhg.	96	30.31 N	119.11 E
Shiqiao, Zhg.	97	30.25 N	104.31 E
Shiqiaopu	97	30.05 N	105.23 E
Shiqiaozhen	90	33.12 N	112.36 E
Shiqiaozi, Zhg.	94	41.27 N	123.43 E
Shiqiaozi, Zhg.	94	41.18 N	123.17 E
Shiqma ≃	122	31.36 N	34.30 E
Shiqu	92	33.04 N	97.45 E
Shiquan, Zhg.	92	32.55 N	108.33 E
Shiquan, Zhg.	96	30.30 N	120.48 E
Shira ≃	82	32.12 N	130.37 E
Shirahama, Nihon	84	34.54 N	139.54 E
Shirahama, Nihon	86	33.40 N	135.20 E
Shirahata-yama ʌ	86	34.54 N	134.23 E
Shiraitono-taki ᒪ	84	35.29 N	139.10 E
Shirakami-saki ≻	82a	41.24 N	140.12 E
Shirakawa, Nihon	84	37.07 N	140.13 E
Shirakawa, Nihon	84	36.16 N	136.54 E
Shirakawa, Nihon	84	35.35 N	137.12 E
Shirakawano-seki ⊥	84	37.03 N	140.15 E
Shirakawa-tōge ʌ[2]	260	34.42 N	135.07 E
Shiraki	86	34.33 N	132.40 E
Shirako	84	35.26 N	140.23 E
Shirākol	116	22.18 N	88.16 E
Shirakura-yama ʌ	84	35.00 N	137.46 E
Shirama-yama ʌ	86	34.01 N	135.23 E
Shiramine	84	36.10 N	136.37 E
Shirane	84	35.38 N	138.28 E
Shirane-san ʌ, Nihon	84	36.38 N	138.32 E
Shirane-san ʌ, Nihon	84	36.48 N	139.22 E
Shirane-san (Kita-dake) ʌ, Nihon	84	35.40 N	138.15 E
Shiranuka, Nihon	82a	42.57 N	144.05 E
Shiranuka, Nihon	82a	41.08 N	141.24 E
Shiraoi	82a	42.33 N	141.21 E
Shiraoka	84	36.01 N	139.40 E
Shiraone	262c	19.03 N	73.01 E
Shirasawa	84	36.40 N	139.08 E
Shirase Glacier ⍌	9	70.10 S	38.35 E
Shīrāz	118	29.36 N	52.32 E
Shirbīn	132	31.11 N	31.32 E
Shirdley Hill	252	53.36 N	2.58 W
Shire (Chire) ≃	144	17.42 S	35.19 E
Shirebrook	42	53.12 N	1.13 W
Shiremanstown	198	40.13 N	76.57 W
Shiretoko-hantō ≻[1]	82a	44.00 N	145.00 E
Shiretoko-kokuritsu-kōen ♠	82a	44.08 N	145.10 E
Shiretoko-misaki ≻[1]	82a	44.14 N	145.17 E
Shīrīn ≃	110	36.49 N	65.01 E
Shiriya-saki ≻	82	41.26 N	141.28 E
Shīr Kūh ʌ	118	31.37 N	54.04 E
Shirland	206	42.27 N	89.12 W
Shirley, B.C., Can.	214	48.23 N	123.54 W
Shirley, Ill., U.S.	206	40.24 N	89.04 W
Shirley, Ind., U.S.	208	39.53 N	85.35 W
Shirley, Mass., U.S.	197	42.33 N	71.39 W
Shirley Plantation ⊥	198	37.21 N	77.15 W
Shirleysburg	204	40.18 N	77.53 W
Shīr Manṣūr, Jabal ⛰	122	33.41 N	36.02 E
Shiro	212	30.37 N	95.53 W
Shiroi	84	35.48 N	140.04 E
Shiroishi	82	38.00 N	140.37 E
Shirokawa	86	33.23 N	132.46 E
Shirone	82	37.46 N	139.01 E
Shirotori, Nihon	84	35.53 N	136.52 E
Shirotori, Nihon	86	34.15 N	134.20 E
Shirouma-dake ʌ	84	36.45 N	137.46 E
Shiroyama	84	35.35 N	139.19 E
Shiro-yama ʌ	260	34.38 N	135.53 E
Shirpur	110	21.21 N	74.53 E
Shirrell Heath	44	50.55 N	1.12 W
Shirshābah	132	30.47 N	31.10 E
Shīrvān	118	37.24 N	57.55 E
Shisaka-jima I	86	34.07 N	133.11 E
Shisanling	95	40.17 N	116.11 E
Shisanzhan	79	51.21 N	125.43 E
Shishaldin Volcano ʌ[1]	170	54.45 N	163.57 W
Shishanshan	94	41.16 N	121.30 E
Shishikui	86	33.34 N	134.18 E
Shishishan ʌ	90	24.44 N	117.54 E
Shishmaref	170	66.14 N	166.09 W
Shishmaref Inlet C	170	66.07 N	165.50 W
Shishou	92	29.43 N	112.19 E
Shisht al-An'ām	132	30.52 N	30.44 E
Shisixian	94	40.53 N	122.59 E
Shisler Point ≻	274a	42.52 N	79.08 W
Shisui	84	35.43 N	140.16 E
Shitan, Zhg.	90	23.10 N	113.47 E
Shitan, Zhg.	90	27.44 N	112.42 E
Shitang, Zhg.	90	28.16 N	121.36 E
Shitang, Zhg.	92	25.38 N	110.50 E
Shitangwan	96	31.40 N	120.13 E
Shitara	84	35.05 N	137.35 E
Shithāthah	118	32.33 N	43.29 E
Shiting, Zhg.	90	27.36 N	113.16 E
Shiting, Zhg.	95	39.31 N	115.41 E
Shitoufangzi	79	48.38 N	126.08 E
Shitougouzi	79	49.19 N	125.55 E
Shitouhe	79	44.50 N	128.44 E
Shitoumiao	92	41.41 N	106.50 E
Shitoumiaozi	94	41.38 N	121.26 E
Shitouqiao	88	41.51 N	119.04 E
Shitoushan	95	40.27 N	116.13 E
Shitoushuangmiao	88	41.28 N	118.55 E
Shituanzhen	97	30.09 N	105.01 E
Shitunwei	94	41.07 N	121.31 E
Shiva, Horvot (Subeita) ⊥	122	30.53 N	34.38 E
Shively	208	38.11 N	85.49 W
Shivering, Mount ʌ	160	34.08 S	150.02 E
Shivpuri	114	25.26 N	77.39 E

Shivpuri □[5]	114	25.20 N	77.40 E
Shiwa	86	34.29 N	132.41 E
Shiwaku-shotō II	86	34.20 N	133.45 E
Shiwan, Zhg.	90	28.12 N	113.49 E
Shiwan, Zhg.	90	27.17 N	112.57 E
Shiwan, Zhg.	90	23.01 N	113.04 E
Shiwanzhen	92	37.35 N	109.01 E
Shiwenchang	94	41.43 N	123.54 E
Shiwu	79	43.48 N	124.13 E
Shiwudu	90	29.44 N	119.10 E
Shixi, Zhg.	90	28.16 N	115.36 E
Shixi, Zhg.	90	28.16 N	117.45 E
Shixia, Zhg.	88	40.15 N	114.54 E
Shixia, Zhg.	95	40.20 N	114.59 E
Shixia, Zhg.	95	40.32 N	117.01 E
Shixian	79	43.05 N	129.47 E
Shixiancun	96	31.12 N	120.29 E
Shixiechang	97	29.51 N	106.41 E
Shixing	90	24.58 N	114.03 E
Shixun	90	24.44 N	118.11 E
Shiyachang	97	30.27 N	106.31 E
Shiyan, Zhg.	92	32.38 N	110.44 E
Shiyan, Zhg.	97	30.22 N	104.27 E
Shiyangchang, Zhg.	97	29.56 N	105.37 E
Shiyangchang, Zhg.	97	30.42 N	105.57 E
Shiyanqiao	97	29.19 N	105.22 E
Shiyu	97	29.46 N	106.06 E
Shizhangzi	88	40.24 N	119.48 E
Shizhen	90	22.37 N	113.11 E
Shizheng	90	24.32 N	115.50 E
Shizhenjie	90	28.51 N	116.56 E
Shizhong, Zhg.	90	24.58 N	117.04 E
Shizhong, Zhg.	96	30.44 N	120.16 E
Shizhongtan	97	30.26 N	104.35 E
Shizhu	92	30.07 N	108.08 E
Shizhuang	96	32.08 N	120.31 E
Shizhuangzi, Zhg.	94	42.24 N	122.53 E
Shizhuangzi, Zhg.	95	40.38 N	116.59 E
Shizhuzi	94	41.18 N	121.35 E
Shizichang	97	29.32 N	106.14 E
Shizigu	95	39.23 N	118.08 E
Shizihe	88	34.07 N	115.33 E
Shizikou	90	24.12 N	113.38 E
Shizilin	96	31.26 N	121.25 E
Shizipo	95	40.21 N	115.07 E
Shizipu	96	30.59 N	119.07 E
Shizugawa	82	38.40 N	141.27 E
Shizui	88	38.52 N	113.42 E
Shizuizi	79	43.08 N	126.06 E
Shizuma ≃	86	35.12 N	132.28 E
Shizunai	82a	42.20 N	142.22 E
Shizuoka	84	34.58 N	138.23 E
Shizuoka □[5]	84	35.00 N	138.00 E
Shizushan	94	41.47 N	121.17 E
Shkodër	38	42.05 N	19.30 E
Shkumbin ≃	38	41.01 N	19.26 E
Shō ≃	84	36.47 N	137.04 E
Shoal ≃	184	30.41 N	86.39 W
Shoal Cape ≻	152	33.53 S	121.07 E
Shoal Creek ≃, U.S.	184	37.05 N	94.42 W
Shoal Creek ≃, U.S.	184	40.28 N	92.42 W
Shoal Creek ≃, Ill., U.S.	209	38.28 N	89.35 W
Shoal Creek ≃, Mo., U.S.	184	39.44 N	93.32 W
Shoal Creek, East Fork ≃	209	38.51 N	89.30 W
Shoal Harbour	176	48.11 N	53.59 W
Shoalhaven ≃	160	34.52 S	150.44 E
Shoalhaven Bight C[3]	160	34.52 S	150.47 E
Shoal Lake	174	50.26 N	100.34 W
Shoal Lake ⊜	174	49.32 N	95.00 W
Shoal Point ≻	266	41.08 N	73.15 W
Shoals	184	38.40 N	86.47 W
Shoals, Bay of C	158b	35.37 S	137.37 E
Shoalwater Bay C	156	22.02 S	150.25 E
Shōbara	86	34.51 N	133.01 E
Shoboku	86	35.06 N	134.07 E
Shobonier	209	38.52 N	89.05 W
Shōdai	260	34.51 N	135.42 E
Shōdo-shima I	86	34.30 N	134.17 E
Shoeburyness	44	51.32 N	0.48 E
Shoe Cove	176	47.45 N	52.44 W
Shoemakersville	198	40.30 N	75.58 W
Shōgawa	84	36.34 N	136.59 E
Shogunle	263a	6.35 N	3.21 E
Shohola	200	41.28 N	74.55 W
Shohola Creek ≃	200	41.28 N	74.55 W
Shokan	200	41.58 N	74.13 W
Shōkawa	84	36.02 N	136.57 E
Sholāpur	112	17.41 N	75.55 E
Sholinghur	112	13.07 N	79.25 E
Shomera	122	33.05 N	35.17 E
Shomolu	263a	6.32 N	3.23 E
Shōmyō-no-taki ᒪ	84	36.35 N	137.31 E
Shōnai, Nihon	84	34.45 N	137.38 E
Shōnai, Nihon	86	33.11 N	131.26 E
Shōnai ≃	84	35.04 N	136.50 E
Shōnan	258	35.50 N	140.02 E
Shongum	266	40.50 N	74.33 W
Shongum Lake ⊜	266	40.51 N	74.32 W
Shongwe	148	27.24 S	32.25 E
Shōō	86	35.02 N	134.08 E
Shooters Hill	160	33.54 S	149.52 E
Shooters Island I	266	40.39 N	74.10 W
Shopiere	206	42.34 N	88.57 W
Shoranūr	112	10.46 N	76.17 E
Shorāpur	112	16.31 N	76.45 E
Shoreacres, B.C., Can.	172	49.26 N	117.32 W
Shore Acres, Calif., U.S.	216	38.02 N	121.58 W
Shore Acres, Mass., U.S.	197	42.13 N	70.44 W
Shore Acres, N.J., U.S.	198	40.02 N	74.06 W
Shoreacres, Tex., U.S.	212	29.37 N	95.01 W
Shoreditch ⬥[8]	250	51.32 N	0.05 W
Shoreham, Eng., U.K.	250	51.20 N	0.11 E
Shoreham, Mich., U.S.	206	42.04 N	86.30 W
Shoreham-by-Sea	44	50.49 N	0.16 W
Shorewood, Ill., U.S.	206	41.32 N	88.12 W
Shorewood, Wis., U.S.	206	43.05 N	87.53 W
Shorewood Hills	206	43.03 N	89.27 W
Shorkot	113	30.50 N	72.04 E
Shorkot Road	113	30.47 N	72.15 E
Shorne	250	51.25 N	0.26 E
Short Acres	216	36.21 N	119.38 W
Short Beach	197	41.15 N	72.52 W
Short Creek	204	40.11 N	80.55 W
Shortland Island I	165e	7.02 S	155.47 E
Short Mountain ʌ	182	36.23 N	83.10 W
Shortsville	200	42.57 N	77.14 W
Shoshone	192	42.56 N	114.24 W
Shoshone ≃	192	44.52 N	108.11 W
Shoshone, North Fork ≃	192	44.29 N	109.18 W
Shoshone, South Fork ≃	192	44.27 N	109.14 W
Shoshone Basin ⊻[1]	192	43.05 N	108.05 W
Shoshone Lake ⊜	192	44.22 N	110.43 W
Shoshone Mountains ⛰	194	39.25 N	117.15 W
Shoshone Peak ʌ	194	36.56 N	116.16 W
Shoshone Range ⛰	194	40.20 N	116.50 W
Shoshong	146	22.59 S	26.30 E
Shoshoni	190	43.14 N	108.07 W
Shostka → Šostka	68	51.52 N	33.30 E
Shotley Gate	44	51.58 N	1.15 E
Shotton	252	53.12 N	3.02 W
Shotton Colliery	42	54.44 N	1.20 W
Shotts	42	55.49 N	3.48 W
Shotwick	252	53.14 N	2.59 W
Shouanzhen	97	30.16 N	103.36 E
Shouchang	90	29.22 N	119.13 E
Shoufeng	90	23.52 N	121.30 E
Shouguang	88	36.53 N	118.42 E
Shoultes	214	48.07 N	122.09 W

≃ River	Fluss	Río	Rivière	Rio
≍ Canal	Kanal	Canal	Canal	Canal
ᒪ Waterfall, Rapids	Wasserfall, Stromschnellen	Cascada, Rápidos	Chute d'eau, Rapides	Cascata, Rápidos
⋃ Strait	Meeresstrasse	Estrecho	Détroit	Estreito
C Bay, Gulf	Bucht, Golf	Bahía, Golfo	Baie, Golfe	Baía, Golfo
⊜ Lake, Lakes	See, Seen	Lago, Lagos	Lac, Lacs	Lago, Lagos
☷ Swamp	Sumpf	Pantano	Marais	Pântano
⍌ Ice Features, Glacier	Eis- und Gletscherformen	Accidentes Glaciales	Formes glaciaires	Acidentes Glaciares
⏚ Other Hydrographic Features	Andere Hydrographische Objekte	Otros Elementos Hidrográficos	Autres données hydrographiques	Outros Elementos Hidrográficos

⟡ Submarine Features	Untermeerische Objekte	Accidentes Submarinos	Formes de relief sous-marin	Acidentes Submarinos
□ Political Unit	Politische Einheit	Unidad Politica	Entité politique	Unidade Política
❦ Cultural Institution	Kulturelle Institution	Institución Cultural	Institution culturelle	Instituição Cultural
⊥ Historical Site	Historische Stätte	Sitio Histórico	Site historique	Sitio Histórico
♠ Recreational Site	Erholungs- und Ferienort	Sitio de Recreo	Centre de loisirs	Sítio de Lazer
⊠ Airport	Flughafen	Aeropuerto	Aéroport	Aeroporto
■ Military Installation	Militäranlage	Instalación Militar	Installation militaire	Instalação Militar
⬥ Miscellaneous	Verschiedenes	Misceláneo	Divers	Miscelânea

Symbols in the index entries represent the broad categories identified in the key at the right. Symbols with superior numbers (⩘[2]) identify subcategories (see complete key on page *I* · *26*).

Kartensymbole in dem Registerverzeichnis stellen die rechts in Schlüssel erklärten Kategorien dar. Symbole mit hochgestellten Ziffern (⩘[2]) bezeichnen Unterabteilungen einer Kategorie (vgl. vollständiger Schlüssel auf Seite *I* · *26*).

Los símbolos incluídos en el texto del índice representan las grandes categorias identificadas con la clave a la derecha. Los símbolos con numeros en su parte superior (⩘[2]) identifican las subcategorías (véase la clave completa en la página *I* · *26*).

Les symboles de l'index représentent les catégories indiquées dans la légende à droite. Les symboles suivis d'un indice (⩘[2]) représentent des sous-catégories (voir légende complète à la page *I* · *26*).

Os símbolos incluídos no texto do índice representam as grandes categorias identificadas com a chave à direita. Os símbolos com números em sua parte superior (⩘[2]) identificam as subcategorias (veja-se a chave completa à página *I* · *26*).

∧ Mountain	Berg	Montaña	Montagne	Montanha
⩘ Mountains	Berge	Montañas	Montagnes	Montanhas
)(Pass	Pass	Paso	Col	Passo
∨ Valley, Canyon	Tal, Cañon	Valle, Cañón	Vallée, Canyon	Vale, Canhão
≚ Plain	Ebene	Llano	Plaine	Planície
≻ Cape	Kap	Cabo	Cap	Cabo
I Island	Insel	Isla	Île	Ilha
II Islands	Inseln	Islas	Îles	Ilhas
⊥ Other Topographic Features	Andere Topographische Objekte	Otros Elementos Topográficos	Autres données topographiques	Outros Elementos Topográficos

Symbol	English	Deutsch	Español	Français	Português
≃	River	Fluss	Río	Rivière	Rio
≌	Canal	Kanal	Canal	Canal	Canal
⌊	Waterfall, Rapids	Wasserfall, Stromschnellen	Cascada, Rápidos	Chute d'eau, Rapides	Cascata, Rápidos
Ʉ	Strait	Meeresstrasse	Estrecho	Détroit	Estreito
C	Bay, Gulf	Bucht, Golf	Bahía, Golfo	Baie, Golfe	Baía, Golfo
⊜	Lake, Lakes	See, Seen	Lago, Lagos	Lac, Lacs	Lago, Lagos
☷	Swamp	Sumpf	Pantano	Marais	Pântano
⍓	Ice Features, Glacier	Eis- und Gletscherformen	Accidentes Glaciales	Formes glaciaires	Acidentes Glaciares
⍑	Other Hydrographic Features	Andere Hydrographische Objekte	Otros Elementos Hidrográficos	Autres données hydrographiques	Outros Elementos Hidrográficos
✢	Submarine Features	Untermeerische Objekte	Accidentes Submarinos	Formes de relief sous-marin	Acidentes Submarinos
□	Political Unit	Politische Einheit	Unidad Política	Entité politique	Unidade Política
ʋ	Cultural Institution	Kulturelle Institution	Institución Cultural	Institution culturelle	Instituição Cultural
⊥	Historical Site	Historische Stätte	Sitio Histórico	Site historique	Sitio Histórico
♠	Recreational Site	Erholungs- und Ferienort	Sitio de Recreo	Centre de loisirs	Sítio de Lazer
⊠	Airport	Flughafen	Aeropuerto	Aéroport	Aeroporto
■	Military Installation	Militäranlage	Instalación Militar	Installation militaire	Instalação Militar
⬥	Miscellaneous	Verschiedenes	Misceláneo	Divers	Miscelânea

Skoghall 40 59.19 N 13.26 E
Skogstorp 40 59.20 N 16.28 E
Skokholm Island I 44 51.42 N 5.16 W
Skoki 30 52.41 N 17.10 E
Skokie 206 42.02 N 87.46 W
Skokie ≃ 206 42.05 N 87.46 W
Skokie Lagoons C 268 42.07 N 87.47 W
Skokloster ⊥ 40 59.42 N 17.37 E
Skokomish, North Fork ≃ 214 47.18 N 123.14 W
Skokomish, South Fork ≃ 214 47.18 N 123.14 W
Skokomish Indian Reservation ◆[4] 214 47.21 N 123.12 W
Sköldinge 40 59.02 N 16.26 E
Skole 68 49.02 N 23.29 E
Sköllersta 40 59.09 N 15.20 E
Skolsta 40 59.40 N 17.14 E
Skolwin 50 53.32 N 14.35 E
Skomer Island I 44 51.44 N 5.17 W
Skomorośki, S.S.S.R. 68 49.20 N 29.26 E
Skomorośki, S.S.S.R. 72 54.05 N 36.57 E
Skón 100 12.04 N 105.04 E
Skookumchuck ≃ 214 46.41 N 123.00 W
Skoonspruit ≃ 148 27.00 S 25.38 E
Skootamatta ≃ 202 44.32 N 77.20 W
Skootamatta Lake ⊜ 202 44.50 N 77.15 W
Skópelos 38 39.07 N 23.43 E
Skópelos I 38 39.10 N 23.40 E
Skopin 66 53.51 N 39.33 E
Skopje 38 41.59 N 21.26 E
Skórcz 30 53.48 N 18.32 E
Skorodnoje, S.S.S.R. 68 51.05 N 37.14 E
Skorodnoje, S.S.S.R. 68 51.38 N 28.49 E
Skørping 26 56.50 N 9.53 E
Skotfoss 26 59.12 N 9.30 E
Skotovataja 73 48.13 N 37.54 E
Skotovo 79 43.20 N 132.21 E
Skotterud 26 59.59 N 12.07 E
Skovby 41 54.53 N 10.00 E
Skövde 26 58.24 N 13.50 E
Skovlund 41 55.44 N 8.43 E
Skovorodino 79 53.59 N 123.55 E
Skowhegan 178 44.46 N 69.43 W
Skownan 174 51.57 N 99.36 W
Skradin 36 43.49 N 15.56 E
Skreia 26 60.39 N 10.56 E
Skriplivka 66 57.32 N 30.38 E
Skrīveri 66 56.39 N 25.08 E
Skromberga 26 56.00 N 12.58 E
Skrudaļiena 66 55.49 N 26.43 E
Skrunda 66 56.41 N 22.01 E
Skruv 26 56.41 N 15.22 E
Skrydstrup 41 55.14 N 9.15 E
Skudeneshavn 26 59.09 N 5.17 E
Skuilte 263d 26.07 S 28.19 E
Skukuza 146 25.01 S 31.38 E
Skuleberget ∧[2] 26 63.05 N 18.21 E
Skulforp 26 58.21 N 13.49 E
Skull Creek ≃ 212 29.32 N 96.24 W
Skull Valley 190 34.30 N 112.41 W
Skull Valley Indian Reservation ◆[4] 190 40.24 N 112.45 W
Skultuna 40 59.43 N 16.25 E
Skuna ≃ 184 33.54 N 89.41 W
Skunk ≃ 180 40.42 N 91.07 W
Skunovka 76 50.45 N 55.27 E
Skuodas 66 56.16 N 21.32 E
Skuratovskij 72 54.07 N 37.36 E
Skurinskaja 68 46.35 N 39.22 E
Skurišenskaja 70 49.52 N 42.57 E
Skurup 41 55.28 N 13.30 E
Skutskär 40 60.38 N 17.25 E
Skvira 68 49.44 N 29.40 E
Skwentna 170 61.58 N 151.11 W
Skwentna ≃ 170 62.00 N 151.08 W
Skye I 28 57.15 N 6.10 W
Skye, Island of I 28 57.15 N 6.10 W
Sky Harbor Airport ⊠ 268 42.09 N 87.51 W
Skykomish 214 47.42 N 121.22 W
Skykomish ≃ 214 47.50 N 122.03 W
Skykomish, North Fork ≃ 214 47.48 N 121.33 W
Skykomish, South Fork ≃ 214 47.47 N 121.33 W
Sky Lake 210 28.28 N 81.24 W
Sky Lake ⊜ 202 44.48 N 81.15 W
Skyland, Nev., U.S. 216 39.01 N 119.57 W
Skyland, N.C., U.S. 182 35.29 N 82.31 W
Skylight 208 38.26 N 85.32 W
Skyline Lakes ⊜ 266 41.04 N 74.16 W
Skyllberg 40 58.57 N 14.59 E
Skyring, Península ≻[1] 244 45.58 S 74.53 W
Skyring, Seno ⋃ 244 52.35 S 72.00 W
Sky Sailing Airport ⊠ 272 37.30 N 121.58 W
Skytop 200 41.14 N 75.15 W
Skyttorp 40 60.05 N 17.44 E
Skyway 214 47.29 N 122.14 W
Slackhall 252 53.20 N 1.53 W
Slackwood 198 40.15 N 74.44 W
Slade Green ◆[8] 250 51.28 N 0.12 E
Sladkij 70 46.10 N 42.17 E
Sladkovo 76 55.32 N 70.20 E
Slagelse 41 55.24 N 11.22 E
Slagnäs 24 65.34 N 18.05 E
Slagoviśći 66 53.57 N 35.54 E
Slaithwaite 252 53.37 N 1.53 W
Slamet, Gunung ∧ 105a 7.14 S 109.12 E
Slancy 66 59.06 N 28.04 E
Slaney ≃ 28 52.21 N 6.30 W
Slangerup 41 55.51 N 12.11 E
Slănic 38 45.15 N 25.57 E
Slănic Moldova 38 46.13 N 26.26 E
Slano 36 42.47 N 17.54 E
Slanské Vrchy ∧ 30 48.50 N 21.30 E
Slaný 30 50.11 N 14.04 E
Slapanice 30 49.10 N 16.44 E
Slaščevskaja 70 49.52 N 42.21 E
Slastucha 70 51.57 N 44.32 E
Slate Bottom Creek ≃ 274a 42.53 N 78.45 W
Slate Creek ≃, Kans., U.S. 188 37.08 N 97.09 W
Slate Creek ≃, Pa., U.S. 269b 40.28 N 79.32 W
Slatedale 198 40.45 N 75.40 W
Slate Hill 200 41.23 N 74.29 W
Slater, Iowa, U.S. 180 41.53 N 93.41 W
Slater, Mo., U.S. 184 39.13 N 93.04 W
Slatersville 197 42.00 N 71.35 W
Slaterville Springs 200 42.24 N 76.21 W
Slatina 38 44.26 N 24.22 E
Slatington 198 40.45 N 75.37 W
Slatino 68 50.12 N 36.11 E
Slaton 186 33.26 N 101.39 W
Slattocks 252 53.35 N 2.10 W
Slaung 105a 8.02 S 111.24 E
Slautnoje 64 63.00 N 167.59 E
Slava 79 52.08 N 129.24 E
Slav'anka, S.S.S.R. 68 48.24 N 36.43 E
Slav'anka, S.S.S.R. 75 40.40 N 68.32 E
Slav'anka, S.S.S.R. 79 42.53 N 131.21 E
Slav'anka ≃ 255a 59.50 N 30.32 E
Slav'anogorsk 73 49.02 N 37.31 E
Slav'anoserbsk 73 48.42 N 38.59 E
Slav'ansk 73 48.52 N 37.37 E
Slav'ansk-na-Kubani 68 45.15 N 38.08 E
Slave ≃ 166 61.18 N 113.39 W
Slave Coast ⊥[2] 140 6.25 N 3.00 E
Slave Lake 172 55.17 N 114.46 W
Slavgorod, S.S.S.R. 66 53.27 N 31.00 E
Slavgorod, S.S.S.R. 68 48.06 N 35.31 E
Slavgorod, S.S.S.R. 68 50.36 N 35.21 E
Slavgorod, S.S.S.R. 76 53.00 N 78.40 E
Slavitino 72 56.41 N 39.13 E
Slavkino 70 52.58 N 47.11 E
Slavkoviči 66 57.39 N 29.05 E
Slavkovský les ∧ 50 50.07 N 12.45 E
Slavkov u Brna 30 49.09 N 16.52 E
Slavnoje 66 54.18 N 29.27 E
Slavonia → Slavonija ◆[1] 36 45.00 N 18.00 E
Slavonice 30 49.00 N 15.21 E
Slavonija ◆[1] 36 45.00 N 18.00 E
Slavonska Požega 36 45.20 N 17.41 E
Slavonski Brod 38 45.10 N 18.01 E
Slavsk (Heinrichswalde) 66 55.03 N 21.41 E
Slavskoje 68 48.49 N 23.24 E
Slavuta 68 50.18 N 26.52 E
Sława 30 51.53 N 16.04 E
Slawi 105a 6.59 S 109.08 E
Sławno 30 54.22 N 16.40 E
Slayton 188 43.59 N 95.45 W
Slea ≃ 44 53.03 N 0.12 W
Sleaford 44 53.00 N 0.24 W
Slea Head ≻ 28 52.06 N 10.27 W
Sledge 184 34.26 N 90.13 W
Sledge Island I 170 64.29 N 166.13 W
Sled Lake ⊜ 174 54.27 N 107.25 W
Sledmere 42 54.04 N 0.35 W
Slednevo 72 56.25 N 38.36 E
Sled'uki 66 53.35 N 30.22 E
Sleen 48 52.46 N 6.48 E
Sleeping Bear Dunes National Lakeshore ♠ 180 44.50 N 86.08 W
Sleeping Giant State Park ♠ 197 41.25 N 72.53 W
Sleepy Eye 188 44.18 N 94.43 W
Sleepy Hollow, Calif., U.S. 216 38.00 N 122.34 W
Sleepy Hollow, Calif., U.S. 270 33.57 N 117.47 W
Sleepy Hollow, Ill., U.S. 206 42.06 N 88.24 W
Sleetmute 170 61.42 N 157.11 W
Sleidinge 46 51.08 N 3.41 E
Sleman 105a 7.42 S 110.20 E
Ślepino 66 59.11 N 29.02 E
Ślesin 30 52.23 N 18.19 E
Slessor Glacier ⊓ 9 79.50 S 28.30 W
Sliabh Gaoil ∧ 42 55.55 N 5.28 W
Slickville 204 40.28 N 79.32 W
Slidell 184 30.17 N 89.47 W
Slide Mountain ∧ 200 42.00 N 74.23 W
Sliderock Mountain ∧ 192 46.35 N 113.33 W
Sliedrecht 48 51.49 N 4.45 E
Slieve Snaght ∧ 42 55.12 N 7.20 W
Sligeach → Sligo 28 54.17 N 8.28 W
Sligo, Eire 28 54.17 N 8.28 W
Sligo, Pa., U.S. 204 41.07 N 79.29 W
Sligo □[6] 28 54.10 N 8.40 W
Sligo Bay C 28 54.20 N 8.40 W
Sligo Creek ≃ 274c 38.57 N 76.58 W
Slikkerveer 48 51.53 N 4.37 E
Slinger 180 43.20 N 88.17 W
Slino, Ozero ⊜ 66 57.40 N 33.23 E
Slippery Rock 204 41.04 N 80.03 W
Slippery Rock Creek ≃ 204 40.51 N 80.15 W
Slite 26 57.43 N 18.48 E
Slīteres Rezervāts ♠ 66 57.38 N 22.25 E
Sliven 38 42.40 N 26.19 E
Slivnica 38 42.51 N 23.02 E
Sloan, Iowa, U.S. 188 42.14 N 96.14 W
Sloan, Nev., U.S. 194 35.57 N 115.13 W
Sloan, N.Y., U.S. 200 42.54 N 78.47 W
Sloan Peak ∧ 214 48.03 N 121.20 W
Sloansville 200 42.46 N 74.20 W
Sloatsburg 200 41.09 N 74.12 W
Sloboda, S.S.S.R. 66 53.58 N 28.08 E
Sloboda, S.S.S.R. 66 55.30 N 31.51 E
Sloboda, S.S.S.R. 66 51.11 N 33.37 E
Sloboda, S.S.S.R. 68 51.09 N 40.17 E
Slobodka, S.S.S.R. 66 55.41 N 27.11 E
Slobodka, S.S.S.R. 68 47.53 N 29.21 E
Slobodka, S.S.S.R. 72 54.22 N 37.33 E
Slobodskoj 76 58.42 N 50.12 E
Slobodzeja 68 46.44 N 29.43 E
Slobodzeja-Prut 68 45.34 N 28.12 E
Slobozia 38 44.34 N 27.23 E
Slocan 172 49.46 N 117.28 W
Slocan Lake ⊜ 172 49.56 N 117.22 W
Slochteren 48 53.12 N 6.47 E
Slocomb 184 31.06 N 85.36 W
Slocum 197 41.32 N 71.31 W
Slocum Mountain ∧ 218 35.18 N 117.13 W
Słomniki 30 50.15 N 20.06 E
Slonim 66 53.06 N 25.19 E
Slonovka 68 50.39 N 37.45 E
Słońsk 50 52.35 N 14.50 E
Sloop Channel ⋃ 266 40.36 N 73.31 W
Sloping Hills 266 40.42 N 74.34 W
Slosh Indian Reserve ◆[4] 172 50.44 N 122.13 W
Sloten 48 52.54 N 5.38 E
Sloten ◆[8] 48 52.21 N 4.48 E
Slotermeer ⊜ 48 52.55 N 5.40 E
Slough 44 51.31 N 0.36 W
Slough □[8] 250 51.30 N 0.35 W
Slough Brook ≃ 266 40.45 N 74.21 W
Sloughhouse 216 38.30 N 121.12 W
Slovakia → Slovensko □[9] 30 48.50 N 20.00 E
Slovan 204 40.22 N 80.23 W
Slovečna ≃ 68 51.41 N 29.41 E
Slovečno 68 51.23 N 28.21 E
Slovenia → Slovenija □[3] 36 46.15 N 15.10 E
Slovenija □[3] 36 46.15 N 15.10 E
Slovenjgradec 36 46.31 N 15.05 E
Slovenska Bistrica 36 46.23 N 15.34 E
Slovenská Socialistická Republika □[3] 30 48.30 N 20.00 E
Slovenské rudohorie ∧ 30 48.45 N 20.00 E
Slovensko □[9] 30 48.50 N 20.00 E
Slovinka 70 58.02 N 43.07 E
Slowakei → Slovensko □[9] 30 48.50 N 20.00 E
Słowiński Park Narodowy ♠ 30 54.40 N 17.25 E
Słubice 50 52.20 N 14.32 E
Sluč', S.S.S.R. 66 52.08 N 27.31 E
Sluč' ≃, S.S.S.R. 68 51.37 N 26.38 E
Sluck 66 53.01 N 27.33 E
Sl'ud'anka 78 51.38 N 103.42 E
Sluderno (Schluderns) 58 46.40 N 10.35 E
Sludy 66 58.52 N 36.52 E
Sluis 48 51.18 N 3.24 E
Sluiskil 48 51.16 N 3.50 E
Šluknov 50 51.00 N 14.27 E
Slunj 36 45.07 N 15.35 E
Słupca 30 52.19 N 17.52 E
Słupia ≃ 30 54.35 N 16.50 E
Słupsk (Stolp) 30 54.28 N 17.01 E
Slurry 146 25.49 S 25.52 E
Šl'uz-Mokr'aki 76 59.17 N 88.50 E
Slyne Head ≻ 28 53.24 N 10.13 W
Smachtino 72 54.51 N 36.25 E
Smackover 184 33.22 N 92.44 W
Smackover Creek ≃ 184 33.22 N 92.24 W
Småland □[9] 26 57.20 N 15.00 E
Smålandsfarvandet ⋃ 41 55.05 N 11.20 E
Smålandsstenar 26 57.10 N 13.24 E
Smalininkai 66 55.05 N 22.35 E
Smallbridge 252 53.38 N 2.08 W
Smalleytown 266 40.39 N 74.28 W
Smallwood 200 41.40 N 74.49 W
Smallwood State Park ♠ 198 38.33 N 77.12 W
Smara → Semara 138 26.44 N 11.41 W
Smartt Syndicate Reservoir ⊜[1] 148 30.40 S 23.18 E
Smartville 216 39.12 N 121.18 W
Smeaton 174 53.30 N 104.49 W
Smeaton Bay C 172 55.20 N 130.50 W
Smečno 50 50.10 N 14.03 E
Smedby 40 58.33 N 16.16 E
Smederevo 38 44.40 N 20.56 E
Smederevska Palanka 38 44.22 N 20.58 E
Smedjebacken 40 60.08 N 15.25 E
Smela 68 49.14 N 31.53 E
Smeloje 68 50.55 N 33.36 E
Šmel'ovka 70 54.47 N 49.11 E
Smelt Brook ≃, Mass., U.S. 273 42.00 N 70.43 W
Smelt Brook ≃, Mass., U.S. 273 42.13 N 70.58 W
Smelt Pond ⊜ 273 41.58 N 70.43 W
Smethport 204 41.49 N 78.27 W
Smethwick (Warley) 44 52.30 N 1.58 W
Smicksburg 204 40.52 N 79.10 W
Šmidovič 79 48.36 N 133.49 E
Šmidta → Mys Šmidta 170 68.56 N 179.26 W
Šmidta, Mys ≻ 170 68.56 N 179.30 W
Šmidta, Ostrov I 64 81.08 N 90.48 E
Šmidta, Poluostrov ≻[1] 79 54.10 N 142.40 E
Šmigiel 30 52.01 N 16.32 E
Smilde 48 52.56 N 5.27 E
Smile 208 38.15 N 83.29 W
Smiley, Sask., Can. 174 51.37 N 109.29 W
Smiley, Tex., U.S. 212 29.16 N 97.38 W
Smilten 66 53.45 N 28.01 E
Smiltene 66 57.26 N 25.56 E
Smirnovskij 76 54.31 N 69.25 E
Smirnych 79 49.43 N 142.38 E
Smite ≃ 44 52.57 N 0.53 W
Smith 172 55.10 N 114.02 W
Smith □[6] 212 32.20 N 95.15 W
Smith ≃, Calif., U.S. 194 41.56 N 124.12 W
Smith ≃, Mont., U.S. 192 47.25 N 111.29 W
Smith ≃, Oreg., U.S. 192 43.43 N 124.05 W
Smith, Cape ≻ 180 45.48 N 81.35 W
Smith Arm C 170 66.15 N 124.00 W
Smith Bay C 170 70.51 N 154.25 W
Smithboro, Ill., U.S. 209 38.54 N 89.20 W
Smithboro, N.Y., U.S. 200 42.02 N 76.24 W
Smith Canyon ∨ 188 37.46 N 103.26 W
Smith Center 188 39.47 N 98.47 W
Smith Creek ≃, S. Dak., U.S. 188 43.58 N 99.20 W
Smith Creek ≃, Wash., U.S. 214 46.45 N 123.53 W
Smithdale 269b 40.14 N 79.48 W
Smithers, B.C., Can. 172 54.47 N 127.10 W
Smithers, W. Va., U.S. 178 38.11 N 81.18 W
Smithfield, Austl. 158b 34.41 S 138.41 E
Smithfield, Austl. 264a 33.51 S 150.57 E
Smithfield, Ont., Can. 202 44.04 N 77.41 W
Smithfield, S. Afr. 148 30.09 S 26.30 E
Smithfield, Eng., U.K. 42 54.59 N 2.52 W
Smithfield, N.C., U.S. 182 35.30 N 78.21 W
Smithfield, Ohio, U.S. 204 40.16 N 80.47 W
Smithfield, Pa., U.S. 204 40.29 N 78.01 W
Smithfield, Utah, U.S. 190 41.50 N 111.50 W
Smithfield, Va., U.S. 198 36.59 N 76.38 W
Smithflat 216 38.44 N 120.45 W
Smith Haven Mall ◆[9] 266 40.52 N 73.08 W
Smithills Hall ⊥ 252 53.36 N 2.27 W
Smith Island I, B.A.T. 9 62.59 S 62.32 W
Smith Island I, N.C., U.S. 182 33.52 N 77.59 W
Smith Island I, Va., U.S. 198 37.10 N 75.51 W
Smith Island I, Wash., U.S. 214 48.19 N 122.50 W
Smith Islands II 198 38.01 N 76.02 W
Smithland 184 37.09 N 88.24 W
Smithmill 204 40.46 N 78.25 W
Smith Mountain ∧ 270 34.17 N 117.52 W
Smith Mountain Lake ⊜ 182 37.10 N 79.40 W
Smith Peak ∧ 192 48.50 N 116.39 W
Smith Peninsula ≻[1] 9 74.25 S 61.15 W
Smith Point 212 29.27 N 94.45 W
Smith Point ≻, N.S., Can. 176 45.51 N 63.25 W
Smith Point ≻, Tex., U.S. 212 29.32 N 94.46 W
Smith Point ≻, Va., U.S. 198 37.53 N 76.14 W
Smithport 204 40.50 N 78.52 W
Smith River 194 41.56 N 124.09 W
Smiths 184 32.32 N 85.06 W
Smiths Creek 204 42.55 N 82.36 W
Smiths Falls 202 44.54 N 76.01 W
Smiths Grove 184 37.03 N 86.12 W
Smiths Mills 266 41.01 N 74.22 W
Smith Sound ⋃ 172 51.18 N 127.48 W
Smithton, Austl. 156 40.51 S 145.07 E
Smithton, Mo., U.S. 184 38.41 N 93.05 W
Smithton, Pa., U.S. 269b 40.09 N 79.44 W
Smithtown 200 40.52 N 73.13 W
Smith Valley 208 39.36 N 86.12 W
Smithville, Ont., Can. 202 43.06 N 79.33 W
Smithville, Ga., U.S. 182 31.54 N 84.15 W
Smithville, Ind., U.S. 208 39.04 N 86.30 W
Smithville, Miss., U.S. 184 33.59 N 88.23 W
Smithville, Mo., U.S. 184 39.23 N 94.35 W
Smithville, N.J., U.S. 198 39.31 N 74.27 W
Smithville, N.J., U.S. 275 39.59 N 74.45 W
Smithville, Ohio, U.S. 204 40.52 N 81.51 W
Smithville, Tenn., U.S. 184 35.58 N 85.49 W
Smithville, Tex., U.S. 212 30.00 N 97.09 W
Smithville Flats 200 42.24 N 75.49 W
Smögen 26 58.21 N 11.13 E
Smoke Creek ≃, Mont., U.S. 188 48.18 N 104.41 W
Smoke Creek ≃, N.Y., U.S. 274a 42.49 N 78.52 W
Smoke Creek, South Branch ≃ 274a 42.49 N 78.49 W
Smoke Creek Desert ◆[2] 194 40.30 N 119.40 W
Smoke Lake ⊜ 202 45.32 N 78.41 W
Smokeless 204 40.24 N 76.02 W
Smokerun 204 40.48 N 78.26 W
Smoketown 198 40.02 N 76.12 W
Smokey Dome ∧ 192 43.29 N 114.56 W
Smoky ≃ 172 56.10 N 117.21 W
Smoky, Cape ≻ 176 46.38 N 60.21 W
Smoky Bay 152 32.22 S 133.56 E
Smoky Cape ≻ 156 30.56 S 153.05 E
Smoky Hill ≃ 188 39.03 N 96.48 W
Smoky Hill, North Fork ≃ 188 39.28 N 98.26 W
Smoky Hills ∧∧[2] 188 39.15 N 99.00 W
Smoky Lake 172 54.07 N 112.28 W
Smøla I, Nor. 24 / 26 63.24 N 8.00 E
Smol'anica 66 52.42 N 24.38 E
Smol'aninovo 79 43.19 N 132.28 E
Smol'any 66 54.36 N 30.04 E
Smolensk 66 54.47 N 32.03 E
Smolenskoje 76 52.20 N 85.05 E
Smolensko-Moskovskaja Vozvyšennost' ∧∧[1] 66 55.00 N 34.00 E
Smoleviči 66 54.02 N 28.05 E
Smólikas ∧ 38 40.06 N 20.52 E
Smoljan 38 41.35 N 24.41 E
Smol'nyj ⌂ 255a 59.57 N 30.24 E
Smolovka 66 55.33 N 30.13 E
Smoot 190 42.37 N 110.55 W
Smoothstone ≃ 174 55.20 N 106.39 W
Smoothstone Lake ⊜ 174 54.40 N 106.50 W
Smorgon' 66 54.29 N 26.24 E
Smorodovka 66 57.08 N 29.52 E
Smotrič 68 48.56 N 26.34 E
Smotrič ≃ 68 48.34 N 26.38 E
Smuskovoje 70 47.19 N 46.02 E
Smyčka 72 56.04 N 35.56 E
Smygehamn 41 55.21 N 13.22 E
Smygehuk ≻ 41 55.21 N 13.23 E
Smyley, Cape ≻ 9 72.26 S 78.10 W
Smyrna → İzmir, Tür. 120 38.25 N 27.09 E
Smyrna, Del., U.S. 198 39.18 N 75.36 W
Smyrna, Ga., U.S. 182 33.53 N 84.31 W
Smyrna, N.Y., U.S. 200 42.41 N 75.34 W
Smyrna, Tenn., U.S. 184 35.59 N 86.31 W
Smyrna ≃ 198 39.22 N 75.31 W
Smyrna Mills 178 46.08 N 68.10 W
Smyšl'ajevka 70 53.15 N 50.22 E
Smyth, Canal ⋃ 244 52.15 S 73.40 W
Smythe Park ♠ 265b 43.41 N 79.30 W
Smythesdale 159 37.38 S 143.41 E
Sn'adin 68 52.04 N 28.19 E
Snæfell ∧, Ísland 24a 64.48 N 15.32 W
Snaefell ∧, I. of Man 42 54.16 N 4.27 W
Snæfellsnes ≻[1] 24a 64.50 N 23.00 W
Snag 170 62.24 N 140.22 W
Snagost' 68 51.21 N 34.54 E
Snahapish ≃ 214 47.38 N 124.11 W
Sn'ajevo 70 52.34 N 46.11 E
Snake ≃, Yukon, Can. 170 65.58 N 134.10 W
Snake ≃, U.S. 192 46.12 N 119.02 W
Snake ≃, Calif., U.S. 216 39.07 N 121.43 W
Snake ≃, Minn., U.S. 180 45.49 N 92.46 W
Snake ≃, Minn., U.S. 188 48.26 N 97.07 W
Snake ≃, Nebr., U.S. 188 42.47 N 100.48 W
Snake Brook ≃ 273 42.18 N 71.22 W
Snake Creek ≃, Mont., U.S. 192 48.32 N 108.53 W
Snake Creek ≃, Nebr., U.S. 188 42.01 N 102.45 W
Snake Creek ≃, S. Dak., U.S. 188 44.58 N 98.29 W
Snake Creek Canal ≃ 210 25.57 N 80.11 W
Snake Indian ≃ 172 53.11 N 118.00 W
Snake Range ∧∧ 194 39.00 N 114.15 W
Snake Rapids ⊥ 202 45.14 N 77.20 W
Snake River Plain ⌣ 192 43.00 N 113.00 W
Snake Valley ∨ 194 39.20 N 113.55 W
Snap Point ≻ 228 23.43 N 77.35 W
Snaptun 41 55.49 N 10.04 E
Snåsahögarna ∧ 26 63.13 N 12.21 E
Sn'atyn 68 48.28 N 25.34 E
Snay Pöl 100 11.40 N 105.13 E
Sneads 182 30.42 N 84.56 W
Snedsted 26 56.54 N 8.32 E
Sneedville 182 36.32 N 83.13 W
Sneek 48 53.02 N 5.40 E
Sneekermeer ⊜ 48 53.02 N 5.45 E
Snee-oosh-Beach 214 48.24 N 122.33 W
Sneeuberg ∧∧ 148 31.46 S 24.20 E
Snekkersten 41 56.00 N 12.36 E
Snelgrove 265b 43.44 N 79.49 W
Snelling 194 37.31 N 120.26 W
Snettisham 44 52.53 N 0.30 E
Snežnaja ≃ 78 51.28 N 104.38 E
Sněžník ∧ 36 45.35 N 14.27 E
Snežnoje 68 48.01 N 38.46 E
Śniardwy, Jezioro ⊜ 30 53.46 N 21.44 E
Snicarte 209 40.07 N 90.14 W
Snicarte Island I 209 40.08 N 90.12 W
Sniga ≃ 72 54.53 N 37.24 E
Snigir'ovka 68 47.06 N 32.47 E
Snina 30 48.59 N 22.07 E
Snipe Keys II 210 24.40 N 81.38 W
Snipe Lake ⊜ 172 55.07 N 116.46 W
Snøde 41 55.05 N 10.55 E
Snodland 44 51.20 N 0.27 E
Snoghøj 41 55.31 N 9.43 E
Snøhetta ∧ 26 62.20 N 9.17 E
Snohomish 214 47.55 N 122.06 W
Snohomish □[6] 214 48.02 N 121.41 W
Snohomish ≃ 214 48.01 N 122.13 W
Snønipa ∧ 26 61.42 N 6.41 E
Snook 212 30.29 N 96.28 W
Snoqualmie 214 47.32 N 121.50 W
Snoqualmie ≃ 214 47.50 N 122.03 W
Snoqualmie, Middle Fork ≃ 214 47.49 N 122.02 W
Snoqualmie, North Fork ≃ 214 47.31 N 121.46 W
Snoqualmie, South Fork ≃ 214 47.49 N 122.02 W
Snoqualmie Falls 214 47.32 N 121.49 W
Snoqualmie Mountain ∧ 214 47.27 N 121.25 W
Snoqualmie Pass)(214 47.25 N 121.25 W
Snøtinden ∧ 24 66.38 N 14.00 E
Snov 66 53.13 N 26.24 E
Snov ≃ 68 51.45 N 31.45 E
Snover 180 43.28 N 82.58 W
Snowbird Lake ⊜ 166 60.41 N 103.00 W
Snow Canyon State Park ♠ 190 37.11 N 113.42 W
Snow Creek ≃ 214 47.59 N 122.53 W
Snowden, Sask., Can. 174 53.30 N 104.41 W
Snowden, Pa., U.S. 269b 40.16 N 79.58 W
Snowdenville 275 40.11 N 75.36 W
Snowdon ∧ 44 53.04 N 4.05 W
Snowdonia National Park ♠ 28 53.00 N 3.57 W
Snowdoun 184 32.15 N 86.18 W
Snowdrift 166 62.23 N 110.47 W
Snowflake 190 34.30 N 110.05 W
Snow Hill, Md., U.S. 198 38.11 N 75.24 W
Snow Hill, N.C., U.S. 182 35.27 N 77.40 W
Snow Hill Island I 9 64.00 S 57.30 W
Snowking Mountain ∧ 214 48.24 N 121.17 W
Snow Lake 174 54.53 N 100.02 W
Snow Lakes ⊜ 214 47.29 N 120.45 W
Snowmass Mountain ∧ 190 39.07 N 107.04 W
Snow Mountain ∧ 216 39.23 N 122.45 W
Snow Peak ∧ 192 48.35 N 118.29 W
Snows Brook ≃ 273 42.47 N 71.06 W
Snow Shoe 204 41.02 N 77.57 W
Snowshoe Butte ∧ 214 47.13 N 121.22 W
Snowshoe Peak ∧ 192 48.13 N 115.41 W
Snowtown 156 33.47 S 138.13 E
Snow Water Lake ⊜ 194 41.00 N 115.00 W
Snowy ≃ 156 37.48 S 148.32 E
Snowy Mountain ∧ 200 43.42 N 74.23 W
Snowy Mountains ∧∧ 156 36.30 S 148.20 E
Snowyside Peak ∧ 192 43.57 N 114.58 W
Snubba Range ∧∧ 161b 35.40 S 148.10 E
Snuŏl 100 12.04 N 106.26 E
Snyder, Okla., U.S. 186 34.40 N 98.57 W
Snyder, Tex., U.S. 186 32.44 N 100.55 W
Snyder □[6] 200 40.47 N 77.03 W
Snydertown 200 40.53 N 76.40 W
So ≃ 66 53.35 N 27.54 E
Soacha 236 4.35 N 74.13 W
Soahanina 147b 18.42 S 44.13 E
Soaker, Mount ∧ 162 45.23 S 167.15 E
Soalala 147b 16.06 S 45.20 E
Soalary 147b 23.36 S 43.44 E
Soaloka 147b 18.32 S 45.15 E
Sŏam 88 38.01 N 126.43 E
Soamanonga 147b 23.52 S 44.47 E
Soān ≃ 113 33.01 N 71.44 E
Soanierana Ivongo 147b 16.55 S 49.35 E
Soanindrariny 147b 19.54 S 47.14 E
Soap Creek ≃ 184 40.55 N 92.14 W
Soap Lake 214 47.23 N 119.29 W
Soasiu → Tidore 98 0.40 N 127.26 E
Soatá 236 6.20 N 72.41 W
Soave 58 45.25 N 11.15 E
Soavina 147b 20.23 S 46.56 E
Soavinandriana 147b 19.09 S 46.45 E
Soay I 28 57.08 N 6.14 W
Soazza 54 46.22 N 9.13 E
Sob ≃ 68 48.42 N 29.17 E
Sobaco, Sierra del ∧∧ 186 26.15 N 103.00 W
Sobaek-sanmaek ∧∧ 88 36.00 N 128.00 E
Sobat ≃ 130 9.22 N 31.33 E
Sobernheim 52 49.47 N 7.38 E
Soběslav 30 49.15 N 14.44 E
Sobger ≃ 154 3.44 S 140.20 E
Sobič 68 51.52 N 33.14 E
Sobinka 70 55.59 N 40.01 E
Soboba Indian Reservation ◆[4] 218 33.47 N 116.54 W
Soboko 130 6.49 N 24.50 E
Sobolekovo 70 55.39 N 51.53 E
Sobolev 70 51.56 N 51.43 E
Sobolevka 68 48.36 N 29.30 E
Sobolevo 72 55.31 N 38.43 E
Sobolino 78 53.23 N 119.42 E
Sobótka 30 50.55 N 16.45 E
Sobradinho 242 29.24 S 53.03 W
Sobrado 34 41.02 N 8.16 W
Sobral 240 3.42 S 40.21 W
Sobrance 30 48.45 N 22.11 E
Sobrante Ridge ∧ 272 37.58 N 122.15 W
Sobrarbe ◆[1] 34 42.22 N 0.10 E
Sobue 84 35.15 N 136.43 E
Søby 41 54.56 N 10.16 E
Soča 58 46.20 N 13.39 E
Soča (Isonzo) ≃ 58 45.47 N 13.32 E
Socaire 242 23.36 S 67.51 W
Socamirim 246 23.37 S 47.12 W
Socchieve 58 46.25 N 12.52 E
Soc-giang 100 22.54 N 106.01 E
Socgorodok 68 50.11 N 38.09 E
Soch 75 39.57 N 71.08 E
Soch ≃ 75 40.20 N 71.02 E
Sochaczew 30 52.14 N 20.14 E
Sochaux 54 47.31 N 6.50 E
Soch'e → Suoche 110 38.25 N 77.16 E
Sochi → Soči 74 43.35 N 39.45 E
Sŏch'ŏn 88 36.05 N 126.41 E
Sochondo 78 51.49 N 112.32 E
Sochondo, Gora ∧ 78 49.44 N 111.05 E
Sochor, Gora ∧ 78 51.18 N 105.15 E
Soči 74 43.35 N 39.45 E
Social Circle 182 33.39 N 83.43 W
Sociedade Hípica Paulista ♠ 277b 23.36 S 46.41 W
Société, Îles de la II 14 17.00 S 150.00 W
Society Hill 182 34.31 N 79.51 W
Society Islands → Société, Îles de la II 14 17.00 S 150.00 W
Society Ridge ◆[3] 14 17.00 S 152.00 W
Soco ≃ 228 18.27 N 69.12 W
Socoltenango 222 16.13 N 92.15 W
Socompa, Paso)(242 24.27 S 68.18 W
Soconusco, Sierra de → Madre, Sierra ∧∧ 226 15.20 N 92.20 W
Socopo, Cerro ∧ 236 10.28 N 70.48 W
Socorro, Bra. 246 22.36 S 46.32 W
Socorro, Col. 236 6.29 N 73.16 W
Socorro, Pil. 106 9.37 N 125.58 E
Socorro, N. Mex., U.S. 190 34.04 N 106.54 W
Socorro, Tex., U.S. 190 31.39 N 106.18 W
Socorro ◆[8] 277b 23.39 S 46.42 W
Socorro, Isla I 222 18.45 N 110.58 W
Sócota 238 6.18 S 78.44 W
Socotora, Isla → Suquṭrā I 108 12.30 N 54.00 E
Socotra → Suquṭrā I 108 12.30 N 54.00 E
Socuéllamos 34 39.17 N 2.48 W
Soda Creek 172 52.21 N 122.18 W
Soda Creek ≃ 216 38.48 N 122.29 W
Soda Lake ⊜, Calif., U.S. 194 35.08 N 116.04 W
Soda Lake ⊜, Calif., U.S. 216 35.15 N 119.53 W
Sodankylä 24 67.29 N 26.32 E
Soda Springs 192 42.39 N 111.36 W
Soddy-Daisy 184 35.17 N 85.10 W
Sodegaura 84 35.26 N 139.57 E
Södel 52 50.23 N 8.48 E
Söderälgen ⊜ 40 59.43 N 14.35 E
Söderåsen ∧∧[2] 41 56.04 N 13.05 E
Söderbärke 40 60.05 N 15.33 E
Söderby-Karl 40 59.53 N 18.41 E
Söderfors 40 60.23 N 17.14 E
Söderhamn 26 61.18 N 17.03 E
Söderköping 26 58.29 N 16.18 E
Södermanland □[9] 41 59.12 N 16.49 E
Södermanlands Län □[6] 40 59.15 N 16.40 E
□[9]Dernmanland 40 59.12 N 16.49
Söderslätt □[9] 41 55.29 N 13.15 E
Södertälje 40 59.12 N 17.37 E
Södertörn ≻[1] 40 59.05 N 18.00 E
Sodhra 113 32.28 N 74.11 E
Sodingen ◆[8] 253 51.32 N 7.15 E
Sodium 148 30.11 S 23.09 E
Sodo 134 6.52 N 37.47 E
Sodpur 262b 22.42 N 88.23 E
Södra Åby 41 55.23 N 13.18 E
Södra Björkfjärden C 40 59.18 N 17.32 E
Södra Hörken ⊜ 40 60.02 N 15.02 E
Södra Kvarken ⋃ 26 60.15 N 19.05 E
Södra Råda 40 59.01 N 14.10 E
Södra Sandby 41 55.43 N 13.20 E
Södra Vi 26 57.45 N 15.48 E
Sodražica 36 45.46 N 14.38 E
Sodus 200 43.14 N 77.04 W
Sodus Bay C 200 43.15 N 76.58 W
Sodus Creek ≃ 200 43.13 N 76.56 W
Sodus Point 200 43.16 N 76.59 W
Sodwalls 160 33.31 S 149.59 E
Soe 102 9.52 S 124.17 E
Soeda 86 33.34 N 130.52 E
Soekmekaar 146 23.28 S 29.58 E
Soela Väin ⋃ 66 58.40 N 22.35 E
Soerabaja → Surabaya 105a 7.15 S 112.45 E
Soest, B.R.D. 48 51.34 N 8.07 E
Soest, Ned. 48 52.09 N 5.18 E
Soestdijk 48 52.11 N 5.18 E
Soestdijk, Paleis ⌂ 48 52.12 N 5.15 E
Soeste ≃ 48 53.10 N 7.44 E
Soesterberg 48 52.07 N 5.17 E
Soeurs, Île des I 265a 45.28 N 73.33 W
Sofádhes 38 39.20 N 22.06 E
Sofala 160 33.05 S 149.42 E
Sofia → Sofija 38 42.41 N 23.19 E
Sofia ≃ 147b 15.27 S 47.23 E
Sofiero 41 56.05 N 12.39 E
Sofija (Sofia) 38 42.41 N 23.19 E
Sofijevka, S.S.S.R. 68 48.04 N 33.52 E
Sofijevka, S.S.S.R. 68 46.33 N 34.03 E
Sofijevskij 73 48.12 N 38.52 E
Sofijsk, S.S.S.R. 79 51.34 N 139.52 E
Sofijsk, S.S.S.R. 79 52.15 N 133.58 E
Sofjanga 24 65.52 N 31.15 E
Sofje-Kondratjevka 73 48.18 N 38.12 E
Sofjino 72 55.30 N 38.11 E
Sofrino 72 56.09 N 37.56 E
Sofronovo 66 59.48 N 36.54 E
Sogakofe 140 6.00 N 0.36 E
Sogamoso 236 5.43 N 72.56 W
Sogamoso ≃ 236 7.13 N 73.56 W
Soğanlı 257b 40.55 N 29.12 E
Soğanlı Dağları ∧∧ 120 40.30 N 40.30 E
Soğanlı Geçidi)(120 40.33 N 40.16 E
Sogcho → Sŏkch'o 88 38.12 N 128.36 E
Sogda 79 50.24 N 132.12 E
Sögel 48 52.50 N 7.31 E
Sogliano al Rubicone 60 44.00 N 12.18 E
Sognafjorden C[2] 26 61.06 N 5.10 E
Søgne 26 58.05 N 7.49 E
Sogne Fjord → Sognafjorden C[2] 26 61.06 N 5.10 E
Sogn og Fjordane □[6] 26 61.30 N 6.50 E
Sogod, Pil. 106 10.45 N 124.00 E
Sogod, Pil. 106 10.23 N 124.59 E
Sogod Bay C 106 10.15 N 125.02 E
Sogoža ≃ 66 58.28 N 39.06 E
Söğüt 120 40.00 N 30.11 E
Söğütalan 120 40.03 N 28.34 E
Söğüt Gölü ⊜ 120 37.03 N 29.53 E
Söğütlü 120 40.54 N 30.29 E
Sohāg → Sawhāj 130 26.33 N 31.42 E
Sohāgpur, Bhārat 114 22.42 N 78.12 E
Sohāgpur, Bhārat 114 23.19 N 81.21 E
Soham 44 52.20 N 0.20 E
Sohano 165e 5.27 S 154.40 E
Soharkha 262a 28.35 N 77.24 E
Soheit-tinlot 52 50.29 N 5.22 E
Sohland 50 51.02 N 14.25 E
Söhlde 48 52.11 N 10.14 E
Sohna 114 28.15 N 77.04 E
Sŏhŭng 88 38.27 N 126.10 E
Sŏhwa-ri 88 38.15 N 128.13 E
Soignes, Forêt de ◆[3] 52 50.47 N 4.25 E
Soignies (Zinnik) 46 50.35 N 4.04 E
Soignolles-en-Brie 251 48.39 N 2.42 E
Soin 140 12.47 N 3.49 W
Soindres 251 48.57 N 1.40 E
Soini 26 62.52 N 24.13 E
Sointula 172 50.38 N 127.01 W
Soisalo ∧ 26 62.40 N 28.10 E
Soissons 46 49.22 N 3.20 E
Soisy-sous-Montmorency 251 48.59 N 2.18 E
Soisy-sur-Seine 251 48.39 N 2.27 E
Sōja 86 34.40 N 133.45 E
Sojana 24 65.48 N 43.20 E
Sojat 110 25.55 N 73.40 E
Sojda 24 61.11 N 37.40 E
Sojiji Temple ⌂[1] 258 35.31 N 139.41 E
Sojitra 110 22.33 N 72.43 E
Šojna 24 67.52 N 44.08 E
Sŏjosŏn-man C 88 39.20 N 124.50 E
Sojoton Point ≻ 106 9.58 N 122.27 E
Sojuz Sovetskich Socialističeskich Respublik → Union of Soviet Socialist Republics □[3] 12 60.00 N 80.00 E
Sok ≃ 70 53.24 N 50.08 E
Sōka, Nihon 84 35.49 N 139.48 E
Soka, Taehan 261b 37.30 N 126.48 E
Sokal' 68 50.29 N 24.17 E
Šokal'skogo, Proliv ⋃ 64 79.00 N 100.25 E
Sŏkch'o 88 38.12 N 128.36 E
Söke 120 37.45 N 27.24 E
Sokele 144 9.55 S 24.36 E
Sokhós 38 40.49 N 23.21 E
Sokir'any 68 48.27 N 27.25 E
Sokirincy 68 50.42 N 32.46 E
Sokna 26 60.14 N 9.54 E
Sokodé 140 8.59 N 1.08 E
Soko Islands II 90 22.10 N 113.54 E
Sokol, S.S.S.R. 66 59.28 N 40.10 E
Sokol, S.S.S.R. 79 47.14 N 142.45 E
Sokółka, Pol. 30 53.25 N 23.31 E
Sokolka, S.S.S.R. 70 55.34 N 51.30 E
Sokol'niki ◆[8] 255b 55.48 N 37.41 E
Sokol'niki, Park ♠ 255b 55.48 N 37.41 E
Sokol'nikovo 72 55.21 N 35.49 E
Sokolo 140 14.44 N 6.08 W
Sokologornoje 68 46.29 N 34.58 E
Sokolov 50 50.09 N 12.40 E
Sokolova-Gora 68 50.19 N 28.36 E
Sokolova Pustyn' 72 54.51 N 38.03 E
Sokolovka, S.S.S.R. 76 55.06 N 69.12 E
Sokolovka, S.S.S.R. 79 42.57 N 133.55 E
Sokolovo, S.S.S.R. 24 65.21 N 56.57 E
Sokolovo, S.S.S.R. 66 52.55 N 34.39 E
Sokolovo, S.S.S.R. 70 52.49 N 42.26 E
Sokolovo, S.S.S.R. 72 56.02 N 36.55 E
Sokolovo, S.S.S.R. 76 52.33 N 84.46 E
Sokolovo-Kundr'učenskij 73 47.50 N 39.57 E
Sokołów 30 50.14 N 22.07 E
Sokołów Podlaski 30 52.25 N 22.15 E
Sokol'skoje 70 57.08 N 43.13 E
Sokone 140 13.53 N 16.22 W
Sokoto 140 13.04 N 5.16 E
Sokoto ≃ 140 11.20 N 4.10 E
Šokpar 75 43.49 N 74.21 E
Sŏkp'o-ri 88 37.46 N 125.27 E
Sokrutovka 70 47.54 N 46.33 E
Šokša 70 58.24 N 42.27 E
Soksa-ri 88 40.40 N 127.17 E
Sokskije Jary ∧∧[2] 70 54.10 N 51.30 E
Sokuluk 75 42.52 N 74.18 E
Sokur, S.S.S.R. 70 52.01 N 45.48 E
Sokur, S.S.S.R. 76 55.13 N 83.13 E
Sol', Česko. 30 48.56 N 21.36 E
Sol', S.S.S.R. 73 48.43 N 38.02 E
Sol, Costa del ⊥[2] 34 36.30 N 4.30 W
Sol, Rio do ≃ 238 6.45 S 67.05 W
Sola, Nor. 26 58.53 N 5.36 E
Sola, Zaïre 144 5.09 S 27.06 E
Soła ≃ 30 50.04 N 19.13 E
Solacolu 38 44.23 N 26.34 E
Sola de Vega 224 16.31 N 96.59 W
Solai 144 0.02 N 36.09 E
Šolaksaj 76 51.45 N 64.48 E
Solana 210 26.57 N 82.01 W
Solana Beach 218 32.59 N 117.16 W
Solander, Cape ≻ 264a 34.01 S 151.14 E
Solander Island I 162 46.34 S 166.53 E
Solânea 240 6.45 S 35.39 W
Solangāri 262b 22.36 N 88.27 E
Sol'anka ≃ 70 50.10 N 51.20 E
Solano 106 16.31 N 121.11 E
Solano □[6] 216 38.15 N 121.52 W
Solar, Morro ∧[2] 276d 12.11 S 77.02 W
Solaro 256b 45.37 N 9.05 E
Solaro, Monte ∧ 60 40.33 N 14.13 E
Solbad Hall in Tirol 58 47.17 N 11.31 E
Solberg 26 63.47 N 17.38 E
Solbiate Arno 56 45.42 N 8.48 E
Solbiate Olona 256b 45.39 N 8.53 E
Solca, Arg. 242 30.46 S 66.28 W
Solca, Rom. 38 47.42 N 25.50 E
Sol'cy 66 58.08 N 30.20 E
Soldados, Cerro ∧ 236 2.54 S 79.10 W
Soldatskaja 74 43.48 N 43.49 E
Soldatskoje 75 40.52 N 68.56 E
Soldatsko-Stepnoje 70 49.32 N 45.30 E
Sölde ◆[8] 253 51.31 N 7.35 E
Sol de Julio 242 29.33 S 63.27 W
Sölden 58 46.58 N 11.00 E
Sölderholz ◆[8] 253 51.29 N 7.35 E
Soldier Creek ≃ 188 39.04 N 95.39 W
Soldier Field ♠ 268 41.52 N 87.37 W
Soldier Key I 210 25.35 N 80.10 W
Soldier Point ≻ 230c 17.02 N 61.41 W
Soldier Pond 176 47.09 N 68.35 W
Soldiers Grove 180 43.24 N 90.47 W
Soldin → Myślibórz 30 52.55 N 14.52 E
Soldotna 170 60.29 N 151.04 W
Sole, Val di ∨ 58 46.20 N 10.45 E
Solebury 198 40.23 N 75.02 W
Solec Kujawski 30 53.06 N 18.14 E
Soledad, Col. 236 10.55 N 74.46 W
Soledad, Calif., U.S. 216 36.26 N 121.19 W
Soledad, Ven. 236 8.10 N 63.34 W
Soledad, Cerro ∧ 186 26.29 N 103.23 W
Soledad de Doblado 224 19.03 N 96.25 W

Symbols in the index entries represent the broad categories identified in the key at the right. Symbols with superior numbers (∧∧[2]) identify subcategories (see complete key on page I · 26).

Kartensymbole in dem Registerverzeichnis stellen die rechts in Schlüssel erklärten Kategorien dar. Symbole mit hochgestellten Ziffern (∧∧[2]) bezeichnen Unterabteilungen einer Kategorie (vgl. vollständiger Schlüssel auf Seite I · 26).

Los símbolos incluídos en el texto del índice representan las grandes categorias identificadas con la clave a la derecha. Los símbolos con numeros en su parte superior (∧∧[2]) identifican las subcategorias (véase la clave completa en la página I · 26).

Les symboles de l'index représentent les catégories indiquées dans la légende à droite. Les symboles suivis d'un indice (∧∧[2]) représentent des sous-catégories (voir légende complète à la page I · 26).

Os símbolos incluídos no texto do índice representam as grandes categorias identificadas com a chave à direita. Os símbolos com números em sua parte superior (∧∧[2]) identificam as subcategorias (veja-se a chave completa à página I · 26).

Symbol	English	Deutsch	Español	Français	Português
∧	Mountain	Berg	Montaña	Montagne	Montanha
∧∧	Mountains	Berge	Montañas	Montagnes	Montanhas
)(	Pass	Pass	Paso	Col	Passo
∨	Valley, Canyon	Tal, Cañon	Valle, Cañón	Vallée, Canyon	Vale, Canhão
⌣	Plain	Ebene	Llano	Plaine	Planície
≻	Cape	Kap	Cabo	Cap	Cabo
I	Island	Insel	Isla	Île	Ilha
II	Islands	Inseln	Islas	Îles	Ilhas
⊥	Other Topographic Features	Andere Topographische Objekte	Otros Elementos Topográficos	Autres données topographiques	Outros Elementos Topográficos

ESPAÑOL / FRANÇAIS / PORTUGUÊS

Nombre / Nom / Nome	Página / Page	Lat.°′	Long.°′ W=Oeste / W=Ouest
Soledad Díez Gutiérrez	224	22.12 N	100.57 W
Soledade	242	28.50 S	52.30 W
Soledade de Minas	246	22.04 S	45.03 W
Soledad Pass)(	218	34.30 N	118.07 W
Soleduck ≃	214	47.55 N	124.35 W
Solen	188	46.23 N	100.48 W
Solenoje	70	46.14 N	42.32 E
Solenoje, Ozero ⊜	76	55.20 N	70.05 E
Solenoje Zajmišče	70	47.56 N	46.07 E
Solentiname, Islas II	226	11.10 N	85.00 W
Solenzara	36	41.51 N	9.23 E
Solenzo	140	12.11 N	4.05 W
Solero	56	44.55 N	8.30 E
Solers	251	48.40 N	2.43 E
Solesmes	46	50.11 N	3.30 E
Soleure → Solothurn	54	47.13 N	7.32 E
Solferino	58	45.23 N	10.34 E
Solginskij	24	61.05 N	41.19 E
Solgne	52	48.58 N	6.18 E
Solgonskij Kr'až ∧	76	55.30 N	91.00 E
Solhan Dağı ∧	74	39.46 N	43.45 E
Solheim, Nor.	26	60.53 N	5.27 E
Solheim, S. Afr.	263d	26.11 S	28.10 E
Soliera	58	44.45 N	10.55 E
Soligalič	66	59.05 N	42.17 E
Solignac-sur-Loire	56	44.58 N	3.53 E
Soligny-la-Trappe	46	48.37 N	0.32 E
Soligorsk	66	52.48 N	27.32 E
Solihull	44	52.25 N	1.45 W
Solikamsk	76	59.39 N	56.47 E
Solila	147b	21.25 S	46.37 E
Sol'-Ileck	76	51.10 N	54.59 E
Soliman	138	36.42 N	10.30 E
Solimões → Amazon ≃	232	0.05 S	50.00 W
Solin ≃	46	48.02 N	2.43 E
Solingen	52		
	253	51.10 N	7.05 E
Solís, Arg.	248	34.18 S	59.20 W
Solís, Ur.	242	34.36 S	55.29 W
Solís, Presa ⊜[1]	224	20.05 N	100.36 W
Soliseño	186	26.01 N	97.48 W
Söll	58	47.30 N	12.11 E
Šollar	74	41.40 N	48.38 E
Sollefteå	26	63.10 N	17.16 E
Sollentuna	40	59.28 N	17.54 E
Sóller	34	39.46 N	2.42 E
Søllerød	41	55.49 N	12.31 E
Sollerön I	26	60.55 N	14.37 E
Søllested	41	54.49 N	11.17 E
Solliès-Pont	56	43.11 N	6.03 E
Solling ⋀	48	51.45 N	9.35 E
Söllingen	50	52.05 N	10.55 E
Solling-Vogler, Naturpark ♠	48	51.45 N	9.40 E
Solln ⬩[8]	58	48.05 N	11.31 E
Sollom	252	53.40 N	2.50 W
Sollstedt	50	51.25 N	10.31 E
Søln ∧	26	61.55 N	11.30 E
Solna	40	59.22 N	18.01 E
Solncedar	68	44.34 N	38.01 E
Solncevo	255b	55.39 N	37.24 E
Solnečnogorsk	72	56.11 N	36.59 E
Solnhofen	52	48.53 N	10.59 E
Solo → Surakarta	105a	7.35 S	110.50 E
Solo ≃	105a	6.47 S	112.33 E
Šolochovskij	70	48.18 N	41.03 E
Solodča	70	49.39 N	44.17 E
Solodniki	70	48.25 N	45.16 E
Solofra	60	40.50 N	14.51 E
Sologne ⬩[1]	46	47.50 N	2.00 E
Šologoncy	64	66.13 N	114.14 E
Solok	102	0.48 S	100.39 E
Sololá, Guat.	226	14.46 N	91.11 W
Solola, Som.	134	0.08 N	41.30 E
Sololá ◻[5]	226	14.40 N	91.15 W
Solomennikova	76	58.20 N	89.02 E
Solomennoje	24	61.51 N	34.19 E
Solomon, Ariz., U.S.	190	32.49 N	109.38 W
Solomon, Kans., U.S.	188	38.55 N	97.22 W
Solomon ≃	188	38.54 N	97.22 W
Solomon, North Fork ≃	188	39.29 N	98.26 W
Solomon, South Fork ≃	188	39.29 N	98.26 W
Solomon Islands ◻[1]	14	7.30 S	152.00 E
Solomon Islands ◻[1]	14	8.00 S	159.00 E
Solomon Islands ◻[1], Oc.	165e	8.00 S	159.00 E
Solomon Islands II	14	8.00 S	159.00 E
Solomon Sea ⬩[2]	14	8.00 S	155.00 E
Solon, Bhārat	113	30.55 N	77.07 E
Solon, Iowa, U.S.	180	41.48 N	91.30 W
Solon, Maine, U.S.	178	44.57 N	69.52 W
Solon, Ohio, U.S.	204	41.22 N	81.55 W
Solonešnoje	76	51.40 N	84.21 E
Solonka	70	50.13 N	41.28 E
Sol'onoje, S.S.S.R.	68	48.13 N	34.52 E
Sol'onoje, S.S.S.R.	73	49.18 N	37.39 E
Sol'onoje, S.S.S.R.	74	44.03 N	40.53 E
Sol'onoje Ozero	68	45.53 N	34.27 E
Solonópole	240	5.44 S	39.01 W
Solon Springs	180	46.22 N	91.48 W
Solopaca	60	41.11 N	14.33 E
Solor, Kepulauan II	102	8.25 S	123.30 E
Solor, Pulau I	102	8.27 S	123.05 E
Solotča	70	54.48 N	39.51 E
Solothurn	54	47.13 N	7.32 E
Solothurn ◻[3]	54	47.25 N	7.35 E
Solotobe	76	44.38 N	66.05 E
Solotvin	68	48.42 N	24.25 E
Solotvina	68	47.57 N	23.52 E
Soloveckije Ostrova II, S.S.S.R.	24	65.05 N	35.40 E
Soloveckije Ostrova II, S.S.S.R.	24	65.07 N	35.53 E
Solovjevsk, S.S.S.R.	78	49.55 N	115.42 E
Solovjevsk, S.S.S.R.	79	54.14 N	124.26 E
Solovjovka	66	60.46 N	30.09 E
Sol'oy	24	58.08 N	30.20 E
Solre-le-Château	46	50.10 N	4.05 E
Solre-sur-Sambre	46	50.18 N	4.08 E
Solsona	34	41.59 N	1.31 E
Şolt	30	46.48 N	19.00 E
Šolta, Otok I	36	43.23 N	16.15 E
Solṭānābād	118	36.23 N	58.02 E
Solṭānīyeh	118	36.26 N	48.48 E
Soltau	48	52.59 N	9.49 E
Solton	76	52.50 N	86.28 E
Solus, Mount ∧	158a	32.28 S	116.13 E
Solutré-Pouilly	54	46.18 N	4.43 E
Solva	44	51.52 N	5.11 W
Solva ≃	44	51.52 N	5.17 W
Solvang	194	34.36 N	120.08 W
Solvarbo	40	60.24 N	15.40 E
Solvay	200	43.04 N	76.12 W
Sölvesborg	26	56.03 N	14.33 E
Sol'vyčegodsk	24	61.21 N	46.52 E
Solway Firth C[1]	42	54.50 N	3.35 W
Solwezi	144	12.11 S	26.25 E
Soly	66	54.31 N	26.11 E
Solymár	254c	47.36 N	18.56 E
Solza	24	64.33 N	39.29 E
Sōma, Nihon	82	37.48 N	140.57 E
Soma, Tür.	120	39.10 N	27.36 E
Somabula	144	19.41 S	29.41 E
Somain	46	50.22 N	3.17 E
Somalia ◻[1]	10		
	134	10.00 N	49.00 E
Somali Basin ✢[1]	12	5.00 N	53.00 E
Somalie → Somalia ◻[1]	134	10.00 N	49.00 E
Somaliland → Somalia ◻[1]	134	10.00 N	49.00 E
Somali Republic → Somalia ◻[1]	134	10.00 N	49.00 E
Somaliya → Somalia ◻[1]	134	10.00 N	49.00 E
Somalomo	142	3.23 N	12.44 E
Sŏman	88	41.20 N	128.54 E
Somanga	144	8.24 S	39.17 E
Sombernon	54	47.18 N	4.42 E
Sombo	142	8.42 S	20.57 E
Sombor	38	45.46 N	19.07 E
Somborn	52	50.08 N	9.07 E
Sombra	204	42.43 N	82.29 W
Sombrerete	224	23.38 N	103.39 W
Sombreretillo	186	26.19 N	99.58 W
Sombrero I	228	18.36 N	63.26 W
Sombrero Channel 𝔘	100	7.41 N	93.35 E
Sombrio	242	29.07 S	49.40 W
Sombrio, Lagoa do C	242	29.12 S	49.42 W
Şomcuta-Mare	38	47.31 N	23.29 E
Somenos	214	48.49 N	123.44 W
Somercotes	44	53.04 N	1.22 W
Somerdale, N.J., U.S.	198	39.51 N	75.01 W
Somerdale, Ohio, U.S.	204	40.34 N	81.22 W
Someren	48	51.24 N	5.44 E
Somero	26	60.37 N	23.32 E
Sõmerpalu	66	57.51 N	26.48 E
Somers, Conn., U.S.	197	41.59 N	72.27 W
Somers, Mont., U.S.	192	48.05 N	114.13 W
Somers, Wis., U.S.	206	42.38 N	87.55 W
Somersby	160	33.25 S	151.17 E
Somerset, Man., Can.	174	49.24 N	98.39 W
Somerset, Colo., U.S.	190	38.56 N	107.16 W
Somerset, Ky., U.S.	182	37.05 N	84.36 W
Somerset, Md., U.S.	274c	38.58 N	77.05 W
Somerset, Mass., U.S.	197	41.45 N	71.09 W
Somerset, N.J., U.S.	198	40.29 N	74.29 W
Somerset, Ohio, U.S.	178	39.48 N	82.18 W
Somerset, Pa., U.S.	178	40.01 N	79.05 W
Somerset, Tex., U.S.	186	29.13 N	98.40 W
Somerset, Wis., U.S.	180	45.08 N	92.40 W
Somerset ◻[6], Eng., U.K.	44	51.08 N	3.00 W
Somerset ◻[6], Md., U.S.	198	38.12 N	75.41 W
Somerset ◻[6], N.J., U.S.	198	40.34 N	74.37 W
Somerset ◻[6], Pa., U.S.	204	40.09 N	79.00 W
Somerset Airport ⊠	266	40.37 N	74.40 W
Somerset Center	206	42.03 N	84.25 W
Somerset East	148	32.42 S	25.35 E
Somerset Hills Airport ⊠	266	40.41 N	74.32 W
Somerset Island I, Ber.	230a	32.17 N	64.52 W
Somerset Island I, N.W. Ter., Can.	166	73.15 N	93.30 W
Somerset West	148	34.08 S	18.50 E
Somersham	44	52.23 N	0.01 E
Somers Point	198	39.20 N	74.36 W
Somersworth	178	43.16 N	70.52 W
Somerton, Eng., U.K.	44	51.03 N	2.44 W
Somerton, Ariz., U.S.	190	32.36 N	114.43 W
Somerton ⬩[8]	275	40.06 N	75.01 W
Somerton Creek ≃	198	36.32 N	76.55 W
Somervell ◻[6]	212	32.15 N	97.45 W
Somerville, Austl.	159	38.13 S	145.10 E
Somerville, Mass., U.S.	197	42.23 N	71.06 W
Somerville, N.J., U.S.	200	40.34 N	74.37 W
Somerville, Ohio, U.S.	208	39.34 N	84.38 W
Somerville, Tenn., U.S.	184	35.15 N	89.21 W
Somerville, Tex., U.S.	212	30.21 N	96.32 W
Somerville Lake ⊜[1]	212	30.18 N	96.40 W
Someș (Szamos) ≃	38	48.07 N	22.22 E
Someșu Cald ≃	38	46.44 N	23.22 E
Someșu Mare ≃	38	47.12 N	24.12 E
Someșu Mic ≃	38	47.09 N	23.55 E
Someșu Rece ≃	38	46.44 N	23.22 E
Somino	66	59.21 N	34.52 E
Somis	218	34.16 N	119.00 W
Sŏmjin-gang ≃	88	34.58 N	127.46 E
Somma, It.	60	42.40 N	12.44 E
Somma, It.	256b	45.41 N	8.42 E
Sommacampagna	58	45.24 N	10.50 E
Somma Lombardo	56	45.41 N	8.42 E
Sommariva	156	26.24 S	146.36 E
Sommariva del Bosco	56	44.46 N	7.47 E
Somma Vesuviana	60	40.52 N	14.26 E
Somme ◻[5]	46	49.55 N	2.30 E
Somme ≃, Fr.	46	49.01 N	4.12 E
Somme ≃, Fr.	46	50.11 N	1.39 E
Somme, Baie de la C	46	50.14 N	1.33 E
Somme, Canal de la ☲	46	50.11 N	1.39 E
Sommedieue	52	49.05 N	5.28 E
Sommelsdijk	48	51.45 N	4.09 E
Sommen ⊜	26	58.01 N	15.15 E
Sommepy-Tahure	52	49.15 N	4.33 E
Sommerberg	253	51.27 N	7.32 E
Sömmerda	50	51.10 N	11.07 E
Sommerfeld → Lubsko	30	51.46 N	14.59 E
Sommersdorf	50	53.17 N	14.11 E
Sommersted	41	55.19 N	9.19 E
Sommesous	46	48.44 N	4.12 E
Somme Woods ♠	268	42.09 N	87.49 W
Somnitel'nyj	79	52.12 N	139.04 E
Somo ≃	180	45.29 N	89.48 W
Somogy ◻[6]	30	46.25 N	17.35 E
Somonauk	206	41.38 N	88.41 W
Somonauk Creek ≃	206	41.32 N	88.41 W
Somosierra, Puerto de)(	34	41.09 N	3.35 W
Somosomo	165g	16.46 S	179.58 W
Somosomo Strait 𝔘	165g	16.47 S	179.58 E
Somotillo	226	13.02 N	86.55 W
Somoto	226	13.28 N	86.35 W
Somovo, S.S.S.R.	66	52.53 N	34.58 E
Somovo, S.S.S.R.	68	51.44 N	39.23 E
Sompeta	112	18.56 N	84.36 E
Somplago	58	46.21 N	13.04 E
Sompolno	30	52.24 N	18.31 E
Somport, Puerto de)(	34	42.48 N	0.31 W
Sompuis	46	48.41 N	4.23 E
Somuncurá, Meseta de ⋀[1]	244	41.30 S	67.15 W
Şomvix	54	46.44 N	8.56 E
Šomyškol'	76	46.30 N	59.53 E
Son, Ned.	48	51.31 N	5.30 E
Son, Nor.	26	59.31 N	10.42 E
Son ≃	114	25.42 N	84.52 E
Soná	226	8.01 N	81.19 W
Sona-Bata	142	4.54 S	15.09 E
Sonādugi	116	22.47 N	90.40 E
Sonaguera	226	15.38 N	86.20 W
Sonahula	114	25.05 N	87.09 E
Sonāmarg	113	34.18 N	75.18 E
Sonāmukhi	116	23.18 N	87.25 E
Sonāmura	110	23.29 N	91.17 E
Sonāpur	116	23.42 N	89.30 E
Sonar	154	2.33 S	133.00 E
Sonār ≃	114	24.24 N	79.56 E
Sonari	262c	18.52 N	72.59 E
Sonārpur	262b	22.26 N	88.25 E
Sonātikri	262b	22.57 N	88.20 E
Sonceboz	54	47.11 N	7.11 E
Sonchamp	251	48.35 N	1.53 E
Sŏnch'ŏn	88	39.48 N	124.55 E
Soncino	56	45.24 N	9.52 E
Sondags ≃	148	33.44 S	25.51 E
Sondalo	58	46.20 N	10.19 E
Sønderå ≃	41	54.53 N	8.59 E
Sønderborg	41	54.55 N	9.47 E
Sønderby	41	55.47 N	10.01 E
Sønder Felding	41	55.57 N	8.47 E
Sønderhav	41	54.51 N	9.30 E
Sønderjylland ◻[6]	41	55.10 N	9.15 E
Sønder Nærå	41	55.18 N	10.30 E
Sønder Omme	41	55.50 N	8.54 E
Sondershausen	50	51.22 N	10.52 E
Søndersø	41	55.29 N	10.16 E
Sondi	104	2.58 N	98.52 E
Søndre Strømfjord	166	66.59 N	50.40 W
Søndre Strømfjord C[2]	166	67.30 N	52.00 W
Sondrio	58	46.10 N	9.52 E
Sondrio ◻[4]	54	46.10 N	10.03 E
Sonduga	66	60.08 N	41.55 E
Sone ≃	116	21.34 N	86.54 E
Sonepur	110	20.50 N	83.55 E
Sonestown	200	41.21 N	76.33 W
Song, Malay.	102	2.01 N	112.33 E
Song, Nig.	136	9.50 N	12.38 E
Song, Thai	100	18.28 N	100.11 E
Songbahutun	94	41.28 N	121.11 E
Song-bay-hap, Cua C	100	8.46 N	104.52 E
Songbu	90	31.05 N	114.48 E
Sŏngbyŏn-ni	88	38.03 N	125.18 E
Song-cau	100	13.27 N	109.13 E
Sŏng-ch'ŏn-gang ≃	88	39.48 N	127.35 E
Songcun	96	30.26 N	119.43 E
Songe	26	58.41 N	9.00 E
Songea	144	10.41 S	35.39 E
Songeons	46	49.33 N	1.52 E
Songfengchang	97	29.44 N	104.13 E
Songgai	97	29.03 N	105.54 E
Songgao	90	29.36 N	121.41 E
Songgato ≃	154	3.26 S	140.22 E
Songhe	90	31.10 N	113.20 E
Songhuahu ⊜	79	43.20 N	127.07 E
Songhuajiang	79	44.46 N	125.54 E
Songhuajiang ≃	79	47.44 N	132.32 E
Songhwa	88	38.21 N	125.08 E
Songino	78	48.54 N	95.49 E
Sŏngjang-ni	88	41.02 N	126.50 E
Songjiachang	97	28.47 N	104.55 E
Songjiacun	97	29.01 N	103.46 E
Songjiang	96	31.01 N	121.14 E
Songjiangzhen	88	42.12 N	126.56 E
Songjiawa	88	37.24 N	122.07 E
Songjiaying	95	40.38 N	115.14 E
Songjiayu	95	38.55 N	114.49 E
Sŏngjin → Kimch'aek	88	40.41 N	129.12 E
Songjŏng	88	35.10 N	126.46 E
Sŏngju	88	35.55 N	128.16 E
Songkan	92	28.27 N	106.50 E
Songkhla	100	7.12 N	100.36 E
Songkou, Zhg.	90	24.32 N	116.24 E
Songkou, Zhg.	90	25.48 N	118.36 E
Songlinba	90	24.00 N	115.59 E
Songlindian	95	39.25 N	115.54 E
Songlingshan ⋀	94	41.30 N	120.30 E
Songlukelujia	110	29.15 N	84.49 E
Songmen	90	28.19 N	121.34 E
Songmenshan I	90	28.18 N	121.37 E
Sŏngnae-ri	88	39.28 N	126.59 E
Sŏng-ni	88	39.38 N	127.06 E
Songnim	88	38.44 N	125.38 E
Songo	142	7.22 S	14.51 E
Songololo	142	5.42 S	14.02 E
Songot ∧	144	3.59 N	34.28 E
Songpan	92	32.40 N	103.24 E
Song Phi Nong	100	14.13 N	100.03 E
Songqigang C	90	26.25 N	119.43 E
Sŏngsa-ri	261b	37.38 N	126.52 E
Songsha	90	30.07 N	120.51 E
Songshancun	94	41.02 N	121.09 E
Songshu	88	39.50 N	122.06 E
Songshugou	95	41.02 N	117.49 E
Songtangmiao	96	31.08 N	119.16 E
Songtao	92	28.06 N	109.05 E
Şongtun	88	39.54 N	123.56 E
Šonguj	24	68.47 N	33.00 E
Songu-ri	88	37.49 N	127.09 E
Songwe, Zaïre	144	3.24 S	26.16 E
Songwe, Zaïre	144	12.25 S	29.40 E
Songxi	90	26.16 N	116.59 E
Songxia	90	25.44 N	119.36 E
Songxian	92	34.10 N	112.05 E
Songyan	88	37.13 N	113.43 E
Songyang	90	28.27 N	119.29 E
Songyangzhen	92	25.24 N	102.59 E
Songyin	96	30.54 N	121.13 E
Songyinxi ≃	90	28.18 N	119.44 E
Songzhangzi	88	41.13 N	119.08 E
Songzheng	90	27.33 N	118.46 E
Songzhuang	96	32.06 N	121.17 E
Songziguan)(	90	31.17 N	115.31 E
Songzong	92	29.45 N	96.10 E
Son-ha	100	15.03 N	108.34 E
Son-hoa	100	13.02 N	108.58 E
Soni, Ehi ∧	136	20.49 N	17.23 E
Sonico	58	46.10 N	10.21 E
Soninho ≃	240	10.13 S	46.56 W
Sonīpat	114	28.59 N	77.01 E
Sonkach	114	22.59 N	76.21 E
Sonk'ol', Ozero ⊜	75	41.50 N	75.08 E
Sonkovo	66	57.47 N	37.09 E
Son-la	100	21.19 N	103.54 E
Sonmiāni	110	25.26 N	66.36 E
Sonmiāni Bay C	110	25.15 N	66.30 E
Sonnberg ∧	254b	48.20 N	16.15 E
Sonneberg	50	50.22 N	11.10 E
Sonnefeld	52	50.13 N	11.08 E
Sonnewalde	50	51.42 N	13.38 E
Sonning	44	51.29 N	0.55 W
Sonningdale	174	52.24 N	107.40 W
Sonnino	60	41.25 N	13.14 E
Sono	260	34.48 N	135.55 E
Sono, Rio do ≃, Bra.	240	8.58 S	48.11 W
Sono, Rio do ≃, Bra.	245	17.02 S	45.32 W
Sonobe	86	35.06 N	135.28 E
Sonogno	54	46.21 N	8.47 E
Sonoita	222	31.51 N	112.50 W
Sonoita Creek ≃	190	31.30 N	110.58 W
Sonoma	216	38.17 N	122.28 W
Sonoma ◻[6]	216	38.26 N	122.35 W
Sonoma Creek ≃	216	38.10 N	122.24 W
Sonoma Mountains ⋀	216	38.17 N	122.35 W
Sonoma Peak ∧	194	40.52 N	117.36 W
Sonoma State Historical Park ♠	216	38.18 N	122.28 W
Sononder	148	29.43 S	21.51 E
Sonop	148	25.39 S	27.42 E
Sonora, Calif., U.S.	216	37.59 N	120.23 W
Sonora, Tex., U.S.	186	30.34 N	100.39 W
Sonora ◻[3]	222	29.20 N	110.40 W
Sonora ≃	222	28.48 N	111.33 W
Sonora Desert ⬩[2]	190	33.00 N	114.00 W
Sonora Pass)(	216	38.19 N	119.37 W
Sonostrov	24	66.09 N	34.10 E
Sonoyta ≃	190	31.16 N	113.26 W
Sonpār Hills ⋀[2]	114	24.20 N	82.15 E
Sonqor	118	34.47 N	47.36 E
Sŏnsan	88	36.16 N	128.17 E
Sonsbeck	48	51.37 N	6.22 E
Sonseca	34	39.42 N	3.57 W
Sonskyn	148	30.47 S	26.28 E
Sonsón	236	5.42 N	75.18 W
Sonsonate	226	13.43 N	89.44 W
Sonsorol Islands II	98	5.20 N	132.13 E
Sonstorp	40	58.45 N	15.36 E
Sonstraal	148	27.07 S	22.28 E
Sontag	184	31.39 N	90.12 W
Son-tay	100	21.08 N	105.30 E
Sontheim	52	49.07 N	9.11 E
Sonthofen	54	47.31 N	10.17 E
Sontra	52	51.04 N	9.56 E
Sonwān	114	27.40 N	81.45 E
Sonyea	200	42.41 N	77.50 W
Soo → Sault Sainte Marie	180	46.30 N	84.21 W
Soochow → Suzhou	96	31.18 N	120.37 E
Sooke	172	48.23 N	123.43 W
Sooke ≃	214	48.23 N	123.42 W
Sooke Basin C	214	48.23 N	123.40 W
Sooke Lake ⊜	214	48.33 N	123.42 W
Soonwald ⋀	52	49.55 N	7.40 E
Sopachuy	238	19.29 S	64.31 W
Sopa Sopa Head ≻	154	1.58 S	146.35 E
Sopchoppy	182	30.04 N	84.29 W
Soperton	182	32.23 N	82.35 W
Sopetrán	236	6.30 N	75.46 W
Sop Hao	100	20.33 N	104.27 E
Sophia	182	37.43 N	81.15 W
Sopki	66	57.06 N	30.55 E
Sopockin	66	53.50 N	23.39 E
Sopot	30	54.28 N	18.34 E
Sop Pong	100	22.04 N	102.03 E
Sop Prap	100	17.53 N	99.20 E
Soprabolzano	58	46.32 N	11.24 E
Şopron	30	47.41 N	16.36 E
Šoptykol'	76	51.16 N	75.45 E
Sopur	113	34.18 N	74.28 E
Sŏp'yŏng-ni	88	35.01 N	127.24 E
Soquel	216	36.59 N	121.57 W
Soquel Creek ≃	216	36.58 N	121.57 W
Sor, Ribeira de ≃	34	39.00 N	8.17 W
Sora	60	41.43 N	13.37 E
Sorada	112	19.45 N	84.26 E
Sorae-san ∧	261b	37.27 N	126.47 E
Soraga	58	46.22 N	11.39 E
Soragna	58	44.56 N	10.07 E
Söråker	26	62.31 N	17.30 E
Şorano	60	42.41 N	11.43 E
Šorapani	74	42.05 N	43.05 E
Soras	238	14.07 S	73.37 W
Sorata	238	15.47 S	68.40 W
Soratte, Monte ∧	60	42.15 N	12.30 E
Sorau → Żary	30	51.38 N	15.09 E
Soraya	238	14.10 S	73.19 W
Şorbas	34	37.07 N	2.07 W
Šorbas, Gora ∧	76	47.25 N	84.12 E
Sörberge	26	62.31 N	17.22 E
Sorbhog	110	26.30 N	90.52 E
Sorbie	42	54.48 N	4.26 W
Sorbo ≃	75	38.45 N	69.20 E
Sorbolo	58	44.51 N	10.28 E
Sorbonne ⋓[2]	251	48.51 N	2.21 E
Sorcier, Lac au ⊜	196	46.42 N	73.24 W
Sordevolo	56	45.34 N	7.59 E
Sordo ≃	224	16.30 N	97.31 W
Sore	32	44.20 N	0.35 W
Sorel	196	46.02 N	73.07 W
Sorell	156	42.47 S	147.33 E
Sorell, Cape ≻	156	42.12 S	145.10 E
Sörenberg	54	46.50 N	8.03 E
Sorento	209	39.00 N	89.34 W
Soreq ≃	122	31.56 N	34.42 E
Soresina	58	45.17 N	9.51 E
Sorezaru Point ≻	165e	7.34 S	156.36 E
Sörfjärden C	40	59.24 N	16.50 E
Sørfjorden C[2]	26	60.24 N	6.40 E
Sørfold	24	67.28 N	15.22 E
Sörforsa	26	61.40 N	17.00 E
Sorge ≃	41	54.21 N	9.25 E
Sorgono	36	40.01 N	9.06 E
Sorgues	56	44.00 N	4.52 E
Sorgun	120	39.49 N	35.11 E
Sori	56	44.22 N	9.06 E
Soria	34	41.46 N	2.28 W
Soriano	242	33.24 S	58.19 W
Soriano ◻[5]	248	33.45 S	57.45 W
Soriano nel Cimino	60	42.25 N	12.14 E
Sorico	54	46.10 N	9.22 E
Sorido	154	1.09 S	136.03 E
Sørli	26	64.15 N	13.45 E
Sormonne ≃	52	49.46 N	4.40 E
Sorn	42	55.30 N	4.18 W
Sorne ≃	54	47.22 N	7.22 E
Soro, Bhārat	110	21.17 N	86.40 E
Sorø, Dan.	41	55.26 N	11.34 E
Soro, Monte ∧	36	37.56 N	14.42 E
Sorocaba	245	23.29 S	47.27 W
Sorocaba ≃	245	22.59 S	47.48 W
Sorocá-Buçu	246	23.44 S	47.09 W
Sorocá-Buçu ≃	246	23.38 S	47.13 W
Soročinka	70	47.30 N	51.44 E
Soročinsk	70	52.26 N	53.10 E
Soročkino	76	57.02 N	68.52 E
Soroco	230m	18.22 N	65.38 W
Sorok	78	52.20 N	100.12 E
Soroki	68	48.09 N	28.17 E
Sorokino, S.S.S.R.	76	54.13 N	91.31 E
Sorokino, S.S.S.R.	76	53.45 N	84.58 E
Sorokino, S.S.S.R.	76	55.52 N	93.15 E
Sorokošiči	68	51.12 N	30.35 E
Soroksár ⬩[8]	254c	47.24 N	19.07 E
Soroksári-Duna ≃[1]	254c	47.19 N	19.02 E
Sorol I[1]	98	8.08 N	140.23 E
Soron	114	27.53 N	78.45 E
Sorong	154	0.53 S	131.15 E
Sororó ≃	240	5.24 S	49.07 W
Sorot' ≃	66	57.04 N	28.50 E
Soroti	144	1.43 N	33.37 E
Sorovskije	76	59.53 N	71.34 E
Sørøya I	24	70.36 N	22.46 E
Sorpestausee ⊜[1]	52	51.20 N	7.56 E
Sorraia ≃	34	38.56 N	8.53 W
Sorrento, Austl.	159	38.20 S	144.45 E
Sorrento, It.	60	40.37 N	14.22 E
Sorrento, Fla., U.S.	210	28.49 N	81.34 W
Sorrento, La., U.S.	184	30.11 N	90.51 W
Sorris Sorris	146	20.57 S	14.50 E
Sør Rondane Mountains ⋀	9	72.00 S	25.00 E
Sorsakoski	26	62.27 N	27.39 E
Sorsatunturi ∧	24	67.24 N	29.38 E
Sorsele	24	65.30 N	17.30 E
Sorsogon	106	12.58 N	124.00 E
Sorsogon ◻[4]	106	12.50 N	123.55 E
Sorsogon Bay C	106	12.55 N	123.55 E
Şörstafors	40	59.35 N	16.13 E
Şorsu	75	40.17 N	70.48 E
Şort	34	42.24 N	1.08 E
Sortandy	76	51.42 N	71.00 E
Sortavala	24	61.42 N	30.41 E
Sortland	24	68.40 N	15.20 E
Sør-Trøndelag ◻[6]	26	63.00 N	10.40 E
Sorūbī	110	34.36 N	69.43 E
Sorunda	40	59.01 N	17.48 E
Sörup	41	54.43 N	9.40 E
Sörvik	40	60.11 N	15.09 E
Sorviži	70	57.52 N	48.32 E
Sosa, D.D.R.	50	50.30 N	12.39 E
Şosa, Taehan	261b	37.29 N	126.47 E
Šoša ≃	72	56.31 N	36.05 E
Sŏsan	88	36.47 N	126.26 E
Şoşar ≃	74	39.22 N	40.59 E
Sösdala	41	56.02 N	13.40 E
Sos del Rey Católico	34	42.30 N	1.13 W
Sosedka	70	53.15 N	42.40 E
Sosedno	66	58.14 N	28.42 E
Sosenka ≃	255b	55.35 N	37.23 E
Sosenki	72	55.34 N	37.26 E
Sösetalsperre ⬩[6]	48	51.44 N	10.20 E
Soshigaya ⬩[8]	258	35.39 N	139.36 E
Şösjöfjällen ⋀	26	63.53 N	13.15 E
Šoška	24	62.42 N	50.40 E
Soskovo	66	52.45 N	35.23 E
Sosna ≃	66	52.42 N	38.55 E
Sosneado, Cerro ∧	242	34.45 S	69.59 W
Sosnica	68	51.32 N	32.28 E
Sosnicy	66	57.38 N	30.25 E
Sosnogorsk	24	63.37 N	53.51 E
Sosnovaja Maza	70	52.30 N	47.53 E
Sosnovaja Pol'ana ⬩[8]	255a	59.50 N	30.09 E
Sosnovec	24	64.26 N	34.27 E
Sosnovica	66	60.21 N	40.50 E
Sosnovka, S.S.S.R.	24	66.30 N	40.32 E
Sosnovka, S.S.S.R.	70	57.48 N	51.43 E
Sosnovka, S.S.S.R.	70	56.17 N	51.17 E
Sosnovka, S.S.S.R.	70	53.14 N	41.22 E
Sosnovka, S.S.S.R.	70	54.06 N	46.38 E
Sosnovka, S.S.S.R.	70	57.16 N	53.31 E
Sosnovka, S.S.S.R.	70	56.13 N	47.13 E
Sosnovka, S.S.S.R.	72	54.31 N	38.08 E
Sosnovka, S.S.S.R.	72	54.54 N	38.41 E
Sosnovka, S.S.S.R.	75	42.40 N	73.55 E
Sosnovka, S.S.S.R.	76	59.10 N	81.18 E
Sosnovka, S.S.S.R.	76	51.26 N	79.28 E
Sosnovka, S.S.S.R.	78	54.09 N	109.35 E
Sosnovo, S.S.S.R.	66	60.33 N	30.15 E
Sosnovo, S.S.S.R.	70	56.42 N	54.35 E
Sosnovoborsk	70	53.18 N	46.16 E
Sosnovoje	68	50.49 N	27.00 E
Sosnovo-Oz'orskoje	78	52.31 N	111.30 E
Sosnovskij	76	54.36 N	73.10 E
Sosnovskoje	70	55.48 N	43.10 E
Sosnovyj Bor, S.S.S.R.	66	59.55 N	29.07 E
Sosnovyj Bor, S.S.S.R.	76	57.07 N	55.03 E
Sosnovyj Solonec	70	53.17 N	49.33 E
Sosnowiec	30	50.18 N	19.08 E
Soso	184	31.45 N	89.16 W
Sosok	102	0.17 N	110.14 E
Sospel	56	43.53 N	7.27 E
Sospirolo	58	46.09 N	12.04 E
Şossusvlei ⊜	146	24.40 S	15.23 E
Šoštanj	36	46.23 N	15.03 E
Šostka	68	51.52 N	33.30 E
Sŏsura	88	42.16 N	130.37 E
Sos'va, S.S.S.R.	62	63.40 N	62.06 E
Sos'va, S.S.S.R.	76	59.10 N	61.50 E
Sos'va ≃	76	59.32 N	62.20 E
Sosyka ≃	68	46.35 N	39.05 E
Sot' ≃	70	58.00 N	40.39 E
Sota ≃	140	11.52 N	3.24 E
Sotério ≃	238	11.36 S	65.10 W
Sotilija ≃	238	11.48 S	71.30 W
Sotkamo	26	64.08 N	28.25 E
Sotnicyno	70	54.17 N	41.49 E
Soto de Aldovea	256a	40.26 N	3.27 W
Soto de Pajares	256a	40.17 N	3.32 W
Soto la Marina	224	23.46 N	98.13 W
Soto la Marina ≃	224	23.45 N	97.45 W
Sotomayor	238	19.18 S	65.03 W
Sotonera, Embalse de la ⊜[1]	34	42.05 N	0.48 W
Sotouboua	140	8.34 N	0.59 E
Sottens	54	46.39 N	6.44 E
Sottern ⊜	40	59.02 N	15.29 E
Sotteville	46	49.25 N	1.06 E
Sottomarina	58	45.13 N	12.17 E
Sottrum	48	53.06 N	9.14 E
Sottunga I	26	60.08 N	20.40 E
Sotuf, Adrar ⋀	138	22.15 N	15.40 W
Souain-Perthes-lès-Hurlus	52	49.11 N	4.32 E
Souanké	142	2.05 N	14.03 E
Soubakaniédougou	140	10.28 N	5.01 W
Soubré	140	5.47 N	6.36 W
Soudan, Austl.	156	20.05 S	137.00 E
Soudan, Minn., U.S.	180	47.49 N	92.10 W
Soudan → Sudan ◻[1]	130	15.00 N	30.00 E
Soude ≃	46	48.52 N	4.10 E
Soudersburg	198	40.01 N	76.09 W
Souderton	198	40.19 N	75.19 W
Souesmes	46	47.27 N	2.10 E
Soufflay	142	2.01 N	14.54 E
Soufflenheim	52	48.50 N	7.58 E
Soufflot, Lac ⊜	180	47.24 N	78.31 W
Souflíon	38	41.12 N	26.18 E
Soufrière	231f	13.52 N	61.04 W
Soufrière ∧, Guad.	231o	16.03 N	61.40 W
Soufrière ∧, St. Vin.	231h	13.20 N	61.11 W
Soufrière Bay C, Dom.	230d	15.14 N	61.22 W
Soufrière Bay C, St. Luc.	231f	13.51 N	61.04 W
Sougahatchee Creek ≃	184	32.38 N	85.50 W
Sougné-Remouchamps	52	50.29 N	5.40 E
Sougueur	138	35.12 N	1.30 E
Souhegan ≃	178	42.51 N	71.29 W
Souillac	32	44.54 N	1.29 E
Souilly	52	49.01 N	5.17 E
Souk Ahras	138	36.23 N	8.00 E
Souk-el-Arba-des-Beni-Hassan	34	35.16 N	5.20 W
Souk-el-Arba-du-Rharb	138	34.43 N	6.01 W
Souk-Khemis-du-Sahel	34	35.17 N	6.05 W
Sŏul (Seoul)	88		
	261b	37.33 N	126.58 E
Sŏul ◻[8]	88	37.34 N	127.00 E
Soulac-sur-Mer	32	45.31 N	1.07 W
Soulaines-Dhuys	54	48.22 N	4.44 E
Soulanges ◻[6]	196	45.20 N	74.15 W
Soulanges, Canal de ☲	265a	45.20 N	73.58 W
Soulougou	140	13.01 N	0.23 E
Soulsbyville	216	37.59 N	120.16 W
Soultzeren	54	48.04 N	7.06 E
Soultz-Haut-Rhin	54	47.53 N	7.14 E
Soultzmatt	54	47.58 N	7.14 E
Soultz-sous-Forêts	52	48.56 N	7.53 E
Soummam, Oued ≃	34	36.45 N	5.04 E
Sound Beach	200	40.58 N	72.58 W
Sounding Creek ≃	174	52.06 N	110.28 W
Sound View Park ♠	266	40.49 N	73.52 W
Soúnion, Ákra ≻	38	37.39 N	24.02 E
Soup Harbour C	202	43.51 N	77.11 W
Souppes-sur-Loing	46	48.11 N	2.44 E
Sources, Mount aux ∧	148	28.46 S	28.52 E
Soure, Bra.	240	0.44 S	48.31 W
Soure, Port.	34	40.03 N	8.38 W
Sour el Ghozlane	138	36.10 N	3.45 E
Souris, Man., Can.	174	49.38 N	100.15 W
Souris, P.E.I., Can.	176	46.21 N	62.15 W
Souris ≃	166	49.39 N	99.34 W
Souris Plain ⩡	188	48.15 N	100.15 W
Sourlake	184	30.09 N	94.25 W
Sourland Mountain ∧[2]	178	40.29 N	74.43 W
Sourou ≃	140	12.45 N	3.25 W
Souroukaha	140	8.13 N	5.08 W
Souš	50	50.32 N	13.34 E
Sous, Oued ∨	138	30.27 N	9.31 W
Sousa	240	6.45 S	38.14 W
Sousânia	245	16.11 S	49.05 W
Sousas	246	22.52 S	46.59 W
Sousel, Bra.	240	2.39 S	51.55 W
Sousel, Port.	34	38.57 N	7.40 W
Sous-le-Vent, Îles → Leeward Islands II	228	17.00 N	63.00 W
Sousse	138	35.49 N	10.38 E
Sousse ◻[8]	36	35.35 N	10.30 E
Sout ≃, S. Afr.	148	33.03 S	23.28 E
Sout ≃, S. Afr.	148	31.35 S	18.24 E
South ≃, Iowa, U.S.	184	41.29 N	93.20 W
South ≃, Md., U.S.	198	38.57 N	76.29 W
South ≃, Mass., U.S.	273	42.10 N	70.43 W
South ≃, Mo., U.S.	209	39.52 N	91.26 W
South ≃, N.J., U.S.	198	40.29 N	74.23 W
South ≃, N.C., U.S.	182	34.20 N	78.03 W
South ≃, Va., U.S.	178	38.18 N	78.49 W
South ≃, Va., U.S.	198	38.02 N	77.23 W
South Acton	197	42.28 N	71.27 W
South Africa ◻[1]	128		
	146	30.00 S	26.00 E
Southall ⬩[8]	250	51.31 N	0.23 W
South Alligator ≃	154	12.15 S	132.24 E
Southam	44	52.15 N	1.23 W
South Amboy	198	40.29 N	74.17 W
South America ●[1]	4		
	18	15.00 S	60.00 W
South Amherst, Mass., U.S.	197	42.21 N	72.30 W
South Amherst, Ohio, U.S.	204	41.22 N	82.14 W
Southampton, N.S., Can.	176	45.35 N	64.15 W
Southampton, Ont., Can.	202	44.29 N	81.23 W
Southampton, Eng., U.K.	44	50.55 N	1.25 W
Southampton, Mass., U.S.	197	42.14 N	72.44 W
Southampton, N.Y., U.S.	197	40.53 N	72.24 W
Southampton, Pa., U.S.	275	40.10 N	75.03 W
Southampton ◻[6]	198	36.42 N	77.05 W
Southampton (Eastleigh) Airport ⊠	44	50.57 N	1.21 W
Southampton, Cape ≻	166	62.09 N	83.40 W
Southampton Island I	166	64.20 N	84.40 W
South Andaman I	100	11.45 N	92.45 E
South Anna ≃	182	37.48 N	77.25 W
South Apopka	210	28.39 N	81.31 W
Southard	198	40.08 N	74.14 W
Southards Pond ⊜	266	40.43 N	73.20 W
South Ashburnham	197	42.37 N	71.57 W
South Aulatsivik Island I	166	56.45 N	61.30 W
South Australia ◻[3]	152	30.00 S	135.00 E
South Australian Basin ✢[1]	14	38.00 S	125.00 E
South Bald Mountain ∧	190	40.45 N	105.41 W
South Baldy ∧	190	33.59 N	107.11 W
South Banda Basin ✢[1]	14	6.30 S	127.00 E
Southbank	172	54.02 N	125.46 W
South Barre	197	42.23 N	72.06 W
South Barrington	268	42.06 N	88.07 W
South Barrule ∧[2]	42	54.12 N	4.40 W
South Barwon	159	38.17 S	144.30 E
South Bass Island I	204	41.39 N	82.49 W
South Bay	210	26.40 N	80.43 W
South Bay C, Man., Can.	174	56.43 N	99.00 W
South Bay C, N.W. Ter., Can.	166	63.58 N	83.30 W
South Bay C, Ont., Can.	180	45.38 N	81.50 W
South Bay C, Ont., Can.	202	43.55 N	77.03 W
South Bay C, Ont., Can.	202	44.52 N	79.47 W
South Bay C, Fla., U.S.	210	26.42 N	80.45 W
South Bay C, Va., U.S.	198	37.14 N	75.52 W
South Bay C, Wash., U.S.	214	46.53 N	124.04 W
South Baymouth	180	45.33 N	82.01 W
South Beach ♠	266	40.35 N	74.05 W
South Beacon Mountain ∧	200	41.29 N	73.57 W
South Bedias Creek ≃	212	30.54 N	95.42 W
South Bellingham	197	42.03 N	71.28 W
South Belmar	198	40.10 N	74.02 W
South Beloit	206	42.29 N	89.02 W
South Bend, Ind., U.S.	206	41.41 N	86.15 W
South Bend, Wash., U.S.	214	46.40 N	123.48 W
South Benfleet	44	51.33 N	0.34 E
South Bentinck Arm C	172	52.15 N	126.15 W
South Bethlehem	204	41.00 N	79.20 W
South Bihar Plains ⩡	114	25.15 N	84.30 E
South Bloomfield	208	39.43 N	82.59 W
Southborough, Eng., U.K.	44	51.10 N	0.15 E
Southborough, Mass., U.S.	197	42.18 N	71.31 W
South Bosque ≃	212	31.29 N	97.16 W
South Boston	182	36.42 N	78.54 W
South Boston ⬩[8]	273	42.20 N	71.03 W
South Bound Brook	266	40.33 N	74.32 W
South Branch, Newf., Can.	176	47.55 N	59.02 W
South Branch, N.J., U.S.	266	40.33 N	74.42 W
South Brent	44	50.25 N	3.50 W
Southbridge, N.Z.	162	43.49 S	172.15 E
Southbridge, Mass., U.S.	197	42.05 N	72.02 W
South Britain	197	41.28 N	73.15 W
Southbrook, Austl.	161a	27.41 S	151.43 E
Southbrook, N.Z.	162	43.20 S	172.36 E
South Brook ≃	275	39.52 N	75.44 W
South Brookfield	176	44.23 N	64.58 W
South Brooklyn ⬩[8]	266	40.41 N	73.59 W
South Bruny I	156	43.23 S	147.17 E
South Burlington	178	44.28 N	73.13 W
Southbury	197	41.29 N	73.13 W
South Butler	200	43.08 N	76.46 W
South Byfield	273	42.45 N	70.54 W
South Byron	200	43.03 N	78.04 W
South Cairo	200	42.17 N	73.57 W
South Canaan	200	41.30 N	75.25 W
South Cape ≻	165g	17.01 S	179.55 E
South Carolina ◻[3]	168		
	182	34.00 N	81.00 W
South Carver	197	41.51 N	70.54 W
South Castor ≃	202	45.15 N	75.23 W
South Cave	42	53.46 N	0.35 W
South Chagrin Reservation ♠	269a	41.25 N	81.25 W
South Channel 𝔘	106	14.20 N	120.37 E
South Channel ≃[1]	271	42.32 N	82.40 W
South Chaplin	197	41.46 N	72.09 W
South Charleston, Ohio, U.S.	208	39.50 N	83.38 W
South Charleston, W. Va., U.S.	178	38.22 N	81.44 W
South Chatham	197	41.41 N	70.01 W
South Chelmsford	273	42.34 N	71.23 W
South Chicago ⬩[8]	268	41.44 N	87.33 W
South China Basin ✢[1]	12	15.00 N	115.00 E
South China Sea ⬩[2]	98	10.00 N	113.00 E
South Cle Elum	214	47.10 N	120.56 W
South Coast Botanic Garden ♠	270	33.47 N	118.21 W
South Coatesville	198	39.58 N	75.49 W
South Concho ≃	186	31.21 N	100.28 W
South Corinth	200	43.12 N	73.51 W
South Corning	200	42.07 N	77.02 W
South Creek ≃	160	33.36 S	150.50 E
Southcrest	263d	26.15 S	28.07 E
South Dakota ◻[3]	168		
	188	44.15 N	100.00 W
South Dandalup ≃	158a	32.35 S	115.53 E
South Darenth	250	51.24 N	0.15 E
South Dartmouth	197	41.36 N	70.57 W
South Dayton	200	42.22 N	79.03 W
South Deerfield	197	42.29 N	72.37 W
South Dennis, Mass., U.S.	197	41.41 N	70.09 W
South Dennis, N.J., U.S.	198	39.11 N	74.49 W
South Dorset	200	43.13 N	73.04 W
South Dorset Downs ⋀[1]	44	50.40 N	2.25 W
South Dos Palos	216	36.58 N	120.39 W
South Downs ⋀[1]	44	50.55 N	0.25 W
South Dum-Dum	116	22.37 N	88.25 E
South Duxbury	197	42.01 N	70.41 W
South East ◻[5]	146	25.00 S	25.45 E
Southeast Asia Treaty Organization Headquarters ⋓	259a	13.45 N	100.31 E
South East Cape ≻, Austl.	156	43.39 S	146.50 E
Southeast Cape ≻, Alaska, U.S.	170	62.55 N	169.42 W
South-Eastern ◻[3]	140	6.00 N	8.30 E

≃ River	Fluss	Río	Rivière	Rio
☲ Canal	Kanal	Canal	Canal	Canal
⦣ Waterfall, Rapids	Wasserfall, Stromschnellen	Cascada, Rápidos	Chute d'eau, Rapides	Cascata, Rápidos
𝔘 Strait	Meeresstrasse	Estrecho	Détroit	Estreito
C Bay, Gulf	Bucht, Golf	Bahía, Golfo	Baie, Golfe	Baía, Golfo
⊜ Lake, Lakes	See, Seen	Lago, Lagos	Lac, Lacs	Lago, Lagos
⩡ Swamp	Sumpf	Pantano	Marais	Pântano
⊞ Ice Features, Glacier	Eis- und Gletscherformen	Accidentes Glaciales	Formes glaciaires	Acidentes Glaciares
⬩ Other Hydrographic Features	Andere Hydrographische Objekte	Otros Elementos Hidrográficos	Autres données hydrographiques	Outros Elementos Hidrográficos

✢ Submarine Features	Untermeerische Objekte	Accidentes Submarinos	Formes de relief sous-marin	Acidentes Submarinos
◻ Political Unit	Politische Einheit	Unidad Politica	Entité politique	Unidade Política
⋓ Cultural Institution	Kulturelle Institution	Institución Cultural	Institution culturelle	Instituição Cultural
⊥ Historical Site	Historische Stätte	Sitio Histórico	Site historique	Sítio Histórico
♠ Recreational Site	Erholungs- und Ferienort	Sitio de Recreo	Centre de loisirs	Sítio de Lazer
⊠ Airport	Flughafen	Aeropuerto	Aéroport	Aeroporto
■ Military Installation	Militäranlage	Instalación Militar	Installation militaire	Instalação Militar
⬩ Miscellaneous	Verschiedenes	Misceláneo	Divers	Miscelânea

Name	Page	Lat.	Long.
South East Mountain ∧	231k	12.05 N	61.40 W
Southeast Newfoundland Ridge ⊹[3]	8	40.00 N	47.00 W
South Easton	197	42.03 N	71.05 W
Southeast Pacific Basin ⊹[1]	6	60.00 S	115.00 W
South East Point ≻	164o	1.40 N	157.10 W
South Egg Harbor	198	39.31 N	74.39 W
South Egremont	197	42.10 N	73.25 W
South Elgin	206	41.59 N	88.18 W
South Elkhorn Creek ≃	208	38.13 N	84.48 W
South El Monte	270	34.03 N	118.02 W
Southend	42	55.20 N	5.38 W
Southend Municipal Airport ⊠	44	51.34 N	0.41 E
Southend-on-Sea	44		
	250	51.33 N	0.43 E
Southend-on-Sea □[8]	250	51.33 N	0.41 E
Southend Pier ◆[5]	250	51.31 N	0.44 E
South English ≃	180	41.30 N	91.56 W
Southern □[4], Malawi	144	15.30 S	35.00 E
Southern □[4], S.L.	140	8.00 N	12.15 W
Southern □[4], Zam.	144	16.00 S	27.00 E
Southern Alps ⛰	162	43.30 S	170.30 E
Southern California, University of ʊ[2]	270	34.02 N	118.17 W
Southern Cross	152	31.13 S	119.19 E
Southern Division □[5]	165f	19.30 S	169.00 E
Southern Ghāts ⛰	112	9.30 N	77.00 E
Southern Highlands □[5]	154	6.00 S	143.30 E
Southern Indian Lake ⊜	166	57.10 N	98.40 W
Southern Leyte □[4]	106	10.50 N	124.55 E
Southern Lueti ≃	142	16.14 S	23.13 E
Southern Pines	182	35.11 N	79.24 W
Southern Ute Indian Reservation ◆[4]	190	37.05 N	107.45 W
Southern View	209	39.46 N	89.39 W
Southern Yemen → Yemen, People's Democratic Republic of □[1]	134	15.00 N	48.00 E
Southery	44	52.32 N	0.23 E
South Esk ≃, Austl.	156	41.25 S	147.08 E
South Esk ≃, Scot., U.K.	42	55.53 N	3.04 W
Southesk Tablelands ⛰[1]	152	20.50 S	126.40 E
South Essex	197	42.38 N	70.46 W
South Euclid	204	41.31 N	81.32 W
Southey	174	50.56 N	104.30 W
South Fabius ≃	209	39.54 N	91.30 W
South Fallsburg	200	41.43 N	74.38 W
South Farmbridge	250	51.38 N	0.41 E
South Farmingdale	266	40.44 N	73.27 W
Southfield, Mass., U.S.	197	42.06 N	73.14 W
Southfield, Mich., U.S.	206	42.29 N	83.17 W
Southfields	200	41.15 N	74.11 W
South Fiji Basin ⊹[1]	14	27.00 S	176.00 E
South Fiji Ridge ⊹[3]	14	23.00 S	179.00 W
Southfleet	250	51.25 N	0.19 E
South Floral Park	266	40.43 N	73.42 W
South Fontana	218	34.05 N	117.24 W
South Foreland ≻	44	51.09 N	1.23 E
South Fork, Colo., U.S.	190	37.40 N	106.37 W
South Fork, Pa., U.S.	204	40.22 N	78.48 W
South Fort George	172	53.54 N	122.45 W
South Forty Foot Drain Ξ	44	52.56 N	0.15 W
South Fox Island I	180	45.25 N	85.50 W
South Fulton	184	36.30 N	88.53 W
South Gate, Calif., U.S.	218	33.57 N	118.12 W
Southgate, Fla., U.S.	210	27.18 N	82.32 W
Southgate, Mich., U.S.	206	42.12 N	83.13 W
Southgate, Wash., U.S.	214	47.10 N	122.30 W
Southgate ◆[8]	250	51.38 N	0.08 W
Southgate ◆[9]	269a	41.25 N	81.32 W
South Georgia I	234	54.15 S	36.45 W
South Georgia Rise ⊹[3]	18	50.00 S	28.00 W
South Germiston	263d	26.15 S	28.10 E
South Gibson	200	41.44 N	75.38 W
South Glamorgan □[6]	44	51.30 N	3.25 W
South Glastonbury	197	41.40 N	72.36 W
South Glens Falls	200	43.18 N	73.39 W
South Grafton	197	42.11 N	71.42 W
South Grand ≃	184	38.18 N	93.28 W
South Grand Island Bridge ◆[5]	274a	43.00 N	78.56 W
South Green	250	51.37 N	0.26 E
South Greensburg	204	40.17 N	79.33 W
South Hackensack	266	40.52 N	74.03 W
South Hadley	197	42.16 N	72.35 W
South Hadley Falls	197	42.14 N	72.36 W
South Hamilton	197	42.37 N	70.53 W
South Hams ⌣	44	50.22 N	3.50 W
South Hanningfield	250	51.39 N	0.31 E
South Hanover	273	42.06 N	70.51 W
South Hartford	200	43.21 N	73.25 W
South Harwich	197	41.41 N	70.03 W
South Hātia Island I	114	22.19 N	91.07 E
South Haven, Ind., U.S.	206	41.33 N	87.08 W
South Haven, Kans., U.S.	188	37.03 N	97.24 W
South Haven, Mich., U.S.	206	42.24 N	86.16 W
South Hayling	44	50.47 N	0.59 W
South Head ≻	264a	33.50 S	151.17 E
South Heart ≃	172	55.34 N	116.11 W
South Hempstead	266	40.41 N	73.37 W
South Henderson	182	36.17 N	78.25 W
South Henik Lake ⊜	166	61.30 N	97.30 W
South Hero	178	44.39 N	73.19 W
South Hill, N.Y., U.S.	200	42.25 N	76.33 W
South Hill, Va., U.S.	182	36.44 N	78.08 W
South Hills ◆[8]	263d	26.15 S	28.05 E
South Hills Village ◆[9]	269b	40.21 N	80.03 W
South Hingham	197	42.11 N	70.53 W
South Hogan Creek ≃	208	39.03 N	84.54 W
South Holland	206	41.37 N	87.37 W
South Holston Lake ⊜[1]	182	36.35 N	82.00 W
South Honcut Creek ≃	216	39.19 N	121.35 W
South Honshu Ridge ⊹[3]	14	18.00 N	143.00 E
South Hopkinton	197	41.24 N	71.45 W
South Horr	144	2.06 N	36.55 E
South Houston	212	29.40 N	95.14 W
South Huntington	266	40.49 N	73.26 W
South Indian Basin ⊹[1]	9	60.00 S	120.00 E
South Indian Lake	174	56.46 N	98.57 W
Southington, Conn., U.S.	197	41.36 N	72.53 W
Southington, Ohio, U.S.	204	41.19 N	80.57 W
South International Falls	180	48.35 N	93.24 W
South Ionia	206	42.57 N	85.04 W
South Island I, Bhārat	112	10.03 N	72.17 E
South Island I, Kenya	144	2.38 N	36.36 E
South Island I, N.Z.	162	43.00 S	171.00 E
South Island I, P.I.T.T.	165c	6.59 N	151.59 E
South Islet I	106	8.44 N	119.49 E
South Jacksonville	209	39.44 N	90.12 W
South Jan Mayen Ridge ⊹[3]	10	68.00 N	10.00 W
South Kemptville Creek ≃	202	44.54 N	75.41 W
South Kenosha	206	42.33 N	87.51 W
South Kensington Museums ʊ	250	51.30 N	0.11 W
South Kent	197	41.41 N	73.28 W
South Kirkby	42	53.34 N	1.20 W
South Konkan Hills ⛰[2]	112	17.00 N	73.30 E
South Korea → Korea, South □[1]	88	36.30 N	128.00 E
South Laguna	218	33.30 N	117.45 W
Southlake	212	32.57 N	97.09 W
South Lake ⊜, Ont., Can.	202	44.26 N	76.13 W
South Lake ⊜, Fla., U.S.	210	28.37 N	80.52 W
South Lake Tahoe	216	38.57 N	119.57 W
South Lancaster	197	42.27 N	71.41 W
Southland, Ky., U.S.	208	38.01 N	84.31 W
Southland, Mich., U.S.	206	42.13 N	84.24 W
Southland, Tex., U.S.	186	33.22 N	101.33 W
Southland ◆[9]	272	37.39 N	122.06 W
Southlawn, Ill., U.S.	209	39.45 N	89.37 W
South Lawn, Md., U.S.	274c	38.48 N	76.59 W
South Lebanon	208	39.22 N	84.13 W
South Lee	197	42.17 N	73.17 W
South Lima	200	42.51 N	77.41 W
South Line Island I	266	40.37 N	73.30 W
South Llano ≃	186	30.30 N	99.46 W
South Lockport	274a	43.09 N	78.42 W
South Loup ≃	188	41.04 N	98.40 W
South Luconia Shoals ⊹[2]	102	5.03 N	112.33 E
South Lynnfield	273	42.31 N	71.00 W
South Lyon	206	42.28 N	83.39 W
South MacMillan ≃	170	63.03 N	133.18 W
South Magnetic Pole ◆	9	66.40 S	140.10 E
South Malosmadulu Atoll I[1]	112	5.10 N	72.58 E
South Manitou Island I	180	45.01 N	86.07 W
South Marsh Island I	198	38.06 N	76.02 W
South Medford	192	42.18 N	122.50 W
South Media	275	39.54 N	75.23 W
South Melbourne	264b	37.50 S	144.57 E
South Merrimack	197	42.49 N	71.34 W
South Miami	210	25.42 N	80.17 W
South Miami Heights	210	25.37 N	80.25 W
South Middleboro	197	41.45 N	70.50 W
South Milford	206	41.32 N	85.16 W
South Mills	182	36.27 N	76.20 W
South Milwaukee	206	42.55 N	87.52 W
South Mimms	250	51.42 N	0.14 W
Southminster	44	51.40 N	0.50 E
South Modesto	216	37.38 N	120.58 W
South Mokelumne ≃	216	38.08 N	121.35 W
South Molton	44	51.01 N	3.50 W
South Monroe	206	41.54 N	83.25 W
Southmont	204	40.18 N	78.56 W
South Montrose	200	41.48 N	75.53 W
South Moose Lake ⊜	174	53.46 N	100.08 W
South Mountain	198	39.51 N	77.29 W
South Mountain ∧, U.S.	198	39.40 N	77.30 W
South Mountain ∧, Idaho, U.S.	192	42.44 N	116.54 W
South Mountain Reservation ♠	266	40.45 N	74.18 W
South Nahanni ≃	166	61.03 N	123.20 W
South Naknek	170	58.43 N	157.05 W
South Nation ≃	196	45.35 N	75.06 W
South New Berlin	200	42.32 N	75.23 W
South New Castle	204	40.58 N	80.21 W
South New River Canal Ξ	210	26.04 N	80.12 W
South Ninepin Island I	261d	22.15 N	114.21 E
South Norfolk → Chesapeake	198	36.43 N	76.15 W
South Normanton	44	52.54 N	1.29 W
South Norwalk Reservoir ⊜[1]	266	41.11 N	73.27 W
South Norwood ◆[8]	250	51.24 N	0.04 W
South Nutfield	250	51.14 N	0.08 W
South Nyack	266	41.05 N	73.55 W
South Ockendon	44	51.32 N	0.18 E
South Ogden	190	41.12 N	111.59 W
Southold	197	41.04 N	72.26 W
South Onondaga	200	42.56 N	76.13 W
South Orange	266	40.45 N	74.15 W
South Orkney Islands II	9	60.35 S	45.30 W
South Oroville	216	39.30 N	121.33 W
South Otselic	200	42.39 N	75.46 W
Southowram	252	53.43 N	1.50 W
South Oxhey	250	51.38 N	0.23 W
South Oyster Bay C	266	40.38 N	73.28 W
South Palo Duro Creek ≃	186	36.06 N	101.29 W
South Para ≃	158b	34.36 S	138.45 E
South Paris	178	44.13 N	70.31 W
South Park, Calif., U.S.	216	38.25 N	122.42 W
South Park, Ill., U.S.	206	41.44 N	88.18 W
South Park ♠, N.Y., U.S.	274a	42.50 N	78.50 W
South Park ♠, Pa., U.S.	269b	40.19 N	80.01 W
South Pasadena, Calif., U.S.	270	34.07 N	118.10 W
South Pasadena, Fla., U.S.	210	27.46 N	82.43 W
South Pass)(	190	42.22 N	108.55 W
South Pass ⊔	165c	7.14 N	151.48 E
South Passage ⊔	161a	27.22 S	153.26 E
South Patrick Shores	210	28.12 N	80.35 W
South Pekin	180	40.30 N	89.39 W
South Pender	214	48.45 N	123.14 W
South Pender Island I	214	48.45 N	123.10 W
South Perth	158a	31.59 S	115.52 E
South Petherton	44	50.58 N	2.49 W
South Philadelphia ◆[8]	275	39.56 N	75.10 W
South Philipsburg	204	40.53 N	78.13 W
South Pittsburg	184	35.01 N	85.42 W
South Plainfield	200	40.35 N	74.25 W
South Platte ≃	188	41.07 N	100.42 W
South Platte, North Fork ≃	190	39.25 N	105.10 W
South Point ≻, Ba.	228	22.50 N	74.52 W
South Point ≻, Barb.	231g	13.02 N	59.31 W
South Point ≻, Pil.	106	10.24 N	122.30 E
South Pole ◆	9	90.00 S	0.00
South Porcupine	180	48.28 N	81.13 W
Southport, Austl.	161a	27.58 S	153.25 E
Southport, Eng., U.K.	42	53.39 N	3.01 W
Southport, Conn., U.S.	197	41.08 N	73.17 W
Southport, Fla., U.S.	184	30.17 N	85.39 W
Southport, Ind., U.S.	208	39.40 N	86.09 W
Southport, N.C., U.S.	182	33.55 N	78.01 W
Southport, N.Y., U.S.	200	42.03 N	76.49 W
South Portland	178	43.38 N	70.15 W
South Portsmouth	208	38.44 N	83.00 W
South Pottstown	198	40.14 N	75.39 W
South Prairie Creek ≃	214	47.08 N	122.10 W
South Raisin ≃	196	45.08 N	74.35 W
South Range	180	47.04 N	88.39 W
South Renovo	204	41.19 N	77.45 W
South Reservoir ⊜[1]	273	42.27 N	71.07 W
South Revelstoke	172	50.48 N	118.11 W
South Ribble □[8]	252	53.45 N	2.42 W
South River, Ont., Can.	180	45.45 N	79.25 W
South River, N.J., U.S.	198	40.27 N	74.23 W
South Rockwood	206	42.04 N	83.16 W
South Ronaldsay I	28	58.46 N	2.50 W
South Roxana	209	38.50 N	90.04 W
South Royalston	197	42.38 N	72.09 W
South Rukuru ≃	144	10.46 S	34.14 E
South Russell	204	41.25 N	81.21 W
South Salmara	114	25.55 N	90.01 E
South Salt Lake	190	40.43 N	111.53 W
South Sand Bluff ≻	148	31.19 S	30.01 E
South Sandwich Islands II	18	57.45 S	26.30 W
South Sandwich Trench ⊹[1]	18	57.00 S	25.00 W
South Sandy Creek ≃	202	43.43 N	76.12 W
South San Francisco	216	37.39 N	122.24 W
South San Gabriel	270	34.04 N	118.05 W
South San Jose Hills	270	34.01 N	117.55 W
South San Ramon Creek ≃	272	37.42 N	121.55 W
South Santiam ≃	192	44.41 N	123.00 W
South Saskatchewan ≃	174	53.15 N	105.05 W
South Saugeen ≃	202	44.08 N	81.02 W
South Seaville	198	39.11 N	74.46 W
South Setauket	200	40.54 N	73.06 W
South Shafter	216	35.28 N	122.42 W
South Shetland Islands II	9	62.00 S	58.00 W
South Shields	42	55.00 N	1.25 W
South Shore	208	38.43 N	82.59 W
South Shore ◆[8]	268	41.46 N	87.35 W
South Shore Mall ◆[9]	266	40.44 N	73.15 W
South Shore Plaza ◆[9]	273	42.13 N	71.01 W
Southside	164h	2.49 S	171.43 W
South Side ◆[8]	269b	40.26 N	79.58 W
Southside Place	212	29.42 N	95.26 W
South Sioux City	188	42.28 N	96.24 W
South Skunk ≃	180	41.15 N	92.02 W
South Slocan	172	49.28 N	117.32 W
South Solon	208	39.44 N	83.37 W
South Spicer Island I	166	68.06 N	79.13 W
South Standard	209	39.21 N	89.47 W
South Sterling	200	41.17 N	75.21 W
South Stickney	268	41.45 N	87.46 W
South Stony Brook	266	40.53 N	73.07 W
South Stradbroke Island I	161a	27.51 S	153.25 E
South Streator	206	41.06 N	88.50 W
South Suburban → Behāla	116	22.31 N	88.19 E
South Sulphur ≃	186	33.23 N	95.18 W
South Sunday Creek ≃	192	46.27 N	105.54 W
South Superior	190	41.46 N	108.58 W
South Swansea	197	41.43 N	71.12 W
South Taranaki Bight C[3]	162	39.40 S	174.10 E
South Tasmania Ridge ⊹[3]	4	46.00 S	147.00 E
South Temple	198	40.24 N	75.55 W
South Thompson ≃	172	50.41 N	120.21 W
South Toms River	198	39.56 N	74.13 W
South Torrington	188	42.03 N	104.11 W
South Towanda	200	41.45 N	76.27 W
South Turkeyfoot Creek ≃	206	41.25 N	83.58 W
South Turlock	216	37.29 N	120.51 W
South Tuscon	190	32.12 N	110.58 W
South Twillingate Island I	176	49.37 N	54.47 W
South Tyne ≃	42	54.59 N	2.08 W
South Ubian	106	5.11 N	120.30 E
South Uist I	28	57.15 N	7.24 W
South Umpqua ≃	192	43.20 N	123.25 W
South Valley	200	42.42 N	74.43 W
South Valley Hills ⛰[2]	275	40.00 N	75.40 W
South Valley Stream	266	40.38 N	73.44 W
South Venice	210	27.03 N	82.24 W
South Ventana Cone ∧	194	36.17 N	121.38 W
South Vernon	204	40.23 N	82.23 W
South Vestal	200	42.01 N	76.00 W
South Vietnam → Vietnam □[1]	100	16.00 N	108.00 E
Southview	204	40.20 N	80.16 W
South Vijayapuri	112	16.49 N	79.33 E
South Wabasca Lake ⊜	172	55.54 N	113.45 W
South Wales	200	42.43 N	78.35 W
South Walpole	273	42.06 N	71.16 W
Southwark ◆[8]	44	51.30 N	0.06 W
South Warren Reservoir ⊜[1]	158b	34.43 S	138.55 E
South Waverly	200	42.00 N	76.32 W
South Weald	250	51.37 N	0.16 E
Southwell	44	53.05 N	0.58 W
South Wellfleet	197	41.55 N	69.58 W
South Wellington	214	49.06 N	123.53 W
Southwest	204	40.12 N	79.32 W
Southwest Bay C	230b	25.00 N	77.32 W
Southwest Branch ≃	274c	38.53 N	76.48 W
South Westbury	266	40.45 N	73.35 W
South West Cape ≻, Austl.	156	43.34 S	146.02 E
Southwest Cape ≻, N.Z.	162	47.17 S	167.28 E
Southwest Cape ≻, Alaska, U.S.	170	63.18 N	171.27 W
Southwest Cape ≻, Vir. Is., U.S.	231n	17.41 N	64.54 W
Southwest Channel ⊔	210	27.34 N	82.45 W
South West City	184	36.31 N	94.37 W
South Westerlo	200	42.27 N	74.02 W
Southwestern Pacific Basin ⊹[1]	14	42.00 S	166.00 W
Southwest Greensburg	204	40.17 N	79.33 W
Southwest Harbor	178	44.17 N	68.20 W
Southwest Indian Ridge ⊹[3]	10	38.00 S	50.00 E
Southwest Miramichi ≃	176	46.58 N	65.35 W
Southwest Museum ʊ	270	34.06 N	118.13 W
Southwest Pacific Basin ⊹[1]	9	55.00 S	180.00 W
Southwest Point ≻, Ba.	228	25.51 N	77.13 W
South West Point ≻, Gilb. Is.	164o	1.52 N	157.33 W
Southwest Point ≻, Pap. N. Gui.	154	2.14 S	146.34 E
Southwest Road ⊔	230m	18.20 N	65.00 W
South Weymouth	273	42.10 N	70.57 W
South Weymouth Naval Air Station ■	197	42.09 N	70.57 W
South Whitley	206	41.05 N	85.38 W
South Whittier	270	33.56 N	118.03 W
South Wichita ≃	186	33.43 N	99.29 W
Southwick, Eng., U.K.	44	50.50 N	0.13 W
Southwick, Mass., U.S.	197	42.03 N	72.46 W
South Williamson	182	37.40 N	82.16 W
South Williamsport	200	41.14 N	77.01 W
South Wilmington	206	41.10 N	88.17 W
South Windham	178	43.44 N	70.26 W
South Windsor	197	41.49 N	72.37 W
Southwold	44	52.20 N	1.40 E
Southwood	200	42.59 N	76.08 W
Southwood Acres	197	41.59 N	72.32 W
South Woodham Ferrers	44	51.39 N	0.37 E
South Woodslee	204	42.14 N	82.43 W
South Woodstock	197	41.56 N	71.58 W
Southworth	214	47.31 N	122.30 W
South Yadkin ≃	182	35.45 N	80.27 W
South Yamhill ≃	214	45.13 N	123.08 W
South Yarmouth	197	41.40 N	70.10 W
South Yorkshire □[6]	42	53.30 N	1.15 W
South Yuba ≃	216	39.17 N	121.12 W
South Zeal	44	50.44 N	3.54 W
Soutpan	148	28.43 S	26.04 E
Soutpansberg ⛰	146	22.55 S	29.30 E
Souvigny	32	46.32 N	3.11 E
Souzy-la-Briche	251	48.32 N	2.09 E
Sovata	38	46.35 N	25.04 E
Soverato	36	38.41 N	16.33 E
Sovere	58	45.49 N	10.01 E
Sovereign Mountain ∧	170	62.08 N	148.36 W
Sövestad	41	55.30 N	13.47 E
Sovetabad	75	40.14 N	69.44 E
Sovetašen, S.S.S.R.	74	40.06 N	44.33 E
Sovetašen, S.S.S.R.	74	39.50 N	45.03 E
Sovetka	73	47.30 N	39.15 E
Sovetsk, S.S.S.R.	66	53.56 N	37.39 E
Sovetsk (Tilsit), S.S.S.R.	66	55.05 N	21.53 E
Sovetsk, S.S.S.R.	70	57.37 N	48.58 E
Sovetskaja, S.S.S.R.	70	49.00 N	42.07 E
Sovetskaja, S.S.S.R.	74	44.02 N	44.03 E
Sovetskaja, S.S.S.R.	74	44.46 N	41.11 E
Sovetskaja Gavan'	79	48.58 N	140.18 E
Sovetskich Oficerov, Pik ∧	75	38.26 N	73.18 E
Sovetskij, S.S.S.R.	66	60.32 N	28.41 E
Sovetskij, S.S.S.R.	68	45.20 N	34.56 E
Sovetskij, S.S.S.R.	70	56.46 N	48.32 E
Sovetskij, S.S.S.R.	75	38.02 N	69.35 E
Sovetskij, S.S.S.R.	76	51.04 N	56.29 E
Sovetskoje, S.S.S.R.	68	50.21 N	39.01 E
Sovetskoje, S.S.S.R.	70	51.27 N	46.44 E
Sovetskoje, S.S.S.R.	74	42.52 N	45.41 E
Sovetskoje, S.S.S.R.	74	43.19 N	43.36 E
Sovetskoje, S.S.S.R.	75	42.17 N	70.15 E
Sovgenovskij	68	45.02 N	40.14 E
Sovicille	60	43.17 N	11.13 E
Sovico	256b	45.39 N	9.16 E
Søvik	26	62.33 N	6.18 E
Søvind	41	55.54 N	10.01 E
Sovpolje	24	65.18 N	43.55 E
Sow ≃	44	52.48 N	2.00 W
Sowek	154	0.49 S	135.30 E
Sowerby, Eng., U.K.	42	54.13 N	1.21 W
Sowerby, Eng., U.K.	252	53.42 N	1.56 W
Sowerby Bridge	42	53.43 N	1.54 W
Soweto ◆[8]	263d	26.14 S	27.54 E
Sowjetisches Ehrenmal ⊥	254a	52.29 N	13.28 E
Soy	52	50.17 N	5.31 E
Soya'	134	0.01 N	42.20 E
Sōya-kaikyō → La Perouse Strait ⊔	79	45.45 N	142.00 E
Sōya-misaki ≻	82a	45.31 N	141.56 E
Soyang-gang ≃	88	37.52 N	127.40 E
Soyapango	226	13.42 N	89.09 W
Soyers Lake ⊜	202	45.02 N	78.37 W
Soyet	114	24.12 N	76.10 E
Soyland Moor ◆[3]	252	53.40 N	2.02 W
Soyons	56	44.53 N	4.51 E
Sož ≃, S.S.S.R.	68	51.57 N	30.48 E
Soz' ≃, S.S.S.R.	72	56.48 N	36.44 E
Şozimskij	24	59.44 N	52.16 E
Šožma	24	61.56 N	40.15 E
Sozopol	38	42.25 N	27.42 E
Sozzago	256b	45.24 N	8.43 E
Spa	52	50.30 N	5.52 E
Space Needle ʊ	214	47.38 N	122.23 W
Spada Lake ⊜[1]	214	47.57 N	121.40 W
Spaden	48	53.34 N	8.38 E
Spahl	52	50.39 N	9.55 E
Spaichingen	54	48.04 N	8.44 E
Spain □[1]	22		
	34	40.00 N	4.00 W
Spakenburg	48	52.15 N	5.23 E
Spalato → Split	36	43.31 N	16.27 E
Spalding, Austl.	156	33.30 S	138.37 E
Spalding, Sask., Can.	174	52.20 N	104.30 W
Spalding, Eng., U.K.	44	52.47 N	0.10 W
Spalding, Mo., U.S.	209	39.38 N	91.32 W
Spalding, Nebr., U.S.	188	41.41 N	98.22 W
Spalt	52	49.10 N	10.55 E
Spam Island I	164h	2.48 S	171.43 W
Spanaway	214	47.06 N	122.26 W
Spandau ◆[8]	254a	52.32 N	13.12 E
Spandau, Berliner Forst ◆[3]	254a	52.35 N	13.11 E
Spang	41	54.56 N	9.50 E
Spangenberg	52	51.07 N	9.40 E
Spangler	204	40.39 N	78.47 W
Spaniard's Bay	176	47.37 N	53.17 W
Spanien → Spain □[1]	34	40.00 N	4.00 W
Spanish	180	46.12 N	82.21 W
Spanish ≃	180	46.11 N	82.19 W
Spanish Camp	212	29.23 N	96.10 W
Spanish Fork	190	40.07 N	111.39 W
Spanish Lake	209	38.47 N	90.13 W
Spanish North Africa □[2]	34		
	124	35.53 N	5.19 W
Spanish Peak ∧	192	44.24 N	119.46 W
Spanish Point ≻	230a	32.18 N	64.48 W
Spanish Sahara → Western Sahara □[2]	124	24.30 N	13.00 W
Spanish Town	231q	17.59 N	76.57 W
Sparbach	254b	48.04 N	16.11 E
Sparkford	44	51.02 N	2.34 W
Sparkill	266	41.02 N	73.56 W
Sparkle Lake	200	41.18 N	73.47 W
Sparkman	184	33.55 N	92.51 W
Sparks, Ga., U.S.	182	31.11 N	83.26 W
Sparks, Nev., U.S.	216	39.32 N	119.45 W
Sparland	180	41.02 N	89.26 W
Sparlingville	204	42.58 N	82.30 W
Sparneck	50	50.09 N	11.50 E
Sparreholm	40	59.04 N	16.49 E
Sparrow Bush	200	41.23 N	74.43 W
Sparrow Lake ⊜	202	44.49 N	79.24 W
Sparrowpit	252	53.19 N	1.52 W
Sparrows Point	198	39.14 N	76.29 W
Sparrows Point ≻	274b	39.12 N	76.30 W
Sparta, Ont., Can.	202	42.42 N	81.05 W
Sparta → Spárti, Ellás	38	37.05 N	22.27 E
Sparta, Ga., U.S.	182	33.17 N	82.58 W
Sparta, Ill., U.S.	184	38.07 N	89.42 W
Sparta, Ky., U.S.	208	38.41 N	84.55 W
Sparta, Mich., U.S.	180	43.10 N	85.42 W
Sparta, N.J., U.S.	200	41.02 N	74.38 W
Sparta, N.C., U.S.	182	36.30 N	81.07 W
Sparta, Ohio, U.S.	204	40.24 N	82.42 W
Sparta, Tenn., U.S.	184	35.56 N	85.29 W
Sparta, Wis., U.S.	180	43.57 N	90.47 W
Sparta Brook ≃	266	41.08 N	73.52 W
Spartak, Sad ♠	255a	59.51 N	30.30 E
Sparta Lake	200	41.03 N	74.34 W
Spartanburg, Ind., U.S.	208	40.04 N	84.51 W
Spartanburg, S.C., U.S.	182	34.57 N	81.55 W
Spartansburg	204	41.49 N	79.41 W
Spartel, Cap ≻	138	35.48 N	5.56 W
Spárti (Sparta)	38	37.05 N	22.27 E
Spartivento, Capo ≻	36	38.53 N	8.50 E
Spas-Demensk	66	54.25 N	34.01 E

ENGLISH

Name	Page	Lat.°′	Long.°′
Spas-Klepiki	70	55.08 N	40.13 E
Spass	72	55.55 N	35.55 E
Spassk-Dal'nij	79	44.37 N	132.48 E
Spasskij	76	53.42 N	59.12 E
Spasskij Zavod	76	49.32 N	73.17 E
Spasskoje, S.S.S.R.	66	53.06 N	36.24 E
Spasskoje, S.S.S.R.	70	55.52 N	45.42 E
Spasskoje, S.S.S.R.	72	54.05 N	38.28 E
Spassk-R'azanskij	70	54.24 N	40.23 E
Spas-Zaulok	72	56.29 N	36.34 E
Spáta	257c	38.00 N	21.31 E
Spátha, Ákra ≻	38	35.42 N	23.44 E
Spaulding	209	39.52 N	89.32 W
Spaulding, Lake ⊜[1]	216	39.20 N	120.37 W
Speaks	212	29.15 N	96.42 W
Spear, Cape ≻	176	47.32 N	52.32 W
Spearfish	188	44.30 N	103.52 W
Spearman	186	36.12 N	101.12 W
Spearsville	208	39.21 N	86.11 W
Spearville	188	37.51 N	99.45 W
Spearwood	158a	32.07 S	115.47 E
Speas Artemidos (Rock Tombs) ⊥	132	27.54 N	30.52 E
Spechtsbrunn	50	50.30 N	11.14 E
Speckhorn ◆[8]	253	51.39 N	7.11 E
Spectacle Island I	273	42.19 N	70.59 W
Spectrum ♠	275	39.54 N	75.10 W
Spectrum Range ⛰	170	57.30 N	130.40 W
Spednic Lake ⊜	176	45.36 N	67.35 W
Speed	208	38.25 N	85.45 W
Speed ≃	202	43.23 N	80.22 W
Speedway	208	39.47 N	86.15 W
Speicher	54	47.24 N	9.27 E
Speichersee ⊜	58	48.13 N	11.45 E
Speightstown	231g	13.15 N	59.39 W
Speigletown	200	42.48 N	73.38 W
Speikkogel ∧	30	47.14 N	15.03 E
Speising ◆[8]	254b	48.10 N	16.17 E
Speke ◆[8]	252	53.21 N	2.51 W
Speke Hall ⊥	252	53.20 N	2.52 W
Speldorf ◆[8]	253	51.25 N	6.52 E
Spellen	253	51.37 N	6.37 E
Spello	60	42.59 N	12.40 E
Spelthorne □[8]	250	51.25 N	0.28 W
Spenard	170	61.11 N	149.55 W
Spence Bay	166	69.32 N	93.31 W
Spencer, Ind., U.S.	184	39.17 N	86.46 W
Spencer, Iowa, U.S.	188	43.09 N	95.09 W
Spencer, Mass., U.S.	197	42.15 N	71.59 W
Spencer, Nebr., U.S.	188	42.53 N	98.42 W
Spencer, N.C., U.S.	182	35.37 N	80.26 W
Spencer, N.Y., U.S.	200	42.13 N	76.30 W
Spencer, Ohio, U.S.	204	41.06 N	82.07 W
Spencer, S. Dak., U.S.	188	43.44 N	97.36 W
Spencer, Tenn., U.S.	184	35.45 N	85.28 W
Spencer, W. Va., U.S.	178	38.48 N	81.21 W
Spencer, Wis., U.S.	180	44.46 N	90.18 W
Spencer, Cape ≻, Austl.	156	35.18 S	136.53 E
Spencer, Cape ≻, N.B., Can.	176	45.12 N	65.55 W
Spencer, Cape ≻, Alaska, U.S.	170	58.14 N	136.40 W
Spencer, Mount ∧	214	49.03 N	124.38 W
Spencer, Point ≻	170	65.18 N	166.50 W
Spencer Brook ≃	273	42.28 N	71.22 W
Spencer Creek ≃, Ont., Can.	202	43.17 N	79.54 W
Spencer Creek ≃, Mo., U.S.	209	39.33 N	91.20 W
Spencer Field ⊠	271	42.31 N	83.33 W
Spencer Gulf C	156	34.00 S	137.00 E
Spencer Lake ⊜	214	47.16 N	122.57 W
Spencerport	200	43.11 N	77.48 W
Spencertown	200	42.20 N	73.33 W
Spencerville, Ont., Can.	202	44.51 N	75.33 W
Spencerville, Ind., U.S.	206	41.19 N	84.54 W
Spencerville, Ohio, U.S.	206	40.42 N	84.21 W
Spences Bridge	172	50.25 N	121.21 W
Spenge	48	52.08 N	8.28 E
Spennymoor	42	54.42 N	1.35 W
Spenser Mountains ⛰	162	42.15 S	172.30 E
Sperenberg	50	52.08 N	13.22 E
Sperillen ⊜	26	60.28 N	10.03 E
Sperkhiós ≃	38	38.52 N	22.34 E
Sperling	214	49.08 N	122.33 W
Sperlonga	60	41.15 N	13.26 E
Spermaceti Cove C	266	40.26 N	73.59 W
Sperry Creek ≃	269a	41.29 N	81.53 W
Sperry Rand Corporation ʊ[3]	266	40.45 N	73.42 W
Sperryville	178	38.39 N	78.14 W
Spessart ◆[1]	52	50.10 N	9.20 E
Spessart, Naturpark ♠	52	49.50 N	9.25 E
Spesutie Island I	198	39.27 N	76.05 W
Spétsai I	38	37.16 N	23.08 E
Spevakovka	73	49.03 N	38.54 E
Spexard	48	51.52 N	8.24 E
Spey ≃	28	57.40 N	3.06 W
Speyer	52	49.19 N	8.26 E
Speyerbach ≃	52	49.19 N	8.27 E
Speyside	231r	11.18 N	60.32 W
Spezia → La Spezia	56	44.07 N	9.50 E
Spezzano Albanese	36	39.40 N	16.19 E
Spiazzo	58	46.07 N	10.40 E
Spiceland	208	39.50 N	85.26 W
Spicer	188	45.14 N	94.56 W
Spicer Creek ≃	274a	43.02 N	78.53 W
Spicer Meadow Reservoir ⊜[1]	216	38.23 N	119.59 W
Spicheren	52	49.12 N	6.58 E
Spickard	184	40.14 N	93.35 W
Spicket ≃	273	42.42 N	71.09 W
Spieka	48	53.45 N	8.35 E
Spiekeroog I	48	53.46 N	7.42 E
Spiess Seamount ⊹[3]	8	54.40 S	0.15 E
Spiez	54	46.41 N	7.39 E
Spijkenisse	48	51.21 N	4.20 E
Špikov	68	48.46 N	28.35 E
Spilamberto	58	44.32 N	11.01 E
Spilimbergo	58	46.07 N	12.54 E
Spillersboda	40	59.42 N	18.51 E
Spillimacheen ≃	172	50.55 N	116.20 W
Spinazzola	36	40.58 N	16.06 E
Spīn Būldak	110	31.01 N	66.24 E
Spincourt	32	49.20 N	5.40 E
Spindale	182	35.22 N	81.55 W
Spindoli	60	43.12 N	12.54 E
Spinea	58	45.29 N	12.10 E
Spinetta Marengo	56	44.53 N	8.41 E
Spinnerstown	198	40.26 N	75.26 W
Spires → Speyer	52	49.19 N	8.26 E
Spirit Lake, Idaho, U.S.	192	47.58 N	116.52 W
Spirit Lake, Iowa, U.S.	188	43.26 N	95.06 W
Spirit Lake, Wash., U.S.	214	46.16 N	122.09 W
Spirit Lake ⊜	214	46.16 N	122.08 W
Spirit River	172	55.47 N	118.50 W
Spiritwood	174	53.22 N	107.31 W
Spiro	184	35.16 N	94.37 W
Spirovo	66	57.26 N	34.59 E
Spišská Nová Ves	30	48.57 N	20.34 E
Spitak	74	40.51 N	44.16 E
Spithead ≻	44	50.45 N	1.05 W
Spit Point ≻	152	20.02 S	119.00 E
Spitsbergen I	12	78.45 N	16.00 E
Spitsbergen Bank ⊹[3]	10	76.00 N	23.00 E
Spittal an der Drau	58	46.48 N	13.30 E
Spitz	30	48.22 N	15.25 E
Spitzbergen und Jan Mayen → Svalbard and Jan Mayen □[2], Eur.	10	78.00 N	20.00 E

DEUTSCH

Name	Seite	Breite°′	Länge°′ E=Ost
Spitzbergen und Jan Mayen → Svalbard and Jan Mayen □[2], Eur.	10	71.00 N	8.20 W
Spitzer-Berg ∧[2]	254a	52.38 N	13.35 E
Spjelkavik	26	62.28 N	6.23 E
Splavnucha	70	51.05 N	45.22 E
Splendora	212	30.14 N	95.10 W
Split	36	43.31 N	16.27 E
Split, Cape ≻	176	45.20 N	64.30 W
Split Lake ⊜	174	56.08 N	96.15 W
Split Rock, Rapides L	265a	45.19 N	73.57 W
Split Rock Creek ≃	188	43.34 N	96.35 W
Splitrock Reservoir ⊜[1]	266	40.58 N	74.27 W
Spluga, Passo della (Splügenpass))(	54	46.30 N	9.20 E
Splügen	54	46.33 N	9.20 E
Splügenpass (Passo della Spluga))(	54	46.30 N	9.20 E
Spodsbjerg	41	54.56 N	10.50 E
Spofford	186	29.11 N	100.25 W
Spoģi	66	56.05 N	26.44 E
Spokane	192	47.40 N	117.23 W
Spokane ≃	192	47.44 N	118.20 W
Spokane, Mount ∧	192	47.55 N	117.07 W
Spokane Indian Reservation ◆[4]	192	47.55 N	118.00 W
Spokojnaja	74	44.15 N	41.25 E
Špola	68	49.01 N	31.24 E
Spoleto	60	42.44 N	12.44 E
Spoltore	60	42.27 N	14.08 E
Spondigna	58	46.38 N	10.37 E
Spondon	44	52.54 N	1.25 W
Sponds Hill ∧[2]	252	53.19 N	2.03 W
Spóng	100	13.27 N	105.34 E
Spoon ≃	180	40.18 N	90.04 W
Spooner	180	45.50 N	91.53 W
Spořice	50	50.26 N	13.25 E
Spornitz	50	53.24 N	11.43 E
Spornoje	64	62.20 N	151.03 E
Sporovo	66	52.25 N	25.20 E
Spørring	41	56.18 N	10.09 E
Sportforum ♠	254a	52.33 N	13.29 E
Sport Hill	197	41.14 N	73.16 W
Sporting Hill	198	40.09 N	76.26 W
Sportsman's Park Race Track ♠	268	41.50 N	87.46 W
Spotorno	56	44.14 N	8.25 E
Spot Pond ⊜	273	42.27 N	71.06 W
Spotswood, Austl.	264b	37.50 S	144.53 E
Spotswood, N.J., U.S.	198	40.23 N	74.23 W
Spotsylvania	198	38.12 N	77.35 W
Spotsylvania □[6]	198	38.15 N	77.30 W
Spotsylvania Court House Battlefield (1864) ⊥	198	38.15 N	77.35 W
Sprague, Man., Can.	174	49.02 N	95.38 W
Sprague, Wash., U.S.	192	47.18 N	117.59 W
Sprague ≃	192	42.34 N	121.51 W
Sprague, North Fork ≃	192	42.26 N	121.07 W
Sprague, South Fork ≃	192	42.26 N	121.07 W
Spragueville	197	41.53 N	71.32 W
Sprain Ridge Park ♠	266	40.59 N	73.51 W
Sprankle Mills	204	41.00 N	79.07 W
Spratly Island I	98	8.38 N	111.55 E
Spratt Point ≻	202	44.36 N	80.01 W
Spray	192	44.50 N	119.48 W
Spray Lakes Reservoir ⊜[1]	172	50.55 N	115.20 W
Spreča ≃	38	44.45 N	18.06 E
Spreckels	216	36.36 N	121.34 W
Spreckelsville	219a	20.54 N	156.25 W
Spree ≃	50	52.32 N	13.13 E
Spreenhagen	50	52.20 N	13.52 E
Spreeufontein	148	33.22 S	20.45 E
Spremberg	50	51.34 N	14.22 E
Sprendlingen, B.R.D.	52	50.01 N	8.41 E
Sprendlingen, B.R.D.	52	49.51 N	7.59 E
Spresiano	58	45.46 N	12.16 E
Spring	212	30.09 N	95.25 W
Spring ≃, U.S.	184	36.52 N	94.44 W
Spring ≃, Ark., U.S.	184	36.08 N	91.05 W
Spring, South Fork ≃	184	36.19 N	91.30 W
Spring Arbor	206	42.12 N	84.34 W
Spring Bay C	190	41.40 N	112.50 W
Springbok	146	29.43 S	17.55 E
Springboro, Ohio, U.S.	208	39.33 N	84.15 W
Springboro, Pa., U.S.	204	41.48 N	80.22 W
Spring Branch ≃	274b	39.26 N	76.35 W
Springbrook, Ont., Can.	265b	43.39 N	79.47 W
Springbrook, Md., U.S.	274c	39.03 N	77.00 W
Spring Brook, N.Y., U.S.	200	42.49 N	78.40 W
Spring Brook ≃, Ill., U.S.	268	41.58 N	87.59 W
Spring Brook ≃, N.J., U.S.	266	40.53 N	74.35 W
Springburn	162	43.40 S	171.28 E
Spring City, Pa., U.S.	198	40.11 N	75.33 W
Spring City, Tenn., U.S.	182	35.42 N	84.52 W
Spring City, Utah, U.S.	190	39.29 N	111.30 W
Spring Coulee ∨	188	48.31 N	100.54 W
Spring Creek, N.Z.	162	41.28 S	173.58 E
Spring Creek, Pa., U.S.	204	41.53 N	79.32 W
Spring Creek ≃, Austl.	156	24.12 S	140.58 E
Spring Creek ≃, U.S.	188	40.30 N	101.21 W
Spring Creek ≃, Ga., U.S.	182	30.54 N	84.45 W
Spring Creek ≃, Ill., U.S.	206	40.49 N	87.50 W
Spring Creek ≃, Ill., U.S.	209	39.52 N	89.37 W
Spring Creek ≃, Ill., U.S.	268	41.32 N	88.04 W
Spring Creek ≃, Mo., U.S.	209	38.21 N	91.10 W
Spring Creek ≃, Nev., U.S.	194	39.55 N	117.50 W
Spring Creek ≃, N. Dak., U.S.	188	47.15 N	101.48 W
Spring Creek ≃, Pa., U.S.	204	40.56 N	77.47 W
Spring Creek ≃, Pa., U.S.	204	41.24 N	78.57 W
Spring Creek ≃, S. Dak., U.S.	188	45.54 N	100.18 W
Spring Creek ≃, S. Dak., U.S.	188	43.52 N	113.00 W
Spring Creek ≃, Tex., U.S.	212	30.02 N	95.16 W
Springdale, Newf., Can.	176	49.30 N	56.04 W
Springdale, Ark., U.S.	184	36.11 N	94.08 W
Springdale, Ohio, U.S.	208	39.17 N	84.28 W
Springdale, Pa., U.S.	204	40.33 N	79.46 W
Springdale, S.C., U.S.	182	33.57 N	81.06 W
Springdale, Utah, U.S.	190	37.11 N	113.00 W
Springdale, Wash., U.S.	192	48.04 N	117.45 W
Spring Dale, W. Va., U.S.	182	37.53 N	80.48 W
Springe	48	52.12 N	9.32 E
Springer	186	36.22 N	104.36 W
Springers Brook ≃	275	39.44 N	74.41 W
Springerville	190	34.08 N	109.17 W
Springfield, N.B., Can.	176	46.01 N	67.03 W

Symbols in the index entries represent the broad categories identified in the key at the right. Symbols with superior numbers (⛰[2]) identify subcategories (see complete key on page I · 26).

Kartensymbole in dem Registerverzeichnis stellen die rechts im Schlüssel erklärten Kategorien dar. Symbole mit hochgestellten Ziffern (⛰[2]) bezeichnen Unterabteilungen einer Kategorie (vgl. vollständiger Schlüssel auf Seite I · 26).

Los símbolos incluídos en el texto del índice representan las grandes categorias identificadas con la clave a la derecha. Los símbolos con numeros en su parte superior (⛰[2]) identifican las subcategorias (véase la clave completa en la página I · 26).

Les symboles de l'index représentent les catégories indiquées dans la légende à droite. Les symboles suivis d'un indice (⛰[2]) représentent des sous-catégories (voir légende complète à la page I · 26).

Os símbolos incluídos no texto do índice representam as grandes categorias identificadas com a chave à direita. Os símbolos com números em sua parte superior (⛰[2]) identificam as subcategorias (veja-se a chave completa à página I · 26).

∧ Mountain	Berg	Montaña	Montagne	Montanha
⛰ Mountains	Berge	Montañas	Montagnes	Montanhas
)(Pass	Pass	Paso	Col	Passo
∨ Valley, Canyon	Tal, Cañon	Valle, Cañón	Vallée, Canyon	Vale, Canhão
⌣ Plain	Ebene	Llano	Plaine	Planície
≻ Cape	Kap	Cabo	Cap	Cabo
I Island	Insel	Isla	Île	Ilha
II Islands	Inseln	Islas	Îles	Ilhas
⊥ Other Topographic Features	Andere Topographische Objekte	Otros Elementos Topográficos	Autres données topographiques	Outros Elementos Topográficos

ESPAÑOL

Nombre	Página	Lat. °′	Long. °′ W=Oeste
Springfield, Ont., Can.	202	42.50 N	80.56 W
Springfield, N.Z.	162	43.20 S	171.55 E
Springfield, S. Afr.	148	29.02 S	22.53 E
Springfield, Colo., U.S.	188	37.24 N	102.37 W
Springfield, Fla., U.S.	184	30.09 N	85.37 W
Springfield, Ga., U.S.	182	32.22 N	81.18 W
Springfield, Ill., U.S.	209	39.47 N	89.40 W
Springfield, Ky., U.S.	184	37.41 N	85.13 W
Springfield, Mass., U.S.	197	42.07 N	72.36 W
Springfield, Mich., U.S.	206	42.20 N	85.15 W
Springfield, Minn., U.S.	188	44.14 N	94.59 W
Springfield, Mo., U.S.	184	37.14 N	93.17 W
Springfield, N.J., U.S.	266	40.43 N	74.19 W
Springfield, Ohio, U.S.	208	39.56 N	83.49 W
Springfield, Oreg., U.S.	192	44.03 N	123.01 W
Springfield, Pa., U.S.	275	39.55 N	75.24 W
Springfield, S.C., U.S.	182	33.30 N	81.17 W
Springfield, S. Dak., U.S.	188	42.49 N	97.54 W
Springfield, Tenn., U.S.	184	36.31 N	86.52 W
Springfield, Vt., U.S.	178	43.18 N	72.29 W
Springfield, Va., U.S.	274c	38.45 N	77.13 W
Springfield, Lake ⊜[1]	209	39.44 N	89.36 W
Springfield Center	200	42.50 N	74.53 W
Springfield Lake ⊜	275	40.11 N	75.00 W
Springfield Lake ⊜[1]	212	31.36 N	96.33 W
Springfield Plateau ⛰[1]	184	37.10 N	93.30 W
Springfontein	148	30.19 S	25.36 E
Spring Garden	236	6.59 N	58.31 W
Spring Garden Brook ≃	266	40.46 N	74.23 W
Spring Garden Township	198	39.57 N	76.44 W
Spring Glen, Fla., U.S.	182	30.18 N	81.36 W
Spring Glen, N.Y., U.S.	200	41.40 N	74.26 W
Spring Glen, Pa., U.S.	198	40.38 N	76.37 W
Spring Green	180	43.11 N	90.04 W
Spring Grove, Ill., U.S.	206	42.26 N	88.13 W
Spring Grove, Minn., U.S.	180	43.33 N	91.38 W
Spring Grove, Pa., U.S.	198	39.52 N	76.52 W
Springhill, N.S., Can.	176	45.39 N	64.03 W
Spring Hill, Calif., U.S.	216	39.15 N	121.03 W
Spring Hill, Fla., U.S.	210	28.29 N	82.35 W
Springhill, La., U.S.	184	33.00 N	93.28 W
Spring Hill, Pa., U.S.	204	40.23 N	78.40 W
Spring Hill, Tenn., U.S.	184	35.45 N	86.56 W
Spring Hill, Tex., U.S.	212	32.34 N	94.48 W
Spring Hills	206	40.16 N	83.22 W
Spring Hope	182	35.57 N	78.06 W
Springhouse	172	51.55 N	122.07 W
Spring Lake, Mich., U.S.	206	43.04 N	86.11 W
Spring Lake, N.J., U.S.	198	40.09 N	74.02 W
Spring Lake, N.C., U.S.	182	35.10 N	78.58 W
Spring Lake ⊜, Mich., U.S.	206	43.06 N	86.11 W
Spring Lake ⊜, N.J., U.S.	266	40.35 N	74.25 W
Spring Lake Heights	198	40.09 N	74.04 W
Spring Mill, Ohio, U.S.	204	40.54 N	82.36 W
Spring Mill, Pa., U.S.	275	40.04 N	75.17 W
Spring Mill Reservoir ⊜[1]	252	53.39 N	2.13 W
Spring Mills	200	40.51 N	77.34 W
Spring Mill State Park ♠	208	38.43 N	86.25 W
Spring Mount	198	40.17 N	75.28 W
Spring Mountains ⛰	194	36.10 N	115.40 W
Spring Pond ⊜	273	42.30 N	70.57 W
Springport, Ind., U.S.	208	40.03 N	85.24 W
Springport, Mich., U.S.	206	42.22 N	84.42 W
Spring Run	204	40.09 N	83.47 W
Springs	148	26.13 S	28.25 E
Springs Aerodrome ⊠	263d	26.15 S	28.24 E
Springside	275	40.04 N	74.51 W
Springs Junction	162	42.19 S	172.11 E
Springs Stadium ♠	263d	26.15 S	28.26 E
Springsure	156	24.07 S	148.05 E
Springton	158b	34.43 S	139.05 E
Springtown	212	32.58 N	97.41 W
Springvale, Austl.	152	17.48 S	127.41 E
Springvale, Austl.	156	23.33 S	140.42 E
Springvale, Austl.	159	37.57 S	145.09 E
Springvale, Maine, U.S.	178	43.28 N	70.48 W
Springvale South	264b	37.58 S	145.09 E
Spring Valley, Calif., U.S.	218	32.45 N	116.59 W
Spring Valley, Ill., U.S.	180	41.20 N	89.12 W
Spring Valley, Minn., U.S.	180	43.41 N	92.23 W
Spring Valley, N.Y., U.S.	200	41.07 N	74.03 W
Spring Valley, Ohio, U.S.	208	39.37 N	84.01 W
Spring Valley, Tex., U.S.	212	29.47 N	95.31 W
Spring Valley, Wis., U.S.	180	44.51 N	92.14 W
Spring Valley ∨	194	39.15 N	114.25 W
Spring Valley Creek ≃	194	39.20 N	114.25 W
Springview	188	42.49 N	99.45 W
Springville, Ala., U.S.	184	33.46 N	86.30 W
Springville, Calif., U.S.	194	36.08 N	118.49 W
Springville, Iowa, U.S.	180	42.03 N	91.27 W
Springville, N.J., U.S.	275	39.56 N	74.52 W
Springville, N.Y., U.S.	200	42.31 N	78.40 W
Springville, Pa., U.S.	200	41.42 N	75.55 W
Springville, Utah, U.S.	190	40.10 N	111.37 W
Springwater	200	42.38 N	77.36 W
Springwood	160	33.42 S	150.33 E
Sprint ≃	42	54.22 N	2.45 W
Sprite Creek ≃	200	43.08 N	74.44 W
Sproat Lake ⊜	172	49.16 N	125.03 W
Sprockhövel	52	51.22 N	7.15 E
Sprogels Run ≃	275	40.14 N	75.37 W
Sprogø I	41	55.20 N	10.58 E
Sprottau → Szprotawa	30	51.34 N	15.33 E
Sprötze	48	53.18 N	9.49 E
Sproul	204	40.16 N	78.28 W
Sprout Brook ≃	266	40.54 N	74.05 W
Spruce Brook	176	48.45 N	58.11 W
Spruce Creek	204	40.37 N	78.08 W
Spruce Creek ≃	200	43.07 N	74.46 W
Spruce Grove	172	53.32 N	113.55 W
Spruce Knob ∧	178	38.42 N	79.32 W
Spruce Knob-Seneca Rocks National Recreation Area ♠	178	38.50 N	79.20 W
Spruce Lake	174	53.32 N	109.14 W
Spruce Mountain ∧, Ariz., U.S.	190	34.28 N	112.24 W
Spruce Mountain ∧, Nev., U.S.	194	40.33 N	114.49 W

FRANÇAIS

Nom	Page	Lat. °′	Long. °′ W=Ouest
Spruce Pine	182	35.55 N	82.04 W
Spruce Run Reservoir ⊜[1]	200	40.40 N	74.57 W
Spruce Run State Park ♠	200	40.40 N	74.56 W
Spruce Woods Provincial Park ♠	174	49.42 N	99.05 W
Spry	198	39.55 N	76.41 W
Spry Lake ⊜	202	44.44 N	81.15 W
Spulico, Capo ≻	36	39.58 N	16.39 E
Spurfield	172	55.13 N	114.16 W
Spurn Head ≻	42	53.34 N	0.07 E
Spurr, Mount ∧	170	61.18 N	152.15 W
Sputendorf	254a	52.20 N	13.13 E
Spuzzum	172	49.41 N	121.25 W
Spy Hill	174	50.36 N	101.41 W
Spy Pond ⊜	273	42.24 N	71.09 W
Squally Channel ⩊	172	53.10 N	129.15 W
Squamish	172	49.42 N	123.09 W
Squamish ≃	172	49.45 N	123.09 W
Squam Lake ⊜	178	43.45 N	71.32 W
Square Butte Creek ≃	188	46.55 N	100.55 W
Square Lake ⊜	176	47.03 N	68.20 W
Squatteck	176	47.53 N	68.43 W
Squaw Cap Mountain ∧	176	47.53 N	66.53 W
Squaw Creek ≃, Idaho, U.S.	192	43.51 N	116.22 W
Squaw Creek ≃, Ill., U.S.	268	42.21 N	88.07 W
Squaw Creek ≃, Oreg., U.S.	192	44.27 N	121.20 W
Squaw Harbor	170	55.11 N	160.30 W
Squaw Hill ∧	190	41.48 N	105.02 W
Squaw Island I	274a	42.56 N	78.54 W
Squaw Peak ∧, Calif., U.S.	216	39.11 N	120.16 W
Squaw Peak ∧, Mont., U.S.	192	47.10 N	114.21 W
Squaw Rapids	174	53.41 N	103.20 W
Squaw Rapids Dam ◆[6]	174	53.40 N	103.25 W
Squaw Run ≃	269b	40.29 N	79.52 W
Squaw Valley State Recreation Area ♠	216	39.12 N	120.15 W
Squibnocket Point ≻	197	41.18 N	70.47 W
Squilax	172	50.52 N	119.35 W
Squillace, Golfo di C	36	38.50 N	16.50 E
Squinzano	36	40.26 N	18.03 E
Squire	182	37.14 N	81.36 W
Squires, Mount ∧	152	26.12 S	127.28 E
Squirrel ≃	170	66.57 N	160.27 W
Squirrel Hill ◆[8]	269b	40.26 N	79.55 W
Squirrel Hill Tunnel ◆[5]	269b	40.26 N	79.55 W
Squirrel's Heath ◆[8]	250	51.35 N	0.13 E
Sragen	105a	7.26 S	111.02 E
Šramkovka	68	50.10 N	32.05 E
Srbija □[3]	38	44.00 N	21.00 E
Srbija □[9]	38	43.00 N	21.00 E
Srbobran	38	45.33 N	19.48 E
Srê Âmběl	100	11.07 N	103.46 E
Sredinnyj Chrebet ⛰	64	56.00 N	158.00 E
Sredna Gora ⛰	38	42.30 N	25.00 E
Sredn'aja Achtuba	70	48.43 N	44.52 E
Sredn'aja Mokla ≃	78	55.01 N	119.37 E
Srednaja Nanaki, Golec ∧	79	52.26 N	132.50 E
Sredn'aja Ol'okma	78	55.26 N	120.33 E
Srednegorje	66	60.34 N	29.25 E
Sredneje Kujto, Ozero ⊜	24	65.08 N	31.15 E
Srednekolymsk	64	67.27 N	153.41 E
Srednerusskaja Vozvyšennost' ⛰[1]	62	52.00 N	38.00 E
Srednesibirskoje Ploskogorje ⛰[1]	64	65.00 N	105.00 E
Srednij Ikorec	68	51.05 N	39.45 E
Srednij Kalar	78	55.51 N	117.24 E
Srednij Oseredok, Ostrov I	70	45.50 N	48.30 E
Srednij Ural ⛰	76	58.00 N	59.00 E
Srednij Urgal	79	51.09 N	132.59 E
Srednij Vas'ugan	76	59.16 N	78.15 E
Srednyj	73	48.09 N	39.50 E
Srê Khtŭm	100	12.10 N	106.52 E
Śrem	30	52.08 N	17.01 E
Srê Moăt	100	13.18 N	107.10 E
Sremska Mitrovica	38	44.58 N	19.37 E
Sremski Karlovci	38	45.12 N	19.57 E
Srêng ≃	100	13.21 N	103.27 E
Srêpŏk ≃	100	13.33 N	106.16 E
Sretensk	78	52.15 N	117.43 E
Sretenskoje	78	56.28 N	96.25 E
Srīdharpur	116	23.04 N	89.25 E
Sri Dūngargarh	110	28.05 N	74.00 E
Sri Gangānagar	113	29.55 N	73.53 E
Sri Hargobindpur	113	31.41 N	75.39 E
Srīkākulam	112	18.18 N	83.54 E
Sri Karanpur	113	29.50 N	73.27 E
Sri Lanka □[1]	108		
	112	7.00 N	81.00 E
Sri Mohangarh	110	27.17 N	71.14 E
Srīnagar, Bhārat	113	34.05 N	74.49 E
Srīnagar, Bhārat	114	30.13 N	78.47 E
Srīnagar, Bngl.	116	23.32 N	90.18 E
Srīnagar Airport ⊠	113	34.00 N	74.52 E
Srīpur, Bngl.	116	23.36 N	89.24 E
Srīpur, Bngl.	116	24.12 N	90.29 E
Srirāmpur	262b	22.49 N	88.29 E
Srīrangam	112	10.52 N	78.41 E
Sri Thep ⊥	100	16.25 N	101.04 E
Srīvardhan	112	18.02 N	73.01 E
Srīvilliputtūr	112	9.31 N	77.38 E
Środa Śląska	30	51.10 N	16.36 E
Środa Wielkopolski	30	52.14 N	17.17 E
Srostki	76	56.20 N	126.00 E
Srpska Crnja	38	45.43 N	20.42 E
Ssangmun-ni ◆[8]	261b	37.39 N	127.02 E
Ssuch'ungch'i	90	22.06 N	120.46 E
Ssup'ing → Siping	79	43.12 N	124.20 E
St. → Saint, Sankt, Sint			
Staaken ◆[8]	254a	52.32 N	13.08 E
Staaken, Flugplatz ⊠	254a	52.32 N	13.06 E
Staaten ≃	154	16.24 S	141.17 E
Staatsburg	200	41.51 N	73.56 W
Stabbursdalen Nasjonalpark ♠	24	70.06 N	24.30 E
Staberhuk ≻	50	54.24 N	11.19 E
Stabroek	46	51.20 N	4.22 E
Stackpoie Head ≻	44	51.37 N	4.54 W
Stacksteads	252	53.41 N	2.13 W
Stacyville	180	43.26 N	92.47 W
Stad-Delden	48	52.16 N	6.42 E
Stade	48	53.36 N	9.28 E
Stade □[6]	48	53.30 N	9.30 E
Staden, Bel.	46	50.59 N	3.01 E
Staden, B.R.D.	52	50.20 N	8.54 E
Städjan ∧	26	61.55 N	12.52 E
Stadlandet ≻[1]	26	62.07 N	5.18 E
Stadlau ◆[8]	254b	48.14 N	16.28 E
Stadl-Paura	58	48.05 N	13.53 E
Stadskanaal	48	53.00 N	6.55 E
Stadt Allendorf	52	50.50 N	9.01 E
Stadtbergen	54	48.22 N	10.50 E
Stadt Haag	30	48.07 N	14.34 E
Stadthagen	48	52.19 N	9.13 E
Stadtilm	50	50.47 N	11.05 E
Städtische Rahmede	253	51.17 N	7.40 E
Stadtkyll	52	50.21 N	6.32 E
Stadtlauringen	52	50.11 N	10.22 E
Stadtlengsfeld	52	50.47 N	10.07 E
Stadtlohn	48	51.59 N	6.55 E
Stadtoldendorf	48	51.53 N	9.37 E

PORTUGUÊS

Nome	Página	Lat. °′	Long. °′ W=Oeste
Stadtprozelten	52	49.47 N	9.25 E
Stadtroda	50	50.51 N	11.44 E
Stadtsteinach	50	50.09 N	11.30 E
Stadt Wehlen	50	50.58 N	14.02 E
Stadum	41	54.44 N	9.03 E
Stäfa	54	47.15 N	8.44 E
Staffanstorp	41	55.38 N	13.13 E
Staffelde	254a	52.44 N	13.00 E
Staffelsee ⊜	58	47.42 N	11.10 E
Staffelstein	52	50.06 N	11.00 E
Staffora ≃	56	45.04 N	9.01 E
Stafford, Eng., U.K.	44	52.48 N	2.07 W
Stafford, Conn., U.S.	197	41.59 N	72.17 W
Stafford, Kans., U.S.	188	37.58 N	98.36 W
Stafford, N.Y., U.S.	200	42.59 N	78.04 W
Stafford, Tex., U.S.	212	29.37 N	95.34 W
Stafford, Va., U.S.	198	38.09 N	76.51 W
Stafford □[6]	198	38.25 N	77.30 W
Staffordshire □[6]	44	52.50 N	2.00 W
Stafford Springs	197	41.57 N	72.18 W
Staffordsville	178	37.50 N	82.50 W
Staffordville	197	42.00 N	72.16 W
Stagen	102	3.18 S	116.10 E
Stag Pond ⊜	266	40.59 N	74.42 W
Stahl-Berg ∧[2]	254a	52.21 N	13.46 E
Stahlbrode	50	54.14 N	13.17 E
Stahle	48	51.50 N	9.25 E
Stahnsdorf	50	52.23 N	13.13 E
Stahringen	54	47.47 N	8.58 E
Staicele	66	57.50 N	24.45 E
Staines	44	51.26 N	0.31 W
Staines Reservoirs ⊜[1]	250	51.27 N	0.30 W
Stainforth	42	53.36 N	1.01 W
Stainland	252	53.40 N	1.53 W
Stainmore Forest ◆[3]	42	54.30 N	2.10 W
Stains	251	48.57 N	2.23 E
Stainz	30	46.54 N	15.16 E
Stairtown	212	29.43 N	97.44 W
Stajki	68	50.05 N	30.54 E
Staked Plain → Estacado, Llano ⩦	186	33.30 N	102.40 W
Stäket	40	59.28 N	17.48 E
Stakroge	41	55.53 N	8.51 E
Stalać	38	43.40 N	21.25 E
Stalbridge	44	50.58 N	2.23 W
Stalden	54	46.14 N	7.52 E
Stalham	44	52.47 N	1.31 E
Stalheim	26	60.50 N	6.40 E
Stalin → Varna, Blg.	38	43.13 N	27.55 E
Stalin → Brașov, Rom.	38	45.39 N	25.37 E
Stalin (Kuçovë), Shq.	38	40.48 N	19.54 E
Stalinabad → Dušanbe	75	38.35 N	68.48 E
Stalino → Doneck	73	48.00 N	37.48 E
Stalinogorsk → Novomoskovsk	72	54.05 N	38.13 W
Stalinogród → Katowice	30	50.16 N	19.00 E
Stalinsk → Novokuzneck	76	53.45 N	87.06 E
Stallarholmen	40	59.22 N	17.12 E
Ställberg	40	59.59 N	14.55 E
Ställdalen	40	59.56 N	14.56 E
Stalowa Wola	30	50.35 N	22.02 E
Stalybridge	252	53.29 N	2.04 W
Stambaugh	180	46.04 N	88.38 W
Stamford, Austl.	156	21.16 S	143.49 E
Stamford, Eng., U.K.	44	52.39 N	0.29 W
Stamford, Conn., U.S.	197	41.03 N	73.32 W
Stamford, N.Y., U.S.	200	42.25 N	74.37 W
Stamford, Tex., U.S.	186	32.57 N	99.48 W
Stamford, Vt., U.S.	197	42.45 N	73.05 W
Stamford, Lake ⊜[1]	186	33.05 N	99.35 W
Stamford Bridge	42	53.59 N	0.55 W
Stamford Brige Stadium ♠	250	51.29 N	0.11 W
Stamford Harbor C	266	41.02 N	73.32 W
Stamford Museum ⚜	266	41.07 N	73.33 W
Stammbach	50	50.09 N	11.41 E
Stammersdorf ◆[8]	254b	48.18 N	16.25 E
Stammheim, B.R.D.	52	48.41 N	8.46 E
Stammheim, Schw.	54	47.38 N	8.47 E
Stampede Pass)(	214	47.17 N	121.21 W
Stampede Reservoir ⊜[1]	216	39.29 N	120.07 W
Stamping Ground	208	38.16 N	84.41 W
Stampriet	146	24.20 S	18.28 E
Stamps	184	33.22 N	93.30 W
Stams	58	47.16 N	10.59 E
Stanaford	178	37.49 N	81.10 W
Stanardsville	178	38.18 N	78.26 W
Stanberry	184	40.13 N	94.35 W
Stanborough	250	51.47 N	0.13 W
Stancija-Gorčakovo	75	40.27 N	71.42 E
Standard, Alta., Can.	172	51.07 N	112.59 W
Standard, Alaska, U.S.	170	64.47 N	148.32 W
Standard, Calif., U.S.	216	37.59 N	120.20 W
Standard, Pa., U.S.	204	40.10 N	79.32 W
Standard Oil Company Refinery ⚜[3]	272	37.57 N	122.24 W
Standard Shaft	269b	40.10 N	79.32 W
Standedge Canal Tunnel ◆[5]	252	53.34 N	2.00 W
Standedge Railway Tunnel ◆[5]	252	53.34 N	2.00 W
Standerton	148	26.58 S	29.07 E
Standiford Field ⊠	208	38.11 N	85.44 W
Standing Buffalo Indian Reserve ◆[4]	174	50.53 N	103.54 W
Standing Rock Indian Reservation ◆[4]	188	45.50 N	101.10 W
Standing Stone Creek ≃	204	40.30 N	78.00 W
Standish, Eng., U.K.	42	53.36 N	2.41 W
Standish, Mich., U.S.	180	43.59 N	83.57 W
Standon	44	51.53 N	0.02 E
Stanfield, Ariz., U.S.	190	32.53 N	111.58 W
Stanfield, Oreg., U.S.	192	45.47 N	119.13 W
Stanford, S. Afr.	148	34.26 S	19.29 E
Stanford, Calif., U.S.	216	37.25 N	122.08 W
Stanford, Ky., U.S.	182	37.32 N	84.40 W
Stanford, Mont., U.S.	192	47.09 N	110.13 W
Stanford Center ◆[9]	272	37.27 N	122.10 W
Stanford Heights	200	42.46 N	73.53 W
Stanford le Hope	44	51.31 N	0.26 E
Stanford Linear Accelerator ⚜[3]	272	37.25 N	122.12 W
Stanford Rivers	250	51.41 N	0.13 E
Stanford University ⚜[2]	272	37.26 N	122.10 W
Stanfordville	200	41.52 N	73.43 W
Stånga	26	57.17 N	18.28 E
Stångån ≃	26	58.27 N	15.37 E
Stångby	41	55.46 N	13.10 E
Stange	26	60.43 N	11.11 E
Stanger	148	29.27 S	31.14 E
Stanghella	58	45.08 N	11.45 E
Stanhope, Eng., U.K.	42	54.45 N	2.01 W
Stanhope, Iowa, U.S.	180	42.17 N	93.48 W
Stanhope, N.J., U.S.	200	40.54 N	74.43 W
Stanično-Luganskoje	73	48.39 N	39.30 E
Stanislaus □[6]	216	37.39 N	121.00 W
Stanislaus ≃	216	37.40 N	121.14 W
Stanislaus, Clark Fork ≃	216	38.22 N	119.52 W
Stanislaus, Middle Fork ≃	216	38.09 N	120.21 W
Stanislaus, North Fork ≃	216	38.09 N	120.21 W
Stanislaus, South Fork ≃	216	38.04 N	120.25 W
Stanislav, S.S.S.R.	68	46.34 N	32.09 E
Stanislav → Ivano-Frankovsk, S.S.S.R.	68	48.55 N	24.43 E
Stanislavčik	68	48.58 N	28.07 E
Stanisławów → Ivano-Frankovsk	68	48.55 N	24.43 E
Stanke Dimitrov	38	42.16 N	23.07 E
Stanley, Austl.	156	40.46 S	145.18 E
Stanley, N.B., Can.	176	46.17 N	66.44 W
Stanley, Falk. Is.	244	51.42 S	57.51 W
Stanley, H.K.	261d	22.13 N	114.12 E
Stanley, Eng., U.K.	42	54.52 N	1.42 W
Stanley, N.C., U.S.	182	35.21 N	81.06 W
Stanley, N. Dak., U.S.	188	48.19 N	102.23 W
Stanley, N.Y., U.S.	200	42.49 N	77.06 W
Stanley, Va., U.S.	178	38.34 N	78.31 W
Stanley, Wis., U.S.	180	44.58 N	90.56 W
Stanley ≃	161a	27.09 S	152.32 E
Stanley, Port C	165f	16.06 S	167.27 E
Stanley Falls ↳	144	0.30 N	25.12 E
Stanley Mills	265b	43.46 N	79.44 W
Stanley Mound ∧[2]	261d	22.14 N	114.12 E
Stanley Park ♠, B.C., Can.	214	49.19 N	123.09 W
Stanley Park ♠, Eng., U.K.	252	53.26 N	2.57 W
Stanley Park ♠, Eng., U.K.	252	53.49 N	3.02 W
Stanley Pool ⊜	142	4.17 S	15.20 E
Stanley Reservoir ⊜[1]	112	11.54 N	77.50 E
Stanleyville → Kisangani	144	0.30 N	25.12 E
Stanlow	42	53.17 N	2.52 W
Stanmore ◆[8]	250	51.37 N	0.19 W
Stannards	200	42.05 N	77.55 W
Stann Creek	222	16.58 N	88.13 W
Stannington	42	55.06 N	1.40 W
Stanoionno-Ojašinskij	76	55.28 N	83.53 E
Stanovoj Chrebet ⛰	64	56.20 N	126.00 E
Stanovoje Nagorje ⛰	78	56.00 N	114.00 E
Stanovoj Kolodez'	66	52.51 N	36.16 E
Stanovoy Mountains → Stanovoje Nagorje ⛰	78	56.00 N	114.00 E
Stans	54	46.57 N	8.22 E
Stansbury	158b	34.55 S	137.47 E
Stansmore Range ⛰	152	21.23 S	128.33 E
Stansstad	54	46.59 N	8.20 E
Stanstead	196	45.01 N	72.05 W
Stanstead □[6]	196	45.10 N	72.00 W
Stanstead Abbots	44	51.47 N	0.01 E
Stansted	250	51.20 N	0.18 E
Stansted Mountfitchet	44	51.54 N	0.12 E
Stanthorpe	156	28.39 S	151.57 E
Stanton, Eng., U.K.	44	52.19 N	0.53 E
Stanton, Calif., U.S.	218	33.48 N	117.59 W
Stanton, Del., U.S.	198	39.43 N	75.37 W
Stanton, Iowa, U.S.	188	40.59 N	95.06 W
Stanton, Ky., U.S.	182	37.54 N	83.52 W
Stanton, Mich., U.S.	180	43.18 N	85.05 W
Stanton, Mo., U.S.	209	38.16 N	91.06 W
Stanton, Nebr., U.S.	188	41.57 N	97.14 W
Stanton, N. Dak., U.S.	188	47.19 N	101.23 W
Stanton, Tenn., U.S.	184	35.28 N	89.24 W
Stanton, Tex., U.S.	186	32.08 N	101.48 W
Stantonsburg	182	35.37 N	77.49 W
Stanwell	250	51.27 N	0.29 W
Stanwell Moor	250	51.28 N	0.30 W
Stanwix	42	54.54 N	2.55 W
Stanwood	214	48.15 N	122.23 W
Stanwood Gardens	275	40.07 N	74.57 W
Stanzach	54	47.23 N	10.34 E
Stapelburg	50	51.53 N	10.40 E
Stapelfeld	48	53.36 N	10.13 E
Staphorst	48	52.37 N	6.12 E
Stapleford	44	52.56 N	1.16 W
Stapleford Abbotts	250	51.38 N	0.10 E
Stapleford Aerodrome ⊠	250	51.39 N	0.08 E
Stapleford Tawney	250	51.40 N	0.11 E
Staplehurst	44	51.10 N	0.33 E
Staples	188	46.21 N	94.48 W
Stapleton, Ala., U.S.	184	30.45 N	87.48 W
Stapleton, Nebr., U.S.	188	41.29 N	100.31 W
Stąporków	30	51.09 N	20.34 E
Star', S.S.S.R.	66	53.37 N	34.09 E
Star, Miss., U.S.	184	32.06 N	90.03 W
Star, N.C., U.S.	182	35.24 N	79.47 W
Stará Boleslav	50	50.12 N	14.42 E
Starachowice	30	51.03 N	21.04 E
Stara Fužina	58	46.17 N	13.54 E
Staraja	255a	59.55 N	30.38 E
Staraja Belica, S.S.S.R.	66	54.42 N	29.38 E
Staraja Belica, S.S.S.R.	68	51.59 N	35.13 E
Staraja Belogorka	70	52.05 N	53.17 E
Staraja Derevn'a ◆[8]	255a	59.59 N	30.15 E
Staraja Duginka	72	54.20 N	38.45 E
Staraja Kriuša	68	50.12 N	41.09 E
Staraja Kulatka	70	52.43 N	47.37 E
Staraja Kupavna	72	55.48 N	38.10 E
Staraja Majačka	68	46.30 N	33.11 E
Staraja Majna	70	54.36 N	48.57 E
Staraja Poltavka	70	50.28 N	46.28 E
Staraja Porubežka	70	52.03 N	49.11 E
Staraja Račejka	70	53.22 N	48.03 E
Staraja Rudn'a	66	52.50 N	30.17 E
Staraja Russa	66	58.00 N	31.23 E
Staraja Ruza	72	55.39 N	36.20 E
Staraja Sachča	70	54.25 N	49.58 E
Staraja Sin'ava	68	49.36 N	27.37 E
Staraja Sitn'a	72	54.56 N	38.09 E
Staraja Terizmorga	70	54.16 N	44.32 E
Staraja Toropa	66	56.17 N	31.40 E
Staraja Ušica	68	48.35 N	27.07 E
Staraja Veduga	68	51.48 N	38.31 E
Staraja Vičuga	70	57.16 N	41.53 E
Staraja Vyževka	68	51.27 N	24.24 E
Staranzano	58	45.49 N	13.30 E
Stara Pazova	38	44.59 N	20.10 E
Stara Planina (Balkan Mountains) ⛰	38	43.15 N	25.00 E
Stará Role	50	50.14 N	12.47 E
Stara Zagora	38	42.25 N	25.38 E
Starbejevo	255b	55.55 N	37.28 E
Starbrick	204	41.50 N	79.12 W
Starbuck, Man., Can.	174	49.46 N	97.36 W
Starbuck, Minn., U.S.	188	45.37 N	95.32 W
Starbuck, Wash., U.S.	192	47.31 N	118.08 W
Starbuck Island I	14	5.37 S	155.53 W
Starčenkovo	68	47.17 N	36.59 E
Star City, Sask., Can.	174	52.53 N	104.21 W
Star City, Ark., U.S.	184	33.56 N	91.51 W
Star City, Ind., U.S.	206	40.58 N	86.33 W
Starcross	44	50.38 N	3.27 W
Stare Czarnowo	50	53.16 N	14.45 E
Starford	204	40.42 N	78.58 W
Stargard Szczeciński (Stargard in Pommern)	30	53.20 N	15.02 E
Stargo	190	33.04 N	109.21 W
Star Harbour C	165e	10.47 S	162.18 E
Stari Bar	38	42.06 N	19.08 E
Starica, S.S.S.R.	66	56.30 N	34.56 E
Starica, S.S.S.R.	66	59.04 N	29.30 E
Starica, S.S.S.R.	70	48.13 N	45.56 E
Stari Grad	36	43.11 N	16.36 E
Starij R'ad	66	58.05 N	34.54 E
Starina	66	59.37 N	44.42 E
Stari Vlah ◆[1]	38	43.35 N	20.15 E
Star Junction	204	40.04 N	79.46 W
Stark □[6]	204	40.48 N	81.22 W
Starke	182	29.57 N	82.07 W
Starke □[6]	206	41.18 N	86.37 W
Starkey	200	42.32 N	76.56 W
Starkville	184	33.28 N	88.48 W
Star Lake	214	47.22 N	122.18 W
Starnberg	58	48.00 N	11.20 E
Starnberger See ⊜	58	47.55 N	11.18 E
Starnikovo	72	55.22 N	38.24 E
Staroalejskoje	76	51.00 N	82.01 E
Starobačaty	76	54.14 N	86.07 E
Starobaltačevo	76	56.01 N	55.56 E
Starobel'sk	73	49.16 N	38.56 E
Starobeševo	73	47.44 N	38.03 E
Starobin	66	52.44 N	27.28 E
Staročerkasskaja	73	47.15 N	40.03 E
Starocuruchajtuj	78	50.12 N	119.15 E
Staroderev'ankovskaja	68	46.08 N	38.58 E
Starodub	66	52.35 N	32.46 E
Starod'umejevo	70	55.16 N	54.22 E
Starogan'kino	70	53.55 N	52.15 E
Starogard Gdański	30	53.59 N	18.33 E
Staroignatjevka	73	47.32 N	37.47 E
Staroje	66	59.16 N	40.40 E
Staroje Bojsarovo	70	55.31 N	53.54 E
Staroje Ibrajkino	70	54.52 N	51.02 E
Staroje Jaškino	70	52.49 N	52.57 E
Staroje Jermakovo	70	54.04 N	51.59 E
Staroje Oleničevo	70	45.34 N	47.11 E
Staroje Rachino	66	58.08 N	32.39 E
Staroje Šajgovo	70	54.18 N	44.26 E
Staroje Šajmurzino	70	54.45 N	47.58 E
Staroje Selo	66	55.14 N	29.54 E
Staroje Sindrovo	70	54.25 N	44.06 E
Staroje Slavkino	70	52.34 N	45.08 E
Staroje Ustje	70	53.28 N	41.51 E
Starojurjevo	70	53.21 N	40.42 E
Starokazačje	68	46.21 N	29.59 E
Starokonstantinov	68	49.46 N	27.13 E
Starokuručevo	70	55.09 N	54.04 E
Starolaspa	73	47.34 N	37.59 E
Staroleuškovskaja	68	45.59 N	39.44 E
Staromichajlovka	73	47.58 N	37.36 E
Starominskaja	68	46.31 N	39.04 E
Staromlinovka	68	47.42 N	36.49 E
Staromušta	70	55.49 N	54.14 E
Staronikolajevo	72	55.37 N	36.16 E
Staro-Podgorodneje	72	54.46 N	38.57 E
Staropokrovka	75	42.50 N	75.18 E
Staroščerbinovskaja	68	46.37 N	38.40 E
Staroseslavino	70	53.12 N	40.25 E
Starošešminsk	70	55.22 N	51.15 E
Starosiedle	50	51.50 N	14.50 E
Starosoldatskoje	76	56.12 N	72.37 E
Starosubchangulovo	76	53.06 N	57.26 E
Starotimoškino	24	53.43 N	47.32 E
Starotitarovskaja	68	45.14 N	37.09 E
Staroutkinsk	76	57.14 N	59.20 E
Staroverovka	68	49.33 N	35.42 E
Starožilovo	70	54.14 N	39.55 E
Starožil'skij	70	56.34 N	47.17 E
Star Peak ∧	194	40.32 N	118.10 W
Starr	204	41.32 N	79.22 W
Starrucca	200	41.54 N	75.28 W
Start Bay C	44	50.17 N	3.36 W
Start Point ≻	44	50.13 N	3.38 W
Startup	214	47.52 N	121.44 W
Starvation Reservoir ⊜[1]	190	40.15 N	110.30 W
Starved Rock State Park ♠	206	41.19 N	88.58 W
Staryj Ajbesi	70	54.57 N	47.03 E
Staryj-Ajdar	73	48.43 N	39.11 E
Staryj Bagr'až	70	54.54 N	51.39 E
Staryj Bir'uz'ak	74	44.47 N	46.54 E
Staryj Bol'ševik	255b	55.57 N	37.47 E
Staryj Čartorijsk	68	51.15 N	25.54 E
Staryj Chop'or	70	51.30 N	42.58 E
Staryj Čindant	78	50.33 N	115.33 E
Staryje Burasy	70	52.16 N	46.09 E
Staryje Dorogi	66	53.02 N	28.16 E
Staryje Maty	70	55.14 N	53.55 E
Staryje Popel'uchi	68	48.18 N	28.55 E
Staryje Senžary	68	49.25 N	34.27 E
Staryje Turdaki	70	53.55 N	45.29 E
Staryje Z'atcy	70	57.21 N	52.39 E
Staryj Kazangal	70	50.15 N	47.39 E
Staryj Krym, S.S.S.R.	68	45.03 N	35.05 E
Staryj Krym, S.S.S.R.	73	47.10 N	37.30 E
Staryj Lesken	74	43.20 N	43.55 E
Staryj Medved'	66	58.18 N	30.30 E
Staryj Merčik	68	49.58 N	35.46 E
Staryj Oskol	68	51.19 N	37.51 E
Staryj Sambor	68	49.27 N	22.59 E
Staryj Terek ≃	74	44.00 N	47.24 E
Staryj Tukšum	70	53.42 N	48.33 E
Starý Plzenec	30	49.42 N	13.28 E
Stary Sącz	30	49.34 N	20.38 E
Stassfurt	50	51.51 N	11.34 E
Staszów	30	50.34 N	21.20 E
State Center	180	42.01 N	93.10 W
State College, Miss., U.S.	184	33.26 N	88.47 W
State College, Pa., U.S.	204	40.48 N	77.52 W
Stateline, Calif., U.S.	216	38.57 N	119.57 W
State Line, Miss., U.S.	184	31.26 N	88.28 W
Stateline, Nev., U.S.	194	38.57 N	119.57 W
Staten Island I	266	40.35 N	74.09 W
Staten Island Mall ◆[9]	266	40.35 N	74.10 W
Statenville	182	30.42 N	83.02 W
State Park Place	209	38.40 N	90.03 W
State Road	182	36.19 N	80.52 W
Statesboro	182	32.27 N	81.47 W
Statesville	182	35.47 N	80.53 W
Stateville State Prison ⚜	268	41.35 N	88.06 W
Station Peak	152	21.10 S	118.11 E
Statue of Liberty National Monument ♠	200	40.41 N	74.03 W
Staufen	54	47.53 N	7.44 E
Staufenberg	52	50.40 N	8.43 E
Staughton Vale	159	37.51 S	144.17 E
Staunton, Ill., U.S.	209	39.01 N	89.47 W
Staunton, Va., U.S.	178	38.09 N	79.04 W
Staunton → Roanoke ≃	182	35.56 N	76.43 W
Stavanger	26	58.58 N	5.45 E
Stave ≃	214	49.10 N	122.26 W
Stave Lake ⊜	172	49.15 N	122.21 W
Staveley	42	53.16 N	1.20 W
Stavelot	52	50.23 N	5.56 E
Stavely	172	50.10 N	113.38 W
Staveren	48	52.53 N	5.22 E
Stavern	26	59.00 N	10.02 E
Stavišče	68	49.23 N	30.12 E
Stavnoje	68	48.59 N	22.40 E
Stavropol', S.S.S.R.	62	45.02 N	41.59 E
Stavropol → Toljatti, S.S.S.R.	70	53.31 N	49.26 E
Stavropol' □[8]	74	44.38 N	43.30 E
Stavrovo	70	56.08 N	40.00 E
Stavsnäs	40	59.17 N	18.41 E
Stawell	156	37.04 S	142.46 E
Stawell ≃	156	20.38 S	142.55 E
Stawiski	30	53.23 N	22.09 E
Stawiszyn	30	51.55 N	18.07 E
Stayner	202	44.25 N	80.05 W
Stayton	192	44.48 N	122.48 W
Stazzema	58	43.59 N	10.19 E
Ste. → Saint			
Steamboat	216	39.23 N	119.44 W
Steamboat Creek ≃	216	39.31 N	119.42 W
Steamboat Mountain ∧	190	41.58 N	108.58 W
Steamboat Slough ≃	216	38.11 N	121.40 W
Steamboat Springs	190	40.29 N	106.50 W
Steamburg	200	42.07 N	78.54 W
Stearns	182	36.42 N	84.28 W
Stearns Pond ⊜	273	42.37 N	71.04 W
Stebbins	170	63.32 N	162.18 W
Stebl'ov	68	49.24 N	31.06 E
Stechow	50	52.38 N	12.28 E
Steckborn	54	47.40 N	8.55 E
Stederdorf	48	52.21 N	10.15 E
Stedten	50	51.26 N	11.41 E
Stedum	48	53.18 N	6.41 E
Steeg	54	47.14 N	10.17 E
Steel ≃	180	48.46 N	86.54 W
Steel City	200	40.38 N	75.20 W
Steele, Mo., U.S.	184	36.05 N	89.50 W
Steele, N. Dak., U.S.	188	46.51 N	99.55 W
Steele ◆[8]	253	51.27 N	7.05 E
Steele, Mount ∧	190	41.50 N	107.00 W
Steele Creek ≃, Tex., U.S.	212	31.13 N	96.19 W
Steele Creek ≃, Tex., U.S.	212	32.01 N	97.28 W
Steeles Corners	265b	43.48 N	79.25 W
Steeleville	184	38.00 N	89.40 W
Steelhead	214	49.13 N	122.19 W
Steel's Drift	148	27.21 S	29.30 E
Steel's Point ≻	164c	29.02 S	168.00 E
Steels Run ≃	269b	40.25 N	79.38 W
Steelton, N.Y., U.S.	274a	42.47 N	78.49 W
Steelton, Pa., U.S.	198	40.14 N	76.49 W
Steelville	184	37.58 N	91.22 W
Steenbergen	48	51.35 N	4.19 E
Steenburg Lake ⊜	202	44.50 N	77.41 W
Steenderen	48	52.04 N	6.11 E
Steenkool	154	2.07 S	133.32 E
Steens Mountain ⛰	192	42.35 N	118.40 W
Steenvoorde	46	50.48 N	2.35 E
Steenwijk	48	52.47 N	6.08 E
Steephill Lake ⊜	174	55.58 N	103.08 W
Steep Holm I	44	51.21 N	3.07 W
Steeping ≃	42	53.06 N	0.18 E
Steep Point ≻	152	26.08 S	113.08 E
Steep Rock	174	51.26 N	98.48 W
Stefanie, Lake (Chew Bahir) ⊜	134	4.40 N	36.50 E
Stefansson Island I	166	73.17 N	106.45 W
Ștefan Vodă	38	44.19 N	27.19 E
Steffisburg	54	46.47 N	7.39 E
Steg	54	47.21 N	8.56 E
Stegalovka	66	52.24 N	38.19 E
Stege	41	54.59 N	12.18 E
Stegeborg	26	58.26 N	16.35 E
Stege Bugt C	41	55.01 N	12.50 E
Stegelitz	50	53.08 N	13.51 E
Steger	206	41.29 N	87.41 W
Stegi	148	26.32 S	31.58 E
Steglitz ◆[8]	254a	52.28 N	13.19 E
Stehag	41	55.54 N	13.23 E
Stehekin	214	48.19 N	120.39 W
Stehekin ≃	214	48.21 N	120.40 W
Steiermark □[3]	30	47.10 N	15.10 E
Steigerwald ⛰	52	49.40 N	10.20 E
Steigra	50	51.18 N	11.39 E
Steilacoom	214	47.10 N	122.36 W
Steimbke	48	52.40 N	9.22 E
Stein, B.R.D.	58	47.59 N	12.32 E
Stein, Ned.	52	50.57 N	5.46 E
Stein, Schw.	54	47.33 N	7.58 E
Steina	50	51.12 N	14.01 E
Steinach, B.R.D.	54	48.18 N	8.04 E
Steinach, D.D.R.	50	50.25 N	11.10 E
Steinach, Öst.	58	47.05 N	11.28 E
Steinach ≃	52	50.11 N	11.12 E
Steinamanger → Szombathely	30	47.14 N	16.38 E
Stein am Rhein	54	47.40 N	8.51 E
Steinau, B.R.D.	52	50.23 N	9.27 E
Steinau → Ścinawa, Pol.	30	51.25 N	16.27 E
Steinbach, B.R.D.	52	48.43 N	8.10 E
Steinbach, B.R.D.	52	50.01 N	9.36 E
Steinbach, Man., Can.	174	49.32 N	96.41 W
Steinbach-Hallenberg	50	50.42 N	10.34 E
Steinberg ∧[2]	253	51.05 N	7.27 E
Steinberger Slough ≃	272	37.33 N	122.13 W
Steinbourg	52	48.46 N	7.25 E
Steinen	54	47.38 N	7.44 E
Steinen ≃	245	12.05 S	53.46 W
Steinernes Meer ⛰	58	47.30 N	12.58 E
Steinfeld, B.R.D.	48	52.35 N	8.12 E
Steinfeld, D.D.R.	50	50.22 N	10.44 E
Steinfeld, Öst.	58	46.45 N	13.15 E
Steinfort	52	49.40 N	5.55 E
Steinforth	253	51.09 N	6.32 E
Steingaden	54	47.42 N	10.51 E
Steinhagen, B.R.D.	48	52.00 N	8.24 E
Steinhagen, D.D.R.	50	54.13 N	12.59 E
Steinhatchie ≃	182	29.40 N	83.24 W
Steinhausen	146	21.49 S	18.20 E
Steinhausen ⚜[1], B.R.D.	58	40.00 N	9.41 E
Steinhausen ⚜[1], B.R.D.	58	48.01 N	9.41 E
Steinheid	50	50.28 N	11.04 E
Steinheim, B.R.D.	48	51.52 N	9.05 E
Steinheim, B.R.D.	52	50.06 N	8.55 E
Steinheim, B.R.D.	52	48.58 N	9.16 E
Steinheim, B.R.D.	54	48.01 N	10.09 E
Steinhöfel	50	52.24 N	14.10 E
Steinhöring	58	48.05 N	12.02 E
Steinhude	48	52.27 N	9.21 E
Steinhuder Meer ⊜	48	52.28 N	9.19 E
Steinkjer	26	64.01 N	11.30 E
Steinkopf	146	29.18 S	17.43 E
Steinloge	48	52.54 N	8.19 E
Stein-Neukirch	52	50.41 N	8.03 E
Steinpass)(	58	47.39 N	12.45 E
Steinpleis	50	50.43 N	12.23 E
Steinsdorf	50	52.02 N	14.40 E
Steinshamn	26	62.47 N	6.29 E
Steinstücken ◆[8]	254a	52.23 N	13.08 E
Steinwiesen	50	50.17 N	11.28 E
Stekene	46	51.12 N	4.02 E
Stekl'anka	66	59.08 N	41.37 E
Steklino	66	56.51 N	32.10 E
Steksovo	70	55.17 N	43.25 E
Stella, It.	56	44.24 N	8.30 E
Stella, S. Afr.	148	26.38 S	24.48 E
Stella, Nebr., U.S.	188	40.14 N	95.46 W
Stella Niagara	200	43.12 N	79.02 W
Stella-Plage	46	50.29 N	1.35 E
Stellaquo Indian Reserve ◆[4]	172	54.03 N	124.55 W
Stellarton	176	45.34 N	62.40 W
Stelle	48	53.23 N	10.06 E
Stellenbosch	148	33.58 S	18.50 E
Steller, Mount ∧	170	60.30 N	143.02 W
Stelvio, Parco Nazionale dello ♠	54	46.20 N	10.40 E
Stelvio, Passo dello)(	54	46.32 N	10.27 E
Stenay	52	49.29 N	5.11 E
Stendal	50	52.36 N	11.51 E
Stende	66	57.09 N	22.33 E
Stenden	253	51.25 N	6.27 E
Stenhammars slott ⊥	40	59.03 N	16.31 E
Stenhousemuir	42	56.02 N	3.48 W
Stenico	58	46.03 N	10.51 E
Stenlille	41	55.32 N	11.36 E
Stenløse	41	55.46 N	12.12 E
Stenón	257c	37.58 N	22.20 E
Stenón Návstathmou ⩊	257c	37.58 N	23.33 E
Stensätra	40	60.36 N	16.44 E
Stensele	24	65.05 N	17.09 E
Stenstorp	26	58.16 N	13.43 E
Stenstrup	41	55.07 N	10.31 E
Stentrop	253	51.30 N	7.49 E
Stenungsund	26	58.05 N	11.49 E
Stepan'	68	51.10 N	26.18 E
Stepanakert	74	39.49 N	46.44 E
Stepanavan	74	41.00 N	44.23 E
Stepancevo, S.S.S.R.	70	56.08 N	41.42 E
Stepancevo, S.S.S.R.	72	56.22 N	36.10 E
Stepancy	68	49.42 N	31.18 E
Stepano-Krynka	73	47.55 N	38.21 E
Stepanovka, S.S.S.R.	68	50.58 N	34.37 E
Stepanovka, S.S.S.R.	70	52.04 N	53.02 E
Stepanovka, S.S.S.R.	76	57.13 N	67.26 E

Symbol	English	Deutsch	Español	Français	Português
≃	River	Fluss	Río	Rivière	Rio
≊	Canal	Kanal	Canal	Canal	Canal
↳	Waterfall, Rapids	Wasserfall, Stromschnellen	Cascada, Rápidos	Chute d'eau, Rapides	Cascata, Rápidos
⩊	Strait	Meeresstrasse	Estrecho	Détroit	Estreito
C	Bay, Gulf	Bucht, Golf	Bahía, Golfo	Baie, Golfe	Baía, Golfo
⊜	Lake, Lakes	See, Seen	Lago, Lagos	Lac, Lacs	Lago, Lagos
☷	Swamp	Sumpf	Pantano	Marais	Pântano
⊼	Ice Features, Glacier	Eis- und Gletscherformen	Accidentes Glaciales	Formes glaciaires	Acidentes Glaciares
⊤	Other Hydrographic Features	Andere Hydrographische Objekte	Otros Elementos Hidrográficos	Autres données hydrographiques	Outros Elementos Hidrográficos
✣	Submarine Features	Untermeerische Objekte	Accidentes Submarinos	Formes de relief sous-marin	Acidentes Submarinos
□	Political Unit	Politische Einheit	Unidad Politica	Entité politique	Unidade Política
⚜	Cultural Institution	Kulturelle Institution	Institución Cultural	Institution culturelle	Instituição Cultural
⊥	Historical Site	Historische Stätte	Sitio Histórico	Site historique	Sitio Histórico
♠	Recreational Site	Erholungs- und Ferienort	Sitio de Recreo	Centre de loisirs	Sítio de Lazer
⊠	Airport	Flughafen	Aeropuerto	Aéroport	Aeroporto
■	Military Installation	Militäranlage	Instalación Militar	Installation militaire	Instalação Militar
◆	Miscellaneous	Verschiedenes	Misceláneo	Divers	Miscelânea

Name	Page	Lat.	Long.
Stepanovo	72	55.43 N	38.28 E
Stepanovskoje	255b	55.47 N	37.10 E
Stepan Razin	74	40.24 N	49.59 E
Stepanščino	72	55.15 N	38.30 E
Stepenitz ≃	50	53.48 N	11.10 E
Stephans-Dom ⊍[1]	254b	48.12 N	16.23 E
Stephanskirchen	58	47.51 N	12.11 E
Stephen	188	48.27 N	96.53 W
Stephen A. Forbes State Park ♠	209	38.44 N	88.46 W
Stephen F. Austin State Historic Park ♠	212	29.48 N	96.05 W
Stephens	184	33.25 N	93.04 W
Stephens, Cape ≻	162	40.42 S	173.57 E
Stephens, Port C	156	32.45 S	152.05 E
Stephens Brook ≃	266	40.54 N	74.35 W
Stephens City	178	39.05 N	78.13 W
Stephens Creek	156	31.50 S	141.30 E
Stephens Island I	172	54.10 N	130.45 W
Stephens Mills	200	42.23 N	77.38 W
Stephenson	180	45.20 N	87.38 W
Stephenson, Lake ⊜	212	29.35 N	94.40 W
Stephenson, Mount ∧	9	69.49 S	69.43 W
Stephens Passage ⊔	170	57.50 N	133.50 W
Stephentown	200	42.33 N	73.23 W
Stephentown Center	200	42.34 N	73.25 W
Stephenville, Newf., Can.	176	48.33 N	58.35 W
Stephenville, Tex., U.S.	186	32.13 N	98.12 W
Stephenville Crossing	176	48.30 N	58.26 W
Stepn'ak	76	52.50 N	70.50 E
Stepney ◂[8]	250	51.31 N	0.02 W
Stepnica	50	53.40 N	14.36 E
Stepnoj	70	48.56 N	45.36 E
Stepnoje, S.S.S.R.	70	51.24 N	46.52 E
Stepnoje, S.S.S.R.	74	44.17 N	44.36 E
Steps Point ≻	164u	14.22 S	170.45 W
Steptoe Valley V	194	39.25 N	114.45 W
Stepurino	66	56.24 N	35.16 E
Sterdyń	30	52.35 N	22.18 E
Sterkaar	148	31.05 S	23.42 E
Sterkrade ◂[8]	253	51.31 N	6.51 E
Sterkspruit	148	30.32 S	27.22 E
Sterkstroom	148	31.32 S	26.32 E
Sterlibaševo	76	53.28 N	55.15 E
Sterling, S. Afr.	148	31.16 S	21.28 E
Sterling, Alaska, U.S.	170	60.28 N	150.08 W
Sterling, Colo., U.S.	188	40.37 N	103.13 W
Sterling, Conn., U.S.	197	41.42 N	71.50 W
Sterling, Ill., U.S.	180	41.48 N	89.42 W
Sterling, Kans., U.S.	188	38.13 N	98.12 W
Sterling, Mass., U.S.	197	42.26 N	71.46 W
Sterling, Mich., U.S.	180	44.02 N	84.02 W
Sterling, Nebr., U.S.	188	40.28 N	96.23 W
Sterling, N.Y., U.S.	200	43.20 N	76.39 W
Sterling, Ohio, U.S.	204	40.58 N	81.51 W
Sterling, Okla., U.S.	186	34.45 N	98.10 W
Sterling, Va., U.S.	198	39.00 N	77.26 W
Sterling City	186	31.50 N	100.59 W
Sterling Creek ≃	200	43.20 N	76.42 W
Sterling Forest Gardens ♠	200	41.14 N	74.16 W
Sterling Forest Lake ⊜	266	41.10 N	74.16 W
Sterling Heights	204	42.35 N	83.02 W
Sterling Junction	197	42.24 N	71.46 W
Sterling Park	272	37.41 N	122.26 W
Sterling Reservoir ⊜[1]	188	40.47 N	103.17 W
Sterling Run	204	41.25 N	78.12 W
Sterlington	184	32.42 N	92.05 W
Sterlitamak	76	53.37 N	55.58 E
Sternberg	50	53.43 N	11.49 E
Sternberg in der Neumark → Torzym	30	52.20 N	15.04 E
Šternberk	30	49.44 N	17.18 E
Šterovka	73	48.19 N	38.57 E
Sterup	41	54.44 N	9.44 E
Sterzing → Vipiteno	58	46.54 N	11.26 E
Stęszew	30	52.18 N	16.42 E
Štětí	50	50.25 N	14.23 E
Stetson Pond ⊜	273	42.02 N	70.50 W
Stetten am kalten Markt	54	48.07 N	9.04 E
Stettin → Szczecin	30	53.24 N	14.32 E
Stettler	172	52.19 N	112.43 W
Steuben □[6], Ind., U.S.	206	41.38 N	85.00 W
Steuben □[6], N.Y., U.S.	200	42.20 N	77.19 W
Steubenville	204	40.22 N	80.37 W
Stevenage	44	51.55 N	0.14 W
Stevens, N.J., U.S.	275	40.05 N	74.49 W
Stevens, Pa., U.S.	198	40.13 N	76.09 W
Stevens, Lake ⊜	214	48.01 N	122.05 W
Stevens, Mount ∧	162	40.48 S	172.27 E
Stevens Creek ≃, Calif., U.S.	272	37.26 N	122.05 W
Stevens Creek ≃, S.C., U.S.	182	33.34 N	82.03 W
Stevens Creek Park ♠	272	37.17 N	122.04 W
Stevens Creek Reservoir ⊜[1]	272	37.17 N	122.05 W
Stevens Institute of Technology ⊍[2]	266	40.44 N	74.02 W
Stevenson, Ala., U.S.	184	34.52 N	85.50 W
Stevenson, Wash., U.S.	214	45.42 N	121.53 W
Stevenson Creek ≃	152	27.06 S	135.33 E
Stevenson Entrance ⊔	170	57.45 N	152.20 W
Stevenson Lake ⊜	174	53.56 N	96.09 W
Stevens Pass)(	214	47.45 N	121.04 W
Stevens Peak ∧	192	47.27 N	115.46 W
Stevens Point	180	44.31 N	89.34 W
Stevenston	42	55.39 N	4.45 W
Stevens Village	170	66.00 N	155.05 W
Stevensville, Ont., Can.	274a	42.57 N	79.04 W
Stevensville, Md., U.S.	198	38.59 N	76.19 W
Stevensville, Mich., U.S.	206	42.01 N	86.31 W
Stevensville, Mont., U.S.	192	46.30 N	114.05 W
Stevensville, Pa., U.S.	200	41.46 N	76.11 W
Stevinson	216	37.20 N	120.51 W
Stevns Klint ⊻[4]	41	55.18 N	12.27 E
Steward	206	41.51 N	89.01 W
Stewardson	209	39.16 N	88.38 W
Stewart, B.C., Can.	172	55.56 N	129.59 W
Stewart, Minn., U.S.	180	44.43 N	94.29 W
Stewart ≃	170	63.18 N	139.25 W
Stewart, Cape ≻	154	11.57 S	134.45 E
Stewart, Isla I	244	54.52 S	71.12 W
Stewart Island I	162	47.00 S	167.50 E
Stewart Lake ⊜	209	40.09 N	90.16 W
Stewart Manor	266	40.43 N	73.41 W
Stewarton	42	55.41 N	4.31 W
Stewartstown, N. Ire., U.K.	42	54.35 N	6.41 W
Stewartstown, Pa., U.S.	198	39.45 N	76.35 W
Stewartsville, Mo., U.S.	184	39.45 N	94.30 W
Stewartsville, N.J., U.S.	198	40.42 N	75.07 W
Stewartsville, Pa., U.S.	269b	40.21 N	79.46 W
Stewart Valley	174	50.36 N	107.50 W
Stewartville	180	43.51 N	92.29 W
Stewiacke	176	45.08 N	63.21 W
Steyerberg	48	52.34 N	9.01 E
Steyning	44	50.53 N	0.20 W
Steynsburg	148	31.15 S	25.49 E
Steynsrus	148	27.58 S	27.33 E
Steyr	30	48.03 N	14.25 E
Steytlerville	148	33.21 S	24.21 E
Stežki	70	53.06 N	41.13 E
Stezzano	56	45.38 N	9.39 E
Sthal	116	24.12 N	89.44 E
Stia	60	43.48 N	11.42 E
Štiavnické vrchy ⩕	30	48.40 N	18.45 E
Stickle Pond ⊜	266	40.59 N	74.25 W
Stickney, Ill., U.S.	206	41.49 N	87.47 W
Stickney, S. Dak., U.S.	188	43.35 N	98.26 W
Stidsvig	41	56.12 N	13.08 E
Stiege	50	51.40 N	10.53 E
Stiene	66	57.26 N	24.34 E
Stienitzfliess ≃	254a	52.33 N	13.43 E
Stienitz-See ⊜	254a	52.30 N	13.49 E
Stiens	48	53.15 N	5.45 E
Stiepel ◂[8]	253	51.25 N	7.15 E
Stiftskirche ⊍[1]	253	51.23 N	7.00 E
Stige	41	55.26 N	10.25 E
Stigler	186	35.15 N	95.08 W
Stigliano	36	40.24 N	16.14 E
Stigtomta	40	58.48 N	16.47 E
Stikine ≃	170	56.40 N	132.30 W
Stikine Ranges ⩕	170	58.45 N	130.00 W
Stiklestad	26	63.48 N	11.33 E
Stilbaai	148	34.24 S	21.26 E
Stile	138	34.20 N	5.51 E
Stiles	200	40.40 N	75.30 W
Stiles Pond ⊜	273	42.41 N	71.02 W
Stilesville	200	42.05 N	75.24 W
Stilfontein	148	26.50 S	26.50 E
Stilís	38	38.55 N	22.36 E
Stillaguamish ≃	214	48.11 N	122.22 W
Stillaguamish, North Fork ≃	214	48.11 N	122.07 W
Stillaguamish, South Fork ≃	214	48.11 N	122.07 W
Stillhouse Hollow Lake ⊜[1]	212	31.00 N	97.35 W
Stilling	41	56.04 N	10.00 E
Stillman Valley	206	42.07 N	89.11 W
Stillmore	182	32.27 N	82.13 W
Still Pond	198	39.20 N	76.03 W
Still Run ≃	275	39.49 N	75.18 W
Stillwater, B.C., Can.	172	49.46 N	124.18 W
Stillwater, Minn., U.S.	180	45.04 N	92.49 W
Stillwater, N.J., U.S.	200	41.02 N	74.52 W
Stillwater, N.Y., U.S.	200	42.57 N	73.39 W
Stillwater, Ohio, U.S.	204	40.20 N	81.18 W
Stillwater, Okla., U.S.	186	36.07 N	97.04 W
Stillwater, Pa., U.S.	200	41.09 N	76.22 W
Stillwater ≃, Mont., U.S.	192	45.38 N	109.17 W
Stillwater ≃, Ohio, U.S.	208	39.47 N	84.12 W
Stillwater Creek ≃	204	40.25 N	81.22 W
Stillwater Range ⩕	194	39.50 N	118.15 W
Stillwell, Ill., U.S.	209	40.13 N	91.11 W
Stillwell, Okla., U.S.	184	35.49 N	94.38 W
Stilo, Punta ≻	36	38.28 N	16.36 E
Stimberg ∧[2]	253	51.40 N	7.15 E
Stimigliano	60	42.18 N	12.34 E
Stimson, Mount ∧	192	48.31 N	113.36 W
Stinchar ≃	42	55.06 N	5.00 W
Stinear Nunataks ⩕	9	69.42 S	64.40 E
Stine Canal ≋	216	35.15 N	119.08 W
Stine Mountain ∧	192	45.44 N	113.07 W
Stingray Point ≻	198	37.33 N	76.18 W
Stînisoara, Munții ⩕	38	47.10 N	26.00 E
Stinking Water Creek ≃	188	40.22 N	101.07 W
Stinnett	186	35.50 N	101.27 W
Ştintonville	263d	26.14 S	28.13 E
Štip	38	41.44 N	22.12 E
Stiperstones ∧	44	52.35 N	2.56 W
Stiring-wendel	52	49.12 N	6.56 E
Stirling, Austl.	152	21.44 S	133.45 E
Stirling, Austl.	158b	35.00 S	138.43 E
Stirling, Alta., Can.	172	49.30 N	112.31 W
Stirling, Ont., Can.	202	44.18 N	77.33 W
Stirling, Scot., U.K.	42	56.07 N	3.57 W
Stirling, N.J., U.S.	200	40.41 N	74.30 W
Stirling, Mount ∧	152	31.50 S	117.38 E
Stirling Castle ⊥	42	56.07 N	3.57 W
Stirling City	194	39.54 N	121.32 W
Stirling Range ⩕	152	34.23 S	117.50 E
Stirling Reservoir ⊜[1]	158a	33.08 S	116.03 E
Stirrat	182	37.44 N	82.00 W
Stissing Mountain ∧	200	41.57 N	73.42 W
Stittsville	202	45.15 N	75.55 W
Stittville	200	43.13 N	75.17 W
Stjärnhov	40	59.05 N	17.00 E
Stjärnsund, Sve.	40	60.26 N	16.12 E
Stjärnsund, Sve.	40	58.51 N	14.55 E
Stjernøya I	24	70.18 N	22.45 E
Stjørdalshalsen	26	63.28 N	10.56 E
Stöberhai ∧	50	51.39 N	10.34 E
Stobi ⊥	38	41.34 N	21.58 E
Stochod ≃	68	51.52 N	25.38 E
Stock	250	51.40 N	0.27 E
Stock, Étang du ⊜	52	48.45 N	6.55 E
Stockach	54	47.51 N	9.00 E
Stöckalp	54	46.48 N	8.17 E
Stockamöllan	41	55.57 N	13.22 E
Stockbridge, Eng., U.K.	44	51.07 N	1.29 W
Stockbridge, Ga., U.S.	182	33.33 N	84.14 W
Stockbridge, Mass., U.S.	197	42.17 N	73.19 W
Stockbridge, Mich., U.S.	206	42.27 N	84.11 W
Stockbridge Bowl ⊜	197	42.20 N	73.19 W
Stockbridge Indian Reservation ◂[4]	180	44.52 N	88.53 W
Stockbury	250	51.20 N	0.39 E
Stockby	40	59.20 N	17.41 E
Stockdale, Ohio, U.S.	208	38.57 N	82.51 W
Stockdale, Tex., U.S.	186	29.14 N	97.58 W
Stockelsdorf	48	53.54 N	10.38 E
Stöcken	50	53.00 N	10.40 E
Stockerau	30	48.23 N	16.13 E
Stockertown	198	40.45 N	75.16 W
Stockett	192	47.21 N	111.10 W
Stockheim	52	50.19 N	9.01 E
Stöckheim bei Braunschweig	48	52.12 N	10.31 E
Stockholm, Sve.	40	59.20 N	18.03 E
Stockholm, Maine, U.S.	176	47.03 N	68.08 W
Stockholm, N.J., U.S.	200	41.05 N	74.31 W
Stockholm, Lake ⊜	266	41.04 N	74.32 W
Stock Island	210	24.34 N	81.45 W
Stockland	206	40.37 N	87.36 W
Stockport, Eng., U.K.	42	53.25 N	2.10 W
Stockport, N.Y., U.S.	200	42.19 N	73.45 W
Stockport □[8]	252	53.23 N	2.08 W
Stocksbridge	42	53.27 N	1.34 W
Stockstadt	52	49.48 N	8.28 E
Stocksund	40	59.23 N	18.04 E
Stockton, Austl.	160	32.55 S	151.47 E
Stockton, Ala., U.S.	184	31.00 N	87.52 W
Stockton, Calif., U.S.	216	37.57 N	121.17 W
Stockton, Ill., U.S.	180	42.21 N	90.01 W
Stockton, Kans., U.S.	188	39.26 N	99.16 W
Stockton, Md., U.S.	198	38.03 N	75.25 W
Stockton, Mo., U.S.	184	37.42 N	93.48 W
Stockton, N.J., U.S.	198	40.24 N	74.58 W
Stockton, N.Y., U.S.	204	42.19 N	79.22 W
Stockton, Utah, U.S.	190	40.27 N	112.22 W
Stockton Heath	252	53.22 N	2.35 W
Stockton Metropolitan Airport ⊠	216	37.54 N	121.15 W
Stockton-on-Tees	42	54.34 N	1.19 W
Stockton Plateau ⩕[1]	186	30.30 N	102.30 W
Stockton Reservoir ⊜[1]	184	37.40 N	93.45 W
Stockton Springs	178	44.29 N	68.52 W
Stockum, B.R.D.	48	51.40 N	7.42 E
Stockum, B.R.D.	253	51.36 N	6.39 E
Stockum, B.R.D.	253	51.32 N	7.47 E
Stockum ◂[8], B.R.D.	253	51.28 N	7.22 E
Stockum ◂[8], B.R.D.	253	51.16 N	6.44 E
Stockville	188	40.32 N	100.23 W
Stockwell	206	40.17 N	86.46 W
Stockwell, Lake ⊜	275	39.51 N	74.47 W
Stoco Lake ⊜	202	44.28 N	77.18 W
Stoczek Łukowski	30	51.58 N	21.58 E
Stoddard Mountain ∧	218	34.42 N	117.07 W
Stöde	26	62.25 N	16.35 E
Stodoliči	68	51.44 N	28.30 E
Stodolišče	66	54.11 N	32.39 E
Stœng Tréng	100	13.31 N	105.58 E
Stoffberg	146	25.29 S	29.49 E
Stoj, Gora ∧	68	48.37 N	23.11 E
Stojba	79	52.49 N	131.43 E
Stoke	250	51.27 N	0.37 E
Stoke ≃	196	45.35 N	71.58 W
Stoke D'Abernon	250	51.19 N	0.23 W
Stoke Golding	44	52.34 N	1.24 W
Stoke Mountains ⩕	196	45.33 N	71.42 W
Stokenchurch	44	51.40 N	0.55 W
Stoke Newington ◂[8]	250	51.34 N	0.05 W
Stoke-on-Trent	44	33.00 N	2.10 W
Stoke Poges	250	51.33 N	0.35 W
Stokes, Mount ∧	162	41.06 S	174.06 E
Stokes Inlet C	152	33.50 S	121.08 E
Stokesley	42	54.28 N	1.11 W
Stokes Point ≻	156	40.10 S	143.56 E
Stokes Range ⩕[2]	154	15.46 S	130.57 E
Stokkemarke	41	54.50 N	11.23 E
Stokksnes ≻	24a	64.17 N	14.54 W
Stol ∧	38	44.13 N	22.14 E
Stolac	36	43.05 N	17.58 E
Stolbcy	66	53.29 N	26.44 E
Stolberg, B.R.D.	52	50.46 N	6.13 E
Stolberg, D.D.R.	50	51.34 N	10.57 E
Stolbišči	70	55.39 N	49.14 E
Stolboucha	76	49.59 N	84.30 E
Stolbovo	66	52.38 N	34.47 E
Stolbovoj, Ostrov I	64	74.05 N	136.00 E
Stolbun	66	52.48 N	31.25 E
Stolby, Zapovednik ♠	78	55.45 N	92.45 E
Stolica ∧	30	48.48 N	20.11 E
Stolin	68	51.53 N	26.51 E
Stollberg	50	50.42 N	12.47 E
Stöllet	26	60.24 N	13.16 E
Stol'noje	68	51.31 N	31.55 E
Stolp → Słupsk	30	54.28 N	17.01 E
Stolpe	254a	52.40 N	13.16 E
Stolpen	50	51.05 N	14.04 E
Stolper Heide ◂[3]	254a	52.39 N	13.14 E
Stolpino	70	57.24 N	42.55 E
Stolpmünde → Ustka	30	54.35 N	16.50 E
Stolzenau	48	52.31 N	9.04 E
Ston	36	42.50 N	17.42 E
Stondon Massey	250	51.41 N	0.18 E
Stone, Eng., U.K.	44	52.54 N	2.10 W
Stone, Eng., U.K.	250	51.27 N	0.16 E
Stoneboro	204	41.20 N	80.07 W
Stone Canyon Reservoir ⊜[1]	270	34.07 N	118.28 W
Stone Corral Creek ≃	216	39.16 N	122.06 W
Stone Creek	204	40.24 N	81.34 W
Stonefort	184	37.37 N	88.42 W
Stoneham, Mass., U.S.	273	42.29 N	71.06 W
Stoneham, Pa., U.S.	204	41.49 N	79.07 W
Stone Harbor	198	39.03 N	74.45 W
Stonehaven	28	56.38 N	2.13 W
Stonehenge	156	24.22 S	143.17 E
Stonehenge ⊥	44	51.11 N	1.49 W
Stonehouse, Eng., U.K.	44	51.45 N	2.17 W
Stonehouse, Scot., U.K.	42	55.43 N	4.00 W
Stone Indian Reserve ◂[4]	172	51.54 N	123.12 W
Stoneleigh	44	52.21 N	1.31 W
Stonelick Creek ≃	208	39.07 N	84.13 W
Stonelick State Park ♠	208	39.13 N	84.04 W
Stone Mountain	182	33.49 N	84.10 W
Stone Mountain ∧	178	44.34 N	71.40 W
Stone Park	268	41.45 N	87.53 W
Stoner	172	53.36 N	122.40 W
Stoner Creek ≃	208	38.18 N	84.14 W
Stone Ridge	200	41.51 N	74.09 W
Stonerstown	204	40.13 N	78.16 W
Stones, East Fork ≃	184	35.59 N	86.27 W
Stones, West Fork ≃	184	35.59 N	86.27 W
Stonestown ◂[9]	272	37.44 N	122.28 W
Stonevilla	269b	40.18 N	79.31 W
Stoneville	182	36.28 N	79.54 W
Stonewall, Man., Can.	174	50.09 N	97.21 W
Stonewall, Miss., U.S.	184	32.08 N	88.47 W
Stonewall, Okla., U.S.	186	34.39 N	96.31 W
Stoney Creek	202	43.13 N	79.46 W
Stoney Point ≻	204	42.18 N	82.34 W
Stonington, Conn., U.S.	197	41.20 N	71.54 W
Stonington, Ill., U.S.	209	39.44 N	89.12 W
Stonington, Maine, U.S.	178	44.09 N	68.40 W
Stony ≃, Alaska, U.S.	170	61.45 N	156.35 W
Stony ≃, Minn., U.S.	180	47.44 N	91.47 W
Stony Brook	200	40.56 N	73.09 W
Stony Brook ≃, Conn., U.S.	266	41.08 N	73.22 W
Stony Brook ≃, Conn., U.S.	266	41.04 N	73.28 W
Stony Brook ≃, Mass., U.S.	273	42.22 N	71.16 W
Stony Brook ≃, Mass., U.S.	273	42.38 N	71.22 W
Stony Brook ≃, N.J., U.S.	266	40.56 N	74.26 W
Stony Brook ≃, N.J., U.S.	266	40.19 N	74.41 W
Stony Brook Harbor C	266	40.54 N	73.10 W
Stony Brook Reservation ♠	273	42.16 N	71.09 W
Stony Creek, Conn., U.S.	197	41.16 N	72.45 W
Stony Creek, Mich., U.S.	271	42.42 N	83.07 W
Stony Creek, Va., U.S.	198	36.57 N	77.24 W
Stony Creek ≃, Calif., U.S.	194	39.41 N	121.58 W
Stony Creek ≃, Ill., U.S.	268	41.41 N	87.51 W
Stony Creek ≃, Mich., U.S.	206	43.00 N	84.55 W
Stony Creek ≃, Mich., U.S.	206	41.57 N	83.18 W
Stony Creek ≃, N.Y., U.S.	202	43.49 N	76.14 W
Stony Creek ≃, Pa., U.S.	204	40.20 N	78.55 W
Stony Creek ≃, Pa., U.S.	275	40.07 N	75.21 W
Stony Creek ≃, Va., U.S.	198	36.56 N	77.23 W
Stony Creek, Middle Fork ≃	216	39.25 N	122.31 W
Stony Creek, North Fork ≃	216	39.22 N	122.37 W
Stony Creek, South Fork ≃	216	39.22 N	122.39 W
Stony Creek Indian Reserve ◂[4]	172	53.57 N	124.07 W
Stony Creek Mills	198	40.21 N	75.52 W
Stony Crossing	156	35.05 S	143.35 E
Stonyford	216	39.23 N	122.33 W
Stony Gorge Reservoir ⊜[1]	216	39.34 N	122.31 W
Stony Indian Reserve ◂[4]	172	51.10 N	114.55 W
Stony Island I, Mich., U.S.	271	42.07 N	83.08 W
Stony Island I, N.Y., U.S.	202	43.53 N	76.25 W
Stony Kill ≃	200	42.24 N	73.38 W
Stony Lake ⊜, Man., Can.	166	58.51 N	98.35 W
Stony Lake ⊜, Ont., Can.	202	44.33 N	78.05 W
Stony Plain	172	53.02 N	114.00 W
Stony Plain Indian Reserve ◂[4]	172	53.30 N	113.45 W
Stony Point, Mich., U.S.	206	41.57 N	83.16 W
Stony Point, N.C., U.S.	182	35.52 N	81.03 W
Stony Point, N.Y., U.S.	200	41.14 N	73.59 W
Stony Point ≻	274a	42.50 N	78.52 W
Stony Point ≻[1]	202	43.52 N	76.15 W
Stony Prairie	204	41.21 N	83.10 W
Stony Rapids	166	59.16 N	105.50 W
Stony Ridge	204	41.31 N	83.30 W
Stony River	170	61.47 N	156.41 W
Stony Run	274b	39.11 N	76.42 W
Stony Run ≃	275	40.09 N	75.32 W
Stony Stratford	44	52.04 N	0.52 W
Stop ≃	273	42.10 N	71.19 W
Stopnica	30	50.27 N	20.57 E
Stoppenberg ◂[8]	253	51.29 N	7.02 E
Stör ≃	50	53.50 N	11.29 E
Storå	40	59.43 N	15.08 E
Storå ≃	26	56.19 N	8.19 E
Stora Alvaret ≚	26	56.30 N	16.30 E
Stora Gla ⊜	26	59.30 N	12.30 E
Stora Kloten ⊜	40	59.52 N	15.16 E
Stora Le ⊜	26	59.05 N	11.53 E
Stora Lulevatten ⊜	24	67.10 N	19.16 E
Stora Mellösa	40	59.13 N	15.30 E
Stora Möja I	40	59.26 N	18.55 E
Stora Norn ⊜	40	60.14 N	15.42 E
Stora Sjöfallets Nationalpark ♠	24	67.44 N	18.16 E
Stora Skedvi	40	60.24 N	15.48 E
Stora Sotra I	26	60.18 N	5.05 E
Stora Sundby	40	59.16 N	16.07 E
Storavan ⊜	24	65.40 N	18.15 E
Stora Vika	40	58.56 N	17.48 E
Storby	26	60.13 N	19.34 E
Stord I	26	59.53 N	5.25 E
Store Andst	41	55.29 N	9.14 E
Store Bælt ⊔	41	55.30 N	11.00 E
Store Heddinge	41	55.19 N	12.25 E
Store Magleby	41	55.36 N	12.38 E
Store Merløse	41	55.33 N	11.40 E
Støren	26	63.02 N	10.18 E
Storeton	252	53.21 N	3.03 W
Storey □[6]	216	39.28 N	119.30 W
Storfjärden ⊜	40	60.30 N	17.23 E
Storfjorden C[2]	26	62.25 N	6.30 E
Storfors	40	59.32 N	14.16 E
Störitzsee ⊜	254a	52.23 N	13.51 E
Störkanal ≋	50	53.36 N	11.30 E
Storkerson Bay C	166	73.00 N	124.50 W
Storkerson Peninsula ≻[1]	166	72.30 N	106.30 W
Storkow, D.D.R.	50	53.19 N	14.17 E
Storkow, D.D.R.	50	52.15 N	13.56 E
Storlien	26	63.19 N	12.06 E
Stormarn ◂[1]	48	53.45 N	10.20 E
Storm Bay C	156	43.10 S	147.32 E
Stormberg ⩕	148	31.27 S	26.55 E
Storm King Mountain ∧	214	46.39 N	122.10 W
Storm Lake	188	42.39 N	95.13 W
Storm Mountain ∧	170	59.37 N	150.35 W
Stormont □[6]	196	45.10 N	75.00 W
Stormovo	73	49.06 N	38.55 E
Stormsrivier	148	33.59 S	23.52 E
Stormsvlei	148	34.05 S	20.06 E
Stormville	200	41.34 N	73.45 W
Stornara	60	41.17 N	15.46 E
Stornarella	60	41.15 N	15.44 E
Stornorrforsen	26	63.52 N	20.03 E
Stornoway	28	58.12 N	6.23 W
Storo	58	45.51 N	10.35 E
Storoževaja	74	43.53 N	41.27 E
Storoževsk	24	61.57 N	52.16 E
Storožinec	68	48.10 N	25.43 E
Storrensjön ⊜	26	63.38 N	12.34 E
Storrington	44	50.55 N	0.28 W
Storrs	197	41.48 N	72.15 W
Storsjøen ⊜, Nor.	26	61.35 N	11.12 E
Storsjøen ⊜, Nor.	26	60.23 N	11.40 E
Storsjön ⊜, Sve.	26	63.12 N	14.18 E
Storsjön ⊜, Sve.	26	62.48 N	13.07 E
Storsjön ⊜, Sve.	40	60.34 N	16.44 E
Storsjön ⊜, Sve.	40	59.04 N	17.12 E
Storskardhøa ∧	26	62.30 N	8.45 E
Storsteinsfjellet ∧	24	68.14 N	17.52 E
Storstrøm □[6]	41	55.00 N	11.55 E
Storstrømmen ⊔	41	54.58 N	11.55 E
Storstrømsbroen ◂[5]	41	54.58 N	11.50 E
Storthoaks	174	49.22 N	101.38 W
Storuman	24	65.06 N	17.06 E
Storuman-See → Storavan ⊜	24	65.40 N	18.15 E
Storvarts gruve	26	62.38 N	11.31 E
Storvätteshågna ∧	26	62.07 N	12.27 E
Storvik	40	60.35 N	16.32 E
Storvindeln ⊜	24	65.43 N	17.05 E
Storvreta	40	59.58 N	17.42 E
Story	192	44.35 N	106.53 W
Story City	180	42.11 N	93.36 W
Storytown, U.S.A. ♠	200	43.22 N	73.42 W
Stössen	50	51.06 N	11.55 E
Stotfold	44	52.01 N	0.14 W
Stotternheim	50	51.03 N	11.02 E
Stottville	200	42.17 N	73.45 W
Stouchsburg	198	40.23 N	76.14 W
Stough Park ♠	270	34.12 N	118.18 W
Stoughton, Sask., Can.	174	49.41 N	103.03 W
Stoughton, Eng., U.K.	250	51.15 N	0.35 W
Stoughton, Mass., U.S.	197	42.07 N	71.06 W
Stoughton, Wis., U.S.	206	42.55 N	89.13 W
Stoumont	52	50.25 N	5.48 E
Stoǔng ≃	100	12.50 N	104.19 E
Stour ≃, Eng., U.K.	44	52.20 N	2.15 W
Stour ≃, Eng., U.K.	44	50.43 N	1.46 W
Stour ≃, Eng., U.K.	44	51.18 N	1.22 E
Stour ≃, Eng., U.K.	44	51.52 N	1.16 E
Stourbridge	44	52.27 N	2.09 W
Stourport-on-Severn	44	52.21 N	2.16 W
Stout Lake ⊜	174	52.08 N	94.33 W
Stoutsville	209	39.33 N	91.51 W
Stover	184	38.27 N	92.59 W
Stow, Mass., U.S.	197	42.26 N	71.30 W
Stow, N.Y., U.S.	204	42.09 N	79.25 W
Stow, Ohio, U.S.	204	41.10 N	81.27 W
Stowe, Pa., U.S.	198	40.15 N	75.39 W
Stowe, Vt., U.S.	178	44.28 N	72.41 W
Stowe Township	269b	40.29 N	80.04 W
Stow Maries	250	51.40 N	0.39 E
Stowmarket	44	52.11 N	1.00 E
Stow-on-the-Wold	44	51.56 N	1.44 W
Stoyoma Mountain ∧	172	49.59 N	121.13 W
Stoystown	204	40.06 N	78.57 W
Stra	58	45.25 N	12.00 E
Straach	50	51.57 N	12.35 E
Strabane, N. Ire., U.K.	28	54.49 N	7.27 W
Strabane, Pa., U.S.	204	40.08 N	80.10 W
Straberg	253	51.05 N	6.45 E
Strachan Island I	154	9.00 S	142.10 E
Stradbroke	44	52.19 N	1.16 E
Stradeč'	68	51.56 N	23.40 E
Stradella	56	45.05 N	9.18 E
Stradovn'a, Ozero ⊜	72	56.53 N	36.18 E
Straelen	52	51.27 N	6.16 E
Strafford	275	40.03 N	75.25 W
Straffordville	202	42.45 N	80.47 W
Strahan	156	42.09 S	145.19 E
Straight Creek ≃	208	38.46 N	83.55 W
Strakonice	30	49.16 N	13.55 E
Stralsund	50	54.19 N	13.05 E
Strambino	56	45.23 N	7.53 E
Strand	148	34.06 S	18.50 E
Stranda	26	62.19 N	6.54 E
Strande	50	54.26 N	10.12 E
Stranger Creek ≃	188	39.00 N	95.01 W
Strangford	42	54.22 N	5.34 W
Strangford Lough ⊜	42	54.28 N	5.35 W
Strängnäs	40	59.23 N	17.02 E
Strångsjö	40	58.54 N	16.12 E
Strangways ≃	154	14.52 S	133.50 E
Strangways, Mount ∧	152	23.02 S	133.51 E
Stranraer	42	54.55 N	5.02 W
Strasbourg, Sask., Can.	174	51.04 N	104.57 W
Strasbourg, Fr.	54	48.35 N	7.45 E
Strasburg, D.D.R.	50	53.30 N	13.44 E
Strasburg, Colo., U.S.	188	39.44 N	104.20 W
Strasburg, N. Dak., U.S.	188	46.08 N	100.10 W
Strasburg, Ohio, U.S.	204	40.36 N	81.32 W
Strasburg, Pa., U.S.	198	39.59 N	76.11 W
Strasburg, Va., U.S.	178	38.59 N	78.22 W
Strašeny	68	47.08 N	28.36 E
Straševiči	66	56.49 N	34.36 E
Stråssa	40	59.45 N	15.13 E
Strass bei Jenbach	58	47.23 N	11.49 E
Strassburg → Strasbourg	54	48.35 N	7.45 E
Strasswalchen	58	47.59 N	13.15 E
Strat Florida Abbey ⊍[1]	44	52.16 N	3.51 W
Stratford, Ont., Can.	202	43.22 N	80.57 W
Stratford, N.Z.	162	39.20 S	174.17 E
Stratford, Calif., U.S.	216	36.11 N	119.49 W
Stratford, Conn., U.S.	197	41.14 N	73.07 W
Stratford, Iowa, U.S.	180	42.16 N	93.56 W
Stratford, N.J., U.S.	198	39.50 N	75.01 W
Stratford, N.Y., U.S.	200	43.11 N	74.42 W
Stratford, Okla., U.S.	186	34.48 N	96.58 W
Stratford, Tex., U.S.	186	36.20 N	102.04 W
Stratford, Wis., U.S.	180	44.48 N	90.04 W
Stratford Centre	196	45.47 N	71.16 W
Stratford Hall ⊥	198	38.10 N	76.49 W
Stratford Point ≻	266	41.09 N	73.06 W
Stratford-upon-Avon	44	52.12 N	1.41 W
Strathalbyn	158b	35.16 S	138.54 E
Strathaven	42	55.40 N	4.04 W
Strathbogie Ranges ⩕	159	36.55 S	145.45 E
Strathclair	174	50.24 N	100.24 W
Strathclyde □[4]	28	56.00 N	5.15 W
Strathcona Provincial Park ♠	172	49.40 N	125.50 W
Strathfield	160	33.52 S	151.06 E
Strathlorne	176	46.11 N	61.17 W
Strathmoor ◂[8]	271	42.23 N	83.11 W
Strathmore, Alta., Can.	172	51.03 N	113.23 W
Strathmore, Calif., U.S.	194	36.09 N	119.04 W
Strathmore, N.J., U.S.	266	40.24 N	74.13 W
Strathpine	161a	27.19 S	152.59 E
Strathroy	204	42.57 N	81.38 W
Strathy Point ≻	28	58.35 N	4.01 W
Strattanville	204	41.12 N	79.20 W
Stratton, Eng., U.K.	44	50.50 N	4.31 W
Stratton, Colo., U.S.	188	39.18 N	102.36 W
Stratton, Maine, U.S.	178	45.08 N	70.26 W
Stratton, Nebr., U.S.	188	40.09 N	101.14 W
Stratton, Ohio, U.S.	204	40.32 N	80.38 W
Stratton Mountain ∧	178	43.05 N	72.56 W
Stratton Saint Margaret	44	51.35 N	1.45 W
Straubing	30	48.53 N	12.34 E
Strauch	253	51.09 N	6.56 E
Straumen	26	63.52 N	11.18 E
Straupitz	50	51.54 N	14.07 E
Strausberg	50	52.35 N	13.53 E
Straus-Berger Stadtforst ♠	254a	52.34 N	13.52 E
Strausberg-Vorstadt	254a	52.32 N	13.51 E
Straussberg	50	51.23 N	10.44 E
Straussee ⊜	254a	52.35 N	13.53 E
Straussfurt	50	51.09 N	10.59 E
Strausstown	198	40.30 N	76.11 W
Stravignano	60	43.05 N	12.49 E
Strawberry	216	38.13 N	118.35 W
Strawberry ≃, Ark., U.S.	184	35.53 N	91.13 W
Strawberry ≃, Utah, U.S.	190	40.10 N	110.24 W
Strawberry Island I	274a	42.57 N	78.55 W
Strawberry Mountain ∧	192	44.19 N	118.43 W
Strawberry Point, Calif., U.S.	272	37.54 N	122.31 W
Strawberry Point, Iowa, U.S.	180	42.41 N	91.32 W
Strawberry Point ≻	273	42.15 N	70.46 W
Strawberry Reservoir ⊜[1]	190	40.11 N	111.08 W
Strawberry Valley	216	39.34 N	121.06 W
Strawbridge Lake ⊜	275	39.57 N	74.57 W
Strawn	186	32.33 N	98.30 W
Straw Pump	269b	40.19 N	79.40 W
Strážnice	30	48.54 N	17.18 E
Strážske	30	48.53 N	21.50 E
Streaky Bay	152	32.48 S	134.13 E
Streaky Bay C	152	32.36 S	134.08 E
Streamwood	206	42.02 N	88.11 W
Streatham, Austl.	159	37.41 S	143.04 E
Streatham, B.C., Can.	172	53.52 N	126.12 W
Streatham ◂[8]	250	51.26 N	0.08 W
Streator	206	41.07 N	88.50 W
Strebersdorf ◂[8]	254b	48.18 N	16.23 E
Streda nad Bodrogem	30	48.23 N	21.46 E
Středočeský Kraj □[4]	30	49.55 N	14.30 E
Stredoslovenský Kraj □[4]	30	48.50 N	19.10 E
Street	44	51.07 N	2.42 W
Streeter	188	46.39 N	99.21 W
Streetman	212	31.53 N	96.19 W
Streetsboro	204	41.14 N	81.21 W
Streets Run ≃	269b	40.23 N	79.56 W
Streetsville	202	43.35 N	79.42 W
Strehaia	38	44.37 N	23.12 E
Strehla	50	51.21 N	13.13 E
Strehlen → Strzelin	30	50.47 N	17.03 E
Střela ≃	50	50.04 N	13.18 E
Strelasund ⊔	50	54.20 N	13.05 E
Strel'covka	73	49.18 N	39.52 E
Streleckaja Step' Zapovednik ♠	73	49.16 N	40.05 E
Streleckije Vyselki	72	54.12 N	38.57 E
Strelica	68	51.37 N	38.55 E
Strelitzalt	50	53.20 N	13.05 E
Strelka	76	58.05 N	93.01 E
Strelka ≃	255a	59.52 N	30.03 E
Strelka-Čun'a	64	61.45 N	102.48 E
Strelkovo	72	55.28 N	37.37 E
Strelkovoje	68	45.54 N	34.53 E
Strelkovskij, Porog ↳	76	58.04 N	93.07 E
Strel'na, S.S.S.R.	24	66.06 N	38.40 E
Strel'na, S.S.S.R.	66	59.51 N	30.02 E
Strel'na ≃	24	66.04 N	38.39 E
Strel'skaja	24	59.28 N	47.47 E
Strembo	58	46.09 N	10.44 E
Stremilovo	72	55.09 N	37.09 E
Strenči	66	57.37 N	25.41 E
Strengen	54	47.08 N	10.27 E
Stresa	56	45.53 N	8.32 E
Strešin	66	52.43 N	30.05 E
Stretford	42	53.27 N	2.19 W
Stretton, Austl.	152	32.32 S	117.41 E
Stretton, Eng., U.K.	42	53.21 N	2.35 W
Stretton, Eng., U.K.	44	52.44 N	0.35 W
Streu ≃	52	50.21 N	10.16 E
Strib	41	55.32 N	9.47 E
Striberg	40	59.33 N	14.56 E
Stříbro	30	49.46 N	13.00 E
Strickherdicke	253	51.29 N	7.43 E
Strickland ≃	154	6.00 S	142.05 E
Striegau → Strzegom	30	50.57 N	16.21 E
Strigno	58	46.04 N	11.31 E
Strijen	48	51.45 N	4.33 E
Striker, Lake ⊜[1]	212	31.57 N	94.59 W
Strimón (Struma) ≃	38	40.47 N	23.51 E
Stringtown, Ind., U.S.	208	40.05 N	86.29 W
Stringtown, Okla., U.S.	186	34.28 N	96.03 W
Striven, Loch C	42	55.58 N	5.09 W
Strižament, Gora ∧	74	44.46 N	42.01 E
Strižavka	68	49.19 N	28.28 E
Striži	70	58.30 N	49.13 E
Strjama ≃	38	42.10 N	24.56 E
Strobel	242	32.03 S	60.37 W
Strobel, Lago ⊜	244	48.22 S	71.12 W
Strobl	58	47.43 N	13.29 E
Strobleton	204	41.22 N	79.25 W
Strøby	41	55.23 N	12.18 E
Stroeder	244	40.11 S	62.37 W
Strogino ◂[8]	255b	55.49 N	37.25 E
Strogonof Point ≻	170	56.53 N	158.49 W
Stroh	206	41.35 N	85.12 W
Ströhen	48	52.32 N	8.41 E
Stroitel'	68	50.47 N	36.26 E
Strom ≃	50	53.15 N	13.50 E
Stroma I	28	58.42 N	3.04 W
Stromberg, B.R.D.	48	51.48 N	8.12 E
Stromberg, B.R.D.	52	49.57 N	7.46 E
Stromboli, Isola I	36	38.48 N	15.13 E
Strome	172	52.48 N	112.04 W
Stromeferry	28	57.21 N	5.34 W
Strömkendorf	50	53.58 N	11.29 E
Stromness	28	58.57 N	3.18 W
Strömsberg	40	60.24 N	17.35 E
Strömsbro	40	60.42 N	17.10 E
Strömsbruk	26	61.53 N	17.19 E
Stromsburg	188	41.07 N	97.36 W
Strömsholm	40	59.32 N	16.15 E
Strömsnäsbruk	26	56.33 N	13.43 E
Strömstad	26	58.56 N	11.10 E
Strömsund	26	63.51 N	15.35 E
Ströms Vattudal V	26	63.56 N	15.28 E
Stromyn'	72	56.03 N	38.29 E
Strong, Ark., U.S.	184	33.07 N	92.21 W
Strong, Maine, U.S.	178	44.48 N	70.13 W
Strong ≃	184	31.51 N	90.08 W
Strong City	188	38.24 N	96.32 W
Stronghurst	180	40.45 N	90.55 W
Strongoli	36	39.15 N	17.03 E
Strongs Creek ≃	266	40.40 N	73.22 W
Strongs Neck ≻[1]	266	40.58 N	73.07 W
Strongstown	204	40.33 N	78.55 W
Strongsville	204	41.19 N	81.50 W
Strongsville Air Park ⊠	269a	41.19 N	81.52 W
Stronsay I	28	59.08 N	2.38 W
Strood	44	51.24 N	0.28 E
Stropkov	30	49.12 N	21.40 E
Stroppiana	56	45.14 N	8.27 E
Stroud, Eng., U.K.	44	51.45 N	2.12 W
Stroud, Okla., U.S.	186	35.45 N	96.40 W
Stroud Road	156	32.20 S	151.56 E
Stroudsburg	200	40.59 N	75.12 W
Strövelstorp	41	56.09 N	12.49 E
Strubenvale	263d	26.16 S	28.28 E
Strücklingen	48	53.07 N	7.40 E
Struer	26	56.29 N	8.37 E
Struga	38	41.11 N	20.40 E
Strugi-Krasnyje	66	58.17 N	29.06 E
Struisbaai	148	34.49 S	20.04 E
Struisbelt	263d	26.19 S	28.29 E
Strum	180	44.33 N	91.24 W
Struma (Strimón) ≃	38	40.47 N	23.51 E
Strumble Head ≻	44	52.02 N	5.04 W
Strumica	38	41.26 N	22.38 E
Strümp	253	51.17 N	6.40 E
Strunino	72	56.23 N	38.34 E
Strupna	72	54.43 N	38.48 E
Struthers	204	41.04 N	80.38 W
Strydenburg	148	29.58 S	23.40 E
Strydomsvlei	148	33.10 S	23.03 E
Strydpoort	148	27.00 S	25.58 E
Stryj	68	49.15 N	23.51 E
Stryj ≃	68	49.24 N	24.13 E
Stryker	206	41.30 N	84.25 W
Strykersville	200	42.42 N	78.27 W
Stryków	30	51.55 N	19.37 E
Stryn	26	61.55 N	6.47 E
Strynø I	41	54.54 N	10.37 E
Strypa ≃	68	48.52 N	25.26 E
Strzegom	30	50.57 N	16.21 E
Strzegowo-Osada	30	52.55 N	20.18 E
Strzelce Krajeńskie	30	52.53 N	15.32 E
Strzelce Opolskie	30	50.31 N	18.19 E
Strzelecki, Mount ∧	152	21.10 S	133.53 E
Strzelecki Creek ≃	156	29.37 S	139.59 E
Strzelin	30	50.47 N	17.03 E
Strzelno	30	52.38 N	18.11 E
Strzyżów	30	49.52 N	21.47 E
Stuart, Fla., U.S.	210	27.12 N	80.15 W
Stuart, Iowa, U.S.	188	41.30 N	94.19 W
Stuart, Nebr., U.S.	188	42.36 N	99.08 W
Stuart, Va., U.S.	182	36.38 N	80.16 W
Stuart ≃	172	54.00 N	123.32 W
Stuart, Mount ∧	214	47.29 N	120.54 W
Stuart Bluff Range ⩕	152	22.47 S	132.13 E
Stuart Channel ⊔	214	48.55 N	123.45 W
Stuart Island I, Alaska, U.S.	170	63.35 N	162.30 W
Stuart Island I, Wash., U.S.	214	48.42 N	123.12 W
Stuart Lake ⊜	172	54.32 N	124.35 W
Stuart Mountains ⩕	162	45.00 S	167.37 E
Stuart Range ⩕	152	29.10 S	134.56 E
Stuarts Draft	182	38.01 N	79.02 W
Stubai V	58	47.06 N	11.19 E
Stubaier Alpen ⩕	58	47.10 N	11.05 E
Stübbecken	253	51.23 N	7.36 E
Stubbekøbing	41	54.53 N	12.03 E
Stubbenfelde	50	54.02 N	14.01 E
Stubbenkammer	50	54.35 N	13.40 E
Stubbins	252	53.39 N	2.19 W
Stubbs Bay C	231h	13.08 N	61.10 W
Stubbs Lake ⊜	202	45.29 N	77.44 W
Stubla ≃	68	50.50 N	26.04 E
Stubner Kogel ∧	58	47.07 N	13.06 E
Stučka	66	56.38 N	25.13 E
Studenec	70	54.52 N	48.16 E
Studenica, Manastir ⊍[1]	38	43.21 N	20.35 E
Studénka	30	49.42 N	18.05 E
Studen Kladenec, Jazovir ⊜[1]	38	41.37 N	25.30 E
Studholme Junction	162	44.44 S	171.08 E
Studland	44	50.39 N	1.58 W
Studley	44	52.16 N	1.52 W

Symbols in the index entries represent the broad categories identified in the key at the right. Symbols with superior numbers (⩕[2]) identify subcategories (see complete key on page *I* · 26).

Kartensymbole in dem Registerverzeichnis stellen die rechts in Schlüssel erklärten Kategorien dar. Symbole mit hochgestellten Ziffern (⩕[2]) bezeichnen Unterabteilungen einer Kategorie (vgl. vollständiger Schlüssel auf Seite *I* · 26).

Los símbolos incluídos en el texto del índice representan las grandes categorias identificadas con la clave a la derecha. Los símbolos con numeros en su parte superior (⩕[2]) identifican las subcategorias (véase la clave completa en la página *I* · 26).

Les symboles de l'index représentent les catégories indiquées dans la légende à droite. Les symboles suivis d'un indice (⩕[2]) représentent des sous-catégories (voir légende complète à la page *I* · 26).

Os símbolos incluídos no texto do índice representam as grandes categorias identificadas com a chave à direita. Os símbolos com números em sua parte superior (⩕[2]) identificam as subcategorias (veja-se a chave completa à página *I* · 26).

∧	Mountain	Berg	Montaña	Montagne	Montanha
⩕	Mountains	Berge	Montañas	Montagnes	Montanhas
)(	Pass	Pass	Paso	Col	Passo
V	Valley, Canyon	Tal, Cañon	Valle, Cañón	Vallée, Canyon	Vale, Canhão
≚	Plain	Ebene	Llano	Plaine	Planície
≻	Cape	Kap	Cabo	Cap	Cabo
I	Island	Insel	Isla	Île	Ilha
II	Islands	Inseln	Islas	Îles	Ilhas
◂	Other Topographic Features	Andere Topographische Objekte	Otros Elementos Topográficos	Autres données topographiques	Outros Elementos Topográficos

ESPAÑOL / FRANÇAIS / PORTUGUÊS

Nombre / Nom / Nome	Página / Page	Lat.°′	Long.°′ W=Oeste / W=Ouest
Stud'onoje, S.S.S.R.	70	51.36 N	53.10 E
Stud'onoje, S.S.S.R.	76	53.37 N	77.31 E
Stud'onok	68	51.42 N	34.07 E
Studsvik	40	58.46 N	17.23 E
Stugudal	26	62.54 N	11.52 E
Stugun	26	63.10 N	15.36 E
Stühlingen	54	47.44 N	8.26 E
Stuhlweissenburg → Székesfehérvár	30	47.12 N	18.25 E
Stuhm → Sztum	30	53.56 N	19.01 E
Stuhr	48	53.01 N	8.45 E
Stuie	172	52.22 N	126.02 W
Stukely Lake ⊜	196	45.22 N	72.15 W
Stukenbrock	48	51.54 N	8.39 E
Stull Lake ⊜	174	54.23 N	92.34 W
Stülpe	50	52.02 N	13.19 E
Stumm	58	47.17 N	11.53 E
Stump Creek	204	41.01 N	78.50 W
Stump Creek ≃	266	40.28 N	74.16 W
Stumpf	253	51.06 N	7.13 E
Stump Lake ⊜	188	47.54 N	98.24 W
Stumsdorf	50	51.37 N	12.03 E
Stuorre Tjöure ∧	26	63.56 N	13.30 E
Stupart ≃	174	56.00 N	93.22 W
Stupino	72	54.53 N	38.05 E
Stuppach	52	49.27 N	9.44 E
Stura di Ala ≃	56	45.18 N	7.24 E
Stura di Demonte ≃	56	44.40 N	7.53 E
Stura di Lanzo ≃	56	45.06 N	7.44 E
Stura di Val Grande ≃	56	45.18 N	7.24 E
Stura di Viù ≃	56	45.16 N	7.26 E
Sturbridge	197	42.07 N	72.05 W
Sturdee	152	31.52 S	132.23 E
Sturge Island I	9	67.27 S	164.18 E
Sturgeon, Mo., U.S.	209	39.14 N	92.17 W
Sturgeon, Pa., U.S.	269b	40.23 N	80.13 W
Sturgeon ≃, Ont., Can.	180	46.19 N	79.58 W
Sturgeon ≃, Sask., Can.	174	53.12 N	105.53 W
Sturgeon ≃, Mich., U.S.	180	45.50 N	86.41 W
Sturgeon ≃, Mich., U.S.	180	45.24 N	84.38 W
Sturgeon ≃, Mich., U.S.	180	47.02 N	88.30 W
Sturgeon Bay	180	44.50 N	87.23 W
Sturgeon Bay C	174	52.00 N	97.50 W
Sturgeon Falls	180	46.22 N	79.55 W
Sturgeon Lake ⊜, Alta., Can.	172	55.06 N	117.30 W
Sturgeon Lake ⊜, Ont., Can.	174	55.25 N	90.55 W
Sturgeon Lake ⊜, Ont., Can.	202	44.28 N	78.42 W
Sturgeon Lake ⊜, Wash., U.S.	214	45.44 N	122.48 W
Sturgeon Lake Indian Reserve ✦[4], Alta., Can.	172	55.04 N	117.29 W
Sturgeon Lake Indian Reserve ✦[4], Sask., Can.	174	53.25 N	106.05 W
Sturgeon Landing	174	54.16 N	101.49 W
Sturgeon Point ≻	202	42.42 N	79.03 W
Sturgis, Sask., Can.	174	51.58 N	102.32 W
Sturgis, Ky., U.S.	184	37.33 N	87.59 W
Sturgis, Mich., U.S.	180	41.48 N	85.25 W
Sturgis, Miss., U.S.	184	33.21 N	89.03 W
Sturgis, S. Dak., U.S.	188	44.25 N	103.31 W
Sturla	56	44.24 N	8.59 E
Sturminster Newton	44	50.50 N	2.19 W
Štúrovo	30	47.48 N	18.49 E
Sturry	44	51.18 N	1.07 E
Sturt, Mount ∧	156	29.33 S	141.42 E
Sturt Creek	152	19.10 S	128.10 E
Sturt Creek ≃	152	20.08 S	127.24 E
Sturt Desert ✦[2]	156	28.30 S	141.00 E
Sturtevant	206	42.42 N	87.54 W
Stürzelberg	253	51.08 N	6.49 E
Stutterheim	148	32.33 S	27.28 E
Stuttgart, B.R.D.	52	48.46 N	9.11 E
Stuttgart, Ark., U.S.	184	34.30 N	91.33 W
Stuttgart □[5]	52	49.00 N	9.45 E
Stuttgart-Echterdingen, Flughafen ⊠	52	48.41 N	9.12 E
Stützengrün	50	50.32 N	12.31 E
Stützerbach	50	50.38 N	10.51 E
Stuyvesant	200	42.24 N	73.47 W
Stuyvesant Falls	200	42.21 N	73.44 W
Stviga ≃	68	52.04 N	27.54 E
Styal	252	53.21 N	2.15 W
Stykkishólmur	24a	65.06 N	22.48 W
Styla	73	47.41 N	37.50 E
Styr' ≃	68	52.07 N	26.35 E
Styrum ✦[8]	253	51.27 N	6.51 E
Styx ≃, Ont., Can.	202	44.11 N	80.57 W
Styx ≃, Ala., U.S.	184	30.31 N	87.27 W
Suaçuí Grande ≃	245	18.50 S	41.46 W
Suai	102	3.48 N	113.38 E
Suain	154	3.20 S	142.55 E
Suaita	236	6.07 N	73.27 W
Suakin Archipelago II	130	18.42 N	38.30 E
Sual	106	16.04 N	120.05 E
Suan	88	38.42 N	126.22 E
Suao, T'aiwan	90	24.36 N	121.51 E
Suao, Zhg.	90	25.38 N	119.42 E
Suaqui Grande	222	28.24 N	109.54 W
Suār	114	29.02 N	79.03 E
Suatá ≃	236	7.52 N	65.22 W
Suātala	114	23.09 N	79.02 E
Šubač	66	60.22 N	38.14 E
Subačius	66	55.46 N	24.47 E
Subah	105a	6.58 S	109.52 E
Subaio	246	22.35 S	42.52 W
Subang	105a	6.34 S	107.45 E
Subansiri ≃	110	26.48 N	93.50 E
Šubarkuduk	76	49.13 N	56.34 E
Subarnapur	262b	22.58 N	88.34 E
Subarnarekha ≃	116	21.34 N	87.24 E
Šubarši	76	48.35 N	57.12 E
Subashi	75	38.22 N	74.57 E
Subasio, Monte ∧	60	43.03 N	12.40 E
Subata	66	56.01 N	25.56 E
Subay', 'Irq as- ✦[2]	134	22.15 N	43.05 E
Subbiano	60	43.34 N	11.52 E
Subbotino	76	53.04 N	91.55 E
Subchankulovo	70	54.34 N	53.49 E
Subei	92	39.27 N	95.03 E
Subhepur	262a	28.45 N	77.16 E
Subiaco	60	41.55 N	13.06 E
Subi Besar, Pulau I	102	2.55 N	108.50 E
Subic	106	14.53 N	120.14 E
Subic Bay C	106	14.45 N	120.13 E
Subic Bay Naval Station (United States) ■	106	14.47 N	120.16 E
Subipur	262b	22.54 N	88.08 E
Subk al-Ahad	132	30.18 N	31.02 E
Sublette	188	37.29 N	100.50 W
Sublett Range ⋀	192	42.20 N	112.50 W
Sublime	212	29.29 N	96.48 W
Subotica	38	46.06 N	19.39 E
Şubr, Jabal ∧	134	13.25 N	44.06 E
Subugo ∧	144	1.40 N	35.49 E
Sučan	79	43.08 N	133.09 E
Sucarnoochee ≃	184	32.25 N	88.02 W
Succasunna	200	40.52 N	74.38 W
Succor Creek ≃	192	43.38 N	116.56 W
Suceava	38	47.39 N	26.19 E
Suceava □[4]	38	47.30 N	25.45 E
Suceava ≃	38	47.32 N	26.32 E
Sucha [beskidzka]	30	49.44 N	19.36 E
Suchaja	78	52.32 N	107.06 E
Suchaja Volnovacha ≃	73	47.37 N	38.01 E
Suchań, Pol.	30	53.17 N	15.19 E
Suchan → Sučan, S.S.S.R.	79	43.08 N	133.09 E
Suchana	64	68.45 N	118.00 E
Suchang	97	30.34 N	103.34 E
Süchbaatar	78	50.17 N	106.10 E
Süchbaatar □[4]	92	45.30 N	114.00 E
Suchdol ✦[8]	50	50.08 N	14.21 E
Suchedniów	30	51.03 N	20.51 E
Suchetgarh	113	32.34 N	74.40 E
Suchiapa	224	16.37 N	93.05 W
Suchiapa ≃	224	16.36 N	93.01 W
Súchil	224	23.38 N	103.55 W
Suchilquitongo	224	17.15 N	96.53 W
Suchiniči	66	54.06 N	35.20 E
Suchitepéquez □[5]	226	14.25 N	91.20 W
Suchitlán	224	19.22 N	103.43 W
Suchitoto	226	13.56 N	89.02 W
Suchobezvodnoje	70	57.03 N	44.50 E
Suchoborka	24	59.06 N	49.58 E
Suchodol	72	54.27 N	37.22 E
Suchodol'skij	66	53.43 N	38.17 E
Suchodrev ≃	72	54.44 N	35.59 E
Suchoj	70	47.06 N	41.21 E
Suchoj Jelančik ≃	73	47.16 N	38.25 E
Suchoj Log	76	56.55 N	62.01 E
Suchoj Pit	76	58.48 N	92.49 E
Suchoj Sambek ≃	73	47.23 N	39.07 E
Suchoj Torec ≃	73	48.49 N	37.36 E
Suchona ≃	24	60.46 N	46.24 E
Suchorečka	70	52.49 N	52.27 E
Suchotinka	70	52.31 N	41.35 E
Suchotinskij	70	47.18 N	44.31 E
Suchou → Suzhou	96	31.18 N	120.37 E
Suchoverkovo	66	56.37 N	35.35 E
Suchov Pervyj	70	49.59 N	43.28 E
Süchow → Xuzhou	88	34.16 N	117.11 E
Süchteln	52	51.17 N	6.22 E
Suchumi	74	43.01 N	41.02 E
Sucio ≃, Col.	236	7.27 N	77.07 W
Sucio ≃, El Sal.	226	14.02 N	89.17 W
Šučje	68	51.45 N	40.29 E
Suck ≃	28	53.16 N	8.03 W
Sucker Creek Indian Reserve ✦[4]	172	55.28 N	116.10 W
Sucker Lake ⊜	202	44.46 N	78.16 W
Suckling, Mount ∧	154	9.45 S	148.55 E
Sucre, Arg.	248	34.30 S	59.07 W
Sucre, Bol.	238	19.02 S	65.17 W
Sucre, Col.	236	8.49 N	74.44 W
Sucre, Ec.	236	1.16 S	80.26 W
Sucre □[3]	236	10.25 N	63.30 W
Sucre □[5], Col.	236	9.00 N	75.00 W
Sucre □[5], Ven.	276c	10.25 N	66.50 W
Sucúa	236	2.28 S	78.10 W
Sucuaro	236	4.34 N	68.50 W
Sucunduri ≃	238	5.50 S	59.32 W
Sucuriju	240	1.39 N	49.57 W
Sucuriú ≃	245	20.47 S	51.38 W
Sucy-en-Brie	46	48.46 N	2.32 E
Sud, Canal du Ʉ	228	18.40 N	73.05 W
Sud, Massif du ⋀	228	18.25 N	73.55 W
Sud, Pointe ≻	147a	11.53 S	43.49 E
Sud, Récif du ✢[2]	165f	23.00 S	167.02 E
Sud, Rivière du ≃	196	45.08 N	73.15 W
Suda	66	59.09 N	37.33 E
Suda ≃	66	59.11 N	37.30 E
Südafrika → South Africa □[1]	146	30.00 S	26.00 E
Sudaj	66	58.58 N	43.08 E
Sudak	68	44.52 N	34.59 E
Sudalsvatnet ⊜	26	59.35 N	6.45 E
Südamerika → South America •[1]	18	15.00 S	60.00 W
Sudan	186	34.04 N	102.32 W
Sudan □[1]	126 / 130	15.00 N	30.00 E
Sudan ✦[1]	126	10.00 N	20.00 E
Sudarsan	262b	22.59 N	88.17 E
Südbahnhof ✦[5]	254b	48.11 N	16.23 E
Sudberg ✦[8]	253	51.11 N	7.08 E
Sudbišči	66	52.57 N	37.39 E
Sud'bodarovka	70	52.19 N	54.07 E
Sudbury, Ont., Can.	180	46.30 N	81.00 W
Sudbury, Eng., U.K.	44	52.02 N	0.44 E
Sudbury, Mass., U.S.	197	42.23 N	71.25 W
Sudbury ≃	273	42.28 N	71.22 W
Sudbury Center	273	42.23 N	71.25 W
Sudbury Reservoir ⊜[1]	197	42.19 N	71.31 W
Südchinesisches Meer → South China Sea ▾[2]	98	10.00 N	113.00 E
Sud Dakota → South Dakota □[3]	188	44.15 N	100.00 W
Sudd an-Na'ām, Jabal ∧	132	29.49 N	31.43 E
Suddie	236	7.07 N	58.29 W
Sude ≃	50	53.22 N	10.45 E
Süderbrarup	41	54.38 N	9.46 E
Süderlügum	41	54.52 N	8.55 E
Suderwich ✦[8]	253	51.37 N	7.15 E
Sudeten → Sudety ⋀	30	50.30 N	16.00 E
Sudety ⋀	30	50.30 N	16.00 E
Süd-Georgien → South Georgia I	234	54.15 S	36.45 W
Südheide, Naturpark ♠	48	52.50 N	10.10 E
Sudi	144	10.06 S	39.57 E
Sudislavl'	70	57.53 N	41.43 E
Südkamen	253	51.35 N	7.39 E
Süd-Korea → Korea, South □[1]	88	36.30 N	128.00 E
Südlengern	48	52.11 N	8.38 E
Sudlersville	198	39.11 N	75.52 W
Südlicher Bug → Južnyj Bug ≃	68	46.59 N	31.58 E
Südlicher Indianer-See → Southern Indian Lake ⊜	166	57.10 N	98.40 W
Südlicher Teutoburger Wald, Naturpark ♠	48	52.10 N	8.15 E
Südlicher Teutoburger Wald-Eggegebirge, Naturpark ♠	48	51.50 N	8.50 E
Sudnikovo	72	55.53 N	36.02 E
Sudočje, Ozero ⊜	76	43.25 N	58.30 E
Sudogda	70	55.57 N	40.50 E
Sudomskaja Vozvyšennost' ⋀[1]	66	57.25 N	29.25 E
Sudong, Pulau I	261c	1.13 N	103.44 E
Süd-Orkney-Inseln → South Orkney Islands II	9	60.35 S	45.30 W
Sudost' ≃	66	52.19 N	33.24 E
Sud-Ouest, Pointe du ≻	176	49.23 N	63.36 W
Sudovaja Višn'a	68	49.49 N	23.22 E
Südradde ≃	48	52.41 N	7.34 E
Süd-Sandwich-Inseln → South Sandwich Islands II	18	57.45 S	26.30 W
Süd-Shetland-Inseln → South Shetland Islands II	9	62.00 S	58.00 W
Sudūd	132	30.25 N	30.54 E
Sudupu	96	31.41 N	119.34 E
Südwest-Kap → South West Cape ≻	156	43.34 S	146.02 E
Sudweyhe	48	52.59 N	8.53 E
Sudža	68	51.12 N	35.16 E
Sudzuche	79	42.52 N	133.45 E
Sue	86	33.35 N	130.30 E
Sue ≃	130	7.41 N	28.03 E
Sueca	34	39.12 N	0.19 W
Suecia → Sweden □[1]	24	62.00 N	15.00 E
Sue Creek C	274b	39.17 N	76.24 W
Suedberg	198	40.32 N	76.28 W
Suède → Sweden □[1]	24	62.00 N	15.00 E
Suemez Island I	170	55.17 N	133.21 W
Suèvres	46	47.40 N	1.28 E
Suez → As-Suways	132	29.58 N	32.33 E
Suez, Gulf of → Suways, Khalīj as- C	130	29.00 N	32.50 E
Suez Canal → Suways, Qanāt as- ☰	132	29.55 N	32.33 E
Sūf	122	32.19 N	35.50 E
Şufaynah	118	23.09 N	40.32 E
Suffern	200	41.07 N	74.09 W
Suffern Park	266	41.07 N	74.07 W
Suffield, Alta., Can.	174	50.12 N	111.10 W
Suffield, Conn., U.S.	197	41.59 N	72.39 W
Suffield, Ohio, U.S.	204	41.01 N	81.21 W
Suffolk	198	36.44 N	76.35 W
Suffolk □[6], Eng., U.K.	44	52.10 N	1.20 E
Suffolk □[6], Mass., U.S.	197	42.21 N	71.04 W
Suffolk □[6], N.Y., U.S.	200	40.55 N	72.40 W
Suffolk, Ruisseau ≃	196	45.48 N	74.59 W
Suffolk Downs Race Track ♠	273	42.23 N	71.00 W
Şūfiān	118	38.17 N	45.59 E
Sufi-Kurgan	75	40.02 N	73.30 E
Sufu → Kashi	75	39.29 N	75.59 E
Sugana, Val V	58	46.00 N	11.40 E
Sugandha	262b	22.54 N	88.20 E
Sugandy	75	43.27 N	74.38 E
Suganhu ⊜	92	38.50 N	94.00 E
Sugano	258	35.44 N	139.56 E
Sugar ≃, U.S.	180	42.26 N	89.12 W
Sugar ≃, N.H., U.S.	178	43.24 N	72.24 W
Sugar ≃, N.Y., U.S.	202	43.31 N	75.19 W
Sugar City	192	43.52 N	111.45 W
Sugarcreek, Ohio, U.S.	204	40.30 N	81.39 W
Sugar Creek, Pa., U.S.	204	41.26 N	79.53 W
Sugar Creek ≃, U.S.	206	40.47 N	87.45 W
Sugar Creek ≃, Ill., U.S.	184	40.09 N	89.38 W
Sugar Creek ≃, Ill., U.S.	209	38.28 N	89.37 W
Sugar Creek ≃, Ill., U.S.	209	39.48 N	89.32 W
Sugar Creek ≃, Ind., U.S.	184	39.51 N	87.21 W
Sugar Creek ≃, Ind., U.S.	208	39.21 N	86.00 W
Sugar Creek ≃, Iowa, U.S.	184	40.23 N	91.28 W
Sugar Creek ≃, Mich., U.S.	271	42.06 N	83.36 W
Sugar Creek ≃, N.Y., U.S.	200	42.38 N	77.09 W
Sugar Creek ≃, Ohio, U.S.	204	40.31 N	81.28 W
Sugar Creek ≃, Ohio, U.S.	206	40.57 N	84.11 W
Sugar Creek ≃, Ohio, U.S.	208	39.27 N	83.25 W
Sugar Creek ≃, Okla., U.S.	186	35.05 N	98.10 W
Sugar Creek ≃, Pa., U.S.	200	41.47 N	76.27 W
Sugar Creek ≃, Wis., U.S.	206	42.43 N	88.19 W
Sugar Grove, Ill., U.S.	206	41.45 N	88.27 W
Sugargrove, Pa., U.S.	204	41.59 N	79.21 W
Sugar Grove, Va., U.S.	182	36.47 N	81.25 W
Sugar Hill	182	34.07 N	84.02 W
Sugar Island I, Ont., Can.	202	44.26 N	77.17 W
Sugar Island I, Mich., U.S.	180	46.25 N	84.12 W
Sugar Land	212	29.37 N	95.38 W
Sugar Loaf	200	41.19 N	74.17 W
Sugar Loaf → Pão de Açúcar ∧	277a	22.57 S	43.09 W
Sugarloaf ∧[2]	204	41.24 N	81.06 W
Sugarloaf Hill ∧[2]	264b	37.58 S	145.19 E
Sugarloaf Key I	210	24.40 N	81.32 W
Sugarloaf Mountain ∧, Ky., U.S.	208	38.13 N	83.32 W
Sugarloaf Mountain ∧, Maine, U.S.	178	45.01 N	70.22 W
Sugar Loaf Mountain ∧, Md., U.S.	198	39.16 N	77.23 W
Sugarloaf Mountain ∧, Okla., U.S.	184	35.02 N	94.28 W
Sugarloaf Mountain ∧[2]	210	28.39 N	81.44 W
Sugarloaf Peak ∧, Calif., U.S.	270	34.14 N	117.38 W
Sugarloaf Peak ∧, Wash., U.S.	214	47.45 N	120.32 W
Sugarloaf Point ≻, Austl.	156	32.26 S	152.33 E
Sugar Loaf Point ≻, Ont., Can.	274a	42.52 N	79.17 W
Sugarloaf Ridge State Park ♠	216	38.26 N	122.29 W
Sugar Notch	200	41.12 N	75.56 W
Sugar Pine Point State Park ♠	216	39.03 N	120.07 W
Sugartown	275	40.00 N	75.31 W
Suga-shima I	84	34.29 N	136.53 E
Sugauli Bazar	114	26.46 N	84.44 E
Sugbai Passage Ʉ	106	5.22 N	120.33 E
Sugbay	106	7.31 N	123.19 E
Sugbuhan Point ≻	106	10.04 N	126.04 E
Suggi Lake ⊜	174	54.22 N	102.47 W
Suginami ✦[8]	258	35.42 N	139.38 E
Sugita ✦[8]	258	35.23 N	139.38 E
Sugito	84	36.02 N	139.44 E
Şūgla Gölü ⊜	120	37.20 N	32.02 E
Sugnou	75	38.35 N	70.20 E
Sugod	106	12.03 N	124.09 E
Sugoj ≃	64	64.15 N	154.29 E
Šugonovo	72	54.41 N	36.41 E
Šugozero	66	59.55 N	34.12 E
Šugurovo, S.S.S.R.	70	54.31 N	52.06 E
Šugurovo, S.S.S.R.	70	53.26 N	46.29 E
Sugut ≃	102	6.26 N	117.43 E
Suguta ≃	144	2.03 N	36.33 E
Suguti	144	1.44 S	33.39 E
Suhaitu	92	44.50 N	93.39 E
Sūhānak	257d	35.48 N	51.32 E
Şuhār	118	24.22 N	56.45 E
Suheli Par I[1]	112	10.03 N	72.17 E
Suhl	50	50.37 N	10.41 E
Suhl □[5]	50	50.40 N	10.30 E
Suhlendorf	50	52.55 N	10.46 E
Suhopolje	36	45.48 N	17.30 E
Suhr	54	47.22 N	8.05 E
Suhr ≃	54	47.25 N	8.04 E
Suhum	140	6.05 N	0.27 W
Şuhut	120	38.32 N	30.33 E
Sūi	110	28.37 N	69.19 E
Suiá-Missu ≃	240	11.13 S	53.15 W
Suian	90	29.28 N	118.44 E
Suianzhan	79	53.07 N	125.20 E
Suiattle ≃	214	48.20 N	121.33 W
Suichang	90	28.34 N	119.14 E
Suichuan	90	26.26 N	114.32 E
Suid-Afrika → South Africa □[1]	146	30.00 S	26.00 E
Suide	92	37.33 N	110.04 E
Suiding	76	44.03 N	80.49 E
Suido-suigenchi ⊜[1]	260	34.54 N	135.17 E
Suidvaal	148	26.52 S	29.47 E
Suifenhe	79	44.24 N	131.10 E
Suifu, Nihon	84	36.37 N	140.29 E
Suifu → Yibin, Zhg.	97	28.47 N	104.38 E
Suigō-kokutei-kōen ♠	84	36.05 N	140.20 E
Suihua	79	46.37 N	127.00 E
Suijiang	92	28.31 N	104.07 E
Suijiang ≃	90	26.30 N	114.45 E
Sui Kau Island I	261d	22.16 N	114.03 E
Suileng	79	47.18 N	127.10 E
Suining, Zhg.	90	33.54 N	117.56 E
Suining, Zhg.	92	26.21 N	110.00 E
Suining, Zhg.	97	30.31 N	105.34 E
Suipacha	242	34.45 S	59.41 W
Suiping	90	33.10 N	113.57 E
Suippe ≃	46	49.25 N	3.57 E
Suippes	52	49.08 N	4.32 E
Suir ≃	28	52.15 N	7.00 W
Suisse → Switzerland □[1]	54	47.00 N	8.00 E
Suisun Bay C	216	38.06 N	122.00 W
Suisun City	216	38.15 N	122.02 W
Suisun Creek ≃	216	38.12 N	122.06 W
Suita	86	34.45 N	135.32 E
Suitland	274c	38.51 N	76.56 W
Suixi, Zhg.	90	33.56 N	116.46 E
Suixi, Zhg.	92	21.25 N	110.15 E
Suixian	90	31.42 N	113.20 E
Suiyang, Zhg.	79	44.26 N	130.53 E
Suiyang, Zhg.	92	27.56 N	107.18 E
Suiyangdian	90	32.04 N	112.55 E
Suiza → Switzerland □[1]	54	47.00 N	8.00 E
Suize ≃	54	48.08 N	5.08 E
Şuizhong	88	40.20 N	120.19 E
Šuja, S.S.S.R.	24	61.55 N	34.12 E
Šuja, S.S.S.R.	70	56.50 N	41.23 E
Šuja ≃, S.S.S.R.	24	61.54 N	34.15 E
Šuja ≃, S.S.S.R.	70	57.56 N	43.15 E
Sujānagar	116	23.57 N	89.25 E
Sūjāngarh	110	27.42 N	74.28 E
Sujāwal	110	24.36 N	68.05 E
Sujeticha	78	55.57 N	97.49 E
Sujfun ≃	79	43.22 N	131.47 E
Suji	97	29.35 N	103.37 E
Sujiabu	90	31.38 N	116.22 E
Sujiaqiao	95	39.24 N	116.10 E
Sujiatun	94	41.40 N	123.22 E
Sujiawan	97	29.48 N	104.57 E
Sujiawu	95	39.17 N	115.55 E
Şujiazui	90	33.40 N	119.29 E
Šujskoje	66	59.22 N	40.59 E
Sujutkina Kosa, Mys ≻	74	44.13 N	47.15 E
Sukabihanawa	102	9.30 S	124.57 E
Sukabumi	105a	6.55 S	106.56 E
Sukadana, Indon.	102	1.15 S	109.57 E
Sukadana, Indon.	105a	5.05 S	105.33 E
Sukadana, Teluk C	102	1.24 S	109.50 E
Sukagawa	82	37.17 N	140.23 E
Sukamandi	105a	6.20 S	107.39 E
Sukamara	102	2.43 S	111.11 E
Sukanegara	105a	7.06 S	107.07 E
Sukapura	105a	7.52 S	113.03 E
Sukaraja, Indon.	102	2.21 S	110.37 E
Sukaraja, Indon.	105a	7.27 S	108.12 E
Sukaraja, Indon.	105a	7.27 S	109.17 E
Sukarno, Pegunungan → Jaya, Puncak ∧	154	4.05 S	137.11 E
Sukau	102	5.32 N	118.17 E
Sukchar	262b	22.42 N	88.22 E
Sukch'ŏn	88	39.24 N	125.38 E
Sukematsu	260	34.31 N	135.26 E
Sukeva	26	63.52 N	27.26 E
Sukhnah, 'Ayn ▾[4]	132	29.35 N	32.15 E
Sukhothai	100	17.01 N	99.49 E
Sukhumi → Suchumi	74	43.01 N	41.02 E
Sukkertoppen	166	65.25 N	52.53 W
Sukkozero	24	63.11 N	32.18 E
Sukkur	110	27.42 N	68.52 E
Sukkwan Island I	170	55.05 N	132.45 W
Suklāra	116	23.11 N	86.21 E
Sukmanovka	68	51.47 N	41.34 E
Sukodadi	105a	7.06 S	112.19 E
Sukoharjo	105a	7.41 S	110.50 E
Sukovo	72	54.54 N	38.19 E
Sukroml'a	66	56.53 N	34.44 E
Sukses	146	21.01 S	16.52 E
Suksun	76	57.07 N	57.24 E
Sukumo	82	32.56 N	132.44 E
Sukun, Pulau I	105b	8.07 S	122.08 E
Sukunka ≃	172	55.37 N	121.37 W
Sul, Baía do C	242	27.40 S	48.35 W
Sul, Canal do Ʉ	240	0.10 S	49.30 W
Sula I	26	61.08 N	4.55 E
Sula ≃, S.S.S.R.	24	67.16 N	52.07 E
Sula ≃, S.S.S.R.	68	49.40 N	32.41 E
Sula, Kepulauan II	102	1.52 S	125.22 E
Sulaco ≃	226	14.58 N	87.45 W
Sulaimān Khel	113	33.41 N	71.01 E
Sulaimān Range ⋀	110	30.30 N	70.10 E
Sulak, S.S.S.R.	70	51.52 N	48.21 E
Sulak, S.S.S.R.	74	43.16 N	47.32 E
Sulak ≃	74	43.20 N	47.34 E
Sulak, Buchta C	74	43.18 N	47.31 E
Sulakyurt	120	40.10 N	33.44 E
Sulancheer	92	42.42 N	109.22 E
Sulang	105a	6.48 S	111.23 E
Sulat	106	11.49 N	125.27 E
Sulauan Point ≻	106	8.37 N	124.29 E
Sulawesi (Celebes) I	102	2.00 S	121.00 E
Sulawesi Selatan □[4]	102	3.30 S	120.00 E
Sulawesi Tengah □[4]	102	1.00 N	123.00 E
Sulaymān, Birak (Solomon's Pools) ⊥	122	31.41 N	35.10 E
Sulby	42	54.18 N	4.29 W
Sulcis ✦[1]	36	39.05 N	8.45 E
Sūldeh	118	36.34 N	52.01 E
Sulechów	30	52.06 N	15.37 E
Sulęcin	30	52.26 N	15.08 E
Suleja	76	55.09 N	58.50 E
Sulejów	30	51.22 N	19.53 E
Sulejówek	30	52.14 N	21.17 E
Sülemaniye Camii ʊ[1]	257b	41.00 N	28.57 E
Sulen, Mount ∧	154	3.25 S	142.15 E
Süleymanlı	120	37.54 N	36.50 E
Sülfeld	48	53.48 N	10.14 E
Şūlgan	257d	35.49 N	51.15 E
Šul'ginka	73	49.08 N	38.56 E
Şulgino, S.S.S.R.	72	55.50 N	35.55 E
Šul'gino, S.S.S.R.	72	54.33 N	37.35 E
Sulia	144	1.32 S	26.33 E
Suliki	102	0.06 S	100.27 E
Sulima	140	6.58 N	11.35 W
Sulin	73	48.54 N	40.07 E
Sulina	38	45.09 N	29.40 E
Sulina, Braţul ≃[1]	38	45.09 N	29.41 E
Sulingen	48	52.41 N	8.47 E
Sulinskij	73	47.52 N	40.06 E
Sulitelma ∧	24	67.08 N	16.24 E
Sulkava	26	61.47 N	28.23 E
Sullana	238	4.53 S	80.41 W
Sulligent	184	33.54 N	88.08 W
Sullivan, Ill., U.S.	184	39.36 N	88.37 W
Sullivan, Ind., U.S.	184	39.06 N	87.24 W
Sullivan, Mo., U.S.	209	38.13 N	91.10 W
Sullivan, Ohio, U.S.	204	41.02 N	82.13 W
Sullivan, Wis., U.S.	206	43.01 N	88.35 W
Sullivan □[6], N.Y., U.S.	200	41.39 N	74.42 W
Sullivan □[6], Pa., U.S.	200	41.25 N	76.29 W
Sullivan Canyon V	270	34.03 N	118.30 W
Sullivan Creek ≃	216	37.53 N	120.25 W
Sullivan Lake ⊜	172	52.00 N	112.00 W
Sullivanville	200	42.14 N	76.46
Sully-sur-Loire	46	47.46 N	2.22 E
Sulmona	60	42.03 N	13.55 E
Sulot' ≃	72	56.41 N	38.01 E
Sulphur, Yukon, Can.	170	63.47 N	138.53 W
Sulphur, Ind., U.S.	208	38.14 N	86.28 W
Sulphur, Ky., U.S.	208	38.30 N	85.17 W
Sulphur, La., U.S.	184	30.14 N	93.23 W
Sulphur, Okla., U.S.	186	34.31 N	96.58 W
Sulphur ≃, Alta., Can.	172	53.50 N	119.10 W
Sulphur ≃, U.S.	184	33.07 N	93.52 W
Sulphur Creek ≃	188	44.46 N	102.25 W
Sulphur Draw V	186	33.12 N	102.17 W
Sulphur Springs, Ind., U.S.	208	40.00 N	85.27 W
Sulphur Springs, Ohio, U.S.	204	40.52 N	82.53 W
Sulphur Springs, Tex., U.S.	212	33.08 N	95.36 W
Sulphur Springs Draw V	186	32.12 N	101.36 W
Sulsul	134	5.06 N	44.55 E
Sultan	214	47.51 N	121.49 W
Sultan ≃	214	47.52 N	121.49 W
Sultana	216	36.33 N	119.20 W
Sultanahmet Camii ʊ[1]	257b	41.00 N	28.58 E
Sultana Point ≻	158b	35.08 S	137.45 E
Sulţanatābād	257d	35.46 N	51.28 E
Sultançiftlikköy	257b	41.02 N	29.11 E
Sultandağı	120	38.32 N	31.14 E
Sultandağı ∧	120	38.58 N	27.26 E
Sultanhanı	120	38.15 N	33.33 E
Sultanhisar	120	37.53 N	28.10 E
Sultan Mosque ʊ[1]	261c	1.18 N	103.52 E
Sultānpur, Bhārat	113	31.13 N	75.11 E
Sultānpur, Bhārat	114	26.16 N	82.04 E
Sultānpur □[5]	114	26.20 N	82.00 E
Sultānpur Dabās ✦[8]	262a	28.46 N	77.03 E
Sultan sa Barongis	106	6.46 N	124.38 E
Sultan-Saly	73	47.21 N	39.35 E
Sulu	154	5.25 S	151.00 E
Sulu □[4]	106	5.30 N	120.30 E
Suluan Island I	106	10.46 N	125.57 E
Sulu Archipelago II	106	6.00 N	121.00 E
Sulu Basin ✢[1]	12	7.30 N	121.00 E
Suluchi ⊜	114	30.12 N	86.20 E
Sülüklü	120	39.05 N	30.58 E
Sul'ukta	75	39.56 N	69.34 E
Sululta	134	9.10 N	38.48 E
Suluntah	136	32.36 N	21.43 E
Suluova (Suluca)	120	40.47 N	35.42 E
Sulūq	136	31.39 N	20.15 E
Sūlūru	112	13.42 N	80.01 E
Sulusaj	75	38.50 N	67.05 E
Sulusaray	120	40.00 N	36.06 E
Sulu Sea ▾[2]	106	8.00 N	120.00 E
Sulusi	92	33.08 N	95.08 E
Suly	76	53.45 N	66.30 E
Sulz	54	48.18 N	7.51 E
Sulz am Neckar	54	48.21 N	8.37 E
Sulzano	58	45.41 N	10.05 E
Sulzbach, B.R.D.	52	49.18 N	7.07 E
Sulzbach, B.R.D.	52	49.21 N	9.13 E
Sulzbach am Kocher	52	48.58 N	9.50 E
Sulzbach-Rosenberg	30	49.30 N	11.45 E
Sulzberger Bay C	9	77.00 S	152.00 W
Sulzbrunn	54	47.41 N	10.20 E
Sulzburg	54	47.50 N	7.42 E
Sülze	48	52.46 N	10.02 E
Šum, S.S.S.R.	66	59.52 N	31.46 E
Šum, S.S.S.R.	78	54.51 N	95.18 E
Şuma ✦[8]	260	34.39 N	135.08 E
Šum'ači	66	53.52 N	32.25 E
Šumadija ✦[1]	38	44.10 N	20.50 E
Sumalata	102	0.59 N	122.30 E
Sumallo ≃	214	49.14 N	121.05 W
Şumampa	242	29.22 S	63.28 W
Šumanaj	76	42.37 N	59.08 E
Sumangat, Tanjong ≻	102	6.35 N	117.33 E
Sumano-ura (Suma Beach) •[2]	86	34.38 N	135.08 E
Sumano-ura ♠	86	34.38 N	135.08 E
Sūmār	118	33.52 N	45.39 E
Sumarokovo	72	55.46 N	35.55 E
Sumas	192	49.00 N	122.13 W
Sumas ≃	214	49.09 N	122.12 W
Sumatera (Sumatra) I	98	0.05 S	102.00 E
Sumatera Barat □[4]	102	0.30 S	100.30 E
Sumatera Selatan □[4]	102	3.00 S	104.00 E
Sumatera Utara □[4]	104	2.20 N	99.00 E
Sum'atino	72	55.00 N	36.21 E
Sumatou	97	30.28 N	104.03 E
Sumatra → Sumatera I	98	0.05 S	102.00 E
Sumaúma	238	7.50 S	60.02 W
Sumava Resorts	206	41.10 N	87.26 W
Sumayh	130	12.43 N	30.50 E
Sumba I	105b	10.00 S	120.00 E
Sumba, Île I	142	1.44 N	19.32 E
Sumba, Selat Ʉ	105b	9.05 S	120.00 E
Sumbang Point ≻	106	5.50 N	125.11 E
Sumbar ≃	118	38.00 N	55.17 E
Sumbawa I	105b	8.40 S	118.00 E
Sumbawa Besar	105b	8.30 S	117.26 E
Sumbawanga	144	7.58 S	31.37 E
Sumbay	238	15.58 S	71.23 W
Sümber	80	46.21 N	108.25 E
Sumbi Head ≻	165e	7.18 S	157.01 E
Sumbilla	34	43.10 N	1.40 W
Sumbing, Gunung ∧	105a	7.23 S	110.04 E
Sumbu Game Reserve ✦[4]	144	8.50 S	30.25 E
Şumburgh Head ≻	28	59.51 N	1.16 W
Šumbut	70	55.33 N	50.41 E
Sumbuya	140	7.39 N	11.58 W
Sumdo	110	35.01 N	78.41 E
Sumé	240	7.39 S	36.55 W
Sumedang	105a	6.52 S	107.55 E
Şümeg	30	46.59 N	17.17 E
Šumek	76	48.42 N	85.32 E
Šumen	38	43.16 N	26.55 E
Sumène	56	43.59 N	3.43 E
Şumenep	105a	7.01 S	113.52 E
Šumerl'a	70	55.30 N	46.26 E
Sumgait	74	40.36 N	49.38 E
Şumgait ≃	74	40.37 N	49.37 E
Šumicha	76	55.14 N	63.19 E
Sumida ✦[8]	258	35.42 N	139.48 E
Sumida ≃	258	35.40 N	139.47 E
Sumidouro	246	22.03 S	42.41 W
Şumilao	106	8.18 N	124.57 E
Šumilino	66	55.18 N	29.37 E
Šumilinskaja	70	49.58 N	41.26 E
Sumisu-jima I	80	31.27 N	140.03 E
Sumiswald	54	47.02 N	7.45 E
Sumiyoshi ✦[8]	260	34.36 N	135.31 E
Sumki	76	55.03 N	65.44 E
Sumkino	76	58.09 N	68.21 E
Sumlug ≃	106	6.53 N	126.02 E
Summer Bridge	42	54.03 N	1.41 W
Summerdale	198	40.18 N	76.56 W
Summerfield, Fla., U.S.	210	29.00 N	82.02 W
Summerfield, Mo., U.S.	209	38.17 N	91.49 W
Summerfield, N.C., U.S.	182	36.12 N	79.54 W
Summerford, Newf., Can.	176	49.29 N	54.47 W
Summerford, Ohio, U.S.	208	39.55 N	83.29 W
Summerhill, Eire	42	53.29 N	6.44 W
Summerhill, Pa., U.S.	204	40.22 N	78.46 W
Summer Island I	180	45.34 N	86.39 W
Summer Lake ⊜	192	42.50 N	120.45 W
Summerland	172	49.39 N	119.33 W
Summerland Reserve ✦[4]	159	38.31 S	145.10 E
Sümmern	52	51.25 N	7.43 E
Summerseat	252	53.38 N	2.19 W
Summerside	176	46.24 N	63.47 W
Summersville, Mo., U.S.	184	37.11 N	91.40 W
Summersville, W. Va., U.S.	178	38.17 N	80.51 W
Summerton	182	33.36 N	80.20 W
Summerville, Ont., Can.	265b	43.37 N	79.34 W
Summerville, Ga., U.S.	182	34.29 N	85.21 W
Summerville, Pa., U.S.	204	41.07 N	79.11 W
Summerville, S.C., U.S.	182	33.01 N	80.11 W
Summit, Eng., U.K.	252	53.40 N	2.05 W
Summit, Alaska, U.S.	170	63.20 N	149.08 W
Summit, Calif., U.S.	218	34.20 N	117.25 W
Summit, Ill., U.S.	206	41.47 N	87.48 W
Summit, Miss., U.S.	184	31.17 N	90.28 W
Summit, N.J., U.S.	200	40.43 N	74.22 W
Summit, N.Y., U.S.	200	42.35 N	74.35 W
Summit, S. Dak., U.S.	188	45.18 N	97.02 W
Summit, Wash., U.S.	214	47.10 N	122.21 W
Summit □[6]	204	41.05 N	81.31 W
Summit Creek ≃	214	46.00 N	121.10 W
Summit Hill	200	40.50 N	75.53 W
Summit Lake	172	54.17 N	122.38 W
Summit Lake ⊜	214	47.04 N	123.07 W
Summit Mountain ∧	194	39.23 N	116.28 W
Summit Park	266	41.09 N	74.03 W
Summit Peak ∧	190	37.21 N	106.42 W
Summit Rock ∧	162	45.25 S	170.04 E
Summit Station	198	40.34 N	76.12 W
Summitville, Ind., U.S.	206	40.20 N	85.39 W
Summitville, N.Y., U.S.	200	41.37 N	74.27 W
Summitville, Ohio, U.S.	204	40.41 N	80.53 W
Summt	254a	52.41 N	13.22 E
Summter See ⊜	254a	52.42 N	13.23 E
Sumnal	110	35.45 N	78.40 E
Sumner, Iowa, U.S.	180	42.51 N	92.06 W
Sumner, Miss., U.S.	184	33.58 N	90.22 W
Sumner, Wash., U.S.	214	47.12 N	122.14 W
Sumner, Lake ⊜	162	42.42 S	172.13 E
Sumner, Lake ⊜[1]	186	34.38 N	104.25 W
Sumner Strait Ʉ	170	56.15 N	133.45 W
Sumoto	86	34.21 N	134.54 E
Şumpangbinangae	102	4.24 S	119.36 E
Šumperk	30	49.58 N	16.58 E
Sumpiuh	105a	7.37 S	109.21 E
Sumprabum	100	26.33 N	97.34 E
Sumpter	271	42.10 N	83.29 W
Sumrall	184	31.25 N	89.33 W
Sumsar	75	41.18 N	71.19 E
Ş'umsi	70	57.07 N	51.37 E
Šumskij	78	54.48 N	99.09 E
Şumskij Posad	24	64.15 N	35.25 E
Šumskoje	68	50.07 N	26.07 E
Šumšu, Ostrov I	64	50.45 N	156.20 E
Sumter	182	33.55 N	80.20 W
Sumter □[6]	210	28.38 N	82.08 W
Sumuştā al-Waqf	132	28.55 N	30.51 E
Sumy, S.S.S.R.	68	50.55 N	34.45 E
Sumy, S.S.S.R.	76	54.48 N	80.26 E
Sumy □[4]	66	52.10 N	33.40 E
S'un' ≃, S.S.S.R.	76	55.43 N	54.17 E
Sun ≃, Mont., U.S.	192	48.29 N	111.55 W
Suna, Kenya	144	1.05 S	34.26 E
Suna, S.S.S.R.	70	57.51 N	50.05 E
Suna ≃	24	62.08 N	34.12 E
Sunagawa	82a	43.29 N	141.55 E
Sun al-Heteimi ▾[4]	122	31.05 N	34.00 E
Sun' al-Menī'i ▾[4]	122	31.07 N	34.12 E
Sunām	113	30.08 N	75.48 E
Sunāmganj	110	25.04 N	91.24 E
Sunami	84	35.25 N	136.40 E
Sunan	88	39.13 N	125.41 E
Sunapee Lake ⊜	178	43.23 N	72.03 W
Sunashinden	258	35.53 N	139.30 E
Sunaysilah ⊜	118	35.35 N	41.53 E
Sunbāṭ	132	30.48 N	31.12 E
Sunbright	182	36.15 N	84.40 W
Sunburst	192	48.53 N	111.55 W
Sunbury, Austl.	159	37.35 S	144.44 E
Sunbury, Eng., U.K.	250	51.25 N	0.26 W
Sunbury, N.C., U.S.	182	36.27 N	76.37 W
Sunbury, Ohio, U.S.	204	40.14 N	82.52 W
Sunbury, Pa., U.S.	200	40.52 N	76.47 W
Sunchales	242	30.56 S	61.34 W
Sunch'ang	88	35.23 N	127.07 E
Sunchild Indian Reserve ✦[4]	172	52.43 N	115.24 W
Suncho Corral	242	27.56 S	63.27 W
Sunch'ŏn, C.M.I.K.	88	39.26 N	125.54 E
Sunch'ŏn, Taehan	88	34.57 N	127.28 E
Sun City, Ariz., U.S.	190	33.36 N	112.17 W
Sun City, Calif., U.S.	218	33.42 N	117.11 W
Sun City, Fla., U.S.	210	27.41 N	82.28 W
Sun City Center	210	27.43 N	82.21 W
Suncook	178	43.08 N	71.27 W
Suncook ≃	178	43.08 N	71.28 W
Sunda, Selat (Sunda Strait) Ʉ	102	6.00 S	105.45 E
Sundance	188	44.24 N	104.23 W
Sundar	102	4.54 N	115.12 E
Sundar ∧	114	28.26 N	84.20 E
Sundarbans ✦[1]	116	22.00 N	89.00 E
Sundargarh	114	22.07 N	84.02 E
Sundargarh □[5]	114	22.18 N	84.30 E
Sundarnagar	113	31.32 N	76.53 E
Sunda Strait → Sunda, Selat Ʉ	102	6.00 S	105.45 E
Sundby, Dan.	41	54.42 N	11.48 E
Sundby, Sve.	40	59.23 N	17.03 E
Sundbyberg	40	59.22 N	17.58 E
Sundbyholm	40	59.27 N	16.37 E
Sundbyholms slott ⊥	40	59.27 N	16.37 E
Sunde	26	59.50 N	5.43 E
Sunderland, Ont., Can.	202	44.16 N	79.04 W
Sunderland, Eng., U.K.	42	54.55 N	1.23 W
Sunderland, Mass., U.S.	197	42.28 N	72.35 W
Sunderland, Vt., U.S.	200	43.08 N	73.08 W
Sundern	52	51.20 N	8.00 E
Sünderup	41	54.46 N	9.27 E
Sundhausen	50	50.56 N	10.40 E
Sundhouse	54	48.15 N	7.36 E
Sundi-Lutete	142	4.34 S	14.14 E
Sundown, Austl.	152	26.14 S	133.12 E
Sundown, N.Y., U.S.	200	41.53 N	74.28 W
Sundown, Tex., U.S.	186	33.27 N	102.29 W
Sundra	263d	26.11 S	28.33 E
Sundre	172	51.48 N	114.38 W
Sundridge, Ont., Can.	180	45.46 N	79.24 W
Sundridge, Eng., U.K.	250	51.17 N	0.18 E
Sunds	41	56.12 N	9.01 E
Sundsbruk	26	62.27 N	17.22 E
Sundsvall	26	62.23 N	17.18 E
Sundwig	253	51.23 N	7.47 E
Suneori	258	35.56 N	139.24 E
Sunfield	206	42.45 N	85.00 W
Sunfish Creek ≃	208	39.01 N	83.03 W
Sunflower	184	33.33 N	90.32 W
Sunflower, Mount ∧	188	39.04 N	102.01 W
Sungaianyar	102	2.55 S	116.18 E
Sungaibamban	104	3.26 N	99.09 E
Sungaibatu	102	0.48 N	110.45 E
Sungai Bayor	104	5.15 N	100.47 E
Sungaibuntu	102	6.03 S	107.24 E
Sungaidareh	102	0.58 S	101.30 E
Sungaigerong	102	2.59 S	104.52 E

Symbol	English	Deutsch	Español	Français	Português
≃	River	Fluss	Río	Rivière	Rio
☰	Canal	Kanal	Canal	Canal	Canal
V	Waterfall, Rapids	Wasserfall, Stromschnellen	Cascada, Rápidos	Chute d'eau, Rapides	Cascata, Rápidos
Ʉ	Strait	Meeresstrasse	Estrecho	Détroit	Estreito
C	Bay, Gulf	Bucht, Golf	Bahía, Golfo	Baie, Golfe	Baía, Golfo
⊜	Lake, Lakes	See, Seen	Lago, Lagos	Lac, Lacs	Lago, Lagos
☷	Swamp	Sumpf	Pantano	Marais	Pântano
⊼	Ice Features, Glacier	Eis- und Gletscherformen	Accidentes Glaciales	Formes glaciaires	Acidentes Glaciares
▾	Other Hydrographic Features	Andere Hydrographische Objekte	Otros Elementos Hidrográficos	Autres données hydrographiques	Outros Elementos Hidrográficos
✢	Submarine Features	Untermeerische Objekte	Accidentes Submarinos	Formes de relief sous-marin	Acidentes Submarinos
□	Political Unit	Politische Einheit	Unidad Politica	Entité politique	Unidade Política
ʊ	Cultural Institution	Kulturelle Institution	Institución Cultural	Institution culturelle	Instituição Cultural
⊥	Historical Site	Historische Stätte	Sitio Histórico	Site historique	Sitio Histórico
♠	Recreational Site	Erholungs- und Ferienort	Sitio de Recreo	Centre de loisirs	Sítio de Lazer
⊠	Airport	Flughafen	Aeropuerto	Aéroport	Aeroporto
■	Military Installation	Militäranlage	Instalación Militar	Installation militaire	Instalação Militar
✦	Miscellaneous	Verschiedenes	Misceláneo	Divers	Miscelânea

ENGLISH — DEUTSCH

Name	Page / Seite	Lat. / Breite °′	Long. / Länge °′ E=Ost
Sungaiguntung	102	0.18 N	103.37 E
Sungaikakap	102	0.04 S	109.10 E
Sungai Kolok	104	6.02 N	101.58 E
Sungailangsat	102	0.52 S	101.18 E
Sungai Lembing	104	3.55 N	103.02 E
Sungailiat	102	1.51 S	106.08 E
Sungailimau	102	0.31 S	100.03 E
Sungaimanasip	104	1.49 N	100.54 E
Sungainipah	104	0.57 N	98.57 E
Sungaipenuh	102	2.05 S	101.23 E
Sungaipenyu	102	0.16 N	109.04 E
Sungai Petani	104	5.39 N	100.30 E
Sungaipinang	102	0.48 S	114.04 E
Sungairampah	104	3.29 N	99.09 E
Sungairotan, Indon.	102	3.06 S	104.18 E
Sungairotan, Indon.	102	1.39 S	102.51 E
Sungaisalak	102	0.27 S	102.59 E
Sungaiselan	102	2.24 S	105.59 E
Sungai Siput	104	4.49 N	101.04 E
Sungaitampang	104	2.20 N	100.07 E
Sungaitiram	102	0.47 S	117.12 E
Šungaj	70	48.32 N	46.46 E
Sungari → Songhuajiang ≃	79	47.44 N	132.32 E
Sungchiang → Songjiang	96	31.01 N	121.14 E
Sungezhuang	95	40.15 N	116.39 E
Sungguminasa	102	5.12 S	119.27 E
Sungi ≃	105b	8.38 S	115.06 E
Sungi Point ≻	106	10.55 N	125.50 E
Sungkai	104	4.00 N	101.19 E
Sung Noen	100	14.54 N	101.50 E
Sungsang	102	2.22 S	104.56 E
Sungurlu	120	40.10 N	34.23 E
Sunharon Roads C	164n	14.57 N	145.36 E
Sunhezhen	95	40.03 N	116.31 E
Suning	88	38.25 N	115.50 E
Suniteyouqi	92	42.32 N	112.58 E
Sunitezouqi (Beilemiao)	92	43.57 N	113.52 E
Sunjiabu	96	30.55 N	118.54 E
Sunjiadizi	94	42.09 N	124.09 E
Sunjiagou	94	40.45 N	120.39 E
Sunjiajiang	95	40.10 N	115.32 E
Sunjiakanzi	94	40.42 N	123.02 E
Sunjiatai	94	42.32 N	124.01 E
Sunjiawan	94	41.59 N	121.42 E
Sunjiazhai	96	30.55 N	121.52 E
Sunjikāy	130	12.20 N	29.46 E
Sunkar, Gora ∧	76	44.15 N	73.50 E
Sun Kosi ≃	114	26.55 N	87.09 E
Sunland ◆[8]	270	34.16 N	118.19 W
Sunland Park	190	32.15 N	106.45 W
Sunlight Creek ≃	192	44.47 N	109.23 W
Sunlongwan	94	41.19 N	122.57 E
Sunman	208	39.14 N	85.06 W
Sunnansjö	40	60.13 N	14.57 E
Sunndalsøra	26	62.40 N	8.33 E
Sunne	26	59.50 N	13.09 E
Sunnemo	40	59.53 N	13.43 E
Sunnersta	40	59.48 N	17.39 E
Sunnī, Khawr V	130	7.09 N	28.41 E
Sunningdale	250	51.24 N	0.38 W
Sunninghill	44	51.25 N	0.40 W
Sunnybrae	176	45.24 N	62.30 W
Sunny Corner	160	33.23 S	149.53 E
Sunny Crest	268	41.33 N	87.42 W
Sunnydale	214	47.28 N	122.20 W
Sunnyland	210	27.17 N	82.29 W
Sunnylvsfjorden C[2]	26	62.17 N	7.01 E
Sunnymead	218	33.56 N	117.15 W
Sunnynook	172	51.17 N	111.40 W
Sunnyridge	263d	26.10 S	28.11 E
Sunnyside, Newf., Can.	176	47.51 N	53.55 W
Sunnyside, Calif., U.S.	216	32.40 N	117.01 W
Sunny Side, Tex., U.S.	212	29.54 N	96.04 W
Sunnyside, Utah, U.S.	190	39.33 N	110.24 W
Sunnyside, Wash., U.S.	192	46.20 N	120.00 W
Sunnyside ⊥	266	41.03 N	73.52 W
Sunnyslope, Alta., Can.	172	51.40 N	113.32 W
Sunnyslope, Wash., U.S.	214	47.30 N	122.44 W
Sunnyvale, Calif., U.S.	216	37.23 N	122.01 W
Sunnyvale, Tex., U.S.	212	32.48 N	96.33 W
Suno ≃	236	0.42 S	77.08 W
Sunol	272	37.36 N	121.53 W
Sunol Ridge ∧	272	37.38 N	121.56 W
Sun Prairie	206	43.11 N	89.13 W
Sunray	186	36.01 N	101.49 W
Sunrise, Fla., U.S.	210	26.08 N	80.14 W
Sunrise, Ky., U.S.	208	38.33 N	84.14 W
Sunrise, Tex., U.S.	212	31.17 N	96.53 W
Sunrise, Wyo., U.S.	190	42.20 N	104.42 W
Sunrise Heights	206	42.18 N	85.09 W
Sunrise Mall ◆[9]	266	40.41 N	73.26 W
Sunrise Peak ∧	214	46.20 N	121.46 W
Sunsas, Serranía de ∧∧	238	17.57 S	59.35 W
Sunset, La., U.S.	184	30.25 N	92.04 W
Sunset, Tex., U.S.	186	33.27 N	97.46 W
Sunset ◆[8]	272	37.45 N	122.30 W
Sunset Bay	204	42.11 N	79.24 W
Sunset Beach, Calif., U.S.	270	33.43 N	118.04 W
Sunset Beach, Haw., U.S.	219c	21.40 N	158.03 W
Sunset Crater National Monument ♠	190	35.18 N	111.21 W
Sunset Hill	266	40.26 N	74.35 W
Sunset Hills	269b	40.35 N	80.15 W
Sunset Peak ∧	270	34.13 N	117.42 W
Sunset Prairie	172	55.50 N	120.48 W
Sunset Trailer Park	268	42.06 N	87.48 W
Sunset Valley	204	40.18 N	79.44 W
Sunshine, Austl.	159	37.47 S	144.50 E
Sunshine, Alaska, U.S.	170	62.10 N	150.04 W
Sunshine Point ≻	271	42.36 N	82.47 W
Sunshine Skyway Bridge ◆[5]	210	27.37 N	82.39 W
Suntai ≃	136	8.05 N	10.04 E
Suntar	64	62.10 N	117.40 E
Suntar-Chajata, Chrebet ∧∧	64	62.00 N	143.00 E
Suntaug Lake @	273	42.32 N	71.00 W
Süntel ∧∧	48	52.12 N	9.25 E
Sunter ◆[8]	259e	6.09 S	106.5. E
Sunter, Kali ≍	259e	6.07 S	106.50 E
Sunti ≃	262b	22.37 N	88.34 E
Suntrana	170	63.51 N	148.51 W
Suntsar	118	25.31 N	62.00 E
Sun Valley, Idaho, U.S.	192	43.42 N	114.21 W
Sun Valley, Nev., U.S.	216	39.34 N	119.47 W
Sun Valley ◆[8]	270	34.14 N	118.21 W
SunValley Center ◆[9]	272	37.58 N	122.03 W
Sunview	212	32.48 N	94.38 W
Sun Village	218	34.35 N	118.03 W
Sunwapta ≃	172	52.32 N	117.41 W
Sunwu	79	49.27 N	127.20 E
Sunwui → Jiangmen	90	22.35 N	113.05 E
Sunxi ≃	97	29.13 N	106.21 E
Sunyani	140	7.20 N	2.20 W
Sunying	88	34.30 N	114.21 E
Sunža ≃	74	43.26 N	46.08 E
Sunženskij Chrebet ∧∧	74	43.21 N	45.00 E
Sunzhongshanling (Tomb of Sun Yat Sen) ⊥	96	32.10 N	118.56 E
Suoche (Yarkand)	110	38.25 N	77.16 E
Suoguohu @	92	42.18 N	101.08 E
Suojarvi	24	62.05 N	32.21 E
Suolahti	26	62.34 N	25.52 E
Suolun	79	46.36 N	121.13 E
Suolunqi (Nantun)	79	49.07 N	119.40 E
Suomenlahti → Finland, Gulf of C	66	60.00 N	27.00 E
Suomenselkä ∧	26	63.59 N	27.00 E
Suomi → Finland □[1]	24	64.00 N	26.00 E
Suomussalmi	26	64.53 N	29.05 E
Suō-nada ⊤[2]	86	33.50 N	131.30 E
Suonenjoki	26	62.37 N	27.08 E
Suonne @	26	61.40 N	26.30 E
Suordach	64	66.43 N	132.04 E
Suoshu	96	31.57 N	119.00 E
Suoxian	110	31.50 N	93.45 E
Supamo ≃	236	6.48 N	61.50 W
Supaul	114	26.07 N	86.36 E
Supe	134	8.37 N	35.38 E
Superbe ≃	46	48.35 N	3.53 E
Superga, Basilica di ✝[1]	56	45.05 N	7.46 E
Superior, Ariz., U.S.	190	33.18 N	111.06 W
Superior, Mont., U.S.	192	47.12 N	114.53 W
Superior, Nebr., U.S.	188	40.01 N	98.04 W
Superior, Wis., U.S.	180	46.44 N	92.05 W
Superior, Laguna C	224	16.20 N	94.55 W
Superior, Lake @	180	48.00 N	88.00 W
Superior Lake @	218	35.15 N	117.02 W
Superior Upland ∧∧[1]	180	46.00 N	90.30 W
Superior Valley V	218	35.16 N	117.00 W
Supetar	36	43.23 N	16.33 E
Suphan Buri	100	14.28 N	100.07 E
Suphan Buri ≃	100	13.29 N	100.17 E
Süphan Dağı ∧	74	38.54 N	42.48 E
Supino	60	41.37 N	13.14 E
Sūpkhār	114	22.12 N	80.56 E
Supoj ≃	68	49.38 N	31.48 E
Suponevo	66	53.12 N	34.18 E
Supoqiao	97	30.40 N	103.59 E
Süpplingen	50	52.14 N	10.54 E
Supraśl	30	53.13 N	23.20 E
Supraśl ≃	30	53.04 N	22.56 E
Sup'ung	88	40.27 N	124.57 E
Sup'ung-chŏsuji @[1]	88	40.30 N	125.05 E
Supur	116	23.01 N	86.52 E
Sūq ash-Shuyūkh	118	30.53 N	46.28 E
Suq'at al-Jamal	130	12.48 N	27.42 E
Suqian	90	33.59 N	118.18 E
Suqiao, Zhg.	90	34.08 N	113.47 E
Suqiao, Zhg.	95	39.03 N	116.29 E
Sūq Suwayq	118	24.23 N	38.27 E
Suquamish	214	47.44 N	122.33 W
Suquṭrā I	108	12.30 N	54.00 E
Ṣūr (Tyre), Lubnān	122	33.16 N	35.11 E
Ṣūr, 'Umān	108	22.35 N	59.31 E
Sur □[4]	138	23.40 N	14.15 W
Sur, Cabo ≻	164z	27.12 S	109.26 W
Sur, Point ≻	216	36.18 N	121.54 W
Sur, Punta ≻	242	36.52 S	56.40 W
Sura	70	53.53 N	45.45 E
Sura ◆[8]	262b	22.33 N	88.25 E
Sura ≃	70	56.06 N	46.00 E
Sura, Ras ≻	134	11.10 N	47.32 E
Şūrāb, Pāk.	110	28.29 N	66.16 E
Šurab, S.S.S.R.	75	40.03 N	70.33 E
Surabaya	105a	7.15 S	112.45 E
Şurad	132	30.59 N	30.54 E
Surag-san ∧	261b	37.42 N	127.04 E
Surahammar	40	59.43 N	16.13 E
Sūrak	118	25.43 N	58.48 E
Surakarta	105a	7.35 S	110.50 E
Suramana	102	0.50 S	119.33 E
Surami	74	42.01 N	43.34 E
Suramskij Chrebet ∧∧	74	42.12 N	43.36 E
Şūrān, Īrān	118	27.18 N	62.04 E
Šuran, S.S.S.R.	70	55.22 N	49.50 E
Şūrān, Sūrīy.	120	36.34 N	37.13 E
Şūrān, Sūrīy.	120	35.17 N	36.45 E
Şuran ≃	54	46.02 N	5.19 E
Šurany	30	48.06 N	18.14 E
Surat, Austl.	156	27.09 S	149.04 E
Surat, Bhārat	110	21.10 N	72.50 E
Sūratgarh	113	29.19 N	73.54 E
Surat Thani (Ban Don)	100	9.08 N	99.19 E
Surava	70	52.57 N	41.18 E
Suraž, Pol.	30	52.58 N	22.58 E
Suraž, S.S.S.R.	66	53.01 N	32.24 E
Suraž, S.S.S.R.	66	55.25 N	30.44 E
Surbiton ◆[8]	250	51.24 N	0.18 W
Surbourg	52	48.55 N	7.51 E
Surchan	70	46.39 N	49.38 E
Surchandarja ≃	75	37.58 N	67.50 E
Surchandarjinskaja Oblast' □[4]	75	38.00 N	67.30 E
Surchdara	75	38.37 N	69.55 E
Şurchob ≃	75	38.53 N	70.03 E
Šurči	75	37.59 N	67.47 E
Surco	276d	12.09 S	77.01 W
Surdulești	38	44.23 N	24.57 E
Surdulica	38	42.41 N	22.10 E
Şûre (Sauer) ≃	52	49.44 N	6.31 E
Šureksor, Ozero @	76	52.16 N	75.50 E
Surendorf	41	54.28 N	10.04 E
Surendranagar	110	22.42 N	71.41 E
Suresnes	251	48.52 N	2.14 E
Suretamati, Mount ∧	165f	13.47 S	167.29 E
Suretka	226	9.34 N	82.56 W
Surf City	198	39.40 N	74.10 W
Surfers Paradise	161a	28.00 S	153.26 E
Surfside, Fla., U.S.	**210**	**25.53 N**	**80.07 W**
Surfside, Fla., U.S.	**212**	**28.57 N**	**95.17 W**
Surgeres	32	46.07 N	0.45 W
Surgidero	230p	22.41 N	82.18 W
Surgoinsville	182	36.27 N	82.59 W
Sürgü	120	38.01 N	37.59 E
Sürgücü	120	37.35 N	40.44 E
Surguja □[5]	114	23.15 N	83.00 E
Surgut, S.S.S.R.	64	61.14 N	73.20 E
Surgut, S.S.S.R.	70	53.55 N	51.14 E
Surhuisterveen	48	53.10 N	6.10 E
Sūri (Bīrbhūm), Bhārat	116	23.55 N	87.32 E
Suri, Pap. N. Gui.	154	7.10 S	143.55 E
Suria	262b	22.51 N	88.33 E
Suriāpet	112	17.09 N	79.37 E
Suribachi-yama ∧[2]	164f	24.45 N	141.17 E
Suribao ≃	106	11.33 N	125.28 E
Surigao	106	9.45 N	125.30 E
Surigao del Norte □[4]	106	9.35 N	125.36 E
Surigao del Sur □[4]	106	9.00 N	126.00 E
Surigao Strait Ⴎ	106	10.15 N	125.23 E
Surin	100	14.53 N	103.29 E
Suriname □[1]	**232**		
	240	**4.00 N**	**56.00 W**
Suriname □[5]	240	5.40 N	54.58 W
Šurinda	78	55.13 N	113.23 E
Suring	180	44.59 N	88.22 W
Surkh Hisār	257d	35.43 N	51.33 E
Surkole	134	10.25 N	34.38 E
S'urkum	79	50.08 N	140.31 E
S'urkum, Mys ≻	79	50.05 N	140.41 E
Šurma	70	56.58 N	50.21 E
Sūrmaq	118	31.03 N	52.48 E
Surmelin ≃	46	49.04 N	3.13 E
Surnadalsøra	26	62.59 N	8.39 E
Surodadi	105a	6.53 S	109.15 E
Surovaticha	70	55.45 N	43.56 E
Surovikino	70	48.36 N	42.51 E
Surovo	78	55.37 N	105.36 E
Surprise	190	33.38 N	112.20 W
Surprise, Lake @	212	29.33 N	94.41 W
Surprise Valley V	194	41.35 N	120.05 W
Surquillo	276d	12.07 S	77.02 W
Surrency	182	31.44 N	82.12 W
Surrey □[6]	44	51.10 N	0.20 W
Surrey Heath □[8]	250	51.23 N	0.35 W
Surry	198	37.08 N	76.50 W
Surry □[6]	198	37.10 N	76.50 W
Sursee	54	47.10 N	8.06 E
Sursés V	54	46.34 N	9.38 E
Sursk	70	53.04 N	45.42 E
Surskij Majdan	70	55.01 N	46.32 E
Surskoje	70	54.30 N	46.44 E
Surt, Khalīj (Gulf of Sidra) C	136	31.30 N	18.00 E
Surtanāhu	110	26.22 N	70.00 E
Surte	26	57.49 N	12.01 E
Surtsey I	24a	63.16 N	20.32 W
Suru	154	6.50 S	144.45 E
Suru ≃	113	34.45 N	76.12 E
Surubim ≃	240	11.15 S	48.27 W
Surubiú ≃	240	3.58 S	48.52 W
Sürüç	120	36.58 N	38.24 E
Surud Ad ∧	134	10.41 N	47.18 E
Suruga-wan C	84	34.51 N	138.33 E
Suruí	246	22.40 S	43.07 W
Suruí ≃	277a	22.42 S	43.07 W
Surulangun	102	2.37 S	102.45 E
Suru-Lere ◆[8]	263a	6.31 N	3.22 E
Surumu ≃	236	3.22 N	60.19 W
Surveyor Point ≻	158b	34.47 S	137.51 E
Survey Pass)(	170	67.51 N	154.06 W
Survilliers	251	49.06 N	2.33 E
Surwold	48	53.00 N	7.30 E
Şury-le-Comtal	56	45.32 N	4.10 E
Šuryškary	64	65.54 N	65.22 E
Susa, It.	56	45.08 N	7.03 E
Susa, Nihon	86	34.37 N	131.36 E
Suså ≃	41	55.11 N	11.46 E
Susa, Valle di V	56	45.09 N	7.10 E
Susak, Otok I	36	44.31 N	14.18 E
Susaki	86	33.22 N	133.17 E
Susami	86	33.33 N	135.30 E
Susamyr	75	42.09 N	73.58 E
Susamyr ≃	75	42.08 N	74.03 E
Susamyrtau, Chrebet ∧∧	75	42.08 N	73.15 E
Susan	198	37.22 N	76.19 W
Susan ≃	194	40.19 N	120.17 W
Susan, Port C	214	48.10 N	122.25 W
Susana Knolls	218	34.16 N	118.41 W
Sūsangerd	118	31.34 N	48.11 E
Susanino, S.S.S.R.	66	59.30 N	30.22 E
Susanino, S.S.S.R.	70	58.09 N	41.36 E
Susanino, S.S.S.R.	79	52.47 N	140.06 E
Susanville	194	40.25 N	120.39 W
Šušary	255a	59.48 N	30.23 E
Susch	54	46.46 N	10.04 E
Susegana	58	45.51 N	12.15 E
Suşehri	120	40.11 N	38.06 E
Süsel	50	54.04 N	10.43 E
Šušenskoje	76	53.19 N	91.58 E
Sušice	30	49.14 N	13.32 E
Susitna	170	61.33 N	150.31 W
Susitna ≃	170	61.16 N	150.30 W
Susleny	68	47.25 N	28.59 E
Suslonger	70	56.18 N	48.13 E
Sušn'aki Pervoje	76	57.53 N	88.47 E
Susobana ≃	84	36.37 N	138.11 E
Susoh	104	3.43 N	96.50 E
Susong	90	30.09 N	116.06 E
Susono	84	35.09 N	138.54 E
Suspiro del Moro, Puerto)(	34	37.04 N	3.39 W
Susquehanna	200	41.57 N	75.36 W
Susquehanna ≃	178	39.33 N	76.05 W
Susquehanna, West Branch ≃	200	40.53 N	76.47 W
Susquehanna State Park ♠	198	39.36 N	76.09 W
Susques	242	23.25 S	66.29 W
Sussa ≃	142	7.22 S	17.05 E
Süssen	52	48.41 N	9.45 E
Süssenbrunn ◆[8]	254b	48.17 N	16.30 E
Süsser See @	50	51.30 N	11.40 E
Sussex, N.B., Can.	176	45.43 N	65.31 W
Sussex, N.J., U.S.	200	41.13 N	74.36 W
Sussex, Va., U.S.	198	36.55 N	77.17 W
Sussex, Wis., U.S.	206	43.08 N	88.13 W
Sussex □[6], Del., U.S.	198	38.42 N	75.23 W
Sussex □[6], N.J., U.S.	200	41.08 N	74.41 W
Sussex □[6], Va., U.S.	198	36.50 N	77.15 W
Sussex, East □[6]	44	50.55 N	0.15 E
Sussex, Vale of V	44	50.57 N	0.17 W
Sussex Inlet	160	35.11 S	150.36 E
Sussey	46	47.13 N	4.22 E
Sustenhorn ∧	54	46.42 N	8.28 E
Susten Pass)(	54	46.44 N	8.27 E
Şusteren	48	51.04 N	5.51 E
Šustikovo	72	55.17 N	35.59 E
Susu	164m	26.47 N	128.19 E
Susubona	165e	8.18 S	159.27 E
Susui	102	4.56 N	116.41 E
Susuman	64	62.47 N	148.10 E
Susurluk	120	39.54 N	28.10 E
Şusuzmüsellim	120	41.06 N	27.03 E
Šušvė ≃	66	55.10 N	23.49 E
Susz	30	53.44 N	19.20 E
Sutāhāta	116	22.06 N	88.07 E
Sutak	113	33.12 N	77.28 E
Sutama	84	35.47 N	138.25 E
Sut-Chol'	76	51.24 N	91.17 E
Sütçüler	120	37.30 N	30.59 E
Sutersville	204	40.14 N	79.48 W
Suthat, Wat ✝[1]	259a	13.45 N	100.30 E
Sutherland, Austl.	160	34.02 S	151.04 E
Sutherland, S. Afr.	148	32.24 S	20.40 E
Sutherland, Iowa, U.S.	188	42.58 N	95.29 W
Sutherland, Nebr., U.S.	188	41.10 N	101.08 W
Sutherland ≃	172	54.29 N	125.05 W
Sutherland, Lake @	214	48.05 N	123.42 W
Sutherlands	158b	34.10 S	139.13 E
Sutherlin	192	43.25 N	123.19 W
Suthiāna	262a	28.31 N	77.26 E
Sutlej (Satluj) (Langchuhe) ≃	110	29.23 N	71.02 E
Sutri	60	42.14 N	12.13 E
Sutrio	58	46.31 N	12.59 E
Sütschou → Xuzhou, Zhg.	88	34.16 N	117.11 E
Sutschou → Suzhou, Zhg.	96	31.18 N	120.37 E
Sutter	216	39.10 N	121.45 W
Sutter □[6]	216	39.08 N	121.37 W
Sutter Buttes ∧	216	39.12 N	121.50 W
Sutter Bypass ≃	216	38.47 N	121.38 W
Sutter Creek	216	38.23 N	120.48 W
Sutter Creek ≃	216	38.22 N	120.59 W
Sutton, Austl.	161b	35.10 S	149.15 E
Sutton, Qué., Can.	196	45.06 N	72.37 W
Sutton, Eng., U.K.	44	52.23 N	0.07 E
Sutton, Eng., U.K.	250	51.12 N	0.26 W
Sutton, Alaska, U.S.	170	61.43 N	148.53 W
Sutton, Mass., U.S.	197	42.09 N	71.45 W
Sutton, Nebr., U.S.	188	40.36 N	97.52 W
Sutton, W. Va., U.S.	178	38.40 N	80.43 W
Sutton ◆[8]	44	51.22 N	0.12 W
Sutton-at-Hone	250	51.25 N	0.14 E
Sutton Bridge	44	52.46 N	0.12 E
Sutton Coldfield	44	52.34 N	1.48 W
Sutton Courtenay	44	51.39 N	1.17 W
Sutton Forest	160	34.35 S	150.19 E
Sutton-in-Ashfield	44	53.08 N	1.15 W
Sutton Lake @[1]	178	38.40 N	80.40 W
Sutton Lane Ends	252	53.14 N	2.06 W
Sutton Leach	252	53.26 N	2.42 W
Sutton Mountains ∧∧	196	45.05 N	72.30 W
Sutton-on-Sea	42	53.19 N	0.17 E
Sutton on Trent	44	53.10 N	0.49 W
Sutton Park	266	40.49 N	74.42 W
Sutton Place ⊥	250	51.16 N	0.33 W
Suttons Bay	180	44.59 N	85.39 W
Sutton Scotney	44	51.10 N	1.21 W
Sutton Valence	44	51.12 N	0.36 E
Sutton Veny	44	51.11 N	2.08 W
Sutton Weaver	252	53.18 N	2.41 W
Sutton West	202	44.18 N	79.22 W
Suttor ≃	156	21.25 S	147.45 E
Suttrop	52	51.27 N	8.22 E
Suttsu	82a	42.48 N	140.14 E
Sutwik Island I	170	56.34 N	157.05 W
Suunduk ≃	76	51.46 N	58.46 E
Suurbekom	263d	26.19 S	27.44 E
Suurberge ∧∧	148	33.18 S	25.32 E
Suurbraak	148	34.00 S	20.39 E
Suure-Jaani	66	58.33 N	25.28 E
Suur Pakri I	66	59.20 N	23.55 E
Suur Väin Ⴎ	66	58.28 N	23.27 E
Suva	165g	18.08 S	178.25 E
Suvainiškis	66	56.10 N	25.17 E
Šuvalovo Oz'orki ◆[8]	255a	60.02 N	30.18 E
Suva Planina ∧∧	38	43.10 N	22.10 E
Suvarlı	120	37.32 N	37.38 E
Suvasvesi @	26	62.39 N	28.12 E
Suvel'an	74	40.30 N	50.09 E
Suvereto	60	43.05 N	10.40 E
Suvo	78	53.39 N	110.00 E
Suvorka	78	56.33 N	103.24 E
Suvorov	72	54.07 N	36.30 E
Suvorovo, S.S.S.R.	68	45.34 N	28.59 E
Suvorovo, S.S.S.R.	72	56.07 N	35.54 E
Suwa	84	36.02 N	138.08 E
Suwa-ko @	84	36.05 N	138.05 E
Suwałki	30	54.07 N	22.56 E
Suwannaphum	100	15.33 N	103.47 E
Suwannee ≃	182	29.18 N	83.09 W
Suwannee Lake @	174	56.08 N	100.10 W
Suwanose-jima I	83b	29.38 N	129.43 E
Suwanose-suidō Ⴎ	83b	29.32 N	129.40 E
Suwarrow I[1]	14	13.15 S	163.05 W
Suwaydah	120	35.46 N	39.38 E
Şuwayliḥ	122	32.02 N	35.50 E
Suways, Khalīj as- (Gulf of Suez) C	130	29.00 N	32.50 E
Suways, Qanāt as- ≍	132	29.55 N	32.33 E
Suwŏn	88	37.17 N	127.01 E
Suwon-dong	88	41.54 N	129.43 E
Suxi	90	29.25 N	120.07 E
Suxian	90	33.38 N	116.58 E
Suykbulak	76	49.48 N	80.50 E
Suyo	236	4.30 S	80.00 W
Suzak	76	44.07 N	68.28 E
Suzaka	84	36.39 N	138.19 E
Suzano	246	23.32 S	46.20 W
Suzano □[7]	277b	23.35 S	46.18 W
Suzdal'	70	56.25 N	40.26 E
Suze ≃	54	47.08 N	7.14 E
Suze-la-Rousse	56	44.17 N	4.51 E
Suzhi	88	42.17 N	113.42 E
Suzhou (Soochow)	96	31.18 N	120.37 E
Suzhuang	95	40.04 N	116.44 E
Suzigou	88	40.25 N	123.25 E
Suzihe ≃	88	41.55 N	124.17 E
S'uzikozero	24	61.48 N	37.20 E
Suz'omka	66	52.19 N	34.05 E
Suzu	82	37.25 N	137.17 E
Suzuka	84	34.51 N	136.35 E
Suzuka ≃	84	34.54 N	136.39 E
Suzuka-sammyaku ∧∧	84	35.00 N	136.25 E
Suzuki-shinden	258	35.43 N	139.31 E
S'uz'um	70	58.02 N	47.32 E
Suzu-misaki ≻	82	37.31 N	137.21 E
Suzun	76	53.47 N	82.19 E
Suzzara	58	45.00 N	10.45 E
Sværdborg	41	55.05 N	11.54 E
Sval'ava	68	48.33 N	22.59 E
Svalbard II	4	78.00 N	20.00 E
Svalbard and Jan Mayen □[2]	10	71.00 N	8.20 W
Svalbard og Jan Mayen → Svalbard and Jan Mayen □[2]	10	78.00 N	20.00 E
Svalöv	41	55.55 N	13.06 E
Svaneholm	41	55.30 N	13.28 E
Svaneke	26	55.08 N	15.09 E
Svanetskij Chrebet ∧∧	74	42.55 N	42.42 E
Svängsta	26	56.16 N	14.46 E
Svanninge	41	55.07 N	10.15 E
Svanskog	26	59.11 N	12.33 E
Svapa ≃	68	51.44 N	34.56 E
Şvappavaara	24	67.39 N	21.04 E
Švarcevskij	72	54.06 N	37.59 E
Şvärdsjö	26	60.45 N	15.55 E
Švaricha	70	57.33 N	49.37 E
Svartå	40	59.08 N	14.31 E
Svartälven ≃	40	59.19 N	14.35 E
Svartån ≃	40	59.37 N	16.33 E
Svarte	41	55.25 N	13.43 E
Svartenhuk ≻[1]	166	71.55 N	55.00 W
Svärtinge	40	58.39 N	16.00 E
Svartisen ⊠	24	66.38 N	14.00 E
Svartlöga I	40	59.34 N	19.03 E
Svartsjölandet I	40	59.22 N	17.41 E
Svataj	64	67.57 N	151.54 E
Svatava	50	50.11 N	12.35 E
Svatava ≃	50	50.32 N	12.07 E
Sv'atica ≃	70	58.22 N	51.43 E
Sv'atogorskaja	73	49.04 N	37.32 E
Sv'atoj Nos, Mys ≻, S.S.S.R.	24	68.10 N	39.45 E
Sv'atoj Nos, Mys ≻, S.S.S.R.	64	72.52 N	140.42 E
Sv'atoj Nos, Poluostrov ≻[1]	78	53.40 N	108.50 E
Sv'atoslavka	70	51.20 N	43.26 E
Svatovo	73	49.23 N	38.13 E
Svay Chék	100	13.48 N	102.58 E
Svay Riĕng	100	11.05 N	105.48 E
Sveafallen L	40	59.10 N	14.22 E
Svebølle	41	55.38 N	11.20 E
Sveča	70	58.16 N	47.32 E
Svedala	41	55.30 N	13.14 E
Svėdasai	66	55.41 N	25.22 E
Şveg	26	62.02 N	14.21 E
Švėkšna	66	55.31 N	21.37 E
Svelgen	26	61.47 N	5.15 E
Svelvik	26	59.37 N	10.24 E
Şven'	66	53.09 N	34.21 E
Švenčionėliai	66	55.10 N	26.00 E
Švenčionys	66	55.07 N	26.10 E
Svendborg	41	55.03 N	10.37 E
Svenljunga	26	57.30 N	13.07 E
Svennevad	40	59.01 N	15.22 E
Svensen	214	46.10 N	123.40 W
Svenstorp	41	55.46 N	13.15 E
Şvenstrup	26	56.59 N	9.52 E
Şventoji	66	56.02 N	21.05 E
Šventoji ≃	66	55.06 N	24.22 E
Sverbejevo	79	53.36 N	123.15 E
Sverdlovo, S.S.S.R.	70	51.16 N	44.34 E
Sverdlovo, S.S.S.R.	72	56.38 N	36.37 E
Sverdlovsk, S.S.S.R.	73	48.05 N	39.40 E
Sverdlovsk, S.S.S.R.	76	56.51 N	60.36 E
Sverdrup, Ostrov I	64	74.35 N	74.30 E
Sverige → Sweden □[1]	24	62.00 N	15.00 E
Şverkestaån ≃	40	59.28 N	15.28 E
Švermov	50	50.09 N	14.05 E
Svessa	68	51.57 N	33.54 E
Sveti Arhandjel Mihajlo ✝[1]	38	42.07 N	21.28 E
Sveti Jovan Bigorski ✝[1]	38	41.38 N	20.37 E
Svetiloviči	66	52.48 N	31.19 E
Sveti Nikole	38	41.52 N	21.58 E
Sveti Petar u Šumi	58	45.11 N	13.52 E
Svetlaja	79	46.33 N	138.18 E
Světlá nad Sázavou	30	49.40 N	15.25 E
Svetlanovo	73	48.42 N	38.28 E
Svetlogorsk, S.S.S.R.	66	52.38 N	29.42 E
Svetlogorsk, S.S.S.R.	66	54.57 N	20.10 E
Svetlograd	62	45.20 N	42.40 E
Svetloje	70	57.03 N	53.38 E
Svetlyj, S.S.S.R.	66	54.41 N	20.08 E
Svetlyj, S.S.S.R.	76	50.47 N	60.53 E
Svetlyj, S.S.S.R.	78	58.26 N	115.55 E
Svetlyj Jar	70	48.29 N	44.46 E
Svetogorsk	24	61.07 N	28.51 E
Svetozarevo	38	43.58 N	21.16 E
Svežen'kaja	70	54.01 N	42.26 E
Svidník	30	49.18 N	21.35 E
Svijaga ≃	70	55.47 N	48.40 E
Svilajnac	38	44.14 N	21.13 E
Svilengrad	38	41.46 N	26.12 E
Svindal	26	58.30 N	7.28 E
Svinecea ∧	38	44.48 N	22.09 E
Svinesund	26	59.06 N	11.16 E
Svinninge	41	55.43 N	11.28 E
Svir'	66	54.51 N	26.24 E
Svir' ≃	66	60.30 N	32.48 E
Svirica	66	60.29 N	32.51 E
Svirsk	78	53.04 N	103.21 E
Svir'stroj	66	60.48 N	33.43 E
Sviščovka	70	52.51 N	43.44 E
Svisloč', S.S.S.R.	66	53.02 N	24.06 E
Svisloč', S.S.S.R.	66	53.26 N	28.59 E
Svisloč' ≃	66	53.26 N	28.59 E
Sviştov	38	43.37 N	25.20 E
Svistunovka	73	49.29 N	38.20 E
Svit	30	49.03 N	20.12 E
Svitávka	30	49.30 N	16.37 E
Svitavy	30	49.45 N	16.27 E
Svitino	72	54.54 N	35.49 E
Svoboda, S.S.S.R.	68	51.58 N	36.17 E
Svoboda, S.S.S.R.	68	47.12 N	40.39 E
Svobodnaja	79	46.48 N	143.23 E
Svobodnoje	73	47.32 N	37.34 E
Svobodnyj, S.S.S.R.	70	52.20 N	46.22 E
Svobodnyj, S.S.S.R.	79	51.24 N	128.07 E
Svobodnyj Port	68	46.20 N	31.51 E
Svoge	38	42.58 N	23.21 E
Svojna	72	54.09 N	36.39 E
Svol'na ≃	66	55.43 N	28.02 E
Svolvær	24	68.14 N	14.34 E
Svor	50	50.47 N	14.36 E
Svorkmo	26	63.10 N	9.45 E
Svratka ≃	30	49.11 N	16.38 E
Svullrya	26	60.25 N	12.24 E
Svyataya Anna Trough ✧[1]	12	80.00 N	70.00 E
Swābi	113	34.07 N	72.28 E
Swadlincote	44	52.47 N	1.33 W
Swaffham	44	52.39 N	0.41 E
Swain	200	42.29 N	77.51 W
Swain Reefs ✧[2]	156	21.40 S	152.15 E
Swainsboro	182	32.36 N	82.20 W
Swains Island I[1]	14	11.03 S	171.05 W
Swakop ≃	146	22.38 S	14.36 E
Swakopmund	146	22.41 S	14.34 E
Swakopmund □[5]	146	22.00 S	14.30 E
Swale □[8]	250	51.21 N	0.41 E
Swale ≃	42	54.06 N	1.20 W
Swale Canyon V	214	45.49 N	121.05 W
Swale Creek ≃	214	45.49 N	121.05 W
Swaledale V	42	54.25 N	1.47 W
Swallowfield	208	38.21 N	84.51 W
Swalmen	48	51.15 N	6.02 E
Swamp City	212	32.29 N	94.56 W
Swampscott	197	42.28 N	70.55 W
Swan	212	32.26 N	95.22 W
Swan ≃, Austl.	158a	32.03 S	115.45 E
Swan ≃, Can.	174	52.30 N	100.47 W
Swan ≃, Alta., Can.	172	55.31 N	115.17 W
Swan ≃, Minn., U.S.	180	47.01 N	93.16 W
Swan Acres	269b	40.33 N	80.02 W
Swanage	44	50.37 N	1.58 W
Swan Bay C	159	38.14 S	144.40 E
Swan Creek ≃, Austl.	161a	28.08 S	152.13 E
Swan Creek ≃, Mich., U.S.	206	41.58 N	85.19 W
Swan Creek ≃, Mich., U.S.	206	41.58 N	83.17 W
Swan Creek ≃, Ohio, U.S.	206	41.39 N	83.32 W
Swan Creek ≃, S. Dak., U.S.	188	45.19 N	100.15 W
Swan Creek, North Branch ≃	271	42.06 N	83.23 W
Swan Creek Point ≻	271	42.40 N	82.39 W
Swan Hill	156	35.21 S	143.34 E
Swan Hills	172	54.52 N	115.45 W
Swan Hills ∧∧[2]	172	54.48 N	115.52 W
Swanington	206	40.35 N	87.17 W
Swan Island I	159	38.15 S	144.41 E
Swan Island II	228	17.25 N	83.55 W
Swank Creek ≃	214	47.07 N	120.45 W
Swan Lake, Man., Can.	174	49.24 N	98.46 W
Swan Lake, Mont., U.S.	192	47.55 N	113.50 W
Swan Lake, N.Y., U.S.	200	41.45 N	74.47 W
Swan Lake @, Man., Can.	174	52.30 N	100.45 W
Swan Lake @, Ont., Can.	174	54.17 N	91.12 W
Swan Lake @, Ill., U.S.	209	38.57 N	90.33 W
Swan Lake @, Minn., U.S.	180	44.19 N	94.15 W
Swanley	44	51.24 N	0.12 E
Swannanda	182	35.36 N	82.23 W
Swannanoa, Lake @	266	41.01 N	74.31 W
Swan Peak ∧	192	47.43 N	113.38 W
Swanquarter	182	35.24 N	76.20 W
Swan Range ∧∧	192	47.50 N	113.40 W
Swan River	174	52.06 N	101.16 W
Swansboro	182	34.36 N	77.07 W
Swanscombe	250	51.26 N	0.18 E
Swansea, Austl.	156	42.08 S	148.04 E
Swansea, Austl.	160	33.05 S	151.38 E
Swansea, Wales, U.K.	44	51.38 N	3.57 W
Swansea, Ill., U.S.	209	38.32 N	89.58 W
Swansea, Mass., U.S.	197	41.45 N	71.11 W
Swansea, S.C., U.S.	182	33.44 N	81.06 W
Swansea ◆[8]	265b	43.38 N	79.28 W
Swansea Bay C	44	51.35 N	3.52 W
Swans Island I	178	44.10 N	68.25 W
Swanson Lake @[1]	188	40.09 N	101.06 W
Swanton, Ohio, U.S.	206	41.35 N	83.53 W
Swanton, Vt., U.S.	178	44.55 N	73.07 W
Swanville	180	45.55 N	94.38 W
Swanzey Center	197	42.52 N	72.17 W
Swartberg	148	30.15 S	29.23 E
Swarthmore	198	39.54 N	75.21 W
Swarthmore College ✝[2]	275	39.54 N	75.21 W
Swart Kei ≃	148	32.09 S	27.24 E
Swartplaas	148	26.08 S	26.57 E
Swartruggens	146	25.40 S	26.42 E
Swartruggens ∧∧	148	33.02 S	19.35 E
Swartswood Lake	200	41.04 N	74.51 W
Swartswood State Park ♠	200	41.05 N	74.50 W
Swartz Creek	206	42.58 N	83.50 W
Swarupkāti	116	22.45 N	90.06 E
Swarupnagar	116	22.49 N	88.52 E
Swarzędz	30	52.26 N	17.05 E
Swasey Wash V	190	39.15 N	112.53 W
Swasiland → Swaziland □[1]	148	26.30 S	31.30 E
Swāt ≃	113	34.20 N	71.34 E
Swatara Creek ≃	198	40.11 N	76.44 W
Swa-Tenda	142	7.09 S	17.07 E
Swatow → Shantou	90	23.23 N	116.41 E
Swauger Creek ≃	216	38.16 N	119.16 W
Swauk Pass)(	214	47.21 N	120.40 W
Sway	44	50.47 N	1.37 W
Swayzee	206	40.30 N	85.49 W
Swaziland □[1]	128		
	148	26.30 S	31.30 E
Swea City	180	43.23 N	94.19 W
Swede Hill	269b	40.17 N	79.34 W
Sweden □[1]	22		
	24	62.00 N	15.00 E
Sweden Valley	204	41.45 N	77.56 W
Swede Run ≃	275	40.02 N	74.58 W
Swedesboro	198	39.45 N	75.15 W
Swedesburg	275	40.06 N	75.20 W
Swedru	140	5.32 N	0.43 W
Sween, Loch C	42	55.59 N	5.39 W
Sweeney Plan	269b	40.11 N	79.48 W
Sweeny	212	29.02 N	85.42 W
Sweeny Park ♠	274a	43.02 N	78.52 W
Sweet Briar	182	37.33 N	79.04 W
Sweet Grass Creek ≃	192	45.47 N	109.47 W
Sweetgrass Hills ∧∧[2]	192	48.55 N	111.30 W
Sweet Grass Indian Reserve ◆[4]	174	52.44 N	108.45 W
Sweetheart Abbey ✝[1]	42	54.59 N	3.38 W
Sweet Home, Oreg., U.S.	192	44.24 N	122.44 W
Sweet Home, Tex., U.S.	212	29.21 N	97.04 W
Sweetsers	206	40.34 N	85.46 W
Sweet Springs	184	38.58 N	93.25 W
Sweet Valley	200	41.17 N	76.09 W
Sweetwater, Fla., U.S.	210	25.46 N	80.21 W
Sweetwater, Ill., U.S.	209	40.03 N	89.42 W
Sweetwater, Tenn., U.S.	182	35.36 N	84.28 W
Sweetwater, Tex., U.S.	186	32.28 N	100.25 W
Sweetwater ≃	190	42.31 N	107.02 W
Sweetwater Creek	210	27.59 N	82.33 W
Sweetwater Creek ≃, U.S.	186	35.18 N	99.57 W
Sweetwater Creek ≃, Tex., U.S.	186	32.40 N	100.06 W
Sweetwater Mountains ∧∧	216	38.30 N	119.25 W
Swellendam	148	34.02 S	20.26 E
Swepsonville	182	36.01 N	79.22 W
Swerdlowsk → Sverdlovsk	76	56.51 N	60.36 E
Świdnica (Schweidnitz)	30	50.51 N	16.29 E
Świdnik	30	51.14 N	22.41 E
Świdwin	30	53.47 N	15.47 E
Świebodzice	30	50.52 N	16.19 E
Świebodzin	30	52.15 N	15.32 E
Świecie	30	53.25 N	18.28 E
Świerzawa	30	51.01 N	15.54 E
Świerzno	50	53.57 N	14.59 E
Święta	50	53.35 N	14.36 E
Świętokrzyskie, Góry ∧∧	30	50.55 N	21.00 E
Świętokrzyski Park Narodowy ♠	30	50.55 N	21.00 E
Swift ≃, Eng., U.K.	44	52.23 N	1.16 W
Swift ≃, Alaska, U.S.	170	61.53 N	156.18 W
Swift ≃, Mass., U.S.	197	42.12 N	72.22 W
Swift Creek ≃, Ala., U.S.	184	32.25 N	86.38 W
Swift Creek ≃, N.C., U.S.	182	35.12 N	77.05 W
Swift Creek ≃, N.C., U.S.	182	35.57 N	77.35 W
Swift Current	174	50.17 N	107.50 W
Swiftcurrent Creek ≃	174	50.40 N	107.44 W
Swifton	184	35.49 N	91.08 W
Swift Reservoir @[1]	214	46.04 N	122.05 W
Swiftwater	200	41.06 N	75.20 W
Swilly, Lough C	28	55.10 N	7.38 W
Swimming ≃	266	40.21 N	74.05 W
Swimming River Reservoir @[1]	266	40.19 N	74.07 W
Świna ≃[1]	50	53.55 N	14.17 E
Swinburne, Cape ≻	166	71.14 N	98.34 W
Swinden Reservoirs @[1]	252	53.48 N	2.10 W
Swindle Island I	172	52.32 N	128.35 W
Swindon	44	51.34 N	1.47 W
Swinemünde → Świnoujście	30	53.53 N	14.14 E
Swinford	28	53.57 N	8.57 W
Swing Bridge ◆[5]	132	30.42 N	32.20 E
Swinging Bridge Reservoir @[1]	200	41.37 N	74.48 W
Swinomish Indian Reservation ◆[4]	214	48.25 N	122.33 W
Świnoujście (Swinemünde)	30	53.53 N	14.14 E
Swinton, Eng., U.K.	42	53.28 N	1.20 W
Swinton, Eng., U.K.	252	53.31 N	2.20 W
Swinton, Scot., U.K.	42	55.43 N	2.15 W
Swissvale	269b	40.25 N	79.53 W
Switzerland □[6]	208	38.45 N	85.04 W
Switzerland □[1]	22		
	54	47.00 N	8.00 E
Swordfish Seamount ✧[3]	14	18.30 N	158.25 W
Swords	28	53.28 N	6.13 W
Swords Range ∧∧	156	21.57 S	141.32 E
Swormville	202	43.02 N	78.42 W
Sworton Heath	252	53.21 N	2.28 W
Swoyerville	200	41.18 N	75.53 W
Syalach	64	66.12 N	124.00 E
Syam	54	46.42 N	5.57 E
Syāmnagar	116	22.21 N	89.07 E
Syāmpur, Bhārat	116	22.18 N	88.02 E
Syampur, Bhārat	262b	22.29 N	88.13 E
Sybille Creek ≃	188	42.07 N	105.02 W
Syburg ◆[8]	253	51.25 N	7.29 E
Sycamore, Ga., U.S.	182	31.40 N	83.38 W
Sycamore, Ill., U.S.	206	41.59 N	88.41 W
Sycamore, Ohio, U.S.	204	40.57 N	83.10 W
Sycamore Creek ≃, Ariz., U.S.	190	33.38 N	111.40 W
Sycamore Creek ≃, Ariz., U.S.	190	34.52 N	112.05 W
Sycamore Creek ≃, Mich., U.S.	206	42.43 N	84.32 W
Sycamore Creek ≃, Ohio, U.S.	204	40.59 N	83.12 W
Sycamore Creek ≃, Tex., U.S.	186	29.14 N	100.48 W
Sycamore Island I	269b	40.29 N	79.52 W
Sycamore Park ♠	270	33.52 N	117.42 W
Sycamore Slough ≃	216	38.48 N	121.44 W
Sycan ≃	192	42.27 N	121.15 W
Sycaway	200	42.44 N	73.39 W
Syčova	76	57.35 N	69.20 E
Syčovka	66	55.50 N	34.17 E
Syców	30	51.19 N	17.43 E
Syda ≃	76	54.22 N	91.23 E
Sydenham, Austl.	264b	37.42 S	144.46 E
Sydenham, Ont., Can.	202	44.25 N	76.36 W
Sydenham ◆[8], S. Afr.	263d	26.09 S	28.06 E
Sydenham ◆[8], Eng., U.K.	250	51.26 N	0.03 W
Sydenham ≃	202	44.35 N	80.57 W
Sydenham Lake @	202	44.25 N	76.35 W
Sydenham West	264b	37.41 S	144.39 E
Sydney	160		
	264a	33.52 S	151.13 E
Sydney, N.S., Can.	176	46.09 N	60.11 W
Sydney, Fla., U.S.	210	27.58 N	82.12 W
Sydney I[1]	14	4.27 S	171.15 W
Sydney, University of ✝[2]	264a	33.53 S	151.11 E
Sydney Bay C, Ont., Can.	202	44.54 N	81.05 W
Sydney Bay C, Norf. I.	164c	29.04 S	167.57 E
Sydney Bay Bluff ⊥[4]	202	44.54 N	81.07 W
Sydney Harbour Bridge ◆[5]	160	33.52 S	151.12 E
Sydney Lake @	174	50.40 N	94.24 W
Sydney Mines	176	46.14 N	60.14 W
Sydney Point ≻	164d	0.53 S	169.36 E
Syferbult	148	26.00 S	27.20 E
Sygan	269b	40.21 N	80.08 W
Syke	48	52.54 N	8.49 E
Sykesville, Md., U.S.	178	39.22 N	76.58 W
Sykesville, Pa., U.S.	204	41.03 N	78.49 W
Sykkylven	26	62.24 N	6.35 E

Symbols in the index entries represent the broad categories identified in the key at the right. Symbols with superior numbers (∧∧[2]) identify subcategories (see complete key on page I · 26).

Kartensymbole in dem Registerverzeichnis stellen die rechts in Schlüssel erklärten Kategorien dar. Symbole mit hochgestellten Ziffern (∧∧[2]) bezeichnen Unterabteilungen einer Kategorie (vgl. vollständiger Schlüssel auf Seite I · 26).

Los símbolos incluídos en el texto del índice representan las grandes categorías identificadas con la clave a la derecha. Los símbolos con numeros en su parte superior (∧∧[2]) identifican las subcategorías (véase la clave completa en la página I · 26).

Les symboles de l'index représentent les catégories indiquées dans la légende à droite. Les symboles suivis d'un indice (∧∧[2]) représentent des sous-catégories (voir légende complète à la page I · 26).

Os símbolos incluídos no texto do índice representam as grandes categorias identificadas com a chave à direita. Os símbolos com números em sua parte superior (∧∧[2]) identificam as subcategorias (veja-se a chave completa à página I · 26).

	English	Deutsch	Español	Français	Português
∧	Mountain	Berg	Montaña	Montagne	Montanha
∧∧	Mountains	Berge	Montañas	Montagnes	Montanhas
)(	Pass	Pass	Paso	Col	Passo
V	Valley, Canyon	Tal, Cañon	Valle, Cañón	Vallée, Canyon	Vale, Canhão
≚	Plain	Ebene	Llano	Plaine	Planície
≻	Cape	Kap	Cabo	Cap	Cabo
I	Island	Insel	Isla	Île	Ilha
II	Islands	Inseln	Islas	Îles	Ilhas
⊥	Other Topographic Features	Andere Topographische Objekte	Otros Elementos Topográficos	Autres données topographiques	Outros Elementos Topográficos

ESPAÑOL / FRANÇAIS / PORTUGUÊS

Nombre / Nom / Nome	Página / Page / Página	Lat.°′	Long.°′ W=Oeste / W=Ouest / W=Oeste
Syktyvkar	24	61.40 N	50.46 E
Sylacauga	184	33.10 N	86.15 W
Sylhet	110	24.54 N	91.52 E
Syloga	24	63.50 N	43.39 E
Sylsjön ⊜	26	62.56 N	12.11 E
Sylt I	30	54.54 N	8.20 E
Sylva	182	35.23 N	83.13 W
Sylvan	214	45.30 N	122.41 W
Sylvan Beach	200	43.12 N	75.44 W
Sylvan Grove	188	39.00 N	98.24 W
Sylvan Hills	184	34.51 N	92.12 W
Sylvania, Austl.	264a	34.01 S	151.07 E
Sylvania, Ga., U.S.	182	32.45 N	81.38 W
Sylvania, Ohio, U.S.	204	41.43 N	83.42 W
Sylvania, Pa., U.S.	200	41.48 N	76.51 W
Sylvania Heights	264a	34.02 S	151.06 E
Sylvan Lake, Alta., Can.	172	52.19 N	114.05 W
Sylvan Lake, Ill., U.S.	268	42.15 N	88.03 W
Sylvan Lake, Mich., U.S.	271	42.37 N	83.20 W
Sylvan Lake ⊜, Alta., Can.	172	52.21 N	114.10 W
Sylvan Lake ⊜, Ind., U.S.	206	41.29 N	85.20 W
Sylvan Lake ⊜, Mich., U.S.	271	42.37 N	83.20 W
Sylvan Pass)(	192	44.28 N	110.08 W
Sylvan Shores	210	28.49 N	81.41 W
Sylvensteinsee ⊜	58	47.34 N	11.32 E
Sylvester, Ga., U.S.	182	31.32 N	83.49 W
Sylvester, Tex., U.S.	186	32.43 N	100.15 W
Sylvester, Mount ∧[2]	176	48.11 N	55.04 W
Sylvia	188	37.57 N	98.24 W
Sylvia Grinnell Lake ⊜	166	64.10 N	69.25 W
Sym	64	60.20 N	88.23 E
Symmes Creek ≃	178	38.26 N	82.27 W
Syn'a	24	65.22 N	57.42 E
Syndal	264b	37.53 S	145.09 E
Synkovo	72	55.21 N	37.38 E
Synnyr, Chrebet ⋏	78	56.50 N	111.10 E
Syntul	70	55.00 N	41.18 E
Synžereja	68	47.38 N	28.09 E
Syon House ⊥	250	51.29 N	0.19 W
Syosset	200	40.50 N	73.30 W
Syracuse → Siracusa, It.	36	37.04 N	15.17 E
Syracuse, Ind., U.S.	206	41.26 N	85.45 W
Syracuse, Kans., U.S.	188	37.59 N	101.45 W
Syracuse, Nebr., U.S.	188	40.39 N	96.11 W
Syracuse, N.Y., U.S.	200	43.03 N	76.09 W
Syrčan	70	57.22 N	50.15 E
Syrdarja	75	40.52 N	68.38 E
Syrdarja (Syr-Darya) ≃	62	46.03 N	61.00 E
Syrdarjinskaja Oblast' □[4]	75	40.40 N	67.40 E
Syrdarjinskij	75	41.15 N	68.00 E
Syr-Darya → Syrdarja ≃	62	46.03 N	61.00 E
Syre ≃	52	49.35 N	6.08 E
Syria □[1]	108		
	118	35.00 N	38.00 E
Syriam	100	16.46 N	96.15 E
Syrian Desert → Shām, Bādiyat ash- ◆[2]	118	32.00 N	40.00 E
Syrie → Syria □[1]	118	35.00 N	38.00 E
Syrien → Syria □[1]	118	35.00 N	38.00 E
Syrskij	66	52.34 N	39.29 E
Sysert'	76	56.29 N	60.49 E
Sysmä	26	61.30 N	25.41 E
Sysola ≃	24	61.42 N	50.53 E
Sysslebäck	26	60.44 N	12.52 E
Syston	44	52.42 N	1.04 W
Systyg Chem	78	52.40 N	95.30 E
Syt'kovo	66	56.31 N	34.01 E
Sytykanskij, Porog ⌊	78	57.49 N	118.33 E
Syukunosho	260	34.50 N	135.32 E
Syväri ⊜	26	63.16 N	28.06 E
Syzran'	70	53.09 N	48.27 E
Syzran' ≃	70	53.04 N	48.26 E
Szabadka → Subotica	38	46.06 N	19.39 E
Szabolcs-Szatmár □[6]	30	48.00 N	22.10 E
Szada	254c	47.38 N	19.19 E
Szamocin	30	53.02 N	17.08 E
Szamos (Someș) ≃	38	48.07 N	22.20 E
Szamotuły	30	52.37 N	16.35 E
Szarvas	30	46.52 N	20.34 E
Szatmárnémeti → Satu Mare	38	47.48 N	22.53 E
Százhalombatta	254c	47.20 N	18.56 E
Szczawnica	30	49.26 N	20.30 E
Szczecin (Stettin)	30	53.24 N	14.32 E
Szczecin □[4]	50	53.15 N	14.45 E
Szczecinek (Neustettin)	30	53.43 N	16.42 E
Szczeciński, Zalew (Oderhaff) C	50	53.46 N	14.14 E
Szczekociny	30	50.38 N	19.50 E
Szczuczyn	30	53.34 N	22.18 E
Szczytno	30	53.34 N	21.00 E
Szechwan → Sichuan □[4]	92	31.00 N	105.00 E
Szécsény	30	48.06 N	19.31 E
Szeged	30	46.15 N	20.09 E
Szeghalom	30	47.01 N	21.11 E
Székesfehérvár	30	47.12 N	18.25 E
Szekszárd	30	46.21 N	18.42 E
Szentendre	30	47.40 N	19.05 E
Szentendrei-Duna ≃[1]	254c	47.36 N	19.05 E
Szentendrei-sziget I	254c	47.39 N	19.07 E
Szentes	30	46.39 N	20.16 E
Szentgotthárd	30	46.57 N	16.17 E
Szeping → Siping	79	43.12 N	124.20 E
Szépművészeti Múzeum ʋ	254c	47.31 N	19.05 E
Szerencs	30	48.09 N	21.13 E
Szigethalom	254c	47.20 N	19.00 E
Szigetszentmiklós	254c	47.21 N	19.03 E
Szilas (Palotai)-patak ≃	254c	47.36 N	19.06 E
Szlichtyngowa	30	51.43 N	16.15 E
Szob	30	47.50 N	18.52 E
Szolnok	30	47.10 N	20.12 E
Szolnok □[6]	30	47.12 N	20.11 E
Szombathely	30	47.14 N	16.38 E
Szprotawa	30	51.34 N	15.33 E
Sztum	30	53.56 N	19.01 E
Szubin	30	53.00 N	17.44 E
Szydłowiec	30	51.14 N	20.51 E
Szypliszki	30	54.15 N	23.05 E
Szzarvíz ≃	30	46.24 N	18.41 E
T			
Ta ≃	84	36.17 N	139.54 E
Taacyn Gol ≃	92	45.09 N	101.27 E
Taakoka I	164k	21.15 S	159.43 W
Taalintehdas → Dalsbruk	26	60.02 N	22.31 E
Taal Lake ⊜	106	13.55 N	121.00 E
Taancan Point ≻	106	10.00 N	125.01 E
Taan Ch'i ≃	90	24.22 N	120.42 E
Taavetti	26	60.55 N	27.34 E
Tabacal	242	23.16 S	64.15 W
Tabacal, Quebrada ≃	276c	10.31 N	67.02 W
Tabaco	106	13.23 N	123.44 E
Tabaco Bay C	106	13.20 N	123.47 E
Tabacundo	236	0.03 N	78.12 W
Tabaí	242	26.07 S	55.32 W
Tabai ≃	154	3.01 S	135.52 E
Tabaloso	238	6.21 S	76.41 W
Tabanan	105b	8.32 S	115.08 E
Tabango	106	11.19 N	124.22 E
Tabankulu	148	30.58 S	29.19 E
Tabaqah	120	35.52 N	38.34 E
Tábara	34	41.49 N	5.57 W
Tabar Island I	154	2.55 S	152.05 E
Tabar Islands II	154	2.50 S	152.00 E
Tabarka	138	36.57 N	8.45 E
Tabarz	50	50.52 N	10.31 E
Ṭabas, Īrān	118	32.48 N	60.14 E
Ṭabas, Īrān	118	33.36 N	56.54 E
Tabasará ≃	226	8.00 N	81.39 W
Tabasará, Serranía de ⋏	226	8.33 N	81.40 W
Tabasco	222	32.35 N	114.55 W
Tabasco □[3]	222	18.15 N	93.00 W
Tabat	76	52.57 N	90.43 E
Tabatinga ≃	245	17.24 S	43.18 W
Tabatinga, Serra da ⋏[2]	240	10.25 S	44.00 W
Tabayama	84	35.47 N	138.55 E
Tabayin	100	22.42 N	95.19 E
Tabb	198	37.08 N	76.29 W
Tabei	88	39.44 N	122.29 E
Tabelbala	138	29.23 N	3.15 W
Tabelbala, Kahal ◆[8]	138	28.30 N	2.00 W
Taber	172	49.47 N	112.08 W
Taberg, Sve.	26	57.41 N	14.05 E
Taberg, Sve.	40	59.50 N	14.08 E
Taberg, N.Y., U.S.	200	43.18 N	75.37 W
Taberis, Laguna C	226	14.18 N	83.15 W
Tabernacle	275	39.50 N	74.43 W
Tabernes de Valldigna	34	39.04 N	0.16 W
Tabi	142	8.10 S	13.18 E
Tabiang, Gilb. Is.	164d	0.52 S	169.35 E
Tabiang, Gilb. Is.	164t	1.26 N	173.06 E
Tabiano Terme	58	44.48 N	10.21 E
Tabira	240	7.35 S	37.33 W
Tabiteuea	164t	1.25 N	173.07 E
Tabiteuea I[1]	14	1.20 S	174.50 E
Tabla	140	13.46 N	3.01 E
Tabla, Cerro de la ∧	230m	18.03 N	66.08 W
Tablada	278	34.42 S	58.32 W
Tablas, Cabo ≻	242	31.51 S	71.34 W
Tablas Island I	106	12.24 N	122.02 E
Tablas Plateau ⋏[1]	106	9.43 N	122.43 E
Tablas Strait ⋃	106	12.40 N	121.48 E
Tablat	34	36.24 N	3.19 E
Table Bay C	148	33.53 S	18.27 E
Table Cape ≻	162	39.06 S	178.00 E
Table Mountain ∧, Newf., Can.	176	47.43 N	59.13 W
Table Mountain ∧, S. Afr.	148	33.57 S	18.25 E
Table Mountain ∧, Ariz., U.S.	190	32.49 N	110.31 W
Table Rock	188	40.11 N	96.06 W
Table Rock Lake ⊜[1]	184	36.35 N	93.30 W
Tabletop ∧, Austl.	152	22.32 S	123.55 E
Table Top ∧, Ariz., U.S.	190	32.46 N	112.07 W
Tabletop Mountain ∧	161b	35.58 S	148.30 E
Tabley Mere ⊜	252	53.17 N	2.25 W
Tabligbo	140	6.35 N	1.30 E
Tablones	230m	18.15 N	65.45 W
Taboan ≃	106	17.57 N	122.11 E
Taboão, Ribeirão do ≃	277b	23.40 S	46.28 W
Taboão da Serra	246	23.38 S	46.46 W
Taboão da Serra □[7]	277b	23.37 S	46.47 W
Taboco ≃	238	19.53 S	55.58 W
Taboga	226	8.48 N	79.33 W
Tabogon	106	10.57 N	124.02 E
Tábor, Česko.	30	49.25 N	14.41 E
Tabor, S.S.S.R.	64	71.16 N	150.12 E
Tabor, Iowa, U.S.	188	40.54 N	95.40 W
Tabor, N.J., U.S.	266	40.52 N	74.29 W
Tabor, S. Dak., U.S.	188	42.57 N	97.39 W
Tabor, Mount → Tavor, Har ∧	122	32.41 N	35.23 E
Tabora	144	5.01 S	32.48 E
Tabora □[4]	144	6.00 S	32.00 E
Tabor City	182	34.09 N	78.52 W
Tabory	76	58.31 N	64.33 E
Tabou	140	4.25 N	7.21 W
Tabrīz	118	38.05 N	46.18 E
Tábua, Riacho da ≃	240	9.12 S	44.25 W
Tabuaço	34	41.07 N	7.34 W
Tabuão	246	21.59 S	44.02 W
Tábuas	246	22.12 S	43.37 W
Tabu-dong	88	36.03 N	128.31 E
Tabuelan	106	10.49 N	123.52 E
Tabūk, Ar. Sa.	118	28.23 N	36.35 E
Tabuk, Pil.	106	17.24 N	121.25 E
Tabuleiro	246	21.22 S	43.15 W
Tabuleiro do Norte	240	5.15 S	38.07 W
Tabunifi	164q	9.28 N	138.05 E
Tabuny	76	52.46 N	78.45 E
Tabuse	86	33.57 N	132.03 E
Tabwemasana, Mount ∧	165f	15.20 S	166.44 E
Täby	40	59.30 N	18.03 E
Tabyn-Bogdo-Ola ⋏	76	49.08 N	87.45 E
Tacacoma	238	15.35 S	68.43 W
Tacagua, Quebrada ≃	276c	10.37 N	67.02 W
Tacaimbó	240	8.19 S	36.18 W
Tacámbaro ≃	224	18.29 N	101.07 W
Tacámbaro de Codallos	224	19.14 N	101.28 W
Tacaná	226	15.14 N	92.05 W
Tacaná, Volcán ∧[1]	226	15.08 N	92.06 W
Tacañitas	242	28.38 S	62.36 W
Tacaratu	240	9.06 S	38.10 W
Taceno	54	46.02 N	9.21 E
T'ačev	68	48.02 N	23.34 E
Taché, Lac ⊜	166	64.00 N	120.00 W
Tacheng	76	46.45 N	82.57 E
Tacherting	58	48.05 N	12.34 E
Tach'i	90	24.57 N	121.53 E
Tachia	90	24.21 N	120.37 E
Tachia Ch'i ≃	90	24.19 N	120.34 E
Tachiataš	62	42.25 N	59.35 E
Tachibana, Nihon	86	33.11 N	130.36 E
Tachibana, Nihon	86	33.54 N	132.17 E
Tachichilte, Isla de I	222	24.59 N	108.04 W
Tachie ≃	172	54.40 N	124.50 W
Tachikawa	84	35.42 N	139.25 E
Tachikawa Air Base (United States) ■	84	35.43 N	139.25 E
Táchira □[3]	236	7.50 N	72.05 W
Tachoshui	90	24.19 N	121.45 E
Tachov	30	49.48 N	12.38 E
Tachta, S.S.S.R.	70	45.54 N	42.07 E
Tachta, S.S.S.R.	79	53.08 N	139.53 E
Tachta-Bazar	118	35.57 N	62.50 E
Tachtakupyr	76	43.02 N	60.17 E
Tachtamygda	79	54.06 N	123.34 E
Tacima	240	6.30 S	35.39 W
Tacinskij	70	48.13 N	41.17 E
Taciuã, Lago ≃	236	4.29 S	60.35 W
Tacloban	106	11.15 N	125.00 E
Taclobo	106	12.20 N	122.34 E
Tacna, Perú	238	18.01 S	70.15 W
Tacna, Ariz., U.S.	190	32.41 N	114.01 W
Tacna □[5]	238	17.40 S	70.20 W
Tacoigmières	251	48.50 N	1.40 E
Tacoma	214	47.15 N	122.27 W
Tacoma Narrows Bridge ◆[5]	214	47.16 N	122.33 W
Taconic	197	42.02 N	73.25 W
Taconic Range ⋏	200	42.30 N	73.20 W
Taconic State Park ♠	200	42.05 N	73.34 W
Tacony ◆[8]	275	40.02 N	75.03 W
Tacony Creek ≃	275	40.01 N	75.06 W
Tacony Creek Park ♠	275	40.02 N	75.07 W
Tacony Palmyra Bridge ◆[5]	275	40.01 N	75.02 W
Taco Pozo	242	25.37 S	63.17 W
Tacotalpa	224	17.36 N	92.49 W
Tacotalpa ≃	224	17.50 N	92.52 W
Tacuarembó	242	31.44 S	55.59 W
Tacuarembó ≃	242	32.25 S	55.29 W
Tacuarí ≃	242	32.46 S	53.18 W
Tacuatí	242	23.27 S	56.35 W
Tacuba ◆[8]	276a	19.28 N	99.12 W
Tacubaya	222	28.20 N	104.34 W
Tacubaya ◆[8]	276a	19.25 N	99.12 W
Tacurong	106	6.42 N	124.42 E
Tacurú, Laguna ⊜	248	34.58 S	58.25 W
Tacutu (Takutu) ≃	236	3.01 N	60.29 W
Tadain	260	34.52 N	135.24 E
Tadami	82	37.21 N	139.19 E
Tadaoka	86	34.29 N	135.24 E
Tadcaster	42	53.53 N	1.16 W
Tademaït, Plateau du ⋏[1]	138	28.30 N	2.00 E
Tadenac Lake ⊜	202	45.03 N	79.56 W
Tādepallegūdem	112	16.50 N	81.30 E
Tadía, Ciénaga de ⊜	236	6.48 N	76.49 W
Tadinou	165f	21.33 S	167.52 E
Tadio, Lagune C	140	5.11 N	5.15 W
Tadjemout	138	25.37 N	3.48 E
Tadjenanet	34	36.08 N	5.59 E
Tadjeraout, Oued ∨	138	21.17 N	1.19 E
Tadjerouine	36	35.54 N	8.34 E
Tadjettaret, Oued ∨	138	21.20 N	7.22 E
Tadjoura	134	11.47 N	42.54 E
Tadjoura, Golfe de C	134	11.42 N	43.00 E
Tadley	44	51.21 N	1.08 W
Tado	84	35.08 N	136.38 E
Tadotsu	86	34.16 N	133.45 E
Tadoule Lake ⊜	166	58.36 N	98.20 W
Tadoussac	176	48.09 N	69.43 W
Tādpatri	112	14.55 N	78.01 E
Taduno	102	1.55 S	123.05 E
Tadworth	44	51.17 N	0.14 W
Tadzhik Soviet Socialist Republic → Tadžikskaja Sovetskaja Socialističeskaja Respublika □[3]	62	39.00 N	71.00 E
Tadžikabad	75	39.07 N	70.50 E
Tadžikskaja Sovetskaja Socialističeskaja Respublika □[3]	62	39.00 N	71.00 E
T'aean	88	36.46 N	126.16 E
T'aebaek-san ∧	88	37.06 N	128.55 E
T'aebaek-sanmaek ⋏	88	37.40 N	128.50 E
Taech'ŏn	88	36.22 N	126.34 E
Taedong	88	39.05 N	125.31 E
Taedong-gang ≃	88	38.42 N	125.15 E
Taegu	88	35.52 N	128.35 E
Taegwan	88	40.13 N	125.12 E
Taehan-Min'guk → Korea, South □[1]	88	36.30 N	128.00 E
Taehŭksan-do I	88	34.40 N	125.25 E
Taehŭng	88	40.06 N	126.56 E
Taehwajŏn	261b	37.36 N	126.52 E
T'aein	88	35.40 N	126.55 E
Taejin	88	36.34 N	129.24 E
Taejŏn	88	36.20 N	127.26 E
Taejujŏm	88	38.24 N	127.58 E
T'aemo-san ∧	261b	37.27 N	127.04 E
Taeng ≃	100	19.06 N	98.57 E
Taer	92	34.09 N	98.50 E
Taerwan	90	31.49 N	113.25 E
Taeryanghwa	88	41.14 N	129.42 E
Tafahi I	14	15.51 S	173.43 W
Tafahnā al-'Azab	132	30.36 N	31.15 E
Tafalla	34	42.31 N	1.40 W
Ṭafas	122	32.44 N	36.04 E
Ṭafāsīkh, Ghurd at- ◆[8]	132	29.43 N	29.45 E
Tafassasset, Oued ∨, Afr.	138	21.20 N	10.10 E
Tafassasset, Oued ∨, Alg.	138	23.00 N	9.20 E
Tafassasset, Ténéré du ◆[2]	136	21.00 N	11.00 E
Tafelbaai → Table Bay C	148	33.53 S	18.27 E
Tafermaar	154	6.51 S	134.06 E
Taff ≃	44	51.27 N	3.09 W
Tafiré	140	9.04 N	5.10 W
Tafí Viejo	242	26.44 S	65.16 W
Taflan	120	41.25 N	36.09 E
Tafna, Oued ≃	34	35.17 N	1.30 W
Tafo	140	6.13 N	0.22 W
Tafraout	138	29.40 N	8.58 W
Taft, Īrān	118	31.45 N	54.14 E
Taft, Pil.	106	11.54 N	125.25 E
Taft, Calif., U.S.	194	35.08 N	119.28 W
Taft, Fla., U.S.	210	28.23 N	81.24 W
Taft, Okla., U.S.	186	35.46 N	95.32 W
Taft, Tex., U.S.	186	27.57 N	97.46 W
Taftān, Kūh-e ∧	118	28.36 N	61.06 E
Tafton	200	41.25 N	75.11 W
Tafuna Airport ⊠	164u	14.20 S	170.43 W
Taga, Nihon	84	35.13 N	136.17 E
Taga, Nihon	260	34.49 N	135.49 E
Taga, W. Sam.	165a	13.46 S	172.28 W
Tagabukid	106	7.00 N	126.21 E
Taga Dzong	114	27.04 N	89.53 E
Tagagawik ≃	170	66.30 N	159.00 W
Tagaj	70	54.18 N	47.39 E
Tagajō	82	38.20 N	141.00 E
Tagama ◆[1]	140	15.50 N	8.12 E
Tagan	76	54.57 N	77.18 E
Tagana-an	106	9.42 N	125.35 E
Taganrog	73	47.12 N	38.56 E
Taganrogskij Zaliv C	68	47.00 N	38.23 E
Tagapula Island I	106	12.04 N	124.12 E
Tågarp	41	55.56 N	12.57 E
Tagauayan Island I	106	10.58 N	121.13 E
Tagaytay	106	14.06 N	120.56 E
Tagbilaran	106	9.39 N	123.51 E
Tagdempt → Tiaret	138	35.28 N	1.21 E
Tage	154	6.20 S	143.20 E
Tageren Canal ≋	164q	9.33 N	138.09 E
Taggia	56	43.52 N	7.51 E
Taghkanic Creek ≃	200	42.13 N	73.45 W
Taghrīfat	136	29.12 N	17.22 E
Tagig	259f	14.32 N	121.04 E
Tagig ≃	259f	14.31 N	121.05 E
T'aginka	68	46.47 N	33.04 E
Tagish Lake ⊜	170	59.45 N	134.15 W
Tagliacozzo	60	42.04 N	13.14 E
Tagliamento ≃	58	45.38 N	13.06 E
Tagliata, Monte della ∧	58	44.34 N	9.48 E
Taglio di Po	58	45.00 N	12.12 E
Tagna	78	53.36 N	101.54 E
Tagna ≃	78	53.38 N	101.53 E
Tagnant, Dhar ◆[4]	140	18.30 N	11.00 W
Tago	106	9.02 N	126.13 E
Tago ≃	106	9.01 N	126.14 E
Tagoloan	106	8.32 N	124.45 E
Tagolo Point ≻	106	8.44 N	123.23 E
Tagon Harbour C	152	33.53 S	123.00 E
Tagounit	138	29.58 N	5.36 W
Tagow Bāy	110	35.42 N	66.03 E
Tagrina, Oued ∨	138	21.00 N	6.16 E
Tagua ≃	236	2.12 N	74.17 W
Taguatinga	245	12.25 S	46.26 W
Tagubanhan Island I	106	11.08 N	123.07 E
Tagudin	106	16.56 N	120.27 E
Taguedoufat ∨	140	14.50 N	7.42 E
Taguke	110	32.07 N	84.35 E
Tagul ≃	78	55.35 N	97.45 E
Tagula Island I	150	11.30 S	153.30 E
Tagum	106	7.28 N	125.48 E
T'agun	76	53.56 N	85.38 E
Tagun Bay C	106	13.55 N	123.46 E
Tagus (Tejo) (Tajo) ≃	34	38.40 N	9.24 W
T'agyŏng-ni	88	38.04 N	126.03 E
Tah, Sebkha ⊜	138	27.45 N	12.42 W
Taha	79	47.33 N	124.14 E
Tahaa I	14	16.38 S	151.30 W
Tahakopa	162	46.31 S	169.23 E
Tahala	138	34.04 N	4.20 W
Tahan, Gunong ∧	104	4.38 N	102.14 E
Tahāneh-ye Ney Basteh	118	32.59 N	30.53 E
Tahara	84	34.40 N	137.16 E
Tahart	138	22.51 N	5.12 E
Tahat ∧	138	23.18 N	5.47 E
Taheke	162	35.27 S	173.39 E
Ṭāherī	118	27.42 N	52.21 E
Tahifet	138	22.58 N	5.55 E
Tahir	120	38.47 N	38.17 E
Tahir Geçidi)(	120	39.54 N	42.22 E
Tahiryuak Lake ⊜	166	70.56 N	112.20 W
Tahiti I	164s	17.37 S	149.27 W
Tahkuna Nina ≻	66	59.07 N	22.36 E
Tahlequah	186	35.55 N	94.58 W
Ṭahmā wa Minshāt 'Abd as-Sayyid	132	29.38 N	31.14 E
Tahmoor	160	34.13 S	150.36 E
Tahnaout	138	31.24 N	7.54 W
Tahneta Pass)(	170	61.53 N	147.20 W
Tahoe, Lake ⊜	216	39.07 N	120.03 W
Tahoe City	216	39.10 N	120.09 W
Tahoe Lake ⊜	166	70.15 N	108.45 W
Tahoe Paradise	216	38.52 N	120.01 W
Tahoe Valley	216	38.55 N	120.00 W
Tahoka	186	33.10 N	101.48 W
Taholah	214	47.21 N	124.17 W
Tahoua	140	14.54 N	5.16 E
Tahoua □[5]	140	16.00 N	5.00 E
Tahquamenon ≃	180	46.34 N	85.02 W
Tahquamenon Falls State Park ♠	180	46.29 N	85.05 W
Tahsis	172	49.55 N	126.39 W
Ta Hsü I	90	23.10 N	119.32 E
Ṭahṭā	130	26.46 N	31.30 E
Tahtaköprü	120	39.57 N	29.39 E
Tahtsa Lake ⊜	172	53.42 N	127.26 W
Tahtsa Peak ∧	172	53.33 N	127.47 W
Tahu	90	24.26 N	120.52 E
Tahuamanu ≃	238	11.06 S	67.36 W
Tahuata I	164x	9.57 S	139.05 W
Tahulandang, Pulau I	102	2.20 N	125.25 E
Tahuna	102	3.37 N	125.29 E
Tahuofang ⊜[1]	94	41.55 N	124.07 E
Tahuya ≃	214	47.23 N	123.03 W
Ṭahwāy	132	30.22 N	30.52 E
Ṭahwīṭat an-Nahr	122	33.52 N	35.31 E
Taï, C. Iv.	140	5.52 N	7.27 W
Tai, It.	58	46.25 N	12.20 E
Tai, Nihon	260	34.31 N	135.26 E
Tai ◆[8]	260	34.45 N	135.00 E
Taiaçupeba	246	23.40 S	46.11 W
Taian, Zhg.	88	36.12 N	117.07 E
Taian, Zhg.	94	41.23 N	122.27 E
Taianchang	97	30.05 N	105.47 E
Taian'gang	96	31.43 N	121.40 E
Taiarapu, Presqu'île de ≻[1]	164s	17.47 S	149.14 W
Taibaiqu	92	34.00 N	107.18 E
Taibaishan ∧, Zhg.	88	39.19 N	114.11 E
Taibaishan ∧, Zhg.	92	33.54 N	107.46 E
Taibilla, Sierra de ⋏	34	38.10 N	2.10 W
Taibon Agordino	58	46.18 N	12.00 E
Taicang	96	31.26 N	121.07 E
T'aichou → Taizhou	90	32.30 N	119.58 E
Taichu → T'aichung	90	24.09 N	120.41 E
T'aichung	90	24.09 N	120.41 E
T'aichunghsien	90	24.15 N	120.43 E
Taicunzhen	96	31.27 N	119.03 E
Taiden → Taejŏn	88	36.20 N	127.26 E
Taiei	84	35.49 N	140.25 E
Taieri ≃	162	46.03 S	170.11 E
Taif → Aṭ-Ṭā'if	134	21.16 N	40.24 E
Taigong	92	26.32 N	108.22 E
Taigu	92	37.28 N	112.30 E
Tai Hang	261d	22.17 N	114.11 E
Taihangshan ⋏	92	36.00 N	113.35 E
Taihape	162	39.40 S	175.48 E
Taihe, Zhg.	90	33.11 N	115.36 E
Taihe, Zhg.	90	26.49 N	114.55 E
Taihechang	97	30.07 N	103.50 E
Taihezhen	79	44.47 N	123.29 E
Taihezhen ⊥	100	25.41 N	100.07 E
Taiho	164m	26.39 N	128.07 E
Taihoku → T'aipei	90	25.03 N	121.30 E
T'aihsi	90	23.42 N	120.11 E
T'aihsien → Taizhou	90	32.30 N	119.58 E
Taihu	90	30.26 N	116.16 E
Taihu ⊜	96	31.15 N	120.10 E
Taihuaizhen	88	38.59 N	113.34 E
Taijimiao	88	40.55 N	113.46 E
Taijinai'erhu ⊜	110	37.15 N	93.20 E
Taijüan → Taiyuan	92	37.55 N	112.30 E
Taikang	88	34.04 N	114.50 E
Taikkyi	100	17.19 N	95.58 E
Taikou	92	31.53 N	111.07 E
Taiko-yama ∧	86	35.46 N	135.12 E
Taikyu → Taegu	88	35.52 N	128.35 E
Tailai	79	46.23 N	123.27 E
Tai Lam Chung	261d	22.22 N	114.01 E
Tai Lam Chung Reservoir ⊜[1]	261d	22.23 N	114.01 E
Tailem Bend	156	35.16 S	139.27 E
Tailfingen	54	48.15 N	9.01 E
Tai Long, H.K.	261d	22.13 N	113.59 E
Tai Long, H.K.	261d	22.25 N	114.23 E
Tai Long Head ≻	261d	22.24 N	114.24 E
Tai Long Wan C	261d	22.24 N	114.24 E
Taima, Nihon	86	34.30 N	135.42 E
T'aima, T'aiwan	90	22.37 N	120.59 E
Taimba	64	60.18 N	98.58 E
Tai Mo Shan ∧	261d	22.25 N	114.07 E
Taimyr-Halbinsel → Tajmyr, Poluostrov ≻[1]	64	76.00 N	104.00 E
Tain	28	57.48 N	4.04 W
Tainaka	260	34.36 N	135.37 E
T'ainan	90	23.00 N	120.11 E
T'ainanhsien	90	23.18 N	120.19 E
Taínaron, Ákra ≻	38	36.22 N	22.30 E
Taining	90	26.54 N	117.09 E
Tain-l'Hermitage	56	45.04 N	4.51 E
Tai O, H.K.	90	22.15 N	113.51 E
Taio, It.	58	46.20 N	11.04 E
Taiobeiras	245	15.49 S	42.14 W
Taiof Island I	165e	5.31 S	154.39 E
Taipas	245	12.15 S	47.09 W
T'aipei	90		
	259d	25.03 N	121.30 E
T'aipei □[6]	259d	25.00 N	121.40 E
Taipei Bridge ◆[5]	259d	24.04 N	121.30 E
T'aipeihsien	90	25.00 N	121.27 E
Taipei Institute of Technology ʋ[2]	259d	25.02 N	121.32 E
Taipei International Airport ⊠	259d	25.04 N	121.33 E
Taipei Park ♠	259d	25.03 N	121.31 E
T'aipei Shih □[7]	259d	25.03 N	121.30 E
Taiping, Malay.	104	4.51 N	100.44 E
Taiping, Zhg.	90	30.18 N	118.12 E
Taiping, Zhg.	92	22.34 N	107.30 E
Taipingchang, Zhg.	92	27.25 N	103.04 E
Taipingchang, Zhg.	97	30.39 N	105.54 E
Taipingchang, Zhg.	97	29.53 N	106.04 E
Taipingchang, Zhg.	97	29.33 N	103.33 E
Taipingchang, Zhg.	97	29.55 N	103.49 E
Taipingchang, Zhg.	97	30.10 N	106.21 E
Taipingchuan, Zhg.	79	44.23 N	123.11 E
Taipingchuan, Zhg.	88	42.36 N	127.20 E
Taipingdian	92	32.08 N	111.45 E
Taipingkou	90	29.50 N	113.35 E
Taipingling	79	43.26 N	128.09 E
Taipingqiao	96	31.26 N	120.42 E
Taipingshan, Zhg.	88	40.34 N	122.25 E
Taipingshan, Zhg.	94	41.36 N	123.41 E
T'aip'ing Shan ∧	90	24.30 N	121.38 E
Taipingshao	88	40.54 N	125.08 E
Taipingsi	97	29.24 N	103.34 E
Taipingxigou	94	42.36 N	121.13 E
Taipingzhai	94	42.14 N	124.07 E
Taipingzhen, Zhg.	79	46.44 N	130.44 E
Taipingzhen, Zhg.	79	51.33 N	120.17 E
Taipingzhen, Zhg.	92	35.42 N	107.37 E
Taipingzhen, Zhg.	97	29.24 N	105.47 E
Taipingzhen, Zhg.	97	30.26 N	104.12 E
Taipingzhuang, Zhg.	94	42.38 N	123.45 E
Taipingzhuang, Zhg.	95	40.03 N	116.24 E
Taipingzhuang, Zhg.	95	40.08 N	117.36 E
Tai Po Hoi C	261d	22.26 N	114.12 E
Tai Po Tsai	261d	22.21 N	114.15 E
Taipu	240	5.37 S	35.36 W
Taipusiqi (Baochang)	88	41.56 N	115.22 E
Taira, Nihon	84	36.26 N	136.57 E
Taira → Iwaki, Nihon	84	37.03 N	140.55 E
Taira, Nihon	164m	26.38 N	128.09 E
Tairetá	246	22.36 S	43.42 W
Tairiqiao	96	30.59 N	121.33 E
Tais	102	4.06 S	102.34 E
Taisen-zan ∧	86	33.06 N	131.17 E
Taisetsu-zan ∧	80	43.30 N	142.57 E
Taisetsu-zan-kokuritsu-kōen ♠	82a	43.30 N	142.57 E
Taisha, Nihon	86	35.24 N	132.40 E
Taisha → Izumo, Nihon	86	35.22 N	132.46 E
Taishaku-kyō ♠	86	34.53 N	133.13 E
Taishaku-zan ∧, Nihon	84	36.58 N	139.28 E
Taishaku-zan ∧, Nihon	260	34.47 N	135.07 E
Taishan	92	22.16 N	112.44 E
Taishan I	90	26.59 N	120.37 E
Taishanchang	97	30.32 N	106.42 E
Taishi, Nihon	86	34.50 N	134.33 E
Taishi, Nihon	260	34.31 N	135.39 E
Taishō	86	33.12 N	132.58 E
Taishō ◆[8]	260	34.38 N	135.27 E
Taishun	90	27.33 N	119.43 E
Taita Hills ⋏[2]	144	3.25 S	38.20 E
Taitao, Península de ≻[1]	244	46.30 S	74.25 W
Taitapu	162	43.40 S	172.33 E
Taitō ◆[8]	258	35.43 N	139.47 E
Tai Tong	261d	22.25 N	114.01 E
Taitouying	88	40.02 N	119.12 E
Taitō-zaki ≻	84	35.18 N	140.29 E
T'aitung	90	22.45 N	121.09 E
Taivalkoski	26	65.34 N	28.15 E
Taiwan □[1]	80		
	90	23.30 N	121.00 E
T'aiwan (Formosa) I	90	23.30 N	121.00 E
Tai Wan Tau	261d	22.18 N	114.17 E
Tai Wan Tsun	261d	22.19 N	114.12 E
Taiwei	90	23.19 N	114.29 E
Taixi	90	24.42 N	116.56 E
Taixing	96	32.11 N	120.01 E
Taixinzhuang	95	38.57 N	115.44 E
Taixizhen	96	31.03 N	119.49 E
Taiyang	90	30.12 N	119.19 E
Taiyanggong	261a	39.58 N	116.25 E
Taiyanghekou	92	31.54 N	101.49 E
Taíyetos Óros ⋏	38	37.16 N	22.12 E
Taiyuan	92	37.55 N	112.30 E
Taizhao	110	30.01 N	93.08 E
Taizhou	90	32.30 N	119.58 E
Taizhouwan C	90	28.38 N	121.40 E
Taizihe ≃	88	41.00 N	122.26 E
Ta'izz	134	13.38 N	44.04 E
Tāj al-'Izz	132	30.57 N	31.35 E
Tajapuru, Furo do ≃[1]	240	1.50 S	50.25 W
Tajarḥī	136	24.21 N	14.28 E
Tajbola	24	68.26 N	33.19 E
Tajdakovo	72	54.29 N	37.32 E
Taježnyj	78	56.13 N	94.55 E
Tajga	76	56.04 N	85.37 E
Tajginka	76	55.37 N	60.30 E
Tajgonos, Poluostrov ≻[1]	64	61.20 N	161.00 E
Tajima	84	37.12 N	139.46 E
Tajimi	84	35.19 N	137.08 E
Tajique	190	34.45 N	106.17 W
Tajiri	260	34.24 N	135.18 E
Tajitos	222	30.58 N	112.18 W
Tajkanskij Chrebet ⋏	79	54.15 N	134.50 E
Tajlakdžegen	76	43.54 N	60.29 E
Tajlakovy	76	59.20 N	74.04 E
Tajmyr, Ozero ⊜	64	74.30 N	102.30 E
Tajmyr, Poluostrov ≻[1]	64	76.00 N	104.00 E
Tajna	78	56.27 N	95.30 E
Tajninka	255b	55.54 N	37.45 E
Tajo → Tagus ≃	34	38.40 N	9.24 W
Tajpur, Bhārat	114	25.51 N	85.41 E
Tajpur, Bhārat	114	29.10 N	78.29 E
Tājpur, Bhārat	262b	22.44 N	88.16 E
Tajpur Khurd ◆[8]	262a	28.35 N	77.03 E
Tajrīsh	118	35.48 N	51.25 E
Tajšet	78	55.57 N	98.00 E
Tajsojgan	70	48.19 N	53.29 E
Tajturka	78	52.51 N	103.28 E
Tajumulco, Volcán ∧[1]	226	15.02 N	91.55 W
Tajuña ≃	34	40.07 N	3.35 W
Tājūrā', Lībīya	136	32.53 N	13.21 E
Tajura, S.S.S.R.	78	57.00 N	106.35 E
Tajura ≃	78	57.00 N	106.35 E
Tajžina	76	53.38 N	87.28 E
Tak	100	16.52 N	99.08 E
Takāb	118	36.24 N	47.07 E
Takabanare-jima I	164m	26.22 N	127.59 E
Takabara	140	11.50 N	11.30 W
Takachiho	82	32.42 N	131.18 E
Takachu	146	22.37 S	21.58 E
Takada, Nihon	84	37.06 N	138.15 E
Takada, Nihon	86	33.06 N	130.28 E
Takada → Bungo-takada, Nihon	86	33.33 N	131.27 E
Takada → Yamato-takada, Nihon	86	34.31 N	135.45 E
Takagi	258	35.56 N	139.35 E
Takahagi	84	36.43 N	140.43 E
Takahama, Nihon	84	34.55 N	136.59 E
Takahama, Nihon	84	37.00 N	136.46 E
Takahama, Nihon	86	35.29 N	135.33 E
Takahara ≃	84	36.28 N	137.15 E
Takahashi	86	34.47 N	133.37 E
Takahashi ≃	86	34.31 N	133.42 E
Takahe, Mount ∧	9	76.16 S	112.14 W
Takaido ◆[8]	258	35.40 N	139.37 E
Takaishi	86	34.32 N	135.26 E
Takaka	162	40.51 S	172.48 E
Takalar	102	5.28 S	119.24 E
Takamatsu, Nihon	84	36.46 N	136.43 E
Takamatsu, Nihon	86	34.20 N	134.03 E
Takamatsu, Nihon	86	34.41 N	133.49 E
Takami-shima I	86	34.19 N	133.41 E
Takamiya	86	34.47 N	132.44 E
Takami-yama ∧	84	34.25 N	136.05 E
Takamori	84	35.33 N	137.53 E
Takanabe	82	32.08 N	131.30 E
Takanawa-hantō ≻[1]	86	33.58 N	132.56 E
Takanawa-san ∧	86	33.56 N	132.51 E
Takane	84	35.50 N	138.25 E
Takanezawa	84	36.37 N	139.59 E
Takano	86	35.02 N	132.55 E
Takanosu	82	40.13 N	140.22 E
Takao → Kaohsiung	90	22.38 N	120.17 E
Takaoka	84	36.45 N	137.01 E
Takao-kokutei-kōen ♠	84	35.38 N	139.15 E
Takao-san ∧	84	35.38 N	139.15 E
Takao-san ∧[2]	260	34.49 N	135.51 E
Takapau	162	40.02 S	176.21 E
Takapoto I[1]	14	14.38 S	145.12 W
Takapuna	162	36.47 S	174.47 E
Takara-jima I	83b	29.09 N	129.13 E
Takarazuka	86	34.49 N	135.21 E
Takartibah	136	26.32 N	13.15 E
Takasago	86	34.45 N	134.48 E
Takasaki	84	36.20 N	139.01 E
Takase	86	34.10 N	133.45 E
Takase ≃	84	36.28 N	137.52 E
Takashima, Nihon	82	32.39 N	129.45 E
Takashima, Nihon	84	35.18 N	136.01 E
Taka-shima I	86	34.50 N	131.50 E
Takashippu	164m	26.24 N	127.44 E
Takasu	84	35.57 N	136.53 E
Takata → Rikuzen-takata, Nihon	82	39.01 N	141.38 E
Takata → Takada, Nihon	84	37.06 N	138.15 E
Takatik I	164r	7.00 N	158.12 E
Takatō	84	35.50 N	138.04 E
Takatomi	84	35.29 N	136.47 E
Takatori	86	34.27 N	135.48 E
Takatori-yama ∧, Nihon	86	33.18 N	130.43 E
Takatori-yama ∧, Nihon	258	35.18 N	139.37 E
Takatsu ≃	86	34.42 N	131.49 E
Takatsuki, Nihon	84	35.28 N	136.14 E
Takatsuki, Nihon	86	34.51 N	135.37 E
Takaungu	144	3.41 S	39.51 E
Ta-kaw	100	21.36 N	98.56 E
Takawa	86	33.38 N	130.49 E
Takaya	86	34.27 N	132.49 E
Takayama, Nihon	84	36.40 N	138.21 E
Takayama, Nihon	84	36.37 N	138.57 E
Takayama, Nihon	84	36.08 N	137.15 E
Takayama, Nihon	260	34.45 N	135.49 E
Takayanagi, Nihon	84	37.13 N	138.38 E
Takayanagi, Nihon	258	35.25 N	139.57 E
Tak Bai	104	6.16 N	102.03 E
Takčijan	75	38.32 N	68.03 E
Takefu	84	35.54 N	136.10 E
Takehara	86	34.21 N	132.55 E
Takela	110	37.54 N	76.44 E
Takeli	75	40.30 N	69.25 E
Takenake	110	34.11 N	81.20 E
Takeno ≃	86	35.45 N	135.06 E
Takenotsuka ◆[8]	258	35.48 N	139.48 E
Takeo	82	33.12 N	130.01 E
Takeoka	258	35.12 N	139.51 E
Tåkern ⊜	26	58.21 N	14.48 E
Takeshi	84	36.17 N	138.14 E
Take-shima I	83b	30.49 N	130.26 E
Tākestān	118	36.04 N	49.43 E
Taketa	86	32.58 N	131.24 E
Taketoyo	84	34.51 N	136.55 E
Takêv	100	10.59 N	104.47 E
Take-yama ∧[2]	258	35.13 N	139.39 E
Takhādīd ⍑[4]	118	29.59 N	44.30 E
Takhār □[4]	110	36.30 N	69.30 E
Takhatpur	114	22.09 N	81.52 E
Ta Khli	100	15.15 N	100.21 E
Ta-khoa	100	21.13 N	104.18 E
Takht-i-Bhāi	113	34.17 N	71.56 E
Takht-i-Sulaiman ∧	113	35.29 N	75.18 E
Tāki, Bhārat	116	22.36 N	88.55 E
Taki, Nihon	84	34.30 N	136.33 E
Taki, Nihon	86	35.16 N	132.38 E
Taki, Pap. N. Gui.	165e	6.29 S	155.50 E
Takijuq Lake ⊜	166	66.15 N	113.05 W
Takikawa	82a	43.33 N	141.54 E
Takingeun	104	4.38 N	96.50 E
Takino	86	34.56 N	134.58 E
Takipur	116	24.19 N	87.58 E
Takitimu Mountains ⋏	162	45.41 S	167.53 E
Takla Lake ⊜	172	55.25 N	125.53 W
Takla Landing	172	55.29 N	125.58 W
Takla Makan → Talimupendi ◆[2]	80	39.00 N	83.00 E
Tako	84	35.44 N	140.28 E
Takob	75	38.50 N	68.57 E
Tako-bana ≻	86	35.36 N	133.06 E
Takolekaju, Pegunungan ⋏	102	2.00 S	121.00 E
Takoma Park	274c	38.59 N	77.01 W
Takoradi → Sekondi-Takoradi	140	4.59 N	1.43 W
Takotna	170	62.56 N	156.04 W
Takow → Kaohsiung	90	22.38 N	120.17 E
Takrouna	36	36.09 N	10.20 E
Taksino	72	56.19 N	36.10 E
Takslesluk Lake ⊜	170	61.04 N	162.55 W
Taksony	254c	47.20 N	19.04 E
Taku	82	33.17 N	130.08 E
Taku ≃	170	58.26 N	133.59 W
Takuam, Mount ∧	165e	6.27 S	155.36 E
Takua Pa	100	8.53 N	98.21 E
Taku Arm ⊜	170	60.00 N	134.10 W
Taku Glacier ⍓	170	58.35 N	134.10 W
Takum	140	7.17 N	9.59 E
Takuma	86	34.13 N	133.40 E
Takundi	142	4.45 S	16.34 E
Takutea I	14	19.49 S	158.18 W
Takut Tangug Bay C	106	6.33 N	122.15 E
Takutu (Tacutu) ≃	236	3.01 N	60.29 W
Takysie Lake	172	53.54 N	125.53 W
Tāl	113	34.55 N	72.13 E
Tala, Arg.	242	26.07 S	65.17 W
Tāla, Bhārat	114	23.43 N	81.02 E
Tala, Bngl.	116	22.46 N	89.16 E
Tala, Méx.	224	20.40 N	103.42 W
Talā, Miṣr	132	30.41 N	30.56 E
Tala, Ur.	242	34.21 S	55.46 W
Tala, Arroyo del ≃	248	33.37 S	56.34 W
Talacogon	106	8.28 N	125.46 E
Talaga	102	2.11 S	125.53 E
Talagang	113	32.55 N	72.25 E
Talagante	242	33.40 S	70.56 W
Talagante □[5]	276e	33.34 S	70.44 W
Talagou	94	41.37 N	120.32 E
Talaimannar	112	9.05 N	79.44 E
Talāja	110	21.21 N	72.03 E
Talak ◆[1]	140	18.20 N	6.00 E
Talakag	106	8.16 N	124.37 E
Talakan	79	49.38 N	133.18 E
Talakovka	73	47.10 N	37.43 E
Tālāla	110	21.02 N	70.32 E
Talalajevka	68	50.51 N	33.08 E
Talamanca, Cordillera de ⋏	226	9.30 N	83.40 W
Talamba	113	30.32 N	72.14 E
Talamone	60	42.33 N	11.08 E
Talana	148	28.10 S	30.15 E
Talandža	79	49.27 N	131.35 E
Talang, Gunung ∧	102	1.11 S	100.43 E
Talangbatu	102	4.06 S	105.29 E
Talangbetutu	102	2.53 S	104.41 E
Talangpadang	102	5.21 S	104.11 E
Talangrimbo	102	3.29 S	105.25 E

≃ River	Fluss	Río	Rivière	Rio	
≋ Canal	Kanal	Canal	Canal	Canal	
⌊ Waterfall, Rapids	Wasserfall, Stromschnellen	Cascada, Rápidos	Chute d'eau, Rapides	Cascata, Rápidos	
⋃ Strait	Meeresstrasse	Estrecho	Détroit	Estreito	
C Bay, Gulf	Bucht, Golf	Bahía, Golfo	Baie, Golfe	Baía, Golfo	
⊜ Lake, Lakes	See, Seen	Lago, Lagos	Lac, Lacs	Lago, Lagos	
☷ Swamp	Sumpf	Pantano	Marais	Pântano	
⍓ Ice Features, Glacier	Eis- und Gletscherformen	Accidentes Glaciales	Formes glaciaires	Acidentes Glaciares	
∨ Other Hydrographic Features	Andere Hydrographische Objekte	Otros Elementos Hidrográficos	Autres données hydrographiques	Outros Elementos Hidrográficos	
✢ Submarine Features	Untermeerische Objekte	Accidentes Submarinos	Formes de relief sous-marin	Acidentes Submarinos	
□ Political Unit	Politische Einheit	Unidad Politica	Entité politique	Unidade Política	
ʋ Cultural Institution	Kulturelle Institution	Institución Cultural	Institution culturelle	Instituição Cultural	
⊥ Historical Site	Historische Stätte	Sitio Histórico	Site historique	Sitio Histórico	
♠ Recreational Site	Erholungs- und Ferienort	Sitio de Recreo	Centre de loisirs	Sítio de Lazer	
⊠ Airport	Flughafen	Aeropuerto	Aéroport	Aeroporto	
■ Military Installation	Militäranlage	Instalación Militar	Installation militaire	Instalação Militar	
◆ Miscellaneous	Verschiedenes	Misceláneo	Divers	Miscelânea	

ENGLISH — Name, Page, Lat.°′, Long.°′ — DEUTSCH — Name, Seite, Breite°′, Länge°′ E=Ost

Talant 54 47.19 N 5.00 E
Talap 70 48.26 N 48.03 E
Talara 236 4.34 S 81.17 W
Talarrubias 34 39.02 N 5.14 W
Talas 75 42.32 N 72.14 E
Talas ≃ 75 44.02 N 69.37 E
Talasea 154 5.20 S 150.05 E
Talatakoh, Pulau I 102 0.22 S 122.05 E
Tal'at al-Jamā'ah, Rujm ∧ 122 30.23 N 35.30 E
Talata Mafara 140 12.35 N 6.04 E
Talaud, Kepulauan II 98 4.20 N 126.50 E
Talavera 106 15.35 N 120.55 E
Talavera de la Reina 34 39.57 N 4.50 W
Talawanta 156 18.38 S 140.16 E
Talawdī 130 10.38 N 30.23 E
Talayan 106 6.55 N 124.24 E
Tālbāndh 116 22.03 N 86.20 E
Talbingo 161b 35.34 S 148.18 E
Talbingo Reservoir ⊜[1] 161b 35.43 S 148.20 E
Talbot 159 37.11 S 143.43 E
Talbot ≃ 202 44.28 N 79.10 W
Talbot, Cape ≻ 154 13.48 S 126.43 E
Talbot Brook 158a 32.01 S 116.40 E
Talbot Islands II 154 9.15 S 142.08 E
Talbot Lake ⊜, Man., Can. 174 54.00 N 99.55 W
Talbot Lake ⊜, Ont., Can. 202 44.42 N 78.51 W
Talbotton 182 32.41 N 84.32 W
Talbotville Royal 204 42.48 N 81.15 W
Talbragar ≃ 156 32.12 S 148.37 E
Talca 242 35.26 S 71.40 W
Talca □[4] 242 35.30 S 71.10 W
Talcahuano 242 36.43 S 73.07 W
Tālcher 110 20.57 N 85.13 E
Talco 186 33.22 N 95.06 W
Talcottville 197 41.49 N 72.30 W
Talcy, Château de ⊥ 46 47.46 N 1.27 E
Taldan 79 53.40 N 124.48 E
Tāldāngra 116 23.02 N 87.06 E
Taldom 72 56.44 N 37.32 E
Taldyapan, S.S.S.R. 70 49.46 N 50.14 E
Taldyapan, S.S.S.R. 70 48.07 N 47.08 E
Taldyk, Pereval)(75 39.47 N 73.11 E
Taldykuduk 70 50.09 N 49.33 E
Taldy-Kurgan 76 45.00 N 78.23 E
Taldy-Kurgan Oblast' □[4] 75 44.00 N 78.00 E
Tale 140 9.26 N 1.07 W
Taleh 134 9.12 N 48.23 E
Tal-e Khosravī 118 30.37 N 51.35 E
Talent 192 42.15 N 122.47 W
Taley 142 6.40 N 16.23 E
Talgar 75 43.18 N 77.18 E
Talgar, Pik ∧ 75 43.05 N 77.20 E
Talgarreg 44 52.08 N 4.18 W
Talgarth 44 52.00 N 3.15 W
Ṭalḥ, 'Ilw aṭ- ∧[2] 132 28.30 N 29.38 E
Talhār 110 24.53 N 68.49 E
Tali, Pointe de ≻ 231o 15.56 N 61.12 W
Talia, Austl. 152 33.19 S 134.54 E
Talia, Méx. 186 25.44 N 102.26 W
Taliabu, Pulau I 102 1.48 S 124.48 E
Taliandao I 88 39.03 N 122.52 E
Talibon 106 10.09 N 124.19 E
Talibong, Ko I 100 7.15 N 99.23 E
Talica, S.S.S.R. 66 58.44 N 41.34 E
Talica, S.S.S.R. 70 58.01 N 51.30 E
Talica, S.S.S.R. 76 57.00 N 63.43 E
Talickij Čamlyk 70 52.02 N 40.32 E
Talien → Lüda 88 38.53 N 121.35 E
Talihina 186 34.45 N 95.03 W
Tālīkota 112 16.29 N 76.19 E
Talikud Island I 106 6.56 N 125.42 E
Talim Island I 106 14.21 N 121.14 E
Talimuashili 75 39.08 N 77.03 E
Talimuhe ≃ 80 41.05 N 86.40 E
Talimupendi (Takla Makan) ◆[2] 80 39.00 N 83.00 E
Taling Chan 259a 13.46 N 100.27 E
Taliouine 138 30.36 N 7.49 W
Taliparamba 112 12.03 N 75.21 E
Tali Post 130 5.54 N 30.47 E
Talisay, Pil. 106 14.08 N 122.55 E
Talisay, Pil. 106 10.44 N 122.58 E
Talisayan 106 9.00 N 124.55 E
Talisei, Pulau I 102 1.51 N 125.05 E
Talish-Mikeyli 74 39.23 N 48.22 E
Talish Mountains (Kūhhā-ye Ṭavālesh) ⛰ 118 38.42 N 48.18 E
Taliwang 105b 8.44 S 116.52 E
Tal'ka 66 53.22 N 28.21 E
Talkeetna 170 62.20 N 150.07 W
Talkeetna Mountains ⛰ 170 62.10 N 148.15 W
Ṭalkhā 132 31.03 N 31.22 E
Talkheh ≃ 118 37.40 N 45.46 E
Tālkot 114 29.37 N 81.19 E
Talladega 184 33.26 N 86.06 W
Tall 'Afar 118 36.22 N 42.27 E
Tal Lah, Bhārat 116 22.19 N 87.18 E
Tallah, Miṣr 132 28.05 N 30.44 E
Tallahaga Creek ≃ 184 32.55 N 88.58 W
Tallahala Creek ≃ 184 31.12 N 89.05 W
Tallahassee 182 30.25 N 84.16 W
Tall al-Abyaḍ 120 36.41 N 38.57 E
Tall al-'Amārnah (Akhetatem) ⊥ 132 27.38 N 30.54 E
Tall al-Maskhūtah (Succotah) ⊥ 132 30.33 N 32.07 E
Tallanalla 158a 33.06 S 116.07 E
Tallangatta 156 36.13 S 147.15 E
Tallangatta Creek ≃ 161b 36.15 S 147.13 E
Tallapoosa 184 33.45 N 85.17 W
Tallapoosa ≃ 184 32.30 N 86.16 W
Tallard 56 44.28 N 6.03 E
Tallarook, Mount ∧ 159 37.22 S 145.19 E
Tall ar-Ratābah (Pithom) ⊥ 132 30.32 N 32.06 E
Tall ar-Rub'(Mendes) ⊥ 132 30.58 N 31.31 E
Tallassee 184 32.27 N 85.54 W
Tall as-Sulṭān ⊥ 122 31.52 N 35.27 E
Tall Banī 'Umrān 132 27.40 N 30.54 E
Tall Basṭah (Bubastis) ⊥ 132 30.34 N 31.31 E
Tällberg 26 60.49 N 15.00 E
Tall Bīsah 120 34.50 N 36.44 E
Talleyville 198 39.48 N 75.33 W
Tallinn 66 59.25 N 24.45 E
Tall Kalakh 120 34.40 N 36.15 E
Tall Kayf 118 36.29 N 43.08 E
Tall Kūshik 120 36.48 N 42.04 E
Tallmadge 204 41.06 N 81.27 W
Tallman 266 41.07 N 74.06 W
Tallman Mountain State Park ♠ 266 41.01 N 73.54 W
Talloires 56 45.51 N 6.13 E
Tallong 160 34.44 S 150.05 E
Tall Rāk 132 30.54 N 31.43 E
Tall Rif'at 120 36.28 N 37.06 E
Tall Salḥab 120 35.15 N 36.22 E
Tall Tamir 120 36.39 N 40.22 E
Tallula 209 39.56 N 89.56 W
Tallulah 184 32.25 N 91.11 W
Tally 70 53.08 N 53.04 E
Tally Ho 264b 37.52 S 145.09 E
Tālma 116 23.29 N 89.54 E
Talmage, Calif., U.S. 194 39.08 N 123.10 W
Talmage, Nebr., U.S. 188 40.32 N 96.01 W
Talmage, Pa., U.S. 198 40.07 N 76.13 W
Talmalmo 161b 35.56 S 147.30 E
Talmas 46 50.02 N 2.20 E
Talmazy 68 46.38 N 29.40 E
Tal'menka 76 53.51 N 83.35 E
Talmont 32 46.28 N 1.37 W
Tal'niki 78 52.47 N 102.24 E
Tal'noje 68 48.53 N 30.42 E
Talo ∧ 134 10.44 N 37.55 E
Taloda 110 21.34 N 74.13 E
Talofofo 164p 13.21 N 144.45 E
Talofofo Bay C 164p 13.20 N 144.46 E
Taloga 186 36.02 N 98.58 W
Taloje 78 55.24 N 95.40 E
Taloje Budrukh 262c 19.05 N 73.05 E
Talok 102 1.03 N 118.48 E
Talomako 165f 15.10 S 166.48 E
Talonan, Tano ≻ 105b 9.07 S 117.02 E
Tāloqān 110 36.44 N 69.33 E
Talovaja 68 51.06 N 40.44 E
Talovka, S.S.S.R. 70 49.58 N 45.01 E
Talovka, S.S.S.R. 70 50.25 N 47.35 E
Talovka, S.S.S.R. 74 44.14 N 46.36 E
Talovka, S.S.S.R. 76 51.27 N 81.54 E
Talovka, S.S.S.R. 76 57.10 N 93.09 E
Talovoje 73 48.18 N 39.40 E
Talpa 186 31.47 N 99.43 W
Talpa de Allende 224 20.23 N 104.51 W
Talpaka Sar ∧ 113 33.42 N 70.31 E
Talquin, Lake ⊜[1] 182 30.26 N 84.33 W
Tālsa 262b 22.49 N 88.33 E
Talsarnau 44 52.54 N 4.03 W
Talsi 66 57.15 N 22.36 E
Talšik 76 53.42 N 71.53 E
Taltal 242 25.24 S 70.29 W
Taltapin Lake ⊜ 172 54.19 N 125.20 W
Taltson ≃ 166 61.23 N 112.45 W
Talu 102 0.14 N 99.59 E
Taludaa 102 0.20 N 123.28 E
Taluk 102 0.32 S 101.35 E
Talumphuk, Laem ≻ 100 8.30 N 100.10 E
Taluti, Teluk C 154 3.21 S 129.45 E
Talvik'ul'a 24 68.45 N 29.19 E
Talwandi Bhāi 113 30.51 N 74.56 E
Talwood 156 28.30 S 149.30 E
Taly 68 49.51 N 40.04 E
Ṭalyā 132 30.16 N 31.00 E
Talybont 44 52.29 N 3.59 W
Talyzino 70 55.06 N 45.49 E
Tama, Arg. 242 30.31 S 66.32 W
Tama, Nihon 84 35.37 N 139.27 E
Tama, Iowa, U.S. 180 41.58 N 92.35 W
Tama ≃ 84 35.32 N 139.47 E
Tama Cemetery ◆ 258 35.41 N 139.31 E
Tamacuarí, Pico ∧ 236 1.15 N 64.45 W
Tamadjert 138 25.36 N 7.20 E
Tamagawa, Nihon 84 37.12 N 140.24 E
Tamagawa, Nihon 86 34.01 N 132.56 E
Tamagawa ◆[8] 258 35.37 N 139.39 E
Tamagawa-josui ≃ 258 35.42 N 139.35 E
Tamakautoga 164v 19.05 S 169.55 W
Tamakawa 84 35.07 N 138.20 E
Tamaki 84 34.29 N 136.38 E
Tama-kyūryō 258 35.35 N 139.30 E
Tamala, Austl. 152 26.42 S 113.45 E
Tamala, S.S.S.R. 70 52.33 N 43.16 E
Tamalameque 236 8.52 N 73.49 W
Ṭamalāy 132 30.30 N 30.51 E
Tamale 140 9.25 N 0.50 W
Tamalea 102 2.29 S 119.19 E
Tamalpais, Mount ∧ 216 37.56 N 122.35 W
Tamalpais Valley 216 37.53 N 122.32 W
Tamamura 84 36.18 N 139.07 E
Taman, Indon. 105a 7.25 S 112.41 E
Taman', S.S.S.R. 68 45.13 N 36.43 E
Tamana 82 32.55 N 130.33 E
Tamana I 14 2.29 S 175.59 E
Tamaná, Cerro ∧ 236 5.02 N 76.17 W
Tamana, Mount ∧[2] 231r 10.28 N 61.12 W
Tamanaco ≃ 236 9.25 N 65.23 W
Tamanan 105a 8.01 S 113.49 E
Tamanar 138 31.00 N 9.35 W
Tamandaré 240 8.45 S 35.06 W
Tamandourirt, Oued ∨ 140 19.39 N 2.04 W
Tamanduatei ≃ 277b 23.36 S 46.35 W
Tamanhint 136 27.13 N 14.36 E
Tamani 140 13.20 N 6.50 W
Tamaniquá 236 2.38 S 65.44 W
Taman Negara ♠ 104 4.43 N 102.23 E
Tamano 86 34.30 N 133.56 E
Tamanrasset 138 22.56 N 5.30 E
Tamanrasset □[5] 138 25.00 N 5.00 E
Tamanrasset, Oued ∨ 138 22.10 N 0.10 E
Tamanskij Zaliv C 68 45.18 N 36.45 E
Tamanthi 100 25.19 N 95.18 E
Tamanusi 102 1.48 S 121.18 E
Tamapatz 224 21.35 N 99.09 W
Tamaqua 198 40.48 N 75.58 W
Tamaquari, Ilha I 236 0.28 S 64.55 W
Tamar 78 50.24 N 107.25 E
Tamar ≃, Austl. 156 41.04 S 146.47 E
Tamar ≃, Col. 236 7.01 N 74.15 W
Tamar ≃, Eng., U.K. 44 50.22 N 4.10 W
Támara 236 5.50 N 72.10 W
Tamarac ≃ 188 48.29 N 97.07 W
Tamarack Lake ⊜[1] 204 41.35 N 80.05 W
Tamarite de Litera 34 41.52 N 0.26 E
Tamaroa 184 38.08 N 89.14 W
Tamarome 154 2.54 S 133.38 E
Tamarugal, Pampa del ⌣ 238 21.00 S 69.25 W
Tamashima 86 34.32 N 133.40 E
Tamási 30 46.38 N 18.18 E
Tamaské 140 14.49 N 5.39 E
Tamatave 147b 18.10 S 49.23 E
Tamatave □[4] 147b 18.00 S 48.40 E
Tamatsukuri 84 36.06 N 140.25 E
Tamaulipas □[3] 222 24.00 N 98.45 W
Tamaya ≃ 238 8.31 S 74.13 W
Tamayu 86 35.25 N 133.01 E
Tamazula 222 24.57 N 106.57 W
Tamazula de Gordiano 224 19.38 N 103.15 W
Tamazulapan [del Progreso] 224 17.41 N 97.34 W
Tamazunchale 224 21.16 N 98.47 W
Tamba 86 35.09 N 135.25 E
Tambach-Dietharz 50 50.48 N 10.36 E
Tambacounda 140 13.47 N 13.40 W
Tamba Dabatou 140 11.48 N 10.40 W
Tambak 105a 5.45 S 112.37 E
Tambakboyo 105a 6.48 S 111.50 E
Tamba-kōchi ⛰[1] 82 35.20 N 135.30 E
Tambakrejo 105a 7.16 S 111.36 E
Tambalan 102 3.08 N 115.34 E
Tambangsawah 102 3.02 S 102.11 E
Tambara 144 16.45 S 34.15 E
Tāmbaram 112 12.55 N 80.07 E
Tamba-sanchi ⛰ 260 34.58 N 135.25 E
Tambaú ≃ 246 21.34 S 47.05 W
Tambault, Île à I 265a 45.20 N 73.51 W
També 240 7.25 S 35.06 W
Tambea 102 4.12 S 121.36 E
Tambej 64 71.30 N 71.50 E
Tambelan, Kepulauan II 102 1.00 N 107.30 E
Tambelan Besar, Pulau I 102 0.58 N 107.34 E
Tambellup 152 34.02 S 117.39 E
Tamberías 242 31.28 S 69.25 W
Tambisan, Pulau I 106 5.27 N 119.10 E
Tambler 106 6.03 N 125.09 E
Tambo, Austl. 156 24.53 S 146.15 E
Tambo, Perú 238 12.56 S 74.01 W
Tambo ≃, Austl. 156 37.51 S 147.48 E
Tambo ≃, Perú 238 10.43 S 73.45 W
Tambo ≃, Perú 238 17.10 S 71.51 W
Tamboara 245 23.09 S 52.33 W
Tambo Grande 238 4.56 S 80.21 W
Tambohorano 147b 17.30 S 43.58 E
Tamboli 102 3.57 S 121.20 E
Tambolongang, Pulau I 102 6.36 S 120.24 E
Tambor 226 9.43 N 85.01 W
Tambora, Gunung ∧ 105b 8.14 S 117.55 E
Tamboril 240 4.50 S 40.20 W
Tamborine 161a 27.53 S 153.08 E
Tamboritha, Mount ∧ 156 37.28 S 146.41 E
Tambor Yacu ≃ 236 2.31 S 73.40 W
Tambov 70 52.43 N 41.25 E
Tambov □[4] 68 51.45 N 41.20 E
Tambovka, S.S.S.R. 70 47.18 N 47.23 E
Tambovka, S.S.S.R. 79 50.06 N 128.04 E
Tambre ≃ 34 42.49 N 8.53 W
Tambu 102 0.02 S 119.52 E
Tambu, Teluk C 102 0.02 N 119.45 E
Tambulian Point ≻ 106 7.22 N 123.27 E
Tambunan 102 5.40 N 116.22 E
Tambura 130 5.36 N 27.28 E
Tamburi 245 13.00 S 40.32 W
Tamchaket 140 17.15 N 10.40 W
Tam Chuak, Laem ≻ 100 8.33 N 98.12 E
Tamčijn Davaa)(92 45.50 N 94.01 E
Tame 236 6.28 N 71.44 W
Tame ≃, Eng., U.K. 44 52.44 N 1.43 W
Tame ≃, Eng., U.K. 252 53.25 N 2.09 W
Tameapa 222 25.39 N 107.22 W
Tamedda, Djebel ∧ 138 32.48 N 0.05 E
Tâmega ≃ 34 41.05 N 8.21 W
Tamel Aike 244 48.19 S 70.58 W
Tamelelt 138 31.50 N 7.29 W
Tamenuen 154 6.27 S 139.48 E
Tamerton Foliot 44 50.26 N 4.08 W
Tamerza 138 34.23 N 7.57 E
Tamesí ≃ 224 22.13 N 97.52 W
Tameside □[8] 252 53.29 N 2.03 W
Tamga, S.S.S.R. 75 42.09 N 77.32 E
Tamga, S.S.S.R. 79 45.34 N 133.36 E
Tamgak, Monts ⛰ 140 19.11 N 8.42 E
Tamgué, Massif du ⛰ 140 12.00 N 12.18 W
Tamiahua 224 21.16 N 97.27 W
Tamiahua, Laguna de C 224 21.35 N 97.35 W
Tamiami Canal ≋ 210 25.47 N 80.15 W
Tamica 24 64.10 N 38.05 E
Tamil Nadu □[3] 112 11.00 N 78.15 E
Tamiment 200 41.09 N 75.02 W
Tamina 212 30.11 N 96.26 W
Tamines 52 50.26 N 4.36 E
Tamiryn ≃ 78 47.48 N 102.36 E
Tamiš (Timiș) ≃ 38 44.51 N 20.39 E
Ṭāmiyah 132 29.29 N 30.58 E
Tamkuhi 114 26.41 N 84.11 E
Tam-ky 100 15.34 N 108.29 E
Tamlūk 116 22.18 N 87.55 E
Tāmma 110 25.11 N 93.42 E
Tammaro ≃ 60 41.09 N 14.50 E
Tammerfors → Tampere 26 61.30 N 23.45 E
Tammisaari → Ekenäs 26 59.58 N 23.26 E
Tamms 184 37.14 N 89.16 W
Ṭammūh 263c 29.56 N 31.16 E
Tāmna 116 23.15 N 86.21 E
Tämnarån ≃ 40 60.31 N 17.39 E
Tämnaren ⊜ 40 60.10 N 17.20 E
Tamon ◆[8] 260 34.39 N 135.04 E
Ta Mong Tsai 261d 22.24 N 114.18 E
Tamoroi 164r 6.51 N 158.19 E
Tamós, Laguna de ⊜ 224 22.10 N 98.02 W
Tampa, Ang. 142 15.30 S 13.27 E
Tampa, Fla., U.S. 210 27.57 N 82.27 W
Tampa Bay C 210 27.45 N 82.35 W
Tampa International Airport ⊠ 210 27.59 N 82.32 W
Tampamachoco, Laguna C 224 21.00 N 97.21 W
Tampang 102 5.54 S 104.43 E
Tampaon ≃ 224 21.59 N 98.36 W
Tamparan 106 8.27 N 117.13 E
Tampere 26 61.30 N 23.45 E
Tampico, Méx. 224 22.13 N 97.51 W
Tampico, Ill., U.S. 180 41.38 N 89.47 W
Tampico, Ind., U.S. 208 38.48 N 85.58 W
Tampin 104 2.28 N 102.14 E
Tampoc ≃ 240 3.27 N 54.00 W
Tampu-lunanjing, Dolok ∧ 104 1.46 N 99.24 E
Tam-quan 100 14.35 N 109.03 E
Tamra 122 32.51 N 35.12 E
Tamrau, Pegunungan ⛰ 154 0.30 S 132.27 E
Tamri 138 30.43 N 9.43 W
Tamsagbulag 78 47.16 N 117.17 E
Tamsalu 66 59.10 N 26.06 E
Tamshiyacu 236 4.05 S 72.58 W
Tamsweg 58 47.08 N 13.48 E
Tamu 100 24.13 N 94.18 E
Tamuín 224 21.59 N 98.45 W
Tamuín ≃ 224 21.59 N 98.36 W
Tamuk Island I 106 6.27 N 121.49 E
Tamulung Point ≻ 106 17.15 N 120.25 E
Tamur ≃ 114 26.55 N 87.10 E
Tamura 258 35.22 N 139.22 E
Tamusuke 75 38.03 N 76.53 E
Tamworth, Austl. 156 31.05 S 150.55 E
Tamworth, Ont., Can. 202 44.29 N 77.00 W
Tamyang 88 35.21 N 126.58 E
Tana, Chile 238 19.27 S 69.57 W
Tana, Nor. 24 70.28 N 28.18 E
Tana I 165f 19.30 S 169.20 E
Tana ≃, Cuba 230p 20.42 N 77.25 W
Tana ≃, Kenya 144 2.32 S 40.31 E
T'an'a ≃, S.S.S.R. 78 58.40 N 120.30 E
Tana, Lake ⊜ 134 12.00 N 37.20 E
Tanabe, Nihon 86 34.49 N 135.46 E
Tanabe, Nihon 86 33.44 N 135.22 E
Tanabi 245 20.37 S 49.37 W
Tanacross 170 63.23 N 143.21 W
Tanafjorden C[2] 24 70.54 N 28.40 E
Tanaga Island I 171a 51.50 N 178.00 W
Tanaga Volcano ∧[1] 171a 51.53 N 178.09 W
Tanaguarena 276c 10.37 N 66.49 W
Tanagura 84 37.02 N 140.23 E
Tanah, Tanjung ≻ 105a 6.29 S 108.32 E
Tanahbala, Pulau I 100 0.25 S 98.25 E
Tanahgrogot 102 1.55 S 116.12 E
Tanahjampea, Pulau I 102 7.05 S 120.42 E
Tanahmasa, Pulau I 100 0.12 S 98.27 E
Tanahmerah, Indon. 102 3.41 N 117.31 E
Tanahmerah, Indon. 154 6.05 S 140.17 E
Tanah Merah, Malay. 104 2.36 N 101.48 E
Tanah Merah, Malay. 104 5.48 N 102.09 E
Tanahputih 104 1.41 N 101.03 E
Tanaka ◆[8] 260 34.42 N 135.00 E
Tanaka Malai ∧ 112 10.21 N 77.04 E
Tanakeke, Pulau I 102 5.30 S 119.16 E
Tanakpur 114 29.05 N 80.07 E
Tan'am 118 23.09 N 56.29 E
Tanami 152 19.59 S 129.43 E
Tanami Desert ◆[2] 152 20.00 S 129.30 E
Tanami Desert Wildlife Sanctuary ◆[4] 152 20.45 S 131.10 E
Ṭanān, Miṣr 132 30.15 N 31.14 E
Tan-an, Viet. 100 8.46 N 105.11 E
Tan-an, Viet. 100 10.32 N 106.25 E
Tanana 170 65.10 N 152.05 W
Tanana ≃ 170 65.09 N 151.55 W
Tananarive → Antananarivo 147b 18.55 S 47.31 E
Tananarive □[4] 147b 19.00 S 47.00 E
Tanapag 164n 15.14 N 145.45 E
Tanapag Harbor C 164n 15.14 N 145.44 E
Tanaro ≃ 56 45.01 N 8.47 E
Tanārūt, Wādī ∨ 136 30.08 N 9.59 E
Tanashi 84 35.44 N 139.33 E
Tanat ≃ 44 52.46 N 3.07 W
Tanauan 106 11.07 N 125.01 E
Tanay 106 14.30 N 121.17 E
Tanba-kōchi ⛰[1] 86 35.17 N 135.30 E
Tanbar 156 25.50 S 141.55 E
Tanbara 86 33.54 N 133.04 E
Ṭanbidī 132 28.38 N 30.47 E
Tan-binh 259c 10.48 N 106.40 E
Tanbu, Zhg. 88 35.51 N 118.17 E
Tanbu, Zhg. 90 28.08 N 114.12 E
Tancarville 46 49.29 N 0.28 E
Tancarville, Canal de ≋ 46 49.28 N 0.28 E
Tancha 164m 26.28 N 121.50 E
Tan-chau 100 10.48 N 105.15 E
Tancheng 88 34.37 N 118.23 E
Tanchipa, Sierra de ⛰ 224 22.20 N 98.50 W
Tanchoj 78 51.33 N 105.07 E
Tanch'ŏn 88 40.27 N 128.54 E
Tancítaro 224 19.20 N 102.22 W
Tancítaro, Pico de ∧ 224 19.23 N 102.13 W
Tancochapa ≃ 224 17.59 N 94.04 W
Tānda, Bhārat 114 26.33 N 82.39 E
Tānda, Bhārat 114 28.59 N 78.56 E
Tanda, C. Iv. 140 7.48 N 3.10 W
Tānda, Pāk. 113 32.42 N 74.22 E
Tandaai 144 19.36 S 32.48 E
Tandag 106 9.04 N 126.12 E
Tandah 132 27.41 N 30.46 E
Tandaj 70 47.33 N 51.30 E
Tandala 144 9.23 S 34.14 E
Tandaltī 130 13.01 N 31.52 E
Ţăndărei 38 44.38 N 27.40 E
Tandian 88 40.39 N 124.46 E
Tandil 242 37.19 S 59.09 W
Tandjiesberg ⛰ 148 32.12 S 25.00 E
Tandjilé □[5] 136 9.45 N 16.30 E
Tandjilé ≃ 136 9.45 N 15.50 E
Tāndliānwāla 113 31.02 N 73.08 E
Tando Ādam 110 25.46 N 68.40 E
Tando Allāhyār 110 25.28 N 68.43 E
Tando Bāgo 110 24.47 N 68.58 E
Tando Muhammad Khān 110 25.08 N 68.32 E
Tandou Lake ⊜ 156 32.38 S 142.05 E
Tandovo, Ozero ⊜ 76 55.07 N 78.02 E
Tando Zinze 142 5.22 S 12.26 E
Tandragee 42 54.22 N 6.25 W
Tandridge 250 51.14 N 0.02 W
Tandridge □[8] 250 51.17 N 0.05 W
Tandslet 41 54.55 N 9.59 E
Tandubas 106 5.10 N 120.20 E
Tandubatu Island I 106 5.13 N 120.17 E
Tandula Tank ⊜[1] 112 20.40 N 81.12 E
Tandun 102 0.36 N 100.38 E
Tāndūr 112 17.14 N 77.35 E
Tanduy ≃ 105a 7.41 S 108.47 E
Taneatua 162 38.04 S 177.01 E
Tanega-shima I 83b 30.40 N 131.00 E
Taneichi 82 40.26 N 141.43 E
Tan Emellel 138 27.30 N 9.45 E
Tanete 102 4.32 S 119.36 E
Taneum Creek ≃ 214 47.10 N 120.40 W
Tanew ≃ 30 50.31 N 22.16 E
Taneytown 178 39.40 N 77.10 W
Tanezrouft ◆[2] 138 24.00 N 0.45 W
Tanezrouft ta n' Ahenet ◆[2] 138 22.15 N 1.30 E
Tanezzuft, Wādī ∨ 136 25.51 N 10.19 E
Tanforan Park ◆[9] 272 37.38 N 122.25 W
Tanga, S.S.S.R. 78 51.02 N 111.33 E
Tånga, Sve. 41 56.12 N 12.46 E
Tanga, Tan. 144 5.04 S 39.06 E
Tanga □[4] 144 5.00 S 38.15 E
Tanga ≃ 142 1.22 N 17.32 E
Tangail 114 24.15 N 89.55 E
Tangainony 147b 22.42 S 47.45 E
Tanga Islands II 14 3.30 S 153.15 E
Tangalla 112 6.01 N 80.48 E
Tangamandapio 222 19.57 N 102.26 W
Tangamong Lake ⊜ 202 44.43 N 77.51 W
Tangancícuaro [de Arista] 224 19.54 N 102.08 W
Tanganika, Lago → Tanganyika, Lake ⊜ 144 6.00 S 29.30 E
Tanganjika-See → Tanganyika, Lake ⊜ 144 6.00 S 29.30 E
Tanganyika, Lake ⊜ 144 6.00 S 29.30 E
Tangará 242 27.08 S 51.13 W
Tangarare 165e 9.35 S 159.39 E
Tanga-shima I 86 34.40 N 134.35 E
Tangbazhen 97 30.00 N 105.46 E
Tangchi 79 47.00 N 123.46 E
Tangchigou 94 41.04 N 124.11 E
Tangcun, Zhg. 90 29.50 N 118.54 E
Tangcun, Zhg. 90 25.26 N 113.10 E
Tanger (Tangier) 138 35.48 N 5.45 W
Tanger ≃ 50 52.33 N 11.59 E
Tangerang 105a 6.11 S 106.37 E
Tangerhütte 50 52.26 N 11.48 E
Tangerine 210 28.47 N 81.38 W
Tangerli 95 39.09 N 116.43 E
Tangermünde 50 52.32 N 11.58 E
Tangfang, Zhg. 92 27.00 N 101.08 E
Tangfang, Zhg. 94 41.20 N 120.34 E
Tangfang, Zhg. 95 39.29 N 118.01 E
Tangfangqiao 96 31.45 N 120.50 E
Tangfeng 88 38.07 N 115.30 E
Tanggangzi 94 41.01 N 122.54 E
Tanggeasinua, Pegunungan ⛰ 102 3.24 S 121.42 E
Tanggengtou 96 30.55 N 119.03 E
Tanggou 90 34.01 N 118.56 E
Tanggu 95 39.01 N 117.40 E
Tangguantun 88 38.43 N 116.55 E
Tanggul 105a 8.10 S 113.26 E
Tanggulahu ⊜ 110 31.00 N 86.20 E
Tanggulashan (Tuotuoheyan) 110 34.05 N 92.45 E
Tanggulashankou)(110 32.59 N 91.45 E
Tanggulashanmai ⛰ 110 33.00 N 90.00 E
Tanggushiluke 110 38.45 N 80.55 E
Tangguxin'gang ≃ 95 39.00 N 117.43 E
Tanghe 90 32.43 N 112.48 E
Tanghe ≃, Zhg. 88 38.45 N 115.35 E
Tanghe ≃, Zhg. 90 32.09 N 112.25 E
Tanghekou 95 40.44 N 116.38 E
Tanghuang 96 31.41 N 119.25 E
Tanghuzhen 95 39.11 N 115.24 E
Tāngi, Bhārat 110 19.56 N 85.24 E
Tangi, Pāk. 113 34.18 N 71.40 E
Tangier → Tanger, Magreb 138 35.48 N 5.45 W
Tangier, Va., U.S. 198 37.49 N 75.59 W
Tangier Island I 198 37.50 N 76.00 W
Tangier Sound ⋃ 198 38.02 N 75.58 W
Tangijatuo 97 29.36 N 106.39 E
Tangipahoa ≃ 184 30.20 N 90.18 W
Tangjia 94 41.40 N 122.14 E
Tangjiagou 90 30.48 N 117.28 E
Tangjiang 90 25.51 N 114.44 E
Tangjiapao 94 40.00 N 122.14 E
Tangjiaqiao 96 31.24 N 119.12 E
Tangjiazha 96 32.05 N 120.49 E
Tangjiazhen 90 22.23 N 113.36 E
Tangjin 88 36.54 N 126.37 E
Tangjiqiaozhen 96 31.13 N 121.31 E
Tangkahan 102 1.36 S 113.52 E
Tangkak 104 2.16 N 102.33 E
Tangkou 90 30.06 N 118.11 E
Tanglad 105b 8.47 S 115.35 E
Tanglewood 212 30.30 N 96.59 W
Tanglewood ♠ 197 42.21 N 73.20 W
Tangling 90 26.14 N 119.24 E
Tanglitun 94 41.45 N 123.57 E
Tangmarg 113 34.02 N 74.26 E
Tangmazhai 94 41.10 N 122.44 E
Tangnang-ni 88 34.12 N 126.52 E
Tang-nhon-phu 259c 10.50 N 106.47 E
Tango 86 35.44 N 135.06 E
Tangowahine 162 35.52 S 173.56 E
Tangpu, Zhg. 90 29.51 N 120.47 E
Tangpu, Zhg. 90 28.28 N 114.58 E
Tangqi 96 30.29 N 120.11 E
Tangqian 90 25.53 N 119.07 E
Tangqiao 96 31.13 N 119.15 E
Tangqipu 94 40.39 N 122.20 E
Tangsanying 88 41.38 N 117.40 E
Tangschan → Tangshan 95 39.38 N 118.11 E
Tangse 104 5.01 N 95.55 E
Tangshan, Zhg. 95 40.10 N 116.22 E
Tangshan, Zhg. 95 39.38 N 118.11 E
Tangshan, Zhg. 96 32.05 N 119.03 E
Tangshan ∧ 96 32.03 N 119.02 E
Tangtou, Zhg. 92 27.42 N 108.17 E
Tangtou, Zhg. 96 31.38 N 120.19 E
Tangtouxia 90 22.50 N 114.06 E
Tangtouzhen 88 35.16 N 118.35 E
Tangtse 110 34.02 N 78.11 E
Tanguá 246 22.44 S 42.43 W
Tangub 106 8.03 N 123.44 E
Tanguiéta 140 10.37 N 1.16 E
Tanguip Point ≻ 106 7.43 N 126.32 E
Tanguisson Point ≻ 164p 13.33 N 144.49 E
Tanguj 78 55.23 N 100.58 E
Tangulbei 144 0.48 N 36.17 E
Tangusu Bay C 106 5.27 N 119.03 E
Tangxi 90 29.04 N 119.23 E
Tangxian 88 38.45 N 114.58 E
Tangxianzhen 90 31.59 N 113.07 E
Tangyan 100 22.29 N 98.24 E
Tangyicheng 88 36.32 N 115.47 E
Tangyin, Zhg. 88 35.55 N 114.21 E
Tangyin, Zhg. 90 27.32 N 116.16 E
Tangyuan 79 46.42 N 129.55 E
Tanhu 114 28.02 N 84.20 E
Tanhuato 224 20.17 N 102.20 W
Tanhushan I 96 30.37 N 121.37 E
Taniantawengshan ⛰ 92 30.15 N 97.32 E
Tanigami ◆[8] 260 34.46 N 135.12 E
Tanigawa-dake ∧ 84 36.50 N 138.56 E
Tanigumi 84 35.31 N 136.36 E
Tanimbar, Kepulauan II 154 7.30 S 131.30 E
Taninges 54 46.07 N 6.36 E
Tanır 120 38.26 N 36.55 E
Tanis (Zoan) ⊥ 132 30.57 N 31.53 E
Tanishpa ∧ 110 31.10 N 68.24 E
Tanjay 106 9.31 N 123.09 E
Tanjiafang 88 36.41 N 118.36 E
Tanjiahe 90 31.58 N 113.56 E
Tanjiang 90 24.07 N 116.32 E
Tanjiang ≃ 90 23.57 N 115.47 E
Tanjiaqiao 90 30.11 N 118.15 E
Tanjil ≃ 159 38.08 S 146.17 E
Tanjong Balai ≻ 261c 1.19 N 103.47 E
Tanjong Dawai 104 5.41 N 100.22 E
Tanjong Malim 104 3.41 N 101.31 E
Tanjore → Thanjāvūr 112 10.48 N 79.09 E
Tanjung, Indon. 102 2.11 S 115.23 E
Tanjung, Indon. 105a 6.52 S 108.52 E
Tanjung, Indon. 105b 8.21 S 116.09 E
Tanjungbalai 104 2.58 N 99.48 E
Tanjungbatu, Indon. 102 0.38 N 103.26 E
Tanjungbatu, Indon. 102 2.17 N 118.05 E
Tanjungbatu, Indon. 102 0.45 N 117.26 E
Tanjungenim 102 3.45 S 103.48 E
Tanjungkarang 105a 5.25 S 105.16 E
Tanjunglabu 102 2.57 S 106.54 E
Tanjungmedan 104 1.26 N 100.34 E
Tanjungmengedar 104 2.39 N 100.01 E
Tanjungpandan 102 2.45 S 107.39 E
Tanjungpinang 102 0.55 N 104.27 E
Tanjungpriok ◆[8] 259e 6.06 S 106.53 E
Tanjungpura 104 3.54 N 98.26 E
Tanjungpusu 102 0.01 S 113.30 E
Tanjungraja 102 3.21 S 104.40 E
Tanjungredep 102 2.09 N 117.29 E
Tanjungselor 102 2.51 N 117.22 E
Tanjungslamat 104 3.49 N 98.20 E
Tanjunguban 102 1.03 N 104.14 E
Tānk 110 32.13 N 70.24 E
Tan Kena 138 26.33 N 9.35 E
Tan-kien 259c 10.42 N 106.35 E
Tankou 90 25.48 N 114.50 E
Tankwa ≃ 148 32.20 S 19.33 E
Tanlay 46 47.50 N 4.05 E
Tann 52 50.38 N 10.01 E
Tanna 50 50.30 N 11.51 E
Tannan 86 35.05 N 135.10 E
Tännäs 26 62.27 N 12.40 E
Tanna-tunnel ◆[5] 84 35.06 N 139.00 E
Tannay 46 47.21 N 3.36 E
Tanne 50 51.41 N 10.42 E
Tannenbergsthal 50 50.26 N 12.27 E
Tanner, Mount ∧ 172 49.40 N 118.34 W
Tannersville, N.Y., U.S. 200 42.12 N 74.08 W
Tannersville, Pa., U.S. 200 41.03 N 75.18 W
Tännforsen ↳ 26 63.27 N 12.44 E
Tannhausen 52 48.59 N 10.21 E
Tannheim 54 47.30 N 10.31 E
Tannila 26 65.29 N 25.59 E
Tannis Bugt C 26 57.40 N 10.15 E
Tannu-Ola, Chrebet ⛰ 64 51.00 N 94.00 E
Tannūrah, Ra's at- ≻ 118 26.40 N 50.30 E
Tano, Nihon 86 33.26 N 134.00 E
Tano, Nihon 260 34.57 N 135.36 E
Tano ≃ 140 5.07 N 2.56 W
Tanon Strait ⋃ 106 10.20 N 123.30 E
Tanoriki 165f 14.59 S 168.09 E
Tânout 140 14.58 N 8.53 E
Tanque de Dolores 224 23.40 N 101.10 W
Tanque Grande, Ribeirão ≃ 277b 23.25 S 46.28 W
Tan-qui-dong 259c 10.44 N 106.42 E
Tanquinho, Bra. 245 11.58 S 39.06 W
Tanquinho, Bra. 246 22.48 S 47.00 W
T'an'šan' → Tien Shan ⛰ 80 42.00 N 80.00 E
Tansania → Tanzania □[1] 144 6.00 S 35.00 E
Tansboro 275 39.46 N 74.55 W
Tanshui 90 25.10 N 121.26 E
Tanshui Ho ≃ 90 25.11 N 121.25 E
Tanshui River Bridge ◆[5] 259d 25.03 N 121.29 E
Tansilla 140 12.26 N 4.23 W
Tansín, Isla de I 226 15.17 N 83.54 W
Tansín, Laguna de C 226 15.13 N 83.55 W
Tānsing 114 27.52 N 83.33 E
Tan Son Nhut Airport ⊠ 259c 10.49 N 106.40 E
Tansyk 76 47.20 N 79.52 E
Ṭanṭā 132 30.47 N 31.00 E
Tantabogue Creek ≃ 212 31.00 N 95.21 W
Tantangara Reservoir ⊜[1] 161b 35.45 S 148.39 E
Tan-thoi-nhut 259c 10.50 N 106.36 E
Tan-thuan-dong 259c 10.45 N 106.44 E
Tāntipāra 116 23.54 N 87.22 E
Tantō 86 35.29 N 135.00 E
Tantonville 54 48.28 N 6.08 E
Tantou, Zhg. 90 26.03 N 119.35 E
Tantou, Zhg. 90 29.07 N 121.09 E
Tantou, Zhg. 90 26.53 N 115.26 E
Tantoushan I 90 23.11 N 122.01 E
Tantoyuca 224 21.21 N 98.14 W
Tanuku 112 16.45 N 81.42 E
Tanuma 84 36.22 N 139.35 E
Tanumshede 26 58.44 N 11.19 E
Tanunda 158b 34.32 S 138.57 E
Tanūr 112 10.58 N 75.52 E
Tan'urer ≃ 170 64.44 N 174.15 E
Tanushimaru 86 33.21 N 130.41 E
Tanvald 30 50.45 N 15.19 E
Tanwax Creek ≃ 214 46.52 N 122.27 W
Tanworth 44 52.20 N 1.50 W
Tanworth-in-Arden 44 52.39 N 1.40 W
Tanxi 90 28.58 N 115.38 E
Tanxia 90 23.58 N 115.34 E
Tanyang 88 36.57 N 128.21 E
Tanyeri 120 39.38 N 39.49 E
Tanyi 88 35.14 N 118.09 E
Tanymas ≃ 75 38.25 N 72.39 E
Tanyp ≃ 76 55.46 N 54.35 E
Tanza 106 14.24 N 120.51 E
Tanzania □[1] 128
Tanzania □[1] 144 6.00 S 35.00 E
Tanzanie → Tanzania □[1] 144 6.00 S 35.00 E
Tanzawa-ō-yama-kokuteikōen ♠ 84 35.30 N 139.30 E
Tanzawa-san ∧ 84 35.28 N 139.10 E
Tao, Ko I 100 10.05 N 99.52 E
Taoan 79 45.22 N 122.47 E
Taochong 90 31.04 N 118.06 E
Taocun, Zhg. 88 37.10 N 121.05 E
Taocun, Zhg. 90 28.44 N 119.36 E
Taodigou 95 40.52 N 116.14 E
Taoerdeng 88 40.44 N 119.02 E
Taoershan 79 44.42 N 120.30 E
Taohe 95 39.12 N 116.50 E
Taohe ≃ 92 35.52 N 103.16 E
Taohua 96 31.23 N 120.04 E
Taohuabao 95 40.04 N 114.59 E
Taohuachiyingzi 94 42.18 N 121.06 E
Taohuadao I 90 29.48 N 122.17 E
Taohuanbuligai 94 42.13 N 122.14 E
Taohuatu 94 41.40 N 120.40 E
Taohuayuan 96 30.34 N 118.42 E
Taojiahe 90 30.55 N 115.56 E
Taojialiang 94 42.36 N 121.25 E
Taojiang ≃ 90 25.56 N 115.06 E
Taojiayan 90 30.02 N 120.44 E
Taolahusu 88 42.34 N 116.48 E
Taolaizhao 79 44.51 N 125.57 E
Taolakepa 110 32.05 N 85.22 E
Taole 92 38.46 N 106.40 E
Taolimin 92 39.38 N 108.40 E
Taolin 88 34.30 N 118.30 E
Taoling 90 30.21 N 118.16 E
Taoluo 88 35.17 N 119.24 E
T'aonan → Taoan 79 45.22 N 122.47 E
Taongi I[1] 14 14.37 N 168.58 E
Taormina 36 37.52 N 15.17 E
Taos, Mo., U.S. 209 38.31 N 92.04 W
Taos, N. Mex., U.S. 190 36.24 N 105.34 W
T'aosai 90 24.16 N 121.30 E
Taouardeï ⍑[4] 140 16.56 N 1.19 E
Taoudenni 138 22.40 N 4.00 W
Taougrite 34 36.15 N 0.55 E
Taounate 138 34.25 N 4.39 W
Taoura 36 36.09 N 8.03 E
Taourirt 138 34.25 N 2.53 W
Taourirt ∧ 138 23.55 N 4.50 E
Taoussa 140 16.55 N 0.35 W
Taowu 96 31.47 N 118.46 E
Taoxi, Zhg. 90 25.18 N 116.05 E
Taoxi, Zhg. 90 31.33 N 117.00 E
Taoxiantun 94 41.39 N 123.27 E
T'aoyüan, T'aiwan 90 25.00 N 121.18 E
Taoyuan, Zhg. 90 25.48 N 117.32 E
Taoyuan, Zhg. 92 28.46 N 111.20 E
Taozhuang 96 30.58 N 120.48 E
Taozhusuo 90 28.50 N 121.31 E
Taozikou ≃[1] 90 34.24 N 120.05 E
Taoziyu 96 31.04 N 121.41 E
Tap 120 38.29 N 41.49 E
Tapa, Bhārat 113 30.19 N 75.21 E
Tapa, S.S.S.R. 66 59.16 N 25.58 E
Tapaan Island I 106 5.28 N 120.44 E
Tapacarí 238 17.31 S 66.36 W
Tapachula 222 14.54 N 92.17 W
Tapaga, Cape ≻ 165a 14.01 S 171.23 W
Tapah 104 4.11 N 101.16 E
Tapah Road 104 4.10 N 101.12 E
Tapaiúna, Ribeirão ≃ 238 10.47 S 55.56 W
Tapaje ≃ 236 2.44 N 78.07 W
Tapajós ≃ 240 2.24 S 54.41 W
Tapak I 164r 6.57 N 158.18 E
Tapaktuan 104 3.16 N 97.11 E
Tapalpa 224 19.57 N 103.46 W
Tapalquén 242 36.21 S 60.01 W
Tapan 102 2.10 S 101.04 E
Tapanahoni ≃ 240 4.22 N 54.27 W
Tapanlieh 90 21.58 N 120.47 E
Tapanui 162 45.57 S 169.16 E
Tapasi 116 23.40 N 87.08 E
Tapauá 238 5.45 S 63.04 W
Tapauá ≃ 238 5.40 S 64.21 W
Tapawera 162 41.24 S 172.49 E
Tapaz 106 11.16 N 122.32 E
Tapejara 242 28.04 S 52.00 W
Tapera 242 28.38 S 52.52 W
Taperas 238 17.54 S 60.23 W
Taperoá, Bra. 240 7.12 S 36.49 W
Taperoá, Bra. 245 13.31 S 39.06 W
Tapes 242 30.40 S 51.23 W
Tapeta 140 6.29 N 8.51 W
Taphan Hin 100 16.13 N 100.26 E
Taphoen ≃ 100 14.07 N 99.25 E
Tāpi ≃, Bhārat 110 21.06 N 72.41 E
Ta Pi ≃, Thai 100 9.05 N 99.12 E
Tapiales 278 34.42 S 58.31 W
Tapiantana Channel ⋃ 106 6.23 N 122.00 E
Tapiantana Group II 106 6.20 N 122.00 E
Tapiantana Island I 106 6.18 N 121.59 E
Tapiau → Gvardejsk 66 54.39 N 21.05 E
Tapiche ≃ 238 4.59 S 73.51 W
Tapili 144 3.25 N 27.40 E
Tapilula 224 17.14 N 93.02 W
Tapini 154 8.20 S 147.00 E
Tapiraí 245 19.52 S 46.01 W
Tapirapé ≃ 240 10.41 S 50.38 W
Tapiratiba 246 21.28 S 46.45 W
Tapis, Gunong ∧ 104 4.03 N 102.54 E
Tapiutan Island I 106 11.12 N 119.16 E
Tapiwa 164d 0.52 S 169.35 E
Tāplejung 114 27.21 N 87.40 E
Tapochau, Mount ∧ 164n 15.11 N 145.45 E
Tapol 136 8.31 N 15.35 E
Tapolca 30 46.53 N 17.27 E
Tappahannock 198 37.56 N 76.52 W
Tappal 114 28.03 N 77.35 E
Tappan 200 41.01 N 73.57 W
Tappan, Lake ⊜ 266 41.01 N 73.59 W
Tappan Lake ⊜[1] 204 40.21 N 81.11 W
Tappan Zee C 266 41.06 N 73.53 W
Tappan Zee Bridge ◆[5] 266 41.04 N 73.54 W
Tappen 188 46.52 N 99.38 W
Tappernøje 41 55.10 N 11.59 E
Tappi-zaki ≻ 82 41.15 N 140.21 E
Tappo 140 10.12 N 2.38 W
Tapps, Lake ⊜ 214 47.13 N 122.09 W
Tapsiā ◆[8] 262b 22.32 N 88.22 E
Tapu, Motu I 164w 21.05 S 175.04 W
Tapuaenuku ∧ 162 42.00 S 173.40 E
Tapuio ≃ 240 3.41 S 44.16 W
Tapul Group II 106 5.30 N 121.00 E
Tapul Island I 106 5.43 N 120.55 E
Tapun 100 18.22 N 95.27 E
Tapurucuara 236 0.24 S 65.02 W
Taputapu, Cape ≻ 164u 14.19 S 170.50 W
Taqāṭu' Hayyā 130 18.20 N 36.22 E
Taqian 90 29.03 N 117.03 E
Taqiao, Zhg. 90 31.28 N 118.25 E
Taqiao, Zhg. 90 28.24 N 117.02 E

Symbols in the index entries represent the broad categories identified in the key at the right. Symbols with superior numbers (⛰[2]) identify subcategories (see complete key on page *I* · 26).

Kartensymbole in dem Registerverzeichnis stellen die rechts in Schlüssel erklärten Kategorien dar. Symbole mit hochgestellten Ziffern (⛰[2]) bezeichnen Unterabteilungen einer Kategorie (vgl. vollständiger Schlüssel auf Seite *I* · 26).

Los símbolos incluídos en el texto del índice representan las grandes categorias identificadas con la clave a la derecha. Los símbolos con numeros en su parte superior (⛰[2]) identifican las subcategorías (véase la clave completa en la página *I* · 26).

Les symboles de l'index représentent les catégories indiquées dans la légende à droite. Les symboles suivis d'un indice (⛰[2]) représentent des sous-catégories (voir légende complète à la page *I* · 26).

Os símbolos incluídos no texto do índice representam as grandes categorias identificadas com a chave à direita. Os símbolos com números em sua parte superior (⛰[2]) identificam as subcategorias (veja-se a chave completa à página *I* · 26).

	English	Deutsch	Español	Français	Português
∧	Mountain	Berg	Montaña	Montagne	Montanha
⛰	Mountains	Berge	Montañas	Montagnes	Montanhas
)(	Pass	Pass	Paso	Col	Passo
∨	Valley, Canyon	Tal, Cañon	Valle, Cañón	Vallée, Canyon	Vale, Canhão
⌣	Plain	Ebene	Llano	Plaine	Planície
≻	Cape	Kap	Cabo	Cap	Cabo
I	Island	Insel	Isla	Île	Ilha
II	Islands	Inseln	Islas	Îles	Ilhas
◆	Other Topographic Features	Andere Topographische Objekte	Otros Elementos Topográficos	Autres données topographiques	Outros Elementos Topográficos

ESPAÑOL — Nombre · Página · Lat.°′ · Long.°′ W=Oeste

Taqin 110 30.57 N 81.20 E
Taqtaq 118 35.53 N 44.35 E
Taquara 242 29.39 S 50.47 W
Taquara ✦8 277a 22.55 S 43.21 W
Taquara, Igarapé ≃ 238 7.40 S 68.12 W
Taquara, Serra da ∧ 246 22.12 S 43.53 W
Taquaral 245 16.01 S 49.38 W
Taquaral, Serra do ⸙ 245 15.42 S 52.30 W
Taquarantã, Ribeirão ≃ 246 22.04 S 47.07 W
Taquaras, Ponta das ≻ 242 27.01 S 48.34 W
Taquari, Bra. 242 29.48 S 51.51 W
Taquari, Bra. 245 17.50 S 53.17 W
Taquari ≃, Bra. 238 19.15 S 57.17 W
Taquari ≃, Bra. 242 29.56 S 51.44 W
Taquari ≃, Bra. 242 23.16 S 49.12 W
Taquari, Pantanal do ☷ 238 18.20 S 56.30 W
Taquaritinga 245 21.24 S 48.30 W
Taquaruçu ≃ 245 21.35 S 52.07 W
Taquaxiara, Ribeirão ≃ 277b 23.44 S 46.47 W
Taquaxiara, Serra da ⸙2 277b 23.46 S 46.52 W
Tar ≃, S.S.S.R. 75 40.38 N 73.26 E
Tar ≃, N.C., U.S. 182 35.33 N 77.05 W
Tara, Austl. 156 27.17 S 150.28 E
Tara, Ont., Can. 202 44.28 N 81.09 W
Tara, S.S.S.R. 76 56.54 N 74.22 E
Tara, Zam. 144 16.56 S 26.47 E
Tara ⸙ 38 43.55 N 19.25 E
Tara ≃, Jugo. 38 43.21 N 18.51 E
Tara ≃, S.S.S.R. 76 56.42 N 74.36 E
Taraba ≃ 136 8.30 N 10.15 E
Tarabuco 238 19.10 S 64.57 W
Ṭarābulus (Tripoli), Lībīya 136 32.54 N 13.11 E
Ṭarābulus (Tripoli), Lubnān 120 34.26 N 35.51 E
Ṭarābulus (Tripolitania) □4 136 31.00 N 15.00 E
Ṭarābulus ✦1 136 31.00 N 15.00 E
Tarabya ✦8 257b 41.08 N 29.03 E
Tarach ≃ 144 4.09 N 34.56 E
Taradale 162 39.32 S 176.51 E
Taragaj ≃ 75 41.35 N 77.42 E
Tarago 160 35.04 S 149.39 E
Tara Hills 272 38.00 N 122.19 W
Tarai ≃ 114 26.35 N 86.40 E
Taraia 114 26.05 N 84.53 E
Taraira (Traíra) ≃ 236 1.04 S 69.26 W
Tara Island I 106 12.17 N 120.22 E
Taraju 105a 7.27 S 107.59 E
Tarakan 102 3.18 N 117.38 E
Tarakan, Pulau I 102 3.21 N 117.36 E
Tarakanovka 72 55.07 N 35.44 E
Tārakeswar 116 22.54 N 88.02 E
Taraklı 120 40.24 N 30.29 E
Taraklija, S.S.S.R. 68 46.34 N 29.06 E
Taraklija, S.S.S.R. 68 45.54 N 28.38 E
Taralga 160 34.24 S 149.49 E
Tarama-jima I 165d 24.39 N 124.42 E
Taramakau ≃ 162 42.34 S 171.08 E
Taramana 102 8.10 S 124.51 E
Tarana 160 33.32 S 149.54 E
Tarancón 34 40.01 N 3.00 W
Tarandacuao 224 19.59 N 100.32 W
Taranga Island I 162 35.58 S 174.43 E
Tarangire National Park ♣ 144 4.00 S 36.00 E
Tarangnan 106 11.54 N 124.45 E
Tarango, Presa @1 276a 19.22 N 99.13 W
Taranovka 68 49.37 N 36.08 E
Taransay I 28 57.55 N 7.10 W
Taranta Peligna 60 42.01 N 14.10 E
Taranto 36 40.28 N 17.15 E
Taranto, Golfo di C 36 40.10 N 17.20 E
Tarapacá 236 2.52 S 69.44 W
Tarapacá □4 238 20.00 S 69.20 W
Tarapoto 238 6.30 S 76.25 W
Ṭaraq al-Hbâri ✦1 120 34.17 N 39.16 E
Ṭaraq an-Na'jah ✦1 120 34.16 N 39.53 E
Ṭaraq Sidâoui ✦1 120 34.33 N 39.54 E
Taraquá 236 0.06 N 68.28 W
Tarara 165e 6.02 S 155.24 E
Tarare 54 45.54 N 4.26 E
Tarariras 248 34.17 S 57.37 W
Tararua Range ⸙ 162 40.46 S 175.23 E
Tarāsa Dwīp I 100 8.15 N 93.10 E
Tarašča 68 49.34 N 30.29 E
Tarascon, Fr. 32 42.51 N 1.36 E
Tarascon, Fr. 56 43.48 N 4.40 E
Tarasht 257d 35.42 N 51.21 E
Tarasovka, S.S.S.R. 73 48.21 N 37.33 E
Tarasovka, S.S.S.R. 73 49.28 N 40.05 E
Tarasovka, S.S.S.R. 73 49.40 N 38.23 E
Tarasovka, S.S.S.R. 255b 55.58 N 37.50 E
Tarasovo, S.S.S.R. 24 62.49 N 41.10 E
Tarasovo, S.S.S.R. 24 66.13 N 46.39 E
Tarasovo, S.S.S.R. 70 58.18 N 48.45 E
Tarasovo, S.S.S.R. 78 55.52 N 107.48 E
Tarasovskij 68 48.43 N 40.22 E
Tarasp 54 46.38 N 10.25 E
Tarat 138 26.13 N 9.18 E
Tarat, Oued ∨ 138 26.09 N 9.20 E
Tarata, Bol. 238 17.37 S 66.01 W
Tarata, Perú 238 17.28 S 70.02 W
Taratakbuluh 102 0.23 N 101.27 E
Tāratanr 116 23.58 N 86.29 E
Tarauacá 238 8.10 S 70.46 W
Tarauacá ≃ 238 6.42 S 69.48 W
Taravao, Baie de C 164s 17.43 S 149.17 W
Taravao, Isthme de •3 164s 17.43 S 149.19 W
Taravo ≃ 36 41.42 N 8.49 E
Tarawa I 164t 1.25 N 173.00 E
Tarawera 162 39.02 S 176.35 E
Tarawera, Lake @ 162 38.12 S 176.27 E
Tarazit, Massif de ⸙ 140 20.00 N 8.25 E
Tarazona 34 41.54 N 1.44 W
Tarazona de la Mancha 34 39.15 N 1.55 W
Tarba 134 0.48 N 42.42 E
Tårbæk 41 55.47 N 12.36 E
Tarbagataj, S.S.S.R. 78 51.12 N 109.05 E
Tarbagataj, S.S.S.R. 78 51.30 N 107.22 E
Tarbagataj, S.S.S.R. 78 52.07 N 109.12 E
Tarbagataj, Chrebet ⸙ 76 47.12 N 83.00 E
Tarbela 113 34.08 N 72.49 E
Tarbert, Scot., U.K. 28 57.54 N 6.49 W
Tarbert, Scot., U.K. 42 55.52 N 5.26 W
Tarbes 32 43.14 N 0.05 E
Tarbock Green 252 53.23 N 2.49 W
Tarbolton 42 55.31 N 4.29 W
Tarboro 182 35.54 N 77.32 W
Tarbū 136 26.02 N 15.10 E
Tarcăului, Munții ⸙ 38 46.45 N 26.20 E
Tarcento 58 46.13 N 13.13 E
Tarchankut, Mys ≻ 68 45.21 N 32.30 E
Tarchankutskaja Vozvyšennost' ⸙1 68 45.30 N 33.10 E
Tarchov Cholm, Gora ∧2 66 57.11 N 38.25 E
Tarchovka 255a 60.04 N 29.58 E
Tarcoola 152 30.41 S 134.33 E
Tarcoon 156 30.16 S 146.43 E
Tarcutta 161b 35.17 S 147.44 E
Tarcutta Creek ≃ 161b 35.08 S 147.36 E
Tārdah 262b 22.27 N 88.31 E
Tardajos 34 42.21 N 3.49 W
Tardoki-Jani, Gora ∧ 79 48.55 N 138.04 E
Tardun 152 28.48 S 115.45 E
Taredo ✦8 262c 19.58 N 72.49 E
Taree 156 31.54 S 152.28 E
Tareja 64 73.20 N 90.37 E
Taremert n' Akli, Oued ∨ 138 25.49 N 5.17 E

FRANÇAIS — Nom · Page · Lat.°′ · Long.°′ W=Ouest

Tärendö 24 67.10 N 22.38 E
Tarent, Golf von → Taranto, Golfo di C 36 40.10 N 17.20 E
Tarentaise ∨ 56 45.30 N 6.30 E
Tarento, Golfo de → Taranto, Golfo di C 36 40.10 N 17.20 E
Tarentum 204 40.36 N 79.45 W
Tarf, Garaet et @ 138 35.40 N 7.10 E
Ṭarfā', Baṭn aṭ- ☷ 118 23.50 N 51.27 E
Ṭarfā', Ra's ≻ 134 17.05 N 42.24 E
Ṭarfā', Wādī aṭ- ∨ 132 28.25 N 30.50 E
Ṭarfāwī, Bi'r ⸗4, Miṣr 130 22.55 N 28.53 E
Ṭarfawi, Bi'r ⸗4, Sūd. 130 21.04 N 34.08 E
Tarfaya 138 27.58 N 12.55 W
Tarf Water ≃ 42 54.55 N 4.35 W
Targa 114 22.27 N 84.40 E
Targan ≃ 75 43.38 N 75.58 E
Target Rock National Wildlife Refuge ✦4 266 40.56 N 73.26 W
Targhee Pass)(192 44.41 N 111.17 W
Targon 32 44.44 N 0.16 W
Târgovište 38 43.15 N 26.34 E
Targuist 138 34.57 N 4.18 W
Târgu-Mureș → Tîrgu Mureș 38 46.33 N 24.33 E
Tarhaouaout 138 22.20 N 5.58 E
Tarhit 138 30.55 N 2.02 W
Tarhjicht 138 29.05 N 9.24 W
Tarhūnah 136 32.26 N 13.38 E
Tari 154 5.50 S 143.00 E
Tarialan 76 49.47 N 91.55 E
Tariat 78 48.06 N 99.32 E
Táriba 236 7.49 N 72.13 W
Tarica 226 12.56 N 84.41 W
Tarifa 34 36.01 N 5.36 W
Tarifa, Punta de ≻ 34 36.00 N 5.37 W
Tariffville 197 41.55 N 72.46 W
Tarija 238 21.31 S 64.45 W
Tarija □5 238 21.30 S 64.00 W
Tarikere 112 13.43 N 75.49 E
Tariki 162 39.14 S 174.15 E
Tariku ≃ 154 3.04 S 138.09 E
Tarīm 134 16.03 N 48.59 E
Tarim → Talimuhe ≃ 80 41.05 N 86.40 E
Tarimoro 224 20.17 N 100.45 W
Taring 104 3.50 N 97.33 E
Tarīn Kowt 110 32.52 N 65.38 E
Taritai 164t 1.32 N 173.00 E
Taritatu ≃ 154 2.54 S 138.27 E
Tarituba 246 23.02 S 44.36 W
Tarka 140 14.37 N 7.55 E
Tarka, Vallée de ∨ 140 14.00 N 6.00 E
Tarkastad 148 32.00 S 26.16 E
Tarkazy 70 53.52 N 53.39 E
Tarkhowrān 118 34.41 N 50.00 E
Tarki 74 42.56 N 47.30 E
Tarkiln 197 41.57 N 71.35 W
Tarkington Bayou ≃ 212 30.10 N 94.59 W
Tarkio 184 40.27 N 95.23 W
Tarkio ≃ 188 40.10 N 95.26 W
Tarko-Sale 64 64.55 N 77.49 E
Tarkwa 140 5.19 N 1.59 W
Tarlac 106 15.29 N 120.35 E
Tarlac □4 106 15.30 N 120.25 E
Tarlac ≃ 106 15.45 N 120.27 E
Tarlee 158b 34.16 S 138.46 E
Tarleton 42 53.41 N 2.50 W
T'arlevo 255a 59.42 N 30.27 E
Tarlscough 252 53.37 N 2.52 W
Tarm 26 55.55 N 8.32 E
Tarma 238 11.25 S 75.42 W
Tarmstedt 48 53.13 N 9.04 E
Tarn □5 32 43.50 N 2.00 E
Tarn ≃ 32 44.05 N 1.06 E
Tarna ≃ 30 47.31 N 19.59 E
Tärnaby 24 65.43 N 15.16 E
Tarnak ≃ 110 31.26 N 65.31 E
Tarna Mare 38 47.29 N 26.20 E
Tårnby 41 55.38 N 12.36 E
Tarneit 264b 37.52 S 144.41 E
Tarn-et-Garonne □5 32 44.05 N 1.20 E
Tarnewitz 50 53.58 N 11.14 E
Tarnica ∧ 30 49.05 N 22.42 E
Tarnobrzeg 30 50.35 N 21.41 E
Tarnogród 30 50.23 N 22.45 E
Tarnogskij Gorodok 24 60.29 N 43.33 E
Tarnopol → Ternopol' 68 49.34 N 25.36 E
Tarnów, Pol. 30 50.01 N 21.00 E
Tarnów, Pol. 50 52.47 N 14.58 E
Tarnowskie Góry 30 50.27 N 18.52 E
Tärnsjö 40 60.09 N 16.56 E
Tarn Tāran 113 31.27 N 74.55 E
Taro ≃ 36 45.00 N 10.15 E
Taron 154 4.25 S 153.05 E
Tarong 156 26.46 S 151.51 E
Taronga Zoological Park ♣ 264a 33.51 S 151.15 E
Taroom 156 25.39 S 149.49 E
Tarouadji, Massif de ⸙ 140 17.15 N 8.33 E
Tarouca 34 41.00 N 7.40 W
Taroudant 138 30.31 N 8.55 W
Ta-roun, Co ∧ 100 17.17 N 106.17 E
Tarp 41 54.40 N 9.23 E
Tarpey 216 36.47 N 119.42 W
Tarpon, Lake @ 210 28.07 N 82.44 W
Tarpon Springs 210 28.09 N 82.45 W
Tarporley 44 53.09 N 2.40 W
Tarquí 236 1.35 S 75.15 W
Tarquinia 60 42.15 N 11.45 E
Tarquinia (Tarquinii) ⊥ 60 42.15 N 11.47 E
Tarqūmiyah 122 31.35 N 35.01 E
Tarra ≃ 236 9.05 N 72.30 W
Tarrafal, C.V. 140a 16.58 N 25.19 W
Tarrafal, C.V. 140a 15.17 N 23.46 W
Tarragona 34 41.07 N 1.15 E
Tarrakoski ⌊ 24 68.10 N 20.00 E
Tarraleah 156 42.18 S 146.27 E
Tarran Hills ⸙2 156 32.27 S 146.27 E
Tarrant 184 33.34 N 86.46 W
Tarrant □6 212 32.47 N 97.18 W
Tarrant Hinton 44 50.53 N 2.05 W
Tarrara Creek ≃ 198 36.33 N 77.10 W
Tarras 162 44.50 S 169.25 E
Tarrasa 34 / 256d 41.34 N 2.01 E
Tárrega 34 41.39 N 1.09 E
Tarri Mashen 134 0.45 N 41.50 E
Tarrs 204 40.10 N 79.35 W
Tarrtown 204 40.51 N 79.31 W
Tarryall Creek ≃ 190 39.05 N 105.19 W
Tarrytown 200 41.05 N 73.52 W
Tarrytown Reservoir @1 266 41.05 N 73.51 W
Tarsus 120 36.55 N 34.53 E
Tarta 118 40.02 N 52.46 E
Tartagal, Arg. 242 22.32 S 63.49 W
Tartagal, Arg. 242 28.40 S 59.52 W
Tartane, Cul-de-Sac C 230e 14.45 N 60.53 W
Tartaro ≃ 58 45.02 N 11.30 E
Tartas 32 43.50 N 0.48 W
Tartas ≃ 76 55.37 N 76.44 E
Tartu 66 58.23 N 26.43 E
Ṭarṭūs 120 34.53 N 35.53 E
Taruaçu 246 21.37 S 42.56 W
Tarui 84 35.22 N 136.32 E
Tarum ≃ 105a 5.59 S 107.03 E
Tarumi ✦8 260 34.38 N 135.03 E
Tarumirim 245 19.16 S 41.59 W
Tarumizu 82 31.29 N 130.42 E
Tarumovka 74 44.03 N 46.33 E
Tarusa 72 54.43 N 37.11 E
Tarusa ≃ 72 54.44 N 37.11 E
Ṭārūṭ 132 30.32 N 31.28 E
Tarutino, S.S.S.R. 68 46.12 N 29.09 E
Tarutino, S.S.S.R. 72 55.07 N 36.56 E

PORTUGUÊS — Nome · Página · Lat.°′ · Long.°′ W=Oeste

Tarutung 104 2.01 N 98.58 E
Tarvagatajn Nuruu ⸙ 78 48.20 N 99.00 E
Tarvisio 58 46.30 N 13.35 E
Tarwin ≃ 159 38.42 S 145.50 E
Tarza 24 62.30 N 40.25 E
Tarzan 186 32.18 N 101.58 W
Tarzana ✦8 270 34.10 N 118.32 W
Tarzo 58 45.58 N 12.14 E
Tas 70 48.27 N 51.02 E
Tas ≃ 44 52.36 N 1.18 E
Taşağıl, Tür. 120 36.55 N 31.14 E
Taşağıl, Tür. 120 41.31 N 27.07 E
Tašanta 76 49.43 N 89.11 E
Tasaral 76 46.20 N 73.58 E
Tašauz 62 41.50 N 59.58 E
Tašauz □4 118 50.15 N 59.00 E
Tasāwah 136 25.58 N 13.30 E
Tasbuget 76 44.48 N 65.33 E
Taschkent → Taškent 75 41.20 N 69.18 E
Taşçı 120 38.13 N 35.48 E
Tasejeva ≃ 76 58.06 N 94.01 E
Tasejevo 76 57.12 N 94.54 E
Taseko ≃ 172 52.00 N 123.40 W
Taseko Lakes @ 172 51.15 N 123.35 W
Taseko Mountain ∧ 172 51.14 N 123.28 W
Tašelan 78 51.45 N 108.55 E
Tasendjanet, Oued ∨ 138 24.36 N 1.07 E
Tāsgaon 112 17.02 N 74.36 E
Tashan, Zhg. 94 40.48 N 122.39 E
Tashan, Zhg. 94 40.51 N 120.56 E
Tashibuhu @ 110 32.10 N 85.05 E
Tashi Gang Dzong 110 27.19 N 91.34 E
Tashikuergan 110 37.49 N 75.14 E
Tashimalike 75 39.06 N 75.41 E
Tashiyi 90 29.43 N 112.48 E
Ṭashk, Daryācheh-ye @ 118 29.45 N 53.35 E
Tashkent → Taškent 75 41.20 N 69.18 E
Tāshkurghān → Kholm 110 36.42 N 67.41 E
Ta Shui Hang 261d 22.25 N 113.56 E
Tashuik'u 259d 25.14 N 121.31 E
Tasikmalaya 105a 7.20 S 108.12 E
Tasīl 122 32.50 N 35.58 E
Tåsinge I 41 55.00 N 10.36 E
Taširovo 72 55.25 N 36.39 E
Tasitan 75 39.17 N 76.07 E
Tåsjö 26 64.13 N 15.54 E
Tåsjön @ 26 64.15 N 15.47 E
Taskajevo 76 55.06 N 78.36 E
Taškent 75 41.20 N 69.18 E
Taškepri 118 36.18 N 62.38 E
Taşkesen 120 39.43 N 41.29 E
Taskesken 76 47.15 N 80.44 E
Tasköprü 120 41.30 N 34.14 E
Taskul 154 2.35 S 150.25 E
Taš-Kumyr 75 41.21 N 72.14 E
Taškyja 75 40.16 N 74.19 E
Tašla 70 51.47 N 52.46 E
Taslina 170 62.04 N 146.27 W
Tasman, Mount ∧ 162 43.34 S 170.09 E
Tasman Basin ✢1 14 44.00 S 157.00 E
Tasman Bay C 162 41.00 S 173.20 E
Tasmania □3 156 43.00 S 147.00 E
Tasmania I 156 42.00 S 147.00 E
Tasmanien → Tasmania I 156 42.00 S 147.00 E
Tasman Mountains ⸙ 162 41.07 S 172.33 E
Tasman Peninsula ≻1 156 43.05 S 147.50 E
Tasman Ridge ✢3 14 46.00 S 147.00 E
Tasman Sea ⸗2 14 40.00 S 163.00 E
Tășnad 38 47.29 N 22.35 E
Tasoba 70 49.47 N 49.52 E
Taşova 120 40.46 N 36.20 E
Tasrār Sharīf 113 33.52 N 74.46 E
Taşrumi 74 38.48 N 44.04 E
Tassajara Creek ≃ 272 37.41 N 121.53 W
Tassdorf 254a 52.30 N 13.47 E
Tassialouc, Lac @ 166 59.03 N 74.00 W
Tassin-la-Demi-Lune 56 45.46 N 4.47 E
Tasso Lake @ 202 45.27 N 78.56 W
Taštagol 76 52.47 N 87.53 E
Tastiota 222 28.22 N 111.23 W
Tåstrup 41 55.39 N 12.19 E
Taštyp 76 52.48 N 89.54 E
Tasucu 120 36.19 N 33.53 E
Tata, Magreb 138 29.44 N 7.56 W
Tata, Magy. 30 47.39 N 18.18 E
Tataa, Pointe ≻ 164s 17.34 S 149.37 W
Tatabánya 30 47.34 N 18.26 E
Tatahuicapan 224 18.14 N 94.45 W
Tatal 70 47.17 N 46.16 E
Tata Mailau, Monte ∧ 102 8.55 S 125.30 E
Tatamy 198 40.44 N 75.15 W
Tataouine 138 32.56 N 10.27 E
Tatarbunary 68 45.49 N 29.36 E
Tatarinka 66 55.58 N 33.54 E
Tatarino 68 50.36 N 39.07 E
Tatarinovo, S.S.S.R. 72 55.13 N 37.56 E
Tatarinovo, S.S.S.R. 72 56.34 N 38.25 E
Tatarischer Sund → Tatarskij Proliv ⋃ 79 50.00 N 141.15 E
Tatarka, S.S.S.R. 66 53.16 N 28.48 E
Tatarka, S.S.S.R. 76 53.58 N 75.05 E
Tatarlar 120 41.46 N 26.55 E
Tatarovo ✦8 255b 55.46 N 37.26 E
Tātārpur ✦8 262a 28.39 N 77.07 E
Tatarsk 76 55.13 N 75.58 E
Tatarskaja Avtonomnaja Sovetskaja Socialističeskaja Respublika □3 70 55.00 N 51.00 E
Tatarskij Kandyz 70 54.07 N 53.07 E
Tatarskij Proliv ⋃ 79 50.00 N 141.15 E
Tatarskij Sajman 70 53.18 N 47.07 E
Tatarskoje-Maklakovo 70 55.48 N 45.34 E
Tatar Strait → Tatarskij Proliv ⋃ 79 50.00 N 141.15 E
Tatau ≃ 102 3.07 N 112.49 E
Tatau Island I 154 2.50 S 152.00 E
Tataurovo, S.S.S.R. 66 58.44 N 43.20 E
Tataurovo, S.S.S.R. 70 57.48 N 49.34 E
Tataurovo, S.S.S.R. 78 51.37 N 112.56 E
Tate 182 34.25 N 84.23 W
Tate ≃ 156 17.22 S 143.44 E
Tatebayashi 84 36.15 N 139.32 E
Tate Gallery ⚜ 250 51.29 N 0.08 W
Tateishi-misaki ≻ 84 35.46 N 136.01 E
Tateiwa 84 37.05 N 139.32 E
Tateiwa-chosuichi @1 86 34.33 N 132.10 E
Tatelang 110 38.28 N 85.35 E
Tatelu 90 22.45 N 120.47 E
Tateshina 84 36.16 N 138.19 E
Tateyama, Nihon 84 34.59 N 139.52 E
Tateyama, Nihon 84 36.40 N 137.19 E
Tate-yama ∧ 84 36.35 N 137.37 E
Tathlina Lake @ 166 60.32 N 117.32 W
Tathlīth, Wādī ∨ 134 20.44 N 44.17 E
Tathong Channel ⋃ 261d 22.15 N 114.15 E
Tathong Point ≻ 261d 22.14 N 114.17 E
Tathra 156 36.44 S 149.59 E
Tatikawa → Tachikawa 84 35.42 N 139.25 E
Tatiščevo, S.S.S.R. 70 51.40 N 45.35 E
Tatiščevo, S.S.S.R. 72 56.24 N 37.31 E
Tatitlek 170 60.52 N 146.41 W
Tatla Lake 172 51.55 N 124.36 W
Tatlayoko Lake 172 51.39 N 124.24 W
Tatlayoko Lake @ 172 51.30 N 124.25 W
Tatlow, Mount ∧ 172 51.23 N 123.52 W
Tatnam, Cape ≻ 166 57.16 N 91.00 W

Tatomi 84 35.36 N 138.31 E
Tatoosh Island I 214 48.24 N 124.44 W
Tatos Dağları ⸙ 120 40.55 N 41.10 E
Tatrzański Park Narodowy ♣ 30 49.15 N 20.00 E
Tatsfield 250 51.18 N 0.02 E
Tatsuno, Nihon 84 35.59 N 137.59 E
Tatsuno, Nihon 86 34.52 N 134.33 E
Tatsunokuchi 84 36.27 N 136.35 E
Tatsuyama 84 34.58 N 137.49 E
Tatta 110 24.45 N 67.55 E
Tattenhall 44 53.06 N 2.46 W
Tatton Hall ⊥ 252 53.20 N 2.23 W
Tatton Mere @ 252 53.19 N 2.22 W
Tatty 75 43.12 N 73.19 E
Tatuapé ✦8 277b 23.32 S 46.34 W
Tatu Ch'i ≃ 90 24.12 N 120.29 E
Tatuk Lake @ 172 53.32 N 124.15 W
Tatum, N. Mex., U.S. 186 33.16 N 103.19 W
Tatum, Tex., U.S. 212 32.19 N 94.31 W
Tat'ung → Datong 92 40.08 N 113.13 E
Tat'un Shan ∧ 90 25.10 N 121.31 E
Tatvan 120 38.30 N 42.16 E
Tatzuli Ch'i ≃ 90 24.08 N 121.40 E
Tau, Nor. 26 59.04 N 5.54 E
Tau, S.S.S.R. 70 49.40 N 47.17 E
Tau I, Am. Sam. 164y 14.15 S 169.30 W
Tau I, Tonga 164w 21.01 S 175.00 W
Tauá 240 6.01 S 40.26 W
Tauak Passage ⋃ 164r 6.55 N 158.06 E
Taualap Pass ⋃ 165c 7.28 N 151.36 E
Tauari 240 1.07 S 47.04 W
Taubaté 246 23.02 S 45.33 W
Tauber ≃ 52 49.46 N 9.31 E
Tauberbischofsheim 52 49.37 N 9.40 E
Taucha 50 51.23 N 12.30 E
Taučik 62 44.21 N 51.19 E
Tauern-Tunnel ✦5 58 47.05 N 13.05 E
Täuffelen 54 47.04 N 7.12 E
Taufstein ∧ 52 50.31 N 9.14 E
Taughannock Creek ≃ 200 42.33 N 76.36 W
Taughannock Falls State Park ♣ 200 42.32 N 76.35 W
Taujskaja Guba C 64 59.20 N 150.20 E
Taukum ✦2 76 44.50 N 75.30 E
Taulabé 226 14.38 N 87.59 W
Taulihawa 114 27.32 N 83.03 E
Taulov 41 55.33 N 9.37 E
Taumarunui 162 38.52 S 175.17 E
Taumaturgo 238 8.57 S 72.48 W
Taum Sauk Mountain ∧ 184 37.34 N 90.44 W
Taunay 238 20.18 S 56.05 W
Taung 148 27.33 S 24.47 E
Taungbon 100 15.25 N 97.50 E
Taungdwingyi 100 20.01 N 95.33 E
Taunggon 100 23.38 N 96.32 E
Taunggyi 100 20.47 N 97.02 E
Taungnyo Range ⸙ 100 15.38 N 97.56 E
Taungup 100 18.51 N 94.14 E
Taungup Pass)(100 18.40 N 94.45 E
Taunoa 164s 17.45 S 149.21 W
Taunsa 113 30.42 N 70.39 E
Taunton, Eng., U.K. 44 51.01 N 3.06 W
Taunton, Mass., U.S. 197 41.54 N 71.06 W
Taunton, N.Y., U.S. 200 43.01 N 76.13 W
Taunton ≃ 197 41.42 N 71.10 W
Taunton, Vale of ∨ 44 51.02 N 3.08 W
Taunton Lake @ 275 39.51 N 74.51 W
Taunton Lakes 275 39.51 N 74.51 W
Taunus ⸙ 52 50.10 N 8.15 E
Taupiri 162 37.37 S 175.11 E
Taupo 162 38.41 S 176.05 E
Taupo, Lake @ 162 38.49 S 175.55 E
Taura 50 50.55 N 12.50 E
Tauragė 66 55.15 N 22.17 E
Taurak 76 51.35 N 85.01 E
Tauranga 162 37.42 S 176.10 E
Taureau, Réservoir @1 196 46.46 N 73.50 W
Tauri ≃ 154 8.08 S 146.06 E
Taurianova 36 38.21 N 16.01 E
Tauripampa 238 12.35 S 76.07 W
Taurisma 238 15.10 S 72.51 W
Tauroa Point ≻ 162 35.10 S 173.04 E
Taurovo 76 59.36 N 73.18 E
Taurus Mountains → Toros Dağları ⸙ 120 37.00 N 33.00 E
Tauste 34 41.55 N 1.15 W
Tautara, Motu I2 164z 27.06 S 109.27 W
Tautira 164s 17.44 S 149.09 W
Tauu Islands II 14 4.45 S 157.00 E
Tauxigny 46 47.13 N 0.50 E
Tauz 74 41.00 N 45.38 E
Tavajvaam ≃ 170 64.56 N 177.30 W
Tavajza 79 45.12 N 136.44 E
Ṭavālesh, Kūhhā-ye → Talish Mountains ⸙ 118 38.42 N 48.18 E
Tavanasa 54 46.45 N 9.04 E
Tavannes 54 47.13 N 7.12 E
Tavant 46 47.07 N 0.23 E
Tavares, Bra. 240 7.38 S 37.54 W
Tavares, Fla., U.S. 210 28.48 N 81.44 W
Tavares, Ilha dos I 277a 22.49 S 43.06 W
Tavarnelle Val di Pesa 60 43.33 N 11.10 E
Tavas 120 37.34 N 29.04 E
Tavastehus → Hämeenlinna 26 61.00 N 24.27 E
Tavaux 54 47.02 N 5.24 E
Tavda 76 58.03 N 65.15 E
Tavda ≃, S.S.S.R. 62 59.20 N 63.28 E
Tavda ≃, S.S.S.R. 76 57.47 N 67.16 E
Tave ≃ 56 44.07 N 4.42 E
Tavera ≃ 58 46.29 N 11.21 E
Tavern Creek ≃ 184 38.19 N 92.18 W
Tavernelle, It. 58 44.18 N 10.04 E
Tavernelle, It. 60 43.00 N 12.09 E
Tavernes 56 43.36 N 6.01 E
Tavernier 210 25.01 N 80.31 W
Tavernole sul Mella 58 45.45 N 10.14 E
Taverny 46 49.02 N 2.13 E
Taveta, Kenya 144 3.24 S 37.41 E
Taveta, Tan. 144 9.01 S 35.37 E
Taveuni I 165g 16.51 S 179.58 W
Tavil'dara 75 38.43 N 70.28 E
Tavira 34 37.07 N 7.39 W
Tavistock, Ont., Can. 202 43.19 N 80.50 W
Tavistock, Eng., U.K. 44 50.33 N 4.08 W
Tavn-Gašun 70 46.01 N 45.55 E
Tavoliere ✦1 36 41.35 N 15.25 E
Tavolžan 76 52.44 N 77.27 E
Tavor, Har (Mount Tabor) ∧ 122 32.41 N 35.23 E
Tavoy 100 14.05 N 98.12 E
Tavoy Point ≻ 100 13.32 N 98.10 E
Tavričanka 79 43.22 N 131.52 E
Tavričeskij Dvorec ⚜ 255a 59.57 N 30.23 E
Tavričeskoje 76 54.35 N 73.38 E
Tavry 255a 59.55 N 30.42 E
Tavsalayihüseyan 120 38.38 N 40.32 E
Tavşanlı 120 39.33 N 29.30 E
Tavsi 120 37.56 N 38.39 E
Tavua 165g 17.27 S 177.51 E
Tavy ≃ 44 50.16 N 4.10 W
Taw ≃ 44 51.04 N 4.11 W
Tawa 162 41.10 S 174.51 E
Tawa ≃ 114 22.48 N 77.48 E
Tawaeli 102 0.43 S 119.51 E
Tawakoni, Lake @1 212 32.55 N 96.00 W
Tawar, Laut @ 104 4.38 N 96.54 E
Tawara 260 34.27 N 135.57 E
Tawarada 258 35.19 N 140.04 E
Tawaramoto 86 34.33 N 135.48 E
Tawas City 180 44.16 N 83.31 W
Tawau 102 4.15 N 117.54 E
Tawd ≃ 252 53.36 N 2.48 W
Tawe ≃ 44 51.37 N 3.55 W

Tāwi ≃ 113 32.40 N 74.41 E
Ṭawīl, Jabal aṭ- ∧2 132 27.22 N 31.07 E
Ṭawīlah, Juzur II 130 27.35 N 33.46 E
Tawitawi Group II 106 5.10 N 120.15 E
Tawitawi Island I 106 5.10 N 120.00 E
Ṭawkar 130 18.26 N 37.44 E
Tawu 90 22.22 N 120.54 E
Ṭāwūq 118 35.08 N 44.27 E
Tāwurghā' 136 32.02 N 15.09 E
Tāwurghā', Sabkhat ☷ 136 31.45 N 15.20 E
Ṭawwah Banī Ibrāhīm 132 28.05 N 30.41 E
Taxco de Alarcón 224 18.33 N 99.36 W
Taxenbach 58 47.17 N 12.58 E
Taxi 79 49.26 N 126.08 E
Taxila 113 33.44 N 72.49 E
Taxisco 226 14.04 N 90.28 W
Taxusi 92 32.58 N 98.10 E
Tay ≃ 202 44.53 N 76.07 W
Tay, Lake @ 152 32.55 S 120.48 E
Tay, Loch @ 28 56.30 N 4.10 W
Tayabamba 238 8.17 S 77.18 W
Tayabas 106 14.01 N 121.35 E
Tayabas Bay C 106 13.45 N 121.45 E
Tayan 102 0.02 S 110.07 E
Tayandu, Kepulauan II 154 5.30 S 132.15 E
Tayangshan I 96 30.35 N 122.00 E
Tayegle 134 4.02 N 44.36 E
Tayin'gou 79 51.27 N 124.16 E
Taylor, B.C., Can. 172 56.10 N 120.41 W
Taylor, Ariz., U.S. 190 34.28 N 110.05 W
Taylor, Ark., U.S. 184 33.06 N 93.28 W
Taylor, Mich., U.S. 206 42.13 N 83.16 W
Taylor, Mo., U.S. 209 39.56 N 91.32 W
Taylor, Nebr., U.S. 188 41.46 N 99.23 W
Taylor, Pa., U.S. 200 41.24 N 75.35 W
Taylor, Tex., U.S. 212 30.34 N 97.25 W
Taylor, Mount ∧, N.Z. 162 43.30 S 171.19 E
Taylor, Mount ∧, N. Mex., U.S. 190 35.14 N 107.37 W
Taylor Creek ≃ 209 39.13 N 90.18 W
Taylor Lake Village 212 29.36 N 95.03 W
Taylor Mountain ∧ 192 44.53 N 114.13 W
Taylor Mountains ⸙ 170 60.50 N 157.20 W
Taylor Run ≃ 275 39.57 N 75.39 W
Taylors 182 34.55 N 82.18 W
Taylors Bush Park ♣ 265b 43.42 N 79.19 W
Taylors Island 198 38.28 N 76.18 W
Taylor Springs 209 39.08 N 89.30 W
Taylors Run ≃ 269b 40.11 N 79.57 W
Taylorstown 204 40.10 N 80.23 W
Taylorsville, Ind., U.S. 208 39.18 N 85.57 W
Taylorsville, Ky., U.S. 184 38.02 N 85.21 W
Taylorsville, Miss., U.S. 184 31.50 N 89.32 W
Taylorsville, N.C., U.S. 182 35.55 N 81.04 W
Taylorsville Reservoir @1 208 40.00 N 84.10 W
Taylortown, N.J., U.S. 266 40.56 N 74.24 W
Taylortown, Ohio, U.S. 204 40.28 N 80.40 W
Taylortown Reservoir @1 266 40.58 N 74.22 W
Taylorville 209 39.33 N 89.18 W
Taylorville, Lake @1 209 39.30 N 89.15 W
Taymā' 118 27.38 N 38.29 E
Taymouth 176 46.11 N 66.37 W
Taymyr Peninsula → Tajmyr, Poluostrov ≻1 64 76.00 N 104.00 E
Tay-ninh 100 11.18 N 106.06 E
Tayoltita 222 24.05 N 105.56 W
Táyros 257c 37.58 N 23.42 E
Tayside □4 28 56.30 N 3.30 W
Taytay, Pil. 106 10.49 N 119.31 E
Taytay, Pil. 106 14.34 N 121.08 E
Taytay Bay C 106 10.55 N 119.35 E
Tayu 105a 6.32 S 111.02 E
Tayüan 90 25.06 N 121.14 E
Tayug 106 16.02 N 120.45 E
Tayyārah 130 13.12 N 30.47 E
Ṭayyebāt 118 34.44 N 60.45 E
Taz ≃ 62 67.32 N 78.40 E
Taza 138 34.16 N 4.01 W
Tazawa-ko @ 82 39.43 N 140.40 E
Tazenakht 138 30.35 N 7.12 W
Tazerbo ⸗4 136 25.45 N 21.00 E
Tazewell, Tenn., U.S. 182 36.27 N 83.34 W
Tazewell, Va., U.S. 182 37.07 N 81.31 W
Tazhuang 95 39.55 N 117.13 E
Tazicheng 79 46.35 N 123.06 E
Tazigouhe ≃ 94 41.44 N 121.30 E
Tazin ≃ 166 60.26 N 110.45 W
Tazin Lake @ 166 59.47 N 109.03 W
T'ažinskij 76 56.07 N 88.31 E
Tazishan 97 29.28 N 104.14 E
Tazlina Lake @ 170 61.50 N 146.30 W
Tazoult-Lambese 34 35.29 N 6.15 E
Tazovskaja Guba C 64 69.05 N 76.00 E
Tazovskij 64 67.28 N 78.42 E
Tazovskij Poluostrov ≻1 62 68.35 N 76.00 E
Tazrouk 138 23.25 N 6.16 E
Tazumal ⊥ 226 13.59 N 89.41 W
Tāzumuddin 116 22.29 N 90.53 E
Tazuruhama 84 37.04 N 136.53 E
Tbilisi 74 41.43 N 44.49 E
Tbilisskaja 68 45.23 N 40.12 E
Tchaba 263b 4.06 S 15.16 E
Tchad → Chad □1 136 15.00 N 19.00 E
Tchad, Lac (Lake Chad) @ 136 13.20 N 14.00 E
Tchagin Golo 136 10.03 N 16.19 E
Tchamba 140 9.02 N 1.25 E
Tch'ang-Cha → Changsha 90 28.11 N 113.01 E
Tchaourou 140 8.53 N 2.36 E
Tchécoslovaquie → Czechoslovakia □1 30 49.30 N 17.00 E
Tchefuncta ≃ 184 30.22 N 90.10 W
Tchékapika 142 1.17 S 16.11 E
Tcheliabinsk → Čel'abinsk 76 55.10 N 61.24 E
Tcheng-Tcheou → Zhengzhou 92 34.48 N 113.39 E
Tchentlo @ 172 55.11 N 125.00 W
Tchériba 140 12.16 N 3.05 W
Tchetti 140 7.50 N 1.40 E
Tchibanga 142 2.51 S 11.02 E
Tchien 140 6.04 N 8.08 W
Tchigaï, Plateau du ⸙1 136 21.30 N 14.50 E
Tchin Tabaraden 140 15.58 N 5.50 E
Tchitondi 142 4.33 S 12.08 E
Tcholliré 136 8.24 N 14.10 E
Tchong-K'ing → Chongqing 97 29.39 N 106.34 E
Tchula 184 33.11 N 90.13 W
⊥C. Steele State Memorial 208 39.08 N 86.20
Tczew 30 54.06 N 18.47 E
Te, Kinh ☰ 259c 10.45 N 106.42 E
Tea ≃ 236 0.30 S 65.09 W
Teaca 38 46.55 N 24.31 E
Teacapán 224 22.33 N 105.45 W
Teaehoa, Pointe ≻ 164x 9.51 S 139.01 W
Teague 212 31.38 N 96.17 W
Te Anau 162 45.25 S 167.43 E
Te Anau, Lake @ 162 45.12 S 167.48 E
Teanaway ≃ 214 47.10 N 120.50 W
Teanaway, Middle Fork ≃ 214 47.15 N 120.53 W
Teanaway, North Fork ≃ 214 47.22 N 120.53 W
Teaneck 200 40.53 N 74.01 W
Teano 60 41.15 N 14.04 E
Teapa 224 17.33 N 92.57 W

Teapa ≃ 224 17.58 N 92.54 W
Te Araroa 162 37.38 S 178.22 E
Tearinibai 164t 1.35 N 172.58 E
Te Aroha 162 37.33 S 175.43 E
Teaticket 197 41.34 N 70.36 W
Tea Tree 152 22.11 S 133.17 E
Teatree Gully 158b 34.49 S 138.44 E
Te Atukura ∧ 164k 21.14 S 159.45 W
Teavaraa, Passe ⋃ 164s 17.46 S 149.28 W
Te Awamutu 162 38.01 S 175.19 E
Teba, Esp. 34 36.58 N 4.56 W
Teba, Indon. 154 1.29 S 137.54 E
Tebakang 102 1.06 N 110.30 E
Tebas 246 21.35 S 42.44 W
Tebay 42 54.26 N 2.35 W
Tebbetts 209 38.37 N 91.58 W
Teberda 74 43.28 N 41.45 E
Teberdinskij Zapovednik ♣ 74 43.20 N 41.45 E
Tebes 276d 12.07 S 77.00 W
Tébessa 138 35.28 N 8.09 E
Tébessa, Monts de ⸙ 138 35.20 N 8.20 E
Tebicuary ≃ 242 26.36 S 58.16 W
Tebicuary-Mí ≃ 242 26.26 S 56.51 W
Tebingbulan 102 3.03 S 103.44 E
Tebingtinggi, Indon. 102 3.36 S 103.05 E
Tebingtinggi, Indon. 102 0.36 N 101.36 E
Tebingtinggi, Indon. 104 3.20 N 99.09 E
Tebingtinggi, Pulau I 104 0.54 N 102.45 E
Tébourba 36 36.49 N 9.51 E
Téboursouk 138 36.28 N 9.15 E
Téboursouk, Monts de ⸙ 36 36.30 N 9.10 E
Tebra ≃ 66 56.51 N 21.12 E
Tebstrup 41 55.59 N 9.53 E
Tebulosmta, Gora ∧ 74 42.33 N 45.19 E
Tebza ≃ 70 58.23 N 41.19 E
Tecalitlán 224 19.26 N 103.15 W
Tecamachalco 224 18.53 N 97.44 W
Tecate 222 32.34 N 116.38 W
Tech ≃ 32 42.36 N 3.03 E
Techendorf 58 46.43 N 13.17 E
Techiman 140 7.35 N 1.56 W
Techimentia 140 7.11 N 2.02 W
Techirghiol 38 44.03 N 28.36 E
Techny 268 42.07 N 87.49 W
Techou → Dezhou 88 37.27 N 116.18 E
Techtin 66 53.51 N 29.44 E
Tecka 244 43.29 S 70.48 W
Tecklenburg 48 52.13 N 7.48 E
Teckomatorp 41 55.52 N 13.05 E
Tecolote Creek ≃ 190 35.22 N 105.15 W
Tecolotlán 224 20.13 N 104.03 W
Tecolutla ≃ 224 20.29 N 97.00 W
Tecomán 224 18.55 N 103.53 W
Tecomate, Laguna C 224 16.35 N 99.25 W
Tecomaxtlahuaca 224 17.21 N 98.02 W
Tecominoacán 224 17.53 N 93.37 W
Tecopa 194 35.51 N 116.13 W
Tecozautla 224 20.32 N 99.38 W
Tecpan de Galeana 224 17.15 N 100.41 W
Tecpán Guatemala 226 14.46 N 91.00 W
Tecpatán 224 17.08 N 93.18 W
Tecuala 224 22.23 N 105.27 W
Tecuamburro, Volcán ∧1 226 14.09 N 90.24 W
Tecuantepec ≃ 224 20.16 N 97.27 W
Tecuci 38 45.50 N 27.26 E
Tecumseh, Ont., Can. 204 42.19 N 82.54 W
Tecumseh, Mich., U.S. 206 42.00 N 83.57 W
Tecumseh, Nebr., U.S. 188 40.22 N 96.11 W
Tecumseh, Okla., U.S. 186 35.15 N 96.56 W
Ted 134 4.26 N 43.55 E
Teddington ✦8 250 51.25 N 0.20 W
Tedesa 134 5.07 N 37.45 E
Tedori ≃ 84 36.29 N 136.28 E
Tedrow 206 41.37 N 84.13 W
Tedžen 118 37.23 N 60.31 E
Tedžen (Harīrūd) ≃ 118 37.24 N 60.38 E
Tedženstroj 118 36.55 N 60.53 E
Teec Nos Pos 190 36.55 N 109.07 W
Tee Creek ≃ 274a 43.02 N 79.06 W
Teels Marsh ☷ 194 38.12 N 118.21 W
Teen @ 40 59.07 N 14.40 E
Teerijärvi → Terjärv 26 63.32 N 23.30 E
Tees ≃ 42 54.34 N 1.16 W
Teesdale ∨ 42 54.38 N 2.07 W
Teesside → Middlesbrough 42 54.35 N 1.14 W
Teesside (Saint George) Airport ⊠ 42 54.31 N 1.25 W
Teeswater 202 44.00 N 81.17 W
Teeswater ≃ 202 44.18 N 81.17 W
Tefé 236 3.22 S 64.42 W
Tefé ≃ 232 3.35 S 64.47 W
Tefé, Lago de @ 236 3.27 S 64.47 W
Tefen 120 41.19 N 32.08 E
Tefenni 120 37.18 N 29.47 E
Tefft 206 41.12 N 86.58 W
Tefle 140 5.59 N 0.35 E
Tegal 105a 6.52 S 109.08 E
Tegalombo 105a 8.04 S 111.17 E
Tega-numa @ 258 35.51 N 140.04 E
Tegel ✦8 254a 52.35 N 13.17 E
Tegel, Berliner Forst ♣ 254a 52.37 N 13.16 E
Tegelen 48 51.21 N 6.09 E
Tegeler See @ 254a 52.35 N 13.15 E
Tegernsee 58 47.43 N 11.45 E
Tegernsee @ 58 47.42 N 11.45 E
Teghra 114 25.29 N 85.57 E
Tegid, Llyn @ 44 52.53 N 3.36 W
Tegina 140 10.05 N 6.14 E
Tegineneng 102 5.12 S 105.10 E
Tegistyk 75 44.02 N 68.22 E
Teglio 58 46.10 N 10.04 E
Tegua I 165f 13.15 S 166.37 E
Tegualda 244 41.02 S 73.26 W
Tegucigalpa 226 14.06 N 87.13 W
Tehachapi 218 35.08 N 118.27 W
Tehachapi Creek ≃ 218 35.17 N 118.38 W
Tehachapi Mountains ⸙ 218 35.00 N 118.40 W
Tehachapi Pass)(218 35.06 N 118.18 W
Tehamiyam 130 18.20 N 36.32 E
Te Hapua 162 34.31 S 172.54 E
Tehar ✦8 262a 28.38 N 77.07 E
Te Haroto 162 39.08 S 176.36 E
Tehata 116 23.43 N 88.32 E
Tehek Lake @ 166 64.55 N 95.38 W
Teheran → Tehrān 118 35.40 N 51.26 E
Téhini 140 9.36 N 3.40 W
Tehoohaivei, Cap ≻ 164x 9.49 S 138.54 W
Te Hope O Te Keho, Cap ≻ 164x 10.02 S 139.06 W
Tehoru 154 3.23 S 129.30 E
Tehrān 118 / 257d 35.40 N 51.26 E
Tehrān □4 118 35.30 N 51.00 E
Tehrān, University of ⚜2 257d 35.42 N 51.24 E
Tehrān Pars ✦8 257d 35.44 N 51.32 E
Tehri 114 30.23 N 78.29 E
Tehri Garhwāl □5 114 30.30 N 78.30 E
Tehri Sar ∧ 113 36.48 N 74.48 E
Tehrthum 114 27.07 N 87.32 E
Tehuacán 224 18.27 N 97.23 W
Tehuacana 212 31.44 N 96.33 W
Tehuacana Creek ≃, Tex., U.S. 212 31.50 N 95.59 W
Tehuacana Creek ≃, Tex., U.S. 212 31.31 N 97.02 W
Tehuantepec, Méx. 224 18.41 N 103.17 W

Symbol	English	Deutsch	Español	Français	Português
≃	River	Fluss	Río	Rivière	Rio
☰	Canal	Kanal	Canal	Canal	Canal
⌊	Waterfall, Rapids	Wasserfall, Stromschnellen	Cascada, Rápidos	Chute d'eau, Rapides	Cascata, Rápidos
⋃	Strait	Meeresstrasse	Estrecho	Détroit	Estreito
C	Bay, Gulf	Bucht, Golf	Bahía, Golfo	Baie, Golfe	Baía, Golfo
@	Lake, Lakes	See, Seen	Lago, Lagos	Lac, Lacs	Lago, Lagos
☷	Swamp	Sumpf	Pantano	Marais	Pântano
⸗	Ice Features, Glacier	Eis- und Gletscherformen	Accidentes Glaciales	Formes glaciaires	Acidentes Glaciares
≃	Other Hydrographic Features	Andere Hydrographische Objekte	Otros Elementos Hidrográficos	Autres données hydrographiques	Outros Elementos Hidrográficos
✢	Submarine Features	Untermeerische Objekte	Accidentes Submarinos	Formes de relief sous-marin	Acidentes Submarinos
□	Political Unit	Politische Einheit	Unidad Politica	Entité politique	Unidade Política
⚜	Cultural Institution	Kulturelle Institution	Institución Cultural	Institution culturelle	Instituição Cultural
⊥	Historical Site	Historische Stätte	Sitio Histórico	Site historique	Sítio Histórico
♣	Recreational Site	Erholungs- und Ferienort	Sitio de Recreo	Centre de loisirs	Sítio de Lazer
⊠	Airport	Flughafen	Aeropuerto	Aéroport	Aeroporto
▪	Military Installation	Militäranlage	Instalación Militar	Installation militaire	Instalação Militar
✦	Miscellaneous	Verschiedenes	Misceláneo	Divers	Miscelânea

ENGLISH — Name · Page · Lat.°′ · Long.°′
DEUTSCH — Name · Seite · Breite°′ · Länge°′ E=Ost

Symbols in the index entries represent the broad categories identified in the key at the right. Symbols with superior numbers (⛰2) identify subcategories (see complete key on page I · 26).

Kartensymbole in dem Registerverzeichnis stellen die rechts in Schlüssel erklärten Kategorien dar. Symbole mit hochgestellten Ziffern (⛰2) bezeichnen Unterabteilungen einer Kategorie (vgl. vollständiger Schlüssel auf Seite I · 26).

Los símbolos incluídos en el texto del índice representan las grandes categorias identificadas con la clave a la derecha. Los símbolos con numeros en su parte superior (⛰2) identifican las subcategorías (véase la clave completa en la página I · 26).

Les symboles de l'index représentent les catégories indiquées dans la légende à droite. Les symboles suivis d'un indice (⛰2) représentent des sous-catégories (voir légende complète à la page I · 26).

Os símbolos incluídos no texto do índice representam as grandes categorias identificadas com a chave à direita. Os símbolos com números em sua parte superior (⛰2) identificam as subcategorias (veja-se a chave completa à página I · 26).

Symbol	English	Deutsch	Español	Français	Português
∧	Mountain	Berg	Montaña	Montagne	Montanha
⛰	Mountains	Berge	Montañas	Montagnes	Montanhas
)(	Pass	Pass	Paso	Col	Passo
∨	Valley, Canyon	Tal, Cañon	Valle, Cañón	Vallée, Canyon	Vale, Canhão
≚	Plain	Ebene	Llano	Plaine	Planície
≻	Cape	Kap	Cabo	Cap	Cabo
I	Island	Insel	Isla	Île	Ilha
II	Islands	Inseln	Islas	Îles	Ilhas
⍛	Other Topographic Features	Andere Topographische Objekte	Otros Elementos Topográficos	Autres données topographiques	Outros Elementos Topográficos

ESPAÑOL: Nombre · Página · Lat.°′ · Long.°′ W=Oeste
FRANÇAIS: Nom · Page · Lat.°′ · Long.°′ W=Ouest
PORTUGUÊS: Nome · Página · Lat.°′ · Long.°′ W=Oeste

Name	Page	Lat.	Long.
Thach-by	100	14.40 N	109.04 E
Thacher Island I	197	42.38 N	70.35 W
Thādiq	118	25.18 N	45.52 E
Thagyettaw	100	13.45 N	98.09 E
Thai-binh	100	20.27 N	106.20 E
Thailand □[1]	98		
	100	15.00 N	100.00 E
Thailand, Gulf of C	100	10.00 N	101.00 E
Thaïlande → Thailand □[1]	100	15.00 N	100.00 E
Thailandia → Thailand □[1]	100	15.00 N	100.00 E
Thai Muang	100	8.24 N	98.16 E
Thai-nguyen	100	21.36 N	105.50 E
Thak	110	30.32 N	70.13 E
Thakhek → Muang Khammouan	100	17.24 N	104.48 E
Thākurdwāra	114	29.12 N	78.51 E
Thākurdwāri	262b	22.34 N	88.28 E
Thākurgaon	114	26.02 N	88.28 E
Thākurpukur	262b	22.28 N	88.19 E
Thākurvādi	262c	18.54 N	73.04 E
Thal, D.D.R.	50	50.55 N	10.23 E
Thal, Pāk.	113	33.22 N	70.33 E
Tha'l, Jabal ∧	130	14.13 N	24.14 E
Thala	36	35.35 N	8.40 E
Thalang	100	8.01 N	98.19 E
Thal-Assling	58	46.47 N	12.38 E
Thal Desert ◆[2]	113	31.30 N	71.40 E
Thale	50	51.45 N	11.02 E
Thalfang	52	49.45 N	6.59 E
Thalgau	58	47.50 N	13.15 E
Thalheim	50	50.42 N	12.51 E
Tha Li	100	17.37 N	101.25 E
Thalia	186	33.59 N	99.32 W
Thalitter	52	51.13 N	8.53 E
Thalkirch	54	46.38 N	9.16 E
Thallon	156	28.38 S	148.52 E
Thallwitz	50	51.26 N	12.40 E
Thalmah, Jabal ∧	132	29.00 N	32.34 E
Thalmah, Marsā C	132	29.03 N	32.38 E
Thalwil	54	47.17 N	8.34 E
Thame	44	51.45 N	0.59 W
Thames	162	37.08 S	175.33 E
Thames ≃, Ont., Can.	180	42.19 N	82.28 W
Thames ≃, Eng., U.K.	44	51.28 N	0.43 E
Thames ≃, Conn., U.S.	197	41.18 N	72.05 W
Thames, Firth Of C	162	37.00 S	175.25 E
Thames Ditton	250	51.23 N	0.21 W
Thames Estuary C[1]	250	51.30 N	0.40 W
Thamesford	202	43.04 N	81.00 W
Thames Haven	250	51.30 N	0.31 E
Thamesville	204	42.33 N	81.59 W
Thāmir, Jabal ∧	134	13.53 N	45.30 E
Thāmit, Wādī V	136	31.15 N	16.06 E
Thammasat, University of ⊎[2]	259a	13.45 N	100.30 E
Thamnūn	134	15.07 N	50.49 E
Thamūd ▿[4]	134	17.15 N	49.54 E
Thāna, Bhārat	112		
	262c	19.12 N	72.58 E
Thāna, Pāk.	118	28.55 N	63.45 E
Thāna □[5]	262c	19.12 N	73.05 E
Thāna Creek C	262c	19.00 N	72.57 E
Thāna Ghāzi	114	27.25 N	76.19 E
Thāna Kasba	114	25.13 N	77.20 E
Thanbyuzayat	100	15.58 N	97.44 E
Thandaung	100	19.04 N	96.41 E
Thānedārwāla	113	32.36 N	71.07 E
Thānesar	114	29.59 N	76.49 E
Thanet, Isle of I	44	51.22 N	1.20 E
Thanet Lake ⊜	202	44.47 N	77.46 W
Thang-binh	100	15.44 N	108.22 E
Thangoo	152	18.10 S	122.22 E
Thangool	156	24.29 S	150.35 E
Thanh-hoa	100	19.48 N	105.46 E
Thanh-my-tay	259c	10.49 N	106.46 E
Thanh-pho Ho Chi Minh (Sai-gon)	100		
	259c	10.45 N	106.40 E
Thanjāvūr	112	10.48 N	79.09 E
Thānkot	114	27.41 N	85.11 E
Thann	54	47.49 N	7.05 E
Thannhausen	54	48.17 N	10.28 E
Thāno Bula Khān	110	25.22 N	67.50 E
Than-uyen	100	22.00 N	103.54 E
Thaon-les-Vosges	54	48.15 N	6.25 E
Tha Pla	100	17.48 N	100.32 E
Thap Than ≃	100	15.21 N	104.06 E
Tharabwin West	100	12.17 N	99.03 E
Tharād	110	24.24 N	71.38 E
Tharandt	50	50.59 N	13.35 E
't Harde	48	52.25 N	5.53 E
Thar Desert (Great Indian Desert) ◆[2]	110	27.00 N	71.00 E
Thargomindah	156	28.00 S	143.49 E
Thāri Pātan ∧	114	28.58 N	82.04 E
Thar Nhom	130	7.26 N	30.29 E
Tharptown	200	40.48 N	76.34 W
Tharr, Wüste → Thar Desert ◆[2]	110	27.00 N	71.00 E
Tharrawaddy	100	17.39 N	95.48 E
Tharrawaw	100	17.41 N	95.28 E
Tharthār, Wādī ath- V	118	33.59 N	43.12 E
Tharwa	161b	35.31 S	149.04 E
Tha Sala	100	8.40 N	99.56 E
Thásos	38	40.47 N	24.42 E
Thásos I	38	40.41 N	24.47 E
Thásos ⊥	38	40.46 N	24.33 E
Tha Tako	100	15.38 N	100.29 E
Thatcham	44	51.25 N	1.15 W
Thatch Cay I	230m	18.22 N	64.52 W
Thatcher	190	32.51 N	109.46 W
Thatch Island I	266	40.38 N	73.23 W
That-khe	100	22.16 N	106.28 E
Thaton	100	16.55 N	97.22 E
That Phanom	100	16.57 N	104.44 E
Thatto Heath	252	53.26 N	2.45 W
Tha Tum	100	15.19 N	103.41 E
Thau, Bassin de C	32	43.23 N	3.36 E
Thaungdut	100	24.26 N	94.42 E
Thaungyin ≃	100	17.50 N	97.42 E
Tha Uthen	100	17.34 N	104.36 E
Thawville	206	40.41 N	88.07 W
Thaxted	44	51.57 N	0.20 E
Thaya (Dyje) ≃	30	48.37 N	16.56 E
Thayawthadangyi Kyun I	100	12.20 N	98.00 E
Thayer, Ill., U.S.	209	39.32 N	89.46 W
Thayer, Ind., U.S.	206	41.10 N	87.20 W
Thayer, Kans., U.S.	188	37.30 N	95.28 W
Thayer, Mo., U.S.	184	36.31 N	91.33 W
Thayetchaung	100	13.52 N	98.16 E
Thayetmyo	100	19.19 N	95.11 E
Thayngen	54	47.45 N	8.42 E
Thazi	100	20.51 N	96.05 E
Theale	44	51.27 N	1.04 W
Thealka	182	37.49 N	82.47 W
The Basin	264b	37.51 S	145.19 E
Thebes	184	37.13 N	89.28 W
Thebes ⊥	130	25.42 N	32.37 E
The Bight	228	24.19 N	75.24 W
The Birket ≃	252	53.24 N	3.01 W
The Bluffs •[4]	200	43.22 N	76.40 W
The Brothers II	108	12.09 N	53.12 E
The Calvados Chain II	154	11.10 S	152.40 E
The Capital ⊎	274c	38.53 N	77.00 W
The Cheviot ∧	42	55.28 N	2.09 W
The Church of the Holy Sepulchre ⊎[1]	122	31.46 N	35.14 E
The Coorong	158b	35.40 S	139.15 E
The Coteau ⛰[2]	174	51.10 N	107.30 W
The Coves Palisades State Park ♠	192	44.34 N	121.15 W
The Dalles	214	45.36 N	121.10 W
The Dalles Dam ◆[6]	214	45.36 N	121.08 W
Thedford	188	41.59 N	100.35 W
Thedinghausen	48	52.58 N	9.01 E
The Downs ▿[3]	44	51.13 N	1.27 E
Theebine	156	25.57 S	152.33 E
The English Companys Islands II	154	11.50 S	136.32 E
The Entrance	160	33.21 S	151.30 E
Theessen	50	52.14 N	12.02 E
The Everglades ≋	210	26.00 N	80.40 W
The Father ∧	154	5.03 S	151.20 E
The Fens ≋	44	52.38 N	0.02 E
The Fiery Range ⛰	161b	35.30 S	148.40 E
The Flash ⊜	252	53.29 N	2.33 W
The Flat Tops ⛰	190	40.00 N	107.10 W
The Forest of Nisene Marks State Park ♠	216	37.03 N	121.53 W
The Glenkens ◆[1]	42	55.10 N	4.15 W
Thègon	100	18.39 N	95.25 E
The Granites	152	20.35 S	130.21 E
The Granites ∧	152	20.35 S	130.20 E
The Graves II	273	42.22 N	70.52 W
The Grove	212	31.16 N	97.32 W
The Hague → 's-Gravenhage	48	52.06 N	4.18 E
The Heads ≻	192	42.44 N	124.31 W
The Hunters Hills ⛰[2]	162	44.30 S	170.50 E
Theinkun	100	11.53 N	99.09 E
The Isles Lagoon C	164o	1.50 N	157.23 W
Theiss → Tisa ≃	38	45.15 N	20.17 E
Theissen	50	51.05 N	12.06 E
The Key Indian Reserve ◆[4]	174	51.45 N	102.08 W
The Lake ⊜	228	21.00 N	73.30 W
The Lake Fleet Islands II	202	44.18 N	76.07 W
Thelon ≃	166	64.16 N	96.05 W
The Long Mynd ∧	44	52.35 N	2.48 W
The Lower Hope ≃[1]	250	51.28 N	0.28 E
Thelwall	252	53.23 N	2.32 W
The Lynd	156	18.56 S	144.30 E
Them	41	56.06 N	9.33 E
The Machars □[8]	42	54.50 N	4.30 W
The Machars ◆[1]	42	55.20 N	4.33 W
Themar	50	50.30 N	10.37 E
The Meadows Race Track ♠	269b	40.13 N	80.12 W
The Mere ⊜	252	53.20 N	2.24 W
Théméricourt	251	49.05 N	1.54 E
The Minch U	28	58.05 N	5.55 W
The Moors ◆[1]	42	54.56 N	4.40 W
The Mumbles	44	51.34 N	4.00 W
Then	113	32.26 N	75.44 E
The Narrows U	266	40.37 N	74.03 W
The Navy Islands II	202	44.21 N	76.03 W
The Naze ≻	44	51.53 N	1.16 E
The Needles ≻	44	50.39 N	1.34 W
Thénezay	32	46.43 N	0.02 W
Thenia	138	36.43 N	3.34 E
The Oa ◆[1]	42	55.37 N	6.16 W
The Oaks, Austl.	160	34.04 S	150.34 E
The Oaks, Calif., U.S.	216	39.13 N	121.05 W
Theodore, Austl.	156	24.57 S	150.05 E
Theodore, Sask., Can.	174	51.25 N	102.54 W
Theodore, Ala., U.S.	184	30.33 N	88.10 W
Theodore Francis Green Airport ⊠	197	41.44 N	71.26 W
Theodore Roosevelt Island I	274c	38.54 N	77.03 W
Theodore Roosevelt Lake ⊜[1]	190	33.42 N	111.07 W
Theodore Roosevelt National Memorial Park (South Unit) ♠, N. Dak., U.S.	188	46.55 N	103.26 W
Theodore Roosevelt National Memorial Park (North Unit) ♠, N. Dak., U.S.	188	47.34 N	103.24 W
Theodor-Heuss-Brücke ◆[5]	253	51.15 N	6.45 E
Theog	113	31.07 N	77.21 E
Theólogos	38	40.39 N	24.41 E
Théoule-sur-Mer	56	43.31 N	6.57 E
The Oval ⊥	250	51.29 N	0.07 W
The Pages II	158b	35.47 S	138.17 E
The Pas	174	53.50 N	101.15 W
The Peak ∧	182	36.24 N	81.39 W
Thepha	100	6.52 N	100.58 E
The Pilot ∧	156	36.45 S	148.13 E
The Pinnacle ∧[2]	209	39.22 N	90.55 W
Thérain ≃	46	49.15 N	2.27 E
The Rajah ∧	172	53.15 N	118.31 W
The Rand → Witwatersrand ◆[1]	148	26.00 S	27.00 E
The Range	144	19.00 S	31.04 E
Theresa	202	44.13 N	75.48 W
Theresa Creek ≃	156	23.26 S	148.09 E
Theresa Park	264a	34.01 S	150.39 E
Theresienstadt → Terezín	50	50.31 N	14.08 E
The Rhins ≻[1]	42	54.50 N	5.00 W
The Rip C	159	38.17 S	144.37 E
The Riverstone Wildlife Refuge ◆[4]	264a	33.42 S	150.51 E
Thermaïkós Kólpos C	38	40.23 N	22.47 E
Thermalito	216	39.31 N	121.36 W
Thermopílai ⊥	38	38.48 N	22.33 E
Thermopolis	190	43.39 N	108.13 W
Thermopylae → Thermopílai ⊥	38	38.48 N	22.33 E
The Rock	156	35.16 S	147.07 E
The Rockies ∧	214	46.39 N	122.22 W
Theron Mountains ⛰	9	79.05 S	28.15 W
The Rope •[4]	164e	25.04 S	130.05 W
Thérouanne	46	50.38 N	2.15 E
The Royal National Park ♠	160	34.10 S	151.05 E
The Savannahs ⊜	210	27.19 N	80.17 W
Theseion ⊥	257c	37.58 N	23.43 E
Thesiger Bay C	166	71.30 N	124.05 W
The Sisters ∧[2]	152	26.17 S	126.40 E
The Slot U	165e	8.00 S	158.10 E
The Sluice ≡	252	53.41 N	2.57 W
The Snares II	9	48.00 S	166.30 E
The Sny ≃	209	39.16 N	90.44 W
The Solent U	44	50.46 N	1.20 W
The Sound U, Austl.	264a	33.49 S	151.17 E
The Sound (Øresund) U, Eur.	41	55.50 N	12.40 E
The Springs	197	41.01 N	72.09 W
Thesprotikón	38	39.15 N	20.47 E
Thessalía ◆[1]	38	39.30 N	22.00 E
Thessalon	180	46.15 N	83.34 W
Thessaloníki (Salonika)	38	40.38 N	22.56 E
Thessalonique → Thessaloníki	38	40.38 N	22.56 E
The Swale U	44	51.22 N	0.56 E
Thet ≃	44	52.27 N	0.33 E
The Terraces •[4]	152	28.40 S	121.30 E
Thetford	44	52.25 N	0.45 E
Thetford Mines	196	46.05 N	71.18 W
The Thumbs ∧	162	43.36 S	170.44 E
Thetis Island	214	49.59 N	123.40 W
Thetis Island I	214	49.00 N	123.41 W
The Twins ∧	162	41.14 S	172.39 E
Theunissen	148	28.30 S	26.41 E
Theux	52	50.32 N	5.49 E
The Valley	228	18.13 N	63.04 W
Thevenard	152	32.09 S	133.38 E
Thevenard Island I	152	21.27 S	115.00 E
The Village	186	35.35 N	97.33 W
The Wash C	44	52.55 N	0.15 E
The Weald ◆[1]	44	51.05 N	0.05 E
The Whirlpool ≃	274a	43.07 N	79.04 W
The Winehead ∧	200	40.58 N	77.28 W
The Wrekin ∧[2]	44	52.41 N	2.34 W
Theydon Bois	250	51.40 N	0.06 E
Theys	56	45.18 N	6.00 E
Thiais	251	48.46 N	2.23 E
Thiant	46	50.18 N	3.27 E
Thiaucourt-Regniéville	52	48.57 N	5.52 E
Thibaudeau	174	57.05 N	94.08 W
Thiberville	46	49.08 N	0.27 E
Thibodaux	184	29.48 N	90.49 W
Thicket	212	30.24 N	94.38 W
Thicket Portage	174	55.19 N	97.42 W
Thiéblemont-Farémont	54	48.41 N	4.44 E
Thief ≃	188	48.08 N	96.10 W
Thief River Falls	188	48.07 N	96.10 W
Thièle ≃	54	47.03 N	7.05 E
Thiel Mountains ⛰	9	85.15 S	91.00 W
Thielsen, Mount ∧	192	43.09 N	122.04 W
Thiendorf	50	51.17 N	13.44 E
Thiene	58	45.42 N	11.29 E
Thiensville	206	43.14 N	87.58 W
Thier	253	51.05 N	7.22 E
Thiérache, Collines de la ⛰[2]	46	49.50 N	3.50 E
Thierhaupten	52	48.34 N	10.54 E
Thiers	56	45.51 N	3.34 E
Thiersheim	50	50.04 N	12.07 E
Thierville-sur-Meuse	52	49.10 N	5.21 E
Thiès	140	14.48 N	16.56 W
Thiès □[4]	140	14.45 N	16.50 W
Thiesi	36	40.31 N	8.43 E
Thiessow	50	54.16 N	13.43 E
Thieux	251	49.01 N	2.40 E
Thieveley Pike ∧[2]	252	53.45 N	2.12 W
Thika	144	1.03 S	37.05 E
Thikombia I	165g	15.44 S	179.55 W
Thilay	52	49.52 N	4.49 E
Thilenius, Cape ≻	154	1.35 S	149.57 E
Thimbu	114	27.28 N	89.39 E
Thines	56	44.29 N	4.03 E
Thingvallavatn ⊜	24a	64.12 N	21.10 W
Thingvellir	24a	64.17 N	21.07 W
Thio	165f	21.37 S	166.14 E
Thionville	52	49.22 N	6.10 E
Thiou	140	13.48 N	2.40 W
Thíra	38	36.25 N	25.26 E
Thíra I	38	36.24 N	25.29 E
Third ≃	266	40.49 N	74.08 W
Third Cataract → Ash-Shallāl ath-Thālith L	130	19.49 N	30.19 E
Third Cliff •[4]	273	42.11 N	70.43 W
Third Creek ≃, Mo., U.S.	209	38.26 N	91.40 W
Third Creek ≃, N.C., U.S.	182	35.47 N	80.31 W
Third Herring Brook ≃	273	42.07 N	70.48 W
Third Lake ⊜	196	45.14 N	71.12 W
Third Street Station ◆[5]	272	37.46 N	122.23 W
Thirlmere	160	34.12 S	150.34 E
Thirlmere ⊜	42	54.33 N	3.04 W
Thiron	46	48.19 N	0.59 E
Thironne ≃	46	48.17 N	1.15 E
Thirroul	160	34.19 S	150.56 E
Thirsk	42	54.14 N	1.20 W
Thirtieth Street Station ◆[5]	275	39.57 N	75.11 W
Thirtymile Creek ≃	188	46.22 N	102.03 W
Thirtymile Point ≻	200	43.22 N	78.29 W
Thisted	26	56.57 N	8.42 E
Thistilfjörđur C	24a	66.20 N	15.25 W
Thistledown Race Track ♠	269a	41.26 N	81.32 W
Thistle Island I	156	35.00 S	136.09 E
Thistletown ◆[8]	265b	43.44 N	79.33 W
Thithia I	165g	17.45 S	179.18 W
Thívai (Thebes)	38	38.21 N	23.19 E
Thiverval-Grignon	251	48.51 N	1.55 E
Thiviers	32	45.25 N	0.56 E
Thizy	32	46.02 N	4.19 E
Thjórsá ≃	24a	63.47 N	20.48 W
Thlewiaza ≃	166	60.28 N	94.45 W
Thoa ≃	166	60.30 N	109.47 W
Thoen	100	17.36 N	99.12 E
Thoi-binh	100	9.21 N	105.05 E
Thoirette	54	46.16 N	5.32 E
Thoiry	251	48.52 N	1.48 E
Thoissey	54	46.10 N	4.48 E
Tholen	48	51.32 N	4.12 E
Tholen I	48	51.35 N	4.05 E
Tholey	52	49.29 N	7.02 E
Thollon	54	46.23 N	6.43 E
Thomas, Okla., U.S.	186	35.45 N	98.45 W
Thomas, Pa., U.S.	269b	40.15 N	80.06 W
Thomas, Wash., U.S.	214	47.21 N	122.14 W
Thomas, W. Va., U.S.	178	39.09 N	79.30 W
Thomasboro	206	40.15 N	88.11 W
Thomas J. O'Brien Lock and Dam ◆[5]	268	41.39 N	87.35 W
Thomas Lake ⊜	174	57.00 N	96.43 W
Thomas Mountains ⛰	9	75.32 S	70.57 W
Thomas Point ≻	198	38.54 N	76.28 W
Thomaston, Ala., U.S.	184	32.11 N	87.37 W
Thomaston, Conn., U.S.	197	41.40 N	73.04 W
Thomaston, Ga., U.S.	182	32.54 N	84.20 W
Thomaston, Maine, U.S.	178	44.05 N	69.10 W
Thomaston, N.Y., U.S.	266	40.47 N	73.43 W
Thomaston, Tex., U.S.	212	28.60 N	97.09 W
Thomastown, Austl.	264b	37.41 S	145.01 E
Thomastown, Eire	28	52.31 N	7.08 W
Thomasville, Ala., U.S.	184	31.55 N	87.51 W
Thomasville, Ga., U.S.	182	30.50 N	83.59 W
Thomasville, N.C., U.S.	182	35.53 N	80.05 W
Thomasville, Pa., U.S.	198	39.56 N	76.51 W
Thom Bay C	166	70.09 N	92.00 W
Thomes Creek ≃	194	39.59 N	122.06 W
Thom Lake ⊜	174	55.24 N	96.08 W
Thomlinson, Mount ∧	172	55.33 N	127.29 W
Thompson, Man., Can.	174	55.45 N	97.45 W
Thompson, Conn., U.S.	197	41.57 N	71.52 W
Thompson, Iowa, U.S.	180	43.22 N	93.46 W
Thompson, Mo., U.S.	209	39.11 N	91.59 W
Thompson, Ohio, U.S.	204	41.41 N	81.03 W
Thompson, Pa., U.S.	200	41.52 N	75.31 W
Thompson ≃, B.C., Can.	172	50.15 N	121.33 W
Thompson ≃, U.S.	184	39.45 N	93.36 W
Thompson Creek ≃, U.S.	188	45.04 N	104.25 W
Thompson Creek ≃, Miss., U.S.	184	31.10 N	88.54 W
Thompson Falls	192	47.36 N	115.21 W
Thompson Island I	273	42.23 N	71.01 W
Thompson Lake ⊜[1]	174	49.45 N	106.35 W
Thompson Pass)(	170	61.08 N	145.45 W
Thompson Peak ∧	194	41.00 N	123.03 W
Thompson Place	214	47.03 N	122.45 W
Thompson Ridge	200	41.34 N	74.20 W
Thompson Run ≃	269b	40.24 N	79.50 W
Thompsons	212	29.30 N	95.36 W
Thompsons Creek ≃	274a	43.03 N	79.08 W
Thompson Sound U	162	45.09 S	166.57 E
Thompsontown	198	40.33 N	77.14 W
Thompsonville	180	44.31 N	85.56 W
Thomsen ≃	166	74.08 N	119.35 W
Thomson, Ga., U.S.	182	33.28 N	82.30 W
Thomson, Ill., U.S.	180	41.58 N	90.06 W
Thomson, N.Y., U.S.	200	43.07 N	73.35 W
Thomson ≃, Austl.	156	25.11 S	142.53 E
Thomson ≃, Austl.	159	37.58 S	146.32 E
Thomson's Falls	144	0.02 N	36.22 E
Thon ≃	46	49.53 N	3.55 E
Thon Buri	100	13.43 N	100.29 E
Thônes	56	45.53 N	6.20 E
Thong	250	51.24 N	0.24 E
Thong Hoe	261c	1.25 N	103.42 E
Thong Pha Phum	100	14.44 N	98.38 E
Thong-tay-hoi	259c	10.50 N	106.39 E
Thongwa	100	16.46 N	96.32 E
Thon-lac-nghiep	100	11.20 N	108.54 E
Thonnance-lès-Joinville	54	48.27 N	5.10 E
Thonon-les-Bains	54	46.22 N	6.29 E
Thonotosassa	210	28.03 N	82.18 W
Thonze	100	17.38 N	95.47 E
Thorah Island I	202	44.27 N	79.14 W
Thorame-Haute	56	44.06 N	6.33 E
Thorburn	176	45.34 N	62.33 W
Thoreau	190	35.24 N	108.13 W
Thorembais-les-Béguines	52	50.40 N	4.49 E
Thorenc	56	43.48 N	6.49 E
Thorens-Glières	54	45.59 N	6.15 E
Thorez → Torez	73	48.01 N	38.37 E
Thorhild	172	54.10 N	113.07 W
Thorial	130	8.40 N	29.56 E
Thorigny	46	48.17 N	3.24 E
Thorigny-sur-Marne	251	48.53 N	2.42 E
Thorigny-sur-Oreuse	46	48.17 N	3.24 E
Thórisvatn ⊜	24a	64.50 N	19.26 W
Thorlákshöfn	24a	63.53 N	21.18 W
Thormanby	42	54.10 N	1.14 W
Thorn, Ned.	48	51.10 N	5.50 E
Thorn → Toruń, Pol.	30	53.02 N	18.35 E
Thornaby-on-Tees	42	54.34 N	1.18 W
Thornapple ≃, Mich., U.S.	206	42.56 N	85.28 W
Thornapple ≃, Wis., U.S.	180	45.28 N	91.16 W
Thornapple Lake ⊜	206	42.37 N	85.11 W
Thornburg	269b	40.26 N	80.05 W
Thornbury, Austl.	264b	37.45 S	145.00 E
Thornbury, Ont., Can.	202	44.34 N	80.26 W
Thornbury, N.Z.	162	46.17 S	168.06 E
Thornbury, Eng., U.K.	44	51.37 N	2.32 W
Thorn Creek ≃	268	41.36 N	87.35 W
Thorndale, Ont., Can.	202	43.06 N	81.08 W
Thorndale, Tex., U.S.	212	30.37 N	97.12 W
Thorndike	197	42.11 N	72.20 W
Thorndon	44	52.17 N	1.08 E
Thorne	42	53.37 N	0.58 W
Thorne ≃	174	54.56 N	90.35 W
Thorne Bay	172	55.44 N	132.32 W
Thorney	44	52.37 N	0.07 W
Thornhill, S. Afr.	263d	26.07 S	28.09 E
Thornhill, Scot., U.K.	42	55.15 N	3.46 W
Thornhurst	200	41.11 N	75.35 W
Thornleigh	264a	33.44 S	151.05 E
Thornton, Austl.	161a	27.49 S	152.23 E
Thornton, Eng., U.K.	42	53.53 N	3.02 W
Thornton, Eng., U.K.	252	53.47 N	1.51 W
Thornton, Ark., U.S.	184	33.47 N	92.29 W
Thornton, Calif., U.S.	216	38.14 N	121.25 W
Thornton, Colo., U.S.	190	39.51 N	104.59 W
Thornton, Pa., U.S.	275	39.54 N	75.32 W
Thornton, Tex., U.S.	212	31.24 N	96.34 W
Thornton Beach ♠	272	37.42 N	122.30 W
Thornton Dale	42	54.14 N	0.43 W
Thornton Hough	252	53.19 N	3.03 W
Thornton-le-Moors	252	53.16 N	2.50 W
Thornwood	200	41.07 N	73.47 W
Thornwood Common	250	51.43 N	0.08 E
Thorny Mountain ∧	184	37.06 N	91.10 W
Thorofare	275	39.51 N	75.12 W
Thorold	202	43.07 N	79.12 W
Thorold South	274a	43.06 N	79.12 W
Thoronet, Abbaye du ⊎[1]	56	43.28 N	6.16 E
Thorp, Wash., U.S.	214	47.04 N	120.40 W
Thorp, Wis., U.S.	180	44.58 N	90.48 W
Thorpe	250	51.24 N	0.32 W
Thorpe-le-Soken	44	51.52 N	1.10 E
Thorpe Saint Andrew	44	52.38 N	1.20 E
Thorp Spring	212	32.28 N	97.49 W
Thorsby, Alta., Can.	172	53.14 N	114.03 W
Thorsby, Ala., U.S.	184	32.55 N	86.43 W
Thorshavn → Tórshavn	22	62.01 N	6.46 W
Thórshöfn	24a	66.13 N	15.17 W
Thorsø	41	56.18 N	9.48 E
Thorsteinson Lake ⊜	174	57.15 N	97.30 W
Thorton Moor Reservoir ⊜[1]	252	53.47 N	1.55 W
Thot-not	100	10.16 N	105.32 E
Thouars	32	46.59 N	0.13 W
Thouin, Cape ≻	152	20.20 S	118.12 E
Thoune → Thun	54	46.45 N	7.37 E
Thourotte	46	49.29 N	2.53 E
Thousand Islands II	202	44.15 N	76.12 W
Thousand Islands International Bridge ◆[5]	202	44.20 N	75.58 W
Thousand Lake Mountain ∧	190	38.25 N	111.29 W
Thousand Oaks	218	34.10 N	118.50 W
Thousand Ships Bay C	165e	8.25 S	159.40 E
Thousand Springs Creek ≃	190	41.17 N	113.51 W
Thowa ≃	144	1.33 S	40.03 E
Thowgla Creek ≃	161b	36.10 S	147.57 E
Thrace □[9]	38	41.20 N	26.45 E
Thrakikón Pélagos ▿[2]	38	40.15 N	24.28 E
Thrall	212	30.35 N	97.18 W
Thrapston	44	52.24 N	0.32 W
Thrasher Lake ⊜	202	44.55 N	78.58 W
Thread Creek ≃	206	43.01 N	83.42 W
Thredbo Village	161b	36.29 S	148.19 E
Three Bridges, Eng., U.K.	44	51.07 N	0.09 W
Three Bridges, N.J., U.S.	198	40.31 N	74.48 W
Three Brothers ∧	214	47.23 N	120.45 W
Three Brothers Mountain ∧	214	49.10 N	120.46 W
Three Creek ≃	198	36.47 N	77.10 W
Three Fingered Jack ∧	192	44.29 N	121.50 W
Three Fingers ∧	214	48.10 N	121.41 W
Three Fools Creek ≃	214	48.53 N	120.57 W
Three Forks	192	45.54 N	111.33 W
Three Hills	172	51.42 N	113.16 W
Three Hummock Island I	156	40.26 S	144.55 E
Three Kings Islands II	162	34.10 S	172.05 E
Three Lakes	180	45.48 N	89.10 W
Three M Airport ⊠	275	40.08 N	74.51 W
Three Mile Bay	202	44.05 N	76.12 W
Three Mile Plains	176	44.58 N	64.07 W
Three Oaks	206	41.48 N	86.36 W
Three Pagodas Pass)(	100	15.18 N	98.23 E
Threepoint Lake ⊜	174	55.41 N	98.56 W
Three Points, Cape ≻	140	4.45 N	2.06 W
Three Rivers, Austl.	152	25.07 S	119.09 E
Three Rivers → Trois-Rivières, Qué., Can.	196	46.21 N	72.33 W
Three Rivers, Mass., U.S.	197	42.11 N	72.22 W
Three Rivers, Mich., U.S.	206	41.57 N	85.38 W
Three Rivers, Tex., U.S.	186	28.28 N	98.11 W
Three Rivers □[8]	250	51.40 N	0.27 W
Three Sisters	148	31.54 S	23.06 E
Three Sisters ∧	192	44.10 N	121.46 W
Three Sisters Pass)(	148	30.08 S	28.32 E
Three Springs, Austl.	152	29.32 S	115.45 E
Three Springs, Pa., U.S.	204	40.12 N	77.59 W
Threlkeld	42	54.38 N	3.03 W
Throat ≃	174	51.48 N	93.30 W
Throckley	42	54.59 N	1.45 W
Throckmorton	186	33.11 N	99.11 W
Throgs Neck ◆[8]	266	40.49 N	73.49 W
Throgs Neck Bridge ◆[5]	266	40.48 N	73.48 W
Throgs Point ≻	266	40.48 N	73.48 W
Throop	200	41.26 N	75.36 W
Throssel, Lake ⊜	152	27.27 S	124.16 E
Throssel Range ⛰	152	22.03 S	121.43 E
Thrushel ≃	44	50.39 N	4.15 W
Thruway Plaza ◆[9]	274a	42.55 N	78.46 W
Thuan-chau	100	21.26 N	103.41 E
Thu-duc	259c	10.51 N	106.45 E
Thueyts	56	44.41 N	4.13 E
Thuilley-aux-Groseilles	54	48.34 N	5.58 E
Thuin	46	50.20 N	4.17 E
Thul	110	28.14 N	68.46 E
Thulaythiwāt, Tilāl ath- ∧	122	30.58 N	36.40 E
Thulba ≃	52	50.11 N	9.52 E
Thule	16	76.34 N	68.47 W
Thum	50	50.40 N	12.57 E
Thumaymah, Jabal ∧[2]	132	30.21 N	30.37 E
Thumb Peak ∧	106	9.48 N	118.36 E
Thumby	41	54.35 N	9.54 E
Thun	54	46.45 N	7.37 E
Thun Chang	100	19.25 N	100.53 E
Thunder Bay	180	48.23 N	89.15 W
Thunder Bay C, Ont., Can.	180	48.24 N	89.00 W
Thunder Bay C, Ont., Can.	202	44.48 N	80.03 W
Thunder Bay ≃	180	45.04 N	83.25 W
Thunder Bay, North Branch ≃	180	45.08 N	83.35 W
Thunderbird, Lake ⊜[1]	186	35.15 N	97.20 W
Thunderbolt	182	32.03 N	81.04 W
Thunder Butte ∧	188	45.19 N	101.53 W
Thunder Butte Creek ≃	188	45.13 N	101.42 W
Thunder Creek ≃	214	48.40 N	121.05 W
Thunder Hills ⛰[2]	174	54.30 N	106.00 W
Thunder Knoll ✧[4]	228	16.25 N	81.20 W
Thunder Mountain ∧[2]	206	42.16 N	86.20 W
Thundersley	250	51.34 N	0.35 E
Thunersee ⊜	54	46.40 N	7.45 E
Thüngen	52	49.56 N	9.51 E
Thung Song	100	8.09 N	99.41 E
Thung Wa	100	7.06 N	99.46 E
Thur ≃, Fr.	54	48.05 N	7.23 E
Thur ≃, Schw.	54	47.36 N	8.35 E
Thurgau □[3]	54	47.35 N	9.00 E
Thurgovie → Thurgau □[3]	54	47.35 N	9.00 E
Thüringen	54	47.12 N	9.45 E
Thüringen □[9]	50	51.00 N	11.00 E
Thüringer Wald ⛰	50	50.30 N	11.00 E
Thürkow	50	53.50 N	12.33 E
Thurles	28	52.41 N	7.49 W
Thurmont	178	39.37 N	77.25 W
Thurn, Pass)(	58	47.19 N	12.24 E
Thurnham	250	51.17 N	0.36 E
Thurnscoe	42	53.31 N	1.19 W
Thurnwald Range ⛰	154	4.45 S	141.15 E
Thurø	41	55.03 N	10.40 E
Thurrock □[8]	250	51.30 N	0.21 E
Thursby	42	54.51 N	3.03 W
Thursday Island	154	10.35 S	142.13 E
Thurso, Qué., Can.	196	45.36 N	75.15 W
Thurso, Scot., U.K.	28	58.35 N	3.32 W
Thurstaston	252	53.21 N	3.08 W
Thurston □[6]	214	46.59 N	122.42 W
Thurston Island I	9	72.20 S	99.00 W
Thury-Harcourt	32	48.59 N	0.29 W
Thusis	54	46.42 N	9.26 E
Thwaites Ice Tongue ⊡	9	74.45 S	106.30 W
Thy ◆[1]	26	57.00 N	8.30 E
Thyborøn	26	56.42 N	8.13 E
Thylungra	156	26.04 S	143.28 E
Thyregod	41	55.54 N	9.16 E
Tiadiaye	140	14.25 N	16.42 W
Tiahuanaco	238	16.33 S	68.42 W
Tía Juana	236	10.16 N	71.22 W
Tiana	256d	44.29 N	2.16 E
Tiananmen ♠	261a	39.55 N	116.23 E
Tian'aoshan I	90	28.48 N	121.51 E
Tianban	90	29.20 N	116.50 E
Tianbao	90	24.36 N	117.35 E
Tiancang	92	41.09 N	100.17 E
Tianchang	90	32.41 N	119.01 E
Tiancunpu	95	39.06 N	115.41 E
Tiandeng	92	23.09 N	107.10 E
Tiandong	92	23.40 N	106.57 E
Tian'e	92	25.01 N	107.20 E
Tianeti	74	42.07 N	44.59 E
Tiangang, Zhg.	79	43.55 N	127.00 E
Tiangang, Zhg.	79	43.24 N	125.54 E
Tiangongsi	95	39.14 N	115.53 E
Tianguá	240	3.44 S	40.59 W
Tianhe	90	27.01 N	114.30 E
Tianhekou	90	32.08 N	113.25 E
Tianhelong	79	43.56 N	120.39 E
Tianhengdao I	88	36.14 N	120.46 E
Tianhuang	88	35.29 N	117.18 E
Tianjara Mountain ∧	160	35.11 S	150.18 E
Tianjia, Zhg.	94	41.07 N	122.03 E
Tianjia, Zhg.	97	29.40 N	105.08 E
Tianjiaba	92	32.08 N	110.03 E
Tianjiatun	94	41.39 N	123.44 E
Tianjiawopu	94	42.28 N	122.38 E
Tianjiazhen	90	29.56 N	115.26 E
Tianjin (Tientsin)	95	39.08 N	117.12 E
Tianjing	96	31.27 N	120.46 E
Tianjun (Tangnaihai)	92	37.25 N	98.58 E
Tiankai	95	39.38 N	115.51 E
Tiankoura	140	10.46 N	3.16 W
Tiankoye	140	12.35 N	12.40 W
Tianlin, Zhg.	92	24.14 N	106.03 E
Tianlin, Zhg.	97	29.49 N	105.19 E
Tianling ∧	79	44.22 N	129.52 E
Tianmashan	96	31.04 N	121.08 E
Tianmen	90	30.40 N	113.08 E
Tianmushan ⛰	90	30.25 N	119.30 E
Tianpu	96	31.56 N	121.07 E
Tianqiaochang	94	40.52 N	121.02 E
Tianqiaoling	79	43.26 N	129.38 E
Tianqiao Theatre ⊎	261a	39.53 N	116.23 E
Tianquan	92	30.10 N	102.48 E
Tianshanmai → Tien Shan ⛰	80	42.00 N	80.00 E
Tianshenggang, Zhg.	96	32.03 N	120.45 E
Tianshenggang, Zhg.	96	32.14 N	121.00 E
Tianshifu	88	41.17 N	124.21 E
Tianshui	92	34.30 N	105.58 E
Tianshuijing, Zhg.	92	40.17 N	95.21 E
Tianshuijing, Zhg.	94	41.19 N	121.48 E
Tianshuituo	95	39.20 N	118.12 E
Tianshuizhan	94	41.00 N	123.34 E
Tianshuizhen	92	34.18 N	105.57 E
Tiantai	90	29.09 N	121.02 E
Tiantaishan ⛰	90	29.22 N	121.10 E
Tiantang	92	22.32 N	111.55 E
Tiantou, Zhg.	90	28.48 N	120.39 E
Tiantou, Zhg.	90	26.19 N	115.57 E
Tianwangsi	96	31.45 N	119.12 E
Tianweijiao ≻	90	22.45 N	115.49 E
Tianxin	92	27.21 N	111.00 E
Tianxinduan	90	27.53 N	113.06 E
Tianxingqiao	96	32.05 N	119.57 E
Tianxinwei	90	28.11 N	114.35 E
Tianxiyang	90	26.31 N	118.33 E
Tianyang	92	23.51 N	106.34 E
Tianyangping	97	29.11 N	105.16 E
Tianyar	105b	8.12 S	115.30 E
Tianzhen	88	40.28 N	114.06 E
Tianzhongying	90	33.13 N	115.22 E
Tianzhu, Zhg.	92	26.50 N	109.00 E
Tianzhu (Anyuanyi), Zhg.	92	37.14 N	102.59 E
Tianzhuang, Zhg.	90	25.43 N	113.40 E
Tianzhuang, Zhg.	95	39.25 N	117.54 E
Tianzhuangtai	94	40.50 N	122.08 E
Tiaodengchang	97	30.47 N	106.22 E
Tiaohe ≃	97	29.53 N	106.10 E
Tiarei	164s	17.32 S	149.20 W
Tiaret	138	35.28 N	1.21 E
Tiarno	58	45.53 N	10.40 E
Tiaro	156	25.44 S	152.35 E
Tiassalé	140	5.54 N	4.50 W
Tiati ∧	144	1.19 N	35.56 E
Tiavea	165a	13.57 S	171.24 W
Tiawichi Creek ≃	212	32.19 N	94.44 W
Tiba → Chiba	84	35.36 N	140.07 E
Ţibābī, Jabal aţ- ∧[2]	132	30.28 N	30.28 E
Tibagi	242	24.30 S	50.24 W
Tibagi ≃	242	22.47 S	51.01 W
Tibari	144	5.01 N	31.43 E
Tibasti, Sarīr ◆[2]	136	24.15 N	17.15 E
Tibati	142	6.27 N	12.38 E
Tibbie	184	31.16 N	88.15 W
Tibe	134	9.03 N	37.08 E
Tibel'ti	78	51.46 N	103.11 E
Tiber → Tevere ≃	60	41.44 N	12.14 E
Tiberias → Teverya	122	32.47 N	35.32 E
Tiberias, Lake → Kinneret, Yam ⊜	122	32.48 N	35.35 E
Tiberina, Val V	60	43.31 N	12.10 E
Tiber Reservoir ⊜[1]	192	48.22 N	111.17 W
Tibesti ⛰	136	21.30 N	17.30 E
Tibet, Lake ⊜	210	28.27 N	81.31 W
Tibiao	106	11.17 N	122.02 E
Tibiao Point ≻	106	11.18 N	122.02 E
Tibidabo ∧	256d	41.25 N	2.07 E
Tibiri	140	13.06 N	4.00 E
Tibiriçá ≃	245	21.43 S	50.15 W
Tibirke	41	56.03 N	12.07 E
Tiblawan	106	6.29 N	126.06 E
Tiblemont, Lac ⊜	180	48.14 N	77.18 W
Ţibleş, Munţii ⛰	38	47.38 N	24.05 E
Tibnah	122	32.59 N	36.13 E
Tibnīn	122	33.12 N	35.25 E
Tibro	26	58.26 N	14.10 E
Tibugá, Golfo de C	236	5.45 N	77.20 W
Tiburon	216	36.04 N	119.19 W
Tiburón, Cabo ≻	236	8.42 N	77.24 W
Tiburón, Isla I	222	29.00 N	112.23 W
Tiburon Peninsula ≻[1]	272	37.53 N	122.28 W
Ticao Island I	106	12.31 N	123.42 E
Ticao Pass U	106	12.38 N	123.47 E
Tice	210	26.41 N	81.49 W
Tice Creek ≃	272	37.53 N	122.03 W
Ticehurst	44	51.03 N	0.25 E
Tichigan	206	42.50 N	88.12 W
Tichigan Lake ⊜	206	42.49 N	88.13 W
Tîchît	140	18.28 N	9.30 W
Tîchît, Dhar •[4]	140	18.30 N	9.25 W
Tichla	138	21.35 N	14.58 W
Tichmenevo, S.S.S.R.	66	58.00 N	38.36 E
Tichmenevo, S.S.S.R.	79	49.12 N	142.54 E
Ticho	134	7.50 N	39.32 E
Tichon	24	59.23 N	46.38 E
Tichonova Pustyn'	72	54.38 N	36.09 E
Tichonoviči	68	51.56 N	32.09 E
Tichonovka	78	53.13 N	104.13 E
Tichoreck	68	45.51 N	40.09 E
Tichtozero	24	65.35 N	30.27 E
Tichvin	66	59.39 N	33.31 E
Tichvinskaja Gr'ada ∧	66	59.30 N	34.30 E
Tichvinskij Kanal ≡	66	59.30 N	34.29 E
Ticino □[3]	54	46.20 N	8.45 E
Ticino ≃	36	45.09 N	9.14 E
Tickfaw	184	30.35 N	90.29 W
Tickfaw ≃	184	30.20 N	90.28 W
Tickhill	42	53.26 N	1.06 W
Ticomán	276a	19.31 N	99.08 W
Ticul	222	20.24 N	89.32 W
Tīdah	132	31.15 N	30.50 E
Tidaholm	26	58.11 N	13.57 E
Tidan ≃	40	58.42 N	13.58 E
Tiddim	100	23.23 N	93.39 E
Tide Lake ⊜	172	50.33 N	111.20 W
Tidewater	198	37.51 N	76.42 W
Tidewater ◆[1]	198	37.45 N	77.00 W
Tidikelt, Plaine du ⌣	138	26.54 N	1.20 E
Tidioute	204	41.41 N	79.24 W
Tidirhine, Jbel ∧	138	34.50 N	4.30 W
Tidjenaouine	138	22.33 N	5.15 E
Tidjidit, Erg ◆[2]	138	23.30 N	1.00 E
Tidjikdja	140	18.33 N	11.25 W
Tidö	40	59.30 N	16.28 E
Tidone ≃	56	45.04 N	9.32 E
Tidore	98	0.40 N	127.26 E
Tidra, Île I	140	19.44 N	16.24 W
Tiébissou	140	7.10 N	5.13 W
Tiechang, Zhg.	88	41.44 N	126.11 E
Tiechang, Zhg.	90	24.10 N	115.30 E
Tiechang, Zhg.	92	26.34 N	103.58 E
Tiechang, Zhg.	95	40.04 N	118.12 E
Tiechangpu	97	29.29 N	104.20 E
Tiefenbroich	253	51.18 N	6.49 E
Tiefencastel	54	46.40 N	9.35 E
Tiefensee	50	52.41 N	13.50 E
Tiefo	97	29.45 N	104.33 E
Tiegenhof → Nowy Dwór Gdański	30	54.13 N	19.06 E
T'iehling → Tieling	94	42.18 N	123.49 E
Tiekou	88	37.16 N	121.13 E
Tiel, Ned.	48	51.54 N	5.25 E
Tièl, Sén.	140	14.56 N	15.04 W
Tielelihu ⊜	80	44.30 N	85.15 E
Tieli	79	46.59 N	128.02 E
Tielinanmuhu ⊜	110	31.05 N	85.35 E
Tieling	94	42.18 N	123.49 E
Tielt	46	51.00 N	3.19 E
Tielutou	90	27.49 N	115.48 E
T'ienching → Tianjin	95	39.08 N	117.12 E
T'ienchung	90	23.53 N	120.34 E
Tienen	52	50.48 N	4.57 E
Tiengen	54	47.38 N	8.16 E
Tiénigbé	140	8.11 N	5.43 W
Tienko	140	10.14 N	7.29 W
Tien Shan ⛰	80	42.00 N	80.00 E
T'ienshui → Tianshui	92	34.30 N	105.58 E
Tientsin → Tianjin	95	39.08 N	117.12 E
Tien-yen	100	21.20 N	107.24 E
Tiepido ≃	58	44.30 N	10.59 E
Tie Plant	184	33.44 N	89.47 W
Tierga	34	41.37 N	1.36 W
Tiergarten ◆[8]	254a	52.31 N	13.21 E
Tiergarten ♠	254a	52.31 N	13.21 E
Tieroko ∧	136	20.45 N	17.52 E
Tierp	40	60.20 N	17.30 E
Tierpark ♠	254a	52.30 N	13.32 E

Symbol	English	Deutsch	Español	Français	Português
≃	River	Fluss	Río	Rivière	Rio
≡	Canal	Kanal	Canal	Canal	Canal
L	Waterfall, Rapids	Wasserfall, Stromschnellen	Cascada, Rápidos	Chute d'eau, Rapides	Cascata, Rápidos
U	Strait	Meeresstrasse	Estrecho	Détroit	Estreito
C	Bay, Gulf	Bucht, Golf	Bahía, Golfo	Baie, Golfe	Baía, Golfo
⊜	Lake, Lakes	See, Seen	Lago, Lagos	Lac, Lacs	Lago, Lagos
≋	Swamp	Sumpf	Pantano	Marais	Pântano
⊡	Ice Features, Glacier	Eis- und Gletscherformen	Accidentes Glaciales	Formes glaciaires	Acidentes Glaciares
▿	Other Hydrographic Features	Andere Hydrographische Objekte	Otros Elementos Hidrográficos	Autres données hydrographiques	Outros Elementos Hidrográficos
✧	Submarine Features	Untermeerische Objekte	Accidentes Submarinos	Formes de relief sous-marin	Acidentes Submarinos
□	Political Unit	Politische Einheit	Unidad Politica	Entité politique	Unidade Política
⊎	Cultural Institution	Kulturelle Institution	Institución Cultural	Institution culturelle	Instituição Cultural
⊥	Historical Site	Historische Stätte	Sitio Histórico	Site historique	Sitio Histórico
♠	Recreational Site	Erholungs- und Ferienort	Sitio de Recreo	Centre de loisirs	Sítio de Lazer
⊠	Airport	Flughafen	Aeropuerto	Aéroport	Aeroporto
■	Military Installation	Militäranlage	Instalación Militar	Installation militaire	Instalação Militar
◆	Miscellaneous	Verschiedenes	Misceláneo	Divers	Miscelânea

ENGLISH — Name | Page | Lat.°′ | Long.°′
DEUTSCH — Name | Seite | Breite°′ | Länge°′ E=Ost

Symbols in the index entries represent the broad categories identified in the key at the right. Symbols with superior numbers (∧∧[2]) identify subcategories (see complete key on page *I* · 26).

Kartensymbole in dem Registerverzeichnis stellen die rechts in Schlüssel erklärten Kategorien dar. Symbole mit hochgestellten Ziffern (∧∧[2]) bezeichnen Unterabteilungen einer Kategorie (vgl. vollständiger Schlüssel auf Seite *I* · 26).

Los símbolos incluídos en el texto del índice representan las grandes categorías identificadas con la clave a la derecha. Los símbolos con numeros en su parte superior (∧∧[2]) identifican las subcategorías (véase la clave completa en la página *I* · 26).

Les symboles de l'index représentent les catégories indiquées dans la légende à droite. Les symboles suivis d'un indice (∧∧[2]) représentent des sous-catégories (voir légende complète à la page *I* · 26).

Os símbolos incluídos no texto do índice representam as grandes categorias identificadas com a chave à direita. Os símbolos com números em sua parte superior (∧∧[2]) identificam as subcategorias (veja-se a chave completa à página *I* · 26).

	English	Deutsch	Español	Français	Português
∧	Mountain	Berg	Montaña	Montagne	Montanha
∧∧	Mountains	Berge	Montañas	Montagnes	Montanhas
)(	Pass	Pass	Paso	Col	Passo
∨	Valley, Canyon	Tal, Cañon	Valle, Cañón	Vallée, Canyon	Vale, Canhão
≚	Plain	Ebene	Llano	Plaine	Planicie
≻	Cape	Kap	Cabo	Cap	Cabo
I	Island	Insel	Isla	Île	Ilha
II	Islands	Inseln	Islas	Îles	Ilhas
⊥	Other Topographic Features	Andere Topographische Objekte	Otros Elementos Topográficos	Autres données topographiques	Outros Elementos Topográficos

ESPAÑOL

Nombre	Página	Lat.°′	Long.°′ W=Oeste
Tohma ≃	120	38.31 N	37.38 E
Toholampi	26	63.46 N	24.15 E
Tohopekaliga, Lake ⊜	210	28.12 N	81.23 W
Tohor, Tanjong ≻	104	1.51 N	102.42 E
T'ohyŏn-ni	88	39.53 N	124.52 E
Toi, Nihon	84	34.54 N	138.47 E
Toi, Niue	164v	18.57 S	169.51 W
Toijala	26	61.10 N	23.52 E
Toili	102	1.27 S	122.24 E
Toi-misaki ≻	82	31.20 N	131.22 E
Tōin	84	35.05 N	136.35 E
Toinya	130	6.17 N	29.44 E
Toi Sar	110	31.06 N	69.54 E
Toiyabe Range ⋀	194	39.10 N	117.10 W
Tojg	118	32.04 N	61.48 E
To-jima I	86	33.12 N	132.22 E
Tojo, Indon.	102	1.17 S	121.11 E
Tōjō, Nihon	86	34.53 N	133.16 E
Tōjō, Nihon	260	34.55 N	135.04 E
Tojtepa	75	41.03 N	69.22 E
Tōju-in ʋ[1]	84	35.19 N	136.04 E
Tok	170	63.20 N	142.59 W
Tok ≃	70	52.46 N	52.22 E
Tokaanu	162	38.58 S	175.46 E
Tokachi ≃	82a	42.44 N	143.42 E
Tokachi-dake ∧	82a	43.25 N	142.41 E
Tokachi-heiya ≡	82a	43.00 N	143.30 E
Tōkagi	258	35.42 N	139.56 E
Tokai, Malay.	104	6.01 N	100.24 E
Tōkai, Nihon	84	36.27 N	140.34 E
Tokaj ≃	68	51.18 N	41.04 E
Tokala	102	1.47 S	121.43 E
Tōkamachi	84	37.08 N	138.46 E
Tokanui	162	46.34 S	168.56 E
Tokara-kaikyō ⋃	83b	30.10 N	130.10 E
Tokara-rettō II	83b	29.36 N	129.43 E
Tokarevka	76	50.08 N	73.12 E
Tokaris	120	37.45 N	38.50 E
Tokar'ovka	70	51.59 N	41.09 E
Tokar'ovo, S.S.S.R.	66	55.17 N	35.04 E
Tokar'ovo, S.S.S.R.	255b	55.38 N	37.55 E
Tokashiki-shima I	83b	26.11 N	127.21 E
Tokat	120	40.19 N	36.34 E
Tokat ☐[4]	120	40.25 N	36.30 E
Tŏkchŏk-kundo II	88	37.14 N	126.07 E
Tŏkch'ŏn	88	39.46 N	126.19 E
Tok-dŏ I	82	37.17 N	131.53 E
Toke	84	35.32 N	140.17 E
Tokeland	214	46.42 N	123.59 W
Tokelau-Inseln → Tokelau Islands ☐[2]	14	9.00 S	171.45 W
Tokelau Islands ☐[2]	14	9.00 S	171.45 W
Tokelau Islands II	4	9.00 S	171.45 W
Tokeneke Brook ≃	266	41.03 N	73.28 W
Tŏkhŭng-ni	88	40.02 N	127.08 E
Toki	84	35.21 N	137.11 E
Toki ≃	84	35.12 N	136.52 E
Tokio → Tōkyō	84	35.42 N	139.46 E
Toki Point ≻	164a	19.19 N	166.35 E
Tokko	64	59.59 N	119.52 E
Tokko ≃	78	58.42 N	119.50 E
Toklar	120	38.26 N	36.01 E
Toklat ≃	170	64.27 N	150.17 W
Tokma	78	58.13 N	105.42 E
Tokmak, S.S.S.R.	68	47.15 N	35.43 E
Tokmak, S.S.S.R.	75	42.55 N	75.18 E
Toko	162	39.20 S	174.24 E
Tököl	254c	47.19 N	18.58 E
Tokolimbu	102	2.48 S	121.34 E
Tokomaru	162	40.28 S	175.30 E
Tokomaru Bay	162	38.08 S	178.18 E
Tokoname	84	34.53 N	136.51 E
Toko Range ⋀	156	23.05 S	138.20 E
Tokoro ≃	82a	44.07 N	144.05 E
Tokoroa	162	38.14 S	175.52 E
Tokorozawa	84	35.47 N	139.28 E
Tokovskoje	68	47.38 N	33.59 E
Toksook Bay	170	60.32 N	165.06 W
Toksovo	66	60.09 N	30.31 E
Toksu Palace ʋ	261b	37.35 N	126.58 E
Toktogul	75	41.50 N	72.50 E
Toku I	14	18.10 S	174.11 W
Tokuji	86	34.09 N	131.45 E
Tokul Creek ≃	214	47.35 N	121.50 W
Tokung	102	0.18 S	114.28 E
Tokuno-shima I	83b	27.45 N	128.58 E
Tokur	79	53.10 N	132.53 E
Tokura	260	34.58 N	135.18 E
Tokura-tōge)(	86	35.17 N	134.31 E
Tokusaga-mine ∧	86	34.26 N	131.41 E
Tokushima	86	34.04 N	134.34 E
Tokushima ☐[5]	86	33.45 N	134.00 E
Tokuyama, Nihon	84	35.42 N	136.29 E
Tokuyama, Nihon	86	34.03 N	131.49 E
Tokwe ≃	144	21.09 S	31.30 E
Tōkyō	84		
	258	35.42 N	139.46 E
Tōkyō ☐[5]	84	35.45 N	139.30 E
Tokyo, University of ʋ[2]	258	35.42 N	139.46 E
Tokyo Bay → Tōkyō-wan C	84	35.30 N	139.54 E
Tōkyō-daigaku-uchūkūkan-kenkyūsho ʋ[3]	82	31.17 N	131.05 E
Tokyo International Airport ⊠	258	35.33 N	139.46 E
Tōkyō-kō C	258	35.37 N	139.47 E
Tōkyō-kokusai-kūkō ⊠	84	35.33 N	139.46 E
Tokyo University of Education ʋ[2]	258	35.43 N	139.44 E
Tōkyō-wan (Tokyo Bay) C	84	35.30 N	139.54 E
Tokzār	110	35.52 N	66.26 E
Tol I	165c	7.22 N	151.37 E
Tolaga Bay	162	38.22 S	178.18 E
Tolala	102	2.56 S	121.06 E
Tolang	104	1.56 N	99.26 E
Tolbert	48	53.10 N	6.21 E
Tolbonuur	76	48.25 N	90.17 E
Tolbuchino	70	57.51 N	40.03 E
Tolbuhin	38	43.34 N	27.50 E
Tolderol Point ≻	158b	35.22 S	139.10 E
Tole, Pan.	226	8.14 N	81.41 W
Tole, S.S.S.R.	75	42.40 N	70.08 E
Toledo, Bol.	238	18.10 S	67.25 W
Toledo, Bra.	242	24.44 S	53.45 W
Toledo, Bra.	246	22.44 S	46.23 W
Toledo, Col.	236	7.19 N	72.28 W
Toledo, Esp.	34	39.52 N	4.01 W
Toledo, Pil.	102	10.23 N	123.38 E
Toledo, Ill., U.S.	184	39.16 N	88.15 W
Toledo, Iowa, U.S.	180	42.00 N	92.35 W
Toledo, Ohio, U.S.	204	41.39 N	83.32 W
Toledo, Oreg., U.S.	192	44.37 N	123.56 W
Toledo, Wash., U.S.	214	46.26 N	122.51 W
Toledo, Ur.	248	34.45 S	56.05 W
Toledo ☐[5]	226	16.20 N	88.55 W
Toledo, Montes de ⋀	34	39.33 N	4.20 W
Toledo Bend Reservoir ⊜[1]	184	31.30 N	93.45 W
Toledo Express Airport ⊠	206	41.35 N	83.49 W
Tolentino	60	43.12 N	13.17 E
Tolfa	60	42.09 N	11.56 E
Tolfa, Monti della ⋀	60	42.08 N	11.54 E
Tolga, Alg.	138	34.46 N	5.22 E
Tolga, Nor.	26	62.25 N	11.00 E
Tolima ☐[5]	236	3.45 N	75.15 W
Tolima, Nevado del ∧	236	4.40 N	75.19 W
Tolimán, Méx.	224	19.36 N	103.55 W
Tolimán, Méx.	224	20.55 N	99.56 W
Tolitoli	102	1.02 N	120.49 E
Toljatti (Togliatti)	70	53.31 N	49.26 E
Tol'ka	64	64.02 N	81.55 E
Tolkmicko	30	54.20 N	19.31 E

FRANÇAIS

Nom	Page	Lat.°′	Long.°′ W=Ouest
Tolland	197	41.52 N	72.22 W
Tolland ☐[6]	197	41.52 N	72.22 W
Tollarp	26	55.56 N	13.59 E
Tollense ≃	50	53.54 N	13.02 E
Tollensesee ⊜	50	53.30 N	13.11 E
Tollesboro	208	38.34 N	83.35 W
Tollesbury	44	51.46 N	0.50 E
Tolleson	190	33.27 N	112.16 W
Tollhouse	216	37.01 N	119.24 W
Tolloche	242	25.30 S	63.32 W
Tølløse	41	55.37 N	11.45 E
Tollygunge ◆[8]	262b	22.30 N	88.21 E
Tolmači	66	57.26 N	35.41 E
Tolmačovo	66	58.52 N	29.55 E
Tolmezzo	58	46.24 N	13.01 E
Tolmin	36	46.11 N	13.44 E
Tolna	30	46.26 N	18.46 E
Tolna ☐[6]	30	46.30 N	18.35 E
Tolo	142	2.56 S	18.34 E
Tolo, Teluk C	102	2.00 S	122.30 E
Toloa, Houma ≻	164w	21.17 S	175.08 W
Toločin	66	54.25 N	29.42 E
Tolokiwa Island I	154	5.20 S	147.40 E
Tolomo	79	50.03 N	137.45 E
Tolong Bay C	106	9.20 N	122.49 E
Tolongoina	147b	21.33 S	47.31 E
Tolono	184	39.59 N	88.16 W
Tolosa	34	43.08 N	2.04 W
Tolosa, Aeródromo ⊠	278	34.53 S	57.58 W
Tolovana ≃	170	64.51 N	149.45 W
Tolpuddle	44	50.45 N	2.18 W
Tol'skij Majdan	70	54.57 N	44.39 E
Tolstoj, Mys ≻	64	59.10 N	155.12 E
Tolstoje	68	48.50 N	25.44 E
Tolstopal'cevo	255b	55.38 N	37.13 E
Tolstyj Byk, Porog ⌊	78	57.59 N	102.42 E
Tolt, North Fork ≃	214	47.42 N	121.49 W
Toltén	244	39.13 S	73.14 W
Tolti	113	35.02 N	76.06 E
Toltry ⋀[1]	68	49.00 N	26.10 E
Tolt-Seattle Water Supply Reservoir ⊜[1]	214	47.42 N	121.39 W
Tolú	236	9.31 N	75.35 W
Toluca	206	41.00 N	89.08 W
Toluca, Nevado de ∧[1]	224	19.08 N	99.44 W
Toluca [de Lerdo]	224	19.17 N	99.40 W
Tolvajarvi	24	62.17 N	31.27 E
Tolvdalselva ≃	26	58.10 N	8.00 E
Tolwa	130	6.38 N	32.37 E
Tolworth ◆[8]	250	51.23 N	0.17 W
Tolyatti → Toljatti	70	53.31 N	49.26 E
Tolybaj	76	50.31 N	62.19 E
Tom' ≃, S.S.S.R.	76	56.50 N	84.27 E
Tom' ≃, S.S.S.R.	79	51.00 N	127.54 E
Toma	140	12.46 N	2.53 W
Tomah	180	43.59 N	90.30 W
Tomahawk	180	45.28 N	89.44 W
Tomakomai	82a	42.38 N	141.36 E
Tomakovka	68	47.48 N	34.44 E
Tomani	102	4.50 N	115.55 E
Tomaniivi, Mount ∧	165g	17.37 S	178.01 E
Tomar, Port.	34	39.36 N	8.25 W
Tomar, S.S.S.R.	76	46.24 N	75.03 E
Tomara	164r	6.54 N	158.08 E
Tomari	79	47.47 N	142.03 E
Tomarovka	68	50.41 N	36.14 E
Tomarza	120	38.27 N	35.49 E
Tomás Barrón (Eucaliptus)	238	17.35 S	67.31 W
Tomasboda ∧[2]	40	59.24 N	14.58 E
Tomás Gomensoro	242	30.26 S	57.26 W
Tomašgorod	68	51.19 N	27.02 E
Tomasina ≃	180	46.40 N	76.16 W
Tomás Jofré	248	34.43 S	59.19 W
Tomašpol'	68	48.33 N	28.31 E
Tomaszów Lubelski	30	50.28 N	23.25 E
Tomaszów Mazowiecki	30	51.32 N	20.01 E
Tomatlán	224	19.56 N	105.15 W
Tomave	238	20.06 S	66.35 W
Tomazina	245	23.46 S	49.58 W
Tomba di Nerone ◆[8]	257a	41.57 N	12.27 E
Tombadonkéa	140	11.00 N	14.23 W
Tombador, Serra do ⋀[1]	238	12.00 S	57.40 W
Tomball	212	30.06 N	95.37 W
Tombara	86	35.05 N	132.47 E
Tombe	130	5.49 N	31.41 E
Tombigbee ≃	184	31.04 N	87.58 W
Tomboco	142	6.48 S	13.18 E
Tombolo	58	45.38 N	11.50 E
Tombos	245	20.55 S	42.02 W
Tombouctou (Timbuktu)	140	16.46 N	3.01 W
Tombs of the Caliphs ⊥	263c	30.03 N	31.17 E
Tombstone	190	31.43 N	110.04 W
Tombstone Mountain ∧	170	64.25 N	138.30 W
Tom Burke	146	23.05 S	28.00 E
Tomé	244	36.37 S	72.57 W
Tomea, Pulau I	102	5.45 S	123.56 E
Tomé-Açu	240	2.25 S	48.09 W
Tomek	120	38.02 N	32.41 E
Tomelilla	26	55.33 N	13.57 E
Tomelloso	34	39.10 N	3.01 W
Tomerong	160	35.04 S	150.35 E
Tomhannock Reservoir ⊜[1]	200	42.51 N	73.33 W
Tomi ≃	142	5.07 N	19.19 E
Tomichi Creek ≃	190	38.31 N	106.58 W
Tomifobia ≃	196	45.11 N	72.02 W
Tomiko Lake ⊜	180	46.32 N	79.49 W
Tomil	164q	9.31 N	138.09 E
Tomil Harbor C	164q	9.30 N	138.09 E
Tomilino	255b	55.39 N	37.57 E
Tomini	102	0.30 N	120.32 E
Tomini, Teluk C	102	0.20 S	121.00 E
Tominian	140	13.17 N	4.35 W
Tomio ≃	260	34.35 N	135.44 E
Tomioka	84	36.15 N	138.54 E
Tomisato	84	35.44 N	140.19 E
Tomiura	84	35.03 N	139.50 E
Tomiyama, Nihon	84	35.11 N	137.48 E
Tomiyama, Nihon	84	35.05 N	139.51 E
Tomizawa	84	35.14 N	138.29 E
T'omkino	66	55.05 N	35.01 E
Tomkins Cove	200	41.15 N	73.59 W
Tomkinson Ranges ⋀	152	26.11 S	129.05 E
Tomlinson Run State Park ♠	204	40.33 N	80.34 W
Tommerup Stationsby	41	55.19 N	10.13 E
Tommot	64	58.58 N	126.19 E
T'omnyj	78	53.24 N	118.31 E
Tomo ≃	236	5.20 N	67.48 W
Tomobe	84	36.20 N	140.20 E
Tomohon	102	1.19 N	124.49 E
Tömörbulag	78	49.16 N	100.15 E
Tomori	164m	26.08 N	127.44 E
Tomori, Teluk C	102	1.58 S	121.28 E
Tomorolong	164r	6.51 N	158.10 E
Tompa	78	55.08 N	109.47 E
Tompkins, Newf., Can.	176	47.48 N	59.13 W
Tompkins, Sask., Can.	174	50.04 N	108.47 W
Tompkins ☐[6]	200	42.27 N	76.30 W
Tompkins County Airport ⊠	200	42.29 N	76.57 W
Tompkinsville	184	36.42 N	85.41 W
Tompo	102	0.56 N	120.20 E
Tom Price, Mount ∧	152	22.39 S	117.40 E
Tomptokan	64	57.06 N	133.59 E
Tomra	26	62.35 N	6.56 E
Toms ≃	198	39.57 N	74.07 W

PORTUGUÊS

Nome	Página	Lat.°′	Long.°′ W=Oeste
Toms, Ridgeway Branch ≃	198	40.00 N	74.14 W
Toms Cove C	198	37.53 N	75.22 W
Toms Creek ≃	198	39.38 N	77.17 W
Tomsk	76	56.30 N	84.58 E
Toms River	198	39.58 N	74.12 W
Tomtabacken ∧[2]	26	57.30 N	14.28 E
Tömük	120	36.41 N	34.22 E
Tomuzlovka ≃	74	44.46 N	44.10 E
Ton	58	46.15 N	11.04 E
Tonadico	58	46.11 N	11.50 E
Tonalá, Méx.	224	16.04 N	93.45 W
Tonalá, Méx.	224	20.37 N	103.14 W
Tonale, Passo del)(	58	46.16 N	10.35 E
Tonami	84	36.38 N	136.54 E
Tonantins	236	2.47 S	67.47 W
Tonantins ≃	236	2.47 S	67.47 W
Tonasket	192	48.42 N	119.26 W
Tonatico	224	18.47 N	99.41 W
Tonawanda	200	43.01 N	78.53 W
Tonawanda, Town of	200	42.59 N	78.52 W
Tonawanda Channel ≃[1]	274a	43.04 N	79.00 W
Tonawanda Creek ≃	200	43.02 N	78.53 W
Tonawanda Indian Reservation ◆[4]	200	43.05 N	78.27 W
Tonawanda Island I	274a	43.02 N	78.53 W
Tonbo	100	18.31 N	95.05 E
Tonbridge	44	51.12 N	0.16 E
Tonbridge and Malling ☐[8]	250	51.16 N	0.20 E
Tonda	260	34.50 N	135.36 E
Tonda ≃	86	33.38 N	135.24 E
Tondabayashi	86	34.30 N	135.36 E
Tondano	102	1.19 N	124.54 E
Tønder	41	54.56 N	8.54 E
Tondhre	262c	19.05 N	73.08 E
Tondi	112	9.44 N	79.01 E
Tondibi	140	16.39 N	0.14 W
Tondidji	140	13.06 N	10.20 W
Tondi Kiwindi	140	14.28 N	2.02 E
Tondoro	146	17.45 S	18.50 E
Tondou, Massif du ∧	136	7.50 N	23.45 E
Tone, Nihon	84	36.42 N	139.23 E
Tone, Nihon	84	35.51 N	140.09 E
Tone ≃	84	35.44 N	140.51 E
Tone-unga ≍	258	35.54 N	139.53 E
Tonež	68	51.49 N	27.48 E
Tonga, Cam.	142	4.58 N	10.42 E
Tonga, Sūd.	130	9.28 N	31.03 E
Tonga ☐[1]	14	20.00 S	175.00 W
Tongaat	148	29.37 S	31.03 E
Tonga Islands II	14	20.00 S	175.00 W
Tong'an, Zhg.	90	24.46 N	118.08 E
Tongan, Zhg.	92	26.23 N	102.18 E
Tonganoxie	188	39.07 N	95.05 W
Tonganqiao	96	31.22 N	120.27 E
Tonga Ridge ✦[3]	14	22.00 S	175.00 W
Tongariki I	165f	17.01 S	168.38 E
Tongariro, Mount ∧	162	39.08 S	175.38 E
Tongariro National Park ♠	162	39.15 S	175.30 E
Tongas	105a	7.44 S	113.06 E
Tongatapu I	164w	21.10 S	175.10 W
Tongatapu Group II	14	21.10 S	175.10 W
Tonga Trench ✦[1]	14	22.00 S	173.00 W
Tongbai, Zhg.	90	32.22 N	113.24 E
Tongbai, Zhg.	95	39.35 N	116.44 E
Tongbaishan ⋀	90	32.20 N	113.15 E
Tongcheng, Zhg.	90	31.03 N	116.58 E
Tongcheng, Zhg.	90	32.53 N	118.58 E
Tongcheng, Zhg.	90	29.11 N	113.49 E
Tongchengzha	90	31.30 N	118.07 E
Tongchengzhuang	95	39.22 N	117.36 E
T'ongch'ŏn	88	38.54 N	127.54 E
Tongchuan	92	35.01 N	109.01 E
Tongdao	92	26.23 N	109.23 E
Tongde	92	35.17 N	100.42 E
Tongerbao	94	41.26 N	123.02 E
Tongeren	52	50.47 N	5.28 E
Tongerlo	52	51.07 N	4.54 E
Tonggou	88	41.53 N	125.46 E
Tonggu, Zhg.	90	28.33 N	114.21 E
Tonggu, Zhg.	90	21.53 N	112.55 E
Tongguan, Zhg.	90	28.29 N	112.48 E
Tongguan, Zhg.	92	23.18 N	101.23 E
Tongguan, Zhg.	92	34.38 N	110.20 E
Tongguanyi	97	29.20 N	106.23 E
Tongguye	110	37.22 N	78.48 E
Tonghai	92	24.07 N	102.49 E
Tonghaikou	90	30.14 N	113.08 E
Tonghe, Zhg.	79	45.59 N	128.45 E
Tonghe, Zhg.	90	32.56 N	112.45 E
Tongho-ri	88	35.49 N	127.54 E
Tonghua	88	41.50 N	125.55 E
Tong Island I	154	2.05 S	147.50 E
Tongjiang	92	31.58 N	107.14 E
Tongjiangchang	97	29.37 N	103.43 E
Tongjiangkou	94	42.37 N	123.41 E
Tongjing	90	31.47 N	118.33 E
Tongjosŏn-man C	88	39.30 N	128.00 E
Tongjuzhen	88	38.36 N	117.11 E
Tongkenhe ≃	79	46.31 N	126.22 E
Tongli	96	31.10 N	120.43 E
Tongliang	97	29.51 N	106.03 E
Tongliao	79	43.39 N	122.14 E
Tongling, Zhg.	90	30.53 N	117.46 E
Tongling, Zhg.	92	23.28 N	109.40 E
Tonglingzhen	90	30.56 N	117.47 E
Tonglu	90	29.48 N	119.40 E
Tongmai	92	30.08 N	95.11 E
Tongmang-ni	88	37.37 N	126.26 E
Tongmu, Zhg.	90	27.57 N	113.55 E
Tongmu, Zhg.	92	24.09 N	110.04 E
Tongnae	88	35.12 N	129.05 E
Tongnan	97	30.11 N	105.48 E
Tongo, Austl.	156	30.30 S	143.45 E
Tongo, Cam.	142	5.11 N	14.00 E
Tong O, H.K.	261d	22.12 N	114.08 E
Tongoa I	165f	16.54 S	168.34 E
Tongobory	147b	23.32 S	44.20 E
Tongololo Creek ≃	152	22.06 S	121.08 E
Tongoy	242	30.15 S	71.30 W
Tongpanshan I	90	27.43 N	120.55 E
Tongqin	90	28.52 N	119.56 E
Tongquansi	97	30.23 N	104.50 E
Tongquil Island I	106	6.02 N	121.51 E
Tongren, Zhg.	92	35.32 N	101.54 E
Tongren, Zhg.	92	27.38 N	109.03 E
Tongrenchang	97	30.02 N	106.42 E
Tongsa ≃	114	26.52 N	90.57 E
Tongsa Dzong	114	27.31 N	90.30 E
Tongsan-ni	261b	37.38 N	126.53 E
Tongshan, Zhg.	88	34.17 N	117.03 E
Tongshan, Zhg.	90	29.38 N	114.29 E
Tongshi	88	35.26 N	117.43 E
Tongshuping	90	27.17 N	114.54 E
Tongta	100	21.20 N	99.16 E
Tongtai	90	32.38 N	120.47 E
Tongtan	97	28.56 N	105.17 E
Tongtianhe ≃	92	33.25 N	96.32 E
Tongtianheyan	110	33.50 N	92.28 E
Tongue	28	58.28 N	4.25 W
Tongue ≃, U.S.	192	46.24 N	105.52 W
Tongue ≃, N. Dak., U.S.	188	48.56 N	97.18 W
Tongue ≃, Tex., U.S.	186	34.07 N	100.25 W
Tongue of the Ocean ✦[1]	228	24.00 N	77.20 W
Tongue River Reservoir ⊜[1]	192	45.06 N	106.47 W
Tongwei	92	35.07 N	105.27 E
Tongxi	97	30.01 N	106.07 E
Tongxi ≃	90	29.49 N	119.41 E
Tongxian, Zhg.	95	39.55 N	116.39 E
Tongxian, Zhg.	97	30.15 N	105.23 E
Tongxiang	96	30.38 N	120.32 E
Tongxin	92	37.02 N	106.09 E
Tongxinchang	97	29.42 N	106.26 E
Tongxing	79	47.45 N	126.46 E
Tongxingchang	97	30.35 N	106.12 E
Tongxu	88	34.29 N	114.28 E
Tongyu	79	44.48 N	123.05 E
Tongyuan	96	30.28 N	120.52 E
Tongyuanbao	94	40.49 N	123.54 E
Tongyuanwei	90	28.04 N	116.08 E
Tongzhaipu	90	32.48 N	112.44 E
Tongzi	92	28.08 N	106.49 E
Tongzidixia	94	41.08 N	120.34 E
Tonica	206	41.13 N	89.04 W
Tónichi	222	28.35 N	109.34 W
Tonila	224	19.26 N	103.31 W
Tönisberg	253	51.25 N	6.30 E
Tönisheide	253	51.19 N	7.03 E
Tönisvort	52	51.19 N	6.29 E
Tonj	130	7.17 N	28.45 E
Tonk	110	26.10 N	75.47 E
Tonk ☐[5]	114	25.55 N	76.10 E
Tonkawa	186	36.41 N	97.18 W
Tonkin, Gulf of C	100	20.00 N	108.00 E
Tonkino	70	57.23 N	46.28 E
Tonkwa	100	23.36 N	96.58 E
Tonnay-Boutonne	32	45.58 N	0.42 W
Tonneins	32	44.23 N	0.19 E
Tonner Canyon ∨	270	33.58 N	117.48 W
Tonnerre	46	47.51 N	3.58 E
Tönnet	40	60.14 N	13.30 E
Tönning	41	54.19 N	8.56 E
Tōno	82	39.19 N	141.32 E
Tonogaya	258	35.46 N	139.22 E
Tonopah	194	38.04 N	117.14 W
Tonoro ≃	236	9.29 N	63.17 W
Tonoshō, Nihon	82	34.29 N	134.11 E
Tōnoshō, Nihon	84	35.49 N	140.42 E
Tonoshō, Nihon	86	34.29 N	134.11 E
Tonosí	236	7.24 N	80.27 W
Tonota	146	21.29 S	27.29 E
Tonquish Creek ≃	271	42.21 N	83.22 W
Tons ≃	114	25.17 N	82.04 E
Tonšajevo	70	57.44 N	47.00 E
Tønsberg	26	59.17 N	10.25 E
Tönsholt	253	51.38 N	6.58 E
Tonstad	26	58.40 N	6.43 E
Tonto ≃	224	18.10 N	96.08 W
Tonto Creek ≃	190	33.46 N	111.15 W
Tontogany	206	41.25 N	83.44 W
Tonto National Monument ♠	190	33.34 N	111.02 W
Tonya	120	40.53 N	39.16 E
Tonyrefail	44	51.36 N	3.25 W
Toobeah	156	28.25 S	149.52 E
Toodyay	158a	31.33 S	116.28 E
Tooele	190	40.32 N	112.18 W
Toogoolawah	161a	27.06 S	152.23 E
Tool	212	32.16 N	96.10 W
Toolik ≃	170	69.55 N	149.30 W
Tooma	161b	35.58 S	148.03 E
Tooma ≃	161b	36.04 S	148.00 E
Tooma Reservoir ⊜[1]	161b	36.04 S	148.16 E
Toomebridge	42	54.45 N	6.27 W
Toompine	156	27.13 S	144.22 E
Toomsboro	182	32.50 N	83.05 W
Toongabbie	264a	33.47 S	150.57 E
Toora	159	38.40 S	146.20 E
Toora-Chem	78	52.28 N	96.17 E
Toosey Indian Reserve ◆[4]	172	51.56 N	122.29 W
Toot Hill	250	51.42 N	0.12 E
Tootie, Mount ∧	160	33.28 S	150.30 E
Tootsi	66	58.34 N	24.47 E
Toowoomba	161a	27.33 S	151.57 E
Topanga	218	34.06 N	118.36 W
Topanga Canyon ∨	270	34.05 N	118.36 W
Topar	76	49.32 N	72.50 E
Topawa	190	31.48 N	111.51 W
Topaz Lake ⊜	216	38.41 N	119.32 W
Topchānchi	116	23.54 N	86.12 E
Töpchin	50	52.10 N	13.34 E
Topčicha	76	52.49 N	83.10 E
Topeka, Ind., U.S.	206	41.32 N	85.32 W
Topeka, Kans., U.S.	188	39.03 N	95.41 W
Töpen	50	50.23 N	11.52 E
Topia	222	25.13 N	106.34 W
Topilejo	276a	19.12 N	99.09 W
Topino ≃	60	43.02 N	12.30 E
Topka, Gora ∧	64	57.08 N	137.24 E
Topkanovo	72	54.43 N	38.29 E
Topkapı ◆[8]	257b	41.02 N	28.54 E
Topkapı Müzesi ⊥	257b	41.00 N	28.59 E
Topki	76	55.16 N	85.36 E
Topl'a ≃	30	48.45 N	21.45 E
Topley	172	54.49 N	126.18 W
Toplica ≃	38	43.13 N	21.49 E
Toplița	38	46.55 N	25.21 E
T'oploje, S.S.S.R.	66	53.13 N	38.53 E
T'oploje, S.S.S.R.	66	53.37 N	37.36 E
T'oploje ≃	73	48.47 N	39.19 E
T'oplyj Stan, S.S.S.R.	70	53.58 N	50.10 E
T'oplyj Stan, S.S.S.R.	72	55.37 N	37.30 E
T'oplyj Stan ◆[8]	255b	55.37 N	37.30 E
Topo, Quebrada ≃	276c	10.33 N	67.00 W
Topocalma, Punta ≻	242	34.08 S	72.01 W
Top of Hebers	252	53.34 N	2.12 W
Topo Infiernito ∧	276c	10.33 N	66.55 W
Topol'čany	30	48.34 N	18.10 E
Topoli	70	47.59 N	51.36 E
Topolnica ≃	38	42.11 N	24.18 E
Topolobampo	222	25.36 N	109.03 W
Topolog	38	44.53 N	28.22 E
Topolovâțu Mare	38	45.46 N	21.37 E
Topolovgrad	38	42.05 N	26.20 E
Toporok	66	58.33 N	33.28 E
Topozero, Ozero ⊜	24	65.40 N	32.00 E
Toppenish	192	46.23 N	120.19 W
Toppenish Creek ≃	192	46.20 N	120.11 W
Toppenish Ridge ∧	214	46.18 N	120.40 W
Toppings	252	53.37 N	2.25 W
Toprakkale	120	37.06 N	36.07 E
Tops, Mount ∧	152	21.50 S	134.00 E
Topsa	24	62.39 N	43.34 E
Topsfield	197	42.38 N	70.57 W
Topsham, Eng., U.K.	44	50.41 N	3.27 W
Topsham, Maine, U.S.	178	43.56 N	69.58 W
Top Springs	154	16.38 S	131.50 E
Topton	198	40.30 N	75.42 W
Toquima Range ⋀	194	39.00 N	117.00 W
Toquop Wash ∨	194	36.45 N	114.11 W
Torahime	84	35.25 N	136.16 E
Torari	165f	17.39 S	168.32 E
Torawitan, Tanjung ≻	102	1.46 N	124.58 E
Toraya	238	14.03 S	73.18 W
Torbalı	120	38.10 N	27.21 E
Torbat-e Ḥeydarīyeh	118	35.16 N	59.13 E
Torbat-e Jām	118	35.14 N	60.36 E
Torbay, Newf., Can.	176	47.40 N	52.44 W
Torbay → Torquay, Eng., U.K.	44	50.28 N	3.30 W
Torbejevo, S.S.S.R.	70	54.05 N	43.15 E
Torbejevo, S.S.S.R.	72	54.44 N	36.11 E
Torbert, Mount ∧	170	61.25 N	152.24 W
Torbino	66	58.35 N	32.53 E
Torbole	58	45.52 N	10.52 E
Torbreck, Mount ∧	159	37.21 S	145.57 E
Torbrook	176	44.55 N	64.59 W
Torch ≃	174	53.50 N	103.05 W
Torchany	70	55.34 N	46.36 E
Torch Lake ⊜	180	45.00 N	85.19 W
Torčin	68	50.46 N	24.59 E
Torcy	251	48.51 N	2.39 E
Torda → Turda	38	46.34 N	23.47 E
Tordera ≃	34	41.39 N	2.47 E
Tordesillas	34	41.30 N	5.00 W
Tordino ≃	60	42.44 N	13.59 E
Tor di Quinto ◆[8]	257a	41.56 N	12.28 E
Töre	26	65.54 N	22.39 E
Töreboda	40	58.43 N	14.08 E
Torej	78	50.33 N	104.50 E
Torekov	26	56.26 N	12.37 E
Toreno	34	42.42 N	6.30 W
Torez	73	48.01 N	38.37 E
Torfou	251	48.32 N	2.14 E
Torgau	50	51.34 N	13.00 E
Torgelow	50	53.37 N	14.00 E
Torgelower See ⊜	50	53.34 N	12.47 E
Torgo	78	58.28 N	119.50 E
Torgun ≃	70	50.15 N	46.18 E
Torhamn	26	56.05 N	15.50 E
Torhout	46	51.04 N	3.06 E
Tori	134	7.53 N	33.40 E
Toribulu	102	0.19 S	120.01 E
Toride	84	35.53 N	140.04 E
Torigakubi-misaki ≻	84	37.10 N	138.06 E
Torigoe	84	36.21 N	136.36 E
Toriido	260	34.25 N	135.43 E
Torii-tōge)(	84	36.29 N	138.24 E
Toriki	255a	59.47 N	30.07 E
Torín	222	27.34 N	110.14 W
Torino (Turin)	56	45.03 N	7.40 E
Torino ☐[4]	56	45.08 N	7.22 E
Torino di Sangro Marina	60	42.11 N	14.32 E
Torio ≃	34	42.35 N	5.34 W
Toriparu	245	16.20 S	53.55 W
Torit	144	4.24 N	32.34 E
Toritama	240	8.01 S	36.04 W
Toriya	84	36.59 N	136.54 E
Torjun	105a	7.10 S	113.13 E
Torkamān	118	37.35 N	47.23 E
Torkestān, Selseleh-ye Band-e ⋀	118	35.25 N	64.15 E
Torkoviči	66	58.52 N	30.20 E
Torlino	76	58.53 N	63.46 E
Torment, Point ≻	152	17.02 S	123.36 E
Tormes ≃	34	41.18 N	6.29 W
Tormestorp	41	56.07 N	13.44 E
Tormey	272	38.03 N	122.15 W
Tormini	58	45.36 N	10.29 E
Tormosin	70	48.12 N	42.42 E
Torna	24	68.04 N	44.10 E
Torna ∧	112	18.16 N	73.37 E
Tornado Mountain ∧	172	49.58 N	114.39 W
Tornareccio	60	42.02 N	14.24 E
Tornberget ∧[2]	40	59.08 N	18.01 E
Torne ≃	42	53.36 N	0.44 W
Torneälven ≃	24	65.48 N	24.08 E
Torne Brook ≃	266	41.08 N	74.10 W
Tornesch	48	53.41 N	9.43 E
Torneträsk ⊜	24	68.20 N	19.10 E
Torngat Mountains ⋀	166	59.00 N	64.00 W
Tornillo	190	31.27 N	106.05 W
Tornillo Creek ≃	186	29.11 N	103.00 W
Tornimparte	60	42.17 N	13.18 E
Torning	41	56.17 N	9.20 E
Tornio	26	65.51 N	24.08 E
Tornquist	242	38.06 S	62.14 W
T'orny, S.S.S.R.	68	50.59 N	33.59 E
T'orny, S.S.S.R.	68	48.09 N	33.33 E
T'orny, S.S.S.R.	73	49.05 N	37.57 E
Toro	34	41.31 N	5.24 W
Toro ☐[5]	144	0.30 N	30.30 E
Torö I	40	58.50 N	17.50 E
Toro, Arroyo ≃	278	34.27 S	58.52 W
Toro, Cañada del ≃	248	35.16 S	59.05 W
Toro, Cerro del ∧	242	29.08 S	69.48 W
Toro, Lago del ⊜	244	51.14 S	72.45 W
Toro, Punta ≻	242	33.47 S	71.49 W
Torobuku	102	4.25 S	122.26 E
Torodi	140	13.18 N	1.40 E
Toro-iseki ⊥	84	34.57 N	138.24 E
Torok	136	10.03 N	14.33 E
Torokina	165e	6.14 S	155.03 E
Törökszentmiklós	30	47.11 N	20.25 E
Torola ≃	226	13.52 N	88.30 W
Torom	79	54.32 N	135.50 E
Torom ≃	79	54.36 N	135.46 E
Toroni, Cerro ∧	238	19.43 S	68.41 W
Toronto, Austl.	160	33.01 S	151.36 E
Toronto, Ont., Can.	202		
	265b	43.39 N	79.23 W
Toronto, Kans., U.S.	188	37.48 N	95.57 W
Toronto, Ohio, U.S.	204	40.28 N	80.36 W
Toronto, S. Dak., U.S.	188	44.34 N	96.39 W
Toronto ☐[6]	265b	43.44 N	79.24 W
Toronto, University of ʋ[2]	265b	43.40 N	79.24 W
Toronto Harbour C	265b	43.38 N	79.22 W
Toronto International Airport ⊠	202	43.41 N	79.38 W
Toronto Island Airport ⊠	265b	43.38 N	79.24 W
Toronto Lake ⊜[1]	188	37.46 N	95.57 W
Toronto Reservoir ⊜[1]	200	41.38 N	74.51 W
Toro Peak ∧	194	33.32 N	116.25 W
Toropec	66	56.30 N	31.39 E
Toropovo	72	54.21 N	36.07 E
Tororo	144	0.42 N	34.11 E
Toros Dağı ∧	120	37.23 N	34.34 E
Toros Dağları ⋀	120	37.00 N	33.00 E
Torošino	66	57.56 N	28.36 E
Torosozero	24	62.30 N	38.10 E
Torotoro	238	18.07 S	65.46 W
Toroume ∧	164k	21.15 S	159.45 W
Torpa ⊥	26	57.39 N	13.16 E
Tor Pignatara ◆[8]	257a	41.52 N	12.32 E
Torpo	26	60.40 N	8.43 E
Torpoint	44	50.22 N	4.11 W
Torquay, Austl.	159	38.21 S	144.19 E
Torquay, Sask., Can.	174	49.08 N	103.31 W
Torquay (Torbay), Eng., U.K.	44	50.28 N	3.30 W
Torquemada	34	42.02 N	4.19 W
Torraccia, Fosso ≃	257a	42.00 N	12.30 E
Torrance, Calif., U.S.	218	33.50 N	118.19 W
Torrance, Pa., U.S.	204	40.25 N	79.14 W
Torrance Lake ⊜	174	57.04 N	98.12 W
Torrance Municipal Airport ⊠	270	33.48 N	118.20 W
Torrão	34	38.18 N	8.13 W
Torre Annunziata	60	40.45 N	14.27 E
Torre Astura ⊥	60	41.24 N	12.46 E
Torre Baja	34	40.07 N	1.15 W
Torrebelvicino	58	45.43 N	11.18 E
Torre Beretti	56	45.04 N	8.40 E
Torreblanca	34	40.13 N	0.12 E
Torrebruna	60	41.52 N	14.33 E
Torrecilla ∧	34	37.36 N	2.31 W
Torrecilla en Cameros	34	42.16 N	2.37 W
Torre del Campo	34	37.46 N	3.53 W
Torre del Greco	60	40.47 N	14.22 E
Torre del Lago Puccini	60	43.50 N	10.17 E
Torre de Moncorvo	34	41.10 N	7.03 W
Torre de'Passeri	60	42.14 N	13.56 E
Torre di Mosto	58	45.41 N	12.43 E
Torre di Santa Maria	58	46.14 N	9.51 E
Torredonjimeno	34	37.46 N	3.57 W
Torre Gaia ◆[8]	257a	41.51 N	12.39 E
Torrejón, Embalse de ⊜[1]	34	39.50 N	5.50 W
Torrejon Air Base ■	256a	40.28 N	3.28 W
Torrejoncillo	34	39.54 N	6.28 W
Torrejón de Ardoz	34	40.27 N	3.29 W
Torrelaguna	34	40.50 N	3.32 W
Torrelavega	34	43.21 N	4.03 W
Torrellas, Riera de ≃	256d	41.23 N	2.01 E
Torrellas de Llobregat	256d	41.21 N	1.59 E
Torremaggiore	60	41.41 N	15.17 E
Torremolinos	34	36.37 N	4.30 W
Torrenieri	60	43.05 N	11.33 E
Torrens ≃	158b	34.56 S	138.30 E
Torrens, Lake ⊜	156	31.00 S	137.50 E
Torrens Creek	156	20.46 S	145.02 E
Torrens Creek ≃	156	22.22 S	145.09 E
Torrens Island I	158b	34.48 S	138.32 E
Torrent	242	28.50 S	56.28 W
Torrente	34	39.26 N	0.28 W
Torreões	246	21.52 S	43.33 W
Torreón	222	25.33 N	103.26 W
Torre Pedrera	60	44.06 N	12.31 E
Torre Pellice	56	44.49 N	7.13 E
Torreperogil	34	38.02 N	3.17 W
Torres	248	34.26 S	59.08 W
Tôrres, Bra.	242	29.21 S	49.44 W
Torres, Arroyo ≃	278	34.39 S	58.45 W
Torresdale ◆[8]	275	40.03 N	75.00 W
Torres de Alcalá	34	35.10 N	4.16 W
Torres Islands II	165f	13.15 S	166.37 E
Torres Martinez Indian Reservation ◆[4]	194	33.35 N	116.02 W
Torres Novas	34	39.29 N	8.32 W
Torres Strait ⋃	154	10.25 S	142.10 E
Torres Vedras	34	39.06 N	9.16 W
Torrette di Fano	60	43.47 N	13.07 E
Torrevieja	34	37.59 N	0.41 W
Torricella in Sabina	60	42.16 N	12.52 E
Torricella Peligna	60	42.01 N	14.15 E
Torricella Sicura	60	42.39 N	13.39 E
Torricelli Mountains ⋀	154	3.25 S	142.20 E
Torridge ≃	44	51.03 N	4.11 W
Torridon	28	57.33 N	5.31 W
Torridon, Loch C	28	57.35 N	5.50 W
Torriglia	56	44.31 N	9.10 E
Torrijos, Esp.	34	39.59 N	4.17 W
Torrijos, Pil.	106	13.19 N	122.05 E
Torrild	41	55.59 N	10.04 E
Torrimpietra ◆[8]	257a	41.56 N	12.13 E
Tørring	41	55.51 N	9.29 E
Torrington, Conn., U.S.	197	41.48 N	73.08 W
Torrington, Wyo., U.S.	188	42.04 N	104.11 W
Torrinha	245	22.26 S	48.09 W
Torrita di Siena	60	43.10 N	11.46 E
Torröjen ⊜	26	63.55 N	12.56 E
Torrox	34	36.46 N	3.58 W
Torrvarpen ⊜	40	59.42 N	14.30 E
Torsåker	40	60.31 N	16.29 E
Tor Sapienza ◆[8]	257a	41.54 N	12.35 E
Torsås	26	56.24 N	16.00 E
Torsburgen ⊥	26	57.25 N	18.43 E
Torsby	26	60.08 N	13.00 E
Tors Cove	176	47.13 N	52.51 W
Torshälla	40	59.25 N	16.28 E
Tórshavn	22	62.01 N	6.46 W
Torside Reservoir ⊜[1]	252	53.29 N	1.54 W
Torsö	40	58.47 N	13.48 E
Torsö I	40	58.48 N	13.50 E
Tortola I	230m	18.27 N	64.36 W
Tortoli	36	39.55 N	9.39 E
Tortona	56	44.54 N	8.52 E
Tortoreto	60	42.48 N	13.55 E
Tortorici	36	38.02 N	14.49 E
Tortosa	34	40.48 N	0.31 E
Tortosa, Cabo de ≻	34	40.43 N	0.55 E
Tortue, Île de la I	228	20.04 N	72.49 W
Tortue, Rivière de la ≃	196	45.24 N	73.32 W
Tortugas, Laguna ⊜	224	22.20 N	98.07 W
Tortuguero, Laguna C	230m	18.28 N	66.26 W
Tortuguero, Puerto del C	230m	18.29 N	66.28 W
Tortuguitas	278	34.28 S	58.46 W
Tortum	120	40.19 N	41.35 E
Toru ≃	104	1.26 N	98.46 E
Toruajgyr	75	42.32 N	76.26 E
Torue	102	0.58 S	120.18 E
Torugart, Pereval)(	75	40.33 N	75.20 E
Toruń	30	53.02 N	18.35 E
Torunos	236	8.30 N	70.04 W
Torup, Sve.	26	56.58 N	13.05 E
Torup, Sve.	41	55.34 N	13.12 E
Tõrva	66	58.00 N	25.56 E
Tory	78	51.47 N	103.00 E
Torysa ≃	30	48.39 N	21.21 E
Toržkovskaja Gr'ada ∧	66	57.00 N	34.44 E
Toržok	66	57.03 N	34.58 E
Torzym	30	52.20 N	15.04 E
Tosa	86	33.29 N	133.25 E
T'osan	88	38.18 N	126.43 E
Tosari	105a	7.53 S	112.54 E
Tosas, Puerto de)(	34	42.19 N	2.01 E
Tosa-shimizu	82	32.46 N	132.57 E
Tosa-wan C	86	33.20 N	133.40 E
Tosayama	86	33.38 N	133.32 E
Tosa-yamada	86	33.36 N	133.41 E
Tosca	146	25.53 S	23.58 E
Toscana ☐[4]	36	43.25 N	11.00 E
Toscolano	58	45.38 N	10.37 E
Tösens	54	47.01 N	10.36 E
Tōshi-jima I	84	34.31 N	136.53 E
Toshima ◆[8]	258	35.44 N	139.43 E
To-shima I, Nihon	82	32.12 N	130.05 E
To-shima I, Nihon	84	34.31 N	139.17 E
Tōshō-gū ʋ[1]	84	36.46 N	139.36 E
Tosi	60	43.45 N	11.31 E
Tosilei	134	1.24 N	41.23 E
Toškalykaja, Gora ∧	76	50.38 N	89.30 E
Toškovskij	73	48.46 N	38.34 E
Tosköy	120	41.27 N	35.54 E
Tosna ≃	255a	59.46 N	30.46 E
Tosno	66	59.33 N	30.53 E
Tosoncengel	78	48.47 N	98.15 E
T'osovo	66	55.37 N	34.30 E
T'osovo-Netyl'skij	66	58.57 N	31.04 E
T'osovskij	66	58.48 N	30.52 E
Töss ≃	54	47.33 N	8.33 E
Tossens	48	53.34 N	8.16 E
Tossi	105b	9.35 S	118.57 E
Tossicia	60	42.33 N	13.39 E
Tost → Toszek	30	50.28 N	18.32 E
Tostado	242	29.14 S	61.46 W
Tõstamaa	66	58.20 N	24.00 E
Tostedt	48	53.17 N	9.42 E
Tosterön I	40	59.25 N	17.00 E
Tostu	75	41.34 N	71.34 E
Tost Uul ⋀	92	43.15 N	100.30 E
Tosu	86	33.22 N	130.31 E
Tosya	120	41.01 N	34.02 E
Toszek	30	50.28 N	18.32 E
Tota, Laguna de ⊜	236	5.33 N	72.55 W
Totagatic ≃	180	46.05 N	92.11 W
Totak ⊜	26	59.42 N	7.57 E
Totana	34	37.46 N	1.30 W
Totānāla	116	22.05 N	87.40 E
Totatiche	224	21.56 N	103.27 W
Totban	70	46.47 N	49.06 E
Toteng	146	20.22 S	22.58 E
Tôtes	46	49.41 N	1.03 E
Totes Gebirge ⋀	30	47.42 N	13.55 E
Totias	134	3.57 N	43.58 E
T'otkino	68	51.17 N	34.16 E
Tot'ma	66	59.57 N	42.45 E
Totnes	44	50.25 N	3.41 W
Totness	240	5.53 N	56.19 W
Totolom ∧	164r	6.52 N	158.14 E
Totonicapán	226	14.55 N	91.22 W
Totonicapán ☐[5]	226	15.00 N	91.20 W
Totopotomoy Creek ≃	198	37.41 N	77.13 W
Totora, Bol.	238	17.49 S	68.07 W
Totora, Bol.	238	17.42 S	65.09 W
Totora Palca	238	19.55 S	65.26 W
Totoras	242	32.35 S	61.11 W
Totos	238	13.31 S	74.30 W
Tototlán	224	20.33 N	102.48 W
Totowa	200	40.54 N	74.13 W

English	Deutsch	Español	Français	Português
≃ River	Fluss	Río	Rivière	Rio
≍ Canal	Kanal	Canal	Canal	Canal
⌊ Waterfall, Rapids	Wasserfall, Stromschnellen	Cascada, Rápidos	Chute d'eau, Rapides	Cascata, Rápidos
⋃ Strait	Meeresstrasse	Estrecho	Détroit	Estreito
C Bay, Gulf	Bucht, Golf	Bahía, Golfo	Baie, Golfe	Baía, Golfo
⊜ Lake, Lakes	See, Seen	Lago, Lagos	Lac, Lacs	Lago, Lagos
≡ Swamp	Sumpf	Pantano	Marais	Pântano
Ice Features, Glacier	Eis- und Gletscherformen	Accidentes Glaciales	Formes glaciaires	Acidentes Glaciares
Other Hydrographic Features	Andere Hydrographische Objekte	Otros Elementos Hidrográficos	Autres données hydrographiques	Outros Elementos Hidrográficos
✦ Submarine Features	Untermeerische Objekte	Accidentes Submarinos	Formes de relief sous-marin	Acidentes Submarinos
☐ Political Unit	Politische Einheit	Unidad Política	Entité politique	Unidade Política
ʋ Cultural Institution	Kulturelle Institution	Institución Cultural	Institution culturelle	Instituição Cultural
⊥ Historical Site	Historische Stätte	Sitio Histórico	Site historique	Sítio Histórico
♠ Recreational Site	Erholungs- und Ferienort	Sitio de Recreo	Centre de loisirs	Sítio de Lazer
⊠ Airport	Flughafen	Aeropuerto	Aéroport	Aeroporto
■ Military Installation	Militäranlage	Instalación Militar	Installation militaire	Instalação Militar
◆ Miscellaneous	Verschiedenes	Misceláneo	Divers	Miscelânea

Name	Page	Lat.	Long.
Totoya I	165g	18.57 S	179.50 W
Totson Mountain ∧	170	64.26 N	157.15 W
Totsuka ⬥[8]	258	35.24 N	139.32 E
Totten Glacier ◸	9	66.45 S	116.10 E
Tottenham, Austl.	156	32.14 S	147.21 E
Tottenham, Ont., Can.	202	44.01 N	79.49 W
Tottenham ⬥[8]	250	51.35 N	0.04 W
Tottenham Hotspur Football Ground ♠	250	51.36 N	0.04 W
Totten Inlet ⊂	214	47.07 N	123.02 W
Tottenville ⬥[8]	266	40.31 N	74.15 W
Totteridge ⬥[8]	250	51.38 N	0.12 W
Tottington	42	53.37 N	2.20 W
Totton	44	50.56 N	1.29 W
Tottori	86	35.30 N	134.14 E
Tottori □[5]	86	35.30 N	134.00 E
Tottori-sakyū ∧[2]	86	35.31 N	134.25 E
Totuskey Creek ≃	198	37.52 N	76.45 W
Tou, Motu I	164k	21.11 S	159.48 W
Touba, C. Iv.	140	8.17 N	7.41 W
Touba, Sén.	140	14.51 N	15.53 W
Touba □[5]	140	8.20 N	7.30 W
Toubéré Bafal	140	14.23 N	13.32 W
Toubkal, Jbel ∧	138	31.05 N	7.55 W
T'ouch'eng	90	24.51 N	121.49 E
Touchet ≃	192	46.02 N	118.41 W
Touchwood Hills ∧∧[2]	174	51.35 N	104.17 W
Touchwood Lake ⊜, Alta., Can.	172	54.50 N	111.23 W
Touchwood Lake ⊜, Man., Can.	174	54.29 N	95.00 W
Toucy	46	47.44 N	3.18 E
Toudaogou, Zhg.	88	42.46 N	129.12 E
Toudaogou, Zhg.	94	41.37 N	121.40 E
Toudaogou, Zhg.	95	40.58 N	117.59 E
Toudaojiang ≃	88	42.36 N	127.11 E
Touët-sur-Var	56	43.57 N	7.00 E
Tougaloo	184	32.24 N	90.09 W
Tougan	140	13.04 N	3.04 W
Touggourt	138	33.10 N	6.00 E
Toughkenamon	275	39.50 N	75.46 W
Tougouri	140	13.19 N	0.31 W
Tougué	140	11.27 N	11.41 W
Tougué □[4]	140	11.28 N	11.36 W
Touho	165f	20.47 S	165.14 E
Touïel, Oued ∨	138	31.30 N	4.46 E
Touil, Oued ∨	138	35.30 N	2.33 E
Touisset	197	41.43 N	71.14 W
Toukansi	90	29.22 N	119.06 E
Toukley	160	33.16 S	151.33 E
Toukoto	140	13.27 N	9.53 W
Toul	54	48.41 N	5.54 E
Toulépleu	140	6.35 N	8.25 W
Toulnustouc ≃	176	49.35 N	68.24 W
Toulnustouc-Nord-Est ≃	176	50.56 N	67.44 W
Toulon, Fr.	56	43.07 N	5.56 E
Toulon, Ill., U.S.	180	41.06 N	89.52 W
Toulon Lake ⊜	194	40.01 N	118.40 W
Toulon-sur-Arroux	32	46.42 N	4.08 E
Touloubre ≃	56	43.33 N	5.02 E
Toulourenc ≃	56	44.14 N	5.09 E
Toulouse	32	43.36 N	1.26 E
Toumenshan I	90	28.41 N	121.46 E
Toumfafi	140	15.02 N	5.38 E
Toumodi	140	7.26 N	5.37 W
Tounan	90	23.41 N	120.28 E
Tounassine, Hamada ⬥[2]	138	28.30 N	5.00 W
Toungoo	100	18.56 N	96.26 E
Toupeng	96	30.19 N	120.31 E
Toupi	90	26.44 N	116.05 E
Touques	46	49.22 N	0.06 E
Touques ≃	46	49.22 N	0.06 E
Tour, Étang de la ⊜	251	48.40 N	1.53 E
Toura, Monts du ∧∧	140	7.40 N	7.25 W
Touraine	178	45.34 N	75.47 W
Touraine □[9]	46	47.12 N	1.30 E
Tourakom	100	18.26 N	102.32 E
Tourane → Da-nang	100	16.04 N	108.13 E
Tourbe ≃	52	49.10 N	4.52 E
Tourcoing	46	50.43 N	3.09 E
Tourinan, Cabo ≻	34	43.03 N	9.18 W
Tournai	46	50.36 N	3.23 E
Tournan-en-Brie	46	48.44 N	2.46 E
Tournesac ≃	46	47.15 N	4.12 E
Tournhout	52	51.19 N	4.57 E
Tournon	56	45.04 N	4.50 E
Tournus	54	46.34 N	4.54 E
Touros	240	5.12 S	35.28 W
Tou-rout	100	16.24 N	107.00 E
Tourouvre	46	48.35 N	0.40 E
Tourrette-Levens	56	43.47 N	7.16 E
Tours	46	47.23 N	0.41 E
Tours-sur-Marne	46	49.03 N	4.07 E
Tours-sur-Meymont	56	45.40 N	3.35 E
Tourteron	52	49.32 N	4.39 E
Tourves	56	43.24 N	5.56 E
Toury	46	48.12 N	1.56 E
Touside, Pic ∧	136	21.02 N	16.25 E
Toussaint Creek ≃	204	41.35 N	83.04 W
Toussus-le-Noble	251	48.45 N	2.07 E
Toussus-le-Noble, Aéroport de ⊠	251	48.45 N	2.10 E
Toustain	36	36.40 N	8.15 E
Toutai, Zhg.	79	45.40 N	124.50 E
Toutai, Zhg.	94	41.41 N	121.11 E
Toutaizi	94	42.19 N	122.49 E
Toutle	214	46.20 N	122.41 W
Toutle ≃	214	46.17 N	122.55 W
Toutle, North Fork ≃	214	46.23 N	122.34 W
Toutle, South Fork ≃	214	46.20 N	122.44 W
Toutle Mountain Range ∧∧	214	46.20 N	122.30 W
Toutuohe	90	31.06 N	116.25 E
Touws ≃	148	33.45 S	21.11 E
Touwsrivier	148	33.20 S	20.00 E
Touzhan	79	49.27 N	129.41 E
Toužim	30	50.04 N	13.00 E
Töv □[4]	78	47.30 N	106.30 E
Tova	24	65.58 N	40.45 E
Tovar	236	8.20 N	71.46 W
Tovarkovo	72	54.42 N	35.57 E
Tovarkovskij	66	53.40 N	38.14 E
Tove ≃	44	52.05 N	0.38 W
Tovey	209	39.35 N	89.27 W
Tow	186	30.53 N	98.28 W
Tōwa	86	33.13 N	132.53 E
Towaco	200	40.56 N	74.21 W
Towada	82	40.37 N	141.13 E
Towada-hachimantai-kokuritsu-kōen ♠	82	40.35 N	140.53 E
Towada-ko ⊜	82	40.28 N	140.55 E
Towai	162	35.29 S	174.08 E
Towamencin Creek ≃	275	40.13 N	75.23 W
Towanda, Ill., U.S.	206	40.34 N	88.54 W
Towanda, Kans., U.S.	188	37.48 N	97.02 W
Towanda, Pa., U.S.	200	41.46 N	76.27 W
Towanda Creek ≃	200	41.45 N	76.26 W
Towan Head ≻	44	50.25 N	5.07 W
Towar Gardens	206	42.45 N	84.28 W
Towari	102	4.36 S	121.29 E
Towcester	44	52.08 N	1.00 W
Tower	180	47.48 N	92.17 W
Tower City, N. Dak., U.S.	188	46.55 N	97.40 W
Tower City, Pa., U.S.	198	40.35 N	76.33 W
Tower Hamlets ⬥[8]	44	51.32 N	0.03 W
Tower Hill, Austl.	156	22.03 S	144.36 E
Tower Hill, Ill., U.S.	209	39.23 N	88.58 W
Towerhill Creek ≃	156	22.29 S	144.39 E
Tower of London ⊥	250	51.30 N	0.05 W
Tower Peak ∧	216	38.09 N	119.33 W
Towers of Silence ʋ[1]	262c	18.58 N	72.48 E
Tower Soudan State Park ♠	180	47.50 N	92.15 W
Towla, Mount ∧	144	21.22 S	29.52 E
Tow Law	42	54.44 N	1.49 W
Towlī	74	39.11 N	47.32 E
Town ≃	273	42.00 N	70.57 W
Town Bank	198	39.00 N	74.56 W
Town Creek ≃, Ala., U.S.	184	34.24 N	86.11 W
Town Creek ≃, Ala., U.S.	184	32.34 N	89.14 W
Town Creek ≃, Ohio, U.S.	206	41.05 N	84.25 W
Town Creek Manor	198	38.19 N	76.27 W
Towneley Hall ⊥	252	53.46 N	2.13 W
Towner	188	48.21 N	100.25 W
Town Estates	275	40.04 N	74.52 W
Town Hill ∧[2]	230a	32.19 N	64.44 W
Town of Pines	206	41.41 N	86.58 W
Townsend, Del., U.S.	198	39.24 N	75.41 W
Townsend, Mass., U.S.	197	42.40 N	71.42 W
Townsend, Mont., U.S.	192	46.19 N	111.31 W
Townsend, Va., U.S.	198	37.11 N	75.57 W
Townsend, Mount ∧	161b	36.25 S	148.15 E
Townsend Island I	266	40.38 N	73.26 W
Townsends Inlet ⊂	198	39.07 N	74.43 W
Townshend Island I	156	22.15 S	150.30 E
Township Line Run ≃	269b	40.13 N	79.33 W
Townsville	156	19.16 S	146.48 E
Townville	204	41.41 N	79.53 W
Towrang	160	34.42 S	149.51 E
Towrang ∧	160	34.46 S	149.51 E
Towra Point ≻	264a	34.00 S	151.10 E
Towr Kham	113	34.08 N	71.05 E
Towrzī, Afg.	110	30.11 N	65.59 E
Towrzī, Afg.	118	32.38 N	65.53 E
Towson	274b	39.24 N	76.36 W
Towson State College ʋ[2]	274b	39.24 N	76.37 W
Towuti, Danau ⊜	102	2.45 S	121.32 E
Toyah	186	31.19 N	103.47 W
Toyah Creek ≃	186	31.18 N	103.27 W
Tōya-ko ⊜	82a	42.35 N	140.51 E
Toyama	84	36.41 N	137.13 E
Toyama □[5]	84	36.30 N	137.30 E
Toyama-heiya ≚	84	36.40 N	137.15 E
Toyama-wan ⊂	84	36.50 N	137.10 E
Toyapakeh	105b	8.41 S	115.29 E
Tōyō	86	33.22 N	134.18 E
Toyo ≃	84	34.47 N	137.20 E
Toyoake	84	35.03 N	137.01 E
Toyoda, Nihon	84	34.45 N	137.49 E
Toyoda, Nihon	258	35.39 N	139.23 E
Toyofuta	258	35.54 N	139.56 E
Toyohama	86	34.04 N	133.38 E
Toyohashi	84	34.46 N	137.23 E
Toyohira	86	34.40 N	132.24 E
Toyokawa	84	34.49 N	137.24 E
Toyo-kawa-yōsui ⩧	84	34.35 N	137.03 E
Toyonaka, Nihon	86	34.47 N	135.28 E
Toyonaka, Nihon	86	34.09 N	133.42 E
Toyone	84	35.09 N	137.43 E
Toyono	84	36.43 N	138.16 E
Toyooka, Nihon	84	35.33 N	137.54 E
Toyooka, Nihon	84	34.50 N	137.52 E
Toyooka, Nihon	86	35.32 N	134.50 E
Toyooka, Nihon	258	35.11 N	139.58 E
Toyosaka	86	34.34 N	132.50 E
Toyosato	84	36.06 N	140.02 E
Toyoshina	84	36.18 N	137.54 E
Toyota, Nihon	84	35.05 N	137.09 E
Toyota, Nihon	84	36.46 N	138.19 E
Toyota, Nihon	86	34.12 N	131.04 E
Toyota-ko ⊜	86	34.14 N	131.08 E
Toyotomi	84	35.34 N	138.33 E
Toyotsu	86	33.40 N	130.58 E
Toyoura	86	34.08 N	130.58 E
Toy's Hill	250	51.14 N	0.06 E
Tozer, Mount ∧	154	12.45 S	143.13 E
Tozeur	138	33.55 N	8.08 E
Tozi, Mount ∧	170	65.41 N	150.58 W
Tozitna ≃	170	65.08 N	152.23 W
Tpig	74	41.47 N	47.36 E
Traar ⬥[8]	253	51.23 N	6.36 E
Trabaria, Bocca)(	60	43.36 N	12.14 E
Traben-Trarbach	52	49.57 N	7.06 E
Trabiju	245	22.03 S	48.18 W
Trabuco, Arroyo ≃	218	33.31 N	117.40 W
Trabzon	120	41.00 N	39.43 E
Trabzon □[4]	120	40.50 N	39.50 E
Tracadie	176	47.31 N	64.54 W
Tracajá, Cachoeira ⌊	238	10.29 S	64.05 W
Trachenberg → Żmigród	30	51.29 N	16.55 E
Trachselwald	54	47.01 N	7.45 E
Tra-cu	100	9.42 N	106.16 E
Tracuateua	240	1.05 S	46.54 W
Tracy, Qué., Can.	196	46.01 N	73.09 W
Tracy, Calif., U.S.	216	37.44 N	121.25 W
Tracy, Minn., U.S.	188	44.14 N	95.37 W
Tracy City	184	35.16 N	85.44 W
Tracyton	214	47.37 N	122.39 W
Tradate	56	45.43 N	8.54 E
Trade Lake ⊜	174	55.22 N	103.44 W
Tradewater ≃	184	37.31 N	88.03 W
Trading Bay ⊂	202	45.15 N	78.55 W
Trælleborg ⊥	41	55.23 N	11.17 E
Traer	180	42.12 N	92.28 W
Trafalgar, Austl.	159	38.12 S	146.09 E
Trafalgar, Ont., Can.	265b	43.29 N	79.43 W
Trafalgar, Ind., U.S.	208	39.25 N	86.09 W
Trafalgar, Cabo ≻	34	36.11 N	6.02 W
Trafaria	256c	38.40 N	9.14 W
Trafford	204	40.23 N	79.45 W
Trafford □[8]	252	53.24 N	2.21 W
Trafford, Lake ⊜	210	26.25 N	81.30 W
Trafford Park	252	53.28 N	2.20 W
Trafoi	58	46.33 N	10.31 E
Tragacete	34	40.21 N	1.51 W
Trāghan	136	25.59 N	14.26 E
Tragliata ⬥[8]	257a	41.58 N	12.15 E
Traição, Córrego ≃	277b	23.36 S	46.41 W
Traid	34	40.40 N	1.49 W
Traíghlí → Tralee	28	52.16 N	9.42 W
Traiguén	242	38.15 S	72.41 W
Traiguén, Isla I	244	45.35 S	73.42 W
Trail	172	49.06 N	117.42 W
Trail Creek	206	41.42 N	86.52 W
Trailer Estates	210	27.24 N	82.34 W
Traînel	46	48.25 N	3.27 E
Trainer	275	39.50 N	75.25 W
Traipu	240	9.58 S	37.01 W
Traira (Taraira) ≃	236	1.04 S	69.26 W
Trairão ≃	240	7.20 S	51.14 W
Traíras ≃	245	14.07 S	48.31 W
Trairi	240	3.17 S	39.15 W
Traiskirchen	254b	48.01 N	16.18 E
Traîtres, Baie des ⊂	164x	9.50 S	139.02 W
Trajouce	256c	38.44 N	9.20 W
Trakai	66	54.38 N	24.56 E
Trakt	24	62.44 N	51.11 E
Träkvista	40	59.16 N	17.47 E
Tralee	28	52.16 N	9.42 W
Tralee Bay ⊂	28	52.15 N	9.59 W
Tramayes	54	46.18 N	4.36 E
Tramelan	54	47.13 N	7.06 E
Tramin → Termeno	58	46.20 N	11.14 E
Trammel	182	37.01 N	82.18 W
Trammel Creek ≃	184	36.52 N	86.23 W
Tramonti di sopra	58	46.18 N	12.47 E
Tramore	28	52.10 N	7.10 W
Tramperos Creek ≃	186	36.05 N	103.15 W
Trân	38	42.50 N	22.39 E
Tranås	26	58.03 N	14.59 E
Trancão ≃	256c	38.48 N	9.06 W
Trancas	242	26.13 S	65.17 W
Trancoso, Méx.	224	22.44 N	102.22 W
Trancoso, Port.	34	40.47 N	7.21 W
Trand	113	34.38 N	72.59 E
Tranderup	41	54.52 N	10.22 E
Tranebjerg	41	55.50 N	10.36 E
Tranekær	41	55.00 N	10.51 E
Tranemo	26	57.29 N	13.21 E
Tranent	42	55.57 N	2.58 W
Tränental	148	27.09 S	19.33 E
Trang	100	7.33 N	99.36 E
Trangahy	147b	19.07 S	44.43 E
Trangan, Pulau I	154	6.35 S	134.20 E
Trangie	156	32.02 S	147.59 E
Tran Grande ≃	106	6.43 N	124.01 E
Trängslet	26	61.25 N	13.40 E
Trani	36	41.17 N	16.26 E
Tranmere	252	53.23 N	3.01 W
Trannon ≃	44	52.31 N	3.25 W
Tranoroa	147b	24.42 S	45.04 E
Tranquebar	112	11.02 N	79.51 E
Tranqueira ≃	240	7.15 S	42.12 W
Tranqueras	242	31.12 S	55.45 W
Tranquility	208	38.58 N	83.32 W
Tranquilla	226	8.30 N	80.14 W
Tranquillity	216	36.39 N	120.15 W
Trans-en-Provence	56	43.30 N	6.29 E
Transfer	204	41.20 N	80.26 W
Transit Airport ⊠	274a	43.06 N	78.44 W
Transkei □[9]	148	31.20 S	29.00 E
Transquaking ≃	198	38.22 N	76.00 W
Transsylvanische Alpen → Carpații Meridionali ∧∧	38	45.30 N	24.15 E
Transtrand	26	61.05 N	13.19 E
Transtrandsfjällen ∧	26	61.17 N	13.00 E
Transvaal □[3]	146	25.00 S	29.00 E
Transylvania □[9]	38	46.30 N	24.00 E
Transylvanian Alps → Carpații Meridionali ∧∧	38	45.30 N	24.15 E
Tranters Creek ≃	182	35.33 N	77.05 W
Traona	54	46.09 N	9.31 E
Trapalcó, Salina ≚	244	39.45 S	66.45 W
Trapani	36	38.01 N	12.31 E
Traphole Brook ≃	273	42.10 N	71.11 W
Trappe, Md., U.S.	198	38.40 N	76.04 W
Trappe, Pa., U.S.	198	40.12 N	75.29 W
Trappenkamp	50	54.03 N	10.16 E
Trapper Peak ∧	192	45.54 N	114.18 W
Trappes	46	48.47 N	2.00 E
Trapuá ≃	277b	23.36 S	46.17 W
Traralgon	159	38.12 S	146.32 E
Traras, Monts des ∧∧	34	35.10 N	1.40 W
Trarza ⬥[1]	140	18.00 N	15.00 W
Trasacco	60	41.57 N	13.32 E
Trasadingen	54	47.40 N	8.26 E
Trăscau, Munții ∧∧	38	46.23 N	23.33 E
Trasimeno, Lago ⊜	60	43.08 N	12.06 E
Trask ≃	214	45.28 N	123.53 W
Träslövsläge	26	57.04 N	12.16 E
Trasna	72	54.45 N	38.42 E
Trás-os-Montes □[9]	34	41.30 N	7.15 W
Trassem	52	49.34 N	6.31 E
Trâstenik	38	43.31 N	24.28 E
Trat	100	12.14 N	102.30 E
Tratzberg, Schloss ⊥	58	47.23 N	11.44 E
Trauchgau	54	47.38 N	10.49 E
Traun	30	48.13 N	14.14 E
Traun ≃, B.R.D.	58	48.00 N	12.32 E
Traun ≃, Öst.	58	48.09 N	14.01 E
Traunkirchen	58	47.50 N	13.47 E
Traunreut	58	47.56 N	12.35 E
Traun-See ⊜	58	47.51 N	13.48 E
Traunstein	58	47.52 N	12.38 E
Traunstein ∧	58	47.52 N	13.50 E
Traunwalchen	58	47.56 N	12.36 E
Trautenstein	50	51.41 N	10.43 E
Travagliato	58	45.31 N	10.05 E
Trave ≃	50	53.54 N	10.50 E
Travedona	56	45.48 N	8.40 E
Travellers Lake ⊜	156	33.18 S	142.00 E
Travemünde ⬥[8]	50	53.57 N	10.52 E
Traver	216	36.27 N	119.29 W
Travers, Mount ∧	162	42.01 S	172.44 E
Travers, Val de ∨	54	46.57 N	6.38 E
Traverse, Lake ⊜	188	45.43 N	96.40 W
Traverse Bay ⊂	174	50.40 N	96.25 W
Traverse City	180	44.46 N	85.37 W
Traversella	56	45.30 N	7.45 E
Traverse Peak ∧	170	65.10 N	159.12 W
Traversetolo	58	44.38 N	10.23 E
Travers Reservoir ⊜[1]	172	50.14 N	112.51 W
Travesía ⊥	226	15.20 N	87.53 W
Travis	212	31.08 N	97.00 W
Travis □[6]	212	30.18 N	97.40 W
Travis, Lake ⊜[1]	186	30.27 N	98.00 W
Travis Air Force Base ■	216	38.16 N	121.55 W
Travnik	36	44.14 N	17.40 E
Trawalla	159	37.26 S	143.29 E
Trawick	212	31.46 N	94.45 W
Trawsfynydd	44	52.54 N	3.55 W
Trayning	152	31.07 S	117.48 E
Trazegnies	46	50.28 N	4.19 E
Trbovlje	36	46.10 N	15.03 E
Treadwell	200	42.21 N	75.03 W
Treales	252	53.47 N	2.51 W
Treasure Island	210	27.46 N	82.46 W
Treasure Island I	216	37.48 N	122.22 W
Treasure Island Naval Station ■	272	37.49 N	122.22 W
Treasury Islands II	165e	7.22 S	155.34 E
Trebatsch	50	52.05 N	14.09 E
Trebbia ≃	56	45.04 N	9.41 E
Trebbin	50	52.13 N	13.13 E
Třebechovice pod Orebem	30	50.12 N	16.00 E
Trebel	50	52.59 N	11.20 E
Trebel ≃	50	53.55 N	13.01 E
Trebelsee ⊜	50	52.28 N	12.47 E
Třebenice	50	50.29 N	14.00 E
Třebíč	30	49.13 N	15.53 E
Trebinje	38	42.43 N	18.20 E
Trebisacce	36	39.52 N	16.32 E
Trebišov	30	48.40 N	21.47 E
Trebitz	50	51.45 N	12.44 E
Trebizond → Trabzon	120	41.00 N	39.43 E
Trebjerg ∧[2]	41	55.10 N	10.14 E
Treble Mountain ∧	172	55.50 N	129.51 W
Treblinka	30	52.39 N	22.03 E
Trebnitz → Trzebnica	30	51.19 N	17.03 E
Třeboň	30	49.00 N	14.47 E
Třeboňská pánev ≚[1]	30	49.00 N	14.50 E
Trebsen	50	51.17 N	12.45 E
Trecate	56	45.26 N	8.44 E
Trece Martires	106	14.16 N	120.50 E
Trecenta	58	45.02 N	11.28 E
Tred Avon River ⊂	198	38.42 N	76.08 W
Tredegar	44	51.47 N	3.16 W
Tredici Archi, Ponte ⬥[5]	60	41.32 N	14.57 E
Treene ≃	41	54.22 N	9.05 E
Trees Mills	269b	40.23 N	80.13 W
Treffen	58	46.40 N	13.52 E
Treffort	54	46.16 N	5.22 E
Treffurt	52	51.08 N	10.14 E
Trèfle, Lac ⊜	196	46.36 N	73.55 W
Tregaron	44	52.13 N	3.55 W
Tregnago	58	45.31 N	11.10 E
Tregosse Islets II	156	17.41 S	150.43 E
Tregubovo	66	58.59 N	31.33 E
Tréguier	32	48.47 N	3.14 W
Treharris	44	51.41 N	3.16 W
Treherne	174	49.38 N	98.41 W
Trehörningsjö	26	63.42 N	18.48 E
Treia, B.R.D.	41	54.30 N	9.17 E
Treia, It.	60	43.19 N	13.19 E
Treinta y Tres	242	33.14 S	54.23 W
Treis	52	50.10 N	7.17 E
Trekkopje	146	22.18 S	14.53 E
Trélazé	32	47.27 N	0.28 W
Trelde Næs ≻	41	55.37 N	9.52 E
Trelew	244	43.15 S	65.18 W
Trelleborg	41	55.22 N	13.10 E
Treloar	209	38.39 N	91.10 W
Trélon	46	50.04 N	4.06 E
Tremadoc	44	52.56 N	4.09 W
Tremblant, Lac ⊜	196	46.15 N	74.38 W
Tremblant, Mont ∧	196	46.16 N	74.35 W
Tremblay, Hippodrome du ♠	251	48.50 N	2.29 E
Tremblay, Île du I	265a	45.31 N	73.45 W
Tremblay-lès-Gonesse	251	48.59 N	2.34 E
Trembleur Lake ⊜	172	54.51 N	125.07 W
Tremedal	245	14.58 S	41.24 W
Tremembé	246	22.58 S	45.33 W
Tremezzo	54	45.59 N	9.15 E
Tremino	78	56.42 N	98.04 E
Tremiti, Isole II	60	42.07 N	15.30 E
Tremo La)(	114	27.44 N	89.12 E
Tremont, Ill., U.S.	180	40.28 N	89.29 W
Tremont, Ind., U.S.	206	41.39 N	87.02 W
Tremont, Pa., U.S.	198	40.38 N	76.23 W
Tremont ⬥[8]	266	40.51 N	73.55 W
Tremont City	208	40.01 N	83.50 W
Tremonton	190	41.43 N	112.10 W
Tremp	34	42.10 N	0.54 E
Trempealeau	180	44.00 N	91.26 W
Trempealeau ≃	180	44.02 N	91.32 W
Trempen → Novostrojevo	66	54.27 N	21.50 E
Tremsbüttel	48	53.44 N	10.18 E
Trena	134	10.45 N	40.38 E
Trenčín	30	48.54 N	18.04 E
Trendelburg	48	51.34 N	9.25 E
Trenel	242	35.42 S	64.08 W
Trêng	100	12.49 N	102.54 E
Trenggalek	105a	8.03 S	111.43 E
Trenque Lauquen	242	35.58 S	62.42 W
Trent, D.D.R.	50	54.31 N	13.15 E
Trent → Trento, It.	58	46.04 N	11.08 E
Trent ≃, Ont., Can.	202	44.06 N	77.34 W
Trent ≃, Eng., U.K.	42	53.42 N	0.41 W
Trent ≃, N.C., U.S.	182	35.05 N	77.02 W
Trent, Vale of ∨	44	52.44 N	1.50 W
Trent and Mersey Canal ⩧	252	53.19 N	2.39 W
Trente-et-un-Milles, Lac des ⊜	178	46.12 N	75.49 W
Trentham	159	37.23 S	144.19 E
Trentino-Alto Adige □[4]	58	46.30 N	11.20 E
Trento	58	46.04 N	11.08 E
Trento □[4]	58	46.08 N	11.07 E
Trentola-Ducenta	60	40.59 N	14.10 E
Trenton, N.S., Can.	176	45.37 N	62.38 W
Trenton, Ont., Can.	202	44.06 N	77.35 W
Trenton, Fla., U.S.	182	29.37 N	82.49 W
Trenton, Ga., U.S.	182	34.52 N	85.31 W
Trenton, Ill., U.S.	209	38.36 N	89.41 W
Trenton, Ky., U.S.	184	36.43 N	87.16 W
Trenton, Mich., U.S.	206	42.09 N	83.11 W
Trenton, Mo., U.S.	184	40.05 N	93.37 W
Trenton, Nebr., U.S.	188	40.11 N	101.01 W
Trenton, N.J., U.S.	198		
	275	40.13 N	74.45 W
Trenton, N.C., U.S.	182	35.04 N	77.21 W
Trenton, Ohio, U.S.	208	39.29 N	84.28 W
Trenton, Tenn., U.S.	184	35.59 N	88.56 W
Trenton, Tex., U.S.	186	33.26 N	96.20 W
Trenton Channel ≃[1]	271	42.06 N	83.11 W
Trentwood	192	47.42 N	117.13 W
Trepalade	58	45.34 N	12.24 E
Trepassey	176	46.44 N	53.22 W
Trepassey Bay ⊂	176	46.40 N	52.20 W
Treptow ⬥[8]	50	52.29 N	13.29 E
Treptow an der Rega → Trzebiatów	30	54.04 N	15.14 E
Trepuzzi	36	40.24 N	18.05 E
Trequanda	60	43.11 N	11.40 E
Tresa ≃	54	46.00 N	8.43 E
Tres Algarrobos	242	35.12 S	62.46 W
Tres Árboles	242	32.24 S	56.43 W
Tres Arroyos	242	38.23 S	60.17 W
Tres Cerros	244	48.13 S	67.33 W
Treščevo	72	54.11 N	37.55 E
Tresckow	200	40.55 N	75.58 W
Três Corações	246	21.42 S	45.16 W
Trescore Balneario	56	45.41 N	9.50 E
Três Coroas	242	29.32 S	50.48 W
Tres de Febrero → Caseros	248	34.36 S	58.33 W
Tres de Febrero □[5]	278	34.36 S	58.35 W
3 de Febrero, Parque ♠	278	34.34 S	58.25 W
Três de Maio	242	27.47 S	54.14 W
Tresenda	58	46.10 N	10.05 E
Tres Esquinas	236	0.43 N	75.16 W
Três Fronteiras	245	20.13 S	50.55 W
Três Ilhas	246	22.04 S	43.29 W
Tresinaro ≃	58	44.39 N	10.47 E
Tres Isletas	242	26.21 S	60.26 W
Treskino	70	52.40 N	44.40 E
Três Lagoas	245	20.48 S	51.43 W
Tres Lagos	244	49.37 S	71.30 W
Tres Marías, Islas II	224	21.25 N	106.28 W
Três Marias, Represa ⊜[1]	245	18.12 S	45.15 W
Tres Montes, Golfo ⊂	244	46.54 S	75.00 W
Tres Montes, Península ≻[1]	244	46.50 S	75.30 W
Tres Montosas ∧	190	34.06 N	107.28 W
Tres Palacio ≃	186	28.45 N	96.09 W
Três Passos	242	27.27 S	53.56 W
Tres Picos	224	15.52 N	93.32 W
Tres Picos, Cerro ∧, Arg.	242	38.09 S	61.57 W
Tres Picos, Cerro ∧, Méx.	224	16.36 N	94.13 W
Tres Pinos	216	36.48 N	121.19 W
Tres Pinos Creek ≃	216	36.47 N	121.21 W
Três Pontas	246	21.22 S	45.31 W
Três Pontas, Cabo das ≻	142	10.23 S	13.32 E
Tres Puntas, Cabo ≻	244	47.06 S	65.53 W
Três Ranchos	245	18.22 S	47.47 W
Tres Reyes Islands II	106	13.14 N	121.51 E
Três Rios, Bra.	246	22.07 S	43.12 W
Tres Ríos, C.R.	226	9.54 N	83.58 W
Tressancourt	251	48.55 N	2.00 E
Třešť	30	49.18 N	15.30 E
Tres Valles	224	18.15 N	96.08 W
Tres Zapotes ⊥	224	18.28 N	95.24 W
Tret'akovskaja Galereja ʋ	255b	55.45 N	37.37 E
Tretet	104	4.40 N	96.51 E
Trets	56	43.27 N	5.41 E
Tretten	26	61.19 N	10.19 E
Treuburg → Olecko	30	54.03 N	22.30 E
Treuchtlingen	52	48.57 N	10.54 E
Treuen	50	50.32 N	12.18 E
Treuenbrietzen	50	52.06 N	12.52 E
Treuhandgebiet Pazifische Inseln → Pacific Islands Trust Territory □[2]	14	10.00 N	155.00 E
Trevelín	244	43.04 S	71.28 W
Trèves → Trier	52	49.45 N	6.38 E
Trevi	60	42.52 N	12.45 E
Treviglio	56	45.31 N	9.35 E
Trevignano Romano	60	42.09 N	12.15 E
Treviño	34	42.44 N	2.45 W
Treviso	58	45.40 N	12.15 E

ENGLISH / DEUTSCH

Name / Name	Page / Seite	Lat.°′ / Breite°′	Long.°′ / Länge°′ E=Ost
Treviso □[4]	58	45.50 N	12.13 E
Trevor	206	42.31 N	88.07 W
Trevorton	198	40.47 N	76.41 W
Trevose	198	40.09 N	74.59 W
Trevose Head ≻	44	50.33 N	5.01 W
Trévoux	54	45.56 N	4.46 E
Trexlertown	198	40.33 N	75.36 W
Treysa	52	50.55 N	9.11 E
Treze Quedas ⌊	240	0.07 N	56.55 W
Trezevant	184	36.01 N	88.37 W
Trezzano	256b	45.25 N	9.04 E
Trezzo sull'Adda	56	45.36 N	9.31 E
Trgovište	38	42.21 N	22.05 E
Trhové Sviny	30	48.51 N	14.39 E
Triabunna	156	42.30 S	147.55 E
Triadelphia Reservoir ⊜[1]	198	39.13 N	77.01 W
Trialeti	74	41.33 N	44.07 E
Trialetskij Chrebet ∧∧	74	41.45 N	43.50 E
Triana	60	42.47 N	11.33 E
Triánda	38	36.24 N	28.10 E
Triangle, Eng., U.K.	252	53.42 N	1.56 W
Triangle, Va., U.S.	198	38.33 N	77.20 W
Triangle Lake	200	42.32 N	74.13 W
Triaucourt-en-Argonne	52	48.59 N	5.04 E
Tribeni	116	22.59 N	88.24 E
Triberg	54	48.08 N	8.13 E
Tribes Hill	200	42.57 N	74.17 W
Tribobó	277a	22.52 S	43.01 W
Triborough Bridge ⬥[5]	266	40.47 N	73.55 W
Tri Brata, Porog ⌊	76	57.25 N	95.39 E
Tribsees	50	54.05 N	12.45 E
Tribune, Sask., Can.	174	49.15 N	103.50 W
Tribune, Kans., U.S.	188	38.28 N	101.45 W
Tribune Channel ⊔	172	50.50 N	126.16 W
Tribuswinkel	254b	48.00 N	16.16 E
Tricao Malal	242	37.03 S	70.19 W
Tricarico	36	40.37 N	16.09 E
Tricase	36	39.56 N	18.22 E
Tricesimo	58	46.10 N	13.13 E
Trichardt	148	26.28 S	29.13 E
Trichiana	58	46.05 N	12.07 E
Trichinopoly → Tiruchchirāppalli	112	10.49 N	78.41 E
Trichūr	112	10.31 N	76.13 E
Tri Cities	212	32.09 N	95.56 W
Tricot	46	49.34 N	2.35 E
Tri County Supply Canal ⩧	188	40.49 N	100.06 W
Trida	156	33.01 S	145.01 E
Trident Peak ∧	194	41.54 N	118.25 W
Triduby	68	48.06 N	30.24 E
Trieben	30	47.29 N	14.30 E
Triebes	50	50.41 N	12.01 E
Triel-sur-Seine	251	48.59 N	2.00 E
Trient → Trento	58	46.04 N	11.08 E
Triepkendorf	50	53.17 N	13.20 E
Trier	52	49.45 N	6.38 E
Trier □[5]	52	50.00 N	6.40 E
Triesen	54	47.06 N	9.31 E
Trieste (Triest)	58	45.40 N	13.46 E
Trieste □[4]	58	45.30 N	13.50 E
Trieste, Gulf of ⊂	58	45.40 N	13.35 E
Trieste Depth ⊹[1]	14	11.21 N	142.12 E
Triesting ≃	254b	48.05 N	16.24 E
Trieux	52	49.20 N	5.56 E
Trigal	238	18.17 S	64.08 W
Triglav ∧	58	46.23 N	13.50 E
Triglitz	50	53.12 N	12.05 E
Trigno ≃	60	42.04 N	14.48 E
Trigo Mountains ∧∧	190	33.15 N	114.35 W
Trigueros	34	37.23 N	6.50 W
Trijangul'atoroje, Pik ∧	78	53.45 N	97.00 E
Tríkala	38	39.34 N	21.46 E
Trikhonís, Límni ⊜	38	38.34 N	21.28 E
Tríkomon	120	35.17 N	33.52 E
Trikora, Puncak (Wilhelmina Peak) ∧	154	4.15 S	138.45 E
Tri Lakes	206	41.15 N	85.27 W
Trilbardou	251	48.57 N	2.48 E
Trilby	210	28.28 N	82.12 W
Trilesy	68	49.59 N	29.50 E
Trilport	46	48.57 N	2.57 E
Trim	28	53.34 N	6.47 W
Triman	110	29.38 N	69.05 E
Trimbach	54	47.22 N	7.54 E
Trimble □[6]	208	38.37 N	85.20 W
Trim Creek ≃	206	41.10 N	87.38 W
Trimonte	246	21.43 S	42.35 W
Trin	54	46.50 N	9.22 E
Trinchera Creek ≃	190	37.19 N	105.45 W
Trincheras, Méx.	186	25.37 N	101.55 W
Trincheras, Méx.	222	30.24 N	111.32 W
Trincomalee	112	8.34 N	81.14 E
Trincomali Channel ⊔	214	48.02 N	123.30 W
Trindade	245	16.40 S	49.30 W
Trindade I	234	20.31 S	29.19 W
Třinec	30	49.41 N	18.40 E
Tring	44	51.48 N	0.40 W
Trinidad, Bol.	238	14.47 S	64.47 W
Trinidad, Col.	236	5.25 N	71.40 W
Trinidad, Cuba	230p	21.48 N	79.59 W
Trinidad, Hond.	226	14.57 N	88.45 W
Trinidad, Para.	242	27.07 S	55.47 W
Trinidad, Colo., U.S.	188	37.10 N	104.31 W
Trinidad, Tex., U.S.	212	32.09 N	96.06 W
Trinidad, Ur.	242	33.32 S	56.54 W
Trinidad I	231r	10.30 N	61.15 W
Trinidad, Golfo ⊂	244	49.55 S	75.25 W
Trinidad, Isla I	242	39.08 S	61.58 W
Trinidad, Río la ≃	224	17.49 N	95.09 W
Trinidad, Sierra de ∧∧	230p	21.56 N	80.00 W
Trinidad and Tobago □[1]	220		
	231r	11.00 N	61.00 W
Trinità	56	44.30 N	7.45 E
Trinitaria	222	16.07 N	92.03 W
Trinité, Havre de la ⊂	230e	14.44 N	60.58 W
Trinity, Newf., Can.	176	48.59 N	53.55 W
Trinity, Tex., U.S.	212	30.57 N	95.22 W
Trinity □[6]	212	31.07 N	95.10 W
Trinity ≃, Calif., U.S.	194	41.11 N	123.42 W
Trinity ≃, Tex., U.S.	212	29.47 N	94.42 W
Trinity, Clear Fork ≃	186	32.46 N	97.21 W
Trinity, East Fork ≃	212	32.30 N	96.30 W
Trinity, Elm Fork ≃	212	32.47 N	96.54 W
Trinity, South Fork ≃	194	40.54 N	123.35 W
Trinity, West Fork ≃	186	32.48 N	96.51 W
Trinity Bay ⊂, Newf., Can.	176	48.00 N	53.40 W
Trinity Bay ⊂, Tex., U.S.	212	29.40 N	94.45 W
Trinity Islands II	170	56.33 N	154.25 W
Trinity Mountain ∧	192	43.36 N	115.26 W
Trinity Mountains ∧∧	194	41.00 N	122.30 W
Trinity Park ♠	265b	43.39 N	79.25 W
Trinity Peak ∧	194	40.14 N	118.45 W
Trinkat Island I	100	8.05 N	93.30 E
Trinkitat	130	18.41 N	37.43 E
Trino	56	45.12 N	8.18 E
Trins	58	47.05 N	11.25 E
Trinway	204	40.09 N	82.01 W
Triolet	147c	20.03 S	57.32 E
Triolo ≃	60	41.40 N	15.34 E
Trion	182	34.33 N	85.19 W
Triora	56	43.59 N	7.46 E
Triplett Creek ≃	208	38.10 N	83.27 W
Triplett Creek, North Fork ≃	208	38.10 N	83.31 W
Tripoli → Ţarābulus, Lībīya	136	32.54 N	13.11 E
Tripoli → Ţarābulus, Lubnān	120	34.26 N	35.51 E
Tripoli, Iowa, U.S.	180	42.48 N	92.16 W
Trípolis, Ellás	38	37.31 N	22.21 E
Tripolis → Ţarābulus, Lībīya	136	32.54 N	13.11 E
Tripolitania → Ţarābulus □[4]	136	31.00 N	15.00 E
Tripolitania → Ţarābulus ⬥[1]	136	31.00 N	15.00 E
Tripolje	68	50.07 N	30.46 E
Triponzo	60	42.50 N	12.56 E
Tripp	188	43.13 N	97.58 W
Trips Subdivision	271	42.34 N	83.25 W
Triptis	50	50.44 N	11.52 E
Tripura □[4]	110	24.00 N	92.00 E
Trisanna ≃	54	47.07 N	10.30 E
Tristan da Cunha Group II	10	37.15 S	12.30 W
Tristan Island I	10	37.05 S	12.17 W
Tristán Suárez	248	34.53 S	58.34 W
Tristao, Îles II	140	10.53 N	14.58 W
Tristate Village	268	41.44 N	87.57 W
Triste	34	42.23 N	0.43 W
Triste, Golfo ⊂	236	10.40 N	68.10 W
Trisūli ≃	114	27.49 N	84.47 E
Tri-ton	100	10.25 N	105.00 E
Triton Island I	98	15.47 N	111.12 E
Tritriva	147b	22.46 S	46.07 E
Trittau	48	53.37 N	10.25 E
Trittenheim	52	49.49 N	6.54 E
Triuggio	256b	45.40 N	9.16 E
Triumph	184	29.20 N	89.30 W
Triunfo	240	7.50 S	38.07 W
Triunfo, Igarapé ≃	240	6.22 S	52.25 W
Triunfo de Madero	224	16.52 N	93.48 W
Trivandrum	112	8.29 N	76.55 E
Trivento	60	41.47 N	14.33 E
Trivero	56	45.40 N	8.10 E
Trnava	30	48.23 N	17.35 E
Trnovo → Veliko Târnovo	38	43.04 N	25.39 E
Troarn	32	49.11 N	0.11 W
Trobriand Island I	154	8.35 S	151.05 E
Trobriand Islands II	154	8.35 S	151.05 E
Tr'ochgolovyj Golec, Gora ∧	78	53.22 N	107.03 E
Tr'ochizbenka	73	48.45 N	38.58 E
Tr'ochsv'atskoje	72	56.29 N	37.03 E
Trochtelfingen	54	48.18 N	9.14 E
Trochu	172	51.50 N	113.13 W
Troense	41	55.02 N	10.39 E
Trofa, Arroyo de ≃	256a	40.30 N	3.45 W
Trofarello	56	44.59 N	7.44 E
Trögd ≻[1]	40	59.31 N	17.15 E
Trogen	54	47.24 N	9.28 E
Trogir	36	43.31 N	16.15 E
Troglav ∧	36	43.57 N	16.36 E
Tröglitz	50	51.04 N	12.11 E
Troia	60	41.22 N	15.18 E
Troica	70	54.24 N	40.14 E
Troice-Lykovo ⬥[8]	255b	55.47 N	37.24 E
Troick, S.S.S.R.	76	54.06 N	61.35 E
Troick, S.S.S.R.	78	57.25 N	94.50 E
Troickaja	68	45.08 N	38.07 E
Troickij, S.S.S.R.	70	50.14 N	43.05 E
Troickij, S.S.S.R.	76	57.03 N	63.43 E
Troickij, S.S.S.R.	76	50.41 N	54.38 E
Troickij, S.S.S.R.	78	54.36 N	113.09 E
Troickije Rosl'ai	70	53.21 N	41.24 E
Troickij Sungur	70	53.17 N	47.37 E
Troickij Zavod	78	53.27 N	102.09 E
Troicko-Charcyzsk	73	47.58 N	38.16 E
Troickoje, S.S.S.R.	68	51.17 N	41.28 E
Troickoje, S.S.S.R.	68	49.55 N	38.19 E
Troickoje, S.S.S.R.	68	47.38 N	30.19 E
Troickoje, S.S.S.R.	70	53.22 N	48.23 E
Troickoje, S.S.S.R.	70	46.26 N	44.15 E
Troickoje, S.S.S.R.	70	53.06 N	52.32 E
Troickoje, S.S.S.R.	70	53.23 N	52.48 E
Troickoje, S.S.S.R.	72	54.52 N	37.07 E
Troickoje, S.S.S.R.	72	55.23 N	37.25 E
Troickoje, S.S.S.R.	73	47.22 N	38.53 E
Troickoje, S.S.S.R.	73	48.32 N	38.23 E
Troickoje, S.S.S.R.	76	52.19 N	56.23 E
Troickoje, S.S.S.R.	76	59.07 N	58.25 E
Troickoje, S.S.S.R.	76	52.58 N	84.40 E
Troickoje, S.S.S.R.	79	49.27 N	136.36 E
Troicko-Pečorsk	24	62.44 N	56.06 E
Troina	36	37.47 N	14.37 E
Troisdorf	52	50.49 N	7.08 E
Trois Fourches, Cap des ≻	138	35.26 N	2.58 W
Trois-Îlets	230e	14.32 N	61.02 W
Trois-Montagnes, Lac des ⊜	196	46.10 N	74.45 W
Trois Pitons, Morne ∧	230d	15.22 N	61.20 W
Trois Ponts	52	50.22 N	5.52 E
Trois-Rivières, Qué., Can.	196	46.21 N	72.33 W
Trois-Rivières, Guad.	231o	15.59 N	61.39 W
Troisvierges	52	50.08 N	6.00 E
Trojan	38	42.51 N	24.43 E
Trojanov	68	50.07 N	28.31 E
Trojanova Tabla ⊥	38	44.37 N	22.20 E
Trojanovka	68	51.20 N	25.17 E
Trojanski prohod)(	38	42.47 N	24.37 E
Trojebratskij	76	54.28 N	66.01 E
Trojekurovo, S.S.S.R.	66	53.25 N	39.43 E
Trojekurovo, S.S.S.R.	66	53.00 N	38.58 E
Troldhede	41	55.59 N	8.45 E
Trolleholm	41	55.54 N	13.15 E
Trollhättan	26	58.16 N	12.18 E
Trollheimen ∧	26	62.51 N	9.05 E
Tromba Grande, Cabo ≻	245	14.18 S	38.58 W
Trombay ⬥[8]	262c	19.02 N	72.57 E
Trombetas ≃	240	1.55 S	55.35 W
Trombudo Central	242	27.18 S	49.47 W
Tromelin I	128	15.52 S	54.25 E
Tromello	56	45.12 N	8.52 E
Tromper Wiek ⊂	50	54.37 N	13.24 E
Trompia, Val ∨	58	45.44 N	10.12 E
Trompsburg	148	30.01 S	25.46 E
Troms □[6]	24	69.15 N	19.40 E
Tromsø	24	69.40 N	18.58 E
Trona	194	35.45 N	117.23 W
Tronador, Monte ∧	244	41.10 S	71.54 W
Trondheim	26	63.25 N	10.25 E
Trondheimsfjorden ⊂[2]	26	63.39 N	10.49 E
Trondheimsleia ⊔	26	63.30 N	9.00 E
Tronto ≃	60	42.54 N	13.55 E
Tronville-en-Barrois	52	48.43 N	5.17 E
Tronzano Vercellese	56	45.21 N	8.10 E
Troo	46	47.47 N	0.47 E
Troödos	120	34.55 N	32.53 E
Trooilapspan	148	28.40 S	21.25 E
Troon	42	55.32 N	4.40 W
Trooper	275	40.09 N	75.24 W
Troparevo	72	55.23 N	35.54 E
Tropar'ovo ⬥[8]	255b	55.39 N	37.29 E
Tropas, Rio das ≃	240	6.07 S	57.28 W
Tropea	36	38.41 N	15.54 E
Trophy Mountain ∧	172	51.47 N	119.48 W
Tropic	190	37.37 N	112.05 W
Tropojë	38	42.24 N	20.10 E
Troppau → Opava	30	49.56 N	17.54 E
Trosa	40	58.54 N	17.33 E
Troškovo	70	57.19 N	46.05 E
Troškūnai	66	55.36 N	24.51 E
Trosna	66	52.26 N	35.46 E
Trossingen	54	48.04 N	8.38 E
Trostan ∧	42	55.03 N	6.09 W
Trost'anec, S.S.S.R.	68	50.28 N	34.59 E

Symbols in the index entries represent the broad categories identified in the key at the right. Symbols with superior numbers (∧∧[2]) identify subcategories (see complete key on page *I* · 26).

Kartensymbole in dem Registerverzeichnis stellen die rechts in Schlüssel erklärten Kategorien dar. Symbole mit hochgestellten Ziffern (∧∧[2]) bezeichnen Unterabteilungen einer Kategorie (vgl. vollständiger Schlüssel auf Seite *I* · 26).

Los símbolos incluídos en el texto del índice representan las grandes categorias identificadas con la clave a la derecha. Los símbolos con numeros en su parte superior (∧∧[2]) identifican las subcategorías (véase la clave completa en la página *I* · 26).

Les symboles de l'index représentent les catégories indiquées dans la légende à droite. Les symboles suivis d'un indice (∧∧[2]) représentent des sous-catégories (voir légende complète à la page *I* · 26).

Os símbolos incluídos no texto do índice representam as grandes categorias identificadas com a chave à direita. Os símbolos com números em sua parte superior (∧∧[2]) identificam as subcategorias (veja-se a chave completa à página *I* · 26).

∧ Mountain	Berg	Montaña	Montagne	Montanha
∧∧ Mountains	Berge	Montañas	Montagnes	Montanhas
)(Pass	Pass	Paso	Col	Passo
∨ Valley, Canyon	Tal, Cañon	Valle, Cañón	Vallée, Canyon	Vale, Canhão
≚ Plain	Ebene	Llano	Plaine	Planície
≻ Cape	Kap	Cabo	Cap	Cabo
I Island	Insel	Isla	Île	Ilha
II Islands	Inseln	Islas	Îles	Ilhas
⊥ Other Topographic Features	Andere Topographische Objekte	Otros Elementos Topográficos	Autres données topographiques	Outros Elementos Topográficos

ESPAÑOL Nombre / FRANÇAIS Nom / PORTUGUÊS Nome	Página / Page	Lat.°'	Long.°' W=Oeste / W=Ouest
Trost'anec, S.S.S.R.	68	48.31 N	29.12 E
Trostberg	58	48.01 N	12.32 E
Trostenskoje Ozero ⊜	72	55.52 N	36.29 E
Trotha ✦[8]	50	51.31 N	11.58 E
Trottiscliffe	250	51.19 N	0.21 E
Trotus ≃	38	46.03 N	27.14 E
Trotwood	208	39.48 N	84.18 W
Troublesome Creek ≃, Ky., U.S.	182	37.29 N	83.21 W
Troublesome Creek ≃, Mo., U.S.	209	39.54 N	91.37 W
Troubridge Point ≻	158b	35.11 S	137.41 E
Trou-du-Nord	228	19.38 N	72.01 W
Troumasse C	231f	13.49 N	60.54 W
Troup	212	32.09 N	95.07 W
Troupsburg	200	42.03 N	77.33 W
Trout	184	31.42 N	92.11 W
Trout ≃, N.W. Ter., Can.	166	61.19 N	119.51 W
Trout ≃, N.A.	196	45.05 N	74.10 W
Trout Brook ≃, Mass., U.S.	273	42.16 N	71.18 W
Trout Brook ≃, Mass., U.S.	273	42.39 N	71.16 W
Trout Creek, Mich., U.S.	180	46.28 N	89.01 W
Trout Creek, N.Y., U.S.	200	42.12 N	75.17 W
Trout Creek ≃, Ariz., U.S.	190	34.56 N	113.36 W
Trout Creek ≃, Oreg., U.S.	192	44.48 N	121.03 W
Trout Creek ≃, Oreg., U.S.	192	42.23 N	118.36 W
Trout Creek ≃, Pa., U.S.	275	40.07 N	75.24 W
Trout Creek ≃, Wash., U.S.	214	46.02 N	121.12 W
Trout Creek Pass)(	190	38.54 N	105.58 W
Troutdale	214	45.32 N	116.23 W
Trout Lake	214	46.00 N	121.32 W
Trout Lake ⊜, B.C., Can.	172	50.35 N	117.26 W
Trout Lake ⊜, N.W. Ter., Can.	166	60.35 N	121.10 W
Trout Lake ⊜, Ont., Can.	174	51.13 N	93.20 W
Trout Lake ⊜, Ont., Can.	180	46.18 N	79.20 W
Trout Lake ⊜, Ont., Can.	180	46.13 N	80.35 W
Trout Lake Creek ≃	214	46.00 N	121.30 W
Trout Peak ∧	192	44.36 N	109.32 W
Trout River	176	49.29 N	58.08 W
Trout Run	200	41.23 N	77.03 W
Troutville, Pa., U.S.	204	41.02 N	78.47 W
Troutville, Va., U.S.	182	37.25 N	79.53 W
Trouville-sur-Mer	46	49.22 N	0.05 E
Trowbridge	44	51.20 N	2.13 W
Troxelville	200	40.48 N	77.12 W
Troy, Ala., U.S.	184	31.48 N	85.58 W
Troy, Idaho, U.S.	192	46.44 N	116.46 W
Troy, Ill., U.S.	209	38.44 N	89.53 W
Troy, Kans., U.S.	188	39.47 N	95.05 W
Troy, Mich., U.S.	204	42.36 N	83.09 W
Troy, Mo., U.S.	209	38.59 N	90.59 W
Troy, Mont., U.S.	192	48.28 N	115.53 W
Troy, N.H., U.S.	178	42.50 N	72.11 W
Troy, N.C., U.S.	182	35.22 N	79.53 W
Troy, N.Y., U.S.	200	42.43 N	73.40 W
Troy, Ohio, U.S.	208	40.02 N	84.13 W
Troy, Pa., U.S.	200	41.47 N	76.47 W
Troy, Tenn., U.S.	194	36.20 N	89.10 W
Troy ⊥	120	39.57 N	26.15 E
Troy Brook ≃	266	40.50 N	74.22 W
Troyes	46	48.18 N	4.05 E
Troy Grove	206	41.28 N	89.05 W
Troy Hills	200	40.51 N	74.23 W
Troy Lake ⊜	194	34.49 N	116.33 W
Troy Meadows ☵	266	40.50 N	74.22 W
Troy Peak ∧	194	38.19 N	115.30 W
Troyville ✦[8]	263d	26.12 S	28.04 E
Trpanj	36	43.00 N	17.17 E
Trst → Trieste	58	45.40 N	13.46 E
Trstená	30	49.22 N	19.37 E
Trstenik	38	43.37 N	21.00 E
Truax	174	49.55 N	104.58 W
Trubč'ovsk	66	52.37 N	33.44 E
Trubetčino	66	52.53 N	39.33 E
Trubino, S.S.S.R.	72	55.59 N	38.08 E
Trubino, S.S.S.R.	72	54.58 N	36.42 E
Trub'ož ≃	72	56.44 N	38.51 E
Truc-giang	100	10.14 N	106.23 E
Truchas	190	36.03 N	105.49 W
Truchas Peak ∧	190	35.58 N	105.39 W
Truchtersheim	54	48.40 N	7.36 E
Trucial States → United Arab Emirates □[1]	118	24.00 N	54.00 E
Truckee	216	39.20 N	120.11 W
Truckee ≃	194	39.51 N	119.24 W
Trucksville	200	41.18 N	75.56 W
Trud	66	57.37 N	33.58 E
Trudfront	70	45.56 N	47.41 E
Trudnovo	76	56.39 N	91.30 E
Trudovaja	73	48.21 N	38.04 E
Trudovoj, S.S.S.R.	70	51.42 N	52.43 E
Trudovoj, S.S.S.R.	76	53.15 N	66.51 E
Trues Creek ≃	266	40.41 N	73.17 W
Truganina	264b	37.49 S	144.43 E
Truite, Lac à la ⊜	180	47.16 N	78.17 W
Trujillo, Col.	236	4.10 N	76.19 W
Trujillo, Esp.	34	39.28 N	5.53 W
Trujillo, Hond.	226	15.55 N	86.00 W
Trujillo, Perú	238	8.07 S	79.02 W
Trujillo, Ven.	236	9.22 N	70.26 W
Trujillo □[3]	236	9.25 N	70.30 W
Trujillo ≃	224	23.39 N	103.08 W
Trujillo Alto	230m	18.22 N	66.01 W
Truk □[5]	165c	7.28 N	151.50 E
Truk Islands II	165c	7.25 N	151.47 E
Trull Brook ≃	273	42.39 N	71.15 W
Truman	188	43.50 N	94.26 W
Trumann	184	35.41 N	90.31 W
Trumansburg	200	42.33 N	76.40 W
Trumbauersville	198	40.25 N	75.23 W
Trumbull	197	41.15 N	73.12 W
Trumbull □[6]	204	41.14 N	80.52 W
Trumbull, Mount ∧	190	36.25 N	113.10 W
Trumon	104	2.49 N	97.38 E
Trun, Fr.	46	48.51 N	0.02 E
Trun, Schw.	54	46.45 N	8.58 E
Trundle	156	32.55 S	147.43 E
Trung-luong	100	13.57 N	109.15 E
Trunovskoje	70	45.29 N	42.08 E
Truro, Austl.	158b	34.25 S	139.07 E
Truro, N.S., Can.	176	45.22 N	63.16 W
Truro, Eng., U.K.	44	50.16 N	5.03 W
Truro, Mass., U.S.	197	42.00 N	70.03 W
Trusan ≃	102	4.58 N	115.11 E
Truscott	186	33.45 N	99.49 W
Trušeny	68	47.04 N	28.41 E
Trușești	38	47.46 N	27.01 E
Trusetal	50	50.47 N	10.25 E
Truskavec	68	49.16 N	23.33 E
Truslejka	70	53.54 N	46.24 E
Truth or Consequences (Hot Springs)	190	33.08 N	107.15 W
Trutnov	30	50.34 N	15.55 E
Truxall	269b	40.33 N	79.33 W
Truxton, Mo., U.S.	209	39.00 N	91.14 W
Truxton, N.Y., U.S.	200	42.43 N	76.02 W
Truxton Wash ∨	190	35.38 N	114.04 W
Truyère ≃	32	44.39 N	2.34 E
Trwyn Cilan ≻	44	52.46 N	4.30 W
Tryon, Nebr., U.S.	188	41.33 N	100.57 W
Tryon, N.C., U.S.	182	35.13 N	82.14 W
Tryonville	204	41.42 N	79.47 W
Trysil	26	61.19 N	12.16 E
Trysilelva (Klarälven) ≃	26	59.23 N	13.32 E
Tryškiai	66	56.04 N	22.35 E
Tryweryn ≃	44	52.24 N	3.35 W
Trzcianka	30	53.03 N	16.28 E
Trzciel	30	52.23 N	15.52 E
Trzcinsko-Zdrój	30	52.58 N	14.35 E
Trzebiatów	30	54.04 N	15.14 E
Trzebiel	30	51.37 N	14.50 E
Trzebież	30	53.42 N	14.31 E
Trzebinia	30	50.10 N	19.18 E
Trzebnica	30	51.19 N	17.03 E
Trzemeszno	30	52.35 N	17.50 E
Trzęsacz	50	54.05 N	14.58 E
Tržič	36	46.22 N	14.19 E
Tsacha Lake ⊜	172	53.05 N	124.40 W
Tsala Apopka Lake ⊜	210	28.52 N	82.20 W
Tsamkong → Zhanjiang	92	21.16 N	110.28 E
Tsangano	144	15.08 S	34.32 E
Ts'anghsien → Cangzhou	88	38.19 N	116.51 E
T'sangwu → Wuzhou	92	23.30 N	111.27 E
Ts'aot'un	90	23.59 N	120.40 E
Tsarabaria	147b	13.46 S	49.58 E
Tsaramandroso	147b	16.22 S	47.02 E
Tsaratanana	147b	16.47 S	47.39 E
Tsaratanana, Massif du ∧	147b	14.00 S	49.00 E
Tsaraxaibis	148	27.25 S	19.22 E
Tsaritsyn → Volgograd	70	48.44 N	44.25 E
Tsau	146	20.12 S	22.22 E
Tsaukaib	146	26.37 S	15.31 E
Tsavo	144	2.59 S	38.28 E
Tsavo National Park ♠	144	3.00 S	38.40 E
Tsawwassen	214	49.01 N	123.06 W
Tsaydaychuz Peak ∧	172	53.02 N	126.35 W
Tschad → Chad □[1]	136	15.00 N	19.00 E
Tschad-See → Chad, Lake ⊜	136	13.20 N	14.00 E
Tschagguns	54	47.05 N	9.54 E
Tschamut	54	46.40 N	8.42 E
Tschangscha → Changsha	90	28.11 N	113.01 E
Tschangtschun → Changchun	79	43.53 N	125.19 E
Tschechoslowakei → Czechoslovakia □[1]	30	49.30 N	17.00 E
Tscheljuskin, Kap → Čel'uskin, Mys ≻	64	77.45 N	104.20 E
Tschengtu → Chengdu	97	30.39 N	104.04 E
Tschenstochau → Częstochowa	30	50.49 N	19.06 E
Tschernitz	50	51.35 N	14.37 E
Tscheschskaja-Bucht → Češskaja Guba C	24	67.30 N	46.30 E
Tschida, Lake ⊜[1]	188	46.36 N	101.54 W
Tschingtau → Qingdao	88	36.06 N	120.19 E
Tschittagong → Chittagong	110	22.20 N	91.50 E
Tschuktschen-Meer → Chukchi Sea ⫧[2]	16	69.00 N	171.00 W
Tschungking → Chongqing	97	29.39 N	106.34 E
Tščikskoje Vodochranilišče ⊜[1]	68	45.06 N	39.31 E
Tsekanyani	146	19.52 S	26.39 E
Tsembeyi	148	31.36 S	27.03 E
Ts'engwen Ch'i ≃	90	23.04 N	120.04 E
Tsenke ≃	263b	4.24 S	15.26 E
Tses	146	25.58 S	18.08 E
Tsethang → Zedang	110	29.16 N	91.46 E
Tsévié	140	6.25 N	1.13 E
Tshabong	146	26.03 S	22.29 E
Tshabuta	142	7.47 S	23.16 E
Tshandi	146	17.42 S	14.50 E
Tshane	146	24.05 S	21.54 E
Tshaneni	148	26.00 S	31.47 E
Tshangalele, Lac ⊜	144	10.55 S	27.03 E
Tshela	142	4.59 S	12.56 E
Tshesebe	146	21.51 S	27.35 E
Tshibeke	144	2.44 S	28.36 E
Tshibinda	144	2.19 S	28.45 E
Tshibomba	142	9.02 S	22.34 E
Tshidilamolomo	146	25.50 S	24.41 E
Tshikapa	142	6.25 S	20.48 E
Tshilenge	142	6.15 S	23.46 E
Tshimbulu	142	6.29 S	22.51 E
Tshimhaka	142	17.20 S	13.51 E
Tshindjamba	142	10.54 S	22.41 E
Tshinota	142	7.01 S	20.57 E
Tshinsenda	144	12.18 S	27.58 E
Tshisuku	142	6.26 S	19.55 E
Tshitadi	142	6.45 S	21.45 E
Tshoa	142	5.34 S	12.41 E
Tshofa	144	5.14 S	25.15 E
Tshopo ≃	144	0.33 N	25.07 E
Tshougu ≃	263b	4.25 S	15.23 E
Tshuapa ≃	142	0.14 S	20.42 E
Tshukudu	146	22.30 S	23.22 E
Tshumbiri	142	2.39 S	16.14 E
Tshwaane	146	22.29 S	22.03 E
Tsiafajavona ∧	147b	19.21 S	47.15 E
Tsiama ≃	263b	4.15 S	15.18 E
Tsianaloka	147b	18.08 S	44.50 E
Tsigara	146	20.10 S	25.18 E
Tsihombe	147b	25.18 S	45.29 E
Tsilmamo	134	6.01 N	35.17 E
Tsimanampetsotsa, Lac ⊜	147b	24.08 S	43.46 E
Tsimilofo	147b	24.59 S	45.10 E
Tsimpsean Indian Reserve ✦[4]	172	54.30 N	130.22 W
Tsinan → Jinan	88	36.40 N	116.57 E
Tsineng	148	27.06 S	23.04 E
Tsinghai → Qinghai □[4]	80	36.00 N	96.00 E
Tsing Island I	261d	22.21 N	114.05 E
Tsingkiang → Huaiyin	90	33.35 N	119.02 E
Tsingtao → Qingdao	88	36.06 N	120.19 E
Tsingyuan → Baoding	95	38.52 N	115.29 E
Tsinh-ho	100	22.22 N	103.14 E
Tsining → Jining	88	35.25 N	116.36 E
Tsinjoarivo	147b	19.37 S	47.40 E
Tsinjomitondraka	147b	15.36 S	47.08 E
Tsinling Shan → Qinlingshanmai ⋀⋀	92	34.00 N	108.00 E
Tsin Shui Wan C	261d	22.13 N	114.10 E
Tsintsabis	146	18.45 S	17.51 E
Tsiribihina ≃	147b	19.42 S	44.31 E
Tsiroanomandidy	147b	18.46 S	46.02 E
Tsitondroina	147b	21.19 S	46.00 E
Tsitsihar → Qiqihaer	79	47.19 N	123.55 E
Tsitsikama Forest and Coastal National Park ♠	148	34.00 S	23.36 E
Tsitsikammaberge ∧	148	33.54 S	23.42 E
Tsitsutl Peak ∧	172	52.43 N	125.47 W
Tsivory	147b	24.04 S	46.05 E
Tskhinvali → Cchinvali	74	42.13 N	43.56 E
Tsna → Cna ≃	70	54.32 N	42.05 E
Tsobis	146	19.27 S	17.30 E
Tsodilo Hill ∧[2]	146	18.45 S	21.45 E
Tsolo	148	31.18 S	28.37 E
Tsomo	148	32.00 S	27.42 E
Tsomo ≃	148	32.25 S	27.50 E
Tsowkêy	113	34.41 N	70.56 E
Tsoying	90	22.41 N	120.17 E
Tsu	84	34.43 N	136.31 E
Tsubakuro-dake ∧	84	36.24 N	137.42 E
Tsubame	82	37.39 N	138.56 E
Tsubata	84	36.40 N	136.44 E
Tsuboro-suigenchi ⊜	260	34.24 N	135.54 E
Tsuchiura	84	36.05 N	140.12 E
Tsuchiyama	84	34.56 N	136.17 E
Tsuda, Nihon	86	34.17 N	134.15 E
Tsuda, Nihon	260	34.49 N	135.43 E
Tsudaka	86	34.44 N	133.55 E
Tsugaru-hantō ≻[1]	82	41.00 N	140.30 E
Tsugaru-heiya ⌣	82	40.49 N	140.27 E
Tsugaru-kaikyō ʯ	82a	41.35 N	141.00 E
Tsuge	84	34.35 N	135.57 E
Tsugu	84	35.10 N	137.37 E
Tsuha	164m	26.14 N	127.47 E
Tsuiki	86	33.40 N	131.03 E
Tsujidō	258	35.20 N	139.27 E
Tsukahara	258	35.18 N	139.58 E
Tsukechi	84	35.38 N	137.26 E
Tsuken-jima I	164m	26.15 N	127.57 E
Tsukinowa-kofun ⊥	86	34.55 N	134.11 E
Tsukise	84	34.42 N	136.02 E
Tsukiyono	84	36.41 N	138.59 E
Tsukuba	84	36.13 N	140.06 E
Tsukuba-san ∧	84	36.13 N	140.06 E
Tsukude	84	34.59 N	137.25 E
Tsukui	84	35.35 N	139.16 E
Tsukumi	86	33.04 N	131.52 E
Tsukumono ✦[8]	260	34.50 N	135.11 E
Tsukushi-heiya ⋀⋀	86	33.40 N	130.25 E
Tsukushi-sanchi ⋀⋀	86	33.30 N	130.30 E
Tsumagoi	84	36.31 N	138.32 E
Tsumeb	146	19.13 S	17.42 E
Tsumeb □[5]	146	19.00 S	17.30 E
Tsumeki-zaki ≻	84	34.39 N	138.59 E
Tsumis Park	146	23.43 S	17.28 E
Tsuna	86	34.26 N	134.54 E
Tsunan	84	37.01 N	138.39 E
Tsunashima ✦[8]	258	35.32 N	139.38 E
Tsunekami-misaki ≻	84	35.38 N	135.49 E
Tsuni → Zunyi	92	27.39 N	106.57 E
Tsuno-shima I	86	34.12 N	130.58 E
Tsun Wan (Quanwan)	261d	22.22 N	114.07 E
Tsuru	84	35.30 N	138.56 E
Tsuruga	84	35.39 N	136.04 E
Tsurugaoka-hachimangu Shrine ʊ[1]	258	35.19 N	139.33 E
Tsurugashima	258	35.56 N	139.24 E
Tsuruga-wan C	84	35.45 N	136.04 E
Tsurugi	84	36.27 N	136.38 E
Tsurugi-dake ∧	84	36.37 N	137.37 E
Tsurugi-saki ≻	258	35.08 N	139.41 E
Tsurugi-san ∧	86	33.51 N	134.06 E
Tsurugi-san-kokutei-kōen ♠	86	33.50 N	134.06 E
Tsuruhara	260	34.26 N	135.20 E
Tsuruma	258	35.51 N	139.33 E
Tsurumi ✦[8]	258	35.30 N	139.41 E
Tsurumi ≃	84	35.29 N	139.41 E
Tsurumi-dake ∧	86	33.17 N	131.26 E
Tsuruoka	82	38.44 N	139.50 E
Tsushima, Nihon	84	35.10 N	136.43 E
Tsushima, Nihon	86	33.05 N	132.30 E
Tsushima II	82	34.30 N	129.22 E
Tsushima-kaikyō ʯ	82	34.00 N	129.00 E
Tsuwano	86	34.28 N	131.46 E
Tsuyama	86	35.03 N	134.00 E
Tsuyazaki	86	33.47 N	130.28 E
Tu → Tsu	84	34.43 N	136.31 E
Tua	142	3.38 S	16.36 E
Tua ≃	34	41.13 N	7.26 W
Tua, Tanjung ≻	102	5.54 S	105.44 E
Tua-chua	100	21.55 N	103.21 E
Tuakau	162	37.16 S	174.57 E
Tual	154	5.40 S	132.45 E
Tualatin	214	45.23 N	122.46 W
Tualatin ≃	214	45.20 N	122.39 W
Tuam	28	53.31 N	8.50 W
Tuamarina	162	41.26 S	173.57 E
Tuamotu, Îles II	14	19.00 S	142.00 W
Tuan, Tanjong ≻	104	2.23 N	101.52 E
Tuanan	102	2.07 S	114.24 E
Tuanfeng	90	30.38 N	114.51 E
Tuan-giao	100	21.35 N	103.25 E
Tuangku, Pulau I	104	2.10 N	97.18 E
Tuanpi	90	30.44 N	115.13 E
Tuanshan	88	40.02 N	123.34 E
Tuanwang	88	36.45 N	120.38 E
Tuanxi	92	27.26 N	106.54 E
Tuapa	164v	18.57 S	169.54 W
Tuapeka Mouth	162	46.01 S	169.31 E
Tuapse	74	44.07 N	39.05 E
Tuaran	102	6.11 N	116.14 E
Tuas	104	1.19 N	103.38 E
Tuasivi	165a	13.40 S	172.07 W
Tuasivi, Cape ≻	165a	13.40 S	172.07 W
Tuatapere	162	46.08 S	167.41 E
Tuba	78	57.24 N	102.48 E
Tuba ≃	76	53.57 N	91.31 E
Tubac	190	31.37 N	111.03 W
Tuba City	190	36.08 N	111.14 W
T'ub'ak-Čekurča	70	56.05 N	49.56 E
Tubalan Head ≻	106	6.30 N	125.35 E
Tuban	105a	6.54 S	112.03 E
Tubarão	242	28.30 S	49.01 W
Ṭūbās	122	32.19 N	35.22 E
Tubas ≃	146	22.55 S	14.37 E
Tubau	102	3.08 N	113.42 E
Ṭubayq, Jabal aṭ- ⋀⋀	118	29.40 N	37.15 E
Tubbataha Reefs ⟡[2]	106	8.51 N	119.56 E
Tubbergen	48	52.25 N	6.46 E
Tubbs Island I	272	38.08 N	122.26 W
Ṭubhār	132	29.19 N	30.42 E
Tubig ≃	106	11.54 N	125.25 E
Tubigan Island I	106	6.26 N	120.47 E
Tubingantan Point ≻	106	5.54 N	120.55 E
Tübingen	54	48.31 N	9.02 E
Tübingen □[5]	54	48.10 N	9.30 E
Tubinskij	76	52.53 N	58.13 E
Tubize	46	50.41 N	4.12 E
T'ub-Karagan, Mys ≻	74	44.39 N	50.18 E
T'ub-Karagan, Poluostrov ≻[1]	74	44.30 N	50.30 E
Tubli	106	13.56 N	124.09 E
Tubod	106	8.03 N	123.48 E
Tubre	58	46.39 N	10.27 E
Ṭubruq (Tobruk)	136	32.05 N	23.59 E
Tuburan, Pil.	106	10.44 N	123.49 W
Tuburan, Pil.	106	6.39 N	122.16 E
Tubutama	190	30.53 N	111.29 W
Tucacas	236	10.48 N	68.19 W
Tucacas, Punta ≻	236	10.50 N	68.14 W
Tucalota Creek ≃	218	33.32 N	117.10 W
Tucannon ≃	192	46.33 N	118.11 W
Tucano	240	10.58 S	38.48 W
Tucavaca ≃	238	18.37 S	58.59 W
T'uch'ang	90	24.34 N	121.29 E
Tucheim	50	52.17 N	12.11 E
Tüchen	50	53.04 N	12.05 E
T'uch'eng, T'aiwan	259d	24.59 N	121.26 E
Tucheng, Zhg.	88	38.53 N	121.15 E
Tuchengchang	92	28.12 N	105.58 E
Tuchengzi, Zhg.	88	41.20 N	116.29 E
Tuchengzi, Zhg.	88	40.29 N	124.24 E
Tuchengzi, Zhg.	94	42.27 N	122.44 E
Tuchengzicun	94	41.52 N	120.41 E
Tuchengziwuhao	88	40.56 N	113.58 E
Tuchlovice	50	50.06 N	14.00 E
Tuchola	30	53.35 N	17.50 E
Tuchów	30	49.54 N	21.03 E
T'uchtet	76	56.32 N	89.19 E
Tuckahoe, N.J., U.S.	198	39.17 N	74.45 W
Tuckahoe, N.Y., U.S.	197	40.54 N	72.25 W
Tuckahoe, N.Y., U.S.	266	40.57 N	73.50 W
Tuckahoe ≃	198	39.17 N	74.39 W
Tuckahoe Creek ≃	198	38.49 N	75.53 W
Tuckanarra	152	27.07 S	118.05 E
Tucker Heights	200	42.55 N	73.55 W
Tuckerman	184	35.44 N	91.12 W
Tuckernuck Island I	197	41.18 N	70.15 W
Tuckerton, N.J., U.S.	198	39.36 N	74.20 W
Tuckerton, Pa., U.S.	198	40.25 N	75.57 W
Tuckfield, Mount ∧	152	18.44 S	124.54 E
Tučkovo	72	55.36 N	36.28 E
Tucson	190	32.13 N	110.58 W
Tucumã, Paraná ≃[1]	236	3.58 S	66.26 W
Tucumán → San Miguel de Tucumán	242	26.49 S	65.13 W
Tucumán □[4]	242	27.00 S	65.30 W
Tucumcari	186	35.10 N	103.44 W
Tucunaré, Cachoeira do ↳	240	5.20 S	55.50 W
Tucunduva	242	27.39 S	54.27 W
Tucunuco	242	30.36 S	68.38 W
Tucupido	236	9.17 N	65.47 W
Tucupita	236	9.04 N	62.03 W
Tucuruí	240	3.42 S	49.27 W
Tucuruvi ✦[8]	277b	23.28 S	46.35 W
Tuczna	30	51.54 N	23.26 E
Tud ≃	44	52.38 N	1.15 E
Tudameda	102	10.52 S	122.55 E
Tudcum	242	30.14 S	69.15 W
Tude Å ≃	41	55.23 N	11.13 E
Tudela, Esp.	34	42.05 N	1.36 W
Tudela, Pil.	106	8.15 N	123.50 E
Tudela de Duero	34	41.35 N	4.35 W
Tudian	96	30.35 N	120.37 E
Tudichang	97	30.06 N	103.56 E
Tuditang	90	30.12 N	114.18 E
Tudmur (Palmyra)	120	34.33 N	38.17 E
Tudu	66	59.11 N	26.51 E
Tudweiliog	44	52.54 N	4.35 W
Tuela ≃	34	41.30 N	7.12 W
Tuenno	58	46.20 N	11.01 E
Tueré ≃	240	2.48 S	50.59 W
Tuergate	75	40.28 N	75.21 E
Tufānganj	114	26.19 N	89.40 E
Tuffé	46	48.07 N	0.31 E
Tufi	154	9.05 S	149.20 E
Tufo	60	41.00 N	14.47 E
Tufts University ʊ[2]	273	42.24 N	71.07 W
Tufukia	164v	19.02 S	169.56 W
Tufu Point ≻	164y	14.13 S	169.32 W
Tug	120	38.27 N	42.16 E
Tugaske	174	50.53 N	106.16 W
Tug Der ≃	134	9.20 N	46.20 E
Tugela	148	29.09 S	31.29 E
Tugela ≃	148	29.14 S	31.30 E
Tugela Beach	148	29.12 S	31.31 E
Tugela Ferry	148	28.44 S	30.27 E
Tuggerah Lake C	160	33.18 S	151.30 E
Tughlakābād ✦[8]	262a	28.31 N	77.16 E
Tugidak Island I	170	56.30 N	154.36 W
Tugolesskij Bor	70	55.33 N	39.49 E
Tugolukovo	70	51.56 N	41.40 E
Tugubun Point ≻	106	7.00 N	126.27 E
Tuguegarao	106	17.37 N	121.44 E
Tugulym	76	57.04 N	64.39 E
Tugun	161a	28.09 S	153.30 E
Tugur	79	53.48 N	136.48 E
Tugur ≃	79	53.48 N	136.44 E
Tugúrio	246	21.15 S	43.35 W
Tugurskij Poluostrov ≻[1]	79	54.00 N	137.24 E
Tuguša	78	55.57 N	96.26 E
Tugutuj	78	52.40 N	104.50 E
Tuguwa	146	17.25 S	18.25 E
Tuhaihe ≃	88	37.55 N	118.05 E
Tuhepu	94	40.54 N	122.49 E
Tuht	120	40.46 N	33.47 E
Tuhuangba	92	31.40 N	108.21 E
Tuibo	79	44.01 N	127.47 E
Tuichi ≃	238	14.36 S	67.35 W
Tuim	76	54.20 N	89.55 E
Tuineje	138	28.19 N	14.03 W
Tuirc, Beinn an ∧	42	55.34 N	5.33 W
Tuitán	224	21.08 N	103.48 W
Tuiutu	246	22.47 S	46.42 W
Tuj ≃	76	57.33 N	72.31 E
T'ujabuguz	75	40.58 N	69.15 E
Tujemojnak	76	49.20 N	62.55 E
Tuji-ri	88	41.31 N	127.12 E
Tujmazy	70	54.36 N	53.42 E
Tüjn Gol ≃	92	45.04 N	100.46 E
Tujunga ✦[8]	270	34.15 N	118.17 W
Tujunga Valley ∨	270	34.17 N	118.20 W
Tujunga Wash ∨	270	34.09 N	118.24 W
Tuka ∧	134	9.07 N	36.47 E
Tukaj	76	55.24 N	90.49 E
T'ukalinsk	76	55.52 N	72.12 E
Tukan	76	53.50 N	57.26 E
Tukangbesi, Kepulauan II	102	5.40 S	123.50 E
Tukayyid	118	29.47 N	45.36 E
Ṭūkh, Miṣr	132	30.21 N	31.12 E
Ṭūkh, Miṣr	132	27.41 N	30.49 E
Ṭūkh al-Aqlām	132	30.52 N	31.26 E
Ṭūkh al-Khayl	132	28.06 N	30.40 E
Ṭūkh Dalakah	132	30.39 N	30.55 E
Tukituki ≃	162	39.36 S	176.57 E
Tuk Méas	100	10.40 N	104.34 E
Tukolon'	78	55.24 N	107.42 E
Tukpo	144	4.25 N	25.52 E
Tūkrah	136	32.32 N	20.34 E
Tuktoyaktuk	170	69.27 N	133.02 W
Tukuj-Mekteb	74	44.20 N	45.11 E
Tukums	66	57.00 N	23.10 E
Tukuran	106	7.51 N	123.35 E
Tukuringra, Chrebet ⋀⋀	79	54.20 N	126.20 E
Tukuyu	144	9.15 S	33.39 E
T'uk'u Yüeh ∧	259d	25.01 N	121.38 E
Tukwila	214	47.29 N	122.16 W
Tula, Am. Sam.	164u	14.15 S	170.34 W
Tula, Méx.	224	23.00 N	99.43 W
Tula, S.S.S.R.	72	54.12 N	37.37 E
Tula □[4]	72	54.23 N	37.47 E
Tula ≃	224	20.40 N	99.30 W
Tula ⊥	224	20.06 N	99.19 W
Tula de Allende	224	20.03 N	99.21 W
Tulagi	165e	9.06 S	160.09 E
Tūlāk	118	33.58 N	63.44 E
Tulalip Indian Reservation ✦[4]	214	48.06 N	122.15 W
Tulancingo	224	20.05 N	98.22 W
Tulangbawang ≃	102	4.24 S	105.52 E
Tulaodian	94	41.13 N	121.27 E
T'ul'apsy	78	57.28 N	89.38 E
Tulare, Calif., U.S.	216	36.13 N	119.21 W
Tulare, S. Dak., U.S.	188	44.44 N	98.31 W
Tulare □[6]	216	36.20 N	119.18 W
Tulare Canal ☰	216	36.08 N	119.25 W
Tulare Lake Bed ⊜	216	36.03 N	119.49 W
Tulare Lake Canal ☰	216	36.04 N	119.39 W
Tularosa	190	33.04 N	106.01 W
Tularosa ≃	190	33.41 N	108.46 W
Tularosa Valley ⌣[1]	190	32.45 N	106.10 W
Tulbagh	148	33.17 S	19.09 E
Tulbing	254b	48.16 N	16.09 E
Tulbinger Kogel ∧	254b	48.17 N	16.09 E
Tulcán	236	0.48 N	77.43 W
Tulcea	38	45.11 N	28.48 E
Tulcea □[4]	38	45.00 N	29.00 E
Tul'čin	68	48.39 N	28.52 E
Tulcingo de Valle	224	18.03 N	98.26 W
Tule ≃, Nic.	226	11.20 N	84.52 W
Tule ≃, Calif., U.S.	216	36.03 N	119.50 W
Tule, North Branch ≃	216	36.06 N	119.22 W
Tule, South Branch ≃	216	36.05 N	119.29 W
Tuléar	147b	23.21 S	43.40 E
Tuléar □[4]	147b	24.00 S	45.00 E
Tule Canal ☰	216	38.37 N	121.35 W
Tule Creek ≃	186	34.40 N	101.14 W
T'ulek	75	41.56 N	75.41 E
Tulelake	194	41.57 N	121.29 W
Tule Lake Sump ⊜	194	41.54 N	121.32 W
T'ulenij, Mys ≻	74	40.12 N	50.22 E
T'ulenij, Ostrov I	74	44.28 N	47.30 E
Tule River Indian Reservation ✦[4]	194	36.02 N	118.42 W
Tulette	56	44.17 N	4.56 E
T'ul'gan	76	52.22 N	56.12 E
Tul'goviči	68	51.47 N	29.38 E
Tuli	144	21.59 S	29.15 E
Tuli ≃	144	21.48 S	29.04 E
Tulia	186	34.32 N	101.46 W
Tulica ≃	72	54.12 N	37.37 E
Tulik Volcano ∧[1]	170	53.22 N	168.03 W
Tulillo	224	22.30 N	104.05 W
Tuling	90	25.11 N	118.50 E
Tuliszków	30	52.05 N	18.17 E
T'uljapsy	76	57.28 N	89.38 E
Ṭūlkarm	122	32.19 N	35.02 E
T'ul'kino	76	59.49 N	56.30 E
T'ul'kubas	75	42.28 N	70.02 E
Tullahoma	184	35.22 N	86.11 W
Tullamarine	264b	37.41 S	144.52 E
Tullamarine Airport ⊠	159	37.40 S	144.50 E
Tullamore, Austl.	156	32.38 S	147.34 E
Tullamore, Ont., Can.	265b	43.47 N	79.46 W
Tullamore, Eire	28	53.16 N	7.30 W
Tullaroop Creek ≃	159	36.53 S	143.53 E
Tull Bay C	198	36.30 N	76.04 W
Tulle	32	45.16 N	1.46 E
Tullgarn	40	58.57 N	17.35 E
Tullibigeal	156	33.25 S	146.44 E
Tullinge	40	59.12 N	17.53 E
Tullins	56	45.18 N	5.29 E
Tulln	30	48.20 N	16.03 E
Tullner Feld ✦[1]	254b	48.19 N	16.10 E
Tulloch Lake ⊜[1]	216	37.53 N	120.35 W
Tullock Creek ≃	192	46.08 N	107.27 W
Tullos	184	31.49 N	92.19 W
Tullow	28	52.48 N	6.44 W
Tullus	130	11.03 N	24.33 E
Tully, Austl.	156	17.56 S	145.56 E
Tully, N.Y., U.S.	200	42.48 N	76.07 W
Tully Lake ⊜[1]	197	42.42 N	72.14 W
Tullytown	198	40.09 N	74.49 W
Ṭulmaythah	136	32.43 N	20.57 E
Tuloma ≃	24	68.52 N	32.49 E
Tulpehocken Creek ≃	198	40.21 N	75.57 W
Tulpfontein	148	32.44 S	19.43 E
Tulsa	186	36.09 N	95.58 W
Tulsequah	166	58.35 N	133.35 W
Tulsī Lake ⊜	262c	19.11 N	72.55 E
Tul'skij	74	44.31 N	40.10 E
Tulstrup	41	56.07 N	9.46 E
Tultepec	224	19.41 N	99.08 W
Tultitlán □[7]	276a	19.39 N	99.09 W
Tultitlán de Mariano Escobedo	276a	19.39 N	99.09 W
Tuluá	236	4.06 N	76.11 W
Tulufan	76	42.56 N	89.10 E
Tulufanpendi ⌣[7]	76	42.40 N	89.10 E
Tuluksak	170	61.06 N	160.58 W
Tulum	222	20.13 N	87.28 W
Tulum ⊥	222	20.12 N	87.26 W
Tulumaya (Lavalle)	242	32.43 S	68.35 W
Tulumayo ≃	238	11.10 S	75.16 W
Tulun	78	54.35 N	100.33 E
Tulungagung	105a	8.04 S	111.54 E
Tulungselapan	102	3.15 S	105.19 E
Tuluran Island I	106	10.59 N	119.17 E
Tulu Welel ∧	134	8.53 N	34.47 E
Tulyehualco	276a	19.15 N	99.01 W
Tum	154	3.38 S	130.23 E
Tuma	70	55.09 N	40.34 E
Tuma ≃	226	13.03 N	84.44 W
Tumacacori National Monument ♠	190	31.25 N	111.01 W
Tumaco	236	1.49 N	78.46 W
Tumaco, Ensenada C	236	1.55 N	78.45 W
Tumak	70	46.14 N	48.31 E
Tumalykol'	76	48.21 N	60.03 E
Tuman'an	74	41.00 N	44.40 E
Tuman-gang (Tumenjiang) ≃	88	42.18 N	130.41 E
Tumannaja, Gora ∧	170	66.33 N	179.43 E
Tumanovo	66	55.25 N	34.39 E
Tumanšet ≃	78	55.53 N	97.30 E
Tumanskij	170	63.58 N	178.12 E
Tumany	64	60.56 N	155.56 E
Tumarbong	106	10.23 N	119.27 E
T'um'ati → Sklad	64	71.55 N	123.33 E
Tumatumari Fall	236	5.22 N	59.00 W
Tumauini	106	17.17 N	121.49 E
Tumba	40	59.12 N	17.49 E
Tumba, Lac ⊜	142	0.48 S	18.03 E
Tumbagaan Island I	106	5.22 N	120.19 E
Tumbarumba	161b	35.47 S	148.01 E
Tumbarumba Creek ≃	161b	35.58 S	148.03 E
Tumbaya	242	23.51 S	65.28 W
Tumbes	236	3.34 S	80.28 W
Tumbes □[4]	236	3.50 N	80.30 W
Tumbes, Punta ≻	242	36.37 S	73.07 W
Tumbiscatio de Ruiz	224	18.31 N	102.21 W
Tumble Mountain ∧	192	45.19 N	110.02 W
Tumblong	161b	35.09 S	148.00 E
Tumbotino	70	55.59 N	43.02 E
Tumbur	144	4.20 N	31.34 E
Tumby Bay	156	34.22 S	136.06 E
Tumča ≃	24	66.36 N	30.48 E
Tŭmch'on-ni ✦[8]	261b	37.34 N	126.51 E
T'umen', S.S.S.R.	76	57.09 N	65.32 E
Tumen, Zhg.	88	42.58 N	129.49 E
T'umen'-Aryk	76	44.02 N	67.01 E
T'umencevo	76	53.20 N	81.31 E
T'umenec, Porog ↳	78	56.38 N	99.00 E
Tumenjiang (Tuman-gang) ≃	88	42.18 N	130.41 E
Tumenpu	97	29.49 N	103.39 E
T'umenskaja Oblast' □[4]	24	65.00 N	62.00 E
Tumenskoje	72	55.00 N	38.32 E
Tumenzi	92	37.43 N	103.09 E
Tumeremo	236	7.18 N	61.30 W
Tumin ≃	79	49.18 N	140.22 E
Tumiritinga	245	18.58 S	41.38 W
Tumkūr	112	13.21 N	77.05 E
Tummo	136	22.40 N	14.10 E
Tumon Bay C	164p	13.31 N	144.48 E
Tumoteqi	92	40.52 N	111.28 E
Tumpang	105a	8.00 S	112.46 E
Tumpat	104	6.12 N	102.10 E
Tumsar	110	21.23 N	79.44 E
Tumu	140	10.52 N	1.59 W
Tumuc-Humac Mountains ⋀⋀	240	2.20 N	55.00 W
Tumupasa	238	14.09 S	67.55 W
Tumu Point ≻	164r	6.56 N	158.07 E
Tumupu	95	40.23 N	115.36 E
Tumut	161b	35.18 S	148.13 E
Tumut ≃	161b	35.07 S	148.13 E
Tumut Pond Reservoir ⊜[1]	161b	35.59 S	148.25 E
Tumutuk	70	55.02 N	53.19 E
Tumwater	214	47.01 N	122.54 W
Tun ≃	100	17.25 N	98.42 E
Tuna Canyon ∨	270	34.03 N	118.36 W
Tunago Lake ⊜	170	66.18 N	125.50 W
Tuna-Hästberg	40	60.20 N	15.11 E
Tunal, Río del ≃	224	24.00 N	104.34 W
Tunapuna	231r	10.38 N	61.23 W
Tunari, Cerro ∧	238	17.18 S	66.22 W
Tunas Creek ≃	186	31.01 N	102.11 W
Tunas de Zaza	230p	21.38 N	79.33 W
Tūnat al-Jabal	132	27.46 N	30.44 E
Tunaydah	130	25.31 N	29.21 E
Tunbridge Wells	44	51.08 N	0.16 E
Tunca (Tundža) ≃	38	41.40 N	26.34 E
Tunçbilek	120	39.37 N	29.29 E
Tunceli	120	39.07 N	39.32 E
Tunceli □[4]	120	39.10 N	39.30 E
Tunchang	100	19.28 N	110.08 E
T'unch'i → Tunxi	90	29.44 N	118.18 E
Tunda, Pulau I	105a	5.49 S	106.16 E
Tundazi ∧	144	17.33 S	28.05 E
Tündern	48	52.04 N	9.22 E
Tūndla	114	27.12 N	78.17 E
Tundubai ⫧[4]	130	18.31 N	28.33 E
Tunduru	144	11.07 S	37.21 E
Tundža (Tunca) ≃	38	41.40 N	26.34 E
Tune	41	55.36 N	12.11 E
Tunesien → Tunisia □[1]	138	34.00 N	9.00 E
T'unež, S.S.S.R.	72	54.37 N	38.29 E
Túnez → Tunis, Tun.	138	36.48 N	10.11 E
Túnez → Tunisia □[1]	138	34.00 N	9.00 E
T'ung ≃	64	63.46 N	121.35 E
Tunga	140	8.00 N	9.19 E
Tunga ≃	112	14.00 N	75.41 E
Tungabhadra ≃	112	15.57 N	78.15 E
Tungabhadra Reservoir ⊜[1]	112	15.16 N	76.21 E
Tungaru	130	10.14 N	30.42 E
Tungauan Bay C	106	7.28 N	122.21 E
Tungchiang	90	22.28 N	120.26 E
Tungchi Hsü I	90	23.15 N	119.40 E
Tungchi University ʊ[2]	259b	31.18 N	121.10 E
T'ungchou → Tongxian	95	39.55 N	116.39 E
T'ungch'uan → Tongchuan	92	35.01 N	109.01 E
Tungch'üan Tao I	90	25.58 N	119.58 E
Tungelsta	40	59.06 N	18.02 E
Tung Hai → East China Sea ⫧[2]	80	30.00 N	126.00 E
Tungho	90	22.58 N	121.18 E
T'unghsien → Tongxian	95	39.55 N	116.39 E
T'unghua → Tonghua	88	41.50 N	125.55 E
Tunghwa → Tonghua	88	41.50 N	125.55 E
Tungi	116	23.53 N	90.24 E
Tungir ≃	78	55.24 N	120.32 E
Tungirskij Chrebet ⋀⋀	78	54.40 N	119.40 E
Tungkal ≃	102	0.48 S	103.29 E
Tungkillo	158b	34.49 S	139.04 E
Tungku	102	5.01 N	118.53 E
Tungla	226	13.18 N	84.26 W
T'ungliao → Tongliao	79	43.39 N	122.14 E
Tung Lung I	261d	22.15 N	114.17 E
Tungokočen	78	53.33 N	115.36 E
Tungshih	90	24.16 N	120.50 E
Tungsten	170	62.00 N	127.40 W
Tungsunga, Jabal ∧	130	11.29 N	23.21 E
Tungting Hsü I	90	24.10 N	118.14 E
Tungurahua □[4]	236	1.15 S	78.35 W
Tungyin Shan I	90	26.22 N	120.30 E
Tuni	112	17.21 N	82.33 E
Tunica	184	34.41 N	90.23 W
Tunis	138	36.48 N	10.11 E
Tunis, Golfe de C	138	37.00 N	10.30 E
Tunis Et Banlieue □[8]	36	36.48 N	10.10 E
Tunisia □[1]	124		
	138	34.00 N	9.00 E
Tunisie → Tunisia □[1]	138	34.00 N	9.00 E
Tunitas Creek ≃	272	37.21 N	122.24 W
Tunja	236	5.31 N	73.22 W
Tunjang	104	6.16 N	100.21 E
Tunka	78	51.45 N	102.32 E
Tunkás	222	20.54 N	88.45 W
Tunkhannock	200	41.32 N	75.57 W
Tunkhannock Creek ≃	200	41.32 N	75.57 W
Tunkhannock Creek, East Branch ≃	200	41.38 N	75.43 W
Tunkinskije Gol'cy ⋀⋀	78	51.50 N	101.40 E
Tunliu	92	36.19 N	112.54 E
Tunnel	200	42.13 N	75.44 W
Tunnelhill	204	40.29 N	78.33 W
Tunnelton, Ind., U.S.	208	38.46 N	86.21 W
Tunnelton, W. Va., U.S.	178	39.24 N	79.45 W
Tunnsjøen ⊜	24	64.43 N	13.24 E
Tunø I	41	55.57 N	10.26 E
Tunstall	44	53.05 N	2.13 W
Tuntenhausen	58	47.56 N	12.01 E
Tuntum	240	5.14 S	44.39 W
Tuntutuliak	170	60.22 N	162.38 W
Tununak	170	60.35 N	165.16 W
Tunungayualok Island I	166	56.05 N	61.05 W
Tunuyán	242	33.34 S	69.01 W
Tunuyán ≃	242	34.03 S	66.45 W
Tunxi	90	29.44 N	118.18 E
Tuoba	92	31.18 N	97.40 E
Tuobalage	110	31.37 N	88.10 E
Tuobuja	64	62.00 N	122.02 E
Tuocheng	90	24.05 N	115.13 E
Tuoeshan ∧	92	24.20 N	103.32 E
Tuohe	90	33.26 N	117.26 E
Tuohu ⊜	90	33.11 N	117.49 E
Tuoj-Chaja	64	62.32 N	111.18 E
Tuojiang ≃	92	28.57 N	105.27 E
Tuojidao I	88	38.09 N	120.14 E
Tuokedingling	110	32.45 N	84.55 E
Tuoketuo	92	40.22 N	111.11 E
Tuokexun	76	42.47 N	88.38 E
Tuokusidawanling ∧	110	37.14 N	85.47 E
Tuoli, Zhg.	76	45.57 N	83.37 E
Tuoli, Zhg.	95	39.46 N	116.01 E
Tuolumne	216	37.58 N	120.14 W
Tuolumne □[6]	216	37.59 N	120.23 W
Tuolumne ≃	216	37.36 N	121.10 W
Tuolumne, Lyell Fork ≃	216	37.53 N	119.23 W
Tuolumne, North Fork ≃	216	37.54 N	120.15 W
Tuolumne, South Fork ≃	216	37.50 N	120.03 W
Tuolunduo	79	50.35 N	120.05 E
Tuoningdao I	90	22.28 N	114.38 E
Tuorong (Tuoyang)	90	27.16 N	119.54 E
Tuoshihanhe (Aksaj) ≃	75	40.55 N	78.16 E
Tuosuohu ⊜, Zhg.	92	35.18 N	98.54 E
Tuosuohu ⊜, Zhg.	92	37.10 N	96.55 E
Tuowu	92	28.58 N	102.13 E
T'up	75	42.44 N	78.22 E
Tupã	245	21.56 S	50.30 W
Tupaciguara	245	18.35 S	48.42 W
Tupa Creek ≃	160	33.05 S	150.37 E
Tupana ≃	236	4.25 S	60.05 W
Tupanciretã	242	29.05 S	53.51 W
Tupelo, Miss., U.S.	184	34.16 N	88.43 W
Tupelo, Okla., U.S.	186	34.37 N	96.26 W

Symbol / English	Deutsch	Español	Français	Português
≃ River	Fluss	Río	Rivière	Rio
☰ Canal	Kanal	Canal	Canal	Canal
↳ Waterfall, Rapids	Wasserfall, Stromschnellen	Cascada, Rápidos	Chute d'eau, Rapides	Cascata, Rápidos
ʯ Strait	Meeresstrasse	Estrecho	Détroit	Estreito
C Bay, Gulf	Bucht, Golf	Bahía, Golfo	Baie, Golfe	Baía, Golfo
⊜ Lake, Lakes	See, Seen	Lago, Lagos	Lac, Lacs	Lago, Lagos
☵ Swamp	Sumpf	Pantano	Marais	Pântano
⊡ Ice Features, Glacier	Eis- und Gletscherformen	Accidentes Glaciales	Formes glaciaires	Acidentes Glaciares
⫧ Other Hydrographic Features	Andere Hydrographische Objekte	Otros Elementos Hidrográficos	Autres données hydrographiques	Outros Elementos Hidrográficos
⟡ Submarine Features	Untermeerische Objekte	Accidentes Submarinos	Formes de relief sous-marin	Acidentes Submarinos
□ Political Unit	Politische Einheit	Unidad Politica	Entité politique	Unidade Política
ʊ Cultural Institution	Kulturelle Institution	Institución Cultural	Institution culturelle	Instituição Cultural
⊥ Historical Site	Historische Stätte	Sitio Histórico	Site historique	Sitio Histórico
♠ Recreational Site	Erholungs- und Ferienort	Sitio de Recreo	Centre de loisirs	Sítio de Lazer
⊠ Airport	Flughafen	Aeropuerto	Aéroport	Aeroporto
■ Military Installation	Militäranlage	Instalación Militar	Installation militaire	Instalação Militar
✦ Miscellaneous	Verschiedenes	Misceláneo	Divers	Miscelânea

Tupelo National Battlefield ⊥ 184 34.13 N 88.44 W
Tupi 106 6.19 N 124.57 E
Tupičov 68 51.46 N 31.26 E
Tupik 78 54.26 N 119.57 E
Tupilac 106 7.40 N 122.30 E
Tupi Paulista 245 21.24 S 51.34 W
Tupiraçaba 245 14.29 S 48.34 W
Tupirama 240 8.58 S 48.12 W
Tupiza 238 21.27 S 65.43 W
Tuplice 30 51.41 N 14.50 E
Tupman 216 35.18 N 119.21 W
Tupper 172 55.31 N 120.02 W
Tupper Lake 178 44.13 N 74.29 W
Tupperville 204 42.36 N 82.16 W
Tupuai, Île I 14 23.18 S 149.30 W
Tupungato 242 33.22 S 69.08 W
Tupungato, Cerro ∧ 242 33.22 S 69.47 W
Tupuseleia 154 9.33 S 147.18 E
Tuqiao, Zhg. 96 31.56 N 119.03 E
Tuqiao, Zhg. 96 31.39 N 120.24 E
Tuqiao, Zhg. 97 30.24 N 105.28 E
Tuqiao, Zhg. 97 30.32 N 104.50 E
Tuqiaochang 97 29.47 N 106.01 E
Tuquan 79 45.26 N 121.50 E
Túquerres 236 1.05 N 77.37 W
Tura, Bhārat 114 25.31 N 90.13 E
Ṭurā, Miṣr 132 29.56 N 31.16 E
Tura, S.S.S.R. 64 64.17 N 100.15 E
Tura ≃, S.S.S.R. 76 57.12 N 66.56 E
Tura ≃, S.S.S.R. 78 51.36 N 114.09 E
Turabah 134 21.13 N 41.39 E
Turabah ⊤[4] 118 28.15 N 42.55 E
Turābah, 'Ayn at- ⊤[4] 122 31.36 N 35.25 E
Turabah, Wādī ∨ 134 21.36 N 41.52 E
Turāg ≃ 116 23.45 N 90.21 E
Turaiyūr 112 11.10 N 78.37 E
Turakina 162 40.02 S 175.13 E
Turakina ≃ 162 40.04 S 175.08 E
Turama ≃ 154 6.50 S 143.05 E
Turambhe 262c 19.04 N 73.01 E
Turan, S.S.S.R. 78 51.38 N 101.40 E
Turan, S.S.S.R. 78 52.08 N 93.55 E
Turangi 162 39.00 S 175.49 E
Turano ≃ 60 42.26 N 12.47 E
Turanskaja Nizmennost' ≡ 76 44.30 N 63.00 E
Turate 256b 45.39 N 9.00 E
Tur'at Ghunaym 132 31.16 N 31.29 E
Turbaco 236 10.20 N 75.25 W
Turbacz ∧ 30 49.33 N 20.08 E
Turbah 134 12.40 N 43.30 E
Turbat 118 25.59 N 63.04 E
Turbenthal 54 47.27 N 8.51 E
Turbigo 56 45.32 N 8.44 E
Turbio ≃ 224 20.19 N 101.37 W
Turbo 236 8.06 N 76.43 W
Turbotville 200 41.06 N 76.46 W
Turbov 68 49.21 N 28.44 E
Turčasovo 24 63.06 N 39.12 E
Turčiansky Svätý Martin → Martin 30 49.05 N 18.55 E
Turckheim 54 48.05 N 7.17 E
Turda 38 46.34 N 23.47 E
Turdej 66 53.22 N 38.01 E
Turee Creek 152 23.37 S 118.39 E
Turee Creek ≃ 152 23.35 S 117.25 E
Turek 30 52.02 N 18.30 E
Turen 105a 8.10 S 112.41 E
Turenki 26 60.55 N 24.38 E
Turfan → Tulufan 76 42.56 N 89.10 E
Turfan Depression → Tulufanpendi ⊥[7] 76 42.40 N 89.10 E
Turffontein ◆[8] 263d 26.15 S 28.02 E
Turffontein Race Course ▲ 263d 26.14 S 28.03 E
Turgaj, S.S.S.R. 76 51.46 N 72.44 E
Turgaj, S.S.S.R. 76 49.38 N 63.28 E
Turgaj ≃ 76 48.01 N 62.45 E
Turgajskaja Dolina ∨ 76 51.00 N 64.30 E
Turgajskaja Stolovaja Strana ∧∧[1] 76 51.00 N 64.00 E
Türgen, Mong. 76 50.04 N 91.36 E
Turgen', S.S.S.R. 75 43.24 N 77.36 E
Turgen' ≃ 75 43.50 N 77.38 E
Turgenevka 78 53.02 N 105.41 E
Turgenevo 70 54.50 N 46.19 E
Turginovo 72 56.30 N 36.00 E
Turgojak 76 55.10 N 60.07 E
Turgoš 66 59.18 N 35.10 E
Tŭrgovishte → Târgovište 38 43.15 N 26.34 E
Turgut 120 38.37 N 31.49 E
Turgutlu 120 38.30 N 27.43 E
Turgwe ≃ 144 20.28 S 32.18 E
Turhal 120 40.24 N 36.06 E
Türi 66 58.48 N 25.26 E
Turia ≃ 34 39.27 N 0.19 W
Turiaçu 240 1.41 S 45.21 W
Turiaçu ≃ 240 1.36 S 45.19 W
Turiančajskij Zapovednik ▲ 74 40.40 N 47.35 E
Turijsk 68 51.07 N 24.31 E
Turij Tog 79 45.14 N 131.58 E
Turilovka 73 49.06 N 40.13 E
Turimetta Head ≻ 264a 33.42 S 151.19 E
Turimiquire, Cerro ∧ 236 10.07 N 63.53 W
Turin, Alta., Can. 172 49.58 N 112.31 W
Turin → Torino, It. 56 45.03 N 7.40 E
Turin, N.Y., U.S. 202 43.38 N 75.25 W
Turinge 40 59.12 N 17.27 E
Turinsk 76 58.03 N 63.42 E
Turinskaja Sloboda 76 57.37 N 64.25 E
Turja ≃ 68 51.48 N 24.52 E
Turka, S.S.S.R. 68 49.10 N 23.02 E
Turka, S.S.S.R. 78 52.57 N 108.13 E
Turka ≃ 78 52.56 N 108.13 E
Türkei → Turkey □[1] 120 39.00 N 35.00 E
Türkeli Adası I 120 40.30 N 27.30 E
Turkestan 75 43.18 N 68.15 E
Turkestanskij Chrebet ∧∧ 75 39.35 N 69.15 E
Túrkeve 30 47.06 N 20.45 E
Turkey 186 34.23 N 100.54 W
Turkey □[1], As., Eur. 22
120 39.00 N 35.00 E
Turkey ≃ 180 42.43 N 91.01 W
Turkey Branch ≃ 274c 38.52 N 76.48 W
Turkey City 204 41.11 N 79.37 W
Turkey Creek 154 17.02 S 128.12 E
Turkey Creek ≃, U.S. 188 39.58 N 96.02 W
Turkey Creek ≃, Ind., U.S. 268 41.31 N 87.18 W
Turkey Creek ≃, Iowa, U.S. 188 41.20 N 95.05 W
Turkey Creek ≃, Kans., U.S. 188 38.53 N 97.11 W
Turkey Creek ≃, Nebr., U.S. 188 40.23 N 96.53 W
Turkey Creek ≃, Okla., U.S. 186 35.58 N 97.56 W
Turkey Creek ≃, Tex., U.S. 186 28.42 N 99.58 W
Turkey Creek ≃, Tex., U.S. 212 30.39 N 97.05 W
Turkey Island I 274c 38.58 N 77.12 W
Turkey Point ≻, Ont., Can. 202 42.40 N 80.21 W
Turkey Point ≻, Fla., U.S. 210 25.26 N 80.19 W
Turkey Point Provincial Park ▲ 202 42.40 N 80.22 W
Turkey Run State Park ▲ 184 39.54 N 87.13 W
Turkeytown 269b 40.12 N 79.44 W
Türkheim 54 48.03 N 10.38 E
Turki 70 51.59 N 43.16 E
Türkiye → Turkey □[1] 120 39.00 N 35.00 E
Turkmān Deh 257d 35.40 N 51.36 E
Turkmen-Kala 118 37.26 N 62.20 E
Turkmenskaja Sovetskaja Socialističeskaja Respublika □[3] 62 40.00 N 60.00 E
Turkmen Soviet Socialist Republic → Turkmenskaja Sovetskaja Socialističeskaja Respublika □[3] 62 40.00 N 60.00 E
Turk Mine 144 19.45 S 28.50 E
Turkoğlu 120 37.31 N 36.49 E
Turks and Caicos Islands □[2] 220
228 21.45 N 71.35 W
Turks Island Passage U 228 21.25 N 71.19 W
Turks Islands II 228 21.24 N 71.07 W
Turks- und Caicos-Inseln → Turks and Caicos Islands □[2] 228 21.45 N 71.35 W
Turku (Åbo) 26 60.27 N 22.17 E
Turkwel ≃ 144 3.06 N 36.06 E
Turlan 75 43.36 N 69.03 E
Turley 186 36.14 N 95.58 W
Turlock 216 37.30 N 120.51 W
Turlock Lake ⊜[1] 216 42.17 N 73.21 W
Turmalina 245 17.17 S 42.45 W
Turmantas 66 55.42 N 26.27 E
Turmerito, Quebrada ≃ 276c 10.26 N 66.55 W
Turnagain ≃ 170 59.06 N 127.35 W
Turnagain, Cape ≻ 162 40.29 S 176.37 E
Turnagain Arm C 170 61.00 N 150.00 W
Turnagain Island I 154 9.34 S 142.18 E
Turna nad Bodvou 30 48.37 N 20.53 E
Turnbull, Mount ∧ 190 33.04 N 110.16 W
Turnbull, Mount ∧[2] 152 21.03 S 131.57 E
Turnbull Dry Lake ⊜ 192 43.10 N 118.00 W
Turneffe Islands II 222 17.22 N 87.51 W
Turner, Austl. 152 17.50 S 128.17 E
Turner, Mont., U.S. 192 48.51 N 108.24 W
Turner, Oreg., U.S. 192 44.51 N 122.57 W
Turner ≃ 152 20.21 S 118.25 E
Turner Field ⊠ 275 40.13 N 75.13 W
Turners Falls 197 42.36 N 72.33 W
Turners Peninsula ≻[1] 140 7.22 N 12.22 W
Turnersville, N.J., U.S. 275 39.46 N 75.03 W
Turnersville, Tex., U.S. 212 31.37 N 97.44 W
Turner Valley 172 50.40 N 114.17 W
Turnhout 48 51.19 N 4.57 E
Türnitz 30 47.57 N 15.30 E
Turnor Lake ⊜ 174 56.32 N 108.38 W
Turnov 30 50.35 N 15.10 E
Tŭrnovo → Veliko Târnovo 38 43.04 N 25.39 E
Turnpike Lake ⊜ 273 42.01 N 71.19 W
Turnu-Măgurele 38 43.45 N 24.53 E
Turnu Roșu, Pasul)(38 45.33 N 24.16 E
Turnu-Severin → Drobeta-Turnu-Severin 38 44.38 N 22.39 E
Turobin 30 50.50 N 22.45 E
Turočak 76 52.16 N 87.08 E
Turon 188 37.48 N 98.26 W
Turon ≃ 160 33.03 S 149.43 E
Turopin 68 51.00 N 24.27 E
Turopolje ≡ 36 45.40 N 16.05 E
Tuross ≃ 161b 36.09 S 149.39 E
Turov 68 52.04 N 27.44 E
Turovo 72 54.52 N 37.49 E
Turques et Caicos Îles → Turks and Caicos Islands □[2] 228 21.45 N 71.35 W
Turquía → Turkey □[1] 120 39.00 N 35.00 E
Turquie → Turkey □[1] 120 39.00 N 35.00 E
Turquino, Pico ∧ 230p 19.59 N 76.50 W
Turrach 58 46.57 N 13.52 E
Turramurra 264a 33.44 S 151.08 E
Turrell 184 35.23 N 90.15 W
Turret Peak ∧ 190 34.15 N 111.53 W
Turriaco 58 45.49 N 13.26 E
Turrialba 226 9.54 N 83.41 W
Turrialba, Volcán ∧[1] 226 10.02 N 83.46 W
Turriers 56 44.24 N 6.10 E
Turriff 28 57.32 N 2.28 W
Turritano ◆[1] 36 40.48 N 8.30 E
Turrubares, Cerro ∧ 226 9.47 N 84.28 W
Turša 70 56.56 N 47.40 E
Turtas ≃ 76 59.06 N 68.52 E
Turtipār 114 26.10 N 83.54 E
Turtle ≃, Man., Can. 174 51.07 N 99.39 W
Turtle ≃, Ont., Can. 174 48.51 N 92.45 W
Turtle ≃, N. Dak., U.S. 188 48.20 N 97.08 W
Turtle, North Branch ≃ 188 47.57 N 97.35 W
Turtle Creek, N.B., Can. 176 45.58 N 64.53 W
Turtle Creek, Pa., U.S. 204 40.25 N 79.49 W
Turtle Creek ≃, Pa., U.S. 269b 40.23 N 79.51 W
Turtle Creek ≃, S. Dak., U.S. 188 44.55 N 98.29 W
Turtle Creek ≃, Wis., U.S. 206 42.29 N 89.03 W
Turtle Flambeau Flowage ⊜[1] 180 46.05 N 90.11 W
Turtleford 174 53.23 N 108.56 W
Turtle Harbor Channel U 210 25.15 N 80.18 W
Turtle Islands II 140 7.37 N 13.02 W
Turtle Lake, N. Dak., U.S. 188 47.31 N 100.53 W
Turtle Lake, Wis., U.S. 180 45.24 N 92.08 W
Turtle Lake ⊜ 174 53.35 N 108.40 W
Turtle Mountain Indian Reservation ◆[4] 188 48.51 N 99.45 W
Turtle Mountain Provincial Park ▲ 174 49.03 N 100.15 W
Turtmann 54 46.18 N 7.41 E
Turton and Entwistle Reservoir ⊜[1] 252 53.39 N 2.25 W
Turton Bottoms 252 53.38 N 2.24 W
Turton Moor ◆[3] 252 53.40 N 2.29 W
Turu ≃ 64 64.38 N 100.00 E
Turua 162 37.14 S 175.34 E
Turuchan ≃ 64 65.56 N 87.42 E
Turuchansk 64 65.49 N 87.59 E
Turuna ≃ 236 0.02 N 56.57 W
Turuntajevo, S.S.S.R. 76 56.38 N 85.59 E
Turuntajevo, S.S.S.R. 78 52.12 N 107.37 E
Türüşmek 120 39.03 N 39.32 E
Turvânia 245 16.39 S 50.09 W
Turvo 242 28.56 S 49.41 W
Turvo ≃, Bra. 242 27.16 S 54.06 W
Turvo ≃, Bra. 245 19.56 S 49.55 W
Turvo ≃, Bra. 245 17.46 S 50.12 W
Turvo ≃, Bra. 246 22.29 S 44.15 W
Turvo ≃, Bra. 246 22.04 S 45.42 W
Turvo ≃, Bra. 246 21.32 S 44.26 W
Turvo ≃, S.A. 238 14.47 S 61.03 W
Turvo Grande ≃ 246 21.42 S 44.22 W
Turvo Pequeno ≃ 246 21.42 S 44.22 W
Turyu-san ∧ 88 41.10 N 128.47 E
Turzovka 30 49.25 N 18.39 E
Tusas, Rio ≃ 190 36.23 N 106.03 W
Tuscaloosa 184 33.13 N 87.33 W
Tuscania 60 42.25 N 11.52 E
Tuscarawas 204 40.24 N 81.25 W
Tuscarawas □[6] 204 40.30 N 81.27 W
Tuscarawas ≃ 204 40.17 N 81.52 W
Tuscarora, N.Y., U.S. 200 42.38 N 77.52 W
Tuscarora, Pa., U.S. 198 40.46 N 76.02 W
Tuscarora Creek ≃, N.Y., U.S. 200 42.07 N 77.14 W
Tuscarora Creek ≃, Pa., U.S. 198 40.32 N 77.23 W
Tuscarora Creek, North Branch ≃ 200 42.05 N 77.18 W
Tuscarora Indian Reservation ◆[4] 200 43.09 N 78.57 W
Tuscarora Mountain ∧ 178 40.10 N 77.45 W
Tuscarora Mountains ∧∧ 194 41.00 N 116.20 W
Tuscarora State Park ▲ 198 40.48 N 76.01 W
Tuscarora Tunnel ◆[5] 204 40.05 N 77.50 W
Tuscola, Ill., U.S. 184 39.48 N 88.17 W
Tuscola, Tex., U.S. 186 32.12 N 99.48 W
Tuscolo ⊥ 257a 41.48 N 12.42 E
Tuscumbia, Ala., U.S. 184 34.44 N 87.42 W
Tuscumbia, Mo., U.S. 184 38.14 N 92.28 W
Tuse 41 55.43 N 11.37 E
Tushanzhen 88 34.14 N 117.51 E
Tušino ◆[8] 255b 55.50 N 37.26 E
Tuskegee 184 32.26 N 85.42 W
Tusker Rock II[1] 44 51.27 N 3.40 W
Tussey Mountain ∧ 204 40.25 N 78.07 W
Tustin 218 33.45 N 117.49 W
Tustumena Lake ⊜ 170 60.12 N 150.50 W
Tuszyn 30 51.37 N 19.34 E
Tut 120 37.48 N 37.55 E
Tuta 142 14.37 S 20.45 E
Tutaekuri ≃ 162 39.30 S 176.54 E
Tutaizi 94 41.01 N 122.38 E
Tutajev 70 57.53 N 39.32 E
Tutak 74 39.32 N 42.46 E
Tutang 90 29.21 N 116.24 E
Tuthills Creek ≃ 266 40.45 N 73.02 W
Tuticorin 112 8.47 N 78.08 E
Tutin 38 42.59 N 20.20 E
Tutkaul 75 38.18 N 69.17 E
T'ut'kovo 72 54.37 N 38.32 E
Tutóia 240 2.45 S 42.16 W
Tutoko, Mount ∧ 162 44.36 S 168.00 E
Tutong 102 4.50 N 114.40 E
Tutova ≃ 38 46.06 N 27.32 E
Tutrakan 38 44.03 N 26.37 E
Tuttle 188 47.09 N 100.00 W
Tuttle Creek Lake ⊜[1] 188 39.22 N 96.40 W
Tuttlingen 54 47.59 N 8.49 E
Tutuala 154 8.24 S 127.15 E
Tutuba I 165f 15.34 S 167.16 E
Tutuban Station ◆[5] 259f 14.37 N 120.58 E
Tutu Bay C 106 5.55 N 121.12 E
Tutubu 144 5.30 S 32.41 E
Tutuila I 164u 14.18 S 170.42 W
Tuṭūn 132 29.09 N 30.46 E
Tutupaca, Volcán ∧[1] 238 17.01 S 70.22 W
Tutura 78 54.46 N 105.15 E
Tutura ≃ 78 54.47 N 105.12 E
Tututalak Mountain ∧ 170 67.46 N 161.10 W
Tututepec 224 16.09 N 97.38 W
Tutwiler 184 34.01 N 90.26 W
Tutzing 58 47.54 N 11.17 E
Tuul ≃ 78 48.57 N 104.48 E
Tuupovaara 26 62.29 N 30.36 E
Tuurun ja Poorin lääni □[4] 26 61.20 N 22.30 E
Tuusniemi 26 62.49 N 28.30 E
Tuutapu, Cerro ∧ 164z 27.08 S 109.24 W
T'uva-Guba 24 69.08 N 33.32 E
Tuvalu □[1] 14 8.00 S 178.00 E
Tuvinskaja Avtonomnaja Sovetskaja Socialističeskaja Respublika □[3] 78 53.00 N 96.00 E
Tuvutha I 165g 17.40 S 178.48 W
Tuwang 97 29.06 N 105.48 E
Ṭuwayq, Jabal ∧∧ 108 23.00 N 46.00 E
Tuxedo Park, Del., U.S. 275 39.43 N 75.37 W
Tuxedo Park, N.Y., U.S. 200 41.11 N 74.11 W
Tuxer Hauptkamm ∧ 58 47.10 N 11.45 E
Tuxer Vorberge ∧∧ 58 47.10 N 11.45 E
Tuxford 174 50.35 N 105.35 W
Tuxiaqiao 90 28.47 N 121.29 E
Tuxpan, Méx. 224 21.57 N 105.18 W
Tuxpan, Méx. 224 19.34 N 100.28 W
Tuxpan, Méx. 224 19.33 N 103.24 W
Tuxpan, Méx. 224 21.37 N 104.07 W
Tuxpan ≃ 224 20.59 N 97.18 W
Tuxpan de Rodríguez Cano 224 20.57 N 97.24 W
Tuxtepec 224 18.06 N 96.07 W
Tuxtla Chico 222 14.57 N 92.10 W
Tuxtla Gutiérrez 224 16.45 N 93.07 W
Túy 34 42.03 N 8.38 W
Tuy ≃ 236 10.24 N 65.59 W
Tuy-an 100 13.17 N 109.16 E
Tuyen-hoa 100 17.50 N 106.10 E
Tuy-hoa 100 13.05 N 109.18 E
Tūysarkān 118 34.33 N 48.27 E
Tuyün → Duyun 92 26.12 N 107.31 E
Ṭuyūr, Burj aṭ- ∧ 130 20.55 N 27.55 E
Tuža 70 57.37 N 47.57 E
Tuzamapan 224 19.24 N 96.51 W
T'uzašu, Pereval)(75 42.21 N 73.48 E
T'uzbel' 75 40.34 N 73.21 E
Tuzdykol', Ozero ⊜ 70 49.36 N 52.20 E
Tuz Gölü ⊜ 120 38.45 N 33.25 E
Tuzigoot National Monument ▲ 190 34.40 N 111.52 W
Tuzkan, Ozero ⊜ 75 40.35 N 67.28 E
Ṭūz Khurmātū 118 34.53 N 44.38 E
Tuzla, Jugo. 38 44.32 N 18.41 E
Tuzla, Tür. 120 36.42 N 35.05 E
Tuzla ≃ 74 39.43 N 40.18 E
Tuzla Gölü ⊜ 120 39.02 N 35.50 E
Tuzlov ≃ 73 47.23 N 40.08 E
Tuzluca 74 40.03 N 43.40 E
Tuzlukçu 120 38.28 N 31.38 E
Tuzly 68 45.52 N 30.05 E
Tvârdica, Blg. 38 43.42 N 25.52 E
Tvardica, S.S.S.R. 68 46.09 N 28.58 E
Tvedestrand 26 58.37 N 8.55 E
Tveitsund 26 59.01 N 8.32 E
Tver → Kalinin 72 56.52 N 35.55 E
Tverca ≃ 66 56.52 N 35.55 E
Twain Harte 216 38.02 N 120.14 W
Twann 54 47.06 N 7.10 E
Twante 100 16.43 N 95.56 E
Twardogóra 30 51.22 N 17.28 E
Tweed 202 44.29 N 77.19 W
Tweed ≃ 42 55.46 N 2.00 W
Tweeddale ∨ 42 55.37 N 2.55 W
Tweede Exloërmond 48 52.55 N 6.58 E
Tweed Heads 161a 28.10 S 153.31 E
Tweedmouth 42 55.45 N 2.01 W
Tweedsmuir Provincial Park ▲ 172 52.55 N 126.05 W
Tweedy Mountain ∧ 192 45.29 N 112.58 W
Tweeling 148 27.38 S 28.31 E
Tweespruit 148 29.11 S 27.01 E
Twello 48 52.14 N 6.06 E
Twelve Mile 206 40.52 N 86.13 W
Twelve Mile Creek ≃, Ont., Can. 202 43.11 N 79.16 W
Twelvemile Creek ≃, N.Y., U.S. 200 43.18 N 78.51 W
Twelvemile Island I 269b 40.32 N 79.51 W
Twelve Mile Lake ⊜, Ont., Can. 202 45.02 N 78.43 W
Twelve Mile Lake ⊜, Sask., Can. 174 49.29 N 106.14 W
Tweng 58 47.11 N 13.36 E
Twente ◆[1] 48 52.17 N 6.40 E
Twentekanaal ≋ 48 52.15 N 6.40 E
Twentieth Century Fox Studios ✝[3] 270 34.03 N 118.25 W
25 de Abril, Ponte ◆[5] 256c 38.41 N 9.11 W
Twentyfive Mile Wash ∨ 190 37.33 N 111.07 W
24-Parganas □[5] 116 22.15 N 88.30 E
24-Parganas ◆[8] 262c 19.00 N 72.51 E
Twenty Mile Creek ≃ 202 43.11 N 79.26 W
Twentynine Palms 194 34.08 N 116.03 W
Twentynine Palms Marine Corps Base ■ 194 34.25 N 116.10 W
Tweya 142 0.54 S 19.05 E
Twickenham ◆[8] 250 51.27 N 0.20 W
Twilight Cove C 152 32.16 S 126.03 E
Twilight Park 200 42.11 N 74.05 W
Twillingate 176 49.39 N 54.46 W
Twin Beach 206 42.34 N 83.24 W
Twin Bridges 192 45.33 N 112.20 W
Twin Butte Creek ≃ 188 38.46 N 100.56 W
Twin Buttes ∧ 192 44.20 N 122.15 W
Twin Buttes Reservoir ⊜[1] 186 31.20 N 100.35 W
Twin City 182 32.35 N 82.10 W
Twin Creek ≃ 208 39.33 N 84.21 W
Twin Falls 192 42.34 N 114.28 W
Twin Heads ∧∧ 152 20.13 S 126.30 E
Twin Hills 170 59.23 N 159.58 W
Twin Lakes, Calif., U.S. 216 36.58 N 122.00 W
Twin Lakes, Ind., U.S. 206 41.19 N 86.23 W
Twin Lakes, Mich., U.S. 206 43.22 N 86.10 W
Twin Lakes, Ohio, U.S. 204 41.11 N 81.21 W
Twin Lakes, Pa., U.S. 200 41.24 N 74.54 W
Twin Lakes, Wis., U.S. 206 42.32 N 88.15 W
Twin Lakes ⊜, Calif., U.S. 216 38.09 N 119.21 W
Twin Lakes ⊜, Conn., U.S. 197 42.02 N 73.26 W
Twin Lakes ⊜, Wash., U.S. 214 47.55 N 120.51 W
Twin Oaks, Ill., U.S. 268 42.03 N 87.50 W
Twin Oaks, Pa., U.S. 198 39.51 N 75.26 W
Twin Peak Islands II 152 34.00 S 122.50 E
Twin Peaks 218 34.12 N 117.12 W
Twin Peaks ∧∧, Calif., U.S. 272 37.45 N 122.27 W
Twin Peaks ∧∧, Idaho, U.S. 192 44.35 N 114.29 W
Twin Rocks, Oreg., U.S. 214 45.36 N 123.57 W
Twin Rocks, Pa., U.S. 204 40.30 N 78.52 W
Twinsburg 204 41.19 N 81.27 W
Twin Valley 188 47.16 N 96.16 W
Twisp 192 48.22 N 120.07 W
Twiss Green 252 53.27 N 2.32 W
Twist 48 52.38 N 7.03 E
Twiste ≃ 48 51.29 N 9.09 E
Twistringen 48 52.48 N 8.38 E
Twitchell Reservoir ⊜[1] 194 35.00 N 120.19 W
Twitya ≃ 170 64.10 N 128.12 W
Two, Channel U 210 24.50 N 80.45 W
Two Butte Creek ≃ 188 38.02 N 102.08 W
Twofold Bay C 156 37.06 S 149.55 E
Two Harbors 180 47.01 N 91.40 W
Two Hills 172 53.43 N 111.45 W
Two Lakes ⊜ 214 46.22 N 121.27 W
Two Medicine ≃ 192 48.29 N 112.14 W
Two Mile Creek ≃, Ont., Can. 274a 43.16 N 79.06 W
Twomile Creek ≃, N.Y., U.S. 274a 43.01 N 78.55 W
Twong 130 8.18 N 28.20 E
Two Penny Run ≃ 275 39.41 N 75.26 W
Two River Lake ⊜ 174 53.52 N 91.27 W
Two Rivers, Bots. 148 26.27 S 20.37 E
Two Rivers, Wis., U.S. 180 44.09 N 87.34 W
Two Rivers ≃ 188 48.49 N 97.09 W
Two Rivers Reservoir ⊜[1] 186 33.17 N 104.45 W
Two Thumb Range ∧∧ 162 43.45 S 170.43 E
Two Wells 158b 34.36 S 138.30 E
Twrch ≃, Wales, U.K. 44 52.42 N 3.29 W
Twrch ≃, Wales, U.K. 44 51.46 N 3.46 W
Twyford, Eng., U.K. 44 51.29 N 0.53 W
Twyford, Eng., U.K. 44 51.01 N 1.19 W
Twymyn ≃ 44 52.38 N 3.44 W
Tyabb 159 38.16 S 145.11 E
Tybju 24 60.37 N 50.20 E
Tybkino 24 54.15 N 43.46 E
Tychy 30 50.09 N 18.59 E
Tyczyn 30 49.58 N 22.02 E
Tydal 26 63.04 N 11.34 E
Tye 186 32.27 N 99.52 W
Tyémé 140 9.33 N 7.19 W
Tyende Creek ≃ 190 36.50 N 109.43 W
Tyendinaga Indian Reserve ◆[4] 202 44.11 N 77.07 W
Tyfors 40 60.09 N 14.12 E
Tygarts Creek ≃ 208 38.43 N 82.57 W
Tygda 79 53.07 N 126.20 E
Tygda ≃ 79 52.35 N 127.55 E
Tygelsjö 41 55.31 N 13.00 E
Tygh Valley 214 45.15 N 121.10 W
Tyin ⊜ 26 61.17 N 8.13 E
Tyja ≃ 78 55.36 N 109.20 E
Tylden 148 32.07 S 27.05 E
Tyldesley 42 53.31 N 2.28 W
Tyler, Minn., U.S. 188 44.17 N 96.08 W
Tyler, Pa., U.S. 204 41.14 N 78.32 W
Tyler, Tex., U.S. 212 32.21 N 95.18 W
Tyler □[6] 212 30.47 N 94.32 W
Tyler, Lake ⊜[1] 212 32.13 N 95.10 W
Tyler East, Lake ⊜[1] 212 32.15 N 95.10 W
Tyler Park 274c 38.52 N 77.12 W
Tylersburg 204 41.23 N 79.19 W
Tyler State Park ▲, Pa., U.S. 198 40.14 N 74.59 W
Tyler State Park ▲, Tex., U.S. 212 32.29 N 95.14 W
Tylersville 200 40.60 N 77.25 W
Tylerton 198 37.58 N 76.01 W
Tylertown 184 31.07 N 90.09 W
Tylla 40 60.28 N 15.33 E
Tylösand 26 56.39 N 12.44 E
Tylöskog ∧∧[2] 40 58.45 N 15.20 E
Tylovaj 70 57.30 N 53.47 E
Tym ≃, S.S.S.R. 64 59.25 N 80.04 E
Tym' ≃, S.S.S.R. 79 51.51 N 143.10 E
Tymna, Laguna C 170 64.00 N 178.30 E
Tymochtee Creek ≃ 204 40.57 N 83.16 W
Tymovskoje 79 50.51 N 142.39 E
Tymsk 76 59.24 N 80.18 E
Tyndall 188 42.59 N 97.52 W
Tyndinskij 64 55.10 N 124.43 E
Tyne ≃, Eng., U.K. 42 55.01 N 1.26 W
Tyne ≃, Scot., U.K. 42 56.00 N 2.31 W
Tyne and Wear □[6] 42 54.55 N 1.35 W
Tynemouth 42 55.01 N 1.24 W
Tyner 206 41.25 N 86.24 W
Tyngsboro 273 42.41 N 71.26 W
Tyngsjö 40 60.18 N 13.53 E
Tynica 68 51.08 N 32.54 E

ENGLISH — Name / Page / Lat.°′ / Long.°′ · DEUTSCH — Name / Seite / Breite°′ / Länge°′ E=Ost

Týn nad Vltavou 30 49.14 N 14.26 E
Tynnelsö 40 59.25 N 17.06 E
Tynset 26 62.17 N 10.47 E
Tyonek 170 61.02 N 151.17 W
Tyoronyaradougou 140 9.21 N 5.38 W
Typta 78 54.35 N 104.31 E
Tyr 79 52.57 N 139.48 E
Tyre → Ṣūr, Lubnān 122 33.16 N 35.11 E
Tyre, Pa., U.S. 204 40.26 N 80.16 W
Tyresö 40 59.14 N 18.18 E
Tyret' 78 53.41 N 102.19 E
Tyrgetuj 78 51.27 N 113.46 E
Tyrifjorden ⊜ 26 60.02 N 10.08 E
Tyringe 41 56.10 N 13.35 E
Tyringham 197 42.15 N 73.12 W
Tyrka 78 54.30 N 107.09 E
Tyrma 79 50.03 N 132.12 E
Tyrma ≃ 79 50.29 N 131.18 E
Tyrnovo 68 48.10 N 27.40 E
Tyrnyauz 74 43.23 N 42.56 E
Tyrone, Ky., U.S. 208 38.02 N 84.51 W
Tyrone, N.Y., U.S. 200 42.25 N 77.03 W
Tyrone, Okla., U.S. 186 36.57 N 101.04 W
Tyrone, Pa., U.S. 204 40.40 N 78.14 W
Tyrone Lake ⊜ 271 42.42 N 83.43 W
Tyrrell, Lake ⊜ 156 35.21 S 142.50 E
Tyrrhenian Sea (Mare Tirreno) ⊤[2] 36 40.00 N 12.00 E
Tyrrhenisches Meer → Tyrrhenian Sea ⊤[2] 36 40.00 N 12.00 E
Tysmenica 68 48.54 N 24.49 E
Tysnesøy I 26 60.00 N 5.35 E
Tysons Corner 274c 38.55 N 77.14 W
Tysons Corner Center ◆[9] 274c 38.55 N 77.13 W
Tysse 26 60.22 N 5.45 E
Tyssedal 26 60.07 N 6.34 E
Tysslingen ⊜ 40 59.19 N 15.02 E
Tystberga 40 58.52 N 17.15 E
Tystrup Sø ⊜ 41 55.22 N 11.35 E
Tytherington 252 53.17 N 2.08 W
Tytuvėnai 66 55.36 N 23.12 E
Ty Ty 182 31.28 N 83.39 W
Tyumen' → T'umen' 76 57.09 N 65.32 E
Tyurginpil'gyn, Laguna C 170 68.30 N 178.00 W
Tyvrov 68 49.01 N 28.30 E
Tywa ≃ 50 53.13 N 14.29 E
Tywardreath 44 50.22 N 4.41 W
Tywi ≃ 44 51.46 N 4.22 W
Tywyn 44 52.35 N 4.05 W
Tzanconeja ≃ 222 16.35 N 91.35 W
Tzaneen 146 23.50 S 30.09 E
Tzekung → Zigong 97 29.22 N 104.46 E
Tzeliutsing → Zigong 97 29.22 N 104.46 E
Tzimol 226 16.16 N 92.16 W
Tzintzuntzan ⊥ 224 19.38 N 101.34 W
Tzucacab 222 20.04 N 89.03 W
Tzukung → Zigong 97 29.22 N 104.46 E
Tzupo → Boshan, Zhg. 88 36.29 N 117.50 E
Tzupo → Zibo, Zhg. 88 36.47 N 118.01 E

U

Uac, Mount ∧ 106 12.12 N 123.40 E
Uaçá ≃ 240 4.13 N 51.32 W
Uagadugu → Ouagadougou 140 12.22 N 1.31 W
Uaiauaka ≃ 236 1.23 N 66.00 W
Uamba 142 7.12 S 16.25 E
Uamba (Wamba) ≃ 142 3.56 S 17.12 E
Uampochane 148 26.23 S 32.41 E
Uaoa Bay C 219a 20.56 N 156.16 W
Uapao, Cap ≻ 165f 21.35 S 167.50 E
Uaran → Ouarane ◆[1] 124 21.00 N 10.30 W
Uatumã ≃ 236 2.26 S 57.37 W
Uauá 240 9.50 S 39.28 W
Uaupés 236 0.08 S 67.05 W
Uaupés (Vaupés) ≃ 236 0.02 N 67.16 W
Ubá 245 21.07 S 42.56 W
Uba ≃ 76 50.15 N 81.41 E
Übach-Palenberg 52 50.55 N 6.07 E
Ubagan ≃ 76 54.24 N 64.45 E
Ubai 154 5.40 S 150.40 E
Ubaidullāhganj 114 22.59 N 77.36 E
Ubaíra 245 13.16 S 39.39 W
Ubaitaba 245 14.18 S 39.20 W
Ubajara 240 3.51 S 40.56 W
Ubajara, Parque Nacional de ▲ 240 3.47 S 40.56 W
Ubangi (Oubangui) ≃ 142 0.30 S 17.42 E
Ubatã 245 14.12 S 39.31 W
Ubaté 236 5.19 N 73.49 W
Ubatuba 246 23.26 S 45.04 W
Ubatuba, Baía de C 246 23.27 S 45.02 W
Ubauro 110 28.10 N 69.44 E
Ubay 106 10.03 N 124.28 E
Ubaye 56 44.28 N 6.22 E
Ubaye ≃ 56 44.28 N 6.18 E
Ubayyiḍ, Wādī al- ∨ 118 32.34 N 43.48 E
Ubby 41 55.37 N 11.13 E
Ube 86 33.56 N 131.15 E
Ubed' ≃ 68 51.27 N 32.29 E
Úbeda 34 38.01 N 3.22 W
Uberaba 245 19.45 S 47.55 W
Uberaba ≃ 245 20.07 S 48.31 W
Uberaba, Lagoa ⊜ 238 17.30 S 57.45 W
Über dem Wind, Inseln → Leeward Islands II 228 17.00 N 63.00 W
Uberlândia 245 18.56 S 48.18 W
Überlingen 54 47.46 N 9.10 E
Überlinger See C 54 47.45 N 9.09 E
Übersee 58 47.49 N 12.28 E
Ubiaja 140 6.38 N 6.21 E
Ubili 144 1.07 S 26.55 E
Ubin, Pulau I 261c 1.24 N 103.58 E
Ubinskoje 76 55.19 N 79.41 E
Ubinskoje, Ozero ⊜ 76 55.30 N 80.05 E
Ubl'a 30 48.55 N 22.23 E
Ubly 180 43.43 N 82.56 W
Uboldo 256b 45.37 N 9.00 E
Ubombo 148 27.33 S 32.00 E
Ubondo 144 0.52 S 25.37 E
Ubon Ratchathani 100 15.14 N 104.54 E
Ubort' ≃ 68 52.06 N 28.28 E
Ubrique 34 36.41 N 5.27 W
Ubudiah, Masjid ✝[1] 104 4.46 N 100.56 E
Ubundi (Ponthierville) 144 0.21 S 25.29 E
Ubur-Tochtor 78 50.06 N 113.37 E
Uča ≃ 72 56.02 N 37.37 E
Ucacha 242 33.02 S 63.31 W
Uč-Adži 118 38.05 N 62.48 E
Učami 64 63.50 N 96.29 E
Učaral 76 46.10 N 80.56 E
Ucayali ≃ 232 4.30 S 73.27 W
Uccellina, Monti dell' ∧∧ 60 42.38 N 11.05 E
Uccle 46 50.48 N 4.19 E
Uch 113 29.14 N 71.03 E
Uchab 146 19.47 S 17.42 E
Uchāna 114 29.28 N 76.10 E
Uchaud 56 43.45 N 4.16 E
Uchee Creek ≃ 182 32.18 N 84.57 W
Uchihara 84 36.22 N 140.21 E
Uchihata 260 34.25 N 135.27 E
Uchiko 86 33.33 N 132.39 E
Uchi Lake 174 51.05 N 92.35 W
Uchinada 84 36.39 N 136.39 E
Uchinomi 86 34.30 N 134.20 E
Uchinoura 82 31.16 N 131.05 E
Uchiumi 86 33.01 N 132.30 E
Uchiura-wan C 82a 42.20 N 140.40 E
Uchiza 238 8.29 S 76.23 W
Uchoa 245 20.56 S 49.13 W
Ucholovo 70 53.47 N 40.29 E
Uchra ≃ 70 58.20 N 39.00 E
Uchta, S.S.S.R. 24 61.12 N 38.32 E
Uchta, S.S.S.R. 24 63.33 N 53.38 E
Uchte 48 52.30 N 8.54 E
Uchte ≃ 50 52.46 N 11.45 E
Uchtoma 66 60.10 N 38.02 E
Uchtspringe 50 52.32 N 11.36 E
Učinskij Ryboučastok 76 60.02 N 65.10 E
Učinskoje Vodochranilišče ⊜[1] 72 56.02 N 37.45 E
Uckange 52 49.18 N 6.09 E
Ückendorf ◆[8] 253 51.30 N 7.07 E
Uckermark □[9] 50 53.10 N 13.35 E
Uckfield 44 50.58 N 0.06 E
Üçköşe 120 40.13 N 41.00 E
Uckro 50 51.51 N 13.37 E
Učkupr'uk 75 40.33 N 71.04 E
Učkurgan 75 41.07 N 72.05 E
Ucluelet 172 48.57 N 125.33 W
Ucon 192 43.36 N 111.58 W
Učterek 75 41.45 N 73.12 E
Úcua ≃ 142 8.35 S 13.40 E
Učujevskij Majdan 70 54.33 N 44.30 E
Učur ≃ 64 58.48 N 130.35 E
Uda ≃, S.S.S.R. 78 56.05 N 99.34 E
Uda ≃, S.S.S.R. 78 51.47 N 107.33 E
Uda ≃, S.S.S.R. 79 54.42 N 135.14 E
Udaipur 110 24.35 N 73.41 E
Udaj ≃ 68 50.05 N 33.07 E
Udala 116 21.35 N 86.34 E
Udalguri 110 26.46 N 92.08 E
Udall 188 37.23 N 97.07 W
Udamalpet 112 10.35 N 77.15 E
Udankudi 112 8.26 N 78.01 E
Udaquiola 242 36.34 S 58.31 W
Udarnyj 79 49.07 N 142.09 E
Udaypur 114 26.56 N 86.31 E
Udbina 36 44.32 N 15.46 E
Udby 41 55.05 N 11.57 E
Uddeholm 40 60.01 N 13.37 E
Uddel 48 52.15 N 5.46 E
Uddevalla 26 58.21 N 11.55 E
Uddingston 42 55.50 N 4.06 W
Uddjaur ⊜ 24 65.55 N 17.49 E
Udel'naja 72 55.38 N 38.03 E
Udel'naja ◆[8] 255a 60.01 N 30.19 E
Uden 48 51.40 N 5.36 E
Udenhout 48 51.37 N 5.08 E
Uder 52 51.22 N 10.05 E
Udgīr 112 18.23 N 77.07 E
Udhampur 113 32.56 N 75.08 E
Udhruḥ 122 30.20 N 35.36 E
Udi 140 6.19 N 7.25 E
Udimskij 24 61.09 N 45.52 E
Udine 58 46.03 N 13.14 E
Udine □[4] 58 46.10 N 13.00 E
Udinskij Chrebet ∧∧ 78 53.20 N 97.50 E
Udipi 112 13.21 N 74.45 E
Udjung-kulon, Menandjung ≻[1] 102 6.45 S 105.20 E
Udmurtskaja Avtonomnaja Sovetskaja Socialističeskaja Respublika □[3] 70 57.00 N 53.00 E
Udokan, Chrebet ∧∧ 78 56.20 N 118.10 E
Udoml'a 66 57.52 N 35.01 E
Udone-jima I 84 34.28 N 139.18 E
Udono 82 33.44 N 136.01 E
Udon Thani 100 17.26 N 102.46 E
Udor, Mount ∧ 152 23.30 S 131.01 E
Udot I 165c 7.23 N 151.43 E
Udskaja Guba C 79 54.50 N 135.45 E
Udskoje 79 54.32 N 134.26 E
Udy 68 50.24 N 36.03 E
Udyl', Ozero ⊜ 79 52.06 N 139.48 E
Udža 64 71.14 N 117.10 E
Udžary 74 40.31 N 47.39 E
Uebaru 165d 24.25 N 123.46 E
Uebigau 50 51.35 N 13.18 E
Uebonti 102 0.55 S 121.38 E
Uebonti, Teluk C 102 0.50 S 121.45 E
Uecker ≃ 50 53.45 N 14.04 E
Ueckeritz 50 54.00 N 14.02 E
Ueckermünde 50 53.44 N 14.03 E
Ueckermünder Heide ◆[3] 50 53.40 N 14.10 E
Ueda 84 36.24 N 138.16 E
Uedem 48 51.40 N 6.16 E
Uedesheim ◆[8] 253 51.10 N 6.48 E
Uegō 258 35.10 N 139.56 E
Uehlfeld 52 49.40 N 10.43 E
Uele ≃ 126 4.09 N 22.26 E
Uelen 170 66.10 N 169.48 W
Uel'kal' 170 65.32 N 179.17 E
Uelsen 48 52.30 N 6.53 E
Uelzen, B.R.D. 48 52.58 N 10.33 E
Uelzen, B.R.D. 253 51.33 N 7.44 E
Ueno, Nihon 84 34.45 N 136.08 E
Ueno, Nihon 84 36.05 N 138.47 E
Ueno, Nihon 84 35.02 N 136.54 E
Ueno, Nihon 260 34.57 N 135.14 E
Uenohara 84 35.37 N 139.07 E
Ueno Park ▲ 258 35.43 N 139.46 E
Uenoshiba 260 34.33 N 135.28 E
Uerdingen ◆[8] 253 51.21 N 6.39 E
Uere ≃ 144 3.42 N 25.24 E
Uetersen 48 53.41 N 9.39 E
Uettingen 52 49.48 N 9.43 E
Uetz 254a 52.28 N 12.56 E
Uetze 48 52.28 N 10.11 E
Ueza ≃ 142 8.03 S 13.11 E
Ufa 76 54.44 N 55.56 E
Ufa ≃ 76 54.40 N 56.00 E
Uffculme 44 50.54 N 3.20 W
Uffenheim 52 49.32 N 10.14 E
Ufita ≃ 60 41.09 N 14.56 E
Ufra 118 40.00 N 53.02 E
Uft'uga ≃ 66 59.46 N 39.21 E
Ugab ≃ 146 21.08 S 13.40 E
Ugak Bay C 170 57.25 N 152.45 W
Ugāle 66 57.16 N 22.02 E
Ugalla ≃ 144 5.08 S 30.42 E
Ugamskij Chrebet ∧∧ 75 42.00 N 70.20 E
Uganda □[1] 10
144 1.00 N 32.00 E
Uganik Island I 170 57.53 N 153.28 W
Ugârčin 38 43.06 N 24.25 E
Ugarit ⊥ 120 35.35 N 35.45 E
Ugashik 170 57.32 N 157.25 W
Ugashik Bay C 170 57.34 N 157.38 W
Ugatkyn ≃ 170 68.24 N 171.30 W
Ugep 140 5.50 N 8.05 E
Ugerløse 41 55.35 N 11.40 E
Ughaybish 130 10.52 N 31.05 E
Ughelli 140 5.29 N 5.59 E
Ugi I 165e 10.15 S 161.45 E
Ugie 148 31.10 S 28.13 E
Ugíjar 34 36.57 N 3.03 W
Ugimi 164m 26.42 N 128.07 E
Ugine 56 45.45 N 6.25 E
Uglegorsk, S.S.S.R. 73 48.19 N 38.17 E
Uglegorsk, S.S.S.R. 79 49.02 N 142.03 E
Uglezavodsk 79 47.21 N 142.38 E
Uglič 66 57.32 N 38.19 E
Ugličskaja Vozvyšennost' ∧∧[1] 66 57.20 N 38.51 E
Ugljan, Otok I 36 44.05 N 15.10 E
Uglovaja 70 57.01 N 52.57 E
Uglovka 66 58.14 N 33.31 E
Uglovoje 79 43.20 N 132.06 E
Uglovskoje 76 51.23 N 80.12 E
Ugly-Zavod 68 52.11 N 32.53 E
Ugnev 68 50.23 N 23.44 E
Ugodiči 70 57.10 N 39.30 E
Ugodskij Zavod 72 55.02 N 36.45 E

Symbols in the index entries represent the broad categories identified in the key at the right. Symbols with superior numbers (∧∧[2]) identify subcategories (see complete key on page *I* · 26).

Kartensymbole in dem Registerverzeichnis stellen die rechts in Schlüssel erklärten Kategorien dar. Symbole mit hochgestellten Ziffern (∧∧[2]) bezeichnen Unterabteilungen einer Kategorie (vgl. vollständiger Schlüssel auf Seite *I* · 26).

Los símbolos incluídos en el texto del índice representan las grandes categorias identificadas con la clave a la derecha. Los símbolos con numeros en su parte superior (∧∧[2]) identifican las subcategorías (véase la clave completa en la página *I* · 26).

Les symboles de l'index représentent les catégories indiquées dans la légende à droite. Les symboles suivis d'un indice (∧∧[2]) représentent des sous-catégories (voir légende complète à la page *I* · 26).

Os símbolos incluídos no texto do índice representam as grandes categorias identificadas com a chave à direita. Os símbolos com números em sua parte superior (∧∧[2]) identificam as subcategorias (veja-se a chave completa à página *I* · 26).

	English	Deutsch	Español	Français	Português
∧	Mountain	Berg	Montaña	Montagne	Montanha
∧∧	Mountains	Berge	Montañas	Montagnes	Montanhas
)(	Pass	Pass	Paso	Col	Passo
∨	Valley, Canyon	Tal, Cañon	Valle, Cañón	Vallée, Canyon	Vale, Canhão
≡	Plain	Ebene	Llano	Plaine	Planície
≻	Cape	Kap	Cabo	Cap	Cabo
I	Island	Insel	Isla	Île	Ilha
II	Islands	Inseln	Islas	Îles	Ilhas
⊥	Other Topographic Features	Andere Topographische Objekte	Otros Elementos Topográficos	Autres données topographiques	Outros Elementos Topográficos

ESPAÑOL

Nombre	Página	Lat.°′	Long.°′ W=Oeste
Ugol'naja, Buchta C	170	63.00 N	179.20 E
Ugolnyy	170	63.03 N	179.03 E
Ugoma ∧	144	4.00 S	28.45 E
Ugovizza	58	46.31 N	13.29 E
Ugra	66	54.47 N	34.17 E
Ugra ≃	72	54.30 N	36.07 E
Ugrojedy	68	50.52 N	35.17 E
Ugr'umovo	72	55.09 N	37.40 E
Ugtaalcajdam	78	48.17 N	105.20 E
Uguj	76	56.02 N	76.03 E
Ug'ut	75	41.24 N	74.50 E
Ugyak, Cape ≻	170	58.17 N	154.04 W
Uh (Už) ≃	30	48.34 N	22.00 E
Uha-dong	88	40.41 N	125.38 E
Uḥayjibah, Jabal al- ∧	122	30.11 N	34.33 E
Uherské Hradiště	30	49.05 N	17.28 E
Uherský Brod	30	49.02 N	17.39 E
Uhingen	52	48.42 N	9.35 E
Uhlenhorst	146	23.45 S	17.55 E
Ühlingen	54	47.43 N	8.19 E
Uhlman Lake @	174	56.40 N	98.23 W
Uhlstädt	50	50.44 N	11.28 E
Uhrichsville	204	40.24 N	81.20 W
Uhyst, D.D.R.	50	51.24 N	14.30 E
Uhyst, D.D.R.	50	51.11 N	14.13 E
Uiche	142	12.03 S	21.02 E
Uíge	142	7.37 S	15.03 E
Uíge □[5]	142	7.00 S	15.30 E
Ŭijŏngbu	88	37.44 N	127.03 E
Ŭiju	88	40.12 N	124.32 E
Uil	76	49.05 N	54.40 E
Uil ≃	70	48.36 N	52.30 E
Uilpata, Gora ∧	74	42.48 N	43.48 E
Uimaharju	26	62.55 N	30.15 E
Uina ≃	136	7.45 N	15.36 E
Uiñaimarca, Lago @	238	16.20 S	68.50 W
Uinebona ≃	236	5.04 N	63.01 W
Uinskoje	76	56.53 N	56.35 E
Uinta ≃	190	40.14 N	109.51 W
Uintah and Ouray Indian Reservation ◆[4]	190	40.20 N	110.20 W
Uinta Mountains ∧∧	190	40.45 N	110.05 W
Uiraúna	240	6.31 S	38.25 W
Uis	146	21.08 S	14.49 E
Ŭisŏng	88	36.22 N	128.41 E
Uitenhage	148	33.40 S	25.28 E
Uitgeest	48	52.32 N	4.43 E
Uithoorn	48	52.14 N	4.50 E
Uithuizen	48	53.24 N	6.40 E
Uithuizermeeden	48	53.24 N	6.42 E
Uitspanning	148	26.46 S	29.56 E
Uj ≃	76	54.17 N	64.58 E
Ujae I[1]	14	9.05 N	165.40 E
Ujaly	76	44.37 N	60.57 E
Ujandina ≃	64	68.23 N	145.50 E
Ujar	76	55.48 N	94.20 E
Ujarrás ⊥	226	9.51 N	83.50 W
Ujazd	30	50.24 N	18.22 E
Ujedinenija, Ostrov I	62	77.28 N	82.28 E
Ujelang I[1]	14	9.49 N	160.55 E
Ujemskij	24	64.29 N	40.50 E
Újezd	50	50.03 N	14.44 E
Újfehértó	30	47.48 N	21.40 E
Ujgursaj	75	40.53 N	71.03 E
Ujhāni	114	28.01 N	79.01 E
Uji	86	34.53 N	135.48 E
Uji ≃	86	34.51 N	135.42 E
Uji-guntō II	82	31.11 N	129.27 E
Ujiie	84	36.41 N	139.58 E
Ujiji	144	4.55 S	29.41 E
Uji-tawara	86	34.51 N	135.31 E
Uji-yamada → Ise	84	34.29 N	136.42 E
Ujjain	110	23.11 N	75.46 E
'Ujmān	118	25.25 N	55.27 E
Ujongtankayji	104	3.32 N	97.13 E
Újpest ◆[8]	254c	47.34 N	19.06 E
Ujście	30	53.04 N	16.43 E
Ujskoje	76	54.22 N	60.00 E
Ujum	75	38.22 N	70.51 E
Ujung	102	7.04 S	120.46 E
Ujungbatu	104	0.43 N	100.31 E
Ujungberung	105a	6.55 S	107.42 E
Ujunggading	100	0.16 N	99.33 E
Ujunggenteng	105a	7.22 S	106.24 E
Ujunglamuru	102	4.40 S	119.58 E
Ujung Pandang (Makasar)	102	5.07 S	119.24 E
Újvidék → Novi Sad	38	45.15 N	19.50 E
Uk	78	55.04 N	98.52 E
Uka, Nihon	164m	26.48 N	128.14 E
Uka, S.S.S.R.	64	57.50 N	162.06 E
Ukamas	148	28.02 S	19.45 E
Ukara Island I	144	1.50 S	33.03 E
'Ukāsh, Wādī ∨	118	34.18 N	40.42 E
Ukaturaka, Île I	142	1.55 N	20.15 E
Ukerewe Island I	144	2.03 S	33.00 E
Ukhayḍir, Jabal ∧	132	29.44 N	32.11 E
Ukhayḍir, Wādī ∨	122	30.55 N	37.01 E
Ukhra	116	23.39 N	87.14 E
Ukhrul	110	25.07 N	94.22 E
Ukhta → Uchta	24	63.33 N	53.38 E
Ukiah, Calif., U.S.	194	39.09 N	123.13 W
Ukiah, Oreg., U.S.	192	45.08 N	118.56 W
Ukibaru-jima I	164m	26.18 N	128.00 E
Ukiha	86	33.19 N	130.47 E
Ukita ◆[8]	258	35.40 N	139.52 E
Ukmergė	66	55.15 N	24.45 E
Ukolnoi Island I	170	55.14 N	161.34 W
Ukrainian Soviet Socialist Republic → Ukrainskaja Sovetskaja Socialističeskaja Respublika □[3]	68	49.00 N	32.00 E
Ukrainka	76	54.39 N	71.20 E
Ukrainsk	73	48.06 N	37.18 E
Ukrainskaja Sovetskaja Socialističeskaja Respublika □[3]	68	49.00 N	32.00 E
Ukrina ≃	36	45.05 N	17.56 E
Uks'anskoje	76	55.57 N	63.01 E
Uktuz	76	55.38 N	68.30 E
Uktym	24	62.38 N	48.52 E
Uku	164m	26.50 N	128.17 E
Ukui	102	0.09 S	102.11 E
Ukurejskij	78	52.24 N	116.49 E
Ukuti	144	3.39 N	33.32 E
Ukyō ◆[8]	260	35.03 N	135.42 E
Ukyr	78	49.28 N	108.52 E
Ula, Bhārat	262b	22.43 N	88.33 E
Ula, Tür.	120	37.05 N	28.26 E
Ula ≃	76	54.40 N	56.00 E
Ulaanbaatar	78	47.55 N	106.53 E
Ulaanbaatar □[8]	78	47.55 N	106.53 E
Ulaanbadrach	92	43.38 N	110.30 E
Ulaanchus	76	49.02 N	89.23 E
Ulaangom	76	49.58 N	92.02 E
Ulaan Nuur @	92	44.30 N	103.35 E
Ulaan Tajga ∧∧	78	50.45 N	98.30 E
'Ulab, Ṭaraq al- ∧∧[2]	120	33.55 N	38.18 E
Ulache ≃	79	44.54 N	133.35 E
Ula-Chuduk	70	47.39 N	45.34 E
Ulak Island I	171a	51.22 N	179.00 W
Ulakmedan	104	2.43 N	99.38 E
Ulamba	142	9.07 S	23.40 E
Ulamona	154	5.00 S	151.15 E
Ulana ≃	226	14.27 N	83.14 W
Ulan Bator → Ulaanbaatar	78	47.55 N	106.53 E
Ulanbel'	76	44.48 N	71.10 E
Ulan-Burgasy, Chrebet ∧∧	78	52.45 N	109.00 E
Ulan-Erge	70	46.19 N	44.53 E
Ulanhot → Wulanhaote	79	46.05 N	122.05 E

FRANÇAIS

Nom	Page	Lat.°′	Long.°′ W=Ouest
Ulānia	116	22.12 N	90.29 E
Ulanov	68	49.42 N	28.08 E
Ulanovo	68	51.46 N	34.18 E
Ulanovskij	72	54.04 N	37.51 E
Ulanów	30	50.30 N	22.16 E
Ulan-Ude	78	51.50 N	107.37 E
Ulan-Ušotej	78	50.45 N	105.29 E
Ulāpāra	116	24.19 N	89.34 E
Ulaş	120	39.27 N	37.03 E
Ul'ašovo	24	65.27 N	56.57 E
Ulatis Creek ≃	216	38.18 N	121.00 W
Ul'atuj	78	51.09 N	116.14 E
Ulawa I	165e	9.46 S	161.57 E
Ulaya	144	7.04 S	36.54 E
Ułazów	30	50.17 N	23.00 E
Ul'ba	76	50.16 N	83.22 E
Ul'banskij Zaliv C	79	53.45 N	137.50 E
Ulchin	88	36.59 N	129.23 E
Ul'chun-Partija	78	49.56 N	112.46 E
Ulcinj	38	41.55 N	19.11 E
Ulco	148	28.21 S	24.15 E
Ulcombe	250	51.12 N	0.39 E
Ulcumayo	238	11.01 S	75.55 W
Uldum	41	55.51 N	9.36 E
Uldz ≃	78	49.56 N	115.31 E
Uleåborg → Oulu	26	65.01 N	25.28 E
Ulefoss	26	59.17 N	9.16 E
Ulen	188	47.05 N	96.16 W
Ulety	78	51.22 N	112.29 E
Ulfborg	26	56.16 N	8.20 E
Ulft	48	51.54 N	6.23 E
Ulgajsyn	76	49.38 N	60.17 E
Ulgueira	256c	38.47 N	9.28 W
Ulhās ≃	262c	19.13 N	73.01 E
Ulhāsnagar	112	19.13 N	73.07 E
Uliast	76	48.57 N	91.17 E
Uliastaj (Džavchlant)	78	47.45 N	96.49 E
Ulindi ≃	144	1.40 S	25.52 E
Ulingan	154	4.30 S	145.25 E
Ulithi I[1]	98	9.58 N	139.40 E
Ulja	64	58.51 N	141.50 E
Uljanino	72	55.21 N	38.26 E
Uljanovka, S.S.S.R.	66	59.38 N	30.46 E
Uljanovka, S.S.S.R.	68	50.58 N	34.18 E
Uljanovka, S.S.S.R.	68	48.20 N	30.13 E
Uljanovo	66	53.43 N	35.32 E
Uljanovsk	70	54.20 N	48.24 E
Uljanovskoje, S.S.S.R.	76	50.02 N	73.42 E
Uljanovskoje, S.S.S.R.	79	46.17 N	142.13 E
Ul'kajak ≃	76	48.54 N	62.00 E
Ul'kan	78	57.14 N	107.19 E
Ul'kan ≃	78	55.53 N	107.45 E
Ul'ken-Karoj, Ozero @	76	54.00 N	71.58 E
Ulla	66	55.14 N	29.15 E
Ulla ≃, Esp.	34	42.39 N	8.44 W
Ulla ≃, S.S.S.R.	66	55.14 N	29.14 E
Ulladulla	160	35.21 S	150.29 E
Ulladulla Trough ✢[1]	14	34.00 S	154.00 E
Ullapool	28	57.54 N	5.10 W
Ullastrell	256d	41.31 N	1.58 E
Üllendahl ◆[8]	253	51.19 N	7.18 E
Ullerslev	41	55.22 N	10.40 E
Ullervad	40	58.40 N	13.52 E
Ullin	184	37.17 N	89.11 W
Üllő	254c	47.23 N	19.21 E
Ullswater @	42	54.34 N	2.54 W
Ullučaj ≃	74	42.18 N	48.08 E
Ullún	242	31.28 S	68.42 W
Ullŭng-do I	82	37.29 N	130.52 E
Ullvettern @	40	59.27 N	14.16 E
Ullvi	40	59.42 N	16.37 E
Ulm, B.R.D.	54	48.24 N	10.00 E
Ulm, Mont., U.S.	192	47.26 N	111.30 W
Ulma	38	47.53 N	25.18 E
Ulmarra	156	29.37 S	153.02 E
Ulmeni	38	45.04 N	26.39 E
Ulmer, Mount ∧	9	77.35 S	86.09 W
Ulmeu-Meisereich	52	50.13 N	6.58 E
Ulpur	116	23.04 N	89.50 E
Ulricehamn	26	57.47 N	13.25 E
Ulrichstein	52	50.34 N	9.11 E
Ulrum	48	53.22 N	6.20 E
Ulsan	88	35.34 N	129.19 E
Ulsteinvik	26	62.20 N	5.53 E
Ulster	200	41.51 N	76.30 W
Ulster □[6]	200	41.56 N	74.00 W
Ulster ≃	52	50.51 N	9.59 E
Ulster Canal ☲	42	54.27 N	6.40 W
Ultimo, Val D' ∨	58	46.35 N	11.00 E
Ultraoriental, Cordillera (Serra do Divisor) ∧∧	238	8.20 S	73.30 W
Ulu, Indon.	102	2.45 N	125.24 E
Ulu, S.S.S.R.	64	60.19 N	127.24 E
Ulu, Sūd.	130	10.43 N	33.29 E
Ulúa ≃	226	15.53 N	87.44 W
Ulubāria	116	22.28 N	88.06 E
Ulubat Gölü @	120	40.10 N	28.35 E
Ulubey	120	38.25 N	29.18 E
Uluborlu	120	38.05 N	30.28 E
Ulu Dağ ∧	120	40.04 N	29.13 E
Uludāngar	262b	22.51 N	88.31 E
Ulugan Bay C	106	10.07 N	118.47 E
Ulug-Chol', Ozero @	78	52.43 N	97.20 E
Uluguru Mountains ∧∧	144	7.10 S	37.40 E
Uluinggalau ∧	165g	16.54 S	179.59 E
Ulu-Jul ≃	76	57.46 N	85.30 E
Ulukışla	120	37.33 N	34.30 E
Ulul I	14	8.35 N	149.40 E
Ulu Laho, Bukit ∧	104	5.43 N	101.27 E
Ulunchan	78	54.51 N	111.02 E
Ulundi	148	28.17 S	31.26 E
Ulunga	79	46.31 N	136.56 E
Ulurijskij-Golec, Gora ∧	78	50.12 N	111.45 E
Ulus	120	41.35 N	32.39 E
Ulusara	116	24.16 N	90.36 E
Ulut ≃	106	12.00 N	125.27 E
Ulutau	76	48.39 N	67.01 E
Ulu Tiram	104	1.36 N	103.49 E
Ulu Yam	104	3.27 N	101.38 E
Ulva ≃	262c	18.59 N	73.02 E
Ulva I	28	56.28 N	6.12 W
Ulvenhout	48	51.34 N	4.48 E
Ulverston	42	54.12 N	3.06 W
Ulverstone	156	41.09 S	146.10 E
Ulvöarna II	26	63.01 N	18.40 E
Ulvshale ≻[1]	41	55.02 N	12.16 E
Ulvshyttan	40	60.18 N	15.22 E
Ulvsund U	41	54.59 N	12.11 E
Ulyanovsk → Uljanovsk	70	54.20 N	48.24 E
Ulysses, Kans., U.S.	188	37.35 N	101.22 W
Ulysses, Nebr., U.S.	188	41.04 N	97.12 W
Ulysses, Pa., U.S.	204	41.54 N	77.46 W
Uly-Žilanšik ≃	76	48.51 N	63.47 E
Ulzë	38	41.41 N	19.54 E
Umag	58	45.25 N	13.32 E
Umaji	86	34.00 N	133.44 E
Umal'tinskij	79	51.56 N	133.36 E
Umán, Méx.	222	20.53 N	89.45 W
Uman', S.S.S.R.	68	48.44 N	30.14 E
'Umān → Oman □[1]	108	22.00 N	58.00 E
Uman I	165c	7.18 N	151.53 E
Umanak	166	70.40 N	52.07 W
Umanak Fjord C[2]	166	70.55 N	53.00 W
Umancevo	70	47.44 N	44.16 E
Umaralla ≃	161b	36.10 S	149.20 E
Umari	240	6.38 S	38.42 W
'Umarī, Qā' al- @	122	31.42 N	36.57 E
Umaria, Bhārat	114	23.48 N	80.56 E
Umaria, Bhārat	114	23.32 N	80.50 E
Umarizal	240	5.59 S	37.49 W
Umarkot	110	25.22 N	69.44 E
Umatac	164p	13.18 N	144.39 E
Umatilla, Fla., U.S.	210	28.55 N	81.40 W

PORTUGUÊS

Nome	Página	Lat.°′	Long.°′ W=Oeste
Umatilla, Oreg., U.S.	192	45.55 N	119.21 W
Umatilla ≃	192	45.55 N	119.20 W
Umatilla Indian Reservation ◆[4]	192	45.41 N	118.31 W
Umayan ≃	106	8.13 N	125.50 E
Umaze	260	34.57 N	135.03 E
Umba	24	66.41 N	34.15 E
Umbai	104	2.10 N	102.20 E
Umbargaon	112	20.12 N	72.45 E
Umbaúba	240	11.22 S	37.39 W
Umbelasha ≃	130	9.51 N	24.50 E
Umbertide	60	43.18 N	12.20 E
Umbogintwini	148	30.00 S	30.58 E
Umboi Island I	154	5.36 S	148.00 E
Umbozero, Ozero @	24	67.43 N	34.25 E
Umbrail, Pass (Giogo di Santa Maria))(	58	46.34 N	10.25 E
Umbria □[4]	60	43.00 N	12.30 E
Umbroli	262c	19.11 N	73.06 E
Umbukul	154	2.30 S	150.00 E
Umbuzeiro	240	7.41 S	35.40 W
Ume ≃	144	16.40 S	28.26 E
Umeå	26	63.50 N	20.15 E
Umeälven ≃	24	63.47 N	20.16 E
Umedani	260	34.44 N	135.51 E
Umedpur	116	22.31 N	89.59 E
Umegashima	84	35.14 N	138.21 E
Umfolozi Game Reserve ◆[4]	148	28.19 S	31.50 E
Umfors	24	65.56 N	15.00 E
Umfreville Lake @	174	50.18 N	94.45 W
Umfuli ≃	144	17.30 S	29.23 E
Umgungundhlovu ⊥	148	28.27 S	31.28 E
Umguza	144	19.25 S	27.51 E
Umhausen	58	47.08 N	10.56 E
Umhlanga Rocks	148	29.43 S	31.06 E
Umhlatuzi ≃	148	28.47 S	32.06 E
Umi	86	33.34 N	130.30 E
Umingan	106	15.56 N	120.50 E
Umiray ≃	106	15.13 N	121.25 E
Umkomaas	148	30.15 S	30.42 E
Umm ad-Daraj, Jabal ∧	122	32.19 N	35.48 E
Umm 'Ajārim ⊽[8]	132	30.50 N	32.49 E
Umm Al-'Abīd	136	27.31 N	15.02 E
Umm al-'Arā'is, Wādī ∨	136	26.26 N	13.55 E
Umm al-Arānib	136	26.08 N	14.45 E
Umm al-Birak	118	23.25 N	39.13 E
Umm al-Ḥawāyā, Jabal ∧	132	28.41 N	31.06 E
Umm al-Jimāl, Khirbat ⊥	122	32.20 N	36.22 E
Umm al-Khashab	134	17.21 N	42.32 E
Umm al-Qaywayn	118	25.35 N	55.34 E
Umm al-Qiṭṭayn	122	32.19 N	36.38 E
Umm al-Quṣūr	132	27.23 N	30.54 E
Ummanz	50	54.28 N	13.10 E
Umm Artah, Wādī ∨	132	28.41 N	32.37 E
Umm as-Sa'd ⊥	122	33.16 N	36.47 E
Umm Badr	130	14.14 N	27.57 E
Umm Balad, Wādī ∨	132	27.40 N	32.39 E
Umm Bayyū'd	130	12.05 N	31.40 E
Umm Bel	130	13.32 N	28.04 E
Umm Boim	130	11.43 N	25.57 E
Umm Dabbī	130	14.37 N	30.23 E
Umm Dam	130	13.45 N	30.59 E
Umm Dhibbān, Sūd.	130	14.14 N	29.37 E
Umm Dhibbān, Sūd.	130	15.26 N	32.51 E
Umm Digulgulaya	130	10.29 N	24.57 E
Umm Dīnār	132	30.12 N	31.04 E
Umm Durmān (Omdurman)	130	15.38 N	32.30 E
Umm el Faḥm	122	32.31 N	35.09 E
Ummeln	48	51.58 N	8.27 E
Ummendorf	50	52.09 N	11.11 E
Umm Habwah, Jabal ∧[2]	132	27.23 N	31.29 E
Umm Ḥamāṭ	122	31.02 N	35.46 E
Umm Jamālah	130	11.27 N	28.12 E
Umm Jurdī, Jabal ∧[2]	132	29.49 N	32.39 E
Umm Kaddādah	130	13.36 N	26.42 E
Umm Khunān	263c	29.55 N	31.15 E
Umm Khushayb, Wādī ∨	132	30.24 N	32.43 E
Umm Kuwaykah	130	13.00 N	32.17 E
Umm Lajj	118	25.04 N	37.13 E
Umm Marahik, Jabal ∧[2]	130	13.40 N	26.53 E
Umm Mirdi	130	18.59 N	33.32 E
Umm Mitmān ⊽[8]	132	30.41 N	32.30 E
Umm Qantur	130	14.17 N	31.22 E
Umm Qurayn	130	9.58 N	28.55 E
Umm Quṣayr	122	31.40 N	35.53 E
Umm Raqabah, Jabal ∧[2]	132	28.58 N	31.08 E
Umm Raqm, Jabal ∧	132	30.14 N	31.52 E
Umm Rīshah, Birkat @	132	30.21 N	30.22 E
Umm Rubūl, Jabal ∧	132	28.20 N	32.37 E
Umm Rumaylah ⊽[4]	130	16.55 N	31.40 E
Umm Ruwābah	130	12.54 N	31.13 E
Umm Saggāt, Wādī ∨	130	15.15 N	23.12 E
Umm Saysabān, Jabal ∧	122	29.45 N	35.10 E
Umm Sayyālah	130	14.25 N	31.10 E
Umm Shalīl	130	10.51 N	23.42 E
Umm Shanqah	130	13.14 N	27.14 E
Umm Shuṭūr	130	7.17 N	33.14 E
Umm Sidr, Wādī ∨	132	27.54 N	32.33 E
Umm Sughra ⊽[4]	130	15.03 N	27.12 E
Umm 'Umayd, Khashm ∧	132	27.39 N	32.37 E
Umm 'Umayd, Ra's ∧	132	27.50 N	32.19 E
Umm 'Umayyid, Bi'r ⊽[4]	132	27.53 N	32.30 E
Umm 'Umayyid, Wādī ∨	132	27.37 N	32.41 E
Umm Urūmah I	118	25.46 N	36.32 E
Umm Walad	122	32.39 N	36.26 E
Umm Zaytah, Jabal ∧[2]	132	29.49 N	32.16 E
Umnak Island I	170	53.25 N	168.10 W
Umnak Pass U	170	53.20 N	167.45 W
Umnäs	24	65.24 N	16.10 E
Umniati	144	18.39 S	29.49 E
Umniati ≃	144	16.49 S	28.45 E
Um'ot, S.S.S.R.	70	54.08 N	42.42 E
Um'ot, S.S.S.R.	70	52.31 N	42.58 E
Umpferstedt	50	50.59 N	11.25 E
Umpqua ≃	192	43.42 N	124.03 W
Umpulo	142	12.38 S	17.42 E
'Umrān	134	15.50 N	43.56 E
'Umrānī, Wādī al- ∨	132	27.37 N	30.53 E
Umraniye, Tür.	120	38.37 N	30.48 E
Umraniye, Tür.	257b	41.01 N	29.05 E
Umrer	112	20.51 N	79.20 E
Umreth	110	22.42 N	73.07 E
Ŭmsŏng	88	36.56 N	127.41 E
Umtali	144	18.58 S	32.40 E
Umtanum Creek ≃	214	46.52 N	120.35 W
Umtata	148	31.35 S	28.47 E
Umtentweni	148	30.42 S	30.28 E
Umuahia	140	5.33 N	7.29 E
Umuarama	245	23.45 S	53.20 W
Umurlu	120	37.50 N	27.58 E
Umvukwe Range ∧∧	144	17.20 S	30.40 E
Umvuma	144	19.19 S	30.35 E
Umzimkulu	148	30.16 S	29.56 E
Umzingwane ≃	144	22.12 S	29.56 E
Umzinto	148	30.22 S	30.33 E
Una, Bhārat	110	20.49 N	71.02 E
Una, Bhārat	113	31.29 N	76.17 E
Una, Bra.	245	15.18 S	39.04 W
Una ≃, Bra.	240	8.50 S	35.08 W
Una ≃, Jugo.	36	45.16 N	16.55 E

Una, Ribeirão ≃	277b	23.31 S	46.18 W
Unac ≃	36	44.30 N	16.09 E
Uña de Gato	186	25.58 N	99.41 W
Unadilla, Ga., U.S.	182	32.16 N	83.44 W
Unadilla, N.Y., U.S.	200	42.20 N	75.19 W
Unadilla ≃	200	42.20 N	75.25 W
Unaí	245	16.23 S	46.53 W
Unakami	84	35.46 N	140.45 E
Unalakleet	170	63.53 N	160.47 W
Unalaska	170	53.52 N	166.32 W
Unalaska Island I	170	53.45 N	166.45 W
Unanderra	160	34.27 S	150.52 E
Unango	144	12.50 S	35.20 E
Unao	114	25.35 N	78.36 E
Unare ≃	236	10.03 N	65.14 W
Unauna, Pulau I	102	0.10 S	121.35 E
Unayyir, Ḥarrat al- ⊽[9]	118	25.20 N	37.45 E
'Unayzah	118	26.06 N	43.56 E
'Unayzah, Jabal ∧	122	30.30 N	35.47 E
Unazuki	84	36.49 N	137.35 E
Uncasville	197	41.26 N	72.07 W
Unchahra	114	24.23 N	80.47 E
Ŭnch'ŏn	88	38.34 N	125.26 E
Uncia	238	18.27 S	66.37 W
Uncompahgre ≃	190	38.45 N	108.06 W
Uncompahgre Peak ∧	190	38.04 N	107.28 W
Uncompahgre Plateau ∧∧[1]	190	38.30 N	108.25 W
Uncukul'	74	42.42 N	46.48 E
Unda	78	51.42 N	116.56 E
Unda ≃	78	51.25 N	116.05 E
Unden @	40	58.47 N	14.26 E
Undenäs	40	58.39 N	14.25 E
Underberg	148	29.50 S	29.22 E
Under River	250	51.15 N	0.14 E
Undersåker	26	63.20 N	13.23 E
Ündersdorf	52	50.09 N	6.49 E
Underwood, Ind., U.S.	208	38.36 N	85.46 W
Underwood, N. Dak., U.S.	188	47.27 N	101.08 W
Underwood, Wash., U.S.	214	45.44 N	121.32 W
Undløse	41	55.36 N	11.35 E
Undory	70	54.37 N	48.25 E
Undu, Tanjung ≻	105b	10.05 S	120.51 E
Undu Cape ≻	165g	16.08 S	179.57 W
Undva Nina ≻	66	58.32 N	21.55 E
Unea Island I	154	4.55 S	149.10 E
Uneča	66	52.50 N	32.40 E
Uneča ≃	66	52.50 N	31.56 E
Uneiuxi ≃	236	0.37 S	65.34 W
Unga Island I	170	55.15 N	160.45 W
Ungaran	105a	7.07 S	110.24 E
Ungarie	156	33.38 S	146.58 E
Ungarn → Hungary □[1]	30	47.00 N	20.00 E
Ungava, Péninsule d' ≻[1]	166	60.00 N	74.00 W
Ungava Bay C	166	59.30 N	67.30 W
Ungay Point ≻	106	13.11 N	124.13 E
Ungch'ŏn	88	35.07 N	128.44 E
Ungeny	68	47.12 N	27.48 E
Unggi	88	42.20 N	130.24 E
Ungurkuj	78	50.27 N	106.58 E
Ungvár → Užgorod	68	48.37 N	22.18 E
Unhos	256c	38.50 N	9.07 W
Unhošť	50	50.04 N	14.08 E
Uni	70	57.46 N	51.30 E
União	240	4.35 S	42.52 W
União da Vitória	242	26.13 S	51.05 W
União dos Palmares	240	9.10 S	36.02 W
Unica	24	62.38 N	34.38 E
Unicoi	182	36.12 N	82.21 W
Unicorn Branch ≃	198	39.15 N	75.52 W
Unicorn Ridge ∧	261d	22.22 N	114.11 E
Unidad Santa Fe	276a	19.23 N	99.15 W
Uniejów	30	51.58 N	18.49 E
Unieux	56	45.24 N	4.16 E
Unije, Otok I	36	44.38 N	14.15 E
Unimak Island I	170	54.50 N	164.00 W
Unimak Pass U	170	54.35 N	164.43 W
Unini ≃	236	1.41 S	61.31 W
Unión, Arg.	242	35.09 S	65.57 W
Union, Ont., Can.	202	42.42 N	81.12 W
Unión, Para.	242	24.48 S	56.33 W
Union, Ill., U.S.	206	42.14 N	88.33 W
Union, Iowa, U.S.	180	42.15 N	93.04 W
Union, Ky., U.S.	208	38.57 N	84.41 W
Union, Maine, U.S.	178	44.13 N	69.17 W
Union, Miss., U.S.	184	32.34 N	89.14 W
Union, Mo., U.S.	209	38.27 N	91.00 W
Union, N.J., U.S.	200	40.42 N	74.16 W
Union, Ohio, U.S.	208	39.54 N	84.18 W
Union, Oreg., U.S.	192	45.13 N	117.52 W
Union, S.C., U.S.	182	34.43 N	81.37 W
Union, Wash., U.S.	214	47.21 N	123.06 W
Union, W. Va., U.S.	182	37.36 N	80.33 W
Unión, Ur.	248	34.53 S	56.08 W
Union □[6], Ind., U.S.	208	39.38 N	84.56 W
Union □[6], N.J., U.S.	198	40.40 N	74.11 W
Union □[6], Ohio, U.S.	204	40.18 N	83.19 W
Union □[6], Pa., U.S.	200	40.58 N	76.54 W
Union Bay	172	49.35 N	124.53 W
Union Beach	198	40.27 N	74.10 W
Union Bridge	198	39.34 N	77.11 W
Union Center	200	42.09 N	76.04 W
Union City, Calif., U.S.	216	37.36 N	122.01 W
Union City, Ga., U.S.	182	33.35 N	84.33 W
Union City, Ind., U.S.	184	40.12 N	84.49 W
Union City, Mich., U.S.	206	42.04 N	85.08 W
Union City, N.J., U.S.	266	40.46 N	74.02 W
Union City, Ohio, U.S.	206	40.10 N	84.48 W
Union City, Pa., U.S.	204	41.54 N	79.51 W
Union City, Tenn., U.S.	184	36.26 N	89.03 W
Union City Reservoir @[1]	204	41.56 N	79.52 W
Uniondale, S. Afr.	148	33.40 S	23.08 E
Uniondale, Ind., U.S.	206	40.50 N	85.15 W
Uniondale, N.Y., U.S.	266	40.43 N	73.36 W
Union Dale, Pa., U.S.	200	41.43 N	75.30 W
Unión de Repúblicas Socialistas Soviéticas → Union of Soviet Socialist Republics □[3]	12	60.00 N	80.00 E
Unión de Reyes	230p	22.48 N	81.32 W
Unión de San Antonio	224	21.06 N	101.58 W
Union des Émirats Arabes → United Arab Emirates □[1]	118	24.00 N	54.00 E
Union des Républiques socialistes soviétiques → Union of Soviet Socialist Republics □[3]	12	60.00 N	80.00 E
Unión de Tula	224	19.58 N	104.16 W
Union Gap	192	46.34 N	120.34 W
Union Grove, Tex., U.S.	212	32.34 N	94.55 W
Union Grove, Wis., U.S.	206	42.41 N	88.03 W
Unión Hidalgo	224	16.28 N	94.50 W
Union Hill	200	43.13 N	77.23 W
Union Lake	206	42.37 N	83.27 W
Union Lake @, Mich., U.S.	206	42.03 N	85.11 W
Union Lake @, Mich., U.S.	271	42.37 N	83.26 W
Union Lake @, N.J., U.S.	198	39.25 N	75.03 W
Union Mills	206	41.30 N	86.47 W
Union of Soviet Socialist Republics □[1], As., Eur.	12	60.00 N	80.00 E
Union Park	210	28.30 N	81.15 W

Union Pier	206	41.50 N	86.42 W
Union Point	182	33.37 N	83.04 W
Unionport, Ind., U.S.	208	40.07 N	85.06 W
Unionport, Ohio, U.S.	204	40.21 N	80.51 W
Union Seamount ✢[3]	16	49.35 N	132.40 W
Union Springs, Ala., U.S.	184	32.09 N	85.49 W
Union Springs, N.Y., U.S.	200	42.50 N	76.42 W
Union Station ◆[5], Calif., U.S.	270	34.04 N	118.14 W
Union Station ◆[5], D.C., U.S.	274c	38.54 N	77.00 W
Union Stock Yards ⱱ[3]	268	41.49 N	87.40 W
Uniontown, Ala., U.S.	184	32.22 N	87.31 W
Uniontown, Ky., U.S.	184	37.46 N	87.56 W
Uniontown, Md., U.S.	198	39.36 N	77.07 W
Uniontown, Ohio, U.S.	204	40.59 N	81.25 W
Uniontown, Pa., U.S.	178	39.54 N	79.44 W
Union Valley Reservoir @[1]	216	38.50 N	120.26 W
Union Village	197	42.00 N	71.32 W
Unionville, Ont., Can.	265b	43.52 N	79.18 W
Unionville, Conn., U.S.	197	41.45 N	72.53 W
Unionville, Ind., U.S.	208	39.14 N	86.25 W
Unionville, Mich., U.S.	180	43.39 N	83.28 W
Unionville, Mo., U.S.	184	40.29 N	93.01 W
Unionville, N.J., U.S.	275	40.01 N	74.46 W
Unionville, N.Y., U.S.	200	41.18 N	74.34 W
Unionville, Ohio, U.S.	204	41.47 N	81.00 W
Unionville, Pa., U.S.	275	39.54 N	75.44 W
Unionville Center	204	40.08 N	83.21 W
Uniopolis	206	40.36 N	84.05 W
Unipouheos Indian Reserve ◆[4]	174	53.52 N	110.21 W
Unisan	106	13.51 N	121.59 E
United	204	40.13 N	79.31 W
United Arab Emirates □[1]	108 / 118	24.00 N	54.00 E
United Arab Republic → Egypt □[1]	130	27.00 N	30.00 E
United Kingdom □[1]	22 / 28	54.00 N	2.00 W
United Nations Headquarters ⱱ	266	40.45 N	73.58 W
United Nations Military Headquarters ■	261b	37.33 N	126.59 E
United States □[1]	168	38.00 N	97.00 W
United States Air Force Academy ■	190	39.00 N	104.55 W
United States Coast Guard Academy ■	197	41.22 N	72.06 W
United States Merchant Marine Academy ⱱ[2]	266	40.48 N	73.46 W
United States Military Academy ■	200	41.23 N	73.28 W
United States Naval Academy ■	198	38.59 N	76.30 W
United States Steel Corporation (Lorain Plant) ⱱ[3], Ohio, U.S.	269a	41.27 N	82.07 W
United States Steel Corporation ⱱ[3], Pa., U.S.	269b	40.20 N	79.54 W
United States Steel Corporation ⱱ[3], Pa., U.S.	269b	40.25 N	79.54 W
United States Steel Corporation Fairless Works ⱱ[3]	275	40.09 N	74.45 W
Unity, Sask., Can.	174	52.27 N	109.10 W
Unity, Maine, U.S.	178	44.40 N	69.14 W
Unity Reservoir @[1]	269b	40.17 N	79.30 W
Universal City	186	29.33 N	98.17 W
Universal City ⱱ[3]	270	34.09 N	118.21 W
Universal Mall ◆[9]	271	42.30 N	83.05 W
Università Degli Studi ⱱ[2]	256b	45.28 N	9.14 E
University	184	34.21 N	89.32 W
University City	209	38.39 N	90.19 W
University Gardens	266	40.46 N	73.44 W
University Heights, Calif., U.S.	216	37.27 N	122.14 W
University Heights, Ohio, U.S.	269a	41.30 N	81.32 W
University Park, Md., U.S.	274c	38.58 N	76.57 W
University Park, N. Mex., U.S.	190	32.17 N	106.45 W
University Park, Tex., U.S.	212	32.52 N	96.47 W
University Place	214	47.14 N	122.34 W
University View	208	40.00 N	83.03 W
Unjha	110	23.48 N	72.24 E
Unkel	52	50.35 N	7.13 E
Unken	58	47.39 N	12.43 E
Unkurda	76	55.48 N	59.24 E
Unley	158b	34.57 S	138.35 E
Un'ma ≃	79	51.54 N	129.18 E
Unna	48	51.32 N	7.41 E
Unna □[8]	253	51.34 N	7.42 E
'Unnāb, Jabal al- ∧	122	29.57 N	36.55 E
'Unnāb, Wādī al- ∨	122	30.11 N	36.39 E
Unnão	114	26.32 N	80.30 E
Unnão □[5]	114	26.30 N	80.30 E
Uno, Ilha de I	140	11.12 N	16.15 W
Unoke	84	36.43 N	136.42 E
Ŭnp'a	88	38.26 N	125.45 E
Unpenji-san ∧	86	34.02 N	133.44 E
Unqua Point ≻	266	40.39 N	73.26 W
Unquillo	242	31.14 S	64.19 W
Ŭnsan	88	39.25 N	126.01 E
Unseburg	50	51.56 N	11.30 E
Unserfrau → Madonna	58	46.43 N	10.52 E
Unsleben	52	50.22 N	10.15 E
Unst I	28	60.45 N	0.55 W
Unstrut ≃	50	51.10 N	11.48 E
Un't	78	49.07 N	102.50 E
Unten	164m	26.41 N	128.00 E
Unterägeri	54	47.08 N	8.35 E
Unterbach, B.R.D.	253	51.12 N	6.54 E
Unterbäch, Schw.	54	46.17 N	7.48 E
Unter dem Wind, Inseln → Windward Islands II	228	13.00 N	61.00 W
Unterelchingen	54	48.27 N	10.07 E
Unterföhring	58	48.12 N	11.38 E
Unterfranken □[5]	52	50.10 N	10.00 E
Untergermaringen	54	47.56 N	10.40 E
Unterglottertal	54	48.03 N	7.56 E
Untergröningen	52	48.55 N	9.53 E
Untergrüne	253	51.22 N	7.39 E
Unterhaching	58	48.04 N	11.38 E
Unterhausen	54	48.26 N	9.16 E
Unter-Inn-Tal ∨	58	47.24 N	11.47 E
Unterjettenberg	58	47.41 N	12.49 E
Unterkirchen	58	47.25 N	11.12 E
Unterlaa ◆[8]	254b	48.08 N	16.25 E
Unterlüss	48	52.50 N	10.17 E
Untermauerbach	254b	48.14 N	16.12 E
Untermünkheim	52	49.09 N	9.44 E
Untermünstertal	54	47.51 N	7.46 E
Unterneuses	52	50.05 N	10.58 E
Unteröwisheim	52	49.08 N	8.40 E
Unterrath ◆[8]	253	51.16 N	6.47 E
Unterschächen	54	46.52 N	8.47 E
Unterschwaningen	52	49.04 N	10.37 E
Unterseen	54	46.41 N	7.51 E
Unterspreewald ◆[1]	50	52.05 N	13.50 E
Untertauern	58	47.18 N	13.30 E
Unterterzen	54	47.07 N	9.15 E
Unterthingau	54	47.46 N	10.31 E
Unterueckersee @	50	53.17 N	13.51 E

Unteruhldingen	54	47.43 N	9.14 E
Unterwalden □[3]	54	46.55 N	8.20 E
Unterwasser	54	47.12 N	9.19 E
Unterweissbach	50	50.37 N	11.10 E
Unterwellenborn	50	50.39 N	11.26 E
Unterwössen	58	47.44 N	12.27 E
Untraverket	40	60.25 N	17.18 E
Unūf, Ra's al- ≻	136	30.31 N	18.34 E
Ünye	120	41.08 N	37.17 E
Unža	70	58.01 N	44.01 E
Unža ≃	70	57.20 N	43.08 E
Unzen-amakusa-kokuritsu-kōen ♠	82	32.45 N	130.17 E
Unzen-dake ∧	82	32.45 N	130.17 E
Unže-Pavinskaja	76	58.53 N	64.02 E
Uojan	78	56.07 N	111.38 E
Uopiane, Serra do ∧∧[1]	238	11.35 S	63.25 W
Uo-shima I	86	34.11 N	133.19 E
Uozu	84	36.48 N	137.24 E
Upa ≃	66	54.02 N	36.15 E
Upala	226	10.47 N	85.02 W
Upanema	240	5.38 S	37.15 W
Upano ≃	236	2.45 S	78.12 W
Upardāng Garhi	114	27.46 N	84.34 E
Upata	236	8.01 N	62.24 W
Upatoi Creek ≃	182	32.22 N	84.58 W
Upavon	44	51.18 N	1.49 W
Ŭpchŏ-ri	88	37.53 N	125.09 E
Upchurch	250	51.23 N	0.39 E
Upemba, Lac @	144	8.36 S	26.26 E
Upemba, Parc National de l' ♠	144	9.10 S	26.35 E
Upernavik	166	72.47 N	56.10 W
Upgant-Schott	48	53.30 N	7.16 E
Uphal	130	6.58 N	34.16 E
Upham	188	48.35 N	100.44 W
Up Holland	42	53.33 N	2.44 W
Uphusen	48	53.01 N	8.58 E
Upi	106	6.57 N	124.09 E
Upía ≃	236	4.18 N	72.45 W
Upington	148	28.25 S	21.15 E
Upire ≃	236	11.27 N	68.58 W
Upland, Calif., U.S.	218	34.06 N	117.39 W
Upland, Ind., U.S.	206	40.28 N	85.30 W
Upland, Nebr., U.S.	188	40.19 N	98.54 W
Upland, Pa., U.S.	275	39.51 N	75.23 W
Upleta	110	21.44 N	70.17 E
Upnuk Lake @	170	60.21 N	158.58 W
Upolu I	165a	13.55 S	171.45 W
Upolu Point ≻	219d	20.16 N	155.51 W
Uporovo	76	56.18 N	66.17 E
Upper □[4]	140	10.30 N	1.30 W
Upper Aetna Lake @	275	39.51 N	74.48 W
Upper Arlington	208	40.00 N	83.03 W
Upper Arrow Lake @	172	50.30 N	117.55 W
Upper Artichoke Reservoir @[1]	273	42.48 N	70.57 W
Upper Beaconsfield	264b	38.01 S	145.25 E
Upper Berkshire Valley	266	40.56 N	74.35 W
Upper Beverley Lake @	202	44.37 N	76.05 W
Upper Black Eddy	200	40.35 N	75.07 W
Upper Blackville	176	46.39 N	65.52 W
Upper Brookville	266	40.51 N	73.34 W
Upper Canada Village ⊥	196	44.57 N	75.03 W
Upper Castlereagh	264a	33.43 S	150.40 E
Upperco	198	39.34 N	76.50 W
Upper Crystal Springs Reservoir @[1]	272	37.30 N	122.20 W
Upper Darby	198	39.58 N	75.16 W
Upper End	252	53.17 N	1.52 W
Upper Erskine Lake @	266	41.06 N	74.15 W
Upper Fairmount	198	38.06 N	75.47 W
Upper Falls	274b	39.26 N	76.24 W
Upper Ferntree Gully	264b	37.54 S	145.19 E
Upper Fraser	172	54.07 N	121.56 W
Upper Ganga Canal ☲	114	29.57 N	78.12 E
Upper Gap U	202	44.06 N	76.50 W
Upper Goose Lake @	174	51.44 N	92.44 W
Upper Greenwood Lake	266	41.11 N	74.24 W
Upper Greenwood Lake @	266	41.11 N	74.23 W
Upper Hat Creek	172	50.38 N	121.35 W
Upper Humber ≃	176	49.10 N	57.28 W
Upper Hutt	162	41.08 S	175.04 E
Upper Iowa ≃	180	43.29 N	91.14 W
Upper Island Cove	176	47.39 N	53.12 W
Upper Juba □[4]	134	3.00 N	43.00 E
Upper Keechi Creek ≃	212	31.23 N	95.42 W
Upper Klamath Lake @	192	42.23 N	122.55 W
Upper Lake	194	39.10 N	122.54 W
Upper Lake @	194	41.44 N	120.08 W
Upper Lehigh	200	41.02 N	75.55 W
Upper Liard	170	60.02 N	128.55 W
Upper Machodoc Creek ≃	198	38.18 N	77.02 W
Upper Manitou Lake @	174	49.24 N	92.48 W
Upper Matecumbe Key I	210	24.55 N	80.39 W
Upper Moutere	162	41.16 S	173.00 E
Upper Musquodoboit	176	45.08 N	62.57 W
Upper Mystic Lake @	273	42.27 N	71.09 W
Upper New York Bay C	266	40.41 N	74.03 W
Upper Nyack	200	41.07 N	73.55 W
Upper Red Lake @	188	48.10 N	94.40 W
Upper Rideau Lake @	202	44.41 N	76.20 W
Upper River Rouge ≃	271	42.23 N	83.16 W
Upper Saddle River	266	41.04 N	74.06 W
Upper Saint Clair	269b	40.21 N	80.05 W
Upper Sandusky	204	40.50 N	83.17 W
Upper San Leandro Reservoir @[1]	216	37.47 N	122.07 W
Upper Sheila	176	47.28 N	64.56 W
Upper Straits Lake @	271	42.35 N	83.24 W
Upper Sumas	214	49.01 N	122.12 W
Upper Takaka	162	41.02 S	172.50 E
Upper Tean	44	52.57 N	1.58 W
Upper Tooting ◆[8]	250	51.26 N	0.10 W
Upper Ugashik Lake @	170	57.40 N	156.43 W
Upper Volta □[1]	124 / 140	13.00 N	2.00 W
Upper Windigo Lake @	174	52.30 N	91.35 W
Upper Yarra Reservoir @[1]	159	37.41 S	145.56 E
Upper Yosemite Fall Ƚ	216	37.45 N	119.36 W
Uppingham	44	52.35 N	0.43 W
Uppland □[9]	40	59.59 N	17.48 E
Upplanda	40	60.14 N	17.44 E
Upplands Väsby	40	59.31 N	17.54 E
Uppsala	40	59.52 N	17.38 E
Uppsala Län □[6]	40	60.00 N	17.50 E
Upright, Cape ≻	170	60.17 N	172.15 W
Upsala → Uppsala	40	59.52 N	17.38 E
Upshi	110	33.50 N	77.49 E
Upshur □[6]	212	32.45 N	94.55 W
Upstart, Cape ≻	156	19.42 S	147.45 E
Upton, Qué., Can.	196	45.39 N	72.41 W
Upton, Eng., U.K.	42	53.13 N	2.52 W
Upton, Eng., U.K.	250	51.30 N	0.35 W
Upton, Mass., U.S.	197	42.11 N	71.36 W
Upton, Wyo., U.S.	188	44.06 N	104.38 W

Symbol	English	Deutsch	Español	Français	Português
≃	River	Fluss	Río	Rivière	Rio
☲	Canal	Kanal	Canal	Canal	Canal
Ƚ	Waterfall, Rapids	Wasserfall, Stromschnellen	Cascada, Rápidos	Chute d'eau, Rapides	Cascata, Rápidos
U	Strait	Meeresstrasse	Estrecho	Détroit	Estreito
C	Bay, Gulf	Bucht, Golf	Bahía, Golfo	Baie, Golfe	Baía, Golfo
@	Lake, Lakes	See, Seen	Lago, Lagos	Lac, Lacs	Lago, Lagos
☷	Swamp	Sumpf	Pantano	Marais	Pântano
⊼	Ice Features, Glacier	Eis- und Gletscherformen	Accidentes Glaciales	Formes glaciaires	Acidentes Glaciares
⊽	Other Hydrographic Features	Andere Hydrographische Objekte	Otros Elementos Hidrográficos	Autres données hydrographiques	Outros Elementos Hidrográficos
✢	Submarine Features	Untermeerische Objekte	Accidentes Submarinos	Formes de relief sous-marin	Acidentes Submarinos
□	Political Unit	Politische Einheit	Unidad Politica	Entité politique	Unidade Política
ⱱ	Cultural Institution	Kulturelle Institution	Institución Cultural	Institution culturelle	Instituição Cultural
⊥	Historical Site	Historische Stätte	Sitio Histórico	Site historique	Sitio Histórico
♠	Recreational Site	Erholungs- und Ferienort	Sitio de Recreo	Centre de loisirs	Sítio de Lazer
⊠	Airport	Flughafen	Aeropuerto	Aéroport	Aeroporto
■	Military Installation	Militäranlage	Instalación Militar	Installation militaire	Instalação Militar
◆	Miscellaneous	Verschiedenes	Misceláneo	Divers	Miscelânea

ENGLISH Name	Page	Lat.°′	Long.°′

V

DEUTSCH Name	Seite	Breite°′	Länge°′ E=Ost

Symbols in the index entries represent the broad categories identified in the key at the right. Symbols with superior numbers (∧∧[2]) identify subcategories (see complete key on page I · 26).

Kartensymbole in dem Registerverzeichnis stellen die rechts in Schlüssel erklärten Kategorien dar. Symbole mit hochgestellten Ziffern (∧∧[2]) bezeichnen Unterabteilungen einer Kategorie (vgl. vollständiger Schlüssel auf Seite I · 26).

Los símbolos incluídos en el texto del índice representan las grandes categorias identificadas con la clave a la derecha. Los símbolos con numeros en su parte superior (∧∧[2]) identifican las subcategorías (véase la clave completa en la página I · 26).

Les symboles de l'index représentent les catégories indiquées dans la légende à droite. Les symboles suivis d'un indice (∧∧[2]) représentent des sous-catégories (voir légende complète à la page I · 26).

Os símbolos incluídos no texto do índice representam as grandes categorias identificadas com a chave à direita. Os símbolos com números em sua parte superior (∧∧[2]) identificam as subcategorias (veja-se a chave completa à página I · 26).

	English	Deutsch	Español	Français	Português
∧	Mountain	Berg	Montaña	Montagne	Montanha
∧∧	Mountains	Berge	Montañas	Montagnes	Montanhas
)(	Pass	Pass	Paso	Col	Passo
∨	Valley, Canyon	Tal, Cañon	Valle, Cañón	Vallée, Canyon	Vale, Canhão
≚	Plain	Ebene	Llano	Plaine	Planície
›	Cape	Kap	Cabo	Cap	Cabo
❙	Island	Insel	Isla	Île	Ilha
❙❙	Islands	Inseln	Islas	Îles	Ilhas
•	Other Topographic Features	Andere Topographische Objekte	Otros Elementos Topográficos	Autres données topographiques	Outros Elementos Topográficos

≃ River	Fluss	Río	Rivière	Rio
≚ Canal	Kanal	Canal	Canal	Canal
L Waterfall, Rapids	Wasserfall, Stromschnellen	Cascada, Rápidos	Chute d'eau, Rapides	Cascata, Rápidos
U Strait	Meeresstrasse	Estrecho	Détroit	Estreito
C Bay, Gulf	Bucht, Golf	Bahía, Golfo	Baie, Golfe	Baía, Golfo
⊜ Lake, Lakes	See, Seen	Lago, Lagos	Lac, Lacs	Lago, Lagos
≍ Swamp	Sumpf	Pantano	Marais	Pântano
⊓ Ice Features, Glacier	Eis- und Gletscherformen	Accidentes Glaciales	Formes glaciaires	Acidentes Glaciares
≈ Other Hydrographic Features	Andere Hydrographische Objekte	Otros Elementos Hidrográficos	Autres données hydrographiques	Outros Elementos Hidrográficos

✢ Submarine Features	Untermeerische Objekte	Accidentes Submarinos	Formes de relief sous-marin	Acidentes Submarinos
□ Political Unit	Politische Einheit	Unidad Politica	Entité politique	Unidade Política
♜ Cultural Institution	Kulturelle Institution	Institución Cultural	Institution culturelle	Instituição Cultural
⊥ Historical Site	Historische Stätte	Sitio Histórico	Site historique	Sitio Histórico
♠ Recreational Site	Erholungs- und Ferienort	Sitio de Recreo	Centre de loisirs	Sítio de Lazer
⊠ Airport	Flughafen	Aeropuerto	Aéroport	Aeroporto
■ Military Installation	Militäranlage	Instalación Militar	Installation militaire	Instalação Militar
↞ Miscellaneous	Verschiedenes	Misceláneo	Divers	Miscelânea

Velikije Korovincy 68 49.59 N 28.17 E
Velikije Krynki 68 49.27 N 33.29 E
Velikije Lučki 68 48.26 N 22.35 E
Velikije Luki 66 56.20 N 30.32 E
Velikije Mosty 68 50.14 N 24.06 E
Velikije Soročincy 68 50.03 N 33.56 E
Velikij Gluboček 68 49.37 N 25.32 E
Velikij Log 73 48.15 N 39.33 E
Velikij Žvančik 68 48.46 N 26.59 E
Veliki kanal ☰ 38 45.45 N 18.50 E
Veliki Vitorog ∧ 36 44.07 N 17.03 E
Velikoanadol'skij Les ♠ 73 47.42 N 37.23 E
Velikoarchangel'skoje 68 50.51 N 40.46 E
Velikockoje 73 49.21 N 40.02 E
Velikodolinskoje 68 46.21 N 30.35 E
Velikodvorskaja 66 60.18 N 41.58 E
Velikodvorskij 70 55.15 N 40.41 E
Veliko Gradište 38 44.45 N 21.32 E
Velikoje, S.S.S.R. 66 59.32 N 36.59 E
Velikoje, S.S.S.R. 70 57.21 N 39.47 E
Velikoje, Ozero ⊜, S.S.S.R. 66 57.02 N 36.34 E
Velikoje, Ozero ⊜, S.S.S.R. 70 55.13 N 40.10 E
Velikonda Hills ⛰2 112 14.45 N 79.10 E
Velikookt'abr'skij 66 57.26 N 33.49 E
Velikoploskoje 68 47.01 N 29.40 E
Velikorusskoje 76 54.39 N 74.38 E
Veliko Tărnovo 38 43.04 N 25.39 E
Velikovisočnoje 24 67.16 N 52.01 E
Velikovo 66 59.18 N 42.08 E
Velilla de San Antonio 256a 40.22 N 3.29 W
Veli Lošinj 36 44.31 N 14.30 E
Velimče 68 51.36 N 24.44 E
Vélingara, Sén. 140 15.00 N 14.40 W
Vélingara, Sén. 140 13.09 N 14.07 W
Velingrad 38 42.04 N 24.00 E
Velino ≃ 60 42.33 N 12.43 E
Velino, Monte ∧ 60 42.09 N 13.23 E
Veliž 66 55.38 N 31.12 E
Veližany 76 57.34 N 65.49 E
Veljaminovo, S.S.S.R. 72 55.12 N 37.52 E
Veljaminovo, S.S.S.R. 72 55.53 N 36.52 E
Velká Bíteš 30 49.17 N 16.13 E
Velká Deštná ∧ 30 50.18 N 16.24 E
Vel'ká Fatra ⛰ 30 49.00 N 19.05 E
Vel'ké Kapušany 30 48.33 N 22.04 E
Velké Meziříčí 30 49.21 N 16.00 E
Velký Šenov 50 51.00 N 14.25 E
Vella Gulf ⊍ 165e 8.00 S 156.50 E
Vella Lavella I 165e 7.45 S 156.40 E
Vellano 60 43.57 N 10.43 E
Vellār ≃ 112 11.29 N 79.46 E
Vellberg 52 49.05 N 9.53 E
Vellechevreux-et-Courbenans 54 47.33 N 6.32 E
Velletri 60 41.41 N 12.47 E
Vellinge 41 55.28 N 13.01 E
Vellmar 52 51.21 N 9.28 E
Vellore, Bhārat 112 12.56 N 79.08 E
Vellore, Ont., Can. 265b 43.50 N 79.34 W
Velm 254b 48.03 N 16.27 E
Velmede 52 51.21 N 8.22 E
Velo d'Astico 58 45.43 N 11.23 E
Velosos 246 23.15 S 45.26 W
Velp 48 52.00 N 5.59 E
Velp ≃ 52 50.58 N 5.05 E
Velpke 50 52.24 N 10.56 E
Velsen 48 52.27 N 4.39 E
Vel'sk 24 61.05 N 42.05 E
Vel't 24 68.03 N 49.55 E
Velten 50 52.41 N 13.10 E
Veltheim 48 52.11 N 8.58 E
Veltrusy 50 50.14 N 14.18 E
Veltrusy ⊥ 32 50.14 N 14.18 E
Veluwe ◆1 48 52.12 N 5.45 E
Veluwemeer ⊜ 48 52.22 N 5.38 E
Velva, It. 56 44.16 N 9.33 E
Velva, N. Dak., U.S. 188 48.04 N 100.56 W
Velvary 50 50.15 N 14.15 E
Vémars 251 49.04 N 2.34 E
Vembādi Shola ∧ 112 10.12 N 77.24 E
Vembanād Lake ⊜ 112 9.35 N 76.25 E
Vemdalen 26 62.27 N 13.52 E
Vemmenæs 41 54.59 N 10.40 E
Vempalle 112 14.22 N 78.28 E
Ven I 41 55.54 N 12.41 E
Venaco 36 42.14 N 9.10 E
Venada, Isla I 226 11.09 N 84.56 W
Venadillo 236 4.43 N 74.55 W
Venado 224 22.56 N 101.05 W
Venado, Isla I, Nic. 226 11.57 N 83.44 W
Venado, Isla I, Ven. 231r 10.00 N 62.25 W
Venado Tuerto 242 33.45 S 61.58 W
Venafro 60 41.29 N 14.02 E
Venalzio 56 45.09 N 7.01 E
Venâncio Aires 242 29.36 S 52.11 W
Venango 204 41.46 N 80.07 W
Venango □6 204 41.24 N 79.50 W
Venanson 56 44.03 N 7.15 E
Venant 251 48.30 N 2.06 E
Venarey-les-Laumes 54 47.32 N 4.26 E
Venaria 56 45.08 N 7.38 E
Venasca 56 44.33 N 7.24 E
Venasque 56 43.59 N 5.09 E
Vence 56 43.43 N 7.07 E
Venceslau Braz 245 23.51 S 49.48 W
Vencimont 52 50.02 N 4.55 E
Venda Nova, Bra. 245 19.49 S 43.58 W
Venda Nova, Port. 34 41.40 N 7.58 W
Vendargues 56 43.39 N 3.58 E
Vendas Novas 34 38.41 N 8.28 W
Vendée □5 32 46.40 N 1.20 W
Vendée ◆1 32 46.40 N 1.10 W
Vendel 40 60.10 N 17.36 E
Vendelsö 40 59.12 N 18.12 E
Vendeuvre-sur-Barse 54 48.14 N 4.28 E
Vendičany 68 48.37 N 27.48 E
Vendin-lès-Béthune 46 50.32 N 2.37 E
Vendin-le-Vieil 46 50.28 N 2.52 E
Vendôme 46 47.48 N 1.04 E
Vendrell 34 41.13 N 1.32 E
Vendsyssel ◆1 26 57.20 N 10.00 E
Venecia, C.R. 226 10.22 N 84.17 W
Venecia → Venezia, It. 58 45.27 N 12.21 E
Venedig → Venezia 58 45.27 N 12.21 E
Venedocia 206 40.44 N 84.25 W
Venedy 209 38.24 N 89.39 W
Veneta, Laguna C 58 45.25 N 12.19 E
Venetia 204 40.15 N 80.03 W
Venetian Village 206 42.24 N 88.02 W
Venetie 170 66.30 N 147.26 W
Veneto □4 58 45.30 N 11.45 E
Venev 72 54.21 N 38.16 E
Venezia (Venice) 58 45.27 N 12.21 E
Venezia □4 58 45.35 N 12.34 E
Venezuela □1 232; 236 8.00 N 66.00 W
Venezuela, Golfo de C 236 11.30 N 71.00 W
Venezuelan Basin ⊹1 16 14.30 N 68.00 W
Veng 41 56.07 N 9.53 E
Vengerovka 73 48.43 N 38.24 E
Vengerovo 76 55.41 N 76.45 E
Vengurla 112 15.52 N 73.38 E
Veniaminof, Mount ∧ 170 56.13 N 159.18 W
Venice → Venezia, It. 58 45.27 N 12.21 E
Venice, Fla., U.S. 210 27.06 N 82.27 W
Venice, Ill., U.S. 209 38.40 N 90.11 W
Venice, La., U.S. 184 29.17 N 89.21 W
Venice, Ohio, U.S. 204 41.27 N 82.46 W
Venice, Pa., U.S. 269b 40.19 N 80.14 W
Venice ◆8 218 34.00 N 118.29 W
Venice, Gulf of C 58 45.15 N 13.00 E
Venise → Venezia 58 45.27 N 12.21 E
Vénissieux 56 45.41 N 4.53 E
Venjan 26 60.57 N 13.55 E
Venjansjön ⊜ 26 60.54 N 14.00 E
Venkatagiri 112 13.58 N 79.35 E
Venlo 48 51.24 N 6.10 E
Vennesla 26 58.17 N 7.59 E
Vennhausen ◆8 253 51.13 N 6.51 E
Venosa 36 40.57 N 15.49 E
Vénosc 56 44.59 N 6.07 E
Venosta, Val ∨ 58 46.40 N 10.35 E
Venoste, Alpi (Ötztaler Alpen) ⛰ 58 46.45 N 10.55 E
Venraij 48 51.32 N 5.59 E
Vent 58 46.52 N 10.56 E
Vent, Îles du → Windward Islands II 228 13.00 N 61.00 W
Venta ≃ 66 57.24 N 21.33 E
Venta, Río de la ≃ 224 16.59 N 93.46 W
Ventanas 236 1.23 S 79.25 W
Ventasso, Monte ∧ 58 44.23 N 10.17 E
Ventenat, Cape ≻ 154 10.10 S 151.15 E
Ventersburg 148 28.09 S 27.08 E
Ventersdorp 148 26.17 S 26.48 E
Venterspos 263d 26.18 S 27.39 E
Venterspos Location 263d 26.18 S 27.42 E
Venterspos West 263d 26.16 S 27.38 E
Venterstad 148 30.47 S 25.48 E
Venticano 60 41.05 N 14.50 E
Ventimiglia 56 43.47 N 7.36 E
Ventnor 44 50.36 N 1.11 W
Ventnor City 198 39.20 N 74.29 W
Ventotene 60 40.48 N 13.26 E
Ventotene, Isola di I 60 40.47 N 13.25 E
Ventoux, Mont ∧ 56 44.10 N 5.17 E
Ventspils 66 57.24 N 21.36 E
Ventuari ≃ 236 3.58 N 67.02 W
Ventura (San Buenaventura) 218 34.17 N 119.18 W
Ventura □6 218 34.30 N 119.00 W
Ventura ≃ 218 34.16 N 119.18 W
Venturina 58 43.02 N 10.36 E
Venus, Fla., U.S. 210 27.04 N 81.21 W
Venus, Pa., U.S. 204 41.22 N 79.29 W
Venus, Tex., U.S. 212 32.26 N 97.06 W
Vénus, Pointe ≻ 164s 17.29 S 149.29 W
Venus Bay C 159 38.40 S 145.43 E
Venustiano Carranza, Méx. 222 16.21 N 92.33 W
Venustiano Carranza, Méx. 224 19.44 N 103.47 W
Venustiano Carranza, Presa ⊜1 222 27.30 N 100.40 W
Venzone 58 46.20 N 13.09 E
Veprik 68 50.23 N 34.11 E
Vepsovskaja Vozvyšennost' ⛰1 66 60.20 N 35.15 E
Ver 165f 14.11 S 167.34 E
Ver ≃ 44 51.42 N 0.20 W
Vera, Esp. 34 37.15 N 1.52 W
Vera, Ill., U.S. 209 39.02 N 89.07 W
Verá, Laguna ⊜ 242 26.05 S 57.39 W
Veracruz, Méx. 190 32.25 N 115.05 W
Vera Cruz, Pa., U.S. 198 40.30 N 75.30 W
Veracruz [Llave] 224 19.12 N 96.08 W
Veracruz □3 222 19.20 N 96.40 W
Veraguas □4 226 8.30 N 81.00 W
Verano Brianza 256b 45.41 N 9.14 E
Veranópolis 242 28.57 S 51.33 W
Verao I 165f 17.30 S 168.15 E
Verava 246 23.47 S 47.05 W
Verāval 110 20.54 N 70.22 E
Verba 68 50.17 N 25.37 E
Verbania 54 45.56 N 8.33 E
Verbank 200 41.44 N 73.43 W
Verbeek, Pegunungan ⛰ 102 2.35 S 121.25 E
Verberg ◆8 253 51.22 N 6.36 E
Verberie 46 49.19 N 2.44 E
Verbier 54 46.06 N 7.13 E
Verbilki 72 56.32 N 37.36 E
Verbinskij 73 47.53 N 40.02 E
Verbl'užka 68 48.23 N 32.54 E
Verbovskij 70 55.32 N 42.00 E
Vercelli 56 45.19 N 8.25 E
Vercelli □4 56 45.37 N 8.10 E
Vercel-Villedieu-le-Camp 54 47.11 N 6.24 E
Verchazovka 70 50.56 N 48.46 E
Verchères 196 45.47 N 73.21 W
Verchères □6 196 45.45 N 73.20 W
Verchn'ačka 68 48.49 N 30.02 E
Verchn'aja Amga 64 59.30 N 126.08 E
Verchn'aja Angara ≃ 78 55.42 N 109.54 E
Verchnaja Balkarija 74 43.06 N 43.24 E
Verchnaja Buzinovka 70 49.04 N 43.12 E
Verchn'aja Čebula 76 56.02 N 87.36 E
Verchn'aja Chava 68 51.50 N 39.56 E
Verchn'aja Chila 78 52.06 N 115.54 E
Verchn'aja Chortica 68 47.51 N 35.01 E
Verchn'aja Čuginka 73 48.55 N 39.39 E
Verchnaja Dobrinka 70 50.46 N 45.03 E
Verchn'aja Gniluša 68 50.16 N 40.23 E
Verchn'aja Grajvoronka 68 51.41 N 37.46 E
Verchn'aja Inta 24 66.00 N 60.20 E
Verchn'aja Irmen' 76 54.35 N 82.14 E
Verchnaja Maza 70 52.58 N 47.56 E
Verchn'aja Orl'anka 70 53.44 N 51.04 E
Verchn'aja Pyšma 76 56.55 N 60.37 E
Verchn'aja Salda 76 58.02 N 60.33 E
Verchn'aja Serebr'akovka 70 47.21 N 42.14 E
Verchn'aja Sin'ačicha 76 57.59 N 61.40 E
Verchn'aja Sysert' 76 56.26 N 60.46 E
Verchn'aja Tajmyra ≃ 64 74.15 N 99.48 E
Verchn'aja Tarka 76 56.37 N 77.30 E
Verchnaja Tereška 70 52.54 N 47.24 E
Verchn'aja Tišanka 68 51.20 N 40.33 E
Verchn'aja Tojma 24 62.13 N 45.00 E
Verchn'aja Troica 66 57.15 N 37.08 E
Verchn'aja Tura 76 58.22 N 59.49 E
Verchn'aja Zaimka 78 55.51 N 110.09 E
Verchn'aja Zima 78 53.48 N 101.47 E
Verchneaks'onovskij 70 48.21 N 42.38 E
Verchne-Angarskij Chrebet ⛰ 78 56.20 N 111.30 E
Verchne-Anikin 73 48.09 N 39.59 E
Verchnebakanskij 68 44.52 N 37.39 E
Verchneber'ozovskij 76 50.17 N 82.13 E
Verchnebuzanskij 70 46.38 N 48.02 E
Verchnecaricynskij 70 48.23 N 43.57 E
Verchnedneprovsk 68 48.39 N 34.21 E
Verchnedneprovskij 66 54.59 N 33.21 E
Verchneduvannyj 68 48.20 N 39.48 E
Verchneduvannyj ◆8 73 48.20 N 39.48 E
Verchnedvinsk 66 55.47 N 27.56 E
Verchneimbatskoje 64 63.11 N 87.58 E
Verchnejarkejev 70 55.27 N 54.19 E
Verchneje 68 48.51 N 38.28 E
Verchneje ◆8 73 48.53 N 38.28 E
Verchneje Šachlovo 72 55.02 N 37.15 E
Verchneje Sinevidnoje 68 49.06 N 23.34 E
Verchne-Kamskaja Vozvyšennost' ⛰1 70 58.15 N 52.30 E
Verchne Karabachskij Kanal ☰ 74 39.44 N 47.57 E
Verchnemakejevka 68 49.10 N 41.03 E
Verchnesadovoje 68 44.42 N 33.42 E
Verchnesjezžeje 70 52.44 N 51.15 E
Verchnespasskoje 70 52.29 N 41.47 E
Verchne-T'oploje 73 48.51 N 39.26 E
Verchnetulomskij 24 68.38 N 31.45 E
Verchneural'sk 76 53.53 N 59.13 E
Verchneusinskoje 76 52.14 N 93.01 E
Verchnevil'ujsk 64 63.27 N 120.18 E
Verchnevolynskoje 75 40.43 N 68.51 E
Verchnij Amyl 78 53.08 N 94.30 E
Verchnij Avz'an 76 53.32 N 57.33 E
Verchnij Balyklej 70 49.34 N 45.10 E
Verchnij Baskunčak 70 48.14 N 46.44 E
Verchnij Byk 68 50.43 N 41.14 E
Verchnije Dvoriki 72 56.28 N 38.22 E
Verchnije Kigi 76 55.28 N 58.37 E
Verchnije Korobki 70 50.19 N 44.38 E
Verchnije Lipki 70 49.38 N 43.51 E
Verchnije Tatyšly 76 56.17 N 55.52 E
Verchnij Ikorec 68 51.11 N 39.46 E
Verchnij-Karačan 70 51.24 N 41.46 E
Verchnij Krasnyj Pereval 79 46.33 N 134.37 E
Verchnij Kužebar 76 53.22 N 93.15 E
Verchnij Landech 70 56.51 N 42.36 E
Verchnij Leb'ažinskij 70 46.45 N 47.50 E
Verchnij Lomov 70 53.28 N 43.34 E
Verchnij Lomovec 66 52.13 N 38.37 E
Verchnij Mamon 68 50.10 N 40.23 E
Verchnij Most 66 57.31 N 28.50 E
Verchnij Nejvinskij 76 57.17 N 60.09 E
Verchnij Petr'ak 76 57.29 N 77.30 E
Verchnij Rogačik 68 47.14 N 34.21 E
Verchnij Šergol'džin 78 50.12 N 108.20 E
Verchnij Tagil 76 57.22 N 59.56 E
Verchnij Takermen' 70 55.39 N 52.43 E
Verchnij Trojanov Val (Upper Trajan's Wall) ⊥ 68 46.35 N 29.00 E
Verchnij Ufalej 76 56.04 N 60.14 E
Verchnij Ul'chun 78 49.34 N 112.32 E
Verchnij Uslon 70 55.47 N 48.57 E
Verchnij Zub, Gora ∧ 76 53.45 N 89.15 E
Verchnyje Nikul'asy 66 60.25 N 30.45 E
Verchnyj Nagol'čik 73 48.05 N 39.06 E
Verchojansk 64 67.35 N 133.27 E
Verchojanskij Chrebet ⛰ 64 67.00 N 129.00 E
Vercholensk 78 54.06 N 105.35 E
Verchopuja 24 61.34 N 41.31 E
Verchošižemje 70 58.01 N 49.07 E
Verchososna 68 50.44 N 38.14 E
Verchoturje 76 58.52 N 60.48 E
Verchoturovo 76 58.22 N 95.21 E
Verchovažje 24 60.45 N 42.00 E
Verchovcevo 68 48.29 N 34.14 E
Verchovino 66 59.33 N 43.19 E
Verchovje 66 52.49 N 37.14 E
Verchovl'an' 72 55.03 N 38.21 E
Verchozim 70 52.56 N 46.23 E
Verchubinka 76 50.29 N 82.26 E
Verclause 56 44.23 N 5.26 E
Vercors □9 56 44.57 N 5.25 E
Verdalsøra 26 63.48 N 11.29 E
Verde ≃, Bra. 238 11.54 S 55.48 W
Verde ≃, Bra. 238 13.33 S 58.01 W
Verde ≃, Bra. 240 10.11 S 42.24 W
Verde ≃, Bra. 245 18.01 S 50.14 W
Verde ≃, Bra. 245 17.05 S 46.05 W
Verde ≃, Bra. 245 15.07 S 48.40 W
Verde ≃, Bra. 245 21.12 S 51.53 W
Verde ≃, Bra. 245 19.55 S 49.45 W
Verde ≃, Bra. 245 19.11 S 50.44 W
Verde ≃, Bra. 246 21.38 S 47.03 W
Verde ≃, Bra. 246 21.34 S 45.31 W
Verde ≃, Méx. 224 21.37 N 99.15 W
Verde ≃, Para. 242 23.09 S 57.37 W
Verde ≃, S.A. 238 13.59 S 60.24 W
Verde ≃, Ariz., U.S. 190 33.33 N 111.40 W
Verde, Arroyo ≃, Arg. 244 41.56 S 65.03 W
Verde, Arroyo ≃, Bol. 238 11.25 S 66.20 W
Verde Grande ≃, Bra. 245 14.35 S 43.53 W
Verde Grande ≃, Méx. 224 20.42 N 103.14 W
Verde Island I 106 13.33 N 121.05 E
Verde Island Passage ⊍ 106 13.34 N 120.51 E
Verdello 56 45.36 N 9.37 E
Verden, B.R.D. 48 52.55 N 9.13 E
Verden, Okla., U.S. 186 35.05 N 98.05 W
Verde Pequeno ≃ 245 14.48 S 43.31 W
Verdesela, Pinhal da ♠ 256c 38.37 N 9.08 W
Verdi 216 39.31 N 119.59 W
Verdigre 188 42.36 N 98.02 W
Verdigre Creek ≃ 188 42.42 N 98.03 W
Verdinho ≃ 245 17.29 S 50.27 W
Verdon 188 40.08 N 95.48 W
Verdon ≃ 56 43.43 N 5.46 E
Verdon, Canal du ☰ 56 43.43 N 5.57 E
Verdoy 200 42.46 N 73.48 W
Verduga 66 58.46 N 29.12 E
Verdugo Mountains ⛰ 270 34.13 N 118.18 W
Verdun, Qué., Can. 196 45.27 N 73.34 W
Verdun, Fr. 32 43.52 N 1.14 E
Verdun, Fr. 52 49.10 N 5.23 E
Verdun-sur-le-Doubs 54 46.54 N 5.01 E
Vereb'jo 66 58.41 N 32.42 E
Vereeniging 148 26.38 S 27.57 E
Vereinigte Arabische Emirate → United Arab Emirates □1 118 24.00 N 54.00 E
Vereinigte Königreich → United Kingdom □1 28 54.00 N 2.00 W
Vereinigte Staaten → United States □1 168 38.00 N 97.00 W
Vereja, S.S.S.R. 72 55.46 N 39.06 E
Vereja, S.S.S.R. 72 55.21 N 36.11 E
Vereja, S.S.S.R. 255b 55.37 N 38.02 E
Veremejki 66 53.46 N 31.15 E
Vereščagino, S.S.S.R. 64 64.14 N 87.37 E
Vereščagino, S.S.S.R. 70 58.05 N 54.40 E
Veresegyház 254c 47.39 N 19.17 E
Veresoč' 68 51.19 N 31.46 E
Veretje 72 54.08 N 36.17 E
Véretz 46 47.22 N 0.48 E
Verga 275 39.52 N 75.10 W
Verga, Cap ≻ 140 10.12 N 14.27 W
Vergara, Esp. 34 43.07 N 2.25 W
Vergara, Ur. 242 32.56 S 53.57 W
Vergato 58 44.17 N 11.07 E
Vergel 186 25.39 N 103.32 W
Vergeletto 54 46.14 N 8.36 E
Vergemont Creek ≃ 156 24.12 S 143.17 E
Vergennes 178 44.10 N 73.15 W
Verghereto 60 43.47 N 12.00 E
Vergiate 56 45.43 N 8.42 E
Vergons 56 43.55 N 6.35 E
Vergt 32 45.02 N 0.43 E
Vergulevka 73 48.24 N 38.32 E
Verigin 174 51.35 N 102.08 W
Verigino 72 56.42 N 38.08 E
Verín 34 41.56 N 7.26 W
Veringenstadt 54 48.11 N 9.12 E
Verin Talin 74 40.23 N 43.53 E
Veriora 66 58.00 N 27.21 E
Veríssimo 245 19.42 S 48.18 W
Veríssimo ≃ 245 18.23 S 48.20 W
Veríssimo Sarmento 142 8.10 S 20.39 E
Verkeerdevlei 148 28.48 S 26.48 E
Verkhneudinsk → Ulan-Ude 78 51.50 N 107.37 E
Verkhniy Ufaley → Verchnij Ufalej 76 56.04 N 60.14 E
Verkhnyaya Salda → Verchn'aja Salda 76 58.02 N 60.33 E
Verkhoyansk → Verchojansk 64 67.35 N 133.27 E
Verkykerskop 148 27.54 S 29.17 E
Verl (Senne I) 48 51.53 N 8.31 E
Vermaaklikheid 148 34.19 S 21.01 E
Vermaas 148 26.30 S 25.59 E
Vermand 46 49.52 N 3.09 E
Verme Falls ⌊ 134 5.20 N 40.16 E
Vermejo ≃ 186 36.30 N 104.33 W
Vermelho ≃, Bra. 240 5.33 S 49.14 W
Vermelho ≃, Bra. 240 7.44 S 47.17 W
Vermelho ≃, Bra. 240 9.16 S 47.23 W
Vermelho ≃, Bra. 245 14.54 S 51.06 W
Vermenton 46 47.40 N 3.44 E
Vermette Lake ⊜ 174 55.40 N 109.05 W
Vermezzo 256b 45.24 N 8.59 E
Vermiglio 58 46.18 N 10.42 E
Vermilion, Alta., Can. 172 53.22 N 110.51 W
Vermilion, Ohio, U.S. 204 41.25 N 82.22 W
Vermilion □6 206 40.08 N 87.37 W
Vermilion ≃, Alta., Can. 174 53.44 N 110.18 W
Vermilion ≃, Ont., Can. 180 46.16 N 81.41 W
Vermilion ≃, Ill., U.S. 206 41.19 N 89.04 W
Vermilion ≃, Minn., U.S. 180 48.16 N 92.30 W
Vermilion ≃, Ohio, U.S. 204 41.26 N 82.22 W
Vermilion, Middle Fork ≃ 206 40.12 N 87.45 W
Vermilion, South Fork ≃ 206 40.49 N 88.30 W
Vermilion Bay 174 49.51 N 93.24 W
Vermilion Bay C 184 29.40 N 92.00 W
Vermilion Hills ⛰2 174 50.43 N 106.50 W
Vermilion Lake ⊜, Ont., Can. 174 50.03 N 92.13 W
Vermilion Lake ⊜, Minn., U.S. 180 47.53 N 92.25 W
Vermilion Range ⛰2 180 47.50 N 92.00 W
Vermillion 188 42.47 N 96.56 W
Vermillion ≃, Minn., U.S. 180 44.45 N 92.51 W
Vermillion ≃, S. Dak., U.S. 188 42.44 N 96.53 W
Vermillion, East Fork ≃ 188 43.44 N 97.03 W
Vermillion, West Fork ≃ 188 43.44 N 97.03 W
Vermillion Creek ≃, U.S. 190 40.46 N 108.53 W
Vermillion Creek ≃, Kans., U.S. 188 39.12 N 96.13 W
Vermont 264b 37.50 S 145.12 E
Vermont □3 168; 178 43.50 N 72.45 W
Vermontville 206 42.38 N 85.02 W
Vernaison 56 45.39 N 4.49 E
Vernal 190 40.27 N 109.32 W
Vernalis 216 37.38 N 121.17 W
Vernante 56 44.15 N 7.32 E
Vernayaz 54 46.08 N 7.02 E
Vernazza 56 44.08 N 9.41 E
Verndale 188 46.24 N 95.01 W
Verne 48 51.41 N 8.34 E
Verner 180 46.25 N 80.07 W
Verneuil 32 48.44 N 0.56 E
Verneuil-l'Étang 251 48.39 N 2.50 E
Verneuil-sur-Avre 46 48.44 N 0.56 E
Verneuil-sur-Seine 46 48.59 N 1.59 E
Verneukpan 148 30.00 S 21.00 E
Verneukpan ⊜ 148 29.58 S 21.10 E
Vernier 54 46.13 N 6.06 E
Verninge 41 55.18 N 10.13 E
Vernio 60 44.03 N 11.09 E
Vernon, B.C., Can. 172 50.16 N 119.16 W
Vernon, Ont., Can. 202 45.10 N 75.28 W
Vernon, Fr. 32 47.48 N 1.38 E
Vernon, Fr. 46 49.05 N 1.29 E
Vernon, Ala., U.S. 184 33.45 N 88.07 W
Vernon, Calif., U.S. 270 34.01 N 118.13 W
Vernon, Conn., U.S. 197 41.50 N 72.28 W
Vernon, Fla., U.S. 184 30.37 N 85.43 W
Vernon, Ill., U.S. 209 38.48 N 89.05 W
Vernon, Ind., U.S. 208 38.59 N 85.36 W
Vernon, Mich., U.S. 206 42.56 N 84.02 W
Vernon, N.J., U.S. 200 41.12 N 74.29 W
Vernon, N.Y., U.S. 200 43.05 N 75.32 W
Vernon, Ohio, U.S. 204 41.23 N 80.34 W
Vernon, Tex., U.S. 186 34.09 N 99.17 W
Vernon, Utah, U.S. 190 40.06 N 112.26 W
Vernon, Lake ⊜ 202 45.20 N 79.17 W
Vernon Dam ◆6 197 42.46 N 72.31 W
Vernon Hills 268 42.13 N 87.58 W
Vernonia 214 45.52 N 123.11 W
Vernon Lake ⊜1 184 31.15 N 93.25 W
Vernon River 176 46.12 N 62.50 W
Vernouillet 251 48.58 N 1.59 E
Vernoux-en-Vivarais 56 44.54 N 4.39 E
Verny 52 49.01 N 6.12 E
Vero ≃ 34 42.00 N 0.10 E
Vero Beach 210 27.38 N 80.24 W
Véroia 38 40.31 N 22.12 E
Verolanuova 58 45.19 N 10.04 E
Verolavecchia 58 45.19 N 10.03 E
Veroli 60 41.41 N 13.25 E
Verona, Ont., Can. 202 44.29 N 76.42 W
Verona, It. 58 45.27 N 11.00 E
Verona, Ky., U.S. 208 38.49 N 84.40 W
Verona, Miss., U.S. 184 34.12 N 88.43 W
Verona, N.J., U.S. 266 40.50 N 74.12 W
Verona, N.Y., U.S. 200 43.08 N 75.34 W
Verona, Ohio, U.S. 208 39.54 N 84.29 W
Verona, Wis., U.S. 206 42.59 N 89.32 W
Verona □4 58 45.25 N 11.02 E
Verona Beach 200 43.12 N 75.44 W
Verona Beach State Park ♠ 200 43.14 N 75.44 W
Verona Park 206 42.21 N 85.09 W
Verónica 248 35.22 S 57.20 W
Verperluda, Ostrov I 255a 59.59 N 30.01 E
Verplanck 200 41.15 N 73.58 W
Verran 156 33.51 S 136.18 E
Verrazano-Narrows Bridge ◆5 200 40.36 N 74.03 W
Verrès 56 45.40 N 7.42 E
Verrettes 228 19.03 N 72.28 W
Verrey-sous-Salmaise 54 47.26 N 4.40 E
Verrières, Bois de ♠ 251 48.45 N 2.15 E
Verrières-le-Buisson 251 48.45 N 2.16 E
Versa ≃ 56 44.54 N 8.16 E
Versailles, Fr. 46 48.48 N 2.08 E
Versailles, Ill., U.S. 184 39.53 N 90.39 W
Versailles, Ind., U.S. 208 39.04 N 85.15 W
Versailles, Ky., U.S. 208 38.03 N 84.44 W
Versailles, Mo., U.S. 184 38.26 N 92.51 W
Versailles, N.Y., U.S. 200 42.31 N 78.59 W
Versailles, Ohio, U.S. 206 40.13 N 84.29 W
Versailles, Pa., U.S. 269b 40.21 N 79.51 W
Versailles ◆8 278 34.38 S 58.31 W
Versailles, Château de ⊥ 251 48.48 N 2.07 E
Versailles, Parc de ♠ 251 48.49 N 2.06 E
Versailles State Park ♠ 208 39.04 N 85.13 W
Verse ≃ 253 51.15 N 7.46 E
Versec → Vršac 38 45.07 N 21.18 E
Versestausee ⊜1 253 51.11 N 7.41 E
Versien 148 27.05 S 27.52 E
Veršina Tei 76 53.20 N 89.36 E
Veršino-Darasunskij 78 52.20 N 115.32 E
Veršino-Šachtaminskij 78 51.21 N 117.50 E
Versmold 48 52.02 N 8.09 E
Versoix 54 46.16 N 6.10 E
Ver-sur-Launette 251 49.06 N 2.41 E
Vert 251 48.57 N 1.41 E
Vert, Cap ≻ 140 14.43 N 17.30 W
Vert'ačij 70 48.57 N 43.53 E
Verte, Île I 265a 45.34 N 73.30 W
Vertedero 230m 18.05 N 66.15 W
Verteillac 32 45.21 N 0.22 E
Vertentes 240 7.54 S 35.59 W
Vertientes 230p 21.16 N 78.09 W
Vertijevka 68 51.10 N 31.51 E
Vertkovo 72 56.07 N 36.25 E
Vert-le-Grand 251 48.34 N 2.22 E
Vert-le-Petit 251 48.33 N 2.22 E
Vertlinskoje 72 56.14 N 36.58 E
Vertou 32 47.10 N 1.29 W
Vertova 56 45.48 N 9.50 E
Vert-Saint-Denis 251 48.34 N 2.37 E
Vertus 46 48.54 N 4.00 E
Verucchio 60 43.59 N 12.25 E
Verulam 148 29.45 S 31.02 E
Verulamium ⊥ 250 51.45 N 0.22 W
Verviers 52 50.35 N 5.52 E
Vervins 46 49.50 N 3.54 E
Verwall Gruppe ⛰ 54 47.02 N 10.10 E
Verwoerd Reservoir ⊜1 148 30.40 S 25.40 E
Verwood 44 50.53 N 1.52 W
Veryan 44 50.13 N 4.54 W
Verzasca ≃ 54 46.09 N 8.52 E
Verzegnis 58 46.25 N 12.59 E
Verzenay 46 49.10 N 4.09 E
Verzuolo 56 44.36 N 7.29 E
Verzy 46 49.09 N 4.10 E
Vesanto 26 62.56 N 26.25 E
Vesava ◆8 262c 19.08 N 72.48 E
Vescovato, Fr. 36 42.30 N 9.26 E
Vescovato, It. 58 45.10 N 10.10 E
Vesdre ≃ 52 50.37 N 5.37 E
Veseja 66 53.04 N 27.41 E
Veselí nad Lužnicí 30 49.11 N 14.43 E
Veselí nad Moravou 30 48.58 N 17.22 E
Veselinovo 68 47.21 N 31.14 E
Veselovskoje 76 54.00 N 78.43 E
Veselovskoje Vodochranilišče ⊜1 70 47.00 N 41.18 E
Vésenaz 54 46.14 N 6.12 E
Vešenskaja 70 49.38 N 41.43 E
Vesgre ≃ 46 48.53 N 1.28 E
Vesijärvi ⊜ 26 61.06 N 25.32 E
Vesjegonsk 66 58.40 N 37.16 E
Veškajma, S.S.S.R. 70 54.04 N 47.02 E
Veškajma, S.S.S.R. 70 54.03 N 47.08 E
Veški 255b 55.56 N 37.37 E
Vesle ≃ 46 49.23 N 3.38 E
Vešn'aki ◆8 255b 55.44 N 37.49 E
Ves'olaja Gora 73 48.43 N 39.16 E
Ves'olaja Rošča 76 53.47 N 76.22 E
Ves'oloje, S.S.S.R. 68 47.01 N 34.55 E
Ves'oloje, S.S.S.R. 70 50.17 N 45.15 E
Ves'oloje, S.S.S.R. 73 47.10 N 38.45 E
Ves'oloje, S.S.S.R. 75 43.19 N 77.06 E
Ves'olo-Voznesenka 73 47.09 N 38.20 E
Ves'olyj, S.S.S.R. 70 47.06 N 40.45 E
Ves'olyj, S.S.S.R. 73 47.20 N 39.18 E
Ves'olyje Terny 68 48.07 N 33.32 E
Ves'olyj Jar, S.S.S.R. 76 51.18 N 81.07 E
Ves'olyj Jar, S.S.S.R. 79 43.57 N 135.28 E
Ves'olyj Podol, S.S.S.R. 68 49.36 N 33.16 E
Ves'olyj Podol, S.S.S.R. 76 53.31 N 65.54 E
Ves'olyj Pos'olok ◆8 255a 59.54 N 30.28 E
Vesoul 54 47.38 N 6.10 E
Vespasiano 245 19.40 S 43.55 W
Vespolate 56 45.21 N 8.40 E
Vesta 226 9.43 N 83.03 W
Vest-Agder □6 26 58.30 N 7.10 E
Vestal 200 42.05 N 76.03 W
Vestal Center 200 42.02 N 76.01 W
Vestavia Hills 184 33.27 N 86.47 W
Vestbygd 26 58.06 N 6.35 E
Vesterålen II 24 68.45 N 15.00 E
Vester Egede 41 55.16 N 11.59 E
Vesterø Havn 26 57.18 N 10.56 E
Vester Skerninge 41 55.03 N 10.28 E
Vester Sottrup 41 54.57 N 9.43 E
Vestfjorden C2 24 68.08 N 15.00 E
Vestfold □6 26 59.15 N 10.10 E
Vestmannaeyjar 24a 63.26 N 20.12 W
Vestone 58 45.42 N 10.24 E
Vestreno 54 46.06 N 9.18 E
Vestsjælland □6 41 55.35 N 11.30 E
Vestvågøya I 24 68.15 N 13.50 E
Vésubie ≃ 56 43.52 N 7.12 E
Vesubio → Vesuvio ∧1 60 40.49 N 14.26 E
Vesuv → Vesuvio ∧1 60 40.49 N 14.26 E
Vesuvio ∧1 60 40.49 N 14.26 E
Vesuvius → Vesuvio ∧1 60 40.49 N 14.26 E
Vesuvius Bay 214 48.53 N 123.35 W
Veszprém 30 47.06 N 17.55 E
Veszprém □6 30 46.50 N 17.30 E
Vésztő 30 46.55 N 21.16 E
Vet ≃ 148 27.40 S 25.40 E
Vetapālem 112 15.47 N 80.19 E
Vétheuil 46 49.04 N 1.42 E
Vetju 24 62.57 N 50.44 E
Vetka 66 52.33 N 31.10 E
Vetlanda 26 57.26 N 15.04 E
Vetl'anka 70 52.52 N 51.09 E
Vetluga 70 57.51 N 45.47 E
Vetluga ≃ 70 56.18 N 46.24 E
Vetlužskij, S.S.S.R. 70 58.23 N 45.26 E
Vetlužskij, S.S.S.R. 70 57.11 N 45.07 E
Vetoškino 70 57.18 N 49.44 E
Vetovo 38 43.42 N 26.16 E
Vetralla 60 42.19 N 12.03 E
Vetren 38 42.16 N 24.03 E
Vetrino 66 55.25 N 28.28 E
Vetriolo 58 46.02 N 11.18 E
Vetrişoaia 38 46.26 N 28.13 E
Vetschau 50 51.47 N 14.04 E
Vettaikkāranpudūr 112 10.34 N 76.56 E
Vettisfossen ⌊ 26 61.22 N 7.55 E
Vetto 58 44.29 N 10.20 E
Vettore, Monte ∧ 60 42.49 N 13.16 E
Vetulonia 60 42.51 N 10.58 E
Veules-les-Roses 46 49.52 N 0.48 E
Veulettes-sur-Mer 46 49.51 N 0.36 E
Veurne (Furnes) 46 51.04 N 2.40 E
Vevay 208 38.45 N 85.04 W
Vevelstad 24 65.43 N 12.30 E
Veveno, Khawr ∨ 130 6.40 N 32.58 E
Vevey 54 46.28 N 6.51 E
Vex 54 46.13 N 7.24 E
Veyle ≃ 54 46.18 N 4.50 E
Veynes 56 44.32 N 5.49 E
Veyrier 56 45.53 N 6.10 E
Vézelay 46 47.28 N 3.44 E
Vézelise 54 48.29 N 6.05 E
Vézénobres 56 44.03 N 4.09 E
Vézère ≃ 32 44.53 N 0.53 E
Vezirköprü 120 41.09 N 35.28 E
Vezouze ≃ 54 48.35 N 6.29 E
Vezza d'Oglio 58 46.14 N 10.24 E
Vezzana, Cima della ∧ 58 46.17 N 11.50 E
Vezzano 58 46.05 N 11.00 E
Vezzano Ligure 58 44.09 N 9.52 E
VI □4 140 19.00 N 15.00 W
Viacha 238 16.39 S 68.18 W
Viadana 58 44.56 N 10.31 E
Viadutos 242 27.34 S 52.01 W
Viai Island I 154 3.20 S 144.25 E
Viale 242 31.53 S 60.01 W
Vialonga 256c 38.52 N 9.05 W
Via Mala ∨ 54 46.40 N 9.26 E
Viamão 242 30.05 S 51.02 W
Viamonte 242 33.44 S 63.06 W
Vian 186 35.30 N 94.58 W
Viana, Bra. 240 3.13 S 45.00 W
Viana, Bra. 245 20.23 S 40.30 W
Viana, Ilha do I 277a 22.52 S 43.08 W
Viana del Bollo 34 42.11 N 7.06 W
Viana do Alentejo 34 38.20 N 8.00 W
Viana do Castelo 34 41.42 N 8.50 W
Vianden 52 49.57 N 6.11 E
Vianen 48 52.00 N 5.05 E
Viangchan (Vientiane) 100 17.58 N 102.36 E
Viangphoukha 100 20.41 N 101.04 E
Viar ≃ 34 37.36 N 5.50 W
Viareggio 58 43.52 N 10.14 E
Viarmes 46 49.08 N 2.22 E
Viatka → Kirov 70 58.38 N 49.42 E
Viaur ≃ 32 44.08 N 2.23 E
Vibank 174 50.20 N 103.55 W
Víboras, Arroyo de las ≃ 248 33.57 S 58.21 W
Viborg, Dan. 26 56.26 N 9.24 E
Viborg → Vyborg, S.S.S.R. 66 60.42 N 28.45 E
Viborg, S. Dak., U.S. 188 43.10 N 97.05 W
Viborg □6 41 56.18 N 9.27 E
Vibo Valentia 36 38.40 N 16.06 E
Vibraye 46 48.03 N 0.44 E
Viburnum 184 37.43 N 91.08 W
Viby 41 55.33 N 12.02 E
Viby ◆8 41 56.07 N 10.10 E
Vic, Étang de C 56 43.29 N 3.50 E
Vicálvaro ◆8 256a 40.24 N 3.36 W
Vicarello 60 42.10 N 12.12 E
Vicchio 60 43.56 N 11.28 E
Vicco 182 37.13 N 83.04 W
Vic-en-Bigorre 32 43.06 N 0.05 E
Vicência 240 7.40 S 35.20 W
Vicente, Point ≻ 270 33.44 N 118.25 W
Vicente Casares 248 34.57 S 58.38 W
Vicente de Carvalho 246 23.56 S 46.19 W
Vicente Guerrero, Méx. 224 18.24 N 92.53 W
Vicente Guerrero, Méx. 224 19.08 N 98.10 W
Vicente López 248 34.32 S 58.28 W
Vicente López □5 278 34.32 S 58.30 W
Vicente Noble 228 18.23 N 71.11 W
Vicente Pérez Rosales, Parque Nacional ♠ 244 41.12 S 72.55 W
Vicenza 58 45.33 N 11.33 E
Vicenza □4 58 45.40 N 11.27 E
Viceroy 174 49.27 N 105.22 W
Vich 34 41.56 N 2.15 E
Vichada □5 236 5.00 N 69.30 W
Vichada ≃ 236 4.55 N 67.50 W
Vichadero 242 31.48 S 54.43 W
Vichayal 238 4.52 S 81.05 W
Vichigasta 242 29.29 S 67.31 W
Vichoreva ≃ 78 56.47 N 101.22 E
Vichorevka 78 56.12 N 101.09 E
Vichra ≃ 66 54.01 N 31.52 E
Vichuga → Vičuga 70 57.13 N 41.56 E
Vichun 90 27.49 N 114.23 E
Vichuquén 242 34.53 S 72.00 W
Vichy 32 46.08 N 3.26 E
Vici 186 36.09 N 99.18 W
Vickery 204 41.23 N 82.56 W
Vicksburg, Mich., U.S. 206 42.06 N 85.32 W
Vicksburg, Miss., U.S. 184 32.14 N 90.56 W
Vicksburg, Pa., U.S. 200 40.56 N 76.59 W
Vicksburg National Military Park ♠ 184 32.24 N 90.52 W
Vico 36 42.10 N 8.48 E
Vico, Lago di ⊜ 60 42.19 N 12.10 E
Vico Canavese 56 45.30 N 7.47 E
Vico del Gargano 60 41.54 N 15.57 E
Vico Equense 60 40.40 N 14.25 E
Vicoforte 56 44.21 N 7.54 E
Vicopisano 60 43.42 N 10.35 E
Viçosa, Bra. 240 9.24 S 36.14 W
Viçosa, Bra. 245 20.45 S 42.53 W
Viçosa, Bra. 246 22.44 S 42.37 W
Viçosa, Ilha I 240 0.27 N 50.00 W
Viçosa do Ceará 240 3.34 S 41.05 W
Vicosoprano 54 46.22 N 9.37 E
Vicovaro 60 42.01 N 12.54 E
Vicq 251 48.49 N 1.50 E
Vic-sur-Aisne 46 49.24 N 3.07 E
Vic-sur-Cère 32 44.59 N 2.37 E
Vic-sur-Seille 52 48.47 N 6.32 E
Victor, Calif., U.S. 216 38.08 N 121.12 W
Victor, Idaho, U.S. 192 43.36 N 111.07 W
Victor, Iowa, U.S. 180 41.44 N 92.18 W
Victor, Mont., U.S. 192 46.25 N 114.09 W
Victor, N.Y., U.S. 200 42.59 N 77.24 W
Victor, Lac ⊜ 176 50.35 N 61.50 W
Victorbur 48 53.29 N 7.20 E
Victor Harbor 158b 35.34 S 138.37 E
Victoria, Arg. 242 32.37 S 60.10 W
Victoria → Vitória, Bra. 245 20.19 S 40.21 W
Victoria, Cam. 142 4.01 N 9.12 E
Victoria, B.C., Can. 172 48.25 N 123.22 W
Victoria, P.E.I., Can. 176 46.13 N 63.29 W
Victoria, Chile 238 20.44 S 69.42 W
Victoria, Chile 242 38.13 S 72.20 W
Victoria, Gren. 231k 12.12 N 61.42 W
Victoria, Guinée 140 10.50 N 14.33 W
Victoria, H.K. 6 22.17 N 114.09 E
Victoria (Xianggang), H.K. 261d 22.17 N 114.09 E
Victoria, Malay. 102 5.17 N 115.15 E
Victoria → Ciudad Victoria, Méx. 224 23.44 N 99.08 W
Victoria, Pil. 106 13.12 N 121.15 E
Victoria, Pil. 106 15.35 N 120.41 E
Victoria, Rom. 38 45.45 N 24.41 E
Victoria, Sey. 128 4.38 S 55.27 E
Victoria, Kans., U.S. 188 38.52 N 99.09 W
Victoria, Tex., U.S. 186 28.48 N 97.00 W
Victoria, Va., U.S. 182 36.59 N 78.14 W
Victoria □3 156 38.00 S 145.00 E
Victoria □4 144 20.54 S 31.21 E
Victoria □6, Ont., Can. 202 44.35 N 78.50 W
Victoria □6, Tex., U.S. 212 28.55 N 97.00 W
Victoria ◆8 278 34.28 S 58.31 W
Victoria ≃, Austl. 150 15.12 S 129.43 E
Victoria ≃, Newf., Can. 176 48.45 N 56.40 W
Victoria, Isla I 244 45.18 S 73.58 W
Victoria, Lake ⊜, Afr. 144 1.00 S 33.00 E
Victoria, Lake ⊜, Austl. 156 34.00 S 141.16 E
Victoria, Mount ∧, Mya. 100 21.14 N 93.55 E
Victoria, Mount ∧, Pap. N. Gui. 154 8.55 S 147.35 E
Victoria, Pont ◆5 265a 45.29 N 73.32 W
Victoria and Albert Museum ⊍ 262c 18.59 N 72.50 E
Victoria Beach 174 50.43 N 96.33 W
Victoria de Durango → Durango 224 24.02 N 104.40 W
Victoria de las Tunas 230p 20.58 N 76.57 W
Victoria Falls 144 17.56 S 25.50 E
Victoria Falls ⌊ 144 17.55 S 25.51 E
Victoria Falls National Park ♠ 144 17.55 S 25.40 E
Victoria Gardens ♠ 262c 18.59 N 72.50 E
Victoria Harbour 202 44.45 N 79.46 W
Victoria International Airport ⊠ 214 48.39 N 123.26 W
Victoria Island I, N.W. Ter., Can. 166 71.00 N 114.00 W
Victoria Island I, Nig. 263a 6.26 N 3.26 E
Victoria Lake ⊜ 263d 26.14 S 28.09 E
Victoria Lake ⊜1 176 48.18 N 57.30 W
Victoria Land ◆1 9 75.00 S 163.00 E
Victoria Lawn Tennis Association Courts ♠ 264b 37.51 S 145.02 E
Victoria Memorial ⊥ 262b 22.33 N 88.21 E
Victoria Memorial Hall ⊍ 261c 1.17 N 103.51 E
Victoria Nile ≃ 144 2.14 N 31.26 E
Victoria Park 158a 31.58 S 115.55 E

Symbols in the index entries represent the broad categories identified in the key at the right. Symbols with superior numbers (⛰2) identify subcategories (see complete key on page *I* · 26).

Kartensymbole in dem Registerverzeichnis stellen die rechts in Schlüssel angeführten Kategorien dar. Symbole mit hochgestellten Ziffern (⛰2) bezeichnen Unterabteilungen einer Kategorie (vgl. vollständiger Schlüssel auf Seite *I* · 26).

Los símbolos incluidos en el texto del índice representan las grandes categorías identificadas con la clave a la derecha. Los símbolos con numeros en su parte superior (⛰2) identifican las subcategorías (véase la clave completa en la página *I* · 26).

Les symboles de l'index représentent les catégories indiquées dans la légende à droite. Les symboles suivis d'un indice (⛰2) représentent des sous-catégories (voir légende complète à la page *I* · 26).

Os símbolos incluídos no texto do índice representam as grandes categorias identificadas com a chave à direita. Os símbolos com números em sua parte superior (⛰2) identificam as subcategorias (veja-se a chave completa à página *I* · 26).

∧ Mountain	Berg	Montaña	Montagne	Montanha
⛰ Mountains	Berge	Montañas	Montagnes	Montanhas
Pass	Pass	Paso	Col	Passo
∨ Valley, Canyon	Tal, Cañon	Valle, Cañón	Vallée, Canyon	Vale, Canhão
Plain	Ebene	Llano	Plaine	Planície
≻ Cape	Kap	Cabo	Cap	Cabo
I Island	Insel	Isla	Île	Ilha
II Islands	Inseln	Islas	Îles	Ilhas
◆ Other Topographic Features	Andere Topographische Objekte	Otros Elementos Topográficos	Autres données topographiques	Outros Elementos Topográficos

ESPAÑOL · FRANÇAIS · PORTUGUÊS

Nombre / Nom / Nome	Página / Page	Lat.°′	Long.°′ W=Oeste / W=Ouest
Victoria Park ♠, H.K.	261d	22.17 N	114.07 E
Victoria Park ♠, Eng., U.K.	252	53.23 N	2.34 W
Victoria Peak ∧, Belize	222	16.48 N	88.37 W
Victoria Peak ∧, B.C., Can.	172	50.03 N	126.06 W
Victoria Peak ∧, H.K.	261d	22.17 N	114.08 E
Victoria Peaks ⋏	106	9.22 N	118.20 E
Victoria Point	161a	27.35 S	153.18 E
Victoria Range ⋏, N.Z.	162	42.09 S	172.08 E
Victoria Range ⋏, Pil.	106	9.32 N	118.23 E
Victoria River Downs	154	16.24 S	131.00 E
Victorias	106	10.54 N	123.05 E
Victoria State Car Club Race Circuit ♠	264b	37.45 S	145.11 E
Victoria Station ◆[5], Eng., U.K.	250	51.29 N	0.09 W
Victoria Station ◆[5], Eng., U.K.	252	53.29 N	2.15 W
Victoria Strait ⊔	166	69.15 N	100.30 W
Victoria University of Manchester ♥[2]	252	53.28 N	2.14 W
Victoriaville	196	46.03 N	71.57 W
Victoria West	148	31.25 S	23.04 E
Victorica	242	36.13 S	65.27 W
Victorino	236	2.48 N	67.50 W
Victorino de la Plaza	242	36.36 S	62.40 W
Victor Manuel Bueno	222	24.20 N	98.58 W
Victorville	218	34.32 N	117.18 W
Victory, Mount ∧	154	9.10 S	149.05 E
Victory Gardens	266	40.52 N	74.32 W
Victory Heights	204	41.22 N	79.46 W
Victory Hills	269b	40.11 N	79.53 W
Victory Mills	200	43.05 N	73.36 W
Victory Monument ⊥	259a	13.46 N	100.33 E
Vičuga	70	57.13 N	41.56 E
Vicuña	242	30.02 S	70.44 W
Vicuña Mackenna	242	33.54 S	64.23 W
Vidal, Cape ≻	148	28.09 S	32.33 E
Vidalia, Ga., U.S.	182	32.13 N	82.25 W
Vidalia, La., U.S.	184	31.34 N	91.26 W
Vidal Ramos	242	27.23 S	49.22 W
Vidauban	56	43.26 N	6.26 E
Videbæk	26	56.05 N	8.38 E
Videira	242	27.00 S	51.08 W
Videle	38	44.16 N	25.31 E
Vidigueira	34	38.13 N	7.48 W
Vidim, Česko.	50	50.28 N	14.31 E
Vidim, S.S.S.R.	78	56.29 N	103.09 E
Vidin	38	43.59 N	22.52 E
Vidisha	114	23.32 N	77.49 E
Vidlica	24	61.10 N	32.21 E
Vidnoje	72	55.34 N	37.41 E
Vidogošči	72	56.42 N	36.23 E
Vidor	184	30.07 N	94.01 W
Vidos ≃	257b	40.58 N	28.53 E
Vidöstern ⊜	26	57.04 N	14.01 E
Vidourle ≃	56	43.32 N	4.08 E
Vidra, Rom.	38	44.16 N	26.11 E
Vidra, Rom.	38	45.55 N	26.54 E
Vidsel	24	65.51 N	20.24 E
Vidzeme ◆[1]	66	57.10 N	25.30 E
Vidzy	66	55.24 N	26.38 E
Vie ≃	46	49.05 N	0.04 E
Viechtach	30	49.05 N	12.53 E
Viechtwang	58	47.55 N	13.57 E
Viedma	244	40.48 S	63.00 W
Viedma, Lago ⊜	244	49.35 S	72.35 W
Vieil Armand ♠	54	47.52 N	7.10 E
Vieillard, Lac du ⊜	180	47.23 N	78.02 W
Vieille Case	230d	15.36 N	61.24 W
Vieira do Minho	34	41.39 N	8.09 W
Viejo ≃	226	12.28 N	86.21 W
Viejo, Cerro ∧	236	4.49 S	79.27 W
Viekšniai	66	56.16 N	22.31 E
Viel, Lac ⊜	196	46.40 N	74.32 W
Vielank	50	53.15 N	11.08 E
Viella	34	42.42 N	0.48 E
Vielle-Eglise-en-Yvelines	251	48.40 N	1.53 E
Vielsalm	52	50.17 N	5.55 E
Viels-Maisons	46	48.54 N	3.24 E
Viena → Vienne ≃	32	47.13 N	0.05 E
Vienenburg	50	51.57 N	10.34 E
Vienna, Ont., Can.	202	42.41 N	80.48 W
Vienna → Wien, Öst.	30	48.13 N	16.20 E
Vienna, Ga., U.S.	182	32.06 N	83.47 W
Vienna, Ill., U.S.	184	37.25 N	88.54 W
Vienna, Ind., U.S.	208	38.39 N	85.46 W
Vienna, Md., U.S.	198	38.29 N	75.49 W
Vienna, Mo., U.S.	184	38.11 N	91.57 W
Vienna, N.J., U.S.	200	40.52 N	74.54 W
Vienna, Ohio, U.S.	204	41.14 N	80.40 W
Vienna, S. Dak., U.S.	188	44.42 N	97.30 W
Vienna, Va., U.S.	198	38.54 N	77.16 W
Vienna, W. Va., U.S.	178	39.20 N	81.26 W
Vienne, Fr.	56	45.31 N	4.52 E
Vienne → Wien, Öst.	30	48.13 N	16.20 E
Vienne □[5]	32	46.35 N	0.30 E
Vienne ≃	32	47.13 N	0.05 E
Vienne-en-Arthies	251	49.04 N	1.44 E
Vienne-le-Château	52	49.11 N	4.53 E
Vientos, Paso de los → Windward Passage ⊔	228	20.00 N	73.50 W
Vieques, Isla de I	230m	18.08 N	65.25 W
Vieques, Pasaje de ⊔	230m	18.11 N	65.37 W
Vieques, Sonda de ⊔	230m	18.15 N	65.23 W
Vière ≃	52	48.46 N	4.41 E
Viereck	50	53.32 N	14.02 E
Vieremä	26	63.45 N	27.01 E
Vierfontein	148	27.03 S	26.46 E
Vierhouten	48	52.20 N	5.50 E
Vieringhausen ◆[8]	253	51.11 N	7.10 E
Vierlande ◆[1]	48	53.26 N	10.14 E
Viernau	50	50.40 N	10.32 E
Viernheim	52	49.32 N	8.34 E
Vierraden	50	53.06 N	14.17 E
Viersen	52	51.15 N	6.23 E
Vierumäki	26	61.06 N	25.57 E
Vierwaldstättersee ⊜	54	47.00 N	8.28 E
Vierzehn-Heiligen ♥[1]	52	50.08 N	11.02 E
Vierzon	46	47.13 N	2.05 E
Viesca	222	25.21 N	102.48 W
Viesecke	50	53.01 N	12.01 E
Vieselbach	50	51.00 N	11.08 E
Viesīte	66	56.21 N	25.33 E
Vieste	60	41.53 N	16.10 E
Vietgest	50	53.45 N	12.20 E
Vietnam □[1]	98	16.00 N	108.00 E
Viet-nam → Vietnam □[1], As.	100	16.00 N	108.00 E
Viet-nam → Vietnam □[1], As.	100	16.00 N	108.00 E
Vietnam □[1]	100	16.00 N	108.00 E
Vietri sul Mare	60	40.40 N	14.44 E
Viet-tri	100	21.18 N	105.26 E
Vietz → Witnica	30	52.40 N	14.55 E
Vieux-Condé	46	50.27 N	3.34 E
Vieux-Ferette	54	47.30 N	7.18 E
Vieux-Fort, Guad.	231o	15.57 N	61.43 W
Vieux Fort, St. Luc.	231f	13.44 N	60.57 W
Vieux-Fort, Pointe du ≻	231o	15.57 N	61.43 W
Vieux Fort Bay C	231f	13.44 N	60.58 W
Vieux-Habitants	231o	16.04 N	61.46 W
Vieux-Thann	54	47.48 N	7.08 E
Vievis	66	54.46 N	24.48 E
View Park	270	34.00 N	118.21 W
Vieytes	248	35.16 S	57.35 W
Vif	56	45.03 N	5.40 E
Vig	41	55.51 N	11.36 E
Viga ≃	66	59.14 N	43.41 E
Vigala	66	58.43 N	24.22 E
Vigan	106	17.34 N	120.23 E
Vigarano Mainarda	58	44.50 N	11.30 E
Vigatto	58	44.43 N	10.20 E
Vigeland	26	58.05 N	7.18 E
Vigentino ◆[8]	256b	45.25 N	9.11 E
Vigersted	41	55.29 N	11.54 E
Vigese, Monte ∧	58	44.12 N	11.06 E
Vigevano	56	45.19 N	8.51 E
Viggiù	56	45.52 N	8.54 E
Vigia	240	0.48 S	48.08 W
Vigie Airport ⊠	231f	14.01 N	60.59 W
Vignacourt	46	50.01 N	2.12 E
Vignale	56	45.01 N	8.24 E
Vignanello	60	42.23 N	12.17 E
Vigneulles-lès-Hattonchâtel	52	48.59 N	5.43 E
Vigneux-sur-Seine	251	48.42 N	2.25 E
Vignola	58	44.29 N	11.00 E
Vignory	54	48.17 N	5.06 E
Vignot	52	48.46 N	5.36 E
Vigny	251	49.05 N	1.56 E
Vigo	34	42.14 N	8.43 W
Vigo, Ría de C[1]	34	42.15 N	8.45 W
Vigodarzere	58	45.27 N	11.53 E
Vigo di Fassa	58	46.25 N	11.40 E
Vigolzone	56	44.55 N	9.40 E
Vigone	56	44.51 N	7.30 E
Vigonovo	58	45.23 N	12.00 E
Vigo-Rendena	58	46.05 N	10.43 E
Vigrestad	26	58.34 N	5.42 E
Viguzzolo	56	44.54 N	8.55 E
Vigy	52	49.12 N	6.18 E
Vihanti	26	64.29 N	25.00 E
Vihāri	113	30.02 N	72.21 E
Vihiers	32	47.09 N	0.32 W
Vihorlat ⋏	30	48.55 N	22.10 E
Vihowa	113	31.08 N	70.30 E
Vihren ∧	38	41.46 N	23.24 E
Vihti	26	60.25 N	24.20 E
VII □[4]	138	22.30 N	10.00 W
Viiala	26	61.13 N	23.47 E
Viinijärvi	26	62.39 N	29.14 E
Viinijärvi ⊜	26	62.44 N	29.17 E
Viipuri → Vyborg	66	60.42 N	28.45 E
Viitasaari	26	63.04 N	25.52 E
Viivikonna	66	59.19 N	27.42 E
Vijāpur	110	23.34 N	72.45 E
Vijayapuri	108	16.52 N	79.35 E
Vijayawāda	112	16.31 N	80.37 E
Vijosë (Aóös) ≃	38	40.37 N	19.20 E
Vik	40	59.44 N	17.28 E
Vik ⊥	40	59.44 N	17.27 E
Vika	40	60.31 N	15.42 E
Vikajärvi	24	66.37 N	26.12 E
Vikārābad	112	17.20 N	77.54 E
Vikbolandet ≻[1]	40	58.32 N	16.40 E
Viken	41	56.09 N	12.34 E
Viken ⊜	26	58.39 N	14.20 E
Vikern ⊜	40	59.30 N	14.55 E
Vikersund	26	59.59 N	10.02 E
Vikhroli ◆[8]	262c	19.07 N	72.56 E
Viking	172	53.06 N	111.46 W
Viking Village	208	39.05 N	84.18 W
Vikmanshyttan	40	60.17 N	15.49 E
Vikna	24	64.57 N	10.58 E
Vikna I	22	64.57 N	10.58 E
Vikramasingapuram	112	8.43 N	77.24 E
Viksøyri	26	61.05 N	6.35 E
Viktor	24	66.09 N	58.07 E
Viktorovka	76	52.51 N	62.32 E
Vikulovo	76	56.49 N	70.37 E
Vila, N. Heb.	165f	17.44 S	168.19 E
Vil'a, S.S.S.R.	70	55.15 N	42.13 E
Vila Alferes Chamusca	146	24.29 S	33.00 E
Vila Armindo Monteiro	102	9.02 S	125.22 E
Vila Arriaga	142	14.46 S	13.21 E
Vila Augusta	277b	23.28 S	46.32 W
Vila Boacaya ◆[8]	277b	23.29 S	46.44 W
Vila Brasil	245	22.22 S	54.34 W
Vila Cabral	144	13.18 S	35.14 E
Vila Caldas Xavier	144	15.59 S	34.12 E
Vila Coutinho	144	14.37 S	34.19 E
Vila da Maganja	144	17.18 S	37.30 E
Vila da Ribeira Brava	140a	16.37 N	24.18 W
Viladecaballs	256d	41.33 N	1.58 E
Viladecáns	256d	41.19 N	2.01 E
Vila de Manabuto	102	8.30 S	126.01 E
Vila de Manica	146	18.56 S	32.53 E
Vila de Rei	34	39.40 N	8.09 W
Vila do Bispo	34	37.05 N	8.55 W
Vila do Conde	34	41.21 N	8.45 W
Vila do Porto	138a	36.56 N	25.09 W
Vila Flor	34	41.18 N	7.09 W
Vila Fontes	146	17.50 S	35.21 E
Vila Formosa ◆[8]	277b	23.34 S	46.33 W
Vilafranca del Panadés	34	41.21 N	1.42 E
Vila Franca de Xira	34	38.57 N	8.59 W
Vila Galvão	277b	23.27 S	46.33 W
Vila Gamito	144	14.12 S	33.00 E
Vila General Carmona	102	8.43 S	125.34 E
Vila Glória	245	22.21 S	54.13 W
Vila Gomes da Costa	146	24.19 S	33.38 E
Vila Gouveia	146	18.03 S	33.11 E
Vila Guilherme ◆[8]	277b	23.30 S	46.36 W
Vilaine ≃	32	47.30 N	2.27 W
Vila Isabel ◆[8]	277a	22.55 S	43.15 W
Vila Jaguára ◆[8]	277b	23.31 S	46.45 W
Vila Junqueiro	144	15.25 S	36.58 E
Viļaka	66	57.11 N	27.41 E
Vila Luísa	146	25.44 S	32.40 E
Vilama, Laguna de ⊜	242	22.36 S	66.55 W
Vila Machado	146	19.18 S	34.11 E
Vila Madalena ◆[8]	277b	23.33 S	46.42 W
Vila Maria ◆[8]	277b	23.31 S	46.34 W
Vila Mariana ◆[8]	277b	23.35 S	46.38 W
Vila Matilde ◆[8]	277b	23.32 S	46.31 W
Vila Muriqui	246	22.56 S	43.57 W
Vilanculos	146	22.01 S	35.19 E
Viļāni	66	56.33 N	26.57 E
Vila Nova	142	12.38 S	16.03 E
Vila Nova ≃	240	0.04 S	51.13 W
Vila Nova de Famalicão	34	41.25 N	8.32 W
Vila Nova de Foz Côa	34	41.05 N	7.12 W
Vila Nova de Gaia	34	41.08 N	8.37 W
Vilanova de la Roca	256d	41.33 N	2.17 E
Vila Nova de Malaca	102	8.22 S	126.54 E
Vila Nova do Seles	142	11.24 S	14.15 E
Vila Novo de Ourém	34	39.39 N	8.35 W
Vila Paiva de Andrada	146	18.44 S	34.03 E
Vila Pery	146	19.08 S	33.29 E
Vila Progresso	277a	22.55 S	43.03 W
Vila Prudente ◆[8]	277b	23.35 S	46.33 W
Vila Real	34	41.18 N	7.45 W
Vila Real de Santo António	34	37.12 N	7.25 W
Vilar Formoso	34	40.37 N	6.50 W
Vila Rica	236	3.40 S	61.02 W
Vilarinho do Monte	240	1.37 S	52.01 W
Vila Salazar	102	8.27 S	126.27 E
Vila Trigo de Morais	146	24.36 S	33.00 E
Vila Vasco da Gama	144	14.54 S	32.14 E
Vila Velha, Bra.	240	3.13 N	51.13 W
Vila Velha, Bra.	245	20.20 S	40.17 W
Vila Velha de Ródão	34	39.38 N	7.40 W
Vila Verde, Port.	34	41.39 N	8.26 W
Vila Verde, Port.	256c	38.50 N	9.22 W
Vila Viçosa	34	38.47 N	8.13 W
Vil'ča	68	51.22 N	29.24 E
Vilcabamba, Cordillera ⋏	238	13.00 S	73.00 W
Vilcanota ≃	238	13.20 S	71.58 W
Vîlcea □[4]	38	45.19 N	24.00 E
Vildbjerg	41	56.12 N	8.46 E
Vilejka	66	54.30 N	26.53 E
Vilelas	242	27.57 S	62.38 W
Vilenki	72	54.16 N	38.55 E
Vil'gort, S.S.S.R.	24	60.34 N	56.24 E
Vil'gort, S.S.S.R.	24	61.35 N	50.40 E
Vilhelmina	26	64.37 N	16.39 E
Vilhena	238	12.43 S	60.07 W
Vilija ≃	66	55.54 N	23.53 E
Viljandi	66	58.22 N	25.36 E
Viljoensdrif	148	26.44 S	27.55 E
Viljoenshof	148	34.40 S	19.42 E
Viljoenskroon	148	27.12 S	27.00 E
Viljoenspos	148	27.35 S	30.30 E
Vilkaviškis	66	54.39 N	23.02 E
Vil'kickogo, Ostrov I, S.S.S.R.	62	73.29 N	75.50 E
Vil'kickogo, Ostrov I, S.S.S.R.	64	75.44 N	152.20 E
Vil'kickogo, Proliv ⊔	64	77.55 N	103.00 E
Vilkija	66	55.03 N	23.35 E
Vilkovo	68	45.25 N	29.35 E
Villa Abecia	238	21.00 S	65.23 W
Villa Aberastain	242	31.39 S	68.35 W
Villa Acuña → Ciudad Acuña	222	29.18 N	100.55 W
Villa Adelina ◆[8]	278	34.31 S	58.32 W
Villa Adriana ⊥	60	41.56 N	12.45 E
Villa Ahumada	222	30.37 N	106.31 W
Villa Alberdi	242	27.35 S	65.37 W
Villa Alejandrina	248	33.46 S	58.21 W
Villa Alemana	242	33.03 S	71.23 W
Villa Allende	242	31.18 S	64.18 W
Villa Alta	224	17.21 N	96.09 W
Villa Ana	242	28.29 S	59.37 W
Villa Ángela	242	27.35 S	60.43 W
Villa Atamisqui	242	28.29 S	63.48 W
Villa Atuel	242	34.50 S	67.54 W
Villaba	106	11.13 N	124.23 E
Villa Ballester ◆[8]	248	34.32 S	58.33 W
Villabassa (Niederdorf)	58	46.44 N	12.10 E
Villabé	251	48.35 N	2.27 E
Villa Bella	238	10.23 S	65.24 W
Villa Berthet	242	27.17 S	60.25 W
Villablino	34	42.56 N	6.19 W
Villa Borghese ♥	257a	41.55 N	12.29 E
Villa Bruzual	236	9.20 N	69.06 W
Villa Bustos	242	29.17 S	67.02 W
Villa Cañás, Arg.	242	34.00 S	61.36 W
Villacañas, Esp.	34	39.38 N	3.20 W
Villa Carlos Paz	242	31.24 S	64.31 W
Villacarriedo	34	43.14 N	3.48 W
Villacarrillo	34	38.07 N	3.05 W
Villa Castelli	242	29.00 S	68.11 W
Villacastín	34	40.47 N	4.25 W
Villach	58	46.36 N	13.50 E
Villachuato, Cerro ∧	224	20.06 N	101.38 W
Villacidro	36	39.27 N	8.44 E
Villa Ciudadela ◆[8]	248	34.38 S	58.34 W
Villa Clara	242	31.50 S	58.49 W
Villa Colón (Caucete), Arg.	242	31.39 S	68.17 W
Villa Colón, Méx.	224	20.48 N	100.03 W
Villa Concepción del Tío	242	31.19 S	62.50 W
Villa Constitución	242	33.14 S	60.20 W
Villa Corona	224	20.25 N	103.41 W
Villa Cortese	256b	45.34 N	8.53 E
Villa Corzo	224	16.10 N	93.15 W
Villacoublay, Aérodrome de ⊠	251	48.45 N	2.10 E
Villa Creek ≃	216	35.27 N	120.58 W
Villa Cuauhtémoc, Méx.	224	19.24 N	99.34 W
Villa Cuauhtémoc, Méx.	224	22.11 N	97.50 W
Villada	34	42.15 N	4.58 W
Villa de Apaseo el Alto	224	20.27 N	100.37 W
Villa de Arriaga	224	21.54 N	101.23 W
Villadeati	56	45.04 N	8.10 E
Villa de Cos	224	23.17 N	102.21 W
Villa de Cura	236	10.02 N	67.29 W
Villa de García	186	25.49 N	100.35 W
Villa de Guadalupe	224	23.22 N	100.46 W
Villa del Carmen	242	32.57 S	65.03 W
Villa Delgado	226	13.43 N	89.10 W
Villa del Pueblito	224	20.32 N	100.27 W
Villa del Río	34	37.59 N	4.17 W
Villa del Rosario, Arg.	242	31.35 S	63.32 W
Villa del Rosario, Arg.	242	30.47 S	57.55 W
Villa del Rosario, Ven.	236	10.19 N	72.19 W
Villa de María	242	29.54 S	63.43 W
Villa de Mayo	248	34.30 S	58.41 W
Villa de Méndez	222	25.07 N	98.34 W
Villa de Nova Sintra	140a	14.52 N	24.43 W
Villa de Reyes	224	21.48 N	100.56 W
Villa de San Antonio	226	14.16 N	87.36 W
Villa de San Francisco	226	14.10 N	86.58 W
Villa de Soto	242	30.51 S	64.59 W
Villa d'Este ⊥	257a	41.57 N	12.48 E
Villa Devoto ◆[8]	278	34.36 S	58.31 W
Villa Diamante ◆[8]	278	34.41 S	58.26 W
Villa di Chiavenna	54	46.20 N	9.29 E
Villa Diego, Arg.	242	33.01 S	60.37 W
Villadiego, Esp.	34	42.31 N	4.00 W
Villa Dolores	242	31.56 S	65.12 W
Villa Domínico ◆[8]	248	34.41 S	58.19 W
Villadose	58	45.04 N	11.53 E
Villadossola	54	46.04 N	8.16 E
Villa El Alto	242	28.18 S	65.22 W
Villa Elisa	242	32.10 S	58.24 W
Villa Elisa ◆[8]	248	34.50 S	58.05 W
Villa Escalante	224	19.24 N	101.39 W
Villa Eufronio Viscarra	238	17.59 S	65.36 W
Villa Flores	224	16.14 N	93.14 W
Villa Florida	242	26.23 S	57.09 W
Villafranca d'Asti	56	44.55 N	8.02 E
Villafranca del Bierzo	34	42.36 N	6.48 W
Villafranca de los Barros	34	38.34 N	6.20 W
Villafranca di Verona	58	45.21 N	10.50 E
Villafranca in Lunigiana	58	44.17 N	9.57 E
Villafranca Piemonte	56	44.47 N	7.33 E
Villa Frontera	222	26.56 N	101.27 W
Villagaracía	34	42.36 N	8.45 W
Villa García	224	22.10 N	101.57 W
Village Creek ≃	184	35.28 N	91.19 W
Village Green	275	39.52 N	75.26 W
Villa General José Maria Arteaga	224	22.10 N	102.21 W
Villa General Ramírez	242	32.11 S	60.12 W
Villa General Roca	242	32.39 S	66.28 W
Village of the Branch	266	40.51 N	73.11 W
Villa González	224	22.50 N	98.27 W
Villa González Ortega	224	22.30 N	101.55 W
Villagrán, Méx.	222	24.29 N	99.29 W
Villagrán, Méx.	224	20.31 N	100.59 W
Villa Grove	184	39.52 N	88.10 W
Villaguay	242	31.51 S	59.01 W
Villa Guerrero, Méx.	224	21.59 N	103.36 W
Villa Guerrero, Méx.	224	18.52 N	99.39 W
Villa Guillermina	242	28.14 S	59.28 W
Villa Hayes	242	25.06 S	57.34 W
Villahermosa	224	17.59 N	92.55 W
Villa Hernandarias	242	31.13 S	59.59 W
Villa Hidalgo, Méx.	194	30.59 N	116.10 W
Villa Hidalgo, Méx.	224	21.44 N	105.15 W
Villa Hidalgo, Méx.	224	21.40 N	102.36 W
Villa Huidobro (Cañada Verde)	242	34.50 S	64.35 W
Villaines-la-Juhel	32	48.21 N	0.17 W
Villa Iris	242	38.10 S	63.15 W
Villa Jiménez	224	19.55 N	101.35 W
Villajoyosa	34	38.30 N	0.14 W
Villa Juárez, Méx.	222	27.10 N	109.50 W
Villa Juárez, Méx.	224	22.20 N	100.17 W
Villa Krause	242	31.34 S	68.32 W
Villa La Angostura	244	40.47 S	71.40 W
Villa Lagarina	58	45.55 N	11.01 E
Villalago	60	41.56 N	13.50 E
Villa La Paz	242	33.27 S	67.38 W
Villa Larca	242	32.37 S	64.59 W
Villa Larroque	242	33.02 S	59.01 W
Villalba, Esp.	34	43.18 N	7.41 W
Villalba, P.R.	230m	18.08 N	66.30 W
Villa Lia	248	34.07 S	59.26 W
Villalon, Cuba	276b	23.03 N	82.26 W
Villalon, Pil.	106	11.31 N	124.22 E
Villalón de Campos	34	42.06 N	5.02 W
Villalonga	244	39.53 S	62.35 W
Villa López	222	27.00 N	105.02 W
Villalpando	34	41.52 N	5.24 W
Villa Lugano ◆[8]	278	34.41 S	58.28 W
Villalvernia	56	44.49 N	8.51 E
Villa Madero, Arg.	278	34.42 S	58.30 W
Villa Madero, Méx.	224	19.24 N	101.16 W
Villa Mainero	222	24.32 N	99.38 W
Villa María, Arg.	242	32.25 S	63.15 W
Villa Maria, Pa., U.S.	204	41.05 N	80.30 W
Villa Martín, Bol.	238	20.46 S	67.47 W
Villamartín, Esp.	34	36.52 N	5.38 W
Villamarzana	58	45.01 N	11.41 E
Villa Matoque	242	25.49 S	63.49 W
Villa Mazár	242	28.40 S	66.34 W
Villa Mercedes	242	30.07 S	68.42 W
Villamil	236a	0.56 S	91.01 W
Villa Minozzo	58	44.22 N	10.28 E
Villa Montes	238	21.15 S	63.30 W
Villa Morelos	224	20.00 N	101.25 W
Villandraut	32	44.28 N	0.23 W
Villandry	46	47.20 N	0.31 E
Villa Nora	146	23.34 S	28.01 E
Villa Nova, Md., U.S.	274b	39.21 N	76.44 W
Villa Nova, Ohio, U.S.	206	40.33 N	84.26 W
Villanova, Pa., U.S.	198	40.02 N	75.21 W
Villanova d'Asti	56	44.57 N	7.56 E
Villanova Mondovì	56	44.21 N	7.45 E
Villanova Monferrato	56	45.11 N	8.28 E
Villanova Monteleone	36	40.30 N	8.28 E
Villanova sull'Arda	58	45.01 N	10.00 E
Villanova University ♥[2]	275	40.02 N	75.21 W
Villa Nueva, Arg.	242	32.26 S	63.15 W
Villanueva, Col.	236	10.37 N	72.59 W
Villa Nueva, Guat.	226	14.31 N	90.35 W
Villanueva, Hond.	226	15.17 N	88.00 W
Villanueva, Méx.	224	22.21 N	102.53 W
Villanueva, Nic.	226	12.58 N	86.49 W
Villanueva, N. Mex., U.S.	190	35.17 N	105.23 W
Villanueva de Córdoba	34	38.20 N	4.37 W
Villa Nueva de Guaymallén → Guaymallén	242	32.54 S	68.47 W
Villanueva de la Serana	34	38.58 N	5.48 W
Villanueva de la Sierra	34	40.12 N	6.24 W
Villanueva de los Infantes	34	38.44 N	2.59 W
Villanueva del Río y Minas	34	37.39 N	5.42 W
Villanueva y Geltrú	34	41.14 N	1.44 E
Villa Numancia	278	34.55 S	58.24 W
Villa Obregón, Méx.	224	21.07 N	102.42 W
Villa Obregón, Méx.	276a	19.21 N	99.12 W
Villa Ocampo	242	28.28 S	59.22 W
Villa Ojo de Agua	242	29.31 S	63.42 W
Villa Oliva	242	26.01 S	57.53 W
Villa Opicina	58	45.40 N	13.49 E
Villa Ottone (Uttenheim)	58	46.52 N	11.57 E
Villa Park, Calif., U.S.	218	33.49 N	117.49 W
Villa Park, Ill., U.S.	268	41.53 N	87.59 W
Villa Park Dam ◆[6]	270	33.48 N	117.46 W
Villa Pedro Montoya	224	21.38 N	99.49 W
Villa Pérez	230m	18.12 N	66.47 W
Villapinzón	236	5.13 N	73.36 W
Villa Potenza	60	43.19 N	13.25 E
Villa Quinteros	242	27.14 S	65.33 W
Villa Quintilio Varo ⊥	257a	41.58 N	12.47 E
Villarcayo	34	42.56 N	3.34 W
Villar-d'Arène	56	45.02 N	6.20 E
Villard-Bonnot	56	45.14 N	5.53 E
Villard-de-Lans	56	45.04 N	5.33 E
Villardefrades	34	41.43 N	5.15 W
Villar del Arzobispo	34	39.44 N	0.49 W
Villareal	106	11.34 N	124.56 E
Villa Real ◆[8]	278	34.37 S	58.31 W
Villa Regina	242	39.06 S	67.04 W
Villa Reynolds	242	33.43 S	65.23 W
Villa Rica	182	33.44 N	84.55 W
Villa Rivero	238	17.37 S	65.48 W
Villaroche	251	48.37 N	2.39 E
Villa Rosa	248	34.25 S	58.52 W
Villar Pellice	56	44.48 N	7.09 E
Villar Perosa	56	44.56 N	7.15 E
Villarreal	34	39.56 N	0.06 W
Villarreales	186	26.07 N	100.20 W
Villarrica, Chile	244	39.16 S	72.13 W
Villarrica, Col.	236	3.58 N	74.37 W
Villarrica, Para.	242	25.45 S	56.26 W
Villarrica, Lago ⊜	244	39.15 S	72.06 W
Villarrobledo	34	39.16 N	2.36 W
Villarrubia de los Ojos	34	39.13 N	3.36 W
Villars	248	34.50 S	58.56 W
Villars, Schw.	54	46.18 N	7.04 E
Villars-Colmars	56	44.10 N	6.36 E
Villars-en-Azois	54	48.04 N	4.45 E
Villars-les-Dombes	54	46.00 N	5.01 E
Villars-sur-Var	56	43.56 N	7.06 E
Villa Ruiz	248	34.25 S	59.15 W
Villas	198	39.02 N	74.56 W
Villa Sáenz Peña ◆[8]	278	34.36 S	58.31 W
Villa San Andrés ◆[8]	278	34.33 S	58.32 W
Villa San Giovanni	36	38.13 N	15.39 E
Villa San José	242	32.12 S	58.13 W
Villa San Martín	242	28.18 S	64.12 W
Villasanta	56	45.37 N	9.18 E
Villa Santa, Montaña ∧	226	14.12 N	86.27 W
Villa Santa Maria	60	41.57 N	14.21 E
Villa Santina	58	46.24 N	12.55 E
Villa Santos Lugares ◆[8]	278	34.36 S	58.32 W
Villasayas	34	41.21 N	2.37 W
Villa Serrano	238	19.06 S	64.22 W
Villasimius	36	39.09 N	9.31 E
Villasis	106	15.54 N	120.35 E
Villa Somoza	226	12.03 N	84.59 W
Villasor	36	39.22 N	8.57 E
Villa Tunari	238	16.55 S	65.25 W
Villa Turdera ◆[8]	278	34.48 S	58.25 W
Villa Unión, Arg.	242	29.24 S	62.47 W
Villa Unión, Arg.	242	29.18 S	68.12 W
Villa Unión, Méx.	222	28.15 N	100.43 W
Villa Unión, Méx.	224	23.12 N	106.14 W
Villa Unión, Méx.	224	23.58 N	104.02 W
Villa Valeria	242	34.20 S	64.55 W
Villa Vallelonga	60	41.52 N	13.37 E
Villa Vásquez	228	19.45 N	71.27 W
Villaverde ◆[8]	256a	40.21 N	3.42 W
Villaverla	58	45.39 N	11.29 E
Villa Verona	216	39.28 N	121.33 W
Villavicencio	236	4.09 N	73.37 W
Villa Vicente Guerrero	224	23.45 N	103.59 W
Villaviciosa	34	43.29 N	5.26 W
Villaviciosa de Córdoba	34	38.05 N	5.01 W
Villa Victoria	224	18.47 N	103.24 W
Villa Vomano	60	42.37 N	13.46 E
Villazón	238	22.06 S	65.36 W
Villa Zorraquín	242	31.19 S	58.02 W
Villé	54	48.20 N	7.18 E
Villebon, Lac ⊜	180	47.58 N	77.17 W
Villebon-sur-Yvette	251	48.42 N	2.15 E
Villeconin	251	48.31 N	2.08 E
Villecresnes	251	48.43 N	2.32 E
Villecroze	56	43.35 N	6.16 E
Ville-d'Avray	251	48.50 N	2.11 E
Ville-de-laval → Laval	196	45.35 N	73.45 W
Villedieu	32	48.50 N	1.13 W
Ville-en-Tardenois	46	49.11 N	3.48 E
Villefort	56	44.26 N	3.56 E
Villefranche	54	45.59 N	4.43 E
Villefranche-de-Rouergue	32	44.21 N	2.02 E
Villefranche-du-Périgord	32	44.38 N	1.05 E
Villefranche-sur-Cher	46	47.18 N	1.46 E
Villefranche-sur-Mer	56	43.42 N	7.19 E
Villejuif	46	48.48 N	2.22 E
Villejust	251	48.41 N	2.14 E
Ville-Marie	180	47.19 N	79.26 W
Villemaur-sur-Vanne	46	48.15 N	3.44 E
Villemeux-sur-Eure	46	48.40 N	1.28 E
Villemoisson-sur-Orge	251	48.40 N	2.19 E
Villemomble	251	48.53 N	2.31 E
Villena	34	38.38 N	0.51 W
Villenauxe-la-Grande	46	48.35 N	3.33 E
Villeneuve, It.	56	45.42 N	7.14 E
Villeneuve, Schw.	54	46.24 N	6.55 E
Villeneuve-d'Ascq	46	50.37 N	3.10 E
Villeneuve-d'Aveyron	32	44.26 N	2.02 E
Villeneuve-de-Berg	56	44.33 N	4.30 E
Villeneuve-la-Garenne	251	48.56 N	2.20 E
Villeneuve-la-Guyard	46	48.20 N	3.04 E
Villeneuve-l'Archevêque	46	48.14 N	3.33 E
Villeneuve-le-Comte	251	48.49 N	2.50 E
Villeneuve-le-Roi	46	48.44 N	2.25 E
Villeneuve-lès-Avignon	56	43.58 N	4.48 E
Villeneuve-lès-Maguelonne	56	43.32 N	3.52 E
Villeneuve-Saint-Denis	251	48.49 N	2.48 E
Villeneuve-Saint-Georges	46	48.44 N	2.27 E
Villeneuve-sous-Dammartin	251	49.02 N	2.39 E
Villeneuve-sur-Lot	32	44.25 N	0.42 E
Villeneuve-sur-Yonne	46	48.05 N	3.18 E
Villennes-sur-Seine	251	48.56 N	2.00 E
Villenoy	46	48.57 N	2.52 E
Villeny	46	47.37 N	1.45 E
Villeparisis	46	48.56 N	2.37 E
Villepinte	251	48.58 N	2.32 E
Ville Platte	184	30.42 N	92.16 W
Villepreux	251	48.50 N	2.01 E
Villequier	46	49.31 N	0.40 E
Villeron	251	49.03 N	2.33 E
Villeroy	46	48.59 N	2.47 E
Villers-Bocage, Fr.	32	49.05 N	0.39 W
Villers-Bocage, Fr.	46	49.59 N	2.20 E
Villers-Bretonneux	46	49.52 N	2.31 E
Villers-Carbonnel	46	49.52 N	2.54 E
Villers-Cotterêts	46	49.15 N	3.05 E
Villers-devant-Orval	52	49.37 N	5.19 E
Villers-en-Arthies	251	49.05 N	1.44 E
Villersexel	54	47.33 N	6.26 E
Villers-Farlay	54	47.00 N	5.45 E
Villers-la-Ville	46	50.35 N	4.32 E
Villers-le-Lac	54	47.04 N	6.40 E
Villers-lès-Nancy	54	48.40 N	6.09 E
Villers-lès-Pots	54	47.13 N	5.21 E
Villers-Outréaux	46	50.02 N	3.18 E
Villers-Saint-Paul	46	49.17 N	2.29 E
Villers-Semeuse	52	49.44 N	4.45 E
Villerupt	52	49.28 N	5.56 E
Villerville	46	49.24 N	0.08 E
Ville-Saint-Georges	178	46.07 N	70.40 W
Villes-sur-Auzon	56	44.03 N	5.14 E
Ville-sur-Tourbe	52	49.11 N	4.47 E
Villeta	236	5.01 N	74.28 W
Villetta Barrea	60	41.47 N	13.56 E
Villeurbanne	56	45.46 N	4.53 E
Villevaudé	251	48.55 N	2.39 E
Villeziers	251	48.40 N	2.10 E
Villiers	148	27.03 S	28.35 E
Villiers-Adam	251	49.04 N	2.14 E
Villiersdorp	148	34.00 S	19.19 E
Villiers-le-Bâcle	251	48.44 N	2.08 E
Villiers-le-Bel	251	49.00 N	2.23 E
Villiers-le-Sec	251	49.04 N	2.23 E
Villiers-Saint-Frédéric	251	48.49 N	1.54 E
Villiers-Saint-Georges	46	48.39 N	3.25 E
Villiers-sur-Marne	46	48.50 N	2.33 E
Villiers-sur-Morin	251	48.52 N	2.53 E
Villigst	253	51.26 N	7.35 E
Villingen-Schwenningen	30	48.04 N	8.28 E
Villisca	188	40.56 N	94.59 W
Villmanstrand → Lappeenranta	26	61.04 N	28.11 E
Villmergen	54	47.21 N	8.15 E
Villorba	58	45.44 N	12.14 E
Villoresi, Canale ☰	56	45.33 N	9.31 E
Villotta	58	45.52 N	12.45 E
Villupuram	112	11.56 N	79.29 E
Vilm I	50	54.19 N	13.32 E
Vilmnitz	50	54.21 N	13.31 E
Vilna, Alta., Can.	172	54.07 N	111.55 W
Vilna → Vilnius, S.S.S.R.	66	54.41 N	25.19 E
Vilnius	66	54.41 N	25.19 E
Vilosnes-sur-Meuse	52	49.20 N	5.14 E
Vilppula	26	62.01 N	24.31 E
Vils	54	47.33 N	10.38 E
Vils ≃	54	47.33 N	10.40 E
Vilsandi I	66	58.23 N	21.52 E
Vilsbiburg	30	48.27 N	12.12 E
Vilshofen	30	48.39 N	13.12 E
Vil'uj ≃	64	64.24 N	126.26 E
Vil'ujsk	64	63.45 N	121.35 E
Vil'va	76	58.37 N	56.52 E
Vilvoorde	46	50.56 N	4.26 E
Vimercate	56	45.37 N	9.22 E
Vimianzo	34	43.07 N	9.02 W
Vimmerby	26	57.40 N	15.51 E
Vimodrone	256b	45.31 N	9.17 E
Vimoutiers	46	48.55 N	0.12 E
Vimpeli	26	63.09 N	23.48 E
Vimperk	30	49.03 N	13.47 E
Vimy	46	50.22 N	2.49 E
Vina	194	39.56 N	122.03 W
Vina ≃	142	7.45 N	15.36 E
Viñac	238	12.56 S	75.47 W
Viña del Mar	242	33.02 S	71.34 W
Vinadi	54	46.55 N	10.29 E
Vinadio	56	44.18 N	7.10 E
Viñales	230p	22.37 N	83.43 W
Vinalhaven	178	44.03 N	68.50 W
Vinalhaven Island I	178	44.05 N	68.52 W
Vina Roni, Mount ∧	165e	8.10 S	157.28 E
Vinaroz	34	40.28 N	0.29 E
Vinay	56	45.13 N	5.24 E
Vinazco ≃	224	20.56 N	97.44 W
Vincennes, Fr.	46	48.51 N	2.26 E
Vincennes, Ind., U.S.	184	38.41 N	87.32 W
Vincennes, Bois de ♠	251	48.50 N	2.25 E
Vincennes, Château de ⊥	251	48.51 N	2.26 E
Vincennes, Étang de ⊜	251	48.47 N	2.45 E
Vincennes Bay C	9	66.30 S	109.30 E
Vincent, Ala., U.S.	184	33.23 N	86.25 W
Vincent, Ohio, U.S.	204	39.23 N	81.40 W
Vincent, Point ≻	164c	29.00 S	167.55 E
Vincentown	198	39.56 N	74.45 W
Vinces	236	1.32 S	79.45 W
Vinces ≃	236	1.39 S	79.47 W
Vincey	54	48.20 N	6.20 E
Vinchiaturo	60	41.29 N	14.35 E
Vinchina	242	28.46 S	68.10 W
Vinchos	238	13.16 S	74.21 W
Vinci	60	43.47 N	10.55 E
Vinco	204	40.25 N	78.52 W
Vindeby	41	55.03 N	10.38 E
Vindelälven ≃	24	63.54 N	19.52 E
Vindeln	26	64.12 N	19.44 E
Vinden, Mount ∧	152	27.01 S	115.38 E
Vinderslev	41	56.15 N	9.26 E
Vinderup	26	56.29 N	8.47 E
Vindhya Range ⋏	110	23.00 N	77.00 E
Vinding	41	55.41 N	9.35 E
Vindinge	41	55.19 N	10.45 E
Vine Brook ≃	273	42.27 N	71.13 W
Vinegar Hill ∧	192	44.43 N	118.34 W
Vine Grove	184	37.49 N	85.59 W
Vine Hill	272	38.00 N	122.06 W
Vineland, Fla., U.S.	210	28.24 N	81.31 W
Vineland, Mich., U.S.	206	42.03 N	86.30 W
Vineland, N.J., U.S.	198	39.29 N	75.02 W
Vinemont	184	34.10 N	86.52 W
Vine Valley	200	42.43 N	77.20 W
Vineyard Canyon ∨	216	35.46 N	120.41 W
Vineyard Haven	197	41.27 N	70.36 W
Vineyard Lake ⊜	206	42.05 N	84.13 W
Vineyard Sound ⊔	197	41.25 N	70.46 W
Vingåker	40	59.02 N	15.52 E
Vingeanne ≃	54	47.21 N	5.29 E
Ving Ngün	100	22.37 N	99.16 E
Vinh	100	18.40 N	105.40 E
Vinhais	34	41.50 N	7.00 W
Vinhas, Ribeira das ≃	256c	38.42 N	9.25 W
Vinh-chau	100	9.19 N	105.59 E
Vinhedo	246	23.01 S	46.59 W
Vinh-linh	100	17.04 N	107.02 E
Vinh-loc	259c	10.49 N	106.34 E
Vinh-long	100	10.15 N	105.58 E
Vinh-tuy, Viet.	100	17.24 N	106.36 E
Vinh-tuy, Viet.	100	9.37 N	105.22 E
Vinica	36	45.28 N	15.15 E
Vinita	186	36.39 N	95.09 W
Vînju Mare	38	44.26 N	22.52 E
Vinkekuil	148	32.42 S	20.27 E
Vinkeveen	48	52.13 N	4.54 E
Vinkovci	38	45.17 N	18.49 E
Vin'kovcy	68	49.02 N	27.14 E
Vinnhorst	48	52.25 N	9.43 E
Vinnica	68	49.14 N	28.29 E
Vinnica □[4]	38	48.30 N	28.30 E
Vinniki	68	49.48 N	24.08 E
Vinnitsa → Vinnica	68	49.14 N	28.29 E
Vinnum	253	51.41 N	7.24 E
Vinogradov	68	48.09 N	23.02 E
Vinogradovo, S.S.S.R.	72	55.25 N	38.23 E
Vinogradovo, S.S.S.R.	72	55.57 N	37.32 E
Vinogrobol'	68	51.51 N	36.26 E
Vinön I	40	59.12 N	15.43 E
Vinon-sur-Verdon	56	43.43 N	5.48 E
Vinovo	56	44.57 N	7.38 E
Vinslöv	26	56.06 N	13.55 E
Vinson Massif ∧	9	78.35 S	85.25 W
Vinstra	26	61.36 N	9.45 E
Vintilă Vodă	38	45.28 N	26.44 E
Vinton, Iowa, U.S.	180	42.10 N	92.01 W
Vinton, Va., U.S.	182	37.17 N	80.01 W
Vintondale	204	40.29 N	78.55 W
Vintrosa	40	59.15 N	14.57 E
Viñuelas, Arroyo de ≃	256a	40.33 N	3.33 W
Viny	66	58.22 N	32.13 E
Vinzelberg	50	52.33 N	11.40 E
Vinzili	76	56.58 N	65.46 E
Viola, Ill., U.S.	180	41.12 N	90.35 W
Viola, N.Y., U.S.	266	41.08 N	74.05 W
Viola, Wis., U.S.	180	43.31 N	90.40 W
Viola, Val ∨	58	46.27 N	10.15 E
Violín, Isla I	226	8.51 N	83.39 W
Viols-le-Fort	56	43.45 N	3.42 E
Viosne ≃	251	49.03 N	2.06 E
Vipava	36	45.51 N	13.58 E
Vipava ≃	58	45.54 N	13.33 E
Vipiteno (Sterzing)	58	46.54 N	11.26 E
Vipos	242	26.29 S	65.22 W
Vipperow	50	53.19 N	12.41 E
Viquique	102	8.52 S	126.22 E
Vir, Otok I	36	44.18 N	15.04 E
Vira	54	46.08 N	8.51 E
Virac, Pil.	106	13.35 N	124.15 E
Virac, Pil.	106	16.22 N	120.39 E
Viracopos, Aeroporto de ⊠	246	23.00 S	47.08 W
Virac Point ≻	106	13.31 N	124.13 E
Viradouro	245	20.53 S	48.18 W
Virago Sound ⊔	172	54.00 N	132.36 W
Virama, Ensenada de C	230p	20.38 N	77.15 W
Viramgām	110	23.07 N	72.02 E
Virandozero	24	64.05 N	35.58 E
Viranşehir, Tür.	120	39.00 N	36.39 E
Viranşehir, Tür.	120	37.13 N	39.45 E
Vīrarājendrapet	112	12.12 N	75.48 E
Virbalis	66	54.38 N	22.49 E
Virden, Man., Can.	174	49.51 N	100.55 W
Virden, Ill., U.S.	209	39.30 N	89.46 W
Virden, N. Mex., U.S.	190	32.42 N	109.00 W
Vire	32	48.50 N	0.53 W
Vire ≃	32	49.20 N	1.07 W
Virelles	46	50.04 N	4.20 E
Virelles, Étang de ⊜	46	50.04 N	4.21 E
Vireši	66	57.27 N	26.23 E
Vireux-Molhain	52	50.05 N	4.43 E
Vîrful, Muntelui ∧	68	46.29 N	23.14 E
Vîrfurile	38	46.19 N	22.31 E
Virgem da Lapa	245	16.49 S	42.21 W
Virgen	58	47.00 N	12.27 E
Vírgen del San Cristóbal ♥[1]	276e	33.26 S	70.39 W
Vírgenes, Cabo ≻	244	52.22 S	68.20 W
Vírgenes, Islas → Virgin Islands □[2], N.A.	228	18.00 N	64.40 W
Vírgenes, Islas → British Virgin Islands □[2], N.A.	230m	18.30 N	64.30 W
Virgen Tal ∨	58	47.00 N	12.25 E
Virgil, Ont., Can.	274a	43.13 N	79.08 W
Virgil, Kans., U.S.	188	37.59 N	96.01 W
Virgil, N.Y., U.S.	200	42.31 N	76.12 W
Virgilina	182	36.33 N	78.52 W
Virgilio	58	45.07 N	10.47 E
Virgin ≃	190	36.31 N	114.20 W
Virginal-Samme	46	50.38 N	4.12 E
Virgin Gorda I	230m	18.30 N	64.24 W
Virgin Gorda Peak ∧	230m	18.30 N	64.24 W
Virginia, Austl.	158b	34.40 S	138.34 E
Virginia, Bra.	246	22.20 S	45.06 W
Virginia, S. Afr.	148	28.12 S	26.49 E
Virginia, Ill., U.S.	209	39.57 N	90.13 W
Virginia, Minn., U.S.	180	47.31 N	92.32 W
Virginia □[3]	168	37.30 N	78.45 W
Virginia Beach	198	36.51 N	75.58 W
Virginia City, Mont., U.S.	192	45.18 N	111.56 W
Virginia City, Nev., U.S.	216	39.19 N	119.39 W
Virginia Creek ≃	216	38.13 N	119.14 W
Virginia Falls ⌊	170	61.38 N	125.42 W
Virginia Gardens	210	25.49 N	80.17 W
Virginia Hills	198	38.47 N	77.06 W
Virginia Key I	210	25.44 N	80.09 W
Virginia Peak ∧	194	39.45 N	119.28 W
Virginia Ranch Reservoir ⊜[1]	216	39.20 N	121.19 W

Symbol	English	Deutsch	Español	Français	Português
≃	River	Fluss	Río	Rivière	Rio
☰	Canal	Kanal	Canal	Canal	Canal
⌊	Waterfall, Rapids	Wasserfall, Stromschnellen	Cascada, Rápidos	Chute d'eau, Rapides	Cascata, Rápidos
⊔	Strait	Meeresstrasse	Estrecho	Détroit	Estreito
C	Bay, Gulf	Bucht, Golf	Bahía, Golfo	Baie, Golfe	Baía, Golfo
⊜	Lake, Lakes	See, Seen	Lago, Lagos	Lac, Lacs	Lago, Lagos
☷	Swamp	Sumpf	Pantano	Marais	Pântano
⩍	Ice Features, Glacier	Eis- und Gletscherformen	Accidentes Glaciales	Formes glaciaires	Acidentes Glaciares
⊤	Other Hydrographic Features	Andere Hydrographische Objekte	Otros Elementos Hidrográficos	Autres données hydrographiques	Outros Elementos Hidrográficos
⬩	Submarine Features	Untermeerische Objekte	Accidentes Submarinos	Formes de relief sous-marin	Acidentes Submarinos
□	Political Unit	Politische Einheit	Unidad Política	Entité politique	Unidade Política
♥	Cultural Institution	Kulturelle Institution	Institución Cultural	Institution culturelle	Instituição Cultural
⊥	Historical Site	Historische Stätte	Sitio Histórico	Site historique	Sítio Histórico
♠	Recreational Site	Erholungs- und Ferienort	Sitio de Recreo	Centre de loisirs	Sítio de Lazer
⊠	Airport	Flughafen	Aeropuerto	Aéroport	Aeroporto
■	Military Installation	Militäranlage	Instalación Militar	Installation militaire	Instalação Militar
◆	Miscellaneous	Verschiedenes	Misceláneo	Divers	Miscelânea

Virginia Range ⛰ 216 39.18 N 119.30 W
Virginiatown 180 48.08 N 79.35 W
Virginia Water 250 51.24 N 0.34 W
Virginie occidentale → West Virginia □3 178 38.45 N 80.30 W
Virgin Islands □2 230m 18.20 N 64.50 W
Virgin Islands II 230m 18.00 N 64.40 W
Virgin Islands National Park ♠ 230m 18.20 N 64.45 W
Virginópolis 245 18.45 S 42.45 W
Virgin Passage C1 230m 18.20 N 65.10 W
Virginville 198 40.31 N 75.52 W
Virgolândia 245 18.27 S 42.18 W
Virieu 56 45.29 N 5.28 E
Virieux-le-Grand 56 45.51 N 5.39 E
Virihaure ⊜ 24 67.20 N 16.35 E
Virje 36 46.04 N 16.59 E
Virkie 28 59.53 N 1.18 W
Virkkala 26 60.12 N 24.01 E
Virklund 41 56.07 N 9.34 E
Virneburg 52 50.20 N 7.04 E
Virôchey 100 13.59 N 106.49 E
Viroflay 46 48.48 N 2.10 E
Viroin ≃ 52 50.05 N 4.43 E
Virojoki 26 60.35 N 27.42 E
Víron 257c 37.57 N 23.45 E
Vironvay 46 49.12 N 1.13 E
Viroqua 180 43.34 N 90.53 W
Virovitica 36 45.50 N 17.23 E
Virpazar 38 42.15 N 19.05 E
Virrat 26 62.14 N 23.47 E
Virsbo 40 59.52 N 16.02 E
Virserum 26 57.19 N 15.35 E
Virtaniemi 24 68.53 N 28.27 E
Virton 52 49.34 N 5.32 E
Vîrtopu 38 44.12 N 23.21 E
Virtsu 66 58.34 N 23.31 E
Virú 238 8.25 S 78.45 W
Virudunagar 112 9.36 N 77.58 E
Viru-Jaagupi 66 59.15 N 26.28 E
Virulento 186 28.52 N 104.21 W
Viru-Nigula 66 59.27 N 26.41 E
Virvyčia ≃ 66 56.13 N 22.34 E
Viry-Châtillon 46 48.40 N 2.23 E
Vis 36 43.03 N 16.12 E
Vis ≃, Fr. 56 43.56 N 3.42 E
Vis ≃, S. Afr. 148 33.30 S 27.08 E
Vis, Otok I 36 43.02 N 16.11 E
Visale 165e 9.15 S 159.42 E
Visalia 216 36.20 N 119.18 W
Visalia Airport ⊠ 216 36.19 N 119.23 W
Visayan Sea ⊤2 106 11.35 N 123.51 E
Visbaai C 148 34.16 S 21.57 E
Visbek 48 52.48 N 8.19 E
Visby 26 57.38 N 18.18 E
Viscaya, Bahía de → Biscay, Bay of C 32 44.00 N 4.00 W
Viscount 174 51.57 N 105.39 W
Viscount Melville Sound Ц 166 74.10 N 113.00 W
Visé 52 50.44 N 5.42 E
Višegrad 38 43.47 N 19.17 E
Vis-en-Artois 46 50.15 N 2.56 E
Višera ≃ 66 58.34 N 31.24 E
Viserba 60 44.05 N 12.32 E
Viseu, Bra. 240 1.12 S 46.07 W
Viseu, Port. 34 40.39 N 7.55 W
Vişeu ≃ 38 46.55 N 23.47 E
Vişeu de Sus 38 47.44 N 24.22 E
Vishākhapatnam 112 17.42 N 83.18 E
Vishoek 148 34.07 S 18.27 E
Visim 76 57.39 N 59.30 E
Visingsö I 26 58.03 N 14.20 E
Visitation, Île de la I 265a 45.35 N 73.40 W
Viskafors 26 57.38 N 12.50 E
Viskan ≃ 26 57.14 N 12.12 E
Viškil' 70 58.05 N 48.19 E
Viskinge 41 55.40 N 11.16 E
Visl'ajevo 72 54.25 N 36.43 E
Vislanda 26 56.47 N 14.27 E
Vislinskij Zaliv C 30 54.27 N 19.40 E
Vismen ⊜ 40 59.17 N 14.17 E
Visnagar 110 23.42 N 72.33 E
Visn'aki 255b 55.47 N 37.54 E
Višn'akovo 72 55.45 N 38.10 E
Višnevčik 68 49.02 N 26.28 E
Visnevo 66 54.08 N 26.14 E
Višnevoje, S.S.S.R. 68 48.27 N 33.56 E
Višnevoje, S.S.S.R. 70 52.38 N 43.26 E
Višn'ovec 68 49.54 N 25.45 E
Višn'ovka, S.S.S.R. 68 46.20 N 28.26 E
Višn'ovka, S.S.S.R. 76 50.49 N 72.12 E
Viso, Monte ∧ 56 44.40 N 7.07 E
Visoki Dečani, Manastir ⊍1 38 42.30 N 20.31 E
Visoko 38 43.59 N 18.11 E
Visokoi Island I 18 56.42 S 27.12 W
Visp 54 46.18 N 7.53 E
Vispa ≃ 54 46.18 N 7.52 E
Vissefjärda 26 56.32 N 15.35 E
Visselhövede 48 52.59 N 9.35 E
Vissenbjerg 41 55.23 N 10.08 E
Visso 60 42.56 N 13.05 E
Vissoie 54 46.13 N 7.36 E
Vista, Calif., U.S. 218 33.12 N 117.15 W
Vista, N.Y., U.S. 200 41.12 N 73.31 W
Vista Alegre, Arg. 242 38.45 S 68.11 W
Vista Alegre, Bra. 246 21.27 S 42.35 W
Vista Alegre, Chile 276e 33.30 S 70.43 W
Vista Alegre, Perú 276d 12.09 S 77.00 W
Vista Flores 242 33.38 S 69.09 W
Vista Hermosa, Méx. 224 19.38 N 103.22 W
Vista Hermosa, Méx. 224 20.16 N 102.29 W
Vista La Mesa 218 32.35 N 117.01 W
Vista Park 218 35.21 N 118.55 W
Vistina 66 59.47 N 28.29 E
Vistre ≃ 56 43.40 N 4.15 E
Vistula → Wisła ≃ 30 54.22 N 18.55 E
Visun' ≃ 68 47.07 N 35.53 E
Vit ≃ 38 43.41 N 24.45 E
Vita 174 49.08 N 96.34 W
Vitacura 276e 33.24 S 70.36 W
Vitali 106 7.22 N 122.18 E
Vitanje 36 46.23 N 15.18 E
Vitarte 238 12.02 S 76.56 W
Vit'azevka 68 48.01 N 31.53 E
Vite 112 17.17 N 74.33 E
Vitebsk 66 55.12 N 30.11 E
Vitebskij Vokzal ⇝5 255a 59.55 N 30.21 E
Viterbo 60 42.25 N 12.06 E
Viterbo □4 60 42.25 N 12.05 E
Vitiaz Strait Ц 154 5.50 S 147.20 E
Vitichi 238 20.13 S 65.29 W
Vitigudino 34 41.01 N 6.26 W
Viti Levu I 165g 18.00 S 178.00 E
Viti Levu Bay C 165g 17.26 S 178.15 E
Vitim 64 59.28 N 112.34 E
Vitim ≃ 64 59.26 N 112.34 E
Vitimskij 78 58.14 N 113.18 E
Vitimskoje Ploskogorje ⛰1 78 54.00 N 113.30 E
Vitinia ⇝8 257a 41.47 N 12.24 E
Vítkov 30 49.46 N 17.45 E
Vitor 238 16.26 S 71.49 W
Vitor ≃ 238 16.37 S 72.19 W
Vitória, Bra. 240 2.54 S 52.01 W
Vitória, Bra. 245 20.19 S 40.21 W
Vitoria, Esp. 34 42.51 N 2.40 W
Vitória, Ilha da I 246 23.45 S 45.01 W
Vitória da Conquista 245 14.51 S 40.51 W
Vitória de Santo Antão 240 8.07 S 35.18 W
Vitória do Mearim 240 3.28 S 44.53 W
Vitorino Freire 240 4.04 S 45.10 W
Vitré 28 48.08 N 1.12 W
Vitrey-sur-Mance 54 47.49 N 5.45 E
Vitry-en-Artois 46 50.20 N 2.59 E
Vitry-la-Ville 46 48.50 N 4.28 E
Vitry-le-François 52 48.44 N 4.35 E
Vitry[-sur-Seine] 46 48.48 N 2.24 E
Vitshumbi 144 0.41 S 29.23 E
Vitte 50 54.34 N 13.06 E
Vitteaux 54 47.24 N 4.32 E
Vittel 54 48.12 N 5.57 E
Vittinge 40 59.54 N 17.04 E
Vittoria, Ont., Can. 202 42.46 N 80.19 W
Vittoria, It. 36 36.57 N 14.32 E
Vittorio Veneto 58 45.59 N 12.18 E
Vittsjö 26 56.20 N 13.40 E
Vitulano 60 41.10 N 14.38 E
Vitznau 54 47.01 N 8.29 E
Viù 56 45.14 N 7.22 E
Vivarais □9 56 44.40 N 4.30 E
Vivarais, Monts du ⛰ 56 44.55 N 4.15 E
Viver 34 39.55 N 0.36 W
Vivero 34 43.38 N 7.35 W
Viverols 56 45.26 N 3.53 E
Viverone, Lago di ⊜ 56 45.25 N 8.02 E
Vivi ≃ 64 63.52 N 97.50 E
Vivian 184 32.53 N 93.59 W
Viviers 56 44.29 N 4.41 E
Viviers-du-Lac 56 45.39 N 5.54 E
Vivione, Passo del)(58 46.02 N 10.12 E
Vivonne 32 46.26 N 0.16 E
Vivoratá 242 37.40 S 57.39 W
Vivorillo, Cayos II 226 15.50 N 83.18 W
Vivsta 26 62.29 N 17.19 E
Viwa I 165g 17.08 S 176.54 E
Vizagapatam → Vishākhapatnam 112 17.42 N 83.18 E
Vizcachas, Meseta de las ⛰1 244 50.35 S 71.55 W
Vizcaíno, Desierto de ⇝2 222 27.40 N 114.40 W
Vizcaya □4 34 43.20 N 2.45 W
Vize 120 41.34 N 27.45 E
Vize, Ostrov I 62 79.30 N 77.00 E
Vizianagaram 112 18.07 N 83.25 E
Vizille 56 45.05 N 5.46 E
Vižinada 36 45.20 N 13.46 E
Vizinga 24 61.05 N 50.04 E
Vižnica 68 48.15 N 25.12 E
Vizzini 36 37.09 N 14.46 E
Vizzola 256b 45.38 N 8.42 E
Vjulka ≃ 72 56.53 N 37.57 E
Vjunka ≃ 255b 55.42 N 38.01 E
Vjuny 76 55.31 N 82.55 E
Vík 24a 63.25 N 19.00 W
Vlaanderen → Flanders □9 46 51.00 N 3.00 E
Vlaardingen 48 51.54 N 4.21 E
Vladař ∧ 50 50.05 N 13.14 E
Vlădeasa ∧ 38 46.45 N 22.48 E
Vlădeni 38 47.25 N 27.20 E
Vladičin Han 38 42.42 N 22.04 E
Vladikavkaz → Ordžonikidze 74 43.03 N 44.40 E
Vladimir 70 56.10 N 40.25 E
Vladimir □4 72 56.15 N 39.00 E
Vladimirec 68 51.25 N 26.08 E
Vladimirovka, S.S.S.R. 68 47.32 N 32.55 E
Vladimirovka, S.S.S.R. 70 50.51 N 51.08 E
Vladimirovka, S.S.S.R. 73 47.44 N 37.23 E
Vladimirovka, S.S.S.R. 76 53.28 N 64.02 E
Vladimirskij Tupik 66 55.42 N 33.18 E
Vladimirskoje 70 56.49 N 45.07 E
Vladimir-Volynskij 68 50.51 N 24.20 E
Vladivostok 79 43.10 N 131.56 E
Vladyčnoje 66 58.49 N 39.29 E
Vladykino ⇝8 255b 55.52 N 37.36 E
Vlárský priesmyk)(30 49.03 N 18.02 E
Vlasenica 38 44.11 N 18.56 E
Vlašim 30 49.42 N 14.54 E
Vlasinsko Jezero ⊜ 38 42.42 N 22.22 E
Vlaskovo 72 56.11 N 36.31 E
Vlasotince 38 42.58 N 22.08 E
Vlasovo 72 56.38 N 38.14 E
Vlatten 52 50.39 N 6.32 E
Vlazoviči 66 53.01 N 32.18 E
Vledder 48 52.52 N 6.12 E
Vleikolk 148 29.43 S 20.50 E
Vleuten 48 52.05 N 5.02 E
Vlieland I 48 53.15 N 5.00 E
Vlijmen 48 51.42 N 5.15 E
Vlissingen (Flushing) 48 51.26 N 3.35 E
Vlodrop 48 51.08 N 6.05 E
Vloesberg → Flobecq 46 50.44 N 3.44 E
Vlonë → Vlorë 38 40.27 N 19.30 E
Vloorskop ∧ 146 25.45 S 20.50 E
Vlorë 38 40.27 N 19.30 E
Vlorës, Gji i C 38 40.25 N 19.25 E
Vlotho 48 52.10 N 8.51 E
Vltava ≃ 30 50.21 N 14.30 E
Vluyn 48 51.26 N 6.32 E
Vnukovo 72 55.38 N 37.16 E
Vnukovo, Aeroport ⊠ 72 55.37 N 37.17 E
Vobarno 58 45.39 N 10.30 E
Voca 186 31.01 N 99.11 W
Vočaž, Porog ⌊ 24 64.55 N 34.22 E
Vochrinka 72 55.24 N 38.18 E
Vochtoga 66 58.47 N 41.07 E
Vočin 36 45.37 N 17.32 E
Vöckla ≃ 58 48.00 N 13.36 E
Vöcklabruck 58 48.01 N 13.39 E
Vöcklamarkt 58 48.00 N 13.29 E
Vodla ≃ 24 61.49 N 36.00 E
Vodlozero, Ozero ⊜ 24 62.20 N 36.55 E
Vodňany 30 49.09 N 14.11 E
Vodnjan 58 44.57 N 13.51 E
Vodnyj 24 63.32 N 53.18 E
Vodo 58 46.25 N 12.14 E
Vodosalma 24 64.29 N 30.44 E
Vodovatovo 70 55.24 N 43.34 E
Vodzimonje 70 56.49 N 51.38 E
Voerde, B.R.D. 48 51.35 N 6.41 E
Voerde, B.R.D. 253 51.18 N 7.24 E
Voesch 253 51.24 N 6.26 E
Vogelenzang 48 52.19 N 4.35 E
Vogelheim ⇝8 253 51.29 N 6.59 E
Vogelkop → Doberai, Jazirah ≻1 154 1.30 S 132.30 E
Vogel Peak → Dimlang ∧ 136 8.24 N 11.47 E
Vogelsang, B.R.D. 52 50.35 N 6.27 E
Vogelsang, D.D.R. 50 53.43 N 14.09 E
Vogelsberg ⛰ 52 50.30 N 9.15 E
Vogelsberg, Naturpark ♠ 52 50.35 N 9.15 E
Vogesen → Vosges ⛰ 54 48.30 N 7.10 E
Voghera 56 44.59 N 9.01 E
Vognema 66 59.59 N 38.10 E
Vogogna 54 46.01 N 8.17 E
Vogtland ⇝1 50 50.30 N 12.05 E
Voh 165f 20.58 S 164.42 E
Vohémar 147b 13.21 S 50.02 E
Vohenstrauss 30 49.37 N 12.21 E
Vohilava 147b 21.04 S 48.00 E
Vohipeno 147b 22.22 S 47.51 E
Vohitsora 147b 23.54 S 44.17 E
Võhma 66 58.38 N 25.33 E
Vöhringen, B.R.D. 54 48.02 N 8.18 E
Vöhringen, B.R.D. 54 48.16 N 10.04 E
Vöhringen, B.R.D. 54 48.20 N 8.40 E
Vöhrum 48 52.20 N 10.10 E
Vohwinkel ⇝8 253 51.14 N 7.09 E
Voi 144 3.23 S 38.34 E
Void 54 48.41 N 5.37 E
Voight Creek ≃ 214 47.06 N 122.10 W
Voikkaa 26 60.56 N 26.37 E
Voinești 38 47.05 N 27.26 E
Voinjama 140 8.25 N 9.45 W
Voinka 68 45.52 N 33.59 E
Voiotía □5 38 38.20 N 23.30 E
Voire ≃ 54 48.27 N 4.25 E
Voiron 56 45.22 N 5.35 E
Voise 46 48.24 N 1.43 E
Voise ≃ 46 48.35 N 1.35 E
Voisenon 251 48.34 N 2.40 E
Voisin, Lac ⊜ 174 54.13 N 107.15 W
Voisins-le-Bretonneux 46 48.45 N 2.03 E
Voiteur 54 46.45 N 5.37 E
Voitsberg 30 47.03 N 15.10 E
Voja ≃ 70 57.23 N 49.55 E
Vojens 41 55.15 N 9.19 E
Vojevodskoje 76 52.47 N 85.35 E
Vojkovice 50 50.15 N 13.02 E
Vojkovo, S.S.S.R. 68 45.31 N 33.52 E
Vojkovo, S.S.S.R. 73 48.00 N 38.02 E
Vojkovskij 73 47.46 N 38.20 E
Vojmsjön ⊜ 26 64.55 N 16.40 E
Vojnić 36 45.19 N 15.42 E
Vojnica 24 65.12 N 30.15 E
Vojnilov 68 49.08 N 24.30 E
Vojtanov 50 50.06 N 12.19 E
Voj-Vož, S.S.S.R. 24 64.20 N 55.03 E
Voj-Vož, S.S.S.R. 24 62.56 N 54.56 E
Vokeo Island I 154 3.10 S 144.05 E
Volano 60 45.55 N 11.03 E
Volant 204 41.07 N 80.16 W
Volary 30 48.55 N 13.54 E
Volcán 242 23.54 S 65.27 W
Volcancillo ∧ 224 19.02 N 103.36 W
Volcán de Colima, Parque Nacional ♠ 224 19.30 N 103.35 W
Volčanka 70 52.33 N 49.59 E
Volcano, Calif., U.S. 216 38.26 N 120.37 W
Volcano, Haw., U.S. 219d 19.26 N 155.14 W
Volcano Islands → Kazan-rettō II 14 25.00 N 141.00 E
Volčansk, S.S.S.R. 68 50.18 N 36.57 E
Volčansk, S.S.S.R. 76 59.56 N 60.04 E
Volčejarovka 73 48.50 N 38.22 E
Volčenskij 73 48.14 N 40.07 E
Volchonka-Zil ⇝8 255b 55.40 N 37.37 E
Volchov 66 59.55 N 32.20 E
Volchov ≃ 66 60.08 N 32.20 E
Volčicha 76 52.02 N 80.23 E
Volčij Nos, Mys ≻ 66 60.31 N 32.35 E
Volčja ≃ 68 48.00 N 36.08 E
Volčje 68 49.14 N 22.53 E
Volčki 70 52.29 N 40.42 E
Volda 26 62.09 N 6.06 E
Volders 58 47.17 N 11.34 E
Volendam 48 52.30 N 5.04 E
Volga, S.S.S.R. 66 57.57 N 38.24 E
Volga, Iowa, U.S. 180 42.48 N 91.33 W
Volga, S. Dak., U.S. 188 44.19 N 96.56 W
Volga ≃, S.S.S.R. 22 45.55 N 47.52 E
Volga ≃, Iowa, U.S. 180 42.45 N 91.17 W
Volga-Baltic Canal → Volgo-Baltijskij Vodnyj Put' ⩸ 24 59.00 N 38.00 E
Volga-Donskoj Kanal ⩸ 70 48.40 N 43.37 E
Volgino 66 58.27 N 33.52 E
Volgo, Ozero ⊜ 66 56.55 N 33.10 E
Volgo-Baltijskij Vodnyj Put' ⩸ 24 59.00 N 38.00 E
Volgodonsk 70 47.33 N 42.08 E
Volgograd (Stalingrad) 70 48.44 N 44.25 E
Volgogradskoje Vodochranilišče ⊜1 70 49.20 N 45.00 E
Volissós 38 38.29 N 25.58 E
Vol'ka 66 52.47 N 25.39 E
Volkach 52 49.52 N 10.13 E
Volkel 48 51.38 N 5.40 E
Völkermarkt 30 46.39 N 14.38 E
Völkerschlachtdenkmal ⊥ 50 51.18 N 12.24 E
Völklingen 52 49.15 N 6.50 E
Volkmarsen 52 51.24 N 9.07 E
Volkovincy 68 49.13 N 27.39 E
Volkovo, S.S.S.R. 66 59.15 N 41.27 E
Volkovo, S.S.S.R. 72 55.46 N 36.15 E
Volkovo, Kladbišče ⇝ 255a 59.54 N 30.22 E
Volkovskoje 72 54.49 N 37.13 E
Volkovysk 66 53.10 N 24.28 E
Volksdorf ⇝8 48 53.39 N 11.00 E
Völksen 48 52.13 N 9.37 E
Volksrust 148 27.24 S 29.53 E
Vollenhove 48 52.41 N 5.58 E
Vollersode 48 53.18 N 8.56 E
Vollme 253 51.10 N 7.36 E
Vollore-Montagne 56 45.47 N 3.41 E
Vollore-Ville 56 45.47 N 3.36 E
Vollsjö 41 55.42 N 13.46 E
Volma ≃ 66 53.35 N 28.19 E
Volmarstein 52 51.22 N 7.23 E
Volme ≃ 253 51.24 N 7.27 E
Volmerange-les-Mines 52 49.27 N 6.05 E
Volmerswerth ⇝8 253 51.11 N 6.46 E
Volmunster 52 49.07 N 7.21 E
Vol'naja Gorka 66 58.43 N 30.51 E
Volnay 54 47.00 N 4.47 E
Vol'nogorsk 68 48.29 N 34.01 E
Vol'noje, S.S.S.R. 70 47.09 N 47.38 E
Vol'noje, S.S.S.R. 76 54.17 N 71.21 E
Volnovacha 73 47.36 N 37.31 E
Vol'nyj 70 45.55 N 45.14 E
Vol'nyj, Ostrov I 255a 59.58 N 30.14 E
Voločajevkall-ja 79 48.34 N 134.34 E
Voločanka 64 71.00 N 94.28 E
Voločisk 68 49.32 N 26.11 E
Volockaja 66 60.17 N 42.59 E
Volodarka, S.S.S.R. 68 49.31 N 29.55 E
Volodarka, S.S.S.R. 76 52.43 N 83.38 E
Volodarsk, S.S.S.R. 66 56.13 N 43.10 E
Volodarsk, S.S.S.R. 73 48.06 N 39.35 E
Volodarskij, S.S.S.R. 70 46.24 N 48.32 E
Volodarskij, S.S.S.R. 72 55.30 N 37.57 E
Volodarskij ⇝8 255a 59.49 N 30.05 E
Volodarskoje, S.S.S.R. 73 47.12 N 37.20 E
Volodarskoje, S.S.S.R. 76 53.18 N 68.08 E
Volodarsk-Volynskij 68 50.37 N 28.25 E
Volodino 76 57.06 N 83.54 E
Vologda 66 59.12 N 39.55 E
Vologda ≃ 66 59.17 N 40.13 E
Voloje 66 54.09 N 34.35 E
Volokolamsk 72 56.02 N 35.57 E
Volokonovka 68 50.29 N 37.51 E
Volokovaja 24 66.28 N 48.10 E
Volonga 24 67.07 N 47.41 E
Volonne 56 44.07 N 6.01 E
Volontirovka 68 46.26 N 29.37 E
Vólos 38 39.21 N 22.56 E
Vološino, S.S.S.R. 73 48.55 N 39.56 E
Vološino, S.S.S.R. 73 47.31 N 39.40 E
Vološka 24 61.20 N 40.06 E
Vološn'a ≃ 72 55.51 N 35.54 E
Vološno 66 58.29 N 28.29 E
Volosoviči 66 54.46 N 28.50 E
Volosovo 66 59.26 N 29.29 E
Volosskaja Balaklejka 73 49.37 N 37.20 E
Volot 66 57.56 N 30.42 E
Volovec 68 48.43 N 23.11 E
Volovo, S.S.S.R. 66 53.35 N 38.02 E
Volovo, S.S.S.R. 68 52.03 N 37.53 E
Voložin 66 54.05 N 26.32 E
Volpago del Montello 58 45.47 N 12.07 E
Volpedo 56 44.53 N 8.59 E
Volpiano 56 45.12 N 7.46 E
Völpke 50 52.08 N 11.09 E
Völs → Fiè 58 46.31 N 11.30 E
Volsini, Monti ⛰ 60 42.40 N 11.55 E
Vol'sk 70 52.02 N 47.23 E
Volta □4 140 7.00 N 0.30 E
Volta ≃ 140 5.46 N 0.41 E
Volta, Lake ⊜1 140 7.30 N 0.15 E
Volta, Riacho da ≃ 240 7.24 S 44.51 W
Volta Blanche (White Volta) ≃ 140 9.10 N 1.15 W
Voltaggio 56 44.37 N 8.50 E
Voltago 58 46.16 N 12.00 E
Volta Grande 246 21.46 S 42.32 W
Volta Mantovana 58 45.19 N 10.39 E
Volta-Noire □5 140 11.00 N 4.00 W
Volta Noire (Black Volta) ≃ 140 8.38 N 1.40 W
Volta Redonda 246 22.32 S 44.07 W
Volta Rouge ≃ 140 10.34 N 0.30 W
Volterra 60 43.24 N 10.51 E
Vol'teva 24 64.30 N 44.12 E
Voltri 56 44.26 N 8.45 E
Volturara Appula 60 41.30 N 15.03 E
Volturara Irpina 60 40.53 N 14.55 E
Volturino 60 41.28 N 15.07 E
Volturino, Monte ∧ 36 40.25 N 15.49 E
Volturno ≃ 60 41.01 N 13.55 E
Volubilis ⊥ 138 34.00 N 5.30 W
Volunteer Point ≻ 244 51.31 S 57.45 W
Voluntown 197 41.34 N 71.52 W
Volusia □6 210 28.51 N 81.05 W
Vólvi, Límni ⊜ 38 40.41 N 23.23 E
Volx 56 43.53 N 5.51 E
Volyncy, S.S.S.R. 66 55.42 N 28.11 E
Volyncy, S.S.S.R. 70 57.48 N 45.28 E
Volyně 30 49.10 N 13.53 E
Volynka 68 51.37 N 32.26 E
Volynskaja Oblast' □4 68 51.00 N 25.00 E
Volynskaya Vozvyšennost' ⛰1 68 50.35 N 25.10 E
Volynskoje Polesje ⇝1 68 51.10 N 26.00 E
Volzhskiy → Volžskij 70 48.50 N 44.44 E
Volžsk 70 55.53 N 48.21 E
Volžskij, S.S.S.R. 70 48.50 N 44.44 E
Volžskij, S.S.S.R. 70 53.27 N 50.07 E
Vom 140 9.41 N 8.42 E
Vomano ≃ 60 42.39 N 14.02 E
Vombsjön ⊜ 41 55.41 N 13.36 E
Vomp 58 47.20 N 11.41 E
Vonda 174 52.19 N 106.06 W
Vondanka 24 59.07 N 47.49 E
Vondrozo 147b 22.49 S 47.20 E
Von Frank Mountain ∧ 170 63.33 N 154.20 W
Võnnu 66 58.17 N 27.05 E
Vonozero 66 60.22 N 34.26 E
Vonsild 41 55.27 N 9.29 E
Von Treuer Tableland ⛰1 152 26.38 S 122.53 E
Voorburg 48 52.05 N 4.23 E
Voordeelspan 148 29.05 S 21.32 E
Voorheesville 200 42.39 N 73.56 W
Voorne I 48 51.55 N 4.00 E
Voorschoten 48 52.07 N 4.27 E
Voorst 48 52.10 N 6.09 E
Voorthuizen 48 52.12 N 5.35 E
Vop' ≃ 66 54.56 N 32.44 E
Vopnafjördur 24a 65.47 N 14.44 W
Vopnafjördur C 24a 65.52 N 14.40 W
Vörå (Vöyri) 26 63.09 N 22.15 E
Vor'a ≃, S.S.S.R. 66 54.54 N 35.01 E
Vor'a ≃, S.S.S.R. 72 55.52 N 38.13 E
Vorarlberg □3 58 47.15 N 9.55 E
Vorau 30 47.25 N 15.54 E
Vorbasse 41 55.38 N 9.05 E
Vorchdorf 58 48.00 N 13.55 E
Vörden, B.R.D. 48 52.28 N 8.05 E
Vorden, Ned. 48 52.07 N 6.18 E
Vorder-Grauspitz ∧ 54 47.03 N 9.36 E
Vorderrhein ≃ 54 46.49 N 9.25 E
Vorderriss 58 47.33 N 11.26 E
Vordingborg 41 55.01 N 11.55 E
Voreifel ⛰ 52 50.15 N 7.10 E
Voreppe 56 45.18 N 5.38 E
Vorey 56 45.11 N 3.54 E
Vorga 66 53.45 N 32.45 E
Vorhalle ⇝8 253 51.23 N 7.28 E
Vorhelm 48 51.48 N 7.56 E
Voríai Sporádhes II 38 39.17 N 23.23 E
Vøringsfossen ⌊ 26 60.26 N 7.15 E
Vórios Evvoïkós Kólpos C 38 38.40 N 23.15 E
Vorkuta 24 67.27 N 63.58 E
Vorma ≃ 26 60.09 N 11.27 E
Vormholz 253 51.24 N 7.18 E
Vormsi I 66 59.00 N 23.20 E
Vorn'any 66 54.44 N 26.01 E
Vorobjevka 70 50.39 N 40.56 E
Vorobjevo, S.S.S.R. 72 56.11 N 35.45 E
Vorobjevo, S.S.S.R. 76 56.08 N 76.32 E
Vorobjevo, S.S.S.R. 78 57.23 N 102.18 E
Vorobji 72 55.09 N 36.48 E
Vorobjovka 68 50.38 N 40.56 E
Vorob'jovo, S.S.S.R. 66 59.38 N 40.53 E
Vorobjovo, S.S.S.R. 68 45.19 N 33.15 E
Vorochta 68 48.18 N 24.36 E
Voron' 66 55.00 N 28.39 E
Voron, Porog ⌊ 78 57.05 N 98.40 E
Vorona ≃ 70 51.22 N 42.03 E
Voroncovka, S.S.S.R. 68 50.37 N 40.21 E
Voroncovka, S.S.S.R. 68 45.51 N 33.47 E
Voroncovka, S.S.S.R. 76 48.49 N 81.32 E
Voroncovka, S.S.S.R. 76 59.39 N 60.14 E
Voroncovka, S.S.S.R. 78 58.51 N 112.56 E
Voroncovo, S.S.S.R. 66 57.18 N 28.42 E
Voroncovo, S.S.S.R. 70 55.16 N 40.27 E
Voronej → Voronež 68 51.40 N 39.10 E
Voronež, S.S.S.R. 68 51.46 N 33.28 E
Voronež, S.S.S.R. 68 51.40 N 39.10 E
Voronež □4, S.S.S.R. 66 51.55 N 40.00 E
Voronež □4, S.S.S.R. 73 49.53 N 40.00 E
Voronež ≃ 66 51.56 N 39.17 E
Voronezh → Voronež 68 51.40 N 39.10 E
Voronežskij Zapovednik ⇝4 66 51.56 N 39.37 E
Voronino 72 56.24 N 36.52 E
Voronin Trough ⇝1 12 82.00 N 85.00 E
Voronja ≃ 24 69.10 N 35.50 E
Voronjo, S.S.S.R. 24 68.27 N 35.21 E
Voronjo, S.S.S.R. 70 58.00 N 42.01 E
Voron'ki, S.S.S.R. 68 50.14 N 33.02 E
Voronki, S.S.S.R. 72 55.48 N 37.16 E
Voronkovo 68 47.43 N 29.08 E
Voronok 66 52.23 N 32.40 E
Voronov, Mys ≻ 66 60.15 N 32.05 E
Voronovica 68 49.06 N 28.41 E
Voronovkova Niva 66 57.04 N 29.16 E
Voronovo, S.S.S.R. 66 54.09 N 25.19 E
Voronovo, S.S.S.R. 72 55.19 N 37.10 E
Voronovo, S.S.S.R. 76 56.01 N 83.52 E
Voropajevo 66 55.09 N 27.13 E
Voroshilov → Ussurijsk 79 43.48 N 131.59 E
Voroshilovsk → Stavropol', S.S.S.R. 62 45.02 N 41.59 E
Voroshilovsk → Kommunarsk, S.S.S.R. 73 48.30 N 38.47 E
Vorošilovgrad 73 48.34 N 39.20 E
Vorošilovgrad Avtonomnaja Sovetskaja Socialističeskaja Respublika □4 73 49.00 N 39.00 E
Vorotajevka 70 51.56 N 47.16 E
Vorotynec 70 56.04 N 45.52 E
Vorotynsk 72 54.25 N 36.05 E
Vorovskolesskaja 74 44.23 N 42.25 E
Vorožba 68 51.12 N 34.14 E
Vorožejka 76 58.12 N 90.02 E

ENGLISH

Name	Page	Lat. °′	Long. °′

Vorpommern □9 50 53.40 N 13.45 E
Vorsfelde 50 52.26 N 10.49 E
Vorskla ≃ 68 48.53 N 34.06 E
Vorsma 70 55.59 N 43.16 E
Vorst, Bel. 52 51.04 N 5.01 E
Vorst, B.R.D. 52 51.18 N 6.25 E
Vørterkaka Nunatak ∧ 9 72.20 S 27.29 E
Võrtsjärv ⊜ 66 58.16 N 26.03 E
Võru 66 57.50 N 27.01 E
Voruch 75 39.52 N 70.35 E
Vorzel' 68 50.33 N 30.09 E
Vosburg 148 30.33 S 22.52 E
Voschod 70 47.24 N 41.50 E
Vösendorf 254b 48.07 N 16.20 E
Vosges □5 54 48.10 N 6.20 E
Vosges ⛰ 54 48.30 N 7.10 E
Vosja 66 59.01 N 41.11 E
Voskresenka, S.S.S.R. 70 51.01 N 46.28 E
Voskresenka, S.S.S.R. 78 53.15 N 119.31 E
Voskresenki 72 54.57 N 38.04 E
Voskresenovskoje 255a 59.43 N 30.47 E
Voskresensk 72 55.19 N 38.42 E
Voskresenskoje, S.S.S.R. 66 57.49 N 37.40 E
Voskresenskoje, S.S.S.R. 66 58.54 N 38.36 E
Voskresenskoje, S.S.S.R. 66 59.26 N 37.56 E
Voskresenskoje, S.S.S.R. 66 53.12 N 38.43 E
Voskresenskoje, S.S.S.R. 68 47.02 N 32.09 E
Voskresenskoje, S.S.S.R. 70 51.51 N 46.56 E
Voskresenskoje, S.S.S.R. 70 56.51 N 45.26 E
Voskresenskoje, S.S.S.R. 72 54.07 N 37.07 E
Voskresenskoje, S.S.S.R. 72 56.20 N 38.29 E
Voskresenskoje, S.S.S.R. 76 53.08 N 56.10 E
Voslapp 48 53.36 N 8.05 E
Voss 26 60.39 N 6.26 E
Vosselaar 52 51.19 N 4.53 E
Vossijatskoje 68 47.41 N 32.07 E
Vossman's Beacon 148 26.11 S 30.40 E
Vostočnaja Kambal'nica 24 68.18 N 46.00 E
Vostočno-Kazachstanskaja Oblast' □4 76 49.00 N 84.00 E
Vostočno-Kounradskij 76 47.02 N 75.07 E
Vostočno-Sibirskoje More ⊤2 12 74.00 N 166.00 E
Vostočnyj, S.S.S.R. 72 55.47 N 37.49 E
Vostočnyj, S.S.S.R. 76 58.48 N 61.52 E
Vostočnyj, S.S.S.R. 79 53.29 N 143.03 E
Vostočnyj, S.S.S.R. 79 48.17 N 142.34 E
Vostočnyj Sajan ⛰ 78 53.00 N 97.00 E
Vostočnyj Tannu-Ola, Chrebet ⛰ 78 50.54 N 94.30 E
Vostok ⊍3 9 78.30 S 106.50 E
Vostok Island I 14 10.06 S 152.23 W
Vostr'akovo 72 55.23 N 37.49 E
Vostrovo 76 52.09 N 80.38 E
Vosves 251 48.31 N 2.36 E
Votaw 212 30.26 N 94.41 W
Votice 30 49.38 N 14.39 E
Votkinsk 70 57.03 N 53.59 E
Votkinskoje Vodochranilišče ⊜1 70 56.45 N 54.08 E
Vot'pa 76 60.13 N 62.57 E
Votuporanga 245 20.24 S 49.59 W
Voué 46 48.28 N 4.07 E
Vouga 142 12.11 S 16.47 E
Vouga ≃ 34 40.41 N 8.40 W
Vougeot 54 47.10 N 4.58 E
Vouillé 32 46.39 N 0.10 E
Voujeaucourt 54 47.28 N 6.46 E
Voulangis 251 48.51 N 2.54 E
Voulou 136 8.33 N 22.36 E
Voulx 46 48.17 N 2.58 E
Voulzie ≃ 46 48.25 N 3.12 E
Voutenay-sur-Cure 46 47.33 N 3.47 E
Vouvray 46 47.25 N 0.48 E
Vouvry 54 46.20 N 6.53 E
Vouziers 52 49.24 N 4.42 E
Voves 46 48.16 N 1.38 E
Vovodo ≃ 130 5.40 N 24.21 E
Vowinckel 204 41.25 N 79.14 W
Voxnan ≃ 26 61.17 N 16.26 E
Voxtrup 48 52.14 N 8.07 E
Voyageurs National Park ♠ 180 48.30 N 93.00 W
Voyeykov Ice Shelf ⊓ 9 66.20 S 124.38 E
Vöyri → Vörå 26 63.09 N 22.15 E
Voža ≃ 72 54.38 N 39.10 E
Vožajol' 24 62.50 N 51.17 E
Vožd' Proletariata 66 55.26 N 39.19 E
Vozdviženka, S.S.S.R. 68 47.46 N 36.05 E
Vozdviženka, S.S.S.R. 70 53.10 N 54.14 E
Vozdviženskoje, S.S.S.R. 70 56.58 N 45.37 E
Vozdviženskoje, S.S.S.R. 70 45.50 N 43.40 E
Vozdviženskoje, S.S.S.R. 72 56.12 N 38.04 E
Vože, Ozero ⊜ 24 60.30 N 39.00 E
Vožega 66 60.29 N 40.12 E
Vožega ≃ 66 60.33 N 39.11 E
Vožgaly 70 58.09 N 50.11 E
Vožgora 24 64.32 N 48.25 E
Voznesenje 24 61.01 N 35.27 E
Voznesenka, S.S.S.R. 68 46.51 N 35.26 E
Voznesenka, S.S.S.R. 76 52.24 N 70.12 E
Voznesenovka 70 46.16 N 44.21 E
Voznesensk 68 47.34 N 31.20 E
Voznesenskoje, S.S.S.R. 70 54.54 N 42.46 E
Voznesenskoje, S.S.S.R. 70 45.49 N 43.25 E
Vozroždenija, Ostrov I 76 45.03 N 59.12 E
Vozroždenije 70 52.42 N 48.12 E
Vozžajevka 79 50.44 N 128.41 E
Vrå 26 57.21 N 9.57 E
Vráble 30 48.15 N 18.19 E
Vraca 38 43.12 N 23.33 E
Vračevo 72 54.53 N 39.10 E
Vrådal 26 59.20 N 8.25 E
Vrancea □4 38 45.45 N 27.00 E
Vrancei, Munții ⛰ 38 46.00 N 26.30 E
Vrangel'a, Mys ≻ 79 54.17 N 138.39 E
Vrangel'a, Ostrov I 64 71.00 N 179.30 W
Vranje 38 42.33 N 21.54 E
Vranov [nad Topl'ou] 30 48.54 N 21.41 E
Vrbas 38 45.35 N 19.39 E
Vrbas ≃ 36 45.06 N 17.31 E
Vrbovec 36 45.53 N 16.25 E
Vrbovsko 36 45.23 N 15.05 E
Vrchlabí 30 50.38 N 15.37 E
Vrede 148 27.30 S 29.06 E
Vredefort 148 27.05 S 27.16 E
Vreden 48 52.02 N 6.52 E
Vredenburg 148 32.54 S 17.59 E
Vredendal 148 31.41 S 18.35 E
Vreed en Hoop 236 6.48 N 58.11 W
Vreeswijk 48 52.01 N 5.05 E
Vrena 40 58.52 N 16.41 E
Vresse 52 49.52 N 4.56 E
Vreta Kloster ⊍1 26 58.28 N 15.29 E
Vretstorp 40 59.02 N 14.52 E
Vrginmost 36 45.21 N 15.52 E

DEUTSCH

Name	Seite	Breite °′	Länge °′ E=Ost

Vrhnika 36 45.58 N 14.18 E
Vriddhāchalam 112 11.30 N 79.20 E
Vriendschaaps ≃ 154 5.28 S 138.53 E
Vries 48 53.04 N 6.35 E
Vriezenveen 48 52.25 N 6.38 E
Vrigne-Meuse 52 49.42 N 4.51 E
Vrigstad 26 57.21 N 14.28 E
Vrilissia 257c 38.02 N 23.50 E
Vrille ≃ 46 47.31 N 2.52 E
Vrin 54 46.39 N 9.06 E
Vrin ≃ 46 48.00 N 3.20 E
Vrindāvan 114 27.35 N 77.42 E
Vrlika 36 43.55 N 16.24 E
Vrnograč 36 45.10 N 15.57 E
Vroeggedeel 148 28.02 S 22.32 E
Vroeunspan 148 27.50 S 20.24 E
Vron 46 50.19 N 1.45 E
Vrondádhes 38 38.24 N 26.08 E
Vroomshoop 48 52.27 N 6.34 E
Vroutek 50 50.08 N 13.24 E
Vršac 38 45.07 N 21.18 E
Vrsar 58 45.08 N 13.37 E
Vršič)(58 46.26 N 13.44 E
Vrubovka 73 48.44 N 38.20 E
Vrubovskij 73 48.26 N 39.07 E
Vrútky 30 49.07 N 18.55 E
Vryburg 148 26.55 S 24.45 E
Vryheid 148 27.52 S 30.38 E
Vschody 66 54.42 N 34.06 E
Vselug, Ozero ⊜ 66 57.03 N 32.42 E
Vsetín 30 49.21 N 17.59 E
Vsevidof, Mount ∧ 170 53.07 N 168.43 W
Vsevoložsk 66 60.01 N 30.40 E
Vtoryje Levyje Lamki 70 53.17 N 41.04 E
Vuadil' 75 40.11 N 71.43 E
Vučitrn 38 42.49 N 20.58 E
Vue-des-Alpes)(54 47.04 N 6.53 E
Vught 48 51.40 N 5.17 E
Vuillafans 54 47.04 N 6.13 E
Vuimasia ∧ 165g 17.59 S 178.07 E
Vuitebœuf 54 46.37 N 6.34 E
Vukovar 38 45.21 N 19.00 E
Vulcan, Alta., Can. 172 50.24 N 113.15 W
Vulcan, Rom. 38 45.23 N 23.17 E
Vulcan, Mich., U.S. 180 45.47 N 87.53 W
Vulcano, Isola I 36 38.27 N 14.58 E
Vulci ⊥ 60 42.25 N 11.35 E
Vu-liet 100 18.43 N 105.23 E
Vulkanešty 68 45.41 N 28.24 E
Vul'vyvejem ≃ 170 66.58 N 179.10 E
Vundúzi ≃ 144 18.56 S 34.01 E
Vung-tau (Cap-Saint-Jacques) 100 10.21 N 107.04 E
Vunindawa 165g 17.49 S 178.19 E
Vunisea 165g 19.03 S 178.09 E
Vunmarama 165f 15.29 S 168.10 E
Vuoggatjålme 24 66.36 N 16.22 E
Vuohijärvi 26 61.05 N 26.48 E
Vuohijärvi ⊜ 26 61.12 N 26.42 E
Vuokatti ∧2 26 64.07 N 28.14 E
Vuoksa, Ozero ⊜ 66 60.40 N 29.50 E
Vuoksenniska 26 61.13 N 28.49 E
Vuoksi ≃ 26 61.03 N 30.11 E
Vuotso 24 68.08 N 27.08 E
Vurnary 70 55.29 N 46.58 E
Vuya 144 5.21 N 29.40 E
Vuyyūru 112 16.22 N 80.51 E
Vvedenka 76 54.03 N 63.45 E
Vvedenovka 79 51.19 N 128.12 E
Vvedenskoje 72 55.42 N 36.54 E
Vyāra 110 21.07 N 73.24 E
Vyatka → Kirov 70 58.38 N 49.42 E
Vyaz'ma → V'az'ma 66 55.13 N 34.18 E
Vyazniki → V'azniki 70 56.15 N 42.10 E
Vyborg 66 60.42 N 28.45 E
Vyborgskij Zaliv C 66 60.35 N 28.24 E
Vyčegda ≃ 24 61.18 N 46.36 E
Vyčegodskij 24 61.16 N 46.48 E
Vychino ⇝8 255b 55.43 N 37.48 E
Východočeský Kraj □4 30 50.10 N 16.00 E
Východoslovenský Kraj □4 30 49.00 N 21.15 E
Vydrino, S.S.S.R. 78 56.50 N 99.02 E
Vydrino, S.S.S.R. 78 51.27 N 104.39 E
Vygoda 68 48.56 N 23.55 E
Vygoniči 66 53.08 N 34.05 E
Vygonišči 66 52.37 N 25.55 E
Vygor' 66 54.49 N 33.59 E
Vygozero, Ozero ⊜ 24 63.35 N 34.42 E
Vyjezdnoje 70 55.23 N 43.47 E
Vyjezžij Log 76 54.58 N 93.57 E
Vyksa 70 55.18 N 42.11 E
Vylkovo 76 53.05 N 81.26 E
Vym' ≃ 24 62.13 N 50.25 E
Vyntja 76 60.31 N 67.18 E
Vypolzovo 66 57.53 N 33.42 E
Vyrica 66 59.25 N 30.21 E
Vyrnwy, Lake ⊜ 44 52.47 N 3.30 W
Vyša 70 53.52 N 42.24 E
Vyša ≃ 70 54.02 N 42.06 E
Vyšehrad ⇝8 50 50.01 N 14.27 E
Vyšelej 70 53.26 N 45.29 E
Vyselki 68 45.35 N 39.38 E
Vyšesteblijevskaja 68 45.12 N 37.00 E
Vyšgorodok 66 57.02 N 28.01 E
Vyška, S.S.S.R. 66 57.31 N 35.57 E
Vyška, S.S.S.R. 118 39.20 N 54.08 E
Vyskod' 66 57.46 N 30.04 E
Vyškov 66 52.29 N 31.41 E
Vyškovskij, Pereval)(68 48.42 N 23.38 E
Vyšná Radvaň 30 49.07 N 21.56 E
Vyšneol'šanoje 66 52.08 N 37.39 E
Vyšnevolockoje Vodochranilišče ⊜1 66 57.35 N 34.28 E
Vyšnij Voločok 66 57.35 N 34.34 E
Vysočany ⇝8 50 50.05 N 14.31 E
Vysock, S.S.S.R. 66 60.36 N 28.34 E
Vysock, S.S.S.R. 68 51.43 N 26.39 E
Vysokaja, Gora ∧ 79 45.59 N 136.35 E
Vysokaja Gora 70 55.56 N 49.19 E
Vysoké Mýto 30 49.57 N 16.10 E
Vysoké Tatry ⛰ 30 49.12 N 20.05 E
Vysokiniči 72 54.54 N 36.55 E
Vysokogornyj 79 50.09 N 139.09 E
Vysokogorsk 79 44.23 N 135.23 E
Vysokoje, S.S.S.R. 66 56.43 N 34.55 E
Vysokoje, S.S.S.R. 66 52.22 N 23.22 E
Vysokoje, S.S.S.R. 66 54.02 N 33.44 E
Vysokoje, S.S.S.R. 72 54.30 N 37.03 E
Vysokoje, S.S.S.R. 75 42.30 N 70.32 E
Vysokoje, S.S.S.R. 255b 55.59 N 37.09 E
Vysokopolje 68 47.29 N 33.32 E
Vysokovsk 72 56.19 N 36.33 E
Vysšaja Dubečn'a 68 50.44 N 30.40 E
Vyšší Brod 30 48.37 N 14.19 E
Vystavka Dostiženij Narodnogo Choz'ajstva S.S.S.R. ⊍ 255b 55.50 N 37.37 E
Vystupoviči 68 51.34 N 29.04 E
Vytebet' ≃ 66 53.53 N 35.38 E
Vytegra 24 61.00 N 36.24 E
Vyževka ≃ 68 51.41 N 24.35 E
Vzmorje 79 47.51 N 142.31 E
Vzvad 66 58.10 N 31.29 E

W

W, Parcs Nationaux du ♠ 140 12.50 N 2.30 W
Wa 140 10.04 N 2.29 W
Waabs 41 54.32 N 9.58 E
Waackaack Creek ≃ 266 40.27 N 74.08 W
Waadt → Vaud □3 54 46.40 N 6.30 E
Waakirchen 58 47.46 N 11.40 E

Symbols in the index entries represent the broad categories identified in the key at the right. Symbols with superior numbers (⛰2) identify subcategories (see complete key on page I · 26).

Kartensymbole in dem Registerverzeichnis stellen die rechts in Schlüssel erklärten Kategorien dar. Symbole mit hochgestellten Ziffern (⛰2) bezeichnen Unterabteilungen einer Kategorie (vgl. vollständiger Schlüssel auf Seite I · 26).

Los símbolos incluídos en el texto del índice representan las grandes categorias identificadas con la clave a la derecha. Los símbolos con numeros en su parte superior (⛰2) identifican las subcategorías (véase la clave completa en la página I · 26).

Les symboles de l'index représentent les catégories indiquées dans la légende à droite. Les symboles suivis d'un indice (⛰2) représentent des sous-catégories (voir légende complète à la page I · 26).

Os símbolos incluídos no texto do índice representam as grandes categorias identificadas com a chave à direita. Os símbolos com números em sua parte superior (⛰2) identificam as subcategorias (veja-se a chave completa à página I · 26).

	English	Deutsch	Español	Français	Português
∧	Mountain	Berg	Montaña	Montagne	Montanha
⛰	Mountains	Berge	Montañas	Montagnes	Montanhas
)(	Pass	Pass	Paso	Col	Passo
∨	Valley, Canyon	Tal, Cañon	Valle, Cañón	Vallée, Canyon	Vale, Canhão
⩸	Plain	Ebene	Llano	Plaine	Planície
≻	Cape	Kap	Cabo	Cap	Cabo
I	Island	Insel	Isla	Île	Ilha
II	Islands	Inseln	Islas	Îles	Ilhas
⊥	Other Topographic Features	Andere Topographische Objekte	Otros Elementos Topográficos	Autres données topographiques	Outros Elementos Topográficos

ESPAÑOL | FRANÇAIS | PORTUGUÊS

Nombre / Nom / Nome	Página / Page	Lat.°′	Long.°′ W=Oeste / W=Ouest
Waal	54	48.00 N	10.46 E
Waal ≃	48	51.55 N	4.30 E
Waalre	48	51.24 N	5.26 E
Waalwijk	48	51.42 N	5.04 E
Waao	92	24.20 N	104.40 E
Waar, Pulau I	154	2.05 S	134.23 E
Waarschoot	46	51.09 N	3.36 E
Waasmunster	46	51.06 N	4.05 E
Wabag	154	5.30 S	143.40 E
Wabamun	172	53.33 N	114.28 W
Wabamun Indian Reserve ◆[4]	172	53.30 N	114.30 W
Wabamun Lake ⊜	172	53.33 N	114.35 W
Waban	273	42.20 N	71.14 W
Waban, Lake ⊜	273	42.17 N	71.17 W
Wabana	176	47.38 N	52.57 W
Wabasca	172	56.00 N	113.53 W
Wabasca ≃	166	58.22 N	115.20 W
Wabasca Indian Reserve ◆[4]	172	55.53 N	113.32 W
Wabash, Ind., U.S.	206	40.48 N	85.49 W
Wabash, Ohio, U.S.	206	40.33 N	84.45 W
Wabash □[6]	206	40.48 N	85.49 W
Wabash ≃	184	37.46 N	88.02 W
Wabasha	180	44.23 N	92.02 W
Wabasso	210	27.45 N	80.26 W
Wabatongushi Lake ⊜	180	48.26 N	84.15 W
Wabeno	180	45.26 N	88.39 W
Wabern	52	51.06 N	9.20 E
Wabigoon Lake ⊜	174	49.44 N	92.44 W
Waboe	164b	0.31 S	166.55 E
Wabowden	174	54.55 N	98.38 W
Wabrah ⍑[4]	118	27.26 N	47.22 E
Wąbrzeźno	30	53.17 N	18.57 E
Wabuhu	90	32.17 N	116.55 E
Wabuska	216	39.09 N	119.11 W
W.A.C. Bennett Dam ◆[6]	172	56.01 N	122.10 W
Waccamaw ≃	182	33.21 N	79.16 W
Waccamaw, Lake ⊜	182	34.17 N	78.30 W
Waccasassa Bay C	182	29.06 N	82.52 W
Wachapreague	198	37.36 N	75.41 W
Wachapreague Inlet C	198	37.35 N	75.36 W
Wachau ◆[1]	30	48.18 N	15.24 E
Wachenheim	52	49.26 N	8.10 E
Wachi	86	35.15 N	135.24 E
Wąchock, Klasztory ʊ[1]	30	51.05 N	21.01 E
Wachtendonk	52	51.24 N	6.20 E
Wächtersbach	52	50.15 N	9.17 E
Wachusett Mountain ∧	197	42.29 N	71.53 W
Wachusett Reservoir ⊜[1]	197	42.23 N	71.43 W
Wachusett Shoal ⊹[2]	14	32.10 S	151.05 W
Wacissa	182	30.21 N	83.59 W
Waco	212	31.55 N	97.08 W
Waco Lake ⊜[1]	212	31.34 N	97.13 W
Waconda Lake ⊜[1]	188	39.30 N	98.35 W
Waconia	180	44.51 N	93.47 W
Wacouno ≃	176	50.54 N	65.57 W
Wacousta	206	42.49 N	84.42 W
Wad	110	27.21 N	66.22 E
Wada, Nihon	84	35.02 N	140.01 E
Wada, Nihon	84	36.12 N	138.13 E
Wada, Nihon	258	35.12 N	139.38 E
Wada, Nihon	260	34.33 N	135.55 E
Wadagou	94	42.27 N	120.58 E
Wad al-Ḥaddād	130	13.49 N	33.32 E
Wadamago	134	8.54 N	46.18 E
Wada-misaki ≻	86	34.39 N	135.11 E
Wādat Ga	110	26.00 N	97.00 E
Wadayama	86	35.19 N	134.52 E
Wad Bandah	130	13.06 N	27.57 E
Wad Ban Naqa	130	16.30 N	33.08 E
Waddān	136	29.10 N	16.08 E
Waddān, Jabal ∧	136	29.20 N	16.20 E
Waddeneilanden II	48	53.26 N	5.30 E
Waddenzee ⍑[2]	48	53.15 N	5.15 E
Wadderin Hill	152	32.00 S	118.27 E
Waddesdon	44	51.51 N	0.56 W
Waddingham	42	53.27 N	0.31 W
Waddington	202	44.52 N	75.12 W
Waddington, Mount ∧	172	51.23 N	125.15 W
Waddinxveen	48	52.03 N	4.40 E
Waddy	208	38.08 N	85.04 W
Wade, Mount ∧	9	84.51 S	174.15 W
Wadebridge	44	50.32 N	4.50 W
Wadena, Sask., Can.	174	51.57 N	103.47 W
Wadena, Ind., U.S.	206	40.43 N	87.16 W
Wadena, Minn., U.S.	188	46.26 N	95.08 W
Wädenswil	54	47.14 N	8.40 E
Wadern	52	49.32 N	6.53 E
Wadersloh	48	51.44 N	8.15 E
Wadesboro	182	34.58 N	80.04 W
Wadeville	263d	26.16 S	28.11 E
Wad Ḥāmid	130	16.30 N	32.48 E
Wadham Islands II	176	49.34 N	53.50 W
Wadhams	172	51.30 N	127.31 W
Wadhurst	44	51.04 N	0.21 E
Wadi	110	28.02 N	96.59 E
Wadian	90	32.48 N	112.30 E
Wādī as-Sīr	122	31.57 N	35.49 E
Wādī Ḥalfā'	130	21.56 N	31.20 E
Wādī Jimāl, Jazīrat I	130	24.40 N	35.10 E
Wādī Mūsā	122	30.19 N	35.29 E
Wading ≃, Mass., U.S.	273	41.56 N	71.13 W
Wading ≃, N.J., U.S.	198	39.33 N	74.28 W
Wading, West Branch ≃	198	39.40 N	74.32 W
Wading River	197	40.57 N	72.51 W
Wādī Rashrāsh, Bi'r ⍑[4]	132	29.26 N	31.31 E
Wadley, Ala., U.S.	184	33.07 N	85.34 W
Wadley, Ga., U.S.	182	32.52 N	82.24 W
Wad Madanī	130	14.25 N	33.28 E
Wadowice	30	49.53 N	19.30 E
Wadsworth, Ill., U.S.	206	42.26 N	87.56 W
Wadsworth, Nev., U.S.	194	39.38 N	119.17 W
Wadsworth, N.Y., U.S.	200	42.49 N	77.54 W
Wadsworth, Ohio, U.S.	204	41.02 N	81.44 W
Wadsworth Moor ◆[3]	252	53.48 N	2.02 W
Wadu I	112	5.51 N	72.58 E
Waegwan	88	35.58 N	128.24 E
Waelder	212	29.42 N	97.18 W
Waenhuiskrans	148	34.41 S	20.14 E
Wafang	88	41.44 N	118.54 E
Wafania	142	1.21 S	20.20 E
Wafrah	118	28.33 N	48.02 E
Wagadugu → Ouagadougou	140	12.22 N	1.31 W
Wāgah	113	31.36 N	74.33 E
Wagait Aboriginal Reserve ◆[4]	154	13.00 S	130.20 E
Wagang	92	28.04 N	103.10 E
Wagenborgen	48	53.15 N	6.56 E
Wagenfeld-Hasslingen	48	52.33 N	8.34 E
Wageningen, Ned.	48	51.58 N	5.40 E
Wageningen, Sur.	240	5.46 N	56.41 W
Wager Bay C	166	65.26 N	88.40 W
Wagerup	158a	32.55 S	115.54 E
Wagga Wagga	161b	35.07 S	147.22 E
Waggoner	209	39.23 N	89.39 W
Wagin	152	33.18 S	117.21 E
Wagina I	165e	7.26 S	157.46 E
Waging am See	58	47.56 N	12.43 E
Waginger See ⊜	58	47.56 N	12.47 E
Wägitaler See ⊜	54	47.06 N	8.55 E
Wagner	188	43.05 N	98.18 W
Wagner College ʊ[2]	266	40.37 N	74.07 W
Wagoner	186	35.58 N	95.22 W
Wagon Mound	186	36.01 N	104.42 W
Wagontire Mountain ∧	192	43.21 N	119.53 W
Wagontown	198	40.01 N	75.51 W
Wagrain	58	47.20 N	13.18 E
Wagrien ◆[1]	50	54.15 N	10.45 E
Wągrowiec	30	52.49 N	17.11 E
Wah	113	33.48 N	72.42 E
Waha	136	28.16 N	19.54 E
Wahai	154	2.48 S	129.30 E
Waharoa	162	37.46 S	175.46 E
Wahiawa	219c	21.30 N	158.01 W
Wahkiakum □[6]	214	46.16 N	123.28 W
Wahlen	52	49.37 N	8.51 E
Wahlstedt	50	53.57 N	10.12 E
Wahn	52	50.52 N	7.05 E
Wahnbachstausee ⊜[1]	52	50.48 N	7.19 E
Wahneta	210	27.57 N	81.44 W
Wahoo	188	41.13 N	96.37 W
Wahpeton	188	46.16 N	96.36 W
Wahrenbrück	50	51.33 N	13.22 E
Wahrenholz	50	52.36 N	10.36 E
Währing ◆[8]	254b	48.14 N	16.21 E
Wahroonga	264a	33.43 S	151.07 E
Wahweap Creek ≃	190	36.57 N	111.29 W
Wai, Bhārat	112	17.56 N	73.54 E
Wai, Indon.	154	1.42 S	127.59 E
Waialailing ⋀	75	39.35 N	74.10 E
Waialeale ∧	219b	22.04 N	159.30 W
Waialua	219c	21.34 N	158.08 W
Waialua Bay C	219c	21.36 N	158.07 W
Waianae	219c	21.27 N	158.11 W
Waianae Mountains ⋀	219c	21.30 N	158.10 W
Waianapanapa Caves State Park ♠	219a	20.47 N	156.01 W
Waiapu ≃	162	37.47 S	178.29 E
Waiatoto ≃	162	43.59 S	168.47 E
Waiau	162	42.39 S	173.03 E
Waiau ≃, N.Z.	162	42.47 S	173.22 E
Waiau ≃, N.Z.	162	38.58 S	177.24 E
Waiau ≃, N.Z.	162	46.12 S	167.38 E
Waibakul	105b	9.36 S	119.35 E
Waibeem	154	0.28 S	132.58 E
Waiblingen	52	48.50 N	9.19 E
Waibstadt	52	49.18 N	8.54 E
Waichagoumen	88	40.54 N	125.45 E
Waidbruck → Ponte Gardena	58	46.36 N	11.32 E
Waidhān	114	24.04 N	82.20 E
Waidhofen an der Thaya	30	48.49 N	15.18 E
Waidhofen an der Ybbs	30	47.58 N	14.47 E
Waidmannslust ◆[8]	254a	52.36 N	13.20 E
Waidring	58	47.35 N	12.34 E
Waiehu	219a	20.55 N	156.30 W
Waigang	96	31.22 N	121.11 E
Waigatsch → Vajgač, Ostrov I	62	70.00 N	59.30 E
Waigeo, Pulau I	154	0.14 S	130.45 E
Waigoumen	88	41.56 N	116.25 E
Waihao Downs	162	44.48 S	170.55 E
Waihee	219a	20.56 N	156.31 W
Waihee Point ≻	219a	20.57 N	156.31 W
Waiheke Island I	162	36.48 S	175.06 E
Waihi	162	37.24 S	175.51 E
Waihola	162	46.02 S	170.06 E
Waihopai ≃	162	41.31 S	173.44 E
Waihou ≃	162	37.10 S	175.32 E
Waihuantan	96	30.25 N	118.40 E
Waika	144	2.21 S	25.43 E
Waikabubak	105b	9.38 S	119.25 E
Waikaia	162	45.44 S	168.51 E
Waikaia ≃	162	45.53 S	168.48 E
Waikanae	162	40.53 S	175.04 E
Waikane	219c	21.30 N	157.51 W
Waikapu	219a	20.51 N	156.30 W
Waikare, Lake ⊜	162	37.26 S	175.13 E
Waikaremoana, Lake ⊜	162	38.46 S	177.07 E
Waikari	162	42.58 S	172.41 E
Waikato ≃	162	37.23 S	174.43 E
Waikelo	105b	9.24 S	119.14 E
Waikerie	156	34.11 S	139.59 E
Waikiki Beach ♠	219c	21.17 N	157.50 W
Waikino	162	37.25 S	175.46 E
Waikouaiti	162	45.36 S	170.41 E
Waikuatang	96	31.20 N	120.41 E
Wailingding I	90	22.07 N	114.05 E
Wailing Wall, The (Kotel Hama'aravi) ⊥	122	31.46 N	35.14 E
Wailua	219b	22.03 N	159.19 W
Wailua River State Park ♠	219b	22.02 N	159.21 W
Wailuku	219a	20.53 N	156.30 W
Waimahaka	162	46.31 S	168.49 E
Waimakariri ≃	162	43.24 S	172.42 E
Waimamaku	162	35.33 S	173.29 E
Waimana	162	38.09 S	177.05 E
Waimana ≃	162	38.04 S	177.00 E
Waimanalo	219c	21.21 N	157.42 W
Waimangaroa	162	41.43 S	171.46 E
Waimangura	105b	9.30 S	119.14 E
Waimarama	162	39.48 S	176.59 E
Waimate	162	44.44 S	171.02 E
Waimea, Haw., U.S.	219c	21.39 N	158.04 W
Waimea, Haw., U.S.	219d	21.58 N	159.42 W
Waimea Canyon V	219b	22.04 N	159.39 W
Waimea Canyon State Park ♠	219b	22.04 N	159.40 W
Waimes	52	50.25 N	6.07 E
Wainfleet All Saints	44	53.07 N	0.14 E
Wainganga ≃	112	18.50 N	79.55 E
Waingapu	105b	9.39 S	120.16 E
Waini ≃	236	8.24 N	59.51 W
Wainscott	250	51.25 N	0.31 E
Wainstalls	252	53.45 N	1.56 W
Wainuiomata	162	41.16 S	174.57 E
Wainunu Bay C	165g	16.55 S	178.53 E
Wainwright, Alta., Can.	172	52.49 N	110.52 W
Wainwright, Alaska, U.S.	170	70.38 N	160.01 W
Wainwright, Ohio, U.S.	204	40.25 N	81.26 W
Waiohau	162	38.14 S	176.51 E
Waiotira	162	35.56 S	174.12 E
Waiouru	162	39.29 S	175.40 E
Waipahi	162	46.07 S	169.15 E
Waipahu	219c	21.23 N	158.01 W
Waipaoa	162	38.32 S	177.54 E
Waipara	162	43.04 S	172.45 E
Waipara ≃	162	43.09 S	172.48 E
Waipawa	162	39.56 S	176.36 E
Waipiata	162	45.11 S	170.10 E
Waipio Acres	219c	21.28 N	158.01 W
Waipio Bay C	219a	20.55 N	156.13 W
Waipiqundao II	90	23.57 N	117.55 E
Waipiro	162	38.01 S	178.20 E
Waipu	162	35.59 S	174.27 E
Waipukurau	162	40.00 S	176.34 E
Wairakei	162	38.38 S	176.06 E
Wairarapa, Lake ⊜	162	41.13 S	175.15 E
Wairau ≃	162	41.30 S	174.04 E
Wairau Valley	162	41.34 S	173.32 E
Wairio	162	46.00 S	168.02 E
Wairoa	162	39.02 S	177.25 E
Wairoa ≃	162	39.04 S	177.26 E
Waisanzao	96	30.57 N	121.52 E
Waitahanui	162	38.47 S	176.05 E
Waitahuna	162	45.59 S	169.46 E
Waitakaruru	162	37.15 S	175.23 E
Waitara, Austl.	264a	33.43 S	151.07 E
Waitara, N.Z.	162	39.00 S	174.13 E
Waitara ≃	162	38.59 S	174.14 E
Waitarere	162	40.33 S	175.12 E
Waita Reservoir ⊜[1]	219b	21.55 N	159.27 W
Waitati	162	45.45 S	170.34 E
Waita-zan ∧	86	33.08 N	131.10 E
Waite Hill	204	41.37 N	81.22 W
Waite Park	180	45.33 N	94.14 W
Waitoa	162	37.37 S	175.38 E
Waitotara	162	39.48 S	174.44 E
Waitotara ≃	162	39.51 S	174.41 E
Waitpinga	158b	35.37 S	138.29 E
Waitsburg	192	46.16 N	118.09 W
Waitzen → Vác	30	47.47 N	19.08 E
Waiuku	162	37.15 S	174.45 E
Waiuta	162	42.18 S	171.49 E
Waiwera South	162	46.13 S	169.30 E
Waiwo	154	0.56 S	131.03 E
Waiya	154	3.13 S	128.55 E
Wajid	134	3.50 N	43.14 E
Wajima	82	37.24 N	136.54 E
Wajir	144	1.45 N	40.04 E
Waka, Tex., U.S.	186	36.17 N	101.03 W
Waka, Yai.	134	7.07 N	37.26 E
Waka, Zaïre	142	1.01 N	20.13 E
Waka, Zaïre	142	0.48 S	20.10 E
Wakajabi	154	5.38 S	134.24 E
Wakakusa	84	35.36 N	138.29 E
Wakakusa-yama ∧[2]	260	34.42 N	135.52 E
Wakalla Wen	134	2.00 N	42.30 E
Wakalla Yero	134	1.47 N	42.42 E
Wakamatsu → Aizu-wakamatsu	82	37.30 N	139.56 E
Wakami ≃	180	47.43 N	82.22 W
Wakami Lake ⊜	180	47.29 N	82.51 W
Wakamiya	86	33.44 N	130.37 E
Wakano-ura ♠	86	34.11 N	135.11 E
Wakarusa	206	41.32 N	86.01 W
Wakarusa ≃	188	38.57 N	95.05 W
Wakasa	86	35.20 N	134.24 E
Wakasa-wan C	86	35.45 N	135.40 E
Wakasa-wan-kokutei-kōen ♠	86	35.35 N	135.30 E
Wakatipu, Lake ⊜	162	45.05 S	168.34 E
Wakatomika Creek ≃	204	40.07 N	82.00 W
Wakato-ohashi ◆[5]	86	33.54 N	130.49 E
Wakaw	174	52.39 N	105.44 W
Wakaya I	165g	17.37 S	179.00 E
Wakayama	86	34.13 N	135.11 E
Wakayama □[5]	86	34.00 N	135.20 E
Wakayanagi	82	38.46 N	141.08 E
Wake	86	34.48 N	134.08 E
Wake Airport ⊠	164a	19.17 N	166.37 E
Wa Keeney	188	39.01 N	99.53 W
Wakefield, N.Z.	162	41.24 S	173.03 E
Wakefield, Eng., U.K.	42	53.42 N	1.29 W
Wakefield, Kans., U.S.	188	39.13 N	97.01 W
Wakefield, Mass., U.S.	197	42.30 N	71.04 W
Wakefield, Nebr., U.S.	188	42.16 N	96.52 W
Wakefield, Ohio, U.S.	208	38.59 N	83.01 W
Wakefield, R.I., U.S.	197	41.26 N	71.30 W
Wakefield, Va., U.S.	182	36.58 N	76.59 W
Wakefield ≃	158b	34.10 S	138.10 E
Wake Forest	182	35.59 N	78.30 W
Wake Island □[2]	14		
	164a	19.17 N	166.36 E
Wakema	100	16.36 N	95.11 E
Wakeman	204	41.15 N	82.24 W
Wakeman ≃	172	51.00 N	126.30 W
Wakenda Creek ≃	184	39.19 N	93.16 W
Wake Village	184	33.26 N	94.07 W
Wakhān → Vākhān ◆[1]	110	37.00 N	73.00 E
Waki	86	34.04 N	134.09 E
Wakis	154	6.13 S	150.17 E
Wakita	186	36.53 N	97.55 W
Wakkanai	82a	45.25 N	141.40 E
Wakkerstroom	148	27.24 S	30.10 E
Wakomata Lake ⊜	180	46.34 N	83.22 W
Wakonassin ≃	180	46.28 N	81.51 W
Wakonda	188	43.00 N	97.06 W
Wakre	154	0.19 S	131.09 E
Waku	154	6.05 S	149.05 E
Wakunai	165e	5.52 S	155.13 E
Wālājāpet	112	12.56 N	79.23 E
Walamba	144	13.29 S	28.45 E
Walamo	224	23.07 N	106.15 W
Walanae ≃	102	4.08 S	119.58 E
Walang	92	28.33 N	100.54 E
Wal Athiang	130	7.42 N	29.40 E
Walawe ≃	112	6.06 N	81.01 E
Walbeck	48	51.30 N	6.15 E
Walberswick	44	52.19 N	1.39 E
Walbran Creek ≃	214	48.34 N	124.40 W
Walbridge	204	41.35 N	83.29 W
Wałbrzych (Waldenburg)	30	50.46 N	16.17 E
Walburg	212	30.44 N	97.35 W
Walbury Hill ∧[2]	44	51.21 N	1.30 W
Walcha	156	30.59 S	151.36 E
Walchensee	58	47.35 N	11.19 E
Walchensee ⊜	58	47.36 N	11.20 E
Walcheren I	48	51.33 N	3.35 E
Walcheren, Kanaal door ≅	46	51.26 N	3.35 E
Walchsee	58	47.39 N	12.19 E
Walcott, B.C., Can.	172	54.31 N	126.51 W
Walcott, Iowa, U.S.	180	41.35 N	90.47 W
Walcott, N. Dak., U.S.	188	46.33 N	90.56 W
Walcott, Lake ⊜[1]	192	42.40 N	113.23 W
Walcourt	46	50.15 N	4.25 E
Wałcz	30	53.17 N	16.28 E
Wald	54	47.17 N	8.55 E
Wald ◆[8]	253	51.11 N	7.03 E
Waldai → Valdajskaja Vozvyšennost' ⋀[2]	24	57.00 N	33.30 E
Waldangelloch	52	49.12 N	8.47 E
Waldbauer ◆[8]	253	51.18 N	7.28 E
Waldbillig	52	49.47 N	6.18 E
Waldböckelheim	52	49.49 N	7.43 E
Waldbröl	52	50.53 N	7.37 E
Waldburg	54	47.45 N	9.43 E
Waldeck	52	51.12 N	9.04 E
Walden, Colo., U.S.	190	40.44 N	106.17 W
Walden, N.Y., U.S.	200	41.34 N	74.11 W
Waldenbuch	52	48.38 N	9.07 E
Waldenburg, B.R.D.	52	49.11 N	9.38 E
Waldenburg, D.D.R.	50	50.52 N	12.36 E
Waldenburg → Wałbrzych, Pol.	30	50.46 N	16.17 E
Waldenburg, Schw.	54	47.23 N	7.45 E
Walden Pond ⊜	273	42.28 N	71.00 W
Walden Ridge ∧	184	35.30 N	85.15 W
Walderslade	250	51.21 N	0.32 E
Waldfischbach	52	49.17 N	7.40 E
Waldheim, Sask., Can.	174	52.37 N	106.38 W
Waldheim, D.D.R.	50	51.04 N	13.01 E
Waldighoffen	54	47.33 N	7.19 E
Wald im Pinzgau	58	47.15 N	12.14 E
Waldkappel	52	51.08 N	9.52 E
Waldkirch	54	48.05 N	7.57 E
Waldkirchen	30	48.44 N	13.37 E
Waldkraiburg	58	48.12 N	12.28 E
Waldmünchen	30	49.23 N	12.43 E
Waldo, B.C., Can.	172	49.13 N	115.13 W
Waldo, Ark., U.S.	184	33.21 N	93.18 W
Waldo, Ohio, U.S.	204	40.28 N	83.05 W
Waldoboro	178	44.06 N	69.23 W
Waldo Lake ⊜	273	42.07 N	71.03 W
Waldon ≃	44	50.22 N	4.14 W
Waldorf	178	38.37 N	76.54 W
Waldport	192	44.26 N	124.04 W
Waldron, Sask., Can.	174	50.51 N	102.30 W
Waldron, Ark., U.S.	184	34.54 N	94.05 W
Waldron, Ind., U.S.	208	39.27 N	85.40 W
Waldron, Mich., U.S.	206	41.44 N	84.25 W
Waldron Island I	214	48.43 N	123.02 W
Waldshut	54	47.37 N	8.13 E
Waldstatt	54	47.21 N	9.17 E
Waldviertel ◆[1]	30	48.40 N	15.40 E
Waldwick	266	41.01 N	74.08 W
Walembele	140	10.30 N	1.58 W
Walensee ⊜	54	47.07 N	9.12 E
Walenstadt	54	47.07 N	9.19 E
Wales, Alaska, U.S.	170	65.36 N	168.05 W
Wales, Mass., U.S.	197	42.04 N	72.13 W
Wales, Wis., U.S.	206	43.00 N	88.23 W
Wales □[8]	28	52.30 N	3.30 W
Wales Center	200	42.46 N	78.32 W
Wales Island I, N.W. Ter., Can.	166	61.50 N	72.05 W
Wales Island I, N.W. Ter., Can.	166	68.00 N	86.43 W
Walewale	140	10.21 N	0.48 W
Walgett	156	30.01 S	148.07 E
Walgreen Coast ⍑[2]	9	75.15 S	105.00 W
Walhachin	172	50.45 N	120.59 W
Walhalla, N. Dak., U.S.	188	48.55 N	97.55 W
Walhalla, S.C., U.S.	182	34.46 N	83.04 W
Walhalla ⊥	30	49.03 N	12.14 E
Walheim	52	50.42 N	6.10 E
Walhonding	204	40.22 N	82.09 W
Walhonding ≃	204	40.18 N	81.53 W
Wali	95	39.42 N	118.20 E
Walia	154	3.47 S	138.32 E
Walikale	144	1.25 S	28.03 E
Walincourt	46	50.04 N	3.20 E
Walis Island I	154	3.15 S	143.20 E
Walkaway	152	28.57 S	114.48 E
Walkden	42	53.32 N	2.24 W
Walkenried	50	51.35 N	10.37 E
Walker, Iowa, U.S.	180	42.17 N	91.47 W
Walker, Mich., U.S.	206	42.58 N	85.46 W
Walker, Minn., U.S.	180	47.06 N	94.35 W
Walker, N.Y., U.S.	200	43.18 N	77.52 W
Walker □[6]	212	30.42 N	95.35 W
Walker ≃	194	38.54 N	118.47 W
Walker, Lac ⊜	176	50.16 N	67.09 W
Walker, Mount ∧[2]	161a	27.48 S	152.34 E
Walker Basin Creek ≃	218	35.20 N	118.47 W
Walker Bay C	148	34.30 S	19.20 E
Walker Creek ≃, Ariz., U.S.	190	36.58 N	109.42 W
Walker Creek ≃, Mass., U.S.	273	42.38 N	70.44 W
Walker Creek ≃, Wyo., U.S.	188	43.09 N	104.52 W
Walker Lake ⊜, Man., Can.	174	54.42 N	96.57 W
Walker Lake ⊜, Alaska, U.S.	170	67.10 N	154.26 W
Walker Lake ⊜, Nev., U.S.	194	38.44 N	118.43 W
Walker Point ≻	148	34.05 S	22.57 E
Walker River Indian Reservation ◆[4]	194	39.00 N	118.40 W
Walkers Mill	269b	40.24 N	80.08 W
Walkersville	178	39.29 N	77.21 W
Walkerton, Ont., Can.	202	44.07 N	81.09 W
Walkerton, Ind., U.S.	206	41.28 N	86.29 W
Walkerton, Va., U.S.	198	37.43 N	77.01 W
Walkertown	182	36.10 N	80.10 W
Walker Valley	200	41.38 N	74.23 W
Walkerville	192	46.01 N	112.30 W
Walk Mill	252	53.46 N	2.12 W
Wall, Pa., U.S.	269b	40.24 N	79.47 W
Wall, S. Dak., U.S.	188	43.59 N	102.14 W
Wallace, Calif., U.S.	216	38.12 N	120.59 W
Wallace, Idaho, U.S.	192	47.28 N	115.56 W
Wallace, Nebr., U.S.	188	40.50 N	101.10 W
Wallace, N.C., U.S.	182	34.44 N	77.59 W
Wallace, N.Y., U.S.	200	42.26 N	77.28 W
Wallaceburg	204	42.36 N	82.23 W
Wallace Lake ⊜	269a	41.22 N	81.52 W
Wallaceton	204	40.57 N	78.17 W
Wallacetown	204	42.38 N	81.28 W
Wallach	253	51.35 N	6.34 E
Wallachia □[9]	38	44.00 N	25.00 E
Wallacia	160	33.52 S	150.39 E
Wallal Downs	152	19.47 S	120.40 E
Wallangarra	156	28.56 S	151.56 E
Wallaroo	158b	33.56 S	137.38 E
Wallaroo Mines	158b	33.57 S	137.41 E
Wallasey	42	53.26 N	3.03 W
Wallau	52	50.56 N	8.28 E
Walla Walla	192	46.08 N	118.20 W
Walla Walla Plateau ⋀[1]	192	46.20 N	117.45 W
Walldorf, B.R.D.	52	49.18 N	8.38 E
Walldorf, D.D.R.	50	50.36 N	10.23 E
Walldürn	52	49.35 N	9.22 E
Walled Lake	206	42.32 N	83.29 W
Walled Lake ⊜	271	42.31 N	83.29 W
Wallen	206	41.10 N	85.11 W
Wallend	250	51.27 N	0.42 E
Wallenfels	50	50.16 N	11.28 E
Wallenpaupack, Lake ⊜	200	41.25 N	75.12 W
Waller	212	30.04 N	95.56 W
Waller □[6]	212	30.00 N	96.00 W
Wallerawang	160	33.25 S	150.04 E
Wallers	46	50.22 N	3.24 E
Wallersee ⊜	58	47.55 N	13.11 E
Wallerstein	52	48.53 N	10.28 E
Wallgau	58	47.31 N	11.16 E
Wallgrove	264a	33.47 S	150.51 E
Wallhead Airport ⊠	269a	41.21 N	82.09 W
Wallibou	231h	13.19 N	61.15 W
Wallilabou Bay C	231h	13.15 N	61.18 W
Wallingford, Eng., U.K.	44	51.37 N	1.08 W
Wallingford, Conn., U.S.	197	41.27 N	72.50 W
Wallingford, Pa., U.S.	275	39.54 N	75.22 W
Wallingford, Vt., U.S.	178	43.28 N	72.59 W
Wallington	266	40.51 N	74.07 W
Wallington ◆[8]	250	51.21 N	0.09 W
Wallis	212	29.38 N	96.04 W
Wallis → Valais □[3]	54	46.10 N	7.30 E
Wallis, Îles II	14	13.18 S	176.10 W
Wallis and Futuna □[2]	14	14.00 S	177.00 W
Wallisellen	54	47.25 N	8.36 E
Wallisville	212	29.50 N	94.44 W
Wallisville Lake ⊜[1]	212	29.50 N	94.45 W
Wallkill	200	41.36 N	74.11 W
Wallkill ≃, U.S.	200	41.51 N	74.03 W
Wallkill ≃, U.S.	266	41.11 N	74.35 W
Wallkill, Wildcat Branch ≃	266	41.07 N	74.36 W
Wall Lake, Iowa, U.S.	188	42.16 N	95.05 W
Wall Lake, Mich., U.S.	206	42.31 N	85.24 W
Wall Lake ⊜	206	42.31 N	85.23 W
Wallmer Bridge	252	53.43 N	2.48 W
Wallmerod	52	50.29 N	7.56 E
Wallops Island I	198	37.52 N	75.27 W
Wallowa	192	45.34 N	117.32 W
Wallowa ≃	192	45.43 N	117.47 W
Wallowa Mountains ⋀	192	45.10 N	117.30 W
Walls	184	34.58 N	90.16 W
Wallsbüll	41	54.47 N	9.14 E
Wallsend, Austl.	160	32.55 S	151.40 E
Wallsend, Eng., U.K.	42	55.00 N	1.31 W
Wallstawe	50	52.47 N	11.01 E
Wall Town Drainage Ditch ≅	206	40.26 N	88.10 W
Wallula, Lake ⊜[1]	192	46.07 N	119.58 W
Walmer	44	51.13 N	1.24 E
Walmersley	252	53.37 N	2.18 W
Walney, Isle of I	42	54.07 N	3.15 W
Walnut, Calif., U.S.	218	34.01 N	117.51 W
Walnut, Ill., U.S.	180	41.33 N	89.36 W
Walnut, Kans., U.S.	188	37.36 N	95.05 W
Walnut, Miss., U.S.	184	34.57 N	88.54 W
Walnut, N.C., U.S.	182	35.51 N	82.44 W
Walnut ≃	186	37.03 N	97.00 W
Walnut Canyon National Monument ♠	190	34.59 N	111.10 W
Walnut Canyon Reservoir ⊜[1]	270	33.50 N	117.45 W
Walnut Cove	182	36.18 N	80.09 W
Walnut Creek, Calif., U.S.	216	37.55 N	122.04 W
Walnut Creek, Ohio, U.S.	204	40.33 N	81.43 W
Walnut Creek ≃, Calif., U.S.	270	34.03 N	118.01 W
Walnut Creek ≃, Calif., U.S.	272	37.54 N	122.03 W
Walnut Creek ≃, Kans., U.S.	188	38.21 N	98.41 W
Walnut Creek ≃, Ohio, U.S.	178	39.41 N	82.59 W
Walnut Creek ≃, Tex., U.S.	212	32.38 N	97.00 W
Walnut Creek, Middle Fork ≃	188	38.32 N	100.08 W
Walnut Grove, B.C., Can.	214	49.11 N	122.39 W
Walnut Grove, Calif., U.S.	216	38.15 N	121.31 W
Walnut Grove, Minn., U.S.	188	44.13 N	95.28 W
Walnut Grove, Miss., U.S.	184	32.36 N	89.28 W
Walnut Heights	272	37.53 N	122.08 W
Walnut Hill	209	38.29 N	89.03 W
Walnut Lake	271	42.33 N	83.19 W
Walnut Lake ⊜	271	42.33 N	83.20 W
Walnut Park	270	33.58 N	118.13 W
Walnutport	198	40.45 N	75.36 W
Walnut Ridge	184	36.04 N	90.57 W
Walnut Springs	212	32.03 N	97.45 W
Walpert Ridge ∧	272	37.38 N	122.00 W
Walpeup	156	35.08 S	142.02 E
Walpole, Austl.	152	34.57 S	116.44 E
Walpole, Mass., U.S.	197	42.08 N	71.15 W
Walpole, N.H., U.S.	178	43.05 N	72.26 W
Walpole, Île I	165f	22.37 S	168.57 E
Walpole Island I	204	42.34 N	82.30 W
Walpole Island Indian Reserve ◆[4]	204	42.32 N	82.37 W
Walpole Saint Peter	44	52.42 N	0.15 E
Walsall	44	52.35 N	1.58 W
Walschleben	50	51.04 N	10.56 E
Walsden	252	53.42 N	2.06 W
Walsenburg	190	37.37 N	104.47 W
Walsh, Austl.	154	16.39 S	143.54 E
Walsh, Alta., Can.	174	49.57 N	110.03 W
Walsh, Colo., U.S.	188	37.23 N	102.17 W
Walsh, Ky., U.S.	208	38.41 N	82.58 W
Walsh ≃	154	16.31 S	143.42 E
Walshaw Dean Reservoirs ⊜[1]	252	53.48 N	2.03 W
Walshville	209	39.04 N	89.37 W
Walsingham	202	42.41 N	80.32 W
Walsoken	44	52.41 N	0.12 E
Walsoorden	48	51.23 N	4.02 E
Walsrode	48	52.52 N	9.35 E
Walston	204	40.58 N	79.01 W
Walsum	48	51.32 N	6.41 E
Walt Disney World ♠	210	28.26 N	81.35 W
Waltenhofen	58	47.40 N	10.17 E
Walterboro	182	32.55 N	80.39 W
Walter F. George Lake ⊜[1]	182	31.49 N	85.08 W
Walter Reed Army Medical Center ʊ	274c	38.58 N	77.02 W
Walters	186	34.22 N	98.19 W
Waltersdorf, D.D.R.	50	50.52 N	14.38 E
Waltersdorf, D.D.R.	254a	52.22 N	13.35 E
Waltershausen	50	50.53 N	10.33 E
Waltershofen	54	47.46 N	9.55 E
Waltersville	184	32.22 N	90.52 W
Walthall	184	33.31 N	89.16 W
Waltham	197	42.23 N	71.14 W
Waltham Abbey	44	51.42 N	0.01 E
Waltham Forest ◆[8]	44	51.35 N	0.01 W
Waltham on the Wolds	44	52.49 N	0.49 W
Walthamstow ◆[8]	250	51.35 N	0.01 W
Walthill	188	42.09 N	96.30 W
Walton, N.S., Can.	176	45.14 N	64.00 W
Walton, Eng., U.K.	44	51.58 N	1.21 E
Walton, Eng., U.K.	44	51.24 N	0.25 W
Walton, Fla., U.S.	210	27.18 N	80.14 W
Walton, Ind., U.S.	206	40.40 N	86.15 W
Walton, Ky., U.S.	208	38.52 N	84.37 W
Walton, N.Y., U.S.	200	42.10 N	75.08 W
Walton Hills	204	41.22 N	81.32 W
Walton-le-Dale	42	53.45 N	2.39 W
Walton on the Hill	250	51.17 N	0.15 W
Walton-on-the-Naze	44	51.51 N	1.16 E
Walton Run ≃	275	40.05 N	74.59 W
Waltonville	209	38.13 N	89.02 W
Waltrop	48	51.37 N	7.23 E
Walt Whitman Center ◆[9]	266	40.50 N	73.25 W
Walt Whitman Homes	275	39.52 N	75.11 W
Walt Whitman House ⊥	266	40.49 N	73.25 W
Waltz	206	42.06 N	83.23 W
Walupt Lake ⊜	214	46.25 N	121.28 W
Walurigi	165f	15.21 S	167.50 E
Walvisbaai (Walvis Bay)	146	22.59 S	14.31 E
Walvis Bay → Walvisbaai	146	22.59 S	14.31 E
Walvis Bay □[8]	146	22.59 S	14.31 E
Walvis Bay C	146	22.57 S	14.30 E
Walvis Ridge ⊹[3]	10	30.00 S	3.00 E
Walwa	161b	35.58 S	147.45 E
Walwen	252	53.14 N	3.15 W
Walworth, N.Y., U.S.	200	43.08 N	77.17 W
Walworth, Wis., U.S.	206	42.32 N	88.36 W
Walworth □[6]	206	42.41 N	88.32 W
Walyungup, Lake ⊜	158a	32.21 S	115.47 E
Walze	253	51.16 N	7.31 E
Walzin, Château de ⊥	52	50.13 N	4.55 E
Wamac	209	38.31 N	89.08 W
Wamba, Kenya	144	0.59 N	37.19 E
Wamba, Nig.	140	8.58 N	8.36 E
Wamba, Zaïre	144	2.09 N	28.00 E
Wamba (Uamba) ≃	142	3.56 S	17.12 E
Wambel ◆[8]	253	51.32 N	7.32 E
Wamego	188	39.12 N	96.18 W
Wamel	48	51.53 N	5.28 E
Wamesit	273	42.37 N	71.16 W
Wami ≃	144	6.08 S	38.49 E
Wamiao	90	30.49 N	112.56 E
Wamic	214	45.14 N	121.21 W
Wamma ≃	154	3.23 S	135.13 E
Wamme ≃	52	50.10 N	5.16 E
Wamplers Lake ⊜	206	42.05 N	84.09 W
Wampool ≃	42	54.54 N	3.14 W
Wampsville	200	43.05 N	75.42 W
Wampum	204	40.54 N	80.21 W
Wampus ≃	266	41.07 N	73.43 W
Wampus Lake Reservoir ⊜[1]	266	41.09 N	73.43 W
Wamsasi	102	3.33 S	126.10 E
Wamsutter	190	41.40 N	107.58 W
Wamuran	161a	27.02 S	152.52 E
Wanaaring	156	29.42 S	144.09 E
Wanaka	162	44.42 S	169.09 E
Wanaka, Lake ⊜	162	44.30 S	169.08 E
Wanakah	200	42.45 N	78.54 W
Wanamassa	198	40.14 N	74.02 W
Wanamie	200	41.10 N	76.02 W
Wanamingo	180	44.18 N	92.47 W
Wan'an, Zhg.	90	26.30 N	114.49 E
Wanan, Zhg.	90	26.56 N	117.22 E
Wan'anchang	97	30.39 N	104.25 E
Wanapiri	154	4.33 S	135.59 E
Wanapitei ≃	180	46.02 N	80.51 W
Wanapitei Lake ⊜	180	46.45 N	80.45 W
Wanapum Lake ⊜[1]	192	47.00 N	120.00 W
Wanaque	200	41.03 N	74.17 W
Wanaque ≃	266	40.58 N	74.17 W
Wanaque Reservoir ⊜[1]	200	41.05 N	74.17 W
Wanatah	206	41.26 N	86.54 W
Wanau	154	1.22 S	132.42 E
Wanawana I	165e	8.15 S	157.05 E
Wanbaoshan	79	44.12 N	125.11 E
Wanbasha	90	22.44 N	113.33 E
Wanbi	156	34.46 S	140.19 E
Wanblee	188	43.34 N	101.40 W
Wanborough	44	51.33 N	1.42 W
Wanchese	182	35.51 N	75.38 W
Wanda	148	29.36 S	24.28 E
Wandai	154	3.41 S	136.41 E
Wandana	152	32.04 S	133.49 E
Wandawega	206	42.45 N	88.40 W
Wande	88	36.21 N	116.56 E
Wanderer	144	19.37 S	29.59 E
Wandering	158a	32.40 S	116.40 E
Wandering ≃	172	55.05 N	112.30 W
Wanderup	41	54.41 N	9.20 E
Wandhofen	253	51.26 N	7.33 E
Wandingzhen	92	24.10 N	98.04 E
Wandlitz	50	52.45 N	13.26 E
Wandlitzer See ⊜	254a	52.46 N	13.27 E
Wando	88	34.18 N	126.47 E
Wandoan	156	26.08 S	149.57 E
Wandsbek ◆[8]	48	53.34 N	10.04 E
Wandsworth ◆[8]	44	51.27 N	0.11 W
Waneta Lake ⊜	200	42.27 N	77.06 W
Wanette	186	34.58 N	97.02 W
Wanfang	94	41.57 N	122.52 E
Wanfoxia	92	40.04 N	95.55 E
Wanfried	52	51.10 N	10.10 E
Wang ≃	100	17.08 N	99.02 E
Wanga	144	2.58 N	29.13 E
Wangal	154	6.10 S	134.12 E
Wanga Mountains ⋀	136	7.06 N	10.22 E
Wanganderry, Mount ∧	160	34.20 S	150.15 E
Wanganella Bank ⊹[4]	14	32.30 S	168.00 E
Wanganui	162	39.56 S	175.03 E
Wanganui ≃	162	39.56 S	175.00 E
Wang'anzhen	95	39.18 N	114.50 E
Wangaratta	156	36.22 S	146.20 E
Wangary	156	34.33 S	135.29 E
Wangbaotaicun	94	41.10 N	123.18 E
Wangbayan ∧	97	28.52 N	106.16 E
Wangbenying	95	40.28 N	116.06 E
Wangbintun	94	41.58 N	123.43 E
Wangchang, Zhg.	97	28.52 N	105.55 E
Wangchang, Zhg.	97	29.05 N	104.40 E
Wangchang, Zhg.	97	29.29 N	103.36 E
Wangchang, Zhg.	97	30.37 N	103.36 E
Wangchangtuizigou	94	41.14 N	120.32 E
Wangcheng, Zhg.	90	29.45 N	120.40 E
Wangcheng, Zhg.	90	28.23 N	112.48 E
Wang Chin	100	17.53 N	99.37 E
Wangcunkou	90	28.22 N	118.59 E
Wangdalong	92	29.25 N	99.03 E
Wangdian	96	30.37 N	120.44 E
Wangdu	88	38.43 N	115.09 E
Wangdu Phodrang	114	27.29 N	89.54 E
Wangels	50	54.16 N	10.45 E
Wangen	58	48.01 N	11.24 E
Wangen an der Aare	54	47.14 N	7.39 E
Wangenbourg	54	48.37 N	7.19 E
Wangen im Allgäu	54	47.41 N	9.50 E
Wangerin → Węgorzyno	30	53.32 N	15.33 E
Wangerooge I	48	53.46 N	7.55 E
Wangersen	48	53.22 N	9.25 E
Wangfu	94	42.05 N	121.29 E
Wanggameti, Gunung ∧	105b	10.07 S	120.14 E
Wanggangpu	94	41.38 N	123.09 E
Wangganji	90	33.11 N	116.04 E
Wanggao	92	24.38 N	111.30 E
Wanggava I	165g	18.52 S	178.54 W
Wanggezhuang	95	40.00 N	117.52 E
Wanggil-li	261b	37.36 N	126.39 E
Wanggoutun	94	41.40 N	121.53 E
Wanggucun	88	39.47 N	113.54 E
Wanghai	88	40.26 N	120.30 E
Wanghechenggou	94	41.52 N	121.13 E
Wang Hin, Khlong ≅	259a	13.48 N	100.35 E
Wanghongbao	92	38.20 N	106.17 E
Wanghuzhuang	95	38.50 N	117.05 E
Wangi, Kenya	144	2.00 S	40.55 E
Wängi, Schw.	54	47.30 N	8.57 E
Wangi Wangi	160	33.04 S	151.35 E
Wangiwangi, Pulau I	102	5.20 S	123.35 E
Wangji	90	33.52 N	118.44 E
Wangjia, Zhg.	96	32.07 N	120.59 E
Wangjia, Zhg.	96	31.59 N	121.13 E
Wangjiachang	97	29.44 N	104.18 E
Wangjiadian, Zhg.	90	31.26 N	113.58 E
Wangjiadian, Zhg.	95	40.03 N	117.29 E
Wangjiagou	94	42.33 N	123.16 E
Wangjiajing	88	39.56 N	122.11 E
Wangjiang	90	30.09 N	116.41 E
Wangjiangjing	96	30.53 N	120.43 E
Wangjianmu (Tomb of Wangjian) ⊥	97	29.51 N	106.31 E
Wangjiaputun	94	40.39 N	122.50 E
Wangjiapuzi, Zhg.	94	40.41 N	122.24 E
Wangjiapuzi, Zhg.	94	41.05 N	123.34 E
Wangjiaqiao	96	30.50 N	119.18 E
Wangjiashan	95	40.19 N	114.45 E
Wangjiashao	92	23.57 N	102.18 E
Wangjiatai	95	39.17 N	117.29 E
Wangjiaying, Zhg.	95	40.36 N	116.34 E
Wangjiaying, Zhg.	95	39.06 N	115.59 E
Wangjiazhai, Zhg.	95	39.31 N	116.43 E
Wangjiazhai, Zhg.	96	31.21 N	121.37 E
Wangjiazui	96	31.16 N	120.18 E
Wangkantou	90	29.12 N	120.09 E
Wangkouzhen	95	38.56 N	116.44 E
Wangkui	79	46.50 N	126.30 E
Wang Lan I	261d	22.11 N	114.18 E
Wanglanzhuang	95	39.26 N	118.01 E
Wangling	90	27.13 N	113.26 E
Wangliuji	90	32.25 N	115.40 E
Wanglongji	88	34.02 N	114.51 E
Wangmiao	90	26.50 N	112.52 E
Wangmulazi	94	41.42 N	124.02 E
Wang Noi	100	14.13 N	100.44 E
Wangong	79	49.10 N	118.53 E
Wangpingchang	97	29.17 N	105.45 E
Wangqing	79	43.20 N	129.48 E
Wangqingmen	88	41.42 N	125.23 E
Wangqingtuo	95	39.11 N	116.53 E
Wangqinzhuang	95	39.15 N	117.05 E
Wangqucun	96	31.22 N	120.19 E
Wangs	54	47.02 N	9.26 E
Wang Saphung	100	17.18 N	101.46 E
Wangshanhutun	94	42.03 N	122.37 E
Wangsi	88	38.00 N	116.55 E
Wangsim-ni ◆[8]	261b	37.36 N	127.03 E
Wangsiying	97	30.34 N	103.29 E
Wangtai, Zhg.	88	36.05 N	119.59 E
Wangtai, Zhg.	90	26.39 N	117.57 E
Wang Thong	100	16.50 N	100.26 E
Wangtian	90	25.59 N	116.04 E
Wangting	96	31.26 N	120.26 E
Wangtong	90	33.12 N	116.21 E
Wangtongshitai	94	42.05 N	123.11 E
Wangtuan, Zhg.	88	37.32 N	116.08 E
Wangtuan, Zhg.	88	37.17 N	122.04 E
Wanguchang	97	29.41 N	105.57 E
Wangwan	96	30.22 N	120.48 E
Wangwenzhuang	95	38.53 N	117.15 E
Wangxiangshang	96	31.29 N	120.15 E
Wangxiangtai	95	40.02 N	115.09 E
Wangxiuqiao	96	31.38 N	121.03 E
Wangyedian	88	41.36 N	118.17 E
Wangyefu	88	41.50 N	118.23 E
Wangyehmiao → Wulanhaote	79	46.05 N	122.05 E
Wangyiguantun	94	42.36 N	123.19 E
Wangzhai	88	34.09 N	116.47 E
Wangzhimawo	95	39.39 N	117.40 E
Wangzhong	88	35.08 N	116.58 E
Wangzhuang, Zhg.	88	34.09 N	118.23 E
Wangzhuang, Zhg.	90	33.07 N	117.29 E
Wangzhuang, Zhg.	95	38.55 N	115.36 E
Wangzhuangbao	88	39.27 N	113.56 E

Symbol	English	Deutsch	Español	Français	Português
≃	River	Fluss	Río	Rivière	Rio
≅	Canal	Kanal	Canal	Canal	Canal
⌊	Waterfall, Rapids	Wasserfall, Stromschnellen	Cascada, Rápidos	Chute d'eau, Rapides	Cascata, Rápidos
⩌	Strait	Meeresstrasse	Estrecho	Détroit	Estreito
C	Bay, Gulf	Bucht, Golf	Bahía, Golfo	Baie, Golfe	Baía, Golfo
⊜	Lake, Lakes	See, Seen	Lago, Lagos	Lac, Lacs	Lago, Lagos
⧣	Swamp	Sumpf	Pantano	Marais	Pântano
⩀	Ice Features, Glacier	Eis- und Gletscherformen	Accidentes Glaciales	Formes glaciaires	Acidentes Glaciares
⍑	Other Hydrographic Features	Andere Hydrographische Objekte	Otros Elementos Hidrográficos	Autres données hydrographiques	Outros Elementos Hidrográficos
⊹	Submarine Features	Untermeerische Objekte	Accidentes Submarinos	Formes de relief sous-marin	Acidentes Submarinos
□	Political Unit	Politische Einheit	Unidad Politica	Entité politique	Unidade Política
ʊ	Cultural Institution	Kulturelle Institution	Institución Cultural	Institution culturelle	Instituição Cultural
⊥	Historical Site	Historische Stätte	Sitio Histórico	Site historique	Sitio Histórico
♠	Recreational Site	Erholungs- und Ferienort	Sitio de Recreo	Centre de loisirs	Sítio de Lazer
⊠	Airport	Flughafen	Aeropuerto	Aéroport	Aeroporto
▪	Military Installation	Militäranlage	Instalación Militar	Installation militaire	Instalação Militar
◆	Miscellaneous	Verschiedenes	Misceláneo	Divers	Miscelânea

Symbols in the index entries represent the broad categories identified in the key at the right. Symbols with superior numbers (²) identify subcategories (see complete key on page I · 26).

Kartensymbole in dem Registerverzeichnis stellen die rechts in Schlüssel erklärten Kategorien dar. Symbole mit hochgestellten Ziffern (²) bezeichnen Unterabteilungen einer Kategorie (vgl. vollständiger Schlüssel auf Seite I · 26).

Los símbolos incluídos en el texto del índice representan las grandes categorías identificadas con la clave a la derecha. Los símbolos con numeros en su parte superior (²) identifican las subcategorías (véase la clave completa en la página I · 26).

Les symboles de l'index représentent les catégories indiquées dans la légende à droite. Les symboles suivis d'un indice (²) représentent des sous-catégories (voir légende complète à la page I · 26).

Os símbolos incluídos no texto do índice representam as grandes categorias identificadas com a chave à direita. Os símbolos com números em sua parte superior (²) identificam as subcategorias (veja-se a chave completa à página I · 26).

Mountain	Berg	Montaña	Montagne	Montanha
Mountains	Berge	Montañas	Montagnes	Montanhas
Pass	Pass	Paso	Col	Passo
Valley, Canyon	Tal, Cañon	Valle, Cañón	Vallée, Canyon	Vale, Canhão
Plain	Ebene	Llano	Plaine	Planície
Cape	Kap	Cabo	Cap	Cabo
Island	Insel	Isla	Île	Ilha
Islands	Inseln	Islas	Îles	Ilhas
Other Topographic Features	Andere Topographische Objekte	Otros Elementos Topográficos	Autres données topographiques	Outros Elementos Topográficos

ESPAÑOL

Nombre	Página	Lat.°′	Long.°′ W=Oeste
Wea Creek ≃	206	40.24 N	86.57 W
Weagamow Lake ⊜	174	52.53 N	91.22 W
Weald Park ♠	250	51.38 N	0.14 E
Wealdstone ⬩[8]	250	51.36 N	0.20 W
Weam	154	8.40 S	141.08 E
Wear ≃	42	54.55 N	1.22 W
Wearhead	42	54.45 N	2.13 W
Wearyan ≃	154	15.57 S	136.51 E
Weatherford, Okla., U.S.	186	35.32 N	98.42 W
Weatherford, Tex., U.S.	212	32.46 N	97.48 W
Weatherford, Lake ⊜[1]	212	32.47 N	97.41 W
Weatherly	200	40.57 N	75.50 W
Weatogue	197	41.51 N	72.49 W
Weaubleau	184	37.54 N	93.32 W
Weaver, Ala., U.S.	184	33.45 N	85.49 W
Weaver, Tex., U.S.	212	33.10 N	95.25 W
Weaver ≃	44	53.19 N	2.45 W
Weaver ☲	252	53.19 N	2.45 W
Weaverham	42	53.16 N	2.35 W
Weaver Lake ⊜	174	52.45 N	96.35 W
Weavertown	269b	40.16 N	80.11 W
Weaverville, Calif., U.S.	194	40.44 N	122.56 W
Weaverville, N.C., U.S.	182	35.42 N	82.34 W
Webau	50	51.10 N	12.04 E
Webb, Sask., Can.	174	50.11 N	108.12 W
Webb, Miss., U.S.	184	33.57 N	90.21 W
Webb Air Force Base ■	186	32.14 N	101.31 W
Webb Brook ≃	273	42.32 N	71.14 W
Webb City	184	37.09 N	94.28 W
Webber Lake ⊜	174	54.28 N	94.00 W
Webberville	206	42.40 N	84.11 W
Webbwood	180	41.16 N	81.53 W
Weber, Mount ∧	172	55.32 N	128.31 W
Webera, Yai.	134	6.25 N	40.45 E
Webera, Yai.	134	9.44 N	39.02 E
Weber City	182	36.37 N	82.34 W
Weber Creek ≃	216	38.46 N	121.00 W
Weber Hill	209	38.27 N	90.34 W
Webi Gof ≃	134	1.07 N	43.45 E
Webi Haharro ≃	134	1.12 N	43.43 E
Webster, Alta., Can.	172	55.26 N	118.42 W
Webster, Fla., U.S.	210	28.37 N	82.03 W
Webster, Ind., U.S.	208	39.54 N	84.57 W
Webster, Mass., U.S.	197	42.03 N	71.53 W
Webster, N.Y., U.S.	200	43.13 N	77.26 W
Webster, Pa., U.S.	204	40.11 N	79.51 W
Webster, S. Dak., U.S.	188	45.20 N	97.31 W
Webster, Wis., U.S.	180	45.53 N	92.22 W
Webster City	180	42.28 N	93.49 W
Webster Crossing	200	42.40 N	77.38 W
Webster Groves	209	38.35 N	90.21 W
Webster Lake ⊜	206	41.19 N	85.41 W
Websters Corners, B.C., Can.	214	49.13 N	122.30 W
Websters Corners, N.Y., U.S.	274a	41.47 N	78.45 W
Webster Springs	178	38.29 N	80.25 W
Weches	212	31.33 N	95.14 W
Wechmar	50	50.53 N	10.47 E
Wechselburg	50	51.00 N	12.47 E
Weda	98	0.21 N	127.52 E
Wedau ⬩[8]	253	51.24 N	6.48 E
Wedau, Sportpark ♠	253	51.25 N	6.47 E
Weddell Island I	244	51.55 S	61.00 W
Weddell Sea ⍑[2]	9	72.00 S	45.00 W
Wedderburn	156	36.25 S	143.37 E
Wedding ⬩[8]	254a	52.33 N	13.22 E
Weddinghofen	253	51.36 N	7.37 E
Wedel	48	53.35 N	9.41 E
Wedge Mountain ∧	172	50.10 N	122.50 W
Wedgeport	176	43.44 N	65.59 W
Wedgewood	209	38.47 N	90.17 W
Wedmore	44	51.14 N	2.49 W
Wednesbury	44	52.34 N	2.00 W
Wednesfield	44	52.36 N	2.04 W
Wedowee	184	33.19 N	85.29 W
Wedron	206	41.26 N	88.46 W
Weduar, Tanjung ≻	154	6.00 S	132.50 E
Wedweil	130	9.00 N	27.12 E
Wedza	144	18.35 S	31.35 E
Weebo	152	28.01 S	121.03 E
Weed	194	41.25 N	122.23 W
Weed Heights	216	38.59 N	119.11 W
Weedon	196	45.42 N	71.28 W
Weedon Beck	44	52.14 N	1.05 W
Weedon Island I	210	27.51 N	82.36 W
Weedon Lake ⊜	196	45.43 N	71.25 W
Weed Patch, Calif., U.S.	216		
	218	30.19 N	118.55 W
Weed Patch Hill ∧[2]	208	39.10 N	86.13 W
Weedsport	200	43.03 N	76.34 W
Weedville	204	41.17 N	78.30 W
Weehawken	266	40.46 N	74.01 W
Weeim, Pulau I	154	1.29 S	130.14 E
Wee Jasper	161b	35.09 S	148.41 E
Weekapauq	197	41.20 N	71.45 W
Weeki Wachee Spring ♠	210	28.32 N	82.35 W
Weeki Wachee Swamp ☷	210	28.31 N	82.37 W
Weeks Point ≻	266	40.53 N	73.39 W
Weekstown	198	39.37 N	74.37 W
Weelde	52	51.25 N	5.00 E
Weems	198	37.39 N	76.27 W
Weende	48	51.33 N	9.55 E
Weenen	148	28.57 S	30.03 E
Weener	48	53.10 N	7.21 E
Weeney Bay C	264a	34.01 S	151.10 E
Weeping Water	188	40.52 N	96.08 W
Weequahic Lake ⊜	266	40.42 N	74.12 W
Weert	48	51.15 N	5.43 E
Weesatche	212	28.51 N	97.27 W
Weesby	41	54.50 N	9.08 E
Weesow	254a	52.39 N	13.43 E
Weesp	48	52.17 N	5.02 E
Weetfeld	253	51.38 N	7.49 E
Weethalle	156	33.53 S	146.38 E
Weeton	252	53.48 N	2.56 W
Wee Waa	156	30.14 S	149.26 E
Weeze	48	51.37 N	6.12 E
Wefensleben	50	52.11 N	11.09 E
Weferlingen	50	52.19 N	11.02 E
Wegberg	52	51.08 N	6.16 E
Wegdras	148	28.50 S	21.52 E
Wegeleben	50	51.53 N	11.10 E
Wegendorf	254a	52.36 N	13.45 E
Wegenstedt	50	52.23 N	11.11 E
Wegeringhausen	52	51.02 N	7.45 E
Weggis	54	47.02 N	8.26 E
Węgliniec	30	51.17 N	15.13 E
Węgorzewo	30	54.14 N	21.44 E
Węgorzyno	30	53.32 N	15.33 E
Węgrów	30	52.25 N	22.01 E
Wegscheid	30	48.36 N	13.48 E
Wehdel	48	53.30 N	8.48 E
Wehingen	54	48.08 N	8.47 E
Wehofen ⬩[8]	253	51.32 N	6.46 E
Wehr	54	47.37 N	7.54 E
Wehringhausen ⬩[8]	253	51.21 N	7.27 E
Wehrsdorf	50	51.03 N	14.22 E
Weichang	88	42.00 N	117.32 E
Weichsel → Wisła ≃	30	54.22 N	18.55 E
Weichuan	88	34.17 N	113.58 E
Weicun	96	31.59 N	119.55 E
Weida	50	50.45 N	12.04 E
Weida ≃	50	50.47 N	12.06 E
Weiden in der Oberpfalz	30	49.41 N	12.10 E
Weidenstetten	52	48.33 N	9.59 E
Weidhausen	52	50.12 N	11.08 E
Weidling	254b	48.17 N	16.19 E
Weidlingau ⬩[8]	254b	48.13 N	16.13 E
Weidlingbach	254b	48.16 N	16.15 E
Weidlinger Bach ≃	254b	48.18 N	16.20 E

FRANÇAIS

Nom	Page	Lat.°′	Long.°′ W=Ouest
Weifang	88	36.42 N	119.04 E
Weigelstown	198	39.59 N	76.49 W
Weihai	88	37.28 N	122.07 E
Weihaiwei → Weihai	88	37.28 N	122.07 E
Weihe ≃, Zhg.	88	37.05 N	119.28 E
Weihe ≃, Zhg.	88	36.51 N	115.43 E
Weihe ≃, Zhg.	92	34.30 N	110.20 E
Weihnachtsinsel → Christmas Island □[2]	102	10.30 S	105.40 E
Weijiagou	95	40.28 N	115.08 E
Weijiatang	96	31.25 N	118.55 E
Weijiawan	88	36.43 N	115.54 E
Weijiazhuang	95	39.37 N	116.22 E
Weijiazui	90	30.29 N	117.20 E
Weijingtang	96	31.27 N	120.39 E
Weikersheim	52	49.29 N	9.54 E
Weil ≃	52	50.28 N	8.16 E
Weil am Rhein	54	47.37 N	7.38 E
Weilbach	52	50.03 N	8.26 E
Weilburg	52	50.29 N	8.15 E
Weil der Stadt	52	48.45 N	8.52 E
Weiler	54	47.36 N	9.55 E
Weilerbach	52	49.29 N	7.37 E
Weilerswist	52	50.45 N	6.50 E
Weilheim	58	47.50 N	11.08 E
Weilheim an der Teck	52	48.37 N	9.32 E
Weilmoringle	156	29.15 S	146.51 E
Weilmünster	52	50.26 N	8.22 E
Weimar, B.R.D.	52	51.22 N	9.23 E
Weimar, D.D.R.	50	50.59 N	11.19 E
Weimar, Calif., U.S.	216	39.02 N	120.58 W
Weimar, Tex., U.S.	212	29.42 N	96.47 W
Weinan	92	34.29 N	109.29 E
Weinböhla	50	51.10 N	13.34 E
Weinel Cross Roads	269b	40.37 N	79.37 W
Weiner	184	35.37 N	90.54 W
Weinfelden	54	47.34 N	9.06 E
Weingarten, B.R.D.	52	49.05 N	8.31 E
Weingarten, B.R.D.	54	47.48 N	9.38 E
Weinheim	52	49.33 N	8.39 E
Weining	92	26.43 N	104.18 E
Weiningying	94	41.21 N	123.49 E
Weinsberg	52	49.10 N	9.17 E
Weipa	154	12.41 S	141.52 E
Weiping	90	29.43 N	118.45 E
Weir, Bhārat	114	27.01 N	77.11 E
Weir, Kans., U.S.	188	37.19 N	94.46 W
Weir, Miss., U.S.	184	33.16 N	89.17 W
Weir ≃, Austl.	156	28.50 S	149.06 E
Weir ≃, Man., Can.	174	56.54 N	93.21 W
Weir ≃, Mass., U.S.	273	42.16 N	70.53 W
Weir, Lake ⊜	210	29.00 N	81.57 W
Weir River	174	56.49 N	94.04 W
Weirsdale	210	28.59 N	81.55 W
Weirton	204	40.25 N	80.35 W
Weisberg → Monguelfo	58	46.45 N	12.06 E
Weisburd	242	27.18 S	62.36 W
Weisburg	208	39.13 N	85.03 W
Weischlitz	50	50.26 N	12.02 E
Weisendorf	52	49.37 N	10.49 E
Weiser	192	44.15 N	116.58 W
Weiser ≃	192	44.15 N	116.59 W
Weishan, Zhg.	88	34.52 N	117.09 E
Weishan, Zhg.	90	29.20 N	120.25 E
Weishan, Zhg.	92	25.15 N	100.20 E
Weishancheng	90	32.34 N	113.24 E
Weishanhe	94	40.47 N	123.31 E
Weishanhu ⊜	88	34.40 N	117.15 E
Weishanzhuang	95	39.40 N	116.25 E
Weishi	88	34.25 N	114.11 E
Weismain	50	50.05 N	11.14 E
Weisner Mountain ∧	184	34.02 N	85.40 W
Weissach, B.R.D.	52	48.50 N	8.55 E
Weissach, B.R.D.	58	47.41 N	11.45 E
Weissbach bei Lofer	58	47.31 N	12.45 E
Weissbriach	58	46.41 N	13.15 E
Weisse Elster ≃	50	51.26 N	11.57 E
Weissenbach	254b	48.05 N	16.13 E
Weissenbach am Attersee	58	47.48 N	13.32 E
Weissenbach am Lech	54	47.26 N	10.39 E
Weissenberg	50	51.11 N	14.40 E
Weissenborn	50	50.52 N	13.25 E
Weissenbrunn	50	50.12 N	11.20 E
Weissenburg	54	46.39 N	7.28 E
Weissenburg in Bayern	52	49.01 N	10.58 E
Weissenfels	50	51.12 N	11.58 E
Weissenhorn	54	48.18 N	10.09 E
Weissensee	50	51.11 N	11.04 E
Weissensee ⬩[8]	254a	52.33 N	13.27 E
Weissensee ⊜	58	46.42 N	13.22 E
Weissenstadt	50	50.06 N	11.53 E
Weissenstein, B.R.D.	52	48.42 N	9.53 E
Weissenstein, Öst.	58	46.41 N	13.44 E
Weissenstein ∧	54	47.15 N	7.31 E
Weissenstein Tunnel ⬩[5]	54	47.12 N	7.23 E
Weissenthurm	52	50.24 N	7.27 E
Weisser Main ≃	50	50.05 N	11.24 E
Weisser Nil → White Nile ≃	130	15.38 N	32.31 E
Weisser See → Beloje, Ozero ⊜	66	60.11 N	37.37 E
Weisser Stein ∧	52	50.23 N	6.20 E
Weisses Meer → Beloje More ⍑[2]	24	65.30 N	38.00 E
Weisse Spitze ∧	58	46.52 N	12.21 E
Weissfluh ∧	54	46.50 N	9.48 E
Weisshorn ∧	54	46.06 N	7.42 E
Weissig	50	51.05 N	13.52 E
Weisskugel (Palla Bianca) ∧	58	46.48 N	10.44 E
Weiss Lake ⊜[1]	182	34.15 N	85.35 W
Weissmeer-Ostsee Kanal → Belomorsko-Baltijskij Kanal ☲	24	62.48 N	34.48 E
Weissport	200	40.50 N	75.42 W
Weisstannen	54	46.59 N	9.21 E
Weisswasser	50	51.30 N	14.38 E
Weisweiler	52	50.50 N	6.19 E
Weitang, Zhg.	95	40.24 N	117.24 E
Weitang, Zhg.	96	31.57 N	119.59 E
Weitendorf	50	53.54 N	12.16 E
Weitian	90	27.43 N	118.46 E
Weitin	50	53.34 N	13.12 E
Weiting	96	31.22 N	120.47 E
Weitmar ⬩[8]	253	51.27 N	7.12 E
Weitnau	54	47.38 N	10.07 E
Weitou	90	24.34 N	118.34 E
Weitouwan C	90	24.34 N	118.30 E
Weitra	30	48.42 N	14.54 E
Weituo	97	30.03 N	106.08 E
Weitzgrund	50	52.11 N	12.32 E
Weixdorf	50	51.09 N	13.48 E
Weixi	92	27.14 N	99.12 E
Weixian, Zhg.	88	36.57 N	115.15 E
Weixian, Zhg.	88	36.22 N	114.56 E
Weixian, Zhg.	88	36.52 N	119.07 E
Weixin	92	27.48 N	105.06 E
Weiyuan, Zhg.	90	30.09 N	115.15 E
Weiyuan, Zhg.	97	29.33 N	104.39 E
Weiyuanbao	88	42.39 N	124.16 E
Weiz	30	47.13 N	15.37 E
Weizhoudao I	92	21.03 N	109.04 E
Weizhuang	95	39.02 N	115.20 E
Weizi	88	40.04 N	123.10 E
Weizigou, Zhg.	94	42.05 N	120.34 E
Weizigou, Zhg.	94	41.05 N	120.38 E
Weizigou, Zhg.	94	42.25 N	122.47 E
Weizigoumen	88	41.58 N	116.49 E
Weizixi	97	30.11 N	106.03 E
Weiziyu	88	41.29 N	124.31 E
Wejherowo	30	54.37 N	18.15 E
Wekiva ≃	210	28.52 N	81.23 W

PORTUGUÊS

Nome	Página	Lat.°′	Long.°′ W=Oeste
Wekiwa Springs State Park ♠	210	28.43 N	81.27 W
Wekoewa Punt ≻	231s	12.14 N	68.24 W
Wekusko Lake ⊜	174	54.45 N	99.50 W
Welaka	182	29.29 N	81.40 W
Welbourn Hill	152	27.21 S	134.06 E
Welch, Okla., U.S.	186	36.52 N	95.06 W
Welch, Tex., U.S.	186	32.56 N	102.08 W
Welch, W. Va., U.S.	182	37.25 N	81.31 W
Welch Creek ≃	272	37.32 N	121.51 W
Welches	214	45.20 N	121.58 W
Welch Peak ∧	214	49.10 N	121.36 W
Welcome, Ont., Can.	202	43.58 N	78.21 W
Welcome, Minn., U.S.	188	43.40 N	94.37 W
Welcome, S.C., U.S.	182	34.49 N	82.26 W
Welcome Lake ⊜	202	45.25 N	78.25 W
Welcome Monument ⊥	259e	6.11 S	106.49 E
Welden	54	48.27 N	10.40 E
Weldon, Sask., Can.	174	53.00 N	105.08 W
Weldon, Ill., U.S.	209	40.07 N	88.45 W
Weldon, N.C., U.S.	182	36.25 N	77.36 W
Weldon, Tex., U.S.	212	31.01 N	95.34 W
Weldon ≃	184	40.06 N	93.38 W
Weldona	188	40.21 N	103.58 W
Weldon Brook ≃	266	40.58 N	74.35 W
Weldya	134	11.50 N	39.36 E
Weleetka	186	35.20 N	96.08 W
Welega □[4]	134	9.40 N	35.50 E
Weleri	105a	6.58 S	110.04 E
Welfare Island I	266	40.45 N	73.57 W
Welgedag	263d	26.12 S	28.30 E
Welhamgreen	250	51.44 N	0.13 W
Welheim ⬩[8]	253	51.32 N	6.59 E
Weligama	112	5.58 N	80.25 E
Welikaja → Velikaja ≃	66	57.48 N	28.20 E
Welkenraedt	52	50.40 N	5.59 E
Welker Seamount ⊹[3]	16	55.10 N	140.20 W
Welkite	134	8.15 N	37.50 E
Wel Koban	134	2.33 N	44.20 E
Welkom	148	27.59 S	26.45 E
Well	48	51.34 N	6.06 E
Welland	202	42.59 N	79.15 W
Welland ≃, Ont., Can.	202	43.04 N	79.03 W
Welland ≃, Eng., U.K.	44	52.53 N	0.02 E
Welland Canal ☲	202	43.14 N	79.13 W
Welland Junction	274a	42.57 N	79.14 W
Wellard	158a	32.19 S	115.50 E
Wellaune	50	51.34 N	12.33 E
Wellborn, Fla., U.S.	182	30.14 N	82.49 W
Wellborn, Tex., U.S.	212	30.32 N	96.18 W
Wellerode	52	51.14 N	9.34 E
Wellers Bay C	202	44.00 N	77.34 W
Wellers Creek ≃	268	42.03 N	87.53 W
Wellesbourne	44	52.12 N	1.35 W
Welles Harbor C	164g	28.12 N	177.26 W
Wellesley, Ont., Can.	202	43.28 N	80.45 W
Wellesley, Mass., U.S.	197	42.18 N	71.17 W
Wellesley College ʊ[2]	273	42.18 N	71.19 W
Wellesley Hills	273	42.19 N	71.17 W
Wellesley Island I	202	44.19 N	75.58 W
Wellesley Islands II, Austl.	152	17.04 S	139.25 E
Wellesley Islands II, Austl.	154	16.42 S	139.30 E
Wellesley Island State Park ♠	202	44.19 N	76.01 W
Wellesley Lake ⊜	170	62.30 N	139.50 W
Wellfleet	197	41.56 N	70.02 W
Well Hill	250	51.21 N	0.09 E
Wellin	52	50.05 N	5.07 E
Welling ⬩[8]	250	51.28 N	0.07 E
Wellingborough	44	52.19 N	0.42 W
Wellinghofen ⬩[8]	253	51.28 N	7.29 E
Wellington, Austl.	156	32.33 S	148.57 E
Wellington, B.C., Can.	214	49.13 N	124.01 W
Wellington, Ont., Can.	202	43.57 N	77.21 W
Wellington, N.Z.	162	41.18 S	174.47 E
Wellington, S. Afr.	148	33.38 S	18.57 E
Wellington, Eng., U.K.	44	52.43 N	2.31 W
Wellington, Eng., U.K.	44	50.59 N	3.14 W
Wellington, Colo., U.S.	190	40.42 N	105.00 W
Wellington, Ill., U.S.	206	40.32 N	87.41 W
Wellington, Kans., U.S.	188	37.16 N	97.24 W
Wellington, Mo., U.S.	184	39.08 N	93.59 W
Wellington, Nev., U.S.	216	38.45 N	119.22 W
Wellington, Ohio, U.S.	204	41.10 N	82.13 W
Wellington, Tex., U.S.	186	34.51 N	100.13 W
Wellington, Utah, U.S.	190	39.32 N	110.44 W
Wellington □[6]	202	43.50 N	80.30 W
Wellington, Isla I	244	49.20 S	74.40 W
Wellington Bay C, N.W. Ter., Can.	166	69.30 N	106.30 W
Wellington Bay C, Ont., Can.	202	43.56 N	77.21 W
Wellington Channel ⩂	166	75.00 N	93.00 W
Wellington Point	161a	27.29 S	153.15 E
Wellington Reservoir ⊜[1]	158a	33.24 S	116.01 E
Wellington Station	176	46.27 N	64.00 W
Wellman, Iowa, U.S.	180	41.28 N	91.50 W
Wellman, Tex., U.S.	186	33.03 N	102.26 W
Wells, B.C., Can.	172	53.06 N	121.34 W
Wells, Eng., U.K.	44	51.13 N	2.39 W
Wells, Mich., U.S.	180	45.47 N	87.04 W
Wells, Minn., U.S.	180	43.44 N	93.44 W
Wells, Nev., U.S.	194	41.07 N	114.58 W
Wells, N.Y., U.S.	200	43.24 N	74.17 W
Wells, Tex., U.S.	212	31.29 N	94.56 W
Wells □[6]	206	40.44 N	85.11 W
Wells, Lake ⊜	152	26.43 S	123.10 E
Wells, Mount ∧[2]	152	17.26 S	127.14 E
Wellsboro	200	41.45 N	77.18 W
Wells Bridge	200	42.22 N	75.15 W
Wellsburg, Iowa, U.S.	180	42.26 N	92.56 W
Wellsburg, N.Y., U.S.	200	42.01 N	76.44 W
Wellsburg, W. Va., U.S.	204	40.16 N	80.37 W
Wells Cathedral ʊ[1]	44	51.13 N	2.39 W
Wellsford	162	36.17 S	174.31 E
Wells Gray Provincial Park ♠	172	52.20 N	120.00 W
Wells Lake ⊜	174	57.15 N	101.00 W
Wells-next-the-Sea	44	52.58 N	0.51 E
Wells Point ≻	274b	39.17 N	76.23 W
Wells State Park ♠	197	42.09 N	72.05 W
Wells Tannery	204	40.05 N	78.10 W
Wellston	178	39.07 N	82.32 W
Wellsville, Kans., U.S.	188	38.43 N	95.05 W
Wellsville, Mo., U.S.	209	39.04 N	91.34 W
Wellsville, N.Y., U.S.	200	42.07 N	77.57 W
Wellsville, Ohio, U.S.	204	40.36 N	80.39 W
Wellsville, Pa., U.S.	198	40.03 N	76.56 W
Wellsville, Utah, U.S.	190	41.38 N	111.56 W
Wellton	190	32.40 N	114.08 W
Welmel ≃	134	5.38 N	40.47 E
Welmen	253	51.39 N	6.41 E
Welney	44	52.31 N	0.15 E
Welo	134	9.27 N	48.57 E
Welo □[4]	134	11.50 N	40.20 E
Wels	30	48.10 N	14.02 E
Welschbillig	52	49.51 N	6.34 E
Welse ≃	50	53.10 N	14.18 E
Welsford	176	45.27 N	66.20 W
Welsh	184	30.14 N	92.49 W
Wel Shimbiro	134	2.22 N	44.20 E
Welshpool, Austl.	159	38.39 S	146.26 E
Welshpool, Wales, U.K.	44	52.40 N	3.09 W
Welsickendorf	50	51.54 N	13.08 E
Welsleben	50	52.00 N	11.38 E
Welverdiend	148	26.23 S	27.16 E
Welwitschia	146	20.21 S	14.57 E
Welwyn Garden City	44	51.50 N	0.13 W
Welwyn Hatfield □[8]	250	51.47 N	0.12 W
Welzheim	52	48.53 N	9.38 E
Welzow	50	51.34 N	14.10 E
Wem	44	52.51 N	2.44 W
Wema	142	0.26 S	21.38 E
Wembere ≃	144	4.10 S	34.11 E
Wembley	172	55.09 N	119.08 W
Wembley ⬩[8]	250	51.33 N	0.18 W
Wembley Stadium ♠, S. Afr.	263d	26.14 S	28.03 E
Wembley Stadium ♠, Eng., U.K.	250	51.33 N	0.17 W
Wemding	52	48.52 N	10.43 E
Wemeldinge	48	51.31 N	4.00 E
Wemme	214	45.21 N	121.58 W
Wemmetsweiler	52	49.22 N	7.05 E
Wemperhardt	52	50.09 N	6.05 E
Wen'an	95	38.52 N	116.28 E
Wenas Creek ≃	214	46.42 N	120.35 W
Wenatchee	192	47.25 N	120.19 W
Wenatchee ≃	192	47.27 N	120.19 W
Wenatchee Lake ⊜	214	47.49 N	120.47 W
Wenatchee Mountains ⩘	192	47.20 N	120.45 W
Wenchang	100	19.41 N	110.48 E
Wencheng	90	27.50 N	120.05 E
Wenchi	140	7.42 N	2.07 W
Wenchow → Wenzhou	90	28.01 N	120.39 E
Wendaohezi	94	41.46 N	124.09 E
Wendel	269b	40.18 N	79.41 W
Wendell, Idaho, U.S.	192	42.46 N	114.42 W
Wendell, N.C., U.S.	182	35.47 N	78.22 W
Wendelsheim	52	49.46 N	7.59 E
Wendelstein	52	49.21 N	11.08 E
Wendelstein ∧	58	47.42 N	12.00 E
Wendelville	274a	43.04 N	78.47 W
Wenden, B.R.D.	48	52.19 N	10.30 E
Wenden, Ariz., U.S.	190	33.49 N	113.32 W
Wendeng	88	37.12 N	122.04 E
Wendesi	154	2.25 S	134.13 E
Wendilou	94	41.13 N	121.08 E
Wendisch Rietz	50	52.13 N	14.01 E
Wendish Baggendorf	50	54.04 N	12.56 E
Wendji	142	0.04 S	18.10 E
Wendlingen am Neckar	52	48.40 N	9.23 E
Wendo	134	6.38 N	38.27 E
Wendover, Eng., U.K.	44	51.46 N	0.46 W
Wendover, Utah, U.S.	190	40.44 N	114.02 W
Wenduine	46	51.18 N	3.05 E
Wenebegon ≃	180	46.53 N	83.12 W
Wenebegon Lake ⊜	180	47.24 N	83.08 W
Wenfang	90	28.02 N	117.19 E
Weng'an	92	26.53 N	107.22 E
Wengbo	110	31.23 N	86.40 E
Wengcheng	90	24.23 N	113.51 E
Wengdang	114	28.50 N	90.03 E
Wenge	142	0.03 N	24.01 E
Wengen, B.R.D.	54	47.41 N	10.09 E
Wengen, Schw.	54	46.36 N	7.56 E
Wengern	253	51.24 N	7.21 E
Wengjiafou	96	30.23 N	120.21 E
Wengjiang ≃	90	24.10 N	113.24 E
Wengongchang	97	30.11 N	104.09 E
Wenguantun	94	41.53 N	123.30 E
Wengyang	90	28.03 N	120.58 E
Wengyuan (Longxianwei)	90	24.21 N	114.08 E
Wenham	197	42.36 N	70.53 W
Wenham Lake ⊜	273	42.35 N	70.53 W
Wenham Swamp ☷	273	42.37 N	70.55 W
Wenhe ≃	88	36.38 N	119.22 E
Wenheng	90	25.42 N	116.45 E
Wenjiachang	97	30.41 N	103.55 E
Wenjiang	97	30.42 N	103.49 E
Wenjiangban	90	26.01 N	117.51 E
Wenjiazhen	90	28.20 N	116.05 E
Wenling	90	28.22 N	121.20 E
Wenlock	154	13.06 S	142.58 E
Wenlock ≃	154	12.02 S	141.55 E
Wenlock Edge ⩘[4]	44	52.30 N	2.40 W
Wenlong	90	24.48 N	114.54 E
Wenmingsi	90	25.33 N	113.20 E
Wennigsen	48	52.16 N	9.34 E
Wenning ≃	42	54.07 N	2.39 W
Wennington ⬩[8]	250	51.30 N	0.13 E
Wenniu	92	24.18 N	104.31 E
Wenns	54	47.10 N	10.44 E
Wenona, Ill., U.S.	206	41.03 N	89.03 W
Wenona, Md., U.S.	198	38.08 N	75.57 W
Wenonah	198	39.48 N	75.09 W
Wenquan, Zhg.	76	44.59 N	81.04 E
Wenquan, Zhg.	90	23.37 N	113.43 E
Wenquansi	94	41.20 N	124.04 E
Wenshan	92	23.30 N	104.20 E
Wenshang	88	35.44 N	116.29 E
Wenshui, Zhg.	92	28.28 N	106.30 E
Wenshui, Zhg.	92	37.28 N	112.01 E
Wensickendorf	254a	52.45 N	13.23 E
Wensleydale ∨	42	54.19 N	2.00 W
Wensum ≃	44	52.37 N	1.19 E
Went ≃	42	53.39 N	0.59 W
Wentorf	48	53.30 N	10.15 E
Wentworth, Austl.	156	34.07 S	141.55 E
Wentworth, N.C., U.S.	182	36.24 N	79.53 W
Wentworth, S. Dak., U.S.	188	44.00 N	96.58 W
Wentworth □[6]	202	43.15 N	80.00 W
Wentworth Falls	160	33.43 S	150.22 E
Wentworth Park	263d	26.07 S	27.48 E
Wentworthville	264a	33.48 S	150.58 E
Wentzville	209	38.49 N	90.51 W
Wenxi	92	35.26 N	111.11 E
Wenxian	92	32.58 N	104.46 E
Wenxiang	92	34.37 N	110.45 E
Wenxingchang	97	29.52 N	106.29 E
Wenyuhe ≃	95	39.59 N	116.38 E
Wenzhou	90	28.01 N	120.39 E
Wenzhouwan C	90	27.56 N	121.00 E
Wenzhu	90	26.58 N	114.04 E
Wenzhuangzicun	94	42.16 N	123.51 E
Weobley	44	52.09 N	2.51 W
Weohyakapka, Lake ⊜	210	27.49 N	81.25 W
Wepener	148	29.46 S	27.00 E
Wépion	52	50.25 N	4.52 E
Wequetequock	197	41.22 N	71.52 W
Wera ≃	105b	8.20 S	120.43 E
Werbellin	50	52.53 N	13.41 E
Werbellinsee ⊜	50	52.54 N	13.40 E
Werben	50	52.52 N	11.58 E
Werbomont	52	50.23 N	5.41 E
Werchojansker Gebirge → Verchojanskij Chrebet ⩘	64	67.00 N	129.00 E
Werda	146	25.15 S	23.16 E
Werdau	50	50.44 N	12.22 E
Werden ⬩[8]	253	51.23 N	7.00 E
Werder	50	52.23 N	12.56 E
Werder ⬩[1]	50	53.40 N	13.25 E
Werdohl	52	51.15 N	7.45 E
Weregta	134	1.30 N	42.28 E
Were Ilu	134	10.37 N	39.28 E
Werfen	58	47.28 N	13.11 E
Weri	154	3.12 S	132.38 E
Werkel	52	51.09 N	9.18 E
Werkendam	48	51.49 N	4.53 E
Werl	48	51.33 N	7.54 E
Werlaburgdorf	50	52.04 N	10.31 E
Werl-Aspe	48	52.04 N	8.43 E
Werleshausen	52	51.19 N	9.54 E
Werlte	48	52.51 N	7.41 E
Wermelskirchen	52	51.08 N	7.13 E
Wermsdorf	50	51.17 N	12.56 E
Wern ≃	52	50.02 N	9.44 E
Wernadinga	156	18.07 S	139.58 E
Wernau	52	48.41 N	9.25 E
Wernberg	58	46.37 N	13.56 E
Werne ⬩[8]	253	51.29 N	7.18 E
Werne an der Lippe	48	51.40 N	7.38 E
Werneck, Bra.	246	22.13 S	43.19 W
Werneck, B.R.D.	52	49.59 N	10.05 E
Werneuchen	50	52.38 N	13.44 E
Wernigerode	50	51.50 N	10.47 E
Wernitz	254a	52.34 N	12.55 E
Wernsdorf	254a	52.22 N	13.43 E
Wernsdorfer See ⊜	254a	52.23 N	13.42 E
Wernshausen	50	50.43 N	10.21 E
Werra ≃	30	51.26 N	9.39 E
Werribee	159	37.54 S	144.40 E
Werribee ≃	159	37.59 S	144.41 E
Werribee Gorge National Park ♠	159	37.40 S	144.21 E
Werribee South	159	37.56 S	144.42 E
Werries	48	51.41 N	7.53 E
Werrimull	156	34.24 S	141.26 E
Werrington	264a	33.45 S	150.46 E
Werris Creek	156	31.21 S	150.39 E
Werschweiler	52	49.27 N	7.13 E
Wersen	48	52.18 N	7.56 E
Wersten ⬩[8]	253	51.11 N	6.49 E
Wertach	54	47.36 N	10.25 E
Wertach ≃	54	48.24 N	10.53 E
Wertheim	52	49.46 N	9.31 E
Werther, B.R.D.	48	52.04 N	8.24 E
Werther, D.D.R.	50	51.29 N	10.46 E
Wertingen	52	48.34 N	10.41 E
Wervershoof	48	52.44 N	5.09 E
Wervik	46	50.47 N	3.02 E
Wervin	252	53.15 N	2.52 W
Werwaru	154	8.13 S	128.11 E
Weschnitz ≃	52	49.43 N	8.24 E
Wesconnett	182	30.14 N	81.44 W
Weseke	48	51.54 N	6.51 E
Wesel	48	51.40 N	6.38 E
Wesel-Datteln-Kanal ☲	253	51.38 N	6.36 E
Wesenberg	50	53.17 N	12.58 E
Wesendahl	254a	52.36 N	13.49 E
Wesendorf	48	52.35 N	10.31 E
Weser ≃	48	53.32 N	8.34 E
Wesergebirge ⩘	48	52.15 N	9.10 E
Wesham	252	53.48 N	2.53 W
Wesickaman Creek ≃	275	39.44 N	74.43 W
Wesiri	102	7.35 S	126.38 E
Weskan	188	38.41 N	101.57 W
Weslaco	186	26.09 N	97.59 W
Weslemkoon Lake ⊜	202	45.02 N	77.25 W
Wesley, Dom.	230d	15.34 N	61.19 W
Wesley, Iowa, U.S.	180	43.05 N	93.59 W
Wesleyville, Newf., Can.	176	49.09 N	53.34 W
Wesleyville, Pa., U.S.	204	42.08 N	80.01 W
Wessel, Cape ≻	154	10.59 S	136.46 E
Wesseling	52	50.49 N	6.58 E
Wessel Islands II	154	11.30 S	136.25 E
Wesselsbron	148	27.50 S	25.23 E
Wesselsvlei	148	27.23 S	23.47 E
Wessington	188	44.27 N	98.42 W
Wessington Springs	188	44.05 N	98.34 W
Wessobrunn	58	47.52 N	11.01 E
Wesson	184	31.42 N	90.23 W
Wessum	48	52.05 N	6.58 E
West, Miss., U.S.	184	33.12 N	89.47 W
West, Tex., U.S.	212	31.48 N	97.06 W
West ≃, N.Y., U.S.	200	42.41 N	77.22 W
West ≃, Vt., U.S.	178	42.52 N	72.33 W
West Abington	197	42.08 N	70.59 W
Westacres	206	42.35 N	83.26 W
West Acton	197	42.29 N	71.28 W
West Alexander	204	40.06 N	80.31 W
West Alexandria	208	39.45 N	84.32 W
Westall, Point ≻	152	32.55 S	134.04 E
West Allen ≃	42	54.55 N	2.19 W
West Allis	206	43.01 N	88.00 W
Westalton	209	38.52 N	90.13 W
West Amityville	266	40.41 N	73.26 W
West Andover	197	42.39 N	71.10 W
West Athens	270	33.55 N	118.18 W
West Atlantic City	198	39.23 N	74.26 W
West Auckland	42	54.38 N	1.43 W
West Australian Basin ⊹[1]	12	20.00 S	100.00 E
West Babylon	200	40.43 N	73.22 W
Westbahnhof ⬩[5]	254b	48.11 N	16.20 E
West Baines ≃	154	15.36 S	129.58 E
West Bangor	200	40.52 N	75.14 W
Westbank	172	49.50 N	119.38 W
West Barnstable	197	41.42 N	70.23 W
West Barrington	197	41.45 N	71.21 W
West Bay, N.S., Can.	176	45.43 N	61.10 W
Westbay, Fla., U.S.	184	30.17 N	85.52 W
West Bay C, Fla., U.S.	184	30.16 N	85.47 W
West Bay C, Tex., U.S.	212	29.15 N	94.57 W
West Bay Shore	266	40.42 N	73.17 W
West Belmar	198	40.10 N	74.02 W
West Bend, Iowa, U.S.	188	42.57 N	94.27 W
West Bend, Wis., U.S.	180	43.25 N	88.11 W
West Bengal □[3]	114	24.00 N	88.00 E
West Berbice □[5]	236	6.10 N	57.45 W
West Bergholt	44	51.55 N	0.51 E
West-Berlin → Berlin (West), B.R.D.	254a	52.31 N	13.24 E
West Berlin, N.J., U.S.	198	39.49 N	74.57 W
West-Berlin □[3]	254a	52.30 N	13.15 E
West Bernard Creek ≃	212	29.23 N	95.58 W
Westbevern	48	52.01 N	7.47 E
West Bhāgīrath Plain ⊻	116	23.30 N	88.00 E
West Bijou Creek ≃	188	39.51 N	104.08 W
West Billerica	273	42.33 N	71.19 W
West Blocton	184	33.07 N	87.07 W
West Bloomfield	200	42.54 N	77.32 W
West Bolivar	204	40.23 N	79.10 W
Westborough	197	42.16 N	71.37 W
Westbourne	174	50.09 N	98.35 W
West Bow Creek ≃	188	42.46 N	97.08 W
West Boxford	273	42.42 N	71.04 W
West Boylston	197	42.22 N	71.47 W
West Bradenton	210	27.30 N	82.37 W
West Branch, Iowa, U.S.	180	41.40 N	91.20 W
West Branch, Mich., U.S.	180	44.17 N	84.14 W
West Branch Reservoir ⊜[1]	200	41.25 N	73.42 W
West Branch State Park ♠	204	41.07 N	81.05 W
Westbridge	172	49.10 N	118.59 W
West Bridgewater	197	42.01 N	71.00 W
West Bridgford	44	52.56 N	1.08 W
West Bristol	275	40.06 N	74.53 W
West Bromwich	44	52.31 N	1.56 W
Westbrook, Austl.	161a	27.36 S	151.52 E
Westbrook, Ont., Can.	202	44.16 N	76.38 W
Westbrook, Conn., U.S.	197	41.17 N	72.27 W
Westbrook, Maine, U.S.	178	43.41 N	70.21 W
Westbrook, Minn., U.S.	188	44.03 N	95.26 W
Westbrook, Tex., U.S.	186	32.21 N	101.01 W
West Brook ≃	266	41.04 N	74.18 W
West Brookfield	197	42.14 N	72.09 W
Westbrookville	200	41.30 N	74.34 W
West Burlington, Iowa, U.S.	180	40.49 N	91.09 W
West Burlington, N.Y., U.S.	200	42.42 N	75.11 W
Westbury, Eng., U.K.	44	51.16 N	2.11 W
Westbury, Eng., U.K.	44	52.41 N	2.57 W
Westbury, N.Y., U.S.	266	40.45 N	73.35 W
Westbury-on-Severn	44	51.50 N	2.24 W
West Butte ∧	192	48.57 N	111.32 W
Westby, Austl.	161b	35.30 S	147.25 E
Westby, Mont., U.S.	188	48.52 N	104.03 W
Westby, Wis., U.S.	180	43.39 N	90.51 W
West Cache Creek ≃	186	34.13 N	98.23 W
West Caicos I	228	21.39 N	72.28 W
West Calder	42	55.52 N	3.35 W
West Caldwell	266	40.51 N	74.17 W
West Cameron	198	40.45 N	76.58 W
West Camp	200	42.07 N	73.56 W
West Canada Creek ≃	200	43.01 N	74.58 W
West Cape ≻	162	45.54 S	166.26 E
West Cape Howe ≻	152	35.08 S	117.36 E
West Cape May	198	38.56 N	74.56 W
West Caroline Basin ⊹[1]	14	5.00 N	139.00 E
West Carrollton	208	39.40 N	84.15 W
West Carson	270	33.50 N	118.18 W
West Carthage	202	43.59 N	75.38 W
West Catfish Creek ≃	202	42.46 N	81.04 W
West Channel ≃[1]	170	68.51 N	136.10 W
Westchester, Ill., U.S.	206	41.51 N	87.53 W
West Chester, Pa., U.S.	275	39.58 N	75.36 W
Westchester, Va., U.S.	274c	38.51 N	77.16 W
Westchester □[6]	200	41.02 N	73.46 W
Westchester ⬩[8], Calif., U.S.	270	33.55 N	118.25 W
Westchester ⬩[8], N.Y., U.S.	266	40.51 N	73.52 W
West Chester Airport ⊠	275	39.59 N	75.35 W
Westchester County Airport ⊠	197	41.04 N	73.43 W
Westchester Creek ≃	266	40.48 N	73.51 W
West Chester State College ʊ[2]	275	39.57 N	75.36 W
West Chicago	206	41.53 N	88.12 W
West Clandon	250	51.15 N	0.30 W
West Clarksville	200	42.08 N	78.15 W
West Clear Creek ≃	190	34.34 N	111.51 W
West Cleddau ≃	44	51.46 N	4.54 W
Westcliff ⬩[8]	263d	26.11 S	28.02 E
Westcliffe	190	38.08 N	105.28 W
Westcliff-on-Sea	250	51.32 N	0.41 E
West College Corner	208	39.34 N	84.49 W
West Collingswood Heights	275	39.59 N	75.07 W
West Columbia, S.C., U.S.	182	34.00 N	81.04 W
West Columbia, Tex., U.S.	212	29.09 N	95.39 W
West Concord, Mass., U.S.	197	42.27 N	71.24 W
West Concord, Minn., U.S.	180	44.09 N	92.54 W
West Conshohocken	275	40.04 N	75.19 W
West Cote Blanche Bay C	184	29.40 N	91.45 W
Westcott	250	51.13 N	0.22 W
Westcott Cove C	266	41.02 N	73.30 W
West Covina	218	34.05 N	117.58 W
West Creek	198	39.38 N	74.18 W
West Creek ≃, Ind., U.S.	206	41.12 N	87.30 W
West Creek ≃, Pa., U.S.	204	41.30 N	78.15 W
Westdale, Ill., U.S.	268	41.56 N	87.55 W
Westdale, Mass., U.S.	273	42.01 N	70.59 W
Westdale, N.Y., U.S.	200	43.23 N	75.49 W
West Danby	200	42.19 N	76.32 W
West Davenport	200	42.27 N	74.58 W
West Deane Park ♠	265b	43.40 N	79.34 W
West Decatur	204	40.56 N	78.17 W
West Demerara □[5]	236	6.00 N	58.15 W
Westdene ⬩[8]	263d	26.11 S	27.59 E
West Dennis	197	41.40 N	70.10 W
West Derby ⬩[8]	252	53.26 N	2.54 W
West Derry	204	40.20 N	79.20 W
West Des Moines	180	41.35 N	93.43 W
West Dinājpur □[5]	114	25.30 N	88.20 E
West Ditch ☲	266	40.56 N	74.19 W
West Dolores ≃	190	37.35 N	108.21 W
West Don ≃	265b	43.43 N	79.20 W
West Drayton ⬩[8]	250	51.30 N	0.29 W
West Duffin Creek ≃	202	43.51 N	79.04 W
West Duxbury	273	42.03 N	70.47 W
West Eaton	200	42.51 N	75.39 W
Westecunk Creek ≃	198	39.37 N	74.16 W
West Edmeston	200	42.46 N	75.17 W
West Elk Mountains ⩘	190	38.40 N	107.15 W
West Elk Peak ∧	190	38.43 N	107.13 W
West Elkton	208	39.35 N	84.33 W
West Ellicott	204	42.05 N	79.16 W
West Elmira	200	42.05 N	76.51 W
West End, Ba.	228	26.41 N	78.58 W
West End, Eng., U.K.	250	51.44 N	0.04 W
West End, Eng., U.K.	250	51.20 N	0.38 W
West End, Ark., U.S.	184	34.13 N	92.03 W
West End, Ill., U.S.	206	42.17 N	89.09 W
West End, N.C., U.S.	182	35.15 N	79.33 W
West End, N.Y., U.S.	200	42.28 N	75.05 W
West End ⬩[8], Eng., U.K.	250	51.32 N	0.24 W
West End ⬩[8], Pa., U.S.	269b	40.27 N	80.02 W
Westende, Bel.	46	51.10 N	2.46 E
Westende, B.R.D.	253	51.25 N	7.24 E
Westendorf	58	47.26 N	12.13 E
Westenfeld ⬩[8]	253	51.28 N	7.09 E
Westenholz	48	51.45 N	8.28 E
Westenschouwen	48	51.41 N	3.42 E
Westerbauer ⬩[8]	253	51.20 N	7.23 E
Westerblokker	48	52.39 N	5.08 E
Westerbönen	253	51.36 N	7.46 E
Westerbork	48	52.51 N	6.37 E
Westerburg	52	50.33 N	7.58 E
Westercelle	48	52.36 N	10.05 E
Westeregeln	50	51.57 N	11.23 E
Westerham	44	51.16 N	0.05 E
Westerhausen	50	51.48 N	11.03 E
Westerholt	48	51.36 N	7.05 E
Westerholz ⬩[3]	253	51.32 N	7.28 E
Westerich □[9]	52	49.15 N	7.20 E
Westerkappeln	48	52.18 N	7.52 E
Westerland	30	54.54 N	8.18 E
Westerlo, Bel.	52	51.05 N	4.55 E
Westerlo, N.Y., U.S.	200	42.31 N	74.03 W
Westerly	197	41.22 N	71.50 W
Western	188	40.24 N	97.12 W
Western □[3]	140	7.45 N	4.00 E
Western □[4], Ghana	140	5.30 N	2.30 W
Western □[4], Kenya	144	0.30 N	34.35 E
Western (Area) □[4], S.L.	140	8.20 N	13.00 W
Western □[4], Zam.	142	16.00 S	24.00 E
Western □[5]	154	7.00 S	142.00 E
Western ≃	156	22.22 S	142.25 E
Western Australia □[3]	150	25.00 S	122.00 E
Western Branch ≃	274c	38.55 N	76.48 W
Western Canal ☲	216	39.28 N	121.35 W
Western Channel ⩂	88	34.40 N	129.00 E
Western Cove C	158b	35.43 S	137.38 E
Western Desert → al-Gharbīyah, Aṣ-Ṣaḥrā' ⬩[2]	130	27.00 N	27.00 E
Western Division □[5], Fiji	165g	18.00 S	177.30 E
Western Division □[5], Sol.is.	165e	8.00 S	157.00 E
Western Ghāts ⩘	112	14.00 N	75.00 E

≃ River	Fluss	Río	Rivière	Rio	
☲ Canal	Kanal	Canal	Canal	Canal	
⌞ Waterfall, Rapids	Wasserfall, Stromschnellen	Cascada, Rápidos	Chute d'eau, Rapides	Cascata, Rápidos	
⩂ Strait	Meeresstrasse	Estrecho	Détroit	Estreito	
C Bay, Gulf	Bucht, Golf	Bahía, Golfo	Baie, Golfe	Baía, Golfo	
⊜ Lake, Lakes	See, Seen	Lago, Lagos	Lac, Lacs	Lago, Lagos	
☷ Swamp	Sumpf	Pantano	Marais	Pântano	
❄ Ice Features, Glacier	Eis- und Gletscherformen	Accidentes Glaciales	Formes glaciaires	Acidentes Glaciares	
⍑ Other Hydrographic Features	Andere Hydrographische Objekte	Otros Elementos Hidrográficos	Autres données hydrographiques	Outros Elementos Hidrográficos	

⊹ Submarine Features	Untermeerische Objekte	Accidentes Submarinos	Formes de relief sous-marin	Acidentes Submarinos
□ Political Unit	Politische Einheit	Unidad Politica	Entité politique	Unidade Política
ʊ Cultural Institution	Kulturelle Institution	Institución Cultural	Institution culturelle	Instituição Cultural
⊥ Historical Site	Historische Stätte	Sitio Histórico	Site historique	Sitio Histórico
♠ Recreational Site	Erholungs- und Ferienort	Sitio de Recreo	Centre de loisirs	Sítio de Lazer
⊠ Airport	Flughafen	Aeropuerto	Aéroport	Aeroporto
■ Military Installation	Militäranlage	Instalación Militar	Installation militaire	Instalação Militar
⬩ Miscellaneous	Verschiedenes	Misceláneo	Divers	Miscelânea

ENGLISH — Name | Page | Lat.°′ | Long.°′
DEUTSCH — Name | Seite | Breite°′ | Länge°′ E=Ost

Western Highlands □[5] 154 5.30 S 143.30 E
Western Isles Islands □[4] 28 57.40 N 7.00 W
Westernport 178 39.29 N 79.03 W
Western Port C 159 38.25 S 145.10 E
Western Sahara □[2] 124
138 24.30 N 13.00 W
Western Samoa □[1] 14
165a 13.55 S 172.00 W
Western Sayans → Zapadnyj Sajan ⛰ 62 53.00 N 94.00 E
Western Shore 176 44.32 N 64.19 W
Western Springs 268 41.47 N 87.53 W
Westernville 200 43.18 N 75.23 W
Westerschelde C[1] 48 51.25 N 3.45 E
Westerstede 48 53.15 N 7.55 E
Westervelt 209 39.29 N 88.52 W
Westerville 204 40.08 N 82.56 W
Westerwald ⛰ 52 50.40 N 7.55 E
West European Basin ✧[1] 10 46.00 N 15.00 W
West Exeter 200 42.48 N 75.09 W
West Fairview 198 40.17 N 76.55 W
Westfalen ◆[1] 48 51.50 N 7.30 E
Westfalenhalle ʊ 253 51.30 N 7.27 E
Westfalenpark ♠ 253 51.30 N 7.28 E
West Falkland I 244 51.50 S 60.00 W
West Falls 200 42.42 N 78.41 W
West Falmouth 197 41.36 N 70.38 W
West Farleigh 250 51.15 N 0.27 E
West Farmington, Maine, U.S. 178 44.40 N 70.10 W
West Farmington, Ohio, U.S. 204 41.23 N 80.59 W
Westfield, Eng., U.K. 44 50.55 N 0.35 E
Westfield, Ill., U.S. 184 39.27 N 88.01 W
Westfield, Ind., U.S. 208 40.02 N 86.08 W
Westfield, Mass., U.S. 197 42.08 N 72.45 W
Westfield, N.J., U.S. 200 40.39 N 74.21 W
Westfield, N.Y., U.S. 204 42.19 N 79.35 W
Westfield, Pa., U.S. 200 41.55 N 77.32 W
Westfield, Tex., U.S. 212 30.01 N 95.24 W
Westfield, Wis., U.S. 180 43.53 N 89.30 W
Westfield ≃ 197 42.05 N 72.35 W
Westfield, Middle Branch ≃ 197 42.16 N 72.52 W
Westfield, West Branch ≃ 197 42.13 N 72.52 W
Westfield Center 204 41.06 N 81.56 W
West Fiord C[2] 166 76.02 N 90.00 W
Westford, Mass., U.S. 273 42.35 N 71.26 W
Westford, N.Y., U.S. 200 42.39 N 74.48 W
West Foxboro 273 42.05 N 71.17 W
West Frankfort 184 37.54 N 88.55 W
West Friesland ◆[1] 48 52.45 N 4.50 E
West Frisian Islands → Waddeneilanden II 48 53.26 N 5.30 E
West Fulton 200 42.34 N 74.28 W
Westgate, Austl. 156 26.35 S 146.12 E
Westgate, Fla., U.S. 210 26.47 N 80.06 W
Westgate, Mich., U.S. 206 43.03 N 85.42 W
Westgate ◆[9] 269a 41.27 N 81.51 W
Westgate-on-Sea 44 51.23 N 1.21 E
West Genesee Terrace 200 43.03 N 76.16 W
West Germany → Germany, Federal Republic Of □[1] 30 51.00 N 9.00 E
West-Ghats → Western Ghāts ⛰ 112 14.00 N 75.00 E
West Gilgo Beach 266 40.37 N 73.25 W
West Glacier 192 48.30 N 113.59 W
West Glamorgan □[6] 44 51.35 N 3.35 W
West Glens Falls 200 43.18 N 73.43 W
West Glenville 200 42.56 N 74.04 W
West Goshen 197 41.50 N 73.15 W
West Granby 197 41.57 N 72.50 W
West Groton 197 42.36 N 71.38 W
West Grove 198 39.49 N 75.50 W
Westham 198 37.35 N 77.33 W
West Ham ◆[8] 250 51.31 N 0.01 E
West Hamburg 198 40.33 N 76.00 W
West Ham Football Club ♠ 250 51.32 N 0.02 E
Westham Island I 214 49.05 N 123.10 W
West Hamlin 178 38.17 N 82.12 W
Westhampton, N.Y., U.S. 197 40.49 N 72.39 W
Westhampton, Va., U.S. 274c 38.54 N 77.11 W
West Hanningfield 250 51.40 N 0.30 E
West Hanover 273 42.07 N 70.53 W
West Harbour 162 45.51 S 170.35 E
West Harrison 208 39.16 N 84.50 W
West Hartford 197 41.46 N 72.45 W
West Hartland 197 42.00 N 72.58 W
Westhausen 52 48.53 N 10.11 E
Westhaven, Calif., U.S. 194 41.03 N 124.06 W
West Haven, Conn., U.S. 197 41.16 N 72.57 W
Westhaven, Ill., U.S. 268 41.35 N 87.51 W
West Haverstraw 200 41.12 N 74.00 W
West Hazleton 200 40.58 N 76.00 W
Westhead 252 53.34 N 2.51 W
West Hebron 200 43.14 N 73.22 W
West Heidelberg 264b 37.45 S 145.02 E
Westheim 52 49.03 N 9.44 E
West Helena 184 34.33 N 90.39 W
Westhemmerde 253 51.33 N 7.47 E
West Hempstead 266 40.42 N 73.39 W
West Henrietta 200 43.02 N 77.40 W
West Hickory 204 41.34 N 79.25 W
West Highland 271 42.38 N 83.39 W
West Highland Creek ≃ 265b 43.46 N 79.08 W
West Hill ◆[8] 265b 43.46 N 79.11 W
West Hills 218 34.27 N 119.17 W
Westhofen 253 51.25 N 7.31 E
Westhoff 212 29.12 N 97.28 W
Westhoffen 54 48.36 N 7.26 E
West Hollywood, Calif., U.S. 218 34.05 N 118.24 W
West Hollywood, Fla., U.S. 210 26.01 N 80.10 W
Westholme 214 49.52 N 123.42 W
West Homestead 269b 40.24 N 79.55 W
Westhope, N. Dak., U.S. 188 48.55 N 101.01 W
Westhope, Ohio, U.S. 206 41.18 N 83.57 W
West Horndon 250 51.34 N 0.21 E
West Horsley 250 51.16 N 0.27 W
Westhoughton 252 53.33 N 2.32 W
West Hoxton 264a 33.55 S 150.49 E
West Humber ≃ 202 43.44 N 79.33 W
West Humble 250 51.15 N 0.20 W
West Huntington 266 40.51 N 73.27 W
West Hurley 200 42.00 N 74.06 W
Westhuyzen 148 27.30 S 25.27 E
West Hyde 250 51.37 N 0.30 W
West Ice Shelf ⛝ 9 67.00 S 85.00 E
Westick 253 51.35 N 7.38 E
Westig 253 51.22 N 7.45 E
West-Indian Ridge ✧[3] 6 26.00 S 50.00 E
West Indies II 220 19.00 N 70.00 W
West Irian → Irian Jaya □[4] 154 5.00 S 138.00 E
West Island I, Austl. 154 15.36 S 136.34 E
West Island I, Mass., U.S. 197 41.36 N 70.50 W
West Islip 200 40.42 N 73.19 W
West Jan Mayen Ridge ✧[3] 10 71.00 N 15.00 W
West Jefferson, N.C., U.S. 182 36.24 N 81.30 W
West Jefferson, Ohio, U.S. 208 39.57 N 83.16 W
Westkapelle, Bel. 46 51.19 N 3.18 E
Westkapelle, Ned. 48 51.32 N 3.27 E
West Keansburg 266 40.27 N 74.09 W
West Kettle ≃ 172 49.07 N 119.00 W
West Kilbride 42 55.42 N 4.51 W
West Kildonan 174 49.56 N 97.07 W
West Kill 200 42.13 N 74.31 W
West Kingsdown 44 51.21 N 0.17 E
West Kingston 197 41.29 N 71.34 W
West Kirby 42 53.22 N 3.10 W
Westkirchen 48 51.53 N 8.02 E
West Kittanning 204 40.49 N 79.32 W
West Lafayette, Ind., U.S. 206 40.27 N 86.55 W
West Lafayette, Ohio, U.S. 204 40.17 N 81.45 W
Westlake, La., U.S. 184 30.15 N 93.15 W
Westlake, Ohio, U.S. 204 41.27 N 81.55 W
Westlake, Tex., U.S. 212 32.59 N 97.12 W
West Lake □[4] 144 2.00 S 31.30 E
West Lake ◎, Ont., Can. 202 43.56 N 77.17 W
West Lake ◎, Fla., U.S. 210 25.12 N 80.49 W
West Lake ◎, N.J., U.S. 266 40.58 N 74.22 W
West Lamma Channel ⋓ 261d 22.13 N 114.04 E
West Lancashire □[8] 252 53.35 N 2.50 W
Westland, Mich., U.S. 206 42.19 N 83.23 W
Westland, Pa., U.S. 204 40.17 N 80.16 W
Westland Center ◆[9] 271 42.20 N 83.23 W
Westland National Park ♠ 162 43.30 S 170.10 E
Westlands 197 42.37 N 71.20 W
West Lawn 274c 38.52 N 77.11 W
West Lebanon, Ind., U.S. 206 40.16 N 87.23 W
West Lebanon, Pa., U.S. 204 40.35 N 79.22 W
West Leechburg 204 40.37 N 79.37 W
Westleigh, S. Afr. 148 27.31 S 27.21 E
Westleigh, Eng., U.K. 252 53.30 N 2.31 W
West Leipsic 206 41.07 N 84.00 W
Westley 216 37.33 N 121.12 W
West Leyden 202 43.28 N 75.28 W
West Liberty, Iowa, U.S. 180 41.34 N 91.16 W
West Liberty, Ky., U.S. 182 37.55 N 83.16 W
West Liberty, Ohio, U.S. 206 40.15 N 83.46 W
West Liberty, Pa., U.S. 204 41.00 N 80.03 W
West Liberty, W. Va., U.S. 204 40.10 N 80.36 W
West Liberty ◆[8] 269b 40.24 N 80.01 W
Westliche Sahara → Western Sahara □[2] 138 24.30 N 13.00 W
Westliche Sierra Madre → Madre Occidental, Sierra ⛰ 222 25.00 N 105.00 W
Westline 204 41.47 N 78.46 W
West Linn 214 45.21 N 122.36 W
West Linton 42 55.46 N 3.22 W
West Little Owyhee ≃ 192 42.28 N 117.15 W
West Loch Tarbert C 42 55.48 N 5.33 W
Westlock 172 54.09 N 113.52 W
West Looe 44 50.21 N 4.28 W
West Lorne 204 42.36 N 81.36 W
West Los Angeles ◆[8] 270 34.03 N 118.28 W
West Lubec 178 44.49 N 67.05 W
West Lulworth 44 50.38 N 2.15 W
West Lunga ≃ 144 13.06 S 24.39 E
Westmalle 52 51.18 N 4.41 E
West Malling 44 51.18 N 0.25 E
West Manayunk 275 40.01 N 75.14 W
West Manchester 208 39.54 N 84.38 W
West Mansfield, Mass., U.S. 197 41.59 N 71.15 W
West Mansfield, Ohio, U.S. 206 40.24 N 83.33 W
West Mayfield 204 40.47 N 80.20 W
West Meadowview 206 41.08 N 87.52 W
Westmeath □[6] 28 53.30 N 7.30 W
West Medway 197 42.09 N 71.26 W
West Melbourne 210 28.04 N 80.38 W
West Memphis 184 35.08 N 90.11 W
West Mengo □[5] 144 0.30 N 32.10 E
West Meon 44 51.01 N 1.05 W
Westmere 200 42.42 N 73.52 W
West Mersea 44 51.47 N 0.55 E
West Miami 210 25.45 N 80.18 W
West Middlesex 204 41.10 N 80.27 W
West Middletown 204 40.15 N 80.25 W
West Midlands □[6] 44 52.30 N 2.00 W
West Mifflin 204 40.22 N 79.52 W
West Milford 200 41.08 N 74.22 W
West Milton, Ohio, U.S. 208 39.58 N 84.20 W
West Milton, Pa., U.S. 200 41.01 N 76.52 W
West Milwaukee 206 42.57 N 87.58 W
West Mineola 212 32.41 N 95.31 W
Westminster, Calif., U.S. 218 33.46 N 118.01 W
Westminster, Colo., U.S. 190 39.50 N 105.02 W
Westminster, Md., U.S. 178 39.35 N 77.00 W
Westminster, Ohio, U.S. 206 40.42 N 83.58 W
Westminster, S.C., U.S. 182 34.40 N 83.06 W
Westminster Abbey ʊ[1] 250 51.30 N 0.07 W
Westminster Mall ◆[9] 270 33.45 N 118.01 W
West Modesto 216 37.37 N 121.02 W
West Monroe 184 32.31 N 92.09 W
Westmont, Calif., U.S. 270 33.56 N 118.18 W
Westmont, Ill., U.S. 268 41.48 N 87.57 W
Westmont, N.J., U.S. 275 39.55 N 75.03 W
Westmont, Pa., U.S. 204 40.19 N 78.57 W
West Monterey 204 41.03 N 79.39 W
West Montreal ≃ 180 47.56 N 80.39 W
West Moors 44 50.49 N 1.55 W
Westmoreland, Kans., U.S. 188 39.24 N 96.25 W
Westmoreland, N.Y., U.S. 200 43.07 N 75.24 W
Westmoreland, Tenn., U.S. 184 36.34 N 86.15 W
Westmoreland, Va., U.S. 198 38.04 N 76.34 W
Westmoreland □[6], Pa., U.S. 204 40.18 N 79.33 W
Westmoreland □[6], Va., U.S. 198 38.10 N 76.50 W
Westmoreland City 204 40.20 N 79.41 W
Westmoreland State Park ♠ 198 38.09 N 76.50 W
Westmorland 194 33.02 N 115.37 W
Westmount 196 45.29 N 73.36 W
West Mountain Λ 178 43.51 N 74.43 W
West Mud Creek ≃ 212 32.07 N 95.10 W
West Mustang Creek ≃ 212 29.04 N 96.26 W
West Nab Λ 252 53.35 N 1.53 W
West Nanticoke 200 40.13 N 76.01 W
West New Britain □[5] 154 5.45 S 149.30 E
West Newbury 197 42.48 N 71.00 W
West Newton, Mass., U.S. 273 42.21 N 71.14 W
West Newton, Pa., U.S. 204 40.13 N 79.46 W
West New York 266 40.47 N 74.04 W
West Nicholson 144 21.06 S 29.25 E
West Nile □[5] 144 3.00 N 31.10 E
West Nishnabotna ≃ 188 40.39 N 95.37 W
West Nodaway ≃ 184 40.38 N 95.01 W
West Norriton 198 40.08 N 75.22 W
West Norwood ◆[8] 250 51.26 N 0.06 W
West Novaya Zemlya Trough ✧[1] 10 73.30 N 50.00 E
West Nueces ≃ 186 29.16 N 99.56 W
West Nyack 200 41.06 N 73.58 W
West Okaw ≃ 209 39.32 N 88.42 W
Weston, Austl. 160 32.49 S 151.28 E
Weston, Malay. 102 5.13 N 115.36 E
Weston, Eng., U.K. 252 53.19 N 2.44 W
Weston, Colo., U.S. 190 37.08 N 104.48 W
Weston, Conn., U.S. 197 41.12 N 73.22 W
Weston, Idaho, U.S. 192 42.02 N 111.59 W
Weston, Mass., U.S. 197 42.22 N 71.18 W
Weston, Mich., U.S. 206 41.46 N 84.06 W
Weston, Mo., U.S. 184 39.25 N 94.54 W
Weston, Nebr., U.S. 188 41.12 N 96.45 W
Weston, Ohio, U.S. 206 41.21 N 83.48 W
Weston, Oreg., U.S. 192 45.49 N 118.26 W
Weston, Pa., U.S. 200 40.57 N 76.09 W
Weston, W. Va., U.S. 178 39.02 N 80.28 W
Weston □[8] 265b 43.43 N 79.31 W
Westonaria 148 26.19 S 27.41 E
West Oneonta 200 42.28 N 75.07 W
Westönnen 48 51.33 N 7.58 E
Weston Reservoir ◎[1] 273 42.21 N 71.18 W
Westons Mill Pond ◎ 266 40.28 N 74.25 W
Westons Mills 200 42.04 N 78.23 W
Weston-super-Mare 44 51.21 N 2.59 W
Weston upon Trent 44 52.45 N 2.02 W
West Orange, N.J., U.S. 266 40.47 N 74.14 W
West Orange, Tex., U.S. 184 30.05 N 93.46 W
Westover, Md., U.S. 198 38.07 N 75.42 W
Westover, Pa., U.S. 204 40.45 N 78.40 W
Westover, W. Va., U.S. 178 39.38 N 79.58 W
Westover Air Force Base ■ 197 42.12 N 72.33 W
West Palm Beach 210 26.43 N 80.04 W
West Palm Beach Canal ⋍ 210 26.38 N 80.03 W
West Paris 178 44.20 N 70.35 W
West Park 200 41.48 N 73.58 W
West Paterson 266 40.54 N 74.12 W
West Pawlet 200 43.21 N 73.15 W
West Peckham 250 51.15 N 0.22 E
West Pembroke 178 44.57 N 67.11 W
West Pensacola 184 30.27 N 87.15 W
West Petersburg 170 56.49 N 132.57 W
Westphalia, Kans., U.S. 188 38.11 N 95.29 W
Westphalia, Mich., U.S. 206 42.56 N 84.48 W
Westphalia, Mo., U.S. 209 38.26 N 92.00 W
West Pittsburg, Calif., U.S. 216 38.02 N 121.54 W
West Pittsburg, Pa., U.S. 204 40.56 N 80.22 W
West Pittston 200 41.20 N 75.49 W
West Plains 184 36.44 N 91.51 W
West Point, Calif., U.S. 216 38.24 N 120.32 W
West Point, Ga., U.S. 182 32.52 N 85.10 W
Westpoint, Ind., U.S. 206 40.21 N 87.03 W
West Point, Iowa, U.S. 180 40.43 N 91.27 W
West Point, Ky., U.S. 184 37.59 N 85.57 W
West Point, Miss., U.S. 184 33.36 N 88.39 W
West Point, Nebr., U.S. 188 41.51 N 96.43 W
West Point, N.Y., U.S. 200 41.23 N 73.57 W
West Point, Ohio, U.S. 204 40.43 N 80.42 W
West Point, Pa., U.S. 275 40.12 N 75.18 W
West Point, Va., U.S. 198 37.32 N 76.48 W
West Point Λ 170 64.57 N 144.40 W
West Point ≻, P.E.I., Can. 176 46.37 N 64.25 W
West Point ≻, Jam. 231q 18.15 N 78.22 W
West Point ≻, N. Heb. 165f 16.30 S 167.25 E
West Pond ◎ 266 40.53 N 73.38 W
Westport, Newf., Can. 176 49.47 N 56.38 W
Westport, N.S., Can. 176 44.16 N 66.21 W
Westport, Ont., Can. 202 44.41 N 76.26 W
Westport, Eire 28 53.48 N 9.32 W
Westport, N.Z. 162 41.45 S 171.36 E
Westport, Conn., U.S. 197 41.09 N 73.22 W
Westport, Ind., U.S. 208 39.11 N 85.34 W
Westport, Ky., U.S. 208 38.29 N 85.29 W
Westport, Mass., U.S. 197 41.37 N 71.04 W
Westport, Oreg., U.S. 214 46.10 N 123.23 W
Westport, Pa., U.S. 204 41.18 N 77.51 W
Westport, Wash., U.S. 214 46.53 N 124.06 W
Westport ≃ 197 41.32 N 71.04 W
West Portland 214 45.25 N 122.45 W
West Portland Park 214 45.21 N 122.37 W
Westport Point 197 41.31 N 71.05 W
West Portsmouth 208 38.46 N 83.02 W
West Prairie ≃ 172 55.30 N 116.31 W
West Puente Valley 270 34.04 N 117.59 W
West Pullman ◆[8] 268 41.41 N 87.39 W
Westpunt ≻ 231s 12.37 N 70.03 W
West Pymble 264a 33.46 S 151.08 E
West Quoddy Head ≻ 176 44.49 N 66.57 W
West Rand 263d 26.07 S 27.45 E
Westray Firth ⋓ 28 59.15 N 3.00 W
West Redding 197 41.20 N 73.26 W
Westrem 46 50.58 N 3.52 E
Westrhauderfehn 48 53.08 N 7.34 E
West Richfield 204 41.14 N 81.39 W
West Richland 192 46.18 N 119.20 W
West River C 198 38.52 N 76.31 W
West Road ≃ 172 53.19 N 122.52 W
West Rosebud Creek ≃ 192 45.29 N 109.27 W
West Roxbury ◆[8] 273 42.17 N 71.09 W
West Rupert 200 43.14 N 73.15 W
West Rutland 178 43.36 N 73.03 W
West Ryde 264a 33.48 S 151.05 E
West Sacramento 216 38.34 N 121.32 W
West Saint Mary's ≃ 176 45.15 N 62.04 W
West Saint Modeste 176 51.36 N 56.42 W
West Salem, Ill., U.S. 184 38.31 N 88.01 W
West Salem, Ohio, U.S. 204 40.58 N 82.06 W
West Salem, Wis., U.S. 180 43.54 N 91.05 W
West Salt Creek ≃ 190 39.13 N 108.54 W
Westsamoa → Western Samoa □[1] 165a 13.55 S 172.00 W
West Sand Lake 200 42.39 N 73.37 W
West Saugerties 200 42.07 N 74.03 W
West Sayville 266 40.44 N 73.06 W
West Sayville County Park ♠ 266 40.43 N 73.06 W
West Scenic Park 210 27.55 N 81.39 W
West Scotia Basin ✧[1] 9 57.00 S 53.00 W
West Seneca 200 42.50 N 78.45 W
West Sepik □[5] 154 4.00 S 141.30 E
West Shoal Lake ◎ 174 50.20 N 97.41 W
West Siberian Plain → Zapadno-Sibirskaja Nizmennost' ≚ 62 60.00 N 75.00 E
Westsibirisches Flachland → Zapadno-Sibirskaja Nizmennost' ≚ 62 60.00 N 75.00 E
West Side Canal ⋍ 216 35.19 N 119.23 W
West Side Tennis Club ♠ 266 40.43 N 73.51 W
West Simsbury 197 41.52 N 72.51 W
West Sister Island I 156 39.42 S 147.55 E
West Slope 214 45.31 N 122.46 W
West Spanish Peak Λ 190 37.23 N 104.59 W
West Springfield, Mass., U.S. 197 42.06 N 72.38 W
West Springfield, Pa., U.S. 204 41.57 N 80.29 W
West Springfield, Va., U.S. 198 38.47 N 77.13 W
West Stewartstown 196 44.59 N 71.32 W
West Stockbridge 197 42.20 N 73.22 W
West Stony Creek ≃ 200 43.15 N 74.13 W
West Suffield 197 41.59 N 72.42 W
West Sunbury 204 41.00 N 79.54 W
West Sussex □[6] 44 50.55 N 0.35 W
West Swanzey 197 42.52 N 72.20 W
West Terre Haute 184 39.28 N 87.27 W
West-Terschelling 48 53.21 N 5.13 E
West Thompson Lake ◎[1] 197 41.57 N 71.54 W
West Thurrock 250 51.29 N 0.16 E
West Tiana 197 40.52 N 72.33 W
West Tilbury 250 51.29 N 0.24 E
West Tisbury 197 41.23 N 70.41 W
West Toodyay 158a 31.33 S 116.27 E
West Torrens 158b 34.56 S 138.32 E
Westtown, N.Y., U.S. 200 41.20 N 74.32 W
Westtown, Pa., U.S. 275 39.56 N 75.33 W
West Townsend 197 42.41 N 71.44 W
West Turffontein ◆[8] 263d 26.16 S 28.02 E
West Twin ≃ 180 44.08 N 87.34 W
West Union, Iowa, U.S. 180 42.57 N 91.49 W
West Union, Ohio, U.S. 208 38.48 N 83.32 W
West Union, W. Va., U.S. 178 39.18 N 80.47 W
West Union Creek ≃ 272 37.25 N 122.16 W
West Unity 206 41.35 N 84.26 W
West University Place 212 29.43 N 95.26 W
West Upton 197 42.10 N 71.37 W
Westvale 200 43.02 N 76.13 W
West Valley, Mont., U.S. 192 46.08 N 113.01 W
West Valley, N.Y., U.S. 200 42.24 N 78.37 W
West Vancouver 172 49.22 N 123.12 W
West View 204 40.31 N 80.02 W
West View Amusement Park ♠ 269b 40.31 N 80.02 W
Westview Heights 197 41.33 N 73.05 W
Westville, N.S., Can. 176 45.34 N 62.43 W
Westville, Ind., U.S. 206 41.33 N 86.54 W
Westville, N.H., U.S. 197 42.49 N 71.07 W
Westville, N.J., U.S. 275 39.52 N 75.08 W
Westville, Ohio, U.S. 208 40.07 N 83.51 W
Westville, Okla., U.S. 184 35.59 N 94.34 W
Westville, Pa., U.S. 204 41.13 N 78.50 W
Westville Center 196 44.57 N 74.24 W
Westville Grove 275 39.51 N 75.07 W
Westville Lake ◎[1] 197 42.05 N 72.05 W
Westville Oaks 275 39.51 N 75.08 W
West Virginia □[3] 168
178 38.45 N 80.30 W
West-Vlaanderen □[4] 46 51.00 N 3.00 E
West Walker ≃ 216 38.53 N 119.10 W
West Wallsend 160 32.54 S 151.35 E
Westward H9o 44 51.02 N 4.15 W
West Wareham 197 41.47 N 70.46 W
West Warren 197 42.13 N 72.14 W
West Warwick 197 41.42 N 71.32 W
West Webster 200 43.12 N 77.30 W
Westwego 184 29.55 N 90.09 W
West Wellow 44 50.58 N 1.35 W
West Whittier 270 33.59 N 118.04 W
West Wickham ◆[8] 250 51.22 N 0.01 W
West Willington 197 41.53 N 72.18 W
West Willow, Mich., U.S. 206
271 42.14 N 83.34 W
West Windsor 200 42.06 N 74.46 W
West Winfield, N.Y., U.S. 200 42.53 N 75.12 W
West Winfield, Pa., U.S. 204 40.48 N 79.42 W
Westwold 172 50.28 N 119.45 W
Westwood, Calif., U.S. 194 40.18 N 121.00 W
Westwood, Ind., U.S. 208 39.55 N 85.25 W
Westwood, Mass., U.S. 197 42.12 N 71.14 W
Westwood, Mich., U.S. 206 42.19 N 85.38 W
Westwood, N.J., U.S. 200 41.59 N 74.02 W
Westwood, Pa., U.S. 204 40.18 N 78.56 W
Westwood ◆[8] 270 34.04 N 118.27 W
Westwood Lakes 210 25.44 N 80.22 W
Westworth Village 212 32.45 N 97.25 W
West Wyalong 156 33.55 S 147.13 E
West Wycombe 44 51.39 N 0.49 W
West Yarmouth 197 41.39 N 70.15 W
West Yegua Creek ≃ 212 30.20 N 96.52 W
West Yellow Creek ≃ 184 39.38 N 93.04 W
West Yellowstone 192 44.30 N 111.05 W
West York 198 39.57 N 76.46 W
West Yorkshire □[6], Eng., U.K. 42 53.45 N 1.40 W
West Yorkshire □[6], Eng., U.K. 252 53.43 N 1.58 W
Wetan, Pulau I 154 7.54 S 129.32 E
Wetar, Pulau I 102 7.48 S 126.18 E
Wetaskiwin 172 52.58 N 113.22 W
Wete 144 5.04 S 39.43 E
Wethau 50 51.08 N 11.52 E
Wetherby 42 53.56 N 1.23 W
Wetherill Park 264a 33.51 S 150.54 E
Wethersfield 197 41.43 N 72.40 W
Wethmar 253 51.37 N 7.33 E
Wetiko Hills ⛰[2] 174 54.30 N 92.20 W
Wetluga → Vetluga ≃ 70 56.18 N 46.24 E
Wetmore 188 39.38 N 95.49 W
Wet Mountains ⛰ 190 38.00 N 105.10 W
Weto 142 7.57 N 7.50 E
Wetten 48 51.34 N 6.17 E
Wetter, B.R.D. 52 51.23 N 7.23 E
Wetter, B.R.D. 52 50.54 N 8.43 E
Wetter ≃ 52 50.18 N 8.49 E
Wetterau □[9] 52 50.15 N 8.50 E
Wetteren 46 51.00 N 3.53 E
Wetterhorn Λ 54 46.39 N 8.08 E
Wetterstein Gebirge ⛰ 58 47.25 N 11.05 E
Wettigan 100 18.57 N 95.21 E
Wettin 50 51.35 N 11.48 E
Wettingen 54 47.28 N 8.19 E
Wettringen 48 52.12 N 7.19 E
Wetumka 186 35.14 N 96.15 W
Wetumpka 184 32.27 N 86.13 W
Wetwang 42 54.01 N 0.34 W
Wetzikon 54 47.19 N 8.47 E
Wetzlar 52 50.33 N 8.29 E
Wetzstein Λ[2] 50 50.27 N 11.27 E
Wevelgem 46 50.48 N 3.10 E
Wevelinghoven 52 51.06 N 6.37 E
Wewahitchka 182 30.07 N 85.12 W
Wewak 154 3.35 S 143.40 E
Wewelsfleth 48 53.50 N 9.24 E
Wewer 48 51.41 N 8.42 E
Wewoka 186 35.09 N 96.30 W
Wexford, Eire 28 52.20 N 6.27 W
Wexford, Pa., U.S. 204 40.38 N 80.03 W
Wexford □[6] 28 52.20 N 6.40 W
Wexford ◆[8] 265b 43.45 N 79.18 W
Wexford Harbour C 28 52.20 N 6.55 W
Wey ≃ 44 51.23 N 0.28 W
Weyakwin Lake ◎ 174 54.30 N 106.00 W
Weyanoke 274c 38.48 N 77.09 W
Weyarn 58 47.51 N 11.48 E
Weyauwega 180 44.19 N 88.56 W
Weybridge 44 51.23 N 0.28 W
Weyburn 174 49.41 N 103.52 W
Weyer ◆[8] 253 51.10 N 7.01 E
Weyer Markt 30 47.52 N 14.41 E
Weyersheim 52 48.43 N 7.48 E
Weyhausen 48 52.47 N 10.23 E
Weyib ≃ 134 4.11 N 42.09 E
Weymouth, N.S., Can. 176 44.25 N 66.00 W
Weymouth, Eng., U.K. 44 50.36 N 2.28 W
Weymouth, Mass., U.S. 197 42.13 N 70.58 W
Weymouth, N.J., U.S. 198 39.31 N 74.47 W
Weymouth Back ≃ 273 42.15 N 70.55 W
Weymouth Fore ≃ 273 42.16 N 70.56 W
Weymouth Great Pond ◎ 273 42.12 N 71.02 W
Wezemaal 52 50.57 N 4.46 E
Wezep 48 52.27 N 6.00 E
Whakatane 162 37.58 S 177.00 E
Whakatane ≃ 162 37.57 S 177.00 E
Whalan 264a 33.45 S 150.49 E
Whale Creek ≃ 266 40.27 N 74.13 W
Whales, Bay of C 9 78.30 S 164.20 W
Whaley Bridge 42 53.20 N 1.59 W
Whaley Lake 200 41.33 N 73.40 W
Whaleysville 198 38.24 N 75.18 W
Whaleyville 198 36.37 N 76.41 W
Whalley 42 53.50 N 2.24 W
Whalom 197 42.34 N 71.45 W
Whalsay I 28 60.22 N 0.59 W
Whangaehu ≃ 162 40.03 S 175.06 E
Whangamata 162 37.12 S 175.52 E
Whangamomona 162 39.09 S 174.44 E
Whangara 162 38.34 S 178.13 E
Whangarei 162 35.43 S 174.19 E
Whangaruru Harbour C 162 35.22 S 174.21 E
Whaplode 44 52.48 N 0.02 W
Wharfe ≃ 42 53.51 N 1.07 W
Wharfedale V 42 54.01 N 1.56 W
Wharles 252 53.49 N 2.50 W
Wharton, N.J., U.S. 200 40.54 N 74.35 W
Wharton, Ohio, U.S. 204 40.52 N 83.21 W
Wharton, Tex., U.S. 212 29.19 N 96.06 W
Wharton, W. Va., U.S. 178 37.55 N 81.40 W
Wharton □[6] 212 29.17 N 96.13 W
Wharton Lake ◎ 166 64.00 N 99.55 W
Wharton State Forest ♠ 275 39.45 N 74.40 W
Whataroa 162 43.17 S 170.25 E
Whatatutu 162 38.23 S 177.50 E
What Cheer 180 41.24 N 92.21 W
Whatcom □[6] 214 48.48 N 121.59 W
Whatcom, Lake ◎ 214 48.43 N 122.20 W
Whately 197 42.26 N 72.38 W
Whatley 184 31.39 N 87.42 W
Whatshan Lake ◎ 172 50.00 N 118.03 W
Whauphill 42 54.49 N 4.29 W
Wheao ≃ 162 38.34 S 176.39 E
Wheatfield 206 41.12 N 87.03 W
Wheathampstead 44 51.49 N 0.17 W
Wheatland, Calif., U.S. 216 39.01 N 121.25 W
Wheatland, Iowa, U.S. 180 41.50 N 90.51 W
Wheatland, Pa., U.S. 204 41.12 N 80.28 W
Wheatland, Wyo., U.S. 190 42.03 N 104.57 W
Wheatland Hills 198 40.02 N 76.21 W
Wheatland Reservoir ◎[1] 190 41.52 N 105.36 W
Wheatley 204 42.06 N 82.27 W
Wheatley Hill 42 54.45 N 1.23 W
Wheaton, Ill., U.S. 206 41.52 N 88.06 W
Wheaton, Md., U.S. 274c 39.03 N 77.03 W
Wheaton, Minn., U.S. 188 45.48 N 96.30 W
Wheaton Plaza ◆[9] 274c 39.02 N 77.03 W
Wheaton Regional Park ♠ 274c 39.03 N 77.02 W
Wheat Ridge 190 39.46 N 105.07 W
Wheelbarrow Peak Λ 194 37.27 N 116.05 W
Wheeler, Ind., U.S. 206 41.31 N 87.11 W
Wheeler, Tex., U.S. 186 35.27 N 100.16 W
Wheeler ≃, Qué., Can. 166 57.02 N 67.13 W
Wheeler ≃, Sask., Can. 174 57.25 N 105.30 W
Wheeler Air Force Base ■ 219c 21.29 N 158.03 W
Wheeler Dam ◆[6] 273 42.48 N 71.12 W
Wheeler Island I 272 38.05 N 121.56 W
Wheeler Lake ◎[1] 184 34.40 N 87.05 W
Wheeler Peak Λ, Calif., U.S. 216 38.25 N 119.17 W
Wheeler Peak Λ, Nev., U.S. 194 38.59 N 114.19 W
Wheeler Peak Λ, N. Mex., U.S. 190 36.34 N 105.25 W
Wheeler Ridge 218 35.06 N 119.01 W
Wheelersburg 208 38.44 N 82.51 W
Wheelers Hill 264b 37.55 S 145.11 E
Wheeling, Ill., U.S. 206 42.09 N 87.55 W
Wheeling, W. Va., U.S. 204 40.05 N 80.42 W
Wheeling Creek ≃ 204 40.03 N 80.41 W
Wheelock 212 30.54 N 96.24 W
Wheelock ≃ 42 53.12 N 2.26 W
Wheelton 252 53.41 N 2.36 W
Wheelwright, Arg. 242 33.47 S 61.13 W
Wheelwright, Ky., U.S. 182 37.20 N 82.43 W
Whela Creek ≃ 152 26.17 S 116.50 E
Whelan, Mount Λ[2] 156 23.25 S 138.54 E
Whelpleyhill 250 51.44 N 0.33 W
Whernside Λ 42 54.14 N 2.23 W
Whetstone Creek ≃ 204 40.23 N 83.03 W
Whetstone Gulf State Park ♠ 202 43.44 N 75.27 W
Whidbey Island I 214 48.15 N 122.40 W
Whidbey Island Naval Air Station ■ 214 48.17 N 122.37 W
Whidbey Islands II 152 34.45 S 135.04 E
Whiddon Down 44 50.43 N 3.51 W
Whigham 182 30.53 N 84.19 W
Whigville 197 41.44 N 72.57 W
Whim Creek 152 20.50 S 117.50 E
Whinham, Mount Λ 152 26.04 S 130.15 E
Whippany 200 40.49 N 74.25 W
Whippany ≃ 266 40.51 N 74.21 W
Whirl Creek ≃ 202 43.28 N 81.12 W
Whirlwind Reefs ✧[2] 154 4.42 S 148.16 E
Whiskey Peak Λ 190 42.18 N 107.35 W
Whiskeytown-Shasta-Trinity National Recreation Area ♠ 194 40.45 N 122.15 W
Whisky Chitto Creek ≃ 184 30.31 N 92.55 W
Whiston 42 53.25 N 2.50 W
Whitacres 197 42.02 N 72.34 W
Whitaker 269b 40.24 N 79.53 W
Whitakers 182 36.06 N 77.43 W
Whitbourne 176 47.25 N 53.32 W
Whitburn 42 55.52 N 3.42 W
Whitby, Ont., Can. 202 43.52 N 78.56 W
Whitby, Eng., U.K. 42 54.29 N 0.37 W
Whitby, Eng., U.K. 252 53.17 N 2.54 W
Whitby Abbey ʊ[1] 42 54.28 N 0.38 W
Whitchurch, Eng., U.K. 44 51.53 N 0.51 W
Whitchurch, Eng., U.K. 44 51.52 N 2.39 W
Whitchurch, Eng., U.K. 44 52.58 N 2.41 W
Whitchurch, Eng., U.K. 44 51.14 N 1.20 W
Whitchurch, Wales, U.K. 44 51.33 N 3.14 W
Whitchurch-Stouffville 202 43.58 N 79.15 W
Whitcombe, Mount Λ 162 43.13 S 170.55 E
White, Ga., U.S. 182 34.17 N 84.45 W
White, S. Dak., U.S. 188 44.26 N 96.39 W
White □[6] 206 40.45 N 86.46 W
White ≃, B.C., Can. 172 50.23 N 115.35 W
White ≃, Ont., Can. 180 48.33 N 86.16 W
White ≃, N.A. 170 63.11 N 139.36 W
White ≃, U.S. 184 33.53 N 91.03 W
White ≃, U.S. 188 43.45 N 99.30 W
White ≃, U.S. 190 40.04 N 109.41 W
White ≃, Ariz., U.S. 190 33.44 N 110.13 W
White ≃, Ind., U.S. 184 38.25 N 87.44 W
White ≃, Nev., U.S. 194 37.42 N 115.10 W
White ≃, Oreg., U.S. 214 45.14 N 121.04 W
White ≃, Tex., U.S. 186 33.14 N 100.56 W
White ≃, Vt., U.S. 178 43.37 N 72.20 W
White ≃, Wash., U.S. 214 47.12 N 122.15 W
White ≃, Wash., U.S. 214 47.50 N 120.49 W
White ≃, Wis., U.S. 180 46.36 N 90.42 W
White ≃, Wis., U.S. 206 42.41 N 88.17 W
White, East Fork ≃, Ariz., U.S. 190 33.47 N 110.00 W
White, East Fork ≃, Ind., U.S. 184 38.33 N 87.14 W
White, Lake ◎ 152 21.05 S 129.00 E
White, Lake ◎[1] 208 39.07 N 83.02 W
White, North Fork ≃, Ariz., U.S. 190 33.47 N 110.00 W
White, North Fork ≃, Colo., U.S. 190 39.58 N 107.38 W
White, South Fork ≃ 190 39.58 N 107.38 W
White, West Fork ≃ 214 47.07 N 121.37 W
White Bay C 176 50.00 N 56.30 W
White Bear Indian Reserve ◆[4] 174 49.15 N 102.15 W
White Bear Lake 180 45.05 N 93.01 W
White Bluff 184 36.06 N 87.13 W
White Breast Creek ≃ 184 41.24 N 93.02 W
White Butte Λ 188 46.23 N 103.19 W
Whitecap Lake ◎ 174 56.54 N 95.14 W
White Cap Mountain Λ 178 45.35 N 69.13 W
White Castle 184 30.10 N 91.09 W
White Center 214 47.31 N 122.21 W
White Chuck ≃ 214 48.11 N 121.27 W
White City, Fla., U.S. 210 27.18 N 80.15 W
White City, Kans., U.S. 188 38.48 N 96.44 W
White City Stadium ♠ 250 51.31 N 0.14 W
White Clay Creek ≃ 188 43.12 N 102.48 W
White Cliffs, Austl. 152 28.26 S 122.57 E
White Cliffs, Austl. 156 30.51 S 143.05 E
White Cloud 180 43.33 N 85.46 W
White Cloud Island I 202 44.50 N 80.58 W
Whitecoomb Λ, N.Z. 162 45.36 S 169.05 E
White Coomb Λ, Scot., U.K. 42 55.26 N 3.20 W
Whitecourt 172 54.09 N 115.41 W
White Creek 200 42.58 N 73.18 W
White Creek ≃, Ind., U.S. 208 38.58 N 86.01 W
White Creek ≃, Wash., U.S. 214 46.01 N 121.08 W
White Deer, Pa., U.S. 200 41.05 N 76.52 W
White Deer, Tex., U.S. 186 35.26 N 101.10 W
White Deer Creek ≃ 200 41.05 N 76.53 W
White Earth ≃ 188 48.09 N 102.42 W
White Earth Indian Reservation ◆[4] 188 47.18 N 95.50 W
White Esk ≃ 42 55.12 N 3.10 W
Whiteface 186 33.36 N 102.37 W
Whiteface ≃ 180 46.58 N 92.48 W
Whiteface, Mount Λ 178 44.22 N 73.54 W
Whitefield, Eng., U.K. 252 53.33 N 2.18 W
Whitefield, Maine, U.S. 178 44.10 N 69.38 W
Whitefield, N.H., U.S. 178 44.22 N 71.36 W
Whitefish 192 48.25 N 114.20 W
Whitefish ≃ 180 45.55 N 86.57 W
Whitefish, East Branch ≃ 180 46.05 N 86.52 W
Whitefish, West Branch ≃ 180 46.05 N 86.52 W
Whitefish Bay 206 43.07 N 87.55 W
Whitefish Bay C, Ont., Can. 174 49.26 N 94.14 W
Whitefish Bay C, N.A. 180 46.40 N 84.50 W
Whitefish Lake ◎, Alta., Can. 172 54.22 N 111.55 W
Whitefish Lake ◎, N.W. Ter., Can. 166 62.41 N 106.48 W
Whitefish Lake ◎, Ont., Can. 180 48.03 N 84.29 W
Whitefish Lake ◎, Ont., Can. 202 44.31 N 76.14 W
Whitefish Lake ◎, Ont., Can. 202 45.18 N 79.47 W
Whitefish Lake ◎, Alaska, U.S. 170 61.21 N 160.00 W
Whitefish Lake ◎, Mont., U.S. 192 48.27 N 114.22 W
White Fish Lake Indian Reserve ◆[4] 172 54.39 N 111.51 W
Whitefish Point 180 46.45 N 84.59 W
Whitefish Point ≻ 180 46.45 N 85.00 W
Whitefish Range ⛰ 192 48.40 N 114.26 W
Whiteford 198 39.42 N 76.21 W
White Fox 174 53.27 N 104.05 W
Whitefox ≃ 174 53.32 N 104.00 W
White Gull Creek ≃ 174 53.44 N 104.20 W
White Hall, Ill., U.S. 209 39.26 N 90.24 W
White Hall, Md., U.S. 198 39.37 N 76.38 W
Whitehall, Mich., U.S. 180 43.24 N 86.21 W
Whitehall, Mont., U.S. 192 45.52 N 112.06 W
Whitehall, N.Y., U.S. 178 43.33 N 73.25 W
Whitehall, Ohio, U.S. 208 39.58 N 82.54 W
White Hall, Pa., U.S. 200 41.07 N 76.38 W
Whitehall, Pa., U.S. 204 40.22 N 79.59 W
Whitehall, Wis., U.S. 180 44.22 N 91.19 W
Whitehaven, Eng., U.K. 42 54.33 N 3.35 W
White Haven, Pa., U.S. 200 41.04 N 75.47 W
Whitehead 42 54.46 N 5.43 W
White Holme Reservoir ◎[1] 252 53.41 N 2.02 W
Whitehorse, Yukon, Can. 170 60.43 N 135.03 W
White Horse, N.J., U.S. 198 40.11 N 74.22 W
White Horse, Vale of V 44 51.37 N 1.37 W
Whitehorse Hill Λ[2] 44 51.34 N 1.34 W
Whitehouse, N.J., U.S. 200 40.37 N 74.46 W
Whitehouse, Ohio, U.S. 206 41.31 N 83.48 W
Whitehouse, Tex., U.S. 212 32.13 N 95.14 W
White House ʊ 274c 38.54 N 77.02 W
White House Station 200 40.37 N 74.46 W
White Island I, Ant. 9 66.44 S 48.35 E
White Island I, N.W. Ter., Can. 166 65.50 N 84.50 W
White Island I, N.Z. 162 37.31 S 177.11 E
White Lake, Mich., U.S. 271 42.41 N 83.33 W
White Lake, N.Y., U.S. 200 41.40 N 74.50 W
White Lake, S. Dak., U.S. 188 43.44 N 98.43 W
White Lake, Wis., U.S. 180 45.09 N 88.46 W
White Lake ◎, Ont., Can. 180 48.48 N 85.36 W
White Lake ◎, Ont., Can. 202 45.18 N 76.31 W

Symbols in the index entries represent the broad categories identified in the key at the right. Symbols with superior numbers (⛰[2]) identify subcategories (see complete key on page *I* · *26*).

Kartensymbole in dem Registerverzeichnis stellen die rechts in Schlüssel erklärten Kategorien dar. Symbole mit hochgestellten Ziffern (⛰[2]) bezeichnen Unterabteilungen einer Kategorie (vgl. vollständiger Schlüssel auf Seite *I* · *26*).

Los símbolos incluidos en el texto del índice representan las grandes categorias identificadas con la clave a la derecha. Los símbolos con numeros en su parte superior (⛰[2]) identifican las subcategorías (véase la clave completa en la página *I* · *26*).

Les symboles de l'index représentent les catégories indiquées dans la légende à droite. Les symboles suivis d'un indice (⛰[2]) représentent des sous-catégories (voir légende complète à la page *I* · *26*).

Os símbolos incluídos no texto do índice representam as grandes categorias identificadas com a chave à direita. Os símbolos com números em sua parte superior (⛰[2]) identificam as subcategorias (veja-se a chave completa à página *I* · *26*).

	English	Deutsch	Español	Français	Português
Λ	Mountain	Berg	Montaña	Montagne	Montanha
⛰	Mountains	Berge	Montañas	Montagnes	Montanhas
⋈	Pass	Pass	Paso	Col	Passo
V	Valley, Canyon	Tal, Cañon	Valle, Cañón	Vallée, Canyon	Vale, Canhão
≚	Plain	Ebene	Llano	Plaine	Planície
≻	Cape	Kap	Cabo	Cap	Cabo
I	Island	Insel	Isla	Île	Ilha
II	Islands	Inseln	Islas	Îles	Ilhas
⩍	Other Topographic Features	Andere Topographische Objekte	Otros Elementos Topográficos	Autres données topographiques	Outros Elementos Topográficos

ESPAÑOL — Nombre · Página · Lat.°′ · Long.°′ W=Oeste

White Lake ⊜, Ont., Can. 202 44.47 N 76.45 W
White Lake ⊜, La., U.S. 184 29.45 N 92.30 W
White Lake ⊜, Mich., U.S. 206 42.40 N 83.34 W
Whiteland 208 39.33 N 86.05 W
Whitelaw 172 56.07 N 118.04 W
Whiteley Village 250 51.21 N 0.26 W
White Lick Creek ≃ 208 39.30 N 86.23 W
White Lick Creek, East Fork ≃ 208 39.35 N 86.22 W
White Lick Creek, West Fork ≃ 208 39.38 N 86.23 W
Whiteman Air Force Base ■ 184 38.44 N 93.34 W
Whiteman Airpark ⊠ 270 34.15 N 118.25 W
Whiteman Range ∧∧ 154 5.50 S 149.55 E
Whitemans Creek ≃ 202 43.10 N 80.21 W
Whitemark 156 40.07 S 148.01 E
White Marsh 274b 39.23 N 76.26 W
Whitemarsh Run ≃ 274b 39.22 N 76.25 W
White Meadow Lake 200 40.55 N 74.31 W
White Meadow Lake ⊜ 266 40.55 N 74.31 W
White Mills 200 41.32 N 75.12 W
White Mountain 170 64.40 N 162.12 W
White Mountain Peak ∧ 194 37.38 N 118.15 W
White Mountains ∧∧, U.S. 194 37.30 N 118.15 W
White Mountains ∧∧, Alaska, U.S. 170 65.30 N 147.00 W
White Mountains ∧∧, Ariz., U.S. 190 33.45 N 109.40 W
White Mountains ∧∧, N.H., U.S. 178 44.10 N 71.35 W
Whitemouth 174 49.57 N 95.59 W
Whitemouth ≃ 174 50.07 N 96.02 W
Whitemouth Lake ⊜ 174 49.14 N 95.40 W
Whitemud ≃ 174 50.15 N 98.37 W
White Nile (Al-Baḥr al-Abyaḍ) ≃ 130 15.38 N 32.31 E
White Nossob ≃ 146 23.05 S 18.45 E
White Oak, Pa., U.S. 269b 40.21 N 79.48 W
White Oak, Tex., U.S. 212 32.32 N 94.52 W
White Oak ≃ 182 34.40 N 77.07 W
White Oak Creek ≃ 184 33.16 N 94.39 W
White Oak Creek, East Fork ≃ 208 39.00 N 83.53 W
White Oak Creek, North Fork ≃ 208 39.00 N 83.53 W
White Oak Lake ⊜[1] 184 33.40 N 93.10 W
White Oak Regional Park ♠ 269a 40.21 N 79.47 W
White Pass)(, N.A. 170 59.38 N 135.05 W
White Pass)(, Wash., U.S. 214 46.38 N 121.24 W
White Pigeon 206 41.48 N 85.38 W
White Pine, Mich., U.S. 180 46.44 N 89.35 W
White Pine, Tenn., U.S. 182 36.07 N 83.17 W
White Pines, Calif., U.S. 216 38.18 N 120.21 W
White Pines, Ill., U.S. 268 41.57 N 87.57 W
White Plains, N.C., U.S. 182 36.27 N 80.38 W
White Plains, N.Y., U.S. 200 41.02 N 73.46 W
White Pond ⊜ 273 42.26 N 71.23 W
White River, Ont., Can. 180 48.35 N 85.15 W
Whiteriver, Ariz., U.S. 190 33.50 N 109.58 W
White River, S. Dak., U.S. 188 43.34 N 100.45 W
White River Junction 178 43.39 N 72.19 W
White Rock 172 49.02 N 122.49 W
White Rock Creek ≃, Kans., U.S. 188 39.55 N 97.51 W
White Rock Creek ≃, Tex., U.S. 212 32.43 N 96.44 W
White Rock Lake ⊜[1] 212 32.50 N 96.44 W
White Rocks ∧ 182 36.40 N 83.27 W
Whiterocks ≃ 190 40.26 N 109.55 W
White Roding 250 51.48 N 0.16 E
Whitesail Lake ⊜ 172 53.30 N 127.00 W
White Salmon 214 45.44 N 121.29 W
White Salmon ≃ 214 45.43 N 121.31 W
Whitesand ≃ 174 51.34 N 101.55 W
Whitesands 165f 19.28 S 169.25 E
White Sands Beach 197 41.18 N 72.09 W
White Sands Missile Range ■ 190 32.23 N 106.28 W
White Sands National Monument ♠ 190 32.46 N 106.20 W
Whitesboro, N.J., U.S. 198 39.03 N 74.51 W
Whitesboro, N.Y., U.S. 200 43.07 N 75.18 W
Whitesboro, Tex., U.S. 186 33.39 N 96.54 W
Whitesburg 182 37.07 N 82.49 W
White Sea → Beloje More ⍑[2] 24 65.30 N 38.00 E
White Settlement 212 32.45 N 97.27 W
Whiteshell Provincial Park ♠ 174 50.00 N 95.25 W
Whiteside 209 39.11 N 91.01 W
Whiteside, Canal ɰ 244 53.55 S 70.15 W
White's Landing 204 41.25 N 82.54 W
White Springs 182 30.20 N 82.45 W
White Stone 198 37.39 N 76.23 W
Whitestone •[8] 266 40.47 N 73.49 W
White Stone Lake ⊜ 174 56.25 N 97.31 W
Whitestown 208 38.59 N 86.21 W
White Sulphur Springs, Mont., U.S. 192 46.33 N 110.54 W
White Sulphur Springs, N.Y., U.S. 200 41.48 N 74.50 W
White Sulphur Springs, W. Va., U.S. 182 37.48 N 80.18 W
Whites Valley 200 41.42 N 75.22 W
Whitesville, Ky., U.S. 184 37.41 N 86.52 W
Whitesville, N.Y., U.S. 200 42.02 N 77.46 W
Whitesville, W. Va., U.S. 178 37.59 N 81.32 W
White Swan 214 46.23 N 120.44 W
White Umbeluzi ≃ 148 26.08 S 31.52 E
White Umfolozi ≃ 148 28.22 S 31.58 E
Whitevale 202 43.53 N 79.09 W
White Valley 204 40.25 N 79.36 W
Whiteville, N.C., U.S. 182 34.20 N 78.42 W
Whiteville, Tenn., U.S. 184 35.20 N 89.11 W
White Volta (Volta Blanche) ≃ 140 9.10 N 1.15 W
Whitewater, Kans., U.S. 188 37.58 N 97.09 W
Whitewater, Mont., U.S. 192 48.46 N 107.38 W
Whitewater, Wis., U.S. 206 42.50 N 88.44 W
Whitewater ≃, U.S. 208 39.10 N 84.47 W
Whitewater ≃, Calif., U.S. 194 33.30 N 116.03 W
Whitewater ≃, Mo., U.S. 184 37.01 N 89.43 W
Whitewater, Dry Fork ≃ 208 39.11 N 84.47 W
Whitewater, East Fork ≃ 208 39.24 N 85.01 W
Whitewater, Greens Fork ≃ 208 39.45 N 85.07 W
Whitewater, Nolands Fork ≃ 208 39.41 N 85.07 W
Whitewater Baldy ∧ 190 33.20 N 108.39 W
Whitewater Bay C 210 25.16 N 81.00 W

FRANÇAIS — Nom · Page · Lat.°′ · Long.°′ W=Ouest

Whitewater Creek ≃, N.A. 192 48.30 N 107.11 W
Whitewater Creek ≃, Ala., U.S. 184 31.25 N 86.04 W
Whitewater Creek ≃, Ga., U.S. 182 32.21 N 84.03 W
Whitewater Creek ≃, Wis., U.S. 206 42.52 N 88.45 W
Whitewater Lake ⊜, Man., Can. 174 49.15 N 100.20 W
Whitewater Lake ⊜, Wis., U.S. 206 42.47 N 88.42 W
Whitewater State Park ♠ 208 39.36 N 84.58 W
White Woman Creek ≃ 188 38.25 N 100.54 W
Whitewood, Austl. 156 21.28 S 143.36 E
Whitewood, Sask., Can. 174 50.20 N 102.15 W
Whitewood, Lake ⊜ 188 44.20 N 97.18 W
Whitewright 186 33.31 N 96.24 W
Whitford Point ≻ 44 51.38 N 4.14 W
Whithorn, Jam. 231q 18.15 N 78.02 W
Whithorn, Scot., U.K. 42 54.44 N 4.25 W
Whitianga 162 36.50 S 175.42 E
Whiting, Ind., U.S. 206 41.40 N 87.29 W
Whiting, Iowa, U.S. 188 42.08 N 96.09 W
Whiting, Kans., U.S. 188 39.35 N 95.37 W
Whiting, N.J., U.S. 198 39.57 N 74.23 W
Whiting, Wis., U.S. 180 44.29 N 89.33 W
Whiting Bay 42 55.29 N 5.06 W
Whitingham 197 42.47 N 72.53 W
Whitinsville 197 42.07 N 71.40 W
Whitland 44 51.50 N 4.37 W
Whitley □[6] 206 41.10 N 85.29 W
Whitley Bay 42 55.03 N 1.25 W
Whitley City 182 36.43 N 84.28 W
Whitley Row 250 51.15 N 0.09 E
Whitman 197 42.05 N 70.56 W
Whitman Mission National Historic Site ⊥ 192 46.01 N 118.30 W
Whitmans Pond ⊜ 273 42.12 N 70.57 W
Whitman Square 198 39.45 N 75.03 W
Whitmire 182 34.30 N 81.37 W
Whitmore Lake 206 42.25 N 83.46 W
Whitmore Lake ⊜ 271 42.26 N 83.45 W
Whitmore Mountains ∧∧ 9 82.35 S 104.30 W
Whitmore Village 219c 21.31 N 158.01 W
Whitner Heights 216 36.37 N 119.32 W
Whitney, Ont., Can. 202 45.30 N 78.14 W
Whitney, Pa., U.S. 204 40.15 N 79.25 W
Whitney, Tex., U.S. 212 31.57 N 97.19 W
Whitney, Lake ⊜[1] 212 31.55 N 97.23 W
Whitney, Mount ∧ 194 36.35 N 118.18 W
Whitney Point 200 42.20 N 75.58 W
Whitney Point Lake ⊜[1] 200 42.25 N 75.55 W
Whitney Woods Reservation ♠ 273 42.13 N 70.51 W
Whitstable 44 51.22 N 1.02 E
Whitsunday Island I 156 20.17 S 148.59 E
Whittaker 206 42.08 N 83.36 W
Whittemore, Iowa, U.S. 188 43.04 N 94.25 W
Whittemore, Mich., U.S. 180 44.14 N 83.48 W
Whittier, Alaska, U.S. 170 60.46 N 148.41 W
Whittier, Calif., U.S. 218 33.59 N 118.02 W
Whittier, N.C., U.S. 182 35.26 N 83.22 W
Whittier Narrows Dam •[6] 270 34.01 N 118.04 W
Whittier Narrows Flood Control Basin ⊜[1] 270 34.02 N 118.04 W
Whittier South 270 33.57 N 118.01 W
Whittingham 42 55.24 N 1.54 W
Whittington 44 52.52 N 3.00 W
Whittle, Cap ≻ 176 50.11 N 60.08 W
Whittle Hill ∧[2] 252 53.40 N 2.16 W
Whittle-le-Woods 252 53.41 N 2.38 W
Whittlesea, Austl. 159 37.31 S 145.07 E
Whittlesea, S. Afr. 148 32.10 S 26.50 E
Whittlesey 44 52.34 N 0.08 W
Whittlesey, Mount ∧[2] 180 46.18 N 90.37 W
Whitwell 184 35.12 N 85.31 W
Whitwick 44 52.44 N 1.21 W
Whitworth 42 53.40 N 2.10 W
Whitworth Peak ∧ 214 49.05 N 121.13 W
Wholdaia Lake ⊜ 166 60.43 N 104.10 W
Whonock 214 49.11 N 122.28 W
W. Howard Frankland Bridge •[5] 210 27.56 N 82.35 W
Whyalla 156 33.02 S 137.35 E
Whycocomagh 176 45.59 N 61.07 W
Whymper, Mount ∧ 214 48.57 N 124.10 W
Wiang Pa Pao 100 19.22 N 99.30 E
Wiang Phan 100 20.26 N 99.53 E
Wiarton 202 44.45 N 81.09 W
Wiasi 140 10.21 N 1.20 W
Wiau Lake ⊜ 172 55.23 N 111.18 W
Wiawso 140 6.12 N 2.29 W
Wiązów 30 50.49 N 17.11 E
Wibaux 188 46.59 N 104.11 W
Wiblingen •[8] 54 48.21 N 9.58 E
Wichian Buri 100 15.39 N 101.07 E
Wichita 188 37.41 N 97.20 W
Wichita Falls 186 33.54 N 98.30 W
Wichita Mountain ∧ 186 34.52 N 99.17 W
Wichita Mountains ∧∧ 186 34.45 N 98.40 W
Wichlinghofen •[8] 253 51.27 N 7.30 E
Wick 28 58.26 N 3.06 W
Wickatunk 266 40.21 N 74.15 W
Wickede 48 51.29 N 7.52 E
Wickede •[8] 253 51.32 N 7.37 E
Wickenburg 190 33.58 N 112.44 W
Wickepin 152 32.46 S 117.30 E
Wicker Memorial Park ♠ 268 41.34 N 87.28 W
Wickett 186 31.34 N 102.59 W
Wickford 44 51.38 N 0.31 E
Wickham, Qué., Can. 196 45.45 N 72.30 W
Wickham, Eng., U.K. 44 50.54 N 1.10 W
Wickham ≃ 154 16.22 S 131.06 E
Wickham, Cape ≻ 156 39.36 S 143.57 E
Wickham Bishops 250 51.47 N 0.40 E
Wickham Market 44 52.09 N 1.22 E
Wickiup Reservoir ⊜[1] 192 43.40 N 121.43 W
Wickliffe, Ky., U.S. 184 36.58 N 89.05 W
Wickliffe, Ohio, U.S. 204 41.36 N 81.28 W
Wickliffe, Ohio, U.S. 204 41.07 N 80.44 W
Wicklow 28 52.59 N 6.03 W
Wicklow □[6] 28 53.00 N 6.30 W
Wicklow Head ≻ 28 52.58 N 6.00 W
Wicklow Mountains ∧∧ 28 53.02 N 6.24 W
Wickrath 52 51.07 N 6.24 E
Wicksteed Lake ⊜ 180 46.46 N 79.40 W
Wicomico 198 37.17 N 76.31 W
Wicomico □[6] 198 38.22 N 75.36 W
Wicomico ≃ 198 38.13 N 75.55 W
Wicomico Church 198 37.49 N 76.23 W
Wiconisco 198 40.34 N 76.41 W
Wiconisco Creek ≃ 198 40.32 N 76.58 W
Wid ≃ 252 51.45 N 0.27 E
Widas ≃ 105a 7.30 S 112.08 E
Widawa ≃ 30 51.13 N 16.55 E
Widdern 52 49.19 N 9.25 E
Widdert •[8] 253 51.08 N 7.04 E
Widdop Reservoir ⊜[1] 252 53.48 N 2.06 W
Wide Bay C, Pap. N. Gui. 154 5.05 S 152.05 E
Wide Bay C, Alaska, U.S. 170 57.20 N 156.25 W
Widecombe in the Moor 44 50.35 N 3.48 W

PORTUGUÊS — Nome · Página · Lat.°′ · Long.°′ W=Oeste

Widemouth Bay 44 50.47 N 4.32 W
Widen 178 38.28 N 80.52 W
Widerøe, Mount ∧ 9 72.08 S 23.30 E
Wide Ruin Wash V 190 35.13 N 109.52 W
Widford 250 51.43 N 0.27 E
Widgeegoara Creek ≃ 156 27.30 S 145.55 E
Widgiemooltha 152 31.30 S 121.34 E
Widnes 42 53.22 N 2.44 W
Widodaren 105a 7.25 S 111.14 E
Widuchowa 50 53.10 N 14.25 E
Wiebelskirchen 52 49.22 N 7.11 E
Więcbork 30 53.22 N 17.30 E
Wieck 50 54.06 N 13.26 E
Wied 212 29.26 N 97.04 W
Wied ≃ 52 50.26 N 7.27 E
Wieda 50 51.38 N 10.34 E
Wiederitzsch 50 51.24 N 12.22 E
Wiedlisbach 54 47.15 N 7.39 E
Wiefelstede 48 53.15 N 8.07 E
Wiehe 50 51.16 N 11.25 E
Wiehengebirge ∧∧ 48 52.20 N 8.40 E
Wiehengebirge, Naturpark ♠ 48 52.20 N 8.20 E
Wiehl 52 50.57 N 7.31 E
Wiek 50 54.37 N 13.17 E
Wieleń 30 52.54 N 16.10 E
Wielichowo 30 52.08 N 16.21 E
Wieliczka 30 49.59 N 20.04 E
Wielkopolska •[1] 30 51.50 N 17.20 E
Wielkopolski Park Narodowy ♠ 30 52.15 N 16.50 E
Wieluń 30 51.14 N 18.34 E
Wiemelhausen •[8] 253 51.28 N 7.13 E
Wien (Vienna) 30
254b 48.13 N 16.20 E
Wien □[3] 254b 41.10 N 16.22 E
Wien ≃ 254b 48.13 N 16.23 E
Wien, Universität ▾[2] 254b 48.13 N 16.22 E
Wiener Berg ∧[2] 254b 48.10 N 16.22 E
Wienerherberg 254b 48.03 N 16.33 E
Wiener Neudorf 254b 48.05 N 16.19 E
Wiener Neustadt 30 47.49 N 16.15 E
Wiener Neustädter Kanal ≋ 254b 48.05 N 16.22 E
Wienerwald ∧∧ 30 48.10 N 16.00 E
Wienhagen ∧[2] 253 51.08 N 7.33 E
Wienhausen 48 52.35 N 10.11 E
Wien-Schwechat, Flughafen ⊠ 254b 48.07 N 16.33 E
Wiepke 50 52.36 N 11.20 E
Wieprz ≃ 30 51.34 N 21.49 E
Wieprza ≃ 30 54.26 N 16.22 E
Wieprz-Krzna, Kanał ≋ 30 51.56 N 22.56 E
Wiera ≃ 52 50.55 N 9.10 E
Wierden 48 52.22 N 6.35 E
Wieren 50 52.53 N 10.39 E
Wiergate 184 31.00 N 93.42 W
Wieringermeer •[1] 48 52.45 N 5.00 E
Wieringerwerf 48 52.51 N 5.02 E
Wieruszów 30 51.18 N 18.08 E
Wierzyca ≃ 30 53.51 N 18.50 E
Wies ▾[1] 54 47.40 N 10.53 E
Wiesa 50 50.36 N 13.01 E
Wiesbaden 52 50.05 N 8.14 E
Wiesbaden □[5] 52 50.20 N 8.20 E
Wiescheid •[8] 253 51.08 N 6.59 E
Wiese ≃ 54 47.35 N 7.35 E
Wiesede 48 53.27 N 7.46 E
Wieselburg 30 48.08 N 15.09 E
Wiesen 54 46.43 N 9.43 E
Wiesenburg 50 52.07 N 12.26 E
Wiesenfeld 52 51.16 N 10.06 E
Wiesensteig 52 48.34 N 9.37 E
Wiesent ≃ 52 49.42 N 11.05 E
Wiesental 52 49.14 N 8.31 E
Wiesentheid 52 49.47 N 10.20 E
Wieseth ≃ 52 49.10 N 10.39 E
Wiesloch 52 49.17 N 8.42 E
Wiesmoor 48 53.25 N 7.43 E
Wietmarschen 48 52.31 N 7.07 E
Wietze 48 52.39 N 9.50 E
Wietzen 48 52.43 N 9.04 E
Wigan 42
252 53.33 N 2.38 W
Wigan □[8] 252 53.32 N 2.35 W
Wiggensbach 54 47.44 N 10.14 E
Wigger ≃ 54 47.18 N 7.53 E
Wiggington 250 51.47 N 0.38 W
Wiggins, Colo., U.S. 188 40.14 N 104.04 W
Wiggins, Miss., U.S. 184 30.51 N 89.08 W
Wigglesworth 42 54.01 N 2.17 W
Wight, Isle of I 44 50.40 N 1.20 W
Wigmore, Eng., U.K. 44 52.19 N 2.51 W
Wigmore, Eng., U.K. 250 51.21 N 0.35 E
Wignehies 46 50.01 N 4.00 E
Wigston Magna 44 52.36 N 1.05 W
Wigton 42 54.49 N 3.09 W
Wigtown 42 54.52 N 4.26 W
Wigtown Bay C 42 54.46 N 4.15 W
Wijchen 48 51.48 N 5.43 E
Wijhe 48 52.24 N 6.07 E
Wijk aan Zee 48 52.29 N 4.35 E
Wijk bij Duurstede 48 51.58 N 5.20 E
Wil 54 47.27 N 9.03 E
Wilbarger Creek ≃ 212 30.11 N 97.23 W
Wilber 188 40.29 N 96.58 W
Wilberforce, Austl. 160 33.33 S 150.50 E
Wilberforce, Ohio, U.S. 208 39.43 N 83.53 W
Wilberforce Falls ↳ 166 67.07 N 108.47 W
Wilbraham 197 42.07 N 72.26 W
Wilbur 192 47.46 N 118.42 W
Wilburton 186 34.55 N 95.19 W
Wilcannia 156 31.34 S 143.23 E
Wilcock, Península ≻[1] 244 50.40 S 74.00 W
Wilcox, Sask., Can. 174 50.07 N 104.44 W
Wilcox, Nebr., U.S. 188 40.22 N 99.10 W
Wilcox, Pa., U.S. 204 41.35 N 78.41 W
Wilcox, Tex., U.S. 212 30.27 N 96.22 W
Wilcox, Mount ∧ 197 42.13 N 73.16 W
Wildau 50 52.19 N 13.38 E
Wildbad im Schwarzwald 52 48.45 N 8.32 E
Wildberg, B.R.D. 52 48.37 N 8.44 E
Wildberg, D.D.R. 50 52.52 N 12.37 E
Wildboarclough 252 53.13 N 2.02 W
Wildcat Canyon Regional Park ♠ 272 37.56 N 122.17 W
Wildcat Creek ≃, Calif., U.S. 272 37.57 N 122.23 W
Wildcat Creek ≃, Ind., U.S. 206 40.28 N 86.52 W
Wildcat Creek, Middle Fork ≃ 206 40.25 N 86.46 W
Wildcat Creek, South Fork ≃ 206 40.26 N 86.48 W
Wildcat Hill ∧[2] 174 53.17 N 102.30 W
Wilde •[8] 278 34.42 S 58.20 W
Wildegg 54 47.25 N 8.11 E
Wildeman ≃ 154 5.33 S 139.13 E
Wildemann 48 51.49 N 10.17 E
Wildenbruch 254a 52.17 N 13.04 E
Wildenfels 50 50.40 N 12.35 E
Wildenstein 54 47.59 N 6.58 E
Wildenthal 50 50.27 N 12.37 E
Wilder 192 43.40 N 116.55 W
Wilderness 148 34.00 S 22.36 E
Wilderness of Judæa (Midbar Yehuda) •[2] 122 31.30 N 35.18 E
Wilderness State Park ♠ 180 45.42 N 84.57 W
Wilder Shoal ✣[2] 14 8.30 N 174.05 W
Wildersville 184 35.48 N 88.22 W
Wildervank 48 53.04 N 6.51 E
Wildeshausen 48 52.54 N 8.26 E
Wildfield 202 43.49 N 79.44 W
Wildflecken 52 50.23 N 9.54 E
Wildfontein 148 31.04 S 24.50 E
Wildhaus 54 47.12 N 9.22 E

Wildhay ≃ 172 54.02 N 117.20 W
Wildhorn ∧ 54 46.21 N 7.22 E
Wildhorse Creek ≃, Okla., U.S. 186 34.32 N 97.10 W
Wild Horse Creek ≃, Wyo., U.S. 188 44.39 N 106.08 W
Wild Horse Draw V 186 31.11 N 104.50 W
Wild Horse Lake ⊜ 192 48.58 N 110.00 W
Wildnest Lake ⊜ 174 55.00 N 102.20 W
Wildon 30 46.53 N 15.31 E
Wild Rice ≃, Minn., U.S. 188 47.20 N 96.50 W
Wild Rice ≃, N. Dak., U.S. 188 46.45 N 96.47 W
Wild Rice, South Branch ≃ 188 47.12 N 96.38 W
Wildrose, N. Dak., U.S. 188 48.38 N 103.11 W
Wild Rose, Wis., U.S. 180 44.11 N 89.15 W
Wildseeloder ∧ 58 47.26 N 12.32 E
Wildspitze ∧ 54 46.53 N 10.52 E
Wildstrubel ∧ 54 46.24 N 7.32 E
Wildwood, Alta., Can. 172 53.37 N 115.14 W
Wildwood, Fla., U.S. 210 28.52 N 82.02 W
Wildwood, Ill., U.S. 206 42.21 N 88.00 W
Wildwood, N.J., U.S. 198 38.59 N 74.49 W
Wildwood, Pa., U.S. 204 40.36 N 79.58 W
Wildwood, Lake ⊜ 266 41.09 N 74.32 W
Wild Wood Beach 274b 39.15 N 76.25 W
Wildwood Canyon Park ♠ 270 34.13 N 118.17 W
Wildwood Crest 198 38.58 N 74.50 W
Wiley 214 46.33 N 120.39 W
Wilferdingen 52 48.56 N 8.35 E
Wilge ≃ 148 27.03 S 28.20 E
Wilgena 152 30.46 S 134.44 E
Wilgersdorf 52 50.49 N 8.09 E
Wilhelm, Lake ⊜[1] 204 41.23 N 80.08 W
Wilhelm, Mount ∧ 154 5.45 S 145.05 E
Wilhelmina ≃ 240 3.51 N 54.32 W
Wilhelmina Gebergte ∧∧ 240 3.45 N 56.30 W
Wilhelminakanaal ≋ 48 51.47 N 4.51 E
Wilhelminaoord 48 52.53 N 6.10 E
Wilhelmina Peak → Trikora, Puncak ∧ 154 4.15 S 138.45 E
Wilhelm-Pieck-Stadt Guben 50 51.57 N 14.43 E
Wilhelmsburg •[8] 48 53.30 N 10.00 E
Wilhelmshaven 48 53.31 N 8.08 E
Wilhelmshöhe, Schloss ⊥ 52 51.21 N 9.22 E
Wilhelmshorst 50 52.19 N 13.03 E
Wilhelmstadt •[8] 254a 52.31 N 13.11 E
Wilhelmstal 146 21.54 S 16.19 E
Wilhelmstein, Schloss ⊥ 48 52.28 N 9.18 E
Wilis, Gunung ∧ 105a 7.48 S 111.45 E
Wilkau-Hasslau 50 50.40 N 12.31 E
Wilkerson Pass)(190 39.02 N 105.32 W
Wilkes ▾[3] 9 66.15 S 110.35 E
Wilkes-Barre 200 41.14 N 75.53 W
Wilkes-Barre Scranton Airport ⊠ 200 41.20 N 75.45 W
Wilkesboro 182 36.09 N 81.09 W
Wilkes Island I 164a 19.18 N 166.34 E
Wilkes Lake ⊜ 180 46.01 N 79.00 W
Wilkes Land •[1] 9 69.00 S 120.00 E
Wilkeson 214 47.06 N 122.03 W
Wilket Creek ≃ 265b 43.43 N 79.21 W
Wilket Creek Park ♠ 265b 43.43 N 79.21 W
Wilkie 174 52.25 N 108.43 W
Wilkinsburg 204 40.27 N 79.53 W
Wilkinson 208 39.53 N 85.36 W
Wilkinson Basin ✣[1] 16 42.30 N 69.30 W
Wilkinson Lakes ⊜ 152 29.40 S 132.39 E
Wilkins Sound ɰ 9 70.15 S 73.00 W
Wilkins Township 269b 40.25 N 79.50 W
Will □[6] 206 41.32 N 88.05 W
Will, Mount ∧ 170 57.31 N 128.46 W
Willacoochee 182 31.20 N 83.03 W
Willacoochee ≃ 182 31.21 N 83.06 W
Willamette ≃ 192 45.39 N 122.46 W
Willamette, Middle Fork ≃ 192 44.01 N 123.01 W
Willamette, North Fork ≃ 192 43.46 N 122.32 W
Willamina 214 45.05 N 123.29 W
Willamina Creek ≃ 214 45.05 N 123.28 W
Willandra Billabong Creek ≃ 156 33.08 S 144.06 E
Willapa 214 46.40 N 123.40 W
Willapa ≃ 214 46.42 N 123.50 W
Willapa Bay C 214 46.37 N 124.00 W
Willard, N. Mex., U.S. 190 34.36 N 106.02 W
Willard, N.Y., U.S. 200 42.41 N 76.52 W
Willard, Ohio, U.S. 204 41.03 N 82.44 W
Willard, Utah, U.S. 190 41.25 N 112.02 W
Willard, Wash., U.S. 214 45.48 N 121.38 W
Willaston, Austl. 158b 34.36 S 138.45 E
Willaston, Eng., U.K. 252 53.18 N 3.00 W
Willaumez Peninsula ≻[1] 154 5.05 S 150.05 E
Willcox 190 32.15 N 109.50 W
Willcox Playa ⊜ 190 32.08 N 109.51 W
Willebadessen 48 51.37 N 9.02 E
Willebroek 46 51.04 N 4.22 E
Willem Pretorius Game Reserve •[4] 146 28.16 S 27.13 E
Willemsoord 48 52.49 N 6.05 E
Willemstad, Ned. 48 51.42 N 4.26 E
Willemstad, Ned. Ant. 231s 12.06 N 68.56 W
Willenhall 44 52.36 N 2.02 W
Willerburn Acres 274c 39.03 N 77.10 W
Willerby 42 53.46 N 0.27 W
Willeroo 154 15.17 S 131.35 E
Willer-sur-Thur 54 47.51 N 7.05 E
Willerswalde 50 54.07 N 13.08 E
Willesden •[8] 250 51.33 N 0.14 W
Willet 200 42.28 N 75.55 W
Willett Pond ⊜ 273 42.11 N 71.14 W
Willey Creek ≃ 269a 41.25 N 81.25 W
William, Lac ⊜ 196 46.07 N 71.34 W
William, Mount ∧, Austl. 156 37.17 S 142.36 E
William, Mount ∧, Austl. 159 37.13 S 144.47 E
William Boyce Regional Park ♠ 269b 40.28 N 79.45 W
William Creek 156 28.55 S 136.21 E
William Girling Reservoir ⊜[1] 250 51.37 N 0.02 W
William Lake ⊜ 174 53.50 N 99.25 W
William Patterson College ▾[2] 266 40.56 N 74.12 W
William P. Gleason Park ♠ 268 41.33 N 87.21 W
William Preston Lane Jr. Memorial Bridge •[5] 198 39.00 N 76.28 W
Williams, Austl. 158a 33.01 S 116.52 E
Williams, Ariz., U.S. 190 35.15 N 112.11 W
Williams, Calif., U.S. 216 39.09 N 122.09 W
Williams, Iowa, U.S. 180 42.29 N 93.33 W
Williams, Minn., U.S. 188 48.45 N 94.54 W
Williams □[6] 206 41.35 N 84.33 W
Williams ≃, Austl. 156 20.04 S 141.08 E
Williams ≃, Austl. 158a 32.59 S 116.24 E
Williams ≃, Austl. 160 32.45 S 151.45 E
Williams, Cape ≻ 9 70.29 S 164.05 E
Williams, Mount ∧ 165f 18.39 S 169.03 E
Williams Bay 206 42.35 N 88.33 W
Williamsburg, Ont., Can. 202 44.58 N 75.15 W
Williamsburg, Ind., U.S. 208 39.57 N 85.01 W
Williamsburg, Iowa, U.S. 180 41.40 N 92.01 W

Williamsburg, Ky., U.S. 182 36.44 N 84.10 W
Williamsburg, Mass., U.S. 197 42.23 N 72.44 W
Williamsburg, Mo., U.S. 209 38.55 N 91.42 W
Williamsburg, Ohio, U.S. 208 39.03 N 84.04 W
Williamsburg, Pa., U.S. 204 40.28 N 78.12 W
Williamsburg, Va., U.S. 198 37.16 N 79.43 W
Williamsburg •[8] 266 40.42 N 73.57 W
Williamsburg Bridge •[5] 266 40.43 N 73.58 W
Williams Center 206 41.26 N 84.36 W
Williams Creek ≃, Austl. 264a 33.57 S 150.58 E
Williams Creek ≃, Ind., U.S. 208 39.36 N 85.09 W
Williamsdale 161b 35.35 S 149.09 E
Williamsfield, Jam. 231q 17.56 N 77.46 W
Williamsfield, Ohio, U.S. 204 41.32 N 80.32 W
Williams Lake 172 52.08 N 122.09 W
Williams Lake Indian Reserve •[4] 172 52.07 N 122.00 W
Williamson, N.Y., U.S. 200 43.13 N 77.11 W
Williamson, W. Va., U.S. 182 37.41 N 82.17 W
Williamson □[6] 212 30.40 N 97.32 W
Williamson ≃ 192 42.28 N 121.57 W
Williamson Head ≻ 9 69.09 S 157.49 E
Williamsport, Newf., Can. 176 50.32 N 56.19 W
Williamsport, Ind., U.S. 206 40.17 N 87.17 W
Williamsport, Ohio, U.S. 204 39.35 N 83.07 W
Williamsport, Pa., U.S. 200 41.14 N 77.00 W
Williamston, Mich., U.S. 206 42.41 N 84.17 W
Williamston, S.C., U.S. 182 34.37 N 82.29 W
Williamstown, Austl. 158b 34.40 S 138.53 E
Williamstown, Austl. 159 37.52 S 144.54 E
Williamstown, Ont., Can. 196 45.08 N 74.35 W
Williamstown, Ky., U.S. 208 38.38 N 84.34 W
Williamstown, Mass., U.S. 197 42.43 N 73.12 W
Williamstown, N.J., U.S. 198 39.41 N 75.01 W
Williamstown, Pa., U.S. 198 40.35 N 76.37 W
Williamstown, Vt., U.S. 178 44.07 N 72.33 W
Williamstown, W. Va., U.S. 178 39.24 N 81.27 W
Williamstown Junction 275 39.45 N 74.56 W
Williamstown Lake ⊜[1] 208 38.41 N 84.32 W
Williamsville, Ill., U.S. 209 39.57 N 89.33 W
Williamsville, N.Y., U.S. 200 42.59 N 78.43 W
Williamtown 160 32.49 S 151.50 E
Willich 52 51.16 N 6.33 E
Willikies 230c 17.05 N 61.42 W
Willimantic 197 41.43 N 72.13 W
Willimantic ≃ 197 41.43 N 72.12 W
Willingale 250 51.44 N 0.19 E
Willingboro 198 40.03 N 74.53 W
Willingboro Plaza •[9] 275 40.03 N 74.53 W
Willingdon, Alta., Can. 172 53.50 N 112.08 W
Willingdon, Eng., U.K. 44 50.47 N 0.15 E
Willingdon, Mount ∧ 172 51.45 N 116.15 W
Willingen 52 51.17 N 8.37 E
Willingham 44 52.19 N 0.04 E
Willington 42 54.43 N 1.41 W
Willis, Mich., U.S. 206 42.09 N 83.34 W
Willis, Tex., U.S. 212 30.25 N 95.29 W
Willis ≃ 182 37.41 N 78.07 W
Willisau 54 47.07 N 8.00 E
Willis Group II 154 16.18 S 150.00 E
Willis Island I 176 48.48 N 53.42 W
Williston, S. Afr. 148 31.20 S 20.53 E
Williston, Fla., U.S. 182 29.23 N 82.27 W
Williston, N. Dak., U.S. 188 48.09 N 103.37 W
Williston, Ohio, U.S. 204 41.36 N 83.20 W
Williston, S.C., U.S. 182 33.24 N 81.25 W
Williston Basin ≚[1] 188 48.15 N 105.00 W
Williston Lake ⊜[1] 172 56.00 N 124.00 W
Williston Park 266 40.45 N 73.39 W
Willisville 184 37.59 N 89.35 W
Willis Wharf 198 37.31 N 75.48 W
Williton 44 51.10 N 3.20 W
Willits 194 39.25 N 123.21 W
Willmar 188 45.07 N 95.03 W
Willmersdorf 254a 52.40 N 13.41 E
Willmore Wilderness Provincial Park ♠ 172 53.45 N 119.00 W
Willoughby, Austl. 160 33.48 S 151.12 E
Willoughby, Ohio, U.S. 204 41.38 N 81.25 W
Willoughby, Cape ≻ 156 35.51 S 138.07 E
Willoughby Bay C 230c 17.02 N 61.44 W
Willoughby Hills 204 41.35 N 81.27 W
Willow, Alaska, U.S. 170 61.45 N 150.03 W
Willow, Mich., U.S. 206 42.07 N 83.24 W
Willow, N.Y., U.S. 200 42.05 N 74.14 W
Willow ≃, Alta., Can. 172 55.58 N 113.55 W
Willow ≃, B.C., Can. 172 54.03 N 122.21 W
Willow ≃, Minn., U.S. 180 46.40 N 93.35 W
Willow ≃, Wis., U.S. 180 44.59 N 92.46 W
Willowbrook, Sask., Can. 174 51.13 N 102.47 W
Willow Brook, Calif., U.S. 270 33.55 N 118.14 W
Willowbrook, Ill., U.S. 268 41.46 N 87.56 W
Willow Brook ≃, Ont., Can. 202 43.53 N 80.16 W
Willow Brook ≃, Eng., U.K. 44 52.32 N 0.24 W
Willow Brook ≃, N.J., U.S. 266 40.20 N 74.10 W
Willowbrook Mall •[9] 266 40.53 N 74.15 W
Willowbrook Park ♠ 266 40.36 N 74.09 W
Willow Bunch 174 49.24 N 105.37 W
Willow Bunch Lake ⊜ 174 49.27 N 105.28 W
Willow City 188 48.36 N 100.18 W
Willow Creek, Calif., U.S. 194 40.56 N 123.38 W
Willow Creek, Mont., U.S. 192 45.49 N 111.39 W
Willow Creek ≃, Alta., Can. 172 49.46 N 113.21 W
Willow Creek ≃, Ont., Can. 202 44.25 N 79.53 W
Willow Creek ≃, Calif., U.S. 216 39.22 N 122.05 W
Willow Creek ≃, Calif., U.S. 216 37.09 N 119.27 W
Willow Creek ≃, Ill., U.S. 206 41.42 N 89.10 W
Willow Creek ≃, Ind., U.S. 206 41.15 N 85.08 W
Willow Creek ≃, Mich., U.S. 271 42.20 N 83.25 W
Willow Creek ≃, Mont., U.S. 192 48.09 N 106.38 W

Willow Creek ≃, Mont., U.S. 192 46.28 N 108.28 W
Willow Creek ≃, Mont., U.S. 192 48.10 N 111.11 W
Willow Creek ≃, Nev., U.S. 194 38.10 N 116.35 W
Willow Creek ≃, Ohio, U.S. 269a 41.20 N 82.03 W
Willow Creek ≃, Oreg., U.S. 192 44.00 N 117.13 W
Willow Creek ≃, Oreg., U.S. 192 45.48 N 120.01 W
Willow Creek ≃, Utah, U.S. 190 40.02 N 109.45 W
Willow Creek, North Fork ≃ 216 37.13 N 119.30 W
Willow Creek, South Fork ≃ 216 39.32 N 122.10 W
Willowdale •[8] 265b 43.47 N 79.26 W
Willowdale State Forest ♠ 273 42.40 N 70.54 W
Willowdene 263d 26.18 S 29.57 E
Willowemac 200 41.55 N 74.41 W
Willow Glen •[8] 272 37.18 N 121.53 W
Willow Grove 198 40.08 N 75.06 W
Willow Grove Naval Air Station ■ 198 40.12 N 75.08 W
Willow Grove Park ♠ 275 40.08 N 75.08 W
Willow Hill 204 40.06 N 77.48 W
Willowick 204 41.38 N 81.28 W
Willow Lake 188 44.38 N 97.38 W
Willow Lake ⊜, N.W. Ter., Can. 166 62.11 N 119.10 W
Willow Lake ⊜, N.Y., U.S. 266 40.43 N 73.50 W
Willowlake ≃ 166 62.52 N 123.08 W
Willowmac Creek ≃ 200 41.53 N 74.48 W
Willow Metropolitan Park ♠ 271 42.08 N 83.22 W
Willowmore 148 33.17 S 23.29 E
Willow Park 212 32.45 N 97.39 W
Willowra 152 21.15 S 132.35 E
Willow Reservoir ⊜[1] 180 45.45 N 89.50 W
Willow River 172 54.04 N 122.28 W
Willow Run, Mich., U.S. 206 42.16 N 83.34 W
Willow Run, Va., U.S. 274c 38.49 N 77.10 W
Willows 216 39.31 N 122.12 W
Willow Springs, Calif., U.S. 218 34.53 N 118.18 W
Willow Springs, Mo., U.S. 184 36.59 N 91.58 W
Willow Springs, Pa., U.S. 269b 40.19 N 79.44 W
Willow Street 198 39.59 N 76.17 W
Willowvale 148 32.16 S 28.30 E
Willow Wall ⊥ 94 42.10 N 122.30 E
Will Rogers State Beach ♠ 270 34.01 N 118.30 W
Will Rogers State Historical Park ♠ 270 34.03 N 118.31 W
Wills Creek ≃, Austl. 156 22.43 S 140.02 E
Wills Creek ≃, Ohio, U.S. 178 40.09 N 81.55 W
Wills Creek Lake ⊜[1] 204 40.08 N 81.45 W
Willseyville 200 42.17 N 76.23 W
Willshire 206 40.45 N 84.48 W
Wills Point 212 32.43 N 96.01 W
Willunga 158b 35.17 S 138.33 E
Wilmar 184 33.38 N 91.56 W
Wilmer, Ala., U.S. 184 30.44 N 88.28 W
Wilmer, Pa., U.S. 275 40.07 N 75.32 W
Wilmer, Tex., U.S. 212 32.35 N 96.41 W
Wilmerding 269b 40.24 N 79.48 W
Wilmersdorf •[8] 254a 52.30 N 13.19 E
Wilmette 206 42.04 N 87.43 W
Wilmington, Austl. 156 32.39 S 138.07 E
Wilmington, Eng., U.K. 250 51.26 N 0.12 E
Wilmington, Del., U.S. 198
275 39.44 N 75.33 W
Wilmington, Ill., U.S. 206 41.18 N 88.09 W
Wilmington, Mass., U.S. 197 42.33 N 71.10 W
Wilmington, N.C., U.S. 182 34.13 N 77.55 W
Wilmington, Ohio, U.S. 208 39.27 N 83.50 W
Wilmington, Vt., U.S. 178 42.52 N 72.52 W
Wilmington •[8] 270 33.47 N 118.16 W
Wilmington Manor 275 39.41 N 75.35 W
Wilmore, Ky., U.S. 182 37.52 N 84.40 W
Wilmore, Pa., U.S. 204 40.23 N 78.43 W
Wilmot, Ark., U.S. 184 33.04 N 91.34 W
Wilmot, Ohio, U.S. 204 40.39 N 81.38 W
Wilmot, S. Dak., U.S. 188 45.25 N 96.52 W
Wilmot, Wis., U.S. 206 42.31 N 88.11 W
Wilmot Woods ♠ 268 42.18 N 87.56 W
Wilmslow 42 53.20 N 2.15 W
Wilna → Vilnius 66 54.41 N 25.19 E
Wilnecote 44 52.36 N 1.40 W
Wilpen 204 40.17 N 79.12 W
Wilpoort 148 27.10 S 26.08 E
Wilpshire 252 53.47 N 2.28 W
Wilrijk 46 51.10 N 4.24 E
Wilsall 192 46.00 N 110.40 W
Wilsdruff 50 51.05 N 13.32 E
Wilseder Berg ∧[2] 48 53.10 N 9.56 E
Wilseyville 216 38.23 N 120.31 W
Wilshamstead 44 52.05 N 0.27 W
Wilson, Austl. 156 32.00 S 138.22 E
Wilson, Ark., U.S. 184 35.34 N 90.03 W
Wilson, Conn., U.S. 197 41.48 N 72.38 W
Wilson, Ill., U.S. 268 42.21 N 87.54 W
Wilson, Kans., U.S. 188 38.50 N 98.29 W
Wilson, N.C., U.S. 182 35.44 N 77.55 W
Wilson, N.Y., U.S. 200 43.19 N 78.50 W
Wilson, Okla., U.S. 186 34.10 N 97.26 W
Wilson, Pa., U.S. 198 40.41 N 75.15 W
Wilson, Tex., U.S. 186 33.19 N 101.44 W
Wilson ≃, Austl. 154 16.47 S 128.17 E
Wilson ≃, Austl. 156 27.38 S 141.24 E
Wilson ≃, Oreg., U.S. 214 45.28 N 123.53 W
Wilson, Cape ≻ 166 66.59 N 81.28 W
Wilson, Mount ∧, Calif., U.S. 270 34.13 N 118.04 W
Wilson, Mount ∧, Colo., U.S. 190 37.51 N 107.59 W
Wilson, Mount ∧, Nev., U.S. 194 38.15 N 114.23 W
Wilson, Mount ∧, Oreg., U.S. 214 45.04 N 121.39 W
Wilson, Mount ∧[2] 152 20.14 S 127.39 E
Wilson, Point ≻ 214 48.08 N 122.45 W
Wilson Cliffs •[4] 152 22.03 S 127.09 E
Wilson Creek ≃, Tex., U.S. 212 33.07 N 96.35 W
Wilson Creek ≃, Wash., U.S. 192 47.25 N 119.07 W
Wilson Lake ⊜[1], Ala., U.S. 184 34.49 N 87.30 W
Wilson Lake ⊜[1], Kans., U.S. 188 38.57 N 98.40 W
Wilson Range ∧∧ 152 28.50 S 124.25 E
Wilson Run ≃, Del., U.S. 275 39.48 N 75.35 W
Wilson Run ≃, Pa., U.S. 269b 40.13 N 79.37 W
Wilsons Beach 176 44.56 N 66.56 W
Wilson's Creek National Battlefield ♠ 184 37.06 N 93.27 W
Wilsons Promontory ≻ 156 38.55 S 146.20 E
Wilsons Promontory National Park ♠ 156 39.00 S 146.25 E
Wilsonville, Ill., U.S. 209 39.04 N 89.51 W
Wilsonville, Nebr., U.S. 188 40.07 N 100.07 W

≃ River	Fluss	Río	Rivière	Rio
≋ Canal	Kanal	Canal	Canal	Canal
↳ Waterfall, Rapids	Wasserfall, Stromschnellen	Cascada, Rápidos	Chute d'eau, Rapides	Cascata, Rápidos
ɰ Strait	Meeresstrasse	Estrecho	Détroit	Estreito
C Bay, Gulf	Bucht, Golf	Bahía, Golfo	Baie, Golfe	Baía, Golfo
⊜ Lake, Lakes	See, Seen	Lago, Lagos	Lac, Lacs	Lago, Lagos
≚ Swamp	Sumpf	Pantano	Marais	Pântano
❄ Ice Features, Glacier	Eis- und Gletscherformen	Accidentes Glaciales	Formes glaciaires	Acidentes Glaciares
⍑ Other Hydrographic Features	Andere Hydrographische Objekte	Otros Elementos Hidrográficos	Autres données hydrographiques	Outros Elementos Hidrográficos

✣ Submarine Features	Untermeerische Objekte	Accidentes Submarinos	Formes de relief sous-marin	Acidentes Submarinos
□ Political Unit	Politische Einheit	Unidad Politica	Entité politique	Unidade Política
▾ Cultural Institution	Kulturelle Institution	Institución Cultural	Institution culturelle	Instituição Cultural
⊥ Historical Site	Historische Stätte	Sitio Histórico	Site historique	Sitio Histórico
♠ Recreational Site	Erholungs- und Ferienort	Sitio de Recreo	Centre de loisirs	Sítio de Lazer
⊠ Airport	Flughafen	Aeropuerto	Aéroport	Aeroporto
■ Military Installation	Militäranlage	Instalación Militar	Installation militaire	Instalação Militar
• Miscellaneous	Verschiedenes	Misceláneo	Divers	Miscelânea

Name	Page	Lat.	Long.
Wilsonville, Oreg., U.S.	214	45.18 N	122.46 W
Wilster	48	53.55 N	9.22 E
Wilthen	50	51.06 N	14.24 E
Wilton, Eng., U.K.	44	51.05 N	1.52 W
Wilton, Conn., U.S.	197	41.12 N	73.26 W
Wilton, Maine, U.S.	178	44.35 N	70.14 W
Wilton, N.H., U.S.	178	42.51 N	71.44 W
Wilton, N. Dak., U.S.	188	47.10 N	100.47 W
Wilton, N.Y., U.S.	200	43.11 N	73.45 W
Wilton, Wis., U.S.	180	43.48 N	90.32 W
Wilton ≃	154	14.45 S	134.33 E
Wilton Creek ≃	202	44.12 N	76.56 W
Wilton Farm Acres	274b	39.18 N	76.50 W
Wilton Junction	184	41.35 N	91.01 W
Wilton Manors	210	26.10 N	80.07 W
Wiltshire □[6]	44	51.15 N	1.50 W
Wiltz	52	49.48 N	5.55 E
Wiluna	152	26.36 S	120.13 E
Wimapedi Lake ⊜	174	55.11 N	99.46 W
Wimauma	210	27.43 N	82.18 W
Wimberley	186	30.00 N	98.06 W
Wimbledon	188	47.10 N	98.28 W
Wimbledon ◆[8]	250	51.25 N	0.12 W
Wimbledon Common ♠	250	51.26 N	0.14 W
Wimborne Minster	44	50.48 N	1.59 W
Wimereux	46	50.46 N	1.37 E
Wimmelburg	50	51.31 N	11.30 E
Wimmenau	52	48.55 N	7.25 E
Wimmera ≃	159	36.55 S	142.56 E
Wimmis	54	46.41 N	7.38 E
Winagami Lake ⊜	172	55.38 N	116.45 W
Winam C	144	0.15 S	34.35 E
Winamac	206	41.03 N	86.36 W
Winburg	148	28.37 S	27.00 E
Winburne	204	40.58 N	78.08 W
Wincanton	44	51.04 N	2.25 W
Wincham	252	53.16 N	2.29 W
Winchcombe	44	51.57 N	1.58 W
Winchelsea, Austl.	159	38.15 S	143.59 E
Winchelsea, Eng., U.K.	44	50.55 N	0.42 E
Winchendon	197	42.41 N	72.03 W
Winchester, Ont., Can.	202	45.06 N	75.21 W
Winchester, N.Z.	162	44.12 S	171.17 E
Winchester, Eng., U.K.	44	51.04 N	1.19 W
Winchester, Calif., U.S.	218	33.42 N	117.05 W
Winchester, Idaho, U.S.	192	46.14 N	116.38 W
Winchester, Ill., U.S.	209	39.38 N	90.27 W
Winchester, Ind., U.S.	208	40.10 N	84.59 W
Winchester, Ky., U.S.	182	37.59 N	84.11 W
Winchester, Mass., U.S.	273	42.28 N	71.10 W
Winchester, N.H., U.S.	178	42.46 N	72.23 W
Winchester, Ohio, U.S.	208	38.57 N	83.39 W
Winchester, Tenn., U.S.	184	35.10 N	86.01 W
Winchester, Tex., U.S.	212	30.01 N	97.01 W
Winchester, Va., U.S.	178	39.11 N	78.10 W
Winchester Cathedral ʋ[1]	44	51.04 N	1.19 W
Winchmore Hill	250	51.39 N	0.39 W
Winchmore Hill ◆[8]	250	51.38 N	0.06 W
Wind ≃, Yukon, Can.	170	65.49 N	135.18 W
Wind ≃, Wash., U.S.	214	45.43 N	121.47 W
Wind ≃, Wyo., U.S.	192	43.35 N	108.13 W
Wind, North Fork ≃	192	43.27 N	109.28 W
Windang	160	34.32 S	150.53 E
Windau → Ventspils	66	57.24 N	21.36 E
Windber	204	40.14 N	78.50 W
Wind Cave National Park ♠	188	43.32 N	103.25 W
Windecken	52	50.13 N	8.52 E
Winder	182	32.59 N	83.43 W
Winder, Lake ⊜	210	28.15 N	80.51 W
Windera	156	26.03 S	151.50 E
Windermere, B.C., Can.	172	50.30 N	115.58 W
Windermere, Eng., U.K.	42	54.23 N	2.54 W
Windermere, Fla., U.S.	210	28.30 N	81.32 W
Windermere ⊜	42	54.22 N	2.56 W
Windermere Lake ⊜	180	47.56 N	83.47 W
Winder Village	275	40.06 N	74.52 W
Windfall, Alta., Can.	172	54.11 N	116.15 W
Windfall, Ind., U.S.	206	40.22 N	85.57 W
Windgap	200	40.51 N	75.18 W
Windham, Conn., U.S.	197	41.42 N	72.10 W
Windham, N.H., U.S.	273	42.49 N	71.19 W
Windham, N.Y., U.S.	200	42.19 N	74.15 W
Windham, Ohio, U.S.	204	41.14 N	81.03 W
Windham □[6], Conn., U.S.	197	41.55 N	71.55 W
Windham □[6], Vt., U.S.	197	42.50 N	72.43 W
Windhoek	146	22.34 S	17.06 E
Windhoek □[5]	146	22.30 S	17.00 E
Windigo ≃	174	53.22 N	91.48 W
Windigo Lake ⊜	174	52.35 N	91.32 W
Windisch	54	47.29 N	8.13 E
Windischgarsten	30	47.44 N	14.20 E
Wind Lake	206	42.50 N	88.09 W
Wind Lake ⊜	206	42.50 N	88.09 W
Windlass Run ≃	274b	39.24 N	76.24 W
Windleite ∧	50	51.22 N	10.56 E
Windlesham	250	51.22 N	0.40 W
Windley Key I	210	24.57 N	80.35 W
Windmill Point ›, Ont., Can.	274a	42.52 N	79.01 W
Windmill Point ›, Mich., U.S.	271	42.22 N	82.55 W
Windmill Point ›, Va., U.S.	198	37.37 N	76.17 W
Windom, Minn., U.S.	188	43.52 N	95.07 W
Windom, N.Y., U.S.	200	42.47 N	78.48 W
Windom Peak ∧	190	37.37 N	107.35 W
Windorah	156	25.26 S	142.39 E
Window Rock	190	35.41 N	109.03 W
Wind Point	206	42.47 N	87.46 W
Wind River Indian Reservation ◆[4]	192	43.26 N	109.00 W
Wind River Peak ∧	190	42.42 N	109.07 W
Wind River Range ∧∧	190	43.05 N	109.25 W
Windrush ≃	44	51.42 N	1.25 W
Windsbach	52	49.14 N	10.50 E
Windsor, Austl.	158b	34.25 S	138.20 E
Windsor, Austl.	160	33.37 S	150.49 E
Windsor, N.B., Can.	176	48.57 N	55.40 W
Windsor, N.S., Can.	176	44.59 N	64.08 W
Windsor, Ont., Can.	204		
	271	42.18 N	83.01 W
Windsor, Qué., Can.	196	45.34 N	72.00 W
Windsor, Eng., U.K.	44	51.29 N	0.38 W
Windsor, Calif., U.S.	194	38.33 N	122.49 W
Windsor, Colo., U.S.	190	40.29 N	104.54 W
Windsor, Conn., U.S.	197	41.51 N	72.39 W
Windsor, Ill., U.S.	184	39.26 N	88.36 W
Windsor, Ind., U.S.	208	40.09 N	85.12 W
Windsor, Mo., U.S.	184	38.32 N	93.31 W
Windsor, N.J., U.S.	198	40.15 N	74.35 W
Windsor, N.C., U.S.	182	36.00 N	76.57 W
Windsor, N.Y., U.S.	200	42.05 N	75.39 W
Windsor, Ohio, U.S.	204	41.32 N	80.56 W
Windsor, Pa., U.S.	198	39.55 N	76.35 W
Windsor, Vt., U.S.	178	43.29 N	72.23 W
Windsor, Va., U.S.	198	36.48 N	76.45 W
Windsor, Wis., U.S.	206	43.13 N	89.20 W
Windsor, Gare ◆[5]	265a	45.30 N	73.34 W
Windsor, University of ʋ[2]	271	42.18 N	83.04 W
Windsor Airport ⊠	204	42.17 N	82.58 W
Windsor and Maidenhead □[8]	250	51.28 N	0.37 W
Windsor Castle ⊥	44	51.29 N	0.36 W
Windsor Dam ◆[6]	178	42.29 N	72.42 W
Windsor Forest ◆[3]	44	51.27 N	0.43 W
Windsor Great Park ♠	250	51.27 N	0.37 W
Windsor Heights	204	40.12 N	80.40 W
Windsor Hills	270	33.59 N	118.21 W
Windsor Locks	197	41.56 N	72.38 W
Windsor Race Course ♠	250	51.29 N	0.39 W
Windsor Raceway ♠	271	42.15 N	83.05 W
Windsorton	148	28.16 S	24.44 E
Windsorville	197	41.53 N	72.32 W
Windthorst	186	33.34 N	98.26 W
Windward Islands II	228	13.00 N	61.00 W
Windward Passage ⋃	228	20.00 N	73.50 W
Windy Hills	275	39.41 N	75.43 W
Windy Lake ⊜	174	54.22 N	102.35 W
Windy Peak ∧	192	48.56 N	119.58 W
Windy Run ≃	274c	38.54 N	77.05 W
Winefred ≃	174	56.02 N	110.36 W
Winefred Lake ⊜	172	55.30 N	110.35 W
Winejok	130	9.01 N	27.34 E
Winesburg	204	40.37 N	81.42 W
Winfield, Alta., Can.	172	52.58 N	114.26 W
Winfield, Ala., U.S.	184	33.56 N	87.49 W
Winfield, Ill., U.S.	206	41.52 N	88.10 W
Winfield, Iowa, U.S.	180	41.07 N	91.26 W
Winfield, Kans., U.S.	188	37.15 N	96.59 W
Winfield, Mo., U.S.	209	38.59 N	90.44 W
Winfield, N.J., U.S.	266	40.39 N	74.17 W
Winfield, Tex., U.S.	212	33.10 N	95.07 W
Winfield, W. Va., U.S.	178	38.32 N	81.53 W
Wing	188	47.09 N	100.17 W
Wing ≃	188	46.29 N	94.58 W
Wingan National Park ♠	156	37.43 S	149.30 E
Wingate, Md., U.S.	198	38.18 N	76.06 W
Wingate, N.C., U.S.	182	34.59 N	80.27 W
Wingate Mountains ∧∧	154	14.29 S	130.42 E
Wingates	252	53.34 N	2.32 W
Wingdale	200	41.39 N	73.34 W
Wingecarribee ≃	160	34.23 S	150.07 E
Wingello	160	34.42 S	150.09 E
Wingene	46	51.04 N	3.16 E
Wingen-sur-Moder	52	48.55 N	7.22 E
Wingham, Austl.	156	31.52 S	152.22 E
Wingham, Ont., Can.	202	43.53 N	81.19 W
Wingham, Eng., U.K.	44	51.17 N	1.13 E
Wing Lake Shores	271	42.33 N	83.17 W
Wingles	46	50.29 N	2.51 E
Wings Airport ⊠	275	40.08 N	75.16 W
Wingst	48	53.43 N	9.03 E
Winhole Channel ⋃	266	43.37 N	73.48 W
Winifred	192	47.04 N	109.23 W
Winifreda	242	36.15 S	64.14 W
Winisk	166	55.15 N	85.12 W
Winisk ≃	166	55.17 N	85.05 W
Winisk Lake ⊜	166	52.55 N	87.22 W
Wink	186	31.45 N	103.09 W
Winkana	100	15.44 N	98.01 E
Winkelman	190	32.59 N	110.46 W
Winkelpos	148	27.35 S	26.49 E
Winkler, Man., Can.	174	49.11 N	97.56 W
Winkler, Tex., U.S.	212	31.56 N	96.13 W
Winklern	58	46.52 N	12.52 E
Winlaw	172	49.37 N	117.34 W
Winlock	214	46.29 N	122.56 W
Winneba	140	5.25 N	0.36 W
Winnebago, Ill., U.S.	180	42.16 N	89.15 W
Winnebago, Minn., U.S.	180	43.46 N	94.10 W
Winnebago, Nebr., U.S.	188	42.14 N	96.28 W
Winnebago □[6]	206	42.17 N	89.06 W
Winnebago ≃	180	43.03 N	92.57 W
Winnebago, Lake ⊜	180	44.00 N	88.25 W
Winnebago Indian Reservation ◆[4], Nebr., U.S.	188	42.15 N	96.31 W
Winnebago Indian Reservation ◆[4], Wis., U.S.	180	44.15 N	90.38 W
Winnecke, Mount ∧[2]	152	18.47 S	130.20 E
Winnecke Creek ≃	152	18.35 S	131.34 E
Winneconne	180	44.07 N	88.43 W
Winneconnet	273	41.59 N	71.08 W
Winneconnet Pond ⊜	273	41.58 N	71.08 W
Winnekendonk	48	51.36 N	6.17 E
Winnemucca	194	40.58 N	117.44 W
Winnemucca Lake ⊜	194	40.09 N	119.20 W
Winnenden	52	48.53 N	9.24 E
Winner	188	43.22 N	99.51 W
Winnetka	206	42.07 N	87.44 W
Winnetka ◆[8]	270	34.13 N	118.35 W
Winnett	192	47.00 N	108.21 W
Winnfield	184	31.55 N	92.38 W
Winnibigoshish, Lake ⊜	180	47.27 N	94.12 W
Winnie	184	29.49 N	94.23 W
Winning	152	23.09 S	114.32 E
Winningen, B.R.D.	52	50.18 N	7.31 E
Winningen, D.D.R.	50	51.49 N	11.26 E
Winnipeg	174	49.53 N	97.09 W
Winnipeg ≃	174	50.38 N	96.19 W
Winnipeg, Lake ⊜	174	52.00 N	97.00 W
Winnipeg Beach	174	50.31 N	96.58 W
Winnipegosis	174	51.39 N	99.56 W
Winnipegosis, Lake ⊜	174	52.30 N	100.00 W
Winnipesaukee, Lake ⊜	178	43.35 N	71.20 W
Winnsboro, La., U.S.	184	32.10 N	91.43 W
Winnsboro, S.C., U.S.	182	34.22 N	81.05 W
Winnsboro, Tex., U.S.	212	32.58 N	95.17 W
Winnsboro Mills	182	34.22 N	81.06 W
Winnweiler	52	49.34 N	7.51 E
Winona, Kans., U.S.	188	39.04 N	101.15 W
Winona, Mich., U.S.	180	46.52 N	88.55 W
Winona, Minn., U.S.	180	44.03 N	91.39 W
Winona, Miss., U.S.	184	33.29 N	89.44 W
Winona, Mo., U.S.	184	37.06 N	91.19 W
Winona, Ohio, U.S.	204	40.50 N	80.54 W
Winona, Tex., U.S.	212	32.29 N	95.10 W
Winona Lake, Ind., U.S.	206	41.14 N	85.49 W
Winona Lake, N.Y., U.S.	200	41.31 N	74.03 W
Winona Lake ⊜	206	41.13 N	85.50 W
Winooski	178	44.29 N	73.11 W
Winooski ≃	178	44.30 N	73.15 W
Winooski, North Branch ≃	178	44.15 N	72.35 W
Winschoten	48	53.08 N	7.02 E
Winsen, B.R.D.	48	53.22 N	10.12 E
Winsen, B.R.D.	48	52.41 N	9.54 E
Winsford, Eng., U.K.	42	53.12 N	2.32 W
Winsford, Eng., U.K.	44	51.06 N	3.33 W
Winshill	44	52.48 N	1.36 W
Winside	188	42.11 N	97.10 W
Winslow, Eng., U.K.	44	51.57 N	0.54 W
Winslow, Ariz., U.S.	190	35.01 N	110.42 W
Winslow, Maine, U.S.	178	44.32 N	69.38 W
Winslow, N.J., U.S.	275	39.39 N	74.52 W
Winslow, Wash., U.S.	214	47.37 N	122.31 W
Winslow Seamount ◆[3]	14	1.35 N	174.55 W
Winsted, Conn., U.S.	197	41.55 N	73.04 W
Winsted, Minn., U.S.	180	44.58 N	94.03 W
Winston, Fla., U.S.	210	28.02 N	82.01 W
Winston, Oreg., U.S.	192	45.07 N	123.25 W
Winston Churchill Memorial ʋ	209	38.52 N	91.58 W
Winston Creek ≃	214	46.30 N	122.40 W
Winston-Salem	182	36.06 N	80.15 W
Winsum	48	53.19 N	6.31 E
Wintego Lake ⊜	174	55.33 N	102.52 W
Winter	180	45.49 N	91.01 W
Winter Beach	210	27.43 N	80.25 W
Winterberg, B.R.D.	52	51.11 N	8.32 E
Winterberg, B.R.D.	253	51.17 N	7.18 E
Winterberg ∧[2]	253	51.20 N	7.13 E
Winterberge ∧∧	148	32.28 S	26.15 E
Winterbourne Abbas	44	50.43 N	2.34 W
Winter Creek ≃	270	34.12 N	118.02 W
Winterfeld	50	52.44 N	11.14 E
Winter Garden	210	28.34 N	81.35 W
Winter Gardens	218	32.50 N	116.56 W
Winter Harbor	178	44.24 N	68.05 W
Winter Harbour	172	50.31 N	128.02 W
Winterhaven, Calif., U.S.	194	32.44 N	114.38 W
Winter Haven, Fla., U.S.	210	28.01 N	81.44 W
Winter Hill ∧[2]	252	53.38 N	2.31 W
Wintering ≃	188	48.12 N	100.34 W
Wintering Lake ⊜	174	55.24 N	97.42 W
Winter Island I, N.W. Ter., Can.	166	66.14 N	83.04 W
Winter Island I, Calif., U.S.	272	38.03 N	121.51 W
Winter Island I, Mass., U.S.	273	42.32 N	70.52 W
Winterlingen	54	48.11 N	9.07 E
Winter Park	210	28.36 N	81.20 W
Winterport	178	44.38 N	68.51 W
Winters, Calif., U.S.	216	38.31 N	121.58 W
Winters, Tex., U.S.	186	31.57 N	99.58 W
Winters Bayou ≃	212	30.22 N	95.06 W
Winters Canal ≍	216	38.32 N	121.58 W
Wintersdorf	50	51.03 N	12.21 E
Winterset, Iowa, U.S.	180	41.20 N	94.01 W
Winterset, Ohio, U.S.	204	40.06 N	81.25 W
Winter Springs	210	28.42 N	81.19 W
Winters Run ≃	198	39.26 N	76.18 W
Winterstown	198	39.50 N	76.37 W
Wintersville	204	40.23 N	80.42 W
Winterswijk	48	51.58 N	6.44 E
Winterthur, Schw.	54	47.30 N	8.43 E
Winterthur, Del., U.S.	275	39.48 N	75.36 W
Winterton, Newf., Can.	176	47.58 N	53.20 W
Winterton, S. Afr.	148	28.46 S	29.35 E
Winterton-on-Sea	44	52.43 N	1.42 E
Winterville, Miss., U.S.	184	33.30 N	91.10 W
Winterville, N.C., U.S.	182	35.32 N	77.24 W
Winthrop, Conn., U.S.	197	41.22 N	72.30 W
Winthrop, Iowa, U.S.	180	42.28 N	91.44 W
Winthrop, Maine, U.S.	178	44.18 N	69.59 W
Winthrop, Mass., U.S.	273	42.23 N	70.59 W
Winthrop, Minn., U.S.	180	44.32 N	94.22 W
Winthrop, Lake ⊜	273	42.11 N	71.25 W
Winthrop Harbor	206	42.29 N	87.49 W
Wintinna	152	27.44 S	134.07 E
Wintinna Creek ≃	152	27.47 S	134.14 E
Winton, Austl.	156	22.23 S	143.02 E
Winton, N.Z.	162	46.09 S	168.20 E
Winton, S. Afr.	148	27.29 S	22.34 E
Winton, Calif., U.S.	216	37.23 N	120.37 W
Winton, N.C., U.S.	182	36.24 N	76.56 W
Winton, Wash., U.S.	214	47.44 N	120.44 W
Wintzenheim	54	48.04 N	7.17 E
Winwick	252	53.26 N	2.36 W
Winzenberg	253	51.06 N	7.38 E
Winzermark	253	51.23 N	7.08 E
Wipper ≃, B.R.D.	253	51.07 N	7.24 E
Wipper ≃, D.D.R.	50	51.47 N	11.42 E
Wipperdorf	50	51.28 N	10.42 E
Wipperfeld	253	51.05 N	7.19 E
Wipperfürth	52	51.07 N	7.23 E
Wippra	50	51.34 N	11.16 E
Wireton, Ill., U.S.	268	41.40 N	87.42 W
Wireton, Pa., U.S.	269b	40.34 N	80.14 W
Wiriaga ≃	154	2.17 S	132.52 E
Wirksworth	44	53.05 N	1.34 W
Wirosari	105a	7.05 S	111.05 E
Wirral □[8]	252	53.22 N	3.05 W
Wirraminna	156	31.12 S	136.15 E
Wirrulla	152	32.24 S	134.31 E
Wisbech	44	52.40 N	0.10 E
Wisby → Visby	26	57.38 N	18.18 E
Wiscasset	178	44.00 N	69.40 W
Wische ◆[1]	50	52.50 N	11.55 E
Wischhafen	48	53.46 N	9.19 E
Wisconsin □[3]	168		
	180	44.45 N	89.30 W
Wisconsin ≃	180	43.00 N	91.15 W
Wisconsin, Lake ⊜[1]	180	43.24 N	89.43 W
Wisconsin Dells	180	43.38 N	89.46 W
Wisconsin Dells ∨	180	43.41 N	89.49 W
Wisconsin Rapids	180	44.23 N	89.49 W
Wiscoy	200	42.30 N	78.05 W
Wisdom	192	45.37 N	113.27 W
Wisdom, Lake ⊜	154	5.20 S	147.05 E
Wise	182	36.59 N	82.34 W
Wise □[6]	212	33.07 N	97.40 W
Wise ≃	192	45.48 N	112.57 W
Wiseman	170	67.25 N	150.06 W
Wisemans Ferry	160	33.24 S	150.59 E
Wises Landing	208	38.35 N	85.25 W
Wishart	174	51.34 N	104.00 W
Wishaw	42	55.47 N	3.56 W
Wishek	188	46.16 N	99.33 W
Wishkah ≃	214	46.58 N	123.45 W
Wishram	214	45.40 N	120.58 W
Wisła	30	49.40 N	18.52 E
Wisła ≃	30	54.22 N	18.55 E
Wisley Gardens ♠	250	51.19 N	0.29 W
Wisłok ≃	30	50.13 N	22.32 E
Wisłoka ≃	30	50.27 N	21.23 E
Wismar, D.D.R.	50	53.53 N	11.28 E
Wismar, Guy.	236	6.00 N	58.18 W
Wismarbucht C	50	53.57 N	11.25 E
Wisner, La., U.S.	184	31.59 N	91.39 W
Wisner, Nebr., U.S.	188	41.59 N	96.55 W
Wissahickon Creek ≃	275	40.01 N	75.12 W
Wissant	46	50.53 N	1.40 E
Wissembourg	52	49.02 N	7.57 E
Wissen	52	50.47 N	7.43 E
Wissenkerke	48	51.35 N	3.45 E
Wissey ≃	44	52.33 N	0.21 E
Wissinoming ◆[8]	275	40.01 N	75.04 W
Wissmar	52	50.38 N	8.41 E
Wissous	251	48.44 N	2.20 E
Wister	184	34.58 N	94.43 W
Wisznice	30	51.48 N	23.12 E
Witbank	148	25.56 S	29.07 E
Witbooisvlei	146	25.04 S	18.27 E
Witchekan Lake ⊜	174	53.25 N	107.35 W
Witch Hazel	214	45.30 N	122.46 W
Witdraai	148	26.58 S	20.45 E
Witfield	263d	26.11 S	28.12 E
Witham	44	51.48 N	0.38 E
Witham ≃	44	52.56 N	0.04 E
Withamsville	208	39.03 N	84.16 W
Withens Clough Reservoir ⊜[1]	252	53.42 N	2.02 W
Witheridge	44	50.55 N	3.42 W
Withernsea	42	53.44 N	0.02 E
Witherspoon, Mount ∧	170	61.23 N	147.12 W
Withington ◆[8]	252	53.26 N	2.14 W
Withington Green	252	53.14 N	2.18 W
Withlacoochee ≃, U.S.	182	30.24 N	83.10 W
Withlacoochee ≃, Fla., U.S.	182	29.00 N	82.45 W
Withnell	252	53.42 N	2.34 W
Withok	263d	26.18 S	28.23 E
Withokspruit ≃	263d	26.19 S	28.21 E
Wit Kei ≃	148	32.09 S	27.24 E
Witkoppies ∧	148	27.44 S	29.20 E
Witkowo	30	52.27 N	17.47 E
Witless Bay	176	47.16 N	52.50 W
Witley	44	51.09 N	0.38 W
Witney	44	51.48 N	1.29 W
Witnica	30	52.40 N	14.55 E
Witpoortje	263d	26.08 S	27.50 E
Witrivier	146	24.40 S	31.00 E
Witry-lès-Reims	46	49.18 N	4.07 E
Witsand	148	34.24 S	20.50 E
Witt	209	39.15 N	89.21 W
Wittabrenna Creek ≃	156	29.20 S	142.43 E
Witteberg ∧∧	148	33.15 S	23.15 E
Witteberge ∧	148	28.40 S	28.02 E
Witteberge ∧∧, S. Afr.	148	33.18 S	20.36 E
Witteberge ∧∧, S. Afr.	148	30.45 S	27.32 E
Wittelsheim	54	47.49 N	7.15 E
Witten	52	51.26 N	7.20 E
Wittenau ◆[8]	254a	52.35 N	13.20 E
Wittenberg, D.D.R.	50	51.52 N	12.39 E
Wittenberg, Wis., U.S.	180	44.49 N	89.10 W
Wittenberge	50	53.00 N	11.44 E
Wittenburg	50	53.31 N	11.04 E
Wittenheim	54	47.49 N	7.20 E
Wittenoom	152	22.17 S	118.19 E
Wittensee ⊜	41	54.23 N	9.45 E
Wittgensdorf	50	50.53 N	12.52 E
Wittichenau	50	51.23 N	14.14 E
Wittingen	50	52.43 N	10.44 E
Wittislingen	52	48.37 N	10.25 E
Wittlaer	52	51.19 N	6.44 E
Wittlich	52	49.59 N	6.53 E
Wittmar	50	52.07 N	10.38 E
Wittmund	48	53.34 N	7.47 E
Witton Park ♠	252	53.45 N	2.31 W
Wittow ›[1]	50	54.38 N	13.19 E
Wittstock	50	53.10 N	12.29 E
Witu	144	2.23 S	40.26 E
Witu Islands II	154	4.40 S	149.25 E
Witvlei	146	22.23 S	18.32 E
Witwatersrand ◆[1]	148	26.00 S	27.00 E
Witwatersrand, University of ʋ[2]	263d	26.12 S	28.02 E
Witwatersrand Gold Mine ◆[7]	263d	26.12 S	28.15 E
Witzenhausen	52	51.20 N	9.51 E
Witzhelden	253	51.07 N	7.06 E
Witzputz	146	27.25 S	17.43 E
Wiveliscombe	44	51.03 N	3.19 W
Wivenhoe	44	51.52 N	0.58 E
Wiwa Creek ≃	174	50.02 N	106.31 W
Wixom	206	42.31 N	83.32 W
Wiżajny	30	54.23 N	22.51 E
Wizernes	46	50.43 N	2.14 E
Wjatka → V'atka ≃	70	55.36 N	51.30 E
Wkra ≃	30	52.27 N	20.44 E
Wladiwostok → Vladivostok	79	43.10 N	131.56 E
Władysławowo	30	54.49 N	18.25 E
Wleń	30	51.01 N	15.40 E
Wlingi	105a	8.05 S	112.19 E
Włocławek	30	52.39 N	19.02 E
Włodawa	30	51.34 N	23.32 E
Włoszczowa	30	50.52 N	19.59 E
Wnion ≃	44	52.45 N	3.54 W
Woady Yaloak ≃	159	38.06 S	143.33 E
Wobaer	75	39.19 N	75.32 E
Wöbbelin	50	53.24 N	11.30 E
Woburn	197	42.29 N	71.09 W
Woburn ◆[8]	265b	43.46 N	79.13 W
Woburn Sands	44	52.01 N	0.39 W
Woden, Austl.	161b	35.22 S	149.08 E
Woden, Tex., U.S.	212	31.30 N	94.32 W
Wodgina	152	21.11 S	118.40 E
Wodonga	156	36.07 S	146.54 E
Wodzisław Śląski	30	50.00 N	18.28 E
Woensdrecht	48	51.26 N	4.18 E
Woerdeke	75	39.41 N	77.53 E
Woerden	48	52.05 N	4.54 E
Woerth	52	48.56 N	7.45 E
Woëvre □[9]	52	49.27 N	5.17 E
Wofoși	95	40.09 N	115.18 E
Wofosi (Temple of the Sleeping Buddha) ʋ[1]	95	40.01 N	116.12 E
Wognum	48	52.41 N	5.01 E
Wohlau → Wołów	30	51.21 N	16.39 E
Wohlde	41	54.24 N	9.17 E
Wohlen	54	47.21 N	8.17 E
Wohlensee ⊜	54	46.58 N	7.20 E
Wohlford, Lake ⊜[1]	218	33.10 N	116.59 W
Wohlthat Mountains ∧∧	9	71.35 S	12.20 E
Wohra ≃	52	50.49 N	8.55 E
Woi	130	7.53 N	31.10 E
Woincourt	46	50.04 N	1.32 E
Wojcieszów	30	50.58 N	15.56 E
Wokalup	158a	33.06 S	115.53 E
Wokam, Pulau I	154	5.37 S	134.30 E
Wokha	110	26.06 N	94.16 E
Woking, Alta., Can.	172	55.35 N	118.46 W
Woking, Eng., U.K.	44	51.20 N	0.34 W
Woking □[8]	250	51.19 N	0.32 W
Wokingham	44	51.25 N	0.51 W
Wokingham Creek ≃	156	22.19 S	142.30 E
Wolbach	188	41.24 N	98.24 W
Wolbeck	48	51.55 N	7.43 E
Wolbrom	30	50.24 N	19.46 E
Wolcott, Conn., U.S.	197	41.36 N	72.59 W
Wolcott, Ind., U.S.	206	40.46 N	87.03 W
Wolcott, N.Y., U.S.	200	43.13 N	76.49 W
Wolcott Creek ≃	200	43.17 N	76.50 W
Wolcottsburg	200	43.04 N	78.38 W
Wolcottsville	200	43.07 N	78.31 W
Wolcottville	184	41.32 N	85.22 W
Wołczyn	30	51.01 N	18.03 E
Woldberg ∧∧[1]	48	52.25 N	5.55 E
Woldegk	50	53.27 N	13.35 E
Woldenburg → Dobiegniew	30	52.59 N	15.47 E
Woldingham	250	51.17 N	0.02 W
Woleai I[1]	98	7.21 N	143.52 E
Woleu-Ntem □[4]	142	2.00 N	12.00 E
Wolf ≃, U.S.	184	35.09 N	90.04 W
Wolf ≃, Kans., U.S.	188	39.54 N	95.11 W
Wolf ≃, Miss., U.S.	184	30.21 N	89.18 W
Wolf ≃, Wis., U.S.	180	44.11 N	88.48 W
Wolf, Isla I	236a	1.23 N	91.49 W
Wolf, Volcán ∧[1]	236a	0.02 N	91.20 W
Wolfach	54	48.17 N	8.13 E
Wolf Bay	176	50.16 N	60.08 W
Wolf Creek, Mont., U.S.	192	47.00 N	112.04 W
Wolf Creek, Oreg., U.S.	192	42.42 N	123.24 W
Wolf Creek ≃, U.S.	186	36.35 N	99.30 W
Wolf Creek ≃, Calif., U.S.	216	39.02 N	121.08 W
Wolf Creek ≃, Ind., U.S.	206	41.15 N	87.07 W
Wolf Creek ≃, Iowa, U.S.	180	42.20 N	92.09 W
Wolf Creek ≃, Mont., U.S.	188	48.05 N	105.40 W
Wolf Creek ≃, Mont., U.S.	192	46.50 N	112.20 W
Wolf Creek ≃, Mont., U.S.	192	47.37 N	109.38 W
Wolf Creek ≃, Ohio, U.S.	204	41.16 N	83.11 W
Wolf Creek ≃, Pa., U.S.	204	41.03 N	80.07 W
Wolf Creek ≃, S. Dak., U.S.	188	43.21 N	97.37 W
Wolf Creek ≃, S. Dak., U.S.	188	44.42 N	98.40 W
Wolf Creek Pass)(	190	37.29 N	106.48 W
Wolf Creek State Park ♠	209	39.30 N	88.41 W
Wolfdale	204	40.12 N	80.17 W
Wolfe □[6]	196	45.45 N	71.30 W
Wolfeboro	178	43.35 N	71.12 W
Wolfegg	54	47.49 N	9.47 E
Wolfe Island	202	44.12 N	76.26 W
Wolfe Island I	202	44.12 N	76.26 W
Wolfe Lake ⊜	202	44.40 N	76.30 W
Wolfen	50	51.40 N	12.16 E
Wolfenbüttel	48	52.10 N	10.32 E
Wolfenden, Mount ∧	172	50.26 N	127.33 W
Wolfenschiessen	54	46.55 N	8.24 E
Wolfertschwenden	54	47.53 N	10.16 E
Wolfforth	186	33.30 N	102.01 W
Wolfhagen	52	51.19 N	9.10 E
Wölfis	50	50.48 N	10.46 E
Wolf Island I	202	44.33 N	78.15 W
Wolflake, Ind., U.S.	206	41.20 N	85.30 W
Wolf Lake, Mich., U.S.	206	43.14 N	86.10 W
Wolf Lake ⊜, Alta., Can.	172	54.42 N	110.59 W
Wolf Lake ⊜, Ont., Can.	202	44.44 N	78.11 W
Wolf Lake ⊜, Yukon, Can.	170	60.40 N	131.40 W
Wolf Lake ⊜, U.S.	268	41.40 N	87.31 W
Wolf Lake ⊜, N.J., U.S.	266	40.57 N	74.42 W
Wolf Mountain ∧	170	65.17 N	154.02 W
Wolfpassing	254b	48.19 N	16.11 E
Wolf Point	192	48.05 N	105.39 W
Wolframs-Eschenbach	52	49.14 N	10.43 E
Wolfratshausen	58	47.54 N	11.25 E
Wolf Rock I[2]	28	49.57 N	5.49 W
Wolf Run	204	40.30 N	80.54 W
Wolfsberg	30	46.51 N	14.51 E
Wolfsberg ∧[2]	253	51.38 N	6.27 E
Wolfsburg	50	52.25 N	10.47 E
Wolf's Castle	44	51.54 N	4.58 W
Wolfsegg am Hausruck	58	48.06 N	13.40 E
Wolfskehlen	52	49.51 N	8.30 E
Wolfstein	52	49.35 N	7.36 E
Wolftrap Creek ≃	274c	38.58 N	77.17 W
Wolfurt	54	47.28 N	9.45 E
Wolfville	176	45.05 N	64.22 W
Wolga → Volga ≃	62	45.55 N	47.52 E
Wolgan ≃	160	33.12 S	150.28 E
Wolgast	50	54.03 N	13.46 E
Wolgograd → Volgograd	70	48.44 N	44.25 E
Wolgograder Stausee → Volgogradskoje Vodochranilišče ⊜[1]	70	49.20 N	45.00 E
Wolhusen	54	47.04 N	8.04 E
Wolin	30	53.50 N	14.35 E
Wolin I	50	53.55 N	14.31 E
Woliński Park Narodowy ♠	30	53.55 N	14.30 E
Wolkenstein	50	50.39 N	13.04 E
Wölkisch	50	51.13 N	13.21 E
Wolkramshausen	50	51.25 N	10.44 E
Wollangambe Creek ≃	160	33.21 S	150.35 E
Wollaston, Cape ›	166	71.04 N	118.07 W
Wollaston, Islas II	244	55.40 S	67.30 W
Wollaston Lake ⊜, Ont., Can.	202	44.50 N	77.50 W
Wollaston Lake ⊜, Sask., Can.	166	58.15 N	103.20 W
Wollaston Peninsula ›[1]	166	70.00 N	115.00 W
Wollemi Creek ≃	160	33.13 S	150.31 E
Wollogorang	156	17.13 S	137.57 E
Wollombi	160	32.56 S	151.09 E
Wollombi Brook ≃	160	32.33 S	151.04 E
Wollondilly ≃	160	33.57 S	150.26 E
Wollongong	160	34.25 S	150.54 E
Wöllstein	52	49.49 N	7.58 E
Wolmaransstad	148	27.12 S	26.13 E
Wolmirsleben	50	51.57 N	11.29 E
Wolmirstedt	50	52.15 N	11.37 E
Wołomin	30	52.21 N	21.14 E
Wołów	30	51.21 N	16.39 E
Wolowaru	105b	8.46 S	121.54 E
Wolseley, Sask., Can.	174	50.25 N	103.19 W
Wolseley, S. Afr.	148	33.26 S	19.12 E
Wolsey	188	44.25 N	98.28 W
Wolsingham	42	54.44 N	1.52 W
Wolsztyn	30	52.08 N	16.06 E
Wolterdingen	48	53.02 N	9.50 E
Woltersdorf, D.D.R.	50	52.24 N	12.22 E
Woltersdorf, D.D.R.	50	52.26 N	13.45 E
Woluogu	95	39.40 N	117.46 E
Woluwe-Saint-Pierre	46	50.50 N	4.25 E
Wolvega	48	52.53 N	6.00 E
Wolvenspruit	148	28.50 S	25.32 E
Wolverhampton	44	52.36 N	2.08 W
Wolverine	180	45.16 N	84.36 W
Wolverine Lake	271	42.33 N	83.29 W
Wolverine Loon Lake ⊜	271	42.33 N	83.30 W
Wolverine Mountain ∧	170	65.20 N	149.51 W
Wolvertem	46	50.57 N	4.18 E
Wolverton	44	52.04 N	0.50 W
Wolwehoek	148	26.55 S	27.48 E
Wolziger See ⊜	50	52.16 N	13.50 E
Woman ≃	180	47.57 N	82.19 W
Wombarra	160	34.16 S	150.58 E
Wombat, Mount ∧	159	36.51 S	145.40 E
Wombeyan Caves •[5]	160	34.18 S	149.56 E
Wombwell	42	53.31 N	1.24 W
Womelsdorf	198	40.22 N	76.11 W
Womerah Range ∧∧	160	33.16 S	150.46 E
Wommels	48	53.06 N	5.36 E
Wonarah	152	19.55 S	136.20 E
Wondai	156	26.19 S	151.52 E
Wondelgem	46	51.05 N	3.43 E
Wonderkop	148	27.50 S	27.26 E
Wonder Lake	206	42.25 N	88.21 W
Wonderland	194	40.24 N	121.19 W
Wonderland Center ◆[9]	271	42.22 N	83.20 W
Wondinong	152	27.52 S	118.25 E
Wŏndong-ni	88	34.23 N	126.40 E
Wonersh	250	51.12 N	0.33 W
Wonewoc	180	43.39 N	90.14 W
Wong ≃	114	27.10 N	89.30 E
Wongan Hills	152	30.53 S	116.42 E
Wonga Park	264b	37.44 S	145.16 E
Wonggarasi	102	0.33 N	121.36 E
Wong Ka Wai	261d	22.24 N	113.58 E
Woniushi	94	42.31 N	123.03 E
Wŏnjang-ni	88	39.05 N	125.32 E
Wŏnju	88	37.22 N	127.58 E
Wono	134	8.31 N	37.30 E
Wonogiri	105a	7.49 S	110.55 E
Wonokromo	105a	7.18 S	112.44 E
Wonosari	105a	7.58 S	110.35 E
Wonosegoro	105a	7.18 S	110.39 E
Wonosobo	105a	7.22 S	109.54 E
Wonotobo Fall ʟ	236	4.22 N	57.55 W
Wonreli	102	8.05 S	127.09 E
Wŏnsan	88	39.09 N	127.25 E
Wonthaggi	159	38.36 S	145.35 E
Woocalla	156	31.42 S	137.13 E
Wood, Pa., U.S.	204	40.10 N	78.08 W
Wood, S. Dak., U.S.	188	43.30 N	100.29 W
Wood □[6], Ohio, U.S.	206	41.22 N	83.39 W
Wood □[6], Tex., U.S.	212	32.48 N	95.20 W
Wood ≃, B.C., Can.	172	52.10 N	118.30 W
Wood ≃, Sask., Can.	174	50.08 N	106.10 W
Wood ≃, U.S.	197	41.26 N	71.43 W
Wood ≃, Nebr., U.S.	188	41.02 N	98.05 W
Wood ≃, Wyo., U.S.	192	44.07 N	108.58 W
Wood, Mount ∧, Yukon, Can.	170	61.14 N	140.31 W
Wood, Mount ∧, Mont., U.S.	192	45.17 N	109.49 W
Woodacre	216	38.05 N	122.36 W
Woodall Mountain ∧[2]	184	34.45 N	88.11 W
Wood Bay C	170	69.45 N	129.00 W
Woodbine, Ga., U.S.	182	30.58 N	81.43 W
Woodbine, Iowa, U.S.	188	41.44 N	95.43 W
Woodbine, Md., U.S.	198	39.22 N	77.04 W
Woodbine, N.J., U.S.	198	39.14 N	74.49 W
Woodbourne, N.Y., U.S.	200	41.46 N	74.35 W
Woodbourne, Ohio, U.S.	208	39.38 N	84.10 W
Woodbourne, Pa., U.S.	275	40.12 N	74.53 W
Woodbridge, Eng., U.K.	44	52.06 N	1.19 E
Woodbridge, Calif., U.S.	216	38.09 N	121.18 W
Woodbridge, Conn., U.S.	197	41.21 N	73.02 W
Woodbridge, N.J., U.S.	200	40.33 N	74.17 W
Woodbridge, Va., U.S.	198	38.39 N	77.15 W
Woodbridge Bay C	230d	15.19 N	61.25 W
Woodbridge Center ◆[9]	266	40.33 N	74.18 W
Woodbridge Creek ≃	266	40.32 N	74.15 W
Woodbridge Island I	273	42.48 N	70.50 W
Woodburn, Ill., U.S.	209	39.03 N	90.00 W
Woodburn, Ind., U.S.	206	41.08 N	84.51 W
Woodburn, Oreg., U.S.	214	45.09 N	122.51 W
Woodbury, Eng., U.K.	44	50.41 N	3.24 W
Woodbury, Conn., U.S.	197	41.33 N	73.13 W
Woodbury, Ga., U.S.	182	32.59 N	84.35 W
Woodbury, Mich., U.S.	206	42.46 N	85.05 W
Woodbury, N.J., U.S.	198	39.50 N	75.10 W
Woodbury, N.Y., U.S.	266	40.49 N	73.28 W
Woodbury, Pa., U.S.	204	40.14 N	78.22 W
Woodbury, Tenn., U.S.	184	35.50 N	86.04 W
Woodbury Creek ≃	275	39.52 N	75.11 W
Woodbury Heights	275	39.49 N	75.09 W
Woodchester	158b	35.13 S	138.57 E
Woodchopper	170	65.03 N	151.00 W
Woodchurch	44	51.05 N	0.46 E
Woodcliff Lake	266	41.01 N	74.03 W
Woodcliff Lake ⊜	266	41.01 N	74.03 W
Woodcock	204	41.45 N	80.05 W
Woodcock, Mount ∧	152	19.16 S	134.02 E
Woodcrest	218	33.52 N	117.21 W
Wood Dale	268	41.58 N	87.58 W
Wooded Bluff •[4]	156	29.22 S	153.22 E
Woodenbong	156	28.23 S	152.37 E
Woodend	159	37.22 S	144.32 E
Woodfibre	172	49.40 N	123.15 W
Woodford, Austl.	161a	26.57 S	152.47 E
Woodford, Eng., U.K.	252	53.21 N	2.10 W
Woodford □[6], Ill., U.S.	206	40.43 N	89.16 W
Woodford □[6], Ky., U.S.	208	38.06 N	84.15 W
Woodford ◆[8]	250	51.36 N	0.02 E
Woodford Aerodrome ⊠	252	53.20 N	2.09 W
Woodford Bridge ◆[8]	250	51.36 N	0.04 E
Woodford Halse	44	52.10 N	1.12 W
Wood Green ◆[8]	250	51.36 N	0.07 W
Woodham	250	51.21 N	0.30 W
Woodham Ferrers	250	51.40 N	0.36 E
Woodham Mortimer	250	51.43 N	0.37 E
Woodham Walter	250	51.44 N	0.37 E
Woodhaven	206	42.08 N	83.14 W
Woodhaven ◆[8]	266	40.41 N	73.51 W
Woodhead Reservoir ⊜[1]	252	53.30 N	1.52 W
Woodhill	265b	43.45 N	79.41 W
Wood Hill ∧[2]	273	42.39 N	71.13 W
Woodhull, Ill., U.S.	180	41.11 N	90.20 W
Woodhull, N.Y., U.S.	200	42.05 N	77.25 W
Woodinville	214	47.45 N	122.09 W
Wood Islands	176	45.58 N	62.45 W
Woodlake, Calif., U.S.	194	36.25 N	119.06 W
Wood Lake, Nebr., U.S.	188	42.38 N	100.14 W
Woodlake, Tex., U.S.	212	31.01 N	95.02 W
Wood Lake ⊜, Ont., Can.	202	45.01 N	79.05 W
Wood Lake ⊜, Sask., Can.	174	55.17 N	103.17 W
Woodland, Calif., U.S.	216	38.41 N	121.46 W
Woodland, Ill., U.S.	206	40.43 N	87.44 W
Woodland, Maine, U.S.	178	45.09 N	67.24 W
Woodland, Mich., U.S.	206	42.43 N	85.08 W
Woodland, Pa., U.S.	204	41.00 N	78.21 W
Woodland, Wash., U.S.	214	45.54 N	122.45 W
Woodland Acres	218	34.24 N	119.18 W
Woodland Beach	206	41.57 N	83.19 W
Woodland Heights	204	41.25 N	79.43 W
Woodland Hills	212	32.39 N	96.55 W
Woodland Hills ◆[8]	270	34.11 N	118.35 W
Woodland Hills Park ♠	269a	41.28 N	81.36 W
Woodland Park, Colo., U.S.	190	39.00 N	105.03 W
Woodland Park, Pa., U.S.	200	41.18 N	77.03 W
Woodlands, N.Z.	162	46.22 S	168.33 E
Woodlands, Sing.	261c	1.27 N	103.46 E
Woodlands, N.Y., U.S.	266	41.01 N	73.50 W
Woodlark Island I	154	9.05 S	152.50 E
Woodlawn, Ill., U.S.	209	38.20 N	89.02 W
Woodlawn, Ky., U.S.	184	37.04 N	85.04 W
Woodlawn, Md., U.S.	274b	39.19 N	76.43 W
Woodlawn, Md., U.S.	274c	38.57 N	76.53 W
Woodlawn, Wash., U.S.	214	47.01 N	123.48 W
Woodlawn ◆[8]	268	41.47 N	87.36 W
Woodlawn Beach	200	42.48 N	78.51 W
Woodlawn Heights	274b	39.11 N	76.39 W
Woodley	44	51.28 N	0.54 W
Woodlyn	275	39.52 N	75.21 W
Woodlynne	275	39.55 N	75.05 W
Woodmansey	42	53.50 N	0.29 W
Woodmansterne	250	51.19 N	0.10 W
Woodmere, N.Y., U.S.	200	40.38 N	73.43 W
Woodmere, Ohio, U.S.	269a	41.28 N	81.29 W
Woodmoor	274b	39.20 N	76.44 W
Wood Mountain ∧	174	49.14 N	106.20 W
Woodplumpton	42	53.48 N	2.47 W
Woodport	266	40.59 N	74.36 W
Woodrarung Range ∧∧	152	27.10 S	115.30 E
Woodridge, Austl.	161a	27.38 S	153.06 E
Woodridge, Man., Can.	174	49.17 N	96.09 W
Woodridge, Ill., U.S.	206	41.46 N	88.04 W
Wood-Ridge, N.J., U.S.	266	40.51 N	74.05 W
Woodridge, N.Y., U.S.	200	41.43 N	74.34 W
Wood River, Alaska, U.S.	170	59.04 N	158.26 W
Wood River, Ill., U.S.	209	38.52 N	90.05 W
Wood River, Nebr., U.S.	188	40.49 N	98.36 W
Wood River Indian Reserve ◆[4]	174	49.21 N	106.24 W
Wood River Lakes ⊜	170	59.30 N	158.45 W
Wood River Mountains ∧∧	170	59.32 N	159.30 W

ENGLISH	DEUTSCH
Name / Page / Lat.°′ / Long.°′	Name / Seite / Breite°′ / Länge°′ E=Ost

Symbols in the index entries represent the broad categories identified in the key at the right. Symbols with superior numbers (∧∧[2]) identify subcategories (see complete key on page I · 26).

Kartensymbole in dem Registerverzeichnis stellen die rechts in Schlüssel erklärten Kategorien dar. Symbole mit hochgestellten Ziffern (∧∧[2]) bezeichnen Unterabteilungen einer Kategorie (vgl. vollständiger Schlüssel auf Seite I · 26).

Los símbolos incluídos en el texto del índice representan las grandes categorias identificadas con la clave a la derecha. Los símbolos con numeros en su parte superior (∧∧[2]) identifican las subcategorías (véase la clave completa en la página I · 26).

Les symboles de l'index représentent les catégories indiquées dans la légende à droite. Les symboles suivis d'un indice (∧∧[2]) représentent des sous-catégories (voir légende complète à la page I · 26).

Os símbolos incluídos no texto do índice representam as grandes categorias identificadas com a chave à direita. Os símbolos com números em sua parte superior (∧∧[2]) identificam as subcategorias (veja-se a chave completa à página I · 26).

Symbol	English	Deutsch	Español	Français	Português
∧	Mountain	Berg	Montaña	Montagne	Montanha
∧∧	Mountains	Berge	Montañas	Montagnes	Montanhas
)(	Pass	Pass	Paso	Col	Passo
∨	Valley, Canyon	Tal, Cañon	Valle, Cañón	Vallée, Canyon	Vale, Canhão
≃	Plain	Ebene	Llano	Plaine	Planície
›	Cape	Kap	Cabo	Cap	Cabo
I	Island	Insel	Isla	Île	Ilha
II	Islands	Inseln	Islas	Îles	Ilhas
♠	Other Topographic Features	Andere Topographische Objekte	Otros Elementos Topográficos	Autres données topographiques	Outros Elementos Topográficos

ESPAÑOL

Nombre	Página	Lat.°′	Long.°′ W=Oeste
Woodroffe ≃	156	21.28 S	137.58 E
Woodroffe, Mount ∧	152	26.20 S	131.45 E
Woodrow Wilson Memorial Bridge ◆[5]	274c	38.48 N	77.02 W
Woodruff, Ariz., U.S.	190	34.47 N	110.03 W
Woodruff, S.C., U.S.	182	34.45 N	82.02 W
Woodruff, Wis., U.S.	180	45.54 N	89.42 W
Woodruff Creek ≃	271	42.21 N	83.43 W
Woods	158b	34.15 S	138.31 E
Woods, Lake ⊜	152	17.50 S	133.30 E
Woods, Lake of the ⊜	174	49.15 N	94.45 W
Woods Bay C	202	45.08 N	80.00 W
Woodsboro, Md., U.S.	198	39.32 N	77.19 W
Woodsboro, Tex., U.S.	186	28.14 N	97.20 W
Woodsburgh	266	40.37 N	73.42 W
Woods Creek ≃, N.Y., U.S.	266	40.39 N	73.24 W
Woods Creek ≃, N.Y., U.S.	274a	43.04 N	78.58 W
Woodsfield	178	39.46 N	81.07 W
Woods Hole	197	41.31 N	70.40 W
Woodside, Austl.	156	38.31 S	146.52 E
Woodside, Austl.	158b	34.57 S	138.52 E
Woodside, Eng., U.K.	250	51.45 N	0.11 W
Woodside, Calif., U.S.	216	37.26 N	122.15 W
Woodside, Del., U.S.	198	39.04 N	75.34 W
Woodside, Pa., U.S.	275	40.13 N	74.53 W
Woodside ◆[8]	266	40.45 N	73.55 W
Woodside National Historic Park ♠	202	43.26 N	80.08 W
Woodson, Ill., U.S.	209	39.38 N	90.13 W
Woodson, Tex., U.S.	186	33.01 N	99.03 W
Woods Point	159	37.35 S	146.15 E
Woodstock, Austl.	156	22.15 S	141.57 E
Woodstock, N.B., Can.	176	46.09 N	67.34 W
Woodstock, Ont., Can.	202	43.08 N	80.45 W
Woodstock, Eng., U.K.	44	51.52 N	1.21 W
Woodstock, Conn., U.S.	197	41.57 N	71.59 W
Woodstock, Ill., U.S.	206	42.19 N	88.27 W
Woodstock, Md., U.S.	274b	39.20 N	76.52 W
Woodstock, N.Y., U.S.	200	42.02 N	74.07 W
Woodstock, Ohio, U.S.	208	40.10 N	83.32 W
Woodstock, Vt., U.S.	178	43.37 N	72.31 W
Woodstock, Va., U.S.	178	38.53 N	78.31 W
Woodstown	198	39.39 N	75.19 W
Wood Street	250	51.15 N	0.38 W
Woodsville	178	44.09 N	72.02 W
Woodvale Airfield ⊠	252	53.35 N	3.03 W
Woodview Manor	268	42.06 N	87.53 W
Wood Village	214	45.32 N	122.19 W
Woodville, Austl.	158b	34.53 S	138.32 E
Woodville, Ont., Can.	202	44.24 N	78.59 W
Woodville, N.Z.	162	40.20 S	175.52 E
Woodville, Ala., U.S.	184	34.38 N	86.16 W
Woodville, Calif., U.S.	216	36.06 N	119.12 W
Woodville, Fla., U.S.	182	30.20 N	84.15 W
Woodville, Ga., U.S.	182	33.40 N	83.06 W
Woodville, Mass., U.S.	197	42.14 N	71.34 W
Woodville, Mich., U.S.	206	42.16 N	84.30 W
Woodville, Miss., U.S.	184	31.01 N	91.18 W
Woodville, N.Y., U.S.	200	42.40 N	77.22 W
Woodville, Ohio, U.S.	204	41.27 N	83.22 W
Woodville, Tex., U.S.	184	30.46 N	94.25 W
Woodward, Iowa, U.S.	180	41.51 N	93.55 W
Woodward, Okla., U.S.	186	36.26 N	99.24 W
Woodward, Pa., U.S.	200	40.54 N	77.21 W
Woodward Reservoir ⊜[1]	216	37.51 N	120.52 W
Woodway, Tex., U.S.	212	31.30 N	97.13 W
Woodway, Wash., U.S.	214	47.47 N	122.23 W
Woodworth, Ohio, U.S.	204	40.59 N	80.40 W
Woodworth, Wis., U.S.	206	42.34 N	88.00 W
Woody ≃	174	52.30 N	100.51 W
Woody Creek ≃	192	47.27 N	106.21 W
Woody Island	170	57.47 N	152.22 W
Wool	44	50.41 N	2.14 W
Woolacombe	44	51.10 N	4.13 W
Woolamai, Cape ≻	159	38.34 S	145.21 E
Wool Bay	158b	35.00 S	137.45 E
Wooldridge	148	33.13 S	27.15 E
Wooler	42	55.33 N	2.01 W
Woolford	198	38.30 N	76.11 W
Woolgangie	152	31.10 S	120.32 E
Woolgoolga	156	30.07 S	153.12 E
Woollahra	264a	33.53 S	151.15 E
Woolooware Bay C	264a	34.02 S	151.09 E
Woolpit	44	52.13 N	0.54 E
Woolrich	200	41.12 N	77.23 W
Woolsey Peak ∧	190	33.10 N	112.53 W
Woolston	252	53.24 N	2.32 W
Woolton	252	53.23 N	2.52 W
Woolwich ◆[8]	250	51.29 N	0.04 E
Woomargama	161b	35.50 S	147.15 E
Woomera	156	31.31 S	137.10 E
Woonona	160	34.21 S	150.55 E
Woonsocket, R.I., U.S.	197	42.00 N	71.31 W
Woonsocket, S. Dak., U.S.	188	44.03 N	98.16 W
Woorabinda	156	24.08 S	149.28 E
Wooramel	152	25.44 S	114.17 E
Wooramel ≃	152	25.47 S	114.10 E
Woorim	161b	27.08 S	153.12 E
Wooroloo	158a	31.48 S	116.19 E
Wooster	204	40.48 N	81.56 W
Wootton Bassett	44	51.33 N	1.54 W
Wootton Wawen	44	52.16 N	1.47 W
Worb	54	46.56 N	7.34 E
Worbis	50	51.25 N	10.21 E
Worcester, S. Afr.	148	33.39 S	19.27 E
Worcester, Eng., U.K.	44	52.11 N	2.13 W
Worcester, Mass., U.S.	197	42.16 N	71.48 W
Worcester, N.Y., U.S.	200	42.36 N	74.45 W
Worcester, Pa., U.S.	275	40.12 N	75.21 W
Worcester □[6], Md., U.S.	198	38.11 N	75.24 W
Worcester □[6], Mass., U.S.	197	42.16 N	71.48 W
Worcester Municipal Airport ⊠	197	42.16 N	71.52 W
Worden, Ill., U.S.	209	38.56 N	89.50 W
Worden, Mont., U.S.	192	45.58 N	108.10 W
Worden Pond ⊜	197	41.26 N	71.35 W
Wördern	254b	48.20 N	16.13 E
Wörgl	58	47.29 N	12.04 E
Workai, Pulau I	154	6.40 S	134.40 E
Work Channel Ɥ	172	54.30 N	130.15 W
Workers' Cultural Palace ❦	259b	31.14 N	121.28 E
Working People's Cultural Palace ❦	261a	39.55 N	116.23 E
Workington	42	54.39 N	3.35 W
Worksop	42	53.18 N	1.07 W
Workum	48	52.57 N	5.26 E
Worland	192	44.01 N	107.57 W
Worli ◆[8]	262c	19.01 N	72.50 E
Wörlitz	50	51.50 N	12.25 E
Wormditt → Orneta	30	54.08 N	20.08 E
Wormerveer	48	52.28 N	4.46 E
Wormhoudt	46	50.53 N	2.28 E
Wormley	250	51.44 N	0.01 W
Worms	52	49.38 N	8.22 E
Worms Head ≻	44	51.34 N	4.20 W
Wormshill	250	51.17 N	0.42 E

FRANÇAIS

Nom	Page	Lat.°′	Long.°′ W=Ouest
Wörnitz ≃	52	48.42 N	10.45 E
Woronesch → Voronež	68	51.40 N	39.10 E
Woronoco	197	42.10 N	72.50 W
Woronora	264a	34.01 S	151.03 E
Woronora ≃	264a	34.00 S	151.04 E
Worplesdon	250	51.16 N	0.37 W
Worpswede	48	53.13 N	8.56 E
Wörrstadt	52	49.50 N	8.07 E
Wörsbach ≃	52	50.22 N	8.09 E
Worsley	252	53.30 N	2.23 W
Worsthorne	252	53.47 N	2.11 W
Wörth, B.R.D.	52	49.48 N	9.09 E
Worth, B.R.D.	253	51.13 N	7.39 E
Worth, Ill., U.S.	206	41.41 N	87.48 W
Worth, Lake ⊜[1]	212	32.48 N	97.28 W
Wortham	212	31.47 N	96.28 W
Wörth am Rhein	52	49.03 N	8.16 E
Worthen	44	52.38 N	3.00 W
Wörther See ⊜	30	46.37 N	14.10 E
Worthing	44	50.48 N	0.23 W
Worthington, Ind., U.S.	184	39.07 N	86.59 W
Worthington, Md., U.S.	274b	39.14 N	76.47 W
Worthington, Minn., U.S.	188	43.37 N	95.36 W
Worthington, N.Y., U.S.	266	41.02 N	73.50 W
Worthington, Ohio, U.S.	204	40.05 N	83.01 W
Worthington, Pa., U.S.	204	40.50 N	79.38 W
Worthington Peak ∧	194	37.55 N	115.37 W
Wörthsee ⊜	58	48.03 N	11.10 E
Worthville, Ky., U.S.	208	38.37 N	85.04 W
Worthville, Pa., U.S.	204	41.02 N	79.08 W
Worton	198	39.17 N	76.06 W
Wŏrun-dong	88	39.36 N	125.20 E
Wosimi	154	2.54 S	134.31 E
Wostok → Vostok ❦[3]	9	78.30 S	106.50 E
Wosu	102	2.21 S	121.50 E
Wotap, Pulau I	154	7.21 S	131.16 E
Wotho I[1]	14	10.06 N	165.59 E
Wotje I[1]	14	9.27 N	170.02 E
Wotton, Qué., Can.	196	45.44 N	71.48 W
Wotton, Eng., U.K.	250	51.13 N	0.23 W
Wotton-under-Edge	44	51.39 N	2.21 W
Wotu	102	2.35 S	120.48 E
Woudenberg	48	52.05 N	5.25 E
Woudrichem	48	51.49 N	5.00 E
Woudsend	48	52.56 N	5.36 E
Wouldham	250	51.21 N	0.28 E
Wounded Knee Creek ≃	188	43.26 N	102.32 W
Wour	136	21.21 N	15.57 E
Wouri ≃	142	4.06 N	9.43 E
Woutchaba	142	5.13 N	13.05 E
Wouw	48	51.32 N	4.24 E
Wowan	156	23.55 S	150.12 E
Wowoni, Pulau I	102	4.08 S	123.06 E
Woy Woy	160	33.30 S	151.20 E
Woźniki	30	50.36 N	19.03 E
Wragby	42	53.18 N	0.19 W
Wrangel Island → Vrangel'a, Ostrov I	64	71.00 N	179.30 W
Wrangell	170	56.28 N	132.23 W
Wrangell, Cape ≻	171a	52.50 N	172.26 E
Wrangell, Mount ∧	170	62.00 N	144.06 W
Wrangell Island I	170	56.15 N	132.10 W
Wrangell Mountains ⩕	170	62.00 N	143.00 W
Wrath, Cape ≻	28	58.37 N	5.01 W
Wray	188	40.05 N	102.13 W
Wraysbury	250	51.27 N	0.33 W
Wrea Green	252	53.46 N	2.55 W
Wreck Bay C	160	35.11 S	150.40 E
Wreck Island I	198	37.16 N	75.48 W
Wreck Reef ✧[2]	156	22.13 S	155.17 E
Wrecks, Bay of C	164o	1.52 N	157.17 W
Wredenhagen	50	53.17 N	12.31 E
Wremen	48	53.39 N	8.30 E
Wren	206	40.48 N	84.46 W
Wrens	182	33.12 N	82.23 W
Wrentham, Alta., Can.	172	49.32 N	112.10 W
Wrentham, Eng., U.K.	44	52.23 N	1.40 E
Wrentham, Mass., U.S.	197	42.04 N	71.20 W
Wrentham State Forest ♠	273	42.02 N	71.20 W
Wrexham	44	53.03 N	3.00 W
Wriezen	50	52.43 N	14.08 E
Wright	268	41.31 N	87.21 W
Wright, Mount ∧, Austl.	156	31.12 S	142.26 E
Wright, Mount ∧, Mont., U.S.	192	47.58 N	112.49 W
Wright Brothers National Memorial ⊥	182	35.55 N	75.50 W
Wright City, Mo., U.S.	209	38.50 N	91.01 W
Wright City, Okla., U.S.	184	34.03 N	95.01 W
Wright City, Tex., U.S.	212	32.12 N	94.59 W
Wrightington Bar	252	53.37 N	2.42 W
Wright Patman Lake ⊜[1]	184	33.16 N	94.14 W
Wright-Patterson Air Force Base ■	208	39.49 N	84.03 W
Wright Peak ∧	194	38.59 N	122.46 W
Wrights	209	39.23 N	90.18 W
Wrightsboro	212	29.22 N	97.34 W
Wrights Corners	200	43.13 N	78.46 W
Wrightson, Mount ∧	190	31.42 N	110.50 W
Wrightstown, N.J., U.S.	198	40.02 N	74.37 W
Wrightstown, Pa., U.S.	198	40.17 N	74.58 W
Wrightstown, Wis., U.S.	180	44.19 N	88.09 W
Wrightsville, Ga., U.S.	182	32.44 N	82.43 W
Wrightsville, Pa., U.S.	204	40.02 N	76.32 W
Wrightwood	218	34.21 N	117.38 W
Wrigley	170	63.16 N	123.37 W
Wrigley Field ♠	268	41.57 N	87.39 W
Wrigley Gulf C	9	74.00 S	129.00 W
Writtle	44	51.44 N	0.26 E
Wrocław (Breslau)	30	51.06 N	17.00 E
Wrong Lake ⊜	174	52.38 N	96.10 W
Wronki	30	52.43 N	16.23 E
Wrotham	44	51.19 N	0.19 E
Wrotham Heath	250	51.18 N	0.21 E
Wroughton	44	51.31 N	1.46 W
Wroxham	44	52.42 N	1.24 E
Wroxton	174	51.14 N	101.53 W
Września	30	52.20 N	17.34 E
Wschowa	30	51.48 N	16.19 E
Wuan	88	36.40 N	114.12 E
Wubao	92	37.33 N	110.39 E
Wubaozhen	97	29.14 N	104.29 E
Wubin	152	30.06 S	116.38 E
Wuchang → Wuhan	90	30.36 N	114.17 E
Wuchang ◆[8]	90	44.54 N	127.08 E
Wucheng, Zhg.	88	37.09 N	115.53 E
Wucheng, Zhg.	90	33.28 N	113.44 E
Wucheng, Zhg.	90	29.36 N	118.10 E
Wuchengzhen	90	29.10 N	115.59 E
Wuch'i	90	24.13 N	120.31 E
Wuchin → Changzhou	96	31.47 N	119.57 E
Wuch'iu Hsü I	90	25.00 N	119.27 E
Wuchow → Wuzhou	92	23.30 N	111.27 E
Wuchuan, Zhg.	92	28.25 N	107.56 E
Wuchuan, Zhg.	92	41.05 N	111.23 E
Wuchuan, Zhg.	92	21.25 N	110.40 E

PORTUGUÊS

Nome	Página	Lat.°′	Long.°′ W=Oeste
Wuchung → Wuzhong	92	37.57 N	106.10 E
Wucun	95	38.57 N	115.19 E
Wuda	92	39.30 N	105.56 E
Wudangshan ⩕	92	32.30 N	110.50 E
Wudaogou, Zhg.	88	41.13 N	116.07 E
Wudaogou, Zhg.	88	42.08 N	125.51 E
Wudaogou, Zhg.	88	41.43 N	127.05 E
Wudaohe ≃	94	42.03 N	122.58 E
Wudaolianggou	94	40.59 N	120.35 E
Wudi	88	37.44 N	117.35 E
Wudian	90	32.42 N	117.18 E
Wuding	92	25.32 N	102.23 E
Wudinna	156	33.03 S	135.28 E
Wudu, Zhg.	90	28.23 N	118.14 E
Wudu, Zhg.	92	33.21 N	105.00 E
Wuduhe	92	31.03 N	111.03 E
Wuerqihan	79	49.37 N	121.45 E
Wuershunhe ≃	78	49.00 N	117.41 E
Wufeng	92	30.11 N	110.33 E
Wufengshan I	96	31.07 N	120.16 E
Wufengxi	97	30.37 N	104.29 E
Wufu	90	30.06 N	120.58 E
Wugang	92	26.40 N	110.31 E
Wugong	92	34.20 N	108.04 E
Wugonghe ≃	95	39.20 N	117.29 E
Wugongshan ∧	90	27.21 N	113.50 E
Wugouying	90	33.28 N	114.08 E
Wugunuoer	79	49.10 N	119.19 E
Wuhan	90	30.36 N	114.17 E
Wuhe, Zhg.	90	24.26 N	115.25 E
Wuhe, Zhg.	90	33.10 N	117.54 E
Wuhe ≃	88	34.25 N	117.55 E
Wuhle ≃	254a	52.29 N	13.34 E
Wuhsi → Wuxi	96	31.35 N	120.18 E
Wuhsing → Huzhou	96	30.52 N	120.06 E
Wuhu	90	31.21 N	118.22 E
Wuhua (Shuizhai)	90	23.57 N	115.48 E
Wuhuanchi	94	42.20 N	121.51 E
Wuhuangchang	97	29.58 N	104.46 E
Wuhudongmiao	92	38.19 N	107.20 E
Wuhushui ≃	90	30.41 N	114.32 E
Wuji, Zhg.	88	38.13 N	114.57 E
Wuji, Zhg.	88	34.12 N	119.02 E
Wuji, Zhg.	90	27.03 N	112.57 E
Wujiabeigou	94	40.57 N	123.50 E
Wujiadian	90	31.57 N	112.46 E
Wujiagou	94	42.01 N	123.52 E
Wujiahe ≃	92	41.10 N	108.45 E
Wujiaku	96	31.06 N	121.11 E
Wujiang, Zhg.	90	31.52 N	118.28 E
Wujiang, Zhg.	90	27.14 N	115.15 E
Wujiang, Zhg.	96	31.10 N	120.38 E
Wujiang ≃, Zhg.	90	27.14 N	115.05 E
Wujiang ≃, Zhg.	90	28.57 N	116.39 E
Wujiangdu	92	27.16 N	106.48 E
Wujianpu	97	29.10 N	105.50 E
Wujiapai	95	39.32 N	117.18 E
Wujiapu, Zhg.	95	38.52 N	117.07 E
Wujiapu, Zhg.	97	29.38 N	105.24 E
Wujiazhuang, Zhg.	95	40.35 N	115.20 E
Wujiazhuang, Zhg.	96	32.18 N	120.10 E
Wujiazi, Zhg.	79	46.27 N	123.34 E
Wujiazi, Zhg.	94	42.13 N	122.08 E
Wujiazi, Zhg.	94	42.30 N	121.10 E
Wujieqiao	96	32.05 N	120.33 E
Wujing	90	25.16 N	114.36 E
Wukang	96	30.33 N	119.58 E
Wukari	140	7.51 N	9.47 E
Wukeshu, Zhg.	79	46.02 N	123.45 E
Wukeshu, Zhg.	79	44.48 N	126.08 E
Wulai	90	24.52 N	121.33 E
Wulajia	79	48.23 N	129.58 E
Wulan	92	36.59 N	98.26 E
Wulandabanshan ⩕	92	38.53 N	96.11 E
Wulanhaote	79	46.05 N	122.05 E
Wulanheduojia	92	42.40 N	113.20 E
Wulanhutong	88	41.44 N	114.49 E
Wulanmuluhne ≃	110	34.15 N	93.11 E
Wulanmutou	94	42.23 N	121.21 E
Wulanwusu, Zhg.	76	44.20 N	85.50 E
Wulanwusu, Zhg.	92	41.39 N	107.48 E
Wular Lake ⊜	113	34.20 N	74.33 E
Wulasitai	79	43.15 N	121.27 E
Wulateqianqi	92	40.39 N	109.05 E
Wulatezhonghouqi	92	41.42 N	108.49 E
Wulaxi	92	28.38 N	101.40 E
Wuleidaowan C	88	36.55 N	122.00 E
Wulfen	48	51.43 N	7.00 E
Wülfrath	52	51.17 N	7.02 E
Wulfsen	48	53.18 N	10.08 E
Wulfsode	48	53.04 N	10.13 E
Wulften	48	51.40 N	10.10 E
Wulian (Hongning)	88	35.47 N	119.15 E
Wulianfeng ⩕	92	28.03 N	103.57 E
Wuliangdian	94	41.52 N	122.16 E
Wuliangshan ⩕	92	24.30 N	100.45 E
Wuliaru, Pulau I	154	7.27 S	131.04 E
Wulichuan	92	33.49 N	111.08 E
Wuling	88	35.53 N	114.36 E
Wuling ⩕	92	27.10 N	108.06 E
Wulingshan ⩕	92	28.48 N	110.15 E
Wulitaizi	94	41.28 N	123.21 E
Wulizhuang	90	33.49 N	118.57 E
Wüllen	48	52.04 N	6.58 E
Wullwye Creek ≃	161b	36.30 S	148.49 E
Wulong, Zhg.	92	29.14 N	107.59 E
Wulong, Zhg.	94	41.39 N	124.13 E
Wulongbei	88	40.21 N	124.16 E
Wulonghe ≃	88	36.35 N	120.56 E
Wulsdorf ◆[8]	48	53.30 N	8.35 E
Wuluhan	105a	8.21 S	113.33 E
Wuluhayingzi	94	42.20 N	121.34 E
Wulumuch'i → Wulumuqi	76	43.48 N	87.35 E
Wulumuqi (Urumchi)	76	43.48 N	87.35 E
Wulunguhe ≃	76	46.59 N	87.27 E
Wuluo	92	26.09 N	108.15 E
Wulur	154	7.09 S	128.39 E
Wulushui ≃	75	39.38 N	74.38 E
Wum	142	6.23 N	10.04 E
Wuma	79	52.36 N	120.37 E
Wumangdao I	88	39.14 N	123.03 E
Wumiaoxiang	97	30.23 N	104.17 E
Wuming	92	23.10 N	108.18 E
Wümme ≃	48	53.10 N	8.44 E
Wunamu	76	46.06 N	85.44 E
Wundowie	158a	31.46 S	116.22 E
Wundwin	100	21.05 N	96.02 E
Wuneba	144	4.50 N	30.20 E
Wuning	90	29.17 N	115.06 E
Wünnenberg	48	51.31 N	8.42 E
Wunnummin Lake ⊜	166	52.55 N	89.10 W
Wun Rog	130	9.00 N	28.21 E
Wünschendorf	50	50.48 N	12.05 E
Wünsdorf	50	52.10 N	13.28 E
Wunstorf	48	52.25 N	9.26 E
Wuntho	100	23.54 N	95.41 E
Wunuer	79	48.53 N	121.15 E
Wupaowan	97	29.50 N	103.59 E
Wupatki National Monument ♠	190	35.24 N	111.14 W
Wuping	90	25.08 N	116.06 E
Wupper ≃	253	51.05 N	7.00 E
Wuppertal, B.R.D.	52		
	253	51.16 N	7.11 E
Wuppertal, S. Afr.	148	32.15 S	19.15 E
Wuqi, Zhg.	90	27.10 N	120.23 E
Wuqi, Zhg.	92	37.08 N	108.10 E
Wuqia	75	39.42 N	75.13 E
Wuqiagou	76	46.48 N	89.45 E
Wuqiang	88	38.03 N	115.58 E
Wuqiangxi ≃	90	29.33 N	118.57 E
Wuqiao	88	37.36 N	116.30 E
Wuqiluofu	79	52.10 N	120.48 E
Wuqing (Yangcun)	95	39.23 N	117.04 E
Wuraming	158a	32.48 S	116.16 E
Wurarga	152	28.25 S	116.17 E
Würenlingen	54	47.32 N	8.16 E
Wurgwitz	50	51.01 N	13.37 E
Wurm ≃, B.R.D.	52	51.08 N	6.10 E
Würm ≃, B.R.D.	58	48.10 N	11.28 E
Wurmberg ∧	50	51.45 N	10.37 E
Wurno	140	13.17 N	5.24 E
Wurong	154	6.07 S	140.47 E
Würselen	52	50.49 N	6.08 E
Wurtsboro	200	41.35 N	74.29 W
Wurtsboro Hills	200	41.36 N	74.30 W
Wurtsmith Air Force Base ■	180	44.27 N	83.23 W
Wuruf	154	6.43 S	146.25 E
Wuryantoro	105a	7.54 S	110.51 E
Wurzbach	50	50.28 N	11.32 E
Würzburg	52	49.48 N	9.56 E
Wurzen	50	51.22 N	12.44 E
Wusanga	142	3.22 S	22.50 E
Wusha	90	30.39 N	117.18 E
Wushan, Zhg.	92	31.05 N	109.48 E
Wushan, Zhg.	92	34.38 N	105.04 E
Wushan, Zhg.	96	31.44 N	118.58 E
Wushanmiao	90	32.04 N	117.03 E
Wushe	90	24.02 N	121.08 E
Wusheng	97	30.21 N	106.17 E
Wushengchang	97	29.00 N	103.43 E
Wushenqi	92	38.58 N	109.01 E
Wushi, Zhg.	92	22.11 N	110.11 E
Wushi, Zhg.	96	31.44 N	120.59 E
Wushishi	140	9.46 N	6.07 E
Wushonkou C[1]	96	31.23 N	121.30 E
Wushui ≃, Zhg.	90	24.48 N	113.35 E
Wushui ≃, Zhg.	92	27.03 N	109.53 E
Wusih → Wuxi	96	31.35 N	120.18 E
Wuskwatim Lake ⊜	174	55.32 N	98.32 W
Wusong	96	31.23 N	121.29 E
Wusongjiang ≃	96	31.15 N	121.29 E
Wusongkou ≃[1]	259b	31.23 N	121.30 E
Wust	50	52.33 N	12.07 E
Wüsten	48	52.06 N	8.47 E
Wüstensachsen	52	50.30 N	10.00 E
Wusterhausen	50	52.54 N	12.28 E
Wusterhusen	50	54.07 N	13.37 E
Wustermark	50	52.33 N	12.56 E
Wüstermarke	50	51.49 N	13.36 E
Wusterwitz	50	52.22 N	12.18 E
Wüsting	48	53.07 N	8.20 E
Wustrow, B.R.D.	50	52.55 N	11.07 E
Wustrow, D.D.R.	50	54.05 N	11.34 E
Wustrow ≻[1]	50	54.05 N	11.34 E
Wusu	76	44.27 N	84.37 E
Wusulijiang (Ussuri) ≃	79	48.27 N	135.04 E
Wusuo, Zhg.	90	26.20 N	114.56 E
Wusuo, Zhg.	90	25.02 N	116.02 E
Wutach ≃	54	47.37 N	8.15 E
Wutai, Zhg.	75	39.28 N	78.09 E
Wutai, Zhg.	76	44.36 N	82.06 E
Wutai, Zhg.	88	41.18 N	113.59 E
Wutai, Zhg.	92	38.44 N	113.17 E
Wutaishan ∧	88	39.04 N	113.35 E
Wutaishan ⩕	92	39.06 N	113.30 E
Wutaizi	94	42.27 N	123.17 E
Wutan	92	28.29 N	111.40 E
Wutanchang	97	29.15 N	106.04 E
Wutang	96	31.31 N	119.10 E
Wutangdun	96	30.38 N	120.08 E
Wutangjie	90	29.59 N	122.22 E
Wutashi	96	31.31 N	120.39 E
Wutianzhen	90	30.23 N	117.12 E
Wutong	92	25.18 N	110.01 E
Wutonghaolai	79	42.55 N	120.15 E
Wutongqiao	97	29.26 N	103.51 E
Wutongwozi	92	42.27 N	95.17 E
Wutsin → Changzhou	96	31.47 N	119.57 E
Wutun	90	27.51 N	118.04 E
Wut'ungch'iao → Wutongqiao	97	29.26 N	103.51 E
Wutuohuo	92	40.51 N	101.48 E
Wuustwezel	46	51.23 N	4.36 E
Wuvulu Island I	154	1.45 S	142.50 E
Wuwei, Zhg.	90	31.18 N	117.54 E
Wuwei (Liangzhou), Zhg.	92	37.58 N	102.49 E
Wuxi, Zhg.	92	31.25 N	109.34 E
Wuxi, Zhg.	96	31.20 N	118.39 E
Wuxi (Wuhsi), Zhg.	96	31.35 N	120.18 E
Wuxi ≃	90	29.00 N	118.56 E
Wuxiang	92	36.51 N	113.00 E
Wuxingchang	96	31.13 N	119.23 E
Wuxuan	92	23.36 N	109.42 E
Wuyang, Zhg.	90	33.26 N	113.34 E
Wuyang, Zhg.	92	26.41 N	110.20 E
Wuyangyuan	90	25.41 N	115.55 E
Wuyi, Zhg.	88	37.49 N	115.54 E
Wuyi, Zhg.	90	32.13 N	118.26 E
Wuyi, Zhg.	90	28.54 N	119.48 E
Wuying	79	48.05 N	129.15 E
Wuyishan ∧	90	27.50 N	117.45 E
Wuyishan ⩕	80	27.52 N	117.40 E
Wuyou ≃	90	33.28 N	120.41 E
Wuyuan, Zhg.	90	29.15 N	117.49 E
Wuyuan, Zhg.	92	41.06 N	108.29 E
Wuyun	79	46.16 N	129.37 E
Wuyunqiao	90	26.02 N	114.52 E
Wuzaizi	94	42.28 N	123.57 E
Wuzhai	92	38.58 N	111.55 E
Wuzhan	79	45.51 N	126.17 E
Wuzhen	96	30.46 N	120.29 E
Wuzhishan ∧	100	18.57 N	109.43 E
Wuzhong	92	37.57 N	106.10 E
Wuzhou (Wuchow)	92	23.30 N	111.27 E
Wuzongbu	96	32.14 N	121.03 E
Wyaaba Creek ≃	154	16.27 S	141.35 E
Wyaconda	184	40.24 N	91.55 W
Wyaconda ≃	184	40.04 N	91.30 W
Wyalkatchem	152	31.10 S	117.22 E
Wyalusing	200	41.40 N	76.16 W
Wyalusing Creek ≃	200	41.40 N	76.16 W
Wyandanch	266	40.45 N	73.22 W
Wyandot	204	40.44 N	83.08 W
Wyandot □[6]	204	40.50 N	83.17 W
Wyandotte	206	42.12 N	83.10 W
Wyandotte Cave ◆[5]	208	38.14 N	86.18 W
Wyandotte National Wildlife Refuge ◆[4]	271	42.14 N	83.08 W
Wyandra	156	27.15 S	145.59 E
Wyangala Reservoir ⊜[1]	156	33.58 S	148.55 E
Wyano	204	40.12 N	79.42 W
Wyatt, Ind., U.S.	206	41.32 N	86.10 W
Wyatt, Mo., U.S.	184	36.55 N	89.13 W
Wycheproof	156	36.05 S	143.14 E
Wyckoff	200	41.01 N	74.10 W
Wydegeleë	148	34.23 S	20.26 E
Wydgee	152	28.51 S	117.49 E
Wy-dit-Joli-Village	251	49.06 N	1.50 E
Wye	44	51.11 N	0.56 E
Wye ≃, Ont., Can.	202	44.44 N	79.52 W
Wye ≃, Eng., U.K.	42	53.12 N	1.37 W
Wye ≃, Eng., U.K.	44	51.37 N	2.39 W
Wyee	160	33.11 S	151.29 E
Wye Lake ⊜	202	44.43 N	79.52 W
Wyemandoo ∧	152	28.31 S	118.32 E
Wyeville	180	44.01 N	90.23 W
Wyhl	54	48.09 N	7.39 E
Wyhra ≃	50	51.09 N	12.27 E
Wyk	30	54.42 N	8.34 E
Wyke Regis	44	50.36 N	2.29 W
Wykoff	180	43.42 N	92.16 W
Wylandville	269b	40.12 N	80.08 W
Wyleswood Lake ⊜	269a	41.20 N	81.55 W
Wylie, Pa., U.S.	269b	40.27 N	79.59 W
Wylie, Tex., U.S.	212	33.01 N	96.32 W
Wylie, Lake ⊜[1]	182	35.07 N	81.02 W
Wylye ≃	44	51.04 N	1.52 W
Wymah	161b	36.02 S	147.17 E
Wymark	174	50.07 N	107.44 W
Wymondham	44	52.34 N	1.07 E
Wymore	188	40.07 N	96.40 W
Wynantskill	200	42.42 N	73.39 W
Wynberg	148	34.02 S	18.28 E
Wynbring	152	30.33 S	133.32 E
Wyncote	275	40.05 N	75.09 W
Wyndham, Austl.	154	15.28 S	128.06 E
Wyndham, N.Z.	162	46.20 S	168.51 E
Wyndmere	188	46.16 N	97.08 W
Wyndmoor	275	40.05 N	75.12 W
Wynigen	54	47.06 N	7.40 E
Wynne	184	35.14 N	90.47 W
Wynnewood, Okla., U.S.	186	34.39 N	97.10 W
Wynnewood, Pa., U.S.	275	40.01 N	75.17 W
Wynniatt Bay C	166	72.55 N	110.30 W
Wynnum	161a	27.27 S	153.10 E
Wynona	186	36.33 N	96.20 W
Wynoochee ≃	214	46.58 N	123.35 W
Wynoochee Lake ⊜[1]	214	47.25 N	123.35 W
Wynot	188	42.45 N	97.10 W
Wynyard, Austl.	156	40.59 S	145.41 E
Wynyard, Sask., Can.	174	51.47 N	104.10 W
Wyocena	180	43.30 N	89.19 W
Wyodak	188	44.18 N	105.24 W
Wyola Lake ⊜	152	29.08 S	130.17 E
Wyoming, Ont., Can.	180	42.57 N	82.07 W
Wyoming, Del., U.S.	198	39.12 N	75.34 W
Wyoming, Ill., U.S.	180	41.04 N	89.47 W
Wyoming, Iowa, U.S.	180	42.04 N	91.00 W
Wyoming, Mich., U.S.	206	42.54 N	85.42 W
Wyoming, N.Y., U.S.	200	42.50 N	78.05 W
Wyoming, Ohio, U.S.	208	39.14 N	84.27 W
Wyoming, Pa., U.S.	200	41.19 N	75.50 W
Wyoming, R.I., U.S.	197	41.31 N	71.42 W
Wyoming □[6], N.Y., U.S.	200	42.44 N	78.08 W
Wyoming □[6], Pa., U.S.	200	41.32 N	75.57 W
Wyoming □[3]	168	43.00 N	107.30 W
Wyoming Peak ∧	190	42.36 N	110.37 W
Wyoming Range ⩕	190	42.00 N	111.00 W
Wyomissing	198	40.20 N	75.58 W
Wyong	160	33.17 S	151.25 E
Wyong Creek ≃	160	33.18 S	151.28 E
Wyperfeld National Park ♠	156	35.30 S	142.00 E
Wyre ≃	42	53.55 N	3.00 W
Wyreema	161a	27.39 S	151.52 E
Wyre Forest ◆[3]	44	52.23 N	2.23 W
Wyrzysk	30	53.10 N	17.15 E
Wyśmierzyce	30	51.38 N	20.49 E
Wysoka	30	53.11 N	17.05 E
Wysokie Mazowieckie	30	52.56 N	22.32 E
Wysox	200	41.46 N	76.24 W
Wyszków	30	52.36 N	21.28 E
Wyszogród	30	52.23 N	20.11 E
Wythenshawe	252	53.24 N	2.17 W
Wythenshawe Hall ⊥	252	53.24 N	2.17 W
Wytheville	182	36.57 N	81.05 W
Wytopitlock	178	45.38 N	68.05 W
Wytschegda → Vyčegda ≃	24	61.18 N	46.36 E
X			
Xabregas ◆[8]	256c	38.44 N	9.07 W
Xá-Cassau	142	9.02 S	20.14 E
Xadani	224	15.56 N	96.04 W
Xalbal ≃	226	16.06 N	90.58 W
Xalpatláhuac	224	17.01 N	99.18 W
Xaltianguis	224	17.04 N	99.50 W
Xambioá	240	6.25 S	48.40 W
Xambrê ≃	245	24.02 S	53.59 W
Xamilpan ≃	224	18.36 N	98.10 W
Xamindele	142	7.08 S	14.16 E
Xam Nua	100	20.25 N	104.02 E
Xa-muong-man	100	10.58 N	108.01 E
Xanten	48	51.39 N	6.26 E
Xánthi	38	41.08 N	24.53 E
Xanxerê	242	26.53 S	52.23 W
Xapuri	238	10.39 S	68.31 W
Xapuri ≃	238	10.39 S	68.30 W
Xarrama ≃	34	38.14 N	8.20 W
Xau, Lake ⊜	146	21.15 S	24.38 E
Xauen → Chechaouene	138	35.10 N	5.16 W
Xavantina	245	21.15 S	52.48 W
Xa-vo-dat	100	11.09 N	107.31 E
Xaxim	242	26.56 S	52.31 W
X-Can	222	20.50 N	87.43 W
Xenia, Ill., U.S.	209	38.38 N	88.38 W
Xenia, Ohio, U.S.	208	39.41 N	83.56 W
Xénô	100	16.35 N	104.50 E
Xercavins, Arroyo de ≃	256d	41.30 N	2.02 E
Xerém	246	22.33 S	43.18 W
Xeres → Jerez de la Frontera	34	36.41 N	6.08 W
Xertigny	54	48.03 N	6.24 E
Xhumo	146	21.07 S	24.42 E
Xiaang	96	30.45 N	120.07 E
Xiaba, Zhg.	90	24.54 N	116.06 E
Xiaba, Zhg.	96	31.18 N	119.05 E
Xiabai, Zhg.	96	30.29 N	120.00 E
Xiabai, Zhg.	96	31.12 N	119.50 E
Xiabancheng	95	40.47 N	118.08 E
Xiabanghu	90	30.31 N	112.38 E
Xiabaocun	96	30.44 N	119.58 E
Xiabeiwo	96	30.06 N	120.02 E
Xiabian	94	40.51 N	120.30 E
Xiabu	90	28.19 N	116.20 E
Xiacang	95	39.47 N	117.24 E
Xiache	90	24.40 N	115.08 E
Xiachengzi	79	44.41 N	130.27 E
Xiachuandao I	92	21.40 N	112.30 E
Xiacun	95	40.21 N	116.14 E
Xiadao	90	26.34 N	118.16 E
Xiadian, Zhg.	88	37.06 N	120.19 E
Xiadian, Zhg.	90	31.26 N	114.17 E
Xiadian, Zhg.	95	39.57 N	116.55 E
Xiadianjie	90	25.13 N	118.27 E
Xiafeidi	88	42.18 N	124.21 E
Xiafu, Zhg.	90	23.52 N	115.45 E
Xiafu, Zhg.	90	25.01 N	113.41 E
Xiagaixin	92	22.36 N	99.59 E
Xiagang	96	31.55 N	120.13 E
Xiage	90	28.52 N	120.52 E
Xiagezhuang	88	36.41 N	120.25 E
Xiaguan, Zhg.	88	39.07 N	114.09 E
Xiaguan, Zhg.	92	25.34 N	100.14 E
Xiaguan, Zhg.	96	32.06 N	118.44 E
Xiaguanjunchang	94	41.28 N	121.40 E
Xiaguanpi	90	24.04 N	117.06 E
Xiagucheng	92	36.47 N	102.53 E
Xiagucun	96	30.56 N	119.09 E
Xiahada	94	41.58 N	124.08 E
Xiahailangzhai	94	41.35 N	123.46 E
Xiahe, Zhg.	88	34.39 N	114.46 E
Xiahe, Zhg.	92	35.06 N	102.40 E
Xiahuangjintun	94	41.57 N	123.48 E
Xiahuayuan	95	40.29 N	115.17 E
Xiajiabaozi	88	42.16 N	124.37 E
Xiajialou	94	42.25 N	123.39 E
Xiajiangdun	96	31.14 N	120.24 E
Xiajiangwu	96	30.29 N	119.00 E
Xiajiayuan	96	32.13 N	120.38 E
Xiajiezi	92	27.28 N	101.35 E
Xiajin	88	36.55 N	115.57 E
Xiakou	90	28.28 N	118.31 E
Xialianggang	95	39.14 N	115.07 E
Xialufang	92	31.11 N	103.38 E
Xiamaguan	92	37.14 N	106.28 E
Xiamen (Amoy)	90	24.28 N	118.07 E
Xiamengang C	90	24.24 N	118.10 E
Xiamin'ansutai	94	41.54 N	120.53 E
Xiamocun	96	31.09 N	119.22 E
Xi'an (Sian)	92	34.15 N	108.52 E
Xianchenggu	88	36.53 N	115.17 E
Xiandu	90	25.04 N	117.44 E
Xianfeng, Zhg.	90	25.42 N	117.53 E
Xianfeng, Zhg.	92	29.41 N	109.02 E
Xianfengpo	95	39.33 N	115.58 E
Xiang'an	90	31.12 N	117.46 E
Xiangcheng, Zhg.	90	33.28 N	114.53 E
Xiangcheng, Zhg.	90	33.53 N	113.29 E
Xiangcheng, Zhg.	92	28.59 N	99.45 E
Xiangcheng, Zhg.	96	31.29 N	120.44 E
Xiangfan	92	32.03 N	112.01 E
Xiangfuguan	90	28.30 N	115.26 E
Xiangfusi	97	30.06 N	104.24 E
Xianggang → Victoria	261d	22.17 N	114.09 E
Xianggongshi	90	28.25 N	113.32 E
Xianggongzhuang	95	39.48 N	118.19 E
Xianghe	95	39.46 N	116.59 E
Xiangheguan	90	33.08 N	113.26 E
Xianghua	96	31.31 N	121.43 E
Xiangjia, Zhg.	96	31.20 N	120.31 E
Xiangjia, Zhg.	96	31.19 N	120.23 E
Xiangjiachang	97	30.08 N	104.18 E
Xiangjiang ≃	92	29.00 N	112.56 E
Xiangkhoang	100	19.20 N	103.22 E
Xiangkhoang, Plateau de ⩕[1]	100	19.30 N	103.10 E
Xianglushan	97	30.17 N	106.09 E
Xiangning	92	36.01 N	110.45 E
Xiangride	92	36.02 N	98.08 E
Xiangshan, Zhg.	88	36.14 N	116.16 E
Xiangshan, Zhg.	90	29.28 N	121.51 E
Xiangshan, Zhg.	95	39.59 N	116.10 E
Xiangshangang C	90	29.38 N	121.48 E
Xiangshanzicun	94	41.06 N	123.13 E
Xiangshishan	97	29.17 N	105.09 E
Xiangshui	90	23.15 N	114.10 E
Xiangshui ≃	90	25.35 N	115.49 E
Xiangshuikou	90	34.13 N	119.37 E
Xiangtan	90	27.51 N	112.54 E
Xiangtang	90	28.26 N	115.58 E
Xiangxiang	92	27.43 N	112.27 E
Xiangyang	95	39.13 N	115.25 E
Xiangyangkou	95	40.06 N	115.47 E
Xiangyin	90	28.40 N	112.53 E
Xiangyuan	92	36.32 N	113.00 E
Xiangyun	92	25.30 N	100.30 E
Xiangzhenpu	90	30.52 N	117.21 E
Xiangzhou, Zhg.	88	36.12 N	119.24 E
Xiangzhou, Zhg.	92	23.55 N	109.49 E
Xiangzhu	90	29.02 N	120.04 E
Xianhe ≃	97	29.22 N	104.44 E
Xianinggang	90	28.20 N	112.56 E
Xianjiang	90	27.48 N	120.30 E
Xianju	90	28.51 N	120.44 E
Xianmübu	90	25.36 N	114.40 E
Xianning	90	29.53 N	114.17 E
Xianru	79	43.11 N	128.02 E
Xianshichang	97	28.43 N	105.44 E
Xianshuigu	95	38.59 N	117.23 E
Xiantan	97	29.21 N	104.53 E
Xiantanchang	97	28.50 N	106.12 E
Xiantang	90	23.48 N	114.46 E
Xianxialing ⩕	90	28.30 N	118.46 E
Xianyang, Zhg.	90	28.02 N	118.30 E
Xianyang, Zhg.	92	34.22 N	108.42 E
Xianyou	90	25.23 N	118.40 E
Xianzhong	90	28.36 N	113.48 E
Xiaoao	90	26.14 N	119.39 E
Xiaoazhang	92	23.42 N	104.58 E
Xiaoba	88	34.32 N	115.29 E
Xiaobangniulu	94	41.34 N	122.46 E
Xiaobazi	88	41.24 N	116.13 E
Xiaobeigou	94	41.55 N	120.46 E
Xiaobeihe, Zhg.	94	42.39 N	123.58 E
Xiaobeihe, Zhg.	94	41.22 N	122.50 E
Xiaocaohu	76	43.06 N	88.30 E
Xiaochangshandao I	88	39.12 N	122.41 E
Xiaocheng	90	26.20 N	119.47 E
Xiaochengdu	96	30.59 N	120.04 E
Xiaochengshan I	88	37.27 N	122.39 E
Xiaochengzi, Zhg.	79	46.33 N	122.54 E
Xiaochengzi, Zhg.	79	42.56 N	123.12 E
Xiaochikou	90	29.46 N	115.59 E
Xiaochiyi	90	30.33 N	116.23 E
Xiaodanyang	96	31.38 N	118.43 E
Xiaodong	92	22.14 N	108.39 E
Xiaoeguan I	90	28.51 N	121.50 E
Xiaofangshen	94	42.13 N	123.54 E
Xiaofangtang	96	31.04 N	118.40 E
Xiaofanshan	95	40.16 N	115.19 E
Xiaofen	96	31.45 N	119.39 E
Xiaofeng	96	30.36 N	119.32 E
Xiaogan	90	30.55 N	113.54 E
Xiaogang	90	28.14 N	115.50 E
Xiaogaojiatun	94	41.02 N	121.59 E
Xiaogencaigangzi	94	41.48 N	122.42 E
Xiaoguai	76	45.13 N	85.02 E
Xiaoguhe ≃	88	36.42 N	120.16 E
Xiaogushan	88	39.49 N	123.12 E
Xiaohai	96	31.58 N	120.59 E
Xiaohaladaokou	88	42.37 N	119.32 E
Xiaohan	88	35.48 N	114.52 E
Xiaohe	96	32.01 N	119.52 E
Xiaoheishan ∧	92	24.42 N	98.55 E
Xiaohekou	92	33.19 N	107.25 E
Xiaoheyan	88	42.26 N	119.38 E
Xiaoheying	92	32.37 N	104.23 E
Xiaohongmen	261a	39.49 N	116.26 E
Xiaohu	90	27.20 N	118.14 E
Xiaohuying	88	41.09 N	117.13 E
Xiaoji, Zhg.	88	36.45 N	121.01 E
Xiaoji, Zhg.	90	32.38 N	119.48 E
Xiaoji, Zhg.	90	27.08 N	113.15 E
Xiaojiachang	97	30.18 N	106.28 E
Xiaojiagang	90	31.06 N	113.55 E
Xiaojialing	90	29.35 N	116.32 E
Xiaojiang	90	25.08 N	114.59 E
Xiaojiawu	95	39.36 N	116.36 E
Xiaojiayingzi	88	40.17 N	118.47 E
Xiaojieling	90	31.36 N	115.09 E
Xiaojin	92	31.00 N	102.21 E
Xiaojingfang	95	39.22 N	116.34 E
Xiaojiu	79	45.15 N	127.47 E
Xiaokaoshantun	94	42.10 N	123.53 E
Xiaokuli	79	50.18 N	120.20 E
Xiaokunshan	96	31.02 N	121.07 E
Xiaolan	90	22.41 N	113.14 E
Xiaoling, Zhg.	79	45.20 N	127.18 E
Xiaoling, Zhg.	94	42.18 N	123.23 E
Xiaolinghe ≃	94	41.06 N	121.07 E
Xiaolingzi	94	41.07 N	123.19 E
Xiaolinzhuang	94	41.36 N	124.01 E
Xiaolongtan	92	23.51 N	103.10 E
Xiaolüzhuang	96	31.57 N	119.25 E
Xiaomei	90	27.50 N	118.58 E
Xiaomeiguan)(	90	25.17 N	114.17 E
Xiaomianxi	97	30.08 N	106.32 E
Xiaomiaozi, Zhg.	88	41.24 N	114.25 E
Xiaomiaozi, Zhg.	88	41.40 N	115.21 E
Xiaonanhai	97	29.23 N	106.27 E
Xiaoniuqun	88	41.59 N	118.20 E
Xiaopikou	88	35.47 N	115.53 E
Xiaopingyang	92	23.22 N	109.13 E
Xiaoqiao	90	26.57 N	118.30 E
Xiaoqiaotou	96	30.43 N	119.27 E
Xiaoqingchuizi	94	42.30 N	123.39 E
Xiaoqinghe ≃, Zhg.	88	37.17 N	118.52 E
Xiaoqinghe ≃, Zhg.	95	39.32 N	116.08 E
Xiaoquan	92	41.14 N	95.26 E
Xiaorun	90	33.23 N	116.29 E
Xiaosanjiazi	94	42.34 N	123.23 E
Xiaosanxia ≃	97	29.34 N	106.35 E
Xiaoshachang	90	29.58 N	113.16 E
Xiaoshan	96	30.10 N	120.15 E
Xiaoshangqiao	90	33.43 N	113.58 E
Xiaoshi, Zhg.	90	27.27 N	116.49 E
Xiaoshi, Zhg.	94	41.17 N	124.06 E
Xiaoshixiang	90	30.36 N	116.38 E
Xiaoshu	96	30.48 N	119.46 E
Xiaoshun	90	29.11 N	119.51 E
Xiaosigou	88	40.53 N	118.33 E
Xiaosijia	94	42.24 N	120.46 E
Xiaotang	88	41.38 N	119.33 E
Xiaotanghe	88	42.04 N	127.10 E
Xiaotao	90	25.46 N	117.08 E
Xiaotianshi	90	32.45 N	115.36 E
Xiaotianzhen	90	31.12 N	116.33 E

≃ River	Fluss	Río	Rivière	Rio	
≅ Canal	Kanal	Canal	Canal	Canal	
Waterfall, Rapids	Wasserfall, Stromschnellen	Cascada, Rápidos	Chute d'eau, Rapides	Cascata, Rápidos	
Ɥ Strait	Meeresstrasse	Estrecho	Détroit	Estreito	
C Bay, Gulf	Bucht, Golf	Bahía, Golfo	Baie, Golfe	Baía, Golfo	
⊜ Lake, Lakes	See, Seen	Lago, Lagos	Lac, Lacs	Lago, Lagos	
Swamp	Sumpf	Pantano	Marais	Pântano	
Ice Features, Glacier	Eis- und Gletscherformen	Accidentes Glaciales	Formes glaciaires	Acidentes Glaciais	
Other Hydrographic Features	Andere Hydrographische Objekte	Otros Elementos Hidrográficos	Autres données hydrographiques	Outros Elementos Hidrográficos	

✧ Submarine Features	Untermeerische Objekte	Accidentes Submarinos	Formes de relief sous-marin	Acidentes Submarinos
□ Political Unit	Politische Einheit	Unidad Politica	Entité politique	Unidade Política
❦ Cultural Institution	Kulturelle Institution	Institución Cultural	Institution culturelle	Instituição Cultural
⊥ Historical Site	Historische Stätte	Sitio Histórico	Site historique	Sitio Histórico
♠ Recreational Site	Erholungs- und Ferienort	Sitio de Recreo	Centre de loisirs	Sítio de Lazer
⊠ Airport	Flughafen	Aeropuerto	Aéroport	Aeroporto
■ Military Installation	Militäranlage	Instalación Militar	Installation militaire	Instalação Militar
◆ Miscellaneous	Verschiedenes	Misceláneo	Divers	Miscelânea

Xiaotun 94 42.24 N 123.44 E
Xiaotunzicun 94 41.14 N 123.20 E
Xiaowa 94 41.03 N 122.04 E
Xiaowan 90 26.53 N 116.36 E
Xiaowangmiao 90 29.41 N 121.21 E
Xiaowenhe ≃ 88 35.59 N 117.11 E
Xiaowugonghe ≃ 95 39.21 N 117.32 E
Xiaowutaishan ∧ 95 39.51 N 115.09 E
Xiaoxi 90 25.48 N 115.21 E
Xiaoxian 88 34.11 N 116.56 E
Xiaoxihe ≃ 96 32.15 N 120.24 E
Xiaoxincheng 95 39.24 N 115.11 E
Xiaoxing'anling-shanmai ∧∧ 79 50.00 N 126.25 E
Xiaoxingshan I 90 22.31 N 114.51 E
Xiaoxintian 261a 39.58 N 116.22 E
Xiaoxizhen 96 30.51 N 119.50 E
Xiaoyangjiadian 94 42.23 N 122.24 E
Xiaoyangkou ≃[1] 90 32.38 N 121.02 E
Xiaoyangqi 79 50.48 N 124.12 E
Xiaoyantai 94 41.26 N 123.10 E
Xiaoyaozhen 90 33.46 N 114.16 E
Xiaoyi 92 37.10 N 111.46 E
Xiaoying, Zhg. 88 37.18 N 118.04 E
Xiaoying, Zhg. 95 40.12 N 116.33 E
Xiaoyingcun 95 39.28 N 116.41 E
Xiaoyushan I 96 30.19 N 121.55 E
Xiaozhanghe ≃ 95 39.47 N 117.22 E
Xiaozhongdian 92 27.40 N 99.46 E
Xiaozhonghe ≃ 261a 39.54 N 116.41 E
Xiaozhuang 94 41.30 N 121.27 E
Xiaozhujiawan 96 31.24 N 121.01 E
Xiapan I 96 30.30 N 121.20 E
Xiapu, Zhg. 90 27.49 N 114.26 E
Xiapu, Zhg. 90 26.52 N 120.01 E
Xiaqialafangzi 94 41.48 N 121.44 E
Xiaqiupu 88 36.59 N 119.55 E
Xiasantumen 95 38.50 N 114.48 E
Xiashe 96 30.33 N 120.11 E
Xiashesi 90 27.46 N 112.57 E
Xiashi 96 30.32 N 120.42 E
Xiashu 96 32.11 N 119.10 E
Xiashuerfowei 79 50.23 N 120.47 E
Xiashuiquan 94 41.52 N 123.38 E
Xiataizi 95 40.37 N 117.45 E
Xiatang, Zhg. 90 33.45 N 112.39 E
Xiatang, Zhg. 96 31.29 N 118.41 E
Xiatangtian 96 30.55 N 120.12 E
Xiataohuatu 94 41.42 N 120.36 E
Xiawa 88 42.39 N 120.35 E
Xiawajiang 96 30.59 N 121.51 E
Xiawaziyu 94 41.15 N 123.38 E
Xiaxi 96 31.43 N 119.45 E
Xiaxian 92 35.11 N 111.15 E
Xiaxiangcheng 92 28.42 N 99.59 E
Xiaxinhe 96 31.40 N 119.31 E
Xiayang, Zhg. 90 24.39 N 116.52 E
Xiayang, Zhg. 90 26.46 N 117.59 E
Xiayang, Zhg. 90 28.48 N 119.41 E
Xiayi 88 34.14 N 116.06 E
Xiaying, Zhg. 88 37.03 N 119.25 E
Xiaying, Zhg. 95 40.10 N 117.25 E
Xiayunling 95 39.43 N 115.44 E
Xiazhang 88 36.08 N 116.57 E
Xiazhen 90 28.39 N 118.21 E
Xiazhi I 90 29.42 N 122.15 E
Xiazhuang, Zhg. 88 35.28 N 118.43 E
Xiazhuang, Zhg. 90 27.22 N 119.01 E
Xiazhuang, Zhg. 95 39.54 N 117.01 E
Xiazhuang, Zhg. 95 39.38 N 115.26 E
Xiazhuang, Zhg. 95 40.18 N 116.21 E
Xiazhuangzhen 88 34.56 N 118.44 E
Xiazikou 95 39.01 N 115.25 E
Xibanchang 97 30.32 N 106.12 E
Xibaqianmou 94 40.59 N 121.35 E
Xibeiyingzi 94 41.55 N 121.38 E
Xibu 90 31.46 N 118.17 E
Xicang 96 31.34 N 120.29 E
Xichang, Zhg. 90 23.53 N 114.29 E
Xichang, Zhg. 92 27.58 N 102.13 E
Xichang, Zhg. 94 42.15 N 124.12 E
Xicheng, Zhg. 79 48.10 N 125.29 E
Xicheng, Zhg. 92 24.09 N 102.39 E
Xichengsi 95 39.36 N 115.45 E
Xichong 92 31.00 N 105.52 E
Xichuan 92 33.02 N 111.30 E
Xicicun 95 39.29 N 116.08 E
Xico 224 19.25 N 97.00 W
Xicotencatl 224 23.00 N 98.56 W
Xicotepec de Juárez 224 20.17 N 97.57 W
Xicun 90 27.46 N 114.14 E
Xidachuan 88 41.46 N 127.34 E
Xidapo 79 43.12 N 130.02 E
Xidaying 95 39.41 N 116.14 E
Xidazhen 88 36.27 N 113.50 E
Xidian 90 29.32 N 121.26 E
Xié ≃ 236 0.54 N 67.11 W
Xiecun 95 39.00 N 115.31 E
Xiedian 90 33.27 N 113.28 E
Xiefang 90 26.12 N 116.41 E
Xiegeer 110 28.38 N 87.04 E
Xiehejian 95 39.58 N 116.03 E
Xiejia 88 42.24 N 125.42 E
Xiejiagangzi 94 41.55 N 122.20 E
Xiejiapu 96 31.15 N 119.09 E
Xiejiaqiao 96 31.44 N 120.45 E
Xiejunmiao 97 30.15 N 103.40 E
Xielipuke 110 31.30 N 82.45 E
Xiemachang 97 29.46 N 106.22 E
Xiemaqiao 96 31.13 N 121.03 E
Xiematashan ∧ 79 50.28 N 120.47 E
Xiepu 90 30.02 N 121.37 E
Xieqiao, Zhg. 96 32.03 N 120.22 E
Xieqiao, Zhg. 96 30.29 N 120.34 E
Xietang 96 31.18 N 120.44 E
Xiexi 96 31.54 N 118.54 E
Xiexinggou 94 41.51 N 121.05 E
Xieyujiangkou C[1] 96 32.10 N 121.23 E
Xiezhen 96 31.35 N 118.38 E
Xifeng, Zhg. 88 42.43 N 124.40 E
Xifeng, Zhg. 92 27.02 N 106.30 E
Xifengkou 95 40.24 N 118.19 E
Xifocun 94 41.26 N 122.33 E
Xigangzi 79 49.58 N 127.20 E
Xigaolizhuangzi 94 41.40 N 122.55 E
Xigaotan 88 38.18 N 116.13 E
Xigaotun 88 40.27 N 122.36 E
Xigouzi 79 53.06 N 120.40 E
Xiguanjiatun 94 42.35 N 123.10 E
Xiguanyingzi 94 41.50 N 120.37 E
Xigui ⊜ 96 31.23 N 119.45 E
Xiguituqi (Yakeshi) 79 49.17 N 120.41 E
Xihaikou 94 40.50 N 121.01 E
Xihamaling ∧∧ 94 42.03 N 124.00 E
Xihe, Zhg. 90 31.01 N 118.28 E
Xihe, Zhg. 92 34.01 N 105.17 E
Xihe ≃ 94 41.44 N 121.30 E
Xiheying 88 39.53 N 114.42 E
Xihezhen 90 31.41 N 113.27 E
Xihezhuang 95 39.20 N 118.02 E
Xihu ⊜ 96 30.15 N 120.08 E
Xihua 90 33.47 N 114.31 E
Xihuangcang 96 31.43 N 121.40 E
Xihuanzidong 94 41.31 N 122.28 E
Xihuashan, Zhg. 90 25.28 N 114.20 E
Xihuashan, Zhg. 95 40.07 N 116.54 E
Xihuishan 94 41.41 N 122.38 E
Xiji, Zhg. 92 35.48 N 105.43 E
Xiji, Zhg. 95 39.49 N 116.52 E
Xijialong 92 23.31 N 103.51 E
Xijiang 90 25.50 N 115.49 E
Xijiang ≃ 92 22.25 N 113.23 E
Xijianshanzi 94 40.47 N 120.48 E
Xijiao Jichang ⊠ 95 39.57 N 116.20 E
Xijiapuzitun 94 41.26 N 123.50 E
Xikou, Zhg. 79 46.40 N 120.40 E
Xikou, Zhg. 90 28.52 N 119.11 E
Xikou, Zhg. 90 25.26 N 118.45 E
Xikou, Zhg. 90 29.14 N 114.24 E
Xikou, Zhg. 90 26.15 N 118.59 E
Xikou, Zhg. 90 25.24 N 117.03 E
Xikou, Zhg. 96 30.40 N 118.41 E
Xilaichang 97 30.20 N 103.29 E
Xilaiqiao 96 32.03 N 119.54 E
Xilaizhen 96 32.07 N 120.25 E
Xilanmulunhe ≃ 92 41.40 N 106.15 E
Xiliaohe ≃ 79 43.10 N 123.37 E
Xilin 110 28.33 N 87.48 E
Xiling ⊥ 95 39.19 N 115.15 E
Xilinhaote 92 43.58 N 116.04 E
Xilintuo 110 30.08 N 88.04 E
Xilitla 224 21.20 N 98.58 W
Xiliuhe 95 38.58 N 116.32 E
Xiliushuyingzi 94 42.25 N 121.54 E
Xilókastron 38 38.05 N 22.38 E
Xiluncun 79 47.08 N 126.26 E
Ximagou 95 40.16 N 117.50 E
Ximakou 90 30.33 N 113.47 E
Ximalatu 79 47.00 N 122.01 E
Ximalin 88 40.48 N 114.29 E
Ximenqiao 96 30.58 N 119.30 E
Ximucheng 94 40.42 N 122.54 E
Xin'an, Zhg. 79 43.46 N 125.40 E
Xin'an, Zhg. 90 26.44 N 116.13 E
Xi'nan, Zhg. 90 25.26 N 117.35 E
Xin'an, Zhg. 95 39.09 N 116.38 E
Xin'an, Zhg. 95 39.45 N 117.32 E
Xin'an, Zhg. 96 31.30 N 120.22 E
Xin'an, Zhg. 96 31.47 N 120.09 E
Xin'andian 90 32.37 N 114.03 E
Xin'andu 90 30.54 N 116.59 E
Xin'anji 90 33.22 N 115.13 E
Xin'anjiang ≃, Zhg. 90 29.33 N 118.58 E
Xin'anjiang ≃, Zhg. 90 29.12 N 119.27 E
Xin'anpu 94 42.39 N 123.27 E
Xin'anqiao 96 32.16 N 121.07 E
Xin'ansuo 92 23.16 N 103.27 E
Xin'anzhen 79 44.06 N 123.46 E
Xi'nanzhuang 95 40.48 N 118.23 E
Xinavane 146 25.02 S 32.47 E
Xinba, Zhg. 88 34.27 N 119.39 E
Xinba, Zhg. 90 30.24 N 116.52 E
Xinba, Zhg. 96 32.16 N 119.45 E
Xinba, Zhg. 96 32.08 N 120.39 E
Xinbaerhuyouqi (Alatan'aola) 78 48.41 N 116.53 E
Xinbaerhuzuoqi (Amugulang) 78 48.14 N 118.18 E
Xinbaoan 95 40.27 N 115.24 E
Xinbin, Zhg. 88 41.42 N 125.02 E
Xinbin, Zhg. 96 30.56 N 121.04 E
Xinbo 88 42.16 N 117.34 E
Xincai 90 32.44 N 114.59 E
Xincang, Zhg. 96 30.25 N 120.42 E
Xincang, Zhg. 96 30.44 N 121.11 E
Xinchang, Zhg. 90 29.30 N 120.53 E
Xinchang, Zhg. 92 28.03 N 103.46 E
Xinchang, Zhg. 92 25.10 N 104.18 E
Xinchang, Zhg. 96 31.42 N 121.46 E
Xinchang, Zhg. 96 31.02 N 121.38 E
Xinchang, Zhg. 97 30.16 N 104.29 E
Xinchang, Zhg. 97 30.29 N 106.21 E
Xinchang, Zhg. 97 29.20 N 104.15 E
Xinchang, Zhg. 97 30.31 N 104.56 E
Xinchang, Zhg. 97 29.38 N 104.33 E
Xinchangzi 97 29.40 N 103.46 E
Xincheng, Zhg. 88 40.37 N 120.43 E
Xincheng, Zhg. 90 25.34 N 114.36 E
Xincheng, Zhg. 92 24.09 N 108.46 E
Xincheng, Zhg. 95 39.15 N 115.59 E
Xincheng, Zhg. 95 38.59 N 117.33 E
Xincheng, Zhg. 96 30.48 N 120.36 E
Xinchengzi 94 42.03 N 123.30 E
Xincunji 90 32.53 N 115.31 E
Xindai 96 30.49 N 121.05 E
Xindeng 90 29.59 N 119.44 E
Xindi 94 42.21 N 120.35 E
Xindian, Zhg. 79 45.55 N 127.50 E
Xindian, Zhg. 88 37.29 N 118.28 E
Xindian, Zhg. 88 37.07 N 114.49 E
Xindian, Zhg. 90 33.38 N 113.51 E
Xindian, Zhg. 90 33.07 N 112.38 E
Xindian, Zhg. 90 29.40 N 113.40 E
Xindian, Zhg. 90 31.33 N 115.16 E
Xindian, Zhg. 95 39.10 N 116.27 E
Xindian, Zhg. 95 40.11 N 116.11 E
Xindian, Zhg. 95 40.47 N 116.49 E
Xindian, Zhg. 97 29.19 N 105.40 E
Xindianbu 90 32.24 N 116.22 E
Xindianji 90 33.33 N 114.50 E
Xindianzhen 97 29.19 N 104.57 E
Xindianzi, Zhg. 95 40.04 N 118.01 E
Xindianzi, Zhg. 97 29.52 N 106.06 E
Xindianzi, Zhg. 97 28.49 N 103.35 E
Xindianzi, Zhg. 97 29.46 N 105.11 E
Xindianzi, Zhg. 97 29.03 N 103.46 E
Xindianzi, Zhg. 97 29.43 N 104.01 E
Xindu 92 23.59 N 111.46 E
Xindukou 92 24.06 N 100.30 E
Xinfatuncun 94 41.13 N 122.28 E
Xinfeng, Zhg. 90 25.24 N 114.56 E
Xinfeng, Zhg. 90 27.26 N 116.40 E
Xinfeng, Zhg. 90 24.04 N 114.12 E
Xinfeng, Zhg. 90 24.05 N 116.53 E
Xinfeng, Zhg. 90 33.19 N 120.30 E
Xinfeng, Zhg. 96 30.43 N 120.55 E
Xinfeng, Zhg. 96 32.05 N 119.34 E
Xinfeng, Zhg. 96 31.09 N 118.40 E
Xinfengshui ≃ 90 23.42 N 114.42 E
Xing'an, Zhg. 79 48.49 N 121.45 E
Xing'an, Zhg. 92 25.37 N 110.31 E
Xin'gang 96 31.56 N 120.57 E
Xing'anlingzhan 79 51.37 N 125.38 E
Xing'antun 79 51.31 N 120.08 E
Xingcheng 94 40.37 N 120.43 E
Xingguo 90 26.21 N 115.19 E
Xinghai 92 35.31 N 99.36 E
Xinghe 88 40.48 N 113.58 E
Xinghua 90 32.57 N 119.50 E
Xinghuawan C 90 25.20 N 119.20 E
Xingkathu (Ozero Chanka) ⊜ 79 45.00 N 132.24 E
Xingliuji 90 33.04 N 115.41 E
Xinglong, Zhg. 95 40.26 N 117.34 E
Xinglong, Zhg. 97 30.36 N 106.20 E
Xinglongchang, Zhg. 97 29.54 N 105.26 E
Xinglongchang, Zhg. 97 30.20 N 106.07 E
Xinglongchang, Zhg. 97 30.25 N 104.06 E
Xinglongchang, Zhg. 97 30.06 N 105.55 E
Xinglongchang, Zhg. 97 29.34 N 106.09 E
Xinglongcun 79 48.50 N 125.12 E
Xinglongdian, Zhg. 94 42.16 N 124.00 E
Xinglongdian, Zhg. 94 41.59 N 123.03 E
Xinglonggou, Zhg. 94 41.46 N 120.38 E
Xinglonggou, Zhg. 94 40.45 N 123.08 E
Xinglongji 90 32.05 N 112.51 E
Xinglongpao 79 46.27 N 125.47 E
Xinglongtai 94 42.30 N 123.48 E
Xinglongtang 95 40.41 N 117.42 E
Xinglongzhen 92 35.38 N 106.08 E
Xingning 90 24.09 N 115.45 E
Xingningjiang ≃ 90 24.00 N 115.54 E
Xin'gou 90 30.41 N 113.57 E
Xin'gouzui 90 30.08 N 112.56 E
Xingren 92 25.27 N 105.13 E
Xingrenbao 92 37.06 N 105.12 E
Xingshanbao 79 45.30 N 125.45 E
Xingtai 88 37.04 N 114.29 E
Xingtan 90 22.46 N 113.07 E
Xingtang 88 38.26 N 114.33 E
Xingtian 90 27.30 N 118.02 E
Xingu ≃ 232 1.30 S 51.53 W
Xinguan 90 33.38 N 118.05 E
Xingwenping 92 29.24 N 103.23 E
Xingxian 92 38.36 N 111.15 E
Xingxing 96 30.39 N 121.09 E
Xingyi, Zhg. 88 38.19 N 114.59 E
Xingyi, Zhg. 92 25.06 N 104.58 E
Xingzhuangzi 95 40.34 N 115.00 E
Xingzi 90 29.28 N 116.01 E
Xinhailian 88 34.39 N 119.16 E
Xinhe, Zhg. 88 37.32 N 115.14 E
Xinhe, Zhg. 90 28.30 N 121.27 E
Xinhe, Zhg. 95 39.03 N 117.37 E
Xinhe, Zhg. 96 31.59 N 121.21 E
Xinhe ≃ 88 35.06 N 116.39 E
Xinhekou 79 48.22 N 130.45 E
Xinheng 90 23.38 N 116.18 E
Xinhezhuang 96 31.09 N 118.45 E
Xinhua 92 27.37 N 111.02 E
Xinhuang 96 30.37 N 120.55 E
Xinhuanghekou ≃[1] 88 38.00 N 119.00 E
Xinhui 90 22.32 N 113.02 E
Xining (Sining) 92 36.38 N 101.55 E
Xiniu 96 31.25 N 120.07 E
Xiniuguchengzi 94 41.01 N 122.24 E
Xiniutan 90 24.10 N 113.07 E
Xinjeji 79 52.08 N 126.24 E
Xinji, Zhg. 88 35.19 N 115.36 E
Xinji, Zhg. 90 33.24 N 114.44 E
Xinji, Zhg. 95 39.52 N 117.10 E
Xinjiaji 88 36.56 N 116.59 E
Xinjian (Shengmi), Zhg. 90 28.34 N 115.47 E
Xinjian, Zhg. 90 28.46 N 120.02 E
Xinjian, Zhg. 96 31.33 N 119.39 E
Xinjiang, Zhg. 90 24.29 N 113.52 E
Xinjiang, Zhg. 92 35.40 N 111.11 E
Xinjiang, Zhg. 96 32.05 N 120.40 E
Xinjiang ≃ 90 28.38 N 116.39 E
Xinjianglang 96 30.58 N 120.54 E
Xinjiang Weiwuer Zizhiqu (Sinkiang) □[4] 80 40.00 N 85.00 E
Xinjiapu 95 40.32 N 115.57 E
Xinjiazhuang 95 40.31 N 114.58 E
Xinjie 92 26.48 N 101.15 E
Xinjin, Bhārat 92 28.59 N 94.50 E
Xinjin, Zhg. 88 39.24 N 121.58 E
Xinjin, Zhg. 97 30.25 N 103.49 E
Xinjingzi 76 42.13 N 87.36 E
Xinkaihe 96 31.35 N 121.31 E
Xinkaihe ≃, Zhg. 79 43.37 N 123.36 E
Xinkaihe ≃, Zhg. 88 41.52 N 122.50 E
Xinkaijing 96 31.09 N 121.00 E
Xinkengdong 90 26.09 N 113.46 E
Xinle 88 38.24 N 114.47 E
Xinlitun, Zhg. 79 44.41 N 126.45 E
Xinlitun, Zhg. 94 42.00 N 122.09 E
Xinlizhuang 95 39.17 N 116.10 E
Xinmin 94 42.00 N 122.48 E
Xinmintun 94 41.39 N 123.02 E
Xinning 92 26.19 N 110.45 E
Xinnongzhen (Xiaozhan) 95 38.55 N 117.25 E
Xinping 92 24.06 N 101.58 E
Xinpu, Zhg. 90 32.50 N 118.45 E
Xinpu, Zhg. 90 24.31 N 116.08 E
Xinqianghe ≃ 90 29.12 N 113.03 E
Xinqianzhen 88 37.59 N 118.15 E
Xinqiao, Zhg. 96 31.32 N 119.04 E
Xinqiao, Zhg. 96 31.04 N 121.18 E
Xinqiao, Zhg. 97 30.33 N 105.33 E
Xinqiao, Zhg. 97 29.32 N 106.28 E
Xinqiao, Zhg. 97 30.10 N 103.50 E
Xinqiaotou 96 31.00 N 119.24 E
Xinqiu 88 41.53 N 119.41 E
Xinqizhou 90 28.56 N 115.50 E
Xinqu 76 44.57 N 85.15 E
Xinquan 90 25.23 N 116.38 E
Xinsanyu 96 31.58 N 120.07 E
Xinshao 92 27.11 N 111.20 E
Xinshenggang 96 32.03 N 120.25 E
Xinshengzhen 97 29.29 N 104.39 E
Xinshi 96 30.37 N 120.19 E
Xinshizhen 97 30.20 N 104.35 E
Xinshuhe ≃ 88 34.41 N 119.12 E
Xintai 88 35.54 N 117.44 E
Xintaimen 88 40.50 N 120.23 E
Xintaizi 94 42.07 N 123.36 E
Xintang, Zhg. 90 23.08 N 113.36 E
Xintang, Zhg. 92 30.13 N 109.30 E
Xintang, Zhg. 96 31.02 N 119.59 E
Xintangcun 96 31.53 N 119.31 E
Xintanpu 90 29.43 N 114.54 E
Xintian 92 25.53 N 112.05 E
Xintun 94 42.11 N 123.45 E
Xinwei, Zhg. 90 22.52 N 114.20 E
Xinwei, Zhg. 90 24.57 N 117.34 E
Xinwei, Zhg. 90 25.21 N 115.48 E
Xinxian, Zhg. 88 36.15 N 115.41 E
Xinxian, Zhg. 90 31.38 N 114.51 E
Xinxian, Zhg. 92 38.25 N 112.48 E
Xinxiang 88 35.20 N 113.51 E
Xinxim ≃ 240 7.57 S 53.20 W
Xinxing, Zhg. 79 43.16 N 129.48 E
Xinxing, Zhg. 90 22.40 N 112.52 E
Xinxing, Zhg. 92 19.57 N 109.32 E
Xinyang 90 32.19 N 114.01 E
Xinyao 90 27.39 N 118.52 E
Xinye 90 32.33 N 112.21 E
Xinyi (Xin'anzhen), Zhg. 88 34.22 N 118.21 E
Xinyi (Dongzhen), Zhg. 92 22.13 N 110.50 E
Xinying 92 36.04 N 105.30 E
Xinyu 90 27.49 N 114.57 E
Xinyuan 76 43.08 N 82.31 E
Xinzao 90 23.02 N 113.26 E
Xinzha 92 23.41 N 101.09 E
Xinzhai, Zhg. 88 39.24 N 118.46 E
Xinzhai, Zhg. 88 36.24 N 118.37 E
Xinzhai, Zhg. 92 24.33 N 99.08 E
Xinzhang 95 39.05 N 116.46 E
Xinzhangzi 95 40.47 N 117.52 E
Xinzhao 92 39.32 N 107.52 E
Xinzhazhen 96 31.50 N 119.52 E
Xinzhen, Zhg. 88 35.37 N 114.03 E
Xinzhen, Zhg. 95 39.01 N 116.22 E
Xinzhen, Zhg. 96 31.24 N 121.24 E
Xinzheng 90 34.25 N 113.43 E
Xinzhenshi 96 32.04 N 120.02 E
Xinzhou, Zhg. 90 30.50 N 114.47 E
Xinzhou, Zhg. 92 19.48 N 109.18 E
Xinzhuang, Zhg. 88 35.05 N 117.56 E
Xinzhuang, Zhg. 96 31.07 N 121.22 E
Xinzhuang, Zhg. 261a 39.56 N 116.31 E
Xinzhuangtou 95 39.25 N 115.45 E
Xinzhuangzi, Zhg. 94 41.05 N 121.23 E
Xinzhuangzi, Zhg. 95 39.20 N 118.25 E
Xinzhuangzi, Zhg. 95 40.14 N 116.59 E
Xinzhuangzi, Zhg. 95 40.32 N 115.10 E
Xinzhuangzi, Zhg. 95 38.52 N 117.21 E
Xinzhuntun 95 39.39 N 117.57 E
Xiongdidao II 90 23.33 N 117.40 E
Xiongershan ∧∧ 92 34.08 N 111.40 E
Xiongjiachang 92 26.31 N 105.39 E
Xiongjiaping 97 29.55 N 106.03 E
Xiongxian 95 38.59 N 116.05 E
Xiongyuecheng 88 40.10 N 122.08 E
Xipamanu ≃ 238 10.43 S 67.50 W
Xiping 90 33.23 N 114.02 E
Xiping'anhe 94 40.47 N 122.01 E
Xipu 90 23.42 N 117.24 E
Xiqi 90 26.45 N 118.42 E
Xiqi ≃ 90 25.14 N 118.03 E
Xiqia 96 31.03 N 119.37 E
Xiqilichiquan 79 49.59 N 119.27 E
Xiqin 90 26.33 N 118.06 E
Xiqingshan ∧∧ 92 35.16 N 101.30 E
Xiqu ≃ 92 31.29 N 100.48 E
Xique-Xique 240 10.50 S 42.44 W
Xiriri, Lago ⊜ 240 1.37 S 55.56 W
Xiruá ≃ 238 6.03 S 67.50 W
Xisanshilipu 90 32.40 N 117.31 E
Xishan, Zhg. 90 28.34 N 115.37 E
Xishan, Zhg. 95 39.38 N 118.10 E
Xishanqiao 96 31.57 N 118.43 E
Xishanxicun 95 40.01 N 116.50 E
Xishijiazi 94 41.46 N 120.55 E
Xishiqiao 96 31.53 N 120.06 E
Xishui 90 30.27 N 115.13 E
Xishui ≃ 90 30.21 N 115.06 E
Xishuiyu 95 40.25 N 116.16 E
Xisuhupu 94 41.41 N 123.14 E
Xitai 88 40.37 N 120.12 E
Xitaihu C 96 31.12 N 120.25 E
Xitan 90 23.47 N 117.08 E
Xitang 96 30.57 N 120.53 E
Xitangqiao, Zhg. 96 31.49 N 120.38 E
Xitangqiao, Zhg. 96 30.37 N 121.01 E
Xitaoyuan 94 40.57 N 122.11 E
Xiti 110 33.27 N 82.48 E
Xitianmushan ∧ 96 30.21 N 119.25 E
Xitiaoxi ≃ 96 30.56 N 120.11 E
Xiting 96 32.08 N 121.02 E
Xititou 95 39.16 N 117.21 E
Xitole 140 11.43 N 14.50 W
Xituan 95 39.29 N 115.47 E
Xiujiangpu 94 41.17 N 123.02 E
Xiuning 90 29.47 N 118.10 E
Xiushan 92 28.29 N 108.52 E
Xiushui 90 29.04 N 114.33 E
Xiushui ≃ 90 29.13 N 115.56 E
Xiushuihe 94 42.22 N 123.01 E
Xiuyan 88 40.17 N 123.18 E
Xiwei 90 25.22 N 117.46 E
Xiweizigou 94 42.01 N 121.59 E
Xiwenquan 97 29.42 N 106.07 E
Xiwu 90 29.40 N 121.30 E
Xiwukou 96 30.24 N 118.54 E
Xixia 92 33.22 N 111.28 E
Xixian, Zhg. 90 32.21 N 114.44 E
Xixian, Zhg. 92 36.43 N 110.52 E
Xixiang 92 32.48 N 107.55 E
Xixiangyang 95 39.33 N 116.02 E
Xixiaojie 94 40.42 N 122.12 E
Xixiaosanjiazi 94 41.22 N 122.32 E
Xixiashu 96 31.57 N 119.49 E
Xixing 96 30.11 N 120.13 E
Xiyang, Zhg. 88 37.37 N 113.42 E
Xiyang, Zhg. 90 33.25 N 116.22 E
Xiyang, Zhg. 90 25.50 N 117.25 E
Xiyang, Zhg. 96 31.49 N 120.43 E
Xiyang, Zhg. 96 31.52 N 119.23 E
Xiyangjiao 96 31.43 N 120.23 E
Xiyangshugou 94 40.41 N 122.44 E
Xiyangzhuang 96 31.50 N 119.22 E
Xiyingzi 94 41.55 N 122.34 E
Xiyinhe ≃ 95 39.08 N 117.43 E
Xiyou 88 37.24 N 119.56 E
Xiyuqiaozhai 94 41.45 N 123.40 E
Xiyushi 96 30.36 N 119.26 E
Xizang Zizhiqu □[4] 80 32.00 N 88.00 E
Xizhou 90 29.29 N 121.39 E
Xizhoushan ∧∧ 92 38.20 N 113.00 E
Xkalak 222 18.16 N 87.50 W
Xlukehu ⊜ 110 31.42 N 89.30 E
Xochapa 224 17.39 N 95.46 W
Xochimilco 224 19.16 N 99.06 W
Xochimilco □[7] 276a 19.14 N 99.05 W
Xochimilco, Lago de ⊜ 276a 19.16 N 99.06 W
Xochipala 224 17.48 N 99.39 W
Xochistlahuaca 224 16.47 N 98.15 W
Xochitlán 224 19.59 N 97.36 W
Xom-binh-phuoc 259c 10.40 N 106.47 E
Xom-long-moc 100 18.51 N 105.01 E
Xom-xoai-minh 259c 10.42 N 106.50 E
Xoxocotla 224 18.41 N 99.15 W
Xuancheng 96 30.58 N 118.45 E
Xuan'en 92 30.00 N 109.20 E
Xuanfeng 90 27.42 N 114.08 E
Xuang ≃ 100 19.58 N 102.15 E
Xuanhan 92 31.24 N 107.43 E
Xuanhua 95 40.37 N 115.03 E
Xuanhuadian 90 31.42 N 114.29 E
Xuanjiabao 96 32.17 N 120.01 E
Xuanjiangying 88 41.25 N 116.45 E
Xuan-loc 100 10.56 N 107.14 E
Xuanping 90 28.36 N 119.34 E
Xuantanchang 97 29.12 N 105.34 E
Xuan-thoi-thuong 259c 10.52 N 106.34 E
Xuanwei 92 26.07 N 104.05 E
Xuanzhuang 95 39.29 N 118.07 E
Xuchang, Zhg. 90 34.03 N 113.49 E
Xuchang, Zhg. 97 29.06 N 104.31 E
Xucheng 88 35.56 N 116.27 E
Xucun 96 30.27 N 120.22 E
Xudazhuang 90 33.44 N 117.53 E
Xueao 90 29.27 N 121.30 E
Xueba 110 29.58 N 93.48 E
Xuebu 96 31.43 N 119.22 E
Xuecheng 88 34.50 N 117.16 E
Xuedian 90 34.30 N 113.44 E
Xuefanggou 94 41.57 N 121.01 E
Xuefeng 90 33.21 N 118.22 E
Xuefengshan ∧∧ 92 27.44 N 111.00 E
Xuejiahu 88 34.08 N 116.27 E
Xueshanzhang 90 24.47 N 113.37 E
Xueshanzhang ∧ 90 24.24 N 113.37 E
Xueshuiwen 79 49.10 N 129.45 E
Xuetangpuzi 94 40.38 N 123.53 E
Xueyanqiao 96 31.30 N 120.06 E
Xuguichenxiaodian 96 32.07 N 121.20 E
Xujiabao 88 40.00 N 113.43 E
Xujiabu 90 29.27 N 116.18 E
Xujiadong 90 25.54 N 113.02 E
Xujiadu 90 28.18 N 114.44 E
Xujiagou 94 42.17 N 124.04 E
Xujiaji 90 31.50 N 116.22 E
Xujiang ≃ 90 28.17 N 116.05 E
Xujiapuzi 94 40.44 N 123.18 E
Xujiatou 96 31.19 N 119.25 E
Xujiazhai 96 31.11 N 121.46 E
Xuliying 95 39.28 N 116.02 E
Xunhe 79 49.18 N 128.04 E
Xunhua 92 35.49 N 102.26 E
Xunjiansi 95 40.50 N 116.04 E
Xunke 79 49.35 N 128.25 E
Xunle 92 25.17 N 108.12 E
Xunmukou 88 34.03 N 114.42 E
Xunshansuo 88 37.10 N 122.29 E
Xunwu 90 24.58 N 115.38 E
Xunwushui ≃ 90 24.28 N 115.26 E
Xunyangba 92 33.19 N 108.49 E
Xupu 92 27.44 N 110.24 E
Xushe 96 31.24 N 119.39 E
Xushui 95 39.02 N 115.39 E
Xutian 88 34.10 N 114.03 E
Xuwen 92 20.21 N 110.11 E
Xuxiandai 96 30.40 N 120.47 E
Xuxiang 96 31.33 N 120.13 E
Xuyen-moc 100 10.34 N 107.25 E
Xuyi 90 33.01 N 118.29 E
Xuyong 92 28.10 N 105.24 E
Xuzhou (Süchow) 88 34.16 N 117.11 E
Xuzhuang, Zhg. 88 35.07 N 117.42 E
Xuzhuang, Zhg. 96 31.09 N 120.32 E

Y

Yaan 92 30.03 N 103.02 E
Yaapeet 156 35.46 S 142.03 E
Ya'aqov Housman, Sede-Te'ufa ⊠ 122 29.33 N 34.59 E
Yaba •[8] 263a 6.30 N 3.23 E
Yaba College of Technology •[2] 263a 6.32 N 3.23 E
Ya'bad 122 32.27 N 35.10 E
Yabakei 86 33.27 N 131.07 E
Yabassi 142 4.28 N 9.58 E
Yabe 86 33.09 N 130.49 E
Yabe ≃ 86 33.06 N 130.26 E
Yabelo 134 4.54 N 38.05 E
Yablis 226 14.10 N 83.49 W
Yablonovy Range → Jablonovyj Chrebet ∧∧ 78 53.30 N 115.00 E
Yabrīn •[4] 118 23.17 N 48.58 E
Yabrūd 120 33.58 N 36.40 E
Yabu, Nihon 86 35.22 N 134.47 E
Yabu, Nihon 164m 26.36 N 127.57 E
Yabucoa 230m 18.03 N 65.53 W
Yabuki 84 37.12 N 140.19 E
Yabuluoni 79 44.55 N 128.35 E
Yacambu, Parque Nacional ♠ 236 9.40 N 68.39 W
Yacaré Norte, Riacho ≃ 242 22.43 S 58.14 W
Yachengzhen 100 18.25 N 109.11 E
Yachimata 84 35.39 N 140.19 E

ENGLISH

Name	Page	Lat. °′	Long. °′

Yachiyo, Nihon 84 36.10 N 139.53 E
Yachiyo, Nihon 84 35.43 N 140.07 E
Yaco 238 17.09 S 67.24 W
Yaco (Iaco) ≃ 238 9.03 S 68.34 W
Yacolt 214 45.52 N 122.25 W
Yacuiba 238 22.02 S 63.45 W
Yacuma ≃ 238 13.38 S 65.23 W
Yacyretá, Isla I 242 27.25 S 56.30 W
Yādgīr 112 16.46 N 77.08 E
Yadkin ≃ 182 35.23 N 80.03 W
Yadkinville 182 36.08 N 80.39 W
Yad Mordekhay 122 31.35 N 34.34 E
Yadong 114 27.29 N 88.55 E
Yādūdah 122 32.40 N 36.04 E
Yaenengu 142 2.28 N 23.15 E
Yaeyama-rettō II 165d 24.20 N 124.00 E
Yāfā 122 32.41 N 35.17 E
Yafran 136 32.04 N 12.31 E
Yaftābād 257d 35.39 N 51.19 E
Yafuquan 75 39.12 N 76.09 E
Yagachi-shima I 164m 26.40 N 128.01 E
Yağcılar 120 39.25 N 28.23 E
Yageg 134 3.24 N 44.00 E
Yageying 88 37.32 N 114.34 E
Yagi 86 35.04 N 135.32 E
Yago 224 21.50 N 105.04 W
Yagonde 142 0.02 N 22.41 E
Yagoona 264a 33.55 S 151.02 E
Yagoua 136 10.20 N 15.14 E
Yaguachi 236 2.07 S 79.41 W
Yaguachi ≃ 236 2.02 S 79.44 W
Yaguajay 230p 22.19 N 79.14 W
Yaguará 236 2.40 N 75.31 W
Yaguaraparo 236 10.34 N 62.49 W
Yaguarí 242 31.31 S 54.58 W
Yaguarón (Jaguarão) ≃ 242 32.39 S 53.12 W
Yaguas ≃ 236 2.45 S 70.04 W
Yaguhu ⊜ 110 28.40 N 91.45 E
Yagur 122 32.44 N 35.04 E
Yahagi ≃ 84 34.50 N 136.59 E
Yahagong 92 28.24 N 99.11 E
Yahara ≃ 180 42.48 N 89.07 W
Yahata → Kitakyūshū 86 33.53 N 130.50 E
Yahe, Zhg. 79 45.24 N 130.24 E
Yahe, Zhg. 96 31.44 N 119.52 E
Yaheladazeshan ∧ 110 35.12 N 95.20 E
Yahila 142 0.13 N 24.28 E
Yahk 172 49.05 N 116.05 W
Yahmūm al-Asmar, Jabal ∧ 132 29.56 N 31.38 E
Yaho 258 35.41 N 139.27 E
Yahōga-take ∧ 86 33.04 N 130.50 E
Yahongqiao 95 39.45 N 117.51 E
Yahualica 224 21.08 N 102.51 W
Yahuma 142 1.05 N 23.13 E
Yahyalı 120 38.07 N 35.22 E
Yai ≃ 104 5.02 N 101.47 E
Yai, Khao ∧ 100 15.25 N 99.20 E
Yainax Butte ∧ 192 42.20 N 121.16 W
Yaita, Nihon 84 36.48 N 139.56 E
Yaita, Nihon 258 35.57 N 140.03 E
Yaitopya → Ethiopia □[1] 134 9.00 N 39.00 E
Yaizu 84 34.52 N 138.20 E
Yajiang 92 30.02 N 101.05 E
Yaka 120 41.15 N 34.01 E
Yakacık 257b 40.55 N 29.13 E
Yakage 86 34.37 N 133.35 E
Yakak, Cape ≻ 170 51.38 N 177.00 W
Yakapınar 120 37.00 N 35.36 E
Yakarta → Jakarta 105a 6.10 S 106.48 E
Yakchāl 118 31.47 N 64.41 E
Yake-dake ∧ 84 36.14 N 137.35 E
Yakehu ⊜ 110 34.55 N 87.20 E
Yake-yama ∧ 84 36.55 N 138.03 E
Yakhchāl 110 31.47 N 64.41 E
Yakima 192 46.36 N 120.31 W
Yakima □[6] 214 46.34 N 121.03 W
Yakima ≃ 192 46.15 N 119.02 W
Yakima Indian Reservation •[4] 214 46.16 N 121.03 W
Yakishiri-jima I 82a 44.26 N 141.25 E
Yakkan ≃ 86 33.34 N 131.22 E
Yakmach 118 28.45 N 63.51 E
Yak Monis 134 0.37 N 41.25 E
Yako 140 12.58 N 2.16 W
Yakō •[8] 258 35.32 N 139.41 E
Yakobi Island I 170 58.00 N 136.30 W
Yakoma 142 4.05 N 22.27 E
Yakotoko 144 5.20 N 25.20 E
Yakou 90 24.46 N 118.46 E
Yakounga ∧∧ 142 5.04 N 11.19 E
Yakuendai 258 35.43 N 140.03 E
Yakuluku 144 4.20 N 28.48 E
Yakumo 82a 42.15 N 140.16 E
Yakuno 86 35.19 N 135.00 E
Yakushi-dake ∧ 84 36.28 N 137.33 E
Yakushi-ji •[1] 84 36.25 N 139.53 E
Yaku-shima I 83b 30.20 N 130.30 E
Yakutat 170 59.33 N 139.44 W
Yakutat Bay C 170 59.45 N 140.45 W
Yakutat Seamount •[3] 16 35.15 N 48.00 W
Yakutsk → Jakutsk 64 62.13 N 129.49 E
Yala, Ghana 140 10.07 N 1.52 W
Yala, Thai 100 6.33 N 101.18 E
Yalaha 210 28.44 N 81.49 W
Yalahán, Laguna de C 222 21.30 N 87.15 W
Yalakdereköy 120 40.36 N 29.33 E
Yalata 152 31.29 S 131.52 E
Yalca, Laguna ⊜ 248 35.34 S 57.55 W
Yalding 250 51.13 N 0.26 E
Yale, B.C., Can. 172 49.34 N 121.26 W
Yale, Mich., U.S. 180 43.08 N 82.48 W
Yale, Va., U.S. 198 36.34 N 77.17 W
Yale, Lake ⊜ 210 28.54 N 81.45 W
Yale, Mount ∧ 190 38.51 N 106.18 W
Yale Lake ⊜[1] 214 46.00 N 122.12 W
Yalgoo 152 28.20 S 116.41 E
Yali, Zaïre 142 0.04 N 21.03 E
Yali, Zhg. 92 24.43 N 106.48 E
Yaliji 88 36.06 N 114.56 E
Yalikomba 142 1.17 S 22.30 E
Yalinga 142 6.31 N 23.15 E
Yalisere 142 0.11 N 22.33 E
Yalleroi 156 24.04 S 145.45 E
Yallourn 159 38.11 S 146.21 E
Yallourn North 159 38.09 S 146.22 E
Yalnızçam Dağları ∧∧ 74 41.10 N 42.25 E
Yalnızçam Geçidi)(120 41.03 N 42.20 E
Yaloke 142 5.19 N 17.05 E
Yalongjiang ≃ 92 30.01 N 101.07 E
Yalova 120 40.39 N 29.15 E
Yalta → Jalta 68 44.30 N 34.10 E
Yalu 79 48.34 N 122.09 E
Yalufi 142 0.45 N 24.26 E
Yalujiang (Amnok-kang) ≃ 88 39.55 N 124.22 E
Yaluzangbujiang → Brahmaputra ≃ 110 24.02 N 90.59 E
Yalvaç 120 38.17 N 31.11 E
Yamachiche 196 46.16 N 72.50 W
Yamachiche ≃ 196 46.16 N 72.48 W
Yamada, Nihon 82 39.28 N 141.57 E
Yamada, Nihon 84 36.34 N 137.05 E
Yamada, Nihon 84 35.49 N 140.36 E
Yamada, Nihon 86 33.33 N 130.47 E
Yamada → Tosa-yamada, Nihon 86 33.36 N 133.41 E
Yamada, Nihon 164m 26.26 N 127.47 E
Yamada, Nihon 260 34.31 N 135.41 E
Yamada ≃ 260 34.47 N 135.04 E
Yamaga, Nihon 86 33.01 N 130.41 E
Yamaga, Nihon 86 33.27 N 131.30 E

DEUTSCH

Name	Seite	Breite °′	Länge °′ E=Ost

Yamagata, Nihon 82 38.15 N 140.15 E
Yamagata, Nihon 84 36.38 N 140.24 E
Yamagata, Nihon 84 36.10 N 137.52 E
Yamagawa 82 31.12 N 130.39 E
Yamaguchi, Nihon 84 35.33 N 137.33 E
Yamaguchi, Nihon 86 34.10 N 131.29 E
Yamaguchi, Nihon 260 34.50 N 135.15 E
Yamaguchi □[5] 86 34.20 N 131.30 E
Yamaguchi-chosuichi ⊜[1] 258 35.46 N 139.25 E
Yamaguni ≃ 86 33.37 N 131.12 E
Yama-hita-hiko-san-kokutei-kōen ♠ 86 33.25 N 131.02 E
Yamakawa 86 34.04 N 134.15 E
Yamakita 84 35.21 N 139.05 E
Yamakuni 86 33.24 N 131.02 E
Yamām, Jabal al- ∧ 122 30.02 N 35.28 E
Yamamoto, Nihon 86 34.07 N 133.44 E
Yamamoto, Nihon 260 34.38 N 135.38 E
Yamanaka 84 36.15 N 136.22 E
Yamanakako 84 35.24 N 138.52 E
Yamanaka-ko ⊜ 84 35.25 N 138.52 E
Yamanashi 84 35.40 N 138.40 E
Yamanashi □[5] 84 35.30 N 138.30 E
Yamanouchi 84 36.44 N 138.25 E
Yamasaki 86 35.00 N 134.33 E
Yamashiro, Nihon 86 33.57 N 133.45 E
Yamashiro, Nihon 86 34.45 N 135.49 E
Yamaska (Saint-Michel) 196 46.00 N 72.55 W
Yamaska □[6] 196 46.00 N 72.45 W
Yamaska ≃ 196 46.06 N 72.56 W
Yamaska Mountain ∧[2] 196 45.27 N 72.52 W
Yamaska-Nord ≃ 196 45.17 N 72.51 W
Yamaska-Sud-Est ≃ 196 45.17 N 72.55 W
Yamate 260 34.30 N 135.27 E
Yamatengwumulu 92 38.38 N 97.05 E
Yamato, Nihon 84 37.10 N 138.56 E
Yamato, Nihon 84 35.48 N 136.54 E
Yamato, Nihon 84 35.29 N 139.29 E
Yamato, Nihon 86 33.08 N 130.30 E
Yamato, Nihon 258 35.44 N 139.26 E
Yamato, Nihon 258 35.47 N 139.37 E
Yamato ≃ 86 34.36 N 135.26 E
Yamato Air Station (United States) ▪ 258 35.44 N 139.25 E
Yamato-kōriyama 86 34.38 N 135.47 E
Yamato-takada 86 34.31 N 135.45 E
Yamatsuri 84 36.52 N 140.25 E
Yamazaki 258 35.56 N 139.54 E
Yamba 156 29.26 S 153.22 E
Yambata 142 2.26 N 21.58 E
Yambéring 140 11.49 N 12.21 W
Yambio 144 4.34 N 28.23 E
Yambol → Jambol 38 42.29 N 26.30 E
Yambou Head ≻ 231h 13.09 N 61.09 W
Yamboyo 142 0.40 N 22.18 E
Yambrasbamba 238 5.45 S 77.54 W
Yambuya 144 1.16 N 24.33 E
Yamdena, Pulau I 154 7.36 S 131.25 E
Yame 86 33.10 N 130.36 E
Yamen C 90 22.08 N 113.06 E
Yamenkou 95 39.53 N 116.12 E
Yamenying 79 43.25 N 122.19 E
Yamethin 100 20.26 N 96.09 E
Yamhill 214 45.21 N 123.11 W
Yamhill □[6] 214 45.15 N 123.20 W
Yamhill ≃ 214 45.14 N 123.00 W
Yamia 140 13.24 N 10.18 E
Y'Ami Island I 98 21.07 N 121.57 E
Yamizo-san ∧ 84 36.56 N 140.17 E
Yamma Yamma, Lake ⊜ 156 26.20 S 141.25 E
Yamoussoukro 140 6.49 N 5.17 W
Yampa 190 40.09 N 106.55 W
Yampa ≃ 190 40.32 N 108.59 W
Yampa, Williams Fork ≃ 190 40.26 N 107.39 W
Yampa Plateau ∧∧[1] 190 40.25 N 109.00 W
Yamparáez 238 19.10 S 65.10 W
Yampi Sound 150 15.15 S 123.30 E
Yamsay Mountain ∧ 192 42.56 N 121.22 W
Yamu 92 43.48 N 94.48 E
Yamuna ≃ 110 25.25 N 81.50 E
Yamuna Bridge •[5] 262a 28.40 N 77.14 E
Yamunānagar 114 30.07 N 77.18 E
Yan 104 5.48 N 100.22 E
Yan ≃ 112 8.55 N 81.01 E
Yanac 156 36.08 S 141.26 E
Yanacachi 238 16.23 S 67.43 W
Yanadani 86 33.32 N 133.01 E
Yanagawa 86 33.10 N 130.24 E
Yanagi 260 34.25 N 135.56 E
Yanagimoto 260 34.34 N 135.51 E
Yanahara 86 34.55 N 134.05 E
Yanaha-shima I 164m 26.54 N 127.56 E
Yanahuara 238 16.24 S 71.33 W
Yanai 86 33.58 N 132.07 E
Yanaka 258 35.24 N 140.01 E
Yanam 112 16.44 N 82.13 E
Yan'an (Yenan) 92 36.41 N 109.19 E
Yanaoca 238 14.13 S 71.26 W
Yanbian 92 26.55 N 101.30 E
Yanbu' 118 24.05 N 38.03 E
Yanbutou 90 29.52 N 115.04 E
Yanceyville 182 36.24 N 79.20 W
Yanchang 92 36.35 N 110.15 E
Yancheng, Zhg. 88 36.48 N 116.44 E
Yancheng, Zhg. 90 33.36 N 113.57 E
Yancheng, Zhg. 90 33.24 N 120.09 E
Yanchep 158a 31.33 S 115.41 E
Yanchep Park and Caves ♠ 158a 31.32 S 115.40 E
Yanchi (Huamachi), Zhg. 92 37.52 N 107.22 E
Yanchi, Zhg. 95 40.02 N 115.53 E
Yanchuan 92 36.56 N 110.05 E
Yanco 156 34.36 S 146.25 E
Yandal 152 27.33 S 121.07 E
Yandama Creek ≃ 156 30.00 S 140.10 E
Yandé, Île I 165f 20.03 S 163.49 E
Yandev 140 7.20 N 9.01 E
Yandina 165e 9.07 S 159.13 E
Yandja 142 1.41 S 17.43 E
Yandongi 142 2.51 N 22.16 E
Yandoon 100 17.02 N 95.39 E
Yandua I 165g 16.49 S 178.18 E
Yandun 92 42.20 N 94.09 E
Yanfeng 92 25.53 N 101.01 E
Yanfolila 140 11.11 N 8.09 W
Yang ≃ 100 15.44 N 104.00 E
Yanga 224 18.50 N 96.48 W
Yangambi 144 0.47 N 24.28 E
Yangan, Austl. 161a 28.12 S 152.13 E
Yang'an, Zhg. 88 37.38 N 117.09 E
Yan'gang 90 26.02 N 116.22 E
Yangarakata 144 3.01 N 30.28 E
Yangasa Levu I 165g 18.57 S 178.26 W
Yangbajing 110 30.06 N 90.33 E
Yangce 90 32.58 N 113.14 E
Yangcha 88 41.11 N 126.15 E
Yangchang 97 30.22 N 103.42 E
Yangcheng, Zhg. 92 35.29 N 112.25 E
Yangcheng, Zhg. 96 31.24 N 120.47 E
Yangchenghu ⊜ 96 31.26 N 120.47 E
Yangchengzi 79 43.59 N 124.25 E
Yangchiang → Yangjiang 92 21.51 N 111.56 E
Yangch'ŏn •[8] 261b 37.34 N 126.51 E
Yangchow → Yangzhou 90 32.24 N 119.26 E
Yangchu 88 37.11 N 120.47 E
Yangch'üan → Yangquan 88 37.52 N 113.36 E
Yangchun 92 22.10 N 111.46 E
Yangcun, Zhg. 90 28.07 N 117.40 E
Yangcun, Zhg. 90 23.26 N 114.30 E
Yangcun, Zhg. 95 39.09 N 115.50 E
Yangcunqiao 90 29.36 N 119.28 E

Symbols in the index entries represent the broad categories identified in the key at the right. Symbols with superior numbers (∧∧²) identify subcategories (see complete key on page *I* · 26).

Kartensymbole in dem Registerverzeichnis stellen die rechts in Schlüssel erklärten Kategorien dar. Symbole mit hochgestellten Ziffern (∧∧²) bezeichnen Unterabteilungen einer Kategorie (vgl. vollständiger Schlüssel auf Seite *I* · 26).

Los símbolos incluidos en el texto del índice representan las grandes categorías identificadas con la clave a la derecha. Los símbolos con numeros en su parte superior (∧∧²) identifican las subcategorías (véase la clave completa en la página *I* · 26).

Les symboles de l'index représentent les catégories indiquées dans la légende à droite. Les symboles suivis d'un indice (∧∧²) représentent des sous-catégories (voir légende complète à la page *I* · 26).

Os símbolos incluídos no texto do índice representam as grandes categorias identificadas com a chave à direita. Os símbolos com números em sua parte superior (∧∧²) identificam as subcategorias (veja-se a chave completa à página *I* · 26).

	English	Deutsch	Español	Français	Português
∧	Mountain	Berg	Montaña	Montagne	Montanha
∧∧	Mountains	Berge	Montañas	Montagnes	Montanhas
)(	Pass	Pass	Paso	Col	Passo
∨	Valley, Canyon	Tal, Cañon	Valle, Cañón	Vallée, Canyon	Vale, Canhão
≚	Plain	Ebene	Llano	Plaine	Planície
≻	Cape	Kap	Cabo	Cap	Cabo
I	Island	Insel	Isla	Île	Ilha
II	Islands	Inseln	Islas	Îles	Ilhas
•	Other Topographic Features	Andere Topographische Objekte	Otros Elementos Topográficos	Autres données topographiques	Outros Elementos Topográficos

ESPAÑOL

Nombre	Página	Lat.°′	Long.°′ W=Oeste
Yangdalinzi	88	42.38 N	125.07 E
Yangdian	96	31.08 N	119.45 E
Yang'erzhuang	88	38.18 N	117.30 E
Yangfangpu	95	40.48 N	115.01 E
Yangfangzhen	95	40.07 N	116.07 E
Yangfen'gang	95	39.07 N	116.52 E
Yangfenzhen	96	30.28 N	120.03 E
Yangganga I	165g	16.35 S	178.35 E
Yanggang Do □[4]	88	41.15 N	128.00 E
Yangganzhen	96	31.00 N	119.15 E
Yanggezhuang	95	40.09 N	116.48 E
Yanggong-ni	261b	37.39 N	126.37 E
Yanggu, Taehan	88	38.06 N	127.59 E
Yanggu, Zhg.	88	34.44 N	114.48 E
Yanggu, Zhg.	88	36.08 N	115.48 E
Yangguan)(	92	39.58 N	94.25 E
Yangguanpu	90	32.13 N	115.31 E
Yanghang	96	31.22 N	121.26 E
Yanghe	90	33.47 N	118.23 E
Yanghe ≃	95	40.24 N	115.20 E
Yanghexi	92	29.39 N	108.40 E
Yanghu	90	32.34 N	116.30 E
Yanghua	97	30.11 N	104.45 E
Yangi-Yul' → Jangijul'	75	41.07 N	69.03 E
Yangji, Zhg.	88	34.00 N	116.13 E
Yangji, Zhg.	88	36.44 N	113.56 E
Yangjia	96	30.41 N	120.15 E
Yangjiachang, Zhg.	97	29.56 N	104.41 E
Yangjiachang, Zhg.	97	29.23 N	104.21 E
Yangjiachang, Zhg.	97	29.45 N	105.21 E
Yangjiadang	90	32.23 N	112.39 E
Yangjiagou, Zhg.	88	37.16 N	118.50 E
Yangjiagou, Zhg.	95	39.18 N	117.54 E
Yangjiaji, Zhg.	88	34.28 N	119.19 E
Yangjiaji, Zhg.	90	34.19 N	119.28 E
Yangjiajiang	90	30.49 N	112.47 E
Yangjiajie	97	30.18 N	104.39 E
Yangjian	96	31.39 N	120.33 E
Yangjiang	92	21.51 N	111.56 E
Yangjiang ≃	90	33.37 N	120.33 E
Yangjiaqiao, Zhg.	90	27.44 N	112.46 E
Yangjiaqiao, Zhg.	96	31.53 N	121.42 E
Yangjiaqiao, Zhg.	96	32.02 N	121.26 E
Yangjiatao	95	39.49 N	117.51 E
Yangjiatun	94	40.57 N	121.41 E
Yangjiawopu	94	42.21 N	122.57 E
Yangjiazeng	95	40.12 N	117.04 E
Yangjiazhangzi	94	40.48 N	120.33 E
Yangjie	92	24.49 N	100.22 E
Yangjishi	90	26.39 N	113.14 E
Yangkou, Zhg.	90	26.47 N	117.51 E
Yangkou, Zhg.	90	28.39 N	118.53 E
Yanglinjie	90	29.07 N	113.27 E
Yangliupu, Zhg.	90	30.52 N	118.37 E
Yangliupu, Zhg.	97	30.09 N	104.03 E
Yangliuqing	95	39.08 N	116.59 E
Yangloudong	90	29.31 N	113.44 E
Yanglousi	90	29.30 N	113.38 E
Yangluomayu	94	40.47 N	122.54 E
Yangmachang	97	30.39 N	103.45 E
Yangmadatun	94	42.35 N	124.13 E
Yangmahe	97	30.29 N	104.31 E
Yangmeisi	90	25.42 N	114.30 E
Yangmiao, Zhg.	88	34.11 N	114.53 E
Yangmiao, Zhg.	96	30.51 N	120.49 E
Yangmingshan	259d	25.09 N	121.33 E
Yangmingshan □[5]	259d	25.09 N	121.32 E
Yangmingshan ∧	92	26.03 N	111.56 E
Yangmugou, Zhg.	88	40.36 N	124.28 E
Yangmugou, Zhg.	94	41.11 N	123.50 E
Yangmulin	95	40.06 N	115.12 E
Yangon → Rangoon	100	16.47 N	96.10 E
Yangor	164b	0.31 S	166.54 E
Yangpingguan	92	32.51 N	106.09 E
Yangpu	90	27.14 N	119.08 E
Yangp'yŏng	88	37.30 N	127.29 E
Yangp'yŏng-ni	88	40.53 N	127.58 E
Yangqi	96	31.23 N	119.57 E
Yangquan	88	37.52 N	113.36 E
Yangquanzi	88	41.17 N	121.39 E
Yangriwan	92	31.37 N	110.49 E
Yangsan	88	35.21 N	129.03 E
Yangshan, Zhg.	88	41.13 N	120.24 E
Yangshan, Zhg.	92	24.28 N	112.38 E
Yangshanji	88	35.13 N	116.13 E
Yangsheying	96	31.52 N	120.32 E
Yangshigangzi	94	41.42 N	122.59 E
Yangshitun	94	42.06 N	123.44 E
Yangshugemen	95	40.55 N	118.18 E
Yangshugoudonggou	94	41.43 N	120.41 E
Yangshuling	88	41.02 N	118.47 E
Yangshuo	92	24.45 N	110.24 E
Yangtianzhang ∧	90	24.37 N	115.38 E
Yangtou	90	23.26 N	115.24 E
Yangtze → Changjiang ≃	80	31.48 N	121.10 E
Yanguan	96	30.26 N	120.32 E
Yangwan, Zhg.	90	28.22 N	116.46 E
Yangwan, Zhg.	96	31.03 N	120.22 E
Yangxi, Zhg.	90	29.31 N	119.18 E
Yangxi, Zhg.	90	27.18 N	114.10 E
Yangxi, Zhg.	90	30.11 N	118.39 E
Yangxian	92	33.03 N	107.47 E
Yangxiang	96	31.29 N	119.35 E
Yangxiangjing	96	31.12 N	121.01 E
Yangxiangtun	94	40.58 N	122.48 E
Yangxiaodian	90	31.46 N	116.45 E
Yangxin, Zhg.	88	37.39 N	117.34 E
Yangxin, Zhg.	90	29.51 N	115.12 E
Yangxing	96	31.37 N	120.34 E
Yangxiudian	261a	39.44 N	116.32 E
Yang Yang, Sén.	140	15.35 N	15.21 W
Yangyang, Taehan	88	38.04 N	128.36 E
Yangyuan	88	40.01 N	114.10 E
Yangze	90	26.57 N	118.23 E
Yangzhong (Sanmaozhen)	96	32.16 N	119.49 E
Yangzhou	90	32.24 N	119.26 E
Yangzhuang, Zhg.	88	34.02 N	117.14 E
Yangzhuang, Zhg.	90	33.36 N	118.58 E
Yangzhujuanzi	94	41.38 N	122.46 E
Yangzhuoyonghu ⊜	110	28.58 N	90.44 E
Yangzishao	88	42.28 N	126.09 E
Yangzizhen	90	31.19 N	112.36 E
Yanhaiyingzi	94	41.52 N	123.05 E
Yanhe	92	28.37 N	108.35 E
Yanhecheng	95	40.04 N	115.43 E
Yanheying	88	40.02 N	119.03 E
Yanhui	88	37.54 N	113.51 E
Yanina → Ioánnina	38	39.40 N	20.50 E
Yanji, Zhg.	88	42.57 N	129.32 E
Yanji, Zhg.	88	34.41 N	115.27 E
Yanji (Longjing), Zhg.	88	42.47 N	129.26 E
Yanjiabao	96	32.19 N	120.07 E
Yanjiahe, Zhg.	90	31.48 N	114.50 E
Yanjiahe, Zhg.	90	31.16 N	115.07 E
Yanjiajie	94	41.02 N	121.32 E
Yanjiao	95	39.56 N	116.48 E
Yanjiatuozi	94	42.27 N	123.47 E
Yanjiawopeng	94	40.59 N	121.17 E
Yanjin	88	35.11 N	114.11 E
Yanjingchi	97	29.56 N	106.21 E
Yankalilla	158b	35.28 S	138.21 E
Yankalilla Bay C	158b	35.28 S	138.15 E
Yankari Game Reserve ⬥[4]	140	9.30 N	10.20 E
Yankdŏk	88	39.14 N	126.41 E
Yankee Lake	200	41.35 N	74.33 W
Yankee Springs State Recreation Area ♠	206	42.38 N	85.30 W
Yankee Stadium ♠	266	40.50 N	73.56 W
Yankeetown	210	29.02 N	82.43 W
Yan Kit	261c	1.22 N	103.58 E
Yankton	188	42.53 N	97.23 W
Yankton Indian Reservation ⬥[4]	188	43.10 N	98.22 W
Yanling, Zhg.	88	34.07 N	114.11 E
Yanling, Zhg.	96	31.54 N	119.30 E

FRANÇAIS

Nom	Page	Lat.°′	Long.°′ W=Ouest
Yanliuji	90	32.01 N	116.52 E
Yanmeimeizi	95	39.42 N	115.03 E
Yanna	156	26.56 S	146.03 E
Yannarie ≃	152	22.28 S	114.48 E
Yanqi	80	42.00 N	86.15 E
Yanqian, Zhg.	90	26.15 N	117.28 E
Yanqian, Zhg.	90	24.54 N	116.14 E
Yanqianhu	94	42.16 N	123.12 E
Yanqiao	96	31.41 N	120.17 E
Yanqidoumen	96	31.17 N	118.42 E
Yanqing	95	40.28 N	115.58 E
Yanque	238	15.39 S	71.39 W
Yanrey	152	22.31 S	114.48 E
Yanshan, Zhg.	88	38.05 N	117.13 E
Yanshan, Zhg.	92	23.41 N	104.21 E
Yanshankou	95	39.59 N	117.42 E
Yanshi	90	25.17 N	117.10 E
Yanshixi ≃	90	25.20 N	117.17 E
Yanshou	79	45.28 N	128.20 E
Yansi	90	29.48 N	118.20 E
Yanṭā	122	33.36 N	35.57 E
Yantabulla	156	29.21 S	145.00 E
Yantai (Chefoo), Zhg.	88	37.33 N	121.20 E
Yantai, Zhg.	95	39.47 N	116.38 E
Yantan, Zhg.	90	28.28 N	120.44 E
Yantan, Zhg.	90	28.55 N	120.11 E
Yantan, Zhg.	97	29.17 N	104.52 E
Yantian, Zhg.	90	27.21 N	114.22 E
Yantian, Zhg.	90	26.53 N	119.53 E
Yantic ≃	197	41.31 N	72.05 W
Yantietang ☲	96	31.49 N	120.46 E
Yanting	92	31.19 N	105.23 E
Yantis	212	32.56 N	95.35 W
Yantongshan, Zhg.	79	43.17 N	126.00 E
Yantongshan, Zhg.	95	40.42 N	115.06 E
Yanwangshan	94	41.36 N	123.57 E
Yanweixiang	88	34.30 N	119.48 E
Yanxi	90	24.46 N	117.47 E
Yanxia	90	29.31 N	114.52 E
Yanxidu	90	26.51 N	114.58 E
Yanxing	92	25.23 N	101.42 E
Yan Yean Reservoir ⊜[1]	159	37.33 S	145.08 E
Yanyegongsi	96	32.02 N	121.41 E
Yanyuan	92	27.29 N	101.32 E
Yanzhou	88	35.33 N	116.50 E
Yanziji	96	32.09 N	118.49 E
Yanzijiao	92	23.38 N	100.12 E
Yanzikou	92	27.31 N	105.21 E
Yao, Nihon	86	34.37 N	135.36 E
Yao, Tchad	136	12.51 N	17.34 E
Yao Airport ⊠	260	34.36 N	135.36 E
Yaoan	92	25.32 N	101.12 E
Yaoba	97	28.45 N	105.39 E
Yaocun, Zhg.	88	35.41 N	116.57 E
Yaocun, Zhg.	88	36.12 N	113.50 E
Yaocun, Zhg.	95	39.09 N	115.32 E
Yaodafangshen	94	42.27 N	122.59 E
Yaoerwan	95	40.49 N	115.27 E
Yaogongbu	90	29.51 N	120.18 E
Yaogutuo	97	29.08 N	104.01 E
Yaohongcaopao	94	40.55 N	122.26 E
Yaohuamen	96	32.08 N	118.52 E
Yaohuangdi	94	41.32 N	122.48 E
Yaojiadian	90	31.14 N	114.22 E
Yaojiaqiao	96	32.10 N	119.46 E
Yaojiatun	94	41.18 N	121.47 E
Yaojiawopeng	94	41.47 N	122.25 E
Yaojie	92	36.26 N	102.59 E
Yaoling	90	24.49 N	113.58 E
Yaolugou	88	40.34 N	119.24 E
Yaoluzi	94	41.26 N	121.34 E
Yao Malikidza	142	5.19 N	19.36 E
Yaopi	90	26.52 N	113.38 E
Yaopu	90	32.14 N	118.20 E
Yaoqianhutun	94	41.32 N	123.36 E
Yaoshizhen	97	30.11 N	105.30 E
Yaotou	90	26.38 N	114.48 E
Yaotsu	84	35.28 N	137.09 E
Yaotun, Zhg.	79	48.28 N	127.30 E
Yaotun, Zhg.	94	40.59 N	122.18 E
Yaotutun	94	42.06 N	123.29 E
Yaoundé	142	3.52 N	11.31 E
Yaowan	88	34.12 N	118.03 E
Yaowangmiao	88	40.47 N	120.10 E
Yaoxian	92	34.56 N	108.53 E
Yao Yai, Ko I	100	8.00 N	98.35 E
Yaozhan, Zhg.	79	52.53 N	125.13 E
Yaozhan, Zhg.	88	37.02 N	116.14 E
Yap	164q	9.31 N	138.08 E
Yap □[5]	164q	9.30 N	138.10 E
Yap I	164q	9.31 N	138.06 E
Yapacani ≃	238	16.00 S	64.25 W
Yapakopra	154	4.24 S	135.05 E
Yapehe	142	0.13 S	24.27 E
Yapei (Tamale Port)	140	9.10 N	1.10 W
Yapen, Pulau I	154	1.45 S	136.15 E
Yapen, Selat ⊔	154	1.30 S	136.10 E
Yapero	154	4.59 S	137.11 E
Yapeyú	242	29.28 S	56.49 W
Yaphank	197	40.50 N	72.56 W
Yappar ≃	156	18.22 S	141.16 E
Yaq Braway	134	2.00 N	43.45 E
Yaqian	90	26.38 N	114.30 E
Ya'qūb	130	12.29 N	25.11 E
Yaque del Norte ≃	228	19.51 N	71.41 W
Yaque del Sur ≃	228	18.17 N	71.06 W
Yaqui ≃	222	27.37 N	110.39 W
Yaquina ≃	192	44.37 N	124.04 W
Yara, Cuba	230p	20.16 N	76.57 W
Yara, Perú	238	16.11 S	71.40 W
Yaracuy □[3]	236	10.20 N	69.10 W
Yaracuy ≃	236	10.33 N	68.15 W
Yaraka	156	24.53 S	144.04 E
Yaratuar	154	2.58 S	134.40 E
Yarbasan	120	38.59 N	28.49 E
Yarcombe	44	50.52 N	3.05 W
Yardea	156	32.23 S	135.32 E
Yardley	198	40.15 N	74.50 W
Yardville	198	40.11 N	74.40 W
Yare ≃	44	52.35 N	1.44 E
Yari	136	13.59 N	12.18 E
Yari ≃	236	0.23 S	72.16 W
Yariga-take ∧	84	36.20 N	137.39 E
Yārik	113	32.06 N	70.47 E
Yarīm	134	14.29 N	44.21 E
Yaring	100	6.52 N	101.22 E
Yaritagua	236	10.05 N	69.08 W
Yarkand → Suoche	110	38.25 N	77.16 E
Yarkand → Yeerqianghe ≃	80	40.28 N	80.52 E
Yarker	202	44.23 N	76.46 W
Yarkhūn ≃	113	36.17 N	72.30 E
Yarlarweelor	152	25.35 S	117.59 E
Yarle Lakes ⊜	152	30.15 S	131.27 E
Yarloop	158a	32.57 S	115.54 E
Yarma	120	37.49 N	32.54 E
Yarmouth, N.S., Can.	176	43.50 N	66.07 W
Yarmouth → Great Yarmouth, Eng., U.K.	44	52.37 N	1.44 E
Yarmouth, Eng., U.K.	44	50.42 N	1.29 W
Yarmouth, Maine, U.S.	178	43.48 N	70.12 W
Yarmouth, Mass., U.S.	197	41.40 N	70.11 W
Yarmu	154	4.18 S	142.17 E
Yarmuk, Nahr al- ≃	122	32.38 N	35.34 E
Yaroupi ≃	240	2.47 N	52.28 W
Yarra ≃	159	37.51 S	144.54 E
Yarra Bend National Park ♠	264b	37.48 S	145.01 E
Yarra Glen	159	37.40 S	145.23 E
Yarragon	159	38.12 S	146.04 E
Yarraloola	152	21.34 S	115.52 E
Yarram	156	38.33 S	146.41 E
Yarraman	161a	26.50 S	151.59 E
Yarrangobilly	161b	35.39 S	148.28 E
Yarrangobilly Caves ⬥[5]	161b	35.44 S	148.29 E
Yarraville	264b	37.49 S	144.53 E

PORTUGUÊS

Nome	Página	Lat.°′	Long.°′ W=Oeste
Yarrawonga	156	36.01 S	146.00 E
Yarra Yarra Lakes ⊜	152	29.40 S	115.47 E
Yarrow, B.C., Can.	214	49.05 N	122.02 W
Yarrow, Scot., U.K.	42	55.32 N	3.01 W
Yarrow ≃	252	53.40 N	2.49 W
Yarrowee ≃	159	38.07 S	144.04 E
Yarrow Point	214	47.39 N	122.13 W
Yarrow Reservoir ⊜[1]	252	53.38 N	2.34 W
Yarrow Water ≃	42	55.34 N	2.51 W
Yarty ≃	44	50.47 N	3.01 W
Yarumal	236	6.58 N	75.24 W
Yarvicoya, Cerro ∧	238	20.07 S	69.00 W
Yasa	142	3.42 S	21.24 E
Yasaka, Nihon	86	34.46 N	132.04 E
Yasaka, Nihon	86	35.39 N	135.07 E
Yasa-Lokwa	142	5.15 S	19.24 E
Yasato	84	36.14 N	140.12 E
Yasawa I	165g	16.47 S	177.31 E
Yasawa Group II	165g	17.00 S	177.23 E
Yasendu	142	0.27 N	24.20 E
Yashanjie	96	30.51 N	119.03 E
Yashbum	134	14.19 N	46.56 E
Yashi	140	12.23 N	7.54 E
Yashikera	140	9.46 N	3.28 E
Ya-shima I	86	33.44 N	132.09 E
Yashio	258	35.49 N	139.51 E
Yashiro	86	34.55 N	134.58 E
Yashiro-jima I	86	33.55 N	132.15 E
Yāsīn	113	33.57 N	72.30 E
Yasku	136	12.20 N	12.30 E
Yasothon	100	15.45 N	104.08 E
Yass	156	34.50 S	148.55 E
Yassy → Iaşi	38	47.10 N	27.35 E
Yasu, Nihon	84	35.03 N	136.01 E
Yasu, Nihon	86	33.32 N	133.45 E
Yasuda	86	33.26 N	133.59 E
Yasufuruichi	86	34.27 N	132.28 E
Yasugi	86	35.26 N	133.15 E
Yasun Burnu ≻	120	41.09 N	37.41 E
Yasuni ≃	236	0.56 S	75.23 W
Yasuoka	84	35.22 N	137.50 E
Yasuura	86	34.15 N	132.50 E
Yasuzuka	84	37.08 N	138.28 E
Yata	238	13.20 S	66.35 W
Yata ≃, Bol.	238	10.29 S	65.26 W
Yata ≃, Nihon	86	35.38 N	134.37 E
Yatabe	84	36.02 N	140.04 E
Yatağan	120	37.20 N	28.09 E
Yatakala	140	14.48 N	0.22 E
Yāṭar	122	33.09 N	35.20 E
Yatate-yama ∧	82	34.10 N	129.10 E
Yaté, N. Cal.	165f	22.09 S	166.57 E
Yate, Eng., U.K.	44	51.32 N	2.25 W
Yates □[6]	200	42.40 N	77.03 W
Yatesboro	204	40.48 N	79.20 W
Yates Center	188	37.53 N	95.44 W
Yates City	180	40.47 N	90.01 W
Yathata I	165g	17.15 S	179.32 W
Yathkyed Lake ⊜	166	62.41 N	98.00 W
Yating	92	25.03 N	106.05 E
Yatomi	84	35.06 N	136.43 E
Yatsuga-take ∧	84	35.59 N	138.23 E
Yatsuga-take-chūshin-kōgen-kokutei-kōen ♠	84	36.03 N	138.20 E
Yatsuka	86	35.17 N	133.52 E
Yatsuo	84	36.34 N	137.08 E
Yatsushiro	82	32.30 N	130.36 E
Yatsushiro-wan C	82	32.20 N	130.25 E
Yaṭṭah	122	31.27 N	35.05 E
Yatta Plateau ⋏[1]	144	2.00 S	38.00 E
Yatton	44	51.24 N	2.49 W
Yatua ≃	236	1.43 N	66.30 W
Yatusiro → Yatsushiro	82	32.30 N	130.36 E
Yauca	238	15.40 S	74.32 W
Yauca ≃	238	15.41 S	74.31 W
Yauco	230m	18.02 N	66.51 W
Yauco ≃	230m	17.59 N	66.48 W
Yauco, Embalse de ⊜[1]	230m	18.07 N	66.50 W
Yauli	238	11.41 S	76.06 W
Yaundé → Yaoundé	142	3.52 N	11.31 E
Yaupi	236	2.59 S	77.50 W
Yauri	238	14.47 S	71.29 W
Yautepec	224	18.53 N	99.04 W
Yauya ≃	226	13.28 N	84.14 W
Yauyos	238	12.24 S	75.57 W
Yāval	110	21.10 N	75.42 E
Yavarí (Javari) ≃	232	4.21 S	70.02 W
Yavarí Mirim ≃	236	4.31 S	71.44 W
Yavaros	222	26.42 N	109.31 W
Yavatmāl	112	20.24 N	78.08 E
Yaven Yaven Creek ≃	161b	35.06 S	147.46 E
Yavero (Paucartambo) ≃	238	12.06 S	72.57 W
Yavi	120	39.48 N	36.13 E
Yaví, Cerro ∧	236	5.32 N	65.59 W
Yavita	236	2.55 N	67.26 W
Yaviza	236	8.11 N	77.41 W
Yavne	122	31.53 N	34.45 E
Yawahara	258	35.59 N	140.01 E
Yawata, Nihon	86	34.52 N	135.42 E
Yawata → Kitakyūshū, Nihon	86	33.53 N	130.50 E
Yawata, Nihon	258	35.32 N	140.08 E
Yawatahama	86	33.27 N	132.24 E
Yawosha I	96	31.23 N	121.41 E
Yaxchilan ⊥	222	16.54 N	90.58 W
Yaxi, Zhg.	92	27.32 N	106.45 E
Yaxi, Zhg.	96	31.23 N	119.10 E
Yaxian	100	18.20 N	109.30 E
Yaxierhu ⊜	110	34.59 N	81.35 E
Yaxley	44	52.31 N	0.16 W
Yayama	142	1.16 S	23.07 E
Yaylak	120	37.23 N	38.20 E
Yayouta	140	8.11 N	8.30 W
Yayuan	88	41.47 N	126.11 E
Yazd	118	31.53 N	54.25 E
Yazi	88	37.04 N	121.17 E
Yazichangcun	94	41.16 N	122.26 E
Yazıhan	120	38.36 N	38.11 E
Yazikou	75	39.48 N	74.21 E
Yazmān	113	29.08 N	71.45 E
Yazoo ≃	184	32.22 N	91.00 W
Yazoo City	184	32.51 N	90.28 W
Ybbs ≃	30	48.10 N	15.06 E
Ybbs an der Donau	30	48.11 N	15.05 E
Ybor City	210	27.57 N	82.27 W
Ybycuí	242	26.01 S	57.03 W
Yding Skovhøj ∧[2]	41	56.00 N	9.48 E
Ydstebøhavn	26	59.08 N	5.15 E
Ydžid Parma ⋏	24	63.06 N	58.15 E
Ye	100	15.15 N	97.51 E
Yé ≃	142	1.25 N	13.14 E
Yea	159	37.13 S	145.26 E
Yea ≃	159	37.11 S	145.23 E
Yeading ⬥[8]	250	51.32 N	0.24 W
Yeadon, Eng., U.K.	42	53.52 N	1.41 W
Yeadon, Pa., U.S.	275	39.56 N	75.15 W
Yeagertown	198	40.39 N	77.35 W
Yealm ≃	44	50.18 N	4.03 W
Yealmpton	44	50.21 N	3.59 W
Yebawgyi	100	18.40 N	94.35 E
Yebbi Bou	136	20.58 N	18.04 E
Yebbi Souma	136	21.08 N	17.56 E
Yébigé, Enneri ∨	136	22.04 N	17.49 E
Yebyu	100	14.15 N	98.12 E
Yecapixtla	224	18.53 N	98.52 W
Yecheng	110	37.54 N	77.25 E
Yech'ŏn	88	36.40 N	128.26 E
Yecla	34	38.37 N	1.07 W
Yécora	222	28.20 N	108.58 W
Yedashe	100	19.09 N	96.21 E
Yedikule ⬥[8]	257b	40.59 N	28.55 E
Yedikule Suriarı ⊥	257b	40.59 N	28.55 E
Yédinga, Ouadi ∨	136	15.46 N	20.05 E
Yedseram ≃	136	12.30 N	14.05 E
Yeeda	152	17.36 S	123.39 E
Yeelanna	156	34.09 S	135.45 E
Yeelirrie	152	27.17 S	120.06 E
Yeernuozhahu ⊜	110	32.30 N	89.30 E
Yeerqianghe (Yarkand) ≃	80	40.28 N	80.52 E
Yegor'yevsk → Jegorjevsk	72	55.23 N	39.02 E
Yegros	242	26.24 S	56.25 W
Yegua Creek ≃	212	30.23 N	96.18 W
Yeguas, Río de las ≃	34	37.22 N	4.45 W
Yehliu	259d	25.12 N	121.41 E
Yehliu Chia ≻	259d	25.13 N	121.42 E
Yehud	122	32.02 N	34.53 E
Yei	144	4.05 N	30.40 E
Yei ≃	130	6.15 N	30.13 E
Yeji	140	8.13 N	0.39 W
Yejiaji	90	31.52 N	115.55 E
Yekaterinburg → Sverdlovsk	76	56.51 N	60.36 E
Yekaterinodar → Krasnodar	68	45.02 N	39.00 E
Yekaterinoslav → Dnepropetrovsk	68	48.27 N	34.59 E
Yekokora ≃	142	1.20 N	20.21 E
Yekumbo	142	1.02 S	23.27 E
Ye Kyun I	100	18.37 N	93.47 E
Yelarbon	156	28.34 S	150.45 E
Yele	140	8.25 N	11.50 W
Yelets → Jelec	66	52.37 N	38.30 E
Yélimané	140	15.08 N	10.34 W
Yell I	28	60.35 N	1.05 W
Yellandu	112	17.36 N	80.20 E
Yellow ≃, U.S.	184	30.33 N	87.00 W
Yellow ≃, Ind., U.S.	206	41.16 N	86.50 W
Yellow ≃, Iowa, U.S.	180	43.05 N	91.11 W
Yellow ≃, Wis., U.S.	180	44.58 N	91.18 W
Yellow ≃, Wis., U.S.	180	46.01 N	92.22 W
Yellow ≃, Wis., U.S.	180	43.59 N	90.03 W
Yellow → Huanghe ≃, Zhg.	80	37.32 N	118.19 E
Yellow Breeches Creek ≃	198	40.13 N	76.51 W
Yellow Creek ≃, U.S.	184	33.34 N	88.20 W
Yellow Creek ≃, Colo., U.S.	190	40.10 N	108.24 W
Yellow Creek ≃, Ohio, U.S.	204	40.34 N	80.40 W
Yellow Creek ≃, Tenn., U.S.	184	36.26 N	87.34 W
Yellow Creek, North Fork ≃	204	40.33 N	80.42 W
Yellow Creek State Park ♠	204	40.35 N	79.02 W
Yellowdine	152	31.18 S	119.39 E
Yellow Grass	174	49.49 N	104.08 W
Yellowhead Pass)(	172	52.53 N	118.28 W
Yellow Housedraw ∨	186	33.35 N	101.50 W
Yellowknife	166	62.27 N	114.21 W
Yellowknife ≃	166	62.31 N	114.19 W
Yellow Lake ⊜	202	44.20 N	75.36 W
Yellow Medicine ≃	188	44.44 N	95.25 W
Yellow Mountain ∧	156	32.30 S	146.51 E
Yellow Sea ✢[2]	80	36.00 N	123.00 E
Yellow Springs	208	39.48 N	83.53 W
Yellowstone ≃	168	47.58 N	103.59 W
Yellowstone, Clarks Fork ≃	192	45.39 N	108.43 W
Yellowstone Falls ↳	192	44.43 N	110.30 W
Yellowstone Lake ⊜	192	44.25 N	110.22 W
Yellowstone National Park	192	44.58 N	110.42 W
Yellowstone National Park ♠	192	44.30 N	110.35 W
Yellowtail Dam ⬥[6]	192	45.12 N	107.57 W
Yell Sound ⊔	28	60.33 N	1.15 W
Yellville	184	36.14 N	92.41 W
Yelm	214	46.56 N	122.36 W
Yelma	152	26.30 S	121.40 E
Yelucá, Cerro ∧	226	14.19 N	84.54 W
Yelusuhu ⊜	110	35.11 N	92.15 E
Yelvertoft	156	20.13 S	138.53 E
Yelverton	44	50.30 N	4.05 W
Yelwa	140	10.51 N	4.46 E
Yemadu	76	43.36 N	81.50 E
Yemagong	114	29.28 N	89.06 E
Yemaoba	97	30.10 N	105.56 E
Yemassee	182	32.41 N	80.51 W
Yematan	92	34.40 N	98.16 E
Yemen □[1]	108 134	15.00 N	44.00 E
Yemen, People's Democratic Republic of □[1]	134 108	15.00 N	48.00 E
Yemen, República Popular Democrática del → Yemen, People's Democratic Republic of □[1]	134	15.00 N	48.00 E
Yémen, République démocratique populaire du → Yemen, People's Democratic Republic of □[1]	134	15.00 N	48.00 E
Yemesguida ∧	138	29.12 N	9.58 W
Yenagoa	140	4.55 N	6.19 E
Yenakiyevo → Jenakijevo	73	48.14 N	38.13 E
Yenangyaung	100	20.28 N	94.52 E
Yenanma	100	19.46 N	94.48 E
Yen-bai	100	21.42 N	104.52 E
Yen-chau	100	21.03 N	104.18 E
Yench'eng → Yancheng	90	33.24 N	120.09 E
Yenchi → Yanji	88	42.57 N	129.32 E
Yenda	156	34.15 S	146.11 E
Yende Millimou	140	8.53 N	10.11 W
Yendéré	140	10.12 N	4.58 W
Yendi	140	9.26 N	0.01 W
Ye-ngan	100	21.09 N	96.27 E
Yenge ≃	142	0.55 S	20.40 E
Yengo	142	0.22 N	15.29 E
Yengo, Mount ∧	160	32.59 S	150.51 E
Yéni	140	13.26 N	2.59 E
Yeniçağa	120	40.46 N	32.02 E
Yenice, Tür.	120	39.55 N	27.18 E
Yenice, Tür.	120	36.59 N	35.03 E
Yenice, Tür.	120	39.45 N	28.55 E
Yenice ≃	120	37.36 N	35.35 E
Yenicekale	120	37.37 N	36.37 E
Yeniceoba	120	38.53 N	32.48 E
Yenifoça	120	38.44 N	26.51 E
Yenikapı ⬥[8]	257b	41.00 N	28.57 E
Yeniköy, Tür.	120	39.46 N	28.00 E
Yeniköy, Tür.	120	37.04 N	30.36 E
Yeniköy ⬥[8]	257b	41.07 N	29.04 E
Yenimehmetli	120	39.26 N	32.10 E
Yenipazar, Tür.	120	37.48 N	28.12 E
Yenipazar, Tür.	120	40.11 N	30.31 E
Yenişehir	120	40.16 N	29.39 E
Yenisey → Jenisej ≃	62	71.50 N	82.40 E
Yennadon	214	49.14 N	122.34 W
Yenne	56	45.42 N	5.46 E
Yennora	264a	33.52 S	150.58 E
Yenshui	90	23.20 N	120.16 E
Yentna ≃	170	61.34 N	150.28 W
Yeo ≃	44	51.02 N	2.49 W
Yeola	112	20.02 N	74.29 E
Yeo Lake ⊜	152	28.04 S	124.23 E
Yeoman	206	40.40 N	86.43 W
Yeoval	156	32.45 S	148.40 E
Yeovil	44	50.57 N	2.39 W
Yeoville ⬥[8]	263d	26.12 S	28.04 E
Yepachic	222	28.26 N	108.23 W
Yeppoon	156	23.08 S	150.45 E
Yerba Buena, Montaña ∧	226	14.05 N	87.26 W
Yerba Buena Island I	272	37.48 N	122.22 W
Yères ≃	46	50.02 N	1.19 E
Yerevan → Jerevan	74	40.11 N	44.30 E
Yerilla	152	29.28 S	121.49 E
Yering	264b	37.41 S	145.23 E
Yerington	216	38.59 N	119.10 W
Yerington Indian Reservation ⬥[4]	216	39.05 N	119.12 W
Yerkes	275	40.10 N	75.27 W
Yerkes Astronomical Observatory ⊍[3]	206	42.34 N	88.34 W
Yerkesik	120	37.07 N	28.17 E
Yerköy	120	39.38 N	34.29 E
Yermasóyia	120	34.43 N	33.05 E
Yermenonville	251	48.33 N	1.37 E
Yermo	194	34.54 N	116.50 W
Yeroḥam	122	31.00 N	34.55 E
Yerolimín	38	36.28 N	22.24 E
Yèrre ≃	46	48.01 N	1.16 E
Yerres	46	48.43 N	2.30 E
Yerres ≃	46	48.43 N	2.27 E
Yerseke	48	51.29 N	4.02 E
Yerupajá, Nevado ∧	238	10.16 S	76.54 W
Yerushalayim (Al-Quds) (Jerusalem)	122	31.46 N	35.14 E
Yerushalayim □[5]	122	31.45 N	35.00 E
Yerushalayim, Sede-Te'ufa ⊠	122	31.52 N	35.12 E
Yerville	46	49.40 N	0.54 E
Yesa, Embalse de ⊜[1]	34	42.36 N	1.09 W
Yesan	88	36.41 N	126.50 E
Yesca, Cerro ∧	224	21.19 N	104.03 W
Yeshenpu	94	40.51 N	122.32 E
Yeshui ≃	88	38.17 N	114.09 E
Yeshvi	262c	18.55 N	73.03 E
Yeşil ≃	120	41.24 N	36.35 E
Yeşilhisar	120	38.21 N	35.06 E
Yeşilkent	120	36.59 N	36.10 E
Yeşilköy	120	40.57 N	28.49 E
Yeşilköy Burnu ≻	257b	40.57 N	28.50 E
Yeşilyurt	120	38.18 N	38.15 E
Yeso	186	34.26 N	104.37 W
Yeso Creek ≃	186	34.13 N	104.15 W
Yesŏng-gang ≃	88	37.53 N	126.24 E
Yessentuki → Jessentuki	74	44.03 N	42.51 E
Yeste	34	38.22 N	2.18 W
Yes Tor ∧	44	50.42 N	4.00 W
Yesud HaMa'ala	122	33.03 N	35.36 E
Yet	134	4.48 N	43.02 E
Yetholme	160	33.27 S	149.49 E
Yetman	156	28.54 S	150.46 E
Yetminster	44	50.53 N	2.33 W
Yetsou	142	2.08 S	10.42 E
Yettem	216	36.29 N	119.16 W
Yetti	154	3.00 S	140.53 E
Yetti ⬥[1]	138	26.10 N	7.50 W
Ye-u	100	22.46 N	95.26 E
Yeu, Île d' I	32	46.42 N	2.20 W
Yevpatoriya → Jevpatorija	68	45.12 N	33.22 E
Yexian, Zhg.	88	37.13 N	119.54 E
Yexian, Zhg.	90	33.37 N	113.20 E
Yexie	96	30.56 N	121.19 E
Yextla ≃	224	18.00 N	100.06 W
Yeysk → Jejsk	68	46.42 N	38.16 E
Yeyuan	88	36.22 N	118.27 E
Yeyupan I	96	30.35 N	121.34 E
Yeywa	100	21.41 N	96.24 E
Yezd → Yazd	118	31.53 N	54.25 E
Yezehu ⊜	96	31.08 N	120.40 E
Yezhuang	95	39.10 N	116.18 E
Yezhuhe	95	40.53 N	118.13 E
Ygnacio Canal ☲	272	37.55 N	122.03 W
Yguazú ≃	242	25.20 S	55.00 W
Yhú	242	24.59 S	55.59 W
Yi ≃	242	33.07 S	57.08 W
Yian	79	47.55 N	125.20 E
Yiannitsá	38	40.48 N	22.25 E
Yibao	96	30.25 N	119.53 E
Yibin (Ipin)	97	28.47 N	104.38 E
Yicanghe	90	32.47 N	120.43 E
Yichang (Ichang)	92	30.42 N	111.11 E
Yichefan	92	26.50 N	103.28 E
Yicheng, Zhg.	88	36.48 N	114.17 E
Yicheng, Zhg.	92	31.43 N	112.07 E
Yichuan, Zhg.	90	34.26 N	112.24 E
Yichuan, Zhg.	92	36.14 N	110.05 E
Yichun	90	27.50 N	114.23 E
Yicun	95	38.57 N	115.37 E
Yidan	79	43.24 N	125.25 E
Yidiezhen	92	37.08 N	110.30 E
Yidu, Zhg.	88	36.41 N	118.28 E
Yidu, Zhg.	92	30.22 N	111.22 E
Yidun	92	29.56 N	99.22 E
Yiershi	79	47.20 N	119.45 E
Yiewsley ⬥[8]	250	51.31 N	0.28 W
Yifag	134	12.02 N	37.44 E
Yifeng, Zhg.	90	33.19 N	113.47 E
Yifeng, Zhg.	90	28.26 N	114.46 E
Yigaolou	96	30.56 N	120.20 E
Yiğitaliler	120	39.52 N	26.37 E
Yigongzong	92	30.17 N	94.51 E
Yigou	88	35.51 N	114.20 E
Yiguqihu ⊜	110	31.05 N	86.55 E
Yihe, Zhg.	88	42.08 N	118.48 E
Yihe, Zhg.	90	23.50 N	114.53 E
Yihe ≃, Zhg.	88	34.13 N	118.03 E
Yihe ≃, Zhg.	90	34.10 N	112.10 E
Yihechang	97	30.23 N	106.24 E
Yiheyuan	261a	40.00 N	116.16 E
Yiheyuan (Summer Palace) ⊍	95	4.00 N	116.16 E
Yihezhen	88	37.53 N	118.23 E
Yihezhuang	94	41.15 N	122.57 E
Yihuang	90	27.34 N	116.10 E
Yihuta	79	43.13 N	122.15 E
Yijiawan	90	27.58 N	113.01 E
Yijiazi	94	42.29 N	122.41 E
Yijin	90	30.54 N	117.12 E
Yijingpu	95	40.08 N	117.47 E
Yijitathu ⊜	110	35.00 N	87.00 E
Yijun	92	35.24 N	109.00 E
Yikechaidamuhu ⊜	92	37.50 N	95.00 E
Yikengaolu	92	42.17 N	98.19 E
Yikou	90	26.45 N	117.00 E
Yilaha	79	48.50 N	125.14 E
Yilan	79	46.19 N	129.34 E
Yilaxi	79	43.47 N	126.08 E
Yıldızdağı ∧	120	40.08 N	36.56 E
Yıldızeli	120	39.52 N	36.38 E
Yilehulishan ⋏	79	51.20 N	124.30 E
Yili	97	30.45 N	105.58 E
Yiliang, Zhg.	92	27.32 N	104.13 E
Yiliang, Zhg.	92	24.58 N	103.07 E
Yiliekede	79	48.51 N	121.37 E
Yilin	90	33.36 N	119.37 E
Yiling	90	32.30 N	119.46 E
Yiliping	110	37.55 N	93.30 E
Yili Zizhizhou □[4]	76	45.00 N	89.00 E
Yilliminning	152	32.54 S	117.22 E
Yilong, Zhg.	79	47.28 N	125.23 E
Yilong, Zhg.	92	31.34 N	106.19 E
Yilong, Zhg.	92	25.20 N	103.14 E
Yimachi	94	42.11 N	122.15 E
Yimatu	94	41.55 N	121.25 E
Yimen, Zhg.	90	33.39 N	116.02 E
Yimen, Zhg.	92	24.43 N	102.10 E
Yimuhe	79	52.45 N	120.07 E
Yin ≃	100	20.04 N	95.01 E
Yinan	88	35.37 N	118.30 E
Yinbaing	100	17.25 N	97.46 E
Yinchuan	92	38.30 N	106.18 E
Yindarlgooda, Lake ⊜	152	30.45 S	121.55 E
Yindi	144	1.35 N	27.40 E
Yinfang	95	39.07 N	114.52 E
Yingcheng	90	30.57 N	113.32 E
Yingchengzi, Zhg.	79	44.08 N	125.56 E
Yingchengzi, Zhg.	88	38.58 N	121.23 E
Yingchengzi, Zhg.	94	41.50 N	124.04 E
Yingchengzi, Zhg.	94	42.22 N	124.14 E
Yingde	90	24.12 N	113.24 E
Yingen	92	41.09 N	104.45 E
Yingfang	95	40.14 N	116.17 E
Yinggehai	100	18.31 N	108.44 E
Yinggen	100	19.04 N	109.48 E
Yinghe ≃	90	32.30 N	116.32 E
Yingheji	90	32.16 N	116.31 E
Yingjisha	75	38.57 N	76.03 E
Yingkou, Zhg.	94	40.40 N	122.14 E
Yingkou (Dashiqiao), Zhg.	94	40.38 N	122.30 E
Yingnahe ≃	88	39.42 N	123.20 E
Yingpan, Zhg.	88	41.54 N	124.15 E
Yingpan, Zhg.	92	24.44 N	99.38 E
Yingpan, Zhg.	92	25.48 N	106.18 E
Yingpanjie	92	25.27 N	98.24 E
Yingqiao	90	33.58 N	113.39 E
Yingshan, Zhg.	90	31.38 N	113.50 E
Yingshan, Zhg.	90	30.45 N	115.39 E
Yingshan, Zhg.	92	31.08 N	106.31 E
Yingshang	90	32.38 N	116.15 E
Yingshouyingzi, Zhg.	95	40.33 N	117.40 E
Yingshouyingzi, Zhg.	95	40.49 N	117.55 E
Yingtan	90	28.14 N	117.00 E
Yingtaogou	94	42.08 N	121.57 E
Yingtaoyuan	94	41.10 N	123.05 E
Yingtian	90	28.50 N	112.56 E
Yingxiangjie	97	29.24 N	105.11 E
Yingxianpu	94	41.20 N	121.31 E
Yining (Kuldja)	76	43.55 N	81.14 E
Yinjia	97	29.34 N	106.01 E
Yinjiadai	96	32.03 N	120.07 E
Yinjiang	92	28.02 N	108.28 E
Yinjiawopeng	94	42.34 N	121.01 E
Yinkanie	156	34.20 S	140.19 E
Yinkeng	90	26.14 N	115.34 E
Yinliu	95	39.59 N	117.23 E
Yinmabin	100	22.05 N	94.54 E
Yinmahe	79	44.07 N	125.44 E
Yinmatuhe ≃	88	40.57 N	117.43 E
Yinnietharra	152	24.39 S	116.11 E
Yinnyein	100	16.48 N	97.23 E
Yinong	92	30.19 N	101.01 E
Yinping	88	34.15 N	118.39 E
Yinqiaotou	96	31.52 N	119.13 E
Yinshanmai ⋏	92	41.48 N	109.00 E
Yinshanzhen	97	29.41 N	104.59 E
Yinwogou	88	41.55 N	117.55 E
Yinxian (Qiuai)	90	29.50 N	121.38 E
Yinxiang	96	31.55 N	118.49 E
Yinxianji	90	32.07 N	116.32 E
Yinyangjie	94	42.16 N	121.23 E
Yinyuan	92	23.26 N	101.54 E
Yinzhan'ao	90	23.33 N	113.07 E
Yio Chu Kang	261c	1.23 N	103.51 E
Yipinchang	97	29.17 N	106.34 E
Yipinglang	92	25.11 N	101.51 E
Yiqian	90	26.34 N	116.11 E
Yirba Moda	134	6.12 N	38.47 E
Yirga Alem	134	6.52 N	38.22 E
Yirkā	122	32.57 N	35.13 E
Yirol	130	6.33 N	30.30 E
Yirrkala Mission	154	12.14 S	136.56 E
Yirwa	130	7.47 N	27.15 E
Yisaduo	92	28.50 N	96.44 E
Yishan, Zhg.	90	27.32 N	120.32 E
Yishan, Zhg.	92	24.40 N	108.35 E
Yishui	88	35.50 N	118.41 E
Yishui ≃, Zhg.	88	35.34 N	116.52 E
Yishui ≃, Zhg.	90	28.05 N	116.18 E
Yishui ≃, Zhg.	95	39.14 N	115.45 E
Yisikan	79	49.09 N	124.47 E
Yisra'el → Israel □[1]	122	31.30 N	34.50 E
Yisuhe	90	27.46 N	112.54 E
Yitajing	92	42.32 N	94.12 E
Yitangji	88	35.10 N	118.16 E
Yitangzhen	90	31.06 N	113.42 E
Yíthion	38	36.45 N	22.34 E
Yiting	90	29.15 N	119.57 E
Yitong	79	43.20 N	125.17 E
Yitonghe ≃	88	42.40 N	125.58 E
Yitulihe	79	50.38 N	121.57 E
Yiwu, Zhg.	90	29.18 N	120.04 E
Yiwu, Zhg.	92	22.00 N	101.28 E
Yiwu, Zhg.	92	43.15 N	94.45 E
Yiwulüshan ⋏	94	41.42 N	121.42 E
Yixi	90	23.45 N	116.38 E
Yixian, Zhg.	88	34.46 N	117.37 E
Yixian, Zhg.	90	29.55 N	117.56 E
Yixian, Zhg.	94	41.32 N	121.15 E
Yixian, Zhg.	95	39.21 N	115.29 E
Yixiken	79	52.57 N	125.40 E
Yixing	96	31.22 N	119.50 E
Yixingbu	95	39.12 N	117.12 E
Yixingchang	97	30.37 N	106.38 E
Yixu	90	26.02 N	119.16 E
Yixunhe ≃	88	41.16 N	117.35 E
Yiyang, Zhg.	90	28.23 N	117.25 E
Yiyang, Zhg.	92	28.36 N	112.20 E
Yiyang, Zhg.	92	34.30 N	112.10 E
Yiyuan	88	36.11 N	118.08 E
Yiyuankou	88	40.13 N	119.32 E
Yizhang	90	25.26 N	112.56 E
Yizheng	96	32.16 N	119.12 E
Yizikong	92	25.38 N	104.28 E
Yizre'el	122	32.33 N	35.20 E
Yizre'el, 'emeq ⊻	122	32.36 N	35.14 E
Ylakiai	66	56.17 N	21.51 E
Yläne	26	60.53 N	22.55 E
Ylig Bay C	164p	13.24 N	144.16 E
Ylihärmä	26	63.09 N	22.47 E
Ylikitka ⊜	26	66.08 N	28.30 E
Ylimarkku → Övermark	26	62.38 N	21.30 E
Ylistaro	26	62.57 N	22.31 E
Ylivieska	26	64.05 N	24.33 E
Ylöjärvi	26	61.33 N	23.36 E
Ymeray	251	48.31 N	1.42 E
Ymir	172	49.17 N	117.13 W
Yndin	24	61.24 N	55.10 E
Yngaren ⊜	40	58.52 N	16.35 E
Yngen ⊜	40	59.44 N	14.18 E
Yngern ⊜	40	59.09 N	17.22 E
Yntaly	76	48.58 N	70.55 E
Ynykčanskij	64	60.15 N	137.43 E
Yoakum	212	29.17 N	97.09 W
Yobi, Indon.	154	1.43 S	138.04 E
Yobi, Indon.	154	1.42 S	136.27 E
Yockanookany ≃	184	32.40 N	89.40 W
Yoco	236	10.36 N	62.24 W
Yōda	258	35.24 N	139.25 E
Yoder	206	40.56 N	85.11 W
Yodo ≃	86	34.41 N	135.25 E
Yodoe	86	35.28 N	133.26 E
Yoe	198	39.55 N	76.39 W
Yōga ⬥[8]	258	35.38 N	139.38 E
Yogo	84	35.33 N	136.12 E
Yog Point ≻	106	14.06 N	124.12 E
Yogyakarta	105a	7.48 S	110.22 E
Yogyakarta □[4]	105a	7.45 S	110.30 E
Yoho National Park ♠	172	51.26 N	116.30 W
Yoichi	82a	43.12 N	140.41 E
Yojoa, Lago de ⊜	226	14.50 N	88.00 W
Yŏju	88	37.18 N	127.37 E
Yōka	86	35.24 N	134.46 E
Yokadouma	142	3.31 N	15.03 E
Yōkaichi	84	35.06 N	136.12 E
Yōkaichiba	84	35.42 N	140.33 E
Yokamba	142	0.01 N	22.17 E
Yokana	142	0.45 N	22.53 E
Yokawa	86	34.52 N	135.06 E

≃ River	Fluss	Río	Rivière	Rio
☲ Canal	Kanal	Canal	Canal	Canal
↳ Waterfall, Rapids	Wasserfall, Stromschnellen	Cascada, Rápidos	Chute d'eau, Rapides	Cascata, Rápidos
⊔ Strait	Meeresstrasse	Estrecho	Détroit	Estreito
C Bay, Gulf	Bucht, Golf	Bahía, Golfo	Baie, Golfe	Baía, Golfo
⊜ Lake, Lakes	See, Seen	Lago, Lagos	Lac, Lacs	Lago, Lagos
☷ Swamp	Sumpf	Pantano	Marais	Pântano
⊿ Ice Features, Glacier	Eis- und Gletscherformen	Accidentes Glaciales	Formes glaciaires	Acidentes Glaciares
⊻ Other Hydrographic Features	Andere Hydrographische Objekte	Otros Elementos Hidrográficos	Autres données hydrographiques	Outros Elementos Hidrográficos
✢ Submarine Features	Untermeerische Objekte	Accidentes Submarinos	Formes de relief sous-marin	Acidentes Submarinos
□ Political Unit	Politische Einheit	Unidad Politica	Entité politique	Unidade Política
⊍ Cultural Institution	Kulturelle Institution	Institución Cultural	Institution culturelle	Instituição Cultural
⊥ Historical Site	Historische Stätte	Sitio Histórico	Site historique	Sitio Histórico
♠ Recreational Site	Erholungs- und Ferienort	Sitio de Recreo	Centre de loisirs	Sítio de Lazer
⊠ Airport	Flughafen	Aeropuerto	Aéroport	Aeroporto
▪ Military Installation	Militäranlage	Instalación Militar	Installation militaire	Instalação Militar
⬥ Miscellaneous	Verschiedenes	Misceláneo	Divers	Miscelânea

ENGLISH

Name	Page	Lat.°′	Long.°′

Z

DEUTSCH

Name	Seite	Breite°′	Länge°′ E=Ost

Symbols in the index entries represent the broad categories identified in the key at the right. Symbols with superior numbers (∧∧[2]) identify subcategories (see complete key on page *I* · 26).

Kartensymbole in dem Registerverzeichnis stellen die rechts in Schlüssel erklärten Kategorien dar. Symbole mit hochgestellten Ziffern (∧∧[2]) bezeichnen Unterabteilungen einer Kategorie (vgl. vollständiger Schlüssel auf Seite *I* · 26).

Los símbolos incluídos en el texto del índice representan las grandes categorias identificadas con la clave a la derecha. Los símbolos con numeros en su parte superior (∧∧[2]) identifican las subcategorías (véase la clave completa en la página *I* · 26).

Les symboles de l'index représentent les catégories indiquées dans la légende à droite. Les symboles suivis d'un indice (∧∧[2]) représentent des sous-catégories (voir légende complète à la page *I* · 26).

Os símbolos incluídos no texto do índice representam as grandes categorias identificadas com a chave à direita. Os símbolos com números em sua parte superior (∧∧[2]) identificam as subcategorias (veja-se a chave completa à página *I* · 26).

Symbol	English	Deutsch	Español	Français	Português
∧	Mountain	Berg	Montaña	Montagne	Montanha
∧∧	Mountains	Berge	Montañas	Montagnes	Montanhas
)(	Pass	Pass	Paso	Col	Passo
∨	Valley, Canyon	Tal, Cañon	Valle, Cañón	Vallée, Canyon	Vale, Canhão
≚	Plain	Ebene	Llano	Plaine	Planície
≻	Cape	Kap	Cabo	Cap	Cabo
I	Island	Insel	Isla	Île	Ilha
II	Islands	Inseln	Islas	Îles	Ilhas
•	Other Topographic Features	Andere Topographische Objekte	Otros Elementos Topográficos	Autres données topographiques	Outros Elementos Topográficos

≃ River	Fluss	Río	Rivière	Rio
Canal	Kanal	Canal	Canal	Canal
Waterfall, Rapids	Wasserfall, Stromschnellen	Cascada, Rápidos	Chute d'eau, Rapides	Cascata, Rápidos
Strait	Meeresstrasse	Estrecho	Détroit	Estreito
C Bay, Gulf	Bucht, Golf	Bahía, Golfo	Baie, Golfe	Baía, Golfo
⊛ Lake, Lakes	See, Seen	Lago, Lagos	Lac, Lacs	Lago, Lagos
≣ Swamp	Sumpf	Pantano	Marais	Pântano
Ice Features, Glacier	Eis- und Gletscherformen	Accidentes Glaciales	Formes glaciaires	Acidentes Glaciares
Other Hydrographic Features	Andere Hydrographische Objekte	Otros Elementos Hidrográficos	Autres données hydrographiques	Outros Elementos Hidrográficos

Submarine Features	Untermeerische Objekte	Accidentes Submarinos	Formes de relief sous-marin	Acidentes Submarinos
□ Political Unit	Politische Einheit	Unidad Politica	Entité politique	Unidade Política
♥ Cultural Institution	Kulturelle Institution	Institución Cultural	Institution culturelle	Instituição Cultural
⊥ Historical Site	Historische Stätte	Sitio Histórico	Site historique	Sitio Histórico
♠ Recreational Site	Erholungs- und Ferienort	Sitio de Recreo	Centre de loisirs	Sítio de Lazer
⊠ Airport	Flughafen	Aeropuerto	Aéroport	Aeroporto
Military Installation	Militäranlage	Instalación Militar	Installation militaire	Instalação Militar
◆ Miscellaneous	Verschiedenes	Misceláneo	Divers	Miscelânea

Zhouzhuang, Zhg. 95 39.09 N 115.18 E
Zhouzhuang, Zhg. 96 31.06 N 120.51 E
Zhouzhuang, Zhg. 96 32.15 N 120.08 E
Zhuangaerpendi ≚[1] 76 45.00 N 88.00 E
Zhuanghang 96 30.54 N 121.23 E
Zhuanghe 88 39.43 N 123.01 E
Zhuangji 88 34.20 N 115.15 E
Zhuangtou 95 40.55 N 117.57 E
Zhuangtouyingzi, Zhg. 94 41.43 N 120.32 E
Zhuangtouyingzi, Zhg. 94 41.50 N 120.43 E
Zhuangxi 97 30.33 N 104.31 E
Zhuangyuanqiao 90 27.54 N 120.48 E
Zhuanmiaoji 88 34.57 N 115.24 E
Zhuanpingshan ∧ 97 29.07 N 103.37 E
Zhuanqiao 96 31.04 N 121.23 E
Zhuantouwan 90 31.29 N 112.24 E
Zhuanwantai 94 41.20 N 122.22 E
Zhuao 90 29.05 N 121.16 E
Zhuchang 92 27.18 N 107.26 E
Zhuchen 88 34.57 N 118.17 E
Zhucheng 88 36.00 N 119.24 E
Zhucikou 90 29.17 N 112.41 E
Zhudian 90 30.33 N 115.12 E
Zhuergan 79 52.04 N 120.48 E
Zhufeng 96 30.35 N 118.56 E
Zhuganhe ≃ 90 32.18 N 114.42 E
Zhuganpu 90 32.13 N 114.39 E
Zhugaosi 97 30.37 N 104.40 E
Zhuge 90 29.15 N 119.18 E
Zhugentan 97 29.25 N 103.50 E
Zhugou, Zhg. 88 36.52 N 120.15 E
Zhugou, Zhg. 90 32.47 N 113.42 E
Zhuguangshan ⋀ 90 26.00 N 114.00 E
Zhugusi 92 37.01 N 102.27 E
Zhuhonggang 90 32.52 N 119.58 E
Zhuhongyu 94 40.48 N 123.00 E
Zhuimuhu ⊜ 110 34.30 N 87.00 E
Zhuji 90 29.43 N 120.14 E
Zhujiabeng 96 31.21 N 120.41 E
Zhujiabian 96 31.38 N 119.11 E
Zhujiachang, Zhg. 97 29.48 N 104.20 E
Zhujiachang, Zhg. 97 30.03 N 104.13 E
Zhujiafang 94 41.20 N 122.40 E
Zhujiahang 96 30.51 N 121.19 E
Zhujiahe, Zhg. 90 29.44 N 113.06 E
Zhujiahe, Zhg. 96 31.08 N 120.53 E
Zhujiajian I 90 29.54 N 122.24 E
Zhujiajiao 96 31.06 N 121.02 E
Zhujiajiaotou 96 31.24 N 121.11 E
Zhujiangkou C[1] 90 23.36 N 113.44 E
Zhujiangkou ≃ 90 23.36 N 113.44 E
Zhujiangqing 90 27.18 N 114.44 E
Zhujiaqiao, Zhg. 96 30.26 N 119.03 E
Zhujiaqiao, Zhg. 96 31.07 N 121.44 E
Zhujiatuo 97 29.02 N 105.51 E
Zhujiawan, Zhg. 90 32.28 N 117.29 E
Zhujiawan, Zhg. 90 30.56 N 114.10 E
Zhujiawan, Zhg. 95 40.08 N 114.56 E
Zhujiawopeng 94 42.27 N 122.13 E
Zhujiesi 92 33.34 N 97.21 E
Zhukeng 90 23.49 N 112.55 E
Zhukou, Zhg. 88 34.07 N 115.04 E
Zhukou, Zhg. 90 26.58 N 117.16 E
Zhukou, Zhg. 90 27.41 N 118.53 E
Zhukovskiy → Žukovskij 72 55.35 N 38.08 E
Zhukuiqiao 96 31.34 N 119.20 E
Zhulanbu 90 25.36 N 115.46 E
Zhulin 96 31.45 N 119.27 E
Zhulinzong 90 32.20 N 113.38 E
Zhulonghe ≃ 88 38.47 N 115.59 E
Zhulongqiao 90 32.21 N 118.09 E
Zhuluke 88 41.36 N 119.54 E
Zhumadian 90 33.00 N 114.01 E
Zhumulangmafeng → Everest, Mount ∧ 114 27.59 N 86.56 E
Zhungeerqi 92 39.49 N 111.10 E
Zhuolu (Baoan) 95 40.22 N 115.12 E
Zhuoni 92 34.32 N 103.24 E
Zhuotian 90 25.38 N 116.13 E
Zhuoxian 95 39.30 N 115.58 E
Zhuozhanghe ≃ 92 36.15 N 115.10 E
Zhuozi 92 40.51 N 112.41 E
Zhuqianzongpuzi 94 42.17 N 123.18 E
Zhuqiao, Zhg. 88 37.22 N 120.05 E
Zhuqiao, Zhg. 96 30.26 N 120.36 E
Zhurushan 90 30.26 N 113.48 E
Zhushan, Zhg. 90 28.43 N 117.01 E
Zhushan, Zhg. 92 32.10 N 110.19 E
Zhusigang 90 31.14 N 118.23 E
Zhutan 90 28.04 N 114.10 E
Zhutang 96 31.06 N 118.39 E
Zhutangqiao 96 31.47 N 120.24 E
Zhuting, Zhg. 90 27.24 N 113.04 E
Zhuting, Zhg. 90 27.48 N 114.02 E
Zhuwasi 92 28.48 N 97.27 E
Zhuwo, Zhg. 92 31.41 N 100.24 E
Zhuwo, Zhg. 95 40.02 N 115.48 E
Zhuwotuo 97 30.31 N 104.34 E
Zhuwumiao 90 30.54 N 116.19 E
Zhuxi, Zhg. 90 28.10 N 118.53 E
Zhuxi, Zhg. 92 32.09 N 109.42 E
Zhuxiang 90 32.19 N 117.12 E
Zhuxianzhen 88 34.37 N 114.16 E
Zhuxichang 90 28.58 N 114.06 E
Zhuya 88 36.38 N 118.12 E
Zhuyang 88 36.16 N 117.22 E
Zhuyangxi 97 29.06 N 105.58 E
Zhuyangzhen 92 34.20 N 110.44 E
Zhuyoucun 88 37.20 N 119.53 E
Zhuyuanpu 97 29.34 N 104.08 E
Zhuzhen 90 32.31 N 118.42 E
Zhuzhou 90 27.50 N 113.09 E
Ziama Mansouria 34 36.40 N 5.29 E
Ziano 58 46.17 N 11.34 E
Ziārat 110 30.23 N 67.43 E
Zīārat-e Shāh Maqṣūd 110 31.59 N 65.30 E
Ziārat Gali Chāh ⊤[4] 118 28.20 N 63.38 E
Žiar nad Hronom 30 48.36 N 18.52 E
Zibā' 118 27.21 N 35.40 E
Zībāk 110 36.32 N 71.21 E
Zibdīn 122 33.22 N 35.28 E
Zibo (Tzupo) 88 36.47 N 118.01 E
Zicapa 224 17.57 N 99.02 W
Zicavo 36 41.54 N 9.08 E
Zicheng 88 36.38 N 117.55 E
Žičicy 66 55.07 N 31.17 E
Zickhusen 50 53.45 N 11.25 E
Židačov 68 49.23 N 24.08 E
Ziddi 75 39.03 N 68.48 E
Žideli 76 48.40 N 70.29 E
Zid'ki 68 49.42 N 36.21 E
Ziębice 30 50.37 N 17.00 E
Ziegelroda 50 51.20 N 11.28 E
Ziegendorf 50 53.18 N 11.49 E
Ziegenhain 52 50.55 N 9.15 E
Ziegenhals, D.D.R. 254a 52.21 N 13.40 E
Ziegenhals → Głuchołazy, Pol. 30 50.20 N 17.22 E
Ziegenort → Trzebież 30 53.42 N 14.31 E
Ziegenrück 50 50.37 N 11.38 E
Zielenzig → Sulęcin 30 52.26 N 15.08 E
Zielona Góra (Grünberg) 30 51.56 N 15.31 E
Ziemetshausen 54 48.18 N 10.31 E
Zierenberg 52 51.22 N 9.18 E
Zierikzee 48 51.38 N 3.55 E
Ziesar 50 52.16 N 12.17 E
Ziesendorf 50 54.00 N 12.02 E
Ziethen 50 53.53 N 13.40 E
Žiežmariai 66 54.48 N 24.27 E
Ziftā 132 30.43 N 31.15 E
Zifta Barrage ⬩[6] 132 30.43 N 31.15 E
Žigajlovka 68 50.38 N 35.07 E
Žigalgan 74 44.36 N 50.46 E
Žigalovo 78 54.48 N 105.08 E
Zigana Dağları ⋀ 120 40.37 N 39.30 E
Žigansk 64 66.45 N 123.20 E
Zigazinskij 76 53.50 N 57.20 E
Zigey 136 14.43 N 15.47 E
Zīghan ⊤[4] 136 25.30 N 22.25 E
Zigong (Tzukung) 97 29.22 N 104.46 E
Zigui 92 31.00 N 110.31 E
Ziguinchor 140 12.35 N 16.16 W
Žigulevsk 70 53.25 N 49.27 E
Žiguli 70 53.22 N 49.19 E
Žiguli ⋀ 70 53.30 N 49.40 E
Zīguri 66 57.16 N 27.40 E
Zigutaicun 94 42.01 N 121.16 E
Zihe ≃ 88 37.12 N 118.34 E
Zihedian 88 36.48 N 118.22 E
Zihuatanejo 224 17.38 N 101.33 W
Zihukou, Zhg. 90 28.55 N 118.08 E
Zihukou, Zhg. 90 28.44 N 112.33 E
Ziichang 92 37.19 N 109.33 E
Ziiyang 92 32.31 N 108.48 E
Ziizhou 92 37.37 N 109.41 E
Zijančurino 76 51.33 N 56.55 E
Žijenkum 75 42.50 N 69.00 E
Zijiao 88 37.21 N 117.25 E
Zijin 90 23.40 N 115.11 E
Zijingguan 95 39.23 N 115.08 E
Zijinshan ∧ 96 32.04 N 118.51 E
Zikejevo 66 53.44 N 34.52 E
Zikhron Ya'aqov 122 32.34 N 34.57 E
Zikoufang 90 26.22 N 117.24 E
Zilair 76 52.14 N 57.30 E
Žilaja Kosa 76 46.49 N 53.12 E
Žilaja Tambica 24 62.32 N 36.09 E
Zile 120 40.18 N 35.54 E
Zili 92 26.50 N 100.27 E
Žilina 30 49.14 N 18.46 E
Žilino 66 54.54 N 21.56 E
Zillah, Lībīya 136 28.33 N 17.35 E
Zillah, Wash., U.S. 192 46.24 N 120.16 W
Ziller ≃ 58 47.24 N 11.50 E
Ziller-Tal ∨ 58 47.20 N 11.50 E
Zillertaler Alpen (Alpi Aurine) ⋀ 58 47.00 N 11.55 E
Zillis 54 46.38 N 9.27 E
Zillisheim 54 47.41 N 7.16 E
Zilly 50 51.56 N 10.49 E
Zilme 134 16.25 N 43.49 E
Žiloj, Ostrov I 118 40.19 N 50.36 E
Žiloj Bor 66 59.06 N 34.37 E
Žil'ovo 72 54.59 N 38.02 E
Ziltendorf 50 52.12 N 14.37 E
Zilupe 66 56.23 N 28.07 E
Zilwaukee 180 43.28 N 83.55 W
Zima 78 53.55 N 102.04 E
Zima ≃ 78 53.52 N 102.02 E
Zimapán 224 20.45 N 99.21 W
Zimatlán de Alvarez 224 16.52 N 96.47 W
Zimba 144 17.19 S 26.13 E
Zimbabwe National Park ♠ 144 20.17 S 30.57 E
Zimbor 38 47.00 N 23.16 E
Zimella 58 45.20 N 11.22 E
Zimi 140 7.19 N 11.18 W
Zimljansker-Stausee → Ciml'anskoje Vodochranilišče ⊜[1] 70 48.00 N 43.00 E
Zimmerman 208 39.42 N 84.02 W
Zimn'ackij 70 49.44 N 42.53 E
Zimnicea 38 43.39 N 25.21 E
Zimogorje 73 48.35 N 38.56 E
Zimonino 66 53.47 N 31.52 E
Zimovniki 70 47.08 N 42.28 E
Zimovskoje 76 57.31 N 86.52 E
Zin, Naḥal ∨ 122 30.57 N 35.19 E
Žina 136 11.16 N 14.58 E
Zinacatepec 224 18.20 N 97.15 W
Zinal 54 46.08 N 7.38 E
Zinapécuaro [de Figueroa] 224 19.52 N 100.49 W
Zinder 140 13.48 N 8.59 E
Zinder □[5] 136 15.00 N 10.30 E
Zinga 142 3.43 N 18.35 E
Zinga Mulike 144 9.09 S 38.44 E
Zingst 50 54.26 N 12.41 E
Zingst ≻[1] 50 54.25 N 12.50 E
Zingwanda 130 7.10 N 27.56 E
Ziniaré 140 12.35 N 1.18 W
Žiniške ≃ 75 43.14 N 78.30 E
Zinkenbach 58 47.44 N 13.25 E
Zinkgruvan 40 58.49 N 15.05 E
Zin'kov 68 49.04 N 27.04 E
Zinnik → Soignies 46 50.35 N 4.04 E
Zinnowitz 50 54.04 N 13.55 E
Zinnwald-Georgenfeld 50 50.44 N 13.46 E
Zinswiller 52 48.55 N 7.35 E
Zion 206 42.27 N 87.50 W
Zionhill 198 40.29 N 75.24 W
Zion National Park ♠ 190 37.10 N 113.00 W
Zionsville 208 39.57 N 86.16 W
Zionz Lake ⊜ 174 51.25 N 91.52 W
Zipaquirá 236 5.02 N 74.00 W
Žipkovšino 78 51.52 N 112.59 E
Zippori 122 32.45 N 35.17 E
Žipsendorf 50 51.02 N 12.16 E
Ziqlāb, Wādī ∨ 122 32.30 N 35.34 E
Zir 120 39.59 N 33.21 E
Zira 113 30.58 N 74.59 E
Zirahuén, Laguna ⊜ 224 19.27 N 101.44 W
Žir'akovo 76 57.53 N 65.37 E
Zirándaro 224 18.27 N 100.59 W
Zirāpur 114 24.01 N 76.22 E
Žir'atino 66 53.15 N 33.44 E
Zirbitzkogel ∧ 30 47.04 N 14.34 E
Zirchow 50 53.53 N 14.08 E
Zirgan 76 53.14 N 55.55 E
Žirje, Otok I 36 43.40 N 15.39 E
Zirl 58 47.17 N 11.14 E
Zirndorf 52 49.26 N 10.58 E
Žirnov 70 48.13 N 41.06 E
Žirnovsk 70 51.00 N 44.46 E
Ziro 110 27.38 N 93.42 E
Žiroškino 72 55.22 N 38.03 E
Žirovnice 30 49.15 N 15.11 E
Zishan 90 25.57 N 115.35 E
Zishui ≃, Zhg. 92 28.45 N 112.25 E
Zishui ≃, Zhg. 97 30.09 N 104.42 E
Zisterzinser Abtei ♉[1] 52 49.01 N 8.47 E
Zisuntang 96 30.38 N 118.42 E
Zitácuaro 224 19.24 N 100.22 W
Zitácuaro ≃ 224 18.51 N 100.44 W
Zitadelle ⊥ 254a 52.33 N 13.13 E
Žiteli 24 65.04 N 47.26 E
Žitenice 50 50.35 N 14.08 E
Žitjevo 66 59.54 N 41.06 E
Žitkoviči 68 52.14 N 27.54 E
Žitkovo 66 60.42 N 29.20 E
Žitkur 70 48.57 N 46.17 E
Zitlala 224 17.38 N 99.05 W
Zitlaltepec 224 19.12 N 97.54 W
Žitnoje 70 45.49 N 47.41 E
Žitomir 68 50.16 N 28.40 E
Žitomirskoje Polesje ⬩[1] 68 50.40 N 28.00 E
Zitong 92 31.43 N 105.10 E
Zittau 50 50.54 N 14.47 E
Zitundo 146 26.45 S 32.50 E
Živa, Gora ∧ 78 53.18 N 107.38 E
Zıvarık 120 38.19 N 32.53 E
Zivint 120 37.13 N 30.18 E
Ziway, Lake ⊜ 134 8.00 N 38.50 E
Ziwuji 90 32.55 N 115.58 E
Zixi 90 27.42 N 117.02 E
Zixing 90 26.00 N 113.23 E
Ziyahe ≃ 95 39.11 N 117.08 E
Ziyang 97 30.07 N 104.39 E
Ziyuan 92 26.01 N 110.31 E
Ziyun 92 25.43 N 106.05 E
Žizdra 66 53.45 N 34.44 E
Žizdra ≃ 72 54.14 N 36.12 E
Zizers 54 46.56 N 9.34 E
Zizhong 97 29.48 N 104.51 E
Zizi 90 28.01 N 117.46 E
Žižica 66 56.17 N 31.21 E
Žižickoje, Ozero ⊜ 66 56.14 N 31.15 E
Žižma ≃ 66 53.54 N 25.36 E
Zlarin 36 43.42 N 15.50 E
Zlatar 36 46.06 N 16.05 E
Zlaté Moravce 30 48.25 N 18.24 E
Zlatica 38 42.43 N 24.08 E
Zlatograd 38 41.23 N 25.06 E
Zlatoust 76 55.10 N 59.40 E
Zlatoustovsk 79 52.58 N 133.38 E
Zlín → Gottwaldov 30 49.13 N 17.41 E
Zlītan 136 32.28 N 14.34 E
Žlobin 66 52.54 N 30.03 E
Złocieniec 30 53.33 N 16.01 E
Złoczew 30 51.25 N 18.36 E
Zlonice 50 50.15 N 14.07 E
Złotoryja 30 51.08 N 15.55 E
Złotów 30 53.22 N 17.02 E
Žlutice 50 50.03 N 13.10 E
Zlydnev 70 48.46 N 45.48 E
Zlynka, S.S.S.R. 66 52.25 N 31.44 E
Zlynka, S.S.S.R. 68 48.28 N 31.32 E
Zmeinogorsk 76 51.10 N 82.13 E
Zmeinyj, Ostrov I 68 45.15 N 30.12 E
Žmerinka 68 49.02 N 28.06 E
Żmigród 30 51.29 N 16.55 E
Zmijov 68 49.40 N 36.19 E
Zmijovka 66 52.40 N 36.23 E
Žminj 36 45.09 N 13.55 E
Zna → Cna ≃ 70 54.32 N 42.05 E
Znamenka, S.S.S.R. 66 54.54 N 34.34 E
Znamenka, S.S.S.R. 68 48.43 N 32.40 E
Znamenka, S.S.S.R. 70 52.24 N 41.26 E
Znamenka, S.S.S.R. 73 48.51 N 37.22 E
Znamenka, S.S.S.R. 76 53.10 N 79.30 E
Znamenka, S.S.S.R. 76 50.05 N 79.32 E
Znamenka, S.S.S.R. 76 53.32 N 91.54 E
Znamenka, S.S.S.R. 78 54.42 N 104.50 E
Znamenka Vtoraja 68 48.43 N 32.35 E
Znamensk 66 54.37 N 21.13 E
Znamenskoje, S.S.S.R. 66 53.17 N 35.41 E
Znamenskoje, S.S.S.R. 70 53.19 N 42.57 E
Znamenskoje, S.S.S.R. 76 57.08 N 73.55 E
Znamenskoje, S.S.S.R. 255b 55.45 N 37.09 E
Żnin 30 52.52 N 17.43 E
Znob'-Novgorodskoje 68 52.16 N 33.36 E
Zoadiba 142 3.04 N 14.02 E
Zoagli 56 44.20 N 9.16 E
Zoar 148 33.30 S 21.28 E
Zoar Village State Memorial ⊥ 204 40.36 N 81.27 W
Zoarville 204 40.35 N 81.24 W
Zobia 144 2.58 N 25.56 E
Zöblitz 50 50.39 N 13.14 E
Zóbuè 144 15.38 S 34.26 E
Zocca 58 44.21 N 10.59 E
Žochova, Ostrov I 64 76.04 N 152.40 E
Zódhia 120 35.10 N 33.00 E
Žodino 66 54.06 N 28.21 E
Žodiški 66 54.38 N 26.26 E
Zoétélé 142 3.15 N 11.53 E
Zoetermeer 48 52.03 N 4.30 E
Zofingen 54 47.18 N 7.57 E
Zogno 56 45.48 N 9.40 E
Zográfos 257c 37.59 N 23.46 E
Zohar 122 31.36 N 34.42 E
Zohreh ≃ 118 30.04 N 49.34 E
Zok 120 38.02 N 41.33 E
Zola Predosa 58 44.29 N 11.12 E
Zolder 52 51.01 N 5.18 E
Zoldo Alto 58 46.22 N 12.06 E
Zolfo Springs 210 27.30 N 81.48 W
Zolka ≃ 74 44.17 N 43.51 E
Żółkiewka 30 50.55 N 22.51 E
Zollhaus 52 50.17 N 8.04 E
Zollikofen 54 47.00 N 7.28 E
Zollikon 54 47.20 N 8.35 E
Zol'noje 70 53.27 N 49.48 E
Zoločov, S.S.S.R. 68 50.17 N 35.59 E
Zoločov, S.S.S.R. 68 49.47 N 24.52 E
Zolotaja Gora 79 54.16 N 126.36 E
Zolotaja Lipa ≃ 68 48.59 N 25.04 E
Zolotari 70 49.46 N 46.21 E
Zolotar'ovka 70 53.04 N 45.20 E
Zolotkovo 70 55.32 N 41.06 E
Zolotniki 68 49.17 N 25.23 E
Zolotoje, S.S.S.R. 70 50.51 N 45.53 E
Zolotoje, S.S.S.R. 73 48.41 N 38.31 E
Zolotoj Kolodec 73 48.32 N 37.15 E
Zolotoj Potok 68 48.54 N 25.20 E
Zolotonoša 68 49.40 N 32.02 E
Zolotucha 70 47.49 N 46.44 E
Zolotuchino 68 52.05 N 36.23 E
Žoltoje, S.S.S.R. 68 47.47 N 33.50 E
Žoltoje, S.S.S.R. 68 48.30 N 33.31 E
Ž'oltoje, S.S.S.R. 73 48.39 N 39.07 E
Žoltyje Vody 68 48.21 N 33.31 E
Žolymbet 76 51.45 N 71.44 E
Zomba 144 15.23 S 35.18 E
Zomergem 46 51.07 N 3.33 E
Zone Point ≻ 44 50.08 N 5.00 W
Zongchang 97 28.52 N 104.36 E
Zongo 142 4.21 N 18.36 E
Zonguldak 120 41.27 N 31.49 E
Zonguldak □[4] 120 41.30 N 32.15 E
Zongwe 144 5.05 S 27.55 E
Zonhoven 52 50.59 N 5.21 E
Zonnebeke 46 50.52 N 2.59 E
Zons 52 51.07 N 6.50 E
Zontehuitz, Cerro ∧ 222 16.50 N 92.38 W
Zonza 36 41.45 N 9.10 E
Zoo, Bahnhof ⬩[5] 254a 52.30 N 13.20 E
Zooafskolk 148 29.56 S 20.24 E
Zoom ≃ 48 51.30 N 4.14 E
Zoppot → Sopot 30 54.28 N 18.34 E
Zopten am Berge → Sobótka 30 50.55 N 16.45 E
Zopui 110 23.39 N 92.14 E
Zörbig 50 51.37 N 12.07 E
Zorge 50 51.38 N 10.38 E
Zorge ≃ 50 51.27 N 10.54 E
Zorgo 140 12.15 N 0.36 W
Zorgongo 140 12.16 N 0.48 W
Zorikovka 73 49.24 N 39.51 E
Zorinsk 73 48.25 N 38.34 E
Zorita 34 39.17 N 5.42 W
Zorkul', Ozero ⊜ 110 37.27 N 73.40 E
Zorn ≃ 52 48.45 N 7.55 E
Zorneding 58 48.05 N 11.49 E
Zornica 38 42.23 N 26.56 E
Zorra, Arroyo de la ≃ 186 29.31 N 101.13 W
Zorritos 236 3.40 S 80.40 W
Zorzor 140 7.46 N 9.28 W
Zöschen 50 51.21 N 12.07 E
Zossen 50 52.13 N 13.27 E
Zoti 74 41.53 N 42.28 E
Zottegem 46 50.52 N 3.48 E
Zou □[5] 140 8.00 N 2.15 E
Zouan-Hounien 140 6.55 N 8.13 W
Zouar 136 20.27 N 16.32 E
Zoug → Zug 54 47.10 N 8.31 E
Zouginindja 142 5.24 N 21.40 E
Zouîrât 138 22.42 N 12.30 W
Zoulabot 142 3.17 N 14.02 E
Zoumagang 97 29.28 N 106.18 E
Zoumatang ≃ 259b 31.18 N 121.23 E
Zoumayi 88 39.07 N 114.34 E
Zouping 88 36.53 N 117.42 E
Zourma -140 11.22 N 0.49 W
Zousfana, Oued ∨ 138 30.29 N 2.17 W
Zoutelande 48 51.30 N 3.30 E
Zoutkamp 48 53.20 N 6.18 E
Zouxian 88 35.24 N 117.00 E
Zovka 66 58.26 N 28.52 E
Žovnino 68 49.23 N 32.41 E
Žovten', S.S.S.R. 68 49.03 N 24.45 E
Žovten', S.S.S.R. 68 47.14 N 30.20 E
Žovtnevoje, S.S.S.R. 68 46.52 N 32.02 E
Žovtnevoje, S.S.S.R. 68 51.15 N 28.07 E
Žovtnevoje, S.S.S.R. 68 50.57 N 34.22 E
Žovtnevoje, S.S.S.R. 68 49.39 N 34.09 E
Zozaya, Picacho de ∧ 222 27.10 N 102.34 W

ENGLISH Name	Page	Lat.°′	Long.°′

Zozov 68 49.19 N 29.01 E
Zreïgat, Bir ⊤[4] 138 22.27 N 8.53 W
Zrenjanin 38 45.23 N 20.24 E
Zriba 36 36.20 N 10.16 E
Zrmanja ≃ 36 44.15 N 15.32 E
Zruč nad Sázavou 30 49.45 N 15.07 E
Zscherndorf 50 51,36 N 12.15 E
Zschieren ⬩[8] 50 51.00 N 13.52 E
Zschopau 50 50.44 N 13.04 E
Zschopau ≃ 50 51.08 N 13.03 E
Zschorlau 50 50.34 N 12.38 E
Zschornewitz 50 51.43 N 12.25 E
Zschortau 50 51.28 N 12.21 E
Žuanbalyk 76 45.04 N 61.51 E
Žuantobe 76 44.45 N 68.54 E
Zuarungu 140 10.47 N 0.48 W
Zubaydīyah, Jabal az- ∧ 122 33.48 N 37.02 E
Zubayr, Jazā'ir az- II 134 15.05 N 42.05 E
Zubayr, Wādī ∨ 132 27.27 N 32.41 E
Zubcov 66 56.10 N 34.34 E
Zubkoviči 68 51.02 N 27.41 E
Zubova Pol'ana 70 54.04 N 42.51 E
Zubovka 70 54.16 N 51.06 E
Zubovo, S.S.S.R. 66 60.19 N 36.57 E
Zubovo, S.S.S.R. 66 54.33 N 35.29 E
Zubovo, S.S.S.R. 70 56.52 N 44.08 E
Zuccarello 56 44.07 N 8.07 E
Zuccone, Monte ∧ 56 44.26 N 9.37 E
Zuchwil 54 47.12 N 7.33 E
Zuckerhütl ∧ 58 46.58 N 11.09 E
Zudañez 238 19.06 S 64.44 W
Zudar 50 54.15 N 13.20 E
Z'udev, Ostrov I 70 45.35 N 47.58 E
Z'udostinskij, Ostrov I 70 45.58 N 48.50 E
Zuel 58 46.31 N 12.08 E
Zuénoula 140 7.26 N 6.03 W
Zuera 34 41.52 N 0.47 W
Zufaytat Mashtūl 132 30.20 N 31.21 E
Zug 54 47.10 N 8.31 E
Zug □[3] 54 47.00 N 8.30 E
Zugdeli 78 55.03 N 111.10 E
Zugdidi 74 42.30 N 41.53 E
Zugersee ⊜ 54 47.08 N 8.30 E
Zug Island I 271 42.17 N 83.07 W
Zugló ⬩[8] 254c 47.31 N 19.08 E
Zugres 73 48.01 N 38.15 E
Zugspitze ∧ 58 47.25 N 10.59 E
Zühlsdorf 254a 52.44 N 13.24 E
Zui 66 57.06 N 31.37 E
Zuid-Beijerland 48 51.45 N 4.22 E
Zuid-Beveland I 48 51.25 N 3.45 E
Zuidbroek 48 53.10 N 6.52 E
Zuidelijk Flevoland ⬩[1] 48 52.22 N 5.20 E
Zuiderzee → IJsselmeer ⊤[2] 48 52.45 N 5.25 E
Zuidholland □[4] 48 52.00 N 4.30 E
Zuidhorn 48 53.14 N 6.24 E
Zuidland 48 51.48 N 4.15 E
Zuidlaren 48 53.05 N 6.41 E
Zuid-Willemsvaart ≍ 48 51.12 N 5.52 E
Zuidwolde 48 53.15 N 6.35 E
Žuja 68 45.03 N 34.20 E
Žuja ≃ 78 58.45 N 118.11 E
Zújar ≃ 34 39.01 N 5.47 W
Zújar, Embalse del ⊜[1] 34 38.50 N 5.20 W
Zujevka, S.S.S.R. 70 58.25 N 51.10 E
Zujevka, S.S.S.R. 73 48.04 N 38.15 E
Z'ukajka 70 58.12 N 54.43 E
Žukopa 66 56.33 N 32.42 E
Žukopa ≃ 66 56.54 N 32.46 E
Žukovka, S.S.S.R. 66 53.32 N 33.44 E
Žukovka, S.S.S.R. 76 56.05 N 91.42 E
Žukovka, S.S.S.R. 255b 55.44 N 37.15 E
Žukovskaja 70 47.37 N 42.28 E
Žukovskij 72 55.35 N 38.08 E
Žukovskoje 70 46.05 N 41.21 E
Žukowo 30 54.21 N 18.22 E
Zula 134 15.11 N 39.41 E
Žulanka 76 54.22 N 80.36 E
Zulayl, Wādī aẓ- ∨ 122 32.09 N 36.03 E
Žuldyz 70 49.16 N 49.30 E
Žulebino 255b 55.42 N 37.51 E
Zulia 144 4.10 N 34.01 E
Zulia □[3] 236 10.00 N 72.10 W
Zulia □[5] 144 3.00 N 32.30 E
Zulia ∧ 144 4.07 N 33.58 E
Zulia ≃ 236 9.04 N 72.18 W
Zulia, Jabal ∧ 144 4.07 N 33.58 E
Züllichau → Sulechów 30 52.06 N 15.37 E
Zülpich 52 50.41 N 6.39 E
Züls → Biała 30 50.23 N 17.40 E
Zulueta 230p 22.22 N 79.34 W
Zululand □[9] 148 28.10 S 32.00 E
Z'ul'z'a 78 52.33 N 116.13 E
Žumala 70 50.29 N 49.47 E
Zumarraga 106 11.38 N 124.50 E
Zumate, Cerro ∧ 224 20.10 N 98.40 W
Zumba 236 4.52 S 79.09 W
Zumbo 144 15.36 S 30.25 E
Zumbro ≃ 180 44.18 N 91.56 W
Zumbro, North Fork ≃ 180 44.15 N 92.29 W
Zumbro, South Fork ≃ 180 44.15 N 92.29 W
Zumbrota 180 44.17 N 92.40 W
Zumpango 224 19.48 N 99.06 W
Zumpango, Lago de ⊜ 224 19.46 N 99.09 W
Zumpango del Rio 224 17.39 N 99.30 W
Zundert 48 51.28 N 4.40 E
Zundi 142 10.28 S 16.48 E
Zune 146 18.59 S 35.18 E
Zungeru 140 9.48 N 6.09 E
Zungur 140 9.58 N 9.47 E
Zungwini 148 27.34 S 30.53 E
Zunhua 95 40.12 N 117.58 E
Zuni, N. Mex., U.S. 190 35.04 N 108.51 W
Zuni, Va., U.S. 198 36.52 N 76.50 W
Zuni ≃ 190 34.39 N 109.40 W

DEUTSCH Name	Seite	Breite°′	Länge°′ E=Ost

Zuni Indian Reservation ⬩[4] 190 35.15 N 108.20 W
Zuni Mountains ⋀ 190 35.10 N 108.15 W
Zun-Murin ≃ 78 51.47 N 102.55 E
Zunsuzhi 92 44.40 N 112.50 E
Zunyi 92 27.39 N 106.57 E
Zuoan 90 26.10 N 114.16 E
Zuodengwei 92 23.27 N 106.57 E
Zuogezhuang 95 39.01 N 116.37 E
Zuojiang ≃ 92 22.50 N 108.06 E
Zuojiazhuang 88 37.40 N 118.35 E
Zuomaozigou 94 42.12 N 120.41 E
Zuomuchedonghu ⊜ 110 28.25 N 88.15 E
Zuoquan 92 37.03 N 113.30 E
Zuoshui 92 33.40 N 109.01 E
Zuosuo 92 27.45 N 100.54 E
Zuotema 110 35.50 N 80.45 E
Zuowei 95 40.41 N 114.43 E
Zuoxiunulemiao 78 48.08 N 115.38 E
Zuoyun 92 40.02 N 112.54 E
Zuoz 54 46.36 N 9.58 E
Županja 38 45.04 N 18.42 E
Zuqar, Jazīrat I 134 14.00 N 42.45 E
Zūq Mīkhā'īl 122 33.58 N 35.37 E
Žura, S.S.S.R. 68 47.31 N 29.04 E
Zura, S.S.S.R. 70 57.37 N 53.26 E
Zūrābād 118 38.49 N 44.35 E
Žuraviči, S.S.S.R. 66 53.15 N 30.33 E
Žuraviči, S.S.S.R. 68 50.59 N 25.43 E
Žuravl'ovka, S.S.S.R. 73 48.13 N 38.58 E
Žuravl'ovka, S.S.S.R. 76 51.57 N 69.56 E
Zurayghiṭ 118 26.29 N 40.33 E
Žurban 79 54.12 N 127.56 E
Zurich, Ont., Can. 180 43.26 N 81.37 W
Zurich, Ned. 48 53.06 N 5.23 E
Zürich, Schw. 54 47.23 N 8.32 E
Zürich □[3] 54 47.25 N 8.40 E
Zurich, Lake ⊜ 268 42.12 N 88.06 W
Zürich-Kloten, Flughafen ⊠ 54 47.27 N 8.33 E
Zürichsee ⊜ 54 47.13 N 8.45 E
Zurigo → Zürich 54 47.23 N 8.32 E
Zurmi 140 12.46 N 6.48 E
Żuromin 30 53.04 N 19.55 E
Zürs 54 47.10 N 10.10 E
Zuru 140 11.27 N 5.12 E
Zurzach 54 47.35 N 8.18 E
Zuša ≃ 66 53.27 N 36.23 E
Zusam ≃ 52 48.42 N 10.45 E
Žusandala ⬩[2] 76 44.20 N 75.00 E
Zushi 84 35.18 N 139.35 E
Zusmarshausen 54 48.24 N 10.35 E
Züssow 50 53.59 N 13.32 E
Žut, Otok I 36 43.52 N 15.19 E
Zutiua ≃ 240 3.43 S 45.29 W
Žutovo Vtoroje 70 47.49 N 43.51 E
Zutphen 48 52.08 N 6.12 E
Zützen 50 51.57 N 13.38 E
Zuurbekom 263d 26.19 S 27.49 E
Zuwārah 136 32.56 N 12.06 E
Zuwayzā 122 31.42 N 35.55 E
Z'uzel'skij 76 56.29 N 60.07 E
Žužemberk 36 45.50 N 14.56 E
Z'uzino 255b 55.40 N 38.07 E
Z'uzino ⬩[8] 255b 55.39 N 37.35 E
Žuzymdyk 75 43.05 N 69.08 E
Zv'agino 255b 55.59 N 37.48 E
Zvannoje 68 51.23 N 34.33 E
Zvenigorod 72 55.44 N 36.51 E
Zvenigorodka 68 49.04 N 30.57 E
Zvenigovo 70 55.58 N 48.02 E
Zverevo 73 48.01 N 40.07 E
Zverinogolovskoje 76 54.28 N 64.50 E
Zvezdec 38 42.07 N 27.25 E
Zvolen 30 48.35 N 19.08 E
Zvornik 38 44.23 N 19.06 E
Zwaag 48 52.40 N 5.05 E
Zwaagwesteinde 48 53.15 N 6.04 E
Zwanenburg 48 52.23 N 4.45 E
Zwartemeer 48 52.43 N 7.03 E
Zwarte Meer ⊜ 48 52.37 N 5.57 E
Zwartsluis 48 52.37 N 6.04 E
Zweckel ⬩[8] 253 51.36 N 6.59 E
Zweibrücken 52 49.15 N 7.21 E
Zweifall 52 50.43 N 6.15 E
Zweisimmen 54 46.33 N 7.22 E
Zwenkau 50 51.13 N 12.19 E
Zwesten 52 51.03 N 9.10 E
Zwettl 30 48.37 N 15.10 E
Zwevegem 46 50.48 N 3.20 E
Zwevezele 46 51.02 N 3.12 E
Zwickau 50 50.44 N 12.29 E
Zwickauer Mulde ≃ 50 51.10 N 12.48 E
Zwiefalten 54 48.14 N 9.28 E
Zwiefaltendorf 54 48.13 N 9.31 E
Zwierzyniec 30 50.37 N 22.58 E
Zwiesel 30 49.01 N 13.14 E
Zwieselstein 58 46.56 N 11.02 E
Zwijndrecht 48 51.49 N 4.39 E
Zwillbrock 48 52.04 N 6.42 E
Zwingen 54 47.26 N 7.32 E
Zwingenberg, B.R.D. 52 49.43 N 8.37 E
Zwingenberg, B.R.D. 52 49.25 N 9.02 E
Zwischenahn 48 53.11 N 8.00 E
Zwischenahner Meer ⊜ 48 53.12 N 8.01 E
Zwochau 50 51.28 N 12.16 E
Zwoleń 30 51.22 N 21.35 E
Zwölfaxing 254b 48.06 N 16.28 E
Zwolle, Ned. 48 52.30 N 6.05 E
Zwolle, La., U.S. 184 31.38 N 93.38 W
Zwönitz 50 50.38 N 12.49 E
Zwota 50 50.21 N 12.25 E
Żychlin 30 52.15 N 19.39 E
Zymoetz ≃ 172 54.33 N 128.26 W
Zyr'anka 64 65.45 N 150.51 E
Zyr'anovsk 76 49.43 N 84.20 E
Zyr'anovskij 76 57.46 N 61.42 E
Zyr'anskoje 76 56.50 N 86.38 E
Żyrardów 30 52.04 N 20.25 E
Zyryanovsk → Zyr'anovsk 76 49.43 N 84.20 E
Żyrzyn 30 51.30 N 22.07 E
Żywiec 30 49.41 N 19.12 E

Symbols in the index entries represent the categories identified in the key on page *I* · 26

Kartensymbole in dem Registerverzeichnis stellen die auf Seite *I* · 26 im Schlüssel erklärten Kategorien dar.

Los símbolos incluídos en el texto del índice representan las categorías identificadas con la clave en la página *I* · 26

Les symboles de l'index représentent les catégories indiquées dans la légende à la page *I* · 26

Os símbolos incluídos no texto do índice representam as categorias identificadas com a chave na página *I* · 26.

Printed in the United States of America